THE ONLY BASEBALL CARD AND COLLECTIBLE
BOOK YOU'LL EVER

BECKETT® ALMANAC

OF BASEBALL CARDS AND COLLECTIBLES

NUMBER

2

Edited by DR. JAMES BECKETT, RICH KLEIN and GRANT SANDGROUND with the Price Guide staff of *BECKETT BASEBALL CARD MONTHLY*

Minor League section edited by BEN ECKLAR

Beckett Publications • Dallas, Texas

Prices in this guide reflect current retail rates determined just prior to printing. They do not reflect for-sale prices by the author, publisher, distributors, advertisers, or any card dealers associated with this guide. Every effort has been made to eliminate errors. Readers are invited to write us noting any errors which may be researched and corrected in subsequent printings. The publisher will not be held responsible for losses which may occur in the sale or purchase of cards because of information contained herein.

BECKETT PUBLICATIONS
DALLAS, TEXAS

Manufactured in the United States of America
First Printing
ISBN 1-887432-34-5

Order with Confidence . . . America's 1st Full-time Dealer—Serving Collectors Since 1948

FREE!! CATALOG (Over 160 Pages) FREE!!

The largest and best catalogs in the hobby.

Our catalogs are jam-packed with baseball, football, basketball and hockey cards. Sets, singles, rookies, superstars, wax packs, reprints and much, much more. If you need any card from 1880 to present, chances are good we have it. Now divided into three separate issues, you will receive our regular catalog, chock full of sets, wax packs, & reprints; our 3-Grade Special catalog highlighting the thousands of cards we have available in 3 different grades & also our "One-of-a-Kind" vintage card sale catalog, listing (with grade and price) over 30,000 cards (1880's to 1970's) ready for shipment. If the cards you are looking for aren't listed, use our "new concept" form which makes over 8 million single cards available to you!

Send $2.00 or seven 32¢ stamps for postage to receive the next 3 issues free!!

REPRINT SETS

WHO BUYS REPRINT SETS? THE TRUE COLLECTOR!

1880'S Old Judge Type Set (80)	$39.80
1909 T204 Ramly (121)	26.95
1909-11 T206 (523)	59.95
1910 Plow Boy (42)	8.95
1911 D304 General Baking (25)	9.95
1911 T205 (208)	64.95
1915 Cracker Jack (176)	29.95
1921 Oxford Confectionary (20)	6.95
1922 E120 American Caramel (240)	29.95
1927 Middy Bread (42)	8.95
1933 Goudey (240)	44.95
1934-36 Diamond Stars (108)	29.95
1938 Horrors of War (288)	44.95
1939 Play Ball (161)	26.95
1940 Play Ball (240)	49.95
1941 Play Ball (72)	17.95
1947 Tip Top Bread (163)	24.95
1948 Bowman (48)	7.95

1948 Bowman Basketball (72)	24.95
1948 Bowman Football (108)	24.95
1949 Bowman (240)	37.95
1950 Bowman (252)	44.95
1950 Bowman Football (144)	34.95
1951 Bowman (324)	74.95
1952 Bowman (252)	149.95
1952 Red Man (52)	19.95
1953 Johnston Cookies (24)	10.95
1954 Johnston Cookies (34)	11.95
1954 Wilson Franks (19)	11.95
1955 Johnston Cookies (34)	11.95

We have many other reprint sets in stock, write for our latest catalog.

T205 Gold Borders

Card	Price
Bender, Phi AL (EX)	195.00
Brown, Chi NL (VG)	120.00
Chance, Chi NL (EX)	240.00
Cicotte, Bos AL (VG-EX)	100.00
Delahanty, Det (EM)	82.50
Doyle, NY NL (EM)	82.50
Evers, Chi NL (VG-EX)	160.00
Frick, Newark (EX)	200.00
Grant, Cin (EX+)	275.00
Joss, Cle (VG)	300.00
Mathewson, NY NL (VG-EX)	400.00
Raymond, NY NL (Abt EX)	235.00
Speaker, Bos AL (VG-EX)	275.00
Tinker, Chi NL (VG-EX)	140.00

More T205 & T206's & thousand's more classics available, call or write for our "One-Of-A-Kind" Catalog

T206 White Borders

Card	Price
Baker, Phi AL (Abt EX)	225.00
Chesbro, NY AL (EX+)	425.00
Cobb, Det (bat off) (EX)	1850.00
Cobb, Det (bat on) (EX)	2000.00
Collins, Phi AL (Abt EX)	250.00
Jennings, Det (dancing) (VG-EX)	110.00
Jennings, Det (yelling) (EX)	200.00
Johnson, Was (port) (EX)	720.00
Lajoie, Cle (bat) (VG)	175.00
Young, Cle (port) (Abt EX)	700.00

WE ARE BUYING!!

Before you sell, talk to us! Our 45 years in card collecting is unchallenges by anyone, and our reputation is beyond reprpach. We do not make wild, unsubstantiated claims: WE BUY CARDS AT A HIGHER PRICE THAN ANYONE! All our purchases made are strictly confidental. Our primary areas of interest are as follows...

- All Tobacco cards (T3 thru T332)
- All "E" Early Candy & Gum Cards
- All 19th Century Cards
- All Goudey & Canadian Goudeys
- Play Ball - 1939-1941
- All cards from the 30's (Batter Up's, Diamond Stars)
- All Meat Cards (Rodeo, Wilson, Kahn's)
- Other Food Cards (Bell Brand, Hage's Dairy)
- Leaf - 1948-49 Baseball & Football
- Topps - 1952
- Sport Kings
- All Sporting News Issues (M101-4, M101-5, M101-6)
- PCL Cards - Zeenuts
- All other unusual cards issued prior to 1965

Call us today for details!

JUST A SAMPLE OF OUR VAST INVENTORY - ALL SETS ARE EM TO NM CONDITION. NOTE: Prices are subject to change without notice.

1997 Topps Series 1 (275)	$31.95
1997 Topps Series 2 (220)	26.95
1997 Donruss (270)	27.95
1997 U.D. Coll. Choice Series 1 Unopened Box (432)	34.95
1996 Topps Series 1 (220)	28.95
1996 Topps Series 2 (220)	27.95
1996 Fleer Complete Set (600)	89.95
1996 Pinnacle Box (240)	44.95
1996 Upper Deck # 1 Box (280)	45.95
1996 U.D. Coll. Choice Series 1 Unopened Box (432)	33.95
1996 Fleer Excel Min. Lg. (250)	47.95
1996 Donruss Series 1 (330)	33.95
1996 Donruss Series 2 (220)	22.95
1995 Topps Traded (165)	36.95
1995 Fleer Update (200)	35.95
1995 Bowman Box (240)	49.95
1995 Upper Deck Collector's Choice (530)	36.95
1995 Topps Series 1 (396)	39.95
1995 Topps Series 2 (264)	32.95
1995 Fleer (660)	66.95
1995 Donruss Series 1 (330)	36.95
1995 Donruss Series 2 (220)	27.95
1995 Score Series 1 Box (432)	37.95
1995 Ultra Series 1 (250)	39.95
1995 Conlon Series 1 (110)	20.95
1994 Ultra 1 (300)	69.95
1994 Upper Deck C.C. (640)	54.95
1994 Topps Factory (792)	59.95
1994 Fleer Baseball (720)	68.95
1994 TWCC Box (432)	55.95
1994 Topps S.C. Ser. 3 Box (288)	36.95
1994 Leaf Series 1 Box (432)	45.00
1994 Finest Series 1 Box (169)	59.95
1994 Conlon Collection Box (432)	33.95
1994 Topps Traded (132)	35.00
1994 Fleer Update (210)	24.00
1994 Bowman Box (288)	49.95
1994 Donruss Series 1 Box (468)	60.95
1994 Donruss Series 2 Box (468)	45.95
1994 Score Series 1 Box (504)	35.00
1994 Score Series 2 Box (504)	35.00
1994 Conlon Set (330)	29.95
1994 TWCC Set (162)	28.95
1993 Topps Factory (825)	48.00
1993 Fleer (720)	49.50
1993 Donruss (792)	57.50
1993 Score (660)	52.50
1993 Upper Deck Factory (840)	46.00
1993 TWCC Set (160)	24.95
1993 TWCC Box (432)	52.95
1993 Leaf 1 Box (504)	44.95
1993 Leaf 2 Box (540)	43.95
1993 Fleer Ultra 1 Box (504)	48.95
1993 Fleer Ultra 2 Box (504)	48.95
1993 Conlon Collection (330)	27.95
1992 Topps Factory (792)	30.00
1992 Fleer Factory (720)	33.95
1992 Donruss Factory (792)	35.00
1992 Score Factory (900)	25.00
1992 Upper Deck Factory (800)	36.00
1992 Fleer Update (132)	160.00
1992 Score Traded (110)	40.00
1992 Conlon Collection (330)	30.95
1992 Conlon Babe Ruth (165)	21.95
1991 Topps Factory (792)	25.00
1991 Fleer Factory (720)	19.50
1991 Score Factory (900)	25.00
1991 Upper Deck Factory (800)	30.00
1991 Bowman Factory (704)	27.95
1990 Upper Deck Factory (800)	31.00
1988 Fleer Factory (660)	30.00
1988 Score Traded (110)	60.00
1987 Fleer Factory (660)	70.00
1987 Donruss Factory (660)	40.00
1986 Topps (792)	35.00
1986 Fleer Factory (660)	110.00
1986 Donruss Factory (660)	120.00
1985 Topps (792)	65.00
1985 Topps Traded (132)	22.50
1985 Fleer Factory (660)	140.00
1985 Fleer Update (132)	27.50
1985 Donruss Factory (660)	185.00
1984 Topps (792)	60.00
1984 Topps Traded (132)	70.00
1984 Fleer (660)	110.00
1984 Fleer Update (132)	875.00
1984 Donruss Factory (660)	300.00
1983 Topps (792)	120.00
1983 Topps Traded (132)	55.00
1983 Fleer (660)	105.00
1983 Donruss Factory (660)	120.00
1982 Topps Traded (132)	360.00
1982 Fleer (660)	80.00
1982 Donruss Factory (660)	90.00
1981 Topps (726)	85.00
1981 Topps Traded (132)	45.00
1981 Fleer (660)	47.50
1981 Donruss (605)	50.00
1980 Topps (726)	200.00
1979 Topps (726)	225.00
1978 Topps (726)	300.00
1977 Topps (660)	400.00
1976 Topps (660)	400.00
1975 Topps (660)	749.95
1974 Topps (660)	650.00
1973 Topps (660)	950.00

THE EXTRAS:

- Add $5.00 shipping and insurance to all orders.
- Personal checks held 15 working days for clearance.
- All prices subject to change. Call to verify prices.
- All orders are subject to manufacturer's delay.
- Master Card & VISA Accepted.
- Phone orders accepted, add 5% to total.
- Wisconsin residents add 5.5% sales tax.

LARRY FRITSCH CARDS, INC.
735 Old Wausau Rd., P.O. Box 863,
Dept. 540
Stevens Point, WI 54481
(715) 344-8687 • Fax: (715) 344-1778

WE ALSO HAVE FOOTBALL, BASKETBALL & HOCKEY SETS! WRITE FOR OUR FREE CATALOG.

Catch us on the Internet at: http://www.fritschcards.com
or email us at: larry@fritschcards.com

Beckett Almanac of Baseball Cards

Table of Contents

Minor League

Kenner Starting Lineup

Advertiser Index

About the Author

Jim Beckett, the leading authority on sport card values in the United States, maintains a wide range of activities in the world of sports. He possesses one of the finest collections of sports cards and autographs in the world, has made numerous appearances on radio and television, and has been frequently cited in many national publications. He was awarded the first "Special Achievement Award" for Contributions to the Hobby by the National Sports Collectors Convention in 1980, the "Jock-Jaspersen Award" for Hobby Dedication in 1983, and the "Buck Barker, Spirit of the Hobby" Award in 1991.

Dr. Beckett is the author of *Beckett Baseball Card Price Guide, The Official Price Guide to Baseball Cards, The Sport Americana Price Guide to Baseball Collectibles, The Sport Americana Baseball Memorabilia and Autograph Price Guide, Beckett Football Card Price Guide, The Official Price Guide to Football Cards, Beckett Hockey Card Price Guide, The Official Price Guide to Hockey Cards, Beckett Basketball Card Price Guide, The Official Price Guide to Basketball Cards, and The Sport Americana Baseball Card Alphabetical Checklist.* In addition, he is the founder, publisher, and editor of *Beckett Baseball Card Monthly, Beckett Basketball Monthly, Beckett Football Card Monthly, Beckett Hockey Monthly, Beckett Future Stars, Beckett Racing Monthly, and Beckett Tribute* magazines.

Jim Beckett received his Ph.D. in Statistics from Southern Methodist University in 1975. Prior to starting Beckett Publications in 1984, Dr. Beckett served as an Associate Professor of Statistics at Bowling Green State University and as a vice president of a consulting firm in Dallas, Texas. He currently resides in Dallas with his wife, Patti, and their daughters, Christina, Rebecca, and Melissa.

Jim Beckett

How To Use This Book

Isn't it great? Every year this book gets bigger and bigger with all the new sets coming out. But even more exciting is that every year there are more collectors, more shows, more stores, and more interest in the cards we love so much. This edition has been enhanced and expanded from the previous edition. The cards you collect — who appears on them, what they look like, where they are from, and (most important to most of you) what their current values are — are enumerated within. Many of the features contained in the other *Beckett Price Guides* have been incorporated into this volume since condition grading, terminology, and many other aspects of collecting are common to the card hobby in general. We hope you find the book both interesting and useful in your collecting pursuits.

The *Beckett Guide* has been successful where other attempts have failed because it is complete, current, and valid. This Price Guide contains not just one, but three prices by condition for all the baseball cards listed. The prices were added to the card lists just prior to printing and reflect not the author's opinions or desires but the going retail prices for each card, based on the marketplace (sports memorabilia conventions and shows, sports card shops, hobby papers, current mail-order catalogs, local club meetings, auction results, and other firsthand reportings of actually realized prices).

What is the best price guide available on the market today? Of course, card sellers prefer the price guide with the highest prices, while card buyers naturally prefer the one with the lowest prices. Accuracy, however, is the true test. Use the price guide trusted by more collectors and dealers than all the others combined. Look for the *Beckett®* name. I won't put my name on anything I won't stake my reputation on. Not the lowest and not the highest — but the most accurate, with integrity.

To facilitate your use of this book, read the complete introductory section on the following pages before going to the pricing pages. Every collectible field has its own terminology; we've tried to capture most of these terms and definitions in our glossary. Please read carefully the section on grading and the condition of your cards, as you cannot determine which price column is appropriate for a given card without first knowing its condition.

Welcome to the world of baseball cards.

Introduction

Welcome to the exciting world of baseball card collecting, America's fastest-growing avocation. You have made a good choice in buying this book, since it will open up to you the entire panorama of this field in the simplest, most concise way.

The growth of *Beckett Baseball Card Monthly, Beckett Basketball Monthly, Beckett Football Card Monthly, Beckett Hockey Monthly, Future Stars/Sports Collectibles, Beckett Racing Monthly and Beckett Vintage Sports* is an indication of the unprecedented popularity of sports cards and collectibles. Founded in 1984 by Dr. James Beckett, the author of this Price Guide, *Beckett Baseball Card Monthly* contains the most extensive and accepted monthly Price Guide, collectible glossy superstar covers, colorful feature articles, "Short Prints," Convention Calendar, tips for beginners, "Readers Write" letters to and responses from the editor, information on errors and varieties, autograph collecting tips and profiles of the sport's Hottest stars. Published every month, *BBCM* is the hobby's largest paid circulation periodical. The other six magazines were built on the success of *BBCM.*

So collecting baseball cards — while still pursued as a hobby with youthful exuberance by kids in the neighborhood — has also taken on the trappings of an industry, with thousands of full- and part-time card dealers, as well as vendors of supplies, clubs and conventions. In fact, each year since 1980 thousands of hobbyists have assembled for a National Sports Collectors Convention, at which hundreds of dealers have displayed their wares, seminars have been conducted, autographs penned by sports notables, and millions of cards changed hands. The Beckett Almanac is the best guide available to the exciting world of baseball cards. Read it and use it. May your enjoyment and your collection increase in the coming months and years.

How to Collect

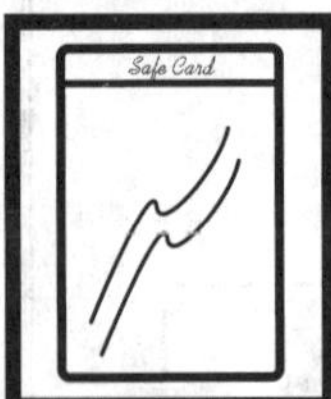

Each collection is personal and reflects the individuality of its owner. There are no set rules on how to collect cards. Since card collecting is a hobby or leisure pastime, what you collect, how much you collect, and how much time and money you spend collecting are entirely up to you. The funds you have available for collecting and your own personal taste should determine how you collect. Information and ideas presented here are intended to help you get the most enjoyment from this hobby.

It is impossible to collect every card ever produced. Therefore, beginners as well as intermediate and advanced collectors usually specialize in some way. One of the reasons this hobby is popular is that individual collectors can define and tailor their collecting methods to match their own tastes. To give you some ideas of the various approaches to collecting, we will list some of the more popular areas of specialization.

Many collectors select complete sets from particular years. For example, they may concentrate on assembling complete sets from all the years since their birth or since they became avid sports fans. They may try to collect a card for every player during that specified period of time.

Many others wish to acquire only certain players. Usually such players are the superstars of the sport, but occasionally collectors will specialize in all the cards of players who attended a particular college or came from a certain town. Some collectors are only interested in the first cards or Rookie Cards of certain players. A handy guide for collectors interested in pursuing the hobby this way is the *Beckett Baseball Card Alphabetical Checklist.*

Another fun way to collect cards is by team. Most fans have a favorite team, and it is natural for that loyalty to be translated into a desire for cards of the players on that favorite team. For most of the recent years, team sets (all the cards from a given team for that year) are readily available at a reasonable price. *The Beckett Team Baseball Card Checklist* will open up this field to the collector.

Obtaining Cards

Several avenues are open to card collectors. Cards still can be purchased in the traditional way: by the pack at the local candy, grocery, drug or major discount stores.

But there are also thousands of card shops across the country that specialize in selling cards individually or by the pack, box, or set. Another alternative is the thousands of card shows held each month around the country, which feature anywhere from eight to 800 tables of sports cards and memorabilia for sale.

For many years, it has been possible to purchase complete sets of baseball cards through mail-order advertisers found in traditional sports media publications, such as *The Sporting News, Baseball Digest, Street & Smith* yearbooks, and others. These sets also are advertised in the card collecting periodicals. Many collectors will begin by subscribing to at least one of the hobby periodicals, all with good up-to-date information. In fact, subscription offers can be found in the advertising section of this book

Most serious card collectors obtain old (and new) cards from one or more of several main sources: (1) trading or buying from other collectors or dealers; (2) responding to sale or auction ads in the hobby publications; (3) buying at a local hobby store; and/or (4) attending sports collectibles shows or conventions.

We advise that you try all four methods since each has its own distinct advantages: (1) trading is a great way to make new friends; (2) hobby periodicals help you keep up with what's going on in the hobby (including when and where the conventions are happening); (3) stores provide the opportunity to enjoy personalized service and consider a great diversity of material in a relaxed sports-oriented atmosphere; and (4) shows allow you to choose from multiple dealers and thousands of cards under one roof in a competitive situation.

Preserving Your Cards

Cards are fragile. They must be handled properly in order to retain their value. Careless handling can easily result in creased or bent cards. It is, however, not recommended that tweezers or tongs be used to pick up your cards since such utensils might mar or indent card surfaces and thus reduce those cards' conditions and values.

In general, your cards should be handled directly as little as possible. This is sometimes easier to say than to do.

Although there are still many who use custom boxes, storage trays, or even shoe boxes, plastic sheets are the preferred method of many collectors for storing cards.

A collection stored in plastic pages in a three-ring album allows you to view your collection at any time without the need to touch the card itself. Cards can also be kept in single holders (of various types and thickness) designed for the enjoyment of each card individually.

For a large collection, some collectors may use a combination of the above methods. When purchasing plastic sheets for your cards, be sure that you find the pocket size that fits the cards snugly. Don't put your 1951 Bowman in a sheet designed to fit 1981 Topps.

Most hobby and collectibles shops and virtually all collectors' conventions will have these plastic pages available in quantity for the various sizes offered, or you can purchase them directly from the advertisers in this book.

Also, remember that pocket size isn't the only factor to consider when looking for plastic sheets. Other factors such as safety, economy, appearance, availability, or personal preference also may indicate which types of sheets a collector may want to buy.

Damp, sunny and/or hot conditions — no, this is not a weather forecast — are three elements to avoid in extremes if you are interested in preserving your collection. Too much (or too little) humidity can cause the gradual deterioration of a card. Direct, bright sun (or fluorescent light) over time will bleach out the color of a card. Extreme heat accelerates the decomposition of the card. On the other hand, many cards have lasted more than 75 years without much scientific intervention. So be cautious, even if the above factors typically present a problem only when present in the extreme. It never hurts to be prudent.

Collecting vs. Investing

Collecting individual players and collecting complete sets are both popular vehicles for investment and speculation.

Most investors and speculators stock up on complete sets or on quantities of players they think have good investment potential.

There is obviously no guarantee in this book, or anywhere else for that matter, that cards will outperform the stock market or other investment alternatives in the future. After all, baseball

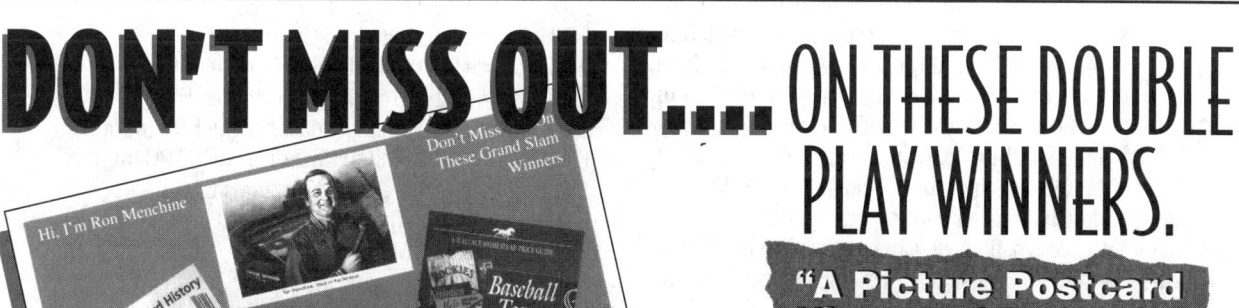

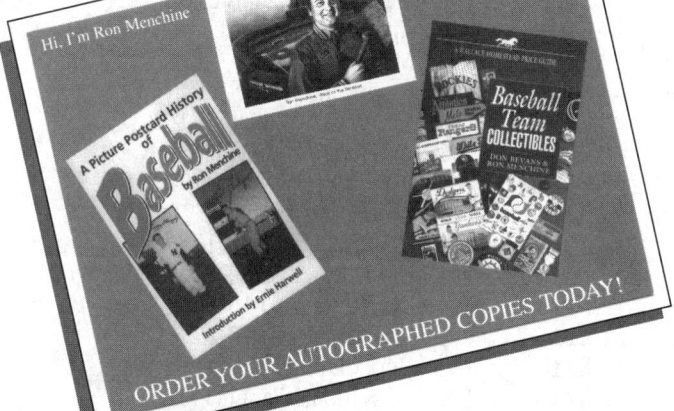

cards do not pay quarterly dividends and cards cannot be sold at their "current values" as easily as stocks or bonds.

Nevertheless, investors have noticed a favorable long-term trend in the past performance of baseball and other sports collectibles, and certain cards and sets have outperformed just about any other investment in some years.

Many hobbyists maintain that the best investment is and always will be the building of a collection, which traditionally has held up better than outright speculation.

Some of the obvious questions are: Which cards? When to buy? When to sell? The best investment you can make is in your own education.

The more you know about your collection and the hobby, the more informed the decisions you will be able to make. We're not selling investment tips. We're selling information about the current value of baseball cards. It's up to you to use that information to your best advantage.

Collectibles/Memorabilia

In recent years more and more hobbyists have diversified their collections to include non-card memorabilia such as autographs, cereal boxes, Highland Mint, Kenner Starting Lineups, programs, publications and tickets. These and other non-card collectibles have been catalogued and priced in this book to aid those collectors who have branched out into these areas. Grading and pricing generally is similar to cards, but factors that are specific to certain types of items may be noted in the set headers.

Terminology

Each hobby has its own language to describe its area of interest. The nomenclature traditionally used for trading cards is derived from the *American Card Catalog*, published in 1960 by Nostalgia Press. That catalog, written by Jefferson Burdick (who is called the "Father of Card Collecting" for his pioneering work), uses letter and number designations for each separate set of cards. The letter used in the ACC designation refers to the generic type of card. While both sport and non-sport issues are classified in the ACC, we shall confine ourselves to the sport issues. The following list defines the letters and their meanings as used by the *American Card Catalog*.

(none) or N - 19th Century U.S. Tobacco
B - Blankets
D - Bakery Inserts Including Bread
E - Early Candy and Gum
F - Food Inserts
H - Advertising
M - Periodicals
PC - Postcards
R - Candy and Gum since 1930

Following the letter prefix and an optional hyphen are one-, two-, or Three- digit numbers, R(-)999. These typically represent the company or entity issuing the cards. In several cases, the ACC number is extended by an additional hyphen and another one- or two-digit numerical suffix. Like other traditional methods of identification, this system provides order to the process of cataloging cards; however, most serious collectors learn the ACC designation of the popular sets by repetition and familiarity, rather than by attempting to "figure out" what they might or should be. From 1948 forward, collectors and dealers commonly refer to all sets by their year, maker, type of issue, and any other distinguishing characteristic. For example, such a characteristic could be an unusual issue or one of several regular issues put out by a specific maker in a single year. Regional issues are usually referred to by year, maker, and sometimes by title or theme of the set.

We've included a comprehensive cross-index for all sets commonly referred to with an ACC catalog number. These sets are all listed alphabetically by maker within the Almanac. Thus if you are wondering why you can't find the 1887 N28 Allen & Ginter set in the "N" section of this book, that's because it is listed in the "A" section as 1887 Allen & Ginter N28. Hopefully, the following cross-index will assist in quickly finding the sets you need to reference.

American Card Catalog Cross Index

C46 = 1912 Imperial Tobacco C46 (minors)
D310 = 1911 Pacific Coast Biscuit D310
D311 = 1911 Pacific Coast Biscuit D311
D322 = 1910 Pirates Tip-Top D322
D327 = 1917 Holsum Bread D327
D381 = 1916 Fleischmann Bread D381
D382 = 1934 Tarzan Thoro Bread D382
D383 = 1921 Koester's Bread World Series Issue D383
E90-1 = 1909-11 American Caramel E90-1
E90-2 = 1910 Pirates American Caramels E90-2
E90-3 = 1910 Chicago E90-3
E91 = 1908-10 American Caramel E91
E92 = 1910 Nadja Caramel E92
E93 = 1910 Standard Caramel E93
E95 = 1909 Philadelphia Caramel E95
E96 = 1912 Philadelphia Caramel E96
E99 = 1910 Bishop Coast League E99 (minors)
E100 = 1911 Bishop Coast League E100 (minors)
E103 = 1910 Williams Caramels E103
E104 = 1910 Nadja E104
E105 = 1910 Mello Mints E105
E106 = 1915 American Caramel E106
E107 = 1903-04 Breisch-Williams E107
E122 = 1922 American Caramel E122
E125 = 1910 American Caramel Die Cuts E125
E126 = 1927 American Caramel E126
E135 = 1916 Collins-McCarthy E135
E136-1 = 1912 Home Run Kisses E136-1 (minors)
E145-1 = 1914 Cracker Jack E145-1
E145-2 = 1915 Cracker Jack E145-2.
E210 = 1927 York Caramel E210
E220 = 1921-23 National Caramel E220
E224 = 1914 Texas Tommy E224
E254 = 1909-11 Colgan's Chips E254
E271 = 1910 Darby Chocolates E271
E285 = 1933 Rittenhouse Candy E285
E286 = 1910 Ju Ju Drums E286
E297 = 1909 Briggs E97
E300 = 1911 Plow's Candy E300
H801-6 = 1950 Four Mighty Heroes H801-6
M101-2 = 1909-13 Sporting News Supplements M101-2
M101-4 = 1916 Sporting News M101-4
M101-5 = 1915 Sporting News M101-5

FREE 100-PAGE CATALOG!

Each catalog offers Star Cards, Rookie Cards, Complete Sets, 1950s & '60s Cards. '70s Cards, Pre-War Cards, Card Lots, Autographs, Rare & Unusual Items, Football & Basketball Cards, and More! Please send your name & address (or call) to receive our **GIANT 100-page fully illustrated catalog!**
"Serving Collectors Since 1976"

KIT YOUNG'S 1997 EARLY WINTER SALE

"IT'S AMERICA'S #1 SPORTS CATALOG!"

1960s TOPPS CARD LOTS

All Cards VG-EX Condition! (Our Choice)

	50 diff.	100 diff.
1960	$60.00	$120.00
1961	45.00	90.00
1962	75.00	150.00
1963	60.00	-
1964	53.00	105.00
1965	30.00	-
1966	30.00	60.00
1967	30.00	60.00
1968	25.00	-
1969	23.00	45.00

1997 TOPPS MICKEY MANTLE INSERTS

For the second year in a row TOPPS has paid tribute to Yankee legend Mickey Mantle with a 16-card insert set. This year's cards feature Mickey's special cards such as his All-Star cards, Duo and Trio cards, and other Bowman

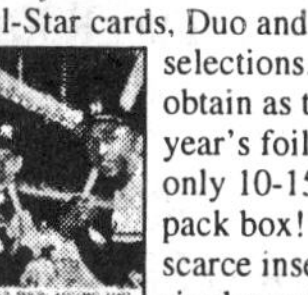

selections. These cards are very difficult to obtain as they were randomly inserted into this year's foil packs, with the average number of only 10-15 cards being pulled out of every 36-pack box! We are pleased to offer these scarce inserts by the complete set and by the single card! Limited quantities available!

COMPLETE 16-CARD SET ONLY
$149.95 each (+$3.95 p/h)

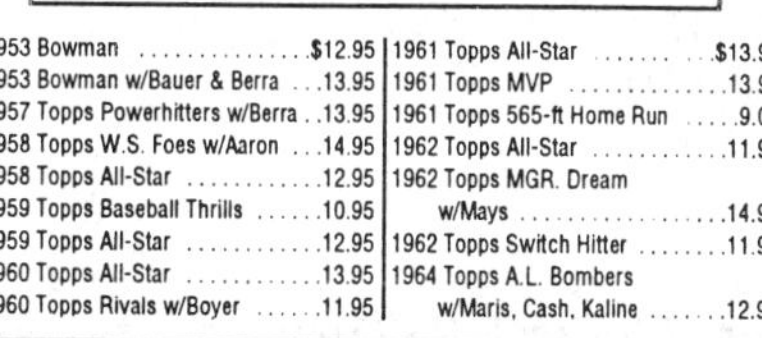

1953 Bowman	$12.95
1953 Bowman w/Bauer & Berra	13.95
1957 Topps Powerhitters w/Berra	13.95
1958 Topps W.S. Foes w/Aaron	14.95
1958 Topps All-Star	12.95
1959 Topps Baseball Thrills	10.95
1959 Topps All-Star	12.95
1960 Topps All-Star	13.95
1960 Topps Rivals w/Boyer	11.95
1961 Topps All-Star	$13.95
1961 Topps MVP	13.95
1961 Topps 565-ft Home Run	9.00
1962 Topps All-Star	11.95
1962 Topps MGR. Dream w/Mays	14.95
1962 Topps Switch Hitter	11.95
1964 Topps A.L. Bombers w/Maris, Cash, Kaline	12.95

INTRODUCTORY OFFER
½ PRICE SPECIAL
Topps Baseball Cards 1955-1991

You can buy a Topps sample card from every year 1955-1991. This is a great chance to learn what cards looked like in the early years!

SPECIAL AUCTIONS

We offer special auctions of new and old cards, sets, lots & memorabilia several times a year. Many at bargain prices. Please send five (5) 32¢ stamps to receive our next three auctions.

BUYING CARDS

We have been buying cards through the mail (or at conventions) since 1976, and make hundreds of purchases each year.

We will buy the following:

A) **Complete Collections** - including accumulations of all sizes
B) **Complete Sets** - from 1983 and older, including partial sets
C) **Star Cards** - Hall of Famers and Rookies, 1983 and older
D) **Older Cards** - All cards (Baseball & Football) before 1970, including Pre-War cards

If you have cards to sell, please call or write us. We will handle all transactions professionally and confidentially.

KIT YOUNG CARDS
11535 SORRENTO VALLEY ROAD #403
DEPT. BAL
SAN DIEGO, CA 92121
Phone (619) 259-1300
Fax (619) 259-1675

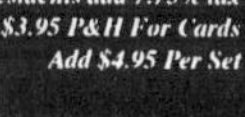

SATISFACTION GUARANTEED

California Residents add 7.75% tax
Add $3.95 P&H For Cards
Add $4.95 Per Set

COMPLETE SETS-TAKE 20% OFF

We are now offering **Complete Topps Sets** from 1954-1975. We can offer them in **VG-EX, Excellent or EX-MINT** conditions. Complete sets have been a great investment in recent years, and are a terrific way to get value for your collecting dollars. In addition to our sets in stock we can also **Build You A Set** to your own specifications from our massive inventory. **Please Call to learn more about our service.**

Set	EX-MT	EX	VG-EX
1954 Topps	$7500.00	4200.00	3650.00
1955Topps	$7500.00	4400.00	3600.00
1956 Topps	$6900.00	3900.00	3500.00
1957 Topps	$7690.00	3900.00	3350.00
1958 Topps	$4800.00	2675.00	2250.00
1959 Topps	$4500.00	2700.00	2200.00
1960 Topps	$3300.00	2100.00	1750.00
1961Topps	$4800.00	2800.00	2395.00
1962 Topps	$4600.00	2675.00	2250.00
1963 Topps	$5000.00	2950.00	2450.00
1964 Topps	$3000.00	1800.00	1500.00
1965 Topps	$3500.00	2150.00	1795.00
1967 Topps	$4600.00	2675.00	2275.00
1968 Topps	$3000.00	1775.00	1495.00
1969 Topps	$2200.00	1350.00	1095.00

MID-ATLANTIC SPORTS CARDS
MORTON, PA (10 MILES WEST OF PHILADELPHIA)

BUYING • SELLING • TRADING
SPECIALIZING IN:

A) BUYING EARLY BASEBALL CARDS
(1880-1975) AND SPORTS MEMORABILIA:
YEARBOOKS, GUIDES, PINS, POSTCARDS, PHOTOGRAPHS, MAGAZINES, ADVERTISING ITEMS, ETC.
B) SELLING ODD-BALL SUPERSTAR CARDS
(SEND STAMPED ENVELOPE TO RECEIVE OUR SELLING LIST OF YOUR FAVORITE CURRENT SUPERSTAR-NAME STAR WANTED)
C) BUY/SELL POLICE SAFETY SETS, REGIONALS, FOOD ISSUES AND OTHER SMALL SETS... SEND FOR LISTING
(WE NEED LARGE QUANTITIES FOR MAIL ORDER)
D) CONTINENTAL INTERNET ON-LINE AUCTIONS
(SEND FOR LISTINGS)

Or you can visit our website: http://www.masc22.com/masc

Bring Cards To Store For Free Appraisal and Sale.
22 South Morton Ave.
Morton, PA 19070
Phone: (610) 544-2171
Fax: (610) 544-2850
E-mail:midatlantic@masc22.com

M101-7 = 1926 Sporting News Supplements M101-7
M116 = 1911 Sporting Life M116
M117 = 1888-89 Sporting Times M117
N28 = 1887 Allen and Ginter N28
N29 = 1888 Allen and Ginter N29
N43 = 1888 Allen and Ginter N43
N135 = 1893 Duke Talk of the Diamond N135
N142 = 1894 Duke Cabinets N142
N162 = 1888 Goodwin N162
N167 = 1888 Old Judge N167
N172 = 1887-90 Old Judge N172
N184 = 1888 Kimball's N184
N284 = 1887 Buchner N284
N300 = 1895 Mayo N300
N321 = 1888 S.F. Hess and Co. Creole N321(minors)
N338-1 = 1893 S.F. Hess and Co. N338-1
N370 = 1887 Lone Jack N370
N403 = 1888 August Beck N403
N566 = 1895 Newsboy N566
N690-1 = 1887 Kalamazoo Bats N690-1
N690-2 = 1887 Kalamazoo Teams N690-2
P2 = 1910 Sweet Caporal Pins P2
PB2 = 1909 Buster Brown Bread Pins PB2
PB3 = 1909 Morton's Pennant Winner Bread Pins PB3
PB4 = 1922-23 Kolbs Mothers' Bread Pins PB4 (minors)
PB5-1 = 1920 Mrs. Sherlock's Pins PB5-1 (minors)
PB5-2 = 1922 Mrs. Sherlock's Pins PB5-2 (minors)
PB5-3 = 1933 Mrs. Sherlock's Pins PB5-3 (minors)
PB6 = 1934 Ward Baking Sporties Pins PB6
PC741 = 1956-60 Braves Bill and Bob Postcards PC741
PC742-1= 1912 Red Sox Boston American Series PC742-1
PC742-2= 1912 Red Sox Boston Daily American Souvenir
PC743 = 1909 H.H. Bregstone PC743
PC744 = 1938-59 George Burke PC744
PC748 = 1953-55 Dormand PC748
PC749 = 1959 Tigers Graphic Arts Service PC749
PC750 = 1959 Hayes Company Bauer PC750
PC751 = 1959 Howard Photo Service PC751
PC753 = 1936-52 Albertype Hall of Fame PC753
PC754-2= 1950-69 J.D. McCarthy PC754-2
PC757 = 1915 Sporting News PC757
PC759 = 1949 Solon Sunbeam/Pureta PC759
PC760 = 1908-09 Rose Company PC760
PC761 = 1947 Indians Van Patrick PC-761
PC762 = 1955-62 Don Wingfield PC762
PC765 = 1907 Cubs A.C. Dietsche Postcards PC765
PC765 = 1907-09 Tigers A.C. Dietsche Postcards PC765
PC768 = 1962 H.F. Gardner Sports Stars PC768
PC770 = 1908 American League Publishing Co. PC770
PC773-1= 1909-10 Tigers Topping and Company PC773-1
PC773-2= 1909-11 Tigers H.M. Taylor PC773-2
PC773-1= 1909 Tigers Topping and Company PC773-1
PC775 = 1907 Cubs G.F. Grignon Co. PC775
PC782 = 1905 Rotograph Co. PC782
PC783 = 1946 Sears-East St. Louis PC783
PC785 = 1905 Souvenir Postcard Shop of Cleveland PC785
PC786 = 1939 Orcajo Photo Art PC786
PC796 = 1910 Sepia Anon PC796
PE4 = 1898 Cameo Pepsin Pins PE4
PM1 = 1910 Ornate Oval Pins PM1
PM8 = 1938 Our National Game Pins PM8
PR1 = 1938 Baseball Tabs PR1
PR2 = 1932-34 Orbit Pins Numbered PR2
PR3 = 1932-34 Orbit Pins Unnumbered PR3
PR4 = 1933 Cracker Jack Pins PR4
PT2 = 1910 Luxello Cigars Pins PT2
PX3 = 1933 Doubleheader Discs PX3
PX7 = 1910 Domino Discs PX7
PM8 = 1939 Our National Game Pins PM8
R300 = 1933 George C. Miller R300
R301 = 1936 Overland Candy R301
R302-1 = 1943 MP and Co. R302-1
R302-2 = 1949 MP and Co. R302-2
R305 = 1933 Tatoo Orbit R305
R308 = 1933 Tatoo Orbit Self Develop R308
R309-1 = 1934 Goudey Premiums R309-1
R309-2 = 1935 Goudey Premiums R309-2
R310 = 1934 Butterfinger R310
R313 = 1936 National Chicle Fine Pens R313
R313A = 1935 Gold Medal Flour R313A
R314 = 1936 Goudey Wide Pens R314
R315 = 1928 Portraits and Action R315
R316 = 1929 Portraits and Action R316
R318 = 1934-36 Batter-Up R318
R319 = 1933 Goudey R319
R320 = 1934 Goudey R320
R321 = 1935 Goudey Puzzle R321
R322 = 1936 Goudey B/W R322
R323 = 1938 Goudey Heads Up R323
R324 = 1941 Goudey R324
R325 = 1937 Goudey Knot Hole R325
R326 = 1937 Goudey Flip Movies R326
R327 = 1934-36 Diamond Stars R327
R328 = 1932 U.S. Caramel R328
R330 = 1941 Double Play R330
R332 = 1930 Schutter-Johnson R332
R333 = 1933 Delong R333
R334 = 1939 Play Ball R334
R335 = 1940 Play Ball R335
R336 = 1941 Play Ball R336
R338 = 1933 Sport Kings R338
R342 = 1937 Goudey Thum Movies R342
R344 = 1936 National Chicle Maranville Secrets R344
R346 = 1948-49 Blue Tint R346
T3 = 1911 Turkey Red T3
T200 = 1913 Fatima T200
T201 = 1911 Mecca Double Folders T201
T202 = 1912 Hassan Triple Folders T202
T203 = 1910 Baseball Comics T203
T204 = 1909 Ramly T204
T208 = 1912 1911 A's Fireside T208
T209 = 1910 Contentnea T209 (minors)
T210 = 1910 Old Mill T210 (minors)
T211 = 1910 Red Sun T211 (minors)
T212 = 1909-11 Obak T212 (minors)
T214 = 1915 Victory T214
T215 = 1910-13 Red Cross T215
T216 = 1910-14 People's T216
T222 = 1914 Fatima Players T222
T330-2 = 1914 Piedmont Stamps T330-2

V61 = 1921 Neilson's V61
V89 = 1922 William Paterson V89
V94 = 1933 Butterfinger Canadian V94
V100 = 1923 Willards Chocolates V100
V117 = 1923 Maple Crispette V117
V300 = 1937 O-Pee-Chee Batter Ups V300
V351-A = 1939 World Wide Gum V351A
V351-B = 1939 World Wide Gum Trimmed Premiums
V353 = 1933 Goudey Canadian V353
V354 = 1934 Goudey Canadian V354
V355 = 1936 World Wide Gum V355
V362 = 1950 World Wide Gum V362
W463-4 = 1934 Exhibits Four-in-One W463-4
W463-5 = 1935 Exhibits Four-in-One W463-5
W463-6 = 1936 Exhibits Four-in-One W463-6
W576 = 1950-56 Callahan HOF W576
W600 = 1911 Sporting Life Cabinets W600
W603 = 1946-49 Sports Exchange W603
W605 = 1955 Robert Gould W605
W711-1 = 1938-39 Cincinnati Orange/Gray W711-1
W711-2 = 1941 Harry Hartman W711-2
W753 = 1941 Browns W753
W754 = 1941 Cardinals W754
WG2 = 1904 Fan Craze AL WG2
WG3 = 1906 Fan Craze NL WG3
WG4 = 1913 Polo Grounds WG4
WG5 = 1913 National Game WG5
WG6 = 1913 Tom Barker WG6
WG7 = 1920 Walter Mails WG7
WG8 = 1936 S and S WG8

Glossary/Legend

Our glossary defines terms used in the card collecting hobby and in this book. Many of these terms are also common to other types of sports memorabilia collecting. Some terms may have several meanings depending on use and context.

ACC - Acronym for American Card Catalog.
ACETATE - A transparent plastic.
ANN- Announcer.
AS - All-Star card. A card portraying an All-Star Player of the previous year that says "All-Star" on its face.
ATG - All-Time Great card.
ATL - All-Time Leaders card.
AU(TO) - Autographed card.
BC - Bonus Card.
BL - Blue letters.
BLANKET - A felt square (normally 5 to 6 inches) portraying a baseball player.
BOX CARD - Card issued on a box (i.e., 1987 Topps Box Bottoms).
BRICK - A group of 50 or more cards having common characteristics that is intended to be bought, sold or traded as a unit.
CABINETS - Popular and highly valuable photographs on thick card stock produced in the 19th and early 20th century.
CHECKLIST - A list of the cards contained in a particular set. The list is always in numerical order if the cards are numbered. Some unnumbered sets are artificially numbered in alphabetical order, by team and alphabetically within the team, or by uniform number for convenience.
CL - Checklist card. A card that lists in order the cards and players in the set or series. Older checklist cards in Mint condition that have not been marked are very desirable and command premiums.
CO - Coach.
COIN - A small disc of metal or plastic portraying a player in its center.
COLLECTOR ISSUE - A set produced for the sake of the card itself with no product or service sponsor. It derives its name from the fact that most of these sets are produced for sale directly to the hobby market.
COM - Card issued by the Post Cereal Company through their mail-in offer.
COMM - Commissioner.
COMMON CARD - The typical card of any set; it has no premium value accruing from subject matter, numerical scarcity, popular demand, or anomaly.
CONVENTION - A gathering of dealers and collectors at a single location for the purpose of buying, selling, and trading sports memorabilia items. Conventions are open to the public and sometimes feature autograph guests, door prizes, contests, seminars, etc. They are frequently referred to simply as "shows."
COOP - Cooperstown.
COR - Corrected card.
COUPON - See Tab.
CY - Cy Young Award.
DEALER - A person who engages in buying, selling, and trading sports collectibles or supplies. A dealer may also be a collector, but as a dealer, his main goal is to earn a profit.
DIECUT - A card with part of its stock partially cut, allowing one or more parts to be folded or removed. After removal or appropriate folding, the remaining part of the card can frequently be made to stand up.
DISC - A circular-shaped card.
DISPLAY CARD - A sheet, usually containing three to nine cards, that is printed and used by the manufacturer to advertise and/or display the packages containing his products and cards. The backs of display cards are blank or contain advertisements.
DK - Diamond King.
DL - Division Leaders.
DP - Double Print (a card that was printed in double the quantity compared to the other cards in the same series) or a Draft Pick card.
DUFEX - A method of card manufacturing technology patented by Pinnacle Brands, Inc. It involves a refractive quality to a card with a foil coating.
EMBOSSED - A raised surface; features of a card that are projected from a flat background.
ERA - Earned Run Average.
ERR - Error card. A card with erroneous information, spelling, or depiction on either side of the card. Most errors are not corrected by the producing card company.
ETCHED - Impressions within the surface of a card.
EXHIBIT - The generic name given to thick-stock, postcard-size cards with single color obverse pictures. The name is derived from the Exhibit Supply Co. of Chicago, the principal manufacturer of this type of card. These also are known as Arcade cards since they were found in many arcades.
FDP - First Draft Pick.
FOIL - Foil embossed stamp on card, or a card printed on pure foil stock.
FOLD - Foldout.

FS - Father/son card.

FULL BLEED - A borderless card; a card containing a photo that encompasses the entire card.

FULL SHEET - A complete sheet of cards that has not been cut up into individual cards by the manufacturer. Also called an uncut sheet.

FUN - Fun Cards.

GL - Green letters.

GLOSS - A card with luster; a shiny finish as in a card with UV coating.

HIGH NUMBER - The cards in the last series of numbers in a year in which such higher-numbered cards were printed or distributed in significantly lesser amounts than the lower-numbered cards. The high-number designation refers to a scarcity of the high-numbered cards. Not all years have high numbers in terms of this definition.

HL - Highlight card.

HOF - Hall of Fame, or a card that portrays a Hall of Famer (HOFer).

HOLOGRAM - A three-dimensional photographic image.

HOR - Horizontal pose on card as opposed to the standard vertical orientation found on most cards.

IA - In Action card.

IF - Infielder.

INSERT - A card of a different type or any other sports collectible (typically a poster or sticker) contained and sold in the same package along with a card or cards of a major set. An insert card is either unnumbered or not numbered in the same sequence as the major set. Sometimes the inserts are randomly distributed and are not found in every pack.

INTERACTIVE - A concept that involves collector participation.

ISSUE - Synonymous with set, but usually used in conjunction with a manufacturer, e.g., a Topps issue.

KARAT - A unit of measure for the fineness of gold; i.e. 24K.

LAYERING - The separation or peeling of one or more layers of the card stock, usually at the corner of the card.

Lenticular - A ribbed plastic creating the illusion of movement or 3-D depth.

LEGITIMATE ISSUE - A set produced to promote or boost sales of a product or service, e.g., bubblegum, cereal, cigarettes, etc. Most collector issues are not legitimate issues in this sense.

LHP - Lefthanded pitcher.

LID - A circular-shaped card (possibly with tab) that forms the top of the container for the product being promoted.

LL - League leaders or large letters on card.

MAJOR SET - A set produced by a national manufacturer of cards containing a large number of cards. Usually 100 or more different cards comprise a major set.

MEM - Memorial card. For example, the 1990 Donruss and Topps Bart Giamatti cards.

METALLIC - A glossy design method that enhances card features.

MG - Manager.

MINI - A small card; for example, a 1975 Topps card of identical design but smaller dimensions than the regular Topps issue of 1975.

ML - Major League.

MULTI-PLAYER CARD - A single card depicting two or more players (but not a team card).

MVP - Most Valuable Player.

NAU - No autograph on card.

NH - No-Hitter.

NNOF - No Name on Front.

NOF - Name on Front.

NON-SPORT CARD - A card from a set whose major theme is a subject other than a sports subject. A card of a sports figure or event that is part of a non-sport set is still a non-sport card, e.g., while the "Look 'N' See" non-sport card set contains a card of Babe Ruth, a sports figure, that card is a non-sport card.

NOTCHING - The grooving of the card, usually caused by fingernails, rubber bands, or bumping card edges against other objects.

OF - Outfield or Outfielder.

OLY - Olympics Card.

ORG - Organist.

P - Pitcher or Pitching pose.

P1 - First Printing.

P2 - Second Printing.

P3 - Third Printing.

PACKS - A means with which cards are issued in terms of pack type (wax, cello, foil, rack, etc.) and channels of distribution (hobby, retail, etc.).

PANEL - An extended card that is composed of two or more individual cards. Often the panel forms the back part of the container for the product being promoted, e.g., a Hostess panel, a Bazooka panel, an Esskay Meat panel.

PARALLEL- A card that is similar in design to its counterpart from a basic set, but offers a distinguishing quality.

PCL - Pacific Coast League.

PF - Profiles.

PLASTIC SHEET - A clear, plastic page that is punched for insertion into a binder (with standard three-ring spacing) containing pockets for displaying cards. Many different styles of sheets exist with pockets of varying sizes to hold the many differing card formats. Also called a display sheet or storage sheet.

PLATINUM - A metallic element used in the process of creating a glossy card.

PR - Printed name on back.

PREMIUM - A card, sometimes on photographic stock, that is purchased or obtained in conjunction with, or redemption for, another card or product. The premium is not packaged in the same unit as the primary item.

PRES - President.

PRISMATIC/PRISM - A glossy or bright design that refracts or disperses light.

PUZZLE CARD - A card whose back contains a part of a picture which, when joined correctly with other puzzle cards, forms the completed picture.

PUZZLE PIECE - A die-cut piece designed to interlock with similar pieces (e.g., early 1980's Donruss).

PVC - Polyvinyl Chloride, a substance used to make many of the popular card display protective sheets. Non-PVC sheets are considered preferable for long-term storage of cards by many.

RARE - A card or series of cards of very limited availability. Unfortunately, "rare" is a subjective term frequently used indiscriminately to hype value. "Rare" cards are harder to obtain than "scarce" cards.

RB - Record Breaker.

REDEMPTION- A program established by multiple card manufacturers that allows collectors to mail in a special card (usually a random insert) in return for special cards, sets or other prizes not available through conventional channels.
REFRACTORS - A card that features a design element which enhances (distorts) its color/appearance through deflecting light.
REGIONAL - A card or set of cards issued and distributed only in a limited geographical area of the country.
REPLICA - An identical copy or reproduction.
REV NEG - Reversed or flopped photo side of the card. This is a major type of error card, but only some are corrected.
RHP - Righthanded pitcher.
ROY - Rookie of the Year.
RP - Relief pitcher.
SA - Super Action card.
SASE - Self-Addressed, Stamped Envelope.
SB - Stolen Bases.
SCARCE - A card or series of cards of limited availability. This subjective term is sometimes used indiscriminately to hype value. "Scarce" cards are not as difficult to obtain as "rare" cards.
SCR - Script name on back.
SD - San Diego Padres.
SEMI-HIGH - A card from the next to last series of a sequentially issued set. It has more value than an average card and generally less value than a high number. A card is not called a semi-high unless the next to last series in which it exists has an additional premium attached to it.
SERIES - The entire set of cards issued by a particular producer in a particular year; e.g., the 1971 Topps series. Also, within a particular set, series can refer to a group of (consecutively numbered) cards printed at the same time; e.g., the first series of the 1957 Topps issue (#1 through #88).
SET - One each of the entire run of cards of the same type produced by a particular manufacturer during a single year. In other words, if you have a complete set of 1976 Topps then you have every card from #1 up to and including #660, i.e., all the different cards that were produced.
SF - Starflics.
SHEEN - Brightness or luster emitted by a card.
SKIP-NUMBERED - A set that has many unissued card numbers between the lowest number in the set and the highest number in the set; e.g., the 1948 Leaf baseball set contains 98 cards skip-numbered from #1 to #168. A major set in which a few numbers were not printed is not considered to be skip-numbered.
SP - Single or Short Print (a card which was printed in lesser quantity compared to the other cards in the same series; see also DP and TP).
SPECIAL CARD - A card that portrays something other than a single player or team; for example, a card that portrays the previous year's statistical leaders or the results from the previous year's World Series.
SS - Shortstop.
STAMP - Adhesive-backed papers depicting a player. The stamp may be individual or in a sheet of many stamps. Moisture must be applied to the adhesive in order for the stamp to be attached to another surface.
STANDARD SIZE - Most modern sports cards measure 2-1/2 by 3-1/2 inches. Exceptions are noted in card descriptions throughout this book.
STAR CARD - A card that portrays a player of some repute, usually determined by his ability, however, sometimes referring to sheer popularity.
STICKER - A card with a removable layer that can be affixed to (stuck onto) another surface.
STOCK - The cardboard or paper on which the card is printed.
STRIP CARDS - A sheet or strip of cards, particularly popular in the 1920s and 1930s, with the individual cards usually separated by broken or dotted lines.
SUPERIMPOSED - To be affixed on top of something, i.e., a player photo over a solid background.
SUPERSTAR CARD - A card that portrays a superstar; e.g., a Hall of Famer or player with strong Hall of Fame potential.
TAB - A card portion set off from the rest of the card, usually with perforations, that may be removed without damaging the central character or event depicted by the card.
TC - Team Checklist.
TEAM CARD - A card that depicts an entire team.
TEST SET - A set, usually containing a small number of cards, issued by a national card producer and distributed in a limited section or sections of the country. Presumably, the purpose of a test set is to test market appeal for a particular type of card.
THREE-DIMENSIONAL (3D) - A visual image that provides an illusion of depth and perspective.
TOPICAL - a subset or group of cards that have a common theme (e.g., MVP award winners).
TP - Triple Print (a card that was printed in triple the quantity compared to the other cards in the same series).
TRANSPARENT - Clear, see through.
TR - Trade reference on card.
TRIMMED A card cut down from its original size.Trimmed cards are undesirable to most collectors.
UDCA - Upper Deck Classic Alumni.
UER - Uncorrected Error.
UMP - Umpire.
UNC - Uncatalogued. In reference to a set that has not been catalogued in the American Card Catalog alpha-numeric listings.
USA - Team USA.
UV - Ultraviolet, a glossy coating used in producing cards.
VAR - Variation card. One of two or more cards from the same series with the same number (or player with identical pose if the series is unnumbered) differing from one another by some aspect, the different feature stemming from the printing or stock of the card. This can be caused when the manufacturer of the cards notices an error in one or more of the cards, makes the changes, and then resumes the print run. In this case there will be two versions or variations of the same card. Sometimes one of the variations is relatively scarce.
VERT - Vertical pose on card.
WAS - Washington National League (1974 Topps).
WC - What's the Call?
WL - White letter on front.
WS - World Series card.
YL - Yellow letters on front
YT - Yellow team name on front.
* - to denote multi-sport sets.

ODDBALL SPECIALIST
"Sets and Singles from College to Pro"
Regionals, Team Issues, Commemorative Sheets, Pins, etc.
Send SASE for listing
29617 N. Waukegan Rd. #103
Lake Bluff, IL 60044
ROBERT ZANZE
(847) 283-8136

BURBANK COINS & SPORTSCARDS
"THE SPORTSCARD SUPERSTORE"
West Coast's Largest Store
Over 4 Million Singles in Number Order
Singles, Inserts, Parallels, Team Sets.
3001 W. Magnolia Blvd.
Burbank, CA 91505
TEL: (818) 843-2600
FAX: (818) 843-8436
Tues-Fri 10-7
Saturday 10-5
Sunday 11-4
Want Lists Welcome
E-Mail: bcs@lainet.com
Internet: http://www.lainet.com/~bcs

NICK PAVLETIC
131 CINDY COURT • LAKE MARY, FL 32746
407-324-5338 • FAX 407-324-5337
ALWAYS BUYING
HIGH QUALITY EARLY MERCHANDISE

ZINDLER'S
Dean & Jennifer Zindler
P.O. Box 1101
Alpharetta, GA 30201
Phone 1-770-410-0021
Fax 1-770-442-8871
BUY/SELL/TRADE

BILL ROSENTHAL
All Sports
Autographs and Memorabilia
Bill Rosenthal
16617 Music Grove Court
Rockville, MD 20853
Telephone & Fax (301) 774-1666

SPORTS MEMORABILIA
BUY - SELL - TRADE
Reflections of Youth
TED ZANIDAKIS
P.O. BOX 4476
Bricktown, NJ 08723
908-349-8556

Dealers... A Business Card Ad in
BECKETT PUBLICATIONS
reaches more collectors than all other card publications combined!
Call (972) 991-6657 and ask for dealer services to get the facts

DAVE & ADAM'S CARD WORLD
2790 Sheridan Drive • Tonawanda, NY 14150
Mon-Sat 1-9pm
★★BUYING★★
Quality Football & Hockey Inserts,
All Unopened Material, SP, Select, Etc.,
Buffalo Bill Team Sets, Inserts, Rookies!!
Call (716) 838-3300

Teletrade Sportscards Auctions
Buy • Sell • Trade
Nationwide exposure
We deal in all sports cards
Everything from T-206's to Topps Finest
27 Main Street, Kingston, NY 12401-5853
(914) 339-2900
Fax: (914) 339-6279
Hours 9-5 EST Weekdays

707 SPORTSCARDS ALWAYS BUYING
875 North Easton Rd. #11P
Doylestown, PA 18901
LEVI BLEAM
(215) 249-0978
Mon.-Fri. 9-5
(215) 230-9080
Fax (215) 230-9082
Specialists in Pre-1970
Stars – Commons – Sets
We do not buy or sell any shiny new cards.
We Carry A Full Line of Allstate Display Cases

SHOEBOX CARDS
Specializing in cards before 1976
22412 Perry Highway
Suite 1A
Zelienople, PA 16063
Ph: (412) 452-8960
Fax: (412) 452-9227
M-F 9:30-5:30
Closed Sat. & Sun.
Send for Our 104 Page Monthly Catalog

Dave's & Alex's Card & Comic Shop
1013 Pecan
McAllen, TX 78501
(210) 682-8891
Fax:(210) 618-5444
TX307
Complete Sets
Traded Sets
Autographed Items
Wax Boxes
Hours: Mon-Fri 10-8, Sat 10-6, Sun 12:30-5:30
★ Buy ★ Sell ★ Trade ★
★ Comics ★ Special Orders
Baseball Cards
Football Cards
Basketball Cards
Pictures • Supplies
Wholesale / Retail Se Habla Español
Now Available • World Cup Soccer Albums

GET CUSTOMIZED PLAYER SEARCHES ONLINE WITH THE BECKWORLD™ INTERACTIVE PRICE GUIDES!

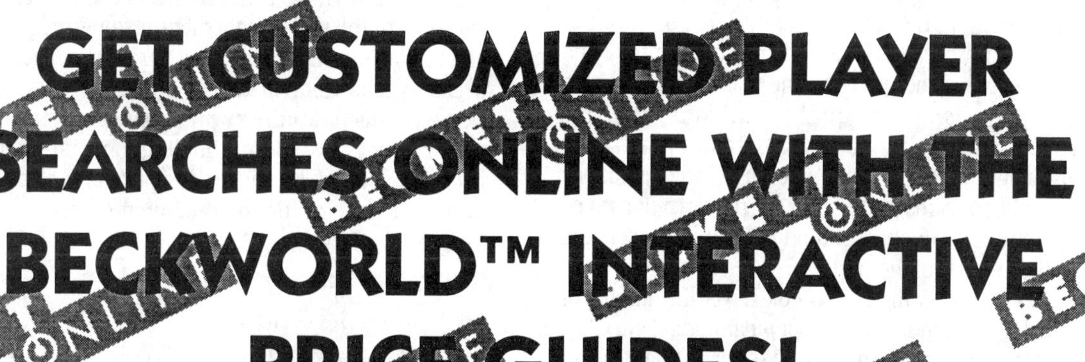

Football, Baseball, Hockey, Basketball, Racing, and Kenner Starting Lineup. Each less than $2 per month!

http://www.beckett.com

Understanding Card Values

Determining Value

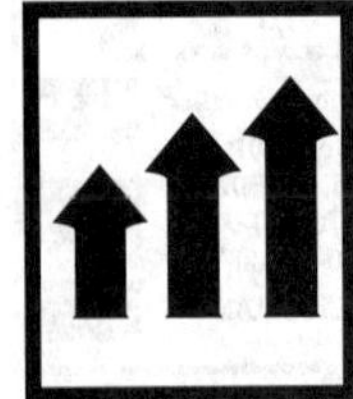

Why are some cards more valuable than others? Obviously, the economic laws of supply and demand are applicable to card collecting just as they are to any other field where a commodity is bought, sold or traded in a free, unregulated market.

Supply (the number of cards available on the market) is less than the total number of cards originally produced since attrition diminishes that original quantity. Each year a percentage of cards is typically thrown away, destroyed or otherwise lost to collectors. This percentage is much, much smaller today than it was in the past because more and more people have become increasingly aware of the value of their cards.

For those who collect only Mint condition cards, the supply of older cards can be quite small indeed. Until recently, collectors were not so conscious of the need to preserve the condition of their cards. For this reason, it is difficult to know exactly how many 1953 Topps are currently available, Mint or otherwise. It is generally accepted that there are fewer 1953 Topps available than 1963, 1973 or 1983 Topps cards. If demand were equal for each of these sets, the law of supply and demand would increase the price for the least available sets. Demand, however, is never equal for all sets, so price correlations can be complicated. The demand for a card is influenced by many factors. These include: (1) the age of the card; (2) the number of cards printed; (3) the player(s) portrayed on the card; (4) the attractiveness and popularity of the set; and (5) the physical condition of the card.

In general, (1) the older the card, (2) the fewer the number of the cards printed, (3) the more famous, popular and talented the player, (4) the more attractive and popular the set, and (5) the better the condition of the card, the higher the value of the card will be. There are exceptions to all but one of these factors: the condition of the card. Given two cards similar in all respects except condition, the one in the best condition will always be valued higher.

While those guidelines help to establish the value of a card, the countless exceptions and peculiarities make any simple, direct mathematical formula to determine card values impossible.

Regional Variation

Since the market varies from region to region, card prices of local players may be higher. This is known as a regional premium. How significant the premium is — and if there is any premium at all — depends on the local popularity of the team and the player.

The largest regional premiums usually do not apply to superstars, who often are so well-known nationwide that the prices of their key cards are too high for local dealers to realize a premium.

Lesser stars often command the strongest premiums. Their popularity is concentrated in their home region, creating local demand that greatly exceeds overall demand.

Regional premiums can apply to popular retired players and sometimes can be found in the areas where the players grew up or starred in college.

A regional discount is the converse of a regional premium. Regional discounts occur when a player has been so popular in his region for so long that local collectors and dealers have accumulated quantities of his key cards. The abundant supply may make the cards available in that area at the lowest prices anywhere.

Set Prices

A somewhat paradoxical situation exists in the price of a complete set vs. the combined cost of the individual cards in the set. In nearly every case, the sum of the prices for the individual cards is higher than the cost for the complete set. This is prevalent especially in the cards of the last few years. The reasons for this apparent anomaly stem from the habits of collectors and from the carrying costs to dealers. Today, each card in a set normally is produced in the same quantity as all other cards in its set.

Many collectors pick up only stars, superstars and particular teams. As a result, the dealer is left with a shortage of certain player cards and an abundance of others. He therefore incurs an expense in simply "carrying" these less desirable cards in stock. On the other hand, if he sells a complete set, he gets rid of large numbers of cards at one time. For this reason, he generally is willing to receive less money for a complete set. By doing this, he recovers all of his costs and also makes a profit.

The disparity between the price of the complete set and the sum of the individual cards also has been influenced by the fact that some of the major manufacturers now are pre-collating card sets. Since "pulling" individual cards from the sets involves a specific type of labor (and cost), the singles or star card market is not affected significantly by pre-collation.

Set prices also do not include rare card varieties, unless specifically stated. Of course, the prices for sets do include one example of each type for the given set, but this is the least expensive variety.

Scarce Series

Scarce series occur because cards issued before 1974 were made available to the public each year in several series of finite numbers of cards, rather than all cards of the set being available for purchase at one time. At some point during the year, usually toward the end of the baseball season, interest in current year baseball cards waned. Consequently, the manufacturers produced smaller numbers of these later-series cards.

Nearly all nationwide issues from post-World War II manufacturers (1948 to 1973) exhibit these series variations. In the past, Topps, for example, may have issued series consisting of many different numbers of cards, including 55, 66, 80, 88 and others. Recently, Topps has settled on what is now its standard sheet size of 132 cards, six of which comprise its 792-card set.

While the number of cards within a given series is usually the same as the number of cards on one printed sheet, this is not always the case. For example, Bowman used 36 cards on its standard printed sheets, but in 1948 substituted 12 cards during later print runs of that year's baseball cards. Twelve of the cards from the initial sheet of 36 cards were removed and replaced by 12 different cards giving, in effect, a first series of 36 cards and a second series of 12 new cards. This replacement produced a scarcity of 24 cards — the 12 cards removed from the original sheet and the 12 new cards added to the sheet. A full sheet of 1948 Bowman cards (second printing) shows that card numbers 37 through 48 have replaced 12 of the cards on the first printing sheet.

The Topps Company also has created scarcities and/or excesses of certain cards in many of its sets. Topps, however, has most frequently gone the other direction by double printing some of the cards. Double printing causes an abundance of cards of the players who are on the same sheet more than one time. During the years from 1978 to 1981, Topps double printed 66 cards out of their large 726-card set. The Topps practice of double printing cards in earlier years is the most logical explanation for the known scarcities of particular cards in some of these Topps sets.

From 1988 through 1990, Donruss short printed and double printed certain cards in its major sets. Ostensibly this was because of its addition of bonus team MVP cards in its regular-issue wax packs.

In recent times several manufactures have started to create contrived scarce series within sets (often under the guise of bronze, silver or gold subsets).

We are always looking for information or photographs of printing sheets of cards for research. Each year, we try to update the hobby's knowledge of distribution anomalies. Please let us know at the address in this book if you have first-hand knowledge that would be helpful in this pursuit.

Grading Your Cards

Each hobby has its own grading terminology — stamps, coins, comic books, record collecting, etc. Collectors of sports cards are no exception. The one invariable criterion for determining the value of a card is its condition: The better the condition of the card, the more valuable it is. Condition grading, however, is subjective. Individual card dealers and collectors differ in the strictness of their grading, but the stated condition of a card should be determined without regard to whether it is being bought or sold.

No allowance is made for age. A 1952 card is judged by the same standards as a 1992 card. But there are specific sets and cards that are condition sensitive (marked with "!" in the Price Guide) because of their border color, consistently poor centering, etc. Such cards and sets sometimes command premiums above the listed percentages in Mint condition.

Centering

Current centering terminology uses numbers representing the percentage of border on either side of the main design. Obviously, centering is diminished in importance for borderless cards such as Stadium Club.

Slightly Off-Center (60/40): A slightly off-center card is one that, upon close inspection, is found to have one border bigger than the opposite border. This degree once was offensive to only purists, but now some hobbyists try to avoid cards that are anything other than perfectly centered.

Off-Center (70/30): An off-center card has one border that is noticeably more than twice as wide as the opposite border.

Badly Off-Center (80/20 or worse): A badly off-center card has virtually no border on one side of the card.

Miscut: A miscut card actually shows part of the adjacent card in its larger border and consequently a corresponding amount of its card is cut off.

Corner Wear

Corner wear is the most scrutinized grading criteria in the hobby. These are the major categories of corner wear:

Corner with a slight touch of wear: The corner still is sharp, but there is a slight touch of wear showing. On a dark-bordered card, this shows as a dot of white.

Fuzzy corner: The corner still comes to a point, but the point has just begun to fray. A slightly "dinged" corner is considered the same as a fuzzy corner.

Slightly rounded corner: The fraying of the corner has increased to where there is only a hint of a point. Mild layering may be evident. A "dinged" corner is considered the same as a slightly rounded corner.

Rounded corner: The point is completely gone. Some layering is noticeable.

Badly rounded corner: The corner is completely round and rough. Severe layering is evident.

Creases

A third common defect is the crease. The degree of creasing in a card is difficult to show in a drawing or picture. On giving the specific condition of an expensive card for sale, the seller should note any creases additionally. Creases can be categorized as to severity according to the following scale:

Light Crease: A light crease is a crease that is barely noticeable upon close inspection. In fact, when cards are in plastic sheets or holders, a light crease may not be seen (until the card is taken out of the holder). A light crease on the front is much more serious than a light crease on the card back only.

Medium Crease: A medium crease is noticeable when held and studied at arm's length by the naked eye, but does not overly detract from the appearance of the card. It is an obvious crease, but not one that breaks the picture surface of the card.

Heavy Crease: A heavy crease is one that has torn or broken through the card's picture surface, e.g., puts a tear in the photo surface.

Alterations

Deceptive Trimming: This occurs when someone alters the card in order (1) to shave off edge wear, (2) to improve the sharpness of the corners, or (3) to improve centering — obviously their objective is to falsely increase the perceived value of the card to an unsuspecting buyer. The shrinkage usually is evident only if the trimmed card is compared to an adjacent full-sized card or if the trimmed card is itself measured.

Obvious Trimming: Obvious trimming is noticeable and unfortunate. It is usually performed by non-collectors who give no thought to the present or future value of their cards.

Deceptively Retouched Borders: This occurs when the borders (especially on those cards with dark borders) are touched up on the edges and corners with magic marker or crayons of appropriate color in order to make the card appear Mint.

Categorization of Defects

Miscellaneous Flaws

The following are common minor flaws that, depending on severity, lower a card's condition by one to four grades and often render it no better than Excellent-Mint: bubbles (lumps in surface), gum and wax stains, diamond cutting (slanted borders), notching, off-centered backs, paper wrinkles, scratched-off cartoons or puzzles on back, rubber band marks, scratches, surface impressions and warping.

The following are common serious flaws that, depending on severity, lower a card's condition at least four grades and often

Centering

Well-centered

Slightly Off-centered

Off-centered

Badly Off-centered

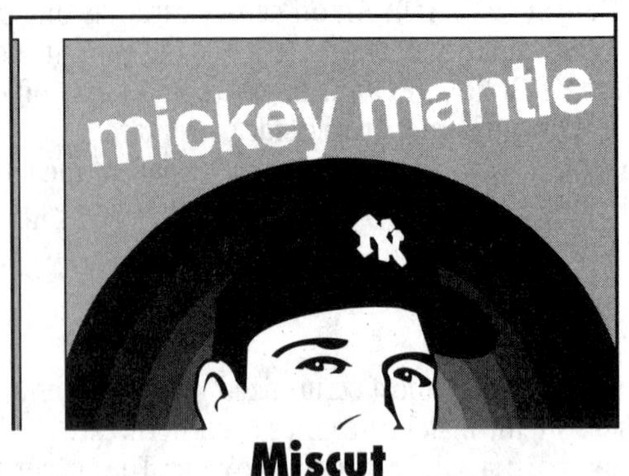

Miscut

Corner Wear

The partial cards shown at right have been photographed at 300%. This was done in order to magnify each card's corner wear to such a degree that differences could be shown on a printed page.

The 1962 Topps Mickey Mantle card definitely has a rounded corner. Some may say that this card is badly rounded, but that is a judgment call.

The 1962 Topps Hank Aaron card has a slighly rounded corner. Note that there is definite corner wear evident by the fraying and that the corner no longer sports a sharp point.

The 1962 Topps Gil Hodges card has corner wear; it is slightly better than the Aaron card above. Nevertheless, some collectors might classify this Hodges corner as slightly rounded.

The 1962 Topps Manager's Dream card showing Mantle and Mays has slight corner wear. This is not a fuzzy corner as very slight wear is noticeable on the card's photo surface.

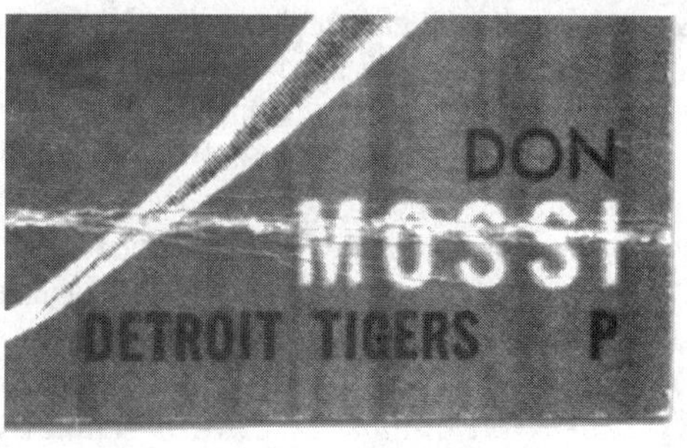

The 1962 Topps Don Mossi card has very slight corner wear such that it might be called a fuzzy corner. A close look at the original card shows the corner is not perfect, but almost. However, note that corner wear is somewhat academic on this card. As you can plainly see, the heavy crease going across his name breaks through the photo surface.

render it no better than Good: chemical or sun fading, erasure marks, mildew, miscutting (severe off-centering), holes, bleached or retouched borders, tape marks, tears, trimming, water or coffee stains and writing.

Condition Guide

Grades

Mint (Mt) - A card with no flaws or wear. The card has four perfect corners, 60/40 or better centering from top to bottom and from left to right, original gloss, smooth edges and original color borders. A Mint card does not have print spots, color or focus imperfections.

Near Mint-Mint (NrMt-Mt) - A card with one minor flaw. Any one of the following would lower a Mint card to Near Mint-Mint: one corner with a slight touch of wear, barely noticeable print spots, color or focus imperfections. The card must have 60/40 or better centering in both directions, original gloss, smooth edges and original color borders.

Near Mint (NrMt) - A card with one minor flaw. Any one of the following would lower a Mint card to Near Mint: one fuzzy corner or two to four corners with slight touches of wear, 70/30 to 60/40 centering, slightly rough edges, minor print spots, color or focus imperfections. The card must have original gloss and original color borders.

Excellent-Mint (ExMt) - A card with two or three fuzzy, but not rounded, corners and centering no worse than 80/20. The card may have no more than two of the following: slightly rough edges, very slightly discolored borders, minor print spots, color or focus imperfections. The card must have original gloss.

Excellent (Ex) - A card with four fuzzy but definitely not rounded corners and centering no worse than 80/20. The card may have a small amount of original gloss lost, rough edges, slightly discolored borders and minor print spots, color or focus imperfections.

Very Good (Vg) - A card that has been handled but not abused: slightly rounded corners with slight layering, slight notching on edges, a significant amount of gloss lost from the surface but no scuffing and moderate discoloration of borders. The card may have a few light creases.

Good (G), Fair (F), Poor (P) - A well-worn, mishandled or abused card: badly rounded and layered corners, scuffing, most or all original gloss missing, seriously discolored borders, moderate or heavy creases, and one or more serious flaws. The grade of Good, Fair or Poor depends on the severity of wear and flaws. Good, Fair and Poor cards generally are used only as fillers.

The most widely used grades are defined above. Obviously, many cards will not perfectly fit one of the definitions.

Therefore, categories between the major grades known as in-between grades are used, such as Good to Very Good (G-Vg), Very Good to Excellent (VgEx), and Excellent-Mint to Near Mint (ExMt-NrMt). Such grades indicate a card with all qualities of the lower category but with at least a few qualities of the higher category.

Beckett Baseball Card Price Guide lists each card and set in three grades, with the middle grade valued at about 40-45% of the top grade, and the bottom grade valued at about 10-15% of the top grade.

The value of cards that fall between the listed columns can also be calculated using a percentage of the top grade. For example, a card that falls between the top and middle grades (Ex, ExMt or NrMt in most cases) will generally be valued at anywhere from 50% to 90% of the top grade.

Similarly, a card that falls between the middle and bottom grades (G-Vg, Vg or VgEx in most cases) will generally be valued at anywhere from 20% to 40% of the top grade.

There are also cases where cards are in better condition than the top grade or worse than the bottom grade. Cards that grade worse than the lowest grade are generally valued at 5-10% of the top grade.

When a card exceeds the top grade by one — such as NrMt-Mt when the top grade is NrMt, or Mint when the top grade is NrMt-Mt — a premium of up to 50% is possible, with 10-20% the usual norm.

When a card exceeds the top grade by two — such as Mint when the top grade is NrMt, or NrMt-Mt when the top grade is ExMt — a premium of 25-50% is the usual norm. But certain condition sensitive cards or sets, particularly those from the pre-war era, can bring premiums of up to 100% or even more.

Unopened packs, boxes and factory-collated sets are considered Mint in their unknown (and presumed perfect) state. Once opened, however, each card can be graded (and valued) in its own right by taking into account any defects that may be present in spite of the fact that the card has never been handled.

Selling Your Cards

Just about every collector sells cards or will sell cards eventually. Someday you may be interested in selling your duplicates or maybe even your whole collection. You may sell to other collectors, friends or dealers. You may even sell cards you purchased from a certain dealer back to that same dealer. In any event, it helps to know some of the mechanics of the typical transaction between buyer and seller.

Dealers will buy cards in order to resell them to other collectors who are interested in the cards. Dealers will always pay a higher percentage for items that (in their opinion) can be resold quickly, and a much lower percentage for those items that are perceived as having low demand and hence are slow moving. In either case, dealers must buy at a price that allows for the expense of doing business and a margin for profit.

If you have cards for sale, the best advice we can give is that you get several offers for your cards — either from card shops or at a card show — and take the best offer, all things considered. Note, the "best" offer may not be the one for the highest amount. And remember, if a dealer really wants your cards, he won't let you get away without making his best competitive offer. Another alternative is to place your cards in an auction as one or several lots.

Many people think nothing of going into a department store and paying $15 for an item of clothing for which the store paid $5. But if you were selling your $15 card to a dealer and he offered you $5 for it, you might consider his mark-up unreasonable. To complete the analogy: Most department stores (and card dealers) that consistently pay $10 for $15 items eventually go out of business. An exception is when the dealer has lined up a willing buyer for the item(s) you are attempting to sell, or if the cards are so Hot that it's likely he'll likely have to hold the cards for just a short period of time.

In those cases, an offer of up to 75 percent of book value still will allow the dealer to make a reasonable profit considering the short time he will need to hold the merchandise. In general, however, most cards and collections will bring offers in the range of 25 to 50 percent of retail price. Also consider that most material from the last five to 10 years is plentiful. If that's what you're selling, don't be surprised if your best offer is well below that range.

Interesting Notes

The first card numerically of an issue is the single card most likely to obtain excessive wear.

Consequently, you typically will find the price on the #1 card (in NrMt or Mint condition) somewhat higher than might otherwise be the case.

Similarly, but to a lesser extent (because normally the less important, reverse side of the card is the one exposed), the last card numerically in an issue also is prone to abnormal wear. This extra wear and tear occurs because the first and last cards are exposed to the elements (human element included) more than any of the other cards. They are generally end cards in any brick formations, rubber bandings, stackings on wet surfaces and like activities.

Sports cards have no intrinsic value. The value of a card, like the value of other collectibles, can be determined only by you and your enjoyment in viewing and possessing these cardboard treasures.

Remember, the buyer ultimately determines the price of each baseball card. You are the determining price factor because you have the ability to say "No" to the price of any card by not exchanging your hard-earned money for a given issue. When the cost of a trading card exceeds the enjoyment you will receive from it, your answer should be "No." We assess and report the prices. You set them!

We are always interested in receiving the price input of collectors and dealers. We happily credit major contributors.

We welcome your opinions, since your contributions assist us in ensuring a better guide each year.

If you would like to join our survey list for the next editions of this book and others authored by Dr. Beckett, please send your name and address to Dr. James Beckett, 15850 Dallas Parkway, Dallas, TX 75248.

History of Baseball Cards

Today's version of the baseball card, with its colorful and oft times high-tech fronts and backs, is a far cry from its earliest predecessors. The issue remains cloudy as to which was the very first baseball card ever produced, but the institution of baseball cards dates from the latter half of the 19th century, more than 100 years ago. Early issues, generally printed on heavy cardboard, were of poor quality, with photographs, drawings, and printing far short of today's standards.

Goodwin & Co., of New York, makers of Gypsy Queen, Old Judge, and other cigarette brands, is considered by many to be the first issuer of baseball and other sports cards. Its issues, predominantly sized 1-1/2 by 2-1/2 inches, generally consisted of photographs of baseball players, boxers, wrestlers, and other subjects mounted on stiff cardboard. More than 2,000 different photos of baseball players alone have been identified. These "Old Judges," a collective name commonly used for the Goodwin & Co. cards, were issued from 1886 to 1890 and are treasured parts of many collections today.

Among the other cigarette companies that issued baseball cards still attracting attention today are Allen & Ginter, D. Buchner & Co. (Gold Coin Chewing Tobacco), and P.H. Mayo & Brother. Cards from the first two companies bear colored line drawings, while the Mayos are sepia photographs on black cardboard. In addition to the small-size cards from this era, several tobacco companies issued cabinet-size baseball cards. These "cabinets" were considerably larger than the small cards, usually about 4-1/4 by 6-1/2 inches, and were printed on heavy stock. Goodwin & Co.'s Old Judge cabinets and the National Tobacco Works' "Newsboy" baseball photos are two that remain popular today.

By 1895, the American Tobacco Company began to dominate its competition. They discontinued baseball card inserts in their cigarette packages (actually slide boxes in those days). The lack of competition in the cigarette market had made these inserts unnecessary. This marked the end of the first era of baseball cards. At the dawn of the 20th century, few baseball cards were being issued. But once again, it was the cigarette companies — particularly, the American Tobacco Company — followed to a lesser extent by the candy and gum makers that revived the practice of including baseball cards with their products. The bulk of these cards, identified in the American Card Catalog (designated hereafter as ACC) as T or E cards for 20th century "Tobacco" or "Early Candy and Gum" issues, respectively, were released from 1909 to 1915.

This romantic and popular era of baseball card collecting produced many desirable items. The most outstanding is the fabled T-206 Honus Wagner card. Other perennial favorites among collectors are the T-206 Eddie Plank card, and the T-206 Magee error card. The former was once the second most valuable card and only recently relinquished that position to a more distinctive and aesthetically pleasing Napoleon Lajoie card from the 1933-34 Goudey Gum series. The latter misspells the player's name as "Magie," the most famous and most valuable blooper card.

The ingenuity and distinctiveness of this era has yet to be surpassed. Highlights include:

- the T-202 Hassan triple-folders, one of the best looking and the most distinctive cards ever issued;
- the durable T-201 Mecca double-folders, one of the first sets with players' records on the reverse;
- the T-3 Turkey Reds, the hobby's most popular cabinet card;
- the E-145 Cracker Jacks, the only major set containing Federal League player cards;
- the T-204 Ramlys, with their distinctive black-and-white oval photos and ornate gold borders.

These are but a few of the varieties issued during this period.

Increasing Popularity

While the American Tobacco Company dominated the field, several other tobacco companies, as well as clothing manufacturers, newspapers and periodicals, game makers, and companies whose identities remain anonymous, also issued cards during this period. In fact, the Collins-McCarthy Candy Company, makers of Zeenuts Pacific Coast League baseball cards, issued cards yearly from 1911 to 1938. Its record for continuous annual card production has been exceeded only by the Topps Chewing Gum Company. The era of the tobacco card issues closed with the onset of World War I, with the exception of the Red Man chewing tobacco sets produced from 1952 to 1955.

The next flurry of card issues broke out in the roaring and prosperous 1920s, the era of the E card. The caramel companies (National Caramel, American Caramel, York Caramel) were the leading distributors of these E cards. In addition, the strip card, a continous strip with several cards divided by dotted lines or other sectioning features, flourished during this time. While the E cards and the strip cards generally are considered less imaginative than the T cards or the recent candy and gum issues, they still are pursued by many advanced collectors.

Another significant event of the 1920s was the introduction of the arcade card. Taking its designation from its issuer, the Exhibit Supply Company of Chicago, it is usually known as the "Exhibit" card. Once a trademark of the penny arcades, amusement parks and county fairs across the country, Exhibit machines dispensed nearly postcard-size photos on thick stock for one penny. These picture cards bore likenesses of a favorite cowboy, actor, actress or baseball player. Exhibit Supply and its associated companies produced baseball cards during a longer time span, although discontinuous, than any other manufacturer. Its first cards appeared in 1921, while its last issue was in 1966. In 1979, the Exhibit Supply Company was bought and somewhat revived by a collector/dealer who has since reprinted Exhibit photos of the past.

If the T card period, from 1909 to 1915, can be designated the "Golden Age" of baseball card collecting, then perhaps the "Silver Age" commenced with the introduction of the Big League Gum series of 239 cards in 1933 (a 240th card was added in 1934). These are the forerunners of today's baseball gum cards, and the Goudey Gum Company of Boston is responsible for their success. This era spanned the period from the Depression days of 1933 to America's formal involvement in World War II in 1941.

Goudey's attractive designs, with full-color line drawings on thick card stock, greatly influenced other cards being issued at that time. As a result, the most attractive and popular vintage cards in history were produced in this "Silver Age." The 1933 Goudey Big League Gum series also owes its popularity to the more than 40 Hall of Fame players in the set. These include four cards of Babe Ruth and two of Lou Gehrig. Goudey's reign continued in 1934, when it issued a 96-card set in color, together with the single remaining card from the 1933 series, #106, the Napoleon Lajoie card.

In addition to Goudey, several other bubblegum manufacturers issued baseball cards during this era. DeLong Gum Company issued an extremely attractive set in 1933. National Chicle Company's 192-card "Batter-Up" series of 1934-1936 became the largest die-cut set in card history. In addition, that company offered the popular "Diamond Stars" series during the same period. Other popular sets included the "Tattoo Orbit" set of 60 color cards issued in 1933 and Gum Products' 75-card "Double Play" set, featuring sepia depictions of two players per card.

In 1939, Gum Inc., which later became Bowman Gum, replaced Goudey Gum as the leading baseball card producer. In 1939 and the following year, it issued two important sets of black-and-white cards. In 1939, its "Play Ball America" set consisted of 162 cards. The larger, 240-card "Play Ball" set of 1940 still is considered by many to be the most attractive black-and-white cards ever produced. That firm introduced its only color set in 1941, consisting of 72 cards titled "Play Ball Sports Hall of Fame." Many of these were colored repeats of poses from the black-and-white 1940 series.

In addition to regular gum cards, many manufacturers distributed premium issues during the 1930s. These premiums were printed on paper or photographic stock, rather than card stock. They were much larger than the regular cards and were sold for a penny across the counter with gum (which was packaged separately from the premium). They often were redeemed at the store or through the mail in exchange for the wrappers of previously purchased gum cards, like proof-of-purchase box-top premiums today. The gum premiums are scarcer than the card issues of the 1930s and in most cases no manufacturer's name is present.

World War II brought an end to this popular era of card collecting when paper and rubber shortages curtailed the production of bubblegum baseball cards. They were resurrected again in 1948 by the Bowman Gum Company (the direct descendent of Gum, Inc.). This marked the beginning of the modern era of card collecting.

In 1948, Bowman Gum issued a 48-card set in black and white consisting of one card and one slab of gum in every 1 cent pack. That same year, the Leaf Gum Company also issued a set of cards. Although rather poor in quality, these cards were issued in color. A squabble over the rights to use players' pictures developed between Bowman and Leaf. Eventually Leaf dropped out of the card market, but not before it had left a lasting heritage to the hobby by issuing some of the rarest cards now in existence. Leaf's baseball card series of 1948-49 contained 98 cards, skip numbered to #168 (not all numbers were printed). Of these 98 cards, 49 are relatively plentiful; the other 49, however, are rare and quite valuable.

Bowman continued its production of cards in 1949 with a color series of 240 cards. Because there are many scarce "high numbers," this series remains the most difficult Bowman regular issue to complete. Although the set was printed in color and commands great interest due to its scarcity, it is considered aesthetically inferior to the Goudey and National Chicle issues of the 1930s. In addition to the regular issue of 1949, Bowman also produced a set of 36 Pacific Coast League players. While this was not a regular issue, it still is prized by collectors. In fact, it has become the most valuable Bowman series.

In 1950 (representing Bowman's one-year monopoly of the baseball card market), the company began a string of top quality cards that continued until its demise in 1955. The 1950 series was itself something of an oddity because the low numbers, rather than the traditional high numbers, were the more difficult cards to obtain.

The year 1951 marked the beginning of the most competitive and perhaps the highest quality period of baseball card production. In that year, Topps Chewing Gum Company of Brooklyn entered the market. Topps' 1951 series consisted of two sets of 52 cards each, one set with red backs and the other with blue backs. In addition, Topps also issued 31 insert cards, three of which remain the rarest Topps cards ("Current All-Stars" Konstanty, Roberts and Stanky). The 1951 Topps cards were unattractive and paled in comparison to the 1951 Bowman issues. They were successful, however, and Topps has continued to produce cards ever since.

Intensified Competition

Topps issued a larger and more attractive card set in 1952. This larger size became standard for the next five years. (Bowman followed with larger-size baseball cards in 1953.) This 1952 Topps set has become, like the 1933 Goudey series and the T-206 white border series, the classic set of its era. The 407-card set is a collector's dream of scarcities, rarities, errors and variations. It also contains the first Topps issues of Mickey Mantle and Willie Mays.

As with Bowman and Leaf in the late 1940s, competition over player rights arose. Ensuing court battles occurred between Topps and Bowman. The market split due to stiff competition, and in January 1956, Topps bought out Bowman. (Topps, using the Bowman name, resurrected Bowman as a later label in 1989.) Topps remained essentially unchallenged as the primary producer of baseball cards through 1980. So, the story of major baseball card sets from 1956 through 1980 is by and large the story of Topps' issues. Notable exceptions include the small sets produced by Fleer Gum in 1959, 1960, 1961 and 1963, and the Kellogg's Cereal and Hostess Cakes baseball cards issued to promote their products.

A court decision in 1980 paved the way for two other large gum companies to enter (or reenter, in Fleer's case) the baseball card arena. Fleer, which had last made photo cards in 1963, and the Donruss Company (then a division of General Mills) secured rights to produce baseball cards of current players, thus breaking Topps' monopoly. Each company issued major card sets in 1981 with bubblegum products.

Then a higher court decision in that year overturned the lower court ruling against Topps. It appeared that Topps had regained its sole position as a producer of baseball cards. Undaunted by the revocation ruling, Fleer and Donruss continued to issue cards in 1982 but without bubblegum or any other edible product. Fleer issued its current player baseball cards with "team logo stickers," while Donruss issued its cards with a piece of a baseball jigsaw puzzle.

Sharing the Pie

Since 1981, these three major baseball card producers all have thrived, sharing relatively equal recognition. Each has steadily increased its involvement in terms of numbers of issues per year. To the delight of collectors, their competition has generated novel, and in some cases exceptional, issues of current Major League Baseball players. Collectors also eagerly accepted the debut efforts of Score (1988) and Upper Deck (1989), the newest companies to enter the baseball card producing derby.

Upper Deck's successful entry into the market turned out to be very important. The company's card stock, photography, packaging and marketing gave baseball cards a new standard for quality, and began the "premium card" trend that continues today. The second premium baseball card set to be issued was the 1990 Leaf set, named for and issued by the parent company of Donruss. To gauge the significance of the premium card trend, one need only note that two of the most valuable post-1986 regular-issue cards in the hobby are the 1989 Upper Deck Ken Griffey Jr. and 1990 Leaf Frank Thomas Rookie Cards.

The impressive debut of Leaf in 1990 was followed by Studio, Ultra, and Stadium Club in 1991. Of those, Stadium Club with it's dramatic borderless photo, Un-coated card fronts made the biggest impact. In 1992, Bowman, and Pinnacle joined the premium fray. In 1992, Donruss and Fleer abandoned the traditional 50-cent pack market and instead produced premium sets comparable to (and presumably designed to compete against) Upper Deck's set. Those moves, combined with the almost instantaneous spread of premium cards to the other major team sports cards, serve as strong indicators that premium cards were here to stay. Bowman had been a lower-level product from 1989 to '91.

In 1993, Fleer, Topps and Upper Deck produced the first "super premium" cards with Flair, Finest and SP, respectively. The success of all three products was an indication the baseball card market was headed toward even higher price levels, and that turned out to be the case in 1994 with the introduction of Bowman's Best (a Topps hybrid of prospect-oriented Bowman and the superpremium Finest) and Leaf Limited. Other 1994 debuts included Upper Deck's entry-level Collector's Choice and Pinnacle's hobby-only Select.

Overall, inserts continued to dominate the hobby scene. Specifically, the parallel chase cards first introduced in 1992 with Topps Gold became the latest major hobby trend. Topps Gold was followed by 1993 Finest Refractors (at the time the scarcest insert ever produced and still a landmark set), and the one-per-box Stadium Club First Day Issue.

Of course, the biggest on-field news of 1994 was the owner-provoked players strike that halted the season prematurely. While the baseball card hobby suffered noticeably from the strike, there was no catastrophic market crash as some had feared. However, the strike pulled the plug on a market that was both strong and growing, and contributed to a serious hobby contraction that continues to this day.

By 1995, parallel insert sets were commonplace and had taken on a new complexion: the most popular ones were those that had announced (or at least suspected) print runs of 500 or less, such as Finest Refractors and Select Artist's Proofs.

As competition to sell cards increased, the manufacturers became more creative than ever in 1996. The most notable trend of last year was the influx of certified autograph cards. Donruss/Leaf made the biggest impact with their Leaf Signature Series brand. Despite a sugested retail price of $9.99 per pack, collectors scooped up the product with fervor in search of Frank Thomas and Alex Rodriguez autographs.

Another notable trend was introduced by Topps in their Finest brand. By splitting their 1996 set into three distinct series of bronze, silver and gold cards (each with a differing level of scarcity), Topps managed to bring an element of their own history similar to the scarce vintage high series cards of the 50's, 60's and 70's.

Finally, the last truly noteworthy trend in 1996 was ever-reducing print runs of scarce parallel sets, most notably featured in the 1996 Select Certified brand. That product featured a whopping six different tiers of parallel cards highlighted by the previously unheard of low print run of only 30 complete sets of Mirror Gold parallels.

Super low print runs like these seem to create disparate opinions amongst hobbyists. Some collectors feel confident knowing that the high dollar cards they're buying are guaranteed to be scarce.

Others, however, balk at the contrived nature of the scarcity and the alarming price tags.

Fortunately, the hobby offers collectors a wide variety. As the 1997 releases continue to hit the market, today's collector enjoys more options and higher quality cards than have ever been made available before.

Finding Out More

The above has been a thumbnail sketch of card collecting from its inception in the 1880s to the present. It is difficult to tell the whole story in just a few pages — there are several other good sources of information. Serious collectors should subscribe to at least one of the excellent hobby periodicals. We also suggest that collectors visit their local card shop(s) and also attend a sports collectibles show in their area. Card collecting is still a young and informal hobby. You can learn more about it in either place. After all, smart dealers realize that spending a few minutes teaching beginners about the hobby often pays off in the long run.

Additional Reading

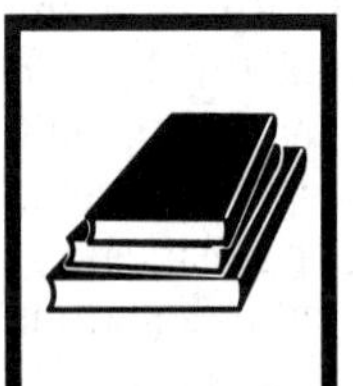

Each year Beckett Publications produces comprehensive annual price guides for each of the four major sports: *Beckett Baseball Card Price Guide, Beckett Basketball Card Price Guide, Beckett Football Card Price Guide, Beckett Hockey Card Price Guide, Beckett Racing Price Guide* and a line of Beckett Alphabetical Checklists Books are being released as well. The aim of these annual guides is to provide information and accurate pricing on a wide array of sports cards, ranging from main issues by the major card manufacturers to various regional, promotional, and food issues. Also alphabetical checklist books are published to assist the collector in identifying all the cards of any particular player. The seasoned collector will find these tools valuable sources of information that will enable him to pursue his hobby interests.

In addition, abridged editions of the Beckett Price Guides have been published for each of the four major sports as part of the House of Collectibles series: *The Official Price Guide to Baseball Cards, The Official Price Guide to Football Cards, The Official Price Guide to Basketball Cards,* and *The Official Price Guide to Hockey Cards.* Published in a convenient mass-market paperback format, these price guides provide information and accurate pricing on all the main issues by the major card manufacturers.

Advertising

Within this Price Guide you will find advertisements for sports memorabilia material, mail order, and retail sports collectibles establishments. All advertisements were accepted in good faith based on the reputation of the advertiser; however, neither the author, the publisher, the distributors, nor the other advertisers in this Price Guide accept any responsibility for any particular advertiser not complying with the terms of his or her ad.

Readers also should be aware that prices in advertisements are subject to change over the annual period before a new edition of this volume is issued each spring. When replying to an advertisement late in the baseball year, the reader should take this into account, and contact the dealer by phone or in writing for up-to-date price information. Should you come into contact with any of the advertisers in this guide as a result of their advertisement herein, please mention this source as your contact.

Prices in this Guide

Prices found in this guide reflect current retail rates just prior to the printing of this book. They do not reflect the FOR SALE prices of the author, the publisher, the distributors, the advertisers, or any card dealers associated with this guide. No one is obligated in any way to buy, sell or trade his or her cards based on these prices. The price listings were compiled by the author from actual buy/sell transactions at sports conventions, sports card shops, buy/sell advertisements in the hobby papers, for sale prices from dealer catalogs and price lists, and discussions with leading hobbyists in the U.S. and Canada. All prices are in U.S. dollars.

Acknowledgments

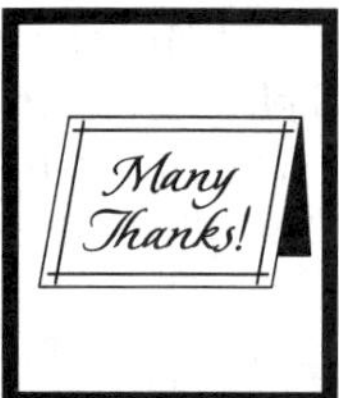

A great deal of diligence, hard work, and dedicated effort went into this year's volume. However, the high standards to which we hold ourselves could not have been met without the expert input and generous amount of time contributed by many people. Our sincere thanks are extended to each and every one of you.

A complete list of these invaluable contributors appears after the Price Guide section.

Work in Progress

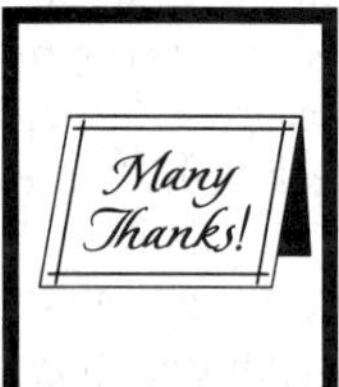

Because we intend the Almanac to be the most comprehensive Price Guide book available, we occasionally include sets with incomplete checklists and/or information. In these cases we have exhausted our resources in an attempt to fill in the missing data but have been unsuccessful. This is where you can help. We always appreciate assistance from our readers to make sure the next edition of this book is even more accurate and more complete. Write to Dr. James Beckett, 15850 Dallas Parkway, Dallas, Texas 75248.

1911 A's Fireside T208

The cards in this 18-card set of color lithographs measure 1 1/2" by 2 5/8"; the cards were marketed in 1911 by Fireside Cigarettes honoring the 1910 World Champion Philadelphia Athletics. This tobacco brand was a product of the Thomas Cullivan Company of Syracuse, New York. The same front designs were also used in the D359 set by Rochester Baking. The players have been alphabetized and numbered for reference in the checklist below since the cards are unnumbered.

	EX-MT	VG-E	GOOD
COMPLETE SET (18)	7500.00	3400.00	950.00
COMMON CARD (1-18)	350.00	160.00	45.00
☐ 1 Frank Baker	500.00	220.00	60.00
☐ 2 Jack Barry	350.00	160.00	45.00
☐ 3 Chief Bender	500.00	220.00	60.00
☐ 4 Eddie Collins	500.00	220.00	60.00
☐ 5 Harry Davis	350.00	160.00	45.00
☐ 6 Jimmy Dygert	350.00	160.00	45.00
☐ 7 Topsy Hartsel	350.00	160.00	45.00
☐ 8 Harry Krause	350.00	160.00	45.00
☐ 9 John Lapp	350.00	160.00	45.00
☐ 10 Paddy Livingston	350.00	160.00	45.00
☐ 11 Bris Lord	350.00	160.00	45.00
☐ 12 Connie Mack MG	1000.00	450.00	125.00
☐ 13 Cy Morgan	350.00	160.00	45.00
☐ 14 Danny Murphy	350.00	160.00	45.00
☐ 15 Rube Oldring	350.00	160.00	45.00
☐ 16 Eddie Plank	1000.00	450.00	125.00
☐ 17 Amos Strunk	350.00	160.00	45.00
☐ 18 Ira Thomas	350.00	160.00	45.00

1955 A's Rodeo Meats

The cards in this 47-card set measure 2 1/2" by 3 1/2". The 1955 Rodeo Meats set contains unnumbered, color cards of the first Kansas City A's team. There are many background color variations noted in the checklist, and the card reverses carry a scrapbook offer. The Grimes and Kryhoski cards listed in the scrapbook album were apparently never issued. The catalog number for this set is F152-1. The cards have been arranged in alphabetical order and assigned numbers for reference.

	NRMT	VG-E	GOOD
COMPLETE SET (47)	4500.00	2000.00	550.00
COMMON CARD (1-47)	75.00	34.00	9.50
☐ 1 Joe Astroth	75.00	34.00	9.50
☐ 2 Harold Bevan	100.00	45.00	12.50
☐ 3 Charles Bishop	100.00	45.00	12.50
☐ 4 Don Bollweg	100.00	45.00	12.50
☐ 5 Lou Boudreau MG	225.00	100.00	28.00
☐ 6 Cloyd Boyer (Salmon)	75.00	34.00	9.50
☐ 7 Cloyd Boyer (Light blue)	125.00	55.00	15.50
☐ 8 Ed Burtschy	150.00	70.00	19.00
☐ 9 Art Ceccarelli	100.00	45.00	12.50
☐ 10 Joe DeMaestri (Yellow)	75.00	34.00	9.50
☐ 11 Joe DeMaestri (Green)	75.00	34.00	9.50
☐ 12 Art Ditmar	75.00	34.00	9.50
☐ 13 John Dixon	100.00	45.00	12.50
☐ 14 Jim Finigan	75.00	34.00	9.50
☐ 15 Marion Fricano	100.00	45.00	12.50
☐ 16 Tom Gorman	75.00	34.00	9.50
☐ 17 John Gray	100.00	45.00	12.50
☐ 18 Ray Herbert	75.00	34.00	9.50
☐ 19 Forrest Jacobs	150.00	70.00	19.00
☐ 20 Alex Kellner	75.00	34.00	9.50
☐ 21 Harry Kraft CO (Craft, sic)	75.00	34.00	9.50
☐ 22 Jack Littrell	75.00	34.00	9.50
☐ 23 Hector Lopez	75.00	34.00	9.50
☐ 24 Oscar Melillo CO	75.00	34.00	9.50
☐ 25 Arnold Portocarrero (Purple)	125.00	55.00	15.50
☐ 26 Arnold Portocarrero (Gray)	75.00	34.00	9.50
☐ 27 Vic Power (Yellow)	75.00	34.00	9.50
☐ 28 Vic Power (Pink)	125.00	55.00	15.50
☐ 29 Vic Raschi	125.00	55.00	15.50
☐ 30 Bill Renna (Lavender)	75.00	34.00	9.50
☐ 31 Bill Renna (Dark pink)	125.00	55.00	15.50
☐ 32 Al Robertson	100.00	45.00	12.50
☐ 33 Johnny Sain	175.00	80.00	22.00
☐ 34 Bobby Schantz ERR (Misspelling)	250.00	110.00	31.00
☐ 35 Bobby Shantz COR	150.00	70.00	19.00
☐ 36 Wilmer Shantz (Orange)	75.00	34.00	9.50
☐ 37 Wilmer Shantz (Lavender)	75.00	34.00	9.50
☐ 38 Harry Simpson	75.00	34.00	9.50
☐ 39 Enos Slaughter	250.00	110.00	31.00
☐ 40 Lou Sleater	75.00	34.00	9.50
☐ 41 George Susce CO	100.00	45.00	12.50
☐ 42 Bob Trice	100.00	45.00	12.50
☐ 43 Elmer Valo (Yellow)	125.00	55.00	15.50
☐ 44 Elmer Valo (Green sky)	90.00	40.00	11.00
☐ 45 Bill Wilson (Yellow)	125.00	55.00	15.50
☐ 46 Bill Wilson (Lavender sky)	75.00	34.00	9.50
☐ 47 Gus Zernial	100.00	45.00	12.50

1956 A's Rodeo Meats

The cards in this 12-card set measure 2 1/2" by 3 1/2". The unnumbered, color cards of the 1956 Rodeo baseball series are easily distinguished from their 1955 counterparts by the absence of the scrapbook offer on the reverse. They were available only in packages of Rodeo All-Meat Wieners. The catalog designation for this set is F152-2, and the cards have been assigned numbers in alphabetical order in the checklist below.

	NRMT	VG-E	GOOD
COMPLETE SET (12)	1200.00	550.00	150.00
COMMON CARD (1-12)	60.00	27.00	7.50
☐ 1 Joe Astroth	60.00	27.00	7.50
☐ 2 Lou Boudreau MG	225.00	100.00	28.00
☐ 3 Joe DeMaestri	60.00	27.00	7.50
☐ 4 Art Ditmar	60.00	27.00	7.50
☐ 5 Jim Finigan	60.00	27.00	7.50
☐ 6 Hector Lopez	60.00	27.00	7.50
☐ 7 Vic Power	60.00	27.00	7.50
☐ 8 Bobby Shantz	125.00	55.00	15.50
☐ 9 Harry Simpson	60.00	27.00	7.50
☐ 10 Enos Slaughter	250.00	110.00	31.00
☐ 11 Elmer Valo	75.00	34.00	9.50
☐ 12 Gus Zernial	75.00	34.00	9.50

1958 A's Jay Publishing

This 12-card set of the Kansas City Athletics measures approximately 5" by 7" and features black-and-white player photos in a white border. These cards were packaged 12 to a packet. The backs are blank. The cards are unnumbered and checklisted below in alphabetical order.

	NRMT	VG-E	GOOD
COMPLETE SET (12)	35.00	16.00	4.40
COMMON CARD (1-12)	3.00	1.35	.35
☐ 1 Harry Craft MG	3.00	1.35	.35
☐ 2 Joe DeMaestri	3.00	1.35	.35
☐ 3 Ned Garver	3.00	1.35	.35
☐ 4 Woody Held	3.00	1.35	.35
☐ 5 Frank House	3.00	1.35	.35
☐ 6 Hector Lopez	3.00	1.35	.35
☐ 7 Vic Power	4.00	1.80	.50
☐ 8 Hal Smith	3.00	1.35	.35
☐ 9 Ralph Terry	3.00	1.35	.35
☐ 10 Virgil Trucks	4.00	1.80	.50
☐ 11 Bill Tuttle	3.00	1.35	.35
☐ 12 Jack Urban	3.00	1.35	.35

1960 A's Jay Publishing

This 11-card set of the Kansas City Athletics measures approximately 5" by 7" and features black-and-white player photos in a white border. These cards were packaged 12 to a packet. The backs are blank. The cards are unnumbered and checklisted below in alphabetical order.

	NRMT	VG-E	GOOD
COMPLETE SET (11)	30.00	13.50	3.70
COMMON CARD (1-11)	2.50	1.10	.30
☐ 1 Hank Bauer	3.00	1.35	.35
☐ 2 Bud Daley	2.50	1.10	.30
☐ 3 Bob Elliott MG	2.50	1.10	.30
☐ 4 Ned Garver	2.50	1.10	.30
☐ 5 Ray Herbert	2.50	1.10	.30
☐ 6 Don Larsen	4.00	1.80	.50
☐ 7 Jerry Lumpe	2.50	1.10	.30
☐ 8 Norm Siebern	2.50	1.10	.30
☐ 9 Marv Throneberry	2.50	1.10	.30
☐ 10 Bill Tuttle	2.50	1.10	.30
☐ 11 Dick Williams	4.00	1.80	.50

1960 A's Team Issue

These 3 1/4" by 5 1/2" blank backed cards feature members of the 1960 A's. The fronts have fascimile autographs and we have sequenced the set in alphabetical order

	NRMT	VG-E	GOOD
COMPLETE SET (18)	35.00	16.00	4.40
COMMON CARD (1-18)	2.50	1.10	.30
☐ 1 Hank Bauer	4.00	1.80	.50
☐ 2 Zeke Bella	2.50	1.10	.30
☐ 3 Bob Cerv	2.50	1.10	.30
☐ 4 Bud Daley	2.50	1.10	.30
☐ 5 Jim Ewell	2.50	1.10	.30
☐ 6 Ken Hamlin	2.50	1.10	.30
☐ 7 Ray Herbert	2.50	1.10	.30
☐ 8 Whitey Herzog	4.00	1.80	.50
☐ 9 Bob Johnson	2.50	1.10	.30
☐ 10 Ken Johnson	2.50	1.10	.30
☐ 11 Johnny Kucks	2.50	1.10	.30
☐ 12 Marty Kutnya	2.50	1.10	.30
☐ 13 Jerry Lumpe	2.50	1.10	.30
☐ 14 Norm Siebern	2.50	1.10	.30
☐ 15 Russ Snyder	2.50	1.10	.30
☐ 16 John Tsitouris	2.50	1.10	.30
☐ 17 Bill Tuttle	2.50	1.10	.30
☐ 18 Dick Williams	4.00	1.80	.50

1961 A's Jay Publishing

This 24-card set of the Kansas City Athletics measures approximately 5" by 7". Originally a 12-card set, updates during the year added more cards. The fronts feature black-and-white posed player photos with the player's and team name printed below in the white border. These cards were packaged 12 to a packet and originally sold for 25 cents. The backs are blank. The cards are unnumbered and checklisted below in alphabetical order.

	NRMT	VG-E	GOOD
COMPLETE SET (24)	50.00	22.00	6.25
COMMON CARD (1-24)	2.00	.90	.25
☐ 1 Jim Archer	2.00	.90	.25
☐ 2 Norm Bass	2.00	.90	.25
☐ 3 Hank Bauer	3.50	1.55	.45
☐ 4 Bob Boyd	2.00	.90	.25
☐ 5 Wayne Causey	3.50	1.55	.45
☐ 6 Frank Cipriani	2.00	.90	.25
☐ 7 Bud Daley	2.00	.90	.25
☐ 8 Joe Gordon MG	3.50	1.55	.45
☐ 9 Ray Herbert	2.00	.90	.25
☐ 10 Dick Howser	3.50	1.55	.45
☐ 11 Manny Jimenez	2.00	.90	.25
☐ 12 Jerry Lumpe (Head photo)	2.00	.90	.25
☐ 13 Jerry Lumpe (At bat)	2.00	.90	.25
☐ 14 Joe Nuxhall	2.00	.90	.25
☐ 15 Joe Pignatano	2.00	.90	.25
☐ 16 Leo Posada	2.00	.90	.25
☐ 17 Ed Rakow	2.00	.90	.25
☐ 18 Norm Siebern (At bat)	2.00	.90	.25
☐ 19 Norm Siebern (Head photo)	2.00	.90	.25
☐ 20 Haywood Sullivan (Waist-up photo)	2.00	.90	.25
☐ 21 Haywood Sullivan Head photo)	2.00	.90	.25
☐ 22 Marv Throneberry	3.50	1.55	.45
☐ 23 Bill Tuttle	2.00	.90	.25
☐ 24 Jerry Walker	2.00	.90	.25

1961 A's Team Issue

These cards measure 3 1/4" by 5 1/2" and are black backs. The fronts have black and white borderless photos with fascimile autographs. We have sequenced this set in alphabetical order.

	NRMT	VG-E	GOOD
COMPLETE SET (21)	35.00	16.00	4.40
COMMON CARD (1-21)	2.00	.90	.25
☐ 1 Bob Boyd	2.00	.90	.25
☐ 2 Andy Carey	2.00	.90	.25
☐ 3 Wayne Causey	2.00	.90	.25
☐ 4 Clint Courtney	2.00	.90	.25
☐ 5 Bud Daley	2.00	.90	.25
☐ 6 Joe Gordon MG	3.00	1.35	.35
☐ 7 Ray Herbert	2.00	.90	.25
☐ 8 Dick Howser	3.00	1.35	.35
☐ 9 Ken Johnson	2.00	.90	.25
☐ 10 Lou Klimchock	2.00	.90	.25
☐ 11 Frank Lane GM	2.00	.90	.25
☐ 12 Don Larsen	4.00	1.80	.50
☐ 13 Jerry Lumpe	2.00	.90	.25
☐ 14 Joe Nuxhall	2.00	.90	.25
☐ 15 Joe Pignatano	2.00	.90	.25
☐ 16 Al Pilarsik	2.00	.90	.25
☐ 17 Leo Posada	2.00	.90	.25
☐ 18 Norm Siebern	2.00	.90	.25
☐ 19 Haywood Sullivan	2.00	.90	.25
☐ 20 Marv Throneberry	2.00	.90	.25
☐ 21 Bill Tuttle	2.00	.90	.25

1963 A's Jay Publishing

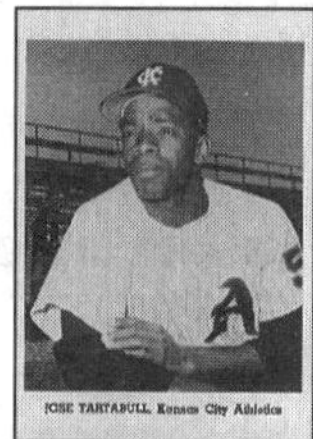

This 12-card set of the Kansas City Athletics measures approximately 5" by 7". The fronts feature black-and-white posed player photos with the player's and team name printed below in the white border. These cards were packaged 12 to a packet. The backs are blank. The cards are unnumbered and checklisted below in alphabetical order.

	NRMT	VG-E	GOOD
COMPLETE SET (12)	25.00	11.00	3.10
COMMON CARD (1-12)	2.00	.90	.25
☐ 1 Jim Archer	2.00	.90	.25
☐ 2 Norm Bass	2.00	.90	.25
☐ 3 Wayne Causey	2.00	.90	.25
☐ 4 Bill Fischer	2.00	.90	.25
☐ 5 Dick Howser	2.50	1.10	.30
☐ 6 Manny Jiminez	2.00	.90	.25
☐ 7 Ed Lopat MG	2.50	1.10	.30
☐ 8 Jerry Lumpe	2.50	1.10	.30
☐ 9 Norm Siebern	2.00	.90	.25
☐ 10 Haywood Sullivan	2.50	1.10	.30
☐ 11 Jose Tartabull	2.00	.90	.25
☐ 12 Jerry Walker	2.00	.90	.25

1964 A's Jay Publishing

This 12-card set of the Kansas City Athletics measures approximately 5" by 7". The fronts feature black-and-white posed player photos with the player's and team name printed below in the white border. These cards were packaged 12 to a packet. The backs are blank. The cards are unnumbered and checklisted below in alphabetical order.

	NRMT	VG-E	GOOD
COMPLETE SET (12)	25.00	11.00	3.10
COMMON CARD (1-12)	2.00	.90	.25

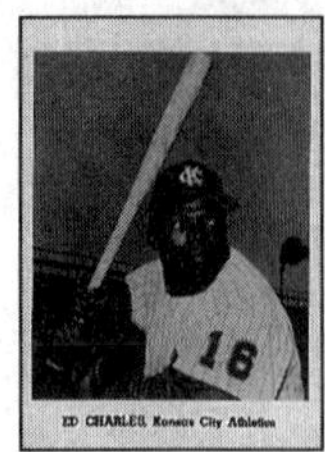

Card	NRMT	VG-E	GOOD
☐ 1 Wayne Causey	2.50	1.10	.30
☐ 2 Ed Charles	2.00	.90	.25
☐ 3 Moe Drabowsky	2.00	.90	.25
☐ 4 Doc Edwards	2.00	.90	.25
☐ 5 Jim Gentile	2.50	1.10	.30
☐ 6 Ken Harrelson	2.50	1.10	.30
☐ 7 Manny Jimenez	2.00	.90	.25
☐ 8 Charlie Lau	2.00	.90	.25
☐ 9 Ed Lopat MG	2.50	1.10	.30
☐ 10 Orlando Pena	2.00	.90	.25
☐ 11 Diego Segui	2.00	.90	.25
☐ 12 Jose Tartabull	2.00	.90	.25

1965 A's Jay Publishing

This 12-card set of the Kansas City Athletics measures approximately 5" by 7". The fronts feature black-and-white posed player photos with the player's and team name printed below in the white border. These cards were packaged 12 to a packet. The backs are blank. The cards are unnumbered and checklisted below in alphabetical order.

	NRMT	VG-E	GOOD
COMPLETE SET (12)	20.00	9.00	2.50
COMMON CARD (1-12)	1.50	.70	.19
☐ 1 Bill Bryan	1.50	.70	.19
☐ 2 Wayne Causey	1.50	.70	.19
☐ 3 Ed Charles	1.50	.70	.19
☐ 4 Doc Edwards	1.50	.70	.19
☐ 5 Jim Gentile	2.50	1.10	.30
☐ 6 Dick Green	1.50	.70	.19
☐ 7 Ken Harrelson	4.00	1.80	.50
☐ 8 Mike Hershberger	1.50	.70	.19
☐ 9 Jim Landis	1.50	.70	.19
☐ 10 Mel McGaha MG	1.50	.70	.19
☐ 11 Wes Stock	1.50	.70	.19
☐ 12 Fred Talbot	1.50	.70	.19

1969 A's Jack in the Box

This 12-card set measures approximately 2 1/16" by 3 5/8" and features black-and-white close-up player photos on a white card face. The player's name and position appears below the picture along with the team name. The backs are blank. The cards are unnumbered and checklisted below in alphabetical order. This set features a card of Joe DiMaggio as an A's coach as well as a card from Reggie Jackson's Rookie Card year. The set is dated by the fact that 1969 was the only year Hank Bauer managed the A's and the only year Tom Reynolds played for the A's.

	NRMT	VG-E	GOOD
COMPLETE SET (12)	60.00	27.00	7.50
COMMON CARD (1-12)	2.50	1.10	.30
☐ 1 Sal Bando	4.00	1.80	.50
☐ 2 Hank Bauer MG	3.50	1.55	.45
☐ 3 Bert Campaneris	3.50	1.55	.45
☐ 4 Danny Cater	2.50	1.10	.30
☐ 5 Joe DiMaggio CO	35.00	16.00	4.40
☐ 6 Chuck Dobson	2.50	1.10	.30
☐ 7 Dick Green	2.50	1.10	.30
☐ 8 Catfish Hunter	10.00	4.50	1.25
☐ 9 Reggie Jackson	20.00	9.00	2.50
☐ 10 Rick Monday	3.50	1.55	.45
☐ 11 Blue Moon Odom	3.50	1.55	.45
☐ 12 Tom Reynolds	2.50	1.10	.30

1976 A's Rodeo Meat Commemorative

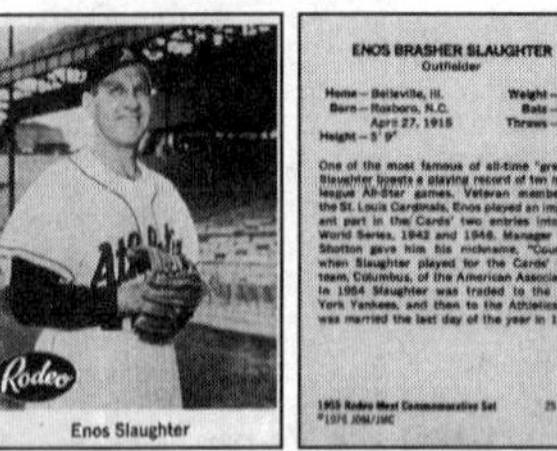

This 30-card standard-sized set commemorates the 1955 Rodeo Meat series. The cards feature posed black-and-white player photos with white borders. The player's name appears in the lower margin. The Rodeo Meat logo is superimposed at the lower left corner of the picture. The backs carry the player's name, biographical information and a player profile. The cards are arranged in alphabetical order and numbered on the back.

	NRMT	VG-E	GOOD
COMPLETE SET (30)	15.00	6.75	1.85
COMMON CARD (1-30)	.50	.23	.06
☐ 1 Title Card	.50	.23	.06
☐ 2 Checklist	.50	.23	.06
☐ 3 Joe Astroth	.50	.23	.06
☐ 4 Lou Boudreau MG	1.00	.45	.12
☐ 5 Cloyd Boyer	1.00	.45	.12
☐ 6 Art Ceccarelli	.50	.23	.06
☐ 7 Harry Craft CO	.50	.23	.06
☐ 8 Joe DeMaestri	.50	.23	.06
☐ 9 Art Ditmar	.75	.35	.09
☐ 10 Jim Finigan	.50	.23	.06
☐ 11 Tom Gorman	.75	.35	.09
☐ 12 Ray Herbert	.50	.23	.06
☐ 13 Alex Kellner	.50	.23	.06
☐ 14 Jack Littrell	.50	.23	.06
☐ 15 Hector Lopez	.75	.35	.09
☐ 16 Oscar Melillo CO	.50	.23	.06
☐ 17 Arnold Portocarrero	.50	.23	.06
☐ 18 Vic Power	.50	.23	.06
☐ 19 Vic Raschi	.75	.35	.09
☐ 20 Bill Renna	.50	.23	.06
☐ 21 John Sain	.75	.35	.09
☐ 22 Bobby Shantz	.75	.35	.09
☐ 23 Wilmer Shantz	.50	.23	.06
☐ 24 Harry Simpson	.50	.23	.06
☐ 25 Enos Slaughter	1.25	.55	.16
☐ 26 Lou Sleator	.50	.23	.06
☐ 27 George Susce CO	.50	.23	.06
☐ 28 Elmer Valo	.75	.35	.09
☐ 29 Bill Wilson	.50	.23	.06
☐ 30 Gus Zernial	.75	.35	.09

1981 A's Granny Goose

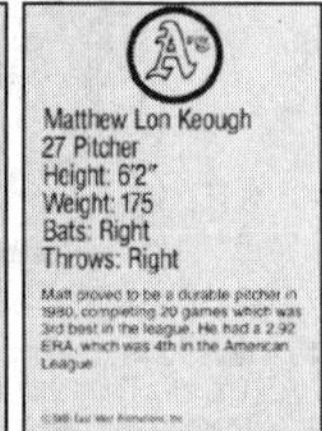

This set is the hardest to obtain of the three years Granny Goose issued cards of the Oakland A's. The Revering card was supposedly destroyed by the printer soon after he was traded away and hence is in shorter supply than the other 14 cards in the set. Wayne Gross is also supposedly available in lesser quantity compared to the other players. The standard-size cards were issued in bags of potato chips. Cards are numbered on the front and back by the player's uniform number.

	NRMT	VG-E	GOOD
COMPLETE SET (15)	75.00	34.00	9.50
COMMON CARD	1.50	.70	.19
☐ 1 Billy Martin MG	10.00	4.50	1.25
☐ 2 Mike Heath	1.50	.70	.19
☐ 5 Jeff Newman	1.50	.70	.19
☐ 6 Mitchell Page	1.50	.70	.19
☐ 8 Rob Picciolo	1.50	.70	.19
☐ 10 Wayne Gross SP	6.00	2.70	.75
☐ 13 Dave Revering SP	35.00	16.00	4.40
☐ 17 Mike Norris	1.50	.70	.19
☐ 20 Tony Armas	2.00	.90	.25
☐ 21 Dwayne Murphy	1.50	.70	.19
☐ 22 Rick Langford	1.50	.70	.19
☐ 27 Matt Keough	1.50	.70	.19
☐ 35 Rickey Henderson	30.00	13.50	3.70
☐ 39 Dave McKay	1.50	.70	.19
☐ 54 Steve McCatty	1.50	.70	.19

1982 A's Granny Goose

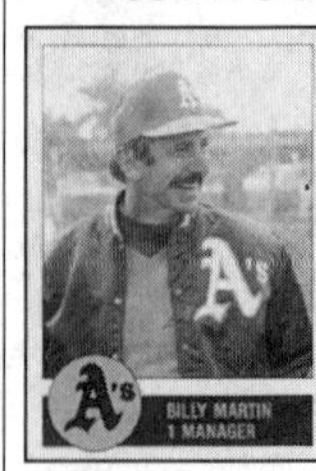

The cards in this 15-card set measure 2 1/2" by 3 1/2". Granny Goose Foods, Inc., a California based company, repeated its successful promotional idea of 1981 by issuing a new set of Oakland A's baseball cards for 1982. Each color player picture is surrounded by white borders and has trim and lettering done in Oakland's green and yellow colors. The cards are, in a sense, numbered according to the uniform number of the player; the card numbering below is according to alphabetical order by name. The card backs carry vital statistics done in black print on a white background. The cards were distributed in packages of potato chips and were also handed out on August 15th at Oakland/Alameda stadium. Although Picciolo was traded, his card was not withdrawn (as was Revering in 1981) and, therefore, its value is no greater than other cards in the set. Blank backs exist for all players; there is no known price differential for these cards.

	NRMT	VG-E	GOOD
COMPLETE SET (15)	15.00	6.75	1.85
COMMON CARD (1-15)	.50	.23	.06
☐ 1 Tony Armas	.75	.35	.09
☐ 2 Wayne Gross	.50	.23	.06
☐ 3 Mike Heath	.50	.23	.06
☐ 4 Rickey Henderson	8.00	3.60	1.00
☐ 5 Cliff Johnson	.75	.35	.09
☐ 6 Matt Keough	.50	.23	.06
☐ 7 Rick Langford	.50	.23	.06
☐ 8 Davey Lopes	1.00	.45	.12
☐ 9 Billy Martin MG	2.50	1.10	.30
☐ 10 Steve McCatty	.50	.23	.06
☐ 11 Dwayne Murphy	.50	.23	.06
☐ 12 Jeff Newman	.50	.23	.06
☐ 13 Mike Norris	.50	.23	.06
☐ 14 Rob Picciolo	.50	.23	.06
☐ 15 Fred Stanley	.50	.23	.06

1983 A's Granny Goose

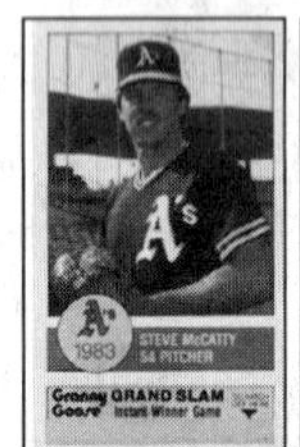

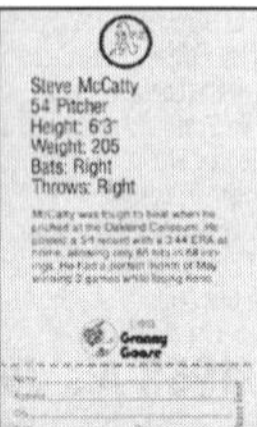

The cards in this 15-card set measure 2 1/2" by 4 1/4". The 1983 Granny Goose Potato Chips set again features Oakland A's players. The cards that were issued in bags of potato chips have a tear off coupon on the bottom with a scratch off section featuring prizes. The grand prize was a World Series trip for two. In addition to their release in bags of potato chips, the Granny Goose cards were also given away (as complete sets with no tabs) to fans attending the Oakland game of July 3, 1983. These give away cards did not contain the coupon on the bottom. Prices listed below are for cards without the detachable tabs that came on the bottom of the cards; cards with tabs intact are valued 50 percent higher than the prices below. The card numbering below is according to uniform number. According to promotional materials, more than one million cards were distributed during the promotion.

	NRMT	VG-E	GOOD
COMPLETE SET (15)	12.00	5.50	1.50
COMMON CARD	.50	.23	.06
☐ 2 Mike Heath	.50	.23	.06
☐ 4 Carney Lansford	1.50	.70	.19
☐ 10 Wayne Gross	.50	.23	.06
☐ 14 Steve Boros MG	.50	.23	.06
☐ 15 Davey Lopes	1.00	.45	.12
☐ 16 Mike Davis	.50	.23	.06
☐ 17 Mike Norris	.50	.23	.06
☐ 21 Dwayne Murphy	.50	.23	.06
☐ 22 Rick Langford	.50	.23	.06
☐ 27 Matt Keough	.50	.23	.06
☐ 31 Tom Underwood	.50	.23	.06
☐ 33 Dave Beard	.50	.23	.06
☐ 35 Rickey Henderson	7.50	3.40	.95
☐ 39 Tom Burgmeier	.50	.23	.06
☐ 54 Steve McCatty	.50	.23	.06

1984 A's Mother's

The cards in this 28-card set measure 2 1/2" by 3 1/2". In 1984, the Los Angeles based Mother's Cookies Co. issued five sets of cards featuring players from major league teams. The Oakland A's set features current players depicted by photos. Similar to the Mother's

Cookies 1952 and 1953 issues, the cards have rounded corners. The backs of the cards contain the Mother's Cookies logo. The cards were distributed in partial sets to fans at the respective stadiums of the teams involved. Whereas 20 cards were given to each patron, a redemption card, redeemable for eight more cards was included. Unfortunately, the eight cards received by redeeming the coupon were not necessarily the eight needed to complete a set. Hobbyist Barry Colla was involved in the production of these sets.

	NRMT	VG-E	GOOD
COMPLETE SET (28)	12.50	5.50	1.55
COMMON CARD (1-28)	.25	.11	.03
☐ 1 Steve Boros MG	.25	.11	.03
☐ 2 Rickey Henderson	5.00	2.20	.60
☐ 3 Joe Morgan	3.00	1.35	.35
☐ 4 Dwayne Murphy	.25	.11	.03
☐ 5 Mike Davis	.25	.11	.03
☐ 6 Bruce Bochte	.25	.11	.03
☐ 7 Carney Lansford	.75	.35	.09
☐ 8 Steve McCatty	.25	.11	.03
☐ 9 Mike Heath	.25	.11	.03
☐ 10 Chris Codiroli	.25	.11	.03
☐ 11 Bill Almon	.25	.11	.03
☐ 12 Bill Caudill	.25	.11	.03
☐ 13 Donnie Hill	.25	.11	.03
☐ 14 Lary Sorensen	.25	.11	.03
☐ 15 Dave Kingman	.75	.35	.09
☐ 16 Garry Hancock	.25	.11	.03
☐ 17 Jeff Burroughs	.25	.11	.03
☐ 18 Tom Burgmeier	.25	.11	.03
☐ 19 Jim Essian	.25	.11	.03
☐ 20 Mike Warren	.25	.11	.03
☐ 21 Davey Lopes	.75	.35	.09
☐ 22 Ray Burris	.25	.11	.03
☐ 23 Tony Phillips	2.00	.90	.25
☐ 24 Tim Conroy	.25	.11	.03
☐ 25 Jeff Bettendorf	.25	.11	.03
☐ 26 Keith Atherton	.25	.11	.03
☐ 27 A's Coaches Ron Schueler Billy Williams Clete Boyer Jackie Moore Bob Didier	.50	.23	.06
☐ 28 A's Checklist Oakland Coliseum	.25	.11	.03

1985 A's Mother's

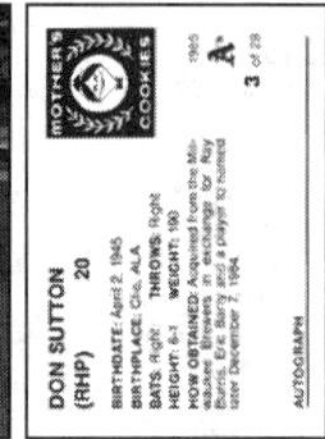

The cards in this 28-card set measure 2 1/2" by 3 1/2". In 1985, the Los Angeles based Mother's Cookies Co. again issued five sets of cards featuring players from major league teams. The Oakland A's set features current players depicted by photos on cards with rounded corners. The backs of the cards contain the Mother's Cookies logo. Cards were passed out at the stadium on July 6.

	NRMT	VG-E	GOOD
COMPLETE SET (28)	10.00	4.50	1.25
COMMON CARD (1-28)	.25	.11	.03
☐ 1 Jackie Moore MG	.25	.11	.03
☐ 2 Dave Kingman	.75	.35	.09
☐ 3 Don Sutton	1.50	.70	.19
☐ 4 Mike Heath	.25	.11	.03
☐ 5 Alfredo Griffin	.25	.11	.03
☐ 6 Dwayne Murphy	.25	.11	.03
☐ 7 Mike Davis	.25	.11	.03
☐ 8 Carney Lansford	.75	.35	.09
☐ 9 Chris Codiroli	.25	.11	.03
☐ 10 Bruce Bochte	.25	.11	.03
☐ 11 Mickey Tettleton	1.50	.70	.19
☐ 12 Donnie Hill	.25	.11	.03
☐ 13 Rob Picciolo	.25	.11	.03
☐ 14 Dave Collins	.25	.11	.03
☐ 15 Dusty Baker	1.00	.45	.12
☐ 16 Tim Conroy	.25	.11	.03
☐ 17 Keith Atherton	.25	.11	.03
☐ 18 Jay Howell	.25	.11	.03

□ 19 Mike Warren	.25	.11	.03
□ 20 Steve McCatty	.25	.11	.03
□ 21 Bill Krueger	.25	.11	.03
□ 22 Curt Young	.25	.11	.03
□ 23 Dan Meyer	.25	.11	.03
□ 24 Mike Gallego	.25	.11	.03
□ 25 Jeff Kaiser	.25	.11	.03
□ 26 Steve Henderson	.25	.11	.03
□ 27 A's Coaches	.50	.23	.06
Clete Boyer			
Bob Didier			
Dave McKay			
Wes Stock			
Billy Williams			
□ 28 A's Checklist	.25	.11	.03
Oakland Stadium			

1986 A's Greats TCMA

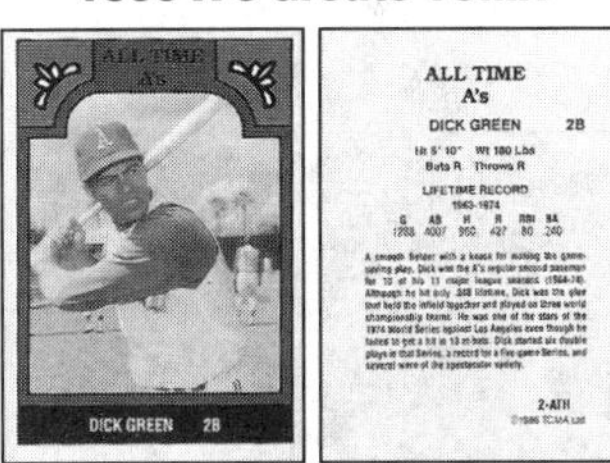

These 12 standard-size cards feature some of the best Oakland A's ever. The fronts feature player photos while the backs have player biographies.

	MINT	NRMT	EXC
COMPLETE SET (12)	5.00	2.20	.60
COMMON CARD (1-12)	.25	.11	.03
□ 1 Gene Tenace	.35	.16	.04
□ 2 Dick Green	.25	.11	.03
□ 3 Bert Campaneris	.50	.23	.06
□ 4 Sal Bando	.50	.23	.06
□ 5 Joe Rudi	.25	.11	.03
□ 6 Rick Monday	.25	.11	.03
□ 7 Billy North	.25	.11	.03
□ 8 Dave Duncan	.25	.11	.03
□ 9 Jim "Catfish" Hunter	1.50	.70	.19
□ 10 Ken Holtzman	.35	.16	.04
□ 11 Rollie Fingers	1.00	.45	.12
□ 12 Alvin Dark MG	.25	.11	.03

1986 A's Mother's

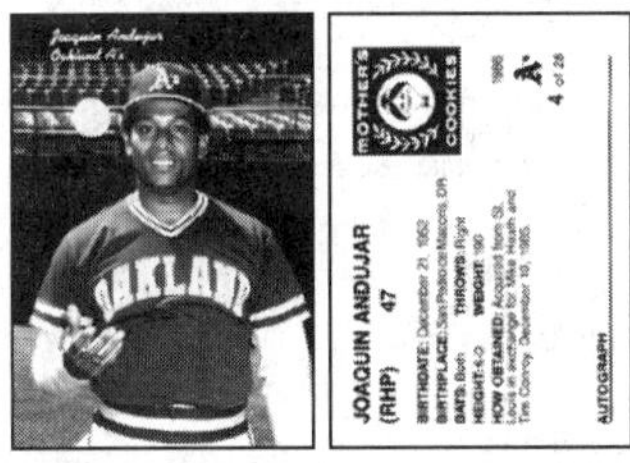

This set consists of 28 full-color, rounded-corner cards each measuring the standard size. Starter sets (only 20 cards but also including a certificate for eight more cards) were given out at the ballpark and collectors were encouraged to trade to fill in the rest of their set. The cards were originally given away on July 20th at Oakland Coliseum. Jose Canseco is featured in his rookie season.

	MINT	NRMT	EXC
COMPLETE SET (28)	18.00	8.00	2.20
COMMON CARD (1-28)	.25	.11	.03
□ 1 Jackie Moore MG	.25	.11	.03
□ 2 Dave Kingman	.75	.35	.09
□ 3 Dusty Baker	1.00	.45	.12
□ 4 Joaquin Andujar	.25	.11	.03
□ 5 Alfredo Griffin	.25	.11	.03
□ 6 Dwayne Murphy	.25	.11	.03
□ 7 Mike Davis	.25	.11	.03
□ 8 Carney Lansford	.75	.35	.09
□ 9 Jose Canseco	10.00	4.50	1.25
□ 10 Bruce Bochte	.25	.11	.03
□ 11 Mickey Tettleton	1.25	.55	.16
□ 12 Donnie Hill	.25	.11	.03
□ 13 Jose Rijo	.50	.23	.06
□ 14 Rick Langford	.25	.11	.03
□ 15 Chris Codiroli	.25	.11	.03
□ 16 Moose Haas	.25	.11	.03
□ 17 Keith Atherton	.25	.11	.03
□ 18 Jay Howell	.25	.11	.03
□ 19 Tony Phillips	1.25	.55	.16
□ 20 Steve Henderson	.25	.11	.03
□ 21 Bill Krueger	.25	.11	.03
□ 22 Steve Ontiveros	.25	.11	.03
□ 23 Bill Bathe	.25	.11	.03
□ 24 Ricky Peters	.25	.11	.03
□ 25 Tim Birtsas	.25	.11	.03
□ 26 A's Trainers and	.25	.11	.03
Equipment Managers			
Frank Ciensczyk			
Steve Vucinich			
Barry Weinberg			
Larry Davis			
□ 27 A's Coaches	.50	.23	.06
Bob Didier			
Dave McKay			
Jeff Newman			
Ron Plaza			
Wes Stock			
Bob Watson			
□ 28 A's Checklist Card	.25	.11	.03
Oakland Coliseum			

1987 A's Mother's

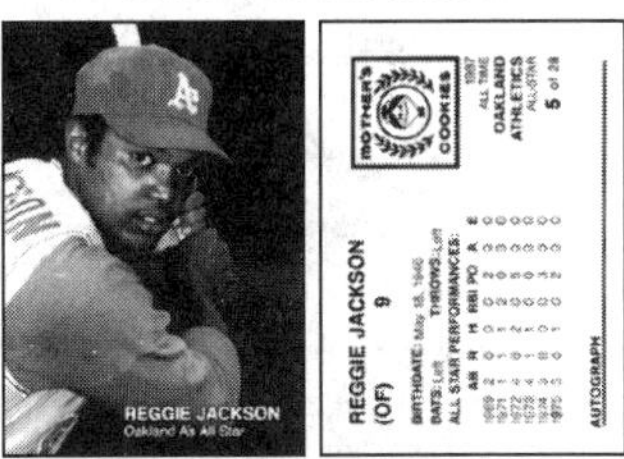

This set consists of 28 full-color, rounded-corner cards each measuring the standard size. Starter sets (only 20 cards but also including a certificate for eight more cards) were given out at the ballpark and collectors were encouraged to trade to fill in the rest of their set. The cards were originally given away on July 5th at Oakland Coliseum during a game against the Boston Red Sox. This set is actually an All-Time All-Star set including every A's All-Star player since 1968 (when the franchise moved to Oakland). The vintage photos (each shot during the year of All-Star appearance) were taken from the collection of Doug McWilliams. The set is sequenced by what year the player first made the All-Star team. The sets were reportedly given out free to the first 25,000 paid admissions at the game.

	MINT	NRMT	EXC
COMPLETE SET (28)	20.00	9.00	2.50
COMMON CARD (1-28)	.25	.11	.03
□ 1 Bert Campaneris	.50	.23	.06
□ 2 Rick Monday	.50	.23	.06
□ 3 John Odom	.25	.11	.03
□ 4 Sal Bando	.50	.23	.06
□ 5 Reggie Jackson	3.00	1.35	.35
□ 6 Jim Hunter	1.50	.70	.19
□ 7 Vida Blue	.75	.35	.09
□ 8 Dave Duncan	.50	.23	.06
□ 9 Joe Rudi	.75	.35	.09
□ 10 Rollie Fingers	1.25	.55	.16
□ 11 Ken Holtzman	.50	.23	.06
□ 12 Dick Williams MG	.25	.11	.03
□ 13 Alvin Dark MG	.25	.11	.03
□ 14 Gene Tenace	.50	.23	.06
□ 15 Claudell Washington	.25	.11	.03
□ 16 Phil Garner	.50	.23	.06
□ 17 Wayne Gross	.25	.11	.03
□ 18 Matt Keough	.25	.11	.03
□ 19 Jeff Newman	.25	.11	.03
□ 20 Rickey Henderson	3.00	1.35	.35
□ 21 Tony Armas	.25	.11	.03
□ 22 Mike Norris	.25	.11	.03
□ 23 Billy Martin MG	1.00	.45	.12
□ 24 Bill Caudill	.25	.11	.03
□ 25 Jay Howell	.25	.11	.03
□ 26 Jose Canseco	4.00	1.80	.50
□ 27 Jose Canseco	3.00	1.35	.35
Reggie Jackson			
□ 28 Checklist Card	.25	.11	.03
A's Logo			

1987 A's Smokey Colorgrams

These cards are actually pages of a booklet featuring members of the Oakland A's and Smokey's fire safety tips. The booklet has 12 pages each containing a black and white photo card (approximately 2 1/2" by 3 3/4") and a black and white player caricature (oversized head) postcard (approximately 3 3/4" by 5 5/8"). The cards are unnumbered but they have biographical information and a fire-prevention cartoon on the back of the card.

	MINT	NRMT	EXC
COMPLETE SET (12)	15.00	6.75	1.85
COMMON CARD (1-12)	.75	.35	.09
□ 1 Joaquin Andujar	.75	.35	.09
□ 2 Jose Canseco	6.00	2.70	.75
□ 3 Mike Davis	.75	.35	.09
□ 4 Alfredo Griffin	.75	.35	.09
□ 5 Moose Haas	.75	.35	.09
□ 6 Jay Howell	.75	.35	.09
□ 7 Reggie Jackson	3.00	1.35	.35
□ 8 Carney Lansford	1.25	.55	.16
□ 9 Dwayne Murphy	.75	.35	.09
□ 10 Tony Phillips	1.25	.55	.16
□ 11 Dave Stewart	1.25	.55	.16
□ 12 Curt Young	.75	.35	.09

1988 A's Mother's

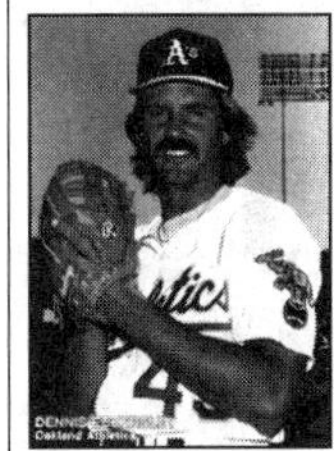

This set consists of 28 full-color, rounded-corner cards each measuring the standard-size. Starter sets (only 20 cards but also including a certificate for eight more cards) were given out at the ballpark and collectors were encouraged to trade to fill in the rest of their set. The cards were originally given away on July 23rd at Oakland Coliseum during a game. Short sets (20 cards plus certificate) were reportedly given out free to the first 35,000 paid admissions at the game.

	MINT	NRMT	EXC
COMPLETE SET (28)	15.00	6.75	1.85
COMMON CARD (1-28)	.25	.11	.03
□ 1 Tony LaRussa MG	1.00	.45	.12
□ 2 Mark McGwire	5.00	2.20	.60
□ 3 Dave Stewart	.75	.35	.09
□ 4 Terry Steinbach	.75	.35	.09
□ 5 Dave Parker	1.00	.45	.12
□ 6 Carney Lansford	.75	.35	.09
□ 7 Jose Canseco	3.00	1.35	.35
□ 8 Don Baylor	.75	.35	.09
□ 9 Bob Welch	.50	.23	.06
□ 10 Dennis Eckersley	2.00	.90	.25
□ 11 Walt Weiss	1.00	.45	.12
□ 12 Tony Phillips	1.00	.45	.12
□ 13 Steve Ontiveros	.25	.11	.03
□ 14 Dave Henderson	.25	.11	.03
□ 15 Stan Javier	.25	.11	.03
□ 16 Ron Hassey	.25	.11	.03
□ 17 Curt Young	.25	.11	.03
□ 18 Glenn Hubbard	.25	.11	.03
□ 19 Storm Davis	.25	.11	.03
□ 20 Eric Plunk	.25	.11	.03
□ 21 Matt Young	.25	.11	.03
□ 22 Mike Gallego	.25	.11	.03
□ 23 Rick Honeycutt	.25	.11	.03
□ 24 Doug Jennings	.25	.11	.03
□ 25 Gene Nelson	.25	.11	.03
□ 26 Greg Cadaret	.25	.11	.03
□ 27 A's Coaches	.50	.23	.06
Dave Duncan			
Rene Lachemann			
Jim Lefebvre			
Dave McKay			
Mike Paul			
Bob Watson			
□ 28 Checklist Card	1.50	.70	.19
Jose Canseco			
Mark McGwire			

1989 A's Mother's

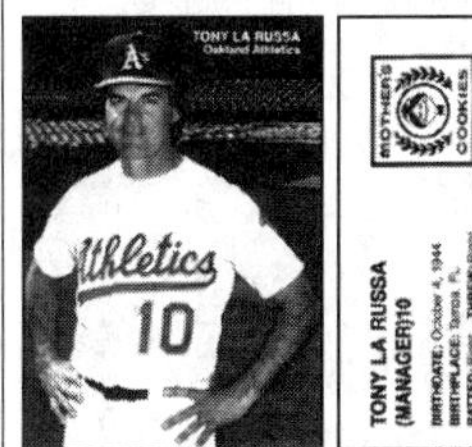

The 1989 Mother's Cookies Oakland A's set contains 28 standard-size cards with rounded corners. The fronts have borderless color photos, and the horizontally oriented backs have biographical information. Starter sets containing 20 of these cards were given away at an A's home game during the 1989 season.

	MINT	NRMT	EXC
COMPLETE SET (28)	15.00	6.75	1.85
COMMON CARD (1-28)	.25	.11	.03
□ 1 Tony LaRussa MG	1.00	.45	.12
□ 2 Mark McGwire	4.00	1.80	.50
□ 3 Terry Steinbach	.75	.35	.09
□ 4 Dave Parker	1.00	.45	.12
□ 5 Carney Lansford	.75	.35	.09
□ 6 Dave Stewart	.75	.35	.09
□ 7 Jose Canseco	2.50	1.10	.30
□ 8 Walt Weiss	.50	.23	.06
□ 9 Bob Welch	.50	.23	.06
□ 10 Dennis Eckersley	1.50	.70	.19
□ 11 Tony Phillips	1.00	.45	.12
□ 12 Mike Moore	.25	.11	.03
□ 13 Dave Henderson	.25	.11	.03
□ 14 Curt Young	.25	.11	.03
□ 15 Ron Hassey	.25	.11	.03
□ 16 Eric Plunk	.25	.11	.03
□ 17 Luis Polonia	.50	.23	.06
□ 18 Storm Davis	.25	.11	.03
□ 19 Glenn Hubbard	.25	.11	.03
□ 20 Greg Cadaret	.25	.11	.03
□ 21 Stan Javier	.25	.11	.03
□ 22 Felix Jose	.25	.11	.03
□ 23 Mike Gallego	.25	.11	.03
□ 24 Todd Burns	.25	.11	.03
□ 25 Rick Honeycutt	.25	.11	.03
□ 26 Gene Nelson	.25	.11	.03
□ 27 A's Coaches	.50	.23	.06
Dave Duncan			
Rene Lachemann			
Art Kusnyer			
Dave McKay			
Tommie Reynolds			
Merv Rettenmund			
□ 28 Checklist Card	1.50	.70	.19
Walt Weiss			
Mark McGwire			
Jose Canseco			

1989 A's Mother's ROY's

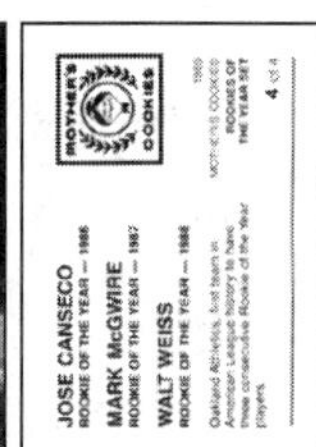

The 1989 Mother's A's ROY's set contains four standard-size cards with rounded corners. The fronts have borderless color photos, and the horizontally oriented backs have biographical information. One card was included in each specially marked box of Mother's Cookies. On the first three cards in the set Rookie of the Year (and year) is mentioned under the player's name.

	MINT	NRMT	EXC
COMPLETE SET (4)	9.00	4.00	1.10
COMMON CARD (1-4)	1.25	.55	.16
□ 1 Jose Canseco	4.00	1.80	.50
1986 ROY			
□ 2 Mark McGwire	3.00	1.35	.35
1987 ROY			
□ 3 Walt Weiss	1.25	.55	.16
1988 ROY			
□ 4 Walt Weiss	3.00	1.35	.35
Mark McGwire			
Jose Canseco			

1989 A's Unocal 76 Pins

These pins were issued by Unocal in conjunction with the Oakland A's. These pins do not feature players, rather they feature symbols or evetnts significant to the A's.

	MINT	NRMT	EXC
COMPLETE SET (5)	15.00	6.75	1.85
COMMON PIN (1-5)	3.00	1.35	.35
□ 1 The Elephant	3.00	1.35	.35
□ 2 Let's Bash	3.00	1.35	.35
□ 3 1988 Western Division	3.00	1.35	.35
Champions			
□ 4 1988 American League	3.00	1.35	.35
Champions			
□ 5 The Pennant	3.00	1.35	.35

1990 A's Mother's

1990 Mother's Cookies Oakland Athletics set contains 28 standard-size cards with rounded corners. The envelope containing the cards honors the 1989 World Championship Oakland Athletics. The A's cards were released at the July 22nd game to the first 35,000 fans to walk through the gates. They were distributed in 20-card random packets at the game and eight more at the redemption booths. However, both groups of cards were random and there was no guarantee of getting a complete set in the cards. The promotional idea was that the only way one could finish the set was to trade for them. The redemption certificates were to be used at the Labor Day San Francisco card show. In addition to this the Mother's Giants cards were also redeemable at that show.

	MINT	NRMT	EXC
COMPLETE SET (28)	11.00	4.90	1.35
COMMON CARD (1-28)	.25	.11	.03
☐ 1 Tony LaRussa MG	.75	.35	.09
☐ 2 Mark McGwire	3.00	1.35	.35
☐ 3 Terry Steinbach	.75	.35	.09
☐ 4 Rickey Henderson	1.50	.70	.19
☐ 5 Dave Stewart	.75	.35	.09
☐ 6 Jose Canseco	2.00	.90	.25
☐ 7 Dennis Eckersley	1.25	.55	.16
☐ 8 Carney Lansford	.75	.35	.09
☐ 9 Mike Moore	.25	.11	.03
☐ 10 Walt Weiss	.50	.23	.06
☐ 11 Scott Sanderson	.25	.11	.03
☐ 12 Ron Hassey	.25	.11	.03
☐ 13 Rick Honeycutt	.25	.11	.03
☐ 14 Ken Phelps	.25	.11	.03
☐ 15 Jamie Quirk	.25	.11	.03
☐ 16 Bob Welch	.50	.23	.06
☐ 17 Felix Jose	.25	.11	.03
☐ 18 Dave Henderson	.25	.11	.03
☐ 19 Mike Norris	.25	.11	.03
☐ 20 Todd Burns	.25	.11	.03
☐ 21 Lance Blankenship	.25	.11	.03
☐ 22 Gene Nelson	.25	.11	.03
☐ 23 Stan Javier	.25	.11	.03
☐ 24 Curt Young	.25	.11	.03
☐ 25 Mike Gallego	.25	.11	.03
☐ 26 Joe Klink	.25	.11	.03
☐ 27 A's Coaches	.50	.23	.06
Rene Lachemann			
Dave Duncan			
Merv Rettenmund			
Tommie Reynolds			
Art Kusnyer			
Dave McKay			
☐ 28 Checklist Card	.25	.11	.03
A's Personnel			
Larry Davis, TR			
Steve Vuchinch,			
Visiting Club Mgr.			
Frank Cienscyk,			
Equipment Mgr.			
Barry Weinberg, TR			

1991 A's Mother's

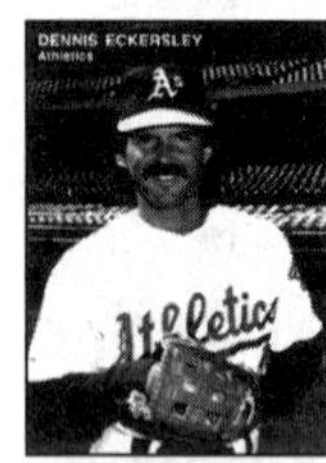

The 1991 Mother's Cookies Oakland Athletics set contains 28 standard-size cards with rounded corners. The set includes an additional card advertising a trading card collectors album. The front design has borderless glossy color player photos from the waist up. The horizontally oriented backs are printed in red and purple, present biographical information, and have blank slots for player autographs.

	MINT	NRMT	EXC
COMPLETE SET (28)	12.00	5.50	1.50
COMMON CARD (1-28)	.25	.11	.03
☐ 1 Tony LaRussa MG	.75	.35	.09
☐ 2 Mark McGwire	2.50	1.10	.30
☐ 3 Terry Steinbach	.75	.35	.09
☐ 4 Rickey Henderson	1.50	.70	.19
☐ 5 Dave Stewart	.75	.35	.09
☐ 6 Jose Canseco	2.00	.90	.25
☐ 7 Dennis Eckersley	1.25	.55	.16
☐ 8 Carney Lansford	.75	.35	.09
☐ 9 Bob Welch	.50	.23	.06
☐ 10 Walt Weiss	.50	.23	.06
☐ 11 Mike Moore	.25	.11	.03
☐ 12 Vance Law	.25	.11	.03
☐ 13 Rick Honeycutt	.25	.11	.03
☐ 14 Harold Baines	.75	.35	.09
☐ 15 Jamie Quirk	.25	.11	.03
☐ 16 Ernest Riles	.25	.11	.03
☐ 17 Willie Wilson	.25	.11	.03
☐ 18 Dave Henderson	.25	.11	.03
☐ 19 Kirk Dressendorfer	.25	.11	.03
☐ 20 Todd Burns	.25	.11	.03
☐ 21 Lance Blankenship	.25	.11	.03
☐ 22 Gene Nelson	.25	.11	.03
☐ 23 Eric Show	.25	.11	.03
☐ 24 Curt Young	.25	.11	.03
☐ 25 Mike Gallego	.25	.11	.03
☐ 26 Joe Klink	.25	.11	.03
☐ 27 Steve Chitren	.25	.11	.03
☐ 28 Checklist Card	.50	.23	.06
Tommie Reynolds CO			
Art Kusnyer CO			
Reggie Jackson CO			
Rick Burleson CO			
Rene Lachemann CO			
Dave Duncan CO			
Dave McKay CO			

1991 A's S.F. Examiner

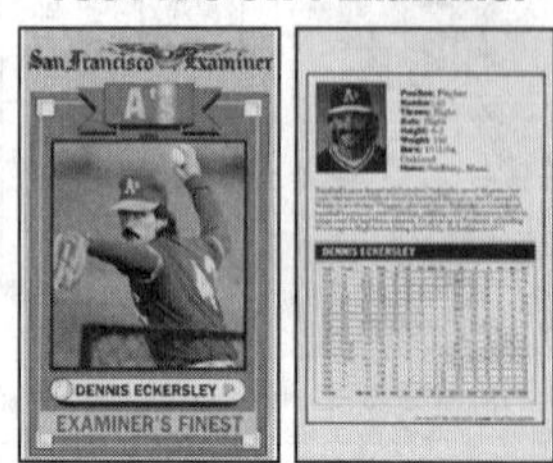

The fifteen 6" by 9" giant-sized cards in this set were issued on yellow cardboard sheets measuring approximately 8 1/2" by 11" and designed for storage in a three-ring binder. The card fronts are green and have color player photos enframed by thin yellow border stripes. The team name appears in a green banner at the top, while the words "Examiner's Finest" appear in a yellow stripe at the bottom of the card. The back has a black and white head shot, biography, career summary, and complete Major League statistics. The cards are unnumbered and checklisted below in alphabetical order.

	MINT	NRMT	EXC
COMPLETE SET (15)	30.00	13.50	3.70
COMMON CARD (1-15)	1.25	.55	.16
☐ 1 Harold Baines	2.00	.90	.25
☐ 2 Jose Canseco	10.00	4.50	1.25
☐ 3 Dennis Eckersley	4.00	1.80	.50
☐ 4 Mike Gallego	1.25	.55	.16
☐ 5 Dave Henderson	1.25	.55	.16
☐ 6 Rickey Henderson	5.00	2.20	.60
☐ 7 Rick Honeycutt	1.25	.55	.16
☐ 8 Mark McGwire	12.50	5.50	1.55
☐ 9 Mike Moore	1.25	.55	.16
☐ 10 Gene Nelson	1.25	.55	.16
☐ 11 Eric Show	1.25	.55	.16
☐ 12 Terry Steinbach	2.00	.90	.25
☐ 13 Dave Stewart	2.50	1.10	.30
☐ 14 Walt Weiss	1.25	.55	.16
☐ 15 Bob Welch	1.50	.70	.19

1992 A's Mother's

This 28-card standard-size set, sponsored by Mother's Cookies, contains borderless posed color player photos of the Oakland Athletics team. The cards have rounded corners. The red and purple backs include biographical information. The set also includes an order-form card for a Mother's Cookies Oakland Athletics collectors album. The album was available for 3.95.

	MINT	NRMT	EXC
COMPLETE SET (28)	10.00	4.50	1.25
COMMON CARD (1-28)	.25	.11	.03
☐ 1 Tony LaRussa MG	.75	.35	.09
☐ 2 Mark McGwire	3.00	1.35	.35
☐ 3 Terry Steinbach	.75	.35	.09
☐ 4 Rickey Henderson	1.50	.70	.19
☐ 5 Dave Stewart	.75	.35	.09
☐ 6 Jose Canseco	2.00	.90	.25
☐ 7 Dennis Eckersley	1.25	.55	.16
☐ 8 Carney Lansford	.75	.35	.09
☐ 9 Bob Welch	.50	.23	.06
☐ 10 Walt Weiss	.50	.23	.06
☐ 11 Mike Moore	.25	.11	.03
☐ 12 Goose Gossage	.75	.35	.09
☐ 13 Rick Honeycutt	.25	.11	.03
☐ 14 Harold Baines	.75	.35	.09
☐ 15 Jamie Quirk	.25	.11	.03
☐ 16 Jeff Parrett	.25	.11	.03
☐ 17 Willie Wilson	.25	.11	.03
☐ 18 Dave Henderson	.25	.11	.03
☐ 19 Joe Slusarski	.25	.11	.03
☐ 20 Mike Bordick	.25	.11	.03
☐ 21 Lance Blankenship	.25	.11	.03
☐ 22 Gene Nelson	.25	.11	.03
☐ 23 Vince Horsman	.25	.11	.03
☐ 24 Ron Darling	.25	.11	.03
☐ 25 Randy Ready	.25	.11	.03
☐ 26 Scott Hemond	.25	.11	.03
☐ 27 Scott Brosius	.50	.23	.06
☐ 28 Checklist	.50	.23	.06
Rene Lachemann CO			
Art Kusnyer CO			
Dave McKay CO			
Tommie Reynolds CO			
Dave Duncan CO			
Doug Rader CO			

1992 A's Unocal 76 Pins

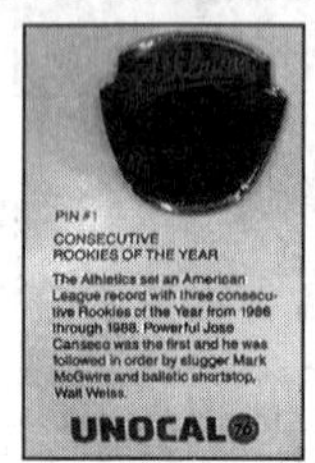

These pins feature important events in the first quarter century of the Oakland A's. Many prominent A's players are pictured on these pins.

	MINT	NRMT	EXC
COMPLETE SET (5)	20.00	9.00	2.50
COMMON PIN (1-5)	4.00	1.80	.50
☐ 1 Jose Canseco	6.00	2.70	.75
Mark McGwire			
Walt Weiss			
Consecutive Rookies			
Of The Year			
☐ 2 Vida Blue	6.00	2.70	.75
Reggie Jackson			
Jose Canseco			
Rickey Henderson			
Athletics MVP's			
☐ 3 Jim "Catfish" Hunter	4.00	1.80	.50
Dave Stewart			
Consecutive 20 Game			
Winners			
☐ 4 Jim "Catfish" Hunter	4.00	1.80	.50
Vida Blue			
Mike Warren			
Dave Stewart			
Oakland No Hitters			
☐ 5 Reggie Jackson	6.00	2.70	.75
Harold Baines			
Dave Henderson			
Three Homers in One Game			

1993 A's Mother's

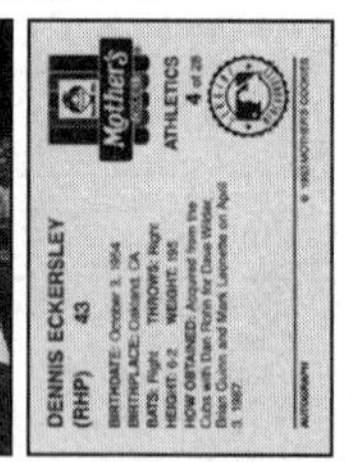

The 1993 Mother's Cookies Athletics set consists of 28 standard-size cards with rounded corners. The fronts display full-bleed color player portraits shot from the waist up in stadium settings. The player's name and team name appear in one of the corners. On a white background in red and purple print, the horizontal backs carry biographical information and the sponsor's logo. A blank slot for the player's autograph rounds out the back.

	MINT	NRMT	EXC
COMPLETE SET (28)	10.00	4.50	1.25
COMMON CARD (1-28)	.25	.11	.03
☐ 1 Tony LaRussa MG	.75	.35	.09
☐ 2 Mark McGwire	2.50	1.10	.30
☐ 3 Terry Steinbach	.75	.35	.09
☐ 4 Dennis Eckersley	1.25	.55	.16
☐ 5 Ruben Sierra	.75	.35	.09
☐ 6 Rickey Henderson	1.50	.70	.19
☐ 7 Mike Bordick	.25	.11	.03
☐ 8 Rick Honeycutt	.25	.11	.03
☐ 9 Dave Henderson	.25	.11	.03
☐ 10 Bob Welch	.50	.23	.06
☐ 11 Dale Sveum	.25	.11	.03
☐ 12 Ron Darling	.25	.11	.03
☐ 13 Jerry Browne	.25	.11	.03
☐ 14 Bobby Witt	.25	.11	.03
☐ 15 Troy Neel	.25	.11	.03
☐ 16 Goose Gossage	.75	.35	.09
☐ 17 Brent Gates	.50	.23	.06
☐ 18 Storm Davis	.25	.11	.03
☐ 19 Scott Hemond	.25	.11	.03
☐ 20 Kelly Downs	.25	.11	.03
☐ 21 Kevin Seitzer	.25	.11	.03
☐ 22 Lance Blankenship	.25	.11	.03
☐ 23 Mike Mohler	.25	.11	.03
☐ 24 Edwin Nunez	.25	.11	.03
☐ 25 Joe Boever	.25	.11	.03
☐ 26 Shawn Hillegas	.25	.11	.03
☐ 27 Coaches Card	.50	.23	.06
Dave McKay			
Dave Duncan			
Tommie Reynolds			
Art Kusnyer			
Greg Luzinski			
☐ 28 Checklist Card	.25	.11	.03
Frank Ciensczyk EQ MG			

1994 A's Mother's

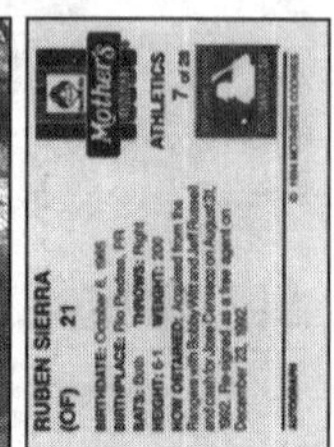

The 1994 Mother's Cookies Athletics set consists of 28 standard-size cards with rounded corners. The fronts display full-bleed color player portraits shot from the waist up against a stadium background. The player's name and team name appear in one of the corners. On a white background in red and purple print, the horizontal backs carry biographical information and the sponsor's logo. A blank slot for the player's autograph rounds out the back.

	MINT	NRMT	EXC
COMPLETE SET (28)	10.00	4.50	1.25
COMMON CARD (1-28)	.25	.11	.03
☐ 1 Tony LaRussa MG	.75	.35	.09
☐ 2 Mark McGwire	2.50	1.10	.30
☐ 3 Terry Steinbach	.75	.35	.09
☐ 4 Dennis Eckersley	1.25	.55	.16
☐ 5 Mike Bordick	.25	.11	.03
☐ 6 Rickey Henderson	1.50	.70	.19
☐ 7 Ruben Sierra	.50	.23	.06
☐ 8 Stan Javier	.25	.11	.03
☐ 9 Todd Van Poppel	.25	.11	.03
☐ 10 Bob Welch	.50	.23	.06
☐ 11 Miguel Jimenez	.25	.11	.03
☐ 12 Steve Karsay	.50	.23	.06
☐ 13 Geronimo Berroa	.50	.23	.06
☐ 14 Bobby Witt	.25	.11	.03
☐ 15 Troy Neel	.25	.11	.03
☐ 16 Ron Darling	.25	.11	.03
☐ 17 Scott Hemond	.25	.11	.03
☐ 18 Steve Ontiveros	.25	.11	.03
☐ 19 Mike Aldrete	.25	.11	.03
☐ 20 Carlos Reyes	.25	.11	.03
☐ 21 Brent Gates	.50	.23	.06
☐ 22 Mark Acre	.25	.11	.03
☐ 23 Eric Helfand	.25	.11	.03
☐ 24 Vince Horsman	.25	.11	.03
☐ 25 Bill Taylor	.25	.11	.03
☐ 26 Scott Brosius	.50	.23	.06
☐ 27 John Briscoe	.25	.11	.03
☐ 28 Checklist/Coaches	.50	.23	.06
Dave Duncan			
Jim Lefebvre			
Carney Lansford			
Tommie Reynolds			
Art Kusnyer			
Dave McKay			

1995 A's CHP

Sponsored by the California Highway Patrol, this eight-card set of the Oakland A's features borderless color action player photos. The backs carry player information and a safety message.

	MINT	NRMT	EXC
COMPLETE SET (8)	15.00	6.75	1.85
COMMON CARD (1-8)	1.00	.45	.12
☐ 1 Brent Gates	1.00	.45	.12
☐ 2 Mark McGwire	7.50	3.40	.95
☐ 3 Geronimo Berroa	1.00	.45	.12
☐ 4 Jason Giambi	2.00	.90	.25
☐ 5 Terry Steinbach	1.50	.70	.19
☐ 6 Mike Bordick	1.50	.70	.19
☐ 7 Todd Van Poppel	1.00	.45	.12
☐ 8 Ariel Prieto	1.00	.45	.12

1995 A's Mother's

The 1995 Mother's Cookies Oakland A's set consists of 30 standard-size cards with rounded corners. The fronts display posed color player portraits in stadium settings. The player's name and team name

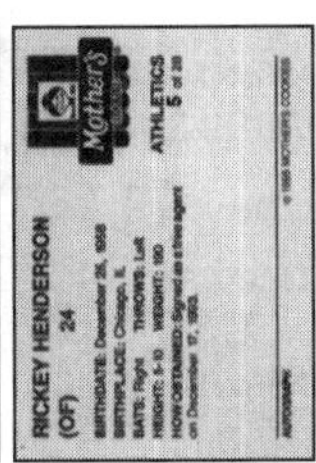

appear in one of the top corners. The backs carry biographical information and the sponsor's logo on a white background in red and purple print. A blank slot for the player's autograph rounds out the back. A special card of Ariel Prieto, as well as a special coupon card, was issued in September as part of Hispanic-American night. The complete set includes the Prieto SP card.

	MINT	NRMT	EXC
COMPLETE SET (30)	20.00	9.00	2.50
COMMON CARD (1-30)	.25	.11	.03
□ 1 Tony LaRussa MG	.75	.35	.09
□ 2 Mark McGwire	2.50	1.10	.30
□ 3 Terry Steinbach	.75	.35	.09
□ 4 Dennis Eckersley	1.25	.55	.16
□ 5 Rickey Henderson	1.50	.70	.19
□ 6 Ron Darling	.25	.11	.03
□ 7 Ruben Sierra	.50	.23	.06
□ 8 Mike Aldrete	.25	.11	.03
□ 9 Stan Javier	.25	.11	.03
□ 10 Mike Bordick	.25	.11	.03
□ 11 Dave Stewart	.75	.35	.09
□ 12 Geronimo Berroa	.50	.23	.06
□ 13 Todd Van Poppel	.25	.11	.03
□ 14 Todd Stottlemyre	.50	.23	.06
□ 15 Eric Helfand	.25	.11	.03
□ 16 Dave Leiper	.25	.11	.03
□ 17 Rick Honeycutt	.25	.11	.03
□ 18 Steve Ontiveros	.25	.11	.03
□ 19 Mike Gallego	.25	.11	.03
□ 20 Carlos Reyes	.25	.11	.03
□ 21 Brent Gates	.50	.23	.06
□ 22 Craig Paquette	.25	.11	.03
□ 23 Mike Harkey	.25	.11	.03
□ 24 Andy Tomberlin	.25	.11	.03
□ 25 Jim Corsi	.25	.11	.03
□ 26 Mark Acre	.25	.11	.03
□ 27 Scott Brosius	.50	.23	.06
□ 28 Coaches/Checklist	.50	.23	.06
Jim Lefebvre			
Tommie Reynolds			
Carney Lansford			
Dave Duncan			
Art Kusnyer			
Dave McKay			
□ 29 Ariel Prieto SP	10.00	4.50	1.25
□ 30 Coupon Card	.25	.11	.03

1996 A's Mother's

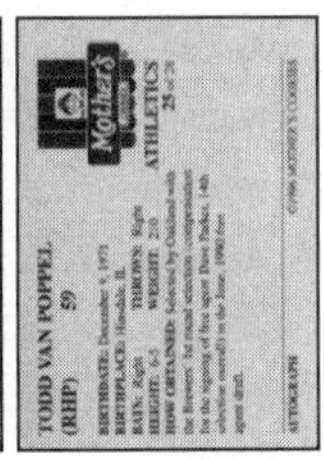

This 28-card set consists of borderless posed color player portraits in stadium settings. The player's and team's names appear in one of the top rounded corners. The backs carry biographical information and the sponsor's logo on a white background in red and purple print. A blank slot for the player's autograph rounds out the back.

	MINT	NRMT	EXC
COMPLETE SET (28)	8.00	3.60	1.00
COMMON CARD (1-28)	.25	.11	.03
□ 1 Art Howe MG	.25	.11	.03
□ 2 Mark McGwire	2.50	1.10	.30
□ 3 Jason Giambi	.75	.35	.09
□ 4 Terry Steinbach	.75	.35	.09
□ 5 Mike Bordick	.25	.11	.03
□ 6 Brent Gates	.25	.11	.03
□ 7 Scott Brosius	.50	.23	.06
□ 8 Doug Johns	.25	.11	.03
□ 9 Jose Herrera	.50	.23	.06
□ 10 John Wasdin	.50	.23	.06
□ 11 Ernie Young	.50	.23	.06
□ 12 Pedro Munoz	.25	.11	.03
□ 13 Steve Wojciechowski	.25	.11	.03
□ 14 Geronimo Berroa	.50	.23	.06
□ 15 Phil Plantier	.25	.11	.03
□ 16 Bobby Chouinard	.25	.11	.03
□ 17 George Williams	.25	.11	.03
□ 18 Jim Corsi	.25	.11	.03
□ 19 Mike Mohler	.25	.11	.03
□ 20 Torey Lovullo	.25	.11	.03
□ 21 Carlos Reyes	.25	.11	.03
□ 22 Buddy Groom	.25	.11	.03
□ 23 Don Wengert	.25	.11	.03
□ 24 Bill Taylor	.25	.11	.03
□ 25 Todd Van Poppel	.25	.11	.03
□ 26 Rafael Bournigal	.25	.11	.03
□ 27 Damon Mashore	.25	.11	.03
□ 28 Coaches Card CL	.25	.11	.03
Bob Cluck			
Brad Fischer			
Duffy Dyer			
Ron Washington			
Bob Alejo			
Denny Walling			

1981 Accel Reggie Jackson

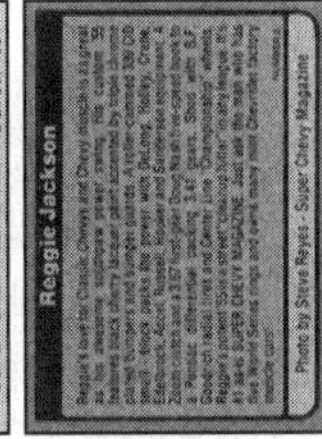

This three-card standard-size set features baseball great Reggie Jackson in front of some of his prize automobiles. The fronts feature Jackson posed with the cars. The backs have details about the cars.

	MINT	NRMT	EXC
COMPLETE SET (3)	15.00	6.75	1.85
COMMON CARD (1-3)	5.00	2.20	.60
□ 1 Reggie Jackson Popular Hot Rodding	5.00	2.20	.60
□ 2 Reggie Jackson Super Chevy Magazine	5.00	2.20	.60
□ 3 Reggie Jackson Hot Rodding	5.00	2.20	.60

1988 Action Packed Test

The 1988 Action Packed Test set contains six standard-size cards with slightly rounded corners. This apparently was the set of cards that Action Packed produced to show their technique to Major League Baseball and the Major League Baseball Players Association in their unsuccessful attempt to seek a baseball card license in 1988. The embossed color player photos on the fronts are bordered in gold. In black lettering, the player's name appears on a gold plaque above the picture, and the team name on a gold plaque beneath the picture. The card backs have the same design as Score issues, with a color head shot, team logo, biography, and major league batting or pitching statistics, again inside a gold border. The face on the front photo of the Ozzie Smith card was apparently considered too dark and thus reportedly not submitted. The cards are unnumbered and checklisted below in alphabetical order.

	MINT	NRMT	EXC
COMPLETE SET (6)	200.00	90.00	25.00
COMMON CARD (1-6)	12.50	5.50	1.55
□ 1 Wade Boggs	25.00	11.00	3.10
□ 2 Andre Dawson	25.00	11.00	3.10
□ 3 Dwight Gooden	25.00	11.00	3.10
□ 4 Carney Lansford	12.50	5.50	1.55
□ 5 Don Mattingly	50.00	22.00	6.25
□ 6 Ozzie Smith SP	75.00	34.00	9.50

1992 Action Packed ASG Prototypes

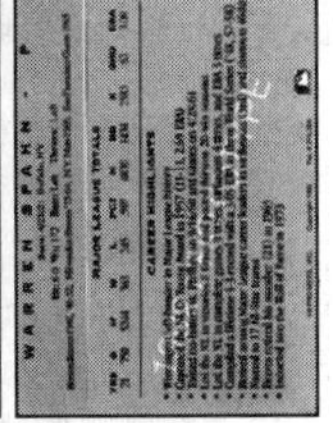

This five-card prototype standard-size set was issued to show the design of the 1992 Action Packed All-Star Gallery regular issue. The prototypes differ from the regular issue in that they are not numbered on the back, and the phrase "1992 Prototype" is printed diagonally in white lettering across the back. The cards are unnumbered and checklisted below in alphabetical order.

	MINT	NRMT	EXC
COMPLETE SET (5)	25.00	11.00	3.10
COMMON CARD (1-5)	4.00	1.80	.50
□ 1 Yogi Berra	7.50	3.40	.95
□ 2 Bob Gibson	4.00	1.80	.50
□ 3 Willie Mays	10.00	4.50	1.25
□ 4 Warren Spahn	4.00	1.80	.50
□ 5 Willie Stargell	4.00	1.80	.50

1992 Action Packed ASG

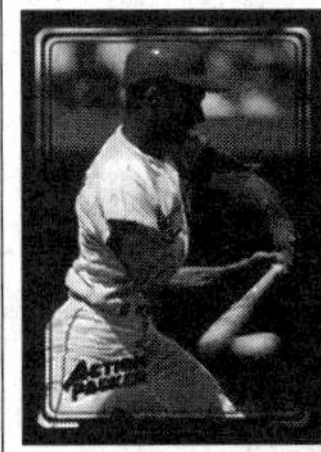
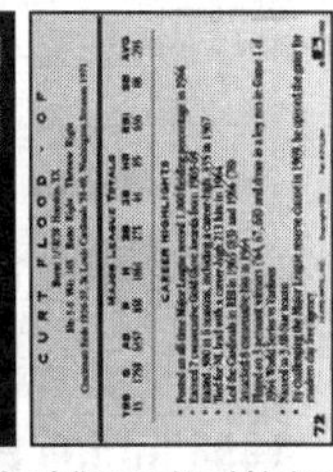

The 1992 Action Packed All-Star Gallery consists of 84 player standard-size cards and pays tribute to former greats of baseball. With the exception of Joe Garagiola, all the players represented appeared in at least one All-Star game. The first 18 cards feature Hall of Famers, and Action Packed guaranteed one Hall of Famer card in each seven-card foil pack. Also 24K gold leaf stamped versions of these Hall of Famer cards were randomly inserted into foil packs. The fronts feature embossed action player photos framed by inner gold border stripes and a black outer border. Most of the photos are color; 13 of them, however, are sepia-toned that have been converted to black and white. On a gray background, the horizontally oriented backs carry biography, career statistics, and a special career highlight section that lists memorable highlights that spanned the players' career.

	MINT	NRMT	EXC
COMPLETE SET (84)	18.00	8.00	2.20
COMMON CARD (1-84)	.25	.11	.03
□ 1 Yogi Berra	1.25	.55	.16
□ 2 Lou Brock	1.00	.45	.12
□ 3 Bob Gibson	1.00	.45	.12
□ 4 Ferguson Jenkins	.75	.35	.09
□ 5 Ralph Kiner	.75	.35	.09
□ 6 Al Kaline	1.00	.45	.12
□ 7 Lou Boudreau	.50	.23	.06
□ 8 Bobby Doerr	.50	.23	.06
□ 9 Billy Herman	.50	.23	.06
□ 10 Monte Irvin	.50	.23	.06
□ 11 George Kell	.50	.23	.06
□ 12 Robin Roberts	.75	.35	.09
□ 13 Johnny Mize	.75	.35	.09
□ 14 Willie Mays	2.50	1.10	.30
□ 15 Enos Slaughter	.50	.23	.06
□ 16 Warren Spahn	.75	.35	.09
□ 17 Willie Stargell	.75	.35	.09
□ 18 Billy Williams	.35	.16	.04
□ 19 Vernon Law	.25	.10	.02
□ 20 Virgil Trucks	.25	.10	.02
□ 21 Mel Parnell	.25	.10	.02
□ 22 Wally Moon	.25	.10	.02
□ 23 Gene Woodling	.25	.10	.02
□ 24 Richie Ashburn	1.00	.45	.12
□ 25 Mark Fidrych	.35	.16	.04
□ 26 Elroy Face	.25	.10	.02
□ 27 Larry Doby	.35	.16	.04
□ 28 Dick Groat	.25	.10	.02
□ 29 Cesar Cedeno	.25	.10	.02
□ 30 Bob Horner	.25	.10	.02
□ 31 Bobby Richardson	.35	.16	.04
□ 32 Bobby Murcer	.35	.16	.04
□ 33 Gil McDougald	.25	.10	.02
□ 34 Roy White	.25	.10	.02
□ 35 Bill Skowron	.35	.16	.04
□ 36 Mickey Lolich	.35	.16	.04
□ 37 Minnie Minoso	.35	.16	.04
□ 38 Bill Pierce	.35	.16	.04
□ 39 Ron Santo	.35	.16	.04
□ 40 Sal Bando	.35	.16	.04
□ 41 Ralph Branca	.35	.16	.04
□ 42 Bert Campaneris	.25	.10	.02
□ 43 Joe Garagiola	.50	.23	.06
□ 44 Vida Blue	.35	.16	.04
□ 45 Frank Crosetti	.50	.23	.06
□ 46 Luis Tiant	.25	.10	.02
□ 47 Maury Wills	.35	.16	.04
□ 48 Sam McDowell	.25	.10	.02
□ 49 Jimmy Piersall	.35	.16	.04
□ 50 Jim Lonborg	.25	.10	.02
□ 51 Don Newcombe	.35	.16	.04
□ 52 Bobby Thomson	.35	.16	.04
□ 53 Wilbur Wood	.25	.10	.02
□ 54 Carl Erskine	.35	.16	.04
□ 55 Chris Chambliss	.25	.10	.02
□ 56 Dave Kingman	.25	.10	.02
□ 57 Ken Holtzman	.25	.10	.02
□ 58 Bud Harrelson	.25	.10	.02
□ 59 Clem Labine	.35	.16	.04
□ 60 Tony Oliva	.35	.16	.04
□ 61 George Foster	.35	.16	.04
□ 62 Bobby Bonds	.35	.16	.04
□ 63 Harvey Haddix	.25	.10	.02
□ 64 Steve Garvey	.35	.16	.04
□ 65 Rocky Colavito	.50	.23	.06
□ 66 Orlando Cepeda	.50	.23	.06
□ 67 Ed Lopat	.35	.16	.04
□ 68 Al Oliver	.35	.16	.04
□ 69 Bill Mazeroski	.35	.16	.04
□ 70 Al Rosen	.35	.16	.04
□ 71 Bob Grich	.35	.16	.04
□ 72 Curt Flood	.35	.16	.04
□ 73 Willie Horton	.35	.16	.04
□ 74 Rico Carty	.25	.10	.02
□ 75 Davey Johnson	.35	.16	.04
□ 76 Don Kessinger	.25	.10	.02
□ 77 Frank Thomas	.25	.10	.02
□ 78 Bobby Shantz	.25	.10	.02
□ 79 Herb Score	.35	.16	.04
□ 80 Boog Powell	.35	.16	.04
□ 81 Rusty Staub	.35	.16	.04
□ 82 Bill Madlock	.35	.16	.04
□ 83 Manny Mota	.25	.10	.02
□ 84 Bill White	.35	.16	.04

1992 Action Packed ASG 24K

The first 18 cards of the 1992 Action Packed All-Star Gallery feature Hall of Famers and were also produced in a 24K version on a limited basis. These 24K gold-leaf stamped versions of these Hall of Famer cards were randomly inserted into foil packs.

	MINT	NRMT	EXC
COMPLETE SET (18)	300.00	135.00	38.00
COMMON CARD (1G-18G)	15.00	6.75	1.85
□ 1G Yogi Berra	40.00	18.00	5.00
□ 2G Lou Brock	25.00	11.00	3.10
□ 3G Bob Gibson	25.00	11.00	3.10
□ 4G Ferguson Jenkins	15.00	6.75	1.85
□ 5G Ralph Kiner	20.00	9.00	2.50
□ 6G Al Kaline	25.00	11.00	3.10
□ 7G Lou Boudreau	15.00	6.75	1.85
□ 8G Bobby Doerr	15.00	6.75	1.85
□ 9G Billy Herman	15.00	6.75	1.85
□ 10G Monte Irvin	15.00	6.75	1.85
□ 11G George Kell	15.00	6.75	1.85
□ 12G Robin Roberts	20.00	9.00	2.50
□ 13G Johnny Mize	20.00	9.00	2.50
□ 14G Willie Mays	50.00	22.00	6.25
□ 15G Enos Slaughter	15.00	6.75	1.85
□ 16G Warren Spahn	20.00	9.00	2.50
□ 17G Willie Stargell	20.00	9.00	2.50
□ 18G Billy Williams	15.00	6.75	1.85

1993 Action Packed ASG

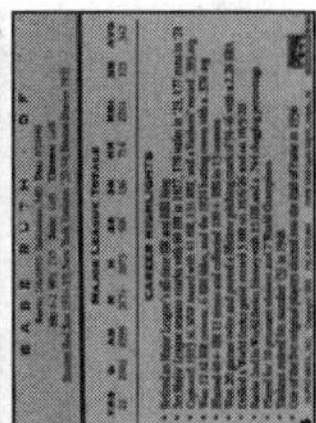

The second series of the Action Packed All-Star Gallery baseball set consists of 84 standard-size cards. Fifty two of the cards are in color, 31 are sepia-tone, and one is a colorized black-and-white. Action Packed included 46 Hall of Famers in the series and guaranteed one of these cards in every pack. Moreover, series II includes randomly inserted 24K cards of these Hall of Famers and contains a card honoring Bud Abbott and Lou Costello, creators of the famous "Who's on First" comedy routine. And as a special bonus for hobby dealers only, each box of cards included two free "Chiptopper" prototype cards of forthcoming Action Packed cards. The fronts feature embossed player photos with gold foil inner border stripes and red outer borders. On a gray background, the horizontal backs carry a biography and career summary.

	MINT	NRMT	EXC
COMPLETE SET (84)	18.00	8.00	2.20
COMMON CARD (85-130)	.50	.23	.06
COMMON CARD (131-168)	.25	.11	.03
□ 85 Cy Young	.75	.35	.09
□ 86 Honus Wagner	1.00	.45	.12
□ 87 Christy Mathewson	1.00	.45	.12
□ 88 Ty Cobb	1.50	.70	.19
□ 89 Eddie Collins	.50	.23	.06
□ 90 Walter Johnson	1.00	.45	.12
□ 91 Tris Speaker	.75	.35	.09
□ 92 Grover Alexander	.75	.35	.09
□ 93 Edd Roush	.50	.23	.06
□ 94 Babe Ruth	2.00	.90	.25
□ 95 Rogers Hornsby	1.00	.45	.12
□ 96 Pie Traynor	.50	.23	.06

☐ 97 Lou Gehrig	1.50	.70	.19
☐ 98 Mickey Cochrane	.75	.35	.09
☐ 99 Lefty Grove	.75	.35	.09
☐ 100 Jimmie Foxx	1.00	.45	.12
☐ 101 Tony Lazzeri	.50	.23	.06
☐ 102 Mel Ott	.75	.35	.09
☐ 103 Carl Hubbell	.50	.23	.06
☐ 104 Al Lopez	.50	.23	.06
☐ 105 Lefty Gomez	.75	.35	.09
☐ 106 Dizzy Dean	1.00	.45	.12
☐ 107 Hank Greenberg	1.00	.45	.12
☐ 108 Joe Medwick	.50	.23	.06
☐ 109 Arky Vaughan	.50	.23	.06
☐ 110 Bob Feller	.75	.35	.09
☐ 111 Hal Newhouser	.50	.23	.06
☐ 112 Early Wynn	.50	.23	.06
☐ 113 Bob Lemon	.50	.23	.06
☐ 114 Red Schoendienst	.50	.23	.06
☐ 115 Satchel Paige	1.00	.45	.12
☐ 116 Whitey Ford	.75	.35	.09
☐ 117 Eddie Mathews	.75	.35	.09
☐ 118 Harmon Killebrew	.75	.35	.09
☐ 119 Roberto Clemente	2.00	.90	.25
☐ 120 Brooks Robinson	.75	.35	.09
☐ 121 Don Drysdale	.75	.35	.09
☐ 122 Luis Aparicio	.50	.23	.06
☐ 123 Willie McCovey	.75	.35	.09
☐ 124 Juan Marichal	.50	.23	.06
☐ 125 Gaylord Perry	.50	.23	.06
☐ 126 Catfish Hunter	.50	.23	.06
☐ 127 Jim Palmer	.75	.35	.09
☐ 128 Rod Carew	.75	.35	.09
☐ 129 Tom Seaver	.75	.35	.09
☐ 130 Rollie Fingers	.50	.23	.06
☐ 131 Joe Jackson	1.50	.70	.19
☐ 132 Pepper Martin	.25	.11	.03
☐ 133 Joe Gordon	.35	.16	.04
☐ 134 Marty Marion	.25	.11	.03
☐ 135 Allie Reynolds	.35	.16	.04
☐ 136 Johnny Sain	.35	.16	.04
☐ 137 Gil Hodges	.75	.35	.09
☐ 138 Ted Kluszewski	.35	.16	.04
☐ 139 Nellie Fox	.75	.35	.09
☐ 140 Billy Martin	.50	.23	.06
☐ 141 Smoky Burgess	.25	.11	.03
☐ 142 Lew Burdette	.35	.16	.04
☐ 143 Joe Black	.25	.11	.03
☐ 144 Don Larsen	.35	.16	.04
☐ 145 Ken Boyer	.35	.16	.04
☐ 146 Johnny Callison	.25	.11	.03
☐ 147 Norm Cash	.35	.16	.04
☐ 148 Keith Hernandez	.25	.11	.03
☐ 149 Jim Kaat	.35	.16	.04
☐ 150 Bill Freehan	.25	.11	.03
☐ 151 Joe Torre	.35	.16	.04
☐ 152 Bob Uecker	.35	.16	.04
☐ 153 Dave McNally	.25	.11	.03
☐ 154 Denny McLain	.35	.16	.04
☐ 155 Dick Allen	.35	.16	.04
☐ 156 Jimmy Wynn	.25	.11	.03
☐ 157 Tommy John	.35	.16	.04
☐ 158 Paul Blair	.25	.11	.03
☐ 159 Reggie Smith	.25	.11	.03
☐ 160 Jerry Koosman	.25	.11	.03
☐ 161 Thurman Munson	.50	.23	.06
☐ 162 Graig Nettles	.35	.16	.04
☐ 163 Ron Cey	.25	.11	.03
☐ 164 Cecil Cooper	.25	.11	.03
☐ 165 Dave Parker	.35	.16	.04
☐ 166 Jim Rice	.35	.16	.04
☐ 167 Kent Tekulve	.25	.11	.03
☐ 168 Who's On First Bud Abbott Lou Costello	.75	.35	.09

1993 Action Packed ASG 24K

The second series of the 1993 Action Packed All-Star Gallery baseball set included 46 Hall of Famers and a special card honoring Bud Abbott and Lou Costello. Action Packed produced 24K gold leaf versions of all these cards and randomly inserted them throughout the foil packs.

	MINT	NRMT	EXC
COMPLETE SET (47)	800.00	350.00	100.00
COMMON CARD (19G-65G)	15.00	6.75	1.85
☐ 19G Cy Young	25.00	11.00	3.10
☐ 20G Honus Wagner	35.00	16.00	4.40
☐ 21G Christy Mathewson	35.00	16.00	4.40
☐ 22G Ty Cobb	50.00	22.00	6.25
☐ 23G Eddie Collins	15.00	6.75	1.85
☐ 24G Walter Johnson	35.00	16.00	4.40
☐ 25G Tris Speaker	25.00	11.00	3.10
☐ 26G Grover Alexander	25.00	11.00	3.10
☐ 27G Ed Roush	15.00	6.75	1.85
☐ 28G Babe Ruth	75.00	34.00	9.50
☐ 29G Rogers Hornsby	35.00	16.00	4.40
☐ 30G Pie Traynor	15.00	6.75	1.85
☐ 31G Lou Gehrig	50.00	22.00	6.25
☐ 32G Mickey Cochrane	25.00	11.00	3.10
☐ 33G Lefty Grove	25.00	11.00	3.10
☐ 34G Jimmie Foxx	35.00	16.00	4.40
☐ 35G Tony Lazzeri	15.00	6.75	1.85
☐ 36G Mel Ott	25.00	11.00	3.10
☐ 37G Carl Hubbell	20.00	9.00	2.50
☐ 38G Al Lopez	15.00	6.75	1.85
☐ 39G Lefty Gomez	25.00	11.00	3.10
☐ 40G Dizzy Dean	35.00	16.00	4.40
☐ 41G Hank Greenberg	35.00	16.00	4.40
☐ 42G Joe Medwick	15.00	6.75	1.85
☐ 43G Arky Vaughan	15.00	6.75	1.85
☐ 44G Bob Feller	35.00	16.00	4.40
☐ 45G Hal Newhouser	15.00	6.75	1.85
☐ 46G Early Wynn	15.00	6.75	1.85
☐ 47G Bob Lemon	15.00	6.75	1.85
☐ 48G Red Schoendienst	15.00	6.75	1.85
☐ 49G Satchel Paige	30.00	13.50	3.70
☐ 50G Whitey Ford	25.00	11.00	3.10
☐ 51G Eddie Mathews	25.00	11.00	3.10
☐ 52G Harmon Killebrew	25.00	11.00	3.10
☐ 53G Roberto Clemente	50.00	22.00	6.25
☐ 54G Brooks Robinson	35.00	16.00	4.40
☐ 55G Don Drysdale	25.00	11.00	3.10
☐ 56G Luis Aparicio	15.00	6.75	1.85
☐ 57G Willie McCovey	20.00	9.00	2.50
☐ 58G Juan Marichal	15.00	6.75	1.85
☐ 59G Gaylord Perry	15.00	6.75	1.85
☐ 60G Catfish Hunter	15.00	6.75	1.85
☐ 61G Jim Palmer	20.00	9.00	2.50
☐ 62G Rod Carew	20.00	9.00	2.50
☐ 63G Tom Seaver	35.00	16.00	4.40
☐ 64G Rollie Fingers	15.00	6.75	1.85
☐ 65G Who's On First	20.00	9.00	2.50

1993 Action Packed ASG Coke/Amoco

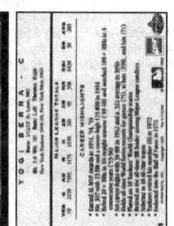

This 18-card standard-size set pays tribute to former greats of baseball. The cards feature Hall of Fame players and were sponsored by Coca Cola and Amoco. The fronts feature embossed action photos framed by inner gold-border stripes and a black outer border. Most of the photos are color; however five of them are sepia-toned. On a gray background, the horizontal back carries biography, career statistics, and special career highlights that list memorable events that spanned the player's career. The cards are numbered on the back. With the purchase of four multi-packs of Coca-Cola products at participating Amoco gas stations, collectors could send in through the mail for a complete set plus a 1.00 off coupon good toward the purchase of Amoco Ultimate gasoline. There was also a pre-promotion set with a red header card, with reportedly only 3000 sets produced, which was not distributed to the public. The red header version was indistinguishable from the gray header set listed below with the exception that Ferguson Jenkins and Billy Herman were replaced in the gray set by Red Schoendienst and Gaylord Perry; Jenkins and Herman were both members of the original 1992 Action Packed ASG set.

	MINT	NRMT	EXC
COMPLETE SET (18)	5.00	2.20	.60
COMMON CARD (1-18)	.25	.11	.03
☐ 1 Yogi Berra	.60	.25	.07
☐ 2 Lou Brock	.35	.16	.04
☐ 3 Bob Gibson	.35	.16	.04
☐ 4 Red Schoendienst	.25	.11	.03
☐ 5 Ralph Kiner	.35	.16	.04
☐ 6 Al Kaline	.50	.23	.06
☐ 7 Lou Boudreau	.25	.11	.03
☐ 8 Bobby Doerr	.25	.11	.03
☐ 9 Gaylord Perry	.25	.11	.03
☐ 10 Monte Irvin	.25	.11	.03
☐ 11 George Kell	.25	.11	.03
☐ 12 Robin Roberts	.35	.16	.04
☐ 13 Johnny Mize	.25	.11	.03
☐ 14 Willie Mays	1.00	.45	.12
☐ 15 Enos Slaughter	.25	.11	.03
☐ 16 Warren Spahn	.35	.16	.04
☐ 17 Willie Stargell	.35	.16	.04
☐ 18 Billy Williams	.25	.11	.03

1993 Action Packed Seaver Promos

This five-card standard-size promo set features embossed color player photos accented by gold foil and red borders. The player's name appears in the gold foil border at the bottom. The horizontal backs are gray and carry biographical and statistical information, and career highlights. The cards are numbered on the back with a "TS" prefix. Random insertions of these cards were also found in packs of Action Packed racing cards.

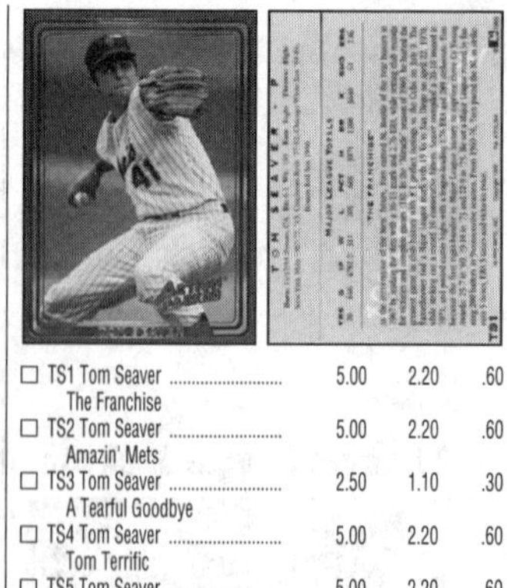

	MINT	NRMT	EXC
COMPLETE SET (5)	20.00	9.00	2.50
COMMON CARD (TS1-TS5)	2.50	1.10	.30
☐ TS1 Tom Seaver The Franchise	5.00	2.20	.60
☐ TS2 Tom Seaver Amazin' Mets	5.00	2.20	.60
☐ TS3 Tom Seaver A Tearful Goodbye	2.50	1.10	.30
☐ TS4 Tom Seaver Tom Terrific	5.00	2.20	.60
☐ TS5 Tom Seaver Dazzling the Windy City	5.00	2.20	.60

1992 AFUD Musial

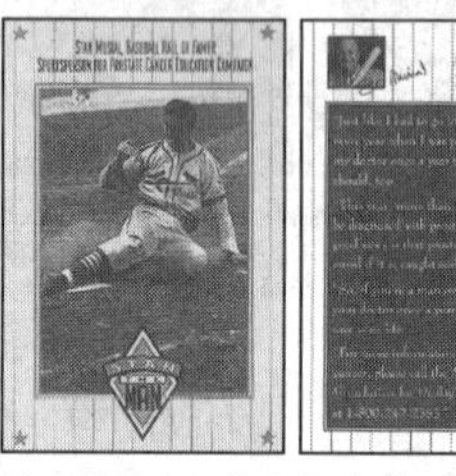

This five-card set, presented by the American Foundation for Urologic Disease, measures approximately 3 1/2" by 5 1/2". The fronts feature black-and-white photos of Stan Musial, spokesperson for the Prostate Cancer Education Campaign, during his career and now. The pictures are bordered in brick-red and rest on a brick-red pin-striped parchment background with red stars in each corner. A "Stan the Man" icon overlaps the bottom of the photo onto the background. The backs have encouraging and informative messages about prostate cancer, including a list of potential symptoms. The messages appear in a brick-red box on a brick-red pinstriped white background. Small pictures of Stan Musial are on all but one card. The set is packaged in a folder that includes information for obtaining materials to promote awareness of prostate cancer. The cards are unnumbered and checklisted.

	MINT	NRMT	EXC
COMPLETE SET (5)	15.00	6.75	1.85
COMMON CARD (1-5)	3.00	1.35	.35
☐ 1 Stan Musial Portrait	3.00	1.35	.35
☐ 2 Stan Musial Running bases	3.00	1.35	.35
☐ 3 Stan Musial Batting	3.00	1.35	.35
☐ 4 Stan Musial Sliding	3.00	1.35	.35
☐ 5 Stan Musial Lifted up by teammates	3.00	1.35	.35

1990 AGFA

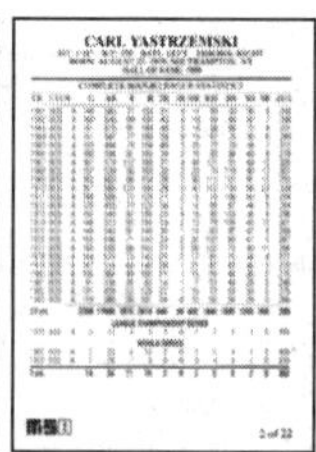

This 22-card standard-size set was issued by MSA (Michael Schechter Associates) for AGFA. The fronts display color head and shoulders shots, with a thin red border on a white card face. In turquoise lettering, the words "Limited Edition Series" appear above the pictures; the player's name is given below the pictures. In black on white, the backs present complete year by year major league statistics. The promotion reportedly consisted of a three-card pack of these cards given away with any purchase of a three-pack of AGFA film.

	MINT	NRMT	EXC
COMPLETE SET (22)	15.00	6.75	1.85
COMMON CARD (1-22)	.25	.11	.03
☐ 1 Willie Mays	1.50	.70	.19
☐ 2 Carl Yastrzemski	1.00	.45	.12
☐ 3 Harmon Killebrew	1.00	.45	.12
☐ 4 Joe Torre	.35	.16	.04
☐ 5 Al Kaline	1.00	.45	.12
☐ 6 Hank Aaron	1.50	.70	.19
☐ 7 Rod Carew	1.00	.45	.12
☐ 8 Roberto Clemente	2.00	.90	.25
☐ 9 Luis Aparicio	.35	.16	.04
☐ 10 Roger Maris	.75	.35	.09
☐ 11 Joe Morgan	.75	.35	.09
☐ 12 Maury Wills	.35	.16	.04
☐ 13 Brooks Robinson	1.00	.45	.12
☐ 14 Tom Seaver	1.00	.45	.12
☐ 15 Steve Carlton	.75	.35	.09
☐ 16 Whitey Ford	1.00	.45	.12
☐ 17 Jim Palmer	1.00	.45	.12
☐ 18 Rollie Fingers	.35	.16	.04
☐ 19 Bruce Sutter	.25	.11	.03
☐ 20 Willie McCovey	1.00	.45	.12
☐ 21 Mike Schmidt	1.00	.45	.12
☐ 22 Yogi Berra	1.00	.45	.12

1936-52 Albertype Hall of Fame PC754-2

The Albertype Company issued postcards of Hall of Fame inductees from 1936 through 1952. This black and white postcard set, the cards being called plaques as they feature the Hall of Fame plaque of the player, was addended to each year by new Hall of Fame inductees. Sixty-two Albertype postcards are known and are listed in the checklist below. The set is sequenced in order of induction into the Hall of Fame.

	MINT	NRMT	EXC
COMPLETE SET (62)	800.00	350.00	100.00
COMMON CARD (1-62)	10.00	4.50	1.25
☐ 1 Ty Cobb	50.00	22.00	6.25
☐ 2 Walter Johnson	40.00	18.00	5.00
☐ 3 Christy Mathewson	40.00	18.00	5.00
☐ 4 Babe Ruth	75.00	34.00	9.50
☐ 5 Honus Wagner	40.00	18.00	5.00
☐ 6 Morgan Bulkeley	10.00	4.50	1.25
☐ 7 Ban Johnson	10.00	4.50	1.25
☐ 8 Nap Lajoie	20.00	9.00	2.50
☐ 9 Connie Mack	20.00	9.00	2.50
☐ 10 John McGraw	20.00	9.00	2.50
☐ 11 Tris Speaker	20.00	9.00	2.50
☐ 12 George Wright	10.00	4.50	1.25
☐ 13 Cy Young	50.00	22.00	6.25
☐ 14 Grover Cleveland Alexander	20.00	9.00	2.50
☐ 15 Alexander Cartwright	15.00	6.75	1.85
☐ 16 Henry Chadwick	10.00	4.50	1.25
☐ 17 Cap Anson	30.00	13.50	3.70
☐ 18 Eddie Collins	20.00	9.00	2.50
☐ 19 Charlie Comiskey	10.00	4.50	1.25
☐ 20 Candy Cummings	10.00	4.50	1.25
☐ 21 Buck Ewing	10.00	4.50	1.25
☐ 22 Lou Gehrig	60.00	27.00	7.50
☐ 23 Willie Keeler	10.00	4.50	1.25
☐ 24 Ole Hoss Radbourne	10.00	4.50	1.25
☐ 25 George Sisler	15.00	6.75	1.85
☐ 26 Albert Spalding	10.00	4.50	1.25
☐ 27 Rogers Hornsby	25.00	11.00	3.10
☐ 28 Kenesaw Mountain Landis	10.00	4.50	1.25
☐ 29 Roger Bresnahan	10.00	4.50	1.25
☐ 30 Dan Brouthers	10.00	4.50	1.25
☐ 31 Fred Clarke	10.00	4.50	1.25
☐ 32 Jimmy Collins	10.00	4.50	1.25
☐ 33 Ed Delahanty	10.00	4.50	1.25
☐ 34 Hugh Duffy	10.00	4.50	1.25
☐ 35 Hugh Jennings	10.00	4.50	1.25
☐ 36 King Kelly	10.00	4.50	1.25
☐ 37 Jimmy O'Rourke	10.00	4.50	1.25
☐ 38 Wilbert Robinson	10.00	4.50	1.25
☐ 39 Jesse Burkett	10.00	4.50	1.25
☐ 40 Frank Chance	20.00	9.00	2.50
☐ 41 Jack Chesbro	10.00	4.50	1.25
☐ 42 Johnny Evers	20.00	9.00	2.50
☐ 43 Clark Griffith	15.00	6.75	1.85
☐ 44 Tom McCarthy	10.00	4.50	1.25
☐ 45 Joe McGinnity	10.00	4.50	1.25
☐ 46 Eddie Plank	20.00	9.00	2.50
☐ 47 Joe Tinker	20.00	9.00	2.50
☐ 48 Rube Waddell	10.00	4.50	1.25
☐ 49 Ed Walsh	15.00	6.75	1.85
☐ 50 Mickey Cochrane	20.00	9.00	2.50
☐ 51 Frankie Frisch	20.00	9.00	2.50
☐ 52 Lefty Grove	25.00	11.00	3.10
☐ 53 Carl Hubbell	25.00	11.00	3.10
☐ 54 Herb Pennock	15.00	6.75	1.85
☐ 55 Pie Traynor	20.00	9.00	2.50
☐ 56 Mordecai Brown	20.00	9.00	2.50
☐ 57 Charlie Gehringer	15.00	6.75	1.85
☐ 58 Kid Nichols	10.00	4.50	1.25
☐ 59 Jimmy Foxx	25.00	11.00	3.10
☐ 60 Mel Ott	20.00	9.00	2.50
☐ 61 Harry Heilmann	10.00	4.50	1.25
☐ 62 Paul Waner	15.00	6.75	1.85

1887 Allen and Ginter N28

This 50-card set of The World's Champions was marketed by Allen and Ginter in 1887. The cards feature color lithographs of champion athletes from seven categories of sport, with baseball, rowing and boxing each having 10 individuals portrayed. Cards numbered 1 to 10 depict baseball players and cards numbered 11 to 20 depict popular boxers of the era. This set is called the first series although no such title appears on the cards. All 50 cards are checklisted on the reverse, and they are unnumbered. An album (catalog: A16) and an advertising banner (catalog: G20) were also issued in conjunction with this set.

	EX-MT	VG-E	GOOD
COMPLETE SET (50)	10000.00	4500.00	1250.00
COMMON BASEBALL (1-10)	300.00	135.00	38.00
COMMON BOXERS (11-20)	125.00	55.00	15.50
COMMON OARSMEN (21-30)	50.00	22.00	6.25
COMMON WRESTLER (31-37)	75.00	34.00	9.50
COMMON SHOOTERS (38-41)	50.00	22.00	6.25
COMMON POOL (42-50)	75.00	34.00	9.50
☐ 1 Adrian C. Anson	2250.00	1000.00	275.00
☐ 2 Chas. W. Bennett	300.00	135.00	38.00
☐ 3 Robert L. Caruthers	350.00	160.00	45.00
☐ 4 John Clarkson	750.00	350.00	95.00
☐ 5 Charles Comiskey	1000.00	450.00	125.00
☐ 6 Capt.Jack Glasscock	350.00	160.00	45.00
☐ 7 Timothy Keefe	900.00	400.00	110.00
☐ 8 Mike Kelly	1250.00	550.00	160.00
☐ 9 Joseph Mulvey	300.00	135.00	38.00
☐ 10 John M. Ward	900.00	400.00	110.00
☐ 11 Jimmy Carney	125.00	55.00	15.50
☐ 12 Jimmy Carroll	125.00	55.00	15.50
☐ 13 Jack Dempsey	200.00	90.00	25.00
☐ 14 Jake Kilrain	150.00	70.00	19.00
☐ 15 Joe Lannon	125.00	55.00	15.50
☐ 16 Jack McAuliffe	125.00	55.00	15.50
☐ 17 Charlie Mitchell	150.00	70.00	19.00
☐ 18 Jem Smith	125.00	55.00	15.50
☐ 19 John L. Sullivan	350.00	160.00	45.00
☐ 20 Ike Weir	125.00	55.00	15.50
☐ 21 Wm. Beach	50.00	22.00	6.25
☐ 22 Geo. Bubear	50.00	22.00	6.25
☐ 23 Jacob Gaudaub	50.00	22.00	6.25
☐ 24 Albert Hamm	50.00	22.00	6.25
☐ 25 Ed. Hanlan	60.00	27.00	7.50
☐ 26 Geo. H. Hosmer	50.00	22.00	6.25
☐ 27 John McKay	50.00	22.00	6.25
☐ 28 Wallace Ross	50.00	22.00	6.25
☐ 29 John Teemer	50.00	22.00	6.25
☐ 30 E.A. Trickett	50.00	22.00	6.25
☐ 31 Joe Acton	75.00	34.00	9.50
☐ 32 Theo. Bauer	75.00	34.00	9.50
☐ 33 Young Bibby (Geo. Mehling)	90.00	40.00	11.00
☐ 34 J.F. McLaughlin	75.00	34.00	9.50
☐ 35 John McMahon	75.00	34.00	9.50
☐ 36 Wm. Muldoon	90.00	40.00	11.00
☐ 37 Matsada Sorakichi	75.00	34.00	9.50
☐ 38 Capt. A.H. Bogardus	50.00	22.00	6.25
☐ 39 Dr. W.F. Carver	50.00	22.00	6.25
☐ 40 Hon. W.F. Cody (Buffalo Bill)	250.00	110.00	31.00
☐ 41 Miss Annie Oakley	250.00	110.00	31.00
☐ 42 Yank Adams	75.00	34.00	9.50
☐ 43 Maurice Daly	75.00	34.00	9.50
☐ 44 Jos. Dion	75.00	34.00	9.50
☐ 45 J. Schaefer	75.00	34.00	9.50
☐ 46 Wm. Sexton	75.00	34.00	9.50
☐ 47 Geo. F. Slosson	75.00	34.00	9.50
☐ 48 M. Vignaux	75.00	34.00	9.50
☐ 49 Albert Frey	75.00	34.00	9.50
☐ 50 J.L. Malone	75.00	34.00	9.50

1888 Allen and Ginter N29

The second series of The World's Champions was probably issued in 1888. Like the first series, the cards are backlisted and unnumbered. However, there are 17 distinct categories of sports represented in this set, with only six baseball players portrayed (as opposed to 10 in the first series). Each card has a color lithograph of the individual set against a white background. An album (catalog: A17) and an advertising banner (catalog: G21) were issued in conjunction with the set. The numbering below is alphabetical within sport, e.g., baseball players (1-6), boxers (7-14), and other sports (15-50).

	EX-MT	VG-E	GOOD
COMPLETE SET (50)	10000.00	4500.00	1250.00
COMMON BASEBALL (1-6)	700.00	325.00	90.00
COMMON BOXERS (7-14)	250.00	110.00	31.00
COMMON ATHLETES (15-17)	90.00	40.00	11.00
COMMON CYCLIST (18-25)	90.00	40.00	11.00
COMMON TENNIS (26-29)	125.00	55.00	15.50
COMMON WRESTLER (30-31)	125.00	55.00	15.50
COMMON SKATER (32-33)	90.00	40.00	11.00
COMMON OTHERS (34-50)	90.00	40.00	11.00
☐ 1 Wm.(Buck) Ewing	1750.00	800.00	220.00
☐ 2 Jas. H. Fogarty	700.00	325.00	90.00
☐ 3 Charles H. Getzien	700.00	325.00	90.00
☐ 4 Geo.F.(Doggie) Miller	700.00	325.00	90.00
☐ 5 John Morrell	700.00	325.00	90.00
☐ 6 James Ryan	750.00	350.00	95.00
☐ 7 Patsey Duffy	250.00	110.00	31.00
☐ 8 Billy Edwards	250.00	110.00	31.00
☐ 9 Jack Havlin	250.00	110.00	31.00
☐ 10 Patsey Kerrigan	250.00	110.00	31.00
☐ 11 George LaBlance	250.00	110.00	31.00
☐ 12 Jack McGee	250.00	110.00	31.00
☐ 13 Frank Murphy	250.00	110.00	31.00
☐ 14 Johnny Murphy	250.00	110.00	31.00
☐ 15 Capt. J.C. Daly	90.00	40.00	11.00
☐ 16 M.W. Ford	90.00	40.00	11.00
☐ 17 Duncan C. Ross	90.00	40.00	11.00
☐ 18 W.E. Crist	90.00	40.00	11.00
☐ 19 H.G. Crocker	90.00	40.00	11.00
☐ 20 Willie Harradon	90.00	40.00	11.00
☐ 21 F.F. Ives	90.00	40.00	11.00
☐ 22 Wm. A. Rowe	90.00	40.00	11.00
☐ 23 Percy Stone	90.00	40.00	11.00
☐ 24 Ralph Temple	90.00	40.00	11.00
☐ 25 Fred Wood	90.00	40.00	11.00
☐ 26 Dr. James Dwight	125.00	55.00	15.50
☐ 27 Thomas Pettit	125.00	55.00	15.50
☐ 28 R.D. Sears	125.00	55.00	15.50
☐ 29 H.W. Slocum Jr.	125.00	55.00	15.50
☐ 30 Theobaud Bauer	125.00	55.00	15.50
☐ 31 Edwin Bibby	125.00	55.00	15.50
☐ 32 Hugh McCormack	90.00	40.00	11.00
☐ 33 Axel Paulsen	90.00	40.00	11.00
☐ 34 T. Ray	90.00	40.00	11.00
☐ 35 C.W.V. Clarke	90.00	40.00	11.00
☐ 36 E.D. Lange	90.00	40.00	11.00
☐ 37 E.C. Carter	90.00	40.00	11.00
☐ 38 Wm. Cummings	90.00	40.00	11.00
☐ 39 W.G. George	90.00	40.00	11.00
☐ 40 L.E. Myers	90.00	40.00	11.00
☐ 41 James Albert	90.00	40.00	11.00
☐ 42 Patrick Fitzgerald	90.00	40.00	11.00
☐ 43 W.B. Page	90.00	40.00	11.00
☐ 44 C.A.J. Queckberner	90.00	40.00	11.00
☐ 45 W.J.M. Barry	90.00	40.00	11.00
☐ 46 Wm. G. East	90.00	40.00	11.00
☐ 47 Wm. O'Connor	90.00	40.00	11.00
☐ 48 Gus Hill	90.00	40.00	11.00
☐ 49 Capt. Paul Boyton	90.00	40.00	11.00
☐ 50 Capt. Matthew Webb	90.00	40.00	11.00

1888 Allen and Ginter N43

The primary designs of this 50-card set are identical to those of N29, but these are placed on a much larger card with extraneous background detail. The set was produced in 1888 by Allen and Ginter as inserts for a larger tobacco package than those in which sets N28 and N29 were marketed. Cards of this set, which is backlisted, are considered to be much scarcer than their counterparts in N29.

	EX-MT	VG-E	GOOD
COMPLETE SET (50)	18000.00	8100.00	2200.00
COMMON BASEBALL (1-6)	1400.00	650.00	180.00
COMMON BOXERS (7-14)	500.00	220.00	60.00
COMMON ATHLETES (15-17)	150.00	70.00	19.00
COMMON CYCLIST (18-25)	150.00	70.00	19.00
COMMON TENNIS (26-29)	200.00	90.00	25.00
COMMON WRESTLER (30-31)	200.00	90.00	25.00
COMMON SKATER (32-33)	150.00	70.00	19.00
COMMON OTHERS (34-50)	150.00	70.00	19.00
☐ 1 William(Buck) Ewing	3000.00	1350.00	375.00
☐ 2 Jas. J. Fogarty	1400.00	650.00	180.00
☐ 3 Charles H. Getzien	1400.00	650.00	180.00
☐ 4 Geo.F.(Doggie) Miller	1400.00	650.00	180.00
☐ 5 John Morrell	1400.00	650.00	180.00
☐ 6 James Ryan	1500.00	700.00	190.00
☐ 7 Patsey Duffy	500.00	220.00	60.00
☐ 8 Billy Edwards	500.00	220.00	60.00
☐ 9 Jack Havlin	500.00	220.00	60.00
☐ 10 Patsey Kerrigan	500.00	220.00	60.00
☐ 11 George LaBlanche	500.00	220.00	60.00
☐ 12 Jack McGee	500.00	220.00	60.00
☐ 13 Frank Murphy	500.00	220.00	60.00
☐ 14 Johnny Murphy	500.00	220.00	60.00
☐ 15 Capt. J.C. Daly	150.00	70.00	19.00
☐ 16 M.W. Ford	150.00	70.00	19.00
☐ 17 Duncan C. Ross	150.00	70.00	19.00
☐ 18 W.E. Crist	150.00	70.00	19.00
☐ 19 H.G. Crocker	150.00	70.00	19.00
☐ 20 Willie Harradon	150.00	70.00	19.00
☐ 21 F.F. Ives	150.00	70.00	19.00
☐ 22 Wm. A. Rowe	150.00	70.00	19.00
☐ 23 Percy Stone	150.00	70.00	19.00
☐ 24 Ralph Temple	150.00	70.00	19.00
☐ 25 Fred Wood	150.00	70.00	19.00
☐ 26 Dr. James Dwight	200.00	90.00	25.00
☐ 27 Thomas Pettitt	200.00	90.00	25.00
☐ 28 R.D. Sears	200.00	90.00	25.00
☐ 29 H.W. Slocum Jr.	200.00	90.00	25.00
☐ 30 Theobaud Bauer	200.00	90.00	25.00
☐ 31 Edwin Bibby	200.00	90.00	25.00
☐ 32 Hugh McCormack	150.00	70.00	19.00
☐ 33 Axel. Paulsen	150.00	70.00	19.00
☐ 34 T. Ray	150.00	70.00	19.00
☐ 35 C.W.V. Clarke	150.00	70.00	19.00
☐ 36 E.D. Lange	150.00	70.00	19.00
☐ 37 E.C. Carter	150.00	70.00	19.00
☐ 38 Wm. Cummings	150.00	70.00	19.00
☐ 39 W.G. George	150.00	70.00	19.00
☐ 40 L.E. Myers	150.00	70.00	19.00
☐ 41 James Albert	150.00	70.00	19.00
☐ 42 Patrick Fitzgerald	150.00	70.00	19.00
☐ 43 W.B. Page	150.00	70.00	19.00
☐ 44 C.A.J. Queckberner	150.00	70.00	19.00
☐ 45 W.J.M. Barry	150.00	70.00	19.00
☐ 46 Wm. G. East	150.00	70.00	19.00
☐ 47 Wm. O'Connor	150.00	70.00	19.00
☐ 48 Gus Hill	150.00	70.00	19.00
☐ 49 Capt. Paul Boyton	150.00	70.00	19.00
☐ 50 Capt. Matthew Webb	150.00	70.00	19.00

1990 All-American Baseball Team

This 24-card, standard-size set was issued by MSA (Michael Schechter Associates) for 7/11, Squirt, and Dr. Pepper, and other carbonated beverages (but there are no markings on the cards whatsoever to indicate who sponsored the set other than MSA). These cards were distributed and issued inside 12-packs of sodas. The 12-packs included a checklist on one panel, and the cards themselves were glued on the inside of the pack so that it was difficult to remove a card without damaging it. The fronts feature a red-white and blue design framing the players photos while the back has major league career statistics and a sentence of career highlights. The back also has a fascimile autograph of the player on the back. Like many of the sets sponsored by MSA there are no team logos on the cards as they have been airbrushed away.

	MINT	NRMT	EXC
COMPLETE SET (24)	25.00	11.00	3.10
COMMON CARD (1-24)	.50	.23	.06
☐ 1 George Brett	2.00	.90	.25
☐ 2 Mark McGwire	2.00	.90	.25
☐ 3 Wade Boggs	1.25	.55	.16
☐ 4 Cal Ripken	5.00	2.20	.60
☐ 5 Rickey Henderson	1.00	.45	.12
☐ 6 Dwight Gooden	.75	.35	.09
☐ 7 Bo Jackson	.75	.35	.09
☐ 8 Roger Clemens	1.50	.70	.19
☐ 9 Orel Hershiser	.75	.35	.09
☐ 10 Ozzie Smith	2.00	.90	.25
☐ 11 Don Mattingly	2.50	1.10	.30
☐ 12 Kirby Puckett	2.50	1.10	.30
☐ 13 Robin Yount	1.00	.45	.12
☐ 14 Tony Gwynn	2.50	1.10	.30
☐ 15 Jose Canseco	1.00	.45	.12
☐ 16 Nolan Ryan	5.00	2.20	.60
☐ 17 Ken Griffey Jr.	6.00	2.70	.75
☐ 18 Will Clark	1.25	.55	.16
☐ 19 Ryne Sandberg	2.00	.90	.25
☐ 20 Kent Hrbek	.50	.23	.06
☐ 21 Carlton Fisk	1.00	.45	.12
☐ 22 Paul Molitor	1.25	.55	.16
☐ 23 Dave Winfield	1.00	.45	.12
☐ 24 Andre Dawson	.75	.35	.09

1908 All-American Ladies Baseball Club

This extremely rare set of printed postcards by an unknown publisher features stars of the All-American Ladies Base Ball Club which toured America early in the 20th century. Although no date is listed on the cards they were produced sometime after 1907 beacuse they have a divided back. Prior to 1907 all postcards backs were undivided and all messages had to be written on the front or picture side of the card. All cards show close up action views of the players on a white background. We have listed the known versions, all additions to this checklist are appreciated.

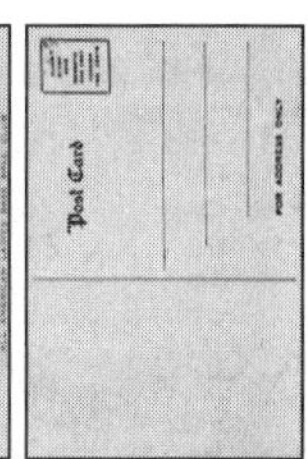

	EX-MT	VG-E	GOOD
COMPLETE SET (5)	1000.00	450.00	125.00
COMMON CARD (1-5)	200.00	90.00	25.00
☐ 1 Bessie Barrett	200.00	90.00	25.00
☐ 2 May Fay	200.00	90.00	25.00
☐ 3 Harriett Murphy	200.00	90.00	25.00
☐ 4 Carrie Nation	200.00	90.00	25.00
☐ 5 Elizabeth Pull	200.00	90.00	25.00

1971 All-Star Baseball Album

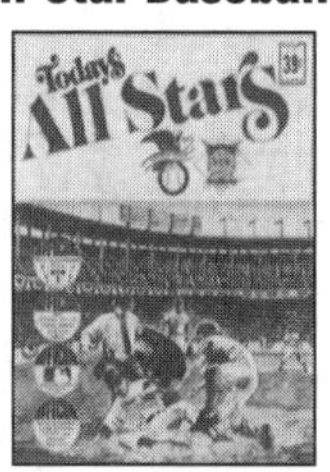

The 1971 All-Star Baseball Album contains two pages of 12 perforated player pictures for a total of 24 cards. Each page has three rows of four cards measuring approximately 7 1/2 by 8 3/4". The individual cards measure 1 7/8" by 2 7/8". The cards are printed on thin paper stock. The fronts feature a posed all star color player photo with the player's autograph facsimile across the bottom of the picture. The backs carry biography, team name, and player profile superimposed over a ghosted team logo. The cards are unnumbered and checklisted below in alphabetical order. On an additional page that follows each of the player picture pages, is a page listing the player's statistics. A 1971 American and National League team schedule appears on the back of the album. The album, titled Today's All-Stars was produced by Dell and originally sold for 39 cents.

	NRMT	VG-E	GOOD
COMPLETE SET (24)	12.50	5.50	1.55
COMMON CARD (1-24)	.10	.05	.01
☐ 1 Hank Aaron	1.00	.45	.12
☐ 2 Luis Aparicio	.50	.23	.06
☐ 3 Ernie Banks	.75	.35	.09
☐ 4 Johnny Bench	.75	.35	.09
☐ 5 Rico Carty	.15	.07	.02
☐ 6 Roberto Clemente	1.50	.70	.19
☐ 7 Bob Gibson	.50	.23	.06
☐ 8 Willie Horton	.20	.09	.03
☐ 9 Frank Howard	.20	.09	.03
☐ 10 Reggie Jackson	.75	.35	.09
☐ 11 Ferguson Jenkins	.50	.23	.06
☐ 12 Alex Johnson	.10	.05	.01
☐ 13 Al Kaline	.50	.23	.06
☐ 14 Harmon Killebrew	.50	.23	.06
☐ 15 Willie Mays	1.00	.45	.12
☐ 16 Sam McDowell	.20	.09	.03
☐ 17 Denny McLain	.20	.09	.03
☐ 18 Boog Powell	.25	.11	.03
☐ 19 Brooks Robinson	.50	.23	.06
☐ 20 Frank Robinson	.50	.23	.06
☐ 21 Pete Rose	.75	.35	.09
☐ 22 Tom Seaver	.75	.35	.09
☐ 23 Rusty Staub	.25	.11	.03
☐ 24 Carl Yastrzemski	.50	.23	.06
☐ XX Album	5.00	2.20	.60

1981 All-Star Game Program Inserts

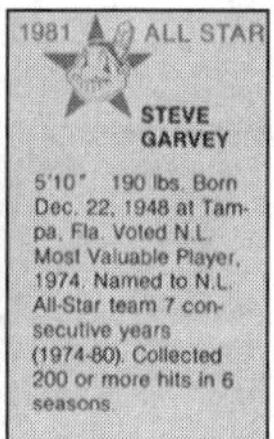

This 180-card set was distributed inside the 1981 All-Star Game Official Program on foldout sheets with each sheet containing 30 cards. Each card measures approximately 1 1/4" by 2" and features color action photos of the American League (#1-90) and the National League All-Star Nominees (#91-181). The cards are unnumbered and checklisted below in alphabetical order by position within each player's respective league.

	NRMT	VG-E	GOOD
COMPLETE SET (180)	10.00	4.50	1.25
COMMON CARD (1-180)	.05	.02	.01
☐ 1 Willie Aikens	.05	.02	.01
☐ 2 Bruce Bochte	.05	.02	.01
☐ 3 Rod Carew	.50	.23	.06
☐ 4 Cecil Cooper	.10	.05	.01
☐ 5 Mike Hargrove	.10	.05	.01
☐ 6 Tony Perez	.25	.11	.03
☐ 7 John Mayberry	.05	.02	.01
☐ 8 Eddie Murray	2.00	.90	.25
☐ 9 Bob Watson	.15	.07	.02
☐ 10 Julio Cruz	.05	.02	.01
☐ 11 Rich Dauer	.05	.02	.01
☐ 12 Damaso Garcia	.05	.02	.01
☐ 13 Bobby Grich	.05	.02	.01
☐ 14 Duane Kuiper	.05	.02	.01
☐ 15 Willie Randolph	.10	.05	.01
☐ 16 Lou Whitaker	.25	.11	.03
☐ 17 Frank White	.10	.05	.01
☐ 18 Bump Wills	.05	.02	.01
☐ 19 Mark Belanger	.05	.02	.01
☐ 20 Rick Burleson	.05	.02	.01
☐ 21 Bucky Dent	.05	.02	.01
☐ 22 Alfredo Griffin	.05	.02	.01
☐ 23 Roy Smalley	.05	.02	.01
☐ 24 Alan Trammell	.50	.23	.06
☐ 25 Tom Veryzer	.05	.02	.01
☐ 26 Robin Yount	1.00	.45	.12
☐ 27 U.L. Washington	.05	.02	.01
☐ 28 Buddy Bell	.10	.05	.01
☐ 29 George Brett	4.00	1.80	.50
☐ 30 John Castino	.05	.02	.01
☐ 31 Doug DeCinces	.10	.05	.01
☐ 32 Wayne Gross	.05	.02	.01
☐ 33 Toby Harrah	.05	.02	.01
☐ 34 Butch Hobson	.05	.02	.01
☐ 35 Carney Lansford	.05	.02	.01
☐ 36 Graig Nettles	.15	.07	.02
☐ 37 Rick Cerone	.05	.02	.01
☐ 38 Rick Dempsey	.05	.02	.01
☐ 39 Brian Downing	.10	.05	.01
☐ 40 Carlton Fisk	1.00	.45	.12
☐ 41 Ron Hassey	.05	.02	.01
☐ 42 Lance Parrish	.10	.05	.01
☐ 43 Ted Simmons	.10	.05	.01
☐ 44 Jim Sundberg	.05	.02	.01
☐ 45 Butch Wynegar	.05	.02	.01
☐ 46 Tony Armas	.05	.02	.01
☐ 47 Don Baylor	.10	.05	.01
☐ 48 Al Bumbry	.05	.02	.01
☐ 49 Joe Charboneau	.05	.02	.01
☐ 50 Miguel Dilone	.05	.02	.01
☐ 51 Dan Ford	.05	.02	.01
☐ 52 Rickey Henderson	2.00	.90	.25
☐ 53 Reggie Jackson	1.00	.45	.12
☐ 54 Steve Kemp	.05	.02	.01
☐ 55 Ron LeFlore	.05	.02	.01
☐ 56 Chet Lemon	.05	.02	.01
☐ 57 Greg Luzinski	.10	.05	.01
☐ 58 Fred Lynn	.10	.05	.01
☐ 59 Hal McRae	.10	.05	.01
☐ 60 Paul Molitor	1.50	.70	.19
☐ 61 Dwayne Murphy	.05	.02	.01
☐ 62 Ben Oglivie	.05	.02	.01
☐ 63 Al Oliver	.15	.07	.02
☐ 64 Jorge Orta	.05	.02	.01
☐ 65 Amos Otis	.05	.02	.01
☐ 66 Jim Rice	.10	.05	.01
☐ 67 Mickey Rivers	.05	.02	.01
☐ 68 Ken Singleton	.05	.02	.01
☐ 69 Gorman Thomas	.05	.02	.01
☐ 70 Willie Wilson	.05	.02	.01
☐ 71 Dave Winfield	1.00	.45	.12
☐ 72 Carl Yastrzemski	1.00	.45	.12
☐ 73 Floyd Bannister	.05	.02	.01
☐ 74 Len Barker	.05	.02	.01
☐ 75 Britt Burns	.05	.02	.01
☐ 76 Richard Dotson	.05	.02	.01
☐ 77 Dennis Eckersley	.75	.35	.09
☐ 78 Rollie Fingers	.50	.23	.06
☐ 79 Mike Flanagan	.05	.02	.01
☐ 80 Ken Forsch	.05	.02	.01
☐ 81 Rich Gossage	.15	.07	.02
☐ 82 Ron Guidry	.10	.05	.01
☐ 83 Larry Gura	.05	.02	.01
☐ 84 Tommy John	.15	.07	.02
☐ 85 Matt Keough	.05	.02	.01
☐ 86 Dennis Leonard	.05	.02	.01
☐ 87 Scott McGregor	.05	.02	.01
☐ 88 Mike Norris	.05	.02	.01
☐ 89 Dave Stieb	.10	.05	.01
☐ 90 Milt Wilcox	.05	.02	.01
☐ 91 Bill Buckner	.05	.02	.01
☐ 92 Enos Cabell	.05	.02	.01
☐ 93 Chris Chambliss	.10	.05	.01
☐ 94 Dan Driessen	.05	.02	.01
☐ 95 Steve Garvey	.50	.23	.06
☐ 96 Keith Hernandez	.10	.05	.01
☐ 97 Willie Montanez	.05	.02	.01
☐ 98 Pete Rose	2.00	.90	.25
☐ 99 Willie Stargell	.75	.35	.09
☐ 100 Doug Flynn	.05	.02	.01
☐ 101 Phil Garner	.05	.02	.01
☐ 102 Glenn Hubbard	.05	.02	.01
☐ 103 Rafael Landestoy	.05	.02	.01
☐ 104 Davey Lopes	.05	.02	.01
☐ 105 Ron Oester	.05	.02	.01
☐ 106 Rodney Scott	.05	.02	.01
☐ 107 Rennie Stennett	.05	.02	.01
☐ 108 Manny Trillo	.05	.02	.01
☐ 109 Larry Bowa	.05	.02	.01
☐ 110 Dave Concepcion	.05	.02	.01
☐ 111 Ivan DeJesus	.05	.02	.01
☐ 112 Tim Foli	.05	.02	.01
☐ 113 Bill Russell	.05	.02	.01
☐ 114 Ozzie Smith	2.50	1.10	.30
☐ 115 Chris Speier	.05	.02	.01
☐ 116 Frank Taveras	.05	.02	.01
☐ 117 Garry Templeton	.05	.02	.01
☐ 118 Ron Cey	.10	.05	.01
☐ 119 Darrell Evans	.10	.05	.01
☐ 120 Bob Horner	.05	.02	.01
☐ 121 Ray Knight	.05	.02	.01
☐ 122 Bill Madlock	.10	.05	.01
☐ 123 Ken Oberkfell	.05	.02	.01
☐ 124 Larry Parrish	.05	.02	.01
☐ 125 Ken Reitz	.05	.02	.01
☐ 126 Mike Schmidt	2.00	.90	.25
☐ 127 Alan Ashby	.05	.02	.01
☐ 128 Johnny Bench	1.50	.70	.19
☐ 129 Bob Boone	.10	.05	.01
☐ 130 Gary Carter	1.50	.70	.19
☐ 131 Terry Kennedy	.05	.02	.01
☐ 132 Milt May	.05	.02	.01
☐ 133 Darrell Porter	.10	.05	.01
☐ 134 John Stearns	.05	.02	.01
☐ 135 Steve Yeager	.05	.02	.01
☐ 136 Dusty Baker	.10	.05	.01
☐ 137 Cesar Cedeno	.05	.02	.01
☐ 138 Jack Clark	.05	.02	.01
☐ 139 Dave Collins	.05	.02	.01
☐ 140 Warren Cromartie	.05	.02	.01
☐ 141 Jose Cruz	.10	.05	.01
☐ 142 Andre Dawson	.75	.35	.09
☐ 143 Mike Easler	.05	.02	.01
☐ 144 George Foster	.05	.02	.01
☐ 145 Ken Griffey	.10	.05	.01
☐ 146 Steve Henderson	.05	.02	.01
☐ 147 George Hendrick	.05	.02	.01
☐ 148 Dave Kingman	.15	.07	.02
☐ 149 Ken Landreaux	.05	.02	.01
☐ 150 Sixto Lezcano	.05	.02	.01
☐ 151 Garry Maddox	.05	.02	.01
☐ 152 Jerry Martin	.05	.02	.01
☐ 153 Gary Matthews	.05	.02	.01
☐ 154 Lee Mazzilli	.05	.02	.01
☐ 155 Bake McBride	.05	.02	.01
☐ 156 Omar Moreno	.05	.02	.01
☐ 157 Dale Murphy	.75	.35	.09
☐ 158 Dave Parker	.10	.05	.01
☐ 159 Terry Puhl	.05	.02	.01
☐ 160 Gene Richards	.05	.02	.01
☐ 161 Reggie Smith	.05	.02	.01
☐ 162 Ellis Valentine	.05	.02	.01
☐ 163 Doyle Alexander	.05	.02	.01
☐ 164 Neil Allen	.05	.02	.01
☐ 165 Jim Bibby	.05	.02	.01
☐ 166 Vida Blue	.10	.05	.01
☐ 167 Steve Carlton	1.00	.45	.12
☐ 168 Juan Eichelberger	.05	.02	.01
☐ 169 Burt Hooton	.05	.02	.01
☐ 170 Bob Knepper	.05	.02	.01
☐ 171 Joe Niekro	.05	.02	.01
☐ 172 Rick Rhoden	.05	.02	.01
☐ 173 Dick Ruthven	.05	.02	.01
☐ 174 Nolan Ryan	4.00	1.80	.50
☐ 175 Scott Sanderson	.05	.02	.01
☐ 176 Tom Seaver	1.00	.45	.12
☐ 177 Lary Sorensen	.05	.02	.01
☐ 178 Bruce Sutter	.15	.07	.02
☐ 179 Don Sutton	.50	.23	.06
☐ 180 Fernando Valenzuela	2.00	.90	.25

1983 All-Star Game Program Inserts

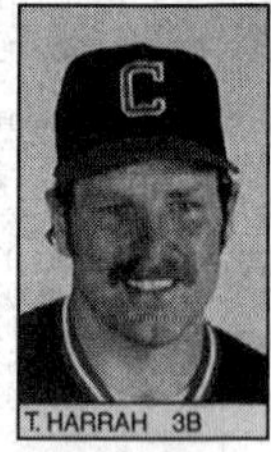

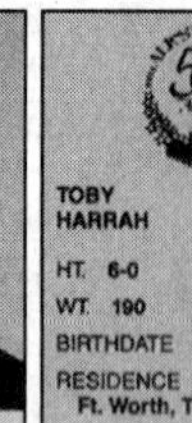

This 180-card set was distributed inside the 1983 All-Star Game Official Program on foldout sheets with each sheet containing 30 cards. Each card measures approximately 1 1/4" by 2" and features color action photos of the American League (#1-90) and the National League All-Star Nominees (#91-181). The cards are unnumbered and checklisted below in alphabetical order by position within each player's respective league.

	NRMT	VG-E	GOOD
COMPLETE SET (180)	10.00	4.50	1.25
COMMON CARD (1-180)	.05	.02	.01
☐ 1 Willie Aikens	.05	.02	.01
☐ 2 Rod Carew	.50	.23	.06
☐ 3 Cecil Cooper	.05	.02	.01
☐ 4 Kent Hrbek	.10	.05	.01
☐ 5 Eddie Murray	1.50	.70	.19
☐ 6 Tom Paciorek	.05	.02	.01
☐ 7 Andre Thornton	.05	.02	.01
☐ 8 Willie Upshaw	.05	.02	.01
☐ 9 Carl Yastrzemski	.75	.35	.09
☐ 10 Rich Dauer	.05	.02	.01
☐ 11 Jim Gantner	.05	.02	.01
☐ 12 Damaso Garcia	.05	.02	.01
☐ 13 Bobby Grich	.10	.05	.01
☐ 14 Willie Randolph	.10	.05	.01
☐ 15 Jerry Remy	.05	.02	.01
☐ 16 Manny Trillo	.05	.02	.01
☐ 17 Lou Whitaker	.50	.23	.06
☐ 18 Frank White	.10	.05	.01
☐ 19 Todd Cruz	.05	.02	.01
☐ 20 Tim Foli	.05	.02	.01
☐ 21 Alfredo Griffin	.05	.02	.01
☐ 22 Glenn Hoffman	.05	.02	.01
☐ 23 Cal Ripken	3.00	1.35	.35
☐ 24 Roy Smalley	.05	.02	.01
☐ 25 Alan Trammell	.50	.23	.06
☐ 26 U.L. Washington	.05	.02	.01
☐ 27 Robin Yount	.50	.23	.06
☐ 28 Buddy Bell	.10	.05	.01
☐ 29 Wade Boggs	4.00	1.80	.50
☐ 30 George Brett	1.50	.70	.19
☐ 31 Doug DeCinces	.05	.02	.01
☐ 32 Gary Gaetti	.75	.35	.09
☐ 33 Toby Harrah	.05	.02	.01
☐ 34 Carney Lansford	.05	.02	.01
☐ 35 Paul Molitor	1.00	.45	.12
☐ 36 Graig Nettles	.25	.11	.03
☐ 37 Bob Boone	.10	.05	.01
☐ 38 Rick Cerone	.05	.02	.01
☐ 39 Rick Dempsey	.05	.02	.01
☐ 40 Carlton Fisk	1.25	.55	.16
☐ 41 Mike Heath	.05	.02	.01
☐ 42 Lance Parrish	.10	.05	.01
☐ 43 Ted Simmons	.10	.05	.01
☐ 44 Jim Sundberg	.05	.02	.01
☐ 45 John Wathan	.05	.02	.01
☐ 46 Tony Armas	.05	.02	.01
☐ 47 Harold Baines	.10	.05	.01
☐ 48 Barry Bonnell	.05	.02	.01
☐ 49 Tom Brunansky	.05	.02	.01
☐ 50 Al Cowens	.05	.02	.01
☐ 51 Brian Downing	.05	.02	.01
☐ 52 Dwight Evans	.10	.05	.01
☐ 53 Kirk Gibson	.15	.07	.02
☐ 54 Rickey Henderson	1.50	.70	.19
☐ 55 Larry Herndon	.05	.02	.01
☐ 56 Reggie Jackson	1.00	.45	.12
☐ 57 Steve Kemp	.05	.02	.01
☐ 58 Chet Lemon	.05	.02	.01
☐ 59 Greg Luzinski	.10	.05	.01
☐ 60 Fred Lynn	.10	.05	.01
☐ 61 Rick Manning	.05	.02	.01
☐ 62 Hal McRae	.05	.02	.01
☐ 63 Jerry Mumphrey	.05	.02	.01
☐ 64 Dwayne Murphy	.05	.02	.01
☐ 65 Ben Oglivie	.05	.02	.01
☐ 66 Amos Otis	.05	.02	.01
☐ 67 Jim Rice	.25	.11	.03
☐ 68 Ken Singleton	.05	.02	.01
☐ 69 Gorman Thomas	.05	.02	.01
☐ 70 Gary Ward	.05	.02	.01
☐ 71 Willie Wilson	.05	.02	.01
☐ 72 Dave Winfield	.75	.35	.09
☐ 73 Bert Blyleven	.10	.05	.01
☐ 74 Bill Caudill	.05	.02	.01
☐ 75 Richard Dotson	.05	.02	.01
☐ 76 Dennis Eckersley	.50	.23	.06
☐ 77 Mike Flanagan	.05	.02	.01
☐ 78 Ken Forsch	.05	.02	.01
☐ 79 Larry Gura	.05	.02	.01
☐ 80 Rick Honeycutt	.05	.02	.01
☐ 81 Dennis Lamp	.05	.02	.01
☐ 82 Mike Norris	.05	.02	.01
☐ 83 Dan Petry	.05	.02	.01
☐ 84 Dan Quisenberry	.05	.02	.01
☐ 85 Shane Rawley	.05	.02	.01
☐ 86 Jim Slaton	.05	.02	.01
☐ 87 Bob Stanley	.05	.02	.01
☐ 88 Dave Stieb	.05	.02	.01
☐ 89 Al Williams	.05	.02	.01
☐ 90 Geoff Zahn	.05	.02	.01
☐ 91 Bill Buckner	.05	.02	.01
☐ 92 Chris Chambliss	.05	.02	.01
☐ 93 Dan Driessen	.05	.02	.01
☐ 94 Steve Garvey	.15	.07	.02
☐ 95 Keith Hernandez	.10	.05	.01
☐ 96 Ray Knight	.10	.05	.01
☐ 97 Al Oliver	.10	.05	.01
☐ 98 Pete Rose	1.00	.45	.12
☐ 99 Jason Thompson	.05	.02	.01
☐ 100 Juan Bonilla	.05	.02	.01
☐ 101 Doug Flynn	.05	.02	.01
☐ 102 Tom Herr	.05	.02	.01
☐ 103 Glenn Hubbard	.05	.02	.01
☐ 104 Joe Morgan	.50	.23	.06
☐ 105 Ron Oester	.05	.02	.01
☐ 106 Johnny Ray	.05	.02	.01
☐ 107 Ryne Sandberg	4.00	1.80	.50
☐ 108 Steve Sax	.10	.05	.01
☐ 109 Larry Bowa	.05	.02	.01
☐ 110 Dave Concepcion	.05	.02	.01
☐ 111 Ivan DeJesus	.05	.02	.01
☐ 112 Rafael Ramirez	.05	.02	.01
☐ 113 Bill Russell	.10	.05	.01
☐ 114 Ozzie Smith	1.50	.70	.19
☐ 115 Chris Speier	.05	.02	.01
☐ 116 Garry Templeton	.05	.02	.01
☐ 117 Dickie Thon	.05	.02	.01
☐ 118 Hubie Brooks	.05	.02	.01
☐ 119 Ron Cey	.10	.05	.01
☐ 120 Phil Garner	.10	.05	.01
☐ 121 Pedro Guerrero	.10	.05	.01
☐ 122 Bob Horner	.05	.02	.01
☐ 123 Bill Madlock	.10	.05	.01
☐ 124 Ken Oberkfell	.05	.02	.01
☐ 125 Mike Schmidt	1.50	.70	.19
☐ 126 Tim Wallach	.05	.02	.01
☐ 127 Alan Ashby	.05	.02	.01
☐ 128 Bruce Benedict	.05	.02	.01
☐ 129 Gary Carter	.50	.23	.06
☐ 130 Jody Davis	.05	.02	.01
☐ 131 Bo Diaz	.05	.02	.01
☐ 132 Terry Kennedy	.05	.02	.01
☐ 133 Tony Pena	.05	.02	.01
☐ 134 Darrell Porter	.05	.02	.01
☐ 135 John Stearns	.05	.02	.01
☐ 136 Dusty Baker	.10	.05	.01
☐ 137 Cesar Cedeno	.05	.02	.01
☐ 138 Jack Clark	.05	.02	.01
☐ 139 Warren Cromartie	.05	.02	.01
☐ 140 Jose Cruz	.10	.05	.01
☐ 141 Chili Davis	.10	.05	.01
☐ 142 Andre Dawson	.50	.23	.06
☐ 143 Leon Durham	.05	.02	.01
☐ 144 Mike Easler	.05	.02	.01
☐ 145 George Foster	.10	.05	.01
☐ 146 Von Hayes	.05	.02	.01
☐ 147 George Hendrick	.05	.02	.01
☐ 148 Ruppert Jones	.05	.02	.01
☐ 149 Ken Landreaux	.05	.02	.01
☐ 150 Sixto Lezcano	.05	.02	.01
☐ 151 Garry Maddox	.05	.02	.01
☐ 152 Gary Matthews	.05	.02	.01
☐ 153 Willie McGee	1.00	.45	.12
☐ 154 Omar Moreno	.05	.02	.01
☐ 155 Dale Murphy	.50	.23	.06
☐ 156 Dave Parker	.10	.05	.01
☐ 157 Terry Puhl	.05	.02	.01
☐ 158 Tim Raines	.15	.07	.02
☐ 159 Gene Richards	.05	.02	.01
☐ 160 Lonnie Smith	.05	.02	.01
☐ 161 Claudell Washington	.05	.02	.01
☐ 162 Mookie Wilson	.05	.02	.01
☐ 163 Joaquin Andujar	.05	.02	.01
☐ 164 Rick Camp	.05	.02	.01
☐ 165 Steve Carlton	.75	.35	.09
☐ 166 Atlee Hammaker	.05	.02	.01
☐ 167 Fergie Jenkins	.50	.23	.06
☐ 168 Bob Knepper	.05	.02	.01
☐ 169 Charlie Lea	.05	.02	.01
☐ 170 Larry McWilliams	.05	.02	.01
☐ 171 Alejandro Pena	.05	.02	.01
☐ 172 Pascual Perez	.05	.02	.01
☐ 173 Jerry Reuss	.10	.05	.01
☐ 174 Steve Rogers	.05	.02	.01
☐ 175 Nolan Ryan	3.00	1.35	.35
☐ 176 Tom Seaver	1.00	.45	.12
☐ 177 Rod Scurry	.05	.02	.01
☐ 178 Eric Show	.05	.02	.01
☐ 179 Mario Soto	.05	.02	.01
☐ 180 Bruce Sutter	.15	.07	.02

1984 All-Star Game Program Inserts

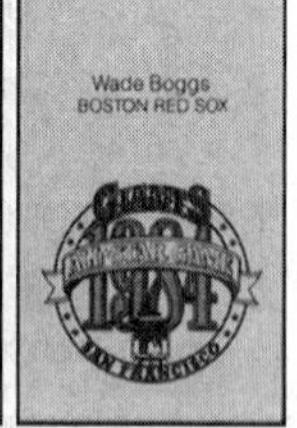

This 180-card set was distributed inside the 1984 All-Star Game Official Program on foldout sheets with each sheet containing 30 cards. Each card measures approximately 1 3/16" by 1 7/8" and features color photos of the National League (#1-90) and the American League All-Star Nominees (#91-181). The cards are unnumbered and checklisted below in alphabetical order by position within each player's respective league.

	NRMT	VG-E	GOOD
COMPLETE SET (180)	10.00	4.50	1.25
COMMON CARD (1-180)	.05	.02	.01

Card			
☐ 1 Bill Buckner	.15	.07	.02
☐ 2 Chris Chambliss	.05	.02	.01
☐ 3 Dan Driessen	.05	.02	.01
☐ 4 Steve Garvey	.25	.11	.03
☐ 5 David Green	.05	.02	.01
☐ 6 Keith Hernandez	.25	.11	.03
☐ 7 Ray Knight	.15	.07	.02
☐ 8 Al Oliver	.15	.07	.02
☐ 9 Jason Thompson	.05	.02	.01
☐ 10 Bill Doran	.05	.02	.01
☐ 11 Tommy Herr	.05	.02	.01
☐ 12 Glenn Hubbard	.05	.02	.01
☐ 13 Ron Oester	.05	.02	.01
☐ 14 Johnny Ray	.05	.02	.01
☐ 15 Ryne Sandberg	3.00	1.35	.35
☐ 16 Steve Sax	.05	.02	.01
☐ 17 Manny Trillo	.05	.02	.01
☐ 18 Alan Wiggins	.05	.02	.01
☐ 19 Dale Berra	.05	.02	.01
☐ 20 Dave Concepcion	.15	.07	.02
☐ 21 Ivan DeJesus	.05	.02	.01
☐ 22 Johnnie LeMaster	.05	.02	.01
☐ 23 Rafael Ramirez	.05	.02	.01
☐ 24 Bill Russell	.15	.07	.02
☐ 25 Ozzie Smith	2.50	1.10	.30
☐ 26 Garry Templeton	.05	.02	.01
☐ 27 Dickie Thon	.05	.02	.01
☐ 28 Ron Cey	.15	.07	.02
☐ 29 Phil Garner	.15	.07	.02
☐ 30 Pedro Guerrero	.05	.02	.01
☐ 31 Bob Horner	.05	.02	.01
☐ 32 Bill Madlock	.05	.02	.01
☐ 33 Graig Nettles	.15	.07	.02
☐ 34 Ken Oberkfell	.05	.02	.01
☐ 35 Mike Schmidt	1.50	.70	.19
☐ 36 Tim Wallach	.05	.02	.01
☐ 37 Alan Ashby	.05	.02	.01
☐ 38 Bruce Benedict	.05	.02	.01
☐ 39 Gary Carter	.50	.23	.06
☐ 40 Jody Davis	.05	.02	.01
☐ 41 Bo Diaz	.05	.02	.01
☐ 42 Terry Kennedy	.05	.02	.01
☐ 43 Tony Pena	.05	.02	.01
☐ 44 Darrell Porter	.05	.02	.01
☐ 45 Steve Yeager	.05	.02	.01
☐ 46 Jack Clark	.15	.07	.02
☐ 47 Jose Cruz	.15	.07	.02
☐ 48 Chili Davis	.15	.07	.02
☐ 49 Andre Dawson	.25	.11	.03
☐ 50 Leon Durham	.05	.02	.01
☐ 51 George Foster	.05	.02	.01
☐ 52 Tony Gwynn	3.00	1.35	.35
☐ 53 George Hendrick	.05	.02	.01
☐ 54 Ken Landreaux	.05	.02	.01
☐ 55 Joe Lefebvre	.05	.02	.01
☐ 56 Jeff Leonard	.05	.02	.01
☐ 57 Willie McGee	.50	.23	.06
☐ 58 Mike Marshall	.05	.02	.01
☐ 59 Gary Matthews	.05	.02	.01
☐ 60 Keith Moreland	.05	.02	.01
☐ 61 Jerry Mumphrey	.05	.02	.01
☐ 62 Dale Murphy	.35	.16	.04
☐ 63 Amos Otis	.05	.02	.01
☐ 64 Dave Parker	.25	.11	.03
☐ 65 Terry Puhl	.05	.02	.01
☐ 66 Tim Raines	.30	.14	.04
☐ 67 Gary Redus	.05	.02	.01
☐ 68 Pete Rose	1.50	.70	.19
☐ 69 Darryl Strawberry	1.00	.45	.12
☐ 70 Lonnie Smith	.05	.02	.01
☐ 71 Claudell Washington	.05	.02	.01
☐ 72 Mookie Wilson	.15	.07	.02
☐ 73 Joaquin Andujar	.05	.02	.01
☐ 74 Steve Bedrosian	.05	.02	.01
☐ 75 John Candelaria	.05	.02	.01
☐ 76 John Denny	.05	.02	.01
☐ 77 Dwight Gooden	2.00	.90	.25
☐ 78 Rich Gossage	.25	.11	.03
☐ 79 Al Holland	.05	.02	.01
☐ 80 Rick Honeycutt	.05	.02	.01
☐ 81 Dave LaPoint	.05	.02	.01
☐ 82 Gary Lavelle	.05	.02	.01
☐ 83 Charlie Lea	.05	.02	.01
☐ 84 Jesse Orosco	.05	.02	.01
☐ 85 Alejandro Pena	.05	.02	.01
☐ 86 Nolan Ryan	4.00	1.80	.50
☐ 87 Eric Show	.05	.02	.01
☐ 88 Bryn Smith	.05	.02	.01
☐ 89 Lee Smith	.25	.11	.03
☐ 90 Mario Soto	.05	.02	.01
☐ 91 Rod Carew	.50	.23	.06
☐ 92 Cecil Cooper	.05	.02	.01
☐ 93 Darrell Evans	.05	.02	.01
☐ 94 Ken Griffey	.15	.07	.02
☐ 95 Kent Hrbek	.05	.02	.01
☐ 96 Eddie Murray	1.00	.45	.12
☐ 97 Tom Paciorek	.05	.02	.01
☐ 98 Andre Thornton	.05	.02	.01
☐ 99 Willie Upshaw	.05	.02	.01
☐ 100 Julio Cruz	.05	.02	.01
☐ 101 Rich Dauer	.05	.02	.01
☐ 102 Jim Gantner	.05	.02	.01
☐ 103 Damasco Garcia	.05	.02	.01
☐ 104 Bobby Grich	.15	.07	.02
☐ 105 Willie Randolph	.15	.07	.02
☐ 106 Jerry Remy	.05	.02	.01
☐ 107 Lou Whitaker	.35	.16	.04
☐ 108 Frank White	.05	.02	.01
☐ 109 Tim Foli	.05	.02	.01
☐ 110 Julio Franco	.25	.11	.03
☐ 111 Alfredo Griffin	.05	.02	.01
☐ 112 Glenn Hoffman	.05	.02	.01
☐ 113 Cal Ripken	4.00	1.80	.50
☐ 114 Dick Schofield	.05	.02	.01
☐ 115 Alan Trammell	.75	.35	.09
☐ 116 Robin Yount	.50	.23	.06
☐ 117 U.L. Washington	.05	.02	.01
☐ 118 Buddy Bell	.15	.07	.02
☐ 119 Wade Boggs	1.50	.70	.19
☐ 120 George Brett	2.50	1.10	.30
☐ 121 John Castino	.05	.02	.01
☐ 122 Doug DeCinces	.05	.02	.01
☐ 123 Toby Harrah	.05	.02	.01
☐ 124 Carney Lansford	.05	.02	.01
☐ 125 Vance Law	.05	.02	.01
☐ 126 Paul Molitor	1.00	.45	.12
☐ 127 Bob Boone	.05	.02	.01
☐ 128 Rick Dempsey	.05	.02	.01
☐ 129 Carlton Fisk	.75	.35	.09
☐ 130 Mike Heath	.05	.02	.01
☐ 131 Lance Parrish	.25	.11	.03
☐ 132 Jim Sundberg	.05	.02	.01
☐ 133 Ted Simmons	.15	.07	.02
☐ 134 John Wathan	.05	.02	.01
☐ 135 Butch Wynegar	.05	.02	.01
☐ 136 Tony Armas	.05	.02	.01
☐ 137 Harold Baines	.15	.07	.02
☐ 138 Don Baylor	.25	.11	.03
☐ 139 Jesse Barfield	.05	.02	.01
☐ 140 Tom Brunansky	.05	.02	.01
☐ 141 Brian Downing	.05	.02	.01
☐ 142 Dwight Evans	.15	.07	.02
☐ 143 Rickey Henderson	1.50	.70	.19
☐ 144 Larry Herndon	.05	.02	.01
☐ 145 Reggie Jackson	1.00	.45	.12
☐ 146 Steve Kemp	.05	.02	.01
☐ 147 Ron Kittle	.05	.02	.01
☐ 148 Chet Lemon	.05	.02	.01
☐ 149 John Lowenstein	.05	.02	.01
☐ 150 Greg Luzinski	.15	.07	.02
☐ 151 Fred Lynn	.15	.07	.02
☐ 152 Hal McRae	.15	.07	.02
☐ 153 Lloyd Moseby	.05	.02	.01
☐ 154 Dwayne Murphy	.05	.02	.01
☐ 155 Larry Parrish	.05	.02	.01
☐ 156 Ben Oglivie	.05	.02	.01
☐ 157 Jim Rice	.25	.11	.03
☐ 158 Gorman Thomas	.05	.02	.01
☐ 159 Ken Singleton	.05	.02	.01
☐ 160 Gary Ward	.05	.02	.01
☐ 161 Dave Winfield	1.00	.45	.12
☐ 162 George Wright	.05	.02	.01
☐ 163 Dave Beard	.05	.02	.01
☐ 164 Bert Blyleven	.25	.11	.03
☐ 165 Mike Boddicker	.05	.02	.01
☐ 166 Mike Caldwell	.05	.02	.01
☐ 167 Bill Caudill	.05	.02	.01
☐ 168 Danny Darwin	.05	.02	.01
☐ 169 Ron Davis	.05	.02	.01
☐ 170 Richard Dotson	.05	.02	.01
☐ 171 Larry Gura	.05	.02	.01
☐ 172 Bruce Hurst	.05	.02	.01
☐ 173 Luis Leal	.05	.02	.01
☐ 174 Jack Morris	.35	.16	.04
☐ 175 Dan Petry	.05	.02	.01
☐ 176 Mike Smithson	.05	.02	.01
☐ 177 Sammy Stewart	.05	.02	.01
☐ 178 Dave Stieb	.15	.07	.02
☐ 179 Milt Wilcox	.05	.02	.01
☐ 180 Geoff Zahn	.05	.02	.01

1985 All-Star Game Program Inserts

This 180-card set was distributed inside the 1985 All-Star Game Official Program on foldout sheets with each sheet containing 30 cards. Each card measures approximately 1 1/4" by 2" and features color photos of the American League (#1-90) and the National League All-Star Nominees (#91-181). The cards are unnumbered and checklisted below in alphabetical order by position within each player's respective league.

	NRMT	VG-E	GOOD
COMPLETE SET (180)	10.00	4.50	1.25
COMMON CARD (1-180)	.05	.02	.01
☐ 1 Bill Buckner	.10	.05	.01
☐ 2 Rod Carew	.75	.35	.09
☐ 3 Cecil Cooper	.10	.05	.01
☐ 4 Alvin Davis	.10	.05	.01
☐ 5 Kent Hrbek	.10	.05	.01
☐ 6 Don Mattingly	2.00	.90	.25
☐ 7 Eddie Murray	.75	.35	.09
☐ 8 Pete O'Brien	.05	.02	.01
☐ 9 Willie Upshaw	.05	.02	.01
☐ 10 Marty Barrett	.05	.02	.01
☐ 11 Julio Cruz	.05	.02	.01
☐ 12 Jim Gantner	.05	.02	.01
☐ 13 Damaso Garcia	.05	.02	.01
☐ 14 Bobby Grich	.10	.05	.01

Card			
☐ 15 Willie Randolph	.10	.05	.01
☐ 16 Tim Teufel	.05	.02	.01
☐ 17 Lou Whitaker	.25	.11	.03
☐ 18 Frank White	.05	.02	.01
☐ 19 Onix Concepcion	.05	.02	.01
☐ 20 Tony Fernandez	.05	.02	.01
☐ 21 Julio Franco	.15	.07	.02
☐ 22 Alfredo Griffin	.05	.02	.01
☐ 23 Jackie Gutierrez	.05	.02	.01
☐ 24 Spike Owen	.05	.02	.01
☐ 25 Cal Ripken	3.00	1.35	.35
☐ 26 Alan Trammell	.50	.23	.06
☐ 27 Robin Yount	.75	.35	.09
☐ 28 Buddy Bell	.10	.05	.01
☐ 29 Wade Boggs	1.50	.70	.19
☐ 30 George Brett	1.50	.70	.19
☐ 31 Doug DeCinces	.10	.05	.01
☐ 32 Darrell Evans	.10	.05	.01
☐ 33 Gary Gaetti	.10	.05	.01
☐ 34 Carney Lansford	.10	.05	.01
☐ 35 Paul Molitor	1.00	.45	.12
☐ 36 Rance Mulliniks	.05	.02	.01
☐ 37 Bob Boone	.05	.02	.01
☐ 38 Rick Dempsey	.10	.05	.01
☐ 39 Carlton Fisk	.75	.35	.09
☐ 40 Rich Gedman	.05	.02	.01
☐ 41 Mike Heath	.05	.02	.01
☐ 42 Lance Parrish	.10	.05	.01
☐ 43 Jim Sundberg	.05	.02	.01
☐ 44 Ernie Whitt	.05	.02	.01
☐ 45 Butch Wynegar	.05	.02	.01
☐ 46 Tony Armas	.05	.02	.01
☐ 47 Harold Baines	.15	.07	.02
☐ 48 Jesse Barfield	.05	.02	.01
☐ 49 Don Baylor	.10	.05	.01
☐ 50 George Bell	.05	.02	.01
☐ 51 Tom Brunansky	.05	.02	.01
☐ 52 Brett Butler	.10	.05	.01
☐ 53 Dave Collins	.05	.02	.01
☐ 54 Brian Downing	.05	.02	.01
☐ 55 Mike Easler	.05	.02	.01
☐ 56 Dwight Evans	.10	.05	.01
☐ 57 Kirk Gibson	.25	.11	.03
☐ 58 Rickey Henderson	1.25	.55	.16
☐ 59 Reggie Jackson	1.00	.45	.12
☐ 60 Ron Kittle	.05	.02	.01
☐ 61 Lee Lacy	.05	.02	.01
☐ 62 Chet Lemon	.05	.02	.01
☐ 63 Fred Lynn	.10	.05	.01
☐ 64 Lloyd Moseby	.05	.02	.01
☐ 65 Dwayne Murphy	.05	.02	.01
☐ 66 Ben Oglivie	.05	.02	.01
☐ 67 Larry Parrish	.05	.02	.01
☐ 68 Kirby Puckett	4.00	1.80	.50
☐ 69 Jim Rice	.10	.05	.01
☐ 70 Gary Ward	.05	.02	.01
☐ 71 Willie Wilson	.05	.02	.01
☐ 72 Dave Winfield	1.00	.45	.12
☐ 73 Doyle Alexander	.05	.02	.01
☐ 74 Mike Boddicker	.05	.02	.01
☐ 75 Oil Can Boyd	.05	.02	.01
☐ 76 Danny Darwin	.05	.02	.01
☐ 77 Ron Guidry	.10	.05	.01
☐ 78 Willie Hernandez	.05	.02	.01
☐ 79 Mark Langston	.25	.11	.03
☐ 80 Charlie Liebrandt	.05	.02	.01
☐ 81 Jack Morris	.10	.05	.01
☐ 82 Dickie Noles	.05	.02	.01
☐ 83 Dan Petry	.05	.02	.01
☐ 84 Dan Quisenberry	.05	.02	.01
☐ 85 Dave Righetti	.05	.02	.01
☐ 86 Don Schulze	.05	.02	.01
☐ 87 Tom Seaver	.50	.23	.06
☐ 88 Jim Slaton	.05	.02	.01
☐ 89 Frank Viola	.10	.05	.01
☐ 90 Geoff Zahn	.05	.02	.01
☐ 91 Greg Brock	.05	.02	.01
☐ 92 Enos Cabell	.05	.02	.01
☐ 93 Dan Driessen	.05	.02	.01
☐ 94 Leon Durham	.05	.02	.01
☐ 95 Steve Garvey	.25	.11	.03
☐ 96 David Green	.05	.02	.01
☐ 97 Keith Hernandez	.10	.05	.01
☐ 98 Pete Rose	1.00	.45	.12
☐ 99 Jason Thompson	.05	.02	.01
☐ 100 Bill Doran	.05	.02	.01
☐ 101 Tommy Herr	.05	.02	.01
☐ 102 Glenn Hubbard	.05	.02	.01
☐ 103 Johnny Ray	.05	.02	.01
☐ 104 Juan Samuel	.05	.02	.01
☐ 105 Ryne Sandberg	1.00	.45	.12
☐ 106 Steve Sax	.10	.05	.01
☐ 107 Manny Trillo	.05	.02	.01
☐ 108 Alan Wiggins	.05	.02	.01
☐ 109 Larry Bowa	.10	.05	.01
☐ 110 Hubie Brooks	.05	.02	.01
☐ 111 Dave Concepcion	.15	.07	.02
☐ 112 Ivan DeJesus	.05	.02	.01
☐ 113 Rafael Ramirez	.05	.02	.01
☐ 114 Craig Reynolds	.05	.02	.01
☐ 115 Bill Russell	.10	.05	.01
☐ 116 Ozzie Smith	1.00	.45	.12
☐ 117 Garry Templeton	.05	.02	.01
☐ 118 Ron Cey	.10	.05	.01
☐ 119 Phil Garner	.10	.05	.01
☐ 120 Bob Horner	.05	.02	.01
☐ 121 Ray Knight	.05	.02	.01
☐ 122 Bill Madlock	.10	.05	.01
☐ 123 Graig Nettles	.15	.07	.02
☐ 124 Terry Pendleton	.25	.11	.03
☐ 125 Mike Schmidt	.75	.35	.09
☐ 126 Tim Wallach	.05	.02	.01
☐ 127 Bob Brenly	.05	.02	.01
☐ 128 Gary Carter	.25	.11	.03
☐ 129 Jody Davis	.05	.02	.01
☐ 130 Mike Fitzgerald	.05	.02	.01
☐ 131 Terry Kennedy	.05	.02	.01
☐ 132 Tony Pena	.05	.02	.01
☐ 133 Darrell Porter	.10	.05	.01
☐ 134 Mike Scioscia	.05	.02	.01
☐ 135 Ozzie Virgil	.05	.02	.01
☐ 136 Jack Clark	.05	.02	.01
☐ 137 Jose Cruz	.10	.05	.01
☐ 138 Chili Davis	.10	.05	.01
☐ 139 Andre Dawson	.15	.07	.02
☐ 140 Bob Dernier	.05	.02	.01
☐ 141 George Foster	.05	.02	.01
☐ 142 Pedro Guerrero	.10	.05	.01
☐ 143 Tony Gwynn	1.50	.70	.19
☐ 144 Von Hayes	.05	.02	.01
☐ 145 George Hendrick	.05	.02	.01
☐ 146 Steve Kemp	.05	.02	.01
☐ 147 Jeff Leonard	.05	.02	.01
☐ 148 Mike Marshall	.05	.02	.01
☐ 149 Gary Matthews	.05	.02	.01
☐ 150 Willie McGee	.25	.11	.03
☐ 151 Kevin McReynolds	.05	.02	.01
☐ 152 Keith Moreland	.05	.02	.01
☐ 153 Jerry Mumphrey	.05	.02	.01
☐ 154 Dale Murphy	.25	.11	.03
☐ 155 Dave Parker	.10	.05	.01
☐ 156 Terry Puhl	.05	.02	.01
☐ 157 Tim Raines	.10	.05	.01
☐ 158 Lonnie Smith	.05	.02	.01
☐ 159 Darryl Strawberry	.25	.11	.03
☐ 160 Claudell Washington	.05	.02	.01
☐ 161 Mookie Wilson	.10	.05	.01
☐ 162 Marvell Wynne	.05	.02	.01
☐ 163 Joaquin Andujar	.05	.02	.01
☐ 164 Steve Bedrosian	.05	.02	.01
☐ 165 John Candelaria	.05	.02	.01
☐ 166 Jose DeLeon	.05	.02	.01
☐ 167 John Denny	.05	.02	.01
☐ 168 Dennis Eckersley	.75	.35	.09
☐ 169 Dwight Gooden	.50	.23	.06
☐ 170 Rich Gossage	.15	.07	.02
☐ 171 Mike Krukow	.05	.02	.01
☐ 172 Rick Mahler	.05	.02	.01
☐ 173 Jesse Orosco	.05	.02	.01
☐ 174 Shane Rawley	.05	.02	.01
☐ 175 Nolan Ryan	3.00	1.35	.35
☐ 176 Bryn Smith	.05	.02	.01
☐ 177 Lee Smith	.15	.07	.02
☐ 178 Mario Soto	.05	.02	.01
☐ 179 Steve Trout	.05	.02	.01
☐ 180 Fernando Valenzuela	.10	.05	.01

1991 Alrak Griffey Gazette

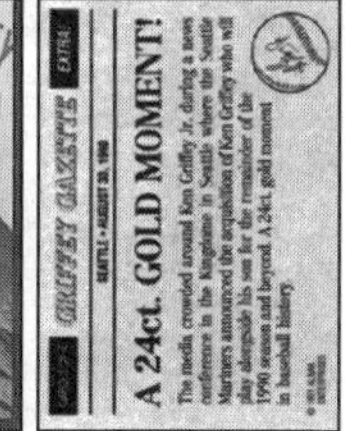

Produced by Alrak Enterprises, these standard-size cards were issued in honor of Ken Griffey Jr. The high gloss color photos on the fronts have gold borders. The horizontally oriented backs have dark blue print on a light blue background and captions to the front pictures. TheThree thousand promo sets were distributed at the SuperBowl Sports Collectors Classic III in Bellevue, Washington (January, 1992). These promos carries the following stamp on their backs: "Promo Card, SuperBowl Sports Collectors Classic III, Bellevue, Washington, January 1992 and are valued at double the prices listed below.

	MINT	NRMT	EXC
COMPLETE SET (4)	6.00	2.70	.75
COMMON CARD (1-4)	1.50	.70	.19
☐ 1 Ken Griffey Jr. Crowd Pleaser	1.50	.70	.19

☐ 2 Ken Griffey Jr. Holdin' On	1.50	.70	.19
☐ 3 Ken Griffey Jr. A 24ct. Gold Moment	1.50	.70	.19
☐ 4 Ken Griffey Jr. Ken Griffey Sr. Next of Ken	1.50	.70	.19

1991 Alrak Griffey Postcard

This one card set measures approximately 5 3/8" by 7 1/4" and was distributed by Alrak Enterprises to advertise their Ken Griffey Jr. Solid Brass Monthly Sportcard Series. The front of the card features Griffey in three different poses. The back tells how to become a member to receive the brass cards and displays a postcard format.

	MINT	NRMT	EXC
COMPLETE SET (1)	2.00	.90	.25
COMMON CARD (1)	2.00	.90	.25
☐ 1 Ken Griffey Jr.	2.00	.90	.25

1992 Alrak Griffey Ace Auto Supply

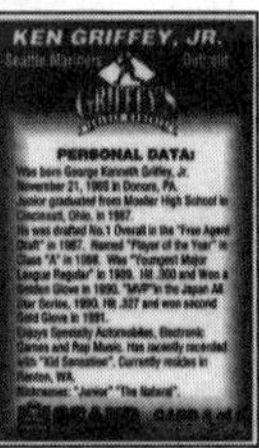

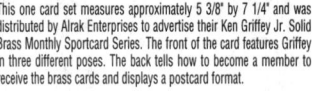

This five-card set, subtitled "Griffey's Golden Moments," was produced by Alrak Enterprises for Ace Auto Supply and Grand Auto Supply stores. The production run was reportedly 85,000 sets and they were sold at 145 stores in northern California, Nevada Washington and Alaska. The plastic cards measure approximately 3 3/8" by 2 1/8" and resemble plastic credit cards. Each front features a color photo of Griffey enclosed by a color inner border (the color differs from card to card) and a black outer border. Each card was sold in a plastic sleeve bearing an orange image of Griffey watching a hit ball after his follow through. The backs are either horizontally or vertically oriented and carry biography, statistics or career highlights.

	MINT	NRMT	EXC
COMPLETE SET (10)	12.00	5.50	1.50
COMMON CARD (1-10)	1.25	.55	.16
☐ 1 Ken Griffey Jr. Complete Minor/Major League Batting Record	1.25	.55	.16
☐ 2 Ken Griffey Jr. Career Highlights	1.25	.55	.16
☐ 3 Ken Griffey Jr. Personal Data	1.25	.55	.16
☐ 4 Ken Griffey Jr. Facts and Figures	1.25	.55	.16
☐ 5 Ken Griffey Jr. Ken Griffey Sr. Father and Son Data	1.25	.55	.16
☐ 6 Ken Griffey Jr. 1991 Highlights	1.25	.55	.16
☐ 7 Ken Griffey Jr. Career Highlights	1.25	.55	.16
☐ 8 Ken Griffey Jr. Facts About Junior	1.25	.55	.16
☐ 9 Ken Griffey Jr. Facts About Junior	1.25	.55	.16
☐ 10 Ken Griffey Jr. Ken Griffey Sr. Father and Son Data	1.25	.55	.16

1992 Alrak Griffey Golden Moments

This ten-card set measures approximately 2 1/8" by 3 3/8" and is similar in design and material to credit cards. The cards feature posed and action color photos of Ken Griffey Jr. and Ken Griffey Sr. with white borders. The backs are white and carry player information, biography or statistics. The cards are numbered on the back. Originally 10,000 sets were to be produced but much less were reportedly actually released. The cards indicate "X of 20" on the back, so a second series of ten more cards was evidently planned.

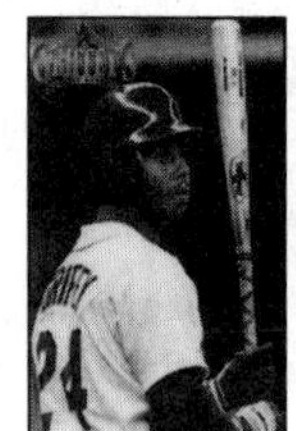
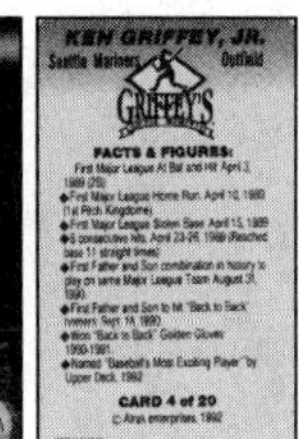

	MINT	NRMT	EXC
COMPLETE SET (10)	15.00	6.75	1.85
COMMON CARD (1-10)	1.50	.70	.19
☐ 1 Ken Griffey Jr. Batting, horizontal shot	1.50	.70	.19
☐ 2 Ken Griffey Jr. Fielding off wall	1.50	.70	.19
☐ 3 Ken Griffey Jr. Sliding	1.50	.70	.19
☐ 4 Ken Griffey Jr. Holding bat	1.50	.70	.19
☐ 5 Ken Griffey Jr. Ken Griffey Sr.	1.50	.70	.19
☐ 6 Ken Griffey Jr. Batting, vertical shot	1.50	.70	.19
☐ 7 Ken Griffey Jr. With All-Star trophy	1.50	.70	.19
☐ 8 Ken Griffey Jr. Close-up	1.50	.70	.19
☐ 9 Ken Griffey Jr. On base	1.50	.70	.19
☐ 10 Ken Griffey Jr. Ken Griffey Sr. In dugout	1.50	.70	.19

1992 Alrak Griffey Golden Moments Sheet

This commemorative sheet measures approximately 8 1/2" by 10 3/4" and features pictures of the Griffey's Golden Moments limited edition plastic baseball cards from Series I and II. The cards appear against star designs. The set name and logo are printed in gold lettering at the top of the sheet. The background fades from black to orange to off-white. Each sheet is individually numbered. Production was limited to 1,000. The back is blank.

	MINT	NRMT	EXC
COMPLETE SET (1)	5.00	2.20	.60
COMMON CARD (1)	5.00	2.20	.60
☐ 1 Ken Griffey Jr.	5.00	2.20	.60

1992 Alrak Griffey McDonald's

This set, sponsored by McDonald's, contains three card and pin combinations. The cards are numbered on the front and measure 2 1/2" X 3 1/2". The card back describes the Ronald McDonald Children's Charities program in Western Washington. The set was produced by Alrak Enterprises with a reported production run of 100,000 for each card and pin combination. They were sold in 117 Western McDonald's Washington restaurants.

	MINT	NRMT	EXC
COMPLETE SET (3)	10.00	4.50	1.25
COMMON CARD (1-3)	3.50	1.55	.45
☐ 1 Ken Griffey Jr. Yellow background	3.50	1.55	.45
☐ 2 Ken Griffey Jr. Black and red background	3.50	1.55	.45
☐ 3 Ken Griffey Jr. Black and blue background	3.50	1.55	.45

1993 Alrak Griffey 24 Taco Time

This six-card standard-size set was issued in the Pacific Northwest at Taco Time restaurants. Three cards have cut-out color player photos against gradated backgrounds of various colors. Color coordinated striped borders edged with gold foil frame the pictures. A gold-foil stamp at the lower right carries the words "Griffey 24" and "One of 24,000." The backs give player profile information and statistics against brightly colored backgrounds with a baseball player icon. The fourth card in the set is a 1992 All-Star MVP commemorative. It features a posed shot of Griffey with the MVP award. The horizontal back carries a color action photo with statistics in a ghosted white box on the left side. The fifth and sixth cards carry the red-foil Taco Time logo in their upper left corners and have red-foil-trimmed borders. The backs carry designs similar to the first three cards described above. The cards are unnumbered.

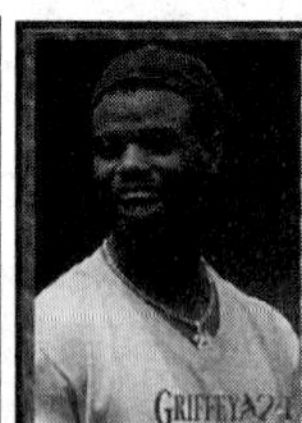

	MINT	NRMT	EXC
COMPLETE SET (6)	10.00	4.50	1.25
COMMON CARD (1-6)	2.00	.90	.25
☐ 1 Ken Griffey Jr. Portrait	2.00	.90	.25
☐ 2 Ken Griffey Jr. Batting	2.00	.90	.25
☐ 3 Ken Griffey Jr. Throwing	2.00	.90	.25
☐ 4 Ken Griffey Jr. All-Star MVP	2.00	.90	.25
☐ 5 Ken Griffey Jr. Leaving batter's box	2.00	.90	.25
☐ 6 Ken Griffey Jr. Head-first slide	2.00	.90	.25

1993 Alrak Griffey Mt. Vernon Ohio

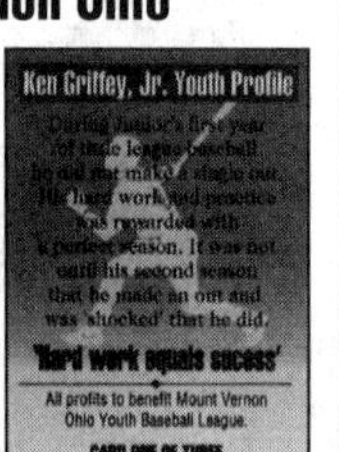

Twenty thousand of these three-card standard-size sets were produced for the city of Mt. Vernon and all profits were to benefit the Mt. Vernon Ohio Youth Baseball League. The cards feature cut-out color player photos (the same ones as in the Griffey 24 set) against gradated backgrounds of various colors. Color coordinated border stripes frame the pictures. The player's name appears in large block letters near one of the top corners. The backs give player profile information against an aqua background that fades to yellow and then white at the bottom and carries a yellow baseball player icon. A motivational message appears in heavy black type below the player profile. Two different versions of the cards exist, one with and one without a gold-foil facsimile autograph inscribed across the picture.

	MINT	NRMT	EXC
COMPLETE SET (3)	6.00	2.70	.75
COMMON CARD (1-3)	2.00	.90	.25
☐ 1 Ken Griffey Jr. Portrait	2.00	.90	.25
☐ 2 Ken Griffey Jr. Batting	2.00	.90	.25
☐ 3 Ken Griffey Jr. Throwing	2.00	.90	.25

1993 Alrak Griffey Triple Play

This tri-fold card measures 7 1/2" by 3 1/2" unfolded and features a full-length color action photo of Griffey on one side with the words "Triple Play" appearing above the photo and statistics below. The other side is divided into three panels. One panel carries a color portrait framed in gold foil. The words "Golden Glove, Golden Smile" appear below the picture. The center panel displays the player's name and the Triple Play name in a horizontal format. The third panel shows a horizontal color action photo of Griffey batting. A black bar at the bottom is edged in gold foil and contains the phrase "1992 All-Star MVP" in gold foil. The production run was reportedly 24,000.

	MINT	NRMT	EXC
COMPLETE SET (1)	3.00	1.35	.35
COMMON CARD	3.00	1.35	.35
☐ 1 Ken Griffey Jr.	3.00	1.35	.35

1993 Alrak Griffey Two-sided

This card measures the standard size and features a cut-out action shot of Griffey batting on one side and three cut-out action photos of Griffey on the other side. The background on each side consists of a dark blue with the player's name printed diagonally in a slightly different shade of blue.

	MINT	NRMT	EXC
COMPLETE SET (1)	3.00	1.35	.35
COMMON CARD	3.00	1.35	.35
☐ 1 Ken Griffey Jr.	3.00	1.35	.35

1994 Alrak Griffey Jr. Taco Time

As part of a "Double Play" combination promotion, these 11 cards were specially offered as foil-wrapped singles to purchasers of a a 44 oz. Coke in a special Ken Griffey Jr. Collector's Cup at Taco Time Restaurants of Western Washington. Production of card numbers 1-6 was limited to 35,000 silver foil-accented sets. Additionally, 5,000 special gold foil-accented versions were created and randomly issued. The production run of the silver-foil SP2, SP4, and SP5 was 15,000, while that of the holographic foil SP1-3 was 20,000. Also, 30,000 cards were distributed to kick off the promotion to fans attending the Mariners-White Sox game of June 24. Measuring 3 1/2" by 5", the fronts feature original caricatures of Griffey by sports artist Larry Weber. The backs carry a description of a memorable moment in the career of the Mariners' star, as well as the Mariners, Alrak, and Taco Time logos.

	MINT	NRMT	EXC
COMPLETE SILVER SET (6)	10.00	4.50	1.25
COMMON SILVER CARD (1-6)	2.00	.90	.25
*GOLD: 3X VALUE			
COMPLETE SP SET (5)	30.00	13.50	3.70
COMMON CARD (SP1-SP5)	6.00	2.70	.75
☐ 1 Ken Griffey Jr. 1990 First Gold Glove	2.00	.90	.25
☐ 2 Ken Griffey Jr. 1993	2.00	.90	.25
☐ 3 Ken Griffey Jr. 1993 AL Defensive Player of the Year	2.00	.90	.25
☐ 4 Ken Griffey Jr. 1992 All-Star MVP	2.00	.90	.25
☐ 5 Ken Griffey Jr. 1994 All-Star	2.00	.90	.25
☐ 6 Ken Griffey Jr. Mariners Care	2.00	.90	.25
☐ SP1 Ken Griffey Jr. 1993 AL Defensive Record	6.00	2.70	.75
☐ SP2 Ken Griffey Jr. 1993 Home Run Streak	8.00	3.60	1.00
☐ SP3 Ken Griffey Jr. 100th Home Run	6.00	2.70	.75
☐ SP4 Ken Griffey Jr. 1993 Off the Wall	8.00	3.60	1.00
☐ SP5 Ken Griffey Jr. 1989 Major League Debut	8.00	3.60	1.00

1908-10 American Caramel E91

The cards in this 99-card set measure 1 1/2" by 2 3/4". E91 encompasses three separate sets of color cards issued in 1908 and 1910. The 33 ballplayer drawings of the 1908 set were also used in the two 1910 sets. Eleven players were dropped and 11 were added for set 3. There are only 75 different players, so that, for example, there are two cards of Bender with identical fronts, but a different player is "named" in the same pose in set 3. Likewise, there can be three different players assigned to the same pose -- one from each set. The set 1 checklist lists "Athletics" first; set 3 "Pittsburgh" first. Because of these drawings (which are generic and do not specifically resemble the actual player's likeness) the set has never been popular with collectors, hence their relatively low price.

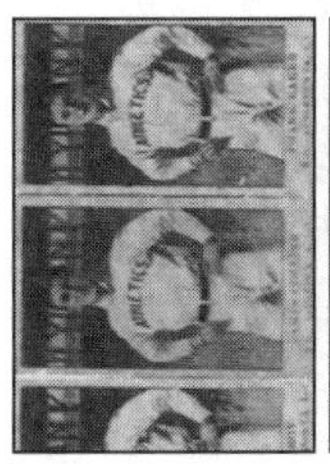
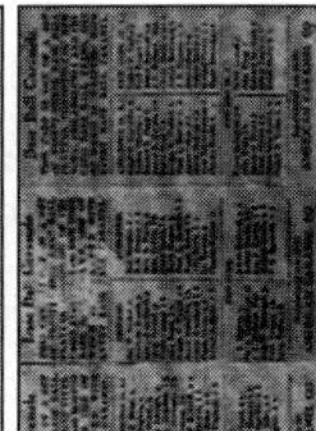

	EX-MT	VG-E	GOOD
COMPLETE SET (99)	6000.00	2700.00	750.00
COMMON CARD (1-99)	40.00	18.00	5.00
☐ 1 Chief Bender	125.00	55.00	15.50
☐ 2 Roger Bresnahan	125.00	55.00	15.50
☐ 3 Al Bridwell	40.00	18.00	5.00
☐ 4 Mordecai Brown	125.00	55.00	15.50
☐ 5 Frank Chance	150.00	70.00	19.00
☐ 6 James Collins	125.00	55.00	15.50
☐ 7 Harry Davis	40.00	18.00	5.00
☐ 8 Art Devlin	40.00	18.00	5.00
☐ 9 Mike Donlin	40.00	18.00	5.00
☐ 10 Johnny Evers	125.00	55.00	15.50
☐ 11 Fred Hartzell	40.00	18.00	5.00
☐ 12 Johnny Kling	40.00	18.00	5.00
☐ 13 Christy Mathewson	200.00	90.00	25.00
☐ 14 Joe McGinnity	125.00	55.00	15.50
☐ 15 John McGraw	150.00	70.00	19.00
☐ 16 Danny Murphy	40.00	18.00	5.00
☐ 17 Simon Nichols	40.00	18.00	5.00
☐ 18 Rube Oldring	40.00	18.00	5.00
☐ 19 Orval Overall	40.00	18.00	5.00
☐ 20 Eddie Plank	125.00	55.00	15.50
☐ 21 Ed Reulbach	40.00	18.00	5.00
☐ 22 Jimmy Scheckard	40.00	18.00	5.00
☐ 23 Ossie Schreckengost	40.00	18.00	5.00
☐ 24 Frank Shulte	40.00	18.00	5.00
☐ 25 Ralph Seybold	40.00	18.00	5.00
☐ 26 J.B. Seymore	40.00	18.00	5.00
☐ 27 Daniel Shay	40.00	18.00	5.00
☐ 28 James Slagle	40.00	18.00	5.00
☐ 29 Harry Steinfeldt	60.00	27.00	7.50
☐ 30 Luther Taylor	40.00	18.00	5.00
☐ 31 Fred Tenney	40.00	18.00	5.00
☐ 32 Joe Tinker	100.00	45.00	12.50
☐ 33 Rube Waddell	125.00	55.00	15.50
☐ 34 Jimmy Archer	40.00	18.00	5.00
☐ 35 Frank Baker	125.00	55.00	15.50
☐ 36 Jack Barry	40.00	18.00	5.00
☐ 37 Chief Bender	125.00	55.00	15.50
☐ 38 Al Bridwell	40.00	18.00	5.00
☐ 39 Mordecai Brown	125.00	55.00	15.50
☐ 40 Frank Chance	150.00	70.00	19.00
☐ 41 Eddie Collins	150.00	70.00	19.00
☐ 42 Harry Davis	40.00	18.00	5.00
☐ 43 Art Devlin	40.00	18.00	5.00
☐ 44 Mike Donlin	40.00	18.00	5.00
☐ 45 Larry Doyle	40.00	18.00	5.00
☐ 46 Johnny Evers	100.00	45.00	12.50
☐ 47 Bob Ganley	40.00	18.00	5.00
☐ 48 Fred Hartzell	40.00	18.00	5.00
☐ 49 Solly Hoffman	40.00	18.00	5.00
☐ 50 Harry Krause	40.00	18.00	5.00
☐ 51 Rube Marquard	125.00	55.00	15.50
☐ 52 Christy Mathewson	200.00	90.00	25.00
☐ 53 John McGraw	100.00	45.00	12.50
☐ 54 Chief Meyers	60.00	27.00	7.50
☐ 55 Danny Murphy	40.00	18.00	5.00
☐ 56 Red Murray	40.00	18.00	5.00
☐ 57 Orval Overall	40.00	18.00	5.00
☐ 58 Eddie Plank	125.00	55.00	15.50
☐ 59 Ed Reulbach	40.00	18.00	5.00
☐ 60 Jimmy Scheckard	40.00	18.00	5.00
☐ 61 Frank Schulte	40.00	18.00	5.00
☐ 62 J.B. Seymore	40.00	18.00	5.00
☐ 63 Harry Steinfeldt	60.00	27.00	7.50
☐ 64 Fred Tenney	40.00	18.00	5.00
☐ 65 Ira Thomas	40.00	18.00	5.00
☐ 66 Joe Tinker	100.00	45.00	12.50
☐ 67 Jap Barbeau	40.00	18.00	5.00
☐ 68 George Browne	40.00	18.00	5.00
☐ 69 Ed Cargar	40.00	18.00	5.00
☐ 70 Robert Chech	40.00	18.00	5.00
☐ 71 Fred Clarke	125.00	55.00	15.50
☐ 72 Wid Conroy	40.00	18.00	5.00
☐ 73 Jim Delehanty	40.00	18.00	5.00
☐ 74 Jiggs Donahue	40.00	18.00	5.00
☐ 75 J.A. Donohue	40.00	18.00	5.00
☐ 76 George Gibson	40.00	18.00	5.00
☐ 77 Bob Groom	40.00	18.00	5.00
☐ 78 Harry Hooper	125.00	55.00	15.50
☐ 79 Tom Hughes	40.00	18.00	5.00
☐ 80 Walter Johnson	200.00	90.00	25.00
☐ 81 Tommy Leach	60.00	27.00	7.50
☐ 82 Sam Leever	40.00	18.00	5.00
☐ 83 Harry Lord	40.00	18.00	5.00
☐ 84 George McBride	40.00	18.00	5.00
☐ 85 Amby McConnell	40.00	18.00	5.00
☐ 86 Clyde Milan	40.00	18.00	5.00
☐ 87 J.B. Miller	40.00	18.00	5.00
☐ 88 Harry Niles	40.00	18.00	5.00
☐ 89 Deacon Phillippe	60.00	27.00	7.50
☐ 90 Tris Speaker	150.00	70.00	19.00
☐ 91 Jack Stahl	60.00	27.00	7.50
☐ 92 Allen Storke	40.00	18.00	5.00
☐ 93 Gabby Street	60.00	27.00	7.50
☐ 94 Bob Unglaub	40.00	18.00	5.00
☐ 95 Charlie Wagner	40.00	18.00	5.00
☐ 96 Honus Wagner	300.00	135.00	38.00
☐ 97 Vic Willis	125.00	55.00	15.50
☐ 98 Owen Wilson	40.00	18.00	5.00
☐ 99 Joe Wood	60.00	27.00	7.50

1909-11 American Caramel E90-1

The cards in this 120-card set measure 1 1/2" by 2 3/4". The E90-1 set contains in order, the Mitchell of Cincinnati, Sweeney of Boston, and Graham cards which are more difficult to obtain than other cards in the set. In fact, there are many differential levels of scarcity in this set which was issued from 1909 through 1911. Several players exist in more than one pose or color background; these cards are noted in the checklist below.

	EX-MT	VG-E	GOOD
COMPLETE SET (120)	40000.00	18000.00	5000.00
COMMON CARD (1-120)	100.00	45.00	12.50
☐ 1 William Bailey	100.00	45.00	12.50
☐ 2 Frank Baker	250.00	110.00	31.00
☐ 3 Jack Barry	100.00	45.00	12.50
☐ 4 George Bell	100.00	45.00	12.50
☐ 5 Harry Bemis	250.00	110.00	31.00
☐ 6 Chief Bender	250.00	110.00	31.00
☐ 7 Bob Bescher	150.00	70.00	19.00
☐ 8 Cliff Blankenship	100.00	45.00	12.50
☐ 9 John Bliss	100.00	45.00	12.50
☐ 10 William J. Bradley	100.00	45.00	12.50
☐ 11 Kitty Bransfield (blue background)	100.00	45.00	12.50
☐ 12 Kitty Bransfield (pink background)	125.00	55.00	15.50
☐ 13 Roger Bresnahan	250.00	110.00	31.00
☐ 14 Al Bridwell	100.00	45.00	12.50
☐ 15 Buster Brown HOR Boston NL	100.00	45.00	12.50
☐ 16 Mordecai Brown Chic NL	300.00	135.00	38.00
☐ 17 Donie Bush	100.00	45.00	12.50
☐ 18 John A. Butler	100.00	45.00	12.50
☐ 19 Howie Camnitz	100.00	45.00	12.50
☐ 20 Frank Chance	300.00	135.00	38.00
☐ 21 Hal Chase	150.00	70.00	19.00
☐ 22 Fred Clarke Phila. NL	250.00	110.00	31.00
☐ 23 Fred Clarke Pitts	1500.00	700.00	190.00
☐ 24 Wallace O. Clement	125.00	55.00	15.50
☐ 25 Ty Cobb	2000.00	900.00	250.00
☐ 26 Eddie Collins	300.00	135.00	38.00
☐ 27 Frank Corridon	100.00	45.00	12.50
☐ 28 Sam Crawford	250.00	110.00	31.00
☐ 29 Lou Criger	100.00	45.00	12.50
☐ 30 Jasper Davis	100.00	45.00	12.50
☐ 31 George Davis	100.00	45.00	12.50
☐ 32 Ray Demmitt	150.00	70.00	19.00
☐ 33 Mike Donlin	100.00	45.00	12.50
☐ 34 Wild Bill Donovan	100.00	45.00	12.50
☐ 35 Red Dooin	100.00	45.00	12.50
☐ 36 Patsy Dougherty	125.00	55.00	15.50
☐ 37 Hugh Duffy	2000.00	900.00	250.00
☐ 38 Jimmy Dygert	100.00	45.00	12.50
☐ 39 Rube Ellis	100.00	45.00	12.50
☐ 40 Clyde Engle	100.00	45.00	12.50
☐ 41 Art Fromme	150.00	70.00	19.00
☐ 42 George Gibson back view	300.00	135.00	38.00
☐ 43 George Gibson front view	100.00	45.00	12.50
☐ 44 George Graham	2000.00	900.00	250.00
☐ 45 Eddie Grant	100.00	45.00	12.50
☐ 46 Dolly Gray	100.00	45.00	12.50
☐ 47 Bob Groom	100.00	45.00	12.50
☐ 48 Charles Hall HOR	100.00	45.00	12.50
☐ 49 Tippy Hartzell green background	100.00	45.00	12.50
☐ 50 Tippy Hartzell pink background	100.00	45.00	12.50
☐ 51 William Heitmuller	100.00	45.00	12.50
☐ 52 Harry Howell follow thru	100.00	45.00	12.50
☐ 53 Harry Howell windup	150.00	70.00	19.00
☐ 54 Tex Erwin Sic, Irwin	100.00	45.00	12.50
☐ 55 Frank Isbell	100.00	45.00	12.50
☐ 56 Joe Jackson	5000.00	2200.00	600.00
☐ 57 Hughie Jennings	250.00	110.00	31.00
☐ 58 Tim Jordan	100.00	45.00	12.50
☐ 59 Addie Joss portrait	250.00	110.00	31.00
☐ 60 Addie Joss HOR pitching	1500.00	700.00	190.00
☐ 61 Ed Karger	750.00	350.00	95.00
☐ 62 Willie Keeler portrait, pink background	250.00	110.00	31.00
☐ 63 Willie Keeler portrait, red background	350.00	160.00	45.00
☐ 64 Willie Keeler HOR throwing	2000.00	900.00	250.00
☐ 65 John Knight	100.00	45.00	12.50
☐ 66 Harry Krause	100.00	45.00	12.50
☐ 67 Napolean Lajoie	500.00	220.00	60.00
☐ 68 Tommy Leach batting	125.00	55.00	15.50
☐ 69 Tommy Leach throwing	125.00	55.00	15.50
☐ 70 Sam Leever	100.00	45.00	12.50
☐ 71 Hans Lobert	150.00	70.00	19.00
☐ 72 Harry Lumley	100.00	45.00	12.50
☐ 73 Rube Marquard	250.00	110.00	31.00
☐ 74 Christy Matthewson (sic, Mathewson)	750.00	350.00	95.00
☐ 75 J. (Stuffy) McInnes	125.00	55.00	15.50
☐ 76 Harry McIntyre (sic, McIntire)	100.00	45.00	12.50
☐ 77 Larry McLean	175.00	80.00	22.00
☐ 78 George McQuillan	100.00	45.00	12.50
☐ 79 Dots Miller	100.00	45.00	12.50
☐ 80 Mike Mitchell Cincinnati	5000.00	2200.00	600.00
☐ 81 Fred Mitchell NY AL	100.00	45.00	12.50
☐ 82 George Mullin	100.00	45.00	12.50
☐ 83 Rebel Oakes	100.00	45.00	12.50
☐ 84 Patrick O'Connor	100.00	45.00	12.50
☐ 85 Charley O'Leary	100.00	45.00	12.50
☐ 86 Orval Overall	125.00	55.00	15.50
☐ 87 Jim Pastorius	100.00	45.00	12.50
☐ 88 Ed Phelps	100.00	45.00	12.50
☐ 89 Eddie Plank	300.00	135.00	38.00
☐ 90 Lew Richie	100.00	45.00	12.50
☐ 91 Germany Schaefer	100.00	45.00	12.50
☐ 92 Victor Schlitzer	125.00	55.00	15.50
☐ 93 Johnny Seigle HOR sic, Siegle	175.00	80.00	22.00
☐ 94 Dave Shean	150.00	70.00	19.00
☐ 95 Jimmy Sheckard	125.00	55.00	15.50
☐ 96 Tris Speaker	1250.00	550.00	160.00
☐ 97 Jake Stahl	1250.00	550.00	160.00
☐ 98 Oscar Stanage	100.00	45.00	12.50
☐ 99 George Stone green background	100.00	45.00	12.50
☐ 100 George Stone sky background	100.00	45.00	12.50
☐ 101 George Stovall	100.00	45.00	12.50
☐ 102 Ed Summers	100.00	45.00	12.50
☐ 103 Bill Sweeney Boston	2000.00	900.00	250.00
☐ 104 Jeff Sweeney	100.00	45.00	12.50
☐ 105 Lee Tannehill Chicago AL	100.00	45.00	12.50
☐ 106 Lee Tannehill Chicago NL	100.00	45.00	12.50
☐ 107 Fred Tenney	100.00	45.00	12.50
☐ 108 Ira Thomas	100.00	45.00	12.50
☐ 109 Roy Thomas	100.00	45.00	12.50
☐ 110 Joe Tinker	250.00	110.00	31.00
☐ 111 Bob Unglaub	100.00	45.00	12.50
☐ 112 Jerry Upp	100.00	45.00	12.50
☐ 113 Honus Wagner batting	750.00	350.00	95.00
☐ 114 Honus Wagner throwing	750.00	350.00	95.00
☐ 115 Bobby Wallace	250.00	110.00	31.00
☐ 116 Ed Walsh	1500.00	700.00	190.00
☐ 117 Vic Willis	250.00	110.00	31.00
☐ 118 Hooks Wiltse	175.00	80.00	22.00
☐ 119 Cy Young Boston AL portrait	350.00	160.00	45.00
☐ 120 Cy Young Cleveland pitching	750.00	350.00	95.00

1915 American Caramel E106

The cards in this 48-card set measure 1 1/2" by 2 3/4". The color cards in this series of "leading Baseball players in the National, American and Federal Leagues" were produced by the American Caramel Company of York, PA. The obverse surfaces appear glazed, a process used in several other sets of this vintage (T213, T216), probably as protection against stain damage. The set was issued in 1915. The cards have been alphabetized and numbered in the checklist below. The complete set price includes all variation cards listed in the checklist below.

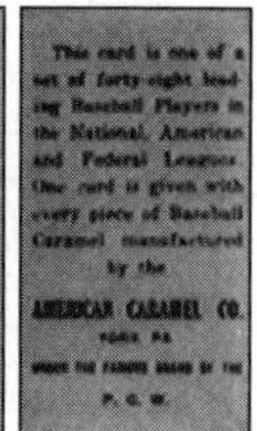

	EX-MT	VG-E	GOOD
COMPLETE SET (48)	10000.00	4500.00	1250.00
COMMON CARD (1-42)	125.00	55.00	15.50
☐ 1 Jack Barry	125.00	55.00	15.50
☐ 2A Chief Bender (blue background)	250.00	110.00	31.00
☐ 2B Chief Bender (green background)	250.00	110.00	31.00
☐ 3 Bob Bescher	125.00	55.00	15.50
☐ 4 Roger Bresnahan	250.00	110.00	31.00
☐ 5 Al Bridwell	125.00	55.00	15.50
☐ 6 Donie Bush	125.00	55.00	15.50
☐ 7A Hal Chase portrait	150.00	70.00	19.00
☐ 7B Hal Chase catching	150.00	70.00	19.00
☐ 8A Ty Cobb batting ft	1250.00	550.00	160.00
☐ 8B Ty Cobb batting sd	1250.00	550.00	160.00
☐ 9 Eddie Collins	300.00	135.00	38.00
☐ 10 Sam Crawford	250.00	110.00	31.00
☐ 11 Ray Demmitt	125.00	55.00	15.50
☐ 12 Bill Donovan	125.00	55.00	15.50
☐ 13 Red Dooin	125.00	55.00	15.50
☐ 14 Mickey Doolan	125.00	55.00	15.50
☐ 15 Larry Doyle	125.00	55.00	15.50
☐ 16 Clyde Engle	125.00	55.00	15.50
☐ 17 Johnny Evers	250.00	110.00	31.00
☐ 18 Art Fromme	125.00	55.00	15.50
☐ 19A George Gibson front	125.00	55.00	15.50
☐ 19B George Gibson back	125.00	55.00	15.50
☐ 20 Topsy Hartzell	125.00	55.00	15.50
☐ 21 Fred Jacklitsch	125.00	55.00	15.50
☐ 22 Hugh Jennings MG	250.00	110.00	31.00
☐ 23 Otto Knabe	125.00	55.00	15.50
☐ 24 Nap Lajoie	350.00	160.00	45.00
☐ 25 Hans Lobert	125.00	55.00	15.50
☐ 26 Rube Marquard	250.00	110.00	31.00
☐ 27 Christy Mathewson	500.00	220.00	60.00
☐ 28 John McGraw MG	300.00	135.00	38.00
☐ 29 George McQuillan	125.00	55.00	15.50
☐ 30 Dots Miller	125.00	55.00	15.50
☐ 31 Danny Murphy	125.00	55.00	15.50
☐ 32 Rebel Oakes	125.00	55.00	15.50
☐ 33 Eddie Plank	300.00	135.00	38.00
☐ 34 Germany Schaefer	125.00	55.00	15.50
☐ 35 Tris Speaker	350.00	160.00	45.00
☐ 36 Oscar Stanage	125.00	55.00	15.50
☐ 37 George Stovall	125.00	55.00	15.50
☐ 38 Jeff Sweeney	125.00	55.00	15.50
☐ 39A Joe Tinker portrait	250.00	110.00	31.00
☐ 39B Joe Tinker batting	250.00	110.00	31.00
☐ 40A Honus Wagner batting	650.00	300.00	80.00
☐ 40B Honus Wagner throwing	650.00	300.00	80.00
☐ 41 Hooks Wiltse	125.00	55.00	15.50
☐ 42 Heinie Zimmerman	125.00	55.00	15.50

1922 American Caramel E122

The cards in this 79-card set measure 2" by 3 1/2". The principal feature of this re-issue of the "80 series" of set E121 is the cross-hatch pattern or "screen" which covers the obverse of the card. The photos are black and white, and the player's name, position and team appear in a panel under his picture, all enclosed within the rectangular frame line. The set, which is unnumbered, was marketed in 1922 by the American Caramel Company. The cards have been alphabetized and numbered in the checklist below.

	EX-MT	VG-E	GOOD
COMPLETE SET (79)	6500.00	2900.00	800.00
COMMON CARD (1-79)	50.00	22.00	6.25

☐ 1 Grover Alexander	200.00	90.00	25.00
☐ 2 Jim Bagby	50.00	22.00	6.25
☐ 3 Frank Baker	125.00	55.00	15.50
☐ 4 Dave Bancroft	125.00	55.00	15.50
☐ 5 Ping Bodie	50.00	22.00	6.25
☐ 6 George Burns	50.00	22.00	6.25
☐ 7 Geo. J. Burns	50.00	22.00	6.25
☐ 8 Owen Bush	50.00	22.00	6.25
☐ 9 Max Carey	125.00	55.00	15.50
☐ 10 Red Causey	50.00	22.00	6.25
☐ 11 Ty Cobb	700.00	325.00	90.00
☐ 12 Eddie Collins	200.00	90.00	25.00
☐ 13 Jake Daubert	75.00	34.00	9.50
☐ 14 Hooks Dauss	50.00	22.00	6.25
☐ 15 Charlie Deal	50.00	22.00	6.25
☐ 16 Bill Doak	50.00	22.00	6.25
☐ 17 Bill Donovan MG	50.00	22.00	6.25
☐ 18 Johnny Evers MG	125.00	55.00	15.50
☐ 19 Urban Faber	125.00	55.00	15.50
☐ 20 Eddie Foster	50.00	22.00	6.25
☐ 21 Larry Gardner	50.00	22.00	6.25
☐ 22 Kid Gleason MG	50.00	22.00	6.25
☐ 23 Hank Gowdy	75.00	34.00	9.50
☐ 24 John Graney	50.00	22.00	6.25
☐ 25 Tom Griffith	50.00	22.00	6.25
☐ 26 Harry Heilmann	150.00	70.00	19.00
☐ 27 Walter Holke	50.00	22.00	6.25
☐ 28 Charley Hollacher	50.00	22.00	6.25
☐ 29 Harry Hooper	125.00	55.00	15.50
☐ 30 Rogers Hornsby	250.00	110.00	31.00
☐ 31 Baby Doll Jacobson	50.00	22.00	6.25
☐ 32 Walter Johnson	250.00	110.00	31.00
☐ 33 James Johnston	50.00	22.00	6.25
☐ 34 Joe Judge	50.00	22.00	6.25
☐ 35 George Kelly	125.00	55.00	15.50
☐ 36 Dick Kerr	75.00	34.00	9.50
☐ 37 Pete Kilduff	50.00	22.00	6.25
☐ 38 Bill Killefer	50.00	22.00	6.25
☐ 39 John Lavan	50.00	22.00	6.25
☐ 40 Duffy Lewis	50.00	22.00	6.25
☐ 41 Al Mamaux	50.00	22.00	6.25
☐ 42 Rabbit Maranville	125.00	55.00	15.50
☐ 43 Carl Mays	75.00	34.00	9.50
☐ 44 John McGraw MG	150.00	70.00	19.00
☐ 45 Snuffy McInnis	75.00	34.00	9.50
☐ 46 Clyde Milan	50.00	22.00	6.25
☐ 47 Otto Miller	50.00	22.00	6.25
☐ 48 Guy Morton	50.00	22.00	6.25
☐ 49 Eddie Murphy	50.00	22.00	6.25
☐ 50 Hy Myers	50.00	22.00	6.25
☐ 51 Steve O'Neill	75.00	34.00	9.50
☐ 52 Roger Peckinpaugh	75.00	34.00	9.50
☐ 53 Jeff Pfeffer	50.00	22.00	6.25
☐ 54 Wally Pipp	75.00	34.00	9.50
☐ 55 Sam Rice	125.00	55.00	15.50
☐ 56 Eppa Rixey	125.00	55.00	15.50
☐ 57 Babe Ruth	1000.00	450.00	125.00
☐ 58 Slim Sallee	50.00	22.00	6.25
☐ 59 Ray Schalk	125.00	55.00	15.50
☐ 60 Walter Schang	50.00	22.00	6.25
☐ 61 Ferd Schupp	50.00	22.00	6.25
☐ 62 Fred Schupp	50.00	22.00	6.25
☐ 63 Everett Scott	75.00	34.00	9.50
☐ 64 Hank Severeid	50.00	22.00	6.25
☐ 65 George Sisler (batting)	200.00	90.00	25.00
☐ 66 George Sisler (throwing)	200.00	90.00	25.00
☐ 67 Tris Speaker	200.00	90.00	25.00
☐ 68 Milton Stock	50.00	22.00	6.25
☐ 69 Amos Strunk	50.00	22.00	6.25
☐ 70 Chester Thomas	50.00	22.00	6.25
☐ 71 George Tyler	50.00	22.00	6.25
☐ 72 Jim Vaughn	50.00	22.00	6.25
☐ 73 Bob Veach	50.00	22.00	6.25
☐ 74 Bill Wambsganss	50.00	22.00	6.25
☐ 75 Zach Wheat	125.00	55.00	15.50
☐ 76 Fred Williams	75.00	34.00	9.50
☐ 77 Ivy B. Wingo	50.00	22.00	6.25
☐ 78 Joe Wood	75.00	34.00	9.50
☐ 79 Pep Young (2ndB. Detroit)	50.00	22.00	6.25

1910 American Caramel Die Cuts E125

These cards have all been discovered since 1969. Cards from this set have been found from the following teams: Philadelphia A's; Boston Red Sox; New York Giants and Pittsburgh Pirates. The best supposition about this set places it being produced during the 1910 season. The cards are black and white and range as high as 7" and as much as 4" wide. While 41 are supposed to exist according to the checklists only about 1/2 of that amount have been found. All cards on the checklist are priced even though not all of them have been found yet.

	EX-MT	VG-E	GOOD
COMPLETE SET (41)	27000.00	12200.00	3400.00
COMMON CARD (1-41)	400.00	180.00	50.00
☐ 1 Babe Adams	400.00	180.00	50.00
☐ 2 Red Ames	400.00	180.00	50.00
☐ 3 Frank Baker	1200.00	550.00	150.00
☐ 4 Jack Barry	400.00	180.00	50.00
☐ 5 Chief Bender	1200.00	550.00	150.00
☐ 6 Al Bridwell	400.00	180.00	50.00
☐ 7 Bobby Byrne	400.00	180.00	50.00
☐ 8 Bill Carrigan	400.00	180.00	50.00
☐ 9 Ed Cicotte	1000.00	450.00	125.00
☐ 10 Fred Clarke Sic, Clark	400.00	180.00	50.00
☐ 11 Eddie Collins	1500.00	700.00	190.00
☐ 12 Harry Davis	400.00	180.00	50.00
☐ 13 Art Devlin	400.00	180.00	50.00
☐ 14 Josh Devore	400.00	180.00	50.00
☐ 15 Larry Doyle	400.00	180.00	50.00
☐ 16 John Flynn	400.00	180.00	50.00
☐ 17 George Gibson	400.00	180.00	50.00
☐ 18 Topsy Hartsel Sic, Hartsell	400.00	180.00	50.00
☐ 19 Harry Hooper	1000.00	450.00	125.00
☐ 20 Harry Krause	400.00	180.00	50.00
☐ 21 Tommy Leach	500.00	220.00	60.00
☐ 22 Harry Lord	400.00	180.00	50.00
☐ 23 Christy Mathewson	3500.00	1600.00	450.00
☐ 24 Ambrose McConnell	400.00	180.00	50.00
☐ 25 Fred Merkle	400.00	180.00	50.00
☐ 26 Dots Miller	400.00	180.00	50.00
☐ 27 Danny Murphy	400.00	180.00	50.00
☐ 28 Red Murray	400.00	180.00	50.00
☐ 29 Harry Niles	400.00	180.00	50.00
☐ 30 Rube Oldring	400.00	180.00	50.00
☐ 31 Eddie Plank	1500.00	700.00	190.00
☐ 32 Cy Seymour	400.00	180.00	50.00
☐ 33 Tris Speaker	1500.00	700.00	190.00
☐ 34 Jake Stahl	400.00	180.00	50.00
☐ 35 Ira Thomas	400.00	180.00	50.00
☐ 36 Heinie Wagner	400.00	180.00	50.00
☐ 37 Honus Wagner Batting	3000.00	1350.00	375.00
☐ 38 Honus Wagner Throwing	3000.00	1350.00	375.00
☐ 39 Art Wilson	400.00	180.00	50.00
☐ 40 Owen Wilson	400.00	180.00	50.00
☐ 41 Hooks Wiltse	400.00	180.00	50.00

1927 American Caramel E126

The cards in this 60-card set measure 1 5/8" by 3 1/4". The American Caramel Company released its set of baseball players in 1927. The cards contain black and white pictures, with the individual's name centered underneath, and his team and position to either side below that. This is the only numbered series of baseball cards to be issued by American Caramel; the backs contain advertising for an album designed to hold the set.

	EX-MT	VG-E	GOOD
COMPLETE SET (60)	7000.00	3200.00	900.00
COMMON CARD (1-60)	75.00	34.00	9.50
☐ 1 John Gooch	75.00	34.00	9.50
☐ 2 Clyde Barnhart	75.00	34.00	9.50
☐ 3 Joe Bush	100.00	45.00	12.50
☐ 4 Lee Meadows	75.00	34.00	9.50
☐ 5 Dick Cox	75.00	34.00	9.50
☐ 6 Red Faber	150.00	70.00	19.00
☐ 7 Aaron Ward	75.00	34.00	9.50
☐ 8 Ray Schalk	150.00	70.00	19.00
☐ 9 Specs Toporcer	75.00	34.00	9.50
☐ 10 Billy Southworth	75.00	34.00	9.50
☐ 11 Allen Sothoron	75.00	34.00	9.50
☐ 12 Will Sherdel	75.00	34.00	9.50
☐ 13 Grover Cleveland Alexander	200.00	90.00	25.00
☐ 14 Jack Quinn	75.00	34.00	9.50
☐ 15 Chick Galloway	75.00	34.00	9.50
☐ 16 Eddie Collins	200.00	90.00	25.00
☐ 17 Ty Cobb	1000.00	450.00	125.00
☐ 18 Percy Jones	75.00	34.00	9.50
☐ 19 Charlie Grimm	100.00	45.00	12.50
☐ 20 Bennie Karr	75.00	34.00	9.50
☐ 21 Charlie Jamieson	75.00	34.00	9.50
☐ 22 Sherrod Smith	75.00	34.00	9.50
☐ 23 Vergil Cheeves	75.00	34.00	9.50
☐ 24 James Ring	75.00	34.00	9.50
☐ 25 Muddy Ruel	75.00	34.00	9.50
☐ 26 Joe Judge	75.00	34.00	9.50
☐ 27 Tris Speaker	250.00	110.00	31.00
☐ 28 Walter Johnson	350.00	160.00	45.00
☐ 29 Sam Rice	150.00	70.00	19.00
☐ 30 Hank DeBerry	75.00	34.00	9.50
☐ 31 Walter Henline	75.00	34.00	9.50
☐ 32 Max Carey	150.00	70.00	19.00
☐ 33 Arnold Statz	75.00	34.00	9.50
☐ 34 Irish Meusel	100.00	45.00	12.50
☐ 35 Pat Collins	75.00	34.00	9.50
☐ 36 Urban Shocker	100.00	45.00	12.50
☐ 37 Bob Shawkey	100.00	45.00	12.50
☐ 38 Babe Ruth	1500.00	700.00	190.00
☐ 39 Bob Meusel	100.00	45.00	12.50
☐ 40 Alex Ferguson	75.00	34.00	9.50
☐ 41 Stuffy McInnis	100.00	45.00	12.50
☐ 42 Cy Williams	100.00	45.00	12.50
☐ 43 Russell Wrightstone	75.00	34.00	9.50
☐ 44 John Tobin photo actually Ed Brown	100.00	45.00	12.50
☐ 45 Baby Doll Jacobson	75.00	34.00	9.50
☐ 46 Bryan Harriss	75.00	34.00	9.50
☐ 47 Elam VanGilder	75.00	34.00	9.50
☐ 48 Ken Williams	100.00	45.00	12.50
☐ 49 George Sisler	200.00	90.00	25.00
☐ 50 Ed Brown photo actually John Tobin	100.00	45.00	12.50
☐ 51 Jack Smith	75.00	34.00	9.50
☐ 52 Dave Bancroft	150.00	70.00	19.00
☐ 53 Larry Woodall	75.00	34.00	9.50
☐ 54 Lu Blue	75.00	34.00	9.50
☐ 55 Johnny Bassler	75.00	34.00	9.50
☐ 56 Jackie May	75.00	34.00	9.50
☐ 57 Horace Ford	75.00	34.00	9.50
☐ 58 Curt Walker	75.00	34.00	9.50
☐ 59 Art Nehf	75.00	34.00	9.50
☐ 60 George Kelly	150.00	70.00	19.00

1908 American League Publishing Co. PC770

This 1908-issued set features a large action shot or pose the player in uniform and also a small portrait of the player in street clothes in an oval at the top of the card. A short biography in a rectangular box is also featured at the base of the front, and the identifying line "American League Pub. Company, Cleveland, O." is located directly below the box.

	EX-MT	VG-E	GOOD
COMPLETE SET (15)	3500.00	1600.00	450.00
COMMON CARD (1-15)	150.00	70.00	19.00
☐ 1 Harry Bay	150.00	70.00	19.00
☐ 2 Charles Berger	150.00	70.00	19.00
☐ 3 Joe Birmingham	150.00	70.00	19.00
☐ 4 Bill Bradley	150.00	70.00	19.00
☐ 5 Walter Clarkson	150.00	70.00	19.00
☐ 6 Ty Cobb	900.00	400.00	110.00
☐ 7 Elmer Flick	250.00	110.00	31.00
☐ 8 Claude Hickman	150.00	70.00	19.00
☐ 9 William Hinchman	150.00	70.00	19.00
☐ 10 Addie Joss	400.00	180.00	50.00
☐ 11 Nap Lajoie	350.00	160.00	45.00
☐ 12 Glen Liebhardt	150.00	70.00	19.00
☐ 13 George Nill	150.00	70.00	19.00
☐ 14 George Perring	150.00	70.00	19.00
☐ 15 Honus Wagner	500.00	220.00	60.00

1950 American Nut And Chocolate Co. Pennant

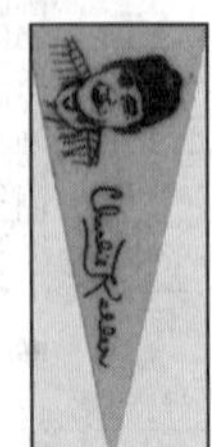

This 22-pennant set was distributed by the American Nut Chocolate Co. and originally sold for 50 cents a set. The pennants card measure approximately 1 7/8" by 4" and feature crude line-art drawings of the players with a facsimile autograph. The pennants are unnumbered and checklisted below in alphabetical order.

	NRMT	VG-E	GOOD
COMPLETE SET (22)	800.00	350.00	100.00
COMMON CARD (1-22)	25.00	11.00	3.10
☐ 1 Ewell Blackwell	25.00	11.00	3.10
☐ 2 Harry Brecheen	25.00	11.00	3.10
☐ 3 Phil Cavarretta	35.00	16.00	4.40
☐ 4 Bobby Doerr	50.00	22.00	6.25
☐ 5 Bob Elliott	25.00	11.00	3.10
☐ 6 Boo Ferriss	25.00	11.00	3.10
☐ 7 Joe Gordon	35.00	16.00	4.40
☐ 8 Tommy Holmes	25.00	11.00	3.10
☐ 9 Charles Keller	35.00	16.00	4.40
☐ 10 Ken Keltner	25.00	11.00	3.10
☐ 11 Whitey Kurowski	25.00	11.00	3.10
☐ 12 Ralph Kiner	75.00	34.00	9.50
☐ 13 Johnny Pesky	35.00	16.00	4.40
☐ 14 Pee Wee Reese	100.00	45.00	12.50
☐ 15 Phil Pizzuto	75.00	34.00	9.50
☐ 16 Johnny Sain	35.00	16.00	4.40
☐ 17 Enos Slaughter	50.00	22.00	6.25
☐ 18 Warren Spahn	60.00	27.00	7.50
☐ 19 Vern Stephens	25.00	11.00	3.10
☐ 20 Earl Torgeson	25.00	11.00	3.10
☐ 21 Dizzy Trout	25.00	11.00	3.10
☐ 22 Ted Williams	200.00	90.00	25.00

1962 American Tract Society

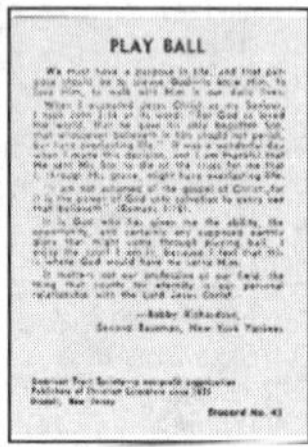

These cards are quite attractive and feature the "pure card" concept that is always popular with collectors, i.e., no borders or anything else on the card front to detract from the color photo. The cards are numbered on the back and the skip-numbering of the cards below is actually due to the fact that these cards are part of a much larger (sport and non-sport) set with a Christian theme. The set features Christian ballplayers giving first-person testimonies on the card backs telling how Jesus has changed their lives. These cards are sometimes referred to as "Tracards." The cards measure approximately 2 3/4" X 3 1/2". The set price below refers to only one of each player, not including any variations.

	NRMT	VG-E	GOOD
COMPLETE SET	30.00	13.50	3.70
COMMON CARD	6.00	2.70	.75
☐ 43A Bobby Richardson black print on back	12.00	5.50	1.50
☐ 43B Bobby Richardson blue print on back	15.00	6.75	1.85
☐ 43C Bobby Richardson black print on back with Play Ball in red	15.00	6.75	1.85
☐ 43D Bobby Richardson black print on back with exclamation point after Play Ball	15.00	6.75	1.85
☐ 51A Jerry Kindall portrait from chest up black print on back	6.00	2.70	.75
☐ 51B Jerry Kindall on one knee with bat blue print on back	6.00	2.70	.75
☐ 52A Felipe Alou on one knee looking up black print on back	10.00	4.50	1.25
☐ 52B Felipe Alou on one knee looking up blue print on back	10.00	4.50	1.25
☐ 52C Felipe Alou Batting pose red lettering "A Tip for You"	10.00	4.50	1.25
☐ 52D Felipe Alou Batting Pose Name on Front of Card	6.00	2.70	.75
☐ 66 Al Worthington (black print on back)	6.00	2.70	.75

1994 Ameritech Yount

This credit card-sized (3 3/8" by 2 1/8") card was issued to fans at Milwaukee County Stadium on Robin Yount Tribute Day, May 29, 1994, to commemorate the retirement of his jersey number (19). It has rounded corners and features on its front a horizontal borderless color action shot of Yount. The card carries a value of 50 cents worth of pay telephone calls. The white back carries instructions for use and the production number out of 63,000 produced.

	MINT	NRMT	EXC
COMPLETE SET	3.00	1.35	.35
COMMON CARD	3.00	1.35	.35
☐ 1 Robin Yount	3.00	1.35	.35

1961 Angels Jay Publishing

This 12-card set of the Los Angeles Angels measures approximately 5" by 7". The fronts feature black-and-white posed player photos with the player's and team name printed below in the white border. These cards were packaged 12 to a packet. The backs are blank. The cards are unnumbered and checklisted below in alphabetical order.

	NRMT	VG-E	GOOD
COMPLETE SET (12)	30.00	13.50	3.70
COMMON CARD (1-12)	2.00	.90	.25
☐ 1 Ken Aspromonte	2.00	.90	.25
☐ 2 Julio Becquer	2.00	.90	.25
☐ 3 Steve Bilko	3.00	1.35	.35
☐ 4 Fritz Brickell	2.00	.90	.25
☐ 5 Bob Cerv	3.00	1.35	.35
☐ 6 Ned Garver	2.00	.90	.25
☐ 7 Ted Kluszewski	5.00	2.20	.60
☐ 8 Tom Morgan	3.00	1.35	.35
☐ 9 Albie Pearson	3.00	1.35	.35
☐ 10 Bill Rigney MG	3.00	1.35	.35
☐ 11 Faye Throneberry	2.00	.90	.25
☐ 12 Ed Yost	2.00	.90	.25

1962 Angels Jay Publishing

This 12-card set of the Los Angeles Angels measures approximately 5" by 7". The fronts feature black-and-white posed player photos with the player's and team name printed below in the white border. These cards were packaged 12 to a packet. The backs are blank. The cards are unnumbered and checklisted below in alphabetical order.

	NRMT	VG-E	GOOD
COMPLETE SET (12)	25.00	11.00	3.10
COMMON CARD (1-12)	2.00	.90	.25
☐ 1 Earl Averill	3.50	1.55	.45
☐ 2 Steve Bilko	3.00	1.35	.35
☐ 3 Ryne Duren	3.00	1.35	.35
☐ 4 Eli Grba	2.00	.90	.25
☐ 5 Ken Hunt	3.00	1.35	.35
☐ 6 Ted Kluszewski	5.00	2.20	.60
☐ 7 Tom Morgan	3.00	1.35	.35
☐ 8 Albie Pearson	3.00	1.35	.35
☐ 9 Bill Rigney MG	3.00	1.35	.35
☐ 10 Ed Sadowski	2.00	.90	.25
☐ 11 Leon Wagner	2.00	.90	.25
☐ 12 Eddie Yost	2.00	.90	.25

1963 Angels Jay Publishing

This 19-card set of the Los Angeles Angels measures approximately 5" by 7". Originally a 12-card set, updates during the year added more cards. The fronts feature black-and-white posed player photos with the player's and team name printed below in the white border. These cards were packaged 12 to a packet. The backs are blank. The cards are unnumbered and checklisted below in alphabetical order.

	NRMT	VG-E	GOOD
COMPLETE SET (19)	50.00	22.00	6.25
COMMON CARD (1-19)	2.50	1.10	.30
☐ 1 Bo Belinsky	3.00	1.35	.35
☐ 2 Dean Chance (Head photo)	3.50	1.55	.45
☐ 3 Dean Chance (Action pose)	3.50	1.55	.45
☐ 4 Charlie Dees	2.50	1.10	.30
☐ 5 Jim Fregosi	3.50	1.55	.45
☐ 6 Ken Hunt	2.50	1.10	.30
☐ 7 Don Lee	2.50	1.10	.30
☐ 8 Ken McBride	2.50	1.10	.30
☐ 9 Billy Moran	2.50	1.10	.30
☐ 10 Tom Morgan	3.00	1.35	.35
☐ 11 Dan Osinski	2.50	1.10	.30
☐ 12 Albie Pearson (Action pose)	3.50	1.55	.45
☐ 13 Albie Pearson (Pose with bat)	3.50	1.55	.45
☐ 14 Bill Rigney MG	3.00	1.35	.35
☐ 15 Bob Rodgers	2.50	1.10	.30
☐ 16 Ed Sadowski	2.50	1.10	.30
☐ 17 Lee Thomas (Pose with bat)	3.50	1.55	.45
☐ 18 Lee Thomas (Closer pose with bat)	3.00	1.35	.35
☐ 19 Leon Wagner	3.00	1.35	.35

1966 Angels Dexter Press

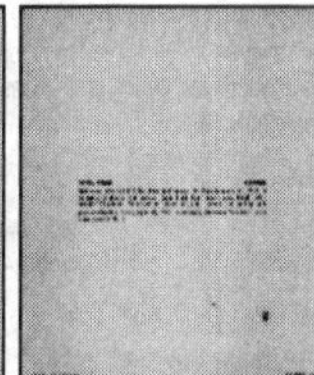

Produced by Dexter Press, Inc. (West Nyack, New York), this seven-card set measures approximately 4" by 5 7/8". The fronts feature glossy posed color player photos with white borders. The player's autograph is inscribed in black across the top of the picture. In blue print, the back has the player's name, position, and biographical information. The cards are unnumbered and checklisted below in alphabetical order.

	NRMT	VG-E	GOOD
COMPLETE SET (7)	15.00	6.75	1.85
COMMON CARD (1-7)	2.00	.90	.25
☐ 1 Dean Chance	2.50	1.10	.30
☐ 2 Bob Knoop	2.00	.90	.25
☐ 3 Marcelino Lopez	2.00	.90	.25
☐ 4 Rick Reichardt	2.00	.90	.25
☐ 5 Bob Rodgers	3.00	1.35	.35
☐ 6 Paul Schaal	2.00	.90	.25
☐ 7 Willie Smith	2.00	.90	.25

1969 Angels Jack in the Box

This 13-card set measures approximately 2 by 3 1/2" and features black-and-white player photos on a white card face. The cards are unnumbered and checklisted below in alphabetical order.

	NRMT	VG-E	GOOD
COMPLETE SET (13)	50.00	22.00	6.25
COMMON CARD (1-13)	2.50	1.10	.30
☐ 1 Sandy Alomar	3.50	1.55	.45
☐ 2 Joe Azcue	2.50	1.10	.30
☐ 3 Jim Fregosi	7.50	3.40	.95
☐ 4 Lou Johnson	3.50	1.55	.45
☐ 5 Jay Johnstone	3.50	1.55	.45
☐ 6 Rudy May	2.50	1.10	.30
☐ 7 Jim McGlothlin	2.50	1.10	.30
☐ 8 Andy Messersmith	5.00	2.20	.60
☐ 9 Tom Murphy	2.50	1.10	.30
☐ 10 Rick Reichardt	2.50	1.10	.30
☐ 11 Aurelio Rodriguez	2.50	1.10	.30
☐ 12 Jim Spencer	2.50	1.10	.30
☐ 13 Hoyt Wilhelm	10.00	4.50	1.25

1971 Angels Jack in the Box

This 10-card set measures approximately 4 by 2 1/2" and features yellowish tone player photos printed on tan paper stock. The cards are unnumbered and checklisted below in alphabetical order.

	NRMT	VG-E	GOOD
COMPLETE SET (10)	25.00	11.00	3.10
COMMON CARD (1-10)	2.00	.90	.25
☐ 1 Sandy Alomar	3.50	1.55	.45
☐ 2 Ken Berry	2.00	.90	.25
☐ 3 Tony Conigliaro	7.50	3.40	.95
☐ 4 Jim Fregosi	5.00	2.20	.60
☐ 5 Alex Johnson	2.00	.90	.25
☐ 6 Rudy May	2.00	.90	.25
☐ 7 Andy Messersmith	3.50	1.55	.45
☐ 8 Lefty Phillips MG	2.00	.90	.25
☐ 9 Jim Spencer	2.00	.90	.25
☐ 10 Clyde Wright	2.00	.90	.25

1978 Angels Family Fun Centers

This 37-card set features members of the 1978 California Angels. These large cards measure approximately 3 1/2" by 5 1/2" and display sepia tone player photos. The cards are unnumbered and checklisted below in alphabetical order.

	NRMT	VG-E	GOOD
COMPLETE SET (37)	50.00	22.00	6.25
COMMON CARD (1-37)	1.50	.70	.19
☐ 1 Don Aase	1.50	.70	.19
☐ 2 Mike Barlow	1.50	.70	.19
☐ 3 Don Baylor	2.50	1.10	.30
☐ 4 Lyman Bostock	5.00	2.20	.60
☐ 5 Ken Brett	2.00	.90	.25
☐ 6 Dave Chalk	1.50	.70	.19
☐ 7 Bob Clear	1.50	.70	.19
☐ 8 Brian Downing	2.50	1.10	.30
☐ 9 Ron Fairly	2.00	.90	.25
☐ 10 Gil Flores	1.50	.70	.19
☐ 11 Dave Frost	1.50	.70	.19
☐ 12 Dave Garcia	1.50	.70	.19
☐ 13 Bobby Grich	2.50	1.10	.30
☐ 14 Tom Griffin	1.50	.70	.19
☐ 15 Marv Grissom	1.50	.70	.19
☐ 16 Ike Hampton	1.50	.70	.19
☐ 17 Paul Hartzell	1.50	.70	.19
☐ 18 Terry Humphrey	1.50	.70	.19
☐ 19 Ron Jackson	1.50	.70	.19
☐ 20 Chris Knapp	1.50	.70	.19
☐ 21 Ken Landreaux	1.50	.70	.19
☐ 22 Carney Lansford	2.50	1.10	.30
☐ 23 Dave LaRoche	1.50	.70	.19
☐ 24 John McNamara MG	2.00	.90	.25
☐ 25 Dyar Miller	1.50	.70	.19
☐ 26 Rick Miller	1.50	.70	.19
☐ 27 Balor Moore	1.50	.70	.19
☐ 28 Rance Mulliniks	1.50	.70	.19
☐ 29 Floyd Rayford	1.50	.70	.19
☐ 30 Jimmie Reese CO	2.00	.90	.25
☐ 31 Merv Rettenmund	1.50	.70	.19
☐ 32 Joe Rudi	2.00	.90	.25
☐ 33 Nolan Ryan	10.00	4.50	1.25
☐ 34 Bob Skinner CO	1.50	.70	.19
☐ 35 Tony Solaita	1.50	.70	.19
☐ 36 Frank Tanana	1.50	.70	.19
☐ 37 Dickie Thon	1.50	.70	.19

1984 Angels Smokey

The cards in this 32-card set measure approximately 2 1/2" by 3 3/4" and feature the California Angels in full color. Sets were given out to persons 15 and under attending the June 16th game against the Indians. Unlike the Padres set of this year, Smokey the Bear is not featured on these cards. The player's photo, the Angels' logo, and the Smokey the Bear logo appear on the front, in addition to the California Department of Forestry and the U.S. Forest Service logos. The abbreviated backs contain short biographical data, career statistics, and an anti-wildfire hint from the player on the front. Since the cards are unnumbered, they are ordered and numbered below alphabetically by the player's name.

	NRMT	VG-E	GOOD
COMPLETE SET (32)	10.00	4.50	1.25
COMMON CARD (1-32)	.25	.11	.03
☐ 1 Don Aase	.25	.11	.03
☐ 2 Juan Beniquez	.25	.11	.03
☐ 3 Bob Boone	1.00	.45	.12
☐ 4 Rick Burleson	.50	.23	.06
☐ 5 Rod Carew	2.50	1.10	.30
☐ 6 John Curtis	.25	.11	.03
☐ 7 Doug DeCinces	.75	.35	.09
☐ 8 Brian Downing	.75	.35	.09
☐ 9 Ken Forsch	.25	.11	.03
☐ 10 Bobby Grich	.75	.35	.09
☐ 11 Reggie Jackson	3.00	1.35	.35
☐ 12 Ron Jackson	.25	.11	.03
☐ 13 Tommy John	1.00	.45	.12
☐ 14 Curt Kaufman	.25	.11	.03
☐ 15 Bruce Kison	.25	.11	.03
☐ 16 Frank LaCorte	.25	.11	.03
☐ 17 Logo Card (Forestry Dept.)	.25	.11	.03
☐ 18 Fred Lynn	.75	.35	.09
☐ 19 John McNamara MG	.25	.11	.03
☐ 20 Jerry Narron	.25	.11	.03
☐ 21 Gary Pettis	.25	.11	.03
☐ 22 Rob Picciolo	.25	.11	.03
☐ 23 Ron Romanick	.25	.11	.03
☐ 24 Luis Sanchez	.25	.11	.03
☐ 25 Dick Schofield	.25	.11	.03
☐ 26 Daryl Sconiers	.25	.11	.03
☐ 27 Jim Slaton	.25	.11	.03
☐ 28 Smokey the Bear	.25	.11	.03
☐ 29 Ellis Valentine	.25	.11	.03
☐ 30 Rob Wilfong	.25	.11	.03
☐ 31 Mike Witt	.25	.11	.03
☐ 32 Geoff Zahn	.25	.11	.03

1985 Angels Smokey

The cards in this 24-card set measure approximately 4 1/4" by 6" and feature the California Angels in full color. The player's photo, the Angels' logo, and the Smokey the Bear logo appear on the front, in addition to the California Department of Forestry and the U.S. Forest Service logos. The abbreviated backs contain short biographical data and an anti-wildfire message.

	NRMT	VG-E	GOOD
COMPLETE SET (24)	8.00	3.60	1.00
COMMON CARD (1-24)	.25	.11	.03
☐ 1 Mike Witt	.25	.11	.03
☐ 2 Reggie Jackson	2.50	1.10	.30
☐ 3 Bob Boone	1.00	.45	.12
☐ 4 Mike Brown	.25	.11	.03
☐ 5 Rod Carew	2.00	.90	.25
☐ 6 Doug DeCinces	.75	.35	.09
☐ 7 Brian Downing	.75	.35	.09
☐ 8 Ken Forsch	.25	.11	.03
☐ 9 Gary Pettis	.25	.11	.03
☐ 10 Jerry Narron	.25	.11	.03
☐ 11 Ron Romanick	.25	.11	.03
☐ 12 Bobby Grich	.75	.35	.09
☐ 13 Dick Schofield	.25	.11	.03
☐ 14 Juan Beniquez	.25	.11	.03
☐ 15 Geoff Zahn	.25	.11	.03
☐ 16 Luis Sanchez	.25	.11	.03
☐ 17 Jim Slaton	.25	.11	.03
☐ 18 Doug Corbett	.25	.11	.03
☐ 19 Ruppert Jones	.25	.11	.03
☐ 20 Rob Wilfong	.25	.11	.03
☐ 21 Donnie Moore	.25	.11	.03
☐ 22 Pat Clements	.25	.11	.03
☐ 23 Tommy John	1.00	.45	.12
☐ 24 Gene Mauch MG	.50	.23	.06

1985 Angels Straw Hat

This 13-card set was distributed by Straw Hat Pizza Restaurants and measures approximately 11" by 16". The fronts feature color player drawings with a white border. The bottom part of the card contains a coupon for pizza and a Silver Anniversary Sweepstakes form. The backs are blank. The cards are unnumbered and checklisted below in alphabetical order.

	MINT	NRMT	EXC
COMPLETE SET (13)	40.00	18.00	5.00
COMMON CARD (1-13)	2.00	.90	.25

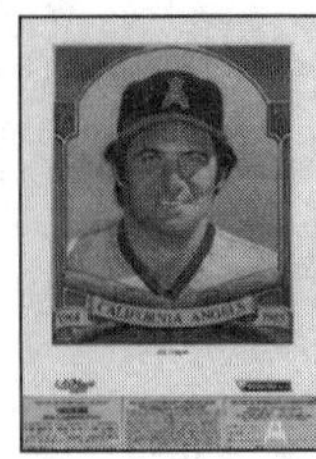

	MINT	NRMT	EXC
□ 1 Gene Autry OWN	3.00	1.35	.35
□ 2 Don Baylor	3.00	1.35	.35
□ 3 Bo Belinsky	2.00	.90	.25
□ 4 Rod Carew	5.00	2.20	.60
□ 5 Dean Chance	2.00	.90	.25
□ 6 Jim Fregosi	2.00	.90	.25
□ 7 Bobby Grich Bobby Knoop	2.00	.90	.25
□ 8 Reggie Jackson	7.50	3.40	.95
□ 9 Alex Johnson	2.00	.90	.25
□ 10 Ted Kluszewski Albie Pearson	3.00	1.35	.35
□ 11 Nolan Ryan	10.00	4.50	1.25
□ 12 Frank Tanana	3.00	1.35	.35
□ 13 Mike Witt	2.00	.90	.25

1986 Angels Greats TCMA

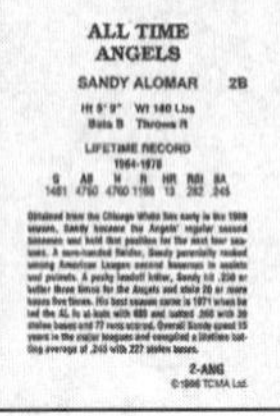

This 12-card standard-size set features some of the leading all-time members of the California Angels. The fronts feature a player photo while the backs have a player biography.

	MINT	NRMT	EXC
COMPLETE SET (12)	5.00	2.20	.60
COMMON CARD (1-12)	.25	.11	.03
□ 1 Rod Carew	2.50	1.10	.30
□ 2 Sandy Alomar	.25	.11	.03
□ 3 Jim Fregosi	.50	.23	.06
□ 4 Dave Chalk	.25	.11	.03
□ 5 Leon Wagner	.25	.11	.03
□ 6 Albie Pearson	.25	.11	.03
□ 7 Rick Reichardt	.25	.11	.03
□ 8 Bob Rodgers	.25	.11	.03
□ 9 Dean Chance	.35	.16	.04
□ 10 Clyde Wright	.25	.11	.03
□ 11 Bob Lee	.25	.11	.03
□ 12 Bill Rigney MG	.25	.11	.03

1986 Angels Smokey

The Forestry Service (in conjunction with the California Angels) produced this large, attractive 24-card set. The cards feature Smokey the Bear pictured in the upper right corner of the card. The card backs give a fire safety tip. The set was given out free at Anaheim Stadium on August 9th. The cards measure approximately 4 1/4" by 6" and are subtitled "Wildfire Prevention" on the front.

	MINT	NRMT	EXC
COMPLETE SET (24)	7.50	3.40	.95
COMMON CARD (1-24)	.25	.11	.03
□ 1 Mike Witt	.25	.11	.03
□ 2 Reggie Jackson	2.50	1.10	.30
□ 3 Bob Boone	1.00	.45	.12
□ 4 Don Sutton	1.50	.70	.19
□ 5 Kirk McCaskill	.25	.11	.03
□ 6 Doug DeCinces	.75	.35	.09
□ 7 Brian Downing	.75	.35	.09
□ 8 Doug Corbett	.25	.11	.03
□ 9 Gary Pettis	.25	.11	.03
□ 10 Jerry Narron	.25	.11	.03
□ 11 Ron Romanick	.25	.11	.03
□ 12 Bobby Grich	.75	.35	.09
□ 13 Dick Schofield	.25	.11	.03
□ 14 George Hendrick	.25	.11	.03
□ 15 Rick Burleson	.25	.11	.03
□ 16 John Candelaria	.25	.11	.03
□ 17 Jim Slaton	.25	.11	.03
□ 18 Darrell Miller	.25	.11	.03
□ 19 Ruppert Jones	.25	.11	.03
□ 20 Rob Wilfong	.25	.11	.03
□ 21 Donnie Moore	.25	.11	.03
□ 22 Wally Joyner	1.50	.70	.19
□ 23 Terry Forster	.25	.11	.03
□ 24 Gene Mauch MG	.50	.23	.06

1987 Angels Grich Sheet

Issued to pay tribute to Bobby Grich's last season, this sheet was issued to fans at Bobby Grich Night, May 1, 1987. The perforated sheet measures approximately 10" by 17 1/2" and features 17 different Topps cards of Grich, from his 1971 Rookie Card (#193) through his 1987 Topps card (#677). When perforated, each card measured the standard size.

	MINT	NRMT	EXC
COMPLETE SET	7.50	3.40	.95
COMMON CARD	.50	.23	.06
□ 1 Bobby Grich 1971	.50	.23	.06
□ 2 Bobby Grich 1972	.50	.23	.06
□ 3 Bobby Grich 1973	.50	.23	.06
□ 4 Bobby Grich 1974	.50	.23	.06
□ 5 Bobby Grich 1975	.50	.23	.06
□ 6 Bobby Grich 1976	.50	.23	.06
□ 7 Bobby Grich 1977	.50	.23	.06
□ 8 Bobby Grich 1978	.50	.23	.06
□ 9 Bobby Grich 1979	.50	.23	.06
□ 10 Bobby Grich 1980	.50	.23	.06
□ 11 Bobby Grich 1981	.50	.23	.06
□ 12 Bobby Grich 1982	.50	.23	.06
□ 13 Bobby Grich 1983	.50	.23	.06
□ 14 Bobby Grich 1984	.50	.23	.06
□ 15 Bobby Grich 1985	.50	.23	.06
□ 16 Bobby Grich 1986	.50	.23	.06
□ 17 Bobby Grich 1987	.50	.23	.06

1987 Angels Smokey

The U.S. Forestry Service (in conjunction with the California Angels) produced this large, attractive 24-card set to commemorate the 43rd birthday of Smokey. The cards feature Smokey the Bear pictured at the bottom of every card. The card backs give a cartoon fire safety tip. The cards measure approximately 4" by 6" and are subtitled "Wildfire Prevention" on the front.

	MINT	NRMT	EXC
COMPLETE SET (24)	7.00	3.10	.85
COMMON CARD (1-24)	.25	.11	.03
□ 1 John Candelaria	.25	.11	.03
□ 2 Don Sutton	1.00	.45	.12
□ 3 Mike Witt	.25	.11	.03
□ 4 Gary Lucas	.25	.11	.03
□ 5 Kirk McCaskill	.25	.11	.03
□ 6 Chuck Finley	1.50	.70	.19
□ 7 Willie Fraser	.25	.11	.03
□ 8 Donnie Moore	.25	.11	.03
□ 9 Urbano Lugo	.25	.11	.03
□ 10 Butch Wynegar	.25	.11	.03
□ 11 Darrell Miller	.25	.11	.03
□ 12 Wally Joyner	1.00	.45	.12
□ 13 Mark McLemore	.75	.35	.09
□ 14 Mark Ryal	.25	.11	.03
□ 15 Dick Schofield	.25	.11	.03
□ 16 Jack Howell	.25	.11	.03
□ 17 Doug DeCinces	.75	.35	.09
□ 18 Gus Polidor	.25	.11	.03
□ 19 Brian Downing	.75	.35	.09
□ 20 Gary Pettis	.25	.11	.03
□ 21 Ruppert Jones	.25	.11	.03
□ 22 George Hendrick	.25	.11	.03
□ 23 Devon White	1.00	.45	.12
□ 24 Checklist Card	.25	.11	.03

1988 Angels Smokey

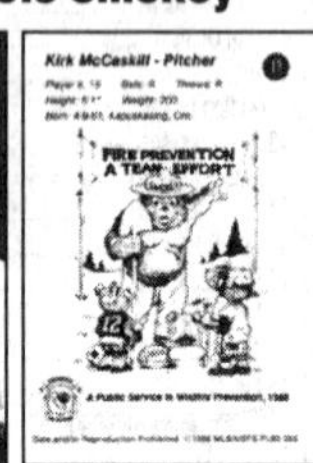

The U.S. Forestry Service (in conjunction with the California Angels) produced this attractive 25-card set. The cards feature Smokey the Bear pictured at the bottom of every card. The card backs give a cartoon fire safety tip. The cards measure approximately 2 1/2" by 3 1/2" and are in full color. The cards are numbered on the back. They were distributed during promotions on August 28, September 4, and September 18.

	MINT	NRMT	EXC
COMPLETE SET (25)	8.00	3.60	1.00
COMMON CARD (1-24)	.25	.11	.03
□ 1 Cookie Rojas MG	.25	.11	.03
□ 2 Johnny Ray	.25	.11	.03
□ 3 Jack Howell	.25	.11	.03
□ 4 Mike Witt	.25	.11	.03
□ 5 Tony Armas	.25	.11	.03
□ 6 Gus Polidor	.25	.11	.03
□ 7 DeWayne Buice	.25	.11	.03
□ 8 Dan Petry	.25	.11	.03
□ 9 Bob Boone	1.00	.45	.12
□ 10 Chili Davis	1.00	.45	.12
□ 11 Greg Minton	.25	.11	.03
□ 12 Kirk McCaskill	.25	.11	.03
□ 13 Devon White	.75	.35	.09
□ 14 Willie Fraser	.25	.11	.03
□ 15 Chuck Finley	1.00	.45	.12
□ 16 Dick Schofield	.25	.11	.03
□ 17 Wally Joyner	1.00	.45	.12
□ 18 Brian Downing	.75	.35	.09
□ 19 Stewart Cliburn	.25	.11	.03
□ 20 Donnie Moore	.25	.11	.03
□ 21 Bryan Harvey	.50	.23	.06
□ 22 Mark McLemore	.50	.23	.06
□ 23 Butch Wynegar	.25	.11	.03
□ 24 George Hendrick	.25	.11	.03
□ NNO Checklist/Logo Card	.25	.11	.03

1989 Angels Smokey

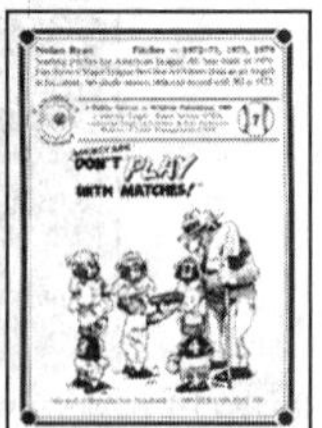

The 1989 Smokey Angels All-Stars set contains 20 standard-size cards. The fronts have red and white borders. The backs are blue and red and feature career highlights. This set, which depicts current and former Angels who appeared in the All-Star game, was given away at the June 25, 1989 Angels home game. The set numbering is ordered chronologically according to when each subject participated in the respective All-Star Game as an Angel representative.

	MINT	NRMT	EXC
COMPLETE SET (20)	12.00	5.50	1.50
COMMON CARD (1-20)	.25	.11	.03
□ 1 Bill Rigney MG	.25	.11	.03
□ 2 Dean Chance	.50	.23	.06
□ 3 Jim Fregosi	.50	.23	.06
□ 4 Bobby Knoop	.25	.11	.03
□ 5 Don Mincher	.25	.11	.03
□ 6 Clyde Wright	.25	.11	.03
□ 7 Nolan Ryan	6.00	2.70	.75
□ 8 Frank Robinson	2.00	.90	.25
□ 9 Frank Tanana	.50	.23	.06
□ 10 Rod Carew	2.00	.90	.25
□ 11 Bobby Grich	.75	.35	.09
□ 12 Brian Downing	.50	.23	.06
□ 13 Don Baylor	1.00	.45	.12
□ 14 Fred Lynn	.50	.23	.06
□ 15 Reggie Jackson	2.00	.90	.25
□ 16 Doug DeCinces	.75	.35	.09
□ 17 Bob Boone	.75	.35	.09
□ 18 Wally Joyner	1.00	.45	.12
□ 19 Mike Witt	.25	.11	.03
□ 20 Johnny Ray	.25	.11	.03

1990 Angels Smokey

The 1990 Smokey Angels set contains standard-size cards which were produced by the U.S. Forest Service and Bureau of Land Management in conjunction with the California Department of Forestry. The first 18 cards in the set are alphabetically arranged. Bailes and McClure were apparently added to the checklist later than these 18, after they were acquired by the Angels.

	MINT	NRMT	EXC
COMPLETE SET (20)	6.00	2.70	.75
COMMON CARD (1-20)	.25	.11	.03
□ 1 Jim Abbott	.75	.35	.09
□ 2 Bert Blyleven	.75	.35	.09
□ 3 Chili Davis	1.00	.45	.12
□ 4 Brian Downing	.50	.23	.06
□ 5 Chuck Finley	.75	.35	.09
□ 6 Willie Fraser	.25	.11	.03
□ 7 Bryan Harvey	.25	.11	.03
□ 8 Jack Howell	.25	.11	.03
□ 9 Wally Joyner	.50	.23	.06
□ 10 Mark Langston	.75	.35	.09
□ 11 Kirk McCaskill	.25	.11	.03
□ 12 Mark McLemore	.25	.11	.03
□ 13 Lance Parrish	.50	.23	.06
□ 14 Johnny Ray	.25	.11	.03
□ 15 Dick Schofield	.25	.11	.03
□ 16 Mike Witt	.25	.11	.03
□ 17 Claudell Washington	.25	.11	.03
□ 18 Devon White	.50	.23	.06
□ 19 Scott Bailes	.25	.11	.03
□ 20 Bob McClure	.25	.11	.03

1991 Angels Smokey

This 20-card standard-size set was sponsored by the USDA Forest Service and USDI Bureau of Land Management in cooperation with the California Department of Forestry. The cards have on their fronts color action player photos with gray borders. Also a dark blue stripe borders the picture above and below. The player's name appears in the white stripe at the card bottom, sandwiched between the team logo and Smokey icon. The player's position is given in a red vertical stripe in the lower left corner. The backs are printed in blue and red on white, and present biography as well as a fire prevention cartoon starring Smokey. The cards are numbered in the upper right corner on the back.

	MINT	NRMT	EXC
COMPLETE SET (20)	6.00	2.70	.75
COMMON CARD (1-20)	.25	.11	.03
□ 1 Luis Polonia	.25	.11	.03
□ 2 Junior Felix	.25	.11	.03
□ 3 Dave Winfield	1.25	.55	.16
□ 4 Dave Parker	.75	.35	.09
□ 5 Lance Parrish	.50	.23	.06
□ 6 Wally Joyner	.75	.35	.09
□ 7 Jim Abbott	.50	.23	.06
□ 8 Mark Langston	.75	.35	.09
□ 9 Chuck Finley	.75	.35	.09
□ 10 Kirk McCaskill	.25	.11	.03
□ 11 Jack Howell	.25	.11	.03
□ 12 Donnie Hill	.25	.11	.03
□ 13 Gary Gaetti	.75	.35	.09

	MINT	NRMT	EXC
☐ 14 Dick Schofield	.25	.11	.03
☐ 15 Luis Sojo	.25	.11	.03
☐ 16 Mark Eichhorn	.25	.11	.03
☐ 17 Bryan Harvey	.25	.11	.03
☐ 18 Jeff D. Robinson	.25	.11	.03
☐ 19 Scott Lewis	.25	.11	.03
☐ 20 John Orton	.25	.11	.03

1992 Angels Police

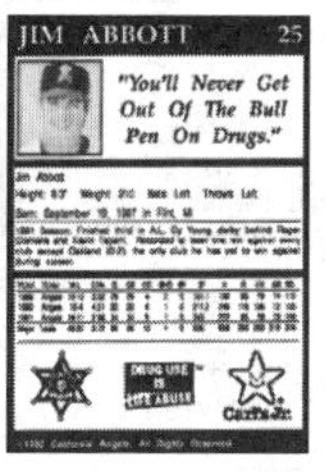

This 18-card standard-size set was cosponsored by the Orange County Sheriff's Department and Carl's Jr. Restaurants in Orange County, California. Deputies and police officers distributed the cards to children in grades K through 6, and 15,000 sets were given out at the September 19 Angel home game. The total number of cards produced was 870,000 individual cards. The cards are printed on thin card stock. The front design has color action player photos inside a red frame and enclosed on three sides by a navy blue outer border studded with six-point white stars. The player's name, team name, and his position appear in the bottom white border along with the anti-drug motto "Drug Use is Life Abuse." On a white background with navy blue print and borders, the backs have a head shot, an anti-drug player quote, biography, statistics, and sponsor logos. The cards are unnumbered and checklisted below in alphabetical order.

	MINT	NRMT	EXC
COMPLETE SET (18)	7.50	3.40	.95
COMMON CARD (1-18)	.25	.11	.03
☐ 1 Jim Abbott	.75	.35	.09
☐ 2 Gene Autry OWN	1.50	.70	.19
☐ 3 Bert Blyleven	.75	.35	.09
☐ 4 Hubie Brooks	.25	.11	.03
☐ 5 Chad Curtis	.50	.23	.06
☐ 6 Alvin Davis	.25	.11	.03
☐ 7 Gary DiSarcina	.25	.11	.03
☐ 8 Junior Felix	.25	.11	.03
☐ 9 Chuck Finley	.75	.35	.09
☐ 10 Gary Gaetti	.50	.23	.06
☐ 11 Rene Gonzales	.25	.11	.03
☐ 12 Von Hayes	.25	.11	.03
☐ 13 Carl Karcher Founder of Carl's Jr. Restaurants	.25	.11	.03
☐ 14 Mark Langston	.75	.35	.09
☐ 15 Luis Polonia	.25	.11	.03
☐ 16 Bobby Rose	.25	.11	.03
☐ 17 Lee Stevens	.25	.11	.03
☐ 18 Happy Star (Title Card)	.25	.11	.03

1993 Angels Adohr Farms Dairy

Adohr Dairy of Santa Ana, Calif., has produced a four-milk carton set featuring California Angels players. Each carton includes a headshot of Tim Salmon, Chad Curtis, J.T. Snow and Damion Easley, along with the player's name, the Angel's logo and a safety tip on the front of the carton. The cartons were issued during the later half of the 1993 season at schools and hospitals in Los Angeles and Orange Counties. It was not available to the general public. According to one collector two million cartons were filled with milk, while 1,500 were left flat and undistributed. This is the first year that Adohr has highlighted Angels players. Previously the company produced cartons with Raiders, Rams and Clippers players.

	MINT	NRMT	EXC
COMPLETE SET (4)	10.00	4.50	1.25
COMMON CARD (1-4)	2.50	1.10	.30
☐ 1 Chad Curtis	3.00	1.35	.35
☐ 2 Damion Easley	2.50	1.10	.30
☐ 3 Tim Salmon	4.00	1.80	.50
☐ 4 J.T. Snow	5.00	2.20	.60

1993 Angels Mother's

The 1993 Mother's Cookies Angels set consists of 28 standard-size cards with rounded corners. The fronts display full-bleed color player portraits shot from the waist up in stadium settings. The player's name and team name appear in one of the corners. On a white background in red and purple print, the horizontal backs carry biographical information and the sponsor's logo.

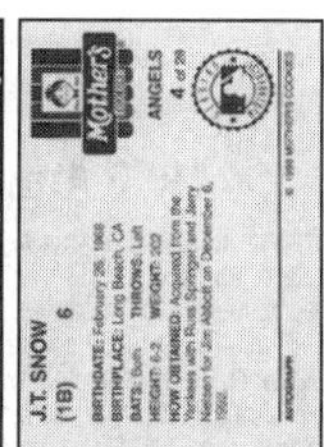

	MINT	NRMT	EXC
COMPLETE SET (28)	12.50	5.50	1.55
COMMON CARD (1-28)	.25	.11	.03
☐ 1 Buck Rodgers MG	.25	.11	.03
☐ 2 Gary DiSarcina	.25	.11	.03
☐ 3 Chuck Finley	.75	.35	.09
☐ 4 J.T. Snow	1.50	.70	.19
☐ 5 Gary Gaetti	.50	.23	.06
☐ 6 Chili Davis	.75	.35	.09
☐ 7 Tim Salmon	3.00	1.35	.35
☐ 8 Mark Langston	.75	.35	.09
☐ 9 Scott Sanderson	.25	.11	.03
☐ 10 John Orton	.25	.11	.03
☐ 11 Julio Valera	.25	.11	.03
☐ 12 Chad Curtis	.75	.35	.09
☐ 13 Kelly Gruber	.25	.11	.03
☐ 14 Rene Gonzales	.25	.11	.03
☐ 15 Luis Polonia	.25	.11	.03
☐ 16 Greg Myers	.25	.11	.03
☐ 17 Gene Nelson	.25	.11	.03
☐ 18 Torey Lovullo	.25	.11	.03
☐ 19 Scott Lewis	.25	.11	.03
☐ 20 Chuck Crim	.25	.11	.03
☐ 21 John Farrell	.25	.11	.03
☐ 22 Steve Frey	.25	.11	.03
☐ 23 Stan Javier	.25	.11	.03
☐ 24 Ken Patterson	.25	.11	.03
☐ 25 Ron Tingley	.25	.11	.03
☐ 26 Damion Easley	.25	.11	.03
☐ 27 Joe Grahe	.25	.11	.03
☐ 28 Checklist/Coaches Chuck Hernandez Jimmie Reese Ken Macha Rod Carew John Wathan Bobby Knoop Rick Turner	.75	.35	.09

1993 Angels Police

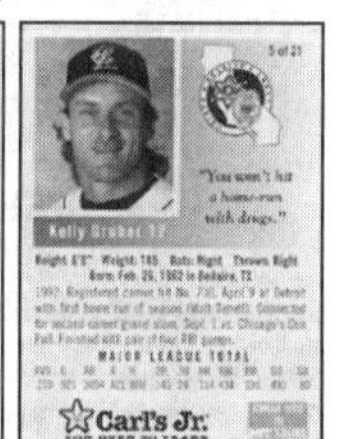

This 21-card standard-size set was sponsored by Carl's Jr. restaurants. The first 11 cards included a paper insert urging the collector to visit any participating Orange Country Carl's Jr. restaurant to receive the rest of the set. On a white card face, the fronts feature color action player photos framed by a purple border. Player information is printed in the wider bottom border between a "Drug Use is Life Abuse" slogan and the team logo. The backs carry a black-and-white headshot, biography, anti-drug message, career summary, and major league statistics. Reportedly only 20,000 sets were produced.

	MINT	NRMT	EXC
COMPLETE SET (21)	25.00	11.00	3.10
COMMON CARD (1-21)	1.00	.45	.12
☐ 1 Gene Autry OWN	5.00	2.20	.60
☐ 2 Carl Karcher (Chairman and Founder, Carl's Jr. Restaurants)	1.00	.45	.12
☐ 3 Buck Rodgers MG	1.00	.45	.12
☐ 4 Rod Carew CO	5.00	2.20	.60
☐ 5 Kelly Gruber	1.00	.45	.12
☐ 6 Chili Davis	1.50	.70	.19
☐ 7 Chad Curtis	1.25	.55	.16
☐ 8 Mark Langston	1.25	.55	.16
☐ 9 Scott Sanderson	1.00	.45	.12
☐ 10 J.T. Snow	1.50	.70	.19
☐ 11 Rene Gonzales	1.00	.45	.12
☐ 12 Jimmie Reese CO	1.50	.70	.19
☐ 13 Damion Easley	1.00	.45	.12
☐ 14 Julio Valera	1.00	.45	.12
☐ 15 Luis Polonia	1.00	.45	.12
☐ 16 John Orton	1.00	.45	.12
☐ 17 Gary DiSarcina	1.00	.45	.12
☐ 18 Greg Myers	1.00	.45	.12
☐ 19 Chuck Finley	1.25	.55	.16
☐ 20 Tim Salmon	8.00	3.60	1.00
☐ 21 Happy Star (Carl's Jr. mascot)	1.00	.45	.12

1994 Angels Adohr Farms

For the second year, Adohr farms produced a set of milk cartons featuring members of the California Angels. These items were not on milk cartons which were distributed in schools and hospitals.

	MINT	NRMT	EXC
COMPLETE SET (4)	10.00	4.50	1.25
COMMON CARD (1-4)	2.50	1.10	.30
☐ 1 Gary DiSarcina	4.00	1.80	.50
☐ 2 Phil Leftwich	2.50	1.10	.30
☐ 3 Joe Magrane	2.50	1.10	.30
☐ 4 Greg Myers	2.50	1.10	.30

1994 Angels L.A. Times

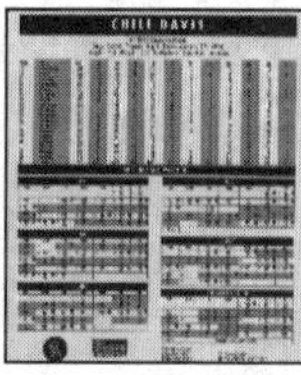

These 26 collector sheets were issued by the Orange County edition of the Los Angeles Times, were printed on semigloss paper, and measure 7 1/2" by 8 3/4". The fronts feature borderless color player action shots. The player's last name appears in large vertical white lettering near the left edge. The Angels' logo rests at the lower right. The back carries the player's name in white lettering within a black stripe near the top, followed below by his uniform number, position, biography, statistics, and '94 Angels game schedule. The sheets are numbered on the front as "X of 26."

	MINT	NRMT	EXC
COMPLETE SET (26)	15.00	6.75	1.85
COMMON CARD (1-26)	.50	.23	.06
☐ 1 Chili Davis	1.00	.45	.12
☐ 2 Chad Curtis	.75	.35	.09
☐ 3 John Dopson	.50	.23	.06
☐ 4 Gary DiSarcina	.50	.23	.06
☐ 5 Jim Edmonds	1.50	.70	.19
☐ 6 Joe Grahe	.50	.23	.06
☐ 7 Bo Jackson	.75	.35	.09
☐ 8 Joe Magrane	.50	.23	.06
☐ 9 Phil Leftwich	.50	.23	.06
☐ 10 Bill Sampen	.50	.23	.06
☐ 11 Chuck Finley	.75	.35	.09
☐ 12 Dwight Smith	.50	.23	.06
☐ 13 Mark Leiter	.50	.23	.06
☐ 14 Mark Langston	.75	.35	.09
☐ 15 Mike Butcher	.50	.23	.06
☐ 16 Rex Hudler	.50	.23	.06
☐ 17 Craig Lefferts	.50	.23	.06
☐ 18 Damion Easley	.50	.23	.06
☐ 19 Greg Myers	.50	.23	.06
☐ 20 Chris Turner	.50	.23	.06
☐ 21 Tim Salmon	2.00	.90	.25
☐ 22 Harold Reynolds	.75	.35	.09
☐ 23 Bob Patterson	.50	.23	.06
☐ 24 Spike Owen	.50	.23	.06
☐ 25 Eduardo Perez	.50	.23	.06
☐ 26 Marcel Lachemann MG	.50	.23	.06

1994 Angels Mother's

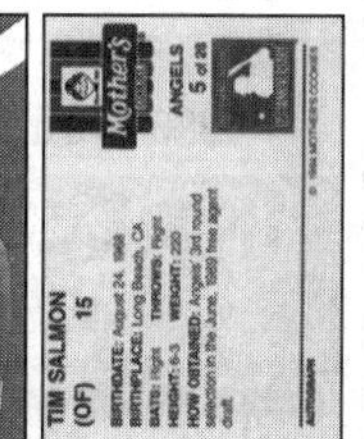

The 1994 Mother's Cookies Angels set consists of 28 standard-size cards with rounded corners. The fronts display full-bleed color player portraits shot from the waist up against a stadium background. The player's name and team name appear in one of the corners. On a white background in red and purple print, the horizontal backs carry biographical information and the sponsor's logo. A blank slot for the player's autograph rounds out the back.

	MINT	NRMT	EXC
COMPLETE SET (28)	12.50	5.50	1.55
COMMON CARD (1-28)	.25	.11	.03
☐ 1 Marcel Lachemann MG	.25	.11	.03
☐ 2 Mark Langston	.75	.35	.09
☐ 3 J.T. Snow	.75	.35	.09
☐ 4 Chad Curtis	.75	.35	.09
☐ 5 Tim Salmon	3.00	1.35	.35
☐ 6 Gary DiSarcina	.25	.11	.03
☐ 7 Bo Jackson	.75	.35	.09
☐ 8 Dwight Smith	.25	.11	.03
☐ 9 Chuck Finley	.75	.35	.09
☐ 10- Rod Correia	.25	.11	.03
☐ 11 Spike Owen	.25	.11	.03
☐ 12 Harold Reynolds	.50	.23	.06
☐ 13 Chris Turner	.25	.11	.03
☐ 14 Chili Davis	.75	.35	.09
☐ 15 Bob Patterson	.25	.11	.03
☐ 16 Jim Edmonds	2.50	1.10	.30
☐ 17 Joe Magrane	.25	.11	.03
☐ 18 Craig Lefferts	.25	.11	.03
☐ 19 Scott Lewis	.25	.11	.03
☐ 20 Rex Hudler	.25	.11	.03
☐ 21 Mike Butcher	.25	.11	.03
☐ 22 Brian Anderson	.25	.11	.03
☐ 23 Greg Myers	.25	.11	.03
☐ 24 Mark Leiter	.25	.11	.03
☐ 25 Joe Grahe	.25	.11	.03
☐ 26 Jorge Fabregas	.25	.11	.03
☐ 27 John Dopson	.25	.11	.03
☐ 28 Checklist/Coaches Chuck Hernandez Ken Macha Bobby Knoop Joe Maddon Rod Carew Max Oliveras	.50	.23	.06

1995 Angels CHP

Sponsored by the California Highway Patrol and commemorating the 35th anniversary of the California Angels, this 16-card set features color action player photos in a silver frame. The backs carry player information and a safety message.

	MINT	NRMT	EXC
COMPLETE SET (16)	20.00	9.00	2.50
COMMON CARD (1-16)	1.00	.45	.12
☐ 1 Tim Salmon	4.00	1.80	.50
☐ 2 Chuck Finley	1.00	.45	.12
☐ 3 Mark Langston	1.00	.45	.12
☐ 4 Gary DiSarcina	1.00	.45	.12
☐ 5 Damion Easley	1.00	.45	.12
☐ 6 Spike Owen	1.00	.45	.12
☐ 7 Troy Percival	1.00	.45	.12
☐ 8 Chili Davis	1.50	.70	.19
☐ 9 Jim Edmonds	2.50	1.10	.30
☐ 10 Rex Hudler	1.00	.45	.12
☐ 11 Greg Myers	1.00	.45	.12
☐ 12 Brian Anderson	1.00	.45	.12
☐ 13 J.T. Snow	1.50	.70	.19
☐ 14 Tony Phillips	1.50	.70	.19
☐ 15 Lee Smith	1.50	.70	.19
☐ 16 Marcel Lachemann MG Chief Don Watkins	1.00	.45	.12

1995 Angels Mother's

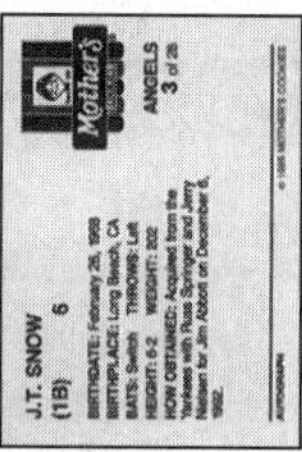

This 1995 Mother's Cookies California Angels set consists of 28 standard-size cards with rounded corners. The fronts display posed color player portraits. The player's name and team name appear in one of the top corners. The horizontal backs carry biographical information and the sponsor's logo on a white background in red and purple print. A blank slot at the bottom for the player's autograph rounds out the back.

	MINT	NRMT	EXC
COMPLETE SET (28)	12.50	5.50	1.55
COMMON CARD (1-28)	.25	.11	.03
☐ 1 Marcel Lachemann MG	.25	.11	.03
☐ 2 Mark Langston	.75	.35	.09
☐ 3 J.T. Snow	.75	.35	.09
☐ 4 Tim Salmon	2.50	1.10	.30
☐ 5 Chili Davis	.75	.35	.09
☐ 6 Gary DiSarcina	.25	.11	.03
☐ 7 Tony Phillips	.75	.35	.09
☐ 8 Jim Edmonds	1.00	.45	.12
☐ 9 Chuck Finley	.75	.35	.09
☐ 10 Mark Dalesandro	.25	.11	.03
☐ 11 Greg Myers	.25	.11	.03
☐ 12 Spike Owen	.25	.11	.03
☐ 13 Lee Smith	.50	.23	.06
☐ 14 Eduardo Perez	.25	.11	.03
☐ 15 Bob Patterson	.25	.11	.03
☐ 16 Mitch Williams	.50	.23	.06

□ 17 Garret Anderson	1.50	.70	.19
□ 18 Mike Bielecki	.25	.11	.03
□ 19 Shawn Boskie	.25	.11	.03
□ 20 Damion Easley	.25	.11	.03
□ 21 Mike Butcher	.25	.11	.03
□ 22 Brian Anderson	.25	.11	.03
□ 23 Andy Allanson	.25	.11	.03
□ 24 Scott Sanderson	.25	.11	.03
□ 25 Troy Percival	.50	.23	.06
□ 26 Rex Hudler	.25	.11	.03
□ 27 Mike James	.25	.11	.03
□ 28 Coaches/Checklist Rod Carew Chuck Hernandez Rick Burleson Bobby Knoop Bill Lachemann Mick Billmeyer Joe Maddon	.75	.35	.09

1995 Angels Team Issue

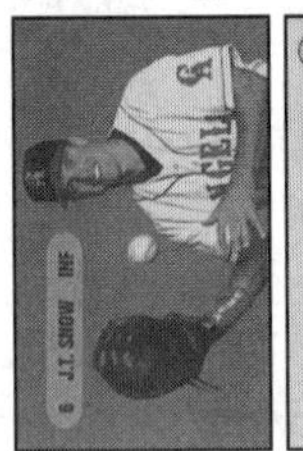

This three-card set features a color player photo on the front with a black-and-white elongated photo, player information, statistics and a facsimile autograph on the back. The cards are unnumbered and checklisted below in alphabetical order.

	MINT	NRMT	EXC
COMPLETE SET (3)	5.00	2.20	.60
COMMON CARD (1-3)	1.00	.45	.12
□ 1 Jim Abbott	2.00	.90	.25
□ 2 Chili Davis	2.00	.90	.25
□ 3 J.T. Snow	1.00	.45	.12

1996 Angels Mother's

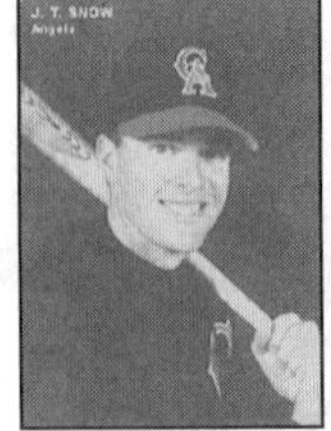

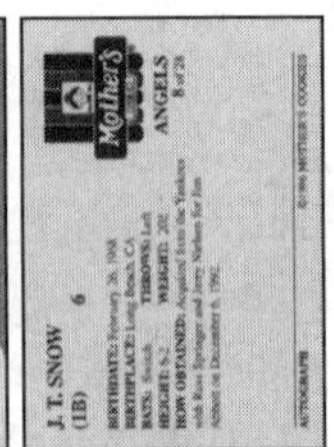

This 28-card set consists of borderless posed color player portraits in stadium settings. The player's and team's names appear in one of the top rounded corners. The backs carry biographical information and the sponsor's logo on a white background in red and purple print. A blank slot for the player's autograph rounds out the back.

	MINT	NRMT	EXC
COMPLETE SET (28)	10.00	4.50	1.25
COMMON CARD (1-28)	.25	.11	.03
□ 1 Marcel Lachemann MG	.25	.11	.03
□ 2 Chili Davis	.75	.35	.09
□ 3 Mark Langston	.75	.35	.09
□ 4 Tim Salmon	1.50	.70	.19
□ 5 Jim Abbott	.25	.11	.03
□ 6 Jim Edmonds	.50	.23	.06
□ 7 Gary DiSarcina	.25	.11	.03
□ 8 J.T. Snow	.50	.23	.06
□ 9 Chuck Finley	.75	.35	.09
□ 10 Tim Wallach	.25	.11	.03
□ 11 Lee Smith	.50	.23	.06
□ 12 George Arias	.50	.23	.06
□ 13 Troy Percival	.50	.23	.06
□ 14 Randy Velarde	.25	.11	.03
□ 15 Garret Anderson	.75	.35	.09
□ 16 Jorge Fabregas	.25	.11	.03
□ 17 Shawn Boskie	.25	.11	.03
□ 18 Mark Eichhorn	.25	.11	.03
□ 19 Jack Howell	.25	.11	.03
□ 20 Jason Grimsley	.25	.11	.03
□ 21 Rex Hudler	.25	.11	.03
□ 22 Mike Aldrete	.25	.11	.03
□ 23 Mike James	.25	.11	.03
□ 24 Scott Sanderson	.25	.11	.03
□ 25 Don Slaught	.25	.11	.03
□ 26 Mark Holzemer	.25	.11	.03
□ 27 Dick Schofield	.25	.11	.03
□ 28 Coaches Card CL Mick Billmeyer Rick Burleson Rod Carew Chuck Hernandez Bobby Knoop Bill Lachemann Joe Maddon	.75	.35	.09

1991 Arena Holograms *

The 1991 Arena hologram cards were distributed through hobby dealers and feature famous football, basketball, and baseball players. According to Arena, production quantities were limited to 250,000 of each card. The cards measure the standard size and display holograms on the fronts. The horizontally oriented backs have a color photo of the player in a tuxedo on the right portion, while the left portion presents player profile in white lettering on black.

	MINT	NRMT	EXC
COMPLETE SET (5)	8.00	3.60	1.00
COMMON CARD (1-5)	1.00	.45	.12
□ 1 Joe Montana	2.00	.90	.25
□ 2 Ken Griffey Jr.	2.50	1.10	.30
□ 3 Frank Thomas	2.50	1.10	.30
□ 4 Barry Sanders	1.00	.45	.12
□ 5 David Robinson	1.00	.45	.12

1992 Arena Kid Griffey Comic Holograms

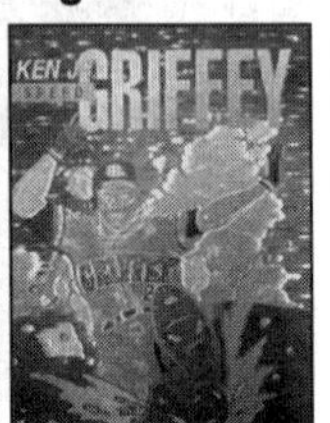

Released in September 1992, this five-card hologram set was produced by Arena Holograms. The production run was reported to be 1,700 individually numbered cases and premium gold edition cards were randomly inserted throughout. The gold versions are valued at five times the values listed below. The holograms measure the standard size. Each foil pack contained one card in a card protector and each protector had a different color border (1-clear, 2-black, 3-red, 4-white and 5-blue). The fronts feature animated holograms, with the player's name and a subtitle appearing across the card top. The backs are white and present head-to-head situations between Kid Griff and Downr Dawg in the opening game of the Inter-Dimensional Universal League.

	MINT	NRMT	EXC
COMPLETE SET (5)	5.00	2.20	.60
COMMON CARD (1-5)	1.00	.45	.12
□ 1 Ken Griffey Jr. The Kid	1.00	.45	.12
□ 2 Ken Griffey Jr. Speed	1.00	.45	.12
□ 3 Ken Griffey Jr. Power	1.00	.45	.12
□ 4 Ken Griffey Jr. Defense	1.00	.45	.12
□ 5 Ken Griffey Jr. Superstar	1.00	.45	.12

1996 Arizona Lottery

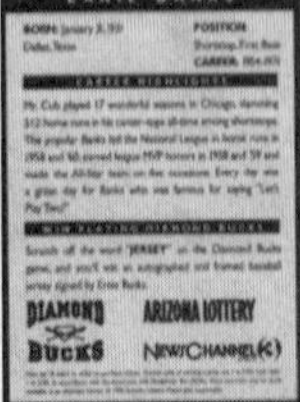

This three-card set features black-and-white action player photos with black borders. The backs carry player information and career highlights as well as information on what the collector can win playing the lottery scratch-off game, "Diamond Bucks." The cards are unnumbered and checklisted below in alphabetical order.

	MINT	NRMT	EXC
COMPLETE SET (3)	8.00	3.60	1.00
COMMON CARD (1-3)	2.00	.90	.25
□ 1 Ernie Banks	3.00	1.35	.35
□ 2 Gaylord Perry	2.00	.90	.25
□ 3 Brooks Robinson	3.00	1.35	.35

1955 Armour Coins

The front of each of the plastic baseball "coins" in this set contains a raised profile of a ballplayer. Each plastic coin measures approximately 1 1/2" in diameter. Although similar in design to the 1959 and 1960 issues by Armour, the 1955 set is distinguished by a number of details: the full team name under the profile, the listing of birthplace and date and batting and throwing preferences on the back and, of course, the 1954 batting or won-loss record located on the reverse. The coins are not numbered and come in colors of black, blue, blue-green, green, orange, red, yellow, tan and gold. Black, tan, and gold are the toughest color coins to find. Mantle and Kuenn exist in two variations each. The set price below includes both variations.

	NRMT	VG-E	GOOD
COMPLETE SET (26)	600.00	275.00	75.00
COMMON COIN (1-26)	10.00	4.50	1.25
□ 1 Johnny Antonelli	10.00	4.50	1.25
□ 2 Yogi Berra	35.00	16.00	4.40
□ 3 Del Crandall	10.00	4.50	1.25
□ 4 Larry Doby	12.00	5.50	1.50
□ 5 Jim Finigan	10.00	4.50	1.25
□ 6 Whitey Ford	30.00	13.50	3.70
□ 7 Jim Gilliam	12.00	5.50	1.50
□ 8 Harvey Haddix	10.00	4.50	1.25
□ 9 Ron Jackson	10.00	4.50	1.25
□ 10 Jackie Jensen	12.00	5.50	1.50
□ 11 Ted Kluszewski	15.00	6.75	1.85
□ 12A Harvey Kuenn (reg.)	15.00	6.75	1.85
□ 12B Harvey Kuenn (cond.)	50.00	22.00	6.25
□ 13A Mickey Mantle ERR name spelled Mantel	125.00	55.00	15.50
□ 13B Mickey Mantle COR	250.00	110.00	31.00
□ 14 Don Mueller	10.00	4.50	1.25
□ 15 Pee Wee Reese	30.00	13.50	3.70
□ 16 Allie Reynolds	15.00	6.75	1.85
□ 17 Al Rosen	15.00	6.75	1.85
□ 18 Curt Simmons	10.00	4.50	1.25
□ 19 Duke Snider	30.00	13.50	3.70
□ 20 Warren Spahn	30.00	13.50	3.70
□ 21 Frank Thomas	10.00	4.50	1.25
□ 22 Virgil Trucks	10.00	4.50	1.25
□ 23 Bob Turley	12.00	5.50	1.50
□ 24 Mickey Vernon	10.00	4.50	1.25

1959 Armour Coins

There are 20 coins in the 1959 Armour set, 10 from each league. Each coin measures 1 1/2" in diameter. In contrast to the 1955 set produced by this company, the raised profiles are not as finely detailed and the lettering is larger. In addition, the team nickname (for example, "Redlegs") is listed below the profile and the reverse does not record birth date and place or batting and throwing preferences. The coins are not numbered and are found in colors of dark and pale blue, dark and pale green, orange, red, pale yellow, pink and gray.

	NRMT	VG-E	GOOD
COMPLETE SET (20)	225.00	100.00	28.00
COMMON COIN (1-20)	6.00	2.70	.75
□ 1 Hank Aaron	50.00	22.00	6.25
□ 2 Johnny Antonelli	6.00	2.70	.75
□ 3 Richie Ashburn	15.00	6.75	1.85
□ 4 Ernie Banks	25.00	11.00	3.10
□ 5 Don Blasingame	6.00	2.70	.75
□ 6 Bob Cerv	6.00	2.70	.75
□ 7 Del Crandall	6.00	2.70	.75
□ 8 Whitey Ford	25.00	11.00	3.10
□ 9 Nellie Fox	15.00	6.75	1.85
□ 10 Jackie Jensen	10.00	4.50	1.25
□ 11 Harvey Kuenn	10.00	4.50	1.25
□ 12 Frank Malzone	6.00	2.70	.75
□ 13 Johnny Podres	10.00	4.50	1.25
□ 14 Frank Robinson	20.00	9.00	2.50
□ 15 Roy Sievers	6.00	2.70	.75
□ 16 Bob Skinner	6.00	2.70	.75
□ 17 Frank Thomas	6.00	2.70	.75
□ 18 Gus Triandos	6.00	2.70	.75
□ 19 Bob Turley	10.00	4.50	1.25
□ 20 Mickey Vernon	6.00	2.70	.75

1960 Armour Coins

Although the 20 plastic baseball player coins produced by Armour in 1960 were identical in style to those of the 1959 set, there was quite a turnover in personnel. Thirteen new subjects were depicted, with Aaron, Banks, Crandall, Ford, Fox, Malzone and Triandos the only returnees. The coins are the same size as the previous year, 1 1/2" in diameter. The reverse of these unnumbered coins lists the 1959 record for each individual. They are found in the following colors: two shades of blue, two shades of green, orange, red, salmon, tan and yellow. The complete set price below includes all variations. The Daley coin is regarded by serious Armour collectors as being quite scarce and has only been seen in two colors, yellow and orange.

	NRMT	VG-E	GOOD
COMPLETE SET (20)	900.00	400.00	110.00
COMMON COIN (1-20)	5.00	2.20	.60
□ 1A Hank Aaron (Milwaukee)	80.00	36.00	10.00
□ 1B Hank Aaron (Braves)	50.00	22.00	6.25
□ 2 Bob Allison	5.00	2.20	.60
□ 3 Ernie Banks	25.00	11.00	3.10
□ 4 Ken Boyer	12.00	5.50	1.50
□ 5 Rocky Colavito	12.00	5.50	1.50
□ 6 Gene Conley	5.00	2.20	.60
□ 7 Del Crandall	5.00	2.20	.60
□ 8 Bud Daley SP	600.00	275.00	75.00
□ 9 Don Drysdale	20.00	9.00	2.50
□ 10 Whitey Ford	25.00	11.00	3.10
□ 11 Nellie Fox	15.00	6.75	1.85
□ 12 Al Kaline	25.00	11.00	3.10
□ 13A Frank Malzone (Boston)	40.00	18.00	5.00
□ 13B Frank Malzone (Red Sox)	5.00	2.20	.60
□ 14 Mickey Mantle	100.00	45.00	12.50
□ 15 Eddie Mathews	20.00	9.00	2.50
□ 16 Willie Mays	50.00	22.00	6.25
□ 17 Vada Pinson	8.00	3.60	1.00
□ 18 Dick Stuart	5.00	2.20	.60
□ 19 Gus Triandos	5.00	2.20	.60
□ 20 Early Wynn	20.00	9.00	2.50

1983 ASA Johnny Mize

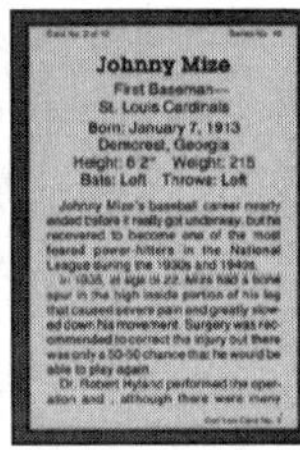

This 12-card set honors the career of Johnny Mize and features fronts of white-bordered and red-trimmed black-and-white photos of him during his career. The backs are red-bordered, trimmed by a black line and carry a story that is continuous from card No. 2 to card No. 9. The backs of cards 10, 11, and 12 carry his lifetime career and World Series records, respectively. Card #1 carries an authentic autograph and is numbered sequentially out of 2,000.

	NRMT	VG-E	GOOD
COMPLETE SET (12)	20.00	9.00	2.50
COMMON CARD (1-12)	.50	.23	.06
□ 1 Johnny Mize (Autograph card)	15.00	6.75	1.85
□ 2 Johnny Mize 1933-35 with Rochester	.50	.23	.06
□ 3 Johnny Mize 1936 Home run in Chicago	.50	.23	.06
□ 4 Johnny Mize 1939 With teammates	.50	.23	.06
□ 5 Johnny Mize 1943 Traded to the Giants	.50	.23	.06
□ 6 Johnny Mize 1948 New York Giants	.50	.23	.06
□ 7 Johnny Mize 1949 Traded to the Yankees	.50	.23	.06
□ 8 Johnny Mize 1949 World Series Game Heroes	.50	.23	.06
□ 9 Johnny Mize 1951 World Series	.50	.23	.06
□ 10 Johnny Mize 1953 Meeting the Duke and Duchess of Windsor	.50	.23	.06
□ 11 Johnny Mize Playing cards with Yogi Berra and Ed Lopat	.50	.23	.06
□ 12 Johnny Mize 1973 Recreation Director	.50	.23	.06

1983 ASA Spahn

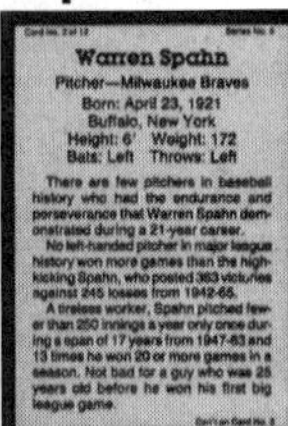

This 12-card standard-size set honors the career of Warren Spahn and features fronts of white-bordered and green-trimmed black-and-white photos of him during his career. The backs are green-bordered, trimmed by a black line and carry a story that is continuous from card No. 2 to card No. 9. The backs of cards 10, 11, and 12 carry his lifetime career and World Series records, respectively. Card #1 is also found in an autographed version; it is valued at between 15 and 25 dollars.

	NRMT	VG-E	GOOD
COMPLETE SET (12)	5.00	2.20	.60
COMMON CARD (1-12)	.50	.23	.06

□ 1 Warren Spahn Title card, color photo	.50	.23	.06
□ 2 Warren Spahn 1947-High Kick	.50	.23	.06
□ 3 Warren Spahn 1948 World Series Pitching to Dale Mitchell	.50	.23	.06
□ 4 Warren Spahn UER Vern Bickford Johnny Sain Misspelled "uupon" on card back	.75	.35	.09
□ 5 Warren Spahn 1951 Spring Training	.50	.23	.06
□ 6 Warren Spahn Fred Haney MG Bobby Thomson Lew Burdette	.75	.35	.09
□ 7 Warren Spahn UER Misspelled Burxette on back	.50	.23	.06
□ 8 Warren Spahn On to '58 World Series	.50	.23	.06
□ 9 Warren Spahn Warren beats Pirates	.50	.23	.06
□ 10 Warren Spahn 1959 Strikeout #2,382	.50	.23	.06
□ 11 Warren Spahn 1965-With the Mets	.50	.23	.06
□ 12 Warren Spahn 1973 Indians Coach-HOF	.50	.23	.06

1967 Ashland Oil

This 12 card set measures 2" by 7 1/2" and the cards are unnumbered. Therefore, we have sequenced the cards in alphabetical order. Jim Maloney is considered tougher and is notated as a SP in the listings below.

	NRMT	VG-E	GOOD
COMPLETE SET	200.00	90.00	25.00
COMMON CARD	10.00	4.50	1.25
□ 1 Jim Bunning	20.00	9.00	2.50
□ 2 Elston Howard	15.00	6.75	1.85
□ 3 Al Kaline	25.00	11.00	3.10
□ 4 Harmon Killebrew	25.00	11.00	3.10
□ 5 Ed Kranepool	10.00	4.50	1.25
□ 6 Jim Maloney SP	50.00	22.00	6.25
□ 7 Bill Mazeroski	20.00	9.00	2.50
□ 8 Frank Robinson	25.00	11.00	3.10
□ 9 Ron Santo	15.00	6.75	1.85
□ 10 Joe Torre	12.50	5.50	1.55
□ 11 Leon Wagner	10.00	4.50	1.25
□ 12 Pete Ward	10.00	4.50	1.25

1967 Astros

These 30 blank-backed cards are irregularly cut, but most measure approximately 1 1/4" by 2". They feature white bordered black-and-white posed player photos and carry the player's name and position in black lettering within the lower white margin. The backs are blank. The cards are unnumbered and checklisted below in alphabetical order.

	NRMT	VG-E	GOOD
COMPLETE SET (30)	60.00	27.00	7.50
COMMMON CARD (1-30)	2.50	1.10	.30
□ 1 Dave Adlesh	2.50	1.10	.30
□ 2 Bob Aspromonte	3.50	1.55	.45
□ 3 John Bateman	2.50	1.10	.30
□ 4 Wade Blasingame	2.50	1.10	.30
□ 5 John Buzhardt	2.50	1.10	.30
□ 6 Danny Coombs	2.50	1.10	.30
□ 7 Mike Cuellar	3.50	1.55	.45
□ 8 Ron Davis	2.50	1.10	.30
□ 9 Larry Dierker	3.50	1.55	.45
□ 10 Dave Giusti	3.00	1.35	.35
□ 11 Fred Gladding	2.50	1.10	.30
□ 12 Julio Gotay	2.50	1.10	.30
□ 13 Buddy Hancken CO	2.50	1.10	.30
□ 14 Grady Hatton MG	2.50	1.10	.30
□ 15 Hal King	2.50	1.10	.30
□ 16 Denny Lemaster	3.00	1.35	.35
□ 17 Mel McGaha CO	2.50	1.10	.30
□ 18 Denis Menke	3.00	1.35	.35
□ 19 Norm Miller	2.50	1.10	.30
□ 20 Joe Morgan	10.00	4.50	1.25
□ 21 Ivan Murrell	2.50	1.10	.30
□ 22 Jim Owens CO	2.50	1.10	.30
□ 23 Salty Parker CO	2.50	1.10	.30
□ 24 Doug Rader	3.50	1.55	.45
□ 25 Jim Ray	2.50	1.10	.30
□ 26 Rusty Staub	6.00	2.70	.75
□ 27 Lee Thomas	2.50	1.10	.30
□ 28 Hector Torres	2.50	1.10	.30
□ 29 Don Wilson	3.00	1.35	.35
□ 30 Jimmy Wynn	5.00	2.20	.60

1967 Astros Team Issue 12

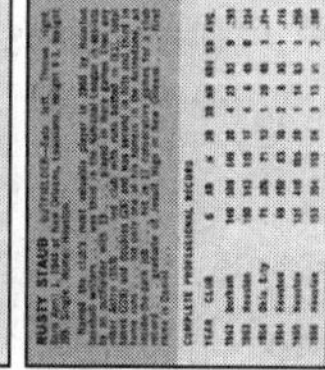

This 12-card team-issued set features the 1967 Houston Astros. The cards measure approximately 2 1/2" by 3" and show signs of perforation on their sides. The posed color player photos have white borders and a facsimile autograph inscribed across them. The horizontally oriented backs have biography and career summary information on a yellow background, and complete statistics. The cards are unnumbered and checklisted below in alphabetical order.

	NRMT	VG-E	GOOD
COMPLETE SET (12)	75.00	34.00	9.50
COMMON CARD (1-12)	3.50	1.55	.45
□ 1 Bob Aspromonte	5.00	2.20	.60
□ 2 John Bateman	5.00	2.20	.60
□ 3 Mike Cuellar	5.00	2.20	.60
□ 4 Larry Dierker	5.00	2.20	.60
□ 5 Dave Giusti	5.00	2.20	.60
□ 6 Grady Hatton MG	3.50	1.55	.45
□ 7 Bill Heath	3.50	1.55	.45
□ 8 Sonny Jackson	3.50	1.55	.45
□ 9 Eddie Mathews	25.00	11.00	3.10
□ 10 Joe Morgan	25.00	11.00	3.10
□ 11 Rusty Staub	7.50	3.40	.95
□ 12 Jim Wynn	7.50	3.40	.95

1967 Astros Team Issue 25

These blank-back black and white photos measure 3 1/4" by 5 1/2". The photos are facsimile autographs on the bottom and we have sequenced them in alphabetical order

	NRMT	VG-E	GOOD
COMPLETE SET (25)	75.00	34.00	9.50
COMMON CARD (1-25)	3.50	1.55	.45
□ 1 Jimmie Adair CO	3.50	1.55	.45
□ 2 Bob Aspromonte	5.00	2.20	.60
□ 3 John Bateman	3.50	1.55	.45
□ 4 Walt Bond	3.50	1.55	.45
□ 5 Bob Bruce	3.50	1.55	.45
□ 6 Jim Busby CO	5.00	2.20	.60
□ 7 Danny Coombs	3.50	1.55	.45
□ 8 Larry Dierker	5.00	2.20	.60
□ 9 Dick Farrell	3.50	1.55	.45
□ 10 Nellie Fox CO	15.00	6.75	1.85
□ 11 Joe Gaines	3.50	1.55	.45
□ 12 Dave Giusti	5.00	2.20	.60
□ 13 Luman Harris MG	5.00	2.20	.60
□ 14 Eddie Kasko	3.50	1.55	.45
□ 15 Bob Lillis	3.50	1.55	.45
□ 16 Ken Mackenzie	3.50	1.55	.45
□ 17 Joe Morgan	10.00	4.50	1.25
□ 18 Don Nottebart	3.50	1.55	.45
□ 19 Jim Owens	3.50	1.55	.45
□ 20 Howie Pollet CO	3.50	1.55	.45
□ 21 Gene Ratliff	3.50	1.55	.45
□ 22 Claude Raymond	3.50	1.55	.45
□ 23 Rusty Staub	7.50	3.40	.95
□ 24 Jim Wynn	6.00	2.70	.75
□ 25 Hal Woodeshick	3.50	1.55	.45

1970 Astros Team Issue

This 12-card set of the Houston Astros measures approximately 4 1/4" by 7". The fronts display black-and-white player portraits bordered in white. The player's name and team are printed in the top margin. The backs are blank. The cards are unnumbered and checklisted below in alphabetical order.

	NRMT	VG-E	GOOD
COMPLETE SET (10)	20.00	9.00	2.50
COMMON CARD (1-10)	1.00	.45	.12
□ 1 Tommy Davis	2.50	1.10	.30
□ 2 Larry Dierker	2.50	1.10	.30
□ 3 John Edwards	1.00	.45	.12
□ 4 Fred Gladding	1.00	.45	.12
□ 5 Tom Griffin	1.00	.45	.12
□ 6 Denny Lemaster	1.00	.45	.12
□ 7 Denis Menke	1.00	.45	.12
□ 8 Joe Morgan	5.00	2.20	.60
□ 9 Joe Pepitone	1.50	.70	.19
□ 10 Doug Rader	1.50	.70	.19
□ 11 Don Wilson	1.50	.70	.19
□ 12 Jim Wynn	2.50	1.10	.30

1971 Astros Coke

Sponsored by the Houston Coca-Cola Bottling Company, these three photos measure approximately 8" by 11" and feature artwork depicting Houston Astro players against stadium backgrounds. The pictures have white borders. A facsimile autograph is printed in black on the picture. The horizontal backs show a pale blue tinted photo of the Astrodome, with player biographical information, statistics and career highlights printed in darker blue over the photo. At the top are the Coca-Cola emblem and slogan. The photos are unnumbered and checklisted below in alphabetical order. Wade Blasingame and Jimmy Wynn are considered to be in shorter supply than the other cards and have been marked with SP in the checklist.

	NRMT	VG-E	GOOD
COMPLETE SET(12)	50.00	22.00	6.25
COMMON CARD (1-12)	2.00	.90	.25
□ 1 Jesus Alou	2.00	.90	.25
□ 2 Wade Blasingame SP	10.00	4.50	1.25
□ 3 Cesar Cedeno	3.00	1.35	.35
□ 4 Larry Dierker	3.00	1.25	.35
□ 5 John Edwards	2.00	.90	.25
□ 6 Denis Menke	2.00	.90	.25
□ 7 Roger Metzger	2.00	.90	.25
□ 8 Joe Morgan	10.00	4.50	1.25
□ 9 Doug Rader	2.00	.90	.25
□ 10 Bob Watson	2.00	.90	.25
□ 11 Don Wilson	2.00	.90	.25
□ 12 Jim Wynn SP	15.00	6.75	1.85

1978 Astros Burger King

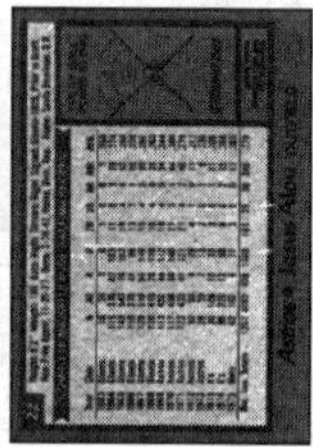

The cards in this 23-card set measure 2 1/2" by 3 1/2". Released in local Houston Burger King outlets during the 1978 season, this Houston Astros series contains the standard 22 numbered player cards and one unnumbered checklist. The player poses found to differ from the regular Topps issue are marked with asterisks.

	NRMT	VG-E	GOOD
COMPLETE SET (23)	16.00	7.25	2.00
COMMON CARD (1-22)	.50	.23	.06
□ 1 Bill Virdon MG	.75	.35	.09
□ 2 Joe Ferguson	.50	.23	.06
□ 3 Ed Herrmann	.50	.23	.06
□ 4 J.R. Richard	1.25	.55	.16
□ 5 Joe Niekro	1.25	.55	.16
□ 6 Floyd Bannister	.75	.35	.09
□ 7 Joaquin Andujar	1.25	.55	.16
□ 8 Ken Forsch	.50	.23	.06
□ 9 Mark Lemongello	.50	.23	.06
□ 10 Joe Sambito	.50	.23	.06
□ 11 Gene Pentz	.50	.23	.06
□ 12 Bob Watson	1.50	.70	.19
□ 13 Julio Gonzalez	.50	.23	.06
□ 14 Enos Cabell	.60	.25	.07
□ 15 Roger Metzger	.50	.23	.06
□ 16 Art Howe	.75	.35	.09
□ 17 Jose Cruz	1.50	.70	.19
□ 18 Cesar Cedeno	1.25	.55	.16
□ 19 Terry Puhl	.75	.35	.09
□ 20 Wilbur Howard	.50	.23	.06
□ 21 Dave Bergman *	.60	.25	.07
□ 22 Jesus Alou *	.75	.35	.09
□ NNO Checklist Card TP	.25	.11	.03

1984 Astros Mother's

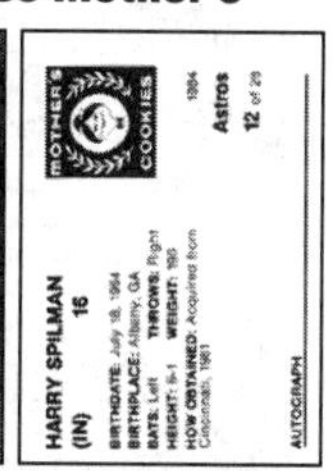

The cards in this 28-card set measure 2 1/2" by 3 1/2". In 1984, the Los Angeles based Mother's Cookies Co. issued five sets of cards featuring players from major league teams. The Houston Astros set features current players depicted by photos. Similar to their 1952 and 1953 issues, the cards have rounded corners. The backs of the cards contain the Mother's Cookies logo. The cards were distributed in partial sets to fans at the respective stadiums of the teams involved. Whereas 20 cards were given to each patron, a redemption card, redeemable for eight more cards was included. Unfortunately, the eight cards received by redeeming the coupon were not necessarily the eight needed to complete a set. Hobbyist Barry Colla was involved in the production of these sets.

	NRMT	VG-E	GOOD
COMPLETE SET (28)	18.00	8.00	2.20
COMMON CARD (1-28)	.25	.11	.03
□ 1 Nolan Ryan	10.00	4.50	1.25
□ 2 Joe Niekro	.75	.35	.09
□ 3 Alan Ashby	.25	.11	.03
□ 4 Bill Doran	.75	.35	.09
□ 5 Phil Garner	1.00	.45	.12
□ 6 Ray Knight	1.00	.45	.12
□ 7 Dickie Thon	.25	.11	.03
□ 8 Jose Cruz	.75	.35	.09
□ 9 Jerry Mumphrey	.25	.11	.03
□ 10 Terry Puhl	.50	.23	.06
□ 11 Enos Cabell	.25	.11	.03
□ 12 Harry Spilman	.25	.11	.03
□ 13 Dave Smith	.50	.23	.06
□ 14 Mike Scott	1.00	.45	.12
□ 15 Bob Lillis MG	.25	.11	.03
□ 16 Bob Knepper	.25	.11	.03
□ 17 Frank DiPino	.25	.11	.03
□ 18 Tom Wieghaus	.25	.11	.03
□ 19 Denny Walling	.25	.11	.03
□ 20 Tony Scott	.25	.11	.03
□ 21 Alan Bannister	.25	.11	.03
□ 22 Bill Dawley	.25	.11	.03
□ 23 Vern Ruhle	.25	.11	.03
□ 24 Mike LaCoss	.25	.11	.03
□ 25 Mike Madden	.25	.11	.03
□ 26 Craig Reynolds	.25	.11	.03
□ 27 Astros' Coaches Cot Deal Don Leppert Denis Menke Les Moss Jerry Walker	.50	.23	.06
□ 28 Astros' Checklist Astros Logo	.25	.11	.03

1985 Astros Mother's

The cards in this 28-card set measure 2 1/2" by 3 1/2". In 1985, the Los Angeles-based Mother's Cookies Co. again issued five sets of cards featuring players from major league teams. The Houston Astros set features current players depicted by photos on cards with rounded corners. The backs of the cards contain the Mother's Cookies logo. Cards were passed out at the stadium on July 13. The checklist card features the Astros logo on the obverse.

	NRMT	VG-E	GOOD
COMPLETE SET (28)	12.50	5.50	1.55
COMMON CARD (1-28)	.25	.11	.03

	MINT	NRMT	EXC
☐ 1 Bob Lillis MG	.25	.11	.03
☐ 2 Nolan Ryan	7.50	3.40	.95
☐ 3 Phil Garner	.75	.35	.09
☐ 4 Jose Cruz	.75	.35	.09
☐ 5 Denny Walling	.25	.11	.03
☐ 6 Joe Niekro	.75	.35	.09
☐ 7 Terry Puhl	.50	.23	.06
☐ 8 Bill Doran	.25	.11	.03
☐ 9 Dickie Thon	.25	.11	.03
☐ 10 Enos Cabell	.25	.11	.03
☐ 11 Frank DiPino	.25	.11	.03
☐ 12 Julio Solano	.25	.11	.03
☐ 13 Alan Ashby	.25	.11	.03
☐ 14 Craig Reynolds	.25	.11	.03
☐ 15 Jerry Mumphrey	.25	.11	.03
☐ 16 Bill Dawley	.25	.11	.03
☐ 17 Mark Bailey	.25	.11	.03
☐ 18 Mike Scott	1.00	.45	.12
☐ 19 Harry Spilman	.25	.11	.03
☐ 20 Bob Knepper	.25	.11	.03
☐ 21 Dave Smith	.50	.23	.06
☐ 22 Kevin Bass	.25	.11	.03
☐ 23 Tim Tolman	.25	.11	.03
☐ 24 Jeff Calhoun	.25	.11	.03
☐ 25 Jim Pankovits	.25	.11	.03
☐ 26 Ron Mathis	.25	.11	.03
☐ 27 Astros' Coaches	.50	.23	.06
Cot Deal			
Matt Galante			
Don Leppert			
Denis Menke			
Jerry Walker			
☐ 28 Astros' Checklist	.25	.11	.03
Astros Logo			

1986 Astros Greats TCMA

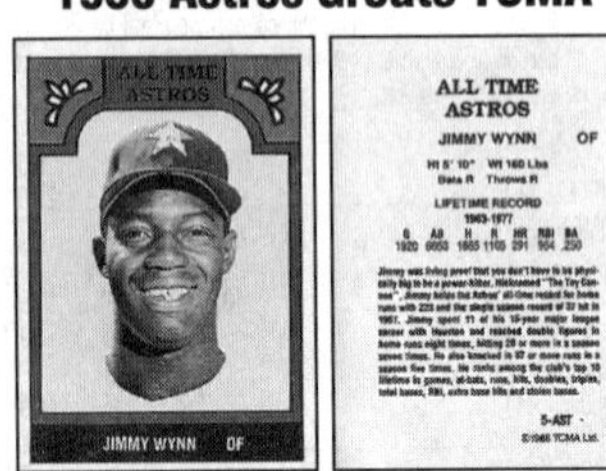

This 12-card standard-size set features some of the best Astros players since their inception in 1962. The cards feature a player photo on the front. Player information as well as statistics are on the back.

	MINT	NRMT	EXC
COMPLETE SET (12)	5.00	2.20	.60
COMMON CARD (1-12)	.25	.11	.03
☐ 1 Bob Watson	.75	.35	.09
☐ 2 Joe Morgan	2.00	.90	.25
☐ 3 Roger Metzger	.25	.11	.03
☐ 4 Doug Rader	.25	.11	.03
☐ 5 Jimmy Wynn	.75	.35	.09
☐ 6 Cesar Cedeno	.75	.35	.09
☐ 7 Rusty Staub	1.00	.45	.12
☐ 8 Johnny Edwards	.25	.11	.03
☐ 9 J.R. Richard	.50	.23	.06
☐ 10 Dave Roberts	.25	.11	.03
☐ 11 Fred Gladding	.25	.11	.03
☐ 12 Bill Virdon MG	.25	.11	.03

1986 Astros Mother's

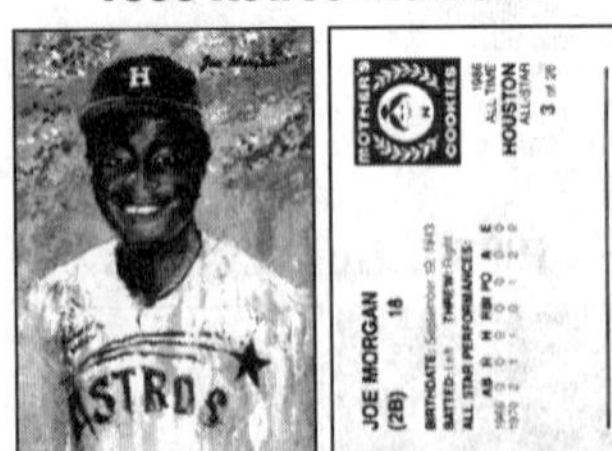

This set consists of 28 full-color, rounded-corner standard-size cards. Starter sets (only 20 cards but also including a certificate for eight more cards) were given out at the ballpark and collectors were encouraged to trade to fill in the rest of their set. Cards were originally given out at the Astrodome on July 10th. Since the 1986 All-Star Game was held in Houston, the set features Astro All-Stars since 1962 as painted by artist Richard Wallich. The set numbering is essentially chronological according to when each player was selected for the All-Star Game as an Astro.

	MINT	NRMT	EXC
COMPLETE SET (28)	12.00	5.50	1.50
COMMON CARD (1-28)	.25	.11	.03
☐ 1 Dick Farrell	.25	.11	.03
☐ 2 Hal Woodeshick	.25	.11	.03
☐ 3 Joe Morgan	2.00	.90	.25
☐ 4 Claude Raymond	.25	.11	.03
☐ 5 Mike Cuellar	.50	.23	.06
☐ 6 Rusty Staub	1.00	.45	.12
☐ 7 Jimmy Wynn	.75	.35	.09
☐ 8 Larry Dierker	.50	.23	.06
☐ 9 Denis Menke	.25	.11	.03
☐ 10 Don Wilson	.25	.11	.03
☐ 11 Cesar Cedeno	.50	.23	.06
☐ 12 Lee May	.50	.23	.06
☐ 13 Bob Watson	1.00	.45	.12
☐ 14 Ken Forsch	.25	.11	.03
☐ 15 Joaquin Andujar	.25	.11	.03
☐ 16 Terry Puhl	.25	.11	.03
☐ 17 Joe Niekro	.75	.35	.09
☐ 18 Craig Reynolds	.25	.11	.03
☐ 19 Joe Sambito	.25	.11	.03
☐ 20 Jose Cruz	.75	.35	.09
☐ 21 J.R. Richard	.75	.35	.09
☐ 22 Bob Knepper	.25	.11	.03
☐ 23 Nolan Ryan	7.50	3.40	.95
☐ 24 Ray Knight	1.00	.45	.12
☐ 25 Bill Dawley	.25	.11	.03
☐ 26 Dickie Thon	.25	.11	.03
☐ 27 Jerry Mumphrey	.25	.11	.03
☐ 28 Checklist Card	.25	.11	.03
Astros' A-S Logo			

1986 Astros Police

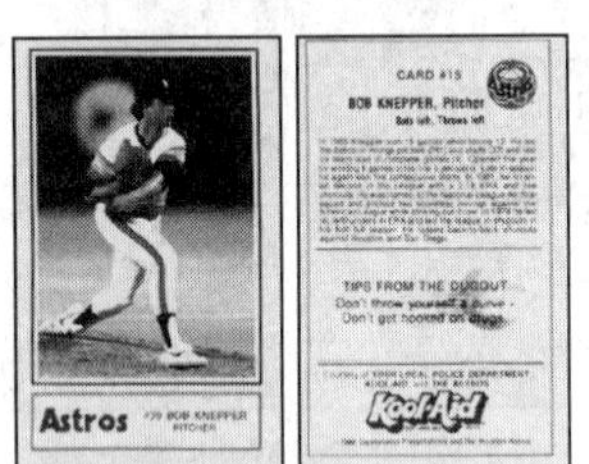

This 26-card safety set was also sponsored by Kool-Aid. The backs contain a biographical paragraph above a "Tip from the Dugout". The front features a full-color photo of the player, his name, and uniform number. The cards are numbered on the back and measure approximately 2 5/8" by 4 1/8". The backs are printed in orange and blue on white card stock. Sets were distributed at the Astrodome on June 14th as well as given away throughout the summer by the Houston Police.

	MINT	NRMT	EXC
COMPLETE SET (26)	8.00	3.60	1.00
COMMON CARD (1-26)	.25	.11	.03
☐ 1 Jim Pankovits	.25	.11	.03
☐ 2 Nolan Ryan	4.00	1.80	.50
☐ 3 Mike Scott	1.00	.45	.12
☐ 4 Kevin Bass	.25	.11	.03
☐ 5 Bill Doran	.25	.11	.03
☐ 6 Hal Lanier MG	.25	.11	.03
☐ 7 Denny Walling	.25	.11	.03
☐ 8 Alan Ashby	.25	.11	.03
☐ 9 Phil Garner	.75	.35	.09
☐ 10 Charlie Kerfeld	.25	.11	.03
☐ 11 Dave Smith	.50	.23	.06
☐ 12 Jose Cruz	.75	.35	.09
☐ 13 Craig Reynolds	.25	.11	.03
☐ 14 Mark Bailey	.25	.11	.03
☐ 15 Bob Knepper	.25	.11	.03
☐ 16 Julio Solano	.25	.11	.03
☐ 17 Dickie Thon	.25	.11	.03
☐ 18 Mike Madden	.25	.11	.03
☐ 19 Jeff Calhoun	.25	.11	.03
☐ 20 Tony Walker	.25	.11	.03
☐ 21 Terry Puhl	.50	.23	.06
☐ 22 Glenn Davis	.75	.35	.09
☐ 23 Billy Hatcher	.25	.11	.03
☐ 24 Jim Deshaies	.25	.11	.03
☐ 25 Frank DiPino	.25	.11	.03
☐ 26 Coaching Staff	.75	.35	.09
Gene Tenace			
Matt Galante			
Denis Menke			
Yogi Berra			
Les Moss			

1986 Astros Team Issue

These 16 photos feature members of the Division Winner '86 Astros. These photos measure 6" by 9" and have full-color photos and a facsimile signature. The photos are unnumbered and we have checklisted them in alphabetical order.

	MINT	NRMT	EXC
COMPLETE SET (16)	10.00	4.50	1.25
COMMON CARD (1-16)	.25	.11	.03
☐ 1 Alan Ashby	.25	.11	.03
☐ 2 Kevin Bass	.25	.11	.03
☐ 3 Jose Cruz	.75	.35	.09
☐ 4 Glenn Davis	.75	.35	.09
☐ 5 Bill Doran	.25	.11	.03
☐ 6 Phil Garner	.75	.35	.09
☐ 7 Billy Hatcher	.25	.11	.03
☐ 8 Charlie Kerfeld	.25	.11	.03
☐ 9 Bob Knepper	.25	.11	.03
☐ 10 Aurelio Lopez	.25	.11	.03
☐ 11 Terry Puhl	.50	.23	.06
☐ 12 Craig Reynolds	.25	.11	.03
☐ 13 Nolan Ryan	6.00	2.70	.75
☐ 14 Mike Scott	.75	.35	.09
☐ 15 Dickie Thon	.25	.11	.03
☐ 16 Denny Walling	.25	.11	.03

1987 Astros Mother's

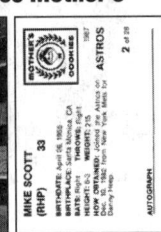

This set consists of 28 full-color, rounded-corner standard-size cards. Starter sets (only 20 cards but also including a certificate for eight more cards) were given out at the ballpark and collectors were encouraged to trade to fill in the rest of their set. Cards were originally given out at the Astrodome on July 17th during a game against the Phillies. Photos were taken by Barry Colla. The sets were reportedly given out free to the first 25,000 paid admissions at the game.

	MINT	NRMT	EXC
COMPLETE SET (28)	12.00	5.50	1.50
COMMON CARD (1-28)	.25	.11	.03
☐ 1 Hal Lanier MG	.25	.11	.03
☐ 2 Mike Scott	.75	.35	.09
☐ 3 Jose Cruz	.75	.35	.09
☐ 4 Bill Doran	.25	.11	.03
☐ 5 Bob Knepper	.25	.11	.03
☐ 6 Phil Garner	.75	.35	.09
☐ 7 Terry Puhl	.50	.23	.06
☐ 8 Nolan Ryan	6.00	2.70	.75
☐ 9 Kevin Bass	.25	.11	.03
☐ 10 Glenn Davis	.50	.23	.06
☐ 11 Alan Ashby	.25	.11	.03
☐ 12 Charlie Kerfeld	.25	.11	.03
☐ 13 Denny Walling	.25	.11	.03
☐ 14 Danny Darwin	.50	.23	.06
☐ 15 Mark Bailey	.25	.11	.03
☐ 16 Davey Lopes	.75	.35	.09
☐ 17 Dave Meads	.25	.11	.03
☐ 18 Aurelio Lopez	.25	.11	.03
☐ 19 Craig Reynolds	.25	.11	.03
☐ 20 Dave Smith	.50	.23	.06
☐ 21 Larry Andersen	.25	.11	.03
☐ 22 Jim Pankovits	.25	.11	.03
☐ 23 Jim Deshaies	.25	.11	.03
☐ 24 Bert Pena	.25	.11	.03
☐ 25 Dickie Thon	.25	.11	.03
☐ 26 Billy Hatcher	.25	.11	.03
☐ 27 Astros' Coaches	1.00	.45	.12
Yogi Berra			
Denis Menke			
Gene Tenace			
Matt Galante			
Les Moss			
☐ 28 Checklist Card	.25	.11	.03
Astrodome			

1987 Astros Police

This 26-card safety set was sponsored by the Astros, Deer Park Hospital, and Sportsmedia Presentations. The backs contain a biographical paragraph above a "Tip from the Dugout". The front features a full-color photo of the player, his name, position, and uniform number. The cards are numbered on the back and measure 2 5/8" by 4 1/8". The first twelve cards were distributed at the Astrodome on July 14th and the rest were given away later in the summer by the Deer Park Hospital.

	MINT	NRMT	EXC
COMPLETE SET (26)	8.00	3.60	1.00
COMMON CARD (1-26)	.25	.11	.03
☐ 1 Larry Andersen	.25	.11	.03
☐ 2 Mark Bailey	.25	.11	.03
☐ 3 Jose Cruz	.50	.23	.06
☐ 4 Danny Darwin	.25	.11	.03
☐ 5 Bill Doran	.25	.11	.03
☐ 6 Billy Hatcher	.25	.11	.03
☐ 7 Hal Lanier MG	.25	.11	.03
☐ 8 Davey Lopes	.50	.23	.06
☐ 9 Dave Meads	.25	.11	.03
☐ 10 Craig Reynolds	.25	.11	.03
☐ 11 Mike Scott	.75	.35	.09
☐ 12 Denny Walling	.25	.11	.03
☐ 13 Aurelio Lopez	.25	.11	.03
☐ 14 Dickie Thon	.25	.11	.03
☐ 15 Terry Puhl	.50	.23	.06
☐ 16 Nolan Ryan	4.00	1.80	.50
☐ 17 Dave Smith	.25	.11	.03
☐ 18 Julio Solano	.25	.11	.03
☐ 19 Jim Deshaies	.25	.11	.03
☐ 20 Bob Knepper	.25	.11	.03
☐ 21 Alan Ashby	.25	.11	.03
☐ 22 Kevin Bass	.25	.11	.03
☐ 23 Glenn Davis	.50	.23	.06
☐ 24 Phil Garner	.75	.35	.09
☐ 25 Jim Pankovits	.25	.11	.03
☐ 26 Coaching Staff	.50	.23	.06
Gene Tenace			
Matt Galante			
Denis Menke			
Yogi Berra			
Les Moss			

1987 Astros-Series One

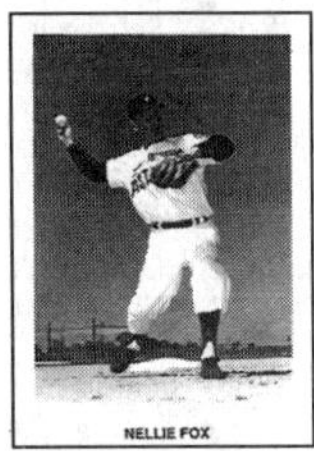
NELLIE FOX

This set features members of the 1965 Houston Astros. The cards are unnumbered, therefore we have sequenced them in alphabetical order.

	MINT	NRMT	EXC
COMPLETE SET (32)	12.00	5.50	1.50
COMMON CARD (1-32)	.25	.11	.03
☐ 1 Bob Aspromonte	.25	.11	.03
☐ 2 John Bateman	.25	.11	.03
☐ 3 Jim Beauchamp	.25	.11	.03
☐ 4 Walt Bond	.25	.11	.03
☐ 5 Ron Brand	.25	.11	.03
☐ 6 Hal Brown	.25	.11	.03
☐ 7 Bob Bruce	.25	.11	.03
☐ 8 Larry Dierker	.50	.23	.06
☐ 9 Dick (Turk) Farrell	.25	.11	.03
☐ 10 Nellie Fox	2.00	.90	.25
☐ 11 Dave Giusti	.25	.11	.03
☐ 12 Sonny Jackson	.25	.11	.03
☐ 13 Ken Johnson	.25	.11	.03
☐ 14 Eddie Kasko	.25	.11	.03
☐ 15 Don Larsen	.50	.23	.06
☐ 16 Bob Lillis	.25	.11	.03
☐ 17 Joe Morgan	3.00	1.35	.35
☐ 18 Don Nottebart	.25	.11	.03
☐ 19 Claude Raymond	.25	.11	.03
☐ 20 Al Spangler	.25	.11	.03
☐ 21 Rusty Staub	1.00	.45	.12
☐ 22 Hal Woodeshick	.25	.11	.03
☐ 23 Jim Wynn	.50	.23	.06
☐ 24 Don Larsen	.50	.23	.06
Bob Turley			
☐ 25 Joe Morgan	2.00	.90	.25
Nellie Fox			
☐ 26 Doug Rader	.25	.11	.03
Norm Miller			
☐ 27 Jim Owens	.75	.35	.09
Nellie Fox			
Turk Farrell			
☐ 28 Al Spangler	.50	.23	.06
Rusty Staub			
Jim Wynn			
☐ 29 Bob Aspromonte	1.00	.45	.12
Eddie Kasko			
Joe Morgan			
Walt Bond			
☐ 30 Lum Harris MG	.25	.11	.03
Clint Courtney CO			
Jim Busby CO			
Jimmy Adair CO			
Howie Pollet CO			
☐ 31 1965 Team Photo	.25	.11	.03
☐ 32 Hats Photo	.25	.11	.03

1987 Astros Shooting Stars-Series One

This set features some of the leading all-time Houston Astros. The cards are unnumbered so we have sequenced them in alphabetical order. The shooting stars refers to the uniform worn by the Astros in the late 60's and early 70's.

	MINT	NRMT	EXC
COMPLETE SET (32)	10.00	4.50	1.25
COMMON CARD (1-32)	.25	.11	.03
☐ 1 Cesar Cedeno	.50	.23	.06
☐ 2 Danny Coombs	.25	.11	.03
☐ 3 Mike Cuellar	.50	.23	.06
☐ 4 Larry Dierker	.50	.23	.06
☐ 5 John Edwards	.25	.11	.03
☐ 6 Dick Farrell	.25	.11	.03
☐ 7 Ken Forsch	.25	.11	.03
☐ 8 Dave Giusti	.25	.11	.03
☐ 9 Fred Gladding	.25	.11	.03
☐ 10 Tom Griffin	.25	.11	.03
☐ 11 Chuck Harrison	.25	.11	.03
☐ 12 Tommy Helms	.25	.11	.03
☐ 13 Sonny Jackson	.25	.11	.03
☐ 14 Denny Lemaster	.25	.11	.03
☐ 15 Lee May	.50	.23	.06
☐ 16 Denis Menke	.25	.11	.03
☐ 17 Norm Miller	.25	.11	.03
☐ 18 Joe Morgan	2.50	1.10	.30
☐ 19 Doug Rader	.25	.11	.03
☐ 20 J.R. Richard	.50	.23	.06
☐ 21 Al Spangler	.25	.11	.03
☐ 22 Rusty Staub	1.00	.45	.12
☐ 23 Bob Watson	.75	.35	.09
☐ 24 Don Wilson	.25	.11	.03
☐ 25 Jim Wynn	.50	.23	.06
☐ 26 Mickey Mantle	3.00	1.35	.35
Don Drysdale			
Rusty Staub			
☐ 27 1969 Pitching Staff	.25	.11	.03
☐ 28 Don Wilson	.25	.11	.03
Harry Walker MG			
☐ 29 Astro Bullpen Car	.25	.11	.03
☐ 30 1966 Team Photo	.25	.11	.03
☐ 31 1967 Team Photo	.25	.11	.03
☐ 32 1968 Team Photo	.25	.11	.03

1987 Astros Shooting Stars-Series Two

This set in another in the continuation of the Astros Shooting Stars. These cards feature more Houston Astros and are unnumbered. Therefore, we have sequenced them in alphabetical order.

	MINT	NRMT	EXC
COMPLETE SET (32)	12.00	5.50	1.50
COMMON CARD (1-32)	.25	.11	.03
☐ 1 Jesus Alou	.25	.11	.03
☐ 2 Jack Billingham	.25	.11	.03
☐ 3 Jim Bouton	1.00	.45	.12
☐ 4 George Culver	.25	.11	.03
☐ 5 Ron Davis	.25	.11	.03
☐ 6 Nellie Fox	1.00	.45	.12
☐ 7 Cesar Geronimo	.25	.11	.03
☐ 8 Julio Gotay	.25	.11	.03
☐ 9 Greg Gross	.25	.11	.03
☐ 10 Cliff Johnson	.25	.11	.03
☐ 11 Dave Nicholson	.25	.11	.03
☐ 12 Claude Osteen	.25	.11	.03
☐ 13 Claude Raymond	.25	.11	.03
☐ 14 Dave Roberts	.25	.11	.03
☐ 15 Fred Scherman	.25	.11	.03
☐ 16 Hector Torres	.25	.11	.03
☐ 17 Bob Stinson	.25	.11	.03
☐ 18 Sandy Valdespino	.25	.11	.03
☐ 19 Jim York	.25	.11	.03
☐ 20 Chris Zachary	.25	.11	.03
☐ 21 Willie Mays	3.00	1.35	.35
Leo Durocher MG			
Cesar Cedeno			
☐ 22 John Mayberry	1.00	.45	.12
Joe Morgan			
☐ 23 Eddie Mathews	.75	.35	.09
Chuck Harrison			
☐ 24 Doug Rader	.25	.11	.03
Harry Walker MG			
Curt Blefary			
Joe Morgan			
Denis Menke			
☐ 25 Rusty Staub	3.00	1.35	.35
Willie Mays			
☐ 26 1973 Outfield Stars	.25	.11	.03
Norm Miller			
Jesus Alou			
Jimmy Stewart			
Jim Wynn			
Bob Watson			
Tommie Agee			
Cesar Cedeno			
☐ 27 1971 Starters	1.00	.45	.12
Cesar Cedeno			
Joe Morgan			
Jim Wynn			
Bob Watson			
Denis Menke			
Doug Rader			
Johnny Edwards			
Roger Metzger			
☐ 28 Don Wilson	.50	.23	.06
Don Larsen			
Bo Belinsky			
☐ 29 Danny Coombs	.50	.23	.06
Dan Schneider			
Bo Belinsky			
Mike Cuellar			
☐ 30 1969 Team Photo	.25	.11	.03
☐ 31 1970 Team Photo	.25	.11	.03
☐ 32 1971 Team Photo	.25	.11	.03

1987 Astros Shooting Stars-Series Three

More Houston Astros of the past are portrayed in this set. These cards are unnumbered so we have sequenced them in alphabetical order.

	MINT	NRMT	EXC
COMPLETE SET (32)	8.00	3.60	1.00
COMMON CARD (1-32)	.25	.11	.03
☐ 1 Dave Adlesh	.25	.11	.03
☐ 2 John Bateman	.25	.11	.03
☐ 3 Bo Belinsky	.75	.35	.09
☐ 4 Nate Colbert	.25	.11	.03
☐ 5 Tommy Davis	.50	.23	.06
☐ 6 Jack DiLauro	.25	.11	.03
☐ 7 Mike Easler	.25	.11	.03
☐ 8 Jim Gentile	.25	.11	.03
☐ 9 Preston Gomez MG	.25	.11	.03
☐ 10 Jim Landis	.25	.11	.03
☐ 11 Barry Latman	.25	.11	.03
☐ 12 Mike Marshall	.25	.11	.03
☐ 13 Marty Martinez	.25	.11	.03
☐ 14 Milt May	.25	.11	.03
☐ 15 John Mayberry	.25	.11	.03
☐ 16 Larry Milbourne	.25	.11	.03
☐ 17 Jim Owens	.25	.11	.03
☐ 18 Joe Pepitone	.50	.23	.06
☐ 19 Jim Ray	.25	.11	.03
☐ 20 Jerry Reuss	.50	.23	.06
☐ 21 Larry Sherry	.25	.11	.03
☐ 22 Dick Simpson	.25	.11	.03
☐ 23 Jimmy Stewart	.25	.11	.03
☐ 24 Robin Roberts	.75	.35	.09
Larry Dierker			
☐ 25 Doug Rader	.25	.11	.03
Roger Metzger			
Tommy Helms			
Lee May			
☐ 26 Jerry Reuss	.25	.11	.03
J.R. Richard			
Tom Griffin			
Jim Owens CO			
Don Wilson			
Dave Roberts			
Ken Forsch			
Larry Dierker			
☐ 27 John Bateman	.25	.11	.03
Dave Adlesh			
Ron Brand			
Bill Heath			
☐ 28 Don Wilson	.25	.11	.03
Tom Griffin			
Larry Dierker			
Denny LeMaster			
☐ 29 Bob Watson	.25	.11	.03
Larry Howard			
John Edwards			
Bob Stinson			
Skip Jutze			
☐ 30 1972 Team Photo	.25	.11	.03
☐ 31 1973 Team Photo	.25	.11	.03
☐ 32 1974 Team Photo	.25	.11	.03

1988 Astros Mother's

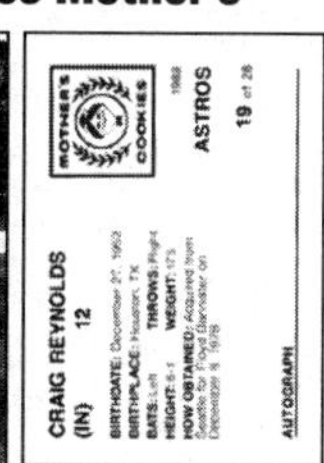

This set consists of 28 full-color, rounded-corner standard-size cards. Starter sets (only 20 cards but also including a certificate for eight more cards) were given out at the ballpark and collectors were encouraged to trade to fill in the rest of their set. Cards were originally given out at the Astrodome on August 26th during a game. The sets were reportedly given out free to the first 25,000 paid admissions at the game.

	MINT	NRMT	EXC
COMPLETE SET (28)	12.00	5.50	1.50
COMMON CARD (1-28)	.25	.11	.03
☐ 1 Hal Lanier MG	.25	.11	.03
☐ 2 Mike Scott	.75	.35	.09
☐ 3 Gerald Young	.25	.11	.03
☐ 4 Bill Doran	.25	.11	.03
☐ 5 Bob Knepper	.25	.11	.03
☐ 6 Billy Hatcher	.25	.11	.03
☐ 7 Terry Puhl	.50	.23	.06
☐ 8 Nolan Ryan	6.00	2.70	.75
☐ 9 Kevin Bass	.25	.11	.03
☐ 10 Glenn Davis	.50	.23	.06
☐ 11 Alan Ashby	.25	.11	.03
☐ 12 Steve Henderson	.25	.11	.03
☐ 13 Denny Walling	.25	.11	.03
☐ 14 Danny Darwin	.50	.23	.06
☐ 15 Mark Bailey	.25	.11	.03
☐ 16 Ernie Camacho	.25	.11	.03
☐ 17 Rafael Ramirez	.25	.11	.03
☐ 18 Jeff Heathcock	.25	.11	.03
☐ 19 Craig Reynolds	.25	.11	.03
☐ 20 Dave Smith	.50	.23	.06
☐ 21 Larry Andersen	.25	.11	.03
☐ 22 Jim Pankovits	.25	.11	.03
☐ 23 Jim Deshaies	.25	.11	.03
☐ 24 Juan Agosto	.25	.11	.03
☐ 25 Chuck Jackson	.25	.11	.03
☐ 26 Joaquin Andujar	.25	.11	.03
☐ 27 Astros' Coaches	1.00	.45	.12
Yogi Berra			
Gene Clines			
Matt Galante			
Marc Hill			
Dennis Menke			
Les Moss			
☐ 28 Checklist Card	.25	.11	.03
Dave Labossiere TR			
Dennis Liborio EQMG			
Doc Ewell TR			

1988 Astros Police

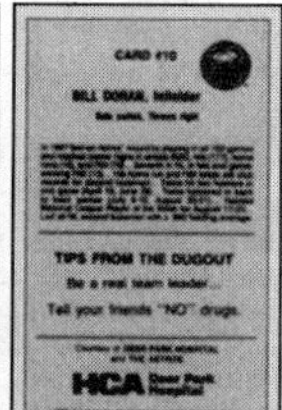

This 26-card safety set was sponsored by the Astros, Deer Park Hospital, and Sportsmedia Presentations. The backs contain a biographical paragraph above "Tips from the Dugout". The front features a full-color photo of the player, his name, position, and uniform number. The cards are numbered on the back and measure 2 5/8" by 4 1/8". The sets were supposedly distributed to the first 15,000 youngsters attending the New York Mets game against the Astros at the Astrodome on July 9th.

	MINT	NRMT	EXC
COMPLETE SET (26)	8.00	3.60	1.00
COMMON CARD (1-26)	.25	.11	.03
☐ 1 Juan Agosto	.25	.11	.03
☐ 2 Larry Andersen	.25	.11	.03
☐ 3 Joaquin Andujar	.25	.11	.03
☐ 4 Alan Ashby	.25	.11	.03
☐ 5 Mark Bailey	.25	.11	.03
☐ 6 Kevin Bass	.25	.11	.03
☐ 7 Danny Darwin	.50	.23	.06
☐ 8 Glenn Davis	.50	.23	.06
☐ 9 Jim Deshaies	.25	.11	.03
☐ 10 Bill Doran	.25	.11	.03
☐ 11 Billy Hatcher	.25	.11	.03
☐ 12 Jeff Heathcock	.25	.11	.03
☐ 13 Steve Henderson	.25	.11	.03
☐ 14 Chuck Jackson	.25	.11	.03
☐ 15 Bob Knepper	.25	.11	.03
☐ 16 Jim Pankovits	.25	.11	.03
☐ 17 Terry Puhl	.50	.23	.06
☐ 18 Rafael Ramirez	.25	.11	.03
☐ 19 Craig Reynolds	.25	.11	.03
☐ 20 Nolan Ryan	4.00	1.80	.50
☐ 21 Mike Scott	.75	.35	.09
☐ 22 Dave Smith	.50	.23	.06
☐ 23 Denny Walling	.25	.11	.03
☐ 24 Gerald Young	.25	.11	.03
☐ 25 Hal Lanier MG	.25	.11	.03
☐ 26 Coaching Staff	.50	.23	.06

1989 Astros Colt .45s Smokey

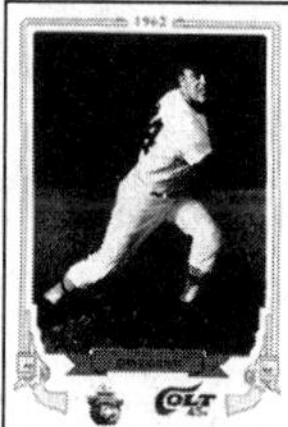
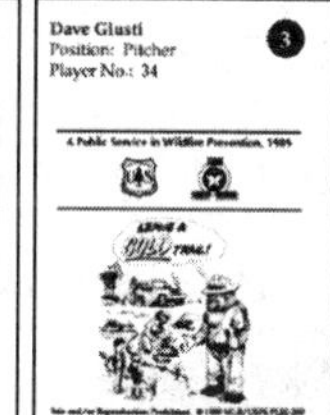

The 1989 Smokey Houston Colt .45s set contains 29 standard-size cards. The Houston Astros were originally called the Houston Colt .45s. The card fronts have black and white photos with white and light blue borders. This set depicts Houston Colt .45s' players from their inaugural 1962 season.

	MINT	NRMT	EXC
COMPLETE SET (29)	6.00	2.70	.75
COMMON CARD (1-29)	.25	.11	.03
☐ 1 Bob Bruce	.25	.11	.03
☐ 2 Al Cicotte	.25	.11	.03
☐ 3 Dave Giusti	.50	.23	.06
☐ 4 Jim Golden	.25	.11	.03
☐ 5 Ken Johnson	.25	.11	.03
☐ 6 Tom Borland	.25	.11	.03
☐ 7 Bobby Shantz	.50	.23	.06
☐ 8 Dick Farrell	.50	.23	.06
☐ 9 Jim Umbricht	.25	.11	.03
☐ 10 Hal Woodeshick	.25	.11	.03
☐ 11 Merritt Ranew	.25	.11	.03
☐ 12 Hal Smith	.25	.11	.03
☐ 13 Jim Campbell	.25	.11	.03
☐ 14 Norm Larker	.25	.11	.03
☐ 15 Joe Amalfitano	.25	.11	.03
☐ 16 Bob Aspromonte	.50	.23	.06
☐ 17 Bob Lillis	.25	.11	.03
☐ 18 Dick Gernert	.25	.11	.03
☐ 19 Don Buddin	.25	.11	.03
☐ 20 Pidge Browne	.25	.11	.03
☐ 21 Von McDaniel	.25	.11	.03
☐ 22 Don Taussig	.25	.11	.03
☐ 23 Al Spangler	.25	.11	.03
☐ 24 Al Heist	.25	.11	.03
☐ 25 Jim Pendleton	.25	.11	.03
☐ 26 Johnny Weekly	.25	.11	.03
☐ 27 Harry Craft MG	.25	.11	.03
☐ 28 Colt Coaches	.25	.11	.03
☐ 29 1962 Houston Colt 45s	.75	.35	.09

1989 Astros Lennox HSE

The 1989 Lennox HSE Astros set contains 26 cards measuring approximately 2 5/8" by 4 1/8". The fronts have color photos with burnt orange and white borders; the backs feature biographical information and career highlights. The set looks very much like the Police Astros sets of the previous years but is not since it was not sponsored by any Police Department and does not have a safety tip anywhere on the card.

	MINT	NRMT	EXC
COMPLETE SET (26)	7.50	3.40	.95
COMMON CARD (1-26)	.25	.11	.03
☐ 1 Billy Hatcher	.25	.11	.03
☐ 2 Greg Gross	.25	.11	.03
☐ 3 Rick Rhoden	.25	.11	.03
☐ 4 Mike Scott	.50	.23	.06
☐ 5 Kevin Bass	.25	.11	.03
☐ 6 Alex Trevino	.25	.11	.03
☐ 7 Jim Clancy	.25	.11	.03
☐ 8 Bill Doran	.25	.11	.03

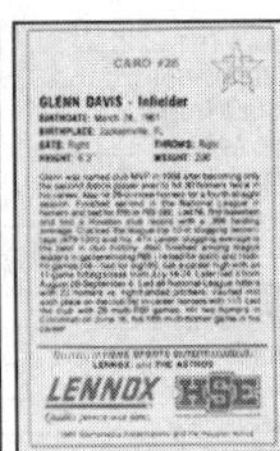

	MINT	NRMT	EXC
□ 9 Dan Schatzeder	.25	.11	.03
□ 10 Bob Knepper	.25	.11	.03
□ 11 Jim Deshaies	.25	.11	.03
□ 12 Eric Yelding	.25	.11	.03
□ 13 Danny Darwin	.25	.11	.03
□ 14 Astros Coaches	.50	.23	.06
Matt Galante			
Yogi Berra			
Ed Napoleon			
Ed Ott			
Phil Garner			
Les Moss			
□ 15 Craig Reynolds	.25	.11	.03
□ 16 Rafael Ramirez	.25	.11	.03
□ 17 Juan Agosto	.25	.11	.03
□ 18 Larry Andersen	.25	.11	.03
□ 19 Dave Smith	.50	.23	.06
□ 20 Gerald Young	.25	.11	.03
□ 21 Ken Caminiti	1.50	.70	.19
□ 22 Terry Puhl	.50	.23	.06
□ 23 Bob Forsch	.25	.11	.03
□ 24 Craig Biggio	2.50	1.10	.30
□ 25 Art Howe MG	.50	.23	.06
□ 26 Glenn Davis	.50	.23	.06

1989 Astros Mother's

The 1989 Mother's Cookies Houston Astros set contains 28 standard-size cards with rounded corners. The fronts have borderless color photos, and the horizontally oriented backs have biographical information. Starter sets containing 20 of these cards were given away at an Astros home game during the 1989 season.

	MINT	NRMT	EXC
COMPLETE SET (28)	10.00	4.50	1.25
COMMON CARD (1-28)	.25	.11	.03
□ 1 Art Howe MG	.25	.11	.03
□ 2 Mike Scott	.75	.35	.09
□ 3 Gerald Young	.25	.11	.03
□ 4 Bill Doran	.25	.11	.03
□ 5 Billy Hatcher	.25	.11	.03
□ 6 Terry Puhl	.50	.23	.06
□ 7 Bob Knepper	.25	.11	.03
□ 8 Kevin Bass	.25	.11	.03
□ 9 Glenn Davis	.50	.23	.06
□ 10 Alan Ashby	.25	.11	.03
□ 11 Bob Forsch	.25	.11	.03
□ 12 Greg Gross	.25	.11	.03
□ 13 Danny Darwin	.50	.23	.06
□ 14 Craig Biggio	3.00	1.35	.35
□ 15 Jim Clancy	.25	.11	.03
□ 16 Rafael Ramirez	.25	.11	.03
□ 17 Alex Trevino	.25	.11	.03
□ 18 Craig Reynolds	.25	.11	.03
□ 19 Dave Smith	.50	.23	.06
□ 20 Larry Andersen	.25	.11	.03
□ 21 Eric Yelding	.25	.11	.03
□ 22 Jim Deshaies	.25	.11	.03
□ 23 Juan Agosto	.25	.11	.03
□ 24 Rick Rhoden	.25	.11	.03
□ 25 Ken Caminiti	3.00	1.35	.35
□ 26 Dave Meads	.25	.11	.03
□ 27 Astros Coaches	1.00	.45	.12
Yogi Berra			
Ed Napoleon			
Matt Galante			
Ed Ott			
Phil Garner			
Les Moss			
□ 28 Checklist Card	.25	.11	.03
Dave Labossiere TR			
Doc Ewell TR			
Dennis Liborio EQMG			

1989 Astros Smokey

These 4" by 6" cards feature members of the Houston Astros. These cards feature player photos on the front and various safety tips on the back. We have sequenced this set in alphabetical order.

	MINT	NRMT	EXC
COMPLETE SET (40)	10.00	4.50	1.25
COMMON CARD (1-40)	.25	.11	.03
□ 1 Juan Agosto	.25	.11	.03
□ 2 Larry Andersen	.25	.11	.03
□ 3 Alan Ashby	.25	.11	.03
□ 4 Kevin Bass	.25	.11	.03
□ 5 Yogi Berra CO	1.00	.45	.12
□ 6 Craig Biggio	2.00	.90	.25
□ 7 Ken Caminiti	2.50	1.10	.30
□ 8 Casey Candaele	.25	.11	.03
□ 9 Jim Clancy	.25	.11	.03
□ 10 Danny Darwin	.50	.23	.06
□ 11 Glenn Davis	.50	.23	.06
□ 12 Jim Deshaies	.25	.11	.03
□ 13 Bill Doran	.25	.11	.03
□ 14 Bob Forsch	.25	.11	.03
□ 15 Matt Galante CO	.25	.11	.03
□ 16 Phil Garner CO	.25	.11	.03
□ 17 Greg Gross	.25	.11	.03
□ 18 Billy Hatcher	.25	.11	.03
□ 19 Art Howe MG	.25	.11	.03
□ 20 Chuck Jackson	.25	.11	.03
□ 21 Charley Kerfeld	.25	.11	.03
□ 22 Bob Knepper	.25	.11	.03
□ 23 Steve Lombardozzi	.25	.11	.03
□ 24 Roger Mason	.25	.11	.03
□ 25 Louie Meadows	.25	.11	.03
□ 26 Dave Meads	.25	.11	.03
□ 27 Brian Meyer	.25	.11	.03
□ 28 Les Moss CO	.25	.11	.03
□ 29 Ed Napoleon CO	.25	.11	.03
□ 30 Ed Ott CO	.25	.11	.03
□ 31 Terry Puhl	.25	.11	.03
□ 32 Rafael Ramirez	.25	.11	.03
□ 33 Craig Reynolds	.25	.11	.03
□ 34 Rick Rhoden	.25	.11	.03
□ 35 Dan Schatzeder	.25	.11	.03
□ 36 Mike Scott	.75	.35	.09
□ 37 Dave Smith	.50	.23	.06
□ 38 Alex Trevino	.25	.11	.03
□ 39 Eric Yelding	.25	.11	.03
□ 40 Gerald Young	.25	.11	.03

1990 Astros Lennox HSE

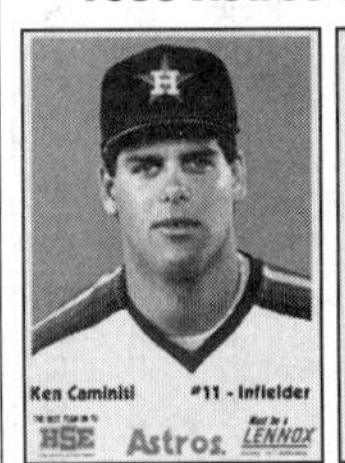

This 28-card, approximately 3 1/2" by 5", set (of 1990 Houston Astros) was issued in conjunction with HSE Cable Network and Lennox Heating and Air Conditioning as indicated on both the front and back of the cards. The front of the cards have full color portraits of the player while the back gives brief information about the player. The set has been checklisted below in alphabetical order.

	MINT	NRMT	EXC
COMPLETE SET (28)	12.00	5.50	1.50
COMMON CARD (1-28)	.50	.23	.06
□ 1 Juan Agosto	.50	.23	.06
□ 2 Larry Andersen	.50	.23	.06
□ 3 Eric Anthony	.50	.23	.06
□ 4 Craig Biggio	2.00	.90	.25
□ 5 Ken Caminiti	2.00	.90	.25
□ 6 Casey Candaele	.50	.23	.06
□ 7 Jose Cano	.50	.23	.06
□ 8 Jim Clancy	.50	.23	.06
□ 9 Danny Darwin	.75	.35	.09
□ 10 Mark Davidson	.50	.23	.06
□ 11 Glenn Davis	.50	.23	.06
□ 12 Jim Deshaies	.50	.23	.06
□ 13 Bill Doran	.50	.23	.06
□ 14 Bill Gullickson	.50	.23	.06
□ 15 Xavier Hernandez	.50	.23	.06
□ 16 Art Howe MG	.50	.23	.06
□ 17 Mark Portugal	.50	.23	.06
□ 18 Terry Puhl	.75	.35	.09
□ 19 Rafael Ramirez	.50	.23	.06
□ 20 David Rohde	.50	.23	.06
□ 21 Dan Schatzeder	.50	.23	.06
□ 22 Mike Scott	1.00	.45	.12
□ 23 Dave Smith	.75	.35	.09
□ 24 Franklin Stubbs	.50	.23	.06
□ 25 Alex Trevino	.50	.23	.06
□ 26 Glenn Wilson	.50	.23	.06
□ 27 Eric Yelding	.50	.23	.06
□ 28 Gerald Young	.50	.23	.06

1990 Astros Mother's

This 28-card standard-size set features members of the 1990 Houston Astros. This set features the traditional rounded corners and has biographical information about each player on the back. These Astros cards were given away on July 15th to the first 25,000 fans at the

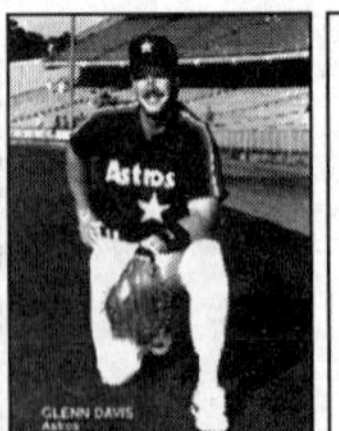
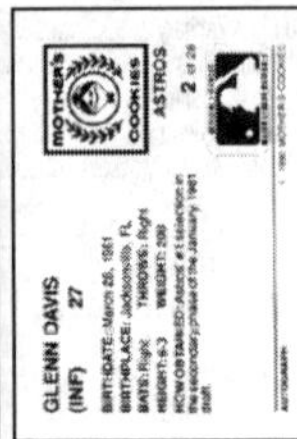

Astrodome. They were distributed in 20 card random packets at the game and eight more at the redemption booths. However, both groups of cards were random and there was no guarantee of getting a complete set in the cards. The promotional idea was that the only way one could finish the set was to trade for them. The certificates of redemption for eight were redeemable at the major card show at the AstroArena on August 24-26, 1990.

	MINT	NRMT	EXC
COMPLETE SET (28)	8.00	3.60	1.00
COMMON CARD (1-28)	.25	.11	.03
□ 1 Art Howe MG	.25	.11	.03
□ 2 Glenn Davis	.50	.23	.06
□ 3 Eric Anthony	.25	.11	.03
□ 4 Mike Scott	.75	.35	.09
□ 5 Craig Biggio	1.50	.70	.19
□ 6 Ken Caminiti	1.50	.70	.19
□ 7 Bill Doran	.25	.11	.03
□ 8 Gerald Young	.25	.11	.03
□ 9 Terry Puhl	.50	.23	.06
□ 10 Mark Portugal	.25	.11	.03
□ 11 Mark Davidson	.25	.11	.03
□ 12 Jim Deshaies	.25	.11	.03
□ 13 Bill Gullickson	.25	.11	.03
□ 14 Franklin Stubbs	.25	.11	.03
□ 15 Danny Darwin	.50	.23	.06
□ 16 Ken Oberkfell	.25	.11	.03
□ 17 Dave Smith	.50	.23	.06
□ 18 Dan Schatzeder	.25	.11	.03
□ 19 Rafael Ramirez	.25	.11	.03
□ 20 Larry Andersen	.25	.11	.03
□ 21 Alex Trevino	.25	.11	.03
□ 22 Glenn Wilson	.25	.11	.03
□ 23 Jim Clancy	.25	.11	.03
□ 24 Eric Yelding	.25	.11	.03
□ 25 Casey Candaele	.25	.11	.03
□ 26 Juan Agosto	.25	.11	.03
□ 27 Coaches Card	.50	.23	.06
Billy Bowman			
Bob Cluck			
Phil Garner			
Matt Galante			
Ed Napoleon			
Rudy Jaramillo			
□ 28 Personnel Card	.25	.11	.03
Dave Labossiere TR			
Dennis Liborio EQ.MG			
Doc Ewell TR			

1991 Astros Mother's

The 1991 Mother's Cookies Houston Astros set contains 28 standard-size cards with rounded corners. The front design has borderless glossy color player photos from the waist up. The horizontally oriented backs are printed in red and purple, present biographical information, and have blank slots for player autographs.

	MINT	NRMT	EXC
COMPLETE SET (28)	12.00	5.50	1.50
COMMON CARD (1-28)	.25	.11	.03
□ 1 Art Howe MG	.25	.11	.03
□ 2 Steve Finley	1.00	.45	.12
□ 3 Pete Harnisch	.25	.11	.03
□ 4 Mike Scott	.75	.35	.09
□ 5 Craig Biggio	1.50	.70	.19
□ 6 Ken Caminiti	2.00	.90	.25
□ 7 Eric Yelding	.25	.11	.03
□ 8 Jeff Bagwell	6.00	2.70	.75
□ 9 Jim Deshaies	.25	.11	.03
□ 10 Mark Portugal	.25	.11	.03
□ 11 Mark Davidson	.25	.11	.03
□ 12 Jimmy Jones	.25	.11	.03
□ 13 Luis Gonzalez	1.00	.45	.12
□ 14 Karl Rhodes	.25	.11	.03
□ 15 Curt Schilling	.25	.11	.03
□ 16 Ken Oberkfell	.25	.11	.03
□ 17 Mark McLemore	.25	.11	.03
□ 18 Dave Rohde	.25	.11	.03
□ 19 Rafael Ramirez	.25	.11	.03
□ 20 Al Osuna	.25	.11	.03
□ 21 Jim Corsi	.25	.11	.03
□ 22 Carl Nichols	.25	.11	.03
□ 23 Jim Clancy	.25	.11	.03
□ 24 Dwayne Henry	.25	.11	.03
□ 25 Casey Candaele	.25	.11	.03
□ 26 Xavier Hernandez	.25	.11	.03
□ 27 Darryl Kile	.75	.35	.09
□ 28 Checklist Card	.50	.23	.06
Phil Garner CO			
Bob Cluck CO			
Ed Ott CO			
Matt Galante CO			
Rudy Jaramillo CO			

1992 Astros Mother's

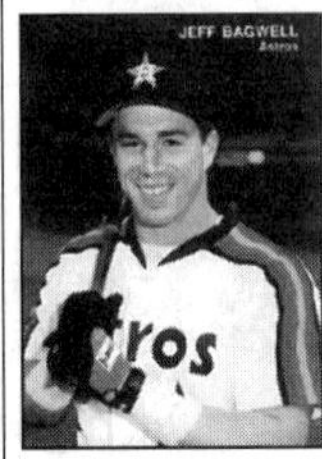

The 1992 Mother's Cookies Astros set contains 28 standard-size cards with rounded corners. The front design has borderless glossy color player photos in which the players are posed with either their glove or a bat. The player's name and team name appear in the upper right corner. The horizontal backs are printed in red and purple, and present biography and a "how obtained" remark where appropriate. A blank slot for the player's autograph rounds out the back.

	MINT	NRMT	EXC
COMPLETE SET (28)	10.00	4.50	1.25
COMMON CARD (1-28)	.25	.11	.03
□ 1 Art Howe MG	.25	.11	.03
□ 2 Steve Finley	1.00	.45	.12
□ 3 Pete Harnisch	.25	.11	.03
□ 4 Pete Incaviglia	.25	.11	.03
□ 5 Craig Biggio	1.50	.70	.19
□ 6 Ken Caminiti	2.00	.90	.25
□ 7 Eric Anthony	.25	.11	.03
□ 8 Jeff Bagwell	5.00	2.20	.60
□ 9 Andujar Cedeno	.25	.11	.03
□ 10 Mark Portugal	.25	.11	.03
□ 11 Eddie Taubensee	.50	.23	.06
□ 12 Jimmy Jones	.25	.11	.03
□ 13 Joe Boever	.25	.11	.03
□ 14 Benny Distefano	.25	.11	.03
□ 15 Juan Guerrero	.25	.11	.03
□ 16 Doug Jones	.25	.11	.03
□ 17 Scott Servais	.25	.11	.03
□ 18 Butch Henry	.25	.11	.03
□ 19 Rafael Ramirez	.25	.11	.03
□ 20 Al Osuna	.25	.11	.03
□ 21 Rob Murphy	.25	.11	.03
□ 22 Chris Jones	.25	.11	.03
□ 23 Rob Mallicoat	.25	.11	.03
□ 24 Darryl Kile	.50	.23	.06
□ 25 Casey Candaele	.25	.11	.03
□ 26 Xavier Hernandez	.25	.11	.03
□ 27 Coaches	.50	.23	.06
Rudy Jaramillo			
Ed Ott			
Matt Galante			
Bob Cluck			
Tom Spencer			
□ 28 Checklist	.25	.11	.03
Dennis Liborio EQMG			
Dave Labossiere TR			
Doc Ewell TR			

1993 Astros Mother's

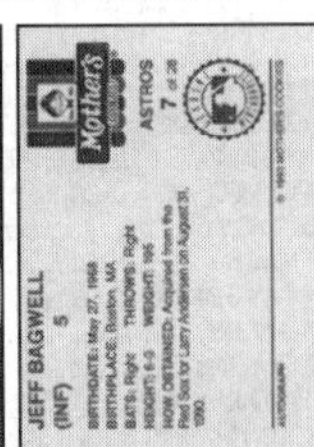

The 1993 Mother's Cookies Astros set consists of 28 standard-size cards with rounded corners. The fronts display full-bleed color player portraits shot from the waist up in stadium settings. The player's name and team name appear in one of the corners. On a white background in red and purple print, the horizontal backs carry biographical information and the sponsor's logo. A blank slot for the player's autograph rounds out the back.

	MINT	NRMT	EXC
COMPLETE SET (28)	10.00	4.50	1.25
COMMON CARD (1-28)	.25	.11	.03
☐ 1 Art Howe MG	.25	.11	.03
☐ 2 Steve Finley	.50	.23	.06
☐ 3 Pete Harnisch	.25	.11	.03
☐ 4 Craig Biggio	1.50	.70	.19
☐ 5 Doug Drabek	.50	.23	.06
☐ 6 Scott Servais	.25	.11	.03
☐ 7 Jeff Bagwell	3.00	1.35	.35
☐ 8 Eric Anthony	.25	.11	.03
☐ 9 Ken Caminiti	2.00	.90	.25
☐ 10 Andujar Cedeno	.25	.11	.03
☐ 11 Mark Portugal	.25	.11	.03
☐ 12 Jose Uribe	.25	.11	.03
☐ 13 Rick Parker	.25	.11	.03
☐ 14 Doug Jones	.25	.11	.03
☐ 15 Luis Gonzalez	.50	.23	.06
☐ 16 Kevin Bass	.25	.11	.03
☐ 17 Greg Swindell	.25	.11	.03
☐ 18 Eddie Taubensee	.25	.11	.03
☐ 19 Darryl Kile	.25	.11	.03
☐ 20 Brian Williams	.25	.11	.03
☐ 21 Chris James	.25	.11	.03
☐ 22 Chris Donnels	.25	.11	.03
☐ 23 Xavier Hernandez	.25	.11	.03
☐ 24 Casey Candaele	.25	.11	.03
☐ 25 Eric Bell	.25	.11	.03
☐ 26 Mark Grant	.25	.11	.03
☐ 27 Tom Edens	.25	.11	.03
☐ 28 Checklist/Coaches	.50	.23	.06
Ed Ott			
Bob Cluck			
Matt Galante			
Billy Joe Bowman			
Rudy Jaramillo			
Tom Spencer			

1994 Astros Mother's

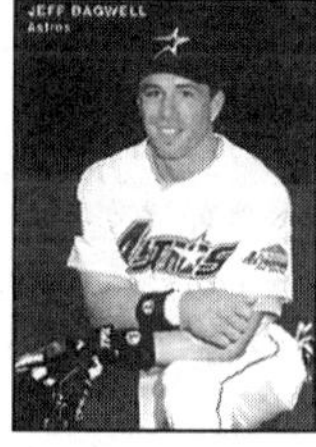

The 1994 Mother's Cookies Astros set consists of 28 standard-size cards with rounded corners. The fronts display full-bleed color player portraits shot from the waist up against a stadium background. The player's name and team name appear in one of the corners. On a white background in red and purple print, the horizontal backs carry biographical information and the sponsor's logo. A blank slot for the player's autograph rounds out the back.

	MINT	NRMT	EXC
COMPLETE SET (28)	10.00	4.50	1.25
COMMON CARD (1-28)	.25	.11	.03
☐ 1 Terry Collins MG	.25	.11	.03
☐ 2 Mitch Williams	.25	.11	.03
☐ 3 Jeff Bagwell	3.00	1.35	.35
☐ 4 Luis Gonzalez	.50	.23	.06
☐ 5 Craig Biggio	1.25	.55	.16
☐ 6 Darryl Kile	.50	.23	.06
☐ 7 Ken Caminiti	2.00	.90	.25
☐ 8 Steve Finley	1.00	.45	.12
☐ 9 Pete Harnisch	.25	.11	.03
☐ 10 Sid Bream	.25	.11	.03
☐ 11 Mike Felder	.25	.11	.03
☐ 12 Tom Edens	.25	.11	.03
☐ 13 James Mouton	.25	.11	.03
☐ 14 Doug Drabek	.25	.11	.03
☐ 15 Greg Swindell	.25	.11	.03
☐ 16 Chris Donnels	.25	.11	.03
☐ 17 John Hudek	.25	.11	.03
☐ 18 Andujar Cedeno	.25	.11	.03
☐ 19 Scott Servais	.25	.11	.03
☐ 20 Todd Jones	.25	.11	.03
☐ 21 Kevin Bass	.25	.11	.03
☐ 22 Shane Reynolds	.50	.23	.06
☐ 23 Brian Williams	.25	.11	.03
☐ 24 Tony Eusebio	.25	.11	.03
☐ 25 Mike Hampton	.50	.23	.06
☐ 26 Andy Stankiewicz	.25	.11	.03
☐ 27 Astros Coaches	.50	.23	.06
Matt Galante			
Steve Henderson			
Ben Hines			
Julio Linares			
Mel Stottlemyre			
☐ 28 Checklist	.25	.11	.03
Dennis Liborio EQMG			
Dave Labossiere TR			
Rex Jones TR			

1995 Astros Mother's

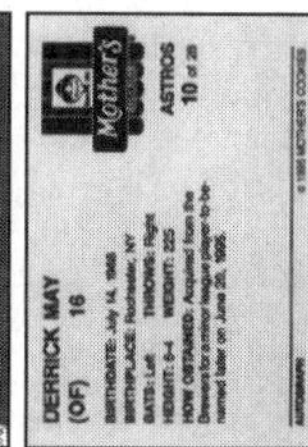

This 1995 Mother's Cookies Houston Astros set consists of 28 standard-size cards with rounded corners. The fronts display posed color player portraits. The player's name and team name appear in one of the top corners. The horizontal backs carry biographical information and the sponsor's logo on a white background in red and purple print. A blank slot at the bottom for the player's autograph rounds out the back.

	MINT	NRMT	EXC
COMPLETE SET (28)	10.00	4.50	1.25
COMMON CARD (1-28)	.25	.11	.03
☐ 1 Terry Collins MG	.25	.11	.03
☐ 2 Jeff Bagwell	3.00	1.35	.35
☐ 3 Luis Gonzalez	.50	.23	.06
☐ 4 Darryl Kile	.50	.23	.06
☐ 5 Derek Bell	.50	.23	.06
☐ 6 Scott Servais	.25	.11	.03
☐ 7 Craig Biggio	1.25	.55	.16
☐ 8 Dave Magadan	.25	.11	.03
☐ 9 Milt Thompson	.25	.11	.03
☐ 10 Derrick May	.25	.11	.03
☐ 11 Doug Drabek	.25	.11	.03
☐ 12 Tony Eusebio	.25	.11	.03
☐ 13 Phil Nevin	.50	.23	.06
☐ 14 James Mouton	.25	.11	.03
☐ 15 Phil Plantier	.25	.11	.03
☐ 16 Pedro Martinez	.50	.23	.06
☐ 17 Orlando Miller	.50	.23	.06
☐ 18 John Hudek	.25	.11	.03
☐ 19 Doug Brocail	.25	.11	.03
☐ 20 Craig Shipley	.25	.11	.03
☐ 21 Shane Reynolds	.50	.23	.06
☐ 22 Mike Hampton	.50	.23	.06
☐ 23 Todd Jones	.25	.11	.03
☐ 24 Greg Swindell	.25	.11	.03
☐ 25 Jim Dougherty	.25	.11	.03
☐ 26 Brian Hunter	1.50	.70	.19
☐ 27 Dave Veres	.25	.11	.03
☐ 28 Coaches/Checklist	.50	.23	.06
Julio Linares			
Matt Galante			
Jesse Barfield			
Mel Stottlemyre			
Steve Henderson			

1996 Astros Mother's

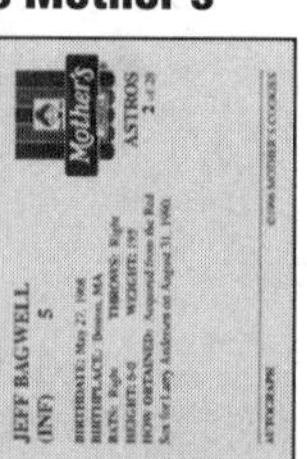

This 28-card set consists of borderless posed color player portraits in stadium settings. The player's and team's names appear in one of the top rounded corners. The backs carry biographical information and the sponsor's logo on a white background in red and purple print. A blank slot for the player's autograph rounds out the back.

	MINT	NRMT	EXC
COMPLETE SET (28)	8.00	3.60	1.00
COMMON CARD (1-28)	.25	.11	.03
☐ 1 Terry Collins MG	.25	.11	.03
☐ 2 Jeff Bagwell	2.50	1.10	.30
☐ 3 Craig Biggio	1.25	.55	.16
☐ 4 Derek Bell	.50	.23	.06
☐ 5 Darryl Kile	.50	.23	.06
☐ 6 Sean Berry	.25	.11	.03
☐ 7 Doug Drabek	.25	.11	.03
☐ 8 Derrick May	.25	.11	.03
☐ 9 Orlando Miller	.25	.11	.03
☐ 10 Mike Hampton	.50	.23	.06
☐ 11 Rick Wilkins	.25	.11	.03
☐ 12 Brian Hunter	.75	.35	.09
☐ 13 Shane Reynolds	.75	.35	.09
☐ 14 James Mouton	.25	.11	.03
☐ 15 Greg Swindell	.25	.11	.03
☐ 16 Bill Spiers	.25	.11	.03
☐ 17 Alvin Morman	.25	.11	.03
☐ 18 Tony Eusebio	.25	.11	.03
☐ 19 John Hudek	.25	.11	.03
☐ 20 Doug Brocail	.25	.11	.03
☐ 21 Anthony Young	.25	.11	.03
☐ 22 John Cangelosi	.25	.11	.03
☐ 23 Jeff Tabaka	.25	.11	.03
☐ 24 Mike Simms	.25	.11	.03
☐ 25 Todd Jones	.25	.11	.03
☐ 26 Ricky Gutierrez	.25	.11	.03
☐ 27 Mark Small	.25	.11	.03
☐ 28 Coaches Card CL	.25	.11	.03
Matt Galante			
Julio Linares			
Rick Sweet			
Brent Strom			
Steve Henderson			

1978 Atlanta Convention

This 24-card set features circular black-and-white player photos framed in light green and bordered in white. The player's name is printed in black across the top with his position, team name, and logo at the bottom. The white backs carry the player's name and career information. The cards are unnumbered and checklisted below in alphabetical order. Almost all of the players in this set played for the Braves at one time.

	NRMT	VG-E	GOOD
COMPLETE SET (24)	15.00	6.75	1.85
COMMON CARD (1-24)	.25	.11	.03
☐ 1 Hank Aaron	5.00	2.20	.60
☐ 2 Joe Adcock	.50	.23	.06
☐ 3 Felipe Alou	1.00	.45	.12
☐ 4 Frank Bolling	.25	.11	.03
☐ 5 Orlando Cepeda	1.00	.45	.12
☐ 6 Ty Cline	.25	.11	.03
☐ 7 Tony Cloninger	.25	.11	.03
☐ 8 Del Crandall	.25	.11	.03
☐ 9 Fred Haney MG	.25	.11	.03
☐ 10 Pat Jarvis	.25	.11	.03
☐ 11 Ernie Johnson	.25	.11	.03
☐ 12 Ken Johnson	.25	.11	.03
☐ 13 Denver Lemaster	.25	.11	.03
☐ 14 Eddie Mathews	2.00	.90	.25
☐ 15 Lee Maye	.25	.11	.03
☐ 16 Denis Menke	.25	.11	.03
☐ 17 Felix Millan	.25	.11	.03
☐ 18 Johnny Mize	1.50	.70	.19
☐ 19 Tommy Nobis	1.00	.45	.12
☐ 20 Gene Oliver	.25	.11	.03
☐ 21 Johnny Sain	.50	.23	.06
☐ 22 Warren Spahn	2.00	.90	.25
☐ 23 Joe Torre	1.00	.45	.12
☐ 24 Bob Turley	.50	.23	.06

1968 Atlantic Oil

This set of 12 perforated game cards measures approximately 2 5/8" by 2 1/8". There are "left side" and "right side" game cards which had to be matched to win a car or a cash prize. The "right side" game cards have a color drawing of a sports personality in a circle on the left, surrounded by laurel leaf twigs, and a short career summary on the right. There is a color bar on the bottom of the game piece carrying a dollar amount and the words "right side". The "left side" game cards carry a rectangular drawing of a sports personality or a photo of a Camaro or a Corvette. A different color bar with a dollar amount and the words "left side" are under the picture. On a dark blue background, the "right side" backs carry the rules of the game, and the "left side" cards show a "Winners Circle". The cards are unnumbered and checklisted below in alphabetical order.

	NRMT	VG-E	GOOD
COMPLETE SET (12)	150.00	70.00	19.00
COMMON CARD (1-12)	3.00	1.35	.35
☐ 1 Julius Boros right side	5.00	2.20	.60
☐ 2 Gay Brewer left side	5.00	2.20	.60
☐ 3 Camaro left side	3.00	1.35	.35
☐ 4 Corvette left side	3.00	1.35	.35
☐ 5 Damascus right side	3.00	1.35	.35
☐ 6 Parnelli Jones left side	5.00	2.20	.60
☐ 7 Mickey Mantle left side	50.00	22.00	6.25
☐ 8 Willie Mays right side	30.00	13.50	3.70
☐ 9 Bob Richards left side	5.00	2.20	.60
☐ 10 Babe Ruth right side	50.00	22.00	6.25
☐ 11 Gale Sayers left side	20.00	9.00	2.50
☐ 12 Bart Starr right side	20.00	9.00	2.50

1968 Atlantic Oil Play Ball Contest Cards

These fifty cards were issued in two-card panels which when split becomes standard-size cards. For easier reference we have sequenced the set in alphabetical order and listed the player number and prize (when applicable) next to the player's name. Winning cards of more than $1 are not priced and not included in the complete set price.

	NRMT	VG-E	GOOD
COMPLETE SET	225.00	100.00	28.00
COMMON CARD	1.50	.70	.19
☐ 1 Hank Aaron-4	25.00	11.00	3.10
☐ 2 Tommy Agee-2 ($2500)			
☐ 3 Felipe Alou-3	2.50	1.10	.30
☐ 4 Max Alvis-2	1.50	.70	.19
☐ 5 Bob Aspromonte-1	1.50	.70	.19
☐ 6 Ernie Banks-5 ($100)			
☐ 7 Lou Brock-1	15.00	6.75	1.85
☐ 8 Jim Bunning-9	4.00	1.80	.50
☐ 9 Johnny Callison-1	2.00	.90	.25
☐ 10 Campy Campaneris-2	2.00	.90	.25
☐ 11 Norm Cash-5	3.00	1.35	.35
☐ 12 Orlando Cepeda-4	2.50	1.10	.30
☐ 13 Dean Chance-9	1.50	.70	.19
☐ 14 Roberto Clemente-7	35.00	16.00	4.40
☐ 15 Tommy Davis-4 ($100)			
☐ 16 Andy Etchebarren-8 ($5)			
☐ 17 Ron Fairly-6 ($10)			
☐ 18 Bill Freehan-3 ($2500)			
☐ 19 Jim Fregosi-2	2.00	.90	.25
☐ 20 Bob Gibson-9	15.00	6.75	1.85
☐ 21 Jim Hart-3	1.50	.70	.19
☐ 22 Joe Horlen-9	1.50	.70	.19
☐ 23 Al Kaline-2	20.00	9.00	2.50
☐ 24 Jim Lonborg-9	2.00	.90	.25
☐ 25 Jim Maloney-9	2.00	.90	.25
☐ 26 Roger Maris-7	15.00	6.75	1.85
☐ 27 Mike McCormick-9	1.50	.70	.19
☐ 28 Willie McCovey-4	15.00	6.75	1.85
☐ 29 Sam McDowell-9	2.00	.90	.25
☐ 30 Tug McGraw-7 ($10)			
☐ 31 Tony Oliva-1	2.50	1.10	.30
☐ 32 Claude Osteen-11 ($1)	5.00	2.20	.60
☐ 33 Milt Pappas-10	2.00	.90	.25
☐ 34 Joe Pepitone-6	2.00	.90	.25
☐ 35 Vada Pinson-3	2.00	.90	.25
☐ 36 Boog Powell-6	3.00	1.35	.35
☐ 37 Brooks Robinson-1	15.00	6.75	1.85
☐ 38 Frank Robinson-5	15.00	6.75	1.85
☐ 39 Pete Rose-1	20.00	9.00	2.50
☐ 40 Jose Santiago-11	1.50	.70	.19
☐ 41 Ron Santo-4	3.00	1.35	.35
☐ 42 George Scott-6	1.50	.70	.19
☐ 43 Ron Swoboda-7	1.50	.70	.19
☐ 44 Tom Tresh-2	1.50	.70	.19
☐ 45 Fred Valentine-6	1.50	.70	.19
☐ 46 Pete Ward-1	1.50	.70	.19
☐ 47 Billy Williams-8 ($5)			
☐ 48 Maury Wills-1	2.00	.90	.25
☐ 49 Earl Wilson-10 ($1)	5.00	2.20	.60
☐ 50 Carl Yastrzemski-5	15.00	6.75	1.85

1888 August Beck N403

The tobacco brand with the unusual name of Yum Yum was marketed by the August Beck Company of Chicago. The cards are blank-backed with sepia fronts and are not numbered. There are ballplayers known, and the series was released to the public in 1887 or 1888. We have sequenced this set in alphabetical order.

	EX-MT	VG-E	GOOD
COMPLETE SET (36)	30000.00	13500.00	3800.00
COMMON CARD (1-36)	800.00	350.00	100.00
☐ 1 Lady Baldwin: Detroit	800.00	350.00	100.00
☐ 2 Dan Brouthers: Detroit	1200.00	550.00	150.00
☐ 3A Tommy Burns: Chicago (civ. portrait)	800.00	350.00	100.00
☐ 3B Tommy Burns: Chicago (standing with bat)	800.00	350.00	100.00
☐ 4A John Clarkson (civ. portrait)	1200.00	550.00	150.00
☐ 4B John Clarkson (throwing)	1200.00	550.00	150.00
☐ 5 Larry Corcoran: New York	800.00	350.00	100.00
☐ 6 Tom Daly: Chicago Picture is Billy Sunday	800.00	350.00	100.00
☐ 7 Tom Deasley: Wash.	800.00	350.00	100.00
☐ 8 Mike Dorgan: New York	800.00	350.00	100.00
☐ 9 Buck Ewing: New York	1200.00	550.00	150.00
☐ 10 Silver Flint: Chicago	800.00	350.00	100.00
☐ 11 Pud Galvin: Pittsburg	1200.00	550.00	150.00
☐ 12 Pete Gillespie: New York	800.00	350.00	100.00
☐ 13 Ed Greer: Brooklyn	800.00	350.00	100.00
☐ 14 Tim Keefe: New York	1200.00	550.00	150.00
☐ 15 Mike (King) Kelly: Boston	1500.00	700.00	190.00

☐ 16 Gus Krock: Chicago	800.00	350.00	100.00
☐ 17 Kid Madden: Boston	800.00	350.00	100.00
☐ 18 George Miller: Pitts.	800.00	350.00	100.00
☐ 19 Bill Nash: Boston	800.00	350.00	100.00
☐ 20A Jim O'Rourke: New York (portrait)	1200.00	550.00	150.00
☐ 20B Jim O'Rourke: no team (New York uniform with bat)	1200.00	550.00	150.00
☐ 21 Danny Richardson. New York	800.00	350.00	100.00
☐ 22 James (Chief) Roseman: Indianapolis	800.00	350.00	100.00
☐ 23 Jimmy Ryan: Chicago	1000.00	450.00	125.00
☐ 24 Bill Sowders: Boston	800.00	350.00	100.00
☐ 25 Billy Sunday: Pitts.	1200.00	550.00	150.00
☐ 26 Ezra Sutton: Boston	800.00	350.00	100.00
☐ 27 Mike Tiernan: New York	800.00	350.00	100.00
☐ 28 George Van Haltren: Chicago	800.00	350.00	100.00
☐ 29A Mickey Welch: New York (portrait)	1200.00	550.00	150.00
☐ 29B Mickey Welch New York Pitching, hands at waist	1200.00	550.00	150.00
☐ 29C Mickey Welch New York Portrait; right arm extended	1200.00	550.00	150.00
☐ 30 Jim Whitney Washington	800.00	350.00	100.00
☐ 31 George Wood Philadelphia	800.00	350.00	100.00

1964 Auravision Records

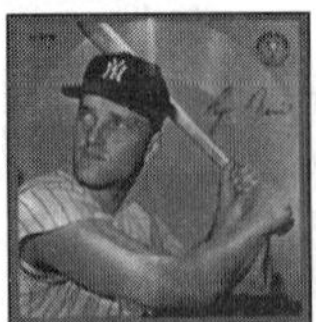

These sixteen 33 1/3 RPM records feature a player photo on the front with biographical and statistical information on the back. When played on a record player, one could hear the player, in his own voice, describing various parts of his career or giving advice. The records were distributed by Columbia Records. The Mays record seems to be in shorter supply and has been given an SP desgination. These unnumbered records have been sequenced in alphabetical order.

	NRMT	VG-E	GOOD
COMPLETE SET (16)	250.00	110.00	31.00
COMMON RECORD	5.00	2.20	.60
☐ 1 Bob Allison	5.00	2.20	.60
☐ 2 Ernie Banks	15.00	6.75	1.85
☐ 3 Ken Boyer	7.50	3.40	.95
☐ 4 Rocky Colavito	10.00	4.50	1.25
☐ 5 Don Drysdale	15.00	6.75	1.85
☐ 6 Whitey Ford	20.00	9.00	2.50
☐ 7 Jim Gentile	5.00	2.20	.60
☐ 8 Al Kaline	10.00	4.50	1.25
☐ 9 Sandy Koufax	15.00	6.75	1.85
☐ 10 Mickey Mantle	75.00	34.00	9.50
☐ 11 Roger Maris	10.00	4.50	1.25
☐ 12 Willie Mays SP	75.00	34.00	9.50
☐ 13 Bill Mazeroski	7.50	3.40	.95
☐ 14 Frank Robinson	15.00	6.75	1.85
☐ 15 Warren Spahn	15.00	6.75	1.85
☐ 16 Pete Ward	5.00	2.20	.60

1914 B18 Blankets

This set of felt-type cloth squares was issed in 1914 with several brands of cigarettes. Each blanket is a 5 1/4" square. Each player exists with two different color combinations based on his team; however, only those variations reflecting price differentials are listed in the checklist below. Cleveland players have either yellow or purple bases; New York Yankees players have either blue or green infields; St. Louis Browns players have either red or purple paths; Washington players have either brown or green bases; Brooklyn players have either blue or green infields; New York Giants players have either brown or green paths; Pittsburgh players have either red or purple bases; and St. Louis Cardinals players have either purple or yellow paths. Some blankets are known to exist in a (third) different color scheme -- those with red infields. These blankets are quite scarce and are listed in the checklist below. The complete set price below reflects a set including all variations listed below. The blankets are unnumbered and are ordered below alphabetically within team, i.e., Cleveland Indians (1-9), Detroit Tigers (10-19), New York Yankees (20-28), St. Louis Browns (29-37), Washington Senators (38-46), Boston Bees NL (47-55), Brooklyn Dodgers (56-64), New York Giants (65-73), Pittsburgh Pirates (74-82) and St. Louis Cardinals (83-91).

	EX-MT	VG-E	GOOD
COMPLETE SET	10000.00	4500.00	1250.00
COMMON PLAYER	15.00	6.75	1.85
☐ 1A Johnny Bassler yellow bases	50.00	22.00	6.25
☐ 1B Johnny Bassler purple bases	30.00	13.50	3.70
☐ 2A Ray Chapman yellow bases	50.00	22.00	6.25
☐ 2B Ray Chapman purple bases	30.00	13.50	3.70
☐ 3A Jack Graney yellow bases	50.00	22.00	6.25
☐ 3B Jack Graney purple bases	30.00	13.50	3.70
☐ 4A Joe Jackson yellow bases	500.00	220.00	60.00
☐ 4B Joe Jackson purple bases	400.00	180.00	50.00
☐ 5A Nemo Leibold yellow bases	50.00	22.00	6.25
☐ 5B Nemo Leibold purple bases	30.00	13.50	3.70
☐ 6A Willie Mitchell yellow bases	50.00	22.00	6.25
☐ 6B Willie Mitchell purple bases	30.00	13.50	3.70
☐ 7A Ivy Olson yellow bases	50.00	22.00	6.25
☐ 7B Ivy Olson purple bases	30.00	13.50	3.70
☐ 8A Steve O'Neil yellow bases	50.00	22.00	6.25
☐ 8B Steve O'Neil purple bases	30.00	13.50	3.70
☐ 9A Terry Turner yellow bases	50.00	22.00	6.25
☐ 9B Terry Turner purple bases	30.00	13.50	3.70
☐ 10A Del Baker white infield	15.00	6.75	1.85
☐ 10B Del Baker brown infield	60.00	27.00	7.50
☐ 10C Del Baker red infield	275.00	125.00	34.00
☐ 11A Paddy Bauman (sic, Baumann) white infield	15.00	6.75	1.85
☐ 11B Paddy Bauman (sic, Baumann) brown infield	60.00	27.00	7.50
☐ 11C Paddy Bauman (sic, Baumann) red infield	275.00	125.00	34.00
☐ 12A George Burns white infield	15.00	6.75	1.85
☐ 12B George Burns brown infield	60.00	27.00	7.50
☐ 12C George Burns red infield	275.00	125.00	34.00
☐ 13A Marty Cavanaugh (sic, Kavanagh) white infield	15.00	6.75	1.85
☐ 13B Marty Cavanaugh (sic, Kavanagh) brown infield	60.00	27.00	7.50
☐ 13C Marty Cavanaugh (sic, Kavanagh) red infield	275.00	125.00	34.00
☐ 14A Ty Cobb white infield	250.00	110.00	31.00
☐ 14B Ty Cobb brown infield	500.00	220.00	60.00
☐ 14C Ty Cobb red infield	1000.00	450.00	125.00
☐ 15A Harry Coveleski white infield	15.00	6.75	1.85
☐ 15B Harry Coveleski brown infield	60.00	27.00	7.50
☐ 15C Harry Coveleski red infield	275.00	125.00	34.00
☐ 16A Ray Demmitt white infield	15.00	6.75	1.85
☐ 16B Ray Demmitt brown infield	60.00	27.00	7.50
☐ 16C Ray Demmitt red infield	275.00	125.00	34.00
☐ 17A Del Gainor white infield	15.00	6.75	1.85
☐ 17B Del Gainor brown infield	60.00	27.00	7.50
☐ 18 Marty Kavanaugh (sic, Kavanagh) white infield	15.00	6.75	1.85
☐ 19A George Moriarty white infield	15.00	6.75	1.85
☐ 19B George Moriarty brown infield	60.00	27.00	7.50
☐ 19C George Moriarty red infield	275.00	125.00	34.00
☐ 20 Luke Boone	15.00	6.75	1.85
☐ 21 Frank Chance (3)	50.00	22.00	6.25
☐ 22 King Cole	15.00	6.75	1.85
☐ 23 Topsy Hartzell	15.00	6.75	1.85
☐ 24 Ray Keating	15.00	6.75	1.85
☐ 25 Fritz Maisel	15.00	6.75	1.85
☐ 26 Roger Peckinpaugh	20.00	9.00	2.50
☐ 27 Jeff Sweeney	15.00	6.75	1.85
☐ 28 Dee Walsh	15.00	6.75	1.85
☐ 29A Sam Agnew red paths	35.00	16.00	4.40
☐ 29B Sam Agnew purple paths	35.00	16.00	4.40
☐ 30A Jimmy Austin red paths	35.00	16.00	4.40
☐ 30B Jimmy Austin purple paths	35.00	16.00	4.40
☐ 31A Earl Hamilton red paths	35.00	16.00	4.40
☐ 31B Earl Hamilton purple paths	35.00	16.00	4.40
☐ 32A Bill McAllister (McAllester) red paths	35.00	16.00	4.40
☐ 32B Bill McAllister (McAllester) purple paths	35.00	16.00	4.40
☐ 33A Del Pratt red paths	35.00	16.00	4.40
☐ 33B Del Pratt purple paths	35.00	16.00	4.40
☐ 34A Burt Shotton red paths	35.00	16.00	4.40
☐ 34B Burt Shotton purple paths	35.00	16.00	4.40
☐ 35A Bobby Wallace red paths	60.00	27.00	7.50
☐ 35B Bobby Wallace purple paths	60.00	27.00	7.50
☐ 36A Jimmy Walsh red paths	35.00	16.00	4.40
☐ 36B Jimmy Walsh purple paths	35.00	16.00	4.40
☐ 37A Gus Williams red paths	35.00	16.00	4.40
☐ 37B Gus Williams purple paths	35.00	16.00	4.40
☐ 38 Eddie Ainsmith	15.00	6.75	1.85
☐ 39 Eddie Foster	15.00	6.75	1.85
☐ 40 Chick Gandil	40.00	18.00	5.00
☐ 41 Walter Johnson	100.00	45.00	12.50
☐ 42 George McBride	15.00	6.75	1.85
☐ 43 Clyde Milan	20.00	9.00	2.50
☐ 44 Danny Moeller	15.00	6.75	1.85
☐ 45 Ray Morgan	15.00	6.75	1.85
☐ 46 Howard Shanks	15.00	6.75	1.85
☐ 47A Joe Connolly white infield	15.00	6.75	1.85
☐ 47B Joe Connolly brown infield	60.00	27.00	7.50
☐ 48A Hank Gowdy white infieldHank	15.00	6.75	1.85
☐ 48B Hank Gowdy brown infield	60.00	27.00	7.50
☐ 48C Hank Gowdy red infield	275.00	125.00	34.00
☐ 49A Tommy Griffith white infield	15.00	6.75	1.85
☐ 49B Tommy Griffith brown infield	60.00	27.00	7.50
☐ 49C Tommy Griffith red infield	275.00	125.00	34.00
☐ 50A Bill James white infield	15.00	6.75	1.85
☐ 50B Bill James brown infield	60.00	27.00	7.50
☐ 51A Les Mann white infield	15.00	6.75	1.85
☐ 51B Les Mann brown infield	60.00	27.00	7.50
☐ 51C Les Mann red infield	275.00	125.00	34.00
☐ 52A Rabbit Maranville white infield	30.00	13.50	3.70
☐ 52B Rabbit Maranville brown infield	100.00	45.00	12.50
☐ 52C Rabbit Maranville red infield	350.00	160.00	45.00
☐ 53A Hub Perdue white infield	15.00	6.75	1.85
☐ 53B Hub Perdue brown infield	60.00	27.00	7.50
☐ 54A Lefty Tyler white infield	15.00	6.75	1.85
☐ 54B Lefty Tyler brown infield	60.00	27.00	7.50
☐ 54C Lefty Tyler red infield	275.00	125.00	34.00
☐ 55A Bart Whaling white infield	15.00	6.75	1.85
☐ 55B Bart Whaling brown infield	60.00	27.00	7.50
☐ 55C Bart Whaling red infield	275.00	125.00	34.00
☐ 56 George Cutshaw	15.00	6.75	1.85
☐ 57 Jake Daubert	20.00	9.00	2.50
☐ 58 John Hummel	15.00	6.75	1.85
☐ 59 Otto Miller	15.00	6.75	1.85
☐ 60 Nap Rucker	20.00	9.00	2.50
☐ 61 Red Smith	15.00	6.75	1.85
☐ 62 Casey Stengel	100.00	45.00	12.50
☐ 63 Bull Wagner	15.00	6.75	1.85
☐ 64 Zach Wheat	30.00	13.50	3.70
☐ 65 George Burns	15.00	6.75	1.85
☐ 66 Larry Doyle	20.00	9.00	2.50
☐ 67 Art Fletcher	15.00	6.75	1.85
☐ 68 Eddie Grant	15.00	6.75	1.85
☐ 69 Chief Meyers	15.00	6.75	1.85
☐ 70 Red Murray	15.00	6.75	1.85
☐ 71 Fred Snodgrass	15.00	6.75	1.85
☐ 72 Jeff Tesreau	15.00	6.75	1.85
☐ 73 Hooks Wiltse	15.00	6.75	1.85
☐ 74A Babe Adams red bases	35.00	16.00	4.40
☐ 74B Babe Adams purple bases	35.00	16.00	4.40
☐ 75A Max Carey red bases	60.00	27.00	7.50
☐ 75B Max Carey purple bases	60.00	27.00	7.50
☐ 76A George Gibson red bases	35.00	16.00	4.40
☐ 76B George Gibson purple bases	35.00	16.00	4.40
☐ 77A Ham Hyatt red bases	35.00	16.00	4.40
☐ 77B Ham Hyatt purple bases	35.00	16.00	4.40
☐ 78A Joe Kelley (Kelly) red bases	35.00	16.00	4.40
☐ 78B Joe Kelley (Kelly) purple bases	35.00	16.00	4.40
☐ 79A Ed Konetchy red bases	35.00	16.00	4.40
☐ 79B Ed Konetchy purple bases	35.00	16.00	4.40
☐ 80A Mowrey red bases	35.00	16.00	4.40
☐ 80B Mike Mowrey purple bases	35.00	16.00	4.40
☐ 81A Marty O'Toole red bases	35.00	16.00	4.40
☐ 81B Marty O'Toole purple bases	35.00	16.00	4.40
☐ 82A Jim Viox red bases	35.00	16.00	4.40
☐ 82B Jim Viox purple bases	35.00	16.00	4.40
☐ 83A Bill Doak purple paths	30.00	13.50	3.70
☐ 83B Bill Doak yellow paths	50.00	22.00	6.25
☐ 84A Cozy Dolan purple paths	25.00	11.00	3.10
☐ 84B Cozy Dolan yellow paths	50.00	22.00	6.25
☐ 85A Miller Huggins purple paths	50.00	22.00	6.25
☐ 85B Miller Huggins yellow paths	75.00	34.00	9.50
☐ 86A Dot's Miller purple paths	30.00	13.50	3.70
☐ 86B Dot's Miller yellow paths	50.00	22.00	6.25
☐ 87A Hank Robinson purple paths	30.00	13.50	3.70
☐ 87B Hank Robinson yellow paths	50.00	22.00	6.25
☐ 88A Slim Sallee purple paths	30.00	13.50	3.70
☐ 88B Slim Sallee yellow paths	50.00	22.00	6.25
☐ 89A Bill Steele purple paths	30.00	13.50	3.70
☐ 89B Bill Steele yellow paths	50.00	22.00	6.25
☐ 90A Possum Whitted purple paths	30.00	13.50	3.70
☐ 90B Possum Whitted yellow paths	50.00	22.00	6.25
☐ 91A Owen Wilson purple paths	30.00	13.50	3.70
☐ 91B Owen Wilson yellow paths	50.00	22.00	6.25

1928 Babe Ruth Candy Company E-Unc.

This six-card set is one of the more obscure candy sets and features cards picturing Babe Ruth which measure approximately 1 7/8" by 4". The cards are sepia in color and depict scenes from either a movie, "Babe Comes Home" (#1, 2 and 4), or scenes from the Yankee Post Season West Coast Exhibition Tour in 1924 (#3 and 6). Each card has "Babe Ruth" below the photo followed by a caption. The backs contain instructions on how to exchange all six cards for a baseball with Babe Ruth's genuine signature on it. The #6 is considerably tougher to find and seems to be a premium card and very difficult to find.

	EX-MT	VG-E	GOOD
COMPLETE SET (6)	2000.00	900.00	250.00
COMMON CARD (1-6)	250.00	110.00	31.00
☐ 1 Babe Ruth (In uniform of Los Angeles)	250.00	110.00	31.00
☐ 2 Babe Ruth (Swinging, follow thru)	250.00	110.00	31.00
☐ 3 Babe Ruth (In uniform with a young boy)	250.00	110.00	31.00
☐ 4 Babe Ruth (In civilian dress with Anna Q. Nilsson)	250.00	110.00	31.00
☐ 5 Babe Ruth (In uniform kissing a small girl)	250.00	110.00	31.00
☐ 6 Babe Ruth (Autographing a ball)	1000.00	450.00	125.00

1948 Babe Ruth Story

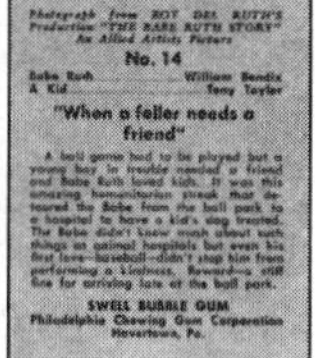

The 1948 Babe Ruth Story set of 28 black and white numbered cards (measuring approximately 2" by 2 1/2") was issued by the Philadelphia Chewing Gum Company to commemorate the 1949 movie of the same name starring William Bendix, Claire Trevor, and Charles Bickford. Babe Ruth himself appears on several cards. The last 12 cards (17 to 28) are more difficult to obtain than other cards in the set and are also more desirable in that most picture actual players as well as actors from the movie. Supposedly these last 12 cards were issued much later after the first 16 cards had already been released and distributed. The last seven cards (22-28) in the set are subtitled "The Babe Ruth Story in the Making" at the top of each reverse. The bottom of every card says "Swell Bubble Gum, Philadelphia Chewing Gum Corporation." The catalog designation for this set is R421.

	NRMT	VG-E	GOOD
COMPLETE SET (28)	1350.00	600.00	170.00
COMMON CARD (1-16)	20.00	9.00	2.50
COMMON CARD (17-24)	50.00	22.00	6.25
COMMON CARD (25-28)	150.00	70.00	19.00
☐ 1 The Babe Ruth Story In the Making (Babe Ruth shown with William Bendix)	150.00	70.00	19.00
☐ 2 Bat Boy Becomes the Babe (Facsimile autographed by William Bendix)	25.00	11.00	3.10
☐ 3 Claire Hodgson played by Claire Trevor	20.00	9.00	2.50
☐ 4 Babe Ruth played by William Bendix; Claire Hodgson played by Claire Trevor	20.00	9.00	2.50
☐ 5 Brother Matthias played by Charles Bickford	20.00	9.00	2.50
☐ 6 Phil Conrad played by Sam Levene	20.00	9.00	2.50
☐ 7 Night Club Singer played by Gertrude Niesen	20.00	9.00	2.50
☐ 8 Baseball's Famous Deal	20.00	9.00	2.50
☐ 9 Babe Ruth played by William Bendix; Mrs.Babe Ruth played by Claire Trevor	20.00	9.00	2.50
☐ 10 Actors for Babe Ruth Mrs. Babe Ruth Brother Matthias	20.00	9.00	2.50
☐ 11 Babe Ruth played by William Bendix; Miller Huggins played by Fred Lightner	20.00	9.00	2.50
☐ 12 Babe Ruth played by William Bendix; Johnny Sylvester played by George Marshall	20.00	9.00	2.50
☐ 13 Actors for Mr., Mrs. and Johnny Sylvester	20.00	9.00	2.50
☐ 14 When A Feller Needs A Friend	20.00	9.00	2.50
☐ 15 Dramatic Home Run	20.00	9.00	2.50
☐ 16 The Homer That Set the Record	20.00	9.00	2.50
☐ 17 The Slap That Started Baseball's Most Famous Career	50.00	22.00	6.25
☐ 18 The Babe Plays Santa Claus	50.00	22.00	6.25
☐ 19 Actors for Ed Barrow Jacob Ruppert Miller Huggins	50.00	22.00	6.25
☐ 20 Broken Window Paid Off	50.00	22.00	6.25
☐ 21 Regardless of the Generation Babe Ruth Bendix shown getting mobbed by crowd	50.00	22.00	6.25
☐ 22 Ted Lyons William Bendix	60.00	27.00	7.50
☐ 23 Charley Grimm William Bendix	50.00	22.00	6.25
☐ 24 Lefty Gomez William Bendix Bucky Harris	75.00	34.00	9.50
☐ 25 Babe Ruth William Bendix Babe Ruth pictured with ball	150.00	70.00	19.00
☐ 26 Babe Ruth William Bendix Babe Ruth pictured with bat	150.00	70.00	19.00
☐ 27 Babe Ruth Claire Trevor	150.00	70.00	19.00
☐ 28 William Bendix Babe Ruth Claire Trevor Babe Ruth pictured autographing ball	150.00	70.00	19.00

1994 Ball Park Franks Will Clark

Measuring the standard-size, this card was sponsored by Ball Park Franks. The front features a full-bleed color action player photo. The player's name and the sponsor name appear at the upper left corner. On a black panel outlined in red, the back carries career highlights. The card is unnumbered.

	MINT	NRMT	EXC
COMPLETE SET	1.00	.45	.12
COMMON CARD	1.00	.45	.12
☐ 1 Will Clark	1.00	.45	.12

1995 Ball Park Franks

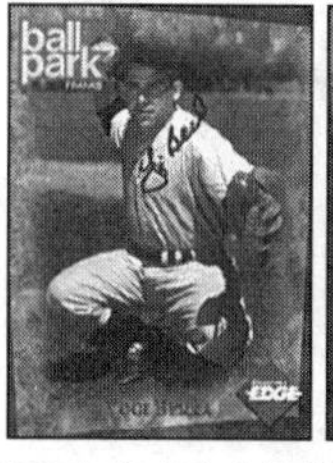

Measuring the standard size, these two autograph cards were produced for Ball Park Franks by Collector's Edge. Collectors could receive the two cards through a mail-in offer for 8 UPC codes from any Ball Park product; for 4 UPC codes and $2.50; or for 2 UPC codes and $5.00. The offer expired on May 31, 1995 or while supplies lasted. The fronts display color action photos that fade to marbleized borders. The player's signature is inscribed across the picture. On a similar design to the front, the backs carry a color head shot and a one-sentence summary of the player's outstanding achievements. The cards are unnumbered and checklisted below in alphabetical order. Each card was accompanied by a second card, featuring a ghosted photo and certifying that the signature is authentic.

	MINT	NRMT	EXC
COMPLETE SET (2)	40.00	18.00	5.00
COMMON CARD (1-2)	20.00	9.00	2.50
☐ 1 Yogi Berra AU	10.00	4.50	1.25
☐ 2 Frank Robinson AU	10.00	4.50	1.25

1911 Baseball Bats E-Unc.

This 44-card set was distributed on candy boxes with the player panel on one side and the name "Baseball Bats" printed on crossed bats and a ball on the opposite side. The two side panels indicate "All Leading Players" and an end flap displays "One Cent." The cards measure approximately 1 3/8" by 2 3/8" and feature a player picture surrounded by either a white or orange border and a thin black line.

	MINT	NRMT	EXC
COMPLETE SET (44)	5000.00	2200.00	600.00
COMMON CARD (1-44)	50.00	22.00	6.25
☐ 1 Frank Baker	200.00	90.00	25.00
☐ 2 Jack Baker	50.00	22.00	6.25
☐ 3 Chief Bender	100.00	45.00	12.50
☐ 4 Al Bridwell	50.00	22.00	6.25
☐ 5 Mordecai Brown	100.00	45.00	12.50
☐ 6 Bill Corrigan UER misspelled Carrigan	50.00	22.00	6.25
☐ 7 Frank Chance	150.00	70.00	19.00
☐ 8 Hal Chase	150.00	70.00	19.00
☐ 9 Eddie Cicotte	150.00	70.00	19.00
☐ 10 Fred Clarke UER misspelled Clark	100.00	45.00	12.50
☐ 11 Ty Cobb	1000.00	450.00	125.00
☐ 12 King Cole	50.00	22.00	6.25
☐ 13 Shano Collins	50.00	22.00	6.25
☐ 14 Sam Crawford	150.00	70.00	19.00
☐ 15 Lou Criger	50.00	22.00	6.25
☐ 16 Harry Davis	50.00	22.00	6.25
☐ 17 Jim Delehanty	50.00	22.00	6.25
☐ 18 Art Devlin	50.00	22.00	6.25
☐ 19 Josh Devore	50.00	22.00	6.25
☐ 20 Patsy Donovan	50.00	22.00	6.25
☐ 21 Larry Doyle	75.00	34.00	9.50
☐ 22 Johnny Evers	150.00	70.00	19.00
☐ 23 John Flynn	50.00	22.00	6.25
☐ 24 Solly Hofman	50.00	22.00	6.25
☐ 25 Walter Johnson	500.00	220.00	60.00
☐ 26 Johnny Kling	50.00	22.00	6.25
☐ 27 Nap Lajoie	250.00	110.00	31.00
☐ 28 Matthew McIntyre	50.00	22.00	6.25
☐ 29 Fred Merkle	75.00	34.00	9.50
☐ 30 Tom Needham	50.00	22.00	6.25
☐ 31 Rube Oldring	50.00	22.00	6.25
☐ 32 Frank Schulte	50.00	22.00	6.25
☐ 33 Cy Seymour	50.00	22.00	6.25
☐ 34 James Sheckard	50.00	22.00	6.25
☐ 35 Tris Speaker	200.00	90.00	25.00
☐ 36 Oscar Stanage (Batting, side)	50.00	22.00	6.25
☐ 37 Oscar Stanage (Batting, front)	50.00	22.00	6.25
☐ 38 Ira Thomas	50.00	22.00	6.25
☐ 39 Joe Tinker	150.00	70.00	19.00
☐ 40 Heinie Wagner	50.00	22.00	6.25
☐ 41 Honus Wagner	300.00	135.00	38.00
☐ 42 Ed Walsh	100.00	45.00	12.50
☐ 43 Chief Wilson	75.00	34.00	9.50
☐ 44 Art Wilson	50.00	22.00	6.25

1910 Baseball Comics T203

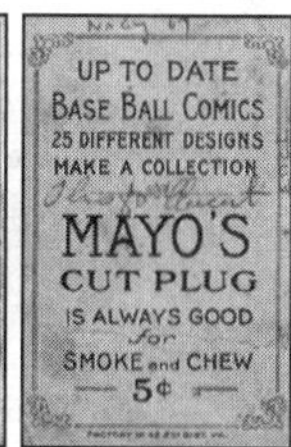

This 25-card set was issued by Winner Cut Plug and Mayo Cut Plug. Measuring 2 1/16" by 3 1/8", each card features a color comic picture relating to a baseball phrase or slogan. The back carries an advertisement inside a picture frame. The cards are unnumbered.

	EX-MT	VG-E	GOOD
COMPLETE SET (25)	350.00	160.00	45.00
COMMON CARD (1-25)	15.00	6.75	1.85
☐ 1 A Crack Outfielder	15.00	6.75	1.85
☐ 2 A Fancy Twirler	15.00	6.75	1.85
☐ 3 A Fine Slide	15.00	6.75	1.85
☐ 4 A Fowl Bawl	15.00	6.75	1.85
☐ 5 A Great Game	15.00	6.75	1.85
☐ 6 A Home Run	15.00	6.75	1.85
☐ 7 An All Star Battery	15.00	6.75	1.85
☐ 8 A Short Stop	15.00	6.75	1.85
☐ 9 A Star Catcher	15.00	6.75	1.85
☐ 10 A White Wash	15.00	6.75	1.85
☐ 11 A Tie Game	15.00	6.75	1.85
☐ 12 A Two Bagger	15.00	6.75	1.85
☐ 13 A Wild Pitch	15.00	6.75	1.85
☐ 14 Caught Napping	15.00	6.75	1.85
☐ 15 On to the Curves	15.00	6.75	1.85
☐ 16 Out	15.00	6.75	1.85
☐ 17 Put Out on 1st	15.00	6.75	1.85
☐ 18 Right over the Plate	15.00	6.75	1.85
☐ 19 Rooting for the Home Team	15.00	6.75	1.85
☐ 20 Stealing a Base	15.00	6.75	1.85
☐ 21 Stealing Home	15.00	6.75	1.85
☐ 22 Strike One	15.00	6.75	1.85
☐ 23 The Bleachers	15.00	6.75	1.85
☐ 24 The Naps	15.00	6.75	1.85
☐ 25 The Red Sox	15.00	6.75	1.85

1979 Baseball Greats

These 2 1/2" by 3 3/4" cards were issued in 1979 by Carl Berg. They have the same design as 53 Bowman Black and White and use photos

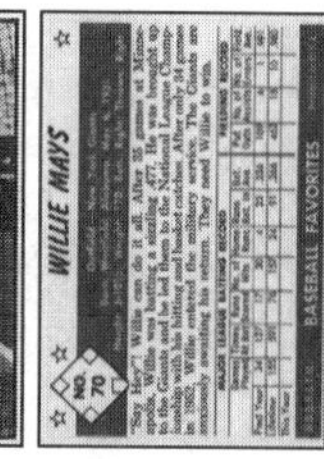

from that era as well. The cards are numbered 65 through 80 as if they were a continuation of the 53 Bowman Black and White set.

	NRMT	VG-E	GOOD
COMPLETE SET (16)	25.00	11.00	3.10
COMMON CARD (65-80)	.50	.23	.06
☐ 65 Monte Irvin	.50	.23	.06
☐ 66 Early Wynn	.50	.23	.06
☐ 67 Robin Roberts	.50	.23	.06
☐ 68 Stan Musial	3.00	1.35	.35
☐ 69 Ernie Banks	2.50	1.10	.30
☐ 70 Willie Mays	5.00	2.20	.60
☐ 71 Yogi Berra	2.50	1.10	.30
☐ 72 Mickey Mantle	7.50	3.40	.95
☐ 73 Whitey Ford	2.00	.90	.25
☐ 74 Bob Feller	2.00	.90	.25
☐ 75 Ted Williams	5.00	2.20	.60
☐ 76 Satchel Paige	3.00	1.35	.35
☐ 77 Jackie Robinson	5.00	2.20	.60
☐ 78 Ed Mathews	.50	.23	.06
☐ 79 Warren Spahn	.50	.23	.06
☐ 80 Ralph Kiner	.50	.23	.06

1982 Baseball Card News

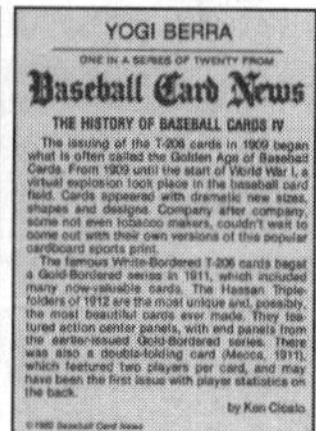

This 20-card standard-size set features glossy, black-and-white posed player photos with rounded corners. Backs display the player's name at the top and below the heading "Baseball Card News," each card carries a portion of a 20-part history of baseball cards by Ken Cicalo. The cards are numbered on the back with Roman numerals.

	NRMT	VG-E	GOOD
COMPLETE SET	20.00	9.00	2.50
COMMON CARD (1-20)	.25	.11	.03
☐ 1 Mickey Mantle	4.00	1.80	.50
☐ 2 Ted Williams	3.00	1.35	.35
☐ 3 Stan Musial	2.00	.90	.25
☐ 4 Yogi Berra	1.00	.45	.12
☐ 5 Roger Maris	1.00	.45	.12
☐ 6 Hank Aaron	2.50	1.10	.30
☐ 7 Willie Mays	2.50	1.10	.30
☐ 8 Joe DiMaggio Bob Feller	1.50	.70	.19
☐ 9 Lou Brock (Portrait)	.50	.23	.06
☐ 10 Roberto Clemente	3.00	1.35	.35
☐ 11 Ernie Banks	1.00	.45	.12
☐ 12 Lou Brock (Holding bat)	.50	.23	.06
☐ 13 Jackie Robinson Roy Campanella	1.50	.70	.19
☐ 14 Maury Wills	.25	.11	.03
☐ 15 Bob Feller	.50	.23	.06
☐ 16 Roy Campanella	1.00	.45	.12
☐ 17 Sandy Koufax	1.00	.45	.12
☐ 18 Joe DiMaggio	3.00	1.35	.35
☐ 19 Satchel Paige	2.00	.90	.25
☐ 20 Babe Ruth	4.00	1.80	.50

1952-53 Baseball Photos

This six-card set features 8" by 10" black-and-white player photos with a white border and blank backs. A facsimile autograph and player information is printed in the wide bottom border. The cards are unnumbered and checklisted below in alphabetical order. There might be more photos so additions to this checklist are appreciated.

	NRMT	VG-E	GOOD
COMPLETE SET (6)	75.00	34.00	9.50
COMMON CARD (1-6)	10.00	4.50	1.25
☐ 1 Richie Ashburn	20.00	9.00	2.50
☐ 2 Nelson Fox	20.00	9.00	2.50
☐ 3 Ted Kluszewski	15.00	6.75	1.85
☐ 4 Allie Reynolds	10.00	4.50	1.25
☐ 5 Red Schoendienst	15.00	6.75	1.85
☐ 6 Warren Spahn	20.00	9.00	2.50

1986 Baseball Star Buttons

This set features color player portraits of 124 Major League Baseball players printed on 1 7/16" diameter button pin-ons. The buttons were distributed two to a package. They are unnumbered and checklisted below in alphabetical order.

	MINT	NRMT	EXC
COMPLETE SET (124)	35.00	16.00	4.40
COMMON CARD (1-124)	.10	.05	.01
☐ 1 Rick Aguilera	.25	.11	.03
☐ 2 Dave Anderson	.10	.05	.01
☐ 3 Alan Ashby	.10	.05	.01
☐ 4 Wally Backman	.10	.05	.01
☐ 5 Steve Balboni	.10	.05	.01
☐ 6 Don Baylor	.25	.11	.03
☐ 7 Buddy Bell	.25	.11	.03
☐ 8 George Bell	.10	.05	.01
☐ 9 Dave Bergman	.10	.05	.01
☐ 10 Buddy Biancalana	.10	.05	.01
☐ 11 Dann Bilardello	.10	.05	.01
☐ 12 Bud Black	.10	.05	.01
☐ 13 Wade Boggs	1.50	.70	.19
☐ 14 Dennis Boyd	.10	.05	.01
☐ 15 George Brett	1.50	.70	.19
☐ 16 Greg Brock	.10	.05	.01
☐ 17 Tom Browning	.10	.05	.01
☐ 18 Bill Buckner	.25	.11	.03
☐ 19 Sal Butera	.10	.05	.01
☐ 20 Gary Carter	.25	.11	.03
☐ 21 Jack Clark	.25	.11	.03
☐ 22 Vince Coleman	.25	.11	.03
☐ 23 Dave Concepcion	.10	.05	.01
☐ 24 Danny Cox	.10	.05	.01
☐ 25 Jose Cruz	.25	.11	.03
☐ 26 Ron Darling	.25	.11	.03
☐ 27 Chili Davis	.25	.11	.03
☐ 28 Glenn Davis	.10	.05	.01
☐ 29 Jody Davis	.10	.05	.01
☐ 30 John Denny	.10	.05	.01
☐ 31 Bob Dernier	.10	.05	.01
☐ 32 Bo Diaz	.10	.05	.01
☐ 33 Bill Doran	.10	.05	.01
☐ 34 Brian Downing	.10	.05	.01
☐ 35 Shawon Dunston	.25	.11	.03
☐ 36 Leon Durham	.10	.05	.01
☐ 37 Lenny Dykstra	.75	.35	.09
☐ 38 Dennis Eckersley	.75	.35	.09
☐ 39 Nick Esasky	.10	.05	.01
☐ 40 Sid Fernandez	.10	.05	.01
☐ 41 Carlton Fisk	1.00	.45	.12
☐ 42 Scott Flecther	.10	.05	.01
☐ 43 Doug Frobel	.10	.05	.01
☐ 44 Phil Garner	.25	.11	.03
☐ 45 Steve Garvey	.50	.23	.06
☐ 46 Kirk Gibson	.25	.11	.03
☐ 47 Dan Gladden	.10	.05	.01
☐ 48 Rich Gossage	.50	.23	.06
☐ 49 Kevin Gross	.10	.05	.01
☐ 50 Pedro Guerrero	.25	.11	.03
☐ 51 Ron Guidry	.25	.11	.03
☐ 52 Tony Gwynn	2.00	.90	.25
☐ 53 Atlee Hammaker	.10	.05	.01
☐ 54 Von Hayes	.10	.05	.01
☐ 55 Rickey Henderson	1.25	.55	.16
☐ 56 Keith Hernandez	.25	.11	.03
☐ 57 Tom Herr	.10	.05	.01
☐ 58 Orel Hershiser	.50	.23	.06
☐ 59 Garth Iorg	.10	.05	.01
☐ 60 Bob James	.10	.05	.01
☐ 61 Tracy Jones	.10	.05	.01
☐ 62 Wally Joyner	.75	.35	.09
☐ 63 Charlie Kerfeld	.10	.05	.01
☐ 64 Dave Kingman	.10	.05	.01
☐ 65 Chet Lemon	.10	.05	.01
☐ 66 Jeff Leonard	.10	.05	.01
☐ 67 Charlie Liebrandt	.10	.05	.01
☐ 68 Fred Lynn	.25	.11	.03
☐ 69 Mike Marshall	.10	.05	.01
☐ 70 Gary Matthews	.10	.05	.01
☐ 71 Don Mattingly	2.00	.90	.25
☐ 72 Roger McDowell	.10	.05	.01
☐ 73 Willie McGee	.25	.11	.03
☐ 74 Keith Moreland	.10	.05	.01
☐ 75 Jack Morris	.25	.11	.03
☐ 76 Dale Murphy	.50	.23	.06
☐ 77 Eddie Murray	1.25	.55	.16
☐ 78 Pete O'Brien	.10	.05	.01
☐ 79 Ron Oester	.10	.05	.01
☐ 80 Bob Ojeda	.10	.05	.01
☐ 81 Jesse Orosco	.10	.05	.01
☐ 82 Tom Paciorek	.10	.05	.01
☐ 83 Dave Parker	.25	.11	.03
☐ 84 Darrell Porter	.10	.05	.01
☐ 85 Terry Puhl	.10	.05	.01
☐ 86 Dan Quisenberry	.10	.05	.01
☐ 87 Willie Randolph	.25	.11	.03
☐ 88 Shane Rawley	.10	.05	.01
☐ 89 Jerry Reuss	.10	.05	.01
☐ 90 Jim Rice	.25	.11	.03
☐ 91 Dave Righetti	.10	.05	.01
☐ 92 Cal Ripken Jr.	3.00	1.35	.35
☐ 93 Pete Rose	1.00	.45	.12
☐ 94 Nolan Ryan	3.00	1.35	.35
☐ 95 Bret Saberhagen	.50	.23	.06
☐ 96 Ryne Sandberg	1.50	.70	.19
☐ 97 Scott Sanderson	.10	.05	.01
☐ 98 Steve Sax	.10	.05	.01
☐ 99 Mike Schmidt	1.00	.45	.12
☐ 100 Ted Simmons	.25	.11	.03
☐ 101 Don Slaught	.10	.05	.01
☐ 102 Lee Smith	.50	.23	.06
☐ 103 Lonnie Smith	.10	.05	.01
☐ 104 Ozzie Smith	1.50	.70	.19
☐ 105 Mario Soto	.10	.05	.01
☐ 106 Darryl Strawberry	.50	.23	.06
☐ 107 Jim Sundberg	.10	.05	.01
☐ 108 Rick Sutcliffe	.10	.05	.01
☐ 109 Bruce Sutter	.10	.05	.01
☐ 110 Jay Tibbs	.10	.05	.01
☐ 111 Alan Trammell	.75	.35	.09
☐ 112 Manny Trillo	.10	.05	.01
☐ 113 John Tudor	.10	.05	.01
☐ 114 Tim Teufel	.10	.05	.01
☐ 115 Fernando Valenzuela	.25	.11	.03
☐ 116 Ozzie Virgil	.10	.05	.01
☐ 117 Tim Wallach	.10	.05	.01
☐ 118 Lou Whitaker	.25	.11	.03
☐ 119 Frank White	.10	.05	.01
☐ 120 Ernie Whitt	.10	.05	.01
☐ 121 Glenn Wilson	.10	.05	.01
☐ 122 Willie Wilson	.10	.05	.01
☐ 123 Dave Winfield	1.00	.45	.12
☐ 124 Robin Yount	.75	.35	.09

1938 Baseball Tabs PR1

The issuer of this set of baseball tabs is unknown. The tabs were produced about 1938 based on the players selected for the set. They measure approximately 3/4" in diameter and are shaped like a baseball with simulated stitching. The printing is in black and white with a solid background color, such as blue, green, orange, red, white or yellow. In the checklist below for these unnumbered tabs, the players are checklisted first (1-27) in alphabetical order, followed by the teams (28-48) given in alphabetical order by team nickname, which is how the tabs are represented on the face of these tabs. The 48 tabs below may constitute the whole set; however any additions to the checklist would be welcome if other tabs from this set exist.

	EX-MT	VG-E	GOOD
COMPLETE SET	1750.00	800.00	220.00
COMMON PLAYER (1-27)	20.00	9.00	2.50
COMMON TEAM (28-48)	6.00	2.70	.75
☐ 1 Luke Appling	35.00	16.00	4.40
☐ 2 Earl Averill	35.00	16.00	4.40
☐ 3 Phil Cavarretta	25.00	11.00	3.10
☐ 4 Dizzy Dean	100.00	45.00	12.50
☐ 5 Paul Derringer	25.00	11.00	3.10
☐ 6 Bill Dickey	60.00	27.00	7.50
☐ 7 Joe DiMaggio	300.00	135.00	38.00
☐ 8 Bob Feller	100.00	45.00	12.50
☐ 9 Lou Fette	20.00	9.00	2.50
☐ 10 Jimmy Foxx	100.00	45.00	12.50
☐ 11 Lou Gehrig	300.00	135.00	38.00
☐ 12 Lefty Gomez	50.00	22.00	6.25
☐ 13 Hank Greenberg	60.00	27.00	7.50
☐ 14 Lefty Grove	70.00	32.00	8.75
☐ 15 Mule Haas	20.00	9.00	2.50
☐ 16 Gabby Hartnett	35.00	16.00	4.40
☐ 17 Rollie Hemsley	20.00	9.00	2.50
☐ 18 Chuck Klein	40.00	18.00	5.00
☐ 19 Red Kress	20.00	9.00	2.50
☐ 20 Tony Lazzeri	35.00	16.00	4.40
☐ 21 Ted Lyons	35.00	16.00	4.40
☐ 22 Joe Medwick	40.00	18.00	5.00
☐ 23 Van Lingle Mungo	20.00	9.00	2.50
☐ 24 Rip Radcliff	20.00	9.00	2.50
☐ 25 Schoolboy Rowe	20.00	9.00	2.50
☐ 26 Al Simmons	35.00	16.00	4.40
☐ 27 Lloyd Waner	35.00	16.00	4.40
☐ 28 Philadelphia Athletics	6.00	2.70	.75
☐ 29 Boston Bees	6.00	2.70	.75
☐ 30 Kansas City Blues	6.00	2.70	.75
☐ 31 Milwaukee Brewers	6.00	2.70	.75
☐ 32 St. Louis Browns	10.00	4.50	1.25
☐ 33 St. Louis Cardinals	10.00	4.50	1.25
☐ 34 Louisville Colonels	6.00	2.70	.75
☐ 35 Chicago Cubs	30.00	13.50	3.70
☐ 36 Brooklyn Dodgers	12.50	5.50	1.55
☐ 37 New York Giants	10.00	4.50	1.25
☐ 38 Indianapolis Indians	6.00	2.70	.75
☐ 39 Washington Nationals	6.00	2.70	.75
☐ 40 Philadelphia Phillies	6.00	2.70	.75
☐ 41 Pittsburgh Pirates	6.00	2.70	.75
☐ 42 Columbus Red Birds	6.00	2.70	.75
☐ 43 Boston Red Sox	10.00	4.50	1.25
☐ 44 Cincinnati Reds	6.00	2.70	.75
☐ 45 St. Paul Saints	6.00	2.70	.75
☐ 46 Detroit Tigers	10.00	4.50	1.25
☐ 47 Chicago White Sox	6.00	2.70	.75
☐ 48 New York Yankees	20.00	9.00	2.50

1990 Baseball Wit

The 1990 Baseball Wit set was issued in complete set form only. This set was dedicated to and featured several ex-members of the Little Leagues. This 108-card, standard-size set was available primarily in retail and chain outlets. Most of the older (retired) players in the set are shown in black and white. The card backs typically give three trivia questions with answers following. The object of the game is to collect points by correctly answering any one of the questions on the back of each card or identifying the picture on the front. The first printing of 10,000 sets had several errors, and the cards were not numbered. The second printing corrected these errors and numbered the cards. The number on the front of the card is used when playing the game and is not to be confused with the card number, which is found on the back of all cards.

	MINT	NRMT	EXC
COMPLETE SET (108)	8.00	3.60	1.00
COMMON CARD (1-108)	.05	.02	.01
☐ 1 Orel Hershiser	.10	.05	.01
☐ 2 Tony Gwynn	.75	.35	.09
☐ 3 Mickey Mantle	1.50	.70	.19
☐ 4 Willie Stargell	.15	.07	.02
☐ 5 Don Baylor	.10	.05	.01
☐ 6 Hank Aaron	.75	.35	.09
☐ 7 Don Larsen	.10	.05	.01
☐ 8 Lee Mazzilli	.05	.02	.01
☐ 9 Boog Powell	.10	.05	.01
☐ 10 Little League World Series	.05	.02	.01
☐ 11 Jose Canseco	.25	.11	.03
☐ 12 Mike Scott	.05	.02	.01
☐ 13 Bob Feller	.20	.09	.03
☐ 14 Ron Santo	.10	.05	.01
☐ 15A Mel Stottlemyer ERR sic, Stottlemyre	.10	.05	.01
☐ 15B Mel Stottlemyre COR	.10	.05	.01
☐ 16 Shea Stadium	.05	.02	.01
☐ 17 Brooks Robinson	.15	.07	.02
☐ 18 Willie Mays	.75	.35	.09
☐ 19 Ernie Banks	.25	.11	.03
☐ 20 Keith Hernandez	.10	.05	.01
☐ 21 Bret Saberhagen	.10	.05	.01
☐ 22 Baseball Hall of Fame	.05	.02	.01
☐ 23 Luis Aparicio	.15	.07	.02
☐ 24 Yogi Berra	.25	.11	.03
☐ 25 Manny Mota	.10	.05	.01
☐ 26 Steve Garvey	.10	.05	.01
☐ 27 Bill Shea	.05	.02	.01
☐ 28 Fred Lynn	.05	.02	.01
☐ 29 Todd Worrell	.05	.02	.01
☐ 30 Roy Campanella	.30	.14	.04
☐ 31 Bob Gibson	.15	.07	.02
☐ 32 Gary Carter	.10	.05	.01
☐ 33 Jim Palmer	.15	.07	.02
☐ 34 Carl Yastrzemski	.15	.07	.02
☐ 35 Dwight Gooden	.10	.05	.01
☐ 36 Stan Musial	.50	.23	.06
☐ 37 Rickey Henderson	.25	.11	.03
☐ 38 Dale Murphy	.15	.07	.02
☐ 39 Mike Schmidt	.25	.11	.03
☐ 40 Gaylord Perry	.15	.07	.02
☐ 41 Ozzie Smith	.50	.23	.06
☐ 42 Reggie Jackson	.25	.11	.03
☐ 43 Steve Carlton	.15	.07	.02
☐ 44 Jim Perry	.05	.02	.01
☐ 45 Vince Coleman	.05	.02	.01
☐ 46 Tom Seaver	.25	.11	.03
☐ 47 Marty Marion	.05	.02	.01
☐ 48 Frank Robinson	.15	.07	.02
☐ 49 Joe DiMaggio	1.00	.45	.12
☐ 50 Ted Williams	1.00	.45	.12
☐ 51 Rollie Fingers	.10	.05	.01
☐ 52 Jackie Robinson	.75	.35	.09
☐ 53 Vic Raschi	.05	.02	.01
☐ 54 Johnny Bench	.20	.09	.03
☐ 55 Nolan Ryan	1.00	.45	.12
☐ 56 Ty Cobb	.75	.35	.09
☐ 57 Harry Steinfeldt	.05	.02	.01
☐ 58 James O'Rourke	.05	.02	.01
☐ 59 John McGraw	.15	.07	.02
☐ 60 Candy Cummings	.10	.05	.01
☐ 61 Jimmie Foxx	.15	.07	.02
☐ 62 Walter Johnson	.15	.07	.02
☐ 63 1903 World Series	.05	.02	.01
☐ 64 Satchel Paige	.25	.11	.03
☐ 65 Bobby Wallace	.10	.05	.01
☐ 66 Cap Anson	.15	.07	.02
☐ 67 Hugh Duffy	.10	.05	.01
☐ 68 William(Buck) Ewing	.10	.05	.01
☐ 69 Bobo Holloman	.05	.02	.01
☐ 70 Ed Delahanty	.10	.05	.01
☐ 71 Dizzy Dean	.20	.09	.03
☐ 72 Tris Speaker	.15	.07	.02
☐ 73 Lou Gehrig	1.00	.45	.12
☐ 74 Wee Willie Keeler	.10	.05	.01
☐ 75 Cal Hubbard	.10	.05	.01
☐ 76 Eddie Collins	.15	.07	.02
☐ 77 Chris Von Der Ahe	.05	.02	.01
☐ 78 Sam Crawford	.15	.07	.02
☐ 79 Cy Young	.15	.07	.02
☐ 80 Johnny Vander Meer	.10	.05	.01
☐ 81 Joey Jay	.05	.02	.01
☐ 82 Zack Wheat	.10	.05	.01
☐ 83 Jim Bottomley	.10	.05	.01
☐ 84 Honus Wagner	.30	.14	.04
☐ 85 Casey Stengel	.25	.11	.03
☐ 86 Babe Ruth	1.50	.70	.19
☐ 87 John Lindemuth Carl Stotz	.05	.02	.01
☐ 88 Max Carey	.10	.05	.01
☐ 89 Mordecai Brown	.10	.05	.01
☐ 90 Cincinnati Red Stockings 1869	.05	.02	.01
☐ 91 Rube Marquard	.10	.05	.01
☐ 92 Charles Radbourne Horse	.10	.05	.01
☐ 93 Hack Wilson	.10	.05	.01
☐ 94 Lefty Grove	.15	.07	.02
☐ 95 Carl Hubbell	.15	.07	.02
☐ 96 A.J. Cartwright	.05	.02	.01
☐ 97 Rogers Hornsby	.20	.09	.03
☐ 98 Ernest Thayer	.05	.02	.01
☐ 99 Connie Mack	.10	.05	.01
☐ 100 Centennial Celebration 1939	.05	.02	.01
☐ 101 Branch Rickey	.10	.05	.01
☐ 102 Dan Brouthers	.10	.05	.01
☐ 103 1st Baseball Uniform	.05	.02	.01
☐ 104 Christy Mathewson	.20	.09	.03
☐ 105 Joe Nuxhall	.05	.02	.01
☐ 106 Centennial Celebration 1939	.05	.02	.01
☐ 107 William H. Taft PRES	.15	.07	.02
☐ 108 Abner Doubleday	.05	.02	.01

1991 Baseball's Best Aces of the Mound

This 8" by 8" sticker album is 24 pages in length and features 18 of MLB's outstanding pitchers. One page is devoted to each player and includes player profile, a black and white photo, and a slot for the sticker. The stickers measure 2 1/2" square and feature glossy color action player photos with white borders. They appear on two insert sheets in the middle of the album and are arranged alphabetically, with the number appearing on the front.

	MINT	NRMT	EXC
COMPLETE SET	8.00	3.60	1.00
COMMON PLAYER (1-18)	.25	.11	.03
☐ 1 Rick Aguilera	.50	.23	.06
☐ 2 Jack Armstrong	.25	.11	.03
☐ 3 Tim Belcher	.25	.11	.03
☐ 4 Roger Clemens	3.00	1.35	.35
☐ 5 Doug Drabek	.50	.23	.06
☐ 6 Dennis Eckersley	2.00	.90	.25
☐ 7 Chuck Finley	.50	.23	.06
☐ 8 Dwight Gooden	1.00	.45	.12
☐ 9 Neal Heaton	.25	.11	.03
☐ 10 Teddy Higuera	.25	.11	.03

☐ 11 Dennis Martinez	.75	.35	.09
☐ 12 Randy Myers	.25	.11	.03
☐ 13 Gregg Olson	.25	.11	.03
☐ 14 Bret Saberhagen	.25	.11	.03
☐ 15 Mike Scott	.25	.11	.03
☐ 16 Dave Stewart	.25	.11	.03
☐ 17 Dave Stieb	.25	.11	.03
☐ 18 Frank Viola	.25	.11	.03

1991 Baseball's Best Hit Men

This 8" by 8" sticker album is 24 pages in length and features 18 of MLB's outstanding hitters. One page is devoted to each player and includes player profile, a black and white photo, and a slot for the sticker. The stickers measure 2 1/2" square and feature glossy color action player photos with white borders. They appear on two insert sheets in the middle of the album and are arranged alphabetically, with the number appearing on the front.

	MINT	NRMT	EXC
COMPLETE SET (18)	15.00	6.75	1.85
COMMON PLAYER (1-18)	.25	.11	.03
☐ 1 George Bell	.25	.11	.03
☐ 2 Wade Boggs	1.25	.55	.16
☐ 3 George Brett	2.50	1.10	.30
☐ 4 Hubie Brooks	.25	.11	.03
☐ 5 Will Clark	1.25	.55	.16
☐ 6 Len Dykstra	.50	.23	.06
☐ 7 Ken Griffey Jr.	4.00	1.80	.50
☐ 8 Pedro Guerrero	.25	.11	.03
☐ 9 Ozzie Guillen	.25	.11	.03
☐ 10 Tony Gwynn	2.50	1.10	.30
☐ 11 Gregg Jefferies	.75	.35	.09
☐ 12 Carney Lansford	.25	.11	.03
☐ 13 Barry Larkin	1.25	.55	.16
☐ 14 Don Mattingly	2.50	1.10	.30
☐ 15 Kirby Puckett	2.50	1.10	.30
☐ 16 Tim Raines	.50	.23	.06
☐ 17 Ryne Sandberg	2.50	1.10	.30
☐ 18 Robin Yount	1.25	.55	.16

1991 Baseball's Best Home Run Kings

This 8" by 8" sticker album is 24 pages in length and features 18 of MLB's home run kings. One page is devoted to each player and includes player profile, a black and white photo, and a slot for the sticker. The stickers measure 2 1/2" square and feature glossy color action player photos with white borders. The stickers are unnumbered and checklisted below in alphabetical order.

	MINT	NRMT	EXC
COMPLETE SET (18)	8.00	3.60	1.00
COMMON PLAYER (1-18)	.25	.11	.03
☐ 1 Jesse Barfield	.25	.11	.03
☐ 2 Jose Canseco	1.25	.55	.16
☐ 3 Eric Davis	.25	.11	.03
☐ 4 Glenn Davis	.25	.11	.03
☐ 5 Andre Dawson	1.00	.45	.12
☐ 6 Dwight Evans	.50	.23	.06
☐ 7 Cecil Fielder	1.50	.70	.19
☐ 8 Kelly Gruber	.25	.11	.03
☐ 9 Von Hayes	.25	.11	.03
☐ 10 Kent Hrbek	.25	.11	.03
☐ 11 Bo Jackson	.50	.23	.06
☐ 12 Howard Johnson	.25	.11	.03
☐ 13 Mark McGwire	2.00	.90	.25
☐ 14 Kevin Mitchell	.25	.11	.03
☐ 15 Eddie Murray	1.50	.70	.19
☐ 16 Ruben Sierra	.25	.11	.03
☐ 17 Darryl Strawberry	.50	.23	.06
☐ 18 Tim Wallach	.25	.11	.03

1991 Baseball's Best Record Breakers

This 8" by 8" sticker album is 24 pages in length and features 18 of MLB's outstanding players. One page is devoted to each player and includes player profile, a black and white photo, and a slot for the sticker. The stickers measure 2 1/2" square and feature glossy color action player photos with white borders. They appear on two insert sheets in the middle of the album and are arranged alphabetically, with the number appearing on the front.

	MINT	NRMT	EXC
COMPLETE SET (18)	15.00	6.75	1.85
COMMON PLAYER (1-18)	.25	.11	.03
☐ 1 Bert Blyleven	.50	.23	.06
☐ 2 Jose Canseco	1.25	.55	.16
☐ 3 Gary Carter	.50	.23	.06
☐ 4 Vince Coleman	.25	.11	.03
☐ 5 Mark Davis	.25	.11	.03
☐ 6 Carlton Fisk	1.25	.55	.16
☐ 7 Rickey Henderson	1.25	.55	.16
☐ 8 Reggie Jackson	1.00	.45	.12
☐ 9 Howard Johnson	.25	.11	.03
☐ 10 Ramon Martinez	.75	.35	.09
☐ 11 Don Mattingly	2.00	.90	.25
☐ 12 Dave Righetti	.25	.11	.03
☐ 13 Cal Ripken Jr.	3.00	1.35	.35
☐ 14 Nolan Ryan	3.00	1.35	.35
☐ 15 Ryne Sandberg	2.00	.90	.25
☐ 16 Mike Schmidt	1.50	.70	.19
☐ 17 Ozzie Smith	2.00	.90	.25
☐ 18 Fernando Valenzuela	.50	.23	.06

1934-36 Batter-Up R318

The 1934-36 Batter-Up set, issued by National Chicle, contains 192 blank-backed die-cut cards. Numbers 1 to 80 are approximately 2 3/8" by 3 1/4" in size while 81 to 192 are 2 3/8" by 3". The latter are more difficult to find than the former. The pictures come in basic black and white or in tints of blue, brown, green, purple, red, or sepia. There are three combination cards (each featuring two players per card) in the high series (98, 111, and 115). Cards with the die-cut backing removed are graded fair at best.

	EX-MT	VG-E	GOOD
COMPLETE SET (192)	18000.00	8100.00	2200.00
COMMON CARD (1-80)	40.00	18.00	5.00
COMMON CARD (81-192)	80.00	36.00	10.00
WRAPPER (1-CENT)	350.00	160.00	45.00
☐ 1 Wally Berger	100.00	45.00	12.50
☐ 2 Ed Brandt	40.00	18.00	5.00
☐ 3 Al Lopez	90.00	40.00	11.00
☐ 4 Dick Bartell	50.00	22.00	6.25
☐ 5 Carl Hubbell	125.00	55.00	15.50
☐ 6 Bill Terry	150.00	70.00	19.00
☐ 7 Pepper Martin	60.00	27.00	7.50
☐ 8 Jim Bottomley	100.00	45.00	12.50
☐ 9 Tom Bridges	50.00	22.00	6.25
☐ 10 Rick Ferrell	90.00	40.00	11.00
☐ 11 Ray Benge	40.00	18.00	5.00
☐ 12 Wes Ferrell	50.00	22.00	6.25
☐ 13 Chalmer Cissell	40.00	18.00	5.00
☐ 14 Pie Traynor	125.00	55.00	15.50
☐ 15 Leroy Mahaffey	40.00	18.00	5.00
☐ 16 Chick Hafey	90.00	40.00	11.00
☐ 17 Lloyd Waner	90.00	40.00	11.00
☐ 18 Jack Burns	40.00	18.00	5.00
☐ 19 Buddy Myer	50.00	22.00	6.25
☐ 20 Bob Johnson	50.00	22.00	6.25
☐ 21 Arky Vaughan	90.00	40.00	11.00
☐ 22 Red Rolfe	50.00	22.00	6.25
☐ 23 Lefty Gomez	150.00	70.00	19.00
☐ 24 Earl Averill	125.00	55.00	15.50
☐ 25 Mickey Cochrane	150.00	70.00	19.00
☐ 26 Van Lingle Mungo	60.00	27.00	7.50
☐ 27 Mel Ott	200.00	90.00	25.00
☐ 28 Jimmy Foxx	250.00	110.00	31.00
☐ 29 Jimmy Dykes	50.00	22.00	6.25
☐ 30 Bill Dickey	200.00	90.00	25.00
☐ 31 Lefty Grove	200.00	90.00	25.00
☐ 32 Joe Cronin	150.00	70.00	19.00
☐ 33 Frank Frisch	125.00	55.00	15.50
☐ 34 Al Simmons	125.00	55.00	15.50
☐ 35 Rogers Hornsby	250.00	110.00	31.00
☐ 36 Ted Lyons	90.00	40.00	11.00
☐ 37 Rabbit Maranville	90.00	40.00	11.00
☐ 38 Jimmy Wilson	50.00	22.00	6.25
☐ 39 Willie Kamm	40.00	18.00	5.00
☐ 40 Bill Hallahan	40.00	18.00	5.00
☐ 41 Gus Suhr	40.00	18.00	5.00
☐ 42 Charlie Gehringer	125.00	55.00	15.50
☐ 43 Joe Heving	40.00	18.00	5.00
☐ 44 Adam Comorosky	40.00	18.00	5.00
☐ 45 Tony Lazzeri	125.00	55.00	15.50
☐ 46 Sam Leslie	40.00	18.00	5.00
☐ 47 Bob Smith	40.00	18.00	5.00
☐ 48 Willis Hudlin	40.00	18.00	5.00
☐ 49 Carl Reynolds	40.00	18.00	5.00
☐ 50 Fred Schulte	40.00	18.00	5.00
☐ 51 Cookie Lavagetto	60.00	27.00	7.50
☐ 52 Hal Schumacher	50.00	22.00	6.25
☐ 53 Roger Cramer	50.00	22.00	6.25
☐ 54 Sylvester Johnson	40.00	18.00	5.00
☐ 55 Ollie Bejma	40.00	18.00	5.00
☐ 56 Sam Byrd	40.00	18.00	5.00
☐ 57 Hank Greenberg	250.00	110.00	31.00
☐ 58 Bill Knickerbocker	40.00	18.00	5.00
☐ 59 Bill Urbanski	40.00	18.00	5.00
☐ 60 Eddie Morgan	40.00	18.00	5.00
☐ 61 Rabbit McNair	40.00	18.00	5.00
☐ 62 Ben Chapman	50.00	22.00	6.25
☐ 63 Roy Johnson	40.00	18.00	5.00
☐ 64 Dizzy Dean	400.00	180.00	50.00
☐ 65 Zeke Bonura	40.00	18.00	5.00
☐ 66 Fred Marberry	40.00	18.00	5.00
☐ 67 Gus Mancuso	40.00	18.00	5.00
☐ 68 Joe Vosmik	40.00	18.00	5.00
☐ 69 Earl Grace	40.00	18.00	5.00
☐ 70 Tony Piet	40.00	18.00	5.00
☐ 71 Rollie Hemsley	40.00	18.00	5.00
☐ 72 Fred Fitzsimmons	50.00	22.00	6.25
☐ 73 Hack Wilson	150.00	70.00	19.00
☐ 74 Chick Fullis	40.00	18.00	5.00
☐ 75 Fred Frankhouse	40.00	18.00	5.00
☐ 76 Ethan Allen	40.00	18.00	5.00
☐ 77 Heinie Manush	90.00	40.00	11.00
☐ 78 Rip Collins	40.00	18.00	5.00
☐ 79 Tony Cuccinello	40.00	18.00	5.00
☐ 80 Joe Kuhel	40.00	18.00	5.00
☐ 81 Tom Bridges	90.00	40.00	11.00
☐ 82 Clint Brown	80.00	36.00	10.00
☐ 83 Albert Blanche	80.00	36.00	10.00
☐ 84 Boze Berger	80.00	36.00	10.00
☐ 85 Goose Goslin	175.00	80.00	22.00
☐ 86 Lefty Gomez	225.00	100.00	28.00
☐ 87 Joe Glenn	80.00	36.00	10.00
☐ 88 Cy Blanton	80.00	36.00	10.00
☐ 89 Tom Carey	80.00	36.00	10.00
☐ 90 Ralph Birkofer	80.00	36.00	10.00
☐ 91 Fred Gabler	80.00	36.00	10.00
☐ 92 Dick Coffman	80.00	36.00	10.00
☐ 93 Ollie Bejma	80.00	36.00	10.00
☐ 94 Leroy Parmelee	80.00	36.00	10.00
☐ 95 Carl Reynolds	80.00	36.00	10.00
☐ 96 Ben Cantwell	80.00	36.00	10.00
☐ 97 Curtis Davis	80.00	36.00	10.00
☐ 98 Earl Webb and Wally Moses	125.00	55.00	15.50
☐ 99 Ray Benge	80.00	36.00	10.00
☐ 100 Pie Traynor	200.00	90.00	25.00
☐ 101 Phil Cavarretta	100.00	45.00	12.50
☐ 102 Pep Young	80.00	36.00	10.00
☐ 103 Willis Hudlin	80.00	36.00	10.00
☐ 104 Mickey Haslin	80.00	36.00	10.00
☐ 105 Oswald Bluege	90.00	40.00	11.00
☐ 106 Paul Andrews	80.00	36.00	10.00
☐ 107 Ed Brandt	80.00	36.00	10.00
☐ 108 Don Taylor	80.00	36.00	10.00
☐ 109 Thornton Lee	90.00	40.00	11.00
☐ 110 Hal Schumacher	90.00	40.00	11.00
☐ 111 Hayes and Ted Lyons	150.00	70.00	19.00
☐ 112 Odell Hale	80.00	36.00	10.00
☐ 113 Earl Averill	175.00	80.00	22.00
☐ 114 Italo Chelini	80.00	36.00	10.00
☐ 115 Andrews and Jim Bottomley	150.00	70.00	19.00
☐ 116 Bill Walker	80.00	36.00	10.00
☐ 117 Bill Dickey	300.00	135.00	38.00
☐ 118 Gerald Walker	80.00	36.00	10.00
☐ 119 Ted Lyons	175.00	80.00	22.00
☐ 120 Eldon Auker	80.00	36.00	10.00
☐ 121 Bill Hallahan	90.00	40.00	11.00
☐ 122 Fred Lindstrom	175.00	80.00	22.00
☐ 123 Oral Hildebrand	80.00	36.00	10.00
☐ 124 Luke Appling	225.00	100.00	28.00
☐ 125 Pepper Martin	100.00	45.00	12.50
☐ 126 Rick Ferrell	175.00	80.00	22.00
☐ 127 Ival Goodman	80.00	36.00	10.00
☐ 128 Joe Kuhel	80.00	36.00	10.00
☐ 129 Ernie Lombardi	175.00	80.00	22.00
☐ 130 Charlie Gehringer	225.00	100.00	28.00
☐ 131 Van Lingle Mungo	90.00	40.00	11.00
☐ 132 Larry French	80.00	36.00	10.00
☐ 133 Buddy Myer	90.00	40.00	11.00
☐ 134 Mel Harder	100.00	45.00	12.50
☐ 135 Augie Galan	80.00	36.00	10.00
☐ 136 Gabby Hartnett	175.00	80.00	22.00
☐ 137 Stan Hack	90.00	40.00	11.00
☐ 138 Billy Herman	175.00	80.00	22.00
☐ 139 Bill Jurges	80.00	36.00	10.00
☐ 140 Bill Lee	90.00	40.00	11.00
☐ 141 Zeke Bonura	80.00	36.00	10.00
☐ 142 Tony Piet	80.00	36.00	10.00
☐ 143 Paul Dean	100.00	45.00	12.50
☐ 144 Jimmy Foxx	400.00	180.00	50.00
☐ 145 Joe Medwick	225.00	100.00	28.00
☐ 146 Rip Collins	80.00	36.00	10.00
☐ 147 Mel Almada	80.00	36.00	10.00
☐ 148 Allan Cooke	80.00	36.00	10.00
☐ 149 Moe Berg	400.00	180.00	50.00
☐ 150 Dolph Camilli	90.00	40.00	11.00
☐ 151 Oscar Melillo	80.00	36.00	10.00
☐ 152 Bruce Campbell	80.00	36.00	10.00
☐ 153 Lefty Grove	300.00	135.00	38.00
☐ 154 Johnny Murphy	100.00	45.00	12.50
☐ 155 Luke Sewell	90.00	40.00	11.00
☐ 156 Leo Durocher	250.00	110.00	31.00
☐ 157 Lloyd Waner	175.00	80.00	22.00
☐ 158 Guy Bush	80.00	36.00	10.00
☐ 159 Jimmy Dykes	90.00	40.00	11.00
☐ 160 Steve O'Neill	90.00	40.00	11.00
☐ 161 General Crowder	80.00	36.00	10.00
☐ 162 Joe Cascarella	80.00	36.00	10.00
☐ 163 Daniel(Bud) Hafey	90.00	40.00	11.00
☐ 164 Gilly Campbell	80.00	36.00	10.00
☐ 165 Ray Hayworth	80.00	36.00	10.00
☐ 166 Frank Demaree	80.00	36.00	10.00
☐ 167 John Babich	80.00	36.00	10.00
☐ 168 Marvin Owen	80.00	36.00	10.00
☐ 169 Ralph Kress	80.00	36.00	10.00
☐ 170 Mule Haas	80.00	36.00	10.00
☐ 171 Frank Higgins	90.00	40.00	11.00
☐ 172 Wally Berger	100.00	45.00	12.50
☐ 173 Frank Frisch	225.00	100.00	28.00
☐ 174 Wes Ferrell	90.00	40.00	11.00
☐ 175 Pete Fox	80.00	36.00	10.00
☐ 176 John Vergez	80.00	36.00	10.00
☐ 177 Billy Rogell	80.00	36.00	10.00
☐ 178 Don Brennan	80.00	36.00	10.00
☐ 179 Jim Bottomley	175.00	80.00	22.00
☐ 180 Travis Jackson	175.00	80.00	22.00
☐ 181 Red Rolfe	100.00	45.00	12.50
☐ 182 Frank Crosetti	125.00	55.00	15.50
☐ 183 Joe Cronin	175.00	80.00	22.00
☐ 184 Schoolboy Rowe	100.00	45.00	12.50
☐ 185 Chuck Klein	225.00	100.00	28.00
☐ 186 Lon Warneke	90.00	40.00	11.00
☐ 187 Gus Suhr	80.00	36.00	10.00
☐ 188 Ben Chapman	90.00	40.00	11.00
☐ 189 Clint Brown	80.00	36.00	10.00
☐ 190 Paul Derringer	100.00	45.00	12.50
☐ 191 John Burns	80.00	36.00	10.00
☐ 192 John Broaca	125.00	55.00	15.50

1959 Bazooka

The 23 full-color, unnumbered cards comprising the 1959 Bazooka set were cut from the bottom of the boxes of gum marketed nationally that year by Topps. Bazooka was the brand name which Topps had been using to sell its one cent bubblegum; this year Topps decided to distribute 25 pieces of Bazooka gum in a box. The cards themselves measure 2 13/16" by 4 15/16". Only nine cards were originally issued; 14 more were added to the set at a later date (these are marked with SP in the checklist). The latter are less plentiful and hence more valuable than the original nine. All the cards are blank backed and the catalog designation is R414-15. The prices below are for the cards cut from the box; complete boxes intact would be worth about 50 percent more.

	NRMT	VG-E	GOOD
COMPLETE SET (23)	7000.00	3200.00	900.00
COMMON CARD (1-23)	50.00	22.00	6.25
COMMON CARD SP	200.00	90.00	25.00
☐ 1 Hank Aaron	550.00	250.00	70.00
☐ 2 Richie Ashburn SP	400.00	180.00	50.00
☐ 3 Ernie Banks SP	600.00	275.00	75.00
☐ 4 Ken Boyer SP	300.00	135.00	38.00
☐ 5 Orlando Cepeda	100.00	45.00	12.50
☐ 6 Bob Cerv SP	200.00	90.00	25.00
☐ 7 Rocco Colavito SP	400.00	180.00	50.00
☐ 8 Del Crandall	50.00	22.00	6.25
☐ 9 Jim Davenport	50.00	22.00	6.25
☐ 10 Don Drysdale SP	500.00	220.00	60.00
☐ 11 Nellie Fox SP	400.00	180.00	50.00
☐ 12 Jackie Jensen SP	300.00	135.00	38.00
☐ 13 Harvey Kuenn SP	250.00	110.00	31.00
☐ 14 Mickey Mantle	1750.00	800.00	220.00
☐ 15 Willie Mays	600.00	275.00	75.00
☐ 16 Bill Mazeroski	100.00	45.00	12.50
☐ 17 Roy McMillan	50.00	22.00	6.25
☐ 18 Billy Pierce SP	200.00	90.00	25.00
☐ 19 Roy Sievers SP	200.00	90.00	25.00
☐ 20 Duke Snider SP	750.00	350.00	95.00
☐ 21 Gus Triandos SP	200.00	90.00	25.00
☐ 22 Bob Turley	50.00	22.00	6.25
☐ 23 Vic Wertz SP	200.00	90.00	25.00

1960 Bazooka

In 1960, Topps introduced a 36-card baseball player set in three card panels on the bottom of Bazooka gum boxes. The cards measure 1 13/16" by 2 3/4" and the panels measure 2 3/4" by 5 1/2". The cards carried full color pictures and were numbered at the bottom underneath the team position. The checklist below contains prices for individual cards. Complete panels of three would have a 50 percent more than the sum of the indiviudal cards (prices) on the panel and complete boxes would command a premium of another 50 percent above those prices.

	NRMT	VG-E	GOOD
COMPLETE INDIV.SET	1000.00	450.00	125.00
COMMON CARD (1-36)	12.00	5.50	1.50

□ 1 Ernie Banks	50.00	22.00	6.25
□ 2 Bud Daley	12.00	5.50	1.50
□ 3 Wally Moon	12.00	5.50	1.50
□ 4 Hank Aaron	100.00	45.00	12.50
□ 5 Milt Pappas	12.00	5.50	1.50
□ 6 Dick Stuart	12.00	5.50	1.50
□ 7 Bob Clemente	150.00	70.00	19.00
□ 8 Yogi Berra	75.00	34.00	9.50
□ 9 Ken Boyer	15.00	6.75	1.85
□ 10 Orlando Cepeda	20.00	9.00	2.50
□ 11 Gus Triandos	12.00	5.50	1.50
□ 12 Frank Malzone	12.00	5.50	1.50
□ 13 Willie Mays	110.00	50.00	14.00
□ 14 Camilo Pascual	12.00	5.50	1.50
□ 15 Bob Cerv	12.00	5.50	1.50
□ 16 Vic Power	12.00	5.50	1.50
□ 17 Larry Sherry	12.00	5.50	1.50
□ 18 Al Kaline	50.00	22.00	6.25
□ 19 Warren Spahn	50.00	22.00	6.25
□ 20 Harmon Killebrew	50.00	22.00	6.25
□ 21 Jackie Jensen	15.00	6.75	1.85
□ 22 Luis Aparicio	30.00	13.50	3.70
□ 23 Gil Hodges	30.00	13.50	3.70
□ 24 Richie Ashburn	40.00	18.00	5.00
□ 25 Nellie Fox	40.00	18.00	5.00
□ 26 Robin Roberts	40.00	18.00	5.00
□ 27 Joe Cunningham	12.00	5.50	1.50
□ 28 Early Wynn	30.00	13.50	3.70
□ 29 Frank Robinson	50.00	22.00	6.25
□ 30 Rocky Colavito	30.00	13.50	3.70
□ 31 Mickey Mantle	275.00	125.00	34.00
□ 32 Glen Hobbie	12.00	5.50	1.50
□ 33 Roy McMillan	12.00	5.50	1.50
□ 34 Harvey Kuenn	12.00	5.50	1.50
□ 35 Johnny Antonelli	12.00	5.50	1.50
□ 36 Del Crandall	12.00	5.50	1.50

1961 Bazooka

The 36 card set issued by Bazooka in 1961 follows the format established in 1960; three full color, numbered cards to each panel found on a Bazooka gum box. The individual cards measure 1 13/16" by 2 3/4" whereas the panels measure 2 3/4" by 5 1/2". The cards of 1960 and 1961 are similar in design but are easily distinguished from one another by their numbers. Complete panels of three would have a value of 40 percent more than the sum of the individual cards (prices) on the panel and complete boxes would command a premium of another 40 percent above those prices.

	NRMT	VG-E	GOOD
COMPLETE INDIV. SET	800.00	350.00	100.00
COMMON CARD (1-36)	12.00	5.50	1.50

□ 1 Art Mahaffey	12.00	5.50	1.50
□ 2 Mickey Mantle	275.00	125.00	34.00
□ 3 Ron Santo	15.00	6.75	1.85
□ 4 Bud Daley	12.00	5.50	1.50
□ 5 Roger Maris	75.00	34.00	9.50
□ 6 Eddie Yost	12.00	5.50	1.50
□ 7 Minnie Minoso	15.00	6.75	1.85
□ 8 Dick Groat	12.00	5.50	1.50
□ 9 Frank Malzone	12.00	5.50	1.50
□ 10 Dick Donovan	12.00	5.50	1.50
□ 11 Ed Mathews	50.00	22.00	6.25
□ 12 Jim Lemon	12.00	5.50	1.50
□ 13 Chuck Estrada	12.00	5.50	1.50
□ 14 Ken Boyer	15.00	6.75	1.85
□ 15 Harvey Kuenn	12.00	5.50	1.50
□ 16 Ernie Broglio	12.00	5.50	1.50
□ 17 Rocky Colavito	30.00	13.50	3.70
□ 18 Ted Kluszewski	30.00	13.50	3.70
□ 19 Ernie Banks	50.00	22.00	6.25
□ 20 Al Kaline	50.00	22.00	6.25
□ 21 Ed Bailey	12.00	5.50	1.50
□ 22 Jim Perry	12.00	5.50	1.50
□ 23 Willie Mays	100.00	45.00	12.50
□ 24 Bill Mazeroski	25.00	11.00	3.10
□ 25 Gus Triandos	12.00	5.50	1.50
□ 26 Don Drysdale	30.00	13.50	3.70
□ 27 Frank Herrera	12.00	5.50	1.50
□ 28 Earl Battey	12.00	5.50	1.50
□ 29 Warren Spahn	50.00	22.00	6.25
□ 30 Gene Woodling	12.00	5.50	1.50
□ 31 Frank Robinson	50.00	22.00	6.25
□ 32 Pete Runnels	12.00	5.50	1.50
□ 33 Woodie Held	12.00	5.50	1.50
□ 34 Norm Larker	12.00	5.50	1.50
□ 35 Luis Aparicio	30.00	13.50	3.70
□ 36 Bill Tuttle	12.00	5.50	1.50

1962 Bazooka

The 1962 Bazooka set of 45 full color, blank backed, unnumbered cards was issued in panels of three on Bazooka bubble gum. The individual cards measure 1 13/16" by 2 3/4" whereas the panels measure 2 3/4" by 5 1/2". The cards below are numbered by panel alphabetically based on the last name of the player pictured on the far left card of the panel. The cards with SP in the checklist below are more difficult to obtain. Complete panels would have a value of 40 percent more than the sum of the individual cards (prices) on the panel and complete boxes would command a premium of another 40 percent above those prices.

	NRMT	VG-E	GOOD
COMPLETE INDIV. SET	3000.00	1350.00	375.00
COMMON CARD (1-45)	12.00	5.50	1.50

□ 1 Bob Allison SP	75.00	34.00	9.50
□ 2 Ed Mathews SP	500.00	220.00	60.00
□ 3 Vada Pinson SP	75.00	34.00	9.50
□ 4 Earl Battey	12.00	5.50	1.50
□ 5 Warren Spahn	50.00	22.00	6.25
□ 6 Lee Thomas	12.00	5.50	1.50
□ 7 Orlando Cepeda	20.00	9.00	2.50
□ 8 Woodie Held	12.00	5.50	1.50
□ 9 Bob Aspromonte	12.00	5.50	1.50
□ 10 Dick Howser	12.00	5.50	1.50
□ 11 Bob Clemente	150.00	70.00	19.00
□ 12 Al Kaline	50.00	22.00	6.25
□ 13 Joe Jay	12.00	5.50	1.50
□ 14 Roger Maris	75.00	34.00	9.50
□ 15 Frank Howard	15.00	6.75	1.85
□ 16 Sandy Koufax	75.00	34.00	9.50
□ 17 Jim Gentile	12.00	5.50	1.50
□ 18 Johnny Callison	12.00	5.50	1.50
□ 19 Jim Landis	12.00	5.50	1.50
□ 20 Ken Boyer	15.00	6.75	1.85
□ 21 Chuck Schilling	12.00	5.50	1.50
□ 22 Art Mahaffey	12.00	5.50	1.50
□ 23 Mickey Mantle	275.00	125.00	34.00
□ 24 Dick Stuart	12.00	5.50	1.50
□ 25 Ken McBride	12.00	5.50	1.50
□ 26 Frank Robinson	50.00	22.00	6.25
□ 27 Gil Hodges	40.00	18.00	5.00
□ 28 Milt Pappas	12.00	5.50	1.50
□ 29 Hank Aaron	100.00	45.00	12.50
□ 30 Luis Aparicio	30.00	13.50	3.70
□ 31 Johnny Romano SP	75.00	34.00	9.50
□ 32 Ernie Banks SP	500.00	220.00	60.00
□ 33 Norm Siebern SP	75.00	34.00	9.50
□ 34 Ron Santo	20.00	9.00	2.50
□ 35 Norm Cash	15.00	6.75	1.85
□ 36 Jim Piersall	15.00	6.75	1.85
□ 37 Don Schwall	12.00	5.50	1.50
□ 38 Willie Mays	110.00	50.00	14.00
□ 39 Norm Larker	12.00	5.50	1.50
□ 40 Bill White	15.00	6.75	1.85
□ 41 Whitey Ford	50.00	22.00	6.25
□ 42 Rocky Colavito	30.00	13.50	3.70
□ 43 Don Zimmer SP	75.00	34.00	9.50
□ 44 Harmon Killebrew SP	500.00	220.00	60.00
□ 45 Gene Woodling SP	75.00	34.00	9.50

1963 Bazooka

The 1963 Bazooka set of 36 full color, blank backed numbered cards was issued on Bazooka bubble gum boxes. This year marked a change in format from previous Bazooka issues with a smaller sized card being issued. The individual cards measure 1 9/16" by 2 1/2" whereas the panels measure 2 1/2" by 4 11/16". The card features a white strip with the player's name printed in black on the card. The number appears in the white border on the bottom of the card. Three cards were issued per panel. Complete panels of three would have a value of 15 percent more thant he sum of the individual cards (prices)on the panel and complete boxes owuld command a premium of another 30 percent above those prices.

	NRMT	VG-E	GOOD
COMPLETE INDIV.SET	800.00	350.00	100.00
COMMON CARD (1-36)	7.50	3.40	.95

□ 1 Mickey Mantle	225.00	100.00	28.00
□ 2 Bob Rodgers	7.50	3.40	.95
□ 3 Ernie Banks	50.00	22.00	6.25
□ 4 Norm Siebern	7.50	3.40	.95
□ 5 Warren Spahn	40.00	18.00	5.00
□ 6 Bill Mazeroski	15.00	6.75	1.85
□ 7 Harmon Killebrew	40.00	18.00	5.00
□ 8 Dick Farrell	7.50	3.40	.95
□ 9 Hank Aaron	75.00	34.00	9.50
□ 10 Dick Donovan	7.50	3.40	.95
□ 11 Jim Gentile	7.50	3.40	.95
□ 12 Willie Mays	85.00	38.00	10.50
□ 13 Camilo Pascual	7.50	3.40	.95
□ 14 Bob Clemente	125.00	55.00	15.50
□ 15 Johnny Callison	7.50	3.40	.95
□ 16 Carl Yastrzemski	40.00	18.00	5.00
□ 17 Don Drysdale	35.00	16.00	4.40
□ 18 Johnny Romano	7.50	3.40	.95
□ 19 Al Jackson	7.50	3.40	.95
□ 20 Ralph Terry	7.50	3.40	.95
□ 21 Bill Monbouquette	7.50	3.40	.95
□ 22 Orlando Cepeda	15.00	6.75	1.85
□ 23 Stan Musial	50.00	22.00	6.25
□ 24 Floyd Robinson	7.50	3.40	.95
□ 25 Chuck Hinton	7.50	3.40	.95
□ 26 Bob Purkey	7.50	3.40	.95
□ 27 Ken Hubbs	10.00	4.50	1.25
□ 28 Bill White	10.00	4.50	1.25
□ 29 Ray Herbert	7.50	3.40	.95
□ 30 Brooks Robinson	50.00	22.00	6.25
□ 31 Frank Robinson	50.00	22.00	6.25
□ 32 Lee Thomas	7.50	3.40	.95
□ 33 Rocky Colavito	20.00	9.00	2.50
□ 34 Al Kaline	50.00	22.00	6.25
□ 35 Art Mahaffey	7.50	3.40	.95
□ 36 Tommy Davis	7.50	3.40	.95

1963 Bazooka ATG

The 1963 Bazooka All Time Greats set contains 41 black and white numbered cards issued as inserts in boxes of Bazooka Bubble gum. The cards feature bust shots with gold trim and measure 1 9/16" by 2 1/2". The backs are yellow with black print containing vital information and a biography of the player. Many of the players are pictured not as they looked during their playing careers but as they looked many years after their playing days were through. The cards also exist in a scarcer variety with silver trim instead of gold; the silver trim variety cards are worth approximately double the prices listed below. Cards are numbered on the back.

	NRMT	VG-E	GOOD
COMPLETE SET (41)	350.00	160.00	45.00
COMMON CARD (1-41)	4.00	1.80	.50

□ 1 Joe Tinker	6.00	2.70	.75
□ 2 Harry Heilmann	6.00	2.70	.75
□ 3 Jack Chesbro	4.00	1.80	.50
□ 4 Christy Mathewson	15.00	6.75	1.85
□ 5 Herb Pennock	6.00	2.70	.75
□ 6 Cy Young	10.00	4.50	1.25
□ 7 Ed Walsh	6.00	2.70	.75
□ 8 Nap Lajoie	10.00	4.50	1.25
□ 9 Eddie Plank	6.00	2.70	.75
□ 10 Honus Wagner	15.00	6.75	1.85
□ 11 Chief Bender	6.00	2.70	.75
□ 12 Walter Johnson	15.00	6.75	1.85
□ 13 Mordecai Brown	6.00	2.70	.75
□ 14 Rabbit Maranville	6.00	2.70	.75
□ 15 Lou Gehrig	50.00	22.00	6.25
□ 16 Ban Johnson	4.00	1.80	.50
□ 17 Babe Ruth	75.00	34.00	9.50
□ 18 Connie Mack	6.00	2.70	.75
□ 19 Hank Greenberg	6.00	2.70	.75
□ 20 John McGraw	6.00	2.70	.75
□ 21 Al Simmons	6.00	2.70	.75
□ 23 Jimmy Collins	6.00	2.70	.75
□ 24 Tris Speaker	8.00	3.60	1.00
□ 25 Frank Chance	6.00	2.70	.75
□ 26 Fred Clarke	6.00	2.70	.75
□ 27 Wilbert Robinson	6.00	2.70	.75
□ 28 Dazzy Vance	6.00	2.70	.75
□ 29 Pete Alexander	8.00	3.60	1.00
□ 30 Judge Landis	6.00	2.70	.75
□ 31 Willie Keeler	6.00	2.70	.75
□ 32 Rogers Hornsby	10.00	4.50	1.25
□ 33 Hugh Duffy	6.00	2.70	.75
□ 34 Mickey Cochrane	6.00	2.70	.75
□ 35 Ty Cobb	50.00	22.00	6.25
□ 36 Mel Ott	10.00	4.50	1.25
□ 37 Clark Griffith	6.00	2.70	.75
□ 38 Ted Lyons	6.00	2.70	.75
□ 39 Cap Anson	6.00	2.70	.75
□ 40 Bill Dickey	6.00	2.70	.75
□ 41 Eddie Collins	6.00	2.70	.75

1964 Bazooka

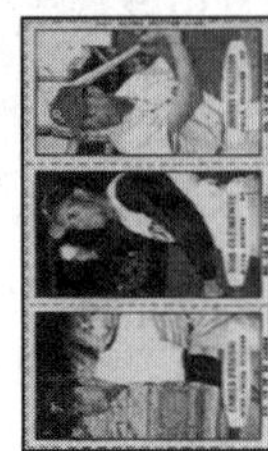

The 1964 Bazooka set of 36 full color, blank backed, numbered cards were issued in panels of three on the backs of Bazooka bubble gum boxes. The individual cards measure 1 9/16" by 2 1/2" whereas the panels measure 2 1/2" by 4 11/16". Many players from the 1963 set have the same numbers; however, the pictures are different. Complete panels of three would have a value of 15 percent more than the sum of the individual cards (prices) on the panel and complete boxes would command a premium of another 40 percent above those prices.

	NRMT	VG-E	GOOD
COMPLETE INDIV. SET	1000.00	450.00	125.00
COMMON CARD (1-36)	10.00	4.50	1.25

□ 1 Mickey Mantle	200.00	90.00	25.00
□ 2 Dick Groat	10.00	4.50	1.25
□ 3 Steve Barber	10.00	4.50	1.25
□ 4 Ken McBride	10.00	4.50	1.25
□ 5 Warren Spahn	40.00	18.00	5.00
□ 6 Bob Friend	10.00	4.50	1.25
□ 7 Harmon Killebrew	40.00	18.00	5.00
□ 8 Dick Farrell	10.00	4.50	1.25
□ 9 Hank Aaron	100.00	45.00	12.50
□ 10 Rich Rollins	10.00	4.50	1.25
□ 11 Jim Gentile	10.00	4.50	1.25
□ 12 Willie Mays	100.00	45.00	12.50
□ 13 Camilo Pascual	10.00	4.50	1.25
□ 14 Bob Clemente	125.00	55.00	15.50
□ 15 Johnny Callison	10.00	4.50	1.25
□ 16 Carl Yastrzemski	50.00	22.00	6.25
□ 17 Billy Williams	30.00	13.50	3.70
□ 18 Johnny Romano	10.00	4.50	1.25
□ 19 Jim Maloney	10.00	4.50	1.25
□ 20 Norm Cash	12.50	5.50	1.55
□ 21 Willie McCovey	30.00	13.50	3.70
□ 22 Jim Fregosi	10.00	4.50	1.25
□ 23 George Altman	10.00	4.50	1.25
□ 24 Floyd Robinson	10.00	4.50	1.25
□ 25 Chuck Hinton	10.00	4.50	1.25
□ 26 Ron Hunt	10.00	4.50	1.25
□ 27 Gary Peters	10.00	4.50	1.25
□ 28 Dick Ellsworth	10.00	4.50	1.25
□ 29 Elston Howard	15.00	6.75	1.85
□ 30 Brooks Robinson	50.00	22.00	6.25
□ 31 Frank Robinson	50.00	22.00	6.25
□ 32 Sandy Koufax	75.00	34.00	9.50
□ 33 Rocky Colavito	25.00	11.00	3.10
□ 34 Al Kaline	50.00	22.00	6.25
□ 35 Ken Boyer	12.50	5.50	1.55
□ 36 Tommy Davis	10.00	4.50	1.25

1965 Bazooka

ANGEL
JIM FREGOSI
L.A. ANGELS SS
NO. 22 OF 36 CARDS

The 1965 Bazooka set of 36 full color, blank backed, numbered cards was issued in panels of three on the backs of Bazooka bubble gum boxes. The individual cards measure 1 9/16" by 2 1/2" whereas the panels measure 2 1/2" by 4 11/16". As in the previous two years some of the players have the same numbers on their cards; however all pictures are different from the previous two years. Complete panels of three would have a value of 15 percent more than the sum of the individual cards (prices) on the panel and complete boxes would command a premium of another 40 percent above those prices.

	NRMT	VG-E	GOOD
COMPLETE INDIV. SET	750.00	350.00	95.00
COMMON CARD (1-36)	7.50	3.40	.95
☐ 1 Mickey Mantle	150.00	70.00	19.00
☐ 2 Larry Jackson	7.50	3.40	.95
☐ 3 Chuck Hinton	7.50	3.40	.95
☐ 4 Tony Oliva	10.00	4.50	1.25
☐ 5 Dean Chance	7.50	3.40	.95
☐ 6 Jim O'Toole	7.50	3.40	.95
☐ 7 Harmon Killebrew	30.00	13.50	3.70
☐ 8 Pete Ward	7.50	3.40	.95
☐ 9 Hank Aaron	75.00	34.00	9.50
☐ 10 Dick Radatz	7.50	3.40	.95
☐ 11 Boog Powell	10.00	4.50	1.25
☐ 12 Willie Mays	75.00	34.00	9.50
☐ 13 Bob Veale	7.50	3.40	.95
☐ 14 Bob Clemente	100.00	45.00	12.50
☐ 15 Johnny Callison	7.50	3.40	.95
☐ 16 Joe Torre	10.00	4.50	1.25
☐ 17 Billy Williams	20.00	9.00	2.50
☐ 18 Bob Chance	7.50	3.40	.95
☐ 19 Bob Aspromonte	7.50	3.40	.95
☐ 20 Joe Christopher	7.50	3.40	.95
☐ 21 Jim Bunning	20.00	9.00	2.50
☐ 22 Jim Fregosi	7.50	3.40	.95
☐ 23 Bob Gibson	30.00	13.50	3.70
☐ 24 Juan Marichal	30.00	13.50	3.70
☐ 25 Dave Wickersham	7.50	3.40	.95
☐ 26 Ron Hunt	7.50	3.40	.95
☐ 27 Gary Peters	7.50	3.40	.95
☐ 28 Ron Santo	15.00	6.75	1.85
☐ 29 Elston Howard	10.00	4.50	1.25
☐ 30 Brooks Robinson	35.00	16.00	4.40
☐ 31 Frank Robinson	35.00	16.00	4.40
☐ 32 Sandy Koufax	50.00	22.00	6.25
☐ 33 Rocky Colavito	15.00	6.75	1.85
☐ 34 Al Kaline	35.00	16.00	4.40
☐ 35 Ken Boyer	10.00	4.50	1.25
☐ 36 Tommy Davis	7.50	3.40	.95

1966 Bazooka

The 1966 Bazooka set of 48 full color, blank backed, numbered cards was issued in panels of three on the backs of Bazooka bubble gum boxes. The individual cardsd measure 1 9/16" by 2 1/2" whereas the complete panels measure 2 1/2" by 4 11/16". The set is distinguishable from the previous years by mention of "48 card set" at the bottom of the card. Complete panels of three would have a value of 15 percent more than the sum of the individual cards (prices) on the panel and complete boxes would command a premium of another 40 percent above those prices.

	NRMT	VG-E	GOOD
COMPLETE INDIV. SET	800.00	350.00	100.00
COMMON CARD (1-48)	7.50	3.40	.95
☐ 1 Sandy Koufax	50.00	22.00	6.25
☐ 2 Willie Horton	7.50	3.40	.95
☐ 3 Frank Howard	10.00	4.50	1.25
☐ 4 Richie Allen	10.00	4.50	1.25
☐ 5 Mel Stottlemyre	7.50	3.40	.95
☐ 6 Tony Conigliaro	12.50	5.50	1.55
☐ 7 Mickey Mantle	150.00	70.00	19.00
☐ 8 Leon Wagner	7.50	3.40	.95
☐ 9 Ed Kranepool	7.50	3.40	.95
☐ 10 Juan Marichal	30.00	13.50	3.70
☐ 11 Harmon Killebrew	30.00	13.50	3.70
☐ 12 Johnny Callison	7.50	3.40	.95
☐ 13 Roy McMillan	7.50	3.40	.95
☐ 14 Willie McCovey	30.00	13.50	3.70
☐ 15 Rocky Colavito	15.00	6.75	1.85
☐ 16 Willie Mays	75.00	34.00	9.50
☐ 17 Sam McDowell	7.50	3.40	.95
☐ 18 Vern Law	7.50	3.40	.95
☐ 19 Jim Fregosi	7.50	3.40	.95
☐ 20 Ron Fairly	7.50	3.40	.95
☐ 21 Bob Gibson	30.00	13.50	3.70
☐ 22 Carl Yastrzemski	40.00	18.00	5.00
☐ 23 Bill White	10.00	4.50	1.25
☐ 24 Bob Aspromonte	7.50	3.40	.95
☐ 25 Dean Chance	7.50	3.40	.95
☐ 26 Bob Clemente	100.00	45.00	12.50
☐ 27 Tony Cloninger	7.50	3.40	.95
☐ 28 Curt Blefary	7.50	3.40	.95
☐ 29 Milt Pappas	7.50	3.40	.95
☐ 30 Hank Aaron	75.00	34.00	9.50
☐ 31 Jim Bunning	15.00	6.75	1.85
☐ 32 Frank Robinson	30.00	13.50	3.70
☐ 33 Bill Skowron	10.00	4.50	1.25
☐ 34 Brooks Robinson	40.00	18.00	5.00
☐ 35 Jim Wynn	7.50	3.40	.95
☐ 36 Joe Torre	10.00	4.50	1.25
☐ 37 Jim Grant	7.50	3.40	.95
☐ 38 Pete Rose	75.00	34.00	9.50
☐ 39 Ron Santo	15.00	6.75	1.85
☐ 40 Tom Tresh	7.50	3.40	.95
☐ 41 Tony Oliva	12.50	5.50	1.55
☐ 42 Don Drysdale	25.00	11.00	3.10
☐ 43 Pete Richert	7.50	3.40	.95
☐ 44 Bert Campaneris	7.50	3.40	.95
☐ 45 Jim Maloney	7.50	3.40	.95
☐ 46 Al Kaline	35.00	16.00	4.40
☐ 47 Eddie Fisher	7.50	3.40	.95
☐ 48 Billy Williams	25.00	11.00	3.10

1967 Bazooka

The 1967 Bazooka set of 48 full color, blank backed, numbered cards was issued in panels of three on the backs of Bazooka bubble gum boxes. The individual cards measure 1 9/16" by 2 1/2" whereas the complete panels measure 2 1/2" by 4 11/16". This set is virtually identical to the 1966 set with the exception of ten new cards as replacements for ten 1966 cards. The remaining 38 cards are identical in pose and number. The replacement cards are listed in the checklist below with an asterisk. Complete panels of three would have a value of 15 percent more than the sum of the individual cards (prices) on the panel and complete boxes would command a premium of another 40 percent above those prices.

	NRMT	VG-E	GOOD
COMPLETE INDIV. SET	800.00	350.00	100.00
COMMON CARD (1-48)	7.50	3.40	.95
☐ 1 Rick Reichardt	7.50	3.40	.95
☐ 2 Tommy Agee	7.50	3.40	.95
☐ 3 Frank Howard	10.00	4.50	1.25
☐ 4 Richie Allen	10.00	4.50	1.25
☐ 5 Mel Stottlemyre	7.50	3.40	.95
☐ 6 Tony Conigliaro	12.50	5.50	1.55
☐ 7 Mickey Mantle	175.00	80.00	22.00
☐ 8 Leon Wagner	7.50	3.40	.95
☐ 9 Gary Peters	7.50	3.40	.95
☐ 10 Juan Marichal	25.00	11.00	3.10
☐ 11 Harmon Killebrew	25.00	11.00	3.10
☐ 12 Johnny Callison	7.50	3.40	.95
☐ 13 Denny McLain	12.50	5.50	1.55
☐ 14 Willie McCovey	20.00	9.00	2.50
☐ 15 Rocky Colavito	20.00	9.00	2.50
☐ 16 Willie Mays	85.00	38.00	10.50
☐ 17 Sam McDowell	7.50	3.40	.95
☐ 18 Jim Kaat	12.00	5.50	1.50
☐ 19 Jim Fregosi	7.50	3.40	.95
☐ 20 Ron Fairly	7.50	3.40	.95
☐ 21 Bob Gibson	25.00	11.00	3.10
☐ 22 Carl Yastrzemski	40.00	18.00	5.00
☐ 23 Bill White	10.00	4.50	1.25
☐ 24 Bob Aspromonte	7.50	3.40	.95
☐ 25 Dean Chance	7.50	3.40	.95
☐ 26 Bob Clemente	125.00	55.00	15.50
☐ 27 Tony Cloninger	7.50	3.40	.95
☐ 28 Curt Blefary	7.50	3.40	.95
☐ 29 Phil Regan	7.50	3.40	.95
☐ 30 Hank Aaron	75.00	34.00	9.50
☐ 31 Jim Bunning	20.00	9.00	2.50
☐ 32 Frank Robinson	30.00	13.50	3.70
☐ 33 Ken Boyer	10.00	4.50	1.25
☐ 34 Brooks Robinson	30.00	13.50	3.70
☐ 35 Jim Wynn	7.50	3.40	.95
☐ 36 Joe Torre	10.00	4.50	1.25
☐ 37 Tommy Davis	7.50	3.40	.95
☐ 38 Pete Rose	75.00	34.00	9.50
☐ 39 Ron Santo	15.00	6.75	1.85
☐ 40 Tom Tresh	7.50	3.40	.95
☐ 41 Tony Oliva	12.50	5.50	1.55
☐ 42 Don Drysdale	25.00	11.00	3.10
☐ 43 Pete Richert	7.50	3.40	.95
☐ 44 Bert Campaneris	7.50	3.40	.95
☐ 45 Jim Maloney	7.50	3.40	.95
☐ 46 Al Kaline	30.00	13.50	3.70
☐ 47 Matty Alou	7.50	3.40	.95
☐ 48 Billy Williams	20.00	9.00	2.50

1968 Bazooka

The 1968 Bazooka Tipps from the Topps is a set of 15 numbered boxes (measuring 5 1/2" by 6 1/4" when detached). each containing on the back panel (measuring 3" by 6 1/4") a baseball playing tip from a star, and on the side panels four mini cards, two per side, in full

color, measuring 1 1/4" by 3 1/8". Although the set contains a total of 60 of these small cards, 4 are repeated; therefore there are only 56 different small cards. Some collectors cut the panels into individual card; however most collectors retain entire panels or boxes. The prices in the checklist therfore reflect only the values of the complete boxes.

	NRMT	VG-E	GOOD
COMPLETE BOX SET	1250.00	550.00	160.00
COMMON BOX (1-15)	60.00	27.00	7.50
COMMON INDIV. PLAYER	3.00	1.35	.35
☐ 1 Maury Wills: Bunting	150.00	70.00	19.00
Al Kaline			
Paul Casanova			
Clete Boyer			
Tom Seaver			
☐ 2 C.Yastrzemski: Batting	100.00	45.00	12.50
Jim Hunter			
Bill Freehan			
Matty Alou			
Jim Lefebvre			
☐ 3 B.Campaneris: Stealing	60.00	27.00	7.50
Tim McCarver			
Bob Veale			
Frank Robinson			
Bobby Knoop			
☐ 4 Maury Wills: Sliding	60.00	27.00	7.50
Ken Holtzman			
Jose Azcue			
Tony Conigliaro			
Bill White			
☐ 5 J.Javier: Double Play	150.00	70.00	19.00
Juan Marichal			
Rico Petrocelli			
Joe Pepitone			
Hank Aaron			
☐ 6 O.Cepeda: 1st Base	100.00	45.00	12.50
Ron Santo			
Don Drysdale			
Pete Rose			
Tommie Agee			
☐ 7 B.Mazeroski: 2nd Base	60.00	27.00	7.50
John Roseboro			
Jim Bunning			
Frank Howard			
George Scott			
☐ 8 B.Robinson: 3rd Base	75.00	34.00	9.50
Tony Gonzalez			
Jim McGlothlin			
Wille Horton			
Harmon Killebrew			
☐ 9 Jim Fregosi: Shortstop	60.00	27.00	7.50
Max Alvis			
Bob Gibson			
Tony Oliva			
Vada Pinson			
☐ 10 Joe Torre: Catching	60.00	27.00	7.50
Dean Chance			
Fergie Jenkins			
Tommy Davis			
Rick Monday			
☐ 11 Jim Lonborg: Pitching	250.00	110.00	31.00
Joel Horlen			
Jim Wynn			
Curt Flood			
Mickey Mantle			
☐ 12 Mike McCormick:	60.00	27.00	7.50
Fielding Pitcher			
Don Mincher			
Tony Perez			
Roberto Clemente			
Al Downing			
☐ 13 F.Crosetti: Coaching	60.00	27.00	7.50
Rod Carew			
Don Wilson			
Ron Swoboda			
Willie McCovey			
☐ 14 Willie Mays: Outfield	150.00	70.00	19.00
Richie Allen			
Gary Peters			
Billy Williams			
Rusty Staub			
☐ 15 L.Brock: Base Running	150.00	70.00	19.00
Tommie Agee			
Pete Rose			
Ron Santo			
Don Drysdale			

1969-70 Bazooka

The 1969-70 Bazooka Baseball Extra News set contains 12 complete panels, each comprising a large action shot of a significant event in

baseball history and four small cards, comparable to those in the Tipps from the Topps set of 1968, of Hall of Famers. Although some collectors cut the panels into individual cards (measuring 3" by 6 1/4" or 1 1/4" by 3 1/8"), most collectors retain the entire panel, or box (measuring 5 1/2" by 6 1/4"). The prices in the checklist below reflect the value for the entire box, as these cards are more widely seen and collected as complete panels or boxes.

	NRMT	VG-E	GOOD
COMPLETE PANEL SET	500.00	220.00	60.00
COMMON PANEL (1-12)	35.00	16.00	4.40
COMMON INDIV. PLAYER	.50	.23	.06
☐ 1 No-Hit Duel by	50.00	22.00	6.25
Fred Toney			
Hippo Vaughn:			
Ty Cobb			
Willie Keeler			
Mordecai Brown			
Eddie Plank			
☐ 2 Alexander Conquers	35.00	16.00	4.40
Yankees:			
Al Simmons			
Ban Johnson			
Walter Johnson			
Rogers Hornsby			
☐ 3 Yanks' Lazzeri Sets	35.00	16.00	4.40
AL Record:			
Christy Mathewson			
Chief Bender			
Grover Alexander			
Cy Young			
☐ 4 Homerun Almost Hit	50.00	22.00	6.25
Out of Stadium:			
Lou Gehrig			
Hugh Duffy			
Tris Speaker			
Joe Tinker			
☐ 5 Four Consecutive	100.00	45.00	12.50
Homers by Lou:			
John McGraw			
Frank Chance			
Babe Ruth			
Mickey Cochrane			
☐ 6 No-Hit Game by	35.00	16.00	4.40
Walter Johnson:			
Cy Young			
Walter Johnson			
Johnny Evers			
John McGraw			
☐ 7 Twelve RBIs by	60.00	27.00	7.50
Jim Bottomley:			
Johnny Evers			
Eddie Collins			
Lou Gehrig			
Ty Cobb			
☐ 8 Ty Cobb Ties Record:	50.00	22.00	6.25
Honus Wagner			
Mickey Cochrane			
Eddie Collins			
Mel Ott			
☐ 9 Babe Ruth Hits Three	60.00	27.00	7.50
Homers in Game:			
Cap Anson			
Tris Speaker			
Jack Chesbro			
Al Simmons			
☐ 10 Babe Ruth Calls Shot	60.00	27.00	7.50
in Series Game:			
Rabbit Maranville			
Ed Walsh			
Nap Lajoie			
Connie Mack			
☐ 11 Babe Ruth's 60th Homer	60.00	27.00	7.50
Sets New Record:			
Joe Tinker			
Nap Lajoie			
Mel Ott			
Frank Chance			
☐ 12 Double Shutout by	35.00	16.00	4.40
Ed Reulbach:			
Rogers Hornsby			
Rabbit Maranville			
Christy Mathewson			
Honus Wagner			

1971 Bazooka Numbered Test

This was supposedly a test issue which was different from the more common unnumbered set and much more difficult to find. There are 48 cards (16 panels) in this numbered set whereas the unnumbered set had only 12 panels or 36 individual cards. Individual cards

measure approximately 2" by 2 5/8" whereas the panels measure 2 5/8" by 5 15/16". Complete panels of three would have a value of 10 percent more than the sum of the individual cards (prices) on the panel and complete boxes would command a premium of another 30 percent above those prices.

	NRMT	VG-E	GOOD
COMPLETE SET (48)	600.00	275.00	75.00
COMMON CARD (1-48)	4.00	1.80	.50
☐ 1 Tim McCarver	10.00	4.50	1.25
☐ 2 Frank Robinson	35.00	16.00	4.40
☐ 3 Bill Mazeroski	10.00	4.50	1.25
☐ 4 Willie McCovey	20.00	9.00	2.50
☐ 5 Carl Yastrzemski	30.00	13.50	3.70
☐ 6 Clyde Wright	4.00	1.80	.50
☐ 7 Jim Merritt	4.00	1.80	.50
☐ 8 Luis Aparicio	20.00	9.00	2.50
☐ 9 Bobby Murcer	5.00	2.20	.60
☐ 10 Rico Petrocelli	4.00	1.80	.50
☐ 11 Sam McDowell	4.00	1.80	.50
☐ 12 Clarence Gaston	4.00	1.80	.50
☐ 13 Fergie Jenkins	15.00	6.75	1.85
☐ 14 Al Kaline	35.00	16.00	4.40
☐ 15 Ken Harrelson	4.00	1.80	.50
☐ 16 Tommie Agee	4.00	1.80	.50
☐ 17 Harmon Killebrew	15.00	6.75	1.85
☐ 18 Reggie Jackson	45.00	20.00	5.50
☐ 19 Juan Marichal	20.00	9.00	2.50
☐ 20 Frank Howard	5.00	2.20	.60
☐ 21 Bill Melton	4.00	1.80	.50
☐ 22 Brooks Robinson	35.00	16.00	4.40
☐ 23 Hank Aaron	45.00	20.00	5.50
☐ 24 Larry Dierker	4.00	1.80	.50
☐ 25 Jim Fregosi	4.00	1.80	.50
☐ 26 Billy Williams	20.00	9.00	2.50
☐ 27 Dave McNally	4.00	1.80	.50
☐ 28 Rico Carty	4.00	1.80	.50
☐ 29 Johnny Bench	40.00	18.00	5.00
☐ 30 Tommy Harper	4.00	1.80	.50
☐ 31 Bert Campaneris	4.00	1.80	.50
☐ 32 Pete Rose	50.00	22.00	6.25
☐ 33 Orlando Cepeda	5.00	2.20	.60
☐ 34 Maury Wills	5.00	2.20	.60
☐ 35 Tom Seaver	40.00	18.00	5.00
☐ 36 Tony Oliva	10.00	4.50	1.25
☐ 37 Bill Freehan	4.00	1.80	.50
☐ 38 Roberto Clemente	85.00	38.00	10.50
☐ 39 Claude Osteen	4.00	1.80	.50
☐ 40 Rusty Staub	5.00	2.20	.60
☐ 41 Bob Gibson	20.00	9.00	2.50
☐ 42 Amos Otis	4.00	1.80	.50
☐ 43 Jim Wynn	10.00	4.50	1.25
☐ 44 Rich Allen	12.50	5.50	1.55
☐ 45 Tony Conigliaro	12.50	5.50	1.55
☐ 46 Randy Hundley	4.00	1.80	.50
☐ 47 Willie Mays	50.00	22.00	6.25
☐ 48 Jim Hunter	20.00	9.00	2.50

1971 Bazooka Unnumbered

The 1971 Bazooka set of 36 full-color, unnumbered cards was issued in 12 panels of three cards each on the backs of boxes containing one cent Bazooka bubble gum. Individual cards measure approximately 2" by 2 5/8" whereas the panels measure 2 5/8" by 5 15/16". The panels are numbered in the checklist alphabetically by the player's last name on the left most card of the panel. Complete panels of three would have a value of 10 percent more than the sum of the individual cards (prices) on the panel and complete boxes would command a premium of another 30 percent above those prices.

	NRMT	VG-E	GOOD
COMPLETE INDIV.SET	350.00	160.00	45.00
COMMON CARD (1-36)	3.00	1.35	.35
☐ 1 Tommie Agee	3.00	1.35	.35
☐ 2 Harmon Killebrew	15.00	6.75	1.85
☐ 3 Reggie Jackson	30.00	13.50	3.70
☐ 4 Bert Campaneris	3.00	1.35	.35
☐ 5 Pete Rose	30.00	13.50	3.70
☐ 6 Orlando Cepeda	5.00	2.20	.60
☐ 7 Rico Carty	3.00	1.35	.35
☐ 8 Johnny Bench	25.00	11.00	3.10
☐ 9 Tommy Harper	3.00	1.35	.35
☐ 10 Bill Freehan	3.00	1.35	.35
☐ 11 Roberto Clemente	60.00	27.00	7.50
☐ 12 Claude Osteen	3.00	1.35	.35
☐ 13 Jim Fregosi	3.00	1.35	.35
☐ 14 Billy Williams	15.00	6.75	1.85
☐ 15 Dave McNally	3.00	1.35	.35
☐ 16 Randy Hundley	3.00	1.35	.35
☐ 17 Willie Mays	35.00	16.00	4.40
☐ 18 Jim Hunter	15.00	6.75	1.85
☐ 19 Juan Marichal	20.00	9.00	2.50
☐ 20 Frank Howard	4.00	1.80	.50
☐ 21 Bill Melton	3.00	1.35	.35
☐ 22 Willie McCovey	20.00	9.00	2.50
☐ 23 Carl Yastrzemski	25.00	11.00	3.10
☐ 24 Clyde Wright	3.00	1.35	.35
☐ 25 Jim Merritt	3.00	1.35	.35
☐ 26 Luis Aparicio	15.00	6.75	1.85
☐ 27 Bobby Murcer	4.00	1.80	.50
☐ 28 Rico Petrocelli	3.00	1.35	.35
☐ 29 Sam McDowell	3.00	1.35	.35
☐ 30 Clarence Gaston	3.00	1.35	.35
☐ 31 Brooks Robinson	20.00	9.00	2.50
☐ 32 Hank Aaron	30.00	13.50	3.70
☐ 33 Larry Dierker	3.00	1.35	.35
☐ 34 Rusty Staub	4.00	1.80	.50
☐ 35 Bob Gibson	20.00	9.00	2.50
☐ 36 Amos Otis	3.00	1.35	.35

1988 Bazooka

There are 22 standard-size cards in the set. The cards have extra thick white borders. Card backs are printed in blue and red on white card stock. Some sets can also be found with gray backs; these gray backs carry no additional value premium. Cards are numbered on the back; they were numbered by Topps alphabetically. The word "Bazooka" only appears faintly as background for the statistics on the back of the card. Cards were available inside specially marked boxes of Bazooka gum retailing between 59 cents and 99 cents. The emphasis in the player selection for this set is on young stars of baseball.

	MINT	NRMT	EXC
COMPLETE SET (22)	8.00	3.60	1.00
COMMON CARD (1-22)	.20	.09	.03
☐ 1 George Bell	.20	.09	.03
☐ 2 Wade Boggs	.50	.23	.06
☐ 3 Jose Canseco	.75	.35	.09
☐ 4 Roger Clemens	.60	.25	.07
☐ 5 Vince Coleman	.20	.09	.03
☐ 6 Eric Davis	.20	.09	.03
☐ 7 Tony Fernandez	.20	.09	.03
☐ 8 Dwight Gooden	.40	.18	.05
☐ 9 Tony Gwynn	1.00	.45	.12
☐ 10 Wally Joyner	.40	.18	.05
☐ 11 Don Mattingly	1.00	.45	.12
☐ 12 Willie McGee	.20	.09	.03
☐ 13 Mark McGwire	1.25	.55	.16
☐ 14 Kirby Puckett	1.00	.45	.12
☐ 15 Tim Raines	.40	.18	.05
☐ 16 Dave Righetti	.20	.09	.03
☐ 17 Cal Ripken	2.00	.90	.25
☐ 18 Juan Samuel	.20	.09	.03
☐ 19 Ryne Sandberg	.75	.35	.09
☐ 20 Benito Santiago	.20	.09	.03
☐ 21 Darryl Strawberry	.40	.18	.05
☐ 22 Todd Worrell	.20	.09	.03

1989 Bazooka

The 1989 Bazooka Shining Stars set contains 22 standard-size cards. The fronts have white borders and a large yellow stripe; the vertically oriented backs are pink, red and white and have career stats. The cards were inserted one per box of Bazooka Gum. The set is sequenced in alphabetical order.

	MINT	NRMT	EXC
COMPLETE SET (22)	8.00	3.60	1.00
COMMON CARD (1-22)	.20	.09	.03
☐ 1 Tim Belcher	.20	.09	.03
☐ 2 Damon Berryhill	.20	.09	.03
☐ 3 Wade Boggs	.50	.23	.06
☐ 4 Jay Buhner	.50	.23	.06
☐ 5 Jose Canseco	.75	.35	.09
☐ 6 Vince Coleman	.20	.09	.03
☐ 7 Cecil Espy	.20	.09	.03
☐ 8 Dave Gallagher	.20	.09	.03
☐ 9 Ron Gant	.50	.23	.06
☐ 10 Kirk Gibson	.40	.18	.05
☐ 11 Paul Gibson	.20	.09	.03
☐ 12 Mark Grace	.75	.35	.09
☐ 13 Tony Gwynn	1.00	.45	.12
☐ 14 Rickey Henderson	.50	.23	.06
☐ 15 Orel Hershiser	.40	.18	.05
☐ 16 Gregg Jefferies	.75	.35	.09
☐ 17 Ricky Jordan	.20	.09	.03
☐ 18 Chris Sabo	.20	.09	.03
☐ 19 Gary Sheffield	1.25	.55	.16
☐ 20 Darryl Strawberry	.40	.18	.05
☐ 21 Frank Viola	.20	.09	.03
☐ 22 Walt Weiss	.20	.09	.03

1990 Bazooka

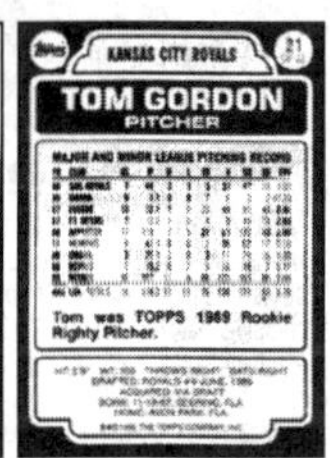

The 1990 Bazooka Shining Stars set contains 22 standard-size cards with a mix of award winners, league leaders, and young stars. This set was issued by Topps using the Bazooka name. Card backs were printed in blue and red on white card stock. The word "Bazooka" appears faintly as background for the statistics on the back of the card as well as appearing prominently on the front of each card.

	MINT	NRMT	EXC
COMPLETE SET (22)	8.00	3.60	1.00
COMMON CARD (1-22)	.15	.07	.02
☐ 1 Kevin Mitchell	.25	.11	.03
☐ 2 Robin Yount	.50	.23	.06
☐ 3 Mark Davis	.15	.07	.02
☐ 4 Bret Saberhagen	.25	.11	.03
☐ 5 Fred McGriff	.75	.35	.09
☐ 6 Tony Gwynn	1.25	.55	.16
☐ 7 Kirby Puckett	1.25	.55	.16
☐ 8 Vince Coleman	.15	.07	.02
☐ 9 Rickey Henderson	.75	.35	.09
☐ 10 Ben McDonald	.50	.23	.06
☐ 11 Gregg Olson	.15	.07	.02
☐ 12 Todd Zeile	.25	.11	.03
☐ 13 Carlos Martinez	.15	.07	.02
☐ 14 Gregg Jefferies	.25	.11	.03
☐ 15 Craig Worthington	.15	.07	.02
☐ 16 Gary Sheffield	1.00	.45	.12
☐ 17 Greg Briley	.15	.07	.02
☐ 18 Ken Griffey Jr.	4.00	1.80	.50
☐ 19 Jerome Walton	.15	.07	.02
☐ 20 Bob Geren	.15	.07	.02
☐ 21 Tom Gordon	.15	.07	.02
☐ 22 Jim Abbott	.25	.11	.03

1991 Bazooka

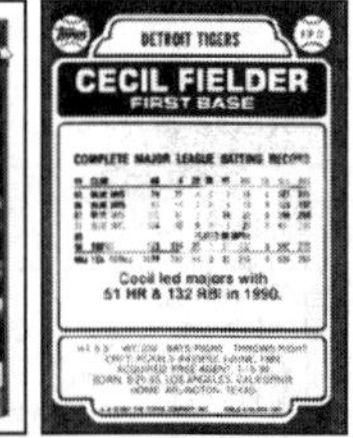

The 1991 Bazooka Shining Stars set contains 22 standard-size cards featuring league leaders and rookie sensations. The set was produced by Topps for Bazooka. One card was inserted in each box of Bazooka Bubble Gum. The fronts are similar to the Topps regular issue, only that the "Shining Star" emblem appears at the card top and the Bazooka logo overlays the lower right corner of the picture. In a blue and red design on white card stock, the backs have statistics and biography.

	MINT	NRMT	EXC
COMPLETE SET (22)	8.00	3.60	1.00
COMMON CARD (1-22)	.15	.07	.02
☐ 1 Barry Bonds	.75	.35	.09
☐ 2 Rickey Henderson	.50	.23	.06
☐ 3 Bob Welch	.15	.07	.02
☐ 4 Doug Drabek	.15	.07	.02
☐ 5 Alex Fernandez	.75	.35	.09
☐ 6 Jose Offerman	.15	.07	.02
☐ 7 Frank Thomas	3.00	1.35	.35
☐ 8 Cecil Fielder	.30	.14	.04
☐ 9 Ryne Sandberg	1.25	.55	.16
☐ 10 George Brett	1.25	.55	.16
☐ 11 Willie McGee	.15	.07	.02
☐ 12 Vince Coleman	.15	.07	.02
☐ 13 Hal Morris	.15	.07	.02
☐ 14 Delino DeShields	.15	.07	.02
☐ 15 Robin Ventura	.75	.35	.09
☐ 16 Jeff Huson	.15	.07	.02
☐ 17 Felix Jose	.15	.07	.02
☐ 18 Dave Justice	.75	.35	.09
☐ 19 Larry Walker	.75	.35	.09
☐ 20 Sandy Alomar Jr.	.30	.14	.04
☐ 21 Kevin Appier	.50	.23	.06
☐ 22 Scott Radinsky	.15	.07	.02

1992 Bazooka Quadracard '53 Archives

This 22-card set was produced by Topps for Bazooka, and the set is subtitled "Topps Archives Quadracard" on the top of the backs. Each standard-size card features four micro-reproductions of 1953 Topps baseball cards. These front and back borders of the cards are blue.

	MINT	NRMT	EXC
COMPLETE SET (22)	12.00	5.50	1.50
COMMON CARD (1-22)	.35	.16	.04
☐ 1 Joe Adcock Bob Lemon Willie Mays Vic Wertz	1.00	.45	.12
☐ 2 Carl Furillo Don Newcombe Phil Rizzuto Hank Sauer	.50	.23	.06
☐ 3 Ferris Fain John Logan Ed Mathews Bobby Shantz	.50	.23	.06
☐ 4 Yogi Berra Del Crandall Howie Pollet Gene Woodling	.75	.35	.09
☐ 5 Richie Ashburn Leo Durocher MG Allie Reynolds Early Wynn	1.00	.45	.12
☐ 6 Hank Aaron Ray Boone Luke Easter Dick Williams	1.50	.70	.19
☐ 7 Ralph Branca Bob Feller Rogers Hornsby Bobby Thomson	.75	.35	.09
☐ 8 Jim Gilliam Billy Martin Minnie Minoso Hal Newhouser	.50	.23	.06
☐ 9 Smoky Burgess John Mize Preacher Roe Warren Spahn	.50	.23	.06
☐ 10 Monte Irvin Bobo Newsom Duke Snider Wes Westrum	.75	.35	.09
☐ 11 Carl Erskine Jackie Jensen George Kell Red Schoendienst	.50	.23	.06
☐ 12 Bill Bruton Whitey Ford Ed Lopat Mickey Vernon	.50	.23	.06
☐ 13 Joe Black Lew Burdette Johnny Pesky Enos Slaughter	.35	.16	.04
☐ 14 Gus Bell Mike Garcia Mel Parnell Jackie Robinson	.75	.35	.09
☐ 15 Alvin Dark Dick Groat	.50	.23	.06

Card	MINT	NRMT	EXC
Pee Wee Reese			
John Sain			
☐ 16 Gil Hodges	.50	.23	.06
Sal Maglie			
Wilmer Mizell			
Billy Pierce			
☐ 17 Nellie Fox	75.00	34.00	9.50
Ralph Kiner			
Ted Kluszewski			
Eddie Stanky			
☐ 18 Ewell Blackwell	.50	.23	.06
Vern Law			
Satchel Paige			
Jim Wilson			
☐ 19 Lou Boudreau MG	.35	.16	.04
Roy Face			
Harvey Haddix			
Bill Rigney			
☐ 20 Roy Campanella	.50	.23	.06
Walt Dropo			
Harvey Kuenn			
Al Rosen			
☐ 21 Joe Garagiola	1.00	.45	.12
Robin Roberts			
Casey Stengel MG			
Hoyt Wilhelm			
☐ 22 John Antonelli	1.00	.45	.12
Bob Friend			
Dixie Walker CO			
Ted Williams			

1993 Bazooka Team USA

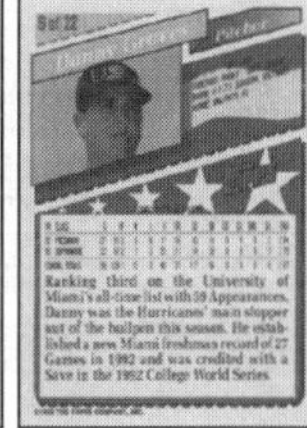

Originally available only in a special Bazooka collector's box, these 22 standard-size cards were produced by Topps and feature the 1993 Team USA players. The card design is similar to that of the '93 Topps series. The white-bordered fronts feature posed color player photos. The player's name appears in a blue stripe near the bottom; the Bazooka logo appears at the upper right. The colorful white-bordered backs carry a color head shot, biography, statistics, and career highlights. The cards are numbered on the back as "X of 22."

	MINT	NRMT	EXC
COMPLETE SET (22)	8.00	3.60	1.00
COMMON CARD (1-22)	.15	.07	.02
☐ 1 Terry Harvey	.15	.07	.02
☐ 2 Dante Powell	1.50	.70	.19
☐ 3 Andy Barkett	.15	.07	.02
☐ 4 Steve Reich	.15	.07	.02
☐ 5 Charlie Nelson	.30	.14	.04
☐ 6 Todd Walker	2.50	1.10	.30
☐ 7 Dustin Hermanson	.50	.23	.06
☐ 8 Pat Clougherty	.15	.07	.02
☐ 9 Danny Graves	.15	.07	.02
☐ 10 Paul Wilson	1.00	.45	.12
☐ 11 Todd Helton	2.50	1.10	.30
☐ 12 Russ Johnson	.75	.35	.09
☐ 13 Darren Grass	.30	.14	.04
☐ 14 A.J. Hinch	.50	.23	.06
☐ 15 Mark Merila	.15	.07	.02
☐ 16 John Powell	.30	.14	.04
☐ 17 Bob Scafa	.15	.07	.02
☐ 18 Matt Beaumont	.50	.23	.06
☐ 19 Todd Dunn	.15	.07	.02
☐ 20 Mike Martin	.30	.14	.04
☐ 21 Carlton Loewer	.50	.23	.06
☐ 22 Bret Wagner	.50	.23	.06

1995 Bazooka

This 132-card standard-size set was issued by Topps. For the previous 35 years, Topps had used the Bazooka label to issue various cards, but this was the first time a mainstream set was issued in pack form. The five-card packs, with a suggested retail price of 50 cents, included an info card as well as a piece of bubble gum. The fronts have an action photo surrounded by white borders. The "Bazooka" label is in the upper left corner, while the player's name and team are on the bottom of the card. The player's position is identified on the right. The backs have a game as well as his previous season and career stats. There are no Rookie Cards in this set. Factory sets included five Red Hots.

	MINT	NRMT	EXC
COMPLETE SET (132)	10.00	4.50	1.25
COMPLETE FACT.SET (137)	15.00	6.75	1.85
COMMON CARD (1-132)	.05	.02	.01
☐ 1 Greg Maddux	1.25	.55	.16
☐ 2 Cal Ripken Jr.	1.50	.70	.19
☐ 3 Lee Smith	.15	.07	.02
☐ 4 Sammy Sosa	.30	.14	.04
☐ 5 Jason Bere	.05	.02	.01
☐ 6 David Justice	.15	.07	.02
☐ 7 Kevin Mitchell	.05	.02	.01
☐ 8 Ozzie Guillen	.05	.02	.01
☐ 9 Roger Clemens	.40	.18	.05
☐ 10 Mike Mussina	.40	.18	.05
☐ 11 Sandy Alomar Jr.	.05	.02	.01
☐ 12 Cecil Fielder	.15	.07	.02
☐ 13 Dennis Martinez	.05	.02	.01
☐ 14 Randy Myers	.05	.02	.01
☐ 15 Jay Buhner	.30	.14	.04
☐ 16 Ivan Rodriguez	.50	.23	.06
☐ 17 Mo Vaughn	.50	.23	.06
☐ 18 Ryan Klesko	.30	.14	.04
☐ 19 Chuck Finley	.05	.02	.01
☐ 20 Barry Bonds	.50	.23	.06
☐ 21 Dennis Eckersley	.15	.07	.02
☐ 22 Kenny Lofton	.50	.23	.06
☐ 23 Rafael Palmeiro	.30	.14	.04
☐ 24 Mike Stanley	.05	.02	.01
☐ 25 Gregg Jefferies	.05	.02	.01
☐ 26 Robin Ventura	.15	.07	.02
☐ 27 Mark McGwire	.60	.25	.07
☐ 28 Ozzie Smith	.50	.23	.06
☐ 29 Troy Neel	.05	.02	.01
☐ 30 Tony Gwynn	.75	.35	.09
☐ 31 Ken Griffey Jr.	2.00	.90	.25
☐ 32 Will Clark	.30	.14	.04
☐ 33 Craig Biggio	.15	.07	.02
☐ 34 Shawon Dunston	.05	.02	.01
☐ 35 Wilson Alvarez	.05	.02	.01
☐ 36 Bobby Bonilla	.15	.07	.02
☐ 37 Marquis Grissom	.15	.07	.02
☐ 38 Ben McDonald	.05	.02	.01
☐ 39 Delino DeShields	.05	.02	.01
☐ 40 Barry Larkin	.30	.14	.04
☐ 41 John Olerud	.05	.02	.01
☐ 42 Jose Canseco	.30	.14	.04
☐ 43 Greg Vaughn	.05	.02	.01
☐ 44 Gary Sheffield	.30	.14	.04
☐ 45 Paul O'Neill	.15	.07	.02
☐ 46 Bob Hamelin	.05	.02	.01
☐ 47 Don Mattingly	1.00	.45	.12
☐ 48 John Franco	.05	.02	.01
☐ 49 Bret Boone	.05	.02	.01
☐ 50 Rick Aguilera	.05	.02	.01
☐ 51 Tim Wallach	.05	.02	.01
☐ 52 Roberto Kelly	.05	.02	.01
☐ 53 Danny Tartabull	.05	.02	.01
☐ 54 Randy Johnson	.30	.14	.04
☐ 55 Greg McMichael	.05	.02	.01
☐ 56 Bip Roberts	.05	.02	.01
☐ 57 David Cone	.15	.07	.02
☐ 58 Raul Mondesi	.30	.14	.04
☐ 59 Travis Fryman	.15	.07	.02
☐ 60 Jeff Conine	.15	.07	.02
☐ 61 Jeff Bagwell	.75	.35	.09
☐ 62 Rickey Henderson	.30	.14	.04
☐ 63 Fred McGriff	.30	.14	.04
☐ 64 Matt Williams	.30	.14	.04
☐ 65 Rick Wilkins	.05	.02	.01
☐ 66 Eric Karros	.15	.07	.02
☐ 67 Mel Rojas	.05	.02	.01
☐ 68 Juan Gonzalez	1.00	.45	.12
☐ 69 Chuck Carr	.05	.02	.01
☐ 70 Moises Alou	.15	.07	.02
☐ 71 Mark Grace	.30	.14	.04
☐ 72 Alex Fernandez	.15	.07	.02
☐ 73 Rod Beck	.05	.02	.01
☐ 74 Ray Lankford	.15	.07	.02
☐ 75 Dean Palmer	.05	.02	.01
☐ 76 Joe Carter	.15	.07	.02
☐ 77 Mike Piazza	1.25	.55	.16
☐ 78 Eddie Murray	.50	.23	.06
☐ 79 Dave Nilsson	.05	.02	.01
☐ 80 Brett Butler	.15	.07	.02
☐ 81 Roberto Alomar	.40	.18	.05
☐ 82 Jeff Kent	.05	.02	.01
☐ 83 Andres Galarraga	.30	.14	.04
☐ 84 Brady Anderson	.30	.14	.04
☐ 85 Jimmy Key	.05	.02	.01
☐ 86 Bret Saberhagen	.05	.02	.01
☐ 87 Chili Davis	.05	.02	.01
☐ 88 Jose Rijo	.05	.02	.01
☐ 89 Wade Boggs	.30	.14	.04
☐ 90 Len Dykstra	.15	.07	.02
☐ 91 Steve Howe	.05	.02	.01
☐ 92 Hal Morris	.05	.02	.01
☐ 93 Larry Walker	.30	.14	.04
☐ 94 Jeff Montgomery	.05	.02	.01
☐ 95 Wil Cordero	.05	.02	.01
☐ 96 Jay Bell	.05	.02	.01
☐ 97 Tom Glavine	.30	.14	.04
☐ 98 Chris Hoiles	.05	.02	.01
☐ 99 Steve Avery	.05	.02	.01
☐ 100 Ruben Sierra	.05	.02	.01
☐ 101 Mickey Tettleton	.05	.02	.01
☐ 102 Paul Molitor	.40	.18	.05
☐ 103 Carlos Baerga	.15	.07	.02
☐ 104 Walt Weiss	.05	.02	.01
☐ 105 Darren Daulton	.15	.07	.02
☐ 106 Jack McDowell	.05	.02	.01
☐ 107 Doug Drabek	.05	.02	.01
☐ 108 Mark Langston	.05	.02	.01
☐ 109 Manny Ramirez	.50	.23	.06
☐ 110 Kevin Appier	.15	.07	.02
☐ 111 Andy Benes	.05	.02	.01
☐ 112 Chuck Knoblauch	.30	.14	.04
☐ 113 Kirby Puckett	.75	.35	.09
☐ 114 Dante Bichette	.30	.14	.04
☐ 115 Deion Sanders	.30	.14	.04
☐ 116 Albert Belle	.75	.35	.09
☐ 117 Todd Zeile	.05	.02	.01
☐ 118 Devon White	.15	.07	.02
☐ 119 Tim Salmon	.30	.14	.04
☐ 120 Frank Thomas	2.00	.90	.25
☐ 121 John Wetteland	.15	.07	.02
☐ 122 James Mouton	.05	.02	.01
☐ 123 Javier Lopez	.30	.14	.04
☐ 124 Carlos Delgado	.15	.07	.02
☐ 125 Cliff Floyd	.15	.07	.02
☐ 126 Alex Gonzalez	.15	.07	.02
☐ 127 Billy Ashley	.05	.02	.01
☐ 128 Rondell White	.15	.07	.02
☐ 129 Rico Brogna	.05	.02	.01
☐ 130 Melvin Nieves	.15	.07	.02
☐ 131 Jose Oliva	.05	.02	.01
☐ 132 J.R. Phillips	.05	.02	.01

1995 Bazooka Red Hot

This 22-card standard-size set, featuring some of the most popular players, is similar to the regular issue. Differences between these cards and the regular issue include the photo being shaded in a red background, the position is also in red and the player's name is stamped in gold foil. The backs are numbered with an "RH" prefix.

	MINT	NRMT	EXC
COMPLETE SET (22)	20.00	9.00	2.50
COMMON CARD (1-22)	.15	.07	.02
☐ RH1 Greg Maddux	2.50	1.10	.30
☐ RH2 Cal Ripken Jr.	3.00	1.35	.35
☐ RH3 Barry Bonds	1.00	.45	.12
☐ RH4 Kenny Lofton	1.00	.45	.12
☐ RH5 Mike Stanley	.15	.07	.02
☐ RH6 Tony Gwynn	1.50	.70	.19
☐ RH7 Ken Griffey Jr.	4.00	1.80	.50
☐ RH8 Barry Larkin	.60	.25	.07
☐ RH9 Jose Canseco	.60	.25	.07
☐ RH10 Paul O'Neill	.30	.14	.04
☐ RH11 Randy Johnson	.60	.25	.07
☐ RH12 David Cone	.30	.14	.04
☐ RH13 Jeff Bagwell	1.50	.70	.19
☐ RH14 Matt Williams	.60	.25	.07
☐ RH15 Mike Piazza	2.50	1.10	.30
☐ RH16 Roberto Alomar	.75	.35	.09
☐ RH17 Jimmy Key	.15	.07	.02
☐ RH18 Wade Boggs	.60	.25	.07
☐ RH19 Paul Molitor	.75	.35	.09
☐ RH20 Carlos Baerga	.30	.14	.04
☐ RH21 Albert Belle	1.50	.70	.19
☐ RH22 Frank Thomas	4.00	1.80	.50

1996 Bazooka

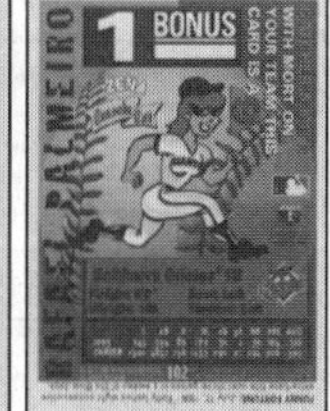

The 1996 Bazooka standard-size set was issued in one series totalling 132 cards. The 5-card packs retail for $.50 each. The set contains baseball's best rookies, rising stars and veterans. The card fronts feature an exciting full-color photo of the player. The back of each card contains one of five different Bazooka Joe characters, along with the Bazooka Ball flipping game, the player's biographical data and 1995 career statistics. Additionally, every card contains a Funny Fortune, which predicts the fate of each player on a particular date. Packs contain five cards plus one chunk of Bazooka gum. Finally, each factory set also included a reprint of Mickey Mantle's 1959 Bazooka card.

	MINT	NRMT	EXC
COMP.FACT.SET (133)	12.00	5.50	1.50
COMPLETE SET (132)	10.00	4.50	1.25
COMMON CARD (1-132)	.05	.02	.01
☐ 1 Ken Griffey, Jr.	2.00	.90	.25
☐ 2 J.T. Snow	.05	.02	.01
☐ 3 Rondell White	.15	.07	.02
☐ 4 Reggie Sanders	.15	.07	.02
☐ 5 Jeff Montgomery	.05	.02	.01
☐ 6 Mike Stanley	.05	.02	.01
☐ 7 Bernie Williams	.40	.18	.05
☐ 8 Mike Piazza	1.25	.55	.16
☐ 9 Brian L.Hunter	.15	.07	.02
☐ 10 Len Dykstra	.15	.07	.02
☐ 11 Ray Lankford	.15	.07	.02
☐ 12 Kenny Lofton	.50	.23	.06
☐ 13 Robin Ventura	.15	.07	.02
☐ 14 Devon White	.05	.02	.01
☐ 15 Cal Ripken	1.50	.70	.19
☐ 16 Heathcliff Slocumb	.05	.02	.01
☐ 17 Ryan Klesko	.30	.14	.04
☐ 18 Terry Steinbach	.05	.02	.01
☐ 19 Travis Fryman	.15	.07	.02
☐ 20 Sammy Sosa	.30	.14	.04
☐ 21 Jim Thome	.40	.18	.05
☐ 22 Kenny Rogers	.05	.02	.01
☐ 23 Don Mattingly	1.00	.45	.12
☐ 24 Kirby Puckett	.75	.35	.09
☐ 25 Matt Williams	.30	.14	.04
☐ 26 Larry Walker	.30	.14	.04
☐ 27 Tim Wakefield	.05	.02	.01
☐ 28 Greg Vaughn	.05	.02	.01
☐ 29 Denny Neagle	.05	.02	.01
☐ 30 Ken Caminiti	.30	.14	.04
☐ 31 Garret Anderson	.05	.02	.01
☐ 32 Brady Anderson	.30	.14	.04
☐ 33 Carlos Baerga	.15	.07	.02
☐ 34 Wade Boggs	.30	.14	.04
☐ 35 Roberto Alomar	.40	.18	.05
☐ 36 Eric Karros	.15	.07	.02
☐ 37 Jay Buhner	.30	.14	.04
☐ 38 Dante Bichette	.30	.14	.04
☐ 39 Darren Daulton	.15	.07	.02
☐ 40 Jeff Bagwell	.75	.35	.09
☐ 41 Jay Bell	.05	.02	.01
☐ 42 Dennis Eckersley	.15	.07	.02
☐ 43 Will Clark	.30	.14	.04
☐ 44 Tom Glavine	.30	.14	.04
☐ 45 Rick Aguilera	.05	.02	.01
☐ 46 Kevin Seitzer	.05	.02	.01
☐ 47 Bret Boone	.05	.02	.01
☐ 48 Mark Grace	.30	.14	.04
☐ 49 Ray Durham	.30	.14	.04
☐ 50 Rico Brogna	.05	.02	.01
☐ 51 Kevin Appier	.15	.07	.02
☐ 52 Moises Alou	.15	.07	.02
☐ 53 Jeff Conine	.15	.07	.02
☐ 54 Marty Cordova	.15	.07	.02
☐ 55 Jose Mesa	.05	.02	.01
☐ 56 Rod Beck	.05	.02	.01
☐ 57 Marquis Grissom	.15	.07	.02
☐ 58 David Cone	.15	.07	.02
☐ 59 Albert Belle	.75	.35	.09
☐ 60 Lee Smith	.15	.07	.02
☐ 61 Frank Thomas	2.00	.90	.25
☐ 62 Roger Clemens	.40	.18	.05
☐ 63 Bobby Bonilla	.15	.07	.02
☐ 64 Paul Molitor	.40	.18	.05
☐ 65 Chuck Knoblauch	.30	.14	.04
☐ 66 Steve Finley	.05	.02	.01
☐ 67 Craig Biggio	.15	.07	.02
☐ 68 Ramon Martinez	.15	.07	.02
☐ 69 Jason Isringhausen	.30	.14	.04
☐ 70 Mark Wohlers	.15	.07	.02
☐ 71 Vinny Castilla	.15	.07	.02
☐ 72 Ron Gant	.15	.07	.02
☐ 73 Juan Gonzalez	1.00	.45	.12
☐ 74 Mark McGwire	.60	.25	.07
☐ 75 Jeff King	.05	.02	.01
☐ 76 Pedro Martinez	.15	.07	.02
☐ 77 Chad Curtis	.05	.02	.01
☐ 78 John Olerud	.05	.02	.01
☐ 79 Greg Maddux	1.25	.55	.16
☐ 80 Derek Jeter	1.25	.55	.16
☐ 81 Mike Mussina	.40	.18	.05
☐ 82 Gregg Jefferies	.05	.02	.01
☐ 83 Jim Edmonds	.15	.07	.02
☐ 84 Carlos Perez	.05	.02	.01
☐ 85 Mo Vaughn	.50	.23	.06
☐ 86 Todd Hundley	.15	.07	.02
☐ 87 Roberto Hernandez	.05	.02	.01
☐ 88 Derek Bell	.15	.07	.02
☐ 89 Andres Galarraga	.30	.14	.04
☐ 90 Brian McRae	.05	.02	.01
☐ 91 Joe Carter	.15	.07	.02
☐ 92 Orlando Merced	.05	.02	.01
☐ 93 Cecil Fielder	.15	.07	.02
☐ 94 Dean Palmer	.05	.02	.01
☐ 95 Randy Johnson	.30	.14	.04

Card	NRMT	VG-E	GOOD
☐ 96 Chipper Jones	1.25	.55	.16
☐ 97 Barry Larkin	.30	.14	.04
☐ 98 Hideo Nomo	.50	.23	.06
☐ 99 Gary Gaetti	.05	.02	.01
☐ 100 Edgar Martinez	.15	.07	.02
☐ 101 John Wetteland	.15	.07	.02
☐ 102 Rafael Palmeiro	.30	.14	.04
☐ 103 Chuck Finley	.05	.02	.01
☐ 104 Ivan Rodriguez	.50	.23	.06
☐ 105 Shawn Green	.05	.02	.01
☐ 106 Manny Ramirez	.50	.23	.06
☐ 107 Lance Johnson	.05	.02	.01
☐ 108 Jose Canseco	.30	.14	.04
☐ 109 Fred McGriff	.30	.14	.04
☐ 110 David Segui	.05	.02	.01
☐ 111 Tim Salmon	.30	.14	.04
☐ 112 Hal Morris	.05	.02	.01
☐ 113 Tino Martinez	.15	.07	.02
☐ 114 Bret Saberhagen	.05	.02	.01
☐ 115 Brian Jordan	.15	.07	.02
☐ 116 David Justice	.05	.02	.01
☐ 117 Jack McDowell	.05	.02	.01
☐ 118 Barry Bonds	.50	.23	.06
☐ 119 Mark Langston	.05	.02	.01
☐ 120 John Valentin	.05	.02	.01
☐ 121 Raul Mondesi	.30	.14	.04
☐ 122 Quilvio Veras	.05	.02	.01
☐ 123 Randy Myers	.05	.02	.01
☐ 124 Tony Gwynn	.75	.35	.09
☐ 125 Johnny Damon	.15	.07	.02
☐ 126 Doug Drabek	.05	.02	.01
☐ 127 Bill Pulsipher	.05	.02	.01
☐ 128 Paul O'Neill	.05	.02	.01
☐ 129 Rickey Henderson	.30	.14	.04
☐ 130 Deion Sanders	.30	.14	.04
☐ 131 Orel Hershiser	.15	.07	.02
☐ 132 Gary Sheffield	.30	.14	.04
☐ NNO 59 Bazooka Mantle	4.00	1.80	.50

1951 Berk Ross *

The 1951 Berk Ross set consists of 72 cards (each measuring approximately 2 1/16" by 2 1/2") with tinted photographs, divided evenly into four series (designated in the checklist as A, B, C and D). The cards were marketed in boxes containing two card panels, without gum, and the set includes stars of other sports as well as baseball players. The set is sometimes still found in the original packaging. Intact panels are worth 25 percent more than the sum of the individual cards. The catalog designation for this set is W532-1. In every series the first ten cards are baseball players; the set has a heavy emphasis on Yankees and Phillies players as they were in the World Series the year before. The set includes the first card of Bob Cousy as well as a card of Whitey Ford in his Rookie Card year.

	NRMT	VG-E	GOOD
COMPLETE SET (72)	1200.00	550.00	150.00
COMMON BASEBALL	10.00	4.50	1.25
COMMON FOOTBALL	10.00	4.50	1.25
COMMON OTHERS	5.00	2.20	.60
☐ A1 Al Rosen	12.00	5.50	1.50
☐ A2 Bob Lemon	20.00	9.00	2.50
☐ A3 Phil Rizzuto	25.00	11.00	3.10
☐ A4 Hank Bauer	15.00	6.75	1.85
☐ A5 Billy Johnson	10.00	4.50	1.25
☐ A6 Jerry Coleman	10.00	4.50	1.25
☐ A7 Johnny Mize	20.00	9.00	2.50
☐ A8 Dom DiMaggio	15.00	6.75	1.85
☐ A9 Richie Ashburn	25.00	11.00	3.10
☐ A10 Del Ennis	10.00	4.50	1.25
☐ A11 Bob Cousy	175.00	80.00	22.00
☐ A12 Dick Schnittker	10.00	4.50	1.25
☐ A13 Ezzard Charles	10.00	4.50	1.25
☐ A14 Leon Hart	12.00	5.50	1.50
☐ A15 James Martin	10.00	4.50	1.25
☐ A16 Ben Hogan	40.00	18.00	5.00
☐ A17 Bill Durnan	25.00	11.00	3.10
☐ A18 Bill Quackenbush	15.00	6.75	1.85
☐ B1 Stan Musial	125.00	55.00	15.50
☐ B2 Warren Spahn	30.00	13.50	3.70
☐ B3 Tom Henrich	12.00	5.50	1.50
☐ B4 Yogi Berra	75.00	34.00	9.50
☐ B5 Joe DiMaggio	175.00	80.00	22.00
☐ B6 Bobby Brown	12.00	5.50	1.50
☐ B7 Granny Hamner	10.00	4.50	1.25
☐ B8 Willie Jones	10.00	4.50	1.25
☐ B9 Stan Lopata	10.00	4.50	1.25
☐ B10 Mike Goliat	10.00	4.50	1.25
☐ B11 Sherman White	10.00	4.50	1.25
☐ B12 Joe Maxim	6.00	2.70	.75
☐ B13 Ray Robinson	25.00	11.00	3.10
☐ B14 Doak Walker	20.00	9.00	2.50
☐ B15 Emil Sitko	10.00	4.50	1.25
☐ B16 Jack Stewart	10.00	4.50	1.25
☐ B17 Dick Button	10.00	4.50	1.25
☐ B18 Melvin Patton	5.00	2.20	.60
☐ C1 Ralph Kiner	20.00	9.00	2.50
☐ C2 Bill Goodman	10.00	4.50	1.25
☐ C3 Allie Reynolds	15.00	6.75	1.85
☐ C4 Vic Raschi	12.00	5.50	1.50
☐ C5 Joe Page	12.00	5.50	1.50
☐ C6 Eddie Lopat	15.00	6.75	1.85
☐ C7 Andy Seminick	10.00	4.50	1.25
☐ C8 Dick Sisler	10.00	4.50	1.25
☐ C9 Eddie Waitkus	10.00	4.50	1.25
☐ C10 Ken Heintzelman	10.00	4.50	1.25
☐ C11 Paul Unruh	10.00	4.50	1.25
☐ C12 Jake LaMotta	20.00	9.00	2.50
☐ C13 Ike Williams	6.00	2.70	.75
☐ C14 Wade Walker	5.00	2.20	.60
☐ C15 Rodney Franz	5.00	2.20	.60
☐ C16 Sid Abel	20.00	9.00	2.50
☐ C17 Claire Sherman	5.00	2.20	.60
☐ C18 Jesse Owens	25.00	11.00	3.10
☐ D1 Gene Woodling	12.00	5.50	1.50
☐ D2 Cliff Mapes	10.00	4.50	1.25
☐ D3 Fred Sanford	10.00	4.50	1.25
☐ D4 Tommy Byrne	10.00	4.50	1.25
☐ D5 Whitey Ford	75.00	34.00	9.50
☐ D6 Jim Konstanty	10.00	4.50	1.25
☐ D7 Russ Meyer	12.00	5.50	1.50
☐ D8 Robin Roberts	25.00	11.00	3.10
☐ D9 Curt Simmons	12.00	5.50	1.50
☐ D10 Sam Jethroe	12.00	5.50	1.50
☐ D11 Bill Sharman	40.00	18.00	5.00
☐ D12 Sandy Saddler	6.00	2.70	.75
☐ D13 Margaret DuPont	5.00	2.20	.60
☐ D14 Arnold Galiffa	10.00	4.50	1.25
☐ D15 Charlie Justice	15.00	6.75	1.85
☐ D16 Glen Cunningham	6.00	2.70	.75
☐ D17 Gregory Rice	5.00	2.20	.60
☐ D18 Harrison Dillard	6.00	2.70	.75

1952 Berk Ross

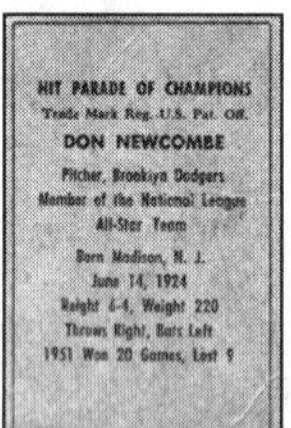

The 1952 Berk Ross set of 72 unnumbered, tinted photocards, each measuring approximately 2" by 3", seems to have been patterned after the highly successful 1951 Bowman set. The reverses of Ewell Blackwell and Nellie Fox are transposed while Phil Rizzuto comes with two different poses. The complete set below includes both poses of Rizzuto. There is a card of Joe DiMaggio even though he retired after the 1951 season. The catalog designation for this set is W532-2, and the cards have been assigned numbers in the alphabetical checklist below.

	NRMT	VG-E	GOOD
COMPLETE SET (72)	5500.00	2500.00	700.00
COMMON CARD (1-71)	20.00	9.00	2.50
☐ 1 Richie Ashburn	60.00	27.00	7.50
☐ 2 Hank Bauer	25.00	11.00	3.10
☐ 3 Yogi Berra	150.00	70.00	19.00
☐ 4 Ewell Blackwell UER (photo actually Nellie Fox)	30.00	13.50	3.70
☐ 5 Bobby Brown	25.00	11.00	3.10
☐ 6 Jim Busby	20.00	9.00	2.50
☐ 7 Roy Campanella	150.00	70.00	19.00
☐ 8 Chico Carrasquel	25.00	11.00	3.10
☐ 9 Jerry Coleman	25.00	11.00	3.10
☐ 10 Joe Collins	20.00	9.00	2.50
☐ 11 Alvin Dark	25.00	11.00	3.10
☐ 12 Dom DiMaggio	30.00	13.50	3.70
☐ 13 Joe DiMaggio	1250.00	550.00	160.00
☐ 14 Larry Doby	30.00	13.50	3.70
☐ 15 Bobby Doerr	40.00	18.00	5.00
☐ 16 Bob Elliott	20.00	9.00	2.50
☐ 17 Del Ennis	20.00	9.00	2.50
☐ 18 Ferris Fain	20.00	9.00	2.50
☐ 19 Bob Feller	100.00	45.00	12.50
☐ 20 Nellie Fox UER (photo actually Ewell Blackwell)	60.00	27.00	7.50
☐ 21 Ned Garver	20.00	9.00	2.50
☐ 22 Clint Hartung	20.00	9.00	2.50
☐ 23 Jim Hearn	20.00	9.00	2.50
☐ 24 Gil Hodges	60.00	27.00	7.50
☐ 25 Monte Irvin	40.00	18.00	5.00
☐ 26 Larry Jansen	20.00	9.00	2.50
☐ 27 Sheldon Jones	20.00	9.00	2.50
☐ 28 George Kell	40.00	18.00	5.00
☐ 29 Monte Kennedy	20.00	9.00	2.50
☐ 30 Ralph Kiner	60.00	27.00	7.50
☐ 31 Dave Koslo	20.00	9.00	2.50
☐ 32 Bob Kuzava	20.00	9.00	2.50
☐ 33 Bob Lemon	40.00	18.00	5.00
☐ 34 Whitey Lockman	20.00	9.00	2.50
☐ 35 Ed Lopat	25.00	11.00	3.10
☐ 36 Sal Maglie	25.00	11.00	3.10
☐ 37 Mickey Mantle	1800.00	800.00	220.00
☐ 38 Billy Martin	60.00	27.00	7.50
☐ 39 Willie Mays	600.00	275.00	75.00
☐ 40 Gil McDougald	25.00	11.00	3.10
☐ 41 Minnie Minoso	30.00	13.50	3.70
☐ 42 Johnny Mize	60.00	27.00	7.50
☐ 43 Tom Morgan	20.00	9.00	2.50
☐ 44 Don Mueller	20.00	9.00	2.50
☐ 45 Stan Musial	300.00	135.00	38.00
☐ 46 Don Newcombe	30.00	13.50	3.70
☐ 47 Ray Noble	20.00	9.00	2.50
☐ 48 Joe Ostrowski	20.00	9.00	2.50
☐ 49 Mel Parnell	25.00	11.00	3.10
☐ 50 Vic Raschi	25.00	11.00	3.10
☐ 51 Pee Wee Reese	75.00	34.00	9.50
☐ 52 Allie Reynolds	25.00	11.00	3.10
☐ 53 Bill Rigney	20.00	9.00	2.50
☐ 54A Phil Rizzuto (bunting)	60.00	27.00	7.50
☐ 54B Phil Rizzuto (swinging)	60.00	27.00	7.50
☐ 55 Robin Roberts	50.00	22.00	6.25
☐ 56 Eddie Robinson	20.00	9.00	2.50
☐ 57 Jackie Robinson	400.00	180.00	50.00
☐ 58 Preacher Roe	25.00	11.00	3.10
☐ 59 Johnny Sain	25.00	11.00	3.10
☐ 60 Red Schoendienst	40.00	18.00	5.00
☐ 61 Duke Snider	150.00	70.00	19.00
☐ 62 George Spencer	20.00	9.00	2.50
☐ 63 Eddie Stanky	25.00	11.00	3.10
☐ 64 Hank Thompson	25.00	11.00	3.10
☐ 65 Bobby Thomson	30.00	13.50	3.70
☐ 66 Vic Wertz	20.00	9.00	2.50
☐ 67 Wally Westlake	20.00	9.00	2.50
☐ 68 Wes Westrum	20.00	9.00	2.50
☐ 69 Ted Williams	400.00	180.00	50.00
☐ 70 Gene Woodling	25.00	11.00	3.10
☐ 71 Gus Zernial	25.00	11.00	3.10

1989 Best Western Ryan

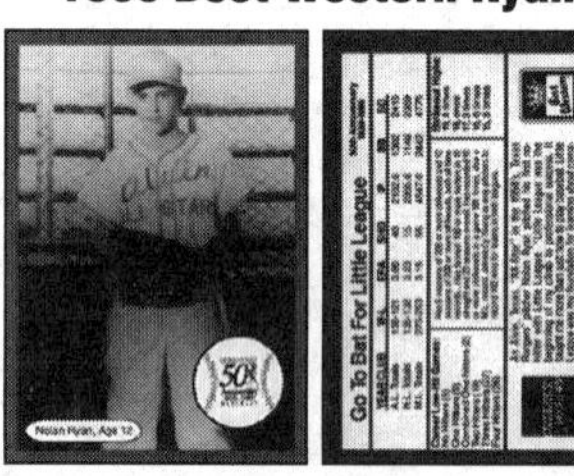

This one-card standard-size set was sponsored by Best Western in conjunction with American Express to commemorate the 50th anniversary of Little League Baseball. The cards were distributed at a Texas Rangers home game in 1989. This card has a black and white photo of Nolan Ryan in his Little League uniform. The photo is bordered in cherry red, and a 50th Anniversary logo appears in the shape of a baseball on the card face. Noaln Ryan's name and age are given toward the bottom of the card. In a horizontal format, the backs have Major League statistics, career highlights, and a player quote regarding the importance of Little League.

	MINT	NRMT	EXC
COMPLETE SET (1)	3.00	1.35	.35
COMMON CARD	3.00	1.35	.35
☐ NNO Nolan Ryan (Little League photo)	3.00	1.35	.35

1916 BF2 Felt Pennants

These small triangular felt pennants were issued around 1916. The pennants themselves are 8 1/4" in length, whereas the unnumbered paper photos (glued on to the felt pennant) are 1 3/4" by 1 1/4". The photos are black and white and appear to have been taken from Sporting News issues of the same era. These unnumbered pennants are ordered below in alphabetical order within team. The teams themselves are ordered alphabetically within league beginning with the American League.

	EX-MT	VG-E	GOOD
COMPLETE SET	9000.00	4000.00	1100.00
COMMON PLAYER	50.00	22.00	6.25
☐ 1 Jack Barry	50.00	22.00	6.25
☐ 2 Hick Cady	50.00	22.00	6.25
☐ 3 Del Gainer	50.00	22.00	6.25
☐ 4 Harry Hooper	100.00	45.00	12.50
☐ 5 Dutch Leonard	50.00	22.00	6.25
☐ 6 Duffy Lewis	50.00	22.00	6.25
☐ 7 Joe Wood	60.00	27.00	7.50
☐ 8 Joe Benz	50.00	22.00	6.25
☐ 9 Eddie Collins	100.00	45.00	12.50
☐ 10 Shano Collins	50.00	22.00	6.25
☐ 11 Charels Comiskey OWN	125.00	55.00	15.50
☐ 12 Red Faber	100.00	45.00	12.50
☐ 13 Joe Jackson	1500.00	700.00	190.00
☐ 14 Jack Lapp	50.00	22.00	6.25
☐ 15 Eddie Murphy	50.00	22.00	6.25
☐ 16 Pants Rowland MG	50.00	22.00	6.25
☐ 17 Reb Russell	50.00	22.00	6.25
☐ 18 Ray Schalk	100.00	45.00	12.50
☐ 19 Jim Scott	50.00	22.00	6.25
☐ 20 Ed Walsh	100.00	45.00	12.50
☐ 21 Buck Weaver	125.00	55.00	15.50
☐ 22 Ray Chapman	60.00	27.00	7.50
☐ 23 Chick Gandil	125.00	55.00	15.50
☐ 24 Guy Morton	50.00	22.00	6.25
☐ 25 Donie Bush	50.00	22.00	6.25
☐ 26 Ty Cobb	1200.00	550.00	150.00
☐ 27 Harry Coveleski	50.00	22.00	6.25
☐ 28 Sam Crawford	100.00	45.00	12.50
☐ 29 Jean Dubuc	50.00	22.00	6.25
☐ 30 Oscar Stanage	50.00	22.00	6.25
☐ 31 Bobby Veach	50.00	22.00	6.25
☐ 32 Ralph Young	50.00	22.00	6.25
☐ 33 Frank Baker	100.00	45.00	12.50
☐ 34 Joe Gideon	50.00	22.00	6.25
☐ 35 Wally Pipp	60.00	27.00	7.50
☐ 36 Napoleon Lajoie	200.00	90.00	25.00
☐ 37 Connie Mack MG	200.00	90.00	25.00
☐ 38 Stuffy McInnis	60.00	27.00	7.50
☐ 39 Rube Oldring	50.00	22.00	6.25
☐ 40 Wally Schang	60.00	27.00	7.50
☐ 41 Earl Hamilton	50.00	22.00	6.25
☐ 42 Fielder Jones	50.00	22.00	6.25
☐ 43 Doc Lavan	50.00	22.00	6.25
☐ 44 George Sisler	125.00	55.00	15.50
☐ 45 Eddie Foster	50.00	22.00	6.25
☐ 46 Walter Johnson	400.00	180.00	50.00
☐ 47 Joe Judge	50.00	22.00	6.25
☐ 48 George McBride	50.00	22.00	6.25
☐ 49 Clyde Milan	60.00	27.00	7.50
☐ 50 Ray Morgan	50.00	22.00	6.25
☐ 51 Johnny Evers	100.00	45.00	12.50
☐ 52 Hank Gowdy	50.00	22.00	6.25
☐ 53 Bill James	50.00	22.00	6.25
☐ 54 Sherry Magee	50.00	22.00	6.25
☐ 55 Rabbit Maranville	100.00	45.00	12.50
☐ 56 Dick Rudolph	50.00	22.00	6.25
☐ 57 George Stallings MG	50.00	22.00	6.25
☐ 58 Lefty Tyler	50.00	22.00	6.25
☐ 59 Jake Daubert	50.00	22.00	6.25
☐ 60 Rube Marquard	100.00	45.00	12.50
☐ 61 Chief Meyers	50.00	22.00	6.25
☐ 62 Otto Miller	50.00	22.00	6.25
☐ 63 Nap Rucker	50.00	22.00	6.25
☐ 64 Jimmy Archer	50.00	22.00	6.25
☐ 65 Mordecai Brown	100.00	45.00	12.50
☐ 66 Claude Hendrix	50.00	22.00	6.25
☐ 67 Jimmy Lavender	50.00	22.00	6.25
☐ 68 Vic Saier	50.00	22.00	6.25
☐ 69 Wildfire Schulte	50.00	22.00	6.25
☐ 70 Joe Tinker	100.00	45.00	12.50
☐ 71 Hippo Vaughn	50.00	22.00	6.25
☐ 72 Heine Zimmerman	50.00	22.00	6.25
☐ 73 Buck Herzog	50.00	22.00	6.25
☐ 74 Ivy Wingo	50.00	22.00	6.25
☐ 75 George Burns	50.00	22.00	6.25
☐ 76 Red Dooin	50.00	22.00	6.25
☐ 77 Larry Doyle	60.00	27.00	7.50
☐ 78 Bennie Kauff	50.00	22.00	6.25
☐ 79 Hans Lobert	50.00	22.00	6.25
☐ 80 John McGraw MG	150.00	70.00	19.00
☐ 81 Fred Merkle	50.00	22.00	6.25
☐ 82 Jeff Tesreau	50.00	22.00	6.25
☐ 83 Grover C. Alexander	150.00	70.00	19.00
☐ 84 Dave Bancroft	100.00	45.00	12.50
☐ 85 Chief Bender	100.00	45.00	12.50
☐ 86 Gavvy Cravath	60.00	27.00	7.50
☐ 87 Josh Devore	50.00	22.00	6.25
☐ 88 Bill Killefer	50.00	22.00	6.25
☐ 89 Fred Luderus	50.00	22.00	6.25
☐ 90 Pat Moran	50.00	22.00	6.25
☐ 91 Dode Paskert	50.00	22.00	6.25
☐ 92 Max Carey	100.00	45.00	12.50
☐ 93 Al Mamaux	50.00	22.00	6.25
☐ 94 Honus Wagner	400.00	180.00	50.00
☐ 95 Miller Huggins	100.00	45.00	12.50
☐ 96 Slim Sallee	50.00	22.00	6.25

1956 Big League Cards

These 3" bronze colored plastic statues were issued in bubble packs. The backing of the package is actually a card of the featured player. Prices below are for cards only. Unopened bubble packs are valued 3 to 5 times the listed prices below. Prices for single cards are listed under Big League in the card section. Players are listed alphabeticly.

	NRMT	VG-E	GOOD
COMPLETE SET (18)	700.00	325.00	90.00
COMMON STATUE (1-18)	20.00	9.00	2.50

☐ 1 John Antonelli	20.00	9.00	2.50
☐ 2 Bobby Avila	20.00	9.00	2.50
☐ 3 Yogi Berra	50.00	22.00	6.25
☐ 4 Roy Campanella	50.00	22.00	6.25
☐ 5 Larry Doby	30.00	13.50	3.70
☐ 6 Del Ennis	20.00	9.00	2.50
☐ 7 Jim Gilliam	30.00	13.50	3.70
☐ 8 Gil Hodges	40.00	18.00	5.00
☐ 9 Harvey Kuenn	20.00	9.00	2.50
☐ 10 Bob Lemon	35.00	16.00	4.40
☐ 11 Mickey Mantle	250.00	110.00	31.00
☐ 12 Eddie Mathews	40.00	18.00	5.00
☐ 13 Minnie Minoso	30.00	13.50	3.70
☐ 14 Stan Musial	50.00	22.00	6.25
☐ 15 Pee Wee Reese	50.00	22.00	6.25
☐ 16 Al Rosen	20.00	9.00	2.50
☐ 17 Duke Snider	40.00	18.00	5.00
☐ 18 Mickey Vernon	25.00	11.00	3.10

1986 Big League Chew

This 12-card standard-size set was produced by Big League Chew and was inserted in with their packages of Big League Chew gum, which were shaped and styled after a pouch of chewing tobacco. The cards were found one per pouch of shredded gum or were available through a mail-in offer of two coupons and $2.00 for a complete set. The cards in the packs often were damaged in the packaging process. The players featured are members of the 500 career home run club. The backs are printed in blue ink on white card stock. The set is subtitled "Home Run Legends". The front of each card shows a year inside a small flag; the year is the year that player passed 500 homers.

	MINT	NRMT	EXC
COMPLETE SET (12)	6.00	2.70	.75
COMMON CARD (1-12)	.25	.11	.03
☐ 1 Hank Aaron	1.50	.70	.19
☐ 2 Babe Ruth	2.00	.90	.25
☐ 3 Willie Mays	1.50	.70	.19
☐ 4 Frank Robinson	.50	.23	.06
☐ 5 Harmon Killebrew	.50	.23	.06
☐ 6 Mickey Mantle	2.00	.90	.25
☐ 7 Jimmie Foxx	.50	.23	.06
☐ 8 Ted Williams	1.50	.70	.19
☐ 9 Ernie Banks	.50	.23	.06
☐ 10 Eddie Mathews	.50	.23	.06
☐ 11 Mel Ott	.50	.23	.06
☐ 12 500 HR Members	.25	.11	.03

1989 Bimbo Bread Discs

The 1989 Bimbo Bread set is a 12-disc set issued in Puerto Rico which measured 2 3/4" in diameter. This set features only Puerto Rican players. The top center of the the front of the disk has the Bimbo Bear logo. The previous years stats are on the back.

	MINT	NRMT	EXC
COMPLETE SET (12)	15.00	6.75	1.85
COMMON DISC (1-12)	.50	.23	.06
☐ 1 Carmelo Martinez	.50	.23	.06
☐ 2 Candy Maldonado	.50	.23	.06
☐ 3 Benito Santiago	.75	.35	.09
☐ 4 Rey Quinones	.50	.23	.06
☐ 5 Jose Oquendo	.50	.23	.06
☐ 6 Ruben Sierra	1.00	.45	.12
☐ 7 Jose Lind	.50	.23	.06
☐ 8 Juan Beniquez	.50	.23	.06
☐ 9 Willie Hernandez	.75	.35	.09
☐ 10 Juan Nieves	.50	.23	.06
☐ 11 Jose Guzman	.50	.23	.06
☐ 12 Roberto Alomar	10.00	4.50	1.25

1975 Blank Back Discs

This six-disc baseball-designed set measures approximately 3 3/8" in diameter. The fronts feature a black-and-white player head photo on a white background in the center with the player's name, position, and team name below. The blue and red sides contain biographical information. The backs are blank. The discs are unnumbered and checklisted below in alphabetical order. Bench and Seaver are available in lesser quantities than other players so they are labeled as SP's in the checklist below

	NRMT	VG-E	GOOD
COMPLETE SET (6)	500.00	220.00	60.00
COMMON DISC (1-6)	5.00	2.20	.60
☐ 1 Henry Aaron	50.00	22.00	6.25
☐ 2 Johnny Bench SP	150.00	70.00	19.00
☐ 3 Catfish Hunter	25.00	11.00	3.10
☐ 4 Fred Lynn	5.00	2.20	.60
☐ 5 Pete Rose	75.00	34.00	9.50
☐ 6 Tom Seaver SP	250.00	110.00	31.00

1991 Bleachers 23K Griffey Jr.

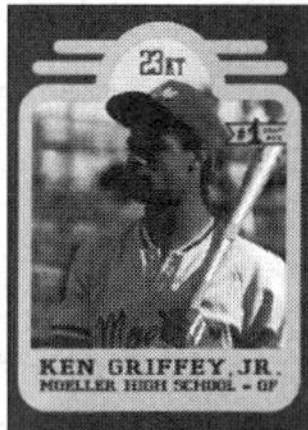

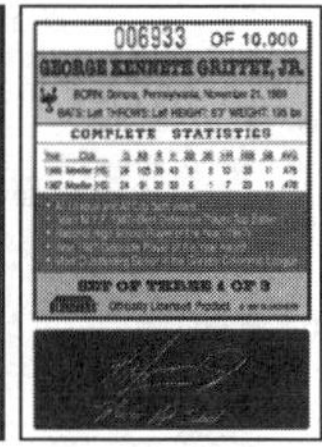

These three 23-karat gold standard-size cards were issued by Bleachers. The production run was reported to be 10,000 numbered sets and 1,500 uncut numbered strips. Extended by a small semi-circle, the color player photos on the fronts capture Griffey in three different phases of his career. Each card has a different color inner border (1-yellow; 2-gray; 3-red) and a gold outer border. On white, green, yellow and blue bars, the backs carry the player's name, biography, statistics, highlights and a serial number ("X of 10,000") inside a black border. The player's name and team name are etched in gold at the card bottom. The cards are numbered on the back.

	MINT	NRMT	EXC
COMPLETE SET (3)	30.00	13.50	3.70
COMMON CARD (1-3)	10.00	4.50	1.25
☐ 1 Ken Griffey Jr. Moeller High	10.00	4.50	1.25
☐ 2 Ken Griffey Jr. Bellingham Mariners	10.00	4.50	1.25
☐ 3 Ken Griffey Jr. San Bernardino Spirit	10.00	4.50	1.25

1991 Bleachers 23K Thomas

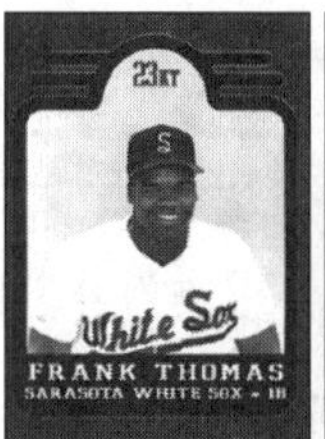

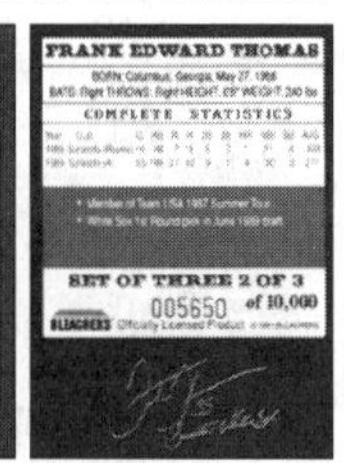

These three 23-karat gold standard-size cards were produced by Bleachers. On a gold card front, posed color player photos are enframed by different color borders (1-blue; 2-black; 3-red). The top of each photo is extended by a small semi-circle that is intersected by two border stripes. The player's name, team name and position are printed in white lettering in the border beneath the picture. On gray, yellow, white and red stripes, the back has the player's name, biography, statistics, highlights and the serial number (1 of 10,000), inside a black border. It was reported that the production run was limited to 10,000 sets and 1,500 uncut numbered strips. The player's signature, team name and jersey number are written in gold at the bottom of the card.

	MINT	NRMT	EXC
COMPLETE SET (3)	35.00	16.00	4.40
COMMON CARD (1-3)	12.00	5.50	1.50
☐ 1 Frank Thomas Auburn Tigers	12.00	5.50	1.50
☐ 2 Frank Thomas Sarasota White Sox	12.00	5.50	1.50
☐ 3 Frank Thomas Birmingham Barons	12.00	5.50	1.50

1991-92 Bleachers Promos

These promo standard-size cards were distributed to dealers to promote the new forthcoming Bleachers 23K card sets. The card backs contain order information as well as information about Bleachers upcoming releases.

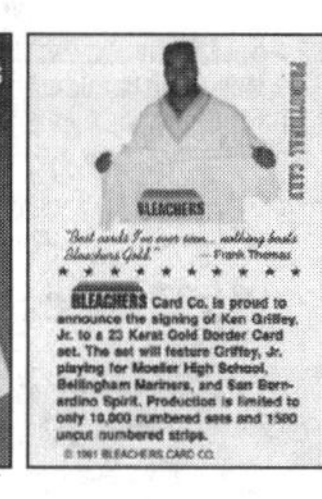

	MINT	NRMT	EXC
COMPLETE SET (6)	18.00	8.00	2.20
COMMON CARD (1-6)	2.00	.90	.25
☐ 1 Ken Griffey Jr. Spirit jersey 1991 copyright Frank Thomas pictured on back	3.00	1.35	.35
☐ 2 Dave Justice 1992 copyright wearing Bleachers t-shirt	2.00	.90	.25
☐ 3 Nolan Ryan 1992 copyright wearing tuxedo green and yellow back no 800 number in border	3.00	1.35	.35
☐ 4 Nolan Ryan 1992 copyright wearing tuxedo blue and yellow back 800 number in border	3.00	1.35	.35
☐ 5 Nolan Ryan 1992 copyright wearing tuxedo gold foil stamped East Coast National '92 on front	3.00	1.35	.35
☐ 6 Nolan Ryan 1992 copyright wearing tuxedo gold foil stamped SF Sports Collectors Card Expo '92 on front	3.00	1.35	.35
☐ 7 Nolan Ryan 1992 copyright wearing tuxedo gold foil stamped Tri-Star St. Louis '92 on front	3.00	1.35	.35

1992 Bleachers 23K Justice

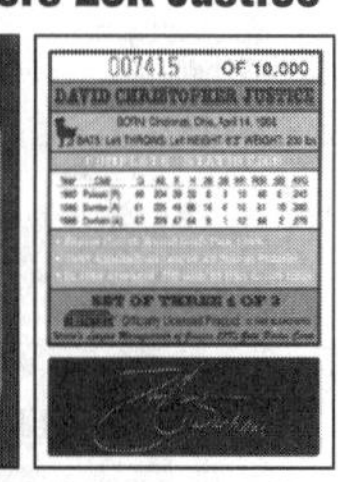

These three 23-karat gold standard-size cards were issued by Bleachers. The production run was reported to be 10,000 numbered sets and 1,500 uncut numbered strips. The color player photos on the fronts capture Justice in three different phases of his career, and the front design differs slightly from that of the previous year's issues. Each card has a different color inner border (1-aqua; 2-black; 3-yellow) and a gold outer border. On white, pink, and orange bars, the backs carry the player's name, biography, statistics, highlights, and a serial number ("X of 10,000") inside a black border. The player's name and team name are etched in gold at the card bottom. The cards are numbered on the back. Prism cards (silver prism border instead of gold) were randomly inserted in sets on a limited basis. These prism versions are valued at double the prices listed below.

	MINT	NRMT	EXC
COMPLETE SET (3)	15.00	6.75	1.85
COMMON CARD (1-3)	5.00	2.20	.60
☐ 1 Dave Justice Durham Bulls	5.00	2.20	.60
☐ 2 Dave Justice Greenville Braves	5.00	2.20	.60
☐ 3 Dave Justice Richmond Braves	5.00	2.20	.60

1992 Bleachers 23K Ryan

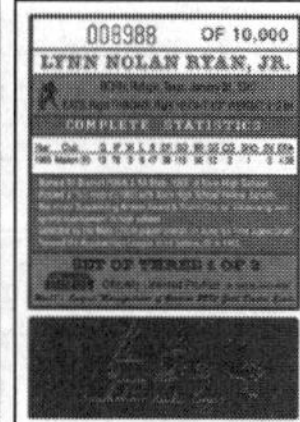

These three 23-karat gold standard-size cards were issued by Bleachers and measure the standard size (2 1/2" by 3 1/2"). The sets were packaged in a cardboard sleeve and shrink wrapped; promo cards and prism cards were randomly inserted. The production run is reported to be 10,000 numbered sets and 1,500 uncut numbered strips. The color player photos on the fronts capture Nolan Ryan in three different phases of his career, and the front design differs slightly from that of the previous year's issues. Each card has a different color inner border (1-blue; 2-gray; 3-orange) and a gold outer border. On white, purple, and orange bars, the backs carry the player's name, biography, statistics, highlights, and a serial number ("X of 10,000") inside a black border. The player's name and team name are etched in gold at the card bottom. The cards are numbered on the back. Prism cards (silver prism border instead of gold) were randomly inserted in sets on a limited basis. These prism versions are valued at double the prices listed below.

	MINT	NRMT	EXC
COMPLETE SET (3)	30.00	13.50	3.70
COMMON CARD (1-3)	10.00	4.50	1.25
☐ 1 Nolan Ryan Marion Mets	10.00	4.50	1.25
☐ 2 Nolan Ryan Greenville Mets	10.00	4.50	1.25
☐ 3 Nolan Ryan Jacksonville Suns	10.00	4.50	1.25

1993 Bleachers Promos

These thirteen promo standard-size cards were distributed to dealers to promote the new upcoming Bleachers 23K card sets. The card backs contain order information as well as information about Bleachers upcoming releases.

	MINT	NRMT	EXC
COMPLETE SET (13)	40.00	18.00	5.00
COMMON CARD (1-13)	3.00	1.35	.35
☐ 1 Barry Bonds 1993 copyright	3.00	1.35	.35
☐ 2 Barry Bonds 1993 copyright Tuff Stuff Buyers Club	3.00	1.35	.35
☐ 3 Barry Bonds 1993 copyright Tri-Star Phoenix '93	3.00	1.35	.35
☐ 4 Nolan Ryan 1992 copyright wearing tuxedo Tri-Star Houston '93 gold stamped on front	3.00	1.35	.35
☐ 5 Nolan Ryan 1993 copyright sitting, western gear	3.00	1.35	.35
☐ 6 Nolan Ryan 1993 copyright sitting; western gear Tuff Stuff Buyers Club	3.00	1.35	.35
☐ 7 Nolan Ryan 1993 copyright wearing tuxedo gold speckled background	6.00	2.70	.75
☐ 8 Nolan Ryan 1993 copyright wearing tuxedo silver-speckled background	6.00	2.70	.75
☐ 9 Nolan Ryan 1993 copyright wearing tuxedo silver wavy background	6.00	2.70	.75
☐ 10 Ryne Sandberg 1993 copyright three photos baseball, basketball and football	3.00	1.35	.35
☐ 11 Ryne Sandberg 1993 copyright three photos baseball, basketball and football Tri-Star Phoenix '93	3.00	1.35	.35
☐ 12 Ryne Sandberg 1993 copyright three photos baseball, basketball and football East Coast National	3.00	1.35	.35
☐ 13 Ryne Sandberg 1993 copyright three photos baseball, basketball and football Tuff Stuff Buyers Club	3.00	1.35	.35

1993 Bleachers 23K Bonds

These three 23-karat gold standard-size cards were issued by Bleachers. The sets were packaged in a cardboard sleeve and shrink wrapped; promo cards and prism cards were randomly inserted. The production run was reported to be 10,000 numbered sets and 1,500 uncut numbered strips. The color player photos on the fronts capture

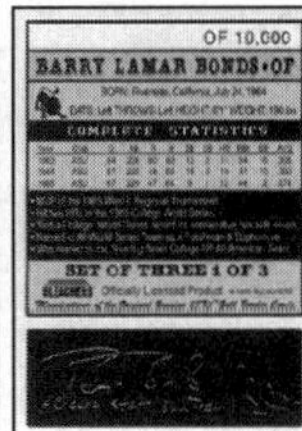

Barry Bonds in three different phases of his career. The backs carry the player's name, biography, statistics, highlights and a serial number ("X of 10,000") inside a black border. The player's name and team name are etched in gold at the card bottom. The cards are numbered on the back. Prism cards (silver prism border instead of gold) were randomly inserted in sets on a limited basis. These prism versions are valued at double the prices listed below.

	MINT	NRMT	EXC
COMPLETE SET (3)	20.00	9.00	2.50
COMMON CARD (1-3)	8.00	3.60	1.00
☐ 1 Barry Bonds Arizona State Sun Devils	8.00	3.60	1.00
☐ 2 Barry Bonds Prince William Pirates	8.00	3.60	1.00
☐ 3 Barry Bonds Hawaii Islanders	8.00	3.60	1.00

1993 Bleachers 23K Griffey Jr.

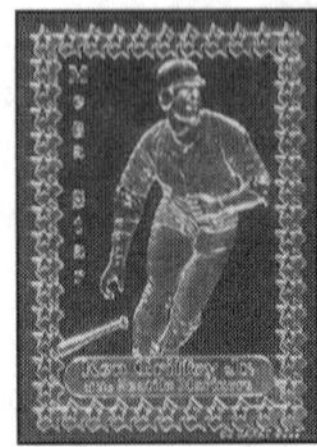

This single sculptured gold standard-size card features on its star-bordered front a raised image of Ken Griffey Jr. dropping his bat after hitting the ball. His name and that of his team, the Seattle Mariners, appear in embossed lettering within a capsule-shaped area beneath his image. The words "Mega Star" appear in raised vertical lettering to the left. The back is framed by a thin embossed line and carries Griffey's name and biography at the top, followed below by career highlights, his uniform number, and a stamped production number out of 10,000 produced. The card was issued in a clear acrylic holder within a gold foil-embossed box. The promo card also measures the standard size (2 1/2" by 3 1/2") and features on its borderless front a posed color photo of Griffey in the uniform of his high school baseball team in Cincinnati (Moeller). Its white back carries information about the sculptured 23K Griffey card.

	MINT	NRMT	EXC
COMPLETE SET (2)	20.00	9.00	2.50
COMMON CARD (1-2)	10.00	4.50	1.25
☐ 1 Ken Griffey Jr. Sculptured card	10.00	4.50	1.25
☐ 2 Ken Griffey Jr. Promo card	10.00	4.50	1.25

1993 Bleachers 23K Sandberg

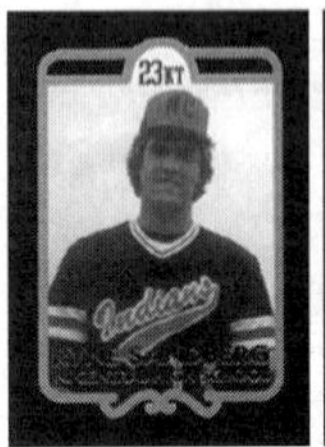
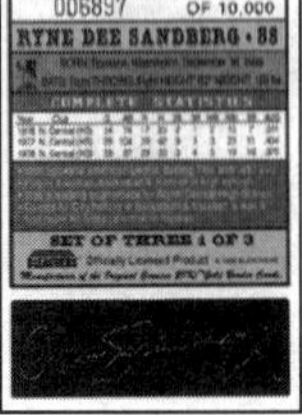

These three 23-karat gold standard-size cards were issued by Bleachers. The sets were packaged in a cardboard sleeve and shrink wrapped; promo cards and prism cards were randomly inserted. The production run was reported to be 10,000 numbered sets and 1,500 uncut numbered strips. The color player photos on the fronts capture Ryne Sandberg in three different phases of his career. The backs carry the player's name, biography, statistics, highlights, and a serial number ("X of 10,000") inside a black border. The player's name and team name are etched in gold at the card bottom. The cards are numbered on the back. Prism cards (silver prism border instead of gold) were randomly inserted in sets on a limited basis. These prism versions are valued at double the prices listed below.

	MINT	NRMT	EXC
COMPLETE SET (3)	20.00	9.00	2.50
COMMON CARD (1-3)	8.00	3.60	1.00
☐ 1 Ryne Sandberg North Central High School	8.00	3.60	1.00
☐ 2 Ryne Sandberg Helena Phillies	8.00	3.60	1.00
☐ 3 Ryne Sandberg Reading Phillies	8.00	3.60	1.00

1993 Bleachers Ryan 6

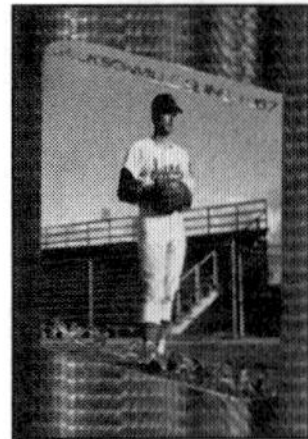

This six-card standard-size set of 1993 Bleachers Nolan Ryan is the premier edition of the holographic prism border cards. The set spotlights future hall of fame pitcher Nolan Ryan appearing in his minor league team uniform, the Jacksonville Suns. Production of this set was limited to 10,000 sets. The fronts display a holographic prism border surrounding a color-tinted black-and-white photo of Ryan with bleachers in the background. In silver foil lettering above the photo is the "Jacksonville Suns 1967" and below the photo is Ryan's name. The backs display the specific set number prominentally at the top. A black and white close-up shot from Ryan's junior high and high school years is near the upper left corner with a black film effect border. To the right of the photo is an orange box with biographical information. The middle section is navy blue with either little league or high school highlights, minor league highlights and statistics, career highlights, and career summary in white lettering. The lower yellow section contains the card number and the Bleachers logo.

	MINT	NRMT	EXC
COMPLETE SET (6)	30.00	13.50	3.70
COMMON CARD (1-6)	5.00	2.20	.60
☐ 1 Nolan Ryan Little League Highlights	5.00	2.20	.60
☐ 2 Nolan Ryan High School Highlights	5.00	2.20	.60
☐ 3 Nolan Ryan Minor League Highlights	5.00	2.20	.60
☐ 4 Nolan Ryan Minor League Statistics	5.00	2.20	.60
☐ 5 Nolan Ryan International Strikeout King	5.00	2.20	.60
☐ 6 Nolan Ryan Career Highlights	5.00	2.20	.60

1979 Blue Jays Bubble Yum

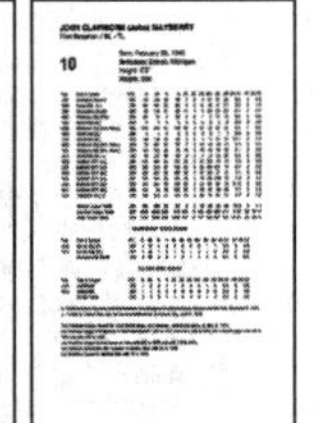

These 20 white-bordered posed black-and-white player photographs measure approximately 5 1/2" by 8 1/2". The player's name and position along with the Blue Jays logo and a picture of a pack of Bubble Yum, appear within the wide lower white margin. The white back carries the player's name and position at the top, followed below by his uniform number, biography and statistics. The photos are unnumbered and checklisted below in alphabetical order.

	NRMT	VG-E	GOOD
COMPLETE SET (20)	30.00	13.50	3.70
COMMON CARD (1-20)	1.50	.70	.19
☐ 1 Bob Bailor	2.50	1.10	.30
☐ 2 Rick Bosetti	1.50	.70	.19
☐ 3 Tom Buskey	1.50	.70	.19
☐ 4 Rico Carty	3.00	1.35	.35
☐ 5 Rick Cerone	2.00	.90	.25
☐ 6 Jim Clancy	2.00	.90	.25
☐ 7 Bobby Doerr CO	4.00	1.80	.50
☐ 8 Dave Freisleben	1.50	.70	.19
☐ 9 Luis Gomez	1.50	.70	.19
☐ 10 Alfredo Griffin	3.00	1.35	.35
☐ 11 Roy Hartsfield MG	1.50	.70	.19
☐ 12 Roy Howell	2.00	.90	.25
☐ 13 Phil Huffman	1.50	.70	.19
☐ 14 Jesse Jefferson	1.50	.70	.19
☐ 15 Dave Lemanczyk	1.50	.70	.19
☐ 16 John Mayberry	3.00	1.35	.35
☐ 17 Balor Moore	1.50	.70	.19
☐ 18 Tom Underwood	1.50	.70	.19
☐ 19 Otto Velez	2.00	.90	.25
☐ 20 Al Woods	1.50	.70	.19

1984 Blue Jays Fire Safety

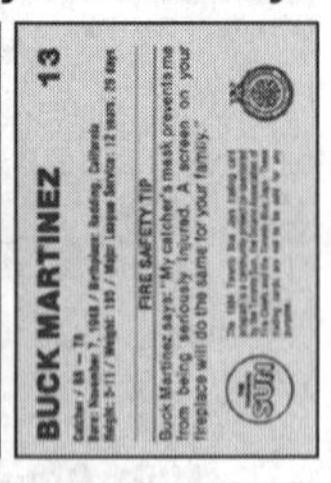

The 35 standard-size cards comprising this 1984 Blue Jays Fire Safety set feature on their fronts blue-bordered, color player action shots. The player's name, position, and uniform number appear in black lettering within the lower blue margin. The circular Blue Jays' logo rests at the bottom right. The horizontal white back carries the player's name and uniform number at the top, followed below by biography and a fire safety tip. The logos at the bottom for the Ontario Association of Fire Chiefs and The Toronto Sun round out the card. The cards are unnumbered and checklisted below in alphabetical order.

	NRMT	VG-E	GOOD
COMPLETE SET (35)	15.00	6.75	1.85
COMMON CARD (1-35)	.50	.23	.06
☐ 1 Jim Acker	.50	.23	.06
☐ 2 Willie Aikens	.50	.23	.06
☐ 3 Doyle Alexander	.75	.35	.09
☐ 4 Jesse Barfield	1.00	.45	.12
☐ 5 George Bell	.75	.35	.09
☐ 6 Jim Clancy	.50	.23	.06
☐ 7 Bryan Clark	.50	.23	.06
☐ 8 Stan Clarke	.50	.23	.06
☐ 9 Dave Collins	.75	.35	.09
☐ 10 Bobby Cox MG	1.00	.45	.12
☐ 11 Tony Fernandez	1.25	.55	.16
☐ 12 Damaso Garcia	.75	.35	.09
☐ 13 Cito Gaston CO	1.25	.55	.16
☐ 14 Jim Gott	.50	.23	.06
☐ 15 Alfredo Griffin	.75	.35	.09
☐ 16 Kelly Gruber	1.00	.45	.12
☐ 17 Garth Iorg	.50	.23	.06
☐ 18 Roy Lee Jackson	.50	.23	.06
☐ 19 Cliff Johnson	.75	.35	.09
☐ 20 Jimmy Key	2.50	1.10	.30
☐ 21 Dennis Lamp	.50	.23	.06
☐ 22 Rick Leach	.50	.23	.06
☐ 23 Luis Leal	.50	.23	.06
☐ 24 Buck Martinez	.75	.35	.09
☐ 25 Lloyd Moseby	1.00	.45	.12
☐ 26 Rance Mulliniks	.75	.35	.09
☐ 27 Billy Smith CO	.50	.23	.06
☐ 28 Dave Stieb	1.00	.45	.12
☐ 29 John Sullivan CO	.50	.23	.06
☐ 30 Willie Upshaw	.75	.35	.09
☐ 31 Mitch Webster	.50	.23	.06
☐ 32 Ernie Whitt	.75	.35	.09
☐ 33 Al Widmar CO	.50	.23	.06
☐ 34 Jimy Williams CO	.50	.23	.06
☐ 35 Blue Jays Logo	.50	.23	.06

1985 Blue Jays Fire Safety

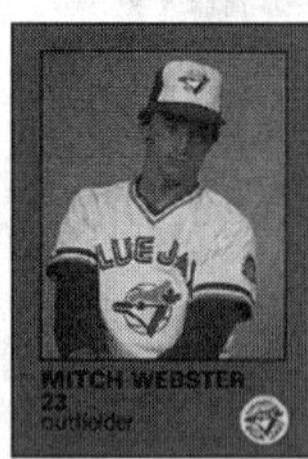

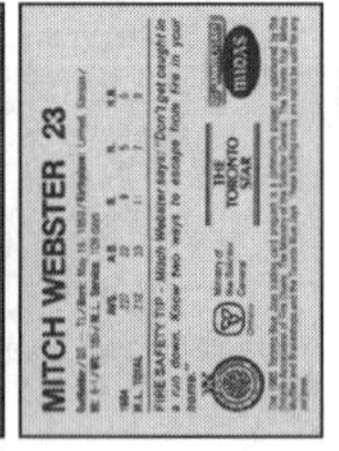

The 36 standard-size cards comprising this 1985 Blue Jays Fire Safety set feature on their fronts blue-bordered posed color player photos. The player's name, position, and uniform number appear in black lettering within the lower blue margin. The circular Blue Jays' logo rests at the bottom right. The horizontal white back carries the player's name and uniform number at the top, followed below by biography, statistics, and a fire safety tip. The logos at the bottom for the Ontario Association of Fire Chiefs, the Ontario Ministry of the Solicitor General, The Toronto Star, and Midas round out the card. The cards are unnumbered and checklisted below in alphabetical order.

	NRMT	VG-E	GOOD
COMPLETE SET (36)	10.00	4.50	1.25
COMMON CARD (1-36)	.25	.11	.03
☐ 1 Jim Acker	.25	.11	.03
☐ 2 Willie Aikens	.25	.11	.03
☐ 3 Doyle Alexander	.50	.23	.06
☐ 4 Jesse Barfield	.75	.35	.09
☐ 5 George Bell	.75	.35	.09
☐ 6 Jeff Burroughs	.50	.23	.06
☐ 7 Bill Caudill	.25	.11	.03
☐ 8 Jim Clancy	.25	.11	.03
☐ 9 Bobby Cox MG	.75	.35	.09
☐ 10 Tony Fernandez	.75	.35	.09
☐ 11 Damaso Garcia	.50	.23	.06
☐ 12 Cito Gaston CO	.75	.35	.09
☐ 13 Kelly Gruber	.75	.35	.09
☐ 14 Tom Henke	1.25	.55	.16
☐ 15 Garth Iorg	.25	.11	.03
☐ 16 Jimmy Key	1.25	.55	.16
☐ 17 Dennis Lamp	.25	.11	.03
☐ 18 Gary Lavelle	.25	.11	.03
☐ 19 Luis Leal	.25	.11	.03
☐ 20 Manny Lee	.25	.11	.03
☐ 21 Buck Martinez	.50	.23	.06
☐ 22 Len Matuszek	.25	.11	.03
☐ 23 Lloyd Moseby	.50	.23	.06
☐ 24 Rance Mulliniks	.25	.11	.03
☐ 25 Ron Musselman	.25	.11	.03
☐ 26 Billy Smith CO	.25	.11	.03
☐ 27 Dave Stieb	.75	.35	.09
☐ 28 John Sullivan CO	.25	.11	.03
☐ 29 Lou Thornton	.25	.11	.03
☐ 30 Willie Upshaw	.50	.23	.06
☐ 31 Mitch Webster	.25	.11	.03
☐ 32 Ernie Whitt	.50	.23	.06
☐ 33 Al Widmar CO	.25	.11	.03
☐ 34 Jimy Williams CO	.25	.11	.03
☐ 35 Blue Jays Logo (Unnumbered checklist back)	.25	.11	.03
☐ 36 Blue Jays Team Photo (Schedule on back)	.50	.23	.06

1985 Blue Jays Pepsi/Frito Lay Pennants

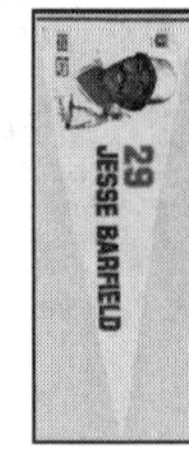

This five-pennant set was produced by Pepsi Cola and Frito Lay and measures approximately 9 1/2" by 26". The fronts display a color drawing of the player's head alongside a full player image with the player's name and jersey number and a facsimile autograph. The cards are unnumbered and checklisted below in alphabetical order.

	MINT	NRMT	EXC
COMPLETE SET (5)	10.00	4.50	1.25
COMMON CARD (1-5)	2.00	.90	.25
☐ 1 Jesse Barfield	3.00	1.35	.35
☐ 2 Bill Caudill	2.00	.90	.25
☐ 3 Dave Stieb	3.00	1.35	.35
☐ 4 Willie Upshaw	2.00	.90	.25
☐ 5 Ernie Whitt	2.00	.90	.25

1986 Blue Jays Ault Foods

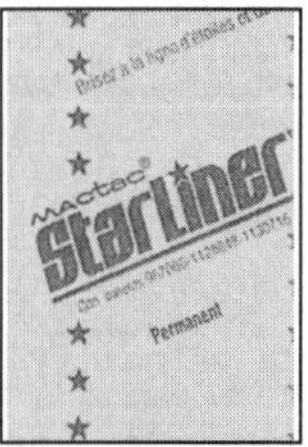

The 24 stickers in this set, featuring members of the Toronto Blue Jays, measure approximately 2" by 3" and were to be pasted in a 9" by 12", 20-page album. On a white background, the fronts feature color player photos, with rounded corners and a thin blue border. The player's last name and number appear under the photo. The backs carry the Starliner logo in light blue letters. Ault Foods were sold under several brands, e.g., Sealtest, Silverwood, Royal Oak, and Copper Cliff. The stickers are unnumbered and checklisted below in alphabetical order. The set is also noteworthy in that it contains Cecil Fielder appearing in his Rookie Card year.

	MINT	NRMT	EXC
COMPLETE SET (24)	20.00	9.00	2.50
COMMON CARD (1-24)	.75	.35	.09
☐ 1 Jim Acker	.75	.35	.09
☐ 2 Doyle Alexander	.75	.35	.09
☐ 3 Jesse Barfield	1.25	.55	.16
☐ 4 George Bell	1.25	.55	.16
☐ 5 Bill Caudill	.75	.35	.09
☐ 6 Jim Clancy	.75	.35	.09
☐ 7 Steve Davis	.75	.35	.09
☐ 8 Tony Fernandez	1.25	.55	.16
☐ 9 Cecil Fielder	7.50	3.40	.95
☐ 10 Damaso Garcia	1.00	.45	.12

	MINT	NRMT	EXC
☐ 11 Don Gordon	.75	.35	.09
☐ 12 Kelly Gruber	1.25	.55	.16
☐ 13 Tom Henke	1.25	.55	.16
☐ 14 Garth Iorg	.75	.35	.09
☐ 15 Cliff Johnson	1.00	.45	.12
☐ 16 Jimmy Key	2.00	.90	.25
☐ 17 Dennis Lamp	.75	.35	.09
☐ 18 Gary Lavelle	.75	.35	.09
☐ 19 Buck Martinez	1.00	.45	.12
☐ 20 Lloyd Moseby	1.25	.55	.16
☐ 21 Rance Mulliniks	1.00	.45	.12
☐ 22 Dave Stieb	1.25	.55	.16
☐ 23 Willie Upshaw	1.00	.45	.12
☐ 24 Ernie Whitt	1.00	.45	.12
☐ xx0 Ault Album	2.50	1.10	.30

1986 Blue Jays Fire Safety

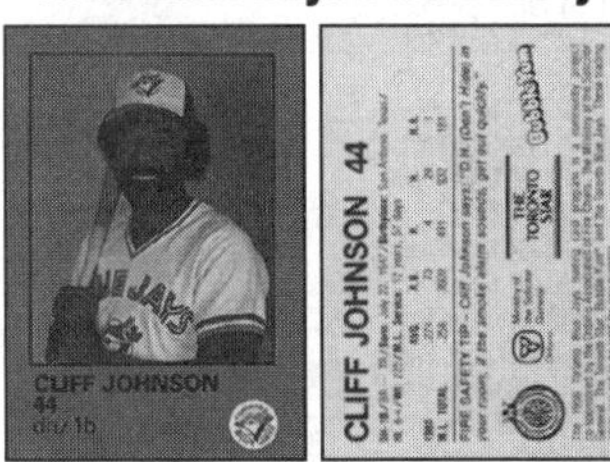

The 36 standard-size cards comprising this 1986 Toronto Blue Jays Fire set feature on their fronts blue-bordered, posed color player photos. The player's name, position, and uniform number appear in black lettering within the lower blue margin. The circular Blue Jays' logo rests at the bottom right. The horizontal white back carries the player's name and uniform number at the top, followed below by biography, statistics, and a fire safety tip. The logos at the bottom for the Ontario Association of Fire Chiefs, the Ontario Ministry of the Solicitor General, The Toronto Star, and Bubble Yum round out the card. The cards are unnumbered and checklisted below in alphabetical order. The set is also noteworthy in that it contains Cecil Fielder appearing in his Rookie Card year.

	MINT	NRMT	EXC
COMPLETE SET (36)	12.00	5.50	1.50
COMMON CARD (1-36)	.25	.11	.03
☐ 1 Jim Acker	.25	.11	.03
☐ 2 Doyle Alexander	.50	.23	.06
☐ 3 Jesse Barfield	.75	.35	.09
☐ 4 George Bell	.75	.35	.09
☐ 5 Bill Caudill	.25	.11	.03
☐ 6 Jim Clancy	.25	.11	.03
☐ 7 Steve Davis	.25	.11	.03
☐ 8 Mark Eichhorn	.50	.23	.06
☐ 9 Tony Fernandez	.75	.35	.09
☐ 10 Cecil Fielder	6.00	2.70	.75
☐ 11 Tom Filer	.25	.11	.03
☐ 12 Damaso Garcia	.50	.23	.06
☐ 13 Cito Gaston CO	.75	.35	.09
☐ 14 Don Gordon	.25	.11	.03
☐ 15 Kelly Gruber	.75	.35	.09
☐ 16 Jeff Hearron	.25	.11	.03
☐ 17 Tom Henke	.75	.35	.09
☐ 18 Garth Iorg	.25	.11	.03
☐ 19 Cliff Johnson	.50	.23	.06
☐ 20 Jimmy Key	1.00	.45	.12
☐ 21 Dennis Lamp	.25	.11	.03
☐ 22 Gary Lavelle	.25	.11	.03
☐ 23 Rick Leach	.25	.11	.03
☐ 24 Buck Martinez	.50	.23	.06
☐ 25 John McLaren CO	.25	.11	.03
☐ 26 Lloyd Moseby	.50	.23	.06
☐ 27 Rance Mulliniks	.25	.11	.03
☐ 28 Billy Smith CO	.25	.11	.03
☐ 29 Dave Stieb	.75	.35	.09
☐ 30 John Sullivan CO	.25	.11	.03
☐ 31 Willie Upshaw	.50	.23	.06
☐ 32 Ernie Whitt	.50	.23	.06
☐ 33 Al Widmar CO	.25	.11	.03
☐ 34 Jimy Williams MG	.25	.11	.03
☐ 35 Blue Jays LOGO (Won-Lost Record)	.25	.11	.03
☐ 36 Blue Jays Team Photo (Checklist back)	.25	.11	.03

1986 Blue Jays Greats TCMA

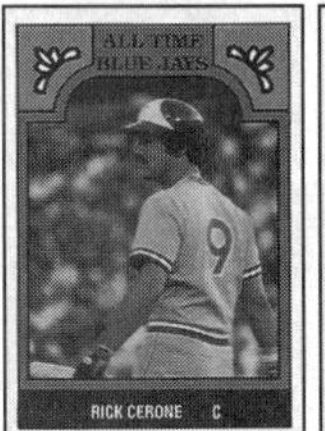

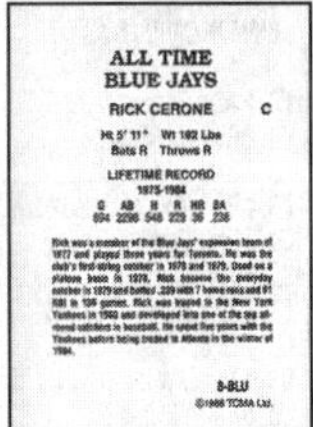

These 12 standard-size cards honor the best players of the Toronto Blue Jays first decade. The players are pictured on the front. The backs have a biography and career statistics.

	MINT	NRMT	EXC
COMPLETE SET (12)	3.00	1.35	.35
COMMON CARD (1-12)	.25	.11	.03
☐ 1 John Mayberry	.35	.16	.04
☐ 2 Bob Bailor	.25	.11	.03
☐ 3 Luis Gomez	.25	.11	.03
☐ 4 Roy Howell	.25	.11	.03
☐ 5 Otto Velez	.25	.11	.03
☐ 6 Rick Bosetti	.25	.11	.03
☐ 7 Al Woods	.25	.11	.03
☐ 8 Rick Cerone	.35	.16	.04
☐ 9 Dave Lemanczyk	.25	.11	.03
☐ 10 Tom Underwood	.25	.11	.03
☐ 11 Joey McLaughlin	.25	.11	.03
☐ 12 Bobby Cox MG	.50	.23	.06

1987 Blue Jays Fire Safety

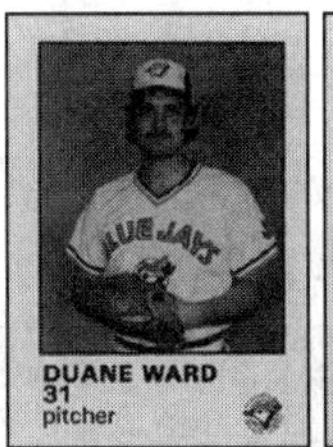

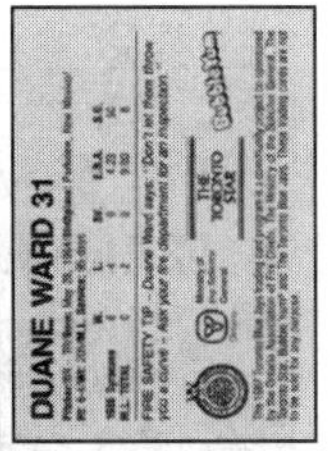

The 36 standard-size cards comprising this 1987 Toronto Blue Jays Fire Safety set feature on their fronts white-bordered, posed color player photos. The player's name, position, and uniform number appear in black lettering within the lower white margin. The circular Blue Jays' logo rests at the bottom right. The horizontal white back carries the player's name and uniform number at the top, followed below by biography, statistics, and a fire safety tip. The logos at the bottom for the Ontario Association of Fire Chiefs, the Ontario Ministry of the Solicitor General, The Toronto Star, and Bubble Yum round out the card. The cards are unnumbered and checklisted below in alphabetical order.

	MINT	NRMT	EXC
COMPLETE SET (36)	8.00	3.60	1.00
COMMON CARD (1-36)	.35	.16	.04
☐ 1 Jesse Barfield	.75	.35	.09
☐ 2 George Bell	1.00	.45	.12
☐ 3 John Cerutti	.35	.16	.04
☐ 4 Checklist Card (Team photo on front)	.50	.23	.06
☐ 5 Jim Clancy	.35	.16	.04
☐ 6 Rob Ducey	.35	.16	.04
☐ 7 Mark Eichhorn	.50	.23	.06
☐ 8 Tony Fernandez	1.00	.45	.12
☐ 9 Cecil Fielder	2.00	.90	.25
☐ 10 Cito Gaston CO	1.00	.45	.12
☐ 11 Kelly Gruber	.50	.23	.06
☐ 12 Tom Henke	.75	.35	.09
☐ 13 Jeff Hearron	.35	.16	.04
☐ 14 Garth Iorg	.35	.16	.04
☐ 15 Joe Johnson	.35	.16	.04
☐ 16 Jimmy Key	.50	.23	.06
☐ 17 Gary Lavelle	.35	.16	.04
☐ 18 Rick Leach	.35	.16	.04
☐ 19 Logo Card (Franchise yearly record on back)	.35	.16	.04
☐ 20 Fred McGriff	4.00	1.80	.50
☐ 21 John McLaren CO	.35	.16	.04
☐ 22 Craig McMurtry	.35	.16	.04
☐ 23 Lloyd Moseby	.50	.23	.06
☐ 24 Rance Mulliniks	.35	.16	.04
☐ 25 Jeff Musselman	.35	.16	.04
☐ 26 Jose Nunez	.35	.16	.04
☐ 27 Mike Sharperson	.35	.16	.04
☐ 28 Billy Smith CO	.35	.16	.04
☐ 29 Matt Stark	.35	.16	.04
☐ 30 Dave Stieb	.75	.35	.09
☐ 31 John Sullivan CO	.35	.16	.04
☐ 32 Willie Upshaw	.50	.23	.06
☐ 33 Duane Ward	.50	.23	.06
☐ 34 Ernie Whitt	.50	.23	.06
☐ 35 Al Widmar CO	.35	.16	.04
☐ 36 Jimy Williams MG	.35	.16	.04

1988 Blue Jays 5x7

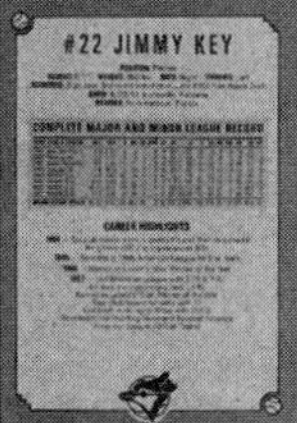

These 14 oversized cards measure approximately 5" by 7" and feature turquoise-bordered retouched posed color player photos. The player's name, along with the Blue Jays name and logo, appears below the photo. Baseball icons highlight the margins at the upper left and lower right. The same border design continues on the back, which carries the player's name and uniform number at the top. Biography, complete major and minor league statistics, and career highlights round out the card. The cards are unnumbered and checklisted below in alphabetical order.

	MINT	NRMT	EXC
COMPLETE SET (14)	16.00	7.25	2.00
COMMON CARD (1-14)	.50	.23	.06
☐ 1 Jesse Barfield	2.00	.90	.25
☐ 2 George Bell	2.00	.90	.25
☐ 3 Jim Clancy	.50	.23	.06
☐ 4 Mark Eichhorn	.50	.23	.06
☐ 5 Tony Fernandez	2.00	.90	.25
☐ 6 Tom Henke	2.00	.90	.25
☐ 7 Jimmy Key	2.50	1.10	.30
☐ 8 Nelson Liriano	.50	.23	.06
☐ 9 Lloyd Moseby	2.00	.90	.25
☐ 10 Dave Stieb	2.00	.90	.25
☐ 11 Willie Upshaw	1.25	.55	.16
☐ 12 Jimy Williams MG	.50	.23	.06
☐ 13 1988 Schedule	.50	.23	.06
☐ 14 1988 Season Ticket Packages/Single Game Ticket Prices	.50	.23	.06

1988 Blue Jays Fire Safety

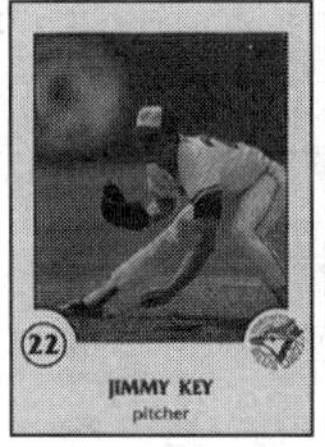

This attractive, white-bordered, 36-card set features Toronto Blue Jays, their coaches and manager. The cards (measuring 3 1/2" by 5") are over-sized. The backs contain brief player data, a Fire Safety Tip (done in question and answer format) emanating from that player and the logos of the sponsoring Toronto Star, Ministry of the Solicitor General, Bubble Yum, and the Ontario Association of Fire Chiefs. The cards are unnumbered and checklisted below in alphabetical order.

	MINT	NRMT	EXC
COMPLETE SET (36)	10.00	4.50	1.25
COMMON CARD (1-36)	.25	.11	.03
☐ 1 Jesse Barfield	.75	.35	.09
☐ 2 George Bell	1.00	.45	.12
☐ 3 Juan Beniquez	.25	.11	.03
☐ 4 Pat Borders	.75	.35	.09
☐ 5 Sil Campusano	.25	.11	.03
☐ 6 John Cerutti	.25	.11	.03
☐ 7 Jim Clancy	.25	.11	.03
☐ 8 Rob Ducey	.25	.11	.03
☐ 9 Mark Eichhorn	.25	.11	.03
☐ 10 Tony Fernandez	1.00	.45	.12
☐ 11 Cecil Fielder	.75	.35	.09
☐ 12 Mike Flanagan	.50	.23	.06
☐ 13 Cito Gaston CO	1.00	.45	.12
☐ 14 Kelly Gruber	.50	.23	.06
☐ 15 Tom Henke	1.00	.45	.12
☐ 16 Jimmy Key	.50	.23	.06
☐ 17 Rick Leach	.25	.11	.03
☐ 18 Manny Lee	.25	.11	.03
☐ 19 Nelson Liriano	.25	.11	.03
☐ 20 Winston Llenas CO	.25	.11	.03
☐ 21 Fred McGriff	3.00	1.35	.35
☐ 22 John McLaren CO	.25	.11	.03
☐ 23 Lloyd Moseby	.50	.23	.06
☐ 24 Rance Mulliniks	.25	.11	.03
☐ 25 Jeff Musselman	.25	.11	.03
☐ 26 Billy Smith CO	.25	.11	.03
☐ 27 Dave Stieb	.75	.35	.09
☐ 28 Todd Stottlemyre	1.50	.70	.19
☐ 29 John Sullivan CO	.25	.11	.03
☐ 30 Duane Ward	.25	.11	.03
☐ 31 David Wells	.75	.35	.09
☐ 32 Ernie Whitt	.50	.23	.06
☐ 33 Al Widmar CO	.25	.11	.03
☐ 34 Jimy Williams MG	.25	.11	.03
☐ 35 Team Card (Checklist back)	.50	.23	.06
☐ 36 Title/Logo Card (Year by year record on back)	.50	.23	.06

1989 Blue Jays Fire Safety

The 36 standard-size cards comprising this 1989 Toronto Blue Jays Fire Safety set feature on their fronts white-bordered, color player action shots. The player's name, position, and uniform number appear in black lettering within the upper white margin. The circular Blue Jays' logo, with the words "On the Move," appears within the lower white margin and also encroaches on the player photo. The horizontal white back carries the player's name and uniform number at the top, followed below by biography, statistics, and a safety tip in the form of a question and inverted answer. The logos at the bottom for the Ontario Association of Fire Chiefs, the Ministry of Solicitor General, A and P/Dominion, and Oh Henry round out the card. The cards are unnumbered and checklisted below in alphabetical order.

	MINT	NRMT	EXC
COMPLETE SET (36)	8.00	3.60	1.00
COMMON CARD (1-36)	.25	.11	.03
☐ 1 Jesse Barfield	.75	.35	.09
☐ 2 George Bell	1.00	.45	.12
☐ 3 Pat Borders	.50	.23	.06
☐ 4 Bob Brenly	.25	.11	.03
☐ 5 Sal Butera	.25	.11	.03
☐ 6 Sil Campusano	.25	.11	.03
☐ 7 John Cerutti	.25	.11	.03
☐ 8 Rob Ducey	.25	.11	.03
☐ 9 Tony Fernandez	.75	.35	.09
☐ 10 Mike Flanagan	.50	.23	.06
☐ 11 Cito Gaston CO	1.00	.45	.12
☐ 12 Kelly Gruber	.75	.35	.09
☐ 13 Tom Henke	.75	.35	.09
☐ 14 Jimmy Key	1.00	.45	.12
☐ 15 Tom Lawless	.25	.11	.03
☐ 16 Manny Lee	.25	.11	.03
☐ 17 Nelson Liriano	.25	.11	.03
☐ 18 Fred McGriff	2.00	.90	.25
☐ 19 John McLaren CO	.25	.11	.03
☐ 20 Lloyd Moseby	.50	.23	.06
☐ 21 Rance Mulliniks	.25	.11	.03
☐ 22 Jeff Musselman	.25	.11	.03
☐ 23 Greg Myers	.25	.11	.03
☐ 24 Jose Nunez	.25	.11	.03
☐ 25 Mike Squires CO	.25	.11	.03
☐ 26 Dave Stieb	.75	.35	.09
☐ 27 Todd Stottlemyre	1.00	.45	.12
☐ 28 John Sullivan CO	.25	.11	.03
☐ 29 Duane Ward	.25	.11	.03
☐ 30 David Wells	.50	.23	.06
☐ 31 Ernie Whitt	.50	.23	.06
☐ 32 Al Widmar CO	.25	.11	.03
☐ 33 Jimy Williams MG	.25	.11	.03
☐ 34 Frank Wills	.25	.11	.03
☐ 35 Team Logo (W-L record on back)	.25	.11	.03
☐ 36 Team Photo (Checklist on back)	.50	.23	.06

1990 Blue Jays Fire Safety

The 36 standard-size cards comprising this 1990 Blue Jays Fan Club set feature on their fronts white-bordered color player action shots. The player's name and position appear in black lettering within the lower white margin. His uniform number appears within a circular white area in the photo's lower right corner. The set's logo appears within a circular white area in the photo's upper left corner. The white back carries the player's uniform number and name near the top, followed below by biography, statistics, and fire safety tip. The logos in each corner for the Ontario Association of Fire Chiefs, the Ministry of Solicitor General, A,P/Dominion, and Oh Henry round out the card. The cards are unnumbered and checklisted below in alphabetical order. The set is also noteworthy in that it contains John Olerud appearing in his Rookie Card year.

	MINT	NRMT	EXC
COMPLETE SET (36)	8.00	3.60	1.00
COMMON CARD (1-36)	.25	.11	.03
☐ 1 Jim Acker	.25	.11	.03
☐ 2 George Bell	1.00	.45	.12
☐ 3 Willie Blair	.25	.11	.03
☐ 4 Pat Borders	.25	.11	.03
☐ 5 John Cerutti	.25	.11	.03
☐ 6 Galen Cisco CO	.25	.11	.03
☐ 7 Junior Felix	.25	.11	.03
☐ 8 Tony Fernandez	1.00	.45	.12
☐ 9 Cito Gaston MG	1.00	.45	.12
☐ 10 Kelly Gruber	.50	.23	.06
☐ 11 Tom Henke	.75	.35	.09

	MINT	NRMT	EXC
☐ 12 Glenallen Hill	.75	.35	.09
☐ 13 Jimmy Key	1.00	.45	.12
☐ 14 Paul Kilgus	.25	.11	.03
☐ 15 Tom Lawless	.25	.11	.03
☐ 16 Manny Lee	.25	.11	.03
☐ 17 Al Leiter	1.00	.45	.12
☐ 18 Nelson Liriano	.25	.11	.03
☐ 19 Fred McGriff	1.50	.70	.19
☐ 20 John McLaren CO	.25	.11	.03
☐ 21 Rance Mulliniks	.25	.11	.03
☐ 22 Greg Myers	.25	.11	.03
☐ 23 John Olerud	2.00	.90	.25
☐ 24 Alex Sanchez	.25	.11	.03
☐ 25 Mike Squires CO	.25	.11	.03
☐ 26 Dave Stieb	.75	.35	.09
☐ 27 Todd Stottlemyre	1.00	.45	.12
☐ 28 John Sullivan CO	.25	.11	.03
☐ 29 Gene Tenace CO	.50	.23	.06
☐ 30 Ozzie Virgil	.25	.11	.03
☐ 31 Duane Ward	.25	.11	.03
☐ 32 David Wells	.50	.23	.06
☐ 33 Frank Wills	.25	.11	.03
☐ 34 Mookie Wilson	.50	.23	.06
☐ 35 Schedule Card	.25	.11	.03
☐ 36 Skydome (Checklist on back)	.50	.23	.06

1990 Blue Jays Hostess Stickers

These six strips of three stickers each feature color player action shots depicting great moments for the Blue Jays. Each strip measures approximately 7" by 3 1/4"; each sticker measures approximately 2 1/4" by 3 1/4". A brief description in English of the great moment, along with the Blue Jays logo, appears within the blue stripe across the top. The same description, in French, appears within the blue stripe at the bottom, along with the Hostess logo. The stickers are unnumbered and checklisted below by strip.

	MINT	NRMT	EXC
COMPLETE SET (6)	20.00	9.00	2.50
COMMON PANEL (1-6)	4.00	1.80	.50
☐ 1 Most Double Plays: Damaso Garcia MVP: George Bell Hits The Cycle: Kelly Gruber	4.00	1.80	.50
☐ 2 First AL East Pennant: Blue Jays Clinch Division Killer Bees Born: George Bell Lloyd Moseby Jesse Barfield AL Home Run Champ: Jesse Barfield	4.00	1.80	.50
☐ 3 First Homer in Skydome: Fred McGriff Club Save Leader: Tom Henke Three Winning Openers In a Row: Jimmy Key	6.00	2.70	.75
☐ 4 First 100 Wins: Jim Clancy ML Home Run Record: Ernie Whitt AL East Champs Again: Tom Henke	4.00	1.80	.50
☐ 5 Stolen Bases: Dave Collins Gold Glove Winners: Jesse Barfield Tony Fernandez Goodbye to Exhibition Stadium: Junior Felix Tony Fernandez Kelly Gruber George Bell Fred McGriff	5.00	2.20	.60
☐ 6 Home Run On First Pitch: Junior Felix Almost Perfect: Dave Stieb First Game at Skydome	4.00	1.80	.50

1991 Blue Jays Fire Safety

This 36-card standard-size set was jointly sponsored by the Ontario Association of Fire Chiefs, the Ministry of the Solicitor General, A and P/Dominion, Oh Henry, and the Toronto Blue Jays. The fronts feature

full-bleed glossy color action player photos. The player's name, uniform number, and position appear in a white stripe beneath the picture. The All-Star Season logo rounds out the card front. The backs have sponsors' logos, biography, statistics, and a fire safety tip. The cards are unnumbered and checklisted below in alphabetical order.

	MINT	NRMT	EXC
COMPLETE SET (36)	10.00	4.50	1.25
COMMON CARD (1-36)	.25	.11	.03
☐ 1 Jim Acker	.25	.11	.03
☐ 2 Roberto Alomar	2.00	.90	.25
☐ 3 Pat Borders	.25	.11	.03
☐ 4 Denis Boucher	.25	.11	.03
☐ 5 Joe Carter	1.50	.70	.19
☐ 6 Galen Cisco CO	.25	.11	.03
☐ 7 Ken Dayley	.25	.11	.03
☐ 8 Rob Ducey	.25	.11	.03
☐ 9 Cito Gaston MG	1.00	.45	.12
☐ 10 Rene Gonzales	.25	.11	.03
☐ 11 Kelly Gruber	.50	.23	.06
☐ 12 Rich Hacker CO	.25	.11	.03
☐ 13 Tom Henke	.75	.35	.09
☐ 14 Glenallen Hill	.75	.35	.09
☐ 15 Jimmy Key	1.00	.45	.12
☐ 16 Manny Lee	.25	.11	.03
☐ 17 Al Leiter	1.00	.45	.12
☐ 18 Rance Mulliniks	.25	.11	.03
☐ 19 Greg Myers	.25	.11	.03
☐ 20 John Olerud	1.00	.45	.12
☐ 21 Mike Squires CO	.25	.11	.03
☐ 22 Dave Stieb	.75	.35	.09
☐ 23 Todd Stottlemyre	1.00	.45	.12
☐ 24 John Sullivan CO	.25	.11	.03
☐ 25 Pat Tabler	.25	.11	.03
☐ 26 Gene Tenace CO	.25	.11	.03
☐ 27 Hector Torres CO	.25	.11	.03
☐ 28 Duane Ward	.25	.11	.03
☐ 29 David Wells	.50	.23	.06
☐ 30 Devon White	1.00	.45	.12
☐ 31 Mark Whiten	.25	.11	.03
☐ 32 Kenny Williams	.25	.11	.03
☐ 33 Frank Wills	.25	.11	.03
☐ 34 Mookie Wilson	.50	.23	.06
☐ 35 B.J. Burdy (Mascot)	.25	.11	.03
☐ 36 Checklist Card	.50	.23	.06

1991 Blue Jays Score

The 1991 Score Toronto Blue Jays set contains 40 player cards plus five magic motion trivia cards. The standard-size cards feature on the fronts glossy color action photos with white borders. The bottom corners of the pictures are cut off by aqua-shaped triangles such that home plate is resembled. The player's name and position appear in an aqua stripe above the picture. The producer's name and the team logo at the bottom round out the card face. The backs have a color head shot of the player, biography, Major League statistics, and a player profile.

	MINT	NRMT	EXC
COMPLETE SET (40)	14.00	6.25	1.75
COMMON CARD (1-40)	.25	.11	.03
☐ 1 Joe Carter	1.50	.70	.19
☐ 2 Tom Henke	.75	.35	.09
☐ 3 Jimmy Key	.75	.35	.09
☐ 4 Al Leiter	1.00	.45	.12
☐ 5 Dave Stieb	.75	.35	.09
☐ 6 Todd Stottlemyre	1.00	.45	.12
☐ 7 Mike Timlin	.50	.23	.06
☐ 8 Duane Ward	.50	.23	.06
☐ 9 David Wells	.50	.23	.06
☐ 10 Frank Wills	.25	.11	.03
☐ 11 Pat Borders	.25	.11	.03
☐ 12 Greg Myers	.25	.11	.03
☐ 13 Roberto Alomar	2.50	1.10	.30
☐ 14 Rene Gonzales	.25	.11	.03
☐ 15 Kelly Gruber	.50	.23	.06
☐ 16 Manny Lee	.25	.11	.03
☐ 17 Rance Mulliniks	.25	.11	.03
☐ 18 John Olerud	1.50	.70	.19
☐ 19 Pat Tabler	.25	.11	.03
☐ 20 Derek Bell	1.25	.55	.16
☐ 21 Jim Acker	.25	.11	.03
☐ 22 Rob Ducey	.25	.11	.03
☐ 23 Devon White	.75	.35	.09
☐ 24 Mookie Wilson	.50	.23	.06
☐ 25 Juan Guzman	2.00	.90	.25
☐ 26 Ed Sprague	.75	.35	.09
☐ 27 Ken Dayley	.25	.11	.03
☐ 28 Tom Candiotti	.25	.11	.03
☐ 29 Candy Maldonado	.25	.11	.03
☐ 30 Eddie Zosky	.25	.11	.03
☐ 31 Steve Karsay	1.25	.55	.16
☐ 32 Bob MacDonald	.25	.11	.03
☐ 33 Ray Giannelli	.25	.11	.03
☐ 34 Jerry Schunk	.25	.11	.03
☐ 35 Dave Weathers	.50	.23	.06
☐ 36 Cito Gaston MG	1.00	.45	.12
☐ 37 Joe Carter AS	.50	.23	.06
☐ 38 Jimmy Key AS	.50	.23	.06
☐ 39 Roberto Alomar AS	1.25	.55	.16
☐ 40 1991 All-Star Game	.25	.11	.03

1992 Blue Jays Fire Safety

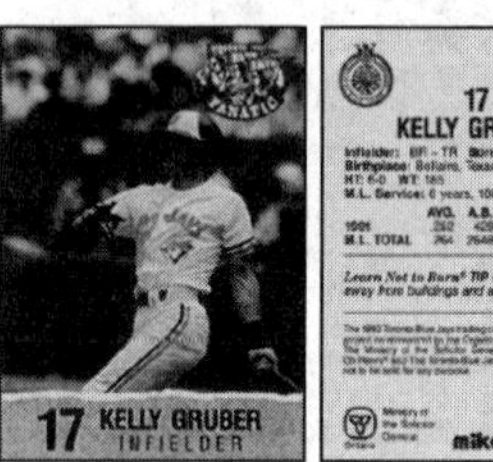

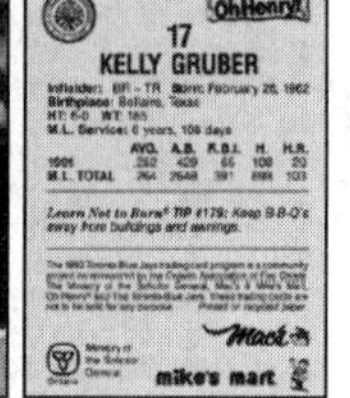

This 36-card standard-size set was jointly sponsored by the Ontario Association of Fire Chiefs, The Ministry of the Solicitor General, Mac's Milk, Mike's Mart, and Oh Henry. The cards are printed on recycled paper and are thinner than most sports cards. Full-bleed color player photos with a torn effect at the bottom enhance the card fronts. The player's name, number, and position appear in a sandy border. The backs feature biographical and statistical player information and fire safety tips. The cards are unnumbered and checklisted below in alphabetical order.

	MINT	NRMT	EXC
COMPLETE SET (36)	12.50	5.50	1.55
COMMON CARD (1-36)	.25	.11	.03
☐ 1 Roberto Alomar	2.00	.90	.25
☐ 2 Bob Bailor CO	.25	.11	.03
☐ 3 Derek Bell	.75	.35	.09
☐ 4 Pat Borders	.25	.11	.03
☐ 5 Joe Carter	1.25	.55	.16
☐ 6 Galen Cisco CO	.25	.11	.03
☐ 7 Ken Dayley	.25	.11	.03
☐ 8 Rob Ducey	.25	.11	.03
☐ 9 Cito Gaston MG	1.00	.45	.12
☐ 10 Alfredo Griffin	.50	.23	.06
☐ 11 Kelly Gruber	.75	.35	.09
☐ 12 Juan Guzman	.50	.23	.06
☐ 13 Rich Hacker CO	.25	.11	.03
☐ 14 Tom Henke	1.00	.45	.12
☐ 15 Larry Hisle CO	.50	.23	.06
☐ 16 Jimmy Key	1.00	.45	.12
☐ 17 Manny Lee	.25	.11	.03
☐ 18 Bob MacDonald	.25	.11	.03
☐ 19 Candy Maldonado	.25	.11	.03
☐ 20 Jack Morris	1.00	.45	.12
☐ 21 Rance Mulliniks	.25	.11	.03
☐ 22 Greg Myers	.25	.11	.03
☐ 23 John Olerud	.75	.35	.09
☐ 24 Dave Stieb	1.00	.45	.12
☐ 25 Todd Stottlemyre	.75	.35	.09
☐ 26 John Sullivan CO	.25	.11	.03
☐ 27 Pat Tabler	.25	.11	.03
☐ 28 Gene Tenace CO	.25	.11	.03
☐ 29 Mike Timlin	.50	.23	.06
☐ 30 Duane Ward	.25	.11	.03
☐ 31 Turner Ward	.25	.11	.03
☐ 32 David Wells	.50	.23	.06
☐ 33 Devon White	.75	.35	.09
☐ 34 Dave Winfield	1.50	.70	.19
☐ 35 Eddie Zosky	.25	.11	.03
☐ 36 Checklist Card	.25	.11	.03

1992 Blue Jays Maxwell House

Sponsored by Maxwell House Coffee, this 18-card standard-size set celebrates the first fifteen years of the Toronto Blue Jays. Each horizontal front has a team photo with a double blue inner border and a white outer border. The team logo appears in a circle at the top while the year and the team name are printed in an oval at the bottom. The horizontal backs list the players' names by rows, manager, record, and highlights or key accomplishments. The set includes a mail-in offer for a commemorative team card album. The cards are unnumbered and checklisted below in alphabetical order.

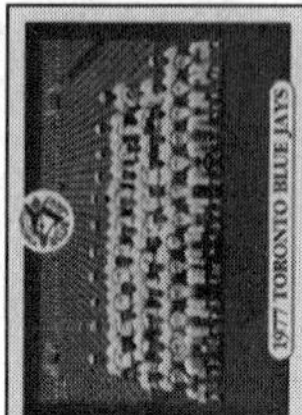

	MINT	NRMT	EXC
COMPLETE SET (18)	15.00	6.75	1.85
COMMON CARD (1-18)	1.00	.45	.12
☐ 1 1977 Team Photo	1.50	.70	.19
☐ 2 1978 Team Photo	1.00	.45	.12
☐ 3 1979 Team Photo	1.00	.45	.12
☐ 4 1980 Team Photo	1.00	.45	.12
☐ 5 1981 Team Photo	1.00	.45	.12
☐ 6 1982 Team Photo	1.00	.45	.12
☐ 7 1983 Team Photo	1.00	.45	.12
☐ 8 1984 Team Photo	1.00	.45	.12
☐ 9 1985 Team Photo	1.50	.70	.19
☐ 10 1986 Team Photo	1.00	.45	.12
☐ 11 1987 Team Photo	1.00	.45	.12
☐ 12 1988 Team Photo	1.00	.45	.12
☐ 13 1989 Team Photo	1.00	.45	.12
☐ 14 1990 Team Photo	1.00	.45	.12
☐ 15 1991 Team Photo	1.00	.45	.12
☐ 16 1992 Team Photo	1.50	.70	.19
☐ 17 Title Card	1.00	.45	.12
☐ 18 Album Offer Card	1.00	.45	.12

1993 Blue Jays Colla Postcards 15

This 15-card set is borderless, without the player's name on the front. Eight cards are marked "WC" for "World Champions", in a border across the front corner. Backs contain the player's name, the Bluejays' logo and are all numbered alphabetically as described below.

	MINT	NRMT	EXC
COMPLETE SET (15)	7.50	3.40	.95
COMMON CARD (1-15)	.50	.23	.06
☐ 1 Roberto Alomar	2.00	.90	.25
☐ 2 Pat Borders	.50	.23	.06
☐ 3 Joe Carter	1.50	.70	.19
☐ 4 Roberto Alomar WC	1.00	.45	.12
☐ 5 Pat Borders WC	.50	.23	.06
☐ 6 Joe Carter WC	.75	.35	.09
☐ 7 Juan Guzman WC	.50	.23	.06
☐ 8 Jack Morris WC	1.00	.45	.12
☐ 9 John Olerud WC	.75	.35	.09
☐ 10 Todd Stottlemyre WC	1.00	.45	.12
☐ 11 Devon White WC	.50	.23	.06
☐ 12 Juan Guzman	.75	.35	.09
☐ 13 Paul Molitor	2.00	.90	.25
☐ 14 Dave Stewart	.75	.35	.09
☐ 15 Devon White	.75	.35	.09

1993 Blue Jays Dempster's

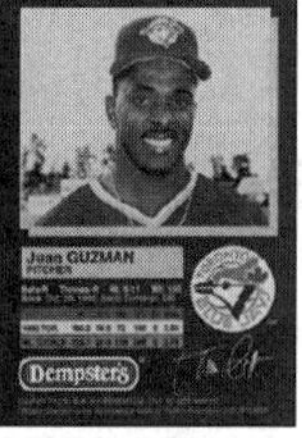

This 25-card standard-size set commemorates the 1992 World Series Champion Toronto Blue Jays and was sponsored by Dempster's. The navy blue with pinstripe fronts feature action color player photos. The player's name and position are printed in white in the lower right. The backs are navy blue and carry a head shot on the top half with biography and 1992 season statistics below. A facsimile autograph is printed in the lower right. The cards are numbered on the front.

	MINT	NRMT	EXC
COMPLETE SET (25)	15.00	6.75	1.85
COMMON CARD (1-25)	.50	.23	.06
☐ 1 Juan Guzman	1.25	.55	.16
☐ 2 Roberto Alomar	2.00	.90	.25
☐ 3 Danny Cox	.50	.23	.06
☐ 4 Paul Molitor	2.00	.90	.25
☐ 5 Todd Stottlemyre	1.00	.45	.12
☐ 6 Joe Carter	1.50	.70	.19
☐ 7 Jack Morris	1.00	.45	.12
☐ 8 Ed Sprague	1.00	.45	.12
☐ 9 Turner Ward	.50	.23	.06
☐ 10 John Olerud	1.00	.45	.12
☐ 11 Duane Ward	.50	.23	.06
☐ 12 Alfredo Griffin	.75	.35	.09
☐ 13 Cito Gaston MG	1.00	.45	.12
☐ 14 Dave Stewart	1.00	.45	.12

☐ 15 Mark Eichhorn	.50	.23	.06
☐ 16 Darnell Coles	.50	.23	.06
☐ 17 Randy Knorr	.50	.23	.06
☐ 18 Al Leiter	1.00	.45	.12
☐ 19 Pat Hentgen	1.50	.70	.19
☐ 20 Devon White	1.25	.55	.16
☐ 21 Pat Borders	.50	.23	.06
☐ 22 Darrin Jackson	.50	.23	.06
☐ 23 Dick Schofield	.50	.23	.06
☐ 24 Luis Sojo	.50	.23	.06
☐ 25 Mike Timlin	.75	.35	.09

1993 Blue Jays Donruss 45

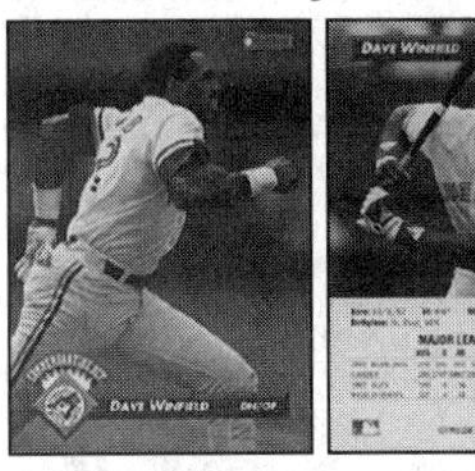

This standard-size 45-card gold-boxed set showcases the 1992 Blue Jays with full-bleed action color photos. The words "Commemorative Set Toronto Blue Jays" appear on a team color-coded logo in the lower right. The player's name is displayed in white lettering along a blue bar at the bottom. The top half of each back carries a color player photo with his name printed on a blue bar at the top. The bottom portion contains biography as well as 1992 and World Series statistics.

	MINT	NRMT	EXC
COMPLETE SET (45)	15.00	6.75	1.85
COMMON CARD (1-45)	.25	.11	.03
☐ 1 Checklist Card	.25	.11	.03
☐ 2 Roberto Alomar	1.50	.70	.19
☐ 3 Derek Bell	.50	.23	.06
☐ 4 Pat Borders	.25	.11	.03
☐ 5 Joe Carter	1.25	.55	.16
☐ 6 Alfredo Griffin	.50	.23	.06
☐ 7 Kelly Gruber	.50	.23	.06
☐ 8 Manny Lee	.25	.11	.03
☐ 9 Candy Maldonado	.25	.11	.03
☐ 10 John Olerud	.75	.35	.09
☐ 11 Ed Sprague	.75	.35	.09
☐ 12 Pat Tabler	.25	.11	.03
☐ 13 Devon White	.75	.35	.09
☐ 14 Dave Winfield	1.50	.70	.19
☐ 15 David Cone	.50	.23	.06
☐ 16 Mark Eichhorn	.25	.11	.03
☐ 17 Juan Guzman	1.00	.45	.12
☐ 18 Tom Henke	.75	.35	.09
☐ 19 Jimmy Key	1.00	.45	.12
☐ 20 Jack Morris	1.00	.45	.12
☐ 21 Todd Stottlemyre	1.00	.45	.12
☐ 22 Mike Timlin	.50	.23	.06
☐ 23 Duane Ward	.25	.11	.03
☐ 24 David Wells	.50	.23	.06
☐ 25 Randy Knorr	.25	.11	.03
☐ 26 Rance Mulliniks	.25	.11	.03
☐ 27 Tom Quinlan	.25	.11	.03
☐ 28 Cito Gaston MG	.75	.35	.09
☐ 29 Dave Stieb	.75	.35	.09
☐ 30 Ken Dayley	.25	.11	.03
☐ 31 Turner Ward	.25	.11	.03
☐ 32 Eddie Zosky	.25	.11	.03
☐ 33 Pat Hentgen	2.00	.90	.25
☐ 34 Al Leiter	1.00	.45	.12
☐ 35 Doug Linton	.25	.11	.03
☐ 36 Bob MacDonald	.25	.11	.03
☐ 37 Rick Trlicek	.25	.11	.03
☐ 38 Domingo Martinez	.25	.11	.03
☐ 39 Mike Maksudian	.25	.11	.03
☐ 40 Rob Ducey	.25	.11	.03
☐ 41 Jeff Kent	1.50	.70	.19
☐ 42 Greg Myers	.25	.11	.03
☐ 43 Dave Weathers	.25	.11	.03
☐ 44 Skydome	.25	.11	.03
☐ 45 Trophy Presentation	.25	.11	.03

1993 Blue Jays Donruss McDonald's

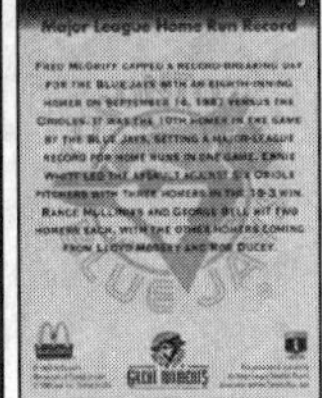

This 36-card standard-size set was produced by Donruss for McDonald's and recognizes "Great Moments" of the Blue Jays. Foil packs sold for 45 cents Canadian with purchase of fries or hash browns. In terms of design, the set subdivides into three sections: 1985-92 Team Highlights (1-13); 1992 World Series (14-26); and regular-issue player cards (27-35). The cards have fronts depicting significant plays and players from 1985 to 1992 in action photos. The McDonald's logo is located in the top left. On cards 1-26, the gold-foil stamped "Great Moments" appears near the bottom with the name of the great moment listed below, while the back describes the event pictured on the front and is superimposed on a ghosted logo of the Blue Jays, with the date in gold lettering across the top. The cards are numbered on the back and are arranged in date sequence.

	MINT	NRMT	EXC
COMPLETE SET (36)	15.00	6.75	1.85
COMMON CARD (1-36)	.25	.11	.03
☐ 1 Willie Upshaw	.50	.23	.06
1985-First Title			
☐ 2 Jesse Barfield	.75	.35	.09
1986-Home Run King			
☐ 3 Fred McGriff	2.50	1.10	.30
1987-Home Run King			
☐ 4 George Bell	.75	.35	.09
1988-Opening Bell			
☐ 5 Kelly Gruber	.50	.23	.06
1989-First Cycle			
☐ 6 Ernie Whitt	.50	.23	.06
1989-Comeback			
☐ 7 Tom Henke	.75	.35	.09
1989-Winners Again			
☐ 8 Dave Stieb	.75	.35	.09
1990-1st No-Hitter			
☐ 9 Jack Morris	.75	.35	.09
1992-1st 20-Gamer			
☐ 10 Team salutes fans	.25	.11	.03
1992-FANtastic			
☐ 11 Pat Borders	.75	.35	.09
Mark McGwire			
1992-Sudden Impact			
☐ 12 Roberto Alomar	2.00	.90	.25
1992-Turning Point			
☐ 13 Candy Maldonado	.25	.11	.03
1992-On to Atlanta			
☐ 14 Ed Sprague	.75	.35	.09
1992-WS Instant Hero			
☐ 15 Bobby Cox MG	.50	.23	.06
Cito Gaston MG			
1992-WS Old Friends			
☐ 16 Devon White	1.00	.45	.12
1992-WS The Catch			
☐ 17 Kelly Gruber	2.00	.90	.25
Deion Sanders			
1992-WS Near Triple Play			
☐ 18A Roberto Alomar ERR	2.00	.90	.25
Winning Welcome			
missing from front)			
Kelly Gruber			
1992-Winning Welcome			
☐ 18B Roberto Alomar COR	2.00	.90	.25
Kelly Gruber			
1992-Winning Welcome			
☐ 19 Kelly Gruber	.25	.11	.03
Damon Berryhill			
1992-WS Winning slide			
☐ 20 Jimmy Key	.75	.35	.09
1992-WS Final Farewell			
☐ 21 Devon White	.50	.23	.06
Candy Maldonado			
1992-WS Winning RBI			
☐ 22 Joe Carter	.50	.23	.06
Otis Nixon; Clincher			
1992-WS Clincher			
☐ 23 Blue Jays COR	.75	.35	.09
1992-World Champions			
☐ 23A Blue Jays ERR	.75	.35	.09
1992-World Champions			
(Front is Jimmy Key			
photo from card 20)			
☐ 24 Paul Beeston PR	.25	.11	.03
Cito Gaston MG			
1992-WS Trophy			
☐ 25 Pat Borders	.25	.11	.03
1992-WS MVP			
☐ 26 SkyDome victory parade	.25	.11	.03
1992-WS Heroes			
☐ 27 John Olerud	.75	.35	.09
☐ 28 Roberto Alomar	2.00	.90	.25
☐ 29 Ed Sprague	.75	.35	.09
☐ 30 Dick Schofield	.25	.11	.03
☐ 31 Devon White	1.00	.45	.12
☐ 32 Joe Carter	1.50	.70	.19
☐ 33 Darrin Jackson	.25	.11	.03
☐ 34 Pat Borders	.25	.11	.03
☐ 35 Paul Molitor	2.00	.90	.25
☐ 36 Checklist 1-36	.25	.11	.03

1993 Blue Jays Donruss World Series

This nine-card horizontally oriented set captures highlights from the 1992 World Series. The standard-size cards feature full-bleed action color pictures with red, white, and blue bunting draped along the top edge. The World Series gold-stamped logo appears below the photo. The backs carry the box score and statistics for each game overlaid on a ghosted Blue Jays' logo. The red, white, and blue bunting design appears at the top with the number of the game and the World Series logo. The cards are numbered on the back with a "WS" prefix.

	MINT	NRMT	EXC
COMPLETE SET (9)	6.00	2.70	.75
COMMON CARD (1-9)	.50	.23	.06
☐ 1 Series Opener	.50	.23	.06
(Blue Jays-Braves)			
☐ 2 Joe Carter	.75	.35	.09
(Home run, Game 1)			
☐ 3 Ed Sprague	.75	.35	.09
Derek Bell			
(Sprague homer, Game 2)			
☐ 4 Candy Maldonado	.50	.23	.06
(Game-winning RBI, Game 3)			
☐ 5 Jimmy Key	1.00	.45	.12
(Key wins Game 4)			
☐ 6 John Olerud	.75	.35	.09
(Scoring run, Game 5)			
☐ 7 Dave Winfield	1.00	.45	.12
Derek Bell			
(Winfield's Series-			
winning double, Game 6)			
☐ 8 Pat Borders	.75	.35	.09
(Series MVP)			
☐ 9 Blue Jays celebrate	.75	.35	.09

1993 Blue Jays Fire Safety

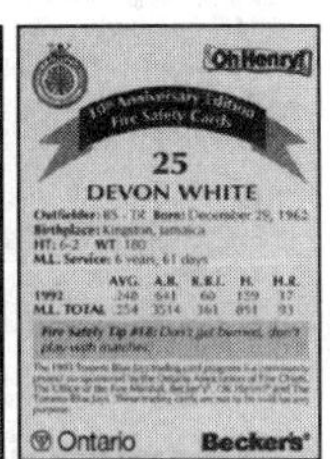

This 36-card standard-size set commemorates the 1992 World Series Champion Toronto Blue Jays. The set was jointly sponsored by the Ontario Association of Fire Chiefs, The Office of the Fire Marshal, Becker's, Oh Henry, and the Blue Jays. The cards are printed on recycled thin paper stock. The full-bleed fronts feature action color shots of the players. The player's name is printed in white script lettering on a navy blue bar across the top. The white backs feature biography, 1992 season statistics, and fire safety tips. This set is the tenth anniversary edition of the fire safety cards. The cards are unnumbered and checklisted below in alphabetical order.

	MINT	NRMT	EXC
COMPLETE SET (36)	10.00	4.50	1.25
COMMON CARD (1-36)	.25	.11	.03
☐ 1 Roberto Alomar	1.50	.70	.19
☐ 2 Bob Bailor CO	.25	.11	.03
☐ 3 Pat Borders	.25	.11	.03
☐ 4 Joe Carter	1.25	.55	.16
☐ 5 Galen Cisco CO	.25	.11	.03
☐ 6 Darnell Coles	.25	.11	.03
☐ 7 Danny Cox	.25	.11	.03
☐ 8 Ken Dayley	.25	.11	.03
☐ 9 Mark Eichhorn	.25	.11	.03
☐ 10 Cito Gaston MG	.75	.35	.09
☐ 11 Alfredo Griffin	.50	.23	.06
☐ 12 Juan Guzman	.75	.35	.09
☐ 13 Rich Hacker CO	.25	.11	.03
☐ 14 Pat Hentgen	1.00	.45	.12
☐ 15 Larry Hisle CO	.25	.11	.03
☐ 16 Darrin Jackson	.25	.11	.03
☐ 17 Randy Knorr	.25	.11	.03
☐ 18 Al Leiter	.75	.35	.09
☐ 19 Domingo Martinez	.25	.11	.03
☐ 20 Paul Molitor	1.50	.70	.19
☐ 21 Jack Morris	.75	.35	.09
☐ 22 John Olerud	.75	.35	.09
☐ 23 Tom Quinlan	.25	.11	.03
☐ 24 Dick Schofield	.25	.11	.03
☐ 25 Luis Sojo	.25	.11	.03
☐ 26 Ed Sprague	.75	.35	.09
☐ 27 Dave Stewart	.75	.35	.09
☐ 28 Todd Stottlemyre	.75	.35	.09
☐ 29 John Sullivan CO	.25	.11	.03
☐ 30 Gene Tenace CO	.25	.11	.03
☐ 31 Mike Timlin	.50	.23	.06
☐ 32 Duane Ward	.25	.11	.03
☐ 33 Turner Ward	.25	.11	.03
☐ 34 Devon White	.75	.35	.09
☐ 35 Eddie Zosky	.25	.11	.03
☐ 36 Checklist 1-36	.25	.11	.03

1994 Blue Jays Postcards

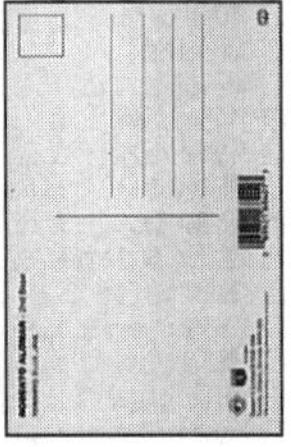

This 12-postcard set of Toronto Blue Jays was issued in a cardboard sleeve. Each postcard measures 4" by 6". The fronts feature a mix of posed and action, borderless color player photos. The backs have a postcard format and carry the player's name, position and team name at the top left. The postcards are unnumbered and checklisted below in alphabetical order.

	MINT	NRMT	EXC
COMPLETE SET (12)	8.00	3.60	1.00
COMMON CARD (1-12)	.50	.23	.06
☐ 1 Roberto Alomar	2.00	.90	.25
☐ 2 Pat Borders	.50	.23	.06
☐ 3 Joe Carter	1.50	.70	.19
☐ 4 Carlos Delgado	2.00	.90	.25
☐ 5 Juan Guzman	1.00	.45	.12
☐ 6 Paul Molitor	2.00	.90	.25
☐ 7 John Olerud	1.00	.45	.12
☐ 8 Ed Sprague	1.00	.45	.12
☐ 9 Devon White	1.00	.45	.12
☐ 10 1992 , 1993 World Series Trophies	.50	.23	.06
☐ 11 World Series Rings	.50	.23	.06
☐ 12 1993 World Series Champions Logo	.50	.23	.06

1994 Blue Jays U.S. Playing Cards

These 56 playing standard-size cards have rounded corners, and feature borderless color posed and action player photos on their fronts. The player's name and position appear near the bottom. The two-tone blue backs carry logos for the Blue Jays, MLB, MLBPA, and Bicycle Sports Collection. The set is checklisted below in playing card order by suits and assigned numbers to aces (1), jacks (11), queens (12), and kings (13).

	MINT	NRMT	EXC
COMPLETE SET (56)	4.00	1.80	.50
COMMON CARD	.05	.02	.01
☐ 1C John Olerud	.20	.09	.03
☐ 1D Roberto Alomar	.50	.23	.06
☐ 1H Joe Carter	.15	.07	.02
☐ 1S Paul Molitor	.40	.18	.05
☐ 2C Al Leiter	.10	.05	.01
☐ 2D Eddie Zosky	.05	.02	.01
☐ 2H Woody Williams	.05	.02	.01
☐ 2S Michael Timlin	.10	.05	.01
☐ 3C Dave Stewart	.10	.05	.01
☐ 3D Rob Butler	.05	.02	.01
☐ 3H Danny Cox	.05	.02	.01
☐ 3S Randy Knorr	.05	.02	.01
☐ 4C Pat Borders	.05	.02	.01
☐ 4D Tony Castillo	.05	.02	.01
☐ 4H Todd Stottlemyre	.10	.05	.01
☐ 4S Pat Hentgen	.30	.14	.04
☐ 5C Devon White	.10	.05	.01
☐ 5D Duane Ward	.05	.02	.01
☐ 5H Ed Sprague	.10	.05	.01
☐ 5S Darnell Coles	.05	.02	.01
☐ 6C Joe Carter	.30	.14	.04
☐ 6D Paul Molitor	.40	.18	.05
☐ 6H John Olerud	.20	.09	.03
☐ 6S Juan Guzman	.20	.09	.03
☐ 7C Roberto Alomar	.50	.23	.06
☐ 7D John Olerud	.20	.09	.03
☐ 7H Paul Molitor	.40	.18	.05
☐ 7S Roberto Alomar	.50	.23	.06
☐ 8C Woody Williams	.05	.02	.01
☐ 8D Carlos Delgado	.75	.35	.09
☐ 8H Scott Brow	.05	.02	.01
☐ 8S Joe Carter	.30	.14	.04
☐ 9C Eddie Zosky	.05	.02	.01
☐ 9D Michael Timlin	.10	.05	.01
☐ 9H Pat Hentgen	.15	.07	.02

☐ 9S Scott Brow	.05	.02	.01
☐ 10C Willie Canate	.05	.02	.01
☐ 10D Randy Knorr	.05	.02	.01
☐ 10H Al Leiter	.10	.05	.01
☐ 10S Dick Schofield	.05	.02	.01
☐ 11C Danny Cox	.05	.02	.01
☐ 11D Pat Hentgen	.30	.14	.04
☐ 11H Dave Stewart	.10	.05	.01
☐ 11S Rob Butler	.05	.02	.01
☐ 12C Todd Stottlemyre	.10	.05	.01
☐ 12D Darnell Coles	.05	.02	.01
☐ 12H Pat Borders	.05	.02	.01
☐ 12S Tony Castillo	.05	.02	.01
☐ 13C Ed Sprague	.20	.09	.03
☐ 13D Juan Guzman	.20	.09	.03
☐ 13H Devon White	.10	.05	.01
☐ 13S Duane Ward	.05	.02	.01
☐ NNO Featured Players	.05	.02	.01

1995 Blue Jays Postcards

This 5-card set of collector postcards comes in a stapled booklet which measures 4" by 8 1/2". The fronts feature borderless color player photos attached by perforation to a sponsor's coupon at the top. After perforation, the postcards measure 4" by 5 1/2". The backs carry a postcard format with the player's name and a fact about the player in the lower right. The cards are unnumbered and checklisted below in alphabetical order.

	MINT	NRMT	EXC
COMPLETE SET (5)	5.00	2.20	.60
COMMON CARD (1-5)	1.00	.45	.12
☐ 1 Roberto Alomar	2.00	.90	.25
☐ 2 Joe Carter	1.50	.70	.19
☐ 3 Juan Guzman	1.00	.45	.12
☐ 4 Paul Molitor	1.50	.70	.19
☐ 5 John Olerud	1.00	.45	.12

1995 Blue Jays U.S. Playing Cards

These 56 standard-size playing cards have rounded corners, and feature color player photos on their white-bordered fronts. The player's name and position appear in a red bar near the bottom. The blue and gray backs carry the logos for the Toronto Blue Jays, MLBPA, and Bicycle Sports Collection. The set is checklisted below in playing card order by suits and assigned numbers to aces (1), jacks (11), queens (12), and kings (13).

	MINT	NRMT	EXC
COMPLETE SET (56)	5.00	2.20	.60
COMMON CARD (1-56)	.05	.02	.01
☐ 1C John Olerud	.25	.11	.03
☐ 1D Joe Carter	.30	.14	.04
☐ 1H Roberto Alomar	.40	.18	.05
☐ 1S Paul Molitor	.40	.18	.05
☐ 2C Pat Hentgen	.30	.14	.04
☐ 2D Duane Ward	.05	.02	.01
☐ 2H Candy Maldonado	.05	.02	.01
☐ 2S Todd Stottlemyre	.15	.07	.02
☐ 3C Juan Guzman	.15	.07	.02
☐ 3D Dave Stewart	.15	.07	.02
☐ 3H Mike Timlin	.05	.02	.01
☐ 3S Rickey Henderson	.40	.18	.05
☐ 4C Cecil Fielder	.30	.14	.04
☐ 4D Tony Fernandez	.15	.07	.02
☐ 4H Ed Sprague	.15	.07	.02
☐ 4S Tom Henke	.15	.07	.02
☐ 5C Roberto Alomar	.40	.18	.05
☐ 5D Jack Morris	.15	.07	.02
☐ 5H Pat Borders	.05	.02	.01
☐ 5S Fred McGriff	.30	.14	.04
☐ 6C Joe Carter	.30	.14	.04
☐ 6D Dave Winfield	.50	.23	.06
☐ 6H Jimmy Key	.05	.02	.01
☐ 6S Devon White	.05	.02	.01
☐ 7C Mark Eichhorn	.05	.02	.01
☐ 7D John Olerud	.25	.11	.03
☐ 7H Paul Molitor	.30	.14	.04
☐ 7S Duane Ward	.05	.02	.01
☐ 8C Carlos Delgado	.40	.18	.05
☐ 8D Manny Lee	.05	.02	.01
☐ 8H Candy Maldonado	.05	.02	.01
☐ 8S David Wells	.05	.02	.01
☐ 9C Tom Candiotti	.05	.02	.01
☐ 9D Pat Hentgen	.30	.14	.04
☐ 9H Danny Cox	.05	.02	.01
☐ 9S David Cone	.25	.11	.03
☐ 10C Dave Stewart	.05	.02	.01
☐ 10D Randy Knorr	.05	.02	.01

☐ 10H Todd Stottlemyre	.15	.07	.02
☐ 10S Mike Timlin	.05	.02	.01
☐ 11C Tony Fernandez	.05	.02	.01
☐ 11D Juan Guzman	.05	.02	.01
☐ 11H Rickey Henderson	.50	.23	.06
☐ 11S Ed Sprague	.05	.02	.01
☐ 12C Pat Borders	.05	.02	.01
☐ 12D Fred McGriff	.40	.18	.05
☐ 12H Tom Henke	.15	.07	.02
☐ 12S Jack Morris	.30	.14	.04
☐ 13C Dave Winfield	.75	.35	.09
☐ 13D Devon White	.05	.02	.01
☐ 13H Cecil Fielder	.25	.11	.03
☐ 13S Jimmy Key	.05	.02	.01
☐ NNO Team Name	.05	.02	.01
☐ NNO Title Card	.05	.02	.01
☐ NNO Featured players	.05	.02	.01
☐ NNO Team Logo	.05	.02	.01

1996 Blue Jays Bookmarks

This six-card set of the Toronto Blue Jays measures approximately 2 1/2" by 6 1/4". One side features a color player portrait with personal statistics in English and a facsimile autograph. The other side displays color action player photos with personal statistics in French and a facsimile autograph. The cards are unnumbered and checklisted below in alphabetical order.

	MINT	NRMT	EXC
COMPLETE SET (6)	5.00	2.20	.60
COMMON CARD (1-6)	.25	.11	.03
☐ 1 Joe Carter	2.00	.90	.25
☐ 2 Pat Hentgen	1.00	.45	.12
☐ 3 Otis Nixon	.25	.11	.03
☐ 4 John Olerud	.50	.23	.06
☐ 5 Ed Sprague	.50	.23	.06
☐ 6 Woody Williams	.25	.11	.03

1996 Blue Jays Oh Henry!

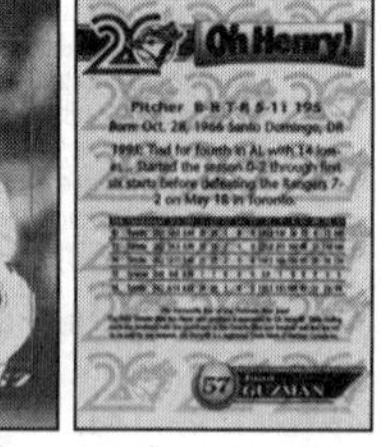

This 36-card set commemorates the 20th anniversary of the Toronto Blue Jays and features color player photos with player information and statistics on the backs.

	MINT	NRMT	EXC
COMPLETE SET (36)	12.00	5.50	1.50
COMMON CARD (1-36)	.25	.11	.03
☐ 1 George Bell	.50	.23	.06
☐ 2 Brian Bohanon	.25	.11	.03
☐ 3 Joe Carter	1.25	.55	.16
☐ 4 Tony Castillo	.25	.11	.03
☐ 5 Domingo Cedeno	.25	.11	.03
☐ 6 Tim Crabtree	.25	.11	.03
☐ 7 Felipe Crespo	.25	.11	.03
☐ 8 Carlos Delgado	1.00	.45	.12
☐ 9 Cito Gaston MG	.25	.11	.03
☐ 10 Alex Gonzalez	.50	.23	.06
☐ 11 Shawn Green	.50	.23	.06
☐ 12 Alfredo Griffin CO	.25	.11	.03
☐ 13 Kelly Gruber	.25	.11	.03
☐ 14 Juan Guzman	.50	.23	.06
☐ 15 Erik Hanson	.25	.11	.03
☐ 16 Pat Hentgen	1.25	.55	.16
☐ 17 Marty Janzen	.50	.23	.06
☐ 18 Nick Leyva CO	.25	.11	.03
☐ 19 Sandy Martinez	.25	.11	.03
☐ 20 Lloyd Moseby	.25	.11	.03
☐ 21 Otis Nixon	.25	.11	.03
☐ 22 Charlie O'Brien	.25	.11	.03
☐ 23 John Olerud	.50	.23	.06
☐ 24 Robert Perez	.25	.11	.03
☐ 25 Mel Queen CO	.25	.11	.03
☐ 26 Paul Quantrill	.25	.11	.03
☐ 27 Bill Risley	.25	.11	.03
☐ 28 Juan Samuel	.25	.11	.03
☐ 29 Ed Sprague	.50	.23	.06
☐ 30 Dave Stieb	.50	.23	.06
☐ 31 Gene Tenace CO	.25	.11	.03
☐ 32 Mike Timlin	.50	.23	.06
☐ 33 Willie Upshaw CO	.25	.11	.03
☐ 34 Jeff Ware	.25	.11	.03
☐ 35 Ernie Whitt	.25	.11	.03
☐ 36 Woody Williams	.25	.11	.03

1997 Blue Jays Sizzler

This 60-card set features color player images on various colored borderless backgrounds with faint baseball images. A facsimile gold autograph is printed across the bottom of the front. The backs carry a small player photo with player information and statistics. Cards #32-50 display "Magic Moments" in the team's history. For $19.95, the collector could obtain a black "Pleather" album with archival-approved sleeves to keep the cards in.

	MINT	NRMT	EXC
COMPLETE SET (60)	25.00	11.00	3.10
COMMON CARD (1-60)	.25	.11	.03
☐ 1 Alex Gonzalez	.50	.23	.06
☐ 2 Pat Hentgen	1.25	.55	.16
☐ 3 Joe Carter	1.00	.45	.12
☐ 4 Ed Sprague	.50	.23	.06
☐ 5 Benito Santiago	.50	.23	.06
☐ 6 Roger Clemens	2.50	1.10	.30
☐ 7 Carlos Garcia	.25	.11	.03
☐ 8 Juan Guzman	.25	.11	.03
☐ 9 Dan Plesac	.25	.11	.03
☐ 10 Carlos Delgado	1.25	.55	.16
☐ 11 Orlando Merced	.25	.11	.03
☐ 12 Woody Williams	.25	.11	.03
☐ 13 Shawn Green	.50	.23	.06
☐ 14 Erik Hanson	.25	.11	.03
☐ 15 Charlie O'Brien	.25	.11	.03
☐ 16 Otis Nixon	.25	.11	.03
☐ 17 Paul Spoljaric	.25	.11	.03
☐ 18 Jacob Brumfield	.25	.11	.03
☐ 19 Mike Timlin	.50	.23	.06
☐ 20 Tilson Brito	.25	.11	.03
☐ 21 Paul Quantrill	.25	.11	.03
☐ 22 Tim Crabtree	.25	.11	.03
☐ 23 Jim Lett	.25	.11	.03
☐ 24 Cito Gaston MG	.25	.11	.03
☐ 25 Alfredo Griffin CO	.25	.11	.03
☐ 26 Nick Leyva CO	.25	.11	.03
☐ 27 Mel Queen CO	.25	.11	.03
☐ 28 Gene Tenace CO	.25	.11	.03
☐ 29 Willie Upshaw CO	.25	.11	.03
☐ 30 Pat Hentgen	.50	.23	.06
☐ 31 Roger Clemens	1.00	.45	.12
☐ 32 First Pitch '77	.25	.11	.03
☐ 33 Dave Stieb's No Hitter	.25	.11	.03
☐ 34 George Bell Lloyd Moseby Jesse Barfield	.25	.11	.03
☐ 35 1992 World Series	.25	.11	.03
☐ 36 1985 Pennant Win	.25	.11	.03
☐ 37 Paul Molitor	1.50	.70	.19
☐ 38 Tom Henke Duane Ward	.25	.11	.03
☐ 39 Ernie Whitt	.25	.11	.03
☐ 40 Joe Carter Home Run, 1993	1.00	.45	.12
☐ 41 Jack Morris	1.00	.45	.12
☐ 42 Pat Borders	.25	.11	.03
☐ 43 Dave Winfield	1.25	.55	.16
☐ 44 Damaso Garcia	.25	.11	.03
☐ 45 Tony Fernandez	.50	.23	.06
☐ 46 Roberto Alomar	1.25	.55	.16
☐ 47 Dave Stewart	.50	.23	.06
☐ 48 John Olerud Paul Molitor Roberto Alomar	1.00	.45	.12
☐ 49 Fred McGriff	1.50	.70	.19
☐ 50 Kelly Gruber	.25	.11	.03
☐ 51 Alex Gonzalez	.25	.11	.03
☐ 52 Huck Flener	.25	.11	.03
☐ 53 Marty Janzen	.25	.11	.03
☐ 54 Sandy Martinez	.25	.11	.03
☐ 55 Felipe Crespo	.25	.11	.03
☐ 56 Tomas Perez	.25	.11	.03
☐ 57 Shannon Stewart	.50	.23	.06
☐ 58 Billy Koch	.50	.23	.06
☐ 59 Roy Halladay	.50	.23	.06
☐ 60 Chris Carpenter	.50	.23	.06

1948-49 Blue Tint R346

The cards in this 48-card set measure 2" by 2 5/8". The "Blue Tint" set derives its name from its distinctive coloration. Collector Ralph Triplette has pointed out in his research that the set was issued during

1948 and 1949, not in 1947 as had been previously commonly thought. The cards are blank-backed and unnumbered, and were issued in strips of six or eight. The set was probably produced in Brooklyn and hence has a heavy emphasis on New York teams, especially the Yankees. Known variations are No. 2, Durocher, listed with Brooklyn or New York Giants, and No. 18, Ott, listed with Giants or no team designation. The set was initially listed in the catalog as R346 as well as being listed as W518. Although the W categorization is undoubtedly the more correct, nevertheless, the R listing has become the popularly referenced designation for the set. The complete set price below includes all listed variations.

	NRMT	VG-E	GOOD
COMPLETE SET	1200.00	550.00	150.00
COMMON CARD (1-48)	10.00	4.50	1.25
☐ 1 Bill Johnson	10.00	4.50	1.25
☐ 2A Leo Durocher (Brooklyn Dodgers)	20.00	9.00	2.50
☐ 2B Leo Durocher (New York Giants)	20.00	9.00	2.50
☐ 3 Marty Marion	12.50	5.50	1.55
☐ 4 Ewell Blackwell	12.50	5.50	1.55
☐ 5 John Lindell	10.00	4.50	1.25
☐ 6 Larry Jansen	10.00	4.50	1.25
☐ 7 Ralph Kiner	20.00	9.00	2.50
☐ 8 Chuck Dressen CO	12.50	5.50	1.55
☐ 9 Bobby Brown	12.50	5.50	1.55
☐ 10 Luke Appling	20.00	9.00	2.50
☐ 11 Bill Nicholson	12.50	5.50	1.55
☐ 12 Phil Masi	10.00	4.50	1.25
☐ 13 Frank Shea	10.00	4.50	1.25
☐ 14 Bob Dillinger	10.00	4.50	1.25
☐ 15 Pete Suder	10.00	4.50	1.25
☐ 16 Joe DiMaggio	200.00	90.00	25.00
☐ 17 John Corriden CO	10.00	4.50	1.25
☐ 18A Mel Ott MG (New York Giants)	40.00	18.00	5.00
☐ 18B Mel Ott (no team designation)	40.00	18.00	5.00
☐ 19 Warren Rosar	10.00	4.50	1.25
☐ 20 Warren Spahn	25.00	11.00	3.10
☐ 21 Allie Reynolds	10.00	4.50	1.25
☐ 22 Lou Boudreau	20.00	9.00	2.50
☐ 23 Hank Majeski (photo actually Randy Gumpert)	10.00	4.50	1.25
☐ 24 Frank Crosetti	15.00	6.75	1.85
☐ 25 Gus Niarhos	10.00	4.50	1.25
☐ 26 Bruce Edwards	10.00	4.50	1.25
☐ 27 Rudy York	10.00	4.50	1.25
☐ 28 Don Black	10.00	4.50	1.25
☐ 29 Lou Gehrig	200.00	90.00	25.00
☐ 30 Johnny Mize	20.00	9.00	2.50
☐ 31 Ed Stanky	12.50	5.50	1.55
☐ 32 Vic Raschi	12.50	5.50	1.55
☐ 33 Cliff Mapes	10.00	4.50	1.25
☐ 34 Enos Slaughter	20.00	9.00	2.50
☐ 35 Hank Greenberg	25.00	11.00	3.10
☐ 36 Jackie Robinson	125.00	55.00	15.50
☐ 37 Frank Hiller	10.00	4.50	1.25
☐ 38 Bob Elliott	12.50	5.50	1.55
☐ 39 Harry Walker	10.00	4.50	1.25
☐ 40 Ed Lopat	15.00	6.75	1.85
☐ 41 Bobby Thomson	15.00	6.75	1.85
☐ 42 Tommy Henrich	12.50	5.50	1.55
☐ 43 Bobby Feller	50.00	22.00	6.25
☐ 44 Ted Williams	150.00	70.00	19.00
☐ 45 Dixie Walker	12.50	5.50	1.55
☐ 46 Johnny Vander Meer	12.50	5.50	1.55
☐ 47 Clint Hartung	10.00	4.50	1.25
☐ 48 Charlie Keller	12.50	5.50	1.55

1987 Boardwalk and Baseball

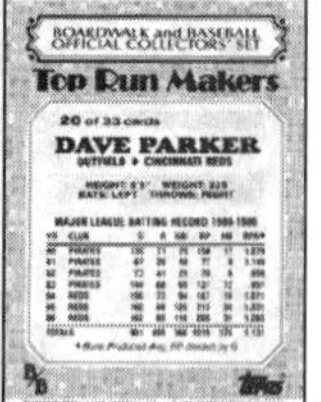

This 33-card standard-size set was produced by Topps for distribution by the "Boardwalk and Baseball" Theme Park which was located in Haines City, Florida. The set comes in a custom blue collector box.

The full-color fronts are surrounded by a pink and black frame border. The card backs are printed in pink and black on white card stock. The set is subtitled "Top Run Makers." Hence no pitchers are included in the set. The checklist for the set is given on the back panel of the box.

	MINT	NRMT	EXC
COMPLETE SET (33)	5.00	2.20	.60
COMMON CARD (1-33)	.05	.02	.01
☐ 1 Mike Schmidt	.60	.25	.07
☐ 2 Eddie Murray	.50	.23	.06
☐ 3 Dale Murphy	.20	.09	.03
☐ 4 Dave Winfield	.25	.11	.03
☐ 5 Jim Rice	.10	.05	.01
☐ 6 Cecil Cooper	.05	.02	.01
☐ 7 Dwight Evans	.05	.02	.01
☐ 8 Rickey Henderson	.30	.14	.04
☐ 9 Robin Yount	.25	.11	.03
☐ 10 Andre Dawson	.25	.11	.03
☐ 11 Gary Carter	.10	.05	.01
☐ 12 Keith Hernandez	.10	.05	.01
☐ 13 George Brett	1.00	.45	.12
☐ 14 Bill Buckner	.05	.02	.01
☐ 15 Tony Armas	.05	.02	.01
☐ 16 Harold Baines	.10	.05	.01
☐ 17 Don Baylor	.10	.05	.01
☐ 18 Steve Garvey	.10	.05	.01
☐ 19 Lance Parrish	.05	.02	.01
☐ 20 Dave Parker	.10	.05	.01
☐ 21 Buddy Bell	.05	.02	.01
☐ 22 Cal Ripken	2.50	1.10	.30
☐ 23 Bob Horner	.05	.02	.01
☐ 24 Tim Raines	.10	.05	.01
☐ 25 Jack Clark	.05	.02	.01
☐ 26 Leon Durham	.05	.02	.01
☐ 27 Pedro Guerrero	.05	.02	.01
☐ 28 Kent Hrbek	.10	.05	.01
☐ 29 Kirk Gibson	.10	.05	.01
☐ 30 Ryne Sandberg	.75	.35	.09
☐ 31 Wade Boggs	.25	.11	.03
☐ 32 Don Mattingly	1.00	.45	.12
☐ 33 Darryl Strawberry	.15	.07	.02

1977 Bob Parker Hall of Fame

These 54 cards measure 3 1/2" by 5 1/2". The cards are checklisted in alphabetical order. Noted sports artist Bob Parker drew these pictures of Hall of Famers.

	NRMT	VG-E	GOOD
COMPLETE SET (54)	50.00	22.00	6.25
COMMON CARD (1-54)	.25	.11	.03
☐ 1 Grover C. Alexander	1.50	.70	.19
☐ 2 Cap Anson	1.50	.70	.19
☐ 3 Luke Appling	.75	.35	.09
☐ 4 Ernie Banks	1.50	.70	.19
☐ 5 Chief Bender	.75	.35	.09
☐ 6 Jim Bottomley	.50	.23	.06
☐ 7 Dan Brouthers	.50	.23	.06
☐ 8 Morgan Bulkeley	.25	.11	.03
☐ 9 Roy Campanella	1.00	.45	.12
☐ 10 Alex Cartwright	.25	.11	.03
☐ 11 Henry Chadwick	.25	.11	.03
☐ 12 John Clarkson	.50	.23	.06
☐ 13 Ty Cobb	5.00	2.20	.60
☐ 14 Eddie Collins	1.00	.45	.12
☐ 15 Jimmy Collins	.50	.23	.06
☐ 16 Charles Comiskey	1.00	.45	.12
☐ 17 Sam Crawford	.75	.35	.09
☐ 18 Jerome "Dizzy" Dean	1.00	.45	.12
☐ 19 Joe DiMaggio	5.00	2.20	.60
☐ 20 Buck Ewing	.75	.35	.09
☐ 21 Bob Feller	1.50	.70	.19
☐ 22 Lou Gehrig	5.00	2.20	.60
☐ 23 Goose Goslin	.75	.35	.09
☐ 24 Burleigh Grimes	.75	.35	.09
☐ 25 Chick Hafey	.50	.23	.06
☐ 26 Rogers Hornsby	1.50	.70	.19
☐ 27 Carl Hubbell	1.00	.45	.12
☐ 28 Miller Huggins	.50	.23	.06
☐ 29 Tim Keefe	.50	.23	.06
☐ 30 Mike Kelly	.75	.35	.09
☐ 31 Larry Lajoie	1.00	.45	.12
☐ 32 Fred Lindstrom	.50	.23	.06
☐ 33 Connie Mack	1.00	.45	.12
☐ 34 Mickey Mantle	7.50	3.40	.95
☐ 35 Heine Manush	.75	.35	.09
☐ 36 Joe McGinnity	.50	.23	.06
☐ 37 John McGraw	1.00	.45	.12
☐ 38 Eddie Plank	.75	.35	.09
☐ 39 Eppa Rixey	.50	.23	.06
☐ 40 Jackie Robinson	4.00	1.80	.50
☐ 41 Eddie Roush	.75	.35	.09
☐ 42 Babe Ruth	7.50	3.40	.95
☐ 43 Al Simmons	.75	.35	.09
☐ 44 Albert Spalding	.50	.23	.06
☐ 45 Tris Speaker	1.50	.70	.19
☐ 46 Casey Stengel	1.00	.45	.12
☐ 47 Bill Terry	.75	.35	.09
☐ 48 Rube Waddell	.50	.23	.06
☐ 49 Hans Wagner	2.00	.90	.25
☐ 50 Paul Waner	.75	.35	.09
☐ 51 John M. Ward	.50	.23	.06
☐ 52 Ted Williams	5.00	2.20	.60
☐ 53 George Wright	.50	.23	.06
☐ 54 Harry Wright	.50	.23	.06

1947 Bond Bread

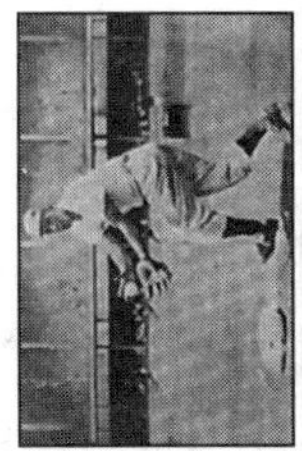

The 1947 Bond Bread Jackie Robinson set features 13 unnumbered cards of Jackie in different action or portrait poses; each card measures approximately 2 1/4" by 3 1/2". Card number 7, which is the only card in the set to contain a facsimile autograph, was apparently issued in greater quantity than other cards in the set and has been noted as a double print (DP) in the checklist below. Several of the cards have a horizontal format; these are marked in the checklist below by HOR. The catalog designation for this set is D302.

	EX-MT	VG-E	GOOD
COMPLETE SET (13)	8500.00	3800.00	1050.00
COMMON CARD (1-13)	450.00	200.00	55.00
☐ 1 Jackie Robinson Sliding into base cap, ump in photo, HOR	750.00	350.00	95.00
☐ 2 Jackie Robinson Running down 3rd base line	750.00	350.00	95.00
☐ 3 Jackie Robinson Batting bat behind head facing camera	750.00	350.00	95.00
☐ 4 Jackie Robinson Moving towards second throw almost to glove HOR	750.00	350.00	95.00
☐ 5 Jackie Robinson Taking throw at first, HOR	750.00	350.00	95.00
☐ 6 Jackie Robinson Jumping high in the air for ball	750.00	350.00	95.00
☐ 7 Jackie Robinson Profile with glove in front of head facsimile autograph DP	450.00	200.00	55.00
☐ 8 Jackie Robinson Leaping over second base ready to throw	750.00	350.00	95.00
☐ 9 Jackie Robinson Portrait holding glove over head	750.00	350.00	95.00
☐ 10 Jackie Robinson Portrait holding bat perpendicular to body	750.00	350.00	95.00
☐ 11 Jackie Robinson Reaching for throw glove near ankle	750.00	350.00	95.00
☐ 12 Jackie Robinson Leaping for throw no scoreboard in background	750.00	350.00	95.00
☐ 13 Jackie Robinson Portrait holding bat parallel to body	750.00	350.00	95.00

1973-96 Book Promotional Cards

This set features various cards used to promote baseball books. We have sequenced them in year order. Cards #2 through #13 all were used to promote "Who was Harry Steinfeldt? and other baseball trivia.". All of these cards measure the standard size. We are not using a complete set price for this set because of the vide variance in years and availability of how these cards were released.

	NRMT	VG-E	GOOD
COMMON CARD	3.00	1.35	.35
☐ 1 Bo Belinsky 1973 Pitching and Wooing	5.00	2.20	.60
☐ 2 Frank Baumholtz	3.00	1.35	.35
☐ 3 Jim Bouton	5.00	2.20	.60
☐ 4 Tony Conigliaro	5.00	2.20	.60
☐ 5 Don Drysdale	10.00	4.50	1.25
☐ 6 Hank Greenberg	10.00	4.50	1.25
☐ 7 Walter Johnson	15.00	6.75	1.85
☐ 8 Billy Loes	3.00	1.35	.35
☐ 9 Johnny Mize	10.00	4.50	1.25
☐ 10 Lefty O'Doul	5.00	2.20	.60
☐ 11 Babe Ruth	25.00	11.00	3.10
☐ 12 Johnny Sain	5.00	2.20	.60
☐ 13 Jim Thorpe	20.00	9.00	2.50
☐ 14 Jim Bouton 1979 Ball Four Plus Ball Five	3.00	1.35	.35
☐ 15 Billy Martin 1980 Number One	5.00	2.20	.60
☐ 16 Mickey Mantle 1986 The Mick	10.00	4.50	1.25
☐ 17 Babe Ruth 1988 Babe Ruth's Book of Basbeall Audio Cassette	3.00	1.35	.35
☐ 18 Orel Hershiser 1989 Out of the Blue	3.00	1.35	.35
☐ 19 Gil Hodges 1992 The Quiet Man	5.00	2.20	.60
☐ 20 Joe Morgan 1993 A Life in Baseball	3.00	1.35	.35

1972-87 Bowery Bank DiMaggio

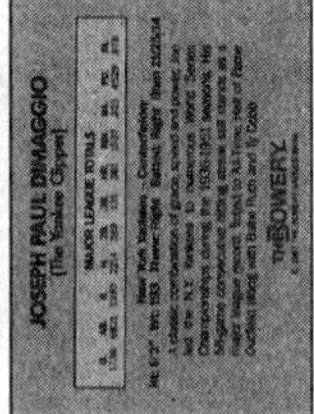

This one-card standard-size set was actually released three times. The first time was is 1972, the second was in 1979 and third was in 1987. We have priced the 1987 version here. The 1979 version is valued at $25 and the 1972 version is at $50. The front features a full-color photo of Dimaggio framed by the words Yankees on top and his name and position on the bottom. The horizontal backs has his career numbers, a brief biography and his vital statistics.

	NRMT	VG-E	GOOD
COMPLETE SET	12.50	5.50	1.55
COMMON CARD	12.50	5.50	1.55
☐ 1 Joe DiMaggio	12.50	5.50	1.55

1948 Bowman

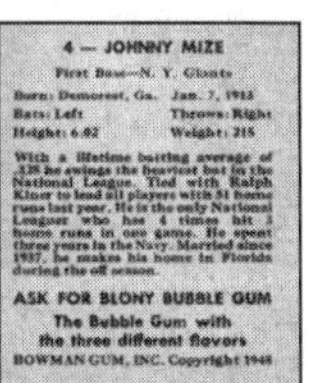

The 48-card Bowman set of 1948 was the first major set of the post-war period. Each 2 1/16" by 2 1/2" card had a black and white photo of a current player, with his biographical information printed in black ink on a gray back. Due to the printing process and the 36-card sheet size upon which Bowman was then printing, the 12 cards marked with an SP in the checklist are scarcer numerically, as they were removed from the printing sheet in order to make room for the 12 high numbers (37-48). Cards were issued in one-card penny packs. Many cards are found with over-printed, transposed, or blank backs. The set features the Rookie Cards of Hall of Famers Yogi Berra, Ralph Kiner, Stan Musial, Red Schoendienst, and Warren Spahn. Half of the cards in the set feature New York players (Yankees or Giants).

	NRMT	VG-E	GOOD
COMPLETE SET (48)	3400.00	1500.00	425.00
COMMON CARD (1-36)	20.00	9.00	2.50
COMMON CARD (37-48)	30.00	13.50	3.70
WRAPPER (1-cent)	700.00	325.00	90.00
☐ 1 Bob Elliott	80.00	12.00	4.00
☐ 2 Ewell Blackwell	40.00	18.00	5.00
☐ 3 Ralph Kiner	150.00	70.00	19.00
☐ 4 Johnny Mize	100.00	45.00	12.50
☐ 5 Bob Feller	225.00	100.00	28.00
☐ 6 Yogi Berra	450.00	200.00	55.00
☐ 7 Pete Reiser SP	120.00	55.00	15.00
☐ 8 Phil Rizzuto SP	300.00	135.00	38.00
☐ 9 Walker Cooper	20.00	9.00	2.50
☐ 10 Buddy Rosar	20.00	9.00	2.50
☐ 11 Johnny Lindell	22.50	10.00	2.80
☐ 12 Johnny Sain	50.00	22.00	6.25
☐ 13 Willard Marshall SP	40.00	18.00	5.00
☐ 14 Allie Reynolds	50.00	22.00	6.25
☐ 15 Eddie Joost	20.00	9.00	2.50
☐ 16 Jack Lohrke SP	40.00	18.00	5.00
☐ 17 Enos Slaughter	100.00	45.00	12.50
☐ 18 Warren Spahn	350.00	160.00	45.00
☐ 19 Tommy Henrich	40.00	18.00	5.00
☐ 20 Buddy Kerr SP	40.00	18.00	5.00
☐ 21 Ferris Fain	25.00	11.00	3.10
☐ 22 Floyd Bevens SP	50.00	22.00	6.25
☐ 23 Larry Jansen	22.50	10.00	2.80
☐ 24 Dutch Leonard SP	40.00	18.00	5.00
☐ 25 Barney McCosky	20.00	9.00	2.50
☐ 26 Frank Shea SP	50.00	22.00	6.25
☐ 27 Sid Gordon	22.50	10.00	2.80
☐ 28 Emil Verban SP	40.00	18.00	5.00
☐ 29 Joe Page SP	75.00	34.00	9.50
☐ 30 Whitey Lockman SP	50.00	22.00	6.25
☐ 31 Bill McCahan	20.00	9.00	2.50
☐ 32 Bill Rigney	20.00	9.00	2.50
☐ 33 Bill Johnson	22.50	10.00	2.80
☐ 34 Sheldon Jones SP	40.00	18.00	5.00
☐ 35 Snuffy Stirnweiss	25.00	11.00	3.10
☐ 36 Stan Musial	800.00	350.00	100.00
☐ 37 Clint Hartung	30.00	13.50	3.70
☐ 38 Red Schoendienst	150.00	70.00	19.00
☐ 39 Augie Galan	30.00	13.50	3.70
☐ 40 Marty Marion	75.00	34.00	9.50
☐ 41 Rex Barney	45.00	20.00	5.50
☐ 42 Ray Poat	30.00	13.50	3.70
☐ 43 Bruce Edwards	30.00	13.50	3.70
☐ 44 Johnny Wyrostek	30.00	13.50	3.70
☐ 45 Hank Sauer	50.00	22.00	6.25
☐ 46 Herman Wehmeier	30.00	13.50	3.70
☐ 47 Bobby Thomson	100.00	45.00	12.50
☐ 48 Dave Koslo	60.00	14.50	4.10

1949 Bowman

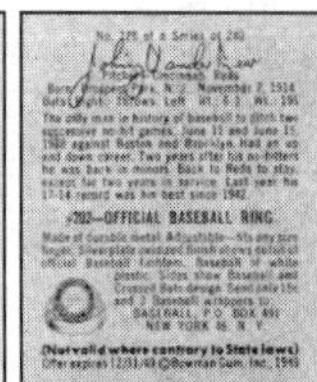

The cards in this 240-card set measure approximately 2 1/16" by 2 1/2". In 1949 Bowman took an intermediate step between black and white and full color with this set of tinted photos on colored backgrounds. Collectors should note the series price variations, which reflect some inconsistencies in the printing process. There are four major varieties in name printing, which are noted in the checklist below: NOF: name on front; NNOF: no name on front; PR: printed name on back; and SCR: script name on back. Cards were issued in five card nickle packs. These variations resulted when Bowman used twelve of the lower numbers to fill out the last press sheet of 36 cards, adding to numbers 217-240. Cards 1-3 and 5-73 can be found with either gray or white backs. The set features the Rookie Cards of Hall of Famers Roy Campanella, Bob Lemon, Robin Roberts, Duke Snider, and Early Wynn as well as Rookie Cards of Richie Ashburn and Gil Hodges.

	NRMT	VG-E	GOOD
COMPLETE SET (240)	13000.00	5800.00	1600.00
COMMON CARD (1-144)	15.00	6.75	1.85
COMMON CARD (145-240)	50.00	22.00	6.25
WRAPPER (5-cent, green)	300.00	135.00	38.00
WRAPPER (5-cent, blue)	200.00	90.00	25.00
☐ 1 Vern Bickford	80.00	16.00	4.80
☐ 2 Whitey Lockman	20.00	9.00	2.50
☐ 3 Bob Porterfield	20.00	9.00	2.50
☐ 4A Jerry Priddy NNOF	15.00	6.75	1.85
☐ 4B Jerry Priddy NOF	40.00	18.00	5.00
☐ 5 Hank Sauer	20.00	9.00	2.50
☐ 6 Phil Cavarretta	20.00	9.00	2.50
☐ 7 Joe Dobson	15.00	6.75	1.85
☐ 8 Murry Dickson	15.00	6.75	1.85
☐ 9 Ferris Fain	20.00	9.00	2.50
☐ 10 Ted Gray	15.00	6.75	1.85
☐ 11 Lou Boudreau	60.00	27.00	7.50
☐ 12 Cass Michaels	15.00	6.75	1.85
☐ 13 Bob Chesnes	15.00	6.75	1.85
☐ 14 Curt Simmons	35.00	16.00	4.40
☐ 15 Ned Garver	15.00	6.75	1.85
☐ 16 Al Kozar	15.00	6.75	1.85
☐ 17 Earl Torgeson	15.00	6.75	1.85
☐ 18 Bobby Thomson	35.00	16.00	4.40
☐ 19 Bobby Brown	35.00	16.00	4.40
☐ 20 Gene Hermanski	15.00	6.75	1.85
☐ 21 Frank Baumholtz	20.00	9.00	2.50
☐ 22 Peanuts Lowrey	15.00	6.75	1.85
☐ 23 Bobby Doerr	60.00	27.00	7.50
☐ 24 Stan Musial	500.00	220.00	60.00

☐ 25 Carl Scheib	15.00	6.75	1.85
☐ 26 George Kell	60.00	27.00	7.50
☐ 27 Bob Feller	175.00	80.00	22.00
☐ 28 Don Kolloway	15.00	6.75	1.85
☐ 29 Ralph Kiner	125.00	55.00	15.50
☐ 30 Andy Seminick	20.00	9.00	2.50
☐ 31 Dick Kokos	15.00	6.75	1.85
☐ 32 Eddie Yost	30.00	13.50	3.70
☐ 33 Warren Spahn	175.00	80.00	22.00
☐ 34 Dave Koslo	15.00	6.75	1.85
☐ 35 Vic Raschi	55.00	25.00	7.00
☐ 36 Pee Wee Reese	175.00	80.00	22.00
☐ 37 Johnny Wyrostek	15.00	6.75	1.85
☐ 38 Emil Verban	15.00	6.75	1.85
☐ 39 Billy Goodman	15.00	6.75	1.85
☐ 40 Red Munger	15.00	6.75	1.85
☐ 41 Lou Brissie	15.00	6.75	1.85
☐ 42 Hoot Evers	15.00	6.75	1.85
☐ 43 Dale Mitchell	20.00	9.00	2.50
☐ 44 Dave Philley	15.00	6.75	1.85
☐ 45 Wally Westlake	15.00	6.75	1.85
☐ 46 Robin Roberts	200.00	90.00	25.00
☐ 47 Johnny Sain	40.00	18.00	5.00
☐ 48 Willard Marshall	15.00	6.75	1.85
☐ 49 Frank Shea	20.00	9.00	2.50
☐ 50 Jackie Robinson	1000.00	450.00	125.00
☐ 51 Herman Wehmeier	15.00	6.75	1.85
☐ 52 Johnny Schmitz	15.00	6.75	1.85
☐ 53 Jack Kramer	15.00	6.75	1.85
☐ 54 Marty Marion	30.00	13.50	3.70
☐ 55 Eddie Joost	15.00	6.75	1.85
☐ 56 Pat Mullin	15.00	6.75	1.85
☐ 57 Gene Bearden	20.00	9.00	2.50
☐ 58 Bob Elliott	20.00	9.00	2.50
☐ 59 Jack Lohrke	15.00	6.75	1.85
☐ 60 Yogi Berra	275.00	125.00	34.00
☐ 61 Rex Barney	20.00	9.00	2.50
☐ 62 Grady Hatton	15.00	6.75	1.85
☐ 63 Andy Pafko	20.00	9.00	2.50
☐ 64 Dom DiMaggio	35.00	16.00	4.40
☐ 65 Enos Slaughter	70.00	32.00	8.75
☐ 66 Elmer Valo	15.00	6.75	1.85
☐ 67 Alvin Dark	35.00	16.00	4.40
☐ 68 Sheldon Jones	15.00	6.75	1.85
☐ 69 Tommy Henrich	35.00	16.00	4.40
☐ 70 Carl Furillo	100.00	45.00	12.50
☐ 71 Vern Stephens	15.00	6.75	1.85
☐ 72 Tommy Holmes	20.00	9.00	2.50
☐ 73 Billy Cox	35.00	16.00	4.40
☐ 74 Tom McBride	15.00	6.75	1.85
☐ 75 Eddie Mayo	15.00	6.75	1.85
☐ 76 Bill Nicholson	15.00	6.75	1.85
☐ 77 Ernie Bonham	15.00	6.75	1.85
☐ 78A Sam Zoldak NNOF	15.00	6.75	1.85
☐ 78B Sam Zoldak NOF	40.00	18.00	5.00
☐ 79 Ron Northey	15.00	6.75	1.85
☐ 80 Bill McCahan	15.00	6.75	1.85
☐ 81 Virgil Stallcup	15.00	6.75	1.85
☐ 82 Joe Page	30.00	13.50	3.70
☐ 83A Bob Scheffing NNOF	15.00	6.75	1.85
☐ 83B Bob Scheffing NOF	40.00	18.00	5.00
☐ 84 Roy Campanella	700.00	325.00	90.00
☐ 85A Johnny Mize NNOF	80.00	36.00	10.00
☐ 85B Johnny Mize NOF	150.00	70.00	19.00
☐ 86 Johnny Pesky	30.00	13.50	3.70
☐ 87 Randy Gumpert	15.00	6.75	1.85
☐ 88A Bill Salkeld NNOF	15.00	6.75	1.85
☐ 88B Bill Salkeld NOF	40.00	18.00	5.00
☐ 89 Mizell Platt	15.00	6.75	1.85
☐ 90 Gil Coan	15.00	6.75	1.85
☐ 91 Dick Wakefield	15.00	6.75	1.85
☐ 92 Willie Jones	20.00	9.00	2.50
☐ 93 Ed Stevens	15.00	6.75	1.85
☐ 94 Mickey Vernon	35.00	16.00	4.40
☐ 95 Howie Pollet	15.00	6.75	1.85
☐ 96 Taft Wright	15.00	6.75	1.85
☐ 97 Danny Litwhiler	15.00	6.75	1.85
☐ 98A Phil Rizzuto NNOF	125.00	55.00	15.50
☐ 98B Phil Rizzuto NOF	200.00	90.00	25.00
☐ 99 Frank Gustine	15.00	6.75	1.85
☐ 100 Gil Hodges	250.00	110.00	31.00
☐ 101 Sid Gordon	15.00	6.75	1.85
☐ 102 Stan Spence	15.00	6.75	1.85
☐ 103 Joe Tipton	15.00	6.75	1.85
☐ 104 Eddie Stanky	35.00	16.00	4.40
☐ 105 Bill Kennedy	15.00	6.75	1.85
☐ 106 Jake Early	15.00	6.75	1.85
☐ 107 Eddie Lake	15.00	6.75	1.85
☐ 108 Ken Heintzelman	15.00	6.75	1.85
☐ 109A Ed Fitzgerald SCR	15.00	6.75	1.85
☐ 109B Ed Fitzgerald PR	40.00	18.00	5.00
☐ 110 Early Wynn	125.00	55.00	15.50
☐ 111 Red Schoendienst	70.00	32.00	8.75
☐ 112 Sam Chapman	20.00	9.00	2.50
☐ 113 Ray LaManno	15.00	6.75	1.85
☐ 114 Allie Reynolds	40.00	18.00	5.00
☐ 115 Dutch Leonard	15.00	6.75	1.85
☐ 116 Joe Hatton	15.00	6.75	1.85
☐ 117 Walker Cooper	15.00	6.75	1.85
☐ 118 Sam Mele	15.00	6.75	1.85
☐ 119 Floyd Baker	15.00	6.75	1.85
☐ 120 Cliff Fannin	15.00	6.75	1.85
☐ 121 Mark Christman	15.00	6.75	1.85
☐ 122 George Vico	15.00	6.75	1.85
☐ 123 Johnny Blatnick	15.00	6.75	1.85
☐ 124A Danny Murtaugh SCR	30.00	13.50	3.70
☐ 124B Danny Murtaugh PR	45.00	20.00	5.50
☐ 125 Ken Keltner	20.00	9.00	2.50
☐ 126A Al Brazle SCR	15.00	6.75	1.85
☐ 126B Al Brazle PR	40.00	18.00	5.00
☐ 127A Hank Majeski SCR	15.00	6.75	1.85
☐ 127B Hank Majeski PR	40.00	18.00	5.00
☐ 128 Johnny VanderMeer	30.00	13.50	3.70
☐ 129 Bill Johnson	20.00	9.00	2.50
☐ 130 Harry Walker	15.00	6.75	1.85
☐ 131 Paul Lehner	15.00	6.75	1.85
☐ 132A Al Evans SCR	15.00	6.75	1.85
☐ 132B Al Evans PR	40.00	18.00	5.00
☐ 133 Aaron Robinson	15.00	6.75	1.85
☐ 134 Hank Borowy	15.00	6.75	1.85
☐ 135 Stan Rojek	15.00	6.75	1.85
☐ 136 Hank Edwards	15.00	6.75	1.85
☐ 137 Ted Wilks	15.00	6.75	1.85
☐ 138 Buddy Rosar	15.00	6.75	1.85
☐ 139 Hank Arft	15.00	6.75	1.85
☐ 140 Ray Scarborough	15.00	6.75	1.85
☐ 141 Tony Lupien	15.00	6.75	1.85
☐ 142 Eddie Waitkus	20.00	9.00	2.50
☐ 143A Bob Dillinger SCR	15.00	6.75	1.85
☐ 143B Bob Dillinger PR	75.00	34.00	9.50
☐ 144 Mickey Haefner	15.00	6.75	1.85
☐ 145 Sylvester Donnelly	50.00	22.00	6.25
☐ 146 Mike McCormick	60.00	27.00	7.50
☐ 147 Bert Singleton	50.00	22.00	6.25
☐ 148 Bob Swift	50.00	22.00	6.25
☐ 149 Roy Partee	50.00	22.00	6.25
☐ 150 Allie Clark	50.00	22.00	6.25
☐ 151 Mickey Harris	50.00	22.00	6.25
☐ 152 Clarence Maddern	50.00	22.00	6.25
☐ 153 Phil Masi	50.00	22.00	6.25
☐ 154 Clint Hartung	75.00	34.00	9.50
☐ 155 Mickey Guerra	50.00	22.00	6.25
☐ 156 Al Zarilla	50.00	22.00	6.25
☐ 157 Walt Masterson	50.00	22.00	6.25
☐ 158 Harry Brecheen	75.00	34.00	9.50
☐ 159 Glen Moulder	50.00	22.00	6.25
☐ 160 Jim Blackburn	50.00	22.00	6.25
☐ 161 Jocko Thompson	50.00	22.00	6.25
☐ 162 Preacher Roe	125.00	55.00	15.50
☐ 163 Clyde McCullough	50.00	22.00	6.25
☐ 164 Vic Wertz	75.00	34.00	9.50
☐ 165 Snuffy Stirnweiss	60.00	27.00	7.50
☐ 166 Mike Tresh	50.00	22.00	6.25
☐ 167 Babe Martin	50.00	22.00	6.25
☐ 168 Doyle Lade	50.00	22.00	6.25
☐ 169 Jeff Heath	60.00	27.00	7.50
☐ 170 Bill Rigney	60.00	27.00	7.50
☐ 171 Dick Fowler	50.00	22.00	6.25
☐ 172 Eddie Pellagrini	50.00	22.00	6.25
☐ 173 Eddie Stewart	50.00	22.00	6.25
☐ 174 Terry Moore	100.00	45.00	12.50
☐ 175 Luke Appling	125.00	55.00	15.50
☐ 176 Ken Raffensberger	50.00	22.00	6.25
☐ 177 Stan Lopata	60.00	27.00	7.50
☐ 178 Tom Brown	60.00	27.00	7.50
☐ 179 Hugh Casey	75.00	34.00	9.50
☐ 180 Connie Berry	50.00	22.00	6.25
☐ 181 Gus Niarhos	50.00	22.00	6.25
☐ 182 Hal Peck	50.00	22.00	6.25
☐ 183 Lou Stringer	50.00	22.00	6.25
☐ 184 Bob Chipman	50.00	22.00	6.25
☐ 185 Pete Reiser	100.00	45.00	12.50
☐ 186 Buddy Kerr	50.00	22.00	6.25
☐ 187 Phil Marchildon	50.00	22.00	6.25
☐ 188 Karl Drews	50.00	22.00	6.25
☐ 189 Earl Wooten	50.00	22.00	6.25
☐ 190 Jim Hearn	50.00	22.00	6.25
☐ 191 Joe Haynes	50.00	22.00	6.25
☐ 192 Harry Gumbert	50.00	22.00	6.25
☐ 193 Ken Trinkle	50.00	22.00	6.25
☐ 194 Ralph Branca	100.00	45.00	12.50
☐ 195 Eddie Bockman	50.00	22.00	6.25
☐ 196 Fred Hutchinson	75.00	34.00	9.50
☐ 197 Johnny Lindell	60.00	27.00	7.50
☐ 198 Steve Gromek	50.00	22.00	6.25
☐ 199 Tex Hughson	50.00	22.00	6.25
☐ 200 Jess Dobernic	50.00	22.00	6.25
☐ 201 Sibby Sisti	50.00	22.00	6.25
☐ 202 Larry Jansen	75.00	34.00	9.50
☐ 203 Barney McCosky	50.00	22.00	6.25
☐ 204 Bob Savage	50.00	22.00	6.25
☐ 205 Dick Sisler	60.00	27.00	7.50
☐ 206 Bruce Edwards	50.00	22.00	6.25
☐ 207 Johnny Hopp	50.00	22.00	6.25
☐ 208 Dizzy Trout	60.00	27.00	7.50
☐ 209 Charlie Keller	100.00	45.00	12.50
☐ 210 Joe Gordon	100.00	45.00	12.50
☐ 211 Boo Ferriss	50.00	22.00	6.25
☐ 212 Ralph Hamner	50.00	22.00	6.25
☐ 213 Red Barrett	50.00	22.00	6.25
☐ 214 Richie Ashburn	550.00	250.00	70.00
☐ 215 Kirby Higbe	50.00	22.00	6.25
☐ 216 Schoolboy Rowe	60.00	27.00	7.50
☐ 217 Marino Pieretti	50.00	22.00	6.25
☐ 218 Dick Kryhoski	50.00	22.00	6.25
☐ 219 Virgil Fire Trucks	60.00	27.00	7.50
☐ 220 Johnny McCarthy	50.00	22.00	6.25
☐ 221 Bob Muncrief	50.00	22.00	6.25
☐ 222 Alex Kellner	50.00	22.00	6.25
☐ 223 Bobby Hofman	50.00	22.00	6.25
☐ 224 Satchell Paige	1000.00	450.00	125.00
☐ 225 Jerry Coleman	100.00	45.00	12.50
☐ 226 Duke Snider	850.00	375.00	105.00
☐ 227 Fritz Ostermueller	50.00	22.00	6.25
☐ 228 Jackie Mayo	50.00	22.00	6.25
☐ 229 Ed Lopat	125.00	55.00	15.50
☐ 230 Augie Galan	60.00	27.00	7.50
☐ 231 Earl Johnson	50.00	22.00	6.25
☐ 232 George McQuinn	60.00	27.00	7.50
☐ 233 Larry Doby	150.00	70.00	19.00
☐ 234 Rip Sewell	50.00	22.00	6.25
☐ 235 Jim Russell	50.00	22.00	6.25
☐ 236 Fred Sanford	50.00	22.00	6.25
☐ 237 Monte Kennedy	50.00	22.00	6.25
☐ 238 Bob Lemon	200.00	90.00	25.00
☐ 239 Frank McCormick	50.00	22.00	6.25
☐ 240 Babe Young UER (Photo actually Bobby Young)	100.00	25.00	6.25

1950 Bowman

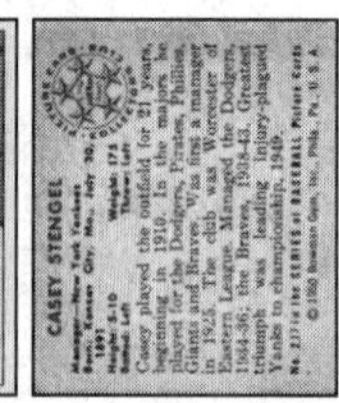

The cards in this 252-card set measure approximately 2 1/16" by 2 1/2". This set, marketed in 1950 by Bowman, represented a major improvement in terms of quality over their previous efforts. Each card was a beautifully colored line drawing developed from a simple photograph. The first 72 cards are the scarcest in the set, while the final 72 cards may be found with or without the copyright line. This was the only Bowman sports set to carry the famous "5-Star" logo. Cards were issued in five-card nickle packs. Key rookies in this set are Hank Bauer, Don Newcombe, and Al Rosen.

	NRMT	VG-E	GOOD
COMPLETE SET (252)	8500.00	3800.00	1050.00
COMMON CARD (1-72)	50.00	22.00	6.25
COMMON CARD (73-252)	16.00	7.25	2.00
WRAPPER (1-cent)	250.00	110.00	31.00
WRAPPER (5-cent)	300.00	135.00	38.00
☐ 1 Mel Parnell	150.00	30.00	9.00
☐ 2 Vern Stephens	55.00	25.00	7.00
☐ 3 Dom DiMaggio	65.00	29.00	8.00
☐ 4 Gus Zernial	60.00	27.00	7.50
☐ 5 Bob Kuzava	50.00	22.00	6.25
☐ 6 Bob Feller	225.00	100.00	28.00
☐ 7 Jim Hegan	55.00	25.00	7.00
☐ 8 George Kell	75.00	34.00	9.50
☐ 9 Vic Wertz	55.00	25.00	7.00
☐ 10 Tommy Henrich	90.00	40.00	11.00
☐ 11 Phil Rizzuto	225.00	100.00	28.00
☐ 12 Joe Page	75.00	34.00	9.50
☐ 13 Ferris Fain	55.00	25.00	7.00
☐ 14 Alex Kellner	50.00	22.00	6.25
☐ 15 Al Kozar	50.00	22.00	6.25
☐ 16 Roy Sievers	65.00	29.00	8.00
☐ 17 Sid Hudson	50.00	22.00	6.25
☐ 18 Eddie Robinson	50.00	22.00	6.25
☐ 19 Warren Spahn	225.00	100.00	28.00
☐ 20 Bob Elliott	55.00	25.00	7.00
☐ 21 Pee Wee Reese	225.00	100.00	28.00
☐ 22 Jackie Robinson	750.00	350.00	95.00
☐ 23 Don Newcombe	150.00	70.00	19.00
☐ 24 Johnny Schmitz	50.00	22.00	6.25
☐ 25 Hank Sauer	60.00	27.00	7.50
☐ 26 Grady Hatton	50.00	22.00	6.25
☐ 27 Herman Wehmeier	50.00	22.00	6.25
☐ 28 Bobby Thomson	65.00	29.00	8.00
☐ 29 Eddie Stanky	55.00	25.00	7.00
☐ 30 Eddie Waitkus	60.00	27.00	7.50
☐ 31 Del Ennis	65.00	29.00	8.00
☐ 32 Robin Roberts	150.00	70.00	19.00
☐ 33 Ralph Kiner	100.00	45.00	12.50
☐ 34 Murry Dickson	50.00	22.00	6.25
☐ 35 Enos Slaughter	100.00	45.00	12.50
☐ 36 Eddie Kazak	55.00	25.00	7.00
☐ 37 Luke Appling	75.00	34.00	9.50
☐ 38 Bill Wight	50.00	22.00	6.25
☐ 39 Larry Doby	75.00	34.00	9.50
☐ 40 Bob Lemon	75.00	34.00	9.50
☐ 41 Hoot Evers	50.00	22.00	6.25
☐ 42 Art Houtteman	50.00	22.00	6.25
☐ 43 Bobby Doerr	75.00	34.00	9.50
☐ 44 Joe Dobson	50.00	22.00	6.25
☐ 45 Al Zarilla	50.00	22.00	6.25
☐ 46 Yogi Berra	325.00	145.00	40.00
☐ 47 Jerry Coleman	75.00	34.00	9.50
☐ 48 Lou Brissie	50.00	22.00	6.25
☐ 49 Elmer Valo	50.00	22.00	6.25
☐ 50 Dick Kokos	50.00	22.00	6.25
☐ 51 Ned Garver	55.00	25.00	7.00
☐ 52 Sam Mele	50.00	22.00	6.25
☐ 53 Clyde Vollmer	50.00	22.00	6.25
☐ 54 Gil Coan	50.00	22.00	6.25
☐ 55 Buddy Kerr	50.00	22.00	6.25
☐ 56 Del Crandall	60.00	27.00	7.50
☐ 57 Vern Bickford	50.00	22.00	6.25
☐ 58 Carl Furillo	90.00	40.00	11.00
☐ 59 Ralph Branca	75.00	34.00	9.50
☐ 60 Andy Pafko	55.00	25.00	7.00
☐ 61 Bob Rush	50.00	22.00	6.25
☐ 62 Ted Kluszewski	100.00	45.00	12.50
☐ 63 Ewell Blackwell	55.00	25.00	7.00
☐ 64 Alvin Dark	60.00	27.00	7.50
☐ 65 Dave Koslo	50.00	22.00	6.25
☐ 66 Larry Jansen	55.00	25.00	7.00
☐ 67 Willie Jones	60.00	27.00	7.50
☐ 68 Curt Simmons	55.00	25.00	7.00
☐ 69 Wally Westlake	50.00	22.00	6.25
☐ 70 Bob Chesnes	50.00	22.00	6.25
☐ 71 Red Schoendienst	75.00	34.00	9.50
☐ 72 Howie Pollet	50.00	22.00	6.25
☐ 73 Willard Marshall	16.00	7.25	2.00
☐ 74 Johnny Antonelli	35.00	16.00	4.40
☐ 75 Roy Campanella	275.00	125.00	34.00
☐ 76 Rex Barney	25.00	11.00	3.10
☐ 77 Duke Snider	275.00	125.00	34.00
☐ 78 Mickey Owen	20.00	9.00	2.50
☐ 79 Johnny VanderMeer	25.00	11.00	3.10
☐ 80 Howard Fox	16.00	7.25	2.00
☐ 81 Ron Northey	16.00	7.25	2.00
☐ 82 Whitey Lockman	20.00	9.00	2.50
☐ 83 Sheldon Jones	16.00	7.25	2.00
☐ 84 Richie Ashburn	100.00	45.00	12.50
☐ 85 Ken Heintzelman	16.00	7.25	2.00
☐ 86 Stan Rojek	16.00	7.25	2.00
☐ 87 Bill Werle	16.00	7.25	2.00
☐ 88 Marty Marion	25.00	11.00	3.10
☐ 89 Red Munger	16.00	7.25	2.00
☐ 90 Harry Brecheen	20.00	9.00	2.50
☐ 91 Cass Michaels	16.00	7.25	2.00
☐ 92 Hank Majeski	16.00	7.25	2.00
☐ 93 Gene Bearden	20.00	9.00	2.50
☐ 94 Lou Boudreau	60.00	27.00	7.50
☐ 95 Aaron Robinson	16.00	7.25	2.00
☐ 96 Virgil Trucks	20.00	9.00	2.50
☐ 97 Maurice McDermott	16.00	7.25	2.00
☐ 98 Ted Williams	825.00	375.00	105.00
☐ 99 Billy Goodman	20.00	9.00	2.50
☐ 100 Vic Raschi	35.00	16.00	4.40
☐ 101 Bobby Brown	35.00	16.00	4.40
☐ 102 Billy Johnson	20.00	9.00	2.50
☐ 103 Eddie Joost	16.00	7.25	2.00
☐ 104 Sam Chapman	16.00	7.25	2.00
☐ 105 Bob Dillinger	16.00	7.25	2.00
☐ 106 Cliff Fannin	16.00	7.25	2.00
☐ 107 Sam Dente	16.00	7.25	2.00
☐ 108 Ray Scarborough	16.00	7.25	2.00
☐ 109 Sid Gordon	16.00	7.25	2.00
☐ 110 Tommy Holmes	20.00	9.00	2.50
☐ 111 Walker Cooper	16.00	7.25	2.00
☐ 112 Gil Hodges	100.00	45.00	12.50
☐ 113 Gene Hermanski	16.00	7.25	2.00
☐ 114 Wayne Terwilliger	16.00	7.25	2.00
☐ 115 Roy Smalley	16.00	7.25	2.00
☐ 116 Virgil Stallcup	16.00	7.25	2.00
☐ 117 Bill Rigney	16.00	7.25	2.00
☐ 118 Clint Hartung	16.00	7.25	2.00
☐ 119 Dick Sisler	20.00	9.00	2.50
☐ 120 John Thompson	16.00	7.25	2.00
☐ 121 Andy Seminick	20.00	9.00	2.50
☐ 122 Johnny Hopp	20.00	9.00	2.50
☐ 123 Dino Restelli	16.00	7.25	2.00
☐ 124 Clyde McCullough	16.00	7.25	2.00
☐ 125 Del Rice	16.00	7.25	2.00
☐ 126 Al Brazle	16.00	7.25	2.00
☐ 127 Dave Philley	16.00	7.25	2.00
☐ 128 Phil Masi	16.00	7.25	2.00
☐ 129 Joe Gordon	20.00	9.00	2.50
☐ 130 Dale Mitchell	20.00	9.00	2.50
☐ 131 Steve Gromek	16.00	7.25	2.00
☐ 132 Mickey Vernon	20.00	9.00	2.50
☐ 133 Don Kolloway	16.00	7.25	2.00
☐ 134 Paul Trout	16.00	7.25	2.00
☐ 135 Pat Mullin	16.00	7.25	2.00
☐ 136 Warren Rosar	16.00	7.25	2.00
☐ 137 Johnny Pesky	20.00	9.00	2.50
☐ 138 Allie Reynolds	35.00	16.00	4.40
☐ 139 Johnny Mize	75.00	34.00	9.50
☐ 140 Pete Suder	16.00	7.25	2.00
☐ 141 Joe Coleman	20.00	9.00	2.50
☐ 142 Sherm Lollar	25.00	11.00	3.10
☐ 143 Eddie Stewart	16.00	7.25	2.00
☐ 144 Al Evans	16.00	7.25	2.00
☐ 145 Jack Graham	16.00	7.25	2.00
☐ 146 Floyd Baker	16.00	7.25	2.00
☐ 147 Mike Garcia	25.00	11.00	3.10
☐ 148 Early Wynn	75.00	34.00	9.50
☐ 149 Bob Swift	16.00	7.25	2.00
☐ 150 George Vico	16.00	7.25	2.00
☐ 151 Fred Hutchinson	20.00	9.00	2.50
☐ 152 Ellis Kinder	16.00	7.25	2.00
☐ 153 Walt Masterson	16.00	7.25	2.00
☐ 154 Gus Niarhos	16.00	7.25	2.00
☐ 155 Frank Shea	20.00	9.00	2.50
☐ 156 Fred Sanford	20.00	9.00	2.50
☐ 157 Mike Guerra	16.00	7.25	2.00
☐ 158 Paul Lehner	16.00	7.25	2.00
☐ 159 Joe Tipton	16.00	7.25	2.00
☐ 160 Mickey Harris	16.00	7.25	2.00

☐ 161 Sherry Robertson	16.00	7.25	2.00
☐ 162 Eddie Yost	20.00	9.00	2.50
☐ 163 Earl Torgeson	16.00	7.25	2.00
☐ 164 Sibby Sisti	16.00	7.25	2.00
☐ 165 Bruce Edwards	16.00	7.25	2.00
☐ 166 Joe Hatton	16.00	7.25	2.00
☐ 167 Preacher Roe	35.00	16.00	4.40
☐ 168 Bob Scheffing	16.00	7.25	2.00
☐ 169 Hank Edwards	16.00	7.25	2.00
☐ 170 Dutch Leonard	16.00	7.25	2.00
☐ 171 Harry Gumbert	16.00	7.25	2.00
☐ 172 Peanuts Lowrey	16.00	7.25	2.00
☐ 173 Lloyd Merriman	16.00	7.25	2.00
☐ 174 Hank Thompson	25.00	11.00	3.10
☐ 175 Monte Kennedy	16.00	7.25	2.00
☐ 176 Sylvester Donnelly	16.00	7.25	2.00
☐ 177 Hank Borowy	16.00	7.25	2.00
☐ 178 Ed Fitzgerald	16.00	7.25	2.00
☐ 179 Chuck Diering	16.00	7.25	2.00
☐ 180 Harry Walker	16.00	7.25	2.00
☐ 181 Marino Pieretti	16.00	7.25	2.00
☐ 182 Sam Zoldak	16.00	7.25	2.00
☐ 183 Mickey Haefner	16.00	7.25	2.00
☐ 184 Randy Gumpert	16.00	7.25	2.00
☐ 185 Howie Judson	16.00	7.25	2.00
☐ 186 Ken Keltner	20.00	9.00	2.50
☐ 187 Lou Stringer	16.00	7.25	2.00
☐ 188 Earl Johnson	16.00	7.25	2.00
☐ 189 Owen Friend	16.00	7.25	2.00
☐ 190 Ken Wood	16.00	7.25	2.00
☐ 191 Dick Starr	16.00	7.25	2.00
☐ 192 Bob Chipman	16.00	7.25	2.00
☐ 193 Pete Reiser	25.00	11.00	3.10
☐ 194 Billy Cox	30.00	13.50	3.70
☐ 195 Phil Cavarretta	25.00	11.00	3.10
☐ 196 Doyle Lade	16.00	7.25	2.00
☐ 197 Johnny Wyrostek	16.00	7.25	2.00
☐ 198 Danny Litwhiler	16.00	7.25	2.00
☐ 199 Jack Kramer	16.00	7.25	2.00
☐ 200 Kirby Higbe	20.00	9.00	2.50
☐ 201 Pete Castiglione	16.00	7.25	2.00
☐ 202 Cliff Chambers	16.00	7.25	2.00
☐ 203 Danny Murtaugh	20.00	9.00	2.50
☐ 204 Granny Hamner	25.00	11.00	3.10
☐ 205 Mike Goliat	16.00	7.25	2.00
☐ 206 Stan Lopata	20.00	9.00	2.50
☐ 207 Max Lanier	16.00	7.25	2.00
☐ 208 Jim Hearn	16.00	7.25	2.00
☐ 209 Johnny Lindell	16.00	7.25	2.00
☐ 210 Ted Gray	16.00	7.25	2.00
☐ 211 Charlie Keller	20.00	9.00	2.50
☐ 212 Jerry Priddy	16.00	7.25	2.00
☐ 213 Carl Scheib	16.00	7.25	2.00
☐ 214 Dick Fowler	16.00	7.25	2.00
☐ 215 Ed Lopat	35.00	16.00	4.40
☐ 216 Bob Porterfield	20.00	9.00	2.50
☐ 217 Casey Stengel MG	125.00	55.00	15.50
☐ 218 Cliff Mapes	20.00	9.00	2.50
☐ 219 Hank Bauer	65.00	29.00	8.00
☐ 220 Leo Durocher MG	60.00	27.00	7.50
☐ 221 Don Mueller	25.00	11.00	3.10
☐ 222 Bobby Morgan	16.00	7.25	2.00
☐ 223 Jim Russell	16.00	7.25	2.00
☐ 224 Jack Banta	16.00	7.25	2.00
☐ 225 Eddie Sawyer MG	20.00	9.00	2.50
☐ 226 Jim Konstanty	40.00	18.00	5.00
☐ 227 Bob Miller	16.00	7.25	2.00
☐ 228 Bill Nicholson	20.00	9.00	2.50
☐ 229 Frank Frisch MG	40.00	18.00	5.00
☐ 230 Bill Serena	16.00	7.25	2.00
☐ 231 Preston Ward	16.00	7.25	2.00
☐ 232 Al Rosen	40.00	18.00	5.00
☐ 233 Allie Clark	16.00	7.25	2.00
☐ 234 Bobby Shantz	40.00	18.00	5.00
☐ 235 Harold Gilbert	16.00	7.25	2.00
☐ 236 Bob Cain	16.00	7.25	2.00
☐ 237 Bill Salkeld	16.00	7.25	2.00
☐ 238 Nippy Jones	16.00	7.25	2.00
☐ 239 Bill Howerton	16.00	7.25	2.00
☐ 240 Eddie Lake	16.00	7.25	2.00
☐ 241 Neil Berry	16.00	7.25	2.00
☐ 242 Dick Kryhoski	16.00	7.25	2.00
☐ 243 Johnny Groth	16.00	7.25	2.00
☐ 244 Dale Coogan	16.00	7.25	2.00
☐ 245 Al Papai	16.00	7.25	2.00
☐ 246 Walt Dropo	25.00	11.00	3.10
☐ 247 Irv Noren	20.00	9.00	2.50
☐ 248 Sam Jethroe	40.00	18.00	5.00
☐ 249 Snuffy Stirnweiss	20.00	9.00	2.50
☐ 250 Ray Coleman	16.00	7.25	2.00
☐ 251 Les Moss	16.00	7.25	2.00
☐ 252 Billy DeMars	40.00	11.00	4.00

1951 Bowman

The cards in this 324-card set measure approximately 2 1/16" by 3 1/8". Many of the obverses of the cards appearing in the 1951 Bowman set are enlargements of those appearing in the previous year. The high number series (253-324) is highly valued and contains the true "Rookie" cards of Mickey Mantle and Willie Mays. Card number 195 depicts Paul Richards in caricature. George Kell's card (number 46) incorrectly lists him as being in the "1941" Bowman series. Cards were issued either in one card penny packs or in five card nickle packs. Player names are found printed in a panel on the front of the card. These cards were supposedly also sold in sheets in variety stores in the Philadelphia area.

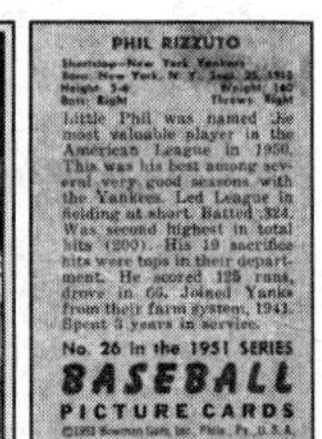

	NRMT	VG-E	GOOD
COMPLETE SET (324)	16000.00	7200.00	2000.00
COMMON CARD (1-252)	18.00	8.00	2.20
COMMON CARD (253-324)	50.00	22.00	6.25
WRAPPER (1-cent)	200.00	90.00	25.00
WRAPPER (5-cent)	250.00	110.00	31.00
☐ 1 Whitey Ford	800.00	200.00	65.00
☐ 2 Yogi Berra	275.00	125.00	34.00
☐ 3 Robin Roberts	75.00	34.00	9.50
☐ 4 Del Ennis	22.00	10.00	2.70
☐ 5 Dale Mitchell	22.00	10.00	2.70
☐ 6 Don Newcombe	50.00	22.00	6.25
☐ 7 Gil Hodges	90.00	40.00	11.00
☐ 8 Paul Lehner	18.00	8.00	2.20
☐ 9 Sam Chapman	18.00	8.00	2.20
☐ 10 Red Schoendienst	55.00	25.00	7.00
☐ 11 Red Munger	18.00	8.00	2.20
☐ 12 Hank Majeski	18.00	8.00	2.20
☐ 13 Eddie Stanky	22.00	10.00	2.70
☐ 14 Alvin Dark	30.00	13.50	3.70
☐ 15 Johnny Pesky	22.00	10.00	2.70
☐ 16 Maurice McDermott	18.00	8.00	2.20
☐ 17 Pete Castiglione	18.00	8.00	2.20
☐ 18 Gil Coan	18.00	8.00	2.20
☐ 19 Sid Gordon	18.00	8.00	2.20
☐ 20 Del Crandall UER (Misspelled Crandell on card)	22.00	10.00	2.70
☐ 21 Snuffy Stirnweiss	22.00	10.00	2.70
☐ 22 Hank Sauer	22.00	10.00	2.70
☐ 23 Hoot Evers	18.00	8.00	2.20
☐ 24 Ewell Blackwell	25.00	11.00	3.10
☐ 25 Vic Raschi	35.00	16.00	4.40
☐ 26 Phil Rizzuto	125.00	55.00	15.50
☐ 27 Jim Konstanty	22.00	10.00	2.70
☐ 28 Eddie Waitkus	18.00	8.00	2.20
☐ 29 Allie Clark	18.00	8.00	2.20
☐ 30 Bob Feller	125.00	55.00	15.50
☐ 31 Roy Campanella	225.00	100.00	28.00
☐ 32 Duke Snider	225.00	100.00	28.00
☐ 33 Bob Hooper	18.00	8.00	2.20
☐ 34 Marty Marion	25.00	11.00	3.10
☐ 35 Al Zarilla	18.00	8.00	2.20
☐ 36 Joe Dobson	18.00	8.00	2.20
☐ 37 Whitey Lockman	25.00	11.00	3.10
☐ 38 Al Evans	18.00	8.00	2.20
☐ 39 Ray Scarborough	18.00	8.00	2.20
☐ 40 Gus Bell	35.00	16.00	4.40
☐ 41 Eddie Yost	22.00	10.00	2.70
☐ 42 Vern Bickford	18.00	8.00	2.20
☐ 43 Billy DeMars	18.00	8.00	2.20
☐ 44 Roy Smalley	18.00	8.00	2.20
☐ 45 Art Houtteman	18.00	8.00	2.20
☐ 46 George Kell 1941 UER	55.00	25.00	7.00
☐ 47 Grady Hatton	18.00	8.00	2.20
☐ 48 Ken Raffensberger	18.00	8.00	2.20
☐ 49 Jerry Coleman	27.00	12.00	3.40
☐ 50 Johnny Mize	55.00	25.00	7.00
☐ 51 Andy Seminick	18.00	8.00	2.20
☐ 52 Dick Sisler	25.00	11.00	3.10
☐ 53 Bob Lemon	55.00	25.00	7.00
☐ 54 Ray Boone	35.00	16.00	4.40
☐ 55 Gene Hermanski	18.00	8.00	2.20
☐ 56 Ralph Branca	35.00	16.00	4.40
☐ 57 Alex Kellner	18.00	8.00	2.20
☐ 58 Enos Slaughter	55.00	25.00	7.00
☐ 59 Randy Gumpert	18.00	8.00	2.20
☐ 60 Chico Carrasquel	30.00	13.50	3.70
☐ 61 Jim Hearn	22.00	10.00	2.70
☐ 62 Lou Boudreau	55.00	25.00	7.00
☐ 63 Bob Dillinger	18.00	8.00	2.20
☐ 64 Bill Werle	18.00	8.00	2.20
☐ 65 Mickey Vernon	25.00	11.00	3.10
☐ 66 Bob Elliott	22.00	10.00	2.70
☐ 67 Roy Sievers	22.00	10.00	2.70
☐ 68 Dick Kokos	18.00	8.00	2.20
☐ 69 Johnny Schmitz	18.00	8.00	2.20
☐ 70 Ron Northey	18.00	8.00	2.20
☐ 71 Jerry Priddy	18.00	8.00	2.20
☐ 72 Lloyd Merriman	18.00	8.00	2.20
☐ 73 Tommy Byrne	18.00	8.00	2.20
☐ 74 Billy Johnson	22.00	10.00	2.70
☐ 75 Russ Meyer	22.00	10.00	2.70
☐ 76 Stan Lopata	22.00	10.00	2.70
☐ 77 Mike Goliat	18.00	8.00	2.20
☐ 78 Early Wynn	55.00	25.00	7.00
☐ 79 Jim Hegan	22.00	10.00	2.70
☐ 80 Pee Wee Reese	125.00	55.00	15.50
☐ 81 Carl Furillo	50.00	22.00	6.25
☐ 82 Joe Tipton	18.00	8.00	2.20
☐ 83 Carl Scheib	18.00	8.00	2.20
☐ 84 Barney McCosky	18.00	8.00	2.20
☐ 85 Eddie Kazak	18.00	8.00	2.20
☐ 86 Harry Brecheen	22.00	10.00	2.70
☐ 87 Floyd Baker	18.00	8.00	2.20
☐ 88 Eddie Robinson	18.00	8.00	2.20
☐ 89 Hank Thompson	22.00	10.00	2.70
☐ 90 Dave Koslo	22.00	10.00	2.70
☐ 91 Clyde Vollmer	18.00	8.00	2.20
☐ 92 Vern Stephens	22.00	10.00	2.70
☐ 93 Danny O'Connell	18.00	8.00	2.20
☐ 94 Clyde McCullough	18.00	8.00	2.20
☐ 95 Sherry Robertson	18.00	8.00	2.20
☐ 96 Sandy Consuegra	18.00	8.00	2.20
☐ 97 Bob Kuzava	18.00	8.00	2.20
☐ 98 Willard Marshall	18.00	8.00	2.20
☐ 99 Earl Torgeson	18.00	8.00	2.20
☐ 100 Sherm Lollar	22.00	10.00	2.70
☐ 101 Owen Friend	18.00	8.00	2.20
☐ 102 Dutch Leonard	18.00	8.00	2.20
☐ 103 Andy Pafko	25.00	11.00	3.10
☐ 104 Virgil Trucks	22.00	10.00	2.70
☐ 105 Don Kolloway	18.00	8.00	2.20
☐ 106 Pat Mullin	18.00	8.00	2.20
☐ 107 Johnny Wyrostek	18.00	8.00	2.20
☐ 108 Virgil Stallcup	18.00	8.00	2.20
☐ 109 Allie Reynolds	35.00	16.00	4.40
☐ 110 Bobby Brown	25.00	11.00	3.10
☐ 111 Curt Simmons	18.00	8.00	2.20
☐ 112 Willie Jones	18.00	8.00	2.20
☐ 113 Bill Nicholson	22.00	10.00	2.70
☐ 114 Sam Zoldak	18.00	8.00	2.20
☐ 115 Steve Gromek	18.00	8.00	2.20
☐ 116 Bruce Edwards	18.00	8.00	2.20
☐ 117 Eddie Miksis	18.00	8.00	2.20
☐ 118 Preacher Roe	35.00	16.00	4.40
☐ 119 Eddie Joost	18.00	8.00	2.20
☐ 120 Joe Coleman	22.00	10.00	2.70
☐ 121 Jerry Staley	18.00	8.00	2.20
☐ 122 Joe Garagiola	75.00	34.00	9.50
☐ 123 Howie Judson	18.00	8.00	2.20
☐ 124 Gus Niarhos	18.00	8.00	2.20
☐ 125 Bill Rigney	22.00	10.00	2.70
☐ 126 Bobby Thomson	35.00	16.00	4.40
☐ 127 Sal Maglie	55.00	25.00	7.00
☐ 128 Ellis Kinder	18.00	8.00	2.20
☐ 129 Matt Batts	18.00	8.00	2.20
☐ 130 Tom Saffell	18.00	8.00	2.20
☐ 131 Cliff Chambers	18.00	8.00	2.20
☐ 132 Cass Michaels	18.00	8.00	2.20
☐ 133 Sam Dente	18.00	8.00	2.20
☐ 134 Warren Spahn	125.00	55.00	15.50
☐ 135 Walker Cooper	18.00	8.00	2.20
☐ 136 Ray Coleman	18.00	8.00	2.20
☐ 137 Dick Starr	18.00	8.00	2.20
☐ 138 Phil Cavarretta	22.00	10.00	2.70
☐ 139 Doyle Lade	18.00	8.00	2.20
☐ 140 Eddie Lake	18.00	8.00	2.20
☐ 141 Fred Hutchinson	22.00	10.00	2.70
☐ 142 Aaron Robinson	18.00	8.00	2.20
☐ 143 Ted Kluszewski	40.00	18.00	5.00
☐ 144 Herman Wehmeier	18.00	8.00	2.20
☐ 145 Fred Sanford	22.00	10.00	2.70
☐ 146 Johnny Hopp	22.00	10.00	2.70
☐ 147 Ken Heintzelman	18.00	8.00	2.20
☐ 148 Granny Hamner	18.00	8.00	2.20
☐ 149 Bubba Church	18.00	8.00	2.20
☐ 150 Mike Garcia	22.00	10.00	2.70
☐ 151 Larry Doby	35.00	16.00	4.40
☐ 152 Cal Abrams	18.00	8.00	2.20
☐ 153 Rex Barney	22.00	10.00	2.70
☐ 154 Pete Suder	18.00	8.00	2.20
☐ 155 Lou Brissie	18.00	8.00	2.20
☐ 156 Del Rice	18.00	8.00	2.20
☐ 157 Al Brazle	18.00	8.00	2.20
☐ 158 Chuck Diering	18.00	8.00	2.20
☐ 159 Eddie Stewart	18.00	8.00	2.20
☐ 160 Phil Masi	18.00	8.00	2.20
☐ 161 Wes Westrum	18.00	8.00	2.20
☐ 162 Larry Jansen	22.00	10.00	2.70
☐ 163 Monte Kennedy	18.00	8.00	2.20
☐ 164 Bill Wight	18.00	8.00	2.20
☐ 165 Ted Williams	700.00	325.00	90.00
☐ 166 Stan Rojek	18.00	8.00	2.20
☐ 167 Murry Dickson	18.00	8.00	2.20
☐ 168 Sam Mele	18.00	8.00	2.20
☐ 169 Sid Hudson	18.00	8.00	2.20
☐ 170 Sibby Sisti	18.00	8.00	2.20
☐ 171 Buddy Kerr	18.00	8.00	2.20
☐ 172 Ned Garver	18.00	8.00	2.20
☐ 173 Hank Arft	18.00	8.00	2.20
☐ 174 Mickey Owen	22.00	10.00	2.70
☐ 175 Wayne Terwilliger	18.00	8.00	2.20
☐ 176 Vic Wertz	25.00	11.00	3.10
☐ 177 Charlie Keller	22.00	10.00	2.70
☐ 178 Ted Gray	18.00	8.00	2.20
☐ 179 Danny Litwhiler	18.00	8.00	2.20
☐ 180 Howie Fox	18.00	8.00	2.20
☐ 181 Casey Stengel MG	75.00	34.00	9.50
☐ 182 Tom Ferrick	18.00	8.00	2.20
☐ 183 Hank Bauer	30.00	13.50	3.70
☐ 184 Eddie Sawyer MG	22.00	10.00	2.70
☐ 185 Jimmy Bloodworth	18.00	8.00	2.20
☐ 186 Richie Ashburn	90.00	40.00	11.00
☐ 187 Al Rosen	25.00	11.00	3.10
☐ 188 Bobby Avila	22.00	10.00	2.70
☐ 189 Erv Palica	18.00	8.00	2.20
☐ 190 Joe Hatten	18.00	8.00	2.20
☐ 191 Billy Hitchcock	18.00	8.00	2.20
☐ 192 Hank Wyse	18.00	8.00	2.20
☐ 193 Ted Wilks	18.00	8.00	2.20
☐ 194 Peanuts Lowrey	18.00	8.00	2.20
☐ 195 Paul Richards MG (Caricature)	22.00	10.00	2.70
☐ 196 Billy Pierce	35.00	16.00	4.40
☐ 197 Bob Cain	18.00	8.00	2.20
☐ 198 Monte Irvin	100.00	45.00	12.50
☐ 199 Sheldon Jones	18.00	8.00	2.20
☐ 200 Jack Kramer	18.00	8.00	2.20
☐ 201 Steve O'Neill MG	18.00	8.00	2.20
☐ 202 Mike Guerra	18.00	8.00	2.20
☐ 203 Vernon Law	30.00	13.50	3.70
☐ 204 Vic Lombardi	18.00	8.00	2.20
☐ 205 Mickey Grasso	18.00	8.00	2.20
☐ 206 Conrado Marrero	18.00	8.00	2.20
☐ 207 Billy Southworth MG	18.00	8.00	2.20
☐ 208 Blix Donnelly	18.00	8.00	2.20
☐ 209 Ken Wood	18.00	8.00	2.20
☐ 210 Les Moss	18.00	8.00	2.20
☐ 211 Hal Jeffcoat	18.00	8.00	2.20
☐ 212 Bob Rush	18.00	8.00	2.20
☐ 213 Neil Berry	18.00	8.00	2.20
☐ 214 Bob Swift	18.00	8.00	2.20
☐ 215 Ken Peterson	18.00	8.00	2.20
☐ 216 Connie Ryan	18.00	8.00	2.20
☐ 217 Joe Page	22.00	10.00	2.70
☐ 218 Ed Lopat	35.00	16.00	4.40
☐ 219 Gene Woodling	40.00	18.00	5.00
☐ 220 Bob Miller	18.00	8.00	2.20
☐ 221 Dick Whitman	18.00	8.00	2.20
☐ 222 Thurman Tucker	18.00	8.00	2.20
☐ 223 Johnny VanderMeer	25.00	11.00	3.10
☐ 224 Billy Cox	27.00	12.00	3.40
☐ 225 Dan Bankhead	25.00	11.00	3.10
☐ 226 Jimmy Dykes MG	22.00	10.00	2.70
☐ 227 Bobby Schantz UER (Sic, Shantz)	22.00	10.00	2.70
☐ 228 Cloyd Boyer	22.00	10.00	2.70
☐ 229 Bill Howerton	18.00	8.00	2.20
☐ 230 Max Lanier	18.00	8.00	2.20
☐ 231 Luis Aloma	18.00	8.00	2.20
☐ 232 Nelson Fox	200.00	90.00	25.00
☐ 233 Leo Durocher MG	60.00	27.00	7.50
☐ 234 Clint Hartung	22.00	10.00	2.70
☐ 235 Jack Lohrke	18.00	8.00	2.20
☐ 236 Warren Rosar	18.00	8.00	2.20
☐ 237 Billy Goodman	22.00	10.00	2.70
☐ 238 Pete Reiser	25.00	11.00	3.10
☐ 239 Bill MacDonald	18.00	8.00	2.20
☐ 240 Joe Haynes	18.00	8.00	2.20
☐ 241 Irv Noren	22.00	10.00	2.70
☐ 242 Sam Jethroe	22.00	10.00	2.70
☐ 243 Johnny Antonelli	22.00	10.00	2.70
☐ 244 Cliff Fannin	18.00	8.00	2.20
☐ 245 John Berardino	30.00	13.50	3.70
☐ 246 Bill Serena	18.00	8.00	2.20
☐ 247 Bob Ramazzotti	18.00	8.00	2.20
☐ 248 Johnny Klippstein	18.00	8.00	2.20
☐ 249 Johnny Groth	18.00	8.00	2.20
☐ 250 Hank Borowy	18.00	8.00	2.20
☐ 251 Willard Ramsdell	18.00	8.00	2.20
☐ 252 Dixie Howell	18.00	8.00	2.20
☐ 253 Mickey Mantle	8000.00	3600.00	1000.00
☐ 254 Jackie Jensen	100.00	45.00	12.50
☐ 255 Milo Candini	50.00	22.00	6.25
☐ 256 Ken Sylvestri	50.00	22.00	6.25
☐ 257 Birdie Tebbetts	60.00	27.00	7.50
☐ 258 Luke Easter	60.00	27.00	7.50
☐ 259 Chuck Dressen MG	75.00	34.00	9.50
☐ 260 Carl Erskine	100.00	45.00	12.50
☐ 261 Wally Moses	60.00	27.00	7.50
☐ 262 Gus Zernial	55.00	25.00	7.00
☐ 263 Howie Pollet	60.00	27.00	7.50
☐ 264 Don Richmond	50.00	22.00	6.25
☐ 265 Steve Bilko	60.00	27.00	7.50
☐ 266 Harry Dorish	50.00	22.00	6.25
☐ 267 Ken Holcombe	50.00	22.00	6.25
☐ 268 Don Mueller	60.00	27.00	7.50
☐ 269 Ray Noble	50.00	22.00	6.25
☐ 270 Willard Nixon	50.00	22.00	6.25
☐ 271 Tommy Wright	50.00	22.00	6.25
☐ 272 Billy Meyer MG	50.00	22.00	6.25
☐ 273 Danny Murtaugh	55.00	25.00	7.00
☐ 274 George Metkovich	50.00	22.00	6.25
☐ 275 Bucky Harris MG	55.00	25.00	7.00
☐ 276 Frank Quinn	50.00	22.00	6.25
☐ 277 Roy Hartsfield	50.00	22.00	6.25
☐ 278 Norman Roy	50.00	22.00	6.25
☐ 279 Jim Delsing	50.00	22.00	6.25
☐ 280 Frank Overmire	50.00	22.00	6.25
☐ 281 Al Widmar	50.00	22.00	6.25
☐ 282 Frank Frisch MG	75.00	34.00	9.50
☐ 283 Walt Dubiel	50.00	22.00	6.25
☐ 284 Gene Bearden	60.00	27.00	7.50
☐ 285 Johnny Lipon	50.00	22.00	6.25
☐ 286 Bob Usher	50.00	22.00	6.25
☐ 287 Jim Blackburn	50.00	22.00	6.25
☐ 288 Bobby Adams	50.00	22.00	6.25
☐ 289 Cliff Mapes	60.00	27.00	7.50
☐ 290 Bill Dickey CO	100.00	45.00	12.50
☐ 291 Tommy Henrich CO	75.00	34.00	9.50

	NRMT	VG-E	GOOD
□ 292 Eddie Pellegrini	50.00	22.00	6.25
□ 293 Ken Johnson	50.00	22.00	6.25
□ 294 Jocko Thompson	50.00	22.00	6.25
□ 295 Al Lopez MG	120.00	55.00	15.00
□ 296 Bob Kennedy	60.00	27.00	7.50
□ 297 Dave Philley	50.00	22.00	6.25
□ 298 Joe Astroth	50.00	22.00	6.25
□ 299 Clyde King	50.00	22.00	6.25
□ 300 Hal Rice	50.00	22.00	6.25
□ 301 Tommy Glaviano	50.00	22.00	6.25
□ 302 Jim Busby	50.00	22.00	6.25
□ 303 Marv Rotblatt	50.00	22.00	6.25
□ 304 Al Gettell	50.00	22.00	6.25
□ 305 Willie Mays	3200.00	1450.00	400.00
□ 306 Jim Piersall	90.00	40.00	11.00
□ 307 Walt Masterson	50.00	22.00	6.25
□ 308 Ted Beard	50.00	22.00	6.25
□ 309 Mel Queen	50.00	22.00	6.25
□ 310 Erv Dusak	50.00	22.00	6.25
□ 311 Mickey Harris	50.00	22.00	6.25
□ 312 Gene Mauch	60.00	27.00	7.50
□ 313 Ray Mueller	50.00	22.00	6.25
□ 314 Johnny Sain	60.00	27.00	7.50
□ 315 Zack Taylor MG	50.00	22.00	6.25
□ 316 Duane Pillette	50.00	22.00	6.25
□ 317 Smoky Burgess	75.00	34.00	9.50
□ 318 Warren Hacker	50.00	22.00	6.25
□ 319 Red Rolfe MG	55.00	25.00	7.00
□ 320 Hal White	50.00	22.00	6.25
□ 321 Earl Johnson	50.00	22.00	6.25
□ 322 Luke Sewell MG	55.00	25.00	7.00
□ 323 Joe Adcock	75.00	34.00	9.50
□ 324 Johnny Pramesa	90.00	27.00	9.00

1952 Bowman

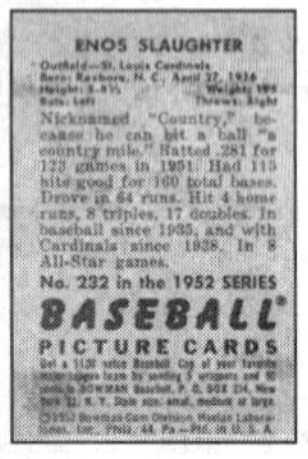

The cards in this 252-card set measure approximately 2 1/16" by 3 1/8". While the Bowman set of 1952 retained the card size introduced in 1951, it employed a modification of color tones from the two preceding years. The cards also appeared with a facsimile autograph on the front and, for the first time since 1949, premium advertising on the back. The 1952 set was apparently sold in sheets as well as in gum packs. Artwork for 15 cards that were never issued was discovered in the early 1980s. Cards were issued in one card penny packs or five card nickle packs. Notable Rookie Cards in this set are Lew Burdette, Gil McDougald, and Minnie Minoso.

	NRMT	VG-E	GOOD
COMPLETE SET (252)	7500.00	3400.00	950.00
COMMON CARD (1-216)	16.00	7.25	2.00
COMMON CARD (217-252)	40.00	18.00	5.00
WRAPPER (1-cent)	200.00	90.00	25.00
WRAPPER (5-cent)	100.00	45.00	12.50

	NRMT	VG-E	GOOD
□ 1 Yogi Berra	400.00	125.00	40.00
□ 2 Bobby Thomson	40.00	18.00	5.00
□ 3 Fred Hutchinson	22.00	10.00	2.70
□ 4 Robin Roberts	60.00	27.00	7.50
□ 5 Minnie Minoso	125.00	55.00	15.50
□ 6 Virgil Stallcup	16.00	7.25	2.00
□ 7 Mike Garcia	25.00	11.00	3.10
□ 8 Pee Wee Reese	125.00	55.00	15.50
□ 9 Vern Stephens	25.00	11.00	3.10
□ 10 Bob Hooper	16.00	7.25	2.00
□ 11 Ralph Kiner	50.00	22.00	6.25
□ 12 Max Surkont	16.00	7.25	2.00
□ 13 Cliff Mapes	16.00	7.25	2.00
□ 14 Cliff Chambers	16.00	7.25	2.00
□ 15 Sam Mele	16.00	7.25	2.00
□ 16 Turk Lown	16.00	7.25	2.00
□ 17 Ed Lopat	40.00	18.00	5.00
□ 18 Don Mueller	25.00	11.00	3.10
□ 19 Bob Cain	16.00	7.25	2.00
□ 20 Willie Jones	16.00	7.25	2.00
□ 21 Nellie Fox	80.00	36.00	10.00
□ 22 Willard Ramsdell	16.00	7.25	2.00
□ 23 Bob Lemon	50.00	22.00	6.25
□ 24 Carl Furillo	40.00	18.00	5.00
□ 25 Mickey McDermott	16.00	7.25	2.00
□ 26 Eddie Joost	16.00	7.25	2.00
□ 27 Joe Garagiola	50.00	22.00	6.25
□ 28 Roy Hartsfield	16.00	7.25	2.00
□ 29 Ned Garver	16.00	7.25	2.00
□ 30 Red Schoendienst	50.00	22.00	6.25
□ 31 Eddie Yost	25.00	11.00	3.10
□ 32 Eddie Miksis	16.00	7.25	2.00
□ 33 Gil McDougald	80.00	36.00	10.00
□ 34 Alvin Dark	25.00	11.00	3.10
□ 35 Granny Hamner	16.00	7.25	2.00
□ 36 Cass Michaels	16.00	7.25	2.00
□ 37 Vic Raschi	25.00	11.00	3.10
□ 38 Whitey Lockman	25.00	11.00	3.10
□ 39 Vic Wertz	25.00	11.00	3.10
□ 40 Bubba Church	16.00	7.25	2.00
□ 41 Chico Carrasquel	25.00	11.00	3.10
□ 42 Johnny Wyrostek	16.00	7.25	2.00
□ 43 Bob Feller	125.00	55.00	15.50
□ 44 Roy Campanella	225.00	100.00	28.00
□ 45 Johnny Pesky	25.00	11.00	3.10
□ 46 Carl Scheib	16.00	7.25	2.00
□ 47 Pete Castiglione	16.00	7.25	2.00
□ 48 Vern Bickford	16.00	7.25	2.00
□ 49 Jim Hearn	16.00	7.25	2.00
□ 50 Jerry Staley	16.00	7.25	2.00
□ 51 Gil Coan	16.00	7.25	2.00
□ 52 Phil Rizzuto	125.00	55.00	15.50
□ 53 Richie Ashburn	90.00	40.00	11.00
□ 54 Billy Pierce	25.00	11.00	3.10
□ 55 Ken Raffensberger	16.00	7.25	2.00
□ 56 Clyde King	25.00	11.00	3.10
□ 57 Clyde Vollmer	16.00	7.25	2.00
□ 58 Hank Majeski	16.00	7.25	2.00
□ 59 Murry Dickson	16.00	7.25	2.00
□ 60 Sid Gordon	22.00	10.00	2.70
□ 61 Tommy Byrne	16.00	7.25	2.00
□ 62 Joe Presko	16.00	7.25	2.00
□ 63 Irv Noren	22.00	10.00	2.70
□ 64 Roy Smalley	16.00	7.25	2.00
□ 65 Hank Bauer	25.00	11.00	3.10
□ 66 Sal Maglie	25.00	11.00	3.10
□ 67 Johnny Groth	16.00	7.25	2.00
□ 68 Jim Busby	16.00	7.25	2.00
□ 69 Joe Adcock	25.00	11.00	3.10
□ 70 Carl Erskine	35.00	16.00	4.40
□ 71 Vernon Law	22.00	10.00	2.70
□ 72 Earl Torgeson	16.00	7.25	2.00
□ 73 Jerry Coleman	25.00	11.00	3.10
□ 74 Wes Westrum	22.00	10.00	2.70
□ 75 George Kell	50.00	22.00	6.25
□ 76 Del Ennis	22.00	10.00	2.70
□ 77 Eddie Robinson	16.00	7.25	2.00
□ 78 Lloyd Merriman	16.00	7.25	2.00
□ 79 Lou Brissie	16.00	7.25	2.00
□ 80 Gil Hodges	90.00	40.00	11.00
□ 81 Billy Goodman	22.00	10.00	2.70
□ 82 Gus Zernial	22.00	10.00	2.70
□ 83 Howie Pollet	16.00	7.25	2.00
□ 84 Sam Jethroe	22.00	10.00	2.70
□ 85 Marty Marion CO	25.00	11.00	3.10
□ 86 Cal Abrams	22.00	10.00	2.70
□ 87 Mickey Vernon	25.00	11.00	3.10
□ 88 Bruce Edwards	16.00	7.25	2.00
□ 89 Billy Hitchcock	16.00	7.25	2.00
□ 90 Larry Jansen	25.00	11.00	3.10
□ 91 Don Kolloway	16.00	7.25	2.00
□ 92 Eddie Waitkus	16.00	7.25	2.00
□ 93 Paul Richards MG	22.00	10.00	2.70
□ 94 Luke Sewell MG	22.00	10.00	2.70
□ 95 Luke Easter	22.00	10.00	2.70
□ 96 Ralph Branca	25.00	11.00	3.10
□ 97 Willard Marshall	16.00	7.25	2.00
□ 98 Jimmy Dykes MG	22.00	10.00	2.70
□ 99 Clyde McCullough	16.00	7.25	2.00
□ 100 Sibby Sisti	16.00	7.25	2.00
□ 101 Mickey Mantle	2500.00	1100.00	300.00
□ 102 Peanuts Lowrey	16.00	7.25	2.00
□ 103 Joe Haynes	16.00	7.25	2.00
□ 104 Hal Jeffcoat	16.00	7.25	2.00
□ 105 Bobby Brown	25.00	11.00	3.10
□ 106 Randy Gumpert	16.00	7.25	2.00
□ 107 Del Rice	16.00	7.25	2.00
□ 108 George Metkovich	22.00	10.00	2.70
□ 109 Tom Morgan	22.00	10.00	2.70
□ 110 Max Lanier	16.00	7.25	2.00
□ 111 Hoot Evers	16.00	7.25	2.00
□ 112 Smoky Burgess	25.00	11.00	3.10
□ 113 Al Zarilla	16.00	7.25	2.00
□ 114 Frank Hiller	16.00	7.25	2.00
□ 115 Larry Doby	40.00	18.00	5.00
□ 116 Duke Snider	200.00	90.00	25.00
□ 117 Bill Wight	16.00	7.25	2.00
□ 118 Ray Murray	16.00	7.25	2.00
□ 119 Bill Howerton	16.00	7.25	2.00
□ 120 Chet Nichols	16.00	7.25	2.00
□ 121 Al Corwin	16.00	7.25	2.00
□ 122 Billy Johnson	16.00	7.25	2.00
□ 123 Sid Hudson	16.00	7.25	2.00
□ 124 Birdie Tebbetts	22.00	10.00	2.70
□ 125 Howie Fox	16.00	7.25	2.00
□ 126 Phil Cavarretta	22.00	10.00	2.70
□ 127 Dick Sisler	16.00	7.25	2.00
□ 128 Don Newcombe	35.00	16.00	4.40
□ 129 Gus Niarhos	16.00	7.25	2.00
□ 130 Allie Clark	16.00	7.25	2.00
□ 131 Bob Swift	16.00	7.25	2.00
□ 132 Dave Cole	16.00	7.25	2.00
□ 133 Dick Kryhoski	16.00	7.25	2.00
□ 134 Al Brazle	16.00	7.25	2.00
□ 135 Mickey Harris	16.00	7.25	2.00
□ 136 Gene Hermanski	16.00	7.25	2.00
□ 137 Stan Rojek	16.00	7.25	2.00
□ 138 Ted Wilks	16.00	7.25	2.00
□ 139 Jerry Priddy	16.00	7.25	2.00
□ 140 Ray Scarborough	16.00	7.25	2.00
□ 141 Hank Edwards	16.00	7.25	2.00
□ 142 Early Wynn	50.00	22.00	6.25
□ 143 Sandy Consuegra	16.00	7.25	2.00
□ 144 Joe Hatton	16.00	7.25	2.00
□ 145 Johnny Mize	50.00	22.00	6.25
□ 146 Leo Durocher MG	50.00	22.00	6.25
□ 147 Marlin Stuart	16.00	7.25	2.00
□ 148 Ken Heintzelman	16.00	7.25	2.00
□ 149 Howie Judson	16.00	7.25	2.00
□ 150 Herman Wehmeier	16.00	7.25	2.00
□ 151 Al Rosen	25.00	11.00	3.10
□ 152 Billy Cox	16.00	7.25	2.00
□ 153 Fred Hatfield	16.00	7.25	2.00
□ 154 Ferris Fain	22.00	10.00	2.70
□ 155 Billy Meyer MG	16.00	7.25	2.00
□ 156 Warren Spahn	125.00	55.00	15.50
□ 157 Jim Delsing	16.00	7.25	2.00
□ 158 Bucky Harris MG	25.00	11.00	3.10
□ 159 Dutch Leonard	16.00	7.25	2.00
□ 160 Eddie Stanky	25.00	11.00	3.10
□ 161 Jackie Jensen	35.00	16.00	4.40
□ 162 Monte Irvin	50.00	22.00	6.25
□ 163 Johnny Lipon	16.00	7.25	2.00
□ 164 Connie Ryan	16.00	7.25	2.00
□ 165 Saul Rogovin	16.00	7.25	2.00
□ 166 Bobby Adams	16.00	7.25	2.00
□ 167 Bobby Avila	25.00	11.00	3.10
□ 168 Preacher Roe	25.00	11.00	3.10
□ 169 Walt Dropo	22.00	10.00	2.70
□ 170 Joe Astroth	16.00	7.25	2.00
□ 171 Mel Queen	16.00	7.25	2.00
□ 172 Ebba St.Claire	16.00	7.25	2.00
□ 173 Gene Bearden	16.00	7.25	2.00
□ 174 Mickey Grasso	16.00	7.25	2.00
□ 175 Randy Jackson	16.00	7.25	2.00
□ 176 Harry Brecheen	22.00	10.00	2.70
□ 177 Gene Woodling	25.00	11.00	3.10
□ 178 Dave Williams	22.00	10.00	2.70
□ 179 Pete Suder	16.00	7.25	2.00
□ 180 Ed Fitzgerald	16.00	7.25	2.00
□ 181 Joe Collins	25.00	11.00	3.10
□ 182 Dave Koslo	16.00	7.25	2.00
□ 183 Pat Mullin	16.00	7.25	2.00
□ 184 Curt Simmons	25.00	11.00	3.10
□ 185 Eddie Stewart	16.00	7.25	2.00
□ 186 Frank Smith	16.00	7.25	2.00
□ 187 Jim Hegan	22.00	10.00	2.70
□ 188 Charlie Dressen MG	25.00	11.00	3.10
□ 189 Jim Piersall	25.00	11.00	3.10
□ 190 Dick Fowler	16.00	7.25	2.00
□ 191 Bob Friend	40.00	18.00	5.00
□ 192 John Cusick	16.00	7.25	2.00
□ 193 Bobby Young	16.00	7.25	2.00
□ 194 Bob Porterfield	16.00	7.25	2.00
□ 195 Frank Baumholtz	16.00	7.25	2.00
□ 196 Stan Musial	600.00	275.00	75.00
□ 197 Charlie Silvera	16.00	7.25	2.00
□ 198 Chuck Diering	16.00	7.25	2.00
□ 199 Ted Gray	16.00	7.25	2.00
□ 200 Ken Silvestri	16.00	7.25	2.00
□ 201 Ray Coleman	16.00	7.25	2.00
□ 202 Harry Perkowski	16.00	7.25	2.00
□ 203 Steve Gromek	16.00	7.25	2.00
□ 204 Andy Pafko	25.00	11.00	3.10
□ 205 Walt Masterson	16.00	7.25	2.00
□ 206 Elmer Valo	16.00	7.25	2.00
□ 207 George Strickland	16.00	7.25	2.00
□ 208 Walker Cooper	16.00	7.25	2.00
□ 209 Dick Littlefield	16.00	7.25	2.00
□ 210 Archie Wilson	16.00	7.25	2.00
□ 211 Paul Minner	16.00	7.25	2.00
□ 212 Solly Hemus	16.00	7.25	2.00
□ 213 Monte Kennedy	16.00	7.25	2.00
□ 214 Ray Boone	22.00	10.00	2.70
□ 215 Sheldon Jones	16.00	7.25	2.00
□ 216 Matt Batts	16.00	7.25	2.00
□ 217 Casey Stengel MG	150.00	70.00	19.00
□ 218 Willie Mays	1200.00	550.00	150.00
□ 219 Neil Berry	40.00	18.00	5.00
□ 220 Russ Meyer	40.00	18.00	5.00
□ 221 Lou Kretlow	40.00	18.00	5.00
□ 222 Dixie Howell	40.00	18.00	5.00
□ 223 Harry Simpson	40.00	18.00	5.00
□ 224 Johnny Schmitz	40.00	18.00	5.00
□ 225 Del Wilber	40.00	18.00	5.00
□ 226 Alex Kellner	40.00	18.00	5.00
□ 227 Clyde Sukeforth CO	40.00	18.00	5.00
□ 228 Bob Chipman	40.00	18.00	5.00
□ 229 Hank Arft	40.00	18.00	5.00
□ 230 Frank Shea	40.00	18.00	5.00
□ 231 Dee Fondy	40.00	18.00	5.00
□ 232 Enos Slaughter	90.00	40.00	11.00
□ 233 Bob Kuzava	40.00	18.00	5.00
□ 234 Fred Fitzsimmons CO	45.00	20.00	5.50
□ 235 Steve Souchock	40.00	18.00	5.00
□ 236 Tommy Brown	40.00	18.00	5.00
□ 237 Sherm Lollar	45.00	20.00	5.50
□ 238 Roy McMillan	40.00	18.00	5.00
□ 239 Dale Mitchell	50.00	22.00	6.25
□ 240 Billy Loes	50.00	22.00	6.25
□ 241 Mel Parnell	50.00	22.00	6.25
□ 242 Everett Kell	40.00	18.00	5.00
□ 243 Red Munger	40.00	18.00	5.00
□ 244 Lew Burdette	50.00	22.00	6.25
□ 245 George Schmees	40.00	18.00	5.00
□ 246 Jerry Snyder	40.00	18.00	5.00
□ 247 Johnny Pramesa	40.00	18.00	5.00
□ 248 Bill Werle	40.00	18.00	5.00
□ 249 Hank Thompson	45.00	20.00	5.50
□ 250 Ike Delock	40.00	18.00	5.00
□ 251 Jack Lohrke	40.00	18.00	5.00
□ 252 Frank Crosetti CO	100.00	25.00	8.00

1953 Bowman B/W

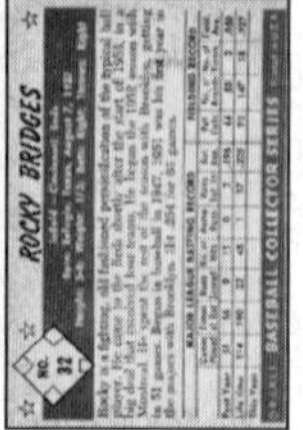

The cards in this 64-card set measure approximately 2 1/2" by 3 3/4". Some collectors believe that the high cost of producing the 1953 color series forced Bowman to issue this set in black and white, since the two sets are identical in design except for the element of color. This set was also produced in fewer numbers than its color counterpart, and is popular among collectors for the challenge involved in completing it. Cards were issued in five-card nickle packs. There are no key Rookie Cards in this set.

	NRMT	VG-E	GOOD
COMPLETE SET (64)	2400.00	1100.00	300.00
COMMON CARD (1-64)	35.00	16.00	4.40
WRAPPER (1-CENT)	350.00	160.00	45.00

	NRMT	VG-E	GOOD
□ 1 Gus Bell	110.00	22.00	8.75
□ 2 Willard Nixon	35.00	16.00	4.40
□ 3 Bill Rigney	35.00	16.00	4.40
□ 4 Pat Mullin	35.00	16.00	4.40
□ 5 Dee Fondy	35.00	16.00	4.40
□ 6 Ray Murray	35.00	16.00	4.40
□ 7 Andy Seminick	35.00	16.00	4.40
□ 8 Pete Suder	35.00	16.00	4.40
□ 9 Walt Masterson	35.00	16.00	4.40
□ 10 Dick Sisler	40.00	18.00	5.00
□ 11 Dick Gernert	35.00	16.00	4.40
□ 12 Randy Jackson	35.00	16.00	4.40
□ 13 Joe Tipton	35.00	16.00	4.40
□ 14 Bill Nicholson	40.00	18.00	5.00
□ 15 Johnny Mize	125.00	55.00	15.50
□ 16 Stu Miller	40.00	18.00	5.00
□ 17 Virgil Trucks	40.00	18.00	5.00
□ 18 Billy Hoeft	35.00	16.00	4.40
□ 19 Paul LaPalme	35.00	16.00	4.40
□ 20 Eddie Robinson	35.00	16.00	4.40
□ 21 Clarence Podbielan	35.00	16.00	4.40
□ 22 Matt Batts	35.00	16.00	4.40
□ 23 Wilmer Mizell	40.00	18.00	5.00
□ 24 Del Wilber	35.00	16.00	4.40
□ 25 Johnny Sain	60.00	27.00	7.50
□ 26 Preacher Roe	60.00	27.00	7.50
□ 27 Bob Lemon	125.00	55.00	15.50
□ 28 Hoyt Wilhelm	125.00	55.00	15.50
□ 29 Sid Hudson	35.00	16.00	4.40
□ 30 Walker Cooper	35.00	16.00	4.40
□ 31 Gene Woodling	60.00	27.00	7.50
□ 32 Rocky Bridges	35.00	16.00	4.40
□ 33 Bob Kuzava	35.00	16.00	4.40
□ 34 Ebba St.Claire	35.00	16.00	4.40
□ 35 Johnny Wyrostek	35.00	16.00	4.40
□ 36 Jim Piersall	60.00	27.00	7.50
□ 37 Hal Jeffcoat	35.00	16.00	4.40
□ 38 Dave Cole	35.00	16.00	4.40
□ 39 Casey Stengel MG	325.00	145.00	40.00
□ 40 Larry Jansen	40.00	18.00	5.00
□ 41 Bob Ramazzotti	35.00	16.00	4.40
□ 42 Howie Judson	35.00	16.00	4.40
□ 43 Hal Bevan	35.00	16.00	4.40
□ 44 Jim Delsing	35.00	16.00	4.40
□ 45 Irv Noren	40.00	18.00	5.00
□ 46 Bucky Harris MG	60.00	27.00	7.50
□ 47 Jack Lohrke	35.00	16.00	4.40
□ 48 Steve Ridzik	35.00	16.00	4.40
□ 49 Floyd Baker	35.00	16.00	4.40
□ 50 Dutch Leonard	35.00	16.00	4.40
□ 51 Lou Burdette	60.00	27.00	7.50
□ 52 Ralph Branca	50.00	22.00	6.25
□ 53 Morrie Martin	35.00	16.00	4.40
□ 54 Bill Miller	35.00	16.00	4.40
□ 55 Don Johnson	35.00	16.00	4.40
□ 56 Roy Smalley	35.00	16.00	4.40
□ 57 Andy Pafko	40.00	18.00	5.00
□ 58 Jim Konstanty	40.00	18.00	5.00
□ 59 Duane Pillette	35.00	16.00	4.40
□ 60 Billy Cox	50.00	22.00	6.25
□ 61 Tom Gorman	35.00	16.00	4.40
□ 62 Keith Thomas	35.00	16.00	4.40
□ 63 Steve Gromek	35.00	16.00	4.40
□ 64 Andy Hansen	60.00	19.00	5.25

1953 Bowman Color

The cards in this 160-card set measure approximately 2 1/2" by 3 3/4". The 1953 Bowman Color set, considered by many to be the best looking set of the modern era, contains Kodachrome photographs with no names or facsimile autographs on the face. Cards were issued

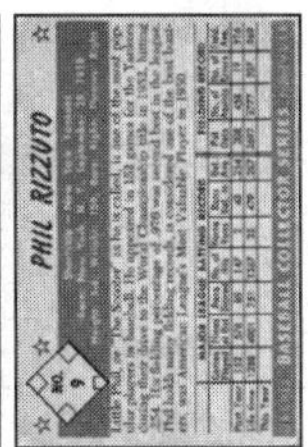

in five-card nickle packs. Numbers 113 to 160 are somewhat more difficult to obtain, with numbers 113 to 128 being the most difficult. There are two cards of Al Corwin (126 and 149). There are no key Rookie Cards in this set.

	NRMT	VG-E	GOOD
COMPLETE SET (160)	12000.00	5400.00	1500.00
COMMON CARD (1-112)	35.00	16.00	4.40
COMMON CARD (113-128)	70.00	32.00	8.75
COMMON CARD (129-160)	60.00	27.00	7.50
WRAPPER (1-cent)	400.00	180.00	50.00
WRAPPER (5-CENT)	300.00	135.00	38.00

	NRMT	VG-E	GOOD
☐ 1 Dave Williams	100.00	20.00	6.00
☐ 2 Vic Wertz	40.00	18.00	5.00
☐ 3 Sam Jethroe	40.00	18.00	5.00
☐ 4 Art Houtteman	35.00	16.00	4.40
☐ 5 Sid Gordon	35.00	16.00	4.40
☐ 6 Joe Ginsberg	35.00	16.00	4.40
☐ 7 Harry Chiti	35.00	16.00	4.40
☐ 8 Al Rosen	40.00	18.00	5.00
☐ 9 Phil Rizzuto	160.00	70.00	20.00
☐ 10 Richie Ashburn	160.00	70.00	20.00
☐ 11 Bobby Shantz	35.00	16.00	4.40
☐ 12 Carl Erskine	45.00	20.00	5.50
☐ 13 Gus Zernial	40.00	18.00	5.00
☐ 14 Billy Loes	40.00	18.00	5.00
☐ 15 Jim Busby	35.00	16.00	4.40
☐ 16 Bob Friend	35.00	16.00	4.40
☐ 17 Gerry Staley	35.00	16.00	4.40
☐ 18 Nellie Fox	100.00	45.00	12.50
☐ 19 Alvin Dark	35.00	16.00	4.40
☐ 20 Don Lenhardt	35.00	16.00	4.40
☐ 21 Joe Garagiola	60.00	27.00	7.50
☐ 22 Bob Porterfield	35.00	16.00	4.40
☐ 23 Herman Wehmeier	35.00	16.00	4.40
☐ 24 Jackie Jensen	40.00	18.00	5.00
☐ 25 Hoot Evers	35.00	16.00	4.40
☐ 26 Roy McMillan	40.00	18.00	5.00
☐ 27 Vic Raschi	45.00	20.00	5.50
☐ 28 Smoky Burgess	35.00	16.00	4.40
☐ 29 Bobby Avila	35.00	16.00	4.40
☐ 30 Phil Cavarretta	35.00	16.00	4.40
☐ 31 Jimmy Dykes MG	35.00	16.00	4.40
☐ 32 Stan Musial	700.00	325.00	90.00
☐ 33 Pee Wee Reese HOR	825.00	375.00	105.00
☐ 34 Gil Coan	35.00	16.00	4.40
☐ 35 Maurice McDermott	35.00	16.00	4.40
☐ 36 Minnie Minoso	60.00	27.00	7.50
☐ 37 Jim Wilson	35.00	16.00	4.40
☐ 38 Harry Byrd	35.00	16.00	4.40
☐ 39 Paul Richards MG	35.00	16.00	4.40
☐ 40 Larry Doby	60.00	27.00	7.50
☐ 41 Sammy White	35.00	16.00	4.40
☐ 42 Tommy Brown	35.00	16.00	4.40
☐ 43 Mike Garcia	40.00	18.00	5.00
☐ 44 Yogi Berra Hank Bauer Mickey Mantle	675.00	300.00	85.00
☐ 45 Walt Dropo	40.00	18.00	5.00
☐ 46 Roy Campanella	275.00	125.00	34.00
☐ 47 Ned Garver	35.00	16.00	4.40
☐ 48 Hank Sauer	35.00	16.00	4.40
☐ 49 Eddie Stanky MG	35.00	16.00	4.40
☐ 50 Lou Kretlow	35.00	16.00	4.40
☐ 51 Monte Irvin	60.00	27.00	7.50
☐ 52 Marty Marion MG	40.00	18.00	5.00
☐ 53 Del Rice	35.00	16.00	4.40
☐ 54 Chico Carrasquel	35.00	16.00	4.40
☐ 55 Leo Durocher MG	70.00	32.00	8.75
☐ 56 Bob Cain	35.00	16.00	4.40
☐ 57 Lou Boudreau MG	60.00	27.00	7.50
☐ 58 Willard Marshall	35.00	16.00	4.40
☐ 59 Mickey Mantle	3000.00	1350.00	375.00
☐ 60 Granny Hamner	35.00	16.00	4.40
☐ 61 George Kell	70.00	32.00	8.75
☐ 62 Ted Kluszewski	60.00	27.00	7.50
☐ 63 Gil McDougald	60.00	27.00	7.50
☐ 64 Curt Simmons	35.00	16.00	4.40
☐ 65 Robin Roberts	80.00	36.00	10.00
☐ 66 Mel Parnell	40.00	18.00	5.00
☐ 67 Mel Clark	35.00	16.00	4.40
☐ 68 Allie Reynolds	45.00	20.00	5.50
☐ 69 Charlie Grimm MG	35.00	16.00	4.40
☐ 70 Clint Courtney	35.00	16.00	4.40
☐ 71 Paul Minner	35.00	16.00	4.40
☐ 72 Ted Gray	35.00	16.00	4.40
☐ 73 Billy Pierce	35.00	16.00	4.40
☐ 74 Don Mueller	40.00	18.00	5.00
☐ 75 Saul Rogovin	35.00	16.00	4.40
☐ 76 Jim Hearn	35.00	16.00	4.40
☐ 77 Mickey Grasso	35.00	16.00	4.40
☐ 78 Carl Furillo	45.00	20.00	5.50
☐ 79 Ray Boone	35.00	16.00	4.40
☐ 80 Ralph Kiner	70.00	32.00	8.75
☐ 81 Enos Slaughter	60.00	27.00	7.50
☐ 82 Joe Astroth	35.00	16.00	4.40
☐ 83 Jack Daniels	35.00	16.00	4.40
☐ 84 Hank Bauer	45.00	20.00	5.50
☐ 85 Solly Hemus	35.00	16.00	4.40
☐ 86 Harry Simpson	35.00	16.00	4.40
☐ 87 Harry Perkowski	35.00	16.00	4.40
☐ 88 Joe Dobson	35.00	16.00	4.40
☐ 89 Sandy Consuegra	35.00	16.00	4.40
☐ 90 Joe Nuxhall	40.00	18.00	5.00
☐ 91 Steve Souchock	35.00	16.00	4.40
☐ 92 Gil Hodges	175.00	80.00	22.00
☐ 93 Phil Rizzuto and Billy Martin	250.00	110.00	31.00
☐ 94 Bob Addis	35.00	16.00	4.40
☐ 95 Wally Moses CO	40.00	18.00	5.00
☐ 96 Sal Maglie	40.00	18.00	5.00
☐ 97 Eddie Mathews	275.00	125.00	34.00
☐ 98 Hector Rodriguez	35.00	16.00	4.40
☐ 99 Warren Spahn	225.00	100.00	28.00
☐ 100 Bill Wight	35.00	16.00	4.40
☐ 101 Red Schoendienst	60.00	27.00	7.50
☐ 102 Jim Hegan	40.00	18.00	5.00
☐ 103 Del Ennis	40.00	18.00	5.00
☐ 104 Luke Easter	40.00	18.00	5.00
☐ 105 Eddie Joost	35.00	16.00	4.40
☐ 106 Ken Raffensberger	35.00	16.00	4.40
☐ 107 Alex Kellner	35.00	16.00	4.40
☐ 108 Bobby Adams	35.00	16.00	4.40
☐ 109 Ken Wood	35.00	16.00	4.40
☐ 110 Bob Rush	35.00	16.00	4.40
☐ 111 Jim Dyck	35.00	16.00	4.40
☐ 112 Toby Atwell	35.00	16.00	4.40
☐ 113 Karl Drews	70.00	32.00	8.75
☐ 114 Bob Feller	300.00	135.00	38.00
☐ 115 Cloyd Boyer	70.00	32.00	8.75
☐ 116 Eddie Yost	75.00	34.00	9.50
☐ 117 Duke Snider	550.00	250.00	70.00
☐ 118 Billy Martin	300.00	135.00	38.00
☐ 119 Dale Mitchell	75.00	34.00	9.50
☐ 120 Marlin Stuart	70.00	32.00	8.75
☐ 121 Yogi Berra	575.00	250.00	70.00
☐ 122 Bill Serena	70.00	32.00	8.75
☐ 123 Johnny Lipon	70.00	32.00	8.75
☐ 124 Charlie Dressen MG	90.00	40.00	11.00
☐ 125 Fred Hatfield	70.00	32.00	8.75
☐ 126 Al Corwin	70.00	32.00	8.75
☐ 127 Dick Kryhoski	70.00	32.00	8.75
☐ 128 Whitey Lockman	75.00	34.00	9.50
☐ 129 Russ Meyer	60.00	27.00	7.50
☐ 130 Cass Michaels	60.00	27.00	7.50
☐ 131 Connie Ryan	60.00	27.00	7.50
☐ 132 Fred Hutchinson	70.00	32.00	8.75
☐ 133 Willie Jones	60.00	27.00	7.50
☐ 134 Johnny Pesky	70.00	32.00	8.75
☐ 135 Bobby Morgan	60.00	27.00	7.50
☐ 136 Jim Brideweser	60.00	27.00	7.50
☐ 137 Sam Dente	60.00	27.00	7.50
☐ 138 Bubba Church	60.00	27.00	7.50
☐ 139 Pete Runnels	70.00	32.00	8.75
☐ 140 Al Brazle	60.00	27.00	7.50
☐ 141 Frank Shea	60.00	27.00	7.50
☐ 142 Larry Miggins	60.00	27.00	7.50
☐ 143 Al Lopez MG	70.00	32.00	8.75
☐ 144 Warren Hacker	60.00	27.00	7.50
☐ 145 George Shuba	70.00	32.00	8.75
☐ 146 Early Wynn	125.00	55.00	15.50
☐ 147 Clem Koshorek	60.00	27.00	7.50
☐ 148 Billy Goodman	70.00	32.00	8.75
☐ 149 Al Corwin	60.00	27.00	7.50
☐ 150 Carl Scheib	60.00	27.00	7.50
☐ 151 Joe Adcock	70.00	32.00	8.75
☐ 152 Clyde Vollmer	60.00	27.00	7.50
☐ 153 Whitey Ford	500.00	220.00	60.00
☐ 154 Turk Lown	60.00	27.00	7.50
☐ 155 Allie Clark	60.00	27.00	7.50
☐ 156 Max Surkont	60.00	27.00	7.50
☐ 157 Sherm Lollar	70.00	32.00	8.75
☐ 158 Howard Fox	60.00	27.00	7.50
☐ 159 Mickey Vernon UER (Photo actually Floyd Baker)	70.00	32.00	8.75
☐ 160 Cal Abrams	100.00	34.00	9.25

1954 Bowman

The cards in this 224-card set measure approximately 2 1/2" by 3 3/4". A contractual problem apparently resulted in the deletion of the number 66 Ted Williams card from this Bowman set, thereby creating a scarcity that is highly valued among collectors. The set price below does NOT include number 66 Williams but does include number 66 Jim Piersall, the apparent replacement for Williams in spite of the fact that Piersall was already number 210 to appear later in the set. Many errors in players' statistics exist (and some were corrected) while a few players' names were printed on the front, instead of appearing as a facsimile autograph. Most of these differences are so minor that there is no price differential for either card. The cards which changes were made on are #'s 12, 22,25,26,35,38, 41, 43, 47, 53, 61, 67, 80, 81, 82, 85, 93, 94, 99, 103, 105, 124, 138, 139, 140, 145, 153, 156, 174, 179, 185, 212, 216 and 217. The set was issued in seven-card nickle packs. The notable Rookie Cards in this set are Harvey Kuenn and Don Larsen.

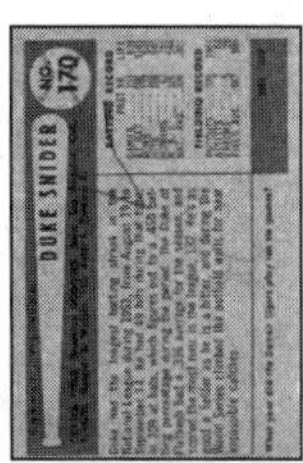

	NRMT	VG-E	GOOD
COMPLETE SET (224)	4000.00	1800.00	500.00
COMMON CARD (1-128)	12.00	5.50	1.50
COMMON CARD (129-224)	14.00	6.25	1.75
WRAPPER (1-CENT, DATED)	150.00	70.00	19.00
WRAPPER (1-CENT, UNDATED)	200.00	90.00	25.00
WRAPPER (5-CENT, DATED)	150.00	70.00	19.00
WRAPPER (5-CENT, UNDATED)	60.00	27.00	7.50

	NRMT	VG-E	GOOD
☐ 1 Phil Rizzuto	150.00	45.00	15.00
☐ 2 Jackie Jensen	16.00	7.25	2.00
☐ 3 Marion Fricano	12.00	5.50	1.50
☐ 4 Bob Hooper	12.00	5.50	1.50
☐ 5 Billy Hunter	12.00	5.50	1.50
☐ 6 Nellie Fox	50.00	22.00	6.25
☐ 7 Walt Dropo	14.00	6.25	1.75
☐ 8 Jim Busby	12.00	5.50	1.50
☐ 9 Dave Williams	12.00	5.50	1.50
☐ 10 Carl Erskine	18.00	8.00	2.20
☐ 11 Sid Gordon	12.00	5.50	1.50
☐ 12 Roy McMillan	14.00	6.25	1.75
☐ 13 Paul Minner	12.00	5.50	1.50
☐ 14 Jerry Staley	12.00	5.50	1.50
☐ 15 Richie Ashburn	75.00	34.00	9.50
☐ 16 Jim Wilson	12.00	5.50	1.50
☐ 17 Tom Gorman	12.00	5.50	1.50
☐ 18 Hoot Evers	12.00	5.50	1.50
☐ 19 Bobby Shantz	14.00	6.25	1.75
☐ 20 Art Houtteman	12.00	5.50	1.50
☐ 21 Vic Wertz	16.00	7.25	2.00
☐ 22 Sam Mele	12.00	5.50	1.50
☐ 23 Harvey Kuenn	35.00	16.00	4.40
☐ 24 Bob Porterfield	12.00	5.50	1.50
☐ 25 Wes Westrum	14.00	6.25	1.75
☐ 26 Billy Cox	18.00	8.00	2.20
☐ 27 Dick Cole	12.00	5.50	1.50
☐ 28 Jim Greengrass	12.00	5.50	1.50
☐ 29 Johnny Klippstein	12.00	5.50	1.50
☐ 30 Del Rice	12.00	5.50	1.50
☐ 31 Smoky Burgess	14.00	6.25	1.75
☐ 32 Del Crandall	14.00	6.25	1.75
☐ 33A Vic Raschi (No mention of trade on back)	20.00	9.00	2.50
☐ 33B Vic Raschi (Traded to St.Louis)	35.00	16.00	4.40
☐ 34 Sammy White	12.00	5.50	1.50
☐ 35 Eddie Joost	12.00	5.50	1.50
☐ 36 George Strickland	12.00	5.50	1.50
☐ 37 Dick Kokos	12.00	5.50	1.50
☐ 38 Minnie Minoso	25.00	11.00	3.10
☐ 39 Ned Garver	12.00	5.50	1.50
☐ 40 Gil Coan	12.00	5.50	1.50
☐ 41 Alvin Dark	16.00	7.25	2.00
☐ 42 Billy Loes	18.00	8.00	2.20
☐ 43 Bob Friend	16.00	7.25	2.00
☐ 44 Harry Perkowski	12.00	5.50	1.50
☐ 45 Ralph Kiner	40.00	18.00	5.00
☐ 46 Rip Repulski	12.00	5.50	1.50
☐ 47 Granny Hamner	12.00	5.50	1.50
☐ 48 Jack Dittmer	12.00	5.50	1.50
☐ 49 Harry Byrd	12.00	5.50	1.50
☐ 50 George Kell	40.00	18.00	5.00
☐ 51 Alex Kellner	12.00	5.50	1.50
☐ 52 Joe Ginsberg	12.00	5.50	1.50
☐ 53 Don Lenhardt	12.00	5.50	1.50
☐ 54 Chico Carrasquel	12.00	5.50	1.50
☐ 55 Jim Delsing	12.00	5.50	1.50
☐ 56 Maurice McDermott	12.00	5.50	1.50
☐ 57 Hoyt Wilhelm	35.00	16.00	4.40
☐ 58 Pee Wee Reese	75.00	34.00	9.50
☐ 59 Bob Schultz	12.00	5.50	1.50
☐ 60 Fred Baczewski	12.00	5.50	1.50
☐ 61 Eddie Miksis	12.00	5.50	1.50
☐ 62 Enos Slaughter	40.00	18.00	5.00
☐ 63 Earl Torgeson	12.00	5.50	1.50
☐ 64 Eddie Mathews	50.00	22.00	6.25
☐ 65 Mickey Mantle	1300.00	575.00	160.00
☐ 66A Ted Williams	4600.00	2100.00	575.00
☐ 66B Jim Piersall	75.00	34.00	9.50
☐ 67 Carl Scheib	12.00	5.50	1.50
☐ 68 Bobby Avila	14.00	6.25	1.75
☐ 69 Clint Courtney	12.00	5.50	1.50
☐ 70 Willard Marshall	12.00	5.50	1.50
☐ 71 Ted Gray	12.00	5.50	1.50
☐ 72 Eddie Yost	14.00	6.25	1.75
☐ 73 Don Mueller	14.00	6.25	1.75
☐ 74 Jim Gilliam	30.00	13.50	3.70
☐ 75 Max Surkont	12.00	5.50	1.50
☐ 76 Joe Nuxhall	14.00	6.25	1.75
☐ 77 Bob Rush	12.00	5.50	1.50
☐ 78 Sal Yvars	12.00	5.50	1.50
☐ 79 Curt Simmons	14.00	6.25	1.75
☐ 80 Johnny Logan	12.00	5.50	1.50
☐ 81 Jerry Coleman	18.00	8.00	2.20
☐ 82 Billy Goodman	14.00	6.25	1.75
☐ 83 Ray Murray	12.00	5.50	1.50
☐ 84 Larry Doby	25.00	11.00	3.10
☐ 85 Jim Dyck	12.00	5.50	1.50
☐ 86 Harry Dorish	12.00	5.50	1.50
☐ 87 Don Lund	12.00	5.50	1.50
☐ 88 Tom Umphlett	12.00	5.50	1.50
☐ 89 Willie Mays	400.00	180.00	50.00
☐ 90 Roy Campanella	175.00	80.00	22.00
☐ 91 Cal Abrams	12.00	5.50	1.50
☐ 92 Ken Raffensberger	12.00	5.50	1.50
☐ 93 Bill Serena	12.00	5.50	1.50
☐ 94 Solly Hemus	12.00	5.50	1.50
☐ 95 Robin Roberts	50.00	22.00	6.25
☐ 96 Joe Adcock	16.00	7.25	2.00
☐ 97 Gil McDougald	20.00	9.00	2.50
☐ 98 Ellis Kinder	12.00	5.50	1.50
☐ 99 Pete Suder	12.00	5.50	1.50
☐ 100 Mike Garcia	14.00	6.25	1.75
☐ 101 Don Larsen	50.00	22.00	6.25
☐ 102 Billy Pierce	16.00	7.25	2.00
☐ 103 Steve Souchock	12.00	5.50	1.50
☐ 104 Frank Shea	12.00	5.50	1.50
☐ 105 Sal Maglie	16.00	7.25	2.00
☐ 106 Clem Labine	18.00	8.00	2.20
☐ 107 Paul LaPalme	12.00	5.50	1.50
☐ 108 Bobby Adams	12.00	5.50	1.50
☐ 109 Roy Smalley	12.00	5.50	1.50
☐ 110 Red Schoendienst	35.00	16.00	4.40
☐ 111 Murry Dickson	12.00	5.50	1.50
☐ 112 Andy Pafko	16.00	7.25	2.00
☐ 113 Allie Reynolds	18.00	8.00	2.20
☐ 114 Willard Nixon	12.00	5.50	1.50
☐ 115 Don Bollweg	12.00	5.50	1.50
☐ 116 Luke Easter	16.00	7.25	2.00
☐ 117 Dick Kryhoski	12.00	5.50	1.50
☐ 118 Bob Boyd	12.00	5.50	1.50
☐ 119 Fred Hatfield	12.00	5.50	1.50
☐ 120 Mel Hoderlein	12.00	5.50	1.50
☐ 121 Ray Katt	12.00	5.50	1.50
☐ 122 Carl Furillo	25.00	11.00	3.10
☐ 123 Toby Atwell	12.00	5.50	1.50
☐ 124 Gus Bell	14.00	6.25	1.75
☐ 125 Warren Hacker	12.00	5.50	1.50
☐ 126 Cliff Chambers	12.00	5.50	1.50
☐ 127 Del Ennis	14.00	6.25	1.75
☐ 128 Ebba St.Claire	12.00	5.50	1.50
☐ 129 Hank Bauer	21.00	9.50	2.60
☐ 130 Milt Bolling	14.00	6.25	1.75
☐ 131 Joe Astroth	14.00	6.25	1.75
☐ 132 Bob Feller	75.00	34.00	9.50
☐ 133 Duane Pillette	14.00	6.25	1.75
☐ 134 Luis Aloma	14.00	6.25	1.75
☐ 135 Johnny Pesky	16.00	7.25	2.00
☐ 136 Clyde Vollmer	14.00	6.25	1.75
☐ 137 Al Corwin	14.00	6.25	1.75
☐ 138 Gil Hodges	75.00	34.00	9.50
☐ 139 Preston Ward	14.00	6.25	1.75
☐ 140 Saul Rogovin	14.00	6.25	1.75
☐ 141 Joe Garagiola	30.00	13.50	3.70
☐ 142 Al Brazle	14.00	6.25	1.75
☐ 143 Willie Jones	14.00	6.25	1.75
☐ 144 Ernie Johnson	25.00	11.00	3.10
☐ 145 Billy Martin	60.00	27.00	7.50
☐ 146 Dick Gernert	14.00	6.25	1.75
☐ 147 Joe DeMaestri	14.00	6.25	1.75
☐ 148 Dale Mitchell	16.00	7.25	2.00
☐ 149 Bob Young	14.00	6.25	1.75
☐ 150 Cass Michaels	14.00	6.25	1.75
☐ 151 Pat Mullin	14.00	6.25	1.75
☐ 152 Mickey Vernon	16.00	7.25	2.00
☐ 153 Whitey Lockman	16.00	7.25	2.00
☐ 154 Don Newcombe	30.00	13.50	3.70
☐ 155 Frank Thomas	20.00	9.00	2.50
☐ 156 Rocky Bridges	14.00	6.25	1.75
☐ 157 Turk Lown	14.00	6.25	1.75
☐ 158 Stu Miller	16.00	7.25	2.00
☐ 159 Johnny Lindell	14.00	6.25	1.75
☐ 160 Danny O'Connell	14.00	6.25	1.75
☐ 161 Yogi Berra	175.00	80.00	22.00
☐ 162 Ted Lepcio	14.00	6.25	1.75
☐ 163A Dave Philley (No mention of trade on back)	20.00	9.00	2.50
☐ 163B Dave Philley (Traded to Cleveland)	36.00	16.00	4.50
☐ 164 Early Wynn	50.00	22.00	6.25
☐ 165 Johnny Groth	14.00	6.25	1.75
☐ 166 Sandy Consuegra	14.00	6.25	1.75
☐ 167 Billy Hoeft	14.00	6.25	1.75
☐ 168 Ed Fitzgerald	14.00	6.25	1.75
☐ 169 Larry Jansen	16.00	7.25	2.00
☐ 170 Duke Snider	125.00	55.00	15.50
☐ 171 Carlos Bernier	14.00	6.25	1.75
☐ 172 Andy Seminick	14.00	6.25	1.75
☐ 173 Dee Fondy	14.00	6.25	1.75
☐ 174 Pete Castiglione	14.00	6.25	1.75
☐ 175 Mel Clark	14.00	6.25	1.75
☐ 176 Vern Bickford	14.00	6.25	1.75
☐ 177 Whitey Ford	100.00	45.00	12.50
☐ 178 Del Wilber	14.00	6.25	1.75

☐ 179 Morrie Martin 14.00 6.25 1.75
☐ 180 Joe Tipton 14.00 6.25 1.75
☐ 181 Les Moss 14.00 6.25 1.75
☐ 182 Sherm Lollar 16.00 7.25 2.00
☐ 183 Matt Batts 14.00 6.25 1.75
☐ 184 Mickey Grasso 14.00 6.25 1.75
☐ 185 Daryl Spencer 14.00 6.25 1.75
☐ 186 Russ Meyer 14.00 6.25 1.75
☐ 187 Vernon Law 16.00 7.25 2.00
☐ 188 Frank Smith 14.00 6.25 1.75
☐ 189 Randy Jackson 14.00 6.25 1.75
☐ 190 Joe Presko 14.00 6.25 1.75
☐ 191 Karl Drews 14.00 6.25 1.75
☐ 192 Lou Burdette 20.00 9.00 2.50
☐ 193 Eddie Robinson 14.00 6.25 1.75
☐ 194 Sid Hudson 14.00 6.25 1.75
☐ 195 Bob Cain 14.00 6.25 1.75
☐ 196 Bob Lemon 40.00 18.00 5.00
☐ 197 Lou Kretlow 14.00 6.25 1.75
☐ 198 Virgil Trucks 16.00 7.25 2.00
☐ 199 Steve Gromek 14.00 6.25 1.75
☐ 200 Conrado Marrero 14.00 6.25 1.75
☐ 201 Bobby Thomson 25.00 11.00 3.10
☐ 202 George Shuba 21.00 9.50 2.60
☐ 203 Vic Janowicz 16.00 7.25 2.00
☐ 204 Jack Collum 14.00 6.25 1.75
☐ 205 Hal Jeffcoat 14.00 6.25 1.75
☐ 206 Steve Bilko 14.00 6.25 1.75
☐ 207 Stan Lopata 14.00 6.25 1.75
☐ 208 Johnny Antonelli 16.00 7.25 2.00
☐ 209 Gene Woodling 14.00 6.25 1.75
☐ 210 Jim Piersall 20.00 9.00 2.50
☐ 211 Al Robertson 14.00 6.25 1.75
☐ 212 Owen Friend 14.00 6.25 1.75
☐ 213 Dick Littlefield 14.00 6.25 1.75
☐ 214 Ferris Fain 16.00 7.25 2.00
☐ 215 Johnny Bucha 14.00 6.25 1.75
☐ 216 Jerry Snyder 14.00 6.25 1.75
☐ 217 Hank Thompson 16.00 7.25 2.00
☐ 218 Preacher Roe 25.00 11.00 3.10
☐ 219 Hal Rice 14.00 6.25 1.75
☐ 220 Hobie Landrith 14.00 6.25 1.75
☐ 221 Frank Baumholtz 14.00 6.25 1.75
☐ 222 Memo Luna 14.00 6.25 1.75
☐ 223 Steve Ridzik 14.00 6.25 1.75
☐ 224 Bill Bruton 40.00 10.00 3.20

1955 Bowman

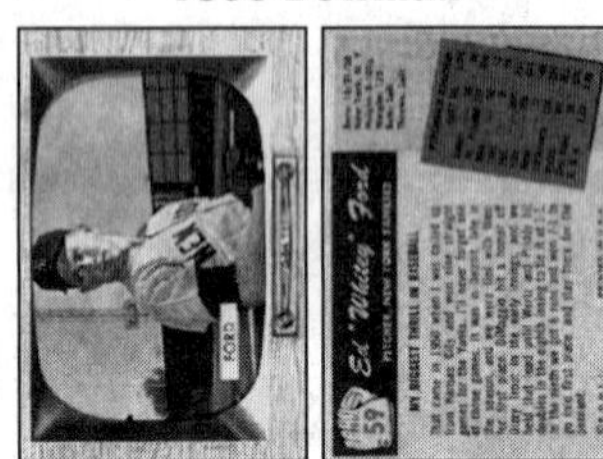

The cards in this 320-card set measure approximately 2 1/2" by 3 3/4". The Bowman set of 1955 is known as the "TV set" because each player photograph is cleverly shown within a television set design. The set contains umpire cards, some transposed pictures (e.g., Johnsons and Bollings), an incorrect spelling for Harvey Kuenn, and a traded line for Palica (all of which are noted in the checklist below). Some three-card advertising strips exist, the backs of these panels contain advertising for Bowman products. Advertising panels seen include Nellie Fox/Carl Furillo/Carl Erskine, Hank Aaron/Johnny Logan/Eddie Miksis, and a panel including Early Wynn and Pee Wee Reese. Cards were issued either in 9-card nickel packs or one card penny packs. The notable Rookie Cards in this set are Elston Howard and Don Zimmer. Hall of Fame umpires pictured in the set are Al Barlick, Jocko Conlon and Cal Hubbard.

	NRMT	VG-E	GOOD
COMPLETE SET (320)	4600.00	2100.00	575.00
COMMON CARD (1-96)	12.00	5.50	1.50
COMMON CARD (97-224)	10.00	4.50	1.25
COMMON CARD (225-320)	16.00	7.25	2.00
WRAPPER (1-CENT)	60.00	27.00	7.50
WRAPPER (5-CENT)	60.00	27.00	7.50

☐ 1 Hoyt Wilhelm 100.00 22.00 6.50
☐ 2 Alvin Dark 14.00 6.25 1.75
☐ 3 Joe Coleman 14.00 6.25 1.75
☐ 4 Eddie Waitkus 14.00 6.25 1.75
☐ 5 Jim Robertson 12.00 5.50 1.50
☐ 6 Pete Suder 12.00 5.50 1.50
☐ 7 Gene Baker 12.00 5.50 1.50
☐ 8 Warren Hacker 12.00 5.50 1.50
☐ 9 Gil McDougald 20.00 9.00 2.50
☐ 10 Phil Rizzuto 65.00 29.00 8.00
☐ 11 Bill Bruton 14.00 6.25 1.75
☐ 12 Andy Pafko 14.00 6.25 1.75
☐ 13 Clyde Vollmer 12.00 5.50 1.50
☐ 14 Gus Keriazakos 12.00 5.50 1.50
☐ 15 Frank Sullivan 12.00 5.50 1.50
☐ 16 Jim Piersall 14.00 6.25 1.75
☐ 17 Del Ennis 14.00 6.25 1.75
☐ 18 Stan Lopata 12.00 5.50 1.50
☐ 19 Bobby Avila 14.00 6.25 1.75
☐ 20 Al Smith 14.00 6.25 1.75
☐ 21 Don Hoak 12.00 5.50 1.50
☐ 22 Roy Campanella 125.00 55.00 15.50
☐ 23 Al Kaline 150.00 70.00 19.00
☐ 24 Al Aber 12.00 5.50 1.50
☐ 25 Minnie Minoso 25.00 11.00 3.10
☐ 26 Virgil Trucks 14.00 6.25 1.75
☐ 27 Preston Ward 12.00 5.50 1.50
☐ 28 Dick Cole 12.00 5.50 1.50
☐ 29 Red Schoendienst 30.00 13.50 3.70
☐ 30 Bill Sarni 12.00 5.50 1.50
☐ 31 Johnny Temple 14.00 6.25 1.75
☐ 32 Wally Post 14.00 6.25 1.75
☐ 33 Nellie Fox 45.00 20.00 5.50
☐ 34 Clint Courtney 12.00 5.50 1.50
☐ 35 Bill Tuttle 12.00 5.50 1.50
☐ 36 Wayne Belardi 12.00 5.50 1.50
☐ 37 Pee Wee Reese 65.00 29.00 8.00
☐ 38 Early Wynn 30.00 13.50 3.70
☐ 39 Bob Darnell 14.00 6.25 1.75
☐ 40 Vic Wertz 14.00 6.25 1.75
☐ 41 Mel Clark 12.00 5.50 1.50
☐ 42 Bob Greenwood 12.00 5.50 1.50
☐ 43 Bob Buhl 14.00 6.25 1.75
☐ 44 Danny O'Connell 12.00 5.50 1.50
☐ 45 Tom Umphlett 12.00 5.50 1.50
☐ 46 Mickey Vernon 14.00 6.25 1.75
☐ 47 Sammy White 12.00 5.50 1.50
☐ 48A Milt Bolling ERR 30.00 13.50 3.70
(Name on back is
Frank Bolling)
☐ 48B Milt Bolling COR 14.00 6.25 1.75
☐ 49 Jim Greengrass 12.00 5.50 1.50
☐ 50 Hobie Landrith 12.00 5.50 1.50
☐ 51 Elvin Tappe 12.00 5.50 1.50
☐ 52 Hal Rice 12.00 5.50 1.50
☐ 53 Alex Kellner 12.00 5.50 1.50
☐ 54 Don Bollweg 12.00 5.50 1.50
☐ 55 Cal Abrams 12.00 5.50 1.50
☐ 56 Billy Cox 14.00 6.25 1.75
☐ 57 Bob Friend 14.00 6.25 1.75
☐ 58 Frank Thomas 14.00 6.25 1.75
☐ 59 Whitey Ford 75.00 34.00 9.50
☐ 60 Enos Slaughter 30.00 13.50 3.70
☐ 61 Paul LaPalme 12.00 5.50 1.50
☐ 62 Royce Lint 12.00 5.50 1.50
☐ 63 Irv Noren 14.00 6.25 1.75
☐ 64 Curt Simmons 14.00 6.25 1.75
☐ 65 Don Zimmer 25.00 11.00 3.10
☐ 66 George Shuba 18.00 8.00 2.20
☐ 67 Don Larsen 20.00 9.00 2.50
☐ 68 Elston Howard 75.00 34.00 9.50
☐ 69 Billy Hunter 12.00 5.50 1.50
☐ 70 Lou Burdette 14.00 6.25 1.75
☐ 71 Dave Jolly 12.00 5.50 1.50
☐ 72 Chet Nichols 12.00 5.50 1.50
☐ 73 Eddie Yost 14.00 6.25 1.75
☐ 74 Jerry Snyder 12.00 5.50 1.50
☐ 75 Brooks Lawrence 12.00 5.50 1.50
☐ 76 Tom Poholsky 12.00 5.50 1.50
☐ 77 Jim McDonald 12.00 5.50 1.50
☐ 78 Gil Coan 12.00 5.50 1.50
☐ 79 Willie Miranda 12.00 5.50 1.50
☐ 80 Lou Limmer 12.00 5.50 1.50
☐ 81 Bobby Morgan 12.00 5.50 1.50
☐ 82 Lee Walls 12.00 5.50 1.50
☐ 83 Max Surkont 12.00 5.50 1.50
☐ 84 George Freese 12.00 5.50 1.50
☐ 85 Cass Michaels 12.00 5.50 1.50
☐ 86 Ted Gray 12.00 5.50 1.50
☐ 87 Randy Jackson 12.00 5.50 1.50
☐ 88 Steve Bilko 12.00 5.50 1.50
☐ 89 Lou Boudreau MG 30.00 13.50 3.70
☐ 90 Art Ditmar 12.00 5.50 1.50
☐ 91 Dick Marlowe 12.00 5.50 1.50
☐ 92 George Zuverink 12.00 5.50 1.50
☐ 93 Andy Seminick 12.00 5.50 1.50
☐ 94 Hank Thompson 14.00 6.25 1.75
☐ 95 Sal Maglie 14.00 6.25 1.75
☐ 96 Ray Narleski 12.00 5.50 1.50
☐ 97 Johnny Podres 25.00 11.00 3.10
☐ 98 Jim Gilliam 25.00 11.00 3.10
☐ 99 Jerry Coleman 15.00 6.75 1.85
☐ 100 Tom Morgan 10.00 4.50 1.25
☐ 101A Don Johnson ERR 30.00 13.50 3.70
(Photo actually
Ernie Johnson)
☐ 101B Don Johnson COR 12.00 5.50 1.50
☐ 102 Bobby Thomson 12.00 5.50 1.50
☐ 103 Eddie Mathews 50.00 22.00 6.25
☐ 104 Bob Porterfield 10.00 4.50 1.25
☐ 105 Johnny Schmitz 10.00 4.50 1.25
☐ 106 Del Rice 10.00 4.50 1.25
☐ 107 Solly Hemus 10.00 4.50 1.25
☐ 108 Lou Kretlow 10.00 4.50 1.25
☐ 109 Vern Stephens 12.00 5.50 1.50
☐ 110 Bob Miller 10.00 4.50 1.25
☐ 111 Steve Ridzik 10.00 4.50 1.25
☐ 112 Granny Hamner 10.00 4.50 1.25
☐ 113 Bob Hall 10.00 4.50 1.25
☐ 114 Vic Janowicz 12.00 5.50 1.50
☐ 115 Roger Bowman 10.00 4.50 1.25
☐ 116 Sandy Consuegra 10.00 4.50 1.25
☐ 117 Johnny Groth 10.00 4.50 1.25
☐ 118 Bobby Adams 10.00 4.50 1.25
☐ 119 Joe Astroth 10.00 4.50 1.25
☐ 120 Ed Burtschy 10.00 4.50 1.25
☐ 121 Rufus Crawford 10.00 4.50 1.25
☐ 122 Al Corwin 10.00 4.50 1.25
☐ 123 Marv Grissom 10.00 4.50 1.25
☐ 124 Johnny Antonelli 12.00 5.50 1.50
☐ 125 Paul Giel 12.00 5.50 1.50
☐ 126 Billy Goodman 12.00 5.50 1.50
☐ 127 Hank Majeski 10.00 4.50 1.25
☐ 128 Mike Garcia 14.00 6.25 1.75
☐ 129 Hal Naragon 10.00 4.50 1.25
☐ 130 Richie Ashburn 45.00 20.00 5.50
☐ 131 Willard Marshall 10.00 4.50 1.25
☐ 132A Harvey Kueen ERR 20.00 9.00 2.50
(Sic, Kuenn)
☐ 132B Harvey Kuenn COR 30.00 13.50 3.70
☐ 133 Charles King 10.00 4.50 1.25
☐ 134 Bob Feller 70.00 32.00 8.75
☐ 135 Lloyd Merriman 10.00 4.50 1.25
☐ 136 Rocky Bridges 10.00 4.50 1.25
☐ 137 Bob Talbot 10.00 4.50 1.25
☐ 138 Davey Williams 12.00 5.50 1.50
☐ 139 Shantz Brothers 12.00 5.50 1.50
Wilmer Shantz
Bobby Shantz
☐ 140 Bobby Shantz 12.00 5.50 1.50
☐ 141 Wes Westrum 12.00 5.50 1.50
☐ 142 Rudy Regalado 10.00 4.50 1.25
☐ 143 Don Newcombe 25.00 11.00 3.10
☐ 144 Art Houtteman 10.00 4.50 1.25
☐ 145 Bob Nieman 10.00 4.50 1.25
☐ 146 Don Liddle 10.00 4.50 1.25
☐ 147 Sam Mele 10.00 4.50 1.25
☐ 148 Bob Chakales 10.00 4.50 1.25
☐ 149 Cloyd Boyer 10.00 4.50 1.25
☐ 150 Billy Klaus 10.00 4.50 1.25
☐ 151 Jim Brideweser 10.00 4.50 1.25
☐ 152 Johnny Klippstein 10.00 4.50 1.25
☐ 153 Eddie Robinson 10.00 4.50 1.25
☐ 154 Frank Lary 12.00 5.50 1.50
☐ 155 Gerry Staley 10.00 4.50 1.25
☐ 156 Jim Hughes 12.00 5.50 1.50
☐ 157A Ernie Johnson ERR 30.00 13.50 3.70
(Photo actually
Don Johnson)
☐ 157B Ernie Johnson COR 30.00 13.50 3.70
☐ 158 Gil Hodges 45.00 20.00 5.50
☐ 159 Harry Byrd 10.00 4.50 1.25
☐ 160 Bill Skowron 25.00 11.00 3.10
☐ 161 Matt Batts 10.00 4.50 1.25
☐ 162 Charlie Maxwell 12.00 5.50 1.50
☐ 163 Sid Gordon 10.00 4.50 1.25
☐ 164 Toby Atwell 10.00 4.50 1.25
☐ 165 Maurice McDermott 10.00 4.50 1.25
☐ 166 Jim Busby 10.00 4.50 1.25
☐ 167 Bob Grim 25.00 11.00 3.10
☐ 168 Yogi Berra 90.00 40.00 11.00
☐ 169 Carl Furillo 25.00 11.00 3.10
☐ 170 Carl Erskine 25.00 11.00 3.10
☐ 171 Robin Roberts 35.00 16.00 4.40
☐ 172 Willie Jones 10.00 4.50 1.25
☐ 173 Chico Carrasquel 10.00 4.50 1.25
☐ 174 Sherm Lollar 12.00 5.50 1.50
☐ 175 Wilmer Shantz 10.00 4.50 1.25
☐ 176 Joe DeMaestri 10.00 4.50 1.25
☐ 177 Willard Nixon 10.00 4.50 1.25
☐ 178 Tom Brewer 10.00 4.50 1.25
☐ 179 Hank Aaron 200.00 90.00 25.00
☐ 180 Johnny Logan 12.00 5.50 1.50
☐ 181 Eddie Miksis 10.00 4.50 1.25
☐ 182 Bob Rush 10.00 4.50 1.25
☐ 183 Ray Katt 10.00 4.50 1.25
☐ 184 Willie Mays 225.00 100.00 28.00
☐ 185 Vic Raschi 10.00 4.50 1.25
☐ 186 Alex Grammas 10.00 4.50 1.25
☐ 187 Fred Hatfield 10.00 4.50 1.25
☐ 188 Ned Garver 10.00 4.50 1.25
☐ 189 Jack Collum 10.00 4.50 1.25
☐ 190 Fred Baczewski 10.00 4.50 1.25
☐ 191 Bob Lemon 30.00 13.50 3.70
☐ 192 George Strickland 10.00 4.50 1.25
☐ 193 Howie Judson 10.00 4.50 1.25
☐ 194 Joe Nuxhall 12.00 5.50 1.50
☐ 195A Erv Palica 12.00 5.50 1.50
(Without trade)
☐ 195B Erv Palica 30.00 13.50 3.70
(With trade)
☐ 196 Russ Meyer 12.00 5.50 1.50
☐ 197 Ralph Kiner 30.00 13.50 3.70
☐ 198 Dave Pope 10.00 4.50 1.25
☐ 199 Vernon Law 12.00 5.50 1.50
☐ 200 Dick Littlefield 10.00 4.50 1.25
☐ 201 Allie Reynolds 15.00 6.75 1.85
☐ 202 Mickey Mantle UER 900.00 400.00 110.00
Birthdate listed as 10/30/31
Should be 10/20/31
☐ 203 Steve Gromek 10.00 4.50 1.25
☐ 204A Frank Bolling ERR 30.00 13.50 3.70
(Name on back is
Milt Bolling)
☐ 204B Frank Bolling COR 12.00 5.50 1.50
☐ 205 Rip Repulski 10.00 4.50 1.25
☐ 206 Ralph Beard 10.00 4.50 1.25
☐ 207 Frank Shea 10.00 4.50 1.25
☐ 208 Ed Fitzgerald 10.00 4.50 1.25
☐ 209 Smoky Burgess 12.00 5.50 1.50
☐ 210 Earl Torgeson 10.00 4.50 1.25
☐ 211 Sonny Dixon 10.00 4.50 1.25
☐ 212 Jack Dittmer 10.00 4.50 1.25
☐ 213 George Kell 30.00 13.50 3.70
☐ 214 Billy Pierce 12.00 5.50 1.50
☐ 215 Bob Kuzava 10.00 4.50 1.25
☐ 216 Preacher Roe 12.00 5.50 1.50
☐ 217 Del Crandall 12.00 5.50 1.50
☐ 218 Joe Adcock 12.00 5.50 1.50
☐ 219 Whitey Lockman 12.00 5.50 1.50
☐ 220 Jim Hearn 10.00 4.50 1.25
☐ 221 Hector Brown 10.00 4.50 1.25
☐ 222 Russ Kemmerer 10.00 4.50 1.25
☐ 223 Hal Jeffcoat 10.00 4.50 1.25
☐ 224 Dee Fondy 10.00 4.50 1.25
☐ 225 Paul Richards MG 16.00 7.25 2.00
☐ 226 Bill McKinley UMP 30.00 13.50 3.70
☐ 227 Frank Baumholtz 16.00 7.25 2.00
☐ 228 John Phillips 16.00 7.25 2.00
☐ 229 Jim Brosnan 20.00 9.00 2.50
☐ 230 Al Brazle 16.00 7.25 2.00
☐ 231 Jim Konstanty 20.00 9.00 2.50
☐ 232 Birdie Tebbetts MG 22.00 10.00 2.70
☐ 233 Bill Serena 16.00 7.25 2.00
☐ 234 Dick Bartell CO 20.00 9.00 2.50
☐ 235 Joe Paparella UMP 30.00 13.50 3.70
☐ 236 Murry Dickson 16.00 7.25 2.00
☐ 237 Johnny Wyrostek 16.00 7.25 2.00
☐ 238 Eddie Stanky MG 20.00 9.00 2.50
☐ 239 Edwin Rommel UMP 30.00 13.50 3.70
☐ 240 Billy Loes 20.00 9.00 2.50
☐ 241 Johnny Pesky CO 20.00 9.00 2.50
☐ 242 Ernie Banks 350.00 160.00 45.00
☐ 243 Gus Bell 20.00 9.00 2.50
☐ 244 Duane Pillette 16.00 7.25 2.00
☐ 245 Bill Miller 16.00 7.25 2.00
☐ 246 Hank Bauer 25.00 11.00 3.10
☐ 247 Dutch Leonard CO 16.00 7.25 2.00
☐ 248 Harry Dorish 16.00 7.25 2.00
☐ 249 Billy Gardner 20.00 9.00 2.50
☐ 250 Larry Napp UMP 30.00 13.50 3.70
☐ 251 Stan Jok 16.00 7.25 2.00
☐ 252 Roy Smalley 16.00 7.25 2.00
☐ 253 Jim Wilson 16.00 7.25 2.00
☐ 254 Bennett Flowers 16.00 7.25 2.00
☐ 255 Pete Runnels 20.00 9.00 2.50
☐ 256 Owen Friend 16.00 7.25 2.00
☐ 257 Tom Alston 16.00 7.25 2.00
☐ 258 John Stevens UMP 30.00 13.50 3.70
☐ 259 Don Mossi 25.00 11.00 3.10
☐ 260 Edwin Hurley UMP 30.00 13.50 3.70
☐ 261 Walt Moryn 20.00 9.00 2.50
☐ 262 Jim Lemon 16.00 7.25 2.00
☐ 263 Eddie Joost 16.00 7.25 2.00
☐ 264 Bill Henry 16.00 7.25 2.00
☐ 265 Albert Barlick UMP 75.00 34.00 9.50
☐ 266 Mike Fornieles 16.00 7.25 2.00
☐ 267 Jim Honochick UMP 75.00 34.00 9.50
☐ 268 Roy Lee Hawes 16.00 7.25 2.00
☐ 269 Joe Amalfitano 22.00 10.00 2.70
☐ 270 Chico Fernandez 20.00 9.00 2.50
☐ 271 Bob Hooper 16.00 7.25 2.00
☐ 272 John Flaherty UMP 30.00 13.50 3.70
☐ 273 Bubba Church 16.00 7.25 2.00
☐ 274 Jim Delsing 16.00 7.25 2.00
☐ 275 William Grieve UMP 30.00 13.50 3.70
☐ 276 Ike Delock 16.00 7.25 2.00
☐ 277 Ed Runge UMP 35.00 16.00 4.40
☐ 278 Charlie Neal 35.00 16.00 4.40
☐ 279 Hank Soar UMP 30.00 13.50 3.70
☐ 280 Clyde McCullough 16.00 7.25 2.00
☐ 281 Charles Berry UMP 30.00 13.50 3.70
☐ 282 Phil Cavarretta 22.00 10.00 2.70
☐ 283 Nestor Chylak UMP 30.00 13.50 3.70
☐ 284 Bill Jackowski UMP 30.00 13.50 3.70
☐ 285 Walt Dropo 20.00 9.00 2.50
☐ 286 Frank Secory UMP 30.00 13.50 3.70
☐ 287 Ron Mrozinski 16.00 7.25 2.00
☐ 288 Dick Smith 16.00 7.25 2.00
☐ 289 Arthur Gore UMP 30.00 13.50 3.70
☐ 290 Hershell Freeman 16.00 7.25 2.00
☐ 291 Frank Dascoli UMP 30.00 13.50 3.70
☐ 292 Marv Blaylock 16.00 7.25 2.00
☐ 293 Thomas Gorman UMP 35.00 16.00 4.40
☐ 294 Wally Moses CO 20.00 9.00 2.50
☐ 295 Lee Ballanfant UMP 30.00 13.50 3.70
☐ 296 Bill Virdon 35.00 16.00 4.40
☐ 297 Dusty Boggess UMP 30.00 13.50 3.70
☐ 298 Charlie Grimm MG 22.00 10.00 2.70
☐ 299 Lon Warneke UMP 35.00 16.00 4.40
☐ 300 Tommy Byrne 20.00 9.00 2.50
☐ 301 William Engeln UMP 30.00 13.50 3.70
☐ 302 Frank Malzone 30.00 13.50 3.70
☐ 303 Jocko Conlan UMP 75.00 34.00 9.50
☐ 304 Harry Chiti 16.00 7.25 2.00
☐ 305 Frank Umont UMP 30.00 13.50 3.70
☐ 306 Bob Cerv 22.00 10.00 2.70
☐ 307 Babe Pinelli UMP 35.00 16.00 4.40
☐ 308 Al Lopez MG 50.00 22.00 6.25
☐ 309 Hal Dixon UMP 30.00 13.50 3.70
☐ 310 Ken Lehman 16.00 7.25 2.00
☐ 311 Lawrence Goetz UMP 30.00 13.50 3.70
☐ 312 Bill Wight 16.00 7.25 2.00
☐ 313 Augie Donatelli UMP 50.00 22.00 6.25
☐ 314 Dale Mitchell 22.00 10.00 2.70
☐ 315 Cal Hubbard UMP 75.00 34.00 9.50

Card	MINT	NRMT	EXC
☐ 316 Marion Fricano	16.00	7.25	2.00
☐ 317 William Summers UMP	30.00	13.50	3.70
☐ 318 Sid Hudson	16.00	7.25	2.00
☐ 319 Al Schroll	16.00	7.25	2.00
☐ 320 George Susce Jr.	45.00	9.00	2.70

1982 Bowman 1952 Extension

In 1980, 15 unissued pieces of artwork initially intended to be used by Bowman Gum in their 1952 baseball card set were discovered. This set consists of 15 cards made from this original artwork. The backs have been created to resemble the original 1952 series, and the set has been numbered 253-267 (the next 15 cards in the 1952 Bowman sequence). The facsimile autograph on the original 1952 Bowmans has been omitted from the cards in this set.

	MINT	NRMT	EXC
COMPLETE SET (15)	5.00	2.20	.60
COMMON CARD (253-267)	.25	.11	.03
☐ 253 Bob Kennedy	.25	.11	.03
☐ 254 Barney McCosky	.25	.11	.03
☐ 255 Chris Van Cuyk	.25	.11	.03
☐ 256 Morrie Martin	.25	.11	.03
☐ 257 Jim Wilson	.25	.11	.03
☐ 258 Bob Thorpe	.25	.11	.03
☐ 259 Bill Henry	.25	.11	.03
☐ 260 Bob Addis	.25	.11	.03
☐ 261 Terry Moore CO	.75	.35	.09
☐ 262 Joe Dobson	.25	.11	.03
☐ 263 John Merson	.25	.11	.03
☐ 264 Virgil Trucks	.50	.23	.06
☐ 265 Johnny Hopp	.25	.11	.03
☐ 266 Cookie Lavagetto CO	.50	.23	.06
☐ 267 George Shuba	.50	.23	.06

1989 Bowman

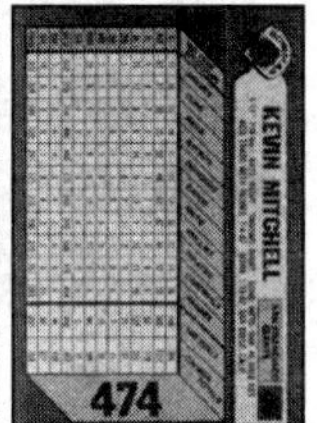

The 1989 Bowman set, produced by Topps, contains 484 slightly oversized cards (measuring 2 1/2" by 3 3/4"). The cards were released in midseason 1989 in wax, rack, cello and factory set formats. The fronts have white-bordered color photos with facsimile autographs and small Bowman logos. The backs feature charts detailing 1988 player performances vs. each team. The cards are ordered alphabetically according to teams in the AL and NL. Cards 258-261 form a father/son subset. Rookie Cards in this set include Andy Benes, Ken Griffey Jr., Tino Martinez, Charles Nagy, Gary Sheffield, John Smoltz and Robin Ventura.

	MINT	NRMT	EXC
COMPLETE SET (484)	12.00	5.50	1.50
COMPLETE FACT.SET (484)	12.00	5.50	1.50
COMMON CARD (1-484)	.05	.02	.01
☐ 1 Oswald Peraza	.05	.02	.01
☐ 2 Brian Holton	.05	.02	.01
☐ 3 Jose Bautista	.05	.02	.01
☐ 4 Pete Harnisch	.10	.05	.01
☐ 5 Dave Schmidt	.05	.02	.01
☐ 6 Gregg Olson	.10	.05	.01
☐ 7 Jeff Ballard	.05	.02	.01
☐ 8 Bob Melvin	.05	.02	.01
☐ 9 Cal Ripken	.75	.35	.09
☐ 10 Randy Milligan	.05	.02	.01
☐ 11 Juan Bell	.05	.02	.01
☐ 12 Billy Ripken	.05	.02	.01
☐ 13 Jim Traber	.05	.02	.01
☐ 14 Pete Stanicek	.05	.02	.01
☐ 15 Steve Finley	.25	.11	.03
☐ 16 Larry Sheets	.05	.02	.01
☐ 17 Phil Bradley	.05	.02	.01
☐ 18 Brady Anderson	.60	.25	.07
☐ 19 Lee Smith	.10	.05	.01
☐ 20 Tom Fischer	.05	.02	.01
☐ 21 Mike Boddicker	.05	.02	.01
☐ 22 Rob Murphy	.05	.02	.01
☐ 23 Wes Gardner	.05	.02	.01
☐ 24 John Dopson	.05	.02	.01
☐ 25 Bob Stanley	.05	.02	.01
☐ 26 Roger Clemens	.20	.09	.03
☐ 27 Rich Gedman	.05	.02	.01
☐ 28 Marty Barrett	.05	.02	.01
☐ 29 Luis Rivera	.05	.02	.01
☐ 30 Jody Reed	.05	.02	.01
☐ 31 Nick Esasky	.05	.02	.01
☐ 32 Wade Boggs	.15	.07	.02
☐ 33 Jim Rice	.15	.07	.02
☐ 34 Mike Greenwell	.05	.02	.01
☐ 35 Dwight Evans	.10	.05	.01
☐ 36 Ellis Burks	.15	.07	.02
☐ 37 Chuck Finley	.10	.05	.01
☐ 38 Kirk McCaskill	.05	.02	.01
☐ 39 Jim Abbott	.15	.07	.02
☐ 40 Bryan Harvey	.10	.05	.01
☐ 41 Bert Blyleven	.10	.05	.01
☐ 42 Mike Witt	.05	.02	.01
☐ 43 Bob McClure	.05	.02	.01
☐ 44 Bill Schroeder	.05	.02	.01
☐ 45 Lance Parrish	.05	.02	.01
☐ 46 Dick Schofield	.05	.02	.01
☐ 47 Wally Joyner	.10	.05	.01
☐ 48 Jack Howell	.05	.02	.01
☐ 49 Johnny Ray	.05	.02	.01
☐ 50 Chili Davis	.10	.05	.01
☐ 51 Tony Armas	.05	.02	.01
☐ 52 Claudell Washington	.05	.02	.01
☐ 53 Brian Downing	.05	.02	.01
☐ 54 Devon White	.10	.05	.01
☐ 55 Bobby Thigpen	.05	.02	.01
☐ 56 Bill Long	.05	.02	.01
☐ 57 Jerry Reuss	.05	.02	.01
☐ 58 Shawn Hillegas	.05	.02	.01
☐ 59 Melido Perez	.05	.02	.01
☐ 60 Jeff Bittiger	.05	.02	.01
☐ 61 Jack McDowell	.10	.05	.01
☐ 62 Carlton Fisk	.15	.07	.02
☐ 63 Steve Lyons	.05	.02	.01
☐ 64 Ozzie Guillen	.05	.02	.01
☐ 65 Robin Ventura	.40	.18	.05
☐ 66 Fred Manrique	.05	.02	.01
☐ 67 Dan Pasqua	.05	.02	.01
☐ 68 Ivan Calderon	.05	.02	.01
☐ 69 Ron Kittle	.05	.02	.01
☐ 70 Daryl Boston	.05	.02	.01
☐ 71 Dave Gallagher	.05	.02	.01
☐ 72 Harold Baines	.10	.05	.01
☐ 73 Charles Nagy	.60	.25	.07
☐ 74 John Farrell	.05	.02	.01
☐ 75 Kevin Wickander	.05	.02	.01
☐ 76 Greg Swindell	.05	.02	.01
☐ 77 Mike Walker	.05	.02	.01
☐ 78 Doug Jones	.05	.02	.01
☐ 79 Rich Yett	.05	.02	.01
☐ 80 Tom Candiotti	.05	.02	.01
☐ 81 Jesse Orosco	.05	.02	.01
☐ 82 Bud Black	.05	.02	.01
☐ 83 Andy Allanson	.05	.02	.01
☐ 84 Pete O'Brien	.05	.02	.01
☐ 85 Jerry Browne	.05	.02	.01
☐ 86 Brook Jacoby	.05	.02	.01
☐ 87 Mark Lewis	.15	.07	.02
☐ 88 Luis Aguayo	.05	.02	.01
☐ 89 Cory Snyder	.05	.02	.01
☐ 90 Oddibe McDowell	.05	.02	.01
☐ 91 Joe Carter	.15	.07	.02
☐ 92 Frank Tanana	.05	.02	.01
☐ 93 Jack Morris	.10	.05	.01
☐ 94 Doyle Alexander	.05	.02	.01
☐ 95 Steve Searcy	.05	.02	.01
☐ 96 Randy Bockus	.05	.02	.01
☐ 97 Jeff M. Robinson	.05	.02	.01
☐ 98 Mike Henneman	.05	.02	.01
☐ 99 Paul Gibson	.05	.02	.01
☐ 100 Frank Williams	.05	.02	.01
☐ 101 Matt Nokes	.05	.02	.01
☐ 102 Rico Brogna UER (Misspelled Ricco on card back)	.20	.09	.03
☐ 103 Lou Whitaker	.10	.05	.01
☐ 104 Al Pedrique	.05	.02	.01
☐ 105 Alan Trammell	.10	.05	.01
☐ 106 Chris Brown	.05	.02	.01
☐ 107 Pat Sheridan	.05	.02	.01
☐ 108 Chet Lemon	.05	.02	.01
☐ 109 Keith Moreland	.05	.02	.01
☐ 110 Mel Stottlemyre Jr.	.05	.02	.01
☐ 111 Bret Saberhagen	.10	.05	.01
☐ 112 Floyd Bannister	.05	.02	.01
☐ 113 Jeff Montgomery	.10	.05	.01
☐ 114 Steve Farr	.05	.02	.01
☐ 115 Tom Gordon UER (Front shows autograph of Don Gordon)	.10	.05	.01
☐ 116 Charlie Leibrandt	.05	.02	.01
☐ 117 Mark Gubicza	.05	.02	.01
☐ 118 Mike Macfarlane	.10	.05	.01
☐ 119 Bob Boone	.10	.05	.01
☐ 120 Kurt Stillwell	.05	.02	.01
☐ 121 George Brett	.40	.18	.05
☐ 122 Frank White	.10	.05	.01
☐ 123 Kevin Seitzer	.05	.02	.01
☐ 124 Willie Wilson	.05	.02	.01
☐ 125 Pat Tabler	.05	.02	.01
☐ 126 Bo Jackson	.15	.07	.02
☐ 127 Hugh Walker	.05	.02	.01
☐ 128 Danny Tartabull	.05	.02	.01
☐ 129 Teddy Higuera	.05	.02	.01
☐ 130 Don August	.05	.02	.01
☐ 131 Juan Nieves	.05	.02	.01
☐ 132 Mike Birkbeck	.05	.02	.01
☐ 133 Dan Plesac	.05	.02	.01
☐ 134 Chris Bosio	.05	.02	.01
☐ 135 Bill Wegman	.05	.02	.01
☐ 136 Chuck Crim	.05	.02	.01
☐ 137 B.J. Surhoff	.15	.07	.02
☐ 138 Joey Meyer	.05	.02	.01
☐ 139 Dale Sveum	.05	.02	.01
☐ 140 Paul Molitor	.20	.09	.03
☐ 141 Jim Gantner	.05	.02	.01
☐ 142 Gary Sheffield	.75	.35	.09
☐ 143 Greg Brock	.05	.02	.01
☐ 144 Robin Yount	.15	.07	.02
☐ 145 Glenn Braggs	.05	.02	.01
☐ 146 Rob Deer	.05	.02	.01
☐ 147 Fred Toliver	.05	.02	.01
☐ 148 Jeff Reardon	.10	.05	.01
☐ 149 Allan Anderson	.05	.02	.01
☐ 150 Frank Viola	.05	.02	.01
☐ 151 Shane Rawley	.05	.02	.01
☐ 152 Juan Berenguer	.05	.02	.01
☐ 153 Johnny Ard	.05	.02	.01
☐ 154 Tim Laudner	.05	.02	.01
☐ 155 Brian Harper	.05	.02	.01
☐ 156 Al Newman	.05	.02	.01
☐ 157 Kent Hrbek	.10	.05	.01
☐ 158 Gary Gaetti	.05	.02	.01
☐ 159 Wally Backman	.05	.02	.01
☐ 160 Gene Larkin	.05	.02	.01
☐ 161 Greg Gagne	.05	.02	.01
☐ 162 Kirby Puckett	.40	.18	.05
☐ 163 Dan Gladden	.05	.02	.01
☐ 164 Randy Bush	.05	.02	.01
☐ 165 Dave LaPoint	.05	.02	.01
☐ 166 Andy Hawkins	.05	.02	.01
☐ 167 Dave Righetti	.05	.02	.01
☐ 168 Lance McCullers	.05	.02	.01
☐ 169 Jimmy Jones	.05	.02	.01
☐ 170 Al Leiter	.10	.05	.01
☐ 171 John Candelaria	.05	.02	.01
☐ 172 Don Slaught	.05	.02	.01
☐ 173 Jamie Quirk	.05	.02	.01
☐ 174 Rafael Santana	.05	.02	.01
☐ 175 Mike Pagliarulo	.05	.02	.01
☐ 176 Don Mattingly	.50	.23	.06
☐ 177 Ken Phelps	.05	.02	.01
☐ 178 Steve Sax	.05	.02	.01
☐ 179 Dave Winfield	.15	.07	.02
☐ 180 Stan Jefferson	.05	.02	.01
☐ 181 Rickey Henderson	.15	.07	.02
☐ 182 Bob Brower	.05	.02	.01
☐ 183 Roberto Kelly	.10	.05	.01
☐ 184 Curt Young	.05	.02	.01
☐ 185 Gene Nelson	.05	.02	.01
☐ 186 Bob Welch	.05	.02	.01
☐ 187 Rick Honeycutt	.05	.02	.01
☐ 188 Dave Stewart	.10	.05	.01
☐ 189 Mike Moore	.05	.02	.01
☐ 190 Dennis Eckersley	.10	.05	.01
☐ 191 Eric Plunk	.05	.02	.01
☐ 192 Storm Davis	.05	.02	.01
☐ 193 Terry Steinbach	.10	.05	.01
☐ 194 Ron Hassey	.05	.02	.01
☐ 195 Stan Royer	.05	.02	.01
☐ 196 Walt Weiss	.05	.02	.01
☐ 197 Mark McGwire	.30	.14	.04
☐ 198 Carney Lansford	.10	.05	.01
☐ 199 Glenn Hubbard	.05	.02	.01
☐ 200 Dave Henderson	.05	.02	.01
☐ 201 Jose Canseco	.15	.07	.02
☐ 202 Dave Parker	.10	.05	.01
☐ 203 Scott Bankhead	.05	.02	.01
☐ 204 Tom Niedenfuer	.05	.02	.01
☐ 205 Mark Langston	.10	.05	.01
☐ 206 Erik Hanson	.15	.07	.02
☐ 207 Mike Jackson	.05	.02	.01
☐ 208 Dave Valle	.05	.02	.01
☐ 209 Scott Bradley	.05	.02	.01
☐ 210 Harold Reynolds	.05	.02	.01
☐ 211 Tino Martinez	.50	.23	.06
☐ 212 Rich Renteria	.05	.02	.01
☐ 213 Rey Quinones	.05	.02	.01
☐ 214 Jim Presley	.05	.02	.01
☐ 215 Alvin Davis	.05	.02	.01
☐ 216 Edgar Martinez	.15	.07	.02
☐ 217 Darnell Coles	.05	.02	.01
☐ 218 Jeffrey Leonard	.05	.02	.01
☐ 219 Jay Buhner	.25	.11	.03
☐ 220 Ken Griffey Jr.	5.00	2.20	.60
☐ 221 Drew Hall	.05	.02	.01
☐ 222 Bobby Witt	.05	.02	.01
☐ 223 Jamie Moyer	.05	.02	.01
☐ 224 Charlie Hough	.10	.05	.01
☐ 225 Nolan Ryan	.75	.35	.09
☐ 226 Jeff Russell	.05	.02	.01
☐ 227 Jim Sundberg	.05	.02	.01
☐ 228 Julio Franco	.10	.05	.01
☐ 229 Buddy Bell	.10	.05	.01
☐ 230 Scott Fletcher	.05	.02	.01
☐ 231 Jeff Kunkel	.05	.02	.01
☐ 232 Steve Buechele	.05	.02	.01
☐ 233 Monty Fariss	.05	.02	.01
☐ 234 Rick Leach	.05	.02	.01
☐ 235 Ruben Sierra	.10	.05	.01
☐ 236 Cecil Espy	.05	.02	.01
☐ 237 Rafael Palmeiro	.15	.07	.02
☐ 238 Pete Incaviglia	.10	.05	.01
☐ 239 Dave Stieb	.05	.02	.01
☐ 240 Jeff Musselman	.05	.02	.01
☐ 241 Mike Flanagan	.05	.02	.01
☐ 242 Todd Stottlemyre	.10	.05	.01
☐ 243 Jimmy Key	.10	.05	.01
☐ 244 Tony Castillo	.05	.02	.01
☐ 245 Alex Sanchez	.05	.02	.01
☐ 246 Tom Henke	.05	.02	.01
☐ 247 John Cerutti	.05	.02	.01
☐ 248 Ernie Whitt	.05	.02	.01
☐ 249 Bob Brenly	.05	.02	.01
☐ 250 Rance Mulliniks	.05	.02	.01
☐ 251 Kelly Gruber	.05	.02	.01
☐ 252 Ed Sprague	.25	.11	.03
☐ 253 Fred McGriff	.20	.09	.03
☐ 254 Tony Fernandez	.05	.02	.01
☐ 255 Tom Lawless	.05	.02	.01
☐ 256 George Bell	.05	.02	.01
☐ 257 Jesse Barfield	.05	.02	.01
☐ 258 Roberto Alomar / Sandy Alomar	.20	.09	.03
☐ 259 Ken Griffey Jr. / Ken Griffey Sr.	1.00	.45	.12
☐ 260 Cal Ripken Jr. / Cal Ripken Sr.	.30	.14	.04
☐ 261 Mel Stottlemyre Jr. / Mel Stottlemyre Sr.	.05	.02	.01
☐ 262 Zane Smith	.05	.02	.01
☐ 263 Charlie Puleo	.05	.02	.01
☐ 264 Derek Lilliquist	.05	.02	.01
☐ 265 Paul Assenmacher	.05	.02	.01
☐ 266 John Smoltz	.75	.35	.09
☐ 267 Tom Glavine	.25	.11	.03
☐ 268 Steve Avery	.25	.11	.03
☐ 269 Pete Smith	.05	.02	.01
☐ 270 Jody Davis	.05	.02	.01
☐ 271 Bruce Benedict	.05	.02	.01
☐ 272 Andres Thomas	.05	.02	.01
☐ 273 Gerald Perry	.05	.02	.01
☐ 274 Ron Gant	.15	.07	.02
☐ 275 Darrell Evans	.10	.05	.01
☐ 276 Dale Murphy	.15	.07	.02
☐ 277 Dion James	.05	.02	.01
☐ 278 Lonnie Smith	.05	.02	.01
☐ 279 Geronimo Berroa	.10	.05	.01
☐ 280 Steve Wilson	.05	.02	.01
☐ 281 Rick Sutcliffe	.05	.02	.01
☐ 282 Kevin Coffman	.05	.02	.01
☐ 283 Mitch Williams	.05	.02	.01
☐ 284 Greg Maddux	.75	.35	.09
☐ 285 Paul Kilgus	.05	.02	.01
☐ 286 Mike Harkey	.05	.02	.01
☐ 287 Lloyd McClendon	.05	.02	.01
☐ 288 Damon Berryhill	.05	.02	.01
☐ 289 Ty Griffin	.05	.02	.01
☐ 290 Ryne Sandberg	.25	.11	.03
☐ 291 Mark Grace	.20	.09	.03
☐ 292 Curt Wilkerson	.05	.02	.01
☐ 293 Vance Law	.05	.02	.01
☐ 294 Shawon Dunston	.05	.02	.01
☐ 295 Jerome Walton	.10	.05	.01
☐ 296 Mitch Webster	.05	.02	.01
☐ 297 Dwight Smith	.10	.05	.01
☐ 298 Andre Dawson	.10	.05	.01
☐ 299 Jeff Sellers	.05	.02	.01
☐ 300 Jose Rijo	.05	.02	.01
☐ 301 John Franco	.10	.05	.01
☐ 302 Rick Mahler	.05	.02	.01
☐ 303 Ron Robinson	.05	.02	.01
☐ 304 Danny Jackson	.05	.02	.01
☐ 305 Rob Dibble	.10	.05	.01
☐ 306 Tom Browning	.05	.02	.01
☐ 307 Bo Diaz	.05	.02	.01
☐ 308 Manny Trillo	.05	.02	.01
☐ 309 Chris Sabo	.05	.02	.01
☐ 310 Ron Oester	.05	.02	.01
☐ 311 Barry Larkin	.20	.09	.03
☐ 312 Todd Benzinger	.05	.02	.01
☐ 313 Paul O'Neill	.10	.05	.01
☐ 314 Kal Daniels	.05	.02	.01
☐ 315 Joel Youngblood	.05	.02	.01
☐ 316 Eric Davis	.10	.05	.01
☐ 317 Dave Smith	.05	.02	.01
☐ 318 Mark Portugal	.05	.02	.01
☐ 319 Brian Meyer	.05	.02	.01
☐ 320 Jim Deshaies	.05	.02	.01
☐ 321 Juan Agosto	.05	.02	.01
☐ 322 Mike Scott	.05	.02	.01
☐ 323 Rick Rhoden	.05	.02	.01
☐ 324 Jim Clancy	.05	.02	.01
☐ 325 Larry Andersen	.05	.02	.01
☐ 326 Alex Trevino	.05	.02	.01
☐ 327 Alan Ashby	.05	.02	.01
☐ 328 Craig Reynolds	.05	.02	.01
☐ 329 Bill Doran	.05	.02	.01
☐ 330 Rafael Ramirez	.05	.02	.01
☐ 331 Glenn Davis	.05	.02	.01
☐ 332 Willie Ansley	.05	.02	.01
☐ 333 Gerald Young	.05	.02	.01
☐ 334 Cameron Drew	.05	.02	.01
☐ 335 Jay Howell	.05	.02	.01
☐ 336 Tim Belcher	.05	.02	.01
☐ 337 Fernando Valenzuela	.10	.05	.01
☐ 338 Ricky Horton	.05	.02	.01
☐ 339 Tim Leary	.05	.02	.01
☐ 340 Bill Bene	.05	.02	.01
☐ 341 Orel Hershiser	.10	.05	.01
☐ 342 Mike Scioscia	.05	.02	.01
☐ 343 Rick Dempsey	.05	.02	.01
☐ 344 Willie Randolph	.10	.05	.01

☐ 345 Alfredo Griffin	.05	.02	.01
☐ 346 Eddie Murray	.25	.11	.03
☐ 347 Mickey Hatcher	.05	.02	.01
☐ 348 Mike Sharperson	.05	.02	.01
☐ 349 John Shelby	.05	.02	.01
☐ 350 Mike Marshall	.05	.02	.01
☐ 351 Kirk Gibson	.15	.07	.02
☐ 352 Mike Davis	.05	.02	.01
☐ 353 Bryn Smith	.05	.02	.01
☐ 354 Pascual Perez	.05	.02	.01
☐ 355 Kevin Gross	.05	.02	.01
☐ 356 Andy McGaffigan	.05	.02	.01
☐ 357 Brian Holman	.05	.02	.01
☐ 358 Dave Wainhouse	.05	.02	.01
☐ 359 Dennis Martinez	.10	.05	.01
☐ 360 Tim Burke	.05	.02	.01
☐ 361 Nelson Santovenia	.05	.02	.01
☐ 362 Tim Wallach	.05	.02	.01
☐ 363 Spike Owen	.05	.02	.01
☐ 364 Rex Hudler	.05	.02	.01
☐ 365 Andres Galarraga	.15	.07	.02
☐ 366 Otis Nixon	.05	.02	.01
☐ 367 Hubie Brooks	.05	.02	.01
☐ 368 Mike Aldrete	.05	.02	.01
☐ 369 Tim Raines	.15	.07	.02
☐ 370 Dave Martinez	.05	.02	.01
☐ 371 Bob Ojeda	.05	.02	.01
☐ 372 Ron Darling	.05	.02	.01
☐ 373 Wally Whitehurst	.05	.02	.01
☐ 374 Randy Myers	.10	.05	.01
☐ 375 David Cone	.15	.07	.02
☐ 376 Dwight Gooden	.10	.05	.01
☐ 377 Sid Fernandez	.05	.02	.01
☐ 378 Dave Proctor	.05	.02	.01
☐ 379 Gary Carter	.10	.05	.01
☐ 380 Keith Miller	.05	.02	.01
☐ 381 Gregg Jefferies	.15	.07	.02
☐ 382 Tim Teufel	.05	.02	.01
☐ 383 Kevin Elster	.10	.05	.01
☐ 384 Dave Magadan	.05	.02	.01
☐ 385 Keith Hernandez	.10	.05	.01
☐ 386 Mookie Wilson	.10	.05	.01
☐ 387 Darryl Strawberry	.10	.05	.01
☐ 388 Kevin McReynolds	.05	.02	.01
☐ 389 Mark Carreon	.05	.02	.01
☐ 390 Jeff Parrett	.05	.02	.01
☐ 391 Mike Maddux	.05	.02	.01
☐ 392 Don Carman	.05	.02	.01
☐ 393 Bruce Ruffin	.05	.02	.01
☐ 394 Ken Howell	.05	.02	.01
☐ 395 Steve Bedrosian	.05	.02	.01
☐ 396 Floyd Youmans	.05	.02	.01
☐ 397 Larry McWilliams	.05	.02	.01
☐ 398 Pat Combs	.05	.02	.01
☐ 399 Steve Lake	.05	.02	.01
☐ 400 Dickie Thon	.05	.02	.01
☐ 401 Ricky Jordan	.05	.02	.01
☐ 402 Mike Schmidt	.20	.09	.03
☐ 403 Tom Herr	.05	.02	.01
☐ 404 Chris James	.05	.02	.01
☐ 405 Juan Samuel	.05	.02	.01
☐ 406 Von Hayes	.05	.02	.01
☐ 407 Ron Jones	.05	.02	.01
☐ 408 Curt Ford	.05	.02	.01
☐ 409 Bob Walk	.05	.02	.01
☐ 410 Jeff D. Robinson	.05	.02	.01
☐ 411 Jim Gott	.05	.02	.01
☐ 412 Scott Medvin	.05	.02	.01
☐ 413 John Smiley	.05	.02	.01
☐ 414 Bob Kipper	.05	.02	.01
☐ 415 Brian Fisher	.05	.02	.01
☐ 416 Doug Drabek	.10	.05	.01
☐ 417 Mike LaValliere	.05	.02	.01
☐ 418 Ken Oberkfell	.05	.02	.01
☐ 419 Sid Bream	.05	.02	.01
☐ 420 Austin Manahan	.05	.02	.01
☐ 421 Jose Lind	.05	.02	.01
☐ 422 Bobby Bonilla	.15	.07	.02
☐ 423 Glenn Wilson	.05	.02	.01
☐ 424 Andy Van Slyke	.10	.05	.01
☐ 425 Gary Redus	.05	.02	.01
☐ 426 Barry Bonds	.40	.18	.05
☐ 427 Don Heinkel	.05	.02	.01
☐ 428 Ken Dayley	.05	.02	.01
☐ 429 Todd Worrell	.05	.02	.01
☐ 430 Brad DuVall	.05	.02	.01
☐ 431 Jose DeLeon	.05	.02	.01
☐ 432 Joe Magrane	.05	.02	.01
☐ 433 John Ericks	.05	.02	.01
☐ 434 Frank DiPino	.05	.02	.01
☐ 435 Tony Pena	.05	.02	.01
☐ 436 Ozzie Smith	.25	.11	.03
☐ 437 Terry Pendleton	.10	.05	.01
☐ 438 Jose Oquendo	.05	.02	.01
☐ 439 Tim Jones	.05	.02	.01
☐ 440 Pedro Guerrero	.10	.05	.01
☐ 441 Milt Thompson	.05	.02	.01
☐ 442 Willie McGee	.05	.02	.01
☐ 443 Vince Coleman	.05	.02	.01
☐ 444 Tom Brunansky	.05	.02	.01
☐ 445 Walt Terrell	.05	.02	.01
☐ 446 Eric Show	.05	.02	.01
☐ 447 Mark Davis	.05	.02	.01
☐ 448 Andy Benes	.15	.07	.02
☐ 449 Ed Whitson	.05	.02	.01
☐ 450 Dennis Rasmussen	.05	.02	.01
☐ 451 Bruce Hurst	.05	.02	.01
☐ 452 Pat Clements	.05	.02	.01
☐ 453 Benito Santiago	.10	.05	.01
☐ 454 Sandy Alomar Jr.	.20	.09	.03
☐ 455 Garry Templeton	.05	.02	.01
☐ 456 Jack Clark	.10	.05	.01
☐ 457 Tim Flannery	.05	.02	.01
☐ 458 Roberto Alomar	.40	.18	.05
☐ 459 Carmelo Martinez	.05	.02	.01
☐ 460 John Kruk	.10	.05	.01
☐ 461 Tony Gwynn	.40	.18	.05
☐ 462 Jerald Clark	.05	.02	.01
☐ 463 Don Robinson	.05	.02	.01
☐ 464 Craig Lefferts	.05	.02	.01
☐ 465 Kelly Downs	.05	.02	.01
☐ 466 Rick Reuschel	.05	.02	.01
☐ 467 Scott Garrelts	.05	.02	.01
☐ 468 Wil Tejada	.05	.02	.01
☐ 469 Kirt Manwaring	.05	.02	.01
☐ 470 Terry Kennedy	.05	.02	.01
☐ 471 Jose Uribe	.05	.02	.01
☐ 472 Royce Clayton	.20	.09	.03
☐ 473 Robby Thompson	.05	.02	.01
☐ 474 Kevin Mitchell	.10	.05	.01
☐ 475 Ernie Riles	.05	.02	.01
☐ 476 Will Clark	.20	.09	.03
☐ 477 Donell Nixon	.05	.02	.01
☐ 478 Candy Maldonado	.05	.02	.01
☐ 479 Tracy Jones	.05	.02	.01
☐ 480 Brett Butler	.10	.05	.01
☐ 481 Checklist 1-121	.05	.02	.01
☐ 482 Checklist 122-242	.05	.02	.01
☐ 483 Checklist 243-363	.05	.02	.01
☐ 484 Checklist 364-484	.05	.02	.01

1989 Bowman Tiffany

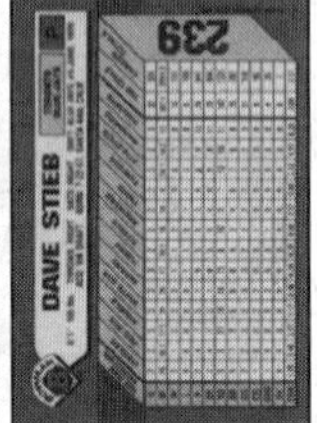

This is a parallel to the regular 1989 Bowman set. This set was issued with a glossy front and clear back, thus joining other Bowman sets known in the Topps family as "Tiffany" sets. The set measure 2 1/2" by 3 3/4" and was issued in factory set form only. In addition to the 484 regular cards, the 11 Reprint inserts were also included in the factory set. Reportedly, only 6,000 factory sets were printed. There are reports within the hobby that no more than 6,000 of these sets were produced.

	MINT	NRMT	EXC
COMPLETE FACT.SET (495)	80.00	36.00	10.00
COMMON CARD (1-484)	.10	.05	.01
COMMON REPRINT (R1-R11)	.30	.14	.04
*STARS: 2X to 4X BASIC CARDS			

1989 Bowman Reprint Inserts

The 1989 Bowman Reprint Inserts set contains 11 cards measuring approximately 2 1/2" by 3 3/4". The fronts depict reproduced actual size "classic" Bowman cards, which are noted as reprints. The backs are devoted to a sweepstakes entry form. One of these reprint cards was included in each 1989 Bowman wax pack thus making these "reprints" quite easy to find. Since the cards are unnumbered, they are ordered below in alphabetical order by player's name and year within player.

	MINT	NRMT	EXC
COMPLETE SET (11)	2.00	.90	.25
COMMON CARD (1-11)	.15	.07	.02
☐ 1 Richie Ashburn '49	.15	.07	.02
☐ 2 Yogi Berra '48	.25	.11	.03
☐ 3 Whitey Ford '51	.20	.09	.03
☐ 4 Gil Hodges '49	.15	.07	.02
☐ 5 Mickey Mantle '51	.75	.35	.09
☐ 6 Mickey Mantle '53	.50	.23	.06
☐ 7 Willie Mays '51	.40	.18	.05
☐ 8 Satchel Paige '49	.25	.11	.03
☐ 9 Jackie Robinson '50	.40	.18	.05
☐ 10 Duke Snider '49	.25	.11	.03
☐ 11 Ted Williams '54	.40	.18	.05

1990 Bowman

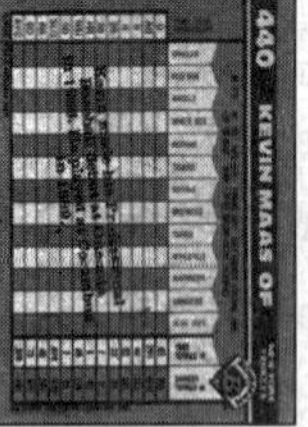

The 1990 Bowman set (produced by Topps) consists of 528 standard-size cards. The cards were issued in wax packs and factory sets. Each wax pack contained one of 11 different 1950's retro art cards. Unlike most sets, player selection focused primarily on rookies instead of proven major leaguers. The cards feature a white border with the player's photo inside and the Bowman logo on top. The card numbering is in team order with the teams themselves being ordered alphabetically within each league. Notable Rookie Cards include Moises Alou, Carlos Baerga, Travis Fryman, Juan Gonzalez, Marquis Grissom, Chuck Knoblauch, Ray Lankford, Ben McDonald, Sammy Sosa, Frank Thomas, Mo Vaughn, Larry Walker, and Bernie Williams.

	MINT	NRMT	EXC
COMPLETE SET (528)	10.00	4.50	1.25
COMPLETE FACT.SET (528)	10.00	4.50	1.25
COMMON CARD (1-528)	.05	.02	.01
☐ 1 Tommy Greene	.05	.02	.01
☐ 2 Tom Glavine	.15	.07	.02
☐ 3 Andy Nezelek	.05	.02	.01
☐ 4 Mike Stanton	.10	.05	.01
☐ 5 Rick Luecken	.05	.02	.01
☐ 6 Kent Mercker	.10	.05	.01
☐ 7 Derek Lilliquist	.05	.02	.01
☐ 8 Charlie Leibrandt	.05	.02	.01
☐ 9 Steve Avery	.15	.07	.02
☐ 10 John Smoltz	.25	.11	.03
☐ 11 Mark Lemke	.10	.05	.01
☐ 12 Lonnie Smith	.05	.02	.01
☐ 13 Oddibe McDowell	.05	.02	.01
☐ 14 Tyler Houston	.15	.07	.02
☐ 15 Jeff Blauser	.10	.05	.01
☐ 16 Ernie Whitt	.05	.02	.01
☐ 17 Alexis Infante	.05	.02	.01
☐ 18 Jim Presley	.05	.02	.01
☐ 19 Dale Murphy	.15	.07	.02
☐ 20 Nick Esasky	.05	.02	.01
☐ 21 Rick Sutcliffe	.05	.02	.01
☐ 22 Mike Bielecki	.05	.02	.01
☐ 23 Steve Wilson	.05	.02	.01
☐ 24 Kevin Blankenship	.05	.02	.01
☐ 25 Mitch Williams	.05	.02	.01
☐ 26 Dean Wilkins	.05	.02	.01
☐ 27 Greg Maddux	.60	.25	.07
☐ 28 Mike Harkey	.05	.02	.01
☐ 29 Mark Grace	.15	.07	.02
☐ 30 Ryne Sandberg	.25	.11	.03
☐ 31 Greg Smith	.05	.02	.01
☐ 32 Dwight Smith	.05	.02	.01
☐ 33 Damon Berryhill	.05	.02	.01
☐ 34 Earl Cunningham UER (Errant * by the word "in")	.05	.02	.01
☐ 35 Jerome Walton	.05	.02	.01
☐ 36 Lloyd McClendon	.05	.02	.01
☐ 37 Ty Griffin	.05	.02	.01
☐ 38 Shawon Dunston	.05	.02	.01
☐ 39 Andre Dawson	.10	.05	.01
☐ 40 Luis Salazar	.05	.02	.01
☐ 41 Tim Layana	.05	.02	.01
☐ 42 Rob Dibble	.05	.02	.01
☐ 43 Tom Browning	.05	.02	.01
☐ 44 Danny Jackson	.05	.02	.01
☐ 45 Jose Rijo	.05	.02	.01
☐ 46 Scott Scudder	.05	.02	.01
☐ 47 Randy Myers UER (Career ERA .274, should be 2.74)	.10	.05	.01
☐ 48 Brian Lane	.05	.02	.01
☐ 49 Paul O'Neill	.10	.05	.01
☐ 50 Barry Larkin	.15	.07	.02
☐ 51 Reggie Jefferson	.15	.07	.02
☐ 52 Jeff Branson	.05	.02	.01
☐ 53 Chris Sabo	.05	.02	.01
☐ 54 Joe Oliver	.05	.02	.01
☐ 55 Todd Benzinger	.05	.02	.01
☐ 56 Rolando Roomes	.05	.02	.01
☐ 57 Hal Morris	.10	.05	.01
☐ 58 Eric Davis	.10	.05	.01
☐ 59 Scott Bryant	.05	.02	.01
☐ 60 Ken Griffey Sr.	.05	.02	.01
☐ 61 Darryl Kile	.10	.05	.01
☐ 62 Dave Smith	.05	.02	.01
☐ 63 Mark Portugal	.05	.02	.01
☐ 64 Jeff Juden	.05	.02	.01
☐ 65 Bill Gullickson	.05	.02	.01
☐ 66 Danny Darwin	.05	.02	.01
☐ 67 Larry Andersen	.05	.02	.01
☐ 68 Jose Cano	.05	.02	.01
☐ 69 Dan Schatzeder	.05	.02	.01
☐ 70 Jim Deshaies	.05	.02	.01
☐ 71 Mike Scott	.05	.02	.01
☐ 72 Gerald Young	.05	.02	.01
☐ 73 Ken Caminiti	.20	.09	.03
☐ 74 Ken Oberkfell	.05	.02	.01
☐ 75 Dave Rohde	.05	.02	.01
☐ 76 Bill Doran	.05	.02	.01
☐ 77 Andujar Cedeno	.05	.02	.01
☐ 78 Craig Biggio	.15	.07	.02
☐ 79 Karl Rhodes	.05	.02	.01
☐ 80 Glenn Davis	.05	.02	.01
☐ 81 Eric Anthony	.10	.05	.01
☐ 82 John Wetteland	.15	.07	.02
☐ 83 Jay Howell	.05	.02	.01
☐ 84 Orel Hershiser	.10	.05	.01
☐ 85 Tim Belcher	.05	.02	.01
☐ 86 Kiki Jones	.05	.02	.01
☐ 87 Mike Hartley	.05	.02	.01
☐ 88 Ramon Martinez	.15	.07	.02
☐ 89 Mike Scioscia	.05	.02	.01
☐ 90 Willie Randolph	.10	.05	.01
☐ 91 Juan Samuel	.05	.02	.01
☐ 92 Jose Offerman	.10	.05	.01
☐ 93 Dave Hansen	.05	.02	.01
☐ 94 Jeff Hamilton	.05	.02	.01
☐ 95 Alfredo Griffin	.05	.02	.01
☐ 96 Tom Goodwin	.15	.07	.02
☐ 97 Kirk Gibson	.10	.05	.01
☐ 98 Jose Vizcaino	.15	.07	.02
☐ 99 Kal Daniels	.05	.02	.01
☐ 100 Hubie Brooks	.05	.02	.01
☐ 101 Eddie Murray	.25	.11	.03
☐ 102 Dennis Boyd	.05	.02	.01
☐ 103 Tim Burke	.05	.02	.01
☐ 104 Bill Sampen	.05	.02	.01
☐ 105 Brett Gideon	.05	.02	.01
☐ 106 Mark Gardner	.05	.02	.01
☐ 107 Howard Farmer	.05	.02	.01
☐ 108 Mel Rojas	.15	.07	.02
☐ 109 Kevin Gross	.05	.02	.01
☐ 110 Dave Schmidt	.05	.02	.01
☐ 111 Denny Martinez	.10	.05	.01
☐ 112 Jerry Goff	.05	.02	.01
☐ 113 Andres Galarraga	.15	.07	.02
☐ 114 Tim Wallach	.05	.02	.01
☐ 115 Marquis Grissom	.50	.23	.06
☐ 116 Spike Owen	.05	.02	.01
☐ 117 Larry Walker	.60	.25	.07
☐ 118 Tim Raines	.15	.07	.02
☐ 119 Delino DeShields	.10	.05	.01
☐ 120 Tom Foley	.05	.02	.01
☐ 121 Dave Martinez	.05	.02	.01
☐ 122 Frank Viola UER (Career ERA .384 should be 3.84)	.05	.02	.01
☐ 123 Julio Valera	.05	.02	.01
☐ 124 Alejandro Pena	.05	.02	.01
☐ 125 David Cone	.15	.07	.02
☐ 126 Dwight Gooden	.10	.05	.01
☐ 127 Kevin D. Brown	.05	.02	.01
☐ 128 John Franco	.05	.02	.01
☐ 129 Terry Bross	.05	.02	.01
☐ 130 Blaine Beatty	.05	.02	.01
☐ 131 Sid Fernandez	.05	.02	.01
☐ 132 Mike Marshall	.05	.02	.01
☐ 133 Howard Johnson	.05	.02	.01
☐ 134 Jaime Roseboro	.05	.02	.01
☐ 135 Alan Zinter	.05	.02	.01
☐ 136 Keith Miller	.05	.02	.01
☐ 137 Kevin Elster	.05	.02	.01
☐ 138 Kevin McReynolds	.05	.02	.01
☐ 139 Barry Lyons	.05	.02	.01
☐ 140 Gregg Jefferies	.10	.05	.01
☐ 141 Darryl Strawberry	.10	.05	.01
☐ 142 Todd Hundley	.60	.25	.07
☐ 143 Scott Service	.05	.02	.01
☐ 144 Chuck Malone	.05	.02	.01
☐ 145 Steve Ontiveros	.05	.02	.01
☐ 146 Roger McDowell	.05	.02	.01
☐ 147 Ken Howell	.05	.02	.01
☐ 148 Pat Combs	.05	.02	.01
☐ 149 Jeff Parrett	.05	.02	.01
☐ 150 Chuck McElroy	.05	.02	.01
☐ 151 Jason Grimsley	.05	.02	.01
☐ 152 Len Dykstra	.10	.05	.01
☐ 153 Mickey Morandini	.10	.05	.01
☐ 154 John Kruk	.10	.05	.01
☐ 155 Dickie Thon	.05	.02	.01
☐ 156 Ricky Jordan	.05	.02	.01
☐ 157 Jeff Jackson	.05	.02	.01
☐ 158 Darren Daulton	.10	.05	.01
☐ 159 Tom Herr	.05	.02	.01
☐ 160 Von Hayes	.05	.02	.01
☐ 161 Dave Hollins	.15	.07	.02
☐ 162 Carmelo Martinez	.05	.02	.01
☐ 163 Bob Walk	.05	.02	.01
☐ 164 Doug Drabek	.05	.02	.01
☐ 165 Walt Terrell	.05	.02	.01
☐ 166 Bill Landrum	.05	.02	.01
☐ 167 Scott Ruskin	.05	.02	.01
☐ 168 Bob Patterson	.05	.02	.01
☐ 169 Bobby Bonilla	.10	.05	.01
☐ 170 Jose Lind	.05	.02	.01
☐ 171 Andy Van Slyke	.10	.05	.01
☐ 172 Mike LaValliere	.05	.02	.01

□ 173 Willie Greene .15 .07 .02
□ 174 Jay Bell .10 .05 .01
□ 175 Sid Bream .05 .02 .01
□ 176 Tom Prince .05 .02 .01
□ 177 Wally Backman .05 .02 .01
□ 178 Moises Alou .40 .18 .05
□ 179 Steve Carter .05 .02 .01
□ 180 Gary Redus .05 .02 .01
□ 181 Barry Bonds .25 .11 .03
□ 182 Don Slaught UER .05 .02 .01
(Card back shows
headings for a pitcher)
□ 183 Joe Magrane .05 .02 .01
□ 184 Bryn Smith .05 .02 .01
□ 185 Todd Worrell .05 .02 .01
□ 186 Jose DeLeon .05 .02 .01
□ 187 Frank DiPino .05 .02 .01
□ 188 John Tudor .05 .02 .01
□ 189 Howard Hilton .05 .02 .01
□ 190 John Ericks .05 .02 .01
□ 191 Ken Dayley .05 .02 .01
□ 192 Ray Lankford .50 .23 .06
□ 193 Todd Zeile .10 .05 .01
□ 194 Willie McGee .05 .02 .01
□ 195 Ozzie Smith .25 .11 .03
□ 196 Milt Thompson .05 .02 .01
□ 197 Terry Pendleton .10 .05 .01
□ 198 Vince Coleman .05 .02 .01
□ 199 Paul Coleman .05 .02 .01
□ 200 Jose Oquendo .05 .02 .01
□ 201 Pedro Guerrero .05 .02 .01
□ 202 Tom Brunansky .05 .02 .01
□ 203 Roger Smithberg .05 .02 .01
□ 204 Eddie Whitson .05 .02 .01
□ 205 Dennis Rasmussen .05 .02 .01
□ 206 Craig Lefferts .05 .02 .01
□ 207 Andy Benes .15 .07 .02
□ 208 Bruce Hurst .05 .02 .01
□ 209 Eric Show .05 .02 .01
□ 210 Rafael Valdez .05 .02 .01
□ 211 Joey Cora .10 .05 .01
□ 212 Thomas Howard .05 .02 .01
□ 213 Rob Nelson .05 .02 .01
□ 214 Jack Clark .10 .05 .01
□ 215 Garry Templeton .05 .02 .01
□ 216 Fred Lynn .05 .02 .01
□ 217 Tony Gwynn .40 .18 .05
□ 218 Benito Santiago .05 .02 .01
□ 219 Mike Pagliarulo .05 .02 .01
□ 220 Joe Carter .10 .05 .01
□ 221 Roberto Alomar .25 .11 .03
□ 222 Bip Roberts .05 .02 .01
□ 223 Rick Reuschel .05 .02 .01
□ 224 Russ Swan .05 .02 .01
□ 225 Eric Gunderson .05 .02 .01
□ 226 Steve Bedrosian .05 .02 .01
□ 227 Mike Remlinger .05 .02 .01
□ 228 Scott Garrelts .05 .02 .01
□ 229 Ernie Camacho .05 .02 .01
□ 230 Andres Santana .05 .02 .01
□ 231 Will Clark .15 .07 .02
□ 232 Kevin Mitchell .10 .05 .01
□ 233 Robby Thompson .05 .02 .01
□ 234 Bill Bathe .05 .02 .01
□ 235 Tony Perezchica .05 .02 .01
□ 236 Gary Carter .10 .05 .01
□ 237 Brett Butler .10 .05 .01
□ 238 Matt Williams .15 .07 .02
□ 239 Earnie Riles .05 .02 .01
□ 240 Kevin Bass .05 .02 .01
□ 241 Terry Kennedy .05 .02 .01
□ 242 Steve Hosey .05 .02 .01
□ 243 Ben McDonald .15 .07 .02
□ 244 Jeff Ballard .05 .02 .01
□ 245 Joe Price .05 .02 .01
□ 246 Curt Schilling .05 .02 .01
□ 247 Pete Harnisch .05 .02 .01
□ 248 Mark Williamson .05 .02 .01
□ 249 Gregg Olson .05 .02 .01
□ 250 Chris Myers .05 .02 .01
□ 251A David Segui ERR .15 .07 .02
(Missing vital stats
at top of card back
under name)
□ 251B David Segui COR .15 .07 .02
□ 252 Joe Orsulak .05 .02 .01
□ 253 Craig Worthington .05 .02 .01
□ 254 Mickey Tettleton .10 .05 .01
□ 255 Cal Ripken .75 .35 .09
□ 256 Billy Ripken .05 .02 .01
□ 257 Randy Milligan .05 .02 .01
□ 258 Brady Anderson .15 .07 .02
□ 259 Chris Hoiles UER .15 .07 .02
Baltimore is spelled Balitmore
□ 260 Mike Devereaux .05 .02 .01
□ 261 Phil Bradley .05 .02 .01
□ 262 Leo Gomez .10 .05 .01
□ 263 Lee Smith .10 .05 .01
□ 264 Mike Rochford .05 .02 .01
□ 265 Jeff Reardon .10 .05 .01
□ 266 Wes Gardner .05 .02 .01
□ 267 Mike Boddicker .05 .02 .01
□ 268 Roger Clemens .20 .09 .03
□ 269 Rob Murphy .05 .02 .01
□ 270 Mickey Pina .05 .02 .01
□ 271 Tony Pena .05 .02 .01
□ 272 Jody Reed .05 .02 .01
□ 273 Kevin Romine .05 .02 .01
□ 274 Mike Greenwell .05 .02 .01
□ 275 Maurice Vaughn 1.50 .70 .19
□ 276 Danny Heep .05 .02 .01
□ 277 Scott Cooper .05 .02 .01
□ 278 Greg Blosser .05 .02 .01
□ 279 Dwight Evans UER .10 .05 .01
(* by "1990 Team
Breakdown")
□ 280 Ellis Burks .15 .07 .02
□ 281 Wade Boggs .15 .07 .02
□ 282 Marty Barrett .05 .02 .01
□ 283 Kirk McCaskill .05 .02 .01
□ 284 Mark Langston .10 .05 .01
□ 285 Bert Blyleven .10 .05 .01
□ 286 Mike Fetters .05 .02 .01
□ 287 Kyle Abbott .05 .02 .01
□ 288 Jim Abbott .10 .05 .01
□ 289 Chuck Finley .10 .05 .01
□ 290 Gary DiSarcina .15 .07 .02
□ 291 Dick Schofield .05 .02 .01
□ 292 Devon White .10 .05 .01
□ 293 Bobby Rose .05 .02 .01
□ 294 Brian Downing .05 .02 .01
□ 295 Lance Parrish .05 .02 .01
□ 296 Jack Howell .05 .02 .01
□ 297 Claudell Washington .05 .02 .01
□ 298 John Orton .05 .02 .01
□ 299 Wally Joyner .10 .05 .01
□ 300 Lee Stevens .05 .02 .01
□ 301 Chili Davis .10 .05 .01
□ 302 Johnny Ray .05 .02 .01
□ 303 Greg Hibbard .05 .02 .01
□ 304 Eric King .05 .02 .01
□ 305 Jack McDowell .15 .07 .02
□ 306 Bobby Thigpen .05 .02 .01
□ 307 Adam Peterson .05 .02 .01
□ 308 Scott Radinsky .05 .02 .01
□ 309 Wayne Edwards .05 .02 .01
□ 310 Melido Perez .05 .02 .01
□ 311 Robin Ventura .15 .07 .02
□ 312 Sammy Sosa .75 .35 .09
□ 313 Dan Pasqua .05 .02 .01
□ 314 Carlton Fisk .15 .07 .02
□ 315 Ozzie Guillen .05 .02 .01
□ 316 Ivan Calderon .05 .02 .01
□ 317 Daryl Boston .05 .02 .01
□ 318 Craig Grebeck .05 .02 .01
□ 319 Scott Fletcher .05 .02 .01
□ 320 Frank Thomas 4.00 1.80 .50
□ 321 Steve Lyons .05 .02 .01
□ 322 Carlos Martinez .05 .02 .01
□ 323 Joe Skalski .05 .02 .01
□ 324 Tom Candiotti .05 .02 .01
□ 325 Greg Swindell .05 .02 .01
□ 326 Steve Olin .10 .05 .01
□ 327 Kevin Wickander .05 .02 .01
□ 328 Doug Jones .05 .02 .01
□ 329 Jeff Shaw .05 .02 .01
□ 330 Kevin Bearse .05 .02 .01
□ 331 Dion James .05 .02 .01
□ 332 Jerry Browne .05 .02 .01
□ 333 Joey Belle .75 .35 .09
□ 334 Felix Fermin .05 .02 .01
□ 335 Candy Maldonado .05 .02 .01
□ 336 Cory Snyder .05 .02 .01
□ 337 Sandy Alomar Jr. .15 .07 .02
□ 338 Mark Lewis .10 .05 .01
□ 339 Carlos Baerga .30 .14 .04
□ 340 Chris James .05 .02 .01
□ 341 Brook Jacoby .05 .02 .01
□ 342 Keith Hernandez .10 .05 .01
□ 343 Frank Tanana .05 .02 .01
□ 344 Scott Aldred .05 .02 .01
□ 345 Mike Henneman .05 .02 .01
□ 346 Steve Wapnick .05 .02 .01
□ 347 Greg Gohr .05 .02 .01
□ 348 Eric Stone .05 .02 .01
□ 349 Brian DuBois .05 .02 .01
□ 350 Kevin Ritz .05 .02 .01
□ 351 Rico Brogna .15 .07 .02
□ 352 Mike Heath .05 .02 .01
□ 353 Alan Trammell .10 .05 .01
□ 354 Chet Lemon .05 .02 .01
□ 355 Dave Bergman .05 .02 .01
□ 356 Lou Whitaker .10 .05 .01
□ 357 Cecil Fielder UER .10 .05 .01
(* by "1990 Team
Breakdown")
□ 358 Milt Cuyler .05 .02 .01
□ 359 Tony Phillips .15 .07 .02
□ 360 Travis Fryman .40 .18 .05
□ 361 Ed Romero .05 .02 .01
□ 362 Lloyd Moseby .05 .02 .01
□ 363 Mark Gubicza .05 .02 .01
□ 364 Bret Saberhagen .10 .05 .01
□ 365 Tom Gordon .05 .02 .01
□ 366 Steve Farr .05 .02 .01
□ 367 Kevin Appier .15 .07 .02
□ 368 Storm Davis .05 .02 .01
□ 369 Mark Davis .05 .02 .01
□ 370 Jeff Montgomery .10 .05 .01
□ 371 Frank White .10 .05 .01
□ 372 Brent Mayne .05 .02 .01
□ 373 Bob Boone .10 .05 .01
□ 374 Jim Eisenreich .05 .02 .01
□ 375 Danny Tartabull .05 .02 .01
□ 376 Kurt Stillwell .05 .02 .01
□ 377 Bill Pecota .05 .02 .01
□ 378 Bo Jackson .10 .05 .01
□ 379 Bob Hamelin .10 .05 .01
□ 380 Kevin Seitzer .05 .02 .01
□ 381 Rey Palacios .05 .02 .01
□ 382 George Brett .40 .18 .05
□ 383 Gerald Perry .05 .02 .01
□ 384 Teddy Higuera .05 .02 .01
□ 385 Tom Filer .05 .02 .01
□ 386 Dan Plesac .05 .02 .01
□ 387 Cal Eldred .15 .07 .02
□ 388 Jaime Navarro .05 .02 .01
□ 389 Chris Bosio .05 .02 .01
□ 390 Randy Veres .05 .02 .01
□ 391 Gary Sheffield .25 .11 .03
□ 392 George Canale .05 .02 .01
□ 393 B.J. Surhoff .10 .05 .01
□ 394 Tim McIntosh .05 .02 .01
□ 395 Greg Brock .05 .02 .01
□ 396 Greg Vaughn .15 .07 .02
□ 397 Darryl Hamilton .10 .05 .01
□ 398 Dave Parker .10 .05 .01
□ 399 Paul Molitor .20 .09 .03
□ 400 Jim Gantner .05 .02 .01
□ 401 Rob Deer .05 .02 .01
□ 402 Billy Spiers .05 .02 .01
□ 403 Glenn Braggs .05 .02 .01
□ 404 Robin Yount .15 .07 .02
□ 405 Rick Aguilera .10 .05 .01
□ 406 Johnny Ard .05 .02 .01
□ 407 Kevin Tapani .10 .05 .01
□ 408 Park Pittman .05 .02 .01
□ 409 Allan Anderson .05 .02 .01
□ 410 Juan Berenguer .05 .02 .01
□ 411 Willie Banks .05 .02 .01
□ 412 Rich Yett .05 .02 .01
□ 413 Dave West .05 .02 .01
□ 414 Greg Gagne .05 .02 .01
□ 415 Chuck Knoblauch .75 .35 .09
□ 416 Randy Bush .05 .02 .01
□ 417 Gary Gaetti .10 .05 .01
□ 418 Kent Hrbek .10 .05 .01
□ 419 Al Newman .05 .02 .01
□ 420 Danny Gladden .05 .02 .01
□ 421 Paul Sorrento .15 .07 .02
□ 422 Derek Parks .05 .02 .01
□ 423 Scott Leius .05 .02 .01
□ 424 Kirby Puckett .40 .18 .05
□ 425 Willie Smith .05 .02 .01
□ 426 Dave Righetti .05 .02 .01
□ 427 Jeff D. Robinson .05 .02 .01
□ 428 Alan Mills .05 .02 .01
□ 429 Tim Leary .05 .02 .01
□ 430 Pascual Perez .05 .02 .01
□ 431 Alvaro Espinoza .05 .02 .01
□ 432 Dave Winfield .15 .07 .02
□ 433 Jesse Barfield .05 .02 .01
□ 434 Randy Velarde .05 .02 .01
□ 435 Rick Cerone .05 .02 .01
□ 436 Steve Balboni .05 .02 .01
□ 437 Mel Hall .05 .02 .01
□ 438 Bob Geren .05 .02 .01
□ 439 Bernie Williams 1.00 .45 .12
□ 440 Kevin Maas .05 .02 .01
□ 441 Mike Blowers .15 .07 .02
□ 442 Steve Sax .05 .02 .01
□ 443 Don Mattingly .50 .23 .06
□ 444 Roberto Kelly .10 .05 .01
□ 445 Mike Moore .05 .02 .01
□ 446 Reggie Harris .05 .02 .01
□ 447 Scott Sanderson .05 .02 .01
□ 448 Dave Otto .05 .02 .01
□ 449 Dave Stewart .10 .05 .01
□ 450 Rick Honeycutt .05 .02 .01
□ 451 Dennis Eckersley .10 .05 .01
□ 452 Carney Lansford .10 .05 .01
□ 453 Scott Hemond .05 .02 .01
□ 454 Mark McGwire .30 .14 .04
□ 455 Felix Jose .05 .02 .01
□ 456 Terry Steinbach .10 .05 .01
□ 457 Rickey Henderson .15 .07 .02
□ 458 Dave Henderson .05 .02 .01
□ 459 Mike Gallego .05 .02 .01
□ 460 Jose Canseco .15 .07 .02
□ 461 Walt Weiss .05 .02 .01
□ 462 Ken Phelps .05 .02 .01
□ 463 Darren Lewis .10 .05 .01
□ 464 Ron Hassey .05 .02 .01
□ 465 Roger Salkeld .05 .02 .01
□ 466 Scott Bankhead .05 .02 .01
□ 467 Keith Comstock .05 .02 .01
□ 468 Randy Johnson .25 .11 .03
□ 469 Erik Hanson .10 .05 .01
□ 470 Mike Schooler .05 .02 .01
□ 471 Gary Eave .05 .02 .01
□ 472 Jeffrey Leonard .05 .02 .01
□ 473 Dave Valle .05 .02 .01
□ 474 Omar Vizquel .15 .07 .02
□ 475 Pete O'Brien .05 .02 .01
□ 476 Henry Cotto .05 .02 .01
□ 477 Jay Buhner .15 .07 .02
□ 478 Harold Reynolds .05 .02 .01
□ 479 Alvin Davis .05 .02 .01
□ 480 Darnell Coles .05 .02 .01
□ 481 Ken Griffey Jr. 1.50 .70 .19
□ 482 Greg Briley .05 .02 .01
□ 483 Scott Bradley .05 .02 .01
□ 484 Tino Martinez .15 .07 .02
□ 485 Jeff Russell .05 .02 .01
□ 486 Nolan Ryan .75 .35 .09
□ 487 Robb Nen .15 .07 .02
□ 488 Kevin Brown
□ 489 Brian Bohanon .05 .02 .01
□ 490 Ruben Sierra .10 .05 .01
□ 491 Pete Incaviglia .05 .02 .01
□ 492 Juan Gonzalez 2.00 .90 .25
□ 493 Steve Buechele .05 .02 .01
□ 494 Scott Coolbaugh .05 .02 .01
□ 495 Geno Petralli .05 .02 .01
□ 496 Rafael Palmeiro .15 .07 .02
□ 497 Julio Franco .10 .05 .01
□ 498 Gary Pettis .05 .02 .01
□ 499 Donald Harris .05 .02 .01
□ 500 Monty Fariss .05 .02 .01
□ 501 Harold Baines .10 .05 .01
□ 502 Cecil Espy .05 .02 .01
□ 503 Jack Daugherty .05 .02 .01
□ 504 Willie Blair .05 .02 .01
□ 505 Dave Stieb .05 .02 .01
□ 506 Tom Henke .05 .02 .01
□ 507 John Cerutti .05 .02 .01
□ 508 Paul Kilgus .05 .02 .01
□ 509 Jimmy Key .10 .05 .01
□ 510 John Olerud .15 .07 .02
□ 511 Ed Sprague .15 .07 .02
□ 512 Manuel Lee .05 .02 .01
□ 513 Fred McGriff .15 .07 .02
□ 514 Glenallen Hill .10 .05 .01
□ 515 George Bell .05 .02 .01
□ 516 Mookie Wilson .05 .02 .01
□ 517 Luis Sojo .05 .02 .01
□ 518 Nelson Liriano .05 .02 .01
□ 519 Kelly Gruber .05 .02 .01
□ 520 Greg Myers .05 .02 .01
□ 521 Pat Borders .05 .02 .01
□ 522 Junior Felix .05 .02 .01
□ 523 Eddie Zosky .05 .02 .01
□ 524 Tony Fernandez .05 .02 .01
□ 525 Checklist 1-132 UER .05 .02 .01
(No copyright mark
on the back)
□ 526 Checklist 133-264 .05 .02 .01
□ 527 Checklist 265-396 .05 .02 .01
□ 528 Checklist 397-528 .05 .02 .01

1990 Bowman Tiffany

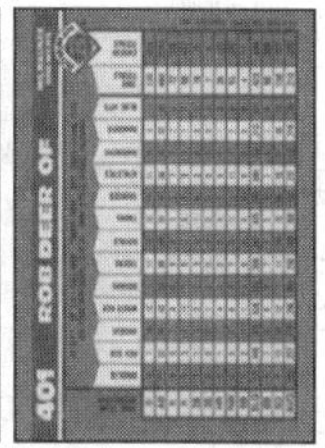

These 539 standard-size cards were issued as a factory set by Topps. These cards parallel the regular Bowman issue except they have glossy fronts and a very easy to read back. In addition to the 528 basic cards, the 11 insert art cards were also included in the factory set.

	MINT	NRMT	EXC
COMPLETE FACT.SET (539)	125.00	55.00	15.50
COMMON CARD (1-528)	.10	.05	.01
COMMON ART CARD (A1-A11)	.20	.09	.03

*STARS: 2.5X to 5X BASIC CARDS
*YOUNG STARS: 2.5X to 5X BASIC CARDS

1990 Bowman Inserts

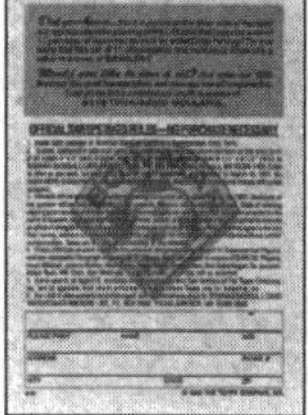

These standard-size cards were included as an insert in every 1990 Bowman pack. This set, which consists of 11 superstars, depicts drawings by Craig Pursley with the backs being descriptions of the 1990 Bowman sweepstakes. We have checklisted the set alphabetically by player. All the cards in this set can be found with either one asterisk or two on the back.

	MINT	NRMT	EXC
COMPLETE SET (11)	2.00	.90	.25
COMMON CARD (1-11)	.10	.05	.01
☐ 1 Will Clark	.15	.07	.02
☐ 2 Mark Davis	.10	.05	.01
☐ 3 Dwight Gooden	.15	.07	.02
☐ 4 Bo Jackson	.15	.07	.02
☐ 5 Don Mattingly	.30	.14	.04
☐ 6 Kevin Mitchell	.10	.05	.01
☐ 7 Gregg Olson	.10	.05	.01
☐ 8 Nolan Ryan	.75	.35	.09
☐ 9 Bret Saberhagen	.10	.05	.01
☐ 10 Jerome Walton	.10	.05	.01
☐ 11 Robin Yount	.25	.11	.03

1991 Bowman

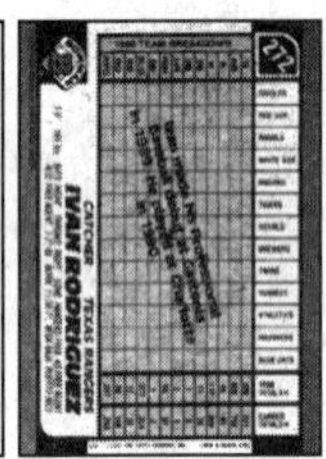

This single-series 704-card standard-size set marked the third straight year that Topps issued a set weighted towards prospects using the Bowman name. Cards were issued in wax packs and factory sets. The cards share a design very similar to the 1990 Bowman set with white borders enframing a color photo. The player name, however, is more prominent than in the previous year set. The cards are arranged in team order by division as follows: AL East, AL West, NL East, and NL West. Subsets include Rod Carew Tribute (1-5), Minor League MVP's (180-185/693-698), AL Silver Sluggers (367-375), NL Silver Sluggers (376-384) and checklists (699-704). Rookie Cards in this set include Jeff Bagwell, Jeff Conine, Carlos Garcia, Pat Hentgen, Chipper Jones, Eric Karros, Ryan Klesko, Kenny Lofton, Javier Lopez, Brian McRae, Raul Mondesi, Mike Mussina, Ivan "Pudge" Rodriguez, Tim Salmon, Reggie Sanders, Jim Thome, Rondell White and Mark Wohlers. There are two instances of misnumbering in the set; Ken Griffey (should be 255) and Ken Griffey Jr. are both numbered 246 and Donovan Osborne (should be 406) and Thomson/Branca share number 410.

	MINT	NRMT	EXC
COMPLETE SET (704)	30.00	13.50	3.70
COMPLETE FACT.SET (704)	30.00	13.50	3.70
COMMON CARD (1-704)	.05	.02	.01
☐ 1 Rod Carew I	.15	.07	.02
☐ 2 Rod Carew II	.15	.07	.02
☐ 3 Rod Carew III	.15	.07	.02
☐ 4 Rod Carew IV	.15	.07	.02
☐ 5 Rod Carew V	.15	.07	.02
☐ 6 Willie Fraser	.05	.02	.01
☐ 7 John Olerud	.10	.05	.01
☐ 8 William Suero	.05	.02	.01
☐ 9 Roberto Alomar	.20	.09	.03
☐ 10 Todd Stottlemyre	.10	.05	.01
☐ 11 Joe Carter	.10	.05	.01
☐ 12 Steve Karsay	.15	.07	.02
☐ 13 Mark Whiten	.10	.05	.01
☐ 14 Pat Borders	.05	.02	.01
☐ 15 Mike Timlin	.05	.02	.01
☐ 16 Tom Henke	.05	.02	.01
☐ 17 Eddie Zosky	.05	.02	.01
☐ 18 Kelly Gruber	.05	.02	.01
☐ 19 Jimmy Key	.10	.05	.01
☐ 20 Jerry Schunk	.05	.02	.01
☐ 21 Manuel Lee	.05	.02	.01
☐ 22 Dave Stieb	.05	.02	.01
☐ 23 Pat Hentgen	.50	.23	.06
☐ 24 Glenallen Hill	.05	.02	.01
☐ 25 Rene Gonzales	.05	.02	.01
☐ 26 Ed Sprague	.10	.05	.01
☐ 27 Ken Dayley	.05	.02	.01
☐ 28 Pat Tabler	.05	.02	.01
☐ 29 Denis Boucher	.05	.02	.01
☐ 30 Devon White	.10	.05	.01
☐ 31 Dante Bichette	.15	.07	.02
☐ 32 Paul Molitor	.20	.09	.03
☐ 33 Greg Vaughn	.10	.05	.01
☐ 34 Dan Plesac	.05	.02	.01
☐ 35 Chris George	.05	.02	.01
☐ 36 Tim McIntosh	.05	.02	.01
☐ 37 Franklin Stubbs	.05	.02	.01
☐ 38 Bo Dodson	.05	.02	.01
☐ 39 Ron Robinson	.05	.02	.01
☐ 40 Ed Nunez	.05	.02	.01
☐ 41 Greg Brock	.05	.02	.01
☐ 42 Jaime Navarro	.05	.02	.01
☐ 43 Chris Bosio	.05	.02	.01
☐ 44 B.J. Surhoff	.10	.05	.01
☐ 45 Chris Johnson	.05	.02	.01
☐ 46 Willie Randolph	.10	.05	.01
☐ 47 Narciso Elvira	.05	.02	.01
☐ 48 Jim Gantner	.05	.02	.01
☐ 49 Kevin Brown	.10	.05	.01
☐ 50 Julio Machado	.05	.02	.01
☐ 51 Chuck Crim	.05	.02	.01
☐ 52 Gary Sheffield	.15	.07	.02
☐ 53 Angel Miranda	.05	.02	.01
☐ 54 Teddy Higuera	.05	.02	.01
☐ 55 Robin Yount	.15	.07	.02
☐ 56 Cal Eldred	.05	.02	.01
☐ 57 Sandy Alomar Jr.	.10	.05	.01
☐ 58 Greg Swindell	.05	.02	.01
☐ 59 Brook Jacoby	.05	.02	.01
☐ 60 Efrain Valdez	.05	.02	.01
☐ 61 Ever Magallanes	.05	.02	.01
☐ 62 Tom Candiotti	.05	.02	.01
☐ 63 Eric King	.05	.02	.01
☐ 64 Alex Cole	.05	.02	.01
☐ 65 Charles Nagy	.15	.07	.02
☐ 66 Mitch Webster	.05	.02	.01
☐ 67 Chris James	.05	.02	.01
☐ 68 Jim Thome	1.50	.70	.19
☐ 69 Carlos Baerga	.15	.07	.02
☐ 70 Mark Lewis	.05	.02	.01
☐ 71 Jerry Browne	.05	.02	.01
☐ 72 Jesse Orosco	.05	.02	.01
☐ 73 Mike Huff	.05	.02	.01
☐ 74 Jose Escobar	.05	.02	.01
☐ 75 Jeff Manto	.05	.02	.01
☐ 76 Turner Ward	.05	.02	.01
☐ 77 Doug Jones	.05	.02	.01
☐ 78 Bruce Egloff	.05	.02	.01
☐ 79 Tim Costo	.05	.02	.01
☐ 80 Beau Allred	.05	.02	.01
☐ 81 Albert Belle	.50	.23	.06
☐ 82 John Farrell	.05	.02	.01
☐ 83 Glenn Davis	.05	.02	.01
☐ 84 Joe Orsulak	.05	.02	.01
☐ 85 Mark Williamson	.05	.02	.01
☐ 86 Ben McDonald	.10	.05	.01
☐ 87 Billy Ripken	.05	.02	.01
☐ 88 Leo Gomez UER Baltimore is spelled Balitmore	.05	.02	.01
☐ 89 Bob Melvin	.05	.02	.01
☐ 90 Jeff M. Robinson	.05	.02	.01
☐ 91 Jose Mesa	.10	.05	.01
☐ 92 Gregg Olson	.05	.02	.01
☐ 93 Mike Devereaux	.05	.02	.01
☐ 94 Luis Mercedes	.05	.02	.01
☐ 95 Arthur Rhodes	.10	.05	.01
☐ 96 Juan Bell	.05	.02	.01
☐ 97 Mike Mussina	1.25	.55	.16
☐ 98 Jeff Ballard	.05	.02	.01
☐ 99 Chris Hoiles	.05	.02	.01
☐ 100 Brady Anderson	.15	.07	.02
☐ 101 Bob Milacki	.05	.02	.01
☐ 102 David Segui	.10	.05	.01
☐ 103 Dwight Evans	.10	.05	.01
☐ 104 Cal Ripken	.75	.35	.09
☐ 105 Mike Linskey	.05	.02	.01
☐ 106 Jeff Tackett	.05	.02	.01
☐ 107 Jeff Reardon	.10	.05	.01
☐ 108 Dana Kiecker	.05	.02	.01
☐ 109 Ellis Burks	.10	.05	.01
☐ 110 Dave Owen	.05	.02	.01
☐ 111 Danny Darwin	.05	.02	.01
☐ 112 Mo Vaughn	.50	.23	.06
☐ 113 Jeff McNeely	.05	.02	.01
☐ 114 Tom Bolton	.05	.02	.01
☐ 115 Greg Blosser	.05	.02	.01
☐ 116 Mike Greenwell	.05	.02	.01
☐ 117 Phil Plantier	.10	.05	.01
☐ 118 Roger Clemens	.20	.09	.03
☐ 119 John Marzano	.05	.02	.01
☐ 120 Jody Reed	.05	.02	.01
☐ 121 Scott Taylor	.05	.02	.01
☐ 122 Jack Clark	.10	.05	.01
☐ 123 Derek Livernois	.05	.02	.01
☐ 124 Tony Pena	.05	.02	.01
☐ 125 Tom Brunansky	.05	.02	.01
☐ 126 Carlos Quintana	.05	.02	.01
☐ 127 Tim Naehring	.10	.05	.01
☐ 128 Matt Young	.05	.02	.01
☐ 129 Wade Boggs	.15	.07	.02
☐ 130 Kevin Morton	.05	.02	.01
☐ 131 Pete Incaviglia	.05	.02	.01
☐ 132 Rob Deer	.05	.02	.01
☐ 133 Bill Gullickson	.05	.02	.01
☐ 134 Rico Brogna	.10	.05	.01
☐ 135 Lloyd Moseby	.05	.02	.01
☐ 136 Cecil Fielder	.10	.05	.01
☐ 137 Tony Phillips	.10	.05	.01
☐ 138 Mark Leiter	.05	.02	.01
☐ 139 John Cerutti	.05	.02	.01
☐ 140 Mickey Tettleton	.10	.05	.01
☐ 141 Milt Cuyler	.05	.02	.01
☐ 142 Greg Gohr	.05	.02	.01
☐ 143 Tony Bernazard	.05	.02	.01
☐ 144 Dan Gakeler	.05	.02	.01
☐ 145 Travis Fryman	.15	.07	.02
☐ 146 Dan Petry	.05	.02	.01
☐ 147 Scott Aldred	.05	.02	.01
☐ 148 John DeSilva	.05	.02	.01
☐ 149 Rusty Meacham	.05	.02	.01
☐ 150 Lou Whitaker	.10	.05	.01
☐ 151 Dave Haas	.05	.02	.01
☐ 152 Luis de los Santos	.05	.02	.01
☐ 153 Ivan Cruz	.05	.02	.01
☐ 154 Alan Trammell	.10	.05	.01
☐ 155 Pat Kelly	.10	.05	.01
☐ 156 Carl Everett	.15	.07	.02
☐ 157 Greg Cadaret	.05	.02	.01
☐ 158 Kevin Maas	.05	.02	.01
☐ 159 Jeff Johnson	.05	.02	.01
☐ 160 Willie Smith	.05	.02	.01
☐ 161 Gerald Williams	.05	.02	.01
☐ 162 Mike Humphreys	.05	.02	.01
☐ 163 Alvaro Espinoza	.05	.02	.01
☐ 164 Matt Nokes	.05	.02	.01
☐ 165 Wade Taylor	.05	.02	.01
☐ 166 Roberto Kelly	.05	.02	.01
☐ 167 John Habyan	.05	.02	.01
☐ 168 Steve Farr	.05	.02	.01
☐ 169 Jesse Barfield	.05	.02	.01
☐ 170 Steve Sax	.05	.02	.01
☐ 171 Jim Leyritz	.10	.05	.01
☐ 172 Robert Eenhoorn	.05	.02	.01
☐ 173 Bernie Williams	.30	.14	.04
☐ 174 Scott Lusader	.05	.02	.01
☐ 175 Torey Lovullo	.05	.02	.01
☐ 176 Chuck Cary	.05	.02	.01
☐ 177 Scott Sanderson	.05	.02	.01
☐ 178 Don Mattingly	.50	.23	.06
☐ 179 Mel Hall	.05	.02	.01
☐ 180 Juan Gonzalez	.75	.35	.09
☐ 181 Hensley Meulens	.05	.02	.01
☐ 182 Jose Offerman	.05	.02	.01
☐ 183 Jeff Bagwell	2.50	1.10	.30
☐ 184 Jeff Conine	.50	.23	.06
☐ 185 Henry Rodriguez	.40	.18	.05
☐ 186 Jimmie Reese CO	.10	.05	.01
☐ 187 Kyle Abbott	.05	.02	.01
☐ 188 Lance Parrish	.05	.02	.01
☐ 189 Rafael Montalvo	.05	.02	.01
☐ 190 Floyd Bannister	.05	.02	.01
☐ 191 Dick Schofield	.05	.02	.01
☐ 192 Scott Lewis	.05	.02	.01
☐ 193 Jeff D. Robinson	.05	.02	.01
☐ 194 Kent Anderson	.05	.02	.01
☐ 195 Wally Joyner	.10	.05	.01
☐ 196 Chuck Finley	.10	.05	.01
☐ 197 Luis Sojo	.05	.02	.01
☐ 198 Jeff Richardson	.05	.02	.01
☐ 199 Dave Parker	.10	.05	.01
☐ 200 Jim Abbott	.10	.05	.01
☐ 201 Junior Felix	.05	.02	.01
☐ 202 Mark Langston	.10	.05	.01
☐ 203 Tim Salmon	1.00	.45	.12
☐ 204 Cliff Young	.05	.02	.01
☐ 205 Scott Bailes	.05	.02	.01
☐ 206 Bobby Rose	.05	.02	.01
☐ 207 Gary Gaetti	.10	.05	.01
☐ 208 Ruben Amaro	.05	.02	.01
☐ 209 Luis Polonia	.05	.02	.01
☐ 210 Dave Winfield	.15	.07	.02
☐ 211 Bryan Harvey	.05	.02	.01
☐ 212 Mike Moore	.05	.02	.01
☐ 213 Rickey Henderson	.15	.07	.02
☐ 214 Steve Chitren	.05	.02	.01
☐ 215 Bob Welch	.05	.02	.01
☐ 216 Terry Steinbach	.10	.05	.01
☐ 217 Earnest Riles	.05	.02	.01
☐ 218 Todd Van Poppel	.10	.05	.01
☐ 219 Mike Gallego	.05	.02	.01
☐ 220 Curt Young	.05	.02	.01
☐ 221 Todd Burns	.05	.02	.01
☐ 222 Vance Law	.05	.02	.01
☐ 223 Eric Show	.05	.02	.01
☐ 224 Don Peters	.05	.02	.01
☐ 225 Dave Stewart	.10	.05	.01
☐ 226 Dave Henderson	.05	.02	.01
☐ 227 Jose Canseco	.15	.07	.02
☐ 228 Walt Weiss	.05	.02	.01
☐ 229 Dann Howitt	.05	.02	.01
☐ 230 Willie Wilson	.05	.02	.01
☐ 231 Harold Baines	.10	.05	.01
☐ 232 Scott Hemond	.05	.02	.01
☐ 233 Joe Slusarski	.05	.02	.01
☐ 234 Mark McGwire	.30	.14	.04
☐ 235 Kirk Dressendorfer	.05	.02	.01
☐ 236 Craig Paquette	.15	.07	.02
☐ 237 Dennis Eckersley	.10	.05	.01
☐ 238 Dana Allison	.05	.02	.01
☐ 239 Scott Bradley	.05	.02	.01
☐ 240 Brian Holman	.05	.02	.01
☐ 241 Mike Schooler	.05	.02	.01
☐ 242 Rich DeLucia	.05	.02	.01
☐ 243 Edgar Martinez	.15	.07	.02
☐ 244 Henry Cotto	.05	.02	.01
☐ 245 Omar Vizquel	.15	.07	.02
☐ 246 Ken Griffey Jr. (See also 255)	1.50	.70	.19
☐ 247 Jay Buhner	.15	.07	.02
☐ 248 Bill Krueger	.05	.02	.01
☐ 249 Dave Fleming	.10	.05	.01
☐ 250 Patrick Lennon	.05	.02	.01
☐ 251 Dave Valle	.05	.02	.01
☐ 252 Harold Reynolds	.05	.02	.01
☐ 253 Randy Johnson	.15	.07	.02
☐ 254 Scott Bankhead	.05	.02	.01
☐ 255 Ken Griffey Sr. UER (Card number is 246)	.05	.02	.01
☐ 256 Greg Briley	.05	.02	.01
☐ 257 Tino Martinez	.15	.07	.02
☐ 258 Alvin Davis	.05	.02	.01
☐ 259 Pete O'Brien	.05	.02	.01
☐ 260 Erik Hanson	.05	.02	.01
☐ 261 Bret Boone	.15	.07	.02
☐ 262 Roger Salkeld	.05	.02	.01
☐ 263 Dave Burba	.05	.02	.01
☐ 264 Kerry Woodson	.05	.02	.01
☐ 265 Julio Franco	.10	.05	.01
☐ 266 Dan Peltier	.05	.02	.01
☐ 267 Jeff Russell	.05	.02	.01
☐ 268 Steve Buechele	.05	.02	.01
☐ 269 Donald Harris	.05	.02	.01
☐ 270 Robb Nen	.10	.05	.01
☐ 271 Rich Gossage	.10	.05	.01
☐ 272 Ivan Rodriguez	1.50	.70	.19
☐ 273 Jeff Huson	.05	.02	.01
☐ 274 Kevin Brown	.10	.05	.01
☐ 275 Dan Smith	.05	.02	.01
☐ 276 Gary Pettis	.05	.02	.01
☐ 277 Jack Daugherty	.05	.02	.01
☐ 278 Mike Jeffcoat	.05	.02	.01
☐ 279 Brad Arnsberg	.05	.02	.01
☐ 280 Nolan Ryan	.75	.35	.09
☐ 281 Eric McCray	.05	.02	.01
☐ 282 Scott Chiamparino	.05	.02	.01
☐ 283 Ruben Sierra	.10	.05	.01
☐ 284 Geno Petralli	.05	.02	.01
☐ 285 Monty Fariss	.05	.02	.01
☐ 286 Rafael Palmeiro	.15	.07	.02
☐ 287 Bobby Witt	.05	.02	.01
☐ 288 Dean Palmer UER (Photo actually Dan Peltier)	.15	.07	.02
☐ 289 Tony Scruggs	.05	.02	.01
☐ 290 Kenny Rogers	.05	.02	.01
☐ 291 Bret Saberhagen	.10	.05	.01
☐ 292 Brian McRae	.25	.11	.03
☐ 293 Storm Davis	.05	.02	.01
☐ 294 Danny Tartabull	.05	.02	.01
☐ 295 David Howard	.05	.02	.01
☐ 296 Mike Boddicker	.05	.02	.01
☐ 297 Joel Johnston	.05	.02	.01
☐ 298 Tim Spehr	.05	.02	.01
☐ 299 Hector Wagner	.05	.02	.01
☐ 300 George Brett	.40	.18	.05
☐ 301 Mike Macfarlane	.05	.02	.01
☐ 302 Kirk Gibson	.10	.05	.01
☐ 303 Harvey Pulliam	.05	.02	.01
☐ 304 Jim Eisenreich	.10	.05	.01
☐ 305 Kevin Seitzer	.05	.02	.01
☐ 306 Mark Davis	.05	.02	.01
☐ 307 Kurt Stillwell	.05	.02	.01
☐ 308 Jeff Montgomery	.10	.05	.01
☐ 309 Kevin Appier	.15	.07	.02
☐ 310 Bob Hamelin	.05	.02	.01
☐ 311 Tom Gordon	.05	.02	.01
☐ 312 Kerwin Moore	.05	.02	.01
☐ 313 Hugh Walker	.05	.02	.01
☐ 314 Terry Shumpert	.05	.02	.01
☐ 315 Warren Cromartie	.05	.02	.01
☐ 316 Gary Thurman	.05	.02	.01
☐ 317 Steve Bedrosian	.05	.02	.01
☐ 318 Danny Gladden	.05	.02	.01
☐ 319 Jack Morris	.10	.05	.01
☐ 320 Kirby Puckett	.40	.18	.05
☐ 321 Kent Hrbek	.10	.05	.01
☐ 322 Kevin Tapani	.05	.02	.01
☐ 323 Denny Neagle	.40	.18	.05
☐ 324 Rich Garces	.05	.02	.01
☐ 325 Larry Casian	.05	.02	.01
☐ 326 Shane Mack	.05	.02	.01
☐ 327 Allan Anderson	.05	.02	.01
☐ 328 Junior Ortiz	.05	.02	.01
☐ 329 Paul Abbott	.05	.02	.01
☐ 330 Chuck Knoblauch	.25	.11	.03
☐ 331 Chili Davis	.10	.05	.01
☐ 332 Todd Ritchie	.05	.02	.01
☐ 333 Brian Harper	.05	.02	.01
☐ 334 Rick Aguilera	.10	.05	.01
☐ 335 Scott Erickson	.10	.05	.01
☐ 336 Pedro Munoz	.10	.05	.01
☐ 337 Scott Leius	.05	.02	.01
☐ 338 Greg Gagne	.05	.02	.01
☐ 339 Mike Pagliarulo	.05	.02	.01
☐ 340 Terry Leach	.05	.02	.01
☐ 341 Willie Banks	.05	.02	.01
☐ 342 Bobby Thigpen	.05	.02	.01
☐ 343 Roberto Hernandez	.15	.07	.02
☐ 344 Melido Perez	.05	.02	.01
☐ 345 Carlton Fisk	.15	.07	.02
☐ 346 Norberto Martin	.05	.02	.01
☐ 347 Johnny Ruffin	.05	.02	.01
☐ 348 Jeff Carter	.05	.02	.01
☐ 349 Lance Johnson	.10	.05	.01
☐ 350 Sammy Sosa	.25	.11	.03
☐ 351 Alex Fernandez	.15	.07	.02
☐ 352 Jack McDowell	.10	.05	.01
☐ 353 Bob Wickman	.05	.02	.01
☐ 354 Wilson Alvarez	.15	.07	.02
☐ 355 Charlie Hough	.05	.02	.01
☐ 356 Ozzie Guillen	.05	.02	.01
☐ 357 Cory Snyder	.05	.02	.01
☐ 358 Robin Ventura	.15	.07	.02
☐ 359 Scott Fletcher	.05	.02	.01
☐ 360 Cesar Bernhardt	.05	.02	.01
☐ 361 Dan Pasqua	.05	.02	.01

☐ 362 Tim Raines .15 .07 .02
☐ 363 Brian Drahman .05 .02 .01
☐ 364 Wayne Edwards .05 .02 .01
☐ 365 Scott Radinsky .05 .02 .01
☐ 366 Frank Thomas 2.00 .90 .25
☐ 367 Cecil Fielder SLUG .10 .05 .01
☐ 368 Julio Franco SLUG .10 .05 .01
☐ 369 Kelly Gruber SLUG .05 .02 .01
☐ 370 Alan Trammell SLUG .10 .05 .01
☐ 371 Rickey Henderson SLUG .15 .07 .02
☐ 372 Jose Canseco SLUG .15 .07 .02
☐ 373 Ellis Burks SLUG .10 .05 .01
☐ 374 Lance Parrish SLUG .05 .02 .01
☐ 375 Dave Parker SLUG .10 .05 .01
☐ 376 Eddie Murray SLUG .15 .07 .02
☐ 377 Ryne Sandberg SLUG .15 .07 .02
☐ 378 Matt Williams SLUG .15 .07 .02
☐ 379 Barry Larkin SLUG .15 .07 .02
☐ 380 Barry Bonds SLUG .15 .07 .02
☐ 381 Bobby Bonilla SLUG .10 .05 .01
☐ 382 Darryl Strawberry SLUG .10 .05 .01
☐ 383 Benny Santiago SLUG .05 .02 .01
☐ 384 Don Robinson SLUG .05 .02 .01
☐ 385 Paul Coleman .05 .02 .01
☐ 386 Milt Thompson .05 .02 .01
☐ 387 Lee Smith .10 .05 .01
☐ 388 Ray Lankford .15 .07 .02
☐ 389 Tom Pagnozzi .05 .02 .01
☐ 390 Ken Hill .10 .05 .01
☐ 391 Jamie Moyer .05 .02 .01
☐ 392 Greg Carmona .05 .02 .01
☐ 393 John Ericks .05 .02 .01
☐ 394 Bob Tewksbury .05 .02 .01
☐ 395 Jose Oquendo .05 .02 .01
☐ 396 Rheal Cormier .05 .02 .01
☐ 397 Mike Milchin .05 .02 .01
☐ 398 Ozzie Smith .25 .11 .03
☐ 399 Aaron Holbert .05 .02 .01
☐ 400 Jose DeLeon .05 .02 .01
☐ 401 Felix Jose .05 .02 .01
☐ 402 Juan Agosto .05 .02 .01
☐ 403 Pedro Guerrero .05 .02 .01
☐ 404 Todd Zeile .10 .05 .01
☐ 405 Gerald Perry .05 .02 .01
☐ 406 Donovan Osborne UER .15 .07 .02
(Card number is 410)
☐ 407 Bryn Smith .05 .02 .01
☐ 408 Bernard Gilkey .10 .05 .01
☐ 409 Rex Hudler .05 .02 .01
☐ 410 Thomson/Branca Shot .15 .07 .02
Bobby Thomson
Ralph Branca
(See also 406)
☐ 411 Lance Dickson .05 .02 .01
☐ 412 Danny Jackson .05 .02 .01
☐ 413 Jerome Walton .05 .02 .01
☐ 414 Sean Cheetham .05 .02 .01
☐ 415 Joe Girardi .10 .05 .01
☐ 416 Ryne Sandberg .25 .11 .03
☐ 417 Mike Harkey .05 .02 .01
☐ 418 George Bell .05 .02 .01
☐ 419 Rick Wilkins .05 .02 .01
☐ 420 Earl Cunningham .05 .02 .01
☐ 421 Heathcliff Slocumb .15 .07 .02
☐ 422 Mike Bielecki .05 .02 .01
☐ 423 Jessie Hollins .05 .02 .01
☐ 424 Shawon Dunston .05 .02 .01
☐ 425 Dave Smith .05 .02 .01
☐ 426 Greg Maddux .60 .25 .07
☐ 427 Jose Vizcaino .05 .02 .01
☐ 428 Luis Salazar .05 .02 .01
☐ 429 Andre Dawson .10 .05 .01
☐ 430 Rick Sutcliffe .05 .02 .01
☐ 431 Paul Assenmacher .05 .02 .01
☐ 432 Erik Pappas .05 .02 .01
☐ 433 Mark Grace .15 .07 .02
☐ 434 Dennis Martinez .10 .05 .01
☐ 435 Marquis Grissom .15 .07 .02
☐ 436 Wil Cordero .15 .07 .02
☐ 437 Tim Wallach .05 .02 .01
☐ 438 Brian Barnes .05 .02 .01
☐ 439 Barry Jones .05 .02 .01
☐ 440 Ivan Calderon .05 .02 .01
☐ 441 Stan Spencer .05 .02 .01
☐ 442 Larry Walker .15 .07 .02
☐ 443 Chris Haney .05 .02 .01
☐ 444 Hector Rivera .05 .02 .01
☐ 445 Delino DeShields .05 .02 .01
☐ 446 Andres Galarraga .15 .07 .02
☐ 447 Gilberto Reyes .05 .02 .01
☐ 448 Willie Greene .10 .05 .01
☐ 449 Greg Colbrunn .10 .05 .01
☐ 450 Rondell White .50 .23 .06
☐ 451 Steve Frey .05 .02 .01
☐ 452 Shane Andrews .15 .07 .02
☐ 453 Mike Fitzgerald .05 .02 .01
☐ 454 Spike Owen .05 .02 .01
☐ 455 Dave Martinez .05 .02 .01
☐ 456 Dennis Boyd .05 .02 .01
☐ 457 Eric Bullock .05 .02 .01
☐ 458 Reid Cornelius .05 .02 .01
☐ 459 Chris Nabholz .05 .02 .01
☐ 460 David Cone .10 .05 .01
☐ 461 Hubie Brooks .05 .02 .01
☐ 462 Sid Fernandez .05 .02 .01
☐ 463 Doug Simons .05 .02 .01
☐ 464 Howard Johnson .05 .02 .01
☐ 465 Chris Donnels .05 .02 .01
☐ 466 Anthony Young .05 .02 .01
☐ 467 Todd Hundley .15 .07 .02
☐ 468 Rick Cerone .05 .02 .01
☐ 469 Kevin Elster .05 .02 .01
☐ 470 Wally Whitehurst .05 .02 .01
☐ 471 Vince Coleman .05 .02 .01
☐ 472 Dwight Gooden .10 .05 .01
☐ 473 Charlie O'Brien .05 .02 .01
☐ 474 Jeromy Burnitz .10 .05 .01
☐ 475 John Franco .05 .02 .01
☐ 476 Daryl Boston .05 .02 .01
☐ 477 Frank Viola .05 .02 .01
☐ 478 D.J. Dozier .05 .02 .01
☐ 479 Kevin McReynolds .05 .02 .01
☐ 480 Tom Herr .05 .02 .01
☐ 481 Gregg Jefferies .10 .05 .01
☐ 482 Pete Schourek .15 .07 .02
☐ 483 Ron Darling .05 .02 .01
☐ 484 Dave Magadan .05 .02 .01
☐ 485 Andy Ashby .15 .07 .02
☐ 486 Dale Murphy .15 .07 .02
☐ 487 Von Hayes .05 .02 .01
☐ 488 Kim Batiste .05 .02 .01
☐ 489 Tony Longmire .05 .02 .01
☐ 490 Wally Backman .05 .02 .01
☐ 491 Jeff Jackson .05 .02 .01
☐ 492 Mickey Morandini .05 .02 .01
☐ 493 Darrel Akerfelds .05 .02 .01
☐ 494 Ricky Jordan .05 .02 .01
☐ 495 Randy Ready .05 .02 .01
☐ 496 Darrin Fletcher .05 .02 .01
☐ 497 Chuck Malone .05 .02 .01
☐ 498 Pat Combs .05 .02 .01
☐ 499 Dickie Thon .05 .02 .01
☐ 500 Roger McDowell .05 .02 .01
☐ 501 Len Dykstra .10 .05 .01
☐ 502 Joe Boever .05 .02 .01
☐ 503 John Kruk .10 .05 .01
☐ 504 Terry Mulholland .05 .02 .01
☐ 505 Wes Chamberlain .05 .02 .01
☐ 506 Mike Lieberthal .15 .07 .02
☐ 507 Darren Daulton .10 .05 .01
☐ 508 Charlie Hayes .05 .02 .01
☐ 509 John Smiley .05 .02 .01
☐ 510 Gary Varsho .05 .02 .01
☐ 511 Curt Wilkerson .05 .02 .01
☐ 512 Orlando Merced .15 .07 .02
☐ 513 Barry Bonds .25 .11 .03
☐ 514 Mike LaValliere .05 .02 .01
☐ 515 Doug Drabek .05 .02 .01
☐ 516 Gary Redus .05 .02 .01
☐ 517 William Pennyfeather .05 .02 .01
☐ 518 Randy Tomlin .05 .02 .01
☐ 519 Mike Zimmerman .05 .02 .01
☐ 520 Jeff King .10 .05 .01
☐ 521 Kurt Miller .05 .02 .01
☐ 522 Jay Bell .10 .05 .01
☐ 523 Bill Landrum .05 .02 .01
☐ 524 Zane Smith .05 .02 .01
☐ 525 Bobby Bonilla .10 .05 .01
☐ 526 Bob Walk .05 .02 .01
☐ 527 Austin Manahan .05 .02 .01
☐ 528 Joe Ausanio .05 .02 .01
☐ 529 Andy Van Slyke .10 .05 .01
☐ 530 Jose Lind .05 .02 .01
☐ 531 Carlos Garcia .15 .07 .02
☐ 532 Don Slaught .05 .02 .01
☐ 533 Gen.Colin Powell .75 .35 .09
☐ 534 Frank Bolick .05 .02 .01
☐ 535 Gary Scott .05 .02 .01
☐ 536 Nikco Riesgo .05 .02 .01
☐ 537 Reggie Sanders .50 .23 .06
☐ 538 Tim Howard .05 .02 .01
☐ 539 Ryan Bowen .05 .02 .01
☐ 540 Eric Anthony .05 .02 .01
☐ 541 Jim Deshaies .05 .02 .01
☐ 542 Tom Nevers .05 .02 .01
☐ 543 Ken Caminiti .15 .07 .02
☐ 544 Karl Rhodes .05 .02 .01
☐ 545 Xavier Hernandez .05 .02 .01
☐ 546 Mike Scott .05 .02 .01
☐ 547 Jeff Juden .05 .02 .01
☐ 548 Darryl Kile .05 .02 .01
☐ 549 Willie Ansley .05 .02 .01
☐ 550 Luis Gonzalez .15 .07 .02
☐ 551 Mike Simms .05 .02 .01
☐ 552 Mark Portugal .05 .02 .01
☐ 553 Jimmy Jones .05 .02 .01
☐ 554 Jim Clancy .05 .02 .01
☐ 555 Pete Harnisch .05 .02 .01
☐ 556 Craig Biggio .15 .07 .02
☐ 557 Eric Yelding .05 .02 .01
☐ 558 Dave Rohde .05 .02 .01
☐ 559 Casey Candaele .05 .02 .01
☐ 560 Curt Schilling .05 .02 .01
☐ 561 Steve Finley .10 .05 .01
☐ 562 Javier Ortiz .05 .02 .01
☐ 563 Andujar Cedeno .05 .02 .01
☐ 564 Rafael Ramirez .05 .02 .01
☐ 565 Kenny Lofton 2.00 .90 .25
☐ 566 Steve Avery .15 .07 .02
☐ 567 Lonnie Smith .05 .02 .01
☐ 568 Kent Mercker .05 .02 .01
☐ 569 Chipper Jones 4.00 1.80 .50
☐ 570 Terry Pendleton .10 .05 .01
☐ 571 Otis Nixon .05 .02 .01
☐ 572 Juan Berenguer .05 .02 .01
☐ 573 Charlie Leibrandt .05 .02 .01
☐ 574 David Justice .15 .07 .02
☐ 575 Keith Mitchell .05 .02 .01
☐ 576 Tom Glavine .15 .07 .02
☐ 577 Greg Olson .05 .02 .01
☐ 578 Rafael Belliard .05 .02 .01
☐ 579 Ben Rivera .05 .02 .01
☐ 580 John Smoltz .15 .07 .02
☐ 581 Tyler Houston .05 .02 .01
☐ 582 Mark Wohlers .40 .18 .05
☐ 583 Ron Gant .10 .05 .01
☐ 584 Ramon Caraballo .05 .02 .01
☐ 585 Sid Bream .05 .02 .01
☐ 586 Jeff Treadway .05 .02 .01
☐ 587 Javier Lopez .75 .35 .09
☐ 588 Deion Sanders .15 .07 .02
☐ 589 Mike Heath .05 .02 .01
☐ 590 Ryan Klesko 1.50 .70 .19
☐ 591 Bob Ojeda .05 .02 .01
☐ 592 Alfredo Griffin .05 .02 .01
☐ 593 Raul Mondesi 1.00 .45 .12
☐ 594 Greg Smith .05 .02 .01
☐ 595 Orel Hershiser .10 .05 .01
☐ 596 Juan Samuel .05 .02 .01
☐ 597 Brett Butler .10 .05 .01
☐ 598 Gary Carter .10 .05 .01
☐ 599 Stan Javier .05 .02 .01
☐ 600 Kal Daniels .05 .02 .01
☐ 601 Jamie McAndrew .05 .02 .01
☐ 602 Mike Sharperson .05 .02 .01
☐ 603 Jay Howell .05 .02 .01
☐ 604 Eric Karros .50 .23 .06
☐ 605 Tim Belcher .05 .02 .01
☐ 606 Dan Opperman .05 .02 .01
☐ 607 Lenny Harris .05 .02 .01
☐ 608 Tom Goodwin .10 .05 .01
☐ 609 Darryl Strawberry .10 .05 .01
☐ 610 Ramon Martinez .15 .07 .02
☐ 611 Kevin Gross .05 .02 .01
☐ 612 Zakary Shinall .05 .02 .01
☐ 613 Mike Scioscia .05 .02 .01
☐ 614 Eddie Murray .25 .11 .03
☐ 615 Ronnie Walden .05 .02 .01
☐ 616 Will Clark .15 .07 .02
☐ 617 Adam Hyzdu .05 .02 .01
☐ 618 Matt Williams .15 .07 .02
☐ 619 Don Robinson .05 .02 .01
☐ 620 Jeff Brantley .05 .02 .01
☐ 621 Greg Litton .05 .02 .01
☐ 622 Steve Decker .05 .02 .01
☐ 623 Robby Thompson .05 .02 .01
☐ 624 Mark Leonard .05 .02 .01
☐ 625 Kevin Bass .05 .02 .01
☐ 626 Scott Garrelts .05 .02 .01
☐ 627 Jose Uribe .05 .02 .01
☐ 628 Eric Gunderson .05 .02 .01
☐ 629 Steve Hosey .05 .02 .01
☐ 630 Trevor Wilson .05 .02 .01
☐ 631 Terry Kennedy .05 .02 .01
☐ 632 Dave Righetti .05 .02 .01
☐ 633 Kelly Downs .05 .02 .01
☐ 634 Johnny Ard .05 .02 .01
☐ 635 Eric Christopherson .05 .02 .01
☐ 636 Kevin Mitchell .10 .05 .01
☐ 637 John Burkett .10 .05 .01
☐ 638 Kevin Rogers .05 .02 .01
☐ 639 Bud Black .05 .02 .01
☐ 640 Willie McGee .05 .02 .01
☐ 641 Royce Clayton .15 .07 .02
☐ 642 Tony Fernandez .05 .02 .01
☐ 643 Ricky Bones .05 .02 .01
☐ 644 Thomas Howard .05 .02 .01
☐ 645 Dave Staton .05 .02 .01
☐ 646 Jim Presley .05 .02 .01
☐ 647 Tony Gwynn .40 .18 .05
☐ 648 Marty Barrett .05 .02 .01
☐ 649 Scott Coolbaugh .05 .02 .01
☐ 650 Craig Lefferts .05 .02 .01
☐ 651 Eddie Whitson .05 .02 .01
☐ 652 Oscar Azocar .05 .02 .01
☐ 653 Wes Gardner .05 .02 .01
☐ 654 Bip Roberts .05 .02 .01
☐ 655 Robbie Beckett .05 .02 .01
☐ 656 Benito Santiago .05 .02 .01
☐ 657 Greg W.Harris .05 .02 .01
☐ 658 Jerald Clark .05 .02 .01
☐ 659 Fred McGriff .15 .07 .02
☐ 660 Larry Andersen .05 .02 .01
☐ 661 Bruce Hurst .05 .02 .01
☐ 662 Steve Martin UER .05 .02 .01
Card said he pitched at Waterloo
He's an outfielder
☐ 663 Rafael Valdez .05 .02 .01
☐ 664 Paul Faries .05 .02 .01
☐ 665 Andy Benes .10 .05 .01
☐ 666 Randy Myers .10 .05 .01
☐ 667 Rob Dibble .05 .02 .01
☐ 668 Glenn Sutko .05 .02 .01
☐ 669 Glenn Braggs .05 .02 .01
☐ 670 Billy Hatcher .05 .02 .01
☐ 671 Joe Oliver .05 .02 .01
☐ 672 Freddy Benavides .05 .02 .01
☐ 673 Barry Larkin .15 .07 .02
☐ 674 Chris Sabo .05 .02 .01
☐ 675 Mariano Duncan .05 .02 .01
☐ 676 Chris Jones .05 .02 .01
☐ 677 Gino Minutelli .05 .02 .01
☐ 678 Reggie Jefferson .10 .05 .01
☐ 679 Jack Armstrong .05 .02 .01
☐ 680 Chris Hammond .05 .02 .01
☐ 681 Jose Rijo .05 .02 .01
☐ 682 Bill Doran .05 .02 .01
☐ 683 Terry Lee .05 .02 .01
☐ 684 Tom Browning .05 .02 .01
☐ 685 Paul O'Neill .10 .05 .01
☐ 686 Eric Davis .10 .05 .01
☐ 687 Dan Wilson .25 .11 .03
☐ 688 Ted Power .05 .02 .01
☐ 689 Tim Layana .05 .02 .01
☐ 690 Norm Charlton .05 .02 .01
☐ 691 Hal Morris .05 .02 .01
☐ 692 Rickey Henderson .15 .07 .02
☐ 693 Sam Militello .05 .02 .01
☐ 694 Matt Mieske .05 .02 .01
☐ 695 Paul Russo .05 .02 .01
☐ 696 Domingo Mota .05 .02 .01
☐ 697 Todd Guggiana .05 .02 .01
☐ 698 Marc Newfield .15 .07 .02
☐ 699 Checklist 1-122 .05 .02 .01
☐ 700 Checklist 123-244 .05 .02 .01
☐ 701 Checklist 245-366 .05 .02 .01
☐ 702 Checklist 367-471 .05 .02 .01
☐ 703 Checklist 472-593 .05 .02 .01
☐ 704 Checklist 594-704 .05 .02 .01

1992 Bowman

This 705-card standard-size set was issued in one comprehensive series. Unlike the previous Bowman issues, the 1992 set was radically upgraded to slick stock with gold foil subset cards in an attempt to reposition the brand as a premium level product. It initially stumbled out of the gate, but it's superior selection of prospects enabled it to eventually gain acceptance in the hobby and now stands as one of the more important issues of the 1990's. Cards were distributed in plastic wrap packs, retail jumbo packs and special 80-card retail carton packs. Card fronts feature posed and action color player photos on a UV-coated white card face. A gradated orange bar accented with black diagonal stripes carries the player's name at the bottom right corner. Interspersed throughout the set are 45 special cards with an identical front design except for a textured gold-foil border. The foil cards were inserted one per wax pack and two per jumbo (23 regular cards) pack. These foil cards feature past and present Team USA players and minor league POY Award winners. Each foil card has an extremely slight variation in that the photos are cropped differently. There is no additional value to either version. Some of the regular and special cards picture players in civilian clothing who are still in the farm system. Rookie Cards in this set include Garret Anderson, Carlos Delgado, Alex Gonzalez, Brian Jordan, Alex Ochoa, Mike Piazza, Manny Ramirez, Mariano Rivera and Michael Tucker.

	MINT	NRMT	EXC
COMPLETE SET (705)	300.00	135.00	38.00
COMMON CARD (1-705)	.15	.07	.02

☐ 1 Ivan Rodriguez 3.00 1.35 .35
☐ 2 Kirk McCaskill .15 .07 .02
☐ 3 Scott Livingstone .15 .07 .02
☐ 4 Salomon Torres .30 .14 .04
☐ 5 Carlos Hernandez .15 .07 .02
☐ 6 Dave Hollins .15 .07 .02
☐ 7 Scott Fletcher .15 .07 .02
☐ 8 Jorge Fabregas .30 .14 .04
☐ 9 Andujar Cedeno .15 .07 .02
☐ 10 Howard Johnson .15 .07 .02
☐ 11 Trevor Hoffman 1.50 .70 .19
☐ 12 Roberto Kelly .15 .07 .02
☐ 13 Gregg Jefferies .30 .14 .04
☐ 14 Marquis Grissom .30 .14 .04
☐ 15 Mike Ignasiak .15 .07 .02
☐ 16 Jack Morris .30 .14 .04
☐ 17 William Pennyfeather .15 .07 .02
☐ 18 Todd Stottlemyre .30 .14 .04
☐ 19 Chito Martinez .15 .07 .02
☐ 20 Roberto Alomar 1.50 .70 .19
☐ 21 Sam Militello .15 .07 .02
☐ 22 Hector Fajardo .15 .07 .02
☐ 23 Paul Quantrill .15 .07 .02
☐ 24 Chuck Knoblauch 2.00 .90 .25
☐ 25 Reggie Jefferson .30 .14 .04
☐ 26 Jeremy McGarity .15 .07 .02
☐ 27 Jerome Walton .15 .07 .02
☐ 28 Chipper Jones 40.00 18.00 5.00

☐ 29 Brian Barber	.30	.14	.04
☐ 30 Ron Darling	.15	.07	.02
☐ 31 Roberto Petagine	.30	.14	.04
☐ 32 Chuck Finley	.15	.07	.02
☐ 33 Edgar Martinez	.30	.14	.04
☐ 34 Napoleon Robinson	.15	.07	.02
☐ 35 Andy Van Slyke	.30	.14	.04
☐ 36 Bobby Thigpen	.15	.07	.02
☐ 37 Travis Fryman	.60	.25	.07
☐ 38 Eric Christopherson	.15	.07	.02
☐ 39 Terry Mulholland	.15	.07	.02
☐ 40 Darryl Strawberry	.30	.14	.04
☐ 41 Manny Alexander	.30	.14	.04
☐ 42 Tracy Sanders	.15	.07	.02
☐ 43 Pete Incaviglia	.15	.07	.02
☐ 44 Kim Batiste	.15	.07	.02
☐ 45 Frank Rodriguez	1.00	.45	.12
☐ 46 Greg Swindell	.15	.07	.02
☐ 47 Delino DeShields	.15	.07	.02
☐ 48 John Ericks	.15	.07	.02
☐ 49 Franklin Stubbs	.15	.07	.02
☐ 50 Tony Gwynn	3.00	1.35	.35
☐ 51 Clifton Garrett	.15	.07	.02
☐ 52 Mike Gardella	.15	.07	.02
☐ 53 Scott Erickson	.30	.14	.04
☐ 54 Gary Caraballo	.15	.07	.02
☐ 55 Jose Oliva	.30	.14	.04
☐ 56 Brook Fordyce	.15	.07	.02
☐ 57 Mark Whiten	.30	.14	.04
☐ 58 Joe Slusarski	.15	.07	.02
☐ 59 J.R. Phillips	.30	.14	.04
☐ 60 Barry Bonds	2.00	.90	.25
☐ 61 Bob Milacki	.15	.07	.02
☐ 62 Keith Mitchell	.15	.07	.02
☐ 63 Angel Miranda	.15	.07	.02
☐ 64 Raul Mondesi	10.00	4.50	1.25
☐ 65 Brian Koelling	.15	.07	.02
☐ 66 Brian McRae	.30	.14	.04
☐ 67 John Patterson	.15	.07	.02
☐ 68 John Wetteland	.30	.14	.04
☐ 69 Wilson Alvarez	.60	.25	.07
☐ 70 Wade Boggs	.60	.25	.07
☐ 71 Darryl Ratliff	.15	.07	.02
☐ 72 Jeff Jackson	.15	.07	.02
☐ 73 Jeremy Hernandez	.15	.07	.02
☐ 74 Darryl Hamilton	.15	.07	.02
☐ 75 Rafael Belliard	.15	.07	.02
☐ 76 Rick Trlicek	.15	.07	.02
☐ 77 Felipe Crespo	.30	.14	.04
☐ 78 Carney Lansford	.30	.14	.04
☐ 79 Ryan Long	.15	.07	.02
☐ 80 Kirby Puckett	3.00	1.35	.35
☐ 81 Earl Cunningham	.15	.07	.02
☐ 82 Pedro Martinez	2.50	1.10	.30
☐ 83 Scott Hatteberg	.15	.07	.02
☐ 84 Juan Gonzalez UER (65 doubles vs. Tigers)	6.00	2.70	.75
☐ 85 Robert Nutting	.15	.07	.02
☐ 86 Calvin Reese	2.00	.90	.25
☐ 87 Dave Silvestri	.15	.07	.02
☐ 88 Scott Ruffcorn	.30	.14	.04
☐ 89 Rick Aguilera	.15	.07	.02
☐ 90 Cecil Fielder	.30	.14	.04
☐ 91 Kirk Dressendorfer	.15	.07	.02
☐ 92 Jerry DiPoto	.15	.07	.02
☐ 93 Mike Felder	.15	.07	.02
☐ 94 Craig Paquette	.30	.14	.04
☐ 95 Elvin Paulino	.15	.07	.02
☐ 96 Donovan Osborne	.30	.14	.04
☐ 97 Hubie Brooks	.15	.07	.02
☐ 98 Derek Lowe	.30	.14	.04
☐ 99 David Zancanaro	.15	.07	.02
☐ 100 Ken Griffey Jr.	12.00	5.50	1.50
☐ 101 Todd Hundley	1.50	.70	.19
☐ 102 Mike Trombley	.15	.07	.02
☐ 103 Ricky Gutierrez	.15	.07	.02
☐ 104 Braulio Castillo	.15	.07	.02
☐ 105 Craig Lefferts	.15	.07	.02
☐ 106 Rick Sutcliffe	.15	.07	.02
☐ 107 Dean Palmer	.30	.14	.04
☐ 108 Henry Rodriguez	2.00	.90	.25
☐ 109 Mark Clark	.40	.18	.05
☐ 110 Kenny Lofton	12.00	5.50	1.50
☐ 111 Mark Carreon	.15	.07	.02
☐ 112 J.T. Bruett	.15	.07	.02
☐ 113 Gerald Williams	.15	.07	.02
☐ 114 Frank Thomas	10.00	4.50	1.25
☐ 115 Kevin Reimer	.15	.07	.02
☐ 116 Sammy Sosa	1.50	.70	.19
☐ 117 Mickey Tettleton	.15	.07	.02
☐ 118 Reggie Sanders	3.00	1.35	.35
☐ 119 Trevor Wilson	.15	.07	.02
☐ 120 Cliff Brantley	.15	.07	.02
☐ 121 Spike Owen	.15	.07	.02
☐ 122 Jeff Montgomery	.30	.14	.04
☐ 123 Alex Sutherland	.15	.07	.02
☐ 124 Brien Taylor	.30	.14	.04
☐ 125 Brian Williams	.15	.07	.02
☐ 126 Kevin Seitzer	.15	.07	.02
☐ 127 Carlos Delgado	10.00	4.50	1.25
☐ 128 Gary Scott	.15	.07	.02
☐ 129 Scott Cooper	.15	.07	.02
☐ 130 Domingo Jean	.15	.07	.02
☐ 131 Pat Mahomes	.15	.07	.02
☐ 132 Mike Boddicker	.15	.07	.02
☐ 133 Roberto Hernandez	.30	.14	.04
☐ 134 Dave Valle	.15	.07	.02
☐ 135 Kurt Stillwell	.15	.07	.02
☐ 136 Brad Pennington	.30	.14	.04
☐ 137 Jermaine Swinton	.30	.14	.04
☐ 138 Ryan Hawblitzel	.15	.07	.02
☐ 139 Tito Navarro	.15	.07	.02
☐ 140 Sandy Alomar	.30	.14	.04
☐ 141 Todd Benzinger	.15	.07	.02
☐ 142 Danny Jackson	.15	.07	.02
☐ 143 Melvin Nieves	2.00	.90	.25
☐ 144 Jim Campanis	.15	.07	.02
☐ 145 Luis Gonzalez	.30	.14	.04
☐ 146 Dave Doorneweerd	.15	.07	.02
☐ 147 Charlie Hayes	.15	.07	.02
☐ 148 Greg Maddux	6.00	2.70	.75
☐ 149 Brian Harper	.15	.07	.02
☐ 150 Brent Miller	.15	.07	.02
☐ 151 Shawn Estes	1.50	.70	.19
☐ 152 Mike Williams	.15	.07	.02
☐ 153 Charlie Hough	.15	.07	.02
☐ 154 Randy Myers	.30	.14	.04
☐ 155 Kevin Young	.15	.07	.02
☐ 156 Rick Wilkins	.15	.07	.02
☐ 157 Terry Shumpert	.15	.07	.02
☐ 158 Steve Karsay	.30	.14	.04
☐ 159 Gary DiSarcina	.15	.07	.02
☐ 160 Deion Sanders	.60	.25	.07
☐ 161 Tom Browning	.15	.07	.02
☐ 162 Dickie Thon	.15	.07	.02
☐ 163 Luis Mercedes	.15	.07	.02
☐ 164 Riccardo Ingram	.15	.07	.02
☐ 165 Tavo Alvarez	.30	.14	.04
☐ 166 Rickey Henderson	.60	.25	.07
☐ 167 Jaime Navarro	.15	.07	.02
☐ 168 Billy Ashley	3.00	1.35	.35
☐ 169 Phil Dauphin	.15	.07	.02
☐ 170 Ivan Cruz	.15	.07	.02
☐ 171 Harold Baines	.30	.14	.04
☐ 172 Bryan Harvey	.15	.07	.02
☐ 173 Alex Cole	.15	.07	.02
☐ 174 Curtis Shaw	.30	.14	.04
☐ 175 Matt Williams	.60	.25	.07
☐ 176 Felix Jose	.15	.07	.02
☐ 177 Sam Horn	.15	.07	.02
☐ 178 Randy Johnson	1.25	.55	.16
☐ 179 Ivan Calderon	.15	.07	.02
☐ 180 Steve Avery	.30	.14	.04
☐ 181 William Suero	.15	.07	.02
☐ 182 Bill Swift	.15	.07	.02
☐ 183 Howard Battle	.30	.14	.04
☐ 184 Ruben Amaro	.15	.07	.02
☐ 185 Jim Abbott	.15	.07	.02
☐ 186 Mike Fitzgerald	.15	.07	.02
☐ 187 Bruce Hurst	.15	.07	.02
☐ 188 Jeff Juden	.15	.07	.02
☐ 189 Jeromy Burnitz	.30	.14	.04
☐ 190 Dave Burba	.15	.07	.02
☐ 191 Kevin Brown	.30	.14	.04
☐ 192 Patrick Lennon	.15	.07	.02
☐ 193 Jeff McNeely	.15	.07	.02
☐ 194 Wil Cordero	2.00	.90	.25
☐ 195 Chili Davis	.30	.14	.04
☐ 196 Milt Cuyler	.15	.07	.02
☐ 197 Von Hayes	.15	.07	.02
☐ 198 Todd Revenig	.15	.07	.02
☐ 199 Joel Johnston	.15	.07	.02
☐ 200 Jeff Bagwell	5.00	2.20	.60
☐ 201 Alex Fernandez	.60	.25	.07
☐ 202 Todd Jones	.50	.23	.06
☐ 203 Charles Nagy	.30	.14	.04
☐ 204 Tim Raines	.60	.25	.07
☐ 205 Kevin Maas	.15	.07	.02
☐ 206 Julio Franco	.30	.14	.04
☐ 207 Randy Velarde	.15	.07	.02
☐ 208 Lance Johnson	.30	.14	.04
☐ 209 Scott Leius	.15	.07	.02
☐ 210 Derek Lee	.15	.07	.02
☐ 211 Joe Sondrini	.15	.07	.02
☐ 212 Royce Clayton	.30	.14	.04
☐ 213 Chris George	.15	.07	.02
☐ 214 Gary Sheffield	1.25	.55	.16
☐ 215 Mark Gubicza	.15	.07	.02
☐ 216 Mike Moore	.15	.07	.02
☐ 217 Rick Huisman	.15	.07	.02
☐ 218 Jeff Russell	.15	.07	.02
☐ 219 D.J. Dozier	.15	.07	.02
☐ 220 Dave Martinez	.15	.07	.02
☐ 221 Alan Newman	.15	.07	.02
☐ 222 Nolan Ryan	6.00	2.70	.75
☐ 223 Teddy Higuera	.15	.07	.02
☐ 224 Damon Buford	.30	.14	.04
☐ 225 Ruben Sierra	.30	.14	.04
☐ 226 Tom Nevers	.15	.07	.02
☐ 227 Tommy Greene	.15	.07	.02
☐ 228 Nigel Wilson	.30	.14	.04
☐ 229 John DeSilva	.15	.07	.02
☐ 230 Bobby Witt	.15	.07	.02
☐ 231 Greg Cadaret	.15	.07	.02
☐ 232 John Vander Wal	.15	.07	.02
☐ 233 Jack Clark	.30	.14	.04
☐ 234 Bill Doran	.15	.07	.02
☐ 235 Bobby Bonilla	.30	.14	.04
☐ 236 Steve Olin	.15	.07	.02
☐ 237 Derek Bell	1.50	.70	.19
☐ 238 David Cone	.30	.14	.04
☐ 239 Victor Cole	.15	.07	.02
☐ 240 Rod Bolton	.15	.07	.02
☐ 241 Tom Pagnozzi	.15	.07	.02
☐ 242 Rob Dibble	.15	.07	.02
☐ 243 Michael Carter	.15	.07	.02
☐ 244 Don Peters	.15	.07	.02
☐ 245 Mike LaValliere	.15	.07	.02
☐ 246 Joe Perona	.15	.07	.02
☐ 247 Mitch Williams	.15	.07	.02
☐ 248 Jay Buhner	.60	.25	.07
☐ 249 Andy Benes	.30	.14	.04
☐ 250 Alex Ochoa	6.00	2.70	.75
☐ 251 Greg Blosser	.15	.07	.02
☐ 252 Jack Armstrong	.15	.07	.02
☐ 253 Juan Samuel	.15	.07	.02
☐ 254 Terry Pendleton	.30	.14	.04
☐ 255 Ramon Martinez	.30	.14	.04
☐ 256 Rico Brogna	.30	.14	.04
☐ 257 John Smiley	.15	.07	.02
☐ 258 Carl Everett	.30	.14	.04
☐ 259 Tim Salmon	6.00	2.70	.75
☐ 260 Will Clark	.60	.25	.07
☐ 261 Ugueth Urbina	1.00	.45	.12
☐ 262 Jason Wood	.15	.07	.02
☐ 263 Dave Magadan	.15	.07	.02
☐ 264 Dante Bichette	.60	.25	.07
☐ 265 Jose DeLeon	.15	.07	.02
☐ 266 Mike Neill	.15	.07	.02
☐ 267 Paul O'Neill	.30	.14	.04
☐ 268 Anthony Young	.15	.07	.02
☐ 269 Greg W. Harris	.15	.07	.02
☐ 270 Todd Van Poppel	.15	.07	.02
☐ 271 Pedro Castellano	.15	.07	.02
☐ 272 Tony Phillips	.30	.14	.04
☐ 273 Mike Gallego	.15	.07	.02
☐ 274 Steve Cooke	.30	.14	.04
☐ 275 Robin Ventura	.30	.14	.04
☐ 276 Kevin Mitchell	.30	.14	.04
☐ 277 Doug Linton	.15	.07	.02
☐ 278 Robert Eenhoorn	.15	.07	.02
☐ 279 Gabe White	.30	.14	.04
☐ 280 Dave Stewart	.30	.14	.04
☐ 281 Mo Sanford	.15	.07	.02
☐ 282 Greg Perschke	.15	.07	.02
☐ 283 Kevin Flora	.15	.07	.02
☐ 284 Jeff Williams	.15	.07	.02
☐ 285 Keith Miller	.15	.07	.02
☐ 286 Andy Ashby	.30	.14	.04
☐ 287 Doug Dascenzo	.15	.07	.02
☐ 288 Eric Karros	3.00	1.35	.35
☐ 289 Glenn Murray	.30	.14	.04
☐ 290 Troy Percival	1.50	.70	.19
☐ 291 Orlando Merced	.30	.14	.04
☐ 292 Peter Hoy	.15	.07	.02
☐ 293 Tony Fernandez	.15	.07	.02
☐ 294 Juan Guzman	.30	.14	.04
☐ 295 Jesse Barfield	.15	.07	.02
☐ 296 Sid Fernandez	.15	.07	.02
☐ 297 Scott Cepicky	.15	.07	.02
☐ 298 Garret Anderson	4.00	1.80	.50
☐ 299 Cal Eldred	.15	.07	.02
☐ 300 Ryne Sandberg	2.00	.90	.25
☐ 301 Jim Gantner	.15	.07	.02
☐ 302 Mariano Rivera	5.00	2.20	.60
☐ 303 Ron Lockett	.15	.07	.02
☐ 304 Jose Offerman	.15	.07	.02
☐ 305 Denny Martinez	.30	.14	.04
☐ 306 Luis Ortiz	.30	.14	.04
☐ 307 David Howard	.15	.07	.02
☐ 308 Russ Springer	.15	.07	.02
☐ 309 Chris Howard	.15	.07	.02
☐ 310 Kyle Abbott	.15	.07	.02
☐ 311 Aaron Sele	1.00	.45	.12
☐ 312 David Justice	1.25	.55	.16
☐ 313 Pete O'Brien	.15	.07	.02
☐ 314 Greg Hansell	.15	.07	.02
☐ 315 Dave Winfield	.60	.25	.07
☐ 316 Lance Dickson	.15	.07	.02
☐ 317 Eric King	.15	.07	.02
☐ 318 Vaughn Eshelman	.30	.14	.04
☐ 319 Tim Belcher	.15	.07	.02
☐ 320 Andres Galarraga	.60	.25	.07
☐ 321 Scott Bullett	.15	.07	.02
☐ 322 Doug Strange	.15	.07	.02
☐ 323 Jerald Clark	.15	.07	.02
☐ 324 Dave Righetti	.15	.07	.02
☐ 325 Greg Hibbard	.15	.07	.02
☐ 326 Eric Hillman	.15	.07	.02
☐ 327 Shane Reynolds	3.00	1.35	.35
☐ 328 Chris Hammond	.15	.07	.02
☐ 329 Albert Belle	4.00	1.80	.50
☐ 330 Rich Becker	1.00	.45	.12
☐ 331 Eddie Williams	.15	.07	.02
☐ 332 Donald Harris	.15	.07	.02
☐ 333 Dave Smith	.15	.07	.02
☐ 334 Steve Fireovid	.15	.07	.02
☐ 335 Steve Buechele	.15	.07	.02
☐ 336 Mike Schooler	.15	.07	.02
☐ 337 Kevin McReynolds	.15	.07	.02
☐ 338 Hensley Meulens	.15	.07	.02
☐ 339 Benji Gil	1.00	.45	.12
☐ 340 Don Mattingly	4.00	1.80	.50
☐ 341 Alvin Davis	.15	.07	.02
☐ 342 Alan Mills	.15	.07	.02
☐ 343 Kelly Downs	.15	.07	.02
☐ 344 Leo Gomez	.15	.07	.02
☐ 345 Tarrik Brock	.15	.07	.02
☐ 346 Ryan Turner	.15	.07	.02
☐ 347 John Smoltz	1.25	.55	.16
☐ 348 Bill Sampen	.15	.07	.02
☐ 349 Paul Byrd	.15	.07	.02
☐ 350 Mike Bordick	.30	.14	.04
☐ 351 Jose Lind	.15	.07	.02
☐ 352 David Wells	.15	.07	.02
☐ 353 Barry Larkin	.60	.25	.07
☐ 354 Bruce Ruffin	.15	.07	.02
☐ 355 Luis Rivera	.15	.07	.02
☐ 356 Sid Bream	.15	.07	.02
☐ 357 Julian Vasquez	.15	.07	.02
☐ 358 Jason Bere	.30	.14	.04
☐ 359 Ben McDonald	.15	.07	.02
☐ 360 Scott Stahoviak	.60	.25	.07
☐ 361 Kirt Manwaring	.15	.07	.02
☐ 362 Jeff Johnson	.15	.07	.02
☐ 363 Rob Deer	.15	.07	.02
☐ 364 Tony Pena	.15	.07	.02
☐ 365 Melido Perez	.15	.07	.02
☐ 366 Clay Parker	.15	.07	.02
☐ 367 Dale Sveum	.15	.07	.02
☐ 368 Mike Scioscia	.15	.07	.02
☐ 369 Roger Salkeld	.15	.07	.02
☐ 370 Mike Stanley	.15	.07	.02
☐ 371 Jack McDowell	.30	.14	.04
☐ 372 Tim Wallach	.15	.07	.02
☐ 373 Billy Ripken	.15	.07	.02
☐ 374 Mike Christopher	.15	.07	.02
☐ 375 Paul Molitor	1.50	.70	.19
☐ 376 Dave Stieb	.15	.07	.02
☐ 377 Pedro Guerrero	.15	.07	.02
☐ 378 Russ Swan	.15	.07	.02
☐ 379 Bob Ojeda	.15	.07	.02
☐ 380 Donn Pall	.15	.07	.02
☐ 381 Eddie Zosky	.15	.07	.02
☐ 382 Darnell Coles	.15	.07	.02
☐ 383 Tom Smith	.15	.07	.02
☐ 384 Mark McGwire	2.50	1.10	.30
☐ 385 Gary Carter	.30	.14	.04
☐ 386 Rich Amaral	.15	.07	.02
☐ 387 Alan Embree	.15	.07	.02
☐ 388 Jonathan Hurst	.15	.07	.02
☐ 389 Bobby Jones	4.00	1.80	.50
☐ 390 Rico Rossy	.15	.07	.02
☐ 391 Dan Smith	.15	.07	.02
☐ 392 Terry Steinbach	.30	.14	.04
☐ 393 Jon Farrell	.15	.07	.02
☐ 394 Dave Anderson	.15	.07	.02
☐ 395 Benny Santiago	.15	.07	.02
☐ 396 Mark Wohlers	1.50	.70	.19
☐ 397 Mo Vaughn	4.00	1.80	.50
☐ 398 Randy Kramer	.15	.07	.02
☐ 399 John Jaha	1.50	.70	.19
☐ 400 Cal Ripken	6.00	2.70	.75
☐ 401 Ryan Bowen	.15	.07	.02
☐ 402 Tim McIntosh	.15	.07	.02
☐ 403 Bernard Gilkey	.30	.14	.04
☐ 404 Junior Felix	.15	.07	.02
☐ 405 Cris Colon	.15	.07	.02
☐ 406 Marc Newfield	2.00	.90	.25
☐ 407 Bernie Williams	3.00	1.35	.35
☐ 408 Jay Howell	.15	.07	.02
☐ 409 Zane Smith	.15	.07	.02
☐ 410 Jeff Shaw	.15	.07	.02
☐ 411 Kerry Woodson	.15	.07	.02
☐ 412 Wes Chamberlain	.15	.07	.02
☐ 413 Dave Mlicki	.15	.07	.02
☐ 414 Benny Distefano	.15	.07	.02
☐ 415 Kevin Rogers	.15	.07	.02
☐ 416 Tim Naehring	.30	.14	.04
☐ 417 Clemente Nunez	1.00	.45	.12
☐ 418 Luis Sojo	.15	.07	.02
☐ 419 Kevin Ritz	.15	.07	.02
☐ 420 Omar Olivares	.15	.07	.02
☐ 421 Manuel Lee	.15	.07	.02
☐ 422 Julio Valera	.15	.07	.02
☐ 423 Omar Vizquel	.30	.14	.04
☐ 424 Darren Burton	.30	.14	.04
☐ 425 Mel Hall	.15	.07	.02
☐ 426 Dennis Powell	.15	.07	.02
☐ 427 Lee Stevens	.15	.07	.02
☐ 428 Glenn Davis	.15	.07	.02
☐ 429 Willie Greene	.30	.14	.04
☐ 430 Kevin Wickander	.15	.07	.02
☐ 431 Dennis Eckersley	.30	.14	.04
☐ 432 Joe Orsulak	.15	.07	.02
☐ 433 Eddie Murray	2.00	.90	.25
☐ 434 Matt Stairs	.15	.07	.02
☐ 435 Wally Joyner	.30	.14	.04
☐ 436 Rondell White	6.00	2.70	.75
☐ 437 Rob Maurer	.15	.07	.02
☐ 438 Joe Redfield	.15	.07	.02
☐ 439 Mark Lewis	.15	.07	.02
☐ 440 Darren Daulton	.30	.14	.04
☐ 441 Mike Henneman	.15	.07	.02
☐ 442 John Cangelosi	.15	.07	.02
☐ 443 Vince Moore	.15	.07	.02
☐ 444 John Wehner	.15	.07	.02
☐ 445 Kent Hrbek	.30	.14	.04
☐ 446 Mark McLemore	.15	.07	.02
☐ 447 Bill Wegman	.15	.07	.02

☐ 448 Robby Thompson .15 .07 .02
☐ 449 Mark Anthony .15 .07 .02
☐ 450 Archi Cianfrocco .15 .07 .02
☐ 451 Johnny Ruffin .15 .07 .02
☐ 452 Javier Lopez 8.00 3.60 1.00
☐ 453 Greg Gohr .15 .07 .02
☐ 454 Tim Scott .15 .07 .02
☐ 455 Stan Belinda .15 .07 .02
☐ 456 Darrin Jackson .15 .07 .02
☐ 457 Chris Gardner .15 .07 .02
☐ 458 Esteban Beltre .15 .07 .02
☐ 459 Phil Plantier .30 .14 .04
☐ 460 Jim Thome 15.00 6.75 1.85
☐ 461 Mike Piazza 60.00 27.00 7.50
☐ 462 Matt Sinatro .15 .07 .02
☐ 463 Scott Servais .15 .07 .02
☐ 464 Brian Jordan 6.00 2.70 .75
☐ 465 Doug Drabek .15 .07 .02
☐ 466 Carl Willis .15 .07 .02
☐ 467 Bret Barberie .15 .07 .02
☐ 468 Hal Morris .15 .07 .02
☐ 469 Steve Sax .15 .07 .02
☐ 470 Jerry Willard .15 .07 .02
☐ 471 Dan Wilson .30 .14 .04
☐ 472 Chris Hoiles .15 .07 .02
☐ 473 Rheal Cormier .15 .07 .02
☐ 474 John Morris .15 .07 .02
☐ 475 Jeff Reardon .30 .14 .04
☐ 476 Mark Leiter .15 .07 .02
☐ 477 Tom Gordon .15 .07 .02
☐ 478 Kent Bottenfield .15 .07 .02
☐ 479 Gene Larkin .15 .07 .02
☐ 480 Dwight Gooden .30 .14 .04
☐ 481 B.J. Surhoff .30 .14 .04
☐ 482 Andy Stankiewicz .15 .07 .02
☐ 483 Tino Martinez .30 .14 .04
☐ 484 Craig Biggio .30 .14 .04
☐ 485 Denny Neagle 1.50 .70 .19
☐ 486 Rusty Meacham .15 .07 .02
☐ 487 Kal Daniels .15 .07 .02
☐ 488 Dave Henderson .15 .07 .02
☐ 489 Tim Costo .15 .07 .02
☐ 490 Doug Davis .15 .07 .02
☐ 491 Frank Viola .15 .07 .02
☐ 492 Cory Snyder .15 .07 .02
☐ 493 Chris Martin .15 .07 .02
☐ 494 Dion James .15 .07 .02
☐ 495 Randy Tomlin .15 .07 .02
☐ 496 Greg Vaughn .30 .14 .04
☐ 497 Dennis Cook .15 .07 .02
☐ 498 Rosario Rodriguez .15 .07 .02
☐ 499 Dave Staton .15 .07 .02
☐ 500 George Brett 3.00 1.35 .35
☐ 501 Brian Barnes .15 .07 .02
☐ 502 Butch Henry .15 .07 .02
☐ 503 Harold Reynolds .15 .07 .02
☐ 504 David Nied .30 .14 .04
☐ 505 Lee Smith .30 .14 .04
☐ 506 Steve Chitren .15 .07 .02
☐ 507 Ken Hill .30 .14 .04
☐ 508 Robbie Beckett .15 .07 .02
☐ 509 Troy Afenir .15 .07 .02
☐ 510 Kelly Gruber .15 .07 .02
☐ 511 Bret Boone .60 .25 .07
☐ 512 Jeff Branson .15 .07 .02
☐ 513 Mike Jackson .15 .07 .02
☐ 514 Pete Harnisch .15 .07 .02
☐ 515 Chad Kreuter .15 .07 .02
☐ 516 Joe Vitko .15 .07 .02
☐ 517 Orel Hershiser .30 .14 .04
☐ 518 John Doherty .15 .07 .02
☐ 519 Jay Bell .30 .14 .04
☐ 520 Mark Langston .30 .14 .04
☐ 521 Dann Howitt .15 .07 .02
☐ 522 Bobby Reed .15 .07 .02
☐ 523 Roberto Munoz .15 .07 .02
☐ 524 Todd Ritchie .30 .14 .04
☐ 525 Bip Roberts .15 .07 .02
☐ 526 Pat Listach .30 .14 .04
☐ 527 Scott Brosius .15 .07 .02
☐ 528 John Roper .30 .14 .04
☐ 529 Phil Hiatt .30 .14 .04
☐ 530 Denny Walling .15 .07 .02
☐ 531 Carlos Baerga .30 .14 .04
☐ 532 Manny Ramirez 25.00 11.00 3.10
☐ 533 Pat Clements UER .15 .07 .02
(Mistakenly numbered 553)
☐ 534 Ron Gant .30 .14 .04
☐ 535 Pat Kelly .15 .07 .02
☐ 536 Billy Spiers .15 .07 .02
☐ 537 Darren Reed .15 .07 .02
☐ 538 Ken Caminiti .60 .25 .07
☐ 539 Butch Huskey 2.50 1.10 .30
☐ 540 Matt Nokes .15 .07 .02
☐ 541 John Kruk .30 .14 .04
☐ 542 John Jaha FOIL .60 .25 .07
☐ 543 Justin Thompson 1.25 .55 .16
☐ 544 Steve Hosey .15 .07 .02
☐ 545 Joe Kmak .15 .07 .02
☐ 546 John Franco .15 .07 .02
☐ 547 Devon White .30 .14 .04
☐ 548 Elston Hansen FOIL .15 .07 .02
☐ 549 Ryan Klesko 12.00 5.50 1.50
☐ 550 Danny Tartabull .15 .07 .02
☐ 551 Frank Thomas FOIL 12.00 5.50 1.50

☐ 552 Kevin Tapani .15 .07 .02
☐ 553 Willie Banks .15 .07 .02
(See also 533)
☐ 554 B.J. Wallace FOIL .30 .14 .04
☐ 555 Orlando Miller .50 .23 .06
☐ 556 Mark Smith .30 .14 .04
☐ 557 Tim Wallach FOIL .15 .07 .02
☐ 558 Bill Gullickson .15 .07 .02
☐ 559 Derek Bell FOIL .60 .25 .07
☐ 560 Joe Randa FOIL .60 .25 .07
☐ 561 Frank Seminara .15 .07 .02
☐ 562 Mark Gardner .15 .07 .02
☐ 563 Rick Greene FOIL .15 .07 .02
☐ 564 Gary Gaetti .30 .14 .04
☐ 565 Ozzie Guillen .15 .07 .02
☐ 566 Charles Nagy FOIL .30 .14 .04
☐ 567 Mike Milchin .15 .07 .02
☐ 568 Ben Shelton .15 .07 .02
☐ 569 Chris Roberts FOIL .30 .14 .04
☐ 570 Ellis Burks .30 .14 .04
☐ 571 Scott Scudder .15 .07 .02
☐ 572 Jim Abbott FOIL .15 .07 .02
☐ 573 Joe Carter .30 .14 .04
☐ 574 Steve Finley .30 .14 .04
☐ 575 Jim Olander FOIL .15 .07 .02
☐ 576 Carlos Garcia .30 .14 .04
☐ 577 Gregg Olson .15 .07 .02
☐ 578 Greg Swindell FOIL .15 .07 .02
☐ 579 Matt Williams FOIL .60 .25 .07
☐ 580 Mark Grace .60 .25 .07
☐ 581 Howard House FOIL .15 .07 .02
☐ 582 Luis Polonia .15 .07 .02
☐ 583 Erik Hanson .15 .07 .02
☐ 584 Salomon Torres FOIL .30 .14 .04
☐ 585 Carlton Fisk .60 .25 .07
☐ 586 Bret Saberhagen .30 .14 .04
☐ 587 Chad McConnell FOIL .30 .14 .04
☐ 588 Jimmy Key .30 .14 .04
☐ 589 Mike Macfarlane .15 .07 .02
☐ 590 Barry Bonds FOIL 2.00 .90 .25
☐ 591 Jamie McAndrew .15 .07 .02
☐ 592 Shane Mack .15 .07 .02
☐ 593 Kerwin Moore .15 .07 .02
☐ 594 Joe Oliver .15 .07 .02
☐ 595 Chris Sabo .15 .07 .02
☐ 596 Alex Gonzalez 4.00 1.80 .50
☐ 597 Brett Butler .30 .14 .04
☐ 598 Mark Hutton .15 .07 .02
☐ 599 Andy Benes FOIL .30 .14 .04
☐ 600 Jose Canseco .60 .25 .07
☐ 601 Darryl Kile .15 .07 .02
☐ 602 Matt Stairs FOIL .15 .07 .02
☐ 603 Robert Butler FOIL .30 .14 .04
☐ 604 Willie McGee .15 .07 .02
☐ 605 Jack McDowell FOIL .30 .14 .04
☐ 606 Tom Candiotti .15 .07 .02
☐ 607 Ed Martel .15 .07 .02
☐ 608 Matt Mieske FOIL .30 .14 .04
☐ 609 Darrin Fletcher .15 .07 .02
☐ 610 Rafael Palmeiro .60 .25 .07
☐ 611 Bill Swift FOIL .15 .07 .02
☐ 612 Mike Mussina 2.50 1.10 .30
☐ 613 Vince Coleman .15 .07 .02
☐ 614 Scott Cepicky FOIL UER .15 .07 .02
(Bats: LEFLT)
☐ 615 Mike Greenwell .15 .07 .02
☐ 616 Kevin McGehee .15 .07 .02
☐ 617 Jeffrey Hammonds FOIL 1.50 .70 .19
☐ 618 Scott Taylor .15 .07 .02
☐ 619 Dave Otto .15 .07 .02
☐ 620 Mark McGwire FOIL 2.50 1.10 .30
☐ 621 Kevin Tatar .15 .07 .02
☐ 622 Steve Farr .15 .07 .02
☐ 623 Ryan Klesko FOIL 2.50 1.10 .30
☐ 624 Dave Fleming .15 .07 .02
☐ 625 Andre Dawson .30 .14 .04
☐ 626 Tino Martinez FOIL .30 .14 .04
☐ 627 Chad Curtis .60 .25 .07
☐ 628 Mickey Morandini .15 .07 .02
☐ 629 Gregg Olson FOIL .15 .07 .02
☐ 630 Lou Whitaker .30 .14 .04
☐ 631 Arthur Rhodes .15 .07 .02
☐ 632 Brandon Wilson .15 .07 .02
☐ 633 Lance Jennings .15 .07 .02
☐ 634 Allen Watson .30 .14 .04
☐ 635 Len Dykstra .30 .14 .04
☐ 636 Joe Girardi .15 .07 .02
☐ 637 Kiki Hernandez FOIL .15 .07 .02
☐ 638 Mike Hampton 1.25 .55 .16
☐ 639 Al Osuna .15 .07 .02
☐ 640 Kevin Appier .30 .14 .04
☐ 641 Rick Helling FOIL .30 .14 .04
☐ 642 Jody Reed .15 .07 .02
☐ 643 Ray Lankford 1.25 .55 .16
☐ 644 John Olerud .30 .14 .04
☐ 645 Paul Molitor FOIL 1.50 .70 .19
☐ 646 Pat Borders .15 .07 .02
☐ 647 Mike Morgan .15 .07 .02
☐ 648 Larry Walker .60 .25 .07
☐ 649 Pedro Castellano FOIL .15 .07 .02
☐ 650 Fred McGriff .60 .25 .07
☐ 651 Walt Weiss .15 .07 .02
☐ 652 Calvin Murray FOIL .30 .14 .04
☐ 653 Dave Nilsson .30 .14 .04
☐ 654 Greg Pirkl .15 .07 .02

☐ 655 Robin Ventura FOIL .30 .14 .04
☐ 656 Mark Portugal .15 .07 .02
☐ 657 Roger McDowell .15 .07 .02
☐ 658 Rick Hirtensteiner FOIL .15 .07 .02
☐ 659 Glenallen Hill .15 .07 .02
☐ 660 Greg Gagne .15 .07 .02
☐ 661 Charles Johnson FOIL 5.00 2.20 .60
☐ 662 Brian Hunter .15 .07 .02
☐ 663 Mark Lemke .15 .07 .02
☐ 664 Tim Belcher FOIL .15 .07 .02
☐ 665 Rich DeLucia .15 .07 .02
☐ 666 Bob Walk .15 .07 .02
☐ 667 Joe Carter FOIL .75 .35 .09
☐ 668 Jose Guzman .15 .07 .02
☐ 669 Otis Nixon .15 .07 .02
☐ 670 Phil Nevin FOIL .30 .14 .04
☐ 671 Eric Davis .30 .14 .04
☐ 672 Damion Easley .30 .14 .04
☐ 673 Will Clark FOIL .60 .25 .07
☐ 674 Mark Kiefer .15 .07 .02
☐ 675 Ozzie Smith 2.00 .90 .25
☐ 676 Manny Ramirez FOIL 5.00 2.20 .60
☐ 677 Gregg Olson .15 .07 .02
☐ 678 Cliff Floyd 2.50 1.10 .30
☐ 679 Duane Singleton .30 .14 .04
☐ 680 Jose Rijo .15 .07 .02
☐ 681 Willie Randolph .30 .14 .04
☐ 682 Michael Tucker FOIL 3.00 1.35 .35
☐ 683 Darren Lewis .15 .07 .02
☐ 684 Dale Murphy .60 .25 .07
☐ 685 Mike Pagliarulo .15 .07 .02
☐ 686 Paul Miller .15 .07 .02
☐ 687 Mike Robertson .15 .07 .02
☐ 688 Mike Devereaux .15 .07 .02
☐ 689 Pedro Astacio .30 .14 .04
☐ 690 Alan Trammell .30 .14 .04
☐ 691 Roger Clemens 1.50 .70 .19
☐ 692 Bud Black .15 .07 .02
☐ 693 Turk Wendell .30 .14 .04
☐ 694 Barry Larkin FOIL .60 .25 .07
☐ 695 Todd Zeile .15 .07 .02
☐ 696 Pat Hentgen 2.50 1.10 .30
☐ 697 Eddie Taubensee .15 .07 .02
☐ 698 Guillermo Velasquez .15 .07 .02
☐ 699 Tom Glavine .60 .25 .07
☐ 700 Robin Yount .60 .25 .07
☐ 701 Checklist 1-141 .15 .07 .02
☐ 702 Checklist 142-282 .15 .07 .02
☐ 703 Checklist 283-423 .15 .07 .02
☐ 704 Checklist 424-564 .15 .07 .02
☐ 705 Checklist 565-705 .15 .07 .02

1993 Bowman

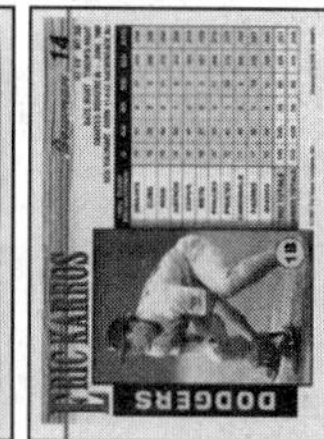

This 708-card standard-size set was issued in one series and features one of the more comprehensive selection of prospects and rookies available that year. Cards were distributed in 14-card plastic wrapped packs and jumbo packs. Each 14-card pack contained one silver foil bordered subset card. The basic issue card fronts feature white-bordered color action player photos. The player's name appears in white lettering at the bottom right, with his last name printed on an ocher rectangle. The 48 foil subset cards (339-374 and 693-704) feature sixteen 1992 MVPs of the Minor Leagues, top prospects and a few father/son combinations. Rookie Cards in this set include James Baldwin, Trey Beamon, Roger Cedeno, Danny Clyburn, Marty Cordova, Brian L. Hunter, Derek Jeter, Jason Kendall and Andy Pettite.

	MINT	NRMT	EXC
COMPLETE SET (708)	70.00	32.00	8.75
COMMON CARD (1-708)	.10	.05	.01

☐ 1 Glenn Davis .10 .05 .01
☐ 2 Hector Roa .10 .05 .01
☐ 3 Ken Ryan .10 .05 .01
☐ 4 Derek Wallace .10 .05 .01
☐ 5 Jorge Fabregas .25 .11 .03
☐ 6 Joe Oliver .10 .05 .01
☐ 7 Brandon Wilson .10 .05 .01
☐ 8 Mark Thompson .25 .11 .03
☐ 9 Tracy Sanders .10 .05 .01
☐ 10 Rich Renteria .10 .05 .01
☐ 11 Lou Whitaker .25 .11 .03
☐ 12 Brian Hunter 2.00 .90 .25
☐ 13 Joe Vitiello .25 .11 .03
☐ 14 Eric Karros .50 .23 .06
☐ 15 Joe Kmak .10 .05 .01
☐ 16 Tavo Alvarez .10 .05 .01
☐ 17 Steve Dunn .25 .11 .03
☐ 18 Tony Fernandez .10 .05 .01
☐ 19 Melido Perez .10 .05 .01
☐ 20 Mike Lieberthal .10 .05 .01

☐ 21 Terry Steinbach .25 .11 .03
☐ 22 Stan Belinda .10 .05 .01
☐ 23 Jay Buhner .50 .23 .06
☐ 24 Allen Watson .10 .05 .01
☐ 25 Daryl Henderson .10 .05 .01
☐ 26 Ray McDavid .25 .11 .03
☐ 27 Shawn Green .75 .35 .09
☐ 28 Bud Black .10 .05 .01
☐ 29 Sherman Obando .10 .05 .01
☐ 30 Mike Hostetler .10 .05 .01
☐ 31 Nate Minchey .25 .11 .03
☐ 32 Randy Myers .25 .11 .03
☐ 33 Brian Grebeck .10 .05 .01
☐ 34 John Roper .10 .05 .01
☐ 35 Larry Thomas .10 .05 .01
☐ 36 Alex Cole .10 .05 .01
☐ 37 Tom Kramer .10 .05 .01
☐ 38 Matt Whisenant .10 .05 .01
☐ 39 Chris Gomez .25 .11 .03
☐ 40 Luis Gonzalez .10 .05 .01
☐ 41 Kevin Appier .25 .11 .03
☐ 42 Omar Daal .25 .11 .03
☐ 43 Duane Singleton .10 .05 .01
☐ 44 Bill Risley .10 .05 .01
☐ 45 Pat Meares .25 .11 .03
☐ 46 Butch Huskey .50 .23 .06
☐ 47 Bobby Munoz .10 .05 .01
☐ 48 Juan Bell .10 .05 .01
☐ 49 Scott Lydy .10 .05 .01
☐ 50 Dennis Moeller .10 .05 .01
☐ 51 Marc Newfield .25 .11 .03
☐ 52 Tripp Cromer .10 .05 .01
☐ 53 Kurt Miller .10 .05 .01
☐ 54 Jim Pena .10 .05 .01
☐ 55 Juan Guzman .25 .11 .03
☐ 56 Matt Williams .50 .23 .06
☐ 57 Harold Reynolds .10 .05 .01
☐ 58 Donnie Elliott .10 .05 .01
☐ 59 Jon Shave .10 .05 .01
☐ 60 Kevin Roberson .10 .05 .01
☐ 61 Hilly Hathaway .10 .05 .01
☐ 62 Jose Rijo .10 .05 .01
☐ 63 Kerry Taylor .10 .05 .01
☐ 64 Ryan Hawblitzel .10 .05 .01
☐ 65 Glenallen Hill .10 .05 .01
☐ 66 Ramon Martinez .25 .11 .03
☐ 67 Travis Fryman .25 .11 .03
☐ 68 Tom Nevers .10 .05 .01
☐ 69 Phil Hiatt .10 .05 .01
☐ 70 Tim Wallach .10 .05 .01
☐ 71 B.J. Surhoff .25 .11 .03
☐ 72 Rondell White .50 .23 .06
☐ 73 Denny Hocking .25 .11 .03
☐ 74 Mike Oquist .10 .05 .01
☐ 75 Paul O'Neill .25 .11 .03
☐ 76 Willie Banks .10 .05 .01
☐ 77 Bob Welch .10 .05 .01
☐ 78 Jose Sandoval .10 .05 .01
☐ 79 Bill Haselman .10 .05 .01
☐ 80 Rheal Cormier .10 .05 .01
☐ 81 Dean Palmer .25 .11 .03
☐ 82 Pat Gomez .10 .05 .01
☐ 83 Steve Karsay .25 .11 .03
☐ 84 Carl Hanselman .10 .05 .01
☐ 85 T.R. Lewis .10 .05 .01
☐ 86 Chipper Jones 4.00 1.80 .50
☐ 87 Scott Hatteberg .10 .05 .01
☐ 88 Greg Hibbard .10 .05 .01
☐ 89 Lance Painter .10 .05 .01
☐ 90 Chad Mottola .25 .11 .03
☐ 91 Jason Bere .25 .11 .03
☐ 92 Dante Bichette .50 .23 .06
☐ 93 Sandy Alomar Jr. .25 .11 .03
☐ 94 Carl Everett .25 .11 .03
☐ 95 Danny Bautista .25 .11 .03
☐ 96 Steve Finley .25 .11 .03
☐ 97 David Cone .25 .11 .03
☐ 98 Todd Hollandsworth 2.00 .90 .25
☐ 99 Matt Mieske .25 .11 .03
☐ 100 Larry Walker .50 .23 .06
☐ 101 Shane Mack .10 .05 .01
☐ 102 Aaron Ledesma .10 .05 .01
☐ 103 Andy Pettite 6.00 2.70 .75
☐ 104 Kevin Stocker .25 .11 .03
☐ 105 Mike Mohler .10 .05 .01
☐ 106 Tony Menendez .10 .05 .01
☐ 107 Derek Lowe .25 .11 .03
☐ 108 Basil Shabazz .10 .05 .01
☐ 109 Dan Smith .10 .05 .01
☐ 110 Scott Sanders .10 .05 .01
☐ 111 Todd Stottlemyre .25 .11 .03
☐ 112 Benji Simonton .10 .05 .01
☐ 113 Rick Sutcliffe .10 .05 .01
☐ 114 Lee Heath .10 .05 .01
☐ 115 Jeff Russell .10 .05 .01
☐ 116 Dave Stevens .25 .11 .03
☐ 117 Mark Holzemer .10 .05 .01
☐ 118 Tim Belcher .10 .05 .01
☐ 119 Bobby Thigpen .10 .05 .01
☐ 120 Roger Bailey .10 .05 .01
☐ 121 Tony Mitchell .10 .05 .01
☐ 122 Junior Felix .10 .05 .01
☐ 123 Rich Robertson .10 .05 .01
☐ 124 Andy Cook .10 .05 .01
☐ 125 Brian Bevil .25 .11 .03

Card			
☐ 126 Darryl Strawberry	.25	.11	.03
☐ 127 Cal Eldred	.10	.05	.01
☐ 128 Cliff Floyd	.25	.11	.03
☐ 129 Alan Newman	.10	.05	.01
☐ 130 Howard Johnson	.10	.05	.01
☐ 131 Jim Abbott	.10	.05	.01
☐ 132 Chad McConnell	.10	.05	.01
☐ 133 Miguel Jimenez	.25	.11	.03
☐ 134 Brett Backlund	.10	.05	.01
☐ 135 John Cummings	.10	.05	.01
☐ 136 Brian Barber	.10	.05	.01
☐ 137 Rafael Palmeiro	.50	.23	.06
☐ 138 Tim Worrell	.10	.05	.01
☐ 139 Jose Pett	.50	.23	.06
☐ 140 Barry Bonds	.75	.35	.09
☐ 141 Damon Buford	.10	.05	.01
☐ 142 Jeff Blauser	.10	.05	.01
☐ 143 Frankie Rodriguez	.25	.11	.03
☐ 144 Mike Morgan	.10	.05	.01
☐ 145 Gary DiSarcina	.10	.05	.01
☐ 146 Calvin Reese	.50	.23	.06
☐ 147 Johnny Ruffin	.10	.05	.01
☐ 148 David Nied	.10	.05	.01
☐ 149 Charles Nagy	.25	.11	.03
☐ 150 Mike Myers	.10	.05	.01
☐ 151 Kenny Carlyle	.10	.05	.01
☐ 152 Eric Anthony	.10	.05	.01
☐ 153 Jose Lind	.10	.05	.01
☐ 154 Pedro Martinez	.50	.23	.06
☐ 155 Mark Kiefer	.10	.05	.01
☐ 156 Tim Laker	.10	.05	.01
☐ 157 Pat Mahomes	.10	.05	.01
☐ 158 Bobby Bonilla	.25	.11	.03
☐ 159 Domingo Jean	.10	.05	.01
☐ 160 Darren Daulton	.25	.11	.03
☐ 161 Mark McGwire	1.00	.45	.12
☐ 162 Jason Kendall	3.00	1.35	.35
☐ 163 Desi Relaford	.25	.11	.03
☐ 164 Ozzie Canseco	.10	.05	.01
☐ 165 Rick Helling	.25	.11	.03
☐ 166 Steve Pegues	.10	.05	.01
☐ 167 Paul Molitor	.60	.25	.07
☐ 168 Larry Carter	.10	.05	.01
☐ 169 Arthur Rhodes	.10	.05	.01
☐ 170 Damon Hollins	.50	.23	.06
☐ 171 Frank Viola	.10	.05	.01
☐ 172 Steve Trachsel	.25	.11	.03
☐ 173 J.T. Snow	.50	.23	.06
☐ 174 Keith Gordon	.10	.05	.01
☐ 175 Carlton Fisk	.50	.23	.06
☐ 176 Jason Bates	.25	.11	.03
☐ 177 Mike Crosby	.10	.05	.01
☐ 178 Benny Santiago	.10	.05	.01
☐ 179 Mike Moore	.10	.05	.01
☐ 180 Jeff Juden	.10	.05	.01
☐ 181 Darren Burton	.10	.05	.01
☐ 182 Todd Williams	.10	.05	.01
☐ 183 John Jaha	.50	.23	.06
☐ 184 Mike Lansing	.25	.11	.03
☐ 185 Pedro Grifol	.10	.05	.01
☐ 186 Vince Coleman	.10	.05	.01
☐ 187 Pat Kelly	.10	.05	.01
☐ 188 Clemente Alvarez	.25	.11	.03
☐ 189 Ron Darling	.10	.05	.01
☐ 190 Orlando Merced	.25	.11	.03
☐ 191 Chris Bosio	.10	.05	.01
☐ 192 Steve Dixon	.10	.05	.01
☐ 193 Doug Dascenzo	.10	.05	.01
☐ 194 Ray Holbert	.10	.05	.01
☐ 195 Howard Battle	.25	.11	.03
☐ 196 Willie McGee	.10	.05	.01
☐ 197 John O'Donoghue	.10	.05	.01
☐ 198 Steve Avery	.25	.11	.03
☐ 199 Greg Blosser	.10	.05	.01
☐ 200 Ryne Sandberg	.75	.35	.09
☐ 201 Joe Grahe	.10	.05	.01
☐ 202 Dan Wilson	.25	.11	.03
☐ 203 Domingo Martinez	.10	.05	.01
☐ 204 Andres Galarraga	.50	.23	.06
☐ 205 Jamie Taylor	.10	.05	.01
☐ 206 Darrell Whitmore	.10	.05	.01
☐ 207 Ben Blomdahl	.10	.05	.01
☐ 208 Doug Drabek	.10	.05	.01
☐ 209 Keith Miller	.10	.05	.01
☐ 210 Billy Ashley	.10	.05	.01
☐ 211 Mike Farrell	.10	.05	.01
☐ 212 John Wetteland	.25	.11	.03
☐ 213 Randy Tomlin	.10	.05	.01
☐ 214 Sid Fernandez	.10	.05	.01
☐ 215 Quilvio Veras	.50	.23	.06
☐ 216 Dave Hollins	.10	.05	.01
☐ 217 Mike Neill	.10	.05	.01
☐ 218 Andy Van Slyke	.25	.11	.03
☐ 219 Bret Boone	.25	.11	.03
☐ 220 Tom Pagnozzi	.10	.05	.01
☐ 221 Mike Welch	.10	.05	.01
☐ 222 Frank Seminara	.10	.05	.01
☐ 223 Ron Villone	.25	.11	.03
☐ 224 D.J. Thielen	.10	.05	.01
☐ 225 Cal Ripken	2.50	1.10	.30
☐ 226 Pedro Borbon Jr.	.25	.11	.03
☐ 227 Carlos Quintana	.10	.05	.01
☐ 228 Tommy Shields	.10	.05	.01
☐ 229 Tim Salmon	.75	.35	.09
☐ 230 John Smiley	.10	.05	.01
☐ 231 Ellis Burks	.25	.11	.03
☐ 232 Pedro Castellano	.10	.05	.01
☐ 233 Paul Byrd	.10	.05	.01
☐ 234 Bryan Harvey	.10	.05	.01
☐ 235 Scott Livingstone	.10	.05	.01
☐ 236 James Mouton	.25	.11	.03
☐ 237 Joe Randa	.25	.11	.03
☐ 238 Pedro Astacio	.10	.05	.01
☐ 239 Darryl Hamilton	.10	.05	.01
☐ 240 Joey Eischen	.25	.11	.03
☐ 241 Edgar Herrera	.25	.11	.03
☐ 242 Dwight Gooden	.25	.11	.03
☐ 243 Sam Militello	.10	.05	.01
☐ 244 Ron Blazier	.25	.11	.03
☐ 245 Ruben Sierra	.25	.11	.03
☐ 246 Al Martin	.25	.11	.03
☐ 247 Mike Felder	.10	.05	.01
☐ 248 Bob Tewksbury	.10	.05	.01
☐ 249 Craig Lefferts	.10	.05	.01
☐ 250 Luis Lopez	.10	.05	.01
☐ 251 Devon White	.10	.05	.01
☐ 252 Will Clark	.50	.23	.06
☐ 253 Mark Smith	.25	.11	.03
☐ 254 Terry Pendleton	.25	.11	.03
☐ 255 Aaron Sele	.25	.11	.03
☐ 256 Jose Viera	.25	.11	.03
☐ 257 Damion Easley	.10	.05	.01
☐ 258 Rod Lofton	.10	.05	.01
☐ 259 Chris Snopek	.50	.23	.06
☐ 260 Quinton McCracken	.25	.11	.03
☐ 261 Mike Matthews	.25	.11	.03
☐ 262 Hector Carrasco	.25	.11	.03
☐ 263 Rick Greene	.25	.11	.03
☐ 264 Chris Holt	.10	.05	.01
☐ 265 George Brett	1.25	.55	.16
☐ 266 Rick Gorecki	.10	.05	.01
☐ 267 Francisco Gamez	.10	.05	.01
☐ 268 Marquis Grissom	.25	.11	.03
☐ 269 Kevin Tapani UER (Misspelled Tapan on card front)	.10	.05	.01
☐ 270 Ryan Thompson	.10	.05	.01
☐ 271 Gerald Williams	.10	.05	.01
☐ 272 Paul Fletcher	.10	.05	.01
☐ 273 Lance Blankenship	.10	.05	.01
☐ 274 Marty Neff	.10	.05	.01
☐ 275 Shawn Estes	.50	.23	.06
☐ 276 Rene Arocha	.10	.05	.01
☐ 277 Scott Eyre	.10	.05	.01
☐ 278 Phil Plantier	.10	.05	.01
☐ 279 Paul Spoljaric	.25	.11	.03
☐ 280 Chris Gambs	.10	.05	.01
☐ 281 Harold Baines	.25	.11	.03
☐ 282 Jose Oliva	.10	.05	.01
☐ 283 Matt Whiteside	.10	.05	.01
☐ 284 Brant Brown	.10	.05	.01
☐ 285 Russ Springer	.10	.05	.01
☐ 286 Chris Sabo	.10	.05	.01
☐ 287 Ozzie Guillen	.10	.05	.01
☐ 288 Marcus Moore	.10	.05	.01
☐ 289 Chad Ogea	.25	.11	.03
☐ 290 Walt Weiss	.10	.05	.01
☐ 291 Brian Edmondson	.10	.05	.01
☐ 292 Jimmy Gonzalez	.10	.05	.01
☐ 293 Danny Miceli	.25	.11	.03
☐ 294 Jose Offerman	.10	.05	.01
☐ 295 Greg Vaughn	.25	.11	.03
☐ 296 Frank Bolick	.10	.05	.01
☐ 297 Mike Maksudian	.10	.05	.01
☐ 298 John Franco	.10	.05	.01
☐ 299 Danny Tartabull	.10	.05	.01
☐ 300 Len Dykstra	.25	.11	.03
☐ 301 Bobby Witt	.10	.05	.01
☐ 302 Trey Beamon	.75	.35	.09
☐ 303 Tino Martinez	.25	.11	.03
☐ 304 Aaron Holbert	.25	.11	.03
☐ 305 Juan Gonzalez	1.50	.70	.19
☐ 306 Billy Hall	.10	.05	.01
☐ 307 Duane Ward	.10	.05	.01
☐ 308 Rod Beck	.25	.11	.03
☐ 309 Jose Mercedes	.10	.05	.01
☐ 310 Otis Nixon	.10	.05	.01
☐ 311 Gettys Glaze	.10	.05	.01
☐ 312 Candy Maldonado	.10	.05	.01
☐ 313 Chad Curtis	.25	.11	.03
☐ 314 Tim Costo	.10	.05	.01
☐ 315 Mike Robertson	.10	.05	.01
☐ 316 Nigel Wilson	.10	.05	.01
☐ 317 Greg McMichael	.25	.11	.03
☐ 318 Scott Pose	.10	.05	.01
☐ 319 Ivan Cruz	.10	.05	.01
☐ 320 Greg Swindell	.10	.05	.01
☐ 321 Kevin McReynolds	.10	.05	.01
☐ 322 Tom Candiotti	.10	.05	.01
☐ 323 Rob Wishnevski	.10	.05	.01
☐ 324 Ken Hill	.25	.11	.03
☐ 325 Kirby Puckett	1.25	.55	.16
☐ 326 Tim Bogar	.10	.05	.01
☐ 327 Mariano Rivera	.75	.35	.09
☐ 328 Mitch Williams	.10	.05	.01
☐ 329 Craig Paquette	.10	.05	.01
☐ 330 Jay Bell	.25	.11	.03
☐ 331 Jose Martinez	.10	.05	.01
☐ 332 Rob Deer	.10	.05	.01
☐ 333 Brook Fordyce	.10	.05	.01
☐ 334 Matt Nokes	.10	.05	.01
☐ 335 Derek Lee	.10	.05	.01
☐ 336 Paul Ellis	.10	.05	.01
☐ 337 Desi Wilson	.10	.05	.01
☐ 338 Roberto Alomar	.60	.25	.07
☐ 339 Jim Tatum FOIL	.10	.05	.01
☐ 340 J.T. Snow FOIL	.50	.23	.06
☐ 341 Tim Salmon FOIL	.75	.35	.09
☐ 342 Russ Davis FOIL	.50	.23	.06
☐ 343 Javier Lopez FOIL	.75	.35	.09
☐ 344 Troy O'Leary FOIL	.50	.23	.06
☐ 345 Marty Cordova FOIL	2.50	1.10	.30
☐ 346 Bubba Smith FOIL	.10	.05	.01
☐ 347 Chipper Jones FOIL	4.00	1.80	.50
☐ 348 Jessie Hollins FOIL	.10	.05	.01
☐ 349 Willie Greene FOIL	.25	.11	.03
☐ 350 Mark Thompson FOIL	.25	.11	.03
☐ 351 Nigel Wilson FOIL	.10	.05	.01
☐ 352 Todd Jones FOIL	.25	.11	.03
☐ 353 Raul Mondesi FOIL	1.00	.45	.12
☐ 354 Cliff Floyd FOIL	.25	.11	.03
☐ 355 Bobby Jones FOIL	.25	.11	.03
☐ 356 Kevin Stocker FOIL	.25	.11	.03
☐ 357 Midre Cummings FOIL	.25	.11	.03
☐ 358 Allen Watson FOIL	.10	.05	.01
☐ 359 Ray McDavid FOIL	.10	.05	.01
☐ 360 Steve Hosey FOIL	.10	.05	.01
☐ 361 Brad Pennington FOIL	.10	.05	.01
☐ 362 Frankie Rodriguez FOIL	.25	.11	.03
☐ 363 Troy Percival FOIL	.25	.11	.03
☐ 364 Jason Bere FOIL	.25	.11	.03
☐ 365 Manny Ramirez FOIL	2.00	.90	.25
☐ 366 Justin Thompson FOIL	.50	.23	.06
☐ 367 Joe Vitiello FOIL	.25	.11	.03
☐ 368 Tyrone Hill FOIL	.10	.05	.01
☐ 369 David McCarty FOIL	.10	.05	.01
☐ 370 Brien Taylor FOIL	.10	.05	.01
☐ 371 Todd Van Poppel FOIL	.10	.05	.01
☐ 372 Marc Newfield FOIL	.25	.11	.03
☐ 373 Terrell Lowery FOIL	.10	.05	.01
☐ 374 Alex Gonzalez FOIL	.50	.23	.06
☐ 375 Ken Griffey Jr.	3.00	1.35	.35
☐ 376 Donovan Osborne	.10	.05	.01
☐ 377 Ritchie Moody	.10	.05	.01
☐ 378 Shane Andrews	.25	.11	.03
☐ 379 Carlos Delgado	.75	.35	.09
☐ 380 Bill Swift	.10	.05	.01
☐ 381 Leo Gomez	.10	.05	.01
☐ 382 Ron Gant	.25	.11	.03
☐ 383 Scott Fletcher	.10	.05	.01
☐ 384 Matt Walbeck	.10	.05	.01
☐ 385 Chuck Finley	.10	.05	.01
☐ 386 Kevin Mitchell	.25	.11	.03
☐ 387 Wilson Alvarez UER (Misspelled Alverez on card front)	.25	.11	.03
☐ 388 John Burke	.10	.05	.01
☐ 389 Alan Embree	.10	.05	.01
☐ 390 Trevor Hoffman	.50	.23	.06
☐ 391 Alan Trammell	.50	.23	.06
☐ 392 Todd Jones	.25	.11	.03
☐ 393 Felix Jose	.10	.05	.01
☐ 394 Orel Hershiser	.25	.11	.03
☐ 395 Pat Listach	.10	.05	.01
☐ 396 Gabe White	.25	.11	.03
☐ 397 Dan Serafini	.50	.23	.06
☐ 398 Todd Hundley	.25	.11	.03
☐ 399 Wade Boggs	.50	.23	.06
☐ 400 Tyler Green	.10	.05	.01
☐ 401 Mike Bordick	.10	.05	.01
☐ 402 Scott Bullett	.10	.05	.01
☐ 403 LaGrande Russell	.10	.05	.01
☐ 404 Ray Lankford	.25	.11	.03
☐ 405 Nolan Ryan	2.50	1.10	.30
☐ 406 Robbie Beckett	.10	.05	.01
☐ 407 Brent Bowers	.25	.11	.03
☐ 408 Adell Davenport	.10	.05	.01
☐ 409 Brady Anderson	.50	.23	.06
☐ 410 Tom Glavine	.50	.23	.06
☐ 411 Doug Hecker	.10	.05	.01
☐ 412 Jose Guzman	.10	.05	.01
☐ 413 Luis Polonia	.10	.05	.01
☐ 414 Brian Williams	.10	.05	.01
☐ 415 Bo Jackson	.50	.23	.06
☐ 416 Eric Young	.50	.23	.06
☐ 417 Kenny Lofton	1.25	.55	.16
☐ 418 Orestes Destrade	.10	.05	.01
☐ 419 Tony Phillips	.25	.11	.03
☐ 420 Jeff Bagwell	1.25	.55	.16
☐ 421 Mark Gardner	.10	.05	.01
☐ 422 Brett Butler	.25	.11	.03
☐ 423 Graeme Lloyd	.10	.05	.01
☐ 424 Delino DeShields	.10	.05	.01
☐ 425 Scott Erickson	.10	.05	.01
☐ 426 Jeff Kent	.25	.11	.03
☐ 427 Jimmy Key	.25	.11	.03
☐ 428 Mickey Morandini	.10	.05	.01
☐ 429 Marcos Armas	.10	.05	.01
☐ 430 Don Slaught	.10	.05	.01
☐ 431 Randy Johnson	.50	.23	.06
☐ 432 Omar Olivares	.10	.05	.01
☐ 433 Charlie Leibrandt	.10	.05	.01
☐ 434 Kurt Stillwell	.10	.05	.01
☐ 435 Scott Brow	.10	.05	.01
☐ 436 Robby Thompson	.10	.05	.01
☐ 437 Ben McDonald	.10	.05	.01
☐ 438 Deion Sanders	.50	.23	.06
☐ 439 Tony Pena	.10	.05	.01
☐ 440 Mark Grace	.50	.23	.06
☐ 441 Eduardo Perez	.10	.05	.01
☐ 442 Tim Pugh	.10	.05	.01
☐ 443 Scott Ruffcorn	.10	.05	.01
☐ 444 Jay Gainer	.10	.05	.01
☐ 445 Albert Belle	1.25	.55	.16
☐ 446 Bret Barberie	.10	.05	.01
☐ 447 Justin Mashore	.10	.05	.01
☐ 448 Pete Harnisch	.10	.05	.01
☐ 449 Greg Gagne	.10	.05	.01
☐ 450 Eric Davis	.25	.11	.03
☐ 451 Dave Mlicki	.10	.05	.01
☐ 452 Moises Alou	.25	.11	.03
☐ 453 Rick Aguilera	.10	.05	.01
☐ 454 Eddie Murray	.75	.35	.09
☐ 455 Bob Wickman	.10	.05	.01
☐ 456 Wes Chamberlain	.10	.05	.01
☐ 457 Brent Gates	.25	.11	.03
☐ 458 Paul Wagner	.10	.05	.01
☐ 459 Mike Hampton	.50	.23	.06
☐ 460 Ozzie Smith	.75	.35	.09
☐ 461 Tom Henke	.10	.05	.01
☐ 462 Ricky Gutierrez	.10	.05	.01
☐ 463 Jack Morris	.25	.11	.03
☐ 464 Joel Chimelis	.10	.05	.01
☐ 465 Gregg Olson	.10	.05	.01
☐ 466 Javier Lopez	.75	.35	.09
☐ 467 Scott Cooper	.10	.05	.01
☐ 468 Willie Wilson	.10	.05	.01
☐ 469 Mark Langston	.25	.11	.03
☐ 470 Barry Larkin	.50	.23	.06
☐ 471 Rod Bolton	.10	.05	.01
☐ 472 Freddie Benavides	.10	.05	.01
☐ 473 Ken Ramos	.10	.05	.01
☐ 474 Chuck Carr	.10	.05	.01
☐ 475 Cecil Fielder	.25	.11	.03
☐ 476 Eddie Taubensee	.10	.05	.01
☐ 477 Chris Eddy	.10	.05	.01
☐ 478 Greg Hansell	.10	.05	.01
☐ 479 Kevin Reimer	.10	.05	.01
☐ 480 Denny Martinez	.25	.11	.03
☐ 481 Chuck Knoblauch	.50	.23	.06
☐ 482 Mike Draper	.10	.05	.01
☐ 483 Spike Owen	.10	.05	.01
☐ 484 Terry Mulholland	.10	.05	.01
☐ 485 Dennis Eckersley	.25	.11	.03
☐ 486 Blas Minor	.10	.05	.01
☐ 487 Dave Fleming	.10	.05	.01
☐ 488 Dan Cholowsky	.10	.05	.01
☐ 489 Ivan Rodriguez	.75	.35	.09
☐ 490 Gary Sheffield	.50	.23	.06
☐ 491 Ed Sprague	.25	.11	.03
☐ 492 Steve Hosey	.10	.05	.01
☐ 493 Jimmy Haynes	.50	.23	.06
☐ 494 John Smoltz	.50	.23	.06
☐ 495 Andre Dawson	.50	.23	.06
☐ 496 Rey Sanchez	.10	.05	.01
☐ 497 Ty Van Burkleo	.10	.05	.01
☐ 498 Bobby Ayala	.25	.11	.03
☐ 499 Tim Raines	.50	.23	.06
☐ 500 Charlie Hayes	.10	.05	.01
☐ 501 Paul Sorrento	.10	.05	.01
☐ 502 Richie Lewis	.10	.05	.01
☐ 503 Jason Pfaff	.10	.05	.01
☐ 504 Ken Caminiti	.50	.23	.06
☐ 505 Mike Macfarlane	.10	.05	.01
☐ 506 Jody Reed	.10	.05	.01
☐ 507 Bobby Hughes	.10	.05	.01
☐ 508 Wil Cordero	.25	.11	.03
☐ 509 George Tsamis	.10	.05	.01
☐ 510 Bret Saberhagen	.25	.11	.03
☐ 511 Derek Jeter	8.00	3.60	1.00
☐ 512 Gene Schall	.10	.05	.01
☐ 513 Curtis Shaw	.10	.05	.01
☐ 514 Steve Cooke	.10	.05	.01
☐ 515 Edgar Martinez	.25	.11	.03
☐ 516 Mike Milchin	.10	.05	.01
☐ 517 Billy Ripken	.10	.05	.01
☐ 518 Andy Benes	.25	.11	.03
☐ 519 Juan de la Rosa	.10	.05	.01
☐ 520 John Burkett	.10	.05	.01
☐ 521 Alex Ochoa	.50	.23	.06
☐ 522 Tony Tarasco	.25	.11	.03
☐ 523 Luis Ortiz	.10	.05	.01
☐ 524 Rick Wilkins	.10	.05	.01
☐ 525 Chris Turner	.10	.05	.01
☐ 526 Rob Dibble	.10	.05	.01
☐ 527 Jack McDowell	.25	.11	.03
☐ 528 Daryl Boston	.10	.05	.01
☐ 529 Bill Wertz	.10	.05	.01
☐ 530 Charlie Hough	.10	.05	.01
☐ 531 Sean Bergman	.10	.05	.01
☐ 532 Doug Jones	.10	.05	.01
☐ 533 Jeff Montgomery	.25	.11	.03
☐ 534 Roger Cedeno	.75	.35	.09
☐ 535 Robin Yount	.50	.23	.06
☐ 536 Mo Vaughn	.75	.35	.09
☐ 537 Brian Harper	.10	.05	.01
☐ 538 Juan Castillo	.10	.05	.01
☐ 539 Steve Farr	.10	.05	.01
☐ 540 John Kruk	.25	.11	.03
☐ 541 Troy Neel	.10	.05	.01

☐ 542 Danny Clyburn	1.00	.45	.12
☐ 543 Jim Converse	.10	.05	.01
☐ 544 Gregg Jefferies	.25	.11	.03
☐ 545 Jose Canseco	.50	.23	.06
☐ 546 Julio Bruno	.10	.05	.01
☐ 547 Rob Butler	.10	.05	.01
☐ 548 Royce Clayton	.25	.11	.03
☐ 549 Chris Hoiles	.10	.05	.01
☐ 550 Greg Maddux	2.00	.90	.25
☐ 551 Joe Ciccarella	.10	.05	.01
☐ 552 Ozzie Timmons	.50	.23	.06
☐ 553 Chili Davis	.25	.11	.03
☐ 554 Brian Koelling	.10	.05	.01
☐ 555 Frank Thomas	3.00	1.35	.35
☐ 556 Vinny Castilla	.50	.23	.06
☐ 557 Reggie Jefferson	.25	.11	.03
☐ 558 Rob Natal	.10	.05	.01
☐ 559 Mike Henneman	.10	.05	.01
☐ 560 Craig Biggio	.25	.11	.03
☐ 561 Billy Brewer	.10	.05	.01
☐ 562 Dan Melendez	.10	.05	.01
☐ 563 Kenny Felder	.10	.05	.01
☐ 564 Miguel Batista	.25	.11	.03
☐ 565 Dave Winfield	.50	.23	.06
☐ 566 Al Shirley	.25	.11	.03
☐ 567 Robert Eenhoorn	.10	.05	.01
☐ 568 Mike Williams	.10	.05	.01
☐ 569 Tanyon Sturtze	.25	.11	.03
☐ 570 Tim Wakefield	.25	.11	.03
☐ 571 Greg Pirkl	.10	.05	.01
☐ 572 Sean Lowe	.25	.11	.03
☐ 573 Terry Burrows	.10	.05	.01
☐ 574 Kevin Higgins	.10	.05	.01
☐ 575 Joe Carter	.25	.11	.03
☐ 576 Kevin Rogers	.10	.05	.01
☐ 577 Manny Alexander	.10	.05	.01
☐ 578 David Justice	.50	.23	.06
☐ 579 Brian Conroy	.10	.05	.01
☐ 580 Jessie Hollins	.10	.05	.01
☐ 581 Ron Watson	.10	.05	.01
☐ 582 Bip Roberts	.10	.05	.01
☐ 583 Tom Urbani	.10	.05	.01
☐ 584 Jason Hutchins	.10	.05	.01
☐ 585 Carlos Baerga	.25	.11	.03
☐ 586 Jeff Mutis	.10	.05	.01
☐ 587 Justin Thompson	.50	.23	.06
☐ 588 Orlando Miller	.25	.11	.03
☐ 589 Brian McRae	.25	.11	.03
☐ 590 Ramon Martinez	.25	.11	.03
☐ 591 Dave Nilsson	.25	.11	.03
☐ 592 Jose Vidro	.50	.23	.06
☐ 593 Rich Becker	.25	.11	.03
☐ 594 Preston Wilson	.50	.23	.06
☐ 595 Don Mattingly	1.50	.70	.19
☐ 596 Tony Longmire	.10	.05	.01
☐ 597 Kevin Seitzer	.10	.05	.01
☐ 598 Midre Cummings	.25	.11	.03
☐ 599 Omar Vizquel	.25	.11	.03
☐ 600 Lee Smith	.25	.11	.03
☐ 601 David Hulse	.10	.05	.01
☐ 602 Darrell Sherman	.10	.05	.01
☐ 603 Alex Gonzalez	.50	.23	.06
☐ 604 Geronimo Pena	.10	.05	.01
☐ 605 Mike Devereaux	.10	.05	.01
☐ 606 Sterling Hitchcock	.50	.23	.06
☐ 607 Mike Greenwell	.10	.05	.01
☐ 608 Steve Buechele	.10	.05	.01
☐ 609 Troy Percival	.25	.11	.03
☐ 610 Roberto Kelly	.10	.05	.01
☐ 611 James Baldwin	2.00	.90	.25
☐ 612 Jerald Clark	.10	.05	.01
☐ 613 Albie Lopez	.25	.11	.03
☐ 614 Dave Magadan	.10	.05	.01
☐ 615 Mickey Tettleton	.10	.05	.01
☐ 616 Sean Runyan	.10	.05	.01
☐ 617 Bob Hamelin	.10	.05	.01
☐ 618 Raul Mondesi	1.00	.45	.12
☐ 619 Tyrone Hill	.10	.05	.01
☐ 620 Darrin Fletcher	.10	.05	.01
☐ 621 Mike Trombley	.10	.05	.01
☐ 622 Jeromy Burnitz	.10	.05	.01
☐ 623 Bernie Williams	.60	.25	.07
☐ 624 Mike Farmer	.10	.05	.01
☐ 625 Rickey Henderson	.50	.23	.06
☐ 626 Carlos Garcia	.10	.05	.01
☐ 627 Jeff Darwin	.10	.05	.01
☐ 628 Todd Zeile	.10	.05	.01
☐ 629 Benji Gil	.25	.11	.03
☐ 630 Tony Gwynn	1.25	.55	.16
☐ 631 Aaron Small	.10	.05	.01
☐ 632 Joe Rosselli	.25	.11	.03
☐ 633 Mike Mussina	.60	.25	.07
☐ 634 Ryan Klesko	1.00	.45	.12
☐ 635 Roger Clemens	.60	.25	.07
☐ 636 Sammy Sosa	.50	.23	.06
☐ 637 Orlando Palmeiro	.10	.05	.01
☐ 638 Willie Greene	.25	.11	.03
☐ 639 George Bell	.10	.05	.01
☐ 640 Garvin Alston	.10	.05	.01
☐ 641 Pete Janicki	.10	.05	.01
☐ 642 Chris Sheff	.10	.05	.01
☐ 643 Felipe Lira	.25	.11	.03
☐ 644 Roberto Petagine	.25	.11	.03
☐ 645 Wally Joyner	.25	.11	.03
☐ 646 Mike Piazza	3.00	1.35	.35
☐ 647 Jaime Navarro	.10	.05	.01
☐ 648 Jeff Hartsock	.10	.05	.01
☐ 649 David McCarty	.10	.05	.01
☐ 650 Bobby Jones	.25	.11	.03
☐ 651 Mark Hutton	.10	.05	.01
☐ 652 Kyle Abbott	.10	.05	.01
☐ 653 Steve Cox	.75	.35	.09
☐ 654 Jeff King	.25	.11	.03
☐ 655 Norm Charlton	.10	.05	.01
☐ 656 Mike Gulan	.10	.05	.01
☐ 657 Julio Franco	.25	.11	.03
☐ 658 Cameron Cairncross	.10	.05	.01
☐ 659 John Olerud	.10	.05	.01
☐ 660 Salomon Torres	.25	.11	.03
☐ 661 Brad Pennington	.10	.05	.01
☐ 662 Melvin Nieves	.50	.23	.06
☐ 663 Ivan Calderon	.10	.05	.01
☐ 664 Turk Wendell	.10	.05	.01
☐ 665 Chris Pritchett	.10	.05	.01
☐ 666 Reggie Sanders	.50	.23	.06
☐ 667 Robin Ventura	.25	.11	.03
☐ 668 Joe Girardi	.10	.05	.01
☐ 669 Manny Ramirez	2.00	.90	.25
☐ 670 Jeff Conine	.25	.11	.03
☐ 671 Greg Gohr	.10	.05	.01
☐ 672 Andujar Cedeno	.10	.05	.01
☐ 673 Les Norman	.10	.05	.01
☐ 674 Mike James	.10	.05	.01
☐ 675 Marshall Boze	.25	.11	.03
☐ 676 B.J. Wallace	.10	.05	.01
☐ 677 Kent Hrbek	.25	.11	.03
☐ 678 Jack Voigt	.10	.05	.01
☐ 679 Brien Taylor	.10	.05	.01
☐ 680 Curt Schilling	.10	.05	.01
☐ 681 Todd Van Poppel	.10	.05	.01
☐ 682 Kevin Young	.10	.05	.01
☐ 683 Tommy Adams	.10	.05	.01
☐ 684 Bernard Gilkey	.25	.11	.03
☐ 685 Kevin Brown	.25	.11	.03
☐ 686 Fred McGriff	.50	.23	.06
☐ 687 Pat Borders	.10	.05	.01
☐ 688 Kirt Manwaring	.10	.05	.01
☐ 689 Sid Bream	.10	.05	.01
☐ 690 John Valentin	.25	.11	.03
☐ 691 Steve Olsen	.10	.05	.01
☐ 692 Roberto Mejia	.10	.05	.01
☐ 693 Carlos Delgado FOIL	.75	.35	.09
☐ 694 Steve Gibralter FOIL	.50	.23	.06
☐ 695 Gary Mota FOIL	.25	.11	.03
☐ 696 Jose Malave FOIL	.25	.11	.03
☐ 697 Larry Sutton FOIL	.25	.11	.03
☐ 698 Dan Frye FOIL	.25	.11	.03
☐ 699 Tim Clark FOIL	.25	.11	.03
☐ 700 Brian Rupp FOIL	.25	.11	.03
☐ 701 Felipe Alou FOIL Moises Alou	.25	.11	.03
☐ 702 Barry Bonds FOIL Bobby Bonds	.50	.23	.06
☐ 703 Ken Griffey Sr. FOIL Ken Griffey Jr.	1.00	.45	.12
☐ 704 Brian McRae FOIL Hal McRae	.25	.11	.03
☐ 705 Checklist 1	.10	.05	.01
☐ 706 Checklist 2	.10	.05	.01
☐ 707 Checklist 3	.10	.05	.01
☐ 708 Checklist 4	.10	.05	.01

1994 Bowman Previews

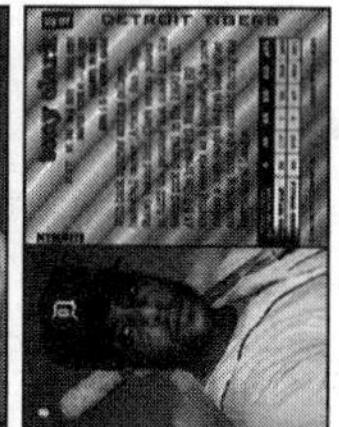

This 10-card standard-size set served as a preview to the 1994 Bowman set. The cards were randomly inserted in 1994 Stadium Club second series packs. Card fronts are similar to the full-bleed basic issue. The differences are a multi-colored foil stripe up the left-hand border with a red stripe at bottom. Red foil also surrounds the Bowman logo. In the upper right-hand corner is a blue foil Bowman Preview logo.The backs are identical to the basic issue with a horizontal layout containing a player photo, text and statistics.

	MINT	NRMT	EXC
COMPLETE SET (10)	40.00	18.00	5.00
COMMON CARD (1-10)	1.00	.45	.12
☐ 1 Frank Thomas	20.00	9.00	2.50
☐ 2 Mike Piazza	12.00	5.50	1.50
☐ 3 Albert Belle	8.00	3.60	1.00
☐ 4 Javier Lopez	3.00	1.35	.35
☐ 5 Cliff Floyd	1.00	.45	.12
☐ 6 Alex Gonzalez	1.00	.45	.12
☐ 7 Ricky Bottalico	1.00	.45	.12
☐ 8 Tony Clark	6.00	2.70	.75
☐ 9 Mac Suzuki	1.00	.45	.12
☐ 10 James Mouton Foil	1.00	.45	.12

1994 Bowman

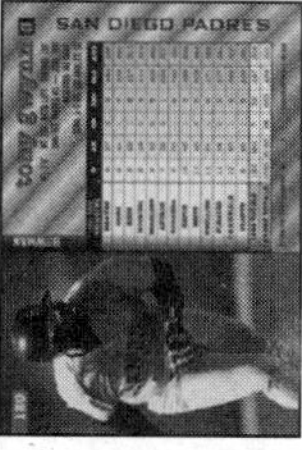

The 1994 Bowman set consists of 682 standard-size, full-bleed cards primarily distributed in plastic wrap packs and jumbo packs. In addition to a color photo on the front, there is a line of gold foil that runs up the far left side and across the bottom of the card. The player's name is also in gold foil at bottom and the Bowman logo at bottom left is enclosed in gold foil. Horizontal backs contain a player photo on the left and statistics and highlights on the right. There are 51 Foil cards (337-388) that include a number of top young stars and prospects. These foil cards were issued one per foil pack and two per jumbo. Rookie Cards of note include Alan Benes, Tony Clark, Jermaine Dye, Jason Isringhausen, Derrek Lee, Chan Ho Park, Edgar Renteria and Ruben Rivera.

	MINT	NRMT	EXC
COMPLETE SET (682)	120.00	55.00	15.00
COMMON CARD (1-682)	.10	.05	.01
☐ 1 Joe Carter	.25	.11	.03
☐ 2 Marcus Moore	.10	.05	.01
☐ 3 Doug Creek	.10	.05	.01
☐ 4 Pedro Martinez	.50	.23	.06
☐ 5 Ken Griffey Jr.	4.00	1.80	.50
☐ 6 Greg Swindell	.10	.05	.01
☐ 7 J.J. Johnson	.25	.11	.03
☐ 8 Homer Bush	.25	.11	.03
☐ 9 Arquimedez Pozo	.50	.23	.06
☐ 10 Bryan Harvey	.10	.05	.01
☐ 11 J.T. Snow	.25	.11	.03
☐ 12 Alan Benes	2.50	1.10	.30
☐ 13 Chad Kreuter	.10	.05	.01
☐ 14 Eric Karros	.25	.11	.03
☐ 15 Frank Thomas	4.00	1.80	.50
☐ 16 Bret Saberhagen	.25	.11	.03
☐ 17 Terrell Lowery	.10	.05	.01
☐ 18 Rod Bolton	.10	.05	.01
☐ 19 Harold Baines	.25	.11	.03
☐ 20 Matt Walbeck	.10	.05	.01
☐ 21 Tom Glavine	.50	.23	.06
☐ 22 Todd Jones	.10	.05	.01
☐ 23 Alberto Castillo	.25	.11	.03
☐ 24 Ruben Sierra	.25	.11	.03
☐ 25 Don Mattingly	2.00	.90	.25
☐ 26 Mike Morgan	.10	.05	.01
☐ 27 Jim Musselwhite	.25	.11	.03
☐ 28 Matt Brunson	.25	.11	.03
☐ 29 Adam Meinershagen	.10	.05	.01
☐ 30 Joe Girardi	.10	.05	.01
☐ 31 Shane Halter	.10	.05	.01
☐ 32 Jose Paniagua	.25	.11	.03
☐ 33 Paul Perkins	.10	.05	.01
☐ 34 John Hudek	.10	.05	.01
☐ 35 Frank Viola	.10	.05	.01
☐ 36 David Lamb	.10	.05	.01
☐ 37 Marshall Boze	.10	.05	.01
☐ 38 Jorge Posada	.25	.11	.03
☐ 39 Brian Anderson	.25	.11	.03
☐ 40 Mark Whiten	.10	.05	.01
☐ 41 Sean Bergman	.25	.11	.03
☐ 42 Jose Parra	.25	.11	.03
☐ 43 Mike Robertson	.10	.05	.01
☐ 44 Pete Walker	.10	.05	.01
☐ 45 Juan Gonzalez	2.00	.90	.25
☐ 46 Cleveland Ladell	.25	.11	.03
☐ 47 Mark Smith	.10	.05	.01
☐ 48 Kevin Jarvis UER (team listed as Yankees on back)	.10	.05	.01
☐ 49 Amaury Telemaco	1.00	.45	.12
☐ 50 Andy Van Slyke	.25	.11	.03
☐ 51 Rikkert Faneyte	.10	.05	.01
☐ 52 Curtis Shaw	.10	.05	.01
☐ 53 Matt Drews	.50	.23	.06
☐ 54 Wilson Alvarez	.25	.11	.03
☐ 55 Manny Ramirez	1.25	.55	.16
☐ 56 Bobby Munoz	.10	.05	.01
☐ 57 Ed Sprague	.25	.11	.03
☐ 58 Jamey Wright	1.50	.70	.19
☐ 59 Jeff Montgomery	.25	.11	.03
☐ 60 Kirk Rueter	.10	.05	.01
☐ 61 Edgar Martinez	.25	.11	.03
☐ 62 Luis Gonzalez	.10	.05	.01
☐ 63 Tim Vanegmond	.10	.05	.01
☐ 64 Bip Roberts	.10	.05	.01
☐ 65 John Jaha	.25	.11	.03
☐ 66 Chuck Carr	.10	.05	.01
☐ 67 Chuck Finley	.10	.05	.01
☐ 68 Aaron Holbert	.25	.11	.03
☐ 69 Cecil Fielder	.25	.11	.03
☐ 70 Tom Engle	.10	.05	.01
☐ 71 Ron Karkovice	.10	.05	.01
☐ 72 Joe Orsulak	.10	.05	.01
☐ 73 Duff Brumley	.10	.05	.01
☐ 74 Craig Clayton	.10	.05	.01
☐ 75 Cal Ripken	3.00	1.35	.35
☐ 76 Brad Fullmer	1.50	.70	.19
☐ 77 Tony Tarasco	.10	.05	.01
☐ 78 Terry Farrar	.10	.05	.01
☐ 79 Matt Williams	.50	.23	.06
☐ 80 Rickey Henderson	.50	.23	.06
☐ 81 Terry Mulholland	.10	.05	.01
☐ 82 Sammy Sosa	.50	.23	.06
☐ 83 Paul Sorrento	.10	.05	.01
☐ 84 Pete Incaviglia	.10	.05	.01
☐ 85 Darren Hall	.10	.05	.01
☐ 86 Scott Klingenbeck	.25	.11	.03
☐ 87 Dario Perez	.10	.05	.01
☐ 88 Ugueth Urbina	.25	.11	.03
☐ 89 Dave Vanhof	.10	.05	.01
☐ 90 Domingo Jean	.10	.05	.01
☐ 91 Otis Nixon	.10	.05	.01
☐ 92 Andres Berumen	.10	.05	.01
☐ 93 Jose Valentin	.25	.11	.03
☐ 94 Edgar Renteria	3.00	1.35	.35
☐ 95 Chris Turner	.10	.05	.01
☐ 96 Ray Lankford	.25	.11	.03
☐ 97 Danny Bautista	.10	.05	.01
☐ 98 Chan Ho Park	2.00	.90	.25
☐ 99 Glenn DiSarcina	.25	.11	.03
☐ 100 Butch Huskey	.25	.11	.03
☐ 101 Ivan Rodriguez	1.00	.45	.12
☐ 102 Johnny Ruffin	.10	.05	.01
☐ 103 Alex Ochoa	.25	.11	.03
☐ 104 Torii Hunter	.50	.23	.06
☐ 105 Ryan Klesko	.75	.35	.09
☐ 106 Jay Bell	.25	.11	.03
☐ 107 Kurt Peltzer	.10	.05	.01
☐ 108 Miguel Jimenez	.10	.05	.01
☐ 109 Russ Davis	.25	.11	.03
☐ 110 Derek Wallace	.10	.05	.01
☐ 111 Keith Lockhart	.10	.05	.01
☐ 112 Mike Lieberthal	.10	.05	.01
☐ 113 Dave Stewart	.25	.11	.03
☐ 114 Tom Schmidt	.10	.05	.01
☐ 115 Brian McRae	.25	.11	.03
☐ 116 Moises Alou	.25	.11	.03
☐ 117 Dave Fleming	.10	.05	.01
☐ 118 Jeff Bagwell	1.50	.70	.19
☐ 119 Luis Ortiz	.10	.05	.01
☐ 120 Tony Gwynn	1.50	.70	.19
☐ 121 Jaime Navarro	.10	.05	.01
☐ 122 Benny Santiago	.10	.05	.01
☐ 123 Darrell Whitmore	.10	.05	.01
☐ 124 John Mabry	.75	.35	.09
☐ 125 Mickey Tettleton	.10	.05	.01
☐ 126 Tom Candiotti	.10	.05	.01
☐ 127 Tim Raines	.50	.23	.06
☐ 128 Bobby Bonilla	.25	.11	.03
☐ 129 John Dettmer	.10	.05	.01
☐ 130 Hector Carrasco	.10	.05	.01
☐ 131 Chris Hoiles	.10	.05	.01
☐ 132 Rick Aguilera	.10	.05	.01
☐ 133 David Justice	.50	.23	.06
☐ 134 Esteban Loaiza	.50	.23	.06
☐ 135 Barry Bonds	1.00	.45	.12
☐ 136 Bob Welch	.10	.05	.01
☐ 137 Mike Stanley	.10	.05	.01
☐ 138 Roberto Hernandez	.25	.11	.03
☐ 139 Sandy Alomar	.25	.11	.03
☐ 140 Darren Daulton	.25	.11	.03
☐ 141 Angel Martinez	.25	.11	.03
☐ 142 Howard Johnson	.10	.05	.01
☐ 143 Bob Hamelin UER (name and card number colors don't match)	.10	.05	.01
☐ 144 J.J. Thobe	.10	.05	.01
☐ 145 Roger Salkeld	.10	.05	.01
☐ 146 Orlando Miller	.10	.05	.01
☐ 147 Dmitri Young	.75	.35	.09
☐ 148 Tim Hyers	.10	.05	.01
☐ 149 Mark Loretta	.10	.05	.01
☐ 150 Chris Hammond	.10	.05	.01
☐ 151 Joel Moore	.10	.05	.01
☐ 152 Todd Zeile	.10	.05	.01
☐ 153 Wil Cordero	.25	.11	.03
☐ 154 Chris Smith	.10	.05	.01
☐ 155 James Baldwin	.75	.35	.09
☐ 156 Edgardo Alfonzo	.50	.23	.06
☐ 157 Kym Ashworth	.25	.11	.03
☐ 158 Paul Bako	.10	.05	.01
☐ 159 Rick Krivda	.10	.05	.01
☐ 160 Pat Mahomes	.10	.05	.01
☐ 161 Damon Hollins	.25	.11	.03
☐ 162 Felix Martinez	.25	.11	.03
☐ 163 Jason Myers	.25	.11	.03
☐ 164 Izzy Molina	.25	.11	.03
☐ 165 Brien Taylor	.10	.05	.01
☐ 166 Kevin Orie	2.00	.90	.25
☐ 167 Casey Whitten	.25	.11	.03
☐ 168 Tony Longmire	.10	.05	.01
☐ 169 John Olerud	.10	.05	.01
☐ 170 Mark Thompson	.25	.11	.03
☐ 171 Jorge Fabregas	.10	.05	.01
☐ 172 John Wetteland	.25	.11	.03
☐ 173 Dan Wilson	.25	.11	.03
☐ 174 Doug Drabek	.10	.05	.01
☐ 175 Jeffrey McNeely	.10	.05	.01
☐ 176 Melvin Nieves	.25	.11	.03

☐ 177 Doug Glanville .25 .11 .03
☐ 178 Javier De La Hoya .10 .05 .01
☐ 179 Chad Curtis .10 .05 .01
☐ 180 Brian Barber .10 .05 .01
☐ 181 Mike Henneman .10 .05 .01
☐ 182 Jose Offerman .10 .05 .01
☐ 183 Robert Ellis .10 .05 .01
☐ 184 John Franco .10 .05 .01
☐ 185 Benji Gil .10 .05 .01
☐ 186 Hal Morris .10 .05 .01
☐ 187 Chris Sabo .10 .05 .01
☐ 188 Blaise Ilsley .10 .05 .01
☐ 189 Steve Avery .25 .11 .03
☐ 190 Rick White .10 .05 .01
☐ 191 Rod Beck .25 .11 .03
☐ 192 Mark McGwire UER 1.25 .55 .16
(No card number on back)
☐ 193 Jim Abbott .10 .05 .01
☐ 194 Randy Myers .10 .05 .01
☐ 195 Kenny Lofton 1.25 .55 .16
☐ 196 Mariano Duncan .10 .05 .01
☐ 197 Lee Daniels .10 .05 .01
☐ 198 Armando Reynoso .10 .05 .01
☐ 199 Joe Randa .25 .11 .03
☐ 200 Cliff Floyd .50 .23 .06
☐ 201 Tim Harkrider .10 .05 .01
☐ 202 Kevin Gallaher .10 .05 .01
☐ 203 Scott Cooper .10 .05 .01
☐ 204 Phil Stidham .10 .05 .01
☐ 205 Jeff D'Amico 1.50 .70 .19
☐ 206 Matt Whisenant .10 .05 .01
☐ 207 De Shawn Warren .25 .11 .03
☐ 208 Rene Arocha .10 .05 .01
☐ 209 Tony Clark 10.00 4.50 1.25
☐ 210 Jason Jacome .25 .11 .03
☐ 211 Scott Christman .25 .11 .03
☐ 212 Bill Pulsipher .25 .11 .03
☐ 213 Dean Palmer .25 .11 .03
☐ 214 Chad Mottola .10 .05 .01
☐ 215 Manny Alexander .10 .05 .01
☐ 216 Rich Becker .25 .11 .03
☐ 217 Andre King .25 .11 .03
☐ 218 Carlos Garcia .10 .05 .01
☐ 219 Ron Pezzoni .10 .05 .01
☐ 220 Steve Karsay .10 .05 .01
☐ 221 Jose Musset .10 .05 .01
☐ 222 Karl Rhodes .10 .05 .01
☐ 223 Frank Cimorelli .10 .05 .01
☐ 224 Kevin Jordan .10 .05 .01
☐ 225 Duane Ward .10 .05 .01
☐ 226 John Burke .10 .05 .01
☐ 227 Mike Macfarlane .10 .05 .01
☐ 228 Mike Lansing .25 .11 .03
☐ 229 Chuck Knoblauch .50 .23 .06
☐ 230 Ken Caminiti .50 .23 .06
☐ 231 Gar Finnvold .10 .05 .01
☐ 232 Derrek Lee 4.00 1.80 .50
☐ 233 Brady Anderson .50 .23 .06
☐ 234 Vic Darensbourg .25 .11 .03
☐ 235 Mark Langston .25 .11 .03
☐ 236 T.J. Mathews .25 .11 .03
☐ 237 Lou Whitaker .25 .11 .03
☐ 238 Roger Cedeno .25 .11 .03
☐ 239 Alex Fernandez .25 .11 .03
☐ 240 Ryan Thompson .10 .05 .01
☐ 241 Kerry Lacy .10 .05 .01
☐ 242 Reggie Sanders .25 .11 .03
☐ 243 Brad Pennington .10 .05 .01
☐ 244 Bryan Eversgerd .10 .05 .01
☐ 245 Greg Maddux 2.50 1.10 .30
☐ 246 Jason Kendall 1.00 .45 .12
☐ 247 J.R. Phillips .10 .05 .01
☐ 248 Bobby Witt .10 .05 .01
☐ 249 Paul O'Neill .25 .11 .03
☐ 250 Ryne Sandberg 1.00 .45 .12
☐ 251 Charles Nagy .25 .11 .03
☐ 252 Kevin Stocker .10 .05 .01
☐ 253 Shawn Green .25 .11 .03
☐ 254 Charlie Hayes .10 .05 .01
☐ 255 Donnie Elliott .10 .05 .01
☐ 256 Rob Fitzpatrick .10 .05 .01
☐ 257 Tim Davis .10 .05 .01
☐ 258 James Mouton .25 .11 .03
☐ 259 Mike Greenwell .10 .05 .01
☐ 260 Ray McDavid .25 .11 .03
☐ 261 Mike Kelly .10 .05 .01
☐ 262 Andy Larkin .25 .11 .03
☐ 263 Marquis Riley UER .10 .05 .01
(No card number on back)
☐ 264 Bob Tewksbury .10 .05 .01
☐ 265 Brian Edmondson .10 .05 .01
☐ 266 Eduardo Lantigua .25 .11 .03
☐ 267 Brandon Wilson .10 .05 .01
☐ 268 Mike Welch .10 .05 .01
☐ 269 Tom Henke .10 .05 .01
☐ 270 Calvin Reese .25 .11 .03
☐ 271 Greg Zaun .25 .11 .03
☐ 272 Todd Ritchie .10 .05 .01
☐ 273 Javier Lopez .50 .23 .06
☐ 274 Kevin Young .10 .05 .01
☐ 275 Kirt Manwaring .10 .05 .01
☐ 276 Bill Taylor .10 .05 .01
☐ 277 Robert Eenhoorn .10 .05 .01
☐ 278 Jessie Hollins .10 .05 .01
☐ 279 Julian Tavarez .25 .11 .03
☐ 280 Gene Schall .25 .11 .03
☐ 281 Paul Molitor .75 .35 .09
☐ 282 Neifi Perez 1.50 .70 .19
☐ 283 Greg Gagne .10 .05 .01
☐ 284 Marquis Grissom .25 .11 .03
☐ 285 Randy Johnson .50 .23 .06
☐ 286 Pete Harnisch .10 .05 .01
☐ 287 Joel Bennett .10 .05 .01
☐ 288 Derek Bell .25 .11 .03
☐ 289 Darryl Hamilton .10 .05 .01
☐ 290 Gary Sheffield .50 .23 .06
☐ 291 Eduardo Perez .10 .05 .01
☐ 292 Basil Shabazz .10 .05 .01
☐ 293 Eric Davis .25 .11 .03
☐ 294 Pedro Astacio .10 .05 .01
☐ 295 Robin Ventura .25 .11 .03
☐ 296 Jeff Kent .10 .05 .01
☐ 297 Rick Helling .10 .05 .01
☐ 298 Joe Oliver .10 .05 .01
☐ 299 Lee Smith .25 .11 .03
☐ 300 Dave Winfield .50 .23 .06
☐ 301 Deion Sanders .50 .23 .06
☐ 302 Ravelo Manzanillo .10 .05 .01
☐ 303 Mark Portugal .10 .05 .01
☐ 304 Brent Gates .10 .05 .01
☐ 305 Wade Boggs .50 .23 .06
☐ 306 Rick Wilkins .10 .05 .01
☐ 307 Carlos Baerga .25 .11 .03
☐ 308 Curt Schilling .10 .05 .01
☐ 309 Shannon Stewart .25 .11 .03
☐ 310 Darren Holmes .10 .05 .01
☐ 311 Robert Toth .25 .11 .03
☐ 312 Gabe White .10 .05 .01
☐ 313 Mac Suzuki .25 .11 .03
☐ 314 Alvin Morman .10 .05 .01
☐ 315 Mo Vaughn 1.00 .45 .12
☐ 316 Bryce Florie .10 .05 .01
☐ 317 Gabby Martinez .25 .11 .03
☐ 318 Carl Everett .10 .05 .01
☐ 319 Kerwin Moore .10 .05 .01
☐ 320 Tom Pagnozzi .10 .05 .01
☐ 321 Chris Gomez .10 .05 .01
☐ 322 Todd Williams .10 .05 .01
☐ 323 Pat Hentgen .25 .11 .03
☐ 324 Kirk Presley .50 .23 .06
☐ 325 Kevin Brown .25 .11 .03
☐ 326 Jason Isringhausen 2.00 .90 .25
☐ 327 Rick Forney .10 .05 .01
☐ 328 Carlos Pulido .10 .05 .01
☐ 329 Terrell Wade 1.00 .45 .12
☐ 330 Al Martin .10 .05 .01
☐ 331 Dan Carlson .10 .05 .01
☐ 332 Mark Acre .10 .05 .01
☐ 333 Sterling Hitchcock .25 .11 .03
☐ 334 Jon Ratliff .25 .11 .03
☐ 335 Alex Ramirez 1.50 .70 .19
☐ 336 Phil Geisler .10 .05 .01
☐ 337 Eddie Zambrano FOIL .10 .05 .01
☐ 338 Jim Thome FOIL 1.00 .45 .12
☐ 339 James Mouton FOIL .25 .11 .03
☐ 340 Cliff Floyd FOIL .50 .23 .06
☐ 341 Carlos Delgado FOIL .50 .23 .06
☐ 342 Roberto Petagine FOIL .25 .11 .03
☐ 343 Tim Clark FOIL .10 .05 .01
☐ 344 Bubba Smith FOIL .10 .05 .01
☐ 345 Randy Curtis FOIL .10 .05 .01
☐ 346 Joe Biasucci FOIL .10 .05 .01
☐ 347 D.J. Boston FOIL .25 .11 .03
☐ 348 Ruben Rivera FOIL 6.00 2.70 .75
☐ 349 Bryan Link FOIL .10 .05 .01
☐ 350 Mike Bell FOIL 1.25 .55 .16
☐ 351 Marty Watson FOIL .10 .05 .01
☐ 352 Jason Myers FOIL .25 .11 .03
☐ 353 Chipper Jones FOIL 3.00 1.35 .35
☐ 354 Brooks Kieschnick FOIL 1.00 .45 .12
☐ 355 Calvin Reese FOIL .25 .11 .03
☐ 356 John Burke FOIL .10 .05 .01
☐ 357 Kurt Miller FOIL .10 .05 .01
☐ 358 Orlando Miller FOIL .10 .05 .01
☐ 359 Todd Hollandsworth FOIL 1.00 .45 .12
☐ 360 Rondell White FOIL .50 .23 .06
☐ 361 Bill Pulsipher FOIL .25 .11 .03
☐ 362 Tyler Green FOIL .10 .05 .01
☐ 363 Midre Cummings FOIL .10 .05 .01
☐ 364 Brian Barber FOIL .10 .05 .01
☐ 365 Melvin Nieves FOIL .25 .11 .03
☐ 366 Salomon Torres FOIL .10 .05 .01
☐ 367 Alex Ochoa FOIL .25 .11 .03
☐ 368 Frankie Rodriguez FOIL .25 .11 .03
☐ 369 Brian Anderson FOIL .25 .11 .03
☐ 370 James Baldwin FOIL .75 .35 .09
☐ 371 Manny Ramirez FOIL 1.25 .55 .16
☐ 372 Justin Thompson FOIL .25 .11 .03
☐ 373 Johnny Damon FOIL .50 .23 .06
☐ 374 Jeff D'Amico FOIL 1.50 .70 .19
☐ 375 Rich Becker FOIL .25 .11 .03
☐ 376 Derek Jeter FOIL 3.00 1.35 .35
☐ 377 Steve Karsay FOIL .10 .05 .01
☐ 378 Mac Suzuki FOIL .25 .11 .03
☐ 379 Benji Gil FOIL .10 .05 .01
☐ 380 Alex Gonzalez FOIL .25 .11 .03
☐ 381 Jason Bere FOIL .25 .11 .03
☐ 382 Brett Butler FOIL .25 .11 .03
☐ 383 Jeff Conine FOIL .25 .11 .03
☐ 384 Darren Daulton FOIL .25 .11 .03
☐ 385 Jeff Kent FOIL .10 .05 .01
☐ 386 Don Mattingly FOIL 2.00 .90 .25
☐ 387 Mike Piazza FOIL 2.50 1.10 .30
☐ 388 Ryne Sandberg FOIL 1.00 .45 .12
☐ 389 Rich Amaral .10 .05 .01
☐ 390 Craig Biggio .25 .11 .03
☐ 391 Jeff Suppan 2.00 .90 .25
☐ 392 Andy Benes .25 .11 .03
☐ 393 Cal Eldred .10 .05 .01
☐ 394 Jeff Conine .25 .11 .03
☐ 395 Tim Salmon .50 .23 .06
☐ 396 Ray Suplee .10 .05 .01
☐ 397 Tony Phillips .25 .11 .03
☐ 398 Ramon Martinez .25 .11 .03
☐ 399 Julio Franco .25 .11 .03
☐ 400 Dwight Gooden .25 .11 .03
☐ 401 Kevin Lomon .10 .05 .01
☐ 402 Jose Rijo .10 .05 .01
☐ 403 Mike Devereaux .10 .05 .01
☐ 404 Mike Zolecki .10 .05 .01
☐ 405 Fred McGriff .50 .23 .06
☐ 406 Danny Clyburn .25 .11 .03
☐ 407 Robby Thompson .10 .05 .01
☐ 408 Terry Steinbach .25 .11 .03
☐ 409 Luis Polonia .10 .05 .01
☐ 410 Mark Grace .50 .23 .06
☐ 411 Albert Belle 1.50 .70 .19
☐ 412 John Kruk .25 .11 .03
☐ 413 Scott Spiezio 1.50 .70 .19
☐ 414 Ellis Burks UER .25 .11 .03
(Name spelled Elkis on front)
☐ 415 Joe Vitiello .25 .11 .03
☐ 416 Tim Costo .10 .05 .01
☐ 417 Marc Newfield .25 .11 .03
☐ 418 Oscar Henriquez .10 .05 .01
☐ 419 Matt Perisho .75 .35 .09
☐ 420 Julio Bruno .10 .05 .01
☐ 421 Kenny Felder .10 .05 .01
☐ 422 Tyler Green .10 .05 .01
☐ 423 Jim Edmonds .75 .35 .09
☐ 424 Ozzie Smith 1.00 .45 .12
☐ 425 Rick Greene .10 .05 .01
☐ 426 Todd Hollandsworth 1.00 .45 .12
☐ 427 Eddie Pearson .50 .23 .06
☐ 428 Quilvio Veras .25 .11 .03
☐ 429 Kenny Rogers .10 .05 .01
☐ 430 Willie Greene .25 .11 .03
☐ 431 Vaughn Eshelman .10 .05 .01
☐ 432 Pat Meares .10 .05 .01
☐ 433 Jermaine Dye 6.00 2.70 .75
☐ 434 Steve Cooke .10 .05 .01
☐ 435 Bill Swift .10 .05 .01
☐ 436 Fausto Cruz .10 .05 .01
☐ 437 Mark Hutton .10 .05 .01
☐ 438 Brooks Kieschnick 1.00 .45 .12
☐ 439 Yorkis Perez .10 .05 .01
☐ 440 Len Dykstra .25 .11 .03
☐ 441 Pat Borders .10 .05 .01
☐ 442 Doug Walls .10 .05 .01
☐ 443 Wally Joyner .25 .11 .03
☐ 444 Ken Hill .10 .05 .01
☐ 445 Eric Anthony .10 .05 .01
☐ 446 Mitch Williams .10 .05 .01
☐ 447 Cory Bailey .10 .05 .01
☐ 448 Dave Staton .10 .05 .01
☐ 449 Greg Vaughn .50 .23 .06
☐ 450 Dave Magadan .10 .05 .01
☐ 451 Chili Davis .25 .11 .03
☐ 452 Gerald Santos .10 .05 .01
☐ 453 Joe Perona .10 .05 .01
☐ 454 Delino DeShields .10 .05 .01
☐ 455 Jack McDowell .25 .11 .03
☐ 456 Todd Hundley .25 .11 .03
☐ 457 Ritchie Moody .10 .05 .01
☐ 458 Bret Boone .25 .11 .03
☐ 459 Ben McDonald .10 .05 .01
☐ 460 Kirby Puckett 1.50 .70 .19
☐ 461 Gregg Olson .10 .05 .01
☐ 462 Rich Aude .25 .11 .03
☐ 463 John Burkett .10 .05 .01
☐ 464 Troy Neel .10 .05 .01
☐ 465 Jimmy Key .25 .11 .03
☐ 466 Ozzie Timmons .25 .11 .03
☐ 467 Eddie Murray 1.00 .45 .12
☐ 468 Mark Tranberg .10 .05 .01
☐ 469 Alex Gonzalez .25 .11 .03
☐ 470 David Nied .10 .05 .01
☐ 471 Barry Larkin .50 .23 .06
☐ 472 Brian Looney .10 .05 .01
☐ 473 Shawn Estes .25 .11 .03
☐ 474 A.J. Sager .10 .05 .01
☐ 475 Roger Clemens .75 .35 .09
☐ 476 Vince Moore .10 .05 .01
☐ 477 Scott Karl .25 .11 .03
☐ 478 Kurt Miller .10 .05 .01
☐ 479 Garret Anderson .50 .23 .06
☐ 480 Allen Watson .10 .05 .01
☐ 481 Jose Lima .25 .11 .03
☐ 482 Rick Gorecki .10 .05 .01
☐ 483 Jimmy Hurst .25 .11 .03
☐ 484 Preston Wilson .25 .11 .03
☐ 485 Will Clark .50 .23 .06
☐ 486 Mike Ferry .10 .05 .01
☐ 487 Curtis Goodwin .25 .11 .03
☐ 488 Mike Myers .10 .05 .01
☐ 489 Chipper Jones 3.00 1.35 .35
☐ 490 Jeff King .25 .11 .03
☐ 491 William VanLandingham .25 .11 .03
☐ 492 Carlos Reyes .10 .05 .01
☐ 493 Andy Pettitte 2.00 .90 .25
☐ 494 Brant Brown .10 .05 .01
☐ 495 Daron Kirkreit .25 .11 .03
☐ 496 Ricky Bottalico .50 .23 .06
☐ 497 Devon White .10 .05 .01
☐ 498 Jason Johnson .10 .05 .01
☐ 499 Vince Coleman .10 .05 .01
☐ 500 Larry Walker .50 .23 .06
☐ 501 Bobby Ayala .10 .05 .01
☐ 502 Steve Finley .50 .23 .06
☐ 503 Scott Fletcher .10 .05 .01
☐ 504 Brad Ausmus .10 .05 .01
☐ 505 Scott Talanoa .10 .05 .01
☐ 506 Orestes Destrade .10 .05 .01
☐ 507 Gary DiSarcina .10 .05 .01
☐ 508 Willie Smith .10 .05 .01
☐ 509 Alan Trammell .25 .11 .03
☐ 510 Mike Piazza 2.50 1.10 .30
☐ 511 Ozzie Guillen .10 .05 .01
☐ 512 Jeromy Burnitz .10 .05 .01
☐ 513 Darren Oliver .75 .35 .09
☐ 514 Kevin Mitchell .25 .11 .03
☐ 515 Rafael Palmeiro .50 .23 .06
☐ 516 David McCarty .10 .05 .01
☐ 517 Jeff Blauser .10 .05 .01
☐ 518 Trey Beamon .25 .11 .03
☐ 519 Royce Clayton .25 .11 .03
☐ 520 Dennis Eckersley .25 .11 .03
☐ 521 Bernie Williams .75 .35 .09
☐ 522 Steve Buechele .10 .05 .01
☐ 523 Denny Martinez .25 .11 .03
☐ 524 Dave Hollins .10 .05 .01
☐ 525 Joey Hamilton .75 .35 .09
☐ 526 Andres Galarraga .50 .23 .06
☐ 527 Jeff Granger .25 .11 .03
☐ 528 Joey Eischen .10 .05 .01
☐ 529 Desi Relaford .10 .05 .01
☐ 530 Roberto Petagine .25 .11 .03
☐ 531 Andre Dawson .25 .11 .03
☐ 532 Ray Holbert .10 .05 .01
☐ 533 Duane Singleton .10 .05 .01
☐ 534 Kurt Abbott .25 .11 .03
☐ 535 Bo Jackson .25 .11 .03
☐ 536 Gregg Jefferies .50 .23 .06
☐ 537 David Mysel .10 .05 .01
☐ 538 Raul Mondesi .50 .23 .06
☐ 539 Chris Snopek .10 .05 .01
☐ 540 Brook Fordyce .10 .05 .01
☐ 541 Ron Frazier .10 .05 .01
☐ 542 Brian Koelling .10 .05 .01
☐ 543 Jimmy Haynes .25 .11 .03
☐ 544 Marty Cordova .75 .35 .09
☐ 545 Jason Green .25 .11 .03
☐ 546 Orlando Merced .25 .11 .03
☐ 547 Lou Pote .10 .05 .01
☐ 548 Todd Van Poppel .10 .05 .01
☐ 549 Pat Kelly .10 .05 .01
☐ 550 Turk Wendell .10 .05 .01
☐ 551 Herbert Perry .25 .11 .03
☐ 552 Ryan Karp .25 .11 .03
☐ 553 Juan Guzman .25 .11 .03
☐ 554 Bryan Rekar .25 .11 .03
☐ 555 Kevin Appier .25 .11 .03
☐ 556 Chris Schwab .50 .23 .06
☐ 557 Jay Buhner .50 .23 .06
☐ 558 Andujar Cedeno .10 .05 .01
☐ 559 Ryan McGuire .25 .11 .03
☐ 560 Ricky Gutierrez .10 .05 .01
☐ 561 Keith Kimsey .10 .05 .01
☐ 562 Tim Clark .10 .05 .01
☐ 563 Damion Easley .10 .05 .01
☐ 564 Clint Davis .10 .05 .01
☐ 565 Mike Moore .10 .05 .01
☐ 566 Orel Hershiser .25 .11 .03
☐ 567 Jason Bere .25 .11 .03
☐ 568 Kevin McReynolds .10 .05 .01
☐ 569 Leland Macon .25 .11 .03
☐ 570 John Courtright .10 .05 .01
☐ 571 Sid Fernandez .10 .05 .01
☐ 572 Chad Roper .10 .05 .01
☐ 573 Terry Pendleton .25 .11 .03
☐ 574 Danny Miceli .10 .05 .01
☐ 575 Joe Rosselli .10 .05 .01
☐ 576 Mike Bordick .10 .05 .01
☐ 577 Danny Tartabull .10 .05 .01
☐ 578 Jose Guzman .10 .05 .01
☐ 579 Omar Vizquel .25 .11 .03
☐ 580 Tommy Greene .10 .05 .01
☐ 581 Paul Spoljaric .10 .05 .01
☐ 582 Walt Weiss .10 .05 .01
☐ 583 Oscar Jimenez .10 .05 .01
☐ 584 Rod Henderson .10 .05 .01
☐ 585 Derek Lowe .10 .05 .01
☐ 586 Richard Hidalgo 3.00 1.35 .35
☐ 587 Shayne Bennett .25 .11 .03
☐ 588 Tim Belk .25 .11 .03
☐ 589 Matt Mieske .10 .05 .01
☐ 590 Nigel Wilson .10 .05 .01
☐ 591 Jeff Knox .25 .11 .03
☐ 592 Bernard Gilkey .25 .11 .03
☐ 593 David Cone .25 .11 .03

☐ 594 Paul LoDuca .25 .11 .03
☐ 595 Scott Ruffcorn .10 .05 .01
☐ 596 Chris Roberts .25 .11 .03
☐ 597 Oscar Munoz .10 .05 .01
☐ 598 Scott Sullivan .25 .11 .03
☐ 599 Matt Jarvis .10 .05 .01
☐ 600 Jose Canseco .50 .23 .06
☐ 601 Tony Graffanino .25 .11 .03
☐ 602 Don Slaught .10 .05 .01
☐ 603 Brett King .25 .11 .03
☐ 604 Jose Herrera .50 .23 .06
☐ 605 Melido Perez .10 .05 .01
☐ 606 Mike Hubbard .10 .05 .01
☐ 607 Chad Ogea .25 .11 .03
☐ 608 Wayne Gomes .25 .11 .03
☐ 609 Roberto Alomar .75 .35 .09
☐ 610 Angel Echevarria .50 .23 .06
☐ 611 Jose Lind .10 .05 .01
☐ 612 Darrin Fletcher .10 .05 .01
☐ 613 Chris Bosio .10 .05 .01
☐ 614 Darryl Kile .10 .05 .01
☐ 615 Frankie Rodriguez .25 .11 .03
☐ 616 Phil Plantier .10 .05 .01
☐ 617 Pat Listach .10 .05 .01
☐ 618 Charlie Hough .10 .05 .01
☐ 619 Ryan Hancock .25 .11 .03
☐ 620 Darrel Deak .10 .05 .01
☐ 621 Travis Fryman .25 .11 .03
☐ 622 Brett Butler .25 .11 .03
☐ 623 Lance Johnson .25 .11 .03
☐ 624 Pete Smith .10 .05 .01
☐ 625 James Hurst .10 .05 .01
☐ 626 Roberto Kelly .10 .05 .01
☐ 627 Mike Mussina .75 .35 .09
☐ 628 Kevin Tapani .10 .05 .01
☐ 629 John Smoltz .50 .23 .06
☐ 630 Midre Cummings .10 .05 .01
☐ 631 Salomon Torres .10 .05 .01
☐ 632 Willie Adams .10 .05 .01
☐ 633 Derek Jeter 3.00 1.35 .35
☐ 634 Steve Trachsel .25 .11 .03
☐ 635 Albie Lopez .25 .11 .03
☐ 636 Jason Moler .10 .05 .01
☐ 637 Carlos Delgado .50 .23 .06
☐ 638 Roberto Mejia .10 .05 .01
☐ 639 Darren Burton .10 .05 .01
☐ 640 B.J. Wallace .10 .05 .01
☐ 641 Brad Clontz .25 .11 .03
☐ 642 Billy Wagner 2.00 .90 .25
☐ 643 Aaron Sele .25 .11 .03
☐ 644 Cameron Cairncross .10 .05 .01
☐ 645 Brian Harper .10 .05 .01
☐ 646 Marc Valdes UER .25 .11 .03
(No card number on back)
☐ 647 Mark Ratekin .10 .05 .01
☐ 648 Terry Bradshaw .25 .11 .03
☐ 649 Justin Thompson .25 .11 .03
☐ 650 Mike Busch .25 .11 .03
☐ 651 Joe Hall .10 .05 .01
☐ 652 Bobby Jones .25 .11 .03
☐ 653 Kelly Stinnett .10 .05 .01
☐ 654 Rod Steph .10 .05 .01
☐ 655 Jay Powell .25 .11 .03
☐ 656 Keith Garagozzo UER .10 .05 .01
(No card number on back)
☐ 657 Todd Dunn .25 .11 .03
☐ 658 Charles Peterson .50 .23 .06
☐ 659 Darren Lewis .10 .05 .01
☐ 660 John Wasdin .50 .23 .06
☐ 661 Tate Seefried .25 .11 .03
☐ 662 Hector Trinidad .25 .11 .03
☐ 663 John Carter .10 .05 .01
☐ 664 Larry Mitchell .10 .05 .01
☐ 665 David Catlett .25 .11 .03
☐ 666 Dante Bichette .50 .23 .06
☐ 667 Felix Jose .10 .05 .01
☐ 668 Rondell White .50 .23 .06
☐ 669 Tino Martinez .25 .11 .03
☐ 670 Brian L. Hunter .50 .23 .06
☐ 671 Jose Malave .25 .11 .03
☐ 672 Archi Cianfrocco .10 .05 .01
☐ 673 Mike Matheny .10 .05 .01
☐ 674 Bret Barberie .10 .05 .01
☐ 675 Andrew Lorraine .10 .05 .01
☐ 676 Brian Jordan .50 .23 .06
☐ 677 Tim Belcher .10 .05 .01
☐ 678 Antonio Osuna .25 .11 .03
☐ 679 Checklist .10 .05 .01
☐ 680 Checklist .10 .05 .01
☐ 681 Checklist .10 .05 .01
☐ 682 Checklist .10 .05 .01

1995 Bowman

Cards from this 439-card standard-size prsopect-oriented set were primarily issued in plastic wrapped packs and jumbo packs. Card fronts feature white broders enframing full color photos. The left border is a reversed negative of the photo. The set includes 54 silver foil subset cards (221-274). The foil subset, largely comprising of minor league stars, have embossed borders and are found one per pack and two per jumbo pack. Rookie Cards of note include Bartolo Colon, Karim Garcia, Derrick Gibson, Vladmir Guerrero, Andrew Jones, Hideo Nomo, Jay Payton and Scott Rolen.

	MINT	NRMT	EXC
COMPLETE SET (439)	180.00	80.00	22.00
COMMON CARD (1-439)	.15	.07	.02

☐ 1 Billy Wagner .60 .25 .07
☐ 2 Chris Widger .15 .07 .02
☐ 3 Brent Bowers .15 .07 .02
☐ 4 Bob Abreu 4.00 1.80 .50
☐ 5 Lou Collier .50 .23 .06
☐ 6 Juan Acevedo .15 .07 .02
☐ 7 Jason Kelley .15 .07 .02
☐ 8 Brian Sackinsky .15 .07 .02
☐ 9 Scott Christman .15 .07 .02
☐ 10 Damon Hollins .30 .14 .04
☐ 11 Willis Otanez .30 .14 .04
☐ 12 Jason Ryan .30 .14 .04
☐ 13 Jason Giambi 1.00 .45 .12
☐ 14 Andy Taulbee .15 .07 .02
☐ 15 Mark Thompson .15 .07 .02
☐ 16 Hugo Pivaral .30 .14 .04
☐ 17 Brien Taylor .15 .07 .02
☐ 18 Antonio Osuna .15 .07 .02
☐ 19 Edgardo Alfonzo .30 .14 .04
☐ 20 Carl Everett .15 .07 .02
☐ 21 Matt Drews .30 .14 .04
☐ 22 Bartolo Colon 4.00 1.80 .50
☐ 23 Andruw Jones 40.00 18.00 5.00
☐ 24 Robert Person .15 .07 .02
☐ 25 Derrek Lee 2.00 .90 .25
☐ 26 John Ambrose .30 .14 .04
☐ 27 Eric Knowles .30 .14 .04
☐ 28 Chris Roberts .15 .07 .02
☐ 29 Don Wengert .15 .07 .02
☐ 30 Marcus Jensen .30 .14 .04
☐ 31 Brian Barber .15 .07 .02
☐ 32 Kevin Brown C 1.00 .45 .12
☐ 33 Benji Gil .15 .07 .02
☐ 34 Mike Hubbard .15 .07 .02
☐ 35 Bart Evans .15 .07 .02
☐ 36 Enrique Wilson 2.00 .90 .25
☐ 37 Brian Buchanan .30 .14 .04
☐ 38 Ken Ray .15 .07 .02
☐ 39 Micah Franklin .30 .14 .04
☐ 40 Ricky Otero .15 .07 .02
☐ 41 Jason Kendall .60 .25 .07
☐ 42 Jimmy Hurst .30 .14 .04
☐ 43 Jerry Wolak .15 .07 .02
☐ 44 Jayson Peterson .30 .14 .04
☐ 45 Allen Battle .15 .07 .02
☐ 46 Scott Stahoviak .15 .07 .02
☐ 47 Steve Schrenk .15 .07 .02
☐ 48 Travis Miller .30 .14 .04
☐ 49 Eddie Rios .15 .07 .02
☐ 50 Mike Hampton .15 .07 .02
☐ 51 Chad Frontera .15 .07 .02
☐ 52 Tom Evans .15 .07 .02
☐ 53 C.J. Nitkowski .30 .14 .04
☐ 54 Clay Caruthers .30 .14 .04
☐ 55 Shannon Stewart .30 .14 .04
☐ 56 Jorge Posada .15 .07 .02
☐ 57 Aaron Holbert .15 .07 .02
☐ 58 Harry Berrios .15 .07 .02
☐ 59 Steve Rodriguez .15 .07 .02
☐ 60 Shane Andrews .15 .07 .02
☐ 61 Will Cunnane .40 .18 .05
☐ 62 Richard Hidalgo 1.25 .55 .16
☐ 63 Bill Selby .15 .07 .02
☐ 64 Jay Cranford .15 .07 .02
☐ 65 Jeff Suppan .60 .25 .07
☐ 66 Curtis Goodwin .30 .14 .04
☐ 67 John Thomson .50 .23 .06
☐ 68 Justin Thompson .30 .14 .04
☐ 69 Troy Percival .15 .07 .02
☐ 70 Matt Wagner .30 .14 .04
☐ 71 Terry Bradshaw .15 .07 .02
☐ 72 Greg Hansell .15 .07 .02
☐ 73 John Burke .15 .07 .02
☐ 74 Jeff D'Amico .60 .25 .07
☐ 75 Ernie Young .30 .14 .04
☐ 76 Jason Bates .15 .07 .02
☐ 77 Chris Stynes .15 .07 .02
☐ 78 Cade Gaspar .30 .14 .04
☐ 79 Melvin Nieves .30 .14 .04
☐ 80 Rick Gorecki .15 .07 .02
☐ 81 Felix Rodriguez .30 .14 .04
☐ 82 Ryan Hancock .15 .07 .02
☐ 83 Chris Carpenter 2.00 .90 .25
☐ 84 Ray McDavid .30 .14 .04
☐ 85 Chris Wimmer .15 .07 .02
☐ 86 Doug Glanville .15 .07 .02
☐ 87 DeShawn Warren .15 .07 .02
☐ 88 Damian Moss 2.00 .90 .25
☐ 89 Rafael Orellano .30 .14 .04
☐ 90 Vladimir Guerrero 25.00 11.00 3.10
☐ 91 Raul Casanova 1.25 .55 .16
☐ 92 Karim Garcia 8.00 3.60 1.00
☐ 93 Bryce Florie .15 .07 .02
☐ 94 Kevin Orie .75 .35 .09
☐ 95 Ryan Nye .30 .14 .04
☐ 96 Matt Sachse .40 .18 .05
☐ 97 Ivan Arteaga .15 .07 .02
☐ 98 Glenn Murray .15 .07 .02
☐ 99 Stacy Hollins .15 .07 .02
☐ 100 Jim Pittsley .60 .25 .07
☐ 101 Craig Mattson .15 .07 .02
☐ 102 Neifi Perez .60 .25 .07
☐ 103 Keith Williams .15 .07 .02
☐ 104 Roger Cedeno .30 .14 .04
☐ 105 Tony Terry .30 .14 .04
☐ 106 Jose Malave .15 .07 .02
☐ 107 Joe Rosselli .15 .07 .02
☐ 108 Kevin Jordan .15 .07 .02
☐ 109 Sid Roberson .15 .07 .02
☐ 110 Alan Embree .15 .07 .02
☐ 111 Terrell Wade .60 .25 .07
☐ 112 Bob Wolcott .30 .14 .04
☐ 113 Carlos Perez .30 .14 .04
☐ 114 Mike Bovee .30 .14 .04
☐ 115 Tommy Davis .30 .14 .04
☐ 116 Jeremey Kendall .15 .07 .02
☐ 117 Rich Aude .15 .07 .02
☐ 118 Rick Huisman .15 .07 .02
☐ 119 Tim Belk .15 .07 .02
☐ 120 Edgar Renteria 1.25 .55 .16
☐ 121 Calvin Maduro .50 .23 .06
☐ 122 Jerry Martin .15 .07 .02
☐ 123 Ramon Fermin .15 .07 .02
☐ 124 Kimera Bartee .30 .14 .04
☐ 125 Mark Farris .30 .14 .04
☐ 126 Frank Rodriguez .30 .14 .04
☐ 127 Bobby Higginson 1.50 .70 .19
☐ 128 Bret Wagner .30 .14 .04
☐ 129 Edwin Diaz .75 .35 .09
☐ 130 Jimmy Haynes .30 .14 .04
☐ 131 Chris Weinke .15 .07 .02
☐ 132 Damian Jackson .30 .14 .04
☐ 133 Felix Martinez .15 .07 .02
☐ 134 Edwin Hurtado .15 .07 .02
☐ 135 Matt Raleigh .15 .07 .02
☐ 136 Paul Wilson 1.25 .55 .16
☐ 137 Ron Villone .15 .07 .02
☐ 138 Eric Stuckenschneider .15 .07 .02
☐ 139 Tate Seefried .15 .07 .02
☐ 140 Rey Ordonez 4.00 1.80 .50
☐ 141 Eddie Pearson .15 .07 .02
☐ 142 Kevin Gallaher .15 .07 .02
☐ 143 Torii Hunter .60 .25 .07
☐ 144 Daron Kirkreit .15 .07 .02
☐ 145 Craig Wilson .15 .07 .02
☐ 146 Ugueth Urbina .15 .07 .02
☐ 147 Chris Snopek .15 .07 .02
☐ 148 Kym Ashworth .30 .14 .04
☐ 149 Wayne Gomes .15 .07 .02
☐ 150 Mark Loretta .15 .07 .02
☐ 151 Ramon Morel .40 .18 .05
☐ 152 Trot Nixon .30 .14 .04
☐ 153 Desi Relaford .30 .14 .04
☐ 154 Scott Sullivan .15 .07 .02
☐ 155 Marc Barcelo .15 .07 .02
☐ 156 Willie Adams .15 .07 .02
☐ 157 Derrick Gibson 6.00 2.70 .75
☐ 158 Brian Meadows .50 .23 .06
☐ 159 Julian Tavarez .15 .07 .02
☐ 160 Bryan Rekar .15 .07 .02
☐ 161 Steve Gibralter .30 .14 .04
☐ 162 Esteban Loaiza .15 .07 .02
☐ 163 John Wasdin .15 .07 .02
☐ 164 Kirk Presley .30 .14 .04
☐ 165 Mariano Rivera .30 .14 .04
☐ 166 Andy Larkin .15 .07 .02
☐ 167 Sean Whiteside .15 .07 .02
☐ 168 Matt Apana .15 .07 .02
☐ 169 Shawn Senior .15 .07 .02
☐ 170 Scott Gentile .15 .07 .02
☐ 171 Quilvio Veras .15 .07 .02
☐ 172 Elieser Marrero .75 .35 .09
☐ 173 Mendy Lopez .50 .23 .06
☐ 174 Homer Bush .15 .07 .02
☐ 175 Brian Stephenson .30 .14 .04
☐ 176 Jon Nunnally .30 .14 .04
☐ 177 Jose Herrera .15 .07 .02
☐ 178 Corey Avrard .50 .23 .06
☐ 179 David Bell .15 .07 .02
☐ 180 Jason Isringhausen 1.00 .45 .12
☐ 181 Jamey Wright .60 .25 .07
☐ 182 Lonell Roberts .15 .07 .02
☐ 183 Marty Cordova .60 .25 .07
☐ 184 Amaury Telemaco .15 .07 .02
☐ 185 John Mabry .60 .25 .07
☐ 186 Andrew Vessel .30 .14 .04
☐ 187 Jim Cole .15 .07 .02
☐ 188 Marquis Riley .15 .07 .02
☐ 189 Todd Dunn .30 .14 .04
☐ 190 John Carter .15 .07 .02
☐ 191 Donnie Sadler 1.00 .45 .12
☐ 192 Mike Bell .60 .25 .07
☐ 193 Chris Cumberland .30 .14 .04
☐ 194 Jason Schmidt .60 .25 .07
☐ 195 Matt Brunson .15 .07 .02
☐ 196 James Baldwin .30 .14 .04
☐ 197 Bill Simas .15 .07 .02
☐ 198 Gus Gandarillas .15 .07 .02
☐ 199 Mac Suzuki .30 .14 .04
☐ 200 Rick Holifield .15 .07 .02
☐ 201 Fernando Lunar .30 .14 .04
☐ 202 Kevin Jarvis .15 .07 .02
☐ 203 Everett Stull .15 .07 .02
☐ 204 Steve Wojciechowski .15 .07 .02
☐ 205 Shawn Estes .15 .07 .02
☐ 206 Jermaine Dye 3.00 1.35 .35
☐ 207 Marc Kroon .15 .07 .02
☐ 208 Peter Munro .40 .18 .05
☐ 209 Pat Watkins .30 .14 .04
☐ 210 Matt Smith .30 .14 .04
☐ 211 Joe Vitiello .15 .07 .02
☐ 212 Gerald Witasick Jr. .15 .07 .02
☐ 213 Freddy Garcia .50 .23 .06
☐ 214 Glenn Dishman .30 .14 .04
☐ 215 Jay Canizaro .30 .14 .04
☐ 216 Angel Martinez .15 .07 .02
☐ 217 Yamil Benitez .50 .23 .06
☐ 218 Fausto Macey .40 .18 .05
☐ 219 Eric Owens .30 .14 .04
☐ 220 Checklist .15 .07 .02
☐ 221 Dwayne Hosey FOIL .30 .14 .04
☐ 222 Brad Woodall FOIL .15 .07 .02
☐ 223 Billy Ashley FOIL .15 .07 .02
☐ 224 Mark Grudzielanek FOIL 1.50 .70 .19
☐ 225 Mark Johnson FOIL .30 .14 .04
☐ 226 Tim Unroe FOIL .30 .14 .04
☐ 227 Todd Greene FOIL .30 .14 .04
☐ 228 Larry Sutton FOIL .15 .07 .02
☐ 229 Derek Jeter FOIL 4.00 1.80 .50
☐ 230 Sal Fasano FOIL .30 .14 .04
☐ 231 Ruben Rivera FOIL 3.00 1.35 .35
☐ 232 Chris Truby FOIL .30 .14 .04
☐ 233 John Donati FOIL .15 .07 .02
☐ 234 Decomba Conner FOIL .50 .23 .06
☐ 235 Sergio Nunez FOIL .75 .35 .09
☐ 236 Ray Brown FOIL .30 .14 .04
☐ 237 Juan Melo FOIL 1.00 .45 .12
☐ 238 Hideo Nomo FOIL 6.00 2.70 .75
☐ 239 Jamie Bluma FOIL .30 .14 .04
☐ 240 Jay Payton FOIL 3.00 1.35 .35
☐ 241 Paul Konerko FOIL 6.00 2.70 .75
☐ 242 Scott Elarton FOIL .75 .35 .09
☐ 243 Jeff Abbott FOIL 1.25 .55 .16
☐ 244 Jim Brower FOIL .30 .14 .04
☐ 245 Geoff Blum FOIL .40 .18 .05
☐ 246 Aaron Boone FOIL 1.00 .45 .12
☐ 247 J.R. Phillips FOIL .15 .07 .02
☐ 248 Alex Ochoa FOIL .30 .14 .04
☐ 249 Nomar Garciaparra FOIL 6.00 2.70 .75
☐ 250 Garret Anderson FOIL .30 .14 .04
☐ 251 Ray Durham FOIL .30 .14 .04
☐ 252 Paul Shuey FOIL .15 .07 .02
☐ 253 Tony Clark FOIL 2.00 .90 .25
☐ 254 Johnny Damon FOIL .30 .14 .04
☐ 255 Duane Singleton FOIL .15 .07 .02
☐ 256 LaTroy Hawkins FOIL .15 .07 .02
☐ 257 Andy Pettitte FOIL 2.50 1.10 .30
☐ 258 Ben Grieve FOIL 5.00 2.20 .60
☐ 259 Marc Newfield FOIL .30 .14 .04
☐ 260 Terrell Lowery FOIL .15 .07 .02
☐ 261 Shawn Green FOIL .30 .14 .04
☐ 262 Chipper Jones FOIL 3.00 1.35 .35
☐ 263 Brooks Kieschnick FOIL .60 .25 .07
☐ 264 Calvin Reese FOIL .15 .07 .02
☐ 265 Doug Million FOIL 1.00 .45 .12
☐ 266 Marc Valdes FOIL .15 .07 .02
☐ 267 Brian L.Hunter FOIL .30 .14 .04
☐ 268 Todd Hollandsworth FOIL 1.00 .45 .12
☐ 269 Rod Henderson FOIL .15 .07 .02
☐ 270 Bill Pulsipher FOIL .30 .14 .04
☐ 271 Scott Rolen FOIL 15.00 6.75 1.85
☐ 272 Trey Beamon FOIL .30 .14 .04
☐ 273 Alan Benes FOIL .60 .25 .07
☐ 274 Dustin Hermanson FOIL .30 .14 .04
☐ 275 Ricky Bottalico .30 .14 .04
☐ 276 Albert Belle 2.00 .90 .25
☐ 277 Deion Sanders .60 .25 .07
☐ 278 Matt Williams .60 .25 .07
☐ 279 Jeff Bagwell 2.00 .90 .25
☐ 280 Kirby Puckett 2.00 .90 .25
☐ 281 Dave Hollins .15 .07 .02
☐ 282 Don Mattingly 2.50 1.10 .30
☐ 283 Joey Hamilton .60 .25 .07
☐ 284 Bobby Bonilla .30 .14 .04
☐ 285 Moises Alou .30 .14 .04
☐ 286 Tom Glavine .60 .25 .07
☐ 287 Brett Butler .30 .14 .04
☐ 288 Chris Hoiles .15 .07 .02
☐ 289 Kenny Rogers .15 .07 .02
☐ 290 Larry Walker .60 .25 .07
☐ 291 Tim Raines .60 .25 .07
☐ 292 Kevin Appier .30 .14 .04
☐ 293 Roger Clemens 1.00 .45 .12
☐ 294 Chuck Carr .15 .07 .02
☐ 295 Randy Myers .15 .07 .02
☐ 296 Dave Nilsson .30 .14 .04
☐ 297 Joe Carter .30 .14 .04
☐ 298 Chuck Finley .30 .14 .04
☐ 299 Ray Lankford .30 .14 .04
☐ 300 Roberto Kelly .15 .07 .02
☐ 301 Jon Lieber .15 .07 .02
☐ 302 Travis Fryman .30 .14 .04

☐ 303 Mark McGwire	1.50	.70	.19
☐ 304 Tony Gwynn	2.00	.90	.25
☐ 305 Kenny Lofton	1.25	.55	.16
☐ 306 Mark Whiten	.15	.07	.02
☐ 307 Doug Drabek	.15	.07	.02
☐ 308 Terry Steinbach	.30	.14	.04
☐ 309 Ryan Klesko	.60	.25	.07
☐ 310 Mike Piazza	3.00	1.35	.35
☐ 311 Ben McDonald	.15	.07	.02
☐ 312 Reggie Sanders	.30	.14	.04
☐ 313 Alex Fernandez	.30	.14	.04
☐ 314 Aaron Sele	.30	.14	.04
☐ 315 Gregg Jefferies	.30	.14	.04
☐ 316 Rickey Henderson	.60	.25	.07
☐ 317 Brian Anderson	.15	.07	.02
☐ 318 Jose Valentin	.30	.14	.04
☐ 319 Rod Beck	.15	.07	.02
☐ 320 Marquis Grissom	.30	.14	.04
☐ 321 Ken Griffey Jr.	5.00	2.20	.60
☐ 322 Bret Saberhagen	.30	.14	.04
☐ 323 Juan Gonzalez	2.50	1.10	.30
☐ 324 Paul Molitor	1.00	.45	.12
☐ 325 Gary Sheffield	.60	.25	.07
☐ 326 Darren Daulton	.30	.14	.04
☐ 327 Bill Swift	.15	.07	.02
☐ 328 Brian McRae	.30	.14	.04
☐ 329 Robin Ventura	.30	.14	.04
☐ 330 Lee Smith	.30	.14	.04
☐ 331 Fred McGriff	.60	.25	.07
☐ 332 Delino DeShields	.15	.07	.02
☐ 333 Edgar Martinez	.30	.14	.04
☐ 334 Mike Mussina	1.00	.45	.12
☐ 335 Orlando Merced	.15	.07	.02
☐ 336 Carlos Baerga	.30	.14	.04
☐ 337 Wil Cordero	.15	.07	.02
☐ 338 Tom Pagnozzi	.15	.07	.02
☐ 339 Pat Hentgen	.30	.14	.04
☐ 340 Chad Curtis	.15	.07	.02
☐ 341 Darren Lewis	.15	.07	.02
☐ 342 Jeff Kent	.15	.07	.02
☐ 343 Bip Roberts	.15	.07	.02
☐ 344 Ivan Rodriguez	1.25	.55	.16
☐ 345 Jeff Montgomery	.30	.14	.04
☐ 346 Hal Morris	.15	.07	.02
☐ 347 Danny Tartabull	.15	.07	.02
☐ 348 Raul Mondesi	.60	.25	.07
☐ 349 Ken Hill	.15	.07	.02
☐ 350 Pedro Martinez	.30	.14	.04
☐ 351 Frank Thomas	5.00	2.20	.60
☐ 352 Manny Ramirez	1.25	.55	.16
☐ 353 Tim Salmon	.60	.25	.07
☐ 354 W. VanLandingham	.15	.07	.02
☐ 355 Andres Galarraga	.60	.25	.07
☐ 356 Paul O'Neill	.30	.14	.04
☐ 357 Brady Anderson	.60	.25	.07
☐ 358 Ramon Martinez	.30	.14	.04
☐ 359 John Olerud	.15	.07	.02
☐ 360 Ruben Sierra	.30	.14	.04
☐ 361 Cal Eldred	.15	.07	.02
☐ 362 Jay Buhner	.60	.25	.07
☐ 363 Jay Bell	.30	.14	.04
☐ 364 Wally Joyner	.30	.14	.04
☐ 365 Chuck Knoblauch	.60	.25	.07
☐ 366 Len Dykstra	.30	.14	.04
☐ 367 John Wetteland	.30	.14	.04
☐ 368 Roberto Alomar	1.00	.45	.12
☐ 369 Craig Biggio	.30	.14	.04
☐ 370 Ozzie Smith	1.25	.55	.16
☐ 371 Terry Pendleton	.30	.14	.04
☐ 372 Sammy Sosa	.60	.25	.07
☐ 373 Carlos Garcia	.15	.07	.02
☐ 374 Jose Rijo	.15	.07	.02
☐ 375 Chris Gomez	.15	.07	.02
☐ 376 Barry Bonds	1.25	.55	.16
☐ 377 Steve Avery	.30	.14	.04
☐ 378 Rick Wilkins	.15	.07	.02
☐ 379 Pete Harnisch	.15	.07	.02
☐ 380 Dean Palmer	.30	.14	.04
☐ 381 Bob Hamelin	.15	.07	.02
☐ 382 Jason Bere	.15	.07	.02
☐ 383 Jimmy Key	.30	.14	.04
☐ 384 Dante Bichette	.60	.25	.07
☐ 385 Rafael Palmeiro	.60	.25	.07
☐ 386 David Justice	.60	.25	.07
☐ 387 Chili Davis	.30	.14	.04
☐ 388 Mike Greenwell	.15	.07	.02
☐ 389 Todd Zeile	.15	.07	.02
☐ 390 Jeff Conine	.30	.14	.04
☐ 391 Rick Aguilera	.15	.07	.02
☐ 392 Eddie Murray	1.25	.55	.16
☐ 393 Mike Stanley	.15	.07	.02
☐ 394 Cliff Floyd UER (numbered 294)	.30	.14	.04
☐ 395 Randy Johnson	.60	.25	.07
☐ 396 David Nied	.15	.07	.02
☐ 397 Devon White	.30	.14	.04
☐ 398 Royce Clayton	.15	.07	.02
☐ 399 Andy Benes	.15	.07	.02
☐ 400 John Hudek	.15	.07	.02
☐ 401 Bobby Jones	.30	.14	.04
☐ 402 Eric Karros	.30	.14	.04
☐ 403 Will Clark	.60	.25	.07
☐ 404 Mark Langston	.15	.07	.02
☐ 405 Kevin Brown	.30	.14	.04
☐ 406 Greg Maddux	3.00	1.35	.35
☐ 407 David Cone	.30	.14	.04
☐ 408 Wade Boggs	.60	.25	.07
☐ 409 Steve Trachsel	.15	.07	.02
☐ 410 Greg Vaughn	.30	.14	.04
☐ 411 Mo Vaughn	1.25	.55	.16
☐ 412 Wilson Alvarez	.30	.14	.04
☐ 413 Cal Ripken	4.00	1.80	.50
☐ 414 Rico Brogna	.15	.07	.02
☐ 415 Barry Larkin	.60	.25	.07
☐ 416 Cecil Fielder	.30	.14	.04
☐ 417 Jose Canseco	.60	.25	.07
☐ 418 Jack McDowell	.30	.14	.04
☐ 419 Mike Lieberthal	.15	.07	.02
☐ 420 Andrew Lorraine	.30	.14	.04
☐ 421 Rich Becker	.15	.07	.02
☐ 422 Tony Phillips	.30	.14	.04
☐ 423 Scott Ruffcorn	.15	.07	.02
☐ 424 Jeff Granger	.15	.07	.02
☐ 425 Greg Pirkl	.15	.07	.02
☐ 426 Dennis Eckersley	.30	.14	.04
☐ 427 Jose Lima	.15	.07	.02
☐ 428 Russ Davis	.15	.07	.02
☐ 429 Armando Benitez	.15	.07	.02
☐ 430 Alex Gonzalez	.15	.07	.02
☐ 431 Carlos Delgado	.30	.14	.04
☐ 432 Chan Ho Park	.60	.25	.07
☐ 433 Mickey Tettleton	.15	.07	.02
☐ 434 Dave Winfield	.60	.25	.07
☐ 435 John Burkett	.30	.14	.04
☐ 436 Orlando Miller	.15	.07	.02
☐ 437 Rondell White	.30	.14	.04
☐ 438 Jose Oliva	.15	.07	.02
☐ 439 Checklist	.15	.07	.02

1995 Bowman Gold Foil

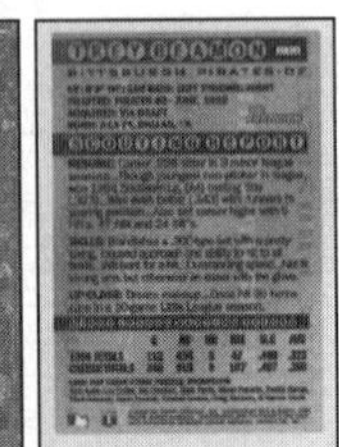

Numbered 221-274, this 54-card standard-size set is the gold insert parallel version of the silver foil subset found in the basic issue. The odds of finding a gold foil version are one in six packs.

	MINT	NRMT	EXC
COMPLETE SET (54)	200.00	90.00	25.00
COMMON CARD (221-274)	2.00	.90	.25
*GOLD: 3X TO 6X BASIC CARDS			
☐ 229 Derek Jeter	25.00	11.00	3.10
☐ 231 Ruben Rivera	12.00	5.50	1.50
☐ 238 Hideo Nomo	20.00	9.00	2.50
☐ 240 Jay Payton	8.00	3.60	1.00
☐ 241 Paul Konerko	20.00	9.00	2.50
☐ 249 Nomar Garciaparra	20.00	9.00	2.50
☐ 253 Tony Clark	8.00	3.60	1.00
☐ 257 Andy Pettitte	12.00	5.50	1.50
☐ 258 Ben Grieve	15.00	6.75	1.85
☐ 262 Chipper Jones	25.00	11.00	3.10
☐ 271 Scott Rolen	30.00	13.50	3.70

1996 Bowman

The 1996 Bowman set was issued in one series totalling 385 cards. The 11-card packs retail for $2.50 each. The fronts feature color action player photos in a tan-checkered frame with the player's name printed in silver foil at the bottom. The backs carry another color player photo with player information, 1995 and career player statistics. Each pack contained 10 regular issue cards plus either one foil parallel or an insert card. In a special promotional program, Topps offered collector's a $100 guarantee on complete sets. To get the guarantee, collector's had to mail in a Guaranteed Value Certificate request form, found in packs, along with a $5 processing and registration fee before the December 31st, 1996 deadline. Collectors would then receive a $100 Guaranteed Value Certificate, of which they could mail back to Topps between August 31st, 1999 and December 31st, 1999, along with their complete set, to receive $100. A reprint version of the 1952 Bowman Mickey Mantle card was randomly inserted into packs.

	MINT	NRMT	EXC
COMPLETE SET (385)	110.00	50.00	14.00
COMMON CARD (1-385)	.15	.07	.02
☐ 1 Cal Ripken	4.00	1.80	.50
☐ 2 Ray Durham	.60	.25	.07
☐ 3 Ivan Rodriguez	1.25	.55	.16
☐ 4 Fred McGriff	.60	.25	.07
☐ 5 Hideo Nomo	1.25	.55	.16
☐ 6 Troy Percival	.30	.14	.04
☐ 7 Moises Alou	.30	.14	.04
☐ 8 Mike Stanley	.15	.07	.02
☐ 9 Jay Buhner	.60	.25	.07
☐ 10 Shawn Green	.15	.07	.02
☐ 11 Ryan Klesko	.60	.25	.07
☐ 12 Andres Galarraga	.60	.25	.07
☐ 13 Dean Palmer	.15	.07	.02
☐ 14 Jeff Conine	.30	.14	.04
☐ 15 Brian L.Hunter	.30	.14	.04
☐ 16 J.T. Snow	.15	.07	.02
☐ 17 Larry Walker	.60	.25	.07
☐ 18 Barry Larkin	.30	.14	.04
☐ 19 Alex Gonzalez	.15	.07	.02
☐ 20 Edgar Martinez	.30	.14	.04
☐ 21 Mo Vaughn	1.25	.55	.16
☐ 22 Mark McGwire	1.50	.70	.19
☐ 23 Jose Canseco	.60	.25	.07
☐ 24 Jack McDowell	.15	.07	.02
☐ 25 Dante Bichette	.60	.25	.07
☐ 26 Wade Boggs	.60	.25	.07
☐ 27 Mike Piazza	3.00	1.35	.35
☐ 28 Ray Lankford	.30	.14	.04
☐ 29 Craig Biggio	.30	.14	.04
☐ 30 Rafael Palmeiro	.60	.25	.07
☐ 31 Ron Gant	.30	.14	.04
☐ 32 Javy Lopez	.30	.14	.04
☐ 33 Brian Jordan	.30	.14	.04
☐ 34 Paul O'Neill	.15	.07	.02
☐ 35 Mark Grace	.60	.25	.07
☐ 36 Matt Williams	.60	.25	.07
☐ 37 Pedro Martinez	.30	.14	.04
☐ 38 Rickey Henderson	.60	.25	.07
☐ 39 Bobby Bonilla	.30	.14	.04
☐ 40 Todd Hollandsworth	.30	.14	.04
☐ 41 Jim Thome	1.00	.45	.12
☐ 42 Gary Sheffield	.60	.25	.07
☐ 43 Tim Salmon	.60	.25	.07
☐ 44 Gregg Jefferies	.15	.07	.02
☐ 45 Roberto Alomar	1.00	.45	.12
☐ 46 Carlos Baerga	.30	.14	.04
☐ 47 Mark Grudzielanek	.30	.14	.04
☐ 48 Randy Johnson	.60	.25	.07
☐ 49 Tino Martinez	.30	.14	.04
☐ 50 Robin Ventura	.30	.14	.04
☐ 51 Ryne Sandberg	1.25	.55	.16
☐ 52 Jay Bell	.15	.07	.02
☐ 53 Jason Schmidt	.60	.25	.07
☐ 54 Frank Thomas	5.00	2.20	.60
☐ 55 Kenny Lofton	1.25	.55	.16
☐ 56 Ariel Prieto	.15	.07	.02
☐ 57 David Cone	.30	.14	.04
☐ 58 Reggie Sanders	.30	.14	.04
☐ 59 Michael Tucker	.30	.14	.04
☐ 60 Vinny Castilla	.30	.14	.04
☐ 61 Len Dykstra	.30	.14	.04
☐ 62 Todd Hundley	.30	.14	.04
☐ 63 Brian McRae	.15	.07	.02
☐ 64 Dennis Eckersley	.30	.14	.04
☐ 65 Rondell White	.30	.14	.04
☐ 66 Eric Karros	.30	.14	.04
☐ 67 Greg Maddux	3.00	1.35	.35
☐ 68 Kevin Appier	.30	.14	.04
☐ 69 Eddie Murray	1.25	.55	.16
☐ 70 John Olerud	.15	.07	.02
☐ 71 Tony Gwynn	2.00	.90	.25
☐ 72 David Justice	.30	.14	.04
☐ 73 Ken Caminiti	.60	.25	.07
☐ 74 Terry Steinbach	.15	.07	.02
☐ 75 Alan Benes	.60	.25	.07
☐ 76 Chipper Jones	3.00	1.35	.35
☐ 77 Jeff Bagwell	2.00	.90	.25
☐ 78 Barry Bonds	1.25	.55	.16
☐ 79 Ken Griffey Jr.	5.00	2.20	.60
☐ 80 Roger Cedeno	.15	.07	.02
☐ 81 Joe Carter	.30	.14	.04
☐ 82 Henry Rodriguez	.30	.14	.04
☐ 83 Jason Isringhausen	.60	.25	.07
☐ 84 Chuck Knoblauch	.60	.25	.07
☐ 85 Manny Ramirez	1.25	.55	.16
☐ 86 Tom Glavine	.60	.25	.07
☐ 87 Jeffrey Hammonds	.15	.07	.02
☐ 88 Paul Molitor	1.00	.45	.12
☐ 89 Roger Clemens	1.00	.45	.12
☐ 90 Greg Vaughn	.15	.07	.02
☐ 91 Marty Cordova	.30	.14	.04
☐ 92 Albert Belle	2.00	.90	.25
☐ 93 Mike Mussina	1.00	.45	.12
☐ 94 Garret Anderson	.15	.07	.02
☐ 95 Juan Gonzalez	2.50	1.10	.30
☐ 96 John Valentin	.15	.07	.02
☐ 97 Jason Giambi	.60	.25	.07
☐ 98 Kirby Puckett	2.00	.90	.25
☐ 99 Jim Edmonds	.30	.14	.04
☐ 100 Cecil Fielder	.30	.14	.04
☐ 101 Mike Aldrete	.15	.07	.02
☐ 102 Marquis Grissom	.30	.14	.04
☐ 103 Derek Bell	.30	.14	.04
☐ 104 Raul Mondesi	.60	.25	.07
☐ 105 Sammy Sosa	.60	.25	.07
☐ 106 Travis Fryman	.30	.14	.04
☐ 107 Rico Brogna	.15	.07	.02
☐ 108 Will Clark	.60	.25	.07
☐ 109 Bernie Williams	1.00	.45	.12
☐ 110 Brady Anderson	.60	.25	.07
☐ 111 Torii Hunter	.30	.14	.04
☐ 112 Derek Jeter	3.00	1.35	.35
☐ 113 Mike Kusiewicz	.50	.23	.06
☐ 114 Scott Rolen	4.00	1.80	.50
☐ 115 Ramon Castro	.30	.14	.04
☐ 116 Jose Guillen	7.00	3.10	.85
☐ 117 Wade Walker	.15	.07	.02
☐ 118 Shawn Senior	.15	.07	.02
☐ 119 Onan Masaoka	.50	.23	.06
☐ 120 Marlon Anderson	.50	.23	.06
☐ 121 Katsuhiro Maeda	1.00	.45	.12
☐ 122 Garrett Stephenson	.15	.07	.02
☐ 123 Butch Huskey	.15	.07	.02
☐ 124 D'Angelo Jimenez	.50	.23	.06
☐ 125 Tony Mounce	.50	.23	.06
☐ 126 Jay Canizaro	.15	.07	.02
☐ 127 Juan Melo	.30	.14	.04
☐ 128 Steve Gibralter	.15	.07	.02
☐ 129 Freddy Garcia	.30	.14	.04
☐ 130 Julio Santana UER Card has him born in 1993	.15	.07	.02
☐ 131 Richard Hidalgo	.60	.25	.07
☐ 132 Jermaine Dye	1.00	.45	.12
☐ 133 Willie Adams	.15	.07	.02
☐ 134 Everett Stull	.15	.07	.02
☐ 135 Ramon Morel	.30	.14	.04
☐ 136 Chan Ho Park	.60	.25	.07
☐ 137 Jamey Wright	.60	.25	.07
☐ 138 Luis Garcia	.15	.07	.02
☐ 139 Dan Serafini	.30	.14	.04
☐ 140 Ryan Dempster	.60	.25	.07
☐ 141 Tate Seefried	.15	.07	.02
☐ 142 Jimmy Hurst	.15	.07	.02
☐ 143 Travis Miller	.15	.07	.02
☐ 144 Curtis Goodwin	.15	.07	.02
☐ 145 Rocky Coppinger	1.00	.45	.12
☐ 146 Enrique Wilson	.60	.25	.07
☐ 147 Jaime Bluma	.15	.07	.02
☐ 148 Andrew Vessel	.30	.14	.04
☐ 149 Damian Moss	.60	.25	.07
☐ 150 Shawn Gallagher	.40	.18	.05
☐ 151 Pat Watkins	.30	.14	.04
☐ 152 Jose Paniagua	.30	.14	.04
☐ 153 Danny Graves	.30	.14	.04
☐ 154 Bryon Gainey	.60	.25	.07
☐ 155 Steve Soderstrom	.15	.07	.02
☐ 156 Cliff Brumbaugh	.15	.07	.02
☐ 157 Eugene Kingsale	.50	.23	.06
☐ 158 Lou Collier	.30	.14	.04
☐ 159 Todd Walker	6.00	2.70	.75
☐ 160 Kris Detmers	.75	.35	.09
☐ 161 Josh Booty	1.00	.45	.12
☐ 162 Greg Whiteman	.15	.07	.02
☐ 163 Damian Jackson	.30	.14	.04
☐ 164 Tony Clark	1.00	.45	.12
☐ 165 Jeff D'Amico	.60	.25	.07
☐ 166 Johnny Damon	.30	.14	.04
☐ 167 Rafael Orellano	.30	.14	.04
☐ 168 Ruben Rivera	1.00	.45	.12
☐ 169 Alex Ochoa	.30	.14	.04
☐ 170 Jay Powell	.15	.07	.02
☐ 171 Tom Evans	.15	.07	.02
☐ 172 Ron Villone	.15	.07	.02
☐ 173 Shawn Estes	.30	.14	.04
☐ 174 John Wasdin	.15	.07	.02
☐ 175 Bill Simas	.15	.07	.02
☐ 176 Kevin Brown	.30	.14	.04
☐ 177 Shannon Stewart	.15	.07	.02
☐ 178 Todd Greene	.30	.14	.04
☐ 179 Bob Wolcott	.15	.07	.02
☐ 180 Chris Snopek	.15	.07	.02
☐ 181 Nomar Garciaparra	2.50	1.10	.30
☐ 182 Cameron Smith	.15	.07	.02
☐ 183 Matt Drews	.30	.14	.04
☐ 184 Jimmy Haynes	.15	.07	.02
☐ 185 Chris Carpenter	.60	.25	.07
☐ 186 Desi Relaford	.15	.07	.02
☐ 187 Ben Grieve	1.50	.70	.19
☐ 188 Mike Bell	.60	.25	.07
☐ 189 Luis Castillo	1.50	.70	.19
☐ 190 Ugueth Urbina	.15	.07	.02
☐ 191 Paul Wilson	.30	.14	.04
☐ 192 Andruw Jones	12.00	5.50	1.50
☐ 193 Wayne Gomes	.15	.07	.02
☐ 194 Craig Counsell	.15	.07	.02
☐ 195 Jim Cole	.15	.07	.02
☐ 196 Brooks Kieschnick	.60	.25	.07
☐ 197 Trey Beamon	.15	.07	.02
☐ 198 Marino Santana	.15	.07	.02
☐ 199 Bob Abreu	.60	.25	.07
☐ 200 Calvin Reese	.15	.07	.02
☐ 201 Dante Powell	2.00	.90	.25
☐ 202 George Arias	.30	.14	.04
☐ 203 Jorge Velandia	.15	.07	.02
☐ 204 George Lombard	2.00	.90	.25
☐ 205 Byron Browne	.15	.07	.02
☐ 206 John Frascatore	.15	.07	.02

☐ 207 Terry Adams	.15	.07	.02
☐ 208 Wilson Delgado	.15	.07	.02
☐ 209 Billy McMillon	.15	.07	.02
☐ 210 Jeff Abbott	.30	.14	.04
☐ 211 Trot Nixon	.15	.07	.02
☐ 212 Amaury Telemaco	.30	.14	.04
☐ 213 Scott Sullivan	.15	.07	.02
☐ 214 Justin Thompson	.30	.14	.04
☐ 215 Decomba Conner	.30	.14	.04
☐ 216 Ryan McGuire	.15	.07	.02
☐ 217 Matt Luke	.15	.07	.02
☐ 218 Doug Million	.60	.25	.07
☐ 219 Jason Dickson	1.00	.45	.12
☐ 220 Ramon Hernandez	.60	.25	.07
☐ 221 Mark Bellhorn	.75	.35	.09
☐ 222 Eric Ludwick	.15	.07	.02
☐ 223 Luke Wilcox	.15	.07	.02
☐ 224 Marty Malloy	.50	.23	.06
☐ 225 Gary Coffee	.50	.23	.06
☐ 226 Wendell Magee	.75	.35	.09
☐ 227 Brett Tomko	.50	.23	.06
☐ 228 Derek Lowe	.15	.07	.02
☐ 229 Jose Rosado	2.00	.90	.25
☐ 230 Steve Bourgeois	.15	.07	.02
☐ 231 Neil Weber	.15	.07	.02
☐ 232 Jeff Ware	.15	.07	.02
☐ 233 Edwin Diaz	.30	.14	.04
☐ 234 Greg Norton	.15	.07	.02
☐ 235 Aaron Boone	.30	.14	.04
☐ 236 Jeff Suppan	.60	.25	.07
☐ 237 Bret Wagner	.15	.07	.02
☐ 238 Elieser Marrero	.30	.14	.04
☐ 239 Will Cunnane	.30	.14	.04
☐ 240 Brian Barkley	.40	.18	.05
☐ 241 Jay Payton	.60	.25	.07
☐ 242 Marcus Jensen	.15	.07	.02
☐ 243 Ryan Nye	.15	.07	.02
☐ 244 Chad Mottola	.15	.07	.02
☐ 245 Scott McClain	.15	.07	.02
☐ 246 Jessie Ibarra	.30	.14	.04
☐ 247 Mike Darr	.50	.23	.06
☐ 248 Bobby Estalella	1.50	.70	.19
☐ 249 Michael Barrett	.30	.14	.04
☐ 250 Jamie Lopiccolo	.40	.18	.05
☐ 251 Shane Spencer	.15	.07	.02
☐ 252 Ben Petrick	1.00	.45	.12
☐ 253 Jason Bell	.40	.18	.05
☐ 254 Arnold Gooch	.50	.23	.06
☐ 255 T.J. Mathews	.15	.07	.02
☐ 256 Jason Ryan	.15	.07	.02
☐ 257 Pat Cline	.75	.35	.09
☐ 258 Rafael Carmona	.15	.07	.02
☐ 259 Carl Pavano	2.50	1.10	.30
☐ 260 Ben Davis	.60	.25	.07
☐ 261 Matt Lawton	.50	.23	.06
☐ 262 Kevin Sefcik	.15	.07	.02
☐ 263 Chris Fussell	.75	.35	.09
☐ 264 Mike Cameron	2.50	1.10	.30
☐ 265 Marty Janzen	.50	.23	.06
☐ 266 Livan Hernandez	.75	.35	.09
☐ 267 Raul Ibanez	.30	.14	.04
☐ 268 Juan Encarnacion	.30	.14	.04
☐ 269 David Yocum	.40	.18	.05
☐ 270 Jonathan Johnson	.50	.23	.06
☐ 271 Reggie Taylor	.30	.14	.04
☐ 272 Danny Buxbaum	.15	.07	.02
☐ 273 Jacob Cruz	.30	.14	.04
☐ 274 Bobby Morris	.15	.07	.02
☐ 275 Andy Fox	.15	.07	.02
☐ 276 Greg Keagle	.15	.07	.02
☐ 277 Charles Peterson	.15	.07	.02
☐ 278 Derrek Lee	.75	.35	.09
☐ 279 Bryant Nelson	.40	.18	.05
☐ 280 Antone Williamson	.75	.35	.09
☐ 281 Scott Elarton	.30	.14	.04
☐ 282 Shad Williams	.15	.07	.02
☐ 283 Rich Hunter	.15	.07	.02
☐ 284 Chris Sheff	.15	.07	.02
☐ 285 Derrick Gibson	1.50	.70	.19
☐ 286 Felix Rodriguez	.15	.07	.02
☐ 287 Brian Banks	.15	.07	.02
☐ 288 Jason McDonald	.15	.07	.02
☐ 289 Glendon Rusch	1.00	.45	.12
☐ 290 Gary Rath	.15	.07	.02
☐ 291 Peter Munro	.30	.14	.04
☐ 292 Tom Fordham	.30	.14	.04
☐ 293 Jason Kendall	.60	.25	.07
☐ 294 Russ Johnson	.75	.35	.09
☐ 295 Joe Long	.15	.07	.02
☐ 296 Robert Smith	1.00	.45	.12
☐ 297 Jarrod Washburn	.50	.23	.06
☐ 298 Dave Coggin	.50	.23	.06
☐ 299 Jeff Yoder	.40	.18	.05
☐ 300 Jed Hansen	.15	.07	.02
☐ 301 Matt Morris	1.00	.45	.12
☐ 302 Josh Bishop	.40	.18	.05
☐ 303 Dustin Hermanson	.15	.07	.02
☐ 304 Mike Gulan	.15	.07	.02
☐ 305 Felipe Crespo	.15	.07	.02
☐ 306 Quinton McCracken	.15	.07	.02
☐ 307 Jim Bonnici	.15	.07	.02
☐ 308 Sal Fasano	.15	.07	.02
☐ 309 Gabe Alvarez	.75	.35	.09
☐ 310 Heath Murray	.40	.18	.05
☐ 311 Jose Valentin	2.50	1.10	.30
☐ 312 Bartolo Colon	1.00	.45	.12
☐ 313 Olmedo Saenz	.15	.07	.02
☐ 314 Norm Hutchins	.40	.18	.05
☐ 315 Chris Holt	.15	.07	.02
☐ 316 David Doster	.15	.07	.02
☐ 317 Robert Person	.15	.07	.02
☐ 318 Donne Wall	.15	.07	.02
☐ 319 Adam Riggs	.30	.14	.04
☐ 320 Homer Bush	.15	.07	.02
☐ 321 Brad Rigby	.15	.07	.02
☐ 322 Lou Merloni	.15	.07	.02
☐ 323 Neifi Perez	.60	.25	.07
☐ 324 Chris Cumberland	.15	.07	.02
☐ 325 Alvie Shepherd	.50	.23	.06
☐ 326 Jarrod Patterson	.15	.07	.02
☐ 327 Ray Ricken	.15	.07	.02
☐ 328 Danny Klassen	.15	.07	.02
☐ 329 David Miller	.50	.23	.06
☐ 330 Chad Alexander	.75	.35	.09
☐ 331 Matt Beaumont	.30	.14	.04
☐ 332 Damon Hollins	.15	.07	.02
☐ 333 Todd Dunn	.15	.07	.02
☐ 334 Mike Sweeney	1.50	.70	.19
☐ 335 Richie Sexson	.60	.25	.07
☐ 336 Billy Wagner	.60	.25	.07
☐ 337 Ron Wright	6.00	2.70	.75
☐ 338 Paul Konerko	2.50	1.10	.30
☐ 339 Tommy Phelps	.40	.18	.05
☐ 340 Karim Garcia	1.25	.55	.16
☐ 341 Mike Grace	.15	.07	.02
☐ 342 Russell Branyan	4.00	1.80	.50
☐ 343 Randy Winn	.40	.18	.05
☐ 344 A.J. Pierzynski	.60	.25	.07
☐ 345 Mike Busby	.15	.07	.02
☐ 346 Matt Beech	.40	.18	.05
☐ 347 Jose Cepeda	.40	.18	.05
☐ 348 Brian Stephenson	.15	.07	.02
☐ 349 Rey Ordonez	.60	.25	.07
☐ 350 Rich Aurilla	.15	.07	.02
☐ 351 Edgard Velazquez	2.00	.90	.25
☐ 352 Raul Casanova	.30	.14	.04
☐ 353 Carlos Guillen	.50	.23	.06
☐ 354 Bruce Aven	.30	.14	.04
☐ 355 Ryan Jones	1.00	.45	.12
☐ 356 Derek Aucoin	.15	.07	.02
☐ 357 Brian Rose	1.00	.45	.12
☐ 358 Richard Almanzar	.40	.18	.05
☐ 359 Fletcher Bates	.40	.18	.05
☐ 360 Russ Ortiz	.15	.07	.02
☐ 361 Wilton Guerrero	4.00	1.80	.50
☐ 362 Geoff Jenkins	1.00	.45	.12
☐ 363 Pete Janicki	.15	.07	.02
☐ 364 Yamil Benitez	.30	.14	.04
☐ 365 Aaron Holbert	.15	.07	.02
☐ 366 Tim Belk	.15	.07	.02
☐ 367 Terrell Wade	.30	.14	.04
☐ 368 Terrence Long	.60	.25	.07
☐ 369 Brad Fullmer	.60	.25	.07
☐ 370 Matt Wagner	.15	.07	.02
☐ 371 Craig Wilson	.15	.07	.02
☐ 372 Mark Loretta	.15	.07	.02
☐ 373 Eric Owens	.15	.07	.02
☐ 374 Vladimir Guerrero	6.00	2.70	.75
☐ 375 Tommy Davis	.15	.07	.02
☐ 376 Donnie Sadler	.30	.14	.04
☐ 377 Edgar Renteria	.60	.25	.07
☐ 378 Todd Helton	5.00	2.20	.60
☐ 379 Ralph Milliard	.15	.07	.02
☐ 380 Darin Blood	1.50	.70	.19
☐ 381 Shayne Bennett	.15	.07	.02
☐ 382 Mark Redman	.30	.14	.04
☐ 383 Felix Martinez	.15	.07	.02
☐ 384 Sean Watkins	.75	.35	.09
☐ 385 Oscar Henriquez	.15	.07	.02
☐ M20 1952 Bowman Mantle Reprint	10.00	4.50	1.25
☐ NNO Unnumbered Checklists	.15	.07	.02

1996 Bowman Foil

These parallel foil cards were seeded at an approximate rate of one per pack. Packs that did not contain a Foil card had a Bowman's Best Preview or Minor League Player of the Year insert card instead. The striking silver foil card fronts differ them from the base 1996 Bowman cards. Please refer to the multipliers provided below to ascertain value for Foil singles.

	MINT	NRMT	EXC
COMPLETE SET (385)	350.00	160.00	45.00
COMMON CARD (1-385)	.50	.23	.06

*STARS: 1.5X TO 3X BASIC CARDS ..
*YOUNG STARS: 1.25X TO 2.5X BASIC CARDS

1996 Bowman Minor League POY

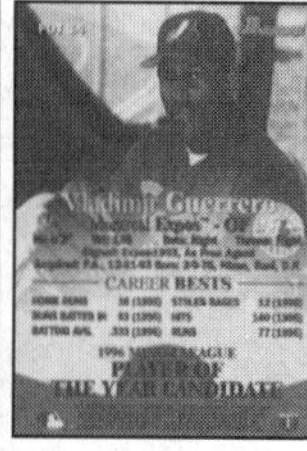

Randomly inserted in packs at a rate of one in 12, this 15-card set features top minor league prospects for Player of the Year Candidates. The fronts carry a color player photo with red-and-silver foil printing. The backs display player information including his career bests.

	MINT	NRMT	EXC
COMPLETE SET (15)	60.00	27.00	7.50
COMMON CARD (1-15)	1.50	.70	.19
☐ 1 Andruw Jones	20.00	9.00	2.50
☐ 2 Derrick Gibson	3.00	1.35	.35
☐ 3 Bob Abreu	2.50	1.10	.30
☐ 4 Todd Walker	10.00	4.50	1.25
☐ 5 Jamey Wright	2.50	1.10	.30
☐ 6 Wes Helms	10.00	4.50	1.25
☐ 7 Karim Garcia	4.00	1.80	.50
☐ 8 Bartolo Colon	2.50	1.10	.30
☐ 9 Alex Ochoa	2.00	.90	.25
☐ 10 Mike Sweeney	3.00	1.35	.35
☐ 11 Ruben Rivera	3.00	1.35	.35
☐ 12 Gabe Alvarez	1.50	.70	.19
☐ 13 Billy Wagner	2.50	1.10	.30
☐ 14 Vladimir Guerrero	12.00	5.50	1.50
☐ 15 Edgard Velazquez	4.00	1.80	.50

1994 Bowman's Best

This 200-card standard-size set consists of 90 veteran stars, 90 rookies and prospects and 20 Mirror Image cards. The veteran cards have red backs and are designated 1R-90R. The rookies and prospects cards have blue backs and are designated 1B-90B. The Mirror Image cards feature a veteran star and a prospect matched by position. These cards are numbered 91-110. Subsets featured are Super Vet (1R-6R), Super Rookie (82R-90R), and Blue Chip (1B-11B). Rookie Cards include Alan Benes, Tony Clark, Chan Ho Park, Edgar Renteria and Ruben Rivera.

	MINT	NRMT	EXC
COMPLETE SET (200)	80.00	36.00	10.00
COMMON BLUE CARD (B1-B90)	.25	.11	.03
COMMON RED CARD (R1-R90)	.25	.11	.03
COMMON MIR.IMAGE (X91-X110)	.25	.11	.03
☐ B1 Chipper Jones	6.00	2.70	.75
☐ B2 Derek Jeter	6.00	2.70	.75
☐ B3 Bill Pulsipher	.50	.23	.06
☐ B4 James Baldwin	1.50	.70	.19
☐ B5 Brooks Kieschnick	1.50	.70	.19
☐ B6 Justin Thompson	.50	.23	.06
☐ B7 Midre Cummings	.25	.11	.03
☐ B8 Joey Hamilton	1.50	.70	.19
☐ B9 Calvin Reese	.50	.23	.06
☐ B10 Brian Barber	.25	.11	.03
☐ B11 John Burke	.25	.11	.03
☐ B12 DeShawn Warren	.25	.11	.03
☐ B13 Edgardo Alfonzo	1.00	.45	.12
☐ B14 Eddie Pearson	.75	.35	.09
☐ B15 Jimmy Haynes	.50	.23	.06
☐ B16 Danny Bautista	.25	.11	.03
☐ B17 Roger Cedeno	.50	.23	.06
☐ B18 Jon Lieber	.25	.11	.03
☐ B19 Billy Wagner	2.50	1.10	.30
☐ B20 Tate Seefried	.50	.23	.06
☐ B21 Chad Mottola	.25	.11	.03
☐ B22 Jose Malave	.50	.23	.06
☐ B23 Terrell Wade	1.50	.70	.19
☐ B24 Shane Andrews	.50	.23	.06
☐ B25 Chan Ho Park	2.50	1.10	.30
☐ B26 Kirk Presley	1.00	.45	.12
☐ B27 Robbie Beckett	.25	.11	.03
☐ B28 Orlando Miller	.25	.11	.03
☐ B29 Jorge Posada	.50	.23	.06
☐ B30 Frankie Rodriguez	.50	.23	.06
☐ B31 Brian L.Hunter	1.25	.55	.16
☐ B32 Billy Ashley	.25	.11	.03
☐ B33 Rondell White	1.00	.45	.12
☐ B34 John Roper	.25	.11	.03
☐ B35 Marc Valdes	.50	.23	.06
☐ B36 Scott Ruffcorn	.25	.11	.03
☐ B37 Rod Henderson	.25	.11	.03
☐ B38 Curtis Goodwin	.50	.23	.06
☐ B39 Russ Davis	.50	.23	.06
☐ B40 Rick Gorecki	.25	.11	.03
☐ B41 Johnny Damon	1.25	.55	.16
☐ B42 Roberto Petagine	.50	.23	.06
☐ B43 Chris Snopek	.25	.11	.03
☐ B44 Mark Acre	.25	.11	.03
☐ B45 Todd Hollandsworth	2.00	.90	.25
☐ B46 Shawn Green	.50	.23	.06
☐ B47 John Carter	.25	.11	.03
☐ B48 Jim Pittsley	1.50	.70	.19
☐ B49 John Wasdin	1.00	.45	.12
☐ B50 D.J.Boston	.25	.11	.03
☐ B51 Tim Clark	.25	.11	.03
☐ B52 Alex Ochoa	.50	.23	.06
☐ B53 Chad Roper	.25	.11	.03
☐ B54 Mike Kelly	.25	.11	.03
☐ B55 Brad Fullmer	2.00	.90	.25
☐ B56 Carl Everett	.25	.11	.03
☐ B57 Tim Belk	.50	.23	.06
☐ B58 Jimmy Hurst	.50	.23	.06
☐ B59 Mac Suzuki	.50	.23	.06
☐ B60 Michael Moore	.25	.11	.03
☐ B61 Alan Benes	3.00	1.35	.35
☐ B62 Tony Clark	10.00	4.50	1.25
☐ B63 Edgar Renteria	5.00	2.20	.60
☐ B64 Trey Beamon	.50	.23	.06
☐ B65 LaTroy Hawkins	.50	.23	.06
☐ B66 Wayne Gomes	.50	.23	.06
☐ B67 Ray McDavid	.50	.23	.06
☐ B68 John Dettmer	.25	.11	.03
☐ B69 Willie Greene	.50	.23	.06
☐ B70 Dave Stevens	.25	.11	.03
☐ B71 Kevin Orie	2.50	1.10	.30
☐ B72 Chad Ogea	.50	.23	.06
☐ B73 Ben Van Ryn	.25	.11	.03
☐ B74 Kym Ashworth	.50	.23	.06
☐ B75 Dmitri Young	1.50	.70	.19
☐ B76 Herbert Perry	.50	.23	.06
☐ B77 Joey Eischen	.25	.11	.03
☐ B78 Arquimedez Pozo	.75	.35	.09
☐ B79 Ugueth Urbina	.50	.23	.06
☐ B80 Keith Williams	.50	.23	.06
☐ B81 John Frascatore	.25	.11	.03
☐ B82 Garey Ingram	.25	.11	.03
☐ B83 Aaron Small	.25	.11	.03
☐ B84 Olmedo Saenz	.25	.11	.03
☐ B85 Jesus Tavarez	.25	.11	.03
☐ B86 Jose Silva	.50	.23	.06
☐ B87 Jay Witasick	.50	.23	.06
☐ B88 Jay Maldonado	.25	.11	.03
☐ B89 Keith Heberling	.25	.11	.03
☐ B90 Rusty Greer	4.00	1.80	.50
☐ R1 Paul Molitor	1.50	.70	.19
☐ R2 Eddie Murray	2.00	.90	.25
☐ R3 Ozzie Smith	2.00	.90	.25
☐ R4 Rickey Henderson	1.00	.45	.12
☐ R5 Lee Smith	.50	.23	.06
☐ R6 Dave Winfield	1.00	.45	.12
☐ R7 Roberto Alomar	1.50	.70	.19
☐ R8 Matt Williams	1.00	.45	.12
☐ R9 Mark Grace	1.00	.45	.12
☐ R10 Lance Johnson	.50	.23	.06
☐ R11 Darren Daulton	.50	.23	.06
☐ R12 Tom Glavine	1.00	.45	.12
☐ R13 Gary Sheffield	1.00	.45	.12
☐ R14 Rod Beck	.50	.23	.06
☐ R15 Fred McGriff	1.00	.45	.12
☐ R16 Joe Carter	.50	.23	.06
☐ R17 Dante Bichette	1.00	.45	.12
☐ R18 Danny Tartabull	.25	.11	.03
☐ R19 Juan Gonzalez	4.00	1.80	.50
☐ R20 Steve Avery	.50	.23	.06
☐ R21 John Wetteland	.50	.23	.06
☐ R22 Ben McDonald	.25	.11	.03
☐ R23 Jack McDowell	.50	.23	.06
☐ R24 Jose Canseco	1.00	.45	.12
☐ R25 Tim Salmon	1.25	.55	.16
☐ R26 Wilson Alvarez	.50	.23	.06
☐ R27 Gregg Jefferies	1.00	.45	.12
☐ R28 John Burkett	.25	.11	.03
☐ R29 Greg Vaughn	1.00	.45	.12
☐ R30 Robin Ventura	.50	.23	.06
☐ R31 Paul O'Neill	.50	.23	.06
☐ R32 Cecil Fielder	.50	.23	.06
☐ R33 Kevin Mitchell	.50	.23	.06
☐ R34 Jeff Conine	.50	.23	.06
☐ R35 Carlos Baerga	.50	.23	.06
☐ R36 Greg Maddux	5.00	2.20	.60
☐ R37 Roger Clemens	1.50	.70	.19
☐ R38 Deion Sanders	1.00	.45	.12
☐ R39 Delino DeShields	.25	.11	.03
☐ R40 Ken Griffey Jr.	8.00	3.60	1.00
☐ R41 Albert Belle	3.00	1.35	.35
☐ R42 Wade Boggs	1.00	.45	.12
☐ R43 Andres Galarraga	1.00	.45	.12
☐ R44 Aaron Sele	.50	.23	.06
☐ R45 Don Mattingly	4.00	1.80	.50
☐ R46 David Cone	.50	.23	.06
☐ R47 Len Dykstra	.50	.23	.06

Card	MINT	NRMT	EXC
□ R48 Brett Butler	.50	.23	.06
□ R49 Bill Swift	.25	.11	.03
□ R50 Bobby Bonilla	.50	.23	.06
□ R51 Rafael Palmeiro	1.00	.45	.12
□ R52 Moises Alou	.50	.23	.06
□ R53 Jeff Bagwell	3.00	1.35	.35
□ R54 Mike Mussina	1.50	.70	.19
□ R55 Frank Thomas	8.00	3.60	1.00
□ R56 Jose Rijo	.25	.11	.03
□ R57 Ruben Sierra	.50	.23	.06
□ R58 Randy Myers	.25	.11	.03
□ R59 Barry Bonds	2.00	.90	.25
□ R60 Jimmy Key	.50	.23	.06
□ R61 Travis Fryman	.50	.23	.06
□ R62 John Olerud	.25	.11	.03
□ R63 David Justice	1.00	.45	.12
□ R64 Ray Lankford	.50	.23	.06
□ R65 Bob Tewksbury	.25	.11	.03
□ R66 Chuck Carr	.25	.11	.03
□ R67 Jay Buhner	1.00	.45	.12
□ R68 Kenny Lofton	2.50	1.10	.30
□ R69 Marquis Grissom	.50	.23	.06
□ R70 Sammy Sosa	1.00	.45	.12
□ R71 Cal Ripken	6.00	2.70	.75
□ R72 Ellis Burks	.50	.23	.06
□ R73 Jeff Montgomery	.50	.23	.06
□ R74 Julio Franco	.50	.23	.06
□ R75 Kirby Puckett	3.00	1.35	.35
□ R76 Larry Walker	1.00	.45	.12
□ R77 Andy Van Slyke	.50	.23	.06
□ R78 Tony Gwynn	3.00	1.35	.35
□ R79 Will Clark	1.00	.45	.12
□ R80 Mo Vaughn	2.00	.90	.25
□ R81 Mike Piazza	5.00	2.20	.60
□ R82 James Mouton	.50	.23	.06
□ R83 Carlos Delgado	1.00	.45	.12
□ R84 Ryan Klesko	1.50	.70	.19
□ R85 Javier Lopez	1.00	.45	.12
□ R86 Raul Mondesi	1.25	.55	.16
□ R87 Cliff Floyd	1.00	.45	.12
□ R88 Manny Ramirez	2.50	1.10	.30
□ R89 Hector Carrasco	.25	.11	.03
□ R90 Jeff Granger	.50	.23	.06
□ X91 Frank Thomas Dmitri Young	4.00	1.80	.50
□ X92 Fred McGriff Brooks Kieschnick	2.50	1.10	.30
□ X93 Matt Williams Shane Andrews	.25	.11	.03
□ X94 Cal Ripken Kevin Orie	3.00	1.35	.35
□ X95 Barry Larkin Derek Jeter	3.00	1.35	.35
□ X96 Ken Griffey Jr. Johnny Damon	4.00	1.80	.50
□ X97 Barry Bonds Rondell White	1.00	.45	.12
□ X98 Albert Belle Jimmy Hurst	1.50	.70	.19
□ X99 Raul Mondesi Ruben Rivera	6.00	2.70	.75
□ X100 Roger Clemens Scott Ruffcorn	.50	.23	.06
□ X101 Greg Maddux John Wasdin	2.50	1.10	.30
□ X102 Tim Salmon Chad Mottola	.50	.23	.06
□ X103 Carlos Baerga Arquimedez Pozo	.50	.23	.06
□ X104 Mike Piazza Bobby Hughes	2.50	1.10	.30
□ X105 Carlos Delgado Melvin Nieves	1.00	.45	.12
□ X106 Javier Lopez Jorge Posada	.50	.23	.06
□ X107 Manny Ramirez Jose Malave	1.25	.55	.16
□ X108 Travis Fryman Chipper Jones	3.00	1.35	.35
□ X109 Steve Avery Bill Pulsipher	.50	.23	.06
□ X110 John Olerud Shawn Green	1.00	.45	.12

1994 Bowman's Best Refractors

This 200-card standard-size set is a parallel to the basic Bowman's Best issue. The cards were randomly inserted in packs at a rate of one in nine Bowman's Best packs. The only difference is the refractive coating that allows for a brighter, shinier appearance.

	MINT	NRMT	EXC
COMPLETE SET (200)	1300.00	575.00	160.00
COMMON CARD	3.00	1.35	.35
*RED STARS: 6X TO 12X BASIC CARDS			
*BLUE STARS: 4X TO 8X BASIC CARDS			
*MIRROR IMAGE STARS: 3X TO 6X BASIC CARDS			
□ B1 Chipper Jones	80.00	36.00	10.00
□ B2 Derek Jeter	80.00	36.00	10.00
□ B4 James Baldwin	15.00	6.75	1.85
□ B5 Brooks Kieschnick	15.00	6.75	1.85
□ B8 Joey Hamilton	18.00	8.00	2.20
□ B19 Billy Wagner	18.00	8.00	2.20
□ B25 Chan Ho Park	20.00	9.00	2.50
□ B41 Johnny Damon	15.00	6.75	1.85
□ B45 Todd Hollandsworth	30.00	13.50	3.70
□ B55 Brad Fullmer	15.00	6.75	1.85
□ B61 Alan Benes	25.00	11.00	3.10
□ B62 Tony Clark	40.00	18.00	5.00
□ B63 Edgar Renteria	30.00	13.50	3.70
□ B71 Kevin Orie	20.00	9.00	2.50
□ B75 Dmitri Young	20.00	9.00	2.50
□ B90 Rusty Greer	25.00	11.00	3.10
□ R1 Paul Molitor	20.00	9.00	2.50
□ R2 Eddie Murray	25.00	11.00	3.10
□ R3 Ozzie Smith	25.00	11.00	3.10
□ R7 Roberto Alomar	20.00	9.00	2.50
□ R19 Juan Gonzalez	50.00	22.00	6.25
□ R25 Tim Salmon	15.00	6.75	1.85
□ R36 Greg Maddux	60.00	27.00	7.50
□ R37 Roger Clemens	20.00	9.00	2.50
□ R40 Ken Griffey Jr.	100.00	45.00	12.50
□ R41 Albert Belle	40.00	18.00	5.00
□ R45 Don Mattingly	50.00	22.00	6.25
□ R53 Jeff Bagwell	40.00	18.00	5.00
□ R54 Mike Mussina	20.00	9.00	2.50
□ R55 Frank Thomas	100.00	45.00	12.50
□ R59 Barry Bonds	25.00	11.00	3.10
□ R68 Kenny Lofton	30.00	13.50	3.70
□ R71 Cal Ripken	80.00	36.00	10.00
□ R75 Kirby Puckett	40.00	18.00	5.00
□ R78 Tony Gwynn	40.00	18.00	5.00
□ R80 Mo Vaughn	25.00	11.00	3.10
□ R81 Mike Piazza	60.00	27.00	7.50
□ R84 Ryan Klesko	20.00	9.00	2.50
□ R86 Raul Mondesi	15.00	6.75	1.85
□ R88 Manny Ramirez	30.00	13.50	3.70
□ X91 Frank Thomas Dmitri Young	30.00	13.50	3.70
□ X94 Cal Ripken Kevin Orie	25.00	11.00	3.10
□ X95 Barry Larkin Derek Jeter	20.00	9.00	2.50
□ X96 Ken Griffey Jr. Johnny Damon	40.00	18.00	5.00
□ X98 Albert Belle Jimmy Hurst	15.00	6.75	1.85
□ X99 Ruben Rivera Raul Mondesi	40.00	18.00	5.00
□ X101 Greg Maddux John Wasdin	20.00	9.00	2.50
□ X104 Mike Piazza Bobby Hughes	20.00	9.00	2.50
□ X108 Travis Fryman Chipper Jones	20.00	9.00	2.50

1995 Bowman's Best

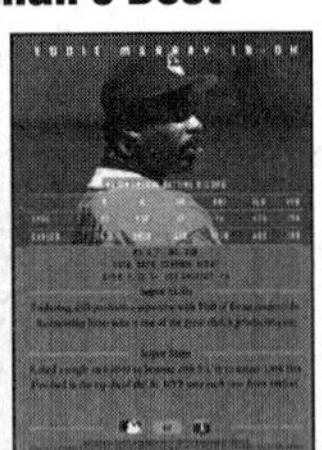

This 195 card standard-size set consists of 90 veteran stars, 90 rookies and prospects and 15 Mirror Image cards. The packs contain seven cards and the suggested retail price was $5. The veteran cards have red backs and are designated R1-R90. Cards of rookies and prospects have blue backs and are designated B1-B90. The Mirror Image cards feature a veteran star and a prospect matched by position. These cards are numbered X1-X15. The fronts have an action photo with the background in silver-foil with the team names at the top and red or blue at the bottom corresponding to the back. The backs have a head shot along with player statistics and information. Rookie Cards include Bartolo Colon, Karim Garcia, Vladimir Guerrero, Andruw Jones, Hideo Nomo, Jay Payton and Scott Rolen.

	MINT	NRMT	EXC
COMPLETE SET (195)	180.00	80.00	22.00
COMMON BLUE CARD (B1-B90)	.25	.11	.03
COMMON RED CARD (R1-R90)	.25	.11	.03
COMMON CARD (X1-X15)	1.00	.45	.12
□ B1 Derek Jeter	5.00	2.20	.60
□ B2 Vladimir Guerrero	30.00	13.50	3.70
□ B3 Bob Abreu	5.00	2.20	.60
□ B4 Chan Ho Park	1.00	.45	.12
□ B5 Paul Wilson	1.50	.70	.19
□ B6 Chad Ogea	.25	.11	.03
□ B7 Andruw Jones	50.00	22.00	6.25
□ B8 Brian Barber	.25	.11	.03
□ B9 Andy Larkin	.25	.11	.03
□ B10 Richie Sexson	3.00	1.35	.35
□ B11 Everett Stull	.25	.11	.03
□ B12 Brooks Kieschnick	1.00	.45	.12
□ B13 Matt Murray	.25	.11	.03
□ B14 John Wasdin	.25	.11	.03
□ B15 Shannon Stewart	.50	.23	.06
□ B16 Luis Ortiz	.25	.11	.03
□ B17 Marc Kroon	.25	.11	.03
□ B18 Todd Greene	.50	.23	.06
□ B19 Juan Acevedo	.25	.11	.03
□ B20 Tony Clark	2.50	1.10	.30
□ B21 Jermaine Dye	4.00	1.80	.50
□ B22 Derrek Lee	2.50	1.10	.30
□ B23 Pat Watkins	.50	.23	.06
□ B24 Calvin Reese	.25	.11	.03
□ B25 Ben Grieve	6.00	2.70	.75
□ B26 Julio Santana	.25	.11	.03
□ B27 Felix Rodriguez	.50	.23	.06
□ B28 Paul Konerko	10.00	4.50	1.25
□ B29 Nomar Garciaparra	8.00	3.60	1.00
□ B30 Pat Ahearne	.25	.11	.03
□ B31 Jason Schmidt	1.00	.45	.12
□ B32 Billy Wagner	1.00	.45	.12
□ B33 Rey Ordonez RC	5.00	2.20	.60
□ B34 Curtis Goodwin	.50	.23	.06
□ B35 Sergio Nunez	1.00	.45	.12
□ B36 Tim Belk	.25	.11	.03
□ B37 Scott Elarton	1.00	.45	.12
□ B38 Jason Isringhausen	1.25	.55	.16
□ B39 Trot Nixon	.50	.23	.06
□ B40 Sid Roberson	.25	.11	.03
□ B41 Ron Villone	.25	.11	.03
□ B42 Ruben Rivera	4.00	1.80	.50
□ B43 Rick Huisman	.25	.11	.03
□ B44 Todd Hollandsworth	1.25	.55	.16
□ B45 Johnny Damon	.50	.23	.06
□ B46 Garret Anderson	.50	.23	.06
□ B47 Jeff D'Amico	1.00	.45	.12
□ B48 Dustin Hermanson	.50	.23	.06
□ B49 Juan Encarnacion	1.50	.70	.19
□ B50 Andy Pettitte	3.00	1.35	.35
□ B51 Chris Stynes	.25	.11	.03
□ B52 Troy Percival	.25	.11	.03
□ B53 LaTroy Hawkins	.25	.11	.03
□ B54 Roger Cedeno	.50	.23	.06
□ B55 Alan Benes	1.00	.45	.12
□ B56 Karim Garcia	10.00	4.50	1.25
□ B57 Andrew Lorraine	.50	.23	.06
□ B58 Gary Rath	.25	.11	.03
□ B59 Bret Wagner	.50	.23	.06
□ B60 Jeff Suppan	1.00	.45	.12
□ B61 Bill Pulsipher	.50	.23	.06
□ B62 Jay Payton	4.00	1.80	.50
□ B63 Alex Ochoa	.50	.23	.06
□ B64 Ugueth Urbina	.25	.11	.03
□ B65 Armando Benitez	.25	.11	.03
□ B66 George Arias	1.00	.45	.12
□ B67 Raul Casanova	1.50	.70	.19
□ B68 Matt Drews	.50	.23	.06
□ B69 Jimmy Haynes	.50	.23	.06
□ B70 Jimmy Hurst	.50	.23	.06
□ B71 C.J. Nitkowski	.50	.23	.06
□ B72 Tommy Davis	.50	.23	.06
□ B73 Bartolo Colon	5.00	2.20	.60
□ B74 Chris Carpenter	2.50	1.10	.30
□ B75 Trey Beamon	.50	.23	.06
□ B76 Bryan Rekar	.25	.11	.03
□ B77 James Baldwin	.50	.23	.06
□ B78 Marc Valdes	.25	.11	.03
□ B79 Tom Fordham	.50	.23	.06
□ B80 Marc Newfield	.25	.11	.03
□ B81 Angel Martinez	.25	.11	.03
□ B82 Brian L. Hunter	.50	.23	.06
□ B83 Jose Herrera	.25	.11	.03
□ B84 Glenn Dishman	.50	.23	.06
□ B85 Jacob Cruz	1.50	.70	.19
□ B86 Paul Shuey	.25	.11	.03
□ B87 Scott Rolen	18.00	8.00	2.20
□ B88 Doug Million	1.00	.45	.12
□ B89 Desi Relaford	.50	.23	.06
□ B90 Michael Tucker	.50	.23	.06
□ R1 Randy Johnson	1.00	.45	.12
□ R2 Joe Carter	.50	.23	.06
□ R3 Chili Davis	.50	.23	.06
□ R4 Moises Alou	.50	.23	.06
□ R5 Gary Sheffield	1.00	.45	.12
□ R6 Kevin Appier	.50	.23	.06
□ R7 Denny Neagle	.50	.23	.06
□ R8 Ruben Sierra	.50	.23	.06
□ R9 Darren Daulton	.50	.23	.06
□ R10 Cal Ripken	6.00	2.70	.75
□ R11 Bobby Bonilla	.50	.23	.06
□ R12 Manny Ramirez	2.00	.90	.25
□ R13 Barry Bonds	2.00	.90	.25
□ R14 Eric Karros	.50	.23	.06
□ R15 Greg Maddux	5.00	2.20	.60
□ R16 Jeff Bagwell	3.00	1.35	.35
□ R17 Paul Molitor	1.50	.70	.19
□ R18 Ray Lankford	.50	.23	.06
□ R19 Mark Grace	1.00	.45	.12
□ R20 Kenny Lofton	2.00	.90	.25
□ R21 Tony Gwynn	3.00	1.35	.35
□ R22 Will Clark	1.00	.45	.12
□ R23 Roger Clemens	1.50	.70	.19
□ R24 Dante Bichette	1.00	.45	.12
□ R25 Barry Larkin	1.00	.45	.12
□ R26 Wade Boggs	1.00	.45	.12
□ R27 Kirby Puckett	3.00	1.35	.35
□ R28 Cecil Fielder	.50	.23	.06
□ R29 Jose Canseco	1.00	.45	.12
□ R30 Juan Gonzalez	4.00	1.80	.50
□ R31 David Cone	.50	.23	.06
□ R32 Craig Biggio	.50	.23	.06
□ R33 Tim Salmon	1.00	.45	.12
□ R34 David Justice	1.00	.45	.12
□ R35 Sammy Sosa	1.00	.45	.12
□ R36 Mike Piazza	5.00	2.20	.60
□ R37 Carlos Baerga	.50	.23	.06
□ R38 Jeff Conine	.50	.23	.06
□ R39 Rafael Palmeiro	1.00	.45	.12
□ R40 Bret Saberhagen	.50	.23	.06
□ R41 Len Dykstra	.50	.23	.06
□ R42 Mo Vaughn	2.00	.90	.25
□ R43 Wally Joyner	.50	.23	.06
□ R44 Chuck Knoblauch	1.00	.45	.12
□ R45 Robin Ventura	.50	.23	.06
□ R46 Don Mattingly	4.00	1.80	.50
□ R47 Dave Hollins	.25	.11	.03
□ R48 Andy Benes	.25	.11	.03
□ R49 Ken Griffey Jr.	8.00	3.60	1.00
□ R50 Albert Belle	3.00	1.35	.35
□ R51 Matt Williams	1.00	.45	.12
□ R52 Rondell White	.50	.23	.06
□ R53 Raul Mondesi	1.00	.45	.12
□ R54 Brian Jordan	1.00	.45	.12
□ R55 Greg Vaughn	.50	.23	.06
□ R56 Fred McGriff	1.00	.45	.12
□ R57 Roberto Alomar	1.50	.70	.19
□ R58 Dennis Eckersley	.50	.23	.06
□ R59 Lee Smith	.50	.23	.06
□ R60 Eddie Murray	2.00	.90	.25
□ R61 Kenny Rogers	.25	.11	.03
□ R62 Ron Gant	.50	.23	.06
□ R63 Larry Walker	1.00	.45	.12
□ R64 Chad Curtis	.25	.11	.03
□ R65 Frank Thomas	8.00	3.60	1.00
□ R66 Paul O'Neill	.50	.23	.06
□ R67 Kevin Seitzer	.25	.11	.03
□ R68 Marquis Grissom	.50	.23	.06
□ R69 Mark McGwire	2.50	1.10	.30
□ R70 Travis Fryman	.50	.23	.06
□ R71 Andres Galarraga	1.00	.45	.12
□ R72 Carlos Perez	.50	.23	.06
□ R73 Tyler Green	.25	.11	.03
□ R74 Marty Cordova	1.00	.45	.12
□ R75 Shawn Green	.50	.23	.06
□ R76 Vaughn Eshelman	.25	.11	.03
□ R77 John Mabry	1.00	.45	.12
□ R78 Jason Bates	.25	.11	.03
□ R79 Jon Nunnally	.50	.23	.06
□ R80 Ray Durham	.50	.23	.06
□ R81 Edgardo Alfonzo	.50	.23	.06
□ R82 Esteban Loaiza	.25	.11	.03
□ R83 Hideo Nomo	8.00	3.60	1.00
□ R84 Orlando Miller	.25	.11	.03
□ R85 Alex Gonzalez	.25	.11	.03
□ R86 Mark Grudzielanek	2.00	.90	.25
□ R87 Julian Tavarez	.25	.11	.03
□ R88 Benji Gil	.25	.11	.03
□ R89 Quilvio Veras	.25	.11	.03
□ R90 Ricky Bottalico	.50	.23	.06
□ X1 Ben Davis Ivan Rodriguez	2.50	1.10	.30
□ X2 Mark Redman Manny Ramirez	1.00	.45	.12
□ X3 Reggie Taylor Deion Sanders	1.50	.70	.19
□ X4 Ryan Jaroncyk Shawn Green	1.25	.55	.16
□ X5 Juan LeBron Juan Gonzalez	2.50	1.10	.30
□ X6 Toby McKnight Craig Biggio	1.25	.55	.16
□ X7 Michael Barrett Travis Fryman	1.25	.55	.16
□ X8 Corey Jenkins Mo Vaughn	2.50	1.10	.30
□ X9 Ruben Rivera Frank Thomas	5.00	2.20	.60
□ X10 Curtis Goodwin Kenny Lofton	1.25	.55	.16
□ X11 Brian L. Hunter Tony Gwynn	1.50	.70	.19
□ X12 Todd Greene Ken Griffey Jr.	4.00	1.80	.50
□ X13 Karim Garcia Matt Williams	2.00	.90	.25
□ X14 Billy Wagner Randy Johnson	1.00	.45	.12
□ X15 Pat Watkins Jeff Bagwell	1.50	.70	.19

1995 Bowman's Best Refractors

Randomly inserted at a rate of one in six packs, this set is a parallel to the basic Bowman's Best issue. As far as the refractive qualities,

the final 15 Mirror Image cards (X1-X15) are considered diffractors which reflects light in a different manner than the typical refractor. The veteran refractor cards have been seen with or without the word refractor on the back. So far, there is no difference in pricing for either variation.

	MINT	NRMT	EXC
COMPLETE SET (195)	2500.00	1100.00	300.00
COMMON BLUE (B1-B90)	4.00	1.80	.50
COMMON RED (R1-R90)	4.00	1.80	.50
COMMON MIR.IMAGE (X1-X15)	5.00	2.20	.60

*STARS: 10X TO 16X BASIC CARDS ..
*YOUNG STARS: 6X TO 12X BASIC CARDS
*RCs: 4X TO 8X BASIC CARDS ....
*MIRROR IMAGE: 2.5X TO 5X BASIC CARDS

☐ B1 Derek Jeter	80.00	36.00	10.00
☐ B2 Vladimir Guerrero	150.00	70.00	19.00
☐ B3 Bob Abreu	30.00	13.50	3.70
☐ B5 Paul Wilson	20.00	9.00	2.50
☐ B7 Andruw Jones	300.00	135.00	38.00
☐ B10 Richie Sexson	25.00	11.00	3.10
☐ B20 Tony Clark	25.00	11.00	3.10
☐ B21 Jermaine Dye	40.00	18.00	5.00
☐ B22 Derrek Lee	25.00	11.00	3.10
☐ B25 Ben Grieve	50.00	22.00	6.25
☐ B28 Paul Konerko	65.00	29.00	8.00
☐ B29 Nomar Garciaparra	65.00	29.00	8.00
☐ B33 Rey Ordonez	40.00	18.00	5.00
☐ B42 Ruben Rivera	40.00	18.00	5.00
☐ B44 Todd Hollandsworth	20.00	9.00	2.50
☐ B50 Andy Pettitte	50.00	22.00	6.25
☐ B56 Karim Garcia	60.00	27.00	7.50
☐ B62 Jay Payton	30.00	13.50	3.70
☐ B73 Bartolo Colon	40.00	18.00	5.00
☐ B87 Scott Rolen	100.00	45.00	12.50
☐ R10 Cal Ripken	80.00	36.00	10.00
☐ R12 Manny Ramirez	25.00	11.00	3.10
☐ R13 Barry Bonds	25.00	11.00	3.10
☐ R15 Greg Maddux	60.00	27.00	7.50
☐ R16 Jeff Bagwell	40.00	18.00	5.00
☐ R17 Paul Molitor	20.00	9.00	2.50
☐ R20 Kenny Lofton	25.00	11.00	3.10
☐ R21 Tony Gwynn	40.00	18.00	5.00
☐ R23 Roger Clemens	20.00	9.00	2.50
☐ R27 Kirby Puckett	40.00	18.00	5.00
☐ R30 Juan Gonzalez	50.00	22.00	6.25
☐ R36 Mike Piazza	60.00	27.00	7.50
☐ R42 Mo Vaughn	25.00	11.00	3.10
☐ R46 Don Mattingly	50.00	22.00	6.25
☐ R49 Ken Griffey Jr.	100.00	45.00	12.50
☐ R50 Albert Belle	40.00	18.00	5.00
☐ R57 Roberto Alomar	20.00	9.00	2.50
☐ R60 Eddie Murray	25.00	11.00	3.10
☐ R65 Frank Thomas	100.00	45.00	12.50
☐ R69 Mark McGwire	30.00	13.50	3.70
☐ R83 Hideo Nomo	50.00	22.00	6.25
☐ X1 Ben Davis Ivan Rodriguez	15.00	6.75	1.85
☐ X9 Ruben Rivera Frank Thomas	25.00	11.00	3.10
☐ X12 Todd Greene Ken Griffey Jr.	20.00	9.00	2.50

1995 Bowman's Best Jumbo Refractors

This ten-card set was produced for various retail outlets. One card was inserted into each specially marked retail Topps box. According to Treat, Inc. there are no more than 9,000 of each card issued. Each over-sized card measures approximately 4" by 6". The most available of these cards are Albert Belle and Greg Maddux since they were distributed nationally. The other eight players were issued on a more regional basis. The cards are an exact parallel of the standard-size Refractor inserts except for their larger size.

	MINT	NRMT	EXC
COMPLETE SET (10)	160.00	70.00	20.00
COMMON CARD (1-10)	8.00	3.60	1.00

☐ 1 Albert Belle DP	8.00	3.60	1.00
☐ 2 Ken Griffey Jr	30.00	13.50	3.70
☐ 3 Tony Gwynn	15.00	6.75	1.85
☐ 4 Greg Maddux DP	10.00	4.50	1.25
☐ 5 Hideo Nomo	15.00	6.75	1.85
☐ 6 Mike Piazza	25.00	11.00	3.10
☐ 7 Cal Ripken	25.00	11.00	3.10
☐ 8 Sammy Sosa	8.00	3.60	1.00
☐ 9 Frank Thomas	30.00	13.50	3.70
☐ 10 Mo Vaughn	10.00	4.50	1.25

1996 Bowman's Best Previews

Printed with Finest technology, this 30-card set features the hottest 15 top prospects and 15 veterans and was randomly inserted in 1996 Bowman packs at the rate of one in 12. The fronts display a color action player photo. The backs carry player information.

	MINT	NRMT	EXC
COMPLETE SET (30)	150.00	70.00	19.00
COMMON CARD (BBP1-BBP30)	2.00	.90	.25

☐ BBP1 Chipper Jones	12.00	5.50	1.50
☐ BBP2 Alan Benes	3.00	1.35	.35
☐ BBP3 Brooks Kieschnick	3.00	1.35	.35
☐ BBP4 Barry Bonds	5.00	2.20	.60
☐ BBP5 Rey Ordonez	3.00	1.35	.35
☐ BBP6 Tim Salmon	3.00	1.35	.35
☐ BBP7 Mike Piazza	12.00	5.50	1.50
☐ BBP8 Billy Wagner	3.00	1.35	.35
☐ BBP9 Andruw Jones	20.00	9.00	2.50
☐ BBP10 Tony Gwynn	8.00	3.60	1.00
☐ BBP11 Paul Wilson	2.50	1.10	.30
☐ BBP12 Calvin Reese	2.00	.90	.25
☐ BBP13 Frank Thomas	20.00	9.00	2.50
☐ BBP14 Greg Maddux	12.00	5.50	1.50
☐ BBP15 Derek Jeter	12.00	5.50	1.50
☐ BBP16 Jeff Bagwell	8.00	3.60	1.00
☐ BBP17 Barry Larkin	2.50	1.10	.30
☐ BBP18 Todd Greene	2.50	1.10	.30
☐ BBP19 Ruben Rivera	3.00	1.35	.35
☐ BBP20 Richard Hidalgo	3.00	1.35	.35
☐ BBP21 Larry Walker	3.00	1.35	.35
☐ BBP22 Carlos Baerga	2.50	1.10	.30
☐ BBP23 Derrick Gibson	3.00	1.35	.35
☐ BBP24 Richie Sexson	3.00	1.35	.35
☐ BBP25 Mo Vaughn	5.00	2.20	.60
☐ BBP26 Hideo Nomo	5.00	2.20	.60
☐ BBP27 Nomar Garciaparra	8.00	3.60	1.00
☐ BBP28 Cal Ripken	15.00	6.75	1.85
☐ BBP29 Karim Garcia	4.00	1.80	.50
☐ BBP30 Ken Griffey Jr.	20.00	9.00	2.50

1996 Bowman's Best Previews Atomic Refractors

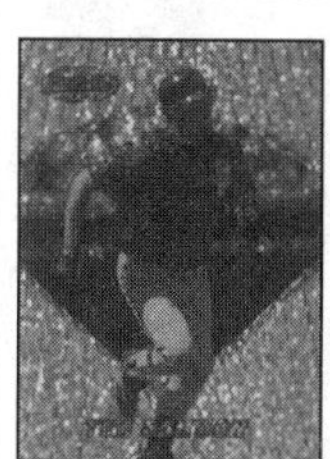
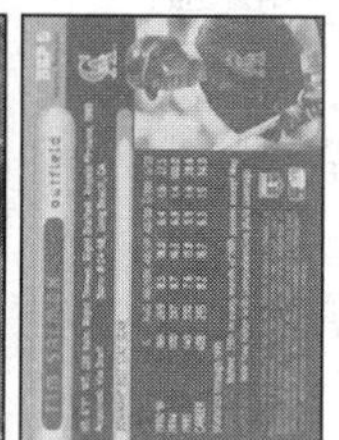

Randomly inserted one in every 48 packs of the 1996 Bowman, these parallel inserts are based upon the more common Bowman's Best Preview inserts. The only difference in design is a sparkling refractive sheen on the card fronts.

	MINT	NRMT	EXC
COMPLETE SET (30)	600.00	275.00	75.00
COMMON CARD (BBP1-BBP30)	8.00	3.60	1.00

*STARS: 2X to 4X BASIC CARDS........

1996 Bowman's Best Previews Refractors

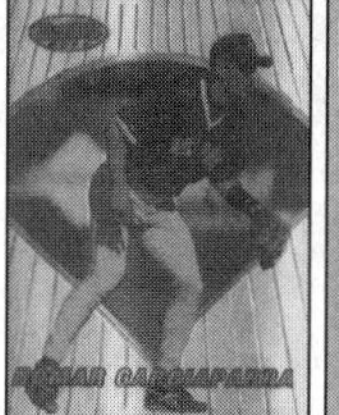

Randomly inserted one in every 24 packs of 1996 Bowman, cards from this 30-card set parallel the more common Bowman's Best Previews inserts. The only difference in design is the refractive sheen on the card fronts.

	MINT	NRMT	EXC
COMPLETE SET (30)	300.00	135.00	38.00
COMMON CARD (BBP1-BBP30)	4.00	1.80	.50

*STARS: 1X TO 2X BASIC CARDS......

1996 Bowman's Best

This 180-card set was issued in packs of six cards at the cost of $4.99 per pack. The fronts feature a color action player cutout of 90 outstanding veteran players on a chromium classic gold background design and 90 up and coming prospects and rookies on a silver design. The backs carry a color player portrait, player information and statistics. Card number 33 was never actually issued. Instead, both Roger Clemens and Rafael Palmeiro are erroneously numbered 32. A chrome reprint of the 1952 Bowman Mickey Mantle was inserted at the rate of one in 24 packs. A Refractor version of the Mantle was seeded at 1:96 packs and an Atomic Refractor version was seeded at 1:192. Notable Rookie Cards include Wes Helms, Jose Guillen and Wilton Guerrero.

	MINT	NRMT	EXC
COMPLETE SET (180)	100.00	45.00	12.50
COMMON GOLD (1-90)	.25	.11	.03
COMMON SILVER (91-180)	.25	.11	.03

☐ 1 Hideo Nomo	2.00	.90	.25
☐ 2 Edgar Martinez	.50	.23	.06
☐ 3 Cal Ripken	6.00	2.70	.75
☐ 4 Wade Boggs	.75	.35	.09
☐ 5 Cecil Fielder	.50	.23	.06
☐ 6 Albert Belle	3.00	1.35	.35
☐ 7 Chipper Jones	5.00	2.20	.60
☐ 8 Ryne Sandberg	2.00	.90	.25
☐ 9 Tim Salmon	.75	.35	.09
☐ 10 Barry Bonds	2.00	.90	.25
☐ 11 Ken Caminiti	.75	.35	.09
☐ 12 Ron Gant	.50	.23	.06
☐ 13 Frank Thomas	8.00	3.60	1.00
☐ 14 Dante Bichette	.75	.35	.09
☐ 15 Jason Kendall	.75	.35	.09
☐ 16 Mo Vaughn	2.00	.90	.25
☐ 17 Rey Ordonez	.75	.35	.09
☐ 18 Henry Rodriguez	.50	.23	.06
☐ 19 Ryan Klesko	.75	.35	.09
☐ 20 Jeff Bagwell	3.00	1.35	.35
☐ 21 Randy Johnson	.75	.35	.09
☐ 22 Jim Edmonds	.50	.23	.06
☐ 23 Kenny Lofton	2.00	.90	.25
☐ 24 Andy Pettitte	2.50	1.10	.30
☐ 25 Brady Anderson	.75	.35	.09
☐ 26 Mike Piazza	5.00	2.20	.60
☐ 27 Greg Vaughn	.75	.35	.09
☐ 28 Joe Carter	.50	.23	.06
☐ 29 Jason Giambi	.75	.35	.09
☐ 30 Ivan Rodriguez	2.00	.90	.25
☐ 31 Jeff Conine	.50	.23	.06
☐ 32 Rafael Palmeiro	.75	.35	.09
☐ 33 Roger Clemens	1.50	.70	.19
☐ 34 Chuck Knoblauch	.75	.35	.09
☐ 35 Reggie Sanders	.50	.23	.06
☐ 36 Andres Galarraga	.75	.35	.09
☐ 37 Paul O'Neill	.25	.11	.03
☐ 38 Tony Gwynn	3.00	1.35	.35
☐ 39 Paul Wilson	.50	.23	.06
☐ 40 Garret Anderson	.50	.23	.06
☐ 41 David Justice	.50	.23	.06
☐ 42 Eddie Murray	2.00	.90	.25
☐ 43 Mike Grace	.25	.11	.03
☐ 44 Marty Cordova	.50	.23	.06
☐ 45 Kevin Appier	.50	.23	.06
☐ 46 Raul Mondesi	.75	.35	.09
☐ 47 Jim Thome	1.50	.70	.19
☐ 48 Sammy Sosa	.75	.35	.09
☐ 49 Craig Biggio	.50	.23	.06
☐ 50 Marquis Grissom	.50	.23	.06
☐ 51 Alan Benes	.75	.35	.09
☐ 52 Manny Ramirez	2.00	.90	.25
☐ 53 Gary Sheffield	.75	.35	.09
☐ 54 Mike Mussina	1.50	.70	.19
☐ 55 Robin Ventura	.50	.23	.06
☐ 56 Johnny Damon	.50	.23	.06
☐ 57 Jose Canseco	.75	.35	.09
☐ 58 Juan Gonzalez	4.00	1.80	.50
☐ 59 Tino Martinez	.50	.23	.06
☐ 60 Brian Hunter	.25	.11	.03
☐ 61 Fred McGriff	.75	.35	.09
☐ 62 Jay Buhner	.75	.35	.09
☐ 63 Carlos Delgado	.50	.23	.06
☐ 64 Moises Alou	.50	.23	.06
☐ 65 Roberto Alomar	1.50	.70	.19
☐ 66 Barry Larkin	.50	.23	.06
☐ 67 Vinny Castilla	.50	.23	.06
☐ 68 Ray Durham	.25	.11	.03
☐ 69 Travis Fryman	.50	.23	.06
☐ 70 Jason Isringhausen	.75	.35	.09
☐ 71 Ken Griffey Jr.	8.00	3.60	1.00
☐ 72 John Smoltz	.75	.35	.09
☐ 73 Matt Williams	.75	.35	.09
☐ 74 Chan Ho Park	.75	.35	.09
☐ 75 Mark McGwire	2.50	1.10	.30
☐ 76 Jeffrey Hammonds	.25	.11	.03
☐ 77 Will Clark	.75	.35	.09
☐ 78 Kirby Puckett	3.00	1.35	.35
☐ 79 Derek Jeter	5.00	2.20	.60
☐ 80 Derek Bell	.50	.23	.06
☐ 81 Eric Karros	.50	.23	.06
☐ 82 Len Dykstra	.50	.23	.06
☐ 83 Larry Walker	.75	.35	.09
☐ 84 Mark Grudzielanek	.50	.23	.06
☐ 85 Greg Maddux	5.00	2.20	.60
☐ 86 Carlos Baerga	.50	.23	.06
☐ 87 Paul Molitor	1.50	.70	.19
☐ 88 John Valentin	.25	.11	.03
☐ 89 Mark Grace	.75	.35	.09
☐ 90 Ray Lankford	.50	.23	.06
☐ 91 Andruw Jones	15.00	6.75	1.85
☐ 92 Nomar Garciaparra	3.00	1.35	.35
☐ 93 Alex Ochoa	.50	.23	.06
☐ 94 Derrick Gibson	2.00	.90	.25
☐ 95 Jeff D'Amico	.75	.35	.09
☐ 96 Ruben Rivera	1.50	.70	.19
☐ 97 Vladimir Guerrero	8.00	3.60	1.00
☐ 98 Calvin Reese	.25	.11	.03
☐ 99 Richard Hidalgo	.75	.35	.09
☐ 100 Bartolo Colon	1.25	.55	.16
☐ 101 Karim Garcia	1.50	.70	.19
☐ 102 Ben Davis	.75	.35	.09
☐ 103 Jay Powell	.25	.11	.03
☐ 104 Chris Snopek	.25	.11	.03
☐ 105 Glendon Rusch	.50	.23	.06
☐ 106 Enrique Wilson	.75	.35	.09
☐ 107 Antonio Alfonseca	.25	.11	.03
☐ 108 Wilton Guerrero	5.00	2.20	.60
☐ 109 Jose Guillen	8.00	3.60	1.00
☐ 110 Miguel Mejia	.25	.11	.03
☐ 111 Jay Payton	.75	.35	.09
☐ 112 Scott Elarton	.50	.23	.06
☐ 113 Brooks Kieschnick	.75	.35	.09
☐ 114 Dustin Hermanson	.25	.11	.03
☐ 115 Roger Cedeno	.50	.23	.06
☐ 116 Matt Wagner	.25	.11	.03
☐ 117 Lee Daniels	.25	.11	.03
☐ 118 Ben Grieve	2.00	.90	.25
☐ 119 Ugueth Urbina	.25	.11	.03
☐ 120 Danny Graves	.50	.23	.06
☐ 121 Dan Donato	.25	.11	.03
☐ 122 Matt Ruebel	.25	.11	.03
☐ 123 Mark Sievert	.25	.11	.03
☐ 124 Chris Stynes	.25	.11	.03
☐ 125 Jeff Abbott	.50	.23	.06
☐ 126 Rocky Coppinger	1.25	.55	.16
☐ 127 Jermaine Dye	1.50	.70	.19
☐ 128 Todd Greene	.50	.23	.06
☐ 129 Chris Carpenter	.75	.35	.09
☐ 130 Edgar Renteria	.75	.35	.09
☐ 131 Matt Drews	.25	.11	.03
☐ 132 Edgard Velazquez	2.50	1.10	.30
☐ 133 Casey Whitten	.25	.11	.03
☐ 134 Ryan Jones	1.25	.55	.16
☐ 135 Todd Walker	8.00	3.60	1.00
☐ 136 Geoff Jenkins	1.25	.55	.16
☐ 137 Matt Morris	1.25	.55	.16
☐ 138 Richie Sexson	.75	.35	.09
☐ 139 Todd Dunwoody	2.50	1.10	.30
☐ 140 Gabe Alvarez	1.00	.45	.12
☐ 141 J.J. Johnson	.25	.11	.03
☐ 142 Shannon Stewart	.25	.11	.03
☐ 143 Brad Fullmer	.75	.35	.09
☐ 144 Julio Santana	.25	.11	.03
☐ 145 Scott Rolen	5.00	2.20	.60
☐ 146 Amaury Telemaco	.50	.23	.06
☐ 147 Trey Beamon	.25	.11	.03
☐ 148 Billy Wagner	.75	.35	.09
☐ 149 Todd Hollandsworth	.50	.23	.06
☐ 150 Doug Million	.75	.35	.09
☐ 151 Jose Valentin	3.00	1.35	.35
☐ 152 Wes Helms	8.00	3.60	1.00
☐ 153 Jeff Suppan	.75	.35	.09
☐ 154 Luis Castillo	2.00	.90	.25
☐ 155 Bob Abreu	.75	.35	.09
☐ 156 Paul Konerko	3.00	1.35	.35
☐ 157 Jamey Wright	.75	.35	.09
☐ 158 Eddie Pearson	.25	.11	.03
☐ 159 Jimmy Haynes	.25	.11	.03
☐ 160 Derrek Lee	1.25	.55	.16
☐ 161 Damian Moss	.75	.35	.09
☐ 162 Carlos Guillen	.25	.11	.03
☐ 163 Chris Fussell	1.00	.45	.12
☐ 164 Mike Sweeney	2.00	.90	.25
☐ 165 Donnie Sadler	.50	.23	.06
☐ 166 Desi Relaford	.25	.11	.03
☐ 167 Steve Gibralter	.25	.11	.03
☐ 168 Neifi Perez	.75	.35	.09
☐ 169 Antone Williamson	1.00	.45	.12
☐ 170 Marty Janzen	.75	.35	.09
☐ 171 Todd Helton	6.00	2.70	.75
☐ 172 Raul Ibanez	.25	.11	.03

	MINT	NRMT	EXC
☐ 173 Bill Selby	.25	.11	.03
☐ 174 Shane Monahan	1.50	.70	.19
☐ 175 Robin Jennings	.25	.11	.03
☐ 176 Bobby Chouinard	.25	.11	.03
☐ 177 Einar Diaz	.25	.11	.03
☐ 178 Jason Thompson	.25	.11	.03
☐ 179 Rafael Medina	1.00	.45	.12
☐ 180 Kevin Orie	.75	.35	.09
☐ NNO 1952 Mantle Atomic Refractor	40.00	18.00	5.00
☐ NNO 1952 Mantle Chrome	8.00	3.60	1.00
☐ NNO 1952 Mantle Refractor	20.00	9.00	2.50

1996 Bowman's Best Atomic Refractors

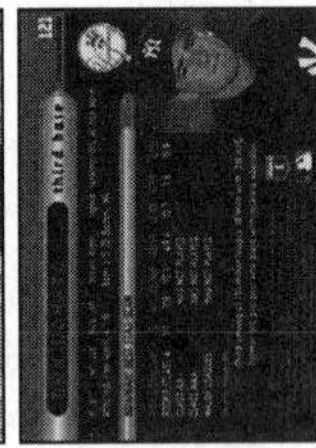

Inserted one in every 48 packs, this 180-card set is parallel to the 1996 Bowman's Best set. It is similar in design to the regular set but was printed with the newest sparkling refractor technology.

	MINT	NRMT	EXC
COMMON CARD (1-180)	12.00	5.50	1.50
*STARS: 18X TO 30X BASIC CARDS			
*YOUNG STARS: 15X TO 25X BASIC CARDS			

	MINT	NRMT	EXC
☐ 1 Hideo Nomo	90.00	40.00	11.00
☐ 3 Cal Ripken	250.00	110.00	31.00
☐ 4 Wade Boggs	40.00	18.00	5.00
☐ 6 Albert Belle	120.00	55.00	15.00
☐ 7 Chipper Jones	175.00	80.00	22.00
☐ 8 Ryne Sandberg	70.00	32.00	8.75
☐ 9 Tim Salmon	40.00	18.00	5.00
☐ 10 Barry Bonds	70.00	32.00	8.75
☐ 11 Ken Caminiti	50.00	22.00	6.25
☐ 13 Frank Thomas	300.00	135.00	38.00
☐ 14 Dante Bichette	40.00	18.00	5.00
☐ 16 Mo Vaughn	70.00	32.00	8.75
☐ 17 Rey Ordonez	40.00	18.00	5.00
☐ 19 Ryan Klesko	50.00	22.00	6.25
☐ 20 Jeff Bagwell	120.00	55.00	15.00
☐ 21 Randy Johnson	50.00	22.00	6.25
☐ 23 Kenny Lofton	70.00	32.00	8.75
☐ 24 Andy Pettitte	70.00	32.00	8.75
☐ 26 Mike Piazza	175.00	80.00	22.00
☐ 30 Ivan Rodriguez	70.00	32.00	8.75
☐ 33 Roger Clemens	60.00	27.00	7.50
☐ 34 Chuck Knoblauch	50.00	22.00	6.25
☐ 36 Andres Galarraga	40.00	18.00	5.00
☐ 38 Tony Gwynn	120.00	55.00	15.00
☐ 42 Eddie Murray	70.00	32.00	8.75
☐ 47 Jim Thome	60.00	27.00	7.50
☐ 48 Sammy Sosa	50.00	22.00	6.25
☐ 52 Manny Ramirez	70.00	32.00	8.75
☐ 53 Gary Sheffield	50.00	22.00	6.25
☐ 54 Mike Mussina	50.00	22.00	6.25
☐ 57 Jose Canseco	40.00	18.00	5.00
☐ 58 Juan Gonzalez	150.00	70.00	19.00
☐ 61 Fred McGriff	40.00	18.00	5.00
☐ 62 Jay Buhner	40.00	18.00	5.00
☐ 65 Roberto Alomar	60.00	27.00	7.50
☐ 66 Barry Larkin	40.00	18.00	5.00
☐ 71 Ken Griffey Jr.	300.00	135.00	38.00
☐ 72 John Smoltz	50.00	22.00	6.25
☐ 73 Matt Williams	40.00	18.00	5.00
☐ 75 Mark McGwire	90.00	40.00	11.00
☐ 77 Will Clark	40.00	18.00	5.00
☐ 78 Kirby Puckett	120.00	55.00	15.00
☐ 79 Derek Jeter	175.00	80.00	22.00
☐ 83 Larry Walker	40.00	18.00	5.00
☐ 85 Greg Maddux	150.00	70.00	19.00
☐ 87 Paul Molitor	60.00	27.00	7.50
☐ 91 Andruw Jones	300.00	135.00	38.00
☐ 92 Nomar Garciaparra	75.00	34.00	9.50
☐ 94 Derrick Gibson	50.00	22.00	6.25
☐ 96 Ruben Rivera	40.00	18.00	5.00
☐ 97 Vladimir Guerrero	175.00	80.00	22.00
☐ 99 Richard Hidalgo	35.00	16.00	4.40
☐ 100 Bartolo Colon	35.00	16.00	4.40
☐ 101 Karim Garcia	60.00	27.00	7.50
☐ 102 Ben Davis	35.00	16.00	4.40
☐ 108 Wilton Guerrero	75.00	34.00	9.50
☐ 109 Jose Guillen	150.00	70.00	19.00
☐ 111 Jay Payton	30.00	13.50	3.70
☐ 118 Ben Grieve	60.00	27.00	7.50
☐ 127 Jermaine Dye	50.00	22.00	6.25
☐ 130 Edgar Renteria	35.00	16.00	4.40
☐ 132 Edgard Velazquez	60.00	27.00	7.50
☐ 135 Todd Walker	185.00	85.00	23.00
☐ 139 Todd Dunwoody	70.00	32.00	8.75
☐ 145 Scott Rolen	125.00	55.00	15.50
☐ 149 Todd Hollandsworth	35.00	16.00	4.40
☐ 151 Jose Valentin	70.00	32.00	8.75
☐ 152 Wes Helms	150.00	70.00	19.00
☐ 154 Luis Castillo	35.00	16.00	4.40
☐ 155 Bob Abreu	30.00	13.50	3.70
☐ 156 Paul Konerko	100.00	45.00	12.50
☐ 160 Derrek Lee	50.00	22.00	6.25
☐ 161 Damian Moss	30.00	13.50	3.70
☐ 169 Antone Williamson	30.00	13.50	3.70
☐ 171 Todd Helton	135.00	60.00	17.00
☐ 174 Shane Monahan	40.00	18.00	5.00
☐ 180 Kevin Orie	30.00	13.50	3.70

1996 Bowman's Best Refractors

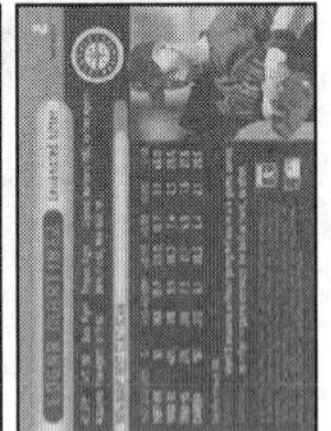

This 180-card set is parallel to the regular 1996 Bowman Best set and is similar in design. The difference is in the refractive quality of the cards. The cards were inserted at the rate of one in every 12 packs.

	MINT	NRMT	EXC
COMPLETE SET (180)	1500.00	700.00	190.00
COMMON CARD (1-180)	2.50	1.10	.30
*STARS: 5X TO 10X BASIC CARDS			
*YOUNG STARS: 4X TO 8X BASIC CARDS			

	MINT	NRMT	EXC
☐ 3 Cal Ripken	60.00	27.00	7.50
☐ 6 Albert Belle	40.00	18.00	5.00
☐ 7 Chipper Jones	50.00	22.00	6.25
☐ 13 Frank Thomas	80.00	36.00	10.00
☐ 20 Jeff Bagwell	30.00	13.50	3.70
☐ 26 Mike Piazza	50.00	22.00	6.25
☐ 38 Tony Gwynn	30.00	13.50	3.70
☐ 58 Juan Gonzalez	40.00	18.00	5.00
☐ 71 Ken Griffey Jr.	80.00	36.00	10.00
☐ 78 Kirby Puckett	30.00	13.50	3.70
☐ 79 Derek Jeter	50.00	22.00	6.25
☐ 85 Greg Maddux	50.00	22.00	6.25
☐ 91 Andruw Jones	100.00	45.00	12.50
☐ 97 Vladimir Guerrero	60.00	27.00	7.50
☐ 109 Jose Guillen	50.00	22.00	6.25
☐ 135 Todd Walker	50.00	22.00	6.25
☐ 145 Scott Rolen	40.00	18.00	5.00
☐ 152 Wes Helms	50.00	22.00	6.25
☐ 156 Paul Konerko	30.00	13.50	3.70
☐ 171 Todd Helton	40.00	18.00	5.00

1996 Bowman's Best Cuts

Randomly inserted in packs at a rate of one in 24, this chromium card die-cut set features 15 top hobby stars. The fronts display color action player cutouts over the team name and a background of swinging bars. The backs carry player information.

	MINT	NRMT	EXC
COMPLETE SET (15)	200.00	90.00	25.00
COMMON CARD (1-15)	5.00	2.20	.60

	MINT	NRMT	EXC
☐ 1 Ken Griffey Jr.	30.00	13.50	3.70
☐ 2 Jason Isringhausen	5.00	2.20	.60
☐ 3 Derek Jeter	20.00	9.00	2.50
☐ 4 Andruw Jones	40.00	18.00	5.00
☐ 5 Chipper Jones	20.00	9.00	2.50
☐ 6 Ryan Klesko	5.00	2.20	.60
☐ 7 Raul Mondesi	5.00	2.20	.60
☐ 8 Hideo Nomo	8.00	3.60	1.00
☐ 9 Mike Piazza	20.00	9.00	2.50
☐ 10 Manny Ramirez	8.00	3.60	1.00
☐ 11 Cal Ripken	25.00	11.00	3.10
☐ 12 Ruben Rivera	6.00	2.70	.75
☐ 13 Tim Salmon	5.00	2.20	.60
☐ 14 Frank Thomas	30.00	13.50	3.70
☐ 15 Jim Thome	6.00	2.70	.75

1996 Bowman's Best Cuts Atomic Refractors

Randomly inserted in packs at a rate of one in 96, this 15-card set is parallel to and is similar in design to the regular Bowman's Best Cuts set except for the sparkling refractive sheen on each card front.

	MINT	NRMT	EXC
COMPLETE SET (15)	800.00	350.00	100.00
COMMON CARD (1-15)	20.00	9.00	2.50
*STARS: 2X to 4X BASIC CARDS			

1996 Bowman's Best Cuts Refractors

Randomly inserted at the rate of one in every 48 packs, this 15-card set is parallel to and is similar in design to the regular Bowman's Best Cuts set. The difference is in the refractive quality of the cards.

	MINT	NRMT	EXC
COMPLETE SET (15)	400.00	180.00	50.00
COMMON CARD (1-15)	10.00	4.50	1.25
*STARS: 1X to 2X BASIC CARDS			

1996 Bowman's Best Mirror Image

Randomly inserted in packs at a rate of one in 48, this 10-card set features four top players on a single card at one of ten different positions. The fronts display a color photo of an AL veteran with a semicircle containing a color portrait of a prospect who plays the same position. The backs carry a color photo of a NL veteran with a semicircle color portrait of a prospect.

	MINT	NRMT	EXC
COMPLETE SET (10)	250.00	110.00	31.00
COMMON CARD (1-10)	20.00	9.00	2.50

	MINT	NRMT	EXC
☐ 1 Jeff Bagwell Todd Helton Frank Thomas Richie Sexson	40.00	18.00	5.00
☐ 2 Craig Biggio Luis Castillo Roberto Alomar Desi Relaford	20.00	9.00	2.50
☐ 3 Chipper Jones Scott Rolen Wade Boggs George Arias	30.00	13.50	3.70
☐ 4 Barry Larkin Neifi Perez Cal Ripken Mark Bellhorn	30.00	13.50	3.70
☐ 5 Larry Walker Karim Garcia Albert Belle Ruben Rivera	20.00	9.00	2.50
☐ 6 Barry Bonds Andruw Jones Kenny Lofton Donnie Sadler	50.00	22.00	6.25
☐ 7 Tony Gwynn Vladimir Guerrero Ken Griffey Ben Grieve	40.00	18.00	5.00
☐ 8 Mike Piazza Ben Davis Ivan Rodriguez Jose Valentin	25.00	11.00	3.10
☐ 9 Greg Maddux Jamey Wright Mike Mussina Bartolo Colon	25.00	11.00	3.10
☐ 10 Tom Glavine Billy Wagner Randy Johnson Jarrod Washburn	20.00	9.00	2.50

1996 Bowman's Best Mirror Image Atomic Refractors

Randomly inserted in packs at a rate of one in 192, this 10-card set is parallel to the regular Bowman's Best Mirror Image set and is the same design. The difference is that these cards were printed with the newest refractor technology.

	MINT	NRMT	EXC
COMPLETE SET (10)	1000.00	450.00	125.00
COMMON CARD (1-10)	80.00	36.00	10.00
*STARS: 2X to 4X BASIC CARDS			

1996 Bowman's Best Mirror Image Refractors

Randomly inserted in packs at a rate of one in 96, this 10-card set is parallel to and is similar in design to the regular Bowman's Best Mirror Image set. The difference is in the refractive quality of the cards.

	MINT	NRMT	EXC
COMPLETE SET (10)	500.00	220.00	60.00
COMMON CARD (1-10)	40.00	18.00	5.00
*STARS: 1X to 2X BASIC CARDS			

1993 Boy Scouts of America Treadway

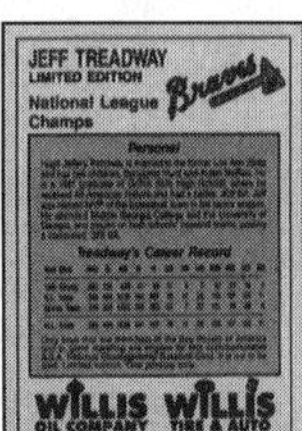

This single standard-size card was distributed by the Flint River Council of the Boy Scouts of America (Griffin, Georgia) to boys who were in scouting as of October 1992. Only 7,000 were produced. The front features a color action photo of Jeff Treadway. The card has black borders. Hot pink lettering sets off the player's name at the bottom and the words "Collector's Edition" at the top. The phrase "Official B.S.A. Baseball Card" is printed in blue just above the player's head. The Flint River Council logo appears in the bottom right corner. The back is white and displays a light blue panel containing personal and career information. Sponsor logos appear at the bottom. The player's name, team logo and the words "Limited Edition" and "National League Champs" are at the top. The bottom has advertisements for Willis Oil Company and Willis Tire and Auto.

	MINT	NRMT	EXC
COMPLETE SET	2.00	.90	.25
COMMON CARD	2.00	.90	.25
☐ 1 Jeff Treadway	2.00	.90	.25

1953 Braves Johnston Cookies

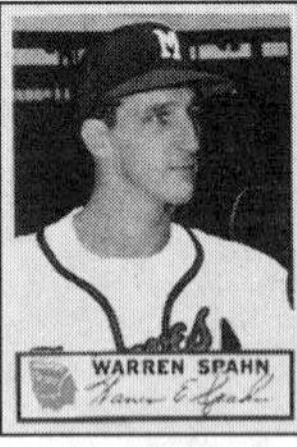

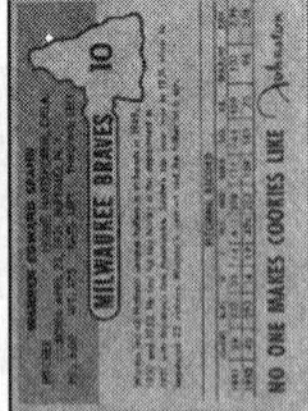

The cards in this 25-card set measure approximately 2 9/16" by 3 5/8". The 1953 Johnston's Cookies set of numbered cards features Milwaukee Braves players only. This set is the most plentiful of the three Johnston's Cookies sets and no known scarcities exist. The catalog designation for this set is D356-1.

	NRMT	VG-E	GOOD
COMPLETE SET (25)	450.00	200.00	55.00
COMMON CARD (1-25)	12.50	5.50	1.55
☐ 1 Charlie Grimm MG	15.00	6.75	1.85
☐ 2 John Antonelli	15.00	6.75	1.85
☐ 3 Vern Bickford	12.50	5.50	1.55
☐ 4 Bob Buhl	15.00	6.75	1.85
☐ 5 Lew Burdette	20.00	9.00	2.50
☐ 6 Dave Cole	12.50	5.50	1.55
☐ 7 Ernie Johnson	15.00	6.75	1.85
☐ 8 Dave Jolly	12.50	5.50	1.55
☐ 9 Don Liddle	12.50	5.50	1.55
☐ 10 Warren Spahn	75.00	34.00	9.50
☐ 11 Max Surkont	12.50	5.50	1.55
☐ 12 Jim Wilson	12.50	5.50	1.55
☐ 13 Sibbi Sisti	12.50	5.50	1.55
☐ 14 Walker Cooper	12.50	5.50	1.55
☐ 15 Del Crandall	15.00	6.75	1.85
☐ 16 Ebba St.Claire	12.50	5.50	1.55
☐ 17 Joe Adcock	20.00	9.00	2.50
☐ 18 George Crowe	12.50	5.50	1.55
☐ 19 Jack Dittmer	12.50	5.50	1.55
☐ 20 Johnny Logan	15.00	6.75	1.85
☐ 21 Ed Mathews	75.00	34.00	9.50
☐ 22 Bill Bruton	15.00	6.75	1.85
☐ 23 Sid Gordon	12.50	5.50	1.55
☐ 24 Andy Pafko	15.00	6.75	1.85
☐ 25 Jim Pendleton	12.50	5.50	1.55

1953-54 Braves Spic and Span 3x5

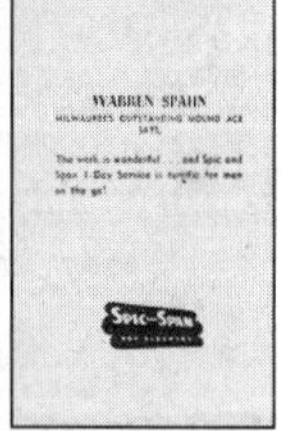

This 27-card set features only members of the Milwaukee Braves. The cards are black and white and approximately 3 1/4" by 5 1/2". Some of the photos in the set are posed against blank backgrounds, but most are posed against seats and a chain link fence, hence the set is sometimes referred to as the "chain link fence" set. There is a facsimile autograph at the bottom of the card. The set was probably issued in 1953 and 1954 since Hank Aaron is not included in the set and Don Liddle, Ebba St.Claire, and Johnny Antonelli were traded from the Braves on February 1, 1954 for Bobby Thomson (who is also in the set). Cards can be found either blank back or with player's name, comment, and logo in blue on the back

	NRMT	VG-E	GOOD
COMPLETE SET (28)	1000.00	450.00	125.00
COMMON CARD (1-28)	25.00	11.00	3.10
☐ 1 Joe Adcock	35.00	16.00	4.40
☐ 2 Johnny Antonelli	30.00	13.50	3.70
☐ 3 Vern Bickford	25.00	11.00	3.10
☐ 4 Bill Bruton	30.00	13.50	3.70
☐ 5 Bob Buhl	30.00	13.50	3.70
☐ 6 Lew Burdette	35.00	16.00	4.40
☐ 7 Dick Cole	25.00	11.00	3.10
☐ 8 Walker Cooper	25.00	11.00	3.10
☐ 9 Del Crandall	30.00	13.50	3.70
☐ 10 George Crowe	25.00	11.00	3.10
☐ 11 Jack Dittmer	25.00	11.00	3.10
☐ 12 Sid Gordon	25.00	11.00	3.10
☐ 13 Ernie Johnson	30.00	13.50	3.70
☐ 14 Dave Jolly	25.00	11.00	3.10
☐ 15 Don Liddle	25.00	11.00	3.10
☐ 16 Johnny Logan	30.00	13.50	3.70
☐ 17 Ed Mathews	150.00	70.00	19.00
☐ 18 Danny O'Connell	25.00	11.00	3.10
☐ 19 Andy Pafko	30.00	13.50	3.70
☐ 20 Jim Pendleton	25.00	11.00	3.10
☐ 21 Ebba St.Claire	25.00	11.00	3.10
☐ 22 Warren Spahn	150.00	70.00	19.00
☐ 23 Max Surkont	25.00	11.00	3.10
☐ 24 Bobby Thomson	35.00	16.00	4.40
☐ 25 Bob Thorpe	25.00	11.00	3.10
☐ 26 Roberto Vargas	25.00	11.00	3.10
☐ 27 Jim Wilson	25.00	11.00	3.10
☐ 28 Hank Aaron	300.00	135.00	38.00

1953-56 Braves Spic and Span 7x10

This 13-card set features only members of the Milwaukee Braves. The set was issued beginning in 1953 but may have been issued for several years as they seem to be the most common of all the Spic and Span issues. In addition, Danny O'Connell and Bobby Thomson were not on the '53 Braves team. The front of each card shows the logo, "Spic and Span Dry Cleaners ... the Choice of Your Favorite Braves." There is a thick white border around the cards with facsimile autograph in black in the bottom border. The cards have blank backs and are approximately 7" by 10".

	NRMT	VG-E	GOOD
COMPLETE SET (13)	200.00	90.00	25.00
COMMON CARD (1-13)	7.50	3.40	.95
☐ 1 Joe Adcock	15.00	6.75	1.85
☐ 2 Billy Bruton	9.00	4.00	1.10
☐ 3 Bob Buhl	9.00	4.00	1.10
☐ 4 Lew Burdette	15.00	6.75	1.85
☐ 5 Del Crandall	10.00	4.50	1.25
☐ 6 Jack Dittmer	7.50	3.40	.95
☐ 7 Johnny Logan	9.00	4.00	1.10
☐ 8 Eddie Mathews	50.00	22.00	6.25
☐ 9 Chet Nichols	7.50	3.40	.95
☐ 10 Danny O'Connell	7.50	3.40	.95
☐ 11 Andy Pafko	9.00	4.00	1.10
☐ 12 Warren Spahn	50.00	22.00	6.25
☐ 13 Bobby Thomson	15.00	6.75	1.85

1954 Braves Johnston Cookies

The cards in this 35-card set measure approximately 2" by 3 7/8". The 1954 Johnston's Cookies set of color cards of Milwaukee Braves are numbered according to the player's uniform number, except for the non-players, Lacks and Taylor, who are found at the end of the set. The Bobby Thomson card was withdrawn early in the year after his injury and is scarce. The catalog number for this set is D356-2. The Hank Aaron card shows him with uniform number 5, rather than the more familiar 44, that he switched to shortly thereafter.

	NRMT	VG-E	GOOD
COMPLETE SET (35)	1100.00	500.00	140.00
COMMON CARD	12.50	5.50	1.55
☐ 1 Del Crandall	18.00	8.00	2.20
☐ 3 Jim Pendleton	12.50	5.50	1.55
☐ 4 Danny O'Connell	12.50	5.50	1.55
☐ 5 Hank Aaron	500.00	220.00	60.00
☐ 6 Jack Dittmer	12.50	5.50	1.55
☐ 9 Joe Adcock	20.00	9.00	2.50
☐ 10 Bob Buhl	15.00	6.75	1.85
☐ 11 Phil Paine	12.50	5.50	1.55
☐ 12 Ben Johnson	12.50	5.50	1.55
☐ 13 Sibbi Sisti	12.50	5.50	1.55
☐ 15 Charles Gorin	12.50	5.50	1.55
☐ 16 Chet Nichols	12.50	5.50	1.55
☐ 17 Dave Jolly	12.50	5.50	1.55
☐ 19 Jim Wilson	12.50	5.50	1.55
☐ 20 Ray Crone	12.50	5.50	1.55
☐ 21 Warren Spahn	75.00	34.00	9.50
☐ 22 Gene Conley	15.00	6.75	1.85
☐ 23 Johnny Logan	18.00	8.00	2.20
☐ 24 Charlie White	12.50	5.50	1.55
☐ 27 George Metkovich	12.50	5.50	1.55
☐ 28 Johnny Cooney CO	12.50	5.50	1.55
☐ 29 Paul Burris	12.50	5.50	1.55
☐ 31 Bucky Walters CO	15.00	6.75	1.85
☐ 32 Ernie Johnson	15.00	6.75	1.85
☐ 33 Lou Burdette	25.00	11.00	3.10
☐ 34 Bobby Thomson SP	200.00	90.00	25.00
☐ 35 Bob Keely	12.50	5.50	1.55
☐ 38 Bill Bruton	15.00	6.75	1.85
☐ 40 Charlie Grimm MG	18.00	8.00	2.20
☐ 41 Eddie Mathews	75.00	34.00	9.50
☐ 42 Sam Calderone	12.50	5.50	1.55
☐ 47 Joey Jay	15.00	6.75	1.85
☐ 48 Andy Pafko	15.00	6.75	1.85
☐ 49 Dr. Charles Lacks (Unnumbered)	12.50	5.50	1.55
☐ 50 Joseph F. Taylor (Unnumbered)	12.50	5.50	1.55

1954 Braves Merrell

This set of the Milwaukee Braves measures approximately 8" by 10" and features black-and-white drawings of players by artist, Marshall Merrell. The cards are unnumbered and checklisted below in alphabetical order. This checklist may be incomplete and additions are welcome.

	NRMT	VG-E	GOOD
COMPLETE SET	60.00	27.00	7.50
COMMON CARD	10.00	4.50	1.25
☐ 1 Bob Buhl	10.00	4.50	1.25
☐ 2 Johnny Logan	10.00	4.50	1.25
☐ 3 Danny O'Connell	10.00	4.50	1.25
☐ 4 Andy Pafko	10.00	4.50	1.25
☐ 5 Warren Spahn	25.00	11.00	3.10
☐ 6 Jim Wilson	10.00	4.50	1.25

1954 Braves Spic and Span Postcards

This black and white set features only members of the Milwaukee Braves. The cards have postcard backs and measure approximately 3 11/16" by 6". The postcards were issued beginning in 1954. There is a facsimile autograph on the front in black or white ink. The set apparently was also issued with white borders in a 5" by 7" size. The catalog designation for this set is PC756. The front of each card shows the logo, "Spic and Span Dry Cleaners ... the Choice of Your Favorite Braves."

	NRMT	VG-E	GOOD
COMPLETE SET (18)	500.00	220.00	60.00
COMMON CARD (1-18)	15.00	6.75	1.85
☐ 1 Henry Aaron	250.00	110.00	31.00
☐ 2 Joe Adcock	25.00	11.00	3.10
☐ 3 Billy Bruton	18.00	8.00	2.20
☐ 4 Bob Buhl	18.00	8.00	2.20
☐ 5 Lew Burdette	25.00	11.00	3.10
☐ 6 Gene Conley	18.00	8.00	2.20
☐ 7 Del Crandall	20.00	9.00	2.50
☐ 8 Ray Crone	15.00	6.75	1.85
☐ 9 Jack Dittmer	15.00	6.75	1.85
☐ 10 Ernie Johnson	18.00	8.00	2.20
☐ 11 Dave Jolly	15.00	6.75	1.85
☐ 12 Johnny Logan	18.00	8.00	2.20
☐ 13 Eddie Mathews	75.00	34.00	9.50
☐ 14 Chet Nichols	15.00	6.75	1.85
☐ 15 Danny O'Connell	15.00	6.75	1.85
☐ 16 Andy Pafko	18.00	8.00	2.20
☐ 17 Warren Spahn	75.00	34.00	9.50
☐ 18 Bobby Thomson	25.00	11.00	3.10

1955 Braves Golden Stamps

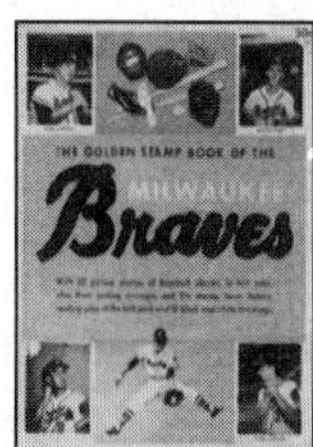

THE GOLDEN STAMP BOOK OF THE
MILWAUKEE
Braves

This 32-stamp set features color photos of the Milwaukee Braves and measures approximately 1 15/16" by 2 5/8". The stamps are designed to be placed in a 32-page album which measures approximately 8 3/8" by 10 15/16". The album contains black-and-white drawings of players with their batting averages and life stories. The team's history and other information is also printed in the album. The stamps are unnumbered and listed below according to where they fall in the album.

	NRMT	VG-E	GOOD
COMPLETE SET (32)	100.00	45.00	12.50
COMMON CARD (1-32)	2.00	.90	.25
☐ 1 1954 Team Photo	7.50	3.40	.95
☐ 2 Charlie Grimm MG	10.00	4.50	1.25
☐ 3 Warren Spahn	15.00	6.75	1.85
☐ 4 Lew Burdette	7.50	3.40	.95
☐ 5 Chet Nichols	2.00	.90	.25
☐ 6 Gene Conley	2.00	.90	.25
☐ 7 Bob Buhl	2.00	.90	.25
☐ 8 Jim Wilson	2.00	.90	.25
☐ 9 Dave Jolly	2.00	.90	.25
☐ 10 Ernie Johnson	4.00	1.80	.50
☐ 11 Joey Jay	2.00	.90	.25
☐ 12 Dave Koslo	2.00	.90	.25
☐ 13 Charlie Gorin	2.00	.90	.25
☐ 14 Ray Crone	2.00	.90	.25
☐ 15 Del Crandall	3.00	1.35	.35
☐ 16 Joe Adcock	4.00	1.80	.50
☐ 17 Jack Dittmer	2.00	.90	.25
☐ 18 Eddie Mathews	20.00	9.00	2.50
☐ 19 Johnny Logan	3.00	1.35	.35
☐ 20 Andy Pafko	3.00	1.35	.35
☐ 21 Bill Bruton	2.00	.90	.25
☐ 22 Bobby Thomson	3.00	1.35	.35
☐ 23 Charlie White	2.00	.90	.25
☐ 24 Danny O'Connell	2.00	.90	.25
☐ 25 Henry Aaron	25.00	11.00	3.10
☐ 26 Jim Pendleton	2.00	.90	.25
☐ 27 George Metkovich	2.00	.90	.25
☐ 28 Mel Roach	2.00	.90	.25
☐ 29 John Cooney CO	2.00	.90	.25
☐ 30 Bucky Walters CO	4.00	1.80	.50
☐ 31 Charles Lacks TR	2.00	.90	.25
☐ 32 Milwaukee County Stadium	7.50	3.40	.95

1955 Braves Johnston Cookies

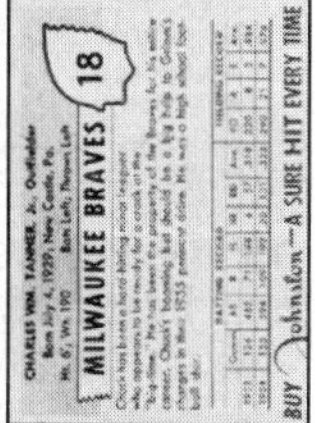

The cards in this 35-card set measure approximately 2 3/4" by 4". This set of Milwaukee Braves issued in 1955 by Johnston Cookies are numbered by the uniform number of the player depicted, except for non-players Lacks, Lewis and Taylor. The cards were issued in strips of six which accounts for the rouletted edges found on single cards. They are larger in size than the two previous sets but are printed on thinner cardboard. Each player in the checklist has been marked to show on which panel or strip he appeared (Pafko appears twice). A complete panel of six cards is worth 25 percent more than the sum of the individual players. The catalog designation for this set is D356-3.

	NRMT	VG-E	GOOD
COMPLETE SET (35)	1100.00	500.00	140.00
COMMON CARD (1-51)	15.00	6.75	1.85
☐ 1 Del Crandall P1	25.00	11.00	3.10
☐ 3 Jim Pendleton P3	15.00	6.75	1.85
☐ 4 Danny O'Connell P1	15.00	6.75	1.85
☐ 6 Jack Dittmer P6	15.00	6.75	1.85
☐ 9 Joe Adcock P2	30.00	13.50	3.70
☐ 10 Bob Buhl P6	20.00	9.00	2.50
☐ 11 Phil Paine P5	15.00	6.75	1.85
☐ 12 Ray Crone P5	15.00	6.75	1.85
☐ 15 Charlie Gorin P1	15.00	6.75	1.85
☐ 16 Dave Jolly P4	15.00	6.75	1.85
☐ 17 Chet Nichols P2	15.00	6.75	1.85
☐ 18 Chuck Tanner P5	30.00	13.50	3.70
☐ 19 Jim Wilson P6	15.00	6.75	1.85
☐ 20 Dave Koslo P4	15.00	6.75	1.85
☐ 21 Warren Spahn P3	75.00	34.00	9.50
☐ 22 Gene Conley P3	20.00	9.00	2.50
☐ 23 Johnny Logan P4	25.00	11.00	3.10
☐ 24 Charlie White P2	15.00	6.75	1.85
☐ 28 Johnny Cooney CO P4	15.00	6.75	1.85
☐ 30 Roy Smalley P3	15.00	6.75	1.85
☐ 31 Bucky Walters CO P6	20.00	9.00	2.50
☐ 32 Ernie Johnson P5	20.00	9.00	2.50
☐ 33 Lew Burdette P1	35.00	16.00	4.40
☐ 34 Bobby Thomson P6	30.00	13.50	3.70
☐ 35 Bob Keely P1	15.00	6.75	1.85
☐ 38 Bill Bruton P4	20.00	9.00	2.50
☐ 39 George Crowe P3	15.00	6.75	1.85
☐ 40 Charlie Grimm MG P6	25.00	11.00	3.10
☐ 41 Eddie Mathews P5	75.00	34.00	9.50
☐ 44 Hank Aaron P1	400.00	180.00	50.00
☐ 47 Joey Jay P2	20.00	9.00	2.50
☐ 48 Andy Pafko P2 P4	15.00	6.75	1.85
☐ 49 Dr. Charles Leaks P2 (Unnumbered)	15.00	6.75	1.85
☐ 50 Duffy Lewis P5 Trav.Sec. (Unnumbered)	15.00	6.75	1.85
☐ 51 Joe Taylor P3 (Unnumbered)	15.00	6.75	1.85

1955 Braves Spic and Span Die-Cut

This 18-card, die-cut, set features only members of the Milwaukee Braves. Each player measures differently according to the pose but they are, on average, approximately 8" by 8". The cards could be

folded together to stand up. Each card contains a logo in the middle at the bottom and a copyright notice, "1955 Spic and Span Cleaners" in the lower right corner.

	NRMT	VG-E	GOOD
COMPLETE SET (18)	2750.00	1250.00	350.00
COMMON CARD (1-18)	100.00	45.00	12.50
☐ 1 Hank Aaron	750.00	350.00	95.00
☐ 2 Joe Adcock	125.00	55.00	15.50
☐ 3 Billy Bruton	100.00	45.00	12.50
☐ 4 Bob Buhl	100.00	45.00	12.50
☐ 5 Lew Burdette	125.00	55.00	15.50
☐ 6 Gene Conley	100.00	45.00	12.50
☐ 7 Del Crandall	100.00	45.00	12.50
☐ 8 Jack Dittmer	100.00	45.00	12.50
☐ 9 Ernie Johnson	100.00	45.00	12.50
☐ 10 Dave Jolly	100.00	45.00	12.50
☐ 11 Johnny Logan	100.00	45.00	12.50
☐ 12 Eddie Mathews	300.00	135.00	38.00
☐ 13 Chet Nichols	100.00	45.00	12.50
☐ 14 Danny O'Connell	100.00	45.00	12.50
☐ 15 Andy Pafko	100.00	45.00	12.50
☐ 16 Warren Spahn	300.00	135.00	38.00
☐ 17 Bob Thomson	125.00	55.00	15.50
☐ 18 Jim Wilson	100.00	45.00	12.50

1956-60 Braves Bill and Bob Postcards PPC-741

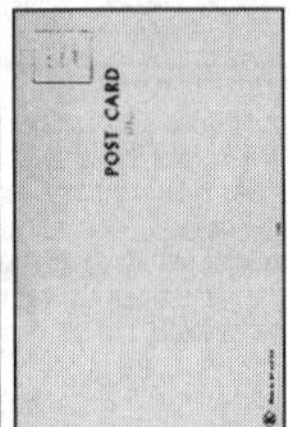

The Bill and Bob postcards issued during the 1956-60 time period features only Milwaukee Braves. The cards are unnumbered, other than the K card number at the middle base on the reverse, and present some of the most attractive color postcards issued in the postwar period. Three poses of Adcock and two poses each of Bruton and Crandall exist. The Torre card has been seen with a Pepsi advertisment on the reverse. The complete set price includes only one of each player.

	NRMT	VG-E	GOOD
COMPLETE SET (15)	1200.00	550.00	150.00
COMMON CARD (1-15)	25.00	11.00	3.10
☐ 1 Hank Aaron	375.00	170.00	47.50
☐ 2 Joe Adcock (3)	50.00	22.00	6.25
☐ 3 Bill Bruton (2)	60.00	27.00	7.50
☐ 4 Bob Buhl	25.00	11.00	3.10
☐ 5 Lew Burdette	35.00	16.00	4.40
☐ 6 Gene Conley	50.00	22.00	6.25
☐ 7 Wes Covington	50.00	22.00	6.25
☐ 8 Del Crandall (2)	25.00	11.00	3.10
☐ 9 Chuck Dressen MG	50.00	22.00	6.25
☐ 10 Charlie Grimm MG	75.00	34.00	9.50
☐ 11 Fred Haney MG	50.00	22.00	6.25
☐ 12 Bobby Keely CO	50.00	22.00	6.25
☐ 13 Ed Mathews	150.00	70.00	19.00
☐ 14 Warren Spahn	150.00	70.00	19.00
☐ 15 Frank Torre	75.00	34.00	9.50

1957 Braves Spic and Span 4x5

This set contains 20 black and white photos each with a blue-printed message such as "Stay in There and Pitch" and blue facsimile autograph The set features only members of the Milwaukee Braves. Red Schoendienst was traded to the Braves on June 15, 1957 in exchange for Danny O'Connell, Ray Crone, and Bobby Thomson. Wes Covington, Felix Mantilla, and Bob Trowbridge are also listed as shorter-printed (SP) cards as they were apparently mid-season call-ups. The cards are approximately 4 5/16" by 5" with a thick white border and are blank backed. Spic and Span appears in blue in the white border in the lower right corner of the card. Since the cards are unnumbered, they are numbered in alphabetical order in the checklist below.

	NRMT	VG-E	GOOD
COMPLETE SET (20)	450.00	200.00	55.00
COMMON CARD (1-20)	10.00	4.50	1.25
COMMON CARD SP	25.00	11.00	3.10
☐ 1 Henry Aaron	150.00	70.00	19.00
☐ 2 Joe Adcock	15.00	6.75	1.85
☐ 3 Billy Bruton	12.00	5.50	1.50
☐ 4 Bob Buhl	12.00	5.50	1.50
☐ 5 Lew Burdette	20.00	9.00	2.50
☐ 6 Gene Conley	12.00	5.50	1.50
☐ 7 Wes Covington SP	30.00	13.50	3.70
☐ 8 Del Crandall	15.00	6.75	1.85
☐ 9 Ray Crone	10.00	4.50	1.25
☐ 10 Fred Haney MG	10.00	4.50	1.25
☐ 11 Ernie Johnson	12.00	5.50	1.50
☐ 12 Johnny Logan	12.00	5.50	1.50
☐ 13 Felix Mantilla SP	25.00	11.00	3.10
☐ 14 Ed Mathews	50.00	22.00	6.25
☐ 15 Danny O'Connell	10.00	4.50	1.25
☐ 16 Andy Pafko	12.00	5.50	1.50
☐ 17 Red Schoendienst SP	50.00	22.00	6.25
☐ 18 Warren Spahn	50.00	22.00	6.25
☐ 19 Bobby Thomson	20.00	9.00	2.50
☐ 20 Bob Trowbridge SP	25.00	11.00	3.10

1958 Braves Jay Publishing

This 12-card set of the Milwaukee Braves measures approximately 5" by 7" and features black-and-white player photos in a white border. These cards were packaged 12 to a packet. The backs are blank. The cards are unnumbered and checklisted below in alphabetical order.

	NRMT	VG-E	GOOD
COMPLETE SET (12)	50.00	22.00	6.25
COMMON CARD (1-12)	3.00	1.35	.35
☐ 1 Hank Aaron	10.00	4.50	1.25
☐ 2 Joe Adcock	4.00	1.80	.50
☐ 3 Lew Burdette	4.00	1.80	.50
☐ 4 Wes Covington	4.00	1.80	.50
☐ 5 Delmar Crandall	3.00	1.35	.35
☐ 6 Robert Hazle	3.00	1.35	.35
☐ 7 John Logan	3.00	1.35	.35
☐ 8 Eddie Mathews	7.50	3.40	.95
☐ 9 Donald McMahon	3.00	1.35	.35
☐ 10 Andy Pafko	3.00	1.35	.35
☐ 11 Red Schoendienst	5.00	2.20	.60
☐ 12 Warren Spahn	10.00	4.50	1.25

1960 Braves Davison's

This set measures approximately 3" by 3 5/8" and features black-and-white player photos. The cards are unnumbered and checklisted below in alphabetical order. The checklist may be incomplete and additions are welcome.

	NRMT	VG-E	GOOD
COMPLETE SET	40.00	18.00	5.00
COMMON CARD	20.00	9.00	2.50
☐ 1 Hank Aaron	25.00	11.00	3.10
☐ 2 Eddie Mathews	20.00	9.00	2.50

1960 Braves Jay Publishing

This 12-card set of the Milwaukee Braves measures approximately 5" by 7" and features black-and-white player photos in a white border. These cards were packaged 12 to a packet. The backs are blank. The cards are unnumbered and checklisted below in alphabetical order.

	NRMT	VG-E	GOOD
COMPLETE SET (12)	40.00	18.00	5.00
COMMON CARD (1-12)	2.50	1.10	.30
☐ 1 Hank Aaron	10.00	4.50	1.25
☐ 2 Billy Bruton	2.50	1.10	.30
☐ 3 Wes Covington	2.50	1.10	.30
☐ 4 Charlie Dressen MG	3.00	1.35	.35
☐ 5 Bob Giggie	2.50	1.10	.30
☐ 6 Joey Jay	2.50	1.10	.30
☐ 7 Stan Lopata	2.50	1.10	.30
☐ 8 Felix Mantilla	2.50	1.10	.30
☐ 9 Bob Rush	2.50	1.10	.30
☐ 10 Red Schoendienst	4.00	1.80	.50
☐ 11 Warren Spahn	7.50	3.40	.95
☐ 12 Frank Torre	3.00	1.35	.35

1960 Braves Lake to Lake

The cards in this 28-card set measure 2 1/2" by 3 1/4". The 1960 Lake to Lake set of unnumbered, blue tinted cards features Milwaukee Braves players only. For some reason, this set of Braves does not include Eddie Mathews. The cards were issued on milk cartons by Lake to Lake Dairy. Most cards have staple holes in the upper right corner. The backs are in red and give details and prizes associated with the card promotion. Cards with staple holes can be considered very good to excellent at best. The catalog designation for this set is F102-1.

	NRMT	VG-E	GOOD
COMPLETE SET (28)	1200.00	550.00	150.00
COMMON CARD (1-28)	15.00	6.75	1.85
☐ 1 Hank Aaron	350.00	160.00	45.00
☐ 2 Joe Adcock	30.00	13.50	3.70
☐ 3 Ray Boone	125.00	55.00	15.50
☐ 4 Bill Bruton	300.00	135.00	38.00
☐ 5 Bob Buhl	25.00	11.00	3.10
☐ 6 Lew Burdette	25.00	11.00	3.10
☐ 7 Chuck Cottier	15.00	6.75	1.85
☐ 8 Wes Covington	25.00	11.00	3.10
☐ 9 Del Crandall	30.00	13.50	3.70
☐ 10 Chuck Dressen MG	25.00	11.00	3.10
☐ 11 Bob Giggie	15.00	6.75	1.85
☐ 12 Joey Jay	30.00	13.50	3.70
☐ 13 Johnny Logan	25.00	11.00	3.10
☐ 14 Felix Mantilla	15.00	6.75	1.85
☐ 15 Lee Maye	15.00	6.75	1.85
☐ 16 Don McMahon	15.00	6.75	1.85
☐ 17 George Myatt CO	15.00	6.75	1.85
☐ 18 Andy Pafko CO	25.00	11.00	3.10
☐ 19 Juan Pizarro	15.00	6.75	1.85
☐ 20 Mel Roach	15.00	6.75	1.85
☐ 21 Bob Rush	15.00	6.75	1.85
☐ 22 Bob Scheffing CO	15.00	6.75	1.85
☐ 23 Red Schoendienst	40.00	18.00	5.00
☐ 24 Warren Spahn	75.00	34.00	9.50
☐ 25 Al Spangler	15.00	6.75	1.85
☐ 26 Frank Torre	25.00	11.00	3.10
☐ 27 Carlton Willey	15.00	6.75	1.85
☐ 28 Whit Wyatt CO	25.00	11.00	3.10

1960 Braves Spic and Span

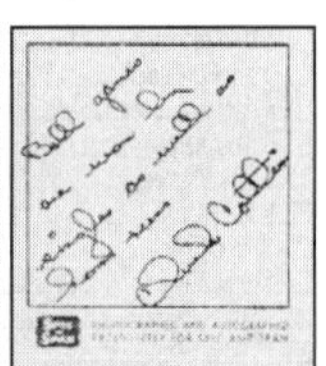

This set features only members of the Milwaukee Braves. These small cards each measure approximately 2 13/16" by 3 1/16". The cards have a thin white border around a black and white photo with no other writing or words on the front. The card backs have the Spic and Span logo at the bottom along with "Photographed and Autographed Exclusively for Spic and Span". A message and facsimile autograph from the player is presented inside a square box all in blue on the card back.

	NRMT	VG-E	GOOD
COMPLETE SET (27)	500.00	220.00	60.00
COMMON CARD (1-26)	10.00	4.50	1.25
☐ 1 Henry Aaron	150.00	70.00	19.00
☐ 2 Joe Adcock	15.00	6.75	1.85
☐ 3 Billy Bruton	12.50	5.50	1.55
☐ 4 Bob Buhl	12.50	5.50	1.55
☐ 5 Lew Burdette	18.00	8.00	2.20
☐ 6 Chuck Cottier	10.00	4.50	1.25
☐ 7A Del Crandall ERR (Reversed negative)	50.00	22.00	6.25
☐ 7B Del Crandall COR	15.00	6.75	1.85
☐ 8 Charlie Dressen MG	12.50	5.50	1.55
☐ 9 Joey Jay	10.00	4.50	1.25
☐ 10 Johnny Logan	12.50	5.50	1.55
☐ 11 Felix Mantilla	10.00	4.50	1.25
☐ 12 Ed Mathews	50.00	22.00	6.25
☐ 13 Lee Maye	10.00	4.50	1.25
☐ 14 Don McMahon	10.00	4.50	1.25
☐ 15 George Myatt CO	10.00	4.50	1.25
☐ 16 Andy Pafko CO	10.00	4.50	1.25
☐ 17 Juan Pizarro	10.00	4.50	1.25
☐ 18 Mel Roach	10.00	4.50	1.25
☐ 19 Bob Rush	10.00	4.50	1.25
☐ 20 Bob Scheffing CO	10.00	4.50	1.25
☐ 21 Red Schoendienst	25.00	11.00	3.10
☐ 22 Warren Spahn	50.00	22.00	6.25
☐ 23 Al Spangler	10.00	4.50	1.25
☐ 24 Frank Torre	12.50	5.50	1.55
☐ 25 Carl Willey	10.00	4.50	1.25
☐ 26 Whit Wyatt CO	12.50	5.50	1.55

1962 Braves Jay Publishing

This 12-card set of the Milwaukee Braves measures approximately 5" by 7". The fronts feature black-and-white posed player photos with the player's and team name printed below in the white border. These cards were packaged 12 to a packet. The backs are blank. The cards are unnumbered and checklisted below in alphabetical order.

	NRMT	VG-E	GOOD
COMPLETE SET (12)	35.00	16.00	4.40
COMMON CARD (1-12)	2.00	.90	.25
☐ 1 Hank Aaron	10.00	4.50	1.25
☐ 2 Joe Adcock	5.00	2.20	.60
☐ 3 Frank Bolling	2.00	.90	.25
☐ 4 Lou Burdette	3.50	1.55	.45
☐ 5 Del Crandall	2.50	1.10	.30
☐ 6 Eddie Mathews	7.50	3.40	.95
☐ 7 Lee Maye	2.00	.90	.25
☐ 8 Roy McMillan	2.00	.90	.25
☐ 9 Warren Spahn	7.50	3.40	.95
☐ 10 George (Birdie) Tebbetts MG	2.50	1.10	.30
☐ 11 Joe Torre	4.50	2.00	.55
☐ 12 Carl Willey	2.00	.90	.25

1963 Braves Jay Publishing

This 12-card set of the Milwaukee Braves measures approximately 5" by 7". The fronts feature black-and-white posed player photos with the player's and team name printed below in the white border. These cards were packaged 12 to a packet. The backs are blank. The cards are unnumbered and checklisted below in alphabetical order.

	NRMT	VG-E	GOOD
COMPLETE SET (12)	35.00	16.00	4.40
COMMON CARD (1-12)	2.00	.90	.25
☐ 1 Hank Aaron	10.00	4.50	1.25
☐ 2 Frank Bolling	2.00	.90	.25
☐ 3 Lew Burdette	3.50	1.55	.45
☐ 4 Del Crandall	2.50	1.10	.30
☐ 5 Bob Hendley	2.00	.90	.25
☐ 6 Norm Larker	2.00	.90	.25
☐ 7 Eddie Mathews	7.50	3.40	.95
☐ 8 Roy McMillan	2.00	.90	.25
☐ 9 Bob Shaw	2.00	.90	.25
☐ 10 Warren Spahn	7.50	3.40	.95
☐ 11 Joe Torre	4.50	2.00	.55
☐ 12 Bob Uecker	4.50	2.00	.55

1964 Braves Jay Publishing

This 12-card set of the Milwaukee Braves measures approximately 5" by 7". The fronts feature black-and-white posed player photos with the player's and team name printed below in the white border. These cards were packaged 12 to a packet. The backs are blank. The cards are unnumbered and checklisted below in alphabetical order.

	NRMT	VG-E	GOOD
COMPLETE SET (12)	35.00	16.00	4.40
COMMON CARD (1-12)	2.00	.90	.25
☐ 1 Hank Aaron	10.00	4.50	1.25
☐ 2 Frank Bolling	2.00	.90	.25
☐ 3 Bobbie Bragan MG	2.50	1.10	.30
☐ 4 Tony Cloninger	2.00	.90	.25
☐ 5 Denny Lemaster	2.00	.90	.25
☐ 6 Eddie Mathews	7.50	3.40	.95
☐ 7 Lee Maye	2.00	.90	.25
☐ 8 Roy McMillan	2.00	.90	.25
☐ 9 Denis Menke	2.00	.90	.25
☐ 10 Bob Sadowski	2.00	.90	.25
☐ 11 Warren Spahn	7.50	3.40	.95
☐ 12 Joe Torre	4.00	1.80	.50

1967 Braves Irvingdale Dairy

Four Atlanta Braves were featured on the back of one milk carton. If each player photo were cut, it would measure 1 3/4" by 2 5/8". The fronts feature a brown-tinted head-and-shoulders shot, with the player's name below. The backs are blank. The cards are unnumbered and checklisted below in alphabetical order.

	NRMT	VG-E	GOOD
COMPLETE SET (4)	30.00	13.50	3.70
COMMON CARD (1-4)	7.50	3.40	.95
☐ 1 Clete Boyer	10.00	4.50	1.25
☐ 2 Mack Jones	7.50	3.40	.95
☐ 3 Denis Menke	7.50	3.40	.95
☐ 4 Joe Torre	15.00	6.75	1.85

1974 Braves Photo Cards

This set of six photo cards was produced by the Atlanta Braves Sales Department. The photos were included in a special brochure promoting the 1974 season. The photo cards measure approximately 7" by 7 1/2" and feature full-bleed color portraits of the Braves' star players. A player autograph facsimile is superimposed on the photo in the upper left corner in white lettering. The backs have a ghosted baseball icon with the words "take 'em out to..." in bold black lettering in the upper left corner. Each card has promotional information regarding season tickets or player highlights from previous seasons. The cards are unnumbered and checklisted below alphabetically.

	NRMT	VG-E	GOOD
COMPLETE SET (6)	18.00	8.00	2.20
COMMON CARD (1-6)	2.50	1.10	.30
☐ 1 Hank Aaron	7.50	3.40	.95
☐ 2 Dusty Baker	3.00	1.35	.35
☐ 3 Darrell Evans	2.50	1.10	.30
☐ 4 Eddie Mathews MG	4.50	2.00	.55
☐ 5 Phil Niekro	3.00	1.35	.35
☐ 6 Johnny Oates	2.50	1.10	.30

1978 Braves Coke

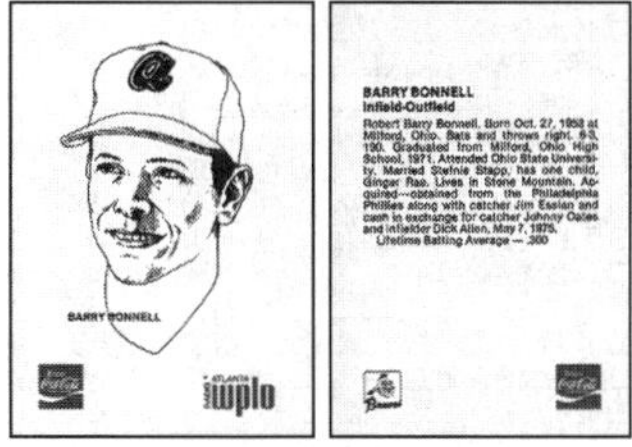

This 14-card set of the Atlanta Braves measures approximately 3" by 4 1/4" and was sponsored by Coca-Cola and Atlanta Radio Station WPLO. The white fronts feature black-and-white drawings of player heads with the player's name and sponsor logos below. The backs carry the player's name, position, biography, and career information with the team and sponsor logos on a white background. The cards are unnumbered and checklisted below in alphabetical order.

	NRMT	VG-E	GOOD
COMPLETE SET (14)	20.00	9.00	2.50
COMMON CARD (1-14)	1.00	.45	.12
☐ 1 Barry Bonnell	1.00	.45	.12
☐ 2 Jeff Burroughs	1.50	.70	.19
☐ 3 Rick Camp	1.00	.45	.12
☐ 4 Gene Garber	1.00	.45	.12
☐ 5 Rod Gilbreath	1.00	.45	.12
☐ 6 Bob Horner	1.50	.70	.19
☐ 7 Glenn Hubbard	1.00	.45	.12
☐ 8 Gary Matthews	2.00	.90	.25
☐ 9 Larry McWilliams	1.00	.45	.12
☐ 10 Dale Murphy	4.50	2.00	.55
☐ 11 Phil Niekro	3.00	1.35	.35
☐ 12 Rowland Office	1.00	.45	.12
☐ 13 Biff Pocoroba	1.00	.45	.12
☐ 14 Jerry Royster	1.00	.45	.12

1978 Braves TCC

These 16 standard-size cards feature past members of the Milwaukee Braves. Although the checklist mentions that uniform and card number are the same we have sequenced this set in alphabetical order.

	NRMT	VG-E	GOOD
COMPLETE SET (16)	7.50	3.40	.95
COMMON CARD (1-16)	.25	.11	.03
☐ 1 Hank Aaron	2.00	.90	.25
☐ 2 Joe Adcock	.75	.35	.09
☐ 3 Billy Bruton	.25	.11	.03
☐ 4 Bob Buhl	.25	.11	.03
☐ 5 Lou Burdette	.50	.23	.06
☐ 6 Wes Covington	.25	.11	.03
☐ 7 Del Crandall	.50	.23	.06
☐ 8 Johnny Logan	.25	.11	.03
☐ 9 Eddie Mathews	1.00	.45	.12
☐ 10 Andy Pafko	.25	.11	.03
☐ 11 Red Schoendienst	.75	.35	.09
☐ 12 Warren Spahn	1.00	.45	.12
☐ 13 Joe Torre	1.25	.55	.16
☐ 14 Bob Uecker	1.00	.45	.12
☐ 15 Carl Willey	.25	.11	.03
☐ 16 Checklist	.25	.11	.03

1981 Braves Police

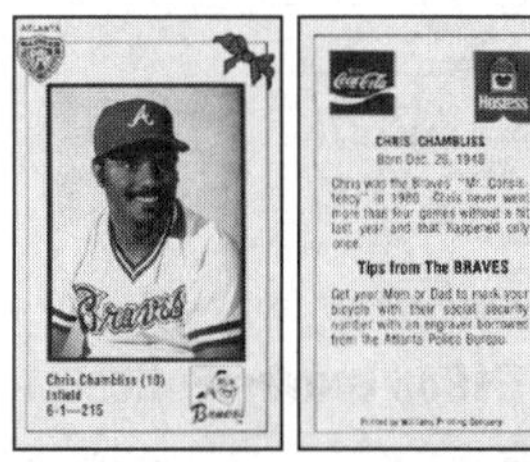

The cards in this 27-card set measure approximately 2 5/8" by 4 1/8". This first Atlanta Police set features full color cards sponsored by the Braves, the Atlanta Police Department, Coca-Cola and Hostess. The cards are numbered by uniform number, which is contained on the front along with an Atlanta Police Athletic League logo, a black and white Braves logo, and a green bow in the upper right corner of the frameline. The backs feature brief player biographies, logos of Coke and Hostess, and Tips from the Braves. It is reported that 33,000 of these sets were printed. The Terry Harper card is supposed to be slightly more difficult to obtain than other cards in the set.

	NRMT	VG-E	GOOD
COMPLETE SET (27)	12.50	5.50	1.55
COMMON CARD	.25	.11	.03
☐ 1 Jerry Royster	.25	.11	.03
☐ 3 Dale Murphy	4.00	1.80	.50
☐ 4 Biff Pocoroba	.25	.11	.03
☐ 5 Bob Horner	.50	.23	.06
☐ 6 Bobby Cox MG	1.00	.45	.12
☐ 9 Luis Gomez	.25	.11	.03
☐ 10 Chris Chambliss	.50	.23	.06
☐ 15 Bill Nahorodny	.25	.11	.03
☐ 16 Rafael Ramirez	.25	.11	.03
☐ 17 Glenn Hubbard	.25	.11	.03
☐ 18 Claudell Washington	.50	.23	.06
☐ 19 Terry Harper SP	1.00	.45	.12
☐ 20 Bruce Benedict	.25	.11	.03
☐ 24 John Montefusco	.25	.11	.03
☐ 25 Rufino Linares	.25	.11	.03
☐ 26 Gene Garber	.50	.23	.06
☐ 30 Brian Asselstine	.25	.11	.03
☐ 34 Larry Bradford	.25	.11	.03
☐ 35 Phil Niekro	2.50	1.10	.30
☐ 37 Rick Camp	.25	.11	.03
☐ 39 Al Hrabosky	.50	.23	.06
☐ 40 Tommy Boggs	.25	.11	.03
☐ 42 Rick Mahler	.25	.11	.03
☐ 44 Hank Aaron CO	4.00	1.80	.50
☐ 45 Ed Miller	.25	.11	.03
☐ 46 Gaylord Perry	2.50	1.10	.30
☐ 49 Preston Hanna	.25	.11	.03

1982 Braves Burger King Lids

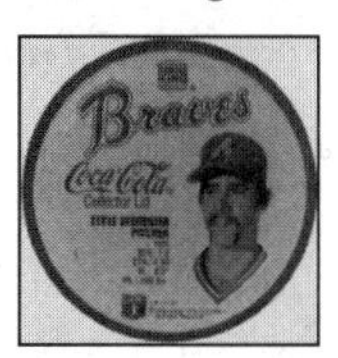

The cards in this 27-card set measure 3 11/16" diameter. During the summer of 1982, the Atlanta-area chain of Burger King restaurants issued a series of 27 "Collector Lids" in honor of the Atlanta Braves baseball team. A special cup listing the scores of the Braves 13-game season-opening win streak and crowned by a baseball player lid was given with the purchase of a large Coca-Cola. The black and white player photos are printed on a sturdy, glazed cardboard disc, the edges of which are attached to a red plastic rim. These lids are blank backed. The individual's name, height, weight and 1981 record are listed, but the lids are not numbered. The MLB and Burger King logos, as well as the Coca-Cola TM line also appear on the disc.

	NRMT	VG-E	GOOD
COMPLETE SET (27)	40.00	18.00	5.00
COMMON PLAYER (1-27)	1.00	.45	.12
☐ 1 Bruce Benedict	1.00	.45	.12
☐ 2 Steve Bedrosian	2.00	.90	.25
☐ 3 Tommy Boggs	1.00	.45	.12
☐ 4 Brett Butler	4.00	1.80	.50
☐ 5 Rick Camp	1.00	.45	.12
☐ 6 Chris Chambliss	2.00	.90	.25
☐ 7 Ken Dayley	1.00	.45	.12
☐ 8 Gene Garber	1.50	.70	.19
☐ 9 Preston Hanna	1.00	.45	.12
☐ 10 Terry Harper	1.00	.45	.12
☐ 11 Bob Horner	2.00	.90	.25
☐ 12 Al Hrabosky	2.00	.90	.25
☐ 13 Glenn Hubbard	1.00	.45	.12
☐ 14 Randy Johnson	1.00	.45	.12
☐ 15 Rufino Linares	1.00	.45	.12
☐ 16 Rick Mahler	1.00	.45	.12
☐ 17 Larry McWilliams	1.00	.45	.12
☐ 18 Dale Murphy	15.00	6.75	1.85
☐ 19 Phil Niekro	7.50	3.40	.95
☐ 20 Biff Pocoroba	1.00	.45	.12
☐ 21 Rafael Ramirez	1.00	.45	.12
☐ 22 Jerry Royster	1.00	.45	.12
☐ 23 Ken Smith	1.00	.45	.12
☐ 24 Bob Walk	1.00	.45	.12
☐ 25 Claudell Washington	1.50	.70	.19
☐ 26 Bob Watson	2.00	.90	.25
☐ 27 Larry Whisenton	1.00	.45	.12

1982 Braves Police

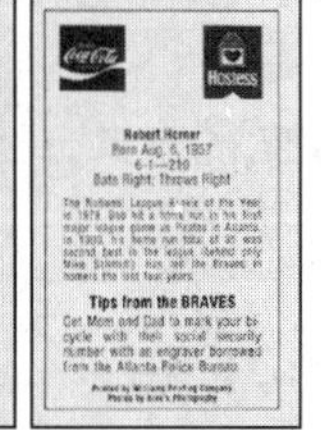

The cards in this 30-card set measure approximately 2 5/8" by 4 1/8". The Atlanta Police Department followed up on their successful 1981 safety set by publishing a new Braves set for 1982. Featured in excellent color photos are manager Joe Torre, 24 players, and 5 coaches. The cards are numbered, by uniform number, on the front only, while the backs contain a short biography of the individual and a Tips from the Braves section. The logos for the Atlanta PAL and the Braves appear on the front; those of Coca-Cola and Hostess are found on the back. A line commemorating Atlanta's record-shattering, season-beginning win streak is located in the upper right corner on every card obverse. The player list on the reverse of the Torre card is a roster list and not a checklist for the set. There were 8,000 sets reportedly printed. The Bob Watson card is supposedly more difficult to obtain than others in this set.

	NRMT	VG-E	GOOD
COMPLETE SET (30)	20.00	9.00	2.50
COMMON CARD	.50	.23	.06
☐ 1 Jerry Royster	.50	.23	.06
☐ 3 Dale Murphy	5.00	2.20	.60
☐ 4 Biff Pocoroba	.50	.23	.06
☐ 5 Bob Horner	.75	.35	.09
☐ 6 Randy Johnson	.50	.23	.06
☐ 8 Bob Watson SP	3.00	1.35	.35
☐ 9 Joe Torre MG	1.25	.55	.16
☐ 10 Chris Chambliss	1.00	.45	.12
☐ 15 Claudell Washington	.75	.35	.09
☐ 16 Rafael Ramirez	.50	.23	.06
☐ 17 Glenn Hubbard	.50	.23	.06
☐ 20 Bruce Benedict	.50	.23	.06
☐ 22 Brett Butler	3.00	1.35	.35
☐ 23 Tommy Aaron CO	.75	.35	.09
☐ 25 Rufino Linares	.50	.23	.06
☐ 26 Gene Garber	.75	.35	.09
☐ 27 Larry McWilliams	.50	.23	.06
☐ 28 Larry Whisenton	.50	.23	.06
☐ 32 Steve Bedrosian	1.00	.45	.12
☐ 35 Phil Niekro	3.00	1.35	.35
☐ 37 Rick Camp	.50	.23	.06
☐ 38 Joe Cowley	.50	.23	.06
☐ 39 Al Hrabosky	.75	.35	.09
☐ 42 Rick Mahler	.50	.23	.06
☐ 43 Bob Walk	.50	.23	.06
☐ 45 Bob Gibson CO	2.00	.90	.25
☐ 49 Preston Hanna	.50	.23	.06
☐ 52 Joe Pignatano CO	.50	.23	.06
☐ 53 Dal Maxvill CO	.50	.23	.06
☐ 54 Rube Walker CO	.50	.23	.06

1983 Braves 53 Fritsch

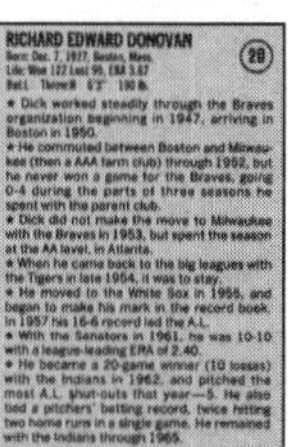

This 32 card set measures approximately 2 5/8" by 3 3/4". These cards commemorated the 30th anniversary of the Braves move to Milwaukee. The player photos are surrounded by blue borders all the way around. They are identified in the bottom right corner. The backs have vital statistics and bulletpoint career highlights. The cards are numbered by uniform number.

	NRMT	VG-E	GOOD
COMPLETE SET (32)	10.00	4.50	1.25
COMMON CARD (1-32)	.25	.11	.03
☐ 1 Del Crandall	.50	.23	.06
☐ 2 Billy Klaus	.25	.11	.03
☐ 4 Sid Gordon	.50	.23	.06
☐ 6 Jack Dittmer	.25	.11	.03
☐ 9 Joe Adcock	.50	.23	.06
☐ 10 Bob Buhl	.50	.23	.06
☐ 11 Murray Wall	.25	.11	.03
☐ 13 Sibby Sisti	.25	.11	.03
☐ 14 Paul Burris	.25	.11	.03
☐ 16 Dave Jolly	.25	.11	.03
☐ 18 Bob Thorpe	.25	.11	.03
☐ 19 Jim Wilson	.25	.11	.03
☐ 20 Dick Donovan	.25	.11	.03
☐ 21 Warren Spahn	2.50	1.10	.30
☐ 22 Virgil Jester	.25	.11	.03
☐ 23 Johnny Logan	.50	.23	.06
☐ 28 Johnny Cooney CO	.25	.11	.03
☐ 29 Luis Marquez	.25	.11	.03
☐ 30 Dave Cole	.25	.11	.03
☐ 31 Bucky Walters CO	.50	.23	.06
☐ 32 Ernie Johnson	.25	.11	.03
☐ 33 Lew Burdette	1.00	.45	.12
☐ 34 John Antonelli	.25	.11	.03
☐ 36 Max Surkont	.25	.11	.03
☐ 37 George Crowe	.25	.11	.03
☐ 38 Billy Bruton	.50	.23	.06
☐ 39 Walker Cooper	.25	.11	.03
☐ 41 Eddie Mathews	2.50	1.10	.30
☐ 42 Ebba St. Claire	.25	.11	.03
☐ 43 Don Liddle	.25	.11	.03
☐ 48 Andy Pafko	.50	.23	.06
☐ 53 Jim Pendleton	.25	.11	.03

1983 Braves Police

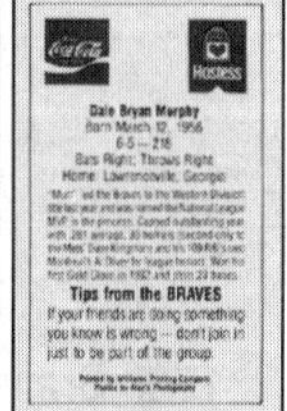

The cards in this 30-card set measure approximately 2 5/8" by 4 1/8". For the third year in a row, the Atlanta Braves, in cooperation with the

Atlanta Police Department, Coca-Cola, and Hostess, issued a full color safety set. The set features Joe Torre, five coaches, and 24 of the Atlanta Braves. Numbered only by uniform number, the statement that the Braves were the 1982 National League Western Division Champions is included on the fronts along with the Braves and Police Athletic biographies, a short narrative on the player, Tips from the Braves, and the Coke and Hostess logos.

	NRMT	VG-E	GOOD
COMPLETE SET (30)	12.50	5.50	1.55
COMMON CARD	.25	.11	.03
☐ 1 Jerry Royster	.25	.11	.03
☐ 3 Dale Murphy	4.00	1.80	.50
☐ 4 Biff Pocoroba	.25	.11	.03
☐ 5 Bob Horner	.50	.23	.06
☐ 6 Randy Johnson	.25	.11	.03
☐ 8 Bob Watson	1.00	.45	.12
☐ 9 Joe Torre MG	1.00	.45	.12
☐ 10 Chris Chambliss	.75	.35	.09
☐ 11 Ken Smith	.25	.11	.03
☐ 15 Claudell Washington	.50	.23	.06
☐ 16 Rafael Ramirez	.25	.11	.03
☐ 17 Glenn Hubbard	.25	.11	.03
☐ 19 Terry Harper	.25	.11	.03
☐ 20 Bruce Benedict	.25	.11	.03
☐ 22 Brett Butler	1.50	.70	.19
☐ 24 Larry Owen	.25	.11	.03
☐ 26 Gene Garber	.50	.23	.06
☐ 27 Pascual Perez	.25	.11	.03
☐ 29 Craig McMurtry	.25	.11	.03
☐ 32 Steve Bedrosian	.50	.23	.06
☐ 33 Pete Falcone	.25	.11	.03
☐ 35 Phil Niekro	2.00	.90	.25
☐ 36 Sonny Jackson CO	.25	.11	.03
☐ 37 Rick Camp	.25	.11	.03
☐ 45 Bob Gibson CO	2.00	.90	.25
☐ 49 Rick Behenna	.25	.11	.03
☐ 51 Terry Forster	.25	.11	.03
☐ 52 Joe Pignatano CO	.25	.11	.03
☐ 53 Dal Maxvill CO	.25	.11	.03
☐ 54 Rube Walker CO	.25	.11	.03

1984 Braves Police

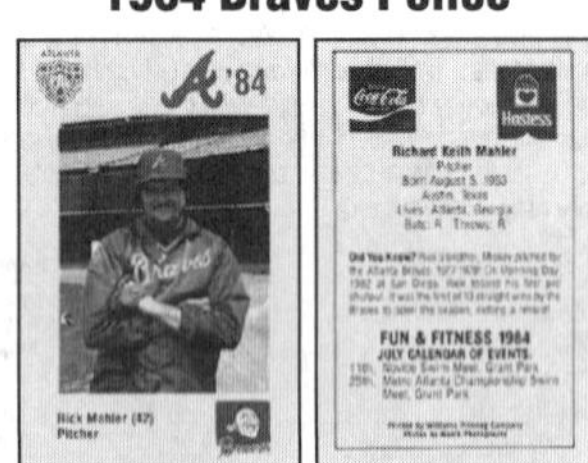

The cards in this 30-card set measure approximately 2 5/8" by 4 1/8". For the fourth straight year, the Atlanta Police Department issued a full color set of Atlanta Braves. The cards were given out two per week by Atlanta police officers. In addition to the police department, the set was sponsored by Coke and Hostess. The backs of the cards of Perez and Ramirez are in Spanish. The Joe Torre card contains the checklist.

	NRMT	VG-E	GOOD
COMPLETE SET (30)	10.00	4.50	1.25
COMMON CARD	.25	.11	.03
☐ 1 Jerry Royster	.25	.11	.03
☐ 3 Dale Murphy	3.00	1.35	.35
☐ 5 Bob Horner	.50	.23	.06
☐ 6 Randy Johnson	.25	.11	.03
☐ 8 Bob Watson	1.00	.45	.12
☐ 9 Joe Torre MG (Checklist back)	1.00	.45	.12
☐ 10 Chris Chambliss	.50	.23	.06
☐ 11 Mike Jorgensen	.25	.11	.03
☐ 15 Claudell Washington	.50	.23	.06
☐ 16 Rafael Ramirez	.25	.11	.03
☐ 17 Glenn Hubbard	.25	.11	.03
☐ 19 Terry Harper	.25	.11	.03
☐ 20 Bruce Benedict	.25	.11	.03
☐ 25 Alex Trevino	.25	.11	.03
☐ 26 Gene Garber	.50	.23	.06
☐ 27 Pascual Perez	.25	.11	.03
☐ 28 Gerald Perry	.25	.11	.03
☐ 29 Craig McMurtry	.25	.11	.03
☐ 31 Donnie Moore	.25	.11	.03
☐ 32 Steve Bedrosian	.50	.23	.06
☐ 33 Pete Falcone	.25	.11	.03
☐ 37 Rick Camp	.25	.11	.03
☐ 39 Len Barker	.25	.11	.03
☐ 42 Rick Mahler	.25	.11	.03
☐ 45 Bob Gibson CO	2.00	.90	.25
☐ 51 Terry Forster	.25	.11	.03
☐ 52 Joe Pignatano CO	.25	.11	.03
☐ 53 Dal Maxvill CO	.25	.11	.03
☐ 54 Rube Walker CO	.25	.11	.03
☐ 55 Luke Appling CO	1.50	.70	.19

1985 Braves Hostess

The cards in this 22-card set measure 2 1/2" by 3 1/2" and feature players of the Atlanta Braves. Cards were produced by Topps for Hostess (Continental Baking Co.) and are quite attractive. The card

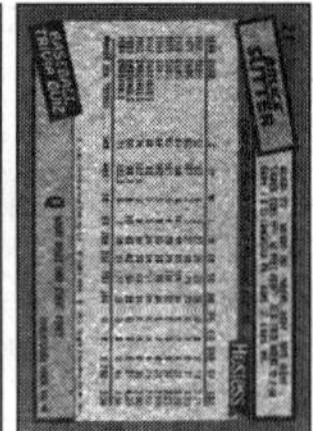

backs are similar in design to the 1985 Topps regular issue; however all photos are different from those that Topps used as these were apparently taken during Spring Training. Cards were available in boxes of Hostess products in packs of four (three players and a contest card). Other than the manager card, the rest of the set is ordered and numbered alphabetically.

	NRMT	VG-E	GOOD
COMPLETE SET (22)	8.00	3.60	1.00
COMMON CARD (1-22)	.25	.11	.03
☐ 1 Eddie Haas MG	.25	.11	.03
☐ 2 Len Barker	.25	.11	.03
☐ 3 Steve Bedrosian	.50	.23	.06
☐ 4 Bruce Benedict	.25	.11	.03
☐ 5 Rick Camp	.25	.11	.03
☐ 6 Rick Cerone	.25	.11	.03
☐ 7 Chris Chambliss	.50	.23	.06
☐ 8 Terry Forster	.25	.11	.03
☐ 9 Gene Garber	.50	.23	.06
☐ 10 Albert Hall	.25	.11	.03
☐ 11 Bob Horner	.50	.23	.06
☐ 12 Glenn Hubbard	.25	.11	.03
☐ 13 Brad Komminsk	.25	.11	.03
☐ 14 Rick Mahler	.25	.11	.03
☐ 15 Craig McMurtry	.25	.11	.03
☐ 16 Dale Murphy	.75	.35	.09
☐ 17 Ken Oberkfell	.25	.11	.03
☐ 18 Pascual Perez	.25	.11	.03
☐ 19 Gerald Perry	.25	.11	.03
☐ 20 Rafael Ramirez	.25	.11	.03
☐ 21 Bruce Sutter	.75	.35	.09
☐ 22 Claudell Washington	.50	.23	.06

1985 Braves Police

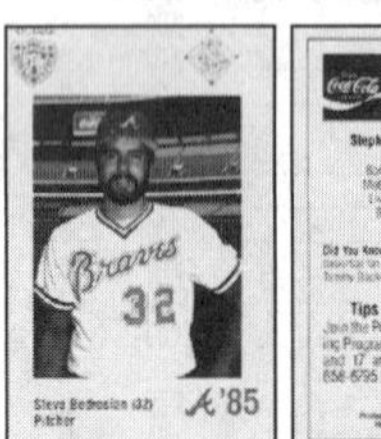

The cards in this 30-card set measure 2 5/8" by 4 1/8". For the fifth straight year, the Atlanta Police Department issued a full color set of Atlanta Braves. The set was also sponsored by Coca Cola and Hostess. In the upper right of the obverse is a logo commemorating the 20th anniversary of the Braves in Atlanta. Cards are numbered by uniform number. Cards feature a safety tip on the back. Each card except for Manager Haas has an interesting "Did You Know" fact about the player.

	NRMT	VG-E	GOOD
COMPLETE SET (30)	10.00	4.50	1.25
COMMON CARD	.25	.11	.03
☐ 2 Albert Hall	.25	.11	.03
☐ 3 Dale Murphy	3.00	1.35	.35
☐ 5 Rick Cerone	.25	.11	.03
☐ 7 Bobby Wine CO	.25	.11	.03
☐ 10 Chris Chambliss	.50	.23	.06
☐ 11 Bob Horner	.50	.23	.06
☐ 12 Paul Runge	.25	.11	.03
☐ 15 Claudell Washington	.50	.23	.06
☐ 16 Rafael Ramirez	.25	.11	.03
☐ 17 Glenn Hubbard	.25	.11	.03
☐ 18 Paul Zuvella	.25	.11	.03
☐ 19 Terry Harper	.25	.11	.03
☐ 20 Bruce Benedict	.25	.11	.03
☐ 22 Eddie Haas MG	.25	.11	.03
☐ 24 Ken Oberkfell	.25	.11	.03
☐ 26 Gene Garber	.50	.23	.06
☐ 27 Pascual Perez	.25	.11	.03
☐ 28 Gerald Perry	.25	.11	.03
☐ 29 Craig McMurtry	.25	.11	.03
☐ 32 Steve Bedrosian	.50	.23	.06
☐ 33 Johnny Sain CO	.75	.35	.09
☐ 34 Zane Smith	.75	.35	.09
☐ 36 Brad Komminsk	.25	.11	.03
☐ 37 Rick Camp	.25	.11	.03
☐ 39 Len Barker	.25	.11	.03
☐ 40 Bruce Sutter	.75	.35	.09
☐ 42 Rick Mahler	.25	.11	.03
☐ 51 Terry Forster	.25	.11	.03
☐ 52 Leo Mazzone CO	.25	.11	.03
☐ 53 Bobby Dews CO	.25	.11	.03

1985 Braves TBS America's Team

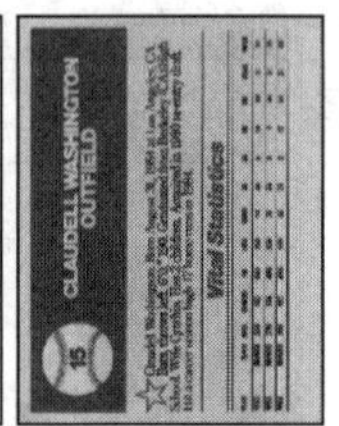

This set features four close-up headshots on painted backgrounds. The photos measure 8 1/4" X 10 3/4". In a star-studded rectangular box, the words "America's Team" are emblazoned across the bottom of each picture. The horizontally oriented backs have biography and statistics for the last three seasons (1982-84). The photos are unnumbered and checklisted below alphabetically.

	NRMT	VG-E	GOOD
COMPLETE SET (4)	6.00	2.70	.75
COMMON CARD (1-4)	1.00	.45	.12
☐ 1 Brad Komminsk	1.00	.45	.12
☐ 2 Dale Murphy	4.00	1.80	.50
☐ 3 Bruce Sutter	2.50	1.10	.30
☐ 4 Claudell Washington	1.50	.70	.19

1986 Braves Greats TCMA

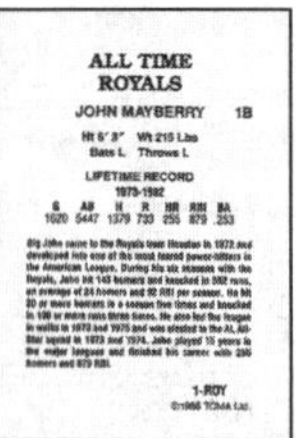

This 12-card standard-size set features leading Braves players from all three cities (Boston, Atlanta and Milwaukee). The fronts have player photos, while the backs have a biography, and career statistics.

	MINT	NRMT	EXC
COMPLETE SET (12)	7.50	3.40	.95
COMMON CARD (1-12)	.25	.11	.03
☐ 1 Joe Adcock	.50	.23	.06
☐ 2 Felix Millan	.25	.11	.03
☐ 3 Rabbit Maranville	.75	.35	.09
☐ 4 Eddie Mathews	1.50	.70	.19
☐ 5 Hank Aaron	3.00	1.35	.35
☐ 6 Wally Berger	.50	.23	.06
☐ 7 Tommy Holmes	.50	.23	.06
☐ 8 Del Crandall	.50	.23	.06
☐ 9 Warren Spahn	1.50	.70	.19
☐ 10 Charles "Kid" Nichols	.75	.35	.09
☐ 11 Cecil Upshaw	.25	.11	.03
☐ 12 Fred Haney MG	.25	.11	.03

1986 Braves Police

This 30-card safety set was also sponsored by Coca-Cola. The backs contain the usual biographical info and safety tip. The front features a full-color photo of the player, his name, and uniform number. The cards measure 2 5/8" by 4 1/8". Cards were freely distributed throughout the summer by the Police Departments in the Atlanta area. Cards are numbered below by uniform number.

	MINT	NRMT	EXC
COMPLETE SET (30)	10.00	4.50	1.25
COMMON CARD	.25	.11	.03
☐ 2 Russ Nixon CO	.25	.11	.03
☐ 3 Dale Murphy	3.00	1.35	.35
☐ 4 Bob Skinner CO	.25	.11	.03
☐ 5 Billy Sample	.25	.11	.03
☐ 7 Chuck Tanner MG	.50	.23	.06
☐ 8 Willie Stargell CO	1.50	.70	.19
☐ 9 Ozzie Virgil	.25	.11	.03
☐ 10 Chris Chambliss	.50	.23	.06
☐ 11 Bob Horner	.50	.23	.06
☐ 14 Andres Thomas	.25	.11	.03
☐ 15 Claudell Washington	.50	.23	.06
☐ 16 Rafael Ramirez	.25	.11	.03
☐ 17 Glenn Hubbard	.25	.11	.03
☐ 18 Omar Moreno	.25	.11	.03
☐ 19 Terry Harper	.25	.11	.03
☐ 20 Bruce Benedict	.25	.11	.03
☐ 23 Ted Simmons	1.00	.45	.12
☐ 24 Ken Oberkfell	.25	.11	.03
☐ 26 Gene Garber	.50	.23	.06
☐ 29 Craig McMurtry	.25	.11	.03
☐ 30 Paul Assenmacher	.25	.11	.03
☐ 33 Johnny Sain CO	.75	.35	.09
☐ 34 Zane Smith	.50	.23	.06
☐ 38 Joe Johnson	.25	.11	.03
☐ 40 Bruce Sutter	.75	.35	.09
☐ 42 Rick Mahler	.25	.11	.03
☐ 46 David Palmer	.25	.11	.03
☐ 48 Duane Ward	.75	.35	.09
☐ 49 Jeff Dedmon	.25	.11	.03
☐ 52 Al Monchak CO	.25	.11	.03

1987 Braves 1957 TCMA

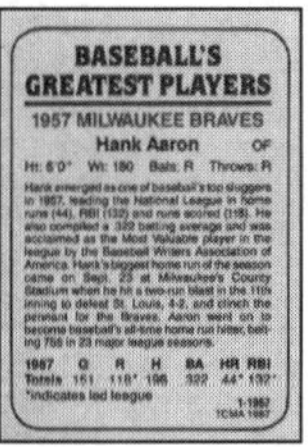

This nine-card standard-size set commemorates the 30th anniversary and members of the 1957 World Champion Milwaukee Braves. The player's name and position are displayed on the front. The backs carry highlights and stats from the 1957 season.

	MINT	NRMT	EXC
COMPLETE SET (9)	6.00	2.70	.75
COMMON CARD (1-9)	.25	.11	.03
☐ 1 Hank Aaron	3.00	1.35	.35
☐ 2 Eddie Mathews	1.50	.70	.19
☐ 3 Bob Hazle	.25	.11	.03
☐ 4 Johnny Logan	.50	.23	.06
☐ 5 Red Schoendienst	1.00	.45	.12
☐ 6 Wes Covington	.35	.16	.04
☐ 7 Lew Burdette	.75	.35	.09
☐ 8 Warren Spahn	1.50	.70	.19
☐ 9 Bob Buhl	.50	.23	.06

1987 Braves Smokey

The U.S. Forestry Service (in conjunction with the Atlanta Braves) produced this large, attractive 27-card set to commemorate the 43rd birthday of Smokey. The cards feature Smokey the Bear pictured in the top right corner of every card. The card backs give a cartoon fire safety tip. The cards measure approximately 4" by 6" and are subtitled "Wildfire Prevention" on the front. Distribution of the cards was gradual at the stadium throughout the summer.

	MINT	NRMT	EXC
COMPLETE SET (27)	30.00	13.50	3.70
COMMON CARD (1-26)	1.00	.45	.12
☐ 1 Zane Smith	1.00	.45	.12
☐ 2 Charlie Puleo	1.00	.45	.12
☐ 3 Randy O'Neal	1.00	.45	.12
☐ 4 David Palmer	1.00	.45	.12
☐ 5 Rick Mahler	1.00	.45	.12
☐ 6 Ed Olwine	1.00	.45	.12
☐ 7 Jeff Dedmon	1.00	.45	.12
☐ 8 Paul Assenmacher	1.50	.70	.19
☐ 9 Gene Garber	1.25	.55	.16
☐ 10 Jim Acker	1.00	.45	.12
☐ 11 Bruce Benedict	1.00	.45	.12
☐ 12 Ozzie Virgil	1.00	.45	.12
☐ 13 Ted Simmons	2.50	1.10	.30
☐ 14 Dale Murphy	10.00	4.50	1.25
☐ 15 Graig Nettles	1.50	.70	.19
☐ 16 Ken Oberkfell	1.00	.45	.12
☐ 17 Gerald Perry	1.00	.45	.12
☐ 18 Rafael Ramirez	1.00	.45	.12
☐ 19 Ken Griffey	1.50	.70	.19
☐ 20 Andres Thomas	1.00	.45	.12

	MINT	NRMT	EXC
☐ 21 Glenn Hubbard	1.00	.45	.12
☐ 22 Damaso Garcia	1.00	.45	.12
☐ 23 Gary Roenicke	1.00	.45	.12
☐ 24 Dion James	1.00	.45	.12
☐ 25 Albert Hall	1.00	.45	.12
☐ 26 Chuck Tanner MG	1.25	.55	.16
☐ NNO Smokey/Checklist	1.00	.45	.12

1989 Braves Dubuque

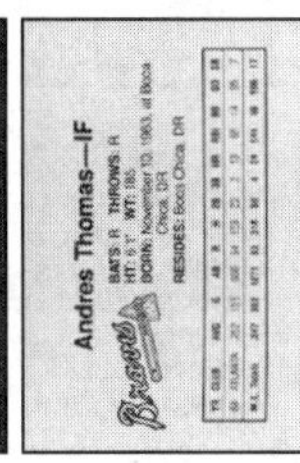

This 30-card set was sponsored by Dubuque, the meat company that makes the hot dogs sold at Atlanta-Fulton County Stadium. The cards were given away at the ballpark on Sundays and at autograph appearances at card stores. Due to the latter, several of these exist in much larger quantities. The cards measure approximately 2 1/4" by 3 1/2". Almost all the photos were taken during spring training, with the exception of Oddibe McDowell, mid-season additions Mark Eichhorn and John Russell, and coach Brian Snitker. The cards are unnumbered and checklisted below in alphabetical order.

	MINT	NRMT	EXC
COMPLETE SET (30)	40.00	18.00	5.00
COMMON CARD (1-30)	1.00	.45	.12
☐ 1 Jim Acker	1.00	.45	.12
☐ 2 Jose Alvarez	1.00	.45	.12
☐ 3 Paul Assenmacher	1.00	.45	.12
☐ 4 Bruce Benedict	1.00	.45	.12
☐ 5 Jeff Blauser	2.00	.90	.25
☐ 6 Joe Boever	1.00	.45	.12
☐ 7 Bruce Dal Canton CO	1.00	.45	.12
☐ 8 Marty Clary	1.00	.45	.12
☐ 9 Jody Davis	1.00	.45	.12
☐ 10 Mark Eichhorn SP	2.00	.90	.25
☐ 11 Ron Gant	4.00	1.80	.50
☐ 12 Tom Glavine	6.00	2.70	.75
☐ 13 Tommy Gregg	1.00	.45	.12
☐ 14 Clarence Jones CO	1.00	.45	.12
☐ 15 Derek Lilliquist	1.00	.45	.12
☐ 16 Roy Majtyka TR	1.00	.45	.12
☐ 17 Oddibe McDowell SP	2.00	.90	.25
☐ 18 Dale Murphy	4.00	1.80	.50
☐ 19 Russ Nixon MG	1.00	.45	.12
☐ 20 Gerald Perry	1.00	.45	.12
☐ 21 John Russell SP	2.00	.90	.25
☐ 22 Lonnie Smith	1.25	.55	.16
☐ 23 Pete Smith	1.00	.45	.12
☐ 24 John Smoltz	10.00	4.50	1.25
☐ 25 Brian Snitker CO SP	2.00	.90	.25
☐ 26 Andres Thomas	1.00	.45	.12
☐ 27 Jeff Treadway	1.00	.45	.12
☐ 28 Jeff Wetherby	1.00	.45	.12
☐ 29 Ed Whited	1.00	.45	.12
☐ 30 Bobby Wine CO	1.00	.45	.12

1990 Braves Dubuque Perforated

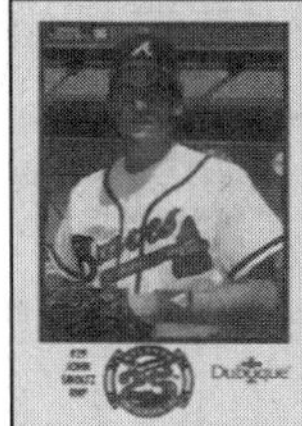

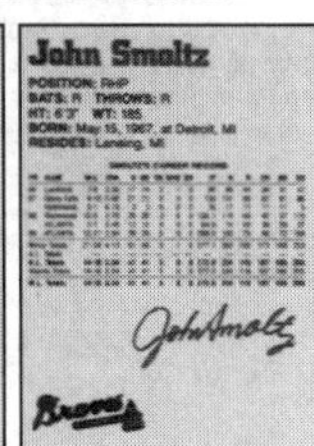

Given out early in the season, this set's 30 cards are slightly smaller than the other Dubuque Singles set, and was part of a perforated sheet that included a team photo. The backs are similar, but the fronts are all different with portrait shots. The cards are unnumbered and checklisted below in alphabetical order.

	MINT	NRMT	EXC
COMPLETE SET (30)	30.00	13.50	3.70
COMMON CARD (1-30)	.75	.35	.09
☐ 1 Jeff Blauser	1.25	.55	.16
☐ 2 Joe Boever	.75	.35	.09
☐ 3 Francisco Cabrera	.75	.35	.09
☐ 4 Tony Castillo	.75	.35	.09
☐ 5 Marty Clary	.75	.35	.09
☐ 6 Nick Esasky	.75	.35	.09
☐ 7 Ron Gant	2.00	.90	.25
☐ 8 Tom Glavine	4.00	1.80	.50
☐ 9 Tommy Gregg	.75	.35	.09
☐ 10 Dwayne Henry	.75	.35	.09
☐ 11 Joe Hesketh	.75	.35	.09
☐ 12 Alexis Infante	.75	.35	.09
☐ 13 David Justice	4.00	1.80	.50
☐ 14 Charlie Kerfeld	.75	.35	.09
☐ 15 Charlie Leibrandt	.75	.35	.09
☐ 16 Mark Lemke	1.25	.55	.16
☐ 17 Derek Lilliquist	.75	.35	.09
☐ 18 Rick Luecken	.75	.35	.09
☐ 19 Oddibe McDowell	.75	.35	.09
☐ 20 Dale Murphy	4.00	1.80	.50
☐ 21 Russ Nixon MG	.75	.35	.09
☐ 22 Greg Olson	.75	.35	.09
☐ 23 Jim Presley	.75	.35	.09
☐ 24 Lonnie Smith	.75	.35	.09
☐ 25 Pete Smith	.75	.35	.09
☐ 26 John Smoltz	5.00	2.20	.60
☐ 27 Mike Stanton	.75	.35	.09
☐ 28 Andres Thomas	.75	.35	.09
☐ 29 Jeff Treadway	.75	.35	.09
☐ 30 Ernie Whitt	.75	.35	.09

1990 Braves Dubuque Singles

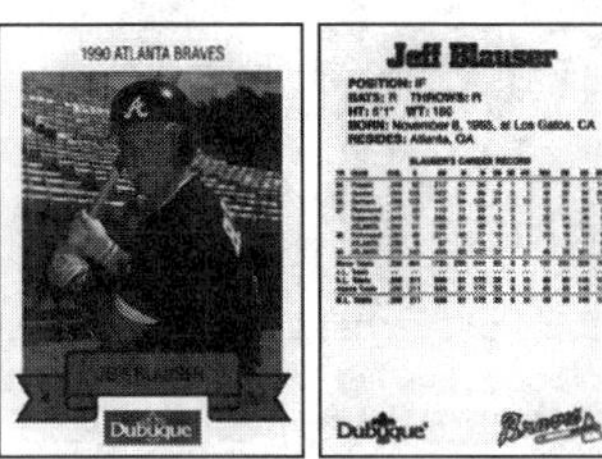

These 35 cards measure approximately 2 1/4" by 3 1/2" and were given out, usually four at a time, on Sundays with subjects available for autographs that day. Several were offered more than once, but Murphy's card was given out once before his trade to the Phillies. The cards issued early in the season featured spring training action shots on their fronts. Those issued later in the season had action photos taken at Atlanta-Fulton County Stadium. The Mark Grant card was given out only on the last Sunday of the season, the only new card to be issued so late. The cards are unnumbered and checklisted below in alphabetical order.

	MINT	NRMT	EXC
COMPLETE SET (35)	50.00	22.00	6.25
COMMON CARD (1-35)	1.00	.45	.12
☐ 1 Steve Avery	3.00	1.35	.35
☐ 2 Jeff Blauser	1.50	.70	.19
☐ 3 Joe Boever	1.00	.45	.12
☐ 4 Francisco Cabrera	1.00	.45	.12
☐ 5 Pat Corrales CO	1.00	.45	.12
☐ 6 Bobby Cox MG	1.50	.70	.19
☐ 7 Nick Esasky	1.00	.45	.12
☐ 8 Ron Gant	3.00	1.35	.35
☐ 9 Tom Glavine	5.00	2.20	.60
☐ 10 Mark Grant SP	5.00	2.20	.60
☐ 11 Tommy Gregg	1.00	.45	.12
☐ 12 Dwayne Henry	1.00	.45	.12
☐ 13 Homer the Brave (Mascot)	1.00	.45	.12
☐ 14 Alexis Infante	1.00	.45	.12
☐ 15 Clarence Jones CO	1.00	.45	.12
☐ 16 David Justice	5.00	2.20	.60
☐ 17 Jimmy Kremers	1.00	.45	.12
☐ 18 Charlie Leibrandt	1.00	.45	.12
☐ 19 Mark Lemke	1.25	.55	.16
☐ 20 Roy Majtyka TR	1.00	.45	.12
☐ 21 Leo Mazzone CO	1.00	.45	.12
☐ 22 Oddibe McDowell	1.00	.45	.12
☐ 23 Dale Murphy SP	1.50	.70	.19
☐ 24 Phil Niekro	2.50	1.10	.30
☐ 25 Greg Olson	1.00	.45	.12
☐ 26 Jim Presley	1.00	.45	.12
☐ 27 Rally (Mascot)	1.00	.45	.12
☐ 28 Lonnie Smith	1.00	.45	.12
☐ 29 Pete Smith	1.00	.45	.12
☐ 30 John Smoltz	5.00	2.20	.60
☐ 31 Brian Snitker CO	1.00	.45	.12
☐ 32 Andres Thomas	1.00	.45	.12
☐ 33 Jeff Treadway	1.00	.45	.12
☐ 34 Ernie Whitt	1.00	.45	.12
☐ 35 Jimy Williams CO	1.00	.45	.12

1991 Braves Dubuque Perforated

The 1991 Atlanta Braves team set was sponsored by Dubuque. The set was issued in three 10 5/8" by 9 3/8" panels that were attached to form a continuous sheet. The first panel features a team photo. The second and third panels have 15 player cards each; after perforation, the cards measure approximately 2 3/16" by 3 3/16". The front design has a posed head and shoulders color photo, with red borders and diamond designs on the corners of the picture. Player information is given in a dark red box below the picture, and the team and sponsor logos in the lower corners round out the card face. In blue and dark red print, the back has biography, Major League statistics, and a facsimile player autograph. The cards are unnumbered and checklisted below in alphabetical order.

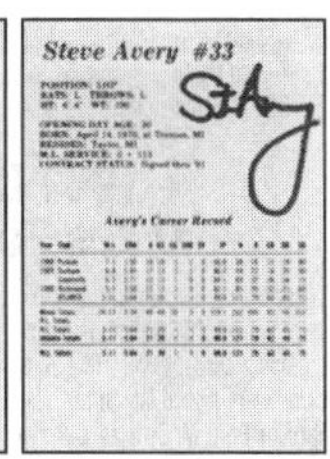

	MINT	NRMT	EXC
COMPLETE SET (30)	18.00	8.00	2.20
COMMON CARD (1-30)	.25	.11	.03
☐ 1 Steve Avery	1.00	.45	.12
☐ 2 Rafael Belliard	.25	.11	.03
☐ 3 Juan Berenguer	.25	.11	.03
☐ 4 Jeff Blauser	.75	.35	.09
☐ 5 Sid Bream	.25	.11	.03
☐ 6 Francisco Cabrera	.25	.11	.03
☐ 7 Bobby Cox MG	.50	.23	.06
☐ 8 Nick Esasky	.25	.11	.03
☐ 9 Marvin Freeman	.25	.11	.03
☐ 10 Ron Gant	1.25	.55	.16
☐ 11 Tom Glavine	3.00	1.35	.35
☐ 12 Mark Grant	.25	.11	.03
☐ 13 Tommy Gregg	.25	.11	.03
☐ 14 Mike Heath	.25	.11	.03
☐ 15 Danny Heep	.25	.11	.03
☐ 16 David Justice	2.00	.90	.25
☐ 17 Charlie Leibrandt	.25	.11	.03
☐ 18 Mark Lemke	.50	.23	.06
☐ 19 Kent Mercker	.25	.11	.03
☐ 20 Otis Nixon	.50	.23	.06
☐ 21 Greg Olson	.25	.11	.03
☐ 22 Jeff Parrett	.25	.11	.03
☐ 23 Terry Pendleton	1.00	.45	.12
☐ 24 Deion Sanders	3.00	1.35	.35
☐ 25 Doug Sisk	.25	.11	.03
☐ 26 Lonnie Smith	.25	.11	.03
☐ 27 Pete Smith	.25	.11	.03
☐ 28 John Smoltz	4.00	1.80	.50
☐ 29 Mike Stanton	.25	.11	.03
☐ 30 Jeff Treadway	.25	.11	.03

1991 Braves Dubuque Standard

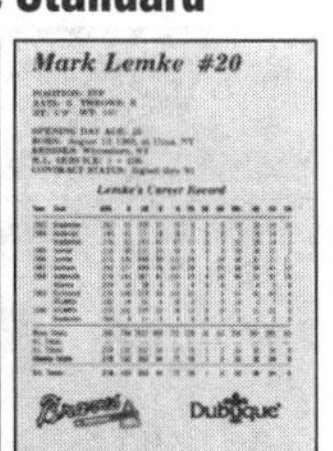

These 39 cards were sponsored by Dubuque Meats and measure approximately 2 1/4" by 3 1/2". They were given out, usually three or six at a time, on Sundays with subjects available for autographs that day. Aside from players' uniform numbers on the back, the cards are unnumbered and checklisted below in alphabetical order. Sunday Aug. 25 had six new cards given out for the first time (Hunter, Mitchell, Clancy, Beauchamp, Esasky, Grant). Sunday Sept. 22 had three new cards issued (Pete Smith, Bell, Reynoso) with three previously released. Two Sundays previous to these had featured three previously issued cards each day. The final day of the season (Oct. 6) featured a Deion Sanders card, along with Glavine, Avery, Cox, Gant, Justice, Pendleton and Treadway. A special "apology" card was issued with the cards this day due to no autographs. Black- and blue-lettered varieties exist on at least 30 cards (different printings). The cards have a mix of posed and action color player photos, bordered by a blue and white pinstripe pattern and a white outer border. In blue print on white, the backs have biography and career statistics.

	MINT	NRMT	EXC
COMPLETE SET (39)	50.00	22.00	6.25
COMMON CARD (1-39)	1.00	.45	.12
☐ 1 Steve Avery	1.50	.70	.19
☐ 2 Jim Beauchamp CO	1.00	.45	.12
☐ 3 Mike Bell	1.00	.45	.12
☐ 4 Rafael Belliard	1.00	.45	.12
☐ 5 Juan Berenguer	1.00	.45	.12
☐ 6 Jeff Blauser	1.50	.70	.19
☐ 7 Sid Bream	1.00	.45	.12
☐ 8 Francisco Cabrera	1.00	.45	.12
☐ 9 Jim Clancy	1.00	.45	.12
☐ 10 Pat Corrales CO	1.00	.45	.12
☐ 11 Bobby Cox MG	1.25	.55	.16
☐ 12 Nick Esasky	1.00	.45	.12
☐ 13 Marvin Freeman	1.00	.45	.12
☐ 14 Ron Gant	2.50	1.10	.30
☐ 15 Tom Glavine	5.00	2.20	.60
☐ 16 Mark Grant	1.00	.45	.12
☐ 17 Tommy Gregg	1.00	.45	.12
☐ 18 Mike Heath	1.00	.45	.12
☐ 19 Brian Hunter	1.00	.45	.12
☐ 20 Clarence Jones CO	1.00	.45	.12
☐ 21 David Justice	3.00	1.35	.35
☐ 22 Charlie Leibrandt	1.00	.45	.12
☐ 23 Mark Lemke	1.25	.55	.16
☐ 24 Leo Mazzone CO	1.00	.45	.12
☐ 25 Kent Mercker	1.00	.45	.12
☐ 26 Keith Mitchell	1.00	.45	.12
☐ 27 Otis Nixon	1.25	.55	.16
☐ 28 Greg Olson	1.00	.45	.12
☐ 29 Jeff Parrett	1.00	.45	.12
☐ 30 Terry Pendleton	2.00	.90	.25
☐ 31 Armando Reynoso	1.50	.70	.19
☐ 32 Deion Sanders	6.00	2.70	.75
☐ 33 Lonnie Smith	1.00	.45	.12
☐ 34 Pete Smith	1.00	.45	.12
☐ 35 John Smoltz	7.50	3.40	.95
☐ 36 Mike Stanton	1.00	.45	.12
☐ 37 Jeff Treadway	1.00	.45	.12
☐ 38 Jimy Williams CO	1.00	.45	.12
☐ 39 Ned Yost CO	1.00	.45	.12

1992 Braves Krystal Postcard

This postcards features two sport athlete Deion Sanders. This postcard was issued by the Krystal food chain.

	MINT	NRMT	EXC
COMPLETE SET	3.00	1.35	.35
COMMON CARD	3.00	1.35	.35
☐ 1 Deion Sanders	3.00	1.35	.35

1992 Braves Lykes Perforated

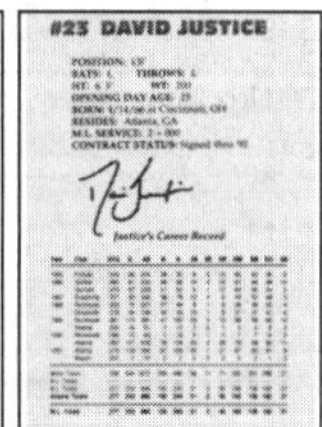

The 1992 Atlanta Braves Team Picture Card set was sponsored by Lykes and distributed as an uncut, perforated sheet before a Braves' home game. It consists of three large sheets (each measuring approximately 10 5/8" by 9 3/8") joined together to form one continuous sheet. The first panel features a team photo, while the second and third panels feature 15 player cards each. After perforation, the cards measure approximately 2 1/8" by 3 1/8". On a white card face, the fronts have posed color player photos with the top corners of the picture rounded off. The player's name appears in a red stripe below the picture with the team and sponsor logos immediately below. In red and blue print on white, the backs have the player's name, jersey number, biography, statistics, and a facsimile autograph. The cards are unnumbered and checklisted below in alphabetical order.

	MINT	NRMT	EXC
COMPLETE SET (30)	14.00	6.25	1.75
COMMON CARD (1-30)	.25	.11	.03
☐ 1 Steve Avery	.75	.35	.09
☐ 2 Rafael Belliard	.25	.11	.03
☐ 3 Juan Berenguer	.25	.11	.03
☐ 4 Damon Berryhill	.25	.11	.03
☐ 5 Mike Bielecki	.25	.11	.03
☐ 6 Jeff Blauser	.75	.35	.09
☐ 7 Sid Bream	.25	.11	.03
☐ 8 Francisco Cabrera	.25	.11	.03
☐ 9 Bobby Cox MG	.50	.23	.06
☐ 10 Nick Esasky	.25	.11	.03
☐ 11 Marvin Freeman	.25	.11	.03
☐ 12 Ron Gant	1.25	.55	.16
☐ 13 Tom Glavine	2.00	.90	.25
☐ 14 Tommy Gregg	.25	.11	.03
☐ 15 Brian Hunter	.25	.11	.03
☐ 16 David Justice	1.25	.55	.16
☐ 17 Charlie Leibrandt	.25	.11	.03
☐ 18 Mark Lemke	.50	.23	.06
☐ 19 Kent Mercker	.25	.11	.03
☐ 20 Otis Nixon	.50	.23	.06
☐ 21 Greg Olson	.25	.11	.03
☐ 22 Alejandro Pena	.25	.11	.03
☐ 23 Terry Pendleton	.75	.35	.09
☐ 24 Deion Sanders	2.50	1.10	.30
☐ 25 Lonnie Smith	.50	.23	.06
☐ 26 John Smoltz	2.50	1.10	.30
☐ 27 Mike Stanton	.25	.11	.03
☐ 28 Jeff Treadway	.25	.11	.03
☐ 29 Jerry Willard	.25	.11	.03
☐ 30 Mark Wohlers	1.25	.55	.16

1992 Braves Lykes Standard

These 37 standard-size cards were given out (some more than once) to fans 12 years old and under on Tuesdays. Two different uncut sheets have surfaced, but no complete sets were sold or given away by the Braves. The mascot cards were available on a daily basis. On a white card face, the fronts feature a mix of posed and action color

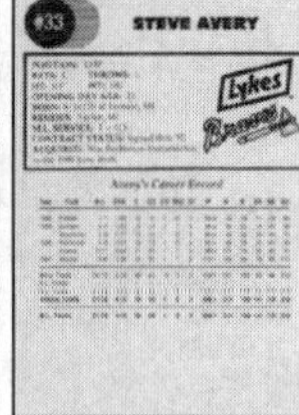

player photos with a white inner border and a red outer border. The year "1992" appears in a dark blue circle at the upper left corner, and the player's name and team name are printed in white lettering in the top red border. In black lettering on white, the backs carry biography and complete career statistics. The cards are unnumbered and checklisted below in alphabetical order.

	MINT	NRMT	EXC
COMPLETE SET (36)	30.00	13.50	3.70
COMMON CARD (1-37)	.75	.35	.09
☐ 1 Steve Avery	1.50	.70	.19
☐ 2 Jim Beauchamp CO	.75	.35	.09
☐ 3 Rafael Belliard	.75	.35	.09
☐ 4 Juan Berenguer	.75	.35	.09
☐ 5 Damon Berryhill	.75	.35	.09
☐ 6 Mike Bielecki	.75	.35	.09
☐ 7 Jeff Blauser	1.50	.70	.19
☐ 8 Sid Bream	.75	.35	.09
☐ 9 Francisco Cabrera	.75	.35	.09
☐ 10 Pat Corrales CO	.75	.35	.09
☐ 11 Bobby Cox MG	1.00	.45	.12
☐ 12 Marvin Freeman	.75	.35	.09
☐ 13 Ron Gant	2.00	.90	.25
☐ 14 Tom Glavine	4.00	1.80	.50
☐ 15 Tommy Gregg	.75	.35	.09
☐ 16 Homer the Brave DP (Mascot)	.50	.23	.06
☐ 17 Brian Hunter	.75	.35	.09
☐ 18 Clarence Jones CO	.75	.35	.09
☐ 19 David Justice	2.00	.90	.25
☐ 20 Charlie Leibrandt	.75	.35	.09
☐ 21 Mark Lemke	1.00	.45	.12
☐ 22 Leo Mazzone CO	.75	.35	.09
☐ 23 Kent Mercker	.75	.35	.09
☐ 24 Otis Nixon	1.00	.45	.12
☐ 25 Greg Olson	.75	.35	.09
☐ 26 Alejandro Pena	.75	.35	.09
☐ 27 Terry Pendleton	1.50	.70	.19
☐ 28 Rally (Mascot) DP	.75	.35	.09
☐ 29 Deion Sanders	2.50	1.10	.30
☐ 30 Lonnie Smith	1.00	.45	.12
☐ 31 John Smoltz	5.00	2.20	.60
☐ 32 Mike Stanton	.75	.35	.09
☐ 33 Jeff Treadway	.75	.35	.09
☐ 34 Jerry Willard	.75	.35	.09
☐ 35 Jimy Williams CO	.75	.35	.09
☐ 36 Mark Wohlers	2.00	.90	.25
☐ 37 Ned Yost CO	.75	.35	.09

1993 Braves Florida Agriculture

These were given out in eight-card perforated sheets at the Sunshine State Games in Tallahassee in July 1993. The sheets measure approximately 7" by 10" and the cards are the standard size. The fronts feature color photos of the players posing with various fruits and vegetables. These pictures are bordered in a serrated blue and red design. The player's name appears at the bottom of the picture within a wavy lime-green panel. The Department's Fresh 2-U logo appears in the upper left. The serrated and wavy panel design continues on the back, but in two different shades of blue. The player's name, uniform number, position, and biography appear in the upper panel, and distinctive Floridian agricultural statistics are shown in the lower panel. Within a baseball icon between the two panels is the result of an "at bat" in a game that used an 11" by 8 1/2" game card, which was also distributed at the Games. The cards are numbered on the back with the numbering essentially following alphabetical order.

	MINT	NRMT	EXC
COMPLETE SET (8)	10.00	4.50	1.25
COMMON CARD (1-8)	1.00	.45	.12
☐ 1 Title Card	1.00	.45	.12
☐ 2 Steve Avery	2.00	.90	.25
☐ 3 Jeff Blauser	1.25	.55	.16
☐ 4 Sid Bream	1.00	.45	.12
☐ 5 Tom Glavine	3.00	1.35	.35
☐ 6 Mark Lemke	1.25	.55	.16
☐ 7 Greg Olson	1.00	.45	.12
☐ 8 Terry Pendleton	1.50	.70	.19

1993 Braves Lykes Perforated

These 30 cards measure approximately 2 1/8" by 3 1/8" and feature color player photos that are the same as the Dubuque Meats Tuesday giveaway cards, except that Ryan Klesko was only in this set. The cards were issued late in the season and as a result include an early card of Fred McGriff as a Brave. The cards are unnumbered and checklisted below in alphabetical order.

	MINT	NRMT	EXC
COMPLETE SET (30)	18.00	8.00	2.20
COMMON CARD (1-30)	.25	.11	.03
☐ 1 Steve Avery	1.00	.45	.12
☐ 2 Steve Bedrosian	.50	.23	.06
☐ 3 Rafael Belliard	.25	.11	.03
☐ 4 Damon Berryhill	.25	.11	.03
☐ 5 Jeff Blauser	.75	.35	.09
☐ 6 Sid Bream	.25	.11	.03
☐ 7 Francisco Cabrera	.25	.11	.03
☐ 8 Bobby Cox MG	.50	.23	.06
☐ 9 Marvin Freeman	.25	.11	.03
☐ 10 Ron Gant	2.00	.90	.25
☐ 11 Tom Glavine	2.50	1.10	.30
☐ 12 Jay Howell	.25	.11	.03
☐ 13 Brian Hunter	.25	.11	.03
☐ 14 David Justice	1.50	.70	.19
☐ 15 Ryan Klesko	4.00	1.80	.50
☐ 16 Mark Lemke	.50	.23	.06
☐ 17 Greg Maddux	6.00	2.70	.75
☐ 18 Fred McGriff	5.00	2.20	.60
☐ 19 Greg McMichael	.25	.11	.03
☐ 20 Kent Mercker	.25	.11	.03
☐ 21 Otis Nixon	.50	.23	.06
☐ 22 Greg Olson	.25	.11	.03
☐ 23 Bill Pecota	.25	.11	.03
☐ 24 Terry Pendleton	1.00	.45	.12
☐ 25 Deion Sanders	2.00	.90	.25
☐ 26 Pete Smith	.25	.11	.03
☐ 27 John Smoltz	3.00	1.35	.35
☐ 28 Mike Stanton	.25	.11	.03
☐ 29 Tony Tarasco	.25	.11	.03
☐ 30 Mark Wohlers	1.00	.45	.12

1993 Braves Lykes Standard

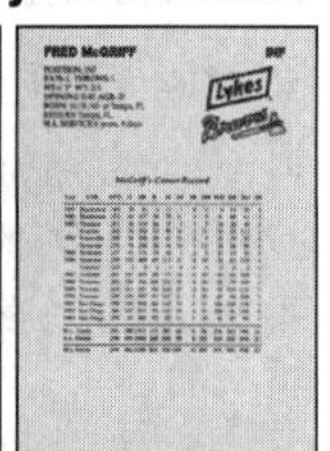

These 38 standard-size cards feature the same portraits as the perforated Dubuque Meats 1993 set, but with a different design. Each Tuesday, the Braves gave out three different cards, and for the first time, did not repeat any player's card during the season. Mascot cards were offered to youngsters on a daily basis. The cards are unnumbered and checklisted below in alphabetical order. Some near-complete sets surfaced following the season, along with some uncut sheets, but neither the near-complete sets nor the sheets included the cards of Javy Lopez, Fred McGriff, and Tony Tarasco, which were the final Tuesday's handout. The uncut sheet had six rows with six slots per row; thirty-five players are featured, and one slot is blank. The printing on the back of these three cards is slightly different from the other 35 cards, indicating a separate printing.

	MINT	NRMT	EXC
COMPLETE SET (38)	40.00	18.00	5.00
COMMON CARD (1-38)	.75	.35	.09
☐ 1 Steve Avery	1.50	.70	.19
☐ 2 Jim Beauchamp CO	.75	.35	.09
☐ 3 Steve Bedrosian	.75	.35	.09
☐ 4 Rafael Belliard	.75	.35	.09
☐ 5 Damon Berryhill	.75	.35	.09
☐ 6 Jeff Blauser	1.00	.45	.12
☐ 7 Sid Bream	.75	.35	.09
☐ 8 Francisco Cabrera	.75	.35	.09
☐ 9 Pat Corrales CO	.75	.35	.09
☐ 10 Bobby Cox MG	1.00	.45	.12
☐ 11 Marvin Freeman	.75	.35	.09
☐ 12 Ron Gant	2.00	.90	.25
☐ 13 Tom Glavine	4.00	1.80	.50
☐ 14 Homer the Brave DP (Mascot)	.50	.23	.06
☐ 15 Jay Howell	.75	.35	.09
☐ 16 Brian Hunter	.75	.35	.09
☐ 17 Clarence Jones CO	.75	.35	.09
☐ 18 David Justice	2.00	.90	.25
☐ 19 Mark Lemke	1.00	.45	.12
☐ 20 Javier Lopez SP	7.50	3.40	.95
☐ 21 Greg Maddux	6.00	2.70	.75
☐ 22 Leo Mazzone CO	.75	.35	.09
☐ 23 Fred McGriff SP	6.00	2.70	.75
☐ 24 Greg McMichael	.75	.35	.09
☐ 25 Kent Mercker	.75	.35	.09
☐ 26 Otis Nixon	1.00	.45	.12
☐ 27 Greg Olson	.75	.35	.09
☐ 28 Bill Pecota	.75	.35	.09
☐ 29 Terry Pendleton	1.50	.70	.19
☐ 30 Rally (Mascot) DP	.75	.35	.09
☐ 31 Deion Sanders	2.50	1.10	.30
☐ 32 Pete Smith	.75	.35	.09
☐ 33 John Smoltz	4.00	1.80	.50
☐ 34 Mike Stanton	.75	.35	.09
☐ 35 Tony Tarasco SP	4.00	1.80	.50
☐ 36 Jimy Williams CO	.75	.35	.09
☐ 37 Mark Wohlers	2.00	.90	.25
☐ 38 Ned Yost CO	.75	.35	.09

1994 Braves Lykes Perforated

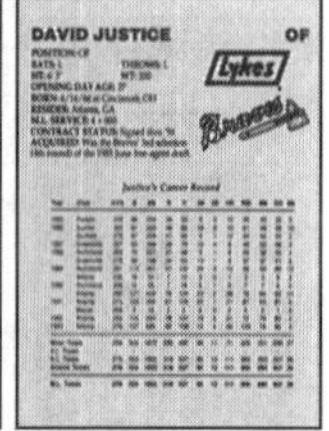

The 1994 Atlanta Braves Team Picture Card set was sponsored by Lykes, the stadium's hot dog maker. It consists of three 10 5/8" by 9 3/8" sheets and one 10 5/8" by 3 1/8" 5-card strip, all joined together to form one continuous sheet. The first panel features a team photo, with each player identified by row. The second and third panels display 15 player cards each, with the 5-card strip for a total of 35 cards. In contrast to the 1994 Braves Standard set, these cards measure 1 1/8" by 3 1/8" and are perforated. The design of these cards is identical to the standard cards, except that the bio and statistics on the card backs are in team color-coded red and blue print rather than black. The difference in player selection between the perforated and standard sets is instructive. The perforated set omits Sanders (traded) but adds Roberto Kelly (acquired), Mike Mordecai (called up), and Jose Oliva (called up). Also Pat Corrales was omitted from the perforated set. The cards are unnumbered but are arranged alphabetically by column beginning in the upper left corner.

	MINT	NRMT	EXC
COMPLETE SET (35)	20.00	9.00	2.50
COMMON CARD (1-35)	.25	.11	.03
☐ 1 Steve Avery	1.00	.45	.12
☐ 2 Jim Beauchamp CO	.25	.11	.03
☐ 3 Steve Bedrosian	.50	.23	.06
☐ 4 Rafael Belliard	.25	.11	.03
☐ 5 Mike Bielecki	.25	.11	.03
☐ 6 Jeff Blauser	.75	.35	.09
☐ 7 Bobby Cox MG	.50	.23	.06
☐ 8 Dave Gallagher	.25	.11	.03
☐ 9 Tom Glavine	2.00	.90	.25
☐ 10 Milt Hill	.25	.11	.03
☐ 11 Chipper Jones	5.00	2.20	.60
☐ 12 Clarence Jones CO	.25	.11	.03
☐ 13 David Justice	1.50	.70	.19
☐ 14 Mike Kelly	.25	.11	.03
☐ 15 Roberto Kelly	.25	.11	.03
☐ 16 Ryan Klesko	3.00	1.35	.35
☐ 17 Mark Lemke	.50	.23	.06
☐ 18 Javier Lopez	3.00	1.35	.35
☐ 19 Greg Maddux	5.00	2.20	.60
☐ 20 Leo Mazzone CO	.25	.11	.03
☐ 21 Fred McGriff	3.00	1.35	.35
☐ 22 Greg McMichael	.25	.11	.03
☐ 23 Kent Mercker	.25	.11	.03
☐ 24 Mike Mordecai	.25	.11	.03
☐ 25 Charlie O'Brien	.25	.11	.03
☐ 26 Jose Oliva	.25	.11	.03
☐ 27 Gregg Olson	.25	.11	.03
☐ 28 Bill Pecota	.25	.11	.03
☐ 29 Terry Pendleton	.75	.35	.09
☐ 30 John Smoltz	2.00	.90	.25
☐ 31 Mike Stanton	.25	.11	.03
☐ 32 Tony Tarasco	.25	.11	.03
☐ 33 Jimy Williams CO	.25	.11	.03
☐ 34 Mark Wohlers	.75	.35	.09
☐ 35 Ned Yost CO	.25	.11	.03

1994 Braves Lykes Standard

This 34-card standard-size set was sponsored by Lykes, the stadium's hot dog maker. Three cards each were to be given out on nine Tuesdays, but three giveaway dates were lost to the strike. The other seven cards were either of players who were traded (Sanders and Hill) or were not given out at games (Cox, Jones, Kelly, Klesko, and McGriff). These seven cards may be scarcer than the others. The fronts display posed color player photos that are edged by a thin black line and also have tan inner borders. The player's name appears vertically in white lettering within a blue bar near the right edge. The player's position and the Braves logo appear within the tan margin beneath the photo. The white back carries the player's name and position at the top, followed below by biography, logos, and statistics. The cards are unnumbered and checklisted below in alphabetical order.

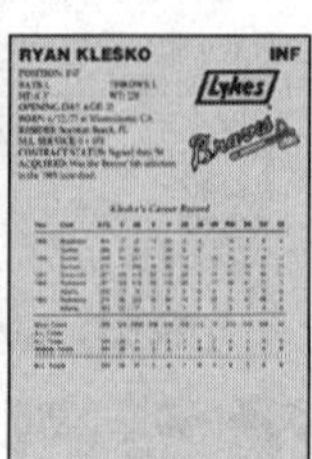

	MINT	NRMT	EXC
COMPLETE SET (34)	35.00	16.00	4.40
COMMON CARD (1-34)	.75	.35	.09
☐ 1 Steve Avery	2.00	.90	.25
☐ 2 Jim Beauchamp CO	.75	.35	.09
☐ 3 Steve Bedrosian	1.00	.45	.12
☐ 4 Rafael Belliard	.75	.35	.09
☐ 5 Mike Bielecki	.75	.35	.09
☐ 6 Jeff Blauser	1.25	.55	.16
☐ 7 Pat Corrales CO	.75	.35	.09
☐ 8 Bobby Cox MG	1.00	.45	.12
☐ 9 Dave Gallagher	.75	.35	.09
☐ 10 Tom Glavine	3.00	1.35	.35
☐ 11 Milt Hill	.75	.35	.09
☐ 12 Chipper Jones	6.00	2.70	.75
☐ 13 Clarence Jones CO	.75	.35	.09
☐ 14 David Justice	2.50	1.10	.30
☐ 15 Mike Kelly	.75	.35	.09
☐ 16 Ryan Klesko	3.00	1.35	.35
☐ 17 Mark Lemke	1.00	.45	.12
☐ 18 Javy Lopez	3.00	1.35	.35
☐ 19 Greg Maddux	4.00	1.80	.50
☐ 20 Leo Mazzone CO	.75	.35	.09
☐ 21 Fred McGriff	4.00	1.80	.50
☐ 22 Greg McMichael	.75	.35	.09
☐ 23 Kent Mercker	.75	.35	.09
☐ 24 Charlie O'Brien	.75	.35	.09
☐ 25 Gregg Olson	.75	.35	.09
☐ 26 Bill Pecota	.75	.35	.09
☐ 27 Terry Pendleton	1.50	.70	.19
☐ 28 Deion Sanders	2.50	1.10	.30
☐ 29 John Smoltz	4.00	1.80	.50
☐ 30 Mike Stanton	.75	.35	.09
☐ 31 Tony Tarasco	.75	.35	.09
☐ 32 Jimy Williams CO	.75	.35	.09
☐ 33 Mark Wohlers	1.50	.70	.19
☐ 34 Ned Yost CO	.75	.35	.09

1994 Braves U.S. Playing Cards

These 56 playing standard-size cards have rounded corners, and feature color posed and action player photos on their white-bordered fronts. The player's name and position appear near the bottom. The blue and red backs carry the logos for the Braves, baseball's 125th Anniversary, MLBPA, and Bicycle Sports Collection. The set is checklisted below in playing card order by suits and assigned numbers to aces (1), jacks (11), queens (12), and kings (13).

	MINT	NRMT	EXC
COMPLETE SET (56)	6.00	2.70	.75
COMMON CARD	.05	.02	.01
☐ 1C Ron Gant	.25	.11	.03
☐ 1D Greg Maddux	1.00	.45	.12
☐ 1H Dave Justice	.25	.11	.03
☐ 1S Jeff Blauser	.05	.02	.01
☐ 2C Chipper Jones	1.00	.45	.12
☐ 2D Ron Gant	.25	.11	.03
☐ 2H Mark Lemke	.05	.02	.01
☐ 2S Mike Stanton	.05	.02	.01
☐ 3C Terry Pendleton	.15	.07	.02
☐ 3D Kent Mercker	.05	.02	.01
☐ 3H Javier Lopez	.30	.14	.04
☐ 3S Ryan Klesko	.50	.23	.06
☐ 4C Mark Wohlers	.15	.07	.02
☐ 4D Greg McMichael	.05	.02	.01
☐ 4H Rafael Belliard	.05	.02	.01
☐ 4S Michael Potts	.05	.02	.01
☐ 5C Pedro Borbon	.05	.02	.01
☐ 5D Tony Tarasco	.05	.02	.01
☐ 5H Bill Pecota	.05	.02	.01
☐ 5S Charlie O'Brien	.05	.02	.01
☐ 6C Steve Avery	.15	.07	.02
☐ 6D John Smoltz	.30	.14	.04
☐ 6H Tom Glavine	.30	.14	.04
☐ 6S Steve Bedrosian	.05	.02	.01
☐ 7C Deion Sanders	.40	.18	.05

☐ 7D Fred McGriff	.30	.14	.04
☐ 7H Milt Hill	.05	.02	.01
☐ 7S Javier Lopez	.30	.14	.04
☐ 8C Dave Justice	.25	.11	.03
☐ 8D Ron Gant	.25	.11	.03
☐ 8H Jeff Blauser	.05	.02	.01
☐ 8S Greg Maddux	1.00	.45	.12
☐ 9C Dave Gallagher	.05	.02	.01
☐ 9D Mike Kelly	.05	.02	.01
☐ 9H Ryan Klesko	.50	.23	.06
☐ 9S Deion Sanders	.40	.18	.05
☐ 10C Rafael Belliard	.05	.02	.01
☐ 10D Steve Bedrosian	.05	.02	.01
☐ 10H Terry Pendleton	.15	.07	.02
☐ 10S Ramon Caraballo	.05	.02	.01
☐ 11C Greg McMichael	.05	.02	.01
☐ 11D Bill Pecota	.05	.02	.01
☐ 11H Mike Stanton	.05	.02	.01
☐ 11S Kent Mercker	.05	.02	.01
☐ 12C John Smoltz	.30	.14	.04
☐ 12D Mark Lemke	.05	.02	.01
☐ 12H Steve Avery	.15	.07	.02
☐ 12S Mark Wohlers	.25	.11	.03
☐ 13C Fred McGriff	.30	.14	.04
☐ 13D Terry Pendleton	.10	.05	.01
☐ 13H Deion Sanders	.40	.18	.05
☐ 13S Tom Glavine	.30	.14	.04
☐ NNO Featured Players	.05	.02	.01

1903-04 Breisch-Williams E107

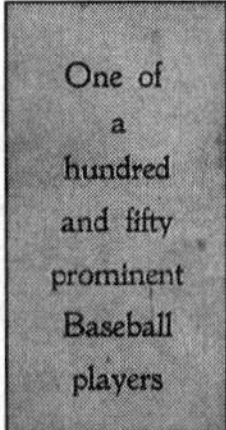

The cards in this 158-card set measure 1 1/4" by 2 1/2". The black and white cards of this series of "prominent baseball players" were marketed by the Breisch-Williams Company. Judging from the team changes for individual players, the set appears to have been issued in 1903-04. Cards have been found with smaller printing front and back and also with the company name hand stamped on back. There are several names misspelled. The cards have been alphabetized and numbered in the checklist below.

	EX-MT	VG-E	GOOD
COMPLETE SET (158)	47000.00	21200.00	5900.00
COMMON CARD (1-158)	250.00	110.00	31.00
☐ 1 John Anderson	250.00	110.00	31.00
St. Louis AL			
☐ 2 John Anderson	250.00	110.00	31.00
NY AL			
☐ 3 Jimmy Barrett: Detroit	250.00	110.00	31.00
(sic, Barret)			
☐ 4 Ginger Beaumont	350.00	160.00	45.00
☐ 5 Erve Beck	250.00	110.00	31.00
☐ 6 Jake Beckley	700.00	325.00	90.00
☐ 7 Harry Bemis: Cleve.	250.00	110.00	31.00
☐ 8 Chief Bender	700.00	325.00	90.00
Phila. AL			
☐ 9 Bill Bernhard	250.00	110.00	31.00
☐ 10 Harry Bay	250.00	110.00	31.00
sic, Bey)			
☐ 11 Bill Bradley	250.00	110.00	31.00
☐ 12 Fritz Buelow	250.00	110.00	31.00
☐ 13 Nixey Callahan	250.00	110.00	31.00
☐ 14 Scoops Carey	250.00	110.00	31.00
☐ 15 Charlie Carr	250.00	110.00	31.00
☐ 16 Bill Carrick	250.00	110.00	31.00
☐ 17 Doc Casey	250.00	110.00	31.00
☐ 18 Frank Chance	700.00	325.00	90.00
☐ 19 Jack Chesbro	700.00	325.00	90.00
☐ 20 Boileryard Clarke	250.00	110.00	31.00
sic, Clark			
☐ 21 Fred Clarke	700.00	325.00	90.00
☐ 22 Jimmy Collins	700.00	325.00	90.00
☐ 23 Duff Cooley	250.00	110.00	31.00
☐ 24 Tommy Corcoran	250.00	110.00	31.00
☐ 25 Bill Coughlin	250.00	110.00	31.00
sic, Coughlan)			
☐ 26 Lou Criger	250.00	110.00	31.00
☐ 27 Lave Cross	250.00	110.00	31.00
☐ 28 Monte Cross	250.00	110.00	31.00
☐ 29 Bill Dahlen	350.00	160.00	45.00
☐ 30 Tom Daly	250.00	110.00	31.00
☐ 31 George Davis	250.00	110.00	31.00
☐ 32 Harry Davis	250.00	110.00	31.00
☐ 33 Ed Delahanty	1000.00	450.00	125.00
☐ 34 Gene DeMontreville	250.00	110.00	31.00
☐ 35 Pop Dillon	250.00	110.00	31.00
Brooklyn			
☐ 36 Pop Dillon	250.00	110.00	31.00
Detroit			
☐ 37 Bill Dinneen	250.00	110.00	31.00
(sic, Dineen)			
☐ 38 Jiggs Donahue	250.00	110.00	31.00
☐ 39 Mike Donlin	250.00	110.00	31.00
☐ 40 Patsy Donovan	250.00	110.00	31.00
☐ 41 Patsy Dougherty	250.00	110.00	31.00
☐ 42 Klondike Douglass	250.00	110.00	31.00
sic, Douglas)			
☐ 43 Jack Doyle	250.00	110.00	31.00
Brooklyn			
☐ 44 Jack Doyle	250.00	110.00	31.00
Phila. NL			
☐ 45 Lew Drill	250.00	110.00	31.00
☐ 46 Jack Dunn	250.00	110.00	31.00
☐ 47 Kid Elberfeld	250.00	110.00	31.00
sic, Elberfield			
☐ 48 Kid Elberfeld	250.00	110.00	31.00
sic, Elberfield			
☐ 49 Duke Farrell	250.00	110.00	31.00
☐ 50 Hobe Ferris	250.00	110.00	31.00
☐ 51 Elmer Flick	700.00	325.00	90.00
☐ 52 Buck Freeman	250.00	110.00	31.00
☐ 53 Bill Friel	250.00	110.00	31.00
sic, Freil			
☐ 54 Dave Fultz	250.00	110.00	31.00
☐ 55 Ned Garvin	250.00	110.00	31.00
☐ 56 Billy Gilbert	250.00	110.00	31.00
☐ 57 Harry Gleason	250.00	110.00	31.00
☐ 58 Kid Gleason	250.00	110.00	31.00
NY NL			
☐ 59 Kid Gleason	250.00	110.00	31.00
Phila. NL			
☐ 60 John Gochnaur	250.00	110.00	31.00
Cleve.			
sic, Gochnauer			
☐ 61 Danny Green	250.00	110.00	31.00
☐ 62 Noodles Hahn	250.00	110.00	31.00
☐ 63 Bill Hallman	250.00	110.00	31.00
☐ 64 Ned Hanlon MG	500.00	220.00	60.00
☐ 65 Dick Harley	250.00	110.00	31.00
☐ 66 Jack Harper	250.00	110.00	31.00
☐ 67 Topsy Hartsel	250.00	110.00	31.00
sic, Hartsell			
☐ 68 Emmett Heidrick	250.00	110.00	31.00
☐ 69 Charlie Hemphill	250.00	110.00	31.00
☐ 70 Weldon Henley	250.00	110.00	31.00
☐ 71 Charlie Hickman	250.00	110.00	31.00
☐ 72 Harry Howell	250.00	110.00	31.00
☐ 73 Frank Isbell	250.00	110.00	31.00
sic, Isabel			
☐ 74 Fred Jacklitsch	250.00	110.00	31.00
sic, Jacklitzch			
☐ 75 Charlie Jones	250.00	110.00	31.00
☐ 76 Fielder Jones	250.00	110.00	31.00
☐ 77 Addie Joss	700.00	325.00	90.00
☐ 78 Mike Kahoe	250.00	110.00	31.00
☐ 79 Willie Keeler	1000.00	450.00	125.00
☐ 80 Joe Kelley	700.00	325.00	90.00
☐ 81 Brickyard Kennedy	250.00	110.00	31.00
☐ 82 Frank Kitson	250.00	110.00	31.00
☐ 83 Malachi Kittredge	250.00	110.00	31.00
Boston NL			
☐ 84 Malachi Kittredge	250.00	110.00	31.00
Wash.			
☐ 85 Candy LaChance	250.00	110.00	31.00
☐ 86 Nap Lajoie	1200.00	550.00	150.00
☐ 87 Tommy Leach	250.00	110.00	31.00
☐ 88 Watty Lee	250.00	110.00	31.00
Pittsburgh			
☐ 89 Watty Lee	250.00	110.00	31.00
Washington			
☐ 90 Sam Leever	250.00	110.00	31.00
☐ 91 Herman Long	250.00	110.00	31.00
☐ 92 Billy Lush	250.00	110.00	31.00
Cleveland			
☐ 93 Billy Lush	250.00	110.00	31.00
Detroit			
☐ 94 Christy Mathewson	1500.00	700.00	190.00
☐ 95 Sport McAllister	250.00	110.00	31.00
☐ 96 Jack McCarthy	250.00	110.00	31.00
☐ 97 Barry McCormick	250.00	110.00	31.00
☐ 98 Ed McFarland	250.00	110.00	31.00
☐ 99 Herm McFarland	250.00	110.00	31.00
☐ 100 Joe McGinnity	700.00	325.00	90.00
☐ 101 John McGraw	1000.00	450.00	125.00
☐ 102 Deacon McGuire	250.00	110.00	31.00
☐ 103 Jock Menefee	250.00	110.00	31.00
☐ 104 Sam Mertes	250.00	110.00	31.00
☐ 105 Roscoe Miller	250.00	110.00	31.00
☐ 106 Fred Mitchell	250.00	110.00	31.00
☐ 107 Earl Moore	250.00	110.00	31.00
☐ 108 Danny Murphy	250.00	110.00	31.00
☐ 109 Jack O'Connor	250.00	110.00	31.00
☐ 110 Al Orth	250.00	110.00	31.00
☐ 111 Dick Padden	250.00	110.00	31.00
☐ 112 Freddy Parent	250.00	110.00	31.00
☐ 113 Roy Patterson	250.00	110.00	31.00
☐ 114 Heinie Peitz	250.00	110.00	31.00
☐ 115 Deacon Phillipe	350.00	160.00	45.00
sic, Phillipi			
☐ 116 Wiley Piatt	250.00	110.00	31.00
☐ 117 Ollie Pickering	250.00	110.00	31.00
☐ 118 Eddie Plank	1000.00	450.00	125.00
☐ 119 Ed Poole	250.00	110.00	31.00
Brooklyn			
☐ 120 Ed Poole	250.00	110.00	31.00
Cinc.			
☐ 121 Jack Powell	250.00	110.00	31.00
New York AL			
☐ 122 Jack Powell	250.00	110.00	31.00
StL AL			
☐ 123 Doc Powers	250.00	110.00	31.00
☐ 124 Claude Ritchey	250.00	110.00	31.00
sic, Ritchie			
☐ 125 Jimmy Ryan	250.00	110.00	31.00
☐ 126 Ossie Schreckengost	250.00	110.00	31.00
☐ 127 Kip Selbach	250.00	110.00	31.00
☐ 128 Socks Seybold	250.00	110.00	31.00
☐ 129 Jimmy Sheckard	250.00	110.00	31.00
☐ 130 Ed Siever	250.00	110.00	31.00
☐ 131 Harry Smith	250.00	110.00	31.00
☐ 132 Tully Sparks	250.00	110.00	31.00
☐ 133 Jake Stahl	350.00	160.00	45.00
☐ 134 Harry Steinfeldt	350.00	160.00	45.00
☐ 135 Sammy Strang	250.00	110.00	31.00
☐ 136 Willie Sudhoff	250.00	110.00	31.00
☐ 137 Joe Sugden	250.00	110.00	31.00
☐ 138 Billy Sullivan	350.00	160.00	45.00
☐ 139 Dummy Taylor	250.00	110.00	31.00
☐ 140 Fred Tenney	250.00	110.00	31.00
☐ 141 Roy Thomas	250.00	110.00	31.00
☐ 142 Jack Thoney	250.00	110.00	31.00
Cleve.			
☐ 143 Jack Thoney	250.00	110.00	31.00
NY AL			
☐ 144 Happy Townsend	250.00	110.00	31.00
☐ 145 George Van Haltren	250.00	110.00	31.00
☐ 146 Rube Waddell	700.00	325.00	90.00
☐ 147 Honus Wagner	2000.00	900.00	250.00
☐ 148 Bobby Wallace	700.00	325.00	90.00
☐ 149 John Warner	250.00	110.00	31.00
☐ 150 Jimmy Wiggs	250.00	110.00	31.00
☐ 151 Jimmy Williams	250.00	110.00	31.00
☐ 152 Vic Willis	500.00	220.00	60.00
☐ 153 Hooks Wiltse	250.00	110.00	31.00
☐ 154 George Winter	250.00	110.00	31.00
sic, Winters			
☐ 155 Bob Wood	350.00	160.00	45.00
☐ 156 Joe Yeager	250.00	110.00	31.00
☐ 157 Cy Young	1200.00	550.00	150.00
☐ 158 Chief Zimmer	250.00	110.00	31.00

1970 Brewers McDonald's

This 31-card set features cards measuring approximately 2 15/16" by 4 3/8" and was issued during the Brewers' first year in Milwaukee after moving from Seattle. The cards are drawings of the members of the 1970 Milwaukee Brewers and underneath the drawings there is information about the players. These cards are still often found in uncut sheet form and hence have no extra value in that form. The backs are blank. The set is checklisted alphabetically with the number of the sheet being listed next to the players name. There were six different sheets of six cards each although only one sheet contained six players; the other sheets depicted five players and a Brewers' logo.

	NRMT	VG-E	GOOD
COMPLETE SET (31)	8.00	3.60	1.00
COMMON CARD (1-31)	.35	.16	.04
☐ 1 Max Alvis 6	.35	.16	.04
☐ 2 Bob Bolin 1	.35	.16	.04
☐ 3 Gene Brabender 3	.35	.16	.04
☐ 4 Dave Bristol 5 MG	.50	.23	.06
☐ 5 Wayne Comer 2	.35	.16	.04
☐ 6 Cal Ermer 3 CO	.35	.16	.04
☐ 7 John Gelnar 4	.35	.16	.04
☐ 8 Greg Goossen 5	.35	.16	.04
☐ 9 Tommy Harper 5	.75	.35	.09
☐ 10 Mike Hegan 3	.50	.23	.06
☐ 11 Mike Hershberger 3	.35	.16	.04
☐ 12 Steve Hovley 2	.35	.16	.04
☐ 13 John Kennedy 2	.35	.16	.04
☐ 14 Lew Krausse 4	.35	.16	.04
☐ 15 Ted Kubiak 1	.35	.16	.04
☐ 16 George Lauzerique 6	.35	.16	.04
☐ 17 Bob Locker 5	.35	.16	.04
☐ 18 Roy McMillan 4 CO	.50	.23	.06
☐ 19 Jerry McNertney 4	.35	.16	.04
☐ 20 Bob Meyer 2	.35	.16	.04
☐ 21 Jackie Moore 6 CO	.50	.23	.06
☐ 22 John Morris 1	.35	.16	.04
☐ 23 John O'Donoghue 1	.35	.16	.04
☐ 24 Marty Pattin 6	.35	.16	.04
☐ 25 Rich Rollins 4	.50	.23	.06
☐ 26 Phil Roof 5	.35	.16	.04
☐ 27 Ted Savage 1	.35	.16	.04
☐ 28 Russ Snyder 6	.35	.16	.04
☐ 29 Wes Stock 2 CO	.50	.23	.06
☐ 30 Sandy Valdespino 2	.35	.16	.04
☐ 31 Danny Walton 3	.35	.16	.04

1970 Brewers Milk

This 24-card set of the Milwaukee Brewers measures approximately 2 5/8" by 4 1/4" and features blue-and-white player photos. The players name is printed in blue in the white wide bottom border. The cards are unnumbered and checklisted below in alphabetical order.

	NRMT	VG-E	GOOD
COMPLETE SET (24)	10.00	4.50	1.25
COMMON CARD (1-24)	.50	.23	.06
☐ 1 Gene Brabender	.50	.23	.06
☐ 2 Dave Bristol MG	.50	.23	.06
☐ 3 Wayne Comer	.50	.23	.06
☐ 4 Cal Ermer CO	.50	.23	.06
☐ 5 Greg Goossen	.50	.23	.06
☐ 6 Tom Harper	.75	.35	.09
☐ 7 Mike Hegan	.50	.23	.06
☐ 8 Mike Hershberger	.50	.23	.06
☐ 9 Steve Hovley	.50	.23	.06
☐ 10 John Kennedy	.50	.23	.06
☐ 11 Lew Krausse	.50	.23	.06
☐ 12 Ted Kubiak	.50	.23	.06
☐ 13 Bob Locker	.50	.23	.06
☐ 14 Roy McMillan CO	.50	.23	.06
☐ 15 Jerry McNertney	.50	.23	.06
☐ 16 Bob Meyer	.50	.23	.06
☐ 17 John Morris	.50	.23	.06
☐ 18 John O'Donoghue	.50	.23	.06
☐ 19 Marty Pattin	.50	.23	.06
☐ 20 Rich Rollins	.50	.23	.06
☐ 21 Phil Roof	.50	.23	.06
☐ 22 Ted Savage	.50	.23	.06
☐ 23 Russ Snyder	.50	.23	.06
☐ 24 Dan Walton	.50	.23	.06

1970 Brewers Team Issue

This 12-card set of the Milwaukee Brewers measures approximately 4 1/4" by 7". The fronts display black-and-white player portraits bordered in white. The player's name and team are printed in the top margin. The backs are blank. The cards are unnumbered and checklisted below in alphabetical order.

	NRMT	VG-E	GOOD
COMPLETE SET (12)	18.00	8.00	2.20
COMMON CARD (1-12)	1.50	.70	.19
☐ 1 Max Alvis	2.00	.90	.25
☐ 2 Dave Bristol MG	1.50	.70	.19
☐ 3 Tommy Harper	2.00	.90	.25
☐ 4 Mike Hegan	1.50	.70	.19
☐ 5 Mike Hershberger	1.50	.70	.19
☐ 6 Lew Krausse	1.50	.70	.19
☐ 7 Ted Kubiak	1.50	.70	.19
☐ 8 Dave May	1.50	.70	.19
☐ 9 Jerry McNertney	1.50	.70	.19
☐ 10 Phil Roof	1.50	.70	.19
☐ 11 Ted Savage	1.50	.70	.19
☐ 12 Danny Walton	1.50	.70	.19

1971 Brewers Team Issue

This 18-photo set features members of the Milwaukee Brewers. The photos are not dated, but can be identified as a 1971 issue since Bill Voss' card is included in the set and this was his first year with the team. Additionally, Tommy Harper's card is included and 1971 was his final year with the Brewers. The photos are printed on thin paper stock that has a pebbled texture. They measure approximately 4 1/4" by 7" and display black-and-white portraits edged in white. The player's name and team are printed in the top margin. The cards have blank backs and are numbered and checklisted alphabetically below.

	NRMT	VG-E	GOOD
COMPLETE SET (18)	20.00	9.00	2.50
COMMON CARD (1-18)	1.50	.70	.19
☐ 1 Max Alvis	1.50	.70	.19
☐ 2 Dave Bristol MG	1.50	.70	.19
☐ 3 Tommy Harper	2.50	1.10	.30
☐ 4 Mike Hegan	2.00	.90	.25
☐ 5 Mike Hershberger	1.50	.70	.19
☐ 6 Lew Krausse	1.50	.70	.19
☐ 7 Ted Kubiak	1.50	.70	.19
☐ 8 Dave May	1.50	.70	.19
☐ 9 Jerry McNertney	1.50	.70	.19
☐ 10 Bill Parsons	1.50	.70	.19
☐ 11 Marty Pattin	1.50	.70	.19
☐ 12 Roberto Pena	1.50	.70	.19
☐ 13 Ellie Rodriguez	1.50	.70	.19
☐ 14 Phil Roof	1.50	.70	.19
☐ 15 Ken Sanders	1.50	.70	.19
☐ 16 Ted Savage	1.50	.70	.19
☐ 17 Bill Voss	1.50	.70	.19
☐ 18 Danny Walton	1.50	.70	.19

1975 Brewers Broadcasters

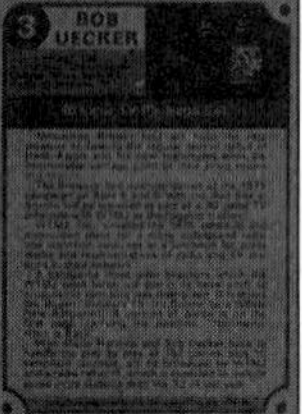

This 7-card standard-size set features 4 announcer cards and 3 schedule cards. All the cards have on the fronts black and white photos, with orange picture frame borders on a white card face. The backs are gray and present either comments on the announcers or broadcast schedules. The first four cards are numbered on the back.

	NRMT	VG-E	GOOD
COMPLETE SET	25.00	11.00	3.10
COMMON CARD	3.50	1.55	.45
☐ 1 Jim Irwin ANN	3.50	1.55	.45
☐ 2 Gary Bender ANN	3.50	1.55	.45
☐ 3 Bob Uecker ANN	10.00	4.50	1.25
☐ 4 Merle Harmon ANN	5.00	2.20	.60
☐ x Television Schedule (unnumbered)	3.50	1.55	.45
☐ x Radio Schedule Part 1 (unnumbered)	3.50	1.55	.45
☐ x Radio Schedule Part 2 (unnumbered)	3.50	1.55	.45

1976 Brewers A and P

This 16-card set of the Milwaukee Brewers measures approximately 5 7/8" by 9". The white-bordered fronts feature color player head photos with a facsimile autograph below. The backs are blank. The cards are unnumbered and checklisted below in alphabetical order.

	NRMT	VG-E	GOOD
COMPLETE SET (16)	20.00	9.00	2.50
COMMON CARD (1-16)	.50	.23	.06
☐ 1 Hank Aaron	10.00	4.50	1.25
☐ 2 Pete Broberg	.50	.23	.06
☐ 3 Jim Colborn	.50	.23	.06
☐ 4 Mike Hegan	.50	.23	.06
☐ 5 Von Joshua	.50	.23	.06
☐ 6 Tim Johnson	.50	.23	.06
☐ 7 Sixto Lezcano	.50	.23	.06
☐ 8 Charlie Moore	.50	.23	.06
☐ 9 Don Money	.50	.23	.06
☐ 10 Darrell Porter	1.50	.70	.19
☐ 11 George Scott	1.50	.70	.19
☐ 12 Bill Sharp	.50	.23	.06
☐ 13 Jim Slaton	.50	.23	.06
☐ 14 Bill Travers	.50	.23	.06
☐ 15 Robin Yount	7.50	3.40	.95
☐ 16 County Stadium	.50	.23	.06

1982 Brewers Police

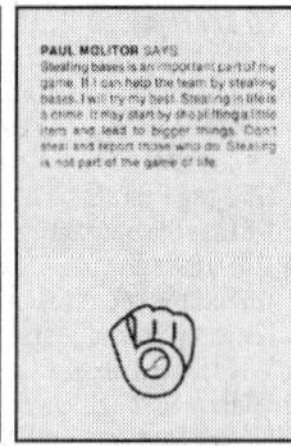

The cards in this 30-card set measure approximately 2 13/16" by 4 1/8". This set of Milwaukee Brewers baseball cards is noted for its excellent color photographs set upon a simple white background. The set was initially distributed at the stadium on May 5th, but was also handed out by several local police departments, and credit lines for the Wisconsin State Fair Park Police (no shield design on reverse), Milwaukee, Brookfield, and Wauwatosa PD's have already been found. The reverses feature advice concerning safety measures, social situations, and crime prevention (Romero card in both Spanish and English). The team card carries a checklist which lists the Brewer's coaches separately although they all appear on a single card; VP/GM Harry Dalton is not mentioned on this list but is included in the set.The prices below are for the basic set without regard to the Police Department listed on the backs. Cards from the more obscure corners and small towns of Wisconsin (where fewer cards were produced) will be valued higher.

	NRMT	VG-E	GOOD
COMPLETE SET (30)	20.00	9.00	2.50
COMMON CARD	.50	.23	.06
☐ 4 Paul Molitor	7.50	3.40	.95
☐ 5 Ned Yost	.50	.23	.06
☐ 7 Don Money	.75	.35	.09
☐ 9 Larry Hisle	.50	.23	.06
☐ 10 Bob McClure	.50	.23	.06
☐ 11 Ed Romero	.50	.23	.06
☐ 13 Roy Howell	.50	.23	.06
☐ 15 Cecil Cooper	1.25	.55	.16
☐ 17 Jim Gantner	1.00	.45	.12
☐ 19 Robin Yount	6.00	2.70	.75
☐ 20 Gorman Thomas	1.00	.45	.12
☐ 22 Charlie Moore	.75	.35	.09
☐ 23 Ted Simmons	1.50	.70	.19
☐ 24 Ben Oglivie	1.00	.45	.12
☐ 26 Kevin Bass	.75	.35	.09
☐ 28 Jamie Easterly	.50	.23	.06
☐ 29 Mark Brouhard	.50	.23	.06
☐ 30 Moose Haas	.75	.35	.09
☐ 34 Rollie Fingers	2.50	1.10	.30
☐ 35 Randy Lerch	.50	.23	.06
☐ 41 Jim Slaton	.50	.23	.06
☐ 45 Doug Jones	1.25	.55	.16
☐ 46 Jerry Augustine	.50	.23	.06
☐ 47 Dwight Bernard	.50	.23	.06
☐ 48 Mike Caldwell	.75	.35	.09
☐ 50 Pete Vuckovich	1.00	.45	.12
☐ NNO Team Card	1.00	.45	.12
☐ NNO Harry Dalton GM	.50	.23	.06
☐ NNO Buck Rodgers MG	.50	.23	.06
☐ NNO Brewer Coaches: Ron Hansen, Bob Rodgers MG, Harry Warner, Larry Haney, Cal McLish	.50	.23	.06

1983 Brewers Gardner's

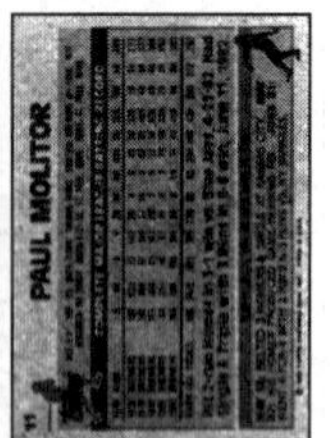

The cards in this 22-card set measure 2 1/2" by 3 1/2". The 1983 Gardner's Brewers set features Milwaukee Brewer players and manager Harvey Kuenn. Topps printed the set for the Madison (Wisconsin) bakery, hence, the backs are identical to the 1983 Topps backs except for the card number. The fronts of the cards, however, feature all new photos and include the Gardner's logo and the Brewers' logo. Many of the cards are grease laden, as they were issued with packages of bread and hamburger and hot-dog buns. The card numbering for this set is essentially in alphabetical order by player's name (after the manager is listed first).

	NRMT	VG-E	GOOD
COMPLETE SET (22)	25.00	11.00	3.10
COMMON CARD (1-22)	.75	.35	.09
☐ 1 Harvey Kuenn MG	1.50	.70	.19
☐ 2 Dwight Bernard	.75	.35	.09
☐ 3 Mark Brouhard	.75	.35	.09
☐ 4 Mike Caldwell	1.00	.45	.12
☐ 5 Cecil Cooper	1.50	.70	.19
☐ 6 Marshall Edwards	.75	.35	.09
☐ 7 Rollie Fingers	3.00	1.35	.35
☐ 8 Jim Gantner	1.50	.70	.19
☐ 9 Moose Haas	.75	.35	.09
☐ 10 Bob McClure	.75	.35	.09
☐ 11 Paul Molitor	8.00	3.60	1.00
☐ 12 Don Money	1.00	.45	.12
☐ 13 Charlie Moore	1.00	.45	.12
☐ 14 Ben Oglivie	1.25	.55	.16
☐ 15 Ed Romero	.75	.35	.09
☐ 16 Ted Simmons	2.00	.90	.25
☐ 17 Jim Slaton	.75	.35	.09
☐ 18 Don Sutton	3.00	1.35	.35
☐ 19 Gorman Thomas	1.50	.70	.19
☐ 20 Pete Vuckovich	1.25	.55	.16
☐ 21 Ned Yost	.75	.35	.09
☐ 22 Robin Yount	6.00	2.70	.75

1983 Brewers Police

The cards in this 30-card set measure approximately 2 13/16" by 4 1/8". The 1983 Police Milwaukee Brewers set contains full color cards issued by the Milwaukee Police Department in conjunction with the Brewers. The cards are numbered on the fronts by the player uniform number and contain the line, "The Milwaukee Police Department Presents the 1983 Milwaukee Braves." The backs contain a brief narrative attributable to the player on the front, the Milwaukee Police logo, and a Milwaukee Brewers logo stating that they were the 1982 American League Champions. In all, 28 variations of these Police sets have been found to date. Prices below are for the basic set without regard to the Police Department listed on the backs of the cards; cards from the more obscure corners and small towns of Wisconsin (whose cards were produced in lesser quantities) will be valued higher.

	NRMT	VG-E	GOOD
COMPLETE SET (30)	12.00	5.50	1.50
COMMON CARD	.25	.11	.03
☐ 4 Paul Molitor	4.00	1.80	.50
☐ 5 Ned Yost	.25	.11	.03
☐ 7 Don Money	.50	.23	.06
☐ 8 Rob Picciolo	.25	.11	.03
☐ 10 Bob McClure	.25	.11	.03
☐ 11 Ed Romero	.25	.11	.03
☐ 13 Roy Howell	.25	.11	.03
☐ 15 Cecil Cooper	.75	.35	.09
☐ 16 Marshall Edwards	.25	.11	.03
☐ 17 Jim Gantner	.75	.35	.09
☐ 19 Robin Yount	3.00	1.35	.35
☐ 20 Gorman Thomas	1.00	.45	.12
☐ 21 Don Sutton	1.50	.70	.19
☐ 22 Charlie Moore	.25	.11	.03
☐ 23 Ted Simmons	1.00	.45	.12
☐ 24 Ben Oglivie	.50	.23	.06
☐ 26 Bob Skube	.25	.11	.03
☐ 27 Pete Ladd	.25	.11	.03
☐ 28 Jamie Easterly	.25	.11	.03
☐ 30 Moose Haas	.25	.11	.03
☐ 32 Harvey Kuenn MG	.50	.23	.06
☐ 34 Rollie Fingers	1.50	.70	.19
☐ 40 Bob L. Gibson	.25	.11	.03
☐ 41 Jim Slaton	.25	.11	.03
☐ 42 Tom Tellmann	.25	.11	.03
☐ 46 Jerry Augustine	.25	.11	.03
☐ 48 Mike Caldwell	.50	.23	.06
☐ 50 Pete Vuckovich	.50	.23	.06
☐ NNO Coaches Card: Pat Dobson, Ron Hansen, Larry Haney, Dave Garcia	.50	.23	.06
☐ NNO Team Photo (Checklist back)	.50	.23	.06

1984 Brewers Gardner's

The cards in this 22-card set measure 2 1/2" by 3 1/2". For the second year in a row, the Gardner Bakery Company issued a set of cards available in packages of Gardner Bakery products. The set was manufactured by Topps, and the backs of the cards are identical to the Topps cards of this year except for the numbers. The Gardner logo appears on the fronts of the cards with the player's name, position abbreviation, the name Brewers, and the words 1984 Series II. The card numbering for this set is essentially in alphabetical order by player's name (after the manager is listed first).

	NRMT	VG-E	GOOD
COMPLETE SET (22)	12.00	5.50	1.50
COMMON CARD (1-22)	.25	.11	.03
☐ 1 Rene Lachemann MG	.25	.11	.03
☐ 2 Mark Brouhard	.25	.11	.03
☐ 3 Mike Caldwell	.50	.23	.06
☐ 4 Bobby Clark	.25	.11	.03
☐ 5 Cecil Cooper	1.00	.45	.12
☐ 6 Rollie Fingers	2.00	.90	.25
☐ 7 Jim Gantner	1.00	.45	.12
☐ 8 Moose Haas	.25	.11	.03
☐ 9 Roy Howell	.25	.11	.03
☐ 10 Pete Ladd	.25	.11	.03
☐ 11 Rick Manning	.25	.11	.03
☐ 12 Bob McClure	.25	.11	.03
☐ 13 Paul Molitor	4.00	1.80	.50
☐ 14 Charlie Moore	.50	.23	.06
☐ 15 Ben Oglivie	.75	.35	.09
☐ 16 Ed Romero	.25	.11	.03
☐ 17 Ted Simmons	1.00	.45	.12
☐ 18 Jim Sundberg	.50	.23	.06
☐ 19 Don Sutton	2.00	.90	.25
☐ 20 Tom Tellmann	.25	.11	.03
☐ 21 Pete Vuckovich	.75	.35	.09
☐ 22 Robin Yount	3.00	1.35	.35

1984 Brewers Police

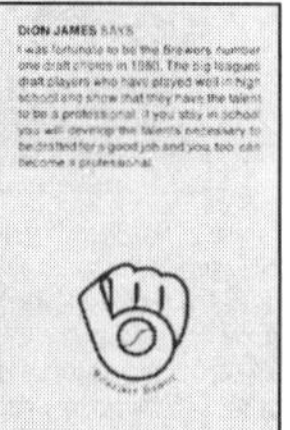

The cards in this 30-card set measure approximately 2 13/16" by 4 1/8". Again this year, the police departments in and around Milwaukee issued sets of the Milwaukee Brewers. Although each set contained the same players and numbers, the individual police departments placed their own name on the fronts of cards to show that they were the particular jurisdiction issuing the set. The backs contain the Brewers logo, a safety tip, and in some cases, a badge of the jurisdiction. To date, 59 variations of this set have been found. Prices below are for the basic set without regard to the Police Department issuing the cards; cards from the more obscure corners and small towns of Wisconsin will be valued higher. Cards are numbered by uniform number.

	NRMT	VG-E	GOOD
COMPLETE SET (30)	10.00	4.50	1.25
COMMON CARD	.25	.11	.03
☐ 2 Randy Ready	.25	.11	.03
☐ 4 Paul Molitor	3.00	1.35	.35
☐ 8 Jim Sundberg	.50	.23	.06
☐ 9 Rene Lachemann MG	.25	.11	.03
☐ 10 Bob McClure	.25	.11	.03
☐ 11 Ed Romero	.25	.11	.03
☐ 13 Roy Howell	.25	.11	.03
☐ 14 Dion James	.25	.11	.03
☐ 15 Cecil Cooper	.75	.35	.09
☐ 17 Jim Gantner	.75	.35	.09
☐ 19 Robin Yount	2.50	1.10	.30
☐ 20 Don Sutton	1.50	.70	.19
☐ 21 Bill Schroeder	.25	.11	.03
☐ 22 Charlie Moore	.25	.11	.03
☐ 23 Ted Simmons	1.00	.45	.12
☐ 24 Ben Oglivie	.75	.35	.09
☐ 25 Bob Clark	.25	.11	.03
☐ 27 Pete Ladd	.25	.11	.03
☐ 28 Rick Manning	.25	.11	.03
☐ 29 Mark Brouhard	.25	.11	.03
☐ 30 Moose Haas	.25	.11	.03
☐ 34 Rollie Fingers	1.50	.70	.19
☐ 42 Tom Tellmann	.25	.11	.03
☐ 43 Chuck Porter	.25	.11	.03
☐ 46 Jerry Augustine	.25	.11	.03
☐ 47 Jaime Cocanower	.25	.11	.03
☐ 48 Mike Caldwell	.50	.23	.06
☐ 50 Pete Vuckovich	.50	.23	.06
☐ NNO Coaches Card: Dave Garcia, Pat Dobson, Andy Etchebarren, Tom Trebelhorn	.25	.11	.03
☐ NNO Team Photo (Checklist back)	.50	.23	.06

1985 Brewers Gardner's

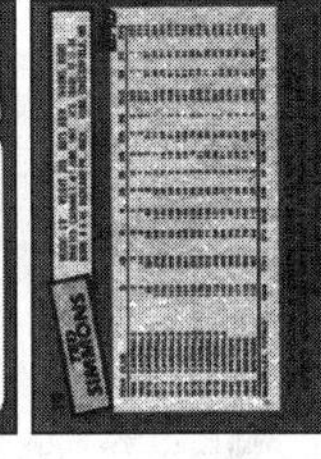

The cards in this 22-card set measure 2 1/2" by 3 1/2". For the third year in a row, the Gardner Bakery Company issued a set of cards available in packages of Gardner Bakery products. The set was manufactured by Topps, and the backs of the cards are identical to the Topps cards of this year except for the card numbers and copyright information. The Gardner logo appears on the fronts of the cards with the player's name, position abbreviation, and the name Brewers. The card numbering for this set is essentially in alphabetical order.

	NRMT	VG-E	GOOD
COMPLETE SET (22)	10.00	4.50	1.25
COMMON CARD (1-22)	.25	.11	.03
□ 1 George Bamberger MG	.50	.23	.06
□ 2 Mark Brouhard	.25	.11	.03
□ 3 Bobby Clark	.25	.11	.03
□ 4 Jaime Cocanower	.25	.11	.03
□ 5 Cecil Cooper	1.00	.45	.12
□ 6 Rollie Fingers	1.50	.70	.19
□ 7 Jim Gantner	1.00	.45	.12
□ 8 Moose Haas	.25	.11	.03
□ 9 Dion James	.25	.11	.03
□ 10 Pete Ladd	.25	.11	.03
□ 11 Rick Manning	.25	.11	.03
□ 12 Bob McClure	.25	.11	.03
□ 13 Paul Molitor	4.00	1.80	.50
□ 14 Charlie Moore	.50	.23	.06
□ 15 Ben Oglivie	.75	.35	.09
□ 16 Chuck Porter	.25	.11	.03
□ 17 Ed Romero	.25	.11	.03
□ 18 Bill Schroeder	.25	.11	.03
□ 19 Ted Simmons	1.00	.45	.12
□ 20 Tom Tellmann	.25	.11	.03
□ 21 Pete Vuckovich	.75	.35	.09
□ 22 Robin Yount	3.00	1.35	.35

1985 Brewers Police

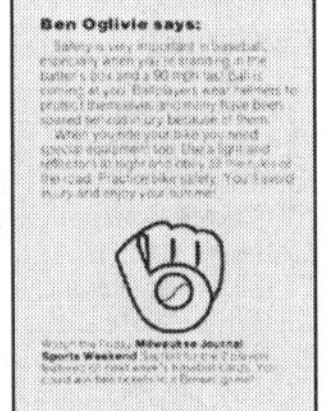

The cards in this 30-card set measure 2 3/4" by 4 1/8". Again this year, the police departments in and around Milwaukee issued sets of the Milwaukee Brewers. The backs contain the Brewers logo, a safety tip, and in some cases, a badge of the jurisdiction. Prices below are for the basic set without regard to the Police Department issuing the cards; cards from the more obscure corners and small towns of Wisconsin (smaller production) will be valued higher. Cards are numbered by uniform number.

	NRMT	VG-E	GOOD
COMPLETE SET (30)	8.00	3.60	1.00
COMMON CARD	.25	.11	.03
□ 2 Randy Ready	.25	.11	.03
□ 4 Paul Molitor	3.00	1.35	.35
□ 5 Doug Loman	.25	.11	.03
□ 7 Paul Householder	.25	.11	.03
□ 10 Bob McClure	.25	.11	.03
□ 11 Ed Romero	.25	.11	.03
□ 14 Dion James	.25	.11	.03
□ 15 Cecil Cooper	1.00	.45	.12
□ 17 Jim Gantner	.75	.35	.09
□ 18 Danny Darwin	.50	.23	.06
□ 19 Robin Yount	2.00	.90	.25
□ 21 Bill Schroeder	.25	.11	.03
□ 22 Charlie Moore	.25	.11	.03
□ 23 Ted Simmons	1.00	.45	.12
□ 24 Ben Oglivie	.75	.35	.09
□ 26 Brian Giles	.25	.11	.03
□ 27 Pete Ladd	.25	.11	.03
□ 28 Rick Manning	.25	.11	.03
□ 29 Mark Brouhard	.25	.11	.03
□ 30 Moose Haas	.25	.11	.03
□ 31 George Bamberger MG	.50	.23	.06
□ 34 Rollie Fingers	1.50	.70	.19
□ 40 Bob L. Gibson	.25	.11	.03
□ 41 Ray Searage	.25	.11	.03
□ 47 Jaime Cocanower	.25	.11	.03
□ 48 Ray Burris	.25	.11	.03
□ 49 Ted Higuera	.50	.23	.06
□ 50 Pete Vuckovich	.50	.23	.06
□ NNO Team Roster	.25	.11	.03
□ NNO Coaches Card Herm Sterrette Tony Muser Frank Howard Larry Haney Andy Etchebarren	.25	.11	.03
□ NNO Newspaper Carrier	.25	.11	.03

1986 Brewers Greats TCMA

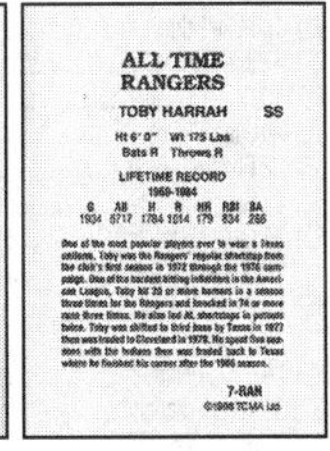

This 12-card standard-size set honors the best retired Brewers of the first two decades. The fronts have a player photo and position while the backs have vital statistics, career information and lifetime statistics.

	MINT	NRMT	EXC
COMPLETE SET (12)	3.00	1.35	.35
COMMON CARD (1-12)	.25	.11	.03
□ 1 George Scott	.35	.16	.04
□ 2 Pedro Garcia	.25	.11	.03
□ 3 Tim Johnson	.25	.11	.03
□ 4 Don Money	.25	.11	.03
□ 5 Sixto Lezcano	.25	.11	.03
□ 6 John Briggs	.25	.11	.03
□ 7 Dave May	.25	.11	.03
□ 8 Darrell Porter	.35	.16	.04
□ 9 Jim Colborn	.25	.11	.03
□ 10 Mike Caldwell	.35	.16	.04
□ 11 Rollie Fingers	1.00	.45	.12
□ 12 Harvey Kuenn MG	.35	.16	.04

1986 Brewers Police

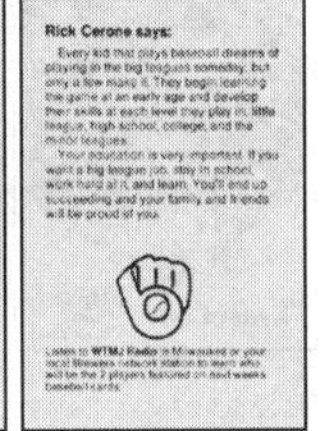

This 32-card safety set was also sponsored by WTMJ Radio and Kinney Shoes. The backs contain the usual biographical info and safety tip. The front features a full-color photo of the player, his name, position, and uniform number. The cards measure approximately 2 5/8" by 4 1/8". Cards were freely distributed throughout the summer by the Police Departments in the Milwaukee area. Cards are numbered below by uniform number.

	MINT	NRMT	EXC
COMPLETE SET (32)	7.00	3.10	.85
COMMON CARD	.25	.11	.03
□ 1 Ernest Riles	.25	.11	.03
□ 2 Randy Ready	.25	.11	.03
□ 3 Juan Castillo	.25	.11	.03
□ 4 Paul Molitor	3.00	1.35	.35
□ 7 Paul Householder	.25	.11	.03
□ 8 Andy Etchebarren CO	.25	.11	.03
□ 10 Bob McClure	.25	.11	.03
□ 11 Rick Cerone	.25	.11	.03
□ 12 Larry Haney CO	.25	.11	.03
□ 13 Billy Joe Robidoux	.25	.11	.03
□ 15 Cecil Cooper	.75	.35	.09
□ 16 Mike Felder	.25	.11	.03
□ 17 Jim Gantner	.75	.35	.09
□ 18 Danny Darwin	.50	.23	.06
□ 19 Robin Yount	1.50	.70	.19
□ 20 Juan Nieves	.25	.11	.03
□ 21 Bill Schroeder	.25	.11	.03
□ 22 Charlie Moore	.25	.11	.03
□ 24 Ben Oglivie	.75	.35	.09
□ 25 Mark Clear	.25	.11	.03
□ 28 Rick Manning	.25	.11	.03
□ 31 George Bamberger MG	.25	.11	.03
□ 33 Frank Howard CO	.50	.23	.06
□ 35 Tony Muser CO	.25	.11	.03
□ 37 Dan Plesac	.50	.23	.06
□ 38 Herm Starrette CO	.25	.11	.03
□ 39 Tim Leary	.25	.11	.03
□ 42 Tom Trebelhorn CO	.25	.11	.03
□ 45 Rob Deer	.50	.23	.06
□ 46 Bill Wegman	.25	.11	.03
□ 47 Jaime Cocanower	.25	.11	.03
□ 49 Teddy Higuera	.50	.23	.06

1987 Brewers Police

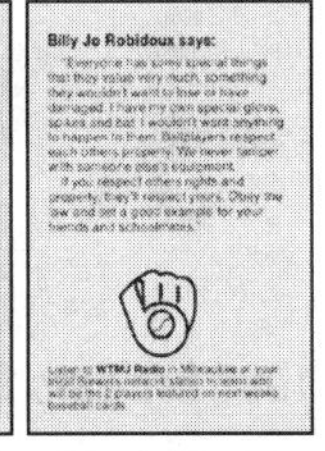

This 30-card safety set was also sponsored by WTMJ Radio and Kinney Shoes. The backs contain the usual biographical info and safety tip. The front features a full-color photo of the player, his name, position, and uniform number. The cards measure approximately 2 5/8" by 4 1/8". Cards were freely distributed throughout the summer by the Police Departments in the Milwaukee area and throughout other parts of Wisconsin. Cards are numbered below by uniform number.

	MINT	NRMT	EXC
COMPLETE SET (30)	7.00	3.10	.85
COMMON CARD	.25	.11	.03
□ 1 Ernest Riles	.25	.11	.03
□ 2 Edgar Diaz	.25	.11	.03
□ 3 Juan Castillo	.25	.11	.03
□ 4 Paul Molitor	2.50	1.10	.30
□ 5 B.J. Surhoff	2.00	.90	.25
□ 7 Dale Sveum	.25	.11	.03
□ 9 Greg Brock	.25	.11	.03
□ 13 Billy Joe Robidoux	.25	.11	.03
□ 14 Jim Paciorek	.25	.11	.03
□ 15 Cecil Cooper	.75	.35	.09
□ 16 Mike Felder	.25	.11	.03
□ 17 Jim Gantner	.75	.35	.09
□ 19 Robin Yount	2.00	.90	.25
□ 20 Juan Nieves	.25	.11	.03
□ 21 Bill Schroeder	.25	.11	.03
□ 25 Mark Clear	.25	.11	.03
□ 26 Glenn Braggs	.25	.11	.03
□ 28 Rick Manning	.25	.11	.03
□ 29 Chris Bosio	.75	.35	.09
□ 32 Chuck Crim	.25	.11	.03
□ 34 Mark Ciardi	.25	.11	.03
□ 37 Dan Plesac	.50	.23	.06
□ 38 John Henry Johnson	.25	.11	.03
□ 40 Mike Birkbeck	.25	.11	.03
□ 42 Tom Trebelhorn MG	.25	.11	.03
□ 45 Rob Deer	.50	.23	.06
□ 46 Bill Wegman	.25	.11	.03
□ 49 Teddy Higuera	.25	.11	.03
□ NNO Coaching Staff Andy Etchebarren Larry Haney Chuck Hartenstein Dave Hilton Tony Muser	.25	.11	.03
□ NNO Brewers Team (Checklist on back)	.50	.23	.06

1987 Brewers Team Issue

These cards feature members of the 1987 Milwaukee Brewers. These cards are unnumbered and we have checklisted them below in alphabetical order.

	MINT	NRMT	EXC
COMPLETE SET (16)	6.00	2.70	.75
COMMON CARD (1-16)	.25	.11	.03
□ 1 Glenn Braggs	.25	.11	.03
□ 2 Greg Brock	.25	.11	.03
□ 3 Mark Clear	.25	.11	.03
□ 4 Cecil Cooper	.75	.35	.09
□ 5 Rob Deer	.25	.11	.03
□ 6 Jim Gantner	.75	.35	.09
□ 7 Teddy Higuera	.25	.11	.03
□ 8 Paul Molitor	2.50	1.10	.30
□ 9 Juan Nieves	.25	.11	.03
□ 10 Dan Plesac	.25	.11	.03
□ 11 Billy Jo Robidoux	.25	.11	.03
□ 12 Bill Schroeder	.25	.11	.03
□ 13 B.J. Surhoff	1.50	.70	.19
□ 14 Dale Sveum	.25	.11	.03
□ 15 Bill Wegman	.25	.11	.03
□ 16 Robin Yount	1.50	.70	.19

1988 Brewers Police

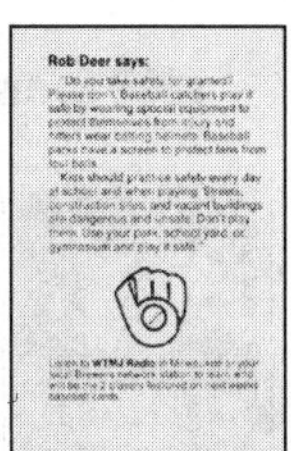

This 30-card safety set was also sponsored by WTMJ Radio and Stadia Athletic Shoes. The backs contain the usual biographical info and safety tip. The front features a full-color photo of the player, his name, position, and uniform number. The cards measure approximately 2 7/8" by 4 1/8". Cards were freely distributed throughout the summer by the Police Departments in the Milwaukee area and throughout other parts of Wisconsin. Cards are numbered below by uniform number.

	MINT	NRMT	EXC
COMPLETE SET (30)	6.00	2.70	.75
COMMON CARD	.25	.11	.03
□ 1 Ernest Riles	.25	.11	.03
□ 3 Juan Castillo	.25	.11	.03
□ 4 Paul Molitor	2.50	1.10	.30
□ 5 B.J. Surhoff	1.25	.55	.16
□ 7 Dale Sveum	.25	.11	.03
□ 9 Greg Brock	.25	.11	.03
□ 11 Charlie O'Brien	.25	.11	.03
□ 14 Jim Adduci	.25	.11	.03
□ 16 Mike Felder	.25	.11	.03
□ 17 Jim Gantner	.75	.35	.09
□ 19 Robin Yount	1.50	.70	.19
□ 20 Juan Nieves	.25	.11	.03
□ 21 Bill Schroeder	.25	.11	.03
□ 23 Joey Meyer	.25	.11	.03
□ 25 Mark Clear	.25	.11	.03
□ 26 Glenn Braggs	.25	.11	.03
□ 28 Odell Jones	.25	.11	.03
□ 29 Chris Bosio	.25	.11	.03
□ 30 Steve Kiefer	.25	.11	.03
□ 32 Chuck Crim	.25	.11	.03
□ 33 Jay Aldrich	.25	.11	.03
□ 37 Dan Plesac	.50	.23	.06
□ 40 Mike Birkbeck	.25	.11	.03
□ 42 Tom Trebelhorn MG	.25	.11	.03
□ 43 Dave Stapleton	.25	.11	.03
□ 45 Rob Deer	.50	.23	.06
□ 46 Bill Wegman	.25	.11	.03
□ 49 Ted Higuera	.25	.11	.03
□ NNO Team Photo HOR	.50	.23	.06
□ NNO Manager/Coaches HOR Andy Etchebarren Larry Haney Chuck Hartenstein Dave Hilton Tony Muser	.25	.11	.03

1989 Brewers Gardner's

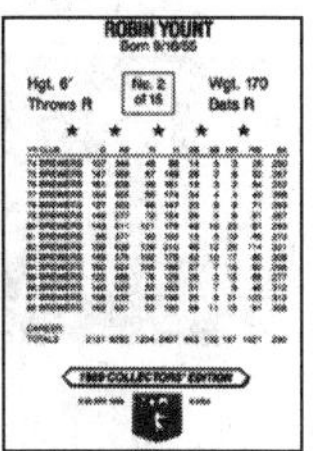

The 1989 Gardner's Brewers set contains 15 standard-size cards. The fronts feature airbrushed mugshots with sky blue backgrounds and white borders. The backs are white and feature career stats. One card was distributed in each specially marked Gardner's bakery product. Cards were issued during the middle of the season. For some reason Riles is included in the set even though he had been traded by the Brewers during the 1988 season.

	MINT	NRMT	EXC
COMPLETE SET (15)	12.50	5.50	1.55
COMMON CARD (1-15)	.50	.23	.06

	MINT	NRMT	EXC
☐ 1 Paul Molitor	6.00	2.70	.75
☐ 2 Robin Yount	4.00	1.80	.50
☐ 3 Jim Gantner	1.00	.45	.12
☐ 4 Rob Deer	.50	.23	.06
☐ 5 B.J. Surhoff	1.50	.70	.19
☐ 6 Dale Sveum	.50	.23	.06
☐ 7 Ted Higuera	.50	.23	.06
☐ 8 Dan Plesac	.75	.35	.09
☐ 9 Bill Wegman	.50	.23	.06
☐ 10 Juan Nieves	.50	.23	.06
☐ 11 Greg Brock	.50	.23	.06
☐ 12 Glenn Braggs	.50	.23	.06
☐ 13 Joey Meyer	.50	.23	.06
☐ 14 Earnest Riles	.50	.23	.06
☐ 15 Don August	.50	.23	.06

1989 Brewers Police

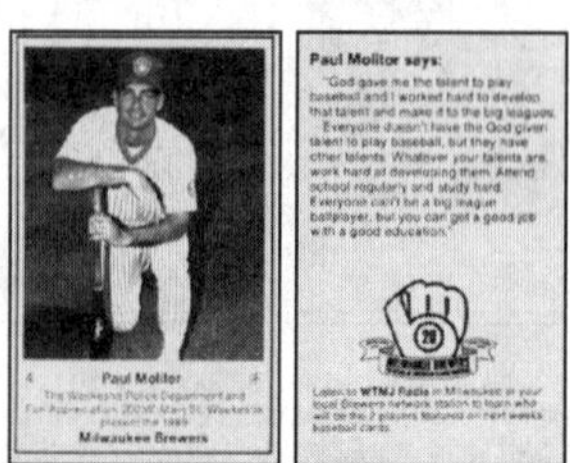

The 1989 Police Milwaukee Brewers set contains 30 cards measuring approximately 2 3/4" by 4 1/4". The fronts have color photos with white borders; the backs feature safety tips. The unnumbered cards were given away by various local Wisconsin police departments. The cards are numbered below by uniform number.

	MINT	NRMT	EXC
COMPLETE SET (30)	7.00	3.10	.85
COMMON CARD	.25	.11	.03
☐ 1 Gary Sheffield	3.50	1.55	.45
☐ 4 Paul Molitor	2.50	1.10	.30
☐ 5 B.J. Surhoff	1.25	.55	.16
☐ 6 Bill Spiers	.25	.11	.03
☐ 7 Dale Sveum	.25	.11	.03
☐ 9 Greg Brock	.25	.11	.03
☐ 14 Gus Polidor	.25	.11	.03
☐ 16 Mike Felder	.25	.11	.03
☐ 17 Jim Gantner	.75	.35	.09
☐ 19 Robin Yount	1.50	.70	.19
☐ 20 Juan Nieves	.25	.11	.03
☐ 22 Charlie O'Brien	.25	.11	.03
☐ 23 Joey Meyer	.25	.11	.03
☐ 25 Dave Engle	.25	.11	.03
☐ 26 Glenn Braggs	.25	.11	.03
☐ 27 Paul Mirabella	.25	.11	.03
☐ 29 Chris Bosio	.25	.11	.03
☐ 30 Terry Francona	.25	.11	.03
☐ 32 Chuck Crim	.25	.11	.03
☐ 37 Dan Plesac	.25	.11	.03
☐ 38 Don August	.25	.11	.03
☐ 40 Mike Birkbeck	.25	.11	.03
☐ 41 Mark Knudson	.25	.11	.03
☐ 42 Tom Trebelhorn MG	.25	.11	.03
☐ 45 Rob Deer	.25	.11	.03
☐ 46 Bill Wegman	.25	.11	.03
☐ 48 Bryan Clutterbuck	.25	.11	.03
☐ 49 Teddy Higuera	.25	.11	.03
☐ NNO Team Card (Checklist on back)	.50	.23	.06
☐ NNO Coaches Card Duffy Dyer Andy Etchebarren Larry Haney Chuck Hartenstein Tony Muser	.25	.11	.03

1989 Brewers Yearbook

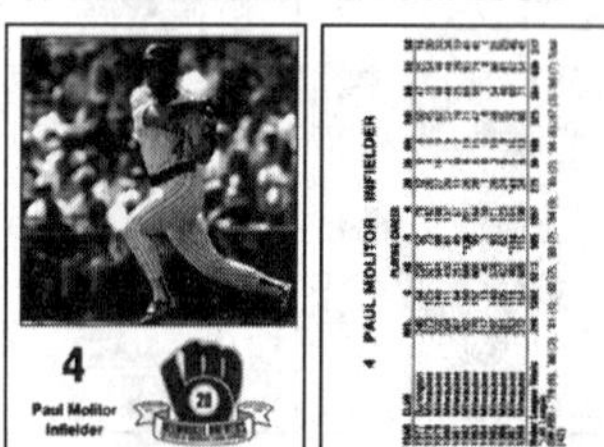

This 18-card standard size set was issued as an insert in the 1989 Milwaukee Brewer Yearbooks. The yearbook itself had a suggested retail price of 4.95. The card set features 17 of the Brewers and their manager. The cards are dominated by a full-color photo of the player on the top two-thirds of the cards along with the uniform number name and position underneath the player. There is also a large logo on the bottom right of the card commemorating the twentieth anniversary of the Brewers in Milwaukee. The backs only contain the player's name and their career statistics. The set is checklisted below by uniform numbers.

	MINT	NRMT	EXC
COMPLETE SET (18)	10.00	4.50	1.25
COMMON CARD	.25	.11	.03
☐ 1 Gary Sheffield	4.00	1.80	.50
☐ 4 Paul Molitor	3.00	1.35	.35
☐ 5 B.J. Surhoff	1.00	.45	.12
☐ 7 Dale Sveum	.25	.11	.03
☐ 9 Greg Brock	.25	.11	.03
☐ 17 Jim Gantner	.75	.35	.09
☐ 19 Robin Yount	2.00	.90	.25
☐ 20 Juan Nieves	.25	.11	.03
☐ 26 Glenn Braggs	.25	.11	.03
☐ 29 Chris Bosio	.50	.23	.06
☐ 32 Chuck Crim	.25	.11	.03
☐ 37 Dan Plesac	.50	.23	.06
☐ 38 Don August	.25	.11	.03
☐ 40 Mike Birkbeck	.25	.11	.03
☐ 42 Tom Trebelhorn MG	.25	.11	.03
☐ 45 Rob Deer	.25	.11	.03
☐ 46 Bill Wegman	.25	.11	.03
☐ 49 Ted Higuera	.25	.11	.03

1990 Brewers Miller Brewing

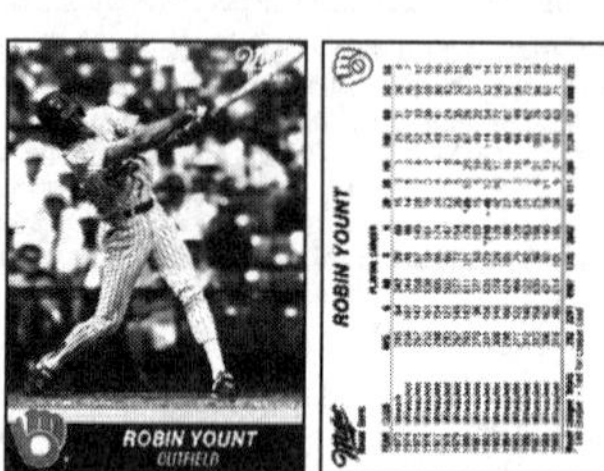

This 32-card standard-size set and a plastic binder were sponsored by Miller Brewing Co. and given away to the first 25,000 adults (21 years and older) attending the Brewers' home game against the White Sox on August 4th. The fronts have either action or posed color player photos, with the player's name and position given in white lettering on a black stripe at the bottom of the card face. The backs have biographical information and player statistics. The cards are unnumbered and checklisted below in alphabetical order. The complete set price below does not include the binder.

	MINT	NRMT	EXC
COMPLETE SET (32)	20.00	9.00	2.50
COMMON CARD (1-32)	.25	.11	.03
☐ 1 Chris Bosio	.50	.23	.06
☐ 2 Greg Brock	.25	.11	.03
☐ 3 Chuck Crim	.25	.11	.03
☐ 4 Rob Deer	.25	.11	.03
☐ 5 Edgar Diaz	.25	.11	.03
☐ 6 Tom Edens	.25	.11	.03
☐ 7 Mike Felder	.25	.11	.03
☐ 8 Tom Filer	.25	.11	.03
☐ 9 Jim Gantner	1.00	.45	.12
☐ 10 Darryl Hamilton	1.00	.45	.12
☐ 11 Teddy Higuera	.25	.11	.03
☐ 12 Mark Knudson	.25	.11	.03
☐ 13 Bill Krueger	.25	.11	.03
☐ 14 Paul Mirabella	.25	.11	.03
☐ 15 Paul Molitor	7.50	3.40	.95
☐ 16 Jaime Navarro	1.00	.45	.12
☐ 17 Charlie O'Brien	.25	.11	.03
☐ 18 Dave Parker	1.00	.45	.12
☐ 19 Dan Plesac	.50	.23	.06
☐ 20 Dennis Powell	.25	.11	.03
☐ 21 Ron Robinson	.25	.11	.03
☐ 22 Bob Sebra	.25	.11	.03
☐ 23 Gary Sheffield	2.50	1.10	.30
☐ 24 Bill Spiers	.25	.11	.03
☐ 25 B.J. Surhoff	1.00	.45	.12
☐ 26 Dale Sveum	.25	.11	.03
☐ 27 Tom Trebelhorn MG	.25	.11	.03
☐ 28 Greg Vaughn	2.00	.90	.25
☐ 29 Randy Veres	.25	.11	.03
☐ 30 Bill Wegman	.25	.11	.03
☐ 31 Robin Yount	5.00	2.20	.60
☐ 32 Coaches Card Don Baylor Ray Burris Duffy Dyer Andy Etchebarren Larry Haney	.50	.23	.06

1990 Brewers Police

This 30-card police set was issued in conjunction with the Fan Appreciation store of Waukesha, Wisconsin and the Waukesha Police department. This set measures approximately 2 13/16" by 4 1/8" and is checklisted by uniform number. The front of the card is a full-color photo surrounded by a blue border while the back has anti-crime tips.

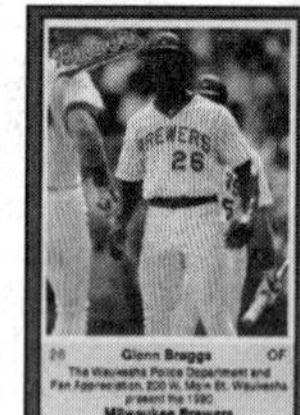

	MINT	NRMT	EXC
COMPLETE SET (30)	7.50	3.40	.95
COMMON CARD	.25	.11	.03
☐ 2 Edgar Diaz	.25	.11	.03
☐ 4 Paul Molitor	2.50	1.10	.30
☐ 7 Dale Sveum	.25	.11	.03
☐ 11 Gary Sheffield	2.00	.90	.25
☐ 14 Gus Polidor	.25	.11	.03
☐ 16 Mike Felder	.25	.11	.03
☐ 17 Jim Gantner	.75	.35	.09
☐ 19 Robin Yount	1.50	.70	.19
☐ 20 Juan Nieves	.25	.11	.03
☐ 22 Charlie O'Brien	.25	.11	.03
☐ 23 Greg Vaughn	1.25	.55	.16
☐ 24 Darryl Hamilton	1.00	.45	.12
☐ 26 Glenn Braggs	.25	.11	.03
☐ 27 Paul Mirabella	.25	.11	.03
☐ 28 Tom Filer	.25	.11	.03
☐ 29 Chris Bosio	.50	.23	.06
☐ 30 Terry Francona	.25	.11	.03
☐ 31 Jaime Navarro	1.00	.45	.12
☐ 32 Chuck Crim	.25	.11	.03
☐ 34 Billy Bates	.25	.11	.03
☐ 36 Tony Fossas	.25	.11	.03
☐ 37 Dan Plesac	.50	.23	.06
☐ 38 Don August	.25	.11	.03
☐ 39 Dave Parker	.75	.35	.09
☐ 40 Mike Birkbeck	.25	.11	.03
☐ 41 Mark Knudson	.25	.11	.03
☐ 42 Tom Trebelhorn MG	.25	.11	.03
☐ 45 Rob Deer	.25	.11	.03
☐ 46 Bill Wegman	.25	.11	.03
☐ 47 Bill Krueger	.25	.11	.03
☐ 49 Teddy Higuera	.25	.11	.03
☐ NNO Coaches Larry Haney Don Baylor Ray Burris Andy Etchebarren Duffy Dyer	.50	.23	.06

1991 Brewers Miller Brewing

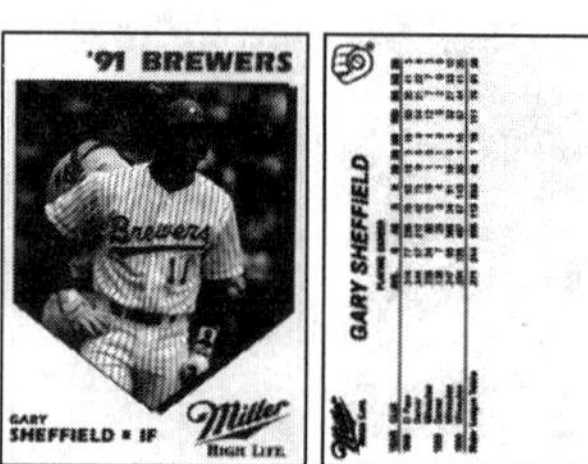

This 32-card set was sponsored by the Miller Brewing Company, and the company logo appears in red lettering at the lower right corner of the front. The sets were given away at the Brewers' home game against the Baltimore Orioles on August 17. The standard-size cards feature on the fronts color action player photos inside a pentagonal-shaped design that resembles home plate. A black border on the right side of the pentagon creates the impression of a shadow. The words '91 Brewers" appears in bluish-purple lettering above the photo, with player information given in black lettering in the lower left corner of the card face. The backs are printed in black and present complete Major League statistics. The cards are unnumbered and checklisted below in alphabetical order, with the coaches' card listed at the end.

	MINT	NRMT	EXC
COMPLETE SET (32)	12.00	5.50	1.50
COMMON CARD (1-32)	.25	.11	.03
☐ 1 Don August	.25	.11	.03
☐ 2 James Austin	.25	.11	.03
☐ 3 Dante Bichette	2.50	1.10	.30
☐ 4 Chris Bosio	.50	.23	.06
☐ 5 Kevin D. Brown	.25	.11	.03
☐ 6 Chuck Crim	.25	.11	.03
☐ 7 Rick Dempsey	.50	.23	.06
☐ 8 Jim Gantner	1.00	.45	.12
☐ 9 Darryl Hamilton	.75	.35	.09
☐ 10 Teddy Higuera	.25	.11	.03
☐ 11 Darren Holmes	.25	.11	.03
☐ 12 Jim Hunter	.25	.11	.03
☐ 13 Mark Knudson	.25	.11	.03
☐ 14 Mark Lee	.25	.11	.03
☐ 15 Julio Machado	.25	.11	.03
☐ 16 Candy Maldonado	.25	.11	.03
☐ 17 Paul Molitor	5.00	2.20	.60
☐ 18 Jaime Navarro	.75	.35	.09
☐ 19 Edwin Nunez	.25	.11	.03
☐ 20 Dan Plesac	.50	.23	.06
☐ 21 Willie Randolph	.50	.23	.06
☐ 22 Ron Robinson	.25	.11	.03
☐ 23 Gary Sheffield	2.50	1.10	.30
☐ 24 Bill Spiers	.25	.11	.03
☐ 25 Franklin Stubbs	.25	.11	.03
☐ 26 B.J. Surhoff	1.50	.70	.19
☐ 27 Dale Sveum	.25	.11	.03
☐ 28 Tom Trebelhorn MG	.25	.11	.03
☐ 29 Greg Vaughn	1.50	.70	.19
☐ 30 Bill Wegman	.25	.11	.03
☐ 31 Robin Yount	4.00	1.80	.50
☐ 32 Coaches Card Don Baylor Fred Stanley Duffy Dyer Larry Haney Andy Etchebarren Ray Burris	.50	.23	.06

1991 Brewers Police

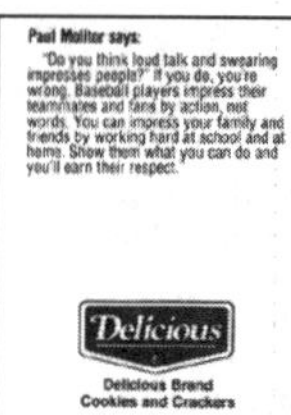

This 30-card standard-size set was sponsored by the Waukesha Police Department, Waukesha Sportscards, and Delicious Brand Cookies and Crackers. These sponsors are mentioned at the bottom of both sides of the card. The fronts feature mostly color action player photos with light gray borders. The team logo is superimposed at the upper right corner. The backs have black print on a white background and feature public service tips by the players.

	MINT	NRMT	EXC
COMPLETE SET (30)	7.50	3.40	.95
COMMON CARD (1-30)	.25	.11	.03
☐ 1 Don August	.25	.11	.03
☐ 2 Dante Bichette	2.00	.90	.25
☐ 3 Chris Bosio	.50	.23	.06
☐ 4 Greg Brock	.25	.11	.03
☐ 5 Kevin D. Brown	.25	.11	.03
☐ 6 Chuck Crim	.25	.11	.03
☐ 7 Rick Dempsey	.50	.23	.06
☐ 8 Jim Gantner	.75	.35	.09
☐ 9 Darryl Hamilton	.75	.35	.09
☐ 10 Teddy Higuera	.25	.11	.03
☐ 11 Mark Lee	.25	.11	.03
☐ 12 Mark Knudson	.25	.11	.03
☐ 13 Julio Machado	.25	.11	.03
☐ 14 Candy Maldonado	.25	.11	.03
☐ 15 Paul Molitor	2.50	1.10	.30
☐ 16 Jaime Navarro	.75	.35	.09
☐ 17 Edwin Nunez	.25	.11	.03
☐ 18 Dan Plesac	.50	.23	.06
☐ 19 Willie Randolph	.50	.23	.06
☐ 20 Ron Robinson	.25	.11	.03
☐ 20 Gary Sheffield	2.00	.90	.25
☐ 21 Bill Spiers	.25	.11	.03
☐ 22 Franklin Stubbs	.25	.11	.03
☐ 23 B.J. Surhoff	1.25	.55	.16
☐ 24 Dale Sveum	.25	.11	.03
☐ 25 Tom Trebelhorn MG	.25	.11	.03
☐ 26 Greg Vaughn	1.25	.55	.16
☐ 27 Bill Wegman	.25	.11	.03
☐ 28 Robin Yount	1.50	.70	.19
☐ NNO Coaches Card Don Baylor Ray Burris Duffy Dyer Andy Etchebarren Larry Haney Fred Stanley	.50	.23	.06

1992 Brewers Carlson Travel

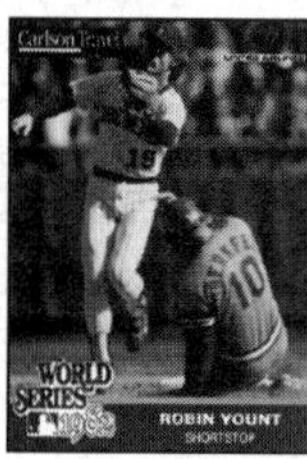

This 31-card standard-size set was sponsored by Carlson Travel in conjunction with United Airlines and TV Channel 6 (WITI in Milwaukee). It was issued to commemorate the 1982 Milwaukee Brewers team who played in the World Series. The set included a travel coupon entitling the holder to 50.00 off per couple on the next cruise vacation. The fronts display color action player photos, with sponsor logos superimposed at the top corners. At the bottom, the player's name and position appear in a blue stripe, which intersects a "World Series 1982" logo in the lower left corner. In blue print on a white background, the backs carry season summary and (batting or pitching) statistics. The cards are unnumbered and checklisted below in alphabetical order.

	MINT	NRMT	EXC
COMPLETE SET (31)	12.50	5.50	1.55
COMMON CARD (1-31)	.25	.11	.03
□ 1 Jerry Augustine	.25	.11	.03
□ 2 Dwight Bernard	.25	.11	.03
□ 3 Mark Brouhard	.25	.11	.03
□ 4 Mike Caldwell	.50	.23	.06
□ 5 Cecil Cooper	.75	.35	.09
□ 6 Marshall Edwards	.25	.11	.03
□ 7 Rollie Fingers	2.00	.90	.25
□ 8 Jim Gantner	.75	.35	.09
□ 9 Moose Haas	.25	.11	.03
□ 10 Roy Howell	.25	.11	.03
□ 11 Harvey Kuenn MG	.50	.23	.06
□ 12 Pete Ladd	.25	.11	.03
□ 13 Bob McClure	.25	.11	.03
□ 14 Doc Medich	.25	.11	.03
□ 15 Paul Molitor	4.00	1.80	.50
□ 16 Don Money	.50	.23	.06
□ 17 Charlie Moore	.25	.11	.03
□ 18 Ben Oglivie	.75	.35	.09
□ 19 Ed Romero	.25	.11	.03
□ 20 Ted Simmons	1.25	.55	.16
□ 21 Jim Slaton	.25	.11	.03
□ 22 Don Sutton	2.00	.90	.25
□ 23 Gorman Thomas	.75	.35	.09
□ 24 Pete Vuckovich	.50	.23	.06
□ 25 Ned Yost	.25	.11	.03
□ 26 Robin Yount	3.00	1.35	.35
□ xx Bernie Brewer (Team Mascot)	.25	.11	.03
□ xx Coaches: Larry Haney, Ron Hansen, Harry Warner, Cal McLish, Pat Dobson	.25	.11	.03
□ xx Post Season Rally	.25	.11	.03
□ xx Team Photo	.50	.23	.06
□ xx Carlson Travel Coupon	.25	.11	.03

1992 Brewers Police

For the second consecutive year, this 30-card standard-size set was sponsored by the Waukesha Police Department, Waukesha Sports Cards, and Delicious Brand Cookies and Crackers. The obverse features a color action photo on a bright yellow card face. The team name and year appear in the border on the top, while the team logo overlaps the photo and border in the upper right corner. The player's name and position are below the picture. The sponsors are mentioned at the bottom of both sides of the card. The backs have black print on a white background and feature public service tips from the players. The cards are unnumbered and checklisted below in alphabetical order.

	MINT	NRMT	EXC
COMPLETE SET (30)	7.50	3.40	.95
COMMON CARD (1-30)	.25	.11	.03
□ 1 Andy Allanson	.25	.11	.03
□ 2 James Austin	.25	.11	.03
□ 3 Dante Bichette	1.25	.55	.16
□ 4 Ricky Bones	.25	.11	.03
□ 5 Chris Bosio	.50	.23	.06
□ 6 Mike Fetters	.25	.11	.03
□ 7 Scott Fletcher	.25	.11	.03
□ 8 Jim Gantner	.75	.35	.09
□ 9 Phil Garner MG	.50	.23	.06
□ 10 Darryl Hamilton	.50	.23	.06
□ 11 Doug Henry	.25	.11	.03
□ 12 Teddy Higuera	.25	.11	.03
□ 13 Pat Listach	.50	.23	.06
□ 14 Tim McIntosh	.25	.11	.03
□ 15 Paul Molitor	2.50	1.10	.30
□ 16 Jaime Navarro	.75	.35	.09
□ 17 Edwin Nunez	.25	.11	.03
□ 18 Jesse Orosco	.25	.11	.03
□ 19 Dan Plesac	.50	.23	.06
□ 20 Ron Robinson	.25	.11	.03
□ 21 Bruce Ruffin	.25	.11	.03
□ 22 Kevin Seitzer	.50	.23	.06
□ 23 Bill Spiers	.25	.11	.03
□ 24 Franklin Stubbs	.25	.11	.03
□ 25 William Suero	.25	.11	.03
□ 26 B.J. Surhoff	1.00	.45	.12
□ 27 Greg Vaughn	1.00	.45	.12
□ 28 Bill Wegman	.25	.11	.03
□ 29 Robin Yount	1.50	.70	.19
□ 30 Coaches Card: Mike Easler, Bill Castro, Don Rowe, Duffy Dyer, Tim Foli	.25	.11	.03

1992 Brewers Sentry Yount

Sponsored by Sentry Foods, this four-card standard-size card captures four moments in the career of Robin Yount, who reached 3,000 career hits during the 1992 season. On a purple marbleized card face, the fronts display color action player photos framed by gold foil borders. A baseball glove icon and the player's name appear in the bottom border. The backs carry text describing Yount's hitting achievement portrayed on the card. The sponsor logo at the bottom rounds out the back. The cards are unnumbered and checklisted below in chronological order.

	MINT	NRMT	EXC
COMPLETE SET (4)	15.00	6.75	1.85
COMMON CARD (1-4)	4.00	1.80	.50
□ 1 Robin Yount First Hit (4/12/74)	4.00	1.80	.50
□ 2 Robin Yount 1,000 Hit (8/16/80)	4.00	1.80	.50
□ 3 Robin Yount 2,000 Hit (9/6/86)	4.00	1.80	.50
□ 4 Robin Yount 3,000 Hit (9/9/92)	4.00	1.80	.50

1992 Brewers U.S. Oil

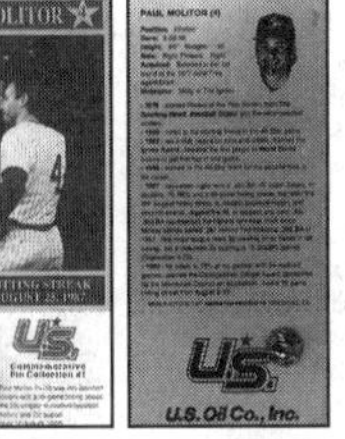

Sponsored by U.S. Oil Co. Inc., this four-card set consists of 2 3/4" by 4 1/4" cards and commemorative pins. The pins are attached to an extension of the card that is perforated for removal. With this section attached, the cards measure 2 3/4" by 5 5/8" inches. The cards feature color action shots with bright yellow borders. The player's name appears in a bright blue stripe across the top. The event being commemorated is printed on a bright blue stripe across the bottom. The pins show a baseball player against a yellow home plate design. Blue banners across the top contain the event, and a blue bar at the bottom contains the player's name. The pin attached to the Milwaukee County Stadium card shows a bat, ball, and glove design, and has the words "American League Champions" at the top. The cards are unnumbered and checklisted below in alphabetical order.

	MINT	NRMT	EXC
COMPLETE SET (4)	6.00	2.70	.75
COMMON CARD (1-4)	1.00	.45	.12
□ 1 Milwaukee County Stadium - 1982	1.00	.45	.12
□ 2 Paul Molitor	3.00	1.35	.35
□ 3 Juan Nieves	1.50	.70	.19
□ 4 Robin Yount	2.00	.90	.25

1993 Brewers Police

This 30-card standard-size set was sponsored by the Waukesha Police Department, Waukesha Sportscards, and Cher-Make. The fronts display a color action photo on a blue background and are edged in blue. The player's name and position appear in white lettering at the top with "93 Brewers" and the team logo printed in yellow along the left edge. The sponsors are listed at the bottom of the card. The backs have black print on a white background and feature public service tips from the players. The Cher-Make logo is

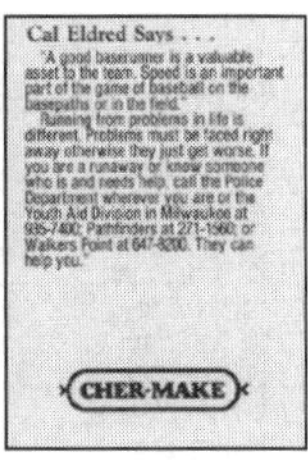

carried on the bottom. The cards are unnumbered and checklisted below in alphabetical order.

	MINT	NRMT	EXC
COMPLETE SET (30)	8.00	3.60	1.00
COMMON CARD (1-29)	.25	.11	.03
□ 1 James Austin	.25	.11	.03
□ 2 Ricky Bones	.25	.11	.03
□ 3 Tom Brunansky	.50	.23	.06
□ 4 Alex Diaz	.25	.11	.03
□ 5 Bill Doran	.25	.11	.03
□ 6 Cal Eldred	.75	.35	.09
□ 7 Mike Fetters	.25	.11	.03
□ 8 Phil Garner MG	.50	.23	.06
□ 9 Darryl Hamilton	.50	.23	.06
□ 10 Doug Henry	.25	.11	.03
□ 11 Ted Higuera	.25	.11	.03
□ 12 John Jaha	.75	.35	.09
□ 13 Mark Kiefer	.25	.11	.03
□ 14 Joe Kmak	.25	.11	.03
□ 15 Pat Listach	.25	.11	.03
□ 16 Graeme Lloyd	.25	.11	.03
□ 17 Tim McIntosh	.25	.11	.03
□ 18 Jaime Navarro	.75	.35	.09
□ 19 Dave Nilsson	1.00	.45	.12
□ 20 Jesse Orosco	.25	.11	.03
□ 21 Kevin Reimer	.25	.11	.03
□ 22 Bill Spiers	.25	.11	.03
□ 23 William Suero	.25	.11	.03
□ 24 B.J. Surhoff	1.00	.45	.12
□ 25 Dickie Thon	.25	.11	.03
□ 26 Greg Vaughn	1.00	.45	.12
□ 27 Bill Wegman	.25	.11	.03
□ 28 Robin Yount	2.00	.90	.25
□ 29 Robin Yount Memorable Moment	.75	.35	.09
□ NNO Title Card	.25	.11	.03

1993 Brewers Sentry

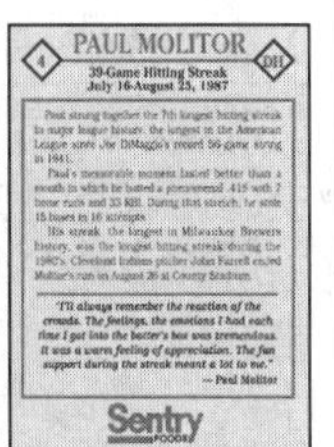

Subtitled "Memorable Moments, this four-card standard-size set was sponsored by Sentry Foods and features color player photos on its fronts. The pictures are edged with dark blue lines and so are the cards. In the light blue area at the top between these darker lines appear the set subtitle and the Brewers logo. Near the bottom of the photo the player's exploit and its date are printed in gold foil. The year of issue appears at the bottom in a gold-foil diamond set off by a gold-foil stripe on either side. The white back carries the player's name, position, uniform number, exploit, and date at the top. The player's career highlights and a quote appear beneath within a red-lined rectangle. The Sentry logo at the bottom rounds out the back. The cards are unnumbered and checklisted below in alphabetical order.

	MINT	NRMT	EXC
COMPLETE SET (4)	8.00	3.60	1.00
COMMON CARD (1-4)	1.00	.45	.12
□ 1 Paul Molitor	4.00	1.80	.50
□ 2 Juan Nieves	1.00	.45	.12
□ 3 Dale Sveum	1.00	.45	.12
□ 4 Robin Yount	3.00	1.35	.35

1994 Brewers Miller Brewing

Produced in perforated booklets, these Brewers cards were supposed to be issued in four sets to fans attending four different Brewers games at Milwaukee County Stadium. Set 1 (1-94) was issued at the April 24 game vs. Kansas City; set 2 (95-188) was issued at the June 26 game vs. Boston. Sets 3 (189-282) and 4 (283-376) were to be issued at later games (August 21 vs. Oakland; September 18 vs. Detroit), but the intervention of the baseball strike postponed their release. All four sets combined would include every player in the Brewers' 25-year history. The perforated booklets measure approximately 13" by 7" and each contains 94 cards; the individual cards measure the standard size. The gold-bordered cards feature on

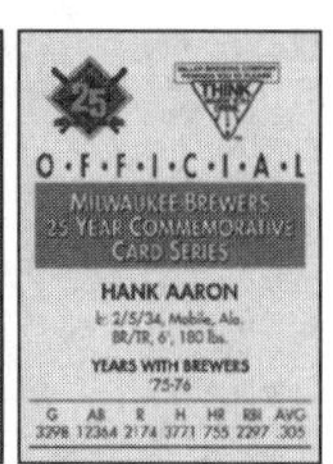

their fronts black-and-white player head shots. The player's name appears in black lettering within a white bar at the bottom. The white back carries the player's name, biography, years with the Brewers, and statistics therefrom. The cards are unnumbered and checklisted below in alphabetical order within each set. The final two series were released early in 1995.

	MINT	NRMT	EXC
COMPLETE SET (376)	40.00	18.00	5.00
COMMON CARD (1-376)	.10	.05	.01
□ 1 Hank Aaron	5.00	2.20	.60
□ 2 Jim Adduci	.10	.05	.01
□ 3 Jay Aldrich	.10	.05	.01
□ 4 Andy Allanson	.10	.05	.01
□ 5 Dave Baldwin	.10	.05	.01
□ 6 Sal Bando	.40	.18	.05
□ 7 Len Barker	.10	.05	.01
□ 8 Kevin Bass	.10	.05	.01
□ 9 Ken Berry	.10	.05	.01
□ 10 George Canale	.10	.05	.01
□ 11 Tom Candiotti	.30	.14	.04
□ 12 Mike Capel	.10	.05	.01
□ 13 Bobby Darwin	.10	.05	.01
□ 14 Danny Darwin	.20	.09	.03
□ 15 Brock Davis	.10	.05	.01
□ 16 Dick Davis	.10	.05	.01
□ 17 Jamie Easterly	.10	.05	.01
□ 18 Tom Edens	.10	.05	.01
□ 19 Marshall Edwards	.10	.05	.01
□ 20 Cal Eldred	.40	.18	.05
□ 21 Rob Ellis	.10	.05	.01
□ 22 Ed Farmer	.10	.05	.01
□ 23 Mike Felder	.10	.05	.01
□ 24 John Felske	.10	.05	.01
□ 25 Mike Ferraro	.10	.05	.01
□ 26 Mike Fetters	.40	.18	.05
□ 27 Danny Frisella	.10	.05	.01
□ 28 Bob Galasso	.10	.05	.01
□ 29 Jim Gantner	.40	.18	.05
□ 30 Pedro Garcia	.10	.05	.01
□ 31 Rob Gardner	.10	.05	.01
□ 32 John Gelnar	.10	.05	.01
□ 33 Moose Haas	.20	.09	.03
□ 34 Darryl Hamilton	.30	.14	.04
□ 35 Larry Haney	.10	.05	.01
□ 36 Jim Hannan	.10	.05	.01
□ 37 Bob Hansen	.10	.05	.01
□ 38 Michael Ignasiak	.10	.05	.01
□ 39 John Jaha	.20	.09	.03
□ 40 Dion James	.10	.05	.01
□ 41 Deron Johnson	.20	.09	.03
□ 42 John Henry Johnson	.10	.05	.01
□ 43 Tim Johnson	.10	.05	.01
□ 44 Rickey Keeton	.10	.05	.01
□ 45 John Kennedy	.10	.05	.01
□ 46 Jim Kern	.10	.05	.01
□ 47 Pete Ladd	.10	.05	.01
□ 48 Joe Lahoud	.10	.05	.01
□ 49 Tom Lampkin	.10	.05	.01
□ 50 Dave LaPoint	.10	.05	.01
□ 51 George Lauzerique	.10	.05	.01
□ 52 Julio Machado	.10	.05	.01
□ 53 Alex Madrid	.10	.05	.01
□ 54 Candy Maldonado	.10	.05	.01
□ 55 Carlos Maldonado	.10	.05	.01
□ 56 Rick Manning	.10	.05	.01
□ 57 Jaime Navarro	.40	.18	.05
□ 58 Ray Newman	.10	.05	.01
□ 59 Juan Nieves	.10	.05	.01
□ 60 Dave Nilsson	.40	.18	.05
□ 61 Charlie O'Brien	.10	.05	.01
□ 62 Syd O'Brien	.10	.05	.01
□ 63 John O'Donoghue	.10	.05	.01
□ 64 Jim Paciorek	.10	.05	.01
□ 65 Dave Parker	.75	.35	.09
□ 66 Bill Parsons	.10	.05	.01
□ 67 Marty Pattin	.10	.05	.01
□ 68 Jamie Quirk	.10	.05	.01
□ 69 Willie Randolph	.20	.09	.03
□ 70 Paul Ratliff	.10	.05	.01
□ 71 Lance Rautzhan	.10	.05	.01
□ 72 Randy Ready	.10	.05	.01
□ 73 Ray Sadecki	.10	.05	.01
□ 74 Lenn Sakata	.10	.05	.01
□ 75 Ken Sanders	.10	.05	.01
□ 76 Ted Savage	.10	.05	.01
□ 77 Dick Schofield	.10	.05	.01
□ 78 Jim Tatum	.10	.05	.01
□ 79 Chuck Taylor	.10	.05	.01
□ 80 Tom Tellmann	.10	.05	.01
□ 81 Frank Tepedino	.10	.05	.01

☐ 82 Sandy Valdespino	.10	.05	.01
☐ 83 Jose Valentin	.40	.18	.05
☐ 84 Greg Vaughn	.75	.35	.09
☐ 85 Carlos Velazquez	.10	.05	.01
☐ 86 Rick Waits	.10	.05	.01
☐ 87 Danny Walton	.10	.05	.01
☐ 88 Floyd Weaver	.10	.05	.01
☐ 89 Bill Wegman	.10	.05	.01
☐ 90 Floyd Wicker	.10	.05	.01
☐ 91 Al Yates	.10	.05	.01
☐ 92 Ned Yost	.10	.05	.01
☐ 93 Mike Young	.10	.05	.01
☐ 94 Robin Yount	3.00	1.35	.35
☐ 95 Hank Allen	.10	.05	.01
☐ 96 Felipe Alou	.40	.18	.05
☐ 97 Max Alvis	.10	.05	.01
☐ 98 Larry Anderson	.10	.05	.01
☐ 99 Rick Auerbach	.10	.05	.01
☐ 100 Don August	.10	.05	.01
☐ 101 Billy Bates	.10	.05	.01
☐ 102 Gary Beare	.10	.05	.01
☐ 103 Larry Bearnarth	.10	.05	.01
☐ 104 Andy Beene	.10	.05	.01
☐ 105 Jerry Bell	.10	.05	.01
☐ 106 Juan Bell	.10	.05	.01
☐ 107 Dwight Bernard	.10	.05	.01
☐ 108 Bernie Carbo	.10	.05	.01
☐ 109 Jose Cardenal	.20	.09	.03
☐ 110 Matias Carrillo	.10	.05	.01
☐ 111 Juan Castillo	.10	.05	.01
☐ 112 Bill Castro	.10	.05	.01
☐ 113 Rick Cerone	.10	.05	.01
☐ 114 Rob Deer	.20	.09	.03
☐ 115 Rick Dempsey	.20	.09	.03
☐ 116 Alex Diaz	.10	.05	.01
☐ 117 Dick Ellsworth	.10	.05	.01
☐ 118 Narciso Elvira	.10	.05	.01
☐ 119 Tom Filer	.10	.05	.01
☐ 120 Rollie Fingers	1.25	.55	.16
☐ 121 Scott Fletcher	.10	.05	.01
☐ 122 John Flinn	.10	.05	.01
☐ 123 Rich Folkers	.10	.05	.01
☐ 124 Tony Fossas	.10	.05	.01
☐ 125 Chris George	.10	.05	.01
☐ 126 Bob L. Gibson	.10	.05	.01
☐ 127 Gus Gil	.10	.05	.01
☐ 128 Tommy Harper	.20	.09	.03
☐ 129 Vic Harris	.10	.05	.01
☐ 130 Paul Hartzell	.10	.05	.01
☐ 131 Tom Hausman	.10	.05	.01
☐ 132 Neal Heaton	.10	.05	.01
☐ 133 Mike Hegan	.10	.05	.01
☐ 134 Jack Heidemann	.10	.05	.01
☐ 135 Doug Jones	.30	.14	.04
☐ 136 Mark Kiefer	.10	.05	.01
☐ 137 Steve Kiefer	.10	.05	.01
☐ 138 Ed Kirkpatrick	.10	.05	.01
☐ 139 Joe Kmak	.10	.05	.01
☐ 140 Mark Knudson	.10	.05	.01
☐ 141 Kevin Kobel	.10	.05	.01
☐ 142 Pete Koegel	.10	.05	.01
☐ 143 Jack Lazorko	.10	.05	.01
☐ 144 Tim Leary	.10	.05	.01
☐ 145 Mark Lee	.10	.05	.01
☐ 146 Jeffrey Leonard	.10	.05	.01
☐ 147 Randy Lerch	.10	.05	.01
☐ 148 Brad Lesley	.10	.05	.01
☐ 149 Sixto Lezcano	.10	.05	.01
☐ 150 Josias Manzanillo	.10	.05	.01
☐ 151 Buck Martinez	.20	.09	.03
☐ 152 Tom Matchick	.10	.05	.01
☐ 153 Dave May	.10	.05	.01
☐ 154 Matt Maysey	.10	.05	.01
☐ 155 Bob McClure	.10	.05	.01
☐ 156 Tim McIntosh	.10	.05	.01
☐ 157 Tim Nordbrook	.10	.05	.01
☐ 158 Ben Oglivie	.30	.14	.04
☐ 159 Troy O'Leary	.40	.18	.05
☐ 160 Jim Olander	.10	.05	.01
☐ 161 Roberto Pena	.10	.05	.01
☐ 162 Jeff Peterek	.10	.05	.01
☐ 163 Ray Peters	.10	.05	.01
☐ 164 Rob Picciolo	.10	.05	.01
☐ 165 Dan Plesac	.20	.09	.03
☐ 166 John Poff	.10	.05	.01
☐ 167 Gus Polidor	.10	.05	.01
☐ 168 Kevin Reimer	.10	.05	.01
☐ 169 Andy Replogle	.10	.05	.01
☐ 170 Jerry Reuss	.20	.09	.03
☐ 171 Archie Reynolds	.10	.05	.01
☐ 172 Bob Reynolds	.10	.05	.01
☐ 173 Ken Reynolds	.10	.05	.01
☐ 174 Tommie Reynolds	.10	.05	.01
☐ 175 Ernest Riles	.10	.05	.01
☐ 176 Bill Schroeder	.10	.05	.01
☐ 177 George Scott	.20	.09	.03
☐ 178 Ray Searage	.10	.05	.01
☐ 179 Bob Sebra	.10	.05	.01
☐ 180 Kevin Seitzer	.30	.14	.04
☐ 181 Dick Selma	.10	.05	.01
☐ 182 Bill Sharp	.10	.05	.01
☐ 183 Ron Theobald	.10	.05	.01
☐ 184 Dan Thomas	.10	.05	.01
☐ 185 Gorman Thomas	.40	.18	.05
☐ 186 Randy Veres	.10	.05	.01
☐ 187 Bill Voss	.10	.05	.01
☐ 188 Jim Wohlford	.10	.05	.01
☐ 189 Jerry Augustine	.10	.05	.01
☐ 190 James Austin	.10	.05	.01
☐ 191 Rick Austin	.10	.05	.01
☐ 192 Kurt Bevacqua	.20	.09	.03
☐ 193 Tommy Bianco	.10	.05	.01
☐ 194 Dante Bichette	1.50	.70	.19
☐ 195 Mike Birkbeck	.10	.05	.01
☐ 196 Dan Boltano	.10	.05	.01
☐ 197 Bobby Bolin	.10	.05	.01
☐ 198 Mark Bomback	.10	.05	.01
☐ 199 Ricky Bones	.10	.05	.01
☐ 200 Chris Bosio	.30	.14	.04
☐ 201 Thad Bosley	.10	.05	.01
☐ 202 Steve Bowling	.10	.05	.01
☐ 203 Gene Brabender	.10	.05	.01
☐ 204 Glenn Braggs	.10	.05	.01
☐ 205 Mike Caldwell	.20	.09	.03
☐ 206 Bill Champion	.10	.05	.01
☐ 207 Mark Ciardi	.10	.05	.01
☐ 208 Bobby Clark	.10	.05	.01
☐ 209 Ron Clark	.10	.05	.01
☐ 210 Mark Clear	.10	.05	.01
☐ 211 Reggie Cleveland	.10	.05	.01
☐ 212 Bryan Clutterbuck	.10	.05	.01
☐ 213 Jaime Cocanower	.10	.05	.01
☐ 214 Jim Colborn	.10	.05	.01
☐ 215 Cecil Cooper	.50	.23	.06
☐ 216 Edgar Diaz	.10	.05	.01
☐ 217 Frank DiPino	.10	.05	.01
☐ 218 Dave Engle	.10	.05	.01
☐ 219 Ray Fosse	.10	.05	.01
☐ 220 Terry Francona	.20	.09	.03
☐ 221 Tito Francona	.10	.05	.01
☐ 222 La Vel Freeman	.10	.05	.01
☐ 223 Brian Giles	.10	.05	.01
☐ 224 Bob Helse	.10	.05	.01
☐ 225 Doug Henry	.10	.05	.01
☐ 226 Mike Hershberger	.10	.05	.01
☐ 227 Teddy Higuera	.20	.09	.03
☐ 228 Sam Hinds	.10	.05	.01
☐ 229 Fred Holdsworth	.10	.05	.01
☐ 230 Darren Holmes	.10	.05	.01
☐ 231 Paul Householder	.10	.05	.01
☐ 232 Odell Jones	.10	.05	.01
☐ 233 Brad Komminsk	.10	.05	.01
☐ 234 Andy Kosco	.10	.05	.01
☐ 235 Lew Krausse	.10	.05	.01
☐ 236 Ray Krawczyk	.10	.05	.01
☐ 237 Bill Krueger	.10	.05	.01
☐ 238 Ted Kubiak	.10	.05	.01
☐ 239 Jack Lind	.10	.05	.01
☐ 240 Frank Linzy	.10	.05	.01
☐ 241 Pat Listach	.20	.09	.03
☐ 242 Graeme Lloyd	.10	.05	.01
☐ 243 Bob Locker	.10	.05	.01
☐ 244 Skip Lockwood	.10	.05	.01
☐ 245 Ken McMullen	.10	.05	.01
☐ 246 Jerry McNertney	.10	.05	.01
☐ 247 Doc Medich	.10	.05	.01
☐ 248 Bob Meyer	.10	.05	.01
☐ 249 Joey Meyer	.10	.05	.01
☐ 250 Matt Mieske	.40	.18	.05
☐ 251 Roger Miller	.10	.05	.01
☐ 252 Paul Mirabella	.10	.05	.01
☐ 253 Angel Miranda	.10	.05	.01
☐ 254 Bobby Mitchell	.10	.05	.01
☐ 255 Paul Mitchell	.10	.05	.01
☐ 256 Paul Molitor	4.00	1.80	.50
☐ 257 Rafael Novoa	.10	.05	.01
☐ 258 Jesse Orosco	.10	.05	.01
☐ 259 Carlos Ponce	.10	.05	.01
☐ 260 Chuck Porter	.10	.05	.01
☐ 261 Darrell Porter	.20	.09	.03
☐ 262 Billy Jo Robidoux	.10	.05	.01
☐ 263 Ron Robinson	.10	.05	.01
☐ 264 Eduardo Rodriguez	.10	.05	.01
☐ 265 Ellie Rodriguez	.10	.05	.01
☐ 266 Rich Rollins	.10	.05	.01
☐ 267 Ed Romero	.10	.05	.01
☐ 268 Gary Sheffield	2.00	.90	.25
☐ 269 Bob Sheldon	.10	.05	.01
☐ 270 Chris Short	.10	.05	.01
☐ 271 Bob Skube	.10	.05	.01
☐ 272 Jim Slaton	.10	.05	.01
☐ 273 Bernie Smith	.10	.05	.01
☐ 274 Russ Snyder	.10	.05	.01
☐ 275 Lary Sorensen	.10	.05	.01
☐ 276 Bill Spiers	.10	.05	.01
☐ 277 Ed Sprague	.10	.05	.01
☐ 278 Dickie Thon	.10	.05	.01
☐ 279 Bill Travers	.10	.05	.01
☐ 280 Pete Vuckovich	.30	.14	.04
☐ 281 Clyde Wright	.10	.05	.01
☐ 282 Jeff Yurak	.10	.05	.01
☐ 283 Joe Azcue	.10	.05	.01
☐ 284 Mike Boddicker	.20	.09	.03
☐ 285 Ken Brett	.10	.05	.01
☐ 286 John Briggs	.10	.05	.01
☐ 287 Pete Broberg	.10	.05	.01
☐ 288 Greg Brock	.10	.05	.01
☐ 289 Jeff Bronkey	.10	.05	.01
☐ 290 Mark Brouhard	.10	.05	.01
☐ 291 Kevin Brown	.20	.09	.03
☐ 292 Ollie Brown	.10	.05	.01
☐ 293 Bruce Brubaker	.10	.05	.01
☐ 294 Tom Brunansky	.20	.09	.03
☐ 295 Steve Brye	.10	.05	.01
☐ 296 Bob Burda	.10	.05	.01
☐ 297 Ray Burris	.10	.05	.01
☐ 298 Jeff Cirillo	.40	.18	.05
☐ 299 Bobby Clark	.10	.05	.01
☐ 300 Bob Coluccio	.10	.05	.01
☐ 301 Wayne Comer	.10	.05	.01
☐ 302 Billy Conigliaro	.10	.05	.01
☐ 303 Cecil Cooper	.50	.23	.06
☐ 304 Barry Cort	.10	.05	.01
☐ 305 Chuck Crim	.10	.05	.01
☐ 306 LaFayette Currence	.10	.05	.01
☐ 307 Kiki Diaz	.10	.05	.01
☐ 308 Bill Doran	.10	.05	.01
☐ 309 Al Downing	.10	.05	.01
☐ 310 Tom Edens	.10	.05	.01
☐ 311 Andy Etchebarren	.10	.05	.01
☐ 312 Rollie Fingers	1.25	.55	.16
☐ 313 Jim Gantner	.40	.18	.05
☐ 314 Greg Goosen	.20	.09	.03
☐ 315 Brian Harper	.20	.09	.03
☐ 316 Larry Hisle	.10	.05	.01
☐ 317 Steve Hovley	.10	.05	.01
☐ 318 Wilbur Howard	.10	.05	.01
☐ 319 Roy Howell	.10	.05	.01
☐ 320 Bob Humphreys	.10	.05	.01
☐ 321 Jim Hunter	.10	.05	.01
☐ 322 Dave Huppert	.10	.05	.01
☐ 323 Von Joshua	.10	.05	.01
☐ 324 Art Kusnyer	.10	.05	.01
☐ 325 Doug Loman	.10	.05	.01
☐ 326 Jim Lonborg	.20	.09	.03
☐ 327 Marcelino Lopez	.10	.05	.01
☐ 328 Willie Lozado	.10	.05	.01
☐ 329 Miko Matheny	.10	.05	.01
☐ 330 Ken McMullen	.10	.05	.01
☐ 331 Jose Mercedes	.10	.05	.01
☐ 332 Paul Molitor	4.00	1.80	.50
☐ 333 Don Money (Head Shot)	.20	.09	.03
☐ 334 Don Money (Action Shot)	.20	.09	.03
☐ 335 Charlie Moore	.20	.09	.03
☐ 336 Donnie Moore	.10	.05	.01
☐ 337 John Morris	.10	.05	.01
☐ 338 Curt Motton	.10	.05	.01
☐ 339 Willie Mueller	.10	.05	.01
☐ 340 Tom Murphy	.10	.05	.01
☐ 341 Tony Muser	.10	.05	.01
☐ 342 Edwin Nunez	.10	.05	.01
☐ 343 Ben Oglivie	.30	.14	.04
☐ 344 Pat Osborn	.10	.05	.01
☐ 345 Dennis Powell	.10	.05	.01
☐ 346 Jody Reed	.20	.09	.03
☐ 347 Phil Roof	.10	.05	.01
☐ 348 Jimmy Rosario	.10	.05	.01
☐ 349 Bruce Ruffin	.10	.05	.01
☐ 350 Gary Ryerson	.10	.05	.01
☐ 351 Bob Scanlan	.10	.05	.01
☐ 352 Ted Simmons (Head Shot)	.75	.35	.09
☐ 353 Ted Simmons (Action Shot)	.75	.35	.09
☐ 354 Duane Singleton	.10	.05	.01
☐ 355 Steve Stanicek	.10	.05	.01
☐ 356 Fred Stanley	.10	.05	.01
☐ 357 Dave Stapleton	.10	.05	.01
☐ 358 Randy Stein	.10	.05	.01
☐ 359 Earl Stephenson	.10	.05	.01
☐ 360 Franklin Stubbs	.10	.05	.01
☐ 361 William Suero	.10	.05	.01
☐ 362 Jim Sundberg	.20	.09	.03
☐ 363 B.J. Surhoff	.75	.35	.09
☐ 364 Gary Sutherland	.10	.05	.01
☐ 365 Don Sutton	1.25	.55	.16
☐ 366 Dale Sveum	.10	.05	.01
☐ 367 Gorman Thomas	.40	.18	.05
☐ 368 Wayne Twitchell	.10	.05	.01
☐ 369 Dave Valle	.10	.05	.01
☐ 370 Greg Vaughn	.50	.23	.06
☐ 371 John Vukovich	.10	.05	.01
☐ 372 Danny Walton	.10	.05	.01
☐ 373 Turner Ward	.10	.05	.01
☐ 374 Rick Wrona	.10	.05	.01
☐ 375 Jim Wynn	.20	.09	.03
☐ 376 Robin Yount	3.00	1.35	.35

1994 Brewers Police

Sponsored by Pick 'n Save and Snickers Ice Cream Bars to celebrate the 25th Anniversary of the Brewers, this 30-card set features, on its fronts, posed color player photos with two-toned green borders. The player's name and uniform number are shown within a blue bar at the top. The Brewers 25th Anniversary logo appears at the lower right. The white and black backs carry the player's name, position, uniform number, and statistics. The Brewers' 25th Anniversary logo and the sponsors' logos at the bottom round out the card. Other than the players' uniform numbers, the cards are unnumbered and checklisted below in alphabetical order.

	MINT	NRMT	EXC
COMPLETE SET (30)	7.50	3.40	.95
COMMON CARD (1-30)	.25	.11	.03
☐ 1 Bernie Brewer Mascot	.25	.11	.03
☐ 2 Ricky Bones	.25	.11	.03
☐ 3 Jeff Bronkey	.25	.11	.03
☐ 4 Tom Brunansky	.25	.11	.03
☐ 5 Jeff D'Amico DP Kelly Wunsch DP	1.00	.45	.12
☐ 6 Cal Eldred	.75	.35	.09
☐ 7 Mike Fetters	.25	.11	.03
☐ 8 Phil Garner MG	.50	.23	.06
☐ 9 Darryl Hamilton	.50	.23	.06
☐ 10 Brian Harper	.25	.11	.03
☐ 11 Doug Henry	.25	.11	.03
☐ 12 Teddy Higuera	.25	.11	.03
☐ 13 Mike Ignasiak	.25	.11	.03
☐ 14 John Jaha	.50	.23	.06
☐ 15 Mark Kiefer	.25	.11	.03
☐ 16 Pat Listach	.25	.11	.03
☐ 17 Graeme Lloyd	.25	.11	.03
☐ 18 Matt Mieske	.50	.23	.06
☐ 19 Jaime Navarro	.25	.11	.03
☐ 20 Dave Nilsson	.50	.23	.06
☐ 21 Jesse Orosco	.25	.11	.03
☐ 22 Jody Reed	.25	.11	.03
☐ 23 Bob Scanlan	.25	.11	.03
☐ 24 Kevin Seitzer	.25	.11	.03
☐ 25 Bill Spiers	.25	.11	.03
☐ 26 B.J. Surhoff	.75	.35	.09
☐ 27 Jose Valentin	.25	.11	.03
☐ 28 Greg Vaughn	.75	.35	.09
☐ 29 Turner Ward	.25	.11	.03
☐ 30 Bill Wegman	.25	.11	.03

1994 Brewers Sentry

This eight-card set was issued to honor outstanding achievements by Milwaukee Brewer players. Though the set is sponsored by Sentry Foods, its logo does not appear on the cards. One card was given out each Tuesday night home game through August 30. The fronts feature color player photos inside a blue border with gold and green. A special Brewers' 25th Anniversary logo appears in the top left, while the player's name is printed on a navy bar beneath the picture. On a white background, the back presents the player's outstanding achievement. The cards are unnumbered and checklisted below in alphabetical order.

	MINT	NRMT	EXC
COMPLETE SET (8)	12.00	5.50	1.50
COMMON CARD (1-8)	1.00	.45	.12
☐ 1 Hank Aaron Final Home Run	4.00	1.80	.50
☐ 2 Rollie Fingers Cy Young/MVP Season	1.50	.70	.19
☐ 3 Pat Listach Rookie of the Year	1.00	.45	.12
☐ 4 Paul Molitor 39-game Hitting Streak	3.00	1.35	.35
☐ 5 Paul Molitor Robin Yount Jim Gantner	3.00	1.35	.35
☐ 6 Juan Nieves No-hitter	1.00	.45	.12
☐ 7 Don Sutton 3,000 Strikeout	1.50	.70	.19
☐ 8 Robin Yount 3,000 Hit	2.50	1.10	.30

1909 Briggs E97

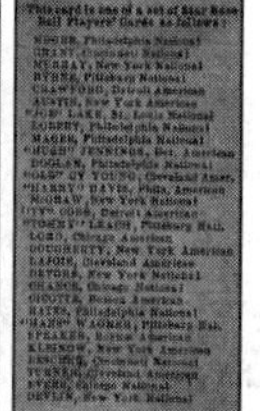

The cards in this 32-card set measure 1 1/2" by 2 3/4". The C.A. Briggs Company distributed this set in 1909, and it is one of the most highly prized of caramel issues. The cards come in two distinct varieties: one group in color with a brown print checklist on back; the other with identical player poses in black and white with blank backs. A comparison of team and name variations suggests that the black and white set pre-dates the color issue. The list below has been correctly alphabetized and hence does not exactly follow the checklist back order.

	EX-MT	VG-E	GOOD
COMPLETE SET (32)	7000.00	3200.00	900.00
COMMON CARD (1-32)	150.00	70.00	19.00
☐ 1 Jimmy Austin	150.00	70.00	19.00
☐ 2 Joe Birmingham	150.00	70.00	19.00

☐ 3 William J. Bradley	150.00	70.00	19.00
☐ 4 Kitty Bransfield	150.00	70.00	19.00
☐ 5 Howie Camnitz	150.00	70.00	19.00
☐ 6 Bill Carrigan	150.00	70.00	19.00
☐ 7 Harry Davis	150.00	70.00	19.00
☐ 8 Josh Devore	150.00	70.00	19.00
☐ 9 Mickey Doolan	150.00	70.00	19.00
☐ 10 Bull Durham	150.00	70.00	19.00
☐ 11 Jimmy Dygert	150.00	70.00	19.00
☐ 12 Topsy Hartsel	150.00	70.00	19.00
☐ 13 Charlie Hemphill	150.00	70.00	19.00
☐ 14 Bill Hinchman	150.00	70.00	19.00
☐ 15 Willie Keeler	500.00	220.00	60.00
☐ 16 Joseph J. Kelly	350.00	160.00	45.00
☐ 17 Red Kleinow	150.00	70.00	19.00
☐ 18 Rube Kroh	150.00	70.00	19.00
☐ 19 Amby McConnell	150.00	70.00	19.00
☐ 20 Matty McIntyre	150.00	70.00	19.00
☐ 21 Chief Meyers	175.00	80.00	22.00
☐ 22 Earl Moore	150.00	70.00	19.00
☐ 23 George Mullin	150.00	70.00	19.00
☐ 24 Red Murray	150.00	70.00	19.00
☐ 25 Simon Nichols (sic)	150.00	70.00	19.00
☐ 26 Claude Rossman	150.00	70.00	19.00
☐ 27 Admiral Schlei	150.00	70.00	19.00
☐ 28 Harry Steinfeldt	175.00	80.00	22.00
☐ 29A Billy Sullivan: Chicago	175.00	80.00	22.00
☐ 29B Billy Sullivan: Boston	1200.00	550.00	150.00
☐ 30A Cy Young: Boston	500.00	220.00	60.00
☐ 30B Cy Young: Cleveland	600.00	275.00	75.00

1953-54 Briggs

The cards in this 37-card set measure 2 1/4" by 3 1/2". The 1953-54 Briggs Hot Dog set of color cards contains 25 Senators and 12 known players from the Dodgers, Yankees and Giants. They were issued in two card panels in the Washington, D.C. area as part of the hot dog package itself. The cards are unnumbered and are printed on waxed cardboard, and the style of the Senator cards differs from that of the New York players. The latter appear in poses which also exist in the Dan Dee and Stahl Meyer card sets. The catalog designation is F154. In the checklist below the Washington players are numbered 1-25 alphabetically by name and the New York players are numbered 26-37 similarly.

	NRMT	VG-E	GOOD
COMPLETE SET (40)	9000.00	4000.00	1100.00
COMMON CARD (1-28)	150.00	70.00	19.00
COMMON CARD (29-40)	150.00	70.00	19.00
☐ 1 Jim Busby	150.00	70.00	19.00
☐ 2 Tommy Byrne	150.00	70.00	19.00
☐ 3 Gilbert Coan	150.00	70.00	19.00
☐ 4 Sonny Dixon	150.00	70.00	19.00
☐ 5 Ed Fitzgerald	150.00	70.00	19.00
☐ 6 Mickey Grasso	150.00	70.00	19.00
☐ 7 Mel Hoderlein	150.00	70.00	19.00
☐ 8 Jackie Jensen	200.00	90.00	25.00
☐ 9 Connie Marrero	150.00	70.00	19.00
☐ 10 Carmen Mauro	150.00	70.00	19.00
☐ 11 Walt Masterson	150.00	70.00	19.00
☐ 12 Mickey McDermott	150.00	70.00	19.00
☐ 13 Julio Moreno	150.00	70.00	19.00
☐ 14 Bob Oldis	150.00	70.00	19.00
☐ 15 Erwin Porterfield	150.00	70.00	19.00
☐ 16 Pete Runnels	175.00	80.00	22.00
☐ 17 Johnny Schmitz	150.00	70.00	19.00
☐ 18 Angel Scull	150.00	70.00	19.00
☐ 19 Spec Shea	150.00	70.00	19.00
☐ 20 Albert Sima	150.00	70.00	19.00
☐ 21 Chuck Stobbs	150.00	70.00	19.00
☐ 22 Wayne Terwilliger	150.00	70.00	19.00
☐ 23 Joe Tipton	150.00	70.00	19.00
☐ 24 Tom Umphlett	150.00	70.00	19.00
☐ 25 Mickey Vernon	175.00	80.00	22.00
☐ 26 Clyde Vollmer	150.00	70.00	19.00
☐ 27 Gene Werbil	150.00	70.00	19.00
☐ 28 Eddie Yost	150.00	70.00	19.00
☐ 29 Hank Bauer	200.00	90.00	25.00
☐ 30 Carl Erskine	200.00	90.00	25.00
☐ 31 Gil Hodges	300.00	135.00	38.00
☐ 32 Monte Irvin	300.00	135.00	38.00
☐ 33 Whitey Lockman	175.00	80.00	22.00
☐ 34 Mickey Mantle	2500.00	1100.00	300.00
☐ 35 Willie Mays	1250.00	550.00	160.00
☐ 36 Gil McDougald	200.00	90.00	25.00
☐ 37 Don Mueller	175.00	80.00	22.00
☐ 38 Don Newcombe	200.00	90.00	25.00
☐ 39 Phil Rizzuto	300.00	135.00	38.00
☐ 40 Duke Snider	500.00	220.00	60.00

1941 Browns W753

The cards in this 29-card set measure approximately 2 1/8" by 2 5/8". The 1941 W753 set features unnumbered cards of the St. Louis Browns. The cards are numbered below alphabetically by player's name. Similar to the W711-2 set, it was issued in a box with a reverse side resembling a mailing label. These sets were also available via mail-order. This set is valued at an extra $100 when still in its original mailing box.

	EX-MT	VG-E	GOOD
COMPLETE SET (30)	450.00	200.00	55.00
COMMON CARD (1-30)	15.00	6.75	1.85
☐ 1 Johnny Allen	18.00	8.00	2.20
☐ 2 Elden Auker	15.00	6.75	1.85
☐ 3 Donald L. Barnes OWN	15.00	6.75	1.85
☐ 4 Johnny Berardino	30.00	13.50	3.70
☐ 5 George Caster	15.00	6.75	1.85
☐ 6 Harland Clift	15.00	6.75	1.85
☐ 7 Roy J. Cullenbine	15.00	6.75	1.85
☐ 8 William O. DeWitt GM	15.00	6.75	1.85
☐ 9 Robert Estalella	15.00	6.75	1.85
☐ 10 Rick Ferrell	60.00	27.00	7.50
☐ 11 Dennis W. Galehouse	18.00	8.00	2.20
☐ 12 Joseph L. Grace	15.00	6.75	1.85
☐ 13 Frank Grube	15.00	6.75	1.85
☐ 14 Robert A. Harris	15.00	6.75	1.85
☐ 15 Donald Heffner	15.00	6.75	1.85
☐ 16 Fred Hofmann	15.00	6.75	1.85
☐ 17 Walter F. Judnich	15.00	6.75	1.85
☐ 18 Jack Kramer	15.00	6.75	1.85
☐ 19 Chester(Chet) Laabs	15.00	6.75	1.85
☐ 20 John Lucadello	15.00	6.75	1.85
☐ 21 George H. McQuinn	15.00	6.75	1.85
☐ 22 Robert Muncrief Jr.	15.00	6.75	1.85
☐ 23 John Niggeling	15.00	6.75	1.85
☐ 24 Fritz Ostermueller	15.00	6.75	1.85
☐ 25 James(Luke) Sewell MG	18.00	8.00	2.20
☐ 26 Alan C. Strange	15.00	6.75	1.85
☐ 27 Bob Swift	15.00	6.75	1.85
☐ 28 James(Zack) Taylor CO	15.00	6.75	1.85
☐ 29 Bill Trotter	15.00	6.75	1.85
☐ 30 Title Card (Order Coupon on back)	15.00	6.75	1.85

1996 Browns '44 Fritsch

This 36-card set of the 1944 American League Champion St. Louis Browns Baseball team with a suggested retail price of $10 features an artist's rendition of the player on the front. The backs carry player information, career statistics, and a small cartoon depicting one aspect of the player's career.

	MINT	NRMT	EXC
COMPLETE SET (36)	10.00	4.50	1.25
COMMON CARD (1-36)	.25	.11	.03
☐ 1 Team Card	.25	.11	.03
☐ 2 Don Gutteridge	.25	.11	.03
☐ 3 Milt Byrnes	.25	.11	.03
☐ 4 Al Hollingsworth	.25	.11	.03
☐ 5 Willis Hudlin	.25	.11	.03
☐ 6 Sid Jakucki	.25	.11	.03
☐ 7 Nelson Potter	.50	.23	.06
☐ 8 Len Schulte	.25	.11	.03
☐ 9 Vern Stephens	.75	.35	.09
☐ 10 Frank Demaree	.25	.11	.03
☐ 11 Al Zarilla	.25	.11	.03
☐ 12 Bob Muncrief	.25	.11	.03
☐ 13 Steve Sundra	.25	.11	.03
☐ 14 Jack Kramer	.25	.11	.03
☐ 15 Lefty West	.25	.11	.03
☐ 16 Denny Galehouse	.25	.11	.03
☐ 17 Luke Sewell MG	.50	.23	.06
☐ 18 Joe Schultz	.50	.23	.06
☐ 19 George McQuinn	.75	.35	.09
☐ 20 Ellis Clary	.25	.11	.03
☐ 21 Babe Martin	.25	.11	.03
☐ 22 Red Hayworth	.25	.11	.03
☐ 23 Frank Mancuso	.25	.11	.03
☐ 24 Tex Shirley	.25	.11	.03
☐ 25 Mike Chartak	.25	.11	.03
☐ 26 Mark Christman	.25	.11	.03
☐ 27 Tom Hafey	.25	.11	.03
☐ 28 Tom Turner	.25	.11	.03
☐ 29 Floyd Baker	.25	.11	.03
☐ 30 Mike Kreevich	.25	.11	.03
☐ 31 George Caster	.25	.11	.03
☐ 32 Gene Moore	.25	.11	.03
☐ 33 Chet Laabs	.25	.11	.03
☐ 34 Sam Zoldak	.25	.11	.03
☐ 35 Hal Epps	.25	.11	.03
☐ 36 Checklist	.25	.11	.03

1887 Buchner N284

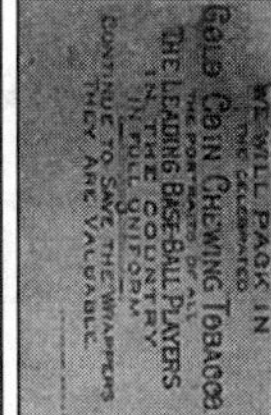

The baseball players found in this Buchner set are a part of a larger group of cards portraying policemen, jockeys and actors, all of which were issued with the tobacco brand "Gold Coin." The set is comprised of three major groupings or types. In the first type, nine players from eight teams, plus three Brooklyn players, are all portrayed in identical poses according to position. In the second type, St. Louis has 14 players depicted in poses which are not repeated. The last group contains 53 additional cards which vary according to pose, team change, spelling, etc. These third type cards are indicated in the checklist below by an asterisk. In all, there are 116 individuals portrayed on 142 cards. The existence of an additional player in the set, McClellan of Brooklyn, has never been verified and the card probably doesn't exist. The set was issued circa 1887. The cards are numbered below in alphabetical order within team with teams themselves listed in alphabetical order: Baltimore (1-4), Boston (5-13), Brooklyn (14-17), Chicago (18-26), Detroit (27-35), Indianapolis (36-47), LaCrosse (48-51), Milwaukee (52-55), New York Mets (56-63), New York (64-73), Philadelphia (74-83), Pittsburg (84-92), St. Louis (93-106), and Washington (107-117).

	EX-MT	VG-E	GOOD
COMPLETE SET (152)	17500.00	7900.00	2200.00
COMMON CARD	100.00	45.00	12.50
COMMON ST. LOUIS	150.00	70.00	19.00
COMMON CARD *	125.00	55.00	15.50
☐ 1 Tommy(Oyster) Burns: Baltimore *	125.00	55.00	15.50
☐ 2 Chris Fulmer: Baltimore *	125.00	55.00	15.50
☐ 3 Matt Kilroy: Baltimore *	125.00	55.00	15.50
☐ 4 Blondie Purcell: Baltimore *	125.00	55.00	15.50
☐ 5 John Burdock: Boston	100.00	45.00	12.50
☐ 6 Bill Daley: Boston	100.00	45.00	12.50
☐ 7 Joe Hornung: Boston	100.00	45.00	12.50
☐ 8 Dick Johnston: Boston	100.00	45.00	12.50
☐ 9A King Kelly: Boston (Right field)	250.00	110.00	31.00
☐ 9B King Kelly: Boston (Catcher) *	300.00	135.00	38.00
☐ 10A John Morrell: Boston (Both hands out-stretched face high)	100.00	45.00	12.50
☐ 10B John Morrell: Boston * (Hands clasped near chin)	125.00	55.00	15.50
☐ 11A Hoss Radbourn: Boston (Sic, Radbourne)	200.00	90.00	25.00
☐ 11B Hoss Radbourn: Boston * (Sic, Radbourne; hands together above waist)	250.00	110.00	31.00
☐ 12 Ezra Sutton: Boston	100.00	45.00	12.50
☐ 13 Sam Wise: Boston	100.00	45.00	12.50
☐ 14 Bill McClellan: Brooklyn (Never confirmed)			
☐ 15 Jimmy Peoples: Brooklyn	100.00	45.00	12.50
☐ 16 Bill Phillips: Brooklyn	100.00	45.00	12.50
☐ 17 Henry Porter: Brooklyn	100.00	45.00	12.50
☐ 18A Adrian Anson: Chicago Both hands out-stretched face high)	400.00	180.00	50.00
☐ 18B Adrian Anson: Chicago * (Left hand on hip right hand down	600.00	275.00	75.00
☐ 19 Tom Burns: Chicago	100.00	45.00	12.50
☐ 20A John Clarkson: Chicago	200.00	90.00	25.00
☐ 20B John Clarkson: Chicago * (Right arm extended, left arm near side)	250.00	110.00	31.00
☐ 21 Silver Flint: Chicago	100.00	45.00	12.50
☐ 22 Fred Pfeffer: Chicago	100.00	45.00	12.50
☐ 23 Jimmy Ryan: Chicago	125.00	55.00	15.50
☐ 24 Billy Sullivan: Chicago	125.00	55.00	15.50
☐ 25 Billy Sunday: Chicago	250.00	110.00	31.00
☐ 26A Ned Williamson: Chicago (Shortstop)	100.00	45.00	12.50
☐ 26B Ned Williamson: Chicago (Second base) *	125.00	55.00	15.50
☐ 27 Charlie Bennett: Detroit	100.00	45.00	12.50
☐ 28A Dan Brouthers: Detroit (Fielding)	200.00	90.00	25.00
☐ 28B Dan Brouthers: Detroit * (Batting)	250.00	110.00	31.00
☐ 29 Fred Dunlap: Detroit	100.00	45.00	12.50
☐ 30 Charlie Getzien: Detroit	100.00	45.00	12.50
☐ 31 Ned Hanlon: Detroit	125.00	55.00	15.50
☐ 32 Jim Manning: Detoit	100.00	45.00	12.50
☐ 33A Hardy Richardson: Detroit (Hands together in front of chest)	100.00	45.00	12.50
☐ 33B Hardy Richardson: Detroit * (Right hand holding ball above head)	125.00	55.00	15.50
☐ 34A Sam Thompson: Detroit (Looking up with hands at waist)	200.00	90.00	25.00
☐ 34B Sam Thompson: Detroit * (Hands chest high)	250.00	110.00	31.00
☐ 35 Deacon White: Detroit	125.00	55.00	15.50
☐ 36 Tug Arundel: Indianapolis	100.00	45.00	12.50
☐ 37 Charley Bassett: Indianapolis	100.00	45.00	12.50
☐ 38 Henry Boyle: Indianapolis *	125.00	55.00	15.50
☐ 39 John Cahill: Indianapolis *	125.00	55.00	15.50
☐ 40A Jerry Denny: Indianapolis (Hands on knees, legs bent)	100.00	45.00	12.50
☐ 40B Jerry Denny: Indianapolis * (Hands on knees, legs not bent)	125.00	55.00	15.50
☐ 41A Jack Glasscock: Indianapolis (Crouching, catching a grounder)	125.00	55.00	15.50
☐ 41B Jack Glasscock: Indianapolis * (Hands on knees)	150.00	70.00	19.00
☐ 42 John Healy: Indianapolis	100.00	45.00	12.50
☐ 43 George Meyers: Indianapolis *	125.00	55.00	15.50
☐ 44 Jack McGeachy: Indianapolis	100.00	45.00	12.50
☐ 45 Mark Polhemus: Indianapolis	100.00	45.00	12.50
☐ 46A Emmett Seery: Indianapolis (Hands together in front of chest)	100.00	45.00	12.50
☐ 46B Emmett Seery: Indianapolis * (Hands outstretched head high)	125.00	55.00	15.50
☐ 47 Shomberg: Indianapolis	100.00	45.00	12.50
☐ 48 Corbett: LaCrosse *	125.00	55.00	15.50
☐ 49 Crowley: LaCrosse *	125.00	55.00	15.50
☐ 50 Kennedy: LaCrosse *	125.00	55.00	15.50
☐ 51 Rooks: LaCrosse *	125.00	55.00	15.50
☐ 52 Forster: Milwaukee *	125.00	55.00	15.50
☐ 53 Hart: Milwaukee *	125.00	55.00	15.50
☐ 54 Morrissy: Milwaukee *	125.00	55.00	15.50
☐ 55 Strauss: Milwaukee *	125.00	55.00	15.50
☐ 56 Ed Cushmann: NY Mets *	125.00	55.00	15.50
☐ 57 Jim Donohue: NY Mets *	125.00	55.00	15.50
☐ 58 Dude Esterbrooke (Sic): NY Mets *	125.00	55.00	15.50
☐ 59 Joe Gerhardt: NY Mets *	125.00	55.00	15.50
☐ 60 Frank Hankinson: NY Mets *	125.00	55.00	15.50
☐ 61 Jack Nelson:	125.00	55.00	15.50

NY Mets *			
☐ 62 Dave Orr: NY Mets *	125.00	55.00	15.50
☐ 63 James Rosemann: NY Mets *	125.00	55.00	15.50
☐ 64A Roger Connor: New York (Both hands out-stretched face high)	200.00	90.00	25.00
☐ 64B Roger Connor: New York * (Hands outstretched, palms up)	250.00	110.00	31.00
☐ 65 Pat Deasley: New York *	125.00	55.00	15.50
☐ 66A Mike Dorgan: New York: Fielding	100.00	45.00	12.50
☐ 66B Mike Dorgan: New York: Batting *	125.00	55.00	15.50
☐ 67A Buck Ewing: New York (Ball in left hand, right arm out shoulder high)	200.00	90.00	25.00
☐ 67B Buck Ewing: New York * Appears ready to clap	250.00	110.00	31.00
☐ 68A Pete Gillespie: New York: Fielding	100.00	45.00	12.50
☐ 68B Pete Gillespie: New York: Batting *	125.00	55.00	15.50
☐ 69 George Gore: New York	100.00	45.00	12.50
☐ 70A Tim Keefe: New York	200.00	90.00	25.00
☐ 70B Tim Keefe: New York * Ball just released from right hand	250.00	110.00	31.00
☐ 71A Jim O'Rourke: New York Hands cupped in front, thigh high	200.00	90.00	25.00
☐ 71B Jim O'Rourke: New York * (Hands on knees, looking right)	250.00	110.00	31.00
☐ 72A Danny Richardson: New York (Third base)	100.00	45.00	12.50
☐ 72B Danny Richardson: New York (Second base) *	125.00	55.00	15.50
☐ 73A John M. Ward: New York (Crouching, catch-ing a grounder)	200.00	90.00	25.00
☐ 73B John M. Ward: New York * (Hands by left knee)	250.00	110.00	31.00
☐ 73C John M. Ward: New York * (Hands on knees)	250.00	110.00	31.00
☐ 74A Ed Andrews: Philadelphia (Hands together in front of neck)	100.00	45.00	12.50
☐ 74B Ed Andrews: Philadelphia * (Catching, hands waist high)	125.00	55.00	15.50
☐ 75 Charlie Bastian: Philadelphia	100.00	45.00	12.50
☐ 76 Dan Casey: Philadelphia *	125.00	55.00	15.50
☐ 77 Jack Clements: Philadelphia	100.00	45.00	12.50
☐ 78 Sid Farrar: Philadelphia	125.00	55.00	15.50
☐ 79 Charlie Ferguson: Philadelphia	100.00	45.00	12.50
☐ 80 Jim Fogarty: Philadelphia	100.00	45.00	12.50
☐ 81 Arthur Irwin: Philadelphia	100.00	45.00	12.50
☐ 82A Joel Mulvey: Philadelphia (Hands on knees)	100.00	45.00	12.50
☐ 82B Joel Mulvey: Philadelphia * (Hands together above head)	125.00	55.00	15.50
☐ 83A Pete Wood: Phila-delphia (Fielding)	100.00	45.00	12.50
☐ 83B Pete Wood: Phila-delphia HOR (Stealing a Base) *	125.00	55.00	15.50
☐ 84 Sam Barkley: Pittsburg	100.00	45.00	12.50
☐ 85 Ed Beecher:	100.00	45.00	12.50
☐ 86 Tom Brown:	100.00	45.00	12.50
☐ 87 Fred Carroll:	100.00	45.00	12.50
☐ 88 John Coleman:	100.00	45.00	12.50
☐ 89 Jim McCormick:	100.00	45.00	12.50
☐ 90 Doggie Miller:	100.00	45.00	12.50
☐ 91 Pop Smith:	100.00	45.00	12.50
☐ 92 Art Whitney:	100.00	45.00	12.50
☐ 93 Sam Barkley: St. Louis	150.00	70.00	19.00
☐ 94 Doc Bushong: St. Louis	150.00	70.00	19.00
☐ 95 Bob Carruthers (Sic): St. Louis	175.00	80.00	22.00
☐ 96 Charles Comiskey: St. Louis	300.00	135.00	38.00
☐ 97 Dave Foutz: St. Louis	150.00	70.00	19.00
☐ 98 William Gleason: St. Louis	175.00	80.00	22.00
☐ 99 Arlie Latham: St. Louis	200.00	90.00	25.00
☐ 100 Jumbo McGinnis: St. Louis	150.00	70.00	19.00
☐ 101 Hugh Nicol: St. Louis	150.00	70.00	19.00
☐ 102 James O'Neil: St. Louis	150.00	70.00	19.00
☐ 103 Yank Robinson: St. Louis	150.00	70.00	19.00
☐ 104 Sullivan: St. Louis	150.00	70.00	19.00
☐ 105 Chris Von Der Ahe OWN St. Louis Actually a photo rather than drawing	300.00	135.00	38.00
☐ 106 Curt Welch: St. Louis	150.00	70.00	19.00
☐ 107 Cliff Carroll: Washington	100.00	45.00	12.50
☐ 108 Craig: Washington *	125.00	55.00	15.50
☐ 109 Sam Crane: Washington *	125.00	55.00	15.50
☐ 110 Ed Dailey: Washington	100.00	45.00	12.50
☐ 111 Jim Donnelly: Washington	100.00	45.00	12.50
☐ 112A Jack Farrell: Washington Ball in left hand right arm out shoulder high)	100.00	45.00	12.50
☐ 112B Jack Farrell: Washington * (Ball in hands near right knee)	125.00	55.00	15.50
☐ 113 Barney Gilligan: Washington	100.00	45.00	12.50
☐ 114A Paul Hines: Washington Fielding	100.00	45.00	12.50
☐ 114B Paul Hines: Washington * (Batting)	125.00	55.00	15.50
☐ 115 Al Myers: Washington	100.00	45.00	12.50
☐ 116 Billy O'Brien: Washington	100.00	45.00	12.50
☐ 117 Jim Whitney: Washington	100.00	45.00	12.50

1988 Bull Durham Movie

These four 4" by 5" cards were issued to promote the 1988 movie "Bull Durham". The fronts have the name of the character as well as two photos. The backs have some of the movie lines as uttered by the characters. Since the cards are unnumbered, we have identified them by their real identites and arranged the set in that order.

	MINT	NRMT	EXC
COMPLETE SET (4)	5.00	2.20	.60
COMMON CARD (1-4)	.50	.23	.06
☐ 1 Kevin Costner Crash Davis	2.00	.90	.25
☐ 2 Tim Robbins Nuke LaLoosh	2.00	.90	.25
☐ 3 Jenny Robertson Millie	.50	.23	.06
☐ 4 Susan Sarandon Annie Savoy	2.00	.90	.25

1977 Burger Chef Discs

The individual discs measure approximately 2 1/2" in diameter and contain a burger-related caricature on the reverse. There were nine discs on each tray; five on the front and four on the back. Each tray contained one team and there were 24 different trays, obviously one for each team. On the tray the copyright notice indicates 1977. The player photos are shown without team logos on their caps. We have sequenced this set in the following order: Houston (1-9), St. Louis (10-18), Texas (19-27), Boston (28-36), Baltimore (37-45), Minnesota

(46-54), Cleveland (55-63), Kansas City (64-72), Chicago White Sox (73-81), Milwaukee (82-90), Detroit (91-99), San Francisco (100-108), Oakland (109-117), California (118-126), San Diego (127-135), New York Mets (136-144), Los Angeles (145-153), Montreal (154-162), Philadelphia (163-171), New York Yankees (172-180), Pirates (181-189), Chicago Cubs (190-198), Cincinnati (199-207), Atlanta (208-216). No 1977 expansion teams were featured in this set.

	NRMT	VG-E	GOOD
COMPLETE SET	150.00	70.00	19.00
COMMON DISC	.25	.11	.03
☐ 1 J.R. Richard	.50	.23	.06
☐ 2 Enos Cabell	.25	.11	.03
☐ 3 Leon Roberts	.25	.11	.03
☐ 4 Ken Forsch	.25	.11	.03
☐ 5 Roger Metzger	.25	.11	.03
☐ 6 Bob Watson	.50	.23	.06
☐ 7 Cesar Cedeno	.50	.23	.06
☐ 8 Joe Ferguson	.25	.11	.03
☐ 9 Jose Cruz	.50	.23	.06
☐ 10 Al Hrabosky	.25	.11	.03
☐ 11 Keith Hernandez	.50	.23	.06
☐ 12 Pete Falcone	.25	.11	.03
☐ 13 Ken Reitz	.25	.11	.03
☐ 14 John Denny	.25	.11	.03
☐ 15 Lou Brock	4.00	1.80	.50
☐ 16 Ted Simmons	1.00	.45	.12
☐ 17 Bake McBride	.25	.11	.03
☐ 18 Mike Tyson	.25	.11	.03
☐ 19 Campy Campaneris	.50	.23	.06
☐ 20 Gaylord Perry	3.00	1.35	.35
☐ 21 Lenny Randle	.25	.11	.03
☐ 22 Bert Blyleven	1.00	.45	.12
☐ 23 Jim Sundberg	.50	.23	.06
☐ 24 Mike Hargrove	.50	.23	.06
☐ 25 Tom Grieve	.25	.11	.03
☐ 26 Toby Harrah	.25	.11	.03
☐ 27 Juan Beniquez	.25	.11	.03
☐ 28 Rick Burleson	.25	.11	.03
☐ 29 Jim Rice	1.50	.70	.19
☐ 30 Dwight Evans	1.00	.45	.12
☐ 31 Fergie Jenkins	3.00	1.35	.35
☐ 32 Bill Lee	.25	.11	.03
☐ 33 Carlton Fisk	6.00	2.70	.75
☐ 34 Luis Tiant	1.00	.45	.12
☐ 35 Fred Lynn	.50	.23	.06
☐ 36 Carl Yastrzemski	4.00	1.80	.50
☐ 37 Al Bumbry	.25	.11	.03
☐ 38 Mark Belanger	.50	.23	.06
☐ 39 Paul Blair	.25	.11	.03
☐ 40 Ross Grimsley	.25	.11	.03
☐ 41 Ken Singleton	.50	.23	.06
☐ 42 Jim Palmer	4.00	1.80	.50
☐ 43 Brooks Robinson	4.00	1.80	.50
☐ 44 Doug DeCinces	.50	.23	.06
☐ 45 Lee May	.50	.23	.06
☐ 46 Tom Johnson	.25	.11	.03
☐ 47 Dave Goltz	.25	.11	.03
☐ 48 Dan Ford	.25	.11	.03
☐ 49 Larry Hisle	.50	.23	.06
☐ 50 Mike Cubbage	.25	.11	.03
☐ 51 Rod Carew	4.00	1.80	.50
☐ 52 Bobby Randall	.25	.11	.03
☐ 53 Butch Wynegar	.25	.11	.03
☐ 54 Lyman Bostock	.50	.23	.06
☐ 55 Duane Kuiper	.25	.11	.03
☐ 56 Rick Manning	.25	.11	.03
☐ 57 Buddy Bell	1.00	.45	.12
☐ 58 Dennis Eckersley	5.00	2.20	.60
☐ 59 Wayne Garland	.25	.11	.03
☐ 60 Dave LaRoche	.25	.11	.03
☐ 61 Rick Waits	.25	.11	.03
☐ 62 Ray Fosse	.25	.11	.03
☐ 63 Frank Duffy	.25	.11	.03
☐ 64 Paul Splittorff	.25	.11	.03
☐ 65 Amos Otis	.50	.23	.06
☐ 66 Tom Poquette	.25	.11	.03
☐ 67 Fred Patek	.25	.11	.03
☐ 68 Doug Bird	.25	.11	.03
☐ 69 John Mayberry	.50	.23	.06
☐ 70 Dennis Leonard	.50	.23	.06
☐ 71 George Brett	25.00	11.00	3.10
☐ 72 Hal McRae	1.00	.45	.12
☐ 73 Chet Lemon	.50	.23	.06
☐ 74 Jorge Orta	.25	.11	.03
☐ 75 Richie Zisk	.25	.11	.03
☐ 76 Lamar Johnson	.25	.11	.03
☐ 77 Bart Johnson	.25	.11	.03
☐ 78 Jack Brohamer	.25	.11	.03
☐ 79 Jim Spencer	.25	.11	.03
☐ 80 Ralph Garr	.50	.23	.06
☐ 81 Bucky Dent	.50	.23	.06
☐ 82 Jerry Augustine	.25	.11	.03
☐ 83 Jim Slaton	.25	.11	.03
☐ 84 Charlie Moore	.25	.11	.03
☐ 85 Von Joshua	.25	.11	.03
☐ 86 Eduardo Rodriquez	.25	.11	.03
☐ 87 Sal Bando	.50	.23	.06
☐ 88 Robin Yount	6.00	2.70	.75
☐ 89 Sixto Lezcano	.25	.11	.03
☐ 90 Bill Travers	.25	.11	.03
☐ 91 Ben Oglivie	.25	.11	.03
☐ 92 Mark Fidrych	5.00	2.20	.60
☐ 93 Aurelio Rodriquez	.25	.11	.03
☐ 94 Bill Freehan	1.00	.45	.12
☐ 95 John Hiller	.25	.11	.03
☐ 96 Rusty Staub	1.00	.45	.12
☐ 97 Willie Horton	.50	.23	.06
☐ 98 Ron LeFlore	.50	.23	.06
☐ 99 Jason Thompson	.25	.11	.03
☐ 100 Marty Perez	.25	.11	.03
☐ 101 Randy Moffitt	.25	.11	.03
☐ 102 Gary Thomasson	.25	.11	.03
☐ 103 Jim Barr	.25	.11	.03
☐ 104 Larry Herndon	.25	.11	.03
☐ 105 Bobby Murcer	1.00	.45	.12
☐ 106 John Montefusco	.25	.11	.03
☐ 107 Willie Crawford	.25	.11	.03
☐ 108 Chris Speier	.25	.11	.03
☐ 109 Phil Garner	1.00	.45	.12
☐ 110 Mike Torrez	.25	.11	.03
☐ 111 Manny Sanguillen	.25	.11	.03
☐ 112 Stan Bahnsen	.25	.11	.03
☐ 113 Mike Norris	.25	.11	.03
☐ 114 Vida Blue	1.00	.45	.12
☐ 115 Claudell Washington	.50	.23	.06
☐ 116 Bill North	.25	.11	.03
☐ 117 Paul Lindblad	.25	.11	.03
☐ 118 Paul Hartzell	.25	.11	.03
☐ 119 Dave Chalk	.25	.11	.03
☐ 120 Ron Jackson	.25	.11	.03
☐ 121 Jerry Remy	.25	.11	.03
☐ 122 Frank Tanana	1.00	.45	.12
☐ 123 Nolan Ryan	25.00	11.00	3.10
☐ 124 Bobby Bonds	.50	.23	.06
☐ 125 Joe Rudi	.50	.23	.06
☐ 126 Bobby Grich	1.00	.45	.12
☐ 127 Butch Metzger	.25	.11	.03
☐ 128 Doug Rader	.25	.11	.03
☐ 129 George Hendrick	.50	.23	.06
☐ 130 David Winfield	7.50	3.40	.95
☐ 131 Gene Tenace	1.00	.45	.12
☐ 132 Randy Jones	.25	.11	.03
☐ 133 Rollie Fingers	3.00	1.35	.35
☐ 134 Mike Ivie	.25	.11	.03
☐ 135 Enzo Hernandez	.25	.11	.03
☐ 136 Ed Kranepool	.25	.11	.03
☐ 137 John Matlack	.25	.11	.03
☐ 138 Felix Millan	.25	.11	.03
☐ 139 Skip Lockwood	.25	.11	.03
☐ 140 John Stearns	.25	.11	.03
☐ 141 Dave Kingman	1.50	.70	.19
☐ 142 Tom Seaver	6.00	2.70	.75
☐ 143 Jerry Koosman	1.00	.45	.12
☐ 144 Bud Harrelson	.25	.11	.03
☐ 145 Davey Lopes	.50	.23	.06
☐ 146 Rick Monday	.25	.11	.03
☐ 147 Don Sutton	2.50	1.10	.30
☐ 148 Rick Rhoden	.25	.11	.03
☐ 149 Doug Rau	.25	.11	.03
☐ 150 Steve Garvey	2.00	.90	.25
☐ 151 Steve Yeager	.25	.11	.03
☐ 152 Reggie Smith	.50	.23	.06
☐ 153 Ron Cey	1.00	.45	.12
☐ 154 Gary Carter	5.00	2.20	.60
☐ 155 Del Unser	.25	.11	.03
☐ 156 Tim Foli	.25	.11	.03
☐ 157 Barry Foote	.25	.11	.03
☐ 158 Ellis Valentine	.25	.11	.03
☐ 159 Steve Rogers	.25	.11	.03
☐ 160 Tony Perez	2.50	1.10	.30
☐ 161 Larry Parrish	.50	.23	.06
☐ 162 Dave Cash	.25	.11	.03
☐ 163 Greg Luzinski	1.00	.45	.12
☐ 164 Bob Boone	1.00	.45	.12
☐ 165 Tug McGraw	1.00	.45	.12
☐ 166 Jay Johnstone	1.00	.45	.12
☐ 167 Garry Maddox	.25	.11	.03
☐ 168 Mike Schmidt	15.00	6.75	1.85
☐ 169 Jim Kaat	1.50	.70	.19
☐ 170 Larry Bowa	1.00	.45	.12
☐ 171 Steve Carlton	6.00	2.70	.75
☐ 172 Don Gullett	.25	.11	.03
☐ 173 Chris Chambliss	.25	.11	.03
☐ 174 Graig Nettles	1.00	.45	.12
☐ 175 Willie Randolph	1.00	.45	.12
☐ 176 Reggie Jackson	6.00	2.70	.75
☐ 177 Thurman Munson	2.50	1.10	.30
☐ 178 Catfish Hunter	4.00	1.80	.50
☐ 179 Roy White	.50	.23	.06
☐ 180 Mickey Rivers	.25	.11	.03
☐ 181 Jerry Reuss	.50	.23	.06
☐ 182 Rennie Stennett	.25	.11	.03
☐ 183 Bill Robinson	.25	.11	.03
☐ 184 Frank Taveras	.25	.11	.03
☐ 185 Duffy Dyer	.25	.11	.03
☐ 186 Willie Stargell	4.00	1.80	.50
☐ 187 Dave Parker	2.50	1.10	.30
☐ 188 John Candelaria	.50	.23	.06
☐ 189 Al Oliver	1.00	.45	.12

☐ 190 Joe Wallis	.25	.11	.03
☐ 191 Manny Trillo	.25	.11	.03
☐ 192 Bill Bonham	.25	.11	.03
☐ 193 Rick Reuschel	.50	.23	.06
☐ 194 Ray Burris	.25	.11	.03
☐ 195 Bill Buckner	.50	.23	.06
☐ 196 Jerry Morales	.25	.11	.03
☐ 197 Jose Cardenal	.25	.11	.03
☐ 198 Bill Madlock	.50	.23	.06
☐ 199 Dan Driessen	.25	.11	.03
☐ 200 Dave Concepcion	1.00	.45	.12
☐ 201 George Foster	1.00	.45	.12
☐ 202 Cesar Geronimo	.25	.11	.03
☐ 203 Gary Nolan	.25	.11	.03
☐ 204 Pete Rose	10.00	4.50	1.25
☐ 205 Johnny Bench	6.00	2.70	.75
☐ 206 Ken Griffey	1.00	.45	.12
☐ 207 Joe Morgan	4.00	1.80	.50
☐ 208 Dick Ruthven	.25	.11	.03
☐ 209 Phil Niekro	3.00	1.35	.35
☐ 210 Gary Matthews	.50	.23	.06
☐ 211 Willie Montanez	.25	.11	.03
☐ 212 Jerry Royster	.25	.11	.03
☐ 213 Andy Messersmith	.25	.11	.03
☐ 214 Jeff Burroughs	.50	.23	.06
☐ 215 Tom Paciorek	.25	.11	.03
☐ 216 Darrel Chaney	.25	.11	.03

1980 Burger King Pitch/Hit/Run

The cards in this 34-card set measure 2 1/2" by 3 1/2". The "Pitch, Hit, and Run" set was a promotion introduced by Burger King in 1980. The cards carry a Burger King logo on the front and those marked by an asterisk in the checklist contain a different photo from that found in the regularly issued Topps series. For example, Nolan Ryan was shown as a California Angel and Joe Morgan was a Cincinnati Red in the 1980 Topps regular set. Cards 1-11 are pitchers, 12-22 are hitters, and 23-33 are speedsters. Within each subgroup, the players are numbered corresponding to the alphabetical order of their names. The unnumbered checklist card was triple printed and is the least valuable card in the set.

	NRMT	VG-E	GOOD
COMPLETE SET (34)	20.00	9.00	2.50
COMMON CARD (1-33)	.10	.05	.01
☐ 1 Vida Blue *	.40	.18	.05
☐ 2 Steve Carlton	1.50	.70	.19
☐ 3 Rollie Fingers	1.00	.45	.12
☐ 4 Ron Guidry *	.25	.11	.03
☐ 5 Jerry Koosman *	.25	.11	.03
☐ 6 Phil Niekro	1.00	.45	.12
☐ 7 Jim Palmer *	2.00	.90	.25
☐ 8 J.R. Richard	.25	.11	.03
☐ 9 Nolan Ryan * Houston Astros	15.00	6.75	1.85
☐ 10 Tom Seaver *	2.00	.90	.25
☐ 11 Bruce Sutter	.25	.11	.03
☐ 12 Don Baylor	.50	.23	.06
☐ 13 George Brett	6.00	2.70	.75
☐ 14 Rod Carew	1.50	.70	.19
☐ 15 George Foster	.25	.11	.03
☐ 16 Keith Hernandez *	.25	.11	.03
☐ 17 Reggie Jackson *	3.00	1.35	.35
☐ 18 Fred Lynn *	.25	.11	.03
☐ 19 Dave Parker	.25	.11	.03
☐ 20 Jim Rice	.25	.11	.03
☐ 21 Pete Rose	4.00	1.80	.50
☐ 22 Dave Winfield *	3.00	1.35	.35
☐ 23 Bobby Bonds *	.40	.18	.05
☐ 24 Enos Cabell	.10	.05	.01
☐ 25 Cesar Cedeno	.25	.11	.03
☐ 26 Julio Cruz	.10	.05	.01
☐ 27 Ron LeFlore *	.25	.11	.03
☐ 28 Dave Lopes *	.25	.11	.03
☐ 29 Omar Moreno *	.25	.11	.03
☐ 30 Joe Morgan * Houston Astros	2.00	.90	.25
☐ 31 Bill North	.10	.05	.01
☐ 32 Frank Taveras	.10	.05	.01
☐ 33 Willie Wilson	.25	.11	.03
☐ NNO Checklist Card TP	.10	.05	.01

1986 Burger King All-Pro

This 20-card standard-size set was distributed in Burger King restaurants across the country. They were produced as panels of three where the middle card was actually a special discount coupon card. The folded panel was given with the purchase of a Whopper. Each individual card measures 2 1/2" by 3 1/2". The team logos have been airbrushed from the pictures. The cards are numbered on the front at the top.

	MINT	NRMT	EXC
COMPLETE SET (20)	10.00	4.50	1.25
COMMON CARD (1-20)	.10	.05	.01
☐ 1 Tony Pena	.10	.05	.01
☐ 2 Dave Winfield	.50	.23	.06
☐ 3 Fernando Valenzuela	.25	.11	.03
☐ 4 Pete Rose	1.00	.45	.12
☐ 5 Mike Schmidt	1.00	.45	.12
☐ 6 Steve Carlton	.50	.23	.06
☐ 7 Glenn Wilson	.10	.05	.01
☐ 8 Jim Rice	.25	.11	.03
☐ 9 Wade Boggs	1.00	.45	.12
☐ 10 Juan Samuel	.10	.05	.01
☐ 11 Dale Murphy	.40	.18	.05
☐ 12 Reggie Jackson	.75	.35	.09
☐ 13 Kirk Gibson	.25	.11	.03
☐ 14 Eddie Murray	1.25	.55	.16
☐ 15 Cal Ripken	3.00	1.35	.35
☐ 16 Willie McGee	.25	.11	.03
☐ 17 Dwight Gooden	.40	.18	.05
☐ 18 Steve Garvey	.40	.18	.05
☐ 19 Don Mattingly	2.00	.90	.25
☐ 20 George Brett	2.00	.90	.25

1987 Burger King All-Pro

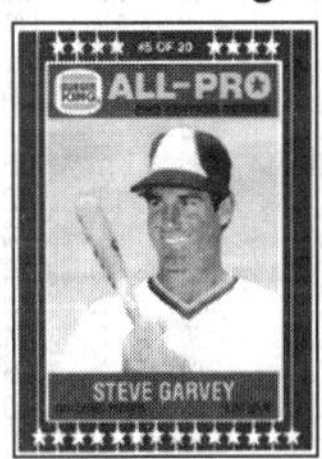

This 20-card set consists of ten panels of two cards each joined together along with a promotional coupon. Individual cards measure 2 1/2" by 3 1/2" whereas the panels measure approximately 3 1/2" by 7 5/8". MSA (Mike Schechter Associates produced the cards for Burger King; there are no Major League logos on the cards. The cards are numbered on the front. The set card numbering is almost (but not quite) in alphabetical order by player's name.

	MINT	NRMT	EXC
COMPLETE SET (20)	4.00	1.80	.50
COMMON CARD (1-20)	.10	.05	.01
☐ 1 Wade Boggs	.40	.18	.05
☐ 2 Gary Carter	.20	.09	.03
☐ 3 Will Clark	.50	.23	.06
☐ 4 Roger Clemens	.50	.23	.06
☐ 5 Steve Garvey	.30	.14	.04
☐ 6 Ron Darling	.10	.05	.01
☐ 7 Pedro Guerrero	.10	.05	.01
☐ 8 Von Hayes	.10	.05	.01
☐ 9 Rickey Henderson	.40	.18	.05
☐ 10 Keith Hernandez	.20	.09	.03
☐ 11 Wally Joyner	.20	.09	.03
☐ 12 Mike Krukow	.10	.05	.01
☐ 13 Don Mattingly	1.00	.45	.12
☐ 14 Ozzie Smith	.75	.35	.09
☐ 15 Tony Pena	.10	.05	.01
☐ 16 Jim Rice	.20	.09	.03
☐ 17 Mike Schmidt	.50	.23	.06
☐ 18 Ryne Sandberg	.75	.35	.09
☐ 19 Darryl Strawberry	.30	.14	.04
☐ 20 Fernando Valenzuela	.20	.09	.03

1994 Burger King Ripken

Co-sponsored by Coca-Cola and Burger King, this nine-card standard-size set was produced by Pinnacle to honor Baltimore Orioles star shortstop, Cal Ripken Jr. Three-card packs were available for 25 cents with the purchase of a large soft drink at Baltimore and Washington, D.C. Burger Kings, beginning May 22. The cards were available until June 19, or while supplies lasted. Each card was issued in two versions: standard and gold-foil, with the three-card packs containing two standard and one gold foil card. Ripken autographed several hundred cards, which were awarded in a drawing held after the promotion to collectors who had mailed in entry forms. The cards feature color photos of Ripken, with the lone black parabolic border on the left carrying his name in white (or gold-foil) lettering at the lower left. A similarly unusual curved border design continues on the back, which carries another color photo and career highlights in white lettering. The cards are numbered on the back as "X of 9." The gold-foil versions are valued at two times the regular cards.

	MINT	NRMT	EXC
COMPLETE SET (9)	5.00	2.20	.60
COMMON CARD (1-9)	.75	.35	.09
☐ 1 Cal Ripken Double Honors	.75	.35	.09
☐ 2 Cal Ripken Perennial All-Star	.75	.35	.09
☐ 3 Cal Ripken Peerless Power	.75	.35	.09
☐ 4 Cal Ripken Fitness Fan	.75	.35	.09
☐ 5 Cal Ripken Prime Concerns	.75	.35	.09
☐ 6 Cal Ripken Home Run Club	.75	.35	.09
☐ 7 Cal Ripken The Ironman	.75	.35	.09
☐ 8 Cal Ripken Heavy Hitter	.75	.35	.09
☐ 9 Cal Ripken Gold Glover	.75	.35	.09

1909 Buster Brown Bread Pins PB2

These pins were produced by Morton's Bakery and have Morton's inside the pennant at the top of the pin. The pins are approximately 1 1/4" in diameter and show a black and white photo of the player surrounded by a yellow background. Also pictured on the pin is Buster Brown in a brightly colored outfit as well as Tige holding a baseball bat. The player on the pin is not explicitly identified on the pin. The pins are unnumbered so they are presented below in alphabetical order.

	EX-MT	VG-E	GOOD
COMPLETE SET (16)	3500.00	1600.00	450.00
COMMON PLAYER	200.00	90.00	25.00
☐ 1 Jimmy Archer	200.00	90.00	25.00
☐ 2 Heinie Beckendorf	200.00	90.00	25.00
☐ 3 Donie Bush	200.00	90.00	25.00
☐ 4 Ty Cobb	1000.00	450.00	125.00
☐ 5 Sam Crawford	200.00	90.00	25.00
☐ 6 Bill Donovan	200.00	90.00	25.00
☐ 7 Hugh Jennings MG	350.00	160.00	45.00
☐ 8 Tom Jones	200.00	90.00	25.00
☐ 9 Red Killefer	200.00	90.00	25.00
☐ 10 Matty McIntyre	200.00	90.00	25.00
☐ 11 George Moriarty	200.00	90.00	25.00
☐ 12 George Mullen (Mullin)	200.00	90.00	25.00
☐ 13 Claude Rossman	200.00	90.00	25.00
☐ 14 Germany Schaefer	250.00	110.00	31.00
☐ 15 Ed Summers	200.00	90.00	25.00
☐ 16 Ed Willett	200.00	90.00	25.00

1933 Butter Cream R306

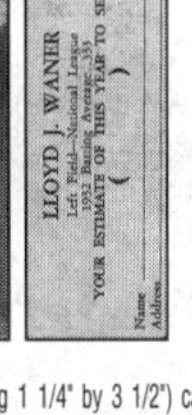

The small, elongated (measuring 1 1/4" by 3 1/2") cards of this 29 card set are unnumbered and contain many cut-down, blurry black and white photos. The producer's name is sometimes printed on the reverse. Despite their limitations, Butter Cream cards are highly prized by collectors. The cards have been alphabetized and numbered for reference in the checklist below. The Babe Ruth card is significantly scarcer than the other cards in the set; although almost never seen, we have priced it in this set. The Ruth card is not included in the set price.

	EX-MT	VG-E	GOOD
COMPLETE SET (29)	7500.00	3400.00	950.00
COMMON CARD (1-29)	200.00	90.00	25.00
☐ 1 Earl Averill	300.00	135.00	38.00
☐ 2 Ed Brandt	200.00	90.00	25.00
☐ 3 Guy T. Bush	200.00	90.00	25.00
☐ 4 Mickey Cochrane	350.00	160.00	45.00
☐ 5 Joe Cronin	350.00	160.00	45.00
☐ 6 George Earnshaw	200.00	90.00	25.00
☐ 7 Wesley Ferrell	200.00	90.00	25.00
☐ 8 Jimmy Foxx	500.00	220.00	60.00
☐ 9 Frank Frisch	350.00	160.00	45.00
☐ 10 Charles M. Gelbert	200.00	90.00	25.00
☐ 11 Lefty Grove	400.00	180.00	50.00
☐ 12 Gabby Hartnett	300.00	135.00	38.00
☐ 13 Babe Herman	300.00	135.00	38.00
☐ 14 Chuck Klein	300.00	135.00	38.00
☐ 15 Ray Kremer	200.00	90.00	25.00
☐ 16 Fred Lindstrom	300.00	135.00	38.00
☐ 17 Ted Lyons	300.00	135.00	38.00
☐ 18 Pepper Martin	250.00	110.00	31.00
☐ 19 Robert O'Farrell	200.00	90.00	25.00
☐ 20 Ed A. Rommell	200.00	90.00	25.00
☐ 21 Charles Root	200.00	90.00	25.00
☐ 22 Harold Ruel	200.00	90.00	25.00
☐ 23 Babe Ruth SP	15000.00	6800.00	1900.00
☐ 24 Al Simmons	350.00	160.00	45.00
☐ 25 Bill Terry	350.00	160.00	45.00
☐ 26 George Uhle	200.00	90.00	25.00
☐ 27 Lloyd Waner	300.00	135.00	38.00
☐ 28 Paul Waner	350.00	160.00	45.00
☐ 29 Hack Wilson	300.00	135.00	38.00
☐ 30 Glenn Wright	200.00	90.00	25.00

1933 Butterfinger Canadian V94

These large photos measure approximately 6 1/2" by 8 1/2" and are printed on thin paper stock. The fronts feature black-and-white posed action shots within white borders. A facsimile autograph is inscribed across the picture. The backs are blank.

	EX-MT	VG-E	GOOD
COMPLETE SET	4000.00	1800.00	500.00
COMMON CARD	40.00	18.00	5.00
☐ 1 Earl Averill	100.00	45.00	12.50
☐ 2 Larry Benton	40.00	18.00	5.00
☐ 3 Jim Bottomley	100.00	45.00	12.50
☐ 4 Tom Bridges	50.00	22.00	6.25
☐ 5 Bob Brown	40.00	18.00	5.00
☐ 6 Owen T. Carroll	40.00	18.00	5.00
☐ 7 Mickey Cochrane	125.00	55.00	15.50
☐ 8 Roger Cramer	50.00	22.00	6.25
☐ 9 Joe Cronin	125.00	55.00	15.50
☐ 10 Alvin Crowder	50.00	22.00	6.25
☐ 11 Dizzy Dean	150.00	70.00	19.00
☐ 12 Edward Delker	40.00	18.00	5.00
☐ 13 Bill Dickey	125.00	55.00	15.50
☐ 14 Rick Ferrell	100.00	45.00	12.50
☐ 15 Lew Fonseca	50.00	22.00	6.25
☐ 16A Jimmy Foxx Name spelled Fox	150.00	70.00	19.00
☐ 16B Jimmie Foxx Name spelled correctly	40.00	18.00	5.00
☐ 17 Chuck Fullis	40.00	18.00	5.00
☐ 18 Lou Gehrig	300.00	135.00	38.00
☐ 19 Charles Gehringer	125.00	55.00	15.50
☐ 20 Lefty Gomez	125.00	55.00	15.50
☐ 21 Lefty Grove	150.00	70.00	19.00
☐ 22 Mule Haas	40.00	18.00	5.00
☐ 23 Chick Hafey	100.00	45.00	12.50
☐ 24 Stanley Harris	100.00	45.00	12.50
☐ 25 Frank Higgins	40.00	18.00	5.00
☐ 26 Shorty Hogan	40.00	18.00	5.00
☐ 27 Ed Holley	40.00	18.00	5.00
☐ 28 Waite Hoyt	100.00	45.00	12.50
☐ 29 Jim Jordan	40.00	18.00	5.00
☐ 30 Hal Lee	40.00	18.00	5.00
☐ 31 Gus Mancuso	50.00	22.00	6.25
☐ 32 Oscar Melillo	40.00	18.00	5.00
☐ 33 Austin Moore	40.00	18.00	5.00
☐ 34 Randy Moore	40.00	18.00	5.00
☐ 35 Joe Morrissey	40.00	18.00	5.00
☐ 36 Joe Mowry	40.00	18.00	5.00
☐ 37 Bobo Newsom	50.00	22.00	6.25
☐ 38 Ernest Orsatti	40.00	18.00	5.00
☐ 39 Carl Reynolds	40.00	18.00	5.00
☐ 40 Walter Roettger	40.00	18.00	5.00
☐ 41 Babe Ruth	400.00	180.00	50.00
☐ 42 Blondy Ryan	40.00	18.00	5.00
☐ 43 John Salveson	40.00	18.00	5.00

☐ 44 Al Simmons	125.00	55.00	15.50
☐ 45 Al Smith	40.00	18.00	5.00
☐ 46 Harold Smith	40.00	18.00	5.00
☐ 47 Allyn Stout	40.00	18.00	5.00
☐ 48 Fresco Thompson	50.00	22.00	6.25
☐ 49 Art Veltman	40.00	18.00	5.00
☐ 50 Johnny Vergez	40.00	18.00	5.00
☐ 51 Gerald Walker	40.00	18.00	5.00
☐ 52 Paul Waner	100.00	45.00	12.50
☐ 53 Burgess Whitehead	40.00	18.00	5.00
☐ 54 Earl Whitehill	40.00	18.00	5.00
☐ 55 Robert Wieland	40.00	18.00	5.00
☐ 56 Jimmy Wilson	50.00	22.00	6.25
☐ 57 Bob Worthington	40.00	18.00	5.00
☐ 58 Tom Zachary	50.00	22.00	6.25

1934 Butterfinger R310

This large-size premium set comes either in paper or on heavy cardboard stock with advertising for Butterfinger or other candy at the top. The heavy cardboard Butterfinger display advertising cards are valued at triple the prices in the list below. The cards are unnumbered and Foxx exists as Fox or Foxx. The cards measure approximately 7 3/4" by 9 3/4" and have a thick off-white border around the player photo.

	EX-MT	VG-E	GOOD
COMPLETE SET (65)	2500.00	1100.00	300.00
COMMON CARD (1-65)	25.00	11.00	3.10
☐ 1 Earl Averill	40.00	18.00	5.00
☐ 2 Richard Bartell	25.00	11.00	3.10
☐ 3 Lawrence Benton	25.00	11.00	3.10
☐ 4 Walter Berger	25.00	11.00	3.10
☐ 5 Jim Bottomley	40.00	18.00	5.00
☐ 6 Ralph Boyle	25.00	11.00	3.10
☐ 7 Tex Carleton	25.00	11.00	3.10
☐ 8 Owen T. Carroll	25.00	11.00	3.10
☐ 9 Ben Chapman	25.00	11.00	3.10
☐ 10 Mickey Cochrane	60.00	27.00	7.50
☐ 11 James Collins	25.00	11.00	3.10
☐ 12 Joe Cronin	60.00	27.00	7.50
☐ 13 Alvin Crowder	25.00	11.00	3.10
☐ 14 Dizzy Dean	125.00	55.00	15.50
☐ 15 Paul Derringer	30.00	13.50	3.70
☐ 16 William Dickey	60.00	27.00	7.50
☐ 17 Leo Durocher	60.00	27.00	7.50
☐ 18 George Earnshaw	25.00	11.00	3.10
☐ 19 Richard Ferrell	40.00	18.00	5.00
☐ 20 Lew Fonseca	30.00	13.50	3.70
☐ 21A Jimmy Fox (sic, Foxx)	125.00	55.00	15.50
☐ 21B Jimmy Foxx	125.00	55.00	15.50
☐ 22 Benny Frey	25.00	11.00	3.10
☐ 23 Frankie Frisch	60.00	27.00	7.50
☐ 24 Lou Gehrig	300.00	135.00	38.00
☐ 25 Chas. Gehringer	60.00	27.00	7.50
☐ 26 Vernon Gomez	60.00	27.00	7.50
☐ 27 Ray Grabowski	25.00	11.00	3.10
☐ 28 Robert Grove	75.00	34.00	9.50
☐ 29 George(Mule) Haas	25.00	11.00	3.10
☐ 30 Chick Hafey	40.00	18.00	5.00
☐ 31 Stanley Harris	40.00	18.00	5.00
☐ 32 Francis J. Hogan	25.00	11.00	3.10
☐ 33 Ed Holley	25.00	11.00	3.10
☐ 34 Rogers Hornsby	100.00	45.00	12.50
☐ 35 Waite Hoyt	40.00	18.00	5.00
☐ 36 Walter Johnson	175.00	80.00	22.00
☐ 37 Jim Jordan	25.00	11.00	3.10
☐ 38 Joe Kuhel	25.00	11.00	3.10
☐ 39 Hal Lee	25.00	11.00	3.10
☐ 40 Gus Mancuso	25.00	11.00	3.10
☐ 41 Henry Manush	40.00	18.00	5.00
☐ 42 Fred Marberry	25.00	11.00	3.10
☐ 43 Pepper Martin	30.00	13.50	3.70
☐ 44 Oscar Melillo	25.00	11.00	3.10
☐ 45 Johnny Moore	25.00	11.00	3.10
☐ 46 Joe Morrisey	25.00	11.00	3.10
☐ 47 Joe Mowrey	25.00	11.00	3.10
☐ 48 Bob O'Farrell	25.00	11.00	3.10
☐ 49 Melvin Ott	75.00	34.00	9.50
☐ 50 Monte Pearson	30.00	13.50	3.70
☐ 51 Carl Reynolds	25.00	11.00	3.10
☐ 52 Chas. Ruffing	40.00	18.00	5.00
☐ 53 Babe Ruth	350.00	160.00	45.00
☐ 54 John(Blondy) Ryan	25.00	11.00	3.10
☐ 55 Al Simmons	40.00	18.00	5.00
☐ 56 Al Spohrer	25.00	11.00	3.10
☐ 57 Gus Suhr	25.00	11.00	3.10
☐ 58 Steve Swetonic	30.00	13.50	3.70
☐ 59 Dazzy Vance	40.00	18.00	5.00
☐ 60 Joe Vosmik	25.00	11.00	3.10
☐ 61 Lloyd Waner	40.00	18.00	5.00
☐ 62 Paul Waner	40.00	18.00	5.00
☐ 63 Sam West	25.00	11.00	3.10
☐ 64 Earl Whitehill	25.00	11.00	3.10
☐ 65 Jimmy Wilson	25.00	11.00	3.10

1989 Cadaco Ellis Discs

The 1989 Cadaco Ellis discs were designed to be used in a game. These are large-sized discs, measuring approximately 3 1/2" in diameter, the standard size which has been used for many decades by the Cadaco Company for the game which was called at one point the Ethan Allen Cadaco game. This set marks the first time that full color photos were used on the front, but with no team logo. The backs contain complete major league statistics on the back. The set is checklisted in alphabetical order.

	MINT	NRMT	EXC
COMPLETE SET (63)	60.00	27.00	7.50
COMMON DISC (1-63)	.25	.11	.03
☐ 1 Harold Baines	1.00	.45	.12
☐ 2 Wade Boggs	1.50	.70	.19
☐ 3 Bobby Bonilla	1.00	.45	.12
☐ 4 George Brett	5.00	2.20	.60
☐ 5 Jose Canseco	1.50	.70	.19
☐ 6 Gary Carter	.50	.23	.06
☐ 7 Joe Carter	1.50	.70	.19
☐ 8 Will Clark	1.50	.70	.19
☐ 9 Roger Clemens	3.00	1.35	.35
☐ 10 Vince Coleman	.25	.11	.03
☐ 11 David Cone	1.00	.45	.12
☐ 12 Eric Davis	.25	.11	.03
☐ 13 Glenn Davis	.25	.11	.03
☐ 14 Andre Dawson	1.50	.70	.19
☐ 15 Shawon Dunston	.25	.11	.03
☐ 16 Dennis Eckersley	.50	.23	.06
☐ 17 Carlton Fisk	1.50	.70	.19
☐ 18 Scott Fletcher	.25	.11	.03
☐ 19 John Franco	.50	.23	.06
☐ 20 Julio Franco	.25	.11	.03
☐ 21 Gary Gaetti	.25	.11	.03
☐ 22 Andres Galarraga	1.00	.45	.12
☐ 23 Kirk Gibson	1.00	.45	.12
☐ 24 Mike Greenwell	.25	.11	.03
☐ 25 Mark Gubicza	.25	.11	.03
☐ 26 Pedro Guerrero	.25	.11	.03
☐ 27 Tony Gwynn	5.00	2.20	.60
☐ 28 Rickey Henderson	1.50	.70	.19
☐ 29 Orel Hershiser	.50	.23	.06
☐ 30 Kent Hrbek	.25	.11	.03
☐ 31 Danny Jackson	.25	.11	.03
☐ 32 Barry Larkin	1.50	.70	.19
☐ 33 Greg Maddux	6.00	2.70	.75
☐ 34 Don Mattingly	5.00	2.20	.60
☐ 35 Fred McGriff	2.00	.90	.25
☐ 36 Mark McGwire	4.00	1.80	.50
☐ 37 Paul Molitor	3.00	1.35	.35
☐ 38 Tony Pena	.25	.11	.03
☐ 39 Gerald Perry	.25	.11	.03
☐ 40 Dan Plesac	.25	.11	.03
☐ 41 Kirby Puckett	4.00	1.80	.50
☐ 42 Johnny Ray	.25	.11	.03
☐ 43 Jeff Reardon	.25	.11	.03
☐ 44 Cal Ripken	10.00	4.50	1.25
☐ 45 Babe Ruth	10.00	4.50	1.25
☐ 46 Nolan Ryan	10.00	4.50	1.25
☐ 47 Juan Samuel	.25	.11	.03
☐ 48 Ryne Sandberg	3.00	1.35	.35
☐ 49 Benito Santiago	.25	.11	.03
☐ 50 Steve Sax	.25	.11	.03
☐ 51 Mike Schmidt	3.00	1.35	.35
☐ 52 Kevin Seitzer	.25	.11	.03
☐ 53 Ozzie Smith	4.00	1.80	.50
☐ 54 Terry Steinbach	.50	.23	.06
☐ 55 Dave Stewart	.25	.11	.03
☐ 56 Darryl Strawberry	.50	.23	.06
☐ 57 Andres Thomas	.25	.11	.03
☐ 58 Alan Trammell	.50	.23	.06
☐ 59 Andy Van Slyke	.25	.11	.03
☐ 60 Frank Viola	.25	.11	.03
☐ 61 Dave Winfield	2.00	.90	.25
☐ 62 Todd Worrell	.50	.23	.06
☐ 63 Strategy Disc	.25	.11	.03

1991 Cadaco Ellis Discs

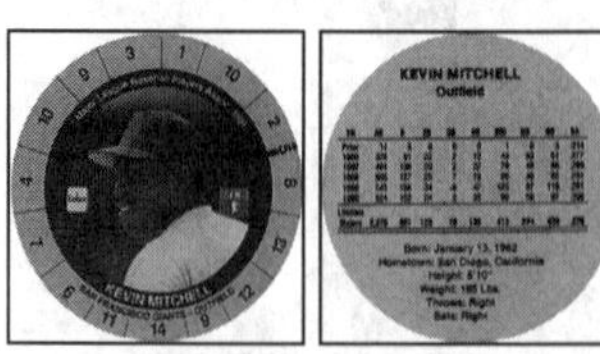

These discs were designed to be used in conjuction with the Cadaco BB game. These discs feature player photos and feature leading stars in the game. Retired superstars Roberto Clemente, Ty Cobb, Lou Gehrig, Babe Ruth and Honus Wagner are also included in this set.

	MINT	NRMT	EXC
COMPLETE SET (62)	75.00	34.00	9.50
COMMON DISC (1-62)	.25	.11	.03
☐ 1 Roberto Alomar	2.00	.90	.25
☐ 2 Harold Baines	1.00	.45	.12
☐ 3 Craig Biggio	1.50	.70	.19
☐ 4 Wade Boggs	2.00	.90	.25
☐ 5 Barry Bonds	2.50	1.10	.30
☐ 6 Bobby Bonilla	.50	.23	.06
☐ 7 Jose Canseco	2.00	.90	.25
☐ 8 Will Clark	2.00	.90	.25
☐ 9 Roger Clemens	3.00	1.35	.35
☐ 10 Roberto Clemente	8.00	3.60	1.00
☐ 11 Ty Cobb	6.00	2.70	.75
☐ 12 Vince Coleman	.25	.11	.03
☐ 13 Eric Davis	.25	.11	.03
☐ 14 Glenn Davis	.25	.11	.03
☐ 15 Andre Dawson	2.00	.90	.25
☐ 16 Delino DeShields	.25	.11	.03
☐ 17 Shawon Dunston	.25	.11	.03
☐ 18 Cecil Fielder	.50	.23	.06
☐ 19 Tony Fernandez	.25	.11	.03
☐ 20 Carlton Fisk	2.00	.90	.25
☐ 21 Julio Franco	.25	.11	.03
☐ 22 Gary Gaetti	.25	.11	.03
☐ 23 Lou Gehrig	8.00	3.60	1.00
☐ 24 Kirk Gibson	.50	.23	.06
☐ 25 Mark Grace	2.50	1.10	.30
☐ 26 Ken Griffey Jr.	10.00	4.50	1.25
☐ 27 Kelly Gruber	.25	.11	.03
☐ 28 Tony Gwynn	4.00	1.80	.50
☐ 29 Rickey Henderson	1.00	.45	.12
☐ 30 Orel Hershiser	.50	.23	.06
☐ 31 David Justice	1.00	.45	.12
☐ 32 Bo Jackson	.50	.23	.06
☐ 33 Howard Johnson	.25	.11	.03
☐ 34 Barry Larkin	1.50	.70	.19
☐ 35 Ramon Martinez	1.00	.45	.12
☐ 36 Don Mattingly	5.00	2.20	.60
☐ 37 Fred McGriff	2.00	.90	.25
☐ 38 Mark McGwire	3.00	1.35	.35
☐ 39 Kevin Mitchell	.25	.11	.03
☐ 40 Lance Parrish	.50	.23	.06
☐ 41 Tony Pena	.25	.11	.03
☐ 42 Kirby Puckett	5.00	2.20	.60
☐ 43 Cal Ripken Jr.	8.00	3.60	1.00
☐ 44 Babe Ruth	10.00	4.50	1.25
☐ 45 Nolan Ryan	8.00	3.60	1.00
☐ 46 Bret Saberhagen	.25	.11	.03
☐ 47 Chris Sabo	.25	.11	.03
☐ 48 Ryne Sandberg	4.00	1.80	.50
☐ 49 Benito Santiago	.25	.11	.03
☐ 50 Steve Sax	.25	.11	.03
☐ 51 Gary Sheffield	1.50	.70	.19
☐ 52 Ruben Sierra	.50	.23	.06
☐ 53 Ozzie Smith	3.00	1.35	.35
☐ 54 Terry Steinbach	.25	.11	.03
☐ 55 Dave Stewart	.25	.11	.03
☐ 56 Mickey Tettleton	.25	.11	.03
☐ 57 Alan Trammell	.50	.23	.06
☐ 58 Jose Uribe	.25	.11	.03
☐ 59 Honus Wagner	3.00	1.35	.35
☐ 60 Lou Whitaker	.50	.23	.06
☐ 61 Matt Williams	2.00	.90	.25
☐ 62 Robin Yount	2.00	.90	.25

1993 Cadaco Discs

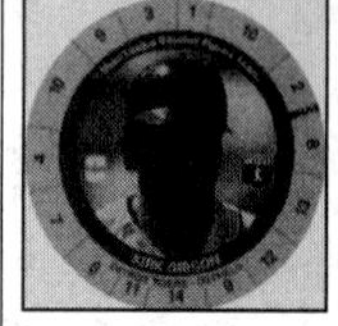

These cards were issued as part of the Cadaco games. These discs feature a mix of active players and a few retired players.

	MINT	NRMT	EXC
COMPLETE SET (62)	75.00	34.00	9.50
COMMON DISC (1-62)	.25	.11	.03
☐ 1 Kevin Appier	.50	.23	.06
☐ 2 Carlos Baerga	2.00	.90	.25
☐ 3 Harold Baines	1.00	.45	.12
☐ 4 Derek Bell	.50	.23	.06
☐ 5 George Bell	.25	.11	.03
☐ 6 Jay Bell	.25	.11	.03
☐ 7 Mike Boddicker	.25	.11	.03
☐ 8 Wade Boggs	2.00	.90	.25
☐ 9 Hubie Brooks	.25	.11	.03
☐ 10 Jose Canseco	2.00	.90	.25
☐ 11 Roger Clemens	2.00	.90	.25
☐ 12 Roberto Clemente	8.00	3.60	1.00
☐ 13 Ty Cobb	6.00	2.70	.75
☐ 14 Alex Cole	.25	.11	.03
☐ 15 Jeff Conine	.50	.23	.06
☐ 16 Andre Dawson	1.50	.70	.19
☐ 17 Shawon Dunston	.25	.11	.03
☐ 18 Len Dykstra	.50	.23	.06
☐ 19 Carlton Fisk	2.00	.90	.25
☐ 20 Darrin Fletcher	.25	.11	.03
☐ 21 Gary Gaetti	.25	.11	.03
☐ 22 Greg Gagne	.25	.11	.03
☐ 23 Mike Gallego	.25	.11	.03
☐ 24 Lou Gehrig	6.00	2.70	.75
☐ 25 Kirk Gibson	.50	.23	.06
☐ 26 Tom Glavine	1.00	.45	.12
☐ 27 Mark Grace	2.50	1.10	.30
☐ 28 Ken Griffey Jr.	10.00	4.50	1.25
☐ 29 Tony Gwynn	4.00	1.80	.50
☐ 30 Charles Hayes	.25	.11	.03
☐ 31 Rickey Henderson	2.00	.90	.25
☐ 32 Orel Hershiser	.50	.23	.06
☐ 33 Bo Jackson	.50	.23	.06
☐ 34 Howard Johnson	.25	.11	.03
☐ 35 Randy Johnson	1.50	.70	.19
☐ 36 Ricky Jordan	.25	.11	.03
☐ 37 David Justice	1.00	.45	.12
☐ 38 Ray Lankford	.50	.23	.06
☐ 39 Ramon Martinez	.50	.23	.06
☐ 40 Don Mattingly	5.00	2.20	.60
☐ 41 Mark McGwire	3.00	1.35	.35
☐ 42 Brian McRae	.25	.11	.03
☐ 43 Joe Oliver	.25	.11	.03
☐ 44 Tony Pena	.25	.11	.03
☐ 45 Kirby Puckett	4.00	1.80	.50
☐ 46 Cal Ripken	8.00	3.60	1.00
☐ 47 Babe Ruth	10.00	4.50	1.25
☐ 48 Nolan Ryan	8.00	3.60	1.00
☐ 49 Bret Saberhagen	.25	.11	.03
☐ 50 Chris Sabo	.25	.11	.03
☐ 51 Ryne Sandberg	4.00	1.80	.50
☐ 52 Benito Santiago	.25	.11	.03
☐ 53 Steve Sax	.25	.11	.03
☐ 54 Gary Sheffield	2.00	.90	.25
☐ 55 Ozzie Smith	4.00	1.80	.50
☐ 56 Dave Stewart	.25	.11	.03
☐ 57 Darryl Strawberry	.50	.23	.06
☐ 58 Frank Thomas	10.00	4.50	1.25
☐ 59 Robin Ventura	.50	.23	.06
☐ 60 Hector Villanueva	.25	.11	.03
☐ 61 Honus Wagner	4.00	1.80	.50
☐ 62 Lou Whitaker	.50	.23	.06

1950-56 Callahan HOF W576

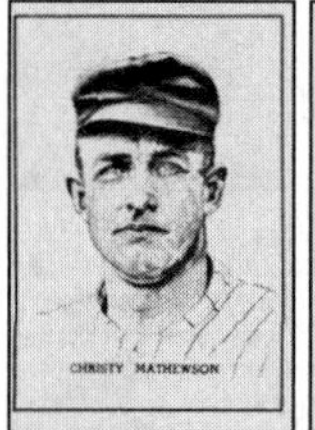

The cards in this 82-card set measure approximately 1 3/4" by 2 1/2". The 1950-56 Callahan Hall of Fame set was issued over a number of years at the Baseball Hall of Fame museum in Cooperstown, New York. New cards were added to the set each year when new members were inducted into the Hall of Fame. The cards with (2) in the checklist exist with two different biographies. The year of each card's first inclusion in the set is also given in parentheses; those not listed parenthetically below were issued in 1950 as well as in all the succeeding years and are hence the most common. Naturally the supply of cards is directly related to how many years a player was included in the set; cards that were not issued until 1955 are much scarcer than those printed all the years between 1950 and 1956. The catalog designation is W576. One frequently finds "complete" sets in the original box; take care to investigate the year of issue, the set may be complete in the sense of all the cards issued up to a certain year, but not all 82 cards below. The box is priced below. For example, a "complete" 1950 set would obviously not include any of the cards marked below with ('52), ('54), or ('55) as none of those cards existed in 1950 since those respective players had not yet been inducted. The complete set price below refers to a set including all 83 cards below. Since the cards are unnumbered, they are numbered below for reference alphabetically by player's name.

	NRMT	VG-E	GOOD
COMPLETE SET (83)	750.00	350.00	95.00
COMMON CARD '50	3.00	1.35	.35
COMMON CARD '52	4.00	1.80	.50
COMMON CARD '54	5.00	2.20	.60
COMMON CARD '55	6.00	2.70	.75
☐ 1 Grover Alexander	5.00	2.20	.60
☐ 2 Cap Anson	4.00	1.80	.50
☐ 3 Frank Baker '55	6.00	2.70	.75
☐ 4 Edward Barrow '54	5.00	2.20	.60
☐ 5 Chief Bender (2) '54	5.00	2.20	.60
☐ 6 Roger Bresnahan	3.00	1.35	.35
☐ 7 Dan Brouthers	3.00	1.35	.35
☐ 8 Mordecai Brown	3.00	1.35	.35
☐ 9 Morgan Bulkeley	3.00	1.35	.35
☐ 10 Jesse Burkett	3.00	1.35	.35
☐ 11 Alexander Cartwright	3.00	1.35	.35
☐ 12 Henry Chadwick	3.00	1.35	.35
☐ 13 Frank Chance	3.00	1.35	.35
☐ 14 Happy Chandler '52	50.00	22.00	6.25
☐ 15 Jack Chesbro	3.00	1.35	.35
☐ 16 Fred Clarke	3.00	1.35	.35
☐ 17 Ty Cobb	75.00	34.00	9.50
☐ 18A Mickey Cochrane ERR Name spelled Cochran	6.00	2.70	.75
☐ 18B Mickey Cochrane COR	30.00	13.50	3.70
☐ 19 Eddie Collins (2)	3.00	1.35	.35
☐ 20 Jimmie Collins	3.00	1.35	.35
☐ 21 Charles Comiskey	3.00	1.35	.35
☐ 22 Tom Connolly '54	5.00	2.20	.60

☐ 23 Candy Cummings	3.00	1.35	.35
☐ 24 Dizzy Dean '54	25.00	11.00	3.10
☐ 25 Ed Delahanty	3.00	1.35	.35
☐ 26 Bill Dickey '54 (2)	10.00	4.50	1.25
☐ 27 Joe DiMaggio '55	200.00	90.00	25.00
☐ 28 Hugh Duffy	3.00	1.35	.35
☐ 29 Johnny Evers	3.00	1.35	.35
☐ 30 Buck Ewing	3.00	1.35	.35
☐ 31 Jimmie Foxx	6.00	2.70	.75
☐ 32 Frank Frisch	3.00	1.35	.35
☐ 33 Lou Gehrig	100.00	45.00	12.50
☐ 34 Charles Gehringer	5.00	2.20	.60
☐ 35 Clark Griffith	3.00	1.35	.35
☐ 36 Lefty Grove	6.00	2.70	.75
☐ 37 Gabby Hartnett '55	6.00	2.70	.75
☐ 38 Harry Heilmann '52	4.00	1.80	.50
☐ 39 Rogers Hornsby	6.00	2.70	.75
☐ 40 Carl Hubbell	4.00	1.80	.50
☐ 41 Hughie Jennings	3.00	1.35	.35
☐ 42 Ban Johnson	3.00	1.35	.35
☐ 43 Walter Johnson	12.00	5.50	1.50
☐ 44 Willie Keeler	3.00	1.35	.35
☐ 45 Mike Kelly	3.00	1.35	.35
☐ 46 Bill Klem '54	5.00	2.20	.60
☐ 47 Napoleon Lajoie	5.00	2.20	.60
☐ 48 Kenesaw Landis	3.00	1.35	.35
☐ 49 Ted Lyons '55	6.00	2.70	.75
☐ 50 Connie Mack	3.00	1.35	.35
☐ 51 Rabbit Maranville '54	5.00	2.20	.60
☐ 52 Christy Mathewson	12.00	5.50	1.50
☐ 53 Tommy McCarthy	3.00	1.35	.35
☐ 54 Joe McGinnity	3.00	1.35	.35
☐ 55 John McGraw	4.00	1.80	.50
☐ 56 Kid Nichols	3.00	1.35	.35
☐ 57 Jim O'Rourke	3.00	1.35	.35
☐ 58 Mel Ott	5.00	2.20	.60
☐ 59 Herb Pennock	3.00	1.35	.35
☐ 60 Eddie Plank	3.00	1.35	.35
☐ 61 Charles Radbourne	3.00	1.35	.35
☐ 62 Wilbert Robinson	3.00	1.35	.35
☐ 63 Babe Ruth	150.00	70.00	19.00
☐ 64 Ray Schalk '55	6.00	2.70	.75
☐ 65 Al Simmons '54	5.00	2.20	.60
☐ 66 George Sisler (2)	3.00	1.35	.35
☐ 67 Albert G. Spalding	3.00	1.35	.35
☐ 68 Tris Speaker	5.00	2.20	.60
☐ 69 Bill Terry '54	6.00	2.70	.75
☐ 70 Joe Tinker	3.00	1.35	.35
☐ 71 Pie Traynor	3.00	1.35	.35
☐ 72 Dazzy Vance '55	6.00	2.70	.75
☐ 73 Rube Waddell	3.00	1.35	.35
☐ 74 Hans Wagner	12.00	5.50	1.50
☐ 75 Bobby Wallace '54	5.00	2.20	.60
☐ 76 Ed Walsh	3.00	1.35	.35
☐ 77 Paul Waner '52	6.00	2.70	.75
☐ 78 George Wright	3.00	1.35	.35
☐ 79 Harry Wright '54	5.00	2.20	.60
☐ 80 Cy Young	7.50	3.40	.95
☐ 81 Museum Interior '54 (2)	5.00	2.20	.60
☐ 82 Museum Exterior '54 (2)	5.00	2.20	.60
☐ XX Presentation Box	3.00	1.35	.35

1898 Cameo Pepsin Pins PE4

The front of the pin is a player head shot with the player's name printed on the edge. The set is checklisted alphabetically below. Additions to this checklist are appreciated.

	EX-MT	VG-E	GOOD
COMPLETE SET	30000.00	13500.00	3800.00
COMMON PIN	300.00	135.00	38.00
☐ 1 Cap Anson	1500.00	700.00	190.00
☐ 2 Jimmy Bannon	300.00	135.00	38.00
☐ 3 Marty Bergen	300.00	135.00	38.00
☐ 4 Lou Bierbauer	300.00	135.00	38.00
☐ 5 Frank Bowerman	300.00	135.00	38.00
☐ 6 Ted Breitenstein	300.00	135.00	38.00
☐ 7 Buttons Briggs	300.00	135.00	38.00
☐ 8 Eddie Burke	300.00	135.00	38.00
☐ 9 Jesse Burkett	600.00	275.00	75.00
☐ 10 Cupid Childs	300.00	135.00	38.00
☐ 11 Willie Clark	300.00	135.00	38.00
☐ 12 Boileryard Clarke	300.00	135.00	38.00
☐ 13 Jack Clements	300.00	135.00	38.00
☐ 14 Cole Cedar Rapids	300.00	135.00	38.00
☐ 14 Cozy Dolan	300.00	135.00	38.00
☐ 15 Tommy Corcoran	300.00	135.00	38.00
☐ 16 Lave Cross	300.00	135.00	38.00
☐ 17 Nig Cuppy	300.00	135.00	38.00
☐ 18 Bill Dammann	300.00	135.00	38.00
☐ 19 Tim Donahue	300.00	135.00	38.00
☐ 20 Donnelley Cedar Rapids	300.00	135.00	38.00
☐ 21 Patsy Donovan	300.00	135.00	38.00
☐ 22 Frank Dwyer	300.00	135.00	38.00
☐ 23 Bones Ely	300.00	135.00	38.00
☐ 24 Buck Ewing	600.00	275.00	75.00
☐ 25 Fisher Cedar Rapids	300.00	135.00	38.00
☐ 26 Tim Flood	300.00	135.00	38.00
☐ 27 Fuller Cedar Rapids	300.00	135.00	38.00
☐ 27 Bill Hoffer	300.00	135.00	38.00
☐ 28 Charlie Ganzel	300.00	135.00	38.00
☐ 29 Jot Goar	300.00	135.00	38.00
☐ 30 Mike Griffin	300.00	135.00	38.00
☐ 31 Billy Hamilton	600.00	275.00	75.00
☐ 32 Bill Hart	300.00	135.00	38.00
☐ 33 Pink Hawley	300.00	135.00	38.00
☐ 34 Belden Hill	300.00	135.00	38.00
☐ 35 Bug Holliday	300.00	135.00	38.00
☐ 36 Dummy Hoy	400.00	180.00	50.00
☐ 37 Jim Hughey	300.00	135.00	38.00
☐ 38 Hutchinson Cedar Rapids	300.00	135.00	38.00
☐ 39 Charlie Irwin	300.00	135.00	38.00
☐ 40 Kennedy Cedar Rapids	300.00	135.00	38.00
☐ 41 Frank Killen	300.00	135.00	38.00
☐ 42 Malachi Kittredge	300.00	135.00	38.00
☐ 43 Candy LaChance	300.00	135.00	38.00
☐ 44 Herman Long	400.00	180.00	50.00
☐ 45 Bobby Lowe	400.00	180.00	50.00
☐ 46 Denny Lyons	300.00	135.00	38.00
☐ 47 Mahaffey Cedar Rapids	300.00	135.00	38.00
☐ 49 Jimmy McAleer	300.00	135.00	38.00
☐ 50 Willard Mains	300.00	135.00	38.00
☐ 51 McDougal Cedar Rapids	300.00	135.00	38.00
☐ 52 Chippy McGarr	300.00	135.00	38.00
☐ 53 Ed McKean	300.00	135.00	38.00
☐ 54 Sadie McMahon	300.00	135.00	38.00
☐ 55 Bid McPhee	300.00	135.00	38.00
☐ 56 Bill Merritt	300.00	135.00	38.00
☐ 56 Dusty Miller	300.00	135.00	38.00
☐ 57 Frank Motz	300.00	135.00	38.00
☐ 58 Kid Nichols	600.00	275.00	75.00
☐ 59 Jack O'Connor	300.00	135.00	38.00
☐ 60 John Pappalau	300.00	135.00	38.00
☐ 61 Heinie Peitz	300.00	135.00	38.00
☐ 62 Jack Powell	300.00	135.00	38.00
☐ 63 Billy Rhines	300.00	135.00	38.00
☐ 64 Claude Ritchey Sic, Richie	300.00	135.00	38.00
☐ 65 Jack Ryan	300.00	135.00	38.00
☐ 66 Pop Schriver	300.00	135.00	38.00
☐ 67 Tom Sharkey Boxer	400.00	180.00	50.00
☐ 68 Billy Shindle	300.00	135.00	38.00
☐ 69 Aleck Smith	300.00	135.00	38.00
☐ 70 Elmer Smith	300.00	135.00	38.00
☐ 71 George Smith	300.00	135.00	38.00
☐ 72 Jake Stenzel	300.00	135.00	38.00
☐ 73 Jack Stivetts	300.00	135.00	38.00
☐ 75 Joe Sudgen	300.00	135.00	38.00
☐ 76 Jim Sullivan	300.00	135.00	38.00
☐ 77 Patsy Tebeau	300.00	135.00	38.00
☐ 78 Fred Tenney	300.00	135.00	38.00
☐ 79 Adonis Terry	300.00	135.00	38.00
☐ 80 Van Buren Cedar Rapids	300.00	135.00	38.00
☐ 81 Farmer Vaughn	300.00	135.00	38.00
☐ 82 Bobby Wallace	600.00	275.00	75.00
☐ 83 Weaver Milwaukee	300.00	135.00	38.00
☐ 84 Cy Young	1500.00	700.00	190.00
☐ 85 Brooklyn Baseball Club 1897	400.00	180.00	50.00
☐ 86 Buffalo Baseball Club 1897	300.00	135.00	38.00
☐ 87 New Castle Baseball Club 1897	300.00	135.00	38.00
☐ 88 Pittsburgh Baseball Club 1897	400.00	180.00	50.00
☐ 89 Toronto Baseball Club 1897	300.00	135.00	38.00

1990 Card Collectors' Justice Boyhood

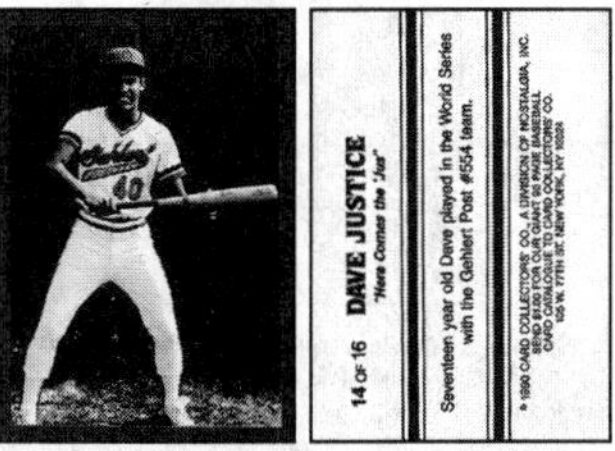

This 16-card set depicts different stages of the boyhood of David Justice. The fronts feature various pictures from his life on a red background. The backs carry information about the picture.

	MINT	NRMT	EXC
COMPLETE SET (16)	4.00	1.80	.50
COMMON CARD (1-16)	.25	.11	.03
☐ 1 David Justice (Age 4)	.25	.11	.03
☐ 2 David Justice (Wearing his Sunday best)	.25	.11	.03
☐ 3 David Justice (Kindergarten graduation)	.25	.11	.03
☐ 4 David Justice (In red party hat)	.25	.11	.03
☐ 5 David Justice (First grade photo)	.25	.11	.03
☐ 6 David Justice (First Communion)	.25	.11	.03
☐ 7 David Justice (Fourth grade photo)	.25	.11	.03
☐ 8 David Justice (At age 10 and 11)	.25	.11	.03
☐ 9 David Justice (Ohio champs in 1976 and 1977)	.25	.11	.03
☐ 10 David Justice (Football team	.25	.11	.03
☐ 11 David Justice (Third grade photo)	.25	.11	.03
☐ 12 David Justice (Senior school picture)	.25	.11	.03
☐ 13 David Justice (At age 16)	.25	.11	.03
☐ 14 David Justice (At age 17)	.25	.11	.03
☐ 15 David Justice (Shooting hoops)	.25	.11	.03
☐ 16 David Justice (Thomas Moore College Baseball Team)	.25	.11	.03

1991 Card Guard Promo Griffey

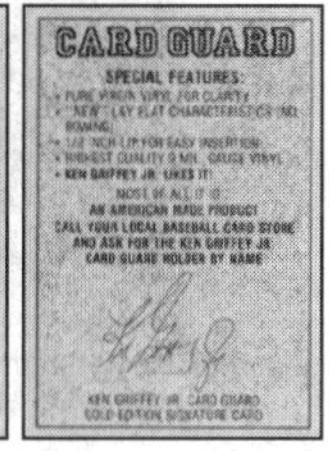

This standard-size is a promo card advertisement for Card Guard. The front has a color photo of Ken Griffey Jr. dressed in a tuxedo and holding a baseball card protected by Card Guard. His autograph is inscribed across the picture in gold ink. The back has an advertisement for Card Guard, highlighting its special features.

	MINT	NRMT	EXC
COMPLETE SET (1)	1.00	.45	.12
COMMON CARD	1.00	.45	.12
☐ 1 Ken Griffey Jr.	1.00	.45	.12

1941 Cardinals W754

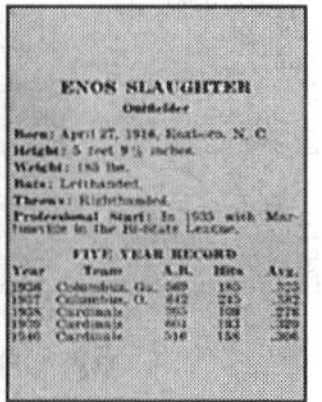

The cards in this 30-card set measure approximately 2 1/8" by 2 5/8". The 1941 W754 set of unnumbered cards features St. Louis Cardinals. The cards are numbered below alphabetically by player's name. This is another set issued in its own box with the other side being a mailing label. This set is worth about $100 more when still in the original box.

	EX-MT	VG-E	GOOD
COMPLETE SET (30)	600.00	275.00	75.00
COMMON CARD (1-30)	15.00	6.75	1.85
☐ 1 Sam Breadon OWN	15.00	6.75	1.85
☐ 2 Jimmy Brown	15.00	6.75	1.85
☐ 3 Mort Cooper	20.00	9.00	2.50
☐ 4 Walker Cooper	18.00	8.00	2.20
☐ 5 Estel Crabtree	15.00	6.75	1.85
☐ 6 Frank Crespi	15.00	6.75	1.85
☐ 7 Bill Crouch	15.00	6.75	1.85
☐ 8 Mike Gonzalez CO	18.00	8.00	2.20
☐ 9 Harry Gumpert	15.00	6.75	1.85
☐ 10 John Hopp	18.00	8.00	2.20
☐ 11 Ira Hutchinson	15.00	6.75	1.85
☐ 12 Howie Krist	15.00	6.75	1.85
☐ 13 Eddie Lake	15.00	6.75	1.85
☐ 14 Max Lanier	20.00	9.00	2.50
☐ 15 Gus Mancuso	15.00	6.75	1.85
☐ 16 Marty Marion	40.00	18.00	5.00
☐ 17 Steve Mesner	15.00	6.75	1.85
☐ 18 John Mize	75.00	34.00	9.50
☐ 19 Terry Moore	25.00	11.00	3.10
☐ 20 Sam Nahem	15.00	6.75	1.85
☐ 21 Don Padgett	15.00	6.75	1.85
☐ 22 Branch Rickey GM	60.00	27.00	7.50
☐ 23 Clyde Shoun	15.00	6.75	1.85
☐ 24 Enos Slaughter	75.00	34.00	9.50
☐ 25 Billy Southworth MG	18.00	8.00	2.20
☐ 26 Coaker Triplett	15.00	6.75	1.85
☐ 27 Buzzy Wares	15.00	6.75	1.85
☐ 28 Lon Warneke	18.00	8.00	2.20
☐ 29 Ernie White	15.00	6.75	1.85
☐ 30 Title Card (Order Coupon on back)	15.00	6.75	1.85

1953 Cardinals Hunter's Wieners

The cards in this 26 card set measure 2 1/4" by 3 1/2". The 1953 Hunter's Wieners set of full color, blank backed unnumbered cards feature St. Louis Cardinal players only. The cards have red borders and were issued in panels of two on hot dog packages. The catalog designation is F 153-1. We have sequenced this set in alphabetical order.

	NRMT	VG-E	GOOD
COMPLETE SET (26)	2200.00	1000.00	275.00
COMMON CARD (1-26)	60.00	27.00	7.50
☐ 1 Steve Bilko	60.00	27.00	7.50
☐ 2 Alpha Brazle	60.00	27.00	7.50
☐ 3 Cloyd Boyer	75.00	34.00	9.50
☐ 4 Cliff Chambers	60.00	27.00	7.50
☐ 5 Mike Clark	60.00	27.00	7.50
☐ 6 Jack Crimian	60.00	27.00	7.50
☐ 7 Les Fusselman	60.00	27.00	7.50
☐ 8 Harvey Haddix	90.00	40.00	11.00
☐ 9 Solly Hemus	60.00	27.00	7.50
☐ 10 Ray Jablonski	60.00	27.00	7.50
☐ 11 Will Johnson	60.00	27.00	7.50
☐ 12 Harry Lowrey	60.00	27.00	7.50
☐ 13 Larry Miggins	60.00	27.00	7.50
☐ 14 Stuart Miller	60.00	27.00	7.50
☐ 15 Wilmer Mizell	60.00	27.00	7.50
☐ 16 Stan Musial	700.00	325.00	90.00
☐ 17 Joe Presko	60.00	27.00	7.50
☐ 18 Del Rice	60.00	27.00	7.50
☐ 19 Hal Rice	60.00	27.00	7.50
☐ 20 Willard Schmidt	60.00	27.00	7.50
☐ 21 Red Schoendienst	125.00	55.00	15.50
☐ 22 Dick Sisler	60.00	27.00	7.50
☐ 23 Enos Slaughter	150.00	70.00	19.00
☐ 24 Gerry Staley	60.00	27.00	7.50
☐ 25 Ed Stanky	90.00	40.00	11.00
☐ 26 John Yuhas	60.00	27.00	7.50

1954 Cardinals Hunter's Wieners

The cards in this 30 card set measure 2 1/4" by 3 1/2". The 1954 Hunter's Weiners set of full color, blank backed unnumbered cards features St. Louis Cardinals. They were issued in pairs on the backs of hot dog packages as in 1953; however one of the cards is a statistical record of the player's career. The poses are very similar to those used in the 1953 set; however, there are captions which read "What's My Name" and "What's My Record". The catalog designation is F153-2.

	NRMT	VG-E	GOOD
COMPLETE SET (30)	2750.00	1250.00	350.00
COMMON CARD (1-30)	75.00	34.00	9.50
☐ 1 Tom Alston	75.00	34.00	9.50
☐ 2 Steve Bilko	75.00	34.00	9.50
☐ 3 Alpha Brazle	75.00	34.00	9.50
☐ 4 Tom Burgess	75.00	34.00	9.50
☐ 5 Cot Deal	75.00	34.00	9.50
☐ 6 Alex Grammas	75.00	34.00	9.50
☐ 7 Harvey Haddix	100.00	45.00	12.50
☐ 8 Solly Hemus	75.00	34.00	9.50
☐ 9 Ray Jablonski	75.00	34.00	9.50
☐ 10 Royce Lint	75.00	34.00	9.50
☐ 11 Harry Lowrey	75.00	34.00	9.50
☐ 12 Memo Luna	75.00	34.00	9.50
☐ 13 Stu Miller	100.00	45.00	12.50
☐ 14 Stan Musial	750.00	350.00	95.00
☐ 15 Tom Poholsky	75.00	34.00	9.50
☐ 16 Bill Posedel CO	75.00	34.00	9.50
☐ 17 Joe Presko	75.00	34.00	9.50
☐ 18 Vic Raschi	125.00	55.00	15.50
☐ 19 Dick Rand	75.00	34.00	9.50
☐ 20 Rip Repulski	75.00	34.00	9.50
☐ 21 Del Rice	75.00	34.00	9.50
☐ 22 John Riddle	75.00	34.00	9.50
☐ 23 Mike Ryba	75.00	34.00	9.50
☐ 24 Red Schoendienst	125.00	55.00	15.50
☐ 25 Dick Schofield	100.00	45.00	12.50
☐ 26 Enos Slaughter	200.00	90.00	25.00
☐ 27 Gerry Staley	75.00	34.00	9.50

☐ 28 Ed Stanky	100.00	45.00	12.50
☐ 29 Ed Yuhas	75.00	34.00	9.50
☐ 30 Sal Yvars	75.00	34.00	9.50

1955 Cardinals Hunter's Wieners

The cards in this 30 card set measure 2" by 4 3/4". The 1955 Hunter's Wieners set of full color, blank backed, unnumbered cards feature St. Louis Cardinals only. This year presented a different format from the previous two years in that there are two pictures on the front of each card, one full figure shot and a close up bust shot. The card was actually the side panel of the hot dog package rather than the back as in the previous two years. The catalog designation of this scarce regional issue is F153-3. Ken Boyer appears in his rookie season.

	NRMT	VG-E	GOOD
COMPLETE SET (30)	3500.00	1600.00	450.00
COMMON CARD (1-30)	100.00	45.00	12.50
☐ 1 Tom Alston	100.00	45.00	12.50
☐ 2 Ken Boyer	150.00	70.00	19.00
☐ 3 Harry Elliott	100.00	45.00	12.50
☐ 4 Jack Faszholz	100.00	45.00	12.50
☐ 5 Joe Frazier	100.00	45.00	12.50
☐ 6 Alex Grammas	100.00	45.00	12.50
☐ 7 Harvey Haddix	125.00	55.00	15.50
☐ 8 Solly Hemus	100.00	45.00	12.50
☐ 9 Larry Jackson	100.00	45.00	12.50
☐ 10 Tony Jacobs	100.00	45.00	12.50
☐ 11 Gordon Jones	100.00	45.00	12.50
☐ 12 Paul LaPalme	100.00	45.00	12.50
☐ 13 Brooks Lawrence	100.00	45.00	12.50
☐ 14 Wally Moon	125.00	55.00	15.50
☐ 15 Stan Musial	1000.00	450.00	125.00
☐ 16 Tom Poholsky	100.00	45.00	12.50
☐ 17 Bill Posedel CO	100.00	45.00	12.50
☐ 18 Vic Raschi	150.00	70.00	19.00
☐ 19 Rip Repulski	100.00	45.00	12.50
☐ 20 Del Rice	100.00	45.00	12.50
☐ 21 John Riddle CO	100.00	45.00	12.50
☐ 22 Bill Sarni	100.00	45.00	12.50
☐ 23 Red Schoendienst	175.00	80.00	22.00
☐ 24 Dick Schofield	125.00	55.00	15.50
☐ 25 Frank Smith	100.00	45.00	12.50
☐ 26 Ed Stanky MG	125.00	55.00	15.50
☐ 27 Bob Tiefenauer	100.00	45.00	12.50
☐ 28 Bill Virdon	150.00	70.00	19.00
☐ 29 Fred Walker CO	100.00	45.00	12.50
☐ 30 Floyd Woolridge	100.00	45.00	12.50

1958 Cardinals Jay Publishing

DEL ENNIS, St. Louis Cardinals

This 12-card set of the St. Louis Cardinals measures approximately 5" by 7" and features black-and-white player photos in a white border. These cards were packaged 12 to a packet. The backs are blank. The cards are unnumbered and checklisted below in alphabetical order.

	NRMT	VG-E	GOOD
COMPLETE SET (12)	35.00	16.00	4.40
COMMON CARD (1-12)	2.50	1.10	.30
☐ 1 Don Blasingame	2.50	1.10	.30
☐ 2 Ken Boyer	4.00	1.80	.50
☐ 3 Joe Cunningham	2.50	1.10	.30
☐ 4 Del Ennis	2.50	1.10	.30
☐ 5 Larry Jackson	2.50	1.10	.30
☐ 6 Sam Jones	2.50	1.10	.30
☐ 7 Eddie Kasko	2.50	1.10	.30
☐ 8 Lindy McDaniel	2.50	1.10	.30
☐ 9 Wilmer Mizell	2.50	1.10	.30
☐ 10 Wally Moon	3.00	1.35	.35
☐ 11 Stan Musial	10.00	4.50	1.25
☐ 12 Hal Smith	2.50	1.10	.30

1960 Cardinals Jay Publishing

This 12-card set of the St. Louis Cardinals measures approximately 5" by 7". The fronts feature black-and-white posed player photos with the player's and team name printed below in the white border. These cards were packaged 12 in a packet. The backs are blank. The cards are unnumbered and checklisted below in alphabetical order.

	NRMT	VG-E	GOOD
COMPLETE SET (12)	35.00	16.00	4.40
COMMON CARD (1-12)	2.50	1.10	.30
☐ 1 Ken Boyer	4.00	1.80	.50
☐ 2 Joe Cunningham	2.50	1.10	.30

JOE CUNNINGHAM, St. Louis Cardinals

☐ 3 Curt Flood	3.50	1.55	.45
☐ 4 Larry Jackson	2.50	1.10	.30
☐ 5 Ronnie Kline	2.50	1.10	.30
☐ 6 Lindy McDaniel	2.50	1.10	.30
☐ 7 Wilmer Mizell	2.50	1.10	.30
☐ 8 Stan Musial	15.00	6.75	1.85
☐ 9 Bob Nieman	2.50	1.10	.30
☐ 10 Hal Smith	2.50	1.10	.30
☐ 11 Daryl Spencer	2.50	1.10	.30
☐ 12 Bill White	3.50	1.55	.45

1961 Cardinals Jay Publishing

HAL SMITH, St. Louis Cardinals

This 13-card set of the St. Louis Cardinals measures approximately 5" by 7". The fronts feature black-and-white posed player photos with the player's and team name printed below in the white border. These cards were packaged 12 in a packet. The backs are blank. The cards are unnumbered and checklisted below in alphabetical order. Thirteen cards are listed for this set as Walt Moryn is included this year. Since these sets were issued throughout the years, sometimes more than the 12 players listed are included. Additions to this or any other team issue set in the book is appreciated.

	NRMT	VG-E	GOOD
COMPLETE SET (13)	35.00	16.00	4.40
COMMON CARD (1-13)	2.00	.90	.25
☐ 1 Ken Boyer	3.50	1.55	.45
☐ 2 Ernie Broglio	2.00	.90	.25
☐ 3 Joe Cunningham	2.00	.90	.25
☐ 4 Curt Flood	3.50	1.55	.45
☐ 5 Solly Hemus MG	2.00	.90	.25
☐ 6 Larry Jackson	2.00	.90	.25
☐ 7 Julian Javier	2.50	1.10	.30
☐ 8 Lindy McDaniel	2.00	.90	.25
☐ 9 Walt Moryn	2.00	.90	.25
☐ 10 Stan Musial	15.00	6.75	1.85
☐ 11 Hal Smith	2.00	.90	.25
☐ 12 Daryl Spencer	2.00	.90	.25
☐ 13 Bill White	3.50	1.55	.45

1962 Cardinals Jay Publishing

BOB GIBSON, St. Louis Cardinals

The 1962 Jay Cardinals set consists of 14 cards produced by Jay Publishing. The Minoso card establishes the year of the set, since 1962 was Minoso's only year with the Cardinals. The cards measure approximately 4 3/4" by 7" and are printed on thin photographic paper stock. The white fronts feature a black-and-white player portrait with the player's name and the team name below. The backs are blank. The cards are packaged 12 to a packet and originally sold for 25 cents. The cards are unnumbered and checklisted below in alphabetical order. Updates during the season account for the additional cards.

	NRMT	VG-E	GOOD
COMPLETE SET (14)	40.00	18.00	5.00
COMMON CARD (1-14)	2.00	.90	.25
☐ 1 Ken Boyer	3.50	1.55	.45
☐ 2 Ernie Broglio	2.00	.90	.25
☐ 3 Curt Flood	3.50	1.55	.45
☐ 4 Bob Gibson	15.00	6.75	1.85
☐ 4 Julio Gotay	2.00	.90	.25
☐ 5 Larry Jackson	2.00	.90	.25
☐ 6 Julian Javier	2.50	1.10	.30
☐ 7 Johnny Keane MG	2.00	.90	.25
☐ 8 Lindy McDaniel	2.00	.90	.25
☐ 9 Minnie Minoso	4.50	2.00	.55
☐ 10 Stan Musial	15.00	6.75	1.85
☐ 11 Curt Simmons	3.50	1.55	.45
☐ 11 Gene Oliver	2.00	.90	.25
☐ 12 Bill White	3.50	1.55	.45

1963 Cardinals Jay Publishing

STAN MUSIAL, St. Louis Cardinals

This set of the St. Louis Cardinals measures approximately 5" by 7". Originally a 12-card set, updates during the year added more cards. The fronts feature black-and-white posed player photos with the player's and team name printed below in the white border. These cards were packaged 12 in a packet. The backs are blank. The cards are unnumbered and checklisted below in alphabetical order.

	NRMT	VG-E	GOOD
COMPLETE SET (20)	60.00	27.00	7.50
COMMON CARD (1-20)	2.00	.90	.25
☐ 1 Ken Boyer (With glove)	3.50	1.55	.45
☐ 2 Ken Boyer (With bat)	3.50	1.55	.45
☐ 3 Ernie Broglio (Above waist pose)	2.00	.90	.25
☐ 4 Ernie Broglio (Action photo with glove)	2.00	.90	.25
☐ 5 Curt Flood (Smiling)	3.50	1.55	.45
☐ 6 Curt Flood	3.50	1.55	.45
☐ 7 Bob Gibson (Head pose)	12.50	5.50	1.55
☐ 8 Bob Gibson (Action pose)	12.50	5.50	1.55
☐ 9 Dick Groat	3.50	1.55	.45
☐ 10 Julian Javier	2.50	1.10	.30
☐ 11 John Keane MG (Above waist pose)	2.00	.90	.25
☐ 12 John Keane MG (Full shot)	2.00	.90	.25
☐ 13 Dal Maxvill	2.00	.90	.25
☐ 14 Tim McCarver	4.00	1.80	.50
☐ 15 Stan Musial	12.50	5.50	1.55
☐ 16 Ray Sadecki (Without glasses)	2.00	.90	.25
☐ 17 Ray Sadecki (With glasses)	2.00	.90	.25
☐ 18 Curt Simmons (Close up head shot)	3.50	1.55	.45
☐ 19 Curt Simmons (With glove)	3.50	1.55	.45
☐ 20 Bill White	3.50	1.55	.45

1964 Cardinals Team Issue

This eight-card set measures approximately 4" by 5" and features black-and-white player portraits in a white border with the player's name and position in the bottom margin. The backs are blank. The cards are unnumbered and checklisted below in alphabetical order.

	MINT	NRMT	EXC
COMPLETE SET (8)	20.00	9.00	2.50
COMMON CARD (1-8)	2.00	.90	.25
☐ 1 Ken Boyer	5.00	2.20	.60
☐ 2 Curt Flood	3.00	1.35	.35
☐ 3 Dick Groat	3.00	1.35	.35
☐ 4 Charley James	2.00	.90	.25
☐ 5 Julian Javier	2.00	.90	.25
☐ 6 Tim McCarver	5.00	2.20	.60
☐ 7 Ray Sadecki	2.00	.90	.25
☐ 8 Bill White	5.00	2.20	.60

1965 Cardinals Jay Publishing

MIKE SHANNON, St. Louis Cardinals

This 12-card set of the St. Louis Cardinals measures approximately 5" by 7". The fronts feature black-and-white posed player photos with the player's and team name printed below in the white border. These cards were packaged 12 in a packet. The backs are blank. The cards are unnumbered and checklisted below in alphabetical order.

	NRMT	VG-E	GOOD
COMPLETE SET (12)	30.00	13.50	3.70
COMMON CARD (1-12)	2.00	.90	.25
☐ 1 Ken Boyer	4.00	1.80	.50
☐ 2 Curt Flood	4.00	1.80	.50
☐ 3 Bob Gibson	7.50	3.40	.95
☐ 4 Dick Groat	3.00	1.35	.35
☐ 5 Julian Javier	2.00	.90	.25
☐ 6 Tim McCarver	4.00	1.80	.50
☐ 7 Bob Purkey	2.00	.90	.25
☐ 8 Red Schoendienst MG	4.00	1.80	.50
☐ 9 Mike Shannon	3.00	1.35	.35
☐ 10 Tracy Stallard	2.00	.90	.25
☐ 11 Carl Warwick	2.00	.90	.25
☐ 12 Bill White	4.00	1.80	.50

1965 Cardinals Team Issue

The 28-card set of the St. Louis Cardinals measures approximately 3 1/4" by 5 1/2" and features black-and-white player photos in a white border with a facsimile autograph in the wide bottom margin. The backs are blank. The cards are unnumbered and checklisted below in alphabetical order.

	NRMT	VG-E	GOOD
COMPLETE SET (28)	75.00	34.00	9.50
COMMON CARD (1-28)	2.00	.90	.25
☐ 1 Dennis Aust	2.00	.90	.25
☐ 2 Joe Becker CO	2.00	.90	.25
☐ 3 Nellie Briles	2.00	.90	.25
☐ 4 Lou Brock	7.50	3.40	.95
☐ 5 Jerry Buchek	2.00	.90	.25
☐ 6 Steve Carlton	15.00	6.75	1.85
☐ 7 Don Dennis	2.00	.90	.25
☐ 8 Curt Flood	4.00	1.80	.50
☐ 9 Bob Gibson	7.50	3.40	.95
☐ 10 Tito Francona	2.00	.90	.25
☐ 11 Phil Gagliano	2.00	.90	.25
☐ 12 Larry Jaster	2.00	.90	.25
☐ 13 Julian Javier	2.00	.90	.25
☐ 14 George Kernek	2.00	.90	.25
☐ 15 Dal Maxvill	2.00	.90	.25
☐ 16 Tim McCarver	4.00	1.80	.50
☐ 17 Bob Milliken	2.00	.90	.25
☐ 18 Bob Purkey	2.00	.90	.25
☐ 19 Ray Sadecki	2.00	.90	.25
☐ 20 Red Schoendienst MG	7.50	3.40	.95
☐ 21 Joe Schultz CO	2.00	.90	.25
☐ 22 Mike Shannon	4.00	1.80	.50
☐ 23 Curt Simmons	4.00	1.80	.50
☐ 24 Bob Skinner	2.00	.90	.25
☐ 25 Tracy Stallard	2.00	.90	.25
☐ 26 Bob Tolan	2.00	.90	.25
☐ 27 Ray Washburn	2.00	.90	.25
☐ 28 Hal Woodeschick	2.00	.90	.25

1966 Cardinals Coins

This 12-coin set measures approximately 1 1/2" in diameter and commemorates some of the all-time great St. Louis Cardinals. The gold coin fronts display a raised player image with the player's name, position, and why he was selected for this set. The backs carry an image of Bush Stadium with the team name and the words "Bush Stadium Immortals."

	NRMT	VG-E	GOOD
COMPLETE SET (12)	60.00	27.00	7.50
COMMON CARD (1-12)	2.00	.90	.25

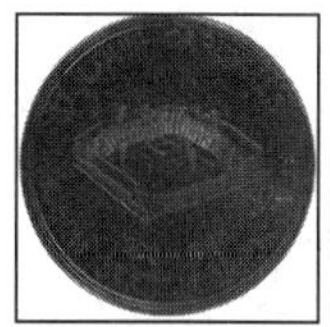

☐ 1 Dizzy Dean	8.00	3.60	1.00
☐ 2 Stan Musial	15.00	6.75	1.85
☐ 3 Johnny Mize	6.00	2.70	.75
☐ 4 Dick Sisler	2.00	.90	.25
☐ 5 Marty Marion	5.00	2.20	.60
☐ 6 Chick Hafey	4.00	1.80	.50
☐ 7 Frankie Frisch	5.00	2.20	.60
☐ 8 Jesse Haines	4.00	1.80	.50
☐ 9 Terry Moore	3.00	1.35	.35
☐ 10 Joe Medwick	5.00	2.20	.60
☐ 11 Enos Slaughter	6.00	2.70	.75
☐ 12 Red Schoendienst	6.00	2.70	.75

1966 Cardinals Team Issue

These 12 black and white photos were available directly from Busch Stadium for twenty-five cents. The cards measure approximately 4 3/4" by 7 and have blank backs. We have dated this set as 1966 was Charlie Smith's last season and Alex Johnson's first season with the Cardinals.

	NRMT	VG-E	GOOD
COMPLETE SET (12)	30.00	13.50	3.70
COMMON CARD (1-12)	2.00	.90	.25
☐ 1 Lou Brock	7.50	3.40	.95
☐ 2 Jerry Buchek	2.00	.90	.25
☐ 3 Curt Flood	3.50	1.55	.45
☐ 4 Phil Gagliano	2.00	.90	.25
☐ 5 Bob Gibson	10.00	4.50	1.25
☐ 6 Julian Javier	2.50	1.10	.30
☐ 7 Alex Johnson	2.00	.90	.25
☐ 8 Tim McCarver	3.50	1.55	.45
☐ 9 Red Schoendienst MG	3.00	1.35	.35
☐ 10 Curt Simmons	3.00	1.35	.35
☐ 11 Charlie Smith	2.00	.90	.25
☐ 12 Tracy Stallard	2.00	.90	.25

1970 Cardinals Team Issue

This 12-card set of the St. Louis Cardinals measures approximately 4 1/4" by 7" and features black-and-white player photos in a white border. These cards were packaged 12 to a packet and some display facsimile autographs. The backs are blank. The cards are unnumbered and checklisted below in alphabetical order.

	NRMT	VG-E	GOOD
COMPLETE SET (12)	40.00	18.00	5.00
COMMON CARD (1-12)	2.00	.90	.25
☐ 1 Richie Allen	5.00	2.20	.60
☐ 2 Lou Brock	7.50	3.40	.95
☐ 3 Jose Cardenal	2.00	.90	.25
☐ 4 Vic Davalillo	2.00	.90	.25
☐ 5 Bob Gibson	7.50	3.40	.95
☐ 6 Joe Hague	2.00	.90	.25
☐ 7 Julian Javier	3.00	1.35	.35
☐ 8 Leron Lee	2.00	.90	.25
☐ 9 Dal Maxvill	2.00	.90	.25
☐ 10 Red Schoendienst MG	5.00	2.20	.60
☐ 11 Mike Shannon	3.00	1.35	.35
☐ 12 Joe Torre	4.00	1.80	.50

1971-72 Cardinals Team Issue

This 44-card set measures 3 1/4" by 5 1/2" and features black-and-white player portraits with white borders. A facsimile autograph appears in the wider white border area at the bottom. The backs are blank. The cards are unnumbered and checklisted below in alphabetical order. The list below probably comprises a combination of 1971 and 1972 sets which are otherwise indistinguishable.

	NRMT	VG-E	GOOD
COMPLETE SET (44)	50.00	22.00	6.25
COMMON CARD (1-44)	1.00	.45	.12
☐ 1 Matty Alou	2.00	.90	.25
☐ 2 Vern Benson CO	1.00	.45	.12
☐ 3 Ken Boyer CO	3.00	1.35	.35
☐ 4 Nelson Briles	1.00	.45	.12
☐ 5 Lou Brock	4.00	1.80	.50
☐ 6 Bob Burda	1.00	.45	.12
☐ 7 Bernie Carbo	1.00	.45	.12
☐ 8 Steve Carlton (Profile)	5.00	2.20	.60
☐ 9 Steve Carlton (Front view)	5.00	2.20	.60
☐ 10 Donn Clendenon	1.00	.45	.12
☐ 11 Reggie Cleveland	1.00	.45	.12
☐ 12 Tony Cloninger	1.00	.45	.12
☐ 13 Ed Crosby	1.00	.45	.12
☐ 14 Jose Cruz	2.00	.90	.25
☐ 15 Moe Drabowsky (Looking up)	1.00	.45	.12
☐ 16 Moe Drabowsky (From right side)	1.00	.45	.12
☐ 17 Bob Gibson (Close-up)	4.00	1.80	.50
☐ 18 Bob Gibson (Team name on jersey showing)	4.00	1.80	.50
☐ 19 Joe Grzenda	1.00	.45	.12
☐ 20 Joe Hague	1.00	.45	.12
☐ 21 Julian Javier	1.50	.70	.19
☐ 22 George Kissell CO (Close-up)	1.00	.45	.12
☐ 23 George Kissell CO (Team name on jersey showing)	1.00	.45	.12
☐ 24 Frank Linzy	1.00	.45	.12
☐ 25 Dal Maxvill (With bat)	1.50	.70	.19
☐ 26 Dal Maxvill (Close-up)	1.50	.70	.19
☐ 27 Luis Melendez	1.00	.45	.12
☐ 28 Jerry McNertney	1.00	.45	.12
☐ 29 Billy Muffett CO	1.00	.45	.12
☐ 30 Jerry Reuss	1.50	.70	.19
☐ 31 Al Santorini	1.00	.45	.12
☐ 32 Red Schoendienst MG	3.00	1.35	.35
☐ 33 Barney Schultz CO	1.00	.45	.12
☐ 34 Don Shaw	1.00	.45	.12
☐ 35 Ted Simmons (Left view)	2.50	1.10	.30
☐ 36 Ted Simmons (Right view)	2.50	1.10	.30
☐ 37 Ted Sizemore	1.00	.45	.12
☐ 38 Scipio Spinks	1.00	.45	.12
☐ 39 Chuck Taylor	1.00	.45	.12
☐ 40 Lee Thomas CO	1.00	.45	.12
☐ 41 Joe Torre	2.50	1.10	.30
☐ 42 Mike Torrez	1.00	.45	.12
☐ 43 Rick Wise	1.00	.45	.12
☐ 44 Chris Zachary	1.00	.45	.12

1974 Cardinals 1934 TCMA

This 31-card set of the 1934 World Champion St. Louis Cardinals measures approximately 2 1/4" by 3 5/8" and features black-and-white player photos. Each set includes four jumbo cards measuring approximately 3 5/8" by 4 1/2" and displaying action photos from the 1934 World Series Games with various information on the backs. The cards are unnumbered and checklisted below with the jumbo cards being the last four cards, numbers 28-31.

	NRMT	VG-E	GOOD
COMPLETE SET (31)	25.00	11.00	3.10
COMMON CARD (1-31)	.50	.23	.06
☐ 1 Tex Carleton	.50	.23	.06
☐ 2 Rip Collins	1.00	.45	.12
☐ 3 Cliff Crawford	.50	.23	.06
☐ 4 Spud Davis	.50	.23	.06
☐ 5 Daffy Dean Dizzy Dean	2.00	.90	.25
☐ 6 Paul Dean	1.00	.45	.12
☐ 7 Dizzy Dean	3.00	1.35	.35
☐ 8 Bill DeLancey	.50	.23	.06
☐ 9 Leo Durocher	3.00	1.35	.35
☐ 10 Frank Frisch P/MG	2.50	1.10	.30
☐ 11 Chick Fullis	.50	.23	.06
☐ 12 Mike Gonzalez CO	.50	.23	.06
☐ 13 Jesse Haines	2.00	.90	.25
☐ 14 Bill Hallahan	1.00	.45	.12
☐ 15 Francis Healy	.50	.23	.06
☐ 16 Jim Lindsey	.50	.23	.06
☐ 17 Pepper Martin	1.50	.70	.19
☐ 18 Joe Medwick	2.50	1.10	.30
☐ 19 Jim Mooney	.50	.23	.06
☐ 20 Ernie Orsatti	.50	.23	.06
☐ 21 Flint Rhem	.50	.23	.06
☐ 22 John Rothrock	.50	.23	.06
☐ 23 Dazzy Vance	2.00	.90	.25
☐ 24 Bill Walker	.50	.23	.06
☐ 25 Buzzy Wares CO	.50	.23	.06
☐ 26 Whitey Whitehead	.50	.23	.06
☐ 27 Jim Winford	.50	.23	.06
☐ 28 Dizzy Dean Leo Durocher Celebrate	2.00	.90	.25
☐ 29 Leo Durocher Scores	2.50	1.10	.30
☐ 30 Joe Medwick Mickey Cochrane	2.00	.90	.25
☐ 31 1934 St. Louis Cardinals World Champions	1.50	.70	.19

1977 Cardinals 5x7

This 30-card set features black-and-white player portraits in a white border with the player's name and position printed in the bottom margin. The backs are blank. The cards are unnumbered and checklisted below in alphabetical order.

	MINT	NRMT	EXC
COMPLETE SET (30)	15.00	6.75	1.85
COMMON CARD (1-30)	.50	.23	.06
☐ 1 Mike Anderson	.50	.23	.06
☐ 2 Lou Brock	2.00	.90	.25
☐ 3 Clay Carroll	.50	.23	.06
☐ 4 Heity Cruz	.50	.23	.06
☐ 5 John Denny	.50	.23	.06
☐ 6 Larry Dierker	.75	.35	.09
☐ 7 Rawly Eastwick	.50	.23	.06
☐ 8 Pete Falcone	.50	.23	.06
☐ 9 Bob Forsch	.50	.23	.06
☐ 10 Roger Freed	.50	.23	.06
☐ 11 Keith Hernandez	1.25	.55	.16
☐ 12 Al Hrabosky	.50	.23	.06
☐ 13 Jack Krol CO	.50	.23	.06
☐ 14 Butch Metzger	.50	.23	.06
☐ 15 Mo Mozzali CO	.50	.23	.06
☐ 16 Jerry Mumphrey	.50	.23	.06
☐ 17 Claude Osteen CO	.50	.23	.06
☐ 18 Mike Phillips	.50	.23	.06
☐ 19 Dave Rader	.50	.23	.06
☐ 20 Vern Rapp MG	.50	.23	.06
☐ 21 Eric Rasmussen	.50	.23	.06
☐ 22 Ken Reitz	.50	.23	.06
☐ 23 Sonny Ruberto CO	.50	.23	.06
☐ 24 Bobby Schultz	.50	.23	.06
☐ 25 Tony Scott	.50	.23	.06
☐ 26 Ted Simmons	1.25	.55	.16
☐ 27 Garry Templeton	1.25	.55	.16
☐ 28 Mike Tyson	.50	.23	.06
☐ 29 Tom Underwood	.50	.23	.06
☐ 30 John Urrea	.50	.23	.06

1977 Cardinals Team Issue

This 28-card set measures approximately 3 1/4" by 5 1/2" and features black-and-white player portraits in a white border. A facsimile autograph is printed in the wide bottom margin. The backs are blank. The cards are unnumbered and checklisted below in alphabetical order.

	MINT	NRMT	EXC
COMPLETE SET (28)	10.00	4.50	1.25
COMMON CARD (1-28)	.25	.11	.03
☐ 1 Mike Anderson	.25	.11	.03
☐ 2 Lou Brock	2.50	1.10	.30
☐ 3 Clay Carroll	.25	.11	.03
☐ 4 Heity Cruz	.25	.11	.03
☐ 5 John Denny	.50	.23	.06
☐ 6 Larry Dierker	.50	.23	.06
☐ 7 Pete Falcone	.25	.11	.03
☐ 8 Bob Forsch	.25	.11	.03
☐ 9 Roger Freed	.25	.11	.03
☐ 10 Keith Hernandez	1.00	.45	.12
☐ 11 Al Hrabosky	.50	.23	.06
☐ 12 Don Kessinger	.25	.11	.03
☐ 13 Jack Krol CO	.25	.11	.03
☐ 14 Butch Metzger	.25	.11	.03
☐ 15 Maurice'Mo' Mozzali CO	.25	.11	.03
☐ 16 Jerry Mumphrey	.25	.11	.03
☐ 17 Claude Osteen CO	.25	.11	.03
☐ 18 Dave Rader	.25	.11	.03
☐ 19 Vern Rapp MG	.25	.11	.03
☐ 20 Eric Rasmussen	.25	.11	.03
☐ 21 Ken Reitz	.25	.11	.03
☐ 22 Sonny Ruberto CO	.25	.11	.03
☐ 23 Buddy Schutz	.25	.11	.03
☐ 24 Tony Scott	.25	.11	.03
☐ 25 Ted Simmons	1.00	.45	.12
☐ 26 Garry Templeton	1.00	.45	.12
☐ 27 Mike Tyson	.25	.11	.03
☐ 28 John Urrea	.25	.11	.03

1978 Cardinals Team Issue

This 26-card set measures approximately 3 1/4" by 5 1/2" and features black-and-white player portraits in a white border. A facsimile autograph is printed in the wide bottom margin. The backs are blank. The cards are unnumbered and checklisted below in alphabetical order.

	MINT	NRMT	EXC
COMPLETE SET (26)	10.00	4.50	1.25
COMMON CARD (1-26)	.25	.11	.03
☐ 1 Ken Boyer MG	1.00	.45	.12
☐ 2 Lou Brock	2.50	1.10	.30
☐ 3 John Denny	.25	.11	.03
☐ 4 Jim Dwyer	.25	.11	.03
☐ 5 Pete Falcone	.25	.11	.03
☐ 6 Bob Forsch	.25	.11	.03
☐ 7 Roger Freed	.25	.11	.03
☐ 8 Keith Hernandez	1.00	.45	.12
☐ 9 Jack Krol CO	.25	.11	.03
☐ 10 Mark Littell	.25	.11	.03
☐ 11 Jerry Morales	.25	.11	.03
☐ 12 Maurice'Mo' Mozzali CO	.25	.11	.03
☐ 13 Jerry Mumphrey	.25	.11	.03
☐ 14 Claude Osteen CO	.25	.11	.03
☐ 15 Mike Phillips	.25	.11	.03
☐ 16 Ken Reitz	.25	.11	.03
☐ 17 Dave Ricketts CO	.25	.11	.03
☐ 18 Sonny Ruberto CO	.25	.11	.03
☐ 19 Buddy Schutz	.25	.11	.03
☐ 20 Tony Scott	.25	.11	.03
☐ 21 Ted Simmons	1.00	.45	.12
☐ 22 Steve Swisher	.25	.11	.03
☐ 23 Garry Templeton	.50	.23	.06
☐ 24 Mike Tyson	.25	.11	.03
☐ 25 Pete Vuckovich	.50	.23	.06
☐ 26 John Urrea	.25	.11	.03

1979 Cardinals 5x7

This 32-card set features black-and-white player portraits in a white border with the player's name and position printed in the bottom margin. The backs are blank. The cards are unnumbered and checklisted below in alphabetical order.

	MINT	NRMT	EXC
COMPLETE SET (31)	20.00	9.00	2.50
COMMON CARD (1-31)	.50	.23	.06

☐ 1 Ken Boyer MG	1.25	.55	.16
☐ 2 Lou Brock	2.50	1.10	.30
☐ 3 Bernie Carbo	.50	.23	.06
☐ 4 John Denny	.50	.23	.06
☐ 5 Bob Forsch	.50	.23	.06
☐ 6 George Frazier	.50	.23	.06
☐ 7 Roger Freed	.50	.23	.06
☐ 8 George Hendrick	.50	.23	.06
☐ 9 John Fulgham	.50	.23	.06
☐ 10 Keith Hernandez	1.25	.55	.16
☐ 11 Dane Iorg	.50	.23	.06
☐ 12 Terry Kennedy	.75	.35	.09
☐ 13 Darold Knowles	.50	.23	.06
☐ 14 Jack Krol CO	.50	.23	.06
☐ 15 Mark Littell	.50	.23	.06
☐ 16 Silvio Martinez	.50	.23	.06
☐ 17 Dal Maxvill CO	.50	.23	.06
☐ 18 Jerry Mumphrey	.50	.23	.06
☐ 19 Ken Oberkfell	.50	.23	.06
☐ 20 Claude Osteen CO	.50	.23	.06
☐ 21 Mike Phillips	.50	.23	.06
☐ 22 Dave Ricketts CO	.50	.23	.06
☐ 23 Tony Scott	.50	.23	.06
☐ 24 Red Schoendienst CO	1.50	.70	.19
☐ 25 Buddy Schultz	.50	.23	.06
☐ 26 Ted Simmons	1.25	.55	.16
☐ 27 Steve Swisher	.50	.23	.06
☐ 28 Bob Sykes	.50	.23	.06
☐ 29 Garry Templeton	.75	.35	.09
☐ 30 Roy Thomas	.50	.23	.06
☐ 31 Mike Tyson	.50	.23	.06
☐ 32 Pete Vuckovich	.75	.35	.09

1981 Cardinals 5x7

This 26-card set features black-and-white player portraits in a white border with the player's name and position printed in the bottom margin. The backs are blank. The cards are unnumbered and checklisted below in alphabetical order.

	MINT	NRMT	EXC
COMPLETE SET (26)	15.00	6.75	1.85
COMMON CARD (1-26)	.50	.23	.06
☐ 1 Steve Braun	.50	.23	.06
☐ 2 Glenn Brummer	.50	.23	.06
☐ 3 Larry Dierker	.75	.35	.09
☐ 4 Bob Forsch	.50	.23	.06
☐ 5 Julio Gonzalez	.50	.23	.06
☐ 6 George Hendrick	.75	.35	.09
☐ 7 Keith Hernandez	1.25	.55	.16
☐ 8 Tom Herr Uniform number visible	.75	.35	.09
☐ 9 Tom Herr No number visible	.75	.35	.09
☐ 10 Whitey Herzog MG	1.25	.55	.16
☐ 11 Chuck Hiller CO	.50	.23	.06
☐ 12 Dane Iorg	.50	.23	.06
☐ 13 Jim Kaat	1.25	.55	.16
☐ 14 Hub Kittle CO	.50	.23	.06
☐ 15 Hal Lanier CO	.50	.23	.06
☐ 16 Dave LaPoint	.50	.23	.06
☐ 17 John Martin	.50	.23	.06
☐ 18 Ken Oberkfell Uniform number 10	.50	.23	.06
☐ 19 Ken Oberkfell Uniform number 20	.50	.23	.06
☐ 20 Jim Otten	.50	.23	.06
☐ 21 Darrell Porter	.75	.35	.09
☐ 22 Dave Ricketts CO	.50	.23	.06
☐ 23 Orlando Sanchez	.50	.23	.06
☐ 24 Red Schoendients CO	1.50	.70	.19
☐ 25 Bob Shirley	.50	.23	.06
☐ 26 Gene Tenace	.75	.35	.09

1983 Cardinals

These cards feature members of the 1983 St. Louis Cardinals. These cards are unnumbered and we have sequenced them in alphabetical order.

	NRMT	VG-E	GOOD
COMPLETE SET (31)	10.00	4.50	1.25
COMMON CARD (1-31)	.25	.11	.03
☐ 1 Joaquin Andujar	.50	.23	.06
☐ 2 Doug Bair	.25	.11	.03
☐ 3 Steve Braun	.25	.11	.03
☐ 4 Glenn Brummer	.25	.11	.03
☐ 5 Bob Forsch	.25	.11	.03
☐ 6 David Green	.25	.11	.03
☐ 7 George Hendrick	.50	.23	.06
☐ 8 Keith Hernandez	.75	.35	.09
☐ 9 Tom Herr	.25	.11	.03
☐ 10 Whitey Herzog MG	.75	.35	.09
☐ 11 Chuck Hiller CO	.25	.11	.03
☐ 12 Jim Kaat	.75	.35	.09
☐ 13 Hub Kittle CO	.25	.11	.03
☐ 14 Jeff Lahti	.25	.11	.03
☐ 15 Hal Lanier CO	.25	.11	.03
☐ 16 David LaPoint	.25	.11	.03
☐ 17 Dane Iorg	.25	.11	.03
☐ 18 John Martin	.25	.11	.03
☐ 19 Willie McGee	2.00	.90	.25
☐ 20 Ken Oberkfell	.25	.11	.03
☐ 21 Darrell Porter	.50	.23	.06
☐ 22 Jamie Quirk	.25	.11	.03
☐ 23 Mike Ramsey	.25	.11	.03
☐ 24 Eric Rasmussen	.25	.11	.03
☐ 25 Dave Ricketts CO	.25	.11	.03
☐ 26 Rafael Santana	.25	.11	.03
☐ 27 Red Schoendienst CO	1.00	.45	.12
☐ 28 Lonnie Smith	.50	.23	.06
☐ 29 Ozzie Smith	3.00	1.35	.35
☐ 30 John Stuper	.25	.11	.03
☐ 31 Bruce Sutter	.75	.35	.09

1983 Cardinals Colonial Bread Porter

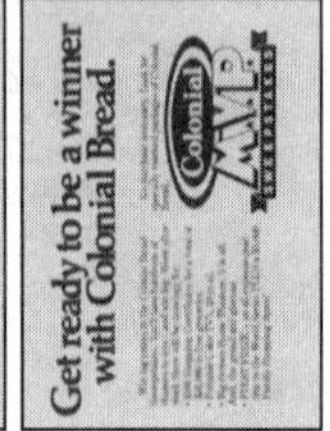

This one-card set features a blue-and-white photo of the 1982 World Series MVP, Darrell Porter of the World Champion St. Louis Cardinals, holding a loaf of Colonial Bread. The back displays sweepstakes rules for a contest sponsored by Colonial Bread.

	NRMT	VG-E	GOOD
COMPLETE SET (1)	3.00	1.35	.35
COMMON CARD (1)	3.00	1.35	.35
☐ 1 Darrell Porter	3.00	1.35	.35

1983 Cardinals Greats TCMA

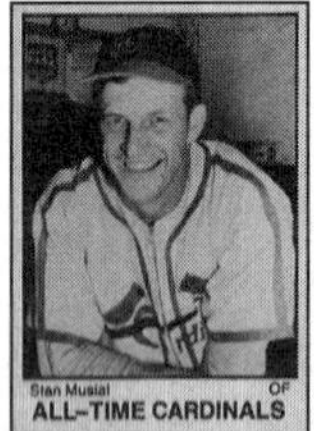

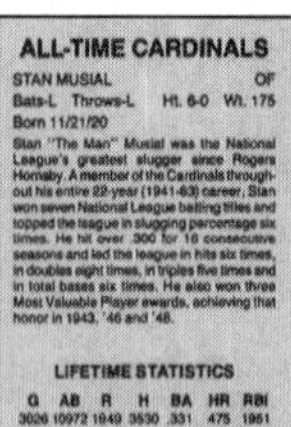

This 12-card standard-size set honors some leading all-time St. Louis Cardinals. These players are noted with their name and position on the front. The backs have vital statistics, a biography as well as career totals.

	NRMT	VG-E	GOOD
COMPLETE SET (12)	6.00	2.70	.75
COMMON CARD (1-12)	.25	.11	.03
☐ 1 Jim Bottomley	.35	.16	.04
☐ 2 Rogers Hornsby	1.25	.55	.16
☐ 3 Ken Boyer	.50	.23	.06
☐ 4 Marty Marion	.50	.23	.06
☐ 5 Ducky Medwick	.35	.16	.04
☐ 6 Chick Hafey	.35	.16	.04
☐ 7 Stan Musial	2.50	1.10	.30
☐ 8 Robert "Bob" Gibson	1.25	.55	.16
☐ 9 Harry Brecheen	.25	.11	.03
☐ 10 Tim McCarver	.50	.23	.06
☐ 11 Alpha Brazle	.25	.11	.03
☐ 12 Red Schoendienst MG	.50	.23	.06

1984 Cardinals

This 32-card set of the St. Louis Cardinals measures approximately 3 1/4" by 5 1/2" and features white-bordered, black-and-white player portraits. A facsimile autograph appears in the wide bottom margin. The backs are blank. Some personnel changes during the season account for more than 30 cards although they were issued in 30 card sets. The cards are unnumbered and checklisted below in alphabetical order.

	NRMT	VG-E	GOOD
COMPLETE SET (30)	7.50	3.40	.95
COMMON CARD (1-30)	.25	.11	.03
☐ 1 Neil Allen	.25	.11	.03
☐ 2 Joaquin Andujar	.50	.23	.06
☐ 3 Steve Braun	.25	.11	.03
☐ 4 Glenn Brummer	.25	.11	.03
☐ 5 Ralph Citarella	.25	.11	.03
☐ 6 Danny Cox	.25	.11	.03
☐ 7 Bob Forsch	.25	.11	.03
☐ 8 David Green	.25	.11	.03
☐ 9 George Hendrick	.50	.23	.06
☐ 10 Tom Herr	.25	.11	.03
☐ 11 Whitey Herzog MG	.75	.35	.09
☐ 12 Rick Horton	.25	.11	.03
☐ 13 Art Howe	.25	.11	.03
☐ 14 Mike Jorgensen	.25	.11	.03
☐ 15 Jeff Lahti	.25	.11	.03
☐ 16 Tito Landrum	.25	.11	.03
☐ 17 Hal Lanier CO	.25	.11	.03
☐ 18 Dave LaPoint	.25	.11	.03
☐ 19 Nick Leyva CO	.25	.11	.03
☐ 20 Bill Lyons	.25	.11	.03
☐ 21 Willie McGee	1.25	.55	.16
☐ 22 Darrell Porter	.50	.23	.06
☐ 23 Dave Ricketts CO	.25	.11	.03
☐ 24 Mike Roarke CO	.25	.11	.03
☐ 25 Dave Rucker	.25	.11	.03
☐ 26 Mark Salas	.25	.11	.03
☐ 27 Red Schoendienst CO	1.00	.45	.12
☐ 28 Lonnie Smith	.25	.11	.03
☐ 29 Ozzie Smith	2.50	1.10	.30
☐ 30 Bruce Sutter	.75	.35	.09
☐ 31 Andy Van Slyke	1.25	.55	.16
☐ 32 Dave Von Ohlen	.25	.11	.03

1984 Cardinals 5x7

This 30-card set features black-and-white player portraits either borderless or in a white border with the player's name and position printed in the bottom margin. The backs are blank. The cards are unnumbered and checklisted below in alphabetical order.

	MINT	NRMT	EXC
COMPLETE SET (30)	20.00	9.00	2.50
COMMON CARD (1-30)	.50	.23	.06
☐ 1 Neil Allen	.50	.23	.06
☐ 2 Joaquin Andujar	.50	.23	.06
☐ 3 Steve Braun	.50	.23	.06
☐ 4 Glenn Brummer	.50	.23	.06
☐ 5 Danny Cox	.50	.23	.06
☐ 6 Bob Forsch	.50	.23	.06
☐ 7 Jose Gonzalez	.50	.23	.06
☐ 8 David Green	.50	.23	.06
☐ 9 George Hendrick	.75	.35	.09
☐ 10 Tom Herr	.50	.23	.06
☐ 11 Whitey Herzog MG	.50	.23	.06
☐ 12 Ricky Horton	.50	.23	.06
☐ 13 Art Howe	.50	.23	.06
☐ 14 Hal Lanier CO	.50	.23	.06
☐ 15 Dave LaPoint	.50	.23	.06
☐ 16 Nick Leyva CO	.50	.23	.06
☐ 17 Bill Lyons	.50	.23	.06
☐ 18 Willie McGee	2.00	.90	.25
☐ 19 Tom Nieto	.50	.23	.06
☐ 20 Terry Pendleton	1.50	.70	.19
☐ 21 Darrell Porter	.75	.35	.09
☐ 22 Dave Ricketts CO	.50	.23	.06
☐ 23 Mike Roarke CO	.50	.23	.06
☐ 24 Dave Rucker	.50	.23	.06
☐ 25 Red Schoendienst CO	1.50	.70	.19
☐ 26 Lonnie Smith	.75	.35	.09
☐ 27 Ozzie Smith	2.50	1.10	.30
☐ 28 John Stuper	.50	.23	.06
☐ 29 Bruce Sutter	1.25	.55	.16
☐ 30 Andy Van Slyke	2.00	.90	.25

1985 Cardinals Team Issue

These 32 cards represent members of the 1985 St. Louis Cardinals. The fronts have black and white photographs and facsimile autographs. The backs are blank. We have checklisted this set in alphabetical order.

	NRMT	VG-E	GOOD
COMPLETE SET (32)	10.00	4.50	1.25
COMMON CARD (1-32)	.25	.11	.03
☐ 1 Neil Allen	.25	.11	.03
☐ 2 Joaquin Andujar	.50	.23	.06
☐ 3 Steve Braun	.25	.11	.03
☐ 4 Bill Campbell	.25	.11	.03
☐ 5 Jack Clark	.75	.35	.09
☐ 6 Vince Coleman	1.25	.55	.16
☐ 7 Danny Cox	.25	.11	.03
☐ 8 Ken Dayley	.25	.11	.03
☐ 9 Ivan DeJesus	.25	.11	.03
☐ 10 Bob Forsch	.25	.11	.03
☐ 11 Brian Harper	.25	.11	.03
☐ 12 Tom Herr	.25	.11	.03
☐ 13 Whitey Herzog MG	.75	.35	.09
☐ 14 Ricky Horton	.25	.11	.03
☐ 15 Mike Jorgensen	.25	.11	.03
☐ 16 Kurt Kepshire	.25	.11	.03
☐ 17 Hal Lanier CO	.25	.11	.03
☐ 18 Jeff Lahti	.25	.11	.03
☐ 19 Tito Landrum	.25	.11	.03
☐ 20 Tom Lawless	.25	.11	.03
☐ 21 Johnny Lewis CO	.25	.11	.03
☐ 22 Nick Leyva CO	.25	.11	.03
☐ 23 Willie McGee	1.00	.45	.12
☐ 24 Tom Nieto	.25	.11	.03
☐ 25 Terry Pendleton	1.25	.55	.16
☐ 26 Darrell Porter	.50	.23	.06
☐ 27 Dave Ricketts CO	.25	.11	.03
☐ 28 Mike Roarke CO	.25	.11	.03
☐ 29 Red Schoendienst CO	1.00	.45	.12
☐ 30 Ozzie Smith	2.50	1.10	.30
☐ 31 John Tudor	.50	.23	.06
☐ 32 Andy Van Slyke	.75	.35	.09

1986 Cardinals Team Issue

This 32-card set of the St. Louis Cardinals measures approximately 3 1/4" by 5 1/2" and features white-bordered, black-and-white player portraits. A facsimile autograph appears in the wide bottom margin. The backs are blank. The cards are unnumbered and checklisted below in alphabetical order.

	MINT	NRMT	EXC
COMPLETE SET (32)	10.00	4.50	1.25
COMMON CARD (1-32)	.25	.11	.03
☐ 1 Nick Allen	.25	.11	.03
☐ 2 Joaquin Andujar	.50	.23	.06
☐ 3 Steve Braun	.25	.11	.03
☐ 4 Bill Campbell	.25	.11	.03
☐ 5 Jack Clark	.75	.35	.09
☐ 6 Vince Coleman	.75	.35	.09
☐ 7 Dan Cox	.25	.11	.03
☐ 8 Ken Dayley	.25	.11	.03
☐ 9 Ivan DeJesus	.25	.11	.03
☐ 10 Bob Forsch	.25	.11	.03
☐ 11 Brian Harper	.25	.11	.03
☐ 12 Tom Herr	.25	.11	.03
☐ 13 Whitey Herzog MG	.75	.35	.09
☐ 14 Rick Horton	.25	.11	.03
☐ 15 Mike Jorgensen	.25	.11	.03
☐ 16 Kurt Kepshire	.25	.11	.03
☐ 17 Jeff Lahti	.25	.11	.03

	MINT	NRMT	EXC
☐ 18 Tito Landrum	.25	.11	.03
☐ 19 Hal Lanier CO	.25	.11	.03
☐ 20 Tom Lawless	.25	.11	.03
☐ 21 Johnny Lewis CO	.25	.11	.03
☐ 22 Nick Leyva CO	.25	.11	.03
☐ 23 Willie McGee	1.00	.45	.12
☐ 24 Tom Nieto	.25	.11	.03
☐ 25 Terry Pendleton	.75	.35	.09
☐ 26 Darrell Porter	.25	.11	.03
☐ 28 Mike Roarke CO	.25	.11	.03
☐ 29 Red Schoendienst CO	1.00	.45	.12
☐ 30 Ozzie Smith	2.50	1.10	.30
☐ 31 John Tudor	.25	.11	.03
☐ 32 Andy Van Slyke	.50	.23	.06

1986 Cardinals IGA Stores

This 14-card set of the St. Louis Cardinals measures approximately 6" by 9". The fronts feature white-framed color player portraits with a facsimile autographed in the lower left. The backs are blank. The cards are unnumbered and checklisted below in alphabetical order.

	MINT	NRMT	EXC
COMPLETE SET (14)	16.00	7.25	2.00
COMMON CARD (1-14)	1.00	.45	.12
☐ 1 Jack Clark	2.00	.90	.25
☐ 2 Vince Coleman	2.50	1.10	.30
☐ 3 Dan Cox	1.00	.45	.12
☐ 4 Bob Forsch	1.00	.45	.12
☐ 5 Mike Heath	1.00	.45	.12
☐ 6 Tom Herr	1.00	.45	.12
☐ 7 Tito Landrum	1.00	.45	.12
☐ 8 Jeff Lahti	1.00	.45	.12
☐ 9 Willie McGee	2.50	1.10	.30
☐ 10 Terry Pendleton	2.00	.90	.25
☐ 11 Ozzie Smith	5.00	2.20	.60
☐ 12 John Tudor	1.00	.45	.12
☐ 13 Andy Van Slyke	2.00	.90	.25
☐ 14 Todd Worrell	2.50	1.10	.30

1986 Cardinals KAS Discs

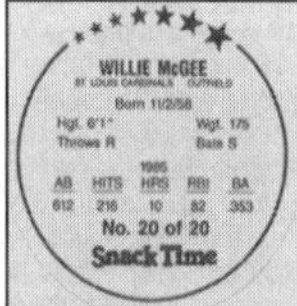

This set of discs was distributed by KAS in 1986 to commemorate the Cardinal's "almost" World Championship in 1985. Each disc measures 2 3/4" in diameter. Each disc has a white border on the front. Inside this white border is a full-color photo of the player with his hat airbrushed to erase the team logo on ther hat. The statistics on back of the disc give the player's 1985 pitching or hitting record as well as his vital statistics. The discs are numbered on the back.

	MINT	NRMT	EXC
COMPLETE SET (20)	12.50	5.50	1.55
COMMON DISC (1-20)	.30	.14	.04
☐ 1 Vince Coleman	.50	.23	.06
☐ 2 Ken Dayley	.30	.14	.04
☐ 3 Tito Landrum	.30	.14	.04
☐ 4 Steve Braun	.30	.14	.04
☐ 5 Danny Cox	.30	.14	.04
☐ 6 Bob Forsch	.30	.14	.04
☐ 7 Ozzie Smith	6.00	2.70	.75
☐ 8 Brian Harper	.30	.14	.04
☐ 9 Jack Clark	.75	.35	.09
☐ 10 Todd Worrell	.75	.35	.09
☐ 11 Joaquin Andujar	.50	.23	.06
☐ 12 Tom Nieto	.30	.14	.04
☐ 13 Kurt Kepshire	.30	.14	.04
☐ 14 Terry Pendleton	1.00	.45	.12
☐ 15 Tom Herr	.30	.14	.04
☐ 16 Darrell Porter	.50	.23	.06
☐ 17 John Tudor	.50	.23	.06
☐ 18 Jeff Lahti	.30	.14	.04
☐ 19 Andy Van Slyke	1.00	.45	.12
☐ 20 Willie McGee	2.00	.90	.25

1986 Cardinals Schnucks Milk

The cards in this set were printed on the sides of Schnucks milk cartons. The set features only members of the St. Louis Cardinals. The cards measure approximately 3 3/4" by 7 1/2" and have black and

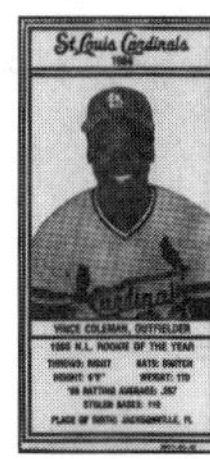

white photos. The cards are unnumbered and blank backed. The cards are ordered below according to alphabetical order except for the mascot and schedule cards which are listed last.

	MINT	NRMT	EXC
COMPLETE SET (26)	40.00	18.00	5.00
COMMON CARD (1-26)	1.50	.70	.19
☐ 1 Jack Clark	3.00	1.35	.35
☐ 2 Vince Coleman	4.00	1.80	.50
☐ 3 Tim Conroy	1.50	.70	.19
☐ 4 Danny Cox	1.50	.70	.19
☐ 5 Ken Dayley	1.50	.70	.19
☐ 6 Bob Forsch	1.50	.70	.19
☐ 7 Mike Heath	1.50	.70	.19
☐ 8 Tom Herr	1.50	.70	.19
☐ 9 Rick Horton	1.50	.70	.19
☐ 10 Clint Hurdle	1.50	.70	.19
☐ 11 Kurt Kepshire	1.50	.70	.19
☐ 12 Jeff Lahti	1.50	.70	.19
☐ 13 Tito Landrum	1.50	.70	.19
☐ 14 Mike Lavalliere	1.50	.70	.19
☐ 15 Tom Lawless	1.50	.70	.19
☐ 16 Willie McGee	5.00	2.20	.60
☐ 17 Jose Oquendo	1.50	.70	.19
☐ 18 Rick Ownbey	1.50	.70	.19
☐ 19 Terry Pendleton	4.00	1.80	.50
☐ 20 Pat Perry	1.50	.70	.19
☐ 21 Ozzie Smith	10.00	4.50	1.25
☐ 22 John Tudor	2.00	.90	.25
☐ 23 Andy Van Slyke	2.00	.90	.25
☐ 24 Todd Worrell	5.00	2.20	.60
☐ 25 Fred Bird (Mascot)	1.50	.70	.19
☐ 26 Cardinals Schedule	1.50	.70	.19

1987 Cardinals 1934 TCMA

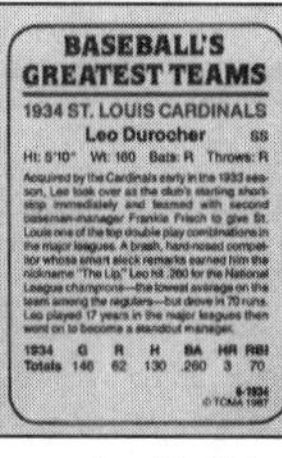

This nine-card standard-size set honors members of the "Gashouse Gang". This team won the world series and was led by the Dean Brothers who combined for 49 wins, 30 by Dizzy. The fronts have a player portrait as well as name and position. The back describes their 1934 season and has stats for that season as well.

	MINT	NRMT	EXC
COMPLETE SET (9)	5.00	2.20	.60
COMMON CARD (1-9)	.25	.11	.03
☐ 1 Dizzy Dean	2.00	.90	.25
☐ 2 Daffy Dean	.50	.23	.06
☐ 3 Pepper Martin	.75	.35	.09
☐ 4 Ripper Collins	.25	.11	.03
☐ 5 Frankie Frisch P/MG	1.00	.45	.12
☐ 6 Leo Durocher	1.00	.45	.12
☐ 7 Ducky Medwick	1.00	.45	.12
☐ 8 Tex Carleton	.25	.11	.03
☐ 9 Spud Davis	.25	.11	.03

1987 Cardinals Smokey

The U.S. Forestry Service (in conjunction with the St. Louis Cardinals) produced this large, attractive 25-card set to commemorate the 43rd birthday of Smokey. The cards feature Smokey the Bear pictured in the top right corner of every card. The card backs give a cartoon fire safety tip. The cards measure approximately 4" by 6" and are subtitled "Wildfire Prevention" on the front. Sets were supposedly available from the Cardinals team for 3.50 postpaid. Also a limited number of 8 1/2" by 12" full-color team photos were available from the team to those who sent in a large SASE. The large team photo is not considered part of the complete set.

	MINT	NRMT	EXC
COMPLETE SET (25)	12.50	5.50	1.55
COMMON CARD (1-25)	.50	.23	.06
☐ 1 Ray Soff	.50	.23	.06
☐ 2 Todd Worrell	1.00	.45	.12
☐ 3 John Tudor	.75	.35	.09
☐ 4 Pat Perry	.50	.23	.06

	MINT	NRMT	EXC
☐ 5 Rick Horton	.50	.23	.06
☐ 6 Danny Cox	.50	.23	.06
☐ 7 Bob Forsch	.75	.35	.09
☐ 8 Greg Mathews	.50	.23	.06
☐ 9 Bill Dawley	.50	.23	.06
☐ 10 Steve Lake	.50	.23	.06
☐ 11 Tony Pena	.75	.35	.09
☐ 12 Tom Pagnozzi	.75	.35	.09
☐ 13 Jack Clark	1.00	.45	.12
☐ 14 Jim Lindeman	.50	.23	.06
☐ 15 Mike Laga	.50	.23	.06
☐ 16 Terry Pendleton	.75	.35	.09
☐ 17 Ozzie Smith	4.00	1.80	.50
☐ 18 Jose Oquendo	.50	.23	.06
☐ 19 Tom Lawless	.50	.23	.06
☐ 20 Tom Herr	.75	.35	.09
☐ 21 Curt Ford	.50	.23	.06
☐ 22 Willie McGee	1.50	.70	.19
☐ 23 Tito Landrum	.50	.23	.06
☐ 24 Vince Coleman	.75	.35	.09
☐ 25 Whitey Herzog MG	1.00	.45	.12
☐ NNO Team Photo (large)	3.00	1.35	.35

1988 Cardinals Smokey

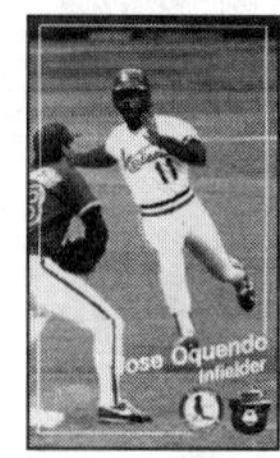

The U.S. Forestry Service (in conjunction with the St. Louis Cardinals) produced this attractive 25-card set. The cards feature Smokey the Bear pictured in the lower right corner of every card. The card backs give a cartoon fire safety tip. The cards measure approximately 3" by 5" and are in full color. The cards are numbered on the backs. The sets were distributed on July 19th during the Cardinals' game against the Los Angeles Dodgers to fans 15 years of age and under.

	MINT	NRMT	EXC
COMPLETE SET (25)	10.00	4.50	1.25
COMMON CARD (1-25)	.25	.11	.03
☐ 1 Whitey Herzog MG	.75	.35	.09
☐ 2 Danny Cox	.25	.11	.03
☐ 3 Ken Dayley	.25	.11	.03
☐ 4 Jose DeLeon	.25	.11	.03
☐ 5 Bob Forsch	.50	.23	.06
☐ 6 Joe Magrane	.25	.11	.03
☐ 7 Greg Mathews	.25	.11	.03
☐ 8 Scott Terry	.25	.11	.03
☐ 9 John Tudor	.50	.23	.06
☐ 10 Todd Worrell	.75	.35	.09
☐ 11 Steve Lake	.25	.11	.03
☐ 12 Tom Pagnozzi	.50	.23	.06
☐ 13 Tony Pena	.50	.23	.06
☐ 14 Bob Horner	.50	.23	.06
☐ 15 Tom Lawless	.25	.11	.03
☐ 16 Jose Oquendo (Ryne Sandberg also shown on card)	1.00	.45	.12
☐ 17 Terry Pendleton	.50	.23	.06
☐ 18 Ozzie Smith	4.00	1.80	.50
☐ 19 Vince Coleman	.50	.23	.06
☐ 20 Curt Ford	.25	.11	.03
☐ 21 Willie McGee	1.25	.55	.16
☐ 22 Larry McWilliams	.25	.11	.03
☐ 23 Steve Peters	.25	.11	.03
☐ 24 Luis Alicea	.25	.11	.03
☐ 25 Tom Brunansky	.25	.11	.03

1989 Cardinals Smokey

The 1989 Smokey Cardinals set contains 24 cards measuring approximately 4" by 6". The fronts have color photos with white and red borders. The backs feature biographical information. The cards are unnumbered so they are listed below in alphabetical order for reference.

	MINT	NRMT	EXC
COMPLETE SET (24)	10.00	4.50	1.25
COMMON CARD (1-24)	.25	.11	.03
☐ 1 Tom Brunansky	.25	.11	.03
☐ 2 Vince Coleman	.75	.35	.09
☐ 3 John Costello	.25	.11	.03

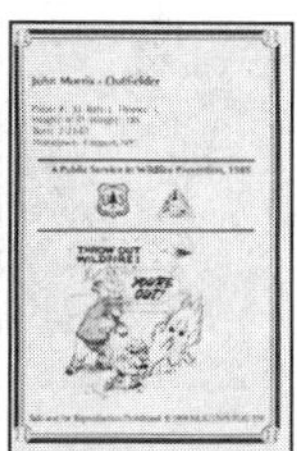

	MINT	NRMT	EXC
☐ 4 Ken Dayley	.25	.11	.03
☐ 5 Jose DeLeon	.25	.11	.03
☐ 6 Frank DiPino	.25	.11	.03
☐ 7 Pedro Guerrero	.75	.35	.09
☐ 8 Whitey Herzog MG	.75	.35	.09
☐ 9 Ken Hill	1.50	.70	.19
☐ 10 Tim Jones	.25	.11	.03
☐ 11 Jim Lindeman	.25	.11	.03
☐ 12 Joe Magrane	.25	.11	.03
☐ 13 Willie McGee	1.25	.55	.16
☐ 14 John Morris	.25	.11	.03
☐ 15 Jose Oquendo	.25	.11	.03
☐ 16 Tom Pagnozzi	.50	.23	.06
☐ 17 Tony Pena	.50	.23	.06
☐ 18 Terry Pendleton	.50	.23	.06
☐ 19 Dan Quisenberry	.75	.35	.09
☐ 20 Ozzie Smith	3.00	1.35	.35
☐ 21 Scott Terry	.25	.11	.03
☐ 22 Milt Thompson	.25	.11	.03
☐ 23 Denny Walling	.25	.11	.03
☐ 24 Todd Worrell	.75	.35	.09

1990 Cardinals Smokey

This 27-card, approximately 3" by 5", set was issued about the 1990 St. Louis Cardinals in conjuction with the US Forest Service which was using the popular character Smokey the Bear. The set has full color action photos of the Cardinals on the front of the card while the back of the card has fire safety tips on the bottom of the card. The set has been checklisted alphabetically for reference. The cards are unnumbered; not even uniform numbers are displayed prominently.

	MINT	NRMT	EXC
COMPLETE SET (27)	12.50	5.50	1.55
COMMON CARD (1-27)	.50	.23	.06
☐ 1 Vince Coleman	1.00	.45	.12
☐ 2 Dave Collins	.50	.23	.06
☐ 3 Danny Cox	.50	.23	.06
☐ 4 Ken Dayley	.50	.23	.06
☐ 5 Frank DiPino	.50	.23	.06
☐ 6 Jose DeLeon	.50	.23	.06
☐ 7 Pedro Guerrero	1.00	.45	.12
☐ 8 Whitey Herzog MG	1.00	.45	.12
☐ 9 Rick Horton	.50	.23	.06
☐ 10 Rex Hudler	.50	.23	.06
☐ 11 Tim Jones	.50	.23	.06
☐ 12 Joe Magrane	.50	.23	.06
☐ 13 Greg Mathews	.50	.23	.06
☐ 14 Willie McGee	1.50	.70	.19
☐ 15 John Morris	.50	.23	.06
☐ 16 Tom Niedenfuer	.50	.23	.06
☐ 17 Jose Oquendo	.50	.23	.06
☐ 18 Tom Pagnozzi	.75	.35	.09
☐ 19 Terry Pendleton	1.25	.55	.16
☐ 20 Bryn Smith	.50	.23	.06
☐ 21 Lee Smith	1.50	.70	.19
☐ 22 Ozzie Smith	3.00	1.35	.35
☐ 23 Scott Terry	.50	.23	.06
☐ 24 Milt Thompson	.50	.23	.06
☐ 25 John Tudor	.50	.23	.06
☐ 26 Denny Walling	.50	.23	.06
☐ 27 Todd Zeile	1.00	.45	.12

1991 Cardinals Police

This 24-card police set was sponsored by the Kansas City Life Insurance Company and distributed by Greater St. Louis Law Enforcement Agencies. The cards measure approximately 2 5/8" by 4 1/8" and feature on the fronts a mix of posed and action color player photos with white borders. The team name, uniform number, and player's name appear in the white border below the pictures. In red print on white, the backs have biography, statistics, a safety cartoon with caption, and sponsor's logo. The cards are checklisted below by uniform number.

	MINT	NRMT	EXC
COMPLETE SET (24)	12.50	5.50	1.55
COMMON CARD	.50	.23	.06

☐ 1 Ozzie Smith	3.00	1.35	.35
☐ 7 Geronimo Pena	.50	.23	.06
☐ 9 Joe Torre MG	1.00	.45	.12
☐ 10 Rex Hudler	.50	.23	.06
☐ 11 Jose Oquendo	.50	.23	.06
☐ 12 Craig Wilson	.50	.23	.06
☐ 16 Ray Lankford	2.00	.90	.25
☐ 19 Tom Pagnozzi	.75	.35	.09
☐ 21 Gerald Perry	.50	.23	.06
☐ 23 Bernard Gilkey	2.00	.90	.25
☐ 25 Milt Thompson	.50	.23	.06
☐ 27 Todd Zeile	1.00	.45	.12
☐ 28 Pedro Guerrero	1.00	.45	.12
☐ 29 Rich Gedman	.50	.23	.06
☐ 34 Felix Jose	.50	.23	.06
☐ 35 Frank DiPino	.50	.23	.06
☐ 36 Bryn Smith	.50	.23	.06
☐ 37 Scott Terry	.50	.23	.06
☐ 38 Todd Worrell	1.00	.45	.12
☐ 39 Bob Tewksbury	.75	.35	.09
☐ 43 Ken Hill	1.25	.55	.16
☐ 47 Lee Smith	1.50	.70	.19
☐ 48 Jose DeLeon	.50	.23	.06
☐ 49 Juan Agosto	.50	.23	.06

1992 Cardinals McDonald's/Pacific

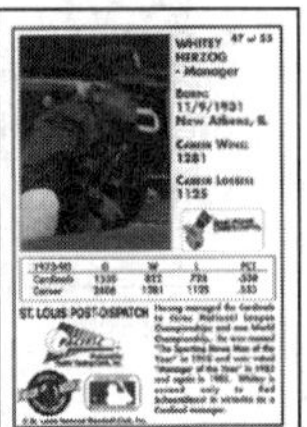

Produced by Pacific, this 55-card standard-size set commemorates the 100th anniversary of the St. Louis Cardinals. The collection was available at McDonald's restaurants in the greater St. Louis area for 1.49 with a purchase, and was distributed to raise money for Ronald McDonald Children's Charities. The set features black-and-white and color action player photos of players throughout Cardinals' history. The pictures are bordered in gold and include the player's name, the Cardinals 100th anniversary logo, and the McDonald's logo. The back design consists of a posed player photo, biographical and statistical information, and a career summary. There was also an album issued to go with this set. The album is not widely available at this time.

	MINT	NRMT	EXC
COMPLETE SET (55)	40.00	18.00	5.00
COMMON CARD (1-55)	.25	.11	.03
☐ 1 Jim Bottomley	1.00	.45	.12
☐ 2 Rip Collins	.25	.11	.03
☐ 3 Johnny Mize	1.50	.70	.19
☐ 4 Rogers Hornsby	3.00	1.35	.35
☐ 5 Miller Huggins	1.00	.45	.12
☐ 6 Marty Marion	.75	.35	.09
☐ 7 Frank Frisch	1.00	.45	.12
☐ 8 Whitey Kurowski	.25	.11	.03
☐ 9 Joe Medwick	1.00	.45	.12
☐ 10 Terry Moore	.75	.35	.09
☐ 11 Chick Hafey	1.00	.45	.12
☐ 12 Pepper Martin	.75	.35	.09
☐ 13 Bob O'Farrell	.25	.11	.03
☐ 14 Walker Cooper	.25	.11	.03
☐ 15 Dizzy Dean	2.00	.90	.25
☐ 16 Grover C. Alexander	1.50	.70	.19
☐ 17 Jesse Haines	1.00	.45	.12
☐ 18 Bill Hallahan	.25	.11	.03
☐ 19 Mort Cooper	.50	.23	.06
☐ 20 Burleigh Grimes	1.00	.45	.12
☐ 21 Red Schoendienst	1.50	.70	.19
☐ 22 Stan Musial	7.50	3.40	.95
☐ 23 Enos Slaughter	1.50	.70	.19
☐ 24 Keith Hernandez	.75	.35	.09
☐ 25 Bill White	.75	.35	.09
☐ 26 Orlando Cepeda	1.00	.45	.12
☐ 27 Julian Javier	.50	.23	.06
☐ 28 Dick Groat	.50	.23	.06
☐ 29 Ken Boyer	.75	.35	.09
☐ 30 Lou Brock	1.50	.70	.19
☐ 31 Mike Shannon	.50	.23	.06
☐ 32 Curt Flood	.75	.35	.09
☐ 33 Joe Cunningham	.25	.11	.03
☐ 34 Reggie Smith	.50	.23	.06
☐ 35 Ted Simmons	.75	.35	.09
☐ 36 Tim McCarver	.75	.35	.09
☐ 37 Tom Herr	.25	.11	.03
☐ 38 Ozzie Smith	5.00	2.20	.60
☐ 39 Joe Torre	1.00	.45	.12
☐ 40 Terry Pendleton	.75	.35	.09
☐ 41 Ken Reitz	.25	.11	.03
☐ 42 Vince Coleman	.25	.11	.03
☐ 43 Willie McGee	.75	.35	.09
☐ 44 Bake McBride	.25	.11	.03
☐ 45 George Hendrick	.25	.11	.03
☐ 46 Bob Gibson	1.50	.70	.19
☐ 47 Whitey Herzog MG	.75	.35	.09
☐ 48 Harry Brecheen	.50	.23	.06
☐ 49 Howard Pollet	.25	.11	.03
☐ 50 John Tudor	.25	.11	.03
☐ 51 Bob Forsch	.25	.11	.03
☐ 52 Bruce Sutter	.75	.35	.09
☐ 53 Lee Smith	.50	.23	.06
☐ 54 Todd Worrell	.75	.35	.09
☐ 55 Al Hrabosky	.50	.23	.06

1992 Cardinals Police

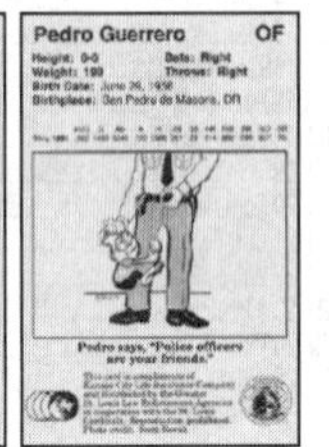

This 26-card set commemorates the 100th anniversary of the Cardinals. The set was sponsored by the Kansas City Life Insurance Company and distributed by the Greater St. Louis Law Enforcement Agencies. The cards measure 2 5/8" by 4 1/8" and feature color action player photos with white borders. One corner of the photo is cut off to create space for the St. Louis Cardinals 100th Anniversary logo. Placement of the logo varies on the cards from the upper right, upper left, or lower right corner. The team name is printed in red on the bottom border, while the player's name and jersey number are in black. The backs are printed in red on a white background and feature biographical and statistical information as well as a cartoon and a corresponding public service player quote. The sponsors are printed at the bottom. The cards are unnumbered and checklisted below in alphabetical order.

	MINT	NRMT	EXC
COMPLETE SET (27)	10.00	4.50	1.25
COMMON CARD (1-27)	.25	.11	.03
☐ 1 Juan Agosto	.25	.11	.03
☐ 2 Cris Carpenter	.25	.11	.03
☐ 3 Jose DeLeon	.25	.11	.03
☐ 4 Andres Galarraga	1.25	.55	.16
☐ 5 Rich Gedman	.25	.11	.03
☐ 6 Bernard Gilkey	1.25	.55	.16
☐ 7 Pedro Guerrero	.50	.23	.06
☐ 8 Rex Hudler	.25	.11	.03
☐ 9 Felix Jose	.25	.11	.03
☐ 10 Ray Lankford	1.25	.55	.16
☐ 11 Joe Magrane	.25	.11	.03
☐ 12 Omar Olivares	.25	.11	.03
☐ 13 Jose Oquendo	.25	.11	.03
☐ 14 Tom Pagnozzi	.50	.23	.06
☐ 15 Geronimo Pena	.25	.11	.03
☐ 16 Gerald Perry	.25	.11	.03
☐ 17 Bryn Smith	.25	.11	.03
☐ 18 Lee Smith	1.25	.55	.16
☐ 19 Ozzie Smith	2.50	1.10	.30
☐ 20 Scott Terry	.25	.11	.03
☐ 21 Bob Tewksbury	.50	.23	.06
☐ 22 Milt Thompson	.25	.11	.03
☐ 23 Joe Torre MG	.75	.35	.09
☐ 24 Craig Wilson	.25	.11	.03
☐ 25 Todd Worrell	.50	.23	.06
☐ 26 Todd Zeile	.50	.23	.06
☐ 27 Checklist	.25	.11	.03

1993 Cardinals Police

Sponsored by the Kansas City Life Insurance Company, the 26 cards comprising this set measure 2 5/8" by 4" and feature on their fronts blue-bordered color player action photos. The player's name, position, and uniform number appear at the bottom in white lettering. The Cardinals name appears at the top in red lettering and the team logo rests in the lower left corner. The white back carries the player's name, position, biography, and statistics at the top. A safety tip appears below. The Kansas City Life and St. Louis Law Enforcement Agencies logos round out the back. The cards are unnumbered and checklisted below in alphabetical order.

	MINT	NRMT	EXC
COMPLETE SET (26)	7.00	3.10	.85
COMMON CARD (1-26)	.25	.11	.03
☐ 1 Luis Alicea	.25	.11	.03
☐ 2 Rene Arocha	.25	.11	.03
☐ 3 Rod Brewer	.25	.11	.03
☐ 4 Ozzie Canseco	.25	.11	.03
☐ 5 Rheal Cormier	.25	.11	.03
☐ 6 Bernard Gilkey	.50	.23	.06
☐ 7 Gregg Jefferies	.50	.23	.06
☐ 8 Brian Jordan	1.00	.45	.12
☐ 9 Ray Lankford	.50	.23	.06
☐ 10 Rob Murphy	.25	.11	.03
☐ 11 Omar Olivares	.25	.11	.03
☐ 12 Jose Oquendo	.25	.11	.03
☐ 13 Donovan Osborne	.75	.35	.09
☐ 14 Tom Pagnozzi	.50	.23	.06
☐ 15 Geronimo Pena	.25	.11	.03
☐ 16 Mike Perez	.25	.11	.03
☐ 17 Gerald Perry	.25	.11	.03
☐ 18 Stan Royer	.25	.11	.03
☐ 19 Lee Smith	1.25	.55	.16
☐ 20 Ozzie Smith	2.50	1.10	.30
☐ 21 Bob Tewksbury	.50	.23	.06
☐ 22 Joe Torre MG	.75	.35	.09
☐ 23 Hector Villanueva	.25	.11	.03
☐ 24 Tracy Woodson	.25	.11	.03
☐ 25 Todd Zeile	.50	.23	.06
☐ 26 Checklist	.25	.11	.03

1994 Cardinals Police

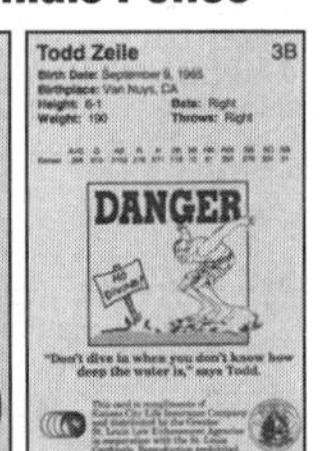

Measuring approximately 2 5/8" by 4", this 26-card set was sponsored by Kansas City Life Insurance Company and distributed by Greater St. Louis Law Enforcement Agencies. The borderless fronts feature an inset color player photo. The player's name and position appear directly underneath the photo. A red stripe runs vertically on the left side and the jersey number is found on a baseball icon in the lower right corner. In red print on white, the backs carry biography, statistics, and a picture illustrating a public service announcement by the player. The cards are unnumbered and checklisted below in alphabetical order.

	MINT	NRMT	EXC
COMPLETE SET (26)	6.00	2.70	.75
COMMON CARD (1-26)	.25	.11	.03
☐ 1 Luis Alicea	.25	.11	.03
☐ 2 Rene Arocha	.25	.11	.03
☐ 3 Rich Batchelor	.25	.11	.03
☐ 4 Rheal Cormier	.25	.11	.03
☐ 5 Bernard Gilkey	1.00	.45	.12
☐ 6 Gregg Jefferies	.75	.35	.09
☐ 7 Brian Jordan	.75	.35	.09
☐ 8 Paul Kilgus	.25	.11	.03
☐ 9 Ray Lankford	1.00	.45	.12
☐ 10 Rob Murphy	.25	.11	.03
☐ 11 Omar Olivares	.25	.11	.03
☐ 12 Jose Oquendo	.25	.11	.03
☐ 13 Tom Pagnozzi	.50	.23	.06
☐ 14 Erik Pappas	.25	.11	.03
☐ 15 Geronimo Pena	.25	.11	.03
☐ 16 Mike Perez	.25	.11	.03
☐ 17 Gerald Perry	.25	.11	.03
☐ 18 Stan Royer	.25	.11	.03
☐ 19 Ozzie Smith	2.00	.90	.25
☐ 20 Rick Sutcliffe	.25	.11	.03
☐ 21 Bob Tewksbury	.25	.11	.03
☐ 22 Joe Torre MG	.75	.35	.09
☐ 23 Tom Urbani	.25	.11	.03
☐ 24 Allen Watson	.75	.35	.09
☐ 25 Mark Whiten	.25	.11	.03
☐ 26 Todd Zeile	.50	.23	.06

1996 Cardinals Police

This 26-card set measures approximately 2 1/2" by 4". The player's photo, name and uniform number are notated on the front. The back has vital statistics, career stats and a safety tip. The cards are unnumberd so we have sequenced them in alphabetical order.

	MINT	NRMT	EXC
COMPLETE SET (26)	7.50	3.40	.95
COMMON CARD (1-26)	.25	.11	.03
☐ 1 Alan Benes	1.00	.45	.12
☐ 2 Andy Benes	.75	.35	.09
☐ 3 Pat Borders	.25	.11	.03

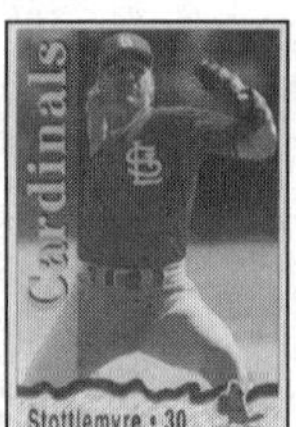

☐ 4 Royce Clayton	.50	.23	.06
☐ 5 Dennis Eckersley	1.00	.45	.12
☐ 6 Tony Fossas	.25	.11	.03
☐ 7 Fredbird CL Mascot	.25	.11	.03
☐ 8 Ron Gant	1.00	.45	.12
☐ 9 Gary Gaetti	.50	.23	.06
☐ 10 Mike Gallego	.25	.11	.03
☐ 11 Rick Honeycutt	.25	.11	.03
☐ 12 Danny Jackson	.25	.11	.03
☐ 13 Brian Jordan	1.00	.45	.12
☐ 14 Ray Lankford	1.00	.45	.12
☐ 15 Tony LaRussa MG	.50	.23	.06
☐ 16 John Mabry	.50	.23	.06
☐ 17 T.J. Mathews	.25	.11	.03
☐ 18 Willie McGee	.75	.35	.09
☐ 19 Mike Morgan	.25	.11	.03
☐ 20 Donovan Osborne	.50	.23	.06
☐ 21 Tom Pagnozzi	.25	.11	.03
☐ 22 Mark Petvosek	.25	.11	.03
☐ 23 Ozzie Smith	2.00	.90	.25
☐ 24 Todd Stottlemyre	.75	.35	.09
☐ 25 Mark Sweeney	.25	.11	.03
☐ 26 Tom Urbani	.25	.11	.03

1993 Cardtoons

This 156-card unlicensed standard-size set was distributed in eight-card packs with a suggested retail of $1.29. The set uses fanciful cartoon caricatures on its fronts to parody major league baseball players. The borderless cartoons are framed by a thin gold-colored line that terminates in gold-colored baseball icons, which set off the "player's" name at the bottom. The backs carry comical "career highlights" within silver-colored panels on the left sides and team logo caricatures on the right sides. Cards #1-95 were drawn by sports artist Dayne Dudley. The checklist below contains five subsets and a Promo Set of three cards.The three Promo cards are numbered on the back with a "P" prefix. Cards F1-F10 belong to the Grand Slam Foil Etched Subset which features U-V coated colors and special effects on each card. Cards R1-R8 belong to a subset titled Cardtoons Awards which could be obtained by a special offer found on one of three replacement cards inserted in packs. Cards S1-S11 features cartoons by cartoonist Dave Simpson and carries his views of baseball in 1993. Cards BB1-BB20 display head caricatures of baseball's highest paid players on dollar bill backgrounds. Cards FOG1-FOG9 belong to the subset Field of Greed which fitted together to form a nine-piece puzzle. Even though this set does not have a liscence, it is listed since the company won a suit that allows it to be released as a parody under first admendment rules. The complete set price includes all the insert cards.

	MINT	NRMT	EXC
COMPLETE SET (156)	75.00	34.00	9.50
COMMON CARD (1-95)	.10	.05	.01
COMMON CARD (P1-P3)	1.00	.45	.12
COMMON CARD (S1-S7)	1.00	.45	.12
COMMON CARD (FOG1-FOG9)	.25	.11	.03
COMMON CARD (BB1-BB20)	1.00	.45	.12
COMMON CARD (F1-F10)	1.00	.45	.12
COMMON CARD (R!-R8)	.50	.23	.06
☐ 1 Hey Abbott	.25	.11	.03
☐ 2 Robin Adventura	.25	.11	.03
☐ 3 Roberto Alamode	.50	.23	.06
☐ 4 Don Battingly	1.00	.45	.12
☐ 5 Cow Belle	1.00	.45	.12
☐ 6 Jay Bellhop	.10	.05	.01
☐ 7 Fowl Boggs	.60	.25	.07
☐ 8 Treasury Bonds	.75	.35	.09
☐ 9 True Brett	1.00	.45	.12
☐ 10 Wild Pitch Mitch	.10	.05	.01
☐ 11 Balou's Brothers	.10	.05	.01
☐ 12 Charlie Bustle	.25	.11	.03
☐ 13 Brett Butter	.10	.05	.01
☐ 14 Rambo Canseco	.50	.23	.06
☐ 15 Roberto Cementie	1.50	.70	.19
☐ 16 Roger Clemency	.75	.35	.09
☐ 17 Will Clock	.10	.05	.01
☐ 18 David Clone	.25	.11	.03
☐ 19 Tom Clowning	.10	.05	.01

☐ 20 Mr. Club	.50	.23	.06
☐ 21 Joe Crater	.25	.11	.03
☐ 22 Doolin' Daulton	.25	.11	.03
☐ 23 Chili Dog Davis	.25	.11	.03
☐ 24 Doug Drawback	.10	.05	.01
☐ 25 Dennis Excellency	.25	.11	.03
☐ 26 Silly Fanatic	.10	.05	.01
☐ 27 Wand Gonzales	1.00	.45	.12
☐ 28 Amazing Grace	.50	.23	.06
☐ 29 Tom Grapevine	.25	.11	.03
☐ 30 Marquis Gruesome	.25	.11	.03
☐ 31 Homerin' Hank	1.00	.45	.12
☐ 32 Kevin Happier	.10	.05	.01
☐ 33 Pete Harness	.10	.05	.01
☐ 34 Charlie Haze	.10	.05	.01
☐ 35 Egotisticky Henderson	.50	.23	.06
☐ 36 Sayanora Infielder	.10	.05	.01
☐ 37 Snoozin' Ted , Tarzan Jane	.10	.05	.01
☐ 38 Cloud Johnson	.10	.05	.01
☐ 39 Sandy K-Fax	.75	.35	.09
☐ 40 The Say What Kid	1.00	.45	.12
☐ 41 Tommy Lasagna	.25	.11	.03
☐ 42 Greg Maddogs	1.25	.55	.16
☐ 43 Stamp the Man	.50	.23	.06
☐ 44 Mark McBash	.60	.25	.07
☐ 45 Fred McGruff	.10	.05	.01
☐ 46 Mount Mick	2.00	.90	.25
☐ 47 Pat Moustache	.10	.05	.01
☐ 48 Ozzie Myth	.75	.35	.09
☐ 49 Bob Nukesbury	.10	.05	.01
☐ 50 Reggie October	.75	.35	.09
☐ 51 Doctor OK	.25	.11	.03
☐ 52 Rafael Palmist	.25	.11	.03
☐ 53 Lose Pinella	.10	.05	.01
☐ 54 Vince Poleman	.10	.05	.01
☐ 55 Charlie Puff	.10	.05	.01
☐ 56 Rob Quibble	.10	.05	.01
☐ 57 Darryl Razzberry	.10	.05	.01
☐ 58 Cal Ripkenwinkle	1.50	.70	.19
☐ 59 Budge Rodriguez	.75	.35	.09
☐ 60 Ryne Sandbox	1.00	.45	.12
☐ 61 Steve Saxophone	.10	.05	.01
☐ 62 Harry Scaray	.10	.05	.01
☐ 63 Scary Shefield	.50	.23	.06
☐ 64 Ruben Siesta	.10	.05	.01
☐ 65 Dennis Smartinez	.10	.05	.01
☐ 66 Lee Smite	.25	.11	.03
☐ 67 Ken Spiffy Jr.	2.00	.90	.25
☐ 68 Nails Spikestra	.10	.05	.01
☐ 69 The Splendid Spinner	1.50	.70	.19
☐ 70 Toad Stottlemyre	.10	.05	.01
☐ 71 Raging Tartabull	.10	.05	.01
☐ 72 Robbery Thompson	.10	.05	.01
☐ 73 Alan Trampoline	.25	.11	.03
☐ 74 Monster Truk	.10	.05	.01
☐ 75 Shawon Tungsten	.10	.05	.01
☐ 76 Tony Twynn	1.00	.45	.12
☐ 77 Andy Van Tyke	.10	.05	.01
☐ 78 Derrick Ventriloquist	.10	.05	.01
☐ 79 Frankie Violin	.10	.05	.01
☐ 80 Rap Winfielder	.75	.35	.09
☐ 81 Robinhood Yount	.50	.23	.06
☐ 82 Swift Justice	.10	.05	.01
☐ 83 Brat Saberhagen	.10	.05	.01
☐ 84 Mike Pizzazz	1.25	.55	.16
☐ 85 Andres Colorado	.25	.11	.03
☐ 86 Money Bagswell	1.25	.55	.16
☐ 87 Video Nomo	1.50	.70	.19
☐ 88 Out of the Park	.10	.05	.01
☐ 89 Tim Wallet	.10	.05	.01
☐ 90 Checklist	.10	.05	.01
☐ 91 Greenback Jack	.10	.05	.01
☐ 92 Mighty Matt Power Hitter	.10	.05	.01
☐ 93 Frankenthomas	2.00	.90	.25
☐ 94 Neon Peon Slanders	1.00	.45	.12
☐ 95 Just Air Jordan	2.50	1.10	.30
☐ F1 Bo Action	1.00	.45	.12
☐ F2 Andre Awesome	1.50	.70	.19
☐ F3 Bobby Bonus	2.50	1.10	.30
☐ F4 Steve Bravery	1.00	.45	.12
☐ F5 Carlton Fist	2.00	.90	.25
☐ F6 E.T. McGee	1.00	.45	.12
☐ F7 Kirbvy Plunkit	3.00	1.35	.35
☐ F8 Jose Rheostat	1.00	.45	.12
☐ F9 Sir Noble Ryan	4.00	1.80	.50
☐ F10 Day-Glo Sabo	1.00	.45	.12
☐ P1 Day-Glo Sabo	1.00	.45	.12
☐ P2 Dennis Excellency	1.50	.70	.19
☐ P3 Pledge of Allegiance	1.00	.45	.12
☐ R1 No Ball Peace Prize	.50	.23	.06
☐ R2 Forrest Grump	.50	.23	.06
☐ R3 Most Virtuous Player	.50	.23	.06
☐ R4 Golden Glove Award	.50	.23	.06
☐ R5 Comedown Player of the Year	.50	.23	.06
☐ R6 Corkville Slugger	.50	.23	.06
☐ R7 Can't Get No Relief	.50	.23	.06
☐ R8 1994 World Series Champ	.50	.23	.06
☐ S1 Pledge of Allegiance	1.00	.45	.12
☐ S2 Th Wave	1.00	.45	.12
☐ S3 Slick Willie	1.00	.45	.12
☐ S4 Umpires Convention	1.00	.45	.12
☐ S5 The Slide	1.00	.45	.12
☐ S6 SH-H-H-H-H-H-H	1.00	.45	.12
☐ S7 Throwing Out the First Contract	1.00	.45	.12
☐ S8 Babe Rush	3.00	1.35	.35
☐ S9 Hot Prospect	1.00	.45	.12
☐ S10 Let's Play Ball	1.00	.45	.12
☐ S11 Role Model	1.00	.45	.12
☐ BB1 Treasury Bonds	2.00	.90	.25
☐ BB2 Sayanora Infielder	1.00	.45	.12
☐ BB3 Cal Ripkenwinkle	4.00	1.80	.50
☐ BB4 Bobby Bonus	1.50	.70	.19
☐ BB5 Joe Crater	1.00	.45	.12
☐ BB6 Kirby Plunkit	2.00	.90	.25
☐ BB7 David Clone	1.00	.45	.12
☐ BB8 Ken Spiffy Jr.	4.00	1.80	.50
☐ BB9 Ruben Siesta	1.00	.45	.12
☐ BB10 Greg Maddogs	2.50	1.10	.30
☐ BB11 Mark McBash	1.50	.70	.19
☐ BB12 Rafael Palmist	1.00	.45	.12
☐ BB13 Roberto Alamode	1.50	.70	.19
☐ BB14 Greenback Jack	1.00	.45	.12
☐ BB15 Raging Tartabull	1.00	.45	.12
☐ BB16 Jimmy Kiwi	1.00	.45	.12
☐ BB17 Roger Clemency	2.50	1.10	.30
☐ BB18 Rambo Canseco	1.50	.70	.19
☐ BB19 Tom Grapevine	1.25	.55	.16
☐ BB20 John Smileyface	1.00	.45	.12
☐ FOG1 Strike 1 (Top left of puzzle)	.25	.11	.03
☐ FOG2 Strike 2 (Top middle of puzzle)	.25	.11	.03
☐ FOG3 Strike 3 (Top right of puzzle)	.25	.11	.03
☐ FOG4 Strike 4 (Middle left of puzzle)	.25	.11	.03
☐ FOG5 Strike 5 (Middle of puzzle)	.25	.11	.03
☐ FOG6 Strike 6 (Middle right of puzzle)	.25	.11	.03
☐ FOG7 Strike 7 (Bottom left of puzzle	.25	.11	.03
☐ FOG8 Strike 8 (Bottom middle of puzzle)	.25	.11	.03
☐ FOG9 Strike 9 (Bottom right of puzzle)	.25	.11	.03

1989 Cereal Superstars

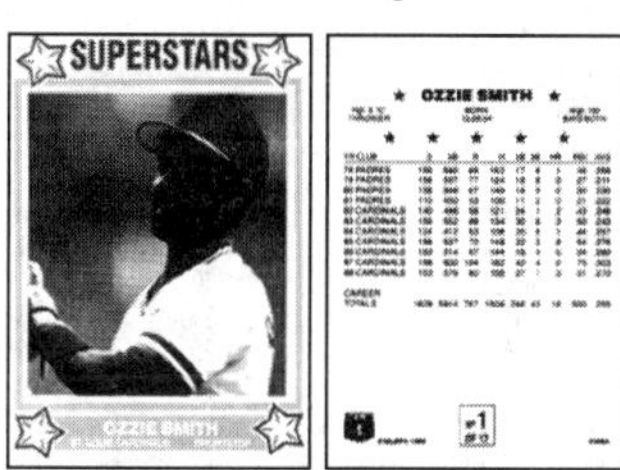

This 12-card, standard-size set was issued by MSA (Michael Schechter Associates) and celebrates some of the baseball's best players as of 1989. The sets have an attractive design of stars in each of the front corners with the word Superstars on the top of the card and players name, team, and position underneath the full color photo of the player. Like most of the MSA sets there are no team logos used. The vertically oriented backs show career statistics. Reportedly two cards were included in each specially marked Ralston Purina cereal box.

	MINT	NRMT	EXC
COMPLETE SET (12)	6.00	2.70	.75
COMMON CARD (1-12)	.25	.11	.03
☐ 1 Ozzie Smith	1.50	.70	.19
☐ 2 Andre Dawson	.50	.23	.06
☐ 3 Darryl Strawberry	.50	.23	.06
☐ 4 Mike Schmidt	1.25	.55	.16
☐ 5 Orel Hershiser	.50	.23	.06
☐ 6 Tim Raines	.50	.23	.06
☐ 7 Roger Clemens	1.25	.55	.16
☐ 8 Kirby Puckett	2.00	.90	.25
☐ 9 George Brett	1.50	.70	.19
☐ 10 Alan Trammell	.50	.23	.06
☐ 11 Don Mattingly	2.00	.90	.25
☐ 12 Jose Canseco	1.00	.45	.12

1964 Challenge The Yankees

These cards were distributed as part of a baseball game produced in 1964. The cards each measure 4" by 5 3/8" and have square corners. The card fronts show a small black and white inset photo of the player, his name, position, vital statistics and the game outcomes associated with that particular player's card. The colors used on the front of the card are a blue border at the top and a yellow background for the game outcomes at the bottom. The game was played by rolling two dice. The outcomes (two through twelve) on the player's card related to the sum of the two dice. The game was noted for slightly inflated offensive production compared to real life. The cards are blank backed. Since the cards are unnumbered, they are listed below in alphabetical order within group. The first 25 cards are Yankees and the next 25 are All-Stars. Sets were put out in two different years, WG9 1964 and WG10 1965, which are difficult to distinguish.

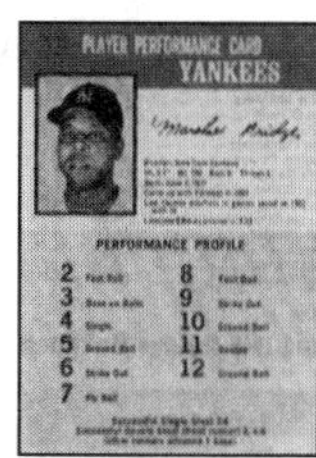

	NRMT	VG-E	GOOD
COMPLETE SET (50)	600.00	275.00	75.00
COMMON CARD (1-50)	5.00	2.20	.60
☐ 1 Yogi Berra	30.00	13.50	3.70
☐ 2 Johnny Blanchard	5.00	2.20	.60
☐ 3 Jim Bouton	7.50	3.40	.95
☐ 4 Clete Boyer	6.00	2.70	.75
☐ 5 Marshall Bridges	5.00	2.20	.60
☐ 6 Harry Bright	5.00	2.20	.60
☐ 7 Al Downing	5.00	2.20	.60
☐ 8 Whitey Ford	25.00	11.00	3.10
☐ 9 Jake Gibbs	5.00	2.20	.60
☐ 10 Pedro Gonzalez	5.00	2.20	.60
☐ 11 Steve Hamilton	5.00	2.20	.60
☐ 12 Elston Howard	10.00	4.50	1.25
☐ 13 Tony Kubek	10.00	4.50	1.25
☐ 14 Phil Linz	5.00	2.20	.60
☐ 15 Hector Lopez	5.00	2.20	.60
☐ 16 Mickey Mantle	150.00	70.00	19.00
☐ 17 Roger Maris	50.00	22.00	6.25
☐ 18 Tom Metcalf	5.00	2.20	.60
☐ 19 Joe Pepitone	6.00	2.70	.75
☐ 20 Hal Reniff	5.00	2.20	.60
☐ 21 Bobby Richardson	10.00	4.50	1.25
☐ 22 Bill Stafford	5.00	2.20	.60
☐ 23 Ralph Terry	6.00	2.70	.75
☐ 24 Tom Tresh	6.00	2.70	.75
☐ 25 Stan Williams	5.00	2.20	.60
☐ 26 Hank Aaron	60.00	27.00	7.50
☐ 27 Tom Cheney	5.00	2.20	.60
☐ 28 Del Crandall	5.00	2.20	.60
☐ 29 Tito Francona	5.00	2.20	.60
☐ 30 Dick Groat	6.00	2.70	.75
☐ 31 Al Kaline	25.00	11.00	3.10
☐ 32 Art Mahaffey	5.00	2.20	.60
☐ 33 Frank Malzone	5.00	2.20	.60
☐ 34 Juan Marichal	15.00	6.75	1.85
☐ 35 Eddie Mathews	15.00	6.75	1.85
☐ 36 Bill Mazeroski	10.00	4.50	1.25
☐ 37 Ken McBride	5.00	2.20	.60
☐ 38 Willie McCovey	15.00	6.75	1.85
☐ 39 Jim O'Toole	5.00	2.20	.60
☐ 40 Milt Pappas	6.00	2.70	.75
☐ 41 Ron Perranoski	5.00	2.20	.60
☐ 42 Johnny Podres	6.00	2.70	.75
☐ 43 Dick Radatz	5.00	2.20	.60
☐ 44 Rich Rollins	5.00	2.20	.60
☐ 45 Ron Santo	10.00	4.50	1.25
☐ 46 Moose Skowron	6.00	2.70	.75
☐ 47 Duke Snider	25.00	11.00	3.10
☐ 48 Pete Ward	5.00	2.20	.60
☐ 49 Carl Warwick	5.00	2.20	.60
☐ 50 Carl Yastrzemski	25.00	11.00	3.10

1965 Challenge The Yankees

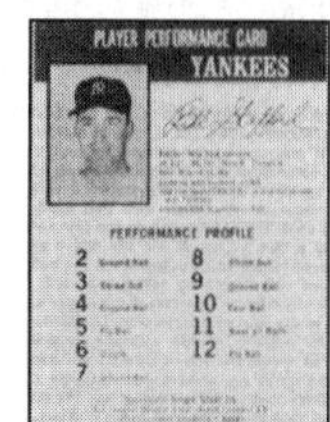

These cards were distributed as part of a baseball game produced in 1965. The cards each measure 4" by 5 3/8" and have square corners. The card fronts show a small black and white inset photo of the player, his name, position, vital statistics and the game outcomes associated with that particular player's card. The colors used on the front of the card are a blue border at the top and a yellow background for the game outcomes at the bottom. The game was played by rolling two dice. The outcomes (two through twelve) on the player's card related to the sum of the two dice. The game was noted for slightly inflated offensive production compared to real life. The cards are blank backed. Since the cards are unnumbered, they are listed below in alphabetical order within group. The first 23 cards are Yankees and the next 25 are All-Stars. There were also 18 blank cards included in the set for extra players of your choice. These "Challenge The Yankees" sets were put out in two different years, WG9 1964 and WG10 1965, which are difficult to distinguish.

	NRMT	VG-E	GOOD
COMPLETE SET (48)	500.00	220.00	60.00
COMMON CARD (1-48)	5.00	2.20	.60
☐ 1 Johnny Blanchard	5.00	2.20	.60
☐ 2 Jim Bouton	7.50	3.40	.95
☐ 3 Clete Boyer	6.00	2.70	.75
☐ 4 Leon Carmel	5.00	2.20	.60
☐ 5 Al Downing	5.00	2.20	.60
☐ 6 Whitey Ford	25.00	11.00	3.10
☐ 7 Jake Gibbs	5.00	2.20	.60
☐ 8 Pedro Gonzalez	5.00	2.20	.60
☐ 9 Steve Hamilton	5.00	2.20	.60
☐ 10 Elston Howard	10.00	4.50	1.25
☐ 11 Tony Kubek	10.00	4.50	1.25
☐ 12 Phil Linz	5.00	2.20	.60
☐ 13 Mickey Mantle	150.00	70.00	19.00
☐ 14 Roger Maris	50.00	22.00	6.25
☐ 15 Tom Metcalf	5.00	2.20	.60
☐ 16 Pete Mikkelsen	5.00	2.20	.60
☐ 17 Joe Pepitone	6.00	2.70	.75
☐ 18 Pedro Ramos	5.00	2.20	.60
☐ 19 Hal Reniff	5.00	2.20	.60
☐ 20 Bobby Richardson	10.00	4.50	1.25
☐ 21 Bill Stafford	5.00	2.20	.60
☐ 22 Mel Stottlemyre	6.00	2.70	.75
☐ 23 Tom Tresh	6.00	2.70	.75
☐ 24 Henry Aaron	60.00	27.00	7.50
☐ 25 Joe Christopher	5.00	2.20	.60
☐ 26 Vic Davalillo	5.00	2.20	.60
☐ 27 Bill Freehan	6.00	2.70	.75
☐ 28 Jim Gentile	5.00	2.20	.60
☐ 29 Dick Groat	6.00	2.70	.75
☐ 30 Al Kaline	25.00	11.00	3.10
☐ 31 Don Lock	5.00	2.20	.60
☐ 32 Art Mahaffey	5.00	2.20	.60
☐ 33 Frank Malzone	5.00	2.20	.60
☐ 34 Juan Marichal	15.00	6.75	1.85
☐ 35 Eddie Mathews	15.00	6.75	1.85
☐ 36 Bill Mazeroski	10.00	4.50	1.25
☐ 37 Ken McBride	5.00	2.20	.60
☐ 38 Tim McCarver	10.00	4.50	1.25
☐ 39 Willie McCovey	15.00	6.75	1.85
☐ 40 Jim O'Toole	5.00	2.20	.60
☐ 41 Milt Pappas	6.00	2.70	.75
☐ 42 Ron Perranoski	5.00	2.20	.60
☐ 43 Johnny Podres	6.00	2.70	.75
☐ 44 Dick Radatz	5.00	2.20	.60
☐ 45 Rich Rollins	5.00	2.20	.60
☐ 46 Ron Santo	10.00	4.50	1.25
☐ 47 Pete Ward	5.00	2.20	.60
☐ 48 Carl Yastrzemski	25.00	11.00	3.10

1982 Charboneau Super Joe's

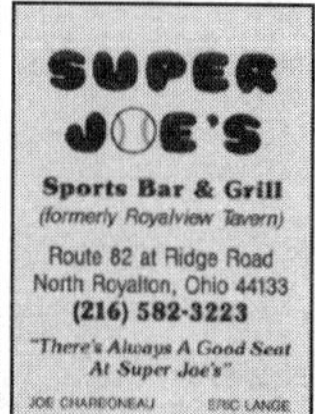

This two-card set features a black-and-white portrait of Cleveland Indians player, Joe Charboneau, on two different size cards. The smaller card is standard size, and the larger one measures approximately 3 1/2" by 5 1/2". The cards are checklisted below with the smaller one listed first.

	MINT	NRMT	EXC
COMPLETE SET (2)	5.00	2.20	.60
COMMON CARD (1-2)	2.00	.90	.25
☐ 1 Joe Charboneau (Standard size card)	2.00	.90	.25
☐ 2 Joe Charboneau (3 1/2" by 5 1/2" size card)	3.00	1.35	.35

1988 Chef Boyardee

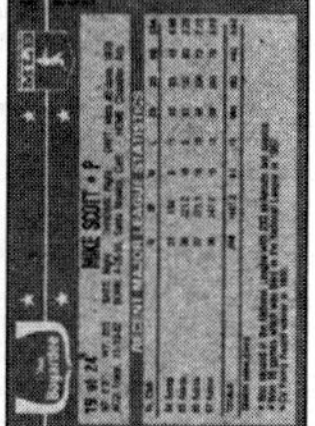

This 24-card set was distributed as a perforated sheet of four rows and six columns of cards in return for ten proofs of purchase of Chef Boyardee products and 1.50 for postage and handling. The card photos on the fronts are in full color with a light blue border but are not shown with team logos. The card backs are numbered and printed in red and blue on gray card stock. Individual cards measure approximately 2 1/2" by 3 1/2" and show the Chef Boyardee logo in the upper right corner of the obverse. Card backs feature year-by-year season statistics since 1984. There is no additional premium for having the sheet intact as opposed to having individual cards neatly cut.

	MINT	NRMT	EXC
COMPLETE SET (24)	10.00	4.50	1.25
COMMON CARD (1-24)	.25	.11	.03

☐ 1 Mark McGwire	2.00	.90	.25
☐ 2 Eric Davis	.50	.23	.06
☐ 3 Jack Morris	.50	.23	.06
☐ 4 George Bell	.25	.11	.03
☐ 5 Ozzie Smith	2.00	.90	.25
☐ 6 Tony Gwynn	2.00	.90	.25
☐ 7 Cal Ripken	3.00	1.35	.35
☐ 8 Todd Worrell	.25	.11	.03
☐ 9 Larry Parrish	.25	.11	.03
☐ 10 Gary Carter	.50	.23	.06
☐ 11 Ryne Sandberg	1.50	.70	.19
☐ 12 Keith Hernandez	.50	.23	.06
☐ 13 Kirby Puckett	2.00	.90	.25
☐ 14 Mike Schmidt	1.00	.45	.12
☐ 15 Frank Viola	.25	.11	.03
☐ 16 Don Mattingly	2.00	.90	.25
☐ 17 Dale Murphy	.75	.35	.09
☐ 18 Andre Dawson	.50	.23	.06
☐ 19 Mike Scott	.25	.11	.03
☐ 20 Rickey Henderson	1.00	.45	.12
☐ 21 Jim Rice	.50	.23	.06
☐ 22 Wade Boggs	1.00	.45	.12
☐ 23 Roger Clemens	1.25	.55	.16
☐ 24 Fernando Valenzuela	.50	.23	.06

1961 Chemstrand Patches

This nine-card set features color star player portraits on 2 1/2" diameter cloth patches which were included with the purchase of a boy's sport shirt for a short period in 1961. The patches were issued one to a cello package with instructions for ironing the patch onto the shirt. The package also offered the opportunity to trade the player patch for a different star. The patches are unnumbered and checklisted below in alphabetical order. Values for unopened cello packs are slightly higher.

	NRMT	VG-E	GOOD
COMPLETE SET (9)	350.00	160.00	45.00
COMMON CARD (1-9)	20.00	9.00	2.50
☐ 1 Ernie Banks	50.00	22.00	6.25
☐ 2 Yogi Berra	50.00	22.00	6.25
☐ 3 Nellie Fox	40.00	18.00	5.00
☐ 4 Dick Groat	20.00	9.00	2.50
☐ 5 Al Kaline	50.00	22.00	6.25
☐ 6 Harmon Killebrew	40.00	18.00	5.00
☐ 7 Frank Malzone	20.00	9.00	2.50
☐ 8 Willie Mays	75.00	34.00	9.50
☐ 9 Warren Spahn	40.00	18.00	5.00

1910 Chicago E90-3

The E90-3 American Caramels "All the Star Players" set contains 20 unnumbered cards (each measuring 1 1/2" by 2 3/4") featuring the Chicago White Sox and Chicago Cubs. The eleven Cubs are listed first in the checklist below in alphabetical order (1-11), followed by the White Sox (12-20). The backs are slightly different from E90-1 cards and the fronts differ in the use of the team nicknames.

	EX-MT	VG-E	GOOD
COMPLETE SET (20)	3000.00	1350.00	375.00
COMMON CARD (1-20)	100.00	45.00	12.50
☐ 1 Jimmy Archer	100.00	45.00	12.50
☐ 2 Mordecai Brown	300.00	135.00	38.00
☐ 3 Frank Chance	400.00	180.00	50.00
☐ 4 King Cole	100.00	45.00	12.50
☐ 5 Johnny Evers	300.00	135.00	38.00
☐ 6 Solly Hoffman	100.00	45.00	12.50
☐ 7 Orval Overall	100.00	45.00	12.50
☐ 8 Frank Schulte	100.00	45.00	12.50
☐ 9 Jimmy Scheckard	100.00	45.00	12.50
☐ 10 Harry Steinfeldt	150.00	70.00	19.00
☐ 11 Joe Tinker	300.00	135.00	38.00
☐ 12 Lena Blackburne	100.00	45.00	12.50
☐ 13 Patsy Dougherty	100.00	45.00	12.50
☐ 14 Chick Gandil	250.00	110.00	31.00
☐ 15 Ed Hahn	100.00	45.00	12.50
☐ 16 Fred Payne	100.00	45.00	12.50
☐ 17 Billy Purtell	100.00	45.00	12.50
☐ 18 Frank (Nig) Smith	100.00	45.00	12.50
☐ 19 Ed Walsh	300.00	135.00	38.00
☐ 20 Rollie Zeider	100.00	45.00	12.50

1930 Chicago Evening American Pins

This set features 10 members of the Chicago Cubs and 10 members of the Chicago White Sox. These unnumbered pins are ordered below alphabetically by team, Chicago Cubs (1-10) and Chicago White Sox (11-20). The pins measure approximately 1 1/4" in diameter. The top of the pin gives the player's position, last name and team nickname. The photos are black and white on a white background. The player photos are head only with no neck shown. The set is thought to have been issued in 1930.

	EX-MT	VG-E	GOOD
COMPLETE SET (20)	2750.00	1250.00	350.00
COMMON PLAYER (1-20)	100.00	45.00	12.50
☐ 1 Les Bell	100.00	45.00	12.50
☐ 2 Kiki Cuyler	200.00	90.00	25.00
☐ 3 Woody English	125.00	55.00	15.50
☐ 4 Charlie Grimm	150.00	70.00	19.00
☐ 5 Gabby Hartnett	200.00	90.00	25.00
☐ 6 Rogers Hornsby	350.00	160.00	45.00
☐ 7 Joe McCarthy MG	200.00	90.00	25.00
☐ 8 Charlie Root	125.00	55.00	15.50
☐ 9 Riggs Stephenson	150.00	70.00	19.00
☐ 10 Hack Wilson	200.00	90.00	25.00
☐ 11 Moe Berg	400.00	180.00	50.00
☐ 12 Donie Bush MG	100.00	45.00	12.50
☐ 13 Bill Cissell	100.00	45.00	12.50
☐ 14 Red Faber	200.00	90.00	25.00
☐ 15 Bill Hunnefield	100.00	45.00	12.50
☐ 16 Smead Jolley	125.00	55.00	15.50
☐ 17 Willie Kamm	100.00	45.00	12.50
☐ 18 Jim Moore	100.00	45.00	12.50
☐ 19 Carl Reynolds	100.00	45.00	12.50
☐ 20 Art Shires	125.00	55.00	15.50

1976 Chicago Greats

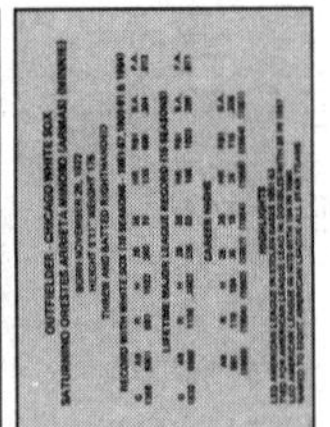

This 19-card standard-size set features black-and-white action player photos with a red baseball and bat border design. A small, square close-up photo is superimposed on one of the upper corners of the picture. "Chicago's Greats" is printed in red at the bottom. The horizontal backs are white and carry the player's name, biographical information, statistics and career highlights. The cards are unnumbered and checklisted below in alphabetical order.

	NRMT	VG-E	GOOD
COMPLETE SET (20)	10.00	4.50	1.25
COMMON CARD (1-20)	.30	.14	.04
☐ 1 Luke Appling	.75	.35	.09
☐ 2 Ernie Banks	1.50	.70	.19
☐ 3 Zeke Bonura	.30	.14	.04
☐ 4 Phil Cavarretta	.50	.23	.06
☐ 5 Jimmie Dykes	.40	.18	.05
☐ 6 Nellie Fox	1.00	.45	.12
☐ 7 Larry French	.30	.14	.04
☐ 8 Charlie Grimm	.50	.23	.06
☐ 9 Billy Herman	.75	.35	.09
☐ 10 Sherm Lollar	.30	.14	.04
☐ 11 Al Lopez	.75	.35	.09
☐ 12 Ted Lyons Red Faber	.40	.18	.05
☐ 13 Minnie Minoso	.75	.35	.09
☐ 14 Bill Nicholson	.30	.14	.04
☐ 15 Claude Passeau	.30	.14	.04
☐ 16 Billy Pierce	.50	.23	.06
☐ 17 Hank Sauer	.30	.14	.04
☐ 18 Riggs Stephenson	.50	.23	.06
☐ 19 Bill Veeck OWN	.50	.23	.06
☐ 20 Philip K. Wrigley OWN	.40	.18	.05

1994 Church's Hometown Stars

A pack containing four standard-size cards from the 28-card Hometown Stars set produced by Pinnacle was offered to consumers who bought a nine-piece family meal at Church's Chicken during April and May. Packs were also sold separately for 69 cents each. Each pack contained three regular cards and one gold foil-stamped card

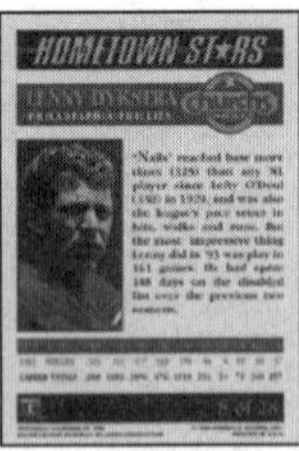

from the set. The gold foil cards are valued at two times the regular cards. A portion of the proceeds from card sales went to Habitat for Humanity, a national volunteer organization that helps families build their own homes. The cards, which are subtitled "Hometown Stars," feature on their fronts borderless color player action shots with team logos airbrushed away. The player's name appears in white lettering (or gold foil for the special cards) at the lower right. The back carries a color player head shot on the left; career highlights appear on the right. The player's name and team are shown near the top; statistics appear near the bottom. The cards are numbered on the back as "X of 28."

	MINT	NRMT	EXC
COMPLETE SET (28)	12.00	5.50	1.50
COMMON CARD (1-28)	.10	.05	.01
☐ 1 Brian McRae	.10	.05	.01
☐ 2 Dwight Gooden	.10	.05	.01
☐ 3 Ruben Sierra	.15	.07	.02
☐ 4 Greg Maddux	2.50	1.10	.30
☐ 5 Kirby Puckett	2.00	.90	.25
☐ 6 Jeff Bagwell	2.00	.90	.25
☐ 7 Cal Ripken	3.00	1.35	.35
☐ 8 Lenny Dykstra	.15	.07	.02
☐ 9 Tim Salmon	.50	.23	.06
☐ 10 Matt Williams	.75	.35	.09
☐ 11 Roberto Alomar	.50	.23	.06
☐ 12 Barry Larkin	.50	.23	.06
☐ 13 Roger Clemens	.60	.25	.07
☐ 14 Mike Piazza	2.50	1.10	.30
☐ 15 Travis Fryman	.20	.09	.03
☐ 16 Ryne Sandberg	1.00	.45	.12
☐ 17 Robin Ventura	.20	.09	.03
☐ 18 Gary Sheffield	.60	.25	.07
☐ 19 Carlos Baerga	.40	.18	.05
☐ 20 Jay Bell	.10	.05	.01
☐ 21 Edgar Martinez	.20	.09	.03
☐ 22 Phil Plantier	.10	.05	.01
☐ 23 Danny Tartabull	.10	.05	.01
☐ 24 Marquis Grissom	.20	.09	.03
☐ 25 Robin Yount	.25	.11	.03
☐ 26 Ozzie Smith	1.00	.45	.12
☐ 27 Ivan Rodriguez	1.00	.45	.12
☐ 28 Dante Bichette	.50	.23	.06

1994 Church's Hometown Stars Gold

This 28 card set is a parallel to the regular Church's Hometown Stars set. These cards were issued one per pack and are valued at a multiple of the regular issue cards listed in the Church's Hometown set.

	MINT	NRMT	EXC
COMPLETE SET (28)	15.00	6.75	1.85
COMMON CARD (1-28)	.25	.11	.03
*STARS: 2X BASIC CARDS			

1994 Church's Show Stoppers

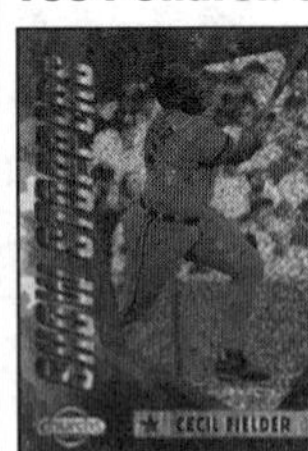

One of ten Show Stoppers cards was inserted in every fourth pack of 1994 Church's Chicken Stars of the Diamond four-card packs. The standard-size inserts were produced by Pinnacle using the "Dufex" printing process and highlight the major leagues' top home run hitters. The colorful metallic fronts feature color player action shots that appear to project from within home plate icons. Team logos are airbrushed away. The player's name appears at the lower right. The light blue back carries a color player head shot on the right, with the player's name, team, and career highlights shown alongside. Statistics for home runs, slugging percentage, and at bat/home run ratio appear near the bottom. The cards are numbered on the back as "X of 10."

	MINT	NRMT	EXC
COMPLETE SET (10)	40.00	18.00	5.00
COMMON CARD (1-10)	1.00	.45	.12
☐ 1 Juan Gonzalez	6.00	2.70	.75
☐ 2 Barry Bonds	3.00	1.35	.35

☐ 3 Ken Griffey Jr.	12.00	5.50	1.50
☐ 4 David Justice	1.50	.70	.19
☐ 5 Frank Thomas	12.00	5.50	1.50
☐ 6 Fred McGriff	2.50	1.10	.30
☐ 7 Albert Belle	6.00	2.70	.75
☐ 8 Joe Carter	1.50	.70	.19
☐ 9 Cecil Fielder	1.50	.70	.19
☐ 10 Mickey Tettleton	1.00	.45	.12

1938-39 Cincinnati Orange/Gray W711-1

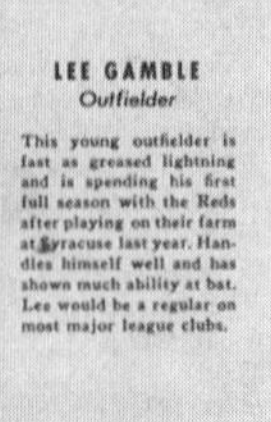

The cards in this 32-card set measure approximately 2" by 3". The 1938-39 Cincinnati Reds Baseball player set was printed in orange and gray tones. Many back variations exist and there are two poses of Johnny VanderMeer, portrait (PORT) and an action (ACT) poses. The set was sold at the ballpark and was printed on thin cardboard stock. The cards are unnumbered but have been alphabetized and numbered in the checklist below.

	EX-MT	VG-E	GOOD
COMPLETE SET (32)	750.00	350.00	95.00
COMMON CARD (1-32)	15.00	6.75	1.85
☐ 1 Wally Berger (2)	20.00	9.00	2.50
☐ 2 Nino Bongiovanni (39)	50.00	22.00	6.25
☐ 3 Stanley Bordagaray Frenchy (39)	50.00	22.00	6.25
☐ 4 Joe Cascarella (38)	15.00	6.75	1.85
☐ 5 Allen Dusty Cooke (38)	15.00	6.75	1.85
☐ 6 Harry Craft	18.00	8.00	2.20
☐ 7 Ray(Peaches) Davis	15.00	6.75	1.85
☐ 8 Paul Derringer (2)	25.00	11.00	3.10
☐ 9 Linus Frey (2)	15.00	6.75	1.85
☐ 10 Lee Gamble (2)	15.00	6.75	1.85
☐ 11 Ival Goodman (2)	15.00	6.75	1.85
☐ 12 Hank Gowdy CO	18.00	8.00	2.20
☐ 13 Lee Grissom (2)	15.00	6.75	1.85
☐ 14 Willard Hershberger (2)	18.00	8.00	2.20
☐ 15 Eddie Joost (39)	18.00	8.00	2.20
☐ 16 Wes Livengood (39)	100.00	45.00	12.50
☐ 17 Ernie Lombardi (2)	60.00	27.00	7.50
☐ 18 Frank McCormick	20.00	9.00	2.50
☐ 19 Bill McKechnie (2) MG	30.00	13.50	3.70
☐ 20 Lloyd Whitey Moore (2)	15.00	6.75	1.85
☐ 21 Billy Myers (2)	15.00	6.75	1.85
☐ 22 Lew Riggs (2)	15.00	6.75	1.85
☐ 23 Eddie Roush CO (38)	45.00	20.00	5.50
☐ 24 Les Scarsella (39)	15.00	6.75	1.85
☐ 25 Gene Schott (38)	15.00	6.75	1.85
☐ 26 Eugene Thompson	15.00	6.75	1.85
☐ 27 Johnny VanderMeer PORT	30.00	13.50	3.70
☐ 28 Johnny VanderMeer ACT	30.00	13.50	3.70
☐ 29 Wm.(Bucky) Walters (2)	20.00	9.00	2.50
☐ 30 Jim Weaver	15.00	6.75	1.85
☐ 31 Bill Werber (39)	15.00	6.75	1.85
☐ 32 Jimmy Wilson (39)	15.00	6.75	1.85

1996 Circa

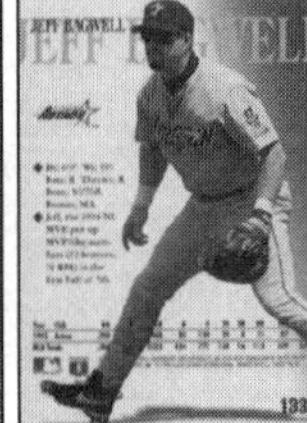

The 1996 Circa set was issued in one series totalling 200 cards. The eight-card packs retail for $1.99 each. The cards feature color action player photos on one of 28 different background designs and colors indicating the player's major league team. The backs carry player information and statistics. The only notable Rookie Card is Darin Erstad.

	MINT	NRMT	EXC
COMPLETE SET (200)	30.00	13.50	3.70
COMMON CARD (1-200)	.10	.05	.01
☐ 1 Roberto Alomar	.60	.25	.07
☐ 2 Brady Anderson	.50	.23	.06
☐ 3 Rocky Coppinger	.60	.25	.07
☐ 4 Eddie Murray	.75	.35	.09
☐ 5 Mike Mussina	.60	.25	.07
☐ 6 Randy Myers	.10	.05	.01

Card	MINT	NRMT	EXC
☐ 7 Rafael Palmeiro	.50	.23	.06
☐ 8 Cal Ripken	2.50	1.10	.30
☐ 9 Jose Canseco	.50	.23	.06
☐ 10 Roger Clemens	.60	.25	.07
☐ 11 Mike Greenwell	.10	.05	.01
☐ 12 Tim Naehring	.10	.05	.01
☐ 13 John Valentin	.25	.11	.03
☐ 14 Mo Vaughn	.75	.35	.09
☐ 15 Tim Wakefield	.10	.05	.01
☐ 16 Jim Abbott	.50	.23	.06
☐ 17 Garret Anderson	.50	.23	.06
☐ 18 Jim Edmonds	.25	.11	.03
☐ 19 Darin Erstad	4.00	1.80	.50
☐ 20 Chuck Finley	.10	.05	.01
☐ 21 Troy Percival	.25	.11	.03
☐ 22 Tim Salmon	.50	.23	.06
☐ 23 J.T. Snow	.25	.11	.03
☐ 24 Wilson Alvarez	.50	.23	.06
☐ 25 Harold Baines	.25	.11	.03
☐ 26 Ray Durham	.50	.23	.06
☐ 27 Alex Fernandez	.25	.11	.03
☐ 28 Tony Phillips	.25	.11	.03
☐ 29 Frank Thomas	3.00	1.35	.35
☐ 30 Robin Ventura	.25	.11	.03
☐ 31 Sandy Alomar Jr.	.10	.05	.01
☐ 32 Albert Belle	1.25	.55	.16
☐ 33 Kenny Lofton	.75	.35	.09
☐ 34 Dennis Martinez	.25	.11	.03
☐ 35 Jose Mesa	.25	.11	.03
☐ 36 Charles Nagy	.25	.11	.03
☐ 37 Manny Ramirez	.75	.35	.09
☐ 38 Jim Thome	.60	.25	.07
☐ 39 Travis Fryman	.25	.11	.03
☐ 40 Bob Higginson	.50	.23	.06
☐ 41 Melvin Nieves	.25	.11	.03
☐ 42 Alan Trammell	.25	.11	.03
☐ 43 Kevin Appier	.25	.11	.03
☐ 44 Johnny Damon	.25	.11	.03
☐ 45 Keith Lockhart	.10	.05	.01
☐ 46 Jeff Montgomery	.10	.05	.01
☐ 47 Joe Randa	.10	.05	.01
☐ 48 Bip Roberts	.10	.05	.01
☐ 49 Ricky Bones	.10	.05	.01
☐ 50 Jeff Cirillo	.10	.05	.01
☐ 51 Marc Newfield	.25	.11	.03
☐ 52 Dave Nilsson	.25	.11	.03
☐ 53 Kevin Seitzer	.10	.05	.01
☐ 54 Ron Coomer	.10	.05	.01
☐ 55 Marty Cordova	.25	.11	.03
☐ 56 Roberto Kelly	.10	.05	.01
☐ 57 Chuck Knoblauch	.50	.23	.06
☐ 58 Paul Molitor	.60	.25	.07
☐ 59 Kirby Puckett	1.25	.55	.16
☐ 60 Scott Stahoviak	.10	.05	.01
☐ 61 Wade Boggs	.50	.23	.06
☐ 62 David Cone	.25	.11	.03
☐ 63 Cecil Fielder	.25	.11	.03
☐ 64 Dwight Gooden	.25	.11	.03
☐ 65 Derek Jeter	2.00	.90	.25
☐ 66 Tino Martinez	.25	.11	.03
☐ 67 Paul O'Neill	.10	.05	.01
☐ 68 Andy Pettitte	1.00	.45	.12
☐ 69 Ruben Rivera	.60	.25	.07
☐ 70 Bernie Williams	.60	.25	.07
☐ 71 Geronimo Berroa	.25	.11	.03
☐ 72 Jason Giambi	.50	.23	.06
☐ 73 Mark McGwire	1.00	.45	.12
☐ 74 Terry Steinbach	.25	.11	.03
☐ 75 Todd Van Poppel	.10	.05	.01
☐ 76 Jay Buhner	.50	.23	.06
☐ 77 Norm Charlton	.10	.05	.01
☐ 78 Ken Griffey Jr.	3.00	1.35	.35
☐ 79 Randy Johnson	.50	.23	.06
☐ 80 Edgar Martinez	.25	.11	.03
☐ 81 Alex Rodriguez	3.00	1.35	.35
☐ 82 Paul Sorrento	.10	.05	.01
☐ 83 Dan Wilson	.10	.05	.01
☐ 84 Will Clark	.50	.23	.06
☐ 85 Kevin Elster	.25	.11	.03
☐ 86 Juan Gonzalez	1.50	.70	.19
☐ 87 Rusty Greer	.50	.23	.06
☐ 88 Ken Hill	.25	.11	.03
☐ 89 Mark McLemore	.10	.05	.01
☐ 90 Dean Palmer	.50	.23	.06
☐ 91 Roger Pavlik	.10	.05	.01
☐ 92 Ivan Rodriguez	.75	.35	.09
☐ 93 Joe Carter	.25	.11	.03
☐ 94 Carlos Delgado	.25	.11	.03
☐ 95 Juan Guzman	.10	.05	.01
☐ 96 John Olerud	.10	.05	.01
☐ 97 Ed Sprague	.25	.11	.03
☐ 98 Jermaine Dye	.60	.25	.07
☐ 99 Tom Glavine	.50	.23	.06
☐ 100 Marquis Grissom	.25	.11	.03
☐ 101 Andruw Jones	5.00	2.20	.60
☐ 102 Chipper Jones	2.00	.90	.25
☐ 103 David Justice	.25	.11	.03
☐ 104 Ryan Klesko	.50	.23	.06
☐ 105 Greg Maddux	2.00	.90	.25
☐ 106 Fred McGriff	.50	.23	.06
☐ 107 John Smoltz	.50	.23	.06
☐ 108 Brant Brown	.10	.05	.01
☐ 109 Mark Grace	.50	.23	.06
☐ 110 Brian McRae	.10	.05	.01
☐ 111 Ryne Sandberg	.75	.35	.09
☐ 112 Sammy Sosa	.50	.23	.06
☐ 113 Steve Trachsel	.10	.05	.01
☐ 114 Bret Boone	.10	.05	.01
☐ 115 Eric Davis	.25	.11	.03
☐ 116 Steve Gibralter	.10	.05	.01
☐ 117 Barry Larkin	.10	.05	.01
☐ 118 Reggie Sanders	.25	.11	.03
☐ 119 John Smiley	.10	.05	.01
☐ 120 Dante Bichette	.50	.23	.06
☐ 121 Ellis Burks	.25	.11	.03
☐ 122 Vinny Castilla	.25	.11	.03
☐ 123 Andres Galarraga	.50	.23	.06
☐ 124 Larry Walker	.50	.23	.06
☐ 125 Eric Young	.25	.11	.03
☐ 126 Kevin Brown	.25	.11	.03
☐ 127 Greg Colbrunn	.10	.05	.01
☐ 128 Jeff Conine	.25	.11	.03
☐ 129 Charles Johnson	.25	.11	.03
☐ 130 Al Leiter	.10	.05	.01
☐ 131 Gary Sheffield	.50	.23	.06
☐ 132 Devon White	.10	.05	.01
☐ 133 Jeff Bagwell	1.25	.55	.16
☐ 134 Derek Bell	.25	.11	.03
☐ 135 Craig Biggio	.25	.11	.03
☐ 136 Doug Drabek	.10	.05	.01
☐ 137 Brian L.Hunter	.25	.11	.03
☐ 138 Darryl Kile	.10	.05	.01
☐ 139 Shane Reynolds	.10	.05	.01
☐ 140 Brett Butler	.10	.05	.01
☐ 141 Eric Karros	.25	.11	.03
☐ 142 Ramon Martinez	.25	.11	.03
☐ 143 Raul Mondesi	.50	.23	.06
☐ 144 Hideo Nomo	.75	.35	.09
☐ 145 Chan Ho Park	.50	.23	.06
☐ 146 Mike Piazza	2.00	.90	.25
☐ 147 Moises Alou	.25	.11	.03
☐ 148 Yamil Benitez	.25	.11	.03
☐ 149 Mark Grudzielanek	.25	.11	.03
☐ 150 Pedro Martinez	.25	.11	.03
☐ 151 Henry Rodriguez	.25	.11	.03
☐ 152 David Segui	.10	.05	.01
☐ 153 Rondell White	.25	.11	.03
☐ 154 Carlos Baerga	.25	.11	.03
☐ 155 John Franco	.10	.05	.01
☐ 156 Bernard Gilkey	.25	.11	.03
☐ 157 Todd Hundley	.25	.11	.03
☐ 158 Jason Isringhausen	.50	.23	.06
☐ 159 Lance Johnson	.25	.11	.03
☐ 160 Alex Ochoa	.25	.11	.03
☐ 161 Rey Ordonez	.50	.23	.06
☐ 162 Paul Wilson	.25	.11	.03
☐ 163 Ron Blazier	.10	.05	.01
☐ 164 Ricky Bottalico	.10	.05	.01
☐ 165 Jim Eisenreich	.10	.05	.01
☐ 166 Pete Incaviglia	.10	.05	.01
☐ 167 Mickey Morandini	.10	.05	.01
☐ 168 Ricky Otero	.10	.05	.01
☐ 169 Curt Schilling	.10	.05	.01
☐ 170 Jay Bell	.25	.11	.03
☐ 171 Charlie Hayes	.10	.05	.01
☐ 172 Jason Kendall	.50	.23	.06
☐ 173 Jeff King	.25	.11	.03
☐ 174 Al Martin	.10	.05	.01
☐ 175 Alan Benes	.50	.23	.06
☐ 176 Royce Clayton	.10	.05	.01
☐ 177 Brian Jordan	.25	.11	.03
☐ 178 Ray Lankford	.25	.11	.03
☐ 179 John Mabry	.25	.11	.03
☐ 180 Willie McGee	.10	.05	.01
☐ 181 Ozzie Smith	.75	.35	.09
☐ 182 Todd Stottlemyre	.10	.05	.01
☐ 183 Andy Ashby	.10	.05	.01
☐ 184 Ken Caminiti	.50	.23	.06
☐ 185 Steve Finley	.50	.23	.06
☐ 186 Tony Gwynn	1.25	.55	.16
☐ 187 Rickey Henderson	.50	.23	.06
☐ 188 Wally Joyner	.10	.05	.01
☐ 189 Fernando Valenzuela	.25	.11	.03
☐ 190 Greg Vaughn	.50	.23	.06
☐ 191 Rod Beck	.10	.05	.01
☐ 192 Barry Bonds	.75	.35	.09
☐ 193 Shawon Dunston	.10	.05	.01
☐ 194 Chris Singleton	.10	.05	.01
☐ 195 Robby Thompson	.10	.05	.01
☐ 196 Matt Williams	.50	.23	.06
☐ 197 Barry Bonds CL	.50	.23	.06
☐ 198 Ken Griffey Jr. CL	1.50	.70	.19
☐ 199 Cal Ripken CL	1.25	.55	.16
☐ 200 Frank Thomas CL	1.50	.70	.19

1996 Circa Rave

Randomly inserted in packs at a rate of one in 60, this 200-card set is parallel and similar in design to the regular set except for sparkling foil lettering on front. Each card is individually numbered on back with 150 of each card produced. No set price is provided due to scarcity.

	MINT	NRMT	EXC
COMMON CARD (1-200)	25.00	11.00	3.10
*STARS: 60X TO 100X BASIC CARDS			
*YOUNG STARS: 50X TO 80X BASIC CARDS			
☐ 1 Roberto Alomar	75.00	34.00	9.50
☐ 2 Brady Anderson	50.00	22.00	6.25
☐ 4 Eddie Murray	100.00	45.00	12.50
☐ 5 Mike Mussina	60.00	27.00	7.50

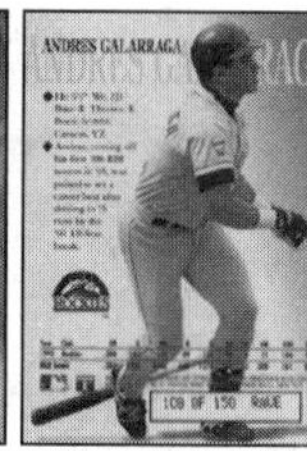

Card	MINT	NRMT	EXC
☐ 7 Rafael Palmeiro	50.00	22.00	6.25
☐ 8 Cal Ripken	300.00	135.00	38.00
☐ 9 Jose Canseco	50.00	22.00	6.25
☐ 10 Roger Clemens	75.00	34.00	9.50
☐ 14 Mo Vaughn	100.00	45.00	12.50
☐ 19 Darin Erstad	150.00	70.00	19.00
☐ 22 Tim Salmon	50.00	22.00	6.25
☐ 29 Frank Thomas	375.00	170.00	47.50
☐ 32 Albert Belle	150.00	70.00	19.00
☐ 33 Kenny Lofton	100.00	45.00	12.50
☐ 37 Manny Ramirez	100.00	45.00	12.50
☐ 38 Jim Thome	75.00	34.00	9.50
☐ 57 Chuck Knoblauch	60.00	27.00	7.50
☐ 58 Paul Molitor	90.00	40.00	11.00
☐ 59 Kirby Puckett	150.00	70.00	19.00
☐ 61 Wade Boggs	50.00	22.00	6.25
☐ 65 Derek Jeter	225.00	100.00	28.00
☐ 68 Andy Pettitte	100.00	45.00	12.50
☐ 69 Ruben Rivera	60.00	27.00	7.50
☐ 70 Bernie Williams	75.00	34.00	9.50
☐ 72 Jason Giambi	50.00	22.00	6.25
☐ 73 Mark McGwire	125.00	55.00	15.50
☐ 76 Jay Buhner	50.00	22.00	6.25
☐ 78 Ken Griffey Jr.	400.00	180.00	50.00
☐ 79 Randy Johnson	60.00	27.00	7.50
☐ 81 Alex Rodriguez	400.00	180.00	50.00
☐ 84 Will Clark	50.00	22.00	6.25
☐ 86 Juan Gonzalez	175.00	80.00	22.00
☐ 92 Ivan Rodriguez	80.00	36.00	10.00
☐ 98 Jermaine Dye	75.00	34.00	9.50
☐ 99 Tom Glavine	50.00	22.00	6.25
☐ 101 Andruw Jones	400.00	180.00	50.00
☐ 102 Chipper Jones	225.00	100.00	28.00
☐ 104 Ryan Klesko	60.00	27.00	7.50
☐ 105 Greg Maddux	200.00	90.00	25.00
☐ 106 Fred McGriff	50.00	22.00	6.25
☐ 107 John Smoltz	60.00	27.00	7.50
☐ 111 Ryne Sandberg	100.00	45.00	12.50
☐ 112 Sammy Sosa	60.00	27.00	7.50
☐ 117 Barry Larkin	50.00	22.00	6.25
☐ 120 Dante Bichette	50.00	22.00	6.25
☐ 123 Andres Galarraga	50.00	22.00	6.25
☐ 124 Larry Walker	50.00	22.00	6.25
☐ 131 Gary Sheffield	60.00	27.00	7.50
☐ 133 Jeff Bagwell	135.00	60.00	17.00
☐ 144 Hideo Nomo	125.00	55.00	15.50
☐ 146 Mike Piazza	225.00	100.00	28.00
☐ 181 Ozzie Smith	100.00	45.00	12.50
☐ 184 Ken Caminiti	60.00	27.00	7.50
☐ 186 Tony Gwynn	150.00	70.00	19.00
☐ 192 Barry Bonds	100.00	45.00	12.50
☐ 196 Matt Williams	50.00	22.00	6.25
☐ 198 Ken Griffey Jr. CL	175.00	80.00	22.00
☐ 199 Cal Ripken CL	150.00	70.00	19.00
☐ 200 Frank Thomas CL	175.00	80.00	22.00

1996 Circa Access

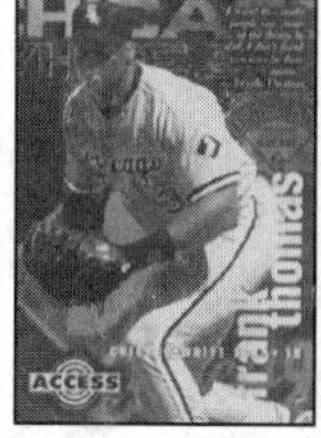

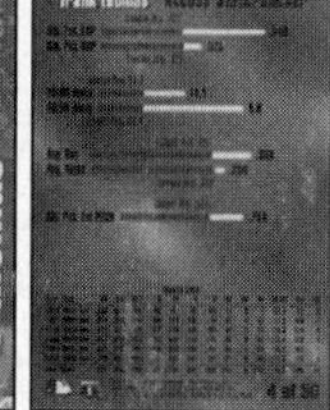

Randomly inserted in packs at a rate of one in 12, this 30-card limited edition set features a fold-out, three-panel card showcasing some of the hottest superstars of the game. The panels display color player photos, player statistics and personal information on team-colored backgrounds. A promotional card featuring Matt Williams was issued to dealers. The card is similar to the basic Access Williams except for the words "Promotional Sample" written across the card front.

	MINT	NRMT	EXC
COMPLETE SET (30)	120.00	55.00	15.00
COMMON CARD (1-30)	2.00	.90	.25
☐ 1 Cal Ripken	15.00	6.75	1.85
☐ 2 Mo Vaughn	5.00	2.20	.60
☐ 3 Tim Salmon	2.50	1.10	.30
☐ 4 Frank Thomas	20.00	9.00	2.50
☐ 5 Albert Belle	8.00	3.60	1.00
☐ 6 Kenny Lofton	5.00	2.20	.60
☐ 7 Manny Ramirez	5.00	2.20	.60
☐ 8 Paul Molitor	4.00	1.80	.50
☐ 9 Kirby Puckett	8.00	3.60	1.00
☐ 10 Paul O'Neill	2.00	.90	.25
☐ 11 Mark McGwire	6.00	2.70	.75
☐ 12 Ken Griffey Jr.	20.00	9.00	2.50
☐ 13 Randy Johnson	3.00	1.35	.35
☐ 14 Greg Maddux	12.00	5.50	1.50
☐ 15 John Smoltz	2.50	1.10	.30
☐ 16 Sammy Sosa	2.50	1.10	.30
☐ 17 Barry Larkin	2.00	.90	.25
☐ 18 Gary Sheffield	2.50	1.10	.30
☐ 19 Jeff Bagwell	8.00	3.60	1.00
☐ 20 Hideo Nomo	5.00	2.20	.60
☐ 21 Mike Piazza	12.00	5.50	1.50
☐ 22 Moises Alou	2.00	.90	.25
☐ 23 Henry Rodriguez	2.00	.90	.25
☐ 24 Rey Ordonez	2.50	1.10	.30
☐ 25 Jay Bell	2.00	.90	.25
☐ 26 Ozzie Smith	5.00	2.20	.60
☐ 27 Tony Gwynn	8.00	3.60	1.00
☐ 28 Rickey Henderson	2.50	1.10	.30
☐ 29 Barry Bonds	5.00	2.20	.60
☐ 30 Matt Williams	2.50	1.10	.30
☐ P30 Matt Williams Promo	1.00	.45	.12

1996 Circa Boss

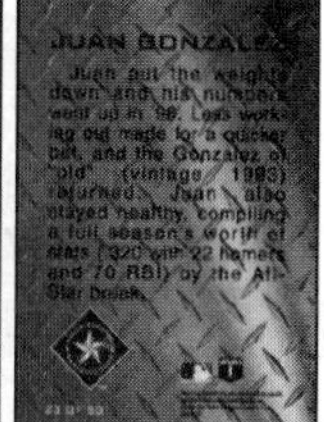

Randomly inserted in packs at a rate of one in six, this 50-card set features a sculpted embossed player image on a team-colored background containing the team logo. The backs carry a information about the player's career. A promotional card featuring Cal Ripken was issued to dealers. The card is similar to the basic Boss Ripken except for the words "Promotional Sample" written across the card front.

	MINT	NRMT	EXC
COMPLETE SET (50)	120.00	55.00	15.00
COMMON CARD (1-50)	1.50	.70	.19
☐ 1 Roberto Alomar	3.00	1.35	.35
☐ 2 Cal Ripken	12.00	5.50	1.50
☐ 3 Jose Canseco	2.50	1.10	.30
☐ 4 Mo Vaughn	4.00	1.80	.50
☐ 5 Tim Salmon	2.50	1.10	.30
☐ 6 Frank Thomas	15.00	6.75	1.85
☐ 7 Robin Ventura	2.00	.90	.25
☐ 8 Albert Belle	6.00	2.70	.75
☐ 9 Kenny Lofton	4.00	1.80	.50
☐ 10 Manny Ramirez	4.00	1.80	.50
☐ 11 Dave Nilsson	1.50	.70	.19
☐ 12 Chuck Knoblauch	2.50	1.10	.30
☐ 13 Paul Molitor	3.00	1.35	.35
☐ 14 Kirby Puckett	6.00	2.70	.75
☐ 15 Wade Boggs	2.50	1.10	.30
☐ 16 Dwight Gooden	2.00	.90	.25
☐ 17 Paul O'Neill	1.50	.70	.19
☐ 18 Mark McGwire	5.00	2.20	.60
☐ 19 Jay Buhner	2.50	1.10	.30
☐ 20 Ken Griffey Jr.	15.00	6.75	1.85
☐ 21 Randy Johnson	2.50	1.10	.30
☐ 22 Will Clark	2.50	1.10	.30
☐ 23 Juan Gonzalez	8.00	3.60	1.00
☐ 24 Joe Carter	2.00	.90	.25
☐ 25 Tom Glavine	2.50	1.10	.30
☐ 26 Ryan Klesko	2.50	1.10	.30
☐ 27 Greg Maddux	10.00	4.50	1.25
☐ 28 John Smoltz	2.50	1.10	.30
☐ 29 Ryne Sandberg	4.00	1.80	.50
☐ 30 Sammy Sosa	2.50	1.10	.30
☐ 31 Barry Larkin	2.00	.90	.25
☐ 32 Reggie Sanders	2.00	.90	.25
☐ 33 Dante Bichette	2.50	1.10	.30
☐ 34 Andres Galarraga	2.50	1.10	.30
☐ 35 Charles Johnson	2.00	.90	.25
☐ 36 Gary Sheffield	2.50	1.10	.30
☐ 37 Jeff Bagwell	6.00	2.70	.75
☐ 38 Hideo Nomo	4.00	1.80	.50
☐ 39 Mike Piazza	10.00	4.50	1.25
☐ 40 Moises Alou	2.00	.90	.25
☐ 41 Henry Rodriguez	2.00	.90	.25
☐ 42 Rey Ordonez	2.50	1.10	.30
☐ 43 Ricky Otero	1.50	.70	.19
☐ 44 Jay Bell	1.50	.70	.19
☐ 45 Royce Clayton	1.50	.70	.19
☐ 46 Ozzie Smith	4.00	1.80	.50
☐ 47 Tony Gwynn	6.00	2.70	.75
☐ 48 Rickey Henderson	2.50	1.10	.30
☐ 49 Barry Bonds	4.00	1.80	.50
☐ 50 Matt Williams	2.50	1.10	.30
☐ P2 Cal Ripken Promo	2.00	.90	.25

1985 Circle K

The cards in this 33-card set measure 2 1/2" by 3 1/2" and were issued with an accompanying custom box. In 1985, Topps produced this set for Circle K; cards were printed in Ireland. Cards are numbered on the back according to each player's rank on the all-time career Home Run list. The backs are printed in blue and red on white card stock. The card fronts are glossy and each player is named in the lower left corner. Most of the obverses are in color, although the older vintage players are pictured in black and white. Joe DiMaggio was not included in the set; card number 31 does not exist. It was intended to be DiMaggio but he apparently would not consent to be included in the set.

	MINT	NRMT	EXC
COMPLETE SET (33)	5.00	2.20	.60
COMMON CARD (1-34)	.10	.05	.01
☐ 1 Hank Aaron	.75	.35	.09
☐ 2 Babe Ruth	1.00	.45	.12
☐ 3 Willie Mays	.75	.35	.09
☐ 4 Frank Robinson	.25	.11	.03
☐ 5 Harmon Killebrew	.25	.11	.03
☐ 6 Mickey Mantle	1.00	.45	.12
☐ 7 Jimmie Foxx	.25	.11	.03
☐ 8 Willie McCovey	.25	.11	.03
☐ 9 Ted Williams	.75	.35	.09
☐ 10 Ernie Banks	.25	.11	.03
☐ 11 Eddie Mathews	.25	.11	.03
☐ 12 Mel Ott	.25	.11	.03
☐ 13 Reggie Jackson	.50	.23	.06
☐ 14 Lou Gehrig	.75	.35	.09
☐ 15 Stan Musial	.50	.23	.06
☐ 16 Willie Stargell	.25	.11	.03
☐ 17 Carl Yastrzemski	.25	.11	.03
☐ 18 Billy Williams	.15	.07	.02
☐ 19 Mike Schmidt	.50	.23	.06
☐ 20 Duke Snider	.25	.11	.03
☐ 21 Al Kaline	.25	.11	.03
☐ 22 Johnny Bench	.25	.11	.03
☐ 23 Frank Howard	.10	.05	.01
☐ 24 Orlando Cepeda	.15	.07	.02
☐ 25 Norm Cash	.10	.05	.01
☐ 26 Dave Kingman	.10	.05	.01
☐ 27 Rocky Colavito	.15	.07	.02
☐ 28 Tony Perez	.15	.07	.02
☐ 29 Gil Hodges	.15	.07	.02
☐ 30 Ralph Kiner	.15	.07	.02
☐ 31 Joe DiMaggio (card does not exist)			
☐ 32 Johnny Mize	.15	.07	.02
☐ 33 Yogi Berra	.25	.11	.03
☐ 34 Lee May	.10	.05	.01

1969 Citgo Metal Coins

This set of metal coins was distributed at Citgo stations in 1969 to commemorate the 100th anniversary of professional baseball. Each metal coin measures 1" in diameter. Although the coins are not numbered, they are arranged in the checklist below according to numbers found on a display card (which could be obtained from the company via mail). Each coin depicts a ballplayer in a raised portrait; the brass-like metal plating is often found discolored due to oxidation.

	NRMT	VG-E	GOOD
COMPLETE SET (20)	45.00	20.00	5.50
COMMON COIN (1-20)	.75	.35	.09
☐ 1 Denny McLain	1.00	.45	.12
☐ 2 Dave McNally	.75	.35	.09
☐ 3 Jim Lonborg	1.00	.45	.12
☐ 4 Harmon Killebrew	6.00	2.70	.75
☐ 5 Mel Stottlemyre	1.00	.45	.12
☐ 6 Willie Horton	1.00	.45	.12
☐ 7 Jim Fregosi	1.00	.45	.12
☐ 8 Rico Petrocelli	.75	.35	.09
☐ 9 Stan Bahnsen	.75	.35	.09
☐ 10 Frank Howard	1.00	.45	.12
☐ 11 Joe Torre	2.00	.90	.25
☐ 12 Jerry Koosman	1.00	.45	.12
☐ 13 Ron Santo	2.00	.90	.25
☐ 14 Pete Rose	15.00	6.75	1.85
☐ 15 Rusty Staub	2.00	.90	.25
☐ 16 Henry Aaron	10.00	4.50	1.25
☐ 17 Richie Allen	2.00	.90	.25
☐ 18 Ron Swoboda	.75	.35	.09
☐ 19 Willie McCovey	5.00	2.20	.60
☐ 20 Jim Bunning	3.00	1.35	.35

1993 City Pride Clemente

One of these standard-size cards was inserted in a protective sleeve attached to City Pride Bakery plastic bread bags. The bread bag itself

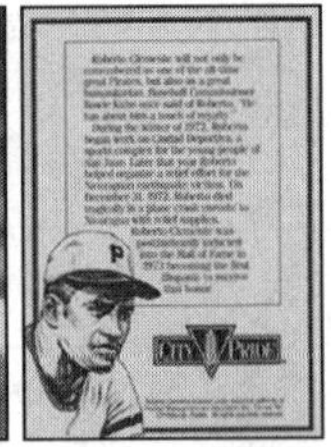

contained a "Help Build The Statue" feature, which stated that proceeds from the sale of this bread would go toward constructing a memorial statue to be unveiled before the 1994 All-Star Game at Three Rivers Stadium. Inside team color-coded border stripes (black and mustard), the fronts display full-bleed color or sepia-toned photos. The backs summarize Clemente's life and career with biography, statistics, and career highlights. The cards are unnumbered.

	MINT	NRMT	EXC
COMPLETE SET (6)	15.00	6.75	1.85
COMMON CARD (1-6)	2.50	1.10	.30
☐ 1 Roberto Clemente Kneeling leaning on one bat	2.50	1.10	.30
☐ 2 Roberto Clemente Kneeling arm resting on 5 bats	2.50	1.10	.30
☐ 3 Roberto Clemente Bat behind beginning to run toward first base	2.50	1.10	.30
☐ 4 Roberto Clemente Portrait	2.50	1.10	.30
☐ 5 Roberto Clemente Bat cocked ready to swing	2.50	1.10	.30
☐ 6 Roberto Clemente Awaiting pitch front leg cocked	2.50	1.10	.30

1987 Classic Game

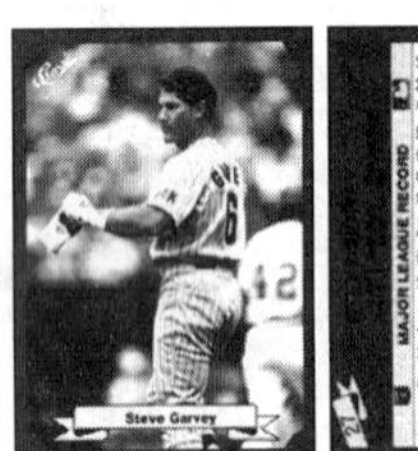

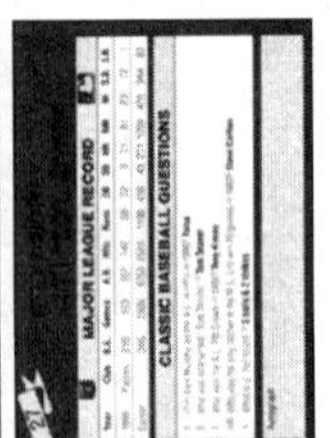

This 100-card standard-size set was actually distributed as part of a trivia board game. The card backs contain several trivia questions (and answers) which are used to play the game. A dark green border frames the full-color photo. The games were produced by Game Time, Ltd. and were available in toy stores as well as from card dealers. According to the producers of this game, only 75,000 sets were distributed. The set features Bo Jackson, Wally Joyner, and Barry Larkin in their Rookie Card year.

	MINT	NRMT	EXC
COMPLETE SET (100)	75.00	34.00	9.50
COMMON CARD (1-100)	.15	.07	.02
☐ 1 Pete Rose	3.00	1.35	.35
☐ 2 Len Dykstra	.50	.23	.06
☐ 3 Darryl Strawberry	.50	.23	.06
☐ 4 Keith Hernandez	.25	.11	.03
☐ 5 Gary Carter	.25	.11	.03
☐ 6 Wally Joyner	.75	.35	.09
☐ 7 Andres Thomas	.15	.07	.02
☐ 8 Pat Dodson	.15	.07	.02
☐ 9 Kirk Gibson	.25	.11	.03
☐ 10 Don Mattingly	5.00	2.20	.60
☐ 11 Dave Winfield	.50	.23	.06
☐ 12 Rickey Henderson	2.00	.90	.25
☐ 13 Dan Pasqua	.15	.07	.02
☐ 14 Don Baylor	.25	.11	.03
☐ 15 Bo Jackson (Swinging bat in Auburn FB uniform)	5.00	2.20	.60
☐ 16 Pete Incaviglia	.25	.11	.03
☐ 17 Kevin Bass	.15	.07	.02
☐ 18 Barry Larkin	4.00	1.80	.50
☐ 19 Dave Magadan	.25	.11	.03
☐ 20 Steve Sax	.15	.07	.02
☐ 21 Eric Davis	.75	.35	.09
☐ 22 Mike Pagliarulo	.15	.07	.02
☐ 23 Fred Lynn	.25	.11	.03
☐ 24 Reggie Jackson	2.00	.90	.25
☐ 25 Larry Parrish	.15	.07	.02
☐ 26 Tony Gwynn	5.00	2.20	.60
☐ 27 Steve Garvey	.50	.23	.06
☐ 28 Glenn Davis	.15	.07	.02
☐ 29 Tim Raines	.25	.11	.03
☐ 30 Vince Coleman	.15	.07	.02
☐ 31 Willie McGee	.25	.11	.03
☐ 32 Ozzie Smith	4.00	1.80	.50
☐ 33 Dave Parker	.25	.11	.03
☐ 34 Tony Pena	.15	.07	.02
☐ 35 Ryne Sandberg	4.00	1.80	.50
☐ 36 Brett Butler	.25	.11	.03
☐ 37 Dale Murphy	.50	.23	.06
☐ 38 Bob Horner	.15	.07	.02
☐ 39 Pedro Guerrero	.15	.07	.02
☐ 40 Brook Jacoby	.15	.07	.02
☐ 41 Carlton Fisk	1.50	.70	.19
☐ 42 Harold Baines	.15	.07	.02
☐ 43 Rob Deer	.15	.07	.02
☐ 44 Robin Yount	2.00	.90	.25
☐ 45 Paul Molitor	2.50	1.10	.30
☐ 46 Jose Canseco	5.00	2.20	.60
☐ 47 George Brett	4.00	1.80	.50
☐ 48 Jim Presley	.15	.07	.02
☐ 49 Rich Gedman	.15	.07	.02
☐ 50 Lance Parrish	.15	.07	.02
☐ 51 Eddie Murray	2.50	1.10	.30
☐ 52 Cal Ripken	8.00	3.60	1.00
☐ 53 Kent Hrbek	.15	.07	.02
☐ 54 Gary Gaetti	.15	.07	.02
☐ 55 Kirby Puckett	6.00	2.70	.75
☐ 56 George Bell	.15	.07	.02
☐ 57 Tony Fernandez	.15	.07	.02
☐ 58 Jesse Barfield	.15	.07	.02
☐ 59 Jim Rice	.25	.11	.03
☐ 60 Wade Boggs	2.00	.90	.25
☐ 61 Marty Barrett	.15	.07	.02
☐ 62 Mike Schmidt	3.00	1.35	.35
☐ 63 Von Hayes	.15	.07	.02
☐ 64 Jeff Leonard	.15	.07	.02
☐ 65 Chris Brown	.15	.07	.02
☐ 66 Dave Smith	.15	.07	.02
☐ 67 Mike Krukow	.15	.07	.02
☐ 68 Ron Guidry	.25	.11	.03
☐ 69 Rob Woodward	.15	.07	.02
☐ 70 Rob Murphy	.15	.07	.02
☐ 71 Andres Galarraga	2.50	1.10	.30
☐ 72 Dwight Gooden	.50	.23	.06
☐ 73 Bob Ojeda	.15	.07	.02
☐ 74 Sid Fernandez	.15	.07	.02
☐ 75 Jesse Orosco	.15	.07	.02
☐ 76 Roger McDowell	.15	.07	.02
☐ 77 John Tudor UER (Misspelled Tutor)	.15	.07	.02
☐ 78 Tom Browning	.15	.07	.02
☐ 79 Rick Aguilera	.25	.11	.03
☐ 80 Lance McCullers	.15	.07	.02
☐ 81 Mike Scott	.15	.07	.02
☐ 82 Nolan Ryan	8.00	3.60	1.00
☐ 83 Bruce Hurst	.15	.07	.02
☐ 84 Roger Clemens	3.00	1.35	.35
☐ 85 Dennis Boyd	.15	.07	.02
☐ 86 Dave Righetti	.15	.07	.02
☐ 87 Dennis Rasmussen	.15	.07	.02
☐ 88 Bret Saberhagen	1.00	.45	.12
☐ 89 Mark Langston	.15	.07	.02
☐ 90 Jack Morris	.25	.11	.03
☐ 91 Fernando Valenzuela	.25	.11	.03
☐ 92 Orel Hershiser	.50	.23	.06
☐ 93 Rick Honeycutt	.15	.07	.02
☐ 94 Jeff Reardon	.15	.07	.02
☐ 95 John Habyan	.15	.07	.02
☐ 96 Goose Gossage	.25	.11	.03
☐ 97 Todd Worrell	.25	.11	.03
☐ 98 Floyd Youmans	.15	.07	.02
☐ 99 Don Aase	.15	.07	.02
☐ 100 John Franco	.25	.11	.03

1987 Classic Update Yellow

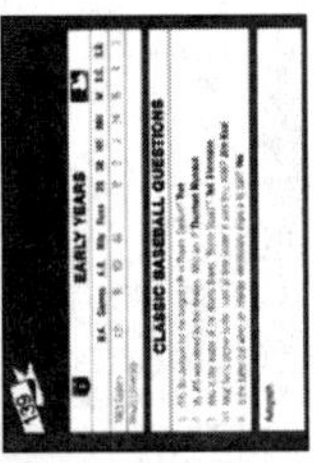

This 50-card standard-size set was actually distributed as part of an update to a trivia board game, but (unlike the original Classic game) was sold without the game. The set is sometimes referred to as the "Travel Edition" of the game. The card backs contain several trivia questions (and answers) which are used to play the game. A yellow border frames the full-color photo. The games were produced by Game Time, Ltd. and were available in toy stores as well as from card dealers. Cards are numbered beginning with 101, as they are an extension of the original set. According to the set's producers, reportedly about 1/3 of the 150,000 sets printed were error sets in that they had green backs instead of yellow backs. This "green back" variation/error set is valued at approximately double the prices listed below.

	MINT	NRMT	EXC
COMPLETE SET (50)	15.00	6.75	1.85
COMMON CARD (101-150)	.10	.05	.01
☐ 101 Mike Schmidt	1.00	.45	.12
☐ 102 Eric Davis	.25	.11	.03
☐ 103 Pete Rose	1.00	.45	.12
☐ 104 Don Mattingly	3.00	1.35	.35
☐ 105 Wade Boggs	1.25	.55	.16
☐ 106 Dale Murphy	.40	.18	.05
☐ 107 Glenn Davis	.10	.05	.01
☐ 108 Wally Joyner	.40	.18	.05
☐ 109 Bo Jackson	1.00	.45	.12
☐ 110 Cory Snyder	.10	.05	.01
☐ 111 Jim Lindeman	.10	.05	.01
☐ 112 Kirby Puckett	3.00	1.35	.35
☐ 113 Barry Bonds	3.00	1.35	.35
☐ 114 Roger Clemens	1.50	.70	.19
☐ 115 Oddibe McDowell	.10	.05	.01
☐ 116 Bret Saberhagen	.20	.09	.03
☐ 117 Joe Magrane	.10	.05	.01
☐ 118 Scott Fletcher	.10	.05	.01
☐ 119 Mark McLemore	.10	.05	.01
☐ 120 Joe Niekro Who Me	.20	.09	.03
☐ 121 Mark McGwire	1.50	.70	.19
☐ 122 Darryl Strawberry	.40	.18	.05
☐ 123 Mike Scott	.10	.05	.01
☐ 124 Andre Dawson	.60	.25	.07
☐ 125 Jose Canseco	2.00	.90	.25
☐ 126 Kevin McReynolds	.10	.05	.01
☐ 127 Joe Carter	1.25	.55	.16
☐ 128 Casey Candaele	.10	.05	.01
☐ 129 Matt Nokes	.10	.05	.01
☐ 130 Kal Daniels	.10	.05	.01
☐ 131 Pete Incaviglia	.20	.09	.03
☐ 132 Benito Santiago	.20	.09	.03
☐ 133 Barry Larkin	2.00	.90	.25
☐ 134 Gary Pettis	.10	.05	.01
☐ 135 B.J. Surhoff	.30	.14	.04
☐ 136 Juan Nieves	.10	.05	.01
☐ 137 Jim Deshaies	.10	.05	.01
☐ 138 Pete O'Brien	.10	.05	.01
☐ 139 Kevin Seitzer	.20	.09	.03
☐ 140 Devon White	.60	.25	.07
☐ 141 Rob Deer	.10	.05	.01
☐ 142 Kurt Stillwell	.10	.05	.01
☐ 143 Edwin Correa	.10	.05	.01
☐ 144 Dion James	.10	.05	.01
☐ 145 Danny Tartabull	.50	.23	.06
☐ 146 Jerry Browne	.10	.05	.01
☐ 147 Ted Higuera	.10	.05	.01
☐ 148 Jack Clark	.10	.05	.01
☐ 149 Ruben Sierra	.75	.35	.09
☐ 150 Mark McGwire and Eric Davis	.75	.35	.09

1988 Classic Blue

This 50-card blue-bordered standard-size set was actually distributed as part of an update to a trivia board game, but (unlike the original Classic game) was sold without the game. The card backs contain several trivia questions (and answers) which are used to play the game. A blue border frames the full color photo. The games were produced by Game Time, Ltd. and were available in toy stores as well as from card dealers. Cards are numbered beginning with 201 as they are an extension of the original sets.

	MINT	NRMT	EXC
COMPLETE SET (50)	10.00	4.50	1.25
COMMON CARD (201-250)	.10	.05	.01
☐ 201 Eric Davis and Dale Murphy	.20	.09	.03
☐ 202 B.J. Surhoff	.10	.05	.01
☐ 203 John Kruk	.40	.18	.05
☐ 204 Sam Horn	.10	.05	.01
☐ 205 Jack Clark	.20	.09	.03
☐ 206 Wally Joyner	.40	.18	.05
☐ 207 Matt Nokes	.10	.05	.01
☐ 208 Bo Jackson	.50	.23	.06
☐ 209 Darryl Strawberry	.20	.09	.03
☐ 210 Ozzie Smith	1.25	.55	.16
☐ 211 Don Mattingly	1.50	.70	.19
☐ 212 Mark McGwire	1.00	.45	.12
☐ 213 Eric Davis	.30	.14	.04
☐ 214 Wade Boggs	.60	.25	.07
☐ 215 Dale Murphy	.40	.18	.05
☐ 216 Andre Dawson	.40	.18	.05
☐ 217 Roger Clemens	.75	.35	.09
☐ 218 Kevin Seitzer	.20	.09	.03
☐ 219 Benito Santiago	.10	.05	.01
☐ 220 Tony Gwynn	1.50	.70	.19
☐ 221 Mike Scott	.10	.05	.01
☐ 222 Steve Bedrosian	.10	.05	.01
☐ 223 Vince Coleman	.10	.05	.01

Card	MINT	NRMT	EXC
☐ 224 Rick Sutcliffe	.10	.05	.01
☐ 225 Will Clark	1.00	.45	.12
☐ 226 Pete Rose	.75	.35	.09
☐ 227 Mike Greenwell	.20	.09	.03
☐ 228 Ken Caminiti	1.25	.55	.16
☐ 229 Ellis Burks	.75	.35	.09
☐ 230 Dave Magadan	.10	.05	.01
☐ 231 Alan Trammell	.40	.18	.05
☐ 232 Paul Molitor	.75	.35	.09
☐ 233 Gary Gaetti	.10	.05	.01
☐ 234 Rickey Henderson	.60	.25	.07
☐ 235 Danny Tartabull UER (Photo actually Hal McRae)	.10	.05	.01
☐ 236 Bobby Bonilla	.50	.23	.06
☐ 237 Mike Dunne	.10	.05	.01
☐ 238 Al Leiter	.40	.18	.05
☐ 239 John Farrell	.10	.05	.01
☐ 240 Joe Magrane	.10	.05	.01
☐ 241 Mike Henneman	.10	.05	.01
☐ 242 George Bell	.10	.05	.01
☐ 243 Gregg Jefferies	.50	.23	.06
☐ 244 Jay Buhner	1.00	.45	.12
☐ 245 Todd Benzinger	.10	.05	.01
☐ 246 Matt Williams	1.00	.45	.12
☐ 247 Mark McGwire and Don Mattingly (Unnumbered; game instructions on back)	1.25	.55	.16
☐ 248 George Brett	1.25	.55	.16
☐ 249 Jimmy Key	.30	.14	.04
☐ 250 Mark Langston	.10	.05	.01

1988 Classic Red

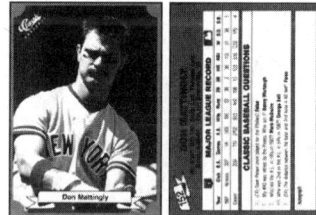

This 50-card red-bordered standard-size set was actually distributed as part of an update to a trivia board game, but (unlike the original Classic game) was sold without the game. The card backs contain several trivia questions (and answers) which are used to play the game. A red border frames the full color photo. The games were produced by Game Time, Ltd. and were available in toy stores as well as from card dealers. Cards are numbered beginning with 151 as they are an extension of the original sets.

	MINT	NRMT	EXC
COMPLETE SET (50)	10.00	4.50	1.25
COMMON CARD (151-200)	.10	.05	.01
☐ 151 Mark McGwire and Don Mattingly	1.25	.55	.16
☐ 152 Don Mattingly	1.50	.70	.19
☐ 153 Mark McGwire	1.25	.55	.16
☐ 154 Eric Davis	.30	.14	.04
☐ 155 Wade Boggs	.60	.25	.07
☐ 156 Dale Murphy	.40	.18	.05
☐ 157 Andre Dawson	.50	.23	.06
☐ 158 Roger Clemens	.75	.35	.09
☐ 159 Kevin Seitzer	.20	.09	.03
☐ 160 Benito Santiago	.10	.05	.01
☐ 161 Kal Daniels	.10	.05	.01
☐ 162 John Kruk	.30	.14	.04
☐ 163 Bill Ripken	.10	.05	.01
☐ 164 Kirby Puckett	1.50	.70	.19
☐ 165 Jose Canseco	1.00	.45	.12
☐ 166 Matt Nokes	.10	.05	.01
☐ 167 Mike Schmidt	.75	.35	.09
☐ 168 Tim Raines	.30	.14	.04
☐ 169 Ryne Sandberg	1.25	.55	.16
☐ 170 Dave Winfield	.50	.23	.06
☐ 171 Dwight Gooden	.20	.09	.03
☐ 172 Bret Saberhagen	.20	.09	.03
☐ 173 Willie McGee	.20	.09	.03
☐ 174 Jack Morris	.10	.05	.01
☐ 175 Jeff Leonard	.10	.05	.01
☐ 176 Cal Ripken	3.00	1.35	.35
☐ 177 Pete Incaviglia	.10	.05	.01
☐ 178 Devon White	.25	.11	.03
☐ 179 Nolan Ryan	3.00	1.35	.35
☐ 180 Ruben Sierra	.30	.14	.04
☐ 181 Todd Worrell	.10	.05	.01
☐ 182 Glenn Davis	.10	.05	.01
☐ 183 Frank Viola	.10	.05	.01
☐ 184 Cory Snyder	.10	.05	.01
☐ 185 Tracy Jones	.10	.05	.01
☐ 186 Terry Steinbach	.30	.14	.04
☐ 187 Julio Franco	.10	.05	.01
☐ 188 Larry Sheets	.10	.05	.01
☐ 189 John Marzano	.10	.05	.01
☐ 190 Kevin Elster	.10	.05	.01
☐ 191 Vicente Palacios	.10	.05	.01
☐ 192 Kent Hrbek	.10	.05	.01
☐ 193 Eric Bell	.10	.05	.01
☐ 194 Kelly Downs	.10	.05	.01
☐ 195 Jose Lind	.10	.05	.01
☐ 196 Dave Stewart	.10	.05	.01
☐ 197 Mark McGwire and Jose Canseco	.60	.25	.07
☐ 198 Phil Niekro Cleveland Indians	.20	.09	.03
☐ 199 Phil Niekro Toronto Blue Jays	.20	.09	.03
☐ 200 Phil Niekro Atlanta Braves	.20	.09	.03

1989 Classic Light Blue

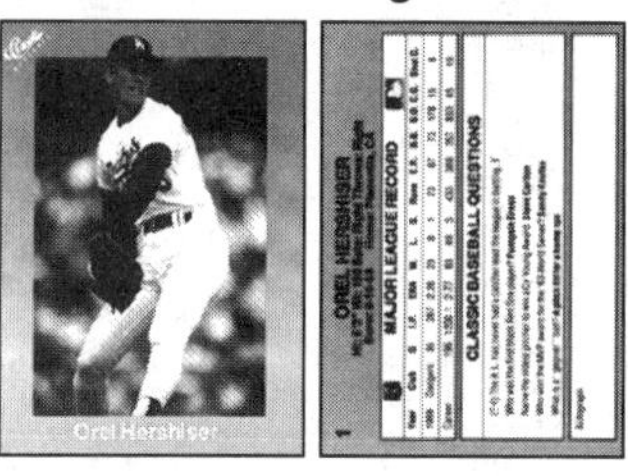

The 1989 Classic set contains 100 standard-size cards. The fronts of these cards have light blue borders. The backs feature 1988 and lifetime stats. The cards were distributed with a baseball boardgame. Reportedly there were 150,000 sets produced.

	MINT	NRMT	EXC
COMPLETE SET (100)	15.00	6.75	1.85
COMMON CARD (1-100)	.10	.05	.01
☐ 1 Orel Hershiser	.20	.09	.03
☐ 2 Wade Boggs	.40	.18	.05
☐ 3 Jose Canseco	.40	.18	.05
☐ 4 Mark McGwire	1.00	.45	.12
☐ 5 Don Mattingly	2.00	.90	.25
☐ 6 Gregg Jefferies	.25	.11	.03
☐ 7 Dwight Gooden	.20	.09	.03
☐ 8 Darryl Strawberry	.20	.09	.03
☐ 9 Eric Davis	.25	.11	.03
☐ 10 Joey Meyer	.10	.05	.01
☐ 11 Joe Carter	.40	.18	.05
☐ 12 Paul Molitor	.75	.35	.09
☐ 13 Mark Grace	.75	.35	.09
☐ 14 Kurt Stillwell	.10	.05	.01
☐ 15 Kirby Puckett	1.50	.70	.19
☐ 16 Keith Miller	.10	.05	.01
☐ 17 Glenn Davis	.10	.05	.01
☐ 18 Will Clark	.75	.35	.09
☐ 19 Cory Snyder	.10	.05	.01
☐ 20 Jose Lind	.10	.05	.01
☐ 21 Andres Thomas	.10	.05	.01
☐ 22 Dave Smith	.10	.05	.01
☐ 23 Mike Scott	.10	.05	.01
☐ 24 Kevin McReynolds	.10	.05	.01
☐ 25 B.J. Surhoff	.20	.09	.03
☐ 26 Mackey Sasser	.10	.05	.01
☐ 27 Chad Kreuter	.10	.05	.01
☐ 28 Hal Morris	.25	.11	.03
☐ 29 Wally Joyner	.20	.09	.03
☐ 30 Tony Gwynn	1.50	.70	.19
☐ 31 Kevin Mitchell	.10	.05	.01
☐ 32 Dave Winfield	.40	.18	.05
☐ 33 Billy Bean	.10	.05	.01
☐ 34 Steve Bedrosian	.10	.05	.01
☐ 35 Ron Gant	.40	.18	.05
☐ 36 Len Dykstra	.30	.14	.04
☐ 37 Andre Dawson	.40	.18	.05
☐ 38 Brett Butler	.20	.09	.03
☐ 39 Rob Deer	.10	.05	.01
☐ 40 Tommy John	.20	.09	.03
☐ 41 Gary Gaetti	.10	.05	.01
☐ 42 Tim Raines	.10	.05	.01
☐ 43 George Bell	.10	.05	.01
☐ 44 Dwight Evans	.20	.09	.03
☐ 45 Dennis Martinez	.10	.05	.01
☐ 46 Andres Galarraga	.60	.25	.07
☐ 47 George Brett	1.50	.70	.19
☐ 48 Mike Schmidt	.50	.23	.06
☐ 49 Dave Stieb	.10	.05	.01
☐ 50 Rickey Henderson	.40	.18	.05
☐ 51 Craig Biggio	1.00	.45	.12
☐ 52 Mark Lemke	.10	.05	.01
☐ 53 Chris Sabo	.10	.05	.01
☐ 54 Jeff Treadway	.10	.05	.01
☐ 55 Kent Hrbek	.10	.05	.01
☐ 56 Cal Ripken	4.00	1.80	.50
☐ 57 Tim Belcher	.10	.05	.01
☐ 58 Ozzie Smith	.75	.35	.09
☐ 59 Keith Hernandez	.10	.05	.01
☐ 60 Pedro Guerrero	.10	.05	.01
☐ 61 Greg Swindell	.10	.05	.01
☐ 62 Bret Saberhagen	.20	.09	.03
☐ 63 John Tudor	.10	.05	.01
☐ 64 Gary Carter	.20	.09	.03
☐ 65 Kevin Seitzer	.10	.05	.01
☐ 66 Jesse Barfield	.10	.05	.01
☐ 67 Luis Medina	.10	.05	.01
☐ 68 Walt Weiss	.10	.05	.01
☐ 69 Terry Steinbach	.20	.09	.03
☐ 70 Barry Larkin	.75	.35	.09
☐ 71 Pete Rose	.50	.23	.06
☐ 72 Luis Salazar	.10	.05	.01
☐ 73 Benito Santiago	.10	.05	.01
☐ 74 Kal Daniels	.10	.05	.01
☐ 75 Kevin Elster	.10	.05	.01
☐ 76 Rob Dibble	.20	.09	.03
☐ 77 Bobby Witt	.10	.05	.01
☐ 78 Steve Searcy	.10	.05	.01
☐ 79 Sandy Alomar Jr.	.75	.35	.09
☐ 80 Chili Davis	.10	.05	.01
☐ 81 Alvin Davis	.10	.05	.01
☐ 82 Charlie Leibrandt	.10	.05	.01
☐ 83 Robin Yount	.40	.18	.05
☐ 84 Mark Carreon	.10	.05	.01
☐ 85 Pascual Perez	.10	.05	.01
☐ 86 Dennis Rasmussen	.10	.05	.01
☐ 87 Ernie Riles	.10	.05	.01
☐ 88 Melido Perez	.10	.05	.01
☐ 89 Doug Jones	.10	.05	.01
☐ 90 Dennis Eckersley	.40	.18	.05
☐ 91 Bob Welch	.10	.05	.01
☐ 92 Bob Milacki	.10	.05	.01
☐ 93 Jeff Robinson	.10	.05	.01
☐ 94 Mike Henneman	.10	.05	.01
☐ 95 Randy Johnson	1.50	.70	.19
☐ 96 Ron Jones	.10	.05	.01
☐ 97 Jack Armstrong	.10	.05	.01
☐ 98 Willie McGee	.20	.09	.03
☐ 99 Ryne Sandberg	.75	.35	.09
☐ 100 David Cone and Danny Jackson			

1989 Classic Travel Orange

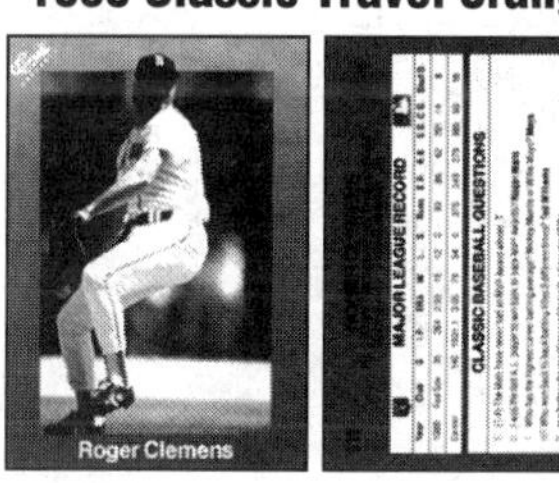

The 1989 Classic Travel Orange set contains 50 standard-size cards. The fronts of the cards have orange borders. The backs feature 1988 and lifetime stats. This subset of cards were distributed as a set in blister packs as "Travel Update I" subsets. Reportedly there were 150,000 sets produced.

	MINT	NRMT	EXC
COMPLETE SET (50)	8.00	3.60	1.00
COMMON CARD (101-150)	.10	.05	.01
☐ 101 Gary Sheffield	.75	.35	.09
☐ 102 Wade Boggs	.40	.18	.05
☐ 103 Jose Canseco	.40	.18	.05
☐ 104 Mark McGwire	1.25	.55	.16
☐ 105 Orel Hershiser	.20	.09	.03
☐ 106 Don Mattingly	2.00	.90	.25
☐ 107 Dwight Gooden	.20	.09	.03
☐ 108 Darryl Strawberry	.20	.09	.03
☐ 109 Eric Davis	.25	.11	.03
☐ 110 Hensley Meulens UER (Listed on card as Bam Bam Muelens)	.10	.05	.01
☐ 111 Andy Van Slyke	.20	.09	.03
☐ 112 Al Leiter	.20	.09	.03
☐ 113 Matt Nokes	.10	.05	.01
☐ 114 Mike Krukow	.10	.05	.01
☐ 115 Tony Fernandez	.10	.05	.01
☐ 116 Fred McGriff	.40	.18	.05
☐ 117 Barry Bonds	1.00	.45	.12
☐ 118 Gerald Perry	.10	.05	.01
☐ 119 Roger Clemens	.50	.23	.06
☐ 120 Kirk Gibson	.30	.14	.04
☐ 121 Greg Maddux	2.00	.90	.25
☐ 122 Bo Jackson	.40	.18	.05
☐ 123 Danny Jackson	.10	.05	.01
☐ 124 Dale Murphy	.30	.14	.04
☐ 125 David Cone	.40	.18	.05
☐ 126 Tom Browning	.10	.05	.01
☐ 127 Roberto Alomar	1.50	.70	.19
☐ 128 Alan Trammell	.20	.09	.03
☐ 129 Ricky Jordan UER (Misspelled Jordon on card back)	.10	.05	.01
☐ 130 Ramon Martinez	.40	.18	.05
☐ 131 Ken Griffey Jr.	4.00	1.80	.50
☐ 132 Gregg Olson	.20	.09	.03
☐ 133 Carlos Quintana	.10	.05	.01
☐ 134 Dave West	.10	.05	.01
☐ 135 Cameron Drew	.10	.05	.01
☐ 136 Teddy Higuera	.10	.05	.01
☐ 137 Sil Campusano	.10	.05	.01
☐ 138 Mark Gubicza	.10	.05	.01
☐ 139 Mike Boddicker	.10	.05	.01
☐ 140 Paul Gibson	.10	.05	.01
☐ 141 Jose Rijo	.10	.05	.01
☐ 142 John Costello	.10	.05	.01
☐ 143 Cecil Espy	.10	.05	.01
☐ 144 Frank Viola	.10	.05	.01
☐ 145 Erik Hanson	.20	.09	.03
☐ 146 Juan Samuel	.10	.05	.01
☐ 147 Harold Reynolds	.10	.05	.01
☐ 148 Joe Magrane	.10	.05	.01
☐ 149 Mike Greenwell	.10	.05	.01
☐ 150 Darryl Strawberry and Will Clark	.40	.18	.05

1989 Classic Travel Purple

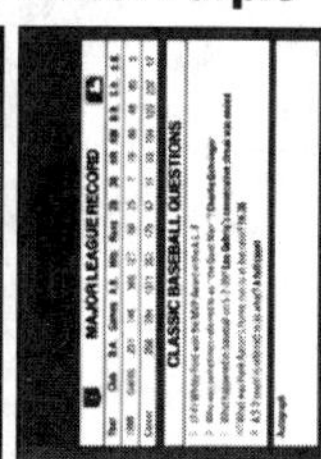

The 1989 Classic "Travel Update II" set contains 50 standard-size cards. The fronts have purple (and gray) borders. The set features "two sport" cards of Bo Jackson and Deion Sanders. The cards were distributed as a set in blister packs.

	MINT	NRMT	EXC
COMPLETE SET (50)	8.00	3.60	1.00
COMMON CARD (151-200)	.10	.05	.01
☐ 151 Jim Abbott	.25	.11	.03
☐ 152 Ellis Burks	.40	.18	.05
☐ 153 Mike Schmidt	.50	.23	.06
☐ 154 Gregg Jefferies	.25	.11	.03
☐ 155 Mark Grace	.60	.25	.07
☐ 156 Jerome Walton	.20	.09	.03
☐ 157 Bo Jackson	.40	.18	.05
☐ 158 Jack Clark	.10	.05	.01
☐ 159 Tom Glavine	.75	.35	.09
☐ 160 Eddie Murray	.75	.35	.09
☐ 161 John Dopson	.10	.05	.01
☐ 162 Ruben Sierra	.25	.11	.03
☐ 163 Rafael Palmeiro	.40	.18	.05
☐ 164 Nolan Ryan	2.00	.90	.25
☐ 165 Barry Larkin	.60	.25	.07
☐ 166 Tommy Herr	.10	.05	.01
☐ 167 Roberto Kelly	.10	.05	.01
☐ 168 Glenn Davis	.10	.05	.01
☐ 169 Glenn Braggs	.10	.05	.01
☐ 170 Juan Bell	.10	.05	.01
☐ 171 Todd Burns	.10	.05	.01
☐ 172 Derek Lilliquist	.10	.05	.01
☐ 173 Orel Hershiser	.20	.09	.03
☐ 174 John Smoltz	.75	.35	.09
☐ 175 Ozzie Guillen and Ellis Burks	.20	.09	.03
☐ 176 Kirby Puckett	1.25	.55	.16
☐ 177 Robin Ventura	.50	.23	.06
☐ 178 Allan Anderson	.10	.05	.01
☐ 179 Steve Sax	.10	.05	.01
☐ 180 Will Clark	.60	.25	.07
☐ 181 Mike Devereaux	.10	.05	.01
☐ 182 Tom Gordon	.20	.09	.03
☐ 183 Rob Murphy	.10	.05	.01
☐ 184 Pete O'Brien	.10	.05	.01
☐ 185 Cris Carpenter	.10	.05	.01
☐ 186 Tom Brunansky	.10	.05	.01
☐ 187 Bob Boone	.20	.09	.03
☐ 188 Lou Whitaker	.20	.09	.03
☐ 189 Dwight Gooden	.20	.09	.03
☐ 190 Mark McGwire	1.00	.45	.12
☐ 191 John Smiley	.10	.05	.01
☐ 192 Tommy Gregg	.10	.05	.01
☐ 193 Ken Griffey Jr.	3.00	1.35	.35
☐ 194 Bruce Hurst	.10	.05	.01
☐ 195 Greg Swindell	.10	.05	.01
☐ 196 Nelson Liriano	.10	.05	.01
☐ 197 Randy Myers	.20	.09	.03
☐ 198 Kevin Mitchell	.10	.05	.01
☐ 199 Dante Bichette	.75	.35	.09
☐ 200 Deion Sanders	.75	.35	.09

1990 Classic Blue

The 1990 Classic Blue (Game) set contains 150 standard-size cards, the largest Classic set to date in terms of player selection. The front borders are blue with magenta splotches. The backs feature 1989 and career total stats. The cards were distributed as a set in blister packs. According to distributors of the set, reportedly there were 200,000 sets produced. Reportedly the Sanders "correction" was made at Sanders own request; less than 10 percent of the sets contain the first version and hence it has the higher value in the checklist below. The complete set price below does not include any of the more difficult variation cards.

	MINT	NRMT	EXC
COMPLETE SET (150)	12.50	5.50	1.55
COMMON CARD (1-150)	.05	.02	.01
☐ 1 Nolan Ryan	1.50	.70	.19
☐ 2 Bo Jackson	.30	.14	.04
☐ 3 Gregg Olson	.05	.02	.01

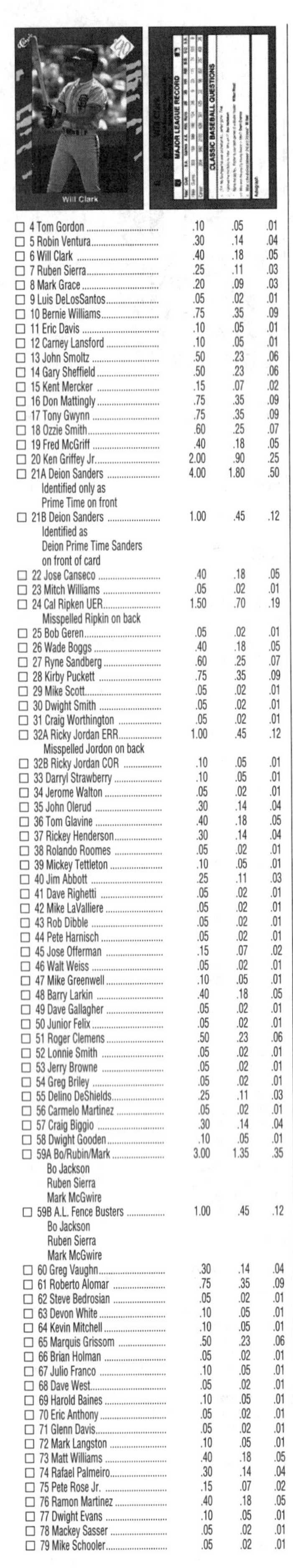

☐ 4 Tom Gordon	.10	.05	.01
☐ 5 Robin Ventura	.30	.14	.04
☐ 6 Will Clark	.40	.18	.05
☐ 7 Ruben Sierra	.25	.11	.03
☐ 8 Mark Grace	.20	.09	.03
☐ 9 Luis DeLosSantos	.05	.02	.01
☐ 10 Bernie Williams	.75	.35	.09
☐ 11 Eric Davis	.10	.05	.01
☐ 12 Carney Lansford	.10	.05	.01
☐ 13 John Smoltz	.50	.23	.06
☐ 14 Gary Sheffield	.50	.23	.06
☐ 15 Kent Mercker	.15	.07	.02
☐ 16 Don Mattingly	.75	.35	.09
☐ 17 Tony Gwynn	.75	.35	.09
☐ 18 Ozzie Smith	.60	.25	.07
☐ 19 Fred McGriff	.40	.18	.05
☐ 20 Ken Griffey Jr.	2.00	.90	.25
☐ 21A Deion Sanders	4.00	1.80	.50
Identified only as			
Prime Time on front			
☐ 21B Deion Sanders	1.00	.45	.12
Identified as			
Deion Prime Time Sanders			
on front of card			
☐ 22 Jose Canseco	.40	.18	.05
☐ 23 Mitch Williams	.05	.02	.01
☐ 24 Cal Ripken UER	1.50	.70	.19
Misspelled Ripkin on back			
☐ 25 Bob Geren	.05	.02	.01
☐ 26 Wade Boggs	.40	.18	.05
☐ 27 Ryne Sandberg	.60	.25	.07
☐ 28 Kirby Puckett	.75	.35	.09
☐ 29 Mike Scott	.05	.02	.01
☐ 30 Dwight Smith	.05	.02	.01
☐ 31 Craig Worthington	.05	.02	.01
☐ 32A Ricky Jordan ERR	1.00	.45	.12
Misspelled Jordon on back			
☐ 32B Ricky Jordan COR	.10	.05	.01
☐ 33 Darryl Strawberry	.10	.05	.01
☐ 34 Jerome Walton	.05	.02	.01
☐ 35 John Olerud	.30	.14	.04
☐ 36 Tom Glavine	.40	.18	.05
☐ 37 Rickey Henderson	.30	.14	.04
☐ 38 Rolando Roomes	.05	.02	.01
☐ 39 Mickey Tettleton	.10	.05	.01
☐ 40 Jim Abbott	.25	.11	.03
☐ 41 Dave Righetti	.05	.02	.01
☐ 42 Mike LaValliere	.05	.02	.01
☐ 43 Rob Dibble	.05	.02	.01
☐ 44 Pete Harnisch	.05	.02	.01
☐ 45 Jose Offerman	.15	.07	.02
☐ 46 Walt Weiss	.05	.02	.01
☐ 47 Mike Greenwell	.10	.05	.01
☐ 48 Barry Larkin	.40	.18	.05
☐ 49 Dave Gallagher	.05	.02	.01
☐ 50 Junior Felix	.05	.02	.01
☐ 51 Roger Clemens	.50	.23	.06
☐ 52 Lonnie Smith	.05	.02	.01
☐ 53 Jerry Browne	.05	.02	.01
☐ 54 Greg Briley	.05	.02	.01
☐ 55 Delino DeShields	.25	.11	.03
☐ 56 Carmelo Martinez	.05	.02	.01
☐ 57 Craig Biggio	.30	.14	.04
☐ 58 Dwight Gooden	.10	.05	.01
☐ 59A Bo/Rubin/Mark	3.00	1.35	.35
Bo Jackson			
Ruben Sierra			
Mark McGwire			
☐ 59B A.L. Fence Busters	1.00	.45	.12
Bo Jackson			
Ruben Sierra			
Mark McGwire			
☐ 60 Greg Vaughn	.30	.14	.04
☐ 61 Roberto Alomar	.75	.35	.09
☐ 62 Steve Bedrosian	.05	.02	.01
☐ 63 Devon White	.10	.05	.01
☐ 64 Kevin Mitchell	.10	.05	.01
☐ 65 Marquis Grissom	.50	.23	.06
☐ 66 Brian Holman	.05	.02	.01
☐ 67 Julio Franco	.10	.05	.01
☐ 68 Dave West	.05	.02	.01
☐ 69 Harold Baines	.10	.05	.01
☐ 70 Eric Anthony	.05	.02	.01
☐ 71 Glenn Davis	.05	.02	.01
☐ 72 Mark Langston	.10	.05	.01
☐ 73 Matt Williams	.40	.18	.05
☐ 74 Rafael Palmeiro	.30	.14	.04
☐ 75 Pete Rose Jr.	.15	.07	.02
☐ 76 Ramon Martinez	.40	.18	.05
☐ 77 Dwight Evans	.10	.05	.01
☐ 78 Mackey Sasser	.05	.02	.01
☐ 79 Mike Schooler	.05	.02	.01
☐ 80 Dennis Cook	.05	.02	.01
☐ 81 Orel Hershiser	.10	.05	.01
☐ 82 Barry Bonds	.50	.23	.06
☐ 83 Geronimo Berroa	.10	.05	.01
☐ 84 George Bell	.05	.02	.01
☐ 85 Andre Dawson	.30	.14	.04
☐ 86 John Franco	.10	.05	.01
☐ 87A Clark/Gwynn	3.00	1.35	.35
Will Clark			
Tony Gwynn			
☐ 87B N.L. Hit Kings	1.00	.45	.12
Will Clark			
Tony Gwynn			
☐ 88 Glenallen Hill	.05	.02	.01
☐ 89 Jeff Ballard	.05	.02	.01
☐ 90 Todd Zeile	.30	.14	.04
☐ 91 Frank Viola	.05	.02	.01
☐ 92 Ozzie Guillen	.10	.05	.01
☐ 93 Jeffrey Leonard	.05	.02	.01
☐ 94 Dave Smith	.05	.02	.01
☐ 95 Dave Parker	.10	.05	.01
☐ 96 Jose Gonzalez	.05	.02	.01
☐ 97 Dave Stieb	.05	.02	.01
☐ 98 Charlie Hayes	.05	.02	.01
☐ 99 Jesse Barfield	.05	.02	.01
☐ 100 Joey Belle	1.00	.45	.12
☐ 101 Jeff Reardon	.10	.05	.01
☐ 102 Bruce Hurst	.05	.02	.01
☐ 103 Luis Medina	.05	.02	.01
☐ 104 Mike Moore	.05	.02	.01
☐ 105 Vince Coleman	.05	.02	.01
☐ 106 Alan Trammell	.30	.14	.04
☐ 107 Randy Myers	.10	.05	.01
☐ 108 Frank Tanana	.05	.02	.01
☐ 109 Craig Lefferts	.05	.02	.01
☐ 110 John Wetteland	.20	.09	.03
☐ 111 Chris Gwynn	.05	.02	.01
☐ 112 Mark Carreon	.10	.05	.01
☐ 113 Von Hayes	.05	.02	.01
☐ 114 Doug Jones	.05	.02	.01
☐ 115 Andres Galarraga	.20	.09	.03
☐ 116 Carlton Fisk UER	.50	.23	.06
Bellows Falls misspelled			
as Bellow Falls on back			
☐ 117 Paul O'Neill	.10	.05	.01
☐ 118 Tim Raines	.05	.02	.01
☐ 119 Tom Brunansky	.05	.02	.01
☐ 120 Andy Benes	.30	.14	.04
☐ 121 Mark Portugal	.05	.02	.01
☐ 122 Willie Randolph	.10	.05	.01
☐ 123 Jeff Blauser	.10	.05	.01
☐ 124 Don August	.05	.02	.01
☐ 125 Chuck Cary	.05	.02	.01
☐ 126 John Smiley	.05	.02	.01
☐ 127 Terry Mulholland	.05	.02	.01
☐ 128 Harold Reynolds	.05	.02	.01
☐ 129 Hubie Brooks	.05	.02	.01
☐ 130 Ben McDonald	.25	.11	.03
☐ 131 Kevin Ritz	.05	.02	.01
☐ 132 Luis Quinones	.05	.02	.01
☐ 133A Hensley Meulens ERR	.75	.35	.09
Misspelled Muelens on front			
☐ 133B Hensley Meulens COR	.20	.09	.03
☐ 134 Bill Spiers UER	.05	.02	.01
Orangeburg misspelled			
as Orangburg on back			
☐ 135 Andy Hawkins	.05	.02	.01
☐ 136 Alvin Davis	.05	.02	.01
☐ 137 Lee Smith	.10	.05	.01
☐ 138 Joe Carter	.30	.14	.04
☐ 139 Bret Saberhagen	.10	.05	.01
☐ 140 Sammy Sosa	.75	.35	.09
☐ 141 Matt Nokes	.05	.02	.01
☐ 142 Bert Blyleven	.10	.05	.01
☐ 143 Bobby Bonilla	.10	.05	.01
☐ 144 Howard Johnson	.10	.05	.01
☐ 145 Joe Magrane	.05	.02	.01
☐ 146 Pedro Guerrero	.10	.05	.01
☐ 147 Robin Yount	.40	.18	.05
☐ 148 Dan Gladden	.05	.02	.01
☐ 149 Steve Sax	.05	.02	.01
☐ 150A Clark/Mitchell	1.50	.70	.19
Will Clark			
Kevin Mitchell			
☐ 150B Bay Bombers	.30	.14	.04
Will Clark			
Kevin Mitchell			

1990 Classic Update

The 1990 Classic Update set was the second set issued by the Classic Game company in 1990. Sometimes referenced as Classic Pink or Red, this set includes a Juan Gonzalez card. This 50-card, standard-size set was issued in late June of 1990. With a few exceptions, the set numbering is in alphabetical order by player's name.

	MINT	NRMT	EXC
COMPLETE SET (50)	6.00	2.70	.75
COMMON CARD (T1-T49)	.10	.05	.01
☐ T1 Gregg Jefferies	.25	.11	.03
☐ T2 Steve Adkins	.10	.05	.01
☐ T3 Sandy Alomar Jr.	.30	.14	.04
☐ T4 Steve Avery	.50	.23	.06
☐ T5 Mike Blowers	.25	.11	.03
☐ T6 George Brett	.60	.25	.07

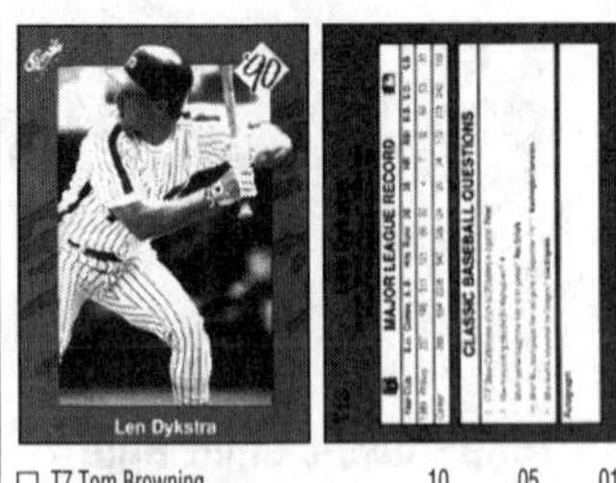

☐ T7 Tom Browning	.10	.05	.01
☐ T8 Ellis Burks	.25	.11	.03
☐ T9 Joe Carter	.30	.14	.04
☐ T10 Jerald Clark	.10	.05	.01
☐ T11 Hot Corners HOR	.50	.23	.06
Matt Williams			
Will Clark			
☐ T12 Pat Combs	.10	.05	.01
☐ T13 Scott Cooper	.10	.05	.01
☐ T14 Mark Davis	.10	.05	.01
☐ T15 Storm Davis	.10	.05	.01
☐ T16 Larry Walker	1.00	.45	.12
☐ T17 Brian DuBois	.10	.05	.01
☐ T18 Len Dykstra	.25	.11	.03
☐ T19 John Franco	.10	.05	.01
☐ T20 Kirk Gibson	.20	.09	.03
☐ T21 Juan Gonzalez	1.50	.70	.19
☐ T22 Tommy Greene	.10	.05	.01
☐ T23 Kent Hrbek	.10	.05	.01
☐ T24 Mike Huff	.10	.05	.01
☐ T25 Bo Jackson	.25	.11	.03
☐ T26 Nolan Ryan	2.00	.90	.25
Nolan Knows Bo			
☐ T27 Roberto Kelly	.10	.05	.01
☐ T28 Mark Langston	.20	.09	.03
☐ T29 Ray Lankford	.75	.35	.09
☐ T30 Kevin Maas	.10	.05	.01
☐ T31 Julio Machado	.10	.05	.01
☐ T32 Greg Maddux	1.50	.70	.19
☐ T33 Mark McGwire	.60	.25	.07
☐ T34 Paul Molitor	.50	.23	.06
☐ T35 Hal Morris	.20	.09	.03
☐ T36 Dale Murphy	.30	.14	.04
☐ T37 Eddie Murray	.50	.23	.06
☐ T38 Jaime Navarro	.10	.05	.01
☐ T39 Dean Palmer	.50	.23	.06
☐ T40 Derek Parks	.10	.05	.01
☐ T41 Bobby Rose	.10	.05	.01
☐ T42 Wally Joyner	.20	.09	.03
☐ T43 Chris Sabo	.10	.05	.01
☐ T44 Benito Santiago	.10	.05	.01
☐ T45 Mike Stanton	.10	.05	.01
☐ T46 Terry Steinbach UER	.20	.09	.03
Career BA .725			
☐ T47 Dave Stewart	.10	.05	.01
☐ T48 Greg Swindell	.10	.05	.01
☐ T49 Jose Vizcaino	.10	.05	.01
☐ NNO Royal Flush			
Mark Davis			
Bret Saberhagen			
(Instructions on back)			

1990 Classic Yellow

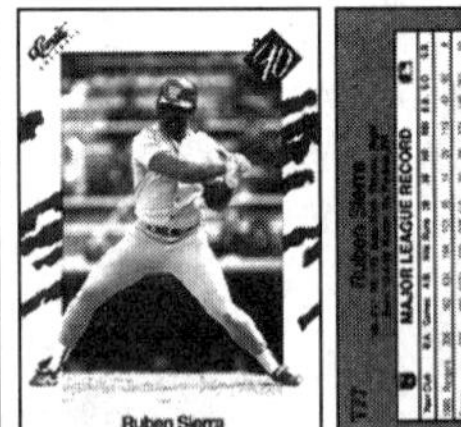

The 1990 Classic III set is also referenced as Classic Yellow. This set also featured number one draft picks of the current year mixed with the other Classic cards. This 100-card standard-size set also contained a special Nolan Ryan commemorative card, Texas Heat. A very early card of Chipper Jones is included in this set. Card T51 was never issued.

	MINT	NRMT	EXC
COMPLETE SET (100)	8.00	3.60	1.00
COMMON CARD (T1-T100)	.05	.02	.01
☐ T1 Ken Griffey Jr.	2.00	.90	.25
☐ T2 John Tudor	.05	.02	.01
☐ T3 John Kruk	.10	.05	.01
☐ T4 Mark Gardner	.05	.02	.01
☐ T5 Scott Radinsky	.05	.02	.01
☐ T6 John Burkett	.10	.05	.01
☐ T7 Will Clark	.40	.18	.05
☐ T8 Gary Carter	.10	.05	.01
☐ T9 Ted Higuera	.05	.02	.01
☐ T10 Dave Parker	.05	.02	.01
☐ T11 Dante Bichette	.40	.18	.05
☐ T12 Don Mattingly	.75	.35	.09
☐ T13 Greg Harris	.05	.02	.01
☐ T14 Dave Hollins	.10	.05	.01
☐ T15 Matt Nokes	.05	.02	.01
☐ T16 Kevin Tapani	.05	.02	.01
☐ T17 Shane Mack	.05	.02	.01
☐ T18 Randy Myers	.05	.02	.01
☐ T19 Greg Olson	.05	.02	.01
☐ T20 Shawn Abner	.05	.02	.01
☐ T21 Jim Presley	.05	.02	.01
☐ T22 Randy Johnson	.50	.23	.06
☐ T23 Edgar Martinez	.50	.23	.06
☐ T24 Scott Coolbaugh	.05	.02	.01
☐ T25 Jeff Treadway	.05	.02	.01
☐ T26 Joe Klink	.05	.02	.01
☐ T27 Rickey Henderson	.30	.14	.04
☐ T28 Sam Horn	.05	.02	.01
☐ T29 Kurt Stillwell	.05	.02	.01
☐ T30 Andy Van Slyke	.05	.02	.01
☐ T31 Willie Banks	.05	.02	.01
☐ T32 Jose Canseco	.40	.18	.05
☐ T33 Felix Jose	.05	.02	.01
☐ T34 Candy Maldonado	.05	.02	.01
☐ T35 Carlos Baerga	.75	.35	.09
☐ T36 Keith Hernandez	.05	.02	.01
☐ T37 Frank Viola	.05	.02	.01
☐ T38 Pete O'Brien	.05	.02	.01
☐ T39 Pat Borders	.05	.02	.01
☐ T40 Mike Heath	.05	.02	.01
☐ T41 Kevin Brown	.20	.09	.03
☐ T42 Chris Bosio	.05	.02	.01
☐ T43 Shawn Boskie	.05	.02	.01
☐ T44 Carlos Quintana	.05	.02	.01
☐ T45 Juan Samuel	.05	.02	.01
☐ T46 Tim Layana	.05	.02	.01
☐ T47 Mike Harkey	.05	.02	.01
☐ T48 Gerald Perry	.05	.02	.01
☐ T49 Mike Witt	.05	.02	.01
☐ T50 Joe Orsulak	.05	.02	.01
☐ T52 Willie Blair	.05	.02	.01
☐ T53 Gene Larkin	.05	.02	.01
☐ T54 Jody Reed	.05	.02	.01
☐ T55 Jeff Reardon	.05	.02	.01
☐ T56 Kevin McReynolds	.05	.02	.01
☐ T57 Mike Marshall	.05	.02	.01
Unnumbered			
game instructions on back			
☐ T58 Eric Yelding	.05	.02	.01
☐ T59 Fred Lynn	.05	.02	.01
☐ T60 Jim Leyritz	.20	.09	.03
☐ T61 John Orton	.05	.02	.01
☐ T62 Mike Lieberthal	.05	.02	.01
☐ T63 Mike Hartley	.05	.02	.01
☐ T64 Kal Daniels	.05	.02	.01
☐ T65 Terry Shumpert	.05	.02	.01
☐ T66 Sil Campusano	.05	.02	.01
☐ T67 Tony Pena	.05	.02	.01
☐ T68 Barry Bonds	.50	.23	.06
☐ T69 Roger McDowell	.05	.02	.01
☐ T70 Kelly Gruber	.05	.02	.01
☐ T71 Willie Randolph	.05	.02	.01
☐ T72 Rick Parker	.05	.02	.01
☐ T73 Bobby Bonilla	.10	.05	.01
☐ T74 Jack Armstrong	.05	.02	.01
☐ T75 Hubie Brooks	.05	.02	.01
☐ T76 Sandy Alomar Jr.	.20	.09	.03
☐ T77 Ruben Sierra	.10	.05	.01
☐ T78 Erik Hanson	.05	.02	.01
☐ T79 Tony Phillips	.10	.05	.01
☐ T80 Rondell White	.75	.35	.09
☐ T81 Bobby Thigpen	.05	.02	.01
☐ T82 Ron Walden	.05	.02	.01
☐ T83 Don Peters	.05	.02	.01
☐ T84 Nolan Ryan 6th	1.50	.70	.19
☐ T85 Lance Dickson	.05	.02	.01
☐ T86 Ryne Sandberg	.60	.25	.07
☐ T87 Eric Christopherson	.05	.02	.01
☐ T88 Shane Andrews	.20	.09	.03
☐ T89 Marc Newfield	.60	.25	.07
☐ T90 Adam Hyzdu	.05	.02	.01
☐ T91 Texas Heat	.75	.35	.09
Nolan Ryan			
Reid Ryan			
☐ T92 Chipper Jones	3.00	1.35	.35
☐ T93 Frank Thomas	2.50	1.10	.30
☐ T94 Cecil Fielder	.30	.14	.04
☐ T95 Delino DeShields	.25	.11	.03
☐ T96 John Olerud	.10	.05	.01
☐ T97 Dave Justice	.75	.35	.09
☐ T98 Joe Oliver	.05	.02	.01
☐ T99 Alex Fernandez	.50	.23	.06
☐ T100 Todd Hundley	.50	.23	.06
☐ NNO0 Micro Players	.50	.23	.06
Frank Viola			
Texas Heat			
Don Mattingly			
Chipper Jones			
(Blue blank back)			

1991 Classic Game

The 1991 Classic Baseball Collector's Edition board game is Classic's first Big Game issue since the 1989 Big Game. Only 100,000 games were produced, and each one included a board game, action spinner, eight stand-up baseball player pieces, action scoreboard, eight-page picture book with tips from five great baseball players (Carew, Spahn, Schmidt, Brock, and Aaron), 200 player cards, and a certificate of limited edition. The standard-size cards have on the fronts glossy

color action photos bordered in purple. The backs are purple and white and have biography, statistics, five trivia questions, and an autograph slot.

	MINT	NRMT	EXC
COMPLETE SET (200)	20.00	9.00	2.50
COMMON CARD (1-200)	.05	.02	.01
☐ 1 Frank Viola	.05	.02	.01
☐ 2 Tim Wallach	.05	.02	.01
☐ 3 Lou Whitaker	.10	.05	.01
☐ 4 Brett Butler	.10	.05	.01
☐ 5 Jim Abbott	.10	.05	.01
☐ 6 Jack Armstrong	.05	.02	.01
☐ 7 Craig Biggio	.20	.09	.03
☐ 8 Brian Barnes	.05	.02	.01
☐ 9 Dennis(Oil Can) Boyd	.05	.02	.01
☐ 10 Tom Browning	.05	.02	.01
☐ 11 Tom Brunansky	.05	.02	.01
☐ 12 Ellis Burks	.15	.07	.02
☐ 13 Harold Baines	.05	.02	.01
☐ 14 Kal Daniels	.05	.02	.01
☐ 15 Mark Davis	.05	.02	.01
☐ 16 Storm Davis	.05	.02	.01
☐ 17 Tom Glavine	.35	.16	.04
☐ 18 Mike Greenwell	.05	.02	.01
☐ 19 Kelly Gruber	.05	.02	.01
☐ 20 Mark Gubicza	.05	.02	.01
☐ 21 Pedro Guerrero	.05	.02	.01
☐ 22 Mike Harkey	.05	.02	.01
☐ 23 Orel Hershiser	.10	.05	.01
☐ 24 Ted Higuera	.05	.02	.01
☐ 25 Von Hayes	.05	.02	.01
☐ 26 Andre Dawson	.30	.14	.04
☐ 27 Shawon Dunston	.05	.02	.01
☐ 28 Roberto Kelly	.05	.02	.01
☐ 29 Joe Magrane	.05	.02	.01
☐ 30 Dennis Martinez	.05	.02	.01
☐ 31 Kevin McReynolds	.05	.02	.01
☐ 32 Matt Nokes	.05	.02	.01
☐ 33 Dan Plesac	.05	.02	.01
☐ 34 Dave Parker	.05	.02	.01
☐ 35 Randy Johnson	.60	.25	.07
☐ 36 Bret Saberhagen	.15	.07	.02
☐ 37 Mackey Sasser	.05	.02	.01
☐ 38 Mike Scott	.05	.02	.01
☐ 39 Ozzie Smith	.75	.35	.09
☐ 40 Kevin Seitzer	.05	.02	.01
☐ 41 Ruben Sierra	.20	.09	.03
☐ 42 Kevin Tapani	.05	.02	.01
☐ 43 Danny Tartabull	.15	.07	.02
☐ 44 Robby Thompson	.05	.02	.01
☐ 45 Andy Van Slyke	.05	.02	.01
☐ 46 Greg Vaughn	.20	.09	.03
☐ 47 Harold Reynolds	.10	.05	.01
☐ 48 Will Clark	.40	.18	.05
☐ 49 Gary Gaetti	.05	.02	.01
☐ 50 Joe Grahe	.05	.02	.01
☐ 51 Carlton Fisk	.30	.14	.04
☐ 52 Robin Ventura	.30	.14	.04
☐ 53 Ozzie Guillen	.05	.02	.01
☐ 54 Tom Candiotti	.05	.02	.01
☐ 55 Doug Jones	.05	.02	.01
☐ 56 Eric King	.05	.02	.01
☐ 57 Kirk Gibson	.10	.05	.01
☐ 58 Tim Costo	.05	.02	.01
☐ 59 Robin Yount	.35	.16	.04
☐ 60 Sammy Sosa	.75	.35	.09
☐ 61 Jesse Barfield	.05	.02	.01
☐ 62 Marc Newfield	.30	.14	.04
☐ 63 Jimmy Key	.05	.02	.01
☐ 64 Felix Jose	.05	.02	.01
☐ 65 Mark Whiten	.05	.02	.01
☐ 66 Tommy Greene	.05	.02	.01
☐ 67 Kent Mercker	.05	.02	.01
☐ 68 Greg Maddux	1.75	.80	.22
☐ 69 Danny Jackson	.05	.02	.01
☐ 70 Reggie Sanders	.50	.23	.06
☐ 71 Eric Yelding	.05	.02	.01
☐ 72 Karl Rhodes	.05	.02	.01
☐ 73 Fernando Valenzuela	.10	.05	.01
☐ 74 Chris Nabholz	.05	.02	.01
☐ 75 Andres Galarraga	.35	.16	.04
☐ 76 Howard Johnson	.05	.02	.01
☐ 77 Hubie Brooks	.05	.02	.01
☐ 78 Terry Mulholland	.05	.02	.01
☐ 79 Paul Molitor	.60	.25	.07
☐ 80 Roger McDowell	.05	.02	.01
☐ 81 Darren Daulton	.10	.05	.01
☐ 82 Zane Smith	.05	.02	.01
☐ 83 Ray Lankford	.30	.14	.04
☐ 84 Bruce Hurst	.05	.02	.01
☐ 85 Andy Benes	.10	.05	.01
☐ 86 John Burkett	.05	.02	.01
☐ 87 Dave Righetti	.05	.02	.01
☐ 88 Steve Karsay	.30	.14	.04
☐ 89 D.J. Dozier	.05	.02	.01
☐ 90 Jeff Bagwell	2.00	.90	.25
☐ 91 Joe Carter	.30	.14	.04
☐ 92 Wes Chamberlain	.05	.02	.01
☐ 93 Vince Coleman	.05	.02	.01
☐ 94 Pat Combs	.05	.02	.01
☐ 95 Jerome Walton	.05	.02	.01
☐ 96 Jeff Conine	.75	.35	.09
☐ 97 Alan Trammell	.10	.05	.01
☐ 98 Don Mattingly	1.50	.70	.19
☐ 99 Ramon Martinez	.20	.09	.03
☐ 100 Dave Magadan	.05	.02	.01
☐ 101 Greg Swindell UER Misnumbered as T10	.05	.02	.01
☐ 102 Dave Stewart	.05	.02	.01
☐ 103 Gary Sheffield	.50	.23	.06
☐ 104 George Bell	.05	.02	.01
☐ 105 Mark Grace	.20	.09	.03
☐ 106 Steve Sax	.05	.02	.01
☐ 107 Ryne Sandberg	1.00	.45	.12
☐ 108 Chris Sabo	.05	.02	.01
☐ 109 Jose Rijo	.05	.02	.01
☐ 110 Cal Ripken	2.00	.90	.25
☐ 111 Kirby Puckett	1.25	.55	.16
☐ 112 Eddie Murray	.75	.35	.09
☐ 113 Roberto Alomar	.60	.25	.07
☐ 114 Randy Myers	.05	.02	.01
☐ 115 Rafael Palmeiro	.35	.16	.04
☐ 116 John Olerud	.20	.09	.03
☐ 117 Gregg Jefferies	.30	.14	.04
☐ 118 Kent Hrbek	.05	.02	.01
☐ 119 Marquis Grissom	.30	.14	.04
☐ 120 Ken Griffey Jr.	3.00	1.35	.35
☐ 121 Dwight Gooden	.10	.05	.01
☐ 122 Juan Gonzalez	1.00	.45	.12
☐ 123 Ron Gant	.10	.05	.01
☐ 124 Travis Fryman	.40	.18	.05
☐ 125 John Franco	.05	.02	.01
☐ 126 Dennis Eckersley	.10	.05	.01
☐ 127 Cecil Fielder	.30	.14	.04
☐ 128 Phil Plantier	.25	.11	.03
☐ 129 Kevin Mitchell	.05	.02	.01
☐ 130 Kevin Maas	.05	.02	.01
☐ 131 Mark McGwire	1.00	.45	.12
☐ 132 Ben McDonald	.20	.09	.03
☐ 133 Len Dykstra	.20	.09	.03
☐ 134 Delino DeShields	.20	.09	.03
☐ 135 Jose Canseco	.40	.18	.05
☐ 136 Eric Davis	.05	.02	.01
☐ 137 George Brett	1.25	.55	.16
☐ 138 Steve Avery	.30	.14	.04
☐ 139 Eric Anthony	.05	.02	.01
☐ 140 Bobby Thigpen	.05	.02	.01
☐ 141 Ken Griffey Sr.	.05	.02	.01
☐ 142 Barry Larkin	.40	.18	.05
☐ 143 Jeff Brantley	.05	.02	.01
☐ 144 Bobby Bonilla	.10	.05	.01
☐ 145 Jose Offerman	.05	.02	.01
☐ 146 Mike Mussina	1.00	.45	.12
☐ 147 Erik Hanson	.05	.02	.01
☐ 148 Dale Murphy	.20	.09	.03
☐ 149 Roger Clemens	.50	.23	.06
☐ 150 Tino Martinez	.25	.11	.03
☐ 151 Todd Van Poppel	.15	.07	.02
☐ 152 Mo Vaughn	.75	.35	.09
☐ 153 Derrick May	.20	.09	.03
☐ 154 Jack Clark	.05	.02	.01
☐ 155 Dave Hansen	.05	.02	.01
☐ 156 Tony Gwynn	1.25	.55	.16
☐ 157 Brian McRae	.30	.14	.04
☐ 158 Matt Williams	.40	.18	.05
☐ 159 Kirk Dressendorfer	.05	.02	.01
☐ 160 Scott Erickson	.05	.02	.01
☐ 161 Tony Fernandez	.05	.02	.01
☐ 162 Willie McGee	.10	.05	.01
☐ 163 Fred McGriff	.40	.18	.05
☐ 164 Leo Gomez	.05	.02	.01
☐ 165 Bernard Gilkey	.20	.09	.03
☐ 166 Bobby Witt	.05	.02	.01
☐ 167 Doug Drabek	.05	.02	.01
☐ 168 Rob Dibble	.05	.02	.01
☐ 169 Glenn Davis	.05	.02	.01
☐ 170 Danny Darwin	.05	.02	.01
☐ 171 Eric Karros	.75	.35	.09
☐ 172 Eddie Zosky	.05	.02	.01
☐ 173 Todd Zeile	.05	.02	.01
☐ 174 Tim Raines	.05	.02	.01
☐ 175 Benito Santiago	.05	.02	.01
☐ 176 Dan Peltier	.05	.02	.01
☐ 177 Darryl Strawberry	.10	.05	.01
☐ 178 Hal Morris	.10	.05	.01
☐ 179 Hensley Meulens	.05	.02	.01
☐ 180 John Smoltz	.60	.25	.07
☐ 181 Frank Thomas	3.00	1.35	.35
☐ 182 Dave Staton	.05	.02	.01
☐ 183 Scott Champarino	.05	.02	.01
☐ 184 Alex Fernandez	.35	.16	.04
☐ 185 Mark Lewis	.15	.07	.02
☐ 186 Bo Jackson	.30	.14	.04
☐ 187 Mickey Morandini UER Photo is Darren Daulton	.10	.05	.01
☐ 188 Cory Snyder	.05	.02	.01
☐ 189 Rickey Henderson	.35	.16	.04
☐ 190 Junior Felix	.05	.02	.01
☐ 191 Milt Cuyler	.05	.02	.01
☐ 192 Wade Boggs	.35	.16	.04
☐ 193 Dave Justice Justice Prevails	.40	.18	.05
☐ 194 Sandy Alomar Jr.	.10	.05	.01
☐ 195 Barry Bonds	.75	.35	.09
☐ 196 Nolan Ryan	2.50	1.10	.30
☐ 197 Rico Brogna	.20	.09	.03
☐ 198 Steve Decker	.05	.02	.01
☐ 199 Bob Welch	.05	.02	.01
☐ 200 Andujar Cedeno	.20	.09	.03

1991 Classic I

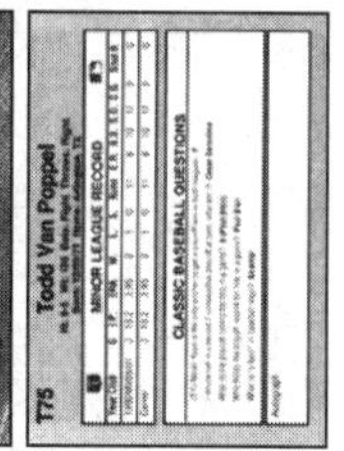

This 100-card standard-size set features many of the most popular players in the game of baseball as well as some of the more exciting prospects. The set includes trivia questions on the backs of the cards. For the most part the set is arranged alphabetically by team and then alphabetically by players within that team.

	MINT	NRMT	EXC
COMPLETE SET (100)	7.50	3.40	.95
COMMON CARD (T1-T99)	.05	.02	.01
☐ T1 John Olerud	.20	.09	.03
☐ T2 Tino Martinez	.15	.07	.02
☐ T3 Ken Griffey Jr.	1.50	.70	.19
☐ T4 Jeromy Burnitz	.10	.05	.01
☐ T5 Ron Gant	.10	.05	.01
☐ T6 Mike Benjamin	.05	.02	.01
☐ T7 Steve Decker	.05	.02	.01
☐ T8 Matt Williams	.30	.14	.04
☐ T9 Rafael Novoa	.05	.02	.01
☐ T10 Kevin Mitchell	.05	.02	.01
☐ T11 Dave Justice	.25	.11	.03
☐ T12 Leo Gomez	.05	.02	.01
☐ T13 Chris Hoiles	.20	.09	.03
☐ T14 Ben McDonald	.10	.05	.01
☐ T15 David Segui	.10	.05	.01
☐ T16 Anthony Telford	.05	.02	.01
☐ T17 Mike Mussina	.50	.23	.06
☐ T18 Roger Clemens	.30	.14	.04
☐ T19 Wade Boggs	.30	.14	.04
☐ T20 Tim Naehring	.10	.05	.01
☐ T21 Joe Carter	.20	.09	.03
☐ T22 Phil Plantier	.20	.09	.03
☐ T23 Rob Dibble	.05	.02	.01
☐ T24 Mo Vaughn	.50	.23	.06
☐ T25 Lee Stevens	.05	.02	.01
☐ T26 Chris Sabo	.05	.02	.01
☐ T27 Mark Grace	.20	.09	.03
☐ T28 Derrick May	.05	.02	.01
☐ T29 Ryne Sandberg	.50	.23	.06
☐ T30 Matt Stark	.05	.02	.01
☐ T31 Bobby Thigpen	.05	.02	.01
☐ T32 Frank Thomas	1.50	.70	.19
☐ T33 Don Mattingly	.60	.25	.07
☐ T34 Eric Davis	.05	.02	.01
☐ T35 Reggie Jefferson	.10	.05	.01
☐ T36 Alex Cole	.05	.02	.01
☐ T37 Mark Lewis	.15	.07	.02
☐ T38 Tim Costo	.05	.02	.01
☐ T39 Sandy Alomar Jr.	.10	.05	.01
☐ T40 Travis Fryman	.20	.09	.03
☐ T41 Cecil Fielder	.30	.14	.04
☐ T42 Milt Cuyler	.05	.02	.01
☐ T43 Andujar Cedeno	.05	.02	.01
☐ T44 Danny Darwin	.05	.02	.01
☐ T45 Randy Hennis	.05	.02	.01
☐ T46 George Brett	.50	.23	.06
☐ T47 Jeff Conine	.40	.18	.05
☐ T48 Bo Jackson	.30	.14	.04
☐ T49 Brian McRae	.30	.14	.04
☐ T50 Brent Mayne	.05	.02	.01
☐ T51 Eddie Murray	.35	.16	.04
☐ T52 Ramon Martinez	.20	.09	.03
☐ T53 Jim Neidlinger	.05	.02	.01
☐ T54 Jim Poole	.05	.02	.01
☐ T55 Tim McIntosh	.05	.02	.01
☐ T56 Randy Veres	.05	.02	.01
☐ T57 Kirby Puckett	.60	.25	.07
☐ T58 Todd Ritchie	.05	.02	.01
☐ T59 Rich Garces	.05	.02	.01
☐ T60 Moises Alou	.20	.09	.03
☐ T61 Delino DeShields	.05	.02	.01
☐ T62 Oscar Azocar	.05	.02	.01
☐ T63 Kevin Maas	.05	.02	.01
☐ T64 Alan Mills	.05	.02	.01
☐ T65 John Franco	.05	.02	.01
☐ T66 Chris Jelic	.05	.02	.01
☐ T67 Dave Magadan	.05	.02	.01
☐ T68 Darryl Strawberry	.10	.05	.01
☐ T69 Hensley Meulens	.05	.02	.01
☐ T70 Juan Gonzalez	.75	.35	.09
☐ T71 Reggie Harris	.05	.02	.01
☐ T72 Rickey Henderson	.25	.11	.03
☐ T73 Mark McGwire	.50	.23	.06
☐ T74 Willie McGee	.10	.05	.01
☐ T75 Todd Van Poppel	.15	.07	.02
☐ T76 Bob Welch	.05	.02	.01
☐ T77 Future Aces Todd Van Poppel Don Peters David Zancanaro Kirk Dressendorfer	.20	.09	.03
☐ T78 Len Dykstra	.20	.09	.03
☐ T79 Mickey Morandini	.05	.02	.01
☐ T80 Wes Chamberlain	.05	.02	.01
☐ T81 Barry Bonds	.40	.18	.05
☐ T82 Doug Drabek	.05	.02	.01
☐ T83 Randy Tomlin	.05	.02	.01
☐ T84 Scott Chiamparino	.05	.02	.01
☐ T85 Rafael Palmeiro	.25	.11	.03
☐ T86 Nolan Ryan	1.25	.55	.16
☐ T87 Bobby Witt	.05	.02	.01
☐ T88 Fred McGriff	.25	.11	.03
☐ T89 Dave Stieb	.05	.02	.01
☐ T90 Ed Sprague	.15	.07	.02
☐ T91 Vince Coleman	.05	.02	.01
☐ T92 Rod Brewer	.05	.02	.01
☐ T93 Bernard Gilkey	.25	.11	.03
☐ T94 Roberto Alomar	.30	.14	.04
☐ T95 Chuck Finley	.05	.02	.01
☐ T96 Dale Murphy	.20	.09	.03
☐ T97 Jose Rijo	.05	.02	.01
☐ T98 Hal Morris	.10	.05	.01
☐ T99 Friendly Foes Darryl Strawberry Dwight Gooden Instructions on back	.10	.05	.01
☐ NNO Todd Van Poppel Dave Justice Ryne Sandberg Kevin Maas (Blank back)	.15	.07	.02

1991 Classic II

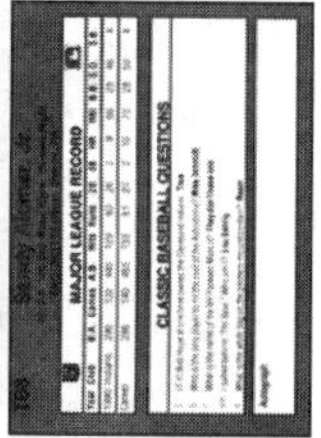

This second issue of the 1991 Classic baseball trivia game contains a small gameboard, accessories, 99 player cards with trivia questions on the backs, and one "4-in-1" micro player card. The cards measure the standard size and have on the fronts glossy color action photos with cranberry red borders. The backs are cranberry and white and have biography, statistics, five trivia questions, and an autograph slot.

	MINT	NRMT	EXC
COMPLETE SET (100)	7.50	3.40	.95
COMMON CARD (T1-T100)	.05	.02	.01
☐ T1 Ken Griffey Jr.	2.00	.90	.25
☐ T2 Wil Cordero	.20	.09	.03
☐ T3 Cal Ripken	1.25	.55	.16
☐ T4 D.J. Dozier	.05	.02	.01
☐ T5 Darrin Fletcher	.05	.02	.01
☐ T6 Glenn Davis	.05	.02	.01
☐ T7 Alex Fernandez	.40	.18	.05
☐ T8 Cory Snyder	.05	.02	.01
☐ T9 Tim Raines	.05	.02	.01
☐ T10 Greg Swindell	.05	.02	.01
☐ T11 Mark Lewis	.10	.05	.01
☐ T12 Rico Brogna	.20	.09	.03
☐ T13 Gary Sheffield	.40	.18	.05
☐ T14 Paul Molitor	.40	.18	.05
☐ T15 Kent Hrbek	.05	.02	.01
☐ T16 Scott Erickson	.05	.02	.01
☐ T17 Steve Sax	.05	.02	.01
☐ T18 Dennis Eckersley	.10	.05	.01
☐ T19 Jose Canseco	.30	.14	.04
☐ T20 Kirk Dressendorfer	.05	.02	.01
☐ T21 Ken Griffey Sr.	.05	.02	.01
☐ T22 Erik Hanson	.05	.02	.01
☐ T23 Dan Peltier	.05	.02	.01
☐ T24 John Olerud	.20	.09	.03
☐ T25 Eddie Zosky	.05	.02	.01
☐ T26 Steve Avery	.25	.11	.03
☐ T27 John Smoltz	.40	.18	.05
☐ T28 Frank Thomas	2.00	.90	.25
☐ T29 Jerome Walton	.05	.02	.01
☐ T30 George Bell	.05	.02	.01
☐ T31 Jose Rijo	.05	.02	.01
☐ T32 Randy Myers	.05	.02	.01
☐ T33 Barry Larkin	.25	.11	.03

	MINT	NRMT	EXC
☐ T34 Eric Anthony	.05	.02	.01
☐ T35 Dave Hansen	.05	.02	.01
☐ T36 Eric Karros	.40	.18	.05
☐ T37 Jose Offerman	.05	.02	.01
☐ T38 Marquis Grissom	.30	.14	.04
☐ T39 Dwight Gooden	.10	.05	.01
☐ T40 Gregg Jefferies	.20	.09	.03
☐ T41 Pat Combs	.05	.02	.01
☐ T42 Todd Zeile	.05	.02	.01
☐ T43 Benito Santiago	.05	.02	.01
☐ T44 Dave Staton	.05	.02	.01
☐ T45 Tony Fernandez	.05	.02	.01
☐ T46 Fred McGriff	.25	.11	.03
☐ T47 Jeff Brantley	.05	.02	.01
☐ T48 Junior Felix	.05	.02	.01
☐ T49 Jack Morris	.05	.02	.01
☐ T50 Chris George	.05	.02	.01
☐ T51 Henry Rodriguez	.25	.11	.03
☐ T52 Paul Marak	.05	.02	.01
☐ T53 Ryan Klesko	1.00	.45	.12
☐ T54 Darren Lewis	.05	.02	.01
☐ T55 Lance Dickson	.05	.02	.01
☐ T56 Anthony Young	.05	.02	.01
☐ T57 Willie Banks	.05	.02	.01
☐ T58 Mike Bordick	.10	.05	.01
☐ T59 Roger Salkeld	.05	.02	.01
☐ T60 Steve Karsay	.30	.14	.04
☐ T61 Bernie Williams	.50	.23	.06
☐ T62 Mickey Tettleton	.05	.02	.01
☐ T63 Dave Justice	.40	.18	.05
☐ T64 Steve Decker	.05	.02	.01
☐ T65 Roger Clemens	.30	.14	.04
☐ T66 Phil Plantier	.15	.07	.02
☐ T67 Ryne Sandberg	.50	.23	.06
☐ T68 Sandy Alomar Jr.	.10	.05	.01
☐ T69 Cecil Fielder	.30	.14	.04
☐ T70 George Brett	.75	.35	.09
☐ T71 Delino DeShields	.20	.09	.03
☐ T72 Dave Magadan	.05	.02	.01
☐ T73 Darryl Strawberry	.10	.05	.01
☐ T74 Juan Gonzalez	.60	.25	.07
☐ T75 Rickey Henderson	.25	.11	.03
☐ T76 Willie McGee	.10	.05	.01
☐ T77 Todd Van Poppel	.15	.07	.02
☐ T78 Barry Bonds	.50	.23	.06
☐ T79 Doug Drabek	.05	.02	.01
☐ T80 Nolan Ryan 300 Game Winner	.75	.35	.09
☐ T81 Roberto Alomar	.40	.18	.05
☐ T82 Ivan Rodriguez	.75	.35	.09
☐ T83 Dan Opperman	.05	.02	.01
☐ T84 Jeff Bagwell	1.50	.70	.19
☐ T85 Braulio Castillo	.05	.02	.01
☐ T86 Doug Simons	.05	.02	.01
☐ T87 Wade Taylor	.05	.02	.01
☐ T88 Gary Scott	.05	.02	.01
☐ T89 Dave Stewart	.05	.02	.01
☐ T90 Mike Simms	.05	.02	.01
☐ T91 Luis Gonzalez	.20	.09	.03
☐ T92 Bobby Bonilla	.10	.05	.01
☐ T93 Tony Gwynn	.75	.35	.09
☐ T94 Will Clark	.25	.11	.03
☐ T95 Rich Rowland	.05	.02	.01
☐ T96 Alan Trammell	.10	.05	.01
☐ T97 Strikeout Kings Nolan Ryan Roger Clemens	.60	.25	.07
☐ T98 Joe Carter	.20	.09	.03
☐ T99 Jack Clark	.05	.02	.01
☐ T100 Steve Decker	.05	.02	.01

1991 Classic III

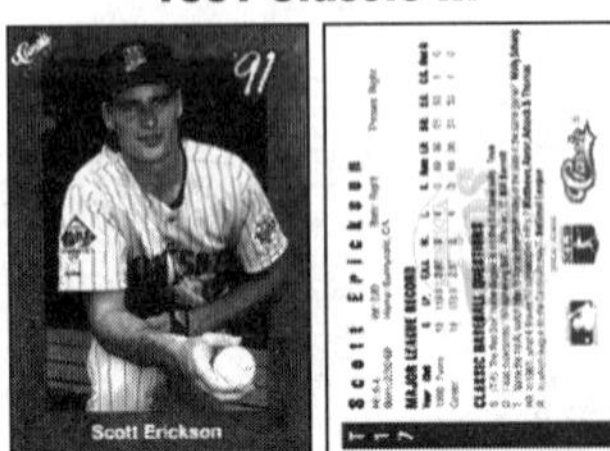

The third issue of the 1991 Classic baseball trivia game contains a small gameboard, accessories, 99 player cards with trivia questions on the backs, and one "4-in-1" micro player card. The cards measure the standard size and have on the fronts glossy color action photos with grayish-green borders. In a horizontal format, the backs feature biography, statistics, and five trivia questions. This information is superimposed over the team logo. The card numbers on the back appear in a green stripe. With few exceptions, the cards are arranged in alphabetical order.

	MINT	NRMT	EXC
COMPLETE SET (100)	10.00	4.50	1.25
COMMON CARD (T1-T99)	.05	.02	.01

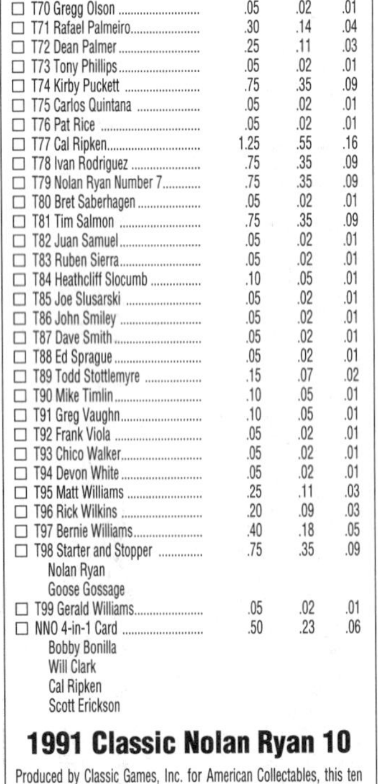

	MINT	NRMT	EXC
☐ T1 Jim Abbott	.20	.09	.03
☐ T2 Craig Biggio	.25	.11	.03
☐ T3 Wade Boggs	.25	.11	.03
☐ T4 Bobby Bonilla	.10	.05	.01
☐ T5 Ivan Calderon	.05	.02	.01
☐ T6 Jose Canseco	.25	.11	.03
☐ T7 Andy Benes	.10	.05	.01
☐ T8 Wes Chamberlain	.05	.02	.01
☐ T9 Will Clark	.25	.11	.03
☐ T10 Royce Clayton	.20	.09	.03
☐ T11 Gerald Alexander	.05	.02	.01
☐ T12 Chili Davis	.05	.02	.01
☐ T13 Eric Davis	.05	.02	.01
☐ T14 Andre Dawson	.20	.09	.03
☐ T15 Rob Dibble	.05	.02	.01
☐ T16 Chris Donnels	.05	.02	.01
☐ T17 Scott Erickson	.05	.02	.01
☐ T18 Monty Fariss	.05	.02	.01
☐ T19 Ruben Amaro Jr.	.05	.02	.01
☐ T20 Chuck Finley	.05	.02	.01
☐ T21 Carlton Fisk	.30	.14	.04
☐ T22 Carlos Baerga	.25	.11	.03
☐ T23 Ron Gant	.20	.09	.03
☐ T24 Dave Justice and Ron Gant	.25	.11	.03
☐ T25 Mike Gardiner	.05	.02	.01
☐ T26 Tom Glavine	.30	.14	.04
☐ T27 Joe Grahe	.05	.02	.01
☐ T28 Derek Bell	.25	.11	.03
☐ T29 Mike Greenwell	.05	.02	.01
☐ T30 Ken Griffey Jr.	2.00	.90	.25
☐ T31 Leo Gomez	.05	.02	.01
☐ T32 Tom Goodwin	.05	.02	.01
☐ T33 Tony Gwynn	.75	.35	.09
☐ T34 Mel Hall	.05	.02	.01
☐ T35 Brian Harper	.05	.02	.01
☐ T36 Dave Henderson	.05	.02	.01
☐ T37 Albert Belle	1.00	.45	.12
☐ T38 Orel Hershiser	.10	.05	.01
☐ T39 Brian Hunter	.05	.02	.01
☐ T40 Howard Johnson	.05	.02	.01
☐ T41 Felix Jose	.05	.02	.01
☐ T42 Wally Joyner	.05	.02	.01
☐ T43 Jeff Juden	.05	.02	.01
☐ T44 Pat Kelly	.05	.02	.01
☐ T45 Jimmy Key	.05	.02	.01
☐ T46 Chuck Knoblauch	.50	.23	.06
☐ T47 John Kruk	.10	.05	.01
☐ T48 Ray Lankford	.25	.11	.03
☐ T49 Ced Landrum	.05	.02	.01
☐ T50 Scott Livingstone	.05	.02	.01
☐ T51 Kevin Maas	.05	.02	.01
☐ T52 Greg Maddux	1.25	.55	.16
☐ T53 Dennis Martinez	.05	.02	.01
☐ T54 Edgar Martinez	.25	.11	.03
☐ T55 Pedro Martinez	.30	.14	.04
☐ T56 Don Mattingly	1.00	.45	.12
☐ T57 Orlando Merced	.25	.11	.03
☐ T58 Keith Mitchell	.05	.02	.01
☐ T59 Kevin Mitchell	.05	.02	.01
☐ T60 Paul Molitor	.40	.18	.05
☐ T61 Jack Morris	.05	.02	.01
☐ T62 Hal Morris	.05	.02	.01
☐ T63 Kevin Morton	.05	.02	.01
☐ T64 Pedro Munoz	.05	.02	.01
☐ T65 Eddie Murray	.50	.23	.06
☐ T66 Jack McDowell	.20	.09	.03
☐ T67 Jeff McNeely	.05	.02	.01
☐ T68 Brian McRae	.25	.11	.03
☐ T69 Kevin McReynolds	.05	.02	.01
☐ T70 Gregg Olson	.05	.02	.01
☐ T71 Rafael Palmeiro	.30	.14	.04
☐ T72 Dean Palmer	.25	.11	.03
☐ T73 Tony Phillips	.05	.02	.01
☐ T74 Kirby Puckett	.75	.35	.09
☐ T75 Carlos Quintana	.05	.02	.01
☐ T76 Pat Rice	.05	.02	.01
☐ T77 Cal Ripken	1.25	.55	.16
☐ T78 Ivan Rodriguez	.75	.35	.09
☐ T79 Nolan Ryan Number 7	.75	.35	.09
☐ T80 Bret Saberhagen	.05	.02	.01
☐ T81 Tim Salmon	.75	.35	.09
☐ T82 Juan Samuel	.05	.02	.01
☐ T83 Ruben Sierra	.05	.02	.01
☐ T84 Heathcliff Slocumb	.10	.05	.01
☐ T85 Joe Slusarski	.05	.02	.01
☐ T86 John Smiley	.05	.02	.01
☐ T87 Dave Smith	.05	.02	.01
☐ T88 Ed Sprague	.05	.02	.01
☐ T89 Todd Stottlemyre	.15	.07	.02
☐ T90 Mike Timlin	.10	.05	.01
☐ T91 Greg Vaughn	.10	.05	.01
☐ T92 Frank Viola	.05	.02	.01
☐ T93 Chico Walker	.05	.02	.01
☐ T94 Devon White	.05	.02	.01
☐ T95 Matt Williams	.25	.11	.03
☐ T96 Rick Wilkins	.20	.09	.03
☐ T97 Bernie Williams	.40	.18	.05
☐ T98 Starter and Stopper Nolan Ryan Goose Gossage	.75	.35	.09
☐ T99 Gerald Williams	.05	.02	.01
☐ NNO 4-in-1 Card Bobby Bonilla Will Clark Cal Ripken Scott Erickson	.50	.23	.06

1991 Classic Nolan Ryan 10

Produced by Classic Games, Inc. for American Collectables, this ten card limited edition career celebration standard size set highlights

Nolan Ryan's achievements. The fronts display posed and action shots with a split design border. The left half of the card has a mottled green and yellow border and the right half displays a teal green one. A black bar overlaid on the photo lists the team he is portrayed playing for, and the years Nolan was a member of that team. The light green horizontal backs carry biography, statistics, and career summary.

	MINT	NRMT	EXC
COMPLETE SET (10)	20.00	9.00	2.50
COMMON CARD (1-10)	2.00	.90	.25

	MINT	NRMT	EXC
☐ 1 Nolan Ryan Mets '66-'71	2.00	.90	.25
☐ 2 Nolan Ryan Angels '72-'79	2.00	.90	.25
☐ 3 Nolan Ryan Astros '80-'88	2.00	.90	.25
☐ 4 Nolan Ryan Rangers '89-'90	2.00	.90	.25
☐ 5 Nolan Ryan 5000 K's	2.00	.90	.25
☐ 6 Nolan Ryan 6th No-No	2.00	.90	.25
☐ 7 Nolan Ryan Angels '72-'79	2.00	.90	.25
☐ 8 Nolan Ryan Astros '80-'88	2.00	.90	.25
☐ 9 Nolan Ryan Rangers '89-'90	2.00	.90	.25
☐ 10 Nolan Ryan 300 Certificate of Authenticity	2.00	.90	.25

1992 Classic Game

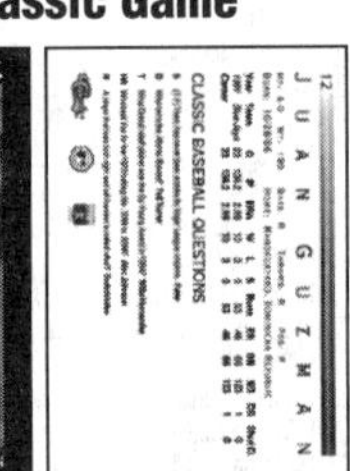

The 1992 Classic Baseball Collector's Edition game contains 200 standard-size cards. The cards were issued in two boxes labeled "Trivia Cards A" and "Trivia Cards B." The game also included an official Major League Action Spinner, eight stand-up baseball hero player pieces, an action scoreboard, a hand-illustrated game board, and a collectible book featuring tips from a new group of baseball legends. According to Classic, production has been limited to 125,000 games. The fronts display glossy color action photos bordered in dark purple. The Classic logo and the year "1992" appear in the top border, while the player's name is given in white lettering in the bottom border. The horizontally oriented backs present biography, statistics (1991 and career), and five baseball trivia questions.

	MINT	NRMT	EXC
COMPLETE SET (200)	18.00	8.00	2.20
COMMON CARD (1-200)	.05	.02	.01

	MINT	NRMT	EXC
☐ 1 Chuck Finley	.05	.02	.01
☐ 2 Craig Biggio	.25	.11	.03
☐ 3 Luis Gonzalez	.05	.02	.01
☐ 4 Pete Harnisch	.05	.02	.01
☐ 5 Jeff Juden	.05	.02	.01
☐ 6 Harold Baines	.05	.02	.01
☐ 7 Kirk Dressendorfer	.05	.02	.01
☐ 8 Dennis Eckersley	.15	.07	.02
☐ 9 Dave Henderson	.05	.02	.01
☐ 10 Dave Stewart	.05	.02	.01
☐ 11 Joe Carter	.25	.11	.03
☐ 12 Juan Guzman	.20	.09	.03
☐ 13 Dave Stieb	.05	.02	.01
☐ 14 Todd Stottlemyre	.15	.07	.02
☐ 15 Ron Gant	.10	.05	.01
☐ 16 Brian Hunter	.05	.02	.01
☐ 17 Dave Justice	.30	.14	.04
☐ 18 John Smoltz	.40	.18	.05
☐ 19 Mike Stanton	.05	.02	.01
☐ 20 Chris George	.05	.02	.01
☐ 21 Paul Molitor	.40	.18	.05
☐ 22 Omar Olivares	.05	.02	.01
☐ 23 Lee Smith	.10	.05	.01
☐ 24 Ozzie Smith	.50	.23	.06
☐ 25 Todd Zeile	.05	.02	.01
☐ 26 George Bell	.05	.02	.01
☐ 27 Andre Dawson	.25	.11	.03
☐ 28 Shawon Dunston	.05	.02	.01
☐ 29 Mark Grace	.20	.09	.03
☐ 30 Greg Maddux	1.25	.55	.16
☐ 31 Dave Smith	.05	.02	.01
☐ 32 Brett Butler	.10	.05	.01
☐ 33 Orel Hershiser	.10	.05	.01
☐ 34 Eric Karros	.40	.18	.05
☐ 35 Ramon Martinez	.10	.05	.01
☐ 36 Jose Offerman	.05	.02	.01
☐ 37 Juan Samuel	.05	.02	.01
☐ 38 Delino DeShields	.05	.02	.01
☐ 39 Marquis Grissom	.25	.11	.03
☐ 40 Tim Wallach	.05	.02	.01
☐ 41 Eric Gunderson	.05	.02	.01
☐ 42 Willie McGee	.05	.02	.01
☐ 43 Dave Righetti	.05	.02	.01
☐ 44 Robby Thompson	.05	.02	.01
☐ 45 Matt Williams	.40	.18	.05
☐ 46 Sandy Alomar Jr.	.10	.05	.01
☐ 47 Reggie Jefferson	.05	.02	.01
☐ 48 Mark Lewis	.05	.02	.01
☐ 49 Robin Ventura	.25	.11	.03
☐ 50 Tino Martinez	.15	.07	.02
☐ 51 Roberto Kelly	.05	.02	.01
☐ 52 Vince Coleman	.05	.02	.01
☐ 53 Dwight Gooden	.10	.05	.01
☐ 54 Todd Hundley	.25	.11	.03
☐ 55 Kevin Maas	.05	.02	.01
☐ 56 Wade Taylor	.05	.02	.01
☐ 57 Bryan Harvey	.05	.02	.01
☐ 58 Leo Gomez	.05	.02	.01
☐ 59 Ben McDonald	.05	.02	.01
☐ 60 Ricky Bones	.05	.02	.01
☐ 61 Tony Gwynn	.60	.25	.07
☐ 62 Benito Santiago	.05	.02	.01
☐ 63 Wes Chamberlain	.05	.02	.01
☐ 64 Tommy Greene	.05	.02	.01
☐ 65 Dale Murphy	.20	.09	.03
☐ 66 Steve Buechele	.05	.02	.01
☐ 67 Doug Drabek	.05	.02	.01
☐ 68 Joe Grahe	.05	.02	.01
☐ 69 Rafael Palmeiro	.25	.11	.03
☐ 70 Wade Boggs	.25	.11	.03
☐ 71 Ellis Burks	.15	.07	.02
☐ 72 Mike Greenwell	.05	.02	.01
☐ 73 Mo Vaughn	.60	.25	.07
☐ 74 Derek Bell	.20	.09	.03
☐ 75 Rob Dibble	.05	.02	.01
☐ 76 Barry Larkin	.25	.11	.03
☐ 77 Jose Rijo	.05	.02	.01
☐ 78 Doug Henry	.05	.02	.01
☐ 79 Chris Sabo	.05	.02	.01
☐ 80 Pedro Guerrero	.05	.02	.01
☐ 81 George Brett	.75	.35	.09
☐ 82 Tom Gordon	.05	.02	.01
☐ 83 Mark Gubicza	.05	.02	.01
☐ 84 Mark Whiten	.05	.02	.01
☐ 85 Brian McRae	.10	.05	.01
☐ 86 Danny Jackson	.05	.02	.01
☐ 87 Milt Cuyler	.05	.02	.01
☐ 88 Travis Fryman	.25	.11	.03
☐ 89 Mickey Tettleton	.05	.02	.01
☐ 90 Alan Trammell	.25	.11	.03
☐ 91 Lou Whitaker	.10	.05	.01
☐ 92 Chili Davis	.05	.02	.01
☐ 93 Scott Erickson	.05	.02	.01
☐ 94 Kent Hrbek	.05	.02	.01
☐ 95 Alex Fernandez	.25	.11	.03
☐ 96 Carlton Fisk	.25	.11	.03
☐ 97 Ramon Garcia	.05	.02	.01
☐ 98 Ozzie Guillen	.05	.02	.01
☐ 99 Tim Raines	.05	.02	.01
☐ 100 Bobby Thigpen	.05	.02	.01
☐ 101 Kirby Puckett	.75	.35	.09
☐ 102 Bernie Williams	.40	.18	.05
☐ 103 Dave Hansen	.05	.02	.01
☐ 104 Kevin Tapani	.05	.02	.01
☐ 105 Don Mattingly	1.00	.45	.12
☐ 106 Frank Thomas	2.00	.90	.25
☐ 107 Monty Fariss	.05	.02	.01
☐ 108 Bo Jackson	.25	.11	.03
☐ 109 Jim Abbott	.10	.05	.01
☐ 110 Jose Canseco	.30	.14	.04
☐ 111 Phil Plantier	.05	.02	.01
☐ 112 Brian Williams	.05	.02	.01
☐ 113 Mark Langston	.05	.02	.01
☐ 114 Wilson Alvarez	.20	.09	.03
☐ 115 Roberto Hernandez	.15	.07	.02
☐ 116 Darryl Kile	.20	.09	.03
☐ 117 Ryan Bowen	.05	.02	.01
☐ 118 Rickey Henderson	.25	.11	.03
☐ 119 Mark McGwire	.60	.25	.07
☐ 120 Devon White	.05	.02	.01
☐ 121 Roberto Alomar	.40	.18	.05
☐ 122 Kelly Gruber	.05	.02	.01
☐ 123 Eddie Zosky	.05	.02	.01
☐ 124 Tom Glavine	.25	.11	.03
☐ 125 Kal Daniels	.05	.02	.01
☐ 126 Cal Eldred	.20	.09	.03
☐ 127 Deion Sanders	.40	.18	.05
☐ 128 Robin Yount	.30	.14	.04
☐ 129 Cecil Fielder	.10	.05	.01
☐ 130 Ray Lankford	.20	.09	.03
☐ 131 Ryne Sandberg	.50	.23	.06
☐ 132 Darryl Strawberry	.10	.05	.01
☐ 133 Chris Haney	.05	.02	.01

	MINT	NRMT	EXC
☐ 134 Dennis Martinez	.05	.02	.01
☐ 135 Bryan Hickerson	.05	.02	.01
☐ 136 Will Clark	.25	.11	.03
☐ 137 Hal Morris	.05	.02	.01
☐ 138 Charles Nagy	.25	.11	.03
☐ 139 Jim Thome	.60	.25	.07
☐ 140 Albert Belle	1.00	.45	.12
☐ 141 Reggie Sanders	.20	.09	.03
☐ 142 Scott Cooper	.05	.02	.01
☐ 143 David Cone	.15	.07	.02
☐ 144 Anthony Young	.05	.02	.01
☐ 145 Howard Johnson	.05	.02	.01
☐ 146 Arthur Rhodes	.05	.02	.01
☐ 147 Scott Aldred	.05	.02	.01
☐ 148 Mike Mussina	.40	.18	.05
☐ 149 Fred McGriff	.30	.14	.04
☐ 150 Andy Benes	.10	.05	.01
☐ 151 Ruben Sierra	.15	.07	.02
☐ 152 Len Dykstra	.20	.09	.03
☐ 153 Andy Van Slyke	.05	.02	.01
☐ 154 Orlando Merced	.05	.02	.01
☐ 155 Barry Bonds	.40	.18	.05
☐ 156 John Smiley	.05	.02	.01
☐ 157 Julio Franco	.05	.02	.01
☐ 158 Juan Gonzalez	.75	.35	.09
☐ 159 Ivan Rodriguez	.50	.23	.06
☐ 160 Willie Banks	.05	.02	.01
☐ 161 Eric Davis	.05	.02	.01
☐ 162 Eddie Murray	.50	.23	.06
☐ 163 Dave Fleming	.05	.02	.01
☐ 164 Wally Joyner	.05	.02	.01
☐ 165 Kevin Mitchell	.05	.02	.01
☐ 166 Ed Taubensee	.05	.02	.01
☐ 167 Danny Tartabull	.05	.02	.01
☐ 168 Ken Hill	.15	.07	.02
☐ 169 Willie Randolph	.05	.02	.01
☐ 170 Kevin McReynolds	.05	.02	.01
☐ 171 Gregg Jefferies	.15	.07	.02
☐ 172 Patrick Lennon	.05	.02	.01
☐ 173 Luis Mercedes	.05	.02	.01
☐ 174 Glenn Davis	.05	.02	.01
☐ 175 Bret Saberhagen	.05	.02	.01
☐ 176 Bobby Bonilla	.10	.05	.01
☐ 177 Kenny Lofton	1.25	.55	.16
☐ 178 Jose Lind	.05	.02	.01
☐ 179 Royce Clayton	.20	.09	.03
☐ 180 Scott Scudder	.05	.02	.01
☐ 181 Chuck Knoblauch	.40	.18	.05
☐ 182 Terry Pendleton	.05	.02	.01
☐ 183 Nolan Ryan	1.50	.70	.19
☐ 184 Rob Maurer	.05	.02	.01
☐ 185 Brian Bohanon	.05	.02	.01
☐ 186 Ken Griffey Jr.	2.00	.90	.25
☐ 187 Jeff Bagwell	1.25	.55	.16
☐ 188 Steve Avery	.25	.11	.03
☐ 189 Roger Clemens	.30	.14	.04
☐ 190 Cal Ripken	1.25	.55	.16
☐ 191 Kim Batiste	.05	.02	.01
☐ 192 Bip Roberts	.05	.02	.01
☐ 193 Greg Swindell	.05	.02	.01
☐ 194 Dave Winfield	.25	.11	.03
☐ 195 Steve Sax	.05	.02	.01
☐ 196 Frank Viola	.05	.02	.01
☐ 197 Mo Sanford	.05	.02	.01
☐ 198 Kyle Abbott	.05	.02	.01
☐ 199 Jack Morris	.05	.02	.01
☐ 200 Andy Ashby	.05	.02	.01

1992 Classic I

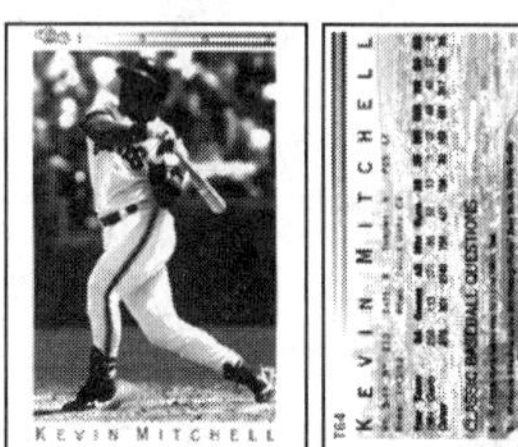

The first issue of the 1992 Classic baseball trivia game contains a small gameboard, accessories, 99 player standard-size cards with trivia questions on the backs, one "4-in-1" micro player card, and four micro player pieces. The cards have on the fronts glossy color action photos bordered in white. A red, gray, and purple stripe with the year "1992" traverses the top of the card. In a horizontal format, the backs feature biography, statistics, and five trivia questions, printed on a ghosted image of the 26 major league city skylines. The cards are numbered on the back and basically arranged in alphabetical order.

	MINT	NRMT	EXC
COMPLETE SET (100)	7.50	3.40	.95
COMMON CARD (T1-T99)	.05	.02	.01
☐ T1 Jim Abbott	.10	.05	.01
☐ T2 Kyle Abbott	.05	.02	.01
☐ T3 Scott Aldred	.05	.02	.01
☐ T4 Roberto Alomar	.40	.18	.05
☐ T5 Wilson Alvarez	.20	.09	.03
☐ T6 Andy Ashby	.05	.02	.01
☐ T7 Steve Avery	.25	.11	.03
☐ T8 Jeff Bagwell	1.25	.55	.16
☐ T9 Bret Barberie	.05	.02	.01
☐ T10 Kim Batiste	.05	.02	.01
☐ T11 Derek Bell	.15	.07	.02
☐ T12 Jay Bell	.05	.02	.01
☐ T13 Albert Belle	1.00	.45	.12
☐ T14 Andy Benes	.10	.05	.01
☐ T15 Sean Berry	.20	.09	.03
☐ T16 Barry Bonds	.40	.18	.05
☐ T17 Ryan Bowen	.05	.02	.01
☐ T18 Trifecta Alejandro Pena Mark Wohlers Kent Mercker	.05	.02	.01
☐ T19 Scott Brosius	.15	.07	.02
☐ T20 Jay Buhner	.25	.11	.03
☐ T21 David Burba	.05	.02	.01
☐ T22 Jose Canseco	.30	.14	.04
☐ T23 Andujar Cedeno	.05	.02	.01
☐ T24 Will Clark	.30	.14	.04
☐ T25 Royce Clayton	.05	.02	.01
☐ T26 Roger Clemens	.30	.14	.04
☐ T27 David Cone	.10	.05	.01
☐ T28 Scott Cooper	.05	.02	.01
☐ T29 Chris Cron	.05	.02	.01
☐ T30 Len Dykstra	.20	.09	.03
☐ T31 Cal Eldred	.05	.02	.01
☐ T32 Hector Fajardo	.05	.02	.01
☐ T33 Cecil Fielder	.10	.05	.01
☐ T34 Dave Fleming	.05	.02	.01
☐ T35 Steve Foster	.05	.02	.01
☐ T36 Julio Franco	.05	.02	.01
☐ T37 Carlos Garcia	.05	.02	.01
☐ T38 Tom Glavine	.20	.09	.03
☐ T39 Tom Goodwin	.05	.02	.01
☐ T40 Ken Griffey Jr.	2.00	.90	.25
☐ T41 Chris Haney	.05	.02	.01
☐ T42 Bryan Harvey	.05	.02	.01
☐ T43 Rickey Henderson 939	.25	.11	.03
☐ T44 Carlos Hernandez	.05	.02	.01
☐ T45 Roberto Hernandez	.10	.05	.01
☐ T46 Brook Jacoby	.05	.02	.01
☐ T47 Howard Johnson	.05	.02	.01
☐ T48 Pat Kelly	.05	.02	.01
☐ T49 Darryl Kile	.05	.02	.01
☐ T50 Chuck Knoblauch	.40	.18	.05
☐ T51 Ray Lankford With Ozzie Smith	.40	.18	.05
☐ T52 Mark Leiter	.05	.02	.01
☐ T53 Darren Lewis	.05	.02	.01
☐ T54 Scott Livingstone	.05	.02	.01
☐ T55 Shane Mack	.05	.02	.01
☐ T56 Chito Martinez	.05	.02	.01
☐ T57 Dennis Martinez The Perfect Game	.05	.02	.01
☐ T58 Don Mattingly	1.00	.45	.12
☐ T59 Paul McClellan	.05	.02	.01
☐ T60 Chuck McElroy	.05	.02	.01
☐ T61 Fred McGriff	.30	.14	.04
☐ T62 Orlando Merced	.05	.02	.01
☐ T63 Luis Mercedes	.05	.02	.01
☐ T64 Kevin Mitchell	.05	.02	.01
☐ T65 Hal Morris	.05	.02	.01
☐ T66 Jack Morris	.05	.02	.01
☐ T67 Mike Mussina	.40	.18	.05
☐ T68 Denny Neagle	.15	.07	.02
☐ T69 Tom Pagnozzi	.05	.02	.01
☐ T70 Terry Pendleton	.05	.02	.01
☐ T71 Phil Plantier	.05	.02	.01
☐ T72 Kirby Puckett	.75	.35	.09
☐ T73 Carlos Quintana	.05	.02	.01
☐ T74 Willie Randolph	.05	.02	.01
☐ T75 Arthur Rhodes	.05	.02	.01
☐ T76 Cal Ripken	1.25	.55	.16
☐ T77 Ivan Rodriguez	.50	.23	.06
☐ T78 Nolan Ryan	1.50	.70	.19
☐ T79 Ryne Sandberg	.50	.23	.06
☐ T80 Deion Sanders Deion Drops In	.30	.14	.04
☐ T81 Reggie Sanders	.20	.09	.03
☐ T82 Mo Sanford	.05	.02	.01
☐ T83 Terry Shumpert	.05	.02	.01
☐ T84 Tim Spehr	.05	.02	.01
☐ T85 Lee Stevens	.05	.02	.01
☐ T86 Darryl Strawberry	.10	.05	.01
☐ T87 Kevin Tapani	.05	.02	.01
☐ T88 Danny Tartabull	.05	.02	.01
☐ T89 Frank Thomas	2.00	.90	.25
☐ T90 Jim Thome	.40	.18	.05
☐ T91 Todd Van Poppel	.15	.07	.02
☐ T92 Andy Van Slyke	.05	.02	.01
☐ T93 John Wehner	.05	.02	.01
☐ T94 John Wetteland	.10	.05	.01
☐ T95 Devon White	.05	.02	.01
☐ T96 Brian Williams	.05	.02	.01
☐ T97 Mark Wohlers	.15	.07	.02
☐ T98 Robin Yount	.30	.14	.04
☐ T99 Eddie Zosky	.05	.02	.01
☐ NNO 4-in-1 Card Barry Bonds Roger Clemens Steve Avery Nolan Ryan	.75	.35	.09

1992 Classic II

The 1992 Series II baseball trivia board game features 99 new player trivia standard-size cards, one "4-in-1" micro player card, a

gameboard, and a spinner. The cards display color action player photos on the fronts. The side borders are either red or blue, shading to white as they merge with the top and bottom borders. The player's name appears in a blue stripe at the bottom of the picture. In a horizontal format, the backs have biography, statistics (1991 and career), five trivia questions, and a color drawing of the team's uniform. According to Classic, the production run was 175,000 games.

	MINT	NRMT	EXC
COMPLETE SET (100)	7.50	3.40	.95
COMMON CARD (T1-T99)	.05	.02	.01
☐ T1 Jim Abbott	.10	.05	.01
☐ T2 Jeff Bagwell	1.25	.55	.16
☐ T3 Jose Canseco	.40	.18	.05
☐ T4 Julio Valera	.05	.02	.01
☐ T5 Scott Brosius	.05	.02	.01
☐ T6 Mark Langston	.05	.02	.01
☐ T7 Andy Stankiewicz	.05	.02	.01
☐ T8 Gary DiSarcina	.05	.02	.01
☐ T9 Pete Harnisch	.05	.02	.01
☐ T10 Mark McGwire	.60	.25	.07
☐ T11 Ricky Bones	.05	.02	.01
☐ T12 Steve Avery	.25	.11	.03
☐ T13 Deion Sanders	.40	.18	.05
☐ T14 Mike Mussina	.40	.18	.05
☐ T15 Dave Justice	.30	.14	.04
☐ T16 Pat Hentgen	.40	.18	.05
☐ T17 Tom Glavine	.25	.11	.03
☐ T18 Juan Guzman	.20	.09	.03
☐ T19 Ron Gant	.10	.05	.01
☐ T20 Kelly Gruber	.05	.02	.01
☐ T21 Eric Karros	.20	.09	.03
☐ T22 Derrick May	.05	.02	.01
☐ T23 Dave Hansen	.05	.02	.01
☐ T24 Andre Dawson	.10	.05	.01
☐ T25 Eric Davis	.05	.02	.01
☐ T26 Ozzie Smith	.50	.23	.06
☐ T27 Sammy Sosa	.40	.18	.05
☐ T28 Lee Smith	.10	.05	.01
☐ T29 Ryne Sandberg	.50	.23	.06
☐ T30 Robin Yount	.30	.14	.04
☐ T31 Matt Williams	.40	.18	.05
☐ T32 John Vander Wal	.05	.02	.01
☐ T33 Bill Swift	.05	.02	.01
☐ T34 Delino DeShields	.05	.02	.01
☐ T35 Royce Clayton	.05	.02	.01
☐ T36 Moises Alou	.15	.07	.02
☐ T37 Will Clark	.30	.14	.04
☐ T38 Darryl Strawberry	.10	.05	.01
☐ T39 Larry Walker	.20	.09	.03
☐ T40 Ramon Martinez	.10	.05	.01
☐ T41 Howard Johnson	.05	.02	.01
☐ T42 Tino Martinez	.15	.07	.02
☐ T43 Dwight Gooden	.10	.05	.01
☐ T44 Ken Griffey Jr.	2.00	.90	.25
☐ T45 David Cone	.10	.05	.01
☐ T46 Kenny Lofton	.75	.35	.09
☐ T47 Bobby Bonilla	.10	.05	.01
☐ T48 Carlos Baerga	.30	.14	.04
☐ T49 Don Mattingly	1.00	.45	.12
☐ T50 Sandy Alomar Jr.	.10	.05	.01
☐ T51 Lenny Dykstra	.20	.09	.03
☐ T52 Tony Gwynn	.75	.35	.09
☐ T53 Felix Jose	.05	.02	.01
☐ T54 Rick Sutcliffe	.05	.02	.01
☐ T55 Wes Chamberlain	.05	.02	.01
☐ T56 Cal Ripken	1.25	.55	.16
☐ T57 Kyle Abbott	.05	.02	.01
☐ T58 Leo Gomez	.05	.02	.01
☐ T59 Gary Sheffield	.30	.14	.04
☐ T60 Anthony Young	.05	.02	.01
☐ T61 Roger Clemens	.30	.14	.04
☐ T62 Rafael Palmeiro	.20	.09	.03
☐ T63 Wade Boggs	.25	.11	.03
☐ T64 Andy Van Slyke	.10	.05	.01
☐ T65 Ruben Sierra	.15	.07	.02
☐ T66 Denny Neagle	.20	.09	.03
☐ T67 Nolan Ryan	1.50	.70	.19
☐ T68 Doug Drabek	.05	.02	.01
☐ T69 Ivan Rodriguez	.50	.23	.06
☐ T70 Barry Bonds	.40	.18	.05
☐ T71 Chuck Knoblauch	.40	.18	.05
☐ T72 Reggie Sanders	.20	.09	.03
☐ T73 Cecil Fielder	.15	.07	.02
☐ T74 Barry Larkin	.30	.14	.04
☐ T75 Scott Aldred	.05	.02	.01
☐ T76 Rob Dibble	.05	.02	.01
☐ T77 Brian McRae	.10	.05	.01
☐ T78 Tim Belcher	.05	.02	.01
☐ T79 George Brett	.75	.35	.09
☐ T80 Frank Viola	.05	.02	.01
☐ T81 Roberto Kelly	.05	.02	.01
☐ T82 Jack McDowell	.20	.09	.03
☐ T83 Mel Hall	.05	.02	.01
☐ T84 Esteban Beltre	.05	.02	.01
☐ T85 Robin Ventura	.15	.07	.02
☐ T86 George Bell	.05	.02	.01
☐ T87 Frank Thomas	2.00	.90	.25
☐ T88 John Smiley	.05	.02	.01
☐ T89 Bobby Thigpen	.05	.02	.01
☐ T90 Kirby Puckett	.75	.35	.09
☐ T91 Kevin Mitchell	.05	.02	.01
☐ T92 Peter Hoy	.05	.02	.01
☐ T93 Russ Springer	.05	.02	.01
☐ T94 Donovan Osborne	.05	.02	.01
☐ T95 Dave Silvestri	.05	.02	.01
☐ T96 Chad Curtis	.30	.14	.04
☐ T97 Pat Mahomes	.05	.02	.01
☐ T98 Danny Tartabull	.05	.02	.01
☐ T99 John Doherty	.05	.02	.01
☐ NNO 4-in-1 Card Ryne Sandberg Mike Mussina Reggie Sanders Jose Canseco	.40	.18	.05

1993 Classic Game

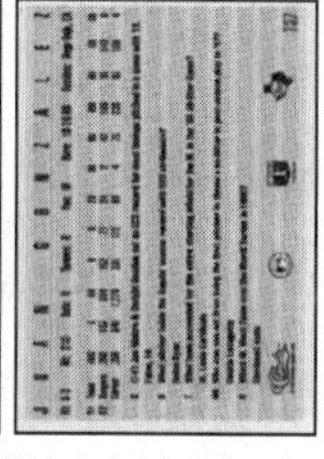

The 1993 Classic Game contains 99 trivia standard-size cards, a micro player card, four micro piece stands, a color game board, and a reusable plastic carrying case. As a special bonus, Classic included highlight trivia cards of George Brett and Robin Yount commemorating their 3,000 hits this past season. The cards feature color action player photos with navy blue borders. The player's name appears in the bottom border. A "1993 Series" logo is superimposed over the photo in the upper left corner. The backs display biographical information, statistics, and trivia questions against a two-tone gray striped background.

	MINT	NRMT	EXC
COMPLETE SET (100)	8.00	3.60	1.00
COMMON CARD (1-99)	.05	.02	.01
☐ 1 Jim Abbott	.10	.05	.01
☐ 2 Roberto Alomar	.40	.18	.05
☐ 3 Moises Alou	.10	.05	.01
☐ 4 Brady Anderson	.20	.09	.03
☐ 5 Eric Anthony	.05	.02	.01
☐ 6 Alex Arias	.05	.02	.01
☐ 7 Pedro Astacio	.05	.02	.01
☐ 8 Steve Avery	.20	.09	.03
☐ 9 Carlos Baerga	.20	.09	.03
☐ 10 Jeff Bagwell	.75	.35	.09
☐ 11 George Bell	.05	.02	.01
☐ 12 Albert Belle	1.00	.45	.12
☐ 13 Craig Biggio	.10	.05	.01
☐ 14 Barry Bonds	.50	.23	.06
☐ 15 Bobby Bonilla	.10	.05	.01
☐ 16 Mike Bordick	.05	.02	.01
☐ 17 George Brett	.75	.35	.09
☐ 18 Jose Canseco	.25	.11	.03
☐ 19 Joe Carter	.25	.11	.03
☐ 20 Royce Clayton	.05	.02	.01
☐ 21 Roger Clemens	.30	.14	.04
☐ 22 Greg Colbrunn	.05	.02	.01
☐ 23 David Cone	.10	.05	.01
☐ 24 Darren Daulton	.10	.05	.01
☐ 25 Delino DeShields	.05	.02	.01
☐ 26 Rob Dibble	.05	.02	.01
☐ 27 Dennis Eckersley	.10	.05	.01
☐ 28 Cal Eldred	.05	.02	.01
☐ 29 Scott Erickson	.05	.02	.01
☐ 30 Junior Felix	.05	.02	.01
☐ 31 Tony Fernandez	.05	.02	.01
☐ 32 Cecil Fielder	.15	.07	.02
☐ 33 Steve Finley	.10	.05	.01
☐ 34 Dave Fleming	.05	.02	.01
☐ 35 Travis Fryman	.25	.11	.03
☐ 36 Tom Glavine	.25	.11	.03
☐ 37 Juan Gonzalez	1.00	.45	.12
☐ 38 Ken Griffey Jr.	2.00	.90	.25
☐ 39 Marquis Grissom	.10	.05	.01
☐ 40 Juan Guzman	.05	.02	.01
☐ 41 Tony Gwynn	.75	.35	.09
☐ 42 Rickey Henderson	.25	.11	.03
☐ 43 Felix Jose	.05	.02	.01
☐ 44 Wally Joyner	.05	.02	.01
☐ 45 David Justice	.25	.11	.03
☐ 46 Eric Karros	.25	.11	.03
☐ 47 Roberto Kelly	.05	.02	.01
☐ 48 Ryan Klesko	.75	.35	.09
☐ 49 Chuck Knoblauch	.30	.14	.04

	MINT	NRMT	EXC
☐ 50 John Kruk	.10	.05	.01
☐ 51 Ray Lankford	.10	.05	.01
☐ 52 Barry Larkin	.25	.11	.03
☐ 53 Pat Listach	.05	.02	.01
☐ 54 Kenny Lofton	.75	.35	.09
☐ 55 Shane Mack	.05	.02	.01
☐ 56 Greg Maddux	1.25	.55	.16
☐ 57 Dave Magadan	.05	.02	.01
☐ 58 Edgar Martinez	.25	.11	.03
☐ 59 Don Mattingly	1.00	.45	.12
☐ 60 Ben McDonald	.05	.02	.01
☐ 61 Jack McDowell	.10	.05	.01
☐ 62 Fred McGriff	.25	.11	.03
☐ 63 Mark McGwire	.60	.25	.07
☐ 64 Kevin McReynolds	.05	.02	.01
☐ 65 Sam Militello	.05	.02	.01
☐ 66 Paul Molitor	.40	.18	.05
☐ 67 Jeff Montgomery	.10	.05	.01
☐ 68 Jack Morris	.05	.02	.01
☐ 69 Eddie Murray	.40	.18	.05
☐ 70 Mike Mussina	.40	.18	.05
☐ 71 Otis Nixon	.05	.02	.01
☐ 72 Donovan Osborne	.05	.02	.01
☐ 73 Terry Pendleton	.05	.02	.01
☐ 74 Mike Piazza	1.50	.70	.19
☐ 75 Kirby Puckett	.75	.35	.09
☐ 76 Cal Ripken Jr.	1.25	.55	.16
☐ 77 Bip Roberts	.05	.02	.01
☐ 78 Ivan Rodriguez	.50	.23	.06
☐ 79 Nolan Ryan	1.50	.70	.19
☐ 80 Ryne Sandberg	.50	.23	.06
☐ 81 Deion Sanders	.25	.11	.03
☐ 82 Reggie Sanders	.20	.09	.03
☐ 83 Frank Seminara	.05	.02	.01
☐ 84 Gary Sheffield	.30	.14	.04
☐ 85 Ruben Sierra	.05	.02	.01
☐ 86 John Smiley	.05	.02	.01
☐ 87 Lee Smith	.10	.05	.01
☐ 88 Ozzie Smith	.50	.23	.06
☐ 89 John Smoltz	.30	.14	.04
☐ 90 Danny Tartabull	.05	.02	.01
☐ 91 Bob Tewksbury	.05	.02	.01
☐ 92 Frank Thomas	2.00	.90	.25
☐ 93 Andy Van Slyke	.05	.02	.01
☐ 94 Mo Vaughn	.50	.23	.06
☐ 95 Robin Ventura	.10	.05	.01
☐ 96 Tim Wakefield	.05	.02	.01
☐ 97 Larry Walker	.25	.11	.03
☐ 98 Dave Winfield	.25	.11	.03
☐ 99 Robin Yount	.25	.11	.03
☐ NNO 4-in-1 Card Mark McGwire Sam Militello Ryan Klesko Greg Maddux	.50	.23	.06

1995 Classic Phone Cards

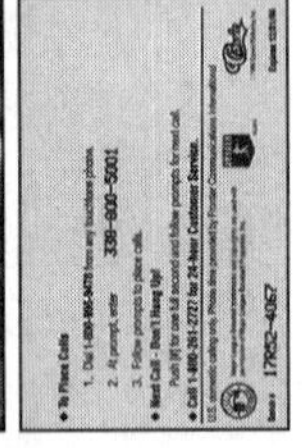

This 57-phone card set measures approximately 2 1/8" by 3 3/8" and features color action player photos with a $10 calling value. The backs carry the instructions on how to use the cards which expired on 12/31/96. The cards are unnumbered and checklisted below alphabetically according to the team's city or state as follows: Atlanta Braves (1-4), Baltimore Orioles (5-6), Boston Red Sox (7-9), California Angels (10), Chicago Cubs (11-12), Chicago White Sox (13-14), Cincinnati Reds (15-17), Cleveland Indians (18-22), Colorado Rockies (23-25), Detroit Tigers (26-27), Florida Marlins (28), Houston Astros (29-30), Kansas City Royals (31), Los Angeles Dodgers (32-34), Minnesota Twins (35), Montreal Expos (36), New York Mets (37), New York Yankees (38-40), Oakland Athletics (41-42), Philadelphia Phillies (43-44), Pittsburgh Pirates (45), San Diego Padres (46), San Francisco Giants (47-49), Seattle Mariners (50-51), St. Louis Cardinals (52), Texas Rangers (53-55), and Toronto Blue Jays (56-57). We have priced the cards as being unused. Cards which has had its PIN used are priced half the value of the unused cards.

	MINT	NRMT	EXC
COMPLETE SET (57)	450.00	200.00	55.00
COMMON CARD (1-57)	5.00	2.20	.60
☐ 1 Chipper Jones	12.50	5.50	1.55
☐ 2 David Justice	7.50	3.40	.95
☐ 3 Greg Maddux	15.00	6.75	1.85
☐ 4 Fred McGriff	7.50	3.40	.95
☐ 5 Cal Ripken	15.00	6.75	1.85
☐ 6 Mike Mussina	10.00	4.50	1.25
☐ 7 Jose Canseco	7.50	3.40	.95
☐ 8 Mo Vaughn	10.00	4.50	1.25
☐ 9 Roger Clemens	10.00	4.50	1.25
☐ 10 Tim Salmon	7.50	3.40	.95
☐ 11 Mark Grace	8.00	3.60	1.00
☐ 12 Sammy Sosa	10.00	4.50	1.25
☐ 13 Frank Thomas	20.00	9.00	2.50
☐ 14 Robin Ventura	6.00	2.70	.75
☐ 15 Barry Larkin	10.00	4.50	1.25
☐ 16 Reggie Sanders	6.00	2.70	.75
☐ 17 Ron Gant	6.00	2.70	.75
☐ 18 Manny Ramirez	10.00	4.50	1.25
☐ 19 Albert Belle	10.00	4.50	1.25
☐ 20 Carlos Baerga	10.00	4.50	1.25
☐ 21 Eddie Murray	10.00	4.50	1.25
☐ 22 Kenny Lofton	10.00	4.50	1.25
☐ 23 Andres Galarraga	7.50	3.40	.95
☐ 24 Dante Bichette	8.00	3.60	1.00
☐ 25 Larry Walker	7.50	3.40	.95
☐ 26 Cecil Fielder	6.00	2.70	.75
☐ 27 Travis Fryman	6.00	2.70	.75
☐ 28 Jeff Conine	6.00	2.70	.75
☐ 29 Craig Biggio	6.00	2.70	.75
☐ 30 Jeff Bagwell	10.00	4.50	1.25
☐ 31 Kevin Appier	6.00	2.70	.75
☐ 32 Hideo Nomo	10.00	4.50	1.25
☐ 33 Mike Piazza	12.50	5.50	1.55
☐ 34 Raul Mondesi	7.50	3.40	.95
☐ 35 Kirby Puckett	10.00	4.50	1.25
☐ 36 Carlos Perez	5.00	2.20	.60
☐ 37 Jeff Kent	5.00	2.20	.60
☐ 38 Don Mattingly	10.00	4.50	1.25
☐ 39 Paul O'Neill	6.00	2.70	.75
☐ 40 Wade Boggs	7.50	3.40	.95
☐ 41 Mark McGwire	10.00	4.50	1.25
☐ 42 Rickey Henderson	7.50	3.40	.95
☐ 43 Darren Daulton	6.00	2.70	.75
☐ 44 Lenny Dykstra	6.00	2.70	.75
☐ 45 Denny Neagle	5.00	2.20	.60
☐ 46 Tony Gwynn	10.00	4.50	1.25
☐ 47 Barry Bonds	10.00	4.50	1.25
☐ 48 Matt Williams	10.00	4.50	1.25
☐ 49 Deion Sanders	7.50	3.40	.95
☐ 50 Ken Griffey Jr.	20.00	9.00	2.50
☐ 51 Randy Johnson	7.50	3.40	.95
☐ 52 Ozzie Smith	10.00	4.50	1.25
☐ 53 Juan Gonzalez	10.00	4.50	1.25
☐ 54 Will Clark	7.50	3.40	.95
☐ 55 Ivan Rodriguez	8.00	3.60	1.00
☐ 56 Joe Carter	6.00	2.70	.75
☐ 57 Roberto Alomar	10.00	4.50	1.25

1995 Classic Phone Cards Promos

These rounded-corner phone cards meaure 2" by 3 1/4". They were handed out at 1995 FanFest as a redemption when a ticket stub was brought to the Classic booth. Packs handed out to dealers also included an usable $10 phone card. The cards are unnumbered and checklisted below in alphabetical order.

	MINT	NRMT	EXC
COMPLETE SET (8)	30.00	13.50	3.70
COMMON CARD (1-8)	1.50	.70	.19
☐ 1 Barry Bonds	2.00	.90	.25
☐ 2 Will Clark	1.50	.70	.19
☐ 3 Juan Gonzalez	4.00	1.80	.50
☐ 4 Ken Griffey Jr.	8.00	3.60	1.00
☐ 5 Mike Piazza	5.00	2.20	.60
☐ 6 Cal Ripken	8.00	3.60	1.00
☐ 7 Ozzie Smith	2.00	.90	.25
☐ 8 Frank Thomas	8.00	3.60	1.00

1996 Classic 7/11 Phone Cards

These eight phone cards feature leading major league players. They were available at all participating 7/11 stores for a cost of $5.99 and are good for 15 minutes of phone time. The cards expire on December 31, 1997. Cards which have been used have half the value of unused cards.

	MINT	NRMT	EXC
COMPLETE SET (8)	75.00	34.00	9.50
COMMON CARD (1-8)	6.00	2.70	.75
☐ 1 Cal Ripken	15.00	6.75	1.85
☐ 2 Frank Thomas	15.00	6.75	1.85
☐ 3 Hideo Nomo	10.00	4.50	1.25
☐ 4 Jeff Conine	6.00	2.70	.75
☐ 5 Ken Griffey Jr.	15.00	6.75	1.85
☐ 6 Greg Maddux	12.00	5.50	1.50
☐ 7 Wade Boggs	7.50	3.40	.95
☐ 8 Ivan Rodriguez	7.50	3.40	.95

1988 CMC Mattingly

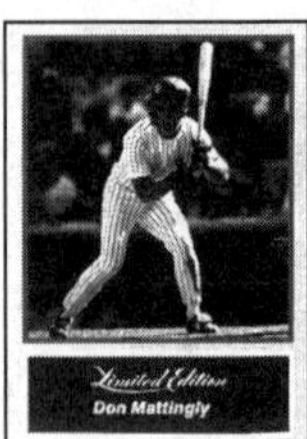

This 20-card set featuring Don Mattingly was distributed as part of a Collecting Kit produced by Collector's Marketing Corp. The cards themselves measure approximately 2 1/2" by 3 1/2" and have a light blue border. The card backs describe some aspect of Mattingly's career. Also in the kit were plastic sheets, a small album, a record, a booklet and information on how to join Don's Fan Club. The set price below is for the whole kit as well as the cards. The set was re-issued with a Line Drive logo in 1993 with a different border.

	MINT	NRMT	EXC
COMPLETE SET (20)	7.50	3.40	.95
COMMON CARD (1-20)	.50	.23	.06
☐ 1 Don Mattingly Game Face	.50	.23	.06
☐ 2 Don Mattingly Columbus Clippers	.50	.23	.06
☐ 3 Don Mattingly 1983 Spring Camp	.50	.23	.06
☐ 4 Don Mattingly AL Batting Crown	.50	.23	.06
☐ 5 Don Mattingly 1981 All-Star Outfielder	.50	.23	.06
☐ 6 Don Mattingly The Batting Tee	.50	.23	.06
☐ 7 Don Mattingly AL MVP Honors	.50	.23	.06
☐ 8 Don Mattingly Gold Glove Winner	.50	.23	.06
☐ 9 Don Mattingly Batting Practice	.50	.23	.06
☐ 10 Don Mattingly Yankee Records	.50	.23	.06
☐ 11 Don Mattingly Baseball On His Mind	.50	.23	.06
☐ 12 Don Mattingly Big Home Runs	.50	.23	.06
☐ 13 Don Mattingly Hustle and Determination	.50	.23	.06
☐ 14 Don Mattingly Delivering In The Clutch	.50	.23	.06
☐ 15 Don Mattingly A Slick First Baseman	.50	.23	.06
☐ 16 Don Mattingly Keep Playing Hard	.50	.23	.06
☐ 17 Don Mattingly Eight-Game Streak	.50	.23	.06
☐ 18 Don Mattingly The Textbook Swing	.50	.23	.06
☐ 19 Don Mattingly It's Time To Go Forward	.50	.23	.06
☐ 20 Don Mattingly Surehanded First Baseman	.50	.23	.06
☐ P1 Don Mattingly Promo	.50	.23	.06

1989 CMC Baseball's Greatest

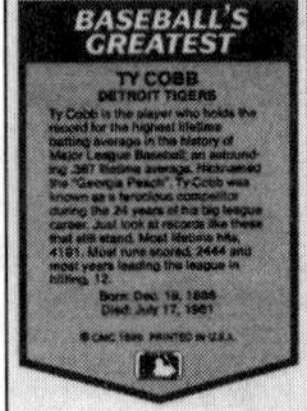

Issued in a cello packs, this four-card, standard-size set was issued by CMC. On a white card face, the fronts feature either color (#1) or sepia-tone (#2-4) player photos inside a red and white border whose shape resembles the home plate. The set's title appears in the red border above the picture while the player's name appears in a turquoise diamond at the bottom. The backs have the same design, only with a career summary presented on a gray panel instead of the front photo. The cards are unnumbered and checklisted below alphabetically.

	MINT	NRMT	EXC
COMPLETE SET	3.00	1.35	.35
COMMON CARD (1-4)	.75	.35	.09
☐ 1 Roberto Clemente	.75	.35	.09
☐ 2 Ty Cobb	.75	.35	.09
☐ 3 Lou Gehrig	.75	.35	.09
☐ 4 Babe Ruth	1.00	.45	.12

1989 CMC Canseco

The 1989 CMC Jose Canseco Collector's Kit set contains 20 numbered standard-size cards. The front borders are Oakland A's green and yellow. The backs are green and white, and feature narratives and facsimile signatures. The cards were distributed as a set in a box along with an album and a booklet as well as other elements by CMC, Collectors Marketing Corporation. Since all the cards in the set feature the same player, cards in the checklist below are differentiated by some other characteristic of the particular card.

	MINT	NRMT	EXC
COMPLETE SET (20)	7.50	3.40	.95
COMMON CARD (1-20)	.50	.23	.06
☐ 1 Jose Canseco Looking up with yellow jersey	.50	.23	.06
☐ 2 Jose Canseco Posing with bat from the waist up	.50	.23	.06
☐ 3 Jose Canseco Portrait with green cap	.50	.23	.06
☐ 4 Jose Canseco Follow-through on swing catcher visible	.50	.23	.06
☐ 5 Jose Canseco Running the bases	.50	.23	.06
☐ 6 Jose Canseco Warming up with bat over head	.50	.23	.06
☐ 7 Jose Canseco Sitting in dugout holding bat	.50	.23	.06
☐ 8 Jose Canseco Standing in outfield with sunglasses up	.50	.23	.06
☐ 9 Jose Canseco Batting stance ready for pitch	.50	.23	.06
☐ 10 Jose Canseco Taking a lead off first base	.50	.23	.06
☐ 11 Jose Canseco Looking to the side elephant logo on left shoulder	.50	.23	.06
☐ 12 Jose Canseco Mark McGwire Bashing after homer	.50	.23	.06
☐ 13 Jose Canseco Looking up with green batting glove in foreground	.50	.23	.06
☐ 14 Jose Canseco Stretching to catch fly ball	.50	.23	.06
☐ 15 Jose Canseco Follow through on swing no catcher visible	.50	.23	.06
☐ 16 Jose Canseco Standing at plate glaring at pitcher	.50	.23	.06
☐ 17 Jose Canseco Follow through on swing stain on pants)	.50	.23	.06
☐ 18 Jose Canseco Signing autographs at the ballpark	.50	.23	.06
☐ 19 Jose Canseco Waiting at first base with hands on hips	.50	.23	.06
☐ 20 Jose Canseco Admiring his hit at plate with tongue out	.50	.23	.06
☐ P1 Jose Canseco Promo			

1989 CMC Mantle

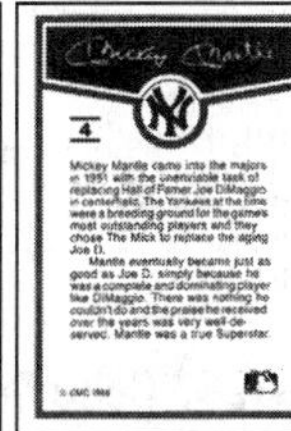

The 1989 CMC Mickey Mantle Collector's Kit set contains 20 numbered standard-size cards. The fronts and backs are white, red and navy. The backs feature narratives and facsimile signatures. The cards were distributed as a set in a box along with an album and a booklet as well as other elements by CMC, Collectors Marketing Corporation. Since all the cards in the set feature the same player, cards in the checklist below are differentiated by some other characteristic of the particular card. Some of the cards in this set are sepia-tone photos as the action predates the widespread use of color film. The set was re-issued with a Line Drive logo in 1993 with a different border.

	MINT	NRMT	EXC
COMPLETE SET (20)	10.00	4.50	1.25
COMMON CARD (1-20)	.50	.23	.06
☐ 1 Mickey Mantle Standing with bat on left shoulder	.50	.23	.06
☐ 2 Mickey Mantle Batting stance lefty back to camera	.50	.23	.06
☐ 3 Mickey Mantle Looking intense in the field waist up	.50	.23	.06
☐ 4 Mickey Mantle Follow through on lefty swing	.50	.23	.06
☐ 5 Mickey Mantle Half smile head and shoulders	.50	.23	.06
☐ 6 Mickey Mantle Roger Maris Posing with bats	1.00	.45	.12
☐ 7 Mickey Mantle Holding up 1962 contract wearing suit and tie	.50	.23	.06
☐ 8 Mickey Mantle Joe Cronin Receiving 1962 MVP	.75	.35	.09
☐ 9 Mickey Mantle Batting stance lefty catcher's glove in picture	.50	.23	.06
☐ 10 Mickey Mantle Roger Maris Yogi Berra	.75	.35	.09
☐ 11 Mickey Mantle Looking away with eyes closed holding bat	.50	.23	.06
☐ 12 Mickey Mantle Swinging righty at pitch	.50	.23	.06
☐ 13 Mickey Mantle Starting to run to first base	.50	.23	.06
☐ 14 Mickey Mantle His Day; September 18, 1965	.75	.35	.09
☐ 15 Mickey Mantle Joe DiMaggio Shaking Hands at Yankee Stadium	1.50	.70	.19
☐ 16 Mickey Mantle Giving speech at Yankee Stadium	.50	.23	.06
☐ 17 Mickey Mantle Backing away from plate after pitch	.50	.23	.06
☐ 18 Mickey Mantle Getting ready at plate with bat in right hand	.50	.23	.06
☐ 19 Mickey Mantle Holding bat in both hands parallel to ground	.50	.23	.06
☐ 20 Mickey Mantle Waiting for pitch with bat on shoulder (lefty)	.50	.23	.06

1989 CMC Ruth

The 1989 CMC Babe Ruth Collector's Kit set contains 20 numbered standard-size cards. The front borders are white, red and navy. The backs are blue and white, and feature narratives and facsimile signatures. The cards were distributed as a set in a box along with an album and a booklet as well as other elements by CMC, Collectors Marketing Corporation. Since all the cards in the set feature the same player, cards in the checklist below are differentiated by some other characteristic of the particular card. All of the cards in this set are sepia-tone photos as the action predates the widespread use of color film.

	MINT	NRMT	EXC
COMPLETE SET (20)	10.00	4.50	1.25
COMMON CARD (1-20)	.50	.23	.06
☐ 1 Babe Ruth Smiling holding three bats	.50	.23	.06
☐ 2 Babe Ruth Posing in Red Sox uniform head and shoulders	.50	.23	.06
☐ 3 Babe Ruth Looking up, waist up	.50	.23	.06
☐ 4 Babe Ruth Holding nine bats in front of him	.50	.23	.06
☐ 5 Babe Ruth Golfing swing follow through	.50	.23	.06
☐ 6 Babe Ruth Oldtimers' game photo holding two bats	.50	.23	.06
☐ 7 Babe Ruth Follow through looking up in Japan	.50	.23	.06
☐ 8 Babe Ruth Looking dapper in fur coat	.50	.23	.06
☐ 9 Babe Ruth On his Day; April 27, 1947	.50	.23	.06
☐ 10 Babe Ruth Bust photo with no background	.50	.23	.06
☐ 11 Babe Ruth Practicing swing photo from knees up	.50	.23	.06
☐ 12 Babe Ruth Watching his hit after swing knees up	.50	.23	.06
☐ 13 Babe Ruth Follow through on swing starting to first base	.50	.23	.06
☐ 14 Babe Ruth Practice swing with photographers in background	.50	.23	.06
☐ 15 Babe Ruth Jacob Ruppert	.75	.35	.09
☐ 16 Babe Ruth Follow through from waist up	.50	.23	.06
☐ 17 Babe Ruth Miller Huggins	.75	.35	.09
☐ 18 Babe Ruth Signing autographs for the kids	.50	.23	.06
☐ 19 Babe Ruth Sitting wearing Braves uniform	.50	.23	.06
☐ 20 Babe Ruth Hall of Fame Plaque	.50	.23	.06
☐ P1 Babe Ruth Promo for Set	1.00	.45	.12

1952 Coke Tips

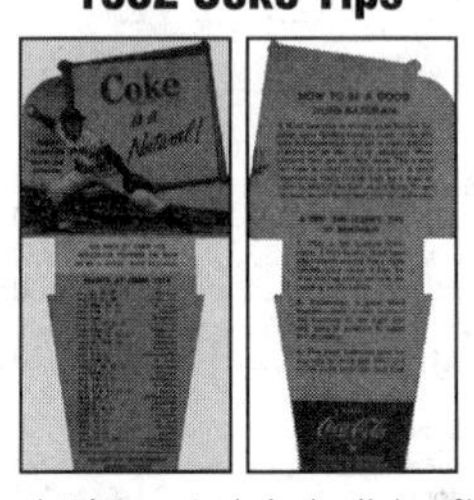

This 10-card set features artwork of various Yankees, Giants and Dodgers and was inserted into regional Coca-Cola bottle cartons. The fronts display the artwork depicting the players and team schedules. The backs carry tips on how to play the pictured player's position and other Big-League tips. The cards are unnumbered and checklisted below in alphabetical order.

	NRMT	VG-E	GOOD
COMPLETE SET (10)	2750.00	1250.00	350.00
COMMON CARD (1-10)	200.00	90.00	25.00
☐ 1 Hank Bauer	300.00	135.00	38.00
☐ 2 Carl Furillo	350.00	160.00	45.00
☐ 3 Gil Hodges	500.00	220.00	60.00
☐ 4 Ed Lopat	250.00	110.00	31.00
☐ 5 Gil McDougald	250.00	110.00	31.00
☐ 6 Don Mueller	200.00	90.00	25.00
☐ 7 Pee Wee Reese	450.00	200.00	55.00
☐ 8 Bobby Thomson (Playing 3rd base)	300.00	135.00	38.00
☐ 9 Bobby Thomson (Hitting)	300.00	135.00	38.00
☐ 10 Wes Westrum	200.00	90.00	25.00

1967 Coke Caps All-Stars

These 1967 Coke caps were found on bottles of Coke, Tab, Sprite, and Fresca and were distributed in areas of the country without major league baseball teams. Collector sheets held 35 caps and could then redeemed at a Thom McAn Shoe Store for six autographed All-Star photos. Five collections could be redeemed for an Official Little League baseball. The caps measure about 1" in diameter and feature player head shots. The caps are numbered and checklisted below.

	NRMT	VG-E	GOOD
COMPLETE SET (35)	140.00	65.00	17.50
COMMON PLAYER (1-35)	2.00	.90	.25
☐ 1 Richie Allen	4.00	1.80	.50
☐ 2 Pete Rose	10.00	4.50	1.25
☐ 3 Brooks Robinson	7.50	3.40	.95
☐ 4 Marcelino Lopez	2.00	.90	.25
☐ 5 Rusty Staub	3.00	1.35	.35
☐ 6 Ron Santo	4.00	1.80	.50
☐ 7 Jim Nash	2.00	.90	.25
☐ 8 Jim Fregosi	3.00	1.35	.35
☐ 9 Paul Casanova	2.00	.90	.25
☐ 10 Willie Mays	12.50	5.50	1.55
☐ 11 Willie Stargell	7.50	3.40	.95
☐ 12 Tony Oliva	5.00	2.20	.60
☐ 13 Joe Pepitone	3.00	1.35	.35
☐ 14 Juan Marichal	7.50	3.40	.95
☐ 15 Jim Bunning	7.50	3.40	.95
☐ 16 Claude Osteen	2.00	.90	.25
☐ 17 Carl Yastrzemski	7.50	3.40	.95
☐ 18 Harmon Killebrew	7.50	3.40	.95
☐ 19 Henry Aaron	12.50	5.50	1.55
☐ 20 Joe Torre	4.00	1.80	.50
☐ 21 Ernie Banks	7.50	3.40	.95
☐ 22 Al Kaline	7.50	3.40	.95
☐ 23 Frank Robinson	7.50	3.40	.95
☐ 24 Max Alvis	2.00	.90	.25
☐ 25 Elston Howard	4.00	1.80	.50
☐ 26 Gaylord Perry	7.50	3.40	.95
☐ 27 Bill Mazeroski	6.00	2.70	.75
☐ 28 Ron Swoboda	2.00	.90	.25
☐ 29 Vada Pinson	3.00	1.35	.35
☐ 30 Joe Morgan	7.50	3.40	.95
☐ 31 Cleon Jones	2.00	.90	.25
☐ 32 Willie Horton	2.00	.90	.25
☐ 33 Leon Wagner	2.00	.90	.25
☐ 34 George Scott	3.00	1.35	.35
☐ 35 Ed Charles	2.00	.90	.25

1967 Coke Caps All-Stars AL

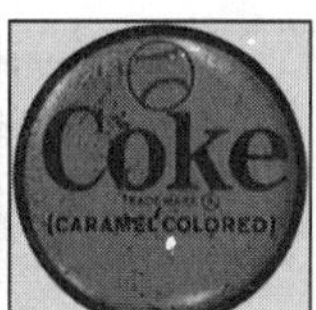

These caps, measuring approximately 1" in diameter feature leading American League players. They were issued in cities which had American league teams. These caps were available on bottles of Coke, Fresca, Sprite and Tab. The caps have an "A" prefix.

	NRMT	VG-E	GOOD
COMPLETE SET (17)	50.00	22.00	6.25
COMMON PLAYER (19-35)	2.00	.90	.25
☐ 19 Al Kaline	7.50	3.40	.95
☐ 20 Frank Howard	3.00	1.35	.35
☐ 21 Brooks Robinson	7.50	3.40	.95
☐ 22 George Scott	2.00	.90	.25
☐ 23 Willie Horton	2.00	.90	.25
☐ 24 Jim Fregosi	3.00	1.35	.35
☐ 25 Ed Charles	2.00	.90	.25
☐ 26 Harmon Killebrew	7.50	3.40	.95
☐ 27 Tony Oliva	5.00	2.20	.60
☐ 28 Joe Pepitone	3.00	1.35	.35
☐ 29 Elston Howard	4.00	1.80	.50
☐ 30 Jim Nash	2.00	.90	.25
☐ 31 Marcelino Lopez	2.00	.90	.25
☐ 32 Frank Robinson	7.50	3.40	.95
☐ 33 Leon Wagner	2.00	.90	.25
☐ 34 Max Alvis	2.00	.90	.25
☐ 35 Paul Casanova	2.00	.90	.25

1967 Coke Caps All-Stars NL

These caps feature leading National League players. They have an "N" prefix and were on Coke, Tab, Sprite and Fresca bottles. These caps were released in National League cities.

	NRMT	VG-E	GOOD
COMPLETE SET (17)	65.00	29.00	8.00
COMMON PLAYER (19-35)	2.00	.90	.25
☐ 19 Hank Aaron	12.50	5.50	1.55
☐ 20 Jim Bunning	6.00	2.70	.75
☐ 21 Joe Torre	5.00	2.20	.60
☐ 22 Claude Osteen	2.00	.90	.25
☐ 23 Ron Santo	4.00	1.80	.50
☐ 24 Joe Morgan	7.50	3.40	.95
☐ 25 Richie Allen	4.00	1.80	.50
☐ 26 Ron Swoboda	2.00	.90	.25
☐ 27 Ernie Banks	7.50	3.40	.95
☐ 28 Bill Mazeroski	4.00	1.80	.50
☐ 29 Willie Stargell	7.50	3.40	.95
☐ 30 Pete Rose	10.00	4.50	1.25
☐ 31 Gaylord Perry	6.00	2.70	.75
☐ 32 Rusty Staub	4.00	1.80	.50
☐ 33 Vada Pinson	3.00	1.35	.35
☐ 34 Juan Marichal	7.50	3.40	.95
☐ 35 Cleon Jones	2.00	.90	.25

1967 Coke Caps Astros

The caps, measuring approximately 1" in diameter feature members of the Houston Astros. They were distributed in the Houston area. The caps have an "H" prefix.

	NRMT	VG-E	GOOD
COMPLETE SET (18)	40.00	18.00	5.00
COMMON PLAYER (1-18)	2.00	.90	.25
☐ 1 Dave Giusti	2.00	.90	.25
☐ 2 Bob Aspromonte	2.00	.90	.25
☐ 3 Ron Davis	2.00	.90	.25
☐ 4 Claude Raymond	2.00	.90	.25
☐ 5 Barry Latman	2.00	.90	.25
☐ 6 Chuck Harrison	2.00	.90	.25
☐ 7 Bill Heath	2.00	.90	.25
☐ 8 Sonny Jackson	2.00	.90	.25
☐ 9 John Bateman	2.00	.90	.25
☐ 10 Ron Brand	2.00	.90	.25
☐ 11 Aaron Pointer	2.00	.90	.25
☐ 12 Joe Morgan	7.50	3.40	.95
☐ 13 Rusty Staub	5.00	2.20	.60
☐ 14 Mike Cuellar	3.00	1.35	.35
☐ 15 Larry Dierker	3.00	1.35	.35
☐ 16 Dick Farrell	2.00	.90	.25
☐ 17 Jim Landis	2.00	.90	.25
☐ 18 Ed Mathews	6.00	2.70	.75

1967 Coke Caps Athletics

These caps, measuring approximately 1" in diameter feature members of the Kansas City Athletics. They were distributed in the Kansas City area. The caps have a "K" prefix

	NRMT	VG-E	GOOD
COMPLETE SET (18)	35.00	16.00	4.40
COMMON PLAYER (1-18)	2.00	.90	.25
☐ 1 Jim Nash	2.00	.90	.25
☐ 2 Bert Campaneris	4.00	1.80	.50
☐ 3 Ed Charles	2.00	.90	.25
☐ 4 Wes Stock	2.00	.90	.25
☐ 5 Johnny Odom	2.00	.90	.25
☐ 6 Ozzie Chavarria	2.00	.90	.25
☐ 7 Jack Aker	2.00	.90	.25
☐ 8 Dick Green	2.00	.90	.25
☐ 9 Phil Roof	2.00	.90	.25
☐ 10 Rene Lachemann	2.00	.90	.25
☐ 11 Mike Hershberger	2.00	.90	.25
☐ 12 Joe Nossek	2.00	.90	.25
☐ 13 Roger Repoz	2.00	.90	.25
☐ 14 Chuck Dobson	2.00	.90	.25
☐ 15 Jim Hunter	6.00	2.70	.75
☐ 16 Lew Krausse	2.00	.90	.25
☐ 17 Danny Cater	2.00	.90	.25
☐ 18 Jim Gosger	2.00	.90	.25

1967 Coke Caps Baseball Tips

These caps, show various plays made on a baseball diamond. These caps were issued in cities which didn't have a major league team.

	NRMT	VG-E	GOOD
COMPLETE SET (8)	15.00	6.75	1.85
COMMON PLAYER (19-26)	2.00	.90	.25
☐ 19 SS fields ball throws to 2b	2.00	.90	.25
☐ 20 2b relays to 1b	2.00	.90	.25
☐ 21 1b completes DP	2.00	.90	.25
☐ 22 Pitcher fields bunt throws to 2b	2.00	.90	.25
☐ 23 2b relays to 1b	2.00	.90	.25
☐ 24 1b completes DP	2.00	.90	.25
☐ 25 CF makes catch throws home	2.00	.90	.25
☐ 26 Catcher tags runner	2.00	.90	.25

1967 Coke Caps Braves

The caps, measuring approximately 1" in diameter, feature members of the Atlanta Braves. The caps were issued in the Atlanta are on bottles of Coke, Fresca, Sprite and Tab. The caps have a "B" prefix

	NRMT	VG-E	GOOD
COMPLETE SET (18)	40.00	18.00	5.00
COMMON PLAYER (1-18)	2.00	.90	.25
☐ 1 Gary Geiger	2.00	.90	.25
☐ 2 Ty Cline	2.00	.90	.25
☐ 3 Hank Aaron	10.00	4.50	1.25
☐ 4 Gene Oliver	2.00	.90	.25
☐ 5 Tony Cloninger	2.00	.90	.25
☐ 6 Denis Menke	2.00	.90	.25
☐ 7 Denny Lemaster	2.00	.90	.25
☐ 8 Woody Woodward	2.00	.90	.25
☐ 9 Joe Torre	5.00	2.20	.60
☐ 10 Ken Johnson	2.00	.90	.25
☐ 11 Bob Bruce	2.00	.90	.25
☐ 12 Felipe Alou	4.00	1.80	.50
☐ 13 Clete Boyer	3.00	1.35	.35
☐ 14 Wade Blasingame	2.00	.90	.25
☐ 15 Don Schwall	2.00	.90	.25
☐ 16 Dick Kelley	2.00	.90	.25
☐ 17 Rico Carty	3.00	1.35	.35
☐ 18 Mack Jones	2.00	.90	.25

1967 Coke Caps Cubs

These 1967 Coke caps were found on bottles of Coke, Tab, Sprite, and Fresca distributed in the Chicago area. The 35 caps could be affixed to a collector sheet and then redeemed at a Chicago area Thom McAn Shoe Store for six autographed Cubs photos. Five collections could be redeemed for an Official Little League baseball. The caps measure about 1" in diameter and feature player headshots. A baseball icon appears on each of the caps' crowns. Caps 1-18 below feature Cubs players and have "C" prefixes.

	NRMT	VG-E	GOOD
COMPLETE SET (18)	45.00	20.00	5.50
COMMON PLAYER (1-18)	2.00	.90	.25
☐ 1 Ferguson Jenkins	5.00	2.20	.60
☐ 2 Ernie Banks	8.00	3.60	1.00
☐ 3 Glenn Beckert	3.00	1.35	.35
☐ 4 Bob Hendley	2.00	.90	.25
☐ 5 John Boccabella	2.00	.90	.25
☐ 6 Ron Campbell	2.00	.90	.25
☐ 7 Ray Culp	2.00	.90	.25
☐ 8 Adolfo Phillips	2.00	.90	.25
☐ 9 Don Bryant	2.00	.90	.25
☐ 10 Randy Hundley	3.00	1.35	.35
☐ 11 Ron Santo	4.00	1.80	.50
☐ 12 Lee Thomas	2.00	.90	.25
☐ 13 Billy Williams	5.00	2.20	.60
☐ 14 Ken Holtzman	3.00	1.35	.35
☐ 15 Cal Koonce	2.00	.90	.25
☐ 16 Curt Simmons	2.00	.90	.25
☐ 17 George Altman	2.00	.90	.25
☐ 18 Byron Browne	2.00	.90	.25

1967 Coke Caps Dodgers

These 1967 caps feature members of the Los Angeles Dodgers. They measure 1" in diameter and have a "D" prefix.

	NRMT	VG-E	GOOD
COMPLETE SET (18)	35.00	16.00	4.40
COMMON PLAYER (1-18)	2.00	.90	.25
☐ 1 Phil Regan	2.00	.90	.25
☐ 2 Bob Bailey	2.00	.90	.25
☐ 3 Ron Fairly	3.00	1.35	.35
☐ 4 Joe Moeller	2.00	.90	.25
☐ 5 Don Sutton	5.00	2.20	.60
☐ 6 Ron Hunt	2.00	.90	.25
☐ 7 Jim Brewer	2.00	.90	.25
☐ 8 Lou Johnson	2.00	.90	.25
☐ 9 John Roseboro	3.00	1.35	.35
☐ 10 Jeff Torborg	2.00	.90	.25
☐ 11 John Kennedy	2.00	.90	.25
☐ 12 Jim Lefebvre	2.00	.90	.25
☐ 13 Wes Parker	2.00	.90	.25
☐ 14 Bob Miller	2.00	.90	.25
☐ 15 Claude Osteen	2.00	.90	.25
☐ 16 Ron Perranoski	2.00	.90	.25
☐ 17 Willie Davis	3.00	1.35	.35
☐ 18 Al Ferrara	2.00	.90	.25

1967 Coke Caps Dodgers/Angels

These caps feature both members of the Los Angeles Dodgers and the California Angels. The caps, which measure approximately 1" in diameter, were issued in bottles of Coke, Fresca, Sprite and Tab. These caps have an "L" prefix.

	NRMT	VG-E	GOOD
COMPLETE SET (35)	65.00	29.00	8.00
COMMON PLAYER (1-35)	2.00	.90	.25
☐ 1 Phil Regan	2.00	.90	.25
☐ 2 Bob Bailey	2.00	.90	.25
☐ 3 Ron Fairly	3.00	1.35	.35
☐ 4 Joe Moeller	2.00	.90	.25
☐ 5 Don Sutton	5.00	2.20	.60
☐ 6 Ron Hunt	2.00	.90	.25
☐ 7 Jim Brewer	2.00	.90	.25
☐ 8 Lou Johnson	2.00	.90	.25
☐ 9 John Roseboro	3.00	1.35	.35
☐ 10 Jeff Torborg	2.00	.90	.25
☐ 11 John Kennedy	2.00	.90	.25
☐ 12 Jim Lefebvre	2.00	.90	.25
☐ 13 Wes Parker	2.00	.90	.25
☐ 14 Bob Miller	2.00	.90	.25
☐ 15 Claude Osteen	2.00	.90	.25
☐ 16 Ron Perranoski	2.00	.90	.25
☐ 17 Willie Davis	3.00	1.35	.35
☐ 18 Al Ferrara	2.00	.90	.25
☐ 19 Len Gabrielson	2.00	.90	.25
☐ 20 Jackie Hernandez	2.00	.90	.25
☐ 21 Paul Schaal	2.00	.90	.25
☐ 22 Lou Burdette	3.00	1.35	.35
☐ 23 Jimmie Hall	2.00	.90	.25
☐ 24 Fred Newman	2.00	.90	.25
☐ 25 Don Mincher	2.00	.90	.25
☐ 26 Bob Rodgers	2.00	.90	.25
☐ 27 Jack Sanford	2.00	.90	.25
☐ 28 Bobby Knoop	2.00	.90	.25
☐ 29 Jose Cardenal	2.00	.90	.25
☐ 30 Jim Fregosi	3.00	1.35	.35
☐ 31 George Brunet	2.00	.90	.25
☐ 32 Marcelino Lopez	2.00	.90	.25
☐ 33 Minnie Rojas	2.00	.90	.25
☐ 34 Jay Johnstone	3.00	1.35	.35
☐ 35 Ed Kirkpatrick	2.00	.90	.25

1967 Coke Caps Giants

These caps featuring members of the San Francisco Giants were issued in the Bay area. The caps have a "G" prefix and measure approximately 1" in diameter.

	NRMT	VG-E	GOOD
COMPLETE SET (18)	50.00	22.00	6.25
COMMON PLAYER (1-18)	2.00	.90	.25
☐ 1 Bob Bolin	2.00	.90	.25
☐ 2 Ollie Brown	2.00	.90	.25
☐ 3 Jim Davenport	2.00	.90	.25
☐ 4 Tito Fuentes	2.00	.90	.25
☐ 5 Norm Siebern	2.00	.90	.25
☐ 6 Jim Hart	2.00	.90	.25
☐ 7 Juan Marichal	6.00	2.70	.75
☐ 8 Hal Lanier	2.00	.90	.25
☐ 9 Tom Haller	2.00	.90	.25
☐ 10 Bob Barton	2.00	.90	.25
☐ 11 Willie McCovey	6.00	2.70	.75
☐ 12 Mike McCormick	3.00	1.35	.35
☐ 13 Frank Linzy	2.00	.90	.25
☐ 14 Ray Sadecki	2.00	.90	.25
☐ 15 Gaylord Perry	6.00	2.70	.75
☐ 16 Lindy McDaniel	2.00	.90	.25
☐ 17 Willie Mays	12.00	5.50	1.50
☐ 18 Jesus Alou	2.00	.90	.25

1967 Coke Caps Indians

These caps feature members of the Cleveland Indians. They measure approximately 1" in diameter. The caps which were included on Coke, Tab, Sprite and Fresca boxes have an "I" prefix.

	NRMT	VG-E	GOOD
COMPLETE SET (18)	35.00	16.00	4.40
COMMON PLAYER (1-18)	2.00	.90	.25
☐ 1 Luis Tiant	4.00	1.80	.50
☐ 2 Max Alvis	2.00	.90	.25
☐ 3 Larry Brown	2.00	.90	.25
☐ 4 Rocky Colavito	6.00	2.70	.75
☐ 5 John O'Donoghue	2.00	.90	.25
☐ 6 Pedro Gonzalez	2.00	.90	.25
☐ 7 Gary Bell	2.00	.90	.25
☐ 8 Sonny Siebert	2.00	.90	.25
☐ 9 Joe Azcue	2.00	.90	.25
☐ 10 Lee Maye	2.00	.90	.25
☐ 11 Chico Salmon	2.00	.90	.25
☐ 12 Leon Wagner	2.00	.90	.25
☐ 13 Fred Whitfield	2.00	.90	.25
☐ 14 Jack Kralick	2.00	.90	.25
☐ 15 Sam McDowell	3.00	1.35	.35
☐ 16 Dick Radatz	2.00	.90	.25
☐ 17 Vic Davalillo	2.00	.90	.25
☐ 18 Chuck Hinton	2.00	.90	.25

1967 Coke Caps Orioles

These caps feature members of the Baltimore Orioles. The caps, which measure approximatley 1" in diameter have an "O" prefix.

	NRMT	VG-E	GOOD
COMPLETE SET (18)	50.00	22.00	6.25
COMMON PLAYER (1-18)	2.00	.90	.25
☐ 1 Dave McNally	3.00	1.35	.35
☐ 2 Luis Aparicio	5.00	2.20	.60
☐ 3 Paul Blair	2.00	.90	.25
☐ 4 Frank Robinson	7.50	3.40	.95
☐ 5 Jim Palmer	7.50	3.40	.95
☐ 6 Russ Snyder	2.00	.90	.25
☐ 7 Stu Miller	2.00	.90	.25
☐ 8 Dave Johnson	4.00	1.80	.50
☐ 9 Andy Etchebarren	2.00	.90	.25
☐ 10 Brooks Robinson	7.50	3.40	.95
☐ 11 Boog Powell	4.00	1.80	.50
☐ 12 Sam Bowens	2.00	.90	.25
☐ 13 Curt Blefary	2.00	.90	.25
☐ 14 Eddie Fisher	2.00	.90	.25
☐ 15 Wally Bunker	2.00	.90	.25
☐ 16 Moe Drabowsky	2.00	.90	.25
☐ 17 Larry Haney	2.00	.90	.25
☐ 18 Tom Phoebus	2.00	.90	.25

1967 Coke Caps Phillies

Included on bottles of Coke, Tab, Sprite and Fresca were these caps. They measured 1" in diameter, featured members of the Philadelphia Phillies and have a "P" prefix.

	NRMT	VG-E	GOOD
COMPLETE SET (18)	40.00	18.00	5.00
COMMON PLAYER (1-18)	2.00	.90	.25
☐ 1 Richie Allen	5.00	2.20	.60
☐ 2 Bob Wine	2.00	.90	.25
☐ 3 John Briggs	2.00	.90	.25
☐ 4 John Callison	2.00	.90	.25
☐ 5 Doug Clemens	2.00	.90	.25
☐ 6 Dick Groat	4.00	1.80	.50
☐ 7 Dick Ellsworth	2.00	.90	.25
☐ 8 Phil Linz	2.00	.90	.25
☐ 9 Clay Dalrymple	2.00	.90	.25
☐ 10 Bob Uecker	5.00	2.20	.60
☐ 11 Cookie Rojas	2.00	.90	.25
☐ 12 Tony Taylor	3.00	1.35	.35
☐ 13 Bill White	4.00	1.80	.50
☐ 14 Larry Jackson	3.00	1.35	.35
☐ 15 Chris Short	2.00	.90	.25
☐ 16 Jim Bunning	6.00	2.70	.75
☐ 17 Tony Gonzalez	2.00	.90	.25
☐ 18 Don Lock	2.00	.90	.25

1967 Coke Caps Pirates

These caps portray members of the 1967 Pittsburgh Pirates. These caps measure 1" in diameter and were on Coke, Fresca, Tab and Sprite bottles. The caps have an "E" prefix.

	NRMT	VG-E	GOOD
COMPLETE SET (18)	50.00	22.00	6.25
COMMON PLAYER (1-18)	2.00	.90	.25
☐ 1 Al McBean	2.00	.90	.25
☐ 2 Gene Alley	2.00	.90	.25
☐ 3 Donn Clendenon	2.00	.90	.25
☐ 4 Bob Veale	2.00	.90	.25
☐ 5 Pete Mikkelsen	2.00	.90	.25
☐ 6 Bill Mazeroski	5.00	2.20	.60
☐ 7 Steve Blass	2.00	.90	.25
☐ 8 Manny Mota	3.00	1.35	.35
☐ 9 Jim Pagliaroni	2.00	.90	.25
☐ 10 Jesse Gonder	2.00	.90	.25
☐ 11 Jose Pagan	2.00	.90	.25
☐ 12 Willie Stargell	6.00	2.70	.75
☐ 13 Maury Wills	5.00	2.20	.60
☐ 14 Roy Face	3.00	1.35	.35
☐ 15 Woodie Fryman	2.00	.90	.25
☐ 16 Vernon Law	3.00	1.35	.35
☐ 17 Matty Alou	3.00	1.35	.35
☐ 18 Roberto Clemente	12.50	5.50	1.55

1967 Coke Caps Red Sox

These caps, issued in various Coke products, featured members of the Boston Red Sox. The caps measure approximately 1" in diameter and have an "R" prefix.

	NRMT	VG-E	GOOD
COMPLETE SET (18)	35.00	16.00	4.40
COMMON PLAYER (1-18)	2.00	.90	.25
☐ 1 Lee Stange	2.00	.90	.25
☐ 2 Carl Yastrzemski	7.50	3.40	.95
☐ 3 Don Demeter	2.00	.90	.25
☐ 4 Jose Santiago	2.00	.90	.25
☐ 5 Darrell Brandon	2.00	.90	.25
☐ 6 Joe Foy	2.00	.90	.25
☐ 7 Don McMahon	2.00	.90	.25
☐ 8 Dalton Jones	2.00	.90	.25
☐ 9 Mike Ryan	2.00	.90	.25
☐ 10 Bob Tillman	2.00	.90	.25
☐ 11 Rico Petrocelli	3.50	1.55	.45
☐ 12 George Scott	3.50	1.55	.45
☐ 13 George Smith	2.00	.90	.25
☐ 14 Dennis Bennett	2.00	.90	.25
☐ 15 Hank Fischer	2.00	.90	.25
☐ 16 Jim Lonborg	3.50	1.55	.45
☐ 17 Jose Tartabull	2.00	.90	.25
☐ 18 George Thomas	2.00	.90	.25

1967 Coke Caps Reds

These caps feature members of the Cincinnati Reds. They were issued in various Coke products, measure approximatley 1" in diameter and have "F" prefixes.

	NRMT	VG-E	GOOD
COMPLETE SET (18)	45.00	20.00	5.50
COMMON PLAYER (1-18)	2.00	.90	.25
☐ 1 Milt Pappas	3.00	1.35	.35
☐ 2 Leo Cardenas	3.00	1.35	.35
☐ 3 Gordy Coleman	2.00	.90	.25
☐ 4 Tommy Harper	2.00	.90	.25
☐ 5 Tommy Helms	3.00	1.35	.35
☐ 6 Deron Johnson	2.00	.90	.25
☐ 7 Jim Maloney	3.00	1.35	.35
☐ 8 Tony Perez	5.00	2.20	.60
☐ 9 Don Pavletich	2.00	.90	.25
☐ 10 John Edwards	2.00	.90	.25
☐ 11 Vada Pinson	4.00	1.80	.50
☐ 12 Chico Ruiz	2.00	.90	.25
☐ 13 Pete Rose	10.00	4.50	1.25
☐ 14 Bill McCool	2.00	.90	.25
☐ 15 Joe Nuxhall	4.00	1.80	.50
☐ 16 Floyd Robinson	2.00	.90	.25
☐ 17 Art Shamsky	2.00	.90	.25
☐ 18 Dick Simpson	2.00	.90	.25

1967 Coke Caps Senators

The 1967 Washington Senators are portrayed in this set. These caps, issued on bottles of Coke, Fresca, Tab and Sprite, measure approximately 1" in diameter. The caps have an "S" prefix.

	NRMT	VG-E	GOOD
COMPLETE SET (18)	35.00	16.00	4.40
COMMON PLAYER (1-18)	2.00	.90	.25
☐ 1 Bob Humphreys	2.00	.90	.25
☐ 2 Bernie Allen	2.00	.90	.25
☐ 3 Ed Brinkman	2.00	.90	.25
☐ 4 Pete Richert	2.00	.90	.25
☐ 5 Camilo Pascual	3.00	1.35	.35
☐ 6 Frank Howard	5.00	2.20	.60
☐ 7 Casey Cox	2.00	.90	.25
☐ 8 Jim King	2.00	.90	.25
☐ 9 Paul Casanova	2.00	.90	.25
☐ 10 Dick Lines	2.00	.90	.25
☐ 11 Dick Nen	2.00	.90	.25
☐ 12 Ken McMullen	2.00	.90	.25
☐ 13 Bob Saverine	2.00	.90	.25
☐ 14 Jim Hannan	2.00	.90	.25
☐ 15 Darold Knowles	2.00	.90	.25

□ 16 Phil Ortega	2.00	.90	.25
□ 17 Ken Harrelson	4.00	1.80	.50
□ 18 Fred Valentine	2.00	.90	.25

1967 Coke Caps Tigers

These caps measure approximately 1" in diameter. Members of the 1967 Detroit Tigers are remembered in this set. The caps have an "T" prefix.

	NRMT	VG-E	GOOD
COMPLETE SET (18)	40.00	18.00	5.00
COMMON PLAYER (1-18)	2.00	.90	.25
□ 1 Larry Sherry	2.00	.90	.25
□ 2 Norm Cash	5.00	2.20	.60
□ 3 Jerry Lumpe	2.00	.90	.25
□ 4 Dave Wickersham	2.00	.90	.25
□ 5 Joe Sparma	2.00	.90	.25
□ 6 Dick McAuliffe	2.00	.90	.25
□ 7 Fred Gladding	2.00	.90	.25
□ 8 Jim Northrup	3.50	1.55	.45
□ 9 Bill Freehan	5.00	2.20	.60
□ 10 Earl Wilson	2.00	.90	.25
□ 11 Dick Tracewski	2.00	.90	.25
□ 12 Don Wert	2.00	.90	.25
□ 13 Jake Wood	2.00	.90	.25
□ 14 Mickey Lolich	5.00	2.20	.60
□ 15 Johnny Podres	3.50	1.55	.45
□ 16 Bill Monbouquette	2.00	.90	.25
□ 17 Al Kaline	7.50	3.40	.95
□ 18 Willie Horton	3.50	1.55	.45

1967 Coke Caps Twins

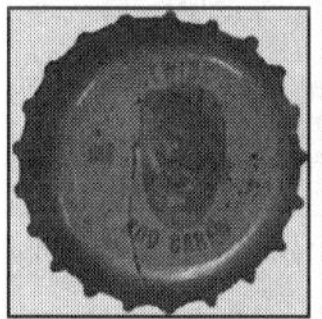

These 1967 Coke Caps feature members of the Minnesota Twins. The caps, which measure approximately 1" in diameter, have an "M" prefix

	NRMT	VG-E	GOOD
COMPLETE SET (18)	40.00	18.00	5.00
COMMON PLAYER (1-18)	2.00	.90	.25
□ 1 Ron Kline	2.00	.90	.25
□ 2 Bob Allison	3.00	1.35	.35
□ 3 Earl Battey	2.00	.90	.25
□ 4 Jim Merritt	2.00	.90	.25
□ 5 Jim Perry	3.00	1.35	.35
□ 6 Harmon Killebrew	6.00	2.70	.75
□ 7 Dave Boswell	2.00	.90	.25
□ 8 Rich Rollins	2.00	.90	.25
□ 9 Jerry Zimmerman	2.00	.90	.25
□ 10 Al Worthington	2.00	.90	.25
□ 11 Cesar Tovar	2.00	.90	.25
□ 12 Sandy Valdespino	2.00	.90	.25
□ 13 Zoilo Versalles	2.00	.90	.25
□ 14 Dean Chance	3.00	1.35	.35
□ 15 Jim Grant	2.00	.90	.25
□ 16 Jim Kaat	5.00	2.20	.60
□ 17 Tony Oliva	5.00	2.20	.60
□ 18 Andy Kosco	2.00	.90	.25

1967 Coke Caps White Sox

These 1967 Coke caps were found on bottles of Coke, Tab, Sprite, and Fresca distributed in the Chicago area. The 35 caps could be affixed to a collector sheet and then redeemed at a Chicago area Thom McAn Shoe Store for six autographed White Sox photos. Five collections could be redeemed for an Official Little League baseball. The caps measure about 1" in diameter and feature player headshots. A baseball icon appears on each of the caps' crowns. The caps are numbered with an "L" prefix.

	NRMT	VG-E	GOOD
COMPLETE SET (18)	35.00	16.00	4.40
COMMON PLAYER(1-18)	2.00	.90	.25
□ 1 Gary Peters	3.00	1.35	.35
□ 2 Jerry Adair	2.00	.90	.25
□ 3 Al Weis	2.00	.90	.25
□ 4 Pete Ward	2.00	.90	.25
□ 5 Hoyt Wilhelm	5.00	2.20	.60
□ 6 Don Buford	2.00	.90	.25
□ 7 John Buzhardt	2.00	.90	.25
□ 8 Wayne Causey	2.00	.90	.25
□ 9 Gerry McNertney	2.00	.90	.25
□ 10 Ron Hansen	2.00	.90	.25
□ 11 Tom McCraw	2.00	.90	.25
□ 12 Jim O'Toole	2.00	.90	.25
□ 13 Bill Skowron	3.00	1.35	.35
□ 14 Joel Horlen	2.00	.90	.25
□ 15 Tommy John	5.00	2.20	.60
□ 16 Bob Locker	2.00	.90	.25
□ 17 Ken Berry	2.00	.90	.25
□ 18 Tommie Agee	2.00	.90	.25

1967 Coke Caps Yankees and Mets

This 35-cap set was found on bottle tops of Coca-Cola and features both the New York Yankees and the Mets. The caps display a small head picture, with the player's name, team, and position surrounding it. The first 18 caps (V1-V18) picture the Yankees, while the last (V19-V35) picture the Mets.

	NRMT	VG-E	GOOD
COMPLETE SET (35)	90.00	40.00	11.00
COMMON PLAYER (1-35)	2.00	.90	.25
□ V1 Mel Stottlemyre	4.00	1.80	.50
□ V2 Ruben Amaro	2.00	.90	.25
□ V3 Jake Gibbs	2.00	.90	.25
□ V4 Dooley Womack	2.00	.90	.25
□ V5 Fred Talbot	2.00	.90	.25
□ V6 Horace Clarke	2.00	.90	.25
□ V7 Jim Bouton	4.00	1.80	.50
□ V8 Mickey Mantle	20.00	9.00	2.50
□ V9 Elston Howard	5.00	2.20	.60
□ V10 Hal Reniff	2.00	.90	.25
□ V11 Charley Smith	2.00	.90	.25
□ V12 Bobby Murcer	5.00	2.20	.60
□ V13 Joe Pepitone	4.00	1.80	.50
□ V14 Al Downing	2.00	.90	.25
□ V15 Steve Hamilton	2.00	.90	.25
□ V16 Fritz Peterson	2.00	.90	.25
□ V17 Tom Tresh	3.00	1.35	.35
□ V18 Roy White	3.00	1.35	.35
□ V19 Chuck Hiller	2.00	.90	.25
□ V20 Johnny Lewis	2.00	.90	.25
□ V21 Ed Kranepool	3.00	1.35	.35
□ V22 Al Luplow	2.00	.90	.25
□ V23 Don Cardwell	2.00	.90	.25
□ V24 Cleon Jones	3.00	1.35	.35
□ V25 Bob Shaw	2.00	.90	.25
□ V26 John Stephenson	2.00	.90	.25
□ V27 Ron Swoboda	3.00	1.35	.35
□ V28 Ken Boyer	4.00	1.80	.50
□ V29 Ed Bressoud	2.00	.90	.25
□ V30 Tommy Davis	3.00	1.35	.35
□ V31 Roy McMillan	2.00	.90	.25
□ V32 Jack Fisher	2.00	.90	.25
□ V33 Tug McGraw	5.00	2.20	.60
□ V34 Jerry Grote	3.00	1.35	.35
□ V35 Jack Hamilton	2.00	.90	.25

1968 Coke Caps Braves

These caps remember members of the 1968 Atlanta Braves. Issued in bottles of Coke, Tab, Fresca and Sprite, these caps measure approximately 1" in diameter. They were issued with the prefix "B".

	NRMT	VG-E	GOOD
COMPLETE SET (18)	45.00	20.00	5.50
COMMON PLAYER (1-18)	2.00	.90	.25
□ 1 Cecil Upshaw	2.00	.90	.25
□ 2 Tito Francona	2.00	.90	.25
□ 3 Henry Aaron	12.50	5.50	1.55
□ 4 Pat Jarvis	2.00	.90	.25
□ 5 Tony Cloninger	2.00	.90	.25
□ 6 Denis Menke	2.00	.90	.25
□ 7 Felix Millan	2.00	.90	.25
□ 8 Woody Woodward	2.00	.90	.25
□ 9 Joe Torre	6.00	2.70	.75
□ 10 Ken Johnson	2.00	.90	.25
□ 11 Marty Martinez	2.00	.90	.25
□ 12 Felipe Alou	5.00	2.20	.60
□ 13 Clete Boyer	2.00	.90	.25
□ 14 Sonny Jackson	2.00	.90	.25
□ 15 Deron Johnson	2.00	.90	.25
□ 16 Dick Kelley	2.00	.90	.25
□ 17 Rico Carty	3.00	1.35	.35
□ 18 Mack Jones	2.00	.90	.25

1968 Coke Caps Orioles

These caps, which measure approximately 1" in diameter, portray members of the Baltimore Orioles. They were issued in various Coke products and have an "O" prefix.

	NRMT	VG-E	GOOD
COMPLETE SET (18)	50.00	22.00	6.25
COMMON PLAYER (1-18)	2.00	.90	.25
□ 1 Dave McNally	2.00	.90	.25
□ 2 Luis Aparicio	6.00	2.70	.75
□ 3 Paul Blair	2.00	.90	.25
□ 4 Frank Robinson	7.50	3.40	.95
□ 5 Jim Palmer	7.50	3.40	.95
□ 6 John O'Donoghue	2.00	.90	.25
□ 7 Dave May	2.00	.90	.25
□ 8 Dave Johnson	3.50	1.55	.45
□ 9 Andy Etchebarren	2.00	.90	.25
□ 10 Brooks Robinson	7.50	3.40	.95
□ 11 Boog Powell	5.00	2.20	.60
□ 12 Pete Richert	2.00	.90	.25
□ 13 Curt Blefary	2.00	.90	.25
□ 14 Mark Belanger	3.50	1.55	.45
□ 15 Wally Bunker	2.00	.90	.25
□ 16 Moe Drabowsky	2.00	.90	.25
□ 17 Larry Haney	2.00	.90	.25
□ 18 Tom Phoebus	2.00	.90	.25

1968 Coke Caps Red Sox

These caps were issued with coke products. They feature members of the Boston Red Sox and measure approximately 1" in diameter. These caps have an "R" prefix. Carl Yastrzemski is not in this set, probably because he is in the National set.

	NRMT	VG-E	GOOD
COMPLETE SET (18)	35.00	16.00	4.40
COMMON PLAYER (1-18)	2.00	.90	.25
□ 1 Lee Stange	2.00	.90	.25
□ 2 Gary Waslewski	2.00	.90	.25
□ 3 Gary Bell	2.00	.90	.25
□ 4 John Wyatt	2.00	.90	.25
□ 5 Darrell Brandon	2.00	.90	.25
□ 6 Joe Foy	2.00	.90	.25
□ 7 Ray Culp	2.00	.90	.25
□ 8 Dalton Jones	2.00	.90	.25
□ 9 Gene Oliver	2.00	.90	.25
□ 10 Jose Santiago	2.00	.90	.25
□ 11 Rico Petrocelli	4.00	1.80	.50
□ 12 George Scott	3.00	1.35	.35
□ 13 Mike Andrews	2.00	.90	.25
□ 14 Dick Ellsworth	2.00	.90	.25
□ 15 Norm Siebern	2.00	.90	.25
□ 16 Jim Lonborg	4.00	1.80	.50
□ 17 Jerry Adair	2.00	.90	.25
□ 18 Elston Howard	4.00	1.80	.50

1968 Coke Caps Tigers

Included as a premium (Cap) with various Coke products (Coke, Tab, Fresca and Sprite), these caps measure approximately 1" in diameter. They have a "T" prefix.

	NRMT	VG-E	GOOD
COMPLETE SET (18)	50.00	22.00	6.25
COMMON PLAYER (1-18)	2.00	.90	.25
□ 1 Ray Oyler	2.00	.90	.25
□ 2 Norm Cash	5.00	2.20	.60
□ 3 Mike Marshall	3.50	1.55	.45
□ 4 Mickey Stanley	2.00	.90	.25
□ 5 Joe Sparma	2.00	.90	.25
□ 6 Dick McAuliffe	3.50	1.55	.45
□ 7 Gates Brown	2.00	.90	.25
□ 8 Jim Northrup	3.50	1.55	.45
□ 9 Bill Freehan	5.00	2.20	.60
□ 10 Earl Wilson	2.00	.90	.25
□ 11 Dick Tracewski	2.00	.90	.25
□ 12 Don Wert	2.00	.90	.25
□ 13 Dennis Ribant	2.00	.90	.25
□ 14 Mickey Lolich	5.00	2.20	.60
□ 15 Denny McLain	5.00	2.20	.60
□ 16 Ed Mathews	6.00	2.70	.75
□ 17 Al Kaline	7.50	3.40	.95
□ 18 Willie Horton	3.50	1.55	.45

1981 Coke Team Sets

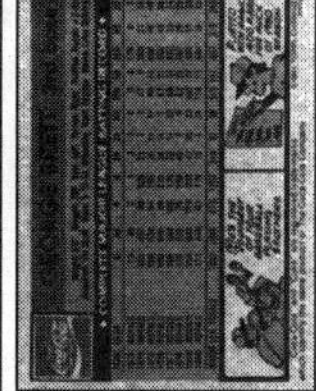

The cards in this 132-card set measure 2 1/2" by 3 1/2". In 1981, Topps produced 11 sets of 12 cards each for the Coca-Cola Company. Each set features 11 star players for a particular team plus an advertising card with the team name on the front. Although the cards are numbered in the upper right corner of the back from 1 to 11, they are re-numbered below within team, i.e., Boston Red Sox (1-12), Chicago Cubs (13-24), Chicago White Sox (25-36), Cincinnati Reds (37-48), Detroit Tigers (49-60), Houston Astros (61-72), Kansas City Royals (73-84), New York Mets (85-96), Philadelphia Phillies (97-108), Pittsburgh Pirates (109-120), and St. Louis Cardinals (121-132). Within each team the player actually numbered number 1 (on the card back) is the first player below and the player numbered number 11 is the last in that team's list. These player cards are quite similar to the 1981 Topps issue but feature a Coca-Cola logo on both the front and the back. The advertising card for each team features, on its back, an offer for obtaining an uncut sheet of 1981 Topps cards. These promotional cards were actually issued by Coke in only a few of the cities, and most of these cards have reached collectors hands through dealers who have purchased the cards through suppliers. Recently, cards of the following New York Yankees have been discovered: Rick Cerone, Rich Gossage and Reggie Jackson. Since these cards are so infrequently found, we have not yet placed a value on them.

	MINT	NRMT	EXC
COMPLETE SET (132)	40.00	18.00	5.00
COMMON CARD (1-132)	.20	.09	.03
COMMON AD CARD	.10	.05	.01
□ 1 Tom Burgmeier	.20	.09	.03
□ 2 Dennis Eckersley	2.00	.90	.25
□ 3 Dwight Evans	.75	.35	.09
□ 4 Bob Stanley	.20	.09	.03
□ 5 Glenn Hoffman	.20	.09	.03
□ 6 Carney Lansford	.30	.14	.04
□ 7 Frank Tanana	.40	.18	.05
□ 8 Tony Perez	1.25	.55	.16
□ 9 Jim Rice	.30	.14	.04
□ 10 Dave Stapleton	.20	.09	.03
□ 11 Carl Yastrzemski	3.50	1.55	.45
□ 12 Red Sox Ad Card (Unnumbered)	.10	.05	.01
□ 13 Tim Blackwell	.20	.09	.03
□ 14 Bill Buckner	.30	.14	.04
□ 15 Ivan DeJesus	.20	.09	.03
□ 16 Leon Durham	.30	.14	.04
□ 17 Steve Henderson	.20	.09	.03
□ 18 Mike Krukow	.20	.09	.03
□ 19 Ken Reitz	.20	.09	.03
□ 20 Rick Reuschel	.30	.14	.04
□ 21 Scot Thompson	.20	.09	.03
□ 22 Dick Tidrow	.20	.09	.03
□ 23 Mike Tyson	.20	.09	.03
□ 24 Cubs Ad Card (Unnumbered)	.10	.05	.01
□ 25 Britt Burns	.20	.09	.03
□ 26 Todd Cruz	.20	.09	.03
□ 27 Rich Dotson	.20	.09	.03
□ 28 Jim Essian	.20	.09	.03
□ 29 Ed Farmer	.20	.09	.03
□ 30 Lamar Johnson	.20	.09	.03
□ 31 Ron LeFlore	.20	.09	.03
□ 32 Chet Lemon	.20	.09	.03
□ 33 Bob Molinaro	.20	.09	.03
□ 34 Jim Morrison	.20	.09	.03
□ 35 Wayne Nordhagen	.20	.09	.03
□ 36 White Sox Ad Card (Unnumbered)	.10	.05	.01
□ 37 Johnny Bench	4.00	1.80	.50
□ 38 Dave Collins	.20	.09	.03
□ 39 Dave Concepcion	.30	.14	.04
□ 40 Dan Driessen	.20	.09	.03
□ 41 George Foster	.50	.23	.06
□ 42 Ken Griffey	.30	.14	.04
□ 43 Tom Hume	.20	.09	.03
□ 44 Ray Knight	.50	.23	.06
□ 45 Ron Oester	.20	.09	.03
□ 46 Tom Seaver	4.00	1.80	.50
□ 47 Mario Soto	.20	.09	.03
□ 48 Reds Ad Card (Unnumbered)	.10	.05	.01
□ 49 Champ Summers	.20	.09	.03
□ 50 Al Cowens	.20	.09	.03
□ 51 Rich Hebner	.30	.14	.04
□ 52 Steve Kemp	.30	.14	.04
□ 53 Aurelio Lopez	.20	.09	.03
□ 54 Jack Morris	1.50	.70	.19
□ 55 Lance Parrish	.75	.35	.09
□ 56 Johnny Wockenfuss	.20	.09	.03
□ 57 Alan Trammell	3.00	1.35	.35
□ 58 Lou Whitaker	2.00	.90	.25
□ 59 Kirk Gibson	3.00	1.35	.35
□ 60 Tigers Ad Card (Unnumbered)	.10	.05	.01
□ 61 Alan Ashby	.20	.09	.03
□ 62 Cesar Cedeno	.30	.14	.04
□ 63 Jose Cruz	.30	.14	.04
□ 64 Art Howe	.20	.09	.03
□ 65 Rafael Landestoy	.20	.09	.03
□ 66 Joe Niekro	.30	.14	.04
□ 67 Terry Puhl	.30	.14	.04
□ 68 J.R. Richard	.30	.14	.04
□ 69 Nolan Ryan	8.00	3.60	1.00
□ 70 Joe Sambito	.30	.14	.04
□ 71 Don Sutton	2.00	.90	.25
□ 72 Astros Ad Card (Unnumbered)	.10	.05	.01
□ 73 Willie Aikens	.20	.09	.03
□ 74 George Brett	7.50	3.40	.95
□ 75 Larry Gura	.20	.09	.03
□ 76 Dennis Leonard	.30	.14	.04
□ 77 Hal McRae	.50	.23	.06
□ 78 Amos Otis	.30	.14	.04
□ 79 Dan Quisenberry	.30	.14	.04
□ 80 U.L. Washington	.20	.09	.03

□ 81 John Wathan	.20	.09	.03
□ 82 Frank White	.30	.14	.04
□ 83 Willie Wilson	.30	.14	.04
□ 84 Royals Ad Card	.10	.05	.01
(Unnumbered)			
□ 85 Neil Allen	.20	.09	.03
□ 86 Doug Flynn	.20	.09	.03
□ 87 Dave Kingman	.30	.14	.04
□ 88 Randy Jones	.20	.09	.03
□ 89 Pat Zachry	.20	.09	.03
□ 90 Lee Mazzilli	.20	.09	.03
□ 91 Rusty Staub	.30	.14	.04
□ 92 Craig Swan	.20	.09	.03
□ 93 Frank Taveras	.20	.09	.03
□ 94 Alex Trevino	.20	.09	.03
□ 95 Joel Youngblood	.20	.09	.03
□ 96 Mets Ad Card	.10	.05	.01
(Unnumbered)			
□ 97 Bob Boone	.30	.14	.04
□ 98 Larry Bowa	.30	.14	.04
□ 99 Steve Carlton	2.00	.90	.25
□ 100 Greg Luzinski	.50	.23	.06
□ 101 Garry Maddox	.30	.14	.04
□ 102 Bake McBride	.20	.09	.03
□ 103 Tug McGraw	.30	.14	.04
□ 104 Pete Rose	4.00	1.80	.50
□ 105 Mike Schmidt	4.00	1.80	.50
□ 106 Lonnie Smith	.30	.14	.04
□ 107 Manny Trillo	.30	.14	.04
□ 108 Phillies Ad Card	.10	.05	.01
(Unnumbered)			
□ 109 Jim Bibby	.20	.09	.03
□ 110 John Candelaria	.30	.14	.04
□ 111 Mike Easler	.30	.14	.04
□ 112 Tim Foli	.20	.09	.03
□ 113 Phil Garner	.30	.14	.04
□ 114 Bill Madlock	.30	.14	.04
□ 115 Omar Moreno	.20	.09	.03
□ 116 Ed Ott	.20	.09	.03
□ 117 Dave Parker	.75	.35	.09
□ 118 Willie Stargell	1.50	.70	.19
□ 119 Kent Tekulve	.30	.14	.04
□ 120 Pirates Ad Card	.10	.05	.01
(Unnumbered)			
□ 121 Bob Forsch	.20	.09	.03
□ 122 George Hendrick	.30	.14	.04
□ 123 Keith Hernandez	.30	.14	.04
□ 124 Tom Herr	.30	.14	.04
□ 125 Sixto Lezcano	.20	.09	.03
□ 126 Ken Oberkfell	.20	.09	.03
□ 127 Darrell Porter	.30	.14	.04
□ 128 Tony Scott	.20	.09	.03
□ 129 Lary Sorensen	.20	.09	.03
□ 130 Bruce Sutter	.30	.14	.04
□ 131 Garry Templeton	.20	.09	.03
□ 132 Cardinals Ad Card	.10	.05	.01
(Unnumbered)			

1991 Coke Mattingly

This 15-card standard-size set was sponsored by Coca-Cola. The front design features mostly color action player photos on a white and blue pinstripe card face. Each card has a year number on the top edge of the picture, and the Coke logo is superimposed at the lower left corner. In a horizontal format the backs are printed in blue and red, and present career highlights and statistics.

	MINT	NRMT	EXC
COMPLETE SET (15)	7.50	3.40	.95
COMMON CARD (1-15)	.50	.23	.06
□ 1 Don Mattingly	.50	.23	.06
1978			
□ 2 Don Mattingly	.50	.23	.06
1979			
□ 3 Don Mattingly	.50	.23	.06
1980			
□ 4 Don Mattingly	.50	.23	.06
1981			
(black and white)			
□ 5 Don Mattingly	.50	.23	.06
1982			
□ 6 Don Mattingly	.50	.23	.06
1983			
□ 7 Don Mattingly	.50	.23	.06
1983-84			
(black and white)			
□ 8 Don Mattingly	.50	.23	.06
1984			
□ 9 Don Mattingly	.50	.23	.06
1985			
□ 10 Don Mattingly	.50	.23	.06
1986			
□ 11 Don Mattingly	.50	.23	.06
1987			
□ 12 Don Mattingly	.50	.23	.06
1990			
□ 13 Don Mattingly	.50	.23	.06
1991 (Photo)			
□ 14 Don Mattingly	.50	.23	.06
1991 (Drawing)			
□ 15 Don Mattingly	.50	.23	.06
1991 (Career stats)			

1993 Coke Case Inserts

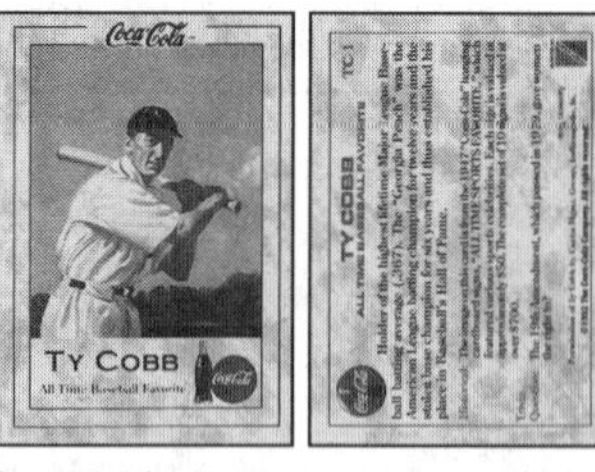

These standard-size cards are one per case inserts in the 1993 Coca-Cola set marketed by Collect-A-Card. The Ty Cobb image on the card is from the 1947 Coca-Cola hanging cardboard signs, "All Time Sports Favorite," which featured various sports celebrities. The variegated gray front has a pair of thin red foil lines surrounding an artist's illustration of the player. Below the picture are the player's name in red foil lettering and the words "All-Time Baseball Favorite." A Coke bottle appears in the lower left corner next to the Coca-Cola logo. The horizontal backs also have a variegated gray background and a thin red line surrounding player profile and a historical trivia question. The card is numbered on the back with a "TC" prefix. The second card features Christy Mathewson in a reprinted ad from 1916. The back describes the ad and gives some more information about Mathewson. The Mathewson card has a "CM" prefix.

	MINT	NRMT	EXC
COMPLETE SET (2)	75.00	34.00	9.50
COMMON CARD	25.00	11.00	3.10
□ CM1 Christy Mathewson	25.00	11.00	3.10
□ TC1 Ty Cobb	50.00	22.00	6.25

1909-11 Colgan's Chips E254

This is list of the players issued by Colgan's chips. This is a combination of the E254. We have separated the Chips into the E254 and E270 listings.The "cards" measure 1 1/2" round and were inserted one per five cent package. The chips are unnumbered and we have sequenced them in alphabetical order.

	EX-MT	VG-E	GOOD
COMPLETE SET	14000.00	6300.00	1800.00
COMMON PLAYER	35.00	16.00	4.40
□ 1 Ed Abbaticchio	35.00	16.00	4.40
□ 2 Fred Abbott	35.00	16.00	4.40
□ 3A Bill Abstein	35.00	16.00	4.40
Pittsburg			
□ 3B Bill Abstein	35.00	16.00	4.40
Jersey City			
□ 4 Babe Adams	35.00	16.00	4.40
□ 5 Doc Adkins	35.00	16.00	4.40
□ 6 Joe Agler	35.00	16.00	4.40
□ 8A Dave Altizer	35.00	16.00	4.40
Cincinnati			
□ 8B Dave Altizer	35.00	16.00	4.40
Minneapolis			
□ 9 Nick Altrock	50.00	22.00	6.25
□ 10B Red Ames	35.00	16.00	4.40
New York Nat'l L			
□ 11 Jimmy Archer	50.00	22.00	6.25
□ 14A Jimmy Austin	50.00	22.00	6.25
New York Am.			
□ 14B Jimmy Austin	50.00	22.00	6.25
St. Louis Am.			
□ 15A Charlie Babb	35.00	16.00	4.40
Memphis			
□ 15B Charlie Babb	35.00	16.00	4.40
Norfolk, Va.			
□ 16 Rudolph Baerwald	35.00	16.00	4.40
□ 17 Bill Bailey	35.00	16.00	4.40
□ 18 Frank Baker	100.00	45.00	12.50
□ 19 Jack Barry	50.00	22.00	6.25
□ 20 Bill Bartley	35.00	16.00	4.40
□ 21A Johnny Bates	35.00	16.00	4.40
Cincinnati			
□ 21B Johnny Bates	35.00	16.00	4.40
Phila Nat'l L			
□ 22 Dick Bayless	35.00	16.00	4.40
Atlanta			
□ 23A Ginger Beaumont	35.00	16.00	4.40
Boston Nat'l L			
□ 23B Ginger Beaumont	35.00	16.00	4.40
Chicago Nat'l			
□ 23C Ginger Beaumont	35.00	16.00	4.40
St. Paul			
□ 24 Beals Becker	35.00	16.00	4.40
□ 26 George Bell	35.00	16.00	4.40
□ 27A Harry Bemis	35.00	16.00	4.40
Cleveland			
□ 27B Harry Bemis	35.00	16.00	4.40
Columbus			
□ 28A Heinie Berger	35.00	16.00	4.40
Cleveland			
□ 28B Heinie Berger	35.00	16.00	4.40
Columbus			
□ 29 Bob Bescher	50.00	22.00	6.25
□ 30 Beumiller	35.00	16.00	4.40
Louisville			
□ 31 Joe Birmingham	35.00	16.00	4.40
□ 32 Kitty Bransfield	35.00	16.00	4.40
□ 33A Roger Bresnahan	100.00	45.00	12.50
St. Louis Nat'l			
□ 34 Al Bridwell	50.00	22.00	6.25
□ 35 Lew Brockett	35.00	16.00	4.40
New York Am L			
□ 37A Al Burch	35.00	16.00	4.40
Brooklyn			
□ 38A William Burke	35.00	16.00	4.40
Ft. Wayne			
□ 38B William Burke	35.00	16.00	4.40
Indianapolis			
□ 40 Donie Bush	50.00	22.00	6.25
□ 41 Bill Byers	35.00	16.00	4.40
Baltimore			
□ 44 Howie Cammitz	35.00	16.00	4.40
□ 46A Charlie Carr	35.00	16.00	4.40
Indianapolis			
□ 46B Charlie Carr	35.00	16.00	4.40
Utica			
□ 48A Frank Chance	100.00	45.00	12.50
□ 49 Hal Chase	75.00	34.00	9.50
□ 51 Clancy	35.00	16.00	4.40
Baltimore			
□ 52 Nig Clarke	100.00	45.00	12.50
□ 53 Fred Clarke	100.00	45.00	12.50
Cincinnati			
□ 56 Clymer	35.00	16.00	4.40
Minneapolis			
□ 57A Ty Cobb	600.00	275.00	75.00
Detroit			
□ 57B Ty Cobb	600.00	275.00	75.00
Detroit			
□ 58 Eddie Collins	100.00	45.00	12.50
□ 59A Buck Congalton	35.00	16.00	4.40
Columbus			
□ 60 Wid Conroy	35.00	16.00	4.40
□ 64 Courtney	35.00	16.00	4.40
Providence			
□ 65A Harry Coveleski	35.00	16.00	4.40
□ 65B Stan Coveleski	35.00	16.00	4.40
□ 66 Doc Crandall	35.00	16.00	4.40
□ 67 Gavvy Cravath	50.00	22.00	6.25
□ 69 Dode Criss	35.00	16.00	4.40
□ 70 Bill Dahlen	35.00	16.00	4.40
□ 72A Jake Daubert	35.00	16.00	4.40
Memphis			
□ 72B Jake Daubert	35.00	16.00	4.40
Brooklyn			
□ 73 Harry Davis	35.00	16.00	4.40
□ 74 George Davis	35.00	16.00	4.40
□ 75 Jim Delahanty	35.00	16.00	4.40
□ 76A Ray Demmett	35.00	16.00	4.40
New York Am. L.			
□ 76B Ray Demmett	35.00	16.00	4.40
Montreal			
□ 76C Ray Demmett	35.00	16.00	4.40
St. Louis Am. L			
□ 77 Art Devlin	35.00	16.00	4.40
□ 80 Bill Donovan	50.00	22.00	6.25
□ 82 Mickey Doolan	35.00	16.00	4.40
□ 83 Patsy Dougherty	35.00	16.00	4.40
□ 84 Tom Downey	35.00	16.00	4.40
□ 85 Larry Doyle	50.00	22.00	6.25
□ 87 Jack Dunn	50.00	22.00	6.25
□ 88 Charles Eagan	35.00	16.00	4.40
□ 89A Kid Elberfield	35.00	16.00	4.40
Washington			
□ 89C Kid Elberfield	35.00	16.00	4.40
New York Am. L			
□ 92 Rube Ellis	35.00	16.00	4.40
□ 94A Clyde Engle	35.00	16.00	4.40
New York Am. L			
□ 94B Clyde Engle	35.00	16.00	4.40
Boston Am.			
□ 96 Steve Evans	35.00	16.00	4.40
□ 97 Johnny Evers	100.00	45.00	12.50
□ 98 George Ferguson	35.00	16.00	4.40
□ 99 Hobe Ferris	35.00	16.00	4.40
□ 100 Field	35.00	16.00	4.40
Montreal			
□ 102 Matthew Fitzgerald	35.00	16.00	4.40
□ 103A Patrick Flaherty	35.00	16.00	4.40
Kansas City			
□ 103B Patrick Flaherty	35.00	16.00	4.40
Atlanta			
□ 104 Flater	35.00	16.00	4.40
Newark			
□ 105A Elmer Flick	100.00	45.00	12.50
Cleveland			
□ 105B Elmer Flick	100.00	45.00	12.50
Toledo			
□ 108A Freck	35.00	16.00	4.40
Baltimore			
□ 108B Freck	35.00	16.00	4.40
Toronto			
□ 109 Freeman	35.00	16.00	4.40
Toledo			
□ 112 Art Froome	35.00	16.00	4.40
Cincinnati			
□ 113A Larry Gardner	35.00	16.00	4.40
Boston Am. L			
□ 113B Larry Gardner	35.00	16.00	4.40
New York Am. L			
□ 114 Harry Gaspar	35.00	16.00	4.40
□ 115A Gus Getz	35.00	16.00	4.40
Boston Nat'l L.			
□ 115B Gus Getz	35.00	16.00	4.40
Pittsburgh			
□ 116 George Gibson	35.00	16.00	4.40
□ 120A Moose Grimshaw	35.00	16.00	4.40
Toronto			
□ 120B Moose Grimshaw	35.00	16.00	4.40
Louisville			
□ 122 Noodles Hahn	35.00	16.00	4.40
□ 123 John Halla	35.00	16.00	4.40
□ 124 Hally	35.00	16.00	4.40
Rochester			
□ 125 Charles Hanford	35.00	16.00	4.40
□ 126A Topsy Hartsel	35.00	16.00	4.40
Phila. Am. L.			
□ 127A Roy Hartzell	35.00	16.00	4.40
St. Louis Am. L.			
□ 127B Roy Hartzell	35.00	16.00	4.40
New York Am.			
□ 128 Weldon Henley	35.00	16.00	4.40
□ 129 Harry Hinchman	35.00	16.00	4.40
□ 131 Solly Hofman	35.00	16.00	4.40
□ 133A Harry Hooper	100.00	45.00	12.50
Boston Am. L			
□ 133B Harry Hooper	100.00	45.00	12.50
Boston Na'l			
□ 134 Del Howard	35.00	16.00	4.40
□ 136B Hughes	35.00	16.00	4.40
Louisville			
□ 136C Hughes	35.00	16.00	4.40
Louisville			
as "c" but name and			
team in uniform			
□ 137 Hughes	35.00	16.00	4.40
Rochester			
□ 138A Rudy Hulswitt	35.00	16.00	4.40
St. Louis Nat'l L			
□ 138B Rudy Hulswitt	35.00	16.00	4.40
Chattanooga			
□ 139 John Hummel	35.00	16.00	4.40
□ 140 George Hunter	35.00	16.00	4.40
□ 141 Joe Jackson	750.00	350.00	95.00
□ 142 Hughie Jennings	100.00	45.00	12.50
□ 144 Davy Jones	50.00	22.00	6.25
□ 145 Tom Jones	35.00	16.00	4.40
□ 146B Jordon	35.00	16.00	4.40
Atlanta			
□ 146C Jordon	35.00	16.00	4.40
Atlanta.			
□ 146D Jordon	35.00	16.00	4.40
Louisville			
□ 147 Joss	100.00	45.00	12.50
Cleveland			
□ 148 Kaiser	35.00	16.00	4.40
Louisville			
□ 150 Willie Keeler	100.00	45.00	12.50
□ 151B Kelly	35.00	16.00	4.40
Toronto			
□ 152A William Killefer	35.00	16.00	4.40
St. Louis Am.			
□ 153A Ed Killian	35.00	16.00	4.40
Detroit			
□ 153B Ed Killian	35.00	16.00	4.40
Toronto			
□ 154 Johnny Kling	50.00	22.00	6.25
□ 156 Otto Knabe	35.00	16.00	4.40
□ 157A John Knight	35.00	16.00	4.40
New York Am L			
□ 158 Ed Konetchy	35.00	16.00	4.40
□ 160 Rube Kroh	35.00	16.00	4.40
□ 161A Doc Lafitte	35.00	16.00	4.40
Rochester			
□ 162 Nap Lajoie	150.00	70.00	19.00
□ 163 Lakoff	35.00	16.00	4.40
Louisville			
□ 164 Frank Lange	35.00	16.00	4.40
□ 165A Frank LaPorte	35.00	16.00	4.40
St. Louis Am			
□ 165B Frank LaPorte	35.00	16.00	4.40
New York Am			
□ 166 Tommy Leach	50.00	22.00	6.25
□ 168 William Lelivelt	35.00	16.00	4.40
□ 169A Lewis	35.00	16.00	4.40

Milwaukee			
☐ 169B Lewis	35.00	16.00	4.40
Indianapolis			
☐ 170A Vivian Lindaman	35.00	16.00	4.40
Boston Nat'l L			
☐ 170B Vivian Lindaman	35.00	16.00	4.40
Louisville			
☐ 170C Vivian Lindaman	35.00	16.00	4.40
Indianapolis			
☐ 171 Bris Lord	35.00	16.00	4.40
☐ 172A Harry Lord	35.00	16.00	4.40
Boston Am L			
☐ 172B Harry Lord	35.00	16.00	4.40
Chicago Am L			
☐ 173A William Ludwig	35.00	16.00	4.40
Milwaukee			
☐ 173B William Ludwig	35.00	16.00	4.40
St. Louis Nat'l L			
☐ 175 Madden	35.00	16.00	4.40
Montreal			
☐ 176A Nicholas Maddox	35.00	16.00	4.40
Pittsburg			
☐ 177A Manser	35.00	16.00	4.40
Jersey City			
☐ 177B Manser	35.00	16.00	4.40
Rochester			
☐ 178 Rube Marquard	100.00	45.00	12.50
☐ 179 Al Mattern	35.00	16.00	4.40
☐ 180 Matthews	35.00	16.00	4.40
Atlanta			
☐ 182 George McBride	35.00	16.00	4.40
☐ 183 Alex McCathy	35.00	16.00	4.40
☐ 184 Ambrose McConnell	35.00	16.00	4.40
Rochester			
☐ 186 Moose McCormick	35.00	16.00	4.40
☐ 187 Dennis McGann	35.00	16.00	4.40
☐ 188 James McGinley	35.00	16.00	4.40
☐ 189 Joe McGinnity	100.00	45.00	12.50
☐ 190A Matty McIntyre	35.00	16.00	4.40
Detroit			
☐ 190B Matty McIntyre	35.00	16.00	4.40
Chicago Am			
☐ 191A Larry McLean	35.00	16.00	4.40
Cincinnati			
☐ 192 Fred Merkle	50.00	22.00	6.25
☐ 193A George Merritt	35.00	16.00	4.40
Buffalo			
☐ 193B George Merritt	35.00	16.00	4.40
Jersey City			
☐ 194 Lee Meyer	35.00	16.00	4.40
☐ 195 Chief Meyers	50.00	22.00	6.25
☐ 196 Clyde Milan	50.00	22.00	6.25
☐ 197 Dots Miller	35.00	16.00	4.40
☐ 199A Michael Mitchell	35.00	16.00	4.40
Cincinnati			
☐ 204 Pat Moran	35.00	16.00	4.40
Atlanta			
☐ 205 George Moriarty	50.00	22.00	6.25
Detroit			
☐ 206A George Moriarty	50.00	22.00	6.25
Louisville			
☐ 206B George Moriarty	50.00	22.00	6.25
Omaha			
☐ 207 Pat Mullen	35.00	16.00	4.40
Detroit			
☐ 208A Simmy Murch	35.00	16.00	4.40
Chattanooga			
☐ 208B Simmy Murch	35.00	16.00	4.40
Indianapolis			
☐ 209 Danny Murphy	35.00	16.00	4.40
☐ 210A Red Murray	35.00	16.00	4.40
☐ 210B Red Murray	35.00	16.00	4.40
St. Paul			
☐ 212 Bill Nattress	35.00	16.00	4.40
Montreal			
☐ 213A Red Nelson	35.00	16.00	4.40
St. Louis Am L			
☐ 213B Red Nelson	35.00	16.00	4.40
Toledo			
☐ 215 Rebel Oakes	35.00	16.00	4.40
☐ 216 Odwell	35.00	16.00	4.40
Columbus			
☐ 219B O'Rourke	35.00	16.00	4.40
Columbus			
☐ 220A Al Orth	35.00	16.00	4.40
New York Am. L.			
☐ 220B Al Orth	35.00	16.00	4.40
Indianapolis			
☐ 221 Wilfred Osborn	35.00	16.00	4.40
☐ 222 Orvie Overall	50.00	22.00	6.25
☐ 223 Frank Owens	35.00	16.00	4.40
☐ 225A Freddie Parent	35.00	16.00	4.40
☐ 226A Dode Paskert	35.00	16.00	4.40
Cincinnati			
☐ 226B Dode Paskert	35.00	16.00	4.40
Phila. Nat'l L			
☐ 227 Heinie Peitz	35.00	16.00	4.40
☐ 229 Robert A. Peterson	35.00	16.00	4.40
☐ 230 John Pfeister	35.00	16.00	4.40
☐ 231 Deacon Phillipe	35.00	16.00	4.40
☐ 232A Pickering	35.00	16.00	4.40
Louisville			
☐ 232B Pickering	35.00	16.00	4.40
Minneapolis			
☐ 232C Pickering	35.00	16.00	4.40
Omaha			
☐ 233A Billy Purtell	35.00	16.00	4.40
Chicago Am L			
☐ 233B Billy Purtell	35.00	16.00	4.40
Boston			
☐ 236 Bugs Raymond	35.00	16.00	4.40
☐ 237 Michael Regan	35.00	16.00	4.40
☐ 238 Thomas Reilly	35.00	16.00	4.40
Chicago Am L			
☐ 239 Thomas Reilly	35.00	16.00	4.40
Louisville			
☐ 240 Ed Reulbach	50.00	22.00	6.25
☐ 241 Claude Ritchey	35.00	16.00	4.40
☐ 242 Lou Ritter	35.00	16.00	4.40
☐ 243 Clyde Robinson	35.00	16.00	4.40
☐ 244 Royal Rock	35.00	16.00	4.40
☐ 245A Rowan	35.00	16.00	4.40
Cincinnati			
☐ 245B Jack Rowan	35.00	16.00	4.40
Phila Nat'l L			
☐ 246 Nap Rucker	50.00	22.00	6.25
☐ 247A Dick Rudolph	35.00	16.00	4.40
New York Nat'l L			
☐ 247B Dick Rudolph	35.00	16.00	4.40
Toronto			
☐ 248 Buddy Ryan	35.00	16.00	4.40
St. Paul			
☐ 250 Slim Sallee	35.00	16.00	4.40
☐ 252A Schardt	35.00	16.00	4.40
Birmingham			
☐ 252B Schardt	35.00	16.00	4.40
Milwaukee			
☐ 253 Jimmy Scheckard	35.00	16.00	4.40
☐ 254A George Schirm	35.00	16.00	4.40
Birmingham			
☐ 254B George Schirm	35.00	16.00	4.40
Buffalo			
☐ 255 Schlafly	35.00	16.00	4.40
Newark			
☐ 256 Frank Schulte	35.00	16.00	4.40
☐ 257 Seabaugh	35.00	16.00	4.40
Nashville			
☐ 258 Selby	35.00	16.00	4.40
Louisville			
☐ 259A Cy Seymour	35.00	16.00	4.40
New York Nat'l L			
☐ 259B Cy Seymour	35.00	16.00	4.40
Baltimore			
☐ 262 Hosea Siner	35.00	16.00	4.40
☐ 263A Smith	35.00	16.00	4.40
Atlanta			
☐ 263B Smith	35.00	16.00	4.40
Buffalo			
☐ 265 George Smith	35.00	16.00	4.40
Montreal			
☐ 266 Fred Snodgrass	50.00	22.00	6.25
☐ 267A Robert Spade	35.00	16.00	4.40
Cincinnati			
☐ 267B Robert Spade	35.00	16.00	4.40
Newark N.J.			
☐ 268A Tully Sparks	35.00	16.00	4.40
Phila. Nat'l L			
☐ 268B Tully Sparks	35.00	16.00	4.40
Richmond, Va.			
☐ 269A Tris Speaker	150.00	70.00	19.00
Boston Am.			
☐ 269B Tris Speaker	150.00	70.00	19.00
Boston Nat'l			
☐ 270 Spencer	35.00	16.00	4.40
St. Paul			
☐ 271 Jake Stahl	35.00	16.00	4.40
☐ 272 Stansberry	35.00	16.00	4.40
Louisville			
☐ 273 Harry Steinfeldt	50.00	22.00	6.25
☐ 274 George R. Stone	35.00	16.00	4.40
☐ 275 George Stovall	35.00	16.00	4.40
Cleveland			
☐ 276 Gabby Street	50.00	22.00	6.25
Washington			
☐ 278A Sullivan	35.00	16.00	4.40
Louisville			
☐ 278B Sullivan	35.00	16.00	4.40
Omaha			
☐ 281 Ed Summers	35.00	16.00	4.40
☐ 285 Lee Tannehill	35.00	16.00	4.40
☐ 286 Taylor	35.00	16.00	4.40
Kansas City			
☐ 289A Joe Tinker	150.00	70.00	19.00
Chicago Nat'l L			
☐ 290A John Titus	35.00	16.00	4.40
Phila. Nat'l			
☐ 291 Terry Turner	35.00	16.00	4.40
☐ 292A Robert Unglaub	35.00	16.00	4.40
Washington Am L			
☐ 292B Robert Unglaub	35.00	16.00	4.40
Lincoln Neb.			
☐ 294A Rube Waddell	100.00	45.00	12.50
St. Louis Am L			
☐ 294B Rube Waddell	100.00	45.00	12.50
Minneapolis			
☐ 294C Rube Waddell	100.00	45.00	12.50
Newark, N.J.			
☐ 295 Honus Wagner	400.00	180.00	50.00
☐ 296 Walker	35.00	16.00	4.40
Atlanta			
☐ 298 Waller	35.00	16.00	4.40
Jersey City			
☐ 301 Wauner	35.00	16.00	4.40
Memphis			
☐ 302 Wiesman	35.00	16.00	4.40
Nashville			
☐ 304 White	35.00	16.00	4.40
Buffalo			
☐ 305 Kirby White	35.00	16.00	4.40
☐ 307 Ed Willett	35.00	16.00	4.40
☐ 308A Williams	35.00	16.00	4.40
Indianapolis			
☐ 308B Williams	35.00	16.00	4.40
Minneapolis			
☐ 309 Owen Wilson	50.00	22.00	6.25
☐ 310 Hooks Wiltse	35.00	16.00	4.40
☐ 312A Orville Woodruff	35.00	16.00	4.40
Indianapolis			
☐ 312B Orville Woodruff	35.00	16.00	4.40
Louisville			
☐ 313 Walter Woods	35.00	16.00	4.40
Buffalo			
☐ 315 Cy Young	200.00	90.00	25.00
Cleveland			
☐ 316 Heinie Zimmerman	75.00	34.00	9.50
Chicago Nat'l L			
☐ 317A Heinie Zimmerman	75.00	34.00	9.50
Newark			

1912 Colgan's Red Border

These chips look the same as the E254's, the only difference is that they have a red border. This set is skip numbered since the checklist is based on the E254 Colgan Chip checklist.

	EX-MT	VG-E	GOOD
COMPLETE SET	18000.00	8100.00	2200.00
COMMON PLAYER	90.00	40.00	11.00
☐ 1 Ed Abbaticchio	90.00	40.00	11.00
☐ 2 Fred Abbott	90.00	40.00	11.00
☐ 4 Babe Adams	125.00	55.00	15.50
☐ 10B Red Ames	90.00	40.00	11.00
New York Nat'l L			
☐ 15B Charlie Babb	90.00	40.00	11.00
Norfolk, Va.			
☐ 17 Bill Bailey	90.00	40.00	11.00
☐ 18 Frank Baker	250.00	110.00	31.00
☐ 19 Jack Barry	125.00	55.00	15.50
☐ 21A Johnny Bates	90.00	40.00	11.00
Cincinnati			
☐ 22 Dick Bayless	90.00	40.00	11.00
☐ 24 Beals Becker	90.00	40.00	11.00
☐ 28B Heinie Berger	90.00	40.00	11.00
Columbus			
☐ 30 Beumiller	90.00	40.00	11.00
Louisville			
☐ 31 Joe Birmingham	90.00	40.00	11.00
Cleveland			
☐ 32 Kitty Bransfield	90.00	40.00	11.00
Phila Nat'l			
☐ 33A Roger Bresnahan	250.00	110.00	31.00
St. Louis Nat'l			
☐ 35 Lew Brockett	90.00	40.00	11.00
☐ 37A Al Burch	90.00	40.00	11.00
Brooklyn			
☐ 40 Donie Bush	125.00	55.00	15.50
☐ 42 Bobby Byrne	90.00	40.00	11.00
☐ 44 Howie Cammitz	90.00	40.00	11.00
☐ 46B Charlie Carr	90.00	40.00	11.00
Utica			
☐ 48A Frank Chance	300.00	135.00	38.00
Chicago Nat'l L.			
☐ 52 Fred Clarke	250.00	110.00	31.00
☐ 53 Tommy Clarke	250.00	110.00	31.00
☐ 56 Clymer	90.00	40.00	11.00
Minneapolis			
☐ 57B Ty Cobb	1750.00	800.00	220.00
Detroit			
☐ 58 Eddie Collins	300.00	135.00	38.00
☐ 60 Wid Conroy	90.00	40.00	11.00
☐ 65B Stan Coveleski	90.00	40.00	11.00
☐ 67 Gavvy Cravath	125.00	55.00	15.50
☐ 69 Dode Criss	90.00	40.00	11.00
☐ 73 Harry Davis	90.00	40.00	11.00
Phila. Am. L.			
☐ 74 George Davis	90.00	40.00	11.00
St. Paul			
☐ 75 Jim Delahanty	90.00	40.00	11.00
Toronto			
☐ 76B Ray Demmett	90.00	40.00	11.00
Montreal			
☐ 78A Josh Devore	90.00	40.00	11.00
Cincinnati			
☐ 80 Billl Donovan	125.00	55.00	15.50
☐ 82 Mickey Doolan	90.00	40.00	11.00
☐ 83 Patsy Dougherty	90.00	40.00	11.00
☐ 84 Tom Downey	90.00	40.00	11.00
☐ 85 Larry Doyle	125.00	55.00	15.50
☐ 87 Jack Dunn	125.00	55.00	15.50
☐ 88 Charles Eagen	90.00	40.00	11.00
Cincinnati			
☐ 89A Kid Elberfield	90.00	40.00	11.00
Washington			
☐ 92 Rube Ellis	90.00	40.00	11.00
St. Louis Nat'l			
☐ 96 Steve Evans	90.00	40.00	11.00
☐ 97 Johnny Evers	300.00	135.00	38.00
☐ 98 George Ferguson	90.00	40.00	11.00
☐ 99 Hobe Ferris	90.00	40.00	11.00
☐ 101 Fisher	90.00	40.00	11.00
Louisville			
☐ 102 Matthew Fitzgerald	90.00	40.00	11.00
☐ 106 Russ Ford	90.00	40.00	11.00
☐ 108A Freck	90.00	40.00	11.00
Baltimore			
☐ 112 Art Froome	90.00	40.00	11.00
☐ 114 Harry Gaspar	90.00	40.00	11.00
☐ 116 George Gibson	90.00	40.00	11.00
☐ 120B Moose Grimshaw	90.00	40.00	11.00
Louisville			
☐ 123 John Halla	90.00	40.00	11.00
Louisville			
☐ 124 Hally	90.00	40.00	11.00
Rochester			
☐ 125 Charles Hanford	90.00	40.00	11.00
Jersey City			
☐ 126A Topsy Hartsel	90.00	40.00	11.00
Phila. Am. L.			
☐ 128 Weldon Henley	90.00	40.00	11.00
Rochester			
☐ 129 Harry Hinchman	90.00	40.00	11.00
Columbus			
☐ 131 Solly Hofman	90.00	40.00	11.00
Chicago Nat'l			
☐ 133A Harry Hooper	250.00	110.00	31.00
Boston Am. L			
☐ 134 Del Howard	90.00	40.00	11.00
☐ 136C Hughes	90.00	40.00	11.00
Louisville			
as "c" but name and			
team in uniform			
☐ 138C Rudy Hulswitt	90.00	40.00	11.00
Louisville			
☐ 139 John Hummel	90.00	40.00	11.00
☐ 140 George Hunter	90.00	40.00	11.00
☐ 142 Hugh Jennings MG	250.00	110.00	31.00
☐ 145 Tom Jones	90.00	40.00	11.00
☐ 146B Jordon	90.00	40.00	11.00
Atlanta			
☐ 152A William Killefer	90.00	40.00	11.00
St. Louis Am.			
☐ 153B Ed Killian	90.00	40.00	11.00
Toronto			
☐ 156 Otto Knabe	90.00	40.00	11.00
☐ 157A John Knight	90.00	40.00	11.00
New York Am L			
☐ 158 Ed Konetchy	90.00	40.00	11.00
☐ 160 Rube Kroh	90.00	40.00	11.00
☐ 166 Tommy Leach	90.00	40.00	11.00
☐ 168 William Lelivelt	90.00	40.00	11.00
☐ 169A Lewis	90.00	40.00	11.00
Milwaukee			
☐ 170B Vivian Lindaman	90.00	40.00	11.00
Louisville			
☐ 171 Bris Lord	90.00	40.00	11.00
☐ 172B Harry Lord	90.00	40.00	11.00
☐ 173A William Ludwig	90.00	40.00	11.00
Milwaukee			
☐ 176A Nicholas Maddox	90.00	40.00	11.00
Pittsburg			
☐ 179 Al Mattern	90.00	40.00	11.00
☐ 182 George McBride	90.00	40.00	11.00
☐ 183 Alex McCathy	90.00	40.00	11.00
☐ 184 Ambrose McConnell	90.00	40.00	11.00
Rochester			
☐ 186 Moose McCormick	90.00	40.00	11.00
☐ 188 James McGinley	90.00	40.00	11.00
☐ 189 Joe McGinnity	250.00	110.00	31.00
☐ 190B Matty McIntyre	90.00	40.00	11.00
Chicago Am			
☐ 192 Fred Merkle	90.00	40.00	11.00
☐ 193A George Merritt	90.00	40.00	11.00
Buffalo			
☐ 195 Chief Meyers	125.00	55.00	15.50
☐ 196 Clyde Milan	125.00	55.00	15.50
☐ 197 Dots Miller	90.00	40.00	11.00
Pittsburg			
☐ 199A Michael Mitchell	90.00	40.00	11.00
Cincinnati			
☐ 205 George Moriarty	90.00	40.00	11.00
Detroit			
☐ 206B Moriarty	90.00	40.00	11.00
Omaha			
☐ 207 Pat Mullen	125.00	55.00	15.50
Detroit			
☐ 208A Murch	90.00	40.00	11.00
Chattanooga			
☐ 209 Danny Murphy	90.00	40.00	11.00
☐ 210A Red Murray	90.00	40.00	11.00
New York Nat'l L			

☐ 213A Red Nelson 90.00 40.00 11.00
St. Louis Am L
☐ 215 Rebel Oakes 90.00 40.00 11.00
☐ 222 Orvie Overall 125.00 55.00 15.50
☐ 223 Frank Owens 90.00 40.00 11.00
☐ 225A Freddie Parent 90.00 40.00 11.00
Chicago Am L
☐ 226B Dode Paskert 90.00 40.00 11.00
Phila. Nat'l L
☐ 227 Heinie Peitz 90.00 40.00 11.00
Louisville
☐ 229 Robert A. Peterson 90.00 40.00 11.00
☐ 232C Pickering 90.00 40.00 11.00
Omaha
☐ 236 Bugs Raymond 90.00 40.00 11.00
☐ 237 Michael Regan 90.00 40.00 11.00
☐ 243 Clyde Robinson 90.00 40.00 11.00
☐ 244 Royal Rock 90.00 40.00 11.00
☐ 245B Jack Rowan 90.00 40.00 11.00
Phila. Nat'l L
☐ 246 Nap Rucker 125.00 55.00 15.50
☐ 247A Dick Rudolph 90.00 40.00 11.00
New York Nat'l L
☐ 250 Slim Sallee 90.00 40.00 11.00
☐ 253 Jimmy Scheckard 90.00 40.00 11.00
☐ 254A George Schirm 90.00 40.00 11.00
Birmingham
☐ 256 Frank Schulte 125.00 55.00 15.50
☐ 257 Seabaugh 90.00 40.00 11.00
Nashville
☐ 258 Selby 90.00 40.00 11.00
Louisville
☐ 262 Hosea Siner 90.00 40.00 11.00
☐ 263A Smith 90.00 40.00 11.00
Atlanta
☐ 266 Fred Snodgrass 125.00 55.00 15.50
☐ 267B Robert Spade 90.00 40.00 11.00
Newark N.J.
☐ 268B Tully Sparks 90.00 40.00 11.00
Richmond, Va.
☐ 269A Tris Speaker 300.00 135.00 38.00
Boston Am.
☐ 274 George R. Stone 90.00 40.00 11.00
St. Louis Am. L.
☐ 275 George Stovall 90.00 40.00 11.00
Cleveland
☐ 276 Gabby Street 90.00 40.00 11.00
Washington
☐ 278B Sullivan 90.00 40.00 11.00
Omaha
☐ 280 J. Sullivan 90.00 40.00 11.00
Louisville
☐ 281 Ed Summers 90.00 40.00 11.00
Detroit
☐ 289A Joe Tinker 300.00 135.00 38.00
Chicago Nat'l L
☐ 290A John Titus 90.00 40.00 11.00
Phila. Nat'l
☐ 291 Terry Turner 90.00 40.00 11.00
Cleveland
☐ 294B Rube Waddell 300.00 135.00 38.00
Minneapolis
☐ 296 Walker 90.00 40.00 11.00
Atlanta
☐ 298 Waller 90.00 40.00 11.00
Jersey City
☐ 302 Wiesman 90.00 40.00 11.00
Nashville
☐ 304 White 90.00 40.00 11.00
Buffalo
☐ 308A Williams 90.00 40.00 11.00
Indianapolis
☐ 310 Hooks Wiltse 90.00 40.00 11.00
☐ 312A Woodruff 90.00 40.00 11.00
Indianapolis
☐ 314 Yeager 90.00 40.00 11.00
National
☐ 315 Cy Young 750.00 350.00 95.00
☐ 316 Heinie Zimmerman 90.00 40.00 11.00
Chicago Nat'l L

1913 Colgans Tin Tops

These chips are nicknames Tin Tops since the redemption offer on these chips asked for the Tin Tops to be included. That is how they are differentiated from the E-254's. This set is skip numbered since the checklist is based on the E-254 Colgan Chip checklist.

	EX-MT	VG-E	GOOD
COMPLETE SET	22500.00	10100.00	2800.00
COMMON PLAYER	100.00	45.00	12.50
☐ 5 Doc Adkins	100.00	45.00	12.50
☐ 7 Whitey Alperman	100.00	45.00	12.50
☐ 10A Red Ames Cincinnati	125.00	55.00	15.50
☐ 10B Red Ames New York Nat'l L	125.00	55.00	15.50
☐ 12A Atkins Atlanta	100.00	45.00	12.50
☐ 12B Atkins Fort Wayne	100.00	45.00	12.50
☐ 13 Atz Providence	100.00	45.00	12.50
☐ 14B Jimmy Austin St. Louis Am.	125.00	55.00	15.50
☐ 18 Frank Baker	250.00	110.00	31.00
☐ 21A Johnny Bates Cincinnati	100.00	45.00	12.50
☐ 25 Fred Beebe	100.00	45.00	12.50
☐ 29 Bob Bescher	125.00	55.00	15.50
☐ 31 Joe Birmingham	100.00	45.00	12.50
☐ 33B Roger Bresnahan Chicago Nat'l	250.00	110.00	31.00
☐ 35 Lew Brockett	100.00	45.00	12.50
☐ 37B Al Burch Louisville	100.00	45.00	12.50
☐ 39 Burns Toledo	100.00	45.00	12.50
☐ 40 Donie Bush	125.00	55.00	15.50
☐ 42 Bobby Byrne	100.00	45.00	12.50
☐ 43 Nixey Callahan	100.00	45.00	12.50
☐ 45 Vin Campbell	100.00	45.00	12.50
☐ 46C Charlie Carr Kansas City	100.00	45.00	12.50
☐ 47 Cashion Washington	100.00	45.00	12.50
☐ 48B Frank Chance	325.00	145.00	40.00
☐ 49 Hal Chase	200.00	90.00	25.00
☐ 50 Eddie Cicotte	250.00	110.00	31.00
☐ 52 Fred Clarke Pittsburgh	250.00	110.00	31.00
☐ 53 Tommy Clarke Cincinnati	250.00	110.00	31.00
☐ 54 Fred Clarke Indianapolis	250.00	110.00	31.00
☐ 55 Clemons Louisville	100.00	45.00	12.50
☐ 56 Clymer Minneapolis	100.00	45.00	12.50
☐ 57A Ty Cobb	1750.00	800.00	220.00
☐ 58 Eddie Collins	300.00	135.00	38.00
☐ 59B Buck Congalton Omaha	100.00	45.00	12.50
☐ 59C Buck Congalton Toledo	100.00	45.00	12.50
☐ 61 Cook Columbus	100.00	45.00	12.50
☐ 62 Jack Coombs	125.00	55.00	15.50
☐ 63 Corcoran Baltimore	100.00	45.00	12.50
☐ 68 Sam Crawford	250.00	110.00	31.00
☐ 70 Bill Dahlen	100.00	45.00	12.50
☐ 71 Bert Daniels	100.00	45.00	12.50
☐ 72B Jake Daubert Brooklyn	125.00	55.00	15.50
☐ 78A Josh Devore Cincinnati	100.00	45.00	12.50
☐ 78B Josh Devore New York Nat'l	100.00	45.00	12.50
☐ 79 Mike Donlin	100.00	45.00	12.50
☐ 81 Red Dooin	100.00	45.00	12.50
☐ 82 Mickey Doolan	100.00	45.00	12.50
☐ 85 Larry Doyle	125.00	55.00	15.50
☐ 86 Drake Kansas City	100.00	45.00	12.50
☐ 89B Kid Elberfield Chattanooga	100.00	45.00	12.50
☐ 90 Ellam Birmingahm	100.00	45.00	12.50
☐ 91 Elliott Nashville	100.00	45.00	12.50
☐ 92 Rube Ellis	100.00	45.00	12.50
☐ 93 Elwert Montgomery	100.00	45.00	12.50
☐ 94B Clyde Engle Boston Am.	100.00	45.00	12.50
☐ 95 Esmond Montreal	100.00	45.00	12.50
☐ 96 Steve Evans	100.00	45.00	12.50
☐ 97 Johnny Evers Chicago Nat'l L	300.00	135.00	38.00
☐ 99 Ferris Minneapolis	100.00	45.00	12.50
☐ 106 Russ Ford	100.00	45.00	12.50
☐ 107 Foster Boston Am	100.00	45.00	12.50
☐ 110 Friel St. Paul	100.00	45.00	12.50
☐ 111 Frill Buffalo	100.00	45.00	12.50
☐ 112 Art Froome	100.00	45.00	12.50
☐ 115B Gus Getz Pittsburgh	100.00	45.00	12.50
☐ 116 George Gibson	100.00	45.00	12.50
☐ 117 Graham Toronto	100.00	45.00	12.50
☐ 118A Eddie Grant Cincinnati	100.00	45.00	12.50
☐ 118B Eddie Grant New York Nat'l	100.00	45.00	12.50
☐ 119 Grief Columbus	100.00	45.00	12.50
☐ 121 Bob Groom	100.00	45.00	12.50
☐ 125 Charles Hanford	100.00	45.00	12.50
☐ 127A Topsy Hartzell	100.00	45.00	12.50
☐ 129 Harry Hinchman	100.00	45.00	12.50
☐ 130 Doc Hoblitzell	100.00	45.00	12.50
☐ 132 Hogan St. Louis Am.	100.00	45.00	12.50
☐ 133A Harry Hooper Boston Am. L	250.00	110.00	31.00
☐ 135 Miller Huggins	250.00	110.00	31.00
☐ 136A Hughes Milwaukee	100.00	45.00	12.50
☐ 137 Hughes Rochester	100.00	45.00	12.50
☐ 138C Hulswitt Louisville	100.00	45.00	12.50
☐ 139 Hummel Brooklyn	100.00	45.00	12.50
☐ 142 Hugh Jennings	250.00	110.00	31.00
☐ 143 Johns Atlanta	100.00	45.00	12.50
☐ 144 Davy Jones	100.00	45.00	12.50
☐ 146A Jordon Toronto	100.00	45.00	12.50
☐ 149 Keefe Rochester	100.00	45.00	12.50
☐ 150 Willie Keeler	250.00	110.00	31.00
☐ 151A Kelly Jersey City	100.00	45.00	12.50
☐ 152B William Killefer Phila. Nat'l L	100.00	45.00	12.50
☐ 153B Ed Killian Toronto	100.00	45.00	12.50
☐ 154A Johnny Kling Boston Nat'l L	125.00	55.00	15.50
☐ 154B Johnny Kling Cincinnati	125.00	55.00	15.50
☐ 155 Klipfer Rochester	100.00	45.00	12.50
☐ 156 Otto Knabe	100.00	45.00	12.50
☐ 157B John Knight Jersey City	100.00	45.00	12.50
☐ 158 Ed Konetchy	100.00	45.00	12.50
☐ 159 Paul Krichell	100.00	45.00	12.50
☐ 161B Doc Lafitte Providence	100.00	45.00	12.50
☐ 162 Nap Lajoie	300.00	135.00	38.00
☐ 167 Lee Newark	100.00	45.00	12.50
☐ 169A Lewis Milwaukee	100.00	45.00	12.50
☐ 172B Harry Lord Chicago Am L	100.00	45.00	12.50
☐ 174 John Lush	100.00	45.00	12.50
☐ 175 Thomas Madden	100.00	45.00	12.50
☐ 176B Nicholas Maddox Louisville	100.00	45.00	12.50
☐ 177A Manser Jersey City	100.00	45.00	12.50
☐ 181 McAllister Atlanta	100.00	45.00	12.50
☐ 183 Alex McCathy	100.00	45.00	12.50
☐ 185 Ambrose McConnell Toronto	100.00	45.00	12.50
☐ 191B Larry McLean St. Louis Nat'l	100.00	45.00	12.50
☐ 192 Fred Merkle	125.00	55.00	15.50
☐ 195 Chief Meyers	125.00	55.00	15.50
☐ 197 Dots Miller Pittsburg	100.00	45.00	12.50
☐ 198 Dots Miller Columbus	100.00	45.00	12.50
☐ 199B Michael Mitchell Chicago Nat'l	100.00	45.00	12.50
☐ 200 Mitchell Providence	100.00	45.00	12.50
☐ 201 Mitchell St. Louis Am.	100.00	45.00	12.50
☐ 202 Carlton Molesworth	100.00	45.00	12.50
☐ 203 Herbie Moran	100.00	45.00	12.50
☐ 205 George Moriarty Detroit	125.00	55.00	15.50
☐ 209 Danny Murphy	100.00	45.00	12.50
☐ 211 Murray Buffalo	100.00	45.00	12.50
☐ 214 Northrop Louisville	100.00	45.00	12.50
☐ 217 Rube Oldring	100.00	45.00	12.50
☐ 218 Steve O'Neil	100.00	45.00	12.50
☐ 219A O'Rourke St. Paul	100.00	45.00	12.50
☐ 225A Freddie Parent Chicago Am L	100.00	45.00	12.50
☐ 226A Dode Paskert Cincinnati	100.00	45.00	12.50
☐ 228 Perry Providence	100.00	45.00	12.50
☐ 234 Bill Rariden	100.00	45.00	12.50
☐ 235 Morrie Rath	100.00	45.00	12.50
☐ 236 Bugs Raymond	100.00	45.00	12.50
☐ 249 Buddy Ryan Cleveland	100.00	45.00	12.50
☐ 250 Slim Sallee	100.00	45.00	12.50
☐ 251 Ray Schalk	250.00	110.00	31.00
☐ 253 Jimmy Scheckard	100.00	45.00	12.50
☐ 260 Bob Shawkey	150.00	70.00	19.00
☐ 261 Shelton Columbus	100.00	45.00	12.50
☐ 263A Smith Atlanta	100.00	45.00	12.50
☐ 264 Smith Newark	100.00	45.00	12.50
☐ 266 Fred Snodgrass	125.00	55.00	15.50
☐ 269A Tris Speaker Boston Am.	300.00	135.00	38.00
☐ 271 Jake Stahl	100.00	45.00	12.50
☐ 272 Stansberry Louisville	100.00	45.00	12.50
☐ 277 Amos Strunk	100.00	45.00	12.50
☐ 279 Sullivan Indianapolis	100.00	45.00	12.50
☐ 282 Swacina Newark	100.00	45.00	12.50
☐ 283 Sweeney New York Am.	100.00	45.00	12.50
☐ 284 Sweeney Boston Nat'l	100.00	45.00	12.50
☐ 287 Taylor Montreal	100.00	45.00	12.50
☐ 288 Jim Thorpe	1500.00	700.00	190.00
☐ 289B Joe Tinker	300.00	135.00	38.00
☐ 290B John Titus Boston Nat'l L	100.00	45.00	12.50
☐ 291 Terry Turner	125.00	55.00	15.50
☐ 292C Robert Unglaub Minneapolis	100.00	45.00	12.50
☐ 293 Viebahn Jersey City	100.00	45.00	12.50
☐ 294B Rube Waddell Minneapolis	250.00	110.00	31.00
☐ 295 Honus Wagner	1000.00	450.00	125.00
☐ 297 Bobby Wallace	250.00	110.00	31.00
☐ 299 Ed Walsh	250.00	110.00	31.00
☐ 300 Jack Warhop	100.00	45.00	12.50
☐ 303 Zach Wheat	250.00	110.00	31.00
☐ 306 Kaiser Wilhelm	100.00	45.00	12.50
☐ 307 Ed Willett	100.00	45.00	12.50
☐ 309 Owen Wilson	100.00	45.00	12.50
☐ 310 Hooks Wiltse	100.00	45.00	12.50
☐ 311 Joe Wood	150.00	70.00	19.00
☐ 312A Woodruff Indianapolis	100.00	45.00	12.50
☐ 314 Yeager National	100.00	45.00	12.50
☐ 317B Heinie Zimmerman Newark	100.00	45.00	12.50
☐ 318 Jameson Buffalo	100.00	45.00	12.50

1989 Colla Postcards Dawson

These postcards measure 3 1/2" by 5 1/2" and showcase Andre Dawson. The fronts feature color action or posed player shots in a postcard format. The typical postcard backs carry the player's name, position and the team name, along with the team logo.

	MINT	NRMT	EXC
COMPLETE SET (8)	5.00	2.20	.60
COMMON CARD (1-8)	.75	.35	.09
☐ 1 Andre Dawson (Standing in front of stadium, bat in both hands)	.75	.35	.09
☐ 2 Andre Dawson (Action shot, batting)	.75	.35	.09
☐ 3 Andre Dawson (Kneeling on base)	.75	.35	.09
☐ 4 Andre Dawson (Close-up photo)	.75	.35	.09
☐ 5 Andre Dawson (Action shot, batting, bat behind head)	.75	.35	.09
☐ 6 Andre Dawson (Action shot, batting, bat in front of face)	.75	.35	.09
☐ 7 Andre Dawson (Standing in outfield)	.75	.35	.09
☐ 8 Andre Dawson (In front of stadium)	.75	.35	.09

1989 Colla Postcards Greenwell

These postcards measure 3 1/2" by 5 1/2" and showcase Mike Greenwell. The fronts feature color action or posed player shots in a postcard format. The typical postcard backs carry the player's name, position and the team name, along with the team logo.

	MINT	NRMT	EXC
COMPLETE SET (8)	4.00	1.80	.50
COMMON CARD (1-8)	.50	.23	.06
☐ 1 Mike Greenwell (Standing in front of	.50	.23	.06

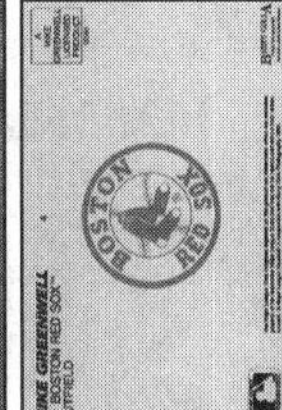

	MINT	NRMT	EXC
stadium, bat in both hands)			
☐ 2 Mike Greenwell (Action shot, batting)	.50	.23	.06
☐ 3 Mike Greenwell (Sitting on steps)	.50	.23	.06
☐ 4 Mike Greenwell (Batting, bat behind shoulders)	.50	.23	.06
☐ 5 Mike Greenwell (Standing in dugout)	.50	.23	.06
☐ 6 Mike Greenwell (Looking over his shoulder)	.50	.23	.06
☐ 7 Mike Greenwell (Action shot, running)	.50	.23	.06
☐ 8 Mike Greenwell (Action shot, bat in right hand)	.50	.23	.06

1989 Colla Postcards McGwire

These postcards measure 3 1/2" by 5 1/2" and showcase Mark McGwire. The fronts feature color action or posed player shots in a postcard format. The typical postcard backs carry the player's name, position and the team name, along with the team logo.

	MINT	NRMT	EXC
COMPLETE SET (8)	7.50	3.40	.95
COMMON CARD (1-8)	1.00	.45	.12
☐ 1 Mark McGwire (Sitting on steps, bat on right shoulder)	1.00	.45	.12
☐ 2 Mark McGwire (Close-up shot, with glove and white uniform)	1.00	.45	.12
☐ 3 Mark McGwire (Close-up shot, green jersey)	1.00	.45	.12
☐ 4 Mark McGwire (Action shot, white uniform)	1.00	.45	.12
☐ 5 Mark McGwire (Action shot, batting, gray uniform)	1.00	.45	.12
☐ 6 Mark McGwire (Close-up shot, bat in both hands)	1.00	.45	.12
☐ 7 Mark McGwire (Action shot, batting, bat behind head)	1.00	.45	.12
☐ 8 Mark McGwire (Action shot, batting bat in front of body)	1.00	.45	.12

1989 Colla Postcards Mitchell

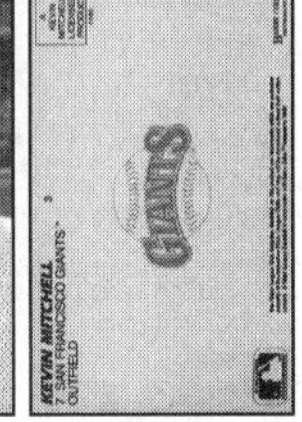

These postcards measure 3 1/2" by 5 1/2" and showcase Kevin Mitchell. The fronts feature color action or posed player shots in a postcard format. The typical postcard backs carry the player's name, position and the team name, along with the team logo.

	MINT	NRMT	EXC
COMPLETE SET (8)	4.00	1.80	.50
COMMON CARD (1-8)	.50	.23	.06
☐ 1 Kevin Mitchell (Action shot, bat in left hand behind body)	.50	.23	.06
☐ 2 Kevin Mitchell (Action shot, bat in left hand, on the ground)	.50	.23	.06
☐ 3 Kevin Mitchell (Close-up head shot)	.50	.23	.06
☐ 4 Kevin Mitchell (Standing, bat on right shoulder)	.50	.23	.06
☐ 5 Kevin Mitchell (Close-up, bat over the shoulders)	.50	.23	.06
☐ 6 Kevin Mitchell (Close-up, black jacket)	.50	.23	.06
☐ 7 Kevin Mitchell (Action shot, batting bat in both hands)	.50	.23	.06
☐ 8 Kevin Mitchell (Standing in front of stadium)	.50	.23	.06

1989 Colla Postcards Ozzie Smith

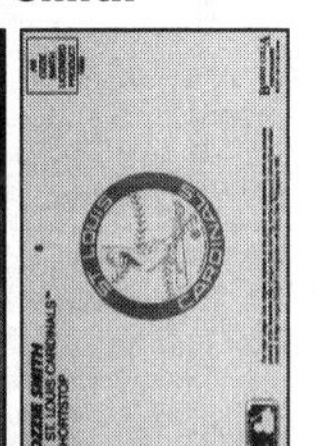

These postcards measure 3 1/2" by 5 1/2" and showcase Ozzie Smith. The fronts feature color action or posed player shots in a postcard format. The typical postcard backs carry the player's name, position and the team name, along with the team logo.

	MINT	NRMT	EXC
COMPLETE SET (8)	10.00	4.50	1.25
COMMON CARD (1-8)	1.25	.55	.16
☐ 1 Ozzie Smith (Close-up, in front of stadium)	1.25	.55	.16
☐ 2 Ozzie Smith (Close-up, bat behind head)	1.25	.55	.16
☐ 3 Ozzie Smith (Close-up, red jersey, glove under left arm)	1.25	.55	.16
☐ 4 Ozzie Smith (Action shot, throwing the ball)	1.25	.55	.16
☐ 5 Ozzie Smith (Action shot, batting, bat in front of body)	1.25	.55	.16
☐ 6 Ozzie Smith (Action shot, batting, bat behind body)	1.25	.55	.16
☐ 7 Ozzie Smith (Close-up, red jersey)	1.25	.55	.16
☐ 8 Ozzie Smith (Close-up, glove in left hand)	1.25	.55	.16

1990 Colla Canseco

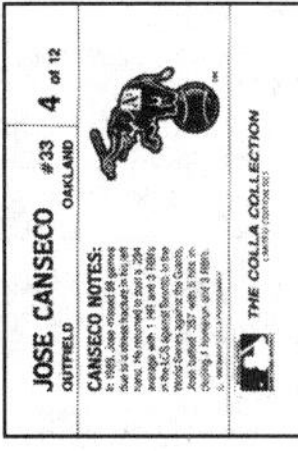

This 12-card standard-size set, issued by noted photographer Barry Colla, features Jose Canseco in various poses. The fronts are beautiful full-color photos while the backs contain notes about Canseco. According to the back of the first card in the set, 20,000 numbered sets were issued.

	MINT	NRMT	EXC
COMPLETE SET (12)	10.00	4.50	1.25
COMMON CARD (1-12)	1.00	.45	.12
☐ 1 Jose Canseco Portrait	1.00	.45	.12
☐ 2 Jose Canseco Follow-Through Bat at Waist	1.00	.45	.12
☐ 3 Jose Canseco Follow-Through Bat at Shoulders	1.00	.45	.12
☐ 4 Jose Canseco Follow-Through Helmetless	1.00	.45	.12
☐ 5 Jose Canseco Dugout Portrait	1.00	.45	.12
☐ 6 Jose Canseco Profile Bat on Shoulder	1.00	.45	.12
☐ 7 Jose Canseco Batting Cage Pose	1.00	.45	.12
☐ 8 Jose Canseco Follow-Through ready to run)	1.00	.45	.12
☐ 9 Jose Canseco Portrait Kneeling	1.00	.45	.12
☐ 10 Jose Canseco Portrait bat under shoulder)	1.00	.45	.12
☐ 11 Jose Canseco At Bat-rack	1.00	.45	.12
☐ 12 Jose Canseco Running Bases	1.00	.45	.12

1990 Colla Maas

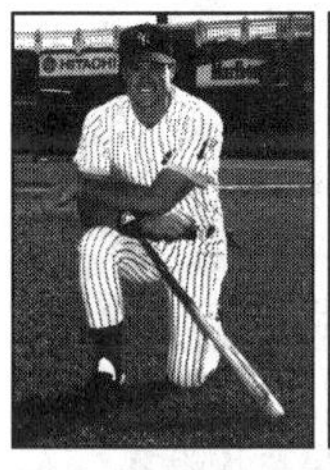

This attractive 12-card standard-size card set was produced by photographer Barry Colla. The set was limited to 7,500 made and each card has some facts relevant to Maas' career on the back of the card. The set was produced to be sold in its own special box and the boxes were issued 24 sets to each bigger box. All of the boxes were produced in the team's colors.

	MINT	NRMT	EXC
COMPLETE SET (12)	6.00	2.70	.75
COMMON CARD (1-12)	.50	.23	.06
☐ 1 Kevin Maas (Batting Pose)	.50	.23	.06
☐ 2 Kevin Maas (Sitting on Dugout Steps)	.50	.23	.06
☐ 3 Kevin Maas (Taking a lead on basepaths)	.50	.23	.06
☐ 4 Kevin Maas (Close-Up)	.50	.23	.06
☐ 5 Kevin Maas (Standing in Dugout)	.50	.23	.06
☐ 6 Kevin Maas (Kneeling with bat)	.50	.23	.06
☐ 7 Kevin Maas (Fielding Pose)	.50	.23	.06
☐ 8 Kevin Maas (Follow Through 24 showing)	.50	.23	.06
☐ 9 Kevin Maas (Portrait with Bat)	.50	.23	.06
☐ 10 Kevin Maas (Follow Through)	.50	.23	.06
☐ 11 Kevin Maas (Side Portrait)	.50	.23	.06
☐ 12 Kevin Maas (Taking Batting Practice)	.50	.23	.06

1990 Colla Mattingly

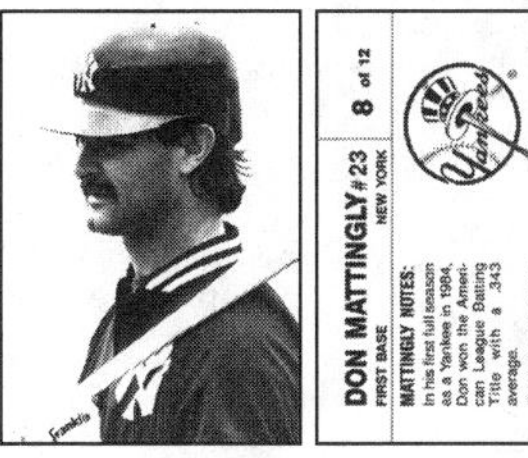

This 12-card standard-size set honoring Yankee great Don Mattingly features the photography of Barry Colla. The set was limited to 15,000 numbered sets and feature full-color photographs on the borderless fronts along with notes about Mattingly on the back.

	MINT	NRMT	EXC
COMPLETE SET (12)	10.00	4.50	1.25
COMMON CARD (1-12)	1.00	.45	.12
☐ 1 Don Mattingly (Head-On Portrait)	1.00	.45	.12
☐ 2 Don Mattingly (Preparing to Swing)	1.00	.45	.12
☐ 3 Don Mattingly (Running Bases)	1.00	.45	.12
☐ 4 Don Mattingly (Portrait with glove in hand)	1.00	.45	.12
☐ 5 Don Mattingly (Backhanding a Ball)	1.00	.45	.12
☐ 6 Don Mattingly (Follow-Through Bat Pointing Up)	1.00	.45	.12
☐ 7 Don Mattingly (Follow-Through bat to be released)	1.00	.45	.12
☐ 8 Don Mattingly (Facing left bat on shoulder)	1.00	.45	.12
☐ 9 Don Mattingly (Portrait facing right)	1.00	.45	.12
☐ 10 Don Mattingly (Practice Swing bat at waist)	1.00	.45	.12
☐ 11 Don Mattingly (Preparing to field ball)	1.00	.45	.12
☐ 12 Don Mattingly (Kneeling)	1.00	.45	.12

1990 Colla Postcards Grace

These postcards measure 3 1/2" by 5 1/2" and showcase Mark Grace. The fronts feature color action or posed player shots in a postcard format. The typical postcard backs carry the player's name, position and the team name, along with the team logo.

	MINT	NRMT	EXC
COMPLETE SET (8)	7.50	3.40	.95
COMMON CARD (1-8)	1.00	.45	.12
☐ 1 Mark Grace (Close-up shot, bat on left shoulder)	1.00	.45	.12
☐ 2 Mark Grace (Action shot, catching the ball)	1.00	.45	.12
☐ 3 Mark Grace (Action shot, waiting for the ball)	1.00	.45	.12
☐ 4 Mark Grace (Action shot, glove in right hand, ball in left)	1.00	.45	.12
☐ 5 Mark Grace (Close-up shot from back)	1.00	.45	.12
☐ 6 Mark Grace (Action shot, batting)	1.00	.45	.12
☐ 7 Mark Grace (Two action shots, batting)	1.00	.45	.12
☐ 8 Mark Grace (Close-up, blue jersey)	1.00	.45	.12

1990 Colla Postcards Will Clark

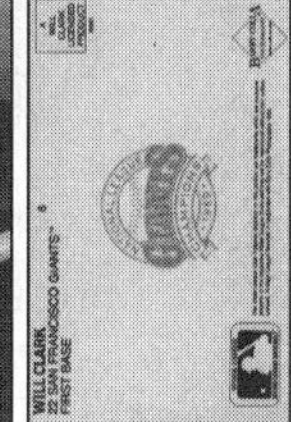

These postcards measure 3 1/2" by 5 1/2" and showcase Will Clark. The fronts feature color action or posed player shots in a postcard format. The typical postcard backs carry the player's name, position and the team name, along with the team logo.

	MINT	NRMT	EXC
COMPLETE SET (8)	10.00	4.50	1.25
COMMON CARD (1-8)	1.25	.55	.16
☐ 1 Will Clark (Close-up shot, bat on left shoulder)	1.25	.55	.16
☐ 2 Will Clark (Kneeling, bat under left arm)	1.25	.55	.16
☐ 3 Will Clark (Action shot, batting)	1.25	.55	.16
☐ 4 Will Clark (Action shot, running)	1.25	.55	.16
☐ 5 Will Clark (Close-up, holding bat on left side)	1.25	.55	.16
☐ 6 Will Clark (Close-up shot, holding bat in both hands)	1.25	.55	.16
☐ 7 Will Clark (Standing in front of dugout)	1.25	.55	.16
☐ 8 Will Clark (Close-up shot, without bat)	1.25	.55	.16

1990 Colla Will Clark

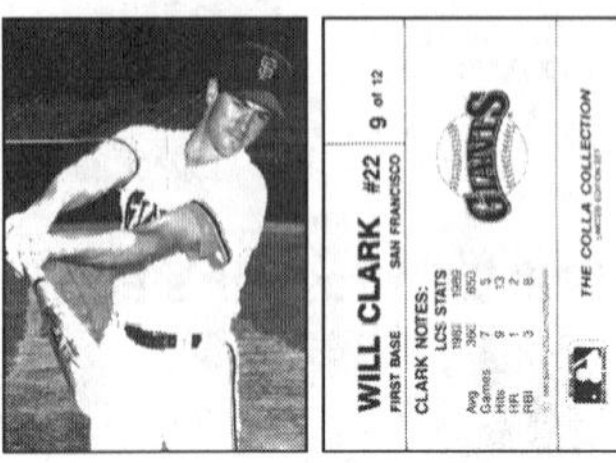

WILL CLARK #22
FIRST BASE SAN FRANCISCO
9 of 12
THE COLLA COLLECTION

This 12-card standard-size set again features the beautiful photography of Barry Colla; this time Will Clark is the featured player. Again the fronts are borderless photos while the back contains notes about Will Clark. According to card number one, 15,000 numbered sets were produced.

	MINT	NRMT	EXC
COMPLETE SET (12)	12.00	5.50	1.50
COMMON CARD (1-12)	1.25	.55	.16
☐ 1 Will Clark Batting Pose Gray Shirt	1.25	.55	.16
☐ 2 Will Clark Bat at Shoulder Short Sleeves	1.25	.55	.16
☐ 3 Will Clark Smiling	1.25	.55	.16
☐ 4 Will Clark Ball in Glove	1.25	.55	.16
☐ 5 Will Clark Batting Pose Long Sleeves	1.25	.55	.16
☐ 6 Will Clark Follow-Through bat over head	1.25	.55	.16
☐ 7 Will Clark Follow-Through hand released	1.25	.55	.16
☐ 8 Will Clark Standing bat on ground	1.25	.55	.16
☐ 9 Will Clark Pose with bat at waist	1.25	.55	.16
☐ 10 Will Clark Portrait with Bat	1.25	.55	.16
☐ 11 Will Clark Kneeling with Glove	1.25	.55	.16
☐ 12 Will Clark Preparing to Field	1.25	.55	.16

1991 Colla Bonds

This 13-card standard size set features colorful photos of Barry Bonds by noted photographer Barry Colla. The high gloss borderless color photos were packed in a full color collector's box. Only 7,500 were produced, with 24 sets per display carton. The first card of each set bears the registration number. In black lettering on a gray background, the horizontally oriented backs feature facts about Bonds. The cards are numbered on the back. This set was issued so late in 1991 that it was actually January 1992 before the set was in general distribution.

	MINT	NRMT	EXC
COMPLETE SET (13)	12.50	5.50	1.55
COMMON CARD (1-12)	1.00	.45	.12
☐ 1 Barry Bonds Posed with bat behind head	1.00	.45	.12
☐ 2 Barry Bonds Kneeling forearm resting on bat	1.00	.45	.12
☐ 3 Barry Bonds Front pose hand in glove	1.00	.45	.12
☐ 4 Barry Bonds Head and shoulders shot	1.00	.45	.12
☐ 5 Barry Bonds Warming up in black warm-up jersey	1.00	.45	.12
☐ 6 Barry Bonds Follow through bat behind head	1.00	.45	.12
☐ 7 Barry Bonds Crouching posture ready to field	1.00	.45	.12
☐ 8 Barry Bonds Seated in dugout	1.00	.45	.12
☐ 9 Barry Bonds Right shoulder forward bat on shoulder	1.00	.45	.12
☐ 10 Barry Bonds Front pose glove in front of chest	1.00	.45	.12
☐ 11 Barry Bonds Right shoulder forward batting pose	1.00	.45	.12
☐ 12 Barry Bonds Front pose arms crossed	1.00	.45	.12
☐ xx Title card Close-up pose forearm resting on bat	1.00	.45	.12

1991 Colla Gooden

This 13-card standard size set features colorful photos of Dwight Gooden by noted photographer Barry Colla. The high gloss borderless color photos were packed in a full color collector's box. Only 15,000 sets were produced, with 24 sets per display carton. The first card of each set bears the registration number. In black lettering on a light gray background, the horizontally oriented backs feature facts about Gooden.

	MINT	NRMT	EXC
COMPLETE SET (13)	10.00	4.50	1.25
COMMON CARD (1-13)	1.00	.45	.12
☐ 1 Dwight Gooden Head and shoulders pose	1.00	.45	.12
☐ 2 Dwight Gooden Pitching, arm behind back	1.00	.45	.12
☐ 3 Dwight Gooden Pitching, arm above head	1.00	.45	.12
☐ 4 Dwight Gooden Posed with glove	1.00	.45	.12
☐ 5 Dwight Gooden Kneeling, glove on knee	1.00	.45	.12
☐ 6 Dwight Gooden Posed, blue uniform	1.00	.45	.12
☐ 7 Dwight Gooden Pitching, just after release	1.00	.45	.12
☐ 8 Dwight Gooden Pose with glove left shoulder forward	1.00	.45	.12
☐ 9 Dwight Gooden Posed in dugout	1.00	.45	.12
☐ 10 Dwight Gooden Head and shoulder pose blue uniform	1.00	.45	.12
☐ 11 Dwight Gooden Kneeling, arms on left knee	1.00	.45	.12
☐ 12 Dwight Gooden Left shoulder pose	1.00	.45	.12
☐ xx Dwight Gooden Title Card Front pose	1.00	.45	.12

1991 Colla Griffey Jr.

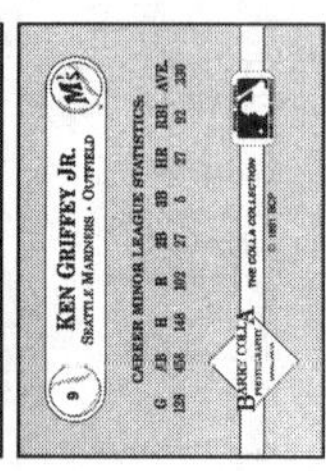

This 12-card standard size set features colorful photos of Ken Griffey Jr. by noted photographer Barry Colla. The high gloss borderless color photos were packed in a full color collector's box. Only 15,000 sets were produced, with 24 sets per display carton. The first card of each set bears the registration number. In black lettering on a light gray background, the horizontally oriented backs feature facts about Ken Griffey.

	MINT	NRMT	EXC
COMPLETE SET (12)	15.00	6.75	1.85
COMMON CARD (1-12)	1.25	.55	.16
☐ 1 Ken Griffey Jr. Bat on shoulder right side	1.25	.55	.16
☐ 2 Ken Griffey Jr. Bat on shoulder straight on	1.25	.55	.16
☐ 3 Ken Griffey Jr. Follow-through	1.25	.55	.16
☐ 4 Ken Griffey Jr. Beside batting cage	1.25	.55	.16
☐ 5 Ken Griffey Jr. In dugout	1.25	.55	.16
☐ 6 Ken Griffey Jr. Batting pose	1.25	.55	.16
☐ 7 Ken Griffey Jr. Adjusting hat	1.25	.55	.16
☐ 8 Ken Griffey Jr. Swinging bat	1.25	.55	.16
☐ 9 Ken Griffey Jr. Pose, middle of swing	1.25	.55	.16
☐ 10 Ken Griffey Jr. Bat at waist	1.25	.55	.16
☐ 11 Ken Griffey Jr. Middle of swing	1.25	.55	.16
☐ 12 Ken Griffey Jr. Hitting fly ball	1.25	.55	.16

1991 Colla Joe Carter

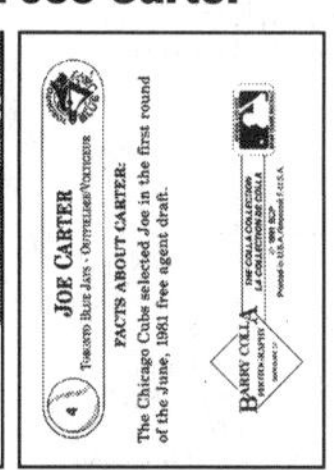

JOE CARTER
FACTS ABOUT CARTER:
The Chicago Cubs selected Joe in the first round of the June, 1981 free agent draft.

This 13-card standard size set features colorful photos of Joe Carter by noted photographer Barry Colla. The high gloss borderless color photos were packed in a full color collector's box. Only 7,500 sets were produced, with 24 sets per display carton. The first card of each set bears the registration number. In black lettering on a light gray background, the horizontally oriented backs feature facts about Carter.

	MINT	NRMT	EXC
COMPLETE SET (13)	10.00	4.50	1.25
COMMON CARD (1-12)	1.00	.45	.12
☐ 1 Joe Carter Posed, bat above shoulder	1.00	.45	.12
☐ 2 Joe Carter Kneeling pose, arm on bat	1.00	.45	.12
☐ 3 Joe Carter Head and shoulders pose	1.00	.45	.12
☐ 4 Joe Carter Posed, bat on right shoulder	1.00	.45	.12
☐ 5 Joe Carter Kneeling pose, close up	1.00	.45	.12
☐ 6 Joe Carter Ready to throw from outfield)	1.00	.45	.12
☐ 7 Joe Carter After throw from outfield	1.00	.45	.12
☐ 8 Joe Carter Watching fly ball after hit	1.00	.45	.12
☐ 9 Joe Carter Bat on shoulder in blue uniform	1.00	.45	.12
☐ 10 Joe Carter Batting helmet in hand	1.00	.45	.12
☐ 11 Joe Carter Posed in blue uniform and sunglasses	1.00	.45	.12
☐ 12 Joe Carter Posed with bat on shoulder from waist up	1.00	.45	.12
☐ xx Joe Carter Title card Front pose, bat on right shoulder	1.00	.45	.12

1991 Colla Justice

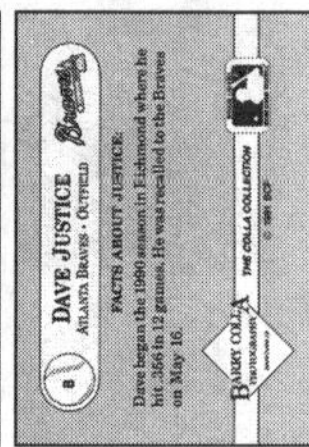

This 13-card standard size set features colorful photos of Dave Justice by noted photographer Barry Colla. The high gloss borderless color photos were packed in a full color collector's box. Only 15,000 sets were produced, with 24 sets per display carton. The first card of each set bears the registration number. In black lettering on a light gray background, the horizontally oriented backs feature facts about Justice.

	MINT	NRMT	EXC
COMPLETE SET (13)	10.00	4.50	1.25
COMMON CARD (1-12)	1.00	.45	.12
☐ 1 Dave Justice Bat on shoulder White jersey	1.00	.45	.12
☐ 2 Dave Justice Leaning on bat	1.00	.45	.12
☐ 3 Dave Justice Running in outfield	1.00	.45	.12
☐ 4 Dave Justice Throwing from the outfield	1.00	.45	.12
☐ 5 Dave Justice Bat over shoulder	1.00	.45	.12
☐ 6 Dave Justice Looking through batting cage	1.00	.45	.12
☐ 7 Dave Justice After ball thrown	1.00	.45	.12
☐ 8 Dave Justice Just before batting	1.00	.45	.12
☐ 9 Dave Justice Watching hit ball	1.00	.45	.12
☐ 10 Dave Justice Running to first	1.00	.45	.12
☐ 11 Dave Justice Warm-up exercises, Stretching	1.00	.45	.12
☐ 12 Dave Justice Bat on shoulder Squatting posture	1.00	.45	.12
☐ xx Title card Bat on shoulder Blue jersey	1.00	.45	.12

1991 Colla Postcards Sandberg

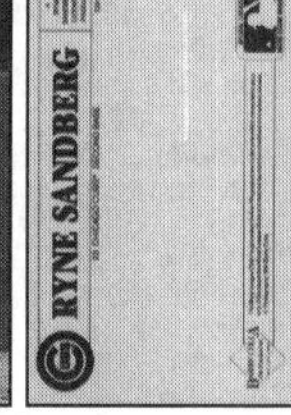

These postcards measure 3 1/2" by 5 1/2" and showcase Ryne Sandberg. The fronts feature color action or posed player shots in a postcard format. The typical postcard backs carry the player's name, position and the team name, along with the team logo.

	MINT	NRMT	EXC
COMPLETE SET (8)	7.50	3.40	.95
COMMON CARD (1-8)	1.00	.45	.12
☐ 1 Ryne Sandberg (Close-up shot, with cap)	1.00	.45	.12
☐ 2 Ryne Sandberg (Close-up shot, with helmet)	1.00	.45	.12
☐ 3 Ryne Sandberg (Action shot, batting)	1.00	.45	.12
☐ 4 Ryne Sandberg (Action shot, from left side)	1.00	.45	.12
☐ 5 Ryne Sandberg (Action shot, from right side)	1.00	.45	.12
☐ 6 Ryne Sandberg (Action shot, batting)	1.00	.45	.12
☐ 7 Ryne Sandberg (Action shot, catching the ball)	1.00	.45	.12
☐ 8 Ryne Sandberg	1.00	.45	.12

(Close-up shot, from the back)

1991 Colla Roberto Alomar

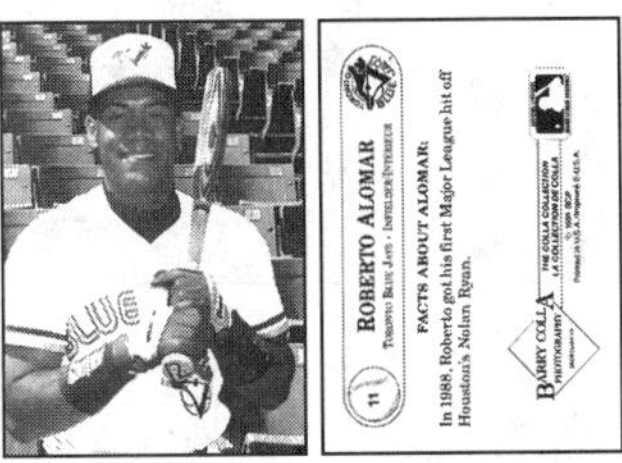

This 13-card standard size set features colorful photos of Roberto Alomar by noted photographer Barry Colla. The high gloss borderless color photos were packed in a full color collector's box. Only 7,500 sets were produced, with 24 sets per display carton. The first card of each set bears the registration number. In black lettering on a light gray background, the horizontally oriented backs feature facts about Alomar.

	MINT	NRMT	EXC
COMPLETE SET (13)	10.00	4.50	1.25
COMMON CARD (1-12)	1.00	.45	.12
☐ 1 Roberto Alomar Headshot	1.00	.45	.12
☐ 2 Roberto Alomar In mid-air at 2nd preparing to throw	1.00	.45	.12
☐ 3 Roberto Alomar In mid-air at 2nd throwing ball	1.00	.45	.12
☐ 4 Roberto Alomar Pose showing right shoulder	1.00	.45	.12
☐ 5 Roberto Alomar Pose showing left shoulder	1.00	.45	.12
☐ 6 Roberto Alomar Watching ball after hit	1.00	.45	.12
☐ 7 Roberto Alomar Follow through hands at waist	1.00	.45	.12
☐ 8 Roberto Alomar Headshot, bat on shoulder	1.00	.45	.12
☐ 9 Roberto Alomar Posed kneeling	1.00	.45	.12
☐ 10 Roberto Alomar Follow through hands at chest	1.00	.45	.12
☐ 11 Roberto Alomar Posed with bat on left shoulder	1.00	.45	.12
☐ 12 Roberto Alomar (Posed with left shoulder forward bat on right shoulder	1.00	.45	.12
☐ xx Roberto Alomar Posed with bat on right shoulder	1.00	.45	.12

1991 Colla Sandberg

This 13-card standard size set features colorful photos of Ryne Sandberg by noted photographer Barry Colla. The high gloss borderless color photos were packed in a full color collector's box. Only 15,000 sets were produced, with 24 sets per display carton. The first card of each set bears the registration number. In black lettering on a light gray background, the horizontally oriented backs feature facts about Ryne Sandberg.

	MINT	NRMT	EXC
COMPLETE SET (13)	10.00	4.50	1.25
COMMON CARD (1-12)	1.00	.45	.12
☐ 1 Ryne Sandberg (Follow-through, bat in motion)	1.00	.45	.12
☐ 2 Ryne Sandberg (Preparing to field blue uniform)	1.00	.45	.12
☐ 3 Ryne Sandberg (Awaiting throw)	1.00	.45	.12
☐ 4 Ryne Sandberg (Follow-Through facing left close up)	1.00	.45	.12
☐ 5 Ryne Sandberg (Holding bat behind back)	1.00	.45	.12
☐ 6 Ryne Sandberg (Pivoting at second)	1.00	.45	.12
☐ 7 Ryne Sandberg (Ready to throw)	1.00	.45	.12
☐ 8 Ryne Sandberg (Left profile shot)	1.00	.45	.12
☐ 9 Ryne Sandberg (Holding bat at waist)	1.00	.45	.12
☐ 10 Ryne Sandberg (Awaiting pitch)	1.00	.45	.12
☐ 11 Ryne Sandberg (Follow-through, bat at shoulders)	1.00	.45	.12
☐ 12 Ryne Sandberg (Batting Cage Pose)	1.00	.45	.12
☐ xx Ryne Sandberg (Header card)	1.00	.45	.12

1991 Colla Strawberry

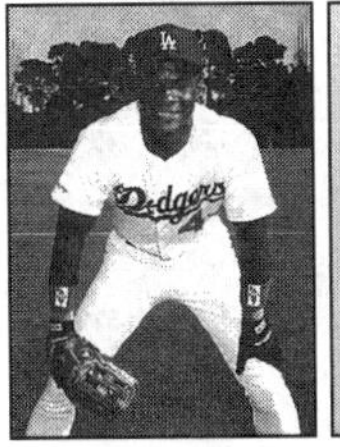

This 13-card standard size set features colorful photos of Darryl Strawberry by noted photographer Barry Colla. The high gloss borderless color photos were packed in a full color collector's box. Only 15,000 sets were produced, with 24 sets per display carton. The first card of each set bears the registration number. In black lettering on a light gray background, the horizontally oriented backs feature facts about Strawberry.

	MINT	NRMT	EXC
COMPLETE SET (13)	8.00	3.60	1.00
COMMON CARD (1-12)	.75	.35	.09
☐ 1 Darryl Strawberry (Posed follow through)	.75	.35	.09
☐ 2 Darryl Strawberry (Bat on shoulder)	.75	.35	.09
☐ 3 Darryl Strawberry (Posed with glove)	.75	.35	.09
☐ 4 Darryl Strawberry (Kneeling with bat)	.75	.35	.09
☐ 5 Darryl Strawberry (Head shot with flip-up sunglasses)	.75	.35	.09
☐ 6 Darryl Strawberry (Ready to run in base path)	.75	.35	.09
☐ 7 Darryl Strawberry (Awaiting fly ball)	.75	.35	.09
☐ 8 Darryl Strawberry (Head shot with batting helmet)	.75	.35	.09
☐ 9 Darryl Strawberry (Follow through after hit)	.75	.35	.09
☐ 10 Darryl Strawberry (Watching hit ball)	.75	.35	.09
☐ 11 Darryl Strawberry (Waiting for at bat)	.75	.35	.09
☐ 12 Darryl Strawberry (Running bases)	.75	.35	.09
☐ xx Title card (Two bats on shoulder)	.75	.35	.09

1992 Colla All-Stars Promos

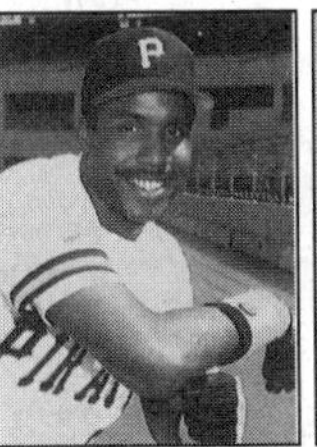

The 1992 Colla All-Stars promo set consists of 25 standard-size cards. The fronts feature full-bleed glossy color photos. The backs carry an advertisement for the cards and logos. Though the cards are unnumbered, they are listed below according to the numbering assigned to them on the checklist card. According to the checklist card, the set was issued July 14, 1992 and limited to 25,000 sets.

	MINT	NRMT	EXC
COMPLETE SET (24)	15.00	6.75	1.85
COMMON CARD (1-24)	.25	.11	.03
☐ 1 Mark McGwire	1.00	.45	.12
☐ 2 Will Clark	.60	.25	.07
☐ 3 Roberto Alomar	.60	.25	.07
☐ 4 Ryne Sandberg	1.25	.55	.16
☐ 5 Cal Ripken	2.50	1.10	.30
☐ 6 Ozzie Smith	1.00	.45	.12
☐ 7 Wade Boggs	.40	.18	.05
☐ 8 Terry Pendleton	.25	.11	.03
☐ 9 Kirby Puckett	1.25	.55	.16
☐ 10 Chuck Knoblauch	.50	.23	.06
☐ 11 Ken Griffey Jr.	3.00	1.35	.35
☐ 12 Joe Carter	.40	.18	.05
☐ 13 Sandy Alomar Jr.	.40	.18	.05
☐ 14 Benito Santiago	.25	.11	.03
☐ 15 Mike Mussina	1.00	.45	.12
☐ 16 Fred McGriff	.60	.25	.07
☐ 17 Dennis Eckersley	.40	.18	.05
☐ 18 Tony Gwynn	1.25	.55	.16
☐ 19 Roger Clemens	.75	.35	.09
☐ 20 Gary Sheffield	.60	.25	.07
☐ 21 Jose Canseco	.75	.35	.09
☐ 22 Barry Bonds	.75	.35	.09
☐ 23 Ivan Rodriguez	.75	.35	.09
☐ 24 Tony Fernandez	.25	.11	.03
☐ NNO Juan Guzman (Checklist)	.25	.11	.03

1992 Colla All-Star Game

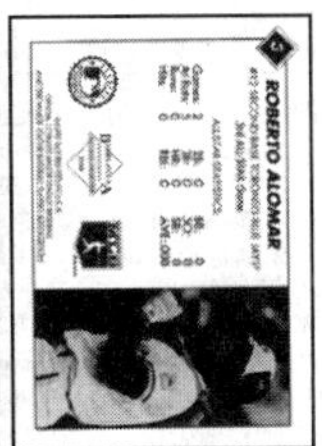

This 24-card standard-size set was made available at the 1992 All-Star game in San Diego. The cards feature 24 All-Stars from the National and American League. Randomly inserted throughout the sets were 200 numbered and autographed Roberto Alomar cards. The production run was limited to 25,000 sets, and the first card (McGwire) of each set bears the set serial number ("X of 25,000"). The fronts display full-bleed glossy color player photos. The All-Star Game logo and the player's name are superimposed across the bottom of the picture. The backs carry a close-up color photo and All-Star statistics. The cards are numbered in a diamond in the upper left corner.

	MINT	NRMT	EXC
COMPLETE SET (24)	12.50	5.50	1.55
COMMON CARD (1-24)	.25	.11	.03
☐ 1 Mark McGwire	1.00	.45	.12
☐ 2 Will Clark	.50	.23	.06
☐ 3 Roberto Alomar	.60	.25	.07
☐ 4 Ryne Sandberg	1.00	.45	.12
☐ 5 Cal Ripken	2.50	1.10	.30
☐ 6 Ozzie Smith	1.00	.45	.12
☐ 7 Wade Boggs	.50	.23	.06
☐ 8 Terry Pendleton	.25	.11	.03
☐ 9 Kirby Puckett	1.25	.55	.16
☐ 10 Chuck Knoblauch	.50	.23	.06
☐ 11 Ken Griffey Jr.	3.00	1.35	.35
☐ 12 Joe Carter	.40	.18	.05
☐ 13 Sandy Alomar Jr.	.40	.18	.05
☐ 14 Benito Santiago	.25	.11	.03
☐ 15 Mike Mussina	.60	.25	.07
☐ 16 Fred McGriff	.60	.25	.07
☐ 17 Dennis Eckersley	.40	.18	.05
☐ 18 Tony Gwynn	1.25	.55	.16
☐ 19 Roger Clemens	.60	.25	.07
☐ 20 Gary Sheffield	.60	.25	.07
☐ 21 Jose Canseco	.50	.23	.06
☐ 22 Barry Bonds	.75	.35	.09
☐ 23 Ivan Rodriguez	.75	.35	.09
☐ 24 Tony Fernandez	.25	.11	.03

1992 Colla Promos

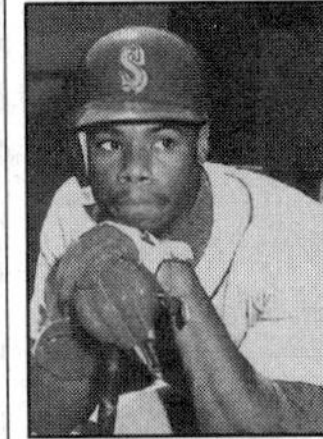

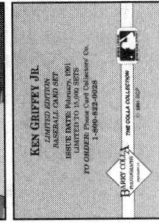

This 17-card standard-size set consists of promo cards to the various Barry Colla limited edition player sets. The cards feature full-bleed glossy color photos on their fronts. Except for the Thomas card, the backs are horizontally oriented. Some of the backs are gray while others are white. Each back gives the player's name, issue date, production quantity and a toll free phone number for ordering the set. The cards are unnumbered and checklisted below in alphabetical order.

	MINT	NRMT	EXC
COMPLETE SET (17)	40.00	18.00	5.00
COMMON CARD (1-15)	1.00	.45	.12
☐ 1A Roberto Alomar (English back)	3.00	1.35	.35
☐ 1B Roberto Alomar (French back)	5.00	2.20	.60
☐ 2 Jeff Bagwell (Bat on right shoulder, dark blue jersey)	2.50	1.10	.30
☐ 3 Barry Bonds	2.00	.90	.25
☐ 4 Jose Canseco	2.50	1.10	.30
☐ 5A Joe Carter (English back)	1.50	.70	.19
☐ 5B Joe Carter (French back)	3.00	1.35	.35
☐ 6 Will Clark	2.50	1.10	.30
☐ 7 Dwight Gooden	1.50	.70	.19
☐ 8 Ken Griffey Jr.	6.00	2.70	.75
☐ 9 Dave Justice	1.50	.70	.19
☐ 10 Kevin Maas	1.00	.45	.12
☐ 11 Don Mattingly	3.00	1.35	.35
☐ 12 Nolan Ryan (Pitching with arm extended behind body)	5.00	2.20	.60
☐ 13 Ryne Sandberg	3.00	1.35	.35
☐ 14 Darryl Strawberry	1.50	.70	.19
☐ 15 Frank Thomas (Leaning forward, right shoulder nearest camera)	6.00	2.70	.75

1992 Colla Bagwell

This 12-card standard-size set features colorful photos of Jeff Bagwell by noted sports photographer Barry Colla. Only 25,000 sets were produced, with 24 sets per display carton. Randomly inserted throughout the sets were 200 numbered and autographed Bagwell cards. There have been very few Bagwell autograph cards appearing in the secondary market, so no value is available for these cards. Also the set included an Allocation Rights card, which entitled the holder to purchase the Colla Rookie set. The high gloss borderless color photos were packed in a full color collector's box. The first card of each set bears the set serial number. In black lettering on a white background, the horizontally oriented backs feature notes about Bagwell and a baseball cartoon picture.

	MINT	NRMT	EXC
COMPLETE SET (12)	10.00	4.50	1.25
COMMON CARD (1-12)	1.00	.45	.12
☐ 1 Jeff Bagwell Front pose in white jersey with bat on shoulder	1.00	.45	.12
☐ 2 Jeff Bagwell Front pose, in shades with two bats on shoulder	1.00	.45	.12
☐ 3 Jeff Bagwell Defensive posture hands on knees	1.00	.45	.12
☐ 4 Jeff Bagwell Close-up photo in dark blue jersey with bat on shoulder	1.00	.45	.12
☐ 5 Jeff Bagwell Preparing to throw with shades on	1.00	.45	.12
☐ 6 Jeff Bagwell Follow through watching flight of ball bat beside body	1.00	.45	.12
☐ 7 Jeff Bagwell Follow through watching flight of ball bat behind body	1.00	.45	.12
☐ 8 Jeff Bagwell Posed action checking bat swing	1.00	.45	.12
☐ 9 Jeff Bagwell Pose from dugout forearms resting on bat	1.00	.45	.12
☐ 10 Jeff Bagwell Front pose holding bat at waist level	1.00	.45	.12
☐ 11 Jeff Bagwell Preparing to field ball	1.00	.45	.12
☐ 12 Jeff Bagwell Front pose with ball in glove	1.00	.45	.12

1992 Colla Gwynn

This 12-card standard size set features colorful photos of Tony Gwynn by noted photographer Barry Colla. The high gloss borderless color photos were packed in a full color collector's box. Only 7,500 sets were produced, with the first card of each set carrying the set number. The "92 The Colla Collection" icon appears in an upper corner and the player's name is printed toward the bottom of the picture. In light black lettering on white, the horizontal backs present biography (1), notes on Gwynn (2-11), or major league statistics (12) on the left portion and baseball cartoons on the right portion.

	MINT	NRMT	EXC
COMPLETE SET (12)	10.00	4.50	1.25
COMMON CARD (1-12)	1.00	.45	.12
☐ 1 Tony Gwynn Head and shoulders pose bat on left shoulder	1.00	.45	.12
☐ 2 Tony Gwynn Batting posture at plate awaiting pitch	1.00	.45	.12
☐ 3 Tony Gwynn Full body shot kneeling with forearm resting on bat	1.00	.45	.12
☐ 4 Tony Gwynn Shot from waist up with bat on shoulder	1.00	.45	.12
☐ 5 Tony Gwynn Full body shot from right side	1.00	.45	.12
☐ 6 Tony Gwynn Running to base	1.00	.45	.12
☐ 7 Tony Gwynn In dugout with shades raised	1.00	.45	.12
☐ 8 Tony Gwynn Carrying baseball equipment bag	1.00	.45	.12
☐ 9 Tony Gwynn Bent over at waist batting weight in hand	1.00	.45	.12
☐ 10 Tony Gwynn Outfield catch ball in glove	1.00	.45	.12
☐ 11 Tony Gwynn Front pose from waist up	1.00	.45	.12
☐ 12 Tony Gwynn Taking off toward first base bat extended behind	1.00	.45	.12

1992 Colla McGwire

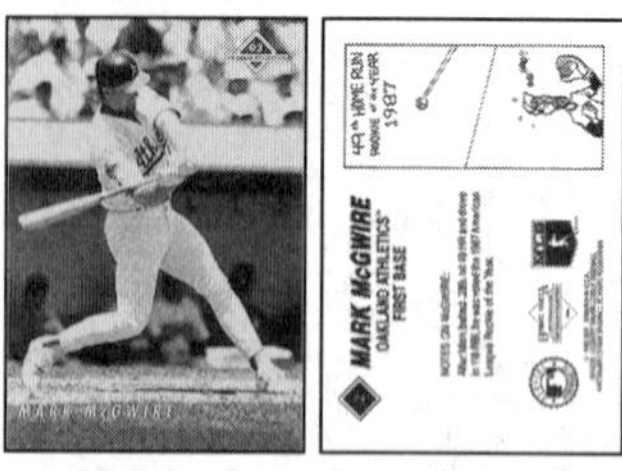

This 12-card standard-size set features colorful photos of Mark McGwire by noted sports photographer Barry Colla. Only 15,000 sets were produced, with 24 sets per display carton. Randomly inserted throughout the sets were 200 numbered and autographed McGwire cards. These autographed cards are rarely seen in the secondary market so no value can be assigned to them. The high gloss borderless color photos were packed in a full color collector's box. The first card of each set bears the set serial number. In black lettering on a white background, the horizontally oriented backs feature notes about McGwire and a baseball cartoon picture.

	MINT	NRMT	EXC
COMPLETE SET (12)	10.00	4.50	1.25
COMMON CARD (1-12)	1.00	.45	.12
☐ 1 Mark McGwire Posing without hat	1.00	.45	.12
☐ 2 Mark McGwire Swinging-unextended	1.00	.45	.12
☐ 3 Mark McGwire Preparing to field	1.00	.45	.12
☐ 4 Mark McGwire Leaving batter's box	1.00	.45	.12
☐ 5 Mark McGwire Watching flight of ball	1.00	.45	.12
☐ 6 Mark McGwire Glaring at umpire	1.00	.45	.12
☐ 7 Mark McGwire Sliding	1.00	.45	.12
☐ 8 Mark McGwire Front pose bat on shoulder	1.00	.45	.12
☐ 9 Mark McGwire Running to dugout	1.00	.45	.12
☐ 10 Mark McGwire Throwing	1.00	.45	.12
☐ 11 Mark McGwire Bat on shoulder in dugout	1.00	.45	.12
☐ 12 Mark McGwire Follow through	1.00	.45	.12

1992 Colla Ryan

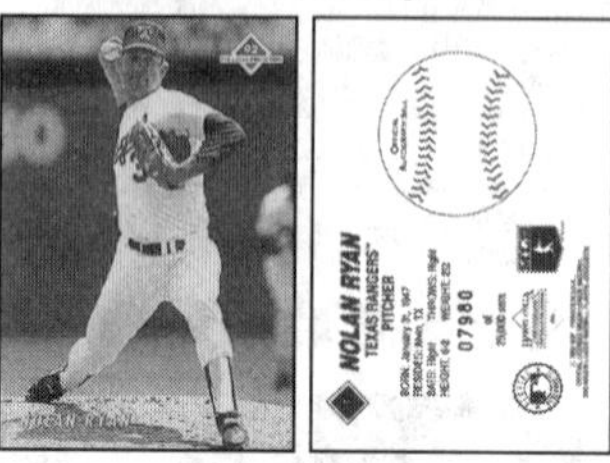

This 12-card standard-size set features colorful photos of Nolan Ryan by noted sports photographer Barry Colla. Only 25,000 sets were produced, with 24 sets per display carton. Randomly inserted throughout the sets were 200 numbered and autographed Ryan cards. These autographed cards are rarely seen; therefore, no market value can be determined. The high-gloss borderless color photos were packed in a full color collector's box. The first card of each set bears the set serial number. In black lettering on a white background, the horizontally oriented backs feature notes about Ryan and a baseball cartoon picture.

	MINT	NRMT	EXC
COMPLETE SET (12)	10.00	4.50	1.25
COMMON CARD (1-12)	1.00	.45	.12
☐ 1 Nolan Ryan Pitching ball behind head	1.00	.45	.12
☐ 2 Nolan Ryan Close-up photo from right side	1.00	.45	.12
☐ 3 Nolan Ryan Pitching just after release of ball	1.00	.45	.12
☐ 4 Nolan Ryan Close-up photo pitching with ball behind head	1.00	.45	.12
☐ 5 Nolan Ryan Sitting on grass, stretching	1.00	.45	.12
☐ 6 Nolan Ryan Wind up, high leg kick	1.00	.45	.12
☐ 7 Nolan Ryan Beginning of pitching motion ball in glove	1.00	.45	.12
☐ 8 Nolan Ryan Walking, staring at ground	1.00	.45	.12
☐ 9 Nolan Ryan Left side shot after release of ball	1.00	.45	.12
☐ 10 Nolan Ryan Throwing football	1.00	.45	.12
☐ 11 Nolan Ryan Close up photo wind up with leg cocked	1.00	.45	.12
☐ 12 Nolan Ryan Walking to batting cage	1.00	.45	.12

1992 Colla Thomas

This 12-card standard-size set features colorful photos of Frank Thomas by noted sports photographer Barry Colla. Only 25,000 sets were produced, with 24 sets per display carton. Randomly inserted throughout the sets were 200 numbered and autographed Frank Thomas cards. Since these autographed cards rarely appear in the secondary market, no value is assigned for these cards. Also the set included an Allocation Rights card, which entitled the holder to purchase the Colla Rookie set. The high gloss borderless color photos were packed in a full color collector's box. The first card of each set bears the set serial number. In black lettering on a white background, the horizontally oriented backs feature notes about Thomas and a baseball cartoon picture.

	MINT	NRMT	EXC
COMPLETE SET (12)	10.00	4.50	1.25
COMMON CARD (1-12)	1.00	.45	.12
☐ 1 Frank Thomas Front pose bat on shoulder	1.00	.45	.12
☐ 2 Frank Thomas Follow through watching flight of ball in black jersey	1.00	.45	.12
☐ 3 Frank Thomas Close-up photo sitting posture	1.00	.45	.12
☐ 4 Frank Thomas On deck lead bat on shoulder	1.00	.45	.12
☐ 5 Frank Thomas Eyeing pop-up into glove	1.00	.45	.12
☐ 6 Frank Thomas Up close with fans	1.00	.45	.12
☐ 7 Frank Thomas Running posture ball in right hand	1.00	.45	.12
☐ 8 Frank Thomas Watching flight of ball white jersey	1.00	.45	.12
☐ 9 Frank Thomas Front pose, kneeling	1.00	.45	.12
☐ 10 Frank Thomas Follow through right hand off bat	1.00	.45	.12
☐ 11 Frank Thomas Back and left shoulder shot glaring	1.00	.45	.12
☐ 12 Frank Thomas Front pose, in locker room	1.00	.45	.12

1993 Colla All-Star Game

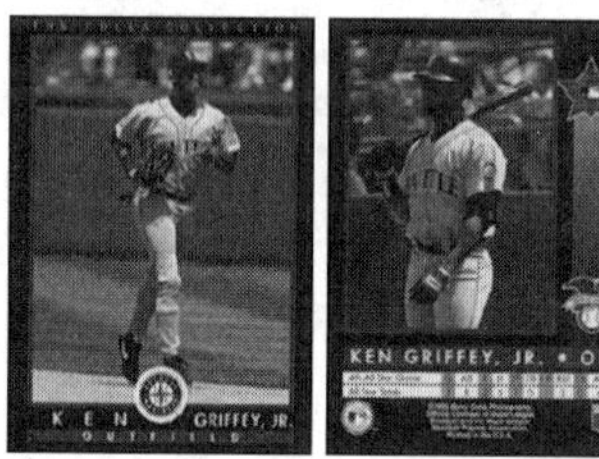

Issued by noted photographer Barry Colla, this 24-card boxed set was made available at the 1993 All-Star game in Baltimore. The standard-size cards feature 24 All-Stars from the National and American Leagues. The fronts display high-gloss, full-action photos framed by variously colored borders with a black outer border. The set's title, "The Colla Collection", appears at the top and the player's name, team logo, and position are printed at the bottom. The backs carry close-up color pictures on a black background with All-Star statistics appearing at the bottom.

	MINT	NRMT	EXC
COMPLETE SET (25)	17.50	8.00	2.20
COMMON CARD (1-24)	.25	.11	.03
☐ 1 Roberto Alomar	.75	.35	.09
☐ 2 Barry Bonds	1.00	.45	.12
☐ 3 Ken Griffey Jr.	4.00	1.80	.50
☐ 4 John Kruk	.40	.18	.05
☐ 5 Kirby Puckett	1.50	.70	.19
☐ 6 Darren Daulton	.40	.18	.05
☐ 7 Wade Boggs	1.00	.45	.12
☐ 8 Matt Williams	.50	.23	.06
☐ 9 Cal Ripken	3.00	1.35	.35
☐ 10 Ryne Sandberg	1.00	.45	.12
☐ 11 Ivan Rodriguez	1.00	.45	.12
☐ 12 Andy Van Slyke	.25	.11	.03
☐ 13 John Olerud	.25	.11	.03
☐ 14 Tom Glavine	.50	.23	.06
☐ 15 Juan Gonzalez	2.00	.90	.25
☐ 16 David Justice	.40	.18	.05
☐ 17 Mike Mussina	.75	.35	.09
☐ 18 Tony Gwynn	1.50	.70	.19
☐ 19 Joe Carter	.40	.18	.05
☐ 20 Barry Larkin	.50	.23	.06
☐ 21 Brian Harper	.25	.11	.03
☐ 22 Ozzie Smith	1.00	.45	.12
☐ 23 Mark McGwire	1.25	.55	.16
☐ 24 Mike Piazza	3.00	1.35	.35
☐ NNO Checklist Card	.25	.11	.03

1993 Colla Postcards Piazza

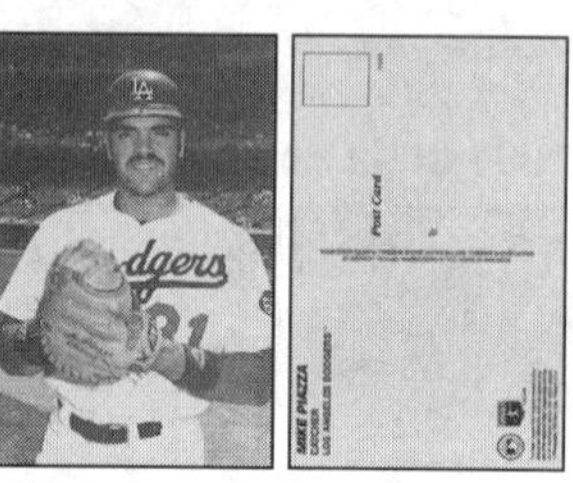

These postcards measure 3 1/2" by 5 1/2" and showcase Mike Piazza. The fronts feature color action or posed player shots in a postcard format. The typical postcard backs carry the player's name, position and the team name, along with the team logo.

	MINT	NRMT	EXC
COMPLETE SET (8)	7.50	3.40	.95
COMMON CARD (1-8)	1.00	.45	.12
☐ 1 Mike Piazza (Close-up shot)	1.00	.45	.12
☐ 2 Mike Piazza (Close-up shot, glove in left hand)	1.00	.45	.12
☐ 3 Mike Piazza (Action shot, batting, bat behind shoulders)	1.00	.45	.12
☐ 4 Mike Piazza (Batting, bat in left hand)	1.00	.45	.12
☐ 5 Mike Piazza (Close-up shot, bat on right shoulder)	1.00	.45	.12
☐ 6 Mike Piazza (Action shot, with catcher's gear)	1.00	.45	.12
☐ 7 Mike Piazza (Close-up shot, bat behind head)	1.00	.45	.12
☐ 8 Mike Piazza (Action shot, with catcher's gear, from the back)	1.00	.45	.12

1993 Colla Postcards Ripken Jr.

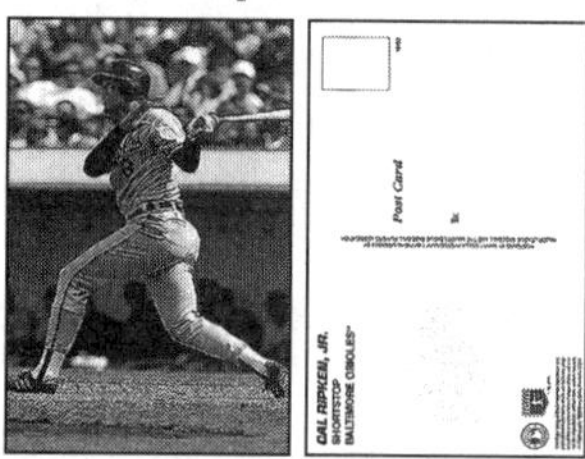

These postcards measure 3 1/2" by 5 1/2" and showcase Cal Ripken Jr. The fronts feature color action or posed player shots in a postcard format. The typical postcard backs carry the player's name, position and the team name, along with the team logo.

	MINT	NRMT	EXC
COMPLETE SET (7)	8.00	3.60	1.00
COMMON CARD (1-7)	1.25	.55	.16
☐ 1 Cal Ripken Jr. (Action shot, batting, bat in left hand)	1.25	.55	.16
☐ 2 Cal Ripken Jr. (Close-up shot, bat in both hands, orange jersey)	1.25	.55	.16
☐ 3 Cal Ripken Jr. (Action shot, catching the ball)	1.25	.55	.16
☐ 4 Cal Ripken Jr. (Action shot, batting, bat in front of body)	1.25	.55	.16
☐ 5 Cal Ripken Jr. (Close-up shot, bat in both hands, gray uniform)	1.25	.55	.16
☐ 6 Cal Ripken Jr. (Action shot, batting, bat behind body)	1.25	.55	.16
☐ 7 Cak Ripken Jr. (Close-up shot, white jersey)	1.25	.55	.16

1990 Collect-A-Books

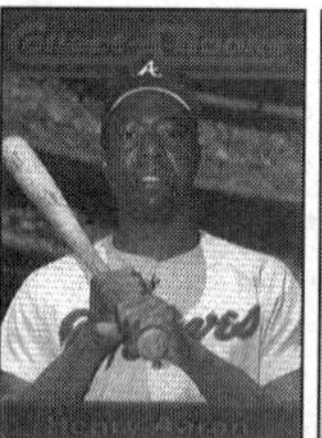

The 1990 Collect-A-Books set was issued by CMC (Collectors Marketing Corp.) in three different sets (boxes) of 12 players apiece. The sets (boxes) were distinguishable by color, red, yellow, or green. The Collect-A-Books were in the style of the 1970 Topps Comic Book inserts but were much more profesionally made. The cards all fit into a nine-pocket sheet (since they are standard size) even though they can be expanded. The set contains an interesting mixture of retired and current players.

	MINT	NRMT	EXC
COMPLETE SET (36)	7.00	3.10	.85
COMMON CARD (1-36)	.10	.05	.01
□ 1 Bo Jackson	.20	.09	.03
□ 2 Dwight Gooden	.20	.09	.03
□ 3 Ken Griffey Jr.	1.50	.70	.19
□ 4 Will Clark	.30	.14	.04
□ 5 Ozzie Smith	.75	.35	.09
□ 6 Orel Hershiser	.20	.09	.03
□ 7 Ruben Sierra	.20	.09	.03
□ 8 Rickey Henderson	.30	.14	.04
□ 9 Robin Yount	.30	.14	.04
□ 10 Babe Ruth	1.50	.70	.19
□ 11 Ernie Banks	.30	.14	.04
□ 12 Carl Yastrzemski	.30	.14	.04
□ 13 Don Mattingly	1.00	.45	.12
□ 14 Nolan Ryan	1.25	.55	.16
□ 15 Jerome Walton	.10	.05	.01
□ 16 Kevin Mitchell	.10	.05	.01
□ 17 Tony Gwynn	1.00	.45	.12
□ 18 Dave Stewart	.10	.05	.01
□ 19 Roger Clemens	.50	.23	.06
□ 20 Darryl Strawberry	.20	.09	.03
□ 21 George Brett	.75	.35	.09
□ 22 Hank Aaron	1.00	.45	.12
□ 23 Ted Williams	1.00	.45	.12
□ 24 Warren Spahn	.30	.14	.04
□ 25 Jose Canseco	.50	.23	.06
□ 26 Wade Boggs	.50	.23	.06
□ 27 Jim Abbott	.20	.09	.03
□ 28 Eric Davis	.20	.09	.03
□ 29 Ryne Sandberg	.75	.35	.09
□ 30 Bret Saberhagen	.20	.09	.03
□ 31 Mark Grace	.40	.18	.05
□ 32 Gregg Olson	.10	.05	.01
□ 33 Kirby Puckett	.50	.23	.06
□ 34 Lou Gehrig	1.25	.55	.16
□ 35 Roberto Clemente	1.25	.55	.16
□ 36 Bob Feller	.30	.14	.04

1991 Collect-A-Books

This 36-card set, which measures the standard size, was issued by Impel for the second consecutive year. Collectors Marketing Corp., the 1990 Collect-a-Book producer, was a division within the Impel Corporation. This 1991 set was issued under Impel's Line Drive brand. Each book consists of eight pages and fits into a standard size plastic sheet. The set features 27 active stars and nine famous retired stars. An action shot of the player is pictured on the first two pages. The next four pages has textual information broken down into biographical information, two pages of more detailed personal information and a page of statistics. The inside back cover has a quote from the player pictured while the back cover has an attractive drawing of the player. Unlike the 1990 issue, the Collect-A-Books were issued in random packs.

	MINT	NRMT	EXC
COMPLETE SET (36)	8.00	3.60	1.00
COMMON CARD (1-36)	.10	.05	.01
□ 1 Roger Clemens	.75	.35	.09
□ 2 Cal Ripken	1.25	.55	.16
□ 3 Nolan Ryan	1.25	.55	.16
□ 4 Ken Griffey Jr.	1.50	.70	.19
□ 5 Bob Welch	.10	.05	.01
□ 6 Kevin Mitchell	.10	.05	.01
□ 7 Kirby Puckett	.75	.35	.09
□ 8 Len Dykstra	.20	.09	.03
□ 9 Ben McDonald	.20	.09	.03
□ 10 Don Drysdale	.30	.14	.04
□ 11 Lou Brock	.30	.14	.04
□ 12 Ralph Kiner	.30	.14	.04
□ 13 Jose Canseco	.50	.23	.06
□ 14 Cecil Fielder	.20	.09	.03
□ 15 Ryne Sandberg	.60	.25	.07
□ 16 Wade Boggs	.40	.18	.05
□ 17 Dwight Gooden	.20	.09	.03
□ 18 Ramon Martinez	.30	.14	.04
□ 19 Tony Gwynn	.75	.35	.09
□ 20 Mark Grace	.50	.23	.06
□ 21 Kevin Maas	.10	.05	.01
□ 22 Thurman Munson	.30	.14	.04
□ 23 Bob Gibson	.30	.14	.04
□ 24 Bill Mazeroski	.30	.14	.04
□ 25 Rickey Henderson	.50	.23	.06
□ 26 Barry Bonds	.40	.18	.05
□ 27 Jose Rijo	.10	.05	.01
□ 28 George Brett	.60	.25	.07
□ 29 Doug Drabek	.10	.05	.01
□ 30 Matt Williams	.40	.18	.05
□ 31 Barry Larkin	.40	.18	.05
□ 32 Dave Stewart	.10	.05	.01
□ 33 Dave Justice	.30	.14	.04
□ 34 Harmon Killebrew	.30	.14	.04
□ 35 Yogi Berra	.30	.14	.04
□ 36 Billy Williams	.30	.14	.04

1994 Collector's Choice

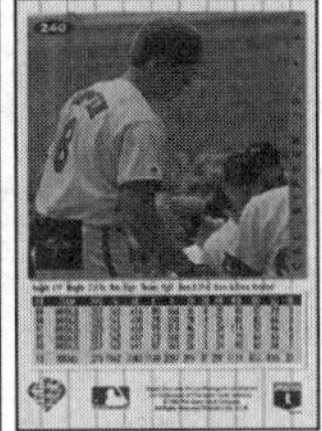

Issued by Upper Deck, this 670 standard-size card set was issued in two series of 320 and 350. Cards were issued in foil-wrapped 12-card packs and factory sets (of which contained five Gold Signature cards for a total of 675 cards). Basic card fronts feature color player action photos with white borders that are highlighted by vertical gray pinstripes. Subsets include Rookie Class (1-20), First Draft Picks (21-30), Top Performers (306-315), Up Close (631-640) and Future Foundation (641-650). Notable Rookie Cards include Michael Jordan, Derrek Lee and Alex Rodriguez.

	MINT	NRMT	EXC
COMPLETE SET (670)	30.00	13.50	3.70
COMPLETE FACT.SET (675)	30.00	13.50	3.70
COMPLETE SERIES 1 (320)	12.00	5.50	1.50
COMPLETE SERIES 2 (350)	18.00	8.00	2.20
COMMON CARD (1-670)	.05	.02	.01
□ 1 Rich Becker	.15	.07	.02
□ 2 Greg Blosser	.05	.02	.01
□ 3 Midre Cummings	.05	.02	.01
□ 4 Carlos Delgado	.30	.14	.04
□ 5 Steve Dreyer	.05	.02	.01
□ 6 Carl Everett	.05	.02	.01
□ 7 Cliff Floyd	.30	.14	.04
□ 8 Alex Gonzalez	.15	.07	.02
□ 9 Shawn Green	.15	.07	.02
□ 10 Butch Huskey	.15	.07	.02
□ 11 Mark Hutton	.05	.02	.01
□ 12 Miguel Jimenez	.05	.02	.01
□ 13 Steve Karsay	.05	.02	.01
□ 14 Marc Newfield	.15	.07	.02
□ 15 Luis Ortiz	.05	.02	.01
□ 16 Manny Ramirez	.60	.25	.07
□ 17 Johnny Ruffin	.05	.02	.01
□ 18 Scott Stahoviak	.05	.02	.01
□ 19 Salomon Torres	.05	.02	.01
□ 20 Gabe White	.05	.02	.01
□ 21 Brian Anderson	.15	.07	.02
□ 22 Wayne Gomes	.15	.07	.02
□ 23 Jeff Granger	.15	.07	.02
□ 24 Steve Soderstrom	.15	.07	.02
□ 25 Trot Nixon	.30	.14	.04
□ 26 Kirk Presley	.30	.14	.04
□ 27 Matt Brunson	.15	.07	.02
□ 28 Brooks Kieschnick	.40	.18	.05
□ 29 Billy Wagner	.60	.25	.07
□ 30 Matt Drews	.60	.25	.07
□ 31 Kurt Abbott	.15	.07	.02
□ 32 Luis Alicea	.05	.02	.01
□ 33 Roberto Alomar	.40	.18	.05
□ 34 Sandy Alomar Jr.	.15	.07	.02
□ 35 Moises Alou	.15	.07	.02
□ 36 Wilson Alvarez	.15	.07	.02
□ 37 Rich Amaral	.05	.02	.01
□ 38 Eric Anthony	.05	.02	.01
□ 39 Luis Aquino	.05	.02	.01
□ 40 Jack Armstrong	.05	.02	.01
□ 41 Rene Arocha	.05	.02	.01
□ 42 Rich Aude	.15	.07	.02
□ 43 Brad Ausmus	.05	.02	.01
□ 44 Steve Avery	.15	.07	.02
□ 45 Bob Ayrault	.05	.02	.01
□ 46 Willie Banks	.05	.02	.01
□ 47 Bret Barberie	.05	.02	.01
□ 48 Kim Batiste	.05	.02	.01
□ 49 Rod Beck	.15	.07	.02
□ 50 Jason Bere	.15	.07	.02
□ 51 Sean Berry	.05	.02	.01
□ 52 Dante Bichette	.30	.14	.04
□ 53 Jeff Blauser	.05	.02	.01
□ 54 Mike Blowers	.05	.02	.01
□ 55 Tim Bogar	.05	.02	.01
□ 56 Tom Bolton	.05	.02	.01
□ 57 Ricky Bones	.05	.02	.01
□ 58 Bobby Bonilla	.15	.07	.02
□ 59 Bret Boone	.15	.07	.02
□ 60 Pat Borders	.05	.02	.01
□ 61 Mike Bordick	.05	.02	.01
□ 62 Daryl Boston	.05	.02	.01
□ 63 Ryan Bowen	.05	.02	.01
□ 64 Jeff Branson	.05	.02	.01
□ 65 George Brett	.75	.35	.09
□ 66 Steve Buechele	.05	.02	.01
□ 67 Dave Burba	.05	.02	.01
□ 68 John Burkett	.05	.02	.01
□ 69 Jeromy Burnitz	.05	.02	.01
□ 70 Brett Butler	.15	.07	.02
□ 71 Rob Butler	.05	.02	.01
□ 72 Ken Caminiti	.30	.14	.04
□ 73 Cris Carpenter	.05	.02	.01
□ 74 Vinny Castilla	.30	.14	.04
□ 75 Andujar Cedeno	.05	.02	.01
□ 76 Wes Chamberlain	.05	.02	.01
□ 77 Archi Cianfrocco	.05	.02	.01
□ 78 Dave Clark	.05	.02	.01
□ 79 Jerald Clark	.05	.02	.01
□ 80 Royce Clayton	.15	.07	.02
□ 81 David Cone	.15	.07	.02
□ 82 Jeff Conine	.15	.07	.02
□ 83 Steve Cooke	.05	.02	.01
□ 84 Scott Cooper	.05	.02	.01
□ 85 Joey Cora	.05	.02	.01
□ 86 Tim Costo	.05	.02	.01
□ 87 Chad Curtis	.05	.02	.01
□ 88 Ron Darling	.05	.02	.01
□ 89 Danny Darwin	.05	.02	.01
□ 90 Rob Deer	.05	.02	.01
□ 91 Jim Deshaies	.05	.02	.01
□ 92 Delino DeShields	.05	.02	.01
□ 93 Rob Dibble	.05	.02	.01
□ 94 Gary DiSarcina	.05	.02	.01
□ 95 Doug Drabek	.05	.02	.01
□ 96 Scott Erickson	.05	.02	.01
□ 97 Rikkert Faneyte	.05	.02	.01
□ 98 Jeff Fassero	.05	.02	.01
□ 99 Alex Fernandez	.15	.07	.02
□ 100 Cecil Fielder	.15	.07	.02
□ 101 Dave Fleming	.05	.02	.01
□ 102 Darrin Fletcher	.05	.02	.01
□ 103 Scott Fletcher	.05	.02	.01
□ 104 Mike Gallego	.05	.02	.01
□ 105 Carlos Garcia	.05	.02	.01
□ 106 Jeff Gardner	.05	.02	.01
□ 107 Brent Gates	.05	.02	.01
□ 108 Benji Gil	.05	.02	.01
□ 109 Bernard Gilkey	.15	.07	.02
□ 110 Chris Gomez	.05	.02	.01
□ 111 Luis Gonzalez	.05	.02	.01
□ 112 Tom Gordon	.05	.02	.01
□ 113 Jim Gott	.05	.02	.01
□ 114 Mark Grace	.30	.14	.04
□ 115 Tommy Greene	.05	.02	.01
□ 116 Willie Greene	.15	.07	.02
□ 117 Ken Griffey Jr.	2.00	.90	.25
□ 118 Bill Gullickson	.05	.02	.01
□ 119 Ricky Gutierrez	.05	.02	.01
□ 120 Juan Guzman	.15	.07	.02
□ 121 Chris Gwynn	.05	.02	.01
□ 122 Tony Gwynn	.75	.35	.09
□ 123 Jeffrey Hammonds	.15	.07	.02
□ 124 Erik Hanson	.05	.02	.01
□ 125 Gene Harris	.05	.02	.01
□ 126 Greg W. Harris	.05	.02	.01
□ 127 Bryan Harvey	.05	.02	.01
□ 128 Billy Hatcher	.05	.02	.01
□ 129 Hilly Hathaway	.05	.02	.01
□ 130 Charlie Hayes	.05	.02	.01
□ 131 Rickey Henderson	.30	.14	.04
□ 132 Mike Henneman	.05	.02	.01
□ 133 Pat Hentgen	.15	.07	.02
□ 134 Roberto Hernandez	.15	.07	.02
□ 135 Orel Hershiser	.15	.07	.02
□ 136 Phil Hiatt	.05	.02	.01
□ 137 Glenallen Hill	.05	.02	.01
□ 138 Ken Hill	.05	.02	.01
□ 139 Eric HIllman	.05	.02	.01
□ 140 Chris Hoiles	.05	.02	.01
□ 141 Dave Hollins	.05	.02	.01
□ 142 David Hulse	.05	.02	.01
□ 143 Todd Hundley	.15	.07	.02
□ 144 Pete Incaviglia	.05	.02	.01
□ 145 Danny Jackson	.05	.02	.01
□ 146 John Jaha	.15	.07	.02
□ 147 Domingo Jean	.05	.02	.01
□ 148 Gregg Jefferies	.30	.14	.04
□ 149 Reggie Jefferson	.15	.07	.02
□ 150 Lance Johnson	.15	.07	.02
□ 151 Bobby Jones	.15	.07	.02
□ 152 Chipper Jones	1.50	.70	.19
□ 153 Todd Jones	.05	.02	.01
□ 154 Brian Jordan	.30	.14	.04
□ 155 Wally Joyner	.15	.07	.02
□ 156 David Justice	.30	.14	.04
□ 157 Ron Karkovice	.05	.02	.01
□ 158 Eric Karros	.15	.07	.02
□ 159 Jeff Kent	.05	.02	.01
□ 160 Jimmy Key	.15	.07	.02
□ 161 Mark Kiefer	.05	.02	.01
□ 162 Darryl Kile	.05	.02	.01
□ 163 Jeff King	.15	.07	.02
□ 164 Wayne Kirby	.05	.02	.01
□ 165 Ryan Klesko	.40	.18	.05
□ 166 Chuck Knoblauch	.30	.14	.04
□ 167 Chad Kreuter	.05	.02	.01
□ 168 John Kruk	.15	.07	.02
□ 169 Mark Langston	.15	.07	.02
□ 170 Mike Lansing	.15	.07	.02
□ 171 Barry Larkin	.30	.14	.04
□ 172 Manuel Lee	.05	.02	.01
□ 173 Phil Leftwich	.05	.02	.01
□ 174 Darren Lewis	.05	.02	.01
□ 175 Derek Lilliquist	.05	.02	.01
□ 176 Jose Lind	.05	.02	.01
□ 177 Albie Lopez	.15	.07	.02
□ 178 Javier Lopez	.30	.14	.04
□ 179 Torey Lovullo	.05	.02	.01
□ 180 Scott Lydy	.05	.02	.01
□ 181 Mike Macfarlane	.05	.02	.01
□ 182 Shane Mack	.05	.02	.01
□ 183 Greg Maddux	1.25	.55	.16
□ 184 Dave Magadan	.05	.02	.01
□ 185 Joe Magrane	.05	.02	.01
□ 186 Kirk Manwaring	.05	.02	.01
□ 187 Al Martin	.05	.02	.01
□ 188 Pedro A. Martinez	.05	.02	.01
□ 189 Pedro J. Martinez	.30	.14	.04
□ 190 Ramon Martinez	.15	.07	.02
□ 191 Tino Martinez	.15	.07	.02
□ 192 Don Mattingly	1.00	.45	.12
□ 193 Derrick May	.05	.02	.01
□ 194 David McCarty	.05	.02	.01
□ 195 Ben McDonald	.05	.02	.01
□ 196 Roger McDowell	.05	.02	.01
□ 197 Fred McGriff UER (Stats on back have 73 stolen bases for 1989; should be 7)	.30	.14	.04
□ 198 Mark McLemore	.05	.02	.01
□ 199 Greg McMichael	.05	.02	.01
□ 200 Jeff McNeely	.05	.02	.01
□ 201 Brian McRae	.15	.07	.02
□ 202 Pat Meares	.05	.02	.01
□ 203 Roberto Mejia	.05	.02	.01
□ 204 Orlando Merced	.15	.07	.02
□ 205 Jose Mesa	.15	.07	.02
□ 206 Blas Minor	.05	.02	.01
□ 207 Angel Miranda	.05	.02	.01
□ 208 Paul Molitor	.40	.18	.05
□ 209 Raul Mondesi	.30	.14	.04
□ 210 Jeff Montgomery	.15	.07	.02
□ 211 Mickey Morandini	.05	.02	.01
□ 212 Mike Morgan	.05	.02	.01
□ 213 Jamie Moyer	.05	.02	.01
□ 214 Bobby Munoz	.05	.02	.01
□ 215 Troy Neel	.05	.02	.01
□ 216 Dave Nilsson	.15	.07	.02
□ 217 John O'Donoghue	.05	.02	.01
□ 218 Paul O'Neill	.15	.07	.02
□ 219 Jose Offerman	.05	.02	.01
□ 220 Joe Oliver	.05	.02	.01
□ 221 Greg Olson	.05	.02	.01
□ 222 Donovan Osborne	.05	.02	.01
□ 223 J. Owens	.05	.02	.01
□ 224 Mike Pagliarulo	.05	.02	.01
□ 225 Craig Paquette	.05	.02	.01
□ 226 Roger Pavlik	.05	.02	.01
□ 227 Brad Pennington	.05	.02	.01
□ 228 Eduardo Perez	.05	.02	.01
□ 229 Mike Perez	.05	.02	.01
□ 230 Tony Phillips	.15	.07	.02
□ 231 Hipolito Pichardo	.05	.02	.01
□ 232 Phil Plantier	.05	.02	.01
□ 233 Curtis Pride	.15	.07	.02
□ 234 Tim Pugh	.05	.02	.01
□ 235 Scott Radinsky	.05	.02	.01
□ 236 Pat Rapp	.05	.02	.01
□ 237 Kevin Reimer	.05	.02	.01
□ 238 Armando Reynoso	.05	.02	.01
□ 239 Jose Rijo	.05	.02	.01
□ 240 Cal Ripken	1.50	.70	.19
□ 241 Kevin Roberson	.05	.02	.01
□ 242 Kenny Rogers	.05	.02	.01
□ 243 Kevin Rogers	.05	.02	.01
□ 244 Mel Rojas	.05	.02	.01
□ 245 John Roper	.05	.02	.01
□ 246 Kirk Rueter	.05	.02	.01
□ 247 Scott Ruffcorn	.05	.02	.01
□ 248 Ken Ryan	.05	.02	.01
□ 249 Nolan Ryan	1.50	.70	.19
□ 250 Bret Saberhagen	.15	.07	.02
□ 251 Tim Salmon	.30	.14	.04
□ 252 Reggie Sanders	.15	.07	.02
□ 253 Curt Schilling	.05	.02	.01
□ 254 David Segui	.05	.02	.01
□ 255 Aaron Sele	.15	.07	.02
□ 256 Scott Servais	.05	.02	.01
□ 257 Gary Sheffield	.30	.14	.04
□ 258 Ruben Sierra	.15	.07	.02
□ 259 Don Slaught	.05	.02	.01
□ 260 Lee Smith	.15	.07	.02
□ 261 Cory Snyder	.05	.02	.01
□ 262 Paul Sorrento	.05	.02	.01
□ 263 Sammy Sosa	.30	.14	.04
□ 264 Bill Spiers	.05	.02	.01
□ 265 Mike Stanley	.05	.02	.01
□ 266 Dave Staton	.05	.02	.01
□ 267 Terry Steinbach	.15	.07	.02
□ 268 Kevin Stocker	.05	.02	.01
□ 269 Todd Stottlemyre	.05	.02	.01

☐ 270 Doug Strange .05 .02 .01
☐ 271 Bill Swift .05 .02 .01
☐ 272 Kevin Tapani .05 .02 .01
☐ 273 Tony Tarasco .05 .02 .01
☐ 274 Julian Tavarez .15 .07 .02
☐ 275 Mickey Tettleton .05 .02 .01
☐ 276 Ryan Thompson .05 .02 .01
☐ 277 Chris Turner .05 .02 .01
☐ 278 John Valentin .15 .07 .02
☐ 279 Todd Van Poppel .05 .02 .01
☐ 280 Andy Van Slyke .15 .07 .02
☐ 281 Mo Vaughn .50 .23 .06
☐ 282 Robin Ventura .15 .07 .02
☐ 283 Frank Viola .05 .02 .01
☐ 284 Jose Vizcaino .05 .02 .01
☐ 285 Omar Vizquel .15 .07 .02
☐ 286 Larry Walker .30 .14 .04
☐ 287 Duane Ward .05 .02 .01
☐ 288 Allen Watson .05 .02 .01
☐ 289 Bill Wegman .05 .02 .01
☐ 290 Turk Wendell .05 .02 .01
☐ 291 Lou Whitaker .15 .07 .02
☐ 292 Devon White .05 .02 .01
☐ 293 Rondell White .30 .14 .04
☐ 294 Mark Whiten .05 .02 .01
☐ 295 Darrel Whitmore .05 .02 .01
☐ 296 Bob Wickman .05 .02 .01
☐ 297 Rick Wilkins .05 .02 .01
☐ 298 Bernie Williams .40 .18 .05
☐ 299 Matt Williams .30 .14 .04
☐ 300 Woody Williams .05 .02 .01
☐ 301 Nigel Wilson .05 .02 .01
☐ 302 Dave Winfield .30 .14 .04
☐ 303 Anthony Young .05 .02 .01
☐ 304 Eric Young .15 .07 .02
☐ 305 Todd Zeile .05 .02 .01
☐ 306 Jack McDowell TP .15 .07 .02
John Burkett
Tom Glavine
☐ 307 Randy Johnson TP .30 .14 .04
☐ 308 Randy Myers TP .05 .02 .01
☐ 309 Jack McDowell TP .05 .02 .01
☐ 310 Mike Piazza TP .60 .25 .07
☐ 311 Barry Bonds TP .30 .14 .04
☐ 312 Andres Galarraga TP .30 .14 .04
☐ 313 Juan Gonzalez TP .50 .23 .06
Barry Bonds
☐ 314 Albert Belle TP .40 .18 .05
☐ 315 Kenny Lofton TP .30 .14 .04
☐ 316 Barry Bonds CL .30 .14 .04
☐ 317 Ken Griffey Jr. CL .50 .23 .06
☐ 318 Mike Piazza CL .30 .14 .04
☐ 319 Kirby Puckett CL .30 .14 .04
☐ 320 Nolan Ryan CL .50 .23 .06
☐ 321 Roberto Alomar CL .30 .14 .04
☐ 322 Roger Clemens CL .30 .14 .04
☐ 323 Juan Gonzalez CL .30 .14 .04
☐ 324 Ken Griffey Jr. CL .50 .23 .06
☐ 325 David Justice CL .15 .07 .02
☐ 326 John Kruk CL .05 .02 .01
☐ 327 Frank Thomas CL .50 .23 .06
☐ 328 Tim Salmon TC .30 .14 .04
☐ 329 Jeff Bagwell TC .40 .18 .05
☐ 330 Mark McGwire TC .30 .14 .04
☐ 331 Roberto Alomar TC .30 .14 .04
☐ 332 David Justice TC .15 .07 .02
☐ 333 Pat Listach TC .05 .02 .01
☐ 334 Ozzie Smith TC .30 .14 .04
☐ 335 Ryne Sandberg TC .30 .14 .04
☐ 336 Mike Piazza TC .60 .25 .07
☐ 337 Cliff Floyd TC .15 .07 .02
☐ 338 Barry Bonds TC .30 .14 .04
☐ 339 Albert Belle TC .40 .18 .05
☐ 340 Ken Griffey Jr. TC 1.00 .45 .12
☐ 341 Gary Sheffield TC .30 .14 .04
☐ 342 Dwight Gooden TC .15 .07 .02
☐ 343 Cal Ripken TC .75 .35 .09
☐ 344 Tony Gwynn TC .40 .18 .05
☐ 345 Lenny Dykstra TC .05 .02 .01
☐ 346 Andy Van Slyke TC .05 .02 .01
☐ 347 Juan Gonzalez TC .50 .23 .06
☐ 348 Roger Clemens TC .30 .14 .04
☐ 349 Barry Larkin TC .30 .14 .04
☐ 350 Andres Galarraga TC .30 .14 .04
☐ 351 Kevin Appier TC .15 .07 .02
☐ 352 Cecil Fielder TC .15 .07 .02
☐ 353 Kirby Puckett TC .30 .14 .04
☐ 354 Frank Thomas TC 1.00 .45 .12
☐ 355 Don Mattingly TC .50 .23 .06
☐ 356 Bo Jackson .15 .07 .02
☐ 357 Randy Johnson .30 .14 .04
☐ 358 Darren Daulton .15 .07 .02
☐ 359 Charlie Hough .05 .02 .01
☐ 360 Andres Galarraga .30 .14 .04
☐ 361 Mike Felder .05 .02 .01
☐ 362 Chris Hammond .05 .02 .01
☐ 363 Shawon Dunston .05 .02 .01
☐ 364 Junior Felix .05 .02 .01
☐ 365 Ray Lankford .15 .07 .02
☐ 366 Darryl Strawberry .15 .07 .02
☐ 367 Dave Magadan .05 .02 .01
☐ 368 Gregg Olson .05 .02 .01
☐ 369 Lenny Dykstra .15 .07 .02
☐ 370 Darrin Jackson .05 .02 .01
☐ 371 Dave Stewart .15 .07 .02
☐ 372 Terry Pendleton .15 .07 .02
☐ 373 Arthur Rhodes .05 .02 .01
☐ 374 Benito Santiago .05 .02 .01
☐ 375 Travis Fryman .15 .07 .02
☐ 376 Scott Brosius .05 .02 .01
☐ 377 Stan Belinda .05 .02 .01
☐ 378 Derek Parks .05 .02 .01
☐ 379 Kevin Seitzer .05 .02 .01
☐ 380 Wade Boggs .30 .14 .04
☐ 381 Wally Whitehurst .05 .02 .01
☐ 382 Scott Leius .05 .02 .01
☐ 383 Danny Tartabull .05 .02 .01
☐ 384 Harold Reynolds .05 .02 .01
☐ 385 Tim Raines .30 .14 .04
☐ 386 Darryl Hamilton .05 .02 .01
☐ 387 Felix Fermin .05 .02 .01
☐ 388 Jim Eisenreich .05 .02 .01
☐ 389 Kurt Abbott .15 .07 .02
☐ 390 Kevin Appier .15 .07 .02
☐ 391 Chris Bosio .05 .02 .01
☐ 392 Randy Tomlin .05 .02 .01
☐ 393 Bob Hamelin .05 .02 .01
☐ 394 Kevin Gross .05 .02 .01
☐ 395 Wil Cordero .15 .07 .02
☐ 396 Joe Girardi .05 .02 .01
☐ 397 Orestes Destrade .05 .02 .01
☐ 398 Chris Haney .05 .02 .01
☐ 399 Xavier Hernandez .05 .02 .01
☐ 400 Mike Piazza 1.25 .55 .16
☐ 401 Alex Arias .05 .02 .01
☐ 402 Tom Candiotti .05 .02 .01
☐ 403 Kirk Gibson .15 .07 .02
☐ 404 Chuck Carr .05 .02 .01
☐ 405 Brady Anderson .30 .14 .04
☐ 406 Greg Gagne .05 .02 .01
☐ 407 Bruce Ruffin .05 .02 .01
☐ 408 Scott Hemond .05 .02 .01
☐ 409 Keith Miller .05 .02 .01
☐ 410 John Wetteland .15 .07 .02
☐ 411 Eric Anthony .05 .02 .01
☐ 412 Andre Dawson .15 .07 .02
☐ 413 Doug Henry .05 .02 .01
☐ 414 John Franco .05 .02 .01
☐ 415 Julio Franco .15 .07 .02
☐ 416 Dave Hansen .05 .02 .01
☐ 417 Mike Harkey .05 .02 .01
☐ 418 Jack Armstrong .05 .02 .01
☐ 419 Joe Orsulak .05 .02 .01
☐ 420 John Smoltz .30 .14 .04
☐ 421 Scott Livingstone .05 .02 .01
☐ 422 Darren Holmes .05 .02 .01
☐ 423 Ed Sprague .15 .07 .02
☐ 424 Jay Buhner .30 .14 .04
☐ 425 Kirby Puckett .75 .35 .09
☐ 426 Phil Clark .05 .02 .01
☐ 427 Anthony Young .05 .02 .01
☐ 428 Reggie Jefferson .15 .07 .02
☐ 429 Mariano Duncan .05 .02 .01
☐ 430 Tom Glavine .30 .14 .04
☐ 431 Dave Henderson .05 .02 .01
☐ 432 Melido Perez .05 .02 .01
☐ 433 Paul Wagner .05 .02 .01
☐ 434 Tim Worrell .05 .02 .01
☐ 435 Ozzie Guillen .05 .02 .01
☐ 436 Mike Butcher .05 .02 .01
☐ 437 Jim Deshaies .05 .02 .01
☐ 438 Kevin Young .05 .02 .01
☐ 439 Tom Browning .05 .02 .01
☐ 440 Mike Greenwell .05 .02 .01
☐ 441 Mike Stanton .05 .02 .01
☐ 442 John Doherty .05 .02 .01
☐ 443 John Dopson .05 .02 .01
☐ 444 Carlos Baerga .15 .07 .02
☐ 445 Jack McDowell .15 .07 .02
☐ 446 Kent Mercker .05 .02 .01
☐ 447 Ricky Jordan .05 .02 .01
☐ 448 Jerry Browne .05 .02 .01
☐ 449 Fernando Vina .05 .02 .01
☐ 450 Jim Abbott .05 .02 .01
☐ 451 Teddy Higuera .05 .02 .01
☐ 452 Tim Naehring .05 .02 .01
☐ 453 Jim Leyritz .05 .02 .01
☐ 454 Frank Castillo .05 .02 .01
☐ 455 Joe Carter .15 .07 .02
☐ 456 Craig Biggio .15 .07 .02
☐ 457 Geronimo Pena .05 .02 .01
☐ 458 Alejandro Pena .05 .02 .01
☐ 459 Mike Moore .05 .02 .01
☐ 460 Randy Myers .05 .02 .01
☐ 461 Greg Myers .05 .02 .01
☐ 462 Greg Hibbard .05 .02 .01
☐ 463 Jose Guzman .05 .02 .01
☐ 464 Tom Pagnozzi .05 .02 .01
☐ 465 Marquis Grissom .15 .07 .02
☐ 466 Tim Wallach .05 .02 .01
☐ 467 Joe Grahe .05 .02 .01
☐ 468 Bob Tewksbury .05 .02 .01
☐ 469 B.J. Surhoff .05 .02 .01
☐ 470 Kevin Mitchell .15 .07 .02
☐ 471 Bobby Witt .05 .02 .01
☐ 472 Milt Thompson .05 .02 .01
☐ 473 John Smiley .05 .02 .01
☐ 474 Alan Trammell .15 .07 .02
☐ 475 Mike Mussina .40 .18 .05
☐ 476 Rick Aguilera .05 .02 .01
☐ 477 Jose Valentin .15 .07 .02
☐ 478 Harold Baines .15 .07 .02
☐ 479 Bip Roberts .05 .02 .01
☐ 480 Edgar Martinez .15 .07 .02
☐ 481 Rheal Cormier .05 .02 .01
☐ 482 Hal Morris .05 .02 .01
☐ 483 Pat Kelly .05 .02 .01
☐ 484 Roberto Kelly .05 .02 .01
☐ 485 Chris Sabo .05 .02 .01
☐ 486 Kent Hrbek .15 .07 .02
☐ 487 Scott Kamieniecki .05 .02 .01
☐ 488 Walt Weiss .05 .02 .01
☐ 489 Karl Rhodes .05 .02 .01
☐ 490 Derek Bell .15 .07 .02
☐ 491 Chili Davis .15 .07 .02
☐ 492 Brian Harper .05 .02 .01
☐ 493 Felix Jose .05 .02 .01
☐ 494 Trevor Hoffman .15 .07 .02
☐ 495 Dennis Eckersley .15 .07 .02
☐ 496 Pedro Astacio .05 .02 .01
☐ 497 Jay Bell .15 .07 .02
☐ 498 Randy Velarde .05 .02 .01
☐ 499 David Wells .05 .02 .01
☐ 500 Frank Thomas 2.00 .90 .25
☐ 501 Mark Lemke .05 .02 .01
☐ 502 Mike Devereaux .05 .02 .01
☐ 503 Chuck McElroy .05 .02 .01
☐ 504 Luis Polonia .05 .02 .01
☐ 505 Damion Easley .05 .02 .01
☐ 506 Greg A. Harris .05 .02 .01
☐ 507 Chris James .05 .02 .01
☐ 508 Terry Mulholland .05 .02 .01
☐ 509 Pete Smith .05 .02 .01
☐ 510 Rickey Henderson .30 .14 .04
☐ 511 Sid Fernandez .05 .02 .01
☐ 512 Al Leiter .15 .07 .02
☐ 513 Doug Jones .05 .02 .01
☐ 514 Steve Farr .05 .02 .01
☐ 515 Chuck Finley .05 .02 .01
☐ 516 Bobby Thigpen .05 .02 .01
☐ 517 Jim Edmonds .40 .18 .05
☐ 518 Graeme Lloyd .05 .02 .01
☐ 519 Dwight Gooden .15 .07 .02
☐ 520 Pat Listach .05 .02 .01
☐ 521 Kevin Bass .05 .02 .01
☐ 522 Willie Banks .05 .02 .01
☐ 523 Steve Finley .30 .14 .04
☐ 524 Delino DeShields .05 .02 .01
☐ 525 Mark McGwire .60 .25 .07
☐ 526 Greg Swindell .05 .02 .01
☐ 527 Chris Nabholz .05 .02 .01
☐ 528 Scott Sanders .05 .02 .01
☐ 529 David Segui .05 .02 .01
☐ 530 Howard Johnson .05 .02 .01
☐ 531 Jaime Navarro .05 .02 .01
☐ 532 Jose Vizcaino .05 .02 .01
☐ 533 Mark Lewis .05 .02 .01
☐ 534 Pete Harnisch .05 .02 .01
☐ 535 Robby Thompson .05 .02 .01
☐ 536 Marcus Moore .05 .02 .01
☐ 537 Kevin Brown .15 .07 .02
☐ 538 Mark Clark .05 .02 .01
☐ 539 Sterling Hitchcock .15 .07 .02
☐ 540 Will Clark .30 .14 .04
☐ 541 Denis Boucher .05 .02 .01
☐ 542 Jack Morris .15 .07 .02
☐ 543 Pedro Munoz .05 .02 .01
☐ 544 Bret Boone .15 .07 .02
☐ 545 Ozzie Smith .50 .23 .06
☐ 546 Dennis Martinez .15 .07 .02
☐ 547 Dan Wilson .15 .07 .02
☐ 548 Rick Sutcliffe .05 .02 .01
☐ 549 Kevin McReynolds .05 .02 .01
☐ 550 Roger Clemens .40 .18 .05
☐ 551 Todd Benzinger .05 .02 .01
☐ 552 Bill Haselman .05 .02 .01
☐ 553 Bobby Munoz .05 .02 .01
☐ 554 Ellis Burks .15 .07 .02
☐ 555 Ryne Sandberg .50 .23 .06
☐ 556 Lee Smith .15 .07 .02
☐ 557 Danny Bautista .05 .02 .01
☐ 558 Rey Sanchez .05 .02 .01
☐ 559 Norm Charlton .05 .02 .01
☐ 560 Jose Canseco .30 .14 .04
☐ 561 Tim Belcher .05 .02 .01
☐ 562 Denny Neagle .15 .07 .02
☐ 563 Eric Davis .15 .07 .02
☐ 564 Jody Reed .05 .02 .01
☐ 565 Kenny Lofton .60 .25 .07
☐ 566 Gary Gaetti .15 .07 .02
☐ 567 Todd Worrell .05 .02 .01
☐ 568 Mark Portugal .05 .02 .01
☐ 569 Dick Schofield .05 .02 .01
☐ 570 Andy Benes .15 .07 .02
☐ 571 Zane Smith .05 .02 .01
☐ 572 Bobby Ayala .05 .02 .01
☐ 573 Chip Hale .05 .02 .01
☐ 574 Bob Welch .05 .02 .01
☐ 575 Deion Sanders .30 .14 .04
☐ 576 Dave Nied .05 .02 .01
☐ 577 Pat Mahomes .05 .02 .01
☐ 578 Charles Nagy .15 .07 .02
☐ 579 Otis Nixon .05 .02 .01
☐ 580 Dean Palmer .15 .07 .02
☐ 581 Roberto Petagine .15 .07 .02
☐ 582 Dwight Smith .05 .02 .01
☐ 583 Jeff Russell .05 .02 .01
☐ 584 Mark Dewey .05 .02 .01
☐ 585 Greg Vaughn .30 .14 .04
☐ 586 Brian Hunter .05 .02 .01
☐ 587 Willie McGee .05 .02 .01
☐ 588 Pedro J. Martinez .30 .14 .04
☐ 589 Roger Salkeld .05 .02 .01
☐ 590 Jeff Bagwell .75 .35 .09
☐ 591 Spike Owen .05 .02 .01
☐ 592 Jeff Reardon .15 .07 .02
☐ 593 Erik Pappas .05 .02 .01
☐ 594 Brian Williams .05 .02 .01
☐ 595 Eddie Murray .50 .23 .06
☐ 596 Henry Rodriguez .15 .07 .02
☐ 597 Erik Hanson .05 .02 .01
☐ 598 Stan Javier .05 .02 .01
☐ 599 Mitch Williams .05 .02 .01
☐ 600 John Olerud .05 .02 .01
☐ 601 Vince Coleman .05 .02 .01
☐ 602 Damon Berryhill .05 .02 .01
☐ 603 Tom Brunansky .05 .02 .01
☐ 604 Robb Nen .15 .07 .02
☐ 605 Rafael Palmeiro .30 .14 .04
☐ 606 Cal Eldred .05 .02 .01
☐ 607 Jeff Brantley .05 .02 .01
☐ 608 Alan Mills .05 .02 .01
☐ 609 Jeff Nelson .05 .02 .01
☐ 610 Barry Bonds .50 .23 .06
☐ 611 Carlos Pulido .05 .02 .01
☐ 612 Tim Hyers .05 .02 .01
☐ 613 Steve Howe .05 .02 .01
☐ 614 Brian Turang .05 .02 .01
☐ 615 Leo Gomez .05 .02 .01
☐ 616 Jesse Orosco .05 .02 .01
☐ 617 Dan Pasqua .05 .02 .01
☐ 618 Marvin Freeman .05 .02 .01
☐ 619 Tony Fernandez .05 .02 .01
☐ 620 Albert Belle .75 .35 .09
☐ 621 Eddie Taubensee .05 .02 .01
☐ 622 Mike Jackson .05 .02 .01
☐ 623 Jose Bautista .05 .02 .01
☐ 624 Jim Thome .50 .23 .06
☐ 625 Ivan Rodriguez .50 .23 .06
☐ 626 Ben Rivera .05 .02 .01
☐ 627 Dave Valle .05 .02 .01
☐ 628 Tom Henke .05 .02 .01
☐ 629 Omar Vizquel .15 .07 .02
☐ 630 Juan Gonzalez 1.00 .45 .12
☐ 631 Roberto Alomar UP .30 .14 .04
☐ 632 Barry Bonds UP .30 .14 .04
☐ 633 Juan Gonzalez UP .50 .23 .06
☐ 634 Ken Griffey Jr. UP 1.00 .45 .12
☐ 635 Michael Jordan UP 4.00 1.80 .50
☐ 636 David Justice UP .15 .07 .02
☐ 637 Mike Piazza UP .60 .25 .07
☐ 638 Kirby Puckett UP .30 .14 .04
☐ 639 Tim Salmon UP .30 .14 .04
☐ 640 Frank Thomas UP 1.00 .45 .12
☐ 641 Alan Benes FF .75 .35 .09
☐ 642 Johnny Damon FF .30 .14 .04
☐ 643 Brad Fullmer FF .50 .23 .06
☐ 644 Derek Jeter FF 1.50 .70 .19
☐ 645 Derrek Lee FF 1.25 .55 .16
☐ 646 Alex Ochoa FF .15 .07 .02
☐ 647 Alex Rodriguez FF 6.00 2.70 .75
☐ 648 Jose Silva FF .15 .07 .02
☐ 649 Terrell Wade FF .40 .18 .05
☐ 650 Preston Wilson FF .15 .07 .02
☐ 651 Shane Andrews .15 .07 .02
☐ 652 James Baldwin .30 .14 .04
☐ 653 Ricky Bottalico .30 .14 .04
☐ 654 Tavo Alvarez .05 .02 .01
☐ 655 Donnie Elliott .05 .02 .01
☐ 656 Joey Eischen .05 .02 .01
☐ 657 Jason Giambi .50 .23 .06
☐ 658 Todd Hollandsworth .50 .23 .06
☐ 659 Brian L. Hunter .30 .14 .04
☐ 660 Charles Johnson .30 .14 .04
☐ 661 Michael Jordan 6.00 2.70 .75
☐ 662 Jeff Juden .05 .02 .01
☐ 663 Mike Kelly .05 .02 .01
☐ 664 James Mouton .15 .07 .02
☐ 665 Ray Holbert .05 .02 .01
☐ 666 Pokey Reese .15 .07 .02
☐ 667 Ruben Santana .05 .02 .01
☐ 668 Paul Spoljaric .05 .02 .01
☐ 669 Luis Lopez .05 .02 .01
☐ 670 Matt Walbeck .05 .02 .01

1994 Collector's Choice Gold Signature

This 670-card Gold Signature set is a parallel to the basic Collector's Choice issue. These cards were randomly inserted into first and second series packs at a rate of one in 36. Gold cards were also issued five per factory set. These cards are identical to the basic issue except for gold foil fronts and a facsimile gold foil player's signature. Some subset cards feature borderless designs (unlike the basic player cards), thus their corresponding borderless Gold Foil Signature cards differ only by the gold foil replica autograph. The Jeffrey Hammonds card has the signature of Orioles General Manager Roland Hemond.

	MINT	NRMT	EXC
COMPLETE SET (670)	2400.00	1100.00	300.00
COMPLETE SERIES 1 (320)	1200.00	550.00	150.00

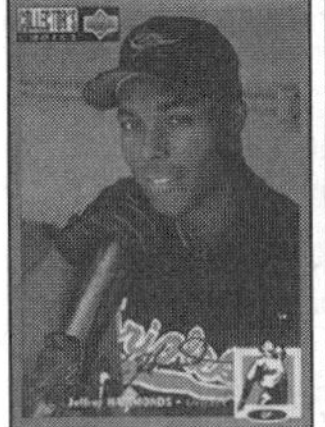

COMPLETE SERIES 2 (350)	1200.00	550.00	150.00
COMMON CARD (1-670)	1.50	.70	.19
*STARS: 20X TO 40X BASIC CARDS..			
*YOUNG STARS: 15X TO 30X BASIC CARDS			

1994 Collector's Choice Silver Signature

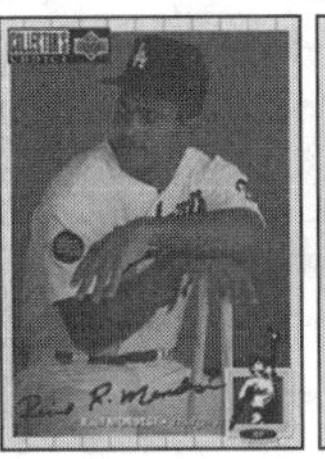

This 670-card set is a parallel to the basic Collector's Choice set. One card was inserted into every first and second series pack. Silver cards were also inserted at different rates in other pack forms. Each Silver Foil Signature card is identical in design to its corresponding regular issue card except for the silver borders and silver replica autograph. As with the gold set, the Jeffrey Hammonds card has the signature of Orioles General Manager Roland Hemond.

	MINT	NRMT	EXC
COMPLETE SET (670)	200.00	90.00	25.00
COMPLETE SERIES 1 (320)	90.00	40.00	11.00
COMPLETE SERIES 2 (350)	110.00	50.00	14.00
COMMON CARD (1-670)	.10	.05	.01
*STARS: 2.5X to 5X BASIC CARDS			
*YOUNG STARS: 1.5X to 3X BASIC CARDS			

1994 Collector's Choice Home Run All-Stars

This 15-card standard-size set served as the eighth place prize in the Crash the Game contest, which was a promotion in both series of Collector's Choice. The series 1 expiration was May 18, 1994; series 2 was Oct. 31, 1994. Horizontal fronts feature holographic images of the player that breaks through a brick wall. A small color photo of the player appears at left or right. The backs, outlined with bricks, features a small photo and text that appears over a stadium background. The cards are numbered with an "HA" prefix.

	MINT	NRMT	EXC
COMPLETE SET (8)	4.00	1.80	.50
COMMON CARD (HA1-HA8)	.25	.11	.03
□ HA1 Juan Gonzalez	1.50	.70	.19
□ HA2 Ken Griffey Jr.	3.00	1.35	.35
□ HA3 Barry Bonds	.75	.35	.09
□ HA4 Bobby Bonilla	.25	.11	.03
□ HA5 Cecil Fielder UER	.50	.23	.06
(Card number is HA4)			
□ HA6 Albert Belle	1.25	.55	.16
□ HA7 David Justice	.50	.23	.06
□ HA8 Mike Piazza	2.00	.90	.25

1994 Collector's Choice Team vs. Team

Issued one per second series pack, these 15 foldout, scratch-off game cards feature one team's lineup against the other. Various prizes were available through these game cards. The most plentiful was the eighth place Home Run All-Stars hologram set. Prizes were redeemable through October 31, 1994. Scratch-off rules and two small player photos are on the front with complete rules and provisions on the back. The cards fold out to expose the game portion. Cards that are scratched are half the values below.

	MINT	NRMT	EXC
COMPLETE SET (15)	5.00	2.20	.60
COMMON FOLDOUT (1-15)	.25	.11	.03
□ 1 Roberto Alomar	1.00	.45	.12
Frank Thomas			
□ 2 Barry Bonds	1.00	.45	.12
Ken Griffey Jr.			
□ 3 Roger Clemens	.50	.23	.06
Don Mattingly			
□ 4 Lenny Dykstra	.25	.11	.03
David Justice			
□ 5 Andres Galarraga	.40	.18	.05
Tony Gwynn			
□ 6 Dwight Gooden	.40	.18	.05
Gary Sheffield			
□ 7 Ken Griffey Jr.	1.00	.45	.12
Juan Gonzalez			
□ 8 Barry Larkin	.40	.18	.05
Jeff Bagwell			
□ 9 Pat Listach	.25	.11	.03
Albert Belle			
□ 10 Mark McGwire	.40	.18	.05
Tim Salmon			
□ 11 Mike Piazza	.60	.25	.07
Barry Bonds			
□ 12 Kirby Puckett	.40	.18	.05
Brian McRae			
□ 13 Cal Ripken	.75	.35	.09
Cecil Fielder			
□ 14 Ryne Sandberg	.50	.23	.06
Ozzie Smith			
□ 15 Andy Van Slyke	.25	.11	.03
Cliff Floyd			

1995 Collector's Choice

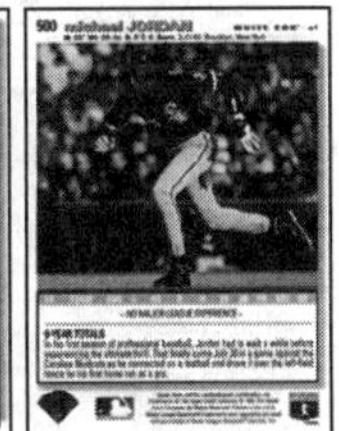

This set contains 530 standard-size cards issued in 12-card foil hobby and retail packs for a suggested price of 99 cents. The fronts have a color photo with a white border and the player's last name at the bottom in his team's color. The backs have an action photo at the top with statistics and information at the bottom with a silver Upper Deck hologram below that. Subsets featured are Rookie Class (1-27), Future Foundation (28-45), Best of the '90s (51-65) and What's the Call? (86-90). Key Rookie Cards in this set include Karim Garcia and Hideo Nomo. The 55-card Trade set represents the cards a collector received when the five randomly inserted trade cards were redeemed. They are numbered in continuation of the regular Collector's Choice cards but have a "T" suffix. The cards numbered 542-552 were also issued as a bonus to dealers who ordered collector's choice factory sets. The trade cards offer expired on February 1, 1996.

	MINT	NRMT	EXC
COMPLETE SET (530)	20.00	9.00	2.50
COMPLETE FACT.SET (545)	30.00	13.50	3.70
COMMON CARD (1-530)	.05	.02	.01
COMPLETE TRADE SET (55)	10.00	4.50	1.25
COMMON TRADE (531-585)	.10	.05	.01
COMMON TRADE DP (542-552)	.05	.02	.01
COMP.TRADE EXCH.SET (5)	4.00	1.80	.50
COMMON TRD.EXCH. (TC1-TC5)	1.00	.45	.12
□ 1 Charles Johnson	.15	.07	.02
□ 2 Scott Ruffcorn	.05	.02	.01
□ 3 Ray Durham	.15	.07	.02
□ 4 Armando Benitez	.05	.02	.01
□ 5 Alex Rodriguez	2.50	1.10	.30
□ 6 Julian Tavarez	.05	.02	.01
□ 7 Chad Ogea	.05	.02	.01
□ 8 Quilvio Veras	.05	.02	.01
□ 9 Phil Nevin	.05	.02	.01
□ 10 Michael Tucker	.15	.07	.02
□ 11 Mark Thompson	.15	.07	.02
□ 12 Rod Henderson	.05	.02	.01
□ 13 Andrew Lorraine	.15	.07	.02
□ 14 Joe Randa	.05	.02	.01
□ 15 Derek Jeter	1.25	.55	.16
□ 16 Tony Clark	.50	.23	.06
□ 17 Juan Castillo	.05	.02	.01
□ 18 Mark Acre	.05	.02	.01
□ 19 Orlando Miller	.05	.02	.01
□ 20 Paul Wilson	.30	.14	.04
□ 21 John Mabry	.30	.14	.04
□ 22 Garey Ingram	.05	.02	.01
□ 23 Garret Anderson	.15	.07	.02
□ 24 Dave Stevens	.05	.02	.01
□ 25 Dustin Hermanson	.15	.07	.02
□ 26 Paul Shuey	.05	.02	.01
□ 27 J.R. Phillips	.05	.02	.01
□ 28 Ruben Rivera FF	.60	.25	.07
□ 29 Nomar Garciaparra FF	1.25	.55	.16
□ 30 John Wasdin FF	.15	.07	.02
□ 31 Jim Pittsley FF	.30	.14	.04
□ 32 Scott Elarton FF	.40	.18	.05
□ 33 Raul Casanova FF	.50	.23	.06
□ 34 Todd Greene FF	.15	.07	.02
□ 35 Bill Pulsipher FF	.15	.07	.02
□ 36 Trey Beamon FF	.15	.07	.02
□ 37 Curtis Goodwin FF	.15	.07	.02
□ 38 Doug Million FF	.30	.14	.04
□ 39 Karim Garcia FF	2.00	.90	.25
□ 40 Ben Grieve FF	1.00	.45	.12
□ 41 Mark Farris FF	.15	.07	.02
□ 42 Juan Acevedo FF	.05	.02	.01
□ 43 C.J. Nitkowski FF	.15	.07	.02
□ 44 Travis Miller FF	.15	.07	.02
□ 45 Reid Ryan FF	.30	.14	.04
□ 46 Nolan Ryan	1.25	.55	.16
□ 47 Robin Yount	.30	.14	.04
□ 48 Ryne Sandberg	.40	.18	.05
□ 49 George Brett	.50	.23	.06
□ 50 Mike Schmidt	.40	.18	.05
□ 51 Cecil Fielder B90	.15	.07	.02
□ 52 Nolan Ryan B90	.60	.25	.07
□ 53 Rickey Henderson B90	.15	.07	.02
□ 54 George Brett B90	.40	.18	.05
Robin Yount			
Dave Winfield			
□ 55 Sid Bream B90	.05	.02	.01
□ 56 Carlos Baerga B90	.15	.07	.02
□ 57 Lee Smith B90	.15	.07	.02
□ 58 Mark Whiten B90	.05	.02	.01
□ 59 Joe Carter B90	.15	.07	.02
□ 60 Barry Bonds B90	.30	.14	.04
□ 61 Tony Gwynn B90	.40	.18	.05
□ 62 Ken Griffey Jr. B90	1.00	.45	.12
□ 63 Greg Maddux B90	.60	.25	.07
□ 64 Frank Thomas B90	1.00	.45	.12
□ 65 Dennis Martinez B90	.05	.02	.01
Kenny Rogers			
□ 66 David Cone	.15	.07	.02
□ 67 Greg Maddux	1.25	.55	.16
□ 68 Jimmy Key	.15	.07	.02
□ 69 Fred McGriff	.30	.14	.04
□ 70 Ken Griffey Jr.	2.00	.90	.25
□ 71 Matt Williams	.30	.14	.04
□ 72 Paul O'Neill	.15	.07	.02
□ 73 Tony Gwynn	.75	.35	.09
□ 74 Randy Johnson	.30	.14	.04
□ 75 Frank Thomas	2.00	.90	.25
□ 76 Jeff Bagwell	.75	.35	.09
□ 77 Kirby Puckett	.75	.35	.09
□ 78 Bob Hamelin	.05	.02	.01
□ 79 Raul Mondesi	.30	.14	.04
□ 80 Mike Piazza	1.25	.55	.16
□ 81 Kenny Lofton	.50	.23	.06
□ 82 Barry Bonds	.50	.23	.06
□ 83 Albert Belle	.75	.35	.09
□ 84 Juan Gonzalez	1.00	.45	.12
□ 85 Cal Ripken Jr.	1.50	.70	.19
□ 86 Barry Bonds WC	.30	.14	.04
□ 87 Mike Piazza WC	.60	.25	.07
□ 88 Ken Griffey Jr. WC	1.00	.45	.12
□ 89 Frank Thomas WC	1.00	.45	.12
□ 90 Juan Gonzalez WC	.50	.23	.06
□ 91 Jorge Fabregas	.05	.02	.01
□ 92 J.T. Snow	.15	.07	.02
□ 93 Spike Owen	.05	.02	.01
□ 94 Eduardo Perez	.05	.02	.01
□ 95 Bo Jackson	.15	.07	.02
□ 96 Damion Easley	.05	.02	.01
□ 97 Gary DiSarcina	.05	.02	.01
□ 98 Jim Edmonds	.30	.14	.04
□ 99 Chad Curtis	.05	.02	.01
□ 100 Tim Salmon	.30	.14	.04
□ 101 Chili Davis	.15	.07	.02
□ 102 Chuck Finley	.15	.07	.02
□ 103 Mark Langston	.05	.02	.01
□ 104 Brian Anderson	.05	.02	.01
□ 105 Lee Smith	.15	.07	.02
□ 106 Phil Leftwich	.05	.02	.01
□ 107 Chris Donnels	.05	.02	.01
□ 108 John Hudek	.05	.02	.01
□ 109 Craig Biggio	.15	.07	.02
□ 110 Luis Gonzalez	.05	.02	.01
□ 111 Brian L. Hunter	.15	.07	.02
□ 112 James Mouton	.05	.02	.01
□ 113 Scott Servais	.05	.02	.01
□ 114 Tony Eusebio	.05	.02	.01
□ 115 Derek Bell	.15	.07	.02
□ 116 Doug Drabek	.05	.02	.01
□ 117 Shane Reynolds	.15	.07	.02
□ 118 Darryl Kile	.05	.02	.01
□ 119 Greg Swindell	.05	.02	.01
□ 120 Phil Plantier	.05	.02	.01
□ 121 Todd Jones	.05	.02	.01
□ 122 Steve Ontiveros	.05	.02	.01
□ 123 Bobby Witt	.05	.02	.01
□ 124 Brent Gates	.05	.02	.01
□ 125 Rickey Henderson	.30	.14	.04
□ 126 Scott Brosius	.05	.02	.01
□ 127 Mike Bordick	.05	.02	.01
□ 128 Fausto Cruz	.05	.02	.01
□ 129 Stan Javier	.05	.02	.01
□ 130 Mark McGwire	.60	.25	.07
□ 131 Geronimo Berroa	.05	.02	.01
□ 132 Terry Steinbach	.15	.07	.02
□ 133 Steve Karsay	.05	.02	.01
□ 134 Dennis Eckersley	.15	.07	.02
□ 135 Ruben Sierra	.15	.07	.02
□ 136 Ron Darling	.05	.02	.01
□ 137 Todd Van Poppel	.05	.02	.01
□ 138 Alex Gonzalez	.15	.07	.02
□ 139 John Olerud	.05	.02	.01
□ 140 Roberto Alomar	.40	.18	.05
□ 141 Darren Hall	.05	.02	.01
□ 142 Ed Sprague	.15	.07	.02
□ 143 Devon White	.15	.07	.02
□ 144 Shawn Green	.15	.07	.02
□ 145 Paul Molitor	.40	.18	.05
□ 146 Pat Borders	.05	.02	.01
□ 147 Carlos Delgado	.15	.07	.02
□ 148 Juan Guzman	.15	.07	.02
□ 149 Pat Hentgen	.15	.07	.02
□ 150 Joe Carter	.15	.07	.02
□ 151 Dave Stewart	.15	.07	.02
□ 152 Todd Stottlemyre	.05	.02	.01
□ 153 Dick Schofield	.05	.02	.01
□ 154 Chipper Jones	1.25	.55	.16
□ 155 Ryan Klesko	.30	.14	.04
□ 156 David Justice	.30	.14	.04
□ 157 Mike Kelly	.05	.02	.01
□ 158 Roberto Kelly	.05	.02	.01
□ 159 Tony Tarasco	.05	.02	.01
□ 160 Javier Lopez	.30	.14	.04
□ 161 Steve Avery	.15	.07	.02
□ 162 Greg McMichael	.05	.02	.01
□ 163 Kent Mercker	.05	.02	.01
□ 164 Mark Lemke	.05	.02	.01
□ 165 Tom Glavine	.30	.14	.04
□ 166 Jose Oliva	.05	.02	.01
□ 167 John Smoltz	.30	.14	.04
□ 168 Jeff Blauser	.05	.02	.01
□ 169 Troy O'Leary	.05	.02	.01
□ 170 Greg Vaughn	.15	.07	.02
□ 171 Jody Reed	.05	.02	.01
□ 172 Kevin Seitzer	.05	.02	.01
□ 173 Jeff Cirillo	.15	.07	.02
□ 174 B.J. Surhoff	.15	.07	.02
□ 175 Cal Eldred	.05	.02	.01
□ 176 Jose Valentin	.15	.07	.02
□ 177 Turner Ward	.05	.02	.01
□ 178 Darryl Hamilton	.05	.02	.01
□ 179 Pat Listach	.05	.02	.01
□ 180 Matt Mieske	.15	.07	.02
□ 181 Brian Harper	.05	.02	.01
□ 182 Dave Nilsson	.15	.07	.02
□ 183 Mike Fetters	.05	.02	.01
□ 184 John Jaha	.15	.07	.02
□ 185 Ricky Bones	.05	.02	.01
□ 186 Geronimo Pena	.05	.02	.01
□ 187 Bob Tewksbury	.05	.02	.01
□ 188 Todd Zeile	.05	.02	.01
□ 189 Danny Jackson	.05	.02	.01
□ 190 Ray Lankford	.15	.07	.02
□ 191 Bernard Gilkey	.15	.07	.02
□ 192 Brian Jordan	.30	.14	.04
□ 193 Tom Pagnozzi	.05	.02	.01
□ 194 Rick Sutcliffe	.05	.02	.01
□ 195 Mark Whiten	.05	.02	.01
□ 196 Tom Henke	.05	.02	.01
□ 197 Rene Arocha	.05	.02	.01
□ 198 Allen Watson	.05	.02	.01
□ 199 Mike Perez	.05	.02	.01
□ 200 Ozzie Smith	.50	.23	.06
□ 201 Anthony Young	.05	.02	.01
□ 202 Rey Sanchez	.05	.02	.01
□ 203 Steve Buechele	.05	.02	.01
□ 204 Shawon Dunston	.05	.02	.01
□ 205 Mark Grace	.30	.14	.04
□ 206 Glenallen Hill	.05	.02	.01
□ 207 Eddie Zambrano	.05	.02	.01
□ 208 Rick Wilkins	.05	.02	.01
□ 209 Derrick May	.05	.02	.01
□ 210 Sammy Sosa	.30	.14	.04
□ 211 Kevin Roberson	.05	.02	.01
□ 212 Steve Trachsel	.05	.02	.01
□ 213 Willie Banks	.05	.02	.01
□ 214 Kevin Foster	.05	.02	.01
□ 215 Randy Myers	.05	.02	.01
□ 216 Mike Morgan	.05	.02	.01
□ 217 Rafael Bournigal	.05	.02	.01
□ 218 Delino DeShields	.05	.02	.01
□ 219 Tim Wallach	.05	.02	.01
□ 220 Eric Karros	.15	.07	.02
□ 221 Jose Offerman	.05	.02	.01
□ 222 Tom Candiotti	.05	.02	.01
□ 223 Ismael Valdes	.15	.07	.02
□ 224 Henry Rodriguez	.15	.07	.02
□ 225 Billy Ashley	.05	.02	.01
□ 226 Darren Dreifort	.05	.02	.01
□ 227 Ramon Martinez	.15	.07	.02
□ 228 Pedro Astacio	.05	.02	.01

Card	Mint	Nrmt	Exc
☐ 229 Orel Hershiser	.15	.07	.02
☐ 230 Brett Butler	.15	.07	.02
☐ 231 Todd Hollandsworth	.30	.14	.04
☐ 232 Chan Ho Park	.30	.14	.04
☐ 233 Mike Lansing	.05	.02	.01
☐ 234 Sean Berry	.05	.02	.01
☐ 235 Rondell White	.15	.07	.02
☐ 236 Ken Hill	.05	.02	.01
☐ 237 Marquis Grissom	.15	.07	.02
☐ 238 Larry Walker	.30	.14	.04
☐ 239 John Wetteland	.15	.07	.02
☐ 240 Cliff Floyd	.15	.07	.02
☐ 241 Joey Eischen	.05	.02	.01
☐ 242 Lou Frazier	.05	.02	.01
☐ 243 Darrin Fletcher	.05	.02	.01
☐ 244 Pedro J. Martinez	.15	.07	.02
☐ 245 Wil Cordero	.05	.02	.01
☐ 246 Jeff Fassero	.05	.02	.01
☐ 247 Butch Henry	.05	.02	.01
☐ 248 Mel Rojas	.05	.02	.01
☐ 249 Kirk Rueter	.05	.02	.01
☐ 250 Moises Alou	.15	.07	.02
☐ 251 Rod Beck	.05	.02	.01
☐ 252 John Patterson	.05	.02	.01
☐ 253 Robby Thompson	.05	.02	.01
☐ 254 Royce Clayton	.05	.02	.01
☐ 255 Wm. VanLandingham	.05	.02	.01
☐ 256 Darren Lewis	.05	.02	.01
☐ 257 Kirt Manwaring	.05	.02	.01
☐ 258 Mark Portugal	.05	.02	.01
☐ 259 Bill Swift	.05	.02	.01
☐ 260 Rikkert Faneyte	.05	.02	.01
☐ 261 Mike Jackson	.05	.02	.01
☐ 262 Todd Benzinger	.05	.02	.01
☐ 263 Bud Black	.05	.02	.01
☐ 264 Salomon Torres	.05	.02	.01
☐ 265 Eddie Murray	.30	.14	.04
☐ 266 Mark Clark	.05	.02	.01
☐ 267 Paul Sorrento	.05	.02	.01
☐ 268 Jim Thome	.40	.18	.05
☐ 269 Omar Vizquel	.15	.07	.02
☐ 270 Carlos Baerga	.15	.07	.02
☐ 271 Jeff Russell	.05	.02	.01
☐ 272 Herbert Perry	.05	.02	.01
☐ 273 Sandy Alomar Jr.	.05	.02	.01
☐ 274 Dennis Martinez	.15	.07	.02
☐ 275 Manny Ramirez	.50	.23	.06
☐ 276 Wayne Kirby	.05	.02	.01
☐ 277 Charles Nagy	.15	.07	.02
☐ 278 Albie Lopez	.05	.02	.01
☐ 279 Jeromy Burnitz	.05	.02	.01
☐ 280 Dave Winfield	.30	.14	.04
☐ 281 Tim Davis	.05	.02	.01
☐ 282 Marc Newfield	.15	.07	.02
☐ 283 Tino Martinez	.15	.07	.02
☐ 284 Mike Blowers	.05	.02	.01
☐ 285 Goose Gossage	.15	.07	.02
☐ 286 Luis Sojo	.05	.02	.01
☐ 287 Edgar Martinez	.15	.07	.02
☐ 288 Rich Amaral	.05	.02	.01
☐ 289 Felix Fermin	.05	.02	.01
☐ 290 Jay Buhner	.30	.14	.04
☐ 291 Dan Wilson	.15	.07	.02
☐ 292 Bobby Ayala	.05	.02	.01
☐ 293 Dave Fleming	.05	.02	.01
☐ 294 Greg Pirkl	.05	.02	.01
☐ 295 Reggie Jefferson	.15	.07	.02
☐ 296 Greg Hibbard	.05	.02	.01
☐ 297 Yorkis Perez	.05	.02	.01
☐ 298 Kurt Miller	.05	.02	.01
☐ 299 Chuck Carr	.05	.02	.01
☐ 300 Gary Sheffield	.30	.14	.04
☐ 301 Jerry Browne	.05	.02	.01
☐ 302 Dave Magadan	.05	.02	.01
☐ 303 Kurt Abbott	.05	.02	.01
☐ 304 Pat Rapp	.05	.02	.01
☐ 305 Jeff Conine	.15	.07	.02
☐ 306 Benito Santiago	.05	.02	.01
☐ 307 Dave Weathers	.05	.02	.01
☐ 308 Robb Nen	.05	.02	.01
☐ 309 Chris Hammond	.05	.02	.01
☐ 310 Bryan Harvey	.05	.02	.01
☐ 311 Charlie Hough	.05	.02	.01
☐ 312 Greg Colbrunn	.05	.02	.01
☐ 313 David Segui	.05	.02	.01
☐ 314 Rico Brogna	.05	.02	.01
☐ 315 Jeff Kent	.05	.02	.01
☐ 316 Jose Vizcaino	.05	.02	.01
☐ 317 Jim Lindeman	.05	.02	.01
☐ 318 Carl Everett	.05	.02	.01
☐ 319 Ryan Thompson	.05	.02	.01
☐ 320 Bobby Bonilla	.15	.07	.02
☐ 321 Joe Orsulak	.05	.02	.01
☐ 322 Pete Harnisch	.05	.02	.01
☐ 323 Doug Linton	.05	.02	.01
☐ 324 Todd Hundley	.15	.07	.02
☐ 325 Bret Saberhagen	.15	.07	.02
☐ 326 Kelly Stinnett	.05	.02	.01
☐ 327 Jason Jacome	.05	.02	.01
☐ 328 Bobby Jones	.15	.07	.02
☐ 329 John Franco	.05	.02	.01
☐ 330 Rafael Palmeiro	.30	.14	.04
☐ 331 Chris Hoiles	.05	.02	.01
☐ 332 Leo Gomez	.05	.02	.01
☐ 333 Chris Sabo	.05	.02	.01
☐ 334 Brady Anderson	.30	.14	.04
☐ 335 Jeffrey Hammonds	.15	.07	.02
☐ 336 Dwight Smith	.05	.02	.01
☐ 337 Jack Voigt	.05	.02	.01
☐ 338 Harold Baines	.15	.07	.02
☐ 339 Ben McDonald	.05	.02	.01
☐ 340 Mike Mussina	.40	.18	.05
☐ 341 Bret Barberie	.05	.02	.01
☐ 342 Jamie Moyer	.05	.02	.01
☐ 343 Mike Oquist	.05	.02	.01
☐ 344 Sid Fernandez	.05	.02	.01
☐ 345 Eddie Williams	.05	.02	.01
☐ 346 Joey Hamilton	.30	.14	.04
☐ 347 Brian Williams	.05	.02	.01
☐ 348 Luis Lopez	.05	.02	.01
☐ 349 Steve Finley	.15	.07	.02
☐ 350 Andy Benes	.05	.02	.01
☐ 351 Andujar Cedeno	.05	.02	.01
☐ 352 Bip Roberts	.05	.02	.01
☐ 353 Ray McDavid	.15	.07	.02
☐ 354 Ken Caminiti	.30	.14	.04
☐ 355 Trevor Hoffman	.15	.07	.02
☐ 356 Mel Nieves	.15	.07	.02
☐ 357 Brad Ausmus	.05	.02	.01
☐ 358 Andy Ashby	.15	.07	.02
☐ 359 Scott Sanders	.05	.02	.01
☐ 360 Gregg Jefferies	.15	.07	.02
☐ 361 Mariano Duncan	.05	.02	.01
☐ 362 Dave Hollins	.05	.02	.01
☐ 363 Kevin Stocker	.05	.02	.01
☐ 364 Fernando Valenzuela	.15	.07	.02
☐ 365 Lenny Dykstra	.15	.07	.02
☐ 366 Jim Eisenreich	.05	.02	.01
☐ 367 Ricky Bottalico	.15	.07	.02
☐ 368 Doug Jones	.05	.02	.01
☐ 369 Ricky Jordan	.05	.02	.01
☐ 370 Darren Daulton	.15	.07	.02
☐ 371 Mike Lieberthal	.05	.02	.01
☐ 372 Bobby Munoz	.05	.02	.01
☐ 373 John Kruk	.15	.07	.02
☐ 374 Curt Schilling	.05	.02	.01
☐ 375 Orlando Merced	.05	.02	.01
☐ 376 Carlos Garcia	.05	.02	.01
☐ 377 Lance Parrish	.05	.02	.01
☐ 378 Steve Cooke	.05	.02	.01
☐ 379 Jeff King	.15	.07	.02
☐ 380 Jay Bell	.15	.07	.02
☐ 381 Al Martin	.15	.07	.02
☐ 382 Paul Wagner	.05	.02	.01
☐ 383 Rick White	.05	.02	.01
☐ 384 Midre Cummings	.05	.02	.01
☐ 385 Jon Lieber	.05	.02	.01
☐ 386 Dave Clark	.05	.02	.01
☐ 387 Don Slaught	.05	.02	.01
☐ 388 Denny Neagle	.15	.07	.02
☐ 389 Zane Smith	.05	.02	.01
☐ 390 Andy Van Slyke	.15	.07	.02
☐ 391 Ivan Rodriguez	.50	.23	.06
☐ 392 David Hulse	.05	.02	.01
☐ 393 John Burkett	.15	.07	.02
☐ 394 Kevin Brown	.15	.07	.02
☐ 395 Dean Palmer	.15	.07	.02
☐ 396 Otis Nixon	.05	.02	.01
☐ 397 Rick Helling	.05	.02	.01
☐ 398 Kenny Rogers	.05	.02	.01
☐ 399 Darren Oliver	.30	.14	.04
☐ 400 Will Clark	.30	.14	.04
☐ 401 Jeff Frye	.05	.02	.01
☐ 402 Kevin Gross	.05	.02	.01
☐ 403 John Dettmer	.05	.02	.01
☐ 404 Manny Lee	.05	.02	.01
☐ 405 Rusty Greer	.30	.14	.04
☐ 406 Aaron Sele	.15	.07	.02
☐ 407 Carlos Rodriguez	.05	.02	.01
☐ 408 Scott Cooper	.05	.02	.01
☐ 409 John Valentin	.15	.07	.02
☐ 410 Roger Clemens	.40	.18	.05
☐ 411 Mike Greenwell	.05	.02	.01
☐ 412 Tim Vanegmond	.05	.02	.01
☐ 413 Tom Brunansky	.05	.02	.01
☐ 414 Steve Farr	.05	.02	.01
☐ 415 Jose Canseco	.30	.14	.04
☐ 416 Joe Hesketh	.05	.02	.01
☐ 417 Ken Ryan	.05	.02	.01
☐ 418 Tim Naehring	.05	.02	.01
☐ 419 Frank Viola	.05	.02	.01
☐ 420 Andre Dawson	.15	.07	.02
☐ 421 Mo Vaughn	.50	.23	.06
☐ 422 Jeff Brantley	.05	.02	.01
☐ 423 Pete Schourek	.15	.07	.02
☐ 424 Hal Morris	.05	.02	.01
☐ 425 Deion Sanders	.30	.14	.04
☐ 426 Brian R. Hunter	.05	.02	.01
☐ 427 Bret Boone	.15	.07	.02
☐ 428 Willie Greene	.05	.02	.01
☐ 429 Ron Gant	.15	.07	.02
☐ 430 Barry Larkin	.30	.14	.04
☐ 431 Reggie Sanders	.15	.07	.02
☐ 432 Eddie Taubensee	.05	.02	.01
☐ 433 Jack Morris	.30	.14	.04
☐ 434 Jose Rijo	.05	.02	.01
☐ 435 Johnny Ruffin	.05	.02	.01
☐ 436 John Smiley	.05	.02	.01
☐ 437 John Roper	.05	.02	.01
☐ 438 Dave Nied	.05	.02	.01
☐ 439 Roberto Mejia	.05	.02	.01
☐ 440 Andres Galarraga	.30	.14	.04
☐ 441 Mike Kingery	.05	.02	.01
☐ 442 Curt Leskanic	.05	.02	.01
☐ 443 Walt Weiss	.05	.02	.01
☐ 444 Marvin Freeman	.05	.02	.01
☐ 445 Charlie Hayes	.05	.02	.01
☐ 446 Eric Young	.15	.07	.02
☐ 447 Ellis Burks	.15	.07	.02
☐ 448 Joe Girardi	.05	.02	.01
☐ 449 Lance Painter	.05	.02	.01
☐ 450 Dante Bichette	.30	.14	.04
☐ 451 Bruce Ruffin	.05	.02	.01
☐ 452 Jeff Granger	.05	.02	.01
☐ 453 Wally Joyner	.15	.07	.02
☐ 454 Jose Lind	.05	.02	.01
☐ 455 Jeff Montgomery	.15	.07	.02
☐ 456 Gary Gaetti	.15	.07	.02
☐ 457 Greg Gagne	.05	.02	.01
☐ 458 Vince Coleman	.05	.02	.01
☐ 459 Mike Macfarlane	.05	.02	.01
☐ 460 Brian McRae	.15	.07	.02
☐ 461 Tom Gordon	.05	.02	.01
☐ 462 Kevin Appier	.15	.07	.02
☐ 463 Billy Brewer	.05	.02	.01
☐ 464 Mark Gubicza	.05	.02	.01
☐ 465 Travis Fryman	.15	.07	.02
☐ 466 Danny Bautista	.05	.02	.01
☐ 467 Sean Bergman	.05	.02	.01
☐ 468 Mike Henneman	.05	.02	.01
☐ 469 Mike Moore	.05	.02	.01
☐ 470 Cecil Fielder	.15	.07	.02
☐ 471 Alan Trammell	.15	.07	.02
☐ 472 Kirk Gibson	.15	.07	.02
☐ 473 Tony Phillips	.15	.07	.02
☐ 474 Mickey Tettleton	.05	.02	.01
☐ 475 Lou Whitaker	.15	.07	.02
☐ 476 Chris Gomez	.05	.02	.01
☐ 477 John Doherty	.05	.02	.01
☐ 478 Greg Gohr	.05	.02	.01
☐ 479 Bill Gullickson	.05	.02	.01
☐ 480 Rick Aguilera	.05	.02	.01
☐ 481 Matt Walbeck	.05	.02	.01
☐ 482 Kevin Tapani	.05	.02	.01
☐ 483 Scott Erickson	.05	.02	.01
☐ 484 Steve Dunn	.05	.02	.01
☐ 485 David McCarty	.05	.02	.01
☐ 486 Scott Leius	.05	.02	.01
☐ 487 Pat Meares	.05	.02	.01
☐ 488 Jeff Reboulet	.05	.02	.01
☐ 489 Pedro Munoz	.05	.02	.01
☐ 490 Chuck Knoblauch	.30	.14	.04
☐ 491 Rich Becker	.05	.02	.01
☐ 492 Alex Cole	.05	.02	.01
☐ 493 Pat Mahomes	.05	.02	.01
☐ 494 Ozzie Guillen	.05	.02	.01
☐ 495 Tim Raines	.30	.14	.04
☐ 496 Kirk McCaskill	.05	.02	.01
☐ 497 Olmedo Saenz	.05	.02	.01
☐ 498 Scott Sanderson	.05	.02	.01
☐ 499 Lance Johnson	.15	.07	.02
☐ 500 Michael Jordan	2.50	1.10	.30
☐ 501 Warren Newson	.05	.02	.01
☐ 502 Ron Karkovice	.05	.02	.01
☐ 503 Wilson Alvarez	.15	.07	.02
☐ 504 Jason Bere	.05	.02	.01
☐ 505 Robin Ventura	.15	.07	.02
☐ 506 Alex Fernandez	.15	.07	.02
☐ 507 Roberto Hernandez	.05	.02	.01
☐ 508 Norberto Martin	.05	.02	.01
☐ 509 Bob Wickman	.05	.02	.01
☐ 510 Don Mattingly	1.00	.45	.12
☐ 511 Melido Perez	.05	.02	.01
☐ 512 Pat Kelly	.05	.02	.01
☐ 513 Randy Velarde	.05	.02	.01
☐ 514 Tony Fernandez	.05	.02	.01
☐ 515 Jack McDowell	.15	.07	.02
☐ 516 Luis Polonia	.05	.02	.01
☐ 517 Bernie Williams	.40	.18	.05
☐ 518 Danny Tartabull	.05	.02	.01
☐ 519 Mike Stanley	.05	.02	.01
☐ 520 Wade Boggs	.30	.14	.04
☐ 521 Jim Leyritz	.05	.02	.01
☐ 522 Steve Howe	.05	.02	.01
☐ 523 Scott Kamieniecki	.05	.02	.01
☐ 524 Russ Davis	.05	.02	.01
☐ 525 Jim Abbott	.05	.02	.01
☐ 526 Eddie Murray CL	.30	.14	.04
☐ 527 Alex Rodriguez CL	1.25	.55	.16
☐ 528 Jeff Bagwell CL	.40	.18	.05
☐ 529 Joe Carter CL	.15	.07	.02
☐ 530 Fred McGriff CL	.30	.14	.04
☐ 531T Tony Phillips TRADE	.10	.05	.01
☐ 532T Dave Magadan TRADE	.10	.05	.01
☐ 533T Mike Gallego TRADE	.10	.05	.01
☐ 534T Dave Stewart TRADE	.15	.07	.02
☐ 535T Todd Stottlemyre TRADE	.15	.07	.02
☐ 536T David Cone TRADE	.15	.07	.02
☐ 537T Marquis Grissom TRADE	.15	.07	.02
☐ 538T Derrick May TRADE	.10	.05	.01
☐ 539T Joe Oliver TRADE	.10	.05	.01
☐ 540T Scott Cooper TRADE	.10	.05	.01
☐ 541T Ken Hill TRADE	.15	.07	.02
☐ 542T Howard Johnson TRADE DP	.05	.02	.01
☐ 543T Brian McRae TRADE DP	.10	.05	.01
☐ 544T Jaime Navarro TRADE DP	.05	.02	.01
☐ 545T Ozzie Timmons TRADE DP	.05	.02	.01
☐ 546T Roberto Kelly TRADE DP	.05	.02	.01
☐ 547T Hideo Nomo TRADE DP	4.00	1.80	.50
☐ 548T Shane Andrews TRADE DP	.10	.05	.01
☐ 549T M.Grudzielanek TRADE DP	1.00	.45	.12
☐ 550T Carlos Perez TRADE DP	.10	.05	.01
☐ 551T Henry Rodriguez TRADE DP	.15	.07	.02
☐ 552T Tony Tarasco TRADE DP	.05	.02	.01
☐ 553T Glenallen Hill TRADE	.10	.05	.01
☐ 554T Terry Mulholland TRADE	.10	.05	.01
☐ 555T Orel Hershiser TRADE	.15	.07	.02
☐ 556T Darren Bragg TRADE	.10	.05	.01
☐ 557T John Burkett TRADE	.15	.07	.02
☐ 558T Bobby Witt TRADE	.10	.05	.01
☐ 559T Terry Pendleton TRADE	.10	.05	.01
☐ 560T Andre Dawson TRADE	.15	.07	.02
☐ 561T Brett Butler TRADE	.15	.07	.02
☐ 562T Kevin Brown TRADE	.10	.05	.01
☐ 563T Doug Jones TRADE	.10	.05	.01
☐ 564T Andy Van Slyke TRADE	.15	.07	.02
☐ 565T Jody Reed TRADE	.10	.05	.01
☐ 566T Fernando Valenzuela TRADE	.15	.07	.02
☐ 567T Charlie Hayes TRADE	.10	.05	.01
☐ 568T Benji Gil TRADE	.10	.05	.01
☐ 569T Mark McLemore TRADE	.10	.05	.01
☐ 570T Mickey Tettleton TRADE	.15	.07	.02
☐ 571T Bob Tewksbury TRADE	.10	.05	.01
☐ 572T Rheal Cormier TRADE	.10	.05	.01
☐ 573T Vaughn Eshelman TRADE	.10	.05	.01
☐ 574T Mike Macfarlane TRADE	.10	.05	.01
☐ 575T Bill Swift TRADE	.10	.05	.01
☐ 576T Mark Whiten TRADE	.10	.05	.01
☐ 577T Benito Santiago TRADE	.10	.05	.01
☐ 578T Jason Bates TRADE	.10	.05	.01
☐ 579T Larry Walker TRADE	.30	.14	.04
☐ 580T Chad Curtis TRADE	.10	.05	.01
☐ 581T Bobby Higginson TRADE	1.25	.55	.16
☐ 582T Marty Cordova TRADE	.50	.23	.06
☐ 583T Mike Devereaux TRADE	.10	.05	.01
☐ 584T John Kruk TRADE	.15	.07	.02
☐ 585T John Wetteland TRADE	.15	.07	.02
☐ TC1 Larry Walker	.30	.14	.04
☐ TC2 David Cone	.15	.07	.02
☐ TC3 Marquis Grissom	.15	.07	.02
☐ TC4 Terry Pendleton	1.00	.45	.12
☐ TC5 Fernando Valenzuela	.15	.07	.02

1995 Collector's Choice Gold Signature

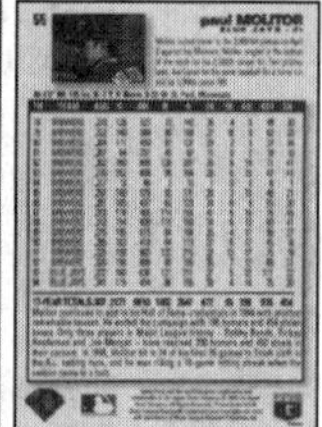

This set is a parallel of the 530 regular cards from the Collector's Choice set. Gold cards were inserted into one in every 35 packs, 12 per gold super pack and 15 per factory set. Unlike regular issue cards, each Gold Signature card features a gold border (except for a selection of borderless subset cards) and gold facsimile signature on front.

	MINT	NRMT	EXC
COMPLETE SET (530)	1000.00	450.00	125.00
COMMON CARD (1-530)	1.00	.45	.12

*STARS: 10X TO 20X BASIC CARDS
*YOUNG STARS: 7.5X TO 15X BASIC CARDS

1995 Collector's Choice Silver Signature

This set is a parallel of the 530 regular cards from the Collector's Choice set. Silver Signature cards were inserted at a rate of one per pack, two per mini jumbo and 12 per silver super pack. Unlike regular issue cards, Silver Signature cards feature silver borders and a silver facsimile signature on front.

	MINT	NRMT	EXC
COMPLETE SET (530)	75.00	34.00	9.50
COMMON CARD (1-530)	.10	.05	.01

*STARS: 2X to 4X BASIC CARDS
*YOUNG STARS: 1.5X to 3X BASIC CARDS

1995 Collector's Choice Crash the All-Star Game

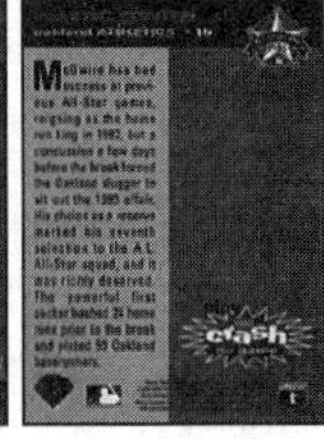

This eight card standard-size set measures the standard size. The cards carry the names of players who participated in the 1995 All-Star game on July 11. The fronts feature color action player photos with a tri-colored border. The player's name and team name are printed in the bottom border. The backs contain the player's name, date of game, and the directions of how to claim a prize if the player hit a home run during the All-Star game. Winner cards could be mailed in, along with 2.00, and redeemed for a gold foil enhanced set. These enhanced cards are valued at the same value as the regular cards. The two winning cards were Mike Piazza and Frank Thomas. The cards are unnumbered and checklisted below in alphabetical order.

	MINT	NRMT	EXC
COMPLETE SET (8)	18.00	8.00	2.20
COMMON CARD (1-8)	1.00	.45	.12
*REDEMPTION WINNERS: 3X VALUE			
☐ 1 Albert Belle	3.00	1.35	.35
☐ 2 Barry Bonds	1.50	.70	.19
☐ 3 Fred McGriff	1.00	.45	.12
☐ 4 Mark McGwire	2.00	.90	.25
☐ 5 Raul Mondesi	1.00	.45	.12
☐ 6 Mike Piazza	5.00	2.20	.60
☐ 7 Manny Ramirez	1.50	.70	.19
☐ 8 Frank Thomas	6.00	2.70	.75

1995 Collector's Choice Crash the Game

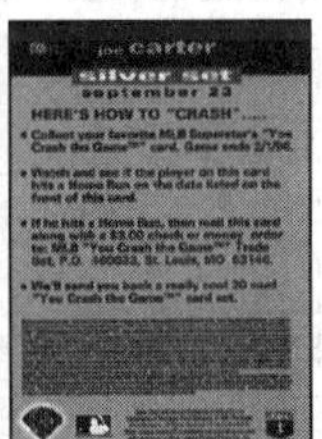

Cards from this 60-card standard-size set were randomly inserted in packs at a rate of one in five. The set is an interactive set in which all 20 players have three cards with a date on it. If the player hit a home run on that date, the collector could redeem the card for a complete enhanced set of all 20 players. The fronts have a color-action photo with the game background in yellow and a large date stamped in silver foil. The expiration date for redeeming these cards was February 1, 1996. Winning cards eligible for redemption at the time have been highlighted with a "W" in our listings below.

	MINT	NRMT	EXC
COMPLETE SET (60)	50.00	22.00	6.25
COMMON CARD (CG1-CG20)	.25	.11	.03
SEMISTARS	.50	.23	.06
UNLISTED STARS	.75	.35	.09
☐ CG1 Jeff Bagwell 7/30	.75	.35	.09
☐ CG1B Jeff Bagwell 8/13	.75	.35	.09
☐ CG1C Jeff Bagwell 9/28	.75	.35	.09
☐ CG2 Albert Belle 6/18	.75	.35	.09
☐ CG2B Albert Belle 8/26	1.00	.45	.12
☐ CG2C Albert Belle 9/20	1.00	.45	.12
☐ CG3 Barry Bonds 6/28	.50	.23	.06
☐ CG3B Barry Bonds 7/9	.50	.23	.06
☐ CG3C Barry Bonds 9/6	.50	.23	.06
☐ CG4 Jose Canseco 6/30 W	.25	.11	.03
☐ CG4B Jose Canseco 7/30 W	.25	.11	.03
☐ CG4C Jose Canseco 9/3	.25	.11	.03
☐ CG5 Joe Carter 7/14	.25	.11	.03
☐ CG5B Joe Carter 8/9	.25	.11	.03
☐ CG5C Joe Carter 9/23	.25	.11	.03
☐ CG6 Cecil Fielder 7/4	.25	.11	.03
☐ CG6B Cecil Fielder 8/2	.25	.11	.03
☐ CG6C Cecil Fielder 10/1	.25	.11	.03
☐ CG7 Juan Gonzalez 6/29	1.00	.45	.12
☐ CG7B Juan Gonzalez 8/13	1.00	.45	.12
☐ CG7C Juan Gonzalez 9/3 W	1.00	.45	.12
☐ CG8 Ken Griffey Jr. 7/2	2.00	.90	.25
☐ CG8B Ken Griffey Jr. 8/24 W	2.00	.90	.25
☐ CG8C Ken Griffey Jr. 9/15	2.00	.90	.25
☐ CG9 Bob Hamelin 7/23	.25	.11	.03
☐ CG9B Bob Hamelin 8/1	.25	.11	.03
☐ CG9C Bob Hamelin 9/29	.25	.11	.03
☐ CG10 David Justice 6/24	.25	.11	.03
☐ CG10B David Justice 7/25	.25	.11	.03
☐ CG10C David Justice 9/17	.25	.11	.03
☐ CG11 Ryan Klesko 7/13	.50	.23	.06
☐ CG11B Ryan Klesko 8/20	.50	.23	.06
☐ CG11C Ryan Klesko 9/10	.50	.23	.06
☐ CG12 Fred McGriff 8/25	.25	.11	.03
☐ CG12B Fred McGriff 9/8	.25	.11	.03
☐ CG12C Fred McGriff 9/24	.25	.11	.03
☐ CG13 Mark McGwire 7/23	.60	.25	.07
☐ CG13B Mark McGwire 8/3 W	.60	.25	.07
☐ CG13C Mark McGwire 9/27	.60	.25	.07
☐ CG14 Raul Mondesi 7/27 W	.25	.11	.03
☐ CG14B Raul Mondesi 8/13	.25	.11	.03
☐ CG14C Raul Mondesi 9/15 W	.25	.11	.03
☐ CG15 Mike Piazza 7/23 W	1.25	.55	.16
☐ CG15B Mike Piazza 8/27	1.25	.55	.16
☐ CG15C Mike Piazza 9/19	1.25	.55	.16
☐ CG16 Manny Ramirez 6/21	.50	.23	.06
☐ CG16B Manny Ramirez 8/13	.50	.23	.06
☐ CG16C Manny Ramirez 9/26	.50	.23	.06
☐ CG17 Alex Rodriguez 9/10	2.00	.90	.25
☐ CG17B Alex Rodriguez 9/18	2.00	.90	.25
☐ CG17C Alex Rodriguez 9/24	2.00	.90	.25
☐ CG18 Gary Sheffield	.25	.11	.03
☐ CG18B Gary Sheffield 8/13	.25	.11	.03
☐ CG18C Gary Sheffield 9/4 W	.25	.11	.03
☐ CG19 Frank Thomas 7/26	2.00	.90	.25
☐ CG19B Frank Thomas 8/17	2.00	.90	.25
☐ CG19C Frank Thomas 9/23	2.00	.90	.25
☐ CG20 Matt Williams 7/29	.25	.11	.03
☐ CG20B Matt Williams 8/12	.25	.11	.03
☐ CG20C Matt Williams 9/19	.25	.11	.03

1995 Collector's Choice Crash the Game Exchange

This 20 card parallel set was received by collectors who had winning cards in the 1995 Collectors Choice Crash the Game contest. The cards are easy to identify from their basic issue counterparts by the card backs, of which contain information on the player rather than rules for the Crash program.

	MINT	NRMT	EXC
COMPLETE SET (20)	10.00	4.50	1.25
COMMON CARD (1-20)	.15	.07	.02
*EXCH.CARDS: .25X TO .5X BASIC CRASH CARDS			

1995 Collector's Choice Crash the Game Gold

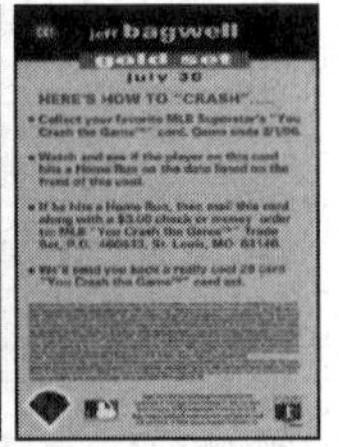

This 60-card set parallels the more common silver foil Crash the Game insert set. The cards are identical in design except for the gold foil stamping on front. These scarce gold interactive cards were seeded at an approximate rate of one in every 49 packs. Winning cards were redeemable for special upgraded 20-card gold sets.

	MINT	NRMT	EXC
COMPLETE SET (60)	250.00	110.00	31.00
COMMON CARD (CG1-CG20)	1.50	.70	.19
*GOLD: 5X BASIC CRASH CARDS			

1995 Collector's Choice Crash the Game Gold Exchange

If a collector had a winning Crash the Game Gold card, that card was redeemable for this 20 card Gold set.

	MINT	NRMT	EXC
COMPLETE SET (20)	50.00	22.00	6.25
COMMON CARD (1-20)	1.00	.45	.12
*GOLDEXCH: 1.25X TO 2.5X BASIC CRASH CARDS			

1996 Collector's Choice

This 790-card standard-size set was issued in 12-card packs with 36 packs per box and 20 boxes per case. Suggested retail price on these packs was 99 cents. The fronts of the regular set feature a player photo, his name and team logo. The backs feature another photo, vital stats and a baseball quiz. The set includes the following subsets: 1995 Stat Leaders (2-9), Rookie Class (10-39), Traditional Threads (100-108), Fantasy Team (268-279), International Flavor (325-342), Series 1 Checklists (358-365), Team Checklists (396-423), First HOF Class (500-504), Award Winners (704-711) and Series 2 Checklists (753-760). Postseason Trade cards were inserted one every 11 packs. These cards had an ordering deadline of May 13 and were each redeemable for 10 cards depicting highlights from the playoffs and

World Series, resulting in a 30-card redemption set. Finally, a 30-card Update set was included in each factory set and was also available through a Series 2 wrapper offer.

	MINT	NRMT	EXC
COMPLETE SET (730)	30.00	13.50	3.70
COMP.FACT.SET (790)	40.00	18.00	5.00
COMPLETE SERIES 1 (365)	15.00	6.75	1.85
COMPLETE SERIES 2 (365)	15.00	6.75	1.85
COMMON CARD (1-360/396-760)	.05	.02	.01
COMP.TRADE SET (30)	15.00	6.75	1.85
COMMON TRADE (366T-395T)	.15	.07	.02
COMPLETE UPDATE SET (30)	8.00	3.60	1.00
COMMON UPDATE (761-790)	.25	.11	.03
☐ 1 Cal Ripken	1.50	.70	.19
☐ 2 Edgar Martinez SL Tony Gwynn	.15	.07	.02
☐ 3 Albert Belle SL Dante Bichette	.30	.14	.04
☐ 4 Albert Belle SL Mo Vaughn Dante Bichette	.30	.14	.04
☐ 5 Kenny Lofton SL Quilvio Veras	.15	.07	.02
☐ 6 Mike Mussina SL Greg Maddux	.50	.23	.06
☐ 7 Randy Johnson SL Hideo Nomo	.30	.14	.04
☐ 8 Randy Johnson SL Greg Maddux	.50	.23	.06
☐ 9 Jose Mesa SL Randy Myers	.05	.02	.01
☐ 10 Johnny Damon	.15	.07	.02
☐ 11 Rick Krivda	.05	.02	.01
☐ 12 Roger Cedeno	.30	.14	.04
☐ 13 Angel Martinez	.05	.02	.01
☐ 14 Ariel Prieto	.05	.02	.01
☐ 15 John Wasdin	.15	.07	.02
☐ 16 Edwin Hurtado	.05	.02	.01
☐ 17 Lyle Mouton	.05	.02	.01
☐ 18 Chris Snopek	.05	.02	.01
☐ 19 Mariano Rivera	.15	.07	.02
☐ 20 Ruben Rivera	.40	.18	.05
☐ 21 Juan Castro	.30	.14	.04
☐ 22 Jimmy Haynes	.30	.14	.04
☐ 23 Bob Wolcott	.05	.02	.01
☐ 24 Brian Barber	.05	.02	.01
☐ 25 Frank Rodriguez	.30	.14	.04
☐ 26 Jesus Tavarez	.15	.07	.02
☐ 27 Glenn Dishman	.15	.07	.02
☐ 28 Jose Herrera	.15	.07	.02
☐ 29 Chan Ho Park	.30	.14	.04
☐ 30 Jason Isringhausen	.30	.14	.04
☐ 31 Doug Johns	.05	.02	.01
☐ 32 Gene Schall	.05	.02	.01
☐ 33 Kevin Jordan	.05	.02	.01
☐ 34 Matt Lawton	.05	.02	.01
☐ 35 Karim Garcia	.40	.18	.05
☐ 36 George Williams	.05	.02	.01
☐ 37 Orlando Palmeiro	.05	.02	.01
☐ 38 Jamie Brewington	.05	.02	.01
☐ 39 Robert Person	.05	.02	.01
☐ 40 Greg Maddux	1.25	.55	.16
☐ 41 Marquis Grissom	.15	.07	.02
☐ 42 Chipper Jones	1.25	.55	.16
☐ 43 David Justice	.15	.07	.02
☐ 44 Mark Lemke	.05	.02	.01
☐ 45 Fred McGriff	.30	.14	.04
☐ 46 Javier Lopez	.30	.14	.04
☐ 47 Mark Wohlers	.15	.07	.02
☐ 48 Jason Schmidt	.30	.14	.04
☐ 49 John Smoltz	.30	.14	.04
☐ 50 Curtis Goodwin	.05	.02	.01
☐ 51 Greg Zaun	.05	.02	.01
☐ 52 Armando Benitez	.05	.02	.01
☐ 53 Manny Alexander	.05	.02	.01
☐ 54 Chris Hoiles	.05	.02	.01
☐ 55 Harold Baines	.15	.07	.02
☐ 56 Ben McDonald	.05	.02	.01
☐ 57 Scott Erickson	.05	.02	.01
☐ 58 Jeff Manto	.05	.02	.01
☐ 59 Luis Alicea	.05	.02	.01
☐ 60 Roger Clemens	.40	.18	.05
☐ 61 Rheal Cormier	.05	.02	.01
☐ 62 Vaughn Eshelman	.05	.02	.01
☐ 63 Zane Smith	.05	.02	.01
☐ 64 Mike Macfarlane	.05	.02	.01
☐ 65 Erik Hanson	.05	.02	.01
☐ 66 Tim Naehring	.15	.07	.02
☐ 67 Lee Tinsley	.05	.02	.01
☐ 68 Troy O'Leary	.15	.07	.02
☐ 69 Garret Anderson	.30	.14	.04
☐ 70 Chili Davis	.05	.02	.01
☐ 71 Jim Edmonds	.15	.07	.02
☐ 72 Troy Percival	.15	.07	.02
☐ 73 Mark Langston	.05	.02	.01
☐ 74 Spike Owen	.05	.02	.01
☐ 75 Tim Salmon	.30	.14	.04
☐ 76 Brian Anderson	.05	.02	.01
☐ 77 Lee Smith	.15	.07	.02
☐ 78 Jim Abbott	.30	.14	.04
☐ 79 Jim Bullinger	.05	.02	.01
☐ 80 Mark Grace	.30	.14	.04
☐ 81 Todd Zeile	.15	.07	.02
☐ 82 Kevin Foster	.05	.02	.01
☐ 83 Howard Johnson	.05	.02	.01
☐ 84 Brian McRae	.05	.02	.01
☐ 85 Randy Myers	.05	.02	.01
☐ 86 Jaime Navarro	.05	.02	.01
☐ 87 Luis Gonzalez	.05	.02	.01
☐ 88 Ozzie Timmons	.05	.02	.01
☐ 89 Wilson Alvarez	.30	.14	.04
☐ 90 Frank Thomas	2.00	.90	.25
☐ 91 James Baldwin	.15	.07	.02
☐ 92 Ray Durham	.30	.14	.04
☐ 93 Alex Fernandez	.15	.07	.02
☐ 94 Ozzie Guillen	.05	.02	.01
☐ 95 Tim Raines	.30	.14	.04
☐ 96 Roberto Hernandez	.15	.07	.02
☐ 97 Lance Johnson	.15	.07	.02
☐ 98 John Kruk	.15	.07	.02
☐ 99 Mark Portugal	.05	.02	.01
☐ 100 Don Mattingly TT	.50	.23	.06
☐ 101 Roger Clemens TT	.30	.14	.04
☐ 102 Raul Mondesi TT	.30	.14	.04
☐ 103 Cecil Fielder TT	.15	.07	.02
☐ 104 Ozzie Smith TT	.30	.14	.04
☐ 105 Frank Thomas TT	1.00	.45	.12
☐ 106 Sammy Sosa TT	.30	.14	.04
☐ 107 Fred McGriff TT	.30	.14	.04
☐ 108 Barry Bonds TT	.30	.14	.04
☐ 109 Thomas Howard	.05	.02	.01
☐ 110 Ron Gant	.15	.07	.02
☐ 111 Eddie Taubensee	.05	.02	.01
☐ 112 Hal Morris	.05	.02	.01
☐ 113 Jose Rijo	.05	.02	.01
☐ 114 Pete Schourek	.15	.07	.02
☐ 115 Reggie Sanders	.15	.07	.02
☐ 116 Benito Santiago	.05	.02	.01
☐ 117 Jeff Brantley	.05	.02	.01
☐ 118 Julian Tavarez	.05	.02	.01
☐ 119 Carlos Baerga	.15	.07	.02
☐ 120 Jim Thome	.40	.18	.05
☐ 121 Jose Mesa	.15	.07	.02
☐ 122 Dennis Martinez	.15	.07	.02
☐ 123 Dave Winfield	.30	.14	.04
☐ 124 Eddie Murray	.50	.23	.06
☐ 125 Manny Ramirez	.50	.23	.06
☐ 126 Paul Sorrento	.05	.02	.01
☐ 127 Kenny Lofton	.50	.23	.06
☐ 128 Eric Young	.15	.07	.02
☐ 129 Jason Bates	.05	.02	.01
☐ 130 Bret Saberhagen	.05	.02	.01
☐ 131 Andres Galarraga	.30	.14	.04
☐ 132 Joe Girardi	.05	.02	.01
☐ 133 John VanderWal	.05	.02	.01
☐ 134 David Nied	.05	.02	.01
☐ 135 Dante Bichette	.30	.14	.04
☐ 136 Vinny Castilla	.15	.07	.02
☐ 137 Kevin Ritz	.05	.02	.01
☐ 138 Felipe Lira	.05	.02	.01
☐ 139 Joe Boever	.05	.02	.01
☐ 140 Cecil Fielder	.15	.07	.02
☐ 141 John Flaherty	.05	.02	.01
☐ 142 Kirk Gibson	.15	.07	.02
☐ 143 Brian Maxcy	.05	.02	.01
☐ 144 Lou Whitaker	.15	.07	.02
☐ 145 Alan Trammell	.15	.07	.02
☐ 146 Bobby Higginson	.15	.07	.02
☐ 147 Chad Curtis	.05	.02	.01
☐ 148 Quilvio Veras	.05	.02	.01
☐ 149 Jerry Browne	.05	.02	.01
☐ 150 Andre Dawson	.15	.07	.02
☐ 151 Robb Nen	.05	.02	.01
☐ 152 Greg Colbrunn	.05	.02	.01
☐ 153 Chris Hammond	.05	.02	.01
☐ 154 Kurt Abbott	.05	.02	.01
☐ 155 Charles Johnson	.15	.07	.02
☐ 156 Terry Pendleton	.15	.07	.02
☐ 157 Dave Weathers	.05	.02	.01
☐ 158 Mike Hampton	.05	.02	.01
☐ 159 Craig Biggio	.15	.07	.02
☐ 160 Jeff Bagwell	.75	.35	.09
☐ 161 Brian L.Hunter	.15	.07	.02
☐ 162 Mike Henneman	.05	.02	.01
☐ 163 Dave Magadan	.05	.02	.01
☐ 164 Shane Reynolds	.15	.07	.02
☐ 165 Derek Bell	.15	.07	.02
☐ 166 Orlando Miller	.05	.02	.01
☐ 167 James Mouton	.05	.02	.01
☐ 168 Melvin Bunch	.05	.02	.01
☐ 169 Tom Gordon	.05	.02	.01
☐ 170 Kevin Appier	.15	.07	.02
☐ 171 Tom Goodwin	.15	.07	.02
☐ 172 Greg Gagne	.05	.02	.01
☐ 173 Gary Gaetti	.15	.07	.02

Card			
☐ 174 Jeff Montgomery	.05	.02	.01
☐ 175 Jon Nunnally	.05	.02	.01
☐ 176 Michael Tucker	.15	.07	.02
☐ 177 Joe Vitiello	.05	.02	.01
☐ 178 Billy Ashley	.05	.02	.01
☐ 179 Tom Candiotti	.05	.02	.01
☐ 180 Hideo Nomo	.50	.23	.06
☐ 181 Chad Fonville	.05	.02	.01
☐ 182 Todd Hollandsworth	.15	.07	.02
☐ 183 Eric Karros	.15	.07	.02
☐ 184 Roberto Kelly	.05	.02	.01
☐ 185 Mike Piazza	1.25	.55	.16
☐ 186 Ramon Martinez	.15	.07	.02
☐ 187 Tim Wallach	.05	.02	.01
☐ 188 Jeff Cirillo	.05	.02	.01
☐ 189 Sid Roberson	.05	.02	.01
☐ 190 Kevin Seitzer	.05	.02	.01
☐ 191 Mike Fetters	.05	.02	.01
☐ 192 Steve Sparks	.05	.02	.01
☐ 193 Matt Mieske	.05	.02	.01
☐ 194 Joe Oliver	.05	.02	.01
☐ 195 B.J. Surhoff	.05	.02	.01
☐ 196 Alberto Reyes	.05	.02	.01
☐ 197 Fernando Vina	.05	.02	.01
☐ 198 LaTroy Hawkins	.05	.02	.01
☐ 199 Marty Cordova	.15	.07	.02
☐ 200 Kirby Puckett	.75	.35	.09
☐ 201 Brad Radke	.05	.02	.01
☐ 202 Pedro Munoz	.05	.02	.01
☐ 203 Scott Klingenbeck	.05	.02	.01
☐ 204 Pat Meares	.05	.02	.01
☐ 205 Chuck Knoblauch	.30	.14	.04
☐ 206 Scott Stahoviak	.05	.02	.01
☐ 207 Dave Stevens	.05	.02	.01
☐ 208 Shane Andrews	.05	.02	.01
☐ 209 Moises Alou	.15	.07	.02
☐ 210 David Segui	.05	.02	.01
☐ 211 Cliff Floyd	.05	.02	.01
☐ 212 Carlos Perez	.05	.02	.01
☐ 213 Mark Grudzielanek	.05	.02	.01
☐ 214 Butch Henry	.05	.02	.01
☐ 215 Rondell White	.15	.07	.02
☐ 216 Mel Rojas	.15	.07	.02
☐ 217 Ugueth Urbina	.05	.02	.01
☐ 218 Edgardo Alfonzo	.15	.07	.02
☐ 219 Carl Everett	.05	.02	.01
☐ 220 John Franco	.05	.02	.01
☐ 221 Todd Hundley	.15	.07	.02
☐ 222 Bobby Jones	.05	.02	.01
☐ 223 Bill Pulsipher	.15	.07	.02
☐ 224 Rico Brogna	.05	.02	.01
☐ 225 Jeff Kent	.05	.02	.01
☐ 226 Chris Jones	.05	.02	.01
☐ 227 Butch Huskey	.15	.07	.02
☐ 228 Robert Eenhoorn	.05	.02	.01
☐ 229 Sterling Hitchcock	.05	.02	.01
☐ 230 Wade Boggs	.30	.14	.04
☐ 231 Derek Jeter	1.25	.55	.16
☐ 232 Tony Fernandez	.05	.02	.01
☐ 233 Jack McDowell	.30	.14	.04
☐ 234 Andy Pettitte	.60	.25	.07
☐ 235 David Cone	.15	.07	.02
☐ 236 Mike Stanley	.05	.02	.01
☐ 237 Don Mattingly	1.00	.45	.12
☐ 238 Geronimo Berroa	.15	.07	.02
☐ 239 Scott Brosius	.15	.07	.02
☐ 240 Rickey Henderson	.30	.14	.04
☐ 241 Terry Steinbach	.15	.07	.02
☐ 242 Mike Gallego	.05	.02	.01
☐ 243 Jason Giambi	.30	.14	.04
☐ 244 Steve Ontiveros	.05	.02	.01
☐ 245 Dennis Eckersley	.15	.07	.02
☐ 246 Dave Stewart	.15	.07	.02
☐ 247 Don Wengert	.05	.02	.01
☐ 248 Paul Quantrill	.05	.02	.01
☐ 249 Ricky Bottalico	.05	.02	.01
☐ 250 Kevin Stocker	.05	.02	.01
☐ 251 Lenny Dykstra	.15	.07	.02
☐ 252 Tony Longmire	.05	.02	.01
☐ 253 Tyler Green	.05	.02	.01
☐ 254 Mike Mimbs	.05	.02	.01
☐ 255 Charlie Hayes	.05	.02	.01
☐ 256 Mickey Morandini	.05	.02	.01
☐ 257 Heathcliff Slocumb	.05	.02	.01
☐ 258 Jeff King	.05	.02	.01
☐ 259 Midre Cummings	.05	.02	.01
☐ 260 Mark Johnson	.05	.02	.01
☐ 261 Freddy Garcia	.05	.02	.01
☐ 262 Jon Lieber	.05	.02	.01
☐ 263 Esteban Loaiza	.05	.02	.01
☐ 264 Dan Miceli	.05	.02	.01
☐ 265 Orlando Merced	.15	.07	.02
☐ 266 Denny Neagle	.15	.07	.02
☐ 267 Steve Parris	.05	.02	.01
☐ 268 Greg Maddux FT	.60	.25	.07
☐ 269 Randy Johnson FT	.30	.14	.04
☐ 270 Hideo Nomo FT	.30	.14	.04
☐ 271 Jose Mesa FT	.05	.02	.01
☐ 272 Mike Piazza FT	.60	.25	.07
☐ 273 Mo Vaughn FT	.30	.14	.04
☐ 274 Craig Biggio FT	.15	.07	.02
☐ 275 Edgar Martinez FT	.15	.07	.02
☐ 276 Barry Larkin FT	.30	.14	.04
☐ 277 Sammy Sosa FT	.30	.14	.04
☐ 278 Dante Bichette FT	.30	.14	.04
☐ 279 Albert Belle FT	.40	.18	.05
☐ 280 Ozzie Smith	.50	.23	.06
☐ 281 Mark Sweeney	.05	.02	.01
☐ 282 Terry Bradshaw	.05	.02	.01
☐ 283 Allen Battle	.05	.02	.01
☐ 284 Danny Jackson	.05	.02	.01
☐ 285 Tom Henke	.15	.07	.02
☐ 286 Scott Cooper	.05	.02	.01
☐ 287 Tripp Cromer	.05	.02	.01
☐ 288 Bernard Gilkey	.15	.07	.02
☐ 289 Brian Jordan	.15	.07	.02
☐ 290 Tony Gwynn	.75	.35	.09
☐ 291 Brad Ausmus	.05	.02	.01
☐ 292 Bryce Florie	.05	.02	.01
☐ 293 Andres Berumen	.05	.02	.01
☐ 294 Ken Caminiti	.30	.14	.04
☐ 295 Bip Roberts	.05	.02	.01
☐ 296 Trevor Hoffman	.15	.07	.02
☐ 297 Roberto Petagine	.05	.02	.01
☐ 298 Jody Reed	.05	.02	.01
☐ 299 Fernando Valenzuela	.15	.07	.02
☐ 300 Barry Bonds	.50	.23	.06
☐ 301 Mark Leiter	.05	.02	.01
☐ 302 Mark Carreon	.05	.02	.01
☐ 303 Royce Clayton	.05	.02	.01
☐ 304 Kirt Manwaring	.05	.02	.01
☐ 305 Glenallen Hill	.15	.07	.02
☐ 306 Deion Sanders	.30	.14	.04
☐ 307 Joe Rosselli	.05	.02	.01
☐ 308 Robby Thompson	.05	.02	.01
☐ 309 W. VanLandingham	.05	.02	.01
☐ 310 Ken Griffey Jr.	2.00	.90	.25
☐ 311 Bobby Ayala	.05	.02	.01
☐ 312 Joey Cora	.05	.02	.01
☐ 313 Mike Blowers	.05	.02	.01
☐ 314 Darren Bragg	.05	.02	.01
☐ 315 Randy Johnson	.30	.14	.04
☐ 316 Alex Rodriguez	2.00	.90	.25
☐ 317 Andy Benes	.05	.02	.01
☐ 318 Tino Martinez	.15	.07	.02
☐ 319 Dan Wilson	.05	.02	.01
☐ 320 Will Clark	.30	.14	.04
☐ 321 Jeff Frye	.05	.02	.01
☐ 322 Benji Gil	.05	.02	.01
☐ 323 Rick Helling	.05	.02	.01
☐ 324 Mark McLemore	.05	.02	.01
☐ 325 Dave Nilsson IF	.05	.02	.01
☐ 326 Larry Walker IF	.30	.14	.04
☐ 327 Jose Canseco IF	.30	.14	.04
☐ 328 Raul Mondesi IF	.30	.14	.04
☐ 329 Manny Ramirez IF	.15	.07	.02
☐ 330 Robert Eenhoorn IF	.05	.02	.01
☐ 331 Chili Davis IF	.05	.02	.01
☐ 332 Hideo Nomo IF	.30	.14	.04
☐ 333 Benji Gil IF	.05	.02	.01
☐ 334 Fernando Valenzuela IF	.15	.07	.02
☐ 335 Dennis Martinez IF	.05	.02	.01
☐ 336 Roberto Kelly IF	.05	.02	.01
☐ 337 Carlos Baerga IF	.15	.07	.02
☐ 338 Juan Gonzalez IF	.50	.23	.06
☐ 339 Roberto Alomar IF	.30	.14	.04
☐ 340 Chan Ho Park IF	.30	.14	.04
☐ 341 Andres Galarraga IF	.30	.14	.04
☐ 342 Midre Cummings IF	.05	.02	.01
☐ 343 Otis Nixon	.05	.02	.01
☐ 344 Jeff Russell	.05	.02	.01
☐ 345 Ivan Rodriguez	.50	.23	.06
☐ 346 Mickey Tettleton	.15	.07	.02
☐ 347 Bob Tewksbury	.05	.02	.01
☐ 348 Domingo Cedeno	.05	.02	.01
☐ 349 Lance Parrish	.15	.07	.02
☐ 350 Joe Carter	.15	.07	.02
☐ 351 Devon White	.05	.02	.01
☐ 352 Carlos Delgado	.15	.07	.02
☐ 353 Alex Gonzalez	.05	.02	.01
☐ 354 Darren Hall	.05	.02	.01
☐ 355 Paul Molitor	.40	.18	.05
☐ 356 Al Leiter	.05	.02	.01
☐ 357 Randy Knorr	.05	.02	.01
☐ 358 Ken Caminiti CL	.05	.02	.01
Steve Finley			
Brian Williams			
Roberto Petagine			
Andujar Cedeno			
Phil Plantier			
Derek Bell			
Pedro A. Martinez			
Doug Brocail			
Craig Shipley			
Ricky Gutierrez			
☐ 359 Hideo Nomo CL	.30	.14	.04
☐ 360 Ramon A.Martinez CL	.05	.02	.01
Ramon J.Martinez			
☐ 361 Robin Ventura CL	.15	.07	.02
☐ 362 Cal Ripken CL	.75	.35	.09
☐ 363 Ken Caminiti CL	.30	.14	.04
☐ 364 Albert Belle CL	.40	.18	.05
Eddie Murray			
☐ 365 Randy Johnson CL	.30	.14	.04
☐ 366T Tony Pena TRADE	60.00	27.00	7.50
☐ 367T Jim Thome TRADE	.75	.35	.09
☐ 368T Don Mattingly TRADE	2.00	.90	.25
☐ 369T Jim Leyritz TRADE	60.00	27.00	7.50
☐ 370T Ken Griffey Jr. TRADE	4.00	1.80	.50
☐ 371T Edgar Martinez TRADE	.15	.07	.02
☐ 372T Pete Schourek TRADE	60.00	27.00	7.50
☐ 373T Mark Lewis TRADE	60.00	27.00	7.50
☐ 374T Chipper Jones TRADE	2.50	1.10	.30
☐ 375T Fred McGriff TRADE	.30	.14	.04
☐ 376T Javy Lopez TRADE	.15	.07	.02
☐ 377T Fred McGriff TRADE	.30	.14	.04
☐ 378T Charlie O'Brien TRADE	60.00	27.00	7.50
☐ 379T Mike Devereaux TRADE	60.00	27.00	7.50
☐ 380T Mark Wohlers TRADE	.30	.14	.04
☐ 381T Bob Wolcott TRADE	60.00	27.00	7.50
☐ 382T Manny Ramirez TRADE	1.00	.45	.12
☐ 383T Jay Buhner TRADE	.30	.14	.04
☐ 384T Orel Hershiser TRADE	.15	.07	.02
☐ 385T Kenny Lofton TRADE	1.00	.45	.12
☐ 386T Greg Maddux TRADE	2.50	1.10	.30
☐ 387T Javier Lopez TRADE	.30	.14	.04
☐ 388T Kenny Lofton TRADE	1.00	.45	.12
☐ 389T Eddie Murray TRADE	1.00	.45	.12
☐ 390T Luis Polonia TRADE	60.00	27.00	7.50
☐ 391T Pedro Borbon TRADE	60.00	27.00	7.50
☐ 392T Jim Thome TRADE	.75	.35	.09
☐ 393T Orel Hershiser TRADE	60.00	27.00	7.50
☐ 394T David Justice TRADE	.30	.14	.04
☐ 395T Tom Glavine TRADE	.30	.14	.04
☐ 396 Greg Maddux TC	.60	.25	.07
☐ 397 Darren Daulton TC	.15	.07	.02
☐ 398 Rico Brogna TC	.05	.02	.01
☐ 399 Gary Sheffield TC	.30	.14	.04
☐ 400 Moises Alou TC	.15	.07	.02
☐ 401 Barry Larkin TC	.30	.14	.04
☐ 402 Jeff Bagwell TC	.40	.18	.05
☐ 403 Sammy Sosa TC	.30	.14	.04
☐ 404 Ozzie Smith TC	.30	.14	.04
☐ 405 Jay Bell TC	.05	.02	.01
☐ 406 Mike Piazza TC	.60	.25	.07
☐ 407 Dante Bichette TC	.30	.14	.04
☐ 408 Tony Gwynn TC	.40	.18	.05
☐ 409 Barry Bonds TC	.30	.14	.04
☐ 410 Kenny Lofton TC	.30	.14	.04
☐ 411 Johnny Damon TC	.15	.07	.02
☐ 412 Frank Thomas TC	1.00	.45	.12
☐ 413 Greg Vaughn TC	.15	.07	.02
☐ 414 Paul Molitor TC	.30	.14	.04
☐ 415 Ken Griffey Jr. TC	1.00	.45	.12
☐ 416 Tim Salmon TC	.30	.14	.04
☐ 417 Juan Gonzalez TC	.50	.23	.06
☐ 418 Mark McGwire TC	.30	.14	.04
☐ 419 Roger Clemens TC	.30	.14	.04
☐ 420 Wade Boggs TC	.30	.14	.04
☐ 421 Cal Ripken TC	.75	.35	.09
☐ 422 Cecil Fielder TC	.15	.07	.02
☐ 423 Joe Carter TC	.15	.07	.02
☐ 424 Osvaldo Fernandez	.30	.14	.04
☐ 425 Billy Wagner	.30	.14	.04
☐ 426 George Arias	.05	.02	.01
☐ 427 Mendy Lopez	.15	.07	.02
☐ 428 Jeff Suppan	.30	.14	.04
☐ 429 Rey Ordonez	.30	.14	.04
☐ 430 Brooks Kieschnick	.30	.14	.04
☐ 431 Raul Ibanez	.15	.07	.02
☐ 432 Livan Hernandez	.30	.14	.04
☐ 433 Shannon Stewart	.05	.02	.01
☐ 434 Steve Cox	.05	.02	.01
☐ 435 Trey Beamon	.15	.07	.02
☐ 436 Sergio Nunez	.15	.07	.02
☐ 437 Jermaine Dye	.30	.14	.04
☐ 438 Mike Sweeney	.40	.18	.05
☐ 439 Richard Hidalgo	.30	.14	.04
☐ 440 Todd Greene	.15	.07	.02
☐ 441 Robert Smith	.40	.18	.05
☐ 442 Rafael Orellano	.05	.02	.01
☐ 443 Wilton Guerrero	1.00	.45	.12
☐ 444 David Doster	.05	.02	.01
☐ 445 Jason Kendall	.30	.14	.04
☐ 446 Edgar Renteria	.30	.14	.04
☐ 447 Scott Spiezio	.30	.14	.04
☐ 448 Jay Canizaro	.05	.02	.01
☐ 449 Enrique Wilson	.30	.14	.04
☐ 450 Bob Abreu	.30	.14	.04
☐ 451 Dwight Smith	.05	.02	.01
☐ 452 Jeff Blauser	.05	.02	.01
☐ 453 Steve Avery	.05	.02	.01
☐ 454 Brad Clontz	.05	.02	.01
☐ 455 Tom Glavine	.30	.14	.04
☐ 456 Mike Mordecai	.05	.02	.01
☐ 457 Rafael Belliard	.05	.02	.01
☐ 458 Greg McMichael	.05	.02	.01
☐ 459 Pedro Borbon	.05	.02	.01
☐ 460 Ryan Klesko	.30	.14	.04
☐ 461 Terrell Wade	.15	.07	.02
☐ 462 Brady Anderson	.30	.14	.04
☐ 463 Roberto Alomar	.50	.23	.06
☐ 464 Bobby Bonilla	.15	.07	.02
☐ 465 Mike Mussina	.40	.18	.05
☐ 466 Cesar Devarez	.05	.02	.01
☐ 467 Jeffrey Hammonds	.05	.02	.01
☐ 468 Mike Devereaux	.05	.02	.01
☐ 469 B.J. Surhoff	.05	.02	.01
☐ 470 Rafael Palmeiro	.30	.14	.04
☐ 471 John Valentin	.15	.07	.02
☐ 472 Mike Greenwell	.05	.02	.01
☐ 473 Dwayne Hosey	.05	.02	.01
☐ 474 Tim Wakefield	.05	.02	.01
☐ 475 Jose Canseco	.30	.14	.04
☐ 476 Aaron Sele	.05	.02	.01
☐ 477 Stan Belinda	.05	.02	.01
☐ 478 Mike Stanley	.05	.02	.01
☐ 479 Jamie Moyer	.05	.02	.01
☐ 480 Mo Vaughn	.50	.23	.06
☐ 481 Randy Velarde	.05	.02	.01
☐ 482 Gary DiSarcina	.05	.02	.01
☐ 483 Jorge Fabregas	.05	.02	.01
☐ 484 Rex Hudler	.05	.02	.01
☐ 485 Chuck Finley	.05	.02	.01
☐ 486 Tim Wallach	.05	.02	.01
☐ 487 Eduardo Perez	.05	.02	.01
☐ 488 Scott Sanderson	.05	.02	.01
☐ 489 J.T. Snow	.15	.07	.02
☐ 490 Sammy Sosa	.30	.14	.04
☐ 491 Terry Adams	.05	.02	.01
☐ 492 Matt Franco	.05	.02	.01
☐ 493 Scott Servais	.05	.02	.01
☐ 494 Frank Castillo	.05	.02	.01
☐ 495 Ryne Sandberg	.50	.23	.06
☐ 496 Rey Sanchez	.05	.02	.01
☐ 497 Steve Trachsel	.05	.02	.01
☐ 498 Jose Hernandez	.05	.02	.01
☐ 499 Dave Martinez	.05	.02	.01
☐ 500 Babe Ruth FC	.50	.23	.06
☐ 501 Ty Cobb FC	.40	.18	.05
☐ 502 Walter Johnson FC	.30	.14	.04
☐ 503 Christy Mathewson FC	.30	.14	.04
☐ 504 Honus Wagner FC	.40	.18	.05
☐ 505 Robin Ventura	.15	.07	.02
☐ 506 Jason Bere	.05	.02	.01
☐ 507 Mike Cameron	.60	.25	.07
☐ 508 Ron Karkovice	.05	.02	.01
☐ 509 Matt Karchner	.05	.02	.01
☐ 510 Harold Baines	.15	.07	.02
☐ 511 Kirk McCaskill	.05	.02	.01
☐ 512 Larry Thomas	.05	.02	.01
☐ 513 Danny Tartabull	.05	.02	.01
☐ 514 Steve Gilbralter	.05	.02	.01
☐ 515 Bret Boone	.05	.02	.01
☐ 516 Jeff Branson	.05	.02	.01
☐ 517 Kevin Jarvis	.05	.02	.01
☐ 518 Xavier Hernandez	.05	.02	.01
☐ 519 Eric Owens	.05	.02	.01
☐ 520 Barry Larkin	.30	.14	.04
☐ 521 Dave Burba	.05	.02	.01
☐ 522 John Smiley	.05	.02	.01
☐ 523 Paul Assenmacher	.05	.02	.01
☐ 524 Chad Ogea	.05	.02	.01
☐ 525 Orel Hershiser	.15	.07	.02
☐ 526 Alan Embree	.05	.02	.01
☐ 527 Tony Pena	.05	.02	.01
☐ 528 Omar Vizquel	.15	.07	.02
☐ 529 Mark Clark	.05	.02	.01
☐ 530 Albert Belle	.75	.35	.09
☐ 531 Charles Nagy	.15	.07	.02
☐ 532 Herbert Perry	.05	.02	.01
☐ 533 Darren Holmes	.05	.02	.01
☐ 534 Ellis Burks	.15	.07	.02
☐ 535 Billy Swift	.05	.02	.01
☐ 536 Armando Reynoso	.05	.02	.01
☐ 537 Curtis Leskanic	.05	.02	.01
☐ 538 Quinton McCracken	.05	.02	.01
☐ 539 Steve Reed	.05	.02	.01
☐ 540 Larry Walker	.30	.14	.04
☐ 541 Walt Weiss	.05	.02	.01
☐ 542 Bryan Rekar	.05	.02	.01
☐ 543 Tony Clark	.40	.18	.05
☐ 544 Steve Rodriguez	.05	.02	.01
☐ 545 C.J. Nitkowski	.05	.02	.01
☐ 546 Todd Steverson	.05	.02	.01
☐ 547 Jose Lima	.05	.02	.01
☐ 548 Phil Nevin	.05	.02	.01
☐ 549 Chris Gomez	.05	.02	.01
☐ 550 Travis Fryman	.15	.07	.02
☐ 551 Mark Lewis	.05	.02	.01
☐ 552 Alex Arias	.05	.02	.01
☐ 553 Marc Valdes	.05	.02	.01
☐ 554 Kevin Brown	.15	.07	.02
☐ 555 Jeff Conine	.15	.07	.02
☐ 556 John Burkett	.05	.02	.01
☐ 557 Devon White	.05	.02	.01
☐ 558 Pat Rapp	.05	.02	.01
☐ 559 Jay Powell	.05	.02	.01
☐ 560 Gary Sheffield	.30	.14	.04
☐ 561 Jim Dougherty	.05	.02	.01
☐ 562 Todd Jones	.05	.02	.01
☐ 563 Tony Eusebio	.05	.02	.01
☐ 564 Darryl Kile	.05	.02	.01
☐ 565 Doug Drabek	.05	.02	.01
☐ 566 Mike Simms	.05	.02	.01
☐ 567 Derrick May	.05	.02	.01
☐ 568 Donne Wall	.05	.02	.01
☐ 569 Greg Swindell	.05	.02	.01
☐ 570 Jim Pittsley	.15	.07	.02
☐ 571 Bob Hamelin	.05	.02	.01
☐ 572 Mark Gubicza	.05	.02	.01
☐ 573 Chris Haney	.05	.02	.01
☐ 574 Keith Lockhart	.05	.02	.01
☐ 575 Mike Macfarlane	.05	.02	.01
☐ 576 Les Norman	.05	.02	.01
☐ 577 Joe Randa	.05	.02	.01
☐ 578 Chris Stynes	.05	.02	.01
☐ 579 Greg Gagne	.05	.02	.01
☐ 580 Raul Mondesi	.30	.14	.04
☐ 581 Delino DeShields	.05	.02	.01

□ 582 Pedro Astacio	.05	.02	.01
□ 583 Antonio Osuna	.05	.02	.01
□ 584 Brett Butler	.05	.02	.01
□ 585 Todd Worrell	.15	.07	.02
□ 586 Mike Blowers	.05	.02	.01
□ 587 Felix Rodriguez	.05	.02	.01
□ 588 Ismael Valdes	.15	.07	.02
□ 589 Ricky Bones	.05	.02	.01
□ 590 Greg Vaughn	.30	.14	.04
□ 591 Mark Loretta	.05	.02	.01
□ 592 Cal Eldred	.05	.02	.01
□ 593 Chuck Carr	.05	.02	.01
□ 594 Dave Nilsson	.15	.07	.02
□ 595 John Jaha	.15	.07	.02
□ 596 Scott Karl	.05	.02	.01
□ 597 Pat Listach	.05	.02	.01
□ 598 Jose Valentin	.05	.02	.01
□ 599 Mike Trombley	.05	.02	.01
□ 600 Paul Molitor	.40	.18	.05
□ 601 Dave Hollins	.05	.02	.01
□ 602 Ron Coomer	.05	.02	.01
□ 603 Matt Walbeck	.05	.02	.01
□ 604 Roberto Kelly	.05	.02	.01
□ 605 Rick Aguilera	.05	.02	.01
□ 606 Pat Mahomes	.05	.02	.01
□ 607 Jeff Reboulet	.05	.02	.01
□ 608 Rich Becker	.15	.07	.02
□ 609 Tim Scott	.05	.02	.01
□ 610 Pedro J. Martinez	.15	.07	.02
□ 611 Kirk Rueter	.05	.02	.01
□ 612 Tavo Alvarez	.05	.02	.01
□ 613 Yamil Benitez	.15	.07	.02
□ 614 Darrin Fletcher	.05	.02	.01
□ 615 Mike Lansing	.05	.02	.01
□ 616 Henry Rodriguez	.15	.07	.02
□ 617 Tony Tarasco	.05	.02	.01
□ 618 Alex Ochoa	.15	.07	.02
□ 619 Tim Bogar	.05	.02	.01
□ 620 Bernard Gilkey	.15	.07	.02
□ 621 Dave Mlicki	.05	.02	.01
□ 622 Brent Mayne	.05	.02	.01
□ 623 Ryan Thompson	.05	.02	.01
□ 624 Pete Harnisch	.05	.02	.01
□ 625 Lance Johnson	.15	.07	.02
□ 626 Jose Vizcaino	.05	.02	.01
□ 627 Doug Henry	.05	.02	.01
□ 628 Scott Kamieniecki	.05	.02	.01
□ 629 Jim Leyritz	.05	.02	.01
□ 630 Ruben Sierra	.05	.02	.01
□ 631 Pat Kelly	.05	.02	.01
□ 632 Joe Girardi	.05	.02	.01
□ 633 John Wetteland	.15	.07	.02
□ 634 Melido Perez	.05	.02	.01
□ 635 Paul O'Neill	.05	.02	.01
□ 636 Jorge Posada	.05	.02	.01
□ 637 Bernie Williams	.40	.18	.05
□ 638 Mark Acre	.05	.02	.01
□ 639 Mike Bordick	.15	.07	.02
□ 640 Mark McGwire	.60	.25	.07
□ 641 Fausto Cruz	.05	.02	.01
□ 642 Ernie Young	.05	.02	.01
□ 643 Todd Van Poppel	.05	.02	.01
□ 644 Craig Paquette	.05	.02	.01
□ 645 Brent Gates	.05	.02	.01
□ 646 Pedro Munoz	.05	.02	.01
□ 647 Andrew Lorraine	.05	.02	.01
□ 648 Sid Fernandez	.05	.02	.01
□ 649 Jim Eisenreich	.05	.02	.01
□ 650 Johnny Damon	.15	.07	.02
□ 651 Dustin Hermanson	.15	.07	.02
□ 652 Joe Randa	.05	.02	.01
□ 653 Michael Tucker	.15	.07	.02
□ 654 Alan Benes	.30	.14	.04
□ 655 Chad Fonville	.05	.02	.01
□ 656 David Bell	.05	.02	.01
□ 657 Jon Nunnally	.05	.02	.01
□ 658 Chan Ho Park	.30	.14	.04
□ 659 LaTroy Hawkins	.05	.02	.01
□ 660 Jamie Brewington	.05	.02	.01
□ 661 Quinton McCracken	.05	.02	.01
□ 662 Tim Unroe	.05	.02	.01
□ 663 Jeff Ware	.05	.02	.01
□ 664 Todd Greene	.30	.14	.04
□ 665 Andrew Lorraine	.05	.02	.01
□ 666 Ernie Young	.05	.02	.01
□ 667 Toby Borland	.05	.02	.01
□ 668 Lenny Webster	.05	.02	.01
□ 669 Benito Santiago	.05	.02	.01
□ 670 Gregg Jefferies	.30	.14	.04
□ 671 Darren Daulton	.15	.07	.02
□ 672 Curt Schilling	.05	.02	.01
□ 673 Mark Whiten	.05	.02	.01
□ 674 Todd Zeile	.15	.07	.02
□ 675 Jay Bell	.05	.02	.01
□ 676 Paul Wagner	.05	.02	.01
□ 677 Dave Clark	.05	.02	.01
□ 678 Nelson Liriano	.05	.02	.01
□ 679 Ramon Morel	.15	.07	.02
□ 680 Charlie Hayes	.05	.02	.01
□ 681 Angelo Encarnacion	.05	.02	.01
□ 682 Al Martin	.05	.02	.01
□ 683 Jacob Brumfield	.05	.02	.01
□ 684 Mike Kingery	.05	.02	.01
□ 685 Carlos Garcia	.05	.02	.01
□ 686 Tom Pagnozzi	.05	.02	.01
□ 687 David Bell	.05	.02	.01
□ 688 Todd Stottlemyre	.05	.02	.01
□ 689 Jose Oliva	.05	.02	.01
□ 690 Ray Lankford	.15	.07	.02
□ 691 Mike Morgan	.05	.02	.01
□ 692 John Frascatore	.05	.02	.01
□ 693 John Mabry	.15	.07	.02
□ 694 Mark Petkovsek	.05	.02	.01
□ 695 Alan Benes	.30	.14	.04
□ 696 Steve Finley	.30	.14	.04
□ 697 Marc Newfield	.15	.07	.02
□ 698 Andy Ashby	.05	.02	.01
□ 699 Marc Kroon	.05	.02	.01
□ 700 Wally Joyner	.05	.02	.01
□ 701 Joey Hamilton	.15	.07	.02
□ 702 Dustin Hermanson	.15	.07	.02
□ 703 Scott Sanders	.05	.02	.01
□ 704 Marty Cordova ROY	.15	.07	.02
□ 705 Hideo Nomo ROY	.30	.14	.04
□ 706 Mo Vaughn MVP	.30	.14	.04
□ 707 Barry Larkin MVP	.30	.14	.04
□ 708 Randy Johnson CY	.30	.14	.04
□ 709 Greg Maddux CY	.60	.25	.07
□ 710 Mark McGwire CB	.30	.14	.04
□ 711 Ron Gant CB	.15	.07	.02
□ 712 Andujar Cedeno	.05	.02	.01
□ 713 Brian Johnson	.05	.02	.01
□ 714 J.R. Phillips	.05	.02	.01
□ 715 Rod Beck	.05	.02	.01
□ 716 Sergio Valdez	.05	.02	.01
□ 717 Marvin Benard	.05	.02	.01
□ 718 Steve Scarsone	.05	.02	.01
□ 719 Rich Aurilia	.05	.02	.01
□ 720 Matt Williams	.30	.14	.04
□ 721 John Patterson	.05	.02	.01
□ 722 Shawn Estes	.15	.07	.02
□ 723 Russ Davis	.05	.02	.01
□ 724 Rich Amaral	.05	.02	.01
□ 725 Edgar Martinez	.15	.07	.02
□ 726 Norm Charlton	.05	.02	.01
□ 727 Paul Sorrento	.05	.02	.01
□ 728 Luis Sojo	.05	.02	.01
□ 729 Arquimedez Pozo	.05	.02	.01
□ 730 Jay Buhner	.30	.14	.04
□ 731 Chris Bosio	.05	.02	.01
□ 732 Chris Widger	.05	.02	.01
□ 733 Kevin Gross	.05	.02	.01
□ 734 Darren Oliver	.15	.07	.02
□ 735 Dean Palmer	.30	.14	.04
□ 736 Matt Whiteside	.05	.02	.01
□ 737 Luis Ortiz	.05	.02	.01
□ 738 Roger Pavlik	.05	.02	.01
□ 739 Damon Buford	.05	.02	.01
□ 740 Juan Gonzalez	1.00	.45	.12
□ 741 Rusty Greer	.30	.14	.04
□ 742 Lou Frazier	.05	.02	.01
□ 743 Pat Hentgen	.15	.07	.02
□ 744 Tomas Perez	.05	.02	.01
□ 745 Juan Guzman	.05	.02	.01
□ 746 Otis Nixon	.05	.02	.01
□ 747 Robert Perez	.05	.02	.01
□ 748 Ed Sprague	.15	.07	.02
□ 749 Tony Castillo	.05	.02	.01
□ 750 John Olerud	.05	.02	.01
□ 751 Shawn Green	.05	.02	.01
□ 752 Jeff Ware	.05	.02	.01
□ 753 Dante Bichette CL Vinny Castilla Andres Galarraga Larry Walker	.15	.07	.02
□ 754 Greg Maddux CL	.60	.25	.07
□ 755 Marty Cordova CL	.15	.07	.02
□ 756 Ozzie Smith CL	.30	.14	.04
□ 757 John Vanderwal CL	.05	.02	.01
□ 758 Andres Galarraga CL	.30	.14	.04
□ 759 Frank Thomas CL	1.00	.45	.12
□ 760 Tony Gwynn CL	.40	.18	.05
□ 761 Randy Myers UPD	.40	.18	.05
□ 762 Kent Mercker UPD	.25	.11	.03
□ 763 David Wells UPD	.25	.11	.03
□ 764 Tom Gordon UPD	.25	.11	.03
□ 765 Wil Cordero UPD	.25	.11	.03
□ 766 Dave Magadan UPD	.25	.11	.03
□ 767 Doug Jones UPD	.25	.11	.03
□ 768 Kevin Tapani UPD	.40	.18	.05
□ 769 Curtis Goodwin UPD	.25	.11	.03
□ 770 Julio Franco UPD	.40	.18	.05
□ 771 Jack McDowell UPD	.75	.35	.09
□ 772 Al Leiter UPD	.40	.18	.05
□ 773 Sean Berry UPD	.25	.11	.03
□ 774 Bip Roberts UPD	.40	.18	.05
□ 775 Jose Offerman UPD	.25	.11	.03
□ 776 Ben McDonald UPD	.40	.18	.05
□ 777 Dan Serafini UPD	.25	.11	.03
□ 778 Ryan McGuire UPD	.40	.18	.05
□ 779 Tim Raines UPD	.75	.35	.09
□ 780 Tino Martinez UPD	.75	.35	.09
□ 781 Kenny Rogers UPD	.25	.11	.03
□ 782 Bob Tewksbury UPD	.25	.11	.03
□ 783 Rickey Henderson UPD	1.00	.45	.12
□ 784 Ron Gant UPD	.75	.35	.09
□ 785 Gary Gaetti UPD	.40	.18	.05
□ 786 Andy Benes UPD	.40	.18	.05
□ 787 Royce Clayton UPD	.40	.18	.05
□ 788 Darryl Hamilton UPD	.25	.11	.03
□ 789 Ken Hill UPD	.25	.11	.03
□ 790 Erik Hanson UPD	.25	.11	.03

1996 Collector's Choice Gold Signature

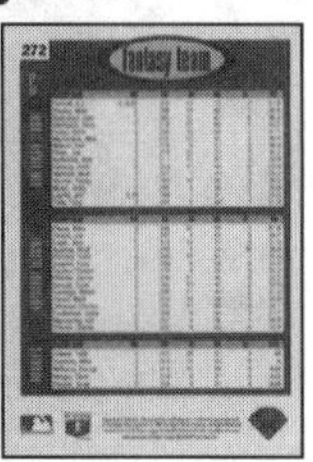

This 730-card set parallels the basic Collector's Choice issue. These cards were inserted approximately one every 35 packs. Cards 1-365 were issued in first series and 396-730 in second series. The cards are similar to the regular issue except they have gold borders and a gold facsimile player's signature on front.

	MINT	NRMT	EXC
COMPLETE SET (730)	1500.00	700.00	190.00
COMPLETE SERIES 1 (365)	800.00	350.00	100.00
COMPLETE SERIES 2 (365)	700.00	325.00	90.00
COMMON CARD (1-360/396-760)	1.00	.45	.12

*STARS: 12.5X TO 25X BASIC CARDS
*YOUNG STARS: 10X TO 20X BASIC CARDS

1996 Collector's Choice Silver Signature

This 730-card set parallels the regular Collector's Choice set. These cards were inserted one per pack in both first and second series packs. The cards are similar to the regular issue except for silver borders and a silver foil facsimile player's signature on the card front. Cards 366-395 do not exist.

	MINT	NRMT	EXC
COMPLETE SET (730)	110.00	50.00	14.00
COMPLETE SERIES 1 (365)	60.00	27.00	7.50
COMPLETE SERIES 2 (365)	50.00	22.00	6.25
COMMON CARD (1-365/396-760)	.10	.05	.01

*STARS: 1.5X TO 3X BASIC CARDS
*YOUNG STARS: 1.25X TO 2.5X BASIC CARDS

1996 Collector's Choice Crash the Game

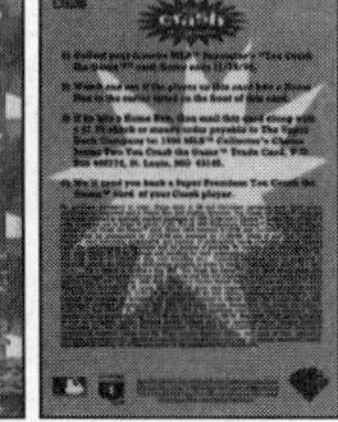

Randomly inserted into one in every five Series 2 packs, silver Crash the Game interactive cards feature a selection of thirty of baseball's top stars. If the featured player hit a home run during the series specified on the card, it was then eligible to be redeemed for a super premium Cell Card of the same player. Winning cards have been highlighted with a "W" in the listings below. The postmark expiration date for exchanging winning cards was November 18th, 1996.

	MINT	NRMT	EXC
COMPLETE SET (90)	50.00	22.00	6.25
COMMON CARD (CG1-CG30)	.40	.18	.05
□ CG1 Chipper Jones 7/11 W	2.00	.90	.25
□ CG1B Chipper Jones 8/27 W	2.00	.90	.25
□ CG1C Chipper Jones 9/19	2.00	.90	.25
□ CG2 Fred McGriff 7/1	.50	.23	.06
□ CG2B Fred McGriff 8/30	.50	.23	.06
□ CG2C Fred McGriff 9/10 W	.50	.23	.06
□ CG3 Rafael Palmeiro 7/4 W	.50	.23	.06
□ CG3B Rafael Palmeiro 8/29	.50	.23	.06
□ CG3C Rafael Palmeiro 9/26	.50	.23	.06
□ CG4 Cal Ripken 6/27	2.50	1.10	.30
□ CG4B Cal Ripken 7/25 W	2.50	1.10	.30
□ CG4C Cal Ripken 9/2	2.50	1.10	.30
□ CG5 Jose Canseco 6/27	.50	.23	.06
□ CG5B Jose Canseco 7/11 W	.50	.23	.06
□ CG5C Jose Canseco 8/23	.50	.23	.06
□ CG6 Mo Vaughn 6/21 W	.75	.35	.09
□ CG6B Mo Vaughn 7/18 W	.75	.35	.09
□ CG6C Mo Vaughn 9/20	.75	.35	.09
□ CG7 Jim Edmonds 7/18 W	.40	.18	.05
□ CG7B Jim Edmonds 8/16 W	.40	.18	.05
□ CG7C Jim Edmonds 9/20	.40	.18	.05
□ CG8 Tim Salmon 6/20	.50	.23	.06
□ CG8B Tim Salmon 7/30	.50	.23	.06
□ CG8C Tim Salmon 9/9	.50	.23	.06
□ CG9 Sammy Sosa 7/4 W	.50	.23	.06
□ CG9B Sammy Sosa 8/1 W	.50	.23	.06
□ CG9C Sammy Sosa 9/2	.50	.23	.06
□ CG10 Frank Thomas 6/27	3.00	1.35	.35
□ CG10B Frank Thomas 7/4	3.00	1.35	.35
□ CG10C Frank Thomas 9/2 W	3.00	1.35	.35
□ CG11 Albert Belle 6/25	1.25	.55	.16
□ CG11B Albert Belle 8/2 W	1.50	.70	.19
□ CG11C Albert Belle 9/6	1.50	.70	.19
□ CG12 Manny Ramirez 7/18 W	.75	.35	.09
□ CG12B Manny Ramirez 8/26	.75	.35	.09
□ CG12C Manny Ramirez 9/9 W	.75	.35	.09
□ CG13 Jim Thome 6/27	.60	.25	.07
□ CG13B Jim Thome 7/4 W	.60	.25	.07
□ CG13C Jim Thome 9/23	.60	.25	.07
□ CG14 Dante Bichette 7/11 W	.50	.23	.06
□ CG14B Dante Bichette 8/9	.50	.23	.06
□ CG14C Dante Bichette 9/9	.50	.23	.06
□ CG15 Vinny Castilla 7/1	.40	.18	.05
□ CG15B Vinny Castilla 8/23 W	.40	.18	.05
□ CG15C Vinny Castilla 9/13 W	.40	.18	.05
□ CG16 Larry Walker 6/24	.50	.23	.06
□ CG16B Larry Walker 7/18	.50	.23	.06
□ CG16C Larry Walker 9/27	.50	.23	.06
□ CG17 Cecil Fielder 6/27	.40	.18	.05
□ CG17B Cecil Fielder 7/30 W	.40	.18	.05
□ CG17C Cecil Fielder 9/17 W	.40	.18	.05
□ CG18 Gary Sheffield 7/4	.50	.23	.06
□ CG18B Gary Sheffield 8/2	.50	.23	.06
□ CG18C Gary Sheffield 9/5 W	.50	.23	.06
□ CG19 Jeff Bagwell 7/4 W	1.25	.55	.16
□ CG19B Jeff Bagwell 8/16	1.25	.55	.16
□ CG19C Jeff Bagwell 9/13	1.25	.55	.16
□ CG20 Eric Karros 7/4 W	.40	.18	.05
□ CG20B Eric Karros 8/13 W	.40	.18	.05
□ CG20C Eric Karros 9/16	.40	.18	.05
□ CG21 Mike Piazza 6/27 W	2.00	.90	.25
□ CG21B Mike Piazza 7/26	2.00	.90	.25
□ CG21C Mike Piazza 9/12 W	2.00	.90	.25
□ CG22 Ken Caminiti 7/11 W	.50	.23	.06
□ CG22B Ken Caminiti 8/16 W	.50	.23	.06
□ CG22C Ken Caminiti 9/19 W	.50	.23	.06
□ CG23 Barry Bonds 6/27 W	.75	.35	.09
□ CG23B Barry Bonds 7/22	.75	.35	.09
□ CG23C Barry Bonds 9/24	.75	.35	.09
□ CG24 Matt Williams 7/11 W	.50	.23	.06
□ CG24B Matt Williams 8/19	.50	.23	.06
□ CG24C Matt Williams 9/27	.50	.23	.06
□ CG25 Jay Buhner 6/20	.50	.23	.06
□ CG25B Jay Buhner 7/25	.50	.23	.06
□ CG25C Jay Buhner 8/29 W	.50	.23	.06
□ CG26 Ken Griffey Jr. 7/18 W	3.00	1.35	.35
□ CG26B Ken Griffey Jr. 8/16 W	3.00	1.35	.35
□ CG26C Ken Griffey Jr. 9/20 W	3.00	1.35	.35
□ CG27 Ron Gant 6/24 W	.40	.18	.05
□ CG27B Ron Gant 7/11 W	.40	.18	.05
□ CG27C Ron Gant 9/27 W	.40	.18	.05
□ CG28 Juan Gonzalez 6/28 W	1.50	.70	.19
□ CG28B Juan Gonzalez 7/15 W	1.50	.70	.19
□ CG28C Juan Gonzalez 8/6	1.50	.70	.19
□ CG29 Mickey Tettleton 7/4 W	.40	.18	.05
□ CG29B Mickey Tettleton 8/6	.40	.18	.05
□ CG29C Mickey Tettleton 9/6 W	.40	.18	.05
□ CG30 Joe Carter 6/25	.40	.18	.05
□ CG30B Joe Carter 8/5	.40	.18	.05
□ CG30C Joe Carter 9/23	.40	.18	.05

1996 Collector's Choice Crash the Game Exchange

This 27-card set features transparent color player images of the homerun hitters from the Collectors Choice Crash the Game regular set in a wood-like frame highlighted with silver foil. The backs carry player statistics. The cards were available via mail on a card-by-card basis in exchange for winning Silver Crash cards.

	MINT	NRMT	EXC
COMPLETE SET (27)	100.00	45.00	12.50
COMMON CARD (CR1-CR29)	2.00	.90	.25

*SILVER EXCH: 5X BASIC CRASH CARDS

1996 Collector's Choice Crash the Game Gold

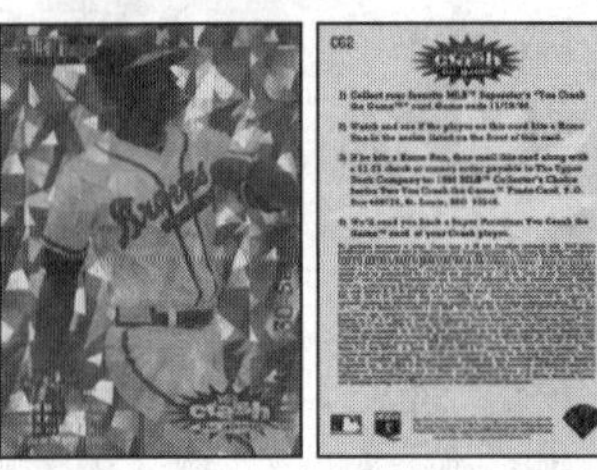

This 90-card set parallels the more common silver Crash the Game cards. Gold cards were randomly inserted into one in every 50 Series 2 packs. Winning cards were redeemable for a super premium Wood Cell Card featuring the same player.

	MINT	NRMT	EXC
COMPLETE SET (90)	250.00	110.00	31.00
COMMON CARD (CG1-CG90)	2.00	.90	.25
*GOLD: 5X BASIC CRASH CARDS			

1996 Collector's Choice Crash the Game Gold Exchange

This set of redeemed cards is a gold parallel to the Crash the Game Silver exchange cards. The cards were available on a card-by-card basis via mail for winning gold Crash cards.

	MINT	NRMT	EXC
COMPLETE SET (27)	300.00	135.00	38.00
COMMON CARD (CR1-CR29)	6.00	2.70	.75
*GOLD EXCH.: 15X BASIC CRASH CARDS			

1996 Collector's Choice Griffey A Cut Above

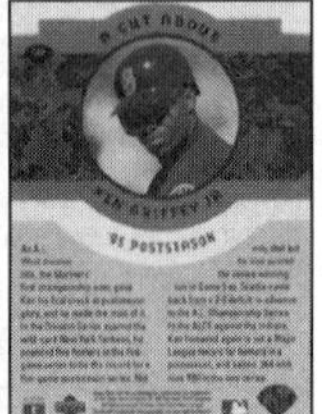

These ten cards focus on Seattle Mariners superstar Ken Griffey Jr. The cards were inserted at a rate of one per pack in special six-card retail packs (five basic CC cards plus one Griffey ACA insert). The packs were sold at Wal-Mart's nationwide and carried a suggested retail price of $0.97.

	MINT	NRMT	EXC
COMPLETE SET (10)	8.00	3.60	1.00
COMMON CARD (CA1-CA10)	1.00	.45	.12
☐ CA1 Ken Griffey Jr.	1.00	.45	.12
☐ CA2 Ken Griffey Jr.	1.00	.45	.12
☐ CA3 Ken Griffey Jr.	1.00	.45	.12
☐ CA4 Ken Griffey Jr.	1.00	.45	.12
☐ CA5 Ken Griffey Jr.	1.00	.45	.12
☐ CA6 Ken Griffey Jr.	1.00	.45	.12
☐ CA7 Ken Griffey Jr.	1.00	.45	.12
☐ CA8 Ken Griffey Jr.	1.00	.45	.12
☐ CA9 Ken Griffey Jr.	1.00	.45	.12
☐ CA10 Ken Griffey Jr.	1.00	.45	.12

1996 Collector's Choice Nomo Scrapbook

This five-card set was randomly inserted one in every 17 second series packs and features season highlights from Rookie of the Year, Hideo Nomo's first year in the Majors. The fronts display color action player cut-outs with yellow and red shadows on a metallic background. The backs carry a career fact about Nomo.

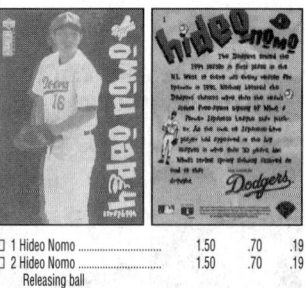

	MINT	NRMT	EXC
COMPLETE SET (5)	6.00	2.70	.75
COMMON NOMO (1-5)	1.50	.70	.19
☐ 1 Hideo Nomo	1.50	.70	.19
☐ 2 Hideo Nomo Releasing ball	1.50	.70	.19
☐ 3 Hideo Nomo Back turned to batter	1.50	.70	.19
☐ 4 Hideo Nomo Hands over head	1.50	.70	.19
☐ 5 Hideo Nomo Glove at side	1.50	.70	.19

1996 Collector's Choice You Make the Play

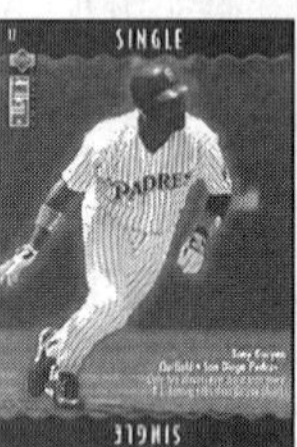

Cards from this 90-card set were inserted one per first series pack. Forty-five players are featured and each player is given two outcomes. The cards measure just about the standard-size but have rounded corners. In addition to being inserted into packs, dealers also were offered extra You Make the Play cards depending on how many cases ordered. A dealer who ordered one case received two 12-card packs of these cards for a total of 24 cards. Meanwhile, a dealer who ordered two cases received six 12-card packs for a total of 72 packs. Customers could also receive 12 of these cards by sending 10 wrappers and $2 to an a mail-in order. This offer expired on May 15, 1996.

	MINT	NRMT	EXC
COMPLETE SET (90)	15.00	6.75	1.85
COMMON CARD (1-45)	.15	.07	.02
☐ 1 Kevin Appier	.25	.11	.03
☐ 1A Kevin Appier	.25	.11	.03
☐ 2 Carlos Baerga	.15	.07	.02
☐ 2A Carlos Baerga	.15	.07	.02
☐ 3 Jeff Bagwell	.75	.35	.09
☐ 3A Jeff Bagwell	.75	.35	.09
☐ 4 Jay Bell	.15	.07	.02
☐ 4A Jay Bell	.15	.07	.02
☐ 5 Albert Belle	.75	.35	.09
☐ 5A Albert Belle	1.00	.45	.12
☐ 6 Craig Biggio	.25	.11	.03
☐ 6A Craig Biggio	.25	.11	.03
☐ 7 Wade Boggs	.35	.16	.04
☐ 7A Wade Boggs	.35	.16	.04
☐ 8 Barry Bonds	.50	.23	.06
☐ 8A Barry Bonds	.50	.23	.06
☐ 9 Bobby Bonilla	.25	.11	.03
☐ 9A Bobby Bonilla	.25	.11	.03
☐ 10 Jose Canseco	.35	.16	.04
☐ 10A Jose Canseco	.35	.16	.04
☐ 11 Joe Carter	.25	.11	.03
☐ 11A Joe Carter	.25	.11	.03
☐ 12 Darren Daulton	.15	.07	.02
☐ 12A Darren Daulton	.15	.07	.02
☐ 13 Cecil Fielder	.25	.11	.03
☐ 13A Cecil Fielder	.25	.11	.03
☐ 14 Ron Gant	.25	.11	.03
☐ 14A Ron Gant	.25	.11	.03
☐ 15 Juan Gonzalez	1.00	.45	.12
☐ 15A Juan Gonzalez	1.00	.45	.12
☐ 16 Ken Griffey Jr.	2.00	.90	.25
☐ 16A Ken Griffey Jr.	2.00	.90	.25
☐ 17 Tony Gwynn	.75	.35	.09
☐ 17A Tony Gwynn	.75	.35	.09
☐ 18 Randy Johnson	.50	.23	.06
☐ 18A Randy Johnson	.50	.23	.06
☐ 19 Chipper Jones	1.25	.55	.16
☐ 19A Chipper Jones	1.25	.55	.16
☐ 20 Barry Larkin	.25	.11	.03
☐ 20A Barry Larkin	.25	.11	.03
☐ 21 Kenny Lofton	.50	.23	.06
☐ 21A Kenny Lofton	.50	.23	.06
☐ 22 Greg Maddux	1.25	.55	.16
☐ 22A Greg Maddux	1.25	.55	.16
☐ 23 Don Mattingly	1.00	.45	.12
☐ 23A Don Mattingly	1.00	.45	.12
☐ 24 Fred McGriff	.35	.16	.04
☐ 24A Fred McGriff	.35	.16	.04
☐ 25 Mark McGwire	.60	.25	.07
☐ 25A Mark McGwire	.60	.25	.07
☐ 26 Paul Molitor	.40	.18	.05
☐ 26A Paul Molitor	.40	.18	.05
☐ 27 Raul Mondesi	.35	.16	.04
☐ 27A Raul Mondesi	.35	.16	.04
☐ 28 Eddie Murray	.50	.23	.06
☐ 28A Eddie Murray	.50	.23	.06
☐ 29 Hideo Nomo	.50	.23	.06
☐ 29A Hideo Nomo	.50	.23	.06
☐ 30 Jon Nunnally	.15	.07	.02
☐ 30A Jon Nunnally	.15	.07	.02
☐ 31 Mike Piazza	1.25	.55	.16
☐ 31A Mike Piazza	1.25	.55	.16
☐ 32 Kirby Puckett	.75	.35	.09
☐ 32A Kirby Puckett	.75	.35	.09
☐ 33 Cal Ripken	1.50	.70	.19
☐ 33A Cal Ripken	1.50	.70	.19
☐ 34 Alex Rodriguez	2.00	.90	.25
☐ 34A Alex Rodriguez	2.00	.90	.25
☐ 35 Tim Salmon	.35	.16	.04
☐ 35A Tim Salmon	.35	.16	.04
☐ 36 Gary Sheffield	.35	.16	.04
☐ 36A Gary Sheffield	.35	.16	.04
☐ 37 Lee Smith	.25	.11	.03
☐ 37A Lee Smith	.25	.11	.03
☐ 38 Ozzie Smith	.50	.23	.06
☐ 38A Ozzie Smith	.50	.23	.06
☐ 39 Sammy Sosa	.35	.16	.04
☐ 39A Sammy Sosa	.35	.16	.04
☐ 40 Frank Thomas	2.00	.90	.25
☐ 40A Frank Thomas	2.00	.90	.25
☐ 41 Greg Vaughn	.15	.07	.02
☐ 41A Greg Vaughn	.15	.07	.02
☐ 42 Mo Vaughn	.50	.23	.06
☐ 42A Mo Vaughn	.50	.23	.06
☐ 43 Larry Walker	.35	.16	.04
☐ 43A Larry Walker	.35	.16	.04
☐ 44 Rondell White	.25	.11	.03
☐ 44A Rondell White	.25	.11	.03
☐ 45 Matt Williams	.35	.16	.04
☐ 45A Matt Williams	.35	.16	.04

1996 Collector's Choice You Make the Play Gold Signature

This 90-card set is a parallel to the regular You Crash the Game cards. These cards are similar to the regular cards except there is a facsimile signature in gold foil. These cards were inserted approximately one every 35 first series packs.

	MINT	NRMT	EXC
COMPLETE SET (90)	225.00	100.00	28.00
COMMON CARD (1-45)	2.00	.90	.25
*GOLD: 7.5X to 15X BASIC CARDS			

1997 Collector's Choice

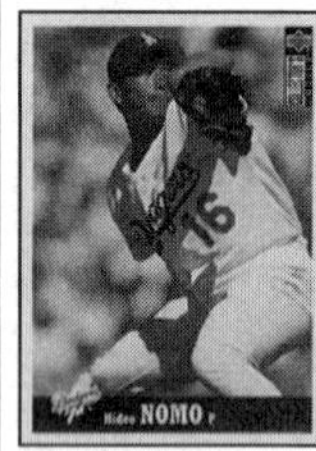

This 246-card first series was distributed in 12-card packs with a suggested retail price of $.99. The fronts feature color action player photos while the backs carry player statistics. The set contains the following subsets: Rookie Class (1-27), League Leaders (56-63), Postseason (218-224) which recaps action from the 1996 playoffs and World Series Games, and Ken Griffey Jr. Checklist (244-246) which also carry collecting tips.

	MINT	NRMT	EXC
COMPLETE SERIES 1 (246)	15.00	6.75	1.85
COMMON CARD (1-246)	.05	.02	.01
☐ 1 Andruw Jones	2.00	.90	.25
☐ 2 Rocky Coppinger	.15	.07	.02
☐ 3 Jeff D'Amico	.15	.07	.02
☐ 4 Dmitri Young	.15	.07	.02
☐ 5 Darin Erstad	1.00	.45	.12
☐ 6 Jermaine Allensworth	.15	.07	.02
☐ 7 Damian Jackson	.05	.02	.01
☐ 8 Bill Mueller	.05	.02	.01
☐ 9 Jacob Cruz	.05	.02	.01
☐ 10 Vladimir Guerrero	1.25	.55	.16
☐ 11 Marty Janzen	.05	.02	.01
☐ 12 Kevin L. Brown	.15	.07	.02
☐ 13 Willie Adams	.05	.02	.01
☐ 14 Wendell Magee	.15	.07	.02
☐ 15 Scott Rolen	.75	.35	.09
☐ 16 Matt Beech	.05	.02	.01
☐ 17 Neifi Perez	.15	.07	.02
☐ 18 Jamey Wright	.15	.07	.02
☐ 19 Jose Paniagua	.05	.02	.01
☐ 20 Todd Walker	.75	.35	.09
☐ 21 Justin Thompson	.15	.07	.02
☐ 22 Robin Jennings	.05	.02	.01
☐ 23 Dario Veras	.05	.02	.01
☐ 24 Brian Lesher	.05	.02	.01
☐ 25 Nomar Garciaparra	.75	.35	.09
☐ 26 Luis Castillo	.25	.11	.03
☐ 27 Brian Giles	.05	.02	.01
☐ 28 Jermaine Dye	.30	.14	.04
☐ 29 Terrell Wade	.05	.02	.01
☐ 30 Fred McGriff	.25	.11	.03
☐ 31 Marquis Grissom	.15	.07	.02
☐ 32 Ryan Klesko	.30	.14	.04
☐ 33 Javier Lopez	.15	.07	.02
☐ 34 Mark Wohlers	.05	.02	.01
☐ 35 Tom Glavine	.25	.11	.03
☐ 36 Denny Neagle	.05	.02	.01
☐ 37 Scott Erickson	.05	.02	.01
☐ 38 Chris Hoiles	.05	.02	.01
☐ 39 Roberto Alomar	.40	.18	.05
☐ 40 Eddie Murray	.50	.23	.06
☐ 41 Cal Ripken	1.50	.70	.19
☐ 42 Randy Myers	.05	.02	.01
☐ 43 B.J. Surhoff	.05	.02	.01
☐ 44 Rick Krivda	.05	.02	.01
☐ 45 Jose Canseco	.25	.11	.03
☐ 46 Heathcliff Slocumb	.05	.02	.01
☐ 47 Jeff Suppan	.15	.07	.02
☐ 48 Tom Gordon	.05	.02	.01
☐ 49 Aaron Sele	.05	.02	.01
☐ 50 Mo Vaughn	.50	.23	.06
☐ 51 Darren Bragg	.05	.02	.01
☐ 52 Wil Cordero	.05	.02	.01
☐ 53 Scott Bullett	.05	.02	.01
☐ 54 Terry Adams	.05	.02	.01
☐ 55 Jackie Robinson	.50	.23	.06
☐ 56 Tony Gwynn LL Alex Rodriguez	.50	.23	.06
☐ 57 Andres Galarraga LL Mark McGwire	.15	.07	.02
☐ 58 Andres Galarraga LL Albert Belle	.15	.07	.02
☐ 59 Eric Young LL Kenny Lofton	.15	.07	.02
☐ 60 John Smoltz LL Andy Pettitte	.15	.07	.02
☐ 61 John Smoltz LL Roger Clemens	.15	.07	.02
☐ 62 Kevin Brown LL Juan Guzman	.05	.02	.01
☐ 63 John Wetteland LL Todd Worrell Jeff Brantley	.05	.02	.01
☐ 64 Scott Servais	.05	.02	.01
☐ 65 Sammy Sosa	.30	.14	.04
☐ 66 Ryne Sandberg	.50	.23	.06
☐ 67 Frank Castillo	.05	.02	.01
☐ 68 Rey Sanchez	.05	.02	.01
☐ 69 Steve Trachsel	.05	.02	.01
☐ 70 Robin Ventura	.15	.07	.02
☐ 71 Wilson Alvarez	.05	.02	.01
☐ 72 Tony Phillips	.05	.02	.01
☐ 73 Lyle Mouton	.05	.02	.01
☐ 74 Mike Cameron	.30	.14	.04
☐ 75 Harold Baines	.05	.02	.01
☐ 76 Albert Belle	.75	.35	.09
☐ 77 Chris Snopek	.05	.02	.01
☐ 78 Reggie Sanders	.15	.07	.02
☐ 79 Jeff Brantley	.05	.02	.01
☐ 80 Barry Larkin	.25	.11	.03
☐ 81 Kevin Jarvis	.05	.02	.01
☐ 82 John Smiley	.05	.02	.01
☐ 83 Pete Schourek	.05	.02	.01
☐ 84 Thomas Howard	.05	.02	.01
☐ 85 Lee Smith	.15	.07	.02
☐ 86 Omar Vizquel	.15	.07	.02
☐ 87 Julio Franco	.05	.02	.01
☐ 88 Orel Hershiser	.15	.07	.02
☐ 89 Charles Nagy	.15	.07	.02
☐ 90 Matt Williams	.25	.11	.03
☐ 91 Dennis Martinez	.05	.02	.01
☐ 92 Jose Mesa	.05	.02	.01
☐ 93 Sandy Alomar Jr.	.05	.02	.01
☐ 94 Jim Thome	.40	.18	.05
☐ 95 Vinny Castilla	.15	.07	.02
☐ 96 Armando Reynoso	.05	.02	.01
☐ 97 Kevin Ritz	.05	.02	.01
☐ 98 Larry Walker	.15	.07	.02
☐ 99 Eric Young	.15	.07	.02
☐ 100 Dante Bichette	.25	.11	.03
☐ 101 Quinton McCracken	.05	.02	.01
☐ 102 John Vander Wal	.05	.02	.01
☐ 103 Phil Nevin	.05	.02	.01
☐ 104 Tony Clark	.25	.11	.03
☐ 105 Alan Trammell	.15	.07	.02

☐ 106 Felipe Lira	.05	.02	.01
☐ 107 Curtis Pride	.05	.02	.01
☐ 108 Bobby Higginson	.15	.07	.02
☐ 109 Mark Lewis	.05	.02	.01
☐ 110 Travis Fryman	.15	.07	.02
☐ 111 Al Leiter	.05	.02	.01
☐ 112 Devon White	.05	.02	.01
☐ 113 Jeff Conine	.15	.07	.02
☐ 114 Charles Johnson	.05	.02	.01
☐ 115 Andre Dawson	.15	.07	.02
☐ 116 Edgar Renteria	.25	.11	.03
☐ 117 Robb Nen	.05	.02	.01
☐ 118 Kevin Brown	.15	.07	.02
☐ 119 Derek Bell	.15	.07	.02
☐ 120 Bob Abreu	.25	.11	.03
☐ 121 Mike Hampton	.05	.02	.01
☐ 122 Todd Jones	.05	.02	.01
☐ 123 Billy Wagner	.15	.07	.02
☐ 124 Shane Reynolds	.05	.02	.01
☐ 125 Jeff Bagwell	.75	.35	.09
☐ 126 Brian L. Hunter	.05	.02	.01
☐ 127 Jeff Montgomery	.05	.02	.01
☐ 128 Rod Myers	.05	.02	.01
☐ 129 Tim Belcher	.05	.02	.01
☐ 130 Kevin Appier	.15	.07	.02
☐ 131 Mike Sweeney	.15	.07	.02
☐ 132 Craig Paquette	.05	.02	.01
☐ 133 Joe Randa	.05	.02	.01
☐ 134 Michael Tucker	.05	.02	.01
☐ 135 Raul Mondesi	.25	.11	.03
☐ 136 Tim Wallach	.05	.02	.01
☐ 137 Brett Butler	.05	.02	.01
☐ 138 Karim Garcia	.30	.14	.04
☐ 139 Todd Hollandsworth	.15	.07	.02
☐ 140 Eric Karros	.15	.07	.02
☐ 141 Hideo Nomo	.50	.23	.06
☐ 142 Ismael Valdes	.15	.07	.02
☐ 143 Cal Eldred	.05	.02	.01
☐ 144 Scott Karl	.05	.02	.01
☐ 145 Matt Mieske	.05	.02	.01
☐ 146 Mike Fetters	.05	.02	.01
☐ 147 Mark Loretta	.05	.02	.01
☐ 148 Fernando Vina	.05	.02	.01
☐ 149 Jeff Cirillo	.05	.02	.01
☐ 150 Dave Nilsson	.05	.02	.01
☐ 151 Kirby Puckett	.75	.35	.09
☐ 152 Rich Becker	.05	.02	.01
☐ 153 Chuck Knoblauch	.30	.14	.04
☐ 154 Marty Cordova	.15	.07	.02
☐ 155 Paul Molitor	.40	.18	.05
☐ 156 Rick Aguilera	.05	.02	.01
☐ 157 Pat Meares	.05	.02	.01
☐ 158 Frank Rodriguez	.05	.02	.01
☐ 159 David Segui	.05	.02	.01
☐ 160 Henry Rodriguez	.15	.07	.02
☐ 161 Shane Andrews	.05	.02	.01
☐ 162 Pedro Martinez	.15	.07	.02
☐ 163 Mark Grudzielanek	.05	.02	.01
☐ 164 Mike Lansing	.05	.02	.01
☐ 165 Rondell White	.05	.02	.01
☐ 166 Ugueth Urbina	.05	.02	.01
☐ 167 Rey Ordonez	.25	.11	.03
☐ 168 Robert Person	.05	.02	.01
☐ 169 Carlos Baerga	.15	.07	.02
☐ 170 Bernard Gilkey	.05	.02	.01
☐ 171 John Franco	.05	.02	.01
☐ 172 Pete Harnisch	.05	.02	.01
☐ 173 Butch Huskey	.05	.02	.01
☐ 174 Paul Wilson	.15	.07	.02
☐ 175 Bernie Williams	.40	.18	.05
☐ 175 Dwight Gooden ERR incorrectly numbered 175	.15	.07	.02
☐ 177 Wade Boggs	.25	.11	.03
☐ 178 Ruben Rivera	.25	.11	.03
☐ 179 Jim Leyritz	.05	.02	.01
☐ 180 Derek Jeter	1.25	.55	.16
☐ 181 Tino Martinez	.15	.07	.02
☐ 182 Tim Raines	.05	.02	.01
☐ 183 Scott Brosius	.05	.02	.01
☐ 184 Jason Giambi	.15	.07	.02
☐ 185 Geronimo Berroa	.05	.02	.01
☐ 186 Ariel Prieto	.05	.02	.01
☐ 187 Scott Spiezio	.15	.07	.02
☐ 188 John Wasdin	.05	.02	.01
☐ 189 Ernie Young	.05	.02	.01
☐ 190 Mark McGwire	.60	.25	.07
☐ 191 Jim Eisenreich	.05	.02	.01
☐ 192 Ricky Bottalico	.05	.02	.01
☐ 193 Darren Daulton	.15	.07	.02
☐ 194 David Doster	.05	.02	.01
☐ 195 Gregg Jefferies	.05	.02	.01
☐ 196 Lenny Dykstra	.15	.07	.02
☐ 197 Curt Schilling	.05	.02	.01
☐ 198 Todd Stottlemyre	.05	.02	.01
☐ 199 Willie McGee	.05	.02	.01
☐ 200 Ozzie Smith	.50	.23	.06
☐ 201 Dennis Eckersley	.15	.07	.02
☐ 202 Ray Lankford	.15	.07	.02
☐ 203 John Mabry	.05	.02	.01
☐ 204 Alan Benes	.15	.07	.02
☐ 205 Ron Gant	.15	.07	.02
☐ 206 Archi Cianfrocco	.05	.02	.01
☐ 207 Fernando Valenzuela	.15	.07	.02
☐ 208 Greg Vaughn	.05	.02	.01
☐ 209 Steve Finley	.05	.02	.01
☐ 210 Tony Gwynn	.75	.35	.09
☐ 211 Rickey Henderson	.25	.11	.03
☐ 212 Trevor Hoffman	.05	.02	.01
☐ 213 Jason Thompson	.05	.02	.01
☐ 214 Osvaldo Fernandez	.05	.02	.01
☐ 215 Glenallen Hill	.05	.02	.01
☐ 216 William VanLandingham	.05	.02	.01
☐ 217 Marvin Benard	.05	.02	.01
☐ 218 Juan Gonzalez POST	.50	.23	.06
☐ 219 Roberto Alomar POST	.25	.11	.03
☐ 220 Brian Jordan POST	.15	.07	.02
☐ 221 John Smoltz POST	.25	.11	.03
☐ 222 Javy Lopez POST	.15	.07	.02
☐ 223 Bernie Williams POST	.15	.07	.02
☐ 224 Jim Leyritz POST John Wetteland	.05	.02	.01
☐ 225 Barry Bonds	.50	.23	.06
☐ 226 Rich Aurilia	.05	.02	.01
☐ 227 Jay Canizaro	.05	.02	.01
☐ 228 Dan Wilson	.05	.02	.01
☐ 229 Bob Wolcott	.05	.02	.01
☐ 230 Ken Griffey Jr.	2.00	.90	.25
☐ 231 Sterling Hitchcock	.05	.02	.01
☐ 232 Edgar Martinez	.15	.07	.02
☐ 233 Joey Cora	.05	.02	.01
☐ 234 Norm Charlton	.05	.02	.01
☐ 235 Alex Rodriguez	2.00	.90	.25
☐ 236 Bobby Witt	.05	.02	.01
☐ 237 Darren Oliver	.05	.02	.01
☐ 238 Kevin Elster	.05	.02	.01
☐ 239 Rusty Greer	.15	.07	.02
☐ 240 Juan Gonzalez	1.00	.45	.12
☐ 241 Will Clark	.25	.11	.03
☐ 242 Dean Palmer	.05	.02	.01
☐ 243 Ivan Rodriguez	.50	.23	.06
☐ 244 Ken Griffey Jr. CL	.50	.23	.06
☐ 245 Ken Griffey Jr. CL	.50	.23	.06
☐ 246 Ken Griffey Jr. CL	.50	.23	.06

1997 Collector's Choice The Big Show

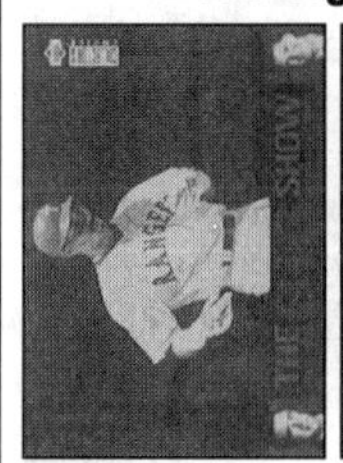
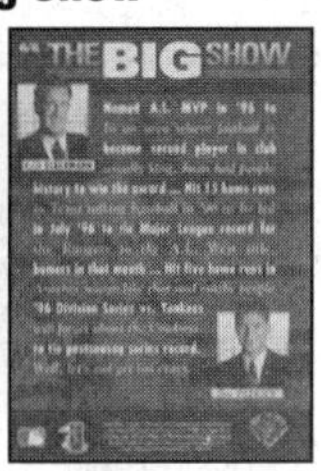

Inserted one in every first series pack, cards from this 45-card set feature color photos of some of the hottest players in baseball. The backs carry comments about the pictured player by ESPN SportsCenter television sportscasters, Keith Olbermann and Dan Patrick.

	MINT	NRMT	EXC
COMPLETE SET (45)	15.00	6.75	1.85
COMMON CARD (1-45)	.10	.05	.01

☐ 1 Greg Maddux	1.25	.55	.16
☐ 2 Chipper Jones	1.25	.55	.16
☐ 3 Andruw Jones	2.00	.90	.25
☐ 4 John Smoltz	.30	.14	.04
☐ 5 Cal Ripken	1.50	.70	.19
☐ 6 Roberto Alomar	.40	.18	.05
☐ 7 Rafael Palmeiro	.25	.11	.03
☐ 8 Eddie Murray	.50	.23	.06
☐ 9 Jose Canseco	.25	.11	.03
☐ 10 Roger Clemens	.40	.18	.05
☐ 11 Mo Vaughn	.50	.23	.06
☐ 12 Jim Edmonds	.20	.09	.03
☐ 13 Tim Salmon	.25	.11	.03
☐ 14 Sammy Sosa	.30	.14	.04
☐ 15 Albert Belle	.75	.35	.09
☐ 16 Frank Thomas	2.00	.90	.25
☐ 17 Barry Larkin	.25	.11	.03
☐ 18 Kenny Lofton	.50	.23	.06
☐ 19 Manny Ramirez	.50	.23	.06
☐ 20 Matt Williams	.25	.11	.03
☐ 21 Dante Bichette	.25	.11	.03
☐ 22 Gary Sheffield	.30	.14	.04
☐ 23 Craig Biggio	.20	.09	.03
☐ 24 Jeff Bagwell	.75	.35	.09
☐ 25 Todd Hollandsworth	.20	.09	.03
☐ 26 Raul Mondesi	.25	.11	.03
☐ 27 Hideo Nomo	.50	.23	.06
☐ 28 Mike Piazza	1.25	.55	.16
☐ 29 Paul Molitor	.40	.18	.05
☐ 30 Kirby Puckett	.75	.35	.09
☐ 31 Rondell White	.10	.05	.01
☐ 32 Rey Ordonez	.25	.11	.03
☐ 33 Paul Wilson	.20	.09	.03
☐ 34 Derek Jeter	1.25	.55	.16
☐ 35 Andy Pettitte	.50	.23	.06
☐ 36 Mark McGwire	.60	.25	.07
☐ 37 Jason Kendall	.20	.09	.03
☐ 38 Ozzie Smith	.50	.23	.06
☐ 39 Tony Gwynn	.75	.35	.09
☐ 40 Barry Bonds	.50	.23	.06
☐ 41 Alex Rodriguez	2.00	.90	.25
☐ 42 Jay Buhner	.25	.11	.03
☐ 43 Ken Griffey Jr.	2.00	.90	.25
☐ 44 Randy Johnson	.30	.14	.04
☐ 45 Juan Gonzalez	1.00	.45	.12

1997 Collector's Choice The Big Show World Headquarters Edition

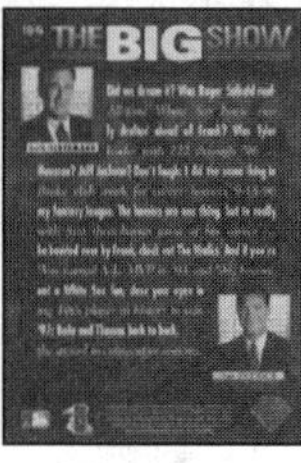

Randomly inserted in first series packs at a rate of one in 35, cards from this 45-card parallel set are a scarcer version of the regular Big Show issue. A large foil "WHQ" embossed logo on front easily differentiates them from their more common counterparts.

	MINT	NRMT	EXC
COMPLETE SET (45)	300.00	135.00	38.00
COMMON CARD (1-45)	2.00	.90	.25
*STARS: 10X TO 20X BASIC CARDS			

1997 Collector's Choice Griffey Clearly Dominant

Randomly inserted in first series packs at a rate of one in 144, this five-card set highlights superstar Ken Griffey Jr. with different color photos and information on each card.

	MINT	NRMT	EXC
COMPLETE SET (5)	80.00	36.00	10.00
COMMON GRIFFEY (CD1-CD5)	20.00	9.00	2.50

☐ CD1 Ken Griffey Jr.	20.00	9.00	2.50
☐ CD2 Ken Griffey Jr.	20.00	9.00	2.50
☐ CD3 Ken Griffey Jr.	20.00	9.00	2.50
☐ CD4 Ken Griffey Jr.	20.00	9.00	2.50
☐ CD5 Ken Griffey Jr.	20.00	9.00	2.50

1997 Collector's Choice Premier Power

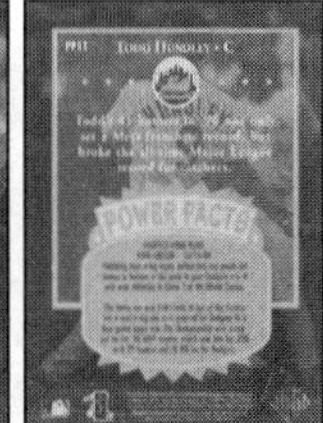

Randomly inserted in first series packs at a rate of one in 15, this silver version 20-card set features borderless color action player photos and information about the 20 top Major League Home Run hitters.

	MINT	NRMT	EXC
COMPLETE SET (20)	40.00	18.00	5.00
COMMON CARD (PP1-PP20)	1.00	.45	.12

☐ PP1 Mark McGwire	3.00	1.35	.35
☐ PP2 Brady Anderson	1.00	.45	.12
☐ PP3 Ken Griffey Jr.	10.00	4.50	1.25
☐ PP4 Albert Belle	4.00	1.80	.50
☐ PP5 Juan Gonzalez	5.00	2.20	.60
☐ PP6 Andres Galarraga	1.25	.55	.16
☐ PP7 Jay Buhner	1.25	.55	.16
☐ PP8 Mo Vaughn	2.50	1.10	.30
☐ PP9 Barry Bonds	2.50	1.10	.30
☐ PP10 Gary Sheffield	1.50	.70	.19
☐ PP11 Todd Hundley	1.00	.45	.12
☐ PP12 Frank Thomas	10.00	4.50	1.25
☐ PP13 Sammy Sosa	1.50	.70	.19
☐ PP14 Ken Caminiti	1.50	.70	.19
☐ PP15 Vinny Castilla	1.00	.45	.12
☐ PP16 Ellis Burks	1.00	.45	.12
☐ PP17 Rafael Palmeiro	1.25	.55	.16
☐ PP18 Alex Rodriguez	10.00	4.50	1.25
☐ PP19 Mike Piazza	6.00	2.70	.75
☐ PP20 Eddie Murray	2.50	1.10	.30

1997 Collector's Choice Premier Power Gold

Randomly inserted in first series packs at a rate of one in 69, cards from this 20-card set are a gold parallel version of the more common silver Premier Power set which honors the Leagues top Home Run hitters. Gold foil features on the card fronts (rather than Silver) differentiate them from their more common counterparts.

	MINT	NRMT	EXC
COMPLETE SET (20)	150.00	70.00	19.00
COMMON CARD (PP1-PP20)	3.00	1.35	.35
*STARS: 1.5X TO 3X BASIC CARDS			

1997 Collector's Choice Stick'Ums

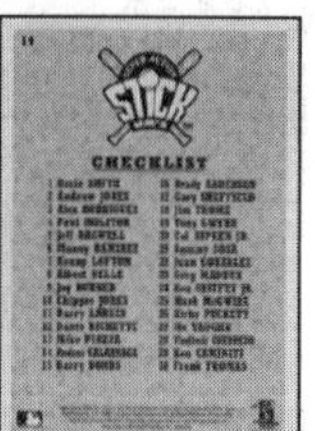

Randomly inserted in first series packs at a rate of one in three, cards from this 30-card set feature color sticker images of star players. These interactive reusable stickers could be used to create mini baseball scenes.

	MINT	NRMT	EXC
COMPLETE SET (30)	15.00	6.75	1.85
COMMON CARD (1-30)	.25	.11	.03

☐ 1 Ozzie Smith	.75	.35	.09
☐ 2 Andruw Jones	3.00	1.35	.35
☐ 3 Alex Rodriguez	3.00	1.35	.35
☐ 4 Paul Molitor	.60	.25	.07
☐ 5 Jeff Bagwell	1.25	.55	.16
☐ 6 Manny Ramirez	.75	.35	.09
☐ 7 Kenny Lofton	.75	.35	.09
☐ 8 Albert Belle	1.25	.55	.16
☐ 9 Jay Buhner	.40	.18	.05
☐ 10 Chipper Jones	2.00	.90	.25
☐ 11 Barry Larkin	.40	.18	.05
☐ 12 Dante Bichette	.40	.18	.05
☐ 13 Mike Piazza	2.00	.90	.25
☐ 14 Andres Galarraga	.40	.18	.05
☐ 15 Barry Bonds	.75	.35	.09
☐ 16 Brady Anderson	.25	.11	.03
☐ 17 Gary Sheffield	.50	.23	.06
☐ 18 Jim Thome	.60	.25	.07
☐ 19 Tony Gwynn	1.25	.55	.16
☐ 20 Cal Ripken	2.50	1.10	.30
☐ 21 Sammy Sosa	.50	.23	.06
☐ 22 Juan Gonzalez	1.50	.70	.19
☐ 23 Greg Maddux	2.00	.90	.25
☐ 24 Ken Griffey Jr.	3.00	1.35	.35
☐ 25 Mark McGwire	1.00	.45	.12
☐ 26 Kirby Puckett	1.25	.55	.16
☐ 27 Mo Vaughn	.75	.35	.09
☐ 28 Vladimir Guerrero	2.00	.90	.25
☐ 29 Ken Caminiti	.50	.23	.06
☐ 30 Frank Thomas	3.00	1.35	.35

1995 Collector's Choice SE

The 1995 Collector's Choice SE set consists of 265 standard-size cards issued in foil packs. The fronts feature color action player photos with blue borders. The player's name, position and the team name are printed on the bottom of the photo. The SE logo in blue-foil appears in a top corner. On a white background, the backs carry another color player photo with a short player biography, career stats and 1994 highlights. Subsets featured include Rookie Class (1-25), Record Pace (26-30), Stat Leaders (137-144), Fantasy Team (249-260). There are no Rookie Cards in this set.

	MINT	NRMT	EXC
COMPLETE SET (265)	20.00	9.00	2.50
COMMON CARD (1-265)	.10	.05	.01

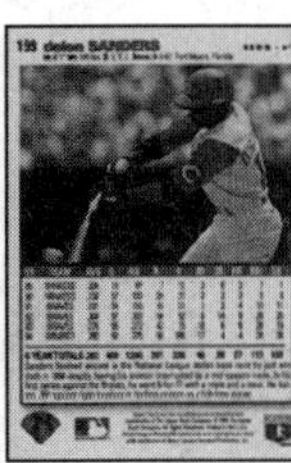

☐ 1 Alex Rodriguez 4.00 1.80 .50
☐ 2 Derek Jeter 2.00 .90 .25
☐ 3 Dustin Hermanson .25 .11 .03
☐ 4 Bill Pulsipher .25 .11 .03
☐ 5 Terrell Wade .50 .23 .06
☐ 6 Darren Dreifort .10 .05 .01
☐ 7 LaTroy Hawkins .10 .05 .01
☐ 8 Alex Ochoa .25 .11 .03
☐ 9 Paul Wilson .50 .23 .06
☐ 10 Rod Henderson .10 .05 .01
☐ 11 Alan Benes .50 .23 .06
☐ 12 Garret Anderson .25 .11 .03
☐ 13 Armando Benitez .10 .05 .01
☐ 14 Mark Thompson .25 .11 .03
☐ 15 Herbert Perry .25 .11 .03
☐ 16 Jose Silva .10 .05 .01
☐ 17 Orlando Miller .10 .05 .01
☐ 18 Russ Davis .10 .05 .01
☐ 19 Jason Isringhausen .50 .23 .06
☐ 20 Ray McDavid .25 .11 .03
☐ 21 Tim VanEgmond .10 .05 .01
☐ 22 Paul Shuey .10 .05 .01
☐ 23 Steve Dunn .10 .05 .01
☐ 24 Mike Lieberthal .10 .05 .01
☐ 25 Chan Ho Park .50 .23 .06
☐ 26 Ken Griffey Jr. RP 1.50 .70 .19
☐ 27 Tony Gwynn RP .60 .25 .07
☐ 28 Chuck Knoblauch RP .50 .23 .06
☐ 29 Frank Thomas RP 1.50 .70 .19
☐ 30 Matt Williams RP .50 .23 .06
☐ 31 Chili Davis .25 .11 .03
☐ 32 Chad Curtis .10 .05 .01
☐ 33 Brian Anderson .10 .05 .01
☐ 34 Chuck Finley .25 .11 .03
☐ 35 Tim Salmon .50 .23 .06
☐ 36 Bo Jackson .25 .11 .03
☐ 37 Doug Drabek .10 .05 .01
☐ 38 Craig Biggio .25 .11 .03
☐ 39 Ken Caminiti .50 .23 .06
☐ 40 Jeff Bagwell 1.25 .55 .16
☐ 41 Darryl Kile .10 .05 .01
☐ 42 John Hudek .10 .05 .01
☐ 43 Brian L. Hunter .25 .11 .03
☐ 44 Dennis Eckersley .25 .11 .03
☐ 45 Mark McGwire 1.00 .45 .12
☐ 46 Brent Gates .10 .05 .01
☐ 47 Steve Karsay .10 .05 .01
☐ 48 Rickey Henderson .50 .23 .06
☐ 49 Terry Steinbach .25 .11 .03
☐ 50 Ruben Sierra .25 .11 .03
☐ 51 Roberto Alomar .60 .25 .07
☐ 52 Carlos Delgado .25 .11 .03
☐ 53 Alex Gonzalez .25 .11 .03
☐ 54 Joe Carter .25 .11 .03
☐ 55 Paul Molitor .60 .25 .07
☐ 56 Juan Guzman .25 .11 .03
☐ 57 John Olerud .10 .05 .01
☐ 58 Shawn Green .25 .11 .03
☐ 59 Tom Glavine .50 .23 .06
☐ 60 Greg Maddux 2.00 .90 .25
☐ 61 Roberto Kelly .10 .05 .01
☐ 62 Ryan Klesko .50 .23 .06
☐ 63 Javier Lopez .50 .23 .06
☐ 64 Jose Oliva .10 .05 .01
☐ 65 Fred McGriff .50 .23 .06
☐ 66 Steve Avery .25 .11 .03
☐ 67 David Justice .50 .23 .06
☐ 68 Ricky Bones .10 .05 .01
☐ 69 Cal Eldred .10 .05 .01
☐ 70 Greg Vaughn .25 .11 .03
☐ 71 Dave Nilsson .25 .11 .03
☐ 72 Jose Valentin .25 .11 .03
☐ 73 Matt Mieske .25 .11 .03
☐ 74 Todd Zeile .10 .05 .01
☐ 75 Ozzie Smith .75 .35 .09
☐ 76 Bernard Gilkey .25 .11 .03
☐ 77 Ray Lankford .25 .11 .03
☐ 78 Bob Tewksbury .10 .05 .01
☐ 79 Mark Whiten .10 .05 .01
☐ 80 Gregg Jefferies .25 .11 .03
☐ 81 Randy Myers .10 .05 .01
☐ 82 Shawon Dunston .10 .05 .01
☐ 83 Mark Grace .50 .23 .06
☐ 84 Derrick May .10 .05 .01
☐ 85 Sammy Sosa .50 .23 .06
☐ 86 Steve Trachsel .10 .05 .01
☐ 87 Brett Butler .25 .11 .03
☐ 88 Delino DeShields .10 .05 .01
☐ 89 Orel Hershiser .25 .11 .03
☐ 90 Mike Piazza 2.00 .90 .25
☐ 91 Todd Hollandsworth .50 .23 .06
☐ 92 Eric Karros .25 .11 .03
☐ 93 Ramon Martinez .25 .11 .03
☐ 94 Tim Wallach .10 .05 .01
☐ 95 Raul Mondesi .50 .23 .06
☐ 96 Larry Walker .50 .23 .06
☐ 97 Wil Cordero .10 .05 .01
☐ 98 Marquis Grissom .25 .11 .03
☐ 99 Ken Hill .10 .05 .01
☐ 100 Cliff Floyd .25 .11 .03
☐ 101 Pedro J. Martinez .25 .11 .03
☐ 102 John Wetteland .25 .11 .03
☐ 103 Rondell White .25 .11 .03
☐ 104 Moises Alou .25 .11 .03
☐ 105 Barry Bonds .75 .35 .09
☐ 106 Darren Lewis .10 .05 .01
☐ 107 Mark Portugal .10 .05 .01
☐ 108 Matt Williams .50 .23 .06
☐ 109 William VanLandingham .10 .05 .01
☐ 110 Bill Swift .10 .05 .01
☐ 111 Robby Thompson .10 .05 .01
☐ 112 Rod Beck .10 .05 .01
☐ 113 Darryl Strawberry .25 .11 .03
☐ 114 Jim Thome .60 .25 .07
☐ 115 Dave Winfield .50 .23 .06
☐ 116 Eddie Murray .75 .35 .09
☐ 117 Manny Ramirez .75 .35 .09
☐ 118 Carlos Baerga .25 .11 .03
☐ 119 Kenny Lofton .75 .35 .09
☐ 120 Albert Belle 1.25 .55 .16
☐ 121 Mark Clark .10 .05 .01
☐ 122 Dennis Martinez .25 .11 .03
☐ 123 Randy Johnson .50 .23 .06
☐ 124 Jay Buhner .50 .23 .06
☐ 125 Ken Griffey Jr. 3.00 1.35 .35
☐ 126 Goose Gossage .25 .11 .03
☐ 127 Tino Martinez .25 .11 .03
☐ 128 Reggie Jefferson .25 .11 .03
☐ 129 Edgar Martinez .25 .11 .03
☐ 130 Gary Sheffield .50 .23 .06
☐ 131 Pat Rapp .10 .05 .01
☐ 132 Bret Barberie .10 .05 .01
☐ 133 Chuck Carr .10 .05 .01
☐ 134 Jeff Conine .25 .11 .03
☐ 135 Charles Johnson .25 .11 .03
☐ 136 Benito Santiago .10 .05 .01
☐ 137 Matt Williams STL .50 .23 .06
☐ 138 Jeff Bagwell STL .60 .25 .07
☐ 139 Kenny Lofton STL .50 .23 .06
☐ 140 Tony Gwynn STL .60 .25 .07
☐ 141 Jimmy Key STL .10 .05 .01
☐ 142 Greg Maddux STL 1.00 .45 .12
☐ 143 Randy Johnson STL .50 .23 .06
☐ 144 Lee Smith STL .25 .11 .03
☐ 145 Bobby Bonilla .25 .11 .03
☐ 146 Jason Jacome .10 .05 .01
☐ 147 Jeff Kent .10 .05 .01
☐ 148 Ryan Thompson .10 .05 .01
☐ 149 Bobby Jones .25 .11 .03
☐ 150 Bret Saberhagen .25 .11 .03
☐ 151 John Franco .10 .05 .01
☐ 152 Lee Smith .25 .11 .03
☐ 153 Rafael Palmeiro .50 .23 .06
☐ 154 Brady Anderson .50 .23 .06
☐ 155 Cal Ripken Jr. 2.50 1.10 .30
☐ 156 Jeffrey Hammonds .25 .11 .03
☐ 157 Mike Mussina .60 .25 .07
☐ 158 Chris Hoiles .10 .05 .01
☐ 159 Ben McDonald .10 .05 .01
☐ 160 Tony Gwynn 1.25 .55 .16
☐ 161 Joey Hamilton .50 .23 .06
☐ 162 Andy Benes .10 .05 .01
☐ 163 Trevor Hoffman .25 .11 .03
☐ 164 Phil Plantier .10 .05 .01
☐ 165 Derek Bell .25 .11 .03
☐ 166 Bip Roberts .10 .05 .01
☐ 167 Eddie Williams .10 .05 .01
☐ 168 Fernando Valenzuela .25 .11 .03
☐ 169 Mariano Duncan .10 .05 .01
☐ 170 Lenny Dykstra .25 .11 .03
☐ 171 Darren Daulton .25 .11 .03
☐ 172 Danny Jackson .10 .05 .01
☐ 173 Bobby Munoz .10 .05 .01
☐ 174 Doug Jones .10 .05 .01
☐ 175 Jay Bell .25 .11 .03
☐ 176 Zane Smith .10 .05 .01
☐ 177 Jon Lieber .10 .05 .01
☐ 178 Carlos Garcia .10 .05 .01
☐ 179 Orlando Merced .10 .05 .01
☐ 180 Andy Van Slyke .25 .11 .03
☐ 181 Rick Helling .10 .05 .01
☐ 182 Rusty Greer .50 .23 .06
☐ 183 Kenny Rogers UER .10 .05 .01
(shows 110 wins in 1990)
☐ 184 Will Clark .50 .23 .06
☐ 185 Jose Canseco .50 .23 .06
☐ 186 Juan Gonzalez 1.50 .70 .19
☐ 187 Dean Palmer .25 .11 .03
☐ 188 Ivan Rodriguez .75 .35 .09
☐ 189 John Valentin .25 .11 .03
☐ 190 Roger Clemens .60 .25 .07
☐ 191 Aaron Sele .25 .11 .03
☐ 192 Scott Cooper .10 .05 .01
☐ 193 Mike Greenwell .10 .05 .01
☐ 194 Mo Vaughn .75 .35 .09
☐ 195 Andre Dawson .25 .11 .03
☐ 196 Ron Gant .25 .11 .03
☐ 197 Jose Rijo .10 .05 .01
☐ 198 Bret Boone .25 .11 .03
☐ 199 Deion Sanders .50 .23 .06
☐ 200 Barry Larkin .50 .23 .06
☐ 201 Hal Morris .10 .05 .01
☐ 202 Reggie Sanders .25 .11 .03
☐ 203 Kevin Mitchell .25 .11 .03
☐ 204 Marvin Freeman .10 .05 .01
☐ 205 Andres Galarraga .50 .23 .06
☐ 206 Walt Weiss .10 .05 .01
☐ 207 Charlie Hayes .10 .05 .01
☐ 208 Dave Nied .10 .05 .01
☐ 209 Dante Bichette .50 .23 .06
☐ 210 David Cone .25 .11 .03
☐ 211 Jeff Montgomery .25 .11 .03
☐ 212 Felix Jose .10 .05 .01
☐ 213 Mike Macfarlane .10 .05 .01
☐ 214 Wally Joyner .25 .11 .03
☐ 215 Bob Hamelin .10 .05 .01
☐ 216 Brian McRae .25 .11 .03
☐ 217 Kirk Gibson .25 .11 .03
☐ 218 Lou Whitaker .25 .11 .03
☐ 219 Chris Gomez .10 .05 .01
☐ 220 Cecil Fielder .25 .11 .03
☐ 221 Mickey Tettleton .10 .05 .01
☐ 222 Travis Fryman .25 .11 .03
☐ 223 Tony Phillips .25 .11 .03
☐ 224 Rick Aguilera .10 .05 .01
☐ 225 Scott Erickson .10 .05 .01
☐ 226 Chuck Knoblauch .50 .23 .06
☐ 227 Kent Hrbek .25 .11 .03
☐ 228 Shane Mack .10 .05 .01
☐ 229 Kevin Tapani .10 .05 .01
☐ 230 Kirby Puckett 1.25 .55 .16
☐ 231 Julio Franco .25 .11 .03
☐ 232 Jack McDowell .25 .11 .03
☐ 233 Jason Bere .10 .05 .01
☐ 234 Alex Fernandez .25 .11 .03
☐ 235 Frank Thomas 3.00 1.35 .35
☐ 236 Ozzie Guillen .10 .05 .01
☐ 237 Robin Ventura .25 .11 .03
☐ 238 Michael Jordan 4.00 1.80 .50
☐ 239 Wilson Alvarez .25 .11 .03
☐ 240 Don Mattingly 1.50 .70 .19
☐ 241 Jim Abbott .10 .05 .01
☐ 242 Jim Leyritz .10 .05 .01
☐ 243 Paul O'Neill .25 .11 .03
☐ 244 Melido Perez .10 .05 .01
☐ 245 Wade Boggs .50 .23 .06
☐ 246 Mike Stanley .10 .05 .01
☐ 247 Danny Tartabull .10 .05 .01
☐ 248 Jimmy Key .25 .11 .03
☐ 249 Greg Maddux FT 1.00 .45 .12
☐ 250 Randy Johnson FT .50 .23 .06
☐ 251 Bret Saberhagen FT .10 .05 .01
☐ 252 John Wetteland FT .25 .11 .03
☐ 253 Mike Piazza FT 1.00 .45 .12
☐ 254 Jeff Bagwell FT .60 .25 .07
☐ 255 Craig Biggio FT .25 .11 .03
☐ 256 Matt Williams FT .50 .23 .06
☐ 257 Wil Cordero FT .10 .05 .01
☐ 258 Kenny Lofton FT .50 .23 .06
☐ 259 Barry Bonds FT .50 .23 .06
☐ 260 Dante Bichette FT .50 .23 .06
☐ 261 Ken Griffey Jr. CL 1.00 .45 .12
☐ 262 Goose Gossage CL .10 .05 .01
☐ 263 Cal Ripken CL 1.00 .45 .12
☐ 264 Kenny Rogers CL .10 .05 .01
☐ 265 John Valentin CL .25 .11 .03

1995 Collector's Choice SE Gold Signature

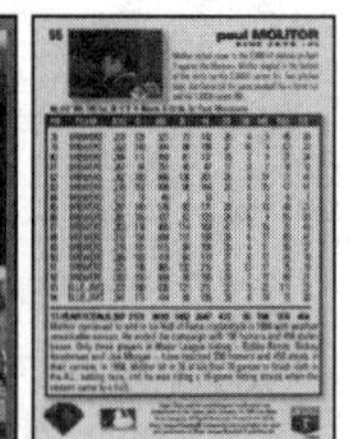

A parallel to the basic 265-card Collector's Choice SE set, each card features a gold-foil replica signature on it. Inserted one in 35 packs, the fronts feature color action player photos with blue borders. Super packs inserted 1:720 contained 12 gold signature cards.

	MINT	NRMT	EXC
COMPLETE SET (265)	1500.00	700.00	190.00
COMMON CARD (1-265)	2.50	1.10	.30

*STARS: 15X TO 30X BASIC CARDS..
*YOUNG STARS: 15X TO 25X BASIC CARDS

1995 Collector's Choice SE Silver Signature

A parallel to the basic 265-card Collector's Choice issue, each card has a silver-foil replica signature on the front. These cards were inserted one in every pack, two per mini jumbo and 12 per super pack (inserted 1:216).

	MINT	NRMT	EXC
COMPLETE SET (265)	60.00	27.00	7.50
COMMON CARD (1-265)	.20	.09	.03

*STARS: 2X to 4X BASIC CARDS........
*YOUNG STARS: 1.5X to 3X BASIC CARDS

1994 Collector's Edge Dial Justice

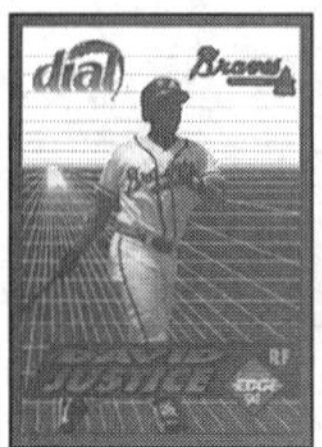

This card measures the standard size. The fronts feature an action player photo on a clear, blue and green background. The Dial logo and team logo appear at the top. The player's name, position and card name are printed in a blue bar at the bottom. The backs are the reverse of the front with career highlights printed in white.

	MINT	NRMT	EXC
COMPLETE SET (1)	3.00	1.35	.35
COMMON CARD	3.00	1.35	.35
☐ 1 David Justice	3.00	1.35	.35

1916 Collins-McCarthy E135

The cards in this 200-card set measure 2" by 3 1/4". Collins-McCarthy, the West Coast manufacturer of Zee Nuts (E137), issued the Baseball's Hall of Fame set of players in 1916. These black and white photos of current players were not only numbered but also listed alphabetically. The set is similar to D328, except that E135 is printed on thinner stock. The complete set price includes all variation cards listed in the checklist below.

	EX-MT	VG-E	GOOD
COMPLETE SET (200)	16000.00	7200.00	2000.00
COMMON CARD (1-200)	50.00	22.00	6.25
☐ 1 Sam Agnew	50.00	22.00	6.25
☐ 2 Grover Alexander	125.00	55.00	15.50
☐ 3 W.E. Alexander	50.00	22.00	6.25
☐ 4 Leon Ames	50.00	22.00	6.25
☐ 5 Fred Anderson	50.00	22.00	6.25
☐ 6 Ed Appleton	50.00	22.00	6.25
☐ 7 Jimmy Archer	50.00	22.00	6.25
☐ 8 Jimmy Austin	50.00	22.00	6.25
☐ 9 Jim Bagby	50.00	22.00	6.25
☐ 10 H.D. Baird	50.00	22.00	6.25
☐ 11 Frank Baker	125.00	55.00	15.50
☐ 12 Dave Bancroft	100.00	45.00	12.50
☐ 13 Jack Barry	50.00	22.00	6.25
☐ 14 Joe Benz	50.00	22.00	6.25
☐ 15 Al Betzel	50.00	22.00	6.25
☐ 16 Ping Bodie	50.00	22.00	6.25
☐ 17 Joe Boehling	50.00	22.00	6.25
☐ 18 Eddie Burns	50.00	22.00	6.25
☐ 19 George Burns (Detroit)	50.00	22.00	6.25
☐ 20 Geo. J. Burns (NY)	50.00	22.00	6.25
☐ 21 Joe Bush	75.00	34.00	9.50
☐ 22 Owen Bush	50.00	22.00	6.25
☐ 23 Bobbie Byrne	50.00	22.00	6.25
☐ 24 Forrest Cady	50.00	22.00	6.25
☐ 25 Max Carey	100.00	45.00	12.50
☐ 26 Ray Chapman	100.00	45.00	12.50
☐ 27 Larry Cheney	50.00	22.00	6.25
☐ 28 Eddie Cicotte	125.00	55.00	15.50
☐ 29 Tom Clarke	50.00	22.00	6.25

☐ 30 Ty Cobb	1000.00	450.00	125.00
☐ 31 Eddie Collins	125.00	55.00	15.50
☐ 32 Shauno Collins	50.00	22.00	6.25
☐ 33 Fred Coumbe	50.00	22.00	6.25
☐ 34 Harry Coveleski	75.00	34.00	9.50
☐ 35 Gavvy Cravath	75.00	34.00	9.50
☐ 36 Sam Crawford	125.00	55.00	15.50
☐ 37 George Cutshaw	75.00	34.00	9.50
☐ 38 Jack Daubert	75.00	34.00	9.50
☐ 39 George Dauss	50.00	22.00	6.25
☐ 40 Charles Deal	50.00	22.00	6.25
☐ 41 Wheezer Dell	50.00	22.00	6.25
☐ 42 William Doak	50.00	22.00	6.25
☐ 43 Bill Donovan	50.00	22.00	6.25
☐ 44 Larry Doyle	75.00	34.00	9.50
☐ 45 Johnny Evers	125.00	55.00	15.50
☐ 46 Urban Faber	100.00	45.00	12.50
☐ 47 Happy Felsch	125.00	55.00	15.50
☐ 48 Bill Fischer	50.00	22.00	6.25
☐ 49 Ray Fisher	50.00	22.00	6.25
☐ 50 Art Fletcher	50.00	22.00	6.25
☐ 51 Eddie Foster	50.00	22.00	6.25
☐ 52 Jacques Fournier	50.00	22.00	6.25
☐ 53 Del Gainer	50.00	22.00	6.25
☐ 54 Bert Gallia	50.00	22.00	6.25
☐ 55 Chick Gandil	125.00	55.00	15.50
☐ 56 Larry Gardner	50.00	22.00	6.25
☐ 57 Joe Gedeon	50.00	22.00	6.25
☐ 58 Gus Getz	50.00	22.00	6.25
☐ 59 Frank Gilhooley	50.00	22.00	6.25
☐ 60 Kid Gleason	75.00	34.00	9.50
☐ 61 Mike Gonzales	50.00	22.00	6.25
☐ 62 Hank Gowdy	75.00	34.00	9.50
☐ 63 John Graney	50.00	22.00	6.25
☐ 64 Tom Griffith	50.00	22.00	6.25
☐ 65 Heinie Groh	75.00	34.00	9.50
☐ 66 Bob Groom	50.00	22.00	6.25
☐ 67 Louis Guisto	50.00	22.00	6.25
☐ 68 Earl Hamilton	50.00	22.00	6.25
☐ 69 Harry Harper	50.00	22.00	6.25
☐ 70 Grover Hartley	50.00	22.00	6.25
☐ 71 Harry Heilmann	100.00	45.00	12.50
☐ 72 Claude Hendrix	50.00	22.00	6.25
☐ 73 Olaf Henriksen	50.00	22.00	6.25
☐ 74 John Henry	50.00	22.00	6.25
☐ 75 Buck Herzog	50.00	22.00	6.25
☐ 76A Hugh High ERR (photo actually Claude Williams, white stockings)	125.00	55.00	15.50
☐ 76B Hugh High COR black stockings)	75.00	34.00	9.50
☐ 77 Dick Hoblitzell	50.00	22.00	6.25
☐ 78 Walter Holke	50.00	22.00	6.25
☐ 79 Harry Hooper	100.00	45.00	12.50
☐ 80 Rogers Hornsby	250.00	110.00	31.00
☐ 81 Ivan Howard	50.00	22.00	6.25
☐ 82 Joe Jackson	1000.00	450.00	125.00
☐ 83 Harold Janvrin	50.00	22.00	6.25
☐ 84 William James	50.00	22.00	6.25
☐ 85 Charlie Jamieson	50.00	22.00	6.25
☐ 86 Hugh Jennings MG	100.00	45.00	12.50
☐ 87 Walter Johnson	250.00	110.00	31.00
☐ 88 James Johnston	50.00	22.00	6.25
☐ 89 Fielder Jones	50.00	22.00	6.25
☐ 90A Joe Judge ERR (photo actually Ray Morgan, bat right shoulder)	125.00	55.00	15.50
☐ 90B Joe Judge COR (bat left shoulder)	75.00	34.00	9.50
☐ 91 Hans Lobert	50.00	22.00	6.25
☐ 92 Benny Kauff	50.00	22.00	6.25
☐ 93 Wm. Killefer Jr.	50.00	22.00	6.25
☐ 94 Ed Konetchy	50.00	22.00	6.25
☐ 95 John Lavan	50.00	22.00	6.25
☐ 96 Jimmy Lavender	50.00	22.00	6.25
☐ 97 Nemo Leibold	50.00	22.00	6.25
☐ 98 Dutch Leonard	75.00	34.00	9.50
☐ 99 Duffy Lewis	50.00	22.00	6.25
☐ 100 Tom Long	50.00	22.00	6.25
☐ 101 Bill Louden	50.00	22.00	6.25
☐ 102 Fred Luderus	50.00	22.00	6.25
☐ 103 Lee Magee	50.00	22.00	6.25
☐ 104 Sherwood Magee	50.00	22.00	6.25
☐ 105 Al Mamaux	50.00	22.00	6.25
☐ 106 Leslie Mann	50.00	22.00	6.25
☐ 107 Rabbit Maranville	100.00	45.00	12.50
☐ 108 Rube Marquard	125.00	55.00	15.50
☐ 109 Armando Marsans	50.00	22.00	6.25
☐ 110 J. Erskine Mayer	50.00	22.00	6.25
☐ 111 George McBride	50.00	22.00	6.25
☐ 112 Lew McCarty	50.00	22.00	6.25
☐ 113 John J. McGraw MG	125.00	55.00	15.50
☐ 114 Jack McInnis	75.00	34.00	9.50
☐ 115 Lee Meadows	50.00	22.00	6.25
☐ 116 Fred Merkle	75.00	34.00	9.50
☐ 117 Chief Meyers	75.00	34.00	9.50
☐ 118 Clyde Milan	50.00	22.00	6.25
☐ 119 Otto Miller	50.00	22.00	6.25
☐ 120 Clarence Mitchell	50.00	22.00	6.25
☐ 121A Ray Morgan ERR (photo actually Joe Judge, bat left shoulder)	125.00	55.00	15.50
☐ 121B Ray Morgan COR (bat right shoulder)	75.00	34.00	9.50
☐ 122 Guy Morton	50.00	22.00	6.25
☐ 123 Mike Mowrey	50.00	22.00	6.25
☐ 124 Elmer Myers	50.00	22.00	6.25
☐ 125 Hy Myers	50.00	22.00	6.25
☐ 126 Greasy Neale	75.00	34.00	9.50
☐ 127 Art Nehf	50.00	22.00	6.25
☐ 128 J.A. Niehoff	50.00	22.00	6.25
☐ 129 Steve O'Neill	75.00	34.00	9.50
☐ 130 Dode Paskert	50.00	22.00	6.25
☐ 131 Roger Peckinpaugh	75.00	34.00	9.50
☐ 132 Pol Perritt	50.00	22.00	6.25
☐ 133 Jeff Pfeffer	50.00	22.00	6.25
☐ 134 Walter Pipp	100.00	45.00	12.50
☐ 135 Derril Pratt	50.00	22.00	6.25
☐ 136 Bill Rariden	50.00	22.00	6.25
☐ 137 Sam Rice	100.00	45.00	12.50
☐ 138 Hank Ritter	50.00	22.00	6.25
☐ 139 Eppa Rixey	100.00	45.00	12.50
☐ 140 Davey Robertson	50.00	22.00	6.25
☐ 141 Bob Roth	50.00	22.00	6.25
☐ 142 Ed Roush	100.00	45.00	12.50
☐ 143 Clarence Rowland MG	50.00	22.00	6.25
☐ 144 Dick Rudolph	50.00	22.00	6.25
☐ 145 William Rumler	50.00	22.00	6.25
☐ 146A Reb Russell ERR (photo actually Mel Wolfgang, pitching, follow through)	125.00	55.00	15.50
☐ 146B Reb Russell COR (standing, hands at side)	75.00	34.00	9.50
☐ 147 Babe Ruth	1200.00	550.00	150.00
☐ 148 Vic Saier	50.00	22.00	6.25
☐ 149 Slim Sallee	50.00	22.00	6.25
☐ 150 Ray Schalk	100.00	45.00	12.50
☐ 151 Walter Schang	50.00	22.00	6.25
☐ 152 Frank Schulte	50.00	22.00	6.25
☐ 153 Ferd Schupp	50.00	22.00	6.25
☐ 154 Everett Scott	75.00	34.00	9.50
☐ 155 Hank Severeid	50.00	22.00	6.25
☐ 156 Howard Shanks	50.00	22.00	6.25
☐ 157 Bob Shawkey	75.00	34.00	9.50
☐ 158 Jimmy Sheckard CO	50.00	22.00	6.25
☐ 159 Ernie Shore	75.00	34.00	9.50
☐ 160 Chick Shorten	50.00	22.00	6.25
☐ 161 Burt Shotton	75.00	34.00	9.50
☐ 162 George Sisler	125.00	55.00	15.50
☐ 163 Elmer Smith	50.00	22.00	6.25
☐ 164 J. Carlisle Smith	50.00	22.00	6.25
☐ 165 Fred Snodgrass	75.00	34.00	9.50
☐ 166 Tris Speaker	125.00	55.00	15.50
☐ 167 Oscar Stanage	50.00	22.00	6.25
☐ 168 Charles Stengel	250.00	110.00	31.00
☐ 169 Milton Stock	50.00	22.00	6.25
☐ 170 Amos Strunk	50.00	22.00	6.25
☐ 171 Zeb Terry	50.00	22.00	6.25
☐ 172 Jeff Tesreau	50.00	22.00	6.25
☐ 173 Chester Thomas	50.00	22.00	6.25
☐ 174 Fred Toney	75.00	34.00	9.50
☐ 175 Terry Turner	50.00	22.00	6.25
☐ 176 George Tyler	50.00	22.00	6.25
☐ 177 Jim Vaughn	50.00	22.00	6.25
☐ 178 Bob Veach	50.00	22.00	6.25
☐ 179 Oscar Vitt	75.00	34.00	9.50
☐ 180 Honus Wagner	500.00	220.00	60.00
☐ 181 Clarence Walker	50.00	22.00	6.25
☐ 182 Jim Walsh	50.00	22.00	6.25
☐ 183 Al Walters	50.00	22.00	6.25
☐ 184 Bill Wambsganss	50.00	22.00	6.25
☐ 185 Buck Weaver	100.00	45.00	12.50
☐ 186 Carl Weilman	50.00	22.00	6.25
☐ 187 Zack Wheat	125.00	55.00	15.50
☐ 188 Geo. Whitted	50.00	22.00	6.25
☐ 189 Joe Wilhoit	50.00	22.00	6.25
☐ 190A Claude Williams ERR (photo actually Hugh High, black stockings)	125.00	55.00	15.50
☐ 190B Claude Williams COR (photo actually Hugh High, black stockings)	75.00	34.00	9.50
☐ 191 Fred Williams	75.00	34.00	9.50
☐ 192 Art Wilson	50.00	22.00	6.25
☐ 193 Lawton Witt	50.00	22.00	6.25
☐ 194 Joe Wood	100.00	45.00	12.50
☐ 195 William Wortman	50.00	22.00	6.25
☐ 196 Steve Yerkes	50.00	22.00	6.25
☐ 197 Earl Yingling	50.00	22.00	6.25
☐ 198 Pep Young (2ndB. Detroit)	50.00	22.00	6.25
☐ 199 Rollie Zeider	50.00	22.00	6.25
☐ 200 Heine Zimmerman	50.00	22.00	6.25

1954 Colonial Meat Products Piersall

These black and white postcards measure 3 1/2" by 5 3/8" and were issued by Colonial Meat Products. Both of these cards feature Jimmy Piersall; however, the cropping and the color of the facsimile autograph on the front of the card are different. The backs of the cards contain a Colonial Meat advertisement and endorsement by Piersall.

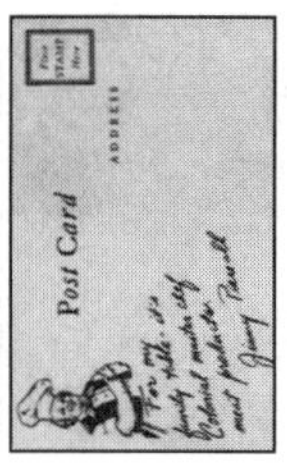

	NRMT	VG-E	GOOD
COMPLETE SET (2)	30.00	13.50	3.70
COMMON CARD (1-2)	15.00	6.75	1.85
☐ 1 Jimmy Piersall Name in black facsimile autograph pictured on chest	15.00	6.75	1.85
☐ 2 Jimmy Piersall Name in blue facsimilie autograph pictured to hips	15.00	6.75	1.85

1962 Colt .45 Booklets

These booklets feature members of the inagural Houston Colt 45's. They were issued and released at various retail outlets. The following booklets are believed to be in shorter supply: Jim Campbell; J.C. Hartman, Roman Mejias, Jim Pendleton, Paul Richards, Bobby Shantz, Jim Umbricht, Hal Woodeshick, Coaches, Announcers. Umbricht is believed to be by far the hardest booklet to acquire.

	NRMT	VG-E	GOOD
COMPLETE SET	250.00	110.00	31.00
COMMON CARD	5.00	2.20	.60
COMMON SP'S	15.00	6.75	1.85
☐ 1 Joe Amalfitano	5.00	2.20	.60
☐ 2 Bob Aspromonte	7.50	3.40	.95
☐ 3 Bob Bruce	5.00	2.20	.60
☐ 4 Jim Campbell SP	15.00	6.75	1.85
☐ 5 Harry Craft MG	5.00	2.20	.60
☐ 6 Dick Farrell	5.00	2.20	.60
☐ 7 Dave Giusti	5.00	2.20	.60
☐ 8 Jim Golden	5.00	2.20	.60
☐ 9 J.C. Hartman SP	15.00	6.75	1.85
☐ 10 Ken Johnson	5.00	2.20	.60
☐ 11 Norm Larker	5.00	2.20	.60
☐ 12 Bob Lillis	7.50	3.40	.95
☐ 13 Don McMahon	5.00	2.20	.60
☐ 14 Roman Mejias SP	15.00	6.75	1.85
☐ 15 Jim Pendleton SP	15.00	6.75	1.85
☐ 16 Paul Richards GM SP	20.00	9.00	2.50
☐ 17 Bobby Shantz SP	20.00	9.00	2.50
☐ 18 Hal Smith	5.00	2.20	.60
☐ 19 Al Spangler	5.00	2.20	.60
☐ 20 Jim Umbricht SP	50.00	22.00	6.25
☐ 21 Carl Warwick	5.00	2.20	.60
☐ 22 Hal Woodeshick SP	20.00	9.00	2.50
☐ 23 The Coaches SP	20.00	9.00	2.50
☐ 24 The Announcers SP	15.00	6.75	1.85

1962 Colt .45's Jay Publishing

This 12-card set of the Houston Colt .45's measures approximately 5" by 7". The fronts feature black-and-white posed player photos with the player's and team name printed below in the white border. These cards were packaged 12 in a packet. The backs are blank. The cards are unnumbered and checklisted below in alphabetical order. A complete set in the original envelope is valued at fifty percent higher.

	NRMT	VG-E	GOOD
COMPLETE SET (12)	40.00	18.00	5.00
COMMON CARD (1-12)	3.00	1.35	.35
☐ 1 Joe Amalfitano	3.50	1.55	.45
☐ 2 Bob Aspromonte	5.00	2.20	.60
☐ 3 Bob Bruce	3.00	1.35	.35
☐ 4 Don Buddin	3.00	1.35	.35
☐ 5 Harry Craft MG	3.00	1.35	.35
☐ 6 Dick Farrell	3.00	1.35	.35
☐ 7 Ken Johnson	3.00	1.35	.35
☐ 8 Norm Larker	3.00	1.35	.35
☐ 9 Roman Mejias	3.50	1.55	.45
☐ 10 Paul Richards GM	5.00	2.20	.60
☐ 11 Hal Smith	3.50	1.55	.45
☐ 12 Al Spangler	3.00	1.35	.35

1963 Colt .45's Jay Publishing

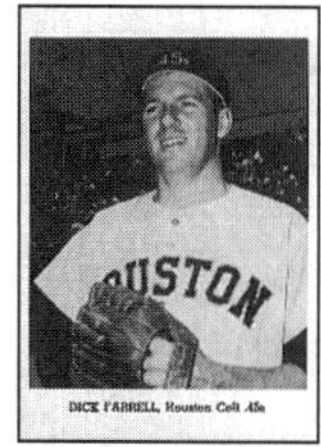

This 12-card set of the Houston Colt .45's measures approximately 5" by 7". The fronts feature black-and-white posed player photos with the player's and team name printed below in the white border. These cards were packaged 12 in a packet. The backs are blank. The cards are unnumbered and checklisted below in alphabetical order.

	NRMT	VG-E	GOOD
COMPLETE SET (12)	35.00	16.00	4.40
COMMON CARD (1-12)	3.00	1.35	.35
☐ 1 Bob Aspromonte	4.00	1.80	.50
☐ 2 Bob Bruce	3.00	1.35	.35
☐ 3 Harry Craft MG	4.00	1.80	.50
☐ 4 Dick Farrell	3.00	1.35	.35
☐ 5 Bob Lillis	4.00	1.80	.50
☐ 6 Don McMahon	3.00	1.35	.35
☐ 7 Jim Pendleton	3.00	1.35	.35
☐ 8 Merritt Ranew	3.00	1.35	.35
☐ 9 Pete Runnels	3.00	1.35	.35
☐ 10 Hal Smith	3.00	1.35	.35
☐ 11 Al Spangler	3.00	1.35	.35
☐ 12 Carl Warwick	3.00	1.35	.35

1964 Colt .45's Jay Publishing

This 12-card set of the Houston Colt .45's measures approximately 5" by 7". The fronts feature black-and-white posed player photos with the player's and team name printed below in the white border. These cards were packaged 12 in a packet. The backs are blank. The cards are unnumbered and checklisted below in alphabetical order.

	NRMT	VG-E	GOOD
COMPLETE SET (12)	35.00	16.00	4.40
COMMON CARD (1-12)	3.00	1.35	.35
☐ 1 Bob Aspromonte	4.00	1.80	.50
☐ 2 Bob Bruce	3.00	1.35	.35
☐ 3 Harry Craft MG	4.00	1.80	.50
☐ 4 Dick Farrell	3.00	1.35	.35
☐ 5 Ken Johnson	3.00	1.35	.35
☐ 6 Pete Runnels	3.00	1.35	.35
☐ 7 Al Spangler	3.00	1.35	.35
☐ 8 Rusty Staub	7.50	3.40	.95
☐ 9 Johnny Temple	4.00	1.80	.50
☐ 10 Carl Warwick	3.00	1.35	.35
☐ 11 Hal Woodeschick	3.00	1.35	.35
☐ 12 Jim Wynn	5.00	2.20	.60

1981 Conlon TSN

Issued by The Sporting News, this 100-card set measures approximately 4" by 5" and features the photography of Charles Martin Conlon. The set consists of baseball portraits from 1915-1935. The set was packaged in a brown leatherette case embossed in silver. The fronts display glossy sepia-tone pictures with white borders on heavy card stock. The words 'The Sporting News" are printed at the top and the player's name, position, the year of the photo and the card number are listed at the bottom. The backs are blank.

	MINT	NRMT	EXC
COMPLETE SET (100)	100.00	45.00	12.50
COMMON CARD (1-100)	.50	.23	.06

☐ 1 Ty Cobb	7.50	3.40	.95
☐ 2 Hugh Jennings	1.50	.70	.19
☐ 3 Miller Huggins	1.50	.70	.19
☐ 4 Babe Ruth	10.00	4.50	1.25
☐ 5 Lou Gehrig	7.50	3.40	.95
☐ 6 John McGraw	4.00	1.80	.50
☐ 7 Bill Terry	2.50	1.10	.30
☐ 8 Stan Baumgartner	.50	.23	.06
☐ 9 Christy Mathewson	4.00	1.80	.50
☐ 10 Grover Alexander	3.00	1.35	.35
☐ 11 Tony Lazzeri	1.50	.70	.19
☐ 12 Frank Chance Joe Tinker	2.50	1.10	.30
☐ 13 Johnny Evers	2.50	1.10	.30
☐ 14 Tris Speaker	2.50	1.10	.30
☐ 15 Harry Hooper	1.50	.70	.19
☐ 16 Duffy Lewis	.50	.23	.06
☐ 17 Smokey Joe Wood	1.00	.45	.12
☐ 18 Hugh Duffy	1.50	.70	.19
☐ 19 Rogers Hornsby	4.00	1.80	.50
☐ 20 Earl Averill	1.50	.70	.19
☐ 21 Dizzy Dean	4.00	1.80	.50
☐ 22 Paul Dean	1.00	.45	.12
☐ 23 Frank Frisch	1.50	.70	.19
☐ 24 Pepper Martin	1.00	.45	.12
☐ 25 Blondy Ryan	.50	.23	.06
☐ 26 Hank Gowdy	.50	.23	.06
☐ 27 Fred Merkle	1.00	.45	.12
☐ 28 Ernie Lombardi	1.50	.70	.19
☐ 29 Greasy Neale	1.00	.45	.12
☐ 30 Morris Badgro	.50	.23	.06
☐ 31 Jim Thorpe	6.00	2.70	.75
☐ 32 Roy Johnson	.50	.23	.06
☐ 33 Bob Johnson	.50	.23	.06
☐ 34 Moose Solters	.50	.23	.06
☐ 35 Specs Toporcer	.50	.23	.06
☐ 36 Jackie Hayes	.50	.23	.06
☐ 37 Walter Johnson	5.00	2.20	.60
☐ 38 Lefty Grove	3.00	1.35	.35
☐ 39 Eddie Collins	3.00	1.35	.35
☐ 40 Buck Weaver	1.50	.70	.19
☐ 41 Cozy Dolan	.50	.23	.06
☐ 42 Emil Meusel	.50	.23	.06
☐ 43 Bob Meusel	1.00	.45	.12
☐ 44 Lefty Gomez	1.50	.70	.19
☐ 45 Rube Marquard	1.50	.70	.19
☐ 46 Jeff Tesreau	.50	.23	.06
☐ 47 Joe Heving	.50	.23	.06
☐ 48 Johnny Heving	.50	.23	.06
☐ 49 Rick Ferrell	1.50	.70	.19
☐ 50 Wes Ferrell	1.00	.45	.12
☐ 51 Bill Wambsganss	.50	.23	.06
☐ 52 Ray Chapman	1.00	.45	.12
☐ 53 Joe Sewell	1.50	.70	.19
☐ 54 Luke Sewell	.50	.23	.06
☐ 55 Odell Hale	.50	.23	.06
☐ 56 Sammy Hale	.50	.23	.06
☐ 57 Earle Mack	.50	.23	.06
☐ 58 Connie Mack	4.00	1.80	.50
☐ 59 Rube Walberg	.50	.23	.06
☐ 60 Mule Haas	.50	.23	.06
☐ 61 Paul Waner	2.50	1.10	.30
☐ 62 Lloyd Waner	1.50	.70	.19
☐ 63 Pie Traynor	2.50	1.10	.30
☐ 64 Honus Wagner	5.00	2.20	.60
☐ 65 Joe Cronin	3.00	1.35	.35
☐ 66 Moon Harris	.50	.23	.06
☐ 67 Sheriff Harris	.50	.23	.06
☐ 68 Bucky Harris	1.50	.70	.19
☐ 69 Alec Gaston	.50	.23	.06
☐ 70 Milt Gaston	.50	.23	.06
☐ 71 Casey Stengel	5.00	2.20	.60
☐ 72 Amos Rusie	1.50	.70	.19
☐ 73 Mickey Welch	1.50	.70	.19
☐ 74 Roger Bresnahan	1.50	.70	.19
☐ 75 Jesse Burkett	1.50	.70	.19
☐ 76 Harry Heilmann	1.50	.70	.19
☐ 77 Heinie Manush	1.50	.70	.19
☐ 78 Charlie Gehringer	2.50	1.10	.30
☐ 79 Hank Greenberg	3.00	1.35	.35
☐ 80 Jimmie Foxx	4.00	1.80	.50
☐ 81 Al Simmons	2.50	1.10	.30
☐ 82 Ed Plank	2.50	1.10	.30
☐ 83 George Sisler	2.50	1.10	.30
☐ 84 Joe Medwick	1.50	.70	.19
☐ 85 Mel Ott	3.00	1.35	.35
☐ 86 Hack Wilson	1.50	.70	.19
☐ 87 Jimmy Wilson	.50	.23	.06
☐ 88 Chuck Klein	1.50	.70	.19
☐ 89 Gabby Hartnett	1.50	.70	.19
☐ 90 Heinie Groh	.50	.23	.06
☐ 91 Ping Bodie	.50	.23	.06
☐ 92 Ted Lyons	1.50	.70	.19
☐ 93 Jack(Picus) Quinn	.50	.23	.06
☐ 94 Oscar Roettger	.50	.23	.06
☐ 95 Wally Roettger	.50	.23	.06
☐ 96 Bubbles Hargrave	.50	.23	.06
☐ 97 Pinky Hargrave	.50	.23	.06
☐ 98 Sam Crawford	1.50	.70	.19
☐ 99 Gee Walker	.50	.23	.06
☐ 100 Homer Summa	.50	.23	.06

1983 Conlon Marketcom

This set of 60 Charles Martin Conlon photo cards was produced by Marketcom in conjunction with The Sporting News. The cards are

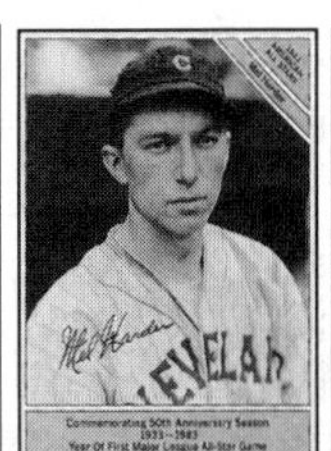

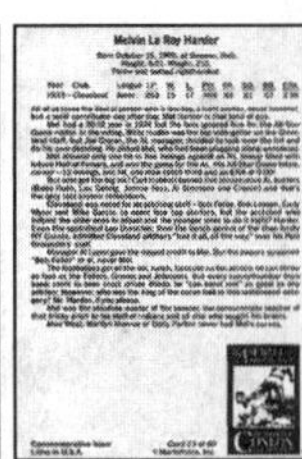

large size, approximately 4 1/2" X 6 1/8" and are in a sepia tone. The players selected for the set are members of the 1933 American and National League All-Star teams as well as Negro League All-Stars. These cards are numbered at the bottom of each reverse. The set numbering is American League (1-24), National League (25-48) and Negro League (49-60). In the upper right corner of each card's obverse is printed "1933 American (National or Negro League as appropriate) All Stars." Each obverse also features a facsimile autograph of the player pictured.

	MINT	NRMT	EXC
COMPLETE SET (60)	25.00	11.00	3.10
COMMON CARD (1-24)	.25	.11	.03
COMMON CARD (25-48)	.25	.11	.03
COMMON CARD (49-60)	.30	.14	.04
☐ 1 Jimmy Foxx	.75	.35	.09
☐ 2 Heinie Manush	.50	.23	.06
☐ 3 Lou Gehrig	2.00	.90	.25
☐ 4 Al Simmons	.50	.23	.06
☐ 5 Charlie Gehringer	.50	.23	.06
☐ 6 Luke Appling	.50	.23	.06
☐ 7 Mickey Cochrane	.50	.23	.06
☐ 8 Joe Kuhel	.25	.11	.03
☐ 9 Bill Dickey	.75	.35	.09
☐ 10 Pinky Higgins	.25	.11	.03
☐ 11 Roy Johnson	.25	.11	.03
☐ 12 Ben Chapman	.25	.11	.03
☐ 13 Urban Hodapp	.25	.11	.03
☐ 14 Joe Cronin	.50	.23	.06
☐ 15 Evar Swanson	.25	.11	.03
☐ 16 Earl Averill	.50	.23	.06
☐ 17 Babe Ruth	3.00	1.35	.35
☐ 18 Tony Lazzeri	.50	.23	.06
☐ 19 Alvin Crowder	.25	.11	.03
☐ 20 Lefty Grove	.75	.35	.09
☐ 21 Earl Whitehill	.25	.11	.03
☐ 22 Lefty Gomez	.75	.35	.09
☐ 23 Mel Harder	.25	.11	.03
☐ 24 Tommy Bridges	.25	.11	.03
☐ 25 Chuck Klein	.50	.23	.06
☐ 26 Spud Davis	.25	.11	.03
☐ 27 Riggs Stephenson	.40	.18	.05
☐ 28 Tony Piet	.25	.11	.03
☐ 29 Bill Terry	.50	.23	.06
☐ 30 Wes Schulmerich	.25	.11	.03
☐ 31 Pepper Martin	.40	.18	.05
☐ 32 Arky Vaughan	.50	.23	.06
☐ 33 Wally Berger	.30	.14	.04
☐ 34 Ripper Collins	.25	.11	.03
☐ 35 Fred Lindstrom	.50	.23	.06
☐ 36 Chick Fullis	.25	.11	.03
☐ 37 Paul Waner	.75	.35	.09
☐ 38 Johnny Frederick	.25	.11	.03
☐ 39 Joe Medwick	.50	.23	.06
☐ 40 Pie Traynor	.50	.23	.06
☐ 41 Frankie Frisch	.50	.23	.06
☐ 42 Chick Hafey	.50	.23	.06
☐ 43 Carl Hubbell	.75	.35	.09
☐ 44 Guy Bush	.25	.11	.03
☐ 45 Dizzy Dean	1.00	.45	.12
☐ 46 Hal Schumacher	.25	.11	.03
☐ 47 Larry French	.25	.11	.03
☐ 48 Lon Warneke	.25	.11	.03
☐ 49 Cool Papa Bell	.75	.35	.09
☐ 50 Oscar Charleston	.60	.25	.07
☐ 51 Josh Gibson	1.25	.55	.16
☐ 52 Satchel Paige	1.25	.55	.16
☐ 53 Dave Malarcher	.30	.14	.04
☐ 54 John Henry Lloyd	.60	.25	.07
☐ 55 Rube Foster	.75	.35	.09
☐ 56 Buck Leonard	.75	.35	.09
☐ 57 Smoky Joe Williams	.30	.14	.04
☐ 58 Willie Wells	.60	.25	.07
☐ 59 Judy Johnson	.75	.35	.09
☐ 60 Martin DiHigo	.60	.25	.07

1986 Conlon Series 1

This 60-card set was produced from the black and white photos in the Charles Martin Conlon collection. Each set comes with a special card which contains the number of that set out of the 12,000 sets which were produced. The cards measure 2 1/2" X 3 1/2" and are printed in sepia tones. The cards are individually numbered on the back.

	MINT	NRMT	EXC
COMPLETE SET (60)	20.00	9.00	2.50
COMMON CARD (1-60)	.15	.07	.02
☐ 1 Lou Gehrig	1.50	.70	.19
☐ 2 Ty Cobb	1.50	.70	.19
☐ 3 Grover C. Alexander	.30	.14	.04

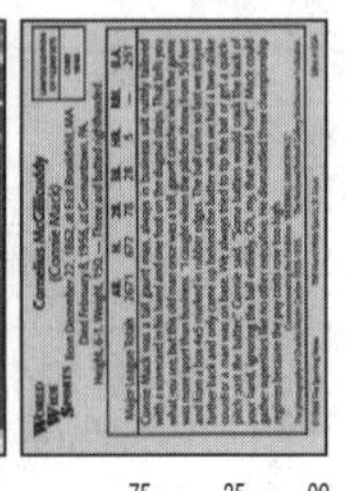

☐ 4 Walter Johnson	.75	.35	.09
☐ 5 Bill Klem	.30	.14	.04
☐ 6 Ty Cobb	1.50	.70	.19
☐ 7 Mickey Cochrane	.30	.14	.04
☐ 8 Paul Waner	.30	.14	.04
☐ 9 Joe Cronin	.30	.14	.04
☐ 10 Dizzy Dean	.50	.23	.06
☐ 11 Leo Durocher	.30	.14	.04
☐ 12 Jimmy Foxx	.50	.23	.06
☐ 13 Babe Ruth	2.00	.90	.25
☐ 14 Mike Gonzalez Frank Frisch Clyde Ellsworth Wares	.15	.07	.02
☐ 15 Carl Hubbell	.30	.14	.04
☐ 16 Miller Huggins	.15	.07	.02
☐ 17 Lou Gehrig	1.50	.70	.19
☐ 18 Connie McGillicuddy (Connie Mack)	.50	.23	.06
☐ 19 Heinie Manush	.30	.14	.04
☐ 20 Babe Ruth	2.00	.90	.25
☐ 22 Pepper Martin	.15	.07	.02
☐ 23 Christy Mathewson	.50	.23	.06
☐ 24 Ty Cobb	1.50	.70	.19
☐ 25 Bucky Harris	.30	.14	.04
☐ 26 Waite Hoyt	.30	.14	.04
☐ 27 Rube Marquard	.30	.14	.04
☐ 28 Joe McCarthy	.30	.14	.04
☐ 29 John McGraw	.50	.23	.06
☐ 30 Tris Speaker	.50	.23	.06
☐ 31 Bill Terry	.30	.14	.04
☐ 32 Christy Mathewson	.75	.35	.09
☐ 33 Casey Stengel	.75	.35	.09
☐ 34 Bob Meusel	.15	.07	.02
☐ 35 Rube Waddell	.30	.14	.04
☐ 36 Mel Ott	.50	.23	.06
☐ 37 Roger Peckinpaugh	.15	.07	.02
☐ 38 Pie Traynor	.50	.23	.06
☐ 39 Chief Bender	.30	.14	.04
☐ 40 Jack Coombs	.15	.07	.02
☐ 41 Ty Cobb	1.50	.70	.19
☐ 42 Harry Heilmann	.30	.14	.04
☐ 43 Charlie Gehringer	.30	.14	.04
☐ 44 Rogers Hornsby	.75	.35	.09
☐ 45 Lefty Gomez	.30	.14	.04
☐ 46 Christy Mathewson	.75	.35	.09
☐ 47 Lefty Grove	.50	.23	.06
☐ 48 Babe Ruth	2.00	.90	.25
☐ 49 Fred Merkle	.15	.07	.02
☐ 50 Babe Ruth	2.00	.90	.25
☐ 51 Herb Pennock	.30	.14	.04
☐ 52 Lou Gehrig	1.50	.70	.19
☐ 53 Fred Clarke	.30	.14	.04
☐ 54 Babe Ruth	2.00	.90	.25
☐ 55 Honus Wagner	.75	.35	.09
☐ 56 Hack Wilson	.30	.14	.04
☐ 57 Lou Gehrig	1.50	.70	.19
☐ 58 Lloyd Waner	.30	.14	.04
☐ 59 Charles Martin Conlon	.15	.07	.02
☐ 60 Conlon and Margie	.15	.07	.02
☐ NNO Set Number Card	.15	.07	.02

1987 Conlon Series 2

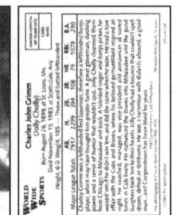

The second series of 60 Charles Martin Conlon photo cards was produced by World Wide Sports in conjunction with The Sporting News. The cards are standard size, 2 1/2" X 3 1/2" and are in a sepia tone. Reportedly 12,000 sets were produced. The photos were selected and background information written by Paul MacFarlane of The Sporting News. The cards are individually numbered on the back.

	MINT	NRMT	EXC
COMPLETE SET (60)	12.00	5.50	1.50
COMMON CARD (1-60)	.15	.07	.02
☐ 1 Lou Gehrig	1.50	.70	.19
☐ 2 Lefty Gomez	.40	.18	.05
☐ 3 Christy Mathewson	.75	.35	.09
☐ 4 Grover Alexander	.50	.23	.06
☐ 5 Ty Cobb	1.50	.70	.19
☐ 6 Walter Johnson	.75	.35	.09
☐ 7 Charles(Babe) Adams	.15	.07	.02
☐ 8 Nick Altrock	.25	.11	.03
☐ 9 Al Schacht	.25	.11	.03
☐ 10 Hugh Critz	.15	.07	.02
☐ 11 Henry Cullop	.15	.07	.02
☐ 12 Jacob Daubert	.15	.07	.02
☐ 13 William Donovan	.15	.07	.02
☐ 14 Chick Hafey	.25	.11	.03
☐ 15 Bill Hallahan	.15	.07	.02
☐ 16 Fred Haney	.15	.07	.02
☐ 17 Charles Hartnett	.25	.11	.03
☐ 18 Walter Henline	.15	.07	.02
☐ 19 Edwin Rommel	.15	.07	.02
☐ 20 Ralph(Babe) Pinelli	.15	.07	.02
☐ 21 Robert Meusel	.25	.11	.03
☐ 22 Emil Meusel	.15	.07	.02
☐ 23 Smead Jolley	.15	.07	.02
☐ 24 Ike Boone	.15	.07	.02
☐ 25 Earl Webb	.15	.07	.02
☐ 26 Charles Comiskey	.40	.18	.05
☐ 27 Eddie Collins	.40	.18	.05
☐ 28 George(Buck) Weaver	.40	.18	.05
☐ 29 Eddie Cicotte	.40	.18	.05
☐ 30 Sam Crawford	.25	.11	.03
☐ 31 Charlie Dressen	.15	.07	.02
☐ 32 Arthur Fletcher	.15	.07	.02
☐ 33 Hugh Duffy	.25	.11	.03
☐ 34 Ira Flagstead	.15	.07	.02
☐ 35 Harry Hooper	.25	.11	.03
☐ 36 George Lewis	.15	.07	.02
☐ 37 Jimmie Dykes	.15	.07	.02
☐ 38 Goose Goslin	.25	.11	.03
☐ 39 Hank Gowdy	.15	.07	.02
☐ 40 Charlie Grimm	.15	.07	.02
☐ 41 Mark Koenig	.15	.07	.02
☐ 42 James Hogan	.15	.07	.02
☐ 43 William Jacobson	.15	.07	.02
☐ 44 Fielder Jones	.15	.07	.02
☐ 45 George Kelly	.25	.11	.03
☐ 46 Adolpho Luque	.25	.11	.03
☐ 47 Rabbit Maranville	.25	.11	.03
☐ 48 Carl Mays	.15	.07	.02
☐ 49 Edward Plank	.25	.11	.03
☐ 50 Hubert Pruett	.15	.07	.02
☐ 51 John(Picus) Quinn	.15	.07	.02
☐ 52 Charles(Flint) Rhem	.15	.07	.02
☐ 53 Amos Rusie	.25	.11	.03
☐ 54 Edd Roush	.25	.11	.03
☐ 55 Ray Schalk	.25	.11	.03
☐ 56 Ernie Shore	.15	.07	.02
☐ 57 Joe Wood	.25	.11	.03
☐ 58 George Sisler	.40	.18	.05
☐ 59 Jim Thorpe	1.50	.70	.19
☐ 60 Earl Whitehill	.15	.07	.02

1988 Conlon American All-Stars

This set of 24 Charles Martin Conlon photo cards was produced by World Wide Sports in conjunction with The Sporting News. The cards are standard size and are in a sepia tone. The photos (members of the 1933 American League All-Star team) were selected and background information written by Paul MacFarlane of The Sporting News. These cards are unnumbered and hence are listed below in alphabetical order. American League is indicated in the lower right corner of each card's reverse. In the upper right corner of each card's obverse is printed "1933 American All Stars."

	MINT	NRMT	EXC
COMPLETE SET (24)	6.00	2.70	.75
COMMON CARD (1-24)	.15	.07	.02
☐ 1 Luke Appling	.30	.14	.04
☐ 2 Earl Averill	.30	.14	.04
☐ 3 Tommy Bridges	.15	.07	.02
☐ 4 Ben Chapman	.15	.07	.02
☐ 5 Mickey Cochrane	.30	.14	.04
☐ 6 Joe Cronin	.30	.14	.04
☐ 7 Alvin Crowder	.15	.07	.02
☐ 8 Bill Dickey	.50	.23	.06
☐ 9 James Emory Foxx	.75	.35	.09
☐ 10 Lou Gehrig	1.50	.70	.19
☐ 11 Charlie Gehringer	.30	.14	.04
☐ 12 Lefty Gomez	.30	.14	.04
☐ 13 Lefty Grove	.50	.23	.06
☐ 14 Mel Harder	.15	.07	.02
☐ 15 Pinky Higgins	.15	.07	.02
☐ 16 Urban Hodapp	.15	.07	.02
☐ 17 Roy Johnson	.15	.07	.02
☐ 18 Joe Kuhel	.15	.07	.02
☐ 19 Tony Lazzeri	.30	.14	.04

	MINT	NRMT	EXC
☐ 20 Heinie Manush	.30	.14	.04
☐ 21 Babe Ruth	2.00	.90	.25
☐ 22 Al Simmons	.30	.14	.04
☐ 23 Evar Swanson	.15	.07	.02
☐ 24 Earl Whitehill	.15	.07	.02

1988 Conlon Hardee's/Coke

This six-card standard-size sepia tone set was issued in 18 central Indiana Hardee's restaurants over a six-week period, a different card per purchase per week. The set features the vintage photography of Charles Martin Conlon, except for the Cool Papa Bell photo which was not shot by Conlon. The card backs contain biographical information, Hardee's logo and a Coca Cola Classic logo. The cards are also copyrighted by The Sporting News.

	MINT	NRMT	EXC
COMPLETE SET (6)	4.50	2.00	.55
COMMON CARD (1-6)	.50	.23	.06
☐ 1 Cool Papa Bell	.75	.35	.09
☐ 2 Ty Cobb	2.00	.90	.25
☐ 3 Lou Gehrig	2.00	.90	.25
☐ 4 Connie Mack	.75	.35	.09
☐ 5 Casey Stengel	.75	.35	.09
☐ 6 Rube Waddell	.50	.23	.06

1988 Conlon National All-Stars

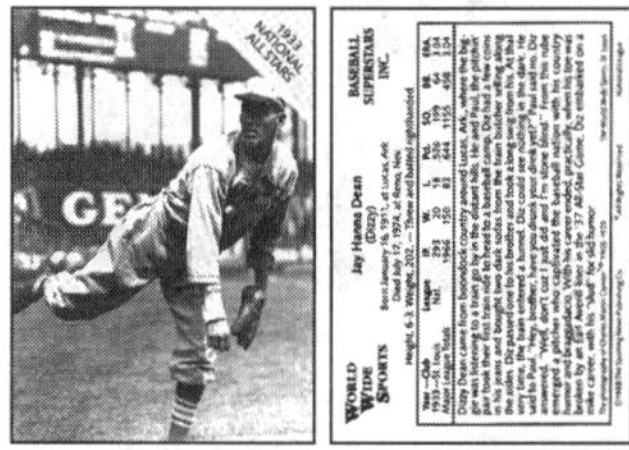

This set of 24 Charles Martin Conlon photo cards was produced by World Wide Sports in conjunction with The Sporting News. The cards are standard size, and are in a sepia tone. The photos (members of the 1933 National League All-Star team) were selected and background information written by Paul MacFarlane of The Sporting News. These cards are unnumbered and hence are listed below in alphabetical order. American League is indicated in the lower right corner of each card's reverse. In the upper right corner of each card's obverse is printed "1933 National All Stars."

	MINT	NRMT	EXC
COMPLETE SET (24)	5.00	2.20	.60
COMMON CARD (1-24)	.15	.07	.02
☐ 1 Wally Berger	.15	.07	.02
☐ 2 Guy Bush	.15	.07	.02
☐ 3 Ripper Collins	.15	.07	.02
☐ 4 Spud Davis	.15	.07	.02
☐ 5 Dizzy Dean	.50	.23	.06
☐ 6 Johnny Frederick	.15	.07	.02
☐ 7 Larry French	.15	.07	.02
☐ 8 Frankie Frisch	.30	.14	.04
☐ 9 Chick Fullis	.15	.07	.02
☐ 10 Chick Hafey	.30	.14	.04
☐ 11 Carl Hubbell	.50	.23	.06
☐ 12 Chuck Klein	.30	.14	.04
☐ 13 Fred Lindstrom	.30	.14	.04
☐ 14 Pepper Martin	.30	.14	.04
☐ 15 Joe Medwick	.30	.14	.04
☐ 16 Tony Piet	.15	.07	.02
☐ 17 Wes Schulmerich	.15	.07	.02
☐ 18 Hal Schumacher	.15	.07	.02
☐ 19 Riggs Stephenson	.30	.14	.04
☐ 20 Bill Terry	.50	.23	.06
☐ 21 Pie Traynor	.50	.23	.06
☐ 22 Arky Vaughan	.30	.14	.04
☐ 23 Paul Waner	.50	.23	.06
☐ 24 Lon Warneke	.15	.07	.02

1988 Conlon Negro All-Stars

This set of 12 photo cards was produced by World Wide Sports in conjunction with The Sporting News. The cards are standard size, and are in a sepia tone. The photos (Negro League All Stars from 1933) were selected and background information written by Paul MacFarlane of The Sporting News. Despite the stylistic similarity of this set with the other Conlon sets, the photos for this set were not taken by Charles Martin Conlon. These cards are unnumbered and hence are listed below in alphabetical order. Negro League is indicated in the

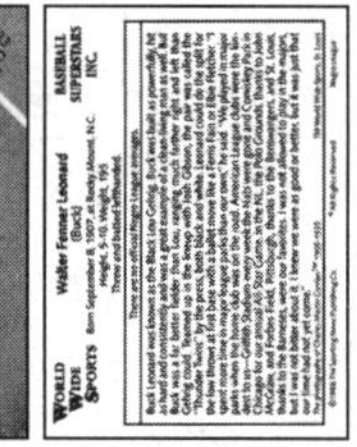

lower right corner of each card's reverse. In the upper right corner of each card's obverse is printed "1933 Negro All Stars." The photo quality on some of the cards is very poor suggesting that the original photo or negative may have been enlarged to an excessive degree.

	MINT	NRMT	EXC
COMPLETE SET (12)	5.00	2.20	.60
COMMON CARD (1-12)	.25	.11	.03
☐ 1 Cool Papa Bell	.75	.35	.09
☐ 2 Oscar Charleston	.50	.23	.06
☐ 3 Martin DiHigo	.50	.23	.06
☐ 4 Rube Foster	.50	.23	.06
☐ 5 Josh Gibson	1.00	.45	.12
☐ 6 Judy Johnson	.50	.23	.06
☐ 7 Buck Leonard	.50	.23	.06
☐ 8 John Henry Lloyd	.50	.23	.06
☐ 9 Dave Malarcher	.25	.11	.03
☐ 10 Satchel Paige	1.00	.45	.12
☐ 11 Willie Wells	.50	.23	.06
☐ 12 Smoky Joe Williams	.25	.11	.03

1988 Conlon Series 3

This third series of 30 Charles Martin Conlon photo cards was produced by World Wide Sports in conjunction with The Sporting News. The cards are standard size, and are in a sepia tone. The photos were selected and background information written by Paul MacFarlane of The Sporting News. These cards are unnumbered and hence are listed below in alphabetical order. Series 3 is indicated in the lower right corner of each card's reverse. A black and white logo for the "Baseball Immortals" and The Conlon Collection is over-printed in the lower left corner of each obverse.

	MINT	NRMT	EXC
COMPLETE SET (30)	6.00	2.70	.75
COMMON CARD (1-30)	.15	.07	.02
☐ 1 Ace Adams	.15	.07	.02
☐ 2 Grover C. Alexander	.50	.23	.06
☐ 3 Elden Auker	.15	.07	.02
☐ 4 Jack Barry	.15	.07	.02
☐ 5 Wally Berger	.15	.07	.02
☐ 6 Ben Chapman	.15	.07	.02
☐ 7 Mickey Cochrane	.30	.14	.04
☐ 8 Frankie Crosetti	.15	.07	.02
☐ 9 Paul Dean	.15	.07	.02
☐ 10 Leo Durocher	.50	.23	.06
☐ 11 Wes Ferrell	.15	.07	.02
☐ 12 Hank Gowdy	.15	.07	.02
☐ 13 Andy High	.15	.07	.02
☐ 14 Rogers Hornsby	.75	.35	.09
☐ 15 Carl Hubbell	.50	.23	.06
☐ 16 Joe Judge	.15	.07	.02
☐ 17 Tony Lazzeri	.30	.14	.04
☐ 18 Pepper Martin	.25	.11	.03
☐ 19 Lee Meadows	.15	.07	.02
☐ 20 Johnny Murphy	.15	.07	.02
☐ 21 Steve O'Neil	.15	.07	.02
☐ 22 Ed Plank	.30	.14	.04
☐ 23 Jack(Picus) Quinn	.15	.07	.02
☐ 24 Charley Root	.15	.07	.02
☐ 25 Babe Ruth	2.00	.90	.25
☐ 26 Fred Snodgrass	.15	.07	.02
☐ 27 Tris Speaker	.50	.23	.06
☐ 28 Bill Terry	.50	.23	.06
☐ 29 Jeff Tesreau	.15	.07	.02
☐ 30 George Toporcer	.15	.07	.02

1988 Conlon Series 4

This fourth series of 30 Charles Martin Conlon photo cards was produced by World Wide Sports in conjunction with The Sporting News. The cards are standard size, and are in a sepia tone. The photos were selected and background information written by Paul MacFarlane of The Sporting News. These cards are unnumbered and hence are listed below in alphabetical order. Series 4 is indicated in the lower right corner of each card's reverse. A black and white logo for the "Baseball Immortals" and The Conlon Collection is over-printed in the lower left corner of each obverse.

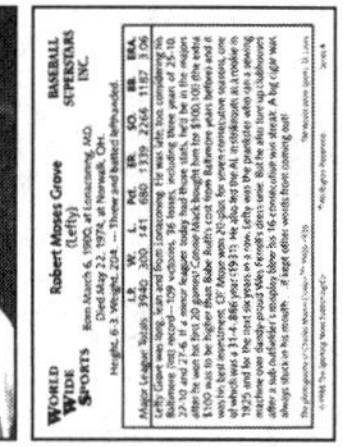

	MINT	NRMT	EXC
COMPLETE SET (30)	6.00	2.70	.75
COMMON CARD (1-30)	.15	.07	.02
☐ 1 Dale Alexander	.15	.07	.02
☐ 2 Morris Badgro	.15	.07	.02
☐ 3 Dick Bartell	.15	.07	.02
☐ 4 Max Bishop	.15	.07	.02
☐ 5 Hal Chase	.30	.14	.04
☐ 6 Ty Cobb	1.50	.70	.19
☐ 7 Nick Cullop	.15	.07	.02
☐ 8 Dizzy Dean	.75	.35	.09
☐ 9 Charlie Dressen	.15	.07	.02
☐ 10 Jimmy Dykes	.15	.07	.02
☐ 11 Art Fletcher	.15	.07	.02
☐ 12 Charlie Grimm	.15	.07	.02
☐ 13 Lefty Grove	.50	.23	.06
☐ 14 Baby Doll Jacobson	.15	.07	.02
☐ 15 Bill Klem UMP	.30	.14	.04
☐ 16 Mark Koenig	.15	.07	.02
☐ 17 Duffy Lewis	.15	.07	.02
☐ 18 Carl Mays	.15	.07	.02
☐ 19 Fred Merkle	.15	.07	.02
☐ 20 Greasy Neale	.30	.14	.04
☐ 21 Mel Ott	.50	.23	.06
☐ 22 Babe Pinelli	.15	.07	.02
☐ 23 Flint Rhem	.15	.07	.02
☐ 24 Slim Sallee UER (Misspelled Salee on card back)	.15	.07	.02
☐ 25 Al Simmons	.30	.14	.04
☐ 26 George Sisler	.30	.14	.04
☐ 27 Riggs Stephenson	.15	.07	.02
☐ 28 Jim Thorpe	1.50	.70	.19
☐ 29 Bill Wambsganss	.15	.07	.02
☐ 30 Cy Young	.50	.23	.06

1988 Conlon Series 5

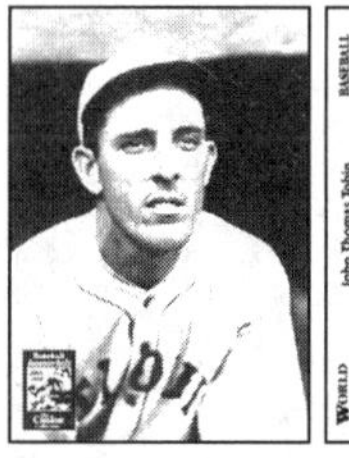

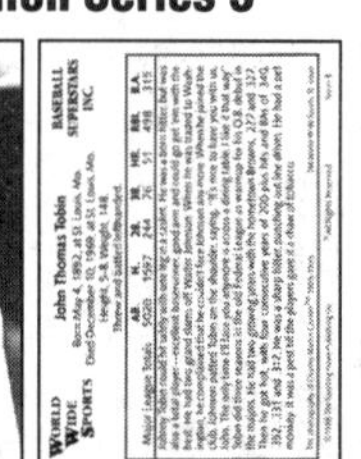

This fifth series of 30 Charles Martin Conlon photo cards was produced by World Wide Sports in conjunction with The Sporting News. The cards are standard size, and are in a sepia tone. The photos were selected and background information written by Paul MacFarlane of The Sporting News. These cards are unnumbered and hence are listed below in alphabetical order. Series 5 is indicated in the lower right corner of each card's reverse. A black and white logo for the "Baseball Immortals" and The Conlon Collection is over-printed in the lower left corner of each obverse.

	MINT	NRMT	EXC
COMPLETE SET (30)	6.00	2.70	.75
COMMON CARD (1-30)	.15	.07	.02
☐ 1 Nick Altrock	.30	.14	.04
☐ 2 Del Baker	.15	.07	.02
☐ 3 Moe Berg	1.00	.45	.12
☐ 4 Zeke Bonura	.15	.07	.02
☐ 5 Eddie Collins	.50	.23	.06
☐ 6 Hughie Critz	.15	.07	.02
☐ 7 George Dauss	.15	.07	.02
☐ 8 Joe Dugan	.15	.07	.02
☐ 9 Howard Ehmke	.15	.07	.02
☐ 10 James Emory Foxx	.75	.35	.09
☐ 11 Frankie Frisch	.30	.14	.04
☐ 12 Lou Gehrig	1.50	.70	.19
☐ 13 Charlie Gehringer	.50	.23	.06
☐ 14 Kid Gleason	.30	.14	.04
☐ 15 Lefty Gomez	.50	.23	.06
☐ 16 Babe Herman	.25	.11	.03
☐ 17 Bill James	.15	.07	.02
☐ 18 Joe Kuhel	.15	.07	.02
☐ 19 Dolf Luque	.30	.14	.04
☐ 20 John McGraw	.50	.23	.06
☐ 21 Stuffy McInnis	.15	.07	.02
☐ 22 Bob Meusel	.15	.07	.02
☐ 23 Lefty O'Doul	.15	.07	.02
☐ 24 Hub Pruett	.15	.07	.02
☐ 25 Paul Richards	.15	.07	.02
☐ 26 Bob Shawkey	.15	.07	.02
☐ 27 Gabby Street	.15	.07	.02
☐ 28 Johnny Tobin	.15	.07	.02
☐ 29 Rube Waddell	.30	.14	.04
☐ 30 Billy Werber	.15	.07	.02

1991 Conlon TSN

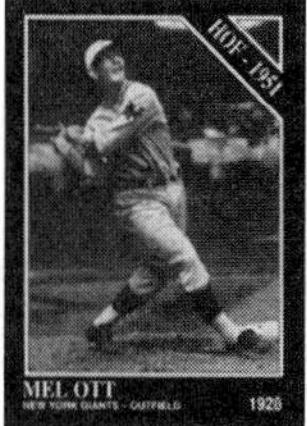

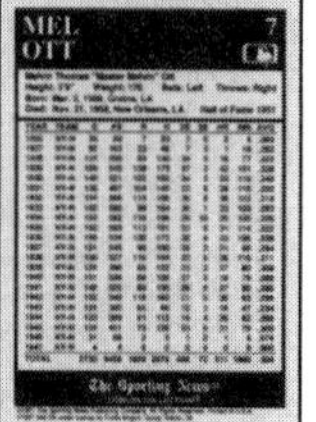

This 330-card standard-size set was issued in black and white and again featured the photography of Charles Conlon. The set was produced by MegaCards in conjunction with The Sporting News. The set was available in both packs as well as factory set form. The card backs contain pertinent information relevant to the front of the cards whether it is career statistics or all-time leaders format or the special cards commemorating the great teams of the first part of the twentieth century.

	MINT	NRMT	EXC
COMPLETE SET (330)	18.00	8.00	2.20
COMMON CARD (1-330)	.05	.02	.01
☐ 1 Rogers Hornsby HOF	.35	.16	.04
☐ 2 Jimmie Foxx HOF	.35	.16	.04
☐ 3 Dizzy Dean HOF	.40	.18	.05
☐ 4 Rabbit Maranville HOF	.20	.09	.03
☐ 5 Paul Waner HOF	.20	.09	.03
☐ 6 Lloyd Waner HOF	.20	.09	.03
☐ 7 Mel Ott HOF	.30	.14	.04
☐ 8 Honus Wagner HOF	.40	.18	.05
☐ 9 Walter Johnson HOF	.40	.18	.05
☐ 10 Carl Hubbell HOF	.25	.11	.03
☐ 11 Frank Frisch HOF	.20	.09	.03
☐ 12 Kiki Cuyler HOF	.20	.09	.03
☐ 13 Red Ruffing HOF	.20	.09	.03
☐ 14 Hank Greenberg HOF	.30	.14	.04
☐ 15 Johnny Evers HOF	.20	.09	.03
☐ 16 Hugh Jennings HOF	.20	.09	.03
☐ 17 Dave Bancroft HOF	.20	.09	.03
☐ 18 Joe Medwick HOF	.20	.09	.03
☐ 19 Ted Lyons HOF	.20	.09	.03
☐ 20 Chief Bender HOF	.20	.09	.03
☐ 21 Eddie Collins HOF	.20	.09	.03
☐ 22 Jim Bottomley HOF	.20	.09	.03
☐ 23 Lefty Grove HOF	.30	.14	.04
☐ 24 Max Carey HOF	.20	.09	.03
☐ 25 Burleigh Grimes HOF	.20	.09	.03
☐ 26 Ross Youngs HOF	.20	.09	.03
☐ 27 Ernie Lombardi HOF	.20	.09	.03
☐ 28 Joe McCarthy HOF	.20	.09	.03
☐ 29 Hack Wilson HOF	.25	.11	.03
☐ 30 Chuck Klein HOF	.20	.09	.03
☐ 31 Earl Averill HOF	.20	.09	.03
☐ 32 Grover C. Alexander HOF	.30	.14	.04
☐ 33 Chick Hafey HOF	.20	.09	.03
☐ 34 Bill McKechnie HOF	.20	.09	.03
☐ 35 Bob Feller HOF	.30	.14	.04
☐ 36 Pie Traynor HOF	.20	.09	.03
☐ 37 Casey Stengel HOF	.30	.14	.04
☐ 38 Arky Vaughan HOF	.20	.09	.03
☐ 39 Eppa Rixey HOF	.20	.09	.03
☐ 40 Joe Sewell HOF	.20	.09	.03
☐ 41 Red Faber HOF	.20	.09	.03
☐ 42 Travis Jackson HOF	.20	.09	.03
☐ 43 Jesse Haines HOF	.20	.09	.03
☐ 44 Tris Speaker HOF	.25	.11	.03
☐ 45 Connie Mack HOF	.25	.11	.03
☐ 46 Connie Mack HOF	.25	.11	.03
☐ 47 Connie Mack HOF	.25	.11	.03
☐ 48 Ray Schalk HOF	.20	.09	.03
☐ 49 Al Simmons HOF	.20	.09	.03
☐ 50 Joe Cronin HOF	.20	.09	.03
☐ 51 Mickey Cochrane HOF	.25	.11	.03
☐ 52 Harry Heilmann HOF	.20	.09	.03
☐ 53 Johnny Mize HOF	.25	.11	.03
☐ 54 Sam Rice HOF	.20	.09	.03
☐ 55 Edd Roush HOF	.20	.09	.03
☐ 56 Enos Slaughter HOF	.20	.09	.03
☐ 57 Christy Mathewson HOF	.40	.18	.05
☐ 58 Fred Lindstrom HOF	.20	.09	.03
☐ 59 Gabby Hartnett HOF	.20	.09	.03
☐ 60 George Kelly HOF	.20	.09	.03
☐ 61 Bucky Harris HOF	.20	.09	.03
☐ 62 Goose Goslin HOF	.20	.09	.03
☐ 63 Heinie Manush HOF	.20	.09	.03
☐ 64 Bill Terry HOF	.25	.11	.03
☐ 65 John McGraw HOF	.25	.11	.03
☐ 66 George Sisler HOF	.20	.09	.03
☐ 67 Lefty Gomez HOF	.25	.11	.03
☐ 68 Joe Judge	.10	.05	.01
☐ 69 Tommy Thevenow	.05	.02	.01
☐ 70 Charlie Gelbert	.05	.02	.01
☐ 71 Jackie Hayes	.05	.02	.01
☐ 72 Bob Fothergill	.05	.02	.01

Card	MINT	NRMT	EXC
□ 73 Adam Comorosky	.05	.02	.01
□ 74 Earl Smith	.05	.02	.01
□ 75 Sam Gray	.05	.02	.01
□ 76 Pete Appleton	.05	.02	.01
□ 77 Gene Moore	.05	.02	.01
□ 78 Art Jorgens	.05	.02	.01
□ 79 Bill Knickerbocker	.05	.02	.01
□ 80 Carl Reynolds	.05	.02	.01
□ 81 Ski Melillo	.05	.02	.01
□ 82 Johnny Burnett	.05	.02	.01
□ 83 Jake Powell	.05	.02	.01
□ 84 Johnny Murphy	.10	.05	.01
□ 85 Roy Parmelee	.05	.02	.01
□ 86 Jimmy Ripple	.05	.02	.01
□ 87 Gee Walker	.05	.02	.01
□ 88 George Earnshaw	.10	.05	.01
□ 89 Billy Southworth	.05	.02	.01
□ 90 Wally Moses	.05	.02	.01
□ 91 Rube Walberg	.05	.02	.01
□ 92 Jimmy Dykes	.10	.05	.01
□ 93 Charlie Root	.05	.02	.01
□ 94 Johnny Cooney	.05	.02	.01
□ 95 Charlie Grimm	.15	.07	.02
□ 96 Bob Johnson	.10	.05	.01
□ 97 Jack Scott	.05	.02	.01
□ 98 Rip Radcliff	.05	.02	.01
□ 99 Fritz Ostermueller	.05	.02	.01
□ 100 Julie Wera '27NY	.05	.02	.01
□ 101 Miller Huggins '27NY	.20	.09	.03
□ 102 Ray Morehart '27NY	.05	.02	.01
□ 103 Benny Bengough '27NY	.10	.05	.01
□ 104 Dutch Ruether '27NY	.05	.02	.01
□ 105 Earle Combs '27NY	.20	.09	.03
□ 106 Myles Thomas '27NY	.05	.02	.01
□ 107 Ben Paschal '27NY	.05	.02	.01
□ 108 Cedric Durst '27NY	.05	.02	.01
□ 109 Wilcy Moore '27NY	.05	.02	.01
□ 110 Babe Ruth '27NY	1.00	.45	.12
□ 111 Lou Gehrig '27NY	.75	.35	.09
□ 112 Joe Dugan '27NY	.10	.05	.01
□ 113 Tony Lazzeri '27NY	.20	.09	.03
□ 114 Urban Shocker '27NY	.10	.05	.01
□ 115 Waite Hoyt '27NY	.20	.09	.03
□ 116 Charley O'Leary '27NY	.05	.02	.01
□ 117 Art Fletcher CO '27NY	.05	.02	.01
□ 118 Pat Collins '27NY	.05	.02	.01
□ 119 Joe Giard '27NY	.05	.02	.01
□ 120 Herb Pennock '27NY	.20	.09	.03
□ 121 Mike Gazella '27NY	.05	.02	.01
□ 122 Bob Meusel '27NY	.15	.07	.02
□ 123 George Pipgras '27NY	.05	.02	.01
□ 124 Johnny Grabowski '27NY	.05	.02	.01
□ 125 Mark Koenig '27NY	.10	.05	.01
□ 126 Stan Hack	.10	.05	.01
□ 127 Earl Whitehill	.05	.02	.01
□ 128 Bill Lee	.05	.02	.01
□ 129 Gus Mancuso	.05	.02	.01
□ 130 Ray Blades	.05	.02	.01
□ 131 Jack Burns	.05	.02	.01
□ 132 Clint Brown	.05	.02	.01
□ 133 Bill Dietrich	.05	.02	.01
□ 134 Cy Blanton	.05	.02	.01
□ 135 Harry Hooper '16 Champs	.20	.09	.03
□ 136 Chick Shorten '16 Champs	.05	.02	.01
□ 137 Tilly Walker '16 Champs	.05	.02	.01
□ 138 Rube Foster '16 Champs	.05	.02	.01
□ 139 Jack Barry '16 Champs	.10	.05	.01
□ 140 Sad Sam Jones '16 Champs	.10	.05	.01
□ 141 Ernie Shore '16 Champs	.10	.05	.01
□ 142 Dutch Leonard '16 Champs	.10	.05	.01
□ 143 Herb Pennock '16 Champs	.20	.09	.03
□ 144 Hal Janvrin '16 Champs	.05	.02	.01
□ 145 Babe Ruth '16 Champs	1.00	.45	.12
□ 146 Duffy Lewis '16 Champs	.10	.05	.01
□ 147 Larry Gardner '16 Champs	.05	.02	.01
□ 148 Doc Hoblitzel '16 Champs	.05	.02	.01
□ 149 Everett Scott '16 Champs	.10	.05	.01
□ 150 Carl Mays '16 Champs	.10	.05	.01
□ 151 Bert Niehoff '16LL	.05	.02	.01
□ 152 Burt Shotton '16LL	.10	.05	.01
□ 153 Red Ames '16LL	.05	.02	.01
□ 154 Cy Williams '16LL	.10	.05	.01
□ 155 Bill Hinchman '16LL	.05	.02	.01
□ 156 Bob Shawkey '16LL	.10	.05	.01
□ 157 Wally Pipp '16LL	.15	.07	.02
□ 158 George J. Burns '16LL	.05	.02	.01
□ 159 Bob Veach '16LL	.05	.02	.01
□ 160 Hal Chase '16LL	.10	.05	.01
□ 161 Tom Hughes '16LL	.05	.02	.01
□ 162 Del Pratt '16LL	.05	.02	.01
□ 163 Heinie Groh '16LL	.10	.05	.01
□ 164 Zack Wheat '16LL	.20	.09	.03
□ 165 Lefty O'Doul Story	.10	.05	.01
□ 166 Willie Kamm Story	.05	.02	.01
□ 167 Paul Waner Story	.20	.09	.03
□ 168 Fred Snodgrass Story	.05	.02	.01
□ 169 Babe Herman Story	.15	.07	.02
□ 170 Al Bridwell Story	.05	.02	.01
□ 171 Chief Meyers Story	.05	.02	.01
□ 172 Hans Lobert Story	.05	.02	.01
□ 173 Rube Bressler Story	.05	.02	.01
□ 174 Sad Sam Jones Story	.10	.05	.01
□ 175 Bob O'Farrell Story	.05	.02	.01
□ 176 Specs Toporcer Story	.05	.02	.01
□ 177 Earl McNeely Story	.05	.02	.01
□ 178 Jack Knott Story	.05	.02	.01
□ 179 Heinie Mueller	.05	.02	.01
□ 180 Tommy Bridges	.10	.05	.01
□ 181 Lloyd Brown	.05	.02	.01
□ 182 Larry Benton	.05	.02	.01
□ 183 Max Bishop	.05	.02	.01
□ 184 Moe Berg	.50	.23	.06
□ 185 Cy Perkins	.05	.02	.01
□ 186 Steve O'Neill	.05	.02	.01
□ 187 Glenn Myatt	.05	.02	.01
□ 188 Joe Kuhel	.05	.02	.01
□ 189 Marty McManus	.05	.02	.01
□ 190 Red Lucas	.05	.02	.01
□ 191 Stuffy McInnis	.05	.02	.01
□ 192 Bing Miller	.05	.02	.01
□ 193 Luke Sewell	.10	.05	.01
□ 194 Bill Sherdel	.05	.02	.01
□ 195 Hal Rhyne	.05	.02	.01
□ 196 Guy Bush	.05	.02	.01
□ 197 Pete Fox	.05	.02	.01
□ 198 Wes Ferrell	.15	.07	.02
□ 199 Roy Johnson	.05	.02	.01
□ 200 Bill Wambsganss Triple Play	.10	.05	.01
□ 201 George H. Burns Triple Play	.05	.02	.01
□ 202 Clarence Mitchell Triple Play	.05	.02	.01
□ 203 Neal Ball Triple Play	.05	.02	.01
□ 204 Johnny Neun Triple Play	.05	.02	.01
□ 205 Homer Summa Triple Play	.05	.02	.01
□ 206 Ernie Padgett Triple Play	.05	.02	.01
□ 207 Walter Holke Triple Play	.05	.02	.01
□ 208 Glenn Wright Triple Play	.05	.02	.01
□ 209 Hank Gowdy	.10	.05	.01
□ 210 Zack Taylor	.05	.02	.01
□ 211 Ben Cantwell	.05	.02	.01
□ 212 Frank Demaree	.05	.02	.01
□ 213 Paul Derringer	.10	.05	.01
□ 214 Bill Hallahan	.05	.02	.01
□ 215 Danny MacFayden	.05	.02	.01
□ 216 Harry Rice	.05	.02	.01
□ 217 Bob Smith	.05	.02	.01
□ 218 Riggs Stephenson	.15	.07	.02
□ 219 Pat Malone	.05	.02	.01
□ 220 Bennie Tate	.05	.02	.01
□ 221 Joe Vosmik	.05	.02	.01
□ 222 George Watkins	.05	.02	.01
□ 223 Jimmie Wilson	.05	.02	.01
□ 224 George Uhle	.05	.02	.01
□ 225 Mel Ott TRIV	.30	.14	.04
□ 226 Nick Altrock TRIV	.05	.02	.01
□ 227 Red Ruffing TRIV	.20	.09	.03
□ 228 Joe Krakauskas TRIV	.05	.02	.01
□ 229 Wally Berger TRIV	.10	.05	.01
□ 230 Bobo Newsom	.15	.07	.02
□ 231 Lon Warneke	.10	.05	.01
□ 232 Frank Snyder	.05	.02	.01
□ 233 Myril Hoag	.05	.02	.01
□ 234 Mel Almada	.05	.02	.01
□ 235 Ivey Wingo	.05	.02	.01
□ 236 Jimmy Austin	.05	.02	.01
□ 237 Zeke Bonura	.05	.02	.01
□ 238 Russ Wrightstone	.05	.02	.01
□ 239 Al Todd	.05	.02	.01
□ 240 Rabbit Warstler	.05	.02	.01
□ 241 Sammy West	.05	.02	.01
□ 242 Art Reinhart	.10	.05	.01
□ 243 Lefty Stewart	.05	.02	.01
□ 244 Johnny Gooch	.05	.02	.01
□ 245 Bubbles Hargrave	.05	.02	.01
□ 246 George Harper	.05	.02	.01
□ 247 Sarge Connally	.05	.02	.01
□ 248 Garland Braxton	.05	.02	.01
□ 249 Wally Schang	.10	.05	.01
□ 250 Ty Cobb ATL	.75	.35	.09
□ 251 Rogers Hornsby ATL	.35	.16	.04
□ 252 Rube Marquard ATL	.20	.09	.03
□ 253 Carl Hubbell ATL	.25	.11	.03
□ 254 Joe Wood ATL	.10	.05	.01
□ 255 Lefty Grove ATL	.30	.14	.04
□ 256 Schoolboy Rowe ATL	.10	.05	.01
□ 257 General Crowder ATL	.05	.02	.01
□ 258 Walter Johnson ATL	.40	.18	.05
□ 259 Chick Hafey ATL	.20	.09	.03
□ 260 Fred Fitzsimmons ATL	.10	.05	.01
□ 261 Earl Webb ATL	.10	.05	.01
□ 262 Earle Combs ATL	.20	.09	.03
□ 263 Ed Konetchy ATL	.05	.02	.01
□ 264 Taylor Douthit ATL	.05	.02	.01
□ 265 Lloyd Waner ATL	.20	.09	.03
□ 266 Mickey Cochrane ATL	.25	.11	.03
□ 267 Hack Wilson ATL	.25	.11	.03
□ 268 Pie Traynor ATL	.20	.09	.03
□ 269 Spud Davis ATL	.05	.02	.01
□ 270 Heinie Manush ATL	.20	.09	.03
□ 271 Pinky Higgins ATL	.05	.02	.01
□ 272 Addie Joss ATL	.20	.09	.03
□ 273 Ed Walsh ATL	.20	.09	.03
□ 274 Pepper Martin ATL	.15	.07	.02
□ 275 Joe Sewell ATL	.20	.09	.03
□ 276 Dutch Leonard ATL	.10	.05	.01
□ 277 Gavvy Cravath ATL	.10	.05	.01
□ 278 Oral Hildebrand	.05	.02	.01
□ 279 Ray Kremer	.05	.02	.01
□ 280 Frankie Pytlak	.05	.02	.01
□ 281 Sammy Byrd	.05	.02	.01
□ 282 Curt Davis	.05	.02	.01
□ 283 Lew Fonseca	.05	.02	.01
□ 284 Muddy Ruel	.05	.02	.01
□ 285 Moose Solters	.05	.02	.01
□ 286 Fred Schulte	.05	.02	.01
□ 287 Jack Quinn	.10	.05	.01
□ 288 Pinky Whitney	.05	.02	.01
□ 289 John Stone	.05	.02	.01
□ 290 Hughie Critz	.05	.02	.01
□ 291 Ira Flagstead	.05	.02	.01
□ 292 George Grantham	.05	.02	.01
□ 293 Sammy Hale	.05	.02	.01
□ 294 Shanty Hogan	.05	.02	.01
□ 295 Ossie Bluege	.05	.02	.01
□ 296 Debs Garms	.05	.02	.01
□ 297 Barney Friberg	.05	.02	.01
□ 298 Ed Brandt	.05	.02	.01
□ 299 Rollie Hemsley	.05	.02	.01
□ 300 Chuck Klein MVP	.20	.09	.03
□ 301 Mort Cooper MVP	.05	.02	.01
□ 302 Jim Bottomley MVP	.20	.09	.03
□ 303 Jimmie Foxx MVP	.35	.16	.04
□ 304 Fred Schulte MVP	.05	.02	.01
□ 305 Frank Frisch MVP	.20	.09	.03
□ 306 Frank McCormick MVP	.10	.05	.01
□ 307 Jake Daubert MVP	.10	.05	.01
□ 308 Roger Peckinpaugh MVP	.05	.02	.01
□ 309 George H. Burns MVP	.05	.02	.01
□ 310 Lou Gehrig MVP	.75	.35	.09
□ 311 Al Simmons MVP	.20	.09	.03
□ 312 Eddie Collins MVP	.20	.09	.03
□ 313 Gabby Hartnett MVP	.20	.09	.03
□ 314 Joe Cronin MVP	.20	.09	.03
□ 315 Paul Waner MVP	.20	.09	.03
□ 316 Bob O'Farrell MVP	.05	.02	.01
□ 317 Larry Doyle MVP	.10	.05	.01
□ 318 Lyn Lary	.05	.02	.01
□ 319 Jakie May	.05	.02	.01
□ 320 Roy Spencer	.05	.02	.01
□ 321 Dick Coffman	.05	.02	.01
□ 322 Pete Donohue	.05	.02	.01
□ 323 Mule Haas	.05	.02	.01
□ 324 Doc Farrell	.05	.02	.01
□ 325 Flint Rhem	.05	.02	.01
□ 326 Firpo Marberry	.05	.02	.01
□ 327 Charles Conlon	.05	.02	.01
□ 328 Checklist 1-110	.05	.02	.01
□ 329 Checklist 111-220	.05	.02	.01
□ 330 Checklist 221-330	.05	.02	.01

1991-92 Conlon TSN Prototypes

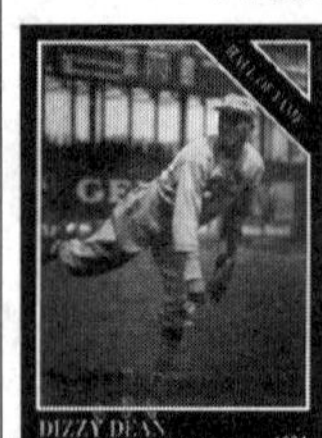

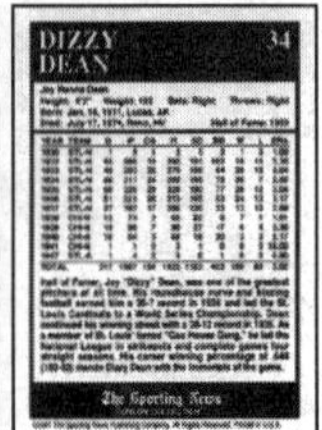

In conjunction with The Sporting News, Megacards issued various prototype cards to preview their soon to be released regular issue sets. All the cards were standard size. The 1991 Conlon prototypes from the first series were not marked as prototypes, and neither did they have the Major League Baseball logo and the Curtis Management logo on their backs. Their numbering was identical with the regular issue cards, with the exception of Dean (number 3 in the regular issue). The production run was reported to be very limited for these first series cards. The 1991 Conlon Color Babe Ruth prototype has the word "prototype" on its reverse. The 50,000 color Ruth prototype cards produced were distributed to collectors and dealers at the 12th National Sports Collectors Convention in Anaheim in July, 1991. Moreover, five prototypes for the second series (1992 Conlon Collection) were distributed at the same time. The production run was announced to be 20,000 for each card, with the exception of Joe Jackson (67,000). All these cards are marked "prototype" on their backs, and with the exception of the Mathewson card, also bear different card numbers from the regular issues. In general, some subtle differences in photos are found with some of the prototype cards. The second series prototypes show a 1992 copyright on the card back. The Cobb and Jackson cards have a computer color-enhanced photo with white and dark blue borders, while the other cards have black and white photos with white and black borders.

	MINT	NRMT	EXC
COMPLETE SET (16)	60.00	27.00	7.50
COMMON CARD	1.00	.45	.12
□ 13 Ty Cobb Color (Card 250)	8.00	3.60	1.00
□ 14 Joe Jackson Color (Card 444 in regular set, prototype)	8.00	3.60	1.00
□ 34 Dizzy Dean	7.50	3.40	.95
□ 111 Lou Gehrig	10.00	4.50	1.25
□ 145 Babe Ruth (Color) DP	15.00	6.75	1.85
□ 250 Ty Cobb	10.00	4.50	1.25
□ 331 Christy Mathewson (Prototype on back)	3.00	1.35	.35
□ 400 Joe Jackson DP (Prototype on back)	5.00	2.20	.60
□ 450 Hughie Jennings (Prototype on back)	1.50	.70	.19
□ 500 Ty Cobb (Prototype on back)	5.00	2.20	.60
□ 520 Goose Goslin (Prototype on back)	1.50	.70	.19
□ 661 Bill Terry	2.50	1.10	.30
□ 662 Lefty Gomez	2.50	1.10	.30
□ 664 Frank Frisch	1.50	.70	.19
□ 710 Red Faber	1.50	.70	.19
□ 905 Lena Blackburne	1.00	.45	.12

1992 Conlon TSN

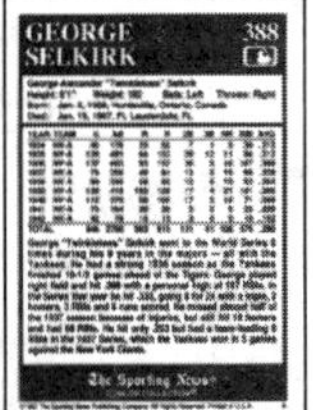

This 330-card standard-size set is numbered in continuation of the previous year's issue and again features the photography of Charles Conlon. The fronts have either posed or action black and white player photos, enframed by a white line on a black card face. A caption in a diagonal stripe cuts across the upper right corner of the picture. The player's name, team, position, and year the photos were taken appear below the pictures in white lettering. The back has biography, statistics, and career summary. The cards are numbered on the back. Special subsets include No-Hitters (331-372), Two Sports (393-407), Great Stories (421-440), Why Not in Hall of Fame (441-450), Hall of Fame (459-474), 75 Years Ago Highlights (483-492), Triple Crown Winners (525-537), Everyday Heroes (538-550), Nicknames (551-566), Trivia (581-601), and St. Louis Cardinals 1892-1992 (618-657). The set was available in packs as well as in a factory set. Four special gold-border cards previewing the 1993 Conlon Sporting News set were available exclusively in the factory sets. Also randomly inserted in the wax packs were a limited number of personally autographed (but not certified) cards of Bobby Doerr, Bob Feller, Marty Marion, Johnny Mize, Enos Slaughter, and Johnny Vander Meer. These autographed cards range in value from 15.00 to 30.00.

	MINT	NRMT	EXC
COMPLETE SET (330)	18.00	8.00	2.20
COMMON CARD (331-660)	.05	.02	.01
□ 331 Christy Mathewson	.40	.18	.05
□ 332 Hooks Wiltse	.05	.02	.01
□ 333 Nap Rucker	.05	.02	.01
□ 334 Red Ames	.05	.02	.01
□ 335 Chief Bender	.20	.09	.03
□ 336 Joe Wood	.10	.05	.01
□ 337 Ed Walsh	.20	.09	.03
□ 338 George Mullin	.05	.02	.01
□ 339 Earl Hamilton	.05	.02	.01
□ 340 Jeff Tesreau	.05	.02	.01
□ 341 Jim Scott	.05	.02	.01
□ 342 Rube Marquard	.20	.09	.03
□ 343 Claude Hendrix	.05	.02	.01
□ 344 Jimmy Lavender	.05	.02	.01
□ 345 Joe Bush	.10	.05	.01
□ 346 Dutch Leonard	.10	.05	.01
□ 347 Fred Toney	.05	.02	.01
□ 348 Hippo Vaughn	.05	.02	.01
□ 349 Ernie Koob	.05	.02	.01
□ 350 Bob Groom	.05	.02	.01
□ 351 Ernie Shore	.10	.05	.01
□ 352 Hod Eller	.05	.02	.01
□ 353 Walter Johnson	.40	.18	.05
□ 354 Charles Robertson	.05	.02	.01
□ 355 Jesse Barnes	.05	.02	.01
□ 356 Sad Sam Jones	.10	.05	.01
□ 357 Howard Ehmke	.05	.02	.01
□ 358 Jesse Haines	.20	.09	.03

☐ 359 Ted Lyons .20 .09 .03
☐ 360 Carl Hubbell .25 .11 .03
☐ 361 Wes Ferrell .15 .07 .02
☐ 362 Bobby Burke .05 .02 .01
☐ 363 Daffy Dean .10 .05 .01
☐ 364 Bobo Newsom .15 .07 .02
☐ 365 Vern Kennedy .05 .02 .01
☐ 366 Bill Dietrich .05 .02 .01
☐ 367 Johnny VanderMeer .15 .07 .02
☐ 368 Johnny VanderMeer .15 .07 .02
☐ 369 Monte Pearson .05 .02 .01
☐ 370 Bob Feller .30 .14 .04
☐ 371 Lon Warneke .10 .05 .01
☐ 372 Jim Tobin .05 .02 .01
☐ 373 Earl Moore .05 .02 .01
☐ 374 Bill Dineen .05 .02 .01
☐ 375 Mal Eason .05 .02 .01
☐ 376 George Mogridge .05 .02 .01
☐ 377 Dazzy Vance .20 .09 .03
☐ 378 Tex Carleton .05 .02 .01
☐ 379 Clyde Shoun .05 .02 .01
☐ 380 Frankie Hayes .05 .02 .01
☐ 381 Benny Frey .05 .02 .01
☐ 382 Hank Johnson .05 .02 .01
☐ 383 Red Kress .05 .02 .01
☐ 384 Johnny Allen .05 .02 .01
☐ 385 Hal Trosky .10 .05 .01
☐ 386 Gene Robertson .05 .02 .01
☐ 387 Pep Young .05 .02 .01
☐ 388 George Selkirk .10 .05 .01
☐ 389 Ed Wells .05 .02 .01
☐ 390 Jim Weaver .05 .02 .01
☐ 391 George McQuinn .05 .02 .01
☐ 392 Hans Lobert .05 .02 .01
☐ 393 Evar Swanson .05 .02 .01
☐ 394 Ernie Nevers .25 .11 .03
☐ 395 Jim Levey .05 .02 .01
☐ 396 Hugo Bezdek .05 .02 .01
☐ 397 Walt French .05 .02 .01
☐ 398 Charlie Berry .10 .05 .01
☐ 399 Frank Grube .05 .02 .01
☐ 400 Chuck Dressen .10 .05 .01
☐ 401 Greasy Neale .10 .05 .01
☐ 402 Ernie Vick .05 .02 .01
☐ 403 Jim Thorpe 1.00 .45 .12
☐ 404 Wally Gilbert .05 .02 .01
☐ 405 Luke Urban .05 .02 .01
☐ 406 Pid Purdy .05 .02 .01
☐ 407 Ab Wright .05 .02 .01
☐ 408 Billy Urbanski .05 .02 .01
☐ 409 Carl Fischer .05 .02 .01
☐ 410 Jack Warner .05 .02 .01
☐ 411 Bill Cissell .05 .02 .01
☐ 412 Merv Shea .05 .02 .01
☐ 413 Dolf Luque .10 .05 .01
☐ 414 Johnny Bassler .05 .02 .01
☐ 415 Odell Hale .05 .02 .01
☐ 416 Larry French .05 .02 .01
☐ 417 Curt Walker .05 .02 .01
☐ 418 Dusty Cooke .05 .02 .01
☐ 419 Phil Todt .05 .02 .01
☐ 420 Poison Andrews .05 .02 .01
☐ 421 Billy Herman .20 .09 .03
☐ 422 Tris Speaker .25 .11 .03
☐ 423 Al Simmons .20 .09 .03
☐ 424 Hack Wilson .25 .11 .03
☐ 425 Ty Cobb .75 .35 .09
☐ 426 Babe Ruth 1.00 .45 .12
☐ 427 Ernie Lombardi .20 .09 .03
☐ 428 Dizzy Dean .40 .18 .05
☐ 429 Lloyd Waner .20 .09 .03
☐ 430 Hank Greenberg .30 .14 .04
☐ 431 Lefty Grove .30 .14 .04
☐ 432 Mickey Cochrane .25 .11 .03
☐ 433 Burleigh Grimes .20 .09 .03
☐ 434 Pie Traynor .20 .09 .03
☐ 435 Johnny Mize .25 .11 .03
☐ 436 Sam Rice .20 .09 .03
☐ 437 Goose Goslin .20 .09 .03
☐ 438 Chuck Klein .20 .09 .03
☐ 439 Connie Mack .25 .11 .03
☐ 440 Jim Bottomley .20 .09 .03
☐ 441 Riggs Stephenson .15 .07 .02
☐ 442 Ken Williams .15 .07 .02
☐ 443 Babe Adams .10 .05 .01
☐ 444 Joe Jackson 1.00 .45 .12
☐ 445 Hal Newhouser .20 .09 .03
☐ 446 Wes Ferrell .15 .07 .02
☐ 447 Lefty O'Doul .10 .05 .01
☐ 448 Wally Schang .10 .05 .01
☐ 449 Sherry Magee .05 .02 .01
☐ 450 Mike Donlin .10 .05 .01
☐ 451 Doc Cramer .10 .05 .01
☐ 452 Dick Bartell .05 .02 .01
☐ 453 Earle Mack .05 .02 .01
☐ 454 Jumbo Brown .05 .02 .01
☐ 455 Johnnie Heving .05 .02 .01
☐ 456 Percy Jones .05 .02 .01
☐ 457 Ted Blankenship .05 .02 .01
☐ 458 Al Wingo .05 .02 .01
☐ 459 Roger Bresnahan .20 .09 .03
☐ 460 Bill Klem .25 .11 .03
☐ 461 Charlie Gehringer .25 .11 .03
☐ 462 Stan Coveleski .20 .09 .03
☐ 463 Eddie Plank .20 .09 .03
☐ 464 Clark Griffith .20 .09 .03
☐ 465 Herb Pennock .20 .09 .03
☐ 466 Earle Combs .20 .09 .03
☐ 467 Bobby Doerr .20 .09 .03
☐ 468 Waite Hoyt .20 .09 .03
☐ 469 Tommy Connolly .20 .09 .03
☐ 470 Harry Hooper .20 .09 .03
☐ 471 Rick Ferrell .20 .09 .03
☐ 472 Billy Evans .15 .07 .02
☐ 473 Billy Herman .20 .09 .03
☐ 474 Bill Dickey .25 .11 .03
☐ 475 Luke Appling .20 .09 .03
☐ 476 Babe Pinelli .10 .05 .01
☐ 477 Eric McNair .05 .02 .01
☐ 478 Sherriff Blake .05 .02 .01
☐ 479 Val Picinich .05 .02 .01
☐ 480 Fred Heimach .05 .02 .01
☐ 481 Jack Graney .05 .02 .01
☐ 482 Reb Russell .05 .02 .01
☐ 483 Red Faber .20 .09 .03
☐ 484 Benny Kauff .10 .05 .01
☐ 485 Pants Rowland .05 .02 .01
☐ 486 Bobby Veach .05 .02 .01
☐ 487 Jim Bagby Sr. .05 .02 .01
☐ 488 Pol Perritt .05 .02 .01
☐ 489 Buck Herzog .05 .02 .01
☐ 490 Art Fletcher .05 .02 .01
☐ 491 Walter Holke .05 .02 .01
☐ 492 Art Nehf .10 .05 .01
☐ 493 Fresco Thompson .05 .02 .01
☐ 494 Jimmy Welsh .05 .02 .01
☐ 495 Ossie Vitt .05 .02 .01
☐ 496 Ownie Carroll .05 .02 .01
☐ 497 Ken O'Dea .05 .02 .01
☐ 498 Fred Frankhouse .05 .02 .01
☐ 499 Jewel Ens .05 .02 .01
☐ 500 Morrie Arnovich .05 .02 .01
☐ 501 Wally Gerber .05 .02 .01
☐ 502 Kiddo Davis .05 .02 .01
☐ 503 Buddy Myer .05 .02 .01
☐ 504 Sam Leslie .05 .02 .01
☐ 505 Cliff Bolton .05 .02 .01
☐ 506 Dixie Walker .10 .05 .01
☐ 507 Jack Smith .05 .02 .01
☐ 508 Bump Hadley .05 .02 .01
☐ 509 Buck Crouse .05 .02 .01
☐ 510 Joe Glenn .05 .02 .01
☐ 511 Chad Kimsey .05 .02 .01
☐ 512 Lou Finney .05 .02 .01
☐ 513 Roxie Lawson .05 .02 .01
☐ 514 Chuck Fullis .05 .02 .01
☐ 515 Earl Sheely .05 .02 .01
☐ 516 George Gibson .05 .02 .01
☐ 517 Johnny Broaca .05 .02 .01
☐ 518 Bibb Falk .05 .02 .01
☐ 519 Don Hurst .05 .02 .01
☐ 520 Grover Hartley .05 .02 .01
☐ 521 Don Heffner .05 .02 .01
☐ 522 Harvey Hendrick .05 .02 .01
☐ 523 Allen Sothoron .05 .02 .01
☐ 524 Tony Piet .05 .02 .01
☐ 525 Ty Cobb .75 .35 .09
☐ 526 Jimmie Foxx .35 .16 .04
☐ 527 Rogers Hornsby .35 .16 .04
☐ 528 Nap Lajoie .35 .16 .04
☐ 529 Lou Gehrig .75 .35 .09
☐ 530 Heinie Zimmerman .05 .02 .01
☐ 531 Chuck Klein .20 .09 .03
☐ 532 Hugh Duffy .20 .09 .03
☐ 533 Lefty Grove .30 .14 .04
☐ 534 Grover C. Alexander .30 .14 .04
☐ 535 Amos Rusie .20 .09 .03
☐ 536 Lefty Gomez .25 .11 .03
☐ 537 Bucky Walters .15 .07 .02
☐ 538 Johnny Hodapp .05 .02 .01
☐ 539 Bruce Campbell .05 .02 .01
☐ 540 Hod Lisenbee .05 .02 .01
☐ 541 Jack Fournier .05 .02 .01
☐ 542 Jim Tabor .05 .02 .01
☐ 543 Johnny Burnett .05 .02 .01
☐ 544 Roy Hartzell .05 .02 .01
☐ 545 Doc Gautreau .05 .02 .01
☐ 546 Emil Yde .05 .02 .01
☐ 547 Bob Johnson .10 .05 .01
☐ 548 Joe Hauser .05 .02 .01
☐ 549 Ed Reulbach .05 .02 .01
☐ 550 Mel Almada .05 .02 .01
☐ 551 Mickey Cochrane .25 .11 .03
☐ 552 Carl Hubbell .25 .11 .03
☐ 553 Charlie Gehringer .25 .11 .03
☐ 554 Al Simmons .20 .09 .03
☐ 555 Mordecai Brown .20 .09 .03
☐ 556 Hugh Jennings .20 .09 .03
☐ 557 Kid Elberfeld .05 .02 .01
☐ 558 Casey Stengel .30 .14 .04
☐ 559 Al Schacht .15 .07 .02
☐ 560 Jimmie Foxx .35 .16 .04
☐ 561 George Kelly .20 .09 .03
☐ 562 Lloyd Waner .20 .09 .03
☐ 563 Paul Waner .20 .09 .03
☐ 564 Walter Johnson .40 .18 .05
☐ 565 Home Run Baker .20 .09 .03
☐ 566 Roy Hughes .05 .02 .01
☐ 567 Lew Riggs .05 .02 .01
☐ 568 John Whitehead .05 .02 .01
☐ 569 Elam Vangilder .05 .02 .01
☐ 570 Billy Zitzmann .05 .02 .01
☐ 571 Walter Schmidt .05 .02 .01
☐ 572 Jackie Tavener .05 .02 .01
☐ 573 Joe Genewich .05 .02 .01
☐ 574 Johnny Marcum .05 .02 .01
☐ 575 Fred Hoffmann .05 .02 .01
☐ 576 Red Rolfe .10 .05 .01
☐ 577 Vic Sorrell .05 .02 .01
☐ 578 Pete Scott .05 .02 .01
☐ 579 Tommy Thomas .05 .02 .01
☐ 580 Al Smith .05 .02 .01
☐ 581 Butch Henline .05 .02 .01
☐ 582 Eddie Collins .20 .09 .03
☐ 583 Earle Combs .20 .09 .03
☐ 584 John McGraw .25 .11 .03
☐ 585 Hack Wilson .25 .11 .03
☐ 586 Gabby Hartnett .20 .09 .03
☐ 587 Kiki Cuyler .20 .09 .03
☐ 588 Bill Terry .25 .11 .03
☐ 589 Joe McCarthy .20 .09 .03
☐ 590 Hank Greenberg .30 .14 .04
☐ 591 Tris Speaker .25 .11 .03
☐ 592 Bill McKechnie .20 .09 .03
☐ 593 Bucky Harris .20 .09 .03
☐ 594 Herb Pennock .20 .09 .03
☐ 595 George Sisler .20 .09 .03
☐ 596 Fred Lindstrom .20 .09 .03
☐ 597 Earl Averill .20 .09 .03
☐ 598 Dave Bancroft .20 .09 .03
☐ 599 Connie Mack .25 .11 .03
☐ 600 Joe Cronin .20 .09 .03
☐ 601 Ken Ash .05 .02 .01
☐ 602 Al Spohrer .05 .02 .01
☐ 603 Roy Mahaffey .05 .02 .01
☐ 604 Frank O'Rourke .05 .02 .01
☐ 605 Lil Stoner .05 .02 .01
☐ 606 Frank Gabler .05 .02 .01
☐ 607 Tom Padden .05 .02 .01
☐ 608 Art Shires .05 .02 .01
☐ 609 Sherry Smith .05 .02 .01
☐ 610 Phil Weintraub .05 .02 .01
☐ 611 Russ Van Atta .05 .02 .01
☐ 612 Jo Jo White .05 .02 .01
☐ 613 Cliff Melton .05 .02 .01
☐ 614 Jimmy Ring .05 .02 .01
☐ 615 Heinie Sand .05 .02 .01
☐ 616 Dale Alexander .05 .02 .01
☐ 617 Kent Greenfield .05 .02 .01
☐ 618 Eddie Dyer .05 .02 .01
☐ 619 Bill Sherdel .05 .02 .01
☐ 620 Max Lanier .05 .02 .01
☐ 621 Bob O'Farrell .05 .02 .01
☐ 622 Rogers Hornsby .35 .16 .04
☐ 623 Bill Beckman .05 .02 .01
☐ 624 Mort Cooper .05 .02 .01
☐ 625 Bill DeLancey .05 .02 .01
☐ 626 Marty Marion .10 .05 .01
☐ 627 Billy Southworth .05 .02 .01
☐ 628 Johnny Mize .25 .11 .03
☐ 629 Joe Medwick .20 .09 .03
☐ 630 Grover C. Alexander .30 .14 .04
☐ 631 Daffy Dean .10 .05 .01
☐ 632 Hi Bell .05 .02 .01
☐ 633 Walker Cooper .05 .02 .01
☐ 634 Frank Frisch .20 .09 .03
☐ 635 Dizzy Dean .40 .18 .05
☐ 636 Don Gutteridge .05 .02 .01
☐ 637 Pepper Martin .15 .07 .02
☐ 638 Ed Konetchy .05 .02 .01
☐ 639 Bill Hallahan .05 .02 .01
☐ 640 Lon Warneke .10 .05 .01
☐ 641 Terry Moore .10 .05 .01
☐ 642 Enos Slaughter .20 .09 .03
☐ 643 Heinie Mueller .05 .02 .01
☐ 644 Specs Toporcer .05 .02 .01
☐ 645 Jim Bottomley .20 .09 .03
☐ 646 Ray Blades .05 .02 .01
☐ 647 Jesse Haines .20 .09 .03
☐ 648 Andy High .05 .02 .01
☐ 649 Miller Huggins .20 .09 .03
☐ 650 Ernie Orsatti .05 .02 .01
☐ 651 Les Bell .05 .02 .01
☐ 652 Gabby Street .05 .02 .01
☐ 653 Wally Roettger .05 .02 .01
☐ 654 Syl Johnson .05 .02 .01
☐ 655 Mike Gonzalez .05 .02 .01
☐ 656 Ripper Collins .05 .02 .01
☐ 657 Chick Hafey .20 .09 .03
☐ 658 Checklist 331-440 .05 .02 .01
☐ 659 Checklist 441-550 .05 .02 .01
☐ 660 Checklist 551-660 .05 .02 .01

1992 Conlon TSN 13th National

In conjunction with The Sporting News, Megacards issued various prototype cards during 1992 to preview their soon to be released regular issue sets. All the cards were standard size. These cards were given away as promotional items at the 13th National Sports Collectors Convention in Atlanta and therefore have "13th National" stamped on their backs.

	MINT	NRMT	EXC
COMPLETE SET (4)	10.00	4.50	1.25
COMMON CARD	1.00	.45	.12

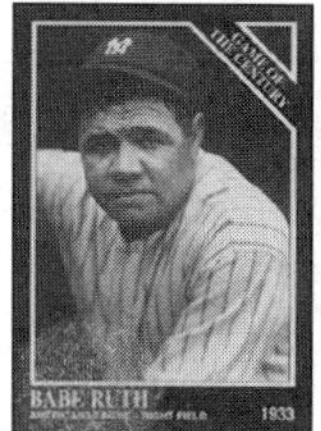

☐ 400 Joe Jackson DP (13th National) 5.00 2.20 .60
☐ 663 Babe Ruth (BW) (13th National) 7.50 3.40 .95
☐ 775 Chief Meyers (13th National) 1.00 .45 .12
☐ 800 Hippo Vaughn (13th National) 1.00 .45 .12

1992 Conlon TSN All-Star Program

In 1992 several gold-foil edition black and white Conlon Collection cards were released to preview the 1993 Conlon Collection. Cards 661G-664G feature four players who played in the first All-Star Game in 1933. Reportedly 34,000 of each of these cards were produced exclusively for and inserted (one per program) in the 1992 All-Star Game program. These standard-size cards have the same design typical of other Conlon issues, only that the vintage black and white player photos are framed in gold foil.

	MINT	NRMT	EXC
COMPLETE SET (4)	20.00	9.00	2.50
COMMON CARD (661G-664G)	3.00	1.35	.35

☐ 661G Bill Terry 5.00 2.20 .60
☐ 662G Lefty Gomez 5.00 2.20 .60
☐ 663G Babe Ruth 10.00 4.50 1.25
☐ 664G Frankie Frisch 3.00 1.35 .35

1992-93 Conlon TSN Color Inserts

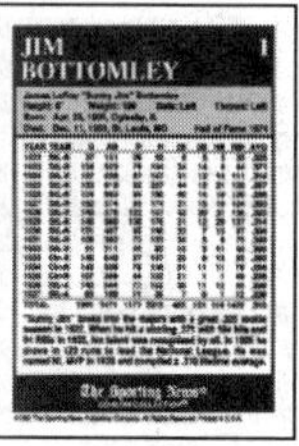

All the cards in this 22-card standard-size set were previously released in black and white in the 1991 or 1992 Conlon regular issue sets. Released on two different occasions, cards 1-6 and 7-12 were issued exclusively as a bonus to collectors who purchased Megacards' hobby accessory products (plastic sheets, card frames, and card sleeves) through retail outlets. The announced production figures for cards 1-6 were 250,000 of each card. For cards 7-12, the announced production run was 252,000 of each card. Cards 13-20 were randomly inserted in 1993 Conlon counter packs and blister packs, with an announced production run of 100,000 of each card. Cards 21-22 were available only through a special send-away offer on the backs of Conlon counter packs and blister packs; 75,000 of each card were produced. There were 60,000 cards of Bob Feller (23) produced exclusively for the Sports Collectors Digest 1993 Price Guide and bound inside copies of that book. The fronts display color player portraits inside a white picture frame on a navy blue card face. A diagonal graphic across the upper right corner of the picture gives the year the player was inducted into the Hall of Fame. The black and white backs are accented in navy blue and provide biography, career statistics, and career summary. The corresponding card number of the black and white regular issue card is given on the line after each player's name.

	MINT	NRMT	EXC
COMPLETE SET (23)	50.00	22.00	6.25
COMMON CARD (1-6)	1.00	.45	.12
COMMON CARD (6-12)	1.00	.45	.12
COMMON CARD (13-20)	2.00	.90	.25
COMMON CARD (21-22)	6.00	2.70	.75
COMMON CARD (23)	5.00	2.20	.60

☐ 1 Jim Bottomley Card 22	1.00	.45	.12
☐ 2 Lefty Grove Card 23	2.00	.90	.25
☐ 3 Lou Gehrig Card 111	4.00	1.80	.50
☐ 4 Babe Ruth Card 145	6.00	2.70	.75
☐ 5 Casey Stengel Card 37	2.00	.90	.25
☐ 6 Rube Marquard Card 252	1.00	.45	.12
☐ 7 Walter Johnson Card 353	2.00	.90	.25
☐ 8 Lou Gehrig Card 310	4.00	1.80	.50
☐ 9 Christy Mathewson Card 331	2.00	.90	.25
☐ 10 Ty Cobb Card 250	4.00	1.80	.50
☐ 11 Mel Ott Card 225	2.00	.90	.25
☐ 12 Carl Hubbell Card 253	1.00	.45	.12
☐ 13 Al Simmons Card 49	2.00	.90	.25
☐ 14 Connie Mack Card 47	3.00	1.35	.35
☐ 15 Grover C. Alexander Card 32	3.00	1.35	.35
☐ 16 Jimmie Foxx Card 303	3.00	1.35	.35
☐ 17 Lloyd Waner Card 6	2.00	.90	.25
☐ 18 Tris Speaker Card 422	3.00	1.35	.35
☐ 19 Dizzy Dean Card 3	4.00	1.80	.50
☐ 20 Rogers Hornsby Card 1	4.00	1.80	.50
☐ 21 Joe Jackson Card 444	6.00	2.70	.75
☐ 22 Jim Thorpe Card 403	6.00	2.70	.75
☐ 23 Bob Feller	5.00	2.20	.60

1992-93 Conlon TSN Gold Inserts

Several gold-foil edition black and white Conlon Collection standard-size cards were released to preview the 1993 Conlon Collection. Card numbers 665, 770, 820, and 880 were included in 1992 Conlon factory sets; reportedly 90,000 of each card were produced. The factory set cases distributed through hobby dealers also included two additional cards (667 and 730) as a bonus (roughly a dozen of each per case), with a stated production run of 20,000 for each card. Card 1000G, of which 100,000 were produced, was inserted in the 65-card jumbo packs sold only at Toys 'R' Us. Likewise, 100,000 of card 934G were produced and inserted into packs sold only at Eckerd's Drugs. The cards have the same design typical of other Conlon issues, only that the vintage black and white player photos are framed in gold foil.

	MINT	NRMT	EXC
COMPLETE SET (8)	12.50	5.50	1.55
COMMON CARD	1.00	.45	.12
☐ 665 Carl Hubbell	1.50	.70	.19
☐ 667 Charlie Gehringer SP	2.50	1.10	.30
☐ 730 Luke Appling SP (Old Aches and Pains)	2.50	1.10	.30
☐ 770 Tommy Henrich	1.00	.45	.12
☐ 820 John McGraw	2.00	.90	.25
☐ 880 Gabby Hartnett	1.50	.70	.19
☐ 934G Walter Johnson and Nolan Ryan	5.00	2.20	.60
☐ 1000G Ty Cobb DP	3.00	1.35	.35

1993 Conlon Masters BW

The 1993 Conlon Collection Master Series premier issue consists of nine cards subtitled "The Best There Was". The set production was limited to 25,000, and each set includes a certificate of authenticity with the serial number. The oversize cards measure approximately 8" by 10" and feature the photography of Charles Martin Conlon, the greatest sports photographer of his time. The Sporting News acquired Conlon's work in 1945, and from this archive, Megacards created the Master Series. The horizontal fronts feature black-and-white glossy action and posed player photos framed by a wide black outer border and a narrow gold inner one. With the exception of the Johnson and Gehrig card (3), the horizontal backs have a black-and-white close-up player shot on the left. Career statistics, biography, and career summary fill out the remainder of the back. A logo for Cooperstown

Collection is printed in the lower right corner and the Conlon Collection Master Series logo appears in the lower left corner. The cards are numbered on the back. Each set was accompanied by a certificate of authenticity that gave the set number out of a production run of 25,000. By returning the original certificate of authenticity along with 9.95, the collector received a protective portfolio to display the cards and a new deluxe certificate. The portfolio and the cards carried a suggested retail price of 29.95.

	MINT	NRMT	EXC
COMPLETE SET (9)	18.00	8.00	2.20
COMMON CARD (1-9)	1.50	.70	.19
☐ 1 The Best There Was 1905 to 1942	1.50	.70	.19
☐ 2 Babe Ruth Outfield	6.00	2.70	.75
☐ 3 Walter Johnson Pitcher Lou Gehrig First base	3.00	1.35	.35
☐ 4 Honus Wagner Shortstop	3.00	1.35	.35
☐ 5 Mickey Cochrane Catcher	2.00	.90	.25
☐ 6 Tris Speaker Outfield	2.00	.90	.25
☐ 7 Ty Cobb Outfield	4.00	1.80	.50
☐ 8 Rogers Hornsby 2nd Base	3.00	1.35	.35
☐ 9 Pie Traynor 3rd Base	2.00	.90	.25

1993 Conlon Masters Color

The 1993 Conlon Collection Color Master Series premier issue consists of nine cards. The set production was limited to 25,000, and each set includes a certificate of authenticity with the serial number. The oversize cards measure approximately 8" by 10" and feature the photography of Charles Martin Conlon, the greatest sports photographer of his time. The Sporting News acquired Conlon's work in 1945, and from this archive, Megacards created the Master Series. Using 1993 technology, one special card (3) features Nolan Ryan transported back in time to Yankee Stadium in 1927 in a fantasy conversation with Walter Johnson. The horizontal fronts feature color enhanced black-and-white glossy action and posed player photos framed by a wide blue-gray outer border and a narrow white inner one. The horizontal backs have a light blue background with a black and white border. The words of sportswriters, past and present, and two poems appear on the back. A logo for Cooperstown Collection is printed in the lower right corner and the Conlon Collection Master Series logo appears in the lower left corner. The cards are numbered on the back. Each set was accompanied by a certificate of authenticity that gave the set number out of a production run of 25,000. By returning the original certificate of authenticity along with 9.95, the collector received a protective portfolio to display the cards and a new deluxe certificate. The portfolio and the cards retailed for 29.95.

	MINT	NRMT	EXC
COMPLETE SET (9)	18.00	8.00	2.20
COMMON CARD (1-9)	1.50	.70	.19
☐ 1 Title Card	1.50	.70	.19
☐ 2 Napoleon Lajoie	2.00	.90	.25
☐ 3 Nolan Ryan Walter Johnson	5.00	2.20	.60
☐ 4 Hilltop Park home of the Highlanders	1.50	.70	.19
☐ 5 Babe Ruth	6.00	2.70	.75
☐ 6 Frank Baker	2.00	.90	.25
☐ 7 John McGraw MG	2.50	1.10	.30
☐ 8 John McGraw Wilbert Robinson Christy Mathewson	2.00	.90	.25
☐ 9 Hughie Jennings MG	2.00	.90	.25

1993 Conlon TSN Prototypes

These two cards are colorized prototypes, with same design as the regular 888 and 934 from the 1993 Conlon TSN set. The production run for each of these two cards was 52,000.

	MINT	NRMT	EXC
COMPLETE SET	10.00	4.50	1.25
COMMON CARD	5.00	2.20	.60
☐ 888 Babe Ruth	5.00	2.20	.60
☐ 934 Walter Johnson with Nolan Ryan	5.00	2.20	.60

1993 Conlon TSN

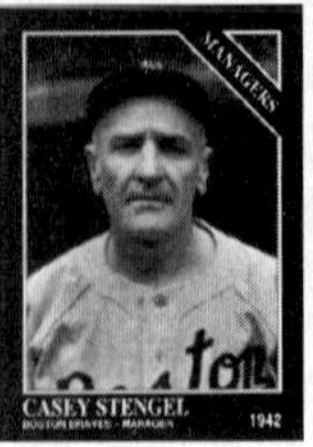
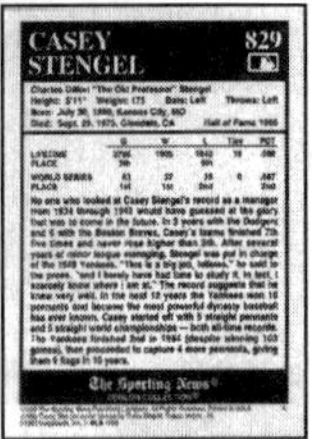

The third 330-card standard-size set of The Sporting News Conlon Collection again features turn-of-the-century to World War II-era players photographed by Charles Conlon, including more than 100 cards of Hall of Famers. Cards from a subset displaying computer color-enhanced photos were randomly inserted in the counter box packs and blister packs. The standard-size cards feature a mix of black-and-white vintage player photos inside a white frame on a black card face. Topical subset titles are printed on a diagonal bar at the upper right corner of the pictures. The backs carry biography, statistics, and extended career summary and highlights. The set contains several subsets continuing from last year's issue and some new subsets unique to this year's set: Game of the Century: 1933 All-Star Game (661-689), Spitballers (702-712), Accused Spitballers (717-725), Nicknames (730-741), Great Stories (751-770), Native Americans: American Indians who played big-league ball (771-777), League Leaders (795-798 and 801-805), Great Managers (817-848), Great Backstops (861-880), Against All Odds (881-894), Trivia (905-918), Nolan Ryan: compares eight Hall of Famers to Ryan (928-935), and First Cards: players for whom cards have never been done before (945-987). The set closes with checklist cards (988-990). The set was also available as a factory set in a special commemorative tin and in the form of three 110-card uncut sheets.

	MINT	NRMT	EXC
COMPLETE SET (330)	18.00	8.00	2.20
COMMON CARD (661-990)	.05	.02	.01
☐ 661 Bill Terry	.25	.11	.03
☐ 662 Lefty Gomez	.25	.11	.03
☐ 663 Babe Ruth	1.00	.45	.12
☐ 664 Frank Frisch	.20	.09	.03
☐ 665 Carl Hubbell	.25	.11	.03
☐ 666 Al Simmons	.20	.09	.03
☐ 667 Charlie Gehringer	.25	.11	.03
☐ 668 Earl Averill	.20	.09	.03
☐ 669 Lefty Grove	.30	.14	.04
☐ 670 Pie Traynor	.20	.09	.03
☐ 671 Chuck Klein	.20	.09	.03
☐ 672 Paul Waner	.20	.09	.03
☐ 673 Lou Gehrig	.75	.35	.09
☐ 674 Rick Ferrell	.20	.09	.03
☐ 675 Gabby Hartnett	.20	.09	.03
☐ 676 Joe Cronin	.20	.09	.03
☐ 677 Chick Hafey	.20	.09	.03
☐ 678 Jimmy Dykes	.10	.05	.01
☐ 679 Sammy West	.05	.02	.01
☐ 680 Pepper Martin	.15	.07	.02
☐ 681 Lefty O'Doul	.10	.05	.01
☐ 682 General Crowder	.05	.02	.01
☐ 683 Jimmie Wilson	.05	.02	.01
☐ 684 Dick Bartell	.05	.02	.01
☐ 685 Bill Hallahan	.05	.02	.01
☐ 686 Wally Berger	.10	.05	.01
☐ 687 Lon Warneke	.10	.05	.01
☐ 688 Ben Chapman	.05	.02	.01
☐ 689 Woody English	.05	.02	.01
☐ 690 Jimmy Reese	.10	.05	.01
☐ 691 Wattie Holm	.05	.02	.01
☐ 692 Charlie Jamieson	.05	.02	.01
☐ 693 Tom Zachary	.05	.02	.01
☐ 694 Blondy Ryan	.05	.02	.01
☐ 695 Sparky Adams	.05	.02	.01
☐ 696 Bill Hunnefield	.05	.02	.01
☐ 697 Lee Meadows	.05	.02	.01
☐ 698 Tom Carey	.05	.02	.01
☐ 699 Johnny Rawlings	.05	.02	.01
☐ 700 Ken Holloway	.05	.02	.01
☐ 701 Lance Richbourg	.05	.02	.01
☐ 702 Ray Fisher	.05	.02	.01
☐ 703 Ed Walsh	.20	.09	.03
☐ 704 Dick Rudolph	.05	.02	.01
☐ 705 Ray Caldwell	.05	.02	.01
☐ 706 Burleigh Grimes	.20	.09	.03
☐ 707 Stan Coveleski	.20	.09	.03
☐ 708 George Hildebrand	.05	.02	.01
☐ 709 Jack Quinn	.10	.05	.01
☐ 710 Red Faber	.20	.09	.03
☐ 711 Urban Shocker	.10	.05	.01
☐ 712 Dutch Leonard	.10	.05	.01
☐ 713 Lou Koupal	.05	.02	.01
☐ 714 Jimmy Wasdell	.05	.02	.01
☐ 715 Johnny Lindell	.05	.02	.01
☐ 716 Don Padgett	.05	.02	.01
☐ 717 Nelson Potter	.05	.02	.01
☐ 718 Schoolboy Rowe	.10	.05	.01
☐ 719 Dave Danforth	.05	.02	.01
☐ 720 Claude Passeau	.05	.02	.01
☐ 721 Harry Kelley	.05	.02	.01
☐ 722 Johnny Allen	.05	.02	.01
☐ 723 Tommy Bridges	.10	.05	.01
☐ 724 Bill Lee	.05	.02	.01
☐ 725 Fred Frankhouse	.05	.02	.01
☐ 726 Johnny McCarthy	.05	.02	.01
☐ 727 Rip Russell	.05	.02	.01
☐ 728 Emory(Topper) Rigney	.05	.02	.01
☐ 729 Howie Shanks	.05	.02	.01
☐ 730 Luke Appling	.20	.09	.03
☐ 731 Bill Byron UMP	.05	.02	.01
☐ 732 Earle Combs	.20	.09	.03
☐ 733 Hank Greenberg	.30	.14	.04
☐ 734 Walter(Boom Boom) Beck	.05	.02	.01
☐ 735 Sloppy Thurston	.05	.02	.01
☐ 736 Hack Wilson	.25	.11	.03
☐ 737 Bill McGowan UMP	.20	.09	.03
☐ 738 Zeke Bonura	.10	.05	.01
☐ 739 Tom Baker	.05	.02	.01
☐ 740 Bill(Baby Doll) Jacobson	.05	.02	.01
☐ 741 Kiki Cuyler	.20	.09	.03
☐ 742 George Blaeholder	.05	.02	.01
☐ 743 Dee Miles	.05	.02	.01
☐ 744 Lee Handley	.05	.02	.01
☐ 745 Shano Collins	.05	.02	.01
☐ 746 Rosy Ryan	.05	.02	.01
☐ 747 Aaron Ward	.05	.02	.01
☐ 748 Monte Pearson	.05	.02	.01
☐ 749 Jake Early	.05	.02	.01
☐ 750 Bill Atwood	.05	.02	.01
☐ 751 Mark Koenig	.10	.05	.01
☐ 752 Buddy Hassett	.05	.02	.01
☐ 753 Davy Jones	.05	.02	.01
☐ 754 Honus Wagner	.40	.18	.05
☐ 755 Bill Dickey	.25	.11	.03
☐ 756 Max Butcher	.05	.02	.01
☐ 757 Waite Hoyt	.20	.09	.03
☐ 758 Walter Johnson	.40	.18	.05
☐ 759 Howard Ehmke	.05	.02	.01
☐ 760 Bobo Newsom	.15	.07	.02
☐ 761 Tony Lazzeri	.20	.09	.03
☐ 762 Tony Lazzeri	.20	.09	.03
☐ 763 Spud Chandler	.10	.05	.01
☐ 764 Kirby Higbe	.05	.02	.01
☐ 765 Paul Richards	.10	.05	.01
☐ 766 Rogers Hornsby	.35	.16	.04
☐ 767 Joe Vosmik	.05	.02	.01
☐ 768 Jesse Haines	.20	.09	.03
☐ 769 Bucky Walters	.15	.07	.02
☐ 770 Tommy Henrich	.15	.07	.02
☐ 771 Jim Thorpe	1.00	.45	.12
☐ 772 Euel Moore	.05	.02	.01
☐ 773 Rudy York	.10	.05	.01
☐ 774 Chief Bender	.20	.09	.03
☐ 775 Chief Meyers	.05	.02	.01
☐ 776 Bob Johnson	.10	.05	.01
☐ 777 Roy Johnson	.05	.02	.01
☐ 778 Dick Porter	.05	.02	.01
☐ 779 Ethan Allen	.10	.05	.01
☐ 780 Slim Sallee	.05	.02	.01
☐ 781 Beau Bell	.05	.02	.01
☐ 782 Jigger Statz	.05	.02	.01
☐ 783 Dutch Henry	.05	.02	.01
☐ 784 Larry Woodall	.05	.02	.01
☐ 785 Phil Collins	.05	.02	.01
☐ 786 Joe Sewell	.20	.09	.03
☐ 787 Billy Herman	.20	.09	.03
☐ 788 Rube Oldring	.05	.02	.01
☐ 789 Bill Walker	.05	.02	.01
☐ 790 Joe Schultz	.05	.02	.01
☐ 791 Fred Maguire	.05	.02	.01
☐ 792 Claude Willoughby	.05	.02	.01
☐ 793 Alex Ferguson	.05	.02	.01
☐ 794 Johnny Morrison	.05	.02	.01
☐ 795 Tris Speaker	.25	.11	.03
☐ 796 Ty Cobb	.75	.35	.09
☐ 797 Max Carey	.20	.09	.03
☐ 798 George Sisler	.20	.09	.03
☐ 799 Charlie Hollocher	.05	.02	.01
☐ 800 Hippo Vaughn	.05	.02	.01
☐ 801 Sad Sam Jones	.10	.05	.01
☐ 802 Harry Hooper	.20	.09	.03
☐ 803 Gavvy Cravath	.10	.05	.01
☐ 804 Walter Johnson	.40	.18	.05
☐ 805 Jake Daubert	.10	.05	.01
☐ 806 Clyde Milan	.10	.05	.01
☐ 807 Hugh McQuillan	.05	.02	.01
☐ 808 Fred Brickell	.05	.02	.01
☐ 809 Joe Stripp	.05	.02	.01
☐ 810 Johnny Hodapp	.05	.02	.01
☐ 811 Johnny Vergez	.05	.02	.01
☐ 812 Lonny Frey	.05	.02	.01
☐ 813 Bill Regan	.05	.02	.01
☐ 814 Babe Young	.05	.02	.01
☐ 815 Charlie Robertson	.05	.02	.01
☐ 816 Walt Judnich	.05	.02	.01
☐ 817 Joe Tinker	.20	.09	.03
☐ 818 Johnny Evers	.20	.09	.03

Card	MINT	NRMT	EXC
☐ 819 Frank Chance	.20	.09	.03
☐ 820 John McGraw	.25	.11	.03
☐ 821 Charlie Grimm	.15	.07	.02
☐ 822 Ted Lyons	.20	.09	.03
☐ 823 Joe McCarthy MG	.20	.09	.03
☐ 824 Connie Mack MG	.25	.11	.03
☐ 825 George Gibson	.05	.02	.01
☐ 826 Steve O'Neill	.05	.02	.01
☐ 827 Tris Speaker	.25	.11	.03
☐ 828 Bill Carrigan	.05	.02	.01
☐ 829 Casey Stengel	.30	.14	.04
☐ 830 Miller Huggins	.20	.09	.03
☐ 831 Bill McKechnie MG	.20	.09	.03
☐ 832 Chuck Dressen	.10	.05	.01
☐ 833 Gabby Street	.05	.02	.01
☐ 834 Mel Ott	.30	.14	.04
☐ 835 Frank Frisch	.20	.09	.03
☐ 836 George Sisler	.20	.09	.03
☐ 837 Nap Lajoie	.35	.16	.04
☐ 838 Ty Cobb	.75	.35	.09
☐ 839 Billy Southworth MG	.05	.02	.01
☐ 840 Clark Griffith	.20	.09	.03
☐ 841 Bill Terry	.25	.11	.03
☐ 842 Rogers Hornsby	.35	.16	.04
☐ 843 Joe Cronin	.20	.09	.03
☐ 844 Al Lopez	.20	.09	.03
☐ 845 Bucky Harris MG	.20	.09	.03
☐ 846 Wilbert Robinson MG	.20	.09	.03
☐ 847 Hughie Jennings	.20	.09	.03
☐ 848 Jimmie Dykes	.10	.05	.01
☐ 849 Roy Cullenbine	.05	.02	.01
☐ 850 Eddie Moore	.05	.02	.01
☐ 851 Jack Rothrock	.05	.02	.01
☐ 852 Bill Lamar	.05	.02	.01
☐ 853 Monte Weaver	.05	.02	.01
☐ 854 Ival Goodman	.05	.02	.01
☐ 855 Hank Severeid	.05	.02	.01
☐ 856 Fred Haney	.05	.02	.01
☐ 857 Joe Shaute	.05	.02	.01
☐ 858 Smead Jolley	.05	.02	.01
☐ 859 Dib Williams	.05	.02	.01
☐ 860 Benny Bengough	.10	.05	.01
☐ 861 Rick Ferrell	.20	.09	.03
☐ 862 Bob O'Farrell	.05	.02	.01
☐ 863 Spud Davis	.05	.02	.01
☐ 864 Frankie Hayes	.05	.02	.01
☐ 865 Muddy Ruel	.05	.02	.01
☐ 866 Mickey Cochrane	.25	.11	.03
☐ 867 Johnny Kling	.05	.02	.01
☐ 868 Ivey Wingo	.05	.02	.01
☐ 869 Bill Dickey	.25	.11	.03
☐ 870 Frank Snyder	.05	.02	.01
☐ 871 Roger Bresnahan	.20	.09	.03
☐ 872 Wally Schang	.10	.05	.01
☐ 873 Al Lopez	.20	.09	.03
☐ 874 Jimmie Wilson	.05	.02	.01
☐ 875 Val Picinich	.05	.02	.01
☐ 876 Steve O'Neill	.05	.02	.01
☐ 877 Ernie Lombardi	.20	.09	.03
☐ 878 Johnny Bassler	.05	.02	.01
☐ 879 Ray Schalk	.20	.09	.03
☐ 880 Gabby Hartnett	.20	.09	.03
☐ 881 Bruce Campbell	.05	.02	.01
☐ 882 Red Ruffing	.20	.09	.03
☐ 883 Mordecai Brown	.20	.09	.03
☐ 884 Jimmy Archer	.05	.02	.01
☐ 885 Dave Keefe	.05	.02	.01
☐ 886 Nate Andrews	.05	.02	.01
☐ 887 Sam Rice	.20	.09	.03
☐ 888 Babe Ruth	1.00	.45	.12
☐ 889 Chick Hafey	.20	.09	.03
☐ 890 Oscar Melillo	.05	.02	.01
☐ 891 Joe Wood	.10	.05	.01
☐ 892 Johnny Evers	.20	.09	.03
☐ 893 Specs Toporcer	.05	.02	.01
☐ 894 Myril Hoag	.05	.02	.01
☐ 895 Bob Weiland	.05	.02	.01
☐ 896 Joe Marty	.05	.02	.01
☐ 897 Sherry Magee	.05	.02	.01
☐ 898 Danny Taylor	.05	.02	.01
☐ 899 Willie Kamm	.05	.02	.01
☐ 900 Jimmy Sheckard	.05	.02	.01
☐ 901 Syl Johnson	.05	.02	.01
☐ 902 Steve Sundra	.05	.02	.01
☐ 903 Doc Cramer	.10	.05	.01
☐ 904 Hub Pruett	.05	.02	.01
☐ 905 Lena Blackburne	.05	.02	.01
☐ 906 Eppa Rixey	.20	.09	.03
☐ 907 Goose Goslin	.20	.09	.03
☐ 908 George Kelly	.20	.09	.03
☐ 909 Jim Bottomley	.20	.09	.03
☐ 910 Christy Mathewson	.40	.18	.05
☐ 911 Tony Lazzeri	.20	.09	.03
☐ 912 Johnny Mostil	.05	.02	.01
☐ 913 Bobby Doerr	.20	.09	.03
☐ 914 Rabbit Maranville	.20	.09	.03
☐ 915 Harry Heilmann	.20	.09	.03
☐ 916 Bobby Wallace	.20	.09	.03
☐ 917 Jimmie Foxx	.35	.16	.04
☐ 918 Johnny Mize	.25	.11	.03
☐ 919 Jack Bentley	.05	.02	.01
☐ 920 Al Schacht	.15	.07	.02
☐ 921 Ed Coleman	.05	.02	.01
☐ 922 Dode Paskert	.05	.02	.01
☐ 923 Hod Ford	.05	.02	.01
☐ 924 Randy Moore	.05	.02	.01
☐ 925 Milt Shoffner	.05	.02	.01
☐ 926 Dick Siebert	.05	.02	.01
☐ 927 Tony Kaufmann	.05	.02	.01
☐ 928 Dizzy Dean with Nolan Ryan	1.00	.45	.12
☐ 929 Dazzy Vance with Nolan Ryan	.60	.25	.07
☐ 930 Lefty Grove with Nolan Ryan	.75	.35	.09
☐ 931 Rube Waddell with Nolan Ryan	.75	.35	.09
☐ 932 Grover C. Alexander with Nolan Ryan	.75	.35	.09
☐ 933 Bob Feller with Nolan Ryan	.75	.35	.09
☐ 934 Walter Johnson with Nolan Ryan	1.50	.70	.19
☐ 935 Ted Lyons with Nolan Ryan	.75	.35	.09
☐ 936 Jim Bagby Jr.	.05	.02	.01
☐ 937 Joe Sugden CO	.05	.02	.01
☐ 938 Earl Grace	.05	.02	.01
☐ 939 Jeff Heath	.05	.02	.01
☐ 940 Ken Williams	.15	.07	.02
☐ 941 Marv Owen	.05	.02	.01
☐ 942 Roy Weatherly	.05	.02	.01
☐ 943 Ed Morgan	.05	.02	.01
☐ 944 Johnny Rizzo	.05	.02	.01
☐ 945 Archie McKain	.05	.02	.01
☐ 946 Bob Garbark	.05	.02	.01
☐ 947 Bob Osborn	.05	.02	.01
☐ 948 Johnny Podgajny	.05	.02	.01
☐ 949 Joe Evans	.05	.02	.01
☐ 950 Tony Rensa	.05	.02	.01
☐ 951 John Humphries	.05	.02	.01
☐ 952 Merritt(Sugar) Cain	.05	.02	.01
☐ 953 Roy(Snipe) Hansen	.05	.02	.01
☐ 954 Johnny Niggeling	.05	.02	.01
☐ 955 Hal Wiltse	.05	.02	.01
☐ 956 Alex Carrasquel	.10	.05	.01
☐ 957 George Grant	.05	.02	.01
☐ 958 Lefty Weinert	.05	.02	.01
☐ 959 Erv Brame	.05	.02	.01
☐ 960 Ray Harrell	.05	.02	.01
☐ 961 Ed Linke	.05	.02	.01
☐ 962 Sam Gibson	.05	.02	.01
☐ 963 Johnny Watwood	.05	.02	.01
☐ 964 Doc Prothro	.05	.02	.01
☐ 965 Julio Bonetti	.05	.02	.01
☐ 966 Lefty Mills	.05	.02	.01
☐ 967 Chick Galloway	.05	.02	.01
☐ 968 Hal Kelleher	.05	.02	.01
☐ 969 Chief Hogsett	.05	.02	.01
☐ 970 Ed Heusser	.05	.02	.01
☐ 971 Ed Baecht	.05	.02	.01
☐ 972 Jack Saltzgaver	.05	.02	.01
☐ 973 Leroy Herrmann	.05	.02	.01
☐ 974 Belve Bean	.05	.02	.01
☐ 975 Harry(Socks) Seibold	.05	.02	.01
☐ 976 Vic Keen	.05	.02	.01
☐ 977 Bill Barrett	.05	.02	.01
☐ 978 Pat McNulty	.05	.02	.01
☐ 979 George Turbeville	.05	.02	.01
☐ 980 Eddie Phillips	.05	.02	.01
☐ 981 Garland Buckeye	.05	.02	.01
☐ 982 Vic Frasier	.05	.02	.01
☐ 983 Gordon Rhodes	.05	.02	.01
☐ 984 Red Barnes	.05	.02	.01
☐ 985 Jim Joe Edwards	.05	.02	.01
☐ 986 Herschel Bennett	.05	.02	.01
☐ 987 Carmen Hill	.05	.02	.01
☐ 988 Checklist 661-770	.05	.02	.01
☐ 989 Checklist 771-880	.05	.02	.01
☐ 990 Checklist 881-990	.05	.02	.01

1994 Conlon TSN Promos

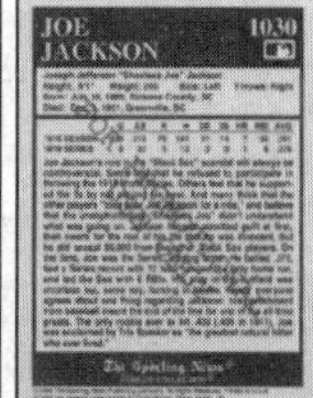

Issued to herald the release of the 330-card 1994 Conlon The Sporting News set, these eight standard-size promos feature black-bordered and white-line-framed black-and-white player photos on their fronts. The player's name, team, position, and year appear in white lettering within the lower black margin. The white and black back carries the player's name, biography, statistics, and career highlights. The faint "For Promotional Use Only" disclaimer appears obliquely. The production run for card numbers 991, 1050, 1105, 1140, 1190, and 1230 was 26,000; for card numbers 1030 and 1170, production was reportedly 52,000.

	MINT	NRMT	EXC
COMPLETE SET (8)	10.00	4.50	1.25
COMMON CARD	1.00	.45	.12
☐ 991 Pepper Martin	1.00	.45	.12
☐ 1030 Joe Jackson DP	3.00	1.35	.35
☐ 1050 Pie Traynor	2.00	.90	.25
☐ 1105 Carl Hubbell	2.00	.90	.25
☐ 1140 Lefty Grove	2.00	.90	.25
☐ 1170 Dizzy Dean and Daffy Dean DP	2.00	.90	.25
☐ 1190 Bill Klem	1.50	.70	.19
☐ 1230 Mark Koenig	1.00	.45	.12

1994 Conlon TSN

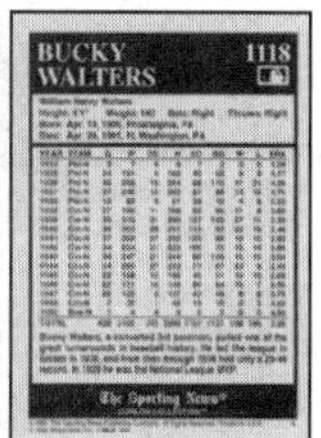

This fourth 330-card standard-size set of The Sporting News Conlon Collection again features the work of noted sports photographer Charles Conlon. The fronts feature black-and-white vintage player photos inside a white frame on a black card face. Subset cards are marked by their title in a black diagonal that cuts across the top right corner. The backs carry biography, statistics, and extended career summary and highlights. Topical subsets featured are Great Stories (991-1007), Hall of Fame (1008-1018), Black Sox Scandal (1019-1042), Nicknames (1050-1066), 1934 All-Star Game (1075-1113), In Memoriam (1121-1128), 1929 Athletics (1135-1159), Double Play Combo (1164-1166), Brothers (1169-1180), Umpires (1185-1212), All-Time Leaders (1217-1223), Switch-Hitters (1229-1237), Trivia (1247-1257), Action (1266-1274), First Card (1282-1317), and Checklists (1318-1320). The cards are numbered on the back in continuation of the previous year's issue. Card 1000 is the famous photo of Ty Cobb sliding. The 1994 Conlon set was issued in 12-card foil packs instead of the 15-card foil packs used in previous years. Reportedly 10,000 gold-bordered burgundy cards were produced for every card in the set. Each foil pack contained one of these cards, while two were inserted in each blister pack. According to Megacards, no more than 200,000 of each card were produced. The set was also available in factory set form.

	MINT	NRMT	EXC
COMPLETE SET (330)	18.00	8.00	2.20
COMPLETE FACT.SET (330)	18.00	8.00	2.20
COMMON CARD (991-1320)	.05	.02	.01
☐ 991 Pepper Martin	.15	.07	.02
☐ 992 Joe Sewell	.20	.09	.03
☐ 993 Edd Roush	.20	.09	.03
☐ 994 Rick Ferrell	.20	.09	.03
☐ 995 Johnny Broaca	.05	.02	.01
☐ 996 Luke Sewell	.10	.05	.01
☐ 997 Burleigh Grimes	.20	.09	.03
☐ 998 Hack Wilson	.25	.11	.03
☐ 999 Lefty Grove	.30	.14	.04
☐ 1000 Ty Cobb	.75	.35	.09
☐ 1001 John McGraw	.25	.11	.03
☐ 1002 Eddie Plank	.20	.09	.03
☐ 1003 Sad Sam Jones	.10	.05	.01
☐ 1004 Jim Bottomley	.20	.09	.03
☐ 1005 Hank Greenberg	.30	.14	.04
☐ 1006 Lloyd Waner	.20	.09	.03
☐ 1007 Wilcy Moore	.05	.02	.01
☐ 1008 Luke Appling	.20	.09	.03
☐ 1009 Hal Newhouser	.20	.09	.03
☐ 1010 Al Lopez	.20	.09	.03
☐ 1011 Ty Cobb	.75	.35	.09
☐ 1012 Kid Nichols	.20	.09	.03
☐ 1013 Ed Walsh	.20	.09	.03
☐ 1014 Hugh Duffy	.20	.09	.03
☐ 1015 Rube Marquard	.20	.09	.03
☐ 1016 Addie Joss	.20	.09	.03
☐ 1017 Bobby Wallace	.20	.09	.03
☐ 1018 Willie Keeler	.25	.11	.03
☐ 1019 Jake Daubert	.10	.05	.01
☐ 1020 Slim Sallee	.05	.02	.01
☐ 1021 Dolf Luque	.10	.05	.01
☐ 1022 Ivey Wingo	.05	.02	.01
☐ 1023 Edd Roush	.20	.09	.03
☐ 1024 Bill Rariden	.05	.02	.01
☐ 1025 Sherry Magee	.05	.02	.01
☐ 1026 Pat Duncan	.05	.02	.01
☐ 1027 Hod Eller	.05	.02	.01
☐ 1028 Greasy Neale	.10	.05	.01
☐ 1029 Buck Weaver	.20	.09	.03
☐ 1030 Joe Jackson	1.00	.45	.12
☐ 1031 Chick Gandil	.25	.11	.03
☐ 1032 Swede Risberg	.20	.09	.03
☐ 1033 Ray Schalk	.20	.09	.03
☐ 1034 Eddie Cicotte	.15	.07	.02
☐ 1035 Bill James	.05	.02	.01
☐ 1036 Nemo Leibold	.05	.02	.01
☐ 1037 Dickie Kerr	.15	.07	.02
☐ 1038 Kid Gleason MG	.10	.05	.01
☐ 1039 Fred McMullin	.05	.02	.01
☐ 1040 Eddie Collins	.20	.09	.03
☐ 1041 Sox Pitchers Lefty Williams Bill James Ed Cicotte Dickie Kerr	.15	.07	.02
☐ 1042 Sox Outfielders Nemo Leibold Happy Felsch Shano Collins Joe Jackson	.25	.11	.03
☐ 1043 Ken Keltner	.05	.02	.01
☐ 1044 Charlie Berry	.10	.05	.01
☐ 1045 Rube Lutzke	.05	.02	.01
☐ 1046 Johnny Schulte	.05	.02	.01
☐ 1047 Johnny Welch	.05	.02	.01
☐ 1048 Jack Russell	.05	.02	.01
☐ 1049 Red Murray	.05	.02	.01
☐ 1050 Pie Traynor	.20	.09	.03
☐ 1051 Mike Donlin	.10	.05	.01
☐ 1052 Gabby Hartnett	.20	.09	.03
☐ 1053 Tony Lazzeri	.20	.09	.03
☐ 1054 Hack Miller	.05	.02	.01
☐ 1055 Dazzy Vance	.20	.09	.03
☐ 1056 Bill Carrigan	.05	.02	.01
☐ 1057 Johnny Murphy	.10	.05	.01
☐ 1058 Cliff Heathcote	.05	.02	.01
☐ 1059 Joe Dugan	.10	.05	.01
☐ 1060 Rabbit Maranville	.20	.09	.03
☐ 1061 Tommy Henrich	.15	.07	.02
☐ 1062 Roy Parmelee	.05	.02	.01
☐ 1063 Lefty Gomez	.25	.11	.03
☐ 1064 Ernie Lombardi	.20	.09	.03
☐ 1065 Dave Bancroft	.20	.09	.03
☐ 1066 Bill McKechnie MG	.20	.09	.03
☐ 1067 Buddy Hassett	.05	.02	.01
☐ 1068 Spud Chandler	.10	.05	.01
☐ 1069 Roy Hughes	.05	.02	.01
☐ 1070 Hooks Dauss	.05	.02	.01
☐ 1071 Joe Hauser	.05	.02	.01
☐ 1072 Spud Davis	.05	.02	.01
☐ 1073 Max Butcher	.05	.02	.01
☐ 1074 Lou Chiozza	.05	.02	.01
☐ 1075 Polo Grounds 1934 All-Star Game	.05	.02	.01
☐ 1076 Charlie Gehringer	.25	.11	.03
☐ 1077 Heinie Manush	.20	.09	.03
☐ 1078 Red Ruffing	.20	.09	.03
☐ 1079 Mel Harder	.10	.05	.01
☐ 1080 Babe Ruth	1.00	.45	.12
☐ 1081 Ben Chapman	.05	.02	.01
☐ 1082 Lou Gehrig	.75	.35	.09
☐ 1083 Jimmie Foxx	.35	.16	.04
☐ 1084 Al Simmons	.20	.09	.03
☐ 1085 Joe Cronin	.20	.09	.03
☐ 1086 Bill Dickey	.25	.11	.03
☐ 1087 Mickey Cochrane	.25	.11	.03
☐ 1088 Lefty Gomez	.25	.11	.03
☐ 1089 Earl Averill Sr.	.20	.09	.03
☐ 1090 Sammy West	.05	.02	.01
☐ 1091 Frank Frisch P/MG	.20	.09	.03
☐ 1092 Billy Herman	.20	.09	.03
☐ 1093 Pie Traynor	.20	.09	.03
☐ 1094 Joe Medwick	.20	.09	.03
☐ 1095 Chuck Klein	.20	.09	.03
☐ 1096 Kiki Cuyler	.20	.09	.03
☐ 1097 Mel Ott	.30	.14	.04
☐ 1098 Wally Berger	.10	.05	.01
☐ 1099 Paul Waner	.20	.09	.03
☐ 1100 Bill Terry	.25	.11	.03
☐ 1101 Travis Jackson	.20	.09	.03
☐ 1102 Arky Vaughan	.20	.09	.03
☐ 1103 Gabby Hartnett	.20	.09	.03
☐ 1104 Al Lopez	.20	.09	.03
☐ 1105 Carl Hubbell	.25	.11	.03
☐ 1106 Lon Warneke	.10	.05	.01
☐ 1107 Van Lingle Mungo	.10	.05	.01
☐ 1108 Pepper Martin	.15	.07	.02
☐ 1109 Dizzy Dean	.40	.18	.05
☐ 1110 Fred Frankhouse	.05	.02	.01
☐ 1111 Bob Quinn J.G. Taylor Spink Mrs. J.G. Taylor Spink	.05	.02	.01
☐ 1112 Joseph Gilleaudeau Mrs. Joseph Gilleaudeau Mrs. J.G. Taylor Spink J.G. Taylor Spink Mrs. John Heydler John Heydler	.05	.02	.01
☐ 1113 Bill Hinchman Edward Keller	.05	.02	.01
☐ 1114 Vic Aldridge	.05	.02	.01
☐ 1115 Pinky Higgins	.05	.02	.01
☐ 1116 Hal Carlson	.05	.02	.01
☐ 1117 Fred Fitzsimmons	.10	.05	.01
☐ 1118 Bucky Walters	.15	.07	.02
☐ 1119 Nick Altrock	.05	.02	.01
☐ 1120 Chuck Dressen	.10	.05	.01
☐ 1121 Mark Koenig	.10	.05	.01
☐ 1122 Charlie Gehringer	.25	.11	.03
☐ 1123 Vern Kennedy	.05	.02	.01
☐ 1124 Harlond Clift	.05	.02	.01
☐ 1125 Babe Phelps	.05	.02	.01
☐ 1126 Johnny Mize	.25	.11	.03
☐ 1127 Hal Schumacher	.10	.05	.01
☐ 1128 Ethan Allen	.10	.05	.01
☐ 1129 Bill Wambsganss	.05	.02	.01
☐ 1130 Freddy Leach	.05	.02	.01

☐ 1131 Bud Clancy .05 .02 .01
☐ 1132 Stuffy Stewart .05 .02 .01
☐ 1133 Bill Brubaker .05 .02 .01
☐ 1134 Les Mann .05 .02 .01
☐ 1135 Howard Ehmke .05 .02 .01
☐ 1136 Al Simmons .20 .09 .03
☐ 1137 George Earnshaw .10 .05 .01
☐ 1138 Mule Haas .05 .02 .01
☐ 1139 Bing Miller .05 .02 .01
☐ 1140 Lefty Grove .30 .14 .04
☐ 1141 Joe Boley .05 .02 .01
☐ 1142 Eddie Collins .20 .09 .03
☐ 1143 Walter French .05 .02 .01
☐ 1144 Eric McNair .05 .02 .01
☐ 1145 Bill Shores .05 .02 .01
☐ 1146 Mickey Cochrane .25 .11 .03
☐ 1147 Homer Summa .05 .02 .01
☐ 1148 Jack Quinn .10 .05 .01
☐ 1149 Max Bishop .05 .02 .01
☐ 1150 Jimmy Dykes .10 .05 .01
☐ 1151 Rube Walberg .05 .02 .01
☐ 1152 Jimmie Foxx .35 .16 .04
☐ 1153 George H. Burns .05 .02 .01
☐ 1154 Doc Cramer .10 .05 .01
☐ 1155 Sammy Hale .05 .02 .01
☐ 1156 Eddie Rommel .05 .02 .01
☐ 1157 Cy Perkins .05 .02 .01
☐ 1158 Jim Cronin .05 .02 .01
☐ 1159 Connie Mack MG .25 .11 .03
☐ 1160 Ray Kolp .05 .02 .01
☐ 1161 Clyde Manion .05 .02 .01
☐ 1162 Frank Grube .05 .02 .01
☐ 1163 Steve Swetonic .05 .02 .01
☐ 1164 Joe Tinker .20 .09 .03
☐ 1165 Johnny Evers .20 .09 .03
☐ 1166 Frank Chance .20 .09 .03
☐ 1167 Emerson Dickman .05 .02 .01
☐ 1168 Jack Tobin .05 .02 .01
☐ 1169 Wes Ferrell .15 .07 .02
Rick Ferrell
☐ 1170 Dizzy Dean .20 .09 .03
Daffy Dean
☐ 1171 Tony Cuccinello .05 .02 .01
Al Cuccinello
☐ 1172 Harry Coveleski .10 .05 .01
Stan Coveleski
☐ 1173 Bob Johnson .05 .02 .01
Roy Johnson
☐ 1174 Andy High .05 .02 .01
Hugh High
☐ 1175 Luke Sewell .15 .07 .02
Joe Sewell
☐ 1176 Johnnie Heving .05 .02 .01
Joe Heving
☐ 1177 Al Wingo .05 .02 .01
Ivy Wingo
☐ 1178 Red Killefer .05 .02 .01
Bill Killefer
☐ 1179 Bubbles Hargrave .05 .02 .01
Pinky Hargrave
☐ 1180 Paul Waner .15 .07 .02
Lloyd Waner
☐ 1181 Johnny VanderMeer .15 .07 .02
☐ 1182 Jo Jo Moore .05 .02 .01
☐ 1183 Bobby Burke .05 .02 .01
☐ 1184 Johnny Moore .05 .02 .01
☐ 1185 Jack Egan UMP .05 .02 .01
☐ 1186 Tommy Connolly UMP .20 .09 .03
☐ 1187 Silk O'Loughlin UMP .05 .02 .01
☐ 1188 Beans Reardon UMP .10 .05 .01
☐ 1189 Charles Moran UMP .05 .02 .01
☐ 1190 Bill Klem UMP .25 .11 .03
☐ 1191 Dolly Stark UMP .10 .05 .01
☐ 1192 Albert Orth UMP .05 .02 .01
☐ 1193 Kitty Bransfield UMP .05 .02 .01
☐ 1194 Roy Van Graflan UMP .05 .02 .01
☐ 1195 Bob Hart UMP .05 .02 .01
☐ 1196 Jocko Conlan UMP .20 .09 .03
☐ 1197 Babe Pinelli UMP .10 .05 .01
☐ 1198 John Sheridan UMP .05 .02 .01
☐ 1199 Dick Nallin UMP .05 .02 .01
☐ 1200 Bill Dineen UMP .05 .02 .01
☐ 1201 Hank O'Day UMP .10 .05 .01
☐ 1202 Cy Rigler UMP .05 .02 .01
☐ 1203 Bob Emslie UMP .05 .02 .01
☐ 1204 Charles Pfirman UMP .05 .02 .01
☐ 1205 Harry Geisel UMP .05 .02 .01
☐ 1206 Ernest Quigley UMP .05 .02 .01
☐ 1207 Red Ormsby UMP .05 .02 .01
☐ 1208 George Hildebrand UMP .05 .02 .01
☐ 1209 George Moriarty UMP .10 .05 .01
☐ 1210 Billy Evans UMP .15 .07 .02
☐ 1211 Brick Owens UMP .05 .02 .01
☐ 1212 Bill McGowan UMP .20 .09 .03
☐ 1213 Kirby Higbe .05 .02 .01
☐ 1214 Taylor Douthit .05 .02 .01
☐ 1215 Del Baker .05 .02 .01
☐ 1216 Al Demaree .05 .02 .01
☐ 1217 Connie Mack MG .25 .11 .03
☐ 1218 Nap Lajoie .35 .16 .04
☐ 1219 Honus Wagner .40 .18 .05
☐ 1220 Christy Mathewson .40 .18 .05
☐ 1221 Sam Crawford .20 .09 .03
☐ 1222 Tris Speaker .25 .11 .03
☐ 1223 Grover C. Alexander .30 .14 .04
☐ 1224 Joe Bowman .05 .02 .01
☐ 1225 Johnny Rigney .05 .02 .01
☐ 1226 Earl Webb .10 .05 .01
☐ 1227 Whitey Moore .05 .02 .01
☐ 1228 Bruce Campbell .05 .02 .01
☐ 1229 Lu Blue .05 .02 .01
☐ 1230 Mark Koenig .10 .05 .01
☐ 1231 Wally Schang .10 .05 .01
☐ 1232 Max Carey .20 .09 .03
☐ 1233 Frank Frisch .20 .09 .03
☐ 1234 Donie Bush .05 .02 .01
☐ 1235 George Davis .05 .02 .01
☐ 1236 Billy Rogell .05 .02 .01
☐ 1237 Ripper Collins .05 .02 .01
☐ 1238 Dick Burrus .05 .02 .01
☐ 1239 Evar Swanson .05 .02 .01
☐ 1240 Woody English .05 .02 .01
☐ 1241 Joe Harris .05 .02 .01
☐ 1242 Harry McCurdy .05 .02 .01
☐ 1243 Dick Bartell .05 .02 .01
☐ 1244 Tommy Thompson .05 .02 .01
☐ 1245 Babe Adams .10 .05 .01
☐ 1246 Art Nehf .10 .05 .01
☐ 1247 Jack Graney .05 .02 .01
☐ 1248 Ted Lyons .20 .09 .03
☐ 1249 Lou Gehrig .75 .35 .09
☐ 1250 Mickey Welch .20 .09 .03
☐ 1251 Red Faber .20 .09 .03
☐ 1252 Joe McGinnity .20 .09 .03
☐ 1253 Rogers Hornsby .35 .16 .04
☐ 1254 Mel Ott .30 .14 .04
☐ 1255 Walter Johnson .40 .18 .05
☐ 1256 Sam Rice .20 .09 .03
☐ 1257 Jim Tobin .05 .02 .01
☐ 1258 Roger Peckinpaugh .05 .02 .01
☐ 1259 George Stovall .05 .02 .01
☐ 1260 Fred Merkle .10 .05 .01
☐ 1261 Rip Collins .05 .02 .01
☐ 1262 Carl Lind .05 .02 .01
☐ 1263 Nap Rucker .05 .02 .01
☐ 1264 Sloppy Thurston .05 .02 .01
☐ 1265 Alex Metzler .05 .02 .01
☐ 1266 Charles Conlon .05 .02 .01
☐ 1267 Lew McCarty IA .05 .02 .01
Sherry Magee
☐ 1268 B.A. Daniels IA .05 .02 .01
☐ 1269 Benny Kauff IA .10 .05 .01
☐ 1270 Heinie Groh IA .10 .05 .01
☐ 1271 Fritz Mollwitz IA .05 .02 .01
☐ 1272 George H. Burns IA .05 .02 .01
☐ 1273 Lee Magee IA .05 .02 .01
☐ 1274 Bill Killefer IA .05 .02 .01
☐ 1275 Jack Warhop .05 .02 .01
☐ 1276 Dutch Leonard .10 .05 .01
☐ 1277 General Crowder .05 .02 .01
☐ 1278 Chet Laabs .05 .02 .01
☐ 1279 Joe Bush .10 .05 .01
☐ 1280 Rube Bressler .05 .02 .01
☐ 1281 Bob Brown .05 .02 .01
☐ 1282 Bernie DeViveiros .05 .02 .01
☐ 1283 Les Tietje .05 .02 .01
☐ 1284 Charlie Devens .05 .02 .01
☐ 1285 Elliott Bigelow .05 .02 .01
☐ 1286 Johnny Dickshot .05 .02 .01
☐ 1287 Buster Chatham .05 .02 .01
☐ 1288 Walter Beall .05 .02 .01
☐ 1289 Dick Attreau .05 .02 .01
☐ 1290 Bunny Brief .05 .02 .01
☐ 1291 Jim Gleeson .05 .02 .01
☐ 1292 Wally Shaner .05 .02 .01
☐ 1293 Pat Crawford .05 .02 .01
☐ 1294 Manny Salvo .05 .02 .01
☐ 1295 Cal Dorsett .05 .02 .01
☐ 1296 Rusty Peters .05 .02 .01
☐ 1297 Johnny Couch .05 .02 .01
☐ 1298 Dutch Ulrich .05 .02 .01
☐ 1299 Jim Bivin .05 .02 .01
☐ 1300 Paul Strand .05 .02 .01
☐ 1301 Johnny Lanning .05 .02 .01
☐ 1302 Bill Brenzel .05 .02 .01
☐ 1303 Don Songer .05 .02 .01
☐ 1304 Dutch Levsen .05 .02 .01
☐ 1305 Otto Bluege .05 .02 .01
☐ 1306 Fabian Gaffke .05 .02 .01
☐ 1307 Flash Archdeacon .05 .02 .01
☐ 1308 Tiny Chaplin .05 .02 .01
☐ 1309 Larry Rosenthal .05 .02 .01
☐ 1310 Bill Bagwell .05 .02 .01
☐ 1311 Joe Dawson .05 .02 .01
☐ 1312 Johnny Sturm .05 .02 .01
☐ 1313 Haskell Billings .05 .02 .01
☐ 1314 Whitey Wilshere .05 .02 .01
☐ 1315 Asby Asbjornson .05 .02 .01
☐ 1316 Hank Steinbacher .05 .02 .01
☐ 1317 Stan Baumgartner .05 .02 .01
☐ 1318 Checklist 991-1100 .05 .02 .01
☐ 1319 Checklist 1101-1210 .05 .02 .01
☐ 1320 Checklist 1211-1320 .05 .02 .01

1994 Conlon TSN Burgundy

This set is a parallel to the regular 1994 Conlon issue. Instead of the black and white borders, the borders had a burgundy color. One of these cards were inserted in each 1994 Conlon pack.

	MINT	NRMT	EXC
COMPLETE SET (330)	50.00	22.00	6.25

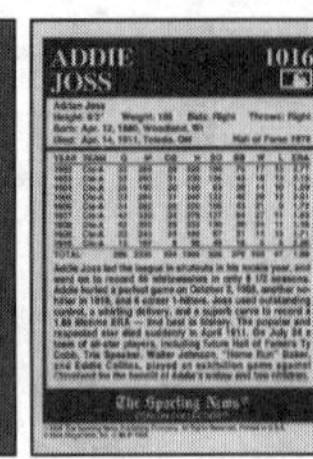

COMMON CARD (991-1320)	.10	.05	.01
*STARS: 2X TO 4X BASIC CARDS			
☐ 1000 Ty Cobb	5.00	2.20	.60
☐ 1011 Ty Cobb	3.00	1.35	.35
☐ 1030 Joe Jackson	5.00	2.20	.60
☐ 1080 Babe Ruth	7.50	3.40	.95
☐ 1082 Lou Gehrig	5.00	2.20	.60
☐ 1109 Dizzy Dean	1.50	.70	.19
☐ 1152 Jimmie Foxx	1.50	.70	.19
☐ 1217 Connie Mack MG	1.00	.45	.12
☐ 1218 Nap Lajoie	1.50	.70	.19
☐ 1219 Honus Wagner	1.50	.70	.19
☐ 1220 Christy Mathewson	1.50	.70	.19
☐ 1249 Lou Gehrig	5.00	2.20	.60
☐ 1253 Rogers Hornsby	1.50	.70	.19
☐ 1255 Walter Johnson	1.50	.70	.19

1994 Conlon TSN Color Inserts

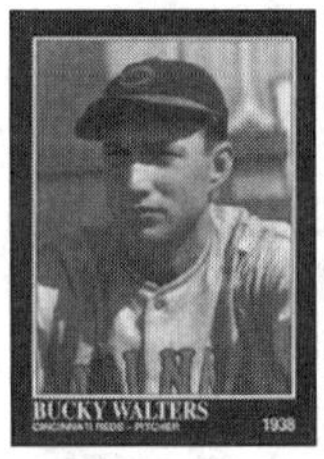

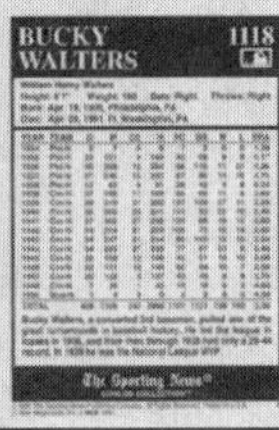

All the cards in this 16-card standard-size set were previously released in black and white in the Conlon regular issue sets. The cards are numbered on the back. The corresponding card number of the black and white regular issue card is given on the line after each player's name. Insert cards 24-39 were issued in 1994. Of these, cards 29-30 were available through a send-away offer, while cards 31-33 were inserted exclusively in hobby foil packs. The production figures for cards 24-39 were as follows: 84,000 for card numbers 24-28; 12,000 for card numbers 29-33; 48,000 for card numbers 34-37; and 12,000 for card numbers 38-39. Cards 34-37 were only available with accessory items purchased at Toys'R'Us. Cards 38-39 were available through special offers to be announced. Finally, 24,000 more of card number 28 were printed and have "Conlon Collection Day, Sept. 11, 1994" printed diagonally across their backs. These cards are specially numbered "28CCD" and were to be given out at a Cardinals game against the Dodgers in St. Louis.

	MINT	NRMT	EXC
COMPLETE SET (16)	40.00	18.00	5.00
COMMON CARD (24-28)	1.50	.70	.19
COMMON CARD (29-33)	2.00	.90	.25
COMMON CARD (34-37)	1.50	.70	.19
COMMON CARD (38-39)	3.00	1.35	.35
☐ 24 Hal Newhouser Card 445	2.00	.90	.25
☐ 25 Hugh Jennings Card 556	1.50	.70	.19
☐ 26 Red Faber	1.50	.70	.19
☐ 27 Enos Slaughter Card 710	2.00	.90	.25
☐ 28 Johnny Mize Card 56	2.00	.90	.25
☐ 29 Pie Traynor Card 628	3.00	1.35	.35
☐ 30 Walter Johnson Nolan Ryan Card 268	6.00	2.70	.75
☐ 31 Lou Gehrig Card 529	6.00	2.70	.75
☐ 32 Benny Bengough Card 860	2.00	.90	.25
☐ 33 Babe Ruth Card 888	7.50	3.40	.95
☐ 34 Charlie Gehringer Card 667	2.00	.90	.25
☐ 35 Babe Ruth Card 426	6.00	2.70	.75
☐ 36 Bill Dickey Card 869	2.50	1.10	.30
☐ 37 Three Finger Brown Card 883	1.50	.70	.19
☐ 38 Ray Schalk Card 48	3.00	1.35	.35
☐ 39 Homerun Baker Card 565	4.00	1.80	.50

1995 Conlon TSN Prototypes

These 10 standard-size prototype cards were issued by Megacards to preview the design of the 1995 Conlon Collection. The card numbers correspond to the same numbers used in the regular set.

	MINT	NRMT	EXC
COMPLETE SET (10)	20.00	9.00	2.50
COMMON CARD	1.00	.45	.12
☐ 3C Babe Ruth 100th Anniversary	5.00	2.20	.60
☐ 1337 Bob Feller	3.00	1.35	.35
☐ 1357 Tris Speaker	2.00	.90	.25
☐ 1397 Charles Comisky OWN	2.00	.90	.25
☐ 1404 Gabby Hartnett	2.00	.90	.25
☐ 1421 Lou Gehrig	4.00	1.80	.50
☐ 1425 Lou Boudreau	2.00	.90	.25
☐ 1464 Ray Chapman	1.00	.45	.12
☐ 1475 Bill Dickey	2.00	.90	.25
☐ 1500 Rabbit Maranville	1.50	.70	.19
☐ 1535 Babe Ruth	5.00	2.20	.60

1995 Conlon TSN

The 1995 Conlon Collection set consists of 110 standard-size cards. This continuation of the Conlon Collection set was supposed to be released in two 110-card series (February and August respectively), but the second series was never released because of the baseball strike. This was the first year that the Conlon Collection did not consist of 330 cards. The set continues to feature the work of noted sports photographer Charles Conlon. No more than 50,000 sets were printed, with a suggested retail price of $19.95 per series. As a special tribute to Conlon and the 100th Anniversary of Babe Ruth's birth, Megacards teamed with Topps to produce a 100th Birthday Card. The card was issued in two forms: a sepia-tone version for 1995 Topps regular series (#3) and an color-enhanced version (#3C) inserted in each 1995 Conlon complete set. On the fronts, each black-and-white photo has a gold foil inner border and a forest green outer border. Topical subsets featured are Veterans of World War I and II (1321-1350), '75 Champs (1354-1367), Great Stories (1371-1378), Nicknames (1382-1390), Behind the Scenes (1394-1400), Great Games (1404-1412), and Beating the Odds (1416-1429). Also groups of three "Generic" cards are scattered throughout the set (1351-1352, 1368-1370, 1379-1381, 1391-1393, 1401-1403, 1413-1415).

	MINT	NRMT	EXC
COMPLETE FACT. SET (110)	15.00	6.75	1.85
COMMON CARD (1321-1430)	.15	.07	.02
☐ 1321 Grover C. Alexander	.50	.23	.06
☐ 1322 Christy Mathewson	.50	.23	.06
☐ 1323 Eddie Grant	.15	.07	.02
☐ 1324 Gabby Street	.15	.07	.02
☐ 1325 Hank Gowdy	.15	.07	.02
☐ 1326 Jack Bentley	.15	.07	.02
☐ 1327 Eppa Rixey	.30	.14	.04
☐ 1328 Bob Shawkey	.30	.14	.04
☐ 1329 Rabbit Maranville	.40	.18	.05
☐ 1330 Casey Stengel	.50	.23	.06
☐ 1331 Herb Pennock	.40	.18	.05
☐ 1332 Eddie Collins Sr.	.40	.18	.05
☐ 1333 Buddy Hassett	.15	.07	.02
☐ 1334 Andy Cohen	.15	.07	.02
☐ 1335 Hank Greenberg	.50	.23	.06
☐ 1336 Andy High	.15	.07	.02
☐ 1337 Bob Feller	.50	.23	.06
☐ 1338 George Earnshaw	.30	.14	.04
☐ 1339 Jack Knott	.15	.07	.02
☐ 1340 Larry French	.15	.07	.02
☐ 1341 Skippy Roberge	.15	.07	.02
☐ 1342 Boze Berger	.15	.07	.02
☐ 1343 Bill Posedel	.15	.07	.02
☐ 1344 Kirby Higbe	.15	.07	.02
☐ 1345 Bob Neighbors	.15	.07	.02
☐ 1346 Hugh Mulcahy	.15	.07	.02
☐ 1347 Harry Walker	.15	.07	.02
☐ 1348 Buddy Lewis	.15	.07	.02
☐ 1349 Cecil Travis	.15	.07	.02
☐ 1350 Moe Berg	1.00	.45	.12
☐ 1351 Nixey Callahan	.15	.07	.02
☐ 1352 Heinie Peitz	.15	.07	.02
☐ 1353 Doc White	.15	.07	.02
☐ 1354 Joe Wood	.30	.14	.04
☐ 1355 Larry Gardner	.15	.07	.02
☐ 1356 Steve O'Neill	.15	.07	.02
☐ 1357 Tris Speaker	.40	.18	.05
☐ 1358 Bill Wambsganss	.15	.07	.02
☐ 1359 George H. Burns	.15	.07	.02
☐ 1360 Charlie Jamieson	.15	.07	.02
☐ 1361 Les Nunamaker	.15	.07	.02
☐ 1362 Stan Coveleski	.40	.18	.05

☐ 1363 Joe Sewell	.40	.18	.05
☐ 1364 Jim Bagby Sr.	.15	.07	.02
☐ 1365 Duster Mails	.15	.07	.02
☐ 1366 Jack Graney	.15	.07	.02
☐ 1367 Elmer Smith	.15	.07	.02
☐ 1368 Tommy Leach	.15	.07	.02
☐ 1369 Russ Ford	.15	.07	.02
☐ 1370 Harry M. Wolter	.15	.07	.02
☐ 1371 Dazzy Vance	.40	.18	.05
☐ 1372 Germany Schaefer	.30	.14	.04
☐ 1373 Elbie Fletcher	.15	.07	.02
☐ 1374 Clark Griffith	.40	.18	.05
☐ 1375 Al Simmons	.40	.18	.05
☐ 1376 Billy Jurges	.15	.07	.02
☐ 1377 Earl Averill Sr.	.40	.18	.05
☐ 1378 Bill Klem	.40	.18	.05
☐ 1379 Armando Marsans	.15	.07	.02
☐ 1380 Mike Gonzalez	.15	.07	.02
☐ 1381 Jack Fournier	.15	.07	.02
☐ 1382 Burleigh Grimes	.40	.18	.05
☐ 1383 Arlie Latham	.15	.07	.02
☐ 1384 Ray Schalk	.40	.18	.05
☐ 1385 Goose Goslin	.40	.18	.05
☐ 1386 Joe Hauser	.15	.07	.02
☐ 1387 Dixie Walker	.30	.14	.04
☐ 1388 Jesse Burkett	.15	.07	.02
☐ 1389 Cliff Melton	.15	.07	.02
☐ 1390 Gee Walker	.15	.07	.02
☐ 1391 Tony Cuccinello	.15	.07	.02
☐ 1392 Vern Kennedy	.15	.07	.02
☐ 1393 Tuck Stainback	.15	.07	.02
☐ 1394 Ed Barrow	.30	.14	.04
☐ 1395 Ford C. Frick	.30	.14	.04
☐ 1396 Ban Johnson	.30	.14	.04
August Herrmann			
☐ 1397 Charles Comiskey	.30	.14	.04
☐ 1398 Jacob Ruppert	.30	.14	.04
Joe McCarthy			
☐ 1399 Branch Rickey	.40	.18	.05
☐ 1400 Jack Kieran	.35	.16	.04
Moe Berg			
☐ 1401 Mike Ryba	.15	.07	.02
☐ 1402 Stan Spence	.15	.07	.02
☐ 1403 Red Barrett	.15	.07	.02
☐ 1404 Gabby Hartnett	.40	.18	.05
☐ 1405 Babe Ruth	2.00	.90	.25
☐ 1406 Fred Merkle	.30	.14	.04
☐ 1407 Claude Passeau	.15	.07	.02
☐ 1408 Joe Wood	.25	.11	.03
☐ 1409 Cliff Heathcote	.15	.07	.02
☐ 1410 Walt Cruise	.15	.07	.02
☐ 1411 Cookie Lavagetto	.15	.07	.02
☐ 1412 Tony Lazzeri	.40	.18	.05
☐ 1413 Atley Donald	.15	.07	.02
☐ 1414 Ken Raffensberger	.15	.07	.02
☐ 1415 Dizzy Trout	.15	.07	.02
☐ 1416 Augie Galan	.15	.07	.02
☐ 1417 Monty Stratton	.15	.07	.02
☐ 1418 Claude Passeau	.15	.07	.02
☐ 1419 Oscar Grimes	.15	.07	.02
☐ 1420 Rollie Hemsley	.15	.07	.02
☐ 1421 Lou Gehrig	1.50	.70	.19
☐ 1422 Tom Sunkel	.15	.07	.02
☐ 1423 Tris Speaker	.40	.18	.05
☐ 1424 Chick Fewster	.15	.07	.02
☐ 1425 Lou Boudreau	.40	.18	.05
☐ 1426 Hank Leiber	.15	.07	.02
☐ 1427 Eddie Mayo	.15	.07	.02
☐ 1428 Charley Gelbert	.15	.07	.02
☐ 1429 Jackie Hayes	.15	.07	.02
☐ 1430 Checklist	.15	.07	.02
☐ NNO Babe Ruth	2.00	.90	.25
100th Birthday			

1995 Conlon TSN Griffey Jr.

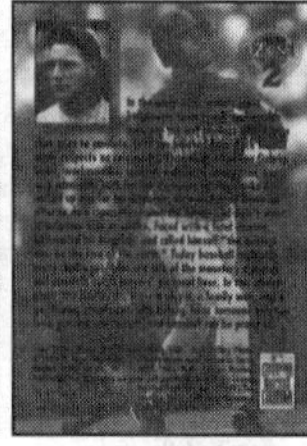

Titled "In the Zone," this eight-card standard-size set commemorates legends of the game from different eras by comparing Ken Griffey, Jr. to eight players from the Conlon era. No more than 50,000 sets were printed. Six cards were in each 110-card clamshell package, three were inserted in the 55-card clamshell, and there is one per 22-card clamshell. The other two cards were available through a mail-in offer. The fronts feature a color action cut-out of Ken Griffey superimposed over a color photo of the player mentioned on the card. Both players' names, along with the set logo, also appear on the fronts. On a ghosted color action Ken Griffey photo, the backs carry a small, black-and-white photo of the past player, along with a description of how those two players are alike.

	MINT	NRMT	EXC
COMPLETE SET (8)	12.50	5.50	1.55
COMMON CARD (1-8)	1.00	.45	.12
☐ 1 Ken Griffey Jr.	3.00	1.35	.35
Babe Ruth			
☐ 2 Ken Griffey Jr.	2.50	1.10	.30
Lou Gehrig			
☐ 3 Ken Griffey Jr.	2.00	.90	.25
Ty Cobb			
☐ 4 Ken Griffey Jr.	1.50	.70	.19
Jimmie Foxx			
☐ 5 Ken Griffey Jr.	1.50	.70	.19
Mel Ott			
☐ 6 Ken Griffey Jr.	2.50	1.10	.30
Shoeless Joe Jackson			
☐ 7 Ken Griffey Jr.	1.50	.70	.19
Tris Speaker			
☐ 8 Ken Griffey Jr.	1.00	.45	.12
Jim(Sunny) Bottomley			

1995 Conlon TSN Club Members Promos

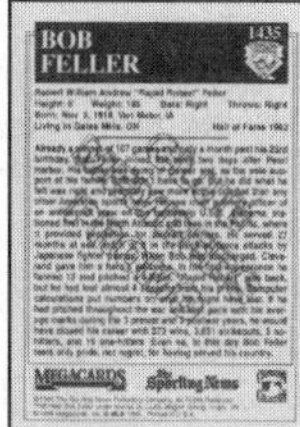

Issued to herald the release of the 1995 Conlon series, these two standard-size promos feature black-bordered and white-line-framed black-and-white player photos on their fronts. The player's name, team, position, and year appear in white lettering within the lower black margin. The white and black back carries the player's name, biography, statistics, and career highlights. The faint "Club Members Promo" disclaimer is printed diagonally across the back.

	MINT	NRMT	EXC
COMPLETE SET (2)	5.00	2.20	.60
COMMON CARD	2.00	.90	.25
☐ 1387 Rabbit Maranville	2.00	.90	.25
☐ 1435 Bob Feller	3.00	1.35	.35

1976 Cool Papa Bell

This 13 card set features highlights in the career of Negro League great Cool Papa Bell. The set was issued soon after his induction into the Hall of Fame.

	NRMT	VG-E	GOOD
COMPLETE SET (13)	12.00	5.50	1.50
COMMON CARD	1.00	.45	.12
☐ 1 Cool Papa Bell	1.50	.70	.19
Amazing Speed			
☐ 2 Cool Papa Bell	1.00	.45	.12
Lou Brock			
Sets S.B. Record			
☐ 3 Cool Papa Bell	1.50	.70	.19
☐ 4 Cool Papa Bell	1.50	.70	.19
Cuba 1928			
☐ 5 Cool Papa Bell	1.00	.45	.12
Great Fielder, Too			
☐ 6 Cool Papa Bell	1.50	.70	.19
HOF, Cooperstown			
☐ 7 Cool Papa Bell	1.50	.70	.19
HOF Favorite			
☐ 8 Cool Papa Bell	1.00	.45	.12
Induction Day, 1974			
☐ 9 Cool Papa Bell	1.00	.45	.12
The Mexican Leagues			
☐ 10 Cool Papa Bell	1.50	.70	.19
On Deck in Cuba			
☐ 11 Cool Papa Bell	1.00	.45	.12
On Deck In Cuba			
☐ 12 Cool Papa Bell	1.50	.70	.19
Touring Havana			
☐ 13 Cool Papa Bell	2.00	.90	.25
Josh Gibson			

1993 Country Time Legends Brooks Robinson

These eight cards measure approximately 2 1/2" by 3 5/8" and feature restored "colorized" black-and-white photos highlighting the 23-season career of HOFer Brooks Robinson. Each photo is overlaid upon a black diamond. The border around the photo is green, red, and black, and the set's logo rests at the lower right. The back carries

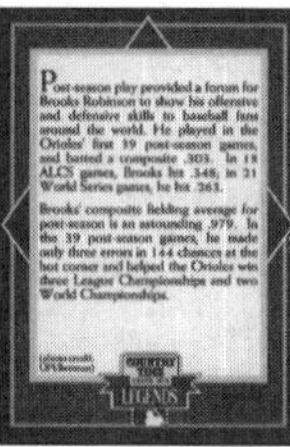

career highlights within a white rectangle framed in yellow and bordered in gray, yellow and black. The cards are unnumbered and checklisted below chronologically and distinguished by pose descriptions.

	MINT	NRMT	EXC
COMPLETE SET	7.00	3.10	.85
COMMON CARD (1-8)	1.00	.45	.12
☐ 1 Brooks Robinson	1.00	.45	.12
Waiting for pitch			
☐ 2 Brooks Robinson	1.00	.45	.12
On his toes at 3rd			
☐ 3 Brooks Robinson	1.00	.45	.12
From back, ending swing			
☐ 4 Brooks Robinson	1.00	.45	.12
Diving for line drive			
☐ 5 Brooks Robinson	1.00	.45	.12
From front, ending swing			
☐ 6 Brooks Robinson	1.00	.45	.12
Fielding grounder			
☐ 7 Brooks Robinson	1.00	.45	.12
Waving cap to crowd			
☐ 8 Title Card	.50	.23	.06

1910-19 Coupon T213

The catalog designation T213, like its predecessor T212, actually contains three separate sets. Set 1 was issued about 1910 and consists of brown-captioned designs taken directly from the T206 set. Set 2 cards are also T206 designs, but with pale blue captions. They were produced in 1914-1915 and contain many team changes and Federal League affiliations. Set 3 cards were produced in 1919 and are physically slightly smaller than the other two sets. Set 1 cards are printed on heavy paper; set 2 cards are printed on cardboard and have a glossy surface, which has resulted in a distinctive type of surface cracking. Each card in Set 1 and 2 measures 1 1/2" by 2 5/8" whereas Set 3 cards are only 2 3/8" by 2 9/16". The "Coupon" brand of cigarettes was manufactured by a branch of the American Tobacco Company located in New Orleans. The different sets can also be distinguished by their back titles, Set 1 (Coupon Mild Cigarettes), Set 2 (Mild and Sweet Coupon Cigarettes 20 for 5 cents), and Set 3 (Coupon Cigarettes 16 for 10 cts.).

	EX-MT	VG-E	GOOD
COMPLETE SET	35000.00	15800.00	4400.00
COMMON TYPE 1 (1-68)	100.00	45.00	12.50
COMMON TYPE 2 (69-255)	60.00	27.00	7.50
COMMON TYPE 3 (256-325)	60.00	27.00	7.50
☐ 1 Harry Bay	150.00	70.00	19.00
Nashville			
☐ 2 Beals Becker	100.00	45.00	12.50
☐ 3 Chief Bender	150.00	70.00	19.00
☐ 4 William H. Bernhard	150.00	70.00	19.00
Nashville			
☐ 5 Ted Breitenstein	150.00	70.00	19.00
New Orleans			
☐ 6 Bobby Byrne	100.00	45.00	12.50
☐ 7 William J. Campbell	100.00	45.00	12.50
☐ 8 Max Carey	150.00	70.00	19.00
Memphis			
☐ 9 Frank Chance	250.00	110.00	31.00
☐ 10 Chappy Charles	100.00	45.00	12.50
☐ 11 Hal Chase (portrait)	150.00	70.00	19.00
☐ 12 Hal Chase (throwing)	150.00	70.00	19.00
☐ 13 Ty Cobb	800.00	350.00	100.00
☐ 14 Cranston	100.00	45.00	12.50
Memphis			
☐ 15 Birdie Cree	100.00	45.00	12.50
☐ 16 Bill Donovan	100.00	45.00	12.50
☐ 17 Mickey Doolan	100.00	45.00	12.50
☐ 18 Jean Dubuc	100.00	45.00	12.50
☐ 19 Joe Dunn	100.00	45.00	12.50
☐ 20 Roy Ellam	150.00	70.00	19.00
Nashville			
☐ 21 Clyde Engle	100.00	45.00	12.50
☐ 22 Johnny Evers	150.00	70.00	19.00
☐ 23 Art Fletcher	100.00	45.00	12.50
☐ 24 Charles Fritz	150.00	70.00	19.00
New Orleans			
☐ 25 Edward Greminger	150.00	70.00	19.00
Montgomery			
☐ 26 Hart	150.00	70.00	19.00
Little Rock			
☐ 27 Hart	150.00	70.00	19.00
Montgomery			
☐ 28 Topsy Hartsel	100.00	45.00	12.50
☐ 29 Charles Hickman	150.00	70.00	19.00
Mobile			
☐ 30 Danny Hoffman	100.00	45.00	12.50
☐ 31 Harry Howell	100.00	45.00	12.50
☐ 32 Miller Huggins	150.00	70.00	19.00
portrait			
☐ 33 Miller Huggins	150.00	70.00	19.00
yelling			
☐ 34 George Hunter	100.00	45.00	12.50
☐ 35 Dutch Jordan	150.00	70.00	19.00
Atlanta			
☐ 36 Ed Killian	100.00	45.00	12.50
☐ 37 Otto Knabe	100.00	45.00	12.50
☐ 38 Frank LaPorte	100.00	45.00	12.50
☐ 39 Ed Lennox	100.00	45.00	12.50
☐ 40 Harry Lentz	150.00	70.00	19.00
Little Rock			
☐ 41 Rube Marquard	150.00	70.00	19.00
☐ 42 Doc Marshall	100.00	45.00	12.50
☐ 43 Christy Mathewson	375.00	170.00	47.50
☐ 44 George McBride	100.00	45.00	12.50
☐ 45 Pryor McElveen	100.00	45.00	12.50
☐ 46 Matty McIntyre	100.00	45.00	12.50
☐ 47 Michael Mitchell	100.00	45.00	12.50
☐ 48 Carlton Molesworth	150.00	70.00	19.00
Birmingham			
☐ 49 Mike Mowrey	100.00	45.00	12.50
☐ 50 Hy Myers	100.00	45.00	12.50
batting			
☐ 51 Hy Myers	100.00	45.00	12.50
fielding			
☐ 52 Dode Paskert	100.00	45.00	12.50
☐ 53 Hub Perdue	150.00	70.00	19.00
Nashville			
☐ 54 Archie Persons	150.00	70.00	19.00
Montgomery			
☐ 55 Edward Reagan	150.00	70.00	19.00
New Orleans			
☐ 56 Robert Rhoades	100.00	45.00	12.50
☐ 57 Isaac Rockenfeld	150.00	70.00	19.00
New Orleans			
☐ 58 Claude Rossman	100.00	45.00	12.50
☐ 59 Boss Schmidt	100.00	45.00	12.50
☐ 60 Sid Smith	150.00	70.00	19.00
Atlanta			
☐ 61 Charles Starr	100.00	45.00	12.50
☐ 62 Gabby Street	100.00	45.00	12.50
☐ 63 Ed Summers	100.00	45.00	12.50
☐ 64 William Sweeney	100.00	45.00	12.50
☐ 65 Chester Thomas	100.00	45.00	12.50
☐ 66 Woodie Thornton	150.00	70.00	19.00
Mobile			
☐ 67 Ed Willett	100.00	45.00	12.50
☐ 68 Owen Wilson	100.00	45.00	12.50
☐ 69 Red Ames	60.00	27.00	7.50
Cincinnati			
☐ 70 Red Ames	60.00	27.00	7.50
St. Louis			
☐ 71 Frank Baker	120.00	55.00	15.00
New York Amer.			
☐ 72 Frank Baker	120.00	55.00	15.00
Philadelphia			
☐ 73 Frank Baker	120.00	55.00	15.00
Phila.			
☐ 74 Cy Barger	60.00	27.00	7.50
☐ 75 Chief Bender	120.00	55.00	15.00
trees			
Baltimore Fed.			
☐ 76 Chief Bender	120.00	55.00	15.00
no trees			
Baltimore Fed.			
☐ 77 Chief Bender	120.00	55.00	15.00
trees			
Philadelphia Amer.			
☐ 78 Chief Bender	120.00	55.00	15.00
no trees			
Philadelphia Amer.			
☐ 79 Chief Bender	120.00	55.00	15.00
trees			
Philadelphia Nat.			
☐ 80 Chief Bender	120.00	55.00	15.00
no trees			
Philadelphia Nat.			
☐ 81 Bill Bradley	60.00	27.00	7.50
☐ 82 Roger Bresnahan	120.00	55.00	15.00
Chicago			
☐ 83 Roger Bresnahan	120.00	55.00	15.00
Toledo			
☐ 84 Al Bridwell	60.00	27.00	7.50
St. Louis			
☐ 85 Al Bridwell	60.00	27.00	7.50
Nashville			
☐ 86 Mordecai Brown	120.00	55.00	15.00
Chicago			
☐ 87 Mordecai Brown	120.00	55.00	15.00
St. Louis Fed.			

☐ 88 Bobby Byrne 60.00 27.00 7.50
☐ 89 Howie Camnitz 60.00 27.00 7.50
hands over
Pittsburgh Fed.
☐ 90 Howie Camnitz 60.00 27.00 7.50
arm at side
Pittsburgh Fed.
☐ 91 Howie Camnitz 60.00 27.00 7.50
Savannah
☐ 92 William J. Campbell 60.00 27.00 7.50
☐ 93 Frank Chance 140.00 65.00 17.50
Los Angeles
batting
☐ 94 Frank Chance 140.00 65.00 17.50
Los Angeles
portrait
☐ 95 Frank Chance 140.00 65.00 17.50
New York Amer.
batting
☐ 96 Frank Chance 140.00 65.00 17.50
New York Amer.
portrait
☐ 97 William Chappelle 60.00 27.00 7.50
Brooklyn
☐ 98 William Chappelle 60.00 27.00 7.50
Cleveland
☐ 99 Hal Chase 120.00 55.00 15.00
Buffalo Fed.
portrait
☐ 100 Hal Chase 120.00 55.00 15.00
Buffalo Fed.
holding cup
☐ 101 Hal Chase 120.00 55.00 15.00
Buffalo Fed.
throwing
☐ 102 Hal Chase 120.00 55.00 15.00
Chicago Amer.
portrait
☐ 103 Hal Chase 120.00 55.00 15.00
Chicago Amer.
holding cup)
☐ 104 Hal Chase 120.00 55.00 15.00
Chicago Amer.
throwing
☐ 105 Ty Cobb 2000.00 900.00 250.00
batting
☐ 106 Ty Cobb 2000.00 900.00 250.00
portrait
☐ 107 Eddie Collins 120.00 55.00 15.00
Chicago Amer.
with A
☐ 108 Eddie Collins 120.00 55.00 15.00
Chicago Amer.
without A
☐ 109 Eddie Collins 120.00 55.00 15.00
Philadelphia
with A
☐ 110 Doc Crandall 60.00 27.00 7.50
St. Louis Amer.
☐ 111 Doc Crandall 60.00 27.00 7.50
St. Louis Fed.
☐ 112 Sam Crawford 120.00 55.00 15.00
☐ 113 Birdie Cree 60.00 27.00 7.50
☐ 114 Harry Davis 60.00 27.00 7.50
Philadelphia
☐ 115 Harry Davis 60.00 27.00 7.50
Phila.
☐ 116 Ray Demmitt 60.00 27.00 7.50
☐ 117 Josh Devore 60.00 27.00 7.50
Philadelphia
☐ 118 Josh Devore 60.00 27.00 7.50
Chillicothe
☐ 119 Mike Donlin 80.00 36.00 10.00
New York Nat.
☐ 120 Mike Donlin 140.00 65.00 17.50
.300 Batter
7 Years
☐ 121 Bill Donovan 60.00 27.00 7.50
☐ 122 Mickey Doolan (batting) 60.00 27.00 7.50
Baltimore Fed.
☐ 123 Mickey Doolan (fielding) 60.00 27.00 7.50
Chicago Nat.
☐ 124 Mickey Doolan (batting) 60.00 27.00 7.50
Baltimore Fed.
☐ 125 Mickey Doolan (fielding) 60.00 27.00 7.50
Chicago Nat.
☐ 126 Tom Downey 60.00 27.00 7.50
☐ 127 Larry Doyle 80.00 36.00 10.00
batting
☐ 128 Larry Doyle 80.00 36.00 10.00
portrait
☐ 129 Jean Dubuc 60.00 27.00 7.50
☐ 130 Jack Dunn 60.00 27.00 7.50
☐ 131 Kid Elberfeld 120.00 55.00 15.00
Brooklyn
☐ 132 Kid Elberfeld 120.00 55.00 15.00
Chattanooga
☐ 133 Steve Evans 60.00 27.00 7.50
☐ 134 Johnny Evers 120.00 55.00 15.00
☐ 135 Russ Ford 60.00 27.00 7.50
☐ 136 Art Fromme 60.00 27.00 7.50
☐ 137 Chick Gandil 120.00 55.00 15.00
Cleveland
☐ 138 Chick Gandil 120.00 55.00 15.00
Washington

☐ 139 Rube Geyer 60.00 27.00 7.50
☐ 140 Clark Griffith 120.00 55.00 15.00
☐ 141 Bob Groom 60.00 27.00 7.50
☐ 142 Buck Herzog 60.00 27.00 7.50
with B
☐ 143 Buck Herzog 60.00 27.00 7.50
without B
☐ 144 Doc Hoblitzell 60.00 27.00 7.50
Boston Amer.
☐ 145 Doc Hoblitzell 60.00 27.00 7.50
Boston Fed.
☐ 146 Doc Hoblitzell 60.00 27.00 7.50
Cincinnati
☐ 147 Solly Hofman 60.00 27.00 7.50
☐ 148 Danny Hofmann 60.00 27.00 7.50
☐ 149 Miller Huggins 120.00 55.00 15.00
portrait
☐ 150 Miller Huggins 120.00 55.00 15.00
yelling
☐ 151 John Hummel 60.00 27.00 7.50
Brooklyn
☐ 152 John Hummel 60.00 27.00 7.50
Brooklyn Nat.
☐ 153 Hugh Jennings 120.00 55.00 15.00
yelling
☐ 154 Hugh Jennings 120.00 55.00 15.00
dancing
☐ 155 Walter Johnson 350.00 160.00 45.00
☐ 156 Tim Jordan 60.00 27.00 7.50
Ft. Worth
☐ 157 Tim Jordan 60.00 27.00 7.50
Toronto
☐ 158 Joe Kelley 120.00 55.00 15.00
New York Amer.
☐ 159 Joe Kelley 120.00 55.00 15.00
Toronto
☐ 160 Otto Knabe 60.00 27.00 7.50
☐ 161 Ed Konetchy 60.00 27.00 7.50
Boston Nat.
☐ 162 Ed Konetchy 60.00 27.00 7.50
Pittsburgh Fed.
☐ 163 Ed Konetchy 60.00 27.00 7.50
Pittsburgh Nat.
☐ 164 Harry Krause 60.00 27.00 7.50
☐ 165 Nap Lajoie 225.00 100.00 28.00
Cleveland
☐ 166 Nap Lajoie 225.00 100.00 28.00
Philadelphia
☐ 167 Nap Lajoie 225.00 100.00 28.00
Phila.
☐ 168 Tommy Leach 60.00 27.00 7.50
Chicago
☐ 169 Tommy Leach 60.00 27.00 7.50
Cincinnati
☐ 170 Tommy Leach 60.00 27.00 7.50
Rochester
☐ 171 Ed Lennox 60.00 27.00 7.50
☐ 172 Sherry Magee 60.00 27.00 7.50
Boston
☐ 173 Sherry Magee 60.00 27.00 7.50
Philadelphia
☐ 174 Sherry Magee 60.00 27.00 7.50
Phila.
☐ 175 Rube Marquard 120.00 55.00 15.00
Brooklyn
pitching
☐ 176 Rube Marquard 120.00 55.00 15.00
Brooklyn
portrait
☐ 177 Rube Marquard 120.00 55.00 15.00
New York
pitching
☐ 178 Rube Marquard 120.00 55.00 15.00
New York
portrait
☐ 179 Christy Mathewson 350.00 160.00 45.00
☐ 180 John McGraw 140.00 65.00 17.50
portrait
☐ 181 John McGraw 140.00 65.00 17.50
glove on hip
☐ 182 Larry McLean 60.00 27.00 7.50
☐ 183 George McQuillan 60.00 27.00 7.50
Philadelphia
☐ 184 George McQuillan 60.00 27.00 7.50
Phila.
☐ 185 George McQuillan 60.00 27.00 7.50
Pittsburgh
☐ 186 Fred Merkle 80.00 36.00 10.00
☐ 187 Chief Meyers 60.00 27.00 7.50
Brooklyn
T206-249 pose
☐ 188 Chief Meyers 60.00 27.00 7.50
Brooklyn
fielding
☐ 189 Chief Meyers 60.00 27.00 7.50
New York
T206-249 pose
☐ 190 Chief Meyers 60.00 27.00 7.50
New York
fielding
☐ 191 Dots Miller 60.00 27.00 7.50
☐ 192 Michael Mitchell 60.00 27.00 7.50
☐ 193 Mike Mowrey 60.00 27.00 7.50
Brooklyn
☐ 194 Mike Mowrey 60.00 27.00 7.50
Pittsburgh Fed.
☐ 195 Mike Mowrey 60.00 27.00 7.50
Pittsburgh Nat.
☐ 196 George Mullin 60.00 27.00 7.50
Indianapolis
☐ 197 George Mullin 60.00 27.00 7.50
Newark
☐ 198 Danny Murphy 60.00 27.00 7.50
☐ 199 Red Murray 60.00 27.00 7.50
Chicago
☐ 200 Red Murray 60.00 27.00 7.50
Kansas City
☐ 201 Red Murray 60.00 27.00 7.50
New York
☐ 202 Tom Needham 60.00 27.00 7.50
☐ 203 Rebel Oakes 60.00 27.00 7.50
☐ 204 Rube Oldring 80.00 36.00 10.00
Philadelphia
☐ 205 Rube Oldring 80.00 36.00 10.00
Phila.
☐ 206 Dode Paskert 60.00 27.00 7.50
Philadelphia
☐ 207 Dode Paskert 60.00 27.00 7.50
Phila.
☐ 208 William Purtell 60.00 27.00 7.50
☐ 209 Jack Quinn 60.00 27.00 7.50
Baltimore
☐ 210 Jack Quinn 60.00 27.00 7.50
Vernon
☐ 211 Ed Reulbach 60.00 27.00 7.50
Brooklyn Fed.
☐ 212 Ed Reulbach 60.00 27.00 7.50
Pittsburgh
☐ 213 Ed Reulbach 60.00 27.00 7.50
Brooklyn Nat.
☐ 214 Nap Rucker 60.00 27.00 7.50
Brooklyn
☐ 215 Nap Rucker 60.00 27.00 7.50
Brooklyn Nat.
☐ 216 Dick Rudolph 60.00 27.00 7.50
☐ 217 Germany Schaefer 60.00 27.00 7.50
Kansas City
☐ 218 Germany Schaefer 60.00 27.00 7.50
New York
☐ 219 Germany Schaefer 60.00 27.00 7.50
Washington
☐ 220 Admiral Schlei 60.00 27.00 7.50
portrait
☐ 221 Admiral Schlei 60.00 27.00 7.50
batting
☐ 222 Boss Schmidt 60.00 27.00 7.50
☐ 223 Frank Schulte 60.00 27.00 7.50
☐ 224 Nig Smith 60.00 27.00 7.50
☐ 225 Tris Speaker 225.00 100.00 28.00
☐ 226 George Stovall 60.00 27.00 7.50
☐ 227 Gabby Street 60.00 27.00 7.50
catching
☐ 228 Gabby Street 60.00 27.00 7.50
portrait
☐ 229 Ed Summers 60.00 27.00 7.50
☐ 230 Ed Sweeney 80.00 36.00 10.00
Boston
☐ 231 Ed Sweeney 80.00 36.00 10.00
Chicago
☐ 232 Ed Sweeney 80.00 36.00 10.00
New York
☐ 233 Ed Sweeney 80.00 36.00 10.00
Richmond
☐ 234 Chester Thomas 60.00 27.00 7.50
Philadelphia
☐ 235 Chester Thomas 60.00 27.00 7.50
Phila.
☐ 236 Joe Tinker 120.00 55.00 15.00
Chicago Fed.
bat on shoulder
☐ 237 Joe Tinker 120.00 55.00 15.00
Chicago Fed.
swinging
☐ 238 Joe Tinker 120.00 55.00 15.00
Chicago Nat.
bat on shoulder
☐ 239 Joe Tinker 120.00 55.00 15.00
Chicago Nat.
swinging
☐ 240 Honus Wagner 250.00 110.00 31.00
☐ 241 Jack Warhop 60.00 27.00 7.50
New York
☐ 242 Jack Warhop 60.00 27.00 7.50
St. Louis
☐ 243 Zack Wheat 120.00 55.00 15.00
Brooklyn
☐ 244 Zack Wheat 120.00 55.00 15.00
Brooklyn Nat.
☐ 245 Kaiser Wilhelm 60.00 27.00 7.50
☐ 246 Ed Willett 60.00 27.00 7.50
Memphis
☐ 247 Ed Willett 60.00 27.00 7.50
St. Louis
☐ 248 Owen Wilson 60.00 27.00 7.50
St. Louis
☐ 249 Hooks Wiltse 60.00 27.00 7.50
Brooklyn Fed.
pitching
☐ 250 Hooks Wiltse 60.00 27.00 7.50
Brooklyn Fed.
portrait

☐ 251 Hooks Wiltse 60.00 27.00 7.50
Jersey City
pitching
☐ 252 Hooks Wiltse 60.00 27.00 7.50
Jersey City
portrait
☐ 253 Hooks Wiltse 60.00 27.00 7.50
New York
pitching
☐ 254 Hooks Wiltse 60.00 27.00 7.50
New York
portrait
☐ 255 Heinie Zimmerman 60.00 27.00 7.50
☐ 256 Red Ames 60.00 27.00 7.50
☐ 257 Frank Baker 120.00 55.00 15.00
New York Amer.
☐ 258 Chief Bender 120.00 55.00 15.00
☐ 259 Chief Bender 120.00 55.00 15.00
☐ 260 Roger Bresnahan 120.00 55.00 15.00
Toledo
☐ 261 Al Bridwell 60.00 27.00 7.50
☐ 262 Mordecai Brown 60.00 27.00 7.50
☐ 263 Bobby Byrne 60.00 27.00 7.50
St.Louis Nat.
☐ 264 Frank Chance 140.00 65.00 17.50
☐ 265 Frank Chance 140.00 65.00 17.50
☐ 266 Hal Chase 120.00 55.00 15.00
N.Y. Nat.
☐ 267 Hal Chase 120.00 55.00 15.00
N.Y. Nat.
☐ 268 Hal Chase 120.00 55.00 15.00
N.Y. Nat.
☐ 269 Ty Cobb 2000.00 900.00 250.00
Detroit
☐ 270 Ty Cobb 2000.00 900.00 250.00
Detroit
☐ 271 Eddie Collins 120.00 55.00 15.00
Chicago Amer.
☐ 272 Sam Crawford 120.00 55.00 15.00
☐ 273 Harry Davis 60.00 27.00 7.50
Philadelphia Amer.
☐ 274 Mike Donlin 80.00 36.00 10.00
☐ 275 Bill Donovan 60.00 27.00 7.50
Jersey City
☐ 276 Mickey Doolan 60.00 27.00 7.50
Reading
☐ 277 Mickey Doolan 60.00 27.00 7.50
Reading
☐ 278 Larry Doyle 80.00 36.00 10.00
N.Y. Nat.
☐ 279 Larry Doyle 80.00 36.00 10.00
N.Y. Nat.
☐ 280 Jean Dubuc 60.00 27.00 7.50
N.Y. Nat.
☐ 281 Jack Dunn 60.00 27.00 7.50
Baltimore
☐ 282 Kid Elberfeld 60.00 27.00 7.50
☐ 283 Johnny Evers 120.00 55.00 15.00
☐ 284 Chick Gandil 120.00 55.00 15.00
Chicago Amer.
☐ 285 Clark Griffith 120.00 55.00 15.00
Washington
☐ 286 Buck Herzog 60.00 27.00 7.50
Boston Nat.
☐ 287 Doc Hoblitzell 60.00 27.00 7.50
Boston Amer.
☐ 288 Miller Huggins 120.00 55.00 15.00
N.Y. Amer.
☐ 289 Miller Huggins 120.00 55.00 15.00
N.Y. Amer.
☐ 290 John Hummel 60.00 27.00 7.50
☐ 291 Hugh Jennings MG 120.00 55.00 15.00
Detroit
☐ 292 Hugh Jennings MG 120.00 55.00 15.00
Detroit
☐ 293 Walter Johnson 350.00 160.00 45.00
Washington
☐ 294 Tim Jordan 60.00 27.00 7.50
☐ 295 Joe Kelley 120.00 55.00 15.00
☐ 296 Ed Konetchy 60.00 27.00 7.50
Brooklyn
☐ 297 Larry Lajoie 225.00 100.00 28.00
☐ 298 Sherry Magee 60.00 27.00 7.50
Cincinnati
☐ 299 Rube Marquard 120.00 55.00 15.00
Brooklyn
☐ 300 Rube Marquard 120.00 55.00 15.00
Brooklyn
☐ 301 Christy Mathewson 350.00 160.00 45.00
New York Nat.
☐ 302 John McGraw MG 140.00 65.00 17.50
New York Nat.
☐ 303 John McGraw MG 140.00 65.00 17.50
New York Nat.
☐ 304 George McQuillan 60.00 27.00 7.50
Boston Nat.
☐ 305 Fred Merkle 80.00 36.00 10.00
Chicago Nat.
☐ 306 Dots Miller 60.00 27.00 7.50
St. Louis Nat.
☐ 307 Mike Mowrey 60.00 27.00 7.50
Brooklyn
☐ 308 Hy Myers 60.00 27.00 7.50
New Haven
☐ 309 Hy Myers 60.00 27.00 7.50

	EX-MT	VG-E	GOOD
Brooklyn			
☐ 310 Dode Paskert	60.00	27.00	7.50
Chicago Nat.			
☐ 311 Jack Quinn	60.00	27.00	7.50
N.Y. Nat.			
☐ 312 Ed Reulbach	80.00	36.00	10.00
☐ 313 Nap Rucker	80.00	36.00	10.00
☐ 314 Dick Rudolph	60.00	27.00	7.50
Boston Nat.			
☐ 315 Germany Schaeffer	60.00	27.00	7.50
☐ 316 Frank Schulte	60.00	27.00	7.50
Binghamton			
☐ 317 Tris Speaker	225.00	100.00	28.00
Cleveland			
☐ 318 Gabby Street	60.00	27.00	7.50
Nashville			
☐ 319 Gabby Street	60.00	27.00	7.50
Nashville			
☐ 320 Ed Sweeney	80.00	36.00	10.00
Pittsburg			
☐ 321 Ira Thomas	60.00	27.00	7.50
☐ 322 Joe Tinker	120.00	55.00	15.00
☐ 323 Zack Wheat	120.00	55.00	15.00
Brooklyn			
☐ 324 Hooks Wiltse	60.00	27.00	7.50
☐ 325 Heinie Zimmerman	60.00	27.00	7.50
N.Y. Nat.			

1914 Cracker Jack E145-1

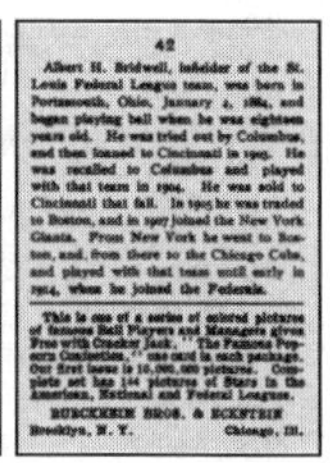
42

Albert H. Bridwell, infielder of the St. Louis Federal League team, was born in Portsmouth, Ohio, January 4, [illegible], and began playing ball when he was eighteen years old. He was tried out by Columbus, and then loaned to Cincinnati in [illegible]. He was recalled to Columbus and played with that team in [illegible]. He was sold to Cincinnati that fall. In [illegible] he was traded to Boston, and in [illegible] joined the New York Giants. From New York he went to Boston, and from there to the Chicago Cubs, and played with that team until early in [illegible], when he joined the Federals.

This is one of a series of colored pictures of famous Ball Players and Managers given Free with Cracker Jack, "The Famous Popcorn Confection," one card in each package. Our first issue is [illegible] pictures. Complete set has 144 pictures of Stars in the American, National and Federal Leagues.

RUECKHEIM BROS. & ECKSTEIN

Brooklyn, N. Y. Chicago, Ill.

The cards in this 144-card set measure approximately 2 1/4" by 3". This "Series of colored pictures of Famous Ball Players and Managers" was issued in packages of Cracker Jack in 1914. The cards have tinted photos set against red backgrounds and many are found with caramel stains. The set also contains Federal League players. The company claims to have printed 15 million cards. The 1914 series can be distinguished from the 1915 issue by the advertising found on the back of the cards. Team names are included for some players to show differences between the 1914 and 1915 issue.

	EX-MT	VG-E	GOOD
COMPLETE SET (144)	45000.00	20200.00	5600.00
COMMON CARD (1-144)	150.00	70.00	19.00
☐ 1 Otto Knabe	200.00	90.00	25.00
☐ 2 Frank Baker	350.00	160.00	45.00
☐ 3 Joe Tinker	350.00	160.00	45.00
☐ 4 Larry Doyle	150.00	70.00	19.00
☐ 5 Ward Miller	150.00	70.00	19.00
☐ 6 Eddie Plank	600.00	275.00	75.00
Phila. AL			
☐ 7 Eddie Collins	450.00	200.00	55.00
Phila. AL			
☐ 8 Rube Oldring	150.00	70.00	19.00
☐ 9 Artie Hoffman	150.00	70.00	19.00
☐ 10 John McInnis	150.00	70.00	19.00
☐ 11 George Stovall	150.00	70.00	19.00
☐ 12 Connie Mack MG	500.00	220.00	60.00
☐ 13 Art Wilson	150.00	70.00	19.00
☐ 14 Sam Crawford	300.00	135.00	38.00
☐ 15 Reb Russell	150.00	70.00	19.00
☐ 16 Howie Camnitz	150.00	70.00	19.00
☐ 17 Roger Bresnahan	350.00	160.00	45.00
Catcher			
☐ 18 Johnny Evers	350.00	160.00	45.00
☐ 19 Chief Bender	450.00	200.00	55.00
Phila. AL			
☐ 20 Cy Falkenberg	150.00	70.00	19.00
☐ 21 Heinie Zimmerman	150.00	70.00	19.00
☐ 22 Joe Wood	300.00	135.00	38.00
☐ 23 Charles Comiskey OWN	300.00	135.00	38.00
☐ 24 George Mullen	150.00	70.00	19.00
☐ 25 Michael Simon	150.00	70.00	19.00
☐ 26 James Scott	150.00	70.00	19.00
☐ 27 Bill Carrigan	150.00	70.00	19.00
☐ 28 Jack Barry	150.00	70.00	19.00
☐ 29 Vean Gregg	175.00	80.00	22.00
Cleveland			
☐ 30 Ty Cobb	6000.00	2700.00	750.00
☐ 31 Heinie Wagner	150.00	70.00	19.00
☐ 32 Mordecai Brown	300.00	135.00	38.00
☐ 33 Amos Strunk	150.00	70.00	19.00
☐ 34 Ira Thomas	150.00	70.00	19.00
☐ 35 Harry Hooper	300.00	135.00	38.00
☐ 36 Ed Walsh	300.00	135.00	38.00
☐ 37 Grover Alexander	800.00	350.00	100.00
☐ 38 Red Dooin	175.00	80.00	22.00
Phila. NL			
☐ 39 Chick Gandil	325.00	145.00	40.00
☐ 40 Jimmy Austin	175.00	80.00	22.00
St.L. AL			
☐ 41 Tommy Leach	150.00	70.00	19.00
☐ 42 Al Bridwell	150.00	70.00	19.00
☐ 43 Rube Marquard	350.00	160.00	45.00
NY NL			
☐ 44 Charles Tesreau	150.00	70.00	19.00
☐ 45 Fred Luderus	150.00	70.00	19.00
☐ 46 Bob Groom	150.00	70.00	19.00
☐ 47 Josh Devore	175.00	80.00	22.00
Phila. NL			
☐ 48 Harry Lord	250.00	110.00	31.00
☐ 49 John Miller	150.00	70.00	19.00
☐ 50 John Hummell	150.00	70.00	19.00
☐ 51 Nap Rucker	150.00	70.00	19.00
☐ 52 Zach Wheat	350.00	160.00	45.00
☐ 53 Otto Miller	150.00	70.00	19.00
☐ 54 Marty O'Toole	150.00	70.00	19.00
☐ 55 Dick Hoblitzel	175.00	80.00	22.00
Cinc.			
☐ 56 Clyde Milan	150.00	70.00	19.00
☐ 57 Walter Johnson	1600.00	700.00	200.00
☐ 58 Wally Schang	150.00	70.00	19.00
☐ 59 Harry Gessler	150.00	70.00	19.00
☐ 60 Rollie Zeider	250.00	110.00	31.00
☐ 61 Ray Schalk	300.00	135.00	38.00
☐ 62 Jay Cashion	300.00	135.00	38.00
☐ 63 Babe Adams	150.00	70.00	19.00
☐ 64 Jimmy Archer	150.00	70.00	19.00
☐ 65 Tris Speaker	700.00	325.00	90.00
☐ 66 Napoleon Lajoie	800.00	350.00	100.00
Cleve.			
☐ 67 Otis Crandall	150.00	70.00	19.00
☐ 68 Honus Wagner	1800.00	800.00	220.00
☐ 69 John McGraw	450.00	200.00	55.00
☐ 70 Fred Clarke	300.00	135.00	38.00
☐ 71 Chief Meyers	150.00	70.00	19.00
☐ 72 John Boehling	150.00	70.00	19.00
☐ 73 Max Carey	300.00	135.00	38.00
☐ 74 Frank Owens	150.00	70.00	19.00
☐ 75 Miller Huggins	300.00	135.00	38.00
☐ 76 Claude Hendrix	150.00	70.00	19.00
☐ 77 Hugh Jennings MG	300.00	135.00	38.00
☐ 78 Fred Merkle	175.00	80.00	22.00
☐ 79 Ping Bodie	150.00	70.00	19.00
☐ 80 Ed Ruelbach	150.00	70.00	19.00
☐ 81 Jim C. Delehanty	150.00	70.00	19.00
☐ 82 Gavvy Cravath	175.00	80.00	22.00
☐ 83 Russ Ford	150.00	70.00	19.00
☐ 84 Elmer E. Knetzer	150.00	70.00	19.00
☐ 85 Buck Herzog	150.00	70.00	19.00
☐ 86 Burt Shotton	150.00	70.00	19.00
☐ 87 Forrest Cady	150.00	70.00	19.00
☐ 88 Christy Mathewson	3000.00	1350.00	375.00
Pitching			
☐ 89 Lawrence Cheney	150.00	70.00	19.00
☐ 90 Frank Smith	150.00	70.00	19.00
☐ 91 Roger Peckinpaugh	150.00	70.00	19.00
☐ 92 Al Demaree N.Y. NL	175.00	80.00	22.00
☐ 93 Del Pratt	250.00	110.00	31.00
Throwing			
☐ 94 Eddie Cicotte	300.00	135.00	38.00
☐ 95 Ray Keating	150.00	70.00	19.00
☐ 96 Beals Becker	150.00	70.00	19.00
☐ 97 John(Rube) Benton	150.00	70.00	19.00
☐ 98 Frank LaPorte	150.00	70.00	19.00
☐ 99 Frank Chance	1500.00	700.00	190.00
☐ 100 Thomas Seaton	150.00	70.00	19.00
☐ 101 Frank Schulte	150.00	70.00	19.00
☐ 102 Ray Fisher	150.00	70.00	19.00
☐ 103 Joe Jackson	8000.00	3600.00	1000.00
☐ 104 Vic Saier	150.00	70.00	19.00
☐ 105 James Lavender	150.00	70.00	19.00
☐ 106 Joe Birmingham	150.00	70.00	19.00
☐ 107 Tom Downey	150.00	70.00	19.00
☐ 108 Sherwood Magee	175.00	80.00	22.00
Phila. NL			
☐ 109 Fred Blanding	150.00	70.00	19.00
☐ 110 Bob Bescher	150.00	70.00	19.00
☐ 111 Jim Callahan	250.00	110.00	31.00
☐ 112 Ed Sweeney	150.00	70.00	19.00
☐ 113 George Suggs	150.00	70.00	19.00
☐ 114 Geo.J. Moriarty	150.00	70.00	19.00
☐ 115 Addison Brennan	150.00	70.00	19.00
☐ 116 Rollie Zeider	150.00	70.00	19.00
☐ 117 Ted Easterly	150.00	70.00	19.00
☐ 118 Ed Konetchy	175.00	80.00	22.00
Pittsburgh			
☐ 119 George Perring	150.00	70.00	19.00
☐ 120 Mike Doolan	150.00	70.00	19.00
☐ 121 Hub Perdue	175.00	80.00	22.00
Boston NL			
☐ 122 Owen Bush	150.00	70.00	19.00
☐ 123 Slim Sallee	150.00	70.00	19.00
☐ 124 Earl Moore	150.00	70.00	19.00
☐ 125 Bert Niehoff	175.00	80.00	22.00
☐ 126 Walter Blair	150.00	70.00	19.00
☐ 127 Butch Schmidt	150.00	70.00	19.00
☐ 128 Steve Evans	150.00	70.00	19.00
☐ 129 Ray Caldwell	150.00	70.00	19.00
☐ 130 Ivy Wingo	150.00	70.00	19.00
☐ 131 George Baumgardner	150.00	70.00	19.00
☐ 132 Les Nunamaker	150.00	70.00	19.00
☐ 133 Branch Rickey	450.00	200.00	55.00
☐ 134 Armando Marsans	175.00	80.00	22.00
Cincinnati			
☐ 135 Bill Killefer	150.00	70.00	19.00
☐ 136 Rabbit Maranville	300.00	135.00	38.00
☐ 137 William Rariden	150.00	70.00	19.00
☐ 138 Hank Gowdy	150.00	70.00	19.00
☐ 139 Rebel Oakes	150.00	70.00	19.00
☐ 140 Danny Murphy	150.00	70.00	19.00
☐ 141 Cy Barger	150.00	70.00	19.00
☐ 142 Eugene Packard	150.00	70.00	19.00
☐ 143 Jake Daubert	150.00	70.00	19.00
☐ 144 James C. Walsh	175.00	80.00	22.00

1915 Cracker Jack E145-2.

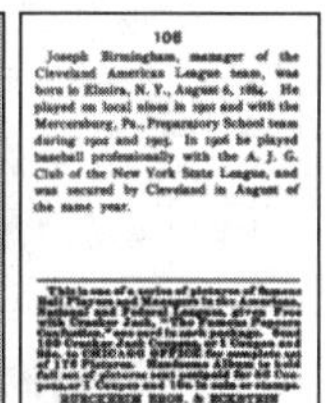
106

Joseph Birmingham, manager of the Cleveland American League team, was born in Elmira, N. Y., August 6, [illegible]. He played on local nines in [illegible] and with the Mercersburg, Pa., Preparatory School team during [illegible] and [illegible]. In [illegible] he played baseball professionally with the A. J. G. Club of the New York State League, and was secured by Cleveland in August of the same year.

[illegible]

RUECKHEIM BROS. & ECKSTEIN

Brooklyn, N. Y. Chicago, Ill.

The cards in this 176-card set measure approximately 2 1/4" by 3". When turned over in a lateral motion, a 1915 "series of 176" Cracker Jack card shows the back printing upside-down. Cards were available in boxes of Cracker Jack or from the company for "100 Cracker Jack coupons, or one coupon and 25 cents." An album was available for "50 coupons or one coupon and 10 cents." Because of this send-in offer, the 1915 Cracker Jack cards are noticeably easier to find than the 1914 Cracker Jack cards, although obviously neither set is plentiful. The set essentially duplicates E145-1 (1914 Cracker Jack) except for some additional cards and new poses. Players in the Federal League are indicated by FED in the checklist below.

	EX-MT	VG-E	GOOD
COMPLETE SET (176)	35000.00	15800.00	4400.00
COMMON CARD (1-144)	100.00	45.00	12.50
COMMON CARD (145-176)	125.00	55.00	15.50
☐ 1 Otto Knabe	175.00	80.00	22.00
☐ 2 Frank Baker	300.00	135.00	38.00
☐ 3 Joe Tinker	300.00	135.00	38.00
☐ 4 Larry Doyle	110.00	50.00	14.00
☐ 5 Ward Miller	100.00	45.00	12.50
☐ 6 Eddie Plank	450.00	200.00	55.00
St.L. FED			
☐ 7 Eddie Collins	350.00	160.00	45.00
Chicago AL			
☐ 8 Rube Oldring	100.00	45.00	12.50
☐ 9 Artie Hoffman	100.00	45.00	12.50
☐ 10 John McInnis	100.00	45.00	12.50
☐ 11 George Stovall	100.00	45.00	12.50
☐ 12 Connie Mack MG	350.00	160.00	45.00
☐ 13 Art Wilson	100.00	45.00	12.50
☐ 14 Sam Crawford	250.00	110.00	31.00
☐ 15 Reb Russell	100.00	45.00	12.50
☐ 16 Howie Camnitz	100.00	45.00	12.50
☐ 17 Roger Bresnahan	250.00	110.00	31.00
☐ 18 Johnny Evers	300.00	135.00	38.00
☐ 19 Chief Bender	350.00	160.00	45.00
Baltimore FED			
☐ 20 Cy Falkenberg	100.00	45.00	12.50
☐ 21 Heinie Zimmerman	100.00	45.00	12.50
☐ 22 Joe Wood	250.00	110.00	31.00
☐ 23 Charles Comiskey OWN	250.00	110.00	31.00
☐ 24 George Mullen	100.00	45.00	12.50
☐ 25 Michael Simon	100.00	45.00	12.50
☐ 26 James Scott	100.00	45.00	12.50
☐ 27 Bill Carrigan	100.00	45.00	12.50
☐ 28 Jack Barry	100.00	45.00	12.50
☐ 29 Vean Gregg	125.00	55.00	15.50
Boston AL			
☐ 30 Ty Cobb	4500.00	2000.00	550.00
☐ 31 Heinie Wagner	100.00	45.00	12.50
☐ 32 Mordecai Brown	250.00	110.00	31.00
☐ 33 Amos Strunk	100.00	45.00	12.50
☐ 34 Ira Thomas	100.00	45.00	12.50
☐ 35 Harry Hooper	250.00	110.00	31.00
☐ 36 Ed Walsh	250.00	110.00	31.00
☐ 37 Grover C. Alexander	600.00	275.00	75.00
☐ 38 Red Dooin	125.00	55.00	15.50
Cincinnati			
☐ 39 Chick Gandil	275.00	125.00	34.00
☐ 40 Jimmy Austin	125.00	55.00	15.50
Pitts. FED			
☐ 41 Tommy Leach	100.00	45.00	12.50
☐ 42 Al Bridwell	100.00	45.00	12.50
☐ 43 Rube Marquard	350.00	160.00	45.00
Brooklyn FED			
☐ 44 Charles(Jeff) Tesreau	100.00	45.00	12.50
☐ 45 Fred Luderus	100.00	45.00	12.50
☐ 46 Bob Groom	100.00	45.00	12.50
☐ 47 Josh Devore	125.00	55.00	15.50
Boston NL			
☐ 48 Steve O'Neill	125.00	55.00	15.50
☐ 49 John Miller	100.00	45.00	12.50
☐ 50 John Hummell	100.00	45.00	12.50
☐ 51 Nap Rucker	110.00	50.00	14.00
☐ 52 Zach Wheat	300.00	135.00	38.00
☐ 53 Otto Miller	100.00	45.00	12.50
☐ 54 Marty O'Toole	100.00	45.00	12.50
☐ 55 Dick Hoblitzel	125.00	55.00	15.50
Boston AL			
☐ 56 Clyde Milan	110.00	50.00	14.00
☐ 57 Walter Johnson	1200.00	550.00	150.00
☐ 58 Wally Schang	110.00	50.00	14.00
☐ 59 Harry Gessler	100.00	45.00	12.50
☐ 60 Oscar Dugey	125.00	55.00	15.50
☐ 61 Ray Schalk	250.00	110.00	31.00
☐ 62 Willie Mitchell	125.00	55.00	15.50
☐ 63 Babe Adams	110.00	50.00	14.00
☐ 64 Jimmy Archer	100.00	45.00	12.50
☐ 65 Tris Speaker	500.00	220.00	60.00
☐ 66 Napoleon Lajoie	600.00	275.00	75.00
Phila. AL			
☐ 67 Otis Crandall	100.00	45.00	12.50
☐ 68 Honus Wagner	1400.00	650.00	180.00
☐ 69 John McGraw MG	300.00	135.00	38.00
☐ 70 Fred Clarke	250.00	110.00	31.00
☐ 71 Chief Meyers	100.00	45.00	12.50
☐ 72 John Boehling	100.00	45.00	12.50
☐ 73 Max Carey	250.00	110.00	31.00
☐ 74 Frank Owens	100.00	45.00	12.50
☐ 75 Miller Huggins	250.00	110.00	31.00
☐ 76 Claude Hendrix	100.00	45.00	12.50
☐ 77 Hugh Jennings MG	250.00	110.00	31.00
☐ 78 Fred Merkle	125.00	55.00	15.50
☐ 79 Ping Bodie	110.00	50.00	14.00
☐ 80 Ed Ruelbach	110.00	50.00	14.00
☐ 81 Jim C. Delehanty	110.00	50.00	14.00
☐ 82 Gavvy Cravath	125.00	55.00	15.50
☐ 83 Russ Ford	100.00	45.00	12.50
☐ 84 Elmer E. Knetzer	100.00	45.00	12.50
☐ 85 Buck Herzog	100.00	45.00	12.50
☐ 86 Burt Shotton	100.00	45.00	12.50
☐ 87 Forrest Cady	100.00	45.00	12.50
☐ 88 Christy Mathewson	1500.00	700.00	190.00
Portrait			
☐ 89 Lawrence Cheney	100.00	45.00	12.50
☐ 90 Frank Smith	100.00	45.00	12.50
☐ 91 Roger Peckinpaugh	110.00	50.00	14.00
☐ 92 Al Demaree	125.00	55.00	15.50
Phila. NL			
☐ 93 Del Pratt	175.00	80.00	22.00
Portrait			
☐ 94 Eddie Cicotte	250.00	110.00	31.00
☐ 95 Ray Keating	100.00	45.00	12.50
☐ 96 Beals Becker	100.00	45.00	12.50
☐ 97 John(Rube) Benton	100.00	45.00	12.50
☐ 98 Frank LaPorte	100.00	45.00	12.50
☐ 99 Hal Chase	300.00	135.00	38.00
☐ 100 Thomas Seaton	100.00	45.00	12.50
☐ 101 Frank Schulte	100.00	45.00	12.50
☐ 102 Ray Fisher	100.00	45.00	12.50
☐ 103 Joe Jackson	6500.00	2900.00	800.00
☐ 104 Vic Saier	100.00	45.00	12.50
☐ 105 James Lavender	100.00	45.00	12.50
☐ 106 Joe Birmingham	100.00	45.00	12.50
☐ 107 Thomas Downey	100.00	45.00	12.50
☐ 108 Sherwood Magee	125.00	55.00	15.50
Boston NL			
☐ 109 Fred Blanding	100.00	45.00	12.50
☐ 110 Bob Bescher	100.00	45.00	12.50
☐ 111 Herbie Moran	125.00	55.00	15.50
☐ 112 Ed Sweeney	100.00	45.00	12.50
☐ 113 George Suggs	100.00	45.00	12.50
☐ 114 Geo.J. Moriarty	110.00	50.00	14.00
☐ 115 Addison Brennan	100.00	45.00	12.50
☐ 116 Rollie Zeider	100.00	45.00	12.50
☐ 117 Ted Easterly	100.00	45.00	12.50
☐ 118 Ed Konetchy	125.00	55.00	15.50
Pitts. FED			
☐ 119 George Perring	100.00	45.00	12.50
☐ 120 Mike Doolan	100.00	45.00	12.50
☐ 121 Hub Perdue	125.00	55.00	15.50
St. Louis NL			
☐ 122 Owen Bush	100.00	45.00	12.50
☐ 123 Slim Sallee	100.00	45.00	12.50
☐ 124 Earl Moore	100.00	45.00	12.50
☐ 125 Bert Niehoff	125.00	55.00	15.50
Phila. NL			
☐ 126 Walter Blair	100.00	45.00	12.50
☐ 127 Butch Schmidt	100.00	45.00	12.50
☐ 128 Steve Evans	100.00	45.00	12.50
☐ 129 Ray Caldwell	100.00	45.00	12.50
☐ 130 Ivy Wingo	100.00	45.00	12.50
☐ 131 Geo. Baumgardner	100.00	45.00	12.50
☐ 132 Les Nunamaker	100.00	45.00	12.50
☐ 133 Branch Rickey	300.00	135.00	38.00
☐ 134 Armando Marsans	125.00	55.00	15.50
St.L. FED			
☐ 135 William Killefer	100.00	45.00	12.50
☐ 136 Rabbit Maranville	250.00	110.00	31.00
☐ 137 William Rariden	100.00	45.00	12.50
☐ 138 Hank Gowdy	100.00	45.00	12.50
☐ 139 Rebel Oakes	100.00	45.00	12.50
☐ 140 Danny Murphy	100.00	45.00	12.50
☐ 141 Cy Barger	100.00	45.00	12.50
☐ 142 Eugene Packard	100.00	45.00	12.50
☐ 143 Jake Daubert	100.00	45.00	12.50
☐ 144 James C. Walsh	100.00	45.00	12.50
☐ 145 Ted Cather	125.00	55.00	15.50
☐ 146 George Tyler	125.00	55.00	15.50
☐ 147 Lee Magee	125.00	55.00	15.50
☐ 148 Owen Wilson	125.00	55.00	15.50
☐ 149 Hal Janvrin	125.00	55.00	15.50
☐ 150 Doc Johnston	125.00	55.00	15.50
☐ 151 George Whitted	125.00	55.00	15.50

☐ 152 George McQuillen	125.00	55.00	15.50
☐ 153 Bill James	125.00	55.00	15.50
☐ 154 Dick Rudolph	125.00	55.00	15.50
☐ 155 Joe Connolly	125.00	55.00	15.50
☐ 156 Jean Dubuc	125.00	55.00	15.50
☐ 157 George Kaiserling	125.00	55.00	15.50
☐ 158 Fritz Maisel	125.00	55.00	15.50
☐ 159 Heinie Groh	135.00	60.00	17.00
☐ 160 Benny Kauff	125.00	55.00	15.50
☐ 161 Edd Roush	300.00	135.00	38.00
☐ 162 George Stallings MG	125.00	55.00	15.50
☐ 163 Bert Whaling	125.00	55.00	15.50
☐ 164 Bob Shawkey	135.00	60.00	17.00
☐ 165 Eddie Murphy	125.00	55.00	15.50
☐ 166 Joe Bush	135.00	60.00	17.00
☐ 167 Clark Griffith	300.00	135.00	38.00
☐ 168 Vin Campbell	125.00	55.00	15.50
☐ 169 Raymond Collins	125.00	55.00	15.50
☐ 170 Hans Lobert	125.00	55.00	15.50
☐ 171 Earl Hamilton	125.00	55.00	15.50
☐ 172 Erskine Mayer	125.00	55.00	15.50
☐ 173 Tilly Walker	125.00	55.00	15.50
☐ 174 Robert Veach	125.00	55.00	15.50
☐ 175 Joseph Benz	125.00	55.00	15.50
☐ 176 Jim Vaughn	175.00	80.00	22.00

1933 Cracker Jack Pins PR4

This 25-pin set is also known as the "PR4 Baseball Drawing Set" as the player portraits are actually line drawings. The pins measure approximately 13/16" in diameter. The pins are printed in gray and blue on a yellow background. The set was probably issued some time in the early thirties based on the selection of players in the set. Be careful not to get these pins wet as the inks are water soluble.

	EX-MT	VG-E	GOOD
COMPLETE SET (25)	500.00	220.00	60.00
COMMON CARD (1-25)	12.00	5.50	1.50
☐ 1 Charles Berry	12.00	5.50	1.50
☐ 2 Bill Cissell	12.00	5.50	1.50
☐ 3 Kiki Cuyler	20.00	9.00	2.50
☐ 4 Dizzy Dean	40.00	18.00	5.00
☐ 5 Wes Ferrell	15.00	6.75	1.85
☐ 6 Frankie Frisch	25.00	11.00	3.10
☐ 7 Lou Gehrig	100.00	45.00	12.50
☐ 8 Lefty Gomez	25.00	11.00	3.10
☐ 9 Goose Goslin	20.00	9.00	2.50
☐ 10 George Grantham	12.00	5.50	1.50
☐ 11 Charlie Grimm	15.00	6.75	1.85
☐ 12 Lefty Grove	25.00	11.00	3.10
☐ 13 Gabby Hartnett	20.00	9.00	2.50
☐ 14 Travis Jackson	20.00	9.00	2.50
☐ 15 Tony Lazzeri	20.00	9.00	2.50
☐ 16 Ted Lyons	20.00	9.00	2.50
☐ 17 Rabbit Maranville	20.00	9.00	2.50
☐ 18 Carl Reynolds	12.00	5.50	1.50
☐ 19 Red Ruffing	20.00	9.00	2.50
☐ 20 Al Simmons	20.00	9.00	2.50
☐ 21 Gus Suhr	12.00	5.50	1.50
☐ 22 Bill Terry	25.00	11.00	3.10
☐ 23 Dazzy Vance	20.00	9.00	2.50
☐ 24 Paul Waner	20.00	9.00	2.50
☐ 25 Lon Warneke	12.00	5.50	1.50

1982 Cracker Jack

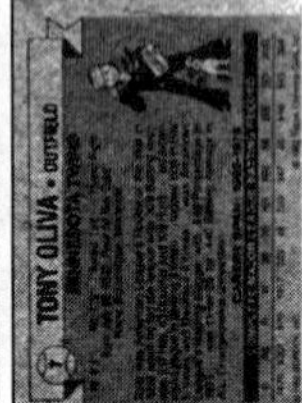

The cards in this 16-card set measure 2 1/2" by 3 1/2"; cards came in two sheets of eight cards, plus an advertising card with a title in the center, which measured approximately 7 1/2" by 10 1/2". Cracker Jack reentered the baseball card market for the first time since 1915 to promote the first "Old Timers Baseball Classic" held July 19, 1982. The color player photos have a Cracker Jack border and have either green (NL) or red (AL) frame lines and name panels. The Cracker Jack logo appears on both sides of each card, with AL players numbered 1-8 and NL players numbered 9-16. Of the 16 ballplayers pictured, five did not appear at the game. At first, the two sheets were available only through the mail but are now commonly found in hobby circles. The set was prepared for Cracker Jack by Topps. The prices below reflect individual card prices; the price for complete panels would be about the same as the sum of the card prices for those players on the panel due to the easy availability of uncut sheets.

	NRMT	VG-E	GOOD
COMPLETE SET (16)	10.00	4.50	1.25
COMMON CARD (1-16)	.25	.11	.03
☐ 1 Larry Doby	.50	.23	.06
☐ 2 Bob Feller	.75	.35	.09
☐ 3 Whitey Ford	1.00	.45	.12
☐ 4 Al Kaline	1.00	.45	.12
☐ 5 Harmon Killebrew	.50	.23	.06
☐ 6 Mickey Mantle	5.00	2.20	.60
☐ 7 Tony Oliva	.25	.11	.03
☐ 8 Brooks Robinson	1.00	.45	.12
☐ 9 Hank Aaron	3.00	1.35	.35
☐ 10 Ernie Banks	1.50	.70	.19
☐ 11 Ralph Kiner	.50	.23	.06
☐ 12 Ed Mathews	.50	.23	.06
☐ 13 Willie Mays	3.00	1.35	.35
☐ 14 Robin Roberts	.75	.35	.09
☐ 15 Duke Snider	1.50	.70	.19
☐ 16 Warren Spahn	.75	.35	.09

1993 Cracker Jack

Cracker Jack
BALL PLAYERS
JOE JACKSON, CLEVELAND - AMERICANS
2 of 24 JOE JACKSON
CLEVELAND-AMERICANS
1915 SET #103
Joseph Jackson, outfielder of the Cleveland American League team, was born in Brandon Mill, S. C., July 16, 1887. In 1905 and 1906 he played with various semi-professional teams in the vicinity of Greenville, S.C. He played with the Greenville Club of the South Carolina League in 1907, and joined the Philadelphia Athletics in 1908. He was farmed out to Savannah in 1909, and in 1910 was released to New Orleans. He joined the Cleveland team late in 1910.
© 1993 Borden Inc.
© 1993 MLB
© 1993 Jackson by Curtis Mngmt., Indpls., IN

To commemorate its 100th anniversary, Cracker Jack issued a 24-card set of miniature replicas of its 1915 set. One mini-card was inserted into each specially marked single, triple, and value-pack box. A mini-card holder album and a fact booklet that includes each player's lifetime stats were available for 6.95 through a mail-in offer. The album features room for 72 cards implying that Cracker Jack would like to continue this series into future years as well. Each minicard measures approximately 1 1/4" by 1 3/4" and features on its front a white-bordered color portrait of the player on a brick-colored background. The player's name, team, and league appear in the white margin below the picture and "Cracker Jack Ball Players" appears at the top. The white back displays the player's name, team, and league at the top, along with his card number from the 1915 set, followed below by a biography.

	MINT	NRMT	EXC
COMPLETE SET (24)	15.00	6.75	1.85
COMMON CARD (1-24)	.25	.11	.03
☐ 1 Ty Cobb	3.00	1.35	.35
☐ 2 Joe Jackson	3.00	1.35	.35
☐ 3 Honus Wagner	1.50	.70	.19
☐ 4 Christy Mathewson	1.25	.55	.16
☐ 5 Walter Johnson	1.50	.70	.19
☐ 6 Tris Speaker	1.00	.45	.12
☐ 7 Grover Alexander	1.00	.45	.12
☐ 8 Nap Lajoie	1.00	.45	.12
☐ 9 Rube Marquard	.50	.23	.06
☐ 10 Connie Mack MG	.75	.35	.09
☐ 11 Johnny Evers	.75	.35	.09
☐ 12 Branch Rickey	.50	.23	.06
☐ 13 Fred Clarke MG	.50	.23	.06
☐ 14 Harry Hooper	.50	.23	.06
☐ 15 Zack Wheat	.50	.23	.06
☐ 16 Joe Tinker	.50	.23	.06
☐ 17 Eddie Collins	1.00	.45	.12
☐ 18 Mordecai Brown	.50	.23	.06
☐ 19 Eddie Plank	.50	.23	.06
☐ 20 Rabbit Maranville	.50	.23	.06
☐ 21 John McGraw MG	.75	.35	.09
☐ 22 Miller Huggins	.50	.23	.06
☐ 23 Ed Walsh	.50	.23	.06
☐ 24 Joe Bush	.25	.11	.03

1976 Crane Discs

Produced by MSA, these discs were distributed by a wide variety of advertisers and can be found in various regions of the country. There are many different versions of this set, however, we are only pricing the Crane version. Several players changed teams during the printing of this set, however only the more commonly found version is included in the complete set price. These sets are unnumbered and sequenced in alphabetical order. Some of the other sponsors include Buchmans, Carousel (of which many different locations are known), Dairy Isle, Isaly, Orbakers, Red Barn, Safelon and Towne Club. All multiplier values are notated before.

	NRMT	VG-E	GOOD
COMPLETE SET (70)	20.00	9.00	2.50
COMMON DISC (1-70)	.10	.05	.01
*BLANKBACK DISCS: SAME VALUE AS BASIC DISCS			
BUCHMANS DISCS: 1.25X BASIC DISCS			
*CAROUSEL: 3X BASIC DISCS			
*DAIRY ISLE: 2X BASIC DISCS			
*ISALYS: SAME VALUE AS BASIC DISCS			
*ORBAKERS: 1.25X BASIC DISCS			
*RED BARN: 15X BASIC DISCS			
*SAFELON: 2X BASIC DISCS			
*TOWNE CLUB: 1.25X BASIC DISCS			
☐ 1 Hank Aaron	2.50	1.10	.30
☐ 2 Johnny Bench	1.50	.70	.19
☐ 3 Vida Blue	.20	.09	.03
☐ 4 Larry Bowa	.20	.09	.03
☐ 5 Lou Brock	1.50	.70	.19
☐ 6 Jeff Burroughs	.10	.05	.01
☐ 7 John Candelaria	.10	.05	.01
☐ 8 Jose Cardenal	.10	.05	.01
☐ 9 Rod Carew	1.50	.70	.19
☐ 10 Steve Carlton	1.50	.70	.19
☐ 11 Dave Cash	.10	.05	.01
☐ 12 Cesar Cedeno	.20	.09	.03
☐ 13 Ron Cey	.20	.09	.03
☐ 14 Carlton Fisk	2.00	.90	.25
☐ 15 Tito Fuentes	.10	.05	.01
☐ 16 Steve Garvey	1.00	.45	.12
☐ 17 Ken Griffey	.20	.09	.03
☐ 18 Don Gullett	.10	.05	.01
☐ 19 Willie Horton	.10	.05	.01
☐ 20 Al Hrabosky	.10	.05	.01
☐ 21 Catfish Hunter	1.50	.70	.19
☐ 22A Reggie Jackson Oakland Athletics	5.00	2.20	.60
☐ 22B Reggie Jackson Baltimore Orioles	1.50	.70	.19
☐ 23 Randy Jones	.10	.05	.01
☐ 24 Jim Kaat	.30	.14	.04
☐ 25 Don Kessinger	.10	.05	.01
☐ 26 Dave Kingman	.30	.14	.04
☐ 27 Jerry Koosman	.20	.09	.03
☐ 28 Mickey Lolich	.20	.09	.03
☐ 29 Greg Luzinski	.30	.14	.04
☐ 30 Fred Lynn	.30	.14	.04
☐ 31 Bill Madlock	.20	.09	.03
☐ 32A Carlos May Chicago White Sox	1.00	.45	.12
☐ 32B Carlos May New York Yankees	.10	.05	.01
☐ 33 John Mayberry	.10	.05	.01
☐ 34 Bake McBride	.10	.05	.01
☐ 35 Doc Medich	.10	.05	.01
☐ 36A Andy Messersmith Los Angeles Dodgers	1.00	.45	.12
☐ 36B Andy Messersmith Atlanta Braves	.10	.05	.01
☐ 37 Rick Monday	.10	.05	.01
☐ 38 John Montefusco	.10	.05	.01
☐ 39 Jerry Morales	.10	.05	.01
☐ 40 Joe Morgan	1.50	.70	.19
☐ 41 Thurman Munson	1.00	.45	.12
☐ 42 Bobby Murcer	.30	.14	.04
☐ 43 Al Oliver	.30	.14	.04
☐ 44 Jim Palmer	1.50	.70	.19
☐ 45 Dave Parker	.30	.14	.04
☐ 46 Tony Perez	1.00	.45	.12
☐ 47 Jerry Reuss	.10	.05	.01
☐ 48 Brooks Robinson	1.50	.70	.19
☐ 49 Frank Robinson	1.50	.70	.19
☐ 50 Steve Rogers	.10	.05	.01
☐ 51 Pete Rose	2.00	.90	.25
☐ 52 Nolan Ryan	4.00	1.80	.50
☐ 53 Manny Sanguillen	.10	.05	.01
☐ 54 Mike Schmidt	2.50	1.10	.30
☐ 55 Tom Seaver	2.50	1.10	.30
☐ 56 Ted Simmons	.30	.14	.04
☐ 57 Reggie Smith	.20	.09	.03
☐ 58 Willie Stargell	1.50	.70	.19
☐ 59 Rusty Staub	.30	.14	.04
☐ 60 Rennie Stennett	.10	.05	.01
☐ 61 Don Sutton	.75	.35	.09
☐ 62A Andre Thornton Chicago Cubs	1.00	.45	.12
☐ 62B Andre Thornton Montreal Expos	.10	.05	.01
☐ 63 Luis Tiant	.30	.14	.04
☐ 64 Joe Torre	.50	.23	.06
☐ 65 Mike Tyson	.10	.05	.01
☐ 66 Bob Watson	.30	.14	.04
☐ 67 Wilbur Wood	.10	.05	.01
☐ 68 Jimmy Wynn	.10	.05	.01
☐ 69 Carl Yastrzemski	1.50	.70	.19
☐ 70 Richie Zisk	.10	.05	.01

1977 MSA Discs

Produced under the auspices of Michael Scheter Associates (MSA) in 1977, the ballplayer on disc format was distributed by a number of different advertisers. There are many different back variations based on the particular area of distribution and sponsor. The discs are approximately 3 3/8" in diameter. Since these discs are unnumbered we have sequenced them in alphabetical order. Some of the other sponsors include Chilly Willie, Customized Sports, Dairy Isle, Detroit Ceasars, Dairy Isle, Holiday Inn, Saga, Wendy's and Zip'z.

	NRMT	VG-E	GOOD
COMPLETE SET (63)	25.00	11.00	3.10
COMMON DISC (1-63)	.25	.11	.03
*CHILLY WILLIE: SAME VALUE AS BASIC DISCS			
*CUSTOMIZED: 15X BASIC DISCS			
*DAIRY ISLE: 5X BASIC DISCS			
*DETROIT CAESARS: 5X BASIC DISCS			
*HOLIDAY INN: 10X BASIC DISCS			
*SAGA: 10X BASIC DISCS			
*WENDYS: 20X BASIC DISCS			
*ZIP'Z: 4X BASIC DISCS			
☐ 1 Sal Bando	.25	.11	.03
☐ 2 Buddy Bell	.50	.23	.06
☐ 3 Johnny Bench	4.00	1.80	.50
☐ 4 Lou Brock	3.00	1.35	.35
☐ 5 Larry Bowa	.50	.23	.06
☐ 6 Steve Braun	.25	.11	.03
☐ 7 George Brett	6.00	2.70	.75
☐ 8 Jeff Burroughs	.25	.11	.03
☐ 9 Campy Campaneris	.50	.23	.06
☐ 10 John Candelaria	.25	.11	.03
☐ 11 Jose Cardenal	.25	.11	.03
☐ 12 Rod Carew	3.00	1.35	.35
☐ 13 Steve Carlton	3.00	1.35	.35
☐ 14 Dave Cash	.25	.11	.03
☐ 15 Ron Cey	.50	.23	.06
☐ 16 Dave Concepcion	.75	.35	.09
☐ 17 Dennis Eckersley	2.00	.90	.25
☐ 18 Mark Fidrych	2.00	.90	.25
☐ 19 Rollie Fingers	2.00	.90	.25
☐ 20 Carlton Fisk	3.00	1.35	.35
☐ 21 George Foster	.75	.35	.09
☐ 22 Wayne Garland	.25	.11	.03
☐ 23 Ralph Garr	.50	.23	.06
☐ 24 Cesar Geronimo	.25	.11	.03
☐ 25 Ken Griffey	.75	.35	.09
☐ 26 Don Gullett	.25	.11	.03
☐ 27 Mike Hargrove	.50	.23	.06
☐ 28 Al Hrabosky	.25	.11	.03
☐ 29 Catfish Hunter	2.00	.90	.25
☐ 30 Reggie Jackson	4.00	1.80	.50
☐ 31 Randy Jones	.25	.11	.03
☐ 32 Dave Kingman	1.00	.45	.12
☐ 33 Jerry Koosman	.50	.23	.06
☐ 34 Dave LaRoche	.25	.11	.03
☐ 35 Greg Luzinski	.75	.35	.09
☐ 36 Fred Lynn	.50	.23	.06
☐ 37 Rick Manning	.25	.11	.03
☐ 38 Jon Matlack	.25	.11	.03
☐ 39 John Mayberry	.25	.11	.03
☐ 40 Hal McRae	.50	.23	.06
☐ 41 Andy Messersmith	.25	.11	.03
☐ 42 Rick Monday	.25	.11	.03
☐ 43 John Montefusco	.25	.11	.03
☐ 44 Joe Morgan	2.00	.90	.25
☐ 45 Thurman Munson	1.50	.70	.19
☐ 46 Bobby Murcer	.75	.35	.09
☐ 47 Bill North	.25	.11	.03
☐ 48 Tony Perez	2.00	.90	.25
☐ 49 Jerry Reuss	.25	.11	.03
☐ 50 Brooks Robinson	3.00	1.35	.35
☐ 51 Pete Rose	4.00	1.80	.50
☐ 52 Joe Rudi	.25	.11	.03
☐ 53 Nolan Ryan	7.50	3.40	.95
☐ 54 Manny Sanguillen	.25	.11	.03
☐ 55 Mike Schmidt	4.00	1.80	.50
☐ 56 Tom Seaver	4.00	1.80	.50
☐ 57 Bill Singer	.25	.11	.03
☐ 58 Willie Stargell	2.00	.90	.25
☐ 59 Rusty Staub	.75	.35	.09
☐ 60 Bob Watson	.75	.35	.09
☐ 61 Butch Wynegar	.25	.11	.03
☐ 62 Carl Yastrzemski	3.00	1.35	.35
☐ 63 Richie Zisk	.25	.11	.03

1907 Cubs A.C. Dietsche Postcards PC765

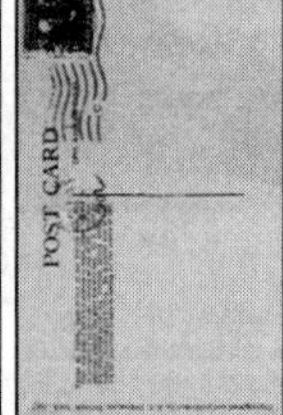

This set of black and white Dietsche postcards was issued in 1907 and feature Chicago Cubs only. Cards have been seen with and without the player's name on the front. There is no current price differential for either variation.

	EX-MT	VG-E	GOOD
COMPLETE SET	1400.00	650.00	180.00
COMMON CARD	75.00	34.00	9.50
☐ 1 Mordecai Brown	150.00	70.00	19.00
☐ 2 Frank Chance	200.00	90.00	25.00
☐ 3 Johnny Evers	175.00	80.00	22.00
☐ 4 Arthur F. Hoffman	75.00	34.00	9.50
☐ 5 John Kling	75.00	34.00	9.50
☐ 6 Carl Lundgren	75.00	34.00	9.50

☐ 7 Patrick J. Moran	75.00	34.00	9.50
☐ 8 Orvall Overall	100.00	45.00	12.50
☐ 9 John A. Pfeister	75.00	34.00	9.50
☐ 10 Ed Reulbach	100.00	45.00	12.50
☐ 11 Frank Schulte	100.00	45.00	12.50
☐ 12 James T. Sheckard	75.00	34.00	9.50
☐ 13 Harry Steinfeldt	100.00	45.00	12.50
☐ 14 James Slagle	75.00	34.00	9.50
☐ 15 Joseph B. Tinker	200.00	90.00	25.00

1907 Cubs G.F. Grignon Co. PC775

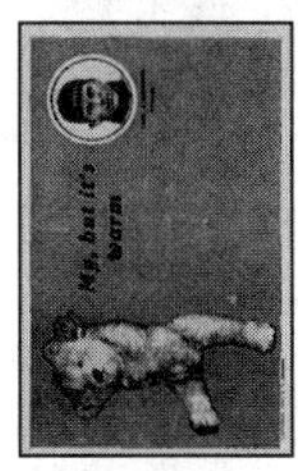

This rather interesting postcard set measures 3 1/2" by 5 1/2", was issued in 1907 and features a Chicago Cub player in a circle in the upper right corner of the front of the card. These cards have green backgrounds featuring a teddy bear in different poses. There is also a head shot in the upper right corner blending comic and photo art. Cards are known to come with an ad for the Boston Oyster House, a popular Chicago restaurant at the time.

	EX-MT	VG-E	GOOD
COMPLETE SET (16)	2000.00	900.00	250.00
COMMON CARD (1-16)	100.00	45.00	12.50
☐ 1 Mordecai Brown	250.00	110.00	31.00
☐ 2 Frank Chance	250.00	110.00	31.00
☐ 3 Johnny Evers	200.00	90.00	25.00
☐ 4 Arthur Hoffman	100.00	45.00	12.50
☐ 5 John Kling	100.00	45.00	12.50
☐ 6 Carl Lundgren	100.00	45.00	12.50
☐ 7 Pat Moran	125.00	55.00	15.50
☐ 8 Orvall Overall	100.00	45.00	12.50
☐ 9 Jack Pfiester	100.00	45.00	12.50
☐ 10 Ed Reulbach	100.00	45.00	12.50
☐ 11 Frank Schulte	100.00	45.00	12.50
☐ 12 Jimmy Sheckard	100.00	45.00	12.50
☐ 13 James Slagle	100.00	45.00	12.50
☐ 14 Harry Steinfeldt	125.00	55.00	15.50
☐ 15 Jack Taylor	100.00	45.00	12.50
☐ 16 Joe Tinker	250.00	110.00	31.00

1908 Cubs Postcards

An unknown Chicago Publisher using a logo of a dollar sign inside a shield produced an attractive set of Cubs players on a gray background in 1908. The known cards in this set are listed below any additions to this checklist are appreciated.

	EX-MT	VG-E	GOOD
COMPLETE SET (4)	725.00	325.00	90.00
COMMON CARD (1-4)	150.00	70.00	19.00
☐ 1 Frank Chance	250.00	110.00	31.00
☐ 2 Artie Hoffman	150.00	70.00	19.00
☐ 3 John Kling	150.00	70.00	19.00
☐ 4 Harry Steinfeldt	175.00	80.00	22.00

1931 Cubs Team Issue

These 30 photos feature players and club personnel involved with the 1931 Chicago Cubs. They measure approximately 6" by 9 1/2" and all the photos have a facsimile autograph as well. All of this is surrounded by white borders. The backs are blank and we have sequenced the photos in alphabetical order.

	EX-MT	VG-E	GOOD
COMPLETE SET (30)	150.00	70.00	19.00
COMMON CARD (1-30)	3.00	1.35	.35
☐ 1 Ed Baecht	3.00	1.35	.35
☐ 2 Les Bell	3.00	1.35	.35
☐ 3 Clarence Blair	3.00	1.35	.35
☐ 4 Sheriff Blake	3.00	1.35	.35
☐ 5 Guy Bush	5.00	2.20	.60
☐ 6 Margaret Donahue FO	3.00	1.35	.35
☐ 7 Woody English	5.00	2.20	.60
☐ 8 Charlie Grimm	7.50	3.40	.95
☐ 9 Gabby Hartnett	15.00	6.75	1.85
☐ 10 Rollie Helmsley	3.00	1.35	.35
☐ 11 Rogers Hornsby	40.00	18.00	5.00
☐ 12 Billy Jurges	5.00	2.20	.60
☐ 13 Bob Lewis TS	3.00	1.35	.35
☐ 14 Andy Lotshaw TR	3.00	1.35	.35
☐ 15 Pat Malone	3.00	1.35	.35
☐ 16 Frank May	3.00	1.35	.35
☐ 17 John Moore	3.00	1.35	.35
☐ 18 Charlie Root	5.00	2.20	.60
☐ 19 Bob Smith	3.00	1.35	.35
☐ 20 Ray Schalk CO	10.00	4.50	1.25
☐ 21 John Seys FO	3.00	1.35	.35
☐ 22 Riggs Stephenson	7.50	3.40	.95
☐ 23 Les Sweetland	3.00	1.35	.35
☐ 24 Zack Taylor	3.00	1.35	.35
☐ 25 Bud Teachout	3.00	1.35	.35
☐ 26 William Veeck PRES	5.00	2.20	.60
☐ 27 W.M. Warner FO	3.00	1.35	.35
☐ 28 Hack Wilson	15.00	6.75	1.85
☐ 29 Phil Wrigley	5.00	2.20	.60
☐ 30 William Wrigley OWN	5.00	2.20	.60

1932 Cubs Team Issue

These 27 photos feature members of the 1932 Chicago Cubs. The photos are shot against a black background and feature a player photo and a facsimile signature. The cards measure approximately 6" by 9" are unnumbered and we have sequenced them in alphabetical order. This set was issued late in the season as Mark Koenig who only spent the last part of the season with the Cubs was included.

	EX-MT	VG-E	GOOD
COMPLETE SET (27)	150.00	70.00	19.00
COMMON CARD (1-27)	3.00	1.35	.35
☐ 1 Guy Bush	5.00	2.20	.60
☐ 2 Red Corriden CO	3.00	1.35	.35
☐ 3 Kiki Cuyler	15.00	6.75	1.85
☐ 4 Frank Demaree	3.00	1.35	.35
☐ 5 Woody English	5.00	2.20	.60
☐ 6 Charlie Grimm	10.00	4.50	1.25
☐ 7 Marv Gudat	3.00	1.35	.35
☐ 8 Burleigh Grimes	15.00	6.75	1.85
☐ 9 Stanley Hack	5.00	2.20	.60
☐ 10 Gabby Hartnett	20.00	9.00	2.50
☐ 11 Rollie Helmsley	3.00	1.35	.35
☐ 12 Billy Herman	15.00	6.75	1.85
☐ 13 Leroy Herrmann	3.00	1.35	.35
☐ 14 Billy Jurges	5.00	2.20	.60
☐ 15 Mark Koenig	5.00	2.20	.60
☐ 16 Pat Malone	3.00	1.35	.35
☐ 17 Jake May	3.00	1.35	.35
☐ 18 Johnny Moore	3.00	1.35	.35
☐ 19 Charley O'Leary CO	3.00	1.35	.35
☐ 20 Charlie Root	5.00	2.20	.60
☐ 21 Bob Smith	3.00	1.35	.35
☐ 22 Riggs Stephenson	10.00	4.50	1.25
☐ 23 Zack Taylor	3.00	1.35	.35
☐ 24 Bud Tinning	3.00	1.35	.35
☐ 25 William Veeck GM	5.00	2.20	.60
☐ 26 Lon Warneke	5.00	2.20	.60
☐ 27 William Wrigley OWN	5.00	2.20	.60

1939 Cubs Team Issue

This set of the Chicago Cubs measures approximately 6 1/2" by 9". The black and white photos display fascimile autographs. The backs are blank. The cards are unnumbered and are checklisted below in alphabetical order.

	EX-MT	VG-E	GOOD
COMPLETE SET (24)	100.00	45.00	12.50
COMMON CARD (1-24)	3.00	1.35	.35
☐ 1 Dick Bartell	5.00	2.20	.60
☐ 2 Phil Cavarretta	5.00	2.20	.60
☐ 3 John Corriden CO	3.00	1.35	.35
☐ 4 Dizzy Dean	15.00	6.75	1.85
☐ 5 Larry French	5.00	2.20	.60
☐ 6 Augie Galan	5.00	2.20	.60
☐ 7 Bob Garbark	3.00	1.35	.35
☐ 8 Jim Gleeson	3.00	1.35	.35
☐ 9 Stanley Hack	5.00	2.20	.60
☐ 10 Leo Hartnett	10.00	4.50	1.25
☐ 11 Billy Herman	10.00	4.50	1.25
☐ 12 Roy Johnson	3.00	1.35	.35
☐ 13 Bill Lee	5.00	2.20	.60
☐ 14 Hank Lieber	3.00	1.35	.35
☐ 15 Gene Lillard	3.00	1.35	.35
☐ 16 Gus Mancuso	3.00	1.35	.35
☐ 17 Bobby Mattick	3.00	1.35	.35
☐ 18 Vance Page	3.00	1.35	.35
☐ 19 Claude Passeau	5.00	2.20	.60
☐ 20 Carl Reynolds	3.00	1.35	.35
☐ 21 Charlie Root	5.00	2.20	.60
☐ 22 Glen "Rip" Russell	3.00	1.35	.35
☐ 23 Jack Russell	3.00	1.35	.35
☐ 24 Earl Whitehill	3.00	1.35	.35

1941 Cubs Team Issue

These photos measure approximately 6 1/2" by 9". They feature members of the 1941 Chicago Cubs. The set is dated by the appearence of Greek George. The backs are blank and we have sequenced them in alphabetical order.

	EX-MT	VG-E	GOOD
COMPLETE SET (25	100.00	45.00	12.50
COMMON CARD (1-25)	3.00	1.35	.35
☐ 1 Phil Cavarretta	7.50	3.40	.95
☐ 2 Dom Dallessandro	3.00	1.35	.35
☐ 3 Paul Erickson	3.00	1.35	.35
☐ 4 Larry French	5.00	2.20	.60
☐ 5 Augie Galan	5.00	2.20	.60
☐ 6 Greek George	3.00	1.35	.35
☐ 7 Charlie Gilbert	3.00	1.35	.35
☐ 8 Stan Hack	5.00	2.20	.60
☐ 9 Johnny Hudson	3.00	1.35	.35
☐ 10 Bill Lee	5.00	2.20	.60
☐ 11 Hank Leiber	3.00	1.35	.35
☐ 12 Clyde McCullough	3.00	1.35	.35
☐ 13 Jake Mooty	3.00	1.35	.35
☐ 14 Bill Myers	3.00	1.35	.35
☐ 15 Bill Nicholson	7.50	3.40	.95
☐ 16 Lou Novikoff	5.00	2.20	.60
☐ 17 Vern Olsen	3.00	1.35	.35
☐ 18 Vance Page	3.00	1.35	.35
☐ 19 Claude Passeau	5.00	2.20	.60
☐ 20 Tot Pressnell	3.00	1.35	.35
☐ 21 Charlie Root	5.00	2.20	.60
☐ 22 Bob Scheffing	3.00	1.35	.35
☐ 23 Lou Stringer	3.00	1.35	.35
☐ 24 Bob Sturgeon	3.00	1.35	.35
☐ 25 Cubs Staff Dick Spalding CO Jimmie Wilson CO Charlie Grimm MG Dizzy Dean CO	15.00	6.75	1.85

1943 Cubs Team Issue

This set of photographs measure approximately 6 1/2" by 9". They feature members of the 1943 Chicago Cubs. The black and white photos also feature fascimile autographs. The backs are blank and we have sequenced this set in alphabetical order.

	EX-MT	VG-E	GOOD
COMPLETE SET (24)	75.00	34.00	9.50
COMMON CARD (1-24)	3.00	1.35	.35
☐ 1 Dick Barrett	3.00	1.35	.35
☐ 2 Heinz Becker	3.00	1.35	.35
☐ 3 Hi Bithorn	3.00	1.35	.35
☐ 4 Phil Cavarretta	10.00	4.50	1.25
☐ 5 Dom Dallessandro	3.00	1.35	.35
☐ 6 Paul Derringer	5.00	2.20	.60
☐ 7 Paul Erickson	3.00	1.35	.35
☐ 8 Bill Fleming	3.00	1.35	.35
☐ 9 Stan Hack	15.00	6.75	1.85
☐ 10 Ed Hanyzewski	3.00	1.35	.35
☐ 11 Chico Hernandez	3.00	1.35	.35
☐ 12 Bill Lee	3.00	1.35	.35
☐ 13 Peanuts Lowery	5.00	2.20	.60
☐ 14 Stu Martin	3.00	1.35	.35
☐ 15 Clyde McCullough	3.00	1.35	.35
☐ 16 Lennie Merullo	3.00	1.35	.35
☐ 17 Bill Nicholson	3.00	1.35	.35
☐ 18 Lou Novikoff	3.00	1.35	.35
☐ 19 Claude Passeau	3.00	1.35	.35
☐ 20 Ray Prim	3.00	1.35	.35
☐ 21 Eddie Stanky	10.00	4.50	1.25
☐ 22 Al Todd	3.00	1.35	.35
☐ 23 Lon Warneke	5.00	2.20	.60
☐ 24 Hank Wyse	3.00	1.35	.35
☐ 25 Cubs Coaches Kiki Cuyler Jimmie Wilson Dick Spalding	7.50	3.40	.95

1944 Cubs Team Issue

These 1944 Chicago Cub team photos are printed on thin paper stock and measure approximately 6" by 8 1/2". The photos feature a black and white head and shoulders shot, with white borders and the player's autograph inscribed across the picture. The backs are blank. The photos are unnumbered and checklisted below in alphabetical order.

	EX-MT	VG-E	GOOD
COMPLETE SET (25)	75.00	34.00	9.50
COMMON CARD (1-25)	3.00	1.35	.35
☐ 1 Heinz Becker	3.00	1.35	.35
☐ 2 John Burrows	3.00	1.35	.35
☐ 3 Phil Cavarretta	5.00	2.20	.60
☐ 4 Dom Dallessandro	3.00	1.35	.35
☐ 5 Paul Derringer	5.00	2.20	.60
☐ 6 Roy Easterwood	3.00	1.35	.35
☐ 7 Paul Erickson	3.00	1.35	.35
☐ 8 Bill Fleming	3.00	1.35	.35
☐ 9 Jimmie Foxx	15.00	6.75	1.85
☐ 10 Ival Goodman	3.00	1.35	.35
☐ 11 Edward Hanyzewski	3.00	1.35	.35
☐ 12 William Holm	3.00	1.35	.35
☐ 13 Don Johnson	3.00	1.35	.35
☐ 14 Garth Mann	3.00	1.35	.35
☐ 15 Lennie Merullo	3.00	1.35	.35
☐ 16 John Miklos	3.00	1.35	.35
☐ 17 Bill Nicholson	5.00	2.20	.60
☐ 18 Lou Novikoff	5.00	2.20	.60
☐ 19 Andy Pafko	5.00	2.20	.60
☐ 20 Eddie Sauer	3.00	1.35	.35
☐ 21 William Schuster	3.00	1.35	.35
☐ 22 Eddie Stanky	5.00	2.20	.60
☐ 23 Hy Vandenberg	3.00	1.35	.35
☐ 24 Hank Wyse	3.00	1.35	.35
☐ 25 Tony York	3.00	1.35	.35

1960 Cubs Jay Publishing

This 12-card set of the Chicago Cubs measures approximately 5" by 7" and features black-and-white player photos in a white border. These cards were packaged 12 to a packet. The backs are blank. The cards are unnumbered and checklisted below in alphabetical order.

	NRMT	VG-E	GOOD
COMPLETE SET (12)	35.00	16.00	4.40
COMMON CARD (1-12)	2.50	1.10	.30
☐ 1 George Altman	2.50	1.10	.30
☐ 2 Bob Anderson	2.50	1.10	.30
☐ 3 Richie Ashburn	6.00	2.70	.75
☐ 4 Ernie Banks	12.50	5.50	1.55
☐ 5 Moe Drabowsky	2.50	1.10	.30
☐ 6 Don Elston	2.50	1.10	.30
☐ 7 Glen Hobbie	2.50	1.10	.30
☐ 8 Dale Long	2.50	1.10	.30
☐ 9 Walt Moryn	2.50	1.10	.30
☐ 10 Sam Taylor	2.50	1.10	.30
☐ 11 Tony Taylor	2.50	1.10	.30
☐ 12 Frank Thomas	3.50	1.55	.45

1961 Cubs Jay Publishing

This 12-card set of the Chicago Cubs measures approximately 5" by 7". The fronts feature black-and-white posed player photos with the player's and team name printed below in the white border. These cards were packaged 12 in a packet. The backs are blank. The cards are unnumbered and checklisted below in alphabetical order.

	NRMT	VG-E	GOOD
COMPLETE SET	35.00	16.00	4.40
COMMON CARD	2.00	.90	.25
☐ 1 George Altman	2.00	.90	.25
☐ 2 Bob Anderson	2.00	.90	.25
☐ 3 Richie Ashburn	5.00	2.20	.60
☐ 4 Ernie Banks	12.50	5.50	1.55
☐ 5 Ed Bouchee	2.00	.90	.25
☐ 6 Dick Ellsworth	2.00	.90	.25
☐ 7 Don Elston	2.00	.90	.25

DICK ELLSWORTH, Chicago Cubs

☐ 8 Glen Hobbie	2.00	.90	.25
☐ 9 Jerry Kindall	2.00	.90	.25
☐ 10 Ron Santo	5.00	2.20	.60
☐ 11 Moe Thacker	2.00	.90	.25
☐ 12 Don Zimmer	3.00	1.35	.35

1962 Cubs Jay Publishing

ERNIE BANKS, Chicago Cubs

This 12-card set of the Chicago Cubs measures approximately 5" by 7". The fronts feature black-and-white posed player photos with the player's and team name printed below in the white border. These cards were packaged 12 in a packet. The backs are blank. The cards are unnumbered and checklisted below in alphabetical order.

	NRMT	VG-E	GOOD
COMPLETE SET (12)	35.00	16.00	4.40
COMMON CARD (1-12)	2.00	.90	.25
☐ 1 George Altman	2.00	.90	.25
☐ 2 Bob Anderson	2.00	.90	.25
☐ 3 Ernie Banks	12.50	5.50	1.55
☐ 4 Don Cardwell	2.00	.90	.25
☐ 5 Jack Curtis	2.00	.90	.25
☐ 6 Don Elston	2.00	.90	.25
☐ 7 Glen Hobbie	2.00	.90	.25
☐ 8 Ken Hubbs	3.50	1.55	.45
☐ 9 Ron Santo	3.00	1.35	.35
☐ 10 Barney Schultz	2.00	.90	.25
☐ 11 Sam Taylor	2.00	.90	.25
☐ 12 Billy Williams	5.00	2.20	.60

1963 Cubs Jay Publishing

LOU BROCK, Chicago Cubs

This 12-card set of the Chicago Cubs measures approximately 5" by 7". The fronts feature black-and-white posed player photos with the player's and team name printed below in the white border. These cards were packaged 12 in a packet. The backs are blank. The cards are unnumbered and checklisted below in alphabetical order.

	NRMT	VG-E	GOOD
COMPLETE SET (12)	35.00	16.00	4.40
COMMON CARD (1-12)	2.00	.90	.25
☐ 1 Ernie Banks	12.50	5.50	1.55
☐ 2 Dick Bertell	2.00	.90	.25
☐ 3 Lou Brock	4.50	2.00	.55
☐ 4 Bob Buhl	2.00	.90	.25
☐ 5 Don Elston	2.00	.90	.25
☐ 6 Ken Hubbs	3.50	1.55	.45
☐ 7 Larry Jackson	2.00	.90	.25
☐ 8 Don Landrum	2.00	.90	.25
☐ 9 Lindy McDaniel	2.00	.90	.25
☐ 10 Andre Rodgers	2.00	.90	.25
☐ 11 Ron Santo	3.00	1.35	.35
☐ 12 Billy Williams	4.50	2.00	.55

1964 Cubs Jay Publishing

This 12-card set of the Chicago Cubs measures approximately 5" by 7". The fronts feature black-and-white posed player photos with the player's and team name printed below in the white border. These cards were packaged 12 in a packet. The backs are blank. The cards are unnumbered and checklisted below in alphabetical order.

DICK ELLSWORTH, Chicago Cubs

	NRMT	VG-E	GOOD
COMPLETE SET (12)	35.00	16.00	4.40
COMMON CARD (1-12)	2.00	.90	.25
☐ 1 Ernie Banks	12.50	5.50	1.55
☐ 2 Dick Bertell	2.00	.90	.25
☐ 3 Lou Brock	4.50	2.00	.55
☐ 4 Bob Buhl	2.00	.90	.25
☐ 5 Dick Ellsworth	2.00	.90	.25
☐ 6 Glen Hobbie	2.00	.90	.25
☐ 7 Larry Jackson	2.00	.90	.25
☐ 8 Bob Kennedy CO	2.00	.90	.25
☐ 9 Lindy McDaniel	2.00	.90	.25
☐ 10 Andre Rodgers	2.00	.90	.25
☐ 11 Ron Santo	3.00	1.35	.35
☐ 12 Billy Williams	4.50	2.00	.55

1965 Cubs Jay Publishing

BOB BUHL, Chicago Cubs

This 12-card set of the Chicago Cubs measures approximately 5" by 7". The fronts feature black-and-white posed player photos with the player's and team name printed below in the white border. These cards were packaged 12 in a packet. The backs are blank. The cards are unnumbered and checklisted below in alphabetical order.

	NRMT	VG-E	GOOD
COMPLETE SET (12)	30.00	13.50	3.70
COMMON CARD (1-12)	2.00	.90	.25
☐ 1 George Altman	2.00	.90	.25
☐ 2 Ernie Banks	10.00	4.50	1.25
☐ 3 Dick Bertell	2.00	.90	.25
☐ 4 Ernie Broglio	2.00	.90	.25
☐ 5 Bob Buhl	2.00	.90	.25
☐ 6 Lou Burdette	3.00	1.35	.35
☐ 7 Dick Ellsworth	2.00	.90	.25
☐ 8 Larry Jackson	2.00	.90	.25
☐ 9 Bob Kennedy CO	2.00	.90	.25
☐ 10 Ron Santo	5.00	2.20	.60
☐ 11 Jim Stewart	2.00	.90	.25
☐ 12 Billy Williams	5.00	2.20	.60

1966 Cubs Team Issue

These 12 cards feature members of the 1966 Chicago Cubs, who by finishing last, enabled the New York Mets to finally not finish in the cellar. The cards are unnumbered and we have sequenced them in alphabetical order.

	NRMT	VG-E	GOOD
COMPLETE SET (12)	35.00	16.00	4.40
COMMON CARD (1-12)	2.00	.90	.25
☐ 1 Ted Abernathy	2.00	.90	.25
☐ 2 George Altman	2.00	.90	.25
☐ 3 Ernie Banks	10.00	4.50	1.25
☐ 4 Glenn Beckert	2.00	.90	.25
☐ 5 Ernie Broglio	2.00	.90	.25
☐ 6 Leo Durocher	4.50	2.00	.55
☐ 7 Dick Ellsworth	2.00	.90	.25
☐ 8 Larry Jackson	2.00	.90	.25
☐ 9 Chris Krug	2.00	.90	.25
☐ 10 Harvey Kuenn	3.50	1.55	.45
☐ 11 Ron Santo	3.50	1.55	.45
☐ 12 Billy Williams	4.50	2.00	.55

1967 Cubs Pro's Pizza Supermarket

This 12-card set features black-and-white player photos of the Chicago Cubs. The cards are unnumbered and checklisted below in alphabetical order.

	NRMT	VG-E	GOOD
COMPLETE SET (12)	3000.00	1350.00	375.00
COMMON CARD (1-12)	100.00	45.00	12.50
☐ 1 Joe Amalfitano	100.00	45.00	12.50
☐ 2 Ernie Banks	1000.00	450.00	125.00
☐ 3 Glenn Beckert	150.00	70.00	19.00
☐ 4 John Boccabella	100.00	45.00	12.50
☐ 5 Bill Hands	100.00	45.00	12.50
☐ 6 Ken Holtzman	150.00	70.00	19.00

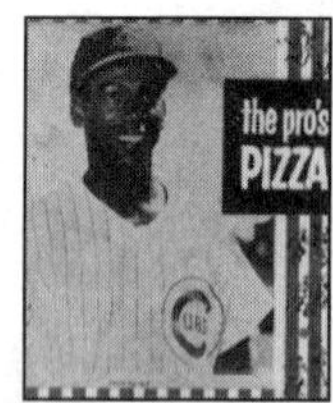

☐ 7 Randy Hundley	150.00	70.00	19.00
☐ 8 Ferguson Jenkins	500.00	220.00	60.00
☐ 9 Don Kessinger	150.00	70.00	19.00
☐ 10 Adolfo Phillips	100.00	45.00	12.50
☐ 11 Ron Santo	500.00	220.00	60.00
☐ 12 Billy Williams	500.00	220.00	60.00

1969 Cubs Jewel Tea

This 20-card set of the Chicago Cubs measures approximately 6" by 9". The white-bordered fronts feature color player action and posed photos with a facsimile autograph across the picture. The backs are blank. The cards are unnumbered and checklisted below in alphabetical order.

	NRMT	VG-E	GOOD
COMPLETE SET (20)	45.00	20.00	5.50
COMMON CARD (1-20)	1.50	.70	.19
☐ 1 Ted Abernathy	1.50	.70	.19
☐ 2 Hank Aguirre	1.50	.70	.19
☐ 3 Ernie Banks	10.00	4.50	1.25
☐ 4 Glenn Beckert	1.50	.70	.19
☐ 5 Bill Hands	1.50	.70	.19
☐ 6 Jim Hickman	1.50	.70	.19
☐ 7 Kenny Holtzman	2.00	.90	.25
☐ 8 Randy Hundley	2.00	.90	.25
☐ 9 Fergie Jenkins	7.50	3.40	.95
☐ 10 Don Kessinger	2.00	.90	.25
☐ 11 Rich Nye	1.50	.70	.19
☐ 12 Paul Popovich	1.50	.70	.19
☐ 13 Jim Qualls	1.50	.70	.19
☐ 14 Phil Regan	1.50	.70	.19
☐ 15 Ron Santo	4.00	1.80	.50
☐ 16 Dick Selma	1.50	.70	.19
☐ 17 Willie Smith	1.50	.70	.19
☐ 18 Al Spangler	1.50	.70	.19
☐ 19 Billy Williams	6.00	2.70	.75
☐ 20 Don Young	1.50	.70	.19

1969 Cubs Photos

These photos feature members of the 1969 Chicago Cubs, best known as the team which lost a huge lead so the Miracle Mets could win the pennant. These photos are unnumbered and we have sequenced them in alphabetical order.

	NRMT	VG-E	GOOD
COMPLETE SET (12)	25.00	11.00	3.10
COMMON CARD (1-12)	1.50	.70	.19
☐ 1 Ted Abernathy	1.50	.70	.19
☐ 2 Ernie Banks	7.50	3.40	.95
☐ 3 Glenn Beckert	1.50	.70	.19
☐ 4 Leo Durocher MG	3.50	1.55	.45
☐ 5 Ken Holtzman	2.00	.90	.25
☐ 6 Randy Hundley	2.00	.90	.25
☐ 7 Ferguson Jenkins	4.50	2.00	.55
☐ 8 Don Kessinger	2.00	.90	.25
☐ 9 Phil Regan	1.50	.70	.19
☐ 10 Ron Santo	3.00	1.35	.35
☐ 11 Al Spangler	1.50	.70	.19
☐ 12 Billy Williams	4.50	2.00	.55

1969 Cubs Team Issue Color

This 10-card set of the Chicago Cubs measures approximately 7" by 8 3/4" with the fronts featuring white-bordered color player photos. The

FERGUSON JENKINS, Cubs

player's name and team is printed in black in the white margin below the picture. The backs are blank. The cards are unnumbered and checklisted below in alphabetical order.

	NRMT	VG-E	GOOD
COMPLETE SET	30.00	13.50	3.70
COMMON CARD	1.75	.80	.22
☐ 1 Ernie Banks	7.50	3.40	.95
☐ 2 Glenn Beckert	1.75	.80	.22
☐ 3 Ken Holtzman	3.00	1.35	.35
☐ 4 Randy Hundley	3.00	1.35	.35
☐ 5 Ferguson Jenkins	5.00	2.20	.60
☐ 6 Don Kessinger	3.00	1.35	.35
☐ 7 Phil Regan	1.75	.80	.22
☐ 8 Ron Santo	4.00	1.80	.50
☐ 9 Willie Smith	1.75	.80	.22
☐ 10 Billy Williams	5.00	2.20	.60

1970 Cubs Dunkin Donuts

This set of six bumper stickers (apparently commemorating the Cubs near-miss in 1969) was produced and distributed by Dunkin Donuts. The stickers are approximately 4 1/16" by 8 1/16" and are in color. Each sticker features a facsimile autograph in the upper left hand corner. The stickers are unnumbered and are listed below in alphabetical order according to the player's name.

	NRMT	VG-E	GOOD
COMPLETE SET (6)	25.00	11.00	3.10
COMMON CARD	1.50	.70	.19
☐ 1 Ernie Banks	15.00	6.75	1.85
☐ 2 Glenn Beckert	1.50	.70	.19
☐ 3 Randy Hundley	1.50	.70	.19
☐ 4 Don Kessinger	2.50	1.10	.30
☐ 5 Ron Santo	4.00	1.80	.50
☐ 6 Billy Williams	7.50	3.40	.95

1972 Cubs Chi-Foursome

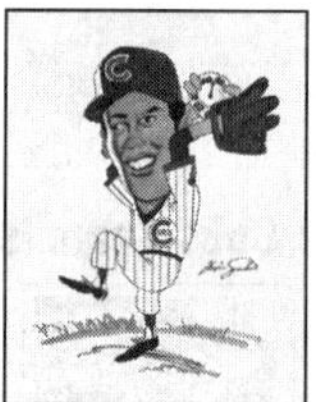

These 11" by 14" drawings feature Chicago Cubs players. The attractive color drawings also have a facimilie signature. The backs are blank and we have sequenced this set in alphabetical order.

	NRMT	VG-E	GOOD
COMPLETE SET (8)	12.50	5.50	1.55
COMMON CARD (1-8)	1.00	.45	.12
☐ 1 Ernie Banks	4.00	1.80	.50
☐ 2 Glenn Beckert	1.00	.45	.12
☐ 3 Fergie Jenkins	2.50	1.10	.30
☐ 4 Don Kessinger	1.00	.45	.12
☐ 5 Milt Pappas	1.00	.45	.12
☐ 6 Joe Pepitone	2.00	.90	.25
☐ 7 Ron Santo	2.50	1.10	.30
☐ 8 Billy Williams	2.50	1.10	.30

1972 Cubs Team Issue

These 12 photos feature members of the 1972 Chicago Cubs. The photos measure approximately 4 1/4" by 7". The black and white photos are surrounded by white borders and feature a facsimile autograph. The backs are blank and we have sequenced this set in alphabetical order.

	NRMT	VG-E	GOOD
COMPLETE SET (12)	20.00	9.00	2.50
COMMON CARD (1-12)	1.50	.70	.19

☐ 1 Ernie Banks CO	5.00	2.20	.60
☐ 2 Glenn Beckert	1.50	.70	.19
☐ 3 Bill Hands	1.50	.70	.19
☐ 4 Jim Hickman	1.50	.70	.19
☐ 5 Randy Hundley	2.00	.90	.25
☐ 6 Fergie Jenkins	3.00	1.35	.35
☐ 7 Don Kessinger	2.00	.90	.25
☐ 8 Rick Monday	2.50	1.10	.30
☐ 9 Milt Pappas	1.50	.70	.19
☐ 10 Joe Pepitone	2.00	.90	.25
☐ 11 Ron Santo	2.50	1.10	.30
☐ 12 Billy Williams	3.00	1.35	.35

1977 Cubs Jewel Tea

This 15-card set of the Chicago Cubs measures approximately 5 7/8" by 9". The white-bordered fronts feature color player head photos with a facsimile autograph. The backs are blank. The cards are unnumbered and checklisted below in alphabetical order.

	NRMT	VG-E	GOOD
COMPLETE SET (15)	12.50	5.50	1.55
COMMON CARD (1-15)	.75	.35	.09
☐ 1 Larry Biittner	.75	.35	.09
☐ 2 Bill Bonham	.75	.35	.09
☐ 3 Bill Buckner	1.25	.55	.16
☐ 4 Ray Burris	.75	.35	.09
☐ 5 Gene Clines	.75	.35	.09
☐ 6 Ivan DeJesus	.75	.35	.09
☐ 7 Willie Hernandez	.75	.35	.09
☐ 8 Mike Krukow	.75	.35	.09
☐ 9 George Mitterwald	.75	.35	.09
☐ 10 Jerry Morales	.75	.35	.09
☐ 11 Bobby Murcer	1.25	.55	.16
☐ 12 Steve Ontiveros	.75	.35	.09
☐ 13 Paul Reuschel	.75	.35	.09
☐ 14 Bruce Sutter	1.25	.55	.16
☐ 15 Manny Trillo	1.25	.55	.16

1980 Cubs Greats TCMA

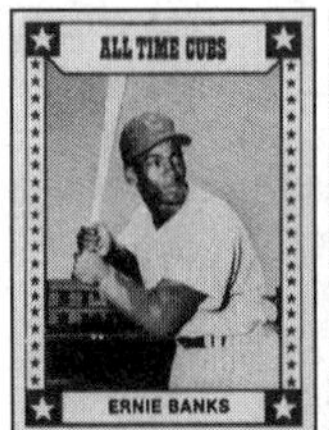

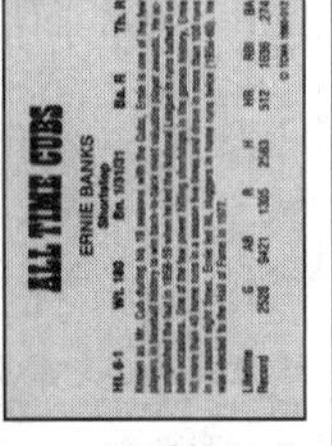

This 12-card standard-size set honors some all-time Cub greats. The fronts have a player photo, his name and position. The backs have vital statistics, career totals and a brief biography.

	NRMT	VG-E	GOOD
COMPLETE SET (12)	5.00	2.20	.60
COMMON CARD (1-12)	.25	.11	.03
☐ 1 Billy Williams	.75	.35	.09
☐ 2 Charlie Root	.35	.16	.04
☐ 3 Ron Santo	.50	.23	.06
☐ 4 Larry French	.25	.11	.03
☐ 5 Gabby Hartnett	.75	.35	.09
☐ 6 Emil Kush	.25	.11	.03
☐ 7 Charlie Grimm	.35	.16	.04
☐ 8 Kiki Cuyler	.75	.35	.09
☐ 9 Billy Herman	.75	.35	.09
☐ 10 Hack Wilson	.75	.35	.09
☐ 11 Rogers Hornsby	1.00	.45	.12
☐ 12 Ernie Banks	1.50	.70	.19

1982 Cubs Red Lobster

The cards in this 28-card set measure 2 1/4" by 3 1/2". This set of Chicago Cubs players was co-produced by the Cubs and Chicago-area

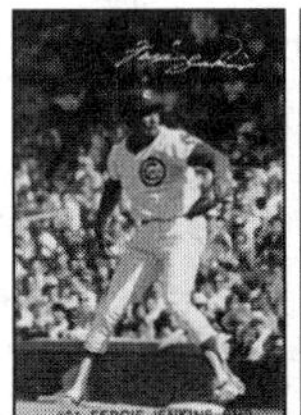

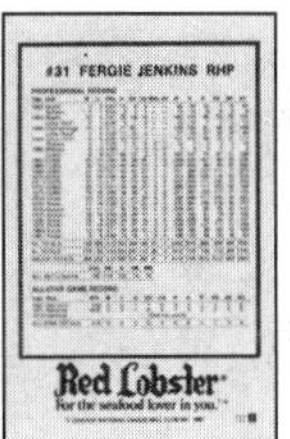

Red Lobster restaurants and was introduced as a promotional giveaway on August 20, 1982, at Wrigley Field. The cards contain borderless color photos of 25 players, manager Lee Elia, the coaching staff, and a team picture. A facsimile autograph appears on the front, and the cards run in sequence by uniform number. While the coaches have a short biographical sketch on back, the player cards simply list the individual's professional record. The key card in the set is obviously Ryne Sandberg's as it predates his Donruss, Fleer, and Topps Rookie Cards by one year. Lee Smith also appears in this set in his Rookie Card year.

	NRMT	VG-E	GOOD
COMPLETE SET (28)	150.00	70.00	19.00
COMMON CARD	1.00	.45	.12
☐ 1 Larry Bowa	2.00	.90	.25
☐ 4 Lee Elia MG	1.00	.45	.12
☐ 6 Keith Moreland	1.25	.55	.16
☐ 7 Jody Davis	1.50	.70	.19
☐ 10 Leon Durham	1.25	.55	.16
☐ 15 Junior Kennedy	1.00	.45	.12
☐ 17 Bump Wills	1.00	.45	.12
☐ 18 Scot Thompson	1.00	.45	.12
☐ 21 Jay Johnstone	2.00	.90	.25
☐ 22 Bill Buckner	3.00	1.35	.35
☐ 23 Ryne Sandberg	100.00	45.00	12.50
☐ 24 Jerry Morales	1.00	.45	.12
☐ 25 Gary Woods	1.00	.45	.12
☐ 28 Steve Henderson	1.00	.45	.12
☐ 29 Bob Molinaro	1.00	.45	.12
☐ 31 Fergie Jenkins	7.50	3.40	.95
☐ 33 Al Ripley	1.00	.45	.12
☐ 34 Randy Martz	1.00	.45	.12
☐ 36 Mike Proly	1.00	.45	.12
☐ 37 Ken Kravec	1.00	.45	.12
☐ 38 Willie Hernandez	1.50	.70	.19
☐ 39 Bill Campbell	1.00	.45	.12
☐ 41 Dick Tidrow	1.00	.45	.12
☐ 46 Lee Smith	10.00	4.50	1.25
☐ 47 Doug Bird	1.00	.45	.12
☐ 48 Dickie Noles	1.00	.45	.12
☐ NNO Team Picture	4.00	1.80	.50
☐ NNO Coaches Card	2.00	.90	.25
John Vukovich			
Gordy MacKenzie			
Billy Williams			
Billy Connors			
Tom Harmon			

1983 Cubs Thorn Apple Valley

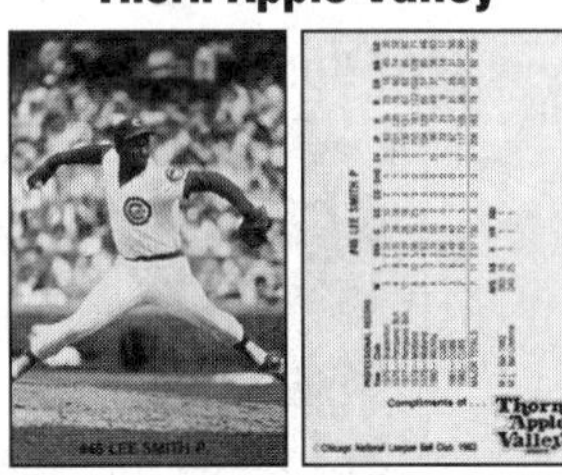

This set of 27 Chicago Cubs features full-color action photos on the front and was sponsored by Thorn Apple Valley. The cards measure approximately 2 1/4" by 3 1/2". The backs provide year-by-year statistics. The cards are unnumbered except for uniform number; they are listed below by uniform with the special cards listed at the end. The card of Joe Carter predates his Donruss Rookie Card by one year.

	NRMT	VG-E	GOOD
COMPLETE SET (27)	50.00	22.00	6.25
COMMON CARD	.50	.23	.06
☐ 1 Larry Bowa	1.00	.45	.12
☐ 6 Keith Moreland	.50	.23	.06
☐ 7 Jody Davis	.75	.35	.09
☐ 10 Leon Durham	.75	.35	.09
☐ 11 Ron Cey	1.00	.45	.12
☐ 16 Steve Lake	.50	.23	.06
☐ 20 Thad Bosley	.50	.23	.06
☐ 21 Jay Johnstone	.75	.35	.09
☐ 22 Bill Buckner	1.00	.45	.12
☐ 23 Ryne Sandberg	20.00	9.00	2.50
☐ 24 Jerry Morales	.50	.23	.06
☐ 25 Gary Woods	.50	.23	.06
☐ 27 Mel Hall	.75	.35	.09
☐ 29 Tom Veryzer	.50	.23	.06
☐ 30 Chuck Rainey	.50	.23	.06
☐ 31 Fergie Jenkins	3.00	1.35	.35
☐ 32 Craig Lefferts	.75	.35	.09
☐ 33 Joe Carter	25.00	11.00	3.10
☐ 34 Steve Trout	.50	.23	.06
☐ 36 Mike Proly	.50	.23	.06
☐ 39 Bill Campbell	.50	.23	.06
☐ 41 Warren Brusstar	.50	.23	.06
☐ 44 Dick Ruthven	.50	.23	.06
☐ 46 Lee Smith	3.00	1.35	.35
☐ 48 Dickie Noles	.50	.23	.06
☐ NNO Manager/Coaches	.50	.23	.06
Lee Elia MG			
Ruben Amaro			
Billy Connors			
Duffy Dyer			
Fred Koenig			
John Vukovich			
☐ NNO Team Photo	2.00	.90	.25

1984 Cubs Chicago Tribune

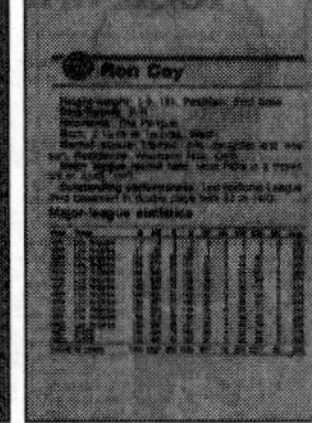

The 1984 Chicago Tribune set was issued in the sports section of the newspaper and features 34 Chicago Cub players. The posed color headshots measure 3 1/4" by 4 5/8" and have blue borders. Next to the photo in a section of equal dimensions appears player information, including position, date of birth, playing experience, baseball career and Major-league playing record. The pictures are unnumbered and checklisted below in alphabetical order.

	NRMT	VG-E	GOOD
COMPLETE SET (34)	25.00	11.00	3.10
COMMON CARD (1-34)	.50	.23	.06
☐ 1 Ruben Amaro CO	.50	.23	.06
☐ 2 Rich Bordi	.50	.23	.06
☐ 3 Thad Bosley	.50	.23	.06
☐ 4 Larry Bowa	1.00	.45	.12
☐ 5 Warren Brusstar	.50	.23	.06
☐ 6 Ron Cey	1.00	.45	.12
☐ 7 Billy Connors CO	.50	.23	.06
☐ 8 Henry Cotto	.50	.23	.06
☐ 9 Jody Davis	.75	.35	.09
☐ 10 Bob Dernier	.50	.23	.06
☐ 11 Dennis Eckersley	1.50	.70	.19
☐ 12 George Frazier	.50	.23	.06
☐ 13 Jim Frey MG	.50	.23	.06
☐ 14 Ron Hassey	.50	.23	.06
☐ 15 Richie Hebner	.75	.35	.09
☐ 16 Steve Lake	.50	.23	.06
☐ 17 Davey Lopes	.75	.35	.09
☐ 18 Gary Matthews	1.00	.45	.12
☐ 19 Keith Moreland	.50	.23	.06
☐ 20 Johnny Oates CO	.50	.23	.06
☐ 21 Dave Owen	.50	.23	.06
☐ 22 Rick Reuschel	1.00	.45	.12
☐ 23 Dan Rohn	.50	.23	.06
☐ 24 Dick Ruthven	.50	.23	.06
☐ 25 Ryne Sandberg	7.50	3.40	.95
☐ 26 Scott Sanderson	.50	.23	.06
☐ 27 Lee Smith	1.50	.70	.19
☐ 28 Tim Stoddard	.50	.23	.06
☐ 29 Rick Sutcliffe	1.50	.70	.19
☐ 30 Steve Trout	.50	.23	.06
☐ 31 Tom Veryzer	.50	.23	.06
☐ 32 John Vukovich CO	.50	.23	.06
☐ 33 Gary Woods	.50	.23	.06
☐ 34 Don Zimmer CO	.50	.23	.06

1984 Cubs Seven-Up

This 28-card set was sponsored by 7-Up. The cards are in full color and measure approximately 2 1/4" by 3 1/2". The card backs are printed in black on white card stock. This set is tougher to find than the other similar Cubs sets since the Cubs were more successful (on the field) in 1984 winning their division, that is, virtually all of the cards printed were distributed during the "Baseball Card Day" promotion (August 12th) which was much better attended that year. There actually were two additional cards produced (in limited quantities) later which some collectors consider part of this set; these late issue cards show four Cubs rookies on each card.

	NRMT	VG-E	GOOD
COMPLETE SET (28)	30.00	13.50	3.70
COMMON CARD	.75	.35	.09
☐ 1 Larry Bowa	1.50	.70	.19
☐ 6 Keith Moreland	.75	.35	.09
☐ 7 Jody Davis	1.00	.45	.12
☐ 10 Leon Durham	1.00	.45	.12
☐ 11 Ron Cey	1.50	.70	.19
☐ 15 Ron Hassey	.75	.35	.09
☐ 18 Richie Hebner	1.00	.45	.12
☐ 19 Dave Owen	.75	.35	.09
☐ 20 Bob Dernier	.75	.35	.09
☐ 21 Jay Johnstone	1.50	.70	.19
☐ 23 Ryne Sandberg	15.00	6.75	1.85
☐ 24 Scott Sanderson	1.00	.45	.12
☐ 25 Gary Woods	.75	.35	.09
☐ 27 Thad Bosley	.75	.35	.09
☐ 28 Henry Cotto	.75	.35	.09
☐ 34 Steve Trout	.75	.35	.09
☐ 36 Gary Matthews	1.50	.70	.19
☐ 39 George Frazier	.75	.35	.09
☐ 40 Rick Sutcliffe	2.00	.90	.25
☐ 41 Warren Brusstar	.75	.35	.09
☐ 42 Rich Bordi	.75	.35	.09
☐ 43 Dennis Eckersley	3.00	1.35	.35
☐ 44 Dick Ruthven	.75	.35	.09
☐ 46 Lee Smith	3.00	1.35	.35
☐ 47 Rick Reuschel	1.50	.70	.19
☐ 49 Tim Stoddard	.75	.35	.09
☐ NNO Coaches Card	.75	.35	.09
Ruben Amaro			
Billy Connors			
Johnny Oates			
John Vukovich			
Don Zimmer			
☐ NNO Jim Frey MG	.75	.35	.09

1984 Cubs Unocal

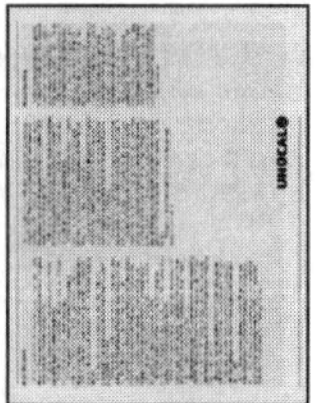

Unocal 76 sponsored this set of 16 color paintings by several different artists. The paintings have white borders and are printed on 11" by 8 1/2" glossy paper. They capture memorable events and players in Chicago Cub history. The backs have an extended caption. The paintings are unnumbered and checklisted below in alphabetical order.

	NRMT	VG-E	GOOD
COMPLETE SET (16)	15.00	6.75	1.85
COMMON CARD (1-16)	.75	.35	.09
☐ 1 Billy Williams	2.00	.90	.25
☐ 2 Bob Dernier	1.50	.70	.19
Ryne Sandberg			
Ernie Banks			
Ken Hubbs			
Larry Jackson			
Ron Santo			
Randy Hundley			
Glenn Beckert			
Don Kessinger			
Gold Glove Winners			
☐ 3 Rogers Hornsby	2.50	1.10	.30
Gabby Hartnett			
Phil Cavarretta			
Hank Sauer			
Ernie Banks			
Ryne Sandberg			
MVP Award Winners			
☐ 4 Ernie Banks	3.00	1.35	.35
☐ 5 Fergie Jenkins	2.00	.90	.25
☐ 6 Gabby Hartnett	1.00	.45	.12
Randy Hundley			
Jody Davis			
Great Catchers			
☐ 7 Frank Chance	2.00	.90	.25
Johnny Evers			
Joe Tinker			
Harry Steinfeldt			
Ernie Banks			
Glenn Beckert			
Don Kessinger			
Ron Santo			
Leon Durham			
Ryne Sandberg			
Larry Bowa			
Ron Cey			
Great Infields			
☐ 8 Frank Chance	1.00	.45	.12
Joe McCarthy			
Charlie Grimm			
Leo Durocher			
Jim Frey			

Great Managers			
☐ 9 Don Elston	1.00	.45	.12
Lindy McDaniel			
Ted Abernathy			
Phil Regan			
Bruce Sutter			
Lee Smith			
Great Relief Pitchers			
☐ 10 Jim Frey	.75	.35	.09
Post-Game Victory Lap			
9/30/84			
☐ 11 Memorable High Scoring	.75	.35	.09
Games			
☐ 12 Ryne Sandberg	1.25	.55	.16
Rick Sutcliffe			
Dallas Green			
Jim Frey			
1984 Award Winners			
☐ 13 '84 Clincher	.75	.35	.09
at Pittsburgh			
☐ 14 Rick Sutcliffe	1.00	.45	.12
Sensational 16-1			
☐ 15 Ryne Sandberg	2.00	.90	.25
June 23, 1984			
☐ 16 Wrigley Field	.75	.35	.09

1985 Cubs Lion Photo

This 27-card set of the Chicago Cubs measures approximately 3 1/2" by 5". The fronts feature color player portraits on a blue background with a white border. The player's name is printed in blue in the wide bottom margin. The white backs carry sponsor information. The cards are unnumbered and checklisted below in alphabetical order.

	NRMT	VG-E	GOOD
COMPLETE SET (27)	12.00	5.50	1.50
COMMON CARD (1-27)	.50	.23	.06
☐ 1 Larry Bowa	1.00	.45	.12
☐ 2 Thad Bosley	.50	.23	.06
☐ 3 Warren Brusstar	.50	.23	.06
☐ 4 Ron Cey	1.00	.45	.12
☐ 5 Jody Davis	.50	.23	.06
☐ 6 Brian Dayett	.50	.23	.06
☐ 7 Bob Dernier	.50	.23	.06
☐ 8 Shawon Dunston	1.50	.70	.19
☐ 9 Leon Durham	.50	.23	.06
☐ 10 Dennis Eckersley	2.00	.90	.25
☐ 11 Ray Fontenot	.50	.23	.06
☐ 12 George Frazier	.50	.23	.06
☐ 13 Jim Frey MG	.50	.23	.06
☐ 14 Steve Lake	.50	.23	.06
☐ 15 Davey Lopes	.75	.35	.09
☐ 16 Gary Matthews	.50	.23	.06
☐ 17 Keith Moreland	.50	.23	.06
☐ 18 Dick Ruthven	.50	.23	.06
☐ 19 Ryne Sandberg	3.00	1.35	.35
☐ 20 Scott Sanderson	.50	.23	.06
☐ 21 Lee Smith	2.00	.90	.25
☐ 22 Lary Sorensen	.50	.23	.06
☐ 23 Chris Speier	.50	.23	.06
☐ 24 Rick Sutcliffe	1.00	.45	.12
☐ 25 Steve Trout	.50	.23	.06
☐ 26 Gary Woods	.50	.23	.06
☐ 27 Don Zimmer CO	.50	.23	.06

1985 Cubs Seven-Up

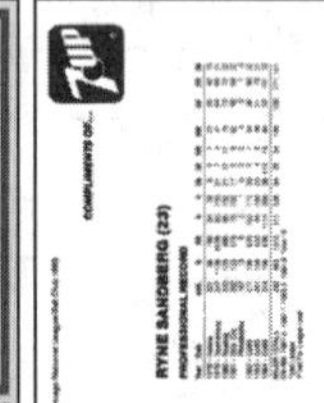

This 28-card set was distributed on August 14th at Wrigley Field for the game against the Expos. The cards measure 2 1/2" by 3 1/2" and were distributed wrapped in cellophane. The cards are unnumbered except for uniform number. The card backs are printed in black on white with a 7-Up logo in the upper right hand corner.

	NRMT	VG-E	GOOD
COMPLETE SET (28)	15.00	6.75	1.85
COMMON CARD	.25	.11	.03
☐ 1 Larry Bowa	.75	.35	.09
☐ 6 Keith Moreland	.25	.11	.03
☐ 7 Jody Davis	.50	.23	.06
☐ 10 Leon Durham	.50	.23	.06
☐ 11 Ron Cey	.75	.35	.09
☐ 15 Davey Lopes	.50	.23	.06
☐ 16 Steve Lake	.25	.11	.03
☐ 18 Rich Hebner	.50	.23	.06
☐ 20 Bob Dernier	.25	.11	.03
☐ 21 Scott Sanderson	.50	.23	.06
☐ 22 Billy Hatcher	.50	.23	.06
☐ 23 Ryne Sandberg	7.50	3.40	.95
☐ 24 Brian Dayett	.25	.11	.03
☐ 25 Gary Woods	.25	.11	.03
☐ 27 Thad Bosley	.25	.11	.03
☐ 28 Chris Speier	.25	.11	.03
☐ 31 Ray Fontenot	.25	.11	.03
☐ 34 Steve Trout	.25	.11	.03
☐ 36 Gary Matthews	.75	.35	.09
☐ 39 George Frazier	.25	.11	.03
☐ 40 Rick Sutcliffe	1.00	.45	.12
☐ 41 Warren Brusstar	.25	.11	.03
☐ 42 Lary Sorensen	.25	.11	.03
☐ 43 Dennis Eckersley	2.50	1.10	.30
☐ 44 Dick Ruthven	.25	.11	.03
☐ 46 Lee Smith	2.50	1.10	.30
☐ NNO Jim Frey MG	.25	.11	.03
☐ NNO Cubs Coaching Staff	.50	.23	.06
Ruben Amaro			
Billy Connors			
Johnny Oates			
John Vukovich			
Don Zimmer			

1986 Cubs Gatorade

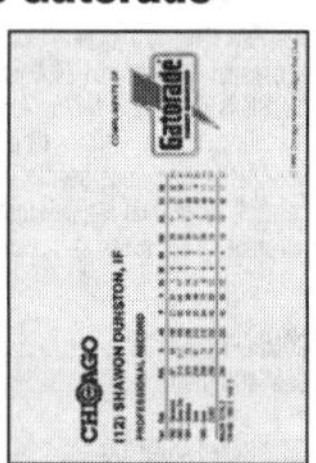

This 28-card set was given out at Wrigley Field on the Cubs' special "baseball card" promotion held July 17th for the game against the Giants. The set was sponsored by Gatorade. The cards are unnumbered except for uniform number. Card backs feature blue print on white card stock. The cards measure approximately 2 7/8" by 4 1/4" and are in full color.

	MINT	NRMT	EXC
COMPLETE SET (28)	12.00	5.50	1.50
COMMON CARD	.25	.11	.03
☐ 4 Gene Michael MG	.25	.11	.03
☐ 6 Keith Moreland	.25	.11	.03
☐ 7 Jody Davis	.50	.23	.06
☐ 10 Leon Durham	.50	.23	.06
☐ 11 Ron Cey	.75	.35	.09
☐ 12 Shawon Dunston	.50	.23	.06
☐ 15 Davey Lopes	.75	.35	.09
☐ 16 Terry Francona	.25	.11	.03
☐ 18 Steve Christmas	.25	.11	.03
☐ 19 Manny Trillo	.25	.11	.03
☐ 20 Bob Dernier	.25	.11	.03
☐ 21 Scott Sanderson	.50	.23	.06
☐ 22 Jerry Mumphrey	.25	.11	.03
☐ 23 Ryne Sandberg	6.00	2.70	.75
☐ 27 Thad Bosley	.25	.11	.03
☐ 28 Chris Speier	.25	.11	.03
☐ 29 Steve Lake	.25	.11	.03
☐ 31 Ray Fontenot	.25	.11	.03
☐ 34 Steve Trout	.25	.11	.03
☐ 36 Gary Matthews	.50	.23	.06
☐ 39 George Frazier	.25	.11	.03
☐ 40 Rick Sutcliffe	.75	.35	.09
☐ 43 Dennis Eckersley	2.00	.90	.25
☐ 46 Lee Smith	2.00	.90	.25
☐ 48 Jay Baller	.25	.11	.03
☐ 49 Jamie Moyer	1.00	.45	.12
☐ 50 Guy Hoffman	.25	.11	.03
☐ NNO Coaches Card	.50	.23	.06
Ruben Amaro			
Billy Connors			
Johnny Oates			
John Vukovich			
Billy Williams			

1986 Cubs Unocal

This set of 20 color action player photos was sponsored by Unocal 76. They are bordered in black and are printed on (approximately) 8 1/2" by 11" glossy paper sheets. A color headshot is superimposed on each front. The backs contain extensive player information, including biography, performance in the 1985 season, complete Major League statistics, and career summary. The player photos are unnumbered and checklisted below in alphabetical order.

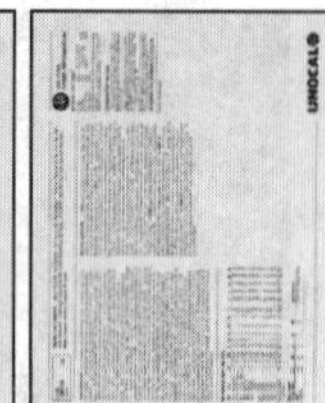

	MINT	NRMT	EXC
COMPLETE SET (20)	10.00	4.50	1.25
COMMON CARD (1-20)	.25	.11	.03
☐ 1 Jay Baller	.25	.11	.03
☐ 2 Thad Bosley	.25	.11	.03
☐ 3 Ron Cey	.75	.35	.09
☐ 4 Jody Davis	.50	.23	.06
☐ 5 Bob Dernier	.25	.11	.03
☐ 6 Shawon Dunston	.50	.23	.06
☐ 7 Leon Durham	.25	.11	.03
☐ 8 Dennis Eckersley	1.50	.70	.19
☐ 9 Ray Fontenot	.25	.11	.03
☐ 10 George Frazier	.25	.11	.03
☐ 11 Davey Lopes	.50	.23	.06
☐ 12 Gary Matthews	.50	.23	.06
☐ 13 Keith Moreland	.25	.11	.03
☐ 14 Jerry Mumphrey	.25	.11	.03
☐ 15 Ryne Sandberg	5.00	2.20	.60
☐ 16 Scott Sanderson	.50	.23	.06
☐ 17 Lee Smith	1.50	.70	.19
☐ 18 Rick Sutcliffe	.75	.35	.09
☐ 19 Manny Trillo	.25	.11	.03
☐ 20 Steve Trout	.25	.11	.03

1987 Cubs 1907 TCMA

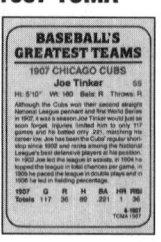

This nine-card standard-size set features some of the 1907 Chicago Cubs stars. The fronts have player photo and identification, while the backs have vital statistics, a biography and 1907 stats.

	MINT	NRMT	EXC
COMPLETE SET (9)	5.00	2.20	.60
COMMON CARD (1-9)	.25	.11	.03
☐ 1 Harry Steinfeldt	.50	.23	.06
☐ 2 Three-Finger Brown	1.00	.45	.12
☐ 3 Ed Reulbach	.50	.23	.06
☐ 4 Johnny Kling	.50	.23	.06
☐ 5 Orvie Overall	.25	.11	.03
☐ 6 Joe Tinker	1.00	.45	.12
☐ 7 Wildfire Schulte	.50	.23	.06
☐ 8 Frank Chance P/MG	1.00	.45	.12
☐ 9 Johnny Evers	1.00	.45	.12

1987 Cubs Canon

This 38 card set features members of the 1987 Chicago Cubs. The fronts have a player photo with his name under the photo. At the bottom are the words "Canon" and "Chicago Cubs" The backs are blank so we have sequenced this set in alphabetical order. An early Greg Maddux item is in this set.

	MINT	NRMT	EXC
COMPLETE SET (38)	20.00	9.00	2.50
COMMON CARD (1-38)	.50	.23	.06
☐ 1 Glenn Brummer	.50	.23	.06
☐ 2 Phil Claussen	.50	.23	.06
☐ 3 Jody Davis	.75	.35	.09
☐ 4 Ron Davis	.50	.23	.06
☐ 5 Andre Dawson	3.00	1.35	.35
☐ 6 Brian Dayett	.50	.23	.06
☐ 7 Bob Dernier	.50	.23	.06
☐ 8 Frank DiPino	.50	.23	.06
☐ 9 Shawon Dunston	.50	.23	.06
☐ 10 Leon Durham	.75	.35	.09
☐ 11 John Fierro TR	.50	.23	.06
☐ 12 Dallas Green GM	.75	.35	.09
☐ 13 Les Lancaster	.50	.23	.06
☐ 14 Frank Lucchesi CO	.50	.23	.06
☐ 15 Ed Lynch	.50	.23	.06
☐ 16 Greg Maddux	10.00	4.50	1.25
☐ 17 David Martinez	1.00	.45	.12
☐ 18 Gary Matthews	1.00	.45	.12
☐ 19 Gene Michael MG	.50	.23	.06
☐ 20 Keith Moreland	.50	.23	.06
☐ 21 Jamie Moyer	.50	.23	.06
☐ 22 Jerry Mumphrey	.50	.23	.06
☐ 23 Dickie Noles	.50	.23	.06
☐ 24 Johnny Oates CO	.75	.35	.09
☐ 25 Jimmy Piersall ANN	1.00	.45	.12
☐ 26 Ryne Sandberg	5.00	2.20	.60
☐ 27 Scott Sanderson	.50	.23	.06
☐ 28 Bob Searles	.50	.23	.06
☐ 29 Lee Smith	1.50	.70	.19
☐ 30 Jim Snyder CO	.50	.23	.06
☐ 31 Herm Starrette CO	.50	.23	.06
☐ 32 Jim Sundberg	.50	.23	.06
☐ 33 Rick Sutcliffe	1.00	.45	.12
☐ 34 Manny Trillo	.50	.23	.06
☐ 35 Steve Trout	.50	.23	.06
☐ 36 John Vukovich CO	.50	.23	.06
☐ 37 Chico Walker	.50	.23	.06
☐ 38 Billy Williams CO	1.50	.70	.19

1987 Cubs David Berg

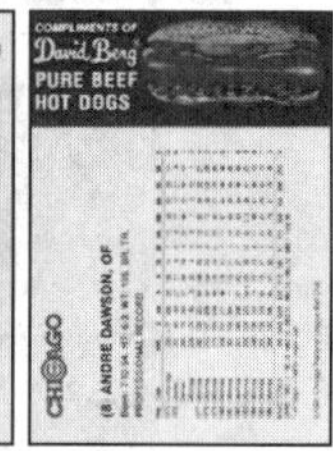

This 26-card set was given out at Wrigley Field on the Cubs' special "baseball card" promotion held July 29th. The set was sponsored by David Berg Pure Beef Hot Dogs. The cards are unnumbered except for uniform number. Card backs feature red and blue print on white card stock. The cards measure approximately 2 7/8" by 4 1/4" and are in full color. The set features Greg Maddux in his Rookie Card year.

	MINT	NRMT	EXC
COMPLETE SET (26)	15.00	6.75	1.85
COMMON CARD	.25	.11	.03
☐ 1 Dave Martinez	.75	.35	.09
☐ 4 Gene Michael MG	.25	.11	.03
☐ 6 Keith Moreland	.25	.11	.03
☐ 7 Jody Davis	.50	.23	.06
☐ 8 Andre Dawson	2.00	.90	.25
☐ 10 Leon Durham	.50	.23	.06
☐ 11 Jim Sundberg	.50	.23	.06
☐ 12 Shawon Dunston	.75	.35	.09
☐ 19 Manny Trillo	.50	.23	.06
☐ 20 Bob Dernier	.25	.11	.03
☐ 21 Scott Sanderson	.50	.23	.06
☐ 22 Jerry Mumphrey	.25	.11	.03
☐ 23 Ryne Sandberg	5.00	2.20	.60
☐ 24 Brian Dayett	.25	.11	.03
☐ 29 Chico Walker	.25	.11	.03
☐ 31 Greg Maddux	7.50	3.40	.95
☐ 33 Frank DiPino	.25	.11	.03
☐ 34 Steve Trout	.25	.11	.03
☐ 36 Gary Matthews	.75	.35	.09
☐ 37 Ed Lynch	.25	.11	.03
☐ 39 Ron Davis	.25	.11	.03
☐ 40 Rick Sutcliffe	.75	.35	.09
☐ 46 Lee Smith	1.50	.70	.19
☐ 47 Dickie Noles	.25	.11	.03
☐ 49 Jamie Moyer	.25	.11	.03
☐ NNO Coaching Staff	.50	.23	.06
Johnny Oates			
Jim Snyder			
Herm Starrette			
John Vukovich			
Billy Williams			

1988 Cubs David Berg

This 27-card set was given out at Wrigley Field with every paid admission on the Cubs' special "baseball card" promotion held August 24th. The set was sponsored by David Berg Pure Beef Hot Dogs and the Venture store chain. The cards are unnumbered except for uniform number. Card backs feature primarily black print on white card stock. The cards measure approximately 2 7/8" by 4 1/4" and are in full color. Mark Grace makes an early card appearance in this set.

	MINT	NRMT	EXC
COMPLETE SET (27)	15.00	6.75	1.85
COMMON CARD	.25	.11	.03
☐ 2 Vance Law	.25	.11	.03
☐ 4 Don Zimmer MG	.50	.23	.06
☐ 7 Jody Davis	.50	.23	.06
☐ 8 Andre Dawson	1.50	.70	.19
☐ 9 Damon Berryhill	.25	.11	.03
☐ 12 Shawon Dunston	.50	.23	.06
☐ 17 Mark Grace	4.00	1.80	.50
☐ 18 Angel Salazar	.25	.11	.03
☐ 19 Manny Trillo	.25	.11	.03
☐ 21 Scott Sanderson	.25	.11	.03
☐ 22 Jerry Mumphrey	.25	.11	.03
☐ 23 Ryne Sandberg	4.00	1.80	.50
☐ 24 Gary Varsho	.25	.11	.03
☐ 25 Rafael Palmeiro	2.50	1.10	.30
☐ 28 Mitch Webster	.25	.11	.03
☐ 30 Darrin Jackson	.25	.11	.03
☐ 31 Greg Maddux	6.00	2.70	.75
☐ 32 Calvin Schiraldi	.25	.11	.03
☐ 33 Frank DiPino	.25	.11	.03
☐ 37 Pat Perry	.25	.11	.03
☐ 40 Rick Sutcliffe	.75	.35	.09
☐ 41 Jeff Pico	.25	.11	.03
☐ 45 Al Nipper	.25	.11	.03
☐ 49 Jamie Moyer	.50	.23	.06
☐ 50 Les Lancaster	.25	.11	.03
☐ 54 Rich Gossage	.75	.35	.09
☐ NNO Cubs Coaching Staff Joe Altobelli Chuck Cottier Larry Cox Jose Martinez Dick Pole	.25	.11	.03

1988 Cubs Vance Law Smokey

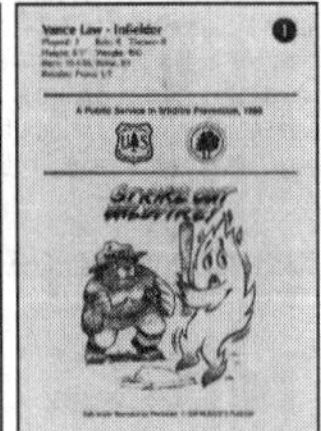

These cards which measure 3 3/4" by 5 1/2" feature Cub player Vance Law. He is in several different poses.

	MINT	NRMT	EXC
COMPLETE SET (4)	4.00	1.80	.50
COMMON CARD (1-4)	1.00	.45	.12
☐ 1 Vance Law Smokey Bear	1.50	.70	.19
☐ 2 Vance Law Fielding	1.25	.55	.16
☐ 3 Vance Law Batting	1.25	.55	.16
☐ 4 Smokey Bear	1.00	.45	.12

1989 Cubs Marathon

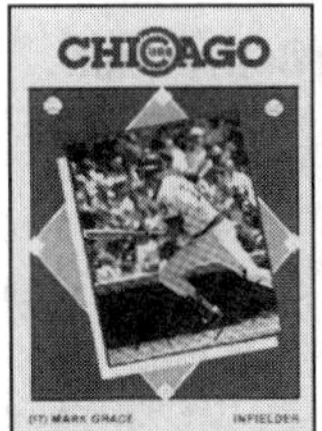

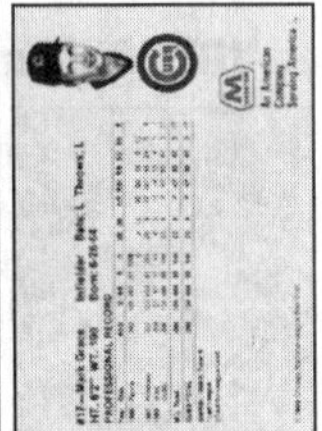

The 1989 Marathon Cubs set features 25 cards measuring approximately 2 3/4" by 4 1/4". The fronts are green and white, and feature facsimile autographs. The backs show black and white mug shots and career stats. The set was given away at the August 10, 1989 Cubs' home game. The cards are numbered by the players' uniform numbers.

	MINT	NRMT	EXC
COMPLETE SET (25)	18.00	8.00	2.20
COMMON CARD	.25	.11	.03
☐ 2 Vance Law	.25	.11	.03
☐ 4 Don Zimmer MG	.50	.23	.06
☐ 7 Joe Girardi	.25	.11	.03
☐ 8 Andre Dawson	2.00	.90	.25
☐ 9 Damon Berryhill	.25	.11	.03
☐ 10 Lloyd McClendon	.25	.11	.03
☐ 12 Shawon Dunston	.75	.35	.09
☐ 15 Domingo Ramos	.25	.11	.03
☐ 17 Mark Grace	5.00	2.20	.60
☐ 18 Dwight Smith	.50	.23	.06
☐ 19 Curt Wilkerson	.25	.11	.03
☐ 20 Jerome Walton	.50	.23	.06
☐ 21 Scott Sanderson	.50	.23	.06
☐ 23 Ryne Sandberg	5.00	2.20	.60
☐ 28 Mitch Williams	.50	.23	.06
☐ 31 Greg Maddux	7.50	3.40	.95
☐ 32 Calvin Schiraldi	.25	.11	.03
☐ 33 Mitch Webster	.25	.11	.03
☐ 36 Mike Bielecki	.25	.11	.03
☐ 39 Paul Kilgus	.25	.11	.03
☐ 40 Rick Sutcliffe	.75	.35	.09
☐ 41 Jeff Pico	.25	.11	.03
☐ 44 Steve Wilson	.25	.11	.03
☐ 50 Les Lancaster	.25	.11	.03
☐ NNO Cubs Coaches Joe Altobelli Chuck Cottier Larry Cox Jose Martinez Dick Pole	.25	.11	.03

1990 Cubs Marathon

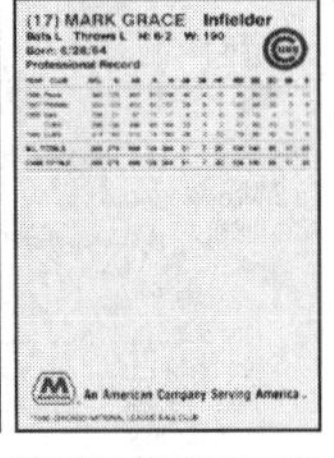

The Marathon Oil Chicago Cubs set contains 28 cards measuring approximately 2 7/8" by 4 1/4" which was given away at the August 17th Cubs' home game. Since the cards are unnumbered, the set is checklisted alphabetically below.

	MINT	NRMT	EXC
COMPLETE SET (28)	12.00	5.50	1.50
COMMON CARD (1-28)	.25	.11	.03
☐ 1 Paul Assenmacher	.25	.11	.03
☐ 2 Mike Bielecki	.25	.11	.03
☐ 3 Shawn Boskie	.75	.35	.09
☐ 4 Dave Clark	.25	.11	.03
☐ 5 Doug Dascenzo	.25	.11	.03
☐ 6 Andre Dawson	1.50	.70	.19
☐ 7 Shawon Dunston	.75	.35	.09
☐ 8 Joe Girardi	.25	.11	.03
☐ 9 Mark Grace	2.00	.90	.25
☐ 10 Mike Harkey	.25	.11	.03
☐ 11 Les Lancaster	.25	.11	.03
☐ 12 Bill Long	.25	.11	.03
☐ 13 Greg Maddux	4.00	1.80	.50
☐ 14 Lloyd McClendon	.25	.11	.03
☐ 15 Jeff Pico	.25	.11	.03
☐ 16 Domingo Ramos	.25	.11	.03
☐ 17 Luis Salazar	.25	.11	.03
☐ 18 Ryne Sandberg	3.00	1.35	.35
☐ 19 Dwight Smith	.25	.11	.03
☐ 20 Rick Sutcliffe	.75	.35	.09
☐ 21 Hector Villanueva	.25	.11	.03
☐ 22 Jerome Walton	.25	.11	.03
☐ 23 Curtis Wilkerson	.25	.11	.03
☐ 24 Mitch Williams	.50	.23	.06
☐ 25 Steve Wilson	.25	.11	.03
☐ 26 Marvell Wynne	.25	.11	.03
☐ 27 Don Zimmer MG	.50	.23	.06
☐ 28 Cubs Coaches Joe Altobelli Jose Martinez Phil Roof Chuck Cottier Dick Pole	.25	.11	.03

1991 Cubs Marathon

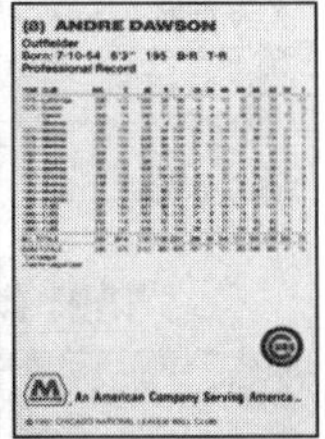

This 28-card set was produced by Marathon Oil, and its company logo appears at the bottom of card back. The cards were given away at the Cubs' home game against Montreal Expos on August 14, 1991. The oversized cards measure approximately 2 7/8" by 4 1/4" and feature on the fronts color action player photos with white borders. The card (uniform) number inside a white diamond and the words "Chicago Cubs" overlay the top portion of the photo. The player's name and position appear in the blue and red stripes traversing the bottom of the card face. The backs are printed in blue, red, and black on a white background and present biographical and statistical information. The set can also be found with blank backs. The cards are skip-numbered by uniform number and checklisted below accordingly.

	MINT	NRMT	EXC
COMPLETE SET (28)	12.00	5.50	1.50
COMMON CARD	.25	.11	.03
☐ 7 Joe Girardi	.25	.11	.03
☐ 8 Andre Dawson	1.25	.55	.16
☐ 9 Damon Berryhill	.25	.11	.03
☐ 10 Luis Salazar	.25	.11	.03
☐ 11 George Bell	.25	.11	.03
☐ 12 Shawon Dunston	.50	.23	.06
☐ 16 Jose Vizcaino	.75	.35	.09
☐ 17 Mark Grace	2.50	1.10	.30
☐ 18 Dwight Smith	.25	.11	.03
☐ 19 Hector Villanueva	.25	.11	.03
☐ 20 Jerome Walton	.25	.11	.03
☐ 22 Mike Harkey	.25	.11	.03
☐ 23 Ryne Sandberg	3.00	1.35	.35
☐ 24 Chico Walker	.25	.11	.03
☐ 29 Doug Dascenzo	.25	.11	.03
☐ 30 Bob Scanlan	.25	.11	.03
☐ 31 Greg Maddux	4.00	1.80	.50
☐ 32 Danny Jackson	.25	.11	.03
☐ 33 Chuck McElroy	.25	.11	.03
☐ 36 Mike Bielecki	.25	.11	.03
☐ 40 Rick Sutcliffe	.50	.23	.06
☐ 41 Jim Essian MG	.25	.11	.03
☐ 42 Dave Smith	.25	.11	.03
☐ 45 Paul Assenmacher	.25	.11	.03
☐ 47 Shawn Boskie	.25	.11	.03
☐ 50 Les Lancaster	.25	.11	.03
☐ 51 Heathcliff Slocumb	.75	.35	.09
☐ NNO Coaches Card Joe Altobelli Chuck Cottier Jose Martinez Billy Connors Phil Roof Richie Zisk	.25	.11	.03

1991 Cubs Vine Line

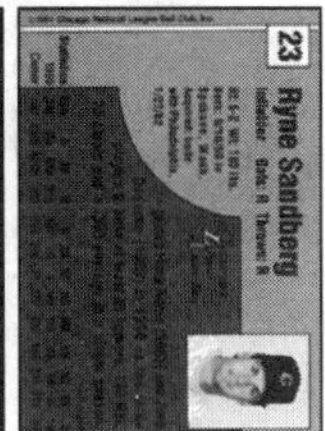

This 36-card set was issued as insert sheets in the Cubs' Vine Line fan news magazine. Each sheet measures approximately 7 1/2" by 10 1/2" and features nine different player cards. After perforation, the cards measure the standard size. On a black card face, the photos are framed by a white border stripes, with the words "Vine Line" above and player information beneath the picture. The color action player photos are cut out and superimposed on indistinct, ghosted action scenes. In a horizontal format, the taupe and green backs present biography, career highlights, and statistics (1990 and career). The cards are unnumbered and checklisted below in alphabetical order.

	MINT	NRMT	EXC
COMPLETE SET (36)	18.00	8.00	2.20
COMMON CARD (1-36)	.25	.11	.03
☐ 1 Paul Assenmacher	.25	.11	.03
☐ 2 Joe Altobelli CO	.25	.11	.03
☐ 3 George Bell	.25	.11	.03
☐ 4 Damon Berryhill	.25	.11	.03
☐ 5 Mike Bielecki	.25	.11	.03
☐ 6 Shawn Boskie	.25	.11	.03
☐ 7 Chuck Cottier CO	.25	.11	.03
☐ 8 Doug Dascenzo	.25	.11	.03
☐ 9 Andre Dawson	2.00	.90	.25
☐ 10 Shawon Dunston	.75	.35	.09
☐ 11 Joe Girardi	.25	.11	.03
☐ 12 Mark Grace	2.50	1.10	.30
☐ 13 Mike Harkey	.25	.11	.03
☐ 14 Danny Jackson	.25	.11	.03
☐ 15 Ferguson Jenkins CO	1.50	.70	.19
☐ 16 Les Lancaster	.25	.11	.03
☐ 17 Greg Maddux	7.50	3.40	.95
☐ 18 Jose Martinez CO	.25	.11	.03
☐ 19 Chuck McElroy	.25	.11	.03
☐ 20 Erik Pappas	.25	.11	.03
☐ 21 Dick Pole CO	.25	.11	.03
☐ 22 Phil Roof CO	.25	.11	.03
☐ 23 Ryne Sandberg	5.00	2.20	.60
☐ 24 Luis Salazar	.25	.11	.03
☐ 25 Gary Scott	.25	.11	.03
☐ 26 Heathcliff Slocumb	1.00	.45	.12
☐ 27 Dave Smith	.50	.23	.06
☐ 28 Dwight Smith	.25	.11	.03
☐ 29 Rick Sutcliffe	.75	.35	.09
☐ 30 Hector Villanueva	.25	.11	.03
☐ 31 Jose Vizcaino	.75	.35	.09
☐ 32 Chico Walker	.25	.11	.03
☐ 33 Jerome Walton	.25	.11	.03
☐ 34 Steve Wilson	.25	.11	.03
☐ 35 Don Zimmer MG	.50	.23	.06
☐ 36 Most Valuable Players Ryne Sandberg Andre Dawson George Bell	1.50	.70	.19

1992 Cubs Marathon

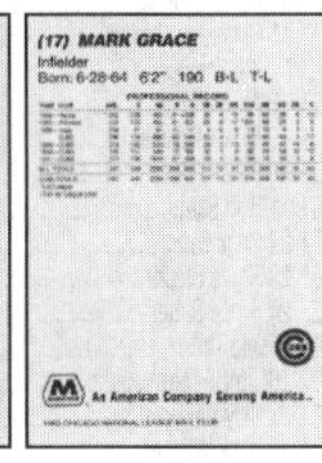

This 28-card set was produced by Marathon Oil, and its company logo appears at the bottom of the card back. The cards measure approximately 2 7/8" by 4 1/4". The fronts display color action player photos bordered in white. The player's name appears in a blue stripe above the picture, while the year is shown in a blue stripe below. The backs are printed in blue, red, and black on a white background and present biographical and statistical information. The cards are skip-numbered on the back by uniform number and checklisted below accordingly.

	MINT	NRMT	EXC
COMPLETE SET (28)	12.00	5.50	1.50
COMMON CARD	.25	.11	.03
☐ 1 Doug Strange	.25	.11	.03
☐ 5 Jim Lefebvre MG	.25	.11	.03
☐ 6 Rey Sanchez	.25	.11	.03
☐ 7 Joe Girardi	.25	.11	.03
☐ 8 Andre Dawson	1.25	.55	.16
☐ 10 Luis Salazar	.25	.11	.03
☐ 12 Shawon Dunston	.75	.35	.09
☐ 16 Jose Vizcaino	.75	.35	.09
☐ 17 Mark Grace	2.00	.90	.25
☐ 18 Dwight Smith	.25	.11	.03
☐ 19 Hector Villanueva	.25	.11	.03
☐ 20 Jerome Walton	.25	.11	.03
☐ 21 Sammy Sosa	2.00	.90	.25
☐ 23 Ryne Sandberg	2.50	1.10	.30
☐ 27 Derrick May	.25	.11	.03
☐ 29 Doug Dascenzo	.25	.11	.03
☐ 30 Bob Scanlan	.25	.11	.03
☐ 31 Greg Maddux	4.00	1.80	.50
☐ 32 Danny Jackson	.25	.11	.03
☐ 34 Ken Patterson	.25	.11	.03
☐ 35 Chuck McElroy	.25	.11	.03
☐ 36 Mike Morgan	.25	.11	.03
☐ 38 Jeff D. Robinson	.25	.11	.03
☐ 42 Dave Smith	.25	.11	.03
☐ 45 Paul Assenmacher	.25	.11	.03
☐ 47 Shawn Boskie	.25	.11	.03
☐ 49 Frank Castillo	.50	.23	.06
☐ NNO Coaches Card Tom Trebelhorn Jose Martinez Billy Williams Sammy Ellis Chuck Cottier Billy Connors	.50	.23	.06

1992 Cubs Old Style

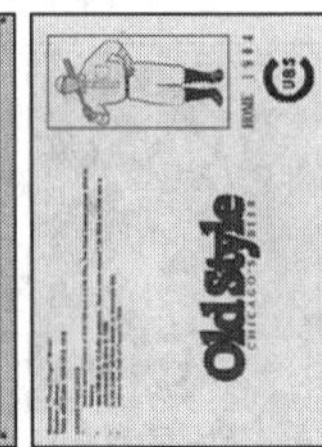

This 28-card set measures the standard size and features sepia-tone player photos with tan borders. The player's name appears below the picture, and the years he played are above it. A thin green line surrounds the text and photo and accents the card front. The horizontal backs are white and carry career highlights and an illustration of the home uniform from the player's first year with the Cubs. Old Style Beer sponsored the set, and the company logo is printed on the back. The cards are unnumbered and checklisted below in alphabetical order.

	MINT	NRMT	EXC
COMPLETE SET (28)	15.00	6.75	1.85
COMMON CARD (1-28)	.25	.11	.03
☐ 1 Grover C. Alexander	1.50	.70	.19
☐ 2 Cap Anson	1.25	.55	.16
☐ 3 Ernie Banks	3.00	1.35	.35
☐ 4 Mordecai Brown	.75	.35	.09
☐ 5 Phil Cavarretta	.50	.23	.06
☐ 6 Frank Chance	1.00	.45	.12
☐ 7 Kiki Cuyler	.75	.35	.09
☐ 8 Johnny Evers	1.00	.45	.12
☐ 9 Charlie Grimm	.50	.23	.06

☐ 10 Stan Hack	.25	.11	.03
☐ 11 Gabby Hartnett	.75	.35	.09
☐ 12 Billy Herman	.75	.35	.09
☐ 13 Rogers Hornsby	1.50	.70	.19
☐ 14 Ken Hubbs	.50	.23	.06
☐ 15 Randy Hundley	.25	.11	.03
☐ 16 Ferguson Jenkins	1.25	.55	.16
☐ 17 Bill Lee	.25	.11	.03
☐ 18 Andy Pafko	.25	.11	.03
☐ 19 Rick Reuschel	.25	.11	.03
☐ 20 Charlie Root	.25	.11	.03
☐ 21 Ron Santo	.75	.35	.09
☐ 22 Hank Sauer	.25	.11	.03
☐ 23 Riggs Stephenson	.50	.23	.06
☐ 24 Bruce Sutter	.50	.23	.06
☐ 25 Joe Tinker	1.00	.45	.12
☐ 26 Jim(Hippo) Vaughn	.25	.11	.03
☐ 27 Billy Williams	1.50	.70	.19
☐ 28 Hack Wilson	1.00	.45	.12

1993 Cubs Marathon

This 32-card set was produced by Marathon Oil, and its company logo appears at the bottom of the card back. The cards measure approximately 2 7/8" by 4 1/4". The backs present biographical and statistical information. The cards are checklisted below in alphabetical order.

	MINT	NRMT	EXC
COMPLETE SET (32)	12.00	5.50	1.50
COMMON CARD (1-32)	.25	.11	.03
☐ 1 Paul Assenmacher	.25	.11	.03
☐ 2 Jose Bautista	.25	.11	.03
☐ 3 Steve Buechele	.25	.11	.03
☐ 4 Frank Castillo	.50	.23	.06
☐ 5 Billy Connors CO	.25	.11	.03
☐ 6 Chuck Cottier CO	.25	.11	.03
☐ 7 Mark Grace	2.50	1.10	.30
☐ 8 Jose Guzman	.25	.11	.03
☐ 9 Mike Harkey	.25	.11	.03
☐ 10 Greg Hibbard	.25	.11	.03
☐ 11 Doug Jennings	.25	.11	.03
☐ 12 Steve Lake	.25	.11	.03
☐ 13 Jim Lefebvre MG	.25	.11	.03
☐ 14 Candy Maldonado	.25	.11	.03
☐ 15 Jose Martinez CO	.25	.11	.03
☐ 16 Derrick May	.25	.11	.03
☐ 17 Mike Morgan	.25	.11	.03
☐ 18 Randy Myers	.75	.35	.09
☐ 19 Tony Muser CO	.25	.11	.03
☐ 20 Dan Plesac	.25	.11	.03
☐ 21 Ryne Sandberg	4.00	1.80	.50
☐ 22 Rey Sanchez	.25	.11	.03
☐ 23 Bob Scanlan	.25	.11	.03
☐ 24 Dan Simonds	.25	.11	.03
☐ 25 Dwight Smith	.25	.11	.03
☐ 26 Sammy Sosa	1.50	.70	.19
☐ 27 Tom Trebelhorn CO	.25	.11	.03
☐ 28 Jose Vizcaino	.75	.35	.09
☐ 29 Rick Wilkins	.25	.11	.03
☐ 30 Billy Williams CO	1.00	.45	.12
☐ 31 Willie Wilson	.25	.11	.03
☐ 32 Eric Yelding	.25	.11	.03

1993 Cubs Old Style Billy Williams

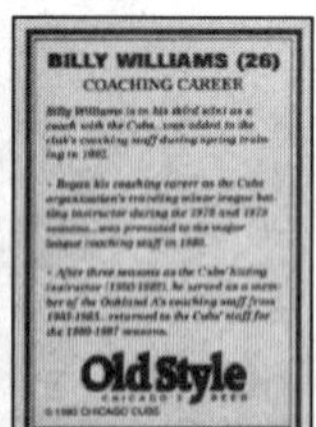

These four standard-size cards feature on their red, white, and blue-bordered fronts black-and-white action shots (except for number 1 below, which carries a posed color photo) of Billy Williams. His first and last name appear in white lettering in blue boxes above and below his image, respectively. The white backs are framed in red and blue lines and carry career highlights. The cards are unnumbered.

	MINT	NRMT	EXC
COMPLETE SET (4)	10.00	4.50	1.25
COMMON CARD (1-4)	3.00	1.35	.35
☐ 1 Billy Williams Coaching Career	3.00	1.35	.35
☐ 2 Billy Williams Playing Career (Making catch at ivy-covered wall)	3.00	1.35	.35
☐ 3 Billy Williams Personal	3.00	1.35	.35
☐ 4 Billy Williams Playing Career (Awaiting pitch)	3.00	1.35	.35

1993 Cubs Rolaids

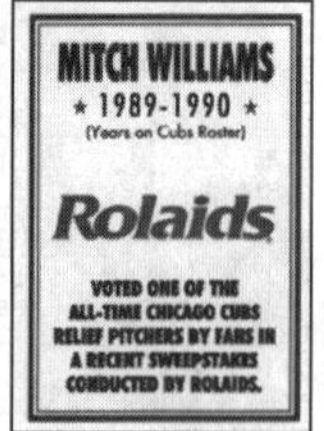

This four-card standard-size set is subtitled "All-Time Cubs Relief Pitchers" and was given away at Wrigley Field on Sept. 4, 1993. Each card features on its front a white-bordered color photo of the pitcher upon a black-and-white background. The white back is framed by red and purple lines and carries the pitcher's name, the years he played for the Cubs, a career highlight, and the Rolaids logo. The cards are unnumbered and checklisted below in alphabetical order.

	MINT	NRMT	EXC
COMPLETE SET (4)	4.00	1.80	.50
COMMON CARD (1-4)	1.00	.45	.12
☐ 1 Randy Myers	1.25	.55	.16
☐ 2 Lee Smith	1.50	.70	.19
☐ 3 Bruce Sutter	1.25	.55	.16
☐ 4 Mitch Williams	1.00	.45	.12

1996 CUI Metal Cards Griffey

This metal card set was issued in a tin box with a suggested retail price of $9.95. The fronts feature color player photos of Ken Griffey Jr. on a blue and green background. The backs carry information about different phases of his life. The cards are unnumbered and checklisted below according to what is taking place on the card.

	MINT	NRMT	EXC
COMPLETE SET (5)	10.00	4.50	1.25
COMMON CARD (1-4)	2.50	1.10	.30
☐ 1 Ken Griffey Jr. (Batting)	2.50	1.10	.30
☐ 2 Ken Griffey Jr. (Watching the ball after it was hit)	2.50	1.10	.30
☐ 3 Ken Griffey Jr. (Running to base)	2.50	1.10	.30
☐ 4 Ken Griffey Jr. (Sliding into base)	2.50	1.10	.30
☐ NNO Ken Griffey Tin Box	2.00	.90	.25

1996 CUI Metal Cards Ripken

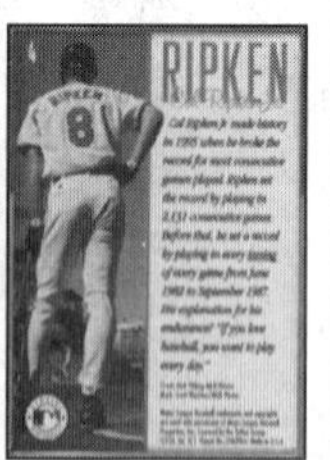

This metal card set was issued in a tin-holder with a suggested retail price of $9.95 and was primarily sold in retail outlets such as K-Mart. The fronts feature color action photos of Cal Ripken Jr. with the backs displaying something about his life. The cards are unnumbered.

	MINT	NRMT	EXC
COMPLETE SET (5)	10.00	4.50	1.25
COMMON CARD (1-4)	2.50	1.10	.30
☐ 1 Cal Ripken (Batting in blue shirt)	2.50	1.10	.30
☐ 2 Cal Ripken (At bat in uniform)	2.50	1.10	.30
☐ 3 Cal Ripken (Running)	2.50	1.10	.30
☐ 4 Cal Ripken (Fielding)	2.50	1.10	.30
☐ NNO Cal Ripken Tin Box	2.00	.90	.25

1995 D3

Manufactured by Topps, this set consists of 59 three-dimension standard-size cards of better players. Utilizing uncluttered fronts, the player's name is at the top with the set logo toward bottom right. The backs offer a small photo with statistical breakdowns in areas such as Home, Away, Day, Night, etc. A second series was planned for this issue but was never issued due to consumer disinterest.

	MINT	NRMT	EXC
COMPLETE SET (59)	15.00	6.75	1.85
COMMON CARD (1-59)	.10	.05	.01
☐ 1 David Justice	.50	.23	.06
☐ 2 Cal Ripken	3.00	1.35	.35
☐ 3 Ruben Sierra	.10	.05	.01
☐ 4 Roberto Alomar	.75	.35	.09
☐ 5 Denny Martinez	.10	.05	.01
☐ 6 Todd Zeile	.10	.05	.01
☐ 7 Albert Belle	2.00	.90	.25
☐ 8 Chuck Knoblauch	.40	.18	.05
☐ 9 Roger Clemens	.75	.35	.09
☐ 10 Cal Eldred	.10	.05	.01
☐ 11 Dennis Eckersley	.25	.11	.03
☐ 12 Andy Benes	.25	.11	.03
☐ 13 Moises Alou	.25	.11	.03
☐ 14 Andres Galarraga	.40	.18	.05
☐ 15 Jim Thome	.75	.35	.09
☐ 16 Tim Salmon	.40	.18	.05
☐ 17 Carlos Garcia	.10	.05	.01
☐ 18 Scott Leius	.10	.05	.01
☐ 19 Jeff Montgomery	.10	.05	.01
☐ 20 Brian Anderson	.10	.05	.01
☐ 21 Will Clark	.50	.23	.06
☐ 22 Bobby Bonilla	.25	.11	.03
☐ 23 Mike Stanley	.10	.05	.01
☐ 24 Barry Bonds	1.00	.45	.12
☐ 25 Jeff Conine	.25	.11	.03
☐ 26 Paul O'Neill	.10	.05	.01
☐ 27 Mike Piazza	2.50	1.10	.30
☐ 28 Tom Glavine	.50	.23	.06
☐ 29 Jim Edmonds	.40	.18	.05
☐ 30 Lou Whitaker	.25	.11	.03
☐ 31 Jeff Frye	.10	.05	.01
☐ 32 Ivan Rodriguez	1.50	.70	.19
☐ 33 Bret Boone	.10	.05	.01
☐ 34 Mike Greenwell	.10	.05	.01
☐ 35 Mark Grace	.50	.23	.06
☐ 36 Darren Lewis	.10	.05	.01
☐ 37 Don Mattingly	2.00	.90	.25
☐ 38 Jose Rijo	.10	.05	.01
☐ 39 Robin Ventura	.25	.11	.03
☐ 40 Bob Hamelin	.10	.05	.01
☐ 41 Tim Wallach	.10	.05	.01
☐ 42 Tony Gwynn	1.50	.70	.19
☐ 43 Ken Griffey Jr.	4.00	1.80	.50
☐ 44 Doug Drabek	.10	.05	.01
☐ 45 Rafael Palmeiro	.50	.23	.06
☐ 46 Dean Palmer	.25	.11	.03
☐ 47 Bip Roberts	.10	.05	.01
☐ 48 Barry Larkin	.40	.18	.05
☐ 49 Dave Nilsson	.10	.05	.01
☐ 50 Wil Cordero	.10	.05	.01
☐ 51 Travis Fryman	.25	.11	.03
☐ 52 Chuck Carr	.10	.05	.01
☐ 53 Rey Sanchez	.10	.05	.01
☐ 54 Walt Weiss	.10	.05	.01
☐ 55 Joe Carter	.40	.18	.05
☐ 56 Len Dykstra	.10	.05	.01
☐ 57 Orlando Merced	.10	.05	.01
☐ 58 Ozzie Smith	1.00	.45	.12
☐ 59 Chris Gomez	.10	.05	.01
☐ PB1 Greg Gagne Baseball Promo	3.00	1.35	.35

1995 D3 Zone

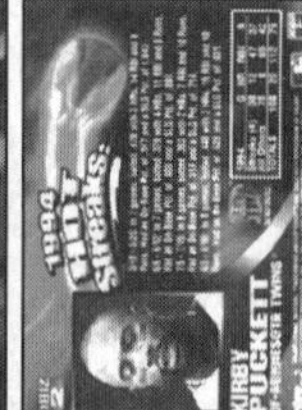

This three-dimensional, six-card set was inserted in Topps D3 packs. They were inserted one in three hobby packs and one in six retail packs. The 3D front has a player photo surrounded by baseballs. The player's name is at the top with the set logo at the bottom. Horizontal backs offer a small player photo and a synopsis of various hot streaks in 1994. Cards are numbered with a "DIII" prefix.

	MINT	NRMT	EXC
COMPLETE SET (6)	15.00	6.75	1.85
COMMON CARD (1-6)	1.00	.45	.12
☐ 1 Frank Thomas	8.00	3.60	1.00
☐ 2 Kirby Puckett	4.00	1.80	.50
☐ 3 Jeff Bagwell	3.00	1.35	.35
☐ 4 Fred McGriff	1.00	.45	.12
☐ 5 Raul Mondesi	1.00	.45	.12
☐ 6 Kenny Lofton	2.00	.90	.25

1994 Dairy Queen Griffey Jr.

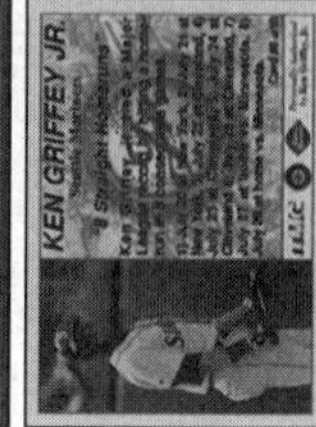

The 1994 Dairy Queen Ken Griffey Jr. set consists of ten standard-size cards. The cards were distributed in 5-card packs at the restaurants, with the gold cards randomly inserted. The fronts feature color action shots of Griffey with the set title's logo appearing in the upper left corner of the picture. Ken Griffey's name is printed below the photo in gold block lettering beside the Dairy Queen logo. The photo is bordered in gold on some sets, and in green on others. The production run on the green-border sets was 90,000, while that of the gold-bordered sets was 10,000. The gold versions are valued at double the values listed below. Except for card number 2, the backs are in a horizontal format, with a posed or action photo on the left side. The right side has a ghosted set logo on a gray marbleized background. The card title and a brief narrative appears on the right side. According to the information on the back, Ken Griffey Jr. personally authorized the set. The cards are numbered on the back.

	MINT	NRMT	EXC
COMPLETE SET (10)	10.00	4.50	1.25
COMMON CARD (1-10)	1.25	.55	.16
☐ 1 Ken Griffey Jr. The Spider Man Catch	1.25	.55	.16
☐ 2 Ken Griffey Jr. Back to Back Home Runs	1.25	.55	.16
☐ 3 Ken Griffey Jr. Hit .327 in 1991	1.25	.55	.16
☐ 4 Ken Griffey Jr. 1992 All-Star MVP	1.25	.55	.16
☐ 5 Ken Griffey Jr. Dialing Long Distance	1.25	.55	.16
☐ 6 Ken Griffey Jr. 8 Straight Home Runs	1.25	.55	.16
☐ 7 Ken Griffey Jr. 4-Time Gold Glove Winner	1.25	.55	.16
☐ 8 Ken Griffey Jr. 45 Home Runs in 1993	1.25	.55	.16
☐ 9 Ken Griffey Jr. Major League Career Hitting Record	1.25	.55	.16
☐ 10 Ken Griffey Jr. Looking to 1994	1.25	.55	.16

1976 Dallas Convention

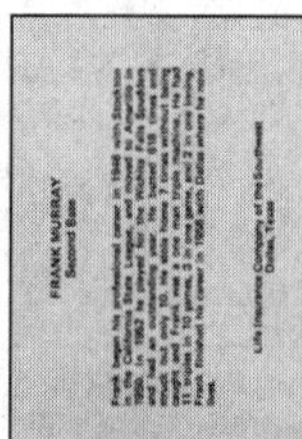

This nine-card slightly oversized set features local Dallas players and was issued in conjunction with the annual Dallas Sports Card Convention hosted by noted hobbyist Gervise Ford. Mr. Ford also produced the set with "Life of the Southwest Insurance Co.".

	NRMT	VG-E	GOOD
COMPLETE SET (9)	2.00	.90	.25
COMMON CARD (1-9)	.25	.11	.03
☐ 1 Paul Aube	.25	.11	.03
☐ 2 Jodie Beeler	.25	.11	.03
☐ 3 Edward Borom (Red)	.25	.11	.03
☐ 4 Sal Gliatto	.25	.11	.03
☐ 5 Richard Herrscher	.25	.11	.03
☐ 6 Joe Kotrany	.25	.11	.03
☐ 7 Joe Macko	.25	.11	.03
☐ 8 Frank Murray	.25	.11	.03
☐ 9 Ron Samford	.25	.11	.03

1985 Dallas National Collectors Convention

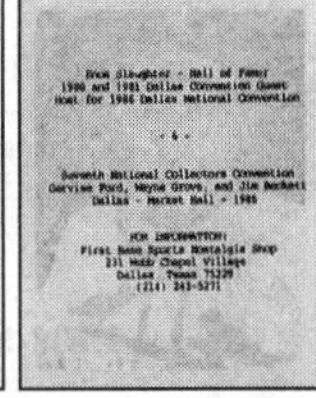

This 12-card set was issued by First Base Sports Nostalgia Shop in Dallas, Texas, to commemorate a bid for the Dallas National Collectors Convention. The black-and-white cards measure approximately 2" by 2 1/2" and include various photos relating to their National Convention bid including a photo of the proposed 1986 Convention hosts (Jim Beckett, Wayne Grove, and Gervise Ford) along with Dallas Maverick star Brad Davis, a shot of the Dallas Marriott, Market Hall and several Baseball legends who were guests of honor of the convention. The backs list the subject of the card front with a brief description and the First Base Sports Nostalgia Shop address. The cards are numbered on the back.

	NRMT	VG-E	GOOD
COMPLETE SET (12)	5.00	2.20	.60
COMMON CARD (1-12)	.25	.11	.03
☐ 1 Stan Musial	1.50	.70	.19
☐ 2 Ted Williams	2.00	.90	.25
☐ 3 Bob Gibson	.75	.35	.09
☐ 4 Brooks Robinson	.75	.35	.09
☐ 5 Warren Spahn	.75	.35	.09
☐ 6 Enos Slaughter	.75	.35	.09
☐ 7 The Famous Chicken	.50	.23	.06
☐ 8 Lou Brock	.75	.35	.09
☐ 9 Market Hall 1986 Dallas Natl. Convention Facility	.25	.11	.03
☐ 10 Texas Ranger Scoreboard	.25	.11	.03
☐ 11 Dallas Marriott Market Center	.25	.11	.03
☐ 12 Jim Beckett Wayne Grove Brad Davis (Dallas Maverick) Gervise Ford Hosts	.50	.23	.06

1954 Dan Dee

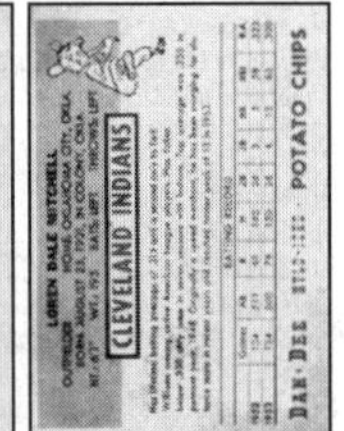

The cards in this 29-card set measure approximately 2 1/2" by 3 5/8". Most of the cards marketed by Dan Dee in bags of potato chips in 1954 depict players from the Cleveland Indians or Pittsburgh Pirates. The Pitttsburgh Pirates players in the set are much tougher to find than the Cleveland Indians players. The pictures used for New York Yankees players were also employed in the Briggs and Stahl-Meyer sets. Dan Dee cards have a waxed surface, but are commonly found with product stains. Paul Smith and Walker Cooper are considered the known scarcities. The catalog designation for this set is F342. These unnumbered cards are listed below in alphabetical order.

	NRMT	VG-E	GOOD
COMPLETE SET (29)	4500.00	2000.00	550.00
COMMON CARD (1-29)	50.00	22.00	6.25
COMMON PIRATE PLAYER	65.00	29.00	8.00
☐ 1 Bobby Avila	50.00	22.00	6.25
☐ 2 Hank Bauer	60.00	27.00	7.50
☐ 3 Walker Cooper SP Pittsburgh Pirates	300.00	135.00	38.00
☐ 4 Larry Doby	75.00	34.00	9.50
☐ 5 Luke Easter	60.00	27.00	7.50
☐ 6 Bob Feller	200.00	90.00	25.00
☐ 7 Bob Friend Pittsburgh Pirates	90.00	40.00	11.00
☐ 8 Mike Garcia	50.00	22.00	6.25
☐ 9 Sid Gordon Pittsburgh Pirates	65.00	29.00	8.00
☐ 10 Jim Hegan	50.00	22.00	6.25
☐ 11 Gil Hodges	125.00	55.00	15.50
☐ 12 Art Houtteman	50.00	22.00	6.25
☐ 13 Monte Irvin	100.00	45.00	12.50
☐ 14 Paul LaPalme Pittsburgh Pirates	65.00	29.00	8.00
☐ 15 Bob Lemon	100.00	45.00	12.50
☐ 16 Al Lopez MG	100.00	45.00	12.50
☐ 17 Mickey Mantle	1800.00	800.00	220.00
☐ 18 Dale Mitchell	50.00	22.00	6.25
☐ 19 Phil Rizzuto	200.00	90.00	25.00
☐ 20 Curt Roberts Pittsburgh Pirates	65.00	29.00	8.00
☐ 21 Al Rosen	60.00	27.00	7.50
☐ 22 Red Schoendienst	100.00	45.00	12.50
☐ 23 Paul Smith SP Pittsburgh Pirates	500.00	220.00	60.00
☐ 24 Duke Snider	225.00	100.00	28.00
☐ 25 George Strickland	50.00	22.00	6.25
☐ 26 Max Surkont Pittsburgh Pirates	65.00	29.00	8.00
☐ 27 Frank Thomas Pittsburgh Pirates	150.00	70.00	19.00
☐ 28 Wally Westlake	50.00	22.00	6.25
☐ 29 Early Wynn	100.00	45.00	12.50

1910 Darby Chocolates E271

These 32 cards listed below are what are known of this very scarce set. A major help in cataloguing this set was a find of 22 cards in 1982. Some new cards are always being discovered. We understand that this checklist may be incomplete therefore verified copies of unlisted cards are appreciated.

	EX-MT	VG-E	GOOD
COMPLETE SET (32)	15000.00	6800.00	1900.00
COMMON CARD (1-32)	300.00	135.00	38.00
☐ 1 Jimmy Archer	300.00	135.00	38.00
☐ 2 Chief Bender	600.00	275.00	75.00
☐ 3 Bob Bescher	300.00	135.00	38.00
☐ 4 Roger Bresnahan	600.00	275.00	75.00
☐ 5 Al Bridwell	300.00	135.00	38.00
☐ 6 Mordecai Brown	600.00	275.00	75.00
☐ 7 Eddie Cicotte	450.00	200.00	55.00
☐ 8 Fred Clarke	600.00	275.00	75.00
☐ 9 Ty Cobb	2500.00	1100.00	300.00
☐ 10 King Cole	300.00	135.00	38.00
☐ 11 Eddie Collins	750.00	350.00	95.00
☐ 12 Wid Conroy	300.00	135.00	38.00
☐ 13 Sam Crawford	600.00	275.00	75.00
☐ 14 Bill Dahlen	300.00	135.00	38.00
☐ 15 Bill Donovan	300.00	135.00	38.00
☐ 16 Patsy Dougherty	300.00	135.00	38.00
☐ 17 Kid Elberfeld	300.00	135.00	38.00
☐ 18 Johnny Evers	600.00	275.00	75.00
☐ 19 Buck Herzog	300.00	135.00	38.00
☐ 20 Walter Johnson	1500.00	700.00	190.00
☐ 21 Ed Konetchy	300.00	135.00	38.00
☐ 22 Tommy Leach	300.00	135.00	38.00
☐ 23 Fred Luderus Sic, Luderous	300.00	135.00	38.00
☐ 24 Mike Mowrey	300.00	135.00	38.00
☐ 25 Jack Powell	300.00	135.00	38.00
☐ 26 Slim Sallee	300.00	135.00	38.00
☐ 27 Jimmy Sheckard Sic, Scheckard	300.00	135.00	38.00
☐ 28 Fred Snodgrass	350.00	160.00	45.00
☐ 29 Tris Speaker	750.00	350.00	95.00
☐ 30 Charlie Suggs	300.00	135.00	38.00
☐ 31 Fred Tenney	300.00	135.00	38.00
☐ 32 Honus Wagner	1600.00	700.00	200.00

1970 Dayton Daily News M137

These 3 3/4" by 3 1/2" cards were issued inside issues of the Dayton Daily News. The newsprint-stock cards were issued on successive days and were numbered in that order.

	NRMT	VG-E	GOOD
COMPLETE SET (160)	400.00	180.00	50.00
COMMON CARD (1-160)	2.00	.90	.25
☐ 1 Pete Rose	15.00	6.75	1.85
☐ 2 Johnny Bench	7.50	3.40	.95
☐ 3 Maury Wills	2.50	1.10	.30
☐ 4 Harmon Killebrew	5.00	2.20	.60
☐ 5 Frank Robinson	7.50	3.40	.95
☐ 7 Hank Aaron	15.00	6.75	1.85
☐ 8 Tom Seaver	7.50	3.40	.95
☐ 9 Sam McDowell	2.00	.90	.25
☐ 10 Rico Petrocelli	2.00	.90	.25
☐ 11 Tony Perez (2)	3.50	1.55	.45
☐ 12 Hoyt Wilhelm	3.50	1.55	.45
☐ 13 Alex Johnson	2.00	.90	.25
☐ 14 Gary Nolan	2.00	.90	.25
☐ 15 Al Kaline	7.50	3.40	.95
☐ 16 Bob Gibson	7.50	3.40	.95
☐ 17 Larry Dierker	2.00	.90	.25
☐ 18 Ernie Banks	7.50	3.40	.95
☐ 19 Lee May	2.00	.90	.25
☐ 20 Claude Osteen	2.00	.90	.25
☐ 21 Tony Horton	2.00	.90	.25
☐ 22 Mack Jones	2.00	.90	.25
☐ 23 Wally Bunker	2.00	.90	.25
☐ 24 Bill Hands	2.00	.90	.25
☐ 25 Bobby Tolan	2.00	.90	.25
☐ 26 Jim Wynn	2.00	.90	.25
☐ 27 Tom Haller	2.00	.90	.25
☐ 28 Carl Yastrzemski	7.50	3.40	.95
☐ 30 Tony Oliva	2.00	.90	.25
☐ 31 Reggie Jackson	15.00	6.75	1.85
☐ 32 Bob Clemente	25.00	11.00	3.10
☐ 33 Tommy Helms	2.00	.90	.25
☐ 34 Boog Powell	3.50	1.55	.45
☐ 35 Mickey Lolich	2.50	1.10	.30
☐ 36 Frank Howard	2.50	1.10	.30
☐ 37 Jim McGlothlin	2.00	.90	.25
☐ 38 Rusty Staub	2.50	1.10	.30
☐ 39 Mel Stottlemyre	2.00	.90	.25
☐ 40 Rico Carty	2.00	.90	.25
☐ 41 Nate Colbert	2.00	.90	.25
☐ 42 Wayne Granger	2.00	.90	.25
☐ 43 Mike Hegan	2.00	.90	.25
☐ 44 Jerry Koosman	2.50	1.10	.30
☐ 45 Jim Perry	2.00	.90	.25
☐ 46 Pat Corrales	2.00	.90	.25
☐ 47 Dick Bosman	2.00	.90	.25
☐ 48 Bert Campaneris	2.00	.90	.25
☐ 49 Larry Hisle	2.00	.90	.25
☐ 50 Bernie Carbo	2.00	.90	.25
☐ 51 Dave McNally	2.00	.90	.25
☐ 53 Andy Messersmith	2.00	.90	.25
☐ 55 Luis Aparicio	3.50	1.55	.45
☐ 56 Mike Cuellar	2.00	.90	.25
☐ 57 Bill Grabarkewitz	2.00	.90	.25
☐ 58 Dick Dietz	2.00	.90	.25
☐ 59 Dave Concepcion	2.50	1.10	.30
☐ 60 Gary Gentry	2.00	.90	.25
☐ 61 Don Money	2.00	.90	.25
☐ 62 Rod Carew	7.50	3.40	.95
☐ 63 Denis Menke	2.00	.90	.25
☐ 64 Hal McRae	2.00	.90	.25
☐ 65 Felipe Alou	2.00	.90	.25
☐ 66 Richie Hebner	2.00	.90	.25
☐ 67 Don Sutton	3.50	1.55	.45
☐ 68 Wayne Simpson	2.00	.90	.25
☐ 69 Art Shamsky	2.00	.90	.25
☐ 70 Luis Tiant	3.00	1.35	.35
☐ 71 Clay Carroll	2.00	.90	.25
☐ 72 Jim Hickman	2.00	.90	.25
☐ 73 Clarence Gaston	2.00	.90	.25
☐ 74 Angel Bravo	2.00	.90	.25
☐ 75 Jim Hunter	3.50	1.55	.45
☐ 76 Lou Piniella	2.00	.90	.25
☐ 77 Jim Bunning	3.50	1.55	.45
☐ 78 Don Gullett	2.00	.90	.25
☐ 80 Richie Allen	3.50	1.55	.45
☐ 81 Jim Bouton	2.00	.90	.25
☐ 82 Jim Palmer	7.50	3.40	.95
☐ 83 Woody Woodward	2.00	.90	.25
☐ 84 Tom Agee	2.00	.90	.25
☐ 85 Carlos May	2.00	.90	.25
☐ 86 Ray Washburn	2.00	.90	.25
☐ 87 Denny McLain	3.50	1.55	.45
☐ 88 Lou Brock	7.50	3.40	.95
☐ 89 Ken Henderson	2.00	.90	.25
☐ 90 Roy White	2.00	.90	.25
☐ 91 Chris Cannizzaro	2.00	.90	.25
☐ 92 Willie Horton	2.00	.90	.25
☐ 93 Jose Cardenal	2.00	.90	.25
☐ 94 Jim Fregosi	2.00	.90	.25
☐ 95 Richie Hebner	2.00	.90	.25
☐ 96 Tony Conigliaro	2.50	1.10	.30
☐ 97 Tony Cloninger	2.00	.90	.25
☐ 98 Mike Epstein	2.00	.90	.25
☐ 99 Ty Cline	2.00	.90	.25
☐ 100 Tommy Harper	2.00	.90	.25
☐ 101 Jose Azcue	2.00	.90	.25
☐ 102a Ray Fosse	2.00	.90	.25
☐ 102b Glenn Beckert	2.00	.90	.25
☐ 103 not issued			
☐ 104 Gerry Moses	2.00	.90	.25
☐ 105 Bud Harrelson	2.00	.90	.25
☐ 106 Joe Torre	3.50	1.55	.45
☐ 107 Dave Johnson	2.00	.90	.25
☐ 108 Don Kessinger	2.00	.90	.25
☐ 110 Sandy Alomar	2.00	.90	.25
☐ 111 Matty Alou	2.00	.90	.25
☐ 112 Joe Morgan	5.00	2.20	.60
☐ 113 John Odom	2.00	.90	.25
☐ 114 Amos Otis	2.00	.90	.25
☐ 115 Jay Johnstone	2.00	.90	.25
☐ 116 Ron Perranoski	2.00	.90	.25
☐ 117 Manny Mota	2.00	.90	.25
☐ 118 Billy Conigliaro	2.00	.90	.25
☐ 119 Leo Cardenas	2.00	.90	.25
☐ 120 Rich Reese	2.00	.90	.25
☐ 121 Ron Santo	3.50	1.55	.45
☐ 122 Gene Michael	2.00	.90	.25
☐ 123 Milt Pappas	2.00	.90	.25
☐ 124 Joe Pepitone	2.00	.90	.25
☐ 125 Jose Cardenal	2.00	.90	.25
☐ 126 Jim Northrup	2.00	.90	.25
☐ 127 Wes Parker	2.00	.90	.25
☐ 128 Fritz Peterson	2.00	.90	.25
☐ 129 Phil Regan	2.00	.90	.25
☐ 130 John Callison	2.00	.90	.25
☐ 131 Cookie Rojas	2.00	.90	.25
☐ 132 Claude Raymond	2.00	.90	.25
☐ 133 Darrell Chaney	2.00	.90	.25
☐ 134 Gary Peters	2.00	.90	.25
☐ 135 Del Unser	2.00	.90	.25
☐ 136 Joey Foy	2.00	.90	.25
☐ 138 Bill Mazeroski	3.50	1.55	.45
☐ 139 Tony Taylor	2.00	.90	.25
☐ 140 Leron Lee	2.00	.90	.25
☐ 141 Jesus Alou	2.00	.90	.25
☐ 142 Donn Clendenon	2.00	.90	.25
☐ 143 Merv Rettenmund	2.00	.90	.25
☐ 144 Bob Moose	2.00	.90	.25
☐ 145 Jim Kaat	3.50	1.55	.45
☐ 146 Randy Hundley	2.00	.90	.25
☐ 147 Jim McAndrew	2.00	.90	.25
☐ 148 Manny Sanguillen	2.00	.90	.25
☐ 149 Bob Allison	2.00	.90	.25
☐ 150 Jim Maloney	2.00	.90	.25
☐ 151 Don Buford	2.00	.90	.25
☐ 152 Gene Alley	2.00	.90	.25
☐ 153 Cesar Tovar	2.00	.90	.25
☐ 154 Brooks Robinson	7.50	3.40	.95
☐ 155 Milt Wilcox	2.00	.90	.25
☐ 156 Willie Stargell	5.00	2.20	.60
☐ 157 Paul Blair	2.00	.90	.25
☐ 158 Andy Etchebarren	2.00	.90	.25
☐ 159 Mark Belanger	2.00	.90	.25
☐ 160 Elrod Hendricks	2.00	.90	.25

1933 Delong R333

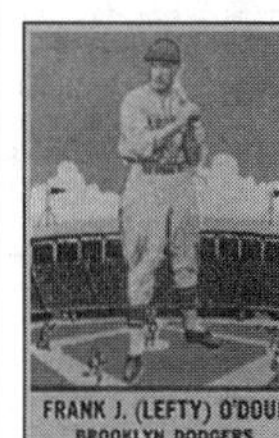

The cards in this 24-card set measure approximately 2" by 3". The 1933 Delong Gum set of 24 multi-colored cards was, along with the 1933 Goudey Big League series, one of the first baseball card sets issued with chewing gum. It was the only card set issued by this company. The reverse text was written by Austen Lake, who also wrote the sports tips found on the Diamond Stars series which began in 1934, leading to speculation that Delong was bought out by National Chicle.

	EX-MT	VG-E	GOOD
COMPLETE SET (24)	8000.00	3600.00	1000.00
COMMON CARD (1-24)	150.00	70.00	19.00
☐ 1 Marty McManus	165.00	75.00	21.00
☐ 2 Al Simmons	350.00	160.00	45.00
☐ 3 Oscar Melillo	150.00	70.00	19.00
☐ 4 Bill Terry	300.00	135.00	38.00
☐ 5 Charlie Gehringer	300.00	135.00	38.00
☐ 6 Mickey Cochrane	350.00	160.00	45.00
☐ 7 Lou Gehrig	3200.00	1450.00	400.00
☐ 8 Kiki Cuyler	275.00	125.00	34.00
☐ 9 Bill Urbanski	150.00	70.00	19.00
☐ 10 Lefty O'Doul	165.00	75.00	21.00
☐ 11 Fred Lindstrom	275.00	125.00	34.00
☐ 12 Pie Traynor	300.00	135.00	38.00
☐ 13 Rabbit Maranville	275.00	125.00	34.00
☐ 14 Lefty Gomez	300.00	135.00	38.00
☐ 15 Riggs Stephenson	165.00	75.00	21.00
☐ 16 Lon Warneke	150.00	70.00	19.00
☐ 17 Pepper Martin	165.00	75.00	21.00
☐ 18 Jimmy Dykes	165.00	75.00	21.00
☐ 19 Chick Hafey	275.00	125.00	34.00
☐ 20 Joe Vosmik	150.00	70.00	19.00
☐ 21 Jimmie Foxx	500.00	220.00	60.00
☐ 22 Chuck Klein	300.00	135.00	38.00
☐ 23 Lefty Grove	450.00	200.00	55.00
☐ 24 Goose Goslin	275.00	125.00	34.00

1992 Delphi Ruth

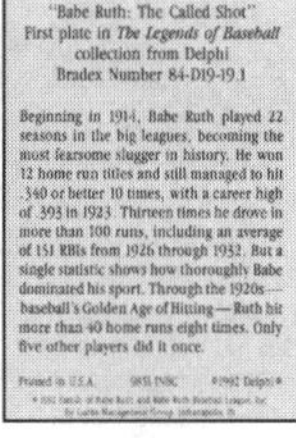

This standard size card was issued to promote the Legends of Baseball plates released by the Delphi company. With each plate in the series, collectors received a free old-fashioned Baseball Legends card depicting the player and recounting the milestones of his career. The front features the artwork of Brent Benger showing Babe Ruth in the batter's box watching the flight of the ball. The picture lies inside a green border in a shape similar to a baseball diamond. The rest of the card face is blue with red borders and contains a white baseball, bat and glove icons. A mustard banner at the bottom contains the words "Babe Ruth: The Called Shot." The back is white and carries promotional text and career highlights. The card is unnumbered.

	MINT	NRMT	EXC
COMPLETE SET(1)	2.00	.90	.25
COMMON CARD	2.00	.90	.25
☐ 1 Babe Ruth	2.00	.90	.25

1991 Denny's Holograms

The 1991 Denny's Grand Slam hologram baseball card set was produced by Upper Deck. The 26-card standard-size set contains one player from each major league team, who was selected on the basis of the number and circumstances of his grand slam home runs. These cards were available at Denny's only with the purchase of a meal from the restaurant's Grand Slam menu; each card came sealed in a plastic bag that prevents prior identification. It is estimated that two million cards were printed. The 3-D cards alternate between silver and full color, and the player appears to stand apart from a background of exploding fireworks. A stripe at the top of the card has the player's name and team, while the Upper Deck and Denny's logos appear toward the bottom of the card face. The back has a descriptive account of the player's grand slams. In 1991, if the contest card was a winner, the collector was entitled to a free meal. By the end of the contest, almost half the teams had hit grand slams during the length of the contest. So many teams hit grand slams that that part of the promotion was never repeated. The cards are numbered on the front.

	MINT	NRMT	EXC
COMPLETE SET (26)	35.00	16.00	4.40
COMMON CARD (1-26)	.75	.35	.09
☐ 1 Ellis Burks	1.00	.45	.12
☐ 2 Cecil Fielder	1.00	.45	.12
☐ 3 Will Clark	2.00	.90	.25
☐ 4 Eric Davis	.75	.35	.09
☐ 5 Dave Parker	1.00	.45	.12
☐ 6 Kelly Gruber	.75	.35	.09
☐ 7 Kent Hrbek	1.00	.45	.12
☐ 8 Don Mattingly	6.00	2.70	.75
☐ 9 Brook Jacoby	.75	.35	.09
☐ 10 Mark McGwire	4.00	1.80	.50
☐ 11 Howard Johnson	.75	.35	.09
☐ 12 Tim Wallach	.75	.35	.09
☐ 13 Ricky Jordan	.75	.35	.09
☐ 14 Andre Dawson	1.00	.45	.12
☐ 15 Eddie Murray	3.00	1.35	.35
☐ 16 Danny Tartabull	.75	.35	.09
☐ 17 Bobby Bonilla	1.00	.45	.12
☐ 18 Benito Santiago	1.00	.45	.12
☐ 19 Alvin Davis	.75	.35	.09
☐ 20 Cal Ripken	10.00	4.50	1.25
☐ 21 Ruben Sierra	1.00	.45	.12
☐ 22 Pedro Guerrero	.75	.35	.09
☐ 23 Wally Joyner	.75	.35	.09
☐ 24 Craig Biggio	1.50	.70	.19
☐ 25 Dave Justice	2.00	.90	.25
☐ 26 Tim Raines	1.00	.45	.12

1992 Denny's Holograms

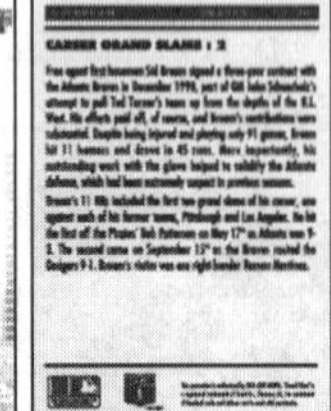

This 26-card standard-size set of holographic cards was produced by Upper Deck for Denny's. The set features one player from each major league team, who was selected on the basis of the number and circumstances of his grand slam home runs. With each order of a Grand Slam meal, the customer received one hologram card. Each hologram shows a cut-out player photo superimposed over a scene from the city in which the team resides. A bar with the words "limited edition" runs along the top of the card, and the words "collector series" run vertically down the right edge. The "1992 Grand Slam" insignia appears in the lower left corner, with the player's name in a bar extending to the right. The backs feature a blue stripe with the player's name across the top. Two red stripes border the top and bottom of a career summary printed in black on a white background.

	MINT	NRMT	EXC
COMPLETE SET (26)	30.00	13.50	3.70
COMMON CARD (1-26)	.50	.23	.06
☐ 1 Marquis Grissom	.75	.35	.09
☐ 2 Ken Caminiti	2.00	.90	.25
☐ 3 Fred McGriff	2.00	.90	.25
☐ 4 Felix Jose	.50	.23	.06
☐ 5 Jack Clark	.50	.23	.06
☐ 6 Albert Belle	6.00	2.70	.75
☐ 7 Sid Bream	.50	.23	.06
☐ 8 Robin Ventura	.75	.35	.09
☐ 9 Cal Ripken	10.00	4.50	1.25
☐ 10 Ryne Sandberg	4.00	1.80	.50
☐ 11 Paul O'Neill	.75	.35	.09
☐ 12 Luis Polonia	.50	.23	.06
☐ 13 Cecil Fielder	.75	.35	.09
☐ 14 Kal Daniels	.50	.23	.06
☐ 15 Brian McRae	.75	.35	.09
☐ 16 Howard Johnson	.50	.23	.06
☐ 17 Greg Vaughn	.75	.35	.09
☐ 18 Dale Murphy	1.00	.45	.12
☐ 19 Kent Hrbek	.75	.35	.09
☐ 20 Barry Bonds	3.00	1.35	.35
☐ 21 Matt Nokes	.50	.23	.06
☐ 22 Jose Canseco	2.00	.90	.25
☐ 23 Jay Buhner	1.00	.45	.12
☐ 24 Will Clark	2.00	.90	.25
☐ 25 Ruben Sierra	.50	.23	.06
☐ 26 Joe Carter	.75	.35	.09

1993 Denny's Holograms

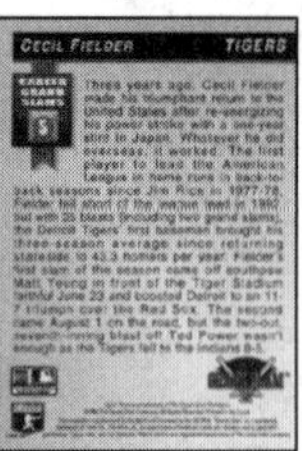

This 28-card standard-size set of holographic cards was produced by Upper Deck for Denny's. The set features one player from each major league team who was selected on the basis of the number and circumstances of his grand slam home runs. With each order of a Grand Slam meal and a Coca-Cola Classic, the customer received one lithogram card. A lithogram card represents the combination of lithography with a hologram. Each hologram shows a cutout player photo superimposed over an action photo. The words "Collector's Series" and the Upper Deck logo are shown along the top. The words "Limited Edition" appear vertically down the left edge. The top, left, and bottom edges are various shades of blue, with the player's name displayed on a team color-coded bar and the Grand Slam insignia in the lower right. The back carries a team color-coded bar with the player's name and team printed across the top. A red box displays the player's career grand slam statistics in the upper left, with a descriptive career summary printed on a light blue background. The cards are numbered on the front. The set ordering follows alphabetical order of team nicknames.

	MINT	NRMT	EXC
COMPLETE SET (28)	30.00	13.50	3.70
COMMON CARD (1-28)	.50	.23	.06
☐ 1 Chili Davis	.50	.23	.06
☐ 2 Eric Anthony	.50	.23	.06
☐ 3 Rickey Henderson	1.00	.45	.12
☐ 4 Joe Carter	.75	.35	.09
☐ 5 Terry Pendleton	.75	.35	.09
☐ 6 Robin Yount	1.50	.70	.19
☐ 7 Ray Lankford	.75	.35	.09
☐ 8 Ryne Sandberg	3.00	1.35	.35
☐ 9 Darryl Strawberry	.75	.35	.09
☐ 10 Marquis Grissom	.75	.35	.09
☐ 11 Will Clark	1.50	.70	.19
☐ 12 Albert Belle	5.00	2.20	.60
☐ 13 Edgar Martinez	.75	.35	.09
☐ 14 Benito Santiago	.50	.23	.06
☐ 15 Eddie Murray	2.50	1.10	.30
☐ 16 Cal Ripken	8.00	3.60	1.00
☐ 17 Gary Sheffield	1.50	.70	.19
☐ 18 Dave Hollins	.50	.23	.06
☐ 19 Andy Van Slyke	.50	.23	.06
☐ 20 Juan Gonzalez	5.00	2.20	.60
☐ 21 John Valentin	.75	.35	.09
☐ 22 Joe Oliver	.50	.23	.06
☐ 23 Dante Bichette	1.50	.70	.19
☐ 24 Wally Joyner	.50	.23	.06
☐ 25 Cecil Fielder	.75	.35	.09
☐ 26 Kirby Puckett	4.00	1.80	.50
☐ 27 Robin Ventura	.75	.35	.09
☐ 28 Danny Tartabull	.50	.23	.06

1994 Denny's Holograms

This 28-card standard-size set of holographic cards was produced by Upper Deck for Denny's and features a star player from each of the 28 Major League baseball teams. With each order of any "Classic Hits" entree, the customer received one hologram card in a blue poly pack. The fronts feature a full-bleed design that is highlighted by a "multi-level" hologram, with a portrait-style hologram at the forefront and an

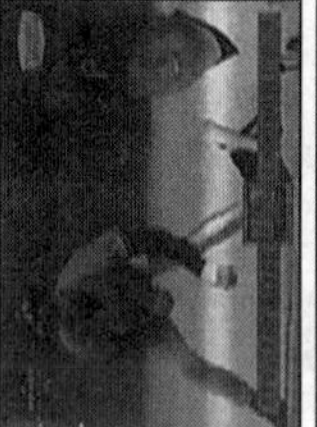

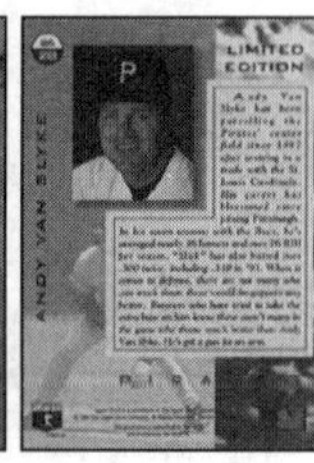

action photo that appears to be "behind" the other photo. The player's name and Major League Baseball's 125th Anniversary logo round out the fronts. The backs carry the player's color photograph and a brief biography. The cards are arranged alphabetically according to player's last name. There was also a Reggie Jackson Hologram printed. The Jackson card was a contest giveaway for each participating Denny's. The Jackson card is currently valued at between $20-30.

	MINT	NRMT	EXC
COMPLETE SET (28)	35.00	16.00	4.40
COMMON CARD (1-28)	.50	.23	.06
☐ 1 Jim Abbott	.50	.23	.06
☐ 2 Roberto Alomar	.75	.35	.09
☐ 3 Kevin Appier	.75	.35	.09
☐ 4 Jeff Bagwell	2.00	.90	.25
☐ 5 Albert Belle	2.50	1.10	.30
☐ 6 Barry Bonds	1.25	.55	.16
☐ 7 Bobby Bonilla	.75	.35	.09
☐ 8 Lenny Dykstra	.50	.23	.06
☐ 9 Cal Eldred	.50	.23	.06
☐ 10 Cecil Fielder	.75	.35	.09
☐ 11 Andres Galarraga	1.00	.45	.12
☐ 12 Ken Griffey Jr.	5.00	2.20	.60
☐ 13 Juan Gonzalez	2.50	1.10	.30
☐ 14 Tony Gwynn	2.50	1.10	.30
☐ 15 Rickey Henderson	1.00	.45	.12
☐ 16 Kent Hrbek	.50	.23	.06
☐ 17 David Justice	1.00	.45	.12
☐ 18 Mike Piazza	3.00	1.35	.35
☐ 19 Jose Rijo	.50	.23	.06
☐ 20 Cal Ripken	4.00	1.80	.50
☐ 21 Tim Salmon	1.00	.45	.12
☐ 22 Ryne Sandberg	2.00	.90	.25
☐ 23 Gary Sheffield	1.00	.45	.12
☐ 24 Ozzie Smith	2.00	.90	.25
☐ 25 Frank Thomas	5.00	2.20	.60
☐ 26 Andy Van Slyke	.50	.23	.06
☐ 27 Mo Vaughn	1.50	.70	.19
☐ 28 Larry Walker	1.50	.70	.19

1995 Denny's Holograms

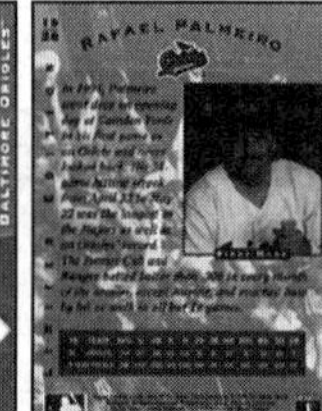

This 28-card standard-size set of holographic cards was produced by Upper Deck for Denny's and features a star player from each of the 28 Major League baseball teams. With each order of an "Classic Hits" entree and a non-alcoholic beverage, the customer received one hologram card in a blue poly pack. Also guests at the restaurants could enter a sweepstakes drawing for a complete set of cards, to be given away by each participating restaurant at the end of the promotion after September 30. The fronts feature a "multilevel" hologram with a portrait-style hologram at the forefront and an action photo that appears to be in front of the rest of the hologram. The player's name, team name and sponsor logos round out the fronts. The backs carry the player's color photograph, a brief biography and statistics.

	MINT	NRMT	EXC
COMPLETE SET (28)	30.00	13.50	3.70
COMMON CARD (1-28)	.50	.23	.06
☐ 1 Roberto Alomar	1.00	.45	.12
☐ 2 Moises Alou	.75	.35	.09
☐ 3 Jeff Bagwell	2.00	.90	.25
☐ 4 Albert Belle	2.50	1.10	.30
☐ 5 Jason Bere	.50	.23	.06
☐ 6 Roger Clemens	1.00	.45	.12
☐ 7 Darren Daulton	.75	.35	.09
☐ 8 Cecil Fielder	.75	.35	.09
☐ 9 Andres Galarraga	1.00	.45	.12
☐ 10 Juan Gonzalez	2.50	1.10	.30
☐ 11 Ken Griffey Jr.	5.00	2.20	.60
☐ 12 Tony Gwynn	2.50	1.10	.30
☐ 13 Barry Larkin	1.00	.45	.12
☐ 14 Greg Maddux	3.00	1.35	.35
☐ 15 Don Mattingly	2.50	1.10	.30
☐ 16 Mark McGwire	2.00	.90	.25
☐ 17 Orlando Merced	.50	.23	.06
☐ 18 Jeff Montgomery	.50	.23	.06
☐ 19 Rafael Palmeiro	1.00	.45	.12
☐ 20 Mike Piazza	3.00	1.35	.35
☐ 21 Kirby Puckett	2.50	1.10	.30
☐ 22 Bret Saberhagen	.50	.23	.06
☐ 23 Tim Salmon	1.00	.45	.12
☐ 24 Gary Sheffield	1.00	.45	.12
☐ 25 Ozzie Smith	2.00	.90	.25
☐ 26 Sammy Sosa	1.00	.45	.12
☐ 27 Greg Vaughn	.50	.23	.06
☐ 28 Matt Williams	1.00	.45	.12

1996 Denny's Holograms

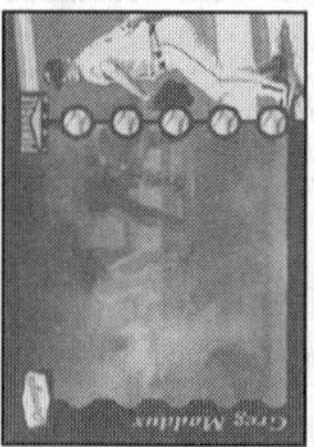

This 28-card set was produced by Pinnacle for Denny's and features a star player from each of the Major League baseball teams. The fronts feature a full motion hologram player image. The backs carry player information. By ordering anything on the menu, a customer could buy two packs. Each Denny's also sponsored a drawing to win all 48 cards (the regular set and both insert sets).

	MINT	NRMT	EXC
COMPLETE SET (28)	25.00	11.00	3.10
COMMON CARD (1-28)	.25	.11	.03
☐ 1 Greg Maddux	2.50	1.10	.30
☐ 2 Cal Ripken	3.00	1.35	.35
☐ 3 Frank Thomas	4.00	1.80	.50
☐ 4 Albert Belle	2.00	.90	.25
☐ 5 Mo Vaughn	1.00	.45	.12
☐ 6 Jeff Bagwell	1.50	.70	.19
☐ 7 Jay Buhner	.75	.35	.09
☐ 8 Barry Bonds	1.00	.45	.12
☐ 9 Ryne Sandberg	1.50	.70	.19
☐ 10 Hideo Nomo	1.50	.70	.19
☐ 11 Kirby Puckett	2.50	1.10	.30
☐ 12 Gary Sheffield	.75	.35	.09
☐ 13 Barry Larkin	.75	.35	.09
☐ 14 Wade Boggs	.75	.35	.09
☐ 15 Tony Gwynn	1.50	.70	.19
☐ 16 Tim Salmon	.75	.35	.09
☐ 17 Jason Isringhausen	.75	.35	.09
☐ 18 Cecil Fielder	.50	.23	.06
☐ 19 Dante Bichette	.75	.35	.09
☐ 20 Ozzie Smith	1.25	.55	.16
☐ 21 Ivan Rodriguez	1.00	.45	.12
☐ 22 Kevin Appier	.50	.23	.06
☐ 23 Joe Carter	.50	.23	.06
☐ 24 Moises Alou	.50	.23	.06
☐ 25 Mark McGwire	1.25	.55	.16
☐ 26 Kevin Seitzer	.25	.11	.03
☐ 27 Darren Daulton	.50	.23	.06
☐ 28 Jay Bell	.25	.11	.03

1996 Denny's Holograms Grand Slam

Randomly inserted in packs, this 10-card set features star players from several of the Major League baseball teams. The fronts display a holographic player image with bursting fireworks in the background, while the backs carry player information.

	MINT	NRMT	EXC
COMPLETE SET (10)	90.00	40.00	11.00
COMMON CARD (1-10)	3.00	1.35	.35
☐ 1 Cal Ripken	20.00	9.00	2.50
☐ 2 Frank Thomas	20.00	9.00	2.50
☐ 3 Mike Piazza	12.50	5.50	1.55
☐ 4 Tony Gwynn	10.00	4.50	1.25
☐ 5 Sammy Sosa	3.00	1.35	.35
☐ 6 Barry Bonds	6.00	2.70	.75
☐ 7 Jeff Bagwell	8.00	3.60	1.00
☐ 8 Albert Belle	10.00	4.50	1.25
☐ 9 Mo Vaughn	5.00	2.20	.60
☐ 10 Kirby Puckett	8.00	3.60	1.00

1996 Denny's Holograms Grand Slam Artist's Proofs

Randomly inserted in packs, this 10-card set is parallel to the regular Denny's Holograms Grand Slam set and are similar in design with the exception of the Artist's Proof logo which is printed on these cards.

	MINT	NRMT	EXC
COMPLETE SET (10)	325.00	145.00	40.00
COMMON CARD (1-10)	12.00	5.50	1.50
☐ 1 Cal Ripken	60.00	27.00	7.50
☐ 2 Frank Thomas	75.00	34.00	9.50
☐ 3 Mike Piazza	45.00	20.00	5.50
☐ 4 Tony Gwynn	30.00	13.50	3.70
☐ 5 Sammy Sosa	12.00	5.50	1.50
☐ 6 Barry Bonds	18.00	8.00	2.20
☐ 7 Jeff Bagwell	30.00	13.50	3.70
☐ 8 Albert Belle	35.00	16.00	4.40
☐ 9 Mo Vaughn	18.00	8.00	2.20
☐ 10 Kirby Puckett	50.00	22.00	6.25

1986 DeSa Commemorative

This one-card set measures approximately 4" by 6 " and commemorates Baseball player Joe DeSa. The front features a color player photo with a red border and the words "Joe DeSa Remembered" printed in white at the top. The back displays information about the player and career statistics.

	MINT	NRMT	EXC
COMPLETE SET (1)	3.00	1.35	.35
COMMON CARD (1)	3.00	1.35	.35
☐ 1 Joe DeSa	3.00	1.35	.35

1967 Dexter Press

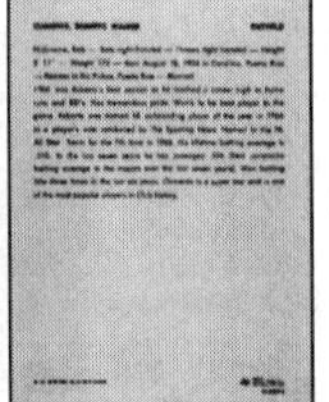

This 228-card set was produced by Dexter Press and issued in team sets as a premium by Coca-Cola Bottling Co. Eighteen Major League teams participated in the promotion. The set measures approximately 5 1/2" by 7" and features glossy color waist-to-cap player photos in a white border with a black facsimile autograph at the top. The white backs display player biographical details and career highlights printed in blue. An all-star set was also produced with these players' cards differentiated from their regular cards in the team sets by the lengthier biographies on the back. The cards are unnumbered and checklisted below in alphabetical order.

	NRMT	VG-E	GOOD
COMPLETE SET (228)	800.00	350.00	100.00
COMMON CARD (1-228)	3.50	1.55	.45
☐ 1 Hank Aaron	20.00	9.00	2.50
☐ 2 Tommie Agee	5.00	2.20	.60
☐ 3 Jack Aker	3.50	1.55	.45
☐ 4 Bernie Allen	3.50	1.55	.45
☐ 5 Rich Allen	5.00	2.20	.60
☐ 6 Gene Alley	3.50	1.55	.45
☐ 7 Bob Allison	5.00	2.20	.60
☐ 8 Felipe Alou	5.00	2.20	.60
☐ 9 Jesus Alou	5.00	2.20	.60
☐ 10 Matty Alou	5.00	2.20	.60
☐ 11 George Altman	3.50	1.55	.45
☐ 12 Max Alvis	3.50	1.55	.45
☐ 13 Luis Aparicio	10.00	4.50	1.25
☐ 14 Bob Aspromonte	3.50	1.55	.45
☐ 15 Joe Azcue	3.50	1.55	.45
☐ 16 Bob Bailey	3.50	1.55	.45
☐ 17 Ernie Banks	15.00	6.75	1.85
☐ 18 John Bateman	3.50	1.55	.45
☐ 19 Earl Battey	3.50	1.55	.45
☐ 20 Glen Beckert	3.50	1.55	.45
☐ 21 Gary Bell	3.50	1.55	.45
☐ 22 Ken Berry	3.50	1.55	.45
☐ 23 Wade Blasingame	3.50	1.55	.45
☐ 24 Curt Blefary	3.50	1.55	.45
☐ 25 John Boccabella	3.50	1.55	.45
☐ 26 Dave Boswell	3.50	1.55	.45
☐ 27 Jim Bouton	5.00	2.20	.60
☐ 28 Clete Boyer	5.00	2.20	.60
☐ 29 Ken Boyer	5.00	2.20	.60
☐ 30 Ed Bressoud	3.50	1.55	.45
☐ 31 John Briggs	3.50	1.55	.45
☐ 32 Ed Brinkman	3.50	1.55	.45
☐ 33 Larry Brown	3.50	1.55	.45
☐ 34 Ollie Brown	3.50	1.55	.45
☐ 35 Bob Bruce	3.50	1.55	.45
☐ 36 Don Buford	3.50	1.55	.45
☐ 37 Wally Bunker	3.50	1.55	.45
☐ 38 Jim Bunning	10.00	4.50	1.25
☐ 39 Jim Bunning AS	5.00	2.20	.60
☐ 40 Johnny Callison	5.00	2.20	.60
☐ 41 Campy Campaneris	3.50	1.55	.45
☐ 42 Leo Cardenas	3.50	1.55	.45
☐ 43 Paul Casanova	3.50	1.55	.45
☐ 44 Norm Cash	5.00	2.20	.60
☐ 45 Danny Cater	3.50	1.55	.45
☐ 46 Dean Chance	3.50	1.55	.45
☐ 47 Ed Charles	3.50	1.55	.45
☐ 48 Ossie Chavarria	3.50	1.55	.45
☐ 49 Horace Clarke	3.50	1.55	.45
☐ 50 Roberto Clemente	25.00	11.00	3.10
☐ 51 Roberto Clemente AS	10.00	4.50	1.25
☐ 52 Donn Clendenon	3.50	1.55	.45
☐ 53 Ty Cline	3.50	1.55	.45
☐ 54 Tony Cloninger	3.50	1.55	.45
☐ 55 Rocky Colavito	7.50	3.40	.95
☐ 56 Gordy Coleman	3.50	1.55	.45
☐ 57 Ray Culp	3.50	1.55	.45
☐ 58 Clay Dalrymple	3.50	1.55	.45
☐ 59 Vic Davalillo	3.50	1.55	.45
☐ 60 Jim Davenport	3.50	1.55	.45
☐ 61 Ron Davis	3.50	1.55	.45
☐ 62 Tommy Davis	5.00	2.20	.60
☐ 63 Willie Davis	5.00	2.20	.60
☐ 64 Willie Davis AS	5.00	2.20	.60
☐ 65 Don Demeter	3.50	1.55	.45
☐ 66 Larry Dierker	5.00	2.20	.60
☐ 67 Al Downing	3.50	1.55	.45
☐ 68 Johnny Edwards	3.50	1.55	.45
☐ 69 Andy Etchebarren	3.50	1.55	.45
☐ 70 Ron Fairly	5.00	2.20	.60
☐ 71 Dick Farrell	3.50	1.55	.45
☐ 72 Bill Fischer	3.50	1.55	.45
☐ 73 Eddie Fisher	3.50	1.55	.45
☐ 74 Jack Fisher	3.50	1.55	.45
☐ 75 Joe Foy	3.50	1.55	.45
☐ 76 Bill Freehan	5.00	2.20	.60
☐ 77 Woodie Fryman	3.50	1.55	.45
☐ 78 Tito Fuentes	3.50	1.55	.45
☐ 79 Dave Giusti	3.50	1.55	.45
☐ 80 Pedro Gonzalez	3.50	1.55	.45
☐ 81 Mudcat Grant	3.50	1.55	.45
☐ 82 Dick Green	3.50	1.55	.45
☐ 83 Dick Groat	5.00	2.20	.60
☐ 84 Jerry Grote	3.50	1.55	.45
☐ 85 Tom Haller	3.50	1.55	.45
☐ 86 Jack Hamilton	3.50	1.55	.45
☐ 87 Steve Hamilton	3.50	1.55	.45
☐ 88 Ron Hansen	3.50	1.55	.45
☐ 89 Tommy Harper	3.50	1.55	.45
☐ 90 Ken Harrelson	5.00	2.20	.60
☐ 91 Chuck Harrison	3.50	1.55	.45
☐ 92 Jim Hart	3.50	1.55	.45
☐ 93 Tommy Helms	3.50	1.55	.45
☐ 94 Mike Hershberger	3.50	1.55	.45
☐ 95 Chuck Hinton	3.50	1.55	.45
☐ 96 Ken Holtzman	3.50	1.55	.45
☐ 97 Joe Horlen	3.50	1.55	.45
☐ 98 Willie Horton	3.50	1.55	.45
☐ 99 Elston Howard	5.00	2.20	.60
☐ 100 Frank Howard	5.00	2.20	.60
☐ 101 Randy Hundley	3.50	1.55	.45
☐ 102 Ron Hunt	3.50	1.55	.45
☐ 103 Larry Jackson	3.50	1.55	.45
☐ 104 Sonny Jackson	3.50	1.55	.45
☐ 105 Tommy John	5.00	2.20	.60
☐ 106 Dave Johnson	5.00	2.20	.60
☐ 107 Deron Johnson	3.50	1.55	.45
☐ 108 Ken Johnson	3.50	1.55	.45
☐ 109 Lou Johnson	3.50	1.55	.45
☐ 110 Cleon Jones	3.50	1.55	.45
☐ 111 Dalton Jones	3.50	1.55	.45
☐ 112 Al Kaline	15.00	6.75	1.85
☐ 113 Al Kaline AS	7.50	3.40	.95
☐ 114 John Kennedy	3.50	1.55	.45
☐ 115 Harmon Killebrew	15.00	6.75	1.85
☐ 116 Harmon Killebrew AS	7.50	3.40	.95
☐ 117 Jim King	3.50	1.55	.45
☐ 118 Cal Koonce	3.50	1.55	.45
☐ 119 Ed Kranepool	3.50	1.55	.45
☐ 120 Lew Krausse	3.50	1.55	.45
☐ 121 Jim Landis	3.50	1.55	.45
☐ 122 Hal Lanier	3.50	1.55	.45
☐ 123 Vern Law	3.50	1.55	.45
☐ 124 Jim Lefebvre	3.50	1.55	.45
☐ 125 Johnny Lewis	3.50	1.55	.45
☐ 126 Don Lock	3.50	1.55	.45
☐ 127 Bob Locker	3.50	1.55	.45
☐ 128 Mickey Lolich	7.50	3.40	.95
☐ 129 Jim Lonborg	5.00	2.20	.60
☐ 130 Jerry Lumpe	3.50	1.55	.45
☐ 131 Jim Maloney	3.50	1.55	.45
☐ 132 Mickey Mantle	50.00	22.00	6.25
☐ 133 Eddie Mathews	15.00	6.75	1.85
☐ 134 Willie Mays	20.00	9.00	2.50
☐ 135 Willie Mays AS	15.00	6.75	1.85
☐ 136 Bill Mazeroski	5.00	2.20	.60
☐ 137 Dick McAuliffe	3.50	1.55	.45
☐ 138 Bill McCool	3.50	1.55	.45
☐ 139 Mike McCormick	3.50	1.55	.45
☐ 140 Willie McCovey	10.00	4.50	1.25
☐ 141 Tommy McCraw	3.50	1.55	.45
☐ 142 Sam McDowell	3.50	1.55	.45
☐ 143 Ken McMullen	3.50	1.55	.45
☐ 144 Dave McNally	3.50	1.55	.45
☐ 145 Jerry McNertney	3.50	1.55	.45
☐ 146 Dennis Menke	3.50	1.55	.45
☐ 147 Jim Merritt	3.50	1.55	.45
☐ 148 Joe Morgan	10.00	4.50	1.25
☐ 149 Manny Mota	5.00	2.20	.60
☐ 150 Jim Nash	3.50	1.55	.45
☐ 151 Dick Nen	3.50	1.55	.45
☐ 152 Joe Nossek	3.50	1.55	.45
☐ 153 Tony Oliva	5.00	2.20	.60
☐ 154 Gene Oliver	3.50	1.55	.45
☐ 155 Phil Ortega	3.50	1.55	.45
☐ 156 Claude Osteen	3.50	1.55	.45
☐ 157 Jim O'Toole	3.50	1.55	.45
☐ 158 Jim Pagliaroni	3.50	1.55	.45
☐ 159 Jim Palmer	15.00	6.75	1.85
☐ 160 Milt Pappas	3.50	1.55	.45
☐ 161 Wes Parker	3.50	1.55	.45
☐ 162 Joe Pepitone	3.50	1.55	.45
☐ 163 Joe Pepitone AS	3.50	1.55	.45
☐ 164 Ron Perranoski	3.50	1.55	.45
☐ 165 Gaylord Perry	10.00	4.50	1.25
☐ 166 Fritz Peterson	3.50	1.55	.45
☐ 167 Rico Petrocelli	3.50	1.55	.45
☐ 168 Adolfo Phillips	3.50	1.55	.45
☐ 169 Vada Pinson	5.00	2.20	.60
☐ 170 Johnny Podres	5.00	2.20	.60
☐ 171 John"Boog" Powell	5.00	2.20	.60
☐ 172 Phil Regan	3.50	1.55	.45
☐ 173 Roger Repoz	3.50	1.55	.45
☐ 174 Pete Richert	3.50	1.55	.45
☐ 175 Brooks Robinson	15.00	6.75	1.85
☐ 176 Brooks Robinson AS	7.50	3.40	.95
☐ 177 Frank Robinson	15.00	6.75	1.85
☐ 178 Frank Robinson AS	7.50	3.40	.95
☐ 179 Cookie Rojas	3.50	1.55	.45
☐ 180 Rich Rollins	3.50	1.55	.45
☐ 181 Phil Roof	3.50	1.55	.45
☐ 182 Pete Rose	20.00	9.00	2.50
☐ 183 Jose Santiago	3.50	1.55	.45
☐ 184 Ron Santo	10.00	4.50	1.25
☐ 185 Ron Santo AS	5.00	2.20	.60
☐ 186 Bob Saverine	3.50	1.55	.45
☐ 187 George Scott	3.50	1.55	.45
☐ 188 Art Shamsky	3.50	1.55	.45
☐ 189 Bob Shaw	3.50	1.55	.45
☐ 190 Chris Short	3.50	1.55	.45
☐ 191 Norman Siebern	3.50	1.55	.45
☐ 192 Bill"Moose" Skowron	5.00	2.20	.60
☐ 193 Charley Smith	3.50	1.55	.45
☐ 194 George Smith	3.50	1.55	.45
☐ 195 Russ Snyder	3.50	1.55	.45
☐ 196 Joe Sparma	3.50	1.55	.45
☐ 197 Willie Stargell	10.00	4.50	1.25
☐ 198 Rusty Staub	5.00	2.20	.60
☐ 199 John Stephenson	3.50	1.55	.45
☐ 200 Mel Stottlemyre	5.00	2.20	.60
☐ 201 Don Sutton	10.00	4.50	1.25
☐ 202 Ron Swoboda	3.50	1.55	.45
☐ 203 Jose Tartabull	3.50	1.55	.45
☐ 204 Tony Taylor	3.50	1.55	.45
☐ 205 Lee Thomas	3.50	1.55	.45
☐ 206 Luis Tiant	5.00	2.20	.60
☐ 207 Bob Tillman	3.50	1.55	.45
☐ 208 Joe Torre	7.50	3.40	.95
☐ 209 Joe Torre AS	4.00	1.80	.50
☐ 210 Tom Tresh	3.50	1.55	.45
☐ 211 Ted Uhlaender	3.50	1.55	.45
☐ 212 Sandy Valdespino	3.50	1.55	.45
☐ 213 Fred Valentine	3.50	1.55	.45
☐ 214 Bob Veale	3.50	1.55	.45
☐ 215 Zoilo Versalles	3.50	1.55	.45
☐ 216 Leon Wagner	3.50	1.55	.45
☐ 217 Pete Ward	3.50	1.55	.45
☐ 218 Don Wert	3.50	1.55	.45
☐ 219 Bill White	5.00	2.20	.60
☐ 220 Roy White	3.50	1.55	.45
☐ 221 Fred Whitfield	3.50	1.55	.45
☐ 222 Dave Wickersham	3.50	1.55	.45
☐ 223 Billy Williams	10.00	4.50	1.25
☐ 224 Maury Wills	5.00	2.20	.60
☐ 225 Earl Wilson	3.50	1.55	.45
☐ 226 Woody Woodward	3.50	1.55	.45
☐ 227 Carl Yastrzemski	15.00	6.75	1.85
☐ 228 Carl Yastrzemski AS	7.50	3.40	.95

1968 Dexter Press

This 77-card set, which measures approximately 3 1/2" by 5 1/2", has beautiful full-color photos on the front of the card with biographical and career information on the back of the card. There are no year by year statistical lines on the back of the card. Dexter Press is another name for cards which the Coca-Cola Company helped to distribute

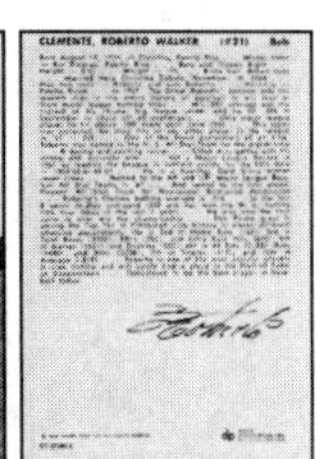

during the mid sixties. The backs of the cards have a facsimile autograph. Dexter Press was located in West Nyack, New York. These unnumbered cards are listed below in alphabetical order.

	NRMT	VG-E	GOOD
COMPLETE SET (77)	250.00	110.00	31.00
COMMON CARD (1-77)	3.00	1.35	.35
☐ 1 Hank Aaron	20.00	9.00	2.50
☐ 2 Jerry Adair	3.00	1.35	.35
☐ 3 Richie Allen	4.00	1.80	.50
☐ 4 Bob Allison	4.00	1.80	.50
☐ 5 Felipe Alou	4.00	1.80	.50
☐ 6 Jesus Alou	3.00	1.35	.35
☐ 7 Mike Andrews	3.00	1.35	.35
☐ 8 Bob Aspromonte	3.00	1.35	.35
☐ 9 Johnny Bateman	3.00	1.35	.35
☐ 10 Mark Belanger	3.00	1.35	.35
☐ 11 Gary Bell	3.00	1.35	.35
☐ 12 Paul Blair	3.00	1.35	.35
☐ 13 Curt Blefary	3.00	1.35	.35
☐ 14 Bobby Bolin	3.00	1.35	.35
☐ 15 Ken Boswell	3.00	1.35	.35
☐ 16 Clete Boyer	4.00	1.80	.50
☐ 17 Ron Brand	3.00	1.35	.35
☐ 18 Darrell Brandon	3.00	1.35	.35
☐ 19 Don Buford	3.00	1.35	.35
☐ 20 Rod Carew	20.00	9.00	2.50
☐ 21 Clay Carroll	3.00	1.35	.35
☐ 22 Rico Carty	4.00	1.80	.50
☐ 23 Dean Chance	3.00	1.35	.35
☐ 24 Roberto Clemente	25.00	11.00	3.10
☐ 25 Tony Cloninger	3.00	1.35	.35
☐ 26 Mike Cuellar	3.00	1.35	.35
☐ 27 Jim Davenport	3.00	1.35	.35
☐ 28 Ron Davis	3.00	1.35	.35
☐ 29 Moe Drabowsky	3.00	1.35	.35
☐ 30 Dick Ellsworth	3.00	1.35	.35
☐ 31 Andy Etchebarren	3.00	1.35	.35
☐ 32 Joe Foy	3.00	1.35	.35
☐ 33 Bill Freehan	3.00	1.35	.35
☐ 34 Jim Fregosi	4.00	1.80	.50
☐ 35 Julio Gotay	3.00	1.35	.35
☐ 36 Dave Giusti	3.00	1.35	.35
☐ 37 Jim Ray Hart	3.00	1.35	.35
☐ 38 Jack Hiatt	3.00	1.35	.35
☐ 39 Ron Hunt	3.00	1.35	.35
☐ 40 Sonny Jackson	3.00	1.35	.35
☐ 41 Pat Jarvis	3.00	1.35	.35
☐ 42 Dave Johnson	4.00	1.80	.50
☐ 43 Ken Johnson	3.00	1.35	.35
☐ 44 Dalton Jones	3.00	1.35	.35
☐ 45 Jim Kaat	5.00	2.20	.60
☐ 46 Harmon Killebrew	12.00	5.50	1.50
☐ 47 Denny Lemaster	3.00	1.35	.35
☐ 48 Frank Linzy	3.00	1.35	.35
☐ 49 Jim Lonborg	4.00	1.80	.50
☐ 50 Juan Marichal	12.00	5.50	1.50
☐ 51 Willie Mays	20.00	9.00	2.50
☐ 52 Bill Mazeroski	4.00	1.80	.50
☐ 53 Mike McCormick	3.00	1.35	.35
☐ 54 Dave McNally	4.00	1.80	.50
☐ 55 Denis Menke	3.00	1.35	.35
☐ 56 Joe Morgan	10.00	4.50	1.25
☐ 57 Dave Morehead	3.00	1.35	.35
☐ 58 Phil Niekro	10.00	4.50	1.25
☐ 59 Russ Nixon	3.00	1.35	.35
☐ 60 Tony Oliva	4.00	1.80	.50
☐ 61 Gaylord Perry	10.00	4.50	1.25
☐ 62 Rico Petrocelli	4.00	1.80	.50
☐ 63 Tom Phoebus	3.00	1.35	.35
☐ 64 Boog Powell	4.00	1.80	.50
☐ 65 Brooks Robinson	12.00	5.50	1.50
☐ 66 Frank Robinson	12.00	5.50	1.50
☐ 67 Rich Rollins	3.00	1.35	.35
☐ 68 John Roseboro	4.00	1.80	.50
☐ 69 Ray Sadecki	3.00	1.35	.35
☐ 70 George Scott	4.00	1.80	.50
☐ 71 Rusty Staub	5.00	2.20	.60
☐ 72 Cesar Tovar	3.00	1.35	.35
☐ 73 Joe Torre	5.00	2.20	.60
☐ 74 Ted Uhlaender	3.00	1.35	.35
☐ 75 Woody Woodward	3.00	1.35	.35
☐ 76 John Wyatt	3.00	1.35	.35
☐ 77 Jimmy Wynn	5.00	2.20	.60

1982 Diamond Classics

These very attractive cards feature drawings of all-time stars on the front. The drawings cover almost all the front of the cards. The backs give a history of the player as well as some important statistics.

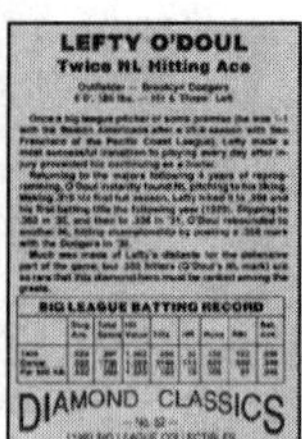

	NRMT	VG-E	GOOD
COMPLETE SET (55)	25.00	11.00	3.10
COMMON CARD (1-55)	.10	.05	.01

	NRMT	VG-E	GOOD
☐ 1 Joe DiMaggio	2.00	.90	.25
☐ 2 Enos Slaughter	.20	.09	.03
☐ 3 Smokey Joe Wood	.20	.09	.03
☐ 4 Roy Campanella	.40	.18	.05
☐ 5 Charlie Gehringer	.20	.09	.03
☐ 6 Carl Hubbell	.30	.14	.04
☐ 7 Rogers Hornsby	.30	.14	.04
☐ 8 Arky Vaughan	.20	.09	.03
☐ 9 Al Simmons	.20	.09	.03
☐ 10 Wally Berger	.10	.05	.01
☐ 11 Sam Rice	.20	.09	.03
☐ 12 Dizzy Dean	.40	.18	.05
☐ 13 Babe Ruth	3.00	1.35	.35
☐ 14 Frankie Frisch	.20	.09	.03
☐ 15 George Kell	.20	.09	.03
☐ 16 Pee Wee Reese	.40	.18	.05
☐ 17 Earl Averill	.20	.09	.03
☐ 18 Willie Mays	1.50	.70	.19
☐ 19 Frank Baker	.20	.09	.03
☐ 20 Hack Wilson	.20	.09	.03
☐ 21 Ted Williams	2.00	.90	.25
☐ 22 Chuck Klein	.20	.09	.03
☐ 23 Bill Dickey	.20	.09	.03
☐ 24 Johnny Mize	.20	.09	.03
☐ 25 Luke Appling	.20	.09	.03
☐ 26 Duke Snider	.40	.18	.05
☐ 27 Wahoo Sam Crawford	.30	.14	.04
☐ 28 Waite Hoyt	.20	.09	.03
☐ 29 Eddie Collins	.30	.14	.04
☐ 30 Warren Spahn	.30	.14	.04
☐ 31 Satchel Paige	.75	.35	.09
☐ 32 Ernie Lombardi	.20	.09	.03
☐ 33 Dom DiMaggio	.20	.09	.03
☐ 34 Joe Garagiola	.30	.14	.04
☐ 35 Lou Gehrig	2.00	.90	.25
☐ 36 Burleigh Grimes	.20	.09	.03
☐ 37 Walter Johnson	.50	.23	.06
☐ 38 Bill Terry	.20	.09	.03
☐ 39 Ty Cobb	2.00	.90	.25
☐ 40 Pie Traynor	.20	.09	.03
☐ 41 Ted Lyons	.20	.09	.03
☐ 42 Richie Ashburn	.30	.14	.04
☐ 43 Lefty Grove	.30	.14	.04
☐ 44 Edd Roush	.20	.09	.03
☐ 45 Phil Rizzuto	.40	.18	.05
☐ 46 Stan Musial	1.00	.45	.12
☐ 47 Bob Feller	.40	.18	.05
☐ 48 Jackie Robinson	2.00	.90	.25
☐ 49 Hank Greenberg	.30	.14	.04
☐ 50 Mel Ott	.30	.14	.04
☐ 51 Joe Cronin	.20	.09	.03
☐ 52 Lefty O'Doul	.20	.09	.03
☐ 53 Indian Bob Johnson	.10	.05	.01
☐ 54 Kiki Cuyler	.20	.09	.03
☐ 55 Mickey Mantle	3.00	1.35	.35

1983 Diamond Classics Series 2

These cards were produced from original art work. They were distributed by collector Steve Mitchell who was also involved in the set production. The drawings on the front cover almost the entire oversized cards while the back have player history as well as important statistics.

	NRMT	VG-E	GOOD
COMPLETE SET (55)	10.00	4.50	1.25
COMMON CARD (56-110)	.10	.05	.01

	NRMT	VG-E	GOOD
☐ 56 Ernie Banks	1.00	.45	.12
☐ 57 Stan Coveleskie	.20	.09	.03
☐ 58 Vince DiMaggio	.20	.09	.03
☐ 59 Jim Bottomley	.20	.09	.03
☐ 60 Sandy Koufax	1.00	.45	.12
☐ 61 Doc Cramer	.10	.05	.01
☐ 62 Ted Kluszewski	.50	.23	.06
☐ 63 Zeke Bonura	.10	.05	.01
☐ 64 Spud Davis	.10	.05	.01
☐ 65 Jackie Jensen	.10	.05	.01
☐ 66 Honus Wagner	.75	.35	.09
☐ 67 Brooks Robinson	.30	.14	.04
☐ 68 Dazzy Vance	.20	.09	.03
☐ 69 George Uhle	.10	.05	.01
☐ 70 Juan Marichal	.30	.14	.04
☐ 71 Bobo Newsom	.10	.05	.01
☐ 72 Billy Herman	.20	.09	.03
☐ 73 Al Rosen	.20	.09	.03
☐ 74 Roberto Clemente	2.00	.90	.25
☐ 75 George Case	.10	.05	.01
☐ 76 Bill Nicholson	.10	.05	.01
☐ 77 Tommy Bridges	.10	.05	.01
☐ 78 Rabbit Maranville	.20	.09	.03
☐ 79 Bob Lemon	.20	.09	.03
☐ 80 Heinie Groh	.10	.05	.01
☐ 81 Tris Speaker	.30	.14	.04
☐ 82 Hank Aaron	1.50	.70	.19
☐ 83 Whitey Ford	.50	.23	.06
☐ 84 Guy Bush	.10	.05	.01
☐ 85 Jimmie Foxx	.30	.14	.04
☐ 86 Marty Marion	.20	.09	.03
☐ 87 Hal Newhouser	.20	.09	.03
☐ 88 George Kelly	.20	.09	.03
☐ 89 Harmon Killebrew	.30	.14	.04
☐ 90 Willie McCovey	.30	.14	.04
☐ 91 Mel Harder	.10	.05	.01
☐ 92 Vada Pinson	.20	.09	.03
☐ 93 Luis Aparicio	.30	.14	.04
☐ 94 Grover Alexander	.50	.23	.06
☐ 95 Joe Kuhel	.10	.05	.01
☐ 96 Casey Stengel	.30	.14	.04
☐ 97 Joe Sewell	.20	.09	.03
☐ 98 Red Lucas	.10	.05	.01
☐ 99 Luke Sewell	.10	.05	.01
☐ 100 Charlie Grimm	.10	.05	.01
☐ 101 Cecil Travis	.10	.05	.01
☐ 102 Travis Jackson	.20	.09	.03
☐ 103 Lou Boudreau	.20	.09	.03
☐ 104 Nap Rucker	.10	.05	.01
☐ 105 Chief Bender	.20	.09	.03
☐ 106 Riggs Stephenson	.10	.05	.01
☐ 107 Red Ruffing	.20	.09	.03
☐ 108 Robin Roberts	.30	.14	.04
☐ 109 Harland Clift	.10	.05	.01
☐ 110 Ralph Kiner	.30	.14	.04
☐ xx Certificate and	.10	.05	.01
☐ NNO Checklist Card	.10	.05	.01

1979 Diamond Greats

This 400-card set features black-and-white player portraits with the player's name, life-time statistics, team name, and playing position printed in black in the white margins. The backs are blank.

	NRMT	VG-E	GOOD
COMPLETE SET (400)	75.00	34.00	9.50
COMMON CARD (1-400)	.10	.05	.01

	NRMT	VG-E	GOOD
☐ 1 Joe DiMaggio	5.00	2.20	.60
☐ 2 Ben Chapman	.10	.05	.01
☐ 3 Joe Dugan	.10	.05	.01
☐ 4 Bob Shawkey	.25	.11	.03
☐ 5 Joe Sewell	.50	.23	.06
☐ 6 George Pipgras	.10	.05	.01
☐ 7 George Selkirk	.10	.05	.01
☐ 8 Babe Dahlgren	.10	.05	.01
☐ 9 Spud Chandler	.25	.11	.03
☐ 10 Duffy Lewis	.10	.05	.01
☐ 11 Lefty Gomez	1.00	.45	.12
☐ 12 Atley Donald	.10	.05	.01
☐ 13 Whitey Witt	.10	.05	.01
☐ 14 Marius Russo	.10	.05	.01
☐ 15 Buddy Rosar	.10	.05	.01
☐ 16 Russ Van Atta	.10	.05	.01
☐ 17 Johnny Lindell	.10	.05	.01
☐ 18 Bobby Brown	.25	.11	.03
☐ 19 Tony Kubek	.25	.11	.03
☐ 20 Joe Beggs	.10	.05	.01
☐ 21 Don Larsen	.25	.11	.03
☐ 22 Andy Carey	.10	.05	.01
☐ 23 Johnny Kucks	.10	.05	.01
☐ 24 Elston Howard	.25	.11	.03
☐ 25 Roger Maris	1.50	.70	.19
☐ 26 Rube Marquard	.75	.35	.09
☐ 27 Sam Leslie	.10	.05	.01
☐ 28 Freddy Leach	.10	.05	.01
☐ 29 Fred Fitzsimmons	.25	.11	.03
☐ 30 Bill Terry	1.00	.45	.12
☐ 31 Joe Moore	.10	.05	.01
☐ 32 Waite Hoyt	.50	.23	.06
☐ 33 Travis Jackson	.50	.23	.06
☐ 34 Gus Mancuso	.10	.05	.01
☐ 35 Carl Hubbell	1.25	.55	.16
☐ 36 Bill Voiselle	.10	.05	.01
☐ 37 Hank Leiber	.10	.05	.01
☐ 38 Burgess Whitehead	.10	.05	.01
☐ 39 Johnny Mize	1.00	.45	.12
☐ 40 Bill Lohrman	.10	.05	.01
☐ 41 Bill Rigney	.10	.05	.01
☐ 42 Cliff Melton	.10	.05	.01
☐ 43 Willard Marshall	.10	.05	.01
☐ 44 Wes Westrum	.10	.05	.01
☐ 45 Monte Irvin	.75	.35	.09
☐ 46 Marv Grissom	.10	.05	.01
☐ 47 Clyde Castleman	.10	.05	.01
☐ 48 Harry Gumbert	.10	.05	.01
☐ 49 Daryl Spencer	.10	.05	.01
☐ 50 Willie Mays	4.00	1.80	.50
☐ 51 Sam West	.10	.05	.01
☐ 52 Fred Schulte	.10	.05	.01
☐ 53 Cecil Travis	.10	.05	.01
☐ 54 Tommy Thomas	.10	.05	.01
☐ 55 Dutch Leonard	.10	.05	.01
☐ 56 Jimmy Wasdell	.10	.05	.01
☐ 57 Doc Cramer	.25	.11	.03
☐ 58 Harland Clift	.10	.05	.01
☐ 59 Ken Chase	.10	.05	.01
☐ 60 Buddy Lewis	.10	.05	.01
☐ 61 Ossie Bluege	.10	.05	.01
☐ 62 Chuck Stobbs	.10	.05	.01
☐ 63 Jimmy DeShong	.10	.05	.01
☐ 64 Roger Wolff	.10	.05	.01
☐ 65 Luke Sewell	.10	.05	.01
☐ 66 Sid Hudson	.10	.05	.01
☐ 67 Jack Russell	.10	.05	.01
☐ 68 Walt Masterson	.10	.05	.01
☐ 69 George Myatt	.10	.05	.01
☐ 70 Monte Weaver	.10	.05	.01
☐ 71 Cliff Bolton	.10	.05	.01
☐ 72 Ray Scarborough	.10	.05	.01
☐ 73 Albie Pearson	.10	.05	.01
☐ 74 Gil Coan	.10	.05	.01
☐ 75 Roy Sievers	.25	.11	.03
☐ 76 Burleigh Grimes	.50	.23	.06
☐ 77 Charlie Hargreaves	.10	.05	.01
☐ 78 Babe Herman	.25	.11	.03
☐ 79 Fred Frankhouse	.10	.05	.01
☐ 80 Al Lopez	.50	.23	.06
☐ 81 Lonny Frey	.10	.05	.01
☐ 82 Dixie Walker	.10	.05	.01
☐ 83 Kirby Higbe	.10	.05	.01
☐ 84 Bobby Bragan	.10	.05	.01
☐ 85 Leo Durocher	.50	.23	.06
☐ 86 Woody English	.10	.05	.01
☐ 87 Preacher Roe	.10	.05	.01
☐ 88 Vic Lombardi	.10	.05	.01
☐ 89 Clyde Sukeforth	.10	.05	.01
☐ 90 Pee Wee Reese	2.00	.90	.25
☐ 91 Joe Hatten	.10	.05	.01
☐ 92 Gene Hermanski	.10	.05	.01
☐ 93 Ray Benge	.10	.05	.01
☐ 94 Duke Snider	2.00	.90	.25
☐ 95 Walter Alston MG	.50	.23	.06
☐ 96 Don Drysdale	1.50	.70	.19
☐ 97 Andy Pafko	.25	.11	.03
☐ 98 Don Zimmer	.25	.11	.03
☐ 99 Carl Erskine	.25	.11	.03
☐ 100 Dick Williams	.25	.11	.03
☐ 101 Charlie Grimm	.25	.11	.03
☐ 102 Clarence Blair	.10	.05	.01
☐ 103 Johnny Moore	.10	.05	.01
☐ 104 Clay Bryant	.10	.05	.01
☐ 105 Billy Herman	.50	.23	.06
☐ 106 Hy Vandenberg	.10	.05	.01
☐ 107 Lennie Merullo	.10	.05	.01
☐ 108 Hank Wyse	.10	.05	.01
☐ 109 Dom Dallessandro	.10	.05	.01
☐ 110 Al Epperly	.10	.05	.01
☐ 111 Bill Nicholson	.10	.05	.01
☐ 112 Vern Olsen	.10	.05	.01
☐ 113 Johnny Schmitz	.10	.05	.01
☐ 114 Bob Scheffing	.10	.05	.01
☐ 115 Bob Rush	.10	.05	.01
☐ 116 Roy Smalley	.10	.05	.01
☐ 117 Ransom Jackson	.10	.05	.01
☐ 118 Cliff Chambers	.10	.05	.01
☐ 119 Harry Chiti	.10	.05	.01
☐ 120 Johnny Klippstein	.10	.05	.01
☐ 121 Gene Baker	.10	.05	.01
☐ 122 Walt Moryn	.10	.05	.01
☐ 123 Dick Littlefield	.10	.05	.01
☐ 124 Bob Speake	.10	.05	.01
☐ 125 Hank Sauer	.10	.05	.01
☐ 126 Monty Stratton	.25	.11	.03
☐ 127 Johnny Kerr	.10	.05	.01
☐ 128 Milt Gaston	.10	.05	.01
☐ 129 Eddie Smith	.10	.05	.01
☐ 130 Larry Rosenthal	.10	.05	.01
☐ 131 Orval Grove	.10	.05	.01
☐ 132 Johnny Hodapp	.10	.05	.01
☐ 133 Johnny Rigney	.10	.05	.01
☐ 134 Willie Kamm	.10	.05	.01
☐ 135 Ed Lopat	.25	.11	.03
☐ 136 Smead Jolley	.10	.05	.01
☐ 137 Ralph Hodgin	.10	.05	.01
☐ 138 Ollie Bejma	.10	.05	.01
☐ 139 Zeke Bonura	.10	.05	.01
☐ 140 Al Hollingsworth	.10	.05	.01
☐ 141 Thurman Tucker	.10	.05	.01
☐ 142 Cass Michaels	.10	.05	.01
☐ 143 Bill Wight	.10	.05	.01
☐ 144 Don Lenhardt	.10	.05	.01
☐ 145 Sammy Esposito	.10	.05	.01
☐ 146 Jack Harshman	.10	.05	.01
☐ 147 Turk Lown	.10	.05	.01
☐ 148 Jim Landis	.10	.05	.01
☐ 149 Bob Shaw	.10	.05	.01
☐ 150 Minnie Minoso	.50	.23	.06
☐ 151 Les Bell	.10	.05	.01
☐ 152 Taylor Douthit	.10	.05	.01
☐ 153 Jack Rothrock	.10	.05	.01
☐ 154 Terry Moore	.25	.11	.03
☐ 155 Max Lanier	.10	.05	.01
☐ 156 Don Gutteridge	.10	.05	.01
☐ 157 Stu Martin	.10	.05	.01
☐ 158 Stan Musial	2.00	.90	.25
☐ 159 Frank Crespi	.10	.05	.01
☐ 160 Johnny Hopp	.10	.05	.01
☐ 161 Ernie Koy	.10	.05	.01
☐ 162 Joe Garagiola	1.25	.55	.16
☐ 163 Joe Orengo	.10	.05	.01
☐ 164 Ed Kazak	.10	.05	.01
☐ 165 Howie Krist	.10	.05	.01
☐ 166 Enos Slaughter	.50	.23	.06
☐ 167 Ray Sanders	.10	.05	.01
☐ 168 Walker Cooper	.10	.05	.01
☐ 169 Nippy Jones	.10	.05	.01
☐ 170 Dick Sisler	.10	.05	.01
☐ 171 Harvey Haddix	.10	.05	.01
☐ 172 Solly Hemus	.10	.05	.01
☐ 173 Ray Jablonski	.10	.05	.01
☐ 174 Alex Grammas	.10	.05	.01
☐ 175 Joe Cunningham	.10	.05	.01
☐ 176 Debs Garms	.10	.05	.01
☐ 177 Chief Hogsett	.10	.05	.01
☐ 178 Alan Strange	.10	.05	.01
☐ 179 Rick Ferrell	.50	.23	.06
☐ 180 Jack Kramer	.10	.05	.01
☐ 181 Jack Knott	.10	.05	.01
☐ 182 Bob Harris	.10	.05	.01
☐ 183 Billy Hitchcock	.10	.05	.01
☐ 184 Jim Walkup	.10	.05	.01
☐ 185 Roy Cullenbine	.10	.05	.01
☐ 186 Bob Muncrief	.10	.05	.01
☐ 187 Chet Laabs	.10	.05	.01
☐ 188 Vern Kennedy	.10	.05	.01
☐ 189 Bill Trotter	.10	.05	.01
☐ 190 Denny Galehouse	.10	.05	.01
☐ 191 Al Zarilla	.10	.05	.01
☐ 192 Hank Arft	.10	.05	.01
☐ 193 Nelson Potter	.10	.05	.01
☐ 194 Ray Coleman	.10	.05	.01
☐ 195 Bob Dillinger	.25	.11	.03
☐ 196 Dick Kokos	.10	.05	.01
☐ 197 Bob Cain	.10	.05	.01
☐ 198 Virgil Trucks	.10	.05	.01
☐ 199 Duane Pillette	.10	.05	.01
☐ 200 Bob Turley	.25	.11	.03
☐ 201 Wally Berger	.10	.05	.01
☐ 202 John Lanning	.10	.05	.01
☐ 203 Buck Jordan	.10	.05	.01
☐ 204 Jim Turner	.10	.05	.01
☐ 205 Johnny Cooney	.10	.05	.01
☐ 206 Hank Majeski	.10	.05	.01
☐ 207 Phil Masi	.10	.05	.01
☐ 208 Tony Cuccinello	.10	.05	.01
☐ 209 Whitey Wietelman	.10	.05	.01
☐ 210 Lou Fette	.10	.05	.01
☐ 211 Vince Di Maggio	.10	.05	.01
☐ 212 Huck Betts	.10	.05	.01
☐ 213 Red Barrett	.10	.05	.01
☐ 214 Pinkey Whitney	.10	.05	.01
☐ 215 Tommy Holmes	.25	.11	.03
☐ 216 Ray Berres	.10	.05	.01
☐ 217 Mike Sandlock	.10	.05	.01
☐ 218 Max Macon	.10	.05	.01
☐ 219 Sibby Sisti	.10	.05	.01
☐ 220 Johnny Beazley	.10	.05	.01
☐ 221 Bill Posedel	.10	.05	.01
☐ 222 Connie Ryan	.10	.05	.01
☐ 223 Del Crandall	.10	.05	.01
☐ 224 Bob Addis	.10	.05	.01
☐ 225 Warren Spahn	1.25	.55	.16
☐ 227 Dom DiMaggio	.25	.11	.03
☐ 228 Emerson Dickman	.10	.05	.01
☐ 229 Bobby Doerr	.50	.23	.06
☐ 230 Tony Lupien	.10	.05	.01
☐ 231 Roy Partee	.10	.05	.01
☐ 232 Stan Spence	.10	.05	.01
☐ 233 Jim Bagby	.10	.05	.01
☐ 234 Buster Mills	.10	.05	.01
☐ 235 Fabian Gaffke	.10	.05	.01
☐ 236 George Metkovich	.10	.05	.01
☐ 237 Tom McBride	.10	.05	.01
☐ 238 Charlie Wagner	.10	.05	.01
☐ 239 Eddie Pellegrini	.10	.05	.01
☐ 240 Harry Dorish	.10	.05	.01
☐ 241 Ike Delock	.10	.05	.01

☐ 242 Mel Parnell	.10	.05	.01
☐ 243 Matt Batts	.10	.05	.01
☐ 244 Gene Stephens	.10	.05	.01
☐ 245 Milt Bolling	.10	.05	.01
☐ 246 Charlie Maxwell	.10	.05	.01
☐ 247 Willard Nixon	.10	.05	.01
☐ 248 Sammy White	.10	.05	.01
☐ 249 Dick Gernert	.10	.05	.01
☐ 250 Rico Petrocelli	.10	.05	.01
☐ 251 Edd Roush	.50	.23	.06
☐ 252 Mark Koenig	.25	.11	.03
☐ 253 Jimmy Outlaw	.10	.05	.01
☐ 254 Ethan Allen	.10	.05	.01
☐ 255 Tony Freitas	.10	.05	.01
☐ 256 Frank McCormick	.10	.05	.01
☐ 257 Bucky Walters	.25	.11	.03
☐ 258 Harry Craft	.10	.05	.01
☐ 259 Nate Andrews	.10	.05	.01
☐ 260 Ed Lukon	.10	.05	.01
☐ 261 Elmer Riddle	.10	.05	.01
☐ 262 Lee Grissom	.10	.05	.01
☐ 263 Johnny Vander Meer	.25	.11	.03
☐ 264 Eddie Joost	.10	.05	.01
☐ 265 Kermit Wahl	.10	.05	.01
☐ 266 Ival Goodman	.10	.05	.01
☐ 267 Clyde Vollmer	.10	.05	.01
☐ 268 Grady Hatten	.10	.05	.01
☐ 269 Ted Kluszewski	.75	.35	.09
☐ 270 Johnny Pramesa	.10	.05	.01
☐ 271 Joe Black	.25	.11	.03
☐ 272 Roy McMillan	.10	.05	.01
☐ 273 Wally Post	.10	.05	.01
☐ 274 Joe Nuxhall	.10	.05	.01
☐ 275 Jerry Lynch	.10	.05	.01
☐ 276 Stan Coveleski	.50	.23	.06
☐ 277 Bill Wambsganss	.25	.11	.03
☐ 278 Bruce Campbell	.10	.05	.01
☐ 279 George Uhle	.10	.05	.01
☐ 280 Earl Averill	.50	.23	.06
☐ 281 Whit Wyatt	.10	.05	.01
☐ 282 Oscar Grimes	.10	.05	.01
☐ 283 Roy Weatherly	.10	.05	.01
☐ 284 Joe Dobson	.10	.05	.01
☐ 285 Bob Feller	1.50	.70	.19
☐ 286 Jim Hegan	.10	.05	.01
☐ 287 Mel Harder	.25	.11	.03
☐ 288 Ken Keltner	.10	.05	.01
☐ 289 Red Embree	.10	.05	.01
☐ 290 Al Milnar	.10	.05	.01
☐ 291 Lou Boudreau	.75	.35	.09
☐ 292 Ed Klieman	.10	.05	.01
☐ 293 Steve Gromek	.10	.05	.01
☐ 294 George Strickland	.10	.05	.01
☐ 295 Gene Woodling	.10	.05	.01
☐ 296 Hank Edwards	.10	.05	.01
☐ 297 Don Mossi	.25	.11	.03
☐ 298 Eddie Robinson	.10	.05	.01
☐ 299 Sam Dente	.10	.05	.01
☐ 300 Herb Score	.25	.11	.03
☐ 301 Dolf Camilli	.10	.05	.01
☐ 302 Jack Warner	.10	.05	.01
☐ 303 Ike Pearson	.10	.05	.01
☐ 304 Johnny Peacock	.10	.05	.01
☐ 305 Gene Corbett	.10	.05	.01
☐ 306 Walt Millies	.10	.05	.01
☐ 307 Vance Dinges	.10	.05	.01
☐ 308 Joe Marty	.10	.05	.01
☐ 309 Hugh Mulcahy	.10	.05	.01
☐ 310 Boom Boom Beck	.10	.05	.01
☐ 311 Charley Schanz	.10	.05	.01
☐ 312 John Bolling	.10	.05	.01
☐ 313 Danny Litwhiler	.10	.05	.01
☐ 314 Emil Verban	.10	.05	.01
☐ 315 Andy Seminick	.10	.05	.01
☐ 316 John Antonelli	.10	.05	.01
☐ 317 Robin Roberts	1.50	.70	.19
☐ 318 Richie Ashburn	1.00	.45	.12
☐ 319 Curt Simmons	.10	.05	.01
☐ 320 Murry Dickson	.10	.05	.01
☐ 321 Jim Greengrass	.10	.05	.01
☐ 322 Gene Freese	.10	.05	.01
☐ 323 Bobby Morgan	.10	.05	.01
☐ 324 Don Demeter	.10	.05	.01
☐ 325 Eddie Sawyer	.10	.05	.01
☐ 326 Bob Johnson	.10	.05	.01
☐ 327 Ace Parker	.50	.23	.06
☐ 328 Joe Hauser	.10	.05	.01
☐ 329 Walt French	.10	.05	.01
☐ 330 Tom Ferrick	.10	.05	.01
☐ 331 Bill Werber	.10	.05	.01
☐ 332 Walt Masters	.10	.05	.01
☐ 333 Les McCrabb	.10	.05	.01
☐ 334 Ben McCoy	.10	.05	.01
☐ 335 Eric Tipton	.10	.05	.01
☐ 336 Al Rubeling	.10	.05	.01
☐ 337 Nick Etten	.10	.05	.01
☐ 338 Carl Scheib	.10	.05	.01
☐ 339 Dario Lodigiani	.10	.05	.01
☐ 340 Earle Brucker	.10	.05	.01
☐ 341 Al Brancato	.10	.05	.01
☐ 342 Lou Limmer	.10	.05	.01
☐ 343 Elmer Valo	.10	.05	.01
☐ 344 Bob Hooper	.10	.05	.01
☐ 345 Joe Astroth	.10	.05	.01
☐ 346 Pete Suder	.10	.05	.01
☐ 347 Dave Philley	.10	.05	.01
☐ 348 Gus Zernial	.10	.05	.01
☐ 349 Bobby Shantz	.10	.05	.01
☐ 350 Joe DeMaestri	.10	.05	.01
☐ 351 Fred Lindstrom	.50	.23	.06
☐ 352 Red Lucas	.10	.05	.01
☐ 353 Clyde Barnhart	.10	.05	.01
☐ 354 Nick Strincevich	.10	.05	.01
☐ 355 Lloyd Waner	.50	.23	.06
☐ 356 Guy Bush	.10	.05	.01
☐ 357 Joe Bowman	.10	.05	.01
☐ 358 Al Todd	.10	.05	.01
☐ 359 Mace Brown	.10	.05	.01
☐ 360 Larry French	.10	.05	.01
☐ 361 Elbie Fletcher	.10	.05	.01
☐ 362 Woody Jensen	.10	.05	.01
☐ 363 Rip Sewell	.10	.05	.01
☐ 364 Johnny Dickshot	.10	.05	.01
☐ 365 Pete Coscarart	.10	.05	.01
☐ 366 Bud Hafey	.10	.05	.01
☐ 367 Ken Heintzelman	.10	.05	.01
☐ 368 Wally Westlake	.10	.05	.01
☐ 369 Frank Gustine	.10	.05	.01
☐ 370 Smoky Burgess	.10	.05	.01
☐ 371 Vernon Law	.25	.11	.03
☐ 372 Dick Groat	.25	.11	.03
☐ 373 Bob Skinner	.10	.05	.01
☐ 374 Don Cardwell	.10	.05	.01
☐ 375 Bob Friend	.10	.05	.01
☐ 376 Frank O'Rourke	.10	.05	.01
☐ 377 Birdie Tebbetts	.10	.05	.01
☐ 378 Charlie Gehringer	.75	.35	.09
☐ 379 Eldon Auker	.10	.05	.01
☐ 380 Tuck Stainback	.10	.05	.01
☐ 381 Chet Morgan	.10	.05	.01
☐ 382 Johnny Lipon	.10	.05	.01
☐ 383 Paul Richards	.10	.05	.01
☐ 384 Johnny Gorsica	.10	.05	.01
☐ 385 Ray Hayworth	.10	.05	.01
☐ 386 Jimmy Bloodworth	.10	.05	.01
☐ 387 Gene Desautels	.10	.05	.01
☐ 388 Jo Jo White	.10	.05	.01
☐ 389 Boots Poffenberger	.10	.05	.01
☐ 390 Barney McCoskey	.10	.05	.01
☐ 391 Dick Wakefield	.10	.05	.01
☐ 392 Johnny Groth	.10	.05	.01
☐ 393 Steve Souchock	.10	.05	.01
☐ 394 George Vico	.10	.05	.01
☐ 395 Hal Newhouser	.50	.23	.06
☐ 396 Ray Herbert	.10	.05	.01
☐ 397 Jim Bunning	.75	.35	.09
☐ 398 Frank Lary	.10	.05	.01
☐ 399 Harvey Kuenn	.25	.11	.03
☐ 400 Eddie Mathews	1.50	.70	.19

1911 Diamond Gum Pins

This set of 29 (the number of pins known at this time) pins is described on each pin as "Free with Diamond Gum." The border of each pin is blue. Since the pins are unnumbered they are ordered below in alphabetical order. The player's name and team are given on the front of the pin on either side of the black and white player photo. Each pin measures approximately 7/8" in diameter.

	EX-MT	VG-E	GOOD
COMPLETE SET	7000.00	3200.00	900.00
COMMON PLAYER (1-29)	150.00	70.00	19.00
☐ 1 Babe Adams	150.00	70.00	19.00
☐ 2 Frank Baker	225.00	100.00	28.00
☐ 3 Chief Bender	225.00	100.00	28.00
☐ 4 Mordecai Brown	225.00	100.00	28.00
☐ 5 Donie Bush	150.00	70.00	19.00
☐ 6 Bill Carrigan	150.00	70.00	19.00
☐ 7 Frank Chance	300.00	135.00	38.00
☐ 8 Hal Chase	250.00	110.00	31.00
☐ 9 Ty Cobb	1250.00	550.00	160.00
☐ 10 Eddie Collins	300.00	135.00	38.00
☐ 11 Harry Davis	150.00	70.00	19.00
☐ 12 Red Dooin	150.00	70.00	19.00
☐ 13 Larry Doyle	175.00	80.00	22.00
☐ 14 Johnny Evers	225.00	100.00	28.00
☐ 15 Miller Huggins	225.00	100.00	28.00
☐ 16 Hugh Jennings	225.00	100.00	28.00
☐ 17 Napolean Lajoie	400.00	180.00	50.00
☐ 18 Harry Lord	150.00	70.00	19.00
☐ 19 Christy Mathewson	500.00	220.00	60.00
☐ 20 Dots Miller	150.00	70.00	19.00
☐ 21 George Mullen (Mullin)	150.00	70.00	19.00
☐ 22 Danny Murphy	150.00	70.00	19.00
☐ 23 Orval Overall	150.00	70.00	19.00
☐ 24 Eddie Plank	300.00	135.00	38.00
☐ 25 Hack Simmons Rochester	150.00	70.00	19.00
☐ 26 Ira Thomas	150.00	70.00	19.00
☐ 27 Joe Tinker	300.00	135.00	38.00
☐ 28 Honus Wagner	500.00	220.00	60.00
☐ 29 Cy Young	400.00	180.00	50.00

1993 Diamond Marks Prototypes

This eight-bookmark prototype set was a collaboration of Barry Colla and Terry Smith. It was produced to gain approval from MLB, and reportedly less than 600 of each card was printed. Dealers who responded to the initial promotional offer from Card Collectors Co., the principal distributor, were given one prototype card with their order. The bookmarks measure approximately 2 1/2" by 5" and feature black-bordered color player shots, some action, others posed, on their fronts. Each photo is framed by a team-colored line, and the photos in this prototype set differ from those in the regular set. The player's name appears in white lettering within the black border above the picture. His team's name and logo are printed over three team color-coded stripes beneath the the picture. The black-bordered horizontal back is designed to resemble an open book. On the left "page" appears a color closeup of the player. On the right "page" is a smaller color player photo and, appearing alongside, a personal profile or career highlight. The backs also state "1993 Diamond Marks Prototype." The bookmarks are unnumbered and checklisted below in alphabetical order.

	MINT	NRMT	EXC
COMPLETE SET (8)	125.00	55.00	15.50
COMMON CARD (1-8)	4.00	1.80	.50
☐ 1 Roberto Alomar	15.00	6.75	1.85
☐ 2 Will Clark	10.00	4.50	1.25
☐ 3 Dennis Eckersley	4.00	1.80	.50
☐ 4 Juan Gonzalez	20.00	9.00	2.50
☐ 5 Ken Griffey Jr.	40.00	18.00	5.00
☐ 6 Kirby Puckett	20.00	9.00	2.50
☐ 7 Ryne Sandberg	20.00	9.00	2.50
☐ 8 Frank Thomas	40.00	18.00	5.00

1993 Diamond Marks

This 120-card bookmark set was a collaboration of Barry Colla and Terry Smith. Ten bookmarks and an ad card came in each cello pack. A total production run of only 2,500 cases were produced, and no factory sets were issued. The bookmarks measure approximately 2 1/2" by 5" and feature black-bordered color player shots, some action, others posed, on their fronts. Each photo is framed by a team color-coded line. The player's name appears in white lettering within the black border above the picture. His team's name and logo are printed over three team-colored stripes beneath the the picture. The black-bordered horizontal back is designed to resemble an open book. On the left "page" appears a color closeup of the player. On the right "page" is a smaller color player photo and, appearing alongside, a personal profile or career highlight. The bookmarks are unnumbered and checklisted below in alphabetical order.

	MINT	NRMT	EXC
COMPLETE SET (120)	20.00	9.00	2.50
COMMON CARD (1-120)	.10	.05	.01
☐ 1 Roberto Alomar	.75	.35	.09
☐ 2 Sandy Alomar Jr.	.20	.09	.03
☐ 3 Moises Alou	.20	.09	.03
☐ 4 Brady Anderson	.40	.18	.05
☐ 5 Steve Avery	.10	.05	.01
☐ 6 Carlos Baerga	.20	.09	.03
☐ 7 Jeff Bagwell	1.50	.70	.19
☐ 8 Derek Bell	.20	.09	.03
☐ 9 Jay Bell	.10	.05	.01
☐ 10 Albert Belle	2.00	.90	.25
☐ 11 Dante Bichette	.40	.18	.05
☐ 12 Craig Biggio	.20	.09	.03
☐ 13 Wade Boggs	.50	.23	.06
☐ 14 Barry Bonds	.75	.35	.09
☐ 15 Bobby Bonilla	.20	.09	.03
☐ 16 Pat Borders	.10	.05	.01
☐ 17 Daryl Boston	.10	.05	.01
☐ 18 George Brett	1.50	.70	.19
☐ 19 John Burkett	.10	.05	.01
☐ 20 Brett Butler	.20	.09	.03
☐ 21 Ken Caminiti	.50	.23	.06
☐ 22 Jose Canseco	.60	.25	.07
☐ 23 Joe Carter	.20	.09	.03
☐ 24 Will Clark	.60	.25	.07
☐ 25 Roger Clemens	.75	.35	.09
☐ 26 Chad Curtis	.10	.05	.01
☐ 27 Darren Daulton	.20	.09	.03
☐ 28 Eric Davis	.20	.09	.03
☐ 29 Andre Dawson	.40	.18	.05
☐ 30 Delino DeShields	.10	.05	.01
☐ 31 Orestes Destrade	.10	.05	.01
☐ 32 Gary DiSarcina	.10	.05	.01
☐ 33 Len Dykstra	.20	.09	.03
☐ 34 Dennis Eckersley	.20	.09	.03
☐ 35 Cecil Fielder	.20	.09	.03
☐ 36 Andres Galarraga	.40	.18	.05
☐ 37 Ron Gant	.20	.09	.03
☐ 38 Tom Glavine	.40	.18	.05
☐ 39 Luis Gonzalez	.10	.05	.01
☐ 40 Juan Gonzalez	2.00	.90	.25
☐ 41 Dwight Gooden	.20	.09	.03
☐ 42 Mark Grace	.50	.23	.06
☐ 43 Mike Greenwell	.10	.05	.01
☐ 44 Ken Griffey Jr.	4.00	1.80	.50
☐ 45 Marquis Grissom	.20	.09	.03
☐ 46 Juan Guzman	.10	.05	.01
☐ 47 Tony Gwynn	2.00	.90	.25
☐ 48 Darryl Hamilton	.10	.05	.01
☐ 49 Charlie Hayes	.10	.05	.01
☐ 50 Rickey Henderson	.50	.23	.06
☐ 51 Orel Hershiser	.20	.09	.03
☐ 52 Dave Hollins	.10	.05	.01
☐ 53 Kent Hrbek	.10	.05	.01
☐ 54 Bo Jackson	.20	.09	.03
☐ 55 Gregg Jefferies	.20	.09	.03
☐ 56 Howard Johnson	.10	.05	.01
☐ 57 Wally Joyner	.20	.09	.03
☐ 58 David Justice	.20	.09	.03
☐ 59 Eric Karros	.40	.18	.05
☐ 60 Roberto Kelly	.10	.05	.01
☐ 61 Chuck Knoblauch	.50	.23	.06
☐ 62 John Kruk	.20	.09	.03
☐ 63 Barry Larkin	.50	.23	.06
☐ 64 Pat Listach	.10	.05	.01
☐ 65 Kenny Lofton	1.25	.55	.16
☐ 66 Mike Macfarlane	.10	.05	.01
☐ 67 Al Martin	.10	.05	.01
☐ 68 Dennis Martinez	.20	.09	.03
☐ 69 Edgar Martinez	.20	.09	.03
☐ 70 Ramon Martinez	.20	.09	.03
☐ 71 Don Mattingly	2.00	.90	.25
☐ 72 Fred McGriff	.40	.18	.05
☐ 73 Mark McGwire	1.25	.55	.16
☐ 74 Brian McRae	.10	.05	.01
☐ 75 Orlando Merced	.10	.05	.01
☐ 76 Kevin Mitchell	.20	.09	.03
☐ 77 Paul Molitor	.75	.35	.09
☐ 78 Eddie Murray	.60	.25	.07
☐ 79 Mike Mussina	.60	.25	.07
☐ 80 Randy Myers	.10	.05	.01
☐ 81 Pete O'Brien	.10	.05	.01
☐ 82 John Olerud	.10	.05	.01
☐ 83 Tom Pagnozzi	.10	.05	.01
☐ 84 Terry Pendleton	.10	.05	.01
☐ 85 Tony Phillips	.10	.05	.01
☐ 86 Mike Piazza	2.50	1.10	.30
☐ 87 Kirby Puckett	2.00	.90	.25
☐ 88 Jose Rijo	.10	.05	.01
☐ 89 Cal Ripken	3.00	1.35	.35
☐ 90 Ivan Rodriguez	1.00	.45	.12
☐ 91 Nolan Ryan	3.00	1.35	.35
☐ 92 Tim Salmon	.50	.23	.06
☐ 93 Ryne Sandberg	1.50	.70	.19
☐ 94 Deion Sanders	.50	.23	.06
☐ 95 Reggie Sanders	.40	.18	.05
☐ 96 Benito Santiago	.10	.05	.01
☐ 97 Gary Sheffield	.50	.23	.06
☐ 98 Ruben Sierra	.10	.05	.01
☐ 99 Ozzie Smith	1.50	.70	.19
☐ 100 John Smoltz	.60	.25	.07
☐ 101 J.T. Snow	.50	.23	.06
☐ 102 Terry Steinbach	.10	.05	.01
☐ 103 Dave Stewart	.10	.05	.01
☐ 104 Darryl Strawberry	.20	.09	.03
☐ 105 B.J. Surhoff	.20	.09	.03
☐ 106 Danny Tartabull	.10	.05	.01
☐ 107 Mickey Tettleton	.10	.05	.01
☐ 108 Frank Thomas	4.00	1.80	.50
☐ 109 Alan Trammell	.40	.18	.05
☐ 110 David Valle	.10	.05	.01
☐ 111 Andy Van Slyke	.10	.05	.01
☐ 112 Mo Vaughn	1.00	.45	.12
☐ 113 Robin Ventura	.20	.09	.03
☐ 114 Jose Vizcaino	.10	.05	.01
☐ 115 Larry Walker	.40	.18	.05
☐ 116 Walt Weiss	.10	.05	.01
☐ 117 Matt Williams	.40	.18	.05
☐ 118 Dave Winfield	.40	.18	.05
☐ 119 Robin Yount	.40	.18	.05
☐ 120 Todd Zeile	.10	.05	.01

1993 Diamond Marks Art

Complimenting the 120-card bookmark set, this eight-bookmark art card set was a collaboration of Barry Colla and Terry Smith. One of

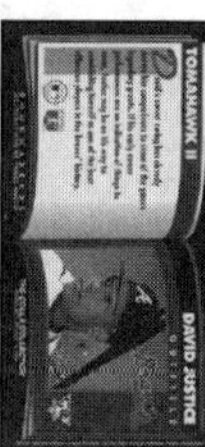

the special art cards is included in each 48-pack carton. The bookmark art cards measure approximately 2 1/2" by 5" and feature black-bordered fanciful color player paintings by Terry Smith on their fronts. The player's name appears in grayish lettering within the black border below the painting. The black-bordered horizontal back is designed to resemble an open book. On the right "page" appears a color closeup player photo. On the left "page" is a personal profile or career highlight. The bookmarks are unnumbered and checklisted below in alphabetical order. There are reports in the hobby that no more than 3,000 of each card were produced.

	MINT	NRMT	EXC
COMPLETE SET (8)	125.00	55.00	15.50
COMMON CARD (1-8)	5.00	2.20	.60
□ 1 Roberto Alomar	15.00	6.75	1.85
□ 2 Barry Bonds	10.00	4.50	1.25
□ 3 Ken Griffey Jr.	50.00	22.00	6.25
□ 4 David Justice	5.00	2.20	.60
□ 5 John Olerud	5.00	2.20	.60
□ 6 Nolan Ryan	40.00	18.00	5.00
□ 7 Frank Thomas	50.00	22.00	6.25
□ 8 Robin Yount	10.00	4.50	1.25

1934 Diamond Matchbooks Series 1 Silver Border

Issued in 1934, the 200-cover Silver-Bordered set includes many of the day's premier ballplayers. Each cover features four different background colors, red, green, blue and orange. Charlie Grimm is shown in two different poses. Players are listed in alphabetical order. All color variations are equally valued. The complete set price includes both Grimm covers. Complete matchbooks are valued fifty percent higher.

	EX-MT	VG-E	GOOD
COMPLETE SET	1000.00	450.00	125.00
COMMON PLAYER	7.50	3.40	.95
□ 1 Earl Adams	7.50	3.40	.95
□ 2 Ethan Allen	7.50	3.40	.95
□ 3 Eldon L. Auker	7.50	3.40	.95
□ 4 Del Baker	7.50	3.40	.95
□ 5 Dick Bartell	7.50	3.40	.95
□ 6 Walter Beck	7.50	3.40	.95
□ 7 Herman Bell	7.50	3.40	.95
□ 8 Ray Benge	10.00	4.50	1.25
□ 9 Larry J. Benton	7.50	3.40	.95
□ 10 Louis W. Berger	7.50	3.40	.95
□ 11 Wally Berger	10.00	4.50	1.25
□ 12 Ray Berres	7.50	3.40	.95
□ 13 Charlie Berry	7.50	3.40	.95
□ 14 Walter (Huck) Betts	7.50	3.40	.95
□ 15 Ralph Birkofer	7.50	3.40	.95
□ 16 George Blaeholder	7.50	3.40	.95
□ 17 Jim Bottomley	20.00	9.00	2.50
□ 18 Ralph Boyle	7.50	3.40	.95
□ 19 Don Brandt	7.50	3.40	.95
□ 20 Don Brennan	7.50	3.40	.95
□ 21 Jack Burns	7.50	3.40	.95
□ 22 Guy Bush	7.50	3.40	.95
□ 23 Dolph Camilli	10.00	4.50	1.25
□ 24 Ben Cantwell	7.50	3.40	.95
□ 25 Tex Carleton	7.50	3.40	.95
□ 26 Owen Carroll	7.50	3.40	.95
□ 27 Louis Chiozza	7.50	3.40	.95
□ 28 Watson Clark	7.50	3.40	.95
□ 29 James A. Collins	10.00	4.50	1.25
□ 30 Phil Collins	7.50	3.40	.95
□ 31 Edward J. Connolly	7.50	3.40	.95
□ 32 Raymond F. Coombs	7.50	3.40	.95
□ 33 Doc Cramer	10.00	4.50	1.25
□ 34 Cliff Crawford	7.50	3.40	.95
□ 35 Hugh Critz	7.50	3.40	.95
□ 36 General Crowder	7.50	3.40	.95
□ 37 Tony Cuccinello	7.50	3.40	.95
□ 38 Kiki Cuyler	20.00	9.00	2.50
□ 39 Virgil Davis	7.50	3.40	.95
□ 40 Dizzy Dean	30.00	13.50	3.70
□ 41 Paul Dean	15.00	6.75	1.85
□ 42 Edward Delker	7.50	3.40	.95
□ 43 Paul Derringer	15.00	6.75	1.85
□ 44 Gene DeSautel	7.50	3.40	.95
□ 45 Bill Dietrich	7.50	3.40	.95
□ 46 Frank F. Doljack	7.50	3.40	.95
□ 47 Edward F. Durham	7.50	3.40	.95
□ 48 Leo Durocher	20.00	9.00	2.50
□ 49 Jim Elliott	7.50	3.40	.95
□ 50 Charles D. English	7.50	3.40	.95
□ 51 Woody English	7.50	3.40	.95
□ 52 Rick Ferrell	15.00	6.75	1.85
□ 53 Wes Ferrell	10.00	4.50	1.25
□ 54 Charles W. Fischer	7.50	3.40	.95
□ 55 Freddy Fitzsimmons	10.00	4.50	1.25
□ 56 Lew Fonseca	10.00	4.50	1.25
□ 57 Fred Frankhouse	10.00	4.50	1.25
□ 58 John Frederick	7.50	3.40	.95
□ 59 Benny Frey	7.50	3.40	.95
□ 60 Linus Frey	7.50	3.40	.95
□ 61 Frankie Frisch	35.00	16.00	4.40
□ 62 Chuck Fullis	7.50	3.40	.95
□ 63 Augie Galan	7.50	3.40	.95
□ 64 Milton Galatzer	7.50	3.40	.95
□ 65 Dennis W. Galehouse	7.50	3.40	.95
□ 66 Milton Gaston	7.50	3.40	.95
□ 67 Charlie Gehringer	20.00	9.00	2.50
□ 68 Edward P. Gharrity	7.50	3.40	.95
□ 69 George Gibson	7.50	3.40	.95
□ 70 Isidore Goldstein	7.50	3.40	.95
□ 71 Hank Gowdy	7.50	3.40	.95
□ 72 Earl Grace	7.50	3.40	.95
□ 73 Chas. (Bust) Grimm	15.00	6.75	1.85
□ 74 Chas. (Reach) Grimm	15.00	6.75	1.85
□ 75 Frank T. Grube	7.50	3.40	.95
□ 76 Richard Gyselman	7.50	3.40	.95
□ 77 Stanley C. Hack	15.00	6.75	1.85
□ 78 Bump Hadley	7.50	3.40	.95
□ 79 Chick Hafey	20.00	9.00	2.50
□ 80 Harold Haid	7.50	3.40	.95
□ 81 Jesse Haines	20.00	9.00	2.50
□ 82 Odell A. Hale	7.50	3.40	.95
□ 83 Bill Hallahan	7.50	3.40	.95
□ 84 Luke Hamlin	7.50	3.40	.95
□ 85 Roy Hansen	7.50	3.40	.95
□ 86 Mel Harder	10.00	4.50	1.25
□ 87 Gabby Hartnett	20.00	9.00	2.50
□ 88 William M. Harris	7.50	3.40	.95
□ 89 Harvey Hendrick	7.50	3.40	.95
□ 90 Babe Herman	15.00	6.75	1.85
□ 91 Billy Herman	20.00	9.00	2.50
□ 92 Shanty Hogan	7.50	3.40	.95
□ 93 Chief Hogsett	7.50	3.40	.95
□ 94 Waite Hoyt	20.00	9.00	2.50
□ 95 Carl Hubbell	25.00	11.00	3.10
□ 96 Si Johnson	7.50	3.40	.95
□ 97 Syl Johnson	7.50	3.40	.95
□ 98 Roy M. Joiner	7.50	3.40	.95
□ 99 Baxter Jordan	7.50	3.40	.95
□ 100 Arndt Jorgens	7.50	3.40	.95
□ 101 William F. Jurges	10.00	4.50	1.25
□ 102 Vernon Kennedy	7.50	3.40	.95
□ 103 John F. Kerr	7.50	3.40	.95
□ 104 Chuck Klein	25.00	11.00	3.10
□ 105 Ted Kleinhans	7.50	3.40	.95
□ 106 Bill Klem UMP	15.00	6.75	1.85
□ 107 Robert G. Kline	7.50	3.40	.95
□ 108 Wm. Knickerbocker	10.00	4.50	1.25
□ 109 Jack H. Knott	7.50	3.40	.95
□ 110 Mark Koenig	7.50	3.40	.95
□ 111 William Lawrence	7.50	3.40	.95
□ 112 Thornton Lee	7.50	3.40	.95
□ 113 Bill Lee	7.50	3.40	.95
□ 114 Dutch Leonard	7.50	3.40	.95
□ 115 Ernie Lombardi	25.00	11.00	3.10
□ 116 Al Lopez	20.00	9.00	2.50
□ 117 Red Lucas	7.50	3.40	.95
□ 118 Ted Lyons	20.00	9.00	2.50
□ 119 Daniel MacFayden	7.50	3.40	.95
□ 120 Ed. Majeski	7.50	3.40	.95
□ 121 Leroy Mahaffey	7.50	3.40	.95
□ 122 Pat Malone	7.50	3.40	.95
□ 123 Leo Mangum	7.50	3.40	.95
□ 124 Rabbit Maranville	25.00	11.00	3.10
□ 125 Charles Marrow	7.50	3.40	.95
□ 126 Bill McKechnie MG	20.00	9.00	2.50
□ 127 Justin McLaughlin	7.50	3.40	.95
□ 128 Marty McManus	7.50	3.40	.95
□ 129 Eric McNair	7.50	3.40	.95
□ 130 Joe Medwick	20.00	9.00	2.50
□ 131 Jim Mooney	7.50	3.40	.95
□ 132 Joe Moore	7.50	3.40	.95
□ 133 John Moore	7.50	3.40	.95
□ 134 Randy Moore	7.50	3.40	.95
□ 135 Joe Morrisey	7.50	3.40	.95
□ 136 Joseph Mowrey	7.50	3.40	.95
□ 137 Fred W. Miller	7.50	3.40	.95
□ 138 Van Lingle Mungo	15.00	6.75	1.85
□ 139 Glenn Myatt	7.50	3.40	.95
□ 140 Lynn Nelson	7.50	3.40	.95
□ 141 Prince Oana	7.50	3.40	.95
□ 142 Lefty O'Doul	15.00	6.75	1.85
□ 143 Robert O'Farrell	7.50	3.40	.95
□ 144 Ernest Orsatti	7.50	3.40	.95
□ 145 Fritz Ostermueller	7.50	3.40	.95
□ 146 Mel Ott	25.00	11.00	3.10
□ 147 Roy Parmelee	10.00	4.50	1.25
□ 148 Ralph Perkins	7.50	3.40	.95
□ 149 Frank Pytlak	7.50	3.40	.95
□ 150 Ernest Quigley	7.50	3.40	.95
□ 151 George Rensa	7.50	3.40	.95
□ 152 Harry Rice	7.50	3.40	.95
□ 153 Walter Roetger	10.00	4.50	1.25
□ 154 William G. Rogell	7.50	3.40	.95
□ 155 Edwin A. Rommel	7.50	3.40	.95
□ 156 Charlie Root	10.00	4.50	1.25
□ 157 John Rothrock	7.50	3.40	.95
□ 158 Jack Russell	7.50	3.40	.95
□ 159 Blondy Ryan	7.50	3.40	.95
□ 160 Al Schacht CO	10.00	4.50	1.25
□ 161 Wes Schultmerick	7.50	3.40	.95
□ 162 Rip Sewell	7.50	3.40	.95
□ 163 Gordon Slade	7.50	3.40	.95
□ 164 Bob Smith	7.50	3.40	.95
□ 165 Moose Solters	7.50	3.40	.95
□ 166 Glenn Spencer	7.50	3.40	.95
□ 167 Al Spohrer	7.50	3.40	.95
□ 168 George Stainback	10.00	4.50	1.25
□ 169 Dolly Stark	15.00	6.75	1.85
□ 170 Casey Stengel MG	30.00	13.50	3.70
□ 171 Riggs Stephenson	15.00	6.75	1.85
□ 172 Walter C. Stewart	7.50	3.40	.95
□ 173 Lin Storti	7.50	3.40	.95
□ 174 Allyn Stout	7.50	3.40	.95
□ 175 Joe Stripp	7.50	3.40	.95
□ 176 Gus Suhr	10.00	4.50	1.25
□ 177 Billy Sullivan Jr.	7.50	3.40	.95
□ 178 Benny Tate	7.50	3.40	.95
□ 179 Danny Taylor	7.50	3.40	.95
□ 180 Tommy Thevenow	7.50	3.40	.95
□ 181 Bud Tinning	7.50	3.40	.95
□ 182 Cecil Travis	7.50	3.40	.95
□ 183 Forest F. Twogood	7.50	3.40	.95
□ 184 Bill Urbanski	7.50	3.40	.95
□ 185 Dazzy Vance	10.00	4.50	1.25
□ 186 Arthur Veltman	7.50	3.40	.95
□ 187 John Vergez	7.50	3.40	.95
□ 188 Gee Walker	7.50	3.40	.95
□ 189 Bill Walker	7.50	3.40	.95
□ 190 Lloyd Waner	20.00	9.00	2.50
□ 191 Paul Waner	20.00	9.00	2.50
□ 192 Lon Warnecke	10.00	4.50	1.25
□ 193 Rabbit Warstler	7.50	3.40	.95
□ 194 Bill Werber	7.50	3.40	.95
□ 195 Jo Jo White	7.50	3.40	.95
□ 196 Pinky Whitney	7.50	3.40	.95
□ 197 Jimmy Wilson	7.50	3.40	.95
□ 198 Hack Wilson	20.00	9.00	2.50
□ 199 Ralph Winegarner	7.50	3.40	.95
□ 200 Thomas Zachary	10.00	4.50	1.25

1935 Diamond Matchbooks Series 2

The Second baseball set was issued circa 1935 by the Diamond Match Company. Each cover in the 24-cover set features a black border on the front and a brief player biography on the reverse. Covers are either green, red or blue in color. A crossed-bat design appears on the front-side of each cover. Players are listed in alphabetical order. Complete matchbooks are valued at fifty percent higher.

	EX-MT	VG-E	GOOD
COMPLETE SET (24)	300.00	135.00	38.00
COMMON PLAYER (1-24)	10.00	4.50	1.25
□ 1 Ethan Allen (red)	15.00	6.75	1.85
□ 2 Wally Berger (red)	15.00	6.75	1.85
□ 3 Tommy Carey (blue)	10.00	4.50	1.25
□ 4 Louis Chiozza (blue)	10.00	4.50	1.25
□ 5 Dizzy Dean (green)	35.00	16.00	4.40
□ 6 Frankie Frisch (red)	30.00	13.50	3.70
□ 7 Charlie Grimm (blue)	20.00	9.00	2.50
□ 8 Chick Hafey (red)	20.00	9.00	2.50
□ 9 J. Francis Hogan (red)	10.00	4.50	1.25
□ 10 Carl Hubbell (green)	25.00	11.00	3.10
□ 11 Chuck Klein (green)	25.00	11.00	3.10
□ 12 Ernie Lombardi (blue)	20.00	9.00	2.50
□ 13 Al Lopez (blue)	25.00	11.00	3.10
□ 14 Rabbit Maranville (green)	25.00	11.00	3.10
□ 15 Joe Moore (red)	10.00	4.50	1.25
□ 16 Van Lingle Mungo green	15.00	6.75	1.85
□ 17 Mel Ott (blue)	30.00	13.50	3.70
□ 18 Gordon Slade (green)	10.00	4.50	1.25
□ 19 Casey Stengel MG green	30.00	13.50	3.70
□ 20 Tommy Thevenow (red)	10.00	4.50	1.25
□ 21 Lloyd Waner (red)	25.00	11.00	3.10
□ 22 Paul Waner (green)	25.00	11.00	3.10
□ 23 Lon Warnecke (blue)	15.00	6.75	1.85
□ 24 James Wilson (blue)	10.00	4.50	1.25

1935-36 Diamond Matchbooks Series 3 Type 1

This set was released over two years (1935-36) by the Diamond Match Company.This set varries from the First and Second set in that the saddle has the "ball" with the players name and team only. Covers come in red, green and blue. Players are listed in alphabetical order. Complete matchbooks are valued fifty percent higher.

	EX-MT	VG-E	GOOD
COMPLETE SET	1000.00	450.00	125.00
COMMON PLAYER	7.50	3.40	.95
□ 1 Ethan Allen	7.50	3.40	.95
□ 2 Melo Almada	7.50	3.40	.95
□ 3 Eldon Auker	7.50	3.40	.95
□ 4 Dick Bartell	7.50	3.40	.95
□ 5 Aloysius Bejma	7.50	3.40	.95
□ 6 Ollie Bejma	7.50	3.40	.95
□ 7 Roy Chester Bell	7.50	3.40	.95
□ 8 Louis Berger	7.50	3.40	.95
□ 9 Wally Berger	10.00	4.50	1.25
□ 10 Ralph Birkofer	10.00	4.50	1.25
□ 11 Max Bishop	10.00	4.50	1.25
□ 12 George Blaeholder	7.50	3.40	.95
□ 13 Zeke Bonura	10.00	4.50	1.25
□ 14 Jim Bottomley	20.00	9.00	2.50
□ 15 Ed Brandt	10.00	4.50	1.25
□ 16 Don Brennan	7.50	3.40	.95
□ 17 Lloyd Brown	7.50	3.40	.95
□ 18 Walter G. Brown	7.50	3.40	.95
□ 19 Claiborne Bryant	7.50	3.40	.95
□ 20 Jim Bucher	10.00	4.50	1.25
□ 21 John Burnett	7.50	3.40	.95
□ 22 Irving Burns	7.50	3.40	.95
□ 23 Merritt Cain	7.50	3.40	.95
□ 24 Ben Cantwell	7.50	3.40	.95
□ 25 Tommy Carey	7.50	3.40	.95
□ 26 Tex Carleton	7.50	3.40	.95
□ 27 Joseph Cascarella	7.50	3.40	.95
□ 28 Thomas H. Casey	7.50	3.40	.95
□ 29 George Caster	7.50	3.40	.95
□ 30 Phil Cavaretta	15.00	6.75	1.85
□ 31 Louis Chiozza	7.50	3.40	.95
□ 32 Edward Cihocki	7.50	3.40	.95
□ 33 Herman E. Clifton	7.50	3.40	.95
□ 34 Richard Coffman	7.50	3.40	.95
□ 35 Edward P. Coleman	7.50	3.40	.95
□ 36 James A. Collins	7.50	3.40	.95
□ 37 Jocko Conlon	15.00	6.75	1.85
□ 38 Roger Cramer	10.00	4.50	1.25
□ 39 Hugh Critz	7.50	3.40	.95
□ 40 Alvin Crowder	7.50	3.40	.95
□ 41 Tony Cuccinello	7.50	3.40	.95
□ 42 Kiki Cuyler	20.00	9.00	2.50
□ 43 Virgil Davis	7.50	3.40	.95
□ 44 Dizzy Dean	30.00	13.50	3.70
□ 45 Paul Derringer	10.00	4.50	1.25
□ 46 James DeShong	7.50	3.40	.95
□ 47 William Dietrich	7.50	3.40	.95
□ 48 Leo Durocher	25.00	11.00	3.10
□ 49 George Earnshaw	15.00	6.75	1.85
□ 50 Elwood English	7.50	3.40	.95
□ 51 Louis Finney	7.50	3.40	.95
□ 52 Charles Fischer	7.50	3.40	.95
□ 53 Freddy Fitzsimmons	10.00	4.50	1.25
□ 54 Linus Benny Frey	10.00	4.50	1.25
□ 55 Frankie Frisch	25.00	11.00	3.10
□ 56 Augie Galan	10.00	4.50	1.25
□ 57 Milton Galatzer	7.50	3.40	.95
□ 58 Dennis Galehouse	7.50	3.40	.95
□ 59 Debs Garms	7.50	3.40	.95
□ 60 Angelo Giuliani	7.50	3.40	.95
□ 61 Earl Grace	7.50	3.40	.95
□ 62 Charlie Grimm	15.00	6.75	1.85
□ 63 Frank Grube	7.50	3.40	.95
□ 64 Stan Hack	20.00	9.00	2.50
□ 65 Irving "Bump" Hadley	7.50	3.40	.95
□ 66 Odell Hale	7.50	3.40	.95
□ 67 Bill Hallahan	7.50	3.40	.95
□ 68 Roy Hanson	7.50	3.40	.95
□ 69 Mel Harder	10.00	4.50	1.25
□ 70 Gabby Hartnett	20.00	9.00	2.50

☐ 71 Clyde Hatter	7.50	3.40	.95
☐ 72 Raymond Hayworth	7.50	3.40	.95
☐ 73 Babe Herman	15.00	6.75	1.85
☐ 74 Gordon Hinkle	7.50	3.40	.95
☐ 75 George Hockette	7.50	3.40	.95
☐ 76 James Holbrook	7.50	3.40	.95
☐ 77 Alex Hooks	7.50	3.40	.95
☐ 78 Waite Hoyt	15.00	6.75	1.85
☐ 79 Carl Hubbell	20.00	9.00	2.50
☐ 80 Roy M. Joiner	7.50	3.40	.95
☐ 81 Sam Jones	7.50	3.40	.95
☐ 82 Baxter Jordan	7.50	3.40	.95
☐ 83 Arndt Jorgens	7.50	3.40	.95
☐ 84 William F. Jurges	10.00	4.50	1.25
☐ 85 William Kamm	10.00	4.50	1.25
☐ 86 Vern Kennedy	7.50	3.40	.95
☐ 87 John Kerr	7.50	3.40	.95
☐ 88 Chuck Klein	20.00	9.00	2.50
☐ 89 Ted Kleinhans	7.50	3.40	.95
☐ 90 Wm. Knickerbocker	7.50	3.40	.95
☐ 91 Jack Knott	7.50	3.40	.95
☐ 92 Mark Koenig	7.50	3.40	.95
☐ 93 Fabian L. Kowalik	7.50	3.40	.95
☐ 94 Red Kress	7.50	3.40	.95
☐ 95 Bill Lee	7.50	3.40	.95
☐ 96 Louis Legett	7.50	3.40	.95
☐ 97 Dutch Leonard	7.50	3.40	.95
☐ 98 Fred Lindstrom	15.00	6.75	1.85
☐ 99 Edward Linke	7.50	3.40	.95
☐ 100 Ernie Lombardi	15.00	6.75	1.85
☐ 101 Al Lopez	20.00	9.00	2.50
☐ 102 John Marcum	7.50	3.40	.95
☐ 103 Bill McKechnie MG	15.00	6.75	1.85
☐ 104 Eric McNair	7.50	3.40	.95
☐ 105 Joe Medwick	20.00	9.00	2.50
☐ 106 Oscar Melillo	7.50	3.40	.95
☐ 107 John Michaels	7.50	3.40	.95
☐ 108 Joe Moore	7.50	3.40	.95
☐ 109 John Moore	7.50	3.40	.95
☐ 110 Wally Moses	12.50	5.50	1.55
☐ 111 Joseph Milligan	7.50	3.40	.95
☐ 112 Van Lingle Mungo	12.50	5.50	1.55
☐ 113 Glenn Myatt	7.50	3.40	.95
☐ 114 James O'Dea	7.50	3.40	.95
☐ 115 Ernest Orsatti	7.50	3.40	.95
☐ 116 Fred Ostermueller	7.50	3.40	.95
☐ 117 Mel Ott	25.00	11.00	3.10
☐ 118 LeRoy Parmelee	10.00	4.50	1.25
☐ 119 Monte Pearson	7.50	3.40	.95
☐ 120 Raymond Pepper	7.50	3.40	.95
☐ 121 Raymond Phelps	7.50	3.40	.95
☐ 122 George Pipgras	7.50	3.40	.95
☐ 123 Frank Pytlak	7.50	3.40	.95
☐ 124 Gordon Rhodes	10.00	4.50	1.25
☐ 125 Charlie Root	10.00	4.50	1.25
☐ 126 John Rothrock	7.50	3.40	.95
☐ 127 Muddy Ruel	7.50	3.40	.95
☐ 128 Jack Saltzgaver	7.50	3.40	.95
☐ 129 Fred Schulte	7.50	3.40	.95
☐ 130 George Selkirk	10.00	4.50	1.25
☐ 131 Mervyn Shea	7.50	3.40	.95
☐ 132 Al Spoher	7.50	3.40	.95
☐ 133 George Stainback	10.00	4.50	1.25
☐ 134 Casey Stengel MG	25.00	11.00	3.10
☐ 135 Walter Stephenson	7.50	3.40	.95
☐ 136 Lee Stine	7.50	3.40	.95
☐ 137 John Stone	7.50	3.40	.95
☐ 138 Gus Suhr	10.00	4.50	1.25
☐ 139 Tommy Thevenow	7.50	3.40	.95
☐ 140 Fay Thomas	7.50	3.40	.95
☐ 141 Leslie Tietje	7.50	3.40	.95
☐ 142 Bill Urbanski	7.50	3.40	.95
☐ 143 William H. Walker	7.50	3.40	.95
☐ 144 Lloyd Waner	20.00	9.00	2.50
☐ 145 Paul Waner	20.00	9.00	2.50
☐ 146 Lon Warnecke	10.00	4.50	1.25
☐ 147 Harold Warstler	7.50	3.40	.95
☐ 148 Bill Werber	10.00	4.50	1.25
☐ 149 Vernon Wiltshere	7.50	3.40	.95
☐ 150 James Wilson	7.50	3.40	.95
☐ 151 Ralph Winegarner	7.50	3.40	.95

1936 Diamond Matchbooks Series 3 Type 2

This 23-player set was issued by the Diamond Match Company around 1936. Each player's cover is featured in three different colors, red, green and blue, All player photos, except "Dizzy" Dean, feature head and shoulders shot. The set was released with two different colors of ink, brown and black. All players are listed in alphabetical order. Complete matchbooks are valued fifty percent higher.

	EX-MT	VG-E	GOOD
COMPLETE SET (23)	200.00	90.00	25.00
COMMON PLAYER (1-23)	7.50	3.40	.95
☐ 1 Claiborne Bryant	7.50	3.40	.95
☐ 2 Tex Carleton	7.50	3.40	.95
☐ 3 Phil Cavaretta	12.50	5.50	1.55
☐ 4 James A. Collins	12.50	5.50	1.55
☐ 5 Curt Davis	7.50	3.40	.95
☐ 6 Dizzy Dean	25.00	11.00	3.10
☐ 7 Frank Demaree	7.50	3.40	.95
☐ 8 Larry French	7.50	3.40	.95
☐ 9 Linus R. Frey	7.50	3.40	.95
☐ 10 August Galan	10.00	4.50	1.25
☐ 11 Bob Garbark	7.50	3.40	.95
☐ 12 Stan Hack	15.00	6.75	1.85
☐ 13 Gabby Hartnett	15.00	6.75	1.85
☐ 14 Billy Herman	15.00	6.75	1.85
☐ 15 William F. Jurges	10.00	4.50	1.25
☐ 16 Wm. C. "Bill" Lee	7.50	3.40	.95
☐ 17 Joe Marty	7.50	3.40	.95
☐ 18 James K. O'Dea	7.50	3.40	.95
☐ 19 LeRoy Parmelee	7.50	3.40	.95
☐ 20 Charlie Root	10.00	4.50	1.25
☐ 21 Clyde Shoun	7.50	3.40	.95
☐ 22 George Stainback	10.00	4.50	1.25
☐ 23 Paul Waner	15.00	6.75	1.85

1936 Diamond Matchbooks Series 4

This is by far the smallest matchcover set released by the Diamond Match Company during the 1930's. The set is similar to the Third Baseball set other than the players team name shows under his name on the back. All of the covers minus Charlie Grimm were printed using brown ink. The three different Grimm cover feature black ink. The players are listed in alphabetical order. Complete matchbooks are valued fifty percent higher.

	EX-MT	VG-E	GOOD
COMPLETE SET (12)	150.00	70.00	19.00
COMMON PLAYER (1-12)	7.50	3.40	.95
☐ 1 Tommy Carey	7.50	3.40	.95
☐ 2 Tony Cuccinello	7.50	3.40	.95
☐ 3 Freddy Fitzsimmons	10.00	4.50	1.25
☐ 4 Frankie Frisch	25.00	11.00	3.10
☐ 5 Charles Grimm (3)	15.00	6.75	1.85
☐ 6 Carl Hubbell	20.00	9.00	2.50
☐ 7 Baxter Jordan	7.50	3.40	.95
☐ 8 Chuck Klein	20.00	9.00	2.50
☐ 9 Al Lopez	18.00	8.00	2.20
☐ 10 Joe Medwick	15.00	6.75	1.85
☐ 11 Van Lingle Mungo	15.00	6.75	1.85
☐ 12 Mel Ott	25.00	11.00	3.10

1934-36 Diamond Stars R327

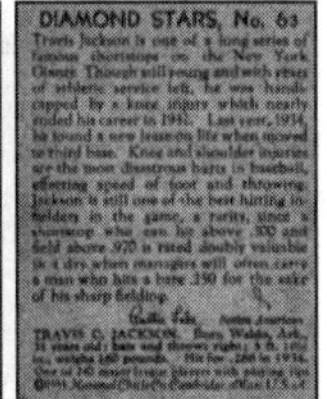

The cards in this 108-card set measure approximately 2 3/8" by 2 7/8". The Diamond Stars set, produced by National Chicle from 1934-36, is also commonly known by its catalog designation, R327. The year of production can be determined by the statistics contained on the back of the card. There are at least 168 possible front/back combinations counting blue (B) and green (G) backs over all three years. The last twelve cards are repeat players and are quite scarce. The checklist below lists the year(s) and back color(s) for the cards. Cards 32 through 72 were issued only in 1935 with green ink on back. Cards 73 through 84 were issued three ways: 35B, 35G, and 36B. Card numbers 85 through 108 were issued only in 1936 with blue ink on back. The complete set price below refers to the set of all variations listed explicitly below. A blank-backed proof sheet of 12 additional (never-issued) cards was discovered in 1980.

	EX-MT	VG-E	GOOD
COMPLETE SET (119)	15000.00	6800.00	1900.00
COMMON CARD (1-31)	45.00	20.00	5.50
COMMON CARD (32-84)	55.00	25.00	7.00
COMMON CARD (85-96)	110.00	50.00	14.00
COMMON CARD (97-108)	225.00	100.00	28.00
WRAPPER (1-CENT, BLUE)	250.00	110.00	31.00
WRAPPER (1-CENT, YELLOW)	200.00	90.00	25.00
WRAPPER (1-CENT, CLEAR)	200.00	90.00	25.00
☐ 1 Lefty Grove (34G, 35G)	700.00	325.00	90.00
☐ 2A Al Simmons (34G, 35G) (Sox on uniform)	125.00	55.00	15.50
☐ 2B Al Simmons (36B) (No name on uniform)	200.00	90.00	25.00
☐ 3 Rabbit Maranville (34G, 35G)	125.00	55.00	15.50
☐ 4 Buddy Myer (34G, 35G, 36B)	55.00	25.00	7.00
☐ 5 Tommy Bridges (34G, 35G, 36B)	55.00	25.00	7.00
☐ 6 Max Bishop (34G, 35G)	45.00	20.00	5.50
☐ 7 Lew Fonseca (34G, 35G)	45.00	20.00	5.50
☐ 8 Joe Vosmik (34G, 35G, 36B)	45.00	20.00	5.50
☐ 9 Mickey Cochrane (34G, 35G, 36B)	175.00	80.00	22.00
☐ 10A Leroy Mahaffey (34G, 35G) (A's on uniform)	45.00	20.00	5.50
☐ 10B Leroy Mahaffey (36B) (No name on uniform)	75.00	34.00	9.50
☐ 11 Bill Dickey (34G, 35G)	225.00	100.00	28.00
☐ 12A Fred Walker (34G) (Ruth retires mentioned on back)	75.00	34.00	9.50
☐ 12B Fred Walker (35G) (Ruth to Boston mentioned on back)	55.00	25.00	7.00
☐ 12C Fred Walker (36B)	90.00	40.00	11.00
☐ 13 George Blaeholder (34G, 35G)	45.00	20.00	5.50
☐ 14 Bill Terry (34G, 35G)	175.00	80.00	22.00
☐ 15A Dick Bartell (34G) (Philadelphia Phillies on card back)	75.00	34.00	9.50
☐ 15B Dick Bartell (35G) (New York Giants on card back)	55.00	25.00	7.00
☐ 16 Lloyd Waner (34G, 35G, 36B)	125.00	55.00	15.50
☐ 17 Frank Frisch (34G, 35G)	125.00	55.00	15.50
☐ 18 Chick Hafey (34G, 35G)	125.00	55.00	15.50
☐ 19 Van Lingle Mungo (34G, 35G)	55.00	25.00	7.00
☐ 20 Frank Hogan (34G, 35G)	45.00	20.00	5.50
☐ 21A Johnny Vergez (34G) (New York Giants on card back)	75.00	34.00	9.50
☐ 21B Johnny Vergez (35G) (Philadelphia Phillies on card back)	55.00	25.00	7.00
☐ 22 Jimmy Wilson (34G, 35G, 36B)	45.00	20.00	5.50
☐ 23 Bill Hallahan (34G, 35G)	45.00	20.00	5.50
☐ 24 Earl Adams (34G, 35G)	45.00	20.00	5.50
☐ 25 Wally Berger (35G)	60.00	27.00	7.50
☐ 26 Pepper Martin 35G, 36B)	75.00	34.00	9.50
☐ 27 Pie Traynor (35G)	150.00	70.00	19.00
☐ 28 Al Lopez (35G)	100.00	45.00	12.50
☐ 29 Red Rolfe (35G)	75.00	34.00	9.50
☐ 30A Heinie Manush (35G) (W on sleeve)	150.00	70.00	19.00
☐ 30B Heinie Manush (36B) (No W on sleeve)	200.00	90.00	25.00
☐ 31A Kiki Cuyler (35G) (Chicago Cubs)	125.00	55.00	15.50
☐ 31B Kiki Cuyler (36B) (Cincinnati Reds)	175.00	80.00	22.00
☐ 32 Sam Rice	125.00	55.00	15.50
☐ 33 Schoolboy Rowe	75.00	34.00	9.50
☐ 34 Stan Hack	75.00	34.00	9.50
☐ 35 Earl Averill	125.00	55.00	15.50
☐ 36A Earnie Lombardi (Sic, Ernie)	300.00	135.00	38.00
☐ 36B Ernie Lombardi	150.00	70.00	19.00
☐ 37 Billy Urbanski	55.00	25.00	7.00
☐ 38 Ben Chapman	75.00	34.00	9.50
☐ 39 Carl Hubbell	165.00	75.00	21.00
☐ 40 Blondy Ryan	55.00	25.00	7.00
☐ 41 Harvey Hendrick	55.00	25.00	7.00
☐ 42 Jimmy Dykes	75.00	34.00	9.50
☐ 43 Ted Lyons	125.00	55.00	15.50
☐ 44 Rogers Hornsby	325.00	145.00	40.00
☐ 45 Jo Jo White	55.00	25.00	7.00
☐ 46 Red Lucas	55.00	25.00	7.00
☐ 47 Bob Bolton	55.00	25.00	7.00
☐ 48 Rick Ferrell	125.00	55.00	15.50
☐ 49 Buck Jordan	55.00	25.00	7.00
☐ 50 Mel Ott	275.00	125.00	34.00
☐ 51 Burgess Whitehead	55.00	25.00	7.00
☐ 52 Tuck Stainback	55.00	25.00	7.00
☐ 53 Oscar Melillo	55.00	25.00	7.00
☐ 54A Hank Greenburg (Sic, Greenberg)	550.00	250.00	70.00
☐ 54B Hank Greenberg	300.00	135.00	38.00
☐ 55 Tony Cuccinello	55.00	25.00	7.00
☐ 56 Gus Suhr	55.00	25.00	7.00
☐ 57 Cy Blanton	55.00	25.00	7.00
☐ 58 Glenn Myatt	55.00	25.00	7.00
☐ 59 Jim Bottomley	125.00	55.00	15.50
☐ 60 Red Ruffing	150.00	70.00	19.00
☐ 61 Bill Werber	55.00	25.00	7.00
☐ 62 Fred Frankhouse	55.00	25.00	7.00
☐ 63 Travis Jackson	125.00	55.00	15.50
☐ 64 Jimmy Foxx	375.00	170.00	47.50
☐ 65 Zeke Bonura	55.00	25.00	7.00
☐ 66 Ducky Medwick	150.00	70.00	19.00
☐ 67 Marvin Owen	55.00	25.00	7.00
☐ 68 Sam Leslie	55.00	25.00	7.00
☐ 69 Earl Grace	55.00	25.00	7.00
☐ 70 Hal Trosky	75.00	34.00	9.50
☐ 71 Ossie Bluege	75.00	34.00	9.50
☐ 72 Tony Piet	55.00	25.00	7.00
☐ 73 Fritz Ostermueller	55.00	25.00	7.00
☐ 74 Tony Lazzeri	175.00	80.00	22.00
☐ 75 Jack Burns	55.00	25.00	7.00
☐ 76 Billy Rogell	55.00	25.00	7.00
☐ 77 Charlie Gehringer	165.00	75.00	21.00
☐ 78 Joe Kuhel	55.00	25.00	7.00
☐ 79 Willis Hudlin	55.00	25.00	7.00
☐ 80 Lou Chiozza	55.00	25.00	7.00
☐ 81 Bill Delancey	55.00	25.00	7.00
☐ 82A Johnny Babich (Dodgers on uniform; 35G, 35B)	55.00	25.00	7.00
☐ 82B Johnny Babich (No name on uniform; 36B)	125.00	55.00	15.50
☐ 83 Paul Waner	150.00	70.00	19.00
☐ 84 Sam Byrd	55.00	25.00	7.00
☐ 85 Moose Solters	110.00	50.00	14.00
☐ 86 Frank Crosetti	125.00	55.00	15.50
☐ 87 Steve O'Neill MG	110.00	50.00	14.00
☐ 88 George Selkirk	125.00	55.00	15.50
☐ 89 Joe Stripp	110.00	50.00	14.00
☐ 90 Ray Hayworth	110.00	50.00	14.00
☐ 91 Bucky Harris MG	225.00	100.00	28.00
☐ 92 Ethan Allen	110.00	50.00	14.00
☐ 93 General Crowder	110.00	50.00	14.00
☐ 94 Wes Ferrell	125.00	55.00	15.50
☐ 95 Luke Appling	275.00	125.00	34.00
☐ 96 Lew Riggs	110.00	50.00	14.00
☐ 97 Al Lopez	350.00	160.00	45.00
☐ 98 Schoolboy Rowe	225.00	100.00	28.00
☐ 99 Pie Traynor	350.00	160.00	45.00
☐ 100 Earl Averill	350.00	160.00	45.00
☐ 101 Dick Bartell	225.00	100.00	28.00
☐ 102 Van Lingle Mungo	225.00	100.00	28.00
☐ 103 Bill Dickey	700.00	325.00	90.00
☐ 104 Red Rolfe	225.00	100.00	28.00
☐ 105 Ernie Lombardi	350.00	160.00	45.00
☐ 106 Red Lucas	225.00	100.00	28.00
☐ 107 Stan Hack	225.00	100.00	28.00
☐ 108 Wally Berger	250.00	110.00	31.00

1981 Diamond Stars Continuation Den's

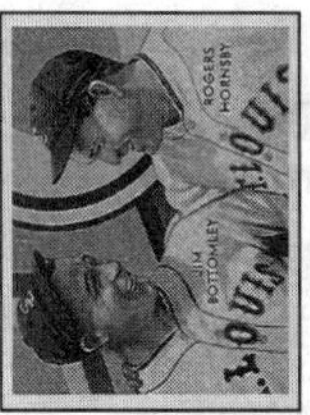

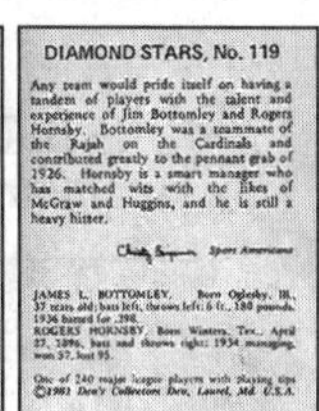

These 2 1/2" by 3" cards feature reproductions of cards which were prepared by Diamond Stars but never printed. These cards were on a twelve-card sheet and continue the numbering of already existing Diamond Stars cards. This set was created and produced by Denny Eckes. Hobbyist Mike Galella was involved in bringing this sheet to the public.

	NRMT	VG-E	GOOD
COMPLETE SET (12)	5.00	2.20	.60
COMMON CARD (109-120)	.25	.11	.03
☐ 109 Benny Frey	.25	.11	.03
☐ 110 Pete Fox	.25	.11	.03
☐ 111 Phil Cavaretta	.50	.23	.06
☐ 112 Goose Goslin	.75	.35	.09
☐ 113 Mel Harder	.50	.23	.06
☐ 114 Doc Cramer	.50	.23	.06
☐ 115 Gene Moore	.25	.11	.03
☐ 116 Rip Collins	.25	.11	.03
☐ 117 Linus Frey	.25	.11	.03
☐ 118 Lefty Gomez	1.00	.45	.12
☐ 119 Jim Bottomley Rogers Hornsby	1.00	.45	.12
☐ 120 Lon Warneke	.50	.23	.06

1993 Diamond Stars Extension Set

This 36-card set measures 2 3/8" by 2 7/8" and was issued by The Chicle Fantasy Company. These cards did not exist in 1936, but might have, had the National Chicle Co. of Cambridge, Mass. not been on

the verge of bankruptcy. Only 108 of a proposed 240 cards were issued from 1934-36. These 36 cards are an idealized version of what might have been. The colorful fronts feature art by D'August Roth Martin and are edged in white. The back carries a descriptive summary of the player's career with biography below. The cards are arranged alphabetically and are numbered on their backs, beginning with number 121. Additionally, three cards (1-3) are included that feature Negro League stars.

	MINT	NRMT	EXC
COMPLETE SET (36)	10.00	4.50	1.25
COMMON CARD (N1-N3)	.50	.23	.06
COMMON CARD (121-153)	.25	.11	.03
□ 121 Moe Berg	1.50	.70	.19
□ 122 Harlond Clift	.25	.11	.03
□ 123 Joe Cronin MG	.75	.35	.09
□ 124 Dizzy Dean	.75	.35	.09
□ 125 Paul Dean	.50	.23	.06
□ 126 Joe DiMaggio	2.00	.90	.25
□ 127 Leo Durocher	.75	.35	.09
□ 128 Bob Feller	1.00	.45	.12
□ 129 Carl Fisher	.25	.11	.03
□ 130 Lou Gehrig	2.00	.90	.25
□ 131 Bump Hadley	.25	.11	.03
□ 132 Jesse Haines	.50	.23	.06
□ 133 Bad News Hale	.25	.11	.03
□ 134 Gabby Hartnett	.75	.35	.09
□ 135 Babe Herman	.50	.23	.06
□ 136 Billy Herman	.75	.35	.09
□ 137 Waite Hoyt	.75	.35	.09
□ 138 Bob Johnson	.50	.23	.06
□ 139 Chuck Klein	.75	.35	.09
□ 140 Mike Kreevich	.25	.11	.03
□ 141 Fred Lindstrom	.50	.23	.06
□ 142 Connie Mack MG	.75	.35	.09
□ 143 Joe McCarthy MG	.75	.35	.09
□ 144 Bill McKechnie MG	.50	.23	.06
□ 145 Johnny Mize	.75	.35	.09
□ 146 Johnny Moore	.25	.11	.03
□ 147 Hugh Mulcahy	.25	.11	.03
□ 148 Buck Newsom	.50	.23	.06
□ 149 Al Smith	.25	.11	.03
□ 150 Casey Stengel MG	.75	.35	.09
□ 151 Arky Vaughan	.75	.35	.09
□ 152 Gee Walker	.25	.11	.03
□ 153 Kenesaw M. Landis COMM	.50	.23	.06
□ N1 Cool Papa Bell	.50	.23	.06
□ N2 Josh Gibson	.75	.35	.09
□ N3 Satchel Paige	.75	.35	.09
□ NNO Title card	.50	.23	.06

1972-79 Dimanche /Derniere Heure

These 145 blank-backed photo sheets in this multi-sport set measure approximately 8 1/2" by 11" and feature white-bordered color sports star photos from Dimanche Derniere Heure, a Montreal newspaper. The player's name, position and biographical information appear within the lower white margin. All text is in French. A white vinyl album was available for storing the photo sheets. Printed on the album's spine are the words, "Mes Vedettes du Sport" (My Stars of Sport).The photos are unnumbered and are checklisted below in alphabetical order according to sport or team as follows: Montreal Expos baseball players (1-52); National League baseball players (53-65); Montreal Canadiens hockey players (66-112); wrestlers (113-137); prize fighters (138-139); auto racing drivers (140-143); and women's golf (144). The set closes with a photo of Patof, a circus clown (145).

	NRMT	VG-E	GOOD
COMPLETE SET (145)	300.00	135.00	38.00
COMMON CARD (1-145)	2.00	.90	.25
□ 1 Bill Atkinson	2.00	.90	.25
□ 2 Dennis Blair	2.00	.90	.25
□ 3 John Boccabella	2.50	1.10	.30
□ 4 Hal Breeden	2.00	.90	.25
□ 5 Dave Bristol CO	2.00	.90	.25
□ 6 Jackie Brown	2.50	1.10	.30
□ 7 Don Carrithers	2.00	.90	.25
□ 8 Jim Cox	2.00	.90	.25
□ 9 Willie Davis	3.00	1.35	.35
□ 10 Don Demola	2.00	.90	.25
□ 11 Larry Doby CO	3.00	1.35	.35
□ 12 Duffy Dyer	2.00	.90	.25
□ 13 Jim Fairey	2.00	.90	.25
□ 14 Ron Fairly	3.00	1.35	.35
□ 15 Tim Foli	2.50	1.10	.30
□ 16 Barry Foote	2.00	.90	.25
□ 17 Barry Foote (Wearing chest protector and shin guards)	2.00	.90	.25
□ 18 Pepe Frias	2.00	.90	.25
□ 19 Wayne Garrett	2.00	.90	.25
□ 20 Terry Humphrey	2.00	.90	.25
□ 21 Ron Hunt	2.50	1.10	.30
□ 22 Tommy Hutton	2.00	.90	.25
□ 23 Mike Jorgensen	2.00	.90	.25
□ 24 Coco Laboy	2.50	1.10	.30
□ 25 Bill Lee	2.50	1.10	.30
□ 26 Larry Lintz	2.00	.90	.25
□ 27 Ken Macha	2.00	.90	.25
□ 28 Mike Marshall	2.00	.90	.25
□ 29 Clyde Mashore	2.00	.90	.25
□ 30 Jim Mason	2.00	.90	.25
□ 31 Gene Mauch MG	3.00	1.35	.35
□ 32 Ernie McAnally	2.00	.90	.25
□ 33 Tim McCarver	4.00	1.80	.50
□ 34 Cal McLish CO	2.00	.90	.25
□ 35 John Montague	2.00	.90	.25
□ 36 Balor Moore	2.00	.90	.25
□ 37 Tony Perez	5.00	2.20	.60
□ 38 Steve Renko	2.00	.90	.25
□ 39 Steve Rogers	3.00	1.35	.35
□ 40 Rodney Scott	2.00	.90	.25
□ 41 Tony Solaita	2.00	.90	.25
□ 42 Elias Sosa	2.00	.90	.25
□ 43 Bill Stoneman	2.50	1.10	.30
□ 44 John Strohmayer	2.00	.90	.25
□ 45 Jeff Terpko	2.00	.90	.25
□ 46 Hector Torres	2.00	.90	.25
□ 47 Mike Torrez	2.50	1.10	.30
□ 48 Mickey Vernon CO	2.50	1.10	.30
□ 49 Tom Walker	2.00	.90	.25
□ 50 Dan Warthen	2.00	.90	.25
□ 51 Bobby Wine	2.00	.90	.25
□ 52 Ron Woods	2.00	.90	.25
□ 53 Hank Aaron	10.00	4.50	1.25
□ 54 Johnny Bench	6.00	2.70	.75
□ 55 Larry Bowa	2.50	1.10	.30
□ 56 Steve Carlton	5.00	2.20	.60
□ 57 Roberto Clemente	10.00	4.50	1.25
□ 58 Willie Davis	2.00	.90	.25
□ 59 Bob Gibson	5.00	2.20	.60
□ 60 Ferguson Jenkins	5.00	2.20	.60
□ 61 Willie McCovey	5.00	2.20	.60
□ 62 Willie Montanez	2.00	.90	.25
□ 63 Pete Rose	7.50	3.40	.95
□ 64 Willie Stargell	5.00	2.20	.60
□ 65 Rusty Staub Mike Jorgensen	3.00	1.35	.35
□ 66 Chuck Arnason	2.50	1.10	.30
□ 67 Jean Beliveau VP	5.00	2.20	.60
□ 68 Pierre Bouchard (Action)	2.50	1.10	.30
□ 69 Pierre Bouchard (Posed)	2.50	1.10	.30
□ 70 Scotty Bowman CO	5.00	2.20	.60
□ 71 Yvan Cournoyer (Action)	5.00	2.20	.60
□ 72 Yvan Cournoyer (Posed)	5.00	2.20	.60
□ 73 Ken Dryden	10.00	4.50	1.25
□ 74 Bob Gainey	5.00	2.20	.60
□ 75 Dale Hoganson	2.50	1.10	.30
□ 76 Rejean Houle	3.00	1.35	.35
□ 77 Guy Lafleur (Action)	10.00	4.50	1.25
□ 78 Guy Lafleur (Posed)	10.00	4.50	1.25
□ 79 Yvon Lambert	3.00	1.35	.35
□ 80 Jacques Laperriere (Action)	5.00	2.20	.60
□ 81 Jacques Laperriere (Posed)	5.00	2.20	.60
□ 82 Guy Lapointe (Action)	5.00	2.20	.60
□ 83 Guy Lapointe (Posed)	5.00	2.20	.60
□ 84 Michel Larocque	4.00	1.80	.50
□ 85 Claude Larose (Action)	3.00	1.35	.35
□ 86 Claude Larose (Posed)	3.00	1.35	.35
□ 87 Chuck Lefley (Action)	2.50	1.10	.30
□ 88 Chuck Lefley (Posed)	2.50	1.10	.30
□ 89 Jacques Lemaire (Action)	5.00	2.20	.60
□ 90 Jacques Lemaire (Posed)	5.00	2.20	.60
□ 91 Frank Mahovlich (Action)	6.00	2.70	.75
□ 92 Frank Mahovlich (Posed)	6.00	2.70	.75
□ 93 Pete Mahovlich (Action)	3.00	1.35	.35
□ 94 Pete Mahovlich (Posed)	3.00	1.35	.35
□ 95 Bob J. Murdoch	2.50	1.10	.30
□ 96 Michel Plasse (Action)	4.00	1.80	.50
□ 97 Michel Plasse (Posed)	4.00	1.80	.50
□ 98 Henri Richard (Action)	6.00	2.70	.75
□ 99 Henri Richard (Posed)	6.00	2.70	.75
□ 100 Jim Roberts (Action)	3.00	1.35	.35
□ 101 Jim Roberts (Posed)	3.00	1.35	.35
□ 102 Larry Robinson (Action)	6.00	2.70	.75
□ 103 Larry Robinson (Posed)	6.00	2.70	.75
□ 104 Serge Savard (Action)	5.00	2.20	.60
□ 105 Serge Savard (Posed)	5.00	2.20	.60
□ 106 Steve Shutt (Action)	5.00	2.20	.60
□ 107 Steve Shutt (Posed)	5.00	2.20	.60
□ 108 Marc Tardif	3.00	1.35	.35
□ 109 Wayne Thomas (Action)	3.00	1.35	.35
□ 110 Wayne Thomas (Posed)	3.00	1.35	.35
□ 111 Murray Wilson (Action)	2.50	1.10	.30
□ 112 Murray Wilson (Posed)	2.50	1.10	.30
□ 113 The Assassins	2.00	.90	.25
□ 114 Dino Bravo Gino Brito	3.00	1.35	.35
□ 115 Edouard Carpentier	4.00	1.80	.50
□ 116 Nick Carte Sweet Williams	2.00	.90	.25
□ 117 Serge Dumont	3.00	1.35	.35
□ 118 Johnny(War) Eagle	2.00	.90	.25
□ 119 Edouard Ethifier	2.00	.90	.25
□ 120 Jean Ferre (Andre The Giant)	10.00	4.50	1.25
□ 121 Bull Gregory	2.00	.90	.25
□ 122 Don Leo Jonathan	3.00	1.35	.35
□ 123 Wladek(Killer) Kowalski	4.00	1.80	.50
□ 124 Leronix et Patonix	2.00	.90	.25
□ 125 Michel Pelletier	2.00	.90	.25
□ 126 Gilles(The Fish) Poisson	2.00	.90	.25
□ 127 Yvon Robert	2.00	.90	.25
□ 128 Yvon Robert (Father and son)	2.00	.90	.25
□ 129 Dale Roberts Gerry Brown	2.00	.90	.25
□ 130 Tokio Joe	2.00	.90	.25
□ 131 Tarzan(La Bottine) Tyler	2.00	.90	.25
□ 132 U.F.O.	2.00	.90	.25
□ 133 Maurice(Mad Dog) Vachon	4.00	1.80	.50
□ 134 Paul(The Butcher) Vachon	4.00	1.80	.50
□ 135 Viviane Vachon	3.00	1.35	.35
□ 136 Frank Valois	2.50	1.10	.30
□ 137 Yagi	2.00	.90	.25
□ 138 Jean-Claude Leclair	2.00	.90	.25
□ 139 Donato Paduano	2.00	.90	.25
□ 140 Emerson Fittipaldi	6.00	2.70	.75
□ 141 Alan Jones	3.00	1.35	.35
□ 142 Jody Scheckter	4.00	1.80	.50
□ 143 Patrick Tambay	3.00	1.35	.35
□ 144 Jocelyne Bourassa (Canadian Women's Golf)	2.00	.90	.25
□ 145 Jacques Desrosiers (Patof, circus clown)	2.00	.90	.25

1937 Dixie Lids

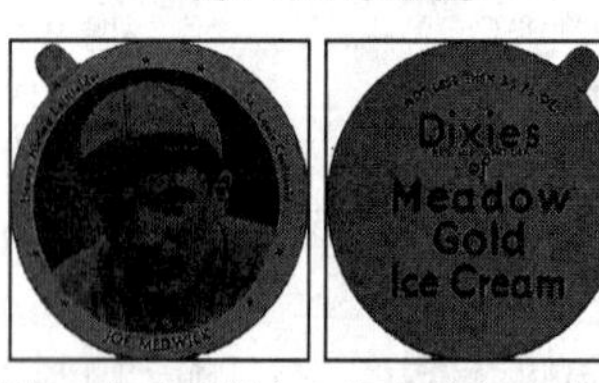

This unnumbered set of lids is actually a combined sport and non-sport set with 24 different lids. The lids are found in more than one size, approximately 2 11/16" in diameter as well as 2 5/16" in diameter. The 1937 lids are distinguished from the 1938 Dixie Lids by the fact that the 1937 lids are printed in black or wine-colored ink where the 1938 lids are printed in blue ink. In the checklist below only the sports subjects are checklisted; non-sport subjects (celebrities) included in this 24-card set are Gene Autry, Freddie Bartholomew, Bill Boyd, Johnny Mack Brown, Madeleine Carroll, Nelson Eddy, Clark Gable, Jean Harlow, Carole Lombard, Myrna Loy, Fred MacMurray, Ken Maynard, Merle Oberon, Eleanor Powell, William Powell, Luisa Rainer, Charles Starrett and Robert Taylor. The catalog designation is F7-1.

	EX-MT	VG-E	GOOD
COMPLETE SPORT (6)	350.00	160.00	45.00
COMMON BASEBALL	65.00	29.00	8.00
COMMON OTHER SPORTS	15.00	6.75	1.85
□ 1 Georgia Coleman	15.00	6.75	1.85
□ 2 Charles Gehringer	90.00	40.00	11.00
□ 3 Charles Hartnett	75.00	34.00	9.50
□ 4 Carl Hubbell	100.00	45.00	12.50
□ 5 Joe Medwick	75.00	34.00	9.50
□ 6 Bill Tilden	25.00	11.00	3.10

1937 Dixie Premiums

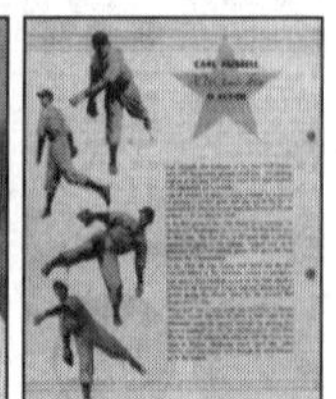

This is a parallel issue to the lids -- an attractive "premium" large picture of each of the subjects in the Dixie Lid set. The premiums are printed on thick stock and feature a large color drawing on the front; each unnumbered premium measures approximately 8" X 10". The 1937 premiums are distinguished from the 1938 Dixie Lid premiums by the fact that the 1937 premiums contain a dark green border whereas the 1938 premiums have a lighter green border completely around the photo. Also, on the reverse, the 1937 premiums have a large gray star and three light gray lines at the top. Only the sports personalities are checklisted below.

	EX-MT	VG-E	GOOD
COMPLETE SPORT SET (6)	350.00	160.00	45.00
COMMON BASEBALL	75.00	34.00	9.50
COMMON OTHER SPORTS	15.00	6.75	1.85
□ 1 Georgia Coleman	15.00	6.75	1.85
□ 2 Charles Gehringer	100.00	45.00	12.50
□ 3 Charles Hartnett	75.00	34.00	9.50
□ 4 Carl Hubbell	100.00	45.00	12.50
□ 5 Joe Medwick	75.00	34.00	9.50
□ 6 Bill Tilden	25.00	11.00	3.10

1938 Dixie Lids

This unnumbered set of lids is actually a combined sport and non-sport set with 24 different lids. The lids are found in more than one size, approximately 2 11/16" in diameter as well as 2 5/16" in diameter. The catalog designation is F7-1. The 1938 lids are distinguished from the 1937 Dixie Lids by the fact that the 1938 lids are printed in blue ink whereas the 1938 lids are printed in black or wine-colored ink. In the checklist below only the sports subjects are checklisted; non-sport subjects (celebrities) included in this 24 card set are Don Ameche, Annabella, Gene Autry, Warner Baxter, William Boyd, Bobby Breen, Gary Cooper, Alice Fay, Sonja Henie, Tommy Kelly, June Lang, Colonel Tim McCoy, Tyrone Power, Tex Ritter, Simone Simon, Bob Steele, The Three Mesquiteers and Jane Withers.

	EX-MT	VG-E	GOOD
COMPLETE SPORT SET (6)	400.00	180.00	50.00
COMMON BASEBALL	40.00	18.00	5.00
COMMON OTHER SPORTS	50.00	22.00	6.25
□ 1 Sam Baugh	50.00	22.00	6.25
□ 2 Bob Feller	100.00	45.00	12.50
□ 3 Jimmie Foxx	100.00	45.00	12.50
□ 4 Carl Hubbell mouth open	90.00	40.00	11.00
□ 5 Wally Moses	40.00	18.00	5.00
□ 6 Bronco Nagurski	60.00	27.00	7.50

1938 Dixie Lids Premiums

This is a parallel issue to the lids -- an attractive "premium" large picture of each of the subjects in the Dixie Lids set. The premiums are printed on thick stock and feature a large color drawing on the front; each unnumbered premium measures approximately 8" X 10". The 1938 premiums are distinguished from the 1937 Dixie Lid premiums by the fact that the 1938 premiums contain a light green border whereas the 1937 premiums have a darker green border completely around the photo. Also, on the reverse, the 1938

premiums have a single gray sline line at the top leading to the player's name in script. Again, we have only checklisted the sports personalities.

	EX-MT	VG-E	GOOD
COMPLETE SET (6)	400.00	180.00	50.00
COMMON BASEBALL	40.00	18.00	5.00
COMMON OTHER SPORTS	50.00	22.00	6.25
☐ 1 Sam Baugh	50.00	22.00	6.25
☐ 2 Bob Feller	100.00	45.00	12.50
☐ 3 Jimmie Foxx	100.00	45.00	12.50
☐ 4 Carl Hubbell	90.00	40.00	11.00
☐ 5 Wally Moses	40.00	18.00	5.00
☐ 6 Bronco Nagurski	60.00	27.00	7.50

1952 Dixie Lids

This scarce 24-lid set features all baseball subjects each measuring 2 11/16". The 1952 set was released very late in the year and in only one size; it is undoubtedly the toughest Dixie baseball set. The lids are found with a blue tint. The catalog designation for this set is F7-2A. Lids found with the tab removed would suffer an approximate 25 percent in value. The asterisked lids below are those that were only available in 1952. The 50s Dixie Lids are distinguished from the 30's lids also by the fact that the 50s lids have the circular picture portion abruptly squared off near the bottom end of the lid where the player's name appears.

	NRMT	VG-E	GOOD
COMPLETE SET (24)	2700.00	1200.00	350.00
COMMON CARD	85.00	38.00	10.50
☐ 1 Richie Ashburn	150.00	70.00	19.00
☐ 2 Tommy Byrne	100.00	45.00	12.50
☐ 3 Chico Carrasquel	85.00	38.00	10.50
☐ 4 Pete Castiglione	100.00	45.00	12.50
☐ 5 Walker Cooper	100.00	45.00	12.50
☐ 6 Billy Cox	85.00	38.00	10.50
☐ 7 Ferris Fain	85.00	38.00	10.50
☐ 8 Bobby Feller	250.00	110.00	31.00
☐ 9 Nellie Fox	150.00	70.00	19.00
☐ 10 Monte Irvin	150.00	70.00	19.00
☐ 11 Ralph Kiner	150.00	70.00	19.00
☐ 12 Cass Michaels	100.00	45.00	12.50
☐ 13 Don Mueller	85.00	38.00	10.50
☐ 14 Mel Parnell	85.00	38.00	10.50
☐ 15 Allie Reynolds	125.00	55.00	15.50
☐ 16 Preacher Roe	125.00	55.00	15.50
☐ 17 Connie Ryan	100.00	45.00	12.50
☐ 18 Hank Sauer	85.00	38.00	10.50
☐ 19 Al Schoendienst	150.00	70.00	19.00
☐ 20 Andy Seminick	100.00	45.00	12.50
☐ 21 Bobby Shantz	100.00	45.00	12.50
☐ 22 Enos Slaughter	150.00	70.00	19.00
☐ 23 Virgil Trucks	85.00	38.00	10.50
☐ 24 Gene Woodling	100.00	45.00	12.50

1952 Dixie Premiums

The catalog designation is F7-2A. The 1952 Dixie Cup Baseball Premiums contain 1951 statistics. There are 24 (sepia-tinted) black and white photos each measuring approximately 8" by 10". Each photo has a facsimile autograph at the bottom. These large premium photos are blank backed and were printed on thick paper stock.

	NRMT	VG-E	GOOD
COMPLETE SET (24)	700.00	325.00	90.00
COMMON CARD (1-24)	25.00	11.00	3.10
☐ 1 Richie Ashburn	60.00	27.00	7.50
☐ 2 Tommy Byrne	25.00	11.00	3.10
☐ 3 Chico Carrasquel	25.00	11.00	3.10
☐ 4 Pete Castiglione	25.00	11.00	3.10
☐ 5 Walker Cooper	25.00	11.00	3.10
☐ 6 Billy Cox	25.00	11.00	3.10
☐ 7 Ferris Fain	25.00	11.00	3.10
☐ 8 Bob Feller	90.00	40.00	11.00
☐ 9 Nelson Fox	60.00	27.00	7.50
☐ 10 Monte Irvin	60.00	27.00	7.50
☐ 11 Ralph Kiner	60.00	27.00	7.50
☐ 12 Cass Michaels	25.00	11.00	3.10
☐ 13 Don Mueller	25.00	11.00	3.10
☐ 14 Mel Parnell	25.00	11.00	3.10
☐ 15 Allie Reynolds	45.00	20.00	5.50
☐ 16 Preacher Roe	30.00	13.50	3.70
☐ 17 Connie Ryan	25.00	11.00	3.10
☐ 18 Hank Sauer	25.00	11.00	3.10
☐ 19 Al Schoendienst	45.00	20.00	5.50
☐ 20 Andy Seminick	25.00	11.00	3.10
☐ 21 Bobby Shantz	30.00	13.50	3.70
☐ 22 Enos Slaughter	60.00	27.00	7.50
☐ 23 Virgil Trucks	25.00	11.00	3.10
☐ 24 Gene Woodling	30.00	13.50	3.70

1953 Dixie Lids

This 24-lid set features all baseball subjects each measuring 2 11/16". There are many different back types in existence. The lids are found with a wine tint. The catalog designation for this set is F7-2. Lids found without the tab attached are considered good condition at best. There is also a smaller size variation, 2 5/16" in diameter. These smaller lids are worth an additional 50 percent more than the prices listed below.

	NRMT	VG-E	GOOD
COMPLETE SET (24)	800.00	350.00	100.00
COMMON CARD (1-24)	25.00	11.00	3.10
☐ 1 Richie Ashburn	60.00	27.00	7.50
☐ 2 Chico Carrasquel	25.00	11.00	3.10
☐ 3 Billy Cox	25.00	11.00	3.10
☐ 4 Ferris Fain	25.00	11.00	3.10
☐ 5 Nellie Fox	60.00	27.00	7.50
☐ 6A Sid Gordon Boston Braves	60.00	27.00	7.50
☐ 6B Sid Gordon Milwaukee Braves	25.00	11.00	3.10
☐ 7 Warren Hacker	25.00	11.00	3.10
☐ 8 Monte Irvin	60.00	27.00	7.50
☐ 9 Jack Jensen	40.00	18.00	5.00
☐ 10 Ralph Kiner	60.00	27.00	7.50
☐ 11 Ted Kluszewski	50.00	22.00	6.25
☐ 12 Bob Lemon	60.00	27.00	7.50
☐ 13 Don Mueller	25.00	11.00	3.10
☐ 14 Mel Parnell	25.00	11.00	3.10
☐ 15 Jerry Priddy	25.00	11.00	3.10
☐ 16 Allie Reynolds	50.00	22.00	6.25
☐ 17 Preacher Roe	50.00	22.00	6.25
☐ 18 Hank Sauer	25.00	11.00	3.10
☐ 19 Al Schoendienst	60.00	27.00	7.50
☐ 20 Bobby Shantz	25.00	11.00	3.10
☐ 21 Enos Slaughter	60.00	27.00	7.50
☐ 22A Warren Spahn Boston Braves	100.00	45.00	12.50
☐ 22B Warren Spahn Milwaukee Braves	90.00	40.00	11.00
☐ 23A Virgil Trucks Chicago White Sox	25.00	11.00	3.10
☐ 23B Virgil Trucks St. Louis Browns	25.00	11.00	3.10
☐ 24 Gene Woodling	25.00	11.00	3.10

1953 Dixie Premiums

The catalog designation is F7-2A. The 1953 Dixie Cup Baseball Premiums contain 1952 statistics. There are 24 (sepia-tinted) black and white photos each measuring approximately 8" by 10". Each photo has a facsimile autograph at the bottom. These large premium photos are blank backed and were printed on thick paper stock.

	NRMT	VG-E	GOOD
COMPLETE SET (24)	400.00	180.00	50.00
COMMON CARD (1-24)	15.00	6.75	1.85
☐ 1 Richie Ashburn	40.00	18.00	5.00
☐ 2 Chico Carrasquel	15.00	6.75	1.85
☐ 3 Billy Cox	15.00	6.75	1.85
☐ 4 Ferris Fain	15.00	6.75	1.85
☐ 5 Nellie Fox	30.00	13.50	3.70
☐ 6 Sid Gordon	15.00	6.75	1.85
☐ 7 Warren Hacker	15.00	6.75	1.85
☐ 8 Monte Irvin	40.00	18.00	5.00
☐ 9 Jack Jensen	25.00	11.00	3.10
☐ 10 Ralph Kiner	40.00	18.00	5.00
☐ 11 Ted Kluszewski	30.00	13.50	3.70
☐ 12 Bob Lemon	40.00	18.00	5.00
☐ 13 Don Mueller	15.00	6.75	1.85
☐ 14 Mel Parnell	15.00	6.75	1.85
☐ 15 Jerry Priddy	15.00	6.75	1.85
☐ 16 Allie Reynolds	30.00	13.50	3.70
☐ 17 Preacher Roe	30.00	13.50	3.70
☐ 18 Hank Sauer	15.00	6.75	1.85
☐ 19 Al Schoendienst	30.00	13.50	3.70
☐ 20 Bobby Shantz	15.00	6.75	1.85
☐ 21 Enos Slaughter	40.00	18.00	5.00
☐ 22 Warren Spahn	50.00	22.00	6.25
☐ 23 Virgil Trucks	15.00	6.75	1.85
☐ 24 Gene Woodling	15.00	6.75	1.85

1954 Dixie Lids

This 18 lid set features all baseball subjects each measuring 2 11/16". There are many different back types in existence. The lids are typically found with a brown sepia tint. The catalog designation for this set is F7-4. Lids found without the tab attached are considered good condition at best. This year is distinguishable by the fact that the lids say "Get Dixie Lid 3-D Starviewer. Send 25 cents, this lid, name, address, to DIXIE, Box 630, New York 17, N.Y." around the border on the front. The lids have an "L" or "R" on the tab, which distinguished which side of the 3-D viewer was to be used for that particular card. The lids are also seen in a small (2 5/16") and large (3 3/16") size; these variations carry approximately double the prices below.

	NRMT	VG-E	GOOD
COMPLETE SET (18)	500.00	220.00	60.00
COMMON CARD (1-18)	18.00	8.00	2.20
☐ 1 Richie Ashburn	50.00	22.00	6.25
☐ 2 Clint Courtney	18.00	8.00	2.20
☐ 3 Sid Gordon	18.00	8.00	2.20
☐ 4 Billy Hoeft	18.00	8.00	2.20
☐ 5 Monte Irvin	50.00	22.00	6.25
☐ 6 Jackie Jensen	25.00	11.00	3.10
☐ 7 Ralph Kiner	50.00	22.00	6.25
☐ 8 Ted Kluszewski	25.00	11.00	3.10
☐ 9 Gil McDougald	25.00	11.00	3.10
☐ 10 Minnie Minoso	40.00	18.00	5.00
☐ 11 Danny O'Connell	18.00	8.00	2.20
☐ 12 Mel Parnell	18.00	8.00	2.20
☐ 13 Preacher Roe	25.00	11.00	3.10
☐ 14 Al Rosen	25.00	11.00	3.10
☐ 15 Al Schoendienst	40.00	18.00	5.00
☐ 16 Enos Slaughter	50.00	22.00	6.25
☐ 17 Gene Woodling	18.00	8.00	2.20
☐ 18 Gus Zernial	18.00	8.00	2.20

1940 Dodgers Team Issue

These photos measure approximately 6 1/2" by 9". They feature members of the 1940 Brooklyn Dodgers. The photos take up nearly all of the card except for a small white border. There is also a facsimile signature of each player. The backs are blank and we have sequenced them in alphabetical order.

	EX-MT	VG-E	GOOD
COMPLETE SET (25)	100.00	45.00	12.50
COMMON CARD (1-25)	3.00	1.35	.35
☐ 1 Dolph Camilli	5.00	2.20	.60
☐ 2 Tex Carleton	3.00	1.35	.35
☐ 3 Hugh Casey	5.00	2.20	.60
☐ 4 Pete Coscarart	3.00	1.35	.35
☐ 5 Curt Davis	3.00	1.35	.35
☐ 6 Leo Durocher	10.00	4.50	1.25
☐ 7 Fred Fitzsimmons	5.00	2.20	.60
☐ 8 Herman Franks	3.00	1.35	.35
☐ 9 Joe Gallagher	3.00	1.35	.35
☐ 10 Charlie Gilbert	3.00	1.35	.35
☐ 11 Luke Hamlin	3.00	1.35	.35
☐ 12 Johnny Hudson	3.00	1.35	.35
☐ 13 Newt Kimball	3.00	1.35	.35
☐ 14 Cookie Lavagetto	5.00	2.20	.60
☐ 15 Gus Mancuso	3.00	1.35	.35
☐ 16 Joe Medwick	10.00	4.50	1.25
☐ 17 Van Lingle Mungo	5.00	2.20	.60
☐ 18 Babe Phelps	3.00	1.35	.35
☐ 19 Tot Pressnell	3.00	1.35	.35
☐ 20 Pee Wee Reese	25.00	11.00	3.10
☐ 21 Vito Tamulis	3.00	1.35	.35
☐ 22 Joe Vosmik	3.00	1.35	.35
☐ 23 Dixie Walker	7.50	3.40	.95
☐ 24 Jimmy Wasdell	3.00	1.35	.35
☐ 25 Whit Wyatt	5.00	2.20	.60

1942 Dodgers Team Issue

This 25-card set of the Brooklyn Dodgers measures approximately 6 1/2" by 9" and features black-and-white player portraits with a facsimile autograph. The cards are unnumbered and checklisted below in alphabetical order.

	EX-MT	VG-E	GOOD
COMPLETE SET (25)	100.00	45.00	12.50
COMMON CARD (1-25)	3.00	1.35	.35
☐ 1 Johnny Allen	3.00	1.35	.35
☐ 2 Frenchy Bordagaray	3.00	1.35	.35
☐ 3 Dolph Camilli	5.00	2.20	.60
☐ 4 Hugh Casey	3.00	1.35	.35
☐ 5 Curt Davis	3.00	1.35	.35
☐ 6 Leo Durocher	15.00	6.75	1.85
☐ 7 Larry French	3.00	1.35	.35
☐ 8 Augie Galan	3.00	1.35	.35
☐ 9 Ed Head	3.00	1.35	.35
☐ 10 Billy Herman	7.50	3.40	.95
☐ 11 Kirby Higbe	3.00	1.35	.35
☐ 12 Alex Kampouris	3.00	1.35	.35
☐ 13 Newell Kimball	3.00	1.35	.35
☐ 14 Joe Medwick	15.00	6.75	1.85
☐ 15 Mickey Owen	7.50	3.40	.95
☐ 16 Pee Wee Reese	20.00	9.00	2.50
☐ 17 Pete Reiser	5.00	2.20	.60
☐ 18 Lew Riggs	3.00	1.35	.35
☐ 19 Johnny Rizzo	3.00	1.35	.35
☐ 20 Schoolboy Rowe	5.00	2.20	.60
☐ 21 Bill Sullivan	3.00	1.35	.35
☐ 22 Arky Vaughn	7.50	3.40	.95
☐ 23 Dixie Walker	3.00	1.35	.35
☐ 24 Les Webber	3.00	1.35	.35
☐ 25 Whitlow Wyatt	3.00	1.35	.35

1943 Dodgers Team Issue

This set of the Brooklyn Dodgers measures approximately 6 1/2" by 9". The black-and-white player photos display fascimile autographs. The backs are blank. The cards are unnumbered and checklisted below in alphabetical order.

	EX-MT	VG-E	GOOD
COMPLETE SET (25)	100.00	45.00	12.50
COMMON CARD (1-25)	3.00	1.35	.35
☐ 1 Johnny Allen	5.00	2.20	.60
☐ 2 Frenchy Bordagaray	3.00	1.35	.35
☐ 3 Bob Bragan	3.00	1.35	.35
☐ 4 Dolph Camilli	5.00	2.20	.60
☐ 5 John Cooney	3.00	1.35	.35
☐ 6 John Corriden	3.00	1.35	.35
☐ 7 Curt Davis	3.00	1.35	.35
☐ 8 Leo Durocher MG	10.00	4.50	1.25
☐ 9 Fred Fitzimmons	5.00	2.20	.60
☐ 10 Augie Galan	5.00	2.20	.60
☐ 11 Al Glossop	3.00	1.35	.35
☐ 12 Ed Head	3.00	1.35	.35
☐ 13 Billy Herman	10.00	4.50	1.25
☐ 14 Kirby Higbe	5.00	2.20	.60

	NRMT	VG-E	GOOD
☐ 15 Max Macon	3.00	1.35	.35
☐ 16 Joe Medwick	7.50	3.40	.95
☐ 17 Rube Melton	3.00	1.35	.35
☐ 18 Dee Moore	3.00	1.35	.35
☐ 19 Bobo Newsom	5.00	2.20	.60
☐ 20 Mickey Owen	5.00	2.20	.60
☐ 21 Arky Vaughan	7.50	3.40	.95
☐ 22 Dixie Walker	5.00	2.20	.60
☐ 23 Paul Waner	12.50	5.50	1.55
☐ 24 Les Webber	3.00	1.35	.35
☐ 25 Whitlow Wyatt	3.00	1.35	.35

1955 Dodgers Golden Stamps

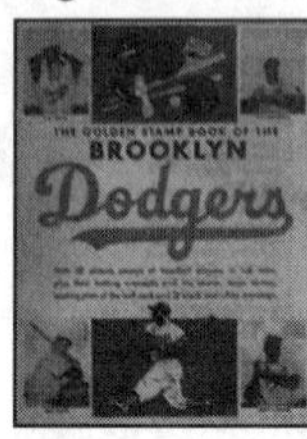

This 32-stamp set features color photos of the Brooklyn Dodgers and measures approximately 2" by 2 5/8". The stamps are designed to be placed in a 32-page album which measures approximately 8 3/8" by 10 15/16". The album contains black-and-white drawings of players with statistics and life stories. The stamps are unnumbered and listed below according to where they fall in the album.

	NRMT	VG-E	GOOD
COMPLETE SET (32)	150.00	70.00	19.00
COMMON CARD (1-32)	2.00	.90	.25
☐ 1 Walt Alston MG	10.00	4.50	1.25
☐ 2 Don Newcombe	4.00	1.80	.50
☐ 3 Carl Erskine	4.00	1.80	.50
☐ 4 Johnny Podres	4.00	1.80	.50
☐ 5 Billy Loes	2.00	.90	.25
☐ 6 Russ Meyer	2.00	.90	.25
☐ 7 Jim Hughes	2.00	.90	.25
☐ 8 Sandy Koufax	25.00	11.00	3.10
☐ 9 Joe Black	4.00	1.80	.50
☐ 10 Karl Spooner	2.00	.90	.25
☐ 11 Clem Labine	3.00	1.35	.35
☐ 12 Roy Campanella	15.00	6.75	1.85
☐ 13 Gil Hodges	10.00	4.50	1.25
☐ 14 Jim Gilliam	7.50	3.40	.95
☐ 15 Jackie Robinson	30.00	13.50	3.70
☐ 16 Pee Wee Reese	10.00	4.50	1.25
☐ 17 Duke Snider	15.00	6.75	1.85
☐ 18 Carl Furillo	7.50	3.40	.95
☐ 19 Sandy Amoros	4.00	1.80	.50
☐ 20 Frank Kellert	2.00	.90	.25
☐ 21 Don Zimmer	4.00	1.80	.50
☐ 22 Al Walker	2.00	.90	.25
☐ 23 Tom Lasorda	10.00	4.50	1.25
☐ 24 Ed Roebuck	2.00	.90	.25
☐ 25 Don Hoak	2.00	.90	.25
☐ 26 George Shuba	3.00	1.35	.35
☐ 27 Billy Herman CO	4.00	1.80	.50
☐ 28 Jake Pitler CO	2.00	.90	.25
☐ 29 Joe Becker CO	2.00	.90	.25
☐ 30 Doc Wendler Carl Furillo	3.00	1.35	.35
☐ 31 Charlie Di Giovanna	2.00	.90	.25
☐ 32 Ebbets Field	10.00	4.50	1.25

1956-57 Dodgers

JACKIE ROBINSON, Dodgers

This 28-piece set features blank-backed, white-bordered, 5 X 7 black-and-white photos. The player's name and team appear in black lettering within the lower margin. The photos are unnumbered and checklisted below in alphabetical order.

	NRMT	VG-E	GOOD
COMPLETE SET (28)	400.00	180.00	50.00
COMMON CARD (1-28)	5.00	2.20	.60
☐ 1 Walter Alston MG	20.00	9.00	2.50
☐ 2 Sandy Amoros	10.00	4.50	1.25
☐ 3 Joe Becker CO	5.00	2.20	.60
☐ 4 Don Bessent	5.00	2.20	.60
☐ 5 Roy Campanella	35.00	16.00	4.40
☐ 6 Roger Craig	7.50	3.40	.95
☐ 7 Don Drysdale	25.00	11.00	3.10
☐ 8 Carl Erskine	15.00	6.75	1.85
☐ 9 Chico Fernandez	5.00	2.20	.60
☐ 10 Carl Furillo	15.00	6.75	1.85
☐ 11 Jim Gilliam	15.00	6.75	1.85
☐ 12 Billy Herman CO	10.00	4.50	1.25
☐ 13 Gil Hodges	25.00	11.00	3.10
☐ 14 Randy Jackson	5.00	2.20	.60
☐ 15 Sandy Koufax	50.00	22.00	6.25
☐ 16 Clem Labine (Uniform)	7.50	3.40	.95
☐ 17 Clem Labine (T-shirt)	7.50	3.40	.95
☐ 18 Sal Maglie	10.00	4.50	1.25
☐ 19 Charlie Neal	7.50	3.40	.95
☐ 20 Don Newcombe (Uniform)	15.00	6.75	1.85
☐ 21 Don Newcombe (T-shirt)	15.00	6.75	1.85
☐ 22 Jake Pitler CO	5.00	2.20	.60
☐ 23 Johnny Podres	10.00	4.50	1.25
☐ 24 Pee Wee Reese	25.00	11.00	3.10
☐ 25 Jackie Robinson	75.00	34.00	9.50
☐ 26 Ed Roebuck	5.00	2.20	.60
☐ 27 Duke Snider	25.00	11.00	3.10
☐ 28 Al Walker	5.00	2.20	.60

1958 Dodgers Bell Brand

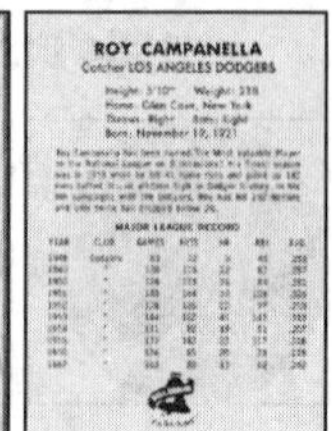

The 1958 Bell Brand Potato Chips set of ten unnumbered cards features members of the Los Angeles Dodgers exclusively. Each card has a 1/4" green border, and the Gino Cimoli, Johnny Podres, Pee Wee Reese and Duke Snider cards are more difficult to find; they are marked with an SP (short printed) in the checklist below. The cards measure approximately 3" by 4". This set marks the first year for the Dodgers in Los Angeles and includes a Campanella card despite the fact that he never played for the team in California. The catalog designation for this set is F339-1. Cards found still inside the original cellophane wrapper are valued at 50 percent more than the prices below. According to printed reports, the promotion went badly for Bell Brand and much of the product was destroyed.

	NRMT	VG-E	GOOD
COMPLETE SET (10)	1350.00	600.00	170.00
COMMON CARD (1-10)	50.00	22.00	6.25
☐ 1 Roy Campanella	175.00	80.00	22.00
☐ 2 Gino Cimoli SP	125.00	55.00	15.50
☐ 3 Don Drysdale	125.00	55.00	15.50
☐ 4 Jim Gilliam	50.00	22.00	6.25
☐ 5 Gil Hodges	90.00	40.00	11.00
☐ 6 Sandy Koufax	225.00	100.00	28.00
☐ 7 Johnny Podres SP	150.00	70.00	19.00
☐ 8 Pee Wee Reese SP	125.00	55.00	15.50
☐ 9 Duke Snider SP	300.00	135.00	38.00
☐ 10 Don Zimmer	50.00	22.00	6.25

1958 Dodgers Jay Publishing

This 12-card set of the Los Angeles Dodgers measures approximately 5" by 7" and features black-and-white player photos in a white border. These cards were packaged 12 to a packet. The backs are blank. The cards are unnumbered and checklisted below in alphabetical order.

	NRMT	VG-E	GOOD
COMPLETE SET (12)	50.00	22.00	6.25
COMMON CARD (1-12)	3.00	1.35	.35
☐ 1 Walt Alston MG	5.00	2.20	.60
☐ 2 Roy Campanella	10.00	4.50	1.25
☐ 3 Gino Cimoli	3.00	1.35	.35
☐ 4 Don Drysdale	7.50	3.40	.95
☐ 5 Carl Furillo	3.00	1.35	.35
☐ 6 Gil Hodges	5.00	2.20	.60
☐ 7 Clem Labine	3.00	1.35	.35
☐ 8 Charley Neal	3.00	1.35	.35
☐ 9 Don Newcombe	3.00	1.35	.35
☐ 10 Johnny Podres	3.00	1.35	.35
☐ 11 Pee Wee Reese	5.00	2.20	.60
☐ 12 Duke Snider	5.00	2.20	.60

1959 Dodgers Morrell

The cards in this 12-card set measure 2 1/2" by 3 1/2". The 1959 Morrell Meats set of full color, unnumbered cards features Los Angeles Dodger players only. The photos used are the same as those selected for the Dodger team issue postcards in 1959. The Morrell Meats logo is on the backs of the cards. The Clem Labine card actually features a picture of Stan Williams and the Norm Larker card actually features a picture of Joe Pignatano as indicated in the checklist below. The catalog designation is F172-1.

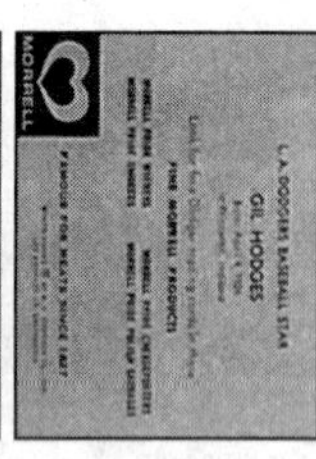

	NRMT	VG-E	GOOD
COMPLETE SET (12)	1250.00	550.00	160.00
COMMON CARD (1-12)	60.00	27.00	7.50
☐ 1 Don Drysdale	125.00	55.00	15.50
☐ 2 Carl Furillo	90.00	40.00	11.00
☐ 3 Jim Gilliam	90.00	40.00	11.00
☐ 4 Gil Hodges	125.00	55.00	15.50
☐ 5 Sandy Koufax	250.00	110.00	31.00
☐ 6 Clem Labine UER (Photo actually Stan Williams)	60.00	27.00	7.50
☐ 7 Norm Larker UER (Photo actually Joe Pignatano)	60.00	27.00	7.50
☐ 8 Charlie Neal	60.00	27.00	7.50
☐ 9 Johnny Podres	90.00	40.00	11.00
☐ 10 John Roseboro	60.00	27.00	7.50
☐ 11 Duke Snider	250.00	110.00	31.00
☐ 12 Don Zimmer	90.00	40.00	11.00

1959 Dodgers Team Issue

This 25-card set of the Los Angeles Dodgers measures approximately 5" by 7" and features black-and-white player photos in a white border. The backs are blank. The cards are unnumbered and checklisted below in alphabetical order.

	NRMT	VG-E	GOOD
COMPLETE SET (25)	60.00	27.00	7.50
COMMON CARD (1-25)	2.50	1.10	.30
☐ 1 Walter Alston MG	5.00	2.20	.60
☐ 2 Don Bessent	2.50	1.10	.30
☐ 3 Roger Craig	2.50	1.10	.30
☐ 4 Charlie Dressen CO	2.50	1.10	.30
☐ 5 Don Drysdale	6.00	2.70	.75
☐ 6 Carl Erskine	3.00	1.35	.35
☐ 7 Carl Furillo	3.00	1.35	.35
☐ 8 Junior Gilliam	4.00	1.80	.50
☐ 9 Gil Hodges	5.00	2.20	.60
☐ 10 Fred Kipp	2.50	1.10	.30
☐ 11 Sandy Koufax	10.00	4.50	1.25
☐ 12 Clem Labine	2.50	1.10	.30
☐ 13 Norm Larker	2.50	1.10	.30
☐ 14 Bob Lillis	2.50	1.10	.30
☐ 15 Danny McDevitt	2.50	1.10	.30
☐ 16 Wally Moon	2.50	1.10	.30
☐ 17 Greg Mulleavy CO	2.50	1.10	.30
☐ 18 Charlie Neal	2.50	1.10	.30
☐ 19 Joe Pignatano	2.50	1.10	.30
☐ 20 Johnny Podres	3.00	1.35	.35
☐ 21 Pee Wee Reese	6.00	2.70	.75
☐ 22 Rip Repulski	2.50	1.10	.30
☐ 23 John Roseboro	2.50	1.10	.30
☐ 24 Duke Snider	5.00	2.20	.60
☐ 25 Don Zimmer	3.00	1.35	.35

1959 Dodgers Volpe

Issued on thin paper stock, these blank-backed reproductions of artist Nicholas Volpe's charcoal portraits of the 1959 Dodgers measure approximately 8" by 10". The player's name appears near the bottom. The portraits are unnumbered and checklisted below in alphabetical order.

	NRMT	VG-E	GOOD
COMPLETE SET (15)	125.00	55.00	15.50
COMMON CARD (1-15)	6.00	2.70	.75
☐ 1 Walter Alston MG	10.00	4.50	1.25
☐ 2 Roy Campnella TRIB	20.00	9.00	2.50
☐ 3 Don Drysdale	15.00	6.75	1.85
☐ 4 Carl Erskine	7.50	3.40	.95
☐ 5 Carl Furillo	7.50	3.40	.95
☐ 6 Jim Gilliam	7.50	3.40	.95
☐ 7 Gil Hodges	15.00	6.75	1.85
☐ 8 Clem Labine	6.00	2.70	.75
☐ 9 Wally Moon	6.00	2.70	.75
☐ 10 Don Newcombe	10.00	4.50	1.25
☐ 11 Johnny Podres	6.00	2.70	.75
☐ 12 Pee Wee Reese CO	15.00	6.75	1.85
☐ 13 Rip Repulski	6.00	2.70	.75
☐ 14 Vin Scully ANN Jerry Doggett ANN	6.00	2.70	.75
☐ 15 Duke Snider	20.00	9.00	2.50

1960 Dodgers Bell Brand

The 1960 Bell Brand Potato Chips set of 20 full color, numbered cards features Los Angeles Dodgers only. Because these cards, measuring approximately 2 1/2" by 3 1/2", were issued in packages of potato chips, many cards suffered from stains. Clem Labine, Johnny Klippstein, and Walt Alston are somewhat more difficult to obtain than other cards in the set; they are marked with SP (short printed) in the checklist below. The catalog designation for this set is F339-2.

	NRMT	VG-E	GOOD
COMPLETE SET (20)	900.00	400.00	110.00
COMMON CARD (1-20)	20.00	9.00	2.50
☐ 1 Norm Larker	20.00	9.00	2.50
☐ 2 Duke Snider	90.00	40.00	11.00
☐ 3 Danny McDevitt	20.00	9.00	2.50
☐ 4 Jim Gilliam	30.00	13.50	3.70
☐ 5 Rip Repulski	20.00	9.00	2.50
☐ 6 Clem Labine SP	100.00	45.00	12.50
☐ 7 John Roseboro	20.00	9.00	2.50
☐ 8 Carl Furillo	25.00	11.00	3.10
☐ 9 Sandy Koufax	150.00	70.00	19.00
☐ 10 Joe Pignatano	20.00	9.00	2.50
☐ 11 Chuck Essegian	20.00	9.00	2.50
☐ 12 John Klippstein SP	100.00	45.00	12.50
☐ 13 Ed Roebuck	20.00	9.00	2.50
☐ 14 Don Demeter	20.00	9.00	2.50
☐ 15 Roger Craig	25.00	11.00	3.10
☐ 16 Stan Williams	20.00	9.00	2.50
☐ 17 Don Zimmer	25.00	11.00	3.10
☐ 18 Walt Alston SP MG	150.00	70.00	19.00
☐ 19 Johnny Podres	30.00	13.50	3.70
☐ 20 Maury Wills	50.00	22.00	6.25

1960 Dodgers Jay Publishing

DON DRYSDALE, Los Angeles Dodgers

This set of the Los Angeles Dodgers measures approximately 5" by 7" and features black-and-white player photos in a white border. The backs are blank. These cards were originally packaged 12 to a packet. The set is more than 12 cards as changes during the season necessitated a second printing. The cards are unnumbered and checklisted below in alphabetical order.

	NRMT	VG-E	GOOD
COMPLETE SET (15)	45.00	20.00	5.50
COMMON CARD (1-15)	2.50	1.10	.30
☐ 1 Roger Craig	2.50	1.10	.30
☐ 2 Don Demeter	2.50	1.10	.30
☐ 3 Don Drysdale	6.00	2.70	.75
☐ 4 Ron Fairly	3.00	1.35	.35
☐ 5 Junior Gilliam	4.00	1.80	.50
☐ 6 Gil Hodges	5.00	2.20	.60
☐ 7 Frank Howard	3.50	1.55	.45
☐ 8 Norm Larker	2.50	1.10	.30
☐ 9 Wally Moon	3.00	1.35	.35
☐ 10 Charlie Neal	2.50	1.10	.30
☐ 11 Johnny Podres	3.00	1.35	.35
☐ 12 John Roseboro	2.50	1.10	.30
☐ 13 Larry Sherry	2.50	1.10	.30
☐ 14 Duke Snider	5.00	2.20	.60
☐ 15 Stan Williams	2.50	1.10	.30
☐ 16 Maury Wills	3.50	1.55	.45

1960 Dodgers Morrell

The cards in this 12-card set measure 2 1/2" by 3 1/2". The 1960 Morrell Meats set of full color, unnumbered cards is similar in format to the 1959 Morrell set but can be distinguished from the 1959 set by a red heart which appears in the Morrell logo on the back. The photos used are the same as those selected for the Dodger team issue postcards in 1960. The Furillo, Hodges, and Snider cards received limited distribution and are hence more scarce. The catalog designation is F172-2. The cards were printed in Japan.

	NRMT	VG-E	GOOD
COMPLETE SET (12)	900.00	400.00	110.00
COMMON CARD (1-12)	20.00	9.00	2.50

☐ 1 Walt Alston MG	45.00	20.00	5.50
☐ 2 Roger Craig	25.00	11.00	3.10
☐ 3 Don Drysdale	60.00	27.00	7.50
☐ 4 Carl Furillo SP	100.00	45.00	12.50
☐ 5 Gil Hodges SP	150.00	70.00	19.00
☐ 6 Sandy Koufax	150.00	70.00	19.00
☐ 7 Wally Moon	20.00	9.00	2.50
☐ 8 Charlie Neal	20.00	9.00	2.50
☐ 9 Johnny Podres	30.00	13.50	3.70
☐ 10 John Roseboro	20.00	9.00	2.50
☐ 11 Larry Sherry	20.00	9.00	2.50
☐ 12 Duke Snider SP	250.00	110.00	31.00

1960 Dodgers Postcards

These 10 postcards feature members of the 1960 Los Angeles Dodgers. These cards are unnumbered and we have sequenced them in alphabetical order.

	NRMT	VG-E	GOOD
COMPLETE SET (10)	25.00	11.00	3.10
COMMON CARD (1-10)	2.00	.90	.25
☐ 1 Walt Alston MG	4.00	1.80	.50
☐ 2 Roger Craig	2.50	1.10	.30
☐ 3 Don Drysdale	5.00	2.20	.60
☐ 4 Gil Hodges	4.00	1.80	.50
☐ 5 Sandy Koufax	7.50	3.40	.95
☐ 6 Wally Moon	2.50	1.10	.30
☐ 7 Charlie Neal	2.00	.90	.25
☐ 8 Johnny Podres	2.50	1.10	.30
☐ 9 Larry Sherry	2.00	.90	.25
☐ 10 Duke Snider	5.00	2.20	.60

1960 Dodgers Team Issue

These 20 blank-backed, black-and-white photos of the 1960 Dodgers have white borders around posed player shots and measure approximately 5" by 7". The pictures came in a manila envelope that carried the year of issue. The player's facsimile autograph appears in the margin below each photo. The photos are unnumbered and checklisted below in alphabetical order.

	NRMT	VG-E	GOOD
COMPLETE SET (20)	75.00	34.00	9.50
COMMON CARD (1-20)	2.50	1.10	.30
☐ 1 Walter Alston MG	4.00	1.80	.50
☐ 2 Bob Bragan CO	2.50	1.10	.30
☐ 3 Roger Craig	3.00	1.35	.35
☐ 4 Don Demeter	2.50	1.10	.30
☐ 5 Don Drysdale	7.50	3.40	.95
☐ 6 Chuck Essegian	2.50	1.10	.30
☐ 7 Jim Gilliam	3.00	1.35	.35
☐ 8 Gil Hodges	7.50	3.40	.95
☐ 9 Frank Howard	3.00	1.35	.35
☐ 10 Sandy Koufax	15.00	6.75	1.85
☐ 11 Norm Larker	2.50	1.10	.30
☐ 12 Wally Moon	2.50	1.10	.30
☐ 13 Charlie Neal	2.50	1.10	.30
☐ 14 Johnny Podres	3.00	1.35	.35
☐ 15 Pete Reiser CO	3.00	1.35	.35
☐ 16 John Roseboro	3.00	1.35	.35
☐ 17 Larry Sherry	3.00	1.35	.35
☐ 18 Duke Snider	7.50	3.40	.95
☐ 19 Stan Williams	2.50	1.10	.30
☐ 20 Maury Wills	5.00	2.20	.60

1960 Dodgers Union Oil

The set contains 23, 16-page unnumbered booklets which describe and give more detailed biographies of the player on the front covers. These booklets were given away at Union Oil gas stations and covered members of the 1960 Los Angeles Dodgers. The back page of the booklets had the Dodger schedule on it along with an ad for Union Oil. They are sometimes referenced as "Meet the Dodger Family" booklets. Each booklet measures approximately 5 3/8" by 7 1/2".

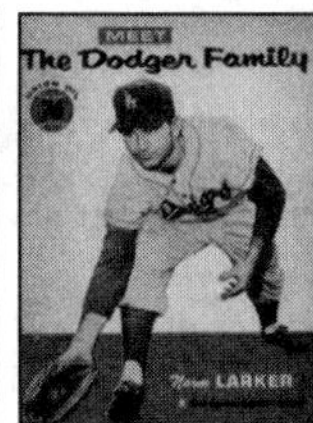

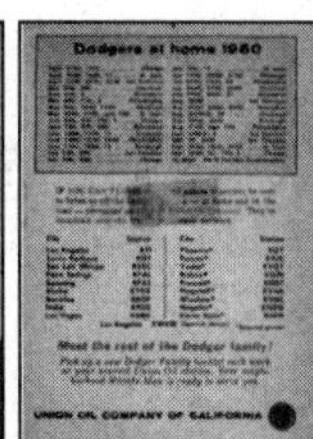

	NRMT	VG-E	GOOD
COMPLETE SET (23)	75.00	34.00	9.50
COMMON CARD (1-23)	2.00	.90	.25
☐ 1 Walt Alston MG	5.00	2.20	.60
☐ 2 Roger Craig	4.00	1.80	.50
☐ 3 Tom Davis	3.00	1.35	.35
☐ 4 Don Demeter	2.00	.90	.25
☐ 5 Don Drysdale	10.00	4.50	1.25
☐ 6 Chuck Essegian	2.00	.90	.25
☐ 7 Jim Gilliam	4.00	1.80	.50
☐ 8 Gil Hodges	10.00	4.50	1.25
☐ 9 Frank Howard	4.00	1.80	.50
☐ 10 Sandy Koufax	18.00	8.00	2.20
☐ 11 Norm Larker	2.00	.90	.25
☐ 12 Wally Moon	3.00	1.35	.35
☐ 13 Charlie Neal	2.00	.90	.25
☐ 14 Johnny Podres	4.00	1.80	.50
☐ 15 Ed Roebuck	2.00	.90	.25
☐ 16 John Roseboro	2.50	1.10	.30
☐ 17 Larry Sherry	2.00	.90	.25
☐ 18 Norm Sherry	2.00	.90	.25
☐ 19 Duke Snider	12.00	5.50	1.50
☐ 20 Stan Williams	2.00	.90	.25
☐ 21 Maury Wills	5.00	2.20	.60
☐ 22 Dodger Broadcasters (Vin Scully and Jerry Doggett)	3.00	1.35	.35
☐ 23 Dodger Coaches Greg Mulleavy CO Joe Becker CO Bobby Bragan CO Pete Reiser CO	2.00	.90	.25

1961 Dodgers Bell Brand

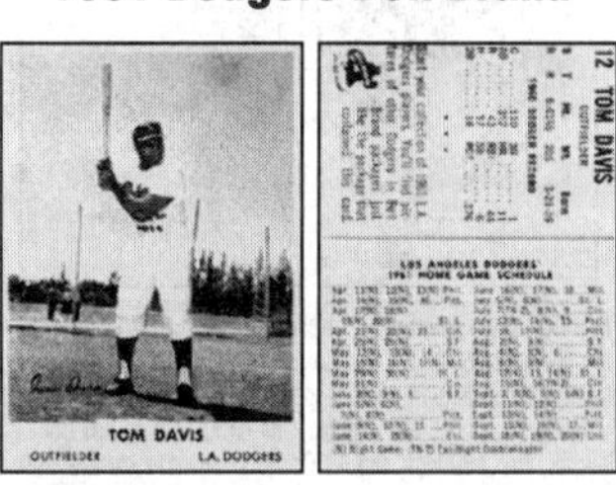

The 1961 Bell Brand Potato Chips set of 20 full color cards features Los Angeles Dodger players only and is numbered by the uniform numbers of the players. The cards are slightly smaller (approximately 2 7/16" by 3 1/2") than the 1960 Bell Brand cards and are on thinner paper stock. The catalog designation is F339-3.

	NRMT	VG-E	GOOD
COMPLETE SET (20)	500.00	220.00	60.00
COMMON CARD	15.00	6.75	1.85
☐ 3 Willie Davis	20.00	9.00	2.50
☐ 4 Duke Snider	75.00	34.00	9.50
☐ 5 Norm Larker	15.00	6.75	1.85
☐ 8 John Roseboro	18.00	8.00	2.20
☐ 9 Wally Moon	18.00	8.00	2.20
☐ 11 Bob Lillis	15.00	6.75	1.85
☐ 12 Tommy Davis	20.00	9.00	2.50
☐ 14 Gil Hodges	30.00	13.50	3.70
☐ 16 Don Demeter	15.00	6.75	1.85
☐ 19 Jim Gilliam	20.00	9.00	2.50
☐ 22 John Podres	20.00	9.00	2.50
☐ 24 Walt Alston MG	25.00	11.00	3.10
☐ 30 Maury Wills	25.00	11.00	3.10
☐ 32 Sandy Koufax	125.00	55.00	15.50
☐ 34 Norm Sherry	15.00	6.75	1.85
☐ 37 Ed Roebuck	15.00	6.75	1.85
☐ 38 Roger Craig	18.00	8.00	2.20
☐ 40 Stan Williams	15.00	6.75	1.85
☐ 43 Charlie Neal	15.00	6.75	1.85
☐ 51 Larry Sherry	15.00	6.75	1.85

1961 Dodgers Jay Publishing

This 12-card set of the Los Angeles Dodgers measures approximately 5" by 7". The fronts feature black-and-white posed player portraits with the player's and team name printed below in the white border. The backs are blank. The cards are unnumbered and checklisted below in alphabetical order.

	NRMT	VG-E	GOOD
COMPLETE SET (12)	30.00	13.50	3.70
COMMON CARD (1-12)	2.00	.90	.25
☐ 1 Walt Alston MG	3.00	1.35	.35
☐ 2 Don Drysdale	7.50	3.40	.95
☐ 3 Junior Gilliam	3.00	1.35	.35
☐ 4 Frank Howard	4.00	1.80	.50
☐ 5 Norm Larker	2.00	.90	.25
☐ 6 Wally Moon	2.00	.90	.25
☐ 7 Charlie Neal	2.00	.90	.25
☐ 8 Johnny Podres	3.00	1.35	.35
☐ 9 John Roseboro	2.00	.90	.25
☐ 10 Larry Sherry	2.00	.90	.25
☐ 11 Stan Williams	2.00	.90	.25
☐ 12 Maury Wills	4.00	1.80	.50

1961 Dodgers Morrell

The cards in this six-card set measure 2 1/2" by 3 1/2". The 1961 Morrell Meats set of full color, unnumbered cards features Los Angeles Dodger players only and contains statistical information on the backs of the cards in brown print. The catalog designation is F172-3.

	NRMT	VG-E	GOOD
COMPLETE SET (6)	275.00	125.00	34.00
COMMON CARD (1-6)	20.00	9.00	2.50
☐ 1 Tommy Davis	22.00	10.00	2.70
☐ 2 Don Drysdale	75.00	34.00	9.50
☐ 3 Frank Howard	25.00	11.00	3.10
☐ 4 Sandy Koufax	150.00	70.00	19.00
☐ 5 Norm Larker	20.00	9.00	2.50
☐ 6 Maury Wills	35.00	16.00	4.40

1961 Dodgers Union Oil

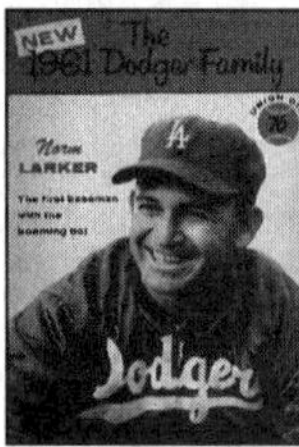

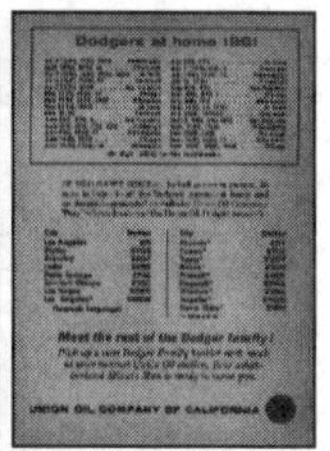

The set contains 24, 16-page unnumbered booklets which describe and give more detailed biographies of the player on the front covers. These booklets were given away by Union Oil at gas stations and covered members of the 1961 Los Angeles Dodgers. The back page of the booklets had the Dodger schedule on it along with an ad for Union Oil. They are sometimes referenced as "Meet the Dodger Family" booklets. Each booklet measures approximately 5 3/8" by 7 1/2".

	NRMT	VG-E	GOOD
COMPLETE SET (24)	75.00	34.00	9.50
COMMON CARD (1-24)	2.00	.90	.25
☐ 1 Walt Alston MG	5.00	2.20	.60
☐ 2 Roger Craig	4.00	1.80	.50
☐ 3 Tommy Davis	3.00	1.35	.35
☐ 4 Willie Davis	3.00	1.35	.35
☐ 5 Don Drysdale	10.00	4.50	1.25
☐ 6 Dick Farrell	2.00	.90	.25
☐ 7 Ron Fairly	2.50	1.10	.30
☐ 8 Jim Gilliam	4.00	1.80	.50
☐ 9 Gil Hodges	10.00	4.50	1.25
☐ 10 Frank Howard	4.00	1.80	.50
☐ 11 Sandy Koufax	18.00	8.00	2.20
☐ 12 Norm Larker	2.00	.90	.25
☐ 13 Wally Moon	3.00	1.35	.35
☐ 14 Charlie Neal	2.00	.90	.25
☐ 15 Ron Perranoski	3.00	1.35	.35
☐ 16 Johnny Podres	4.00	1.80	.50
☐ 17 John Roseboro	2.50	1.10	.30
☐ 18 Larry Sherry	2.00	.90	.25
☐ 19 Norm Sherry	2.00	.90	.25
☐ 20 Duke Snider	12.00	5.50	1.50
☐ 21 Daryl Spencer	2.00	.90	.25
☐ 22 Stan Williams	2.00	.90	.25
☐ 23 Maury Wills	5.00	2.20	.60
☐ 24 Dodger Broadcasters (Vin Scully and Jerry Doggett)	3.00	1.35	.35

1962 Dodgers Bell Brand

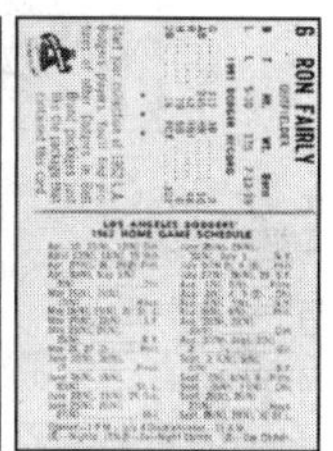

The 1962 Bell Brand Potato Chips set of 20 full color cards features Los Angeles Dodger players only and is numbered by the uniform numbers of the players. These cards were printed on a high quality glossy paper, much better than the previous two years, virtually eliminating the grease stains. This set is distinguished by a 1962 Home schedule on the backs of the cards. The cards measure 2 7/16" by 3 1/2", the same size as the year before. The catalog designation is F339-4.

	NRMT	VG-E	GOOD
COMPLETE SET (20)	500.00	220.00	60.00
COMMON CARD	15.00	6.75	1.85
☐ 3 Willie Davis	20.00	9.00	2.50
☐ 4 Duke Snider	75.00	34.00	9.50
☐ 6 Ron Fairly	18.00	8.00	2.20
☐ 8 John Roseboro	18.00	8.00	2.20
☐ 9 Wally Moon	18.00	8.00	2.20
☐ 12 Tommy Davis	20.00	9.00	2.50
☐ 16 Ron Perranoski	18.00	8.00	2.20
☐ 19 Jim Gilliam	20.00	9.00	2.50
☐ 20 Daryl Spencer	15.00	6.75	1.85
☐ 22 John Podres	20.00	9.00	2.50
☐ 24 Walt Alston MG	25.00	11.00	3.10
☐ 25 Frank Howard	20.00	9.00	2.50
☐ 30 Maury Wills	25.00	11.00	3.10
☐ 32 Sandy Koufax	125.00	55.00	15.50
☐ 34 Norm Sherry	15.00	6.75	1.85
☐ 37 Ed Roebuck	15.00	6.75	1.85
☐ 40 Stan Williams	15.00	6.75	1.85
☐ 51 Larry Sherry	15.00	6.75	1.85
☐ 53 Don Drysdale	50.00	22.00	6.25
☐ 56 Lee Walls	15.00	6.75	1.85

1962 Dodgers Jay Publishing

This 12-card set of the Los Angeles Dodgers measures approximately 5" by 7". The fronts feature black-and-white posed player photos with the player's and team name printed below in the white border. These cards were packaged 12 in a packet. The backs are blank. The cards are unnumbered and checklisted below in alphabetical order.

	NRMT	VG-E	GOOD
COMPLETE SET (12)	45.00	20.00	5.50
COMMON CARD (1-12)	2.50	1.10	.30
☐ 1 Walt Alston MG	3.50	1.55	.45
☐ 2 Don Drysdale	7.50	3.40	.95
☐ 3 Ron Fairly	3.00	1.35	.35
☐ 4 Jim Gilliam	3.50	1.55	.45
☐ 5 Frank Howard	3.00	1.35	.35
☐ 6 Sandy Koufax	15.00	6.75	1.85
☐ 7 Wally Moon	2.50	1.10	.30
☐ 8 John Podres	3.00	1.35	.35
☐ 9 John Roseboro	3.50	1.55	.45
☐ 10 Duke Snider	7.50	3.40	.95
☐ 11 Stan Williams	2.50	1.10	.30
☐ 12 Maury Wills	3.50	1.55	.45

1963 Dodgers Jay Publishing

The 1963 Dodgers Jay set consists of 12 cards produced by Jay Publishing. The Skowron card establishes the year of the set, since 1963 was Skowron's only year with the Dodgers. The cards measure approximately 4 3/4" by 7 1/4" and are printed on thin photographic paper stock. The white fronts feature a black-and-white player portrait with the player's name and the team name below. The backs are blank. The cards are packaged 12 to a packet. The cards are unnumbered and checklisted below in alphabetical order.

	NRMT	VG-E	GOOD
COMPLETE SET (12)	40.00	18.00	5.00
COMMON CARD (1-12)	2.50	1.10	.30
☐ 1 Walt Alston MG	3.00	1.35	.35
☐ 2 Tom Davis	3.00	1.35	.35
☐ 3 Willie Davis	3.00	1.35	.35
☐ 4 Don Drysdale	6.00	2.70	.75
☐ 5 Ron Fairly	3.00	1.35	.35
☐ 6 Jim Gilliam	3.00	1.35	.35
☐ 7 Frank Howard	3.50	1.55	.45
☐ 8 Sandy Koufax	12.50	5.50	1.55
☐ 9 Johnny Podres	3.00	1.35	.35
☐ 10 John Roseboro	2.50	1.10	.30
☐ 11 Bill Skowron	3.00	1.35	.35
☐ 12 Maury Wills	3.00	1.35	.35

1964 Dodgers Heads-Up

This ten-card blank-backed set was issued in 1964 as a way to further merchandise some of the Los Angeles stars. This set features a large full-color head shot of a player which came with instructiions on how to push out the players face and the rest of the torso. The whole cardboard sheet measures approximately 7 1/4" by 8 1/2". There was a quantity of these items found in the late 1980's. Since these are unnummbered, they are checklisted below alphabetically.

	NRMT	VG-E	GOOD
COMPLETE SET (10)	40.00	18.00	5.00
COMMON CARD (1-10)	2.50	1.10	.30
☐ 1 Tom Davis	3.50	1.55	.45
☐ 2 Willie Davis	3.00	1.35	.35
☐ 3 Don Drysdale	7.50	3.40	.95
☐ 4 Ron Fairly	3.00	1.35	.35
☐ 5 Frank Howard	3.50	1.55	.45
☐ 6 Sandy Koufax	15.00	6.75	1.85
☐ 7 Joe Moeller	2.50	1.10	.30
☐ 8 Ron Perranoski	3.00	1.35	.35
☐ 9 John Roseboro	3.00	1.35	.35
☐ 10 Maury Wills	5.00	2.20	.60

1965 Dodgers Jay Publishing

These 12 cards feature members of the World Champion Los Angeles Dodgers. They were issued in a pack as a set and the cards are unnumbered and checklisted below in alphabetical order.

	NRMT	VG-E	GOOD
COMPLETE SET (12)	35.00	16.00	4.40
COMMON CARD (1-12)	2.00	.90	.25
☐ 1 Walter Alston MG	3.50	1.55	.45
☐ 2 Tommy Davis	2.00	.90	.25
☐ 3 Willie Davis	3.50	1.55	.45
☐ 4 Don Drysdale	7.50	3.40	.95
☐ 5 Ron Fairly	2.50	1.10	.30
☐ 6 Lou Johnson	2.00	.90	.25
☐ 7 Sandy Koufax	15.00	6.75	1.85
☐ 8 Jim Lefebvre	2.00	.90	.25
☐ 9 Claude Osteen	2.00	.90	.25
☐ 10 Wes Parker	3.50	1.55	.45
☐ 11 John Roseboro	2.50	1.10	.30
☐ 12 Maury Wills	4.00	1.80	.50

1965 Dodgers Team Issue

These 20, blank-backed, black-and-white photos of the 1965 Los Angeles Dodgers have white borders around posed player shots and measure approximately 5" by 7". The player's facsimile autograph appears in the bottom margin on each photo. The pictures came in an undated manila envelope. The year of issue was determined to be 1965 because that was Dick Tracewski's last year with the Dodgers and Lou Johnson's first. The photos are unnumbered and checklisted below in alphabetical order.

	NRMT	VG-E	GOOD
COMPLETE SET (20)	35.00	16.00	4.40
COMMON CARD (1-20)	1.50	.70	.19
☐ 1 Walter Alston MG	3.00	1.35	.35
☐ 2 Tommy Davis	2.50	1.10	.30
☐ 3 Willie Davis	2.50	1.10	.30
☐ 4 Don Drysdale	6.00	2.70	.75
☐ 5 Ron Fairly	2.00	.90	.25
☐ 6 Derrell Griffith	1.50	.70	.19
☐ 7 Lou Johnson	2.00	.90	.25
☐ 8 John Kennedy	1.50	.70	.19
☐ 9 Sandy Koufax	12.50	5.50	1.55
☐ 10 Bob Miller	1.50	.70	.19
☐ 11 Nate Oliver	1.50	.70	.19
☐ 12 Claude Osteen	2.00	.90	.25
☐ 13 Wes Parker	2.00	.90	.25
☐ 14 Ron Perranoski	2.00	.90	.25
☐ 15 Johnny Podres	2.50	1.10	.30
☐ 16 John Purdin	1.50	.70	.19
☐ 17 Howie Reed	1.50	.70	.19
☐ 18 John Roseboro	2.00	.90	.25
☐ 19 Dick Tracewski	1.50	.70	.19
☐ 20 Maury Wills	3.00	1.35	.35

1971 Dodgers Ticketron

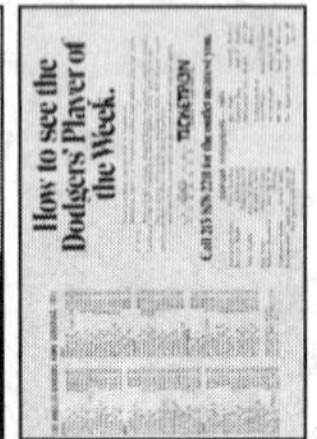

The 1971 Ticketron Los Angeles Dodgers set is a 20-card set with cards measuring approximately 4" by 6". This set has a 1971 Garvey rookie year card as well as 18 other players including Richie Allen in his only year as a Dodger. The fronts are beautiful full-color photos which also have a facsimile autograph on the front and are borderless while the backs contain an advertisement for Ticketron, the 1971 Dodger home schedule and a list of promotional events scheduled for 1971. These unnumbered cards are listed in alphabetical order for convenience.

	NRMT	VG-E	GOOD
COMPLETE SET (20)	75.00	34.00	9.50
COMMON CARD (1-20)	2.00	.90	.25
☐ 1 Richie Allen	6.00	2.70	.75
☐ 2 Walt Alston MG	6.00	2.70	.75
☐ 3 Jim Brewer	2.00	.90	.25
☐ 4 Willie Crawford	2.00	.90	.25
☐ 5 Willie Davis	3.50	1.55	.45
☐ 6 Steve Garvey	20.00	9.00	2.50
☐ 7 Bill Grabarkewitz	2.00	.90	.25
☐ 8 Jim Lefebvre	3.50	1.55	.45
☐ 9 Pete Mikkelsen	2.00	.90	.25
☐ 10 Joe Moeller	2.00	.90	.25
☐ 11 Manny Mota	3.50	1.55	.45
☐ 12 Claude Osteen	3.50	1.55	.45
☐ 13 Wes Parker	3.50	1.55	.45
☐ 14 Bill Russell	6.00	2.70	.75
☐ 15 Duke Sims	2.00	.90	.25
☐ 16 Bill Singer	2.00	.90	.25
☐ 17 Bill Sudakis	2.00	.90	.25
☐ 18 Don Sutton	7.50	3.40	.95
☐ 19 Maury Wills	5.00	2.20	.60
☐ 20 Vic Scully ANN and Jerry Doggett ANN	3.50	1.55	.45

1979 Dodgers Blue

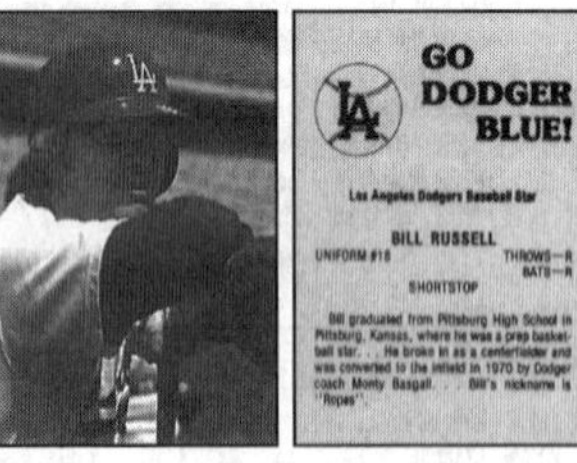

GO
DODGER
BLUE!
Los Angeles Dodgers Baseball Star
BILL RUSSELL
UNIFORM #18
THROWS—R
BATS—R
SHORTSTOP

This 13-card standard-size set features full-bleed posed color player photos. The backs are white and carry the slogan "Go Dodger Blue," the player's name, uniform number, batting and throwing preference and a player profile. The cards are unnumbered and checklisted below in alphabetical order.

	NRMT	VG-E	GOOD
COMPLETE SET (13)	10.00	4.50	1.25
COMMON CARD (1-13)	.25	.11	.03
☐ 1 Dusty Baker	1.25	.55	.16
☐ 2 Ron Cey	.75	.35	.09
☐ 3 Terry Forster	.50	.23	.06
☐ 4 Steve Garvey	1.25	.55	.16
☐ 5 Burt Hooton	.50	.23	.06
☐ 6 Charlie Hough	.75	.35	.09
☐ 7 Tom Lasorda MG	1.25	.55	.16
☐ 8 Davey Lopes	.60	.25	.07
☐ 9 Manny Mota	.50	.23	.06
☐ 10 Doug Rau	.25	.11	.03
☐ 11 Bill Russell	.75	.35	.09
☐ 12 Don Sutton	1.25	.55	.16
☐ 13 Steve Yeager	.50	.23	.06

1980 Dodgers Greats TCMA

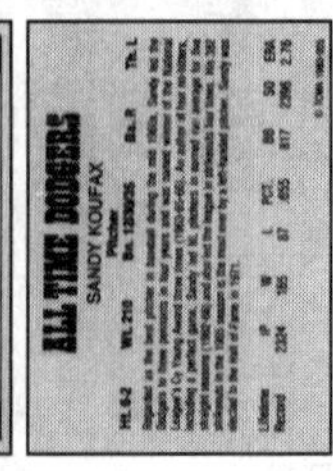

This 12-card standard-size set features some leading all-time Dodgers. The fronts have a player photo in the middle with the words "All-Time Dodgers" on top and his name on the bottom. The backs have vital statistics, a biography as well as career totals.

	NRMT	VG-E	GOOD
COMPLETE SET (12)	7.50	3.40	.95
COMMON CARD (1-12)	.25	.11	.03
☐ 1 Gil Hodges	1.00	.45	.12
☐ 2 Jim Gilliam	.50	.23	.06
☐ 3 Pee Wee Reese	1.50	.70	.19
☐ 4 Jackie Robinson	2.50	1.10	.30
☐ 5 Sandy Koufax	2.00	.90	.25
☐ 6 Zach Wheat	.50	.23	.06
☐ 7 Dixie Walker	.50	.23	.06
☐ 8 Hugh Casey	.25	.11	.03
☐ 9 Dazzy Vance	.50	.23	.06
☐ 10 Duke Snider	1.50	.70	.19
☐ 11 Roy Campanella	1.50	.70	.19
☐ 12 Walter Alston MG	.50	.23	.06

1980 Dodgers Police

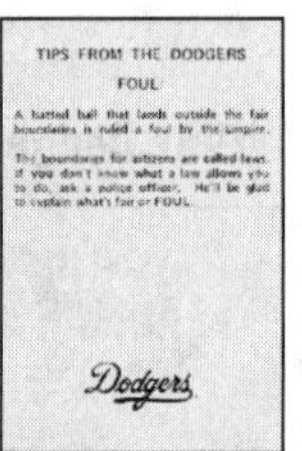

The cards in this 30-card set measure approximately 2 13/16" by 4 1/8". The full color 1980 Police Los Angeles Dodgers set features the player's name, uniform number, position, and biographical data on the fronts in addition to the photo. The backs feature Tips from the Dodgers, the LAPD logo, and the Dodgers' logo. The cards are listed below according to uniform number.

	NRMT	VG-E	GOOD
COMPLETE SET (30)	12.00	5.50	1.50
COMMON CARD	.25	.11	.03
☐ 5 Johnny Oates	.50	.23	.06
☐ 6 Steve Garvey	1.50	.70	.19
☐ 7 Steve Yeager	.50	.23	.06
☐ 8 Reggie Smith	.75	.35	.09
☐ 9 Gary Thomasson	.25	.11	.03
☐ 10 Ron Cey	.75	.35	.09
☐ 12 Dusty Baker	1.00	.45	.12
☐ 13 Joe Ferguson	.25	.11	.03
☐ 15 Davey Lopes	.75	.35	.09
☐ 16 Rick Monday	.50	.23	.06
☐ 18 Bill Russell	1.00	.45	.12
☐ 20 Don Sutton	1.50	.70	.19
☐ 21 Jay Johnstone	.75	.35	.09
☐ 23 Teddy Martinez	.25	.11	.03
☐ 27 Joe Beckwith	.25	.11	.03
☐ 28 Pedro Guerrero	1.25	.55	.16
☐ 29 Don Stanhouse	.25	.11	.03
☐ 30 Derrel Thomas	.25	.11	.03
☐ 31 Doug Rau	.25	.11	.03
☐ 34 Ken Brett	.25	.11	.03
☐ 35 Bob Welch	.50	.23	.06
☐ 37 Robert Castillo	.25	.11	.03
☐ 38 Dave Goltz	.25	.11	.03
☐ 41 Jerry Reuss	.50	.23	.06
☐ 43 Rick Sutcliffe	1.50	.70	.19
☐ 44 Mickey Hatcher	.50	.23	.06
☐ 46 Burt Hooton	.50	.23	.06
☐ 49 Charlie Hough	.75	.35	.09
☐ 51 Terry Forster	.50	.23	.06
☐ NNO Team Card	.50	.23	.06

1981 Dodgers

This 12-card set of the Los Angeles Dodgers measures approximately 8" by 10" and features white-bordered color action player photos with a facsimile autograph on the front. The backs are blank. The cards are unnumbered and checklisted below in alphabetical order.

	NRMT	VG-E	GOOD
COMPLETE SET (12)	10.00	4.50	1.25
COMMON CARD (1-12)	.50	.23	.06
☐ 1 Dusty Baker	1.00	.45	.12
☐ 2 Ron Cey	1.00	.45	.12
☐ 3 Terry Forster	.50	.23	.06
☐ 4 Steve Garvey	1.50	.70	.19
☐ 5 Pedro Guerrero	1.50	.70	.19
☐ 6 Burt Hooton	.50	.23	.06
☐ 7 Davey Lopes	1.00	.45	.12
☐ 8 Rick Monday	.75	.35	.09
☐ 9 Jerry Reuss	1.00	.45	.12
☐ 10 Don Sutton	2.00	.90	.25
☐ 11 Derrel Thomas	.50	.23	.06
☐ 12 Fernando Valenzuela	3.00	1.35	.35

1981 Dodgers Police

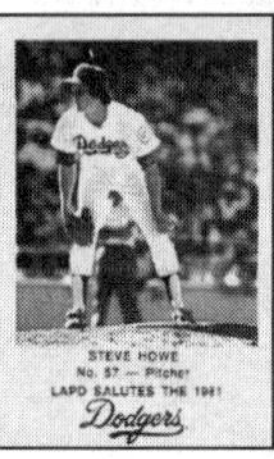

STEVE HOWE
No. 57 — Pitcher
LAPD SALUTES THE 1981
Dodgers

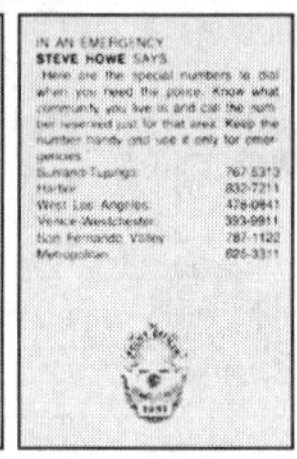

The cards in this 32-card set measure approximately 2 13/16" by 4 1/8". The full color set of 1981 Los Angeles Dodgers features the player's name, number, position and a line stating that the LAPD salutes the 1981 Dodgers, in addition to the player's photo. The backs feature the LAPD logo and short narratives, attributable to the player on the front of the card, revealing police associated tips. The cards of Ken Landreaux and Dave Stewart are reported to be more difficult to obtain than other cards in this set due to the fact that they are replacements for Stanhouse (released 4/17/81) and Hatcher (traded for Landreaux 3/30/81). The complete set price below refers to all 32 cards, i.e., including the variations. The Dave Stewart card pre-dates his Rookie Card.

	NRMT	VG-E	GOOD
COMPLETE SET (32)	15.00	6.75	1.85
COMMON CARD	.25	.11	.03
☐ 2 Tom Lasorda MG	1.50	.70	.19
☐ 3 Rudy Law	.25	.11	.03
☐ 6 Steve Garvey	1.50	.70	.19
☐ 7 Steve Yeager	.50	.23	.06
☐ 8 Reggie Smith	.75	.35	.09
☐ 10 Ron Cey	.75	.35	.09
☐ 12 Dusty Baker	.75	.35	.09
☐ 13 Joe Ferguson	.25	.11	.03
☐ 14 Mike Scioscia	.75	.35	.09
☐ 15 Davey Lopes	.75	.35	.09
☐ 16 Rick Monday	.50	.23	.06
☐ 18 Bill Russell	1.00	.45	.12
☐ 21 Jay Johnstone	.75	.35	.09
☐ 26 Don Stanhouse	.25	.11	.03
☐ 27 Joe Beckwith	.25	.11	.03
☐ 28 Pedro Guerrero	1.00	.45	.12
☐ 30 Derrel Thomas	.25	.11	.03
☐ 34 Fernando Valenzuela	2.00	.90	.25
☐ 35 Bob Welch	.75	.35	.09
☐ 36 Pepe Frias	.25	.11	.03
☐ 37 Robert Castillo	.25	.11	.03
☐ 38 Dave Goltz	.25	.11	.03
☐ 41 Jerry Reuss	.50	.23	.06
☐ 43 Rick Sutcliffe	1.00	.45	.12
☐ 44A Mickey Hatcher	.25	.11	.03
☐ 44B Ken Landreaux SP	2.50	1.10	.30
☐ 46 Burt Hooton	.50	.23	.06
☐ 48 Dave Stewart SP	5.00	2.20	.60
☐ 51 Terry Forster	.25	.11	.03
☐ 57 Steve Howe	.25	.11	.03
☐ NNO Team Photo/Checklist	.50	.23	.06
☐ NNO Coaching Staff Monty Basgall Tom Lasorda MG Danny Ozark Ron Perranoski Manny Mota Mark Creese	.50	.23	.06

1982 Dodgers Builders Emporium

This seven-card set of the Los Angeles Dodgers was sponsored by Builders Emporium. The fronts feature black-and-white player action

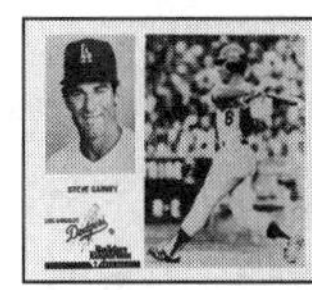

pictures with a small black-and-white head photo of the player on the left. The player's name, team, and sponsor name are printed below this small photo. The backs are blank. The cards are unnumbered and checklisted below in alphabetical order.

	NRMT	VG-E	GOOD
COMPLETE SET (7)	7.50	3.40	.95
COMMON CARD (1-7)	1.00	.45	.12
☐ 1 Dusty Baker	1.50	.70	.19
☐ 2 Ron Cey	1.50	.70	.19
☐ 3 Steve Garvey	2.50	1.10	.30
☐ 4 Pedro Guerrero	1.25	.55	.16
☐ 5 Tommy Lasorda MG	1.50	.70	.19
☐ 6 Jerry Reuss	1.00	.45	.12
☐ 7 Steve Sax	2.00	.90	.25

1982 Dodgers Police

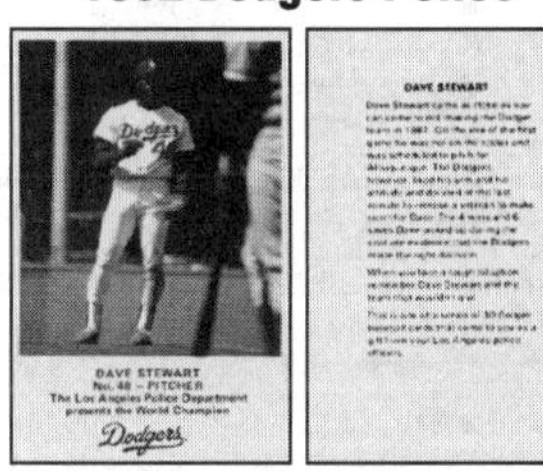

The cards in this 30-card set measure approximately 2 13/16" by 4 1/8". The 1982 Los Angeles Dodgers police set depicts the players and events of the 1981 season. There is a World Series trophy card, three cards commemorating the Division, League, and World Series wins, one manager card, and 25 player cards. The obverses have brilliant color photos set on white, and the player cards are numbered according to the uniform number of the individual. The reverses contain biographical material, information about stadium events, and a safety feature emphasizing "the team that wouldn't quit."

	NRMT	VG-E	GOOD
COMPLETE SET (30)	10.00	4.50	1.25
COMMON CARD	.25	.11	.03
☐ 2 Tom Lasorda MG	1.25	.55	.16
☐ 6 Steve Garvey	1.50	.70	.19
☐ 7 Steve Yeager	.50	.23	.06
☐ 8 Mark Belanger	.50	.23	.06
☐ 10 Ron Cey	.75	.35	.09
☐ 12 Dusty Baker	1.00	.45	.12
☐ 14 Mike Scioscia	.50	.23	.06
☐ 16 Rick Monday	.50	.23	.06
☐ 18 Bill Russell	1.00	.45	.12
☐ 21 Jay Johnstone	.50	.23	.06
☐ 26 Alejandro Pena	.75	.35	.09
☐ 28 Pedro Guerrero	1.00	.45	.12
☐ 30 Derrel Thomas	.25	.11	.03
☐ 31 Jorge Orta	.25	.11	.03
☐ 34 Fernando Valenzuela	1.50	.70	.19
☐ 35 Bob Welch	.75	.35	.09
☐ 38 Dave Goltz	.25	.11	.03
☐ 40 Ron Roenicke	.25	.11	.03
☐ 41 Jerry Reuss	.50	.23	.06
☐ 44 Ken Landreaux	.25	.11	.03
☐ 46 Burt Hooton	.50	.23	.06
☐ 48 Dave Stewart	2.00	.90	.25
☐ 49 Tom Niedenfuer	.25	.11	.03
☐ 51 Terry Forster	.25	.11	.03
☐ 52 Steve Sax	1.50	.70	.19
☐ 57 Steve Howe	.25	.11	.03
☐ NNO World Series Trophy (Checklist back)	.50	.23	.06
☐ NNO World Series Commemorative	.25	.11	.03
☐ NNO NL Champions	.25	.11	.03
☐ NNO Division Champs	.25	.11	.03

1982 Dodgers Postcards

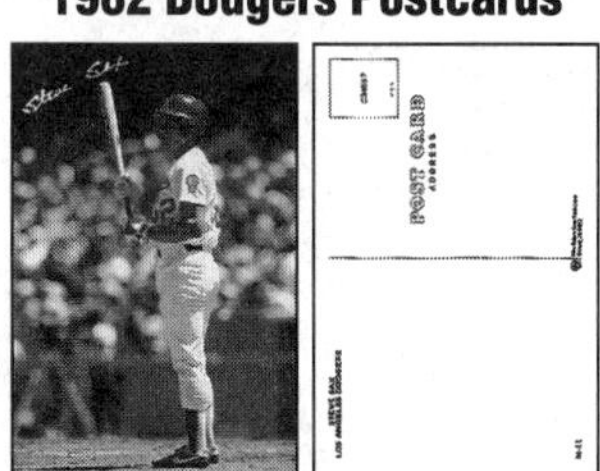

These postcards feature members of the 1982 Los Angeles Dodgers. These cards are unnumbered and we have sequenced them in alphabetical order.

	NRMT	VG-E	GOOD
COMPLETE SET (10)	6.00	2.70	.75
COMMON CARD (1-10)	.50	.23	.06
☐ 1 Terry Forster	.50	.23	.06
☐ 2 Steve Garvey	1.50	.70	.19
☐ 3 Pedro Guerrero	1.00	.45	.12
☐ 4 Steve Howe	.50	.23	.06
☐ 5 Tom Lasorda MG	1.25	.55	.16
☐ 6 Tom Neidenfuer	.50	.23	.06
☐ 7 Steve Sax	1.50	.70	.19
☐ 8 Mike Scioscia	.75	.35	.09
☐ 9 Bob Welch	.75	.35	.09
☐ 10 Steve Yeager	.75	.35	.09

1982 Dodgers Union Oil Volpe

Artist Nicholas Volpe drew members of the Dodgers for a Union Oil giveaway. These color portraits are painted in pastel; one portrait a week was given away at the stations;. The cards measure 8 1/2" x 11", and the backs contain statistics and other biographical inforamtion.

	NRMT	VG-E	GOOD
COMPLETE SET	12.00	5.50	1.50
COMMON CARD	.50	.23	.06
☐ 1 Dusty Baker	1.00	.45	.12
☐ 2 Mark Belanger	.75	.35	.09
☐ 3 Ron Cey	1.00	.45	.12
☐ 4 Terry Forster	.50	.23	.06
☐ 5 Steve Garvey	1.50	.70	.19
☐ 6 Pedro Guerrero	1.25	.55	.16
☐ 7 Burt Hooton	.50	.23	.06
☐ 8 Steve Howe	.50	.23	.06
☐ 9 Ken Landreaux	.50	.23	.06
☐ 10 Tom Lasorda MG	1.25	.55	.16
☐ 11 Mike Marshall	.75	.35	.09
☐ 12 Rick Monday	.75	.35	.09
☐ 13 Jose Morales	.50	.23	.06
☐ 14 Tom Niedenfuer	.50	.23	.06
☐ 15 Jorge Orta	.50	.23	.06
☐ 16 Jerry Reuss	.75	.35	.09
☐ 17 Ron Roenicke	.50	.23	.06
☐ 18 Bill Russell	.75	.35	.09
☐ 19 Steve Sax	1.25	.55	.16
☐ 20 Mike Scioscia	.75	.35	.09
☐ 21 Vin Scully ANN	1.50	.70	.19
☐ 22 Dave Stewart	2.00	.90	.25
☐ 23 Derrell Thomas	.50	.23	.06
☐ 24 Fernando Valenzuela	1.00	.45	.12
☐ 25 Bob Welch	.75	.35	.09
☐ 26 Steve Yeager	.50	.23	.06

1983 Dodgers Police

The cards in this 30-card set measure approximately 2 13/16" by 4 1/8". The full color Police Los Angeles Dodgers set of 1983 features the player's name and uniform number on the front along with the Dodger's logo, the year, and the player's photo. The backs feature a small insert portrait picture of the player, player biographies, and career statistics. The logo of the Los Angeles Police Department, the sponsor of the set, is found on the backs of the cards.

	NRMT	VG-E	GOOD
COMPLETE SET (30)	8.00	3.60	1.00
COMMON CARD	.25	.11	.03
☐ 2 Tom Lasorda MG	.75	.35	.09
☐ 3 Steve Sax	.35	.16	.04
☐ 5 Mike Marshall	.35	.16	.04
☐ 7 Steve Yeager	.35	.16	.04
☐ 12 Dusty Baker	.50	.23	.06
☐ 14 Mike Scioscia	.35	.16	.04
☐ 16 Rick Monday	.35	.16	.04
☐ 17 Greg Brock	.25	.11	.03
☐ 18 Bill Russell	.50	.23	.06
☐ 20 Candy Maldonado	.25	.11	.03
☐ 21 Ricky Wright	.25	.11	.03
☐ 22 Mark Bradley	.25	.11	.03
☐ 23 Dave Sax	.25	.11	.03
☐ 26 Alejandro Pena	.25	.11	.03
☐ 27 Joe Beckwith	.25	.11	.03
☐ 28 Pedro Guerrero	.50	.23	.06
☐ 30 Derrel Thomas	.25	.11	.03
☐ 34 Fernando Valenzuela	.75	.35	.09
☐ 35 Bob Welch	.50	.23	.06
☐ 38 Pat Zachry	.25	.11	.03
☐ 40 Ron Roenicke	.25	.11	.03
☐ 41 Jerry Reuss	.35	.16	.04
☐ 43 Jose Morales	.25	.11	.03
☐ 44 Ken Landreaux	.25	.11	.03
☐ 46 Burt Hooton	.35	.16	.04
☐ 47 Larry White	.25	.11	.03
☐ 48 Dave Stewart	.75	.35	.09
☐ 49 Tom Niedenfuer	.25	.11	.03
☐ 57 Steve Howe	.25	.11	.03
☐ NNO Coaching Staff Ron Perranoski Joe Amalfitano Monty Basgall Mark Cresse Manny Mota	.25	.11	.03

1983 Dodgers Postcards

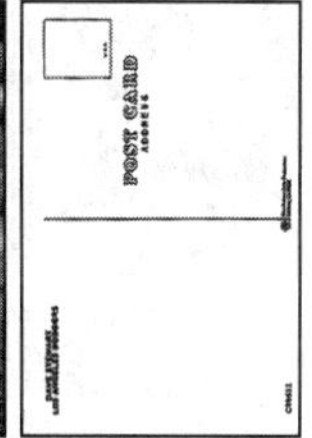

These postcards feature members of the 1983 Los Angeles Dodgers. These cards are unnumbered and checklisted below in alphabetical order.

	NRMT	VG-E	GOOD
COMPLETE SET	10.00	4.50	1.25
COMMON CARD	.50	.23	.06
☐ 1 Dusty Baker	1.00	.45	.12
☐ 2 Greg Brock	.50	.23	.06
☐ 3 Pedro Guerrero	.75	.35	.09
☐ 4 Burt Hooton	.50	.23	.06
☐ 5 Steve Howe	.50	.23	.06
☐ 6 Ken Landreaux	.50	.23	.06
☐ 7 Tommy Lasorda MG	1.25	.55	.16
☐ 8 Mike Marshall	.50	.23	.06
☐ 9 Rick Monday	.75	.35	.09
☐ 10 Manny Mota CO	.75	.35	.09
☐ 11 Tom Neidenfuer	.50	.23	.06
☐ 12 Jerry Reuss	1.00	.45	.12
☐ 13 Bill Russell	1.00	.45	.12
☐ 14 Steve Sax	1.00	.45	.12
☐ 15 Mike Scioscia	.75	.35	.09
☐ 16 Dave Stewart	.75	.35	.09
☐ 17 Derrel Thomas	.50	.23	.06
☐ 18 Fernando Valenzuela	1.00	.45	.12
☐ 19 Bob Welch	.75	.35	.09
☐ 20 Steve Yeager	.50	.23	.06

1984 Dodgers Police

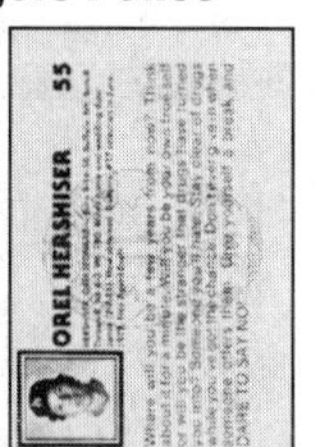

The cards in this 30-card set measure 2 13/16" by 4 1/8". For the fifth straight year, the Los Angeles Police Department sponsored a set of Dodger baseball cards. The set is numbered by player uniform number, which is featured on both the fronts and backs of the cards. The Dodgers' logo appears on the front, and the LAPD logo is superimposed on the backs of the cards. The backs are printed in Dodger blue ink and contain a small photo of the player on the front. Player biographical data and "Dare to Say No" antidrug information are featured on the back. The set features an early card of Orel Hershiser predating his Rookie Cards issued the following year.

	NRMT	VG-E	GOOD
COMPLETE SET (30)	8.00	3.60	1.00
COMMON CARD	.25	.11	.03
☐ 2 Tom Lasorda MG	1.00	.45	.12
☐ 3 Steve Sax	.75	.35	.09
☐ 5 Mike Marshall	.25	.11	.03
☐ 7 Steve Yeager	.50	.23	.06
☐ 9 Greg Brock	.25	.11	.03
☐ 10 Dave Anderson	.25	.11	.03
☐ 14 Mike Scioscia	.50	.23	.06
☐ 16 Rick Monday	.50	.23	.06
☐ 17 Rafael Landestoy	.25	.11	.03
☐ 18 Bill Russell	.75	.35	.09
☐ 20 Candy Maldonado	.25	.11	.03
☐ 21 Bob Bailor	.25	.11	.03
☐ 25 German Rivera	.25	.11	.03
☐ 26 Alejandro Pena	.25	.11	.03
☐ 27 Carlos Diaz	.25	.11	.03
☐ 28 Pedro Guerrero	.75	.35	.09
☐ 31 Jack Fimple	.25	.11	.03
☐ 34 Fernando Valenzuela	1.00	.45	.12
☐ 35 Bob Welch	.75	.35	.09
☐ 38 Pat Zachry	.25	.11	.03
☐ 40 Rick Honeycutt	.25	.11	.03
☐ 41 Jerry Reuss	.50	.23	.06
☐ 43 Jose Morales	.25	.11	.03
☐ 44 Ken Landreaux	.25	.11	.03
☐ 45 Terry Whitfield	.25	.11	.03
☐ 46 Burt Hooton	.50	.23	.06
☐ 49 Tom Niedenfuer	.25	.11	.03
☐ 55 Orel Hershiser	4.00	1.80	.50
☐ 56 Richard Rodas	.25	.11	.03
☐ NNO Coaching Staff Monty Basgall Joe Amalfitano Mark Cresse Manny Mota Ron Perranoski	.25	.11	.03

1984 Dodgers Smokey

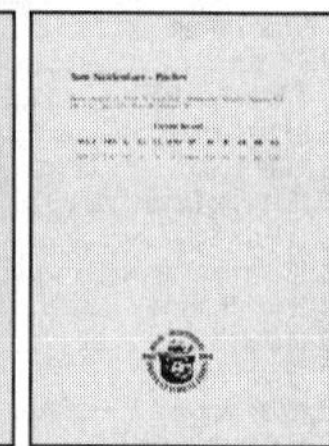

This four-card set was not widely distributed and has not proven to be very popular with collectors. Cards were supposedly distributed by fire agencies in Southern California at fairs, mall displays, and special events. Cards measure approximately 5" by 7" and feature a color picture of Smokey the Bear with a Dodger. The cards were printed on relatively thin card stock; printing on the back is black on white.

	NRMT	VG-E	GOOD
COMPLETE SET (4)	18.00	8.00	2.20
COMMON CARD (1-4)	4.00	1.80	.50
☐ 1 Ken Landreaux with Smokey	5.00	2.20	.60
☐ 2 Tom Niedenfuer with Smokey	5.00	2.20	.60
☐ 3 Steve Sax with Smokey	6.00	2.70	.75
☐ 4 Smokey the Bear (Batting pose)	4.00	1.80	.50

1984 Dodgers Union Oil Photos

Distributed by Union Oil, this 16-card set measures approximately 8 1/2" by 11" and features color drawings of some of the great moments in Dodgers history. The backs carry text discribing the significance of the drawing.

	NRMT	VG-E	GOOD
COMPLETE SET (16)	25.00	11.00	3.10
COMMON CARD (1-16)	1.00	.45	.12
☐ 1 Baseball's Record-Setting Infield	1.00	.45	.12
☐ 2 Roy Campanella Tribute	5.00	2.20	.60
☐ 3 Willie Davis 31-Game Hitting Streak	1.50	.70	.19
☐ 4 Don Drysdale 58 2/3 Scoreless Inning Streak	3.00	1.35	.35
☐ 5 Manny Mota 145th Pinch Hit	1.50	.70	.19
☐ 6 Jerry Reuss Bill Singer No-Hitters	1.50	.70	.19
☐ 7 The Tenth Player	1.00	.45	.12
☐ 8 Dusty Baker Ron Cey Steve Garvey Reggie Smith 30-Homer Foursome	2.00	.90	.25
☐ 9 Fernando Valenzuela Cy Young Award Season 1981	2.50	1.10	.30
☐ 10 Bob Welch Strikes Out Reggie Jackson	1.50	.70	.19
☐ 11 Maury Wills 104th Stolen Base-1962	2.50	1.10	.30
☐ 12 1959 World Championship	1.00	.45	.12
☐ 13 1963 World Championship	1.00	.45	.12
☐ 14 1965 World Championship	1.00	.45	.12
☐ 15 1977 National League Champ. Series	1.00	.45	.12
☐ 16 1981 World Championship	1.00	.45	.12

1985 Dodgers Coke Postcards

This 34-card set was sponsored by Coke, and the company logo appears on the back of the cards. These oversized cards measure approximately 3 1/2" by 5 1/2". The front design features glossy color player photos, bordered in white and with the player's name below the pictures. Except for the sponsor's logo, the backs are blank. The cards are unnumbered and checklisted below in alphabetical order.

	NRMT	VG-E	GOOD
COMPLETE SET (34)	20.00	9.00	2.50
COMMON CARD (1-34)	.50	.23	.06

□ 1 Joe Amalfitano CO	.50	.23	.06
□ 2 Dave Anderson	.50	.23	.06
□ 3 Bob Bailor	.50	.23	.06
□ 4 Monty Basgall CO	.50	.23	.06
□ 5 Tom Brennan	.50	.23	.06
□ 6 Greg Brock	.50	.23	.06
□ 7 Bobby Castillo	.50	.23	.06
□ 8 Mark Cresse CO	.50	.23	.06
□ 9 Carlos Diaz	.50	.23	.06
□ 10 Mariano Duncan	2.00	.90	.25
□ 11 Pedro Guerrero	1.50	.70	.19
□ 12 Orel Hershiser	3.00	1.35	.35
□ 13 Rick Honeycutt	.50	.23	.06
□ 14 Steve Howe	.50	.23	.06
□ 15 Ken Howell	.50	.23	.06
□ 16 Jay Johnstone	1.00	.45	.12
□ 17 Ken Landreaux	.50	.23	.06
□ 18 Tom Lasorda MG	2.00	.90	.25
□ 19 Candy Maldonado	.50	.23	.06
□ 20 Mike Marshall	.50	.23	.06
□ 21 Manny Mota CO	.50	.23	.06
□ 22 Tom Niedenfuer	.50	.23	.06
□ 23 Al Oliver	1.00	.45	.12
□ 24 Alejandro Pena	.50	.23	.06
□ 25 Ron Perranoski CO	.50	.23	.06
□ 26 Jerry Reuss	1.00	.45	.12
□ 27 R.J. Reynolds	.50	.23	.06
□ 28 Bill Russell	1.00	.45	.12
□ 29 Steve Sax	1.00	.45	.12
□ 30 Mike Scioscia	1.00	.45	.12
□ 31 Fernando Valenzuela	1.00	.45	.12
□ 32 Bob Welch	1.00	.45	.12
□ 33 Terry Whitfield	.50	.23	.06
□ 34 Steve Yeager	.50	.23	.06

1986 Dodgers Coke Postcards

This 33-card Dodger set was sponsored by Coke, and the company logo appears on the back of the cards. The oversized cards measure approximately 3 1/2" by 5 1/2". The front design features glossy color player photos (mostly action), bordered in white and with the player's name below the picture. The backs are blank except for a small Coca-Cola logo. The cards are unnumbered and checklisted below in alphabetical order.

	MINT	NRMT	EXC
COMPLETE SET (33)	15.00	6.75	1.85
COMMON CARD (1-33)	.50	.23	.06
□ 1 Joe Amalfitano CO	.50	.23	.06
□ 2 Dave Anderson	.50	.23	.06
□ 3 Monty Basgall CO	.50	.23	.06
□ 4 Greg Brock	.50	.23	.06
□ 5 Enos Cabell	.50	.23	.06
□ 6 Cesar Cedeno	.75	.35	.09
□ 7 Mark Cresse CO	.50	.23	.06
□ 8 Mariano Duncan	1.00	.45	.12
□ 9 Carlos Diaz	.50	.23	.06
□ 10 Pedro Guerrero	1.00	.45	.12
□ 11 Orel Hershiser	2.50	1.10	.30
□ 12 Ben Hines TR	.50	.23	.06
□ 13 Rick Honeycutt	.50	.23	.06
□ 14 Ken Howell	.50	.23	.06
□ 15 Ken Landreaux	.50	.23	.06
□ 16 Tom Lasorda MG	1.25	.55	.16
□ 17 Bill Madlock	.75	.35	.09
□ 18 Mike Marshall	.50	.23	.06
□ 19 Len Matuszek	.50	.23	.06
□ 20 Manny Mota CO	.50	.23	.06
□ 21 Tom Niedenfuer	.50	.23	.06
□ 22 Alejandro Pena	.50	.23	.06
□ 23 Ron Perranoski CO	.50	.23	.06
□ 24 Dennis Powell	.50	.23	.06
□ 25 Jerry Reuss	.75	.35	.09
□ 26 Bill Russell	.75	.35	.09
□ 27 Steve Sax	.75	.35	.09
□ 28 Mike Scioscia	.75	.35	.09
□ 29 Alex Trevino	.50	.23	.06
□ 30 Fernando Valenzuela	.75	.35	.09
□ 31 Ed VandeBerg	.50	.23	.06
□ 32 Bob Welch	.75	.35	.09
□ 33 Terry Whitfield	.50	.23	.06

1986 Dodgers Police

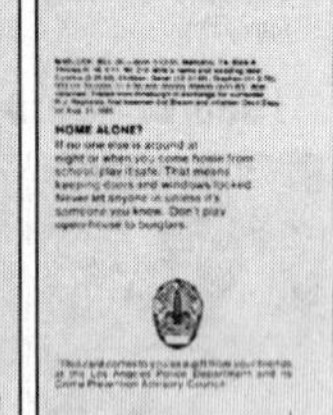

This 30-card set features full-color cards each measuring 2 13/16" by 4 1/8". The cards are unnumbered except for uniform numbers. The backs give a safety tip as well as a short capsule biography. The sets were given away at Dodger Stadium on May 18th.

	MINT	NRMT	EXC
COMPLETE SET (30)	6.00	2.70	.75
COMMON CARD	.25	.11	.03
□ 2 Tom Lasorda MG	1.00	.45	.12
□ 3 Steve Sax	.75	.35	.09
□ 5 Mike Marshall	.25	.11	.03
□ 9 Greg Brock	.25	.11	.03
□ 10 Dave Anderson	.25	.11	.03
□ 12 Bill Madlock	.50	.23	.06
□ 14 Mike Scioscia	.50	.23	.06
□ 17 Len Matuszek	.25	.11	.03
□ 18 Bill Russell	.75	.35	.09
□ 22 Franklin Stubbs	.25	.11	.03
□ 23 Enos Cabell	.25	.11	.03
□ 25 Mariano Duncan	.75	.35	.09
□ 26 Alejandro Pena	.25	.11	.03
□ 27 Carlos Diaz	.25	.11	.03
□ 28 Pedro Guerrero	.75	.35	.09
□ 29 Alex Trevino	.25	.11	.03
□ 31 Ed VandeBerg	.25	.11	.03
□ 34 Fernando Valenzuela	.50	.23	.06
□ 35 Bob Welch	.75	.35	.09
□ 40 Rick Honeycutt	.25	.11	.03
□ 41 Jerry Reuss	.50	.23	.06
□ 43 Ken Howell	.25	.11	.03
□ 44 Ken Landreaux	.25	.11	.03
□ 45 Terry Whitfield	.25	.11	.03
□ 48 Dennis Powell	.25	.11	.03
□ 49 Tom Niedenfuer	.25	.11	.03
□ 51 Reggie Williams	.25	.11	.03
□ 55 Orel Hershiser	1.25	.55	.16
□ NNO Coaching Staff Don McMahon Mark Cresse Ben Hines Ron Perranoski Monty Basgall Manny Mota Joe Amalfitano	.25	.11	.03
□ NNO Team Photo (Checklist back)	.50	.23	.06

1986 Dodgers Union Oil Photos

This 24-card set features color photos of the 1986 Los Angeles Dodgers and measures approximately 8 1/2" by 11". Player information is printed on the backs. The cards are unnumbered and checklisted below in alphabetical order.

	MINT	NRMT	EXC
COMPLETE SET (24)	10.00	4.50	1.25
COMMON CARD (1-24)	.25	.11	.03
□ 1 Dave Anderson	.25	.11	.03
□ 2 Greg Brock	.25	.11	.03
□ 3 Enos Cabell	.25	.11	.03
□ 4 Carlos Diaz	.25	.11	.03
□ 5 Mariano Duncan	.75	.35	.09
□ 6 Pedro Guerrero	.75	.35	.09
□ 7 Orel Hershiser	1.25	.55	.16
□ 8 Rick Honeycutt	.25	.11	.03
□ 9 Ken Howell	.25	.11	.03
□ 10 Tommy Lasorda MG	1.25	.55	.16
□ 11 Ken Landreaux	.25	.11	.03
□ 12 Bill Madlock	.50	.23	.06
□ 13 Mike Marshall	.25	.11	.03
□ 14 Tom Niedenfuer	.25	.11	.03
□ 15 Jerry Reuss	.50	.23	.06
□ 16 Bill Russell	.75	.35	.09
□ 17 Steve Sax	.50	.23	.06
□ 18 Mike Scioscia	.25	.11	.03
□ 19 Franklin Stubbs	.25	.11	.03
□ 20 Alex Trevino	.25	.11	.03
□ 21 Fernando Valenzuela	.50	.23	.06
□ 22 Ed Vandeberg	.25	.11	.03
□ 23 Bob Welch	.50	.23	.06
□ 24 Reggie Williams	.25	.11	.03

1987 Dodgers 1955 TCMA

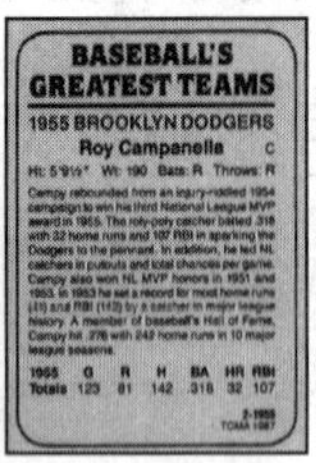

This nine-card standard-size set feature members of the 1955 Brooklyn Dodgers. That team was the only Brooklyn Dodger team to win the World Series. The fronts have player photos, while the backs have information about the players as well as their 1955 statistics.

	MINT	NRMT	EXC
COMPLETE SET (9)	5.00	2.20	.60
COMMON CARD (1-9)	.25	.11	.03
□ 1 Duke Snider Walter Alston MG	.75	.35	.09
□ 2 Roy Campanella	1.00	.45	.12
□ 3 Jackie Robinson	2.00	.90	.25
□ 4 Carl Furillo	.75	.35	.09
□ 5 Gil Hodges	1.00	.45	.12
□ 6 Pee Wee Reese Jim Gilliam	.75	.35	.09
□ 7 Don Newcombe	.75	.35	.09
□ 8 Ed Roebuck Clem Labine	.25	.11	.03
□ 9 Carl Erskine	.50	.23	.06

1987 Dodgers Mother's

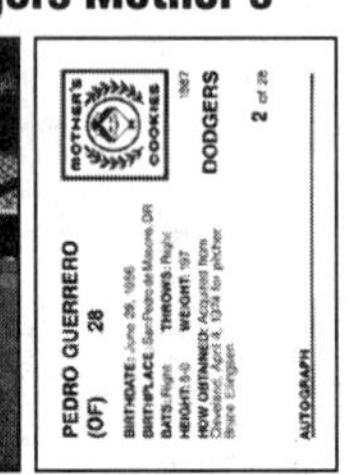

This set consists of 28 full-color, rounded-corner cards each measuring 2 1/2" by 3 1/2". Starter sets (only 20 cards but also including a certificate for eight more cards) were given out at the ballpark and collectors were encouraged to trade to fill in the rest of their set. Cards were originally given out at Dodger Stadium on August 9th. Photos were taken by Barry Colla. The sets were reportedly given out free to all game attendees 14 years of age and under.

	MINT	NRMT	EXC
COMPLETE SET (28)	8.00	3.60	1.00
COMMON CARD (1-28)	.25	.11	.03
□ 1 Tom Lasorda MG	1.00	.45	.12
□ 2 Pedro Guerrero	.75	.35	.09
□ 3 Steve Sax	.75	.35	.09
□ 4 Fernando Valenzuela	.50	.23	.06
□ 5 Mike Marshall	.25	.11	.03
□ 6 Orel Hershiser	1.00	.45	.12
□ 7 Mariano Duncan	.50	.23	.06
□ 8 Bill Madlock	.25	.11	.03
□ 9 Bob Welch	.25	.11	.03
□ 10 Mike Scioscia	.50	.23	.06
□ 11 Mike Ramsey	.25	.11	.03
□ 12 Matt Young	.25	.11	.03
□ 13 Franklin Stubbs	.25	.11	.03
□ 14 Tom Niedenfuer	.25	.11	.03
□ 15 Reggie Williams	.25	.11	.03
□ 16 Rick Honeycutt	.25	.11	.03
□ 17 Dave Anderson	.25	.11	.03
□ 18 Alejandro Pena	.25	.11	.03
□ 19 Ken Howell	.25	.11	.03
□ 20 Len Matuszek	.25	.11	.03
□ 21 Tim Leary	.25	.11	.03
□ 22 Tracy Woodson	.25	.11	.03
□ 23 Alex Trevino	.25	.11	.03
□ 24 Ken Landreaux	.25	.11	.03
□ 25 Mickey Hatcher	.25	.11	.03
□ 26 Brian Holton	.25	.11	.03
□ 27 Dodgers' Coaches	.25	.11	.03
□ 28 Checklist Card	.25	.11	.03

1987 Dodgers Police

This 30-card set features full-color cards each measuring approximately 2 13/16" by 4 1/8". The cards are unnumbered except for uniform numbers. The backs give a safety tip as well as a short capsule biography. Cards were given away at Dodger Stadium on April 24th and later during the summer by LAPD officers at a rate of two cards per week.

	MINT	NRMT	EXC
COMPLETE SET (30)	6.00	2.70	.75
COMMON CARD (1-30)	.25	.11	.03

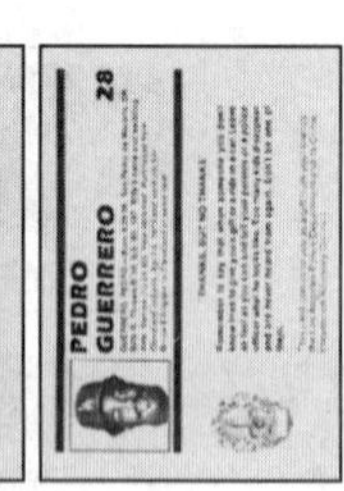

□ 1 Tom Lasorda MG	1.00	.45	.12
□ 2 Steve Sax	.75	.35	.09
□ 3 Mike Marshall	.25	.11	.03
□ 4 Dave Anderson	.25	.11	.03
□ 5 Bill Madlock	.50	.23	.06
□ 6 Mike Scioscia	.50	.23	.06
□ 7 Gilberto Reyes	.25	.11	.03
□ 8 Len Matuszek	.25	.11	.03
□ 9 Reggie Williams	.25	.11	.03
□ 10 Franklin Stubbs	.25	.11	.03
□ 11 Tim Leary	.25	.11	.03
□ 12 Mariano Duncan	.50	.23	.06
□ 13 Alejandro Pena	.25	.11	.03
□ 14 Pedro Guerrero	.75	.35	.09
□ 15 Alex Trevino	.25	.11	.03
□ 16 Jeff Hamilton	.25	.11	.03
□ 17 Fernando Valenzuela	.50	.23	.06
□ 18 Bob Welch	.75	.35	.09
□ 19 Matt Young	.25	.11	.03
□ 20 Rick Honeycutt	.25	.11	.03
□ 21 Jerry Reuss	.50	.23	.06
□ 22 Ken Howell	.25	.11	.03
□ 23 Ken Landreaux	.25	.11	.03
□ 24 Ralph Bryant	.25	.11	.03
□ 25 Jose Gonzalez	.25	.11	.03
□ 26 Tom Niedenfuer	.25	.11	.03
□ 27 Brian Holton	.25	.11	.03
□ 28 Orel Hershiser	1.00	.45	.12
□ 29 Coaching Staff Ron Perranoski Tom Lasorda Joe Amalfitano Don McMahon Manny Mota Bill Russell Mark Cresse (Unnumbered)	.50	.23	.06
□ 30 Dodgers Stadium (25th Anniversary)	.25	.11	.03

1987 Dodgers Smokey All-Stars

This 40-card set was issued by the U.S. Forestry Service to commemorate the Los Angeles Dodgers selected for the All-Star game over the past 25 years. The cards measure approximately 2 1/2" by 3 3/4" and have full-color fronts. The card fronts are distinguished by their thick silver borders and the bats, balls, and stadium design layout. The 25th anniversary logo for Dodger Stadium is in the lower right corner of each card. The set numbering is alphabetical by subject's name.

	MINT	NRMT	EXC
COMPLETE SET (40)	15.00	6.75	1.85
COMMON CARD (1-40)	.25	.11	.03
□ 1 Walt Alston MG	1.00	.45	.12
□ 2 Dusty Baker	.75	.35	.09
□ 3 Jim Brewer	.25	.11	.03
□ 4 Ron Cey	.75	.35	.09
□ 5 Tommy Davis	.50	.23	.06
□ 6 Willie Davis	.50	.23	.06
□ 7 Don Drysdale	1.50	.70	.19
□ 8 Steve Garvey	1.00	.45	.12
□ 9 Bill Grabarkewitz	.25	.11	.03
□ 10 Pedro Guerrero	.75	.35	.09
□ 11 Tom Haller	.25	.11	.03
□ 12 Orel Hershiser	.75	.35	.09
□ 13 Burt Hooton	.25	.11	.03
□ 14 Steve Howe	.25	.11	.03
□ 15 Tommy John	.75	.35	.09
□ 16 Sandy Koufax	2.00	.90	.25
□ 17 Tom Lasorda MG	1.00	.45	.12
□ 18 Jim Lefebvre	.25	.11	.03
□ 19 Davey Lopes	.50	.23	.06
□ 20 Mike G. Marshall	.25	.11	.03
□ 21 Mike A. Marshall	.25	.11	.03
□ 22 Andy Messersmith	.25	.11	.03
□ 23 Rick Monday	.25	.11	.03

	MINT	NRMT	EXC
☐ 24 Manny Mota	.50	.23	.06
☐ 25 Claude Osteen	.25	.11	.03
☐ 26 Johnny Podres	.50	.23	.06
☐ 27 Phil Regan	.25	.11	.03
☐ 28 Jerry Reuss	.25	.11	.03
☐ 29 Rick Rhoden	.25	.11	.03
☐ 30 John Roseboro	.50	.23	.06
☐ 31 Bill Russell	.50	.23	.06
☐ 32 Steve Sax	.50	.23	.06
☐ 33 Bill Singer	.25	.11	.03
☐ 34 Reggie Smith	.50	.23	.06
☐ 35 Don Sutton	1.00	.45	.12
☐ 36 Fernando Valenzuela	.75	.35	.09
☐ 37 Bob Welch	.50	.23	.06
☐ 38 Maury Wills	.75	.35	.09
☐ 39 Jim Wynn	.25	.11	.03
☐ 40 Checklist Card	.25	.11	.03

1988 Dodgers Mother's

This set consists of 28 full-color, rounded-corner cards each measuring 2 1/2" by 3 1/2". Starter sets (only 20 cards but also including a certificate for eight more cards) were given out at the ballpark and collectors were encouraged to trade to fill in the rest of their set. Cards were originally given out at Dodger Stadium on July 31st. Photos were taken by Barry Colla. The sets were reportedly given out free to the first 25,000 game attendees 14 years of age and under.

	MINT	NRMT	EXC
COMPLETE SET (28)	10.00	4.50	1.25
COMMON CARD (1-28)	.25	.11	.03
☐ 1 Tom Lasorda MG	1.00	.45	.12
☐ 2 Pedro Guerrero	.75	.35	.09
☐ 3 Steve Sax	.75	.35	.09
☐ 4 Fernando Valenzuela	.50	.23	.06
☐ 5 Mike Marshall	.25	.11	.03
☐ 6 Orel Hershiser	.50	.23	.06
☐ 7 Alfredo Griffin	.25	.11	.03
☐ 8 Kirk Gibson	.50	.23	.06
☐ 9 Don Sutton	1.00	.45	.12
☐ 10 Mike Scioscia	.50	.23	.06
☐ 11 Franklin Stubbs	.25	.11	.03
☐ 12 Mike Davis	.25	.11	.03
☐ 13 Jesse Orosco	.25	.11	.03
☐ 14 John Shelby	.25	.11	.03
☐ 15 Rick Dempsey	.50	.23	.06
☐ 16 Jay Howell	.25	.11	.03
☐ 17 Dave Anderson	.25	.11	.03
☐ 18 Alejandro Pena	.25	.11	.03
☐ 19 Jeff Hamilton	.25	.11	.03
☐ 20 Danny Heep	.25	.11	.03
☐ 21 Tim Leary	.25	.11	.03
☐ 22 Brad Havens	.25	.11	.03
☐ 23 Tim Belcher	.50	.23	.06
☐ 24 Ken Howell	.25	.11	.03
☐ 25 Mickey Hatcher	.25	.11	.03
☐ 26 Brian Holton	.25	.11	.03
☐ 27 Mike Devereaux	.50	.23	.06
☐ 28 Checklist Card Joe Ferguson CO Mark Cresse CO Ron Perranoski CO Bill Russell CO Joe Amalfitano CO Manny Mota CO Ben Hines CO	.50	.23	.06

1988 Dodgers Police

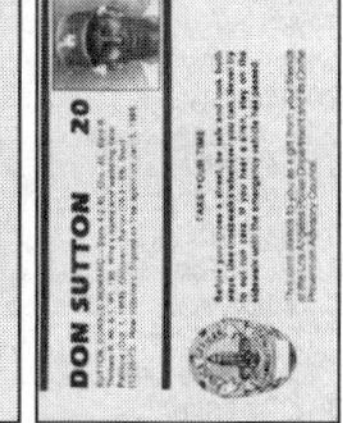

This 30-card set features full-color cards each measuring approximately 2 13/16" by 4 1/8". The cards are unnumbered except for uniform numbers. The backs give a safety tip as well as a short capsule biography. Cards were given during the summer by LAPD officers. The set is very similar to the 1987 set, the 1988 set is distinguished by the fact that it does not have the 25th anniversary (of Dodger Stadium) logo on the card front.

	MINT	NRMT	EXC
COMPLETE SET (30)	6.00	2.70	.75
COMMON CARD	.25	.11	.03
☐ 2 Tom Lasorda MG	1.25	.55	.16
☐ 3 Steve Sax	.50	.23	.06
☐ 5 Mike Marshall	.25	.11	.03
☐ 7 Alfredo Griffin	.25	.11	.03
☐ 9 Mickey Hatcher	.25	.11	.03
☐ 10 Dave Anderson	.25	.11	.03
☐ 12 Danny Heep	.25	.11	.03
☐ 14 Mike Scioscia	.50	.23	.06
☐ 20 Don Sutton	.75	.35	.09
☐ 21 Tito Landrum and 17 Len Matuszek	.25	.11	.03
☐ 22 Franklin Stubbs	.25	.11	.03
☐ 23 Kirk Gibson	.50	.23	.06
☐ 25 Mariano Duncan	.50	.23	.06
☐ 26 Alejandro Pena	.25	.11	.03
☐ 27 Mike Sharperson and 52 Tim Crews	.25	.11	.03
☐ 28 Pedro Guerrero	.75	.35	.09
☐ 29 Alex Trevino	.25	.11	.03
☐ 31 John Shelby	.25	.11	.03
☐ 33 Jeff Hamilton	.25	.11	.03
☐ 34 Fernando Valenzuela	.75	.35	.09
☐ 37 Mike Davis	.25	.11	.03
☐ 41 Brad Havens	.25	.11	.03
☐ 43 Ken Howell	.25	.11	.03
☐ 47 Jesse Orosco	.25	.11	.03
☐ 49 Tim Belcher and 57 Shawn Hillegas	.50	.23	.06
☐ 50 Jay Howell	.25	.11	.03
☐ 51 Brian Holton	.25	.11	.03
☐ 54 Tim Leary	.25	.11	.03
☐ 55 Orel Hershiser	1.00	.45	.12
☐ NNO Tom Lasorda MG and Coaches	1.00	.45	.12

1988 Dodgers Smokey

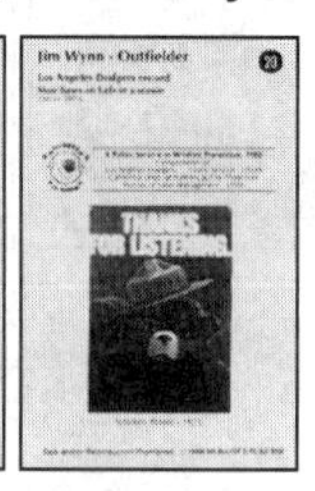

This 32-card set was issued by the U.S. Forestry Service as a perforated sheet that could be separated into individual cards. The set commemorates Los Angeles Dodgers who hold various team and league records, i.e., "L.A. Dodgers Record-Breakers." The cards measure approximately 2 1/2" by 4" and have full-color fronts. The card fronts are distinguished by their thick light blue borders and the bats, balls, and stadium design layout. The sheets of cards were distributed at the Dodgers' Smokey Bear Day game on September 9th.

	MINT	NRMT	EXC
COMPLETE SET (32)	12.00	5.50	1.50
COMMON CARD (1-32)	.25	.11	.03
☐ 1 Walter Alston MG	.75	.35	.09
☐ 2 John Roseboro	.25	.11	.03
☐ 3 Frank Howard	.50	.23	.06
☐ 4 Sandy Koufax	2.00	.90	.25
☐ 5 Manny Mota	.50	.23	.06
☐ 6 Sandy Koufax Jerry Reuss Bill Singer	.75	.35	.09
☐ 7 Maury Wills	.75	.35	.09
☐ 8 Tommy Davis	.50	.23	.06
☐ 9 Phil Regan	.25	.11	.03
☐ 10 Wes Parker	.25	.11	.03
☐ 11 Don Drysdale	1.00	.45	.12
☐ 12 Willie Davis	.50	.23	.06
☐ 13 Bill Russell	.50	.23	.06
☐ 14 Jim Brewer	.25	.11	.03
☐ 15 Steve Garvey Davey Lopes Bill Russell Ron Cey	.75	.35	.09
☐ 16 Mike Marshall	.25	.11	.03
☐ 17 Steve Garvey	1.00	.45	.12
☐ 18 Davey Lopes	.50	.23	.06
☐ 19 Burt Hooton	.25	.11	.03
☐ 20 Jim Wynn	.25	.11	.03
☐ 21 Dusty Baker Ron Cey Steve Garvey Reggie Smith	.50	.23	.06
☐ 22 Dusty Baker	.75	.35	.09
☐ 23 Tommy Lasorda MG	1.00	.45	.12
☐ 24 Fernando Valenzuela	.75	.35	.09
☐ 25 Steve Sax	.50	.23	.06
☐ 26 Dodger Stadium	.25	.11	.03
☐ 27 Ron Cey	.50	.23	.06
☐ 28 Pedro Guerrero	.50	.23	.06
☐ 29 Mike Marshall	.25	.11	.03
☐ 30 Don Sutton	.75	.35	.09
☐ NNO Checklist Card	.50	.23	.06
☐ NNO Smokey Bear	.25	.11	.03

1989 Dodgers Mother's

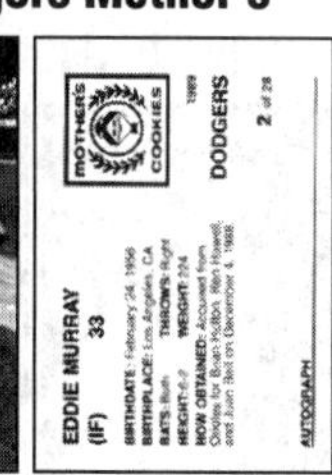

The 1989 Mother's Los Angeles Dodgers set contains 28 standard-size cards with rounded corners. The fronts have borderless color photos, and the horizontally oriented backs have biographical information. Starter sets containing 20 of these cards were given away at a Dodgers home game during the 1989 season.

	MINT	NRMT	EXC
COMPLETE SET (28)	8.00	3.60	1.00
COMMON CARD (1-28)	.25	.11	.03
☐ 1 Tom Lasorda MG	1.00	.45	.12
☐ 2 Eddie Murray	1.25	.55	.16
☐ 3 Mike Scioscia	.50	.23	.06
☐ 4 Fernando Valenzuela	.50	.23	.06
☐ 5 Mike Marshall	.25	.11	.03
☐ 6 Orel Hershiser	.50	.23	.06
☐ 7 Alfredo Griffin	.25	.11	.03
☐ 8 Kirk Gibson	.75	.35	.09
☐ 9 John Tudor	.25	.11	.03
☐ 10 Willie Randolph	.50	.23	.06
☐ 11 Franklin Stubbs	.25	.11	.03
☐ 12 Mike Davis	.25	.11	.03
☐ 13 Mike Morgan	.25	.11	.03
☐ 14 John Shelby	.25	.11	.03
☐ 15 Rick Dempsey	.50	.23	.06
☐ 16 Jay Howell	.25	.11	.03
☐ 17 Dave Anderson	.25	.11	.03
☐ 18 Alejandro Pena	.25	.11	.03
☐ 19 Jeff Hamilton	.25	.11	.03
☐ 20 Ricky Horton	.25	.11	.03
☐ 21 Tim Leary	.25	.11	.03
☐ 22 Ray Searage	.25	.11	.03
☐ 23 Tim Belcher	.50	.23	.06
☐ 24 Tim Crews	.25	.11	.03
☐ 25 Mickey Hatcher	.25	.11	.03
☐ 26 Mariano Duncan	.50	.23	.06
☐ 27 Dodgers Coaches Joe Amalfitano Manny Mota Joe Ferguson Ron Perranoski Bill Russell Mark Cresse Ben Hines	.50	.23	.06
☐ 28 Checklist Card World Championship Trophy	.50	.23	.06

1989 Dodgers Police

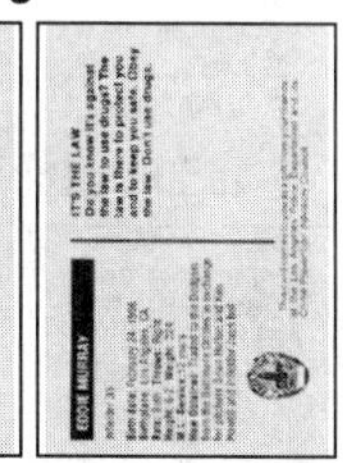

The 1989 Police Los Angeles Dodgers set contains 30 cards measuring approximately 2 5/8" by 4 1/4". The fronts have color photos with white borders; the backs feature safety tips and biographical information. The unnumbered cards were given away by various Los Angeles-area police departments. The cards were also issued as an uncut, perforated sheet to children (age 14 and under) at Dodger Stadium on Baseball Card Night, May 5, 1989.

	MINT	NRMT	EXC
COMPLETE SET (30)	6.00	2.70	.75
COMMON CARD (1-30)	.25	.11	.03
☐ 1 Dodger Coaches (Unnumbered) Ben Hines Ron Perranoski Tom Lasorda MG Joe Amalfitano Joe Ferguson Mark Cresse Bill Russell Manny Mota	.50	.23	.06
☐ 2 Tom Lasorda MG	1.00	.45	.12
☐ 3 Jeff Hamilton	.25	.11	.03
☐ 4 Mike Marshall	.25	.11	.03
☐ 5 Alfredo Griffin	.25	.11	.03
☐ 6 Mickey Hatcher	.25	.11	.03
☐ 7 Dave Anderson	.25	.11	.03
☐ 8 Willie Randolph	.50	.23	.06
☐ 9 Mike Scioscia	.50	.23	.06
☐ 10 Rick Dempsey	.50	.23	.06
☐ 11 Mike Davis	.25	.11	.03
☐ 12 Tracy Woodson	.25	.11	.03
☐ 13 Franklin Stubbs	.25	.11	.03
☐ 14 Kirk Gibson	.75	.35	.09
☐ 15 Mariano Duncan	.50	.23	.06
☐ 16 Alejandro Pena	.25	.11	.03
☐ 17 Mike Sharperson	.25	.11	.03
☐ 18 Ricky Horton	.25	.11	.03
☐ 19 John Tudor	.25	.11	.03
☐ 20 John Shelby	.25	.11	.03
☐ 21 Eddie Murray	1.25	.55	.16
☐ 22 Fernando Valenzuela	.75	.35	.09
☐ 23 Mike Morgan	.25	.11	.03
☐ 24 Ramon Martinez	2.00	.90	.25
☐ 25 Tim Belcher	.25	.11	.03
☐ 26 Jay Howell	.25	.11	.03
☐ 27 Tim Crews	.25	.11	.03
☐ 28 Tim Leary	.25	.11	.03
☐ 29 Orel Hershiser	.50	.23	.06
☐ 30 Ray Searage	.25	.11	.03

1989 Dodgers Smokey Greats

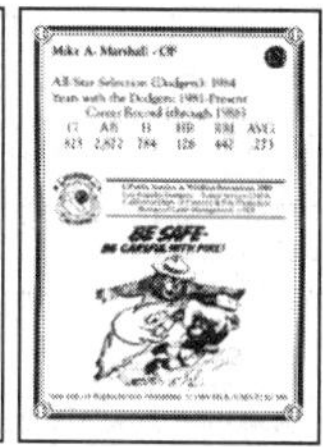

The 1989 Smokey Dodger Greats set contains 104 standard-size cards. The fronts and backs have white and blue borders. The backs are vertically oriented and feature career totals and fire prevention cartoons. The set depicts notable Dodgers of all eras, and was distributed in perforated sheet format. Cards 1-36 are ordered alphabetically and (except for number 31) depict Dodger members of the Hall of Fame. Cards 37-64 (except for number 57) represent Brooklyn Dodgers whereas cards 65-101 represent Los Angeles Dodgers. The last three cards in the set (102-104) are Hall of Famers apparently overlooked in the first group.

	MINT	NRMT	EXC
COMPLETE SET (104)	20.00	9.00	2.50
COMMON CARD (1-100)	.10	.05	.01
COMMON CARD (101-104)	.40	.18	.05
☐ 1 Walter Alston MG	.50	.23	.06
☐ 2 David Bancroft	.30	.14	.04
☐ 3 Dan Brouthers	.30	.14	.04
☐ 4 Roy Campanella	1.00	.45	.12
☐ 5 Max Carey	.30	.14	.04
☐ 6 Hazen(Kiki) Cuyler	.30	.14	.04
☐ 7 Don Drysdale	.75	.35	.09
☐ 8 Burleigh Grimes	.30	.14	.04
☐ 9 Billy Herman	.30	.14	.04
☐ 10 Waite Hoyt	.30	.14	.04
☐ 11 Hughie Jennings	.30	.14	.04
☐ 12 Willie Keeler	.30	.14	.04
☐ 13 Joseph Kelley	.30	.14	.04
☐ 14 George Kelly	.30	.14	.04
☐ 15 Sandy Koufax	1.50	.70	.19
☐ 16 Heinie Manush	.30	.14	.04
☐ 17 Juan Marichal	.50	.23	.06
☐ 18 Rabbit Maranville	.30	.14	.04
☐ 19 Rube Marquard	.30	.14	.04
☐ 20 Thomas McCarthy	.30	.14	.04
☐ 21 Joseph McGinnity	.30	.14	.04
☐ 22 Joe Medwick	.30	.14	.04
☐ 23 Pee Wee Reese	.75	.35	.09
☐ 24 Frank Robinson	.75	.35	.09
☐ 25 Jackie Robinson	2.00	.90	.25
☐ 26 Babe Ruth	3.00	1.35	.35
☐ 27 Duke Snider	1.00	.45	.12
☐ 28 Casey Stengel	.75	.35	.09
☐ 29 Dazzy Vance	.30	.14	.04
☐ 30 Arky Vaughan	.30	.14	.04
☐ 31 Mike Scioscia	.10	.05	.01
☐ 32 Lloyd Waner	.30	.14	.04
☐ 33 John Montgemery Ward	.30	.14	.04
☐ 34 Zack Wheat	.30	.14	.04
☐ 35 Hoyt Wilhelm	.30	.14	.04
☐ 36 Hack Wilson	.30	.14	.04
☐ 37 Tony Cuccinello	.10	.05	.01
☐ 38 Al Lopez	.30	.14	.04
☐ 39 Leo Durocher	.30	.14	.04
☐ 40 Cookie Lavagetto	.10	.05	.01
☐ 41 Babe Phelps	.10	.05	.01
☐ 42 Dolph Camilli	.20	.09	.03
☐ 43 Whitlow Wyatt	.10	.05	.01
☐ 44 Mickey Owen	.10	.05	.01
☐ 45 Van Mungo	.10	.05	.01
☐ 46 Pete Coscarart	.10	.05	.01

☐ 47 Pete Reiser	.20	.09	.03
☐ 48 Augie Galan	.10	.05	.01
☐ 49 Dixie Walker	.20	.09	.03
☐ 50 Kirby Higbe	.10	.05	.01
☐ 51 Ralph Branca	.20	.09	.03
☐ 52 Bruce Edwards	.10	.05	.01
☐ 53 Eddie Stanky	.20	.09	.03
☐ 54 Gil Hodges	.30	.14	.04
☐ 55 Don Newcombe	.20	.09	.03
☐ 56 Preacher Roe	.20	.09	.03
☐ 57 Willie Randolph	.20	.09	.03
☐ 58 Carl Furillo	.20	.09	.03
☐ 59 Charlie Dressen	.10	.05	.01
☐ 60 Carl Erskine	.20	.09	.03
☐ 61 Clem Labine	.10	.05	.01
☐ 62 Gino Cimoli	.10	.05	.01
☐ 63 Johnny Podres	.20	.09	.03
☐ 64 Johnny Roseboro	.10	.05	.01
☐ 65 Wally Moon	.20	.09	.03
☐ 66 Charlie Neal	.10	.05	.01
☐ 67 Norm Larker	.10	.05	.01
☐ 68 Stan Williams	.10	.05	.01
☐ 69 Maury Wills	.30	.14	.04
☐ 70 Tommy Davis	.20	.09	.03
☐ 71 Jim Lefebvre	.10	.05	.01
☐ 72 Phil Regan	.10	.05	.01
☐ 73 Claude Osteen	.10	.05	.01
☐ 74 Tom Haller	.10	.05	.01
☐ 75 Bill Singer	.10	.05	.01
☐ 76 Bill Grabarkewitz	.10	.05	.01
☐ 77 Willie Davis	.20	.09	.03
☐ 78 Don Sutton	.30	.14	.04
☐ 79 Jim Brewer	.10	.05	.01
☐ 80 Manny Mota	.20	.09	.03
☐ 81 Bill Russell	.30	.14	.04
☐ 82 Ron Cey	.20	.09	.03
☐ 83 Steve Garvey	.30	.14	.04
☐ 84 Mike G. Marshall	.10	.05	.01
☐ 85 Andy Messersmith	.10	.05	.01
☐ 86 Jimmy Wynn	.10	.05	.01
☐ 87 Rick Rhoden	.10	.05	.01
☐ 88 Reggie Smith	.20	.09	.03
☐ 89 Jay Howell	.10	.05	.01
☐ 90 Rick Monday	.20	.09	.03
☐ 91 Tommy John	.20	.09	.03
☐ 92 Bob Welch	.20	.09	.03
☐ 93 Dusty Baker	.20	.09	.03
☐ 94 Pedro Guerrero	.20	.09	.03
☐ 95 Burt Hooton	.10	.05	.01
☐ 96 Davey Lopes	.20	.09	.03
☐ 97 Fernando Valenzuela	.30	.14	.04
☐ 98 Steve Howe	.10	.05	.01
☐ 99 Steve Sax	.20	.09	.03
☐ 100 Orel Hershiser	.30	.14	.04
☐ 101 Mike A. Marshall	.40	.18	.05
☐ 102 Ernie Lombardi	.75	.35	.09
☐ 103 Fred Lindstrom	.75	.35	.09
☐ 104 Wilbert Robinson	.75	.35	.09

1989 Dodgers Stamps St. Vincent

This 18-stamp set was issued by the government of the Caribbean Island of St. Vincent and distributed by Empire of America Federal Savings Bank. The stamps were designed to be placed in a commemorative folder with the 1989 Dodgers team photo printed in the center section. Two players' photos appear on most of the stamps. The stamps are unnumbered and checklisted below in alphabetical order according to the name of the player on the left of the stamp.

	MINT	NRMT	EXC
COMPLETE SET (18)	10.00	4.50	1.25
COMMON STAMP (1-18)	.50	.23	.06
☐ 1 Dave Anderson	.50	.23	.06
Alfredo Griffin			
☐ 2 Tim Belcher	.50	.23	.06
Tim Crews			
☐ 3 Coaches Stamp	.50	.23	.06
☐ 4 Kal Daniels	.50	.23	.06
Mike Marshall			
☐ 5 Mike Davis	1.00	.45	.12
Kirk Gibson			
☐ 6 Jeff Hamilton	.50	.23	.06
Franklin Stubbs			
☐ 7 Lenny Harris	.50	.23	.06
Chris Gwynn			
Billy Bean			
☐ 8 Orel Hershiser	.75	.35	.09
Mike Morgan			
☐ 9 Jay Howell	.50	.23	.06
Alejandro Pena			
☐ 10 Tom Lasorda MG	.75	.35	.09
Jose Gonzalez			
☐ 11 Eddie Murray	1.50	.70	.19
Willie Randolph			
☐ 12 Mike Scioscia	.50	.23	.06
Rick Dempsey			
☐ 13 Ray Searage	.50	.23	.06
John Tudor			
☐ 14 Mike Sharperson	.50	.23	.06
Mickey Hatcher			
☐ 15 Fernando Valenzuela	.60	.25	.07
John Shelby			
☐ 16 John Wetteland	1.25	.55	.16
Ramon Martinez			
☐ 17 Stadium Stamp	.50	.23	.06
☐ 18 Team Logo	.50	.23	.06

1990 Dodgers Mother's

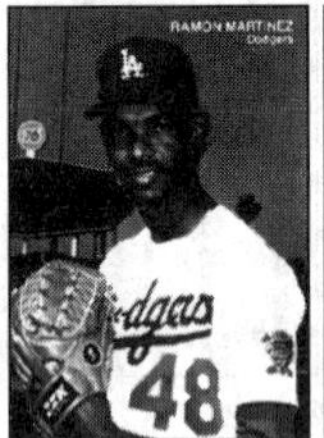
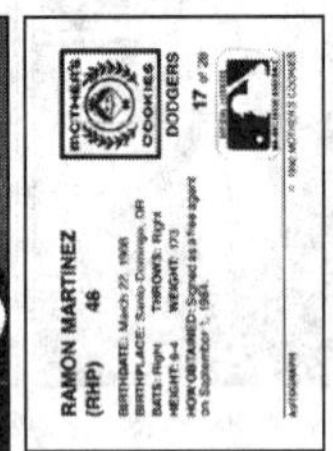

The 1990 Mother's Cookies Los Angeles Dodgers set contains 28 standard-size cards issued with rounded corners and beautiful full color fronts with biographical information on the back. These Dodgers cards were given away at Chavez Ravine to all fans fourteen and under at the August 19th game. They were distributed in 20-card random packets at the game and eight more at the redemption booths. However, both groups of cards were random and there was no guarantee of getting a complete set in the cards. The promotional idea was that the only way one could finish the set was to trade for them. The redemption for eight more cards was done at the 22nd Annual Labor Day card show at the Anaheim Convention Center.

	MINT	NRMT	EXC
COMPLETE SET (28)	8.00	3.60	1.00
COMMON CARD (1-28)	.25	.11	.03
☐ 1 Tom Lasorda MG	1.00	.45	.12
☐ 2 Fernando Valenzuela	.75	.35	.09
☐ 3 Kal Daniels	.25	.11	.03
☐ 4 Mike Scioscia	.50	.23	.06
☐ 5 Eddie Murray	1.50	.70	.19
☐ 6 Mickey Hatcher	.25	.11	.03
☐ 7 Juan Samuel	.25	.11	.03
☐ 8 Alfredo Griffin	.25	.11	.03
☐ 9 Tim Belcher	.50	.23	.06
☐ 10 Hubie Brooks	.25	.11	.03
☐ 11 Jose Gonzalez	.25	.11	.03
☐ 12 Orel Hershiser	.50	.23	.06
☐ 13 Kirk Gibson	.75	.35	.09
☐ 14 Chris Gwynn	.25	.11	.03
☐ 15 Jay Howell	.25	.11	.03
☐ 16 Rick Dempsey	.50	.23	.06
☐ 17 Ramon Martinez	1.50	.70	.19
☐ 18 Lenny Harris	.25	.11	.03
☐ 19 John Wetteland	1.25	.55	.16
☐ 20 Mike Sharperson	.25	.11	.03
☐ 21 Mike Morgan	.25	.11	.03
☐ 22 Ray Searage	.25	.11	.03
☐ 23 Jeff Hamilton	.25	.11	.03
☐ 24 Jim Gott	.25	.11	.03
☐ 25 John Shelby	.25	.11	.03
☐ 26 Tim Crews	.25	.11	.03
☐ 27 Don Aase	.25	.11	.03
☐ 28 Dodger Coaches	.25	.11	.03
Joe Ferguson			
Ron Perranoski			
Mark Cresse			
Ben Hines			
Joe Amalfitano			
Bill Russell			
Manny Mota			

1990 Dodgers Police

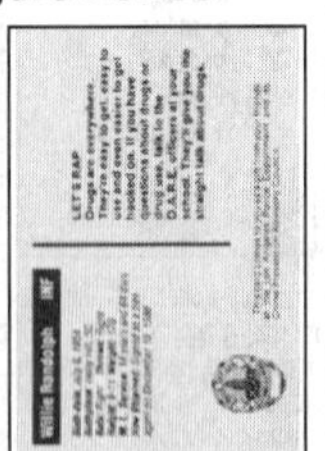

This 30-card set measures approximately 2 13/16" by 4 1/8" and was distributed by both the Los Angeles Police Department and at a pre-season Dodger-Angel exhibition game. This set also commemorated the 100th anniversary of the Dodgers existence. The front has a full-color photo of the player on the front while the back has a brief profile of the player with an anti-crime message. This set is checklisted below by uniform number.

	MINT	NRMT	EXC
COMPLETE SET (30)	6.00	2.70	.75
COMMON CARD	.25	.11	.03
☐ 1 Tommy Lasorda MG	1.00	.45	.12
☐ 3 Jeff Hamilton	.25	.11	.03
☐ 7 Alfredo Griffin	.25	.11	.03
☐ 8 Mickey Hatcher	.25	.11	.03
☐ 10 Juan Samuel	.25	.11	.03
☐ 12 Willie Randolph	.50	.23	.06
☐ 14 Mike Scioscia	.50	.23	.06
☐ 15 Chris Gwynn	.25	.11	.03
☐ 17 Rick Dempsey	.25	.11	.03
☐ 21 Hubie Brooks	.25	.11	.03
☐ 22 Franklin Stubbs	.25	.11	.03
☐ 23 Kirk Gibson	.75	.35	.09
☐ 27 Mike Sharperson	.25	.11	.03
☐ 28 Kal Daniels	.25	.11	.03
☐ 29 Lenny Harris	.25	.11	.03
☐ 31 John Shelby	.25	.11	.03
☐ 33 Eddie Murray	1.50	.70	.19
☐ 34 Fernando Valenzuela	.75	.35	.09
☐ 35 Jim Gott	.25	.11	.03
☐ 36 Mike Morgan	.25	.11	.03
☐ 38 Jose Gonzalez	.25	.11	.03
☐ 39 Jim Neidlinger	.25	.11	.03
☐ 46 Mike Hartley	.25	.11	.03
☐ 49 Tim Belcher	.25	.11	.03
☐ 50 Jay Howell	.25	.11	.03
☐ 52 Tim Crews	.25	.11	.03
☐ 55 Orel Hershiser	.50	.23	.06
☐ 57 John Wetteland	1.00	.45	.12
☐ 59 Ray Searage	.25	.11	.03
☐ NNO Coaches Card	.50	.23	.06
Ben Hines			
Ron Perranowski			
Mark Cresse			
Manny Mota			
Tommy Lasorda MG			
Joe Amalfitano			
Joe Ferguson			
Bill Russell			

1990 Dodgers Target

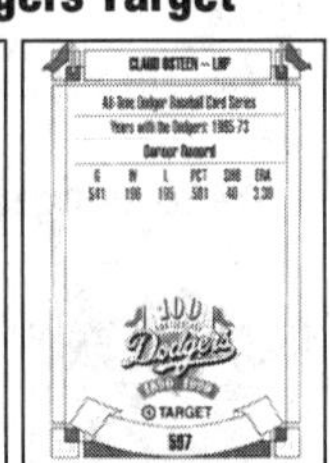

The 1990 Target Dodgers is one of the largest sets ever made. This (more than) 1000-card set features cards each measuring approximately 2" by 3" individually and was issued in large perforated sheets of 15 cards. Players in the set played at one time or another for one of the Dodgers franchises. As such many of the players in the set are older and relatively unknown to today's younger collectors. The set was apparently intended to be arranged in alphabetical order. There were several numbers not used (408, 458, 463, 792, 902, 907, 969, 996, 1031, 1054, 1061, and 1098) as well as a few instances of duplicated numbers.

	MINT	NRMT	EXC
COMPLETE SET (1106)	125.00	55.00	15.50
COMMON CARD	.10	.05	.01
☐ 1 Bert Abbey	.10	.05	.01
☐ 2 Cal Abrams	.10	.05	.01
☐ 3 Hank Aguirre	.10	.05	.01
☐ 4 Eddie Ainsmith	.10	.05	.01
☐ 5 Ed Albosta	.10	.05	.01
☐ 6 Luis Alcaraz	.10	.05	.01
☐ 7 Doyle Alexander	.15	.07	.02
☐ 8 Dick Allen	.50	.23	.06
☐ 9 Frank Allen	.10	.05	.01
☐ 10 Johnny Allen	.15	.07	.02
☐ 11 Mel Almada	.10	.05	.01
☐ 12 Walt Alston	1.00	.45	.12
☐ 13 Ed Amelung	.10	.05	.01
☐ 14 Sandy Amoros	.20	.09	.03
☐ 15 Dave Anderson	.10	.05	.01
☐ 16 Ferrell Anderson	.10	.05	.01
☐ 17 John Anderson	.10	.05	.01
☐ 18 Stan Andrews	.10	.05	.01
☐ 19 Bill Antonello	.10	.05	.01
☐ 20 Jimmy Archer	.15	.07	.02
☐ 21 Bob Aspromonte	.10	.05	.01
☐ 22 Rick Auerbach	.10	.05	.01
☐ 23 Charlie Babb	.10	.05	.01
☐ 24 Johnny Babich	.10	.05	.01
☐ 25 Bob Bailey	.10	.05	.01
☐ 26 Bob Bailor	.10	.05	.01
☐ 27 Dusty Baker	.50	.23	.06
☐ 28 Tom Baker	.10	.05	.01
☐ 29 Dave Bancroft	.50	.23	.06
☐ 30 Dan Bankhead	.10	.05	.01
☐ 31 Jack Banta	.10	.05	.01
☐ 32 Jim Barbieri	.10	.05	.01
☐ 33 Red Barkley	.10	.05	.01
☐ 34 Jesse Barnes	.10	.05	.01
☐ 35 Rex Barney	.15	.07	.02
☐ 36 Billy Barnie	.10	.05	.01
☐ 37 Bob Barrett	.10	.05	.01
☐ 38 Jim Baxes	.10	.05	.01
☐ 39 Billy Bean	.10	.05	.01
☐ 40 BoomBoom Beck	.10	.05	.01
☐ 41 Joe Beckwith	.10	.05	.01
☐ 42 Hank Behrman	.10	.05	.01
☐ 43 Mark Belanger	.20	.09	.03
☐ 44 Wayne Belardi	.10	.05	.01
☐ 45 Tim Belcher	.10	.05	.01
☐ 46 George Bell	.10	.05	.01
☐ 47 Ray Benge	.10	.05	.01
☐ 48 Moe Berg	2.00	.90	.25
☐ 49 Bill Bergen	.10	.05	.01
☐ 50 Ray Berres	.10	.05	.01
☐ 51 Don Bessent	.10	.05	.01
☐ 52 Steve Bilko	.10	.05	.01
☐ 53 Jack Billingham	.10	.05	.01
☐ 54 Babe Birrer	.10	.05	.01
☐ 55 Del Bissonette	.10	.05	.01
☐ 56 Joe Black	.20	.09	.03
☐ 57 Lu Blue	.10	.05	.01
☐ 58 George Boehler	.10	.05	.01
☐ 59 Sammy Bohne	.10	.05	.01
☐ 60 John Bolling	.10	.05	.01
☐ 61 Ike Boone	.10	.05	.01
☐ 62 Frenchy Bordagaray	.10	.05	.01
☐ 63 Ken Boyer	.35	.16	.04
☐ 64 Buzz Boyle	.10	.05	.01
☐ 65 Mark Bradley	.10	.05	.01
☐ 66 Bobby Bragan	.15	.07	.02
☐ 67 Ralph Branca	.35	.16	.04
☐ 68 Ed Brandt	.10	.05	.01
☐ 69 Sid Bream	.10	.05	.01
☐ 70 Marv Breeding	.10	.05	.01
☐ 71 Tom Brennan	.10	.05	.01
☐ 72 William Brennan	.10	.05	.01
☐ 73 Rube Bressler	.10	.05	.01
☐ 74 Ken Brett	.10	.05	.01
☐ 75 Jim Brewer	.10	.05	.01
☐ 76 Tony Brewer	.10	.05	.01
☐ 77 Rocky Bridges	.10	.05	.01
☐ 78 Greg Brock	.10	.05	.01
☐ 79 Dan Brouthers	.50	.23	.06
☐ 80 Eddie Brown	.10	.05	.01
☐ 81 Elmer Brown	.10	.05	.01
☐ 82 Lindsay Brown	.10	.05	.01
☐ 83 Lloyd Brown	.10	.05	.01
☐ 84 Mace Brown	.10	.05	.01
☐ 85 Tommy Brown	.10	.05	.01
☐ 86 Pete Browning	.50	.23	.06
☐ 87 Ralph Bryant	.10	.05	.01
☐ 88 Jim Bucher	.10	.05	.01
☐ 89 Bill Buckner	.35	.16	.04
☐ 90 Jim Bunning	.50	.23	.06
☐ 91 Jack Burdock	.10	.05	.01
☐ 92 Glenn Burke	.10	.05	.01
☐ 93 Buster Burrell	.10	.05	.01
☐ 94 Larry Burright	.10	.05	.01
☐ 95 Doc Bushong	.10	.05	.01
☐ 96 Max Butcher	.10	.05	.01
☐ 97 Johnny Butler	.10	.05	.01
☐ 98 Enos Cabell	.10	.05	.01
☐ 99 Leon Cadore	.10	.05	.01
☐ 100 Bruce Caldwell	.10	.05	.01
☐ 101 Dick Calmus	.10	.05	.01
☐ 102 Dolf Camilli	.20	.09	.03
☐ 103 Doug Camilli	.10	.05	.01
☐ 104 Roy Campanella	5.00	2.20	.60
☐ 105 Al Campanis	.15	.07	.02
☐ 106 Jim Campanis	.10	.05	.01
☐ 107A Leo Callahan	.10	.05	.01
☐ 107B Gilly Campbell	.10	.05	.01
☐ 108 Jimmy Canavan	.10	.05	.01
☐ 109 Chris Cannizzaro	.10	.05	.01
☐ 110 Guy Cantrell	.10	.05	.01
☐ 111 Ben Cantwell	.10	.05	.01
☐ 112 Andy Carey	.10	.05	.01
☐ 113 Max Carey	.50	.23	.06
☐ 114 Tex Carleton	.10	.05	.01
☐ 115 Ownie Carroll	.10	.05	.01
☐ 116 Bob Caruthers	.15	.07	.02
☐ 117 Doc Casey	.10	.05	.01
☐ 118 Hugh Casey	.15	.07	.02
☐ 119 Bobby Castillo	.10	.05	.01
☐ 120 Cesar Cedeno	.20	.09	.03
☐ 121 Ron Cey	.35	.16	.04
☐ 122 Ed Chandler	.10	.05	.01
☐ 123 Ben Chapman	.20	.09	.03
☐ 124 Larry Cheney	.10	.05	.01
☐ 125 Bob Chipman	.10	.05	.01
☐ 126 Chuck Churn	.10	.05	.01
☐ 127 Gino Cimoli	.10	.05	.01
☐ 128 Moose Clabaugh	.10	.05	.01
☐ 129 Bud Clancy	.10	.05	.01
☐ 130 Bob Clark	.10	.05	.01
☐ 131 Watty Clark	.10	.05	.01
☐ 132 Alta Cohen	.10	.05	.01
☐ 133 Rocky Colavito	1.00	.45	.12
☐ 134 Jackie Collum	.10	.05	.01
☐ 135 Chuck Connors	1.50	.70	.19
☐ 136 Jack Coombs	.35	.16	.04
☐ 137 Johnny Cooney	.10	.05	.01
☐ 138 Tommy Corcoran	.10	.05	.01
☐ 139 Pop Corkhill	.10	.05	.01
☐ 140 John Corriden	.10	.05	.01
☐ 141 Pete Coscarart	.10	.05	.01
☐ 142 Wes Covington	.10	.05	.01
☐ 143 Billy Cox	.20	.09	.03
☐ 144 Roger Craig	.20	.09	.03
☐ 146 Willie Crawford	.10	.05	.01
☐ 147 Tim Crews	.10	.05	.01

☐ 148 John Cronin	.10	.05	.01
☐ 149 Lave Cross	.10	.05	.01
☐ 150 Bill Crouch	.10	.05	.01
☐ 151 Don Crow	.10	.05	.01
☐ 152 Henry Cruz	.10	.05	.01
☐ 153 Tony Cuccinello	.10	.05	.01
☐ 154 Roy Cullenbine	.10	.05	.01
☐ 155 George Culver	.10	.05	.01
☐ 156 Nick Cullop	.10	.05	.01
☐ 157 George Cutshaw	.10	.05	.01
☐ 158 Kiki Cuyler	.50	.23	.06
☐ 159 Bill Dahlen	.20	.09	.03
☐ 160 Babe Dahlgren	.20	.09	.03
☐ 161 Jack Dalton	.10	.05	.01
☐ 162 Tom Daly	.10	.05	.01
☐ 163 Cliff Dapper	.10	.05	.01
☐ 164 Bob Darnell	.10	.05	.01
☐ 165 Bobby Darwin	.10	.05	.01
☐ 166 Jake Daubert	.15	.07	.02
☐ 167 Vic Davalillo	.15	.07	.02
☐ 168 Curt Davis	.10	.05	.01
☐ 169 Mike Davis	.10	.05	.01
☐ 170 Ron Davis	.10	.05	.01
☐ 171 Tommy Davis	.35	.16	.04
☐ 172 Willie Davis	.20	.09	.03
☐ 173 Pea Ridge Day	.10	.05	.01
☐ 174 Tommy Dean	.10	.05	.01
☐ 175 Hank DeBerry	.10	.05	.01
☐ 176 Art Decatur	.10	.05	.01
☐ 177 Raoul(Rod) Dedeaux	1.00	.45	.12
☐ 178 Ivan DeJesus	.10	.05	.01
☐ 179 Don Demeter	.10	.05	.01
☐ 180 Gene DeMontreville	.10	.05	.01
☐ 181 Rick Dempsey	.15	.07	.02
☐ 182 Eddie Dent	.10	.05	.01
☐ 183 Mike Devereaux	.15	.07	.02
☐ 184 Carlos Diaz	.10	.05	.01
☐ 185 Dick Dietz	.10	.05	.01
☐ 186 Pop Dillon	.10	.05	.01
☐ 187 Bill Doak	.10	.05	.01
☐ 188 John Dobbs	.10	.05	.01
☐ 189 George Dockins	.10	.05	.01
☐ 190 Cozy Dolan	.10	.05	.01
☐ 191 Patsy Donovan	.10	.05	.01
☐ 192 Wild Bill Donovan	.10	.05	.01
☐ 193 Mickey Doolan	.10	.05	.01
☐ 194 Jack Doscher	.10	.05	.01
☐ 195 Phil Douglas	.10	.05	.01
☐ 196 Snooks Dowd	.10	.05	.01
☐ 197 Al Downing	.15	.07	.02
☐ 198 Red Downs	.10	.05	.01
☐ 199 Jack Doyle	.10	.05	.01
☐ 200 Solly Drake	.10	.05	.01
☐ 201 Tom Drake	.10	.05	.01
☐ 202 Chuck Dressen	.15	.07	.02
☐ 203 Don Drysdale	2.50	1.10	.30
☐ 204 Clise Dudley	.10	.05	.01
☐ 205 Mariano Duncan	.20	.09	.03
☐ 206 Jack Dunn	.10	.05	.01
☐ 207 Bull Durham	.15	.07	.02
☐ 208 Leo Durocher	1.00	.45	.12
☐ 209 Billy Earle	.10	.05	.01
☐ 210 George Earnshaw	.15	.07	.02
☐ 211 Ox Eckhardt	.10	.05	.01
☐ 212 Bruce Edwards	.10	.05	.01
☐ 213 Hank Edwards	.10	.05	.01
☐ 214 Dick W. Egan	.10	.05	.01
☐ 215 Harry Eisenstat	.10	.05	.01
☐ 216 Kid Elberfeld	.10	.05	.01
☐ 217 Jumbo Elliot	.10	.05	.01
☐ 218 Don Elston	.10	.05	.01
☐ 219 Gil English	.10	.05	.01
☐ 220 Johnny Enzmann	.10	.05	.01
☐ 221 Al Epperly	.10	.05	.01
☐ 222 Carl Erskine	.25	.11	.03
☐ 223 Tex Erwin	.10	.05	.01
☐ 224 Cecil Espy	.10	.05	.01
☐ 225 Chuck Essegian	.10	.05	.01
☐ 226 Dude Esterbrook	.10	.05	.01
☐ 227 Red Evans	.10	.05	.01
☐ 228 Bunny Fabrique	.10	.05	.01
☐ 229 Jim Fairey	.10	.05	.01
☐ 230 Ron Fairly	.20	.09	.03
☐ 231 George Fallon	.10	.05	.01
☐ 232 Turk Farrell	.15	.07	.02
☐ 233 Duke Farrel	.10	.05	.01
☐ 234 Jim Faulkner	.10	.05	.01
☐ 235 Alex Ferguson	.10	.05	.01
☐ 236 Joe Ferguson	.10	.05	.01
☐ 237 Chico Fernandez	.10	.05	.01
☐ 238 Sid Fernandez	.25	.11	.03
☐ 239 Al Ferrara	.10	.05	.01
☐ 240 Wes Ferrell	.20	.09	.03
☐ 241 Lou Fette	.10	.05	.01
☐ 242 Chick Fewster	.10	.05	.01
☐ 243 Jack Fimple	.10	.05	.01
☐ 244 Neal Mickey Finn	.10	.05	.01
☐ 245 Bob Fisher	.10	.05	.01
☐ 246 Freddie Fitzsimmons	.15	.07	.02
☐ 247 Tim Flood	.10	.05	.01
☐ 248 Jake Flowers	.10	.05	.01
☐ 249 Hod Ford	.10	.05	.01
☐ 250 Terry Forster	.15	.07	.02
☐ 251 Alan Foster	.10	.05	.01
☐ 252 Jack Fournier	.10	.05	.01
☐ 253 Dave Foutz	.10	.05	.01
☐ 254 Art Fowler	.10	.05	.01
☐ 255 Fred Frankhouse	.10	.05	.01
☐ 256 Herman Franks	.10	.05	.01
☐ 257 Johnny Frederick	.10	.05	.01
☐ 258 Larry French	.10	.05	.01
☐ 259 Lonny Frey	.10	.05	.01
☐ 260 Pepe Frias	.10	.05	.01
☐ 261 Charlie Fuchs	.10	.05	.01
☐ 262 Carl Furillo	.25	.11	.03
☐ 263 Len Gabrielson	.10	.05	.01
☐ 264 Augie Galan	.10	.05	.01
☐ 265 Joe Gallagher	.10	.05	.01
☐ 266 Phil Gallivan	.10	.05	.01
☐ 267 Balvino Galvez	.10	.05	.01
☐ 268 Mike Garman	.10	.05	.01
☐ 269 Phil Garner	.20	.09	.03
☐ 270 Steve Garvey	1.00	.45	.12
☐ 271 Ned Garvin	.10	.05	.01
☐ 272 Hank Gastright	.10	.05	.01
☐ 273 Sid Gautreaux	.10	.05	.01
☐ 274 Jim Gentile	.15	.07	.02
☐ 275 Greek George	.10	.05	.01
☐ 276 Ben Geraghty	.10	.05	.01
☐ 277 Gus Getz	.10	.05	.01
☐ 278 Bob Giallombardo	.10	.05	.01
☐ 279 Kirk Gibson	.35	.16	.04
☐ 280 Charlie Gilbert	.10	.05	.01
☐ 281 Jim Gilliam	.20	.09	.03
☐ 282 Al Gionfriddo	.15	.07	.02
☐ 283 Tony Giuliani	.10	.05	.01
☐ 284 Al Glossop	.10	.05	.01
☐ 285 John Gochnaur	.10	.05	.01
☐ 286 Jim Golden	.10	.05	.01
☐ 287 Dave Goltz	.10	.05	.01
☐ 288 Jose Gonzalez	.10	.05	.01
☐ 289 Johnny Gooch	.10	.05	.01
☐ 290 Ed Goodson	.10	.05	.01
☐ 291 Billy Grabarkewitz	.10	.05	.01
☐ 292 Jack Graham	.10	.05	.01
☐ 293 Mudcat Grant	.15	.07	.02
☐ 294 Dick Gray	.10	.05	.01
☐ 295 Kent Greenfield	.10	.05	.01
☐ 296 Hal Gregg	.10	.05	.01
☐ 297 Alfredo Griffin	.10	.05	.01
☐ 298 Mike Griffin	.10	.05	.01
☐ 299 Derrell Griffith	.10	.05	.01
☐ 300 Tommy Griffith	.10	.05	.01
☐ 301 Burleigh Grimes	.50	.23	.06
☐ 302 Lee Grissom	.10	.05	.01
☐ 303 Jerry Grote	.15	.07	.02
☐ 304 Pedro Guerrero	.25	.11	.03
☐ 305 Brad Gulden	.10	.05	.01
☐ 306 Ad Gumbert	.10	.05	.01
☐ 307 Chris Gwynn	.10	.05	.01
☐ 308 Bert Haas	.10	.05	.01
☐ 309 John Hale	.10	.05	.01
☐ 310 Tom Haller	.15	.07	.02
☐ 311 Bill Hallman	.10	.05	.01
☐ 312 Jeff Hamilton	.10	.05	.01
☐ 313 Luke Hamlin	.10	.05	.01
☐ 314 Ned Hanlon	.50	.23	.06
☐ 315 Gerald Hannahs	.10	.05	.01
☐ 316 Charlie Hargreaves	.10	.05	.01
☐ 317 Tim Harkness	.10	.05	.01
☐ 318 Harry Harper	.10	.05	.01
☐ 319 Joe Harris	.10	.05	.01
☐ 320 Lenny Harris	.10	.05	.01
☐ 321 Bill F. Hart	.10	.05	.01
☐ 322 Buddy Hassett	.10	.05	.01
☐ 323 Mickey Hatcher	.10	.05	.01
☐ 324 Joe Hatten	.10	.05	.01
☐ 325 Phil Haugstad	.10	.05	.01
☐ 326 Brad Havens	.10	.05	.01
☐ 327 Ray Hayworth	.10	.05	.01
☐ 328 Ed Head	.10	.05	.01
☐ 329 Danny Heep	.10	.05	.01
☐ 330 Fred Heimach	.10	.05	.01
☐ 331 Harvey Hendrick	.10	.05	.01
☐ 332 Weldon Henley	.10	.05	.01
☐ 333 Butch Henline	.10	.05	.01
☐ 334 Dutch Henry	.10	.05	.01
☐ 335 Roy Henshaw	.10	.05	.01
☐ 336 Babe Herman	.20	.09	.03
☐ 337 Billy Herman	.50	.23	.06
☐ 338 Gene Hermanski	.10	.05	.01
☐ 339 Enzo Hernandez	.10	.05	.01
☐ 340 Art Herring	.10	.05	.01
☐ 341 Orel Hershiser	.75	.35	.09
☐ 342 Dave J. Hickman	.10	.05	.01
☐ 343 Jim Hickman	.10	.05	.01
☐ 344 Kirby Higbe	.15	.07	.02
☐ 345 Andy High	.10	.05	.01
☐ 346 George Hildebrand	.10	.05	.01
☐ 347 Hunkey Hines	.10	.05	.01
☐ 348 Don Hoak	.15	.07	.02
☐ 349 Oris Hockett	.10	.05	.01
☐ 350 Gil Hodges	2.50	1.10	.30
☐ 351 Glenn Hoffman	.10	.05	.01
☐ 352 Al Hollingsworth	.10	.05	.01
☐ 353 Tommy Holmes	.20	.09	.03
☐ 354 Brian Holton	.10	.05	.01
☐ 355 Rick Honeycutt	.10	.05	.01
☐ 356 Burt Hooton	.15	.07	.02
☐ 357 Gail Hopkins	.10	.05	.01
☐ 358 Johnny Hopp	.10	.05	.01
☐ 359 Charlie Hough	.25	.11	.03
☐ 360 Frank Howard	.35	.16	.04
☐ 361 Steve Howe	.10	.05	.01
☐ 362 Dixie Howell	.10	.05	.01
☐ 363 Harry Howell	.10	.05	.01
☐ 364 Jay Howell	.15	.07	.02
☐ 365 Ken Howell	.10	.05	.01
☐ 366 Waite Hoyt	.50	.23	.06
☐ 367 Johnny Hudson	.10	.05	.01
☐ 368 Jim J. Hughes	.10	.05	.01
☐ 369 Jim R. Hughes	.10	.05	.01
☐ 370 Mickey Hughes	.10	.05	.01
☐ 371 John Hummel	.10	.05	.01
☐ 372 Ron Hunt	.10	.05	.01
☐ 373 Willard Hunter	.10	.05	.01
☐ 374 Ira Hutchinson	.10	.05	.01
☐ 375 Tom Hutton	.10	.05	.01
☐ 376 Charlie Irwin	.10	.05	.01
☐ 377 Fred Jacklitsch	.10	.05	.01
☐ 378 Randy Jackson	.10	.05	.01
☐ 379 Merwin Jacobson	.10	.05	.01
☐ 380 Cleo James	.10	.05	.01
☐ 381 Hal Janvrin	.10	.05	.01
☐ 382 Roy Jarvis	.10	.05	.01
☐ 383 George Jeffcoat	.10	.05	.01
☐ 384 Jack Jenkins	.10	.05	.01
☐ 385 Hughie Jennings	.50	.23	.06
☐ 386 Tommy John	.50	.23	.06
☐ 387 Lou Johnson	.15	.07	.02
☐ 388 Fred Ivy Johnston	.10	.05	.01
☐ 389 Jimmy Johnston	.10	.05	.01
☐ 390 Jay Johnstone	.25	.11	.03
☐ 391 Fielder Jones	.10	.05	.01
☐ 392 Oscar Jones	.10	.05	.01
☐ 393 Tim Jordan	.10	.05	.01
☐ 394 Spider Jorgensen	.10	.05	.01
☐ 395 Von Joshua	.10	.05	.01
☐ 396 Bill Joyce	.10	.05	.01
☐ 397 Joe Judge	.15	.07	.02
☐ 398 Alex Kampouris	.10	.05	.01
☐ 399 Willie Keeler	.50	.23	.06
☐ 400 Mike Kekich	.10	.05	.01
☐ 401 John Kelleher	.10	.05	.01
☐ 402 Frank Kellert	.10	.05	.01
☐ 403 Joe Kelley	.50	.23	.06
☐ 404 George Kelly	.50	.23	.06
☐ 405 Bob Kennedy	.10	.05	.01
☐ 406 Brickyard Kennedy	.10	.05	.01
☐ 407 John Kennedy	.10	.05	.01
☐ 408 Not issued			
☐ 409 Newt Kimball	.10	.05	.01
☐ 410 Clyde King	.10	.05	.01
☐ 411 Enos Kirkpatrick	.10	.05	.01
☐ 412 Frank Kitson	.10	.05	.01
☐ 413 Johnny Klippstein	.10	.05	.01
☐ 414 Elmer Klumpp	.10	.05	.01
☐ 415 Len Koenecke	.10	.05	.01
☐ 416 Ed Konetchy	.10	.05	.01
☐ 417 Andy Kosco	.10	.05	.01
☐ 418 Sandy Koufax	7.50	3.40	.95
☐ 419 Ernie Koy	.15	.07	.02
☐ 420 Charlie Kress	.10	.05	.01
☐ 421 Bill Krueger	.10	.05	.01
☐ 422 Ernie Krueger	.10	.05	.01
☐ 423 Clem Labine	.20	.09	.03
☐ 424 Candy LaChance	.10	.05	.01
☐ 425 Lee Lacy	.10	.05	.01
☐ 426 Lerrin LaGrow	.10	.05	.01
☐ 427 Bill Lamar	.10	.05	.01
☐ 428 Wayne LaMaster	.10	.05	.01
☐ 429 Ray Lamb	.10	.05	.01
☐ 430 Rafael Landestoy	.10	.05	.01
☐ 431 Ken Landreaux	.10	.05	.01
☐ 432 Tito Landrum	.10	.05	.01
☐ 433 Norm Larker	.10	.05	.01
☐ 434 Lyn Lary	.10	.05	.01
☐ 435 Tom Lasorda	2.00	.90	.25
☐ 436 Cookie Lavagetto	.20	.09	.03
☐ 437 Rudy Law	.10	.05	.01
☐ 438 Tony Lazzeri	.75	.35	.09
☐ 439 Tim Leary	.10	.05	.01
☐ 440 Bob Lee	.10	.05	.01
☐ 441 Hal Lee	.10	.05	.01
☐ 442 Leron Lee	.10	.05	.01
☐ 443 Jim Lefebvre	.15	.07	.02
☐ 444 Ken Lehman	.10	.05	.01
☐ 445 Don LeJohn	.10	.05	.01
☐ 446 Steve Lembo	.10	.05	.01
☐ 447 Ed Lennox	.10	.05	.01
☐ 448 Dutch Leonard	.20	.09	.03
☐ 449 Jeffrey Leonard	.15	.07	.02
☐ 451 Dennis Lewallyn	.10	.05	.01
☐ 452 Bob Lillis	.10	.05	.01
☐ 453 Jim Lindsey	.10	.05	.01
☐ 454 Fred Lindstrom	.50	.23	.06
☐ 455 Billy Loes	.15	.07	.02
☐ 456 Bob Logan	.10	.05	.01
☐ 457 Bill Lohrman	.10	.05	.01
☐ 458 Not issued			
☐ 459 Vic Lombardi	.10	.05	.01
☐ 460 Davey Lopes	.25	.11	.03
☐ 461 Al Lopez	.50	.23	.06
☐ 462 Ray Lucas	.10	.05	.01
☐ 463 Not issued			
☐ 464 Harry Lumley	.10	.05	.01
☐ 465 Don Lund	.10	.05	.01
☐ 466 Dolf Luque	.25	.11	.03
☐ 467 Jim Lyttle	.10	.05	.01
☐ 468 Max Macon	.10	.05	.01
☐ 469 Bill Madlock	.20	.09	.03
☐ 470 Lee Magee	.10	.05	.01
☐ 471 Sal Maglie	.35	.16	.04
☐ 472 George Magoon	.10	.05	.01
☐ 473 Duster Mails	.10	.05	.01
☐ 474 Candy Maldonado	.10	.05	.01
☐ 475 Tony Malinosky	.10	.05	.01
☐ 476 Lew Malone	.10	.05	.01
☐ 477 Al Mamaux	.10	.05	.01
☐ 478 Gus Mancuso	.10	.05	.01
☐ 479 Charlie Manuel	.10	.05	.01
☐ 480 Heinie Manush	.50	.23	.06
☐ 481 Rabbit Maranville	.50	.23	.06
☐ 482 Juan Marichal	1.00	.45	.12
☐ 483 Rube Marquard	.50	.23	.06
☐ 484 Bill Marriott	.10	.05	.01
☐ 485 Buck Marrow	.10	.05	.01
☐ 486 Mike A. Marshall	.20	.09	.03
☐ 487 Mike G. Marshall	.20	.09	.03
☐ 488 Morrie Martin	.10	.05	.01
☐ 489 Ramon Martinez	.75	.35	.09
☐ 490 Teddy Martinez	.10	.05	.01
☐ 491 Earl Mattingly	.10	.05	.01
☐ 492 Len Matuszek	.10	.05	.01
☐ 493 Gene Mauch	.15	.07	.02
☐ 494 Al Maul	.10	.05	.01
☐ 495 Carmen Mauro	.10	.05	.01
☐ 496 Alvin McBean	.10	.05	.01
☐ 497 Bill McCarren	.10	.05	.01
☐ 498 Jack McCarthy	.10	.05	.01
☐ 499 Tommy McCarthy	.50	.23	.06
☐ 500 Lew McCarty	.10	.05	.01
☐ 501 Mike J. McCormick	.10	.05	.01
☐ 502 Judge McCreedie	.10	.05	.01
☐ 503 Tom McCreery	.10	.05	.01
☐ 504 Danny McDevitt	.10	.05	.01
☐ 505 Chappie McFarland	.10	.05	.01
☐ 506 Joe McGinnity	.50	.23	.06
☐ 507 Bob McGraw	.10	.05	.01
☐ 508 Deacon McGuire	.10	.05	.01
☐ 509 Bill McGunnigle	.10	.05	.01
☐ 510 Harry McIntire	.10	.05	.01
☐ 511 Cal McLish	.10	.05	.01
☐ 512 Ken McMullen	.10	.05	.01
☐ 513 Doug McWeeny	.10	.05	.01
☐ 514 Joe Medwick	.50	.23	.06
☐ 515 Rube Melton	.10	.05	.01
☐ 516 Fred Merkle	.20	.09	.03
☐ 517 Orlando Mercado	.10	.05	.01
☐ 518 Andy Messersmith	.15	.07	.02
☐ 519 Irish Meusel	.10	.05	.01
☐ 520 Benny Meyer	.10	.05	.01
☐ 521 Russ Meyer	.10	.05	.01
☐ 522 Chief Meyers	.15	.07	.02
☐ 523 Gene Michael	.15	.07	.02
☐ 524 Pete Mikkelsen	.10	.05	.01
☐ 525 Eddie Miksis	.10	.05	.01
☐ 526 Johnny Miljus	.10	.05	.01
☐ 527 Bob Miller	.10	.05	.01
☐ 528 Larry Miller Wearing a N.Y. Mets uniform	.10	.05	.01
☐ 529 Otto Miller	.10	.05	.01
☐ 530 Ralph Miller	.10	.05	.01
☐ 531 Walt Miller	.10	.05	.01
☐ 532 Wally Millies	.10	.05	.01
☐ 533 Bob Milliken	.10	.05	.01
☐ 534 Buster Mills	.10	.05	.01
☐ 535 Paul Minner	.10	.05	.01
☐ 536 Bobby Mitchell	.10	.05	.01
☐ 537 Clarence Mitchell	.10	.05	.01
☐ 538 Dale Mitchell	.15	.07	.02
☐ 539 Fred Mitchell	.10	.05	.01
☐ 540 Johnny Mitchell	.10	.05	.01
☐ 541 Joe Moeller	.10	.05	.01
☐ 542 Rick Monday	.15	.07	.02
☐ 543 Wally Moon	.15	.07	.02
☐ 544 Cy Moore	.10	.05	.01
☐ 545 Dee Moore	.10	.05	.01
☐ 546 Eddie Moore	.10	.05	.01
☐ 547 Gene Moore	.10	.05	.01
☐ 548 Randy Moore	.10	.05	.01
☐ 549 Ray Moore	.10	.05	.01
☐ 550 Jose Morales	.10	.05	.01
☐ 551 Bobby Morgan	.10	.05	.01
☐ 552 Eddie Morgan	.10	.05	.01
☐ 553 Mike Morgan	.10	.05	.01
☐ 554 Johnny Morrison	.10	.05	.01
☐ 555 Walt Moryn	.10	.05	.01
☐ 556 Ray Moss	.10	.05	.01
☐ 557 Manny Mota	.15	.07	.02
☐ 558 Joe Mulvey	.10	.05	.01
☐ 559 Van Lingle Mungo	.15	.07	.02
☐ 560 Les Munns	.10	.05	.01
☐ 561 Mike Munoz	.10	.05	.01
☐ 562 Simmy Murch	.10	.05	.01
☐ 563 Eddie Murray	1.50	.70	.19
☐ 564 Hy Myers	.10	.05	.01
☐ 565 Sam Nahem	.10	.05	.01
☐ 566 Earl Naylor	.10	.05	.01
☐ 567 Charlie Neal	.15	.07	.02

☐ 568 Ron Negray	.10	.05	.01
☐ 569 Bernie Neis	.10	.05	.01
☐ 570 Rocky Nelson	.10	.05	.01
☐ 571 Dick Nen	.10	.05	.01
☐ 572 Don Newcombe	.50	.23	.06
☐ 573 Bobo Newsom	.15	.07	.02
☐ 574 Doc Newton	.10	.05	.01
☐ 575 Tom Niedenfuer	.10	.05	.01
☐ 576 Otho Nitcholas	.10	.05	.01
☐ 577 Al Nixon	.10	.05	.01
☐ 578 Jerry Nops	.10	.05	.01
☐ 579 Irv Noren	.10	.05	.01
☐ 580 Fred Norman	.10	.05	.01
☐ 581 Bill North	.10	.05	.01
☐ 582 Johnny Oates	.25	.11	.03
☐ 583 Bob O'Brien	.10	.05	.01
☐ 584 John O'Brien	.10	.05	.01
☐ 585 Lefty O'Doul	.20	.09	.03
☐ 586 Joe Oeschger	.10	.05	.01
☐ 587 Al Oliver	.25	.11	.03
☐ 588 Nate Oliver	.10	.05	.01
☐ 589 Luis Olmo	.10	.05	.01
☐ 590 Ivy Olson	.10	.05	.01
☐ 591 Mickey O'Neil	.10	.05	.01
☐ 592 Joe Orengo	.10	.05	.01
☐ 593 Jesse Orosco	.10	.05	.01
☐ 594 Frank O'Rourke	.10	.05	.01
☐ 595 Jorge Orta	.10	.05	.01
☐ 596 Phil Ortega	.10	.05	.01
☐ 597 Claude Osteen	.15	.07	.02
☐ 598 Fritz Ostermueller	.10	.05	.01
☐ 599 Mickey Owen	.15	.07	.02
☐ 600 Tom Paciorek	.20	.09	.03
☐ 601 Don Padgett	.10	.05	.01
☐ 602 Andy Pafko	.15	.07	.02
☐ 603 Erv Palica	.10	.05	.01
☐ 604 Ed Palmquist	.10	.05	.01
☐ 605 Wes Parker	.20	.09	.03
☐ 606 Jay Partridge	.10	.05	.01
☐ 607 Camilo Pascual	.15	.07	.02
☐ 608 Kevin Pasley	.10	.05	.01
☐ 609 Dave Patterson	.10	.05	.01
☐ 610 Harley Payne	.10	.05	.01
☐ 611 Johnny Peacock	.10	.05	.01
☐ 612 Hal Peck	.10	.05	.01
☐ 613 Stu Pederson	.10	.05	.01
☐ 614 Alejandro Pena	.10	.05	.01
☐ 615 Jose Pena	.10	.05	.01
☐ 616 Jack Perconte	.10	.05	.01
☐ 617 Charlie Perkins	.10	.05	.01
☐ 618 Ron Perranoski	.15	.07	.02
☐ 619 Jim Peterson	.10	.05	.01
☐ 620 Jesse Petty	.10	.05	.01
☐ 621 Jeff Pfeffer	.10	.05	.01
☐ 622 Babe Phelps	.10	.05	.01
☐ 623 Val Picinich	.10	.05	.01
☐ 624 Joe Pignatano	.10	.05	.01
☐ 625 George Pinkney	.10	.05	.01
☐ 626 Ed Pipgras	.10	.05	.01
☐ 627 Bud Podbielan	.10	.05	.01
☐ 628 Johnny Podres	.20	.09	.03
☐ 629 Boots Poffenberger	.10	.05	.01
☐ 630 Nick Polly	.10	.05	.01
☐ 631 Paul Popovich	.10	.05	.01
☐ 632 Bill Posedel	.10	.05	.01
☐ 633 Boog Powell	.35	.16	.04
☐ 634 Dennis Powell	.10	.05	.01
☐ 635 Paul Ray Powell	.10	.05	.01
☐ 636 Ted Power	.10	.05	.01
☐ 637 Tot Pressnell	.10	.05	.01
☐ 638 John Purdin	.10	.05	.01
☐ 639 Jack Quinn	.15	.07	.02
☐ 640 Marv Rackley	.10	.05	.01
☐ 641 Jack Radtke	.10	.05	.01
☐ 642 Pat Ragan	.10	.05	.01
☐ 643 Ed Rakow	.10	.05	.01
☐ 644 Bob Ramazzotti	.10	.05	.01
☐ 645 Willie Ramsdell	.10	.05	.01
☐ 646 Mike James Ramsey	.10	.05	.01
☐ 647 Mike Jeffery Ramsey	.10	.05	.01
☐ 648 Willie Randolph	.20	.09	.03
☐ 649 Doug Rau	.10	.05	.01
☐ 650 Lance Rautzhan	.10	.05	.01
☐ 651 Howie Reed	.10	.05	.01
☐ 652 Pee Wee Reese	3.00	1.35	.35
☐ 653 Phil Regan	.15	.07	.02
☐ 654 Bill Reidy	.10	.05	.01
☐ 655 Bobby Reis	.10	.05	.01
☐ 656 Pete Reiser	.35	.16	.04
☐ 657 Rip Repulski	.10	.05	.01
☐ 658 Ed Reulbach	.15	.07	.02
☐ 659 Jerry Reuss	.15	.07	.02
☐ 660 R.J. Reynolds	.10	.05	.01
☐ 661 Billy Rhiel	.10	.05	.01
☐ 662 Rick Rhoden	.10	.05	.01
☐ 663 Paul Richards	.15	.07	.02
☐ 664 Danny Richardson	.10	.05	.01
☐ 665 Pete Richert	.10	.05	.01
☐ 666 Harry Riconda	.10	.05	.01
☐ 667 Joe Riggert	.10	.05	.01
☐ 668 Lew Riggs	.10	.05	.01
☐ 669 Jimmy Ripple	.10	.05	.01
☐ 670 Lou Ritter	.10	.05	.01
☐ 671 German Rivera	.10	.05	.01
☐ 672 Johnny Rizzo	.10	.05	.01
☐ 673 Jim Roberts	.10	.05	.01
☐ 674 Earl Robinson	.10	.05	.01
☐ 675 Frank Robinson	3.00	1.35	.35
☐ 676 Jackie Robinson	7.50	3.40	.95
☐ 677A Wilbert Robinson	1.00	.45	.12
☐ 678 Rich Rodas	.10	.05	.01
☐ 678B Sergio Robles	.10	.05	.01
☐ 679 Ellie Rodriguez	.10	.05	.01
☐ 680 Preacher Roe	.25	.11	.03
☐ 681 Ed Roebuck	.15	.07	.02
☐ 682 Ron Hoenicke	.10	.05	.01
☐ 683 Oscar Roettger	.10	.05	.01
☐ 684 Lee Rogers	.10	.05	.01
☐ 685 Packy Rogers	.10	.05	.01
☐ 686 Stan Rojek	.10	.05	.01
☐ 687 Vicente Romo	.10	.05	.01
☐ 688 Johnny Roseboro	.15	.07	.02
☐ 689 Goody Rosen	.10	.05	.01
☐ 690 Don Ross	.10	.05	.01
☐ 691 Ken Rowe	.10	.05	.01
☐ 692 Schoolboy Rowe	.15	.07	.02
☐ 693 Luther Roy	.10	.05	.01
☐ 694 Jerry Royster	.10	.05	.01
☐ 695 Nap Rucker	.20	.09	.03
☐ 696 Dutch Ruether	.10	.05	.01
☐ 697 Bill Russell	.35	.16	.04
☐ 698 Jim Russell	.10	.05	.01
☐ 699 John Russell UER (Photo actually current catcher John Russell)	.10	.05	.01
☐ 700 Johnny Rutherford	.10	.05	.01
☐ 701 John Ryan	.10	.05	.01
☐ 702 Rosy Ryan	.10	.05	.01
☐ 703 Mike Sandlock	.10	.05	.01
☐ 704 Ted Savage	.10	.05	.01
☐ 705 Dave Sax	.10	.05	.01
☐ 706 Steve Sax	.25	.11	.03
☐ 707 Bill Sayles	.10	.05	.01
☐ 708 Bill Schardt	.10	.05	.01
☐ 709 Johnny Schmitz	.10	.05	.01
☐ 710 Dick Schofield	.10	.05	.01
☐ 711 Howie Schultz	.10	.05	.01
☐ 712 Ferdie Schupp	.10	.05	.01
☐ 713 Mike Scioscia	.20	.09	.03
☐ 714 Dick Scott	.10	.05	.01
☐ 715 Tom Seats	.10	.05	.01
☐ 716 Jimmy Sebring	.10	.05	.01
☐ 717 Larry See	.10	.05	.01
☐ 718 Dave Sells	.10	.05	.01
☐ 719 Greg Shanahan	.10	.05	.01
☐ 720 Mike Sharperson	.10	.05	.01
☐ 721 Joe Shaute	.10	.05	.01
☐ 722 Merv Shea	.10	.05	.01
☐ 723 Jimmy Sheckard	.10	.05	.01
☐ 724 Jack Sheehan	.10	.05	.01
☐ 725 John Shelby	.10	.05	.01
☐ 726 Vince Sherlock	.10	.05	.01
☐ 727 Larry Sherry	.20	.09	.03
☐ 728 Norm Sherry	.10	.05	.01
☐ 729 Bill Shindle	.10	.05	.01
☐ 730 Craig Shipley	.10	.05	.01
☐ 731 Bart Shirley	.10	.05	.01
☐ 732 Steve Shirley	.10	.05	.01
☐ 733 Burt Shotton	.15	.07	.02
☐ 734 George Shuba	.15	.07	.02
☐ 735 Dick Siebert	.10	.05	.01
☐ 736 Joe Simpson	.10	.05	.01
☐ 737 Duke Sims	.10	.05	.01
☐ 738 Bill Singer	.15	.07	.02
☐ 739 Fred Sington	.10	.05	.01
☐ 740 Ted Sizemore	.15	.07	.02
☐ 741 Frank Skaff	.10	.05	.01
☐ 742 Bill Skowron	.20	.09	.03
☐ 743 Gordon Slade	.10	.05	.01
☐ 744 Dwain Lefty Sloat	.10	.05	.01
☐ 745 Charley Smith	.10	.05	.01
☐ 746 Dick Smith (Wearing a N.Y Mets uniform)	.10	.05	.01
☐ 747 George Smith	.10	.05	.01
☐ 748 Germany Smith	.10	.05	.01
☐ 749 Jack Smith	.10	.05	.01
☐ 750 Reggie Smith	.25	.11	.03
☐ 751 Sherry Smith	.10	.05	.01
☐ 752 Harry Smythe	.10	.05	.01
☐ 753 Duke Snider	4.00	1.80	.50
☐ 754 Eddie Solomon	.10	.05	.01
☐ 755 Elias Sosa	.10	.05	.01
☐ 756 Daryl Spencer	.10	.05	.01
☐ 757 Roy Spencer	.10	.05	.01
☐ 758 Karl Spooner	.15	.07	.02
☐ 759 Eddie Stack	.10	.05	.01
☐ 760 Tuck Stainback	.10	.05	.01
☐ 761 George Stallings	.15	.07	.02
☐ 762 Jerry Standaert	.10	.05	.01
☐ 763 Don Stanhouse	.10	.05	.01
☐ 764 Eddie Stanky	.20	.09	.03
☐ 765 Dolly Stark	.15	.07	.02
☐ 766 Jigger Statz	.10	.05	.01
☐ 767 Casey Stengel	1.50	.70	.19
☐ 768 Jerry Stephenson	.10	.05	.01
☐ 769 Ed Stevens	.10	.05	.01
☐ 770 Dave Stewart	.25	.11	.03
☐ 771 Stuffy Stewart	.10	.05	.01
☐ 772 Bob Stinson	.10	.05	.01
☐ 773 Milt Stock	.10	.05	.01
☐ 774 Harry Stovey	.20	.09	.03
☐ 775 Mike Strahler	.10	.05	.01
☐ 776 Sammy Strang	.10	.05	.01
☐ 777 Elmer Stricklett	.10	.05	.01
☐ 778 Joe Stripp	.10	.05	.01
☐ 779 Dick Stuart (Wearing a N.Y. Mets uniform)	.20	.09	.03
☐ 780 Franklin Stubbs	.10	.05	.01
☐ 781 Bill Sudakis	.10	.05	.01
☐ 782 Clyde Sukeforth	.10	.05	.01
☐ 783 Billy Sullivan	.20	.09	.03
☐ 784 Tom Sunkel	.10	.05	.01
☐ 785 Rick Sutcliffe	.20	.09	.03
☐ 786 Don Sutton	1.00	.45	.12
☐ 787 Bill Swift	.10	.05	.01
☐ 788 Vito Tamulis	.10	.05	.01
☐ 789 Danny Taylor	.10	.05	.01
☐ 790 Harry Taylor	.10	.05	.01
☐ 791 Zack Taylor	.10	.05	.01
☐ 792 Not issued			
☐ 793 Chuck Templeton	.10	.05	.01
☐ 794 Wayne Terwilliger	.10	.05	.01
☐ 795 Derrel Thomas	.10	.05	.01
☐ 796 Fay Thomas	.10	.05	.01
☐ 797 Gary Thomasson	.10	.05	.01
☐ 798 Don Thompson	.10	.05	.01
☐ 799 Fresco Thompson	.20	.09	.03
☐ 800 Tim Thompson	.10	.05	.01
☐ 801 Hank Thormahlen	.10	.05	.01
☐ 802 Sloppy Thurston	.10	.05	.01
☐ 803 Cotton Tierney	.10	.05	.01
☐ 804 Al Todd	.10	.05	.01
☐ 805 Bert Tooley	.10	.05	.01
☐ 806 Jeff Torborg	.15	.07	.02
☐ 807 Dick Tracewski	.10	.05	.01
☐ 808 Nick Tremark	.10	.05	.01
☐ 809 Alex Trevino	.10	.05	.01
☐ 810 Tommy Tucker	.10	.05	.01
☐ 811 John Tudor	.10	.05	.01
☐ 812 Mike Vail	.10	.05	.01
☐ 813 Rene Valdes	.10	.05	.01
☐ 814 Bobby Valentine	.20	.09	.03
☐ 815 Fernando Valenzuela	.35	.16	.04
☐ 816 Elmer Valo	.10	.05	.01
☐ 817 Dazzy Vance	.50	.23	.06
☐ 818 Sandy Vance	.10	.05	.01
☐ 819 Chris Van Cuyk	.10	.05	.01
☐ 820 Ed VandeBerg	.10	.05	.01
☐ 821 Arky Vaughan	.50	.23	.06
☐ 822 Zoilo Versalles	.20	.09	.03
☐ 823 Joe Vosmik	.10	.05	.01
☐ 824 Ben Wade	.10	.05	.01
☐ 825 Dixie Walker	.20	.09	.03
☐ 826 Rube Walker	.10	.05	.01
☐ 827 Stan Wall	.10	.05	.01
☐ 828 Lee Walls	.10	.05	.01
☐ 829 Danny Walton	.10	.05	.01
☐ 830 Lloyd Waner	.50	.23	.06
☐ 831 Paul Waner	.50	.23	.06
☐ 832 Chuck Ward	.10	.05	.01
☐ 833 John Monte Ward	.50	.23	.06
☐ 834 Preston Ward	.10	.05	.01
☐ 835 Jack Warner	.10	.05	.01
☐ 836 Tommy Warren	.10	.05	.01
☐ 837 Carl Warwick	.10	.05	.01
☐ 838 Jimmy Wasdell	.10	.05	.01
☐ 839 Ron Washington	.10	.05	.01
☐ 840 George Watkins	.10	.05	.01
☐ 841 Hank Webb	.10	.05	.01
☐ 842 Les Webber	.10	.05	.01
☐ 843 Gary Weiss	.10	.05	.01
☐ 844 Bob Welch	.20	.09	.03
☐ 845 Brad Wellman	.10	.05	.01
☐ 846 John Werhas	.10	.05	.01
☐ 847 Max West	.10	.05	.01
☐ 848 Gus Weyhing	.10	.05	.01
☐ 849 Mack Wheat	.10	.05	.01
☐ 850 Zack Wheat	.50	.23	.06
☐ 851 Ed Wheeler	.10	.05	.01
☐ 852 Larry White	.10	.05	.01
☐ 853 Myron White	.10	.05	.01
☐ 854 Terry Whitfield	.10	.05	.01
☐ 855 Dick Whitman	.10	.05	.01
☐ 856 Possum Whitted	.10	.05	.01
☐ 857 Kemp Wicker	.10	.05	.01
☐ 858 Hoyt Wilhelm	.50	.23	.06
☐ 859 Kaiser Wilhelm	.10	.05	.01
☐ 860 Nick Willhite	.10	.05	.01
☐ 861 Dick Williams	.15	.07	.02
☐ 862 Reggie Williams	.10	.05	.01
☐ 863 Stan Williams	.15	.07	.02
☐ 864 Woody Williams	.10	.05	.01
☐ 865 Maury Wills	1.00	.45	.12
☐ 866 Hack Wilson	.75	.35	.09
☐ 867 Robert Wilson	.10	.05	.01
☐ 868 Gordon Windhorn	.10	.05	.01
☐ 869 Jim Winford	.10	.05	.01
☐ 870 Lave Winham	.10	.05	.01
☐ 871 Tom Winsett	.10	.05	.01
☐ 872 Hank Winston	.10	.05	.01
☐ 873 Whitey Witt	.10	.05	.01
☐ 874 Pete Wojey	.10	.05	.01
☐ 875 Tracy Woodson	.10	.05	.01
☐ 876 Clarence Wright	.10	.05	.01
☐ 877 Glenn Wright	.20	.09	.03
☐ 878 Ricky Wright	.10	.05	.01
☐ 879 Whit Wyatt	.20	.09	.03
☐ 880 Jimmy Wynn	.20	.09	.03
☐ 881 Joe Yeager	.10	.05	.01
☐ 882 Steve Yeager	.20	.09	.03
☐ 883 Matt Young	.10	.05	.01
☐ 884 Tom Zachary	.10	.05	.01
☐ 885 Pat Zachry	.10	.05	.01
☐ 886 Geoff Zahn	.10	.05	.01
☐ 887 Don Zimmer	.20	.09	.03
☐ 888 Morrie Aderholt	.10	.05	.01
☐ 889 Raleigh Aitchison	.10	.05	.01
☐ 890 Whitey Alperman	.10	.05	.01
☐ 891 Orlando Alvarez	.10	.05	.01
☐ 892 Pat Ankenman	.10	.05	.01
☐ 893 Ed Appleton	.10	.05	.01
☐ 894 Doug Baird	.10	.05	.01
☐ 895 Lady Baldwin	.10	.05	.01
☐ 896 Win Ballou	.10	.05	.01
☐ 897 Bob Barr	.10	.05	.01
☐ 898 Boyd Bartley	.10	.05	.01
☐ 899 Eddie Basinski	.10	.05	.01
☐ 900 Erve Beck	.10	.05	.01
☐ 901 Ralph Birkofer	.10	.05	.01
☐ 902 Not issued			
☐ 903 Joe Bradshaw	.10	.05	.01
☐ 904 Bruce Brubaker	.10	.05	.01
☐ 905 Oyster Burns	.10	.05	.01
☐ 906 John Butler	.10	.05	.01
☐ 907 Not issued			
☐ 908 Kid Carsey	.10	.05	.01
☐ 909 Pete Cassidy	.10	.05	.01
☐ 910 Tom Catterson	.10	.05	.01
☐ 911 Glenn Chapman	.10	.05	.01
☐ 912 Paul Chervinko	.10	.05	.01
☐ 913 George Cisar	.10	.05	.01
☐ 914 Wally Clement	.10	.05	.01
☐ 915 Bill Collins	.10	.05	.01
☐ 916 Chuck Corgan	.10	.05	.01
☐ 917 Dick Cox	.10	.05	.01
☐ 918 George Crable	.10	.05	.01
☐ 919 Sam Crane	.10	.05	.01
☐ 920 Cliff Curtis	.10	.05	.01
☐ 921 Fats Dantonio	.10	.05	.01
☐ 922 Con Daily	.10	.05	.01
☐ 923 Jud Daley	.10	.05	.01
☐ 924 Jake Daniel	.10	.05	.01
☐ 925 Kal Daniels	.10	.05	.01
☐ 926 Dan Daub	.10	.05	.01
☐ 927 Lindsay Deal	.10	.05	.01
☐ 928 Artie Dede	.10	.05	.01
☐ 929 Pat Deisel	.10	.05	.01
☐ 930 Bert Delmas	.10	.05	.01
☐ 931 Rube Dessau	.10	.05	.01
☐ 932 Leo Dickerman	.10	.05	.01
☐ 933 John Douglas	.10	.05	.01
☐ 934 Red Downey	.10	.05	.01
☐ 935 Carl Doyle	.10	.05	.01
☐ 936 John Duffie	.10	.05	.01
☐ 937 Dick Durning	.10	.05	.01
☐ 938 Red Durrett	.10	.05	.01
☐ 939 Mal Eason	.10	.05	.01
☐ 940 Charlie Ebbetts	.20	.09	.03
☐ 941 Rube Ehardt	.10	.05	.01
☐ 942 Rowdy Elliot	.10	.05	.01
☐ 943 Bones Ely	.10	.05	.01
☐ 944 Woody English	.15	.07	.02
☐ 945 Roy Evans	.10	.05	.01
☐ 946 Gus Felix	.10	.05	.01
☐ 947 Bill Fischer	.10	.05	.01
☐ 948 Jeff Fischer	.10	.05	.01
☐ 949 Chauncey Fisher	.10	.05	.01
☐ 950 Tom Fitzsimmons	.10	.05	.01
☐ 951 Darrin Fletcher	.10	.05	.01
☐ 952 Wes Flowers	.10	.05	.01
☐ 953 Howard Freigau	.10	.05	.01
☐ 954 Nig Fuller	.10	.05	.01
☐ 955 John Gaddy	.10	.05	.01
☐ 956 Welcome Gaston	.10	.05	.01
☐ 957 Frank Gatins	.10	.05	.01
☐ 958 Pete Gilbert	.10	.05	.01
☐ 959 Wally Gilbert	.10	.05	.01
☐ 960 Carden Gillenwater	.10	.05	.01
☐ 961 Roy Gleason	.10	.05	.01
☐ 962 Harvey Green	.10	.05	.01
☐ 963 Nelson Greene	.10	.05	.01
☐ 964 John Grim	.10	.05	.01
☐ 965 Dan Griner	.10	.05	.01
☐ 967 Bill Hall	.10	.05	.01
☐ 968 Johnny Hall	.10	.05	.01
☐ 969 Not issued			
☐ 970 Pat Hanifin	.10	.05	.01
☐ 971 Bill Harris	.10	.05	.01
☐ 972 Bill W. Hart	.10	.05	.01
☐ 973 Chris Hartje	.10	.05	.01
☐ 974 Mike Hartley	.10	.05	.01
☐ 975 Gil Hatfield	.10	.05	.01
☐ 976 Chris Haughey	.10	.05	.01
☐ 977 Hugh Hearne	.10	.05	.01
☐ 978 Mike Hechinger	.10	.05	.01
☐ 979 Jake Hehl	.10	.05	.01
☐ 980 Bob Higgins	.10	.05	.01
☐ 981 Still Bill Hill	.10	.05	.01
☐ 982 Shawn Hillegas	.10	.05	.01

	MINT	NRMT	EXC
☐ 983 Wally Hood	.10	.05	.01
☐ 984 Lefty Hopper	.10	.05	.01
☐ 985 Ricky Horton	.10	.05	.01
☐ 986 Ed Householder	.10	.05	.01
☐ 987 Bill Hubbell	.10	.05	.01
☐ 988 Al Humphrey	.10	.05	.01
☐ 989 Bernie Hungling	.10	.05	.01
☐ 990 George Hunter	.10	.05	.01
☐ 991 Pat Hurley	.10	.05	.01
☐ 992 Joe Hutcheson	.10	.05	.01
☐ 993 Roy Hutson	.10	.05	.01
☐ 994 Bert Inks	.10	.05	.01
☐ 995 Dutch Jordan	.10	.05	.01
☐ 996 Not issued			
☐ 997 Frank Kane	.10	.05	.01
☐ 998 Chet Kehn	.10	.05	.01
☐ 999 Maury Kent	.10	.05	.01
☐ 1000 Tom Kinslow	.10	.05	.01
☐ 1001 Fred Kipp	.10	.05	.01
☐ 1002 Joe Klugman	.10	.05	.01
☐ 1003 Elmer Knetzer	.10	.05	.01
☐ 1004 Barney Koch	.10	.05	.01
☐ 1005 Jim Korwan	.10	.05	.01
☐ 1006 Joe Koukalik	.10	.05	.01
☐ 1007 Lou Koupal	.10	.05	.01
☐ 1008 Joe Kustus	.10	.05	.01
☐ 1009 Frank Lamanske	.10	.05	.01
☐ 1010 Tacks Latimer	.10	.05	.01
☐ 1011 Bill Leard	.10	.05	.01
☐ 1012 Phil Lewis	.10	.05	.01
☐ 1013 Mickey Livingston	.10	.05	.01
☐ 1014 Dick Loftus	.10	.05	.01
☐ 1015 Charlie Loudenslager	.10	.05	.01
☐ 1016 Tom Lovett	.10	.05	.01
☐ 1017 Charlie Malay	.10	.05	.01
☐ 1018 Mal Mallette	.10	.05	.01
☐ 1019 Ralph Mauriello	.10	.05	.01
☐ 1020 Bill McCabe	.10	.05	.01
☐ 1021 Gene McCann	.10	.05	.01
☐ 1022 Mike W. McCormick	.10	.05	.01
☐ 1023 Terry McDermott	.10	.05	.01
☐ 1024 John McDougal	.10	.05	.01
☐ 1025 Pryor McElveen	.10	.05	.01
☐ 1026 Dan McGann	.10	.05	.01
☐ 1027 Pat McGlothin	.10	.05	.01
☐ 1028 Doc McJames	.10	.05	.01
☐ 1029 Kit McKenna	.10	.05	.01
☐ 1030 Sadie McMahon	.10	.05	.01
☐ 1031 Not issued			
☐ 1032 Tommy McMillan	.10	.05	.01
☐ 1033 Glenn Mickens	.10	.05	.01
☐ 1034 Don Miles	.10	.05	.01
☐ 1035 Hack Miller	.10	.05	.01
☐ 1036 John Miller	.10	.05	.01
☐ 1037 Lemmie Miller	.10	.05	.01
☐ 1038 George Mohart	.10	.05	.01
☐ 1039 Gary Moore	.10	.05	.01
☐ 1040 Herbie Moran	.10	.05	.01
☐ 1041 Earl Mossor	.10	.05	.01
☐ 1042 Glen Moulder	.10	.05	.01
☐ 1043 Billy Mullen	.10	.05	.01
☐ 1045 Curly Onis	.10	.05	.01
☐ 1046 Tiny Osborne	.10	.05	.01
☐ 1047 Jim Pastorius	.10	.05	.01
☐ 1048 Art Parks	.10	.05	.01
☐ 1049 Chink Outen	.10	.05	.01
☐ 1050 Jimmy Pattison	.10	.05	.01
☐ 1051 Norman Plitt	.10	.05	.01
☐ 1052 Doc Reisling	.10	.05	.01
☐ 1053 Gilberto Reyes	.10	.05	.01
☐ 1054 Not issued			
☐ 1055 Lou Rochelli	.10	.05	.01
☐ 1056 Jim Romano	.10	.05	.01
☐ 1057 Max Rosenfeld	.10	.05	.01
☐ 1058 Andy Rush	.10	.05	.01
☐ 1059 Jack Ryan	.10	.05	.01
☐ 1060 Jack Savage	.10	.05	.01
☐ 1061 Not issued			
☐ 1062 Ray Schmandt	.10	.05	.01
☐ 1063 Henry Schmidt	.10	.05	.01
☐ 1064 Charlie Schmutz	.10	.05	.01
☐ 1065 Joe Schultz	.10	.05	.01
☐ 1066 Ray Searage	.10	.05	.01
☐ 1067 Elmer Sexauer	.10	.05	.01
☐ 1068 George Sharrott	.10	.05	.01
☐ 1069 Tommy Sheehan	.10	.05	.01
☐ 1071 George Shoch	.10	.05	.01
☐ 1072 Broadway Aleck Smith	.10	.05	.01
☐ 1073 Hap Smith	.10	.05	.01
☐ 1074 Red Smith	.10	.05	.01
☐ 1075 Tony Smith	.10	.05	.01
☐ 1076 Gene Snyder	.10	.05	.01
☐ 1077 Denny Sothern	.10	.05	.01
☐ 1078 Bill Steele	.10	.05	.01
☐ 1080 Farmer Steelman	.10	.05	.01
☐ 1081 Dutch Stryker	.10	.05	.01
☐ 1082 Tommy Tatum	.10	.05	.01
☐ 1084 Adonis Terry	.10	.05	.01
☐ 1085 Ray Thomas	.10	.05	.01
☐ 1086 George Treadway	.10	.05	.01
☐ 1087 Overton Tremper	.10	.05	.01
☐ 1088 Ty Tyson	.10	.05	.01
☐ 1089 Rube Vickers	.10	.05	.01
☐ 1090 Jose Vizcaino	.50	.23	.06
☐ 1091 Bull Wagner	.10	.05	.01
☐ 1092 Butts Wagner	.10	.05	.01
☐ 1093 Rube Ward	.10	.05	.01
☐ 1094 John Wetteland	1.00	.45	.12
☐ 1095 Eddie Wilson	.10	.05	.01
☐ 1096 Tex Wilson	.10	.05	.01
☐ 1097 Zeke Wrigley	.10	.05	.01
☐ 1098 Not issued			
☐ 1099 Rube Yarrison	.10	.05	.01
☐ 1100 Earl Yingling	.10	.05	.01
☐ 1101 Chink Zachary	.10	.05	.01
☐ 1102 Lefty Davis	.10	.05	.01
☐ 1103 Bob Hall	.10	.05	.01
☐ 1104 Darby O'Brien	.10	.05	.01
☐ 1105 Larry LeJeune	.10	.05	.01
☐ 1144 Hub Northen	.10	.05	.01

1991 Dodgers Mother's

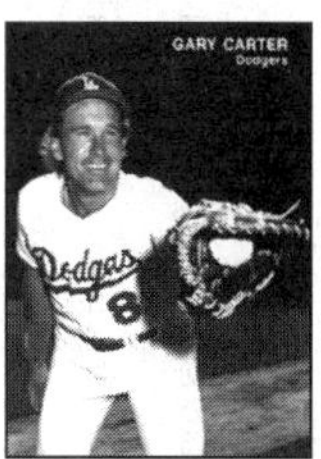

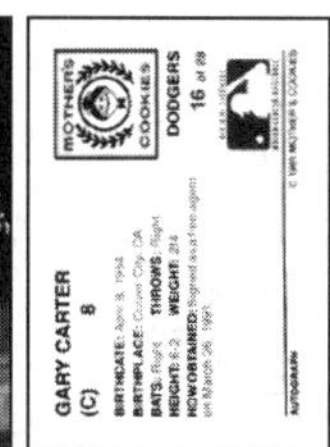

The 1991 Mother's Cookies Los Angeles Dodgers set contains 28 standard-size cards with rounded corners. The front design has borderless glossy color player photos. The horizontally oriented backs are printed in red and purple, present biographical information, and have blank slots for player autographs.

	MINT	NRMT	EXC
COMPLETE SET (28)	8.00	3.60	1.00
COMMON CARD (1-28)	.25	.11	.03
☐ 1 Tom Lasorda MG	1.00	.45	.12
☐ 2 Darryl Strawberry	.50	.23	.06
☐ 3 Kal Daniels	.25	.11	.03
☐ 4 Mike Scioscia	.50	.23	.06
☐ 5 Eddie Murray	1.25	.55	.16
☐ 6 Brett Butler	1.00	.45	.12
☐ 7 Juan Samuel	.25	.11	.03
☐ 8 Alfredo Griffin	.25	.11	.03
☐ 9 Tim Belcher	.50	.23	.06
☐ 10 Ramon Martinez	.75	.35	.09
☐ 11 Jose Gonzalez	.25	.11	.03
☐ 12 Orel Hershiser	.50	.23	.06
☐ 13 Bob Ojeda	.25	.11	.03
☐ 14 Chris Gwynn	.25	.11	.03
☐ 15 Jay Howell	.25	.11	.03
☐ 16 Gary Carter	.50	.23	.06
☐ 17 Kevin Gross	.25	.11	.03
☐ 18 Lenny Harris	.25	.11	.03
☐ 19 Mike Hartley	.25	.11	.03
☐ 20 Mike Sharperson	.25	.11	.03
☐ 21 Mike Morgan	.25	.11	.03
☐ 22 John Candelaria	.25	.11	.03
☐ 23 Jeff Hamilton	.25	.11	.03
☐ 24 Jim Gott	.25	.11	.03
☐ 25 Barry Lyons	.25	.11	.03
☐ 26 Tim Crews	.25	.11	.03
☐ 27 Stan Javier	.25	.11	.03
☐ 28 Checklist Card	.50	.23	.06
Joe Ferguson CO			
Ben Hines CO			
Mark Cresse CO			
Joe Amalfitano CO			
Ron Perranoski CO			
Manny Mota CO			
Bill Russell CO			

1991 Dodgers Police

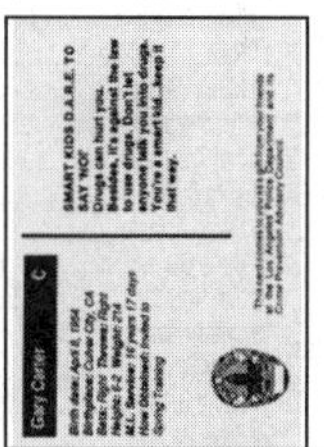

This 30-card set was sponsored by the Los Angeles Police Department and its Crime Prevention Advisory Council. The cards measure approximately 2 13/16" by 4 1/8". The fronts feature color action player photos with the top corners rounded off and white borders on all sides. A black line divides the horizontally oriented back into two halves. While the left half presents biographical information, the right half has an anti-drug or alcohol message. The cards are skip-numbered by uniform number on the fronts.

	MINT	NRMT	EXC
COMPLETE SET (30)	6.00	2.70	.75
COMMON CARD	.25	.11	.03
☐ 3 Jeff Hamilton	.25	.11	.03
☐ 5 Stan Javier	.25	.11	.03
☐ 7 Alfredo Griffin	.25	.11	.03
☐ 10 Juan Samuel	.25	.11	.03
☐ 12 Gary Carter	.50	.23	.06
☐ 14 Mike Scioscia	.50	.23	.06
☐ 15 Chris Gwynn	.25	.11	.03
☐ 17 Bob Ojeda	.25	.11	.03
☐ 22 Brett Butler	.75	.35	.09
☐ 25 Dennis Cook	.25	.11	.03
☐ 27 Mike Sharperson	.25	.11	.03
☐ 28 Kal Daniels	.25	.11	.03
☐ 29 Lenny Harris	.25	.11	.03
☐ 30 Jose Offerman	.25	.11	.03
☐ 31 Jim Neidlinger	.25	.11	.03
☐ 33 Eddie Murray	1.00	.45	.12
☐ 35 Jim Gott	.25	.11	.03
☐ 36 Mike Morgan	.25	.11	.03
☐ 38 Jose Gonzalez	.25	.11	.03
☐ 40 Barry Lyons	.25	.11	.03
☐ 44 Darryl Strawberry	.50	.23	.06
☐ 45 Kevin Gross	.25	.11	.03
☐ 46 Mike Hartley	.25	.11	.03
☐ 48 Ramon Martinez	.75	.35	.09
☐ 49 Tim Belcher	.50	.23	.06
☐ 50 Jay Howell	.25	.11	.03
☐ 52 Tim Crews	.25	.11	.03
☐ 54 John Candelaria	.25	.11	.03
☐ 55 Orel Hershiser	.50	.23	.06
☐ NNO Coaches Card	.50	.23	.06
Ben Hines			
Ron Perranoski			
Mark Cresse			
Manny Mota			
Tommy Lasorda MG			
Joe Amalfitano			
Joe Ferguson			
Bill Russell			

1991 Dodgers Unocal 76 Pins

Some leading events in Dodger history are featured in this set. Many leading Dodger players are featured in this set. This set was issued in conjunction with the Unocal 76 gas station chain.

	MINT	NRMT	EXC
COMPLETE SET (6)	15.00	6.75	1.85
COMMON PIN (1-6)	2.00	.90	.25
☐ 1 Ron Cey Steve Garvey Davey Lopes Bill Russell Record-Setting Infield	3.00	1.35	.35
☐ 2 Manny Mota Lee Lacy Pinch-Hitting Records	2.00	.90	.25
☐ 3 Don Drysdale Orel Hershiser Fernando Valenzuela Consecutive Shutout Innings	3.00	1.35	.35
☐ 4 Sandy Koufax Bill Singer Jerry Reuss Fernando Valenzuela No-Hitters in L.A.	5.00	2.20	.60
☐ 5 Steve Garvey Reggie Smith Ron Cey Dusty Baker Four Teammates with 30 HR's	3.00	1.35	.35
☐ 6 Sandy Koufax Ramon Martinez 18 Strikeouts in a Game	5.00	2.20	.60

1992 Dodgers Mother's

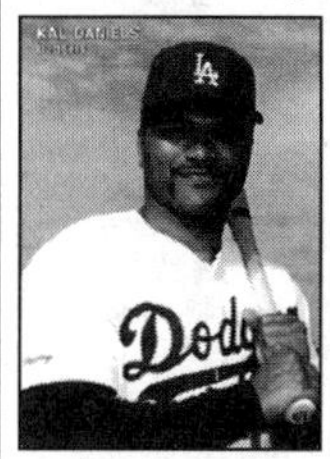

The 1992 Mother's Cookies Los Angeles Dodgers set contains 28 standard size cards with rounded corners. The front design features borderless color player photos with the baseball stadium as the background. The horizontally oriented backs display biographical information printed in purple and red.

	MINT	NRMT	EXC
COMPLETE SET (28)	10.00	4.50	1.25
COMMON CARD (1-28)	.25	.11	.03
☐ 1 Tom Lasorda MG	1.00	.45	.12
☐ 2 Brett Butler	.75	.35	.09
☐ 3 Tom Candiotti	.25	.11	.03
☐ 4 Eric Davis	.50	.23	.06
☐ 5 Lenny Harris	.25	.11	.03
☐ 6 Orel Hershiser	.50	.23	.06
☐ 7 Ramon Martinez	.50	.23	.06
☐ 8 Jose Offerman	.25	.11	.03
☐ 9 Mike Scioscia	.50	.23	.06
☐ 10 Darryl Strawberry	.50	.23	.06
☐ 11 Todd Benzinger	.25	.11	.03
☐ 12 John Candelaria	.25	.11	.03
☐ 13 Tim Crews	.25	.11	.03
☐ 14 Kal Daniels	.25	.11	.03
☐ 15 Jim Gott	.25	.11	.03
☐ 16 Kevin Gross	.25	.11	.03
☐ 17 Dave Hansen	.25	.11	.03
☐ 18 Carlos Hernandez	.25	.11	.03
☐ 19 Jay Howell	.25	.11	.03
☐ 20 Stan Javier	.25	.11	.03
☐ 21 Eric Karros	3.00	1.35	.35
☐ 22 Roger McDowell	.25	.11	.03
☐ 23 Bob Ojeda	.25	.11	.03
☐ 24 Juan Samuel	.25	.11	.03
☐ 25 Mike Sharperson	.25	.11	.03
☐ 26 Mitch Webster	.25	.11	.03
☐ 27 Steve Wilson	.25	.11	.03
☐ 28 Checklist Card	.50	.23	.06
Mark Cresse CO			
Ron Perranoski CO			
Ben Hines CO			
Manny Mota CO			
Joe Amalfitano CO			
Joe Ferguson CO			
Ron Roenicke CO			

1992 Dodgers Police

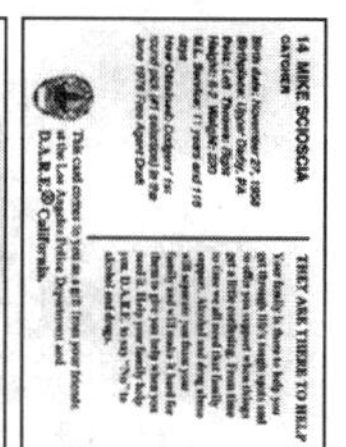

This 30-card standard size set was given out as a promotion at the ball park and was sponsored by the Los Angeles Police Department and D.A.R.E. California. The set, which commemorates the 30th anniversary of Dodger Stadium, features color action photos with rounded corners on a white card face with a navy blue stripe bordering the photos. A commemorative logo is superimposed on the photo at the lower left corner and overlaps onto the white card face. The player's name and uniform number appear at the bottom. The horizontally oriented backs display biographical information and anti-drug or alcohol messages. The cards are skip-numbered by uniform number on the front and back.

	MINT	NRMT	EXC
COMPLETE SET (30)	6.00	2.70	.75
COMMON CARD	.25	.11	.03
☐ 2 Tommy Lasorda MG	1.00	.45	.12
☐ 3 Jeff Hamilton	.25	.11	.03
☐ 5 Stan Javier	.25	.11	.03
☐ 10 Juan Samuel	.25	.11	.03
☐ 14 Mike Scioscia	.50	.23	.06
☐ 15 Dave Hansen	.25	.11	.03
☐ 17 Bob Ojeda	.25	.11	.03
☐ 20 Mitch Webster	.25	.11	.03
☐ 22 Brett Butler	.75	.35	.09
☐ 23 Eric Karros	1.50	.70	.19
☐ 27 Mike Sharperson	.25	.11	.03
☐ 28 Kal Daniels	.25	.11	.03
☐ 29 Lenny Harris	.25	.11	.03
☐ 30 Jose Offerman	.25	.11	.03
☐ 31 Roger McDowell	.25	.11	.03
☐ 33 Eric Davis	.50	.23	.06
☐ 35 Jim Gott	.25	.11	.03
☐ 36 Todd Benzinger	.25	.11	.03
☐ 38 Steve Wilson	.25	.11	.03
☐ 41 Carlos Hernandez	.25	.11	.03
☐ 44 Darryl Strawberry	.50	.23	.06
☐ 46 Kevin Gross	.25	.11	.03
☐ 48 Ramon Martinez	.75	.35	.09
☐ 49 Tom Candiotti	.25	.11	.03
☐ 50 Jay Howell	.25	.11	.03
☐ 52 Tim Crews	.25	.11	.03
☐ 54 John Candelaria	.25	.11	.03
☐ 55 Orel Hershiser	.50	.23	.06
☐ 57 Kip Gross	.25	.11	.03
☐ NNO Coaching Staff	.50	.23	.06
Ben Hines			
Ron Perranoski			
Tommy Lasorda MG			
Joe Amalfitano			
Ron Roenicke			
Joe Ferguson			
Manny Mota			
Mark Cresse			

1992 Dodgers Smokey

This set measures 3 1/2" by 5 1/2". The cards are numbered in various sequences but the last two numbers are always 92.

	MINT	NRMT	EXC
COMPLETE SET (30)	15.00	6.75	1.85
COMMON CARD	.50	.23	.06
☐ 10092 Stan Javier	.50	.23	.06
☐ 10192 Roger McDowell	.50	.23	.06
☐ 10292 Jose Offerman	.50	.23	.06
☐ 10392 Bob Ojeda	.50	.23	.06
☐ 10492 Juan Samuel	.50	.23	.06
☐ 10592 Mike Sharperson	.50	.23	.06
☐ 10692 Mitch Webster	.50	.23	.06
☐ 4192 Dodger Coaches	.50	.23	.06
☐ 4292 Brett Butler	1.00	.45	.12
☐ 4392 Eric Davis	.75	.35	.09
☐ 4492 Orel Hershiser	.75	.35	.09
☐ 4592 Ramon Martinez	.75	.35	.09
☐ 4692 Darryl Strawberry	.75	.35	.09
☐ 4792 Tom Candiotti	.50	.23	.06
☐ 4892 Jim Gott	.50	.23	.06
☐ 4992 Eric Karros	4.00	1.80	.50
☐ 5092 Tom Lasorda MG	1.25	.55	.16
☐ 5192 Mike Scioscia	.50	.23	.06
☐ 5292 Steve Wilson	.50	.23	.06
☐ 5392 Dave Anderson	.50	.23	.06
☐ 5492 Todd Benzinger	.50	.23	.06
☐ 5592 John Candelaria	.50	.23	.06
☐ 5692 Tim Crews	.50	.23	.06
☐ 5792 Kal Daniels	.50	.23	.06
☐ 5892 Kevin Gross	.50	.23	.06
☐ 5992 Kip Gross	.50	.23	.06
☐ 9692 Dave Hansen	.50	.23	.06
☐ 9792 Lenny Harris	.50	.23	.06
☐ 9892 Carlos Hernandez	.50	.23	.06
☐ 9992 Jay Howell	.50	.23	.06

1992 Dodgers Stamps Trak Auto

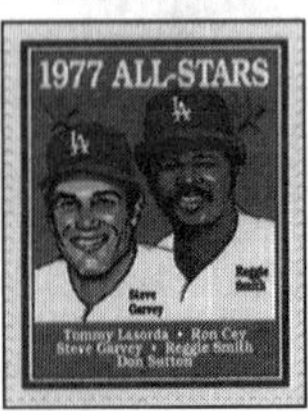

This 32-stamp set salutes the Los Angeles Dodgers All-Stars from 1962 through 1992. They were presented by Trak Auto and Valvoline. The stamps were designed to go into a folder making a frameable print. The stamps are listed below in chronological order according to their all-star years.

	MINT	NRMT	EXC
COMPLETE SET (32)	10.00	4.50	1.25
COMMON STAMP (1-32)	.25	.11	.03
☐ 1 Johnny Podres	.25	.11	.03
John Roseboro			
☐ 2 Tommy Davis	.50	.23	.06
Maury Wills			
☐ 3 Don Drysdale	.75	.35	.09
☐ 4 Sandy Koufax	1.50	.70	.19
☐ 5 Jim Lefebvre	.25	.11	.03
Phil Regan			
☐ 6 Walter Alston MG	.50	.23	.06
☐ 7 Tom Haller	.25	.11	.03
☐ 8 Bill Singer	.25	.11	.03
☐ 9 Bill Grabarkewitz	.25	.11	.03
Claude Osteen			
☐ 10 Willie Davis	.35	.16	.04
☐ 11 Don Sutton	.50	.23	.06
☐ 12 Jim Brewer	.25	.11	.03
Manny Mota			
☐ 13 Mike Marshall	.25	.11	.03
Jimmy Wynn			
☐ 14 Ron Cey	.35	.16	.04
Andy Messersmith			
☐ 15 Rick Rhoden	.25	.11	.03
Bill Russell			
☐ 16 Steve Garvey	.50	.23	.06
Reggie Smith			
☐ 17 Tommy John	.25	.11	.03
Rick Monday			
☐ 18 Tommy Lasorda MG	.50	.23	.06
☐ 19 Jerry Reuss	.35	.16	.04
Bob Welch			
☐ 20 Burt Hooton	.25	.11	.03
Davey Lopes			
☐ 21 Dusty Baker	.35	.16	.04
Steve Howe			
☐ 22 Tommy Lasorda CO	.50	.23	.06
☐ 23 Mike Marshall	.25	.11	.03
☐ 24 Fernando Valenzuela	.35	.16	.04
☐ 25 Steve Sax	.25	.11	.03
☐ 26 Pedro Guerrero	.35	.16	.04
☐ 27 Orel Hershiser	.50	.23	.06
☐ 28 Jay Howell	.25	.11	.03
Willie Randolph			
☐ 29 Ramon Martinez	.50	.23	.06
Mike Scioscia			
☐ 30 Brett Butler	.35	.16	.04
Mike Morgan			
Eddie Murray			
Juan Samuel			
Darryl Strawberry			
☐ 31 Mike Sharperson	.25	.11	.03
☐ 32 Special Stamp	.25	.11	.03

1992 Dodgers Unocal 76 Pins

For the second straight year, Unocal 76 in conjunction with the Dodgers issued a set of pins featuring highlights of Dodger history. This set is less player specific than the previous season's set.

	MINT	NRMT	EXC
COMPLETE SET (6)	12.00	5.50	1.50
COMMON PIN (1-6)	2.00	.90	.25
☐ 1 Four World	2.00	.90	.25
Championships			
1962-1991			
☐ 2 30th Anniversary Logo	2.00	.90	.25
☐ 3 Total Wins; 2,621 Wins	2.00	.90	.25
☐ 4 The 10th Player	2.00	.90	.25
Salute to Dodger Fans			
☐ 5 Walter Alston	3.00	1.35	.35
Tommy Lasorda			
Dodger Managers			
☐ 6 Eight NL Pennants	2.00	.90	.25
1962-1991			

1993 Dodgers Mother's

The 1993 Mother's Cookies Dodgers set consists of 28 standard-size cards with rounded corners. The fronts display full-bleed color player portraits shot from the waist up. The player's name and team name appear in one of the corners. On a white background in red and purple print, the horizontal backs carry biographical information and the sponsor's logo. A blank slot for the player's autograph rounds out the back.

	MINT	NRMT	EXC
COMPLETE SET (28)	15.00	6.75	1.85
COMMON CARD (1-28)	.25	.11	.03
☐ 1 Tommy Lasorda MG	1.00	.45	.12
☐ 2 Eric Karros	1.50	.70	.19
☐ 3 Brett Butler	.75	.35	.09
☐ 4 Mike Piazza	7.50	3.40	.95
☐ 5 Jose Offerman	.25	.11	.03
☐ 6 Tim Wallach	.50	.23	.06
☐ 7 Eric Davis	.50	.23	.06
☐ 8 Darryl Strawberry	.50	.23	.06
☐ 9 Jody Reed	.25	.11	.03
☐ 10 Orel Hershiser	.50	.23	.06
☐ 11 Tom Candiotti	.25	.11	.03
☐ 12 Ramon Martinez	.75	.35	.09
☐ 13 Lenny Harris	.25	.11	.03
☐ 14 Mike Sharperson	.25	.11	.03
☐ 15 Omar Daal	.25	.11	.03
☐ 16 Pedro Martinez	.75	.35	.09
☐ 17 Jim Gott	.25	.11	.03
☐ 18 Carlos Hernandez	.25	.11	.03
☐ 19 Kevin Gross	.25	.11	.03
☐ 20 Cory Snyder	.25	.11	.03
☐ 21 Todd Worrell	.75	.35	.09
☐ 22 Mitch Webster	.25	.11	.03
☐ 23 Steve Wilson	.25	.11	.03
☐ 24 Dave Hansen	.25	.11	.03
☐ 25 Roger McDowell	.25	.11	.03
☐ 26 Pedro Astacio	.75	.35	.09
☐ 27 Rick Trlicek	.25	.11	.03
☐ 28 Checklist/Coaches	.50	.23	.06
Joe Ferguson			
Ben Hines			
Manny Mota			
Mark Cresse			
Ron Perranoski			
Joe Amalfitano			
Ron Roenicke			

1993 Dodgers Police

This 30-card standard size set was sponsored by the Los Angeles Police Department, the L.A. Dodgers, and D.A.R.E. The fronts feature color action photos with blue borders. The Dodger logo overlaps onto the photo at the lower left corner. The player's name is printed in white on the lower edge. The horizontal backs are printed in black on a white background and display biographical information and anti-drug or alcohol messages. Other than the uniform numbers on front and back, the cards are unnumbered and checklisted below in alphabetical order.

	MINT	NRMT	EXC
COMPLETE SET (30)	7.50	3.40	.95
COMMON CARD (1-30)	.25	.11	.03
☐ 1 Pedro Astacio	.75	.35	.09
☐ 2 Brett Butler	.75	.35	.09
☐ 3 Tom Candiotti	.25	.11	.03
☐ 4 Eric Davis	.50	.23	.06
☐ 5 Tom Goodwin	.25	.11	.03
☐ 6 Jim Gott	.25	.11	.03
☐ 7 Kevin Gross	.25	.11	.03
☐ 8 Kip Gross	.25	.11	.03
☐ 9 Dave Hansen	.25	.11	.03
☐ 10 Lenny Harris	.25	.11	.03
☐ 11 Carlos Hernandez	.25	.11	.03
☐ 12 Orel Hershiser	.50	.23	.06
☐ 13 Eric Karros	1.00	.45	.12
☐ 14 Tommy Lasorda MG	1.00	.45	.12
☐ 15 Pedro Martinez	.75	.35	.09
☐ 16 Ramon Martinez	.75	.35	.09
☐ 17 Roger McDowell	.25	.11	.03
☐ 18 Jose Offerman	.25	.11	.03
☐ 19 Lance Parrish	.50	.23	.06
☐ 20 Mike Piazza	3.00	1.35	.35
☐ 21 Jody Reed	.25	.11	.03
☐ 22 Henry Rodriguez	.75	.35	.09
☐ 23 Mike Sharperson	.25	.11	.03
☐ 24 Cory Snyder	.25	.11	.03
☐ 25 Darryl Strawberry	.50	.23	.06
☐ 26 Tim Wallach	.50	.23	.06
☐ 27 Mitch Webster	.25	.11	.03
☐ 28 Steve Wilson	.25	.11	.03
☐ 29 Todd Worrell	.50	.23	.06
☐ 30 Coaches Card	.50	.23	.06
Joe Amalfitano			
Ron Perranoski			
Ben Hines			
Manny Mota			
Mark Cresse			
Joe Ferguson			
Ron Roenicke			
Tommy Lasorda MG			

1994 Dodgers Mother's

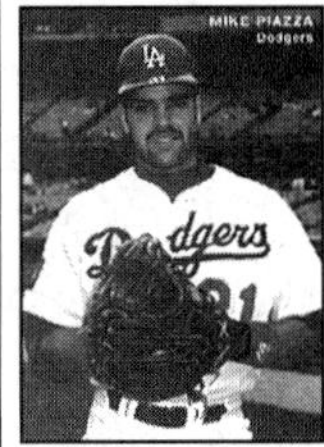

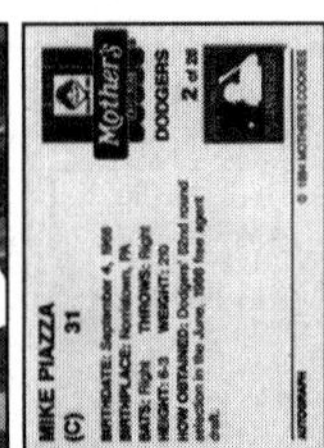

The 1994 Mother's Cookies Dodgers set consists of 28 standard-size cards with rounded corners. The fronts display full-bleed color player portraits shot from the waist up against a stadium background. The player's name and team name appear in one of the corners. On a white background in red and purple print, the horizontal backs carry biographical information and the sponsor's logo. A blank slot for the player's autograph rounds out lthe back.

	MINT	NRMT	EXC
COMPLETE SET (28)	15.00	6.75	1.85
COMMON CARD (1-28)	.25	.11	.03
☐ 1 Tommy Lasorda MG	1.00	.45	.12
☐ 2 Mike Piazza	6.00	2.70	.75
☐ 3 Delino DeShields	.50	.23	.06
☐ 4 Eric Karros	1.50	.70	.19
☐ 5 Jose Offerman	.25	.11	.03
☐ 6 Brett Butler	.75	.35	.09
☐ 7 Orel Hershiser	.50	.23	.06
☐ 8 Henry Rodriguez	.50	.23	.06
☐ 9 Raul Mondesi	4.00	1.80	.50
☐ 10 Tim Wallach	.50	.23	.06
☐ 11 Ramon Martinez	.75	.35	.09
☐ 12 Mitch Webster	.25	.11	.03
☐ 13 Todd Worrell	.75	.35	.09
☐ 14 Jeff Treadway	.25	.11	.03
☐ 15 Tom Candiotti	.25	.11	.03
☐ 16 Pedro Astacio	.50	.23	.06
☐ 17 Chris Gwynn	.25	.11	.03
☐ 18 Jim Gott	.25	.11	.03
☐ 19 Omar Daal	.25	.11	.03
☐ 20 Cory Snyder	.25	.11	.03
☐ 21 Kevin Gross	.25	.11	.03
☐ 22 Dave Hansen	.25	.11	.03
☐ 23 Al Osuna	.25	.11	.03
☐ 24 Darren Dreifort	.50	.23	.06
☐ 25 Roger McDowell	.25	.11	.03
☐ 26 Carlos Hernandez	.25	.11	.03
☐ 27 Gary Wayne	.25	.11	.03
☐ 28 Checklist/Coaches	.50	.23	.06
Ron Perranoski			
Joe Amalfitano			
Reggie Smith			
Joe Ferguson			
Bill Russell			
Mark Cresse			

1994 Dodgers Police

As part of an annual promotion, this 30-card standard-size set was given out at the home game vs. the Pirates on May 27, 1994. All fans in attendance were given a perforated, uncut sheet of the 30-card set. The set was also available as individual cards. The blue-bordered fronts feature color player action shots. The player's name appears in a yellow bar in the blue margin at the bottom. His uniform number appears in a baseball icon at the upper left. The white horizontal back carries the player's name, uniform number, and biographical information on the left side; an antidrug message appears on the right. The cards are unnumbered and checklisted below in alphabetical order.

	MINT	NRMT	EXC
COMPLETE SET (30)	6.00	2.70	.75
COMMON CARD (1-30)	.25	.11	.03
☐ 1 Billy Ashley	.25	.11	.03
☐ 2 Pedro Astacio	.50	.23	.06
☐ 3 Rafael Bournigal	.25	.11	.03
☐ 4 Brett Butler	.75	.35	.09
☐ 5 Tom Candiotti	.25	.11	.03
☐ 6 Delino DeShields	.50	.23	.06
☐ 7 Darren Dreifort	.50	.23	.06
☐ 8 Jim Gott	.25	.11	.03
☐ 9 Kevin Gross	.25	.11	.03
☐ 10 Chris Gwynn	.25	.11	.03
☐ 11 Dave Hansen	.25	.11	.03
☐ 12 Carlos Hernandez	.25	.11	.03
☐ 13 Orel Hershiser	.50	.23	.06
☐ 14 Chan Ho Park	1.00	.45	.12
☐ 15 Tommy Lasorda MG	1.00	.45	.12
☐ 16 Eric Karros	.50	.23	.06
☐ 17 Ramon Martinez	.75	.35	.09
☐ 18 Roger McDowell	.25	.11	.03
☐ 19 Raul Mondesi	1.50	.70	.19
☐ 20 Jose Offerman	.25	.11	.03
☐ 21 Mike Piazza	2.00	.90	.25
☐ 22 Tom Prince	.25	.11	.03
☐ 23 Henry Rodriguez	.50	.23	.06
☐ 24 Cory Snyder	.25	.11	.03
☐ 25 Jeff Treadway	.25	.11	.03
☐ 26 Tim Wallach	.50	.23	.06
☐ 27 Gary Wayne	.25	.11	.03
☐ 28 Mitch Webster	.25	.11	.03
☐ 29 Todd Worrell	.50	.23	.06
☐ 30 Coaches	.50	.23	.06
Mark Cresse			
Manny Mota			
Bill Russell			
Reggie Smith			
Joe Ferguson			
Ron Perranoski			
Tommy Lasorda MG			
Joe Amalfitano			

1995 Dodgers Mother's

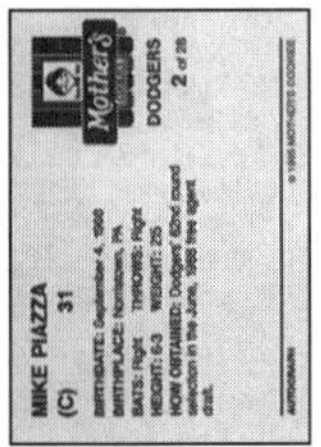

The 1995 Mother's Cookies Los Angeles Dodgers set consists of 28 standard-size cards with rounded corners. The fronts display posed color player portraits in stadium settings. The player's name and team name appear in one of the top corners. The backs carry biographical information and the sponsor's logo on a white background in red and purple print. A blank slot for the player's autograph rounds out the back. A rookie year card of Hideo Nomo is in this set.

	MINT	NRMT	EXC
COMPLETE SET (28)	15.00	6.75	1.85
COMMON CARD (1-28)	.25	.11	.03
☐ 1 Tommy Lasorda MG	1.00	.45	.12
☐ 2 Mike Piazza	3.00	1.35	.35
☐ 3 Raul Mondesi	1.50	.70	.19
☐ 4 Ramon Martinez	.75	.35	.09
☐ 5 Eric Karros	1.00	.45	.12
☐ 6 Roberto Kelly	.25	.11	.03
☐ 7 Tim Wallach	.50	.23	.06
☐ 8 Jose Offerman	.25	.11	.03

□ 9 Delino DeShields	.50	.23	.06
□ 10 Dave Hansen	.25	.11	.03
□ 11 Pedro Astacio	.50	.23	.06
□ 12 Mitch Webster	.25	.11	.03
□ 13 Hideo Nomo	7.50	3.40	.95
□ 14 Billy Ashley	.25	.11	.03
□ 15 Chris Gwynn	.25	.11	.03
□ 16 Todd Hollandsworth	1.00	.45	.12
□ 17 Omar Daal	.25	.11	.03
□ 18 Todd Worrell	.75	.35	.09
□ 19 Todd Williams	.25	.11	.03
□ 20 Carlos Hernandez	.25	.11	.03
□ 21 Tom Candiotti	.25	.11	.03
□ 22 Antonio Osuna	.50	.23	.06
□ 23 Ismael Valdes	.75	.35	.09
□ 24 Rudy Seanez	.25	.11	.03
□ 25 Joey Eischen	.25	.11	.03
□ 26 Greg Hansell	.25	.11	.03
□ 27 Rick Parker	.25	.11	.03
□ 28 Coaches/Checklist	.50	.23	.06
Dave Wallace			
Bill Russell			
Reggie Smith			
Joe Amalfitano			
Manny Mota			
Mark Cresse			

1995 Dodgers Police

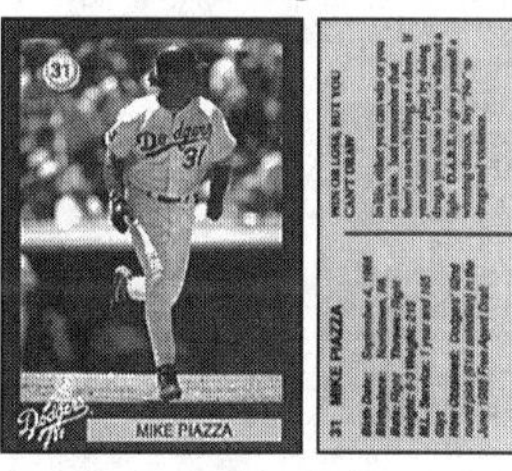

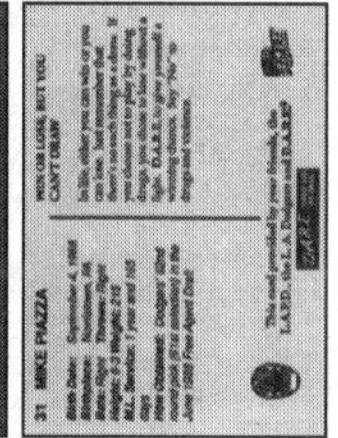

As part of an annual promotion, this 30-card standard-size set was given out at the home game vs. Atlanta on April 30, 1995. All fans in attendance were given a perforated, uncut sheet of this 30-card set. (40,785 sets were handed out.) The fronts feature color action player photos with blue borders. The team logo appears in the lower left, with the player's name inside a yellow bar next to it, while the player's uniform number is printed inside a baseball in the upper left corner. The backs carry player biography and a safety tip, along with the LAPD and D.A.R.E. logos. The cards are unnumbered and checklisted below in alphabetical order. The key card in this set is a rookie year card of international sensation Hideo Nomo.

	MINT	NRMT	EXC
COMPLETE SET (30)	10.00	4.50	1.25
COMMON CARD (1-30)	.25	.11	.03
□ 1 Billy Ashley	.25	.11	.03
□ 2 Pedro Astacio	.50	.23	.06
□ 3 Rafael Bournigal	.25	.11	.03
□ 4 Tom Candiotti	.25	.11	.03
□ 5 Ron Coomer	.25	.11	.03
□ 6 Omar Daal	.25	.11	.03
□ 7 Delino DeShields	.50	.23	.06
□ 8 Greg Hansell	.25	.11	.03
□ 9 Dave Hansen	.25	.11	.03
□ 10 Carlos Hernandez	.25	.11	.03
□ 11 Todd Hollandsworth	.75	.35	.09
□ 12 Eric Karros	.50	.23	.06
□ 13 Tommy Lasorda MG	.50	.23	.06
□ 14 Ramon Martinez	.75	.35	.09
□ 15 Raul Mondesi	1.50	.70	.19
□ 16 Hideo Nomo	5.00	2.20	.60
□ 17 Jose Offerman	.25	.11	.03
□ 18 Al Osuna	.50	.23	.06
□ 19 Antonio Osuna	.50	.23	.06
□ 20 Chan Ho Park	.75	.35	.09
□ 21 Mike Piazza	2.50	1.10	.30
□ 22 Eddie Pye	.25	.11	.03
□ 23 Henry Rodriguez	.50	.23	.06
□ 24 Rudy Seanez	.25	.11	.03
□ 25 Jeff Treadway	.25	.11	.03
□ 26 Ismael Valdes	.75	.35	.09
□ 27 Tim Wallach	.50	.23	.06
□ 28 Todd Williams	.25	.11	.03
□ 29 Todd Worrell	.50	.23	.06
□ 30 Coaches	.50	.23	.06
Mark Cresse			
Manny Mota			
Bill Russell			
Reggie Smith			
Tommy Lasorda MG			
Joe Amalfitano			
Dave Wallace			
Ralph Avila			

1995 Dodgers ROYs

Consisting of 14 standard-size cards, this team-issued boxed set features all 14 Dodger National League Rookie of the Year winners. The set was not sold but was made available to Dodger season ticket holders and preseason mail order customers. The cards are chromium-plated and feature on their fronts player action cutouts on colorful background designs. The words "Limited Edition," the year the

player received the award, and his name are printed on bars superposed on the picture. The horizontal backs carry an oval-shaped portrait, biography, player profile, and statistics, all on a color background (red, green, turquoise, or purple) that varies from card to card. The cards are numbered on the back "X of 14."

	MINT	NRMT	EXC
COMPLETE SET (14)	250.00	110.00	31.00
COMMON CARD (1-14)	10.00	4.50	1.25
□ 1 Jackie Robinson	75.00	34.00	9.50
□ 2 Don Newcombe	15.00	6.75	1.85
□ 3 Joe Black	10.00	4.50	1.25
□ 4 Jim Gilliam	15.00	6.75	1.85
□ 5 Frank Howard	15.00	6.75	1.85
□ 6 Jim Lefebvre	10.00	4.50	1.25
□ 7 Ted Sizemore	10.00	4.50	1.25
□ 8 Rick Sutcliffe	10.00	4.50	1.25
□ 9 Steve Howe	10.00	4.50	1.25
□ 10 Fernando Valenzuela	20.00	9.00	2.50
□ 11 Steve Sax	15.00	6.75	1.85
□ 12 Eric Karros	20.00	9.00	2.50
□ 13 Mike Piazza	60.00	27.00	7.50
□ 14 Raul Mondesi	30.00	13.50	3.70

1996 Dodgers Mother's

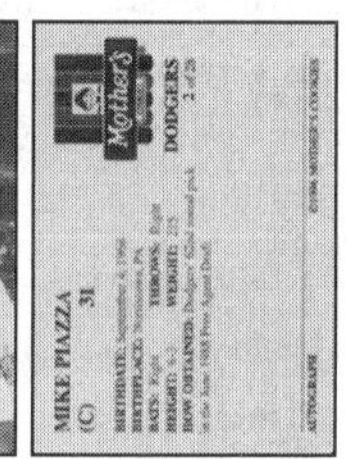

This 28-card set consists of borderless posed color player portraits in stadium settings. The player's and team's names appear in one of the top rounded corners. The backs carry biographical information and the sponsor's logo on a white background in red and purple print. A blank slot for the player's autograph rounds out the back.

	MINT	NRMT	EXC
COMPLETE SET (28)	12.00	5.50	1.50
COMMON CARD (1-28)	.25	.11	.03
□ 1 Tommy Lasorda MG	1.00	.45	.12
□ 2 Mike Piazza	2.50	1.10	.30
□ 3 Hideo Nomo	2.50	1.10	.30
□ 4 Raul Mondesi	1.00	.45	.12
□ 5 Eric Karros	1.00	.45	.12
□ 6 Delino DeShields	.50	.23	.06
□ 7 Greg Gagne	.25	.11	.03
□ 8 Brett Butler	.75	.35	.09
□ 9 Todd Hollandsworth	.50	.23	.06
□ 10 Mike Blowers	.25	.11	.03
□ 11 Ismael Valdes	.75	.35	.09
□ 12 Pedro Astacio	.50	.23	.06
□ 13 Billy Ashley	.25	.11	.03
□ 14 Tom Candiotti	.25	.11	.03
□ 15 Dave Hansen	.25	.11	.03
□ 16 Joey Eischen	.25	.11	.03
□ 17 Milt Thompson	.25	.11	.03
□ 18 Chan Ho Park	1.00	.45	.12
□ 19 Antonio Osuna	.25	.11	.03
□ 20 Carlos Hernandez	.25	.11	.03
□ 21 Ramon Martinez	.50	.23	.06
□ 22 Scott Radinsky	.25	.11	.03
□ 23 Chad Fonville	.25	.11	.03
□ 24 Darren Hall	.25	.11	.03
□ 25 Todd Worrell	.75	.35	.09
□ 26 Mark Guthrie	.25	.11	.03
□ 27 Roger Cedeno	.25	.11	.03
□ 28 Coaches Card CL	.25	.11	.03
Joe Amalfitano			
Mark Cresse			
Manny Mota			
Bill Russell			
Dave Wallace			
Reggie Smith			

1996 Dodgers Police

This 30-card set was distributed as a perforated sheet. The fronts feature color action player photos in blue borders while the backs carry player biography and a safety tip. The cards are unnumbered and checklisted below in alphabetical order.

	MINT	NRMT	EXC
COMPLETE SET (30)	10.00	4.50	1.25
COMMON CARD (1-30)	.10	.05	.01
□ 1 Billy Ashley	.10	.05	.01
□ 2 Pedro Astacio	.25	.11	.03
□ 3 Mike Blowers	.10	.05	.01
□ 4 Mike Busch	.10	.05	.01
□ 5 Brett Butler	.25	.11	.03
□ 6 Tom Candiotti	.10	.05	.01
□ 7 Roger Cedeno	.25	.11	.03
□ 8 Coaches Card	.10	.05	.01
Mark Cresse			
Manny Mota			
Bill Russell			
Reggie Smith			
Tommy Lasorda MG			
Joe Amalfitano			
Dave Wallace			
□ 9 John Cummings	.10	.05	.01
□ 10 Delino DeShields	.25	.11	.03
□ 11 Joey Eischen	.10	.05	.01
□ 12 Chad Fonville	.10	.05	.01
□ 13 Greg Gagne	.10	.05	.01
□ 14 Karim Garcia	2.00	.90	.25
□ 15 Mark Guthrie	.10	.05	.01
□ 16 Darren Hall	.10	.05	.01
□ 17 Dave Hansen	.10	.05	.01
□ 18 Carlos Hernandez	.10	.05	.01
□ 19 Todd Hollandsworth	1.00	.45	.12
□ 20 Garey Ingram	.10	.05	.01
□ 21 Eric Karros	.75	.35	.09
□ 22 Tommy Lasorda MG	.75	.35	.09
□ 23 Ramon Martinez	.25	.11	.03
□ 24 Raul Mondesi	.50	.23	.06
□ 25 Hideo Nomo	2.50	1.10	.30
□ 26 Antonio Osuna	.10	.05	.01
□ 27 Mike Piazza	3.00	1.35	.35
□ 28 Milt Thompson	.10	.05	.01
□ 29 Ismael Valdes	.50	.23	.06
□ 30 Todd Worrell	.25	.11	.03

1910 Domino Discs PX7

These discs were issued by Sweet Caporal Cigarettes and consist of a metal rim around cardboard. The discs come in a variety of colors: black, blue, brown, green and red. The player's picture, name, and team are on the front whereas the back shows a domino. Each disc is approximately 1 1/16" in diameter. The catalog designation for this set is PX7. Many variations exist. The set price below does not include variations.

	EX-MT	VG-E	GOOD
COMPLETE SET (136)	3500.00	1600.00	450.00
COMMON PLAYER (1-129)	15.00	6.75	1.85
□ 1 Red Ames	15.00	6.75	1.85
□ 2 Jimmy Archer	15.00	6.75	1.85
□ 3 Jimmy Austin	15.00	6.75	1.85
□ 4 Frank Baker	40.00	18.00	5.00
□ 5 Neal Ball	15.00	6.75	1.85
□ 6 Cy Barger	15.00	6.75	1.85
□ 7 Jack Barry	15.00	6.75	1.85
□ 8 John Bates	15.00	6.75	1.85
□ 9 Beals Becker	15.00	6.75	1.85
□ 10 George Bell	15.00	6.75	1.85
□ 11 Chief Bender	35.00	16.00	4.40
□ 12 Bill Bergen	15.00	6.75	1.85
□ 13 Bob Bescher	20.00	9.00	2.50
□ 14 Dode Birmingham	15.00	6.75	1.85
□ 15 Roger Bresnahan	35.00	16.00	4.40
□ 16 Al Bridwell	15.00	6.75	1.85
□ 17 Mordecai Brown	35.00	16.00	4.40
□ 18 Robert Byrne	15.00	6.75	1.85
□ 19 Nixey Callahan	15.00	6.75	1.85
□ 20 Howie Camnitz	15.00	6.75	1.85
□ 21 Bill Carrigan	15.00	6.75	1.85
□ 22 Frank Chance	50.00	22.00	6.25
□ 23 Hal Chase	35.00	16.00	4.40
□ 24 Ed Cicotte	35.00	16.00	4.40
□ 25 Fred Clarke	40.00	18.00	5.00
□ 26A Ty Cobb D on cap	500.00	220.00	60.00
□ 26B Ty Cobb No D on cap	500.00	220.00	60.00
□ 27 Eddie Collins	40.00	18.00	5.00
□ 28 Doc Crandall	15.00	6.75	1.85
□ 29 Birdie Cree	15.00	6.75	1.85
□ 30 Bill Dahlen	20.00	9.00	2.50
□ 31 Jim Delahanty	20.00	9.00	2.50
□ 32 Art Devlin	15.00	6.75	1.85
□ 33 Josh Devore	15.00	6.75	1.85
□ 34 Red Dooin	15.00	6.75	1.85
□ 35 Mickey Doolan	15.00	6.75	1.85
□ 36 Patsy Dougherty	15.00	6.75	1.85
□ 37 Tom Downey	15.00	6.75	1.85
□ 38 Larry Doyle	20.00	9.00	2.50
□ 39 Louis Drucke	15.00	6.75	1.85
□ 40 Clyde Engle	15.00	6.75	1.85
□ 41 Tex Erwin	15.00	6.75	1.85
□ 42 Steve Evans	15.00	6.75	1.85
□ 43 Johnny Evers	50.00	22.00	6.25
□ 44 Cecil Ferguson	15.00	6.75	1.85
□ 45 Russ Ford	15.00	6.75	1.85
□ 46 Art Fromme	15.00	6.75	1.85
□ 47 Harry Gaspar	15.00	6.75	1.85
□ 48 George Gibson	15.00	6.75	1.85
□ 49 Eddie Grant	15.00	6.75	1.85
□ 50 Clark Griffith	40.00	18.00	5.00
□ 51 Bob Groom	15.00	6.75	1.85
□ 52 Bob Harmon	15.00	6.75	1.85
□ 53 Topsy Hartsel	15.00	6.75	1.85
□ 54 Arnold Hauser	15.00	6.75	1.85
□ 55 Dick Hoblitzel	15.00	6.75	1.85
□ 56 Danny Hoffman	15.00	6.75	1.85
□ 57 Miller Huggins	40.00	18.00	5.00
□ 58 John Hummell	15.00	6.75	1.85
□ 59 Hugh Jennings	40.00	18.00	5.00
□ 60 Walter Johnson	175.00	80.00	22.00
□ 61 Ed Karger	15.00	6.75	1.85
□ 62A John Knight Senators	35.00	16.00	4.40
□ 62B John Knight Yankees	35.00	16.00	4.40
□ 63 Ed Konetchy	15.00	6.75	1.85
□ 64 Harry Krause	15.00	6.75	1.85
□ 65 Napoleon Lajoie	100.00	45.00	12.50
□ 66 Frank LaPorte	15.00	6.75	1.85
□ 67 Tommy Leach	15.00	6.75	1.85
□ 68 Sam Leever	15.00	6.75	1.85
□ 69 Lefty Leifield	15.00	6.75	1.85
□ 70 Paddy Livingston	15.00	6.75	1.85
□ 71 Hans Lobert	15.00	6.75	1.85
□ 72 Harry Lord	15.00	6.75	1.85
□ 73 Nick Maddox	15.00	6.75	1.85
□ 74 Sherry McGee	15.00	6.75	1.85
□ 75 Rube Marquard	40.00	18.00	5.00
□ 76 Christy Mathewson	175.00	80.00	22.00
□ 77 Al Mattern	15.00	6.75	1.85
□ 78 George McBride	15.00	6.75	1.85
□ 79 John McGraw	50.00	22.00	6.25
□ 80 Larry McLean	15.00	6.75	1.85
□ 81 John McIntire	15.00	6.75	1.85
□ 82 Matty McIntyre	15.00	6.75	1.85
□ 83 Fred Merkle	20.00	9.00	2.50
□ 84 Chief Meyers	20.00	9.00	2.50
□ 85 Clyde Milan	20.00	9.00	2.50
□ 86 Dots Miller	15.00	6.75	1.85
□ 87 Mike Mitchell	15.00	6.75	1.85
□ 88A Pat Moran	35.00	16.00	4.40
Chicago Cubs			
□ 88B Pat Moran	35.00	16.00	4.40
Philadelphia Phillies			
□ 89 George Mullen (Mullin)	15.00	6.75	1.85
□ 90 Danny Murphy	15.00	6.75	1.85
□ 91 Red Murray	15.00	6.75	1.85
□ 92 Tom Needham	15.00	6.75	1.85
□ 93 Rebel Oakes	15.00	6.75	1.85
□ 94 Rube Oldring	15.00	6.75	1.85
□ 95 Fred Parent	15.00	6.75	1.85
□ 96 Dode Paskert	15.00	6.75	1.85
□ 97 Barney Pelty	15.00	6.75	1.85
□ 98 Eddie Phelps	15.00	6.75	1.85
□ 99 Deacon Phillippe	20.00	9.00	2.50
□ 100 Jack Quinn	15.00	6.75	1.85
□ 101 Ed Reulbach	20.00	9.00	2.50
□ 102 Lew Richie	15.00	6.75	1.85
□ 103 Jack Rowan	15.00	6.75	1.85
□ 104 Nap Rucker	20.00	9.00	2.50
□ 105A Doc Scanlan Superbas	35.00	16.00	4.40
□ 105B Doc Scanlan Phillies	35.00	16.00	4.40
□ 106 Germany Schaefer	20.00	9.00	2.50
□ 107 Boss Schmidt	15.00	6.75	1.85
□ 108 Wildfire Schulte	20.00	9.00	2.50
□ 109 Jimmy Sheckard	15.00	6.75	1.85
□ 110 Hap Smith	15.00	6.75	1.85
□ 111 Tris Speaker	125.00	55.00	15.50
□ 112 Gabby Stovall	15.00	6.75	1.85
□ 113A Gabby Street	35.00	16.00	4.40
Washington Senators			
□ 113B Gabby Street	35.00	16.00	4.40
New York Yankees			
□ 114 George Suggs	15.00	6.75	1.85
□ 115 Ira Thomas	15.00	6.75	1.85
□ 116 Joe Tinker	50.00	22.00	6.25
□ 117 John Titus	15.00	6.75	1.85
□ 118 Terry Turner	15.00	6.75	1.85
□ 119 Heine Wagner	20.00	9.00	2.50
□ 120 Bobby Wallace	35.00	16.00	4.40
□ 121 Ed Walsh	40.00	18.00	5.00
□ 122 Jack Warhop	15.00	6.75	1.85
□ 123 Zach Wheat	40.00	18.00	5.00
□ 124 Doc White	15.00	6.75	1.85
□ 125A Art Wilson Pirates	20.00	9.00	2.50
□ 125B Art Wilson Giants	15.00	6.75	1.85
□ 126A Owen Wilson Pirates	15.00	6.75	1.85
□ 126B Owen Wilson Giants	15.00	6.75	1.85
□ 127 Hooks Wiltse	15.00	6.75	1.85
□ 128 Harry Wolter	15.00	6.75	1.85
□ 129 Cy Young	125.00	55.00	15.50

1955-62 Don Wingfield PC762

This set of black and white and color postcards was first issued in 1955 and consists of three diffferent types. Type 1 postcards consist of Washington Senatos only and feature the player's name - Washington Nationals, copyright 1955 - Don Wingfield, Griffith Stadium, Washington, D.C., at the base of the front. The type 2 postcards feature players from many teams and present the player's name on the back down the center of the card. The type 3 postcard is in color and consist of but one card (Killebrew). Multiple player poses of several of the Type 2 postcards exist. Cards 1-9 are Type 1 card, Cards 10-42 are Type 2 and Card 43 is Type 3.

	NRMT	VG-E	GOOD
COMPLETE SET (43)	500.00	220.00	60.00
COMMON CARD (1-43)	5.00	2.20	.60
☐ 1 Jim Busby	5.00	2.20	.60
☐ 2 Charley Dressen MG	20.00	9.00	2.50
☐ 3 Ed Fitzgerald	20.00	9.00	2.50
☐ 4 Bob Porterfield	5.00	2.20	.60
☐ 5 Roy Sievers	20.00	9.00	2.50
☐ 6 Chuck Stobbs	20.00	9.00	2.50
☐ 7 Dean Stone	20.00	9.00	2.50
☐ 8 Mickey Vernon	20.00	9.00	2.50
☐ 9 Eddie Yost	20.00	9.00	2.50
☐ 10 Bob Allison (2)	10.00	4.50	1.25
☐ 11 Ernie Banks	25.00	11.00	3.10
☐ 12 Earl Battey	5.00	2.20	.60
☐ 13 Norm Cash	10.00	4.50	1.25
☐ 14 Jim Coates	5.00	2.20	.60
☐ 15 Rocky Colavito	15.00	6.75	1.85
☐ 16 Chuck Cottier	5.00	2.20	.60
☐ 17 Bennie Daniels	5.00	2.20	.60
☐ 18 Dan Dobbek	5.00	2.20	.60
☐ 19 Nellie Fox	15.00	6.75	1.85
☐ 20 Jim Gentile	5.00	2.20	.60
☐ 21 Gene Green	5.00	2.20	.60
☐ 22 Steve Hamilton	5.00	2.20	.60
☐ 23 Ken Hamlin	5.00	2.20	.60
☐ 24 Rudy Hernandez	5.00	2.20	.60
☐ 25 Ed Hobaugh	5.00	2.20	.60
☐ 26 Elston Howard	15.00	6.75	1.85
☐ 27 Bob Johnson	5.00	2.20	.60
☐ 28 Russ Kemmerer	5.00	2.20	.60
☐ 29 Harmon Killebrew (3)	20.00	9.00	2.50
☐ 30 Dale Long	5.00	2.20	.60
☐ 31 Mickey Mantle	50.00	22.00	6.25
☐ 32 Roger Maris	25.00	11.00	3.10
☐ 33 Willie Mays	30.00	13.50	3.70
☐ 34 Stan Musial	30.00	13.50	3.70
☐ 35 Claude Osteen	5.00	2.20	.60
☐ 36 Ken Retzer	5.00	2.20	.60
☐ 37 Brooks Robinson	20.00	9.00	2.50
☐ 38 Dick Rudolph	5.00	2.20	.60
☐ 39 Dave Stenhouse	5.00	2.20	.60
☐ 40 Jose Valdivielso	5.00	2.20	.60
☐ 41 Gene Woodling	10.00	4.50	1.25
☐ 42 Bud Zipfel	5.00	2.20	.60
☐ 43 Harmon Killebrew	15.00	6.75	1.85

1981 Donruss

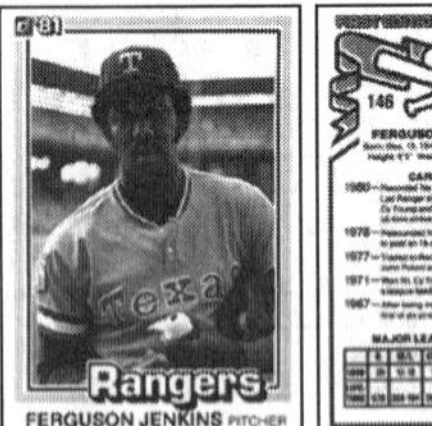

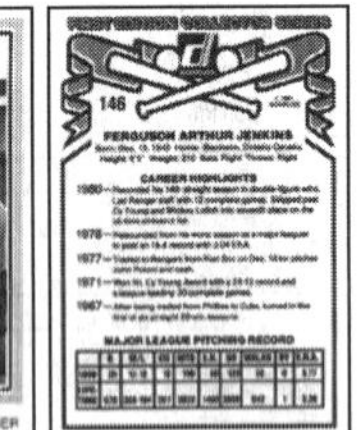

In 1981 Donruss launched itself into the baseball card market with a 600-card set. Wax packs contained 15 cards as well as a piece of gum. This would be the only year that Donruss was allowed to have any confectionary product in their packs. The standard-size cards are printed on thin stock and more than one pose exists for several popular players. Numerous errors of the first print run were later corrected by the company. These are marked P1 and P2 in the checklist below. The key Rookie Cards in this set are Danny Ainge, Tim Raines, and Jeff Reardon.

	NRMT	VG-E	GOOD
COMPLETE SET (605)	40.00	18.00	5.00
COMMON CARD (1-605)	.10	.05	.01
☐ 1 Ozzie Smith	4.00	1.80	.50
☐ 2 Rollie Fingers	.50	.23	.06
☐ 3 Rick Wise	.10	.05	.01
☐ 4 Gene Richards	.10	.05	.01
☐ 5 Alan Trammell	1.25	.55	.16
☐ 6 Tom Brookens	.10	.05	.01
☐ 7A Duffy Dyer P1	.25	.11	.03
1980 batting average			
has decimal point			
☐ 7B Duffy Dyer P2	.10	.05	.01
1980 batting average			
has no decimal point			
☐ 8 Mark Fidrych	.50	.23	.06
☐ 9 Dave Rozema	.10	.05	.01
☐ 10 Ricky Peters	.10	.05	.01
☐ 11 Mike Schmidt	2.00	.90	.25
☐ 12 Willie Stargell	.60	.25	.07
☐ 13 Tim Foli	.10	.05	.01
☐ 14 Manny Sanguillen	.25	.11	.03
☐ 15 Grant Jackson	.10	.05	.01
☐ 16 Eddie Solomon	.10	.05	.01
☐ 17 Omar Moreno	.10	.05	.01
☐ 18 Joe Morgan	.60	.25	.07
☐ 19 Rafael Landestoy	.10	.05	.01
☐ 20 Bruce Bochy	.10	.05	.01
☐ 21 Joe Sambito	.10	.05	.01
☐ 22 Manny Trillo	.10	.05	.01
☐ 23A Dave Smith P1	.25	.11	.03
Line box around stats			
is not complete			
☐ 23B Dave Smith P2	.25	.11	.03
Box totally encloses			
stats at top			
☐ 24 Terry Puhl	.10	.05	.01
☐ 25 Bump Wills	.10	.05	.01
☐ 26A John Ellis P1 ERR	.50	.23	.06
Danny Walton photo on front			
☐ 26B John Ellis P2 COR	.25	.11	.03
☐ 27 Jim Kern	.10	.05	.01
☐ 28 Richie Zisk	.10	.05	.01
☐ 29 John Mayberry	.10	.05	.01
☐ 30 Bob Davis	.10	.05	.01
☐ 31 Jackson Todd	.10	.05	.01
☐ 32 Alvis Woods	.10	.05	.01
☐ 33 Steve Carlton	1.00	.45	.12
☐ 34 Lee Mazzilli	.10	.05	.01
☐ 35 John Stearns	.10	.05	.01
☐ 36 Roy Lee Jackson	.10	.05	.01
☐ 37 Mike Scott	.25	.11	.03
☐ 38 Lamar Johnson	.10	.05	.01
☐ 39 Kevin Bell	.10	.05	.01
☐ 40 Ed Farmer	.10	.05	.01
☐ 41 Ross Baumgarten	.10	.05	.01
☐ 42 Leo Sutherland	.10	.05	.01
☐ 43 Dan Meyer	.10	.05	.01
☐ 44 Ron Reed	.10	.05	.01
☐ 45 Mario Mendoza	.10	.05	.01
☐ 46 Rick Honeycutt	.10	.05	.01
☐ 47 Glenn Abbott	.10	.05	.01
☐ 48 Leon Roberts	.10	.05	.01
☐ 49 Rod Carew	.75	.35	.09
☐ 50 Bert Campaneris	.25	.11	.03
☐ 51A Tom Donahue P1 ERR	.25	.11	.03
Name on front			
misspelled Donahue			
☐ 51B Tom Donohue	.10	.05	.01
P2 COR			
☐ 52 Dave Frost	.10	.05	.01
☐ 53 Ed Halicki	.10	.05	.01
☐ 54 Dan Ford	.10	.05	.01
☐ 55 Garry Maddox	.10	.05	.01
☐ 56A Steve Garvey P1	.50	.23	.06
Surpassed 25 HR			
☐ 56B Steve Garvey P2	.50	.23	.06
Surpassed 21 HR			
☐ 57 Bill Russell	.25	.11	.03
☐ 58 Don Sutton	.50	.23	.06
☐ 59 Reggie Smith	.25	.11	.03
☐ 60 Rick Monday	.25	.11	.03
☐ 61 Ray Knight	.25	.11	.03
☐ 62 Johnny Bench	1.25	.55	.16
☐ 63 Mario Soto	.10	.05	.01
☐ 64 Doug Bair	.10	.05	.01
☐ 65 George Foster	.25	.11	.03
☐ 66 Jeff Burroughs	.10	.05	.01
☐ 67 Keith Hernandez	.25	.11	.03
☐ 68 Tom Herr	.25	.11	.03
☐ 69 Bob Forsch	.10	.05	.01
☐ 70 John Fulgham	.10	.05	.01
☐ 71A Bobby Bonds P1 ERR	.50	.23	.06
986 lifetime HR			
☐ 71B Bobby Bonds P2 COR	.25	.11	.03
326 lifetime HR			
☐ 72A Rennie Stennett P1	.25	.11	.03
Breaking broke leg			
☐ 72B Rennie Stennett P2	.10	.05	.01
Word "broke" deleted			
☐ 73 Joe Strain	.10	.05	.01
☐ 74 Ed Whitson	.10	.05	.01
☐ 75 Tom Griffin	.10	.05	.01
☐ 76 Billy North	.10	.05	.01
☐ 77 Gene Garber	.10	.05	.01
☐ 78 Mike Hargrove	.25	.11	.03
☐ 79 Dave Rosello	.10	.05	.01
☐ 80 Ron Hassey	.10	.05	.01
☐ 81 Sid Monge	.10	.05	.01
☐ 82A Joe Charboneau P1	.25	.11	.03
'78 highlights			
For some reason			
☐ 82B Joe Charboneau P2	.25	.11	.03
Phrase "For some reason" deleted			
☐ 83 Cecil Cooper	.25	.11	.03
☐ 84 Sal Bando	.25	.11	.03
☐ 85 Moose Haas	.10	.05	.01
☐ 86 Mike Caldwell	.10	.05	.01
☐ 87A Larry Hisle P1	.25	.11	.03
'77 highlights			
line ends with "28 RBI"			
☐ 87B Larry Hisle P2	.10	.05	.01
Correct line "28 HR"			
☐ 88 Luis Gomez	.10	.05	.01
☐ 89 Larry Parrish	.10	.05	.01
☐ 90 Gary Carter	.25	.11	.03
☐ 91 Bill Gullickson	.50	.23	.06
☐ 92 Fred Norman	.10	.05	.01
☐ 93 Tommy Hutton	.10	.05	.01
☐ 94 Carl Yastrzemski	1.00	.45	.12
☐ 95 Glenn Hoffman	.10	.05	.01
☐ 96 Dennis Eckersley	.75	.35	.09
☐ 97A Tom Burgmeier P1	.25	.11	.03
ERR Throws: Right			
☐ 97B Tom Burgmeier P2	.10	.05	.01
COR Throws: Left			
☐ 98 Win Remmerswaal	.10	.05	.01
☐ 99 Bob Horner	.25	.11	.03
☐ 100 George Brett	4.00	1.80	.50
☐ 101 Dave Chalk	.10	.05	.01
☐ 102 Dennis Leonard	.10	.05	.01
☐ 103 Renie Martin	.10	.05	.01
☐ 104 Amos Otis	.25	.11	.03
☐ 105 Graig Nettles	.25	.11	.03
☐ 106 Eric Soderholm	.10	.05	.01
☐ 107 Tommy John	.50	.23	.06
☐ 108 Tom Underwood	.10	.05	.01
☐ 109 Lou Piniella	.25	.11	.03
☐ 110 Mickey Klutts	.10	.05	.01
☐ 111 Bobby Murcer	.25	.11	.03
☐ 112 Eddie Murray	4.00	1.80	.50
☐ 113 Rick Dempsey	.25	.11	.03
☐ 114 Scott McGregor	.10	.05	.01
☐ 115 Ken Singleton	.25	.11	.03
☐ 116 Gary Roenicke	.10	.05	.01
☐ 117 Dave Revering	.10	.05	.01
☐ 118 Mike Norris	.10	.05	.01
☐ 119 Rickey Henderson	3.00	1.35	.35
☐ 120 Mike Heath	.10	.05	.01
☐ 121 Dave Cash	.10	.05	.01
☐ 122 Randy Jones	.10	.05	.01
☐ 123 Eric Rasmussen	.10	.05	.01
☐ 124 Jerry Mumphrey	.10	.05	.01
☐ 125 Richie Hebner	.10	.05	.01
☐ 126 Mark Wagner	.10	.05	.01
☐ 127 Jack Morris	.50	.23	.06
☐ 128 Dan Petry	.25	.11	.03
☐ 129 Bruce Robbins	.10	.05	.01
☐ 130 Champ Summers	.10	.05	.01
☐ 131 Pete Rose P1	1.50	.70	.19
Last line ends with			
see card 251			
☐ 131B Pete Rose P2	1.50	.70	.19
Last line corrected			
see card 371			
☐ 132 Willie Stargell	.60	.25	.07
☐ 133 Ed Ott	.10	.05	.01
☐ 134 Jim Bibby	.10	.05	.01
☐ 135 Bert Blyleven	.50	.23	.06
☐ 136 Dave Parker	.25	.11	.03
☐ 137 Bill Robinson	.25	.11	.03
☐ 138 Enos Cabell	.10	.05	.01
☐ 139 Dave Bergman	.10	.05	.01
☐ 140 J.R. Richard	.25	.11	.03
☐ 141 Ken Forsch	.10	.05	.01
☐ 142 Larry Bowa UER	.25	.11	.03
Shortshop on front			
☐ 143 Frank LaCorte UER	.10	.05	.01
Photo actually Randy Niemann			
☐ 144 Denny Walling	.10	.05	.01
☐ 145 Buddy Bell	.25	.11	.03
☐ 146 Ferguson Jenkins	.50	.23	.06
☐ 147 Dannny Darwin	.10	.05	.01
☐ 148 John Grubb	.10	.05	.01
☐ 149 Alfredo Griffin	.10	.05	.01
☐ 150 Jerry Garvin	.10	.05	.01
☐ 151 Paul Mirabella	.10	.05	.01
☐ 152 Rick Bosetti	.10	.05	.01
☐ 153 Dick Ruthven	.10	.05	.01
☐ 154 Frank Taveras	.10	.05	.01
☐ 155 Craig Swan	.10	.05	.01
☐ 156 Jeff Reardon	1.00	.45	.12
☐ 157 Steve Henderson	.10	.05	.01
☐ 158 Jim Morrison	.10	.05	.01
☐ 159 Glenn Borgmann	.10	.05	.01
☐ 160 LaMarr Hoyt	.25	.11	.03
☐ 161 Rich Wortham	.10	.05	.01
☐ 162 Thad Bosley	.10	.05	.01
☐ 163 Julio Cruz	.10	.05	.01
☐ 164A Del Unser P1	.25	.11	.03
No "3B" heading			
☐ 164B Del Unser P2	.10	.05	.01
Batting record on back			
corrected "3B"			
☐ 165 Jim Anderson	.10	.05	.01
☐ 166 Jim Beattie	.10	.05	.01
☐ 167 Shane Rawley	.10	.05	.01
☐ 168 Joe Simpson	.10	.05	.01
☐ 169 Rod Carew	.75	.35	.09
☐ 170 Fred Patek	.10	.05	.01
☐ 171 Frank Tanana	.25	.11	.03
☐ 172 Alfredo Martinez	.10	.05	.01
☐ 173 Chris Knapp	.10	.05	.01
☐ 174 Joe Rudi	.25	.11	.03
☐ 175 Greg Luzinski	.25	.11	.03
☐ 176 Steve Garvey	.50	.23	.06
☐ 177 Joe Ferguson	.10	.05	.01
☐ 178 Bob Welch	.25	.11	.03
☐ 179 Dusty Baker	.50	.23	.06
☐ 180 Rudy Law	.10	.05	.01
☐ 181 Dave Concepcion	.25	.11	.03
☐ 182 Johnny Bench	1.25	.55	.16
☐ 183 Mike LaCoss	.10	.05	.01
☐ 184 Ken Griffey	.25	.11	.03
☐ 185 Dave Collins	.10	.05	.01
☐ 186 Brian Asselstine	.10	.05	.01
☐ 187 Garry Templeton	.10	.05	.01
☐ 188 Mike Phillips	.10	.05	.01
☐ 189 Pete Vuckovich	.25	.11	.03
☐ 190 John Urrea	.10	.05	.01
☐ 191 Tony Scott	.10	.05	.01
☐ 192 Darrell Evans	.25	.11	.03
☐ 193 Milt May	.10	.05	.01
☐ 194 Bob Knepper	.10	.05	.01
☐ 195 Randy Moffitt	.10	.05	.01
☐ 196 Larry Herndon	.10	.05	.01
☐ 197 Rick Camp	.10	.05	.01
☐ 198 Andre Thornton	.25	.11	.03
☐ 199 Tom Veryzer	.10	.05	.01
☐ 200 Gary Alexander	.10	.05	.01
☐ 201 Rick Waits	.10	.05	.01
☐ 202 Rick Manning	.10	.05	.01
☐ 203 Paul Molitor	2.50	1.10	.30
☐ 204 Jim Gantner	.25	.11	.03
☐ 205 Paul Mitchell	.10	.05	.01
☐ 206 Reggie Cleveland	.10	.05	.01
☐ 207 Sixto Lezcano	.10	.05	.01
☐ 208 Bruce Benedict	.10	.05	.01
☐ 209 Rodney Scott	.10	.05	.01
☐ 210 John Tamargo	.10	.05	.01
☐ 211 Bill Lee	.25	.11	.03
☐ 212 Andre Dawson UER	1.25	.55	.16
Middle name Fernando			
should be Nolan			
☐ 213 Rowland Office	.10	.05	.01
☐ 214 Carl Yastrzemski	1.00	.45	.12
☐ 215 Jerry Remy	.10	.05	.01
☐ 216 Mike Torrez	.10	.05	.01
☐ 217 Skip Lockwood	.10	.05	.01
☐ 218 Fred Lynn	.25	.11	.03
☐ 219 Chris Chambliss	.25	.11	.03
☐ 220 Willie Aikens	.10	.05	.01
☐ 221 John Wathan	.10	.05	.01
☐ 222 Dan Quisenberry	.25	.11	.03
☐ 223 Willie Wilson	.25	.11	.03
☐ 224 Clint Hurdle	.10	.05	.01
☐ 225 Bob Watson	.25	.11	.03
☐ 226 Jim Spencer	.10	.05	.01
☐ 227 Ron Guidry	.25	.11	.03
☐ 228 Reggie Jackson	1.25	.55	.16
☐ 229 Oscar Gamble	.10	.05	.01
☐ 230 Jeff Cox	.10	.05	.01
☐ 231 Luis Tiant	.25	.11	.03
☐ 232 Rich Dauer	.10	.05	.01
☐ 233 Dan Graham	.10	.05	.01
☐ 234 Mike Flanagan	.25	.11	.03
☐ 235 John Lowenstein	.10	.05	.01
☐ 236 Benny Ayala	.10	.05	.01
☐ 237 Wayne Gross	.10	.05	.01
☐ 238 Rick Langford	.10	.05	.01
☐ 239 Tony Armas	.25	.11	.03
☐ 240A Bob Lacey P1 ERR	.50	.23	.06
Name misspelled Lacy			
☐ 240B Bob Lacey P2 COR	.10	.05	.01
☐ 241 Gene Tenace	.25	.11	.03
☐ 242 Bob Shirley	.10	.05	.01
☐ 243 Gary Lucas	.10	.05	.01
☐ 244 Jerry Turner	.10	.05	.01
☐ 245 John Wockenfuss	.10	.05	.01
☐ 246 Stan Papi	.10	.05	.01
☐ 247 Milt Wilcox	.10	.05	.01
☐ 248 Dan Schatzeder	.10	.05	.01
☐ 249 Steve Kemp	.10	.05	.01
☐ 250 Jim Lentine	.10	.05	.01
☐ 251 Pete Rose	1.50	.70	.19
☐ 252 Bill Madlock	.25	.11	.03
☐ 253 Dale Berra	.10	.05	.01
☐ 254 Kent Tekulve	.25	.11	.03
☐ 255 Enrique Romo	.10	.05	.01
☐ 256 Mike Easler	.10	.05	.01
☐ 257 Chuck Tanner MG	.25	.11	.03
☐ 258 Art Howe	.10	.05	.01
☐ 259 Alan Ashby	.10	.05	.01
☐ 260 Nolan Ryan	5.00	2.20	.60
☐ 261A Vern Ruhle P1 ERR	.50	.23	.06
Ken Forsch photo on front			
☐ 261B Vern Ruhle P2 COR	.25	.11	.03
☐ 262 Bob Boone	.25	.11	.03
☐ 263 Cesar Cedeno	.25	.11	.03
☐ 264 Jeff Leonard	.25	.11	.03
☐ 265 Pat Putnam	.10	.05	.01
☐ 266 Jon Matlack	.10	.05	.01
☐ 267 Dave Rajsich	.10	.05	.01
☐ 268 Billy Sample	.10	.05	.01
☐ 269 Damaso Garcia	.10	.05	.01
☐ 270 Tom Buskey	.10	.05	.01
☐ 271 Joey McLaughlin	.10	.05	.01
☐ 272 Barry Bonnell	.10	.05	.01
☐ 273 Tug McGraw	.25	.11	.03
☐ 274 Mike Jorgensen	.10	.05	.01
☐ 275 Pat Zachry	.10	.05	.01

Card			
☐ 276 Neil Allen	.10	.05	.01
☐ 277 Joel Youngblood	.10	.05	.01
☐ 278 Greg Pryor	.10	.05	.01
☐ 279 Britt Burns	.10	.05	.01
☐ 280 Rich Dotson	.10	.05	.01
☐ 281 Chet Lemon	.10	.05	.01
☐ 282 Rusty Kuntz	.10	.05	.01
☐ 283 Ted Cox	.10	.05	.01
☐ 284 Sparky Lyle	.25	.11	.03
☐ 285 Larry Cox	.10	.05	.01
☐ 286 Floyd Bannister	.10	.05	.01
☐ 287 Byron McLaughlin	.10	.05	.01
☐ 288 Rodney Craig	.10	.05	.01
☐ 289 Bobby Grich	.25	.11	.03
☐ 290 Dickie Thon	.25	.11	.03
☐ 291 Mark Clear	.10	.05	.01
☐ 292 Dave Lemanczyk	.10	.05	.01
☐ 293 Jason Thompson	.10	.05	.01
☐ 294 Rick Miller	.10	.05	.01
☐ 295 Lonnie Smith	.25	.11	.03
☐ 296 Ron Cey	.25	.11	.03
☐ 297 Steve Yeager	.10	.05	.01
☐ 298 Bobby Castillo	.10	.05	.01
☐ 299 Manny Mota	.25	.11	.03
☐ 300 Jay Johnstone	.25	.11	.03
☐ 301 Dan Driessen	.10	.05	.01
☐ 302 Joe Nolan	.10	.05	.01
☐ 303 Paul Householder	.10	.05	.01
☐ 304 Harry Spilman	.10	.05	.01
☐ 305 Cesar Geronimo	.10	.05	.01
☐ 306A Gary Mathews P1 ERR	.50	.23	.06
Name misspelled			
☐ 306B Gary Matthews P2	.25	.11	.03
COR			
☐ 307 Ken Reitz	.10	.05	.01
☐ 308 Ted Simmons	.25	.11	.03
☐ 309 John Littlefield	.10	.05	.01
☐ 310 George Frazier	.10	.05	.01
☐ 311 Dane Iorg	.10	.05	.01
☐ 312 Mike Ivie	.10	.05	.01
☐ 313 Dennis Littlejohn	.10	.05	.01
☐ 314 Gary Lavelle	.10	.05	.01
☐ 315 Jack Clark	.25	.11	.03
☐ 316 Jim Wohlford	.10	.05	.01
☐ 317 Rick Matula	.10	.05	.01
☐ 318 Toby Harrah	.25	.11	.03
☐ 319A Dwane Kuiper P1 ERR	.25	.11	.03
Name misspelled			
☐ 319B Duane Kuiper P2 COR	.10	.05	.01
☐ 320 Len Barker	.10	.05	.01
☐ 321 Victor Cruz	.10	.05	.01
☐ 322 Dell Alston	.10	.05	.01
☐ 323 Robin Yount	1.50	.70	.19
☐ 324 Charlie Moore	.10	.05	.01
☐ 325 Lary Sorensen	.10	.05	.01
☐ 326A Gorman Thomas P1	.50	.23	.06
2nd line on back:			
"30 HR mark 4th"			
☐ 326B Gorman Thomas P2	.25	.11	.03
30 HR mark 3rd			
☐ 327 Bob Rodgers MG	.10	.05	.01
☐ 328 Phil Niekro	.50	.23	.06
☐ 329 Chris Speier	.10	.05	.01
☐ 330A Steve Rodgers P1	.25	.11	.03
ERR Name misspelled			
☐ 330B Steve Rogers P2 COR	.10	.05	.01
☐ 331 Woodie Fryman	.10	.05	.01
☐ 332 Warren Cromartie	.10	.05	.01
☐ 333 Jerry White	.10	.05	.01
☐ 334 Tony Perez	.50	.23	.06
☐ 335 Carlton Fisk	1.25	.55	.16
☐ 336 Dick Drago	.10	.05	.01
☐ 337 Steve Renko	.10	.05	.01
☐ 338 Jim Rice	.25	.11	.03
☐ 339 Jerry Royster	.10	.05	.01
☐ 340 Frank White	.25	.11	.03
☐ 341 Jamie Quirk	.10	.05	.01
☐ 342A Paul Spittorff P1 ERR	.25	.11	.03
Name misspelled			
☐ 342B Paul Splittorff	.10	.05	.01
P2 COR			
☐ 343 Marty Pattin	.10	.05	.01
☐ 344 Pete LaCock	.10	.05	.01
☐ 345 Willie Randolph	.25	.11	.03
☐ 346 Rick Cerone	.10	.05	.01
☐ 347 Rich Gossage	.50	.23	.06
☐ 348 Reggie Jackson	1.25	.55	.16
☐ 349 Ruppert Jones	.10	.05	.01
☐ 350 Dave McKay	.10	.05	.01
☐ 351 Yogi Berra CO	.50	.23	.06
☐ 352 Doug DeCinces	.25	.11	.03
☐ 353 Jim Palmer	.60	.25	.07
☐ 354 Tippy Martinez	.10	.05	.01
☐ 355 Al Bumbry	.25	.11	.03
☐ 356 Earl Weaver MG	.50	.23	.06
☐ 357A Bob Picciolo P1 ERR	.25	.11	.03
Name misspelled			
☐ 357B Rob Picciolo P2 COR	.10	.05	.01
☐ 358 Matt Keough	.10	.05	.01
☐ 359 Dwayne Murphy	.10	.05	.01
☐ 360 Brian Kingman	.10	.05	.01
☐ 361 Bill Fahey	.10	.05	.01
☐ 362 Steve Mura	.10	.05	.01
☐ 363 Dennis Kinney	.10	.05	.01
☐ 364 Dave Winfield	1.50	.70	.19
☐ 365 Lou Whitaker	1.00	.45	.12
☐ 366 Lance Parrish	.25	.11	.03
☐ 367 Tim Corcoran	.10	.05	.01
☐ 368 Pat Underwood	.10	.05	.01
☐ 369 Al Cowens	.10	.05	.01
☐ 370 Sparky Anderson MG	.25	.11	.03
☐ 371 Pete Rose	1.50	.70	.19
☐ 372 Phil Garner	.25	.11	.03
☐ 373 Steve Nicosia	.10	.05	.01
☐ 374 John Candelaria	.25	.11	.03
☐ 375 Don Robinson	.10	.05	.01
☐ 376 Lee Lacy	.10	.05	.01
☐ 377 John Milner	.10	.05	.01
☐ 378 Craig Reynolds	.10	.05	.01
☐ 379A Luis Pujols P1 ERR	.25	.11	.03
Name misspelled Pujois			
☐ 379B Luis Pujols P2 COR	.10	.05	.01
☐ 380 Joe Niekro	.25	.11	.03
☐ 381 Joaquin Andujar	.25	.11	.03
☐ 382 Keith Moreland	.25	.11	.03
☐ 383 Jose Cruz	.25	.11	.03
☐ 384 Bill Virdon MG	.10	.05	.01
☐ 385 Jim Sundberg	.25	.11	.03
☐ 386 Doc Medich	.10	.05	.01
☐ 387 Al Oliver	.25	.11	.03
☐ 388 Jim Norris	.10	.05	.01
☐ 389 Bob Bailor	.10	.05	.01
☐ 390 Ernie Whitt	.10	.05	.01
☐ 391 Otto Velez	.10	.05	.01
☐ 392 Roy Howell	.10	.05	.01
☐ 393 Bob Walk	.25	.11	.03
☐ 394 Doug Flynn	.10	.05	.01
☐ 395 Pete Falcone	.10	.05	.01
☐ 396 Tom Hausman	.10	.05	.01
☐ 397 Elliott Maddox	.10	.05	.01
☐ 398 Mike Squires	.10	.05	.01
☐ 399 Marvis Foley	.10	.05	.01
☐ 400 Steve Trout	.10	.05	.01
☐ 401 Wayne Nordhagen	.10	.05	.01
☐ 402 Tony LaRussa MG	.25	.11	.03
☐ 403 Bruce Bochte	.10	.05	.01
☐ 404 Bake McBride	.10	.05	.01
☐ 405 Jerry Narron	.10	.05	.01
☐ 406 Rob Dressler	.10	.05	.01
☐ 407 Dave Heaverlo	.10	.05	.01
☐ 408 Tom Paciorek	.10	.05	.01
☐ 409 Carney Lansford	.25	.11	.03
☐ 410 Brian Downing	.10	.05	.01
☐ 411 Don Aase	.10	.05	.01
☐ 412 Jim Barr	.10	.05	.01
☐ 413 Don Baylor	.50	.23	.06
☐ 414 Jim Fregosi MG	.10	.05	.01
☐ 415 Dallas Green MG	.10	.05	.01
☐ 416 Dave Lopes	.25	.11	.03
☐ 417 Jerry Reuss	.25	.11	.03
☐ 418 Rick Sutcliffe	.25	.11	.03
☐ 419 Derrel Thomas	.10	.05	.01
☐ 420 Tom Lasorda MG	.25	.11	.03
☐ 421 Charlie Leibrandt	.50	.23	.06
☐ 422 Tom Seaver	1.25	.55	.16
☐ 423 Ron Oester	.10	.05	.01
☐ 424 Junior Kennedy	.10	.05	.01
☐ 425 Tom Seaver	1.25	.55	.16
☐ 426 Bobby Cox MG	.25	.11	.03
☐ 427 Leon Durham	.25	.11	.03
☐ 428 Terry Kennedy	.10	.05	.01
☐ 429 Silvio Martinez	.10	.05	.01
☐ 430 George Hendrick	.10	.05	.01
☐ 431 Red Schoendienst MG	.50	.23	.06
☐ 432 Johnnie LeMaster	.10	.05	.01
☐ 433 Vida Blue	.25	.11	.03
☐ 434 John Montefusco	.10	.05	.01
☐ 435 Terry Whitfield	.10	.05	.01
☐ 436 Dave Bristol MG	.10	.05	.01
☐ 437 Dale Murphy	.75	.35	.09
☐ 438 Jerry Dybzinski	.10	.05	.01
☐ 439 Jorge Orta	.10	.05	.01
☐ 440 Wayne Garland	.10	.05	.01
☐ 441 Miguel Dilone	.10	.05	.01
☐ 442 Dave Garcia MG	.10	.05	.01
☐ 443 Don Money	.10	.05	.01
☐ 444A Buck Martinez P1 ERR	.25	.11	.03
Reverse negative			
☐ 444B Buck Martinez	.10	.05	.01
P2 COR			
☐ 445 Jerry Augustine	.10	.05	.01
☐ 446 Ben Oglivie	.25	.11	.03
☐ 447 Jim Slaton	.10	.05	.01
☐ 448 Doyle Alexander	.10	.05	.01
☐ 449 Tony Bernazard	.10	.05	.01
☐ 450 Scott Sanderson	.10	.05	.01
☐ 451 David Palmer	.10	.05	.01
☐ 452 Stan Bahnsen	.10	.05	.01
☐ 453 Dick Williams MG	.10	.05	.01
☐ 454 Rick Burleson	.10	.05	.01
☐ 455 Gary Allenson	.10	.05	.01
☐ 456 Bob Stanley	.10	.05	.01
☐ 457A John Tudor P1 ERR	.25	.11	.03
Lifetime W-L 9.7			
☐ 457B John Tudor P2 COR	.25	.11	.03
Lifetime W-L 9-7			
☐ 458 Dwight Evans	.50	.23	.06
☐ 459 Glenn Hubbard	.10	.05	.01
☐ 460 U.L. Washington	.10	.05	.01
☐ 461 Larry Gura	.10	.05	.01
☐ 462 Rich Gale	.10	.05	.01
☐ 463 Hal McRae	.50	.23	.06
☐ 464 Jim Frey MG	.10	.05	.01
☐ 465 Bucky Dent	.25	.11	.03
☐ 466 Dennis Werth	.10	.05	.01
☐ 467 Ron Davis	.10	.05	.01
☐ 468 Reggie Jackson UER	1.25	.55	.16
32 HR in 1970			
should be 23			
☐ 469 Bobby Brown	.10	.05	.01
☐ 470 Mike Davis	.10	.05	.01
☐ 471 Gaylord Perry	.50	.23	.06
☐ 472 Mark Belanger	.25	.11	.03
☐ 473 Jim Palmer	.60	.25	.07
☐ 474 Sammy Stewart	.10	.05	.01
☐ 475 Tim Stoddard	.10	.05	.01
☐ 476 Steve Stone	.25	.11	.03
☐ 477 Jeff Newman	.10	.05	.01
☐ 478 Steve McCatty	.10	.05	.01
☐ 479 Billy Martin MG	.50	.23	.06
☐ 480 Mitchell Page	.10	.05	.01
☐ 481 Steve Carlton CY	1.00	.45	.12
☐ 482 Bill Buckner	.25	.11	.03
☐ 483A Ivan DeJesus P1 ERR	.25	.11	.03
Lifetime hits 702			
☐ 483B Ivan DeJesus P2 COR	.10	.05	.01
Lifetime hits 642			
☐ 484 Cliff Johnson	.10	.05	.01
☐ 485 Lenny Randle	.10	.05	.01
☐ 486 Larry Milbourne	.10	.05	.01
☐ 487 Roy Smalley	.10	.05	.01
☐ 488 John Castino	.10	.05	.01
☐ 489 Ron Jackson	.10	.05	.01
☐ 490A Dave Roberts P1	.25	.11	.03
Career Highlights			
Showed pop in			
☐ 490B Dave Roberts P2	.10	.05	.01
Declared himself			
☐ 491 George Brett MVP	2.50	1.10	.30
☐ 492 Mike Cubbage	.10	.05	.01
☐ 493 Rob Wilfong	.10	.05	.01
☐ 494 Danny Goodwin	.10	.05	.01
☐ 495 Jose Morales	.10	.05	.01
☐ 496 Mickey Rivers	.25	.11	.03
☐ 497 Mike Edwards	.10	.05	.01
☐ 498 Mike Sadek	.10	.05	.01
☐ 499 Lenn Sakata	.10	.05	.01
☐ 500 Gene Michael MG	.10	.05	.01
☐ 501 Dave Roberts	.10	.05	.01
☐ 502 Steve Dillard	.10	.05	.01
☐ 503 Jim Essian	.10	.05	.01
☐ 504 Rance Mulliniks	.10	.05	.01
☐ 505 Darrell Porter	.10	.05	.01
☐ 506 Joe Torre MG	.25	.11	.03
☐ 507 Terry Crowley	.10	.05	.01
☐ 508 Bill Travers	.10	.05	.01
☐ 509 Nelson Norman	.10	.05	.01
☐ 510 Bob McClure	.10	.05	.01
☐ 511 Steve Howe	.25	.11	.03
☐ 512 Dave Rader	.10	.05	.01
☐ 513 Mick Kelleher	.10	.05	.01
☐ 514 Kiko Garcia	.10	.05	.01
☐ 515 Larry Biittner	.10	.05	.01
☐ 516A Willie Norwood P1	.25	.11	.03
Career Highlights			
Spent most of			
☐ 516B Willie Norwood P2	.10	.05	.01
Traded to Seattle			
☐ 517 Bo Diaz	.10	.05	.01
☐ 518 Juan Beniquez	.10	.05	.01
☐ 519 Scot Thompson	.10	.05	.01
☐ 520 Jim Tracy	.10	.05	.01
☐ 521 Carlos Lezcano	.10	.05	.01
☐ 522 Joe Amalfitano MG	.10	.05	.01
☐ 523 Preston Hanna	.10	.05	.01
☐ 524A Ray Burris P1	.25	.11	.03
Career Highlights			
Went on 0			
☐ 524B Ray Burris P2	.10	.05	.01
Drafted by 0			
☐ 525 Broderick Perkins	.10	.05	.01
☐ 526 Mickey Hatcher	.25	.11	.03
☐ 527 John Goryl MG	.10	.05	.01
☐ 528 Dick Davis	.10	.05	.01
☐ 529 Butch Wynegar	.10	.05	.01
☐ 530 Sal Butera	.10	.05	.01
☐ 531 Jerry Koosman	.25	.11	.03
☐ 532A Geoff Zahn P1	.25	.11	.03
(Career Highlights			
Was 2nd in			
☐ 532B Geoff Zahn P2	.10	.05	.01
Signed a 3 year			
☐ 533 Dennis Martinez	.50	.23	.06
☐ 534 Gary Thomasson	.10	.05	.01
☐ 535 Steve Macko	.10	.05	.01
☐ 536 Jim Kaat	.50	.23	.06
☐ 537 Best Hitters	2.50	1.10	.30
George Brett			
Rod Carew			
☐ 538 Tim Raines	4.00	1.80	.50
☐ 539 Keith Smith	.10	.05	.01
☐ 540 Ken Macha	.10	.05	.01
☐ 541 Burt Hooton	.10	.05	.01
☐ 542 Butch Hobson	.10	.05	.01
☐ 543 Bill Stein	.10	.05	.01
☐ 544 Dave Stapleton	.10	.05	.01
☐ 545 Bob Pate	.10	.05	.01
☐ 546 Doug Corbett	.10	.05	.01
☐ 547 Darrell Jackson	.10	.05	.01
☐ 548 Pete Redfern	.10	.05	.01
☐ 549 Roger Erickson	.10	.05	.01
☐ 550 Al Hrabosky	.10	.05	.01
☐ 551 Dick Tidrow	.10	.05	.01
☐ 552 Dave Ford	.10	.05	.01
☐ 553 Dave Kingman	.25	.11	.03
☐ 554A Mike Vail P1	.25	.11	.03
Career Highlights			
After two			
☐ 554B Mike Vail P2	.10	.05	.01
Traded to			
☐ 555A Jerry Martin P1	.25	.11	.03
Career Highlights			
Overcame a			
☐ 555B Jerry Martin P2	.10	.05	.01
Traded to			
☐ 556A Jesus Figueroa P1	.25	.11	.03
Career Highlights			
Had an			
☐ 556B Jesus Figueroa P2	.10	.05	.01
Traded to			
☐ 557 Don Stanhouse	.10	.05	.01
☐ 558 Barry Foote	.10	.05	.01
☐ 559 Tim Blackwell	.10	.05	.01
☐ 560 Bruce Sutter	.25	.11	.03
☐ 561 Rick Reuschel	.25	.11	.03
☐ 562 Lynn McGlothen	.10	.05	.01
☐ 563A Bob Owchinko P1	.25	.11	.03
Career Highlights			
Traded to			
☐ 563B Bob Owchinko P2	.10	.05	.01
Involved in a			
☐ 564 John Verhoeven	.10	.05	.01
☐ 565 Ken Landreaux	.10	.05	.01
☐ 566A Glen Adams P1 ERR	.25	.11	.03
Name misspelled			
☐ 566B Glenn Adams P2 COR	.10	.05	.01
☐ 567 Hosken Powell	.10	.05	.01
☐ 568 Dick Noles	.10	.05	.01
☐ 569 Danny Ainge	3.00	1.35	.35
☐ 570 Bobby Mattick MG	.10	.05	.01
☐ 571 Joe Lefebvre	.10	.05	.01
☐ 572 Bobby Clark	.10	.05	.01
☐ 573 Dennis Lamp	.10	.05	.01
☐ 574 Randy Lerch	.10	.05	.01
☐ 575 Mookie Wilson	.50	.23	.06
☐ 576 Ron LeFlore	.25	.11	.03
☐ 577 Jim Dwyer	.10	.05	.01
☐ 578 Bill Castro	.10	.05	.01
☐ 579 Greg Minton	.10	.05	.01
☐ 580 Mark Littell	.10	.05	.01
☐ 581 Andy Hassler	.10	.05	.01
☐ 582 Dave Stieb	.25	.11	.03
☐ 583 Ken Oberkfell	.10	.05	.01
☐ 584 Larry Bradford	.10	.05	.01
☐ 585 Fred Stanley	.10	.05	.01
☐ 586 Bill Caudill	.10	.05	.01
☐ 587 Doug Capilla	.10	.05	.01
☐ 588 George Riley	.10	.05	.01
☐ 589 Willie Hernandez	.25	.11	.03
☐ 590 Mike Schmidt MVP	1.50	.70	.19
☐ 591 Steve Stone CY	.10	.05	.01
☐ 592 Rick Sofield	.10	.05	.01
☐ 593 Bombo Rivera	.10	.05	.01
☐ 594 Gary Ward	.10	.05	.01
☐ 595A Dave Edwards P1	.25	.11	.03
Career Highlights			
Sidelined the			
☐ 595B Dave Edwards P2	.10	.05	.01
Traded to			
☐ 596 Mike Proly	.10	.05	.01
☐ 597 Tommy Boggs	.10	.05	.01
☐ 598 Greg Gross	.10	.05	.01
☐ 599 Elias Sosa	.10	.05	.01
☐ 600 Pat Kelly	.10	.05	.01
☐ 601A Checklist 1-120 P1	.25	.11	.03
ERR Unnumbered			
51 Donahue			
☐ 601B Checklist 1-120 P2	.50	.23	.06
COR Unnumbered			
51 Donohue			
☐ 602 Checklist 121-240	.25	.11	.03
Unnumbered			
☐ 603A Checklist 241-360 P1	.25	.11	.03
ERR Unnumbered			
306 Mathews			
☐ 603B Checklist 241-360 P2	.25	.11	.03
COR Unnumbered			
306 Matthews			
☐ 604A Checklist 361-480 P1	.25	.11	.03
ERR Unnumbered			
379 Pujois			
☐ 604B Checklist 361-480 P2	.25	.11	.03
COR Unnumbered			
379 Pujols			
☐ 605A Checklist 481-600 P1	.25	.11	.03
ERR Unnumbered			
566 Glen Adams			
☐ 605B Checklist 481-600 P2	.25	.11	.03
COR Unnumbered			
566 Glenn Adams			

1982 Donruss

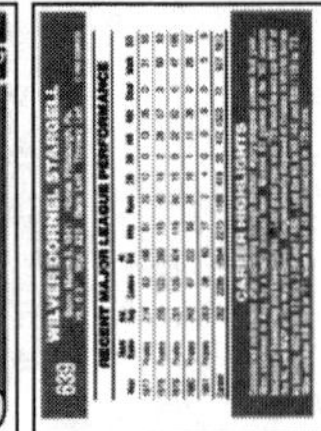

The 1982 Donruss set contains 653 numbered standard-size cards and seven unnumbered checklists. The first 26 cards of this set are entitled Diamond Kings (DK) and feature the artwork of Dick Perez of Perez-Steele Galleries. The set was marketed with puzzle pieces in 15-card packs rather than with bubble gum. There are 63 pieces to the puzzle, which, when put together, make a collage of Babe Ruth entitled "Hall of Fame Diamond King." The card stock in this year's Donruss cards is considerably thicker than the 1981 cards. The seven unnumbered checklist cards are arbitrarily assigned numbers 654 through 660 and are listed at the end of the list below. Notable Rookie Cards in this set include Brett Butler, Cal Ripken Jr., Lee Smith and Dave Stewart.

	NRMT	VG-E	GOOD
COMPLETE SET (660)	70.00	32.00	8.75
COMPLETE FACT.SET (660)	75.00	34.00	9.50
COMMON CARD (1-660)	.10	.05	.01
☐ 1 Pete Rose DK	2.00	.90	.25
☐ 2 Gary Carter DK	.20	.09	.03
☐ 3 Steve Garvey DK	.40	.18	.05
☐ 4 Vida Blue DK	.20	.09	.03
☐ 5 Alan Trammell DK COR	.50	.23	.06
☐ 5A Alan Trammel DK ERR (Name misspelled)	.50	.23	.06
☐ 6 Len Barker DK	.20	.09	.03
☐ 7 Dwight Evans DK	.40	.18	.05
☐ 8 Rod Carew DK	.60	.25	.07
☐ 9 George Hendrick DK	.20	.09	.03
☐ 10 Phil Niekro DK	.40	.18	.05
☐ 11 Richie Zisk DK	.20	.09	.03
☐ 12 Dave Parker DK	.20	.09	.03
☐ 13 Nolan Ryan DK	4.00	1.80	.50
☐ 14 Ivan DeJesus DK	.20	.09	.03
☐ 15 George Brett DK	2.00	.90	.25
☐ 16 Tom Seaver DK	.75	.35	.09
☐ 17 Dave Kingman DK	.20	.09	.03
☐ 18 Dave Winfield DK	1.50	.70	.19
☐ 19 Mike Norris DK	.20	.09	.03
☐ 20 Carlton Fisk DK	.40	.18	.05
☐ 21 Ozzie Smith DK	2.00	.90	.25
☐ 22 Roy Smalley DK	.20	.09	.03
☐ 23 Buddy Bell DK	.20	.09	.03
☐ 24 Ken Singleton DK	.20	.09	.03
☐ 25 John Mayberry DK	.20	.09	.03
☐ 26 Gorman Thomas DK	.20	.09	.03
☐ 27 Earl Weaver MG	.40	.18	.05
☐ 28 Rollie Fingers	.40	.18	.05
☐ 29 Sparky Anderson MG	.20	.09	.03
☐ 30 Dennis Eckersley	.40	.18	.05
☐ 31 Dave Winfield	1.50	.70	.19
☐ 32 Burt Hooton	.10	.05	.01
☐ 33 Rick Waits	.10	.05	.01
☐ 34 George Brett	3.50	1.55	.45
☐ 35 Steve McCatty	.10	.05	.01
☐ 36 Steve Rogers	.10	.05	.01
☐ 37 Bill Stein	.10	.05	.01
☐ 38 Steve Renko	.10	.05	.01
☐ 39 Mike Squires	.10	.05	.01
☐ 40 George Hendrick	.10	.05	.01
☐ 41 Bob Knepper	.10	.05	.01
☐ 42 Steve Carlton	.75	.35	.09
☐ 43 Larry Biittner	.10	.05	.01
☐ 44 Chris Welsh	.10	.05	.01
☐ 45 Steve Nicosia	.10	.05	.01
☐ 46 Jack Clark	.20	.09	.03
☐ 47 Chris Chambliss	.20	.09	.03
☐ 48 Ivan DeJesus	.10	.05	.01
☐ 49 Lee Mazzilli	.10	.05	.01
☐ 50 Julio Cruz	.10	.05	.01
☐ 51 Pete Redfern	.10	.05	.01
☐ 52 Dave Stieb	.20	.09	.03
☐ 53 Doug Corbett	.10	.05	.01
☐ 54 Jorge Bell	.75	.35	.09
☐ 55 Joe Simpson	.10	.05	.01
☐ 56 Rusty Staub	.20	.09	.03
☐ 57 Hector Cruz	.10	.05	.01
☐ 58 Claudell Washington	.10	.05	.01
☐ 59 Enrique Romo	.10	.05	.01
☐ 60 Gary Lavelle	.10	.05	.01
☐ 61 Tim Flannery	.10	.05	.01
☐ 62 Joe Nolan	.10	.05	.01
☐ 63 Larry Bowa	.20	.09	.03
☐ 64 Sixto Lezcano	.10	.05	.01
☐ 65 Joe Sambito	.10	.05	.01
☐ 66 Bruce Kison	.10	.05	.01
☐ 67 Wayne Nordhagen	.10	.05	.01
☐ 68 Woodie Fryman	.10	.05	.01
☐ 69 Billy Sample	.10	.05	.01
☐ 70 Amos Otis	.20	.09	.03
☐ 71 Matt Keough	.10	.05	.01
☐ 72 Toby Harrah	.20	.09	.03
☐ 73 Dave Righetti	.40	.18	.05
☐ 74 Carl Yastrzemski	.75	.35	.09
☐ 75 Bob Welch	.20	.09	.03
☐ 76 Alan Trammell COR	1.00	.45	.12
☐ 76A Alan Trammel ERR (Name misspelled)	1.00	.45	.12
☐ 77 Rick Dempsey	.20	.09	.03
☐ 78 Paul Molitor	2.00	.90	.25
☐ 79 Dennis Martinez	.20	.09	.03
☐ 80 Jim Slaton	.10	.05	.01
☐ 81 Champ Summers	.10	.05	.01
☐ 82 Carney Lansford	.20	.09	.03
☐ 83 Barry Foote	.10	.05	.01
☐ 84 Steve Garvey	.40	.18	.05
☐ 85 Rick Manning	.10	.05	.01
☐ 86 John Wathan	.10	.05	.01
☐ 87 Brian Kingman	.10	.05	.01
☐ 88 Andre Dawson UER (Middle name Fernando should be Nolan)	1.00	.45	.12
☐ 89 Jim Kern	.10	.05	.01
☐ 90 Bobby Grich	.20	.09	.03
☐ 91 Bob Forsch	.10	.05	.01
☐ 92 Art Howe	.10	.05	.01
☐ 93 Marty Bystrom	.10	.05	.01
☐ 94 Ozzie Smith	3.00	1.35	.35
☐ 95 Dave Parker	.20	.09	.03
☐ 96 Doyle Alexander	.10	.05	.01
☐ 97 Al Hrabosky	.10	.05	.01
☐ 98 Frank Taveras	.10	.05	.01
☐ 99 Tim Blackwell	.10	.05	.01
☐ 100 Floyd Bannister	.10	.05	.01
☐ 101 Alfredo Griffin	.10	.05	.01
☐ 102 Dave Engle	.10	.05	.01
☐ 103 Mario Soto	.10	.05	.01
☐ 104 Ross Baumgarten	.10	.05	.01
☐ 105 Ken Singleton	.20	.09	.03
☐ 106 Ted Simmons	.20	.09	.03
☐ 107 Jack Morris	.20	.09	.03
☐ 108 Bob Watson	.20	.09	.03
☐ 109 Dwight Evans	.40	.18	.05
☐ 110 Tom Lasorda MG	.20	.09	.03
☐ 111 Bert Blyleven	.40	.18	.05
☐ 112 Dan Quisenberry	.20	.09	.03
☐ 113 Rickey Henderson	2.50	1.10	.30
☐ 114 Gary Carter	.20	.09	.03
☐ 115 Brian Downing	.10	.05	.01
☐ 116 Al Oliver	.20	.09	.03
☐ 117 LaMarr Hoyt	.10	.05	.01
☐ 118 Cesar Cedeno	.20	.09	.03
☐ 119 Keith Moreland	.10	.05	.01
☐ 120 Bob Shirley	.10	.05	.01
☐ 121 Terry Kennedy	.10	.05	.01
☐ 122 Frank Pastore	.10	.05	.01
☐ 123 Gene Garber	.10	.05	.01
☐ 124 Tony Pena	.20	.09	.03
☐ 125 Allen Ripley	.10	.05	.01
☐ 126 Randy Martz	.10	.05	.01
☐ 127 Richie Zisk	.10	.05	.01
☐ 128 Mike Scott	.20	.09	.03
☐ 129 Lloyd Moseby	.10	.05	.01
☐ 130 Rob Wilfong	.10	.05	.01
☐ 131 Tim Stoddard	.10	.05	.01
☐ 132 Gorman Thomas	.20	.09	.03
☐ 133 Dan Petry	.10	.05	.01
☐ 134 Bob Stanley	.10	.05	.01
☐ 135 Lou Piniella	.20	.09	.03
☐ 136 Pedro Guerrero	.20	.09	.03
☐ 137 Len Barker	.10	.05	.01
☐ 138 Rich Gale	.10	.05	.01
☐ 139 Wayne Gross	.10	.05	.01
☐ 140 Tim Wallach	.50	.23	.06
☐ 141 Gene Mauch MG	.10	.05	.01
☐ 142 Doc Medich	.10	.05	.01
☐ 143 Tony Bernazard	.10	.05	.01
☐ 144 Bill Virdon MG	.10	.05	.01
☐ 145 John Littlefield	.10	.05	.01
☐ 146 Dave Bergman	.10	.05	.01
☐ 147 Dick Davis	.10	.05	.01
☐ 148 Tom Seaver	.75	.35	.09
☐ 149 Matt Sinatro	.10	.05	.01
☐ 150 Chuck Tanner MG	.10	.05	.01
☐ 151 Leon Durham	.20	.09	.03
☐ 152 Gene Tenace	.20	.09	.03
☐ 153 Al Bumbry	.20	.09	.03
☐ 154 Mark Brouhard	.10	.05	.01
☐ 155 Rick Peters	.10	.05	.01
☐ 156 Jerry Remy	.10	.05	.01
☐ 157 Rick Reuschel	.20	.09	.03
☐ 158 Steve Howe	.10	.05	.01
☐ 159 Alan Bannister	.10	.05	.01
☐ 160 U.L. Washington	.10	.05	.01
☐ 161 Rick Langford	.10	.05	.01
☐ 162 Bill Gullickson	.10	.05	.01
☐ 163 Mark Wagner	.10	.05	.01
☐ 164 Geoff Zahn	.10	.05	.01
☐ 165 Ron LeFlore	.20	.09	.03
☐ 166 Dane Iorg	.10	.05	.01
☐ 167 Joe Niekro	.20	.09	.03
☐ 168 Pete Rose	1.50	.70	.19
☐ 169 Dave Collins	.10	.05	.01
☐ 170 Rick Wise	.10	.05	.01
☐ 171 Jim Bibby	.10	.05	.01
☐ 172 Larry Herndon	.10	.05	.01
☐ 173 Bob Horner	.20	.09	.03
☐ 174 Steve Dillard	.10	.05	.01
☐ 175 Mookie Wilson	.20	.09	.03
☐ 176 Dan Meyer	.10	.05	.01
☐ 177 Fernando Arroyo	.10	.05	.01
☐ 178 Jackson Todd	.10	.05	.01
☐ 179 Darrell Jackson	.10	.05	.01
☐ 180 Alvis Woods	.10	.05	.01
☐ 181 Jim Anderson	.10	.05	.01
☐ 182 Dave Kingman	.20	.09	.03
☐ 183 Steve Henderson	.10	.05	.01
☐ 184 Brian Asselstine	.10	.05	.01
☐ 185 Rod Scurry	.10	.05	.01
☐ 186 Fred Breining	.10	.05	.01
☐ 187 Danny Boone	.10	.05	.01
☐ 188 Junior Kennedy	.10	.05	.01
☐ 189 Sparky Lyle	.20	.09	.03
☐ 190 Whitey Herzog MG	.20	.09	.03
☐ 191 Dave Smith	.10	.05	.01
☐ 192 Ed Ott	.10	.05	.01
☐ 193 Greg Luzinski	.20	.09	.03
☐ 194 Bill Lee	.20	.09	.03
☐ 195 Don Zimmer MG	.10	.05	.01
☐ 196 Hal McRae	.20	.09	.03
☐ 197 Mike Norris	.10	.05	.01
☐ 198 Duane Kuiper	.10	.05	.01
☐ 199 Rick Cerone	.10	.05	.01
☐ 200 Jim Rice	.20	.09	.03
☐ 201 Steve Yeager	.10	.05	.01
☐ 202 Tom Brookens	.10	.05	.01
☐ 203 Jose Morales	.10	.05	.01
☐ 204 Roy Howell	.10	.05	.01
☐ 205 Tippy Martinez	.10	.05	.01
☐ 206 Moose Haas	.10	.05	.01
☐ 207 Al Cowens	.10	.05	.01
☐ 208 Dave Stapleton	.10	.05	.01
☐ 209 Bucky Dent	.20	.09	.03
☐ 210 Ron Cey	.20	.09	.03
☐ 211 Jorge Orta	.10	.05	.01
☐ 212 Jamie Quirk	.10	.05	.01
☐ 213 Jeff Jones	.10	.05	.01
☐ 214 Tim Raines	1.50	.70	.19
☐ 215 Jon Matlack	.10	.05	.01
☐ 216 Rod Carew	.75	.35	.09
☐ 217 Jim Kaat	.20	.09	.03
☐ 218 Joe Pittman	.10	.05	.01
☐ 219 Larry Christenson	.10	.05	.01
☐ 220 Juan Bonilla	.10	.05	.01
☐ 221 Mike Easler	.10	.05	.01
☐ 222 Vida Blue	.20	.09	.03
☐ 223 Rick Camp	.10	.05	.01
☐ 224 Mike Jorgensen	.10	.05	.01
☐ 225 Jody Davis	.10	.05	.01
☐ 226 Mike Parrott	.10	.05	.01
☐ 227 Jim Clancy	.10	.05	.01
☐ 228 Hosken Powell	.10	.05	.01
☐ 229 Tom Hume	.10	.05	.01
☐ 230 Britt Burns	.10	.05	.01
☐ 231 Jim Palmer	.60	.25	.07
☐ 232 Bob Rodgers MG	.10	.05	.01
☐ 233 Milt Wilcox	.10	.05	.01
☐ 234 Dave Revering	.10	.05	.01
☐ 235 Mike Torrez	.10	.05	.01
☐ 236 Robert Castillo	.10	.05	.01
☐ 237 Von Hayes	.20	.09	.03
☐ 238 Renie Martin	.10	.05	.01
☐ 239 Dwayne Murphy	.10	.05	.01
☐ 240 Rodney Scott	.10	.05	.01
☐ 241 Fred Patek	.10	.05	.01
☐ 242 Mickey Rivers	.10	.05	.01
☐ 243 Steve Trout	.10	.05	.01
☐ 244 Jose Cruz	.20	.09	.03
☐ 245 Manny Trillo	.10	.05	.01
☐ 246 Lary Sorensen	.10	.05	.01
☐ 247 Dave Edwards	.10	.05	.01
☐ 248 Dan Driessen	.10	.05	.01
☐ 249 Tommy Boggs	.10	.05	.01
☐ 250 Dale Berra	.10	.05	.01
☐ 251 Ed Whitson	.10	.05	.01
☐ 252 Lee Smith	6.00	2.70	.75
☐ 253 Tom Paciorek	.10	.05	.01
☐ 254 Pat Zachry	.10	.05	.01
☐ 255 Luis Leal	.10	.05	.01
☐ 256 John Castino	.10	.05	.01
☐ 257 Rich Dauer	.10	.05	.01
☐ 258 Cecil Cooper	.20	.09	.03
☐ 259 Dave Rozema	.10	.05	.01
☐ 260 John Tudor	.20	.09	.03
☐ 261 Jerry Mumphrey	.10	.05	.01
☐ 262 Jay Johnstone	.20	.09	.03
☐ 263 Bo Diaz	.10	.05	.01
☐ 264 Dennis Leonard	.10	.05	.01
☐ 265 Jim Spencer	.10	.05	.01
☐ 266 John Milner	.10	.05	.01
☐ 267 Don Aase	.10	.05	.01
☐ 268 Jim Sundberg	.20	.09	.03
☐ 269 Lamar Johnson	.10	.05	.01
☐ 270 Frank LaCorte	.10	.05	.01
☐ 271 Barry Evans	.10	.05	.01
☐ 272 Enos Cabell	.10	.05	.01
☐ 273 Del Unser	.10	.05	.01
☐ 274 George Foster	.20	.09	.03
☐ 275 Brett Butler	2.00	.90	.25
☐ 276 Lee Lacy	.10	.05	.01
☐ 277 Ken Reitz	.10	.05	.01
☐ 278 Keith Hernandez	.20	.09	.03
☐ 279 Doug DeCinces	.20	.09	.03
☐ 280 Charlie Moore	.10	.05	.01
☐ 281 Lance Parrish	.40	.18	.05
☐ 282 Ralph Houk MG	.20	.09	.03
☐ 283 Rich Gossage	.40	.18	.05
☐ 284 Jerry Reuss	.20	.09	.03
☐ 285 Mike Stanton	.10	.05	.01
☐ 286 Frank White	.20	.09	.03
☐ 287 Bob Owchinko	.10	.05	.01
☐ 288 Scott Sanderson	.10	.05	.01
☐ 289 Bump Wills	.10	.05	.01
☐ 290 Dave Frost	.10	.05	.01
☐ 291 Chet Lemon	.10	.05	.01
☐ 292 Tito Landrum	.10	.05	.01
☐ 293 Vern Ruhle	.10	.05	.01
☐ 294 Mike Schmidt	2.00	.90	.25
☐ 295 Sam Mejias	.10	.05	.01
☐ 296 Gary Lucas	.10	.05	.01
☐ 297 John Candelaria	.10	.05	.01
☐ 298 Jerry Martin	.10	.05	.01
☐ 299 Dale Murphy	.40	.18	.05
☐ 300 Mike Lum	.10	.05	.01
☐ 301 Tom Hausman	.10	.05	.01
☐ 302 Glenn Abbott	.10	.05	.01
☐ 303 Roger Erickson	.10	.05	.01
☐ 304 Otto Velez	.10	.05	.01
☐ 305 Danny Goodwin	.10	.05	.01
☐ 306 John Mayberry	.10	.05	.01
☐ 307 Lenny Randle	.10	.05	.01
☐ 308 Bob Bailor	.10	.05	.01
☐ 309 Jerry Morales	.10	.05	.01
☐ 310 Rufino Linares	.10	.05	.01
☐ 311 Kent Tekulve	.20	.09	.03
☐ 312 Joe Morgan	.60	.25	.07
☐ 313 John Urrea	.10	.05	.01
☐ 314 Paul Householder	.10	.05	.01
☐ 315 Garry Maddox	.10	.05	.01
☐ 316 Mike Ramsey	.10	.05	.01
☐ 317 Alan Ashby	.10	.05	.01
☐ 318 Bob Clark	.10	.05	.01
☐ 319 Tony LaRussa MG	.20	.09	.03
☐ 320 Charlie Lea	.10	.05	.01
☐ 321 Danny Darwin	.10	.05	.01
☐ 322 Cesar Geronimo	.10	.05	.01
☐ 323 Tom Underwood	.10	.05	.01
☐ 324 Andre Thornton	.10	.05	.01
☐ 325 Rudy May	.10	.05	.01
☐ 326 Frank Tanana	.20	.09	.03
☐ 327 Dave Lopes	.20	.09	.03
☐ 328 Richie Hebner	.20	.09	.03
☐ 329 Mike Flanagan	.20	.09	.03
☐ 330 Mike Caldwell	.10	.05	.01
☐ 331 Scott McGregor	.10	.05	.01
☐ 332 Jerry Augustine	.10	.05	.01
☐ 333 Stan Papi	.10	.05	.01
☐ 334 Rick Miller	.10	.05	.01
☐ 335 Graig Nettles	.20	.09	.03
☐ 336 Dusty Baker	.40	.18	.05
☐ 337 Dave Garcia MG	.10	.05	.01
☐ 338 Larry Gura	.10	.05	.01
☐ 339 Cliff Johnson	.10	.05	.01
☐ 340 Warren Cromartie	.10	.05	.01
☐ 341 Steve Comer	.10	.05	.01
☐ 342 Rick Burleson	.10	.05	.01
☐ 343 John Martin	.10	.05	.01
☐ 344 Craig Reynolds	.10	.05	.01
☐ 345 Mike Proly	.10	.05	.01
☐ 346 Ruppert Jones	.10	.05	.01
☐ 347 Omar Moreno	.10	.05	.01
☐ 348 Greg Minton	.10	.05	.01
☐ 349 Rick Mahler	.10	.05	.01
☐ 350 Alex Trevino	.10	.05	.01
☐ 351 Mike Krukow	.10	.05	.01
☐ 352A Shane Rawley ERR (Photo actually Jim Anderson)	.40	.18	.05
☐ 352B Shane Rawley COR	.10	.05	.01
☐ 353 Garth Iorg	.10	.05	.01
☐ 354 Pete Mackanin	.10	.05	.01
☐ 355 Paul Moskau	.10	.05	.01
☐ 356 Richard Dotson	.10	.05	.01
☐ 357 Steve Stone	.20	.09	.03
☐ 358 Larry Hisle	.10	.05	.01
☐ 359 Aurelio Lopez	.10	.05	.01
☐ 360 Oscar Gamble	.10	.05	.01
☐ 361 Tom Burgmeier	.10	.05	.01
☐ 362 Terry Forster	.10	.05	.01
☐ 363 Joe Charboneau	.10	.05	.01
☐ 364 Ken Brett	.10	.05	.01
☐ 365 Tony Armas	.10	.05	.01
☐ 366 Chris Speier	.10	.05	.01
☐ 367 Fred Lynn	.20	.09	.03
☐ 368 Buddy Bell	.20	.09	.03
☐ 369 Jim Essian	.10	.05	.01
☐ 370 Terry Puhl	.10	.05	.01
☐ 371 Greg Gross	.10	.05	.01
☐ 372 Bruce Sutter	.20	.09	.03
☐ 373 Joe Lefebvre	.10	.05	.01
☐ 374 Ray Knight	.20	.09	.03
☐ 375 Bruce Benedict	.10	.05	.01
☐ 376 Tim Foli	.10	.05	.01
☐ 377 Al Holland	.10	.05	.01

☐ 378 Ken Kravec .10 .05 .01
☐ 379 Jeff Burroughs .10 .05 .01
☐ 380 Pete Falcone .10 .05 .01
☐ 381 Ernie Whitt .10 .05 .01
☐ 382 Brad Havens .10 .05 .01
☐ 383 Terry Crowley .10 .05 .01
☐ 384 Don Money .10 .05 .01
☐ 385 Dan Schatzeder .10 .05 .01
☐ 386 Gary Allenson .10 .05 .01
☐ 387 Yogi Berra CO .50 .23 .06
☐ 388 Ken Landreaux .10 .05 .01
☐ 389 Mike Hargrove .20 .09 .03
☐ 390 Darryl Motley .10 .05 .01
☐ 391 Dave McKay .10 .05 .01
☐ 392 Stan Bahnsen .10 .05 .01
☐ 393 Ken Forsch .10 .05 .01
☐ 394 Mario Mendoza .10 .05 .01
☐ 395 Jim Morrison .10 .05 .01
☐ 396 Mike Ivie .10 .05 .01
☐ 397 Broderick Perkins .10 .05 .01
☐ 398 Darrell Evans .20 .09 .03
☐ 399 Ron Reed .10 .05 .01
☐ 400 Johnny Bench .75 .35 .09
☐ 401 Steve Bedrosian .20 .09 .03
☐ 402 Bill Robinson .10 .05 .01
☐ 403 Bill Buckner .20 .09 .03
☐ 404 Ken Oberkfell .10 .05 .01
☐ 405 Cal Ripken 50.00 22.00 6.25
☐ 406 Jim Gantner .20 .09 .03
☐ 407 Kirk Gibson .75 .35 .09
☐ 408 Tony Perez .40 .18 .05
☐ 409 Tommy John UER .40 .18 .05
(Text says 52-56 as Yankee, should be 52-26)
☐ 410 Dave Stewart 1.50 .70 .19
☐ 411 Dan Spillner .10 .05 .01
☐ 412 Willie Aikens .10 .05 .01
☐ 413 Mike Heath .10 .05 .01
☐ 414 Ray Burris .10 .05 .01
☐ 415 Leon Roberts .10 .05 .01
☐ 416 Mike Witt .20 .09 .03
☐ 417 Bob Molinaro .10 .05 .01
☐ 418 Steve Braun .10 .05 .01
☐ 419 Nolan Ryan UER 5.00 2.20 .60
(Nisnumbering of Nolan's no-hitters on card back)
☐ 420 Tug McGraw .20 .09 .03
☐ 421 Dave Concepcion .20 .09 .03
☐ 422A Juan Eichelberger .40 .18 .05
ERR (Photo actually Gary Lucas)
☐ 422B Juan Eichelberger .10 .05 .01
COR
☐ 423 Rick Rhoden .10 .05 .01
☐ 424 Frank Robinson MG .40 .18 .05
☐ 425 Eddie Miller .10 .05 .01
☐ 426 Bill Caudill .10 .05 .01
☐ 427 Doug Flynn .10 .05 .01
☐ 428 Larry Andersen UER .10 .05 .01
(Misspelled Anderson on card front)
☐ 429 Al Williams .10 .05 .01
☐ 430 Jerry Garvin .10 .05 .01
☐ 431 Glenn Adams .10 .05 .01
☐ 432 Barry Bonnell .10 .05 .01
☐ 433 Jerry Narron .10 .05 .01
☐ 434 John Stearns .10 .05 .01
☐ 435 Mike Tyson .10 .05 .01
☐ 436 Glenn Hubbard .10 .05 .01
☐ 437 Eddie Solomon .10 .05 .01
☐ 438 Jeff Leonard .10 .05 .01
☐ 439 Randy Bass .20 .09 .03
☐ 440 Mike LaCoss .10 .05 .01
☐ 441 Gary Matthews .20 .09 .03
☐ 442 Mark Littell .10 .05 .01
☐ 443 Don Sutton .40 .18 .05
☐ 444 John Harris .10 .05 .01
☐ 445 Vada Pinson CO .20 .09 .03
☐ 446 Elias Sosa .10 .05 .01
☐ 447 Charlie Hough .20 .09 .03
☐ 448 Willie Wilson .20 .09 .03
☐ 449 Fred Stanley .10 .05 .01
☐ 450 Tom Veryzer .10 .05 .01
☐ 451 Ron Davis .10 .05 .01
☐ 452 Mark Clear .10 .05 .01
☐ 453 Bill Russell .20 .09 .03
☐ 454 Lou Whitaker .40 .18 .05
☐ 455 Dan Graham .10 .05 .01
☐ 456 Reggie Cleveland .10 .05 .01
☐ 457 Sammy Stewart .10 .05 .01
☐ 458 Pete Vuckovich .10 .05 .01
☐ 459 John Wockenfuss .10 .05 .01
☐ 460 Glenn Hoffman .10 .05 .01
☐ 461 Willie Randolph .20 .09 .03
☐ 462 Fernando Valenzuela .40 .18 .05
☐ 463 Ron Hassey .10 .05 .01
☐ 464 Paul Splittorff .10 .05 .01
☐ 465 Rob Picciolo .10 .05 .01
☐ 466 Larry Parrish .10 .05 .01
☐ 467 Johnny Grubb .10 .05 .01
☐ 468 Dan Ford .10 .05 .01
☐ 469 Silvio Martinez .10 .05 .01
☐ 470 Kiko Garcia .10 .05 .01
☐ 471 Bob Boone .20 .09 .03
☐ 472 Luis Salazar .10 .05 .01
☐ 473 Randy Niemann .10 .05 .01
☐ 474 Tom Griffin .10 .05 .01
☐ 475 Phil Niekro .40 .18 .05
☐ 476 Hubie Brooks .20 .09 .03
☐ 477 Dick Tidrow .10 .05 .01
☐ 478 Jim Beattie .10 .05 .01
☐ 479 Damaso Garcia .10 .05 .01
☐ 480 Mickey Hatcher .10 .05 .01
☐ 481 Joe Price .10 .05 .01
☐ 482 Ed Farmer .10 .05 .01
☐ 483 Eddie Murray 3.00 1.35 .35
☐ 484 Ben Oglivie .20 .09 .03
☐ 485 Kevin Saucier .10 .05 .01
☐ 486 Bobby Murcer .20 .09 .03
☐ 487 Bill Campbell .10 .05 .01
☐ 488 Reggie Smith .20 .09 .03
☐ 489 Wayne Garland .10 .05 .01
☐ 490 Jim Wright .10 .05 .01
☐ 491 Billy Martin MG .20 .09 .03
☐ 492 Jim Fanning MG .10 .05 .01
☐ 493 Don Baylor .40 .18 .05
☐ 494 Rick Honeycutt .10 .05 .01
☐ 495 Carlton Fisk .75 .35 .09
☐ 496 Denny Walling .10 .05 .01
☐ 497 Bake McBride .10 .05 .01
☐ 498 Darrell Porter .20 .09 .03
☐ 499 Gene Richards .10 .05 .01
☐ 500 Ron Oester .10 .05 .01
☐ 501 Ken Dayley .10 .05 .01
☐ 502 Jason Thompson .10 .05 .01
☐ 503 Milt May .10 .05 .01
☐ 504 Doug Bird .10 .05 .01
☐ 505 Bruce Bochte .10 .05 .01
☐ 506 Neil Allen .10 .05 .01
☐ 507 Joey McLaughlin .10 .05 .01
☐ 508 Butch Wynegar .10 .05 .01
☐ 509 Gary Roenicke .10 .05 .01
☐ 510 Robin Yount 1.50 .70 .19
☐ 511 Dave Tobik .10 .05 .01
☐ 512 Rich Gedman .20 .09 .03
☐ 513 Gene Nelson .10 .05 .01
☐ 514 Rick Monday .10 .05 .01
☐ 515 Miguel Dilone .10 .05 .01
☐ 516 Clint Hurdle .10 .05 .01
☐ 517 Jeff Newman .10 .05 .01
☐ 518 Grant Jackson .10 .05 .01
☐ 519 Andy Hassler .10 .05 .01
☐ 520 Pat Putnam .10 .05 .01
☐ 521 Greg Pryor .10 .05 .01
☐ 522 Tony Scott .10 .05 .01
☐ 523 Steve Mura .10 .05 .01
☐ 524 Johnnie LeMaster .10 .05 .01
☐ 525 Dick Ruthven .10 .05 .01
☐ 526 John McNamara MG .10 .05 .01
☐ 527 Larry McWilliams .10 .05 .01
☐ 528 Johnny Ray .20 .09 .03
☐ 529 Pat Tabler .20 .09 .03
☐ 530 Tom Herr .20 .09 .03
☐ 531A San Diego Chicken .75 .35 .09
ERR (Without TM)
☐ 531B San Diego Chicken .75 .35 .09
COR (With TM)
☐ 532 Sal Butera .10 .05 .01
☐ 533 Mike Griffin .10 .05 .01
☐ 534 Kelvin Moore .10 .05 .01
☐ 535 Reggie Jackson 1.00 .45 .12
☐ 536 Ed Romero .10 .05 .01
☐ 537 Derrel Thomas .10 .05 .01
☐ 538 Mike O'Berry .10 .05 .01
☐ 539 Jack O'Connor .10 .05 .01
☐ 540 Bob Ojeda .40 .18 .05
☐ 541 Roy Lee Jackson .10 .05 .01
☐ 542 Lynn Jones .10 .05 .01
☐ 543 Gaylord Perry .40 .18 .05
☐ 544A Phil Garner ERR .40 .18 .05
(Reverse negative)
☐ 544B Phil Garner COR .20 .09 .03
☐ 545 Garry Templeton .10 .05 .01
☐ 546 Rafael Ramirez .10 .05 .01
☐ 547 Jeff Reardon .40 .18 .05
☐ 548 Ron Guidry .20 .09 .03
☐ 549 Tim Laudner .10 .05 .01
☐ 550 John Henry Johnson .10 .05 .01
☐ 551 Chris Bando .10 .05 .01
☐ 552 Bobby Brown .10 .05 .01
☐ 553 Larry Bradford .10 .05 .01
☐ 554 Scott Fletcher .40 .18 .05
☐ 555 Jerry Royster .10 .05 .01
☐ 556 Shooty Babitt UER .10 .05 .01
(Spelled Babbitt on front)
☐ 557 Kent Hrbek 1.00 .45 .12
☐ 558 Yankee Winners .20 .09 .03
Ron Guidry
Tommy John
☐ 559 Mark Bomback .10 .05 .01
☐ 560 Julio Valdez .10 .05 .01
☐ 561 Buck Martinez .10 .05 .01
☐ 562 Mike A. Marshall .20 .09 .03
☐ 563 Rennie Stennett .10 .05 .01
☐ 564 Steve Crawford .10 .05 .01
☐ 565 Bob Babcock .10 .05 .01
☐ 566 Johnny Podres CO .20 .09 .03
☐ 567 Paul Serna .10 .05 .01
☐ 568 Harold Baines .40 .18 .05
☐ 569 Dave LaRoche .10 .05 .01
☐ 570 Lee May .20 .09 .03
☐ 571 Gary Ward .10 .05 .01
☐ 572 John Denny .10 .05 .01
☐ 573 Roy Smalley .10 .05 .01
☐ 574 Bob Brenly .10 .05 .01
☐ 575 Bronx Bombers 1.50 .70 .19
Reggie Jackson
Dave Winfield
☐ 576 Luis Pujols .10 .05 .01
☐ 577 Butch Hobson .10 .05 .01
☐ 578 Harvey Kuenn MG .20 .09 .03
☐ 579 Cal Ripken Sr. CO .20 .09 .03
☐ 580 Juan Berenguer .10 .05 .01
☐ 581 Benny Ayala .10 .05 .01
☐ 582 Vance Law .10 .05 .01
☐ 583 Rick Leach .10 .05 .01
☐ 584 George Frazier .10 .05 .01
☐ 585 Phillies Finest 1.50 .70 .19
Pete Rose
Mike Schmidt
☐ 586 Joe Rudi .10 .05 .01
☐ 587 Juan Beniquez .10 .05 .01
☐ 588 Luis DeLeon .10 .05 .01
☐ 589 Craig Swan .10 .05 .01
☐ 590 Dave Chalk .10 .05 .01
☐ 591 Billy Gardner MG .10 .05 .01
☐ 592 Sal Bando .20 .09 .03
☐ 593 Bert Campaneris .20 .09 .03
☐ 594 Steve Kemp .10 .05 .01
☐ 595A Randy Lerch ERR .40 .18 .05
(Braves)
☐ 595B Randy Lerch COR .10 .05 .01
(Brewers)
☐ 596 Bryan Clark .10 .05 .01
☐ 597 Dave Ford .10 .05 .01
☐ 598 Mike Scioscia .20 .09 .03
☐ 599 John Lowenstein .10 .05 .01
☐ 600 Rene Lachemann MG .10 .05 .01
☐ 601 Mick Kelleher .10 .05 .01
☐ 602 Ron Jackson .10 .05 .01
☐ 603 Jerry Koosman .20 .09 .03
☐ 604 Dave Goltz .10 .05 .01
☐ 605 Ellis Valentine .10 .05 .01
☐ 606 Lonnie Smith .20 .09 .03
☐ 607 Joaquin Andujar .20 .09 .03
☐ 608 Garry Hancock .10 .05 .01
☐ 609 Jerry Turner .10 .05 .01
☐ 610 Bob Bonner .10 .05 .01
☐ 611 Jim Dwyer .10 .05 .01
☐ 612 Terry Bulling .10 .05 .01
☐ 613 Joel Youngblood .10 .05 .01
☐ 614 Larry Milbourne .10 .05 .01
☐ 615 Gene Roof UER .10 .05 .01
(Name on front is Phil Roof)
☐ 616 Keith Drumwright .10 .05 .01
☐ 617 Dave Rosello .10 .05 .01
☐ 618 Rickey Keeton .10 .05 .01
☐ 619 Dennis Lamp .10 .05 .01
☐ 620 Sid Monge .10 .05 .01
☐ 621 Jerry White .10 .05 .01
☐ 622 Luis Aguayo .10 .05 .01
☐ 623 Jamie Easterly .10 .05 .01
☐ 624 Steve Sax .40 .18 .05
☐ 625 Dave Roberts .10 .05 .01
☐ 626 Rick Bosetti .10 .05 .01
☐ 627 Terry Francona .10 .05 .01
☐ 628 Pride of Reds 1.00 .45 .12
Tom Seaver
Johnny Bench
☐ 629 Paul Mirabella .10 .05 .01
☐ 630 Rance Mulliniks .10 .05 .01
☐ 631 Kevin Hickey .10 .05 .01
☐ 632 Reid Nichols .10 .05 .01
☐ 633 Dave Geisel .10 .05 .01
☐ 634 Ken Griffey .20 .09 .03
☐ 635 Bob Lemon MG .40 .18 .05
☐ 636 Orlando Sanchez .10 .05 .01
☐ 637 Bill Almon .10 .05 .01
☐ 638 Danny Ainge 1.00 .45 .12
☐ 639 Willie Stargell .40 .18 .05
☐ 640 Bob Sykes .10 .05 .01
☐ 641 Ed Lynch .10 .05 .01
☐ 642 John Ellis .10 .05 .01
☐ 643 Ferguson Jenkins .40 .18 .05
☐ 644 Lenn Sakata .10 .05 .01
☐ 645 Julio Gonzalez .10 .05 .01
☐ 646 Jesse Orosco .10 .05 .01
☐ 647 Jerry Dybzinski .10 .05 .01
☐ 648 Tommy Davis CO .20 .09 .03
☐ 649 Ron Gardenhire .10 .05 .01
☐ 650 Felipe Alou CO .20 .09 .03
☐ 651 Harvey Haddix CO .20 .09 .03
☐ 652 Willie Upshaw .10 .05 .01
☐ 653 Bill Madlock .20 .09 .03
☐ 654A DK Checklist 1-26 .40 .18 .05
ERR (Unnumbered) (With Trammel)
☐ 654B DK Checklist 1-26 .20 .09 .03
COR (Unnumbered) (With Trammell)
☐ 655 Checklist 27-130 .20 .09 .03
(Unnumbered)
☐ 656 Checklist 131-234 .20 .09 .03
(Unnumbered)
☐ 657 Checklist 235-338 .20 .09 .03
(Unnumbered)
☐ 658 Checklist 339-442 .20 .09 .03
(Unnumbered)
☐ 659 Checklist 443-544 .20 .09 .03
(Unnumbered)
☐ 660 Checklist 545-653 .20 .09 .03
(Unnumbered)

1983 Donruss

The 1983 Donruss baseball set leads off with a 26-card Diamond Kings (DK) series. Of the remaining 634 standard-size cards, two are combination cards, one portrays the San Diego Chicken, one shows the completed Ty Cobb puzzle, and seven are unnumbered checklist cards. The seven unnumbered checklist cards are arbitrarily assigned numbers 654 through 660 and are listed at the end of the list below. All cards measure the standard size. Card fronts feature full color photos around a framed white broder. Several printing variations are available but the complete set price below includes only the more common of each variation pair. Cards were issued in 15-card packs which included a three-piece Ty Cobb puzzle panel (21 different panels were needed to complete the puzzle). Notable Rookie Cards include Wade Boggs, Tony Gwynn and Ryne Sandberg.

	NRMT	VG-E	GOOD
COMPLETE SET (660)	80.00	36.00	10.00
COMPLETE FACT.SET (660)	90.00	40.00	11.00
COMMON CARD (1-660)	.10	.05	.01

☐ 1 Fernando Valenzuela DK .40 .18 .05
☐ 2 Rollie Fingers DK .40 .18 .05
☐ 3 Reggie Jackson DK .75 .35 .09
☐ 4 Jim Palmer DK .40 .18 .05
☐ 5 Jack Morris DK .20 .09 .03
☐ 6 George Foster DK .20 .09 .03
☐ 7 Jim Sundberg DK .20 .09 .03
☐ 8 Willie Stargell DK .40 .18 .05
☐ 9 Dave Stieb DK .20 .09 .03
☐ 10 Joe Niekro DK .20 .09 .03
☐ 11 Rickey Henderson DK 1.25 .55 .16
☐ 12 Dale Murphy DK .40 .18 .05
☐ 13 Toby Harrah DK .20 .09 .03
☐ 14 Bill Buckner DK .20 .09 .03
☐ 15 Willie Wilson DK .20 .09 .03
☐ 16 Steve Carlton DK .40 .18 .05
☐ 17 Ron Guidry DK .20 .09 .03
☐ 18 Steve Rogers DK .20 .09 .03
☐ 19 Kent Hrbek DK .20 .09 .03
☐ 20 Keith Hernandez DK .20 .09 .03
☐ 21 Floyd Bannister DK .20 .09 .03
☐ 22 Johnny Bench DK .40 .18 .05
☐ 23 Britt Burns DK .20 .09 .03
☐ 24 Joe Morgan DK .40 .18 .05
☐ 25 Carl Yastrzemski DK .40 .18 .05
☐ 26 Terry Kennedy DK .20 .09 .03
☐ 27 Gary Roenicke .10 .05 .01
☐ 28 Dwight Bernard .10 .05 .01
☐ 29 Pat Underwood .10 .05 .01
☐ 30 Gary Allenson .10 .05 .01
☐ 31 Ron Guidry .20 .09 .03
☐ 32 Burt Hooton .10 .05 .01
☐ 33 Chris Bando .10 .05 .01
☐ 34 Vida Blue .20 .09 .03
☐ 35 Rickey Henderson 1.50 .70 .19
☐ 36 Ray Burris .10 .05 .01
☐ 37 John Butcher .10 .05 .01
☐ 38 Don Aase .10 .05 .01
☐ 39 Jerry Koosman .20 .09 .03
☐ 40 Bruce Sutter .20 .09 .03
☐ 41 Jose Cruz .20 .09 .03
☐ 42 Pete Rose 1.25 .55 .16
☐ 43 Cesar Cedeno .20 .09 .03
☐ 44 Floyd Chiffer .10 .05 .01
☐ 45 Larry McWilliams .10 .05 .01
☐ 46 Alan Fowlkes .10 .05 .01
☐ 47 Dale Murphy .40 .18 .05
☐ 48 Doug Bird .10 .05 .01
☐ 49 Hubie Brooks .20 .09 .03
☐ 50 Floyd Bannister .10 .05 .01
☐ 51 Jack O'Connor .10 .05 .01
☐ 52 Steve Senteney .10 .05 .01
☐ 53 Gary Gaetti .75 .35 .09
☐ 54 Damaso Garcia .10 .05 .01
☐ 55 Gene Nelson .10 .05 .01
☐ 56 Mookie Wilson .20 .09 .03
☐ 57 Allen Ripley .10 .05 .01
☐ 58 Bob Horner .10 .05 .01
☐ 59 Tony Pena .20 .09 .03

☐ 60 Gary Lavelle .10 .05 .01
☐ 61 Tim Lollar .10 .05 .01
☐ 62 Frank Pastore .10 .05 .01
☐ 63 Garry Maddox .10 .05 .01
☐ 64 Bob Forsch .10 .05 .01
☐ 65 Harry Spilman .10 .05 .01
☐ 66 Geoff Zahn .10 .05 .01
☐ 67 Salome Barojas .10 .05 .01
☐ 68 David Palmer .10 .05 .01
☐ 69 Charlie Hough .20 .09 .03
☐ 70 Dan Quisenberry .20 .09 .03
☐ 71 Tony Armas .10 .05 .01
☐ 72 Rick Sutcliffe .20 .09 .03
☐ 73 Steve Balboni .10 .05 .01
☐ 74 Jerry Remy .10 .05 .01
☐ 75 Mike Scioscia .20 .09 .03
☐ 76 John Wockenfuss .10 .05 .01
☐ 77 Jim Palmer .50 .23 .06
☐ 78 Rollie Fingers .40 .18 .05
☐ 79 Joe Nolan .10 .05 .01
☐ 80 Pete Vuckovich .10 .05 .01
☐ 81 Rick Leach .10 .05 .01
☐ 82 Rick Miller .10 .05 .01
☐ 83 Graig Nettles .20 .09 .03
☐ 84 Ron Cey .20 .09 .03
☐ 85 Miguel Dilone .10 .05 .01
☐ 86 John Wathan .10 .05 .01
☐ 87 Kelvin Moore .10 .05 .01
☐ 88A Byrn Smith ERR .20 .09 .03
(Sic, Bryn)
☐ 88B Bryn Smith COR .40 .18 .05
☐ 89 Dave Hostetler .10 .05 .01
☐ 90 Rod Carew .60 .25 .07
☐ 91 Lonnie Smith .10 .05 .01
☐ 92 Bob Knepper .10 .05 .01
☐ 93 Marty Bystrom .10 .05 .01
☐ 94 Chris Welsh .10 .05 .01
☐ 95 Jason Thompson .10 .05 .01
☐ 96 Tom O'Malley .10 .05 .01
☐ 97 Phil Niekro .40 .18 .05
☐ 98 Neil Allen .10 .05 .01
☐ 99 Bill Buckner .20 .09 .03
☐ 100 Ed VandeBerg .10 .05 .01
☐ 101 Jim Clancy .10 .05 .01
☐ 102 Robert Castillo .10 .05 .01
☐ 103 Bruce Berenyi .10 .05 .01
☐ 104 Carlton Fisk .75 .35 .09
☐ 105 Mike Flanagan .20 .09 .03
☐ 106 Cecil Cooper .20 .09 .03
☐ 107 Jack Morris .20 .09 .03
☐ 108 Mike Morgan .10 .05 .01
☐ 109 Luis Aponte .10 .05 .01
☐ 110 Pedro Guerrero .20 .09 .03
☐ 111 Len Barker .10 .05 .01
☐ 112 Willie Wilson .20 .09 .03
☐ 113 Dave Beard .10 .05 .01
☐ 114 Mike Gates .10 .05 .01
☐ 115 Reggie Jackson 1.00 .45 .12
☐ 116 George Wright .10 .05 .01
☐ 117 Vance Law .10 .05 .01
☐ 118 Nolan Ryan 4.00 1.80 .50
☐ 119 Mike Krukow .10 .05 .01
☐ 120 Ozzie Smith 2.00 .90 .25
☐ 121 Broderick Perkins .10 .05 .01
☐ 122 Tom Seaver .75 .35 .09
☐ 123 Chris Chambliss .20 .09 .03
☐ 124 Chuck Tanner MG .20 .09 .03
☐ 125 Johnnie LeMaster .10 .05 .01
☐ 126 Mel Hall .20 .09 .03
☐ 127 Bruce Bochte .10 .05 .01
☐ 128 Charlie Puleo .10 .05 .01
☐ 129 Luis Leal .10 .05 .01
☐ 130 John Pacella .10 .05 .01
☐ 131 Glenn Gulliver .10 .05 .01
☐ 132 Don Money .10 .05 .01
☐ 133 Dave Rozema .10 .05 .01
☐ 134 Bruce Hurst .20 .09 .03
☐ 135 Rudy May .10 .05 .01
☐ 136 Tom Lasorda MG .20 .09 .03
☐ 137 Dan Spillner UER .10 .05 .01
(Photo actually
Ed Whitson)
☐ 138 Jerry Martin .10 .05 .01
☐ 139 Mike Norris .10 .05 .01
☐ 140 Al Oliver .20 .09 .03
☐ 141 Daryl Sconiers .10 .05 .01
☐ 142 Lamar Johnson .10 .05 .01
☐ 143 Harold Baines .20 .09 .03
☐ 144 Alan Ashby .10 .05 .01
☐ 145 Garry Templeton .10 .05 .01
☐ 146 Al Holland .10 .05 .01
☐ 147 Bo Diaz .10 .05 .01
☐ 148 Dave Concepcion .20 .09 .03
☐ 149 Rick Camp .10 .05 .01
☐ 150 Jim Morrison .10 .05 .01
☐ 151 Randy Martz .10 .05 .01
☐ 152 Keith Hernandez .20 .09 .03
☐ 153 John Lowenstein .10 .05 .01
☐ 154 Mike Caldwell .10 .05 .01
☐ 155 Milt Wilcox .10 .05 .01
☐ 156 Rich Gedman .10 .05 .01
☐ 157 Rich Gossage .40 .18 .05
☐ 158 Jerry Reuss .20 .09 .03
☐ 159 Ron Hassey .10 .05 .01
☐ 160 Larry Gura .10 .05 .01
☐ 161 Dwayne Murphy .10 .05 .01
☐ 162 Woodie Fryman .10 .05 .01
☐ 163 Steve Comer .10 .05 .01
☐ 164 Ken Forsch .10 .05 .01
☐ 165 Dennis Lamp .10 .05 .01
☐ 166 David Green .10 .05 .01
☐ 167 Terry Puhl .10 .05 .01
☐ 168 Mike Schmidt 1.50 .70 .19
(Wearing 37
rather than 20)
☐ 169 Eddie Milner .10 .05 .01
☐ 170 John Curtis .10 .05 .01
☐ 171 Don Robinson .10 .05 .01
☐ 172 Rich Gale .10 .05 .01
☐ 173 Steve Bedrosian .20 .09 .03
☐ 174 Willie Hernandez .20 .09 .03
☐ 175 Ron Gardenhire .10 .05 .01
☐ 176 Jim Beattie .10 .05 .01
☐ 177 Tim Laudner .10 .05 .01
☐ 178 Buck Martinez .10 .05 .01
☐ 179 Kent Hrbek .20 .09 .03
☐ 180 Alfredo Griffin .10 .05 .01
☐ 181 Larry Andersen .10 .05 .01
☐ 182 Pete Falcone .10 .05 .01
☐ 183 Jody Davis .10 .05 .01
☐ 184 Glenn Hubbard .10 .05 .01
☐ 185 Dale Berra .10 .05 .01
☐ 186 Greg Minton .10 .05 .01
☐ 187 Gary Lucas .10 .05 .01
☐ 188 Dave Van Gorder .10 .05 .01
☐ 189 Bob Dernier .10 .05 .01
☐ 190 Willie McGee .40 .18 .05
☐ 191 Dickie Thon .10 .05 .01
☐ 192 Bob Boone .20 .09 .03
☐ 193 Britt Burns .10 .05 .01
☐ 194 Jeff Reardon .20 .09 .03
☐ 195 Jon Matlack .10 .05 .01
☐ 196 Don Slaught .40 .18 .05
☐ 197 Fred Stanley .10 .05 .01
☐ 198 Rick Manning .10 .05 .01
☐ 199 Dave Righetti .20 .09 .03
☐ 200 Dave Stapleton .10 .05 .01
☐ 201 Steve Yeager .10 .05 .01
☐ 202 Enos Cabell .10 .05 .01
☐ 203 Sammy Stewart .10 .05 .01
☐ 204 Moose Haas .10 .05 .01
☐ 205 Lenn Sakata .10 .05 .01
☐ 206 Charlie Moore .10 .05 .01
☐ 207 Alan Trammell .40 .18 .05
☐ 208 Jim Rice .20 .09 .03
☐ 209 Roy Smalley .10 .05 .01
☐ 210 Bill Russell .20 .09 .03
☐ 211 Andre Thornton .10 .05 .01
☐ 212 Willie Aikens .10 .05 .01
☐ 213 Dave McKay .10 .05 .01
☐ 214 Tim Blackwell .10 .05 .01
☐ 215 Buddy Bell .20 .09 .03
☐ 216 Doug DeCinces .20 .09 .03
☐ 217 Tom Herr .20 .09 .03
☐ 218 Frank LaCorte .10 .05 .01
☐ 219 Steve Carlton .75 .35 .09
☐ 220 Terry Kennedy .10 .05 .01
☐ 221 Mike Easler .10 .05 .01
☐ 222 Jack Clark .20 .09 .03
☐ 223 Gene Garber .10 .05 .01
☐ 224 Scott Holman .10 .05 .01
☐ 225 Mike Proly .10 .05 .01
☐ 226 Terry Bulling .10 .05 .01
☐ 227 Jerry Garvin .10 .05 .01
☐ 228 Ron Davis .10 .05 .01
☐ 229 Tom Hume .10 .05 .01
☐ 230 Marc Hill .10 .05 .01
☐ 231 Dennis Martinez .20 .09 .03
☐ 232 Jim Gantner .20 .09 .03
☐ 233 Larry Pashnick .10 .05 .01
☐ 234 Dave Collins .10 .05 .01
☐ 235 Tom Burgmeier .10 .05 .01
☐ 236 Ken Landreaux .10 .05 .01
☐ 237 John Denny .10 .05 .01
☐ 238 Hal McRae .20 .09 .03
☐ 239 Matt Keough .10 .05 .01
☐ 240 Doug Flynn .10 .05 .01
☐ 241 Fred Lynn .20 .09 .03
☐ 242 Billy Sample .10 .05 .01
☐ 243 Tom Paciorek .10 .05 .01
☐ 244 Joe Sambito .10 .05 .01
☐ 245 Sid Monge .10 .05 .01
☐ 246 Ken Oberkfell .10 .05 .01
☐ 247 Joe Pittman UER .10 .05 .01
(Photo actually
Juan Eichelberger)
☐ 248 Mario Soto .10 .05 .01
☐ 249 Claudell Washington .10 .05 .01
☐ 250 Rick Rhoden .10 .05 .01
☐ 251 Darrell Evans .20 .09 .03
☐ 252 Steve Henderson .10 .05 .01
☐ 253 Manny Castillo .10 .05 .01
☐ 254 Craig Swan .10 .05 .01
☐ 255 Joey McLaughlin .10 .05 .01
☐ 256 Pete Redfern .10 .05 .01
☐ 257 Ken Singleton .20 .09 .03
☐ 258 Robin Yount 1.25 .55 .16
☐ 259 Elias Sosa .10 .05 .01
☐ 260 Bob Ojeda .10 .05 .01
☐ 261 Bobby Murcer .20 .09 .03
☐ 262 Candy Maldonado .20 .09 .03
☐ 263 Rick Waits .10 .05 .01
☐ 264 Greg Pryor .10 .05 .01
☐ 265 Bob Owchinko .10 .05 .01
☐ 266 Chris Speier .10 .05 .01
☐ 267 Bruce Kison .10 .05 .01
☐ 268 Mark Wagner .10 .05 .01
☐ 269 Steve Kemp .10 .05 .01
☐ 270 Phil Garner .20 .09 .03
☐ 271 Gene Richards .10 .05 .01
☐ 272 Renie Martin .10 .05 .01
☐ 273 Dave Roberts .10 .05 .01
☐ 274 Dan Driessen .10 .05 .01
☐ 275 Rufino Linares .10 .05 .01
☐ 276 Lee Lacy .10 .05 .01
☐ 277 Ryne Sandberg 15.00 6.75 1.85
☐ 278 Darrell Porter .10 .05 .01
☐ 279 Cal Ripken 16.00 7.25 2.00
☐ 280 Jamie Easterly .10 .05 .01
☐ 281 Bill Fahey .10 .05 .01
☐ 282 Glenn Hoffman .10 .05 .01
☐ 283 Willie Randolph .20 .09 .03
☐ 284 Fernando Valenzuela .40 .18 .05
☐ 285 Alan Bannister .10 .05 .01
☐ 286 Paul Splittorff .10 .05 .01
☐ 287 Joe Rudi .10 .05 .01
☐ 288 Bill Gullickson .20 .09 .03
☐ 289 Danny Darwin .10 .05 .01
☐ 290 Andy Hassler .10 .05 .01
☐ 291 Ernesto Escarrega .10 .05 .01
☐ 292 Steve Mura .10 .05 .01
☐ 293 Tony Scott .10 .05 .01
☐ 294 Manny Trillo .10 .05 .01
☐ 295 Greg Harris .10 .05 .01
☐ 296 Luis DeLeon .10 .05 .01
☐ 297 Kent Tekulve .20 .09 .03
☐ 298 Atlee Hammaker .10 .05 .01
☐ 299 Bruce Benedict .10 .05 .01
☐ 300 Fergie Jenkins .40 .18 .05
☐ 301 Dave Kingman .20 .09 .03
☐ 302 Bill Caudill .10 .05 .01
☐ 303 John Castino .10 .05 .01
☐ 304 Ernie Whitt .10 .05 .01
☐ 305 Randy Johnson .10 .05 .01
☐ 306 Garth Iorg .10 .05 .01
☐ 307 Gaylord Perry .40 .18 .05
☐ 308 Ed Lynch .10 .05 .01
☐ 309 Keith Moreland .10 .05 .01
☐ 310 Rafael Ramirez .10 .05 .01
☐ 311 Bill Madlock .20 .09 .03
☐ 312 Milt May .10 .05 .01
☐ 313 John Montefusco .10 .05 .01
☐ 314 Wayne Krenchicki .10 .05 .01
☐ 315 George Vukovich .10 .05 .01
☐ 316 Joaquin Andujar .10 .05 .01
☐ 317 Craig Reynolds .10 .05 .01
☐ 318 Rick Burleson .10 .05 .01
☐ 319 Richard Dotson .10 .05 .01
☐ 320 Steve Rogers .10 .05 .01
☐ 321 Dave Schmidt .10 .05 .01
☐ 322 Bud Black .20 .09 .03
☐ 323 Jeff Burroughs .10 .05 .01
☐ 324 Von Hayes .20 .09 .03
☐ 325 Butch Wynegar .10 .05 .01
☐ 326 Carl Yastrzemski .75 .35 .09
☐ 327 Ron Roenicke .10 .05 .01
☐ 328 Howard Johnson .50 .23 .06
☐ 329 Rick Dempsey UER .20 .09 .03
(Posing as a left-
handed batter)
☐ 330A Jim Slaton .10 .05 .01
(Bio printed
black on white)
☐ 330B Jim Slaton .20 .09 .03
(Bio printed
black on yellow)
☐ 331 Benny Ayala .10 .05 .01
☐ 332 Ted Simmons .20 .09 .03
☐ 333 Lou Whitaker .20 .09 .03
☐ 334 Chuck Rainey .10 .05 .01
☐ 335 Lou Piniella .20 .09 .03
☐ 336 Steve Sax .20 .09 .03
☐ 337 Toby Harrah .10 .05 .01
☐ 338 George Brett 3.00 1.35 .35
☐ 339 Dave Lopes .20 .09 .03
☐ 340 Gary Carter .20 .09 .03
☐ 341 John Grubb .10 .05 .01
☐ 342 Tim Foli .10 .05 .01
☐ 343 Jim Kaat .20 .09 .03
☐ 344 Mike LaCoss .10 .05 .01
☐ 345 Larry Christenson .10 .05 .01
☐ 346 Juan Bonilla .10 .05 .01
☐ 347 Omar Moreno .10 .05 .01
☐ 348 Chili Davis .20 .09 .03
☐ 349 Tommy Boggs .10 .05 .01
☐ 350 Rusty Staub .20 .09 .03
☐ 351 Bump Wills .10 .05 .01
☐ 352 Rick Sweet .10 .05 .01
☐ 353 Jim Gott .10 .05 .01
☐ 354 Terry Felton .10 .05 .01
☐ 355 Jim Kern .10 .05 .01
☐ 356 Bill Almon UER .10 .05 .01
(Expos/Mets in 1983,
not Padres/Mets)
☐ 357 Tippy Martinez .10 .05 .01
☐ 358 Roy Howell .10 .05 .01
☐ 359 Dan Petry .10 .05 .01
☐ 360 Jerry Mumphrey .10 .05 .01
☐ 361 Mark Clear .10 .05 .01
☐ 362 Mike Marshall .10 .05 .01
☐ 363 Lary Sorensen .10 .05 .01
☐ 364 Amos Otis .20 .09 .03
☐ 365 Rick Langford .10 .05 .01
☐ 366 Brad Mills .10 .05 .01
☐ 367 Brian Downing .10 .05 .01
☐ 368 Mike Richardt .10 .05 .01
☐ 369 Aurelio Rodriguez .10 .05 .01
☐ 370 Dave Smith .10 .05 .01
☐ 371 Tug McGraw .20 .09 .03
☐ 372 Doug Bair .10 .05 .01
☐ 373 Ruppert Jones .10 .05 .01
☐ 374 Alex Trevino .10 .05 .01
☐ 375 Ken Dayley .10 .05 .01
☐ 376 Rod Scurry .10 .05 .01
☐ 377 Bob Brenly .10 .05 .01
☐ 378 Scot Thompson .10 .05 .01
☐ 379 Julio Cruz .10 .05 .01
☐ 380 John Stearns .10 .05 .01
☐ 381 Dale Murray .40 .18 .05
☐ 382 Frank Viola .50 .23 .06
☐ 383 Al Bumbry .20 .09 .03
☐ 384 Ben Oglivie .10 .05 .01
☐ 385 Dave Tobik .10 .05 .01
☐ 386 Bob Stanley .10 .05 .01
☐ 387 Andre Robertson .10 .05 .01
☐ 388 Jorge Orta .10 .05 .01
☐ 389 Ed Whitson .10 .05 .01
☐ 390 Don Hood .10 .05 .01
☐ 391 Tom Underwood .10 .05 .01
☐ 392 Tim Wallach .20 .09 .03
☐ 393 Steve Renko .10 .05 .01
☐ 394 Mickey Rivers .10 .05 .01
☐ 395 Greg Luzinski .20 .09 .03
☐ 396 Art Howe .10 .05 .01
☐ 397 Alan Wiggins .10 .05 .01
☐ 398 Jim Barr .10 .05 .01
☐ 399 Ivan DeJesus .10 .05 .01
☐ 400 Tom Lawless .10 .05 .01
☐ 401 Bob Walk .10 .05 .01
☐ 402 Jimmy Smith .10 .05 .01
☐ 403 Lee Smith 2.00 .90 .25
☐ 404 George Hendrick .10 .05 .01
☐ 405 Eddie Murray 2.00 .90 .25
☐ 406 Marshall Edwards .10 .05 .01
☐ 407 Lance Parrish .20 .09 .03
☐ 408 Carney Lansford .20 .09 .03
☐ 409 Dave Winfield 1.25 .55 .16
☐ 410 Bob Welch .20 .09 .03
☐ 411 Larry Milbourne .10 .05 .01
☐ 412 Dennis Leonard .10 .05 .01
☐ 413 Dan Meyer .10 .05 .01
☐ 414 Charlie Lea .10 .05 .01
☐ 415 Rick Honeycutt .10 .05 .01
☐ 416 Mike Witt .10 .05 .01
☐ 417 Steve Trout .10 .05 .01
☐ 418 Glenn Brummer .10 .05 .01
☐ 419 Denny Walling .10 .05 .01
☐ 420 Gary Matthews .20 .09 .03
☐ 421 Charlie Leibrandt UER .10 .05 .01
(Liebrandt on
front of card)
☐ 422 Juan Eichelberger UER .10 .05 .01
(Photo actually
Joe Pittman)
☐ 423 Cecilio Guante UER .20 .09 .03
(Listed as Matt
on card)
☐ 424 Bill Laskey .10 .05 .01
☐ 425 Jerry Royster .10 .05 .01
☐ 426 Dickie Noles .10 .05 .01
☐ 427 George Foster .20 .09 .03
☐ 428 Mike Moore .20 .09 .03
☐ 429 Gary Ward .10 .05 .01
☐ 430 Barry Bonnell .10 .05 .01
☐ 431 Ron Washington .10 .05 .01
☐ 432 Rance Mulliniks .10 .05 .01
☐ 433 Mike Stanton .10 .05 .01
☐ 434 Jesse Orosco .10 .05 .01
☐ 435 Larry Bowa .20 .09 .03
☐ 436 Biff Pocoroba .10 .05 .01
☐ 437 Johnny Ray .10 .05 .01
☐ 438 Joe Morgan .40 .18 .05
☐ 439 Eric Show .10 .05 .01
☐ 440 Larry Biittner .10 .05 .01
☐ 441 Greg Gross .10 .05 .01
☐ 442 Gene Tenace .20 .09 .03
☐ 443 Danny Heep .10 .05 .01
☐ 444 Bobby Clark .10 .05 .01
☐ 445 Kevin Hickey .10 .05 .01
☐ 446 Scott Sanderson .10 .05 .01
☐ 447 Frank Tanana .20 .09 .03
☐ 448 Cesar Geronimo .10 .05 .01
☐ 449 Jimmy Sexton .10 .05 .01
☐ 450 Mike Hargrove .20 .09 .03
☐ 451 Doyle Alexander .10 .05 .01
☐ 452 Dwight Evans .20 .09 .03
☐ 453 Terry Forster .10 .05 .01
☐ 454 Tom Brookens .10 .05 .01
☐ 455 Rich Dauer .10 .05 .01
☐ 456 Rob Picciolo .10 .05 .01

☐ 457 Terry Crowley	.10	.05	.01
☐ 458 Ned Yost	.10	.05	.01
☐ 459 Kirk Gibson	.40	.18	.05
☐ 460 Reid Nichols	.10	.05	.01
☐ 461 Oscar Gamble	.10	.05	.01
☐ 462 Dusty Baker	.20	.09	.03
☐ 463 Jack Perconte	.10	.05	.01
☐ 464 Frank White	.20	.09	.03
☐ 465 Mickey Klutts	.10	.05	.01
☐ 466 Warren Cromartie	.10	.05	.01
☐ 467 Larry Parrish	.10	.05	.01
☐ 468 Bobby Grich	.20	.09	.03
☐ 469 Dane Iorg	.10	.05	.01
☐ 470 Joe Niekro	.20	.09	.03
☐ 471 Ed Farmer	.10	.05	.01
☐ 472 Tim Flannery	.10	.05	.01
☐ 473 Dave Parker	.20	.09	.03
☐ 474 Jeff Leonard	.10	.05	.01
☐ 475 Al Hrabosky	.10	.05	.01
☐ 476 Ron Hodges	.10	.05	.01
☐ 477 Leon Durham	.10	.05	.01
☐ 478 Jim Essian	.10	.05	.01
☐ 479 Roy Lee Jackson	.10	.05	.01
☐ 480 Brad Havens	.10	.05	.01
☐ 481 Joe Price	.10	.05	.01
☐ 482 Tony Bernazard	.10	.05	.01
☐ 483 Scott McGregor	.10	.05	.01
☐ 484 Paul Molitor	1.25	.55	.16
☐ 485 Mike Ivie	.10	.05	.01
☐ 486 Ken Griffey	.20	.09	.03
☐ 487 Dennis Eckersley	.40	.18	.05
☐ 488 Steve Garvey	.40	.18	.05
☐ 489 Mike Fischlin	.10	.05	.01
☐ 490 U.L. Washington	.10	.05	.01
☐ 491 Steve McCatty	.10	.05	.01
☐ 492 Roy Johnson	.10	.05	.01
☐ 493 Don Baylor	.40	.18	.05
☐ 494 Bobby Johnson	.10	.05	.01
☐ 495 Mike Squires	.10	.05	.01
☐ 496 Bert Roberge	.10	.05	.01
☐ 497 Dick Ruthven	.10	.05	.01
☐ 498 Tito Landrum	.10	.05	.01
☐ 499 Sixto Lezcano	.10	.05	.01
☐ 500 Johnny Bench	.75	.35	.09
☐ 501 Larry Whisenton	.10	.05	.01
☐ 502 Manny Sarmiento	.10	.05	.01
☐ 503 Fred Breining	.10	.05	.01
☐ 504 Bill Campbell	.10	.05	.01
☐ 505 Todd Cruz	.10	.05	.01
☐ 506 Bob Bailor	.10	.05	.01
☐ 507 Dave Stieb	.20	.09	.03
☐ 508 Al Williams	.10	.05	.01
☐ 509 Dan Ford	.10	.05	.01
☐ 510 Gorman Thomas	.10	.05	.01
☐ 511 Chet Lemon	.10	.05	.01
☐ 512 Mike Torrez	.10	.05	.01
☐ 513 Shane Rawley	.10	.05	.01
☐ 514 Mark Belanger	.10	.05	.01
☐ 515 Rodney Craig	.10	.05	.01
☐ 516 Onix Concepcion	.10	.05	.01
☐ 517 Mike Heath	.10	.05	.01
☐ 518 Andre Dawson UER (Middle name Fernando, should be Nolan)	.75	.35	.09
☐ 519 Luis Sanchez	.10	.05	.01
☐ 520 Terry Bogener	.10	.05	.01
☐ 521 Rudy Law	.10	.05	.01
☐ 522 Ray Knight	.20	.09	.03
☐ 523 Joe Lefebvre	.10	.05	.01
☐ 524 Jim Wohlford	.10	.05	.01
☐ 525 Julio Franco	2.00	.90	.25
☐ 526 Ron Oester	.10	.05	.01
☐ 527 Rick Mahler	.10	.05	.01
☐ 528 Steve Nicosia	.10	.05	.01
☐ 529 Junior Kennedy	.10	.05	.01
☐ 530A Whitey Herzog MG (Bio printed black on white)	.20	.09	.03
☐ 530B Whitey Herzog MG (Bio printed black on yellow)	.20	.09	.03
☐ 531A Don Sutton (Blue border on photo)	.40	.18	.05
☐ 531B Don Sutton (Green border on photo)	.40	.18	.05
☐ 532 Mark Brouhard	.10	.05	.01
☐ 533A Sparky Anderson MG (Bio printed black on white)	.20	.09	.03
☐ 533B Sparky Anderson MG (Bio printed black on yellow)	.20	.09	.03
☐ 534 Roger LaFrancois	.10	.05	.01
☐ 535 George Frazier	.10	.05	.01
☐ 536 Tom Niedenfuer	.10	.05	.01
☐ 537 Ed Glynn	.10	.05	.01
☐ 538 Lee May	.20	.09	.03
☐ 539 Bob Kearney	.10	.05	.01
☐ 540 Tim Raines	.40	.18	.05
☐ 541 Paul Mirabella	.10	.05	.01
☐ 542 Luis Tiant	.20	.09	.03
☐ 543 Ron LeFlore	.20	.09	.03
☐ 544 Dave LaPoint	.10	.05	.01
☐ 545 Randy Moffitt	.10	.05	.01
☐ 546 Luis Aguayo	.10	.05	.01
☐ 547 Brad Lesley	.20	.09	.03
☐ 548 Luis Salazar	.10	.05	.01
☐ 549 John Candelaria	.10	.05	.01
☐ 550 Dave Bergman	.10	.05	.01
☐ 551 Bob Watson	.20	.09	.03
☐ 552 Pat Tabler	.10	.05	.01
☐ 553 Brent Gaff	.10	.05	.01
☐ 554 Al Cowens	.10	.05	.01
☐ 555 Tom Brunansky	.20	.09	.03
☐ 556 Lloyd Moseby	.10	.05	.01
☐ 557A Pascual Perez ERR (Twins in glove)	2.00	.90	.25
☐ 557B Pascual Perez COR (Braves in glove)	.20	.09	.03
☐ 558 Willie Upshaw	.10	.05	.01
☐ 559 Richie Zisk	.10	.05	.01
☐ 560 Pat Zachry	.10	.05	.01
☐ 561 Jay Johnstone	.20	.09	.03
☐ 562 Carlos Diaz	.10	.05	.01
☐ 563 John Tudor	.10	.05	.01
☐ 564 Frank Robinson MG	.40	.18	.05
☐ 565 Dave Edwards	.10	.05	.01
☐ 566 Paul Householder	.10	.05	.01
☐ 567 Ron Reed	.10	.05	.01
☐ 568 Mike Ramsey	.10	.05	.01
☐ 569 Kiko Garcia	.10	.05	.01
☐ 570 Tommy John	.40	.18	.05
☐ 571 Tony LaRussa MG	.20	.09	.03
☐ 572 Joel Youngblood	.10	.05	.01
☐ 573 Wayne Tolleson	.10	.05	.01
☐ 574 Keith Creel	.10	.05	.01
☐ 575 Billy Martin MG	.20	.09	.03
☐ 576 Jerry Dybzinski	.10	.05	.01
☐ 577 Rick Cerone	.10	.05	.01
☐ 578 Tony Perez	.40	.18	.05
☐ 579 Greg Brock	.10	.05	.01
☐ 580 Glenn Wilson	.20	.09	.03
☐ 581 Tim Stoddard	.10	.05	.01
☐ 582 Bob McClure	.10	.05	.01
☐ 583 Jim Dwyer	.10	.05	.01
☐ 584 Ed Romero	.10	.05	.01
☐ 585 Larry Herndon	.10	.05	.01
☐ 586 Wade Boggs	10.00	4.50	1.25
☐ 587 Jay Howell	.20	.09	.03
☐ 588 Dave Stewart	.20	.09	.03
☐ 589 Bert Blyleven	.40	.18	.05
☐ 590 Dick Howser MG	.20	.09	.03
☐ 591 Wayne Gross	.10	.05	.01
☐ 592 Terry Francona	.10	.05	.01
☐ 593 Don Werner	.10	.05	.01
☐ 594 Bill Stein	.10	.05	.01
☐ 595 Jesse Barfield	.20	.09	.03
☐ 596 Bob Molinaro	.10	.05	.01
☐ 597 Mike Vail	.10	.05	.01
☐ 598 Tony Gwynn	20.00	9.00	2.50
☐ 599 Gary Rajsich	.10	.05	.01
☐ 600 Jerry Ujdur	.10	.05	.01
☐ 601 Cliff Johnson	.10	.05	.01
☐ 602 Jerry White	.10	.05	.01
☐ 603 Bryan Clark	.10	.05	.01
☐ 604 Joe Ferguson	.10	.05	.01
☐ 605 Guy Sularz	.10	.05	.01
☐ 606A Ozzie Virgil (Green border on photo)	.20	.09	.03
☐ 606B Ozzie Virgil (Orange border on photo)	.20	.09	.03
☐ 607 Terry Harper	.10	.05	.01
☐ 608 Harvey Kuenn MG	.20	.09	.03
☐ 609 Jim Sundberg	.20	.09	.03
☐ 610 Willie Stargell	.40	.18	.05
☐ 611 Reggie Smith	.20	.09	.03
☐ 612 Rob Wilfong	.10	.05	.01
☐ 613 The Niekro Brothers Joe Niekro Phil Niekro	.40	.18	.05
☐ 614 Lee Elia MG	.10	.05	.01
☐ 615 Mickey Hatcher	.10	.05	.01
☐ 616 Jerry Hairston	.10	.05	.01
☐ 617 John Martin	.10	.05	.01
☐ 618 Wally Backman	.10	.05	.01
☐ 619 Storm Davis	.10	.05	.01
☐ 620 Alan Knicely	.10	.05	.01
☐ 621 John Stuper	.10	.05	.01
☐ 622 Matt Sinatro	.10	.05	.01
☐ 623 Geno Petralli	.20	.09	.03
☐ 624 Duane Walker	.10	.05	.01
☐ 625 Dick Williams MG	.10	.05	.01
☐ 626 Pat Corrales MG	.10	.05	.01
☐ 627 Vern Ruhle	.10	.05	.01
☐ 628 Joe Torre MG	.20	.09	.03
☐ 629 Anthony Johnson	.10	.05	.01
☐ 630 Steve Howe	.10	.05	.01
☐ 631 Gary Woods	.10	.05	.01
☐ 632 LaMarr Hoyt	.20	.09	.03
☐ 633 Steve Swisher	.10	.05	.01
☐ 634 Terry Leach	.10	.05	.01
☐ 635 Jeff Newman	.10	.05	.01
☐ 636 Brett Butler	.40	.18	.05
☐ 637 Gary Gray	.10	.05	.01
☐ 638 Lee Mazzilli	.10	.05	.01
☐ 639A Ron Jackson ERR (A's in glove)	10.00	4.50	1.25
☐ 639B Ron Jackson COR (Angels in glove, red border on photo)	.10	.05	.01
☐ 639C Ron Jackson COR (Angels in glove, green border on photo)	.40	.18	.05
☐ 640 Juan Beniquez	.10	.05	.01
☐ 641 Dave Rucker	.10	.05	.01
☐ 642 Luis Pujols	.10	.05	.01
☐ 643 Rick Monday	.10	.05	.01
☐ 644 Hosken Powell	.10	.05	.01
☐ 645 The Chicken	.40	.18	.05
☐ 646 Dave Engle	.10	.05	.01
☐ 647 Dick Davis	.10	.05	.01
☐ 648 Frank Robinson Vida Blue Joe Morgan	.20	.09	.03
☐ 649 Al Chambers	.10	.05	.01
☐ 650 Jesus Vega	.10	.05	.01
☐ 651 Jeff Jones	.10	.05	.01
☐ 652 Marvis Foley	.10	.05	.01
☐ 653 Ty Cobb Puzzle Card	.40	.18	.05
☐ 654A Dick Perez/Diamond King Checklist 1-26 (Unnumbered) ERR (Word "checklist" omitted from back)	.40	.18	.05
☐ 654B Dick Perez/Diamond King Checklist 1-26 (Unnumbered) COR (Word "checklist" is on back)	.40	.18	.05
☐ 655 Checklist 27-130 (Unnumbered)	.20	.09	.03
☐ 656 Checklist 131-234 (Unnumbered)	.20	.09	.03
☐ 657 Checklist 235-338 (Unnumbered)	.20	.09	.03
☐ 658 Checklist 339-442 (Unnumbered)	.20	.09	.03
☐ 659 Checklist 443-544 (Unnumbered)	.20	.09	.03
☐ 660 Checklist 545-653 (Unnumbered)	.20	.09	.03

1983 Donruss Action All-Stars

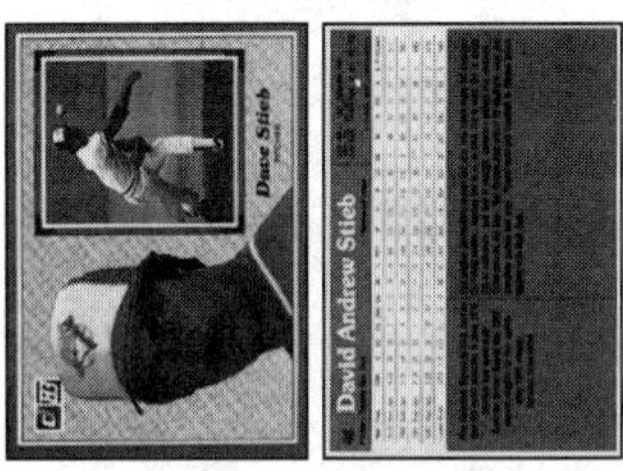

The cards in this 60-card set measure approximately 3 1/2" by 5". The 1983 Action All-Stars series depicts 60 major leagers in a distinctive new style. Each card contains a large close-up on the left and an action photo on the right. Team affiliations appear as part of the background design, and the cards have cranberry color borders. The backs contain the card number, the player's major league line record, and biographical material. A 63-piece Mickey Mantle puzzle (three pieces on one card per pack) was marketed as an insert premium; the complete puzzle card set is one of the more difficult of the Donruss insert puzzles and is currently valued at 20.00.

	NRMT	VG-E	GOOD
COMPLETE SET (60)	6.00	2.70	.75
COMMON CARD (1-60)	.05	.02	.01
☐ 1 Eddie Murray	.60	.25	.07
☐ 2 Dwight Evans	.10	.05	.01
☐ 3A Reggie Jackson ERR (Red screen on back covers some stats)	3.00	1.35	.35
☐ 3B Reggie Jackson COR	.50	.23	.06
☐ 4 Greg Luzinski	.10	.05	.01
☐ 5 Larry Herndon	.05	.02	.01
☐ 6 Al Oliver	.10	.05	.01
☐ 7 Bill Buckner	.10	.05	.01
☐ 8 Jason Thompson	.05	.02	.01
☐ 9 Andre Dawson	.40	.18	.05
☐ 10 Greg Minton	.05	.02	.01
☐ 11 Terry Kennedy	.05	.02	.01
☐ 12 Phil Niekro	.20	.09	.03
☐ 13 Willie Wilson	.05	.02	.01
☐ 14 Johnny Bench	.50	.23	.06
☐ 15 Ron Guidry	.10	.05	.01
☐ 16 Hal McRae	.05	.02	.01
☐ 17 Damaso Garcia	.05	.02	.01
☐ 18 Gary Ward	.05	.02	.01
☐ 19 Cecil Cooper	.10	.05	.01
☐ 20 Keith Hernandez	.10	.05	.01
☐ 21 Ron Cey	.10	.05	.01
☐ 22 Rickey Henderson	.50	.23	.06
☐ 23 Nolan Ryan	2.00	.90	.25
☐ 24 Steve Carlton	.40	.18	.05
☐ 25 John Stearns	.05	.02	.01
☐ 26 Jim Sundberg	.05	.02	.01
☐ 27 Joaquin Andujar	.05	.02	.01
☐ 28 Gaylord Perry	.20	.09	.03
☐ 29 Jack Clark	.10	.05	.01
☐ 30 Bill Madlock	.10	.05	.01
☐ 31 Pete Rose	.75	.35	.09
☐ 32 Mookie Wilson	.10	.05	.01
☐ 33 Rollie Fingers	.10	.05	.01
☐ 34 Lonnie Smith	.05	.02	.01
☐ 35 Tony Pena	.05	.02	.01
☐ 36 Dave Winfield	.40	.18	.05
☐ 37 Tim Lollar	.05	.02	.01
☐ 38 Rod Carew	.40	.18	.05
☐ 39 Toby Harrah	.05	.02	.01
☐ 40 Buddy Bell	.10	.05	.01
☐ 41 Bruce Sutter	.10	.05	.01
☐ 42 George Brett	1.25	.55	.16
☐ 43 Carlton Fisk	.50	.23	.06
☐ 44 Carl Yastrzemski	.50	.23	.06
☐ 45 Dale Murphy	.25	.11	.03
☐ 46 Bob Horner	.05	.02	.01
☐ 47 Dave Concepcion	.10	.05	.01
☐ 48 Dave Stieb	.05	.02	.01
☐ 49 Kent Hrbek	.10	.05	.01
☐ 50 Lance Parrish	.10	.05	.01
☐ 51 Joe Niekro	.05	.02	.01
☐ 52 Cal Ripken	3.00	1.35	.35
☐ 53 Fernando Valenzuela	.25	.11	.03
☐ 54 Richie Zisk	.05	.02	.01
☐ 55 Leon Durham	.05	.02	.01
☐ 56 Robin Yount	.50	.23	.06
☐ 57 Mike Schmidt	.75	.35	.09
☐ 58 Gary Carter	.25	.11	.03
☐ 59 Fred Lynn	.10	.05	.01
☐ 60 Checklist Card	.05	.02	.01

1983 Donruss HOF Heroes

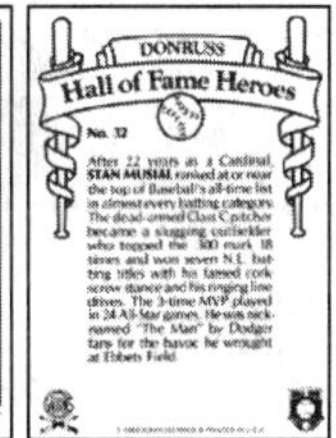

The cards in this 44-card set measure 2 1/2" by 3 1/2". Although it was issued with the same Mantle puzzle as the Action All Stars set, the Donruss Hall of Fame Heroes set is completely different in content and design. Of the 44 cards in the set, 42 are Dick Perez artwork portraying Hall of Fame members, while one card depicts the completed Mantle puzzle and the last card is a checklist. The red, white, and blue backs contain the card number and a short player biography. The cards were packaged eight cards plus one puzzle card (three pieces) for 30 cents in the summer of 1983.

	NRMT	VG-E	GOOD
COMPLETE SET (44)	7.50	3.40	.95
COMMON CARD (1-44)	.05	.02	.01
☐ 1 Ty Cobb	1.00	.45	.12
☐ 2 Walter Johnson	.50	.23	.06
☐ 3 Christy Mathewson	.50	.23	.06
☐ 4 Josh Gibson	.50	.23	.06
☐ 5 Honus Wagner	.75	.35	.09
☐ 6 Jackie Robinson	.75	.35	.09
☐ 7 Mickey Mantle	2.00	.90	.25
☐ 8 Luke Appling	.05	.02	.01
☐ 9 Ted Williams	1.00	.45	.12
☐ 10 Johnny Mize	.20	.09	.03
☐ 11 Satchel Paige	.50	.23	.06
☐ 12 Lou Boudreau	.05	.02	.01
☐ 13 Jimmie Foxx	.20	.09	.03
☐ 14 Duke Snider	.30	.14	.04
☐ 15 Monte Irvin	.20	.09	.03
☐ 16 Hank Greenberg	.20	.09	.03
☐ 17 Roberto Clemente	1.00	.45	.12
☐ 18 Al Kaline	.30	.14	.04
☐ 19 Frank Robinson	.30	.14	.04
☐ 20 Joe Cronin	.20	.09	.03
☐ 21 Burleigh Grimes	.05	.02	.01
☐ 22 The Waner Brothers Paul Waner Lloyd Waner	.05	.02	.01
☐ 23 Grover Alexander	.20	.09	.03
☐ 24 Yogi Berra	.30	.14	.04
☐ 25 Cool Papa Bell	.20	.09	.03
☐ 26 Bill Dickey	.20	.09	.03
☐ 27 Cy Young	.30	.14	.04
☐ 28 Charlie Gehringer	.05	.02	.01
☐ 29 Dizzy Dean	.30	.14	.04
☐ 30 Bob Lemon	.20	.09	.03
☐ 31 Red Ruffing	.05	.02	.01
☐ 32 Stan Musial	.75	.35	.09
☐ 33 Carl Hubbell	.20	.09	.03
☐ 34 Hank Aaron	.75	.35	.09
☐ 35 John McGraw	.05	.02	.01
☐ 36 Bob Feller	.30	.14	.04

Card	NRMT	VG-E	GOOD
☐ 37 Casey Stengel	.30	.14	.04
☐ 38 Ralph Kiner	.20	.09	.03
☐ 39 Roy Campanella	.50	.23	.06
☐ 40 Mel Ott	.20	.09	.03
☐ 41 Robin Roberts	.20	.09	.03
☐ 42 Early Wynn	.05	.02	.01
☐ 43 Mantle Puzzle Card	2.00	.90	.25
☐ 44 Checklist Card	.05	.02	.01

1984 Donruss

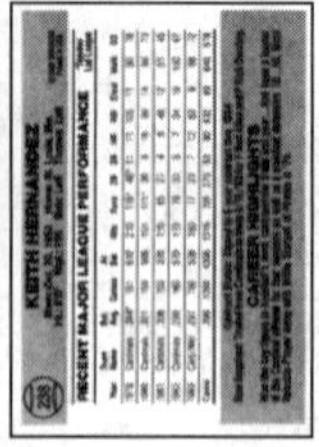

The 1984 Donruss set contains a total of 660 standard-size cards; however, only 658 are numbered. The first 26 cards in the set are again Diamond Kings (DK). A new feature, Rated Rookies (RR), was introduced with this set with Bill Madden's 20 selections comprising numbers 27 through 46. Two "Living Legend" cards designated A (featuring Gaylord Perry and Rollie Fingers) and B (featuring Johnny Bench and Carl Yastrzemski) were issued as bonus cards in wax packs, but were not issued in the factory sets sold to hobby dealers. The seven unnumbered checklist cards are arbitrarily assigned numbers 652 through 658 and are listed at the end of the list below. The attractive card front designs changed considerably from the previous two years. The backs contain statistics and are printed in green and black ink. The cards were distributed with a 3-piece puzzle panel of Duke Snider. There are no extra variation cards included in the complete set price below. The variation cards apparently resulted from a different printing for the factory sets as the Darling and Stenhouse no number variations as well as the Perez-Steele errors were corrected in the factory sets which were released later in the year. The Diamond King cards found in packs spelled Perez-Steele as Perez-Steel. Notable Rookie Cards in this set include Joe Carter, Don Mattingly, Tony Phillips, Darryl Strawberry, and Andy Van Slyke. The Joe Carter card is almost never found well centered.

	NRMT	VG-E	GOOD
COMPLETE SET (660)	225.00	100.00	28.00
COMPLETE FACT.SET (658)	260.00	115.00	32.00
COMMON CARD (1-658)	.25	.11	.03
☐ 1 Robin Yount DK COR	5.00	2.20	.60
☐ 1A Robin Yount DK ERR	5.00	2.20	.60
☐ 2 Dave Concepcion DK COR	1.00	.45	.12
☐ 2A Dave Concepcion DK ERR	.50	.23	.06
☐ 3 Dwayne Murphy DK COR	.40	.18	.05
☐ 3A Dwayne Murphy DK ERR	.25	.11	.03
☐ 4 John Castino DK COR	.40	.18	.05
☐ 4A John Castino DK ERR	.25	.11	.03
☐ 5 Leon Durham DK COR	.40	.18	.05
☐ 5A Leon Durham DK ERR	.25	.11	.03
☐ 6 Rusty Staub DK COR	.50	.23	.06
☐ 6A Rusty Staub DK ERR	.40	.18	.05
☐ 7 Jack Clark DK COR	.50	.23	.06
☐ 7A Jack Clark DK ERR	.40	.18	.05
☐ 8 Dave Dravecky DK COR	.50	.23	.06
☐ 8A Dave Dravecky DK ERR	.40	.18	.05
☐ 9 Al Oliver DK COR	.50	.23	.06
☐ 9A Al Oliver DK ERR	.40	.18	.05
☐ 10 Dave Righetti DK COR	.50	.23	.06
☐ 10A Dave Righetti DK ERR	.40	.18	.05
☐ 11 Hal McRae DK COR	.50	.23	.06
☐ 11A Hal McRae DK ERR	.40	.18	.05
☐ 12 Ray Knight DK COR	.50	.23	.06
☐ 12A Ray Knight DK ERR	.40	.18	.05
☐ 13 Bruce Sutter DK COR	.50	.23	.06
☐ 13A Bruce Sutter DK ERR	.40	.18	.05
☐ 14 Bob Horner DK COR	.50	.23	.06
☐ 14A Bob Horner DK ERR	.40	.18	.05
☐ 15 Lance Parrish DK COR	.40	.18	.05
☐ 15A Lance Parrish DK ERR	.40	.18	.05
☐ 16 Matt Young DK COR	.40	.18	.05
☐ 16A Matt Young DK ERR	.25	.11	.03
☐ 17 Fred Lynn DK COR	.40	.18	.05
☐ 17A Fred Lynn DK ERR	.40	.18	.05
☐ 18 Ron Kittle DK COR	.40	.18	.05
☐ 18A Ron Kittle DK ERR	.25	.11	.03
☐ 19 Jim Clancy DK COR	.40	.18	.05
☐ 19A Jim Clancy DK ERR	.25	.11	.03
☐ 20 Bill Madlock DK COR	.50	.23	.06
☐ 20A Bill Madlock DK ERR	.40	.18	.05
☐ 21 Larry Parrish DK COR	.40	.18	.05
☐ 21A Larry Parrish DK ERR	.25	.11	.03
☐ 22 Eddie Murray DK COR	3.00	1.35	.35
☐ 22A Eddie Murray DK ERR	3.00	1.35	.35
☐ 23 Mike Schmidt DK COR	5.00	2.20	.60
☐ 23A Mike Schmidt DK ERR	5.00	2.20	.60
☐ 24 Pedro Guerrero DK COR	.50	.23	.06
☐ 24A Pedro Guerrero DK ERR	.40	.18	.05
☐ 25 Andre Thornton DK COR	.50	.23	.06
☐ 25A Andre Thornton DK ERR	.40	.18	.05
☐ 26 Wade Boggs DK COR	3.50	1.55	.45
☐ 26A Wade Boggs DK ERR	3.50	1.55	.45
☐ 27 Joel Skinner RR	.25	.11	.03
☐ 28 Tommy Dunbar RR	.25	.11	.03
☐ 29A Mike Stenhouse RR ERR No number on back	.25	.11	.03
☐ 29B Mike Stenhouse RR COR Numbered on back	2.00	.90	.25
☐ 30A Ron Darling RR ERR (No number on back)	.75	.35	.09
☐ 30B Ron Darling RR COR (Numbered on back)	3.00	1.35	.35
☐ 31 Dion James RR	.40	.18	.05
☐ 32 Tony Fernandez RR	1.00	.45	.12
☐ 33 Angel Salazar RR	.25	.11	.03
☐ 34 Kevin McReynolds RR	1.00	.45	.12
☐ 35 Dick Schofield RR	.40	.18	.05
☐ 36 Brad Komminsk RR	.25	.11	.03
☐ 37 Tim Teufel RR	.25	.11	.03
☐ 38 Doug Frobel RR	.25	.11	.03
☐ 39 Greg Gagne RR	.50	.23	.06
☐ 40 Mike Fuentes RR	.25	.11	.03
☐ 41 Joe Carter RR	35.00	16.00	4.40
☐ 42 Mike Brown RR (Angels OF)	.25	.11	.03
☐ 43 Mike Jeffcoat RR	.25	.11	.03
☐ 44 Sid Fernandez RR	1.00	.45	.12
☐ 45 Brian Dayett RR	.25	.11	.03
☐ 46 Chris Smith RR	.25	.11	.03
☐ 47 Eddie Murray	8.00	3.60	1.00
☐ 48 Robin Yount	5.00	2.20	.60
☐ 49 Lance Parrish	.40	.18	.05
☐ 50 Jim Rice	.40	.18	.05
☐ 51 Dave Winfield	5.00	2.20	.60
☐ 52 Fernando Valenzuela	.40	.18	.05
☐ 53 George Brett	10.00	4.50	1.25
☐ 54 Rickey Henderson	5.00	2.20	.60
☐ 55 Gary Carter	.40	.18	.05
☐ 56 Buddy Bell	.40	.18	.05
☐ 57 Reggie Jackson	4.00	1.80	.50
☐ 58 Harold Baines	.40	.18	.05
☐ 59 Ozzie Smith	8.00	3.60	1.00
☐ 60 Nolan Ryan UER (Text on back refers to 1972 as the year he struck out 383; the year was 1973)	20.00	9.00	2.50
☐ 61 Pete Rose	5.00	2.20	.60
☐ 62 Ron Oester	.25	.11	.03
☐ 63 Steve Garvey	1.00	.45	.12
☐ 64 Jason Thompson	.25	.11	.03
☐ 65 Jack Clark	.40	.18	.05
☐ 66 Dale Murphy	.50	.23	.06
☐ 67 Leon Durham	.25	.11	.03
☐ 68 Darryl Strawberry	12.00	5.50	1.50
☐ 69 Richie Zisk	.25	.11	.03
☐ 70 Kent Hrbek	.40	.18	.05
☐ 71 Dave Stieb	.25	.11	.03
☐ 72 Ken Schrom	.25	.11	.03
☐ 73 George Bell	.40	.18	.05
☐ 74 John Moses	.25	.11	.03
☐ 75 Ed Lynch	.25	.11	.03
☐ 76 Chuck Rainey	.25	.11	.03
☐ 77 Biff Pocoroba	.25	.11	.03
☐ 78 Cecilio Guante	.25	.11	.03
☐ 79 Jim Barr	.25	.11	.03
☐ 80 Kurt Bevacqua	.25	.11	.03
☐ 81 Tom Foley	.25	.11	.03
☐ 82 Joe Lefebvre	.25	.11	.03
☐ 83 Andy Van Slyke	2.50	1.10	.30
☐ 84 Bob Lillis MG	.25	.11	.03
☐ 85 Ricky Adams	.25	.11	.03
☐ 86 Jerry Hairston	.25	.11	.03
☐ 87 Bob James	.25	.11	.03
☐ 88 Joe Altobelli MG	.25	.11	.03
☐ 89 Ed Romero	.25	.11	.03
☐ 90 John Grubb	.25	.11	.03
☐ 91 John Henry Johnson	.25	.11	.03
☐ 92 Juan Espino	.25	.11	.03
☐ 93 Candy Maldonado	.25	.11	.03
☐ 94 Andre Thornton	.25	.11	.03
☐ 95 Onix Concepcion	.25	.11	.03
☐ 96 Donnie Hill UER (Listed as P, should be 2B)	.40	.18	.05
☐ 97 Andre Dawson UER (Wrong middle name, should be Nolan)	4.00	1.80	.50
☐ 98 Frank Tanana	.40	.18	.05
☐ 99 Curt Wilkerson	.25	.11	.03
☐ 100 Larry Gura	.25	.11	.03
☐ 101 Dwayne Murphy	.25	.11	.03
☐ 102 Tom Brennan	.25	.11	.03
☐ 103 Dave Righetti	.40	.18	.05
☐ 104 Steve Sax	.40	.18	.05
☐ 105 Dan Petry	.40	.18	.05
☐ 106 Cal Ripken	30.00	13.50	3.70
☐ 107 Paul Molitor UER ('83 stats should say .270 BA, 608 AB, and 164 hits)	5.00	2.20	.60
☐ 108 Fred Lynn	.40	.18	.05
☐ 109 Neil Allen	.25	.11	.03
☐ 110 Joe Niekro	.40	.18	.05
☐ 111 Steve Carlton	3.00	1.35	.35
☐ 112 Terry Kennedy	.25	.11	.03
☐ 113 Bill Madlock	.25	.11	.03
☐ 114 Chili Davis	.40	.18	.05
☐ 115 Jim Gantner	.40	.18	.05
☐ 116 Tom Seaver	4.00	1.80	.50
☐ 117 Bill Buckner	.40	.18	.05
☐ 118 Bill Caudill	.25	.11	.03
☐ 119 Jim Clancy	.25	.11	.03
☐ 120 John Castino	.25	.11	.03
☐ 121 Dave Concepcion	.40	.18	.05
☐ 122 Greg Luzinski	.40	.18	.05
☐ 123 Mike Boddicker	.25	.11	.03
☐ 124 Pete Ladd	.25	.11	.03
☐ 125 Juan Berenguer	.25	.11	.03
☐ 126 John Montefusco	.25	.11	.03
☐ 127 Ed Jurak	.25	.11	.03
☐ 128 Tom Niedenfuer	.25	.11	.03
☐ 129 Bert Blyleven	.40	.18	.05
☐ 130 Bud Black	.25	.11	.03
☐ 131 Gorman Heimueller	.25	.11	.03
☐ 132 Dan Schatzeder	.25	.11	.03
☐ 133 Ron Jackson	.25	.11	.03
☐ 134 Tom Henke	1.00	.45	.12
☐ 135 Kevin Hickey	.25	.11	.03
☐ 136 Mike Scott	.40	.18	.05
☐ 137 Bo Diaz	.25	.11	.03
☐ 138 Glenn Brummer	.25	.11	.03
☐ 139 Sid Monge	.25	.11	.03
☐ 140 Rich Gale	.25	.11	.03
☐ 141 Brett Butler	.50	.23	.06
☐ 142 Brian Harper	.50	.23	.06
☐ 143 John Rabb	.25	.11	.03
☐ 144 Gary Woods	.25	.11	.03
☐ 145 Pat Putnam	.25	.11	.03
☐ 146 Jim Acker	.25	.11	.03
☐ 147 Mickey Hatcher	.25	.11	.03
☐ 148 Todd Cruz	.25	.11	.03
☐ 149 Tom Tellmann	.25	.11	.03
☐ 150 John Wockenfuss	.25	.11	.03
☐ 151 Wade Boggs UER 1983 runs 10; should be 100	7.00	3.10	.85
☐ 152 Don Baylor	.50	.23	.06
☐ 153 Bob Welch	.25	.11	.03
☐ 154 Alan Bannister	.25	.11	.03
☐ 155 Willie Aikens	.25	.11	.03
☐ 156 Jeff Burroughs	.25	.11	.03
☐ 157 Bryan Little	.25	.11	.03
☐ 158 Bob Boone	.40	.18	.05
☐ 159 Dave Hostetler	.25	.11	.03
☐ 160 Jerry Dybzinski	.25	.11	.03
☐ 161 Mike Madden	.25	.11	.03
☐ 162 Luis DeLeon	.25	.11	.03
☐ 163 Willie Hernandez	.40	.18	.05
☐ 164 Frank Pastore	.25	.11	.03
☐ 165 Rick Camp	.25	.11	.03
☐ 166 Lee Mazzilli	.25	.11	.03
☐ 167 Scot Thompson	.25	.11	.03
☐ 168 Bob Forsch	.25	.11	.03
☐ 169 Mike Flanagan	.25	.11	.03
☐ 170 Rick Manning	.25	.11	.03
☐ 171 Chet Lemon	.40	.18	.05
☐ 172 Jerry Remy	.25	.11	.03
☐ 173 Ron Guidry	.40	.18	.05
☐ 174 Pedro Guerrero	.40	.18	.05
☐ 175 Willie Wilson	.25	.11	.03
☐ 176 Carney Lansford	.40	.18	.05
☐ 177 Al Oliver	.40	.18	.05
☐ 178 Jim Sundberg	.40	.18	.05
☐ 179 Bobby Grich	.40	.18	.05
☐ 180 Rich Dotson	.25	.11	.03
☐ 181 Joaquin Andujar	.25	.11	.03
☐ 182 Jose Cruz	.40	.18	.05
☐ 183 Mike Schmidt	8.00	3.60	1.00
☐ 184 Gary Redus	.25	.11	.03
☐ 185 Garry Templeton	.25	.11	.03
☐ 186 Tony Pena	.25	.11	.03
☐ 187 Greg Minton	.25	.11	.03
☐ 188 Phil Niekro	1.00	.45	.12
☐ 189 Ferguson Jenkins	1.00	.45	.12
☐ 190 Mookie Wilson	.40	.18	.05
☐ 191 Jim Beattie	.25	.11	.03
☐ 192 Gary Ward	.25	.11	.03
☐ 193 Jesse Barfield	.40	.18	.05
☐ 194 Pete Filson	.25	.11	.03
☐ 195 Roy Lee Jackson	.25	.11	.03
☐ 196 Rick Sweet	.25	.11	.03
☐ 197 Jesse Orosco	.25	.11	.03
☐ 198 Steve Lake	.25	.11	.03
☐ 199 Ken Dayley	.25	.11	.03
☐ 200 Manny Sarmiento	.25	.11	.03
☐ 201 Mark Davis	.25	.11	.03
☐ 202 Tim Flannery	.25	.11	.03
☐ 203 Bill Scherrer	.25	.11	.03
☐ 204 Al Holland	.25	.11	.03
☐ 205 Dave Von Ohlen	.25	.11	.03
☐ 206 Mike LaCoss	.25	.11	.03
☐ 207 Juan Beniquez	.25	.11	.03
☐ 208 Juan Agosto	.25	.11	.03
☐ 209 Bobby Ramos	.25	.11	.03
☐ 210 Al Bumbry	.40	.18	.05
☐ 211 Mark Brouhard	.25	.11	.03
☐ 212 Howard Bailey	.25	.11	.03
☐ 213 Bruce Hurst	.25	.11	.03
☐ 214 Bob Shirley	.25	.11	.03
☐ 215 Pat Zachry	.25	.11	.03
☐ 216 Julio Franco	1.00	.45	.12
☐ 217 Mike Armstrong	.25	.11	.03
☐ 218 Dave Beard	.25	.11	.03
☐ 219 Steve Rogers	.25	.11	.03
☐ 220 John Butcher	.25	.11	.03
☐ 221 Mike Smithson	.25	.11	.03
☐ 222 Frank White	.40	.18	.05
☐ 223 Mike Heath	.25	.11	.03
☐ 224 Chris Bando	.25	.11	.03
☐ 225 Roy Smalley	.25	.11	.03
☐ 226 Dusty Baker	.50	.23	.06
☐ 227 Lou Whitaker	.40	.18	.05
☐ 228 John Lowenstein	.25	.11	.03
☐ 229 Ben Oglivie	.25	.11	.03
☐ 230 Doug DeCinces	.25	.11	.03
☐ 231 Lonnie Smith	.25	.11	.03
☐ 232 Ray Knight	.40	.18	.05
☐ 233 Gary Matthews	.25	.11	.03
☐ 234 Juan Bonilla	.25	.11	.03
☐ 235 Rod Scurry	.25	.11	.03
☐ 236 Atlee Hammaker	.25	.11	.03
☐ 237 Mike Caldwell	.25	.11	.03
☐ 238 Keith Hernandez	.40	.18	.05
☐ 239 Larry Bowa	.40	.18	.05
☐ 240 Tony Bernazard	.25	.11	.03
☐ 241 Damaso Garcia	.25	.11	.03
☐ 242 Tom Brunansky	.40	.18	.05
☐ 243 Dan Driessen	.25	.11	.03
☐ 244 Ron Kittle	.25	.11	.03
☐ 245 Tim Stoddard	.25	.11	.03
☐ 246 Bob L. Gibson (Brewers Pitcher)	.25	.11	.03
☐ 247 Marty Castillo	.25	.11	.03
☐ 248 Don Mattingly UER ("Traiing" on back)	50.00	22.00	6.25
☐ 249 Jeff Newman	.25	.11	.03
☐ 250 Alejandro Pena	.40	.18	.05
☐ 251 Toby Harrah	.40	.18	.05
☐ 252 Cesar Geronimo	.25	.11	.03
☐ 253 Tom Underwood	.25	.11	.03
☐ 254 Doug Flynn	.25	.11	.03
☐ 255 Andy Hassler	.25	.11	.03
☐ 256 Odell Jones	.25	.11	.03
☐ 257 Rudy Law	.25	.11	.03
☐ 258 Harry Spilman	.25	.11	.03
☐ 259 Marty Bystrom	.25	.11	.03
☐ 260 Dave Rucker	.25	.11	.03
☐ 261 Ruppert Jones	.25	.11	.03
☐ 262 Jeff R. Jones (Reds OF)	.25	.11	.03
☐ 263 Gerald Perry	.40	.18	.05
☐ 264 Gene Tenace	.40	.18	.05
☐ 265 Brad Wellman	.25	.11	.03
☐ 266 Dickie Noles	.25	.11	.03
☐ 267 Jamie Allen	.25	.11	.03
☐ 268 Jim Gott	.25	.11	.03
☐ 269 Ron Davis	.25	.11	.03
☐ 270 Benny Ayala	.25	.11	.03
☐ 271 Ned Yost	.25	.11	.03
☐ 272 Dave Rozema	.25	.11	.03
☐ 273 Dave Stapleton	.25	.11	.03
☐ 274 Lou Piniella	.40	.18	.05
☐ 275 Jose Morales	.25	.11	.03
☐ 276 Broderick Perkins	.25	.11	.03
☐ 277 Butch Davis	.25	.11	.03
☐ 278 Tony Phillips	4.00	1.80	.50
☐ 279 Jeff Reardon	.40	.18	.05
☐ 280 Ken Forsch	.25	.11	.03
☐ 281 Pete O'Brien	.40	.18	.05
☐ 282 Tom Paciorek	.25	.11	.03
☐ 283 Frank LaCorte	.25	.11	.03
☐ 284 Tim Lollar	.25	.11	.03
☐ 285 Greg Gross	.25	.11	.03
☐ 286 Alex Trevino	.25	.11	.03
☐ 287 Gene Garber	.25	.11	.03
☐ 288 Dave Parker	.40	.18	.05
☐ 289 Lee Smith	2.00	.90	.25
☐ 290 Dave LaPoint	.25	.11	.03
☐ 291 John Shelby	.25	.11	.03
☐ 292 Charlie Moore	.25	.11	.03
☐ 293 Alan Trammell	.50	.23	.06
☐ 294 Tony Armas	.25	.11	.03
☐ 295 Shane Rawley	.25	.11	.03
☐ 296 Greg Brock	.25	.11	.03
☐ 297 Hal McRae	.40	.18	.05
☐ 298 Mike Davis	.25	.11	.03
☐ 299 Tim Raines	.50	.23	.06
☐ 300 Bucky Dent	.40	.18	.05
☐ 301 Tommy John	.50	.23	.06
☐ 302 Carlton Fisk	3.00	1.35	.35
☐ 303 Darrell Porter	.25	.11	.03
☐ 304 Dickie Thon	.25	.11	.03
☐ 305 Garry Maddox	.25	.11	.03
☐ 306 Cesar Cedeno	.40	.18	.05

☐ 307 Gary Lucas .25 .11 .03
☐ 308 Johnny Ray .25 .11 .03
☐ 309 Andy McGaffigan .25 .11 .03
☐ 310 Claudell Washington .25 .11 .03
☐ 311 Ryne Sandberg 15.00 6.75 1.85
☐ 312 George Foster .40 .18 .05
☐ 313 Spike Owen .40 .18 .05
☐ 314 Gary Gaetti .50 .23 .06
☐ 315 Willie Upshaw .25 .11 .03
☐ 316 Al Williams .25 .11 .03
☐ 317 Jorge Orta .25 .11 .03
☐ 318 Orlando Mercado .25 .11 .03
☐ 319 Junior Ortiz .25 .11 .03
☐ 320 Mike Proly .25 .11 .03
☐ 321 Randy Johnson UER .25 .11 .03
('72-'82 stats are from Twins' Randy Johnson, '83 stats are from Braves' Randy Johnson)
☐ 322 Jim Morrison .25 .11 .03
☐ 323 Max Venable .25 .11 .03
☐ 324 Tony Gwynn 20.00 9.00 2.50
☐ 325 Duane Walker .25 .11 .03
☐ 326 Ozzie Virgil .25 .11 .03
☐ 327 Jeff Lahti .25 .11 .03
☐ 328 Bill Dawley .25 .11 .03
☐ 329 Rob Wilfong .25 .11 .03
☐ 330 Marc Hill .25 .11 .03
☐ 331 Ray Burris .25 .11 .03
☐ 332 Allan Ramirez .25 .11 .03
☐ 333 Chuck Porter .25 .11 .03
☐ 334 Wayne Krenchicki .25 .11 .03
☐ 335 Gary Allenson .25 .11 .03
☐ 336 Bobby Meacham .25 .11 .03
☐ 337 Joe Beckwith .25 .11 .03
☐ 338 Rick Sutcliffe .40 .18 .05
☐ 339 Mark Huismann .25 .11 .03
☐ 340 Tim Conroy .25 .11 .03
☐ 341 Scott Sanderson .25 .11 .03
☐ 342 Larry Biittner .25 .11 .03
☐ 343 Dave Stewart .40 .18 .05
☐ 344 Darryl Motley .25 .11 .03
☐ 345 Chris Codiroli .25 .11 .03
☐ 346 Rich Behenna .25 .11 .03
☐ 347 Andre Robertson .25 .11 .03
☐ 348 Mike Marshall .25 .11 .03
☐ 349 Larry Herndon .40 .18 .05
☐ 350 Rich Dauer .25 .11 .03
☐ 351 Cecil Cooper .40 .18 .05
☐ 352 Rod Carew 2.00 .90 .25
☐ 353 Willie McGee .50 .23 .06
☐ 354 Phil Garner .40 .18 .05
☐ 355 Joe Morgan 1.50 .70 .19
☐ 356 Luis Salazar .25 .11 .03
☐ 357 John Candelaria .25 .11 .03
☐ 358 Bill Laskey .25 .11 .03
☐ 359 Bob McClure .25 .11 .03
☐ 360 Dave Kingman .40 .18 .05
☐ 361 Ron Cey .40 .18 .05
☐ 362 Matt Young .25 .11 .03
☐ 363 Lloyd Moseby .25 .11 .03
☐ 364 Frank Viola .50 .23 .06
☐ 365 Eddie Milner .25 .11 .03
☐ 366 Floyd Bannister .25 .11 .03
☐ 367 Dan Ford .25 .11 .03
☐ 368 Moose Haas .25 .11 .03
☐ 369 Doug Bair .25 .11 .03
☐ 370 Ray Fontenot .25 .11 .03
☐ 371 Luis Aponte .25 .11 .03
☐ 372 Jack Fimple .25 .11 .03
☐ 373 Neal Heaton .25 .11 .03
☐ 374 Greg Pryor .25 .11 .03
☐ 375 Wayne Gross .25 .11 .03
☐ 376 Charlie Lea .25 .11 .03
☐ 377 Steve Lubratich .25 .11 .03
☐ 378 Jon Matlack .25 .11 .03
☐ 379 Julio Cruz .25 .11 .03
☐ 380 John Mizerock .25 .11 .03
☐ 381 Kevin Gross .40 .18 .05
☐ 382 Mike Ramsey .25 .11 .03
☐ 383 Doug Gwosdz .25 .11 .03
☐ 384 Kelly Paris .25 .11 .03
☐ 385 Pete Falcone .25 .11 .03
☐ 386 Milt May .25 .11 .03
☐ 387 Fred Breining .25 .11 .03
☐ 388 Craig Lefferts .25 .11 .03
☐ 389 Steve Henderson .25 .11 .03
☐ 390 Randy Moffitt .25 .11 .03
☐ 391 Ron Washington .25 .11 .03
☐ 392 Gary Roenicke .25 .11 .03
☐ 393 Tom Candiotti 1.00 .45 .12
☐ 394 Larry Pashnick .25 .11 .03
☐ 395 Dwight Evans .40 .18 .05
☐ 396 Goose Gossage .50 .23 .06
☐ 397 Derrel Thomas .25 .11 .03
☐ 398 Juan Eichelberger .25 .11 .03
☐ 399 Leon Roberts .25 .11 .03
☐ 400 Dave Lopes .40 .18 .05
☐ 401 Bill Gullickson .25 .11 .03
☐ 402 Geoff Zahn .25 .11 .03
☐ 403 Billy Sample .25 .11 .03
☐ 404 Mike Squires .25 .11 .03
☐ 405 Craig Reynolds .25 .11 .03
☐ 406 Eric Show .25 .11 .03
☐ 407 John Denny .25 .11 .03
☐ 408 Dann Bilardello .25 .11 .03
☐ 409 Bruce Benedict .25 .11 .03
☐ 410 Kent Tekulve .40 .18 .05
☐ 411 Mel Hall .40 .18 .05
☐ 412 John Stuper .25 .11 .03
☐ 413 Rick Dempsey .25 .11 .03
☐ 414 Don Sutton .50 .23 .06
☐ 415 Jack Morris .40 .18 .05
☐ 416 John Tudor .25 .11 .03
☐ 417 Willie Randolph .40 .18 .05
☐ 418 Jerry Reuss .25 .11 .03
☐ 419 Don Slaught .40 .18 .05
☐ 420 Steve McCatty .25 .11 .03
☐ 421 Tim Wallach .40 .18 .05
☐ 422 Larry Parrish .25 .11 .03
☐ 423 Brian Downing .25 .11 .03
☐ 424 Britt Burns .25 .11 .03
☐ 425 David Green .25 .11 .03
☐ 426 Jerry Mumphrey .25 .11 .03
☐ 427 Ivan DeJesus .25 .11 .03
☐ 428 Mario Soto .25 .11 .03
☐ 429 Gene Richards .25 .11 .03
☐ 430 Dale Berra .25 .11 .03
☐ 431 Darrell Evans .40 .18 .05
☐ 432 Glenn Hubbard .25 .11 .03
☐ 433 Jody Davis .25 .11 .03
☐ 434 Danny Heep .25 .11 .03
☐ 435 Ed Nunez .25 .11 .03
☐ 436 Bobby Castillo .25 .11 .03
☐ 437 Ernie Whitt .25 .11 .03
☐ 438 Scott Ullger .25 .11 .03
☐ 439 Doyle Alexander .25 .11 .03
☐ 440 Domingo Ramos .25 .11 .03
☐ 441 Craig Swan .25 .11 .03
☐ 442 Warren Brusstar .25 .11 .03
☐ 443 Len Barker .25 .11 .03
☐ 444 Mike Easler .25 .11 .03
☐ 445 Renie Martin .25 .11 .03
☐ 446 Dennis Rasmussen .25 .11 .03
☐ 447 Ted Power .25 .11 .03
☐ 448 Charles Hudson .25 .11 .03
☐ 449 Danny Cox .25 .11 .03
☐ 450 Kevin Bass .25 .11 .03
☐ 451 Daryl Sconiers .25 .11 .03
☐ 452 Scott Fletcher .25 .11 .03
☐ 453 Bryn Smith .25 .11 .03
☐ 454 Jim Dwyer .25 .11 .03
☐ 455 Rob Picciolo .25 .11 .03
☐ 456 Enos Cabell .25 .11 .03
☐ 457 Dennis Boyd .40 .18 .05
☐ 458 Butch Wynegar .25 .11 .03
☐ 459 Burt Hooton .25 .11 .03
☐ 460 Ron Hassey .25 .11 .03
☐ 461 Danny Jackson 1.00 .45 .12
☐ 462 Bob Kearney .25 .11 .03
☐ 463 Terry Francona .25 .11 .03
☐ 464 Wayne Tolleson .25 .11 .03
☐ 465 Mickey Rivers .25 .11 .03
☐ 466 John Wathan .25 .11 .03
☐ 467 Bill Almon .25 .11 .03
☐ 468 George Vukovich .25 .11 .03
☐ 469 Steve Kemp .25 .11 .03
☐ 470 Ken Landreaux .25 .11 .03
☐ 471 Milt Wilcox .25 .11 .03
☐ 472 Tippy Martinez .25 .11 .03
☐ 473 Ted Simmons .40 .18 .05
☐ 474 Tim Foli .25 .11 .03
☐ 475 George Hendrick .25 .11 .03
☐ 476 Terry Puhl .25 .11 .03
☐ 477 Von Hayes .25 .11 .03
☐ 478 Bobby Brown .25 .11 .03
☐ 479 Lee Lacy .25 .11 .03
☐ 480 Joel Youngblood .25 .11 .03
☐ 481 Jim Slaton .25 .11 .03
☐ 482 Mike Fitzgerald .25 .11 .03
☐ 483 Keith Moreland .25 .11 .03
☐ 484 Ron Roenicke .25 .11 .03
☐ 485 Luis Leal .25 .11 .03
☐ 486 Bryan Oelkers .25 .11 .03
☐ 487 Bruce Berenyi .25 .11 .03
☐ 488 LaMarr Hoyt .25 .11 .03
☐ 489 Joe Nolan .25 .11 .03
☐ 490 Marshall Edwards .25 .11 .03
☐ 491 Mike Laga .40 .18 .05
☐ 492 Rick Cerone .25 .11 .03
☐ 493 Rick Miller UER .25 .11 .03
(Listed as Mike on card front)
☐ 494 Rick Honeycutt .25 .11 .03
☐ 495 Mike Hargrove .40 .18 .05
☐ 496 Joe Simpson .25 .11 .03
☐ 497 Keith Atherton .25 .11 .03
☐ 498 Chris Welsh .25 .11 .03
☐ 499 Bruce Kison .25 .11 .03
☐ 500 Bobby Johnson .25 .11 .03
☐ 501 Jerry Koosman .40 .18 .05
☐ 502 Frank DiPino .25 .11 .03
☐ 503 Tony Perez 1.00 .45 .12
☐ 504 Ken Oberkfell .25 .11 .03
☐ 505 Mark Thurmond .25 .11 .03
☐ 506 Joe Price .25 .11 .03
☐ 507 Pascual Perez .25 .11 .03
☐ 508 Marvell Wynne .25 .11 .03
☐ 509 Mike Krukow .25 .11 .03
☐ 510 Dick Ruthven .25 .11 .03
☐ 511 Al Cowens .25 .11 .03
☐ 512 Cliff Johnson .25 .11 .03
☐ 513 Randy Bush .25 .11 .03
☐ 514 Sammy Stewart .25 .11 .03
☐ 515 Bill Schroeder .25 .11 .03
☐ 516 Aurelio Lopez .40 .18 .05
☐ 517 Mike G. Brown .25 .11 .03
☐ 518 Graig Nettles .40 .18 .05
☐ 519 Dave Sax .25 .11 .03
☐ 520 Jerry Willard .25 .11 .03
☐ 521 Paul Splittorff .25 .11 .03
☐ 522 Tom Burgmeier .25 .11 .03
☐ 523 Chris Speier .25 .11 .03
☐ 524 Bobby Clark .25 .11 .03
☐ 525 George Wright .25 .11 .03
☐ 526 Dennis Lamp .25 .11 .03
☐ 527 Tony Scott .25 .11 .03
☐ 528 Ed Whitson .25 .11 .03
☐ 529 Ron Reed .25 .11 .03
☐ 530 Charlie Puleo .25 .11 .03
☐ 531 Jerry Royster .25 .11 .03
☐ 532 Don Robinson .25 .11 .03
☐ 533 Steve Trout .25 .11 .03
☐ 534 Bruce Sutter .40 .18 .05
☐ 535 Bob Horner .25 .11 .03
☐ 536 Pat Tabler .25 .11 .03
☐ 537 Chris Chambliss .25 .11 .03
☐ 538 Bob Ojeda .25 .11 .03
☐ 539 Alan Ashby .25 .11 .03
☐ 540 Jay Johnstone .40 .18 .05
☐ 541 Bob Dernier .25 .11 .03
☐ 542 Brook Jacoby .40 .18 .05
☐ 543 U.L. Washington .25 .11 .03
☐ 544 Danny Darwin .25 .11 .03
☐ 545 Kiko Garcia .25 .11 .03
☐ 546 Vance Law UER .25 .11 .03
(Listed as P on card front)
☐ 547 Tug McGraw .40 .18 .05
☐ 548 Dave Smith .25 .11 .03
☐ 549 Len Matuszek .25 .11 .03
☐ 550 Tom Hume .25 .11 .03
☐ 551 Dave Dravecky .40 .18 .05
☐ 552 Rick Rhoden .25 .11 .03
☐ 553 Duane Kuiper .25 .11 .03
☐ 554 Rusty Staub .40 .18 .05
☐ 555 Bill Campbell .25 .11 .03
☐ 556 Mike Torrez .25 .11 .03
☐ 557 Dave Henderson .40 .18 .05
☐ 558 Len Whitehouse .25 .11 .03
☐ 559 Barry Bonnell .25 .11 .03
☐ 560 Rick Lysander .25 .11 .03
☐ 561 Garth Iorg .25 .11 .03
☐ 562 Bryan Clark .25 .11 .03
☐ 563 Brian Giles .25 .11 .03
☐ 564 Vern Ruhle .25 .11 .03
☐ 565 Steve Bedrosian .25 .11 .03
☐ 566 Larry McWilliams .25 .11 .03
☐ 567 Jeff Leonard UER .25 .11 .03
(Listed as P on card front)
☐ 568 Alan Wiggins .25 .11 .03
☐ 569 Jeff Russell .50 .23 .06
☐ 570 Salome Barojas .25 .11 .03
☐ 571 Dane Iorg .25 .11 .03
☐ 572 Bob Knepper .25 .11 .03
☐ 573 Gary Lavelle .25 .11 .03
☐ 574 Gorman Thomas .25 .11 .03
☐ 575 Manny Trillo .25 .11 .03
☐ 576 Jim Palmer 2.00 .90 .25
☐ 577 Dale Murray .25 .11 .03
☐ 578 Tom Brookens .40 .18 .05
☐ 579 Rich Gedman .25 .11 .03
☐ 580 Bill Doran .40 .18 .05
☐ 581 Steve Yeager .25 .11 .03
☐ 582 Dan Spillner .25 .11 .03
☐ 583 Dan Quisenberry .25 .11 .03
☐ 584 Rance Mulliniks .25 .11 .03
☐ 585 Storm Davis .25 .11 .03
☐ 586 Dave Schmidt .25 .11 .03
☐ 587 Bill Russell .25 .11 .03
☐ 588 Pat Sheridan .25 .11 .03
☐ 589 Rafael Ramirez .25 .11 .03
UER (A's on front)
☐ 590 Bud Anderson .25 .11 .03
☐ 591 George Frazier .25 .11 .03
☐ 592 Lee Tunnell .25 .11 .03
☐ 593 Kirk Gibson .50 .23 .06
☐ 594 Scott McGregor .25 .11 .03
☐ 595 Bob Bailor .25 .11 .03
☐ 596 Tommy Herr .40 .18 .05
☐ 597 Luis Sanchez .25 .11 .03
☐ 598 Dave Engle .25 .11 .03
☐ 599 Craig McMurtry .25 .11 .03
☐ 600 Carlos Diaz .25 .11 .03
☐ 601 Tom O'Malley .25 .11 .03
☐ 602 Nick Esasky .25 .11 .03
☐ 603 Ron Hodges .25 .11 .03
☐ 604 Ed VandeBerg .25 .11 .03
☐ 605 Alfredo Griffin .25 .11 .03
☐ 606 Glenn Hoffman .25 .11 .03
☐ 607 Hubie Brooks .25 .11 .03
☐ 608 Richard Barnes UER .25 .11 .03
(Photo actually Neal Heaton)
☐ 609 Greg Walker .40 .18 .05
☐ 610 Ken Singleton .25 .11 .03
☐ 611 Mark Clear .25 .11 .03
☐ 612 Buck Martinez .25 .11 .03
☐ 613 Ken Griffey .40 .18 .05
☐ 614 Reid Nichols .25 .11 .03
☐ 615 Doug Sisk .25 .11 .03
☐ 616 Bob Brenly .25 .11 .03
☐ 617 Joey McLaughlin .25 .11 .03
☐ 618 Glenn Wilson .40 .18 .05
☐ 619 Bob Stoddard .25 .11 .03
☐ 620 Lenn Sakata UER .25 .11 .03
(Listed as Len on card front)
☐ 621 Mike Young .25 .11 .03
☐ 622 John Stefero .25 .11 .03
☐ 623 Carmelo Martinez .25 .11 .03
☐ 624 Dave Bergman .25 .11 .03
☐ 625 Runnin' Reds UER 2.00 .90 .25
(Sic, Redbirds)
David Green
Willie McGee
Lonnie Smith
Ozzie Smith
☐ 626 Rudy May .25 .11 .03
☐ 627 Matt Keough .25 .11 .03
☐ 628 Jose DeLeon .25 .11 .03
☐ 629 Jim Essian .25 .11 .03
☐ 630 Darnell Coles .25 .11 .03
☐ 631 Mike Warren .25 .11 .03
☐ 632 Del Crandall MG .25 .11 .03
☐ 633 Dennis Martinez .40 .18 .05
☐ 634 Mike Moore .40 .18 .05
☐ 635 Lary Sorensen .25 .11 .03
☐ 636 Ricky Nelson .25 .11 .03
☐ 637 Omar Moreno .25 .11 .03
☐ 638 Charlie Hough .40 .18 .05
☐ 639 Dennis Eckersley 2.50 1.10 .30
☐ 640 Walt Terrell .25 .11 .03
☐ 641 Denny Walling .25 .11 .03
☐ 642 Dave Anderson .25 .11 .03
☐ 643 Jose Oquendo .40 .18 .05
☐ 644 Bob Stanley .25 .11 .03
☐ 645 Dave Geisel .25 .11 .03
☐ 646 Scott Garrelts .25 .11 .03
☐ 647 Gary Pettis .25 .11 .03
☐ 648 Duke Snider .50 .23 .06
Puzzle Card
☐ 649 Johnnie LeMaster .25 .11 .03
☐ 650 Dave Collins .25 .11 .03
☐ 651 The Chicken 1.00 .45 .12
☐ 652 DK Checklist 1-26 .40 .18 .05
(Unnumbered)
☐ 653 Checklist 27-130 .40 .18 .05
(Unnumbered)
☐ 654 Checklist 131-234 .40 .18 .05
(Unnumbered)
☐ 655 Checklist 235-338 .40 .18 .05
(Unnumbered)
☐ 656 Checklist 339-442 .40 .18 .05
(Unnumbered)
☐ 657 Checklist 443-546 .40 .18 .05
(Unnumbered)
☐ 658 Checklist 547-651 .40 .18 .05
(Unnumbered)
☐ A Living Legends A 4.00 1.80 .50
Gaylord Perry
Rollie Fingers
☐ B Living Legends B 8.00 3.60 1.00
Carl Yastrzemski
Johnny Bench

1984 Donruss Action All-Stars

The cards in this 60-card set measure approximately 3 1/2" by 5". For the second year in a row, Donruss issued a postcard-size card set. The set was distributed with a 63-piece Ted Williams puzzle. Unlike last year, when the fronts of the cards contained both an action and a portrait shot of the player, the fronts of this year's cards contain only an action photo. On the backs, the top section contains the card number and a full-color portrait of the player pictured on the front. The bottom half features the player's career statistics.

	NRMT	VG-E	GOOD
COMPLETE SET (60)	6.00	2.70	.75
COMMON CARD (1-60)	.05	.02	.01
☐ 1 Gary Lavelle	.05	.02	.01
☐ 2 Willie McGee	.30	.14	.04
☐ 3 Tony Pena	.05	.02	.01
☐ 4 Lou Whitaker	.10	.05	.01

Card	NRMT	VG-E	GOOD
☐ 5 Robin Yount	.40	.18	.05
☐ 6 Doug DeCinces	.05	.02	.01
☐ 7 John Castino	.05	.02	.01
☐ 8 Terry Kennedy	.05	.02	.01
☐ 9 Rickey Henderson	.50	.23	.06
☐ 10 Bob Horner	.05	.02	.01
☐ 11 Harold Baines	.10	.05	.01
☐ 12 Buddy Bell	.10	.05	.01
☐ 13 Fernando Valenzuela	.10	.05	.01
☐ 14 Nolan Ryan	2.00	.90	.25
☐ 15 Andre Thornton	.05	.02	.01
☐ 16 Gary Redus	.05	.02	.01
☐ 17 Pedro Guerrero	.10	.05	.01
☐ 18 Andre Dawson	.40	.18	.05
☐ 19 Dave Stieb	.05	.02	.01
☐ 20 Cal Ripken	2.50	1.10	.30
☐ 21 Ken Griffey	.10	.05	.01
☐ 22 Wade Boggs	.50	.23	.06
☐ 23 Keith Hernandez	.10	.05	.01
☐ 24 Steve Carlton	.50	.23	.06
☐ 25 Hal McRae	.05	.02	.01
☐ 26 John Lowenstein	.05	.02	.01
☐ 27 Fred Lynn	.10	.05	.01
☐ 28 Bill Buckner	.10	.05	.01
☐ 29 Chris Chambliss	.05	.02	.01
☐ 30 Richie Zisk	.05	.02	.01
☐ 31 Jack Clark	.10	.05	.01
☐ 32 George Hendrick	.05	.02	.01
☐ 33 Bill Madlock	.05	.02	.01
☐ 34 Lance Parrish	.10	.05	.01
☐ 35 Paul Molitor	.50	.23	.06
☐ 36 Reggie Jackson	.50	.23	.06
☐ 37 Kent Hrbek	.10	.05	.01
☐ 38 Steve Garvey	.10	.05	.01
☐ 39 Carney Lansford	.10	.05	.01
☐ 40 Dale Murphy	.30	.14	.04
☐ 41 Greg Luzinski	.10	.05	.01
☐ 42 Larry Parrish	.05	.02	.01
☐ 43 Ryne Sandberg	1.25	.55	.16
☐ 44 Dickie Thon	.05	.02	.01
☐ 45 Bert Blyleven	.10	.05	.01
☐ 46 Ron Oester	.05	.02	.01
☐ 47 Dusty Baker	.10	.05	.01
☐ 48 Steve Rogers	.05	.02	.01
☐ 49 Jim Clancy	.05	.02	.01
☐ 50 Eddie Murray	.60	.25	.07
☐ 51 Ron Guidry	.10	.05	.01
☐ 52 Jim Rice	.10	.05	.01
☐ 53 Tom Seaver	.50	.23	.06
☐ 54 Pete Rose	.75	.35	.09
☐ 55 George Brett	1.25	.55	.16
☐ 56 Dan Quisenberry	.05	.02	.01
☐ 57 Mike Schmidt	.60	.25	.07
☐ 58 Ted Simmons	.10	.05	.01
☐ 59 Dave Righetti	.05	.02	.01
☐ 60 Checklist Card	.05	.02	.01

1984 Donruss Champions

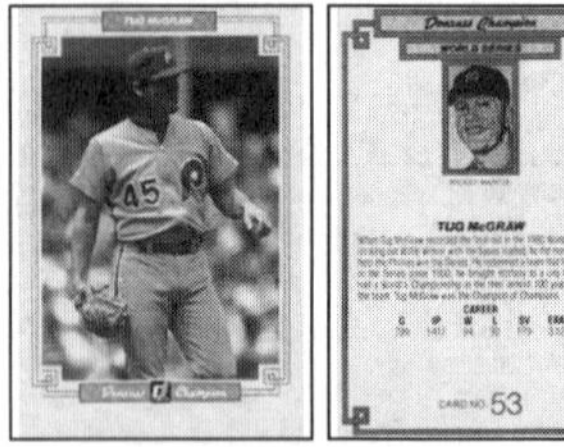

The cards in this 60-card set measure approximately 3 1/2" by 5". The 1984 Donruss Champions set is a hybrid photo/artwork issue. Grand Champions, listed GC in the checklist below, feature the artwork of Dick Perez of Perez-Steele Galleries. Current players in the set feature photographs. The theme of this postcard-size set features a Grand Champion and those current players that are directly behind him in a baseball statistical category, for example, Season Home Runs (1-7), Career Home Runs (8-13), Season Batting Average (14-19), Career Batting Average (20-25), Career Hits (26-30), Career Victories (31-36), Career Strikeouts (37-42), Most Valuable Players (43-49), World Series stars (50-54), and All-Star heroes (55-59). The cards were issued in cello packs with pieces of the Duke Snider puzzle.

	NRMT	VG-E	GOOD
COMPLETE SET (60)	10.00	4.50	1.25
COMMON CARD (1-60)	.05	.02	.01
☐ 1 Babe Ruth GC	2.00	.90	.25
☐ 2 George Foster	.10	.05	.01
☐ 3 Dave Kingman	.10	.05	.01
☐ 4 Jim Rice	.10	.05	.01
☐ 5 Gorman Thomas	.05	.02	.01
☐ 6 Ben Oglivie	.05	.02	.01
☐ 7 Jeff Burroughs	.05	.02	.01
☐ 8 Hank Aaron GC	.75	.35	.09
☐ 9 Reggie Jackson	.50	.23	.06
☐ 10 Carl Yastrzemski	.50	.23	.06
☐ 11 Mike Schmidt	.60	.25	.07
☐ 12 Graig Nettles	.10	.05	.01
☐ 13 Greg Luzinski	.10	.05	.01
☐ 14 Ted Williams GC	1.50	.70	.19
☐ 15 George Brett	1.25	.55	.16
☐ 16 Wade Boggs	.50	.23	.06
☐ 17 Hal McRae	.05	.02	.01
☐ 18 Bill Buckner	.10	.05	.01
☐ 19 Eddie Murray	.60	.25	.07
☐ 20 Rogers Hornsby GC	.50	.23	.06
☐ 21 Rod Carew	.40	.18	.05
☐ 22 Bill Madlock	.05	.02	.01
☐ 23 Lonnie Smith	.05	.02	.01
☐ 24 Cecil Cooper	.10	.05	.01
☐ 25 Ken Griffey	.10	.05	.01
☐ 26 Ty Cobb GC	1.00	.45	.12
☐ 27 Pete Rose	.75	.35	.09
☐ 28 Rusty Staub	.10	.05	.01
☐ 29 Tony Perez	.10	.05	.01
☐ 30 Al Oliver	.10	.05	.01
☐ 31 Cy Young GC	.50	.23	.06
☐ 32 Gaylord Perry	.20	.09	.03
☐ 33 Ferguson Jenkins	.20	.09	.03
☐ 34 Phil Niekro	.20	.09	.03
☐ 35 Jim Palmer	.40	.18	.05
☐ 36 Tommy John	.10	.05	.01
☐ 37 Walter Johnson GC	.50	.23	.06
☐ 38 Steve Carlton	.40	.18	.05
☐ 39 Nolan Ryan	2.00	.90	.25
☐ 40 Tom Seaver	.40	.18	.05
☐ 41 Don Sutton	.10	.05	.01
☐ 42 Bert Blyleven	.10	.05	.01
☐ 43 Frank Robinson GC	.40	.18	.05
☐ 44 Joe Morgan	.20	.09	.03
☐ 45 Rollie Fingers	.10	.05	.01
☐ 46 Keith Hernandez	.10	.05	.01
☐ 47 Robin Yount	.40	.18	.05
☐ 48 Cal Ripken	2.50	1.10	.30
☐ 49 Dale Murphy	.20	.09	.03
☐ 50 Mickey Mantle GC	3.00	1.35	.35
☐ 51 Johnny Bench	.50	.23	.06
☐ 52 Carlton Fisk	.50	.23	.06
☐ 53 Tug McGraw	.10	.05	.01
☐ 54 Paul Molitor	.50	.23	.06
☐ 55 Carl Hubbell GC	.10	.05	.01
☐ 56 Steve Garvey	.10	.05	.01
☐ 57 Dave Parker	.10	.05	.01
☐ 58 Gary Carter	.10	.05	.01
☐ 59 Fred Lynn	.10	.05	.01
☐ 60 Checklist Card	.05	.02	.01

1985 Donruss

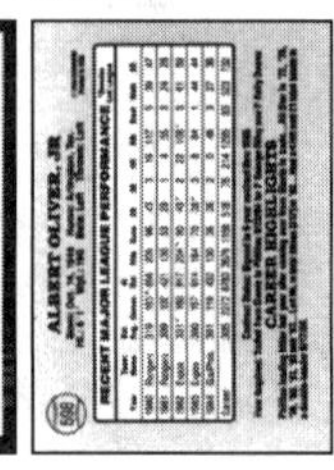

The 1985 Donruss set consists of 660 standard-size cards. Wax packs contained 15 cards and a Lou Gehrig puzzle panel. The fronts feature full color photos framed by jet black borders (making the cards condition sensitive). The first 26 cards of the set feature Diamond Kings (DK), for the fourth year in a row; the artwork on the Diamond Kings was again produced by the Perez-Steele Galleries. Cards 27-46 feature Rated Rookies (RR). The unnumbered checklist cards are arbitrarily numbered below as numbers 654 through 660. Rookie Cards in this set include Roger Clemens, Eric Davis, Shawon Dunston, Dwight Gooden, Orel Hershiser, Jimmy Key, Mark Langston, Terry Pendleton, Kirby Puckett, Jose Rijo, Bret Saberhagen, and Danny Tartabull.

	NRMT	VG-E	GOOD
COMPLETE SET (660)	120.00	55.00	15.00
COMPLETE FACT.SET (660)	140.00	65.00	17.50
COMMON CARD (1-660)	.10	.05	.01
☐ 1 Ryne Sandberg DK	2.50	1.10	.30
☐ 2 Doug DeCinces DK	.10	.05	.01
☐ 3 Richard Dotson DK	.10	.05	.01
☐ 4 Bert Blyleven DK	.20	.09	.03
☐ 5 Lou Whitaker DK	.40	.18	.05
☐ 6 Dan Quisenberry DK	.10	.05	.01
☐ 7 Don Mattingly DK	4.00	1.80	.50
☐ 8 Carney Lansford DK	.20	.09	.03
☐ 9 Frank Tanana DK	.10	.05	.01
☐ 10 Willie Upshaw DK	.10	.05	.01
☐ 11 Claudell Washington DK	.10	.05	.01
☐ 12 Mike Marshall DK	.10	.05	.01
☐ 13 Joaquin Andujar DK	.10	.05	.01
☐ 14 Cal Ripken DK	5.00	2.20	.60
☐ 15 Jim Rice DK	.20	.09	.03
☐ 16 Don Sutton DK	.20	.09	.03
☐ 17 Frank Viola DK	.20	.09	.03
☐ 18 Alvin Davis DK	.10	.05	.01
☐ 19 Mario Soto DK	.10	.05	.01
☐ 20 Jose Cruz DK	.10	.05	.01
☐ 21 Charlie Lea DK	.10	.05	.01
☐ 22 Jesse Orosco DK	.10	.05	.01
☐ 23 Juan Samuel DK	.10	.05	.01
☐ 24 Tony Pena DK	.10	.05	.01
☐ 25 Tony Gwynn DK	3.00	1.35	.35
☐ 26 Bob Brenly DK	.10	.05	.01
☐ 27 Danny Tartabull RR	1.00	.45	.12
☐ 28 Mike Bielecki RR	.10	.05	.01
☐ 29 Steve Lyons RR	.20	.09	.03
☐ 30 Jeff Reed RR	.10	.05	.01
☐ 31 Tony Brewer RR	.10	.05	.01
☐ 32 John Morris RR	.10	.05	.01
☐ 33 Daryl Boston RR	.10	.05	.01
☐ 34 Al Pulido RR	.10	.05	.01
☐ 35 Steve Kiefer RR	.10	.05	.01
☐ 36 Larry Sheets RR	.10	.05	.01
☐ 37 Scott Bradley RR	.10	.05	.01
☐ 38 Calvin Schiraldi RR	.10	.05	.01
☐ 39 Shawon Dunston RR	1.00	.45	.12
☐ 40 Charlie Mitchell RR	.10	.05	.01
☐ 41 Billy Hatcher RR	.40	.18	.05
☐ 42 Russ Stephans RR	.10	.05	.01
☐ 43 Alejandro Sanchez RR	.10	.05	.01
☐ 44 Steve Jeltz RR	.10	.05	.01
☐ 45 Jim Traber RR	.10	.05	.01
☐ 46 Doug Loman RR	.10	.05	.01
☐ 47 Eddie Murray	2.50	1.10	.30
☐ 48 Robin Yount	2.00	.90	.25
☐ 49 Lance Parrish	.20	.09	.03
☐ 50 Jim Rice	.20	.09	.03
☐ 51 Dave Winfield	1.50	.70	.19
☐ 52 Fernando Valenzuela	.20	.09	.03
☐ 53 George Brett	4.00	1.80	.50
☐ 54 Dave Kingman	.20	.09	.03
☐ 55 Gary Carter	.20	.09	.03
☐ 56 Buddy Bell	.20	.09	.03
☐ 57 Reggie Jackson	1.50	.70	.19
☐ 58 Harold Baines	.20	.09	.03
☐ 59 Ozzie Smith	2.50	1.10	.30
☐ 60 Nolan Ryan UER (Set strikeout record in 1973, not 1972)	8.00	3.60	1.00
☐ 61 Mike Schmidt	2.50	1.10	.30
☐ 62 Dave Parker	.20	.09	.03
☐ 63 Tony Gwynn	6.00	2.70	.75
☐ 64 Tony Pena	.10	.05	.01
☐ 65 Jack Clark	.20	.09	.03
☐ 66 Dale Murphy	.40	.18	.05
☐ 67 Ryne Sandberg	5.00	2.20	.60
☐ 68 Keith Hernandez	.20	.09	.03
☐ 69 Alvin Davis	.20	.09	.03
☐ 70 Kent Hrbek	.20	.09	.03
☐ 71 Willie Upshaw	.10	.05	.01
☐ 72 Dave Engle	.10	.05	.01
☐ 73 Alfredo Griffin	.10	.05	.01
☐ 74A Jack Perconte (Career Highlights takes four lines)	.10	.05	.01
☐ 74B Jack Perconte (Career Highlights takes three lines)	.10	.05	.01
☐ 75 Jesse Orosco	.10	.05	.01
☐ 76 Jody Davis	.10	.05	.01
☐ 77 Bob Horner	.10	.05	.01
☐ 78 Larry McWilliams	.10	.05	.01
☐ 79 Joel Youngblood	.10	.05	.01
☐ 80 Alan Wiggins	.10	.05	.01
☐ 81 Ron Oester	.10	.05	.01
☐ 82 Ozzie Virgil	.10	.05	.01
☐ 83 Ricky Horton	.10	.05	.01
☐ 84 Bill Doran	.10	.05	.01
☐ 85 Rod Carew	.60	.25	.07
☐ 86 LaMarr Hoyt	.10	.05	.01
☐ 87 Tim Wallach	.20	.09	.03
☐ 88 Mike Flanagan	.10	.05	.01
☐ 89 Jim Sundberg	.10	.05	.01
☐ 90 Chet Lemon	.10	.05	.01
☐ 91 Bob Stanley	.10	.05	.01
☐ 92 Willie Randolph	.20	.09	.03
☐ 93 Bill Russell	.10	.05	.01
☐ 94 Julio Franco	.40	.18	.05
☐ 95 Dan Quisenberry	.20	.09	.03
☐ 96 Bill Caudill	.10	.05	.01
☐ 97 Bill Gullickson	.10	.05	.01
☐ 98 Danny Darwin	.10	.05	.01
☐ 99 Curtis Wilkerson	.10	.05	.01
☐ 100 Bud Black	.10	.05	.01
☐ 101 Tony Phillips	.40	.18	.05
☐ 102 Tony Bernazard	.10	.05	.01
☐ 103 Jay Howell	.10	.05	.01
☐ 104 Burt Hooton	.10	.05	.01
☐ 105 Milt Wilcox	.10	.05	.01
☐ 106 Rich Dauer	.10	.05	.01
☐ 107 Don Sutton	.40	.18	.05
☐ 108 Mike Witt	.10	.05	.01
☐ 109 Bruce Sutter	.20	.09	.03
☐ 110 Enos Cabell	.10	.05	.01
☐ 111 John Denny	.10	.05	.01
☐ 112 Dave Dravecky	.20	.09	.03
☐ 113 Marvell Wynne	.10	.05	.01
☐ 114 Johnnie LeMaster	.10	.05	.01
☐ 115 Chuck Porter	.10	.05	.01
☐ 116 John Gibbons	.10	.05	.01
☐ 117 Keith Moreland	.10	.05	.01
☐ 118 Darnell Coles	.10	.05	.01
☐ 119 Dennis Lamp	.10	.05	.01
☐ 120 Ron Davis	.10	.05	.01
☐ 121 Nick Esasky	.10	.05	.01
☐ 122 Vance Law	.10	.05	.01
☐ 123 Gary Roenicke	.10	.05	.01
☐ 124 Bill Schroeder	.10	.05	.01
☐ 125 Dave Rozema	.10	.05	.01
☐ 126 Bobby Meacham	.10	.05	.01
☐ 127 Marty Barrett	.10	.05	.01
☐ 128 R.J. Reynolds	.10	.05	.01
☐ 129 Ernie Camacho UER (Photo actually Rich Thompson)	.10	.05	.01
☐ 130 Jorge Orta	.10	.05	.01
☐ 131 Lary Sorensen	.10	.05	.01
☐ 132 Terry Francona	.10	.05	.01
☐ 133 Fred Lynn	.20	.09	.03
☐ 134 Bob Jones	.10	.05	.01
☐ 135 Jerry Hairston	.10	.05	.01
☐ 136 Kevin Bass	.10	.05	.01
☐ 137 Garry Maddox	.10	.05	.01
☐ 138 Dave LaPoint	.10	.05	.01
☐ 139 Kevin McReynolds	.20	.09	.03
☐ 140 Wayne Krenchicki	.10	.05	.01
☐ 141 Rafael Ramirez	.10	.05	.01
☐ 142 Rod Scurry	.10	.05	.01
☐ 143 Greg Minton	.10	.05	.01
☐ 144 Tim Stoddard	.10	.05	.01
☐ 145 Steve Henderson	.10	.05	.01
☐ 146 George Bell	.20	.09	.03
☐ 147 Dave Meier	.10	.05	.01
☐ 148 Sammy Stewart	.10	.05	.01
☐ 149 Mark Brouhard	.10	.05	.01
☐ 150 Larry Herndon	.10	.05	.01
☐ 151 Oil Can Boyd	.10	.05	.01
☐ 152 Brian Dayett	.10	.05	.01
☐ 153 Tom Niedenfuer	.10	.05	.01
☐ 154 Brook Jacoby	.10	.05	.01
☐ 155 Onix Concepcion	.10	.05	.01
☐ 156 Tim Conroy	.10	.05	.01
☐ 157 Joe Hesketh	.10	.05	.01
☐ 158 Brian Downing	.10	.05	.01
☐ 159 Tommy Dunbar	.10	.05	.01
☐ 160 Marc Hill	.10	.05	.01
☐ 161 Phil Garner	.10	.05	.01
☐ 162 Jerry Davis	.10	.05	.01
☐ 163 Bill Campbell	.10	.05	.01
☐ 164 John Franco	1.00	.45	.12
☐ 165 Len Barker	.10	.05	.01
☐ 166 Benny Distefano	.10	.05	.01
☐ 167 George Frazier	.10	.05	.01
☐ 168 Tito Landrum	.10	.05	.01
☐ 169 Cal Ripken	8.00	3.60	1.00
☐ 170 Cecil Cooper	.20	.09	.03
☐ 171 Alan Trammell	.40	.18	.05
☐ 172 Wade Boggs	2.50	1.10	.30
☐ 173 Don Baylor	.40	.18	.05
☐ 174 Pedro Guerrero	.20	.09	.03
☐ 175 Frank White	.20	.09	.03
☐ 176 Rickey Henderson	1.50	.70	.19
☐ 177 Charlie Lea	.10	.05	.01
☐ 178 Pete O'Brien	.10	.05	.01
☐ 179 Doug DeCinces	.10	.05	.01
☐ 180 Ron Kittle	.10	.05	.01
☐ 181 George Hendrick	.10	.05	.01
☐ 182 Joe Niekro	.10	.05	.01
☐ 183 Juan Samuel	.10	.05	.01
☐ 184 Mario Soto	.10	.05	.01
☐ 185 Goose Gossage	.20	.09	.03
☐ 186 Johnny Ray	.10	.05	.01
☐ 187 Bob Brenly	.10	.05	.01
☐ 188 Craig McMurtry	.10	.05	.01
☐ 189 Leon Durham	.10	.05	.01
☐ 190 Dwight Gooden	4.00	1.80	.50
☐ 191 Barry Bonnell	.10	.05	.01
☐ 192 Tim Teufel	.10	.05	.01
☐ 193 Dave Stieb	.20	.09	.03
☐ 194 Mickey Hatcher	.10	.05	.01
☐ 195 Jesse Barfield	.10	.05	.01
☐ 196 Al Cowens	.10	.05	.01
☐ 197 Hubie Brooks	.10	.05	.01
☐ 198 Steve Trout	.10	.05	.01
☐ 199 Glenn Hubbard	.10	.05	.01
☐ 200 Bill Madlock	.10	.05	.01
☐ 201 Jeff D. Robinson	.10	.05	.01
☐ 202 Eric Show	.10	.05	.01
☐ 203 Dave Concepcion	.20	.09	.03
☐ 204 Ivan DeJesus	.10	.05	.01
☐ 205 Neil Allen	.10	.05	.01
☐ 206 Jerry Mumphrey	.10	.05	.01
☐ 207 Mike C. Brown	.10	.05	.01
☐ 208 Carlton Fisk	.75	.35	.09
☐ 209 Bryn Smith	.10	.05	.01
☐ 210 Tippy Martinez	.10	.05	.01
☐ 211 Dion James	.10	.05	.01
☐ 212 Willie Hernandez	.10	.05	.01
☐ 213 Mike Easler	.10	.05	.01
☐ 214 Ron Guidry	.20	.09	.03
☐ 215 Rick Honeycutt	.10	.05	.01
☐ 216 Brett Butler	.20	.09	.03
☐ 217 Larry Gura	.10	.05	.01
☐ 218 Ray Burris	.10	.05	.01
☐ 219 Steve Rogers	.10	.05	.01
☐ 220 Frank Tanana UER (Bats Left listed twice on card back)	.10	.05	.01
☐ 221 Ned Yost	.10	.05	.01
☐ 222 Bret Saberhagen UER (18 career IP on back)	1.50	.70	.19
☐ 223 Mike Davis	.10	.05	.01
☐ 224 Bert Blyleven	.40	.18	.05
☐ 225 Steve Kemp	.10	.05	.01

□ 226 Jerry Reuss .10 .05 .01
□ 227 Darrell Evans UER .20 .09 .03
(80 homers in 1980)
□ 228 Wayne Gross .10 .05 .01
□ 229 Jim Gantner .10 .05 .01
□ 230 Bob Boone .20 .09 .03
□ 231 Lonnie Smith .10 .05 .01
□ 232 Frank DiPino .10 .05 .01
□ 233 Jerry Koosman .10 .05 .01
□ 234 Graig Nettles .20 .09 .03
□ 235 John Tudor .10 .05 .01
□ 236 John Rabb .10 .05 .01
□ 237 Rick Manning .10 .05 .01
□ 238 Mike Fitzgerald .10 .05 .01
□ 239 Gary Matthews .10 .05 .01
□ 240 Jim Presley .20 .09 .03
□ 241 Dave Collins .10 .05 .01
□ 242 Gary Gaetti .20 .09 .03
□ 243 Dann Bilardello .10 .05 .01
□ 244 Rudy Law .10 .05 .01
□ 245 John Lowenstein .10 .05 .01
□ 246 Tom Tellmann .10 .05 .01
□ 247 Howard Johnson .20 .09 .03
□ 248 Ray Fontenot .10 .05 .01
□ 249 Tony Armas .10 .05 .01
□ 250 Candy Maldonado .10 .05 .01
□ 251 Mike Jeffcoat .10 .05 .01
□ 252 Dane Iorg .10 .05 .01
□ 253 Bruce Bochte .10 .05 .01
□ 254 Pete Rose 2.00 .90 .25
□ 255 Don Aase .10 .05 .01
□ 256 George Wright .10 .05 .01
□ 257 Britt Burns .10 .05 .01
□ 258 Mike Scott .10 .05 .01
□ 259 Len Matuszek .10 .05 .01
□ 260 Dave Rucker .10 .05 .01
□ 261 Craig Lefferts .10 .05 .01
□ 262 Jay Tibbs .10 .05 .01
□ 263 Bruce Benedict .10 .05 .01
□ 264 Don Robinson .10 .05 .01
□ 265 Gary Lavelle .10 .05 .01
□ 266 Scott Sanderson .10 .05 .01
□ 267 Matt Young .10 .05 .01
□ 268 Ernie Whitt .10 .05 .01
□ 269 Houston Jimenez .10 .05 .01
□ 270 Ken Dixon .10 .05 .01
□ 271 Pete Ladd .10 .05 .01
□ 272 Juan Berenguer .10 .05 .01
□ 273 Roger Clemens 18.00 8.00 2.20
□ 274 Rick Cerone .10 .05 .01
□ 275 Dave Anderson .10 .05 .01
□ 276 George Vukovich .10 .05 .01
□ 277 Greg Pryor .10 .05 .01
□ 278 Mike Warren .10 .05 .01
□ 279 Bob James .10 .05 .01
□ 280 Bobby Grich .20 .09 .03
□ 281 Mike Mason .10 .05 .01
□ 282 Ron Reed .10 .05 .01
□ 283 Alan Ashby .10 .05 .01
□ 284 Mark Thurmond .10 .05 .01
□ 285 Joe Lefebvre .10 .05 .01
□ 286 Ted Power .10 .05 .01
□ 287 Chris Chambliss .10 .05 .01
□ 288 Lee Tunnell .10 .05 .01
□ 289 Rich Bordi .10 .05 .01
□ 290 Glenn Brummer .10 .05 .01
□ 291 Mike Boddicker .10 .05 .01
□ 292 Rollie Fingers .40 .18 .05
□ 293 Lou Whitaker .40 .18 .05
□ 294 Dwight Evans .20 .09 .03
□ 295 Don Mattingly 8.00 3.60 1.00
□ 296 Mike Marshall .10 .05 .01
□ 297 Willie Wilson .10 .05 .01
□ 298 Mike Heath .10 .05 .01
□ 299 Tim Raines .20 .09 .03
□ 300 Larry Parrish .10 .05 .01
□ 301 Geoff Zahn .10 .05 .01
□ 302 Rich Dotson .10 .05 .01
□ 303 David Green .10 .05 .01
□ 304 Jose Cruz .20 .09 .03
□ 305 Steve Carlton .75 .35 .09
□ 306 Gary Redus .10 .05 .01
□ 307 Steve Garvey .40 .18 .05
□ 308 Jose DeLeon .10 .05 .01
□ 309 Randy Lerch .10 .05 .01
□ 310 Claudell Washington .10 .05 .01
□ 311 Lee Smith 1.00 .45 .12
□ 312 Darryl Strawberry 1.00 .45 .12
□ 313 Jim Beattie .10 .05 .01
□ 314 John Butcher .10 .05 .01
□ 315 Damaso Garcia .10 .05 .01
□ 316 Mike Smithson .10 .05 .01
□ 317 Luis Leal .10 .05 .01
□ 318 Ken Phelps .10 .05 .01
□ 319 Wally Backman .10 .05 .01
□ 320 Ron Cey .20 .09 .03
□ 321 Brad Komminsk .10 .05 .01
□ 322 Jason Thompson .10 .05 .01
□ 323 Frank Williams .10 .05 .01
□ 324 Tim Lollar .10 .05 .01
□ 325 Eric Davis 1.50 .70 .19
□ 326 Von Hayes .10 .05 .01
□ 327 Andy Van Slyke .40 .18 .05
□ 328 Craig Reynolds .10 .05 .01
□ 329 Dick Schofield .10 .05 .01
□ 330 Scott Fletcher .10 .05 .01
□ 331 Jeff Reardon .20 .09 .03
□ 332 Rick Dempsey .10 .05 .01
□ 333 Ben Oglivie .10 .05 .01
□ 334 Dan Petry .10 .05 .01
□ 335 Jackie Gutierrez .10 .05 .01
□ 336 Dave Righetti .20 .09 .03
□ 337 Alejandro Pena .10 .05 .01
□ 338 Mel Hall .10 .05 .01
□ 339 Pat Sheridan .10 .05 .01
□ 340 Keith Atherton .10 .05 .01
□ 341 David Palmer .10 .05 .01
□ 342 Gary Ward .10 .05 .01
□ 343 Dave Stewart .20 .09 .03
□ 344 Mark Gubicza .40 .18 .05
□ 345 Carney Lansford .20 .09 .03
□ 346 Jerry Willard .10 .05 .01
□ 347 Ken Griffey .20 .09 .03
□ 348 Franklin Stubbs .10 .05 .01
□ 349 Aurelio Lopez .10 .05 .01
□ 350 Al Bumbry .10 .05 .01
□ 351 Charlie Moore .10 .05 .01
□ 352 Luis Sanchez .10 .05 .01
□ 353 Darrell Porter .10 .05 .01
□ 354 Bill Dawley .10 .05 .01
□ 355 Charles Hudson .10 .05 .01
□ 356 Garry Templeton .10 .05 .01
□ 357 Cecilio Guante .10 .05 .01
□ 358 Jeff Leonard .10 .05 .01
□ 359 Paul Molitor 2.00 .90 .25
□ 360 Ron Gardenhire .10 .05 .01
□ 361 Larry Bowa .20 .09 .03
□ 362 Bob Kearney .10 .05 .01
□ 363 Garth Iorg .10 .05 .01
□ 364 Tom Brunansky .20 .09 .03
□ 365 Brad Gulden .10 .05 .01
□ 366 Greg Walker .10 .05 .01
□ 367 Mike Young .10 .05 .01
□ 368 Rick Waits .10 .05 .01
□ 369 Doug Bair .10 .05 .01
□ 370 Bob Shirley .10 .05 .01
□ 371 Bob Ojeda .10 .05 .01
□ 372 Bob Welch .10 .05 .01
□ 373 Neal Heaton .10 .05 .01
□ 374 Danny Jackson UER .10 .05 .01
(Photo actually
Frank Wills)
□ 375 Donnie Hill .10 .05 .01
□ 376 Mike Stenhouse .10 .05 .01
□ 377 Bruce Kison .10 .05 .01
□ 378 Wayne Tolleson .10 .05 .01
□ 379 Floyd Bannister .10 .05 .01
□ 380 Vern Ruhle .10 .05 .01
□ 381 Tim Corcoran .10 .05 .01
□ 382 Kurt Kepshire .10 .05 .01
□ 383 Bobby Brown .10 .05 .01
□ 384 Dave Van Gorder .10 .05 .01
□ 385 Rick Mahler .10 .05 .01
□ 386 Lee Mazzilli .10 .05 .01
□ 387 Bill Laskey .10 .05 .01
□ 388 Thad Bosley .10 .05 .01
□ 389 Al Chambers .10 .05 .01
□ 390 Tony Fernandez .20 .09 .03
□ 391 Ron Washington .10 .05 .01
□ 392 Bill Swaggerty .10 .05 .01
□ 393 Bob L. Gibson .10 .05 .01
□ 394 Marty Castillo .10 .05 .01
□ 395 Steve Crawford .10 .05 .01
□ 396 Clay Christiansen .10 .05 .01
□ 397 Bob Bailor .10 .05 .01
□ 398 Mike Hargrove .20 .09 .03
□ 399 Charlie Leibrandt .10 .05 .01
□ 400 Tom Burgmeier .10 .05 .01
□ 401 Razor Shines .10 .05 .01
□ 402 Rob Wilfong .10 .05 .01
□ 403 Tom Henke .40 .18 .05
□ 404 Al Jones .10 .05 .01
□ 405 Mike LaCoss .10 .05 .01
□ 406 Luis DeLeon .10 .05 .01
□ 407 Greg Gross .10 .05 .01
□ 408 Tom Hume .10 .05 .01
□ 409 Rick Camp .10 .05 .01
□ 410 Milt May .10 .05 .01
□ 411 Henry Cotto .10 .05 .01
□ 412 David Von Ohlen .10 .05 .01
□ 413 Scott McGregor .10 .05 .01
□ 414 Ted Simmons .20 .09 .03
□ 415 Jack Morris .20 .09 .03
□ 416 Bill Buckner .20 .09 .03
□ 417 Butch Wynegar .10 .05 .01
□ 418 Steve Sax .20 .09 .03
□ 419 Steve Balboni .10 .05 .01
□ 420 Dwayne Murphy .10 .05 .01
□ 421 Andre Dawson 1.25 .55 .16
□ 422 Charlie Hough .20 .09 .03
□ 423 Tommy John .40 .18 .05
□ 424A Tom Seaver ERR 1.25 .55 .16
(Photo actually
Floyd Bannister)
□ 424B Tom Seaver COR 25.00 11.00 3.10
□ 425 Tommy Herr .20 .09 .03
□ 426 Terry Puhl .10 .05 .01
□ 427 Al Holland .10 .05 .01
□ 428 Eddie Milner .10 .05 .01
□ 429 Terry Kennedy .10 .05 .01
□ 430 John Candelaria .10 .05 .01
□ 431 Manny Trillo .10 .05 .01
□ 432 Ken Oberkfell .10 .05 .01
□ 433 Rick Sutcliffe .10 .05 .01
□ 434 Ron Darling .20 .09 .03
□ 435 Spike Owen .10 .05 .01
□ 436 Frank Viola .20 .09 .03
□ 437 Lloyd Moseby .10 .05 .01
□ 438 Kirby Puckett 30.00 13.50 3.70
□ 439 Jim Clancy .10 .05 .01
□ 440 Mike Moore .10 .05 .01
□ 441 Doug Sisk .10 .05 .01
□ 442 Dennis Eckersley .40 .18 .05
□ 443 Gerald Perry .10 .05 .01
□ 444 Dale Berra .10 .05 .01
□ 445 Dusty Baker .20 .09 .03
□ 446 Ed Whitson .10 .05 .01
□ 447 Cesar Cedeno .20 .09 .03
□ 448 Rick Schu .10 .05 .01
□ 449 Joaquin Andujar .10 .05 .01
□ 450 Mark Bailey .10 .05 .01
□ 451 Ron Romanick .10 .05 .01
□ 452 Julio Cruz .10 .05 .01
□ 453 Miguel Dilone .10 .05 .01
□ 454 Storm Davis .10 .05 .01
□ 455 Jaime Cocanower .10 .05 .01
□ 456 Barbaro Garbey .10 .05 .01
□ 457 Rich Gedman .10 .05 .01
□ 458 Phil Niekro .40 .18 .05
□ 459 Mike Scioscia .10 .05 .01
□ 460 Pat Tabler .10 .05 .01
□ 461 Darryl Motley .10 .05 .01
□ 462 Chris Codiroli .10 .05 .01
□ 463 Doug Flynn .10 .05 .01
□ 464 Billy Sample .10 .05 .01
□ 465 Mickey Rivers .10 .05 .01
□ 466 John Wathan .10 .05 .01
□ 467 Bill Krueger .10 .05 .01
□ 468 Andre Thornton .10 .05 .01
□ 469 Rex Hudler .10 .05 .01
□ 470 Sid Bream .40 .18 .05
□ 471 Kirk Gibson .20 .09 .03
□ 472 John Shelby .10 .05 .01
□ 473 Moose Haas .10 .05 .01
□ 474 Doug Corbett .10 .05 .01
□ 475 Willie McGee .20 .09 .03
□ 476 Bob Knepper .10 .05 .01
□ 477 Kevin Gross .10 .05 .01
□ 478 Carmelo Martinez .10 .05 .01
□ 479 Kent Tekulve .10 .05 .01
□ 480 Chili Davis .20 .09 .03
□ 481 Bobby Clark .10 .05 .01
□ 482 Mookie Wilson .20 .09 .03
□ 483 Dave Owen .10 .05 .01
□ 484 Ed Nunez .10 .05 .01
□ 485 Rance Mulliniks .10 .05 .01
□ 486 Ken Schrom .10 .05 .01
□ 487 Jeff Russell .20 .09 .03
□ 488 Tom Paciorek .10 .05 .01
□ 489 Dan Ford .10 .05 .01
□ 490 Mike Caldwell .10 .05 .01
□ 491 Scottie Earl .10 .05 .01
□ 492 Jose Rijo 1.00 .45 .12
□ 493 Bruce Hurst .10 .05 .01
□ 494 Ken Landreaux .10 .05 .01
□ 495 Mike Fischlin .10 .05 .01
□ 496 Don Slaught .10 .05 .01
□ 497 Steve McCatty .10 .05 .01
□ 498 Gary Lucas .10 .05 .01
□ 499 Gary Pettis .10 .05 .01
□ 500 Marvis Foley .10 .05 .01
□ 501 Mike Squires .10 .05 .01
□ 502 Jim Pankovits .10 .05 .01
□ 503 Luis Aguayo .10 .05 .01
□ 504 Ralph Citarella .10 .05 .01
□ 505 Bruce Bochy .10 .05 .01
□ 506 Bob Owchinko .10 .05 .01
□ 507 Pascual Perez .10 .05 .01
□ 508 Lee Lacy .10 .05 .01
□ 509 Atlee Hammaker .10 .05 .01
□ 510 Bob Dernier .10 .05 .01
□ 511 Ed VandeBerg .10 .05 .01
□ 512 Cliff Johnson .10 .05 .01
□ 513 Len Whitehouse .10 .05 .01
□ 514 Dennis Martinez .20 .09 .03
□ 515 Ed Romero .10 .05 .01
□ 516 Rusty Kuntz .10 .05 .01
□ 517 Rick Miller .10 .05 .01
□ 518 Dennis Rasmussen .10 .05 .01
□ 519 Steve Yeager .10 .05 .01
□ 520 Chris Bando .10 .05 .01
□ 521 U.L. Washington .10 .05 .01
□ 522 Curt Young .10 .05 .01
□ 523 Angel Salazar .10 .05 .01
□ 524 Curt Kaufman .10 .05 .01
□ 525 Odell Jones .10 .05 .01
□ 526 Juan Agosto .10 .05 .01
□ 527 Denny Walling .10 .05 .01
□ 528 Andy Hawkins .10 .05 .01
□ 529 Sixto Lezcano .10 .05 .01
□ 530 Skeeter Barnes .10 .05 .01
□ 531 Randy Johnson .10 .05 .01
□ 532 Jim Morrison .10 .05 .01
□ 533 Warren Brusstar .10 .05 .01
□ 534A Jeff Pendleton ERR 1.50 .70 .19
(Wrong first name)
□ 534B Terry Pendleton COR 8.00 3.60 1.00
□ 535 Vic Rodriguez .10 .05 .01
□ 536 Bob McClure .10 .05 .01
□ 537 Dave Bergman .10 .05 .01
□ 538 Mark Clear .10 .05 .01
□ 539 Mike Pagliarulo .10 .05 .01
□ 540 Terry Whitfield .10 .05 .01
□ 541 Joe Beckwith .10 .05 .01
□ 542 Jeff Burroughs .10 .05 .01
□ 543 Dan Schatzeder .10 .05 .01
□ 544 Donnie Scott .10 .05 .01
□ 545 Jim Slaton .10 .05 .01
□ 546 Greg Luzinski .20 .09 .03
□ 547 Mark Salas .10 .05 .01
□ 548 Dave Smith .10 .05 .01
□ 549 John Wockenfuss .10 .05 .01
□ 550 Frank Pastore .10 .05 .01
□ 551 Tim Flannery .10 .05 .01
□ 552 Rick Rhoden .10 .05 .01
□ 553 Mark Davis .10 .05 .01
□ 554 Jeff Dedmon .10 .05 .01
□ 555 Gary Woods .10 .05 .01
□ 556 Danny Heep .10 .05 .01
□ 557 Mark Langston 1.25 .55 .16
□ 558 Darrell Brown .10 .05 .01
□ 559 Jimmy Key 1.00 .45 .12
□ 560 Rick Lysander .10 .05 .01
□ 561 Doyle Alexander .10 .05 .01
□ 562 Mike Stanton .10 .05 .01
□ 563 Sid Fernandez .40 .18 .05
□ 564 Richie Hebner .10 .05 .01
□ 565 Alex Trevino .10 .05 .01
□ 566 Brian Harper .20 .09 .03
□ 567 Dan Gladden .20 .09 .03
□ 568 Luis Salazar .10 .05 .01
□ 569 Tom Foley .10 .05 .01
□ 570 Larry Andersen .10 .05 .01
□ 571 Danny Cox .10 .05 .01
□ 572 Joe Sambito .10 .05 .01
□ 573 Juan Beniquez .10 .05 .01
□ 574 Joel Skinner .10 .05 .01
□ 575 Randy St.Claire .10 .05 .01
□ 576 Floyd Rayford .10 .05 .01
□ 577 Roy Howell .10 .05 .01
□ 578 John Grubb .10 .05 .01
□ 579 Ed Jurak .10 .05 .01
□ 580 John Montefusco .10 .05 .01
□ 581 Orel Hershiser 2.50 1.10 .30
□ 582 Tom Waddell .10 .05 .01
□ 583 Mark Huismann .10 .05 .01
□ 584 Joe Morgan .50 .23 .06
□ 585 Jim Wohlford .10 .05 .01
□ 586 Dave Schmidt .10 .05 .01
□ 587 Jeff Kunkel .10 .05 .01
□ 588 Hal McRae .20 .09 .03
□ 589 Bill Almon .10 .05 .01
□ 590 Carmen Castillo .10 .05 .01
□ 591 Omar Moreno .10 .05 .01
□ 592 Ken Howell .10 .05 .01
□ 593 Tom Brookens .10 .05 .01
□ 594 Joe Nolan .10 .05 .01
□ 595 Willie Lozado .10 .05 .01
□ 596 Tom Nieto .10 .05 .01
□ 597 Walt Terrell .10 .05 .01
□ 598 Al Oliver .20 .09 .03
□ 599 Shane Rawley .10 .05 .01
□ 600 Denny Gonzalez .10 .05 .01
□ 601 Mark Grant .10 .05 .01
□ 602 Mike Armstrong .10 .05 .01
□ 603 George Foster .20 .09 .03
□ 604 Dave Lopes .20 .09 .03
□ 605 Salome Barojas .10 .05 .01
□ 606 Roy Lee Jackson .10 .05 .01
□ 607 Pete Filson .10 .05 .01
□ 608 Duane Walker .10 .05 .01
□ 609 Glenn Wilson .10 .05 .01
□ 610 Rafael Santana .10 .05 .01
□ 611 Roy Smith .10 .05 .01
□ 612 Ruppert Jones .10 .05 .01
□ 613 Joe Cowley .10 .05 .01
□ 614 Al Nipper UER .10 .05 .01
(Photo actually
Mike Brown)
□ 615 Gene Nelson .10 .05 .01
□ 616 Joe Carter 5.00 2.20 .60
□ 617 Ray Knight .20 .09 .03
□ 618 Chuck Rainey .10 .05 .01
□ 619 Dan Driessen .10 .05 .01
□ 620 Daryl Sconiers .10 .05 .01
□ 621 Bill Stein .10 .05 .01
□ 622 Roy Smalley .10 .05 .01
□ 623 Ed Lynch .10 .05 .01
□ 624 Jeff Stone .10 .05 .01
□ 625 Bruce Berenyi .10 .05 .01
□ 626 Kelvin Chapman .10 .05 .01
□ 627 Joe Price .10 .05 .01
□ 628 Steve Bedrosian .10 .05 .01
□ 629 Vic Mata .10 .05 .01
□ 630 Mike Krukow .10 .05 .01
□ 631 Phil Bradley .20 .09 .03
□ 632 Jim Gott .10 .05 .01
□ 633 Randy Bush .10 .05 .01
□ 634 Tom Browning .40 .18 .05
□ 635 Lou Gehrig .50 .23 .06
Puzzle Card

☐ 636 Reid Nichols	.10	.05	.01
☐ 637 Dan Pasqua	.20	.09	.03
☐ 638 German Rivera	.10	.05	.01
☐ 639 Don Schulze	.10	.05	.01
☐ 640A Mike Jones (Career Highlights, takes five lines)	.10	.05	.01
☐ 640B Mike Jones (Career Highlights, takes four lines)	.10	.05	.01
☐ 641 Pete Rose	2.50	1.10	.30
☐ 642 Wade Rowdon	.10	.05	.01
☐ 643 Jerry Narron	.10	.05	.01
☐ 644 Darrell Miller	.10	.05	.01
☐ 645 Tim Hulett	.10	.05	.01
☐ 646 Andy McGaffigan	.10	.05	.01
☐ 647 Kurt Bevacqua	.10	.05	.01
☐ 648 John Russell	.10	.05	.01
☐ 649 Ron Robinson	.10	.05	.01
☐ 650 Donnie Moore	.10	.05	.01
☐ 651A Two for the Title Dave Winfield Don Mattingly (Yellow letters)	3.00	1.35	.35
☐ 651B Two for the Title Dave Winfield Don Mattingly (White letters)	8.00	3.60	1.00
☐ 652 Tim Laudner	.10	.05	.01
☐ 653 Steve Farr	.20	.09	.03
☐ 654 DK Checklist 1-26 (Unnumbered)	.20	.09	.03
☐ 655 Checklist 27-130 (Unnumbered)	.20	.09	.03
☐ 656 Checklist 131-234 (Unnumbered)	.20	.09	.03
☐ 657 Checklist 235-338 (Unnumbered)	.20	.09	.03
☐ 658 Checklist 339-442 (Unnumbered)	.20	.09	.03
☐ 659 Checklist 443-546 (Unnumbered)	.20	.09	.03
☐ 660 Checklist 547-653 (Unnumbered)	.20	.09	.03

1985 Donruss Wax Box Cards

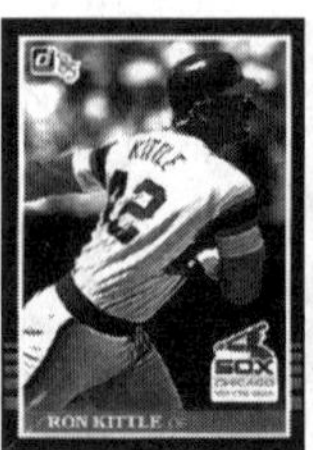
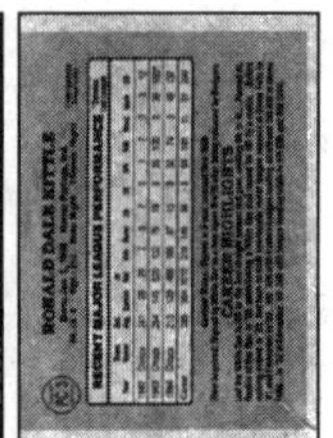

The boxes of the 1985 Donruss regular issue baseball cards, in which the wax packs were contained, featured four standard-size cards, with backs. The complete set price of the regular issue set does not include these cards; they are considered a separate set. The cards and are styled the same as the regular Donruss cards. The cards are numbered but with the prefix PC before the number. The value of the panel uncut is slightly greater, perhaps by 25 percent greater, than the value of the individual cards cut up carefully.

	NRMT	VG-E	GOOD
COMPLETE SET (4)	4.00	1.80	.50
COMMON CARD	.25	.11	.03
☐ PC1 Dwight Gooden	1.25	.55	.16
☐ PC2 Ryne Sandberg	2.00	.90	.25
☐ PC3 Ron Kittle	.25	.11	.03
☐ PUZ Lou Gehrig Puzzle Card	.75	.35	.09

1985 Donruss Action All-Stars

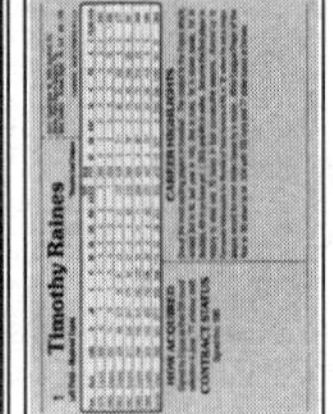

The cards in this 60-card set measure approximately 3 1/2" by 5". For the third year in a row, Donruss issued a set of Action All-Stars. This set features action photos on the obverse which also contains a portrait inset of the player. The backs, unlike the year before, do not contain a full color picture of the player but list, if space is available, full statistical data, biographical data, career highlights, and acquisition and contract status. The cards were issued with a Lou Gehrig puzzle card.

	NRMT	VG-E	GOOD
COMPLETE SET (60)	6.00	2.70	.75
COMMON CARD (1-60)	.05	.02	.01
☐ 1 Tim Raines	.10	.05	.01
☐ 2 Jim Gantner	.05	.02	.01
☐ 3 Mario Soto	.05	.02	.01
☐ 4 Spike Owen	.05	.02	.01
☐ 5 Lloyd Moseby	.05	.02	.01
☐ 6 Damaso Garcia	.05	.02	.01
☐ 7 Cal Ripken	2.50	1.10	.30
☐ 8 Dan Quisenberry	.05	.02	.01
☐ 9 Eddie Murray	.60	.25	.07
☐ 10 Tony Pena	.05	.02	.01
☐ 11 Buddy Bell	.10	.05	.01
☐ 12 Dave Winfield	.40	.18	.05
☐ 13 Ron Kittle	.05	.02	.01
☐ 14 Rich Gossage	.10	.05	.01
☐ 15 Dwight Evans	.10	.05	.01
☐ 16 Alvin Davis	.05	.02	.01
☐ 17 Mike Schmidt	.60	.25	.07
☐ 18 Pascual Perez	.05	.02	.01
☐ 19 Tony Gwynn	1.25	.55	.16
☐ 20 Nolan Ryan	2.00	.90	.25
☐ 21 Robin Yount	.40	.18	.05
☐ 22 Mike Marshall	.05	.02	.01
☐ 23 Brett Butler	.10	.05	.01
☐ 24 Ryne Sandberg	.75	.35	.09
☐ 25 Dale Murphy	.20	.09	.03
☐ 26 George Brett	1.25	.55	.16
☐ 27 Jim Rice	.10	.05	.01
☐ 28 Ozzie Smith	1.00	.45	.12
☐ 29 Larry Parrish	.05	.02	.01
☐ 30 Jack Clark	.10	.05	.01
☐ 31 Manny Trillo	.05	.02	.01
☐ 32 Dave Kingman	.10	.05	.01
☐ 33 Geoff Zahn	.05	.02	.01
☐ 34 Pedro Guerrero	.10	.05	.01
☐ 35 Dave Parker	.10	.05	.01
☐ 36 Rollie Fingers	.20	.09	.03
☐ 37 Fernando Valenzuela	.10	.05	.01
☐ 38 Wade Boggs	.40	.18	.05
☐ 39 Reggie Jackson	.50	.23	.06
☐ 40 Kent Hrbek	.10	.05	.01
☐ 41 Keith Hernandez	.10	.05	.01
☐ 42 Lou Whitaker	.20	.09	.03
☐ 43 Tom Herr	.10	.05	.01
☐ 44 Alan Trammell	.20	.09	.03
☐ 45 Butch Wynegar	.05	.02	.01
☐ 46 Leon Durham	.05	.02	.01
☐ 47 Dwight Gooden	.50	.23	.06
☐ 48 Don Mattingly	1.50	.70	.19
☐ 49 Phil Niekro	.20	.09	.03
☐ 50 Johnny Ray	.05	.02	.01
☐ 51 Doug DeCinces	.05	.02	.01
☐ 52 Willie Upshaw	.05	.02	.01
☐ 53 Lance Parrish	.10	.05	.01
☐ 54 Jody Davis	.05	.02	.01
☐ 55 Steve Carlton	.40	.18	.05
☐ 56 Juan Samuel	.05	.02	.01
☐ 57 Gary Carter	.10	.05	.01
☐ 58 Harold Baines	.10	.05	.01
☐ 59 Eric Show	.05	.02	.01
☐ 60 Checklist Card	.05	.02	.01

1985 Donruss Highlights

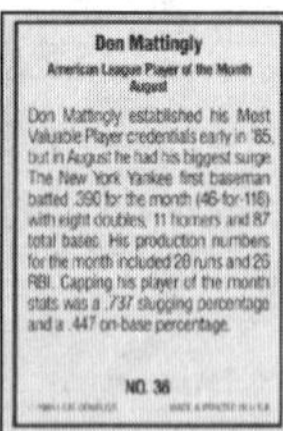

This 56-card standard-size set features the players and pitchers of the month for each league as well as a number of highlight cards commemorating the 1985 season. The Donruss Company dedicated the last two cards to their own selections for Rookies of the Year (ROY). This set proved to be more popular than the Donruss Company had predicted, as their first and only print run was exhausted before card dealers' initial orders were filled.

	NRMT	VG-E	GOOD
COMPLETE FACT. SET (56)	15.00	6.75	1.85
COMMON CARD (1-55)	.10	.05	.01
CHECKLIST (NNO)	.10	.05	.01
☐ 1 Tom Seaver Sets Opening Day Record	.50	.23	.06
☐ 2 Rollie Fingers Sets AL Save Mark	.30	.14	.04
☐ 3 Mike Davis AL Player April	.10	.05	.01
☐ 4 Charlie Leibrandt AL Pitcher April	.10	.05	.01
☐ 5 Dale Murphy NL Player April	.30	.14	.04
☐ 6 Fernando Valenzuela NL Pitcher April	.20	.09	.03
☐ 7 Larry Bowa NL Shortstop Record	.20	.09	.03
☐ 8 Dave Concepcion Joins Reds' 2000 Hit Club	.20	.09	.03
☐ 9 Tony Perez Eldest Grand Slammer	.30	.14	.04
☐ 10 Pete Rose NL Career Run Leader	1.25	.55	.16
☐ 11 George Brett AL Player May	1.50	.70	.19
☐ 12 Dave Stieb AL Pitcher May	.10	.05	.01
☐ 13 Dave Parker NL Player May	.20	.09	.03
☐ 14 Andy Hawkins NL Pitcher May	.10	.05	.01
☐ 15 Andy Hawkins Records 11th Straight Win	.10	.05	.01
☐ 16 Von Hayes Two Homers in First Inning	.10	.05	.01
☐ 17 Rickey Henderson AL Player June	.50	.23	.06
☐ 18 Jay Howell AL Pitcher June	.10	.05	.01
☐ 19 Pedro Guerrero NL Player June	.20	.09	.03
☐ 20 John Tudor NL Pitcher June	.10	.05	.01
☐ 21 Keith Hernandez Gary Carter Marathon Game Iron Men	.20	.09	.03
☐ 22 Nolan Ryan Records 4000th K	4.00	1.80	.50
☐ 23 LaMarr Hoyt All-Star Game MVP	.10	.05	.01
☐ 24 Oddibe McDowell 1st Ranger to Hit for Cycle	.10	.05	.01
☐ 25 George Brett AL Player July	1.50	.70	.19
☐ 26 Bret Saberhagen AL Pitcher July	.20	.09	.03
☐ 27 Keith Hernandez NL Player July	.20	.09	.03
☐ 28 Fernando Valenzuela NL Pitcher July	.20	.09	.03
☐ 29 Willie McGee Vince Coleman Record Setting Base Stealers	.20	.09	.03
☐ 30 Tom Seaver Notches 300th Career Win	.50	.23	.06
☐ 31 Rod Carew Strokes 3000th Hit	.40	.18	.05
☐ 32 Dwight Gooden Establishes Met Record	1.00	.45	.12
☐ 33 Dwight Gooden Achieves Strikeout Milestone	1.00	.45	.12
☐ 34 Eddie Murray Explodes for 9 RBI	1.00	.45	.12
☐ 35 Don Baylor AL Career HBP Leader	.20	.09	.03
☐ 36 Don Mattingly AL Player August	2.50	1.10	.30
☐ 37 Dave Righetti AL Pitcher August	.20	.09	.03
☐ 38 Willie McGee NL Player August	.20	.09	.03
☐ 39 Shane Rawley NL Pitcher August	.10	.05	.01
☐ 40 Pete Rose Ty-Breaking Hit	1.50	.70	.19
☐ 41 Andre Dawson Hits 3 HR's, Drives in 8 Runs	.40	.18	.05
☐ 42 Rickey Henderson Sets Yankee Theft Mark	.50	.23	.06
☐ 43 Tom Browning 20 Wins in Rookie Season	.20	.09	.03
☐ 44 Don Mattingly Yankee Milestone for Hits	2.50	1.10	.30
☐ 45 Don Mattingly AL Player September	2.50	1.10	.30
☐ 46 Charlie Leibrandt AL Pitcher September	.10	.05	.01
☐ 47 Gary Carter NL Player September	.20	.09	.03
☐ 48 Dwight Gooden NL Pitcher September	1.00	.45	.12
☐ 49 Wade Boggs Major League Record Setter	.50	.23	.06
☐ 50 Phil Niekro Hurls Shutout for 300th Win	.40	.18	.05
☐ 51 Darrell Evans Venerable HR King	.20	.09	.03
☐ 52 Willie McGee NL Switch-Hitting Record	.20	.09	.03
☐ 53 Dave Winfield Equals DiMaggio Feat	.50	.23	.06
☐ 54 Vince Coleman Donruss NL ROY	.20	.09	.03
☐ 55 Ozzie Guillen Donruss AL ROY	.25	.11	.03
☐ NNO Checklist Card	.10	.05	.01

1985 Donruss HOF Sluggers

This eight-card set of Hall of Fame players features the artwork of resident Donruss artist Dick Perez. These oversized (3 1/2" by 6 1/2", blank backed cards actually form part of a box of gum distributed by the Donruss Company through supermarket type outlets. These cards are reminiscent of the Bazooka issues. The players in the set were ostensibly chosen based on their career slugging percentage, which is listed below each player. The cards themselves are numbered by (slugging percentage) rank. The boxes are also numbered on one of the white side tabs of the complete box; this completely different numbering system is not used.

	NRMT	VG-E	GOOD
COMPLETE SET (8)	7.00	3.10	.85
COMMON CARD (1-8)	.50	.23	.06
☐ 1 Babe Ruth Slugging Percent .690	2.00	.90	.25
☐ 2 Ted Williams Slugging Percent .634	1.50	.70	.19
☐ 3 Lou Gehrig Slugging Percent .632	1.50	.70	.19
☐ 4 Johnny Mize Slugging Percent .562	.50	.23	.06
☐ 5 Stan Musial Slugging Percent .559	.75	.35	.09
☐ 6 Mickey Mantle Slugging Percent .557	2.50	1.10	.30
☐ 7 Hank Aaron Slugging Percent .555	1.00	.45	.12
☐ 8 Frank Robinson Slugging Percent .537	.50	.23	.06

1985 Donruss Super DK's

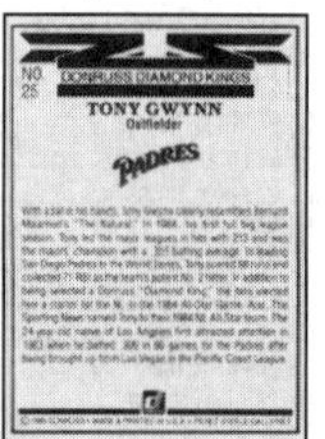

The cards in this 28-card set measure approximately 4 15/16 by 6 3/4". The 1985 Donruss Diamond Kings Supers set contains enlarged cards of the first 26 cards of the Donruss regular set of this year. In addition, the Diamond Kings checklist card, a card of artist Dick Perez and a Lou Gehrig puzzle card are included in the set. The set was the brain-child of the Perez-Steele Galleries and could be obtained via a write-in offer on the wrappers of the Donruss regular cards of this year. The Gehrig puzzle card is actually a 12-piece jigsaw puzzle. The back of the checklist card is blank; however, the Dick Perez card back gives a short history of Dick Perez and the Perez-Steele Galleries. The offer for obtaining this set was detailed on the wax pack wrappers; three wrappers plus $9.00 was required for this mail-in offer.

	NRMT	VG-E	GOOD
COMPLETE SET (28)	15.00	6.75	1.85
COMMON CARD (1-28)	.50	.23	.06
☐ 1 Ryne Sandberg	2.50	1.10	.30
☐ 2 Doug DeCinces	.50	.23	.06
☐ 3 Richard Dotson	.50	.23	.06
☐ 4 Bert Blyleven	1.00	.45	.12
☐ 5 Lou Whitaker	1.50	.70	.19
☐ 6 Dan Quisenberry	.50	.23	.06
☐ 7 Don Mattingly	4.00	1.80	.50
☐ 8 Carney Lansford	1.00	.45	.12
☐ 9 Frank Tanana	.50	.23	.06
☐ 10 Willie Upshaw	.50	.23	.06
☐ 11 Claudell Washington	.50	.23	.06
☐ 12 Mike Marshall	.50	.23	.06
☐ 13 Joaquin Andujar	.50	.23	.06
☐ 14 Cal Ripken	6.00	2.70	.75
☐ 15 Jim Rice	1.00	.45	.12
☐ 16 Don Sutton	1.50	.70	.19
☐ 17 Frank Viola	1.00	.45	.12
☐ 18 Alvin Davis	.50	.23	.06
☐ 19 Mario Soto	.50	.23	.06
☐ 20 Jose Cruz	.50	.23	.06
☐ 21 Charlie Lea	.50	.23	.06
☐ 22 Jesse Orosco	.50	.23	.06
☐ 23 Juan Samuel	.50	.23	.06
☐ 24 Tony Pena	.50	.23	.06
☐ 25 Tony Gwynn	3.00	1.35	.35
☐ 26 Bob Brenly	.50	.23	.06

☐ NNO Checklist Card	.50	.23	.06
☐ NNO Dick Perez (History of DK's)	.50	.23	.06

1986 Donruss

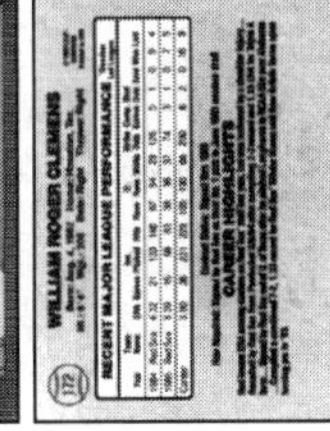

The 1986 Donruss set consists of 660 standard-size cards. Wax packs contained 15 cards plus a Hank Aaron puzzle panel. The card fronts feature blue borders, the standard team logo, player's name, position, and Donruss logo. The first 26 cards of the set are Diamond Kings (DK), for the fifth year in a row; the artwork on the Diamond Kings was again produced by the Perez-Steele Galleries. Cards 27-46 again feature Rated Rookies (RR). The unnumbered checklist cards are arbitrarily numbered below as numbers 654 through 660. Rookie Cards in this set include Jose Canseco, Darren Daulton, Len Dykstra, Cecil Fielder, Andres Galarraga, Fred McGriff, Paul O'Neill, and Mickey Tettleton.

	MINT	NRMT	EXC
COMPLETE SET (660)	70.00	32.00	8.75
COMPLETE FACT.SET (660)	75.00	34.00	9.50
COMMON CARD (1-660)	.10	.05	.01
☐ 1 Kirk Gibson DK	.20	.09	.03
☐ 2 Goose Gossage DK	.40	.18	.05
☐ 3 Willie McGee DK	.20	.09	.03
☐ 4 George Bell DK	.10	.05	.01
☐ 5 Tony Armas DK	.10	.05	.01
☐ 6 Chili Davis DK	.40	.18	.05
☐ 7 Cecil Cooper DK	.10	.05	.01
☐ 8 Mike Boddicker DK	.10	.05	.01
☐ 9 Dave Lopes DK	.10	.05	.01
☐ 10 Bill Doran DK	.10	.05	.01
☐ 11 Bret Saberhagen DK	.40	.18	.05
☐ 12 Brett Butler DK	.20	.09	.03
☐ 13 Harold Baines DK	.40	.18	.05
☐ 14 Mike Davis DK	.10	.05	.01
☐ 15 Tony Perez DK	.40	.18	.05
☐ 16 Willie Randolph DK	.20	.09	.03
☐ 17 Bob Boone DK	.20	.09	.03
☐ 18 Orel Hershiser DK	.40	.18	.05
☐ 19 Johnny Ray DK	.10	.05	.01
☐ 20 Gary Ward DK	.10	.05	.01
☐ 21 Rick Mahler DK	.10	.05	.01
☐ 22 Phil Bradley DK	.10	.05	.01
☐ 23 Jerry Koosman DK	.20	.09	.03
☐ 24 Tom Brunansky DK	.10	.05	.01
☐ 25 Andre Dawson DK	.40	.18	.05
☐ 26 Dwight Gooden DK	.40	.18	.05
☐ 27 Kal Daniels RR	.20	.09	.03
☐ 28 Fred McGriff RR	15.00	6.75	1.85
☐ 29 Cory Snyder RR	.10	.05	.01
☐ 30 Jose Guzman RR	.10	.05	.01
☐ 31 Ty Gainey RR	.10	.05	.01
☐ 32 Johnny Abrego RR	.10	.05	.01
☐ 33 Andres Galarraga RR (No accent)	6.00	2.70	.75
☐ 33B Andre's Galarraga RR (Accent over e)	6.00	2.70	.75
☐ 34 Dave Shipanoff RR	.10	.05	.01
☐ 35 Mark McLemore RR	.50	.23	.06
☐ 36 Marty Clary RR	.10	.05	.01
☐ 37 Paul O'Neill RR	2.50	1.10	.30
☐ 38 Danny Tartabull RR	.20	.09	.03
☐ 39 Jose Canseco RR	12.00	5.50	1.50
☐ 40 Juan Nieves RR	.10	.05	.01
☐ 41 Lance McCullers RR	.10	.05	.01
☐ 42 Rick Surhoff RR	.10	.05	.01
☐ 43 Todd Worrell RR	.40	.18	.05
☐ 44 Bob Kipper RR	.10	.05	.01
☐ 45 John Habyan RR	.10	.05	.01
☐ 46 Mike Woodard RR	.10	.05	.01
☐ 47 Mike Boddicker	.10	.05	.01
☐ 48 Robin Yount	.75	.35	.09
☐ 49 Lou Whitaker	.20	.09	.03
☐ 50 Oil Can Boyd	.10	.05	.01
☐ 51 Rickey Henderson	.75	.35	.09
☐ 52 Mike Marshall	.10	.05	.01
☐ 53 George Brett	2.00	.90	.25
☐ 54 Dave Kingman	.20	.09	.03
☐ 55 Hubie Brooks	.10	.05	.01
☐ 56 Oddibe McDowell	.10	.05	.01
☐ 57 Doug DeCinces	.10	.05	.01
☐ 58 Britt Burns	.10	.05	.01
☐ 59 Ozzie Smith	1.25	.55	.16
☐ 60 Jose Cruz	.10	.05	.01
☐ 61 Mike Schmidt	1.00	.45	.12
☐ 62 Pete Rose	.75	.35	.09
☐ 63 Steve Garvey	.40	.18	.05
☐ 64 Tony Pena	.10	.05	.01
☐ 65 Chili Davis	.40	.18	.05
☐ 66 Dale Murphy	.40	.18	.05
☐ 67 Ryne Sandberg	2.00	.90	.25
☐ 68 Gary Carter	.20	.09	.03
☐ 69 Alvin Davis	.10	.05	.01
☐ 70 Kent Hrbek	.20	.09	.03
☐ 71 George Bell	.20	.09	.03
☐ 72 Kirby Puckett	5.00	2.20	.60
☐ 73 Lloyd Moseby	.10	.05	.01
☐ 74 Bob Kearney	.10	.05	.01
☐ 75 Dwight Gooden	.60	.25	.07
☐ 76 Gary Matthews	.10	.05	.01
☐ 77 Rick Mahler	.10	.05	.01
☐ 78 Benny Distefano	.10	.05	.01
☐ 79 Jeff Leonard	.10	.05	.01
☐ 80 Kevin McReynolds	.20	.09	.03
☐ 81 Ron Oester	.10	.05	.01
☐ 82 John Russell	.10	.05	.01
☐ 83 Tommy Herr	.10	.05	.01
☐ 84 Jerry Mumphrey	.10	.05	.01
☐ 85 Ron Romanick	.10	.05	.01
☐ 86 Daryl Boston	.10	.05	.01
☐ 87 Andre Dawson	.40	.18	.05
☐ 88 Eddie Murray	1.25	.55	.16
☐ 89 Dion James	.10	.05	.01
☐ 90 Chet Lemon	.10	.05	.01
☐ 91 Bob Stanley	.10	.05	.01
☐ 92 Willie Randolph	.20	.09	.03
☐ 93 Mike Scioscia	.10	.05	.01
☐ 94 Tom Waddell	.10	.05	.01
☐ 95 Danny Jackson	.10	.05	.01
☐ 96 Mike Davis	.10	.05	.01
☐ 97 Mike Fitzgerald	.10	.05	.01
☐ 98 Gary Ward	.10	.05	.01
☐ 99 Pete O'Brien	.10	.05	.01
☐ 100 Bret Saberhagen	.40	.18	.05
☐ 101 Alfredo Griffin	.10	.05	.01
☐ 102 Brett Butler	.20	.09	.03
☐ 103 Ron Guidry	.20	.09	.03
☐ 104 Jerry Reuss	.10	.05	.01
☐ 105 Jack Morris	.20	.09	.03
☐ 106 Rick Dempsey	.10	.05	.01
☐ 107 Ray Burris	.10	.05	.01
☐ 108 Brian Downing	.10	.05	.01
☐ 109 Willie McGee	.20	.09	.03
☐ 110 Bill Doran	.10	.05	.01
☐ 111 Kent Tekulve	.10	.05	.01
☐ 112 Tony Gwynn	2.50	1.10	.30
☐ 113 Marvell Wynne	.10	.05	.01
☐ 114 David Green	.10	.05	.01
☐ 115 Jim Gantner	.10	.05	.01
☐ 116 George Foster	.20	.09	.03
☐ 117 Steve Trout	.10	.05	.01
☐ 118 Mark Langston	.20	.09	.03
☐ 119 Tony Fernandez	.10	.05	.01
☐ 120 John Butcher	.10	.05	.01
☐ 121 Ron Robinson	.10	.05	.01
☐ 122 Dan Spillner	.10	.05	.01
☐ 123 Mike Young	.10	.05	.01
☐ 124 Paul Molitor	1.00	.45	.12
☐ 125 Kirk Gibson	.20	.09	.03
☐ 126 Ken Griffey	.20	.09	.03
☐ 127 Tony Armas	.10	.05	.01
☐ 128 Mariano Duncan	.40	.18	.05
☐ 129 Pat Tabler	.10	.05	.01
☐ 130 Frank White	.20	.09	.03
☐ 131 Carney Lansford	.20	.09	.03
☐ 132 Vance Law	.10	.05	.01
☐ 133 Dick Schofield	.10	.05	.01
☐ 134 Wayne Tolleson	.10	.05	.01
☐ 135 Greg Walker	.10	.05	.01
☐ 136 Denny Walling	.10	.05	.01
☐ 137 Ozzie Virgil	.10	.05	.01
☐ 138 Ricky Horton	.10	.05	.01
☐ 139 LaMarr Hoyt	.10	.05	.01
☐ 140 Wayne Krenchicki	.10	.05	.01
☐ 141 Glenn Hubbard	.10	.05	.01
☐ 142 Cecilio Guante	.10	.05	.01
☐ 143 Mike Krukow	.10	.05	.01
☐ 144 Lee Smith	.40	.18	.05
☐ 145 Edwin Nunez	.10	.05	.01
☐ 146 Dave Stieb	.10	.05	.01
☐ 147 Mike Smithson	.10	.05	.01
☐ 148 Ken Dixon	.10	.05	.01
☐ 149 Danny Darwin	.10	.05	.01
☐ 150 Chris Pittaro	.10	.05	.01
☐ 151 Bill Buckner	.20	.09	.03
☐ 152 Mike Pagliarulo	.10	.05	.01
☐ 153 Bill Russell	.10	.05	.01
☐ 154 Brook Jacoby	.10	.05	.01
☐ 155 Pat Sheridan	.10	.05	.01
☐ 156 Mike Gallego	.20	.09	.03
☐ 157 Jim Wohlford	.10	.05	.01
☐ 158 Gary Pettis	.10	.05	.01
☐ 159 Toby Harrah	.10	.05	.01
☐ 160 Richard Dotson	.10	.05	.01
☐ 161 Bob Knepper	.10	.05	.01
☐ 162 Dave Dravecky	.20	.09	.03
☐ 163 Greg Gross	.10	.05	.01
☐ 164 Eric Davis	.20	.09	.03
☐ 165 Gerald Perry	.10	.05	.01
☐ 166 Rick Rhoden	.10	.05	.01
☐ 167 Keith Moreland	.10	.05	.01
☐ 168 Jack Clark	.20	.09	.03
☐ 169 Storm Davis	.10	.05	.01
☐ 170 Cecil Cooper	.20	.09	.03
☐ 171 Alan Trammell	.40	.18	.05
☐ 172 Roger Clemens	2.50	1.10	.30
☐ 173 Don Mattingly	3.00	1.35	.35
☐ 174 Pedro Guerrero	.20	.09	.03
☐ 175 Willie Wilson	.10	.05	.01
☐ 176 Dwayne Murphy	.10	.05	.01
☐ 177 Tim Raines	.20	.09	.03
☐ 178 Larry Parrish	.10	.05	.01
☐ 179 Mike Witt	.10	.05	.01
☐ 180 Harold Baines	.40	.18	.05
☐ 181 Vince Coleman UER (BA 2.67 on back)	.40	.18	.05
☐ 182 Jeff Heathcock	.10	.05	.01
☐ 183 Steve Carlton	.50	.23	.06
☐ 184 Mario Soto	.10	.05	.01
☐ 185 Goose Gossage	.20	.09	.03
☐ 186 Johnny Ray	.10	.05	.01
☐ 187 Dan Gladden	.10	.05	.01
☐ 188 Bob Horner	.10	.05	.01
☐ 189 Rick Sutcliffe	.10	.05	.01
☐ 190 Keith Hernandez	.20	.09	.03
☐ 191 Phil Bradley	.10	.05	.01
☐ 192 Tom Brunansky	.10	.05	.01
☐ 193 Jesse Barfield	.10	.05	.01
☐ 194 Frank Viola	.20	.09	.03
☐ 195 Willie Upshaw	.10	.05	.01
☐ 196 Jim Beattie	.10	.05	.01
☐ 197 Darryl Strawberry	.40	.18	.05
☐ 198 Ron Cey	.20	.09	.03
☐ 199 Steve Bedrosian	.10	.05	.01
☐ 200 Steve Kemp	.10	.05	.01
☐ 201 Manny Trillo	.10	.05	.01
☐ 202 Garry Templeton	.10	.05	.01
☐ 203 Dave Parker	.20	.09	.03
☐ 204 John Denny	.10	.05	.01
☐ 205 Terry Pendleton	.40	.18	.05
☐ 206 Terry Puhl	.10	.05	.01
☐ 207 Bobby Grich	.20	.09	.03
☐ 208 Ozzie Guillen	.40	.18	.05
☐ 209 Jeff Reardon	.20	.09	.03
☐ 210 Cal Ripken	4.00	1.80	.50
☐ 211 Bill Schroeder	.10	.05	.01
☐ 212 Dan Petry	.10	.05	.01
☐ 213 Jim Rice	.20	.09	.03
☐ 214 Dave Righetti	.10	.05	.01
☐ 215 Fernando Valenzuela	.20	.09	.03
☐ 216 Julio Franco	.40	.18	.05
☐ 217 Darryl Motley	.10	.05	.01
☐ 218 Dave Collins	.10	.05	.01
☐ 219 Tim Wallach	.10	.05	.01
☐ 220 George Wright	.10	.05	.01
☐ 221 Tommy Dunbar	.10	.05	.01
☐ 222 Steve Balboni	.10	.05	.01
☐ 223 Jay Howell	.10	.05	.01
☐ 224 Joe Carter	2.00	.90	.25
☐ 225 Ed Whitson	.10	.05	.01
☐ 226 Orel Hershiser	.40	.18	.05
☐ 227 Willie Hernandez	.10	.05	.01
☐ 228 Lee Lacy	.10	.05	.01
☐ 229 Rollie Fingers	.40	.18	.05
☐ 230 Bob Boone	.20	.09	.03
☐ 231 Joaquin Andujar	.10	.05	.01
☐ 232 Craig Reynolds	.10	.05	.01
☐ 233 Shane Rawley	.10	.05	.01
☐ 234 Eric Show	.10	.05	.01
☐ 235 Jose DeLeon	.10	.05	.01
☐ 236 Jose Uribe	.10	.05	.01
☐ 237 Moose Haas	.10	.05	.01
☐ 238 Wally Backman	.10	.05	.01
☐ 239 Dennis Eckersley	.40	.18	.05
☐ 240 Mike Moore	.10	.05	.01
☐ 241 Damaso Garcia	.10	.05	.01
☐ 242 Tim Teufel	.10	.05	.01
☐ 243 Dave Concepcion	.20	.09	.03
☐ 244 Floyd Bannister	.10	.05	.01
☐ 245 Fred Lynn	.20	.09	.03
☐ 246 Charlie Moore	.10	.05	.01
☐ 247 Walt Terrell	.10	.05	.01
☐ 248 Dave Winfield	.60	.25	.07
☐ 249 Dwight Evans	.20	.09	.03
☐ 250 Dennis Powell	.10	.05	.01
☐ 251 Andre Thornton	.10	.05	.01
☐ 252 Onix Concepcion	.10	.05	.01
☐ 253 Mike Heath	.10	.05	.01
☐ 254A David Palmer ERR (Position 2B)	.10	.05	.01
☐ 254B David Palmer COR (Position P)	.40	.18	.05
☐ 255 Donnie Moore	.10	.05	.01
☐ 256 Curtis Wilkerson	.10	.05	.01
☐ 257 Julio Cruz	.10	.05	.01
☐ 258 Nolan Ryan	4.00	1.80	.50
☐ 259 Jeff Stone	.10	.05	.01
☐ 260 John Tudor	.10	.05	.01
☐ 261 Mark Thurmond	.10	.05	.01
☐ 262 Jay Tibbs	.10	.05	.01
☐ 263 Rafael Ramirez	.10	.05	.01
☐ 264 Larry McWilliams	.10	.05	.01
☐ 265 Mark Davis	.10	.05	.01
☐ 266 Bob Dernier	.10	.05	.01
☐ 267 Matt Young	.10	.05	.01
☐ 268 Jim Clancy	.10	.05	.01
☐ 269 Mickey Hatcher	.10	.05	.01
☐ 270 Sammy Stewart	.10	.05	.01
☐ 271 Bob L. Gibson	.10	.05	.01
☐ 272 Nelson Simmons	.10	.05	.01
☐ 273 Rich Gedman	.10	.05	.01
☐ 274 Butch Wynegar	.10	.05	.01
☐ 275 Ken Howell	.10	.05	.01
☐ 276 Mel Hall	.10	.05	.01
☐ 277 Jim Sundberg	.10	.05	.01
☐ 278 Chris Codiroli	.10	.05	.01
☐ 279 Herm Winningham	.10	.05	.01
☐ 280 Rod Carew	.50	.23	.06
☐ 281 Don Slaught	.10	.05	.01
☐ 282 Scott Fletcher	.10	.05	.01
☐ 283 Bill Dawley	.10	.05	.01
☐ 284 Andy Hawkins	.10	.05	.01
☐ 285 Glenn Wilson	.10	.05	.01
☐ 286 Nick Esasky	.10	.05	.01
☐ 287 Claudell Washington	.10	.05	.01
☐ 288 Lee Mazzilli	.10	.05	.01
☐ 289 Jody Davis	.10	.05	.01
☐ 290 Darrell Porter	.20	.09	.03
☐ 291 Scott McGregor	.10	.05	.01
☐ 292 Ted Simmons	.20	.09	.03
☐ 293 Aurelio Lopez	.10	.05	.01
☐ 294 Marty Barrett	.10	.05	.01
☐ 295 Dale Berra	.10	.05	.01
☐ 296 Greg Brock	.10	.05	.01
☐ 297 Charlie Leibrandt	.10	.05	.01
☐ 298 Bill Krueger	.10	.05	.01
☐ 299 Bryn Smith	.10	.05	.01
☐ 300 Burt Hooton	.10	.05	.01
☐ 301 Stu Cliburn	.10	.05	.01
☐ 302 Luis Salazar	.10	.05	.01
☐ 303 Ken Dayley	.10	.05	.01
☐ 304 Frank DiPino	.10	.05	.01
☐ 305 Von Hayes	.10	.05	.01
☐ 306 Gary Redus	.10	.05	.01
☐ 307 Craig Lefferts	.10	.05	.01
☐ 308 Sammy Khalifa	.10	.05	.01
☐ 309 Scott Garrelts	.10	.05	.01
☐ 310 Rick Cerone	.10	.05	.01
☐ 311 Shawon Dunston	.20	.09	.03
☐ 312 Howard Johnson	.20	.09	.03
☐ 313 Jim Presley	.10	.05	.01
☐ 314 Gary Gaetti	.20	.09	.03
☐ 315 Luis Leal	.10	.05	.01
☐ 316 Mark Salas	.10	.05	.01
☐ 317 Bill Caudill	.10	.05	.01
☐ 318 Dave Henderson	.10	.05	.01
☐ 319 Rafael Santana	.10	.05	.01
☐ 320 Leon Durham	.10	.05	.01
☐ 321 Bruce Sutter	.20	.09	.03
☐ 322 Jason Thompson	.10	.05	.01
☐ 323 Bob Brenly	.10	.05	.01
☐ 324 Carmelo Martinez	.10	.05	.01
☐ 325 Eddie Milner	.10	.05	.01
☐ 326 Juan Samuel	.10	.05	.01
☐ 327 Tom Nieto	.10	.05	.01
☐ 328 Dave Smith	.10	.05	.01
☐ 329 Urbano Lugo	.10	.05	.01
☐ 330 Joel Skinner	.10	.05	.01
☐ 331 Bill Gullickson	.10	.05	.01
☐ 332 Floyd Rayford	.10	.05	.01
☐ 333 Ben Oglivie	.10	.05	.01
☐ 334 Lance Parrish	.20	.09	.03
☐ 335 Jackie Gutierrez	.10	.05	.01
☐ 336 Dennis Rasmussen	.10	.05	.01
☐ 337 Terry Whitfield	.10	.05	.01
☐ 338 Neal Heaton	.10	.05	.01
☐ 339 Jorge Orta	.10	.05	.01
☐ 340 Donnie Hill	.10	.05	.01
☐ 341 Joe Hesketh	.10	.05	.01
☐ 342 Charlie Hough	.20	.09	.03
☐ 343 Dave Rozema	.10	.05	.01
☐ 344 Greg Pryor	.10	.05	.01
☐ 345 Mickey Tettleton	2.00	.90	.25
☐ 346 George Vukovich	.10	.05	.01
☐ 347 Don Baylor	.40	.18	.05
☐ 348 Carlos Diaz	.10	.05	.01
☐ 349 Barbaro Garbey	.10	.05	.01
☐ 350 Larry Sheets	.10	.05	.01
☐ 351 Ted Higuera	.20	.09	.03
☐ 352 Juan Beniquez	.10	.05	.01
☐ 353 Bob Forsch	.10	.05	.01
☐ 354 Mark Bailey	.10	.05	.01
☐ 355 Larry Andersen	.10	.05	.01
☐ 356 Terry Kennedy	.10	.05	.01
☐ 357 Don Robinson	.10	.05	.01
☐ 358 Jim Gott	.10	.05	.01
☐ 359 Earnie Riles	.10	.05	.01
☐ 360 John Christensen	.10	.05	.01
☐ 361 Ray Fontenot	.10	.05	.01
☐ 362 Spike Owen	.10	.05	.01
☐ 363 Jim Acker	.10	.05	.01
☐ 364 Ron Davis	.10	.05	.01
☐ 365 Tom Hume	.10	.05	.01
☐ 366 Carlton Fisk	.40	.18	.05
☐ 367 Nate Snell	.10	.05	.01
☐ 368 Rick Manning	.10	.05	.01
☐ 369 Darrell Evans	.20	.09	.03
☐ 370 Ron Hassey	.10	.05	.01
☐ 371 Wade Boggs	1.00	.45	.12
☐ 372 Rick Honeycutt	.10	.05	.01
☐ 373 Chris Bando	.10	.05	.01
☐ 374 Bud Black	.10	.05	.01
☐ 375 Steve Henderson	.10	.05	.01
☐ 376 Charlie Lea	.10	.05	.01
☐ 377 Reggie Jackson	.75	.35	.09

☐ 378 Dave Schmidt	.10	.05	.01
☐ 379 Bob James	.10	.05	.01
☐ 380 Glenn Davis	.20	.09	.03
☐ 381 Tim Corcoran	.10	.05	.01
☐ 382 Danny Cox	.10	.05	.01
☐ 383 Tim Flannery	.10	.05	.01
☐ 384 Tom Browning	.10	.05	.01
☐ 385 Rick Camp	.10	.05	.01
☐ 386 Jim Morrison	.10	.05	.01
☐ 387 Dave LaPoint	.10	.05	.01
☐ 388 Dave Lopes	.20	.09	.03
☐ 389 Al Cowens	.10	.05	.01
☐ 390 Doyle Alexander	.10	.05	.01
☐ 391 Tim Laudner	.10	.05	.01
☐ 392 Don Aase	.10	.05	.01
☐ 393 Jaime Cocanower	.10	.05	.01
☐ 394 Randy O'Neal	.10	.05	.01
☐ 395 Mike Easler	.10	.05	.01
☐ 396 Scott Bradley	.10	.05	.01
☐ 397 Tom Niedenfuer	.10	.05	.01
☐ 398 Jerry Willard	.10	.05	.01
☐ 399 Lonnie Smith	.10	.05	.01
☐ 400 Bruce Bochte	.10	.05	.01
☐ 401 Terry Francona	.10	.05	.01
☐ 402 Jim Slaton	.10	.05	.01
☐ 403 Bill Stein	.10	.05	.01
☐ 404 Tim Hulett	.10	.05	.01
☐ 405 Alan Ashby	.10	.05	.01
☐ 406 Tim Stoddard	.10	.05	.01
☐ 407 Garry Maddox	.10	.05	.01
☐ 408 Ted Power	.10	.05	.01
☐ 409 Len Barker	.10	.05	.01
☐ 410 Denny Gonzalez	.10	.05	.01
☐ 411 George Frazier	.10	.05	.01
☐ 412 Andy Van Slyke	.20	.09	.03
☐ 413 Jim Dwyer	.10	.05	.01
☐ 414 Paul Householder	.10	.05	.01
☐ 415 Alejandro Sanchez	.10	.05	.01
☐ 416 Steve Crawford	.10	.05	.01
☐ 417 Dan Pasqua	.10	.05	.01
☐ 418 Enos Cabell	.10	.05	.01
☐ 419 Mike Jones	.10	.05	.01
☐ 420 Steve Kiefer	.10	.05	.01
☐ 421 Tim Burke	.10	.05	.01
☐ 422 Mike Mason	.10	.05	.01
☐ 423 Ruppert Jones	.10	.05	.01
☐ 424 Jerry Hairston	.10	.05	.01
☐ 425 Tito Landrum	.10	.05	.01
☐ 426 Jeff Calhoun	.10	.05	.01
☐ 427 Don Carman	.10	.05	.01
☐ 428 Tony Perez	.40	.18	.05
☐ 429 Jerry Davis	.10	.05	.01
☐ 430 Bob Walk	.10	.05	.01
☐ 431 Brad Wellman	.10	.05	.01
☐ 432 Terry Forster	.10	.05	.01
☐ 433 Billy Hatcher	.20	.09	.03
☐ 434 Clint Hurdle	.10	.05	.01
☐ 435 Ivan Calderon	.20	.09	.03
☐ 436 Pete Filson	.10	.05	.01
☐ 437 Tom Henke	.20	.09	.03
☐ 438 Dave Engle	.10	.05	.01
☐ 439 Tom Filer	.10	.05	.01
☐ 440 Gorman Thomas	.10	.05	.01
☐ 441 Rick Aguilera	.50	.23	.06
☐ 442 Scott Sanderson	.10	.05	.01
☐ 443 Jeff Dedmon	.10	.05	.01
☐ 444 Joe Orsulak	.10	.05	.01
☐ 445 Atlee Hammaker	.10	.05	.01
☐ 446 Jerry Royster	.10	.05	.01
☐ 447 Buddy Bell	.20	.09	.03
☐ 448 Dave Rucker	.10	.05	.01
☐ 449 Ivan DeJesus	.10	.05	.01
☐ 450 Jim Pankovits	.10	.05	.01
☐ 451 Jerry Narron	.10	.05	.01
☐ 452 Bryan Little	.10	.05	.01
☐ 453 Gary Lucas	.10	.05	.01
☐ 454 Dennis Martinez	.20	.09	.03
☐ 455 Ed Romero	.10	.05	.01
☐ 456 Bob Melvin	.10	.05	.01
☐ 457 Glenn Hoffman	.10	.05	.01
☐ 458 Bob Shirley	.10	.05	.01
☐ 459 Bob Welch	.10	.05	.01
☐ 460 Carmen Castillo	.10	.05	.01
☐ 461 Dave Leeper	.10	.05	.01
☐ 462 Tim Birtsas	.10	.05	.01
☐ 463 Randy St.Claire	.10	.05	.01
☐ 464 Chris Welsh	.10	.05	.01
☐ 465 Greg Harris	.10	.05	.01
☐ 466 Lynn Jones	.10	.05	.01
☐ 467 Dusty Baker	.20	.09	.03
☐ 468 Roy Smith	.10	.05	.01
☐ 469 Andre Robertson	.10	.05	.01
☐ 470 Ken Landreaux	.10	.05	.01
☐ 471 Dave Bergman	.10	.05	.01
☐ 472 Gary Roenicke	.10	.05	.01
☐ 473 Pete Vuckovich	.10	.05	.01
☐ 474 Kirk McCaskill	.20	.09	.03
☐ 475 Jeff Lahti	.10	.05	.01
☐ 476 Mike Scott	.10	.05	.01
☐ 477 Darren Daulton	2.50	1.10	.30
☐ 478 Graig Nettles	.20	.09	.03
☐ 479 Bill Almon	.10	.05	.01
☐ 480 Greg Minton	.10	.05	.01
☐ 481 Randy Ready	.10	.05	.01
☐ 482 Len Dykstra	2.00	.90	.25
☐ 483 Thad Bosley	.10	.05	.01
☐ 484 Harold Reynolds	.50	.23	.06
☐ 485 Al Oliver	.20	.09	.03
☐ 486 Roy Smalley	.10	.05	.01
☐ 487 John Franco	.40	.18	.05
☐ 488 Juan Agosto	.10	.05	.01
☐ 489 Al Pardo	.10	.05	.01
☐ 490 Bill Wegman	.10	.05	.01
☐ 491 Frank Tanana	.10	.05	.01
☐ 492 Brian Fisher	.10	.05	.01
☐ 493 Mark Clear	.10	.05	.01
☐ 494 Len Matuszek	.10	.05	.01
☐ 495 Ramon Romero	.10	.05	.01
☐ 496 John Wathan	.10	.05	.01
☐ 497 Rob Picciolo	.10	.05	.01
☐ 498 U.L. Washington	.10	.05	.01
☐ 499 John Candelaria	.10	.05	.01
☐ 500 Duane Walker	.10	.05	.01
☐ 501 Gene Nelson	.10	.05	.01
☐ 502 John Mizerock	.10	.05	.01
☐ 503 Luis Aguayo	.10	.05	.01
☐ 504 Kurt Kepshire	.10	.05	.01
☐ 505 Ed Wojna	.10	.05	.01
☐ 506 Joe Price	.10	.05	.01
☐ 507 Milt Thompson	.20	.09	.03
☐ 508 Junior Ortiz	.10	.05	.01
☐ 509 Vida Blue	.20	.09	.03
☐ 510 Steve Engel	.10	.05	.01
☐ 511 Karl Best	.10	.05	.01
☐ 512 Cecil Fielder	6.00	2.70	.75
☐ 513 Frank Eufemia	.10	.05	.01
☐ 514 Tippy Martinez	.10	.05	.01
☐ 515 Billy Joe Robidoux	.10	.05	.01
☐ 516 Bill Scherrer	.10	.05	.01
☐ 517 Bruce Hurst	.10	.05	.01
☐ 518 Rich Bordi	.10	.05	.01
☐ 519 Steve Yeager	.10	.05	.01
☐ 520 Tony Bernazard	.10	.05	.01
☐ 521 Hal McRae	.20	.09	.03
☐ 522 Jose Rijo	.20	.09	.03
☐ 523 Mitch Webster	.10	.05	.01
☐ 524 Jack Howell	.10	.05	.01
☐ 525 Alan Bannister	.10	.05	.01
☐ 526 Ron Kittle	.10	.05	.01
☐ 527 Phil Garner	.10	.05	.01
☐ 528 Kurt Bevacqua	.10	.05	.01
☐ 529 Kevin Gross	.10	.05	.01
☐ 530 Bo Diaz	.10	.05	.01
☐ 531 Ken Oberkfell	.10	.05	.01
☐ 532 Rick Reuschel	.10	.05	.01
☐ 533 Ron Meridith	.10	.05	.01
☐ 534 Steve Braun	.10	.05	.01
☐ 535 Wayne Gross	.10	.05	.01
☐ 536 Ray Searage	.10	.05	.01
☐ 537 Tom Brookens	.10	.05	.01
☐ 538 Al Nipper	.10	.05	.01
☐ 539 Billy Sample	.10	.05	.01
☐ 540 Steve Sax	.10	.05	.01
☐ 541 Dan Quisenberry	.10	.05	.01
☐ 542 Tony Phillips	.20	.09	.03
☐ 543 Floyd Youmans	.10	.05	.01
☐ 544 Steve Buechele	.20	.09	.03
☐ 545 Craig Gerber	.10	.05	.01
☐ 546 Joe DeSa	.10	.05	.01
☐ 547 Brian Harper	.10	.05	.01
☐ 548 Kevin Bass	.10	.05	.01
☐ 549 Tom Foley	.10	.05	.01
☐ 550 Dave Van Gorder	.10	.05	.01
☐ 551 Bruce Bochy	.10	.05	.01
☐ 552 R.J. Reynolds	.10	.05	.01
☐ 553 Chris Brown	.10	.05	.01
☐ 554 Bruce Benedict	.10	.05	.01
☐ 555 Warren Brusstar	.10	.05	.01
☐ 556 Danny Heep	.10	.05	.01
☐ 557 Darnell Coles	.10	.05	.01
☐ 558 Greg Gagne	.20	.09	.03
☐ 559 Ernie Whitt	.10	.05	.01
☐ 560 Ron Washington	.10	.05	.01
☐ 561 Jimmy Key	.40	.18	.05
☐ 562 Billy Swift	.20	.09	.03
☐ 563 Ron Darling	.10	.05	.01
☐ 564 Dick Ruthven	.10	.05	.01
☐ 565 Zane Smith	.10	.05	.01
☐ 566 Sid Bream	.10	.05	.01
☐ 567A Joel Youngblood ERR	.10	.05	.01
(Position P)			
☐ 567B Joel Youngblood COR	.40	.18	.05
(Position IF)			
☐ 568 Mario Ramirez	.10	.05	.01
☐ 569 Tom Runnells	.10	.05	.01
☐ 570 Rick Schu	.10	.05	.01
☐ 571 Bill Campbell	.10	.05	.01
☐ 572 Dickie Thon	.10	.05	.01
☐ 573 Al Holland	.10	.05	.01
☐ 574 Reid Nichols	.10	.05	.01
☐ 575 Bert Roberge	.10	.05	.01
☐ 576 Mike Flanagan	.10	.05	.01
☐ 577 Tim Leary	.10	.05	.01
☐ 578 Mike Laga	.10	.05	.01
☐ 579 Steve Lyons	.10	.05	.01
☐ 580 Phil Niekro	.40	.18	.05
☐ 581 Gilberto Reyes	.10	.05	.01
☐ 582 Jamie Easterly	.10	.05	.01
☐ 583 Mark Gubicza	.20	.09	.03
☐ 584 Stan Javier	.20	.09	.03
☐ 585 Bill Laskey	.10	.05	.01
☐ 586 Jeff Russell	.10	.05	.01
☐ 587 Dickie Noles	.10	.05	.01
☐ 588 Steve Farr	.20	.09	.03
☐ 589 Steve Ontiveros	.20	.09	.03
☐ 590 Mike Hargrove	.20	.09	.03
☐ 591 Marty Bystrom	.10	.05	.01
☐ 592 Franklin Stubbs	.10	.05	.01
☐ 593 Larry Herndon	.10	.05	.01
☐ 594 Bill Swaggerty	.10	.05	.01
☐ 595 Carlos Ponce	.10	.05	.01
☐ 596 Pat Perry	.10	.05	.01
☐ 597 Ray Knight	.20	.09	.03
☐ 598 Steve Lombardozzi	.10	.05	.01
☐ 599 Brad Havens	.10	.05	.01
☐ 600 Pat Clements	.10	.05	.01
☐ 601 Joe Niekro	.10	.05	.01
☐ 602 Hank Aaron	.30	.14	.04
Puzzle Card			
☐ 603 Dwayne Henry	.10	.05	.01
☐ 604 Mookie Wilson	.20	.09	.03
☐ 605 Buddy Biancalana	.10	.05	.01
☐ 606 Rance Mulliniks	.10	.05	.01
☐ 607 Alan Wiggins	.10	.05	.01
☐ 608 Joe Cowley	.10	.05	.01
☐ 609 Tom Seaver	.50	.23	.06
(Green borders on name)			
☐ 609B Tom Seaver	2.00	.90	.25
(Yellow borders on name)			
☐ 610 Neil Allen	.10	.05	.01
☐ 611 Don Sutton	.40	.18	.05
☐ 612 Fred Toliver	.10	.05	.01
☐ 613 Jay Baller	.10	.05	.01
☐ 614 Marc Sullivan	.10	.05	.01
☐ 615 John Grubb	.10	.05	.01
☐ 616 Bruce Kison	.10	.05	.01
☐ 617 Bill Madlock	.10	.05	.01
☐ 618 Chris Chambliss	.20	.09	.03
☐ 619 Dave Stewart	.20	.09	.03
☐ 620 Tim Lollar	.10	.05	.01
☐ 621 Gary Lavelle	.10	.05	.01
☐ 622 Charles Hudson	.10	.05	.01
☐ 623 Joel Davis	.10	.05	.01
☐ 624 Joe Johnson	.10	.05	.01
☐ 625 Sid Fernandez	.20	.09	.03
☐ 626 Dennis Lamp	.10	.05	.01
☐ 627 Terry Harper	.10	.05	.01
☐ 628 Jack Lazorko	.10	.05	.01
☐ 629 Roger McDowell	.20	.09	.03
☐ 630 Mark Funderburk	.10	.05	.01
☐ 631 Ed Lynch	.10	.05	.01
☐ 632 Rudy Law	.10	.05	.01
☐ 633 Roger Mason	.10	.05	.01
☐ 634 Mike Felder	.10	.05	.01
☐ 635 Ken Schrom	.10	.05	.01
☐ 636 Bob Ojeda	.10	.05	.01
☐ 637 Ed VandeBerg	.10	.05	.01
☐ 638 Bobby Meacham	.10	.05	.01
☐ 639 Cliff Johnson	.10	.05	.01
☐ 640 Garth Iorg	.10	.05	.01
☐ 641 Dan Driessen	.10	.05	.01
☐ 642 Mike Brown OF	.10	.05	.01
☐ 643 John Shelby	.10	.05	.01
☐ 644 Pete Rose	.60	.25	.07
(Ty-Breaking)			
☐ 645 The Knuckle Brothers	.20	.09	.03
Phil Niekro			
Joe Niekro			
☐ 646 Jesse Orosco	.10	.05	.01
☐ 647 Billy Beane	.10	.05	.01
☐ 648 Cesar Cedeno	.20	.09	.03
☐ 649 Bert Blyleven	.40	.18	.05
☐ 650 Max Venable	.10	.05	.01
☐ 651 Fleet Feet	.20	.09	.03
Vince Coleman			
Willie McGee			
☐ 652 Calvin Schiraldi	.10	.05	.01
☐ 653 King of Kings	1.00	.45	.12
(Pete Rose)			
☐ 654 Diamond Kings CL 1-26	.20	.09	.03
(Unnumbered)			
☐ 655A CL 1: 27-130	.20	.09	.03
(Unnumbered)			
(45 Beane ERR)			
☐ 655B CL 1: 27-130	.20	.09	.03
(Unnumbered)			
(45 Habyan COR)			
☐ 656 CL 2: 131-234	.20	.09	.03
(Unnumbered)			
☐ 657 CL 3: 235-338	.20	.09	.03
(Unnumbered)			
☐ 658 CL 4: 339-442	.20	.09	.03
(Unnumbered)			
☐ 659 CL 5: 443-546	.20	.09	.03
(Unnumbered)			
☐ 660 CL 6: 547-653	.20	.09	.03
(Unnumbered)			

1986 Donruss Wax Box Cards

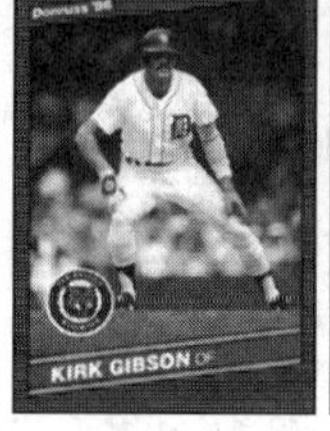

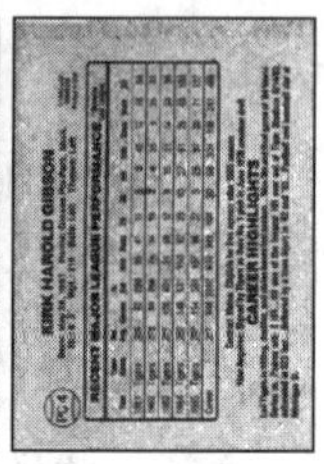

The cards in this four-card set measure the standard 2 1/2" by 3 1/2". Cards have essentially the same design as the 1986 Donruss regular issue set. The cards were printed on the bottoms of the regular issue wax pack boxes. The four cards (PC4 to PC6 plus a Hank Aaron puzzle card) are considered a separate set in their own right and are not typically included in a complete set of the regular issue 1986 Donruss cards. The value of the panel uncut is slightly greater, perhaps by 25 percent greater, than the value of the individual cards cut up carefully.

	MINT	NRMT	EXC
COMPLETE SET (4)	1.00	.45	.12
COMMON CARD	.10	.05	.01
☐ PC4 Kirk Gibson	.40	.18	.05
☐ PC5 Willie Hernandez	.10	.05	.01
☐ PC6 Doug DeCinces	.10	.05	.01
☐ PUZ Hank Aaron	.75	.35	.09
Puzzle Card			

1986 Donruss Rookies

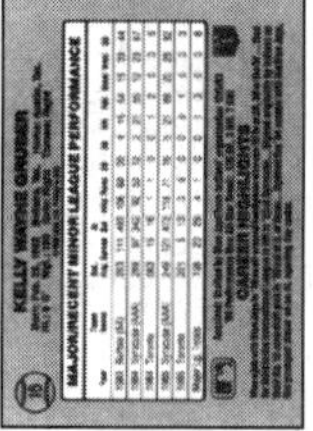

The 1986 Donruss "The Rookies" set features 56 full-color standard-size cards plus a 15-piece puzzle of Hank Aaron. The set was distributed through hobby dealers in a small green, cellophane wrapped factory box. Although the set was wrapped in cellophane, the top card was number 1 Joyner, resulting in a percentage of the Joyner cards arriving in less than perfect condition. Donruss fixed the problem after it was called to their attention and even went so far as to include a customer service phone number in their second printing. Card fronts are similar in design to the 1986 Donruss regular issue except for the presence of "The Rookies" logo in the lower left corner and a bluish green border instead of a blue border. The key extended Rookie Cards in this set are Barry Bonds, Bobby Bonilla, Will Clark, Bo Jackson, Wally Joyner, John Kruk, Kevin Mitchell, and Ruben Sierra.

	MINT	NRMT	EXC
COMPLETE FACT.SET (56)	25.00	11.00	3.10
COMMON CARD (1-56)	.10	.05	.01
☐ 1 Wally Joyner	1.00	.45	.12
☐ 2 Tracy Jones	.10	.05	.01
☐ 3 Allan Anderson	.10	.05	.01
☐ 4 Ed Correa	.10	.05	.01
☐ 5 Reggie Williams	.10	.05	.01
☐ 6 Charlie Kerfeld	.10	.05	.01
☐ 7 Andres Galarraga	3.00	1.35	.35
☐ 8 Bob Tewksbury	.25	.11	.03
☐ 9 Al Newman	.25	.11	.03
☐ 10 Andres Thomas	.10	.05	.01
☐ 11 Barry Bonds	7.00	3.10	.85
☐ 12 Juan Nieves	.10	.05	.01
☐ 13 Mark Eichhorn	.10	.05	.01
☐ 14 Dan Plesac	.10	.05	.01
☐ 15 Cory Snyder	.10	.05	.01
☐ 16 Kelly Gruber	.10	.05	.01
☐ 17 Kevin Mitchell	.40	.18	.05
☐ 18 Steve Lombardozzi	.10	.05	.01
☐ 19 Mitch Williams	.25	.11	.03
☐ 20 John Cerutti	.10	.05	.01
☐ 21 Todd Worrell	.40	.18	.05
☐ 22 Jose Canseco	4.00	1.80	.50
☐ 23 Pete Incaviglia	.40	.18	.05
☐ 24 Jose Guzman	.10	.05	.01
☐ 25 Scott Bailes	.10	.05	.01
☐ 26 Greg Mathews	.10	.05	.01
☐ 27 Eric King	.10	.05	.01
☐ 28 Paul Assenmacher	.10	.05	.01
☐ 29 Jeff Sellers	.10	.05	.01
☐ 30 Bobby Bonilla	1.50	.70	.19
☐ 31 Doug Drabek	.60	.25	.07
☐ 32 Will Clark UER	3.00	1.35	.35
(Listed as throwing right, should be left)			
☐ 33 Bip Roberts	.40	.18	.05
☐ 34 Jim Deshaies	.10	.05	.01
☐ 35 Mike LaValliere	.10	.05	.01
☐ 36 Scott Bankhead	.10	.05	.01
☐ 37 Dale Sveum	.10	.05	.01
☐ 38 Bo Jackson	2.00	.90	.25
☐ 39 Robby Thompson	.25	.11	.03
☐ 40 Eric Plunk	.10	.05	.01
☐ 41 Bill Bathe	.10	.05	.01
☐ 42 John Kruk	1.00	.45	.12

	MINT	NRMT	EXC
☐ 43 Andy Allanson	.10	.05	.01
☐ 44 Mark Portugal	.25	.11	.03
☐ 45 Danny Tartabull	.25	.11	.03
☐ 46 Bob Kipper	.10	.05	.01
☐ 47 Gene Walter	.10	.05	.01
☐ 48 Rey Quinones UER	.10	.05	.01
(Misspelled Quinonez)			
☐ 49 Bobby Witt	.25	.11	.03
☐ 50 Bill Mooneyham	.10	.05	.01
☐ 51 John Cangelosi	.10	.05	.01
☐ 52 Ruben Sierra	2.00	.90	.25
☐ 53 Rob Woodward	.10	.05	.01
☐ 54 Ed Hearn	.10	.05	.01
☐ 55 Joel McKeon	.10	.05	.01
☐ 56 Checklist 1-56	.10	.05	.01

1986 Donruss All-Stars

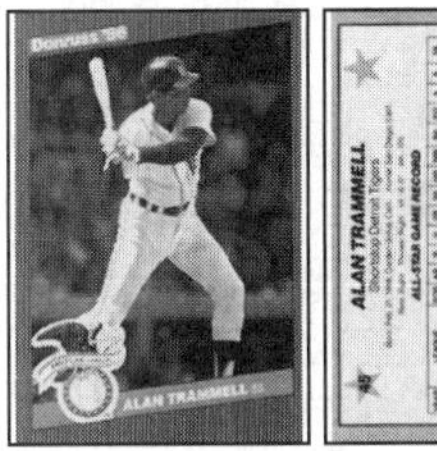

The cards in this 60-card set measure approximately 3 1/2" by 5". Players featured were involved in the 1985 All-Star game played in Minnesota. Cards are very similar in design to the 1986 Donruss regular issue set. The backs give each player's All-Star game statistics and have an orange-yellow border.

	MINT	NRMT	EXC
COMPLETE SET (60)	6.00	2.70	.75
COMMON CARD (1-59)	.05	.02	.01
☐ 1 Tony Gwynn	1.25	.55	.16
☐ 2 Tommy Herr	.05	.02	.01
☐ 3 Steve Garvey	.20	.09	.03
☐ 4 Dale Murphy	.20	.09	.03
☐ 5 Darryl Strawberry	.20	.09	.03
☐ 6 Graig Nettles	.10	.05	.01
☐ 7 Terry Kennedy	.05	.02	.01
☐ 8 Ozzie Smith	1.00	.45	.12
☐ 9 LaMarr Hoyt	.05	.02	.01
☐ 10 Rickey Henderson	.40	.18	.05
☐ 11 Lou Whitaker	.10	.05	.01
☐ 12 George Brett	1.25	.55	.16
☐ 13 Eddie Murray	.60	.25	.07
☐ 14 Cal Ripken	2.00	.90	.25
☐ 15 Dave Winfield	.40	.18	.05
☐ 16 Jim Rice	.10	.05	.01
☐ 17 Carlton Fisk	.40	.18	.05
☐ 18 Jack Morris	.10	.05	.01
☐ 19 Jose Cruz	.05	.02	.01
☐ 20 Tim Raines	.10	.05	.01
☐ 21 Nolan Ryan	2.50	1.10	.30
☐ 22 Tony Pena	.05	.02	.01
☐ 23 Jack Clark	.10	.05	.01
☐ 24 Dave Parker	.10	.05	.01
☐ 25 Tim Wallach	.05	.02	.01
☐ 26 Ozzie Virgil	.05	.02	.01
☐ 27 Fernando Valenzuela	.10	.05	.01
☐ 28 Dwight Gooden	.20	.09	.03
☐ 29 Glenn Wilson	.05	.02	.01
☐ 30 Garry Templeton	.05	.02	.01
☐ 31 Goose Gossage	.10	.05	.01
☐ 32 Ryne Sandberg	.75	.35	.09
☐ 33 Jeff Reardon	.05	.02	.01
☐ 34 Pete Rose	.75	.35	.09
☐ 35 Scott Garrelts	.05	.02	.01
☐ 36 Willie McGee	.10	.05	.01
☐ 37 Ron Darling	.05	.02	.01
☐ 38 Dick Williams MG	.05	.02	.01
☐ 39 Paul Molitor	.50	.23	.06
☐ 40 Damaso Garcia	.05	.02	.01
☐ 41 Phil Bradley	.05	.02	.01
☐ 42 Dan Petry	.05	.02	.01
☐ 43 Willie Hernandez	.05	.02	.01
☐ 44 Tom Brunansky	.05	.02	.01
☐ 45 Alan Trammell	.25	.11	.03
☐ 46 Donnie Moore	.05	.02	.01
☐ 47 Wade Boggs	.40	.18	.05
☐ 48 Ernie Whitt	.05	.02	.01
☐ 49 Harold Baines	.10	.05	.01
☐ 50 Don Mattingly	1.00	.45	.12
☐ 51 Gary Ward	.05	.02	.01
☐ 52 Bert Blyleven	.10	.05	.01
☐ 53 Jimmy Key	.20	.09	.03
☐ 54 Cecil Cooper	.10	.05	.01
☐ 55 Dave Stieb	.05	.02	.01
☐ 56 Rich Gedman	.05	.02	.01
☐ 57 Jay Howell	.05	.02	.01
☐ 58 Sparky Anderson MG	.05	.02	.01
☐ 59 Minneapolis Metrodome	.05	.02	.01
☐ NNO Checklist Card	.05	.02	.01

1986 Donruss All-Star Box

The cards in this four-card set measure the standard size in spite of the fact that they form the bottom of the wax pack box for the larger

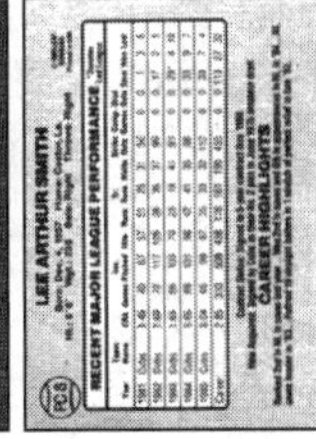

Donruss All-Star cards. These box cards have essentially the same design as the 1986 Donruss regular issue set. The cards were printed on the bottoms of the Donruss All-Star (3 1/2" by 5") wax pack boxes. The four cards (PC7 to PC9 plus a Hank Aaron puzzle card) are considered a separate set in their own right and are not typically included in a complete set of the regular issue 1986 Donruss All-Star (or regular) cards. The value of the panel uncut is slightly greater, perhaps by 25 percent greater, than the value of the individual cards cut up carefully.

	MINT	NRMT	EXC
COMPLETE SET (4)	2.00	.90	.25
COMMON CARD	.25	.11	.03
☐ PC7 Wade Boggs	1.00	.45	.12
☐ PC8 Lee Smith	.50	.23	.06
☐ PC9 Cecil Cooper	.50	.23	.06
☐ PUZ Hank Aaron	.75	.35	.09
Puzzle Card			

1986 Donruss Highlights

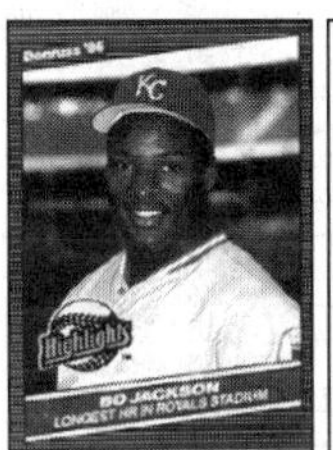

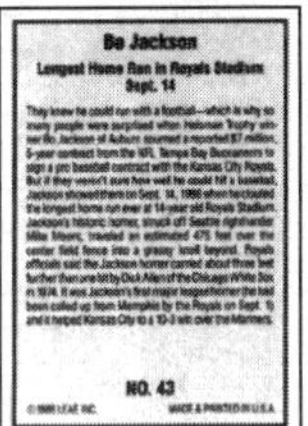

Donruss' second edition of Highlights was released late in 1986. These glossy-coated cards are standard size. Cards commemorate events during the 1986 season, as well as players and pitchers of the month from each league. The set was distributed in its own red, white, blue, and gold box along with a small Hank Aaron puzzle. Card fronts are similar to the regular 1986 Donruss issue except that the Highlights logo is positioned in the lower left-hand corner and the borders are in gold instead of blue. The backs are printed in black and gold on white card stock.

	MINT	NRMT	EXC
COMPLETE FACT. SET (56)	3.00	1.35	.35
COMMON CARD (1-56)	.05	.02	.01
☐ 1 Will Clark	.40	.18	.05
Homers in First At-Bat			
☐ 2 Jose Rijo	.10	.05	.01
Oakland Milestone for Strikeouts			
☐ 3 George Brett	.50	.23	.06
Royals All-Time Hit Man			
☐ 4 Mike Schmidt	.30	.14	.04
Phillies RBI Leader			
☐ 5 Roger Clemens	.40	.18	.05
KKKKKKKKKKKKKKKKKKKK			
☐ 6 Roger Clemens	.40	.18	.05
AL Pitcher April			
☐ 7 Kirby Puckett	.60	.25	.07
AL Player April			
☐ 8 Dwight Gooden	.15	.07	.02
NL Pitcher April			
☐ 9 Johnny Ray	.05	.02	.01
NL Player April			
☐ 10 Reggie Jackson	.75	.35	.09
Mickey Mantle			
Mantle's HR Record			
☐ 11 Wade Boggs	.20	.09	.03
First Five-Hit Game of Career			
☐ 12 Don Aase	.05	.02	.01
AL Pitcher May			
☐ 13 Wade Boggs	.20	.09	.03
AL Player May			
☐ 14 Jeff Reardon	.05	.02	.01
NL Pitcher May			
☐ 15 Hubie Brooks	.05	.02	.01
NL Player May			
☐ 16 Don Sutton	.10	.05	.01
Notches 300th			
☐ 17 Roger Clemens	.40	.18	.05
Starts 14-0			
☐ 18 Roger Clemens	.40	.18	.05
AL Pitcher June			
☐ 19 Kent Hrbek	.10	.05	.01
AL Player June			
☐ 20 Rick Rhoden	.05	.02	.01
NL Pitcher June			
☐ 21 Kevin Bass	.05	.02	.01
NL Player June			
☐ 22 Bob Horner	.05	.02	.01
Blasts Four HRs in One Game			
☐ 23 Wally Joyner	.15	.07	.02
Starting All-Star Rookie			
☐ 24 Darryl Strawberry	.15	.07	.02
Starts Third Straight A-S Game			
☐ 25 Fernando Valenzuela	.10	.05	.01
Ties A-S Game Record			
☐ 26 Roger Clemens	.40	.18	.05
All-Star Game MVP			
☐ 27 Jack Morris	.10	.05	.01
AL Pitcher July			
☐ 28 Scott Fletcher	.05	.02	.01
AL Player July			
☐ 29 Todd Worrell	.15	.07	.02
NL Pitcher July			
☐ 30 Eric Davis	.10	.05	.01
NL Player July			
☐ 31 Bert Blyleven	.10	.05	.01
Records 3000th Strikeout			
☐ 32 Bobby Doerr	.10	.05	.01
'86 HOF Inductee			
☐ 33 Ernie Lombardi	.10	.05	.01
'86 HOF Inductee			
☐ 34 Willie McCovey	.15	.07	.02
'86 HOF Inductee			
☐ 35 Steve Carlton	.20	.09	.03
Notches 4000th K			
☐ 36 Mike Schmidt	.30	.14	.04
Surpasses DiMaggio Record			
☐ 37 Juan Samuel	.05	.02	.01
Third Quadruple Double			
☐ 38 Mike Witt	.05	.02	.01
AL Pitcher August			
☐ 39 Doug DeCinces	.05	.02	.01
AL Player August			
☐ 40 Bill Gullickson	.05	.02	.01
NL Pitcher August			
☐ 41 Dale Murphy	.15	.07	.02
NL Player August			
☐ 42 Joe Carter	.15	.07	.02
Sets Tribe Offensive Record			
☐ 43 Bo Jackson	.15	.07	.02
Longest HR in Royals Stadium			
☐ 44 Joe Cowley	.05	.02	.01
Majors 1st No-Hitter in 2 Years			
☐ 45 Jim Deshaies	.05	.02	.01
Sets ML Strikeout Record			
☐ 46 Mike Scott	.05	.02	.01
No-Hitter Clinches Division			
☐ 47 Bruce Hurst	.05	.02	.01
AL Pitcher September			
☐ 48 Don Mattingly	.75	.35	.09
AL Player September			
☐ 49 Mike Krukow	.05	.02	.01
NL Pitcher September			
☐ 50 Steve Sax	.05	.02	.01
NL Player September			
☐ 51 John Cangelosi	.05	.02	.01
AL Rookie Steals Record			
☐ 52 Dave Righetti	.05	.02	.01
ML Save Mark			
☐ 53 Don Mattingly	.75	.35	.09
Yankee Record for Hits and Doubles			
☐ 54 Todd Worrell	.15	.07	.02
Donruss NL ROY			
☐ 55 Jose Canseco	.40	.18	.05
Donruss AL ROY			
☐ 56 Checklist Card	.05	.02	.01

1986 Donruss Pop-Ups

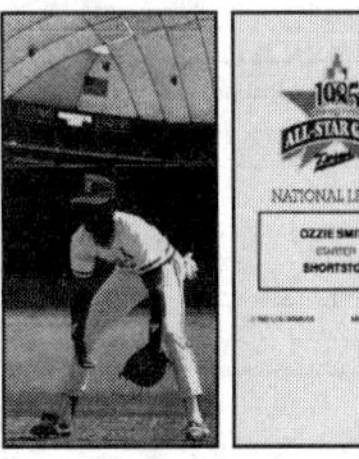

This set is the companion of the 1986 Donruss All-Star (60) set; as such it features the first 18 cards of that set (the All-Star starting line-ups) in a pop-up, die-cut type of card. These cards (measuring (2 1/2" X 5") can be "popped up" to feature a standing card showing the player in action in front of the Metrodome ballpark background. Although this set is unnumbered it is numbered in the same order as its companion set, presumably according to the respective batting orders of the starting line-ups. The first nine numbers below are National Leaguers and the last nine are American Leaguers. See also the Donruss All-Star checklist card which contains a checklist for the Pop-Ups as well.

	MINT	NRMT	EXC
COMPLETE SET (18)	5.00	2.20	.60
COMMON CARD (1-18)	.05	.02	.01
☐ 1 Tony Gwynn	1.25	.55	.16
☐ 2 Tommy Herr	.05	.02	.01
☐ 3 Steve Garvey	.20	.09	.03
☐ 4 Dale Murphy	.20	.09	.03
☐ 5 Darryl Strawberry	.40	.18	.05
☐ 6 Graig Nettles	.10	.05	.01
☐ 7 Terry Kennedy	.05	.02	.01
☐ 8 Ozzie Smith	1.00	.45	.12
☐ 9 LaMarr Hoyt	.05	.02	.01
☐ 10 Rickey Henderson	.40	.18	.05
☐ 11 Lou Whitaker	.10	.05	.01
☐ 12 George Brett	1.25	.55	.16
☐ 13 Eddie Murray	.60	.25	.07
☐ 14 Cal Ripken	2.50	1.10	.30
☐ 15 Dave Winfield	.40	.18	.05
☐ 16 Jim Rice	.10	.05	.01
☐ 17 Carlton Fisk	.40	.18	.05
☐ 18 Jack Morris	.10	.05	.01

1986 Donruss Super DK's

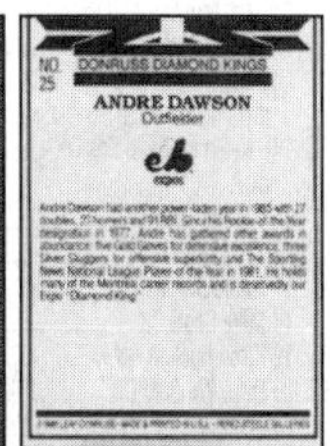

This 29-card set of large Diamond Kings features the full-color artwork of Dick Perez. The set could be obtained from Perez-Steele Galleries by sending three Donruss wrappers and $9.00. The cards measure 4 7/8" by 6 13/16" and are identical in design to the Diamond King cards in the Donruss regular issue.

	MINT	NRMT	EXC
COMPLETE SET (27)	12.50	5.50	1.55
COMMON CARD (1-27)	.50	.23	.06
☐ 1 Kirk Gibson	.75	.35	.09
☐ 2 Goose Gossage	.75	.35	.09
☐ 3 Willie McGee	.75	.35	.09
☐ 4 George Bell	.75	.35	.09
☐ 5 Tony Armas	.50	.23	.06
☐ 6 Chili Davis	.75	.35	.09
☐ 7 Cecil Cooper	.75	.35	.09
☐ 8 Mike Boddicker	.50	.23	.06
☐ 9 Dave Lopes	.50	.23	.06
☐ 10 Bill Doran	.50	.23	.06
☐ 11 Bret Saberhagen	1.00	.45	.12
☐ 12 Brett Butler	.75	.35	.09
☐ 13 Harold Baines	.75	.35	.09
☐ 14 Mike Davis	.50	.23	.06
☐ 15 Tony Perez	1.00	.45	.12
☐ 16 Willie Randolph	.75	.35	.09
☐ 17 Bob Boone	.75	.35	.09
☐ 18 Orel Hershiser	1.00	.45	.12
☐ 19 Johnny Ray	.50	.23	.06
☐ 20 Gary Ward	.50	.23	.06
☐ 21 Rick Mahler	.50	.23	.06
☐ 22 Phil Bradley	.50	.23	.06
☐ 23 Jerry Koosman	.75	.35	.09
☐ 24 Tom Brunansky	.50	.23	.06
☐ 25 Andre Dawson	1.00	.45	.12
☐ 26 Dwight Gooden	2.00	.90	.25
☐ 27 Pete Rose	3.00	1.35	.35
King of Kings			
☐ NNO Checklist Card	.50	.23	.06
☐ NNO Aaron Large Puzzle	2.00	.90	.25

1987 Donruss

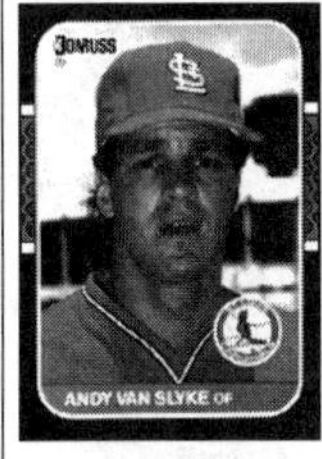

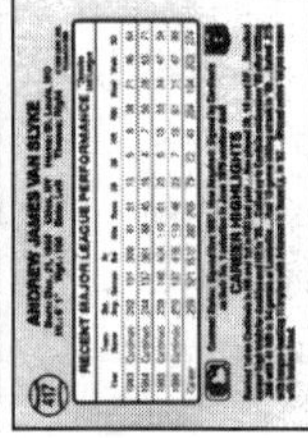

This set consists of 660 standard-size cards. Cards were primarily distributed in 15-card wax packs, rack packs and a factory set. All packs included a Roberto Clemente puzzle panel and the factory sets contained a complete puzzle.The regular-issue cards feature a black and gold border on the front. The backs of the cards in the factory sets are oriented differently than cards taken from wax packs, giving the appearance that one version or the other is upside down when sorting from the card backs. There are no premiums or discounts for either version. The popular Diamond King subset returns for the sixth consecutive year. Some of the Diamond King (1-26) selections are repeats from prior years; Perez-Steele Galleries had indicated in 1987 that a five-year rotation would be maintained in order to avoid depleting the pool of available worthy "kings" on some of the teams. Rookie Cards in this set include Barry Bonds, Bobby Bonilla, Kevin Brown, Will Clark, David Cone, Chuck Finley, Mike Greenwell, Bo Jackson, Wally Joyner, Barry Larkin, Greg Maddux, Kevin Mitchell, Rafael Palmeiro, Ruben Sierra, and Devon White. The Greg Maddux card has been noted to have a premium for perfectly centered copies.

	MINT	NRMT	EXC
COMPLETE SET (660)	30.00	13.50	3.70
COMPLETE FACT.SET (660)	30.00	13.50	3.70
COMMON CARD (1-660)	.05	.02	.01
☐ 1 Wally Joyner DK	.30	.14	.04
☐ 2 Roger Clemens DK	.30	.14	.04
☐ 3 Dale Murphy DK	.30	.14	.04
☐ 4 Darryl Strawberry DK	.30	.14	.04
☐ 5 Ozzie Smith DK	.30	.14	.04
☐ 6 Jose Canseco DK	.50	.23	.06
☐ 7 Charlie Hough DK	.05	.02	.01
☐ 8 Brook Jacoby DK	.05	.02	.01
☐ 9 Fred Lynn DK	.15	.07	.02
☐ 10 Rick Rhoden DK	.05	.02	.01
☐ 11 Chris Brown DK	.05	.02	.01
☐ 12 Von Hayes DK	.05	.02	.01
☐ 13 Jack Morris DK	.15	.07	.02
☐ 14A Kevin McReynolds DK ERR (Yellow strip missing on back)	.30	.14	.04
☐ 14B Kevin McReynolds DK COR	.05	.02	.01
☐ 15 George Brett DK	.40	.18	.05
☐ 16 Ted Higuera DK	.05	.02	.01
☐ 17 Hubie Brooks DK	.05	.02	.01
☐ 18 Mike Scott DK	.05	.02	.01
☐ 19 Kirby Puckett DK	.75	.35	.09
☐ 20 Dave Winfield DK	.30	.14	.04
☐ 21 Lloyd Moseby DK	.05	.02	.01
☐ 22A Eric Davis DK ERR (Yellow strip missing on back)	.30	.14	.04
☐ 22B Eric Davis DK COR	.15	.07	.02
☐ 23 Jim Presley DK	.05	.02	.01
☐ 24 Keith Moreland DK	.05	.02	.01
☐ 25A Greg Walker DK ERR (Yellow strip missing on back)	.30	.14	.04
☐ 25B Greg Walker DK COR	.05	.02	.01
☐ 26 Steve Sax DK	.05	.02	.01
☐ 27 DK Checklist 1-26	.15	.07	.02
☐ 28 B.J. Surhoff RR	.40	.18	.05
☐ 29 Randy Myers RR	.50	.23	.06
☐ 30 Ken Gerhart RR	.05	.02	.01
☐ 31 Benito Santiago RR	.15	.07	.02
☐ 32 Greg Swindell RR	.30	.14	.04
☐ 33 Mike Birkbeck RR	.05	.02	.01
☐ 34 Terry Steinbach RR	.40	.18	.05
☐ 35 Bo Jackson RR	1.00	.45	.12
☐ 36 Greg Maddux UER (middle name misspelled "Allen")	20.00	9.00	2.50
☐ 37 Jim Lindeman RR	.05	.02	.01
☐ 38 Devon White RR	.40	.18	.05
☐ 39 Eric Bell RR	.05	.02	.01
☐ 40 Willie Fraser RR	.05	.02	.01
☐ 41 Jerry Browne RR	.15	.07	.02
☐ 42 Chris James RR	.05	.02	.01
☐ 43 Rafael Palmeiro RR	2.50	1.10	.30
☐ 44 Pat Dodson RR	.05	.02	.01
☐ 45 Duane Ward RR	.15	.07	.02
☐ 46 Mark McGwire RR	4.00	1.80	.50
☐ 47 Bruce Fields RR UER (Photo actually Darnell Coles)	.05	.02	.01
☐ 48 Eddie Murray	.50	.23	.06
☐ 49 Ted Higuera	.05	.02	.01
☐ 50 Kirk Gibson	.15	.07	.02
☐ 51 Oil Can Boyd	.05	.02	.01
☐ 52 Don Mattingly	1.00	.45	.12
☐ 53 Pedro Guerrero	.15	.07	.02
☐ 54 George Brett	.75	.35	.09
☐ 55 Jose Rijo	.05	.02	.01
☐ 56 Tim Raines	.15	.07	.02
☐ 57 Ed Correa	.05	.02	.01
☐ 58 Mike Witt	.05	.02	.01
☐ 59 Greg Walker	.05	.02	.01
☐ 60 Ozzie Smith	.50	.23	.06
☐ 61 Glenn Davis	.05	.02	.01
☐ 62 Glenn Wilson	.05	.02	.01
☐ 63 Tom Browning	.05	.02	.01
☐ 64 Tony Gwynn	.75	.35	.09
☐ 65 R.J. Reynolds	.05	.02	.01
☐ 66 Will Clark	2.00	.90	.25
☐ 67 Ozzie Virgil	.05	.02	.01
☐ 68 Rick Sutcliffe	.05	.02	.01
☐ 69 Gary Carter	.15	.07	.02
☐ 70 Mike Moore	.05	.02	.01
☐ 71 Bert Blyleven	.15	.07	.02
☐ 72 Tony Fernandez	.05	.02	.01
☐ 73 Kent Hrbek	.30	.14	.04
☐ 74 Lloyd Moseby	.05	.02	.01
☐ 75 Alvin Davis	.05	.02	.01
☐ 76 Keith Hernandez	.15	.07	.02
☐ 77 Ryne Sandberg	.50	.23	.06
☐ 78 Dale Murphy	.30	.14	.04
☐ 79 Sid Bream	.05	.02	.01
☐ 80 Chris Brown	.05	.02	.01
☐ 81 Steve Garvey	.30	.14	.04
☐ 82 Mario Soto	.05	.02	.01
☐ 83 Shane Rawley	.05	.02	.01
☐ 84 Willie McGee	.05	.02	.01
☐ 85 Jose Cruz	.05	.02	.01
☐ 86 Brian Downing	.05	.02	.01
☐ 87 Ozzie Guillen	.30	.14	.04
☐ 88 Hubie Brooks	.05	.02	.01
☐ 89 Cal Ripken	1.50	.70	.19
☐ 90 Juan Nieves	.05	.02	.01
☐ 91 Lance Parrish	.15	.07	.02
☐ 92 Jim Rice	.15	.07	.02
☐ 93 Ron Guidry	.15	.07	.02
☐ 94 Fernando Valenzuela	.15	.07	.02
☐ 95 Andy Allanson	.05	.02	.01
☐ 96 Willie Wilson	.05	.02	.01
☐ 97 Jose Canseco	1.00	.45	.12
☐ 98 Jeff Reardon	.15	.07	.02
☐ 99 Bobby Witt	.15	.07	.02
☐ 100 Checklist 28-133	.15	.07	.02
☐ 101 Jose Guzman	.05	.02	.01
☐ 102 Steve Balboni	.05	.02	.01
☐ 103 Tony Phillips	.15	.07	.02
☐ 104 Brook Jacoby	.05	.02	.01
☐ 105 Dave Winfield	.30	.14	.04
☐ 106 Orel Hershiser	.15	.07	.02
☐ 107 Lou Whitaker	.15	.07	.02
☐ 108 Fred Lynn	.15	.07	.02
☐ 109 Bill Wegman	.05	.02	.01
☐ 110 Donnie Moore	.05	.02	.01
☐ 111 Jack Clark	.15	.07	.02
☐ 112 Bob Knepper	.05	.02	.01
☐ 113 Von Hayes	.05	.02	.01
☐ 114 Bip Roberts	.30	.14	.04
☐ 115 Tony Pena	.05	.02	.01
☐ 116 Scott Garrelts	.05	.02	.01
☐ 117 Paul Molitor	.40	.18	.05
☐ 118 Darryl Strawberry	.30	.14	.04
☐ 119 Shawon Dunston	.15	.07	.02
☐ 120 Jim Presley	.05	.02	.01
☐ 121 Jesse Barfield	.05	.02	.01
☐ 122 Gary Gaetti	.05	.02	.01
☐ 123 Kurt Stillwell	.05	.02	.01
☐ 124 Joel Davis	.05	.02	.01
☐ 125 Mike Boddicker	.05	.02	.01
☐ 126 Robin Yount	.30	.14	.04
☐ 127 Alan Trammell	.30	.14	.04
☐ 128 Dave Righetti	.05	.02	.01
☐ 129 Dwight Evans	.15	.07	.02
☐ 130 Mike Scioscia	.05	.02	.01
☐ 131 Julio Franco	.15	.07	.02
☐ 132 Bret Saberhagen	.15	.07	.02
☐ 133 Mike Davis	.05	.02	.01
☐ 134 Joe Hesketh	.05	.02	.01
☐ 135 Wally Joyner	.50	.23	.06
☐ 136 Don Slaught	.05	.02	.01
☐ 137 Daryl Boston	.05	.02	.01
☐ 138 Nolan Ryan	1.50	.70	.19
☐ 139 Mike Schmidt	.40	.18	.05
☐ 140 Tommy Herr	.05	.02	.01
☐ 141 Garry Templeton	.05	.02	.01
☐ 142 Kal Daniels	.05	.02	.01
☐ 143 Billy Sample	.05	.02	.01
☐ 144 Johnny Ray	.05	.02	.01
☐ 145 Rob Thompson	.15	.07	.02
☐ 146 Bob Dernier	.05	.02	.01
☐ 147 Danny Tartabull	.15	.07	.02
☐ 148 Ernie Whitt	.05	.02	.01
☐ 149 Kirby Puckett	1.50	.70	.19
☐ 150 Mike Young	.05	.02	.01
☐ 151 Ernest Riles	.05	.02	.01
☐ 152 Frank Tanana	.05	.02	.01
☐ 153 Rich Gedman	.05	.02	.01
☐ 154 Willie Randolph	.15	.07	.02
☐ 155 Bill Madlock	.05	.02	.01
☐ 156 Joe Carter	.40	.18	.05
☐ 157 Danny Jackson	.05	.02	.01
☐ 158 Carney Lansford	.15	.07	.02
☐ 159 Bryn Smith	.05	.02	.01
☐ 160 Gary Pettis	.05	.02	.01
☐ 161 Oddibe McDowell	.05	.02	.01
☐ 162 John Cangelosi	.05	.02	.01
☐ 163 Mike Scott	.05	.02	.01
☐ 164 Eric Show	.05	.02	.01
☐ 165 Juan Samuel	.05	.02	.01
☐ 166 Nick Esasky	.05	.02	.01
☐ 167 Zane Smith	.05	.02	.01
☐ 168 Mike C. Brown OF	.05	.02	.01
☐ 169 Keith Moreland	.05	.02	.01
☐ 170 John Tudor	.05	.02	.01
☐ 171 Ken Dixon	.05	.02	.01
☐ 172 Jim Gantner	.05	.02	.01
☐ 173 Jack Morris	.15	.07	.02
☐ 174 Bruce Hurst	.05	.02	.01
☐ 175 Dennis Rasmussen	.05	.02	.01
☐ 176 Mike Marshall	.05	.02	.01
☐ 177 Dan Quisenberry	.05	.02	.01
☐ 178 Eric Plunk	.05	.02	.01
☐ 179 Tim Wallach	.05	.02	.01
☐ 180 Steve Buechele	.05	.02	.01
☐ 181 Don Sutton	.30	.14	.04
☐ 182 Dave Schmidt	.05	.02	.01
☐ 183 Terry Pendleton	.15	.07	.02
☐ 184 Jim Deshaies	.05	.02	.01
☐ 185 Steve Bedrosian	.05	.02	.01
☐ 186 Pete Rose	.40	.18	.05
☐ 187 Dave Dravecky	.15	.07	.02
☐ 188 Rick Reuschel	.05	.02	.01
☐ 189 Dan Gladden	.05	.02	.01
☐ 190 Rick Mahler	.05	.02	.01
☐ 191 Thad Bosley	.05	.02	.01
☐ 192 Ron Darling	.05	.02	.01
☐ 193 Matt Young	.05	.02	.01
☐ 194 Tom Brunansky	.05	.02	.01
☐ 195 Dave Stieb	.05	.02	.01
☐ 196 Frank Viola	.05	.02	.01
☐ 197 Tom Henke	.05	.02	.01
☐ 198 Karl Best	.05	.02	.01
☐ 199 Dwight Gooden	.30	.14	.04
☐ 200 Checklist 134-239	.15	.07	.02
☐ 201 Steve Trout	.05	.02	.01
☐ 202 Rafael Ramirez	.05	.02	.01
☐ 203 Bob Walk	.05	.02	.01
☐ 204 Roger Mason	.05	.02	.01
☐ 205 Terry Kennedy	.05	.02	.01
☐ 206 Ron Oester	.05	.02	.01
☐ 207 John Russell	.05	.02	.01
☐ 208 Greg Mathews	.05	.02	.01
☐ 209 Charlie Kerfeld	.05	.02	.01
☐ 210 Reggie Jackson	.40	.18	.05
☐ 211 Floyd Bannister	.05	.02	.01
☐ 212 Vance Law	.05	.02	.01
☐ 213 Rich Bordi	.05	.02	.01
☐ 214 Dan Plesac	.05	.02	.01
☐ 215 Dave Collins	.05	.02	.01
☐ 216 Bob Stanley	.05	.02	.01
☐ 217 Joe Niekro	.05	.02	.01
☐ 218 Tom Niedenfuer	.05	.02	.01
☐ 219 Brett Butler	.15	.07	.02
☐ 220 Charlie Leibrandt	.05	.02	.01
☐ 221 Steve Ontiveros	.05	.02	.01
☐ 222 Tim Burke	.05	.02	.01
☐ 223 Curtis Wilkerson	.05	.02	.01
☐ 224 Pete Incaviglia	.15	.07	.02
☐ 225 Lonnie Smith	.05	.02	.01
☐ 226 Chris Codiroli	.05	.02	.01
☐ 227 Scott Bailes	.05	.02	.01
☐ 228 Rickey Henderson	.30	.14	.04
☐ 229 Ken Howell	.05	.02	.01
☐ 230 Darnell Coles	.05	.02	.01
☐ 231 Don Aase	.05	.02	.01
☐ 232 Tim Leary	.05	.02	.01
☐ 233 Bob Boone	.15	.07	.02
☐ 234 Ricky Horton	.05	.02	.01
☐ 235 Mark Bailey	.05	.02	.01
☐ 236 Kevin Gross	.05	.02	.01
☐ 237 Lance McCullers	.05	.02	.01
☐ 238 Cecilio Guante	.05	.02	.01
☐ 239 Bob Melvin	.05	.02	.01
☐ 240 Billy Joe Robidoux	.05	.02	.01
☐ 241 Roger McDowell	.05	.02	.01
☐ 242 Leon Durham	.05	.02	.01
☐ 243 Ed Nunez	.05	.02	.01
☐ 244 Jimmy Key	.15	.07	.02
☐ 245 Mike Smithson	.05	.02	.01
☐ 246 Bo Diaz	.05	.02	.01
☐ 247 Carlton Fisk	.30	.14	.04
☐ 248 Larry Sheets	.05	.02	.01
☐ 249 Juan Castillo	.05	.02	.01
☐ 250 Eric King	.05	.02	.01
☐ 251 Doug Drabek	.40	.18	.05
☐ 252 Wade Boggs	.30	.14	.04
☐ 253 Mariano Duncan	.05	.02	.01
☐ 254 Pat Tabler	.05	.02	.01
☐ 255 Frank White	.15	.07	.02
☐ 256 Alfredo Griffin	.05	.02	.01
☐ 257 Floyd Youmans	.05	.02	.01
☐ 258 Rob Wilfong	.05	.02	.01
☐ 259 Pete O'Brien	.05	.02	.01
☐ 260 Tim Hulett	.05	.02	.01
☐ 261 Dickie Thon	.05	.02	.01
☐ 262 Darren Daulton	.30	.14	.04
☐ 263 Vince Coleman	.05	.02	.01
☐ 264 Andy Hawkins	.05	.02	.01
☐ 265 Eric Davis	.15	.07	.02
☐ 266 Andres Thomas	.05	.02	.01
☐ 267 Mike Diaz	.05	.02	.01
☐ 268 Chili Davis	.15	.07	.02
☐ 269 Jody Davis	.05	.02	.01
☐ 270 Phil Bradley	.05	.02	.01
☐ 271 George Bell	.05	.02	.01
☐ 272 Keith Atherton	.05	.02	.01
☐ 273 Storm Davis	.05	.02	.01
☐ 274 Rob Deer	.05	.02	.01
☐ 275 Walt Terrell	.05	.02	.01
☐ 276 Roger Clemens	.75	.35	.09
☐ 277 Mike Easler	.05	.02	.01
☐ 278 Steve Sax	.05	.02	.01
☐ 279 Andre Thornton	.05	.02	.01
☐ 280 Jim Sundberg	.05	.02	.01
☐ 281 Bill Bathe	.05	.02	.01
☐ 282 Jay Tibbs	.05	.02	.01
☐ 283 Dick Schofield	.05	.02	.01
☐ 284 Mike Mason	.05	.02	.01
☐ 285 Jerry Hairston	.05	.02	.01
☐ 286 Bill Doran	.05	.02	.01
☐ 287 Tim Flannery	.05	.02	.01
☐ 288 Gary Redus	.05	.02	.01
☐ 289 John Franco	.15	.07	.02
☐ 290 Paul Assenmacher	.05	.02	.01
☐ 291 Joe Orsulak	.05	.02	.01
☐ 292 Lee Smith	.30	.14	.04
☐ 293 Mike Laga	.05	.02	.01
☐ 294 Rick Dempsey	.15	.07	.02
☐ 295 Mike Felder	.05	.02	.01
☐ 296 Tom Brookens	.05	.02	.01
☐ 297 Al Nipper	.05	.02	.01
☐ 298 Mike Pagliarulo	.05	.02	.01
☐ 299 Franklin Stubbs	.05	.02	.01
☐ 300 Checklist 240-345	.15	.07	.02
☐ 301 Steve Farr	.05	.02	.01
☐ 302 Bill Mooneyham	.05	.02	.01
☐ 303 Andres Galarraga	.50	.23	.06
☐ 304 Scott Fletcher	.05	.02	.01
☐ 305 Jack Howell	.05	.02	.01
☐ 306 Russ Morman	.05	.02	.01
☐ 307 Todd Worrell	.15	.07	.02
☐ 308 Dave Smith	.05	.02	.01
☐ 309 Jeff Stone	.05	.02	.01
☐ 310 Ron Robinson	.05	.02	.01
☐ 311 Bruce Bochy	.05	.02	.01
☐ 312 Jim Winn	.05	.02	.01
☐ 313 Mark Davis	.05	.02	.01
☐ 314 Jeff Dedmon	.05	.02	.01
☐ 315 Jamie Moyer	.15	.07	.02
☐ 316 Wally Backman	.05	.02	.01
☐ 317 Ken Phelps	.05	.02	.01
☐ 318 Steve Lombardozzi	.05	.02	.01
☐ 319 Rance Mulliniks	.05	.02	.01
☐ 320 Tim Laudner	.05	.02	.01
☐ 321 Mark Eichhorn	.05	.02	.01
☐ 322 Lee Guetterman	.05	.02	.01
☐ 323 Sid Fernandez	.05	.02	.01
☐ 324 Jerry Mumphrey	.05	.02	.01
☐ 325 David Palmer	.05	.02	.01
☐ 326 Bill Almon	.05	.02	.01
☐ 327 Candy Maldonado	.05	.02	.01
☐ 328 John Kruk	.50	.23	.06
☐ 329 John Denny	.05	.02	.01
☐ 330 Milt Thompson	.05	.02	.01
☐ 331 Mike LaValliere	.05	.02	.01
☐ 332 Alan Ashby	.05	.02	.01
☐ 333 Doug Corbett	.05	.02	.01
☐ 334 Ron Karkovice	.15	.07	.02
☐ 335 Mitch Webster	.05	.02	.01
☐ 336 Lee Lacy	.05	.02	.01
☐ 337 Glenn Braggs	.05	.02	.01
☐ 338 Dwight Lowry	.05	.02	.01
☐ 339 Don Baylor	.30	.14	.04
☐ 340 Brian Fisher	.05	.02	.01
☐ 341 Reggie Williams	.05	.02	.01
☐ 342 Tom Candiotti	.05	.02	.01
☐ 343 Rudy Law	.05	.02	.01
☐ 344 Curt Young	.05	.02	.01
☐ 345 Mike Fitzgerald	.05	.02	.01
☐ 346 Ruben Sierra	1.00	.45	.12
☐ 347 Mitch Williams	.15	.07	.02
☐ 348 Jorge Orta	.05	.02	.01
☐ 349 Mickey Tettleton	.15	.07	.02
☐ 350 Ernie Camacho	.05	.02	.01
☐ 351 Ron Kittle	.05	.02	.01
☐ 352 Ken Landreaux	.05	.02	.01
☐ 353 Chet Lemon	.05	.02	.01
☐ 354 John Shelby	.05	.02	.01
☐ 355 Mark Clear	.05	.02	.01
☐ 356 Doug DeCinces	.05	.02	.01
☐ 357 Ken Dayley	.05	.02	.01
☐ 358 Phil Garner	.05	.02	.01
☐ 359 Steve Jeltz	.05	.02	.01
☐ 360 Ed Whitson	.05	.02	.01
☐ 361 Barry Bonds	4.00	1.80	.50
☐ 362 Vida Blue	.15	.07	.02
☐ 363 Cecil Cooper	.15	.07	.02
☐ 364 Bob Ojeda	.05	.02	.01
☐ 365 Dennis Eckersley	.30	.14	.04
☐ 366 Mike Morgan	.05	.02	.01
☐ 367 Willie Upshaw	.05	.02	.01
☐ 368 Allan Anderson	.05	.02	.01
☐ 369 Bill Gullickson	.05	.02	.01
☐ 370 Bobby Thigpen	.15	.07	.02
☐ 371 Juan Beniquez	.05	.02	.01
☐ 372 Charlie Moore	.05	.02	.01
☐ 373 Dan Petry	.05	.02	.01
☐ 374 Rod Scurry	.05	.02	.01
☐ 375 Tom Seaver	.30	.14	.04
☐ 376 Ed VandeBerg	.05	.02	.01
☐ 377 Tony Bernazard	.05	.02	.01
☐ 378 Greg Pryor	.05	.02	.01
☐ 379 Dwayne Murphy	.05	.02	.01
☐ 380 Andy McGaffigan	.05	.02	.01
☐ 381 Kirk McCaskill	.05	.02	.01
☐ 382 Greg Harris	.05	.02	.01
☐ 383 Rich Dotson	.05	.02	.01
☐ 384 Craig Reynolds	.05	.02	.01
☐ 385 Greg Gross	.05	.02	.01
☐ 386 Tito Landrum	.05	.02	.01
☐ 387 Craig Lefferts	.05	.02	.01
☐ 388 Dave Parker	.15	.07	.02
☐ 389 Bob Horner	.05	.02	.01
☐ 390 Pat Clements	.05	.02	.01
☐ 391 Jeff Leonard	.05	.02	.01
☐ 392 Chris Speier	.05	.02	.01
☐ 393 John Moses	.05	.02	.01
☐ 394 Garth Iorg	.05	.02	.01
☐ 395 Greg Gagne	.05	.02	.01
☐ 396 Nate Snell	.05	.02	.01
☐ 397 Bryan Clutterbuck	.05	.02	.01
☐ 398 Darrell Evans	.15	.07	.02
☐ 399 Steve Crawford	.05	.02	.01
☐ 400 Checklist 346-451	.05	.02	.01
☐ 401 Phil Lombardi	.05	.02	.01
☐ 402 Rick Honeycutt	.05	.02	.01
☐ 403 Ken Schrom	.05	.02	.01

☐ 404 Bud Black .05 .02 .01
☐ 405 Donnie Hill .05 .02 .01
☐ 406 Wayne Krenchicki .05 .02 .01
☐ 407 Chuck Finley .40 .18 .05
☐ 408 Toby Harrah .05 .02 .01
☐ 409 Steve Lyons .05 .02 .01
☐ 410 Kevin Bass .05 .02 .01
☐ 411 Marvell Wynne .05 .02 .01
☐ 412 Ron Roenicke .05 .02 .01
☐ 413 Tracy Jones .05 .02 .01
☐ 414 Gene Garber .05 .02 .01
☐ 415 Mike Bielecki .05 .02 .01
☐ 416 Frank DiPino .05 .02 .01
☐ 417 Andy Van Slyke .15 .07 .02
☐ 418 Jim Dwyer .05 .02 .01
☐ 419 Ben Oglivie .05 .02 .01
☐ 420 Dave Bergman .05 .02 .01
☐ 421 Joe Sambito .05 .02 .01
☐ 422 Bob Tewksbury .15 .07 .02
☐ 423 Len Matuszek .05 .02 .01
☐ 424 Mike Kingery .15 .07 .02
☐ 425 Dave Kingman .15 .07 .02
☐ 426 Al Newman .05 .02 .01
☐ 427 Gary Ward .05 .02 .01
☐ 428 Ruppert Jones .05 .02 .01
☐ 429 Harold Baines .15 .07 .02
☐ 430 Pat Perry .05 .02 .01
☐ 431 Terry Puhl .05 .02 .01
☐ 432 Don Carman .05 .02 .01
☐ 433 Eddie Milner .05 .02 .01
☐ 434 LaMarr Hoyt .05 .02 .01
☐ 435 Rick Rhoden .05 .02 .01
☐ 436 Jose Uribe .05 .02 .01
☐ 437 Ken Oberkfell .05 .02 .01
☐ 438 Ron Davis .05 .02 .01
☐ 439 Jesse Orosco .05 .02 .01
☐ 440 Scott Bradley .05 .02 .01
☐ 441 Randy Bush .05 .02 .01
☐ 442 John Cerutti .05 .02 .01
☐ 443 Roy Smalley .05 .02 .01
☐ 444 Kelly Gruber .05 .02 .01
☐ 445 Bob Kearney .05 .02 .01
☐ 446 Ed Hearn .05 .02 .01
☐ 447 Scott Sanderson .05 .02 .01
☐ 448 Bruce Benedict .05 .02 .01
☐ 449 Junior Ortiz .05 .02 .01
☐ 450 Mike Aldrete .15 .07 .02
☐ 451 Kevin McReynolds .05 .02 .01
☐ 452 Rob Murphy .05 .02 .01
☐ 453 Kent Tekulve .05 .02 .01
☐ 454 Curt Ford .05 .02 .01
☐ 455 Dave Lopes .15 .07 .02
☐ 456 Bob Grich .15 .07 .02
☐ 457 Jose DeLeon .05 .02 .01
☐ 458 Andre Dawson .30 .14 .04
☐ 459 Mike Flanagan .05 .02 .01
☐ 460 Joey Meyer .05 .02 .01
☐ 461 Chuck Cary .05 .02 .01
☐ 462 Bill Buckner .15 .07 .02
☐ 463 Bob Shirley .05 .02 .01
☐ 464 Jeff Hamilton .05 .02 .01
☐ 465 Phil Niekro .30 .14 .04
☐ 466 Mark Gubicza .05 .02 .01
☐ 467 Jerry Willard .05 .02 .01
☐ 468 Bob Sebra .05 .02 .01
☐ 469 Larry Parrish .05 .02 .01
☐ 470 Charlie Hough .05 .02 .01
☐ 471 Hal McRae .15 .07 .02
☐ 472 Dave Leiper .05 .02 .01
☐ 473 Mel Hall .05 .02 .01
☐ 474 Dan Pasqua .05 .02 .01
☐ 475 Bob Welch .05 .02 .01
☐ 476 Johnny Grubb .05 .02 .01
☐ 477 Jim Traber .05 .02 .01
☐ 478 Chris Bosio .15 .07 .02
☐ 479 Mark McLemore .05 .02 .01
☐ 480 John Morris .05 .02 .01
☐ 481 Billy Hatcher .05 .02 .01
☐ 482 Dan Schatzeder .05 .02 .01
☐ 483 Rich Gossage .15 .07 .02
☐ 484 Jim Morrison .05 .02 .01
☐ 485 Bob Brenly .05 .02 .01
☐ 486 Bill Schroeder .05 .02 .01
☐ 487 Mookie Wilson .15 .07 .02
☐ 488 Dave Martinez .15 .07 .02
☐ 489 Harold Reynolds .05 .02 .01
☐ 490 Jeff Hearron .05 .02 .01
☐ 491 Mickey Hatcher .05 .02 .01
☐ 492 Barry Larkin 2.50 1.10 .30
☐ 493 Bob James .05 .02 .01
☐ 494 John Habyan .05 .02 .01
☐ 495 Jim Adduci .05 .02 .01
☐ 496 Mike Heath .05 .02 .01
☐ 497 Tim Stoddard .05 .02 .01
☐ 498 Tony Armas .05 .02 .01
☐ 499 Dennis Powell .05 .02 .01
☐ 500 Checklist 452-557 .05 .02 .01
☐ 501 Chris Bando .05 .02 .01
☐ 502 David Cone 1.50 .70 .19
☐ 503 Jay Howell .05 .02 .01
☐ 504 Tom Foley .05 .02 .01
☐ 505 Ray Chadwick .05 .02 .01
☐ 506 Mike Loynd .05 .02 .01
☐ 507 Neil Allen .05 .02 .01
☐ 508 Danny Darwin .05 .02 .01
☐ 509 Rick Schu .05 .02 .01
☐ 510 Jose Oquendo .05 .02 .01
☐ 511 Gene Walter .05 .02 .01
☐ 512 Terry McGriff .05 .02 .01
☐ 513 Ken Griffey .15 .07 .02
☐ 514 Benny Distefano .05 .02 .01
☐ 515 Terry Mulholland .15 .07 .02
☐ 516 Ed Lynch .05 .02 .01
☐ 517 Bill Swift .05 .02 .01
☐ 518 Manny Lee .05 .02 .01
☐ 519 Andre David .05 .02 .01
☐ 520 Scott McGregor .05 .02 .01
☐ 521 Rick Manning .05 .02 .01
☐ 522 Willie Hernandez .05 .02 .01
☐ 523 Marty Barrett .05 .02 .01
☐ 524 Wayne Tolleson .05 .02 .01
☐ 525 Jose Gonzalez .05 .02 .01
☐ 526 Cory Snyder .05 .02 .01
☐ 527 Buddy Biancalana .05 .02 .01
☐ 528 Moose Haas .05 .02 .01
☐ 529 Wilfredo Tejada .05 .02 .01
☐ 530 Stu Cliburn .05 .02 .01
☐ 531 Dale Mohorcic .05 .02 .01
☐ 532 Ron Hassey .05 .02 .01
☐ 533 Ty Gainey .05 .02 .01
☐ 534 Jerry Royster .05 .02 .01
☐ 535 Mike Maddux .05 .02 .01
☐ 536 Ted Power .05 .02 .01
☐ 537 Ted Simmons .15 .07 .02
☐ 538 Rafael Belliard .05 .02 .01
☐ 539 Chico Walker .05 .02 .01
☐ 540 Bob Forsch .05 .02 .01
☐ 541 John Stefero .05 .02 .01
☐ 542 Dale Sveum .05 .02 .01
☐ 543 Mark Thurmond .05 .02 .01
☐ 544 Jeff Sellers .05 .02 .01
☐ 545 Joel Skinner .05 .02 .01
☐ 546 Alex Trevino .05 .02 .01
☐ 547 Randy Kutcher .05 .02 .01
☐ 548 Joaquin Andujar .05 .02 .01
☐ 549 Casey Candaele .05 .02 .01
☐ 550 Jeff Russell .05 .02 .01
☐ 551 John Candelaria .05 .02 .01
☐ 552 Joe Cowley .05 .02 .01
☐ 553 Danny Cox .05 .02 .01
☐ 554 Denny Walling .05 .02 .01
☐ 555 Bruce Ruffin .05 .02 .01
☐ 556 Buddy Bell .15 .07 .02
☐ 557 Jimmy Jones .05 .02 .01
☐ 558 Bobby Bonilla .75 .35 .09
☐ 559 Jeff D. Robinson .05 .02 .01
☐ 560 Ed Olwine .05 .02 .01
☐ 561 Glenallen Hill .30 .14 .04
☐ 562 Lee Mazzilli .05 .02 .01
☐ 563 Mike G. Brown P .05 .02 .01
☐ 564 George Frazier .05 .02 .01
☐ 565 Mike Sharperson .05 .02 .01
☐ 566 Mark Portugal .15 .07 .02
☐ 567 Rick Leach .05 .02 .01
☐ 568 Mark Langston .15 .07 .02
☐ 569 Rafael Santana .05 .02 .01
☐ 570 Manny Trillo .05 .02 .01
☐ 571 Cliff Speck .05 .02 .01
☐ 572 Bob Kipper .05 .02 .01
☐ 573 Kelly Downs .05 .02 .01
☐ 574 Randy Asadoor .05 .02 .01
☐ 575 Dave Magadan .15 .07 .02
☐ 576 Marvin Freeman .15 .07 .02
☐ 577 Jeff Lahti .05 .02 .01
☐ 578 Jeff Calhoun .05 .02 .01
☐ 579 Gus Polidor .05 .02 .01
☐ 580 Gene Nelson .05 .02 .01
☐ 581 Tim Teufel .05 .02 .01
☐ 582 Odell Jones .05 .02 .01
☐ 583 Mark Ryal .05 .02 .01
☐ 584 Randy O'Neal .05 .02 .01
☐ 585 Mike Greenwell .30 .14 .04
☐ 586 Ray Knight .15 .07 .02
☐ 587 Ralph Bryant .05 .02 .01
☐ 588 Carmen Castillo .05 .02 .01
☐ 589 Ed Wojna .05 .02 .01
☐ 590 Stan Javier .05 .02 .01
☐ 591 Jeff Musselman .05 .02 .01
☐ 592 Mike Stanley .30 .14 .04
☐ 593 Darrell Porter .05 .02 .01
☐ 594 Drew Hall .05 .02 .01
☐ 595 Rob Nelson .05 .02 .01
☐ 596 Bryan Oelkers .05 .02 .01
☐ 597 Scott Nielsen .05 .02 .01
☐ 598 Brian Holton .05 .02 .01
☐ 599 Kevin Mitchell .30 .14 .04
☐ 600 Checklist 558-660 .05 .02 .01
☐ 601 Jackie Gutierrez .05 .02 .01
☐ 602 Barry Jones .05 .02 .01
☐ 603 Jerry Narron .05 .02 .01
☐ 604 Steve Lake .05 .02 .01
☐ 605 Jim Pankovits .05 .02 .01
☐ 606 Ed Romero .05 .02 .01
☐ 607 Dave LaPoint .05 .02 .01
☐ 608 Don Robinson .05 .02 .01
☐ 609 Mike Krukow .05 .02 .01
☐ 610 Dave Valle .05 .02 .01
☐ 611 Len Dykstra .30 .14 .04
☐ 612 Roberto Clemente PUZ .40 .18 .05
☐ 613 Mike Trujillo .05 .02 .01
☐ 614 Damaso Garcia .05 .02 .01
☐ 615 Neal Heaton .05 .02 .01
☐ 616 Juan Berenguer .05 .02 .01
☐ 617 Steve Carlton .30 .14 .04
☐ 618 Gary Lucas .05 .02 .01
☐ 619 Geno Petralli .05 .02 .01
☐ 620 Rick Aguilera .15 .07 .02
☐ 621 Fred McGriff 1.50 .70 .19
☐ 622 Dave Henderson .05 .02 .01
☐ 623 Dave Clark .15 .07 .02
☐ 624 Angel Salazar .05 .02 .01
☐ 625 Randy Hunt .05 .02 .01
☐ 626 John Gibbons .05 .02 .01
☐ 627 Kevin Brown 1.00 .45 .12
☐ 628 Bill Dawley .05 .02 .01
☐ 629 Aurelio Lopez .05 .02 .01
☐ 630 Charles Hudson .05 .02 .01
☐ 631 Ray Soff .05 .02 .01
☐ 632 Ray Hayward .05 .02 .01
☐ 633 Spike Owen .05 .02 .01
☐ 634 Glenn Hubbard .05 .02 .01
☐ 635 Kevin Elster .30 .14 .04
☐ 636 Mike LaCoss .05 .02 .01
☐ 637 Dwayne Henry .05 .02 .01
☐ 638 Rey Quinones .05 .02 .01
☐ 639 Jim Clancy .05 .02 .01
☐ 640 Larry Andersen .05 .02 .01
☐ 641 Calvin Schiraldi .05 .02 .01
☐ 642 Stan Jefferson .05 .02 .01
☐ 643 Marc Sullivan .05 .02 .01
☐ 644 Mark Grant .05 .02 .01
☐ 645 Cliff Johnson .05 .02 .01
☐ 646 Howard Johnson .05 .02 .01
☐ 647 Dave Sax .05 .02 .01
☐ 648 Dave Stewart .15 .07 .02
☐ 649 Danny Heep .05 .02 .01
☐ 650 Joe Johnson .05 .02 .01
☐ 651 Bob Brower .05 .02 .01
☐ 652 Rob Woodward .05 .02 .01
☐ 653 John Mizerock .05 .02 .01
☐ 654 Tim Pyznarski .05 .02 .01
☐ 655 Luis Aquino .05 .02 .01
☐ 656 Mickey Brantley .05 .02 .01
☐ 657 Doyle Alexander .05 .02 .01
☐ 658 Sammy Stewart .05 .02 .01
☐ 659 Jim Acker .05 .02 .01
☐ 660 Pete Ladd .05 .02 .01

1987 Donruss Wax Box Cards

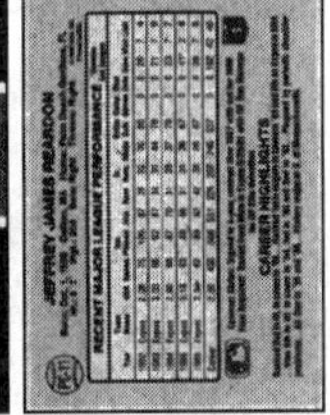

The cards in this four-card set measure the standard 2 1/2" by 3 1/2". Cards have essentially the same design as the 1987 Donruss regular issue set. The cards were printed on the bottoms of the regular issue wax pack boxes. The four cards (PC10 to PC12 plus a Roberto Clemente puzzle card) are considered a separate set in their own right and are not typically included in a complete set of the regular issue 1987 Donruss cards. The value of the panel uncut is slightly greater, perhaps by 25 percent greater, than the value of the individual cards cut up carefully.

	MINT	NRMT	EXC
COMPLETE SET (4)	.75	.35	.09
COMMON CARD	.25	.11	.03

☐ PC10 Dale Murphy .50 .23 .06
☐ PC11 Jeff Reardon .25 .11 .03
☐ PC12 Jose Canseco 1.00 .45 .12
☐ PUZ Roberto Clemente (Puzzle Card) .75 .35 .09

1987 Donruss Rookies

The 1987 Donruss "The Rookies" set features 56 full-color standard-size cards plus a 15-piece puzzle of Roberto Clemente. The set was distributed in factory set form packaged in a small green and black box through hobby dealers. Card fronts are similar in design to the 1987 Donruss regular issue except for the presence of "The Rookies" logo in the lower left corner and a green border instead of a black border. The key extended Rookie Cards in this set are Ellis Burks and Matt Williams. The second Donruss-issued cards of Greg Maddux and Rafael Palmeiro are also in this set.

	MINT	NRMT	EXC
COMPLETE FACT.SET (56)	20.00	9.00	2.50
COMMON CARD (1-56)	.10	.05	.01

☐ 1 Mark McGwire 3.00 1.35 .35
☐ 2 Eric Bell .10 .05 .01
☐ 3 Mark Williamson .10 .05 .01
☐ 4 Mike Greenwell .20 .09 .03
☐ 5 Ellis Burks 1.50 .70 .19
☐ 6 DeWayne Buice .10 .05 .01
☐ 7 Mark McLemore .10 .05 .01
☐ 8 Devon White .20 .09 .03
☐ 9 Willie Fraser .10 .05 .01
☐ 10 Les Lancaster .10 .05 .01
☐ 11 Ken Williams .10 .05 .01
☐ 12 Matt Nokes .15 .07 .02
☐ 13 Jeff M. Robinson .10 .05 .01
☐ 14 Bo Jackson 1.00 .45 .12
☐ 15 Kevin Seitzer .30 .14 .04
☐ 16 Billy Ripken .10 .05 .01
☐ 17 B.J. Surhoff .20 .09 .03
☐ 18 Chuck Crim .10 .05 .01
☐ 19 Mike Birkbeck .10 .05 .01
☐ 20 Chris Bosio .15 .07 .02
☐ 21 Les Straker .10 .05 .01
☐ 22 Mark Davidson .10 .05 .01
☐ 23 Gene Larkin .10 .05 .01
☐ 24 Ken Gerhart .10 .05 .01
☐ 25 Luis Polonia .20 .09 .03
☐ 26 Terry Steinbach .20 .09 .03
☐ 27 Mickey Brantley .10 .05 .01
☐ 28 Mike Stanley .20 .09 .03
☐ 29 Jerry Browne .10 .05 .01
☐ 30 Todd Benzinger .10 .05 .01
☐ 31 Fred McGriff 2.50 1.10 .30
☐ 32 Mike Henneman .20 .09 .03
☐ 33 Casey Candaele .10 .05 .01
☐ 34 Dave Magadan .15 .07 .02
☐ 35 David Cone 1.50 .70 .19
☐ 36 Mike Jackson .15 .07 .02
☐ 37 John Mitchell .10 .05 .01
☐ 38 Mike Dunne .10 .05 .01
☐ 39 John Smiley .15 .07 .02
☐ 40 Joe Magrane .10 .05 .01
☐ 41 Jim Lindeman .10 .05 .01
☐ 42 Shane Mack .15 .07 .02
☐ 43 Stan Jefferson .10 .05 .01
☐ 44 Benito Santiago .15 .07 .02
☐ 45 Matt Williams 5.00 2.20 .60
☐ 46 Dave Meads .10 .05 .01
☐ 47 Rafael Palmeiro 2.50 1.10 .30
☐ 48 Bill Long .10 .05 .01
☐ 49 Bob Brower .10 .05 .01
☐ 50 James Steels .10 .05 .01
☐ 51 Paul Noce .10 .05 .01
☐ 52 Greg Maddux 14.00 6.25 1.75
☐ 53 Jeff Musselman .10 .05 .01
☐ 54 Brian Holton .10 .05 .01
☐ 55 Chuck Jackson .10 .05 .01
☐ 56 Checklist 1-56 .10 .05 .01

1987 Donruss All-Stars

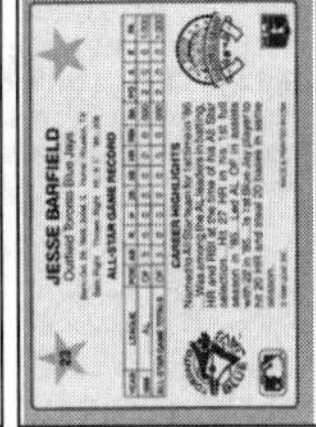

This 60-card set features cards measuring approximately 3 1/2" by 5". Card fronts are in full color with a black border. The card backs are printed in black and blue on white card stock. Cards are numbered on the back. Card backs feature statistical information about the player's performance in past All-Star games. The set was distributed in packs which also contained a Pop-Up.

	MINT	NRMT	EXC
COMPLETE SET (60)	6.00	2.70	.75
COMMON CARD (1-60)	.05	.02	.01

☐ 1 Wally Joyner .10 .05 .01
☐ 2 Dave Winfield .20 .09 .03
☐ 3 Lou Whitaker .10 .05 .01
☐ 4 Kirby Puckett 1.25 .55 .16
☐ 5 Cal Ripken 2.00 .90 .25
☐ 6 Rickey Henderson .40 .18 .05
☐ 7 Wade Boggs .40 .18 .05
☐ 8 Roger Clemens .50 .23 .06
☐ 9 Lance Parrish .10 .05 .01
☐ 10 Dick Howser MG .05 .02 .01
☐ 11 Keith Hernandez .10 .05 .01
☐ 12 Darryl Strawberry .20 .09 .03
☐ 13 Ryne Sandberg .75 .35 .09
☐ 14 Dale Murphy .20 .09 .03

	MINT	NRMT	EXC
☐ 15 Ozzie Smith	1.00	.45	.12
☐ 16 Tony Gwynn	1.25	.55	.16
☐ 17 Mike Schmidt	.60	.25	.07
☐ 18 Dwight Gooden	.20	.09	.03
☐ 19 Gary Carter	.10	.05	.01
☐ 20 Whitey Herzog MG	.05	.02	.01
☐ 21 Jose Canseco	.60	.25	.07
☐ 22 John Franco	.10	.05	.01
☐ 23 Jesse Barfield	.05	.02	.01
☐ 24 Rick Rhoden	.05	.02	.01
☐ 25 Harold Baines	.10	.05	.01
☐ 26 Sid Fernandez	.05	.02	.01
☐ 27 George Brett	1.25	.55	.16
☐ 28 Steve Sax	.05	.02	.01
☐ 29 Jim Presley	.05	.02	.01
☐ 30 Dave Smith	.05	.02	.01
☐ 31 Eddie Murray	.60	.25	.07
☐ 32 Mike Scott	.05	.02	.01
☐ 33 Don Mattingly	1.00	.45	.12
☐ 34 Dave Parker	.10	.05	.01
☐ 35 Tony Fernandez	.05	.02	.01
☐ 36 Tim Raines	.10	.05	.01
☐ 37 Brook Jacoby	.05	.02	.01
☐ 38 Chili Davis	.10	.05	.01
☐ 39 Rich Gedman	.05	.02	.01
☐ 40 Kevin Bass	.05	.02	.01
☐ 41 Frank White	.10	.05	.01
☐ 42 Glenn Davis	.05	.02	.01
☐ 43 Willie Hernandez	.05	.02	.01
☐ 44 Chris Brown	.05	.02	.01
☐ 45 Jim Rice	.10	.05	.01
☐ 46 Tony Pena	.05	.02	.01
☐ 47 Don Aase	.05	.02	.01
☐ 48 Hubie Brooks	.05	.02	.01
☐ 49 Charlie Hough	.05	.02	.01
☐ 50 Jody Davis	.05	.02	.01
☐ 51 Mike Witt	.05	.02	.01
☐ 52 Jeff Reardon	.05	.02	.01
☐ 53 Ken Schrom	.05	.02	.01
☐ 54 Fernando Valenzuela	.10	.05	.01
☐ 55 Dave Righetti	.05	.02	.01
☐ 56 Shane Rawley	.05	.02	.01
☐ 57 Ted Higuera	.05	.02	.01
☐ 58 Mike Krukow	.05	.02	.01
☐ 59 Lloyd Moseby	.05	.02	.01
☐ 60 Checklist Card	.05	.02	.01

1987 Donruss All-Star Box

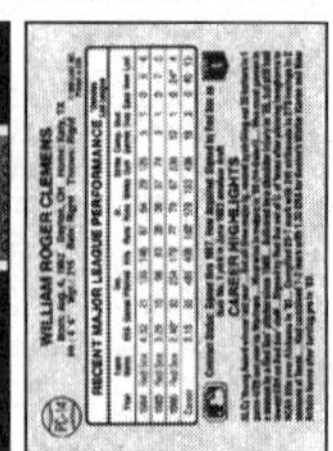

The cards in this four-card set measure the standard 2 1/2" by 3 1/2" in spite of the fact that they form the bottom of the wax pack box for the larger Donruss All-Star cards. These box cards have essentially the same design as the 1987 Donruss regular issue set. The cards were printed on the bottoms of the Donruss All-Star (3 1/2" by 5") wax pack boxes. The four cards (PC13 to PC15 plus a Roberto Clemente puzzle card) are considered a separate set in their own right and are not typically included in a complete set of the 1987 Donruss All-Star (or regular) cards. The value of the panel uncut is slightly greater, perhaps by 25 percent greater, than the value of the individual cards cut up carefully.

	MINT	NRMT	EXC
COMPLETE SET (4)	2.50	1.10	.30
COMMON CARD	.25	.11	.03
☐ PC13 Mike Scott	.25	.11	.03
☐ PC14 Roger Clemens	1.00	.45	.12
☐ PC15 Mike Krukow	.25	.11	.03
☐ PUZ Roberto Clemente Puzzle Card	1.00	.45	.12

1987 Donruss Highlights

Donruss' third (and last) edition of Highlights was released late in 1987. The cards are standard size and are glossy in appearance. Cards commemorate events during the 1987 season, as well as players and pitchers of the month from each league. The set was distributed in its own red, black, blue, and gold box along with a small Roberto Clemente puzzle. Card fronts are similar to the regular 1987 Donruss issue except that the Highlights logo is positioned in the lower right-hand corner and the borders are in blue instead of black. The backs are printed in black and gold on white card stock.

	MINT	NRMT	EXC
COMPLETE SET (56)	4.00	1.80	.50
COMMON CARD (1-56)	.50	.23	.06
☐ 1 Juan Nieves First No-Hitter	.50	.23	.06
☐ 2 Mike Schmidt Hits 500th Homer	.25	.11	.03
☐ 3 Eric Davis NL Player April	.10	.05	.01
☐ 4 Sid Fernandez NL Pitcher April	.50	.23	.06
☐ 5 Brian Downing AL Player April	.50	.23	.06
☐ 6 Bret Saberhagen AL Pitcher April	.10	.05	.01
☐ 7 Tim Raines Free Agent Returns	.10	.05	.01
☐ 8 Eric Davis NL Player May	.50	.23	.06
☐ 9 Steve Bedrosian NL Pitcher May	.50	.23	.06
☐ 10 Larry Parrish AL Player May	.50	.23	.06
☐ 11 Jim Clancy AL Pitcher May	.50	.23	.06
☐ 12 Tony Gwynn UER NL Player June over 20 hits	.40	.18	.05
☐ 13 Orel Hershiser NL Pitcher June	.10	.05	.01
☐ 14 Wade Boggs AL Player June	.15	.07	.02
☐ 15 Steve Ontiveros AL Pitcher June	.50	.23	.06
☐ 16 Tim Raines All Star Game Hero	.10	.05	.01
☐ 17 Don Mattingly Consecutive Game HR Streak	.50	.23	.06
☐ 18 Ray Dandridge 1987 HOF Inductee	.10	.05	.01
☐ 19 Jim "Catfish" Hunter 1987 HOF Inductee	.15	.07	.02
☐ 20 Billy Williams 1987 HOF Inductee	.15	.07	.02
☐ 21 Bo Diaz NL Player July	.50	.23	.06
☐ 22 Floyd Youmans NL Pitcher July	.50	.23	.06
☐ 23 Don Mattingly AL Player July	.50	.23	.06
☐ 24 Frank Viola AL Pitcher July	.50	.23	.06
☐ 25 Bobby Witt K's Four Batters in One Inning	.10	.05	.01
☐ 26 Kevin Seitzer Ties AL 9-Inning Game Hit Mark	.15	.07	.02
☐ 27 Mark McGwire Sets Rookie HR Record	.75	.35	.09
☐ 28 Andre Dawson Sets Cubs' 1st Year Homer Mark	.15	.07	.02
☐ 29 Paul Molitor Hits in 39 Straight Games	.30	.14	.04
☐ 30 Kirby Puckett Record Weekend	.50	.23	.06
☐ 31 Andre Dawson NL Player August	.15	.07	.02
☐ 32 Doug Drabek NL Pitcher August	.10	.05	.01
☐ 33 Dwight Evans AL Player August	.10	.05	.01
☐ 34 Mark Langston AL Pitcher August	.10	.05	.01
☐ 35 Wally Joyner 100 RBI in 1st Two Major League Seasons	.10	.05	.01
☐ 36 Vince Coleman 100 SB in 1st Three Major League Seasons	.50	.23	.06
☐ 37 Eddie Murray Orioles' All Time Homer King	.25	.11	.03
☐ 38 Cal Ripken Ends Consecutive Innings Streak	1.00	.45	.12
☐ 39 Fred McGriff Rob Ducey Ernie Whitt Blue Jays Hit Record 10 Homers In One Game	.50	.23	.06
☐ 40 Mark McGwire Jose Canseco Equal A's RBI Marks	.50	.23	.06
☐ 41 Bob Boone Sets All-Time Catching Record	.10	.05	.01
☐ 42 Darryl Strawberry Sets Mets' One-Season HR Mark	.15	.07	.02
☐ 43 Howard Johnson NL's All-Time Switchhit HR King	.50	.23	.06
☐ 44 Wade Boggs Five Straight 200 Hit Seasons	.15	.07	.02
☐ 45 Benito Santiago Rookie Game Hitting Streak	.10	.05	.01
☐ 46 Mark McGwire Eclipses (Reggie) Jackson's A's HR Record	.75	.35	.09
☐ 47 Kevin Seitzer 13th Rookie to Collect 200 Hits	.15	.07	.02
☐ 48 Don Mattingly Sets Slam Record	.50	.23	.06
☐ 49 Darryl Strawberry NL Player September	.15	.07	.02
☐ 50 Pascual Perez NL Pitcher September	.50	.23	.06
☐ 51 Alan Trammell AL Player September	.15	.07	.02
☐ 52 Doyle Alexander AL Pitcher September	.50	.23	.06
☐ 53 Nolan Ryan Strikeout King Again	1.25	.55	.16
☐ 54 Mark McGwire Donruss AL ROY	.75	.35	.09
☐ 55 Benito Santiago Donruss NL ROY	.10	.05	.01
☐ 56 Checklist 1-56	.50	.23	.06

1987 Donruss Opening Day

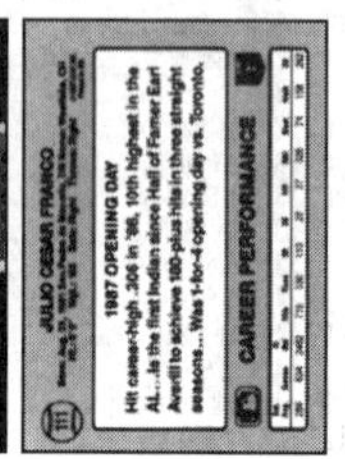

This innovative set of 272 standard-size cards features a card for each of the players in the starting line-ups of all the teams on Opening Day 1987. The set was packaged in a specially designed box. Cards are very similar in design to the 1987 regular Donruss issue except that these "OD" cards have a maroon border instead of a black border. Teams in the same city share a checklist card. A 15-piece puzzle of Roberto Clemente is also included with every complete set. The error on Barry Bonds (picturing Johnny Ray by mistake) was corrected very early in the press run; supposedly less than one percent of the sets have the error. Players in this set in their Rookie Card year include Will Clark, Bo Jackson, Wally Joyner and Barry Larkin.

	MINT	NRMT	EXC
COMPLETE FACT. SET (272)	10.00	4.50	1.25
COMMON CARD (1-248)	.05	.02	.01
COMMON LOGO (249-272)	.03	.01	.01
☐ 1 Doug DeCinces	.05	.02	.01
☐ 2 Mike Witt	.05	.02	.01
☐ 3 George Hendrick	.05	.02	.01
☐ 4 Dick Schofield	.05	.02	.01
☐ 5 Devon White	.15	.07	.02
☐ 6 Butch Wynegar	.05	.02	.01
☐ 7 Wally Joyner	.40	.18	.05
☐ 8 Mark McLemore	.05	.02	.01
☐ 9 Brian Downing	.05	.02	.01
☐ 10 Gary Pettis	.05	.02	.01
☐ 11 Bill Doran	.05	.02	.01
☐ 12 Phil Garner	.05	.02	.01
☐ 13 Jose Cruz	.05	.02	.01
☐ 14 Kevin Bass	.05	.02	.01
☐ 15 Mike Scott	.05	.02	.01
☐ 16 Glenn Davis	.05	.02	.01
☐ 17 Alan Ashby	.05	.02	.01
☐ 18 Billy Hatcher	.05	.02	.01
☐ 19 Craig Reynolds	.05	.02	.01
☐ 20 Carney Lansford	.10	.05	.01
☐ 21 Mike Davis	.05	.02	.01
☐ 22 Reggie Jackson	.40	.18	.05
☐ 23 Mickey Tettleton	.10	.05	.01
☐ 24 Jose Canseco	.75	.35	.09
☐ 25 Rob Nelson	.05	.02	.01
☐ 26 Tony Phillips	.10	.05	.01
☐ 27 Dwayne Murphy	.05	.02	.01
☐ 28 Alfredo Griffin	.05	.02	.01
☐ 29 Curt Young	.05	.02	.01
☐ 30 Willie Upshaw	.05	.02	.01
☐ 31 Mike Sharperson	.05	.02	.01
☐ 32 Rance Mulliniks	.05	.02	.01
☐ 33 Ernie Whitt	.05	.02	.01
☐ 34 Jesse Barfield	.05	.02	.01
☐ 35 Tony Fernandez	.05	.02	.01
☐ 36 Lloyd Moseby	.05	.02	.01
☐ 37 Jimmy Key	.10	.05	.01
☐ 38 Fred McGriff	.75	.35	.09
☐ 39 George Bell	.05	.02	.01
☐ 40 Dale Murphy	.15	.07	.02
☐ 41 Rick Mahler	.05	.02	.01
☐ 42 Ken Griffey	.10	.05	.01
☐ 43 Andres Thomas	.05	.02	.01
☐ 44 Dion James	.05	.02	.01
☐ 45 Ozzie Virgil	.05	.02	.01
☐ 46 Ken Oberkfell	.05	.02	.01
☐ 47 Gary Roenicke	.05	.02	.01
☐ 48 Glenn Hubbard	.05	.02	.01
☐ 49 Bill Schroeder	.05	.02	.01
☐ 50 Greg Brock	.05	.02	.01
☐ 51 Billy Joe Robidoux	.05	.02	.01
☐ 52 Glenn Braggs	.05	.02	.01
☐ 53 Jim Gantner	.05	.02	.01
☐ 54 Paul Molitor	.50	.23	.06
☐ 55 Dale Sveum	.05	.02	.01
☐ 56 Ted Higuera	.05	.02	.01
☐ 57 Rob Deer	.05	.02	.01
☐ 58 Robin Yount	.40	.18	.05
☐ 59 Jim Lindeman	.05	.02	.01
☐ 60 Vince Coleman	.05	.02	.01
☐ 61 Tommy Herr	.05	.02	.01
☐ 62 Terry Pendleton	.10	.05	.01
☐ 63 John Tudor	.05	.02	.01
☐ 64 Tony Pena	.05	.02	.01
☐ 65 Ozzie Smith	1.00	.45	.12
☐ 66 Tito Landrum	.05	.02	.01
☐ 67 Jack Clark	.10	.05	.01
☐ 68 Bob Dernier	.05	.02	.01
☐ 69 Rick Sutcliffe	.05	.02	.01
☐ 70 Andre Dawson	.30	.14	.04
☐ 71 Keith Moreland	.05	.02	.01
☐ 72 Jody Davis	.05	.02	.01
☐ 73 Brian Dayett	.05	.02	.01
☐ 74 Leon Durham	.05	.02	.01
☐ 75 Ryne Sandberg	1.25	.55	.16
☐ 76 Shawon Dunston	.10	.05	.01
☐ 77 Mike Marshall	.05	.02	.01
☐ 78 Bill Madlock	.05	.02	.01
☐ 79 Orel Hershiser	.10	.05	.01
☐ 80 Mike Ramsey	.05	.02	.01
☐ 81 Ken Landreaux	.05	.02	.01
☐ 82 Mike Scioscia	.05	.02	.01
☐ 83 Franklin Stubbs	.05	.02	.01
☐ 84 Mariano Duncan	.05	.02	.01
☐ 85 Steve Sax	.05	.02	.01
☐ 86 Mitch Webster	.05	.02	.01
☐ 87 Reid Nichols	.05	.02	.01
☐ 88 Tim Wallach	.05	.02	.01
☐ 89 Floyd Youmans	.05	.02	.01
☐ 90 Andres Galarraga	.75	.35	.09
☐ 91 Hubie Brooks	.05	.02	.01
☐ 92 Jeff Reed	.05	.02	.01
☐ 93 Alonzo Powell	.05	.02	.01
☐ 94 Vance Law	.05	.02	.01
☐ 95 Bob Brenly	.05	.02	.01
☐ 96 Will Clark	1.50	.70	.19
☐ 97 Chili Davis	.10	.05	.01
☐ 98 Mike Krukow	.05	.02	.01
☐ 99 Jose Uribe	.05	.02	.01
☐ 100 Chris Brown	.05	.02	.01
☐ 101 Robby Thompson	.05	.02	.01
☐ 102 Candy Maldonado	.05	.02	.01
☐ 103 Jeff Leonard	.05	.02	.01
☐ 104 Tom Candiotti	.05	.02	.01
☐ 105 Chris Bando	.05	.02	.01
☐ 106 Cory Snyder	.05	.02	.01
☐ 107 Pat Tabler	.05	.02	.01
☐ 108 Andre Thornton	.05	.02	.01
☐ 109 Joe Carter	.15	.07	.02
☐ 110 Tony Bernazard	.05	.02	.01
☐ 111 Julio Franco	.10	.05	.01
☐ 112 Brook Jacoby	.05	.02	.01
☐ 113 Brett Butler	.10	.05	.01
☐ 114 Donell Nixon	.05	.02	.01
☐ 115 Alvin Davis	.05	.02	.01
☐ 116 Mark Langston	.10	.05	.01
☐ 117 Harold Reynolds	.10	.05	.01
☐ 118 Ken Phelps	.05	.02	.01
☐ 119 Mike Kingery	.05	.02	.01
☐ 120 Dave Valle	.05	.02	.01
☐ 121 Rey Quinones	.05	.02	.01
☐ 122 Phil Bradley	.05	.02	.01
☐ 123 Jim Presley	.05	.02	.01
☐ 124 Keith Hernandez	.10	.05	.01
☐ 125 Kevin McReynolds	.05	.02	.01
☐ 126 Rafael Santana	.05	.02	.01
☐ 127 Bob Ojeda	.05	.02	.01
☐ 128 Darryl Strawberry	.15	.07	.02
☐ 129 Mookie Wilson	.10	.05	.01
☐ 130 Gary Carter	.10	.05	.01
☐ 131 Tim Teufel	.05	.02	.01
☐ 132 Howard Johnson	.05	.02	.01
☐ 133 Cal Ripken	2.50	1.10	.30
☐ 134 Rick Burleson	.05	.02	.01
☐ 135 Fred Lynn	.10	.05	.01
☐ 136 Eddie Murray	.75	.35	.09
☐ 137 Ray Knight	.10	.05	.01
☐ 138 Alan Wiggins	.05	.02	.01
☐ 139 John Shelby	.05	.02	.01
☐ 140 Mike Boddicker	.05	.02	.01
☐ 141 Ken Gerhart	.05	.02	.01
☐ 142 Terry Kennedy	.05	.02	.01
☐ 143 Steve Garvey	.10	.05	.01
☐ 144 Marvell Wynne	.05	.02	.01
☐ 145 Kevin Mitchell	.15	.07	.02
☐ 146 Tony Gwynn	1.50	.70	.19
☐ 147 Joey Cora	.20	.09	.03
☐ 148 Benito Santiago	.10	.05	.01
☐ 149 Eric Show	.05	.02	.01
☐ 150 Garry Templeton	.05	.02	.01
☐ 151 Carmelo Martinez	.05	.02	.01
☐ 152 Von Hayes	.05	.02	.01
☐ 153 Lance Parrish	.10	.05	.01
☐ 154 Milt Thompson	.05	.02	.01
☐ 155 Mike Easler	.05	.02	.01
☐ 156 Juan Samuel	.05	.02	.01
☐ 157 Steve Jeltz	.05	.02	.01

Card	MINT	NRMT	EXC
□ 158 Glenn Wilson	.05	.02	.01
□ 159 Shane Rawley	.05	.02	.01
□ 160 Mike Schmidt	.75	.35	.09
□ 161 Andy Van Slyke	.10	.05	.01
□ 162 Johnny Ray	.05	.02	.01
□ 163A Barry Bonds ERR (Photo actually Johnny Ray wearing a black shirt)	200.00	90.00	25.00
□ 163B Barry Bonds COR	3.00	1.35	.35
□ 164 Junior Ortiz	.05	.02	.01
□ 165 Rafael Belliard	.05	.02	.01
□ 166 Bob Patterson	.05	.02	.01
□ 167 Bobby Bonilla	.75	.35	.09
□ 168 Sid Bream	.05	.02	.01
□ 169 Jim Morrison	.05	.02	.01
□ 170 Jerry Browne	.05	.02	.01
□ 171 Scott Fletcher	.05	.02	.01
□ 172 Ruben Sierra	.25	.11	.03
□ 173 Larry Parrish	.05	.02	.01
□ 174 Pete O'Brien	.05	.02	.01
□ 175 Pete Incaviglia	.10	.05	.01
□ 176 Don Slaught	.05	.02	.01
□ 177 Oddibe McDowell	.05	.02	.01
□ 178 Charlie Hough	.05	.02	.01
□ 179 Steve Buechele	.05	.02	.01
□ 180 Bob Stanley	.05	.02	.01
□ 181 Wade Boggs	.40	.18	.05
□ 182 Jim Rice	.10	.05	.01
□ 183 Bill Buckner	.10	.05	.01
□ 184 Dwight Evans	.10	.05	.01
□ 185 Spike Owen	.05	.02	.01
□ 186 Don Baylor	.10	.05	.01
□ 187 Marc Sullivan	.05	.02	.01
□ 188 Marty Barrett	.05	.02	.01
□ 189 Dave Henderson	.05	.02	.01
□ 190 Bo Diaz	.05	.02	.01
□ 191 Barry Larkin	1.50	.70	.19
□ 192 Kal Daniels	.05	.02	.01
□ 193 Terry Francona	.05	.02	.01
□ 194 Tom Browning	.05	.02	.01
□ 195 Ron Oester	.05	.02	.01
□ 196 Buddy Bell	.10	.05	.01
□ 197 Eric Davis	.15	.07	.02
□ 198 Dave Parker	.10	.05	.01
□ 199 Steve Balboni	.05	.02	.01
□ 200 Danny Tartabull	.10	.05	.01
□ 201 Ed Hearn	.05	.02	.01
□ 202 Buddy Biancalana	.05	.02	.01
□ 203 Danny Jackson	.05	.02	.01
□ 204 Frank White	.10	.05	.01
□ 205 Bo Jackson	.25	.11	.03
□ 206 George Brett	1.50	.70	.19
□ 207 Kevin Seitzer	.15	.07	.02
□ 208 Willie Wilson	.05	.02	.01
□ 209 Orlando Mercado	.05	.02	.01
□ 210 Darrell Evans	.10	.05	.01
□ 211 Larry Herndon	.05	.02	.01
□ 212 Jack Morris	.10	.05	.01
□ 213 Chet Lemon	.05	.02	.01
□ 214 Mike Heath	.05	.02	.01
□ 215 Darnell Coles	.05	.02	.01
□ 216 Alan Trammell	.15	.07	.02
□ 217 Terry Harper	.05	.02	.01
□ 218 Lou Whitaker	.10	.05	.01
□ 219 Gary Gaetti	.05	.02	.01
□ 220 Tom Nieto	.05	.02	.01
□ 221 Kirby Puckett	1.50	.70	.19
□ 222 Tom Brunansky	.05	.02	.01
□ 223 Greg Gagne	.05	.02	.01
□ 224 Dan Gladden	.05	.02	.01
□ 225 Mark Davidson	.05	.02	.01
□ 226 Bert Blyleven	.10	.05	.01
□ 227 Steve Lombardozzi	.05	.02	.01
□ 228 Kent Hrbek	.10	.05	.01
□ 229 Gary Redus	.05	.02	.01
□ 230 Ivan Calderon	.05	.02	.01
□ 231 Tim Hulett	.05	.02	.01
□ 232 Carlton Fisk	.40	.18	.05
□ 233 Greg Walker	.05	.02	.01
□ 234 Ron Karkovice	.05	.02	.01
□ 235 Ozzie Guillen	.05	.02	.01
□ 236 Harold Baines	.10	.05	.01
□ 237 Donnie Hill	.05	.02	.01
□ 238 Rich Dotson	.05	.02	.01
□ 239 Mike Pagliarulo	.05	.02	.01
□ 240 Joel Skinner	.05	.02	.01
□ 241 Don Mattingly	1.25	.55	.16
□ 242 Gary Ward	.05	.02	.01
□ 243 Dave Winfield	.40	.18	.05
□ 244 Dan Pasqua	.05	.02	.01
□ 245 Wayne Tolleson	.05	.02	.01
□ 246 Willie Randolph	.10	.05	.01
□ 247 Dennis Rasmussen	.05	.02	.01
□ 248 Rickey Henderson	.40	.18	.05
□ 249 Angels Logo	.03	.01	.01
□ 250 Astros Logo	.03	.01	.01
□ 251 A's Logo	.03	.01	.01
□ 252 Blue Jays Logo	.03	.01	.01
□ 253 Braves Logo	.03	.01	.01
□ 254 Brewers Logo	.03	.01	.01
□ 255 Cardinals Logo	.03	.01	.01
□ 256 Dodgers Logo	.03	.01	.01
□ 257 Expos Logo	.03	.01	.01
□ 258 Giants Logo	.03	.01	.01
□ 259 Indians Logo	.03	.01	.01
□ 260 Mariners Logo	.03	.01	.01
□ 261 Orioles Logo	.03	.01	.01
□ 262 Padres Logo	.03	.01	.01
□ 263 Phillies Logo	.03	.01	.01
□ 264 Pirates Logo	.03	.01	.01
□ 265 Rangers Logo	.03	.01	.01
□ 266 Red Sox Logo	.03	.01	.01
□ 267 Reds Logo	.03	.01	.01
□ 268 Royals Logo	.03	.01	.01
□ 269 Tigers Logo	.03	.01	.01
□ 270 Twins Logo	.05	.02	.01
□ 271 Chicago Logos	.03	.01	.01
□ 272 New York Logos	.03	.01	.01

1987 Donruss Pop-Ups

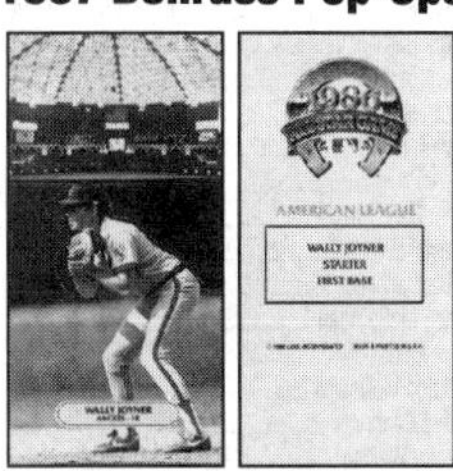

This 20-card set features "fold-out" cards measuring approximately 2 1/2" X 5". Card fronts are in full color. Cards are unnumbered but are listed in the same order as the Donruss All-Stars on the All-Star checklist card. Card backs present essentially no information about the player. The set was distributed in packs which also contained All-Star cards (3 1/2" by 5").

	MINT	NRMT	EXC
COMPLETE SET (20)	5.00	2.20	.60
COMMON CARD (1-20)	.05	.02	.01
□ 1 Wally Joyner	.40	.18	.05
□ 2 Dave Winfield	.50	.23	.06
□ 3 Lou Whitaker	.10	.05	.01
□ 4 Kirby Puckett	1.25	.55	.16
□ 5 Cal Ripken	2.50	1.10	.30
□ 6 Rickey Henderson	.50	.23	.06
□ 7 Wade Boggs	.50	.23	.06
□ 8 Roger Clemens	.75	.35	.09
□ 9 Lance Parrish	.10	.05	.01
□ 10 Dick Howser MG	.05	.02	.01
□ 11 Keith Hernandez	.10	.05	.01
□ 12 Darryl Strawberry	.15	.07	.02
□ 13 Ryne Sandberg	.75	.35	.09
□ 14 Dale Murphy	.15	.07	.02
□ 15 Ozzie Smith	1.00	.45	.12
□ 16 Tony Gwynn	1.25	.55	.16
□ 17 Mike Schmidt	.75	.35	.09
□ 18 Dwight Gooden	.15	.07	.02
□ 19 Gary Carter	.10	.05	.01
□ 20 Whitey Herzog MG	.05	.02	.01

1987 Donruss Super DK's

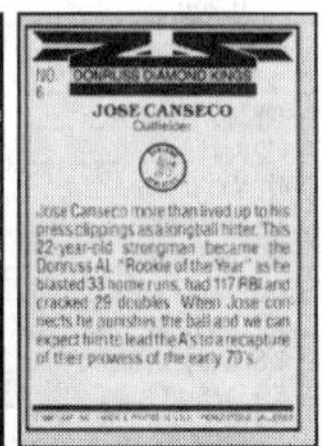

This 28-card set was available through a mail-in offer detailed on the wax packs. The set was sent in return for $8.00 and three wrappers plus $1.50 postage and handling. The set features the popular Diamond King subseries in large (approximately 4 7/8" X 6 13/16") form. Dick Perez of Perez-Steele Galleries did the original artwork from which these cards were taken. The cards are essentially a large version of the Donruss regular issue Diamond Kings.

	MINT	NRMT	EXC
COMPLETE SET (26)	12.00	5.50	1.50
COMMON CARD (1-26)	.50	.23	.06
□ 1 Wally Joyner	.75	.35	.09
□ 2 Roger Clemens	1.50	.70	.19
□ 3 Dale Murphy	1.00	.45	.12
□ 4 Darryl Strawberry	1.00	.45	.12
□ 5 Ozzie Smith	1.50	.70	.19
□ 6 Jose Canseco	2.00	.90	.25
□ 7 Charlie Hough	.50	.23	.06
□ 8 Brook Jacoby	.50	.23	.06
□ 9 Fred Lynn	.75	.35	.09
□ 10 Rick Rhoden	.50	.23	.06
□ 11 Chris Brown	.50	.23	.06
□ 12 Von Hayes	.50	.23	.06
□ 13 Jack Morris	.75	.35	.09
□ 14 Kevin McReynolds	.50	.23	.06
□ 15 George Brett	3.00	1.35	.35
□ 16 Ted Higuera	.50	.23	.06
□ 17 Hubie Brooks	.50	.23	.06
□ 18 Mike Scott	.50	.23	.06
□ 19 Kirby Puckett	3.00	1.35	.35
□ 20 Dave Winfield	1.25	.55	.16
□ 21 Lloyd Moseby	.50	.23	.06
□ 22 Eric Davis	.75	.35	.09
□ 23 Jim Presley	.50	.23	.06
□ 24 Keith Moreland	.50	.23	.06
□ 25 Greg Walker	.50	.23	.06
□ 26 Steve Sax	.50	.23	.06
□ NNO Roberto Clemente Large Puzzle	1.00	.45	.12
□ NNO DK Checklist 1-26	.50	.23	.06

1988 Donruss

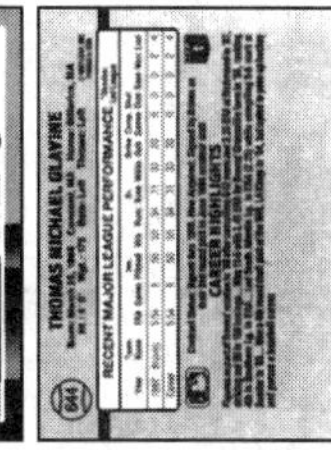

This set consists of 660 standard-size cards. For the seventh straight year, wax packs consisted of 15 cards plus a puzzle panel (featuring Stan Musial this time around). Cards were also distributed in rack packs and retail and hobby factory sets. Card fronts feature a distinctive black and blue border on the front. The card front border design pattern of the factory set card fronts is oriented differently from that of the regular wax pack cards. No premium or discount exists for either version. Subsets include Diamond Kings (1-27) and Rated Rookies (28-47). Cards marked as SP (short printed) from 648-660 are more difficult to find than the other 13 SP's in the lower 600s. These 26 cards listed as SP were apparently pulled from the printing sheet to make room for the 26 Bonus MVP cards. Numbered with the prefix "BC" for bonus card, this 26-card set featuring the most valuable player from each of the 26 teams was randomly inserted in the wax and rack packs. The cards are distinguished by the MVP logo in the upper left corner of the obverse, and cards BC14-BC26 are considered to be more difficult to find than cards BC1-BC13. Six of the checklist cards were done two different ways to reflect the inclusion or exclusion of the Bonus MVP cards in the wax packs. In the checklist below, the A variations (for the checklist cards) are from the wax packs and the B variations are from the factory-collated sets. The key Rookie Cards in this set are Roberto Alomar, Jay Bell, Jay Buhner, Ellis Burks, Ken Caminiti, Ron Gant, Tom Glavine, Mark Grace, Gregg Jefferies, Jack McDowell, and Matt Williams. There was also a Kirby Puckett card issued as the package back of Donruss blister packs; it uses a different photo from both of Kirby's regular and Bonus MVP cards and is unnumbered on the back.

	MINT	NRMT	EXC
COMPLETE SET (660)	8.00	3.60	1.00
COMPLETE FACT.SET (660)	8.00	3.60	1.00
COMMON CARD (1-647)	.05	.02	.01
COMMON CARD SP (648-660)	.07	.03	.01
□ 1 Mark McGwire DK	.30	.14	.04
□ 2 Tim Raines DK	.10	.05	.01
□ 3 Benito Santiago DK	.05	.02	.01
□ 4 Alan Trammell DK	.10	.05	.01
□ 5 Danny Tartabull DK	.05	.02	.01
□ 6 Ron Darling DK	.05	.02	.01
□ 7 Paul Molitor DK	.15	.07	.02
□ 8 Devon White DK	.15	.07	.02
□ 9 Andre Dawson DK	.10	.05	.01
□ 10 Julio Franco DK	.10	.05	.01
□ 11 Scott Fletcher DK	.05	.02	.01
□ 12 Tony Fernandez DK	.05	.02	.01
□ 13 Shane Rawley DK	.05	.02	.01
□ 14 Kal Daniels DK	.05	.02	.01
□ 15 Jack Clark DK	.05	.02	.01
□ 16 Dwight Evans DK	.10	.05	.01
□ 17 Tommy John DK	.10	.05	.01
□ 18 Andy Van Slyke DK	.05	.02	.01
□ 19 Gary Gaetti DK	.05	.02	.01
□ 20 Mark Langston DK	.10	.05	.01
□ 21 Will Clark DK	.15	.07	.02
□ 22 Glenn Hubbard DK	.05	.02	.01
□ 23 Billy Hatcher DK	.05	.02	.01
□ 24 Bob Welch DK	.05	.02	.01
□ 25 Ivan Calderon DK	.05	.02	.01
□ 26 Cal Ripken DK	.40	.18	.05
□ 27 DK Checklist 1-26	.05	.02	.01
□ 28 Mackey Sasser RR	.05	.02	.01
□ 29 Jeff Treadway RR	.05	.02	.01
□ 30 Mike Campbell RR	.05	.02	.01
□ 31 Lance Johnson RR	.30	.14	.04
□ 32 Nelson Liriano RR	.05	.02	.01
□ 33 Shawn Abner RR	.05	.02	.01
□ 34 Roberto Alomar RR	1.50	.70	.19
□ 35 Shawn Hillegas RR	.05	.02	.01
□ 36 Joey Meyer RR	.05	.02	.01
□ 37 Kevin Elster RR	.10	.05	.01
□ 38 Jose Lind RR	.10	.05	.01
□ 39 Kirt Manwaring RR	.10	.05	.01
□ 40 Mark Grace RR	.60	.25	.07
□ 41 Jody Reed RR	.10	.05	.01
□ 42 John Farrell RR	.05	.02	.01
□ 43 Al Leiter RR	.15	.07	.02
□ 44 Gary Thurman RR	.05	.02	.01
□ 45 Vicente Palacios RR	.05	.02	.01
□ 46 Eddie Williams RR	.10	.05	.01
□ 47 Jack McDowell RR	.30	.14	.04
□ 48 Ken Dixon	.05	.02	.01
□ 49 Mike Birkbeck	.05	.02	.01
□ 50 Eric King	.05	.02	.01
□ 51 Roger Clemens	.20	.09	.03
□ 52 Pat Clements	.05	.02	.01
□ 53 Fernando Valenzuela	.10	.05	.01
□ 54 Mark Gubicza	.05	.02	.01
□ 55 Jay Howell	.05	.02	.01
□ 56 Floyd Youmans	.05	.02	.01
□ 57 Ed Correa	.05	.02	.01
□ 58 DeWayne Buice	.05	.02	.01
□ 59 Jose DeLeon	.05	.02	.01
□ 60 Danny Cox	.05	.02	.01
□ 61 Nolan Ryan	.75	.35	.09
□ 62 Steve Bedrosian	.05	.02	.01
□ 63 Tom Browning	.05	.02	.01
□ 64 Mark Davis	.05	.02	.01
□ 65 R.J. Reynolds	.05	.02	.01
□ 66 Kevin Mitchell	.10	.05	.01
□ 67 Ken Oberkfell	.05	.02	.01
□ 68 Rick Sutcliffe	.05	.02	.01
□ 69 Dwight Gooden	.10	.05	.01
□ 70 Scott Bankhead	.05	.02	.01
□ 71 Bert Blyleven	.10	.05	.01
□ 72 Jimmy Key	.10	.05	.01
□ 73 Les Straker	.05	.02	.01
□ 74 Jim Clancy	.05	.02	.01
□ 75 Mike Moore	.05	.02	.01
□ 76 Ron Darling	.05	.02	.01
□ 77 Ed Lynch	.05	.02	.01
□ 78 Dale Murphy	.15	.07	.02
□ 79 Doug Drabek	.10	.05	.01
□ 80 Scott Garrelts	.05	.02	.01
□ 81 Ed Whitson	.05	.02	.01
□ 82 Rob Murphy	.05	.02	.01
□ 83 Shane Rawley	.05	.02	.01
□ 84 Greg Mathews	.05	.02	.01
□ 85 Jim Deshaies	.05	.02	.01
□ 86 Mike Witt	.05	.02	.01
□ 87 Donnie Hill	.05	.02	.01
□ 88 Jeff Reed	.05	.02	.01
□ 89 Mike Boddicker	.05	.02	.01
□ 90 Ted Higuera	.05	.02	.01
□ 91 Walt Terrell	.05	.02	.01
□ 92 Bob Stanley	.05	.02	.01
□ 93 Dave Righetti	.05	.02	.01
□ 94 Orel Hershiser	.10	.05	.01
□ 95 Chris Bando	.05	.02	.01
□ 96 Bret Saberhagen	.10	.05	.01
□ 97 Curt Young	.05	.02	.01
□ 98 Tim Burke	.05	.02	.01
□ 99 Charlie Hough	.10	.05	.01
□ 100A Checklist 28-137	.05	.02	.01
□ 100B Checklist 28-133	.05	.02	.01
□ 101 Bobby Witt	.05	.02	.01
□ 102 George Brett	.40	.18	.05
□ 103 Mickey Tettleton	.10	.05	.01
□ 104 Scott Bailes	.05	.02	.01
□ 105 Mike Pagliarulo	.05	.02	.01
□ 106 Mike Scioscia	.05	.02	.01
□ 107 Tom Brookens	.05	.02	.01
□ 108 Ray Knight	.10	.05	.01
□ 109 Dan Plesac	.05	.02	.01
□ 110 Wally Joyner	.15	.07	.02
□ 111 Bob Forsch	.05	.02	.01
□ 112 Mike Scott	.05	.02	.01
□ 113 Kevin Gross	.05	.02	.01
□ 114 Benito Santiago	.10	.05	.01
□ 115 Bob Kipper	.05	.02	.01
□ 116 Mike Krukow	.05	.02	.01
□ 117 Chris Bosio	.05	.02	.01
□ 118 Sid Fernandez	.05	.02	.01
□ 119 Jody Davis	.05	.02	.01
□ 120 Mike Morgan	.05	.02	.01
□ 121 Mark Eichhorn	.05	.02	.01
□ 122 Jeff Reardon	.10	.05	.01
□ 123 John Franco	.10	.05	.01
□ 124 Richard Dotson	.05	.02	.01
□ 125 Eric Bell	.05	.02	.01
□ 126 Juan Nieves	.05	.02	.01
□ 127 Jack Morris	.15	.07	.02
□ 128 Rick Rhoden	.05	.02	.01
□ 129 Rich Gedman	.05	.02	.01
□ 130 Ken Howell	.05	.02	.01
□ 131 Brook Jacoby	.05	.02	.01
□ 132 Danny Jackson	.05	.02	.01
□ 133 Gene Nelson	.05	.02	.01
□ 134 Neal Heaton	.05	.02	.01
□ 135 Willie Fraser	.05	.02	.01
□ 136 Jose Guzman	.05	.02	.01
□ 137 Ozzie Guillen	.10	.05	.01
□ 138 Bob Knepper	.05	.02	.01
□ 139 Mike Jackson	.10	.05	.01
□ 140 Joe Magrane	.05	.02	.01
□ 141 Jimmy Jones	.05	.02	.01
□ 142 Ted Power	.05	.02	.01
□ 143 Ozzie Virgil	.05	.02	.01
□ 144 Felix Fermin	.05	.02	.01
□ 145 Kelly Downs	.05	.02	.01
□ 146 Shawon Dunston	.05	.02	.01

☐ 147 Scott Bradley .05 .02 .01
☐ 148 Dave Stieb .10 .05 .01
☐ 149 Frank Viola .05 .02 .01
☐ 150 Terry Kennedy .05 .02 .01
☐ 151 Bill Wegman .05 .02 .01
☐ 152 Matt Nokes .05 .02 .01
☐ 153 Wade Boggs .15 .07 .02
☐ 154 Wayne Tolleson .05 .02 .01
☐ 155 Mariano Duncan .05 .02 .01
☐ 156 Julio Franco .10 .05 .01
☐ 157 Charlie Leibrandt .05 .02 .01
☐ 158 Terry Steinbach .15 .07 .02
☐ 159 Mike Fitzgerald .05 .02 .01
☐ 160 Jack Lazorko .05 .02 .01
☐ 161 Mitch Williams .10 .05 .01
☐ 162 Greg Walker .05 .02 .01
☐ 163 Alan Ashby .05 .02 .01
☐ 164 Tony Gwynn .40 .18 .05
☐ 165 Bruce Ruffin .05 .02 .01
☐ 166 Ron Robinson .05 .02 .01
☐ 167 Zane Smith .05 .02 .01
☐ 168 Junior Ortiz .05 .02 .01
☐ 169 Jamie Moyer .05 .02 .01
☐ 170 Tony Pena .05 .02 .01
☐ 171 Cal Ripken .75 .35 .09
☐ 172 B.J. Surhoff .10 .05 .01
☐ 173 Lou Whitaker .10 .05 .01
☐ 174 Ellis Burks .40 .18 .05
☐ 175 Ron Guidry .05 .02 .01
☐ 176 Steve Sax .05 .02 .01
☐ 177 Danny Tartabull .05 .02 .01
☐ 178 Carney Lansford .10 .05 .01
☐ 179 Casey Candaele .05 .02 .01
☐ 180 Scott Fletcher .05 .02 .01
☐ 181 Mark McLemore .05 .02 .01
☐ 182 Ivan Calderon .05 .02 .01
☐ 183 Jack Clark .10 .05 .01
☐ 184 Glenn Davis .05 .02 .01
☐ 185 Luis Aguayo .05 .02 .01
☐ 186 Bo Diaz .05 .02 .01
☐ 187 Stan Jefferson .05 .02 .01
☐ 188 Sid Bream .05 .02 .01
☐ 189 Bob Brenly .05 .02 .01
☐ 190 Dion James .05 .02 .01
☐ 191 Leon Durham .05 .02 .01
☐ 192 Jesse Orosco .05 .02 .01
☐ 193 Alvin Davis .05 .02 .01
☐ 194 Gary Gaetti .05 .02 .01
☐ 195 Fred McGriff .30 .14 .04
☐ 196 Steve Lombardozzi .05 .02 .01
☐ 197 Rance Mulliniks .05 .02 .01
☐ 198 Rey Quinones .05 .02 .01
☐ 199 Gary Carter .10 .05 .01
☐ 200A Checklist 138-247 .05 .02 .01
☐ 200B Checklist 134-239 .05 .02 .01
☐ 201 Keith Moreland .05 .02 .01
☐ 202 Ken Griffey .05 .02 .01
☐ 203 Tommy Gregg .05 .02 .01
☐ 204 Will Clark .25 .11 .03
☐ 205 John Kruk .15 .07 .02
☐ 206 Buddy Bell .10 .05 .01
☐ 207 Von Hayes .05 .02 .01
☐ 208 Tommy Herr .05 .02 .01
☐ 209 Craig Reynolds .05 .02 .01
☐ 210 Gary Pettis .05 .02 .01
☐ 211 Harold Baines .10 .05 .01
☐ 212 Vance Law .05 .02 .01
☐ 213 Ken Gerhart .05 .02 .01
☐ 214 Jim Gantner .05 .02 .01
☐ 215 Chet Lemon .05 .02 .01
☐ 216 Dwight Evans .10 .05 .01
☐ 217 Don Mattingly .50 .23 .06
☐ 218 Franklin Stubbs .05 .02 .01
☐ 219 Pat Tabler .05 .02 .01
☐ 220 Bo Jackson .15 .07 .02
☐ 221 Tony Phillips .15 .07 .02
☐ 222 Tim Wallach .05 .02 .01
☐ 223 Ruben Sierra .15 .07 .02
☐ 224 Steve Buechele .05 .02 .01
☐ 225 Frank White .10 .05 .01
☐ 226 Alfredo Griffin .05 .02 .01
☐ 227 Greg Swindell .05 .02 .01
☐ 228 Willie Randolph .10 .05 .01
☐ 229 Mike Marshall .05 .02 .01
☐ 230 Alan Trammell .10 .05 .01
☐ 231 Eddie Murray .25 .11 .03
☐ 232 Dale Sveum .05 .02 .01
☐ 233 Dick Schofield .05 .02 .01
☐ 234 Jose Oquendo .05 .02 .01
☐ 235 Bill Doran .05 .02 .01
☐ 236 Milt Thompson .05 .02 .01
☐ 237 Marvell Wynne .05 .02 .01
☐ 238 Bobby Bonilla .15 .07 .02
☐ 239 Chris Speier .05 .02 .01
☐ 240 Glenn Braggs .05 .02 .01
☐ 241 Wally Backman .05 .02 .01
☐ 242 Ryne Sandberg .25 .11 .03
☐ 243 Phil Bradley .05 .02 .01
☐ 244 Kelly Gruber .05 .02 .01
☐ 245 Tom Brunansky .05 .02 .01
☐ 246 Ron Oester .05 .02 .01
☐ 247 Bobby Thigpen .05 .02 .01
☐ 248 Fred Lynn .05 .02 .01
☐ 249 Paul Molitor .20 .09 .03
☐ 250 Darrell Evans .10 .05 .01
☐ 251 Gary Ward .05 .02 .01
☐ 252 Bruce Hurst .05 .02 .01
☐ 253 Bob Welch .05 .02 .01
☐ 254 Joe Carter .15 .07 .02
☐ 255 Willie Wilson .05 .02 .01
☐ 256 Mark McGwire .60 .25 .07
☐ 257 Mitch Webster .05 .02 .01
☐ 258 Brian Downing .05 .02 .01
☐ 259 Mike Stanley .10 .05 .01
☐ 260 Carlton Fisk .15 .07 .02
☐ 261 Billy Hatcher .05 .02 .01
☐ 262 Glenn Wilson .05 .02 .01
☐ 263 Ozzie Smith .25 .11 .03
☐ 264 Randy Ready .05 .02 .01
☐ 265 Kurt Stillwell .05 .02 .01
☐ 266 David Palmer .05 .02 .01
☐ 267 Mike Diaz .05 .02 .01
☐ 268 Robby Thompson .05 .02 .01
☐ 269 Andre Dawson .10 .05 .01
☐ 270 Lee Guetterman .05 .02 .01
☐ 271 Willie Upshaw .05 .02 .01
☐ 272 Randy Bush .05 .02 .01
☐ 273 Larry Sheets .05 .02 .01
☐ 274 Rob Deer .05 .02 .01
☐ 275 Kirk Gibson .10 .05 .01
☐ 276 Marty Barrett .05 .02 .01
☐ 277 Rickey Henderson .15 .07 .02
☐ 278 Pedro Guerrero .10 .05 .01
☐ 279 Brett Butler .10 .05 .01
☐ 280 Kevin Seitzer .10 .05 .01
☐ 281 Mike Davis .05 .02 .01
☐ 282 Andres Galarraga .15 .07 .02
☐ 283 Devon White .15 .07 .02
☐ 284 Pete O'Brien .05 .02 .01
☐ 285 Jerry Hairston .05 .02 .01
☐ 286 Kevin Bass .05 .02 .01
☐ 287 Carmelo Martinez .05 .02 .01
☐ 288 Juan Samuel .05 .02 .01
☐ 289 Kal Daniels .05 .02 .01
☐ 290 Albert Hall .05 .02 .01
☐ 291 Andy Van Slyke .10 .05 .01
☐ 292 Lee Smith .10 .05 .01
☐ 293 Vince Coleman .05 .02 .01
☐ 294 Tom Niedenfuer .05 .02 .01
☐ 295 Robin Yount .15 .07 .02
☐ 296 Jeff M. Robinson .05 .02 .01
☐ 297 Todd Benzinger .10 .05 .01
☐ 298 Dave Winfield .15 .07 .02
☐ 299 Mickey Hatcher .05 .02 .01
☐ 300A Checklist 248-357 .05 .02 .01
☐ 300B Checklist 240-345 .05 .02 .01
☐ 301 Bud Black .05 .02 .01
☐ 302 Jose Canseco .25 .11 .03
☐ 303 Tom Foley .05 .02 .01
☐ 304 Pete Incaviglia .05 .02 .01
☐ 305 Bob Boone .10 .05 .01
☐ 306 Bill Long .05 .02 .01
☐ 307 Willie McGee .05 .02 .01
☐ 308 Ken Caminiti .75 .35 .09
☐ 309 Darren Daulton .10 .05 .01
☐ 310 Tracy Jones .05 .02 .01
☐ 311 Greg Booker .05 .02 .01
☐ 312 Mike LaValliere .05 .02 .01
☐ 313 Chili Davis .15 .07 .02
☐ 314 Glenn Hubbard .05 .02 .01
☐ 315 Paul Noce .05 .02 .01
☐ 316 Keith Hernandez .10 .05 .01
☐ 317 Mark Langston .10 .05 .01
☐ 318 Keith Atherton .05 .02 .01
☐ 319 Tony Fernandez .05 .02 .01
☐ 320 Kent Hrbek .10 .05 .01
☐ 321 John Cerutti .05 .02 .01
☐ 322 Mike Kingery .05 .02 .01
☐ 323 Dave Magadan .05 .02 .01
☐ 324 Rafael Palmeiro .25 .11 .03
☐ 325 Jeff Dedmon .05 .02 .01
☐ 326 Barry Bonds .60 .25 .07
☐ 327 Jeffrey Leonard .05 .02 .01
☐ 328 Tim Flannery .05 .02 .01
☐ 329 Dave Concepcion .10 .05 .01
☐ 330 Mike Schmidt .20 .09 .03
☐ 331 Bill Dawley .05 .02 .01
☐ 332 Larry Andersen .05 .02 .01
☐ 333 Jack Howell .05 .02 .01
☐ 334 Ken Williams .05 .02 .01
☐ 335 Bryn Smith .05 .02 .01
☐ 336 Billy Ripken .10 .05 .01
☐ 337 Greg Brock .05 .02 .01
☐ 338 Mike Heath .05 .02 .01
☐ 339 Mike Greenwell .15 .07 .02
☐ 340 Claudell Washington .05 .02 .01
☐ 341 Jose Gonzalez .05 .02 .01
☐ 342 Mel Hall .05 .02 .01
☐ 343 Jim Eisenreich .10 .05 .01
☐ 344 Tony Bernazard .05 .02 .01
☐ 345 Tim Raines .10 .05 .01
☐ 346 Bob Brower .05 .02 .01
☐ 347 Larry Parrish .05 .02 .01
☐ 348 Thad Bosley .05 .02 .01
☐ 349 Dennis Eckersley .10 .05 .01
☐ 350 Cory Snyder .05 .02 .01
☐ 351 Rick Cerone .05 .02 .01
☐ 352 John Shelby .05 .02 .01
☐ 353 Larry Herndon .05 .02 .01
☐ 354 John Habyan .05 .02 .01
☐ 355 Chuck Crim .05 .02 .01
☐ 356 Gus Polidor .05 .02 .01
☐ 357 Ken Dayley .05 .02 .01
☐ 358 Danny Darwin .05 .02 .01
☐ 359 Lance Parrish .05 .02 .01
☐ 360 James Steels .05 .02 .01
☐ 361 Al Pedrique .05 .02 .01
☐ 362 Mike Aldrete .05 .02 .01
☐ 363 Juan Castillo .05 .02 .01
☐ 364 Len Dykstra .10 .05 .01
☐ 365 Luis Quinones .05 .02 .01
☐ 366 Jim Presley .05 .02 .01
☐ 367 Lloyd Moseby .05 .02 .01
☐ 368 Kirby Puckett .40 .18 .05
☐ 369 Eric Davis .10 .05 .01
☐ 370 Gary Redus .05 .02 .01
☐ 371 Dave Schmidt .05 .02 .01
☐ 372 Mark Clear .05 .02 .01
☐ 373 Dave Bergman .05 .02 .01
☐ 374 Charles Hudson .05 .02 .01
☐ 375 Calvin Schiraldi .05 .02 .01
☐ 376 Alex Trevino .05 .02 .01
☐ 377 Tom Candiotti .05 .02 .01
☐ 378 Steve Farr .05 .02 .01
☐ 379 Mike Gallego .05 .02 .01
☐ 380 Andy McGaffigan .05 .02 .01
☐ 381 Kirk McCaskill .05 .02 .01
☐ 382 Oddibe McDowell .05 .02 .01
☐ 383 Floyd Bannister .05 .02 .01
☐ 384 Denny Walling .05 .02 .01
☐ 385 Don Carman .05 .02 .01
☐ 386 Todd Worrell .05 .02 .01
☐ 387 Eric Show .05 .02 .01
☐ 388 Dave Parker .15 .07 .02
☐ 389 Rick Mahler .05 .02 .01
☐ 390 Mike Dunne .05 .02 .01
☐ 391 Candy Maldonado .05 .02 .01
☐ 392 Bob Dernier .05 .02 .01
☐ 393 Dave Valle .05 .02 .01
☐ 394 Ernie Whitt .05 .02 .01
☐ 395 Juan Berenguer .05 .02 .01
☐ 396 Mike Young .05 .02 .01
☐ 397 Mike Felder .05 .02 .01
☐ 398 Willie Hernandez .05 .02 .01
☐ 399 Jim Rice .15 .07 .02
☐ 400A Checklist 358-467 .05 .02 .01
☐ 400B Checklist 346-451 .05 .02 .01
☐ 401 Tommy John .10 .05 .01
☐ 402 Brian Holton .05 .02 .01
☐ 403 Carmen Castillo .05 .02 .01
☐ 404 Jamie Quirk .05 .02 .01
☐ 405 Dwayne Murphy .05 .02 .01
☐ 406 Jeff Parrett .05 .02 .01
☐ 407 Don Sutton .15 .07 .02
☐ 408 Jerry Browne .05 .02 .01
☐ 409 Jim Winn .05 .02 .01
☐ 410 Dave Smith .05 .02 .01
☐ 411 Shane Mack .05 .02 .01
☐ 412 Greg Gross .05 .02 .01
☐ 413 Nick Esasky .05 .02 .01
☐ 414 Damaso Garcia .05 .02 .01
☐ 415 Brian Fisher .05 .02 .01
☐ 416 Brian Dayett .05 .02 .01
☐ 417 Curt Ford .05 .02 .01
☐ 418 Mark Williamson .05 .02 .01
☐ 419 Bill Schroeder .05 .02 .01
☐ 420 Mike Henneman .10 .05 .01
☐ 421 John Marzano .05 .02 .01
☐ 422 Ron Kittle .05 .02 .01
☐ 423 Matt Young .05 .02 .01
☐ 424 Steve Balboni .05 .02 .01
☐ 425 Luis Polonia .15 .07 .02
☐ 426 Randy St.Claire .05 .02 .01
☐ 427 Greg Harris .05 .02 .01
☐ 428 Johnny Ray .05 .02 .01
☐ 429 Ray Searage .05 .02 .01
☐ 430 Ricky Horton .05 .02 .01
☐ 431 Gerald Young .05 .02 .01
☐ 432 Rick Schu .05 .02 .01
☐ 433 Paul O'Neill .10 .05 .01
☐ 434 Rich Gossage .15 .07 .02
☐ 435 John Cangelosi .05 .02 .01
☐ 436 Mike LaCoss .05 .02 .01
☐ 437 Gerald Perry .05 .02 .01
☐ 438 Dave Martinez .05 .02 .01
☐ 439 Darryl Strawberry .10 .05 .01
☐ 440 John Moses .05 .02 .01
☐ 441 Greg Gagne .05 .02 .01
☐ 442 Jesse Barfield .05 .02 .01
☐ 443 George Frazier .05 .02 .01
☐ 444 Garth Iorg .05 .02 .01
☐ 445 Ed Nunez .05 .02 .01
☐ 446 Rick Aguilera .10 .05 .01
☐ 447 Jerry Mumphrey .05 .02 .01
☐ 448 Rafael Ramirez .05 .02 .01
☐ 449 John Smiley .15 .07 .02
☐ 450 Atlee Hammaker .05 .02 .01
☐ 451 Lance McCullers .05 .02 .01
☐ 452 Guy Hoffman .05 .02 .01
☐ 453 Chris James .05 .02 .01
☐ 454 Terry Pendleton .10 .05 .01
☐ 455 Dave Meads .05 .02 .01
☐ 456 Bill Buckner .10 .05 .01
☐ 457 John Pawlowski .05 .02 .01
☐ 458 Bob Sebra .05 .02 .01
☐ 459 Jim Dwyer .05 .02 .01
☐ 460 Jay Aldrich .05 .02 .01
☐ 461 Frank Tanana .05 .02 .01
☐ 462 Oil Can Boyd .05 .02 .01
☐ 463 Dan Pasqua .05 .02 .01
☐ 464 Tim Crews .10 .05 .01
☐ 465 Andy Allanson .05 .02 .01
☐ 466 Bill Pecota .05 .02 .01
☐ 467 Steve Ontiveros .05 .02 .01
☐ 468 Hubie Brooks .05 .02 .01
☐ 469 Paul Kilgus .05 .02 .01
☐ 470 Dale Mohorcic .05 .02 .01
☐ 471 Dan Quisenberry .05 .02 .01
☐ 472 Dave Stewart .10 .05 .01
☐ 473 Dave Clark .05 .02 .01
☐ 474 Joel Skinner .05 .02 .01
☐ 475 Dave Anderson .05 .02 .01
☐ 476 Dan Petry .05 .02 .01
☐ 477 Carl Nichols .05 .02 .01
☐ 478 Ernest Riles .05 .02 .01
☐ 479 George Hendrick .05 .02 .01
☐ 480 John Morris .05 .02 .01
☐ 481 Manny Hernandez .05 .02 .01
☐ 482 Jeff Stone .05 .02 .01
☐ 483 Chris Brown .05 .02 .01
☐ 484 Mike Bielecki .05 .02 .01
☐ 485 Dave Dravecky .10 .05 .01
☐ 486 Rick Manning .05 .02 .01
☐ 487 Bill Almon .05 .02 .01
☐ 488 Jim Sundberg .05 .02 .01
☐ 489 Ken Phelps .05 .02 .01
☐ 490 Tom Henke .05 .02 .01
☐ 491 Dan Gladden .05 .02 .01
☐ 492 Barry Larkin .30 .14 .04
☐ 493 Fred Manrique .05 .02 .01
☐ 494 Mike Griffin .05 .02 .01
☐ 495 Mark Knudson .05 .02 .01
☐ 496 Bill Madlock .05 .02 .01
☐ 497 Tim Stoddard .05 .02 .01
☐ 498 Sam Horn .05 .02 .01
☐ 499 Tracy Woodson .05 .02 .01
☐ 500A Checklist 468-577 .05 .02 .01
☐ 500B Checklist 452-557 .05 .02 .01
☐ 501 Ken Schrom .05 .02 .01
☐ 502 Angel Salazar .05 .02 .01
☐ 503 Eric Plunk .05 .02 .01
☐ 504 Joe Hesketh .05 .02 .01
☐ 505 Greg Minton .05 .02 .01
☐ 506 Geno Petralli .05 .02 .01
☐ 507 Bob James .05 .02 .01
☐ 508 Robbie Wine .05 .02 .01
☐ 509 Jeff Calhoun .05 .02 .01
☐ 510 Steve Lake .05 .02 .01
☐ 511 Mark Grant .05 .02 .01
☐ 512 Frank Williams .05 .02 .01
☐ 513 Jeff Blauser .15 .07 .02
☐ 514 Bob Walk .05 .02 .01
☐ 515 Craig Lefferts .05 .02 .01
☐ 516 Manny Trillo .05 .02 .01
☐ 517 Jerry Reed .05 .02 .01
☐ 518 Rick Leach .05 .02 .01
☐ 519 Mark Davidson .05 .02 .01
☐ 520 Jeff Ballard .05 .02 .01
☐ 521 Dave Stapleton .05 .02 .01
☐ 522 Pat Sheridan .05 .02 .01
☐ 523 Al Nipper .05 .02 .01
☐ 524 Steve Trout .05 .02 .01
☐ 525 Jeff Hamilton .05 .02 .01
☐ 526 Tommy Hinzo .05 .02 .01
☐ 527 Lonnie Smith .05 .02 .01
☐ 528 Greg Cadaret .05 .02 .01
☐ 529 Bob McClure UER .05 .02 .01
(Rob on front)
☐ 530 Chuck Finley .10 .05 .01
☐ 531 Jeff Russell .05 .02 .01
☐ 532 Steve Lyons .05 .02 .01
☐ 533 Terry Puhl .05 .02 .01
☐ 534 Eric Nolte .05 .02 .01
☐ 535 Kent Tekulve .05 .02 .01
☐ 536 Pat Pacillo .05 .02 .01
☐ 537 Charlie Puleo .05 .02 .01
☐ 538 Tom Prince .05 .02 .01
☐ 539 Greg Maddux 1.25 .55 .16
☐ 540 Jim Lindeman .05 .02 .01
☐ 541 Pete Stanicek .05 .02 .01
☐ 542 Steve Kiefer .05 .02 .01
☐ 543A Jim Morrison ERR .15 .07 .02
(No decimal before
lifetime average)
☐ 543B Jim Morrison COR .05 .02 .01
☐ 544 Spike Owen .05 .02 .01
☐ 545 Jay Buhner .75 .35 .09
☐ 546 Mike Devereaux .15 .07 .02
☐ 547 Jerry Don Gleaton .05 .02 .01
☐ 548 Jose Rijo .05 .02 .01
☐ 549 Dennis Martinez .10 .05 .01
☐ 550 Mike Loynd .05 .02 .01
☐ 551 Darrell Miller .05 .02 .01
☐ 552 Dave LaPoint .05 .02 .01
☐ 553 John Tudor .05 .02 .01
☐ 554 Rocky Childress .05 .02 .01
☐ 555 Wally Ritchie .05 .02 .01
☐ 556 Terry McGriff .05 .02 .01
☐ 557 Dave Leiper .05 .02 .01
☐ 558 Jeff D. Robinson .05 .02 .01

☐ 559 Jose Uribe	.05	.02	.01
☐ 560 Ted Simmons	.10	.05	.01
☐ 561 Les Lancaster	.05	.02	.01
☐ 562 Keith A. Miller	.05	.02	.01
☐ 563 Harold Reynolds	.05	.02	.01
☐ 564 Gene Larkin	.05	.02	.01
☐ 565 Cecil Fielder	.15	.07	.02
☐ 566 Roy Smalley	.05	.02	.01
☐ 567 Duane Ward	.10	.05	.01
☐ 568 Bill Wilkinson	.05	.02	.01
☐ 569 Howard Johnson	.05	.02	.01
☐ 570 Frank DiPino	.05	.02	.01
☐ 571 Pete Smith	.05	.02	.01
☐ 572 Darnell Coles	.05	.02	.01
☐ 573 Don Robinson	.05	.02	.01
☐ 574 Rob Nelson UER (Career 0 RBI, but 1 RBI in '87)	.05	.02	.01
☐ 575 Dennis Rasmussen	.05	.02	.01
☐ 576 Steve Jeltz UER (Photo actually Juan Samuel; Samuel noted for one batting glove and black bat)	.05	.02	.01
☐ 577 Tom Pagnozzi	.10	.05	.01
☐ 578 Ty Gainey	.05	.02	.01
☐ 579 Gary Lucas	.05	.02	.01
☐ 580 Ron Hassey	.05	.02	.01
☐ 581 Herm Winningham	.05	.02	.01
☐ 582 Rene Gonzales	.05	.02	.01
☐ 583 Brad Komminsk	.05	.02	.01
☐ 584 Doyle Alexander	.05	.02	.01
☐ 585 Jeff Sellers	.05	.02	.01
☐ 586 Bill Gullickson	.05	.02	.01
☐ 587 Tim Belcher	.05	.02	.01
☐ 588 Doug Jones	.10	.05	.01
☐ 589 Melido Perez	.10	.05	.01
☐ 590 Rick Honeycutt	.05	.02	.01
☐ 591 Pascual Perez	.05	.02	.01
☐ 592 Curt Wilkerson	.05	.02	.01
☐ 593 Steve Howe	.05	.02	.01
☐ 594 John Davis	.05	.02	.01
☐ 595 Storm Davis	.05	.02	.01
☐ 596 Sammy Stewart	.05	.02	.01
☐ 597 Neil Allen	.05	.02	.01
☐ 598 Alejandro Pena	.05	.02	.01
☐ 599 Mark Thurmond	.05	.02	.01
☐ 600A Checklist 578-660/BC1-BC26		.05	.02
.01			
☐ 600B Checklist 558-660	.05	.02	.01
☐ 601 Jose Mesa	.30	.14	.04
☐ 602 Don August	.05	.02	.01
☐ 603 Terry Leach SP	.07	.03	.01
☐ 604 Tom Newell	.05	.02	.01
☐ 605 Randall Byers SP	.07	.03	.01
☐ 606 Jim Gott	.05	.02	.01
☐ 607 Harry Spilman	.05	.02	.01
☐ 608 John Candelaria	.05	.02	.01
☐ 609 Mike Brumley	.05	.02	.01
☐ 610 Mickey Brantley	.05	.02	.01
☐ 611 Jose Nunez SP	.07	.03	.01
☐ 612 Tom Nieto	.05	.02	.01
☐ 613 Rick Reuschel	.05	.02	.01
☐ 614 Lee Mazzilli SP	.07	.03	.01
☐ 615 Scott Lusader	.05	.02	.01
☐ 616 Bobby Meacham	.05	.02	.01
☐ 617 Kevin McReynolds SP	.07	.03	.01
☐ 618 Gene Garber	.05	.02	.01
☐ 619 Barry Lyons SP	.07	.03	.01
☐ 620 Randy Myers	.15	.07	.02
☐ 621 Donnie Moore	.05	.02	.01
☐ 622 Domingo Ramos	.05	.02	.01
☐ 623 Ed Romero	.05	.02	.01
☐ 624 Greg Myers	.05	.02	.01
☐ 625 Ripken Family (Cal Ripken Sr. Cal Ripken Jr. Billy Ripken)	.40	.18	.05
☐ 626 Pat Perry	.05	.02	.01
☐ 627 Andres Thomas SP	.07	.03	.01
☐ 628 Matt Williams SP	1.00	.45	.12
☐ 629 Dave Hengel	.05	.02	.01
☐ 630 Jeff Musselman SP	.07	.03	.01
☐ 631 Tim Laudner	.05	.02	.01
☐ 632 Bob Ojeda SP	.07	.03	.01
☐ 633 Rafael Santana	.05	.02	.01
☐ 634 Wes Gardner	.05	.02	.01
☐ 635 Roberto Kelly SP	.15	.07	.02
☐ 636 Mike Flanagan SP	.07	.03	.01
☐ 637 Jay Bell	.20	.09	.03
☐ 638 Bob Melvin	.05	.02	.01
☐ 639 Damon Berryhill UER (Bats: Swithch)	.05	.02	.01
☐ 640 David Wells SP	.15	.07	.02
☐ 641 Stan Musial PUZ	.15	.07	.02
☐ 642 Doug Sisk	.05	.02	.01
☐ 643 Keith Hughes	.05	.02	.01
☐ 644 Tom Glavine	.75	.35	.09
☐ 645 Al Newman	.05	.02	.01
☐ 646 Scott Sanderson	.05	.02	.01
☐ 647 Scott Terry	.05	.02	.01
☐ 648 Tim Teufel SP	.07	.03	.01
☐ 649 Garry Templeton SP	.07	.03	.01
☐ 650 Manny Lee SP	.07	.03	.01
☐ 651 Roger McDowell SP	.07	.03	.01
☐ 652 Mookie Wilson SP	.15	.07	.02
☐ 653 David Cone SP	.30	.14	.04
☐ 654 Ron Gant SP	.50	.23	.06
☐ 655 Joe Price SP	.07	.03	.01
☐ 656 George Bell SP	.10	.05	.01
☐ 657 Gregg Jefferies SP	.40	.18	.05
☐ 658 Todd Stottlemyre SP	.30	.14	.04
☐ 659 Geronimo Berroa SP	.40	.18	.05
☐ 660 Jerry Royster SP	.07	.03	.01

1988 Donruss Bonus MVP's

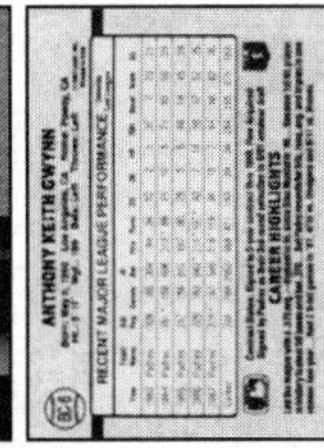

Numbered with the prefix "BC" for bonus card, this 26-card set featuring the most valuable player from each major league team was randomly inserted in the wax and rack packs. The cards are distinguished by the MVP logo in the upper left corner of the obverse, and cards BC14-BC26 are considered to be more difficult to find than cards BC1-BC13.

	MINT	NRMT	EXC
COMPLETE SET (26)	3.00	1.35	.35
COMMON CARD (BC1-BC13)	.05	.02	.01
COMMON CARD (BC14-BC26)	.10	.05	.01
☐ BC1 Cal Ripken	.50	.23	.06
☐ BC2 Eric Davis	.10	.05	.01
☐ BC3 Paul Molitor	.20	.09	.03
☐ BC4 Mike Schmidt	.25	.11	.03
☐ BC5 Ivan Calderon	.05	.02	.01
☐ BC6 Tony Gwynn	.25	.11	.03
☐ BC7 Wade Boggs	.15	.07	.02
☐ BC8 Andy Van Slyke	.10	.05	.01
☐ BC9 Joe Carter	.15	.07	.02
☐ BC10 Andre Dawson	.10	.05	.01
☐ BC11 Alan Trammell	.10	.05	.01
☐ BC12 Mike Scott	.05	.02	.01
☐ BC13 Wally Joyner	.15	.07	.02
☐ BC14 Dale Murphy SP	.15	.07	.02
☐ BC15 Kirby Puckett SP	.40	.18	.05
☐ BC16 Pedro Guerrero SP	.10	.05	.01
☐ BC17 Kevin Seitzer SP	.10	.05	.01
☐ BC18 Tim Raines SP	.10	.05	.01
☐ BC19 George Bell SP	.10	.05	.01
☐ BC20 Darryl Strawberry SP	.10	.05	.01
☐ BC21 Don Mattingly SP	.50	.23	.06
☐ BC22 Ozzie Smith SP	.30	.14	.04
☐ BC23 Mark McGwire SP	.30	.14	.04
☐ BC24 Will Clark SP	.15	.07	.02
☐ BC25 Alvin Davis SP	.10	.05	.01
☐ BC26 Ruben Sierra SP	.15	.07	.02

1988 Donruss Rookies

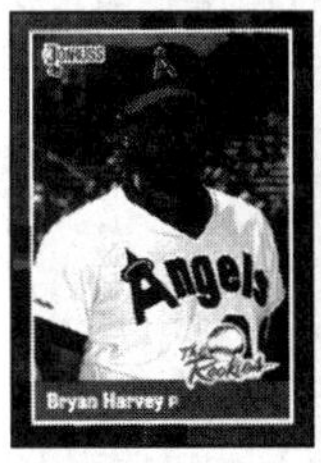

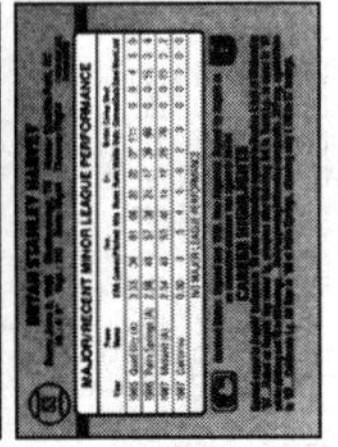

The 1988 Donruss "The Rookies" set features 56 standard-size full-color cards plus a 15-piece puzzle of Stan Musial. This set was distributed exclusively in factory set form in a small, cellophane-wrapped, green and black through hobby dealers. Card fronts are similar in design to the 1988 Donruss regular issue except for the presence of "The Rookies" logo in the lower right corner and a green and black border instead of a blue and black border on the fronts. Extended Rookie Cards in this set include Brady Anderson, Edgar Martinez, and Walt Weiss. Notable second cards were issued of Roberto Alomar and Jay Buhner.

	MINT	NRMT	EXC
COMPLETE FACT.SET (56)	15.00	6.75	1.85
COMMON CARD (1-56)	.07	.03	.01
☐ 1 Mark Grace	1.50	.70	.19
☐ 2 Mike Campbell	.07	.03	.01
☐ 3 Todd Frohwirth	.07	.03	.01
☐ 4 Dave Stapleton	.07	.03	.01
☐ 5 Shawn Abner	.07	.03	.01
☐ 6 Jose Cecena	.07	.03	.01
☐ 7 Dave Gallagher	.07	.03	.01
☐ 8 Mark Parent	.07	.03	.01
☐ 9 Cecil Espy	.07	.03	.01
☐ 10 Pete Smith	.07	.03	.01
☐ 11 Jay Buhner	2.50	1.10	.30
☐ 12 Pat Borders	.10	.05	.01
☐ 13 Doug Jennings	.07	.03	.01
☐ 14 Brady Anderson	2.50	1.10	.30
☐ 15 Pete Stanicek	.07	.03	.01
☐ 16 Roberto Kelly	.15	.07	.02
☐ 17 Jeff Treadway	.07	.03	.01
☐ 18 Walt Weiss	.15	.07	.02
☐ 19 Paul Gibson	.07	.03	.01
☐ 20 Tim Crews	.10	.05	.01
☐ 21 Melido Perez	.10	.05	.01
☐ 22 Steve Peters	.07	.03	.01
☐ 23 Craig Worthington	.07	.03	.01
☐ 24 John Trautwein	.07	.03	.01
☐ 25 DeWayne Vaughn	.07	.03	.01
☐ 26 David Wells	.10	.05	.01
☐ 27 Al Leiter	.15	.07	.02
☐ 28 Tim Belcher	.10	.05	.01
☐ 29 Johnny Paredes	.07	.03	.01
☐ 30 Chris Sabo	.10	.05	.01
☐ 31 Damon Berryhill	.07	.03	.01
☐ 32 Randy Milligan	.07	.03	.01
☐ 33 Gary Thurman	.07	.03	.01
☐ 34 Kevin Elster	.10	.05	.01
☐ 35 Roberto Alomar	5.00	2.20	.60
☐ 36 Edgar Martinez UER (Photo actually Edwin Nunez)	2.00	.90	.25
☐ 37 Todd Stottlemyre	.50	.23	.06
☐ 38 Joey Meyer	.07	.03	.01
☐ 39 Carl Nichols	.07	.03	.01
☐ 40 Jack McDowell	.75	.35	.09
☐ 41 Jose Bautista	.07	.03	.01
☐ 42 Sil Campusano	.07	.03	.01
☐ 43 John Dopson	.07	.03	.01
☐ 44 Jody Reed	.10	.05	.01
☐ 45 Darrin Jackson	.07	.03	.01
☐ 46 Mike Capel	.07	.03	.01
☐ 47 Ron Gant	1.00	.45	.12
☐ 48 John Davis	.07	.03	.01
☐ 49 Kevin Coffman	.07	.03	.01
☐ 50 Cris Carpenter	.07	.03	.01
☐ 51 Mackey Sasser	.07	.03	.01
☐ 52 Luis Alicea	.10	.05	.01
☐ 53 Bryan Harvey	.10	.05	.01
☐ 54 Steve Ellsworth	.07	.03	.01
☐ 55 Mike Macfarlane	.15	.07	.02
☐ 56 Checklist 1-56	.07	.03	.01

1988 Donruss All-Stars

This 64-card set features cards measures the standard size. Card fronts are in full color with a solid blue and black border. The card backs are printed in black and blue on white card stock. Cards are numbered on the back inside a blue star in the upper right hand corner. Card backs feature statistical information about the player's performance in past All-Star games. The set was distributed in packs which also contained a Pop-Up. The AL Checklist card number 32 has two uncorrected errors on it, Wade Boggs is erroneously listed as the AL Leftfielder and Dan Plesac is erroneously listed as being on the Tigers.

	MINT	NRMT	EXC
COMPLETE SET (64)	8.00	3.60	1.00
COMMON CARD (1-64)	.05	.02	.01
☐ 1 Don Mattingly	1.50	.70	.19
☐ 2 Dave Winfield	.20	.09	.03
☐ 3 Willie Randolph	.05	.02	.01
☐ 4 Rickey Henderson	.20	.09	.03
☐ 5 Cal Ripken	2.50	1.10	.30
☐ 6 George Bell	.05	.02	.01
☐ 7 Wade Boggs	.50	.23	.06
☐ 8 Bret Saberhagen	.10	.05	.01
☐ 9 Terry Kennedy	.05	.02	.01
☐ 10 John McNamara MG	.05	.02	.01
☐ 11 Jay Howell	.05	.02	.01
☐ 12 Harold Baines	.10	.05	.01
☐ 13 Harold Reynolds	.10	.05	.01
☐ 14 Bruce Hurst	.05	.02	.01
☐ 15 Kirby Puckett	1.25	.55	.16
☐ 16 Matt Nokes	.05	.02	.01
☐ 17 Pat Tabler	.05	.02	.01
☐ 18 Dan Plesac	.05	.02	.01
☐ 19 Mark McGwire	1.00	.45	.12
☐ 20 Mike Witt	.05	.02	.01
☐ 21 Larry Parrish	.05	.02	.01
☐ 22 Alan Trammell	.10	.05	.01
☐ 23 Dwight Evans	.10	.05	.01
☐ 24 Jack Morris	.10	.05	.01
☐ 25 Tony Fernandez	.05	.02	.01
☐ 26 Mark Langston	.10	.05	.01
☐ 27 Kevin Seitzer	.10	.05	.01
☐ 28 Tom Henke	.05	.02	.01
☐ 29 Dave Righetti	.05	.02	.01
☐ 30 Oakland Stadium	.05	.02	.01
☐ 31 Wade Boggs (Top AL Vote Getter)	.50	.23	.06
☐ 32 AL Checklist UER	.05	.02	.01
☐ 33 Jack Clark	.10	.05	.01
☐ 34 Darryl Strawberry	.10	.05	.01
☐ 35 Ryne Sandberg	.75	.35	.09
☐ 36 Andre Dawson	.10	.05	.01
☐ 37 Ozzie Smith	1.00	.45	.12
☐ 38 Eric Davis	.10	.05	.01
☐ 39 Mike Schmidt	.75	.35	.09
☐ 40 Mike Scott	.05	.02	.01
☐ 41 Gary Carter	.10	.05	.01
☐ 42 Davey Johnson MG	.05	.02	.01
☐ 43 Rick Sutcliffe	.05	.02	.01
☐ 44 Willie McGee	.05	.02	.01
☐ 45 Hubie Brooks	.05	.02	.01
☐ 46 Dale Murphy	.20	.09	.03
☐ 47 Bo Diaz	.05	.02	.01
☐ 48 Pedro Guerrero	.05	.02	.01
☐ 49 Keith Hernandez	.10	.05	.01
☐ 50 Ozzie Virgil UER (Phillies logo on card back, wrong birth year)	.05	.02	.01
☐ 51 Tony Gwynn	1.25	.55	.16
☐ 52 Rick Reuschel UER (Pirates logo on card back)	.05	.02	.01
☐ 53 John Franco	.10	.05	.01
☐ 54 Jeffrey Leonard	.05	.02	.01
☐ 55 Juan Samuel	.05	.02	.01
☐ 56 Orel Hershiser	.10	.05	.01
☐ 57 Tim Raines	.10	.05	.01
☐ 58 Sid Fernandez	.05	.02	.01
☐ 59 Tim Wallach	.05	.02	.01
☐ 60 Lee Smith	.10	.05	.01
☐ 61 Steve Bedrosian	.05	.02	.01
☐ 62 Tim Raines	.10	.05	.01
☐ 63 Ozzie Smith (Top NL Vote Getter)	1.00	.45	.12
☐ 64 NL Checklist	.05	.02	.01

1988 Donruss Baseball's Best

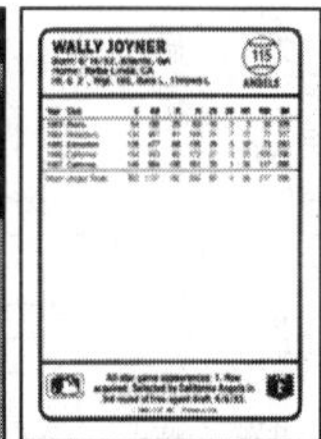

This innovative set of 336 standard-size cards was released by Donruss very late in the 1988 season to be sold in large national retail chains as a complete packaged set. The set was packaged in a specially designed box. Cards are very similar in design to the 1988 regular Donruss issue except that these cards have orange and black borders instead of blue and black borders. The set is also sometimes referred to as the Halloween set because of the orange box and design of the cards. Six (2 1/2" by 3 1/2") 15-piece puzzles of Stan Musial are also included with every complete set.

	MINT	NRMT	EXC
COMPLETE SET (336)	15.00	6.75	1.85
COMMON CARD (1-336)	.05	.02	.01
☐ 1 Don Mattingly	1.25	.55	.16
☐ 2 Ron Gant	.50	.23	.06
☐ 3 Bob Boone	.10	.05	.01
☐ 4 Mark Grace	1.50	.70	.19
☐ 5 Andy Allanson	.05	.02	.01
☐ 6 Kal Daniels	.05	.02	.01
☐ 7 Floyd Bannister	.05	.02	.01
☐ 8 Alan Ashby	.05	.02	.01
☐ 9 Marty Barrett	.05	.02	.01
☐ 10 Tim Belcher	.05	.02	.01
☐ 11 Harold Baines	.10	.05	.01
☐ 12 Hubie Brooks	.05	.02	.01
☐ 13 Doyle Alexander	.05	.02	.01
☐ 14 Gary Carter	.10	.05	.01
☐ 15 Glenn Braggs	.05	.02	.01
☐ 16 Steve Bedrosian	.05	.02	.01
☐ 17 Barry Bonds	1.00	.45	.12
☐ 18 Bert Blyleven	.10	.05	.01
☐ 19 Tom Brunansky	.05	.02	.01
☐ 20 John Candelaria	.05	.02	.01
☐ 21 Shawn Abner	.05	.02	.01
☐ 22 Jose Canseco	.25	.11	.03
☐ 23 Brett Butler	.10	.05	.01
☐ 24 Scott Bradley	.05	.02	.01
☐ 25 Ivan Calderon	.05	.02	.01
☐ 26 Rich Gossage	.10	.05	.01
☐ 27 Brian Downing	.05	.02	.01
☐ 28 Jim Rice	.10	.05	.01
☐ 29 Dion James	.05	.02	.01
☐ 30 Terry Kennedy	.05	.02	.01
☐ 31 George Bell	.05	.02	.01

☐ 32 Scott Fletcher	.05	.02	.01
☐ 33 Bobby Bonilla	.15	.07	.02
☐ 34 Tim Burke	.05	.02	.01
☐ 35 Darrell Evans	.10	.05	.01
☐ 36 Mike Davis	.05	.02	.01
☐ 37 Shawon Dunston	.05	.02	.01
☐ 38 Kevin Bass	.05	.02	.01
☐ 39 George Brett	1.25	.55	.16
☐ 40 David Cone	.25	.11	.03
☐ 41 Ron Darling	.05	.02	.01
☐ 42 Roberto Alomar	2.00	.90	.25
☐ 43 Dennis Eckersley	.10	.05	.01
☐ 44 Vince Coleman	.05	.02	.01
☐ 45 Sid Bream	.05	.02	.01
☐ 46 Gary Gaetti	.05	.02	.01
☐ 47 Phil Bradley	.05	.02	.01
☐ 48 Jim Clancy	.05	.02	.01
☐ 49 Jack Clark	.10	.05	.01
☐ 50 Mike Krukow	.05	.02	.01
☐ 51 Henry Cotto	.05	.02	.01
☐ 52 Rich Dotson	.05	.02	.01
☐ 53 Jim Gantner	.05	.02	.01
☐ 54 John Franco	.10	.05	.01
☐ 55 Pete Incaviglia	.05	.02	.01
☐ 56 Joe Carter	.25	.11	.03
☐ 57 Roger Clemens	.60	.25	.07
☐ 58 Gerald Perry	.05	.02	.01
☐ 59 Jack Howell	.05	.02	.01
☐ 60 Vance Law	.05	.02	.01
☐ 61 Jay Bell	.15	.07	.02
☐ 62 Eric Davis	.10	.05	.01
☐ 63 Gene Garber	.05	.02	.01
☐ 64 Glenn Davis	.05	.02	.01
☐ 65 Wade Boggs	.25	.11	.03
☐ 66 Kirk Gibson	.10	.05	.01
☐ 67 Carlton Fisk	.25	.11	.03
☐ 68 Casey Candaele	.05	.02	.01
☐ 69 Mike Heath	.05	.02	.01
☐ 70 Kevin Elster	.15	.07	.02
☐ 71 Greg Brock	.05	.02	.01
☐ 72 Don Carman	.05	.02	.01
☐ 73 Doug Drabek	.10	.05	.01
☐ 74 Greg Gagne	.05	.02	.01
☐ 75 Danny Cox	.05	.02	.01
☐ 76 Rickey Henderson	.25	.11	.03
☐ 77 Chris Brown	.05	.02	.01
☐ 78 Terry Steinbach	.15	.07	.02
☐ 79 Will Clark	.40	.18	.05
☐ 80 Mickey Brantley	.05	.02	.01
☐ 81 Ozzie Guillen	.10	.05	.01
☐ 82 Greg Maddux	2.50	1.10	.30
☐ 83 Kirk McCaskill	.05	.02	.01
☐ 84 Dwight Evans	.10	.05	.01
☐ 85 Ozzie Virgil	.05	.02	.01
☐ 86 Mike Morgan	.05	.02	.01
☐ 87 Tony Fernandez	.05	.02	.01
☐ 88 Jose Guzman	.05	.02	.01
☐ 89 Mike Dunne	.05	.02	.01
☐ 90 Andres Galarraga	.25	.11	.03
☐ 91 Mike Henneman	.10	.05	.01
☐ 92 Alfredo Griffin	.05	.02	.01
☐ 93 Rafael Palmeiro	.40	.18	.05
☐ 94 Jim Deshaies	.05	.02	.01
☐ 95 Mark Gubicza	.05	.02	.01
☐ 96 Dwight Gooden	.10	.05	.01
☐ 97 Howard Johnson	.05	.02	.01
☐ 98 Mark Davis	.05	.02	.01
☐ 99 Dave Stewart	.10	.05	.01
☐ 100 Joe Magrane	.05	.02	.01
☐ 101 Brian Fisher	.05	.02	.01
☐ 102 Kent Hrbek	.10	.05	.01
☐ 103 Kevin Gross	.05	.02	.01
☐ 104 Tom Henke	.05	.02	.01
☐ 105 Mike Pagliarulo	.05	.02	.01
☐ 106 Kelly Downs	.05	.02	.01
☐ 107 Alvin Davis	.05	.02	.01
☐ 108 Willie Randolph	.05	.02	.01
☐ 109 Rob Deer	.05	.02	.01
☐ 110 Bo Diaz	.05	.02	.01
☐ 111 Paul Kilgus	.05	.02	.01
☐ 112 Tom Candiotti	.05	.02	.01
☐ 113 Dale Murphy	.15	.07	.02
☐ 114 Rick Mahler	.05	.02	.01
☐ 115 Wally Joyner	.15	.07	.02
☐ 116 Ryne Sandberg	1.00	.45	.12
☐ 117 John Farrell	.05	.02	.01
☐ 118 Nick Esasky	.05	.02	.01
☐ 119 Bo Jackson	.15	.07	.02
☐ 120 Bill Doran	.05	.02	.01
☐ 121 Ellis Burks	.40	.18	.05
☐ 122 Pedro Guerrero	.05	.02	.01
☐ 123 Dave LaPoint	.05	.02	.01
☐ 124 Neal Heaton	.05	.02	.01
☐ 125 Willie Hernandez	.05	.02	.01
☐ 126 Roger McDowell	.05	.02	.01
☐ 127 Ted Higuera	.05	.02	.01
☐ 128 Von Hayes	.05	.02	.01
☐ 129 Mike LaValliere	.05	.02	.01
☐ 130 Dan Gladden	.05	.02	.01
☐ 131 Willie McGee	.05	.02	.01
☐ 132 Al Leiter	.15	.07	.02
☐ 133 Mark Grant	.05	.02	.01
☐ 134 Bob Welch	.05	.02	.01
☐ 135 Dave Dravecky	.05	.02	.01
☐ 136 Mark Langston	.10	.05	.01
☐ 137 Dan Pasqua	.05	.02	.01
☐ 138 Rick Sutcliffe	.10	.05	.01
☐ 139 Dan Petry	.05	.02	.01
☐ 140 Rich Gedman	.05	.02	.01
☐ 141 Ken Griffey Sr.	.05	.02	.01
☐ 142 Eddie Murray	.50	.23	.06
☐ 143 Jimmy Key	.10	.05	.01
☐ 144 Dale Mohorcic	.05	.02	.01
☐ 145 Jose Lind	.05	.02	.01
☐ 146 Dennis Martinez	.10	.05	.01
☐ 147 Chet Lemon	.05	.02	.01
☐ 148 Orel Hershiser	.10	.05	.01
☐ 149 Dave Martinez	.05	.02	.01
☐ 150 Billy Hatcher	.05	.02	.01
☐ 151 Charlie Leibrandt	.05	.02	.01
☐ 152 Keith Hernandez	.10	.05	.01
☐ 153 Kevin McReynolds	.05	.02	.01
☐ 154 Tony Gwynn	1.25	.55	.16
☐ 155 Stan Javier	.05	.02	.01
☐ 156 Tony Pena	.05	.02	.01
☐ 157 Andy Van Slyke	.10	.05	.01
☐ 158 Gene Larkin	.05	.02	.01
☐ 159 Chris James	.05	.02	.01
☐ 160 Fred McGriff	.25	.11	.03
☐ 161 Rick Rhoden	.05	.02	.01
☐ 162 Scott Garrelts	.05	.02	.01
☐ 163 Mike Campbell	.05	.02	.01
☐ 164 Dave Righetti	.05	.02	.01
☐ 165 Paul Molitor	.40	.18	.05
☐ 166 Danny Jackson	.05	.02	.01
☐ 167 Pete O'Brien	.05	.02	.01
☐ 168 Julio Franco	.10	.05	.01
☐ 169 Mark McGwire	1.25	.55	.16
☐ 170 Zane Smith	.05	.02	.01
☐ 171 Johnny Ray	.05	.02	.01
☐ 172 Les Lancaster	.05	.02	.01
☐ 173 Mel Hall	.05	.02	.01
☐ 174 Tracy Jones	.05	.02	.01
☐ 175 Kevin Seitzer	.10	.05	.01
☐ 176 Bob Knepper	.05	.02	.01
☐ 177 Mike Greenwell	.10	.05	.01
☐ 178 Mike Marshall	.05	.02	.01
☐ 179 Melido Perez	.05	.02	.01
☐ 180 Tim Raines	.10	.05	.01
☐ 181 Jack Morris	.10	.05	.01
☐ 182 Darryl Strawberry	.10	.05	.01
☐ 183 Robin Yount	.25	.11	.03
☐ 184 Lance Parrish	.05	.02	.01
☐ 185 Darnell Coles	.05	.02	.01
☐ 186 Kirby Puckett	1.00	.45	.12
☐ 187 Terry Pendleton	.10	.05	.01
☐ 188 Don Slaught	.05	.02	.01
☐ 189 Jimmy Jones	.05	.02	.01
☐ 190 Dave Parker	.10	.05	.01
☐ 191 Mike Aldrete	.05	.02	.01
☐ 192 Mike Moore	.05	.02	.01
☐ 193 Greg Walker	.05	.02	.01
☐ 194 Calvin Schiraldi	.05	.02	.01
☐ 195 Dick Schofield	.05	.02	.01
☐ 196 Jody Reed	.10	.05	.01
☐ 197 Pete Smith	.05	.02	.01
☐ 198 Cal Ripken	2.50	1.10	.30
☐ 199 Lloyd Moseby	.05	.02	.01
☐ 200 Ruben Sierra	.15	.07	.02
☐ 201 R.J. Reynolds	.05	.02	.01
☐ 202 Bryn Smith	.05	.02	.01
☐ 203 Gary Pettis	.05	.02	.01
☐ 204 Steve Sax	.05	.02	.01
☐ 205 Frank DiPino	.05	.02	.01
☐ 206 Mike Scott UER (1977 Jackson losses say 1.10, should be 1)	.05	.02	.01
☐ 207 Kurt Stillwell	.05	.02	.01
☐ 208 Mookie Wilson	.10	.05	.01
☐ 209 Lee Mazzilli	.05	.02	.01
☐ 210 Lance McCullers	.05	.02	.01
☐ 211 Rick Honeycutt	.05	.02	.01
☐ 212 John Tudor	.05	.02	.01
☐ 213 Jim Gott	.05	.02	.01
☐ 214 Frank Viola	.05	.02	.01
☐ 215 Juan Samuel	.05	.02	.01
☐ 216 Jesse Barfield	.05	.02	.01
☐ 217 Claudell Washington	.05	.02	.01
☐ 218 Rick Reuschel	.05	.02	.01
☐ 219 Jim Presley	.05	.02	.01
☐ 220 Tommy John	.10	.05	.01
☐ 221 Dan Plesac	.05	.02	.01
☐ 222 Barry Larkin	.40	.18	.05
☐ 223 Mike Stanley	.05	.02	.01
☐ 224 Cory Snyder	.05	.02	.01
☐ 225 Andre Dawson	.10	.05	.01
☐ 226 Ken Oberkfell	.05	.02	.01
☐ 227 Devon White	.15	.07	.02
☐ 228 Jamie Moyer	.05	.02	.01
☐ 229 Brook Jacoby	.05	.02	.01
☐ 230 Rob Murphy	.05	.02	.01
☐ 231 Bret Saberhagen	.10	.05	.01
☐ 232 Nolan Ryan	2.00	.90	.25
☐ 233 Bruce Hurst	.05	.02	.01
☐ 234 Jesse Orosco	.05	.02	.01
☐ 235 Bobby Thigpen	.05	.02	.01
☐ 236 Pascual Perez	.05	.02	.01
☐ 237 Matt Nokes	.05	.02	.01
☐ 238 Bob Ojeda	.05	.02	.01
☐ 239 Joey Meyer	.05	.02	.01
☐ 240 Shane Rawley	.05	.02	.01
☐ 241 Jeff Robinson	.05	.02	.01
☐ 242 Jeff Reardon	.05	.02	.01
☐ 243 Ozzie Smith	.75	.35	.09
☐ 244 Dave Winfield	.25	.11	.03
☐ 245 John Kruk	.20	.09	.03
☐ 246 Carney Lansford	.10	.05	.01
☐ 247 Candy Maldonado	.05	.02	.01
☐ 248 Ken Phelps	.05	.02	.01
☐ 249 Ken Williams	.05	.02	.01
☐ 250 Al Nipper	.05	.02	.01
☐ 251 Mark McLemore	.05	.02	.01
☐ 252 Lee Smith	.10	.05	.01
☐ 253 Albert Hall	.05	.02	.01
☐ 254 Billy Ripken	.05	.02	.01
☐ 255 Kelly Gruber	.05	.02	.01
☐ 256 Charlie Hough	.05	.02	.01
☐ 257 John Smiley	.10	.05	.01
☐ 258 Tim Wallach	.05	.02	.01
☐ 259 Frank Tanana	.05	.02	.01
☐ 260 Mike Scioscia	.05	.02	.01
☐ 261 Damon Berryhill	.05	.02	.01
☐ 262 Dave Smith	.05	.02	.01
☐ 263 Willie Wilson	.05	.02	.01
☐ 264 Len Dykstra	.10	.05	.01
☐ 265 Randy Myers	.10	.05	.01
☐ 266 Keith Moreland	.05	.02	.01
☐ 267 Eric Plunk	.05	.02	.01
☐ 268 Todd Worrell	.05	.02	.01
☐ 269 Bob Walk	.05	.02	.01
☐ 270 Keith Atherton	.05	.02	.01
☐ 271 Mike Schmidt	.50	.23	.06
☐ 272 Mike Flanagan	.05	.02	.01
☐ 273 Rafael Santana	.05	.02	.01
☐ 274 Robby Thompson	.05	.02	.01
☐ 275 Rey Quinones	.05	.02	.01
☐ 276 Cecilio Guante	.05	.02	.01
☐ 277 B.J. Surhoff	.15	.07	.02
☐ 278 Chris Sabo	.10	.05	.01
☐ 279 Mitch Williams	.05	.02	.01
☐ 280 Greg Swindell	.05	.02	.01
☐ 281 Alan Trammell	.10	.05	.01
☐ 282 Storm Davis	.05	.02	.01
☐ 283 Chuck Finley	.10	.05	.01
☐ 284 Dave Stieb	.05	.02	.01
☐ 285 Scott Bailes	.05	.02	.01
☐ 286 Larry Sheets	.05	.02	.01
☐ 287 Danny Tartabull	.05	.02	.01
☐ 288 Checklist Card	.05	.02	.01
☐ 289 Todd Benzinger	.05	.02	.01
☐ 290 John Shelby	.05	.02	.01
☐ 291 Steve Lyons	.05	.02	.01
☐ 292 Mitch Webster	.05	.02	.01
☐ 293 Walt Terrell	.05	.02	.01
☐ 294 Pete Stanicek	.05	.02	.01
☐ 295 Chris Bosio	.05	.02	.01
☐ 296 Milt Thompson	.05	.02	.01
☐ 297 Fred Lynn	.05	.02	.01
☐ 298 Juan Berenguer	.05	.02	.01
☐ 299 Ken Dayley	.05	.02	.01
☐ 300 Joel Skinner	.05	.02	.01
☐ 301 Benito Santiago	.05	.02	.01
☐ 302 Ron Hassey	.05	.02	.01
☐ 303 Jose Uribe	.05	.02	.01
☐ 304 Harold Reynolds	.10	.05	.01
☐ 305 Dale Sveum	.05	.02	.01
☐ 306 Glenn Wilson	.05	.02	.01
☐ 307 Mike Witt	.05	.02	.01
☐ 308 Ron Robinson	.05	.02	.01
☐ 309 Denny Walling	.05	.02	.01
☐ 310 Joe Orsulak	.05	.02	.01
☐ 311 David Wells	.05	.02	.01
☐ 312 Steve Buechele	.05	.02	.01
☐ 313 Jose Oquendo	.05	.02	.01
☐ 314 Floyd Youmans	.05	.02	.01
☐ 315 Lou Whitaker	.10	.05	.01
☐ 316 Fernando Valenzuela	.10	.05	.01
☐ 317 Mike Boddicker	.05	.02	.01
☐ 318 Gerald Young	.05	.02	.01
☐ 319 Frank White	.10	.05	.01
☐ 320 Bill Wegman	.05	.02	.01
☐ 321 Tom Niedenfuer	.05	.02	.01
☐ 322 Ed Whitson	.05	.02	.01
☐ 323 Curt Young	.05	.02	.01
☐ 324 Greg Mathews	.05	.02	.01
☐ 325 Doug Jones	.10	.05	.01
☐ 326 Tommy Herr	.05	.02	.01
☐ 327 Kent Tekulve	.05	.02	.01
☐ 328 Rance Mulliniks	.05	.02	.01
☐ 329 Checklist Card	.05	.02	.01
☐ 330 Craig Lefferts	.05	.02	.01
☐ 331 Franklin Stubbs	.05	.02	.01
☐ 332 Rick Cerone	.05	.02	.01
☐ 333 Dave Schmidt	.05	.02	.01
☐ 334 Larry Parrish	.05	.02	.01
☐ 335 Tom Browning	.05	.02	.01
☐ 336 Checklist Card	.05	.02	.01

1988 Donruss Pop-Ups

This 20-card set features "fold-out" cards measures the standard size. Card fronts are in full color. Cards are unnumbered but are listed in the same order as the Donruss All-Stars on the All-Star checklist card. Card backs present essentially no information about the player. The set was distributed in packs which also contained All-Star cards. In order to remain in mint condition, the cards should not be popped up.

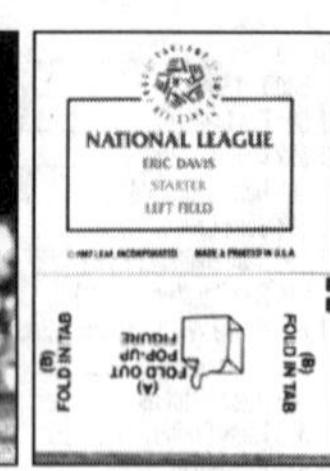

	MINT	NRMT	EXC
COMPLETE SET (20)	5.00	2.20	.60
COMMON CARD (1-20)	.05	.02	.01
☐ 1 Don Mattingly	1.50	.70	.19
☐ 2 Dave Winfield	.50	.23	.06
☐ 3 Willie Randolph	.10	.05	.01
☐ 4 Rickey Henderson	.50	.23	.06
☐ 5 Cal Ripken	2.50	1.10	.30
☐ 6 George Bell	.05	.02	.01
☐ 7 Wade Boggs	.50	.23	.06
☐ 8 Bret Saberhagen	.10	.05	.01
☐ 9 Terry Kennedy	.05	.02	.01
☐ 10 John McNamara MG	.05	.02	.01
☐ 11 Jack Clark	.10	.05	.01
☐ 12 Darryl Strawberry	.10	.05	.01
☐ 13 Ryne Sandberg	.75	.35	.09
☐ 14 Andre Dawson	.10	.05	.01
☐ 15 Ozzie Smith	1.00	.45	.12
☐ 16 Eric Davis	.10	.05	.01
☐ 17 Mike Schmidt	.75	.35	.09
☐ 18 Mike Scott	.05	.02	.01
☐ 19 Gary Carter	.10	.05	.01
☐ 20 Davey Johnson MG	.05	.02	.01

1988 Donruss Super DK's

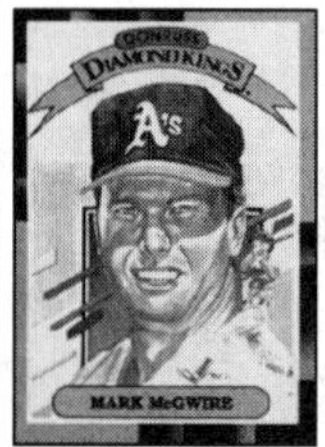

This 26-player card set was available through a mail-in offer detailed on the wax packs. The set was sent in return for 8.00 and three wrappers plus 1.50 postage and handling. The set features the popular Diamond King subseries in large (approximately 4 7/8" by 6 13/16") form. Dick Perez of Perez-Steele Galleries did another outstanding job on the artwork. The cards are essentially a large version of the Donruss regular issue Diamond Kings.

	MINT	NRMT	EXC
COMPLETE SET (26)	12.00	5.50	1.50
COMMON CARD (1-26)	.50	.23	.06
☐ 1 Mark McGwire	2.00	.90	.25
☐ 2 Tim Raines	.75	.35	.09
☐ 3 Benito Santiago	.75	.35	.09
☐ 4 Alan Trammell	.75	.35	.09
☐ 5 Danny Tartabull	.50	.23	.06
☐ 6 Ron Darling	.50	.23	.06
☐ 7 Paul Molitor	1.50	.70	.19
☐ 8 Devon White	1.00	.45	.12
☐ 9 Andre Dawson	.75	.35	.09
☐ 10 Julio Franco	.75	.35	.09
☐ 11 Scott Fletcher	.50	.23	.06
☐ 12 Tony Fernandez	.50	.23	.06
☐ 13 Shane Rawley	.50	.23	.06
☐ 14 Kal Daniels	.50	.23	.06
☐ 15 Jack Clark	.75	.35	.09
☐ 16 Dwight Evans	.75	.35	.09
☐ 17 Tommy John	.75	.35	.09
☐ 18 Andy Van Slyke	.75	.35	.09
☐ 19 Gary Gaetti	.50	.23	.06
☐ 20 Mark Langston	.75	.35	.09
☐ 21 Will Clark	1.50	.70	.19
☐ 22 Glenn Hubbard	.50	.23	.06
☐ 23 Billy Hatcher	.50	.23	.06
☐ 24 Bob Welch	.50	.23	.06
☐ 25 Ivan Calderon	.50	.23	.06
☐ 26 Cal Ripken	5.00	2.20	.60

1988 Donruss Team Book Athletics

The 1988 Donruss Athletics Team Book set features 27 cards (three pages with nine cards on each page) plus a large full-page puzzle of Stan Musial. Cards are in full color and are standard size. The set was distributed as a four-page book; although the puzzle page was perforated, the card pages were not. The cover of the "Team Collection" book is primarily bright red. Card fronts are very similar in design to the 1988 Donruss regular issue. The card numbers on the backs are the same for those players that are the same as in the regular Donruss set; the new players pictured are numbered on the

back as "NEW." In fact 1988 A.L. Rookie of the Year Walt Weiss makes his first Donruss appearance in this set as a "NEW" card. The book is usually sold intact. When cut from the book into individual cards, these cards are distinguishable from the regular 1988 Donruss cards since these have a 1988 copyright on the back whereas the regular issue has a 1987 copyright on the back.

	MINT	NRMT	EXC
COMPLETE SET (27)	4.00	1.80	.50
COMMON CARD	.10	.05	.01
☐ 97 Curt Young	.10	.05	.01
☐ 133 Gene Nelson	.10	.05	.01
☐ 158 Terry Steinbach	.40	.18	.05
☐ 178 Carney Lansford	.25	.11	.03
☐ 221 Tony Phillips	.25	.11	.03
☐ 256 Mark McGwire	1.25	.55	.16
☐ 302 Jose Canseco	1.00	.45	.12
☐ 349 Dennis Eckersley	.25	.11	.03
☐ 379 Mike Gallego	.10	.05	.01
☐ 425 Luis Polonia	.25	.11	.03
☐ 467 Steve Ontiveros	.10	.05	.01
☐ 472 Dave Stewart	.25	.11	.03
☐ 503 Eric Plunk	.10	.05	.01
☐ 528 Greg Cadaret	.10	.05	.01
☐ 590 Rick Honeycutt	.10	.05	.01
☐ 595 Storm Davis	.10	.05	.01
☐ NEW Don Baylor UER (Career stats are incorrect)	.25	.11	.03
☐ NEW Ron Hassey	.10	.05	.01
☐ NEW Dave Henderson	.25	.11	.03
☐ NEW Glenn Hubbard	.10	.05	.01
☐ NEW Stan Javier	.10	.05	.01
☐ NEW Doug Jennings	.10	.05	.01
☐ NEW Ed Jurak	.10	.05	.01
☐ NEW Dave Parker	.25	.11	.03
☐ NEW Walt Weiss	.40	.18	.05
☐ NEW Bob Welch	.10	.05	.01
☐ NEW Matt Young	.10	.05	.01

1988 Donruss Team Book Cubs

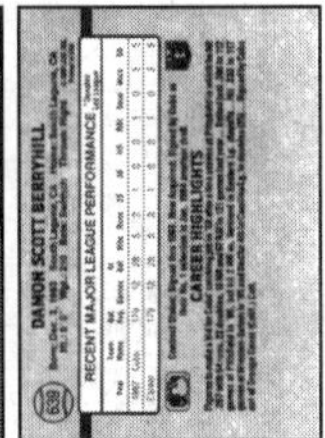

The 1988 Donruss Cubs Team Book set features 27 cards (three pages with nine cards on each page) plus a large full-page puzzle of Stan Musial. Cards are in full color and are standard size. The set was distributed as a four-page book; although the puzzle page was perforated, the card pages were not. The cover of the "Team Collection" book is primarily bright red. Card fronts are very similar in design to the 1988 Donruss regular issue. The card numbers on the backs are the same for those players that are the same as in the regular Donruss set; the new players pictured are numbered on the back as "NEW." The book is usually sold intact. When cut from the book into individual cards, these cards are distinguishable from the regular 1988 Donruss cards since these have a 1988 copyright on the back whereas the regular issue has a 1987 copyright on the back.

	MINT	NRMT	EXC
COMPLETE SET (27)	6.00	2.70	.75
COMMON CARD	.10	.05	.01
☐ 40 Mark Grace RR	2.00	.90	.25
☐ 68 Rick Sutcliffe	.10	.05	.01
☐ 119 Jody Davis	.10	.05	.01
☐ 146 Shawon Dunston	.25	.11	.03
☐ 169 Jamie Moyer	.10	.05	.01
☐ 191 Leon Durham	.10	.05	.01
☐ 242 Ryne Sandberg	1.00	.45	.12
☐ 269 Andre Dawson	.25	.11	.03
☐ 315 Paul Noce	.10	.05	.01
☐ 324 Rafael Palmeiro	1.00	.45	.12
☐ 438 Dave Martinez	.10	.05	.01
☐ 447 Jerry Mumphrey	.10	.05	.01
☐ 488 Jim Sundberg	.25	.11	.03
☐ 516 Manny Trillo	.10	.05	.01
☐ 539 Greg Maddux	4.00	1.80	.50
☐ 561 Les Lancaster	.10	.05	.01
☐ 570 Frank DiPino	.10	.05	.01
☐ 639 Damon Berryhill	.10	.05	.01
☐ 646 Scott Sanderson	.10	.05	.01
☐ NEW Mike Bielecki	.10	.05	.01
☐ NEW Rich Gossage	.25	.11	.03
☐ NEW Drew Hall	.10	.05	.01
☐ NEW Darrin Jackson	.10	.05	.01
☐ NEW Vance Law	.10	.05	.01
☐ NEW Al Nipper	.10	.05	.01
☐ NEW Angel Salazar	.10	.05	.01
☐ NEW Calvin Schiraldi	.10	.05	.01

1988 Donruss Team Book Mets

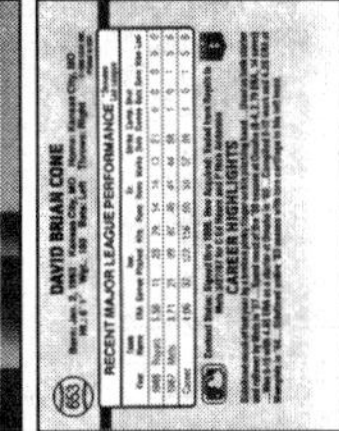

The 1988 Donruss Mets Team Book set features 27 cards (three pages with nine cards on each page) plus a large full-page puzzle of Stan Musial. Cards are in full color and are standard size. The set was distributed as a four-page book; although the puzzle page was perforated, the card pages were not. The cover of the "Team Collection" book is primarily bright red. Card fronts are very similar in design to the 1988 Donruss regular issue. The card numbers on the backs are the same for those players that are the same as in the regular Donruss set; the new players pictured are numbered on the back as "NEW." The book is usually sold intact. When cut from the book into individual cards, these cards are distinguishable from the regular 1988 Donruss cards since these have a 1988 copyright on the back whereas the regular issue has a 1987 copyright on the back.

	MINT	NRMT	EXC
COMPLETE SET (27)	3.00	1.35	.35
COMMON CARD	.10	.05	.01
☐ 37 Kevin Elster RR	.50	.23	.06
☐ 69 Dwight Gooden	.25	.11	.03
☐ 76 Ron Darling	.10	.05	.01
☐ 118 Sid Fernandez	.10	.05	.01
☐ 199 Gary Carter	.25	.11	.03
☐ 241 Wally Backman	.10	.05	.01
☐ 316 Keith Hernandez	.25	.11	.03
☐ 323 Dave Magadan	.10	.05	.01
☐ 364 Len Dykstra	.25	.11	.03
☐ 439 Darryl Strawberry	.25	.11	.03
☐ 446 Rick Aguilera	.25	.11	.03
☐ 562 Keith Miller	.10	.05	.01
☐ 569 Howard Johnson	.25	.11	.03
☐ 603 Terry Leach	.10	.05	.01
☐ 614 Lee Mazzilli	.10	.05	.01
☐ 617 Kevin McReynolds	.10	.05	.01
☐ 619 Barry Lyons	.10	.05	.01
☐ 620 Randy Myers	.25	.11	.03
☐ 632 Bob Ojeda	.10	.05	.01
☐ 648 Tim Teufel	.10	.05	.01
☐ 651 Roger McDowell	.10	.05	.01
☐ 652 Mookie Wilson	.25	.11	.03
☐ 653 David Cone	.75	.35	.09
☐ 657 Gregg Jefferies	.75	.35	.09
☐ NEW Jeff Innis	.10	.05	.01
☐ NEW Mackey Sasser	.10	.05	.01
☐ NEW Gene Walter	.10	.05	.01

1988 Donruss Team Book Red Sox

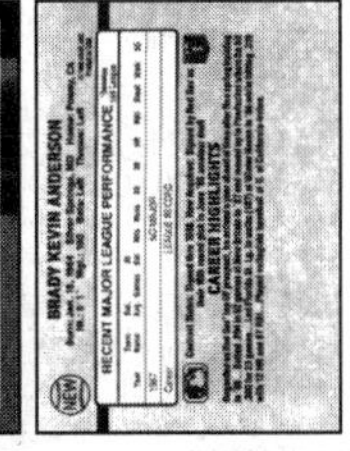

The 1988 Donruss Red Sox Team Book set features 27 cards (three pages with nine cards on each page) plus a large full-page puzzle of Stan Musial. Cards are in full color and are standard size. The set was distributed as a four-page book; although the puzzle page was perforated, the card pages were not. The cover of the "Team Collection" book is primarily bright red. Card fronts are very similar in design to the 1988 Donruss regular issue. The card numbers on the backs are the same for those players that are the same as in the regular Donruss set; the new players pictured are numbered on the back as "NEW." The book is usually sold intact. When cut from the book into individual cards, these cards are distinguishable from the regular 1988 Donruss cards since these have a 1988 copyright on the back whereas the regular issue has a 1987 copyright on the back.

	MINT	NRMT	EXC
COMPLETE SET (27)	4.00	1.80	.50
COMMON CARD	.10	.05	.01
☐ 41 Jody Reed RR	.25	.11	.03
☐ 51 Roger Clemens	1.00	.45	.12
☐ 92 Bob Stanley	.10	.05	.01
☐ 129 Rich Gedman	.10	.05	.01
☐ 153 Wade Boggs	.75	.35	.09
☐ 174 Ellis Burks	1.00	.45	.12
☐ 216 Dwight Evans	.25	.11	.03
☐ 252 Bruce Hurst	.10	.05	.01
☐ 276 Marty Barrett	.10	.05	.01
☐ 297 Todd Benzinger	.10	.05	.01
☐ 339 Mike Greenwell	.25	.11	.03
☐ 399 Jim Rice	.25	.11	.03
☐ 421 John Marzano	.10	.05	.01
☐ 462 Oil Can Boyd	.10	.05	.01
☐ 498 Sam Horn	.10	.05	.01
☐ 544 Spike Owen	.10	.05	.01
☐ 585 Jeff Sellers	.10	.05	.01
☐ 623 Ed Romero	.10	.05	.01
☐ 634 Wes Gardner	.10	.05	.01
☐ NEW Brady Anderson	2.00	.90	.25
☐ NEW Rick Cerone	.10	.05	.01
☐ NEW Steve Ellsworth	.10	.05	.01
☐ NEW Dennis Lamp	.10	.05	.01
☐ NEW Kevin Romine	.10	.05	.01
☐ NEW Lee Smith	.50	.23	.06
☐ NEW Mike Smithson	.10	.05	.01
☐ NEW John Trautwein	.10	.05	.01

1988 Donruss Team Book Yankees

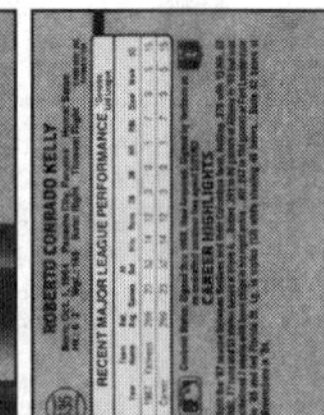

The 1988 Donruss Yankees Team Book set features 27 cards (three pages with nine cards on each page) plus a large full-page puzzle of Stan Musial. Cards are in full color and are standard size. The set was distributed as a four-page book; although the puzzle page was perforated, the card pages were not. The cover of the "Team Collection" book is primarily bright red. Card fronts are very similar in design to the 1988 Donruss regular issue. The card numbers on the backs are the same for those players that are the same as in the regular Donruss set; the new players pictured are numbered on the back as "NEW." The book is usually sold intact. When cut from the book into individual cards, these cards are distinguishable from the regular 1988 Donruss cards since these have a 1988 copyright on the back whereas the regular issue has a 1987 copyright on the back.

	MINT	NRMT	EXC
COMPLETE SET (27)	4.00	1.80	.50
COMMON CARD	.10	.05	.01
☐ 43 Al Leiter RR	.50	.23	.06
☐ 93 Dave Righetti	.10	.05	.01
☐ 105 Mike Pagliarulo	.10	.05	.01
☐ 128 Rick Rhoden	.10	.05	.01
☐ 175 Ron Guidry	.25	.11	.03
☐ 217 Don Mattingly	2.00	.90	.25
☐ 228 Willie Randolph	.25	.11	.03
☐ 251 Gary Ward	.10	.05	.01
☐ 277 Rickey Henderson	.75	.35	.09
☐ 278 Dave Winfield	.75	.35	.09
☐ 340 Claudell Washington	.10	.05	.01
☐ 374 Charles Hudson	.10	.05	.01
☐ 401 Tommy John	.25	.11	.03
☐ 474 Joel Skinner	.10	.05	.01
☐ 497 Tim Stoddard	.10	.05	.01
☐ 545 Jay Buhner	2.00	.90	.25
☐ 616 Bobby Meacham	.10	.05	.01
☐ 635 Roberto Kelly	.25	.11	.03
☐ NEW John Candelaria	.10	.05	.01
☐ NEW Jack Clark	.10	.05	.01
☐ NEW Jose Cruz	.10	.05	.01
☐ NEW Richard Dotson	.10	.05	.01
☐ NEW Cecilio Guante	.10	.05	.01
☐ NEW Lee Guetterman	.10	.05	.01
☐ NEW Rafael Santana	.10	.05	.01
☐ NEW Steve Shields	.10	.05	.01
☐ NEW Don Slaught	.10	.05	.01

1989 Donruss

This set consists of 660 standard-size cards. The cards were primarily issued 15-card wax packs, rack packs and hobby and retail factory sets. Each wax pack also contained a puzzle panel (featuring Warren Spahn this year). The cards feature a distinctive black side border with an alternating coating. Subsets include Diamond Kings (1-27) and Rated Rookies (28-47). There are two variations that occur throughout most of the set. On the card backs "Denotes Led League" can be found with one asterisk to the left or with an asterisk on each side. On the card fronts the horizontal lines on the left and right

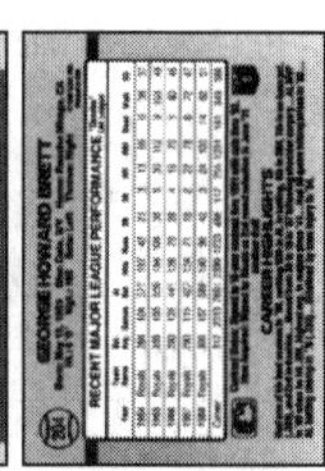

borders can be glossy or non-glossy. Since both of these variation types are relatively minor and seem equally common, there is no premium value for either type. Rather than short-printing 26 cards in order to make room for printing the Bonus MVP's this year, Donruss apparently chose to double print 106 cards. These double prints are listed below by DP. Numbered with the prefix "BC" for bonus card, the 26-card set featuring the most valuable player from each of the 26 teams was randomly inserted in the wax and rack packs. These cards are distinguished by the bold MVP logo in the upper background of the obverse. Rookie Cards in this set include Sandy Alomar Jr., Brady Anderson, Dante Bichette, Craig Biggio, Ken Griffey Jr., Ken Hill, Randy Johnson, Ramon Martinez, Hal Morris, Gary Sheffield, and John Smoltz.

	MINT	NRMT	EXC
COMPLETE SET (660)	10.00	4.50	1.25
COMPLETE FACT.SET (672)	12.00	5.50	1.50
COMMON CARD (1-660)	.05	.02	.01
☐ 1 Mike Greenwell DK	.05	.02	.01
☐ 2 Bobby Bonilla DK DP	.15	.07	.02
☐ 3 Pete Incaviglia DK	.05	.02	.01
☐ 4 Chris Sabo DK DP	.05	.02	.01
☐ 5 Robin Yount DK	.15	.07	.02
☐ 6 Tony Gwynn DK DP	.15	.07	.02
☐ 7 Carlton Fisk DK UER (OF on back)	.15	.07	.02
☐ 8 Cory Snyder DK	.05	.02	.01
☐ 9 David Cone DK UER ("hurdlers")	.15	.07	.02
☐ 10 Kevin Seitzer DK	.05	.02	.01
☐ 11 Rick Reuschel DK	.05	.02	.01
☐ 12 Johnny Ray DK	.05	.02	.01
☐ 13 Dave Schmidt DK	.05	.02	.01
☐ 14 Andres Galarraga DK	.15	.07	.02
☐ 15 Kirk Gibson DK	.15	.07	.02
☐ 16 Fred McGriff DK	.15	.07	.02
☐ 17 Mark Grace DK	.15	.07	.02
☐ 18 Jeff M. Robinson DK	.05	.02	.01
☐ 19 Vince Coleman DK DP	.05	.02	.01
☐ 20 Dave Henderson DK	.05	.02	.01
☐ 21 Harold Reynolds DK	.05	.02	.01
☐ 22 Gerald Perry DK	.05	.02	.01
☐ 23 Frank Viola DK	.05	.02	.01
☐ 24 Steve Bedrosian DK	.05	.02	.01
☐ 25 Glenn Davis DK	.05	.02	.01
☐ 26 Don Mattingly DK UER (Doesn't mention Don's previous DK in 1985)	.25	.11	.03
☐ 27 DK Checklist 1-26 DP	.05	.02	.01
☐ 28 Sandy Alomar Jr. RR	.20	.09	.03
☐ 29 Steve Searcy RR	.05	.02	.01
☐ 30 Cameron Drew RR	.05	.02	.01
☐ 31 Gary Sheffield RR	.75	.35	.09
☐ 32 Erik Hanson RR	.15	.07	.02
☐ 33 Ken Griffey Jr. RR	5.00	2.20	.60
☐ 34 Greg W. Harris RR	.05	.02	.01
☐ 35 Gregg Jefferies RR	.15	.07	.02
☐ 36 Luis Medina RR	.05	.02	.01
☐ 37 Carlos Quintana RR	.05	.02	.01
☐ 38 Felix Jose RR	.05	.02	.01
☐ 39 Cris Carpenter RR	.05	.02	.01
☐ 40 Ron Jones RR	.05	.02	.01
☐ 41 Dave West RR	.05	.02	.01
☐ 42 Randy Johnson RR UER Card says born in 1964 he was born in 1963	.75	.35	.09
☐ 43 Mike Harkey RR	.05	.02	.01
☐ 44 Pete Harnisch RR DP	.10	.05	.01
☐ 45 Tom Gordon RR DP	.10	.05	.01
☐ 46 Gregg Olson RR DP	.10	.05	.01
☐ 47 Alex Sanchez RR DP	.05	.02	.01
☐ 48 Ruben Sierra	.10	.05	.01
☐ 49 Rafael Palmeiro	.15	.07	.02
☐ 50 Ron Gant	.15	.07	.02
☐ 51 Cal Ripken	.75	.35	.09
☐ 52 Wally Joyner	.10	.05	.01
☐ 53 Gary Carter	.10	.05	.01
☐ 54 Andy Van Slyke	.10	.05	.01
☐ 55 Robin Yount	.15	.07	.02
☐ 56 Pete Incaviglia	.10	.05	.01
☐ 57 Greg Brock	.05	.02	.01
☐ 58 Melido Perez	.05	.02	.01
☐ 59 Craig Lefferts	.05	.02	.01
☐ 60 Gary Pettis	.05	.02	.01
☐ 61 Danny Tartabull	.05	.02	.01
☐ 62 Guillermo Hernandez	.05	.02	.01
☐ 63 Ozzie Smith	.25	.11	.03
☐ 64 Gary Gaetti	.05	.02	.01
☐ 65 Mark Davis	.05	.02	.01
☐ 66 Lee Smith	.10	.05	.01
☐ 67 Dennis Eckersley	.10	.05	.01
☐ 68 Wade Boggs	.15	.07	.02

☐ 69 Mike Scott .05 .02 .01
☐ 70 Fred McGriff .20 .09 .03
☐ 71 Tom Browning .05 .02 .01
☐ 72 Claudell Washington .05 .02 .01
☐ 73 Mel Hall .05 .02 .01
☐ 74 Don Mattingly .50 .23 .06
☐ 75 Steve Bedrosian .05 .02 .01
☐ 76 Juan Samuel .05 .02 .01
☐ 77 Mike Scioscia .05 .02 .01
☐ 78 Dave Righetti .05 .02 .01
☐ 79 Alfredo Griffin .05 .02 .01
☐ 80 Eric Davis UER .10 .05 .01
(165 games in 1988, should be 135)
☐ 81 Juan Berenguer .05 .02 .01
☐ 82 Todd Worrell .05 .02 .01
☐ 83 Joe Carter .15 .07 .02
☐ 84 Steve Sax .05 .02 .01
☐ 85 Frank White .10 .05 .01
☐ 86 John Kruk .10 .05 .01
☐ 87 Rance Mulliniks .05 .02 .01
☐ 88 Alan Ashby .05 .02 .01
☐ 89 Charlie Leibrandt .05 .02 .01
☐ 90 Frank Tanana .05 .02 .01
☐ 91 Jose Canseco .15 .07 .02
☐ 92 Barry Bonds .40 .18 .05
☐ 93 Harold Reynolds .05 .02 .01
☐ 94 Mark McLemore .05 .02 .01
☐ 95 Mark McGwire .30 .14 .04
☐ 96 Eddie Murray .25 .11 .03
☐ 97 Tim Raines .15 .07 .02
☐ 98 Robby Thompson .05 .02 .01
☐ 99 Kevin McReynolds .05 .02 .01
☐ 100 Checklist 28-137 .05 .02 .01
☐ 101 Carlton Fisk .15 .07 .02
☐ 102 Dave Martinez .05 .02 .01
☐ 103 Glenn Braggs .05 .02 .01
☐ 104 Dale Murphy .15 .07 .02
☐ 105 Ryne Sandberg .25 .11 .03
☐ 106 Dennis Martinez .10 .05 .01
☐ 107 Pete O'Brien .05 .02 .01
☐ 108 Dick Schofield .05 .02 .01
☐ 109 Henry Cotto .05 .02 .01
☐ 110 Mike Marshall .05 .02 .01
☐ 111 Keith Moreland .05 .02 .01
☐ 112 Tom Brunansky .05 .02 .01
☐ 113 Kelly Gruber UER .05 .02 .01
(Wrong birthdate)
☐ 114 Brook Jacoby .05 .02 .01
☐ 115 Keith Brown .05 .02 .01
☐ 116 Matt Nokes .05 .02 .01
☐ 117 Keith Hernandez .10 .05 .01
☐ 118 Bob Forsch .05 .02 .01
☐ 119 Bert Blyleven UER .10 .05 .01
(... 3000 strikeouts in 1987, should be 1986)
☐ 120 Willie Wilson .05 .02 .01
☐ 121 Tommy Gregg .05 .02 .01
☐ 122 Jim Rice .15 .07 .02
☐ 123 Bob Knepper .05 .02 .01
☐ 124 Danny Jackson .05 .02 .01
☐ 125 Eric Plunk .05 .02 .01
☐ 126 Brian Fisher .05 .02 .01
☐ 127 Mike Pagliarulo .05 .02 .01
☐ 128 Tony Gwynn .40 .18 .05
☐ 129 Lance McCullers .05 .02 .01
☐ 130 Andres Galarraga .15 .07 .02
☐ 131 Jose Uribe .05 .02 .01
☐ 132 Kirk Gibson UER .15 .07 .02
(Wrong birthdate)
☐ 133 David Palmer .05 .02 .01
☐ 134 R.J. Reynolds .05 .02 .01
☐ 135 Greg Walker .05 .02 .01
☐ 136 Kirk McCaskill UER .05 .02 .01
(Wrong birthdate)
☐ 137 Shawon Dunston .05 .02 .01
☐ 138 Andy Allanson .05 .02 .01
☐ 139 Rob Murphy .05 .02 .01
☐ 140 Mike Aldrete .05 .02 .01
☐ 141 Terry Kennedy .05 .02 .01
☐ 142 Scott Fletcher .05 .02 .01
☐ 143 Steve Balboni .05 .02 .01
☐ 144 Bret Saberhagen .10 .05 .01
☐ 145 Ozzie Virgil .05 .02 .01
☐ 146 Dale Sveum .05 .02 .01
☐ 147 Darryl Strawberry .10 .05 .01
☐ 148 Harold Baines .10 .05 .01
☐ 149 George Bell .05 .02 .01
☐ 150 Dave Parker .10 .05 .01
☐ 151 Bobby Bonilla .15 .07 .02
☐ 152 Mookie Wilson .10 .05 .01
☐ 153 Ted Power .05 .02 .01
☐ 154 Nolan Ryan .75 .35 .09
☐ 155 Jeff Reardon .10 .05 .01
☐ 156 Tim Wallach .05 .02 .01
☐ 157 Jamie Moyer .05 .02 .01
☐ 158 Rich Gossage .15 .07 .02
☐ 159 Dave Winfield .15 .07 .02
☐ 160 Von Hayes .05 .02 .01
☐ 161 Willie McGee .05 .02 .01
☐ 162 Rich Gedman .05 .02 .01
☐ 163 Tony Pena .05 .02 .01
☐ 164 Mike Morgan .05 .02 .01
☐ 165 Charlie Hough .10 .05 .01
☐ 166 Mike Stanley .05 .02 .01
☐ 167 Andre Dawson .10 .05 .01
☐ 168 Joe Boever .05 .02 .01
☐ 169 Pete Stanicek .05 .02 .01
☐ 170 Bob Boone .10 .05 .01
☐ 171 Ron Darling .05 .02 .01
☐ 172 Bob Walk .05 .02 .01
☐ 173 Rob Deer .05 .02 .01
☐ 174 Steve Buechele .05 .02 .01
☐ 175 Ted Higuera .05 .02 .01
☐ 176 Ozzie Guillen .05 .02 .01
☐ 177 Candy Maldonado .05 .02 .01
☐ 178 Doyle Alexander .05 .02 .01
☐ 179 Mark Gubicza .05 .02 .01
☐ 180 Alan Trammell .10 .05 .01
☐ 181 Vince Coleman .05 .02 .01
☐ 182 Kirby Puckett .40 .18 .05
☐ 183 Chris Brown .05 .02 .01
☐ 184 Marty Barrett .05 .02 .01
☐ 185 Stan Javier .05 .02 .01
☐ 186 Mike Greenwell .05 .02 .01
☐ 187 Billy Hatcher .05 .02 .01
☐ 188 Jimmy Key .10 .05 .01
☐ 189 Nick Esasky .05 .02 .01
☐ 190 Don Slaught .05 .02 .01
☐ 191 Cory Snyder .05 .02 .01
☐ 192 John Candelaria .05 .02 .01
☐ 193 Mike Schmidt .20 .09 .03
☐ 194 Kevin Gross .05 .02 .01
☐ 195 John Tudor .05 .02 .01
☐ 196 Neil Allen .05 .02 .01
☐ 197 Orel Hershiser .10 .05 .01
☐ 198 Kal Daniels .05 .02 .01
☐ 199 Kent Hrbek .10 .05 .01
☐ 200 Checklist 138-247 .05 .02 .01
☐ 201 Joe Magrane .05 .02 .01
☐ 202 Scott Bailes .05 .02 .01
☐ 203 Tim Belcher .05 .02 .01
☐ 204 George Brett .40 .18 .05
☐ 205 Benito Santiago .10 .05 .01
☐ 206 Tony Fernandez .05 .02 .01
☐ 207 Gerald Young .05 .02 .01
☐ 208 Bo Jackson .15 .07 .02
☐ 209 Chet Lemon .05 .02 .01
☐ 210 Storm Davis .05 .02 .01
☐ 211 Doug Drabek .10 .05 .01
☐ 212 Mickey Brantley UER .05 .02 .01
(Photo actually Nelson Simmons)
☐ 213 Devon White .10 .05 .01
☐ 214 Dave Stewart .10 .05 .01
☐ 215 Dave Schmidt .05 .02 .01
☐ 216 Bryn Smith .05 .02 .01
☐ 217 Brett Butler .10 .05 .01
☐ 218 Bob Ojeda .05 .02 .01
☐ 219 Steve Rosenberg .05 .02 .01
☐ 220 Hubie Brooks .05 .02 .01
☐ 221 B.J. Surhoff .15 .07 .02
☐ 222 Rick Mahler .05 .02 .01
☐ 223 Rick Sutcliffe .05 .02 .01
☐ 224 Neal Heaton .05 .02 .01
☐ 225 Mitch Williams .05 .02 .01
☐ 226 Chuck Finley .10 .05 .01
☐ 227 Mark Langston .10 .05 .01
☐ 228 Jesse Orosco .05 .02 .01
☐ 229 Ed Whitson .05 .02 .01
☐ 230 Terry Pendleton .10 .05 .01
☐ 231 Lloyd Moseby .05 .02 .01
☐ 232 Greg Swindell .05 .02 .01
☐ 233 John Franco .10 .05 .01
☐ 234 Jack Morris .10 .05 .01
☐ 235 Howard Johnson .05 .02 .01
☐ 236 Glenn Davis .05 .02 .01
☐ 237 Frank Viola .05 .02 .01
☐ 238 Kevin Seitzer .05 .02 .01
☐ 239 Gerald Perry .05 .02 .01
☐ 240 Dwight Evans .10 .05 .01
☐ 241 Jim Deshaies .05 .02 .01
☐ 242 Bo Diaz .05 .02 .01
☐ 243 Carney Lansford .10 .05 .01
☐ 244 Mike LaValliere .05 .02 .01
☐ 245 Rickey Henderson .15 .07 .02
☐ 246 Roberto Alomar .40 .18 .05
☐ 247 Jimmy Jones .05 .02 .01
☐ 248 Pascual Perez .05 .02 .01
☐ 249 Will Clark .20 .09 .03
☐ 250 Fernando Valenzuela .10 .05 .01
☐ 251 Shane Rawley .05 .02 .01
☐ 252 Sid Bream .05 .02 .01
☐ 253 Steve Lyons .05 .02 .01
☐ 254 Brian Downing .05 .02 .01
☐ 255 Mark Grace .20 .09 .03
☐ 256 Tom Candiotti .05 .02 .01
☐ 257 Barry Larkin .20 .09 .03
☐ 258 Mike Krukow .05 .02 .01
☐ 259 Billy Ripken .05 .02 .01
☐ 260 Cecilio Guante .05 .02 .01
☐ 261 Scott Bradley .05 .02 .01
☐ 262 Floyd Bannister .05 .02 .01
☐ 263 Pete Smith .05 .02 .01
☐ 264 Jim Gantner UER .05 .02 .01
(Wrong birthdate)
☐ 265 Roger McDowell .05 .02 .01
☐ 266 Bobby Thigpen .05 .02 .01
☐ 267 Jim Clancy .05 .02 .01
☐ 268 Terry Steinbach .10 .05 .01
☐ 269 Mike Dunne .05 .02 .01
☐ 270 Dwight Gooden .10 .05 .01
☐ 271 Mike Heath .05 .02 .01
☐ 272 Dave Smith .05 .02 .01
☐ 273 Keith Atherton .05 .02 .01
☐ 274 Tim Burke .05 .02 .01
☐ 275 Damon Berryhill .05 .02 .01
☐ 276 Vance Law .05 .02 .01
☐ 277 Rich Dotson .05 .02 .01
☐ 278 Lance Parrish .05 .02 .01
☐ 279 Denny Walling .05 .02 .01
☐ 280 Roger Clemens .20 .09 .03
☐ 281 Greg Mathews .05 .02 .01
☐ 282 Tom Niedenfuer .05 .02 .01
☐ 283 Paul Kilgus .05 .02 .01
☐ 284 Jose Guzman .05 .02 .01
☐ 285 Calvin Schiraldi .05 .02 .01
☐ 286 Charlie Puleo UER .05 .02 .01
(Career ERA 4.24, should be 4.23)
☐ 287 Joe Orsulak .05 .02 .01
☐ 288 Jack Howell .05 .02 .01
☐ 289 Kevin Elster .10 .05 .01
☐ 290 Jose Lind .05 .02 .01
☐ 291 Paul Molitor .20 .09 .03
☐ 292 Cecil Espy .05 .02 .01
☐ 293 Bill Wegman .05 .02 .01
☐ 294 Dan Pasqua .05 .02 .01
☐ 295 Scott Garrelts UER .05 .02 .01
(Wrong birthdate)
☐ 296 Walt Terrell .05 .02 .01
☐ 297 Ed Hearn .05 .02 .01
☐ 298 Lou Whitaker .10 .05 .01
☐ 299 Ken Dayley .05 .02 .01
☐ 300 Checklist 248-357 .05 .02 .01
☐ 301 Tommy Herr .05 .02 .01
☐ 302 Mike Brumley .05 .02 .01
☐ 303 Ellis Burks .15 .07 .02
☐ 304 Curt Young UER .05 .02 .01
(Wrong birthdate)
☐ 305 Jody Reed .05 .02 .01
☐ 306 Bill Doran .05 .02 .01
☐ 307 David Wells .05 .02 .01
☐ 308 Ron Robinson .05 .02 .01
☐ 309 Rafael Santana .05 .02 .01
☐ 310 Julio Franco .10 .05 .01
☐ 311 Jack Clark .10 .05 .01
☐ 312 Chris James .05 .02 .01
☐ 313 Milt Thompson .05 .02 .01
☐ 314 John Shelby .05 .02 .01
☐ 315 Al Leiter .10 .05 .01
☐ 316 Mike Davis .05 .02 .01
☐ 317 Chris Sabo .05 .02 .01
☐ 318 Greg Gagne .05 .02 .01
☐ 319 Jose Oquendo .05 .02 .01
☐ 320 John Farrell .05 .02 .01
☐ 321 Franklin Stubbs .05 .02 .01
☐ 322 Kurt Stillwell .05 .02 .01
☐ 323 Shawn Abner .05 .02 .01
☐ 324 Mike Flanagan .05 .02 .01
☐ 325 Kevin Bass .05 .02 .01
☐ 326 Pat Tabler .05 .02 .01
☐ 327 Mike Henneman .05 .02 .01
☐ 328 Rick Honeycutt .05 .02 .01
☐ 329 John Smiley .05 .02 .01
☐ 330 Rey Quinones .05 .02 .01
☐ 331 Johnny Ray .05 .02 .01
☐ 332 Bob Welch .05 .02 .01
☐ 333 Larry Sheets .05 .02 .01
☐ 334 Jeff Parrett .05 .02 .01
☐ 335 Rick Reuschel UER .05 .02 .01
(For Don Robinson, should be Jeff)
☐ 336 Randy Myers .10 .05 .01
☐ 337 Ken Williams .05 .02 .01
☐ 338 Andy McGaffigan .05 .02 .01
☐ 339 Joey Meyer .05 .02 .01
☐ 340 Dion James .05 .02 .01
☐ 341 Les Lancaster .05 .02 .01
☐ 342 Tom Foley .05 .02 .01
☐ 343 Geno Petralli .05 .02 .01
☐ 344 Dan Petry .05 .02 .01
☐ 345 Alvin Davis .05 .02 .01
☐ 346 Mickey Hatcher .05 .02 .01
☐ 347 Marvell Wynne .05 .02 .01
☐ 348 Danny Cox .05 .02 .01
☐ 349 Dave Stieb .05 .02 .01
☐ 350 Jay Bell .15 .07 .02
☐ 351 Jeff Treadway .05 .02 .01
☐ 352 Luis Salazar .05 .02 .01
☐ 353 Len Dykstra .10 .05 .01
☐ 354 Juan Agosto .05 .02 .01
☐ 355 Gene Larkin .05 .02 .01
☐ 356 Steve Farr .05 .02 .01
☐ 357 Paul Assenmacher .05 .02 .01
☐ 358 Todd Benzinger .05 .02 .01
☐ 359 Larry Andersen .05 .02 .01
☐ 360 Paul O'Neill .10 .05 .01
☐ 361 Ron Hassey .05 .02 .01
☐ 362 Jim Gott .05 .02 .01
☐ 363 Ken Phelps .05 .02 .01
☐ 364 Tim Flannery .05 .02 .01
☐ 365 Randy Ready .05 .02 .01
☐ 366 Nelson Santovenia .05 .02 .01
☐ 367 Kelly Downs .05 .02 .01
☐ 368 Danny Heep .05 .02 .01
☐ 369 Phil Bradley .05 .02 .01
☐ 370 Jeff D. Robinson .05 .02 .01
☐ 371 Ivan Calderon .05 .02 .01
☐ 372 Mike Witt .05 .02 .01
☐ 373 Greg Maddux .75 .35 .09
☐ 374 Carmen Castillo .05 .02 .01
☐ 375 Jose Rijo .05 .02 .01
☐ 376 Joe Price .05 .02 .01
☐ 377 Rene Gonzales .05 .02 .01
☐ 378 Oddibe McDowell .05 .02 .01
☐ 379 Jim Presley .05 .02 .01
☐ 380 Brad Wellman .05 .02 .01
☐ 381 Tom Glavine .25 .11 .03
☐ 382 Dan Plesac .05 .02 .01
☐ 383 Wally Backman .05 .02 .01
☐ 384 Dave Gallagher .05 .02 .01
☐ 385 Tom Henke .05 .02 .01
☐ 386 Luis Polonia .10 .05 .01
☐ 387 Junior Ortiz .05 .02 .01
☐ 388 David Cone .15 .07 .02
☐ 389 Dave Bergman .05 .02 .01
☐ 390 Danny Darwin .05 .02 .01
☐ 391 Dan Gladden .05 .02 .01
☐ 392 John Dopson .05 .02 .01
☐ 393 Frank DiPino .05 .02 .01
☐ 394 Al Nipper .05 .02 .01
☐ 395 Willie Randolph .10 .05 .01
☐ 396 Don Carman .05 .02 .01
☐ 397 Scott Terry .05 .02 .01
☐ 398 Rick Cerone .05 .02 .01
☐ 399 Tom Pagnozzi .05 .02 .01
☐ 400 Checklist 358-467 .05 .02 .01
☐ 401 Mickey Tettleton .10 .05 .01
☐ 402 Curtis Wilkerson .05 .02 .01
☐ 403 Jeff Russell .05 .02 .01
☐ 404 Pat Perry .05 .02 .01
☐ 405 Jose Alvarez .05 .02 .01
☐ 406 Rick Schu .05 .02 .01
☐ 407 Sherman Corbett .05 .02 .01
☐ 408 Dave Magadan .05 .02 .01
☐ 409 Bob Kipper .05 .02 .01
☐ 410 Don August .05 .02 .01
☐ 411 Bob Brower .05 .02 .01
☐ 412 Chris Bosio .05 .02 .01
☐ 413 Jerry Reuss .05 .02 .01
☐ 414 Atlee Hammaker .05 .02 .01
☐ 415 Jim Walewander .05 .02 .01
☐ 416 Mike Macfarlane .10 .05 .01
☐ 417 Pat Sheridan .05 .02 .01
☐ 418 Pedro Guerrero .10 .05 .01
☐ 419 Allan Anderson .05 .02 .01
☐ 420 Mark Parent .05 .02 .01
☐ 421 Bob Stanley .05 .02 .01
☐ 422 Mike Gallego .05 .02 .01
☐ 423 Bruce Hurst .05 .02 .01
☐ 424 Dave Meads .05 .02 .01
☐ 425 Jesse Barfield .05 .02 .01
☐ 426 Rob Dibble .10 .05 .01
☐ 427 Joel Skinner .05 .02 .01
☐ 428 Ron Kittle .05 .02 .01
☐ 429 Rick Rhoden .05 .02 .01
☐ 430 Bob Dernier .05 .02 .01
☐ 431 Steve Jeltz .05 .02 .01
☐ 432 Rick Dempsey .05 .02 .01
☐ 433 Roberto Kelly .10 .05 .01
☐ 434 Dave Anderson .05 .02 .01
☐ 435 Herm Winningham .05 .02 .01
☐ 436 Al Newman .05 .02 .01
☐ 437 Jose DeLeon .05 .02 .01
☐ 438 Doug Jones .05 .02 .01
☐ 439 Brian Holton .05 .02 .01
☐ 440 Jeff Montgomery .10 .05 .01
☐ 441 Dickie Thon .05 .02 .01
☐ 442 Cecil Fielder .10 .05 .01
☐ 443 John Fishel .05 .02 .01
☐ 444 Jerry Don Gleaton .05 .02 .01
☐ 445 Paul Gibson .05 .02 .01
☐ 446 Walt Weiss .05 .02 .01
☐ 447 Glenn Wilson .05 .02 .01
☐ 448 Mike Moore .05 .02 .01
☐ 449 Chili Davis .10 .05 .01
☐ 450 Dave Henderson .05 .02 .01
☐ 451 Jose Bautista .05 .02 .01
☐ 452 Rex Hudler .05 .02 .01
☐ 453 Bob Brenly .05 .02 .01
☐ 454 Mackey Sasser .05 .02 .01
☐ 455 Daryl Boston .05 .02 .01
☐ 456 Mike R. Fitzgerald .05 .02 .01
☐ 457 Jeffrey Leonard .05 .02 .01
☐ 458 Bruce Sutter .05 .02 .01
☐ 459 Mitch Webster .05 .02 .01
☐ 460 Joe Hesketh .05 .02 .01
☐ 461 Bobby Witt .05 .02 .01
☐ 462 Stew Cliburn .05 .02 .01
☐ 463 Scott Bankhead .05 .02 .01
☐ 464 Ramon Martinez .25 .11 .03
☐ 465 Dave Leiper .05 .02 .01
☐ 466 Luis Alicea .05 .02 .01
☐ 467 John Cerutti .05 .02 .01
☐ 468 Ron Washington .05 .02 .01
☐ 469 Jeff Reed .05 .02 .01
☐ 470 Jeff M. Robinson .05 .02 .01
☐ 471 Sid Fernandez .05 .02 .01
☐ 472 Terry Puhl .05 .02 .01

☐ 473 Charlie Lea	.05	.02	.01
☐ 474 Israel Sanchez	.05	.02	.01
☐ 475 Bruce Benedict	.05	.02	.01
☐ 476 Oil Can Boyd	.05	.02	.01
☐ 477 Craig Reynolds	.05	.02	.01
☐ 478 Frank Williams	.05	.02	.01
☐ 479 Greg Cadaret	.05	.02	.01
☐ 480 Randy Kramer	.05	.02	.01
☐ 481 Dave Eiland	.05	.02	.01
☐ 482 Eric Show	.05	.02	.01
☐ 483 Garry Templeton	.05	.02	.01
☐ 484 Wallace Johnson	.05	.02	.01
☐ 485 Kevin Mitchell	.10	.05	.01
☐ 486 Tim Crews	.05	.02	.01
☐ 487 Mike Maddux	.05	.02	.01
☐ 488 Dave LaPoint	.05	.02	.01
☐ 489 Fred Manrique	.05	.02	.01
☐ 490 Greg Minton	.05	.02	.01
☐ 491 Doug Dascenzo UER (Photo actually Damon Berryhill)	.05	.02	.01
☐ 492 Willie Upshaw	.05	.02	.01
☐ 493 Jack Armstrong	.05	.02	.01
☐ 494 Kirt Manwaring	.05	.02	.01
☐ 495 Jeff Ballard	.05	.02	.01
☐ 496 Jeff Kunkel	.05	.02	.01
☐ 497 Mike Campbell	.05	.02	.01
☐ 498 Gary Thurman	.05	.02	.01
☐ 499 Zane Smith	.05	.02	.01
☐ 500 Checklist 468-577 DP	.05	.02	.01
☐ 501 Mike Birkbeck	.05	.02	.01
☐ 502 Terry Leach	.05	.02	.01
☐ 503 Shawn Hillegas	.05	.02	.01
☐ 504 Manny Lee	.05	.02	.01
☐ 505 Doug Jennings	.05	.02	.01
☐ 506 Ken Oberkfell	.05	.02	.01
☐ 507 Tim Teufel	.05	.02	.01
☐ 508 Tom Brookens	.05	.02	.01
☐ 509 Rafael Ramirez	.05	.02	.01
☐ 510 Fred Toliver	.05	.02	.01
☐ 511 Brian Holman	.05	.02	.01
☐ 512 Mike Bielecki	.05	.02	.01
☐ 513 Jeff Pico	.05	.02	.01
☐ 514 Charles Hudson	.05	.02	.01
☐ 515 Bruce Ruffin	.05	.02	.01
☐ 516 Larry McWilliams UER (New Richland, should be North Richland)	.05	.02	.01
☐ 517 Jeff Sellers	.05	.02	.01
☐ 518 John Costello	.05	.02	.01
☐ 519 Brady Anderson	.60	.25	.07
☐ 520 Craig McMurtry	.05	.02	.01
☐ 521 Ray Hayward DP	.05	.02	.01
☐ 522 Drew Hall DP	.05	.02	.01
☐ 523 Mark Lemke DP	.10	.05	.01
☐ 524 Oswald Peraza DP	.05	.02	.01
☐ 525 Bryan Harvey DP	.10	.05	.01
☐ 526 Rick Aguilera DP	.15	.07	.02
☐ 527 Tom Prince DP	.05	.02	.01
☐ 528 Mark Clear DP	.05	.02	.01
☐ 529 Jerry Browne DP	.05	.02	.01
☐ 530 Juan Castillo DP	.05	.02	.01
☐ 531 Jack McDowell DP	.10	.05	.01
☐ 532 Chris Speier DP	.05	.02	.01
☐ 533 Darrell Evans DP	.10	.05	.01
☐ 534 Luis Aquino DP	.05	.02	.01
☐ 535 Eric King DP	.05	.02	.01
☐ 536 Ken Hill DP	.40	.18	.05
☐ 537 Randy Bush DP	.05	.02	.01
☐ 538 Shane Mack DP	.05	.02	.01
☐ 539 Tom Bolton DP	.05	.02	.01
☐ 540 Gene Nelson DP	.05	.02	.01
☐ 541 Wes Gardner DP	.05	.02	.01
☐ 542 Ken Caminiti DP	.20	.09	.03
☐ 543 Duane Ward DP	.05	.02	.01
☐ 544 Norm Charlton DP	.10	.05	.01
☐ 545 Hal Morris DP	.15	.07	.02
☐ 546 Rich Yett DP	.05	.02	.01
☐ 547 Hensley Meulens DP	.05	.02	.01
☐ 548 Greg A. Harris DP	.05	.02	.01
☐ 549 Darren Daulton DP (Posing as right-handed hitter)	.10	.05	.01
☐ 550 Jeff Hamilton DP	.05	.02	.01
☐ 551 Luis Aguayo DP	.05	.02	.01
☐ 552 Tim Leary DP (Resembles M.Marshall)	.05	.02	.01
☐ 553 Ron Oester DP	.05	.02	.01
☐ 554 Steve Lombardozzi DP	.05	.02	.01
☐ 555 Tim Jones DP	.05	.02	.01
☐ 556 Bud Black DP	.05	.02	.01
☐ 557 Alejandro Pena DP	.05	.02	.01
☐ 558 Jose DeJesus DP	.05	.02	.01
☐ 559 Dennis Rasmussen DP	.05	.02	.01
☐ 560 Pat Borders DP	.10	.05	.01
☐ 561 Craig Biggio DP	.40	.18	.05
☐ 562 Luis DeLosSantos DP	.05	.02	.01
☐ 563 Fred Lynn DP	.05	.02	.01
☐ 564 Todd Burns DP	.05	.02	.01
☐ 565 Felix Fermin DP	.05	.02	.01
☐ 566 Darnell Coles DP	.05	.02	.01
☐ 567 Willie Fraser DP	.05	.02	.01
☐ 568 Glenn Hubbard DP	.05	.02	.01
☐ 569 Craig Worthington DP	.05	.02	.01
☐ 570 Johnny Paredes DP	.05	.02	.01
☐ 571 Don Robinson DP	.05	.02	.01
☐ 572 Barry Lyons DP	.05	.02	.01
☐ 573 Bill Long DP	.05	.02	.01
☐ 574 Tracy Jones DP	.05	.02	.01
☐ 575 Juan Nieves DP	.05	.02	.01
☐ 576 Andres Thomas DP	.05	.02	.01
☐ 577 Rolando Roomes DP	.05	.02	.01
☐ 578 Luis Rivera UER DP (Wrong birthdate)	.05	.02	.01
☐ 579 Chad Kreuter DP	.05	.02	.01
☐ 580 Tony Armas DP	.05	.02	.01
☐ 581 Jay Buhner	.25	.11	.03
☐ 582 Ricky Horton DP	.05	.02	.01
☐ 583 Andy Hawkins DP	.05	.02	.01
☐ 584 Sil Campusano	.05	.02	.01
☐ 585 Dave Clark	.05	.02	.01
☐ 586 Van Snider DP	.05	.02	.01
☐ 587 Todd Frohwirth DP	.05	.02	.01
☐ 588 Warren Spahn DP PUZ	.15	.07	.02
☐ 589 William Brennan	.05	.02	.01
☐ 590 German Gonzalez	.05	.02	.01
☐ 591 Ernie Whitt DP	.05	.02	.01
☐ 592 Jeff Blauser	.10	.05	.01
☐ 593 Spike Owen DP	.05	.02	.01
☐ 594 Matt Williams	.25	.11	.03
☐ 595 Lloyd McClendon DP	.05	.02	.01
☐ 596 Steve Ontiveros	.05	.02	.01
☐ 597 Scott Medvin	.05	.02	.01
☐ 598 Hipolito Pena DP	.05	.02	.01
☐ 599 Jerald Clark DP	.05	.02	.01
☐ 600A Checklist 578-660 DP (635 Kurt Schilling)	.05	.02	.01
☐ 600B Checklist 578-660 DP (635 Curt Schilling; MVP's not listed on checklist card)	.05	.02	.01
☐ 600C Checklist 578-660 DP (635 Curt Schilling; MVP's listed following 660)	.05	.02	.01
☐ 601 Carmelo Martinez DP	.05	.02	.01
☐ 602 Mike LaCoss	.05	.02	.01
☐ 603 Mike Devereaux	.05	.02	.01
☐ 604 Alex Madrid DP	.05	.02	.01
☐ 605 Gary Redus DP	.05	.02	.01
☐ 606 Lance Johnson	.15	.07	.02
☐ 607 Terry Clark DP	.05	.02	.01
☐ 608 Manny Trillo DP	.05	.02	.01
☐ 609 Scott Jordan	.10	.05	.01
☐ 610 Jay Howell DP	.05	.02	.01
☐ 611 Francisco Melendez	.05	.02	.01
☐ 612 Mike Boddicker	.05	.02	.01
☐ 613 Kevin Brown DP	.15	.07	.02
☐ 614 Dave Valle	.05	.02	.01
☐ 615 Tim Laudner DP	.05	.02	.01
☐ 616 Andy Nezelek UER (Wrong birthdate)	.05	.02	.01
☐ 617 Chuck Crim	.05	.02	.01
☐ 618 Jack Savage DP	.05	.02	.01
☐ 619 Adam Peterson	.05	.02	.01
☐ 620 Todd Stottlemyre	.10	.05	.01
☐ 621 Lance Blankenship	.05	.02	.01
☐ 622 Miguel Garcia DP	.05	.02	.01
☐ 623 Keith A. Miller DP	.05	.02	.01
☐ 624 Ricky Jordan DP	.10	.05	.01
☐ 625 Ernest Riles DP	.05	.02	.01
☐ 626 John Moses DP	.05	.02	.01
☐ 627 Nelson Liriano DP	.05	.02	.01
☐ 628 Mike Smithson DP	.05	.02	.01
☐ 629 Scott Sanderson	.05	.02	.01
☐ 630 Dale Mohorcic	.05	.02	.01
☐ 631 Marvin Freeman DP	.05	.02	.01
☐ 632 Mike Young DP	.05	.02	.01
☐ 633 Dennis Lamp	.05	.02	.01
☐ 634 Dante Bichette DP	.60	.25	.07
☐ 635 Curt Schilling DP	.15	.07	.02
☐ 636 Scott May DP	.05	.02	.01
☐ 637 Mike Schooler	.05	.02	.01
☐ 638 Rick Leach	.05	.02	.01
☐ 639 Tom Lampkin UER (Throws Left, should be Throws Right)	.05	.02	.01
☐ 640 Brian Meyer	.05	.02	.01
☐ 641 Brian Harper	.05	.02	.01
☐ 642 John Smoltz	.75	.35	.09
☐ 643 Jose Canseco (40/40 Club)	.15	.07	.02
☐ 644 Bill Schroeder	.05	.02	.01
☐ 645 Edgar Martinez	.15	.07	.02
☐ 646 Dennis Cook	.05	.02	.01
☐ 647 Barry Jones	.05	.02	.01
☐ 648 Orel Hershiser (59 and Counting)	.10	.05	.01
☐ 649 Rod Nichols	.05	.02	.01
☐ 650 Jody Davis	.05	.02	.01
☐ 651 Bob Milacki	.05	.02	.01
☐ 652 Mike Jackson	.05	.02	.01
☐ 653 Derek Lilliquist	.05	.02	.01
☐ 654 Paul Mirabella	.05	.02	.01
☐ 655 Mike Diaz	.05	.02	.01
☐ 656 Jeff Musselman	.05	.02	.01
☐ 657 Jerry Reed	.05	.02	.01
☐ 658 Kevin Blankenship	.05	.02	.01
☐ 659 Wayne Tolleson	.05	.02	.01
☐ 660 Eric Hetzel	.05	.02	.01

1989 Donruss Bonus MVP's

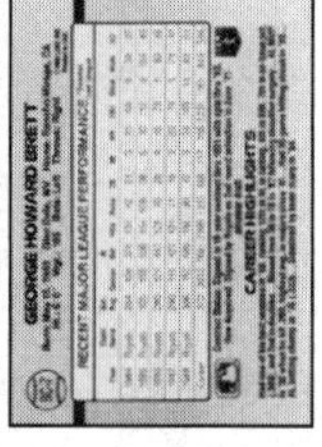

Rather than short-printing 26 cards in order to make room for printing the Bonus MVP's this year, Donruss apparently chose to double print 106 cards. Numbered with the prefix "BC" for bonus card, the 26-card set featuring the most valuable player from each of the 26 teams was randomly inserted in the wax and rack packs. These cards are distinguished by the bold MVP logo in the upper background of the obverse, and the four doubleprinted cards are denoted by "DP" in the checklist below.

	MINT	NRMT	EXC
COMPLETE SET (26)	1.50	.70	.19
COMMON CARD (BC1-BC26)	.05	.02	.01
☐ BC1 Kirby Puckett	.40	.18	.05
☐ BC2 Mike Scott	.05	.02	.01
☐ BC3 Joe Carter	.10	.05	.01
☐ BC4 Orel Hershiser	.10	.05	.01
☐ BC5 Jose Canseco	.15	.07	.02
☐ BC6 Darryl Strawberry	.10	.05	.01
☐ BC7 George Brett	.40	.18	.05
☐ BC8 Andre Dawson	.10	.05	.01
☐ BC9 Paul Molitor UER (Brewers logo missing the word Milwaukee)	.20	.09	.03
☐ BC10 Andy Van Slyke	.05	.02	.01
☐ BC11 Dave Winfield	.15	.07	.02
☐ BC12 Kevin Gross	.05	.02	.01
☐ BC13 Mike Greenwell	.05	.02	.01
☐ BC14 Ozzie Smith	.30	.14	.04
☐ BC15 Cal Ripken	.75	.35	.09
☐ BC16 Andres Galarraga	.15	.07	.02
☐ BC17 Alan Trammell	.10	.05	.01
☐ BC18 Kal Daniels	.05	.02	.01
☐ BC19 Fred McGriff	.15	.07	.02
☐ BC20 Tony Gwynn	.40	.18	.05
☐ BC21 Wally Joyner DP	.10	.05	.01
☐ BC22 Will Clark DP	.15	.07	.02
☐ BC23 Ozzie Guillen	.05	.02	.01
☐ BC24 Gerald Perry DP	.05	.02	.01
☐ BC25 Alvin Davis DP	.05	.02	.01
☐ BC26 Ruben Sierra	.10	.05	.01

1989 Donruss Grand Slammers

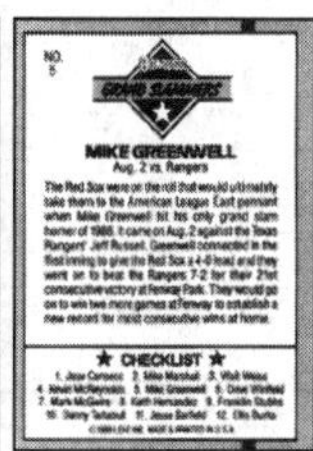

The 1989 Donruss Grand Slammers set contains 12 standard-size cards. Each card in the set can be found with five different colored border combinations, but no color combination of borders appears to be scarcer than any other. The set includes cards for each player who hit one or more grand slams in 1988. The backs detail the players' grand slams. The cards were distributed one per cello pack as well as an insert (complete) set in each factory set.

	MINT	NRMT	EXC
COMPLETE SET (12)	2.00	.90	.25
COMMON CARD (1-12)	.05	.02	.01
☐ 1 Jose Canseco	.30	.14	.04
☐ 2 Mike Marshall	.05	.02	.01
☐ 3 Walt Weiss	.05	.02	.01
☐ 4 Kevin McReynolds	.05	.02	.01
☐ 5 Mike Greenwell	.05	.02	.01
☐ 6 Dave Winfield	.30	.14	.04
☐ 7 Mark McGwire	.60	.25	.07
☐ 8 Keith Hernandez	.15	.07	.02
☐ 9 Franklin Stubbs	.05	.02	.01
☐ 10 Danny Tartabull	.05	.02	.01
☐ 11 Jesse Barfield	.05	.02	.01
☐ 12 Ellis Burks	.30	.14	.04

1989 Donruss Rookies

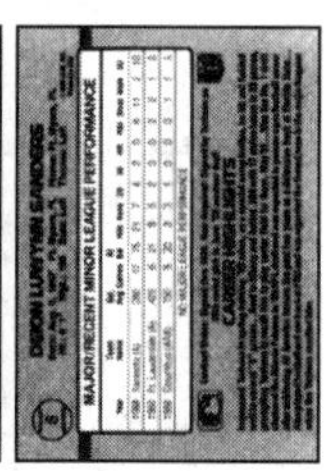

The 1989 Donruss Rookies set contains 56 standard-size cards. The cards were distributed exclusively in factory set form in small, emerald green, cellophane-wrapped boxes through hobby dealers. The cards are almost identical in design to geular 1989 Donruss except for the green borders. Rookie Cards in this set include Jim Abbott, Steve Finley, Kenny Rogers and Deion Sanders. Ken Griffey Jr. is also featured on a card within the set.

	MINT	NRMT	EXC
COMPLETE FACT.SET (56)	8.00	3.60	1.00
COMMON CARD (1-56)	.05	.02	.01
☐ 1 Gary Sheffield	.75	.35	.09
☐ 2 Gregg Jefferies	.15	.07	.02
☐ 3 Ken Griffey Jr.	5.00	2.20	.60
☐ 4 Tom Gordon	.10	.05	.01
☐ 5 Billy Spiers	.05	.02	.01
☐ 6 Deion Sanders	.75	.35	.09
☐ 7 Donn Pall	.05	.02	.01
☐ 8 Steve Carter	.05	.02	.01
☐ 9 Francisco Oliveras	.05	.02	.01
☐ 10 Steve Wilson	.05	.02	.01
☐ 11 Bob Geren	.05	.02	.01
☐ 12 Tony Castillo	.05	.02	.01
☐ 13 Kenny Rogers	.10	.05	.01
☐ 14 Carlos Martinez	.05	.02	.01
☐ 15 Edgar Martinez	.15	.07	.02
☐ 16 Jim Abbott	.15	.07	.02
☐ 17 Torey Lovullo	.05	.02	.01
☐ 18 Mark Carreon	.05	.02	.01
☐ 19 Geronimo Berroa	.10	.05	.01
☐ 20 Luis Medina	.05	.02	.01
☐ 21 Sandy Alomar Jr.	.10	.05	.01
☐ 22 Bob Milacki	.05	.02	.01
☐ 23 Joe Girardi	.15	.07	.02
☐ 24 German Gonzalez	.05	.02	.01
☐ 25 Craig Worthington	.05	.02	.01
☐ 26 Jerome Walton	.10	.05	.01
☐ 27 Gary Wayne	.05	.02	.01
☐ 28 Tim Jones	.05	.02	.01
☐ 29 Dante Bichette	.60	.25	.07
☐ 30 Alexis Infante	.05	.02	.01
☐ 31 Ken Hill	.40	.18	.05
☐ 32 Dwight Smith	.10	.05	.01
☐ 33 Luis de los Santos	.05	.02	.01
☐ 34 Eric Yelding	.05	.02	.01
☐ 35 Gregg Olson	.10	.05	.01
☐ 36 Phil Stephenson	.05	.02	.01
☐ 37 Ken Patterson	.05	.02	.01
☐ 38 Rick Wrona	.05	.02	.01
☐ 39 Mike Brumley	.05	.02	.01
☐ 40 Cris Carpenter	.05	.02	.01
☐ 41 Jeff Brantley	.15	.07	.02
☐ 42 Ron Jones	.05	.02	.01
☐ 43 Randy Johnson	.75	.35	.09
☐ 44 Kevin Brown	.15	.07	.02
☐ 45 Ramon Martinez	.25	.11	.03
☐ 46 Greg W.Harris	.05	.02	.01
☐ 47 Steve Finley	.25	.11	.03
☐ 48 Randy Kramer	.05	.02	.01
☐ 49 Erik Hanson	.15	.07	.02
☐ 50 Matt Merullo	.05	.02	.01
☐ 51 Mike Devereaux	.05	.02	.01
☐ 52 Clay Parker	.05	.02	.01
☐ 53 Omar Vizquel	.40	.18	.05
☐ 54 Derek Lilliquist	.05	.02	.01
☐ 55 Junior Felix	.05	.02	.01
☐ 56 Checklist 1-56	.05	.02	.01

1989 Donruss All-Stars

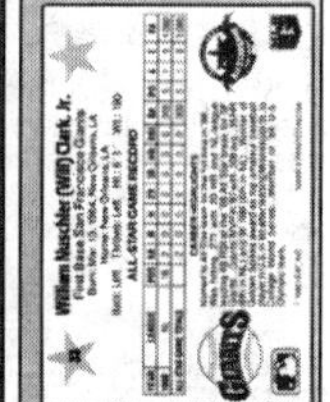

These All-Stars are standard size and very similar in design to the regular issue of 1989 Donruss. The set is distinguished by the presence of the respective League logos in the lower right corner of each obverse. The cards are numbered on the backs. The players chosen for the set are essentially the participants at the previous year's All-Star Game. Individual wax packs of All Stars (suggested retail price of 35 cents) contained one Pop-Up, five All-Star cards, and a Warren Spahn puzzle card.

	MINT	NRMT	EXC
COMPLETE SET (64)	8.00	3.60	1.00
COMMON CARD (1-64)	.05	.02	.01

☐ 1 Mark McGwire	1.25	.55	.16
☐ 2 Jose Canseco	.20	.09	.03
☐ 3 Paul Molitor	.40	.18	.05
☐ 4 Rickey Henderson	.25	.11	.03
☐ 5 Cal Ripken	2.00	.90	.25
☐ 6 Dave Winfield	.30	.14	.04
☐ 7 Wade Boggs	.25	.11	.03
☐ 8 Frank Viola	.05	.02	.01
☐ 9 Terry Steinbach	.10	.05	.01
☐ 10 Tom Kelly MG	.05	.02	.01
☐ 11 George Brett	1.00	.45	.12
☐ 12 Doyle Alexander	.05	.02	.01
☐ 13 Gary Gaetti	.05	.02	.01
☐ 14 Roger Clemens	.50	.23	.06
☐ 15 Mike Greenwell	.05	.02	.01
☐ 16 Dennis Eckersley	.10	.05	.01
☐ 17 Carney Lansford	.10	.05	.01
☐ 18 Mark Gubicza	.05	.02	.01
☐ 19 Tim Laudner	.05	.02	.01
☐ 20 Doug Jones	.05	.02	.01
☐ 21 Don Mattingly	1.25	.55	.16
☐ 22 Dan Plesac	.05	.02	.01
☐ 23 Kirby Puckett	1.25	.55	.16
☐ 24 Jeff Reardon	.10	.05	.01
☐ 25 Johnny Ray	.05	.02	.01
☐ 26 Jeff Russell	.05	.02	.01
☐ 27 Harold Reynolds	.05	.02	.01
☐ 28 Dave Stieb	.05	.02	.01
☐ 29 Kurt Stillwell	.05	.02	.01
☐ 30 Jose Canseco (Top AL Vote Getter)	.20	.09	.03
☐ 31 Terry Steinbach (All-Star Game MVP)	.10	.05	.01
☐ 32 AL Checklist 1-32	.05	.02	.01
☐ 33 Will Clark	.20	.09	.03
☐ 34 Darryl Strawberry	.10	.05	.01
☐ 35 Ryne Sandberg	1.00	.45	.12
☐ 36 Andre Dawson	.10	.05	.01
☐ 37 Ozzie Smith	1.00	.45	.12
☐ 38 Vince Coleman	.05	.02	.01
☐ 39 Bobby Bonilla	.20	.09	.03
☐ 40 Dwight Gooden	.10	.05	.01
☐ 41 Gary Carter	.10	.05	.01
☐ 42 Whitey Herzog MG	.05	.02	.01
☐ 43 Shawon Dunston	.05	.02	.01
☐ 44 David Cone	.20	.09	.03
☐ 45 Andres Galarraga	.20	.09	.03
☐ 46 Mark Davis	.05	.02	.01
☐ 47 Barry Larkin	.20	.09	.03
☐ 48 Kevin Gross	.05	.02	.01
☐ 49 Vance Law	.05	.02	.01
☐ 50 Orel Hershiser	.10	.05	.01
☐ 51 Willie McGee	.05	.02	.01
☐ 52 Danny Jackson	.05	.02	.01
☐ 53 Rafael Palmeiro	.40	.18	.05
☐ 54 Bob Knepper	.05	.02	.01
☐ 55 Lance Parrish	.05	.02	.01
☐ 56 Greg Maddux	2.00	.90	.25
☐ 57 Gerald Perry	.05	.02	.01
☐ 58 Bob Walk	.05	.02	.01
☐ 59 Chris Sabo	.05	.02	.01
☐ 60 Todd Worrell	.05	.02	.01
☐ 61 Andy Van Slyke	.10	.05	.01
☐ 62 Ozzie Smith (Top AL Vote Getter)	.75	.35	.09
☐ 63 Riverfront Stadium	.05	.02	.01
☐ 64 NL Checklist 33-64	.05	.02	.01

1989 Donruss Baseball's Best

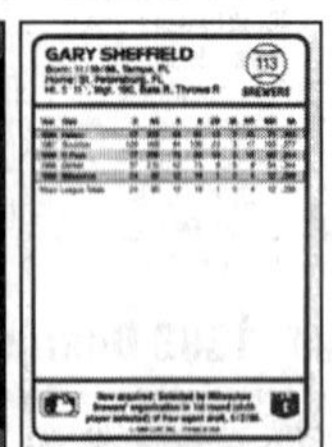

The 1989 Donruss Baseball's Best set contains 336 standard-size glossy cards. The fronts are green and yellow, and the backs feature career highlight information. The backs are green, and feature vertically oriented career stats. The cards were distributed as a set in a blister pack through various retail and department store chains. The Sammy Sosa card in this set is the only card issued of him in 1989.

	MINT	NRMT	EXC
COMPLETE SET (336)	6.00	2.70	.75
COMMON CARD (1-336)	.05	.02	.01

☐ 1 Don Mattingly	1.00	.45	.12
☐ 2 Tom Glavine	.50	.23	.06
☐ 3 Bert Blyleven	.10	.05	.01
☐ 4 Andre Dawson	.10	.05	.01
☐ 5 Pete O'Brien	.05	.02	.01
☐ 6 Eric Davis	.10	.05	.01
☐ 7 George Brett	.75	.35	.09
☐ 8 Glenn Davis	.05	.02	.01
☐ 9 Ellis Burks	.15	.07	.02
☐ 10 Kirk Gibson	.15	.07	.02
☐ 11 Carlton Fisk	.25	.11	.03
☐ 12 Andres Galarraga	.15	.07	.02
☐ 13 Alan Trammell	.10	.05	.01
☐ 14 Dwight Gooden	.10	.05	.01
☐ 15 Paul Molitor	.40	.18	.05
☐ 16 Roger McDowell	.05	.02	.01
☐ 17 Doug Drabek	.05	.02	.01
☐ 18 Kent Hrbek	.10	.05	.01
☐ 19 Vince Coleman	.05	.02	.01
☐ 20 Steve Sax	.05	.02	.01
☐ 21 Roberto Alomar	.50	.23	.06
☐ 22 Carney Lansford	.10	.05	.01
☐ 23 Will Clark	.15	.07	.02
☐ 24 Alvin Davis	.05	.02	.01
☐ 25 Bobby Thigpen	.05	.02	.01
☐ 26 Ryne Sandberg	.75	.35	.09
☐ 27 Devon White	.10	.05	.01
☐ 28 Mike Greenwell	.05	.02	.01
☐ 29 Dale Murphy	.15	.07	.02
☐ 30 Jeff Ballard	.05	.02	.01
☐ 31 Kelly Gruber	.05	.02	.01
☐ 32 Julio Franco	.10	.05	.01
☐ 33 Bobby Bonilla	.15	.07	.02
☐ 34 Tim Wallach	.05	.02	.01
☐ 35 Lou Whitaker	.10	.05	.01
☐ 36 Jay Howell	.05	.02	.01
☐ 37 Greg Maddux	1.50	.70	.19
☐ 38 Bill Doran	.05	.02	.01
☐ 39 Danny Tartabull	.05	.02	.01
☐ 40 Darryl Strawberry	.10	.05	.01
☐ 41 Ron Darling	.05	.02	.01
☐ 42 Tony Gwynn	1.00	.45	.12
☐ 43 Mark McGwire	1.25	.55	.16
☐ 44 Ozzie Smith	.60	.25	.07
☐ 45 Andy Van Slyke	.10	.05	.01
☐ 46 Juan Berenguer	.05	.02	.01
☐ 47 Von Hayes	.05	.02	.01
☐ 48 Tony Fernandez	.05	.02	.01
☐ 49 Eric Plunk	.05	.02	.01
☐ 50 Ernest Riles	.05	.02	.01
☐ 51 Harold Reynolds	.10	.05	.01
☐ 52 Andy Hawkins	.05	.02	.01
☐ 53 Robin Yount	.15	.07	.02
☐ 54 Danny Jackson	.05	.02	.01
☐ 55 Nolan Ryan	1.50	.70	.19
☐ 56 Joe Carter	.25	.11	.03
☐ 57 Jose Canseco	.30	.14	.04
☐ 58 Jody Davis	.05	.02	.01
☐ 59 Lance Parrish	.05	.02	.01
☐ 60 Mitch Williams	.05	.02	.01
☐ 61 Brook Jacoby	.05	.02	.01
☐ 62 Tom Browning	.05	.02	.01
☐ 63 Kurt Stillwell	.05	.02	.01
☐ 64 Rafael Ramirez	.05	.02	.01
☐ 65 Roger Clemens	.30	.14	.04
☐ 66 Mike Scioscia	.05	.02	.01
☐ 67 Dave Gallagher	.05	.02	.01
☐ 68 Mark Langston	.10	.05	.01
☐ 69 Chet Lemon	.05	.02	.01
☐ 70 Kevin McReynolds	.05	.02	.01
☐ 71 Rob Deer	.05	.02	.01
☐ 72 Tommy Herr	.05	.02	.01
☐ 73 Barry Bonds	.40	.18	.05
☐ 74 Frank Viola	.05	.02	.01
☐ 75 Pedro Guerrero	.05	.02	.01
☐ 76 Dave Righetti UER (ML total of 7 wins incorrect)	.05	.02	.01
☐ 77 Bruce Hurst	.05	.02	.01
☐ 78 Rickey Henderson	.25	.11	.03
☐ 79 Robby Thompson	.05	.02	.01
☐ 80 Randy Johnson	1.25	.55	.16
☐ 81 Harold Baines	.10	.05	.01
☐ 82 Calvin Schiraldi	.05	.02	.01
☐ 83 Kirk McCaskill	.05	.02	.01
☐ 84 Lee Smith	.10	.05	.01
☐ 85 John Smoltz	1.00	.45	.12
☐ 86 Mickey Tettleton	.05	.02	.01
☐ 87 Jimmy Key	.10	.05	.01
☐ 88 Rafael Palmeiro	.30	.14	.04
☐ 89 Sid Bream	.05	.02	.01
☐ 90 Dennis Martinez	.10	.05	.01
☐ 91 Frank Tanana	.05	.02	.01
☐ 92 Eddie Murray	.40	.18	.05
☐ 93 Shawon Dunston	.05	.02	.01
☐ 94 Mike Scott	.05	.02	.01
☐ 95 Bret Saberhagen	.10	.05	.01
☐ 96 David Cone	.20	.09	.03
☐ 97 Kevin Elster	.05	.02	.01
☐ 98 Jack Clark	.10	.05	.01
☐ 99 Dave Stewart	.10	.05	.01
☐ 100 Jose Oquendo	.05	.02	.01
☐ 101 Jose Lind	.05	.02	.01
☐ 102 Gary Gaetti	.05	.02	.01
☐ 103 Ricky Jordan	.05	.02	.01
☐ 104 Fred McGriff	.40	.18	.05
☐ 105 Don Slaught	.05	.02	.01
☐ 106 Jose Uribe	.05	.02	.01
☐ 107 Jeffrey Leonard	.05	.02	.01
☐ 108 Lee Guetterman	.05	.02	.01
☐ 109 Chris Bosio	.05	.02	.01
☐ 110 Barry Larkin	.15	.07	.02
☐ 111 Ruben Sierra	.10	.05	.01
☐ 112 Greg Swindell	.05	.02	.01
☐ 113 Gary Sheffield	1.00	.45	.12
☐ 114 Lonnie Smith	.05	.02	.01
☐ 115 Chili Davis	.10	.05	.01
☐ 116 Damon Berryhill	.05	.02	.01
☐ 117 Tom Candiotti	.05	.02	.01
☐ 118 Kal Daniels	.05	.02	.01
☐ 119 Mark Gubicza	.05	.02	.01
☐ 120 Jim Deshaies	.05	.02	.01
☐ 121 Dwight Evans	.10	.05	.01
☐ 122 Mike Morgan	.05	.02	.01
☐ 123 Dan Pasqua	.05	.02	.01
☐ 124 Bryn Smith	.05	.02	.01
☐ 125 Doyle Alexander	.05	.02	.01
☐ 126 Howard Johnson	.05	.02	.01
☐ 127 Chuck Crim	.05	.02	.01
☐ 128 Darren Daulton	.20	.09	.03
☐ 129 Jeff Robinson	.05	.02	.01
☐ 130 Kirby Puckett	1.00	.45	.12
☐ 131 Joe Magrane	.05	.02	.01
☐ 132 Jesse Barfield	.05	.02	.01
☐ 133 Mark Davis UER (Photo actually Dave Leiper)	.05	.02	.01
☐ 134 Dennis Eckersley	.10	.05	.01
☐ 135 Mike Krukow	.05	.02	.01
☐ 136 Jay Buhner	.40	.18	.05
☐ 137 Ozzie Guillen	.05	.02	.01
☐ 138 Rick Sutcliffe	.05	.02	.01
☐ 139 Wally Joyner	.10	.05	.01
☐ 140 Wade Boggs	.25	.11	.03
☐ 141 Jeff Treadway	.05	.02	.01
☐ 142 Cal Ripken	1.50	.70	.19
☐ 143 Dave Stieb	.05	.02	.01
☐ 144 Pete Incaviglia	.05	.02	.01
☐ 145 Bob Walk	.05	.02	.01
☐ 146 Nelson Santovenia	.05	.02	.01
☐ 147 Mike Heath	.05	.02	.01
☐ 148 Willie Randolph	.10	.05	.01
☐ 149 Paul Kilgus	.05	.02	.01
☐ 150 Billy Hatcher	.05	.02	.01
☐ 151 Steve Farr	.05	.02	.01
☐ 152 Gregg Jefferies	.25	.11	.03
☐ 153 Randy Myers	.10	.05	.01
☐ 154 Garry Templeton	.05	.02	.01
☐ 155 Walt Weiss	.05	.02	.01
☐ 156 Terry Pendleton	.10	.05	.01
☐ 157 John Smiley	.05	.02	.01
☐ 158 Greg Gagne	.05	.02	.01
☐ 159 Len Dykstra	.10	.05	.01
☐ 160 Nelson Liriano	.05	.02	.01
☐ 161 Alvaro Espinoza	.05	.02	.01
☐ 162 Rick Reuschel	.05	.02	.01
☐ 163 Omar Vizquel UER (Photo actually Darnell Coles)	.25	.11	.03
☐ 164 Clay Parker	.05	.02	.01
☐ 165 Dan Plesac	.05	.02	.01
☐ 166 John Franco	.10	.05	.01
☐ 167 Scott Fletcher	.05	.02	.01
☐ 168 Cory Snyder	.05	.02	.01
☐ 169 Bo Jackson	.15	.07	.02
☐ 170 Tommy Gregg	.05	.02	.01
☐ 171 Jim Abbott	.25	.11	.03
☐ 172 Jerome Walton	.10	.05	.01
☐ 173 Doug Jones	.05	.02	.01
☐ 174 Todd Benzinger	.05	.02	.01
☐ 175 Frank White	.10	.05	.01
☐ 176 Craig Biggio	.40	.18	.05
☐ 177 John Dopson	.05	.02	.01
☐ 178 Alfredo Griffin	.05	.02	.01
☐ 179 Melido Perez	.05	.02	.01
☐ 180 Tim Burke	.05	.02	.01
☐ 181 Matt Nokes	.05	.02	.01
☐ 182 Gary Carter	.10	.05	.01
☐ 183 Ted Higuera	.05	.02	.01
☐ 184 Ken Howell	.05	.02	.01
☐ 185 Rey Quinones	.05	.02	.01
☐ 186 Wally Backman	.05	.02	.01
☐ 187 Tom Brunansky	.05	.02	.01
☐ 188 Steve Balboni	.05	.02	.01
☐ 189 Marvell Wynne	.05	.02	.01
☐ 190 Dave Henderson	.05	.02	.01
☐ 191 Don Robinson	.05	.02	.01
☐ 192 Ken Griffey Jr.	3.00	1.35	.35
☐ 193 Ivan Calderon	.05	.02	.01
☐ 194 Mike Bielecki	.05	.02	.01
☐ 195 Johnny Ray	.05	.02	.01
☐ 196 Rob Murphy	.05	.02	.01
☐ 197 Andres Thomas	.05	.02	.01
☐ 198 Phil Bradley	.05	.02	.01
☐ 199 Junior Felix	.05	.02	.01
☐ 200 Jeff Russell	.05	.02	.01
☐ 201 Mike LaValliere	.05	.02	.01
☐ 202 Kevin Gross	.05	.02	.01
☐ 203 Keith Moreland	.05	.02	.01
☐ 204 Mike Marshall	.05	.02	.01
☐ 205 Dwight Smith	.10	.05	.01
☐ 206 Jim Clancy	.05	.02	.01
☐ 207 Kevin Seitzer	.05	.02	.01
☐ 208 Keith Hernandez	.10	.05	.01
☐ 209 Bob Ojeda	.05	.02	.01
☐ 210 Ed Whitson	.05	.02	.01
☐ 211 Tony Phillips	.10	.05	.01
☐ 212 Milt Thompson	.05	.02	.01
☐ 213 Randy Kramer	.05	.02	.01
☐ 214 Randy Bush	.05	.02	.01
☐ 215 Randy Ready	.05	.02	.01
☐ 216 Duane Ward	.05	.02	.01
☐ 217 Jimmy Jones	.05	.02	.01
☐ 218 Scott Garrelts	.05	.02	.01
☐ 219 Scott Bankhead	.05	.02	.01
☐ 220 Lance McCullers	.05	.02	.01
☐ 221 B.J. Surhoff	.10	.05	.01
☐ 222 Chris Sabo	.05	.02	.01
☐ 223 Steve Buechele	.05	.02	.01
☐ 224 Joel Skinner	.05	.02	.01
☐ 225 Orel Hershiser	.10	.05	.01
☐ 226 Derek Lilliquist	.05	.02	.01
☐ 227 Claudell Washington	.05	.02	.01
☐ 228 Lloyd McClendon	.05	.02	.01
☐ 229 Felix Fermin	.05	.02	.01
☐ 230 Paul O'Neill	.10	.05	.01
☐ 231 Charlie Leibrandt	.05	.02	.01
☐ 232 Dave Smith	.05	.02	.01
☐ 233 Bob Stanley	.05	.02	.01
☐ 234 Tim Belcher	.05	.02	.01
☐ 235 Eric King	.05	.02	.01
☐ 236 Spike Owen	.05	.02	.01
☐ 237 Mike Henneman	.05	.02	.01
☐ 238 Juan Samuel	.05	.02	.01
☐ 239 Greg Brock	.05	.02	.01
☐ 240 John Kruk	.20	.09	.03
☐ 241 Glenn Wilson	.05	.02	.01
☐ 242 Jeff Reardon	.10	.05	.01
☐ 243 Todd Worrell	.05	.02	.01
☐ 244 Dave LaPoint	.05	.02	.01
☐ 245 Walt Terrell	.05	.02	.01
☐ 246 Mike Moore	.05	.02	.01
☐ 247 Kelly Downs	.05	.02	.01
☐ 248 Dave Valle	.05	.02	.01
☐ 249 Ron Kittle	.05	.02	.01
☐ 250 Steve Wilson	.05	.02	.01
☐ 251 Dick Schofield	.05	.02	.01
☐ 252 Marty Barrett	.05	.02	.01
☐ 253 Dion James	.05	.02	.01
☐ 254 Bob Milacki	.05	.02	.01
☐ 255 Ernie Whitt	.05	.02	.01
☐ 256 Kevin Brown	.15	.07	.02
☐ 257 R.J. Reynolds	.05	.02	.01
☐ 258 Tim Raines	.10	.05	.01
☐ 259 Frank Williams	.05	.02	.01
☐ 260 Jose Gonzalez	.05	.02	.01
☐ 261 Mitch Webster	.05	.02	.01
☐ 262 Ken Caminiti	.40	.18	.05
☐ 263 Bob Boone	.10	.05	.01
☐ 264 Dave Magadan	.05	.02	.01
☐ 265 Rick Aguilera	.10	.05	.01
☐ 266 Chris James	.05	.02	.01
☐ 267 Bob Welch	.05	.02	.01
☐ 268 Ken Dayley	.05	.02	.01
☐ 269 Junior Ortiz	.05	.02	.01
☐ 270 Allan Anderson	.05	.02	.01
☐ 271 Steve Jeltz	.05	.02	.01
☐ 272 George Bell	.05	.02	.01
☐ 273 Roberto Kelly	.05	.02	.01
☐ 274 Brett Butler	.10	.05	.01
☐ 275 Mike Schooler	.05	.02	.01
☐ 276 Ken Phelps	.05	.02	.01
☐ 277 Glenn Braggs	.05	.02	.01
☐ 278 Jose Rijo	.05	.02	.01
☐ 279 Bobby Witt	.05	.02	.01
☐ 280 Jerry Browne	.05	.02	.01
☐ 281 Kevin Mitchell	.10	.05	.01
☐ 282 Craig Worthington	.05	.02	.01
☐ 283 Greg Minton	.05	.02	.01
☐ 284 Nick Esasky	.05	.02	.01
☐ 285 John Farrell	.05	.02	.01
☐ 286 Rick Mahler	.05	.02	.01
☐ 287 Tom Gordon	.10	.05	.01
☐ 288 Gerald Young	.05	.02	.01
☐ 289 Jody Reed	.05	.02	.01
☐ 290 Jeff Hamilton	.05	.02	.01
☐ 291 Gerald Perry	.05	.02	.01
☐ 292 Hubie Brooks	.05	.02	.01
☐ 293 Bo Diaz	.05	.02	.01
☐ 294 Terry Puhl	.05	.02	.01
☐ 295 Jim Gantner	.05	.02	.01
☐ 296 Jeff Parrett	.05	.02	.01
☐ 297 Mike Boddicker	.05	.02	.01
☐ 298 Dan Gladden	.05	.02	.01
☐ 299 Tony Pena	.05	.02	.01
☐ 300 Checklist Card	.05	.02	.01
☐ 301 Tom Henke	.05	.02	.01
☐ 302 Pascual Perez	.05	.02	.01
☐ 303 Steve Bedrosian	.05	.02	.01
☐ 304 Ken Hill	.25	.11	.03
☐ 305 Jerry Reuss	.05	.02	.01
☐ 306 Jim Eisenreich	.10	.05	.01
☐ 307 Jack Howell	.05	.02	.01
☐ 308 Rick Cerone	.05	.02	.01
☐ 309 Tim Leary	.05	.02	.01
☐ 310 Joe Orsulak	.05	.02	.01
☐ 311 Jim Dwyer	.05	.02	.01
☐ 312 Geno Petralli	.05	.02	.01
☐ 313 Rick Honeycutt	.05	.02	.01
☐ 314 Tom Foley	.05	.02	.01
☐ 315 Kenny Rogers	.25	.11	.03
☐ 316 Mike Flanagan	.05	.02	.01
☐ 317 Bryan Harvey	.10	.05	.01
☐ 318 Billy Ripken	.05	.02	.01
☐ 319 Jeff Montgomery	.10	.05	.01
☐ 320 Erik Hanson	.15	.07	.02

	MINT	NRMT	EXC
☐ 321 Brian Downing	.05	.02	.01
☐ 322 Gregg Olson	.10	.05	.01
☐ 323 Terry Steinbach	.10	.05	.01
☐ 324 Sammy Sosa	1.50	.70	.19
☐ 325 Gene Harris	.05	.02	.01
☐ 326 Mike Devereaux	.05	.02	.01
☐ 327 Dennis Cook	.05	.02	.01
☐ 328 David Wells	.05	.02	.01
☐ 329 Checklist Card	.05	.02	.01
☐ 330 Kirt Manwaring	.05	.02	.01
☐ 331 Jim Presley	.05	.02	.01
☐ 332 Checklist Card	.05	.02	.01
☐ 333 Chuck Finley	.10	.05	.01
☐ 334 Rob Dibble	.05	.02	.01
☐ 335 Cecil Espy	.05	.02	.01
☐ 336 Dave Parker	.10	.05	.01

1989 Donruss Pop-Ups

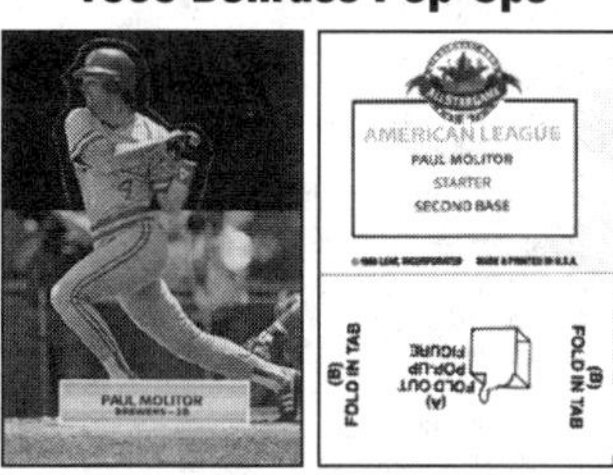

These Pop-Ups are borderless and standard size. The cards are unnumbered; however the All Star checklist card lists the same numbers as the All Star cards. Those numbers are used below for reference. The players chosen for the set are essentially the starting lineups for the previous year's All-Star Game. Individual wax packs of All Stars (suggested retail price of 35 cents) contained one Pop-Up, five All-Star cards and a puzzle card.

	MINT	NRMT	EXC
COMPLETE SET (20)	5.00	2.20	.60
COMMON AL (1-10)	.10	.05	.01
COMMON NL (33-42)	.10	.05	.01
☐ 1 Mark McGwire	1.25	.55	.16
☐ 2 Jose Canseco	.50	.23	.06
☐ 3 Paul Molitor	.50	.23	.06
☐ 4 Rickey Henderson	.30	.14	.04
☐ 5 Cal Ripken	2.50	1.10	.30
☐ 6 Dave Winfield	.30	.14	.04
☐ 7 Wade Boggs	.40	.18	.05
☐ 8 Frank Viola	.10	.05	.01
☐ 9 Terry Steinbach	.20	.09	.03
☐ 10 Tom Kelly MG	.10	.05	.01
☐ 33 Will Clark	.30	.14	.04
☐ 34 Darryl Strawberry	.20	.09	.03
☐ 35 Ryne Sandberg	1.00	.45	.12
☐ 36 Andre Dawson	.20	.09	.03
☐ 37 Ozzie Smith	1.00	.45	.12
☐ 38 Vince Coleman	.10	.05	.01
☐ 39 Bobby Bonilla	.30	.14	.04
☐ 40 Dwight Gooden	.20	.09	.03
☐ 41 Gary Carter	.20	.09	.03
☐ 42 Whitey Herzog MG	.10	.05	.01

1989 Donruss Super DK's

This 26-player card set was available through a mail-in offer detailed on the wax packs. The set was sent in return for $8.00 and three wrappers plus $2.00 postage and handling. The set features the popular Diamond King subseries in large (approximately 4 7/8" X 6 13/16") form. Dick Perez of Perez-Steele Galleries did another outstanding job on the artwork. The cards are essentially a large version of the Donruss regular issue Diamond Kings.

	MINT	NRMT	EXC
COMPLETE SET (26)	15.00	6.75	1.85
COMMON CARD (1-26)	.25	.11	.03
☐ 1 Mike Greenwell	.25	.11	.03
☐ 2 Bobby Bonilla	.75	.35	.09
☐ 3 Pete Incaviglia	.25	.11	.03
☐ 4 Chris Sabo	.25	.11	.03
☐ 5 Robin Yount	.75	.35	.09
☐ 6 Tony Gwynn	2.50	1.10	.30
☐ 7 Carlton Fisk	1.25	.55	.16
☐ 8 Cory Snyder	.25	.11	.03
☐ 9 David Cone	1.25	.55	.16
☐ 10 Kevin Seitzer	.25	.11	.03
☐ 11 Rick Reuschel	.25	.11	.03
☐ 12 Johnny Ray	.25	.11	.03
☐ 13 Dave Schmidt	.25	.11	.03
☐ 14 Andres Galarraga	.75	.35	.09
☐ 15 Kirk Gibson	.75	.35	.09
☐ 16 Fred McGriff	2.00	.90	.25
☐ 17 Mark Grace	2.00	.90	.25
☐ 18 Jeff M. Robinson	.25	.11	.03
☐ 19 Vince Coleman	.25	.11	.03
☐ 20 Dave Henderson	.25	.11	.03
☐ 21 Harold Reynolds	.50	.23	.06
☐ 22 Gerald Perry	.25	.11	.03
☐ 23 Frank Viola	.25	.11	.03
☐ 24 Steve Bedrosian	.25	.11	.03
☐ 25 Glenn Davis	.25	.11	.03
☐ 26 Don Mattingly	3.00	1.35	.35

1989 Donruss Traded

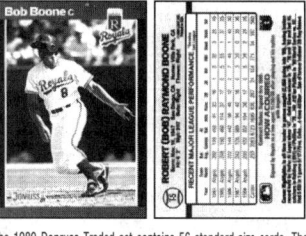

The 1989 Donruss Traded set contains 56 standard-size cards. The fronts have yellowish-orange borders; the backs are yellow and feature recent statistics. The cards were distributed as a boxed set. The set was never very popular with collectors since it included (as the name implies) only traded players rather than rookies. The cards are numbered with a "T" prefix.

	MINT	NRMT	EXC
COMPLETE SET (56)	4.00	1.80	.50
COMMON CARD (1-56)	.05	.02	.01
☐ 1 Jeffrey Leonard	.05	.02	.01
☐ 2 Jack Clark	.10	.05	.01
☐ 3 Kevin Gross	.05	.02	.01
☐ 4 Tommy Herr	.05	.02	.01
☐ 5 Bob Boone	.10	.05	.01
☐ 6 Rafael Palmeiro	.75	.35	.09
☐ 7 John Dopson	.05	.02	.01
☐ 8 Willie Randolph	.10	.05	.01
☐ 9 Chris Brown	.05	.02	.01
☐ 10 Wally Backman	.05	.02	.01
☐ 11 Steve Ontiveros	.05	.02	.01
☐ 12 Eddie Murray	.75	.35	.09
☐ 13 Lance McCullers	.05	.02	.01
☐ 14 Spike Owen	.05	.02	.01
☐ 15 Rob Murphy	.05	.02	.01
☐ 16 Pete O'Brien	.05	.02	.01
☐ 17 Ken Williams	.05	.02	.01
☐ 18 Nick Esasky	.05	.02	.01
☐ 19 Nolan Ryan	2.50	1.10	.30
☐ 20 Brian Holton	.05	.02	.01
☐ 21 Mike Moore	.05	.02	.01
☐ 22 Joel Skinner	.05	.02	.01
☐ 23 Steve Sax	.05	.02	.01
☐ 24 Rick Mahler	.05	.02	.01
☐ 25 Mike Aldrete	.05	.02	.01
☐ 26 Jesse Orosco	.05	.02	.01
☐ 27 Dave LaPoint	.05	.02	.01
☐ 28 Walt Terrell	.05	.02	.01
☐ 29 Eddie Williams	.05	.02	.01
☐ 30 Mike Devereaux	.05	.02	.01
☐ 31 Julio Franco	.10	.05	.01
☐ 32 Jim Clancy	.05	.02	.01
☐ 33 Felix Fermin	.05	.02	.01
☐ 34 Curt Wilkerson	.05	.02	.01
☐ 35 Bert Blyleven	.10	.05	.01
☐ 36 Mel Hall	.05	.02	.01
☐ 37 Eric King	.05	.02	.01
☐ 38 Mitch Williams	.05	.02	.01
☐ 39 Jamie Moyer	.05	.02	.01
☐ 40 Rick Rhoden	.05	.02	.01
☐ 41 Phil Bradley	.05	.02	.01
☐ 42 Paul Kilgus	.05	.02	.01
☐ 43 Milt Thompson	.05	.02	.01
☐ 44 Jerry Browne	.05	.02	.01
☐ 45 Bruce Hurst	.05	.02	.01
☐ 46 Claudell Washington	.05	.02	.01
☐ 47 Todd Benzinger	.05	.02	.01
☐ 48 Steve Balboni	.05	.02	.01
☐ 49 Oddibe McDowell	.05	.02	.01
☐ 50 Charles Hudson	.05	.02	.01
☐ 51 Ron Kittle	.05	.02	.01
☐ 52 Andy Hawkins	.05	.02	.01
☐ 53 Tom Brookens	.05	.02	.01
☐ 54 Tom Niedenfuer	.05	.02	.01
☐ 55 Jeff Parrett	.05	.02	.01
☐ 56 Checklist Card	.05	.02	.01

1990 Donruss Previews

The 1990 Donruss Previews set contains 12 standard-size cards. The bright red borders are exactly like the regular 1990 Donruss cards, but many of the photos are different. The horizontally oriented backs are plain white with career highlights in black lettering. Two cards were sent to each dealer in the Donruss dealer network thus making it quite difficult to put together a set.

	MINT	NRMT	EXC
COMPLETE SET (12)	400.00	180.00	50.00
COMMON CARD (1-12)	15.00	6.75	1.85
☐ 1 Todd Zeile (Not shown as Rated Rookie on front)	15.00	6.75	1.85
☐ 2 Ben McDonald	15.00	6.75	1.85
☐ 3 Bo Jackson	20.00	9.00	2.50
☐ 4 Will Clark	30.00	13.50	3.70
☐ 5 Dave Stewart	15.00	6.75	1.85
☐ 6 Kevin Mitchell	15.00	6.75	1.85
☐ 7 Nolan Ryan	200.00	90.00	25.00
☐ 8 Howard Johnson	15.00	6.75	1.85
☐ 9 Tony Gwynn	75.00	34.00	9.50
☐ 10 Jerome Walton (Shown ready to bunt)	15.00	6.75	1.85
☐ 11 Wade Boggs	30.00	13.50	3.70
☐ 12 Kirby Puckett	75.00	34.00	9.50

1990 Donruss

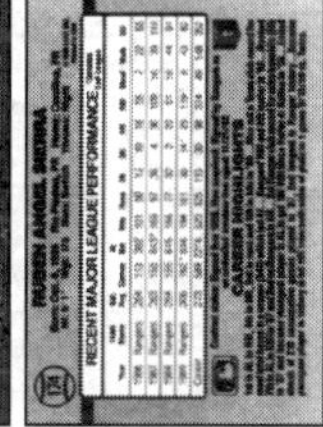

The 1990 Donruss set contains 716 standard-size cards. Cards were issued in wax packs and hobby and retail factory sets. The card fronts feature bright red borders. Subsets include Diamond Kings (1-27) and Rated Rookies (28-47). The set was the largest ever produced by Donruss, unfortunately it also had a large number of errors which were corrected after the cards were released. Most of these feature minor printing flaws and insignificant variations that collectors have found unworthy of price differentials. There are several double-printed cards within the set indicated in the checklists below with a "DP" coding. Rookie Cards of note include Juan Gonzalez, Marquis Grissom, Dave Justice, Ben McDonald, Dean Palmer, Sammy Sosa, Larry Walker and Bernie Williams. Numbered with the prefix "BC", Special Bonus Cards from a set featuring one most valuable player from each of the 26 teams were randomly inserted in all 1990 Donruss unopened pack formats. The factory sets were distributed without the Bonus Cards.

	MINT	NRMT	EXC
COMPLETE SET (716)	8.00	3.60	1.00
COMPLETE FACT.SET (728)	8.00	3.60	1.00
COMMON CARD (1-716)	.05	.02	.01
☐ 1 Bo Jackson DK	.10	.05	.01
☐ 2 Steve Sax DK	.05	.02	.01
☐ 3A Ruben Sierra DK ERR (No small line on top border on card back)	.20	.09	.03
☐ 3B Ruben Sierra DK COR	.15	.07	.02
☐ 4 Ken Griffey Jr. DK	.75	.35	.09
☐ 5 Mickey Tettleton DK	.05	.02	.01
☐ 6 Dave Stewart DK	.10	.05	.01
☐ 7 Jim Deshaies DK DP	.05	.02	.01
☐ 8 John Smoltz DK	.15	.07	.02
☐ 9 Mike Bielecki DK	.05	.02	.01
☐ 10A Brian Downing DK ERR (Reverse negative on card front)	.15	.07	.02
☐ 10B Brian Downing DK COR	.05	.02	.01
☐ 11 Kevin Mitchell DK	.05	.02	.01
☐ 12 Kelly Gruber DK	.05	.02	.01
☐ 13 Joe Magrane DK	.05	.02	.01
☐ 14 John Franco DK	.05	.02	.01
☐ 15 Ozzie Guillen DK	.05	.02	.01
☐ 16 Lou Whitaker DK	.10	.05	.01
☐ 17 John Smiley DK	.05	.02	.01
☐ 18 Howard Johnson DK	.05	.02	.01
☐ 19 Willie Randolph DK	.10	.05	.01
☐ 20 Chris Bosio DK	.05	.02	.01
☐ 21 Tommy Herr DK DP	.05	.02	.01
☐ 22 Dan Gladden DK	.05	.02	.01
☐ 23 Ellis Burks DK	.15	.07	.02
☐ 24 Pete O'Brien DK	.05	.02	.01
☐ 25 Bryn Smith DK	.05	.02	.01
☐ 26 Ed Whitson DK DP	.05	.02	.01
☐ 27 DK Checklist 1-27 DP (Comments on Perez-Steele on back)	.05	.02	.01
☐ 28 Robin Ventura RR	.15	.07	.02
☐ 29 Todd Zeile RR	.10	.05	.01
☐ 30 Sandy Alomar Jr. RR	.15	.07	.02
☐ 31 Kent Mercker RR	.10	.05	.01
☐ 32 Ben McDonald RR UER (Middle name Benard, not Benjamin)	.15	.07	.02
☐ 33A Juan Gonzalez RR ERR (Reverse negative)	5.00	2.20	.60
☐ 33B Juan Gonzalez RR COR	2.00	.90	.25
☐ 34 Eric Anthony RR	.10	.05	.01
☐ 35 Mike Fetters RR	.10	.05	.01
☐ 36 Marquis Grissom RR	.50	.23	.06
☐ 37 Greg Vaughn RR	.15	.07	.02
☐ 38 Brian DuBois RR	.05	.02	.01
☐ 39 Steve Avery RR UER (Born in MI, not NJ)	.15	.07	.02
☐ 40 Mark Gardner RR	.05	.02	.01
☐ 41 Andy Benes RR	.15	.07	.02
☐ 42 Delino DeShields RR	.10	.05	.01
☐ 43 Scott Coolbaugh RR	.05	.02	.01
☐ 44 Pat Combs RR DP	.05	.02	.01
☐ 45 Alex Sanchez RR DP	.05	.02	.01
☐ 46 Kelly Mann RR DP	.05	.02	.01
☐ 47 Julio Machado RR DP	.05	.02	.01
☐ 48 Pete Incaviglia	.05	.02	.01
☐ 49 Shawon Dunston	.05	.02	.01
☐ 50 Jeff Treadway	.05	.02	.01
☐ 51 Jeff Ballard	.05	.02	.01
☐ 52 Claudell Washington	.05	.02	.01
☐ 53 Juan Samuel	.05	.02	.01
☐ 54 John Smiley	.10	.05	.01
☐ 55 Rob Deer	.05	.02	.01
☐ 56 Geno Petralli	.05	.02	.01
☐ 57 Chris Bosio	.05	.02	.01
☐ 58 Carlton Fisk	.15	.07	.02
☐ 59 Kirt Manwaring	.05	.02	.01
☐ 60 Chet Lemon	.05	.02	.01
☐ 61 Bo Jackson	.10	.05	.01
☐ 62 Doyle Alexander	.05	.02	.01
☐ 63 Pedro Guerrero	.05	.02	.01
☐ 64 Allan Anderson	.05	.02	.01
☐ 65 Greg W. Harris	.05	.02	.01
☐ 66 Mike Greenwell	.05	.02	.01
☐ 67 Walt Weiss	.05	.02	.01
☐ 68 Wade Boggs	.15	.07	.02
☐ 69 Jim Clancy	.05	.02	.01
☐ 70 Junior Felix	.05	.02	.01
☐ 71 Barry Larkin	.15	.07	.02
☐ 72 Dave LaPoint	.05	.02	.01
☐ 73 Joel Skinner	.05	.02	.01
☐ 74 Jesse Barfield	.05	.02	.01
☐ 75 Tommy Herr	.05	.02	.01
☐ 76 Ricky Jordan	.05	.02	.01
☐ 77 Eddie Murray	.25	.11	.03
☐ 78 Steve Sax	.05	.02	.01
☐ 79 Tim Belcher	.05	.02	.01
☐ 80 Danny Jackson	.05	.02	.01
☐ 81 Kent Hrbek	.10	.05	.01
☐ 82 Milt Thompson	.05	.02	.01
☐ 83 Brook Jacoby	.05	.02	.01
☐ 84 Mike Marshall	.05	.02	.01
☐ 85 Kevin Seitzer	.05	.02	.01
☐ 86 Tony Gwynn	.40	.18	.05
☐ 87 Dave Stieb	.05	.02	.01
☐ 88 Dave Smith	.05	.02	.01
☐ 89 Bret Saberhagen	.10	.05	.01
☐ 90 Alan Trammell	.10	.05	.01
☐ 91 Tony Phillips	.15	.07	.02
☐ 92 Doug Drabek	.05	.02	.01
☐ 93 Jeffrey Leonard	.05	.02	.01
☐ 94 Wally Joyner	.10	.05	.01
☐ 95 Carney Lansford	.10	.05	.01
☐ 96 Cal Ripken	.75	.35	.09
☐ 97 Andres Galarraga	.15	.07	.02
☐ 98 Kevin Mitchell	.10	.05	.01
☐ 99 Howard Johnson	.05	.02	.01
☐ 100A Checklist 28-129	.05	.02	.01
☐ 100B Checklist 28-125	.05	.02	.01
☐ 101 Melido Perez	.05	.02	.01
☐ 102 Spike Owen	.05	.02	.01
☐ 103 Paul Molitor	.20	.09	.03
☐ 104 Geronimo Berroa	.10	.05	.01
☐ 105 Ryne Sandberg	.25	.11	.03
☐ 106 Bryn Smith	.05	.02	.01
☐ 107 Steve Buechele	.05	.02	.01
☐ 108 Jim Abbott	.10	.05	.01
☐ 109 Alvin Davis	.05	.02	.01
☐ 110 Lee Smith	.10	.05	.01
☐ 111 Roberto Alomar	.25	.11	.03
☐ 112 Rick Reuschel	.05	.02	.01
☐ 113A Kelly Gruber ERR (Born 2/22)	.05	.02	.01
☐ 113B Kelly Gruber COR (Born 2/26; corrected in factory sets)	.05	.02	.01
☐ 114 Joe Carter	.10	.05	.01
☐ 115 Jose Rijo	.05	.02	.01
☐ 116 Greg Minton	.05	.02	.01
☐ 117 Bob Ojeda	.05	.02	.01
☐ 118 Glenn Davis	.05	.02	.01
☐ 119 Jeff Reardon	.10	.05	.01
☐ 120 Kurt Stillwell	.05	.02	.01
☐ 121 John Smoltz	.25	.11	.03
☐ 122 Dwight Evans	.10	.05	.01

Card			
☐ 123 Eric Yelding	.05	.02	.01
☐ 124 John Franco	.05	.02	.01
☐ 125 Jose Canseco	.15	.07	.02
☐ 126 Barry Bonds	.25	.11	.03
☐ 127 Lee Guetterman	.05	.02	.01
☐ 128 Jack Clark	.10	.05	.01
☐ 129 Dave Valle	.05	.02	.01
☐ 130 Hubie Brooks	.05	.02	.01
☐ 131 Ernest Riles	.05	.02	.01
☐ 132 Mike Morgan	.05	.02	.01
☐ 133 Steve Jeltz	.05	.02	.01
☐ 134 Jeff D. Robinson	.05	.02	.01
☐ 135 Ozzie Guillen	.05	.02	.01
☐ 136 Chili Davis	.10	.05	.01
☐ 137 Mitch Webster	.05	.02	.01
☐ 138 Jerry Browne	.05	.02	.01
☐ 139 Bo Diaz	.05	.02	.01
☐ 140 Robby Thompson	.05	.02	.01
☐ 141 Craig Worthington	.05	.02	.01
☐ 142 Julio Franco	.10	.05	.01
☐ 143 Brian Holman	.05	.02	.01
☐ 144 George Brett	.40	.18	.05
☐ 145 Tom Glavine	.15	.07	.02
☐ 146 Robin Yount	.15	.07	.02
☐ 147 Gary Carter	.10	.05	.01
☐ 148 Ron Kittle	.05	.02	.01
☐ 149 Tony Fernandez	.05	.02	.01
☐ 150 Dave Stewart	.10	.05	.01
☐ 151 Gary Gaetti	.10	.05	.01
☐ 152 Kevin Elster	.05	.02	.01
☐ 153 Gerald Perry	.05	.02	.01
☐ 154 Jesse Orosco	.05	.02	.01
☐ 155 Wally Backman	.05	.02	.01
☐ 156 Dennis Martinez	.10	.05	.01
☐ 157 Rick Sutcliffe	.05	.02	.01
☐ 158 Greg Maddux	.60	.25	.07
☐ 159 Andy Hawkins	.05	.02	.01
☐ 160 John Kruk	.10	.05	.01
☐ 161 Jose Oquendo	.05	.02	.01
☐ 162 John Dopson	.05	.02	.01
☐ 163 Joe Magrane	.05	.02	.01
☐ 164 Bill Ripken	.05	.02	.01
☐ 165 Fred Manrique	.05	.02	.01
☐ 166 Nolan Ryan UER	.75	.35	.09
(Did not lead NL in K's in '89 as he was in AL in '89)			
☐ 167 Damon Berryhill	.05	.02	.01
☐ 168 Dale Murphy	.15	.07	.02
☐ 169 Mickey Tettleton	.10	.05	.01
☐ 170A Kirk McCaskill ERR	.05	.02	.01
(Born 4/19)			
☐ 170B Kirk McCaskill COR	.05	.02	.01
(Born 4/9; corrected in factory sets)			
☐ 171 Dwight Gooden	.10	.05	.01
☐ 172 Jose Lind	.05	.02	.01
☐ 173 B.J. Surhoff	.10	.05	.01
☐ 174 Ruben Sierra	.10	.05	.01
☐ 175 Dan Plesac	.05	.02	.01
☐ 176 Dan Pasqua	.05	.02	.01
☐ 177 Kelly Downs	.05	.02	.01
☐ 178 Matt Nokes	.05	.02	.01
☐ 179 Luis Aquino	.05	.02	.01
☐ 180 Frank Tanana	.05	.02	.01
☐ 181 Tony Pena	.05	.02	.01
☐ 182 Dan Gladden	.05	.02	.01
☐ 183 Bruce Hurst	.05	.02	.01
☐ 184 Roger Clemens	.20	.09	.03
☐ 185 Mark McGwire	.30	.14	.04
☐ 186 Rob Murphy	.05	.02	.01
☐ 187 Jim Deshaies	.05	.02	.01
☐ 188 Fred McGriff	.15	.07	.02
☐ 189 Rob Dibble	.05	.02	.01
☐ 190 Don Mattingly	.50	.23	.06
☐ 191 Felix Fermin	.05	.02	.01
☐ 192 Roberto Kelly	.10	.05	.01
☐ 193 Dennis Cook	.05	.02	.01
☐ 194 Darren Daulton	.10	.05	.01
☐ 195 Alfredo Griffin	.05	.02	.01
☐ 196 Eric Plunk	.05	.02	.01
☐ 197 Orel Hershiser	.10	.05	.01
☐ 198 Paul O'Neill	.10	.05	.01
☐ 199 Randy Bush	.05	.02	.01
☐ 200A Checklist 130-231	.05	.02	.01
☐ 200B Checklist 126-223	.05	.02	.01
☐ 201 Ozzie Smith	.25	.11	.03
☐ 202 Pete O'Brien	.05	.02	.01
☐ 203 Jay Howell	.05	.02	.01
☐ 204 Mark Gubicza	.05	.02	.01
☐ 205 Ed Whitson	.05	.02	.01
☐ 206 George Bell	.05	.02	.01
☐ 207 Mike Scott	.05	.02	.01
☐ 208 Charlie Leibrandt	.05	.02	.01
☐ 209 Mike Heath	.05	.02	.01
☐ 210 Dennis Eckersley	.10	.05	.01
☐ 211 Mike LaValliere	.05	.02	.01
☐ 212 Darnell Coles	.05	.02	.01
☐ 213 Lance Parrish	.05	.02	.01
☐ 214 Mike Moore	.05	.02	.01
☐ 215 Steve Finley	.15	.07	.02
☐ 216 Tim Raines	.15	.07	.02
☐ 217A Scott Garrelts ERR	.05	.02	.01
(Born 10/20)			
☐ 217B Scott Garrelts COR	.05	.02	.01
(Born 10/30; corrected in factory sets)			
☐ 218 Kevin McReynolds	.05	.02	.01
☐ 219 Dave Gallagher	.05	.02	.01
☐ 220 Tim Wallach	.05	.02	.01
☐ 221 Chuck Crim	.05	.02	.01
☐ 222 Lonnie Smith	.05	.02	.01
☐ 223 Andre Dawson	.10	.05	.01
☐ 224 Nelson Santovenia	.05	.02	.01
☐ 225 Rafael Palmeiro	.15	.07	.02
☐ 226 Devon White	.10	.05	.01
☐ 227 Harold Reynolds	.05	.02	.01
☐ 228 Ellis Burks	.15	.07	.02
☐ 229 Mark Parent	.05	.02	.01
☐ 230 Will Clark	.15	.07	.02
☐ 231 Jimmy Key	.10	.05	.01
☐ 232 John Farrell	.05	.02	.01
☐ 233 Eric Davis	.10	.05	.01
☐ 234 Johnny Ray	.05	.02	.01
☐ 235 Darryl Strawberry	.10	.05	.01
☐ 236 Bill Doran	.05	.02	.01
☐ 237 Greg Gagne	.05	.02	.01
☐ 238 Jim Eisenreich	.05	.02	.01
☐ 239 Tommy Gregg	.05	.02	.01
☐ 240 Marty Barrett	.05	.02	.01
☐ 241 Rafael Ramirez	.05	.02	.01
☐ 242 Chris Sabo	.05	.02	.01
☐ 243 Dave Henderson	.05	.02	.01
☐ 244 Andy Van Slyke	.10	.05	.01
☐ 245 Alvaro Espinoza	.05	.02	.01
☐ 246 Garry Templeton	.05	.02	.01
☐ 247 Gene Harris	.05	.02	.01
☐ 248 Kevin Gross	.05	.02	.01
☐ 249 Brett Butler	.10	.05	.01
☐ 250 Willie Randolph	.10	.05	.01
☐ 251 Roger McDowell	.05	.02	.01
☐ 252 Rafael Belliard	.05	.02	.01
☐ 253 Steve Rosenberg	.05	.02	.01
☐ 254 Jack Howell	.05	.02	.01
☐ 255 Marvell Wynne	.05	.02	.01
☐ 256 Tom Candiotti	.05	.02	.01
☐ 257 Todd Benzinger	.05	.02	.01
☐ 258 Don Robinson	.05	.02	.01
☐ 259 Phil Bradley	.05	.02	.01
☐ 260 Cecil Espy	.05	.02	.01
☐ 261 Scott Bankhead	.05	.02	.01
☐ 262 Frank White	.10	.05	.01
☐ 263 Andres Thomas	.05	.02	.01
☐ 264 Glenn Braggs	.05	.02	.01
☐ 265 David Cone	.15	.07	.02
☐ 266 Bobby Thigpen	.05	.02	.01
☐ 267 Nelson Liriano	.05	.02	.01
☐ 268 Terry Steinbach	.10	.05	.01
☐ 269 Kirby Puckett UER	.40	.18	.05
(Back doesn't consider Joe Torre's .363 in '71)			
☐ 270 Gregg Jefferies	.10	.05	.01
☐ 271 Jeff Blauser	.10	.05	.01
☐ 272 Cory Snyder	.05	.02	.01
☐ 273 Roy Smith	.05	.02	.01
☐ 274 Tom Foley	.05	.02	.01
☐ 275 Mitch Williams	.05	.02	.01
☐ 276 Paul Kilgus	.05	.02	.01
☐ 277 Don Slaught	.05	.02	.01
☐ 278 Von Hayes	.05	.02	.01
☐ 279 Vince Coleman	.05	.02	.01
☐ 280 Mike Boddicker	.05	.02	.01
☐ 281 Ken Dayley	.05	.02	.01
☐ 282 Mike Devereaux	.05	.02	.01
☐ 283 Kenny Rogers	.10	.05	.01
☐ 284 Jeff Russell	.05	.02	.01
☐ 285 Jerome Walton	.05	.02	.01
☐ 286 Derek Lilliquist	.05	.02	.01
☐ 287 Joe Orsulak	.05	.02	.01
☐ 288 Dick Schofield	.05	.02	.01
☐ 289 Ron Darling	.05	.02	.01
☐ 290 Bobby Bonilla	.10	.05	.01
☐ 291 Jim Gantner	.05	.02	.01
☐ 292 Bobby Witt	.05	.02	.01
☐ 293 Greg Brock	.05	.02	.01
☐ 294 Ivan Calderon	.05	.02	.01
☐ 295 Steve Bedrosian	.05	.02	.01
☐ 296 Mike Henneman	.05	.02	.01
☐ 297 Tom Gordon	.05	.02	.01
☐ 298 Lou Whitaker	.10	.05	.01
☐ 299 Terry Pendleton	.10	.05	.01
☐ 300A Checklist 232-333	.05	.02	.01
☐ 300B Checklist 224-321	.05	.02	.01
☐ 301 Juan Berenguer	.05	.02	.01
☐ 302 Mark Davis	.05	.02	.01
☐ 303 Nick Esasky	.05	.02	.01
☐ 304 Rickey Henderson	.15	.07	.02
☐ 305 Rick Cerone	.05	.02	.01
☐ 306 Craig Biggio	.15	.07	.02
☐ 307 Duane Ward	.05	.02	.01
☐ 308 Tom Browning	.05	.02	.01
☐ 309 Walt Terrell	.05	.02	.01
☐ 310 Greg Swindell	.05	.02	.01
☐ 311 Dave Righetti	.05	.02	.01
☐ 312 Mike Maddux	.05	.02	.01
☐ 313 Len Dykstra	.10	.05	.01
☐ 314 Jose Gonzalez	.05	.02	.01
☐ 315 Steve Balboni	.05	.02	.01
☐ 316 Mike Scioscia	.05	.02	.01
☐ 317 Ron Oester	.05	.02	.01
☐ 318 Gary Wayne	.05	.02	.01
☐ 319 Todd Worrell	.05	.02	.01
☐ 320 Doug Jones	.05	.02	.01
☐ 321 Jeff Hamilton	.05	.02	.01
☐ 322 Danny Tartabull	.05	.02	.01
☐ 323 Chris James	.05	.02	.01
☐ 324 Mike Flanagan	.05	.02	.01
☐ 325 Gerald Young	.05	.02	.01
☐ 326 Bob Boone	.10	.05	.01
☐ 327 Frank Williams	.05	.02	.01
☐ 328 Dave Parker	.10	.05	.01
☐ 329 Sid Bream	.05	.02	.01
☐ 330 Mike Schooler	.05	.02	.01
☐ 331 Bert Blyleven	.10	.05	.01
☐ 332 Bob Welch	.05	.02	.01
☐ 333 Bob Milacki	.05	.02	.01
☐ 334 Tim Burke	.05	.02	.01
☐ 335 Jose Uribe	.05	.02	.01
☐ 336 Randy Myers	.10	.05	.01
☐ 337 Eric King	.05	.02	.01
☐ 338 Mark Langston	.10	.05	.01
☐ 339 Teddy Higuera	.05	.02	.01
☐ 340 Oddibe McDowell	.05	.02	.01
☐ 341 Lloyd McClendon	.05	.02	.01
☐ 342 Pascual Perez	.05	.02	.01
☐ 343 Kevin Brown UER	.15	.07	.02
(Signed is misspelled as signeed on back)			
☐ 344 Chuck Finley	.10	.05	.01
☐ 345 Erik Hanson	.10	.05	.01
☐ 346 Rich Gedman	.05	.02	.01
☐ 347 Bip Roberts	.05	.02	.01
☐ 348 Matt Williams	.15	.07	.02
☐ 349 Tom Henke	.05	.02	.01
☐ 350 Brad Komminsk	.05	.02	.01
☐ 351 Jeff Reed	.05	.02	.01
☐ 352 Brian Downing	.05	.02	.01
☐ 353 Frank Viola	.05	.02	.01
☐ 354 Terry Puhl	.05	.02	.01
☐ 355 Brian Harper	.05	.02	.01
☐ 356 Steve Farr	.05	.02	.01
☐ 357 Joe Boever	.05	.02	.01
☐ 358 Danny Heep	.05	.02	.01
☐ 359 Larry Andersen	.05	.02	.01
☐ 360 Rolando Roomes	.05	.02	.01
☐ 361 Mike Gallego	.05	.02	.01
☐ 362 Bob Kipper	.05	.02	.01
☐ 363 Clay Parker	.05	.02	.01
☐ 364 Mike Pagliarulo	.05	.02	.01
☐ 365 Ken Griffey Jr. UER	1.50	.70	.19
(Signed through 1990, should be 1991)			
☐ 366 Rex Hudler	.05	.02	.01
☐ 367 Pat Sheridan	.05	.02	.01
☐ 368 Kirk Gibson	.10	.05	.01
☐ 369 Jeff Parrett	.05	.02	.01
☐ 370 Bob Walk	.05	.02	.01
☐ 371 Ken Patterson	.05	.02	.01
☐ 372 Bryan Harvey	.05	.02	.01
☐ 373 Mike Bielecki	.05	.02	.01
☐ 374 Tom Magrann	.05	.02	.01
☐ 375 Rick Mahler	.05	.02	.01
☐ 376 Craig Lefferts	.05	.02	.01
☐ 377 Gregg Olson	.05	.02	.01
☐ 378 Jamie Moyer	.05	.02	.01
☐ 379 Randy Johnson	.25	.11	.03
☐ 380 Jeff Montgomery	.10	.05	.01
☐ 381 Marty Clary	.05	.02	.01
☐ 382 Bill Spiers	.05	.02	.01
☐ 383 Dave Magadan	.05	.02	.01
☐ 384 Greg Hibbard	.05	.02	.01
☐ 385 Ernie Whitt	.05	.02	.01
☐ 386 Rick Honeycutt	.05	.02	.01
☐ 387 Dave West	.05	.02	.01
☐ 388 Keith Hernandez	.10	.05	.01
☐ 389 Jose Alvarez	.05	.02	.01
☐ 390 Joey Belle	.75	.35	.09
☐ 391 Rick Aguilera	.10	.05	.01
☐ 392 Mike Fitzgerald	.05	.02	.01
☐ 393 Dwight Smith	.05	.02	.01
☐ 394 Steve Wilson	.05	.02	.01
☐ 395 Bob Geren	.05	.02	.01
☐ 396 Randy Ready	.05	.02	.01
☐ 397 Ken Hill	.15	.07	.02
☐ 398 Jody Reed	.05	.02	.01
☐ 399 Tom Brunansky	.05	.02	.01
☐ 400A Checklist 334-435	.05	.02	.01
☐ 400B Checklist 322-419	.05	.02	.01
☐ 401 Rene Gonzales	.05	.02	.01
☐ 402 Harold Baines	.10	.05	.01
☐ 403 Cecilio Guante	.05	.02	.01
☐ 404 Joe Girardi	.10	.05	.01
☐ 405A Sergio Valdez ERR	.05	.02	.01
(Card front shows black line crossing S in Sergio)			
☐ 405B Sergio Valdez COR	.05	.02	.01
☐ 406 Mark Williamson	.05	.02	.01
☐ 407 Glenn Hoffman	.05	.02	.01
☐ 408 Jeff Innis	.05	.02	.01
☐ 409 Randy Kramer	.05	.02	.01
☐ 410 Charlie O'Brien	.05	.02	.01
☐ 411 Charlie Hough	.05	.02	.01
☐ 412 Gus Polidor	.05	.02	.01
☐ 413 Ron Karkovice	.05	.02	.01
☐ 414 Trevor Wilson	.05	.02	.01
☐ 415 Kevin Ritz	.05	.02	.01
☐ 416 Gary Thurman	.05	.02	.01
☐ 417 Jeff M. Robinson	.05	.02	.01
☐ 418 Scott Terry	.05	.02	.01
☐ 419 Tim Laudner	.05	.02	.01
☐ 420 Dennis Rasmussen	.05	.02	.01
☐ 421 Luis Rivera	.05	.02	.01
☐ 422 Jim Corsi	.05	.02	.01
☐ 423 Dennis Lamp	.05	.02	.01
☐ 424 Ken Caminiti	.20	.09	.03
☐ 425 David Wells	.05	.02	.01
☐ 426 Norm Charlton	.05	.02	.01
☐ 427 Deion Sanders	.20	.09	.03
☐ 428 Dion James	.05	.02	.01
☐ 429 Chuck Cary	.05	.02	.01
☐ 430 Ken Howell	.05	.02	.01
☐ 431 Steve Lake	.05	.02	.01
☐ 432 Kal Daniels	.05	.02	.01
☐ 433 Lance McCullers	.05	.02	.01
☐ 434 Lenny Harris	.05	.02	.01
☐ 435 Scott Scudder	.05	.02	.01
☐ 436 Gene Larkin	.05	.02	.01
☐ 437 Dan Quisenberry	.05	.02	.01
☐ 438 Steve Olin	.10	.05	.01
☐ 439 Mickey Hatcher	.05	.02	.01
☐ 440 Willie Wilson	.05	.02	.01
☐ 441 Mark Grant	.05	.02	.01
☐ 442 Mookie Wilson	.05	.02	.01
☐ 443 Alex Trevino	.05	.02	.01
☐ 444 Pat Tabler	.05	.02	.01
☐ 445 Dave Bergman	.05	.02	.01
☐ 446 Todd Burns	.05	.02	.01
☐ 447 R.J. Reynolds	.05	.02	.01
☐ 448 Jay Buhner	.15	.07	.02
☐ 449 Lee Stevens	.05	.02	.01
☐ 450 Ron Hassey	.05	.02	.01
☐ 451 Bob Melvin	.05	.02	.01
☐ 452 Dave Martinez	.05	.02	.01
☐ 453 Greg Litton	.05	.02	.01
☐ 454 Mark Carreon	.05	.02	.01
☐ 455 Scott Fletcher	.05	.02	.01
☐ 456 Otis Nixon	.05	.02	.01
☐ 457 Tony Fossas	.05	.02	.01
☐ 458 John Russell	.05	.02	.01
☐ 459 Paul Assenmacher	.05	.02	.01
☐ 460 Zane Smith	.05	.02	.01
☐ 461 Jack Daugherty	.05	.02	.01
☐ 462 Rich Monteleone	.05	.02	.01
☐ 463 Greg Briley	.05	.02	.01
☐ 464 Mike Smithson	.05	.02	.01
☐ 465 Benito Santiago	.05	.02	.01
☐ 466 Jeff Brantley	.10	.05	.01
☐ 467 Jose Nunez	.05	.02	.01
☐ 468 Scott Bailes	.05	.02	.01
☐ 469 Ken Griffey Sr.	.05	.02	.01
☐ 470 Bob McClure	.05	.02	.01
☐ 471 Mackey Sasser	.05	.02	.01
☐ 472 Glenn Wilson	.05	.02	.01
☐ 473 Kevin Tapani	.10	.05	.01
☐ 474 Bill Buckner	.05	.02	.01
☐ 475 Ron Gant	.15	.07	.02
☐ 476 Kevin Romine	.05	.02	.01
☐ 477 Juan Agosto	.05	.02	.01
☐ 478 Herm Winningham	.05	.02	.01
☐ 479 Storm Davis	.05	.02	.01
☐ 480 Jeff King	.10	.05	.01
☐ 481 Kevin Mmahat	.05	.02	.01
☐ 482 Carmelo Martinez	.05	.02	.01
☐ 483 Omar Vizquel	.15	.07	.02
☐ 484 Jim Dwyer	.05	.02	.01
☐ 485 Bob Knepper	.05	.02	.01
☐ 486 Dave Anderson	.05	.02	.01
☐ 487 Ron Jones	.05	.02	.01
☐ 488 Jay Bell	.10	.05	.01
☐ 489 Sammy Sosa	.75	.35	.09
☐ 490 Kent Anderson	.05	.02	.01
☐ 491 Domingo Ramos	.05	.02	.01
☐ 492 Dave Clark	.05	.02	.01
☐ 493 Tim Birtsas	.05	.02	.01
☐ 494 Ken Oberkfell	.05	.02	.01
☐ 495 Larry Sheets	.05	.02	.01
☐ 496 Jeff Kunkel	.05	.02	.01
☐ 497 Jim Presley	.05	.02	.01
☐ 498 Mike Macfarlane	.05	.02	.01
☐ 499 Pete Smith	.05	.02	.01
☐ 500A Checklist 436-537 DP	.05	.02	.01
☐ 500B Checklist 420-517	.05	.02	.01
☐ 501 Gary Sheffield	.25	.11	.03
☐ 502 Terry Bross	.05	.02	.01
☐ 503 Jerry Kutzler	.05	.02	.01
☐ 504 Lloyd Moseby	.05	.02	.01
☐ 505 Curt Young	.05	.02	.01
☐ 506 Al Newman	.05	.02	.01
☐ 507 Keith Miller	.05	.02	.01
☐ 508 Mike Stanton	.10	.05	.01
☐ 509 Rich Yett	.05	.02	.01
☐ 510 Tim Drummond	.05	.02	.01
☐ 511 Joe Hesketh	.05	.02	.01
☐ 512 Rick Wrona	.05	.02	.01
☐ 513 Luis Salazar	.05	.02	.01
☐ 514 Hal Morris	.10	.05	.01
☐ 515 Terry Mulholland	.05	.02	.01
☐ 516 John Morris	.05	.02	.01
☐ 517 Carlos Quintana	.05	.02	.01
☐ 518 Frank DiPino	.05	.02	.01

□ 519 Randy Milligan .05 .02 .01
□ 520 Chad Kreuter .05 .02 .01
□ 521 Mike Jeffcoat .05 .02 .01
□ 522 Mike Harkey .05 .02 .01
□ 523A Andy Nezelek ERR .05 .02 .01
(Wrong birth year)
□ 523B Andy Nezelek COR .15 .07 .02
(Finally corrected
in factory sets)
□ 524 Dave Schmidt .05 .02 .01
□ 525 Tony Armas .05 .02 .01
□ 526 Barry Lyons .05 .02 .01
□ 527 Rick Reed .05 .02 .01
□ 528 Jerry Reuss .05 .02 .01
□ 529 Dean Palmer .40 .18 .05
□ 530 Jeff Peterek .05 .02 .01
□ 531 Carlos Martinez .05 .02 .01
□ 532 Atlee Hammaker .05 .02 .01
□ 533 Mike Brumley .05 .02 .01
□ 534 Terry Leach .05 .02 .01
□ 535 Doug Strange .05 .02 .01
□ 536 Jose DeLeon .05 .02 .01
□ 537 Shane Rawley .05 .02 .01
□ 538 Joey Cora .10 .05 .01
□ 539 Eric Hetzel .05 .02 .01
□ 540 Gene Nelson .05 .02 .01
□ 541 Wes Gardner .05 .02 .01
□ 542 Mark Portugal .05 .02 .01
□ 543 Al Leiter .10 .05 .01
□ 544 Jack Armstrong .05 .02 .01
□ 545 Greg Cadaret .05 .02 .01
□ 546 Rod Nichols .05 .02 .01
□ 547 Luis Polonia .05 .02 .01
□ 548 Charlie Hayes .10 .05 .01
□ 549 Dickie Thon .05 .02 .01
□ 550 Tim Crews .05 .02 .01
□ 551 Dave Winfield .15 .07 .02
□ 552 Mike Davis .05 .02 .01
□ 553 Ron Robinson .05 .02 .01
□ 554 Carmen Castillo .05 .02 .01
□ 555 John Costello .05 .02 .01
□ 556 Bud Black .05 .02 .01
□ 557 Rick Dempsey .05 .02 .01
□ 558 Jim Acker .05 .02 .01
□ 559 Eric Show .05 .02 .01
□ 560 Pat Borders .05 .02 .01
□ 561 Danny Darwin .05 .02 .01
□ 562 Rick Luecken .05 .02 .01
□ 563 Edwin Nunez .05 .02 .01
□ 564 Felix Jose .05 .02 .01
□ 565 John Cangelosi .05 .02 .01
□ 566 Bill Swift .05 .02 .01
□ 567 Bill Schroeder .05 .02 .01
□ 568 Stan Javier .05 .02 .01
□ 569 Jim Traber .05 .02 .01
□ 570 Wallace Johnson .05 .02 .01
□ 571 Donell Nixon .05 .02 .01
□ 572 Sid Fernandez .05 .02 .01
□ 573 Lance Johnson .10 .05 .01
□ 574 Andy McGaffigan .05 .02 .01
□ 575 Mark Knudson .05 .02 .01
□ 576 Tommy Greene .05 .02 .01
□ 577 Mark Grace .15 .07 .02
□ 578 Larry Walker .60 .25 .07
□ 579 Mike Stanley .05 .02 .01
□ 580 Mike Witt DP .05 .02 .01
□ 581 Scott Bradley .05 .02 .01
□ 582 Greg A. Harris .05 .02 .01
□ 583A Kevin Hickey ERR .15 .07 .02
□ 583B Kevin Hickey COR .05 .02 .01
□ 584 Lee Mazzilli .05 .02 .01
□ 585 Jeff Pico .05 .02 .01
□ 586 Joe Oliver .05 .02 .01
□ 587 Willie Fraser DP .05 .02 .01
□ 588 Carl Yastrzemski .15 .07 .02
Puzzle Card DP
□ 589 Kevin Bass DP .05 .02 .01
□ 590 John Moses DP .05 .02 .01
□ 591 Tom Pagnozzi DP .05 .02 .01
□ 592 Tony Castillo DP .05 .02 .01
□ 593 Jerald Clark DP .05 .02 .01
□ 594 Dan Schatzeder .05 .02 .01
□ 595 Luis Quinones DP .05 .02 .01
□ 596 Pete Harnisch DP .05 .02 .01
□ 597 Gary Redus .05 .02 .01
□ 598 Mel Hall .05 .02 .01
□ 599 Rick Schu .05 .02 .01
□ 600A Checklist 538-639 .05 .02 .01
□ 600B Checklist 518-617 .05 .02 .01
□ 601 Mike Kingery DP .05 .02 .01
□ 602 Terry Kennedy DP .05 .02 .01
□ 603 Mike Sharperson DP .05 .02 .01
□ 604 Don Carman DP .05 .02 .01
□ 605 Jim Gott .05 .02 .01
□ 606 Donn Pall DP .05 .02 .01
□ 607 Rance Mulliniks .05 .02 .01
□ 608 Curt Wilkerson DP .05 .02 .01
□ 609 Mike Felder DP .05 .02 .01
□ 610 Guillermo Hernandez DP .05 .02 .01
□ 611 Candy Maldonado DP .05 .02 .01
□ 612 Mark Thurmond DP .05 .02 .01
□ 613 Rick Leach DP .05 .02 .01
□ 614 Jerry Reed DP .05 .02 .01
□ 615 Franklin Stubbs .05 .02 .01
□ 616 Billy Hatcher DP .05 .02 .01
□ 617 Don August DP .05 .02 .01
□ 618 Tim Teufel .05 .02 .01
□ 619 Shawn Hillegas DP .05 .02 .01
□ 620 Manny Lee .05 .02 .01
□ 621 Gary Ward DP .05 .02 .01
□ 622 Mark Guthrie DP .05 .02 .01
□ 623 Jeff Musselman DP .05 .02 .01
□ 624 Mark Lemke DP .10 .05 .01
□ 625 Fernando Valenzuela .10 .05 .01
□ 626 Paul Sorrento DP .15 .07 .02
□ 627 Glenallen Hill DP .10 .05 .01
□ 628 Les Lancaster DP .05 .02 .01
□ 629 Vance Law DP .05 .02 .01
□ 630 Randy Velarde DP .05 .02 .01
□ 631 Todd Frohwirth DP .05 .02 .01
□ 632 Willie McGee .05 .02 .01
□ 633 Dennis Boyd DP .05 .02 .01
□ 634 Cris Carpenter DP .05 .02 .01
□ 635 Brian Holton .05 .02 .01
□ 636 Tracy Jones DP .05 .02 .01
□ 637A Terry Steinbach AS .10 .05 .01
(Recent Major
League Performance)
□ 637B Terry Steinbach AS .10 .05 .01
(All-Star Game
Performance)
□ 638 Brady Anderson .15 .07 .02
□ 639A Jack Morris ERR .10 .05 .01
(Card front shows
black line crossing
J in Jack)
□ 639B Jack Morris COR .10 .05 .01
□ 640 Jaime Navarro .05 .02 .01
□ 641 Darrin Jackson .05 .02 .01
□ 642 Mike Dyer .05 .02 .01
□ 643 Mike Schmidt .20 .09 .03
□ 644 Henry Cotto .05 .02 .01
□ 645 John Cerutti .05 .02 .01
□ 646 Francisco Cabrera .05 .02 .01
□ 647 Scott Sanderson .05 .02 .01
□ 648 Brian Meyer .05 .02 .01
□ 649 Ray Searage .05 .02 .01
□ 650A Bo Jackson AS .10 .05 .01
(Recent Major
League Performance)
□ 650B Bo Jackson AS .10 .05 .01
(All-Star Game
Performance)
□ 651 Steve Lyons .05 .02 .01
□ 652 Mike LaCoss .05 .02 .01
□ 653 Ted Power .05 .02 .01
□ 654A Howard Johnson AS .10 .05 .01
(Recent Major
League Performance)
□ 654B Howard Johnson AS .05 .02 .01
(All-Star Game
Performance)
□ 655 Mauro Gozzo .05 .02 .01
□ 656 Mike Blowers .15 .07 .02
□ 657 Paul Gibson .05 .02 .01
□ 658 Neal Heaton .05 .02 .01
□ 659 Nolan Ryan 5000K .40 .18 .05
COR (Still an error as
Ryan did not lead AL
in K's in '75)
□ 659A Nolan Ryan 5000K 1.50 .70 .19
(665 King of
Kings back) ERR
□ 660A Harold Baines AS .75 .35 .09
(Black line through
star on front;
Recent Major
League Performance)
□ 660B Harold Baines AS 1.00 .45 .12
(Black line through
star on front;
All-Star Game
Performance)
□ 660C Harold Baines AS .15 .07 .02
(Black line behind
star on front;
Recent Major
League Performance)
□ 660D Harold Baines AS .05 .02 .01
(Black line behind
star on front;
All-Star Game
Performance)
□ 661 Gary Pettis .05 .02 .01
□ 662 Clint Zavaras .05 .02 .01
□ 663A Rick Reuschel AS .10 .05 .01
(Recent Major
League Performance)
□ 663B Rick Reuschel AS .05 .02 .01
(All-Star Game
Performance)
□ 664 Alejandro Pena .05 .02 .01
□ 665 Nolan Ryan KING COR .40 .18 .05
□ 665A Nolan Ryan KING 1.50 .70 .19
(659 5000 K
back) ERR
□ 665C Nolan Ryan KING ERR .75 .35 .09
(No number on back;
in factory sets)
□ 666 Ricky Horton .05 .02 .01
□ 667 Curt Schilling .05 .02 .01
□ 668 Bill Landrum .05 .02 .01
□ 669 Todd Stottlemyre .10 .05 .01
□ 670 Tim Leary .05 .02 .01
□ 671 John Wetteland .15 .07 .02
□ 672 Calvin Schiraldi .05 .02 .01
□ 673A Ruben Sierra AS .10 .05 .01
(Recent Major
League Performance)
□ 673B Ruben Sierra AS .10 .05 .01
(All-Star Game
Performance)
□ 674A Pedro Guerrero AS .10 .05 .01
(Recent Major
League Performance)
□ 674B Pedro Guerrero AS .05 .02 .01
(All-Star Game
Performance)
□ 675 Ken Phelps .05 .02 .01
□ 676 Cal Ripken AS .40 .18 .05
(All-Star Game
Performance)
□ 676A Cal Ripken AS .75 .35 .09
(Recent Major
League Performance)
□ 677 Denny Walling .05 .02 .01
□ 678 Goose Gossage .10 .05 .01
□ 679 Gary Mielke .05 .02 .01
□ 680 Bill Bathe .05 .02 .01
□ 681 Tom Lawless .05 .02 .01
□ 682 Xavier Hernandez .05 .02 .01
□ 683A Kirby Puckett AS .25 .11 .03
(Recent Major
League Performance)
□ 683B Kirby Puckett AS .25 .11 .03
(All-Star Game
Performance)
□ 684 Mariano Duncan .05 .02 .01
□ 685 Ramon Martinez .15 .07 .02
□ 686 Tim Jones .05 .02 .01
□ 687 Tom Filer .05 .02 .01
□ 688 Steve Lombardozzi .05 .02 .01
□ 689 Bernie Williams 1.00 .45 .12
□ 690 Chip Hale .05 .02 .01
□ 691 Beau Allred .05 .02 .01
□ 692A Ryne Sandberg AS .25 .11 .03
(Recent Major
League Performance)
□ 692B Ryne Sandberg AS .15 .07 .02
(All-Star Game
Performance)
□ 693 Jeff Huson .05 .02 .01
□ 694 Curt Ford .05 .02 .01
□ 695A Eric Davis AS .10 .05 .01
(Recent Major
League Performance)
□ 695B Eric Davis AS .10 .05 .01
(All-Star Game
Performance)
□ 696 Scott Lusader .05 .02 .01
□ 697A Mark McGwire AS .15 .07 .02
(Recent Major
League Performance)
□ 697B Mark McGwire AS .10 .05 .01
(All-Star Game
Performance)
□ 698 Steve Cummings .05 .02 .01
□ 699 George Canale .05 .02 .01
□ 700A Checklist 640-715 .15 .07 .02
and BC1-BC26
□ 700B Checklist 640-716 .10 .05 .01
and BC1-BC26
□ 700C Checklist 618-716 .05 .02 .01
□ 701A Julio Franco AS .10 .05 .01
(Recent Major
League Performance)
□ 701B Julio Franco AS .05 .02 .01
(All-Star Game
Performance)
□ 702 Dave Johnson (P) .05 .02 .01
□ 703A Dave Stewart AS .10 .05 .01
(Recent Major
League Performance)
□ 703B Dave Stewart AS .10 .05 .01
(All-Star Game
Performance)
□ 704 Dave Justice .50 .23 .06
□ 705 Tony Gwynn AS .20 .09 .03
(All-Star Game
Performance)
□ 705A Tony Gwynn AS .25 .11 .03
(Recent Major
League Performance)
□ 706 Greg Myers .05 .02 .01
□ 707A Will Clark AS .15 .07 .02
(Recent Major
League Performance)
□ 707B Will Clark AS .15 .07 .02
(All-Star Game
Performance)
□ 708A Benito Santiago AS .10 .05 .01
(Recent Major
League Performance)
□ 708B Benito Santiago AS .05 .02 .01
(All-Star Game
Performance)
□ 709 Larry McWilliams .05 .02 .01
□ 710A Ozzie Smith AS .15 .07 .02
(Recent Major
League Performance)
□ 710B Ozzie Smith AS .10 .05 .01
(All-Star Game
Performance)
□ 711 John Olerud .15 .07 .02
□ 712A Wade Boggs AS .15 .07 .02
(Recent Major
League Performance)
□ 712B Wade Boggs AS .15 .07 .02
(All-Star Game
Performance)
□ 713 Gary Eave .05 .02 .01
□ 714 Bob Tewksbury .05 .02 .01
□ 715A Kevin Mitchell AS .10 .05 .01
(Recent Major
League Performance)
□ 715B Kevin Mitchell AS .05 .02 .01
(All-Star Game
Performance)
□ 716 Bart Giamatti COMM .15 .07 .02
(In Memoriam)

1990 Donruss Bonus MVP's

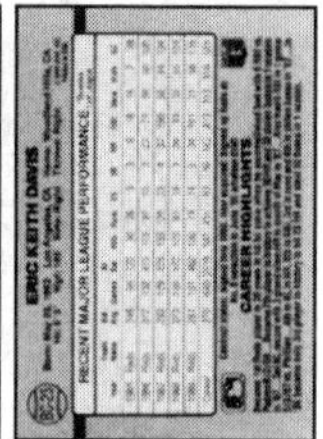

Numbered with the prefix "BC" for bonus card, a 26-card set featuring the most valuable player from each of the 26 teams was randomly inserted in all 1990 Donruss unopened pack formats. The factory sets were distributed without the Bonus Cards; thus there were again new checklist cards printed to reflect the exclusion of the Bonus Cards.

	MINT	NRMT	EXC
COMPLETE SET (26)	1.50	.70	.19
COMMON CARD (BC1-BC26)	.05	.02	.01

□ BC1 Bo Jackson .10 .05 .01
□ BC2 Howard Johnson .05 .02 .01
□ BC3 Dave Stewart .10 .05 .01
□ BC4 Tony Gwynn .25 .11 .03
□ BC5 Orel Hershiser .10 .05 .01
□ BC6 Pedro Guerrero .05 .02 .01
□ BC7 Tim Raines .10 .05 .01
□ BC8 Kirby Puckett .25 .11 .03
□ BC9 Alvin Davis .05 .02 .01
□ BC10 Ryne Sandberg .25 .11 .03
□ BC11 Kevin Mitchell .10 .05 .01
□ BC12A John Smoltz ERR .15 .07 .02
(Photo actually
Tom Glavine)
□ BC12B John Smoltz COR .75 .35 .09
□ BC13 George Bell .05 .02 .01
□ BC14 Julio Franco .10 .05 .01
□ BC15 Paul Molitor .20 .09 .03
□ BC16 Bobby Bonilla .10 .05 .01
□ BC17 Mike Greenwell .05 .02 .01
□ BC18 Cal Ripken .60 .25 .07
□ BC19 Carlton Fisk .15 .07 .02
□ BC20 Chili Davis .10 .05 .01
□ BC21 Glenn Davis .05 .02 .01
□ BC22 Steve Sax .05 .02 .01
□ BC23 Eric Davis DP .10 .05 .01
□ BC24 Greg Swindell DP .05 .02 .01
□ BC25 Von Hayes DP .05 .02 .01
□ BC26 Alan Trammell .10 .05 .01

1990 Donruss Grand Slammers

This 12-card standard size set was in the 1990 Donruss set as a special card deliniating each 55-card section of the 1990 Factory Set. This set honors those players who connected for grand slam homers during the 1989 season. The cards are in the 1990 Donruss design and the back describes the grand slam homer hit by each player.

	MINT	NRMT	EXC
COMPLETE SET (12)	1.50	.70	.19
COMMON CARD (1-12)	.05	.02	.01

Card	MINT	NRMT	EXC
□ 1 Matt Williams	.25	.11	.03
□ 2 Jeffrey Leonard	.05	.02	.01
□ 3 Chris James	.05	.02	.01
□ 4 Mark McGwire	.75	.35	.09
□ 5 Dwight Evans	.10	.05	.01
□ 6 Will Clark	.25	.11	.03
□ 7 Mike Scioscia	.05	.02	.01
□ 8 Todd Benzinger	.05	.02	.01
□ 9 Fred McGriff	.25	.11	.03
□ 10 Kevin Bass	.05	.02	.01
□ 11 Jack Clark	.10	.05	.01
□ 12 Bo Jackson	.10	.05	.01

1990 Donruss Rookies

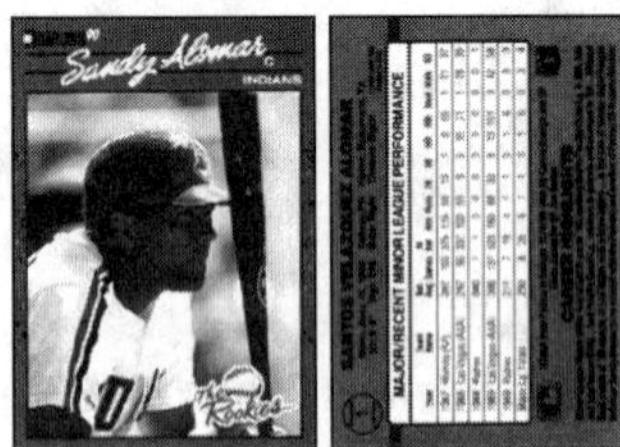

The 1990 Donruss Rookies set marked the fifth consecutive year that Donruss issued a boxed set honoring the best rookies of the season. This set, which used the 1990 Donruss design but featured a green border, was issued exclusively through the Donruss dealer network to hobby dealers. This 56-card, standard size set came in its own box and the words 'The Rookies' are featured prominently on the front of the cards. The only notable Rookie Card in this set is Carlos Baerga.

	MINT	NRMT	EXC
COMPLETE FACT.SET (56)	2.00	.90	.25
COMMON CARD (1-56)	.05	.02	.01
□ 1 Sandy Alomar Jr. UER (No stitches on baseball on Donruss logo on card front)	.25	.11	.03
□ 2 John Olerud	.25	.11	.03
□ 3 Pat Combs	.05	.02	.01
□ 4 Brian DuBois	.05	.02	.01
□ 5 Felix Jose	.05	.02	.01
□ 6 Delino DeShields	.15	.07	.02
□ 7 Mike Stanton	.15	.07	.02
□ 8 Mike Munoz	.05	.02	.01
□ 9 Craig Grebeck	.05	.02	.01
□ 10 Joe Kraemer	.05	.02	.01
□ 11 Jeff Huson	.05	.02	.01
□ 12 Bill Sampen	.05	.02	.01
□ 13 Brian Bohanon	.05	.02	.01
□ 14 Dave Justice	.50	.23	.06
□ 15 Robin Ventura	.25	.11	.03
□ 16 Greg Vaughn	.25	.11	.03
□ 17 Wayne Edwards	.05	.02	.01
□ 18 Shawn Boskie	.05	.02	.01
□ 19 Carlos Baerga	.30	.14	.04
□ 20 Mark Gardner	.05	.02	.01
□ 21 Kevin Appier	.25	.11	.03
□ 22 Mike Harkey	.05	.02	.01
□ 23 Tim Layana	.05	.02	.01
□ 24 Glenallen Hill	.15	.07	.02
□ 25 Jerry Kutzler	.05	.02	.01
□ 26 Mike Blowers	.25	.11	.03
□ 27 Scott Ruskin	.05	.02	.01
□ 28 Dana Kiecker	.05	.02	.01
□ 29 Willie Blair	.05	.02	.01
□ 30 Ben McDonald	.15	.07	.02
□ 31 Todd Zeile	.15	.07	.02
□ 32 Scott Coolbaugh	.05	.02	.01
□ 33 Xavier Hernandez	.05	.02	.01
□ 34 Mike Hartley	.05	.02	.01
□ 35 Kevin Tapani	.15	.07	.02
□ 36 Kevin Wickander	.05	.02	.01
□ 37 Carlos Hernandez	.05	.02	.01
□ 38 Brian Traxler	.05	.02	.01
□ 39 Marty Brown	.05	.02	.01
□ 40 Scott Radinsky	.05	.02	.01
□ 41 Julio Machado	.05	.02	.01
□ 42 Steve Avery	.15	.07	.02
□ 43 Mark Lemke	.15	.07	.02
□ 44 Alan Mills	.05	.02	.01
□ 45 Marquis Grissom	.50	.23	.06
□ 46 Greg Olson	.05	.02	.01
□ 47 Dave Hollins	.15	.07	.02
□ 48 Jerald Clark	.05	.02	.01
□ 49 Eric Anthony	.15	.07	.02
□ 50 Tim Drummond	.05	.02	.01
□ 51 John Burkett	.15	.07	.02
□ 52 Brent Knackert	.05	.02	.01
□ 53 Jeff Shaw	.05	.02	.01
□ 54 John Orton	.05	.02	.01
□ 55 Terry Shumpert	.05	.02	.01
□ 56 Checklist 1-56	.05	.02	.01

1990 Donruss Best AL

The 1990 Donruss Best of the American League set consists of 144 standard-size cards. This was Donruss' latest version of what had been titled the previous two years as Baseball's Best. In 1990, the sets were split into National and American League and marketed separately. The front design was similar to the regular issue Donruss set except for the front borders being blue while the backs have complete major and minor league statistics as compared to the regular Donruss cards which only cover the past five major-league seasons.

	MINT	NRMT	EXC
COMPLETE SET (144)	10.00	4.50	1.25
COMMON CARD (1-144)	.05	.02	.01
□ 1 Ken Griffey Jr.	3.00	1.35	.35
□ 2 Bob Milacki	.05	.02	.01
□ 3 Mike Boddicker	.05	.02	.01
□ 4 Bert Blyleven	.10	.05	.01
□ 5 Carlton Fisk	.40	.18	.05
□ 6 Greg Swindell	.05	.02	.01
□ 7 Alan Trammell	.10	.05	.01
□ 8 Mark Davis	.05	.02	.01
□ 9 Chris Bosio	.05	.02	.01
□ 10 Gary Gaetti	.05	.02	.01
□ 11 Matt Nokes	.05	.02	.01
□ 12 Dennis Eckersley	.10	.05	.01
□ 13 Kevin Brown	.15	.07	.02
□ 14 Tom Henke	.05	.02	.01
□ 15 Mickey Tettleton	.05	.02	.01
□ 16 Jody Reed	.05	.02	.01
□ 17 Mark Langston	.10	.05	.01
□ 18 Melido Perez UER (Listed as an Expo rather than White Sox)	.05	.02	.01
□ 19 John Farrell	.05	.02	.01
□ 20 Tony Phillips	.10	.05	.01
□ 21 Bret Saberhagen	.10	.05	.01
□ 22 Robin Yount	.15	.07	.02
□ 23 Kirby Puckett	1.25	.55	.16
□ 24 Steve Sax	.05	.02	.01
□ 25 Dave Stewart	.10	.05	.01
□ 26 Alvin Davis	.05	.02	.01
□ 27 Geno Petralli	.05	.02	.01
□ 28 Mookie Wilson	.05	.02	.01
□ 29 Jeff Ballard	.05	.02	.01
□ 30 Ellis Burks	.15	.07	.02
□ 31 Wally Joyner	.10	.05	.01
□ 32 Bobby Thigpen	.05	.02	.01
□ 33 Keith Hernandez	.10	.05	.01
□ 34 Jack Morris	.10	.05	.01
□ 35 George Brett	1.25	.55	.16
□ 36 Dan Plesac	.05	.02	.01
□ 37 Brian Harper	.05	.02	.01
□ 38 Don Mattingly	1.50	.70	.19
□ 39 Dave Henderson	.05	.02	.01
□ 40 Scott Bankhead UER (Asheboro misspelled as Ashboro on card)	.05	.02	.01
□ 41 Rafael Palmeiro	.25	.11	.03
□ 42 Jimmy Key	.10	.05	.01
□ 43 Gregg Olson	.05	.02	.01
□ 44 Tony Pena	.05	.02	.01
□ 45 Jack Howell	.05	.02	.01
□ 46 Eric King	.05	.02	.01
□ 47 Cory Snyder	.05	.02	.01
□ 48 Frank Tanana	.05	.02	.01
□ 49 Nolan Ryan	2.50	1.10	.30
□ 50 Bob Boone	.10	.05	.01
□ 51 Dave Parker	.10	.05	.01
□ 52 Allan Anderson	.05	.02	.01
□ 53 Tim Leary	.05	.02	.01
□ 54 Mark McGwire	1.00	.45	.12
□ 55 Dave Valle	.05	.02	.01
□ 56 Fred McGriff	.40	.18	.05
□ 57 Cal Ripken	2.00	.90	.25
□ 58 Roger Clemens	.50	.23	.06
□ 59 Lance Parrish	.10	.05	.01
□ 60 Robin Ventura	.15	.07	.02
□ 61 Doug Jones	.05	.02	.01
□ 62 Lloyd Moseby	.05	.02	.01
□ 63 Bo Jackson	.10	.05	.01
□ 64 Paul Molitor	.50	.23	.06
□ 65 Kent Hrbek	.10	.05	.01
□ 66 Mel Hall	.05	.02	.01
□ 67 Bob Welch	.05	.02	.01
□ 68 Erik Hanson	.05	.02	.01
□ 69 Harold Baines	.10	.05	.01
□ 70 Junior Felix	.05	.02	.01
□ 71 Craig Worthington	.05	.02	.01
□ 72 Jeff Reardon	.05	.02	.01
□ 73 Johnny Ray	.05	.02	.01
□ 74 Ozzie Guillen	.05	.02	.01
□ 75 Brook Jacoby	.05	.02	.01
□ 76 Chet Lemon	.05	.02	.01
□ 77 Mark Gubicza	.05	.02	.01
□ 78 B.J. Surhoff	.05	.02	.01
□ 79 Rick Aguilera	.05	.02	.01
□ 80 Pascual Perez	.05	.02	.01
□ 81 Jose Canseco	.40	.18	.05
□ 82 Mike Schooler	.05	.02	.01
□ 83 Jeff Huson	.05	.02	.01
□ 84 Kelly Gruber	.05	.02	.01
□ 85 Randy Milligan	.05	.02	.01
□ 86 Wade Boggs	.40	.18	.05
□ 87 Dave Winfield	.15	.07	.02
□ 88 Scott Fletcher	.05	.02	.01
□ 89 Tom Candiotti	.05	.02	.01
□ 90 Mike Heath	.05	.02	.01
□ 91 Kevin Seitzer	.05	.02	.01
□ 92 Ted Higuera	.05	.02	.01
□ 93 Kevin Tapani	.10	.05	.01
□ 94 Roberto Kelly	.05	.02	.01
□ 95 Walt Weiss	.05	.02	.01
□ 96 Checklist Card	.05	.02	.01
□ 97 Sandy Alomar Jr.	.15	.07	.02
□ 98 Pete O'Brien	.05	.02	.01
□ 99 Jeff Russell	.05	.02	.01
□ 100 John Olerud	.25	.11	.03
□ 101 Pete Harnisch	.05	.02	.01
□ 102 Dwight Evans	.10	.05	.01
□ 103 Chuck Finley	.10	.05	.01
□ 104 Sammy Sosa	1.25	.55	.16
□ 105 Mike Henneman	.05	.02	.01
□ 106 Kurt Stillwell	.05	.02	.01
□ 107 Greg Vaughn	.15	.07	.02
□ 108 Dan Gladden	.05	.02	.01
□ 109 Jesse Barfield	.05	.02	.01
□ 110 Willie Randolph	.10	.05	.01
□ 111 Randy Johnson	.60	.25	.07
□ 112 Julio Franco	.10	.05	.01
□ 113 Tony Fernandez	.05	.02	.01
□ 114 Ben McDonald	.15	.07	.02
□ 115 Mike Greenwell	.05	.02	.01
□ 116 Luis Polonia	.05	.02	.01
□ 117 Carney Lansford	.10	.05	.01
□ 118 Bud Black	.05	.02	.01
□ 119 Lou Whitaker	.10	.05	.01
□ 120 Jim Eisenreich	.10	.05	.01
□ 121 Gary Sheffield	.75	.35	.09
□ 122 Shane Mack	.05	.02	.01
□ 123 Alvaro Espinoza	.05	.02	.01
□ 124 Rickey Henderson	.15	.07	.02
□ 125 Jeffrey Leonard	.05	.02	.01
□ 126 Gary Pettis	.05	.02	.01
□ 127 Dave Stieb	.05	.02	.01
□ 128 Danny Tartabull	.10	.05	.01
□ 129 Joe Orsulak	.05	.02	.01
□ 130 Tom Brunansky	.05	.02	.01
□ 131 Dick Schofield	.05	.02	.01
□ 132 Candy Maldonado	.05	.02	.01
□ 133 Cecil Fielder	.10	.05	.01
□ 134 Terry Shumpert	.05	.02	.01
□ 135 Greg Gagne	.05	.02	.01
□ 136 Dave Righetti	.05	.02	.01
□ 137 Terry Steinbach	.10	.05	.01
□ 138 Harold Reynolds	.10	.05	.01
□ 139 George Bell	.05	.02	.01
□ 140 Carlos Quintana	.05	.02	.01
□ 141 Ivan Calderon	.05	.02	.01
□ 142 Greg Brock	.05	.02	.01
□ 143 Ruben Sierra	.10	.05	.01
□ 144 Checklist Card	.05	.02	.01

1990 Donruss Best NL

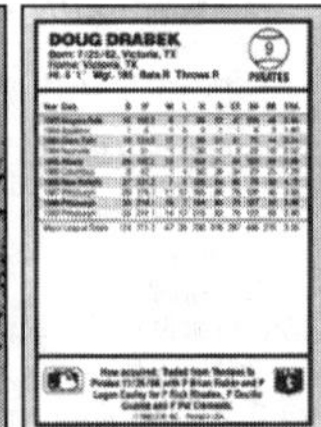

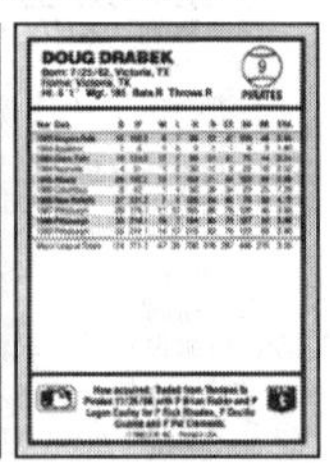

The 1990 Donruss Best of the National League set consists of 144 standard-size cards. This was Donruss' latest version of what had been titled the previous two years as Baseball's Best. In 1990, the sets were split into National and American League and marketed separately. The front design was similar to the regular issue Donruss set except for the front borders being blue while the backs have complete major and minor league statistics as compared to the regular Donruss cards which only cover the past five major-league seasons.

	MINT	NRMT	EXC
COMPLETE SET (144)	8.00	3.60	1.00
COMMON CARD (1-144)	.05	.02	.01
□ 1 Eric Davis	.05	.02	.01
□ 2 Tom Glavine	.40	.18	.05
□ 3 Mike Bielecki	.05	.02	.01
□ 4 Jim Deshaies	.05	.02	.01
□ 5 Mike Scioscia	.05	.02	.01
□ 6 Spike Owen	.05	.02	.01
□ 7 Dwight Gooden	.10	.05	.01
□ 8 Ricky Jordan	.05	.02	.01
□ 9 Doug Drabek	.05	.02	.01
□ 10 Bryn Smith	.05	.02	.01
□ 11 Tony Gwynn	1.00	.45	.12
□ 12 John Burkett	.05	.02	.01
□ 13 Nick Esasky	.05	.02	.01
□ 14 Greg Maddux	1.50	.70	.19
□ 15 Joe Oliver	.05	.02	.01
□ 16 Mike Scott	.05	.02	.01
□ 17 Tim Belcher	.05	.02	.01
□ 18 Kevin Gross	.05	.02	.01
□ 19 Howard Johnson	.05	.02	.01
□ 20 Darren Daulton	.10	.05	.01
□ 21 John Smiley	.05	.02	.01
□ 22 Ken Dayley	.05	.02	.01
□ 23 Craig Lefferts	.05	.02	.01
□ 24 Will Clark	.15	.07	.02
□ 25 Greg Olson	.05	.02	.01
□ 26 Ryne Sandberg	.75	.35	.09
□ 27 Tom Browning	.05	.02	.01
□ 28 Eric Anthony	.05	.02	.01
□ 29 Juan Samuel	.05	.02	.01
□ 30 Dennis Martinez	.10	.05	.01
□ 31 Kevin Elster	.05	.02	.01
□ 32 Tom Herr	.05	.02	.01
□ 33 Sid Bream	.05	.02	.01
□ 34 Terry Pendleton	.10	.05	.01
□ 35 Roberto Alomar	.75	.35	.09
□ 36 Kevin Bass	.05	.02	.01
□ 37 Jim Presley	.05	.02	.01
□ 38 Les Lancaster	.05	.02	.01
□ 39 Paul O'Neill	.10	.05	.01
□ 40 Dave Smith	.05	.02	.01
□ 41 Kirk Gibson	.10	.05	.01
□ 42 Tim Burke	.05	.02	.01
□ 43 David Cone	.15	.07	.02
□ 44 Ken Howell	.05	.02	.01
□ 45 Barry Bonds	.60	.25	.07
□ 46 Joe Magrane	.05	.02	.01
□ 47 Andy Benes	.15	.07	.02
□ 48 Gary Carter	.10	.05	.01
□ 49 Pat Combs	.05	.02	.01
□ 50 John Smoltz	.60	.25	.07
□ 51 Mark Grace	.15	.07	.02
□ 52 Barry Larkin	.15	.07	.02
□ 53 Danny Darwin	.05	.02	.01
□ 54 Orel Hershiser	.10	.05	.01
□ 55 Tim Wallach	.05	.02	.01
□ 56 Dave Magadan	.05	.02	.01
□ 57 Roger McDowell	.05	.02	.01
□ 58 Bill Landrum	.05	.02	.01
□ 59 Jose DeLeon	.05	.02	.01
□ 60 Bip Roberts	.05	.02	.01
□ 61 Matt Williams	.40	.18	.05
□ 62 Dale Murphy	.15	.07	.02
□ 63 Dwight Smith	.05	.02	.01
□ 64 Chris Sabo	.10	.05	.01
□ 65 Glenn Davis	.05	.02	.01
□ 66 Jay Howell	.05	.02	.01
□ 67 Andres Galarraga	.15	.07	.02
□ 68 Frank Viola	.05	.02	.01
□ 69 John Kruk	.10	.05	.01
□ 70 Bobby Bonilla	.10	.05	.01
□ 71 Todd Zeile	.05	.02	.01
□ 72 Joe Carter	.10	.05	.01
□ 73 Robby Thompson	.05	.02	.01
□ 74 Jeff Blauser	.05	.02	.01
□ 75 Mitch Williams	.05	.02	.01
□ 76 Rob Dibble	.05	.02	.01
□ 77 Rafael Ramirez	.05	.02	.01
□ 78 Eddie Murray	.60	.25	.07
□ 79 Dave Martinez	.05	.02	.01
□ 80 Darryl Strawberry	.10	.05	.01
□ 81 Dickie Thon	.05	.02	.01
□ 82 Jose Lind	.05	.02	.01
□ 83 Ozzie Smith	.75	.35	.09
□ 84 Bruce Hurst	.05	.02	.01
□ 85 Kevin Mitchell	.10	.05	.01
□ 86 Lonnie Smith	.05	.02	.01
□ 87 Joe Girardi	.05	.02	.01
□ 88 Randy Myers	.05	.02	.01
□ 89 Craig Biggio	.15	.07	.02
□ 90 Fernando Valenzuela	.10	.05	.01
□ 91 Larry Walker	1.25	.55	.16
□ 92 John Franco	.05	.02	.01
□ 93 Dennis Cook	.05	.02	.01
□ 94 Bob Walk	.05	.02	.01
□ 95 Pedro Guerrero	.05	.02	.01
□ 96 Checklist Card	.05	.02	.01
□ 97 Andre Dawson	.10	.05	.01
□ 98 Ed Whitson	.05	.02	.01
□ 99 Steve Bedrosian	.05	.02	.01
□ 100 Oddibe McDowell	.05	.02	.01
□ 101 Todd Benzinger	.05	.02	.01
□ 102 Bill Doran	.05	.02	.01
□ 103 Alfredo Griffin	.05	.02	.01
□ 104 Tim Raines	.10	.05	.01
□ 105 Sid Fernandez	.05	.02	.01
□ 106 Charlie Hayes	.05	.02	.01
□ 107 Mike LaValliere	.05	.02	.01
□ 108 Jose Oquendo	.05	.02	.01
□ 109 Jack Clark	.10	.05	.01
□ 110 Scott Garrelts	.05	.02	.01
□ 111 Ron Gant	.15	.07	.02
□ 112 Shawon Dunston	.05	.02	.01
□ 113 Mariano Duncan	.05	.02	.01
□ 114 Eric Yelding	.05	.02	.01

☐ 115 Hubie Brooks	.05	.02	.01
☐ 116 Delino DeShields	.15	.07	.02
☐ 117 Gregg Jefferies	.10	.05	.01
☐ 118 Len Dykstra	.10	.05	.01
☐ 119 Andy Van Slyke	.10	.05	.01
☐ 120 Lee Smith	.10	.05	.01
☐ 121 Benito Santiago	.05	.02	.01
☐ 122 Jose Uribe	.05	.02	.01
☐ 123 Jeff Treadway	.05	.02	.01
☐ 124 Jerome Walton	.05	.02	.01
☐ 125 Billy Hatcher	.05	.02	.01
☐ 126 Ken Caminiti	.15	.07	.02
☐ 127 Kal Daniels	.05	.02	.01
☐ 128 Marquis Grissom	.75	.35	.09
☐ 129 Kevin McReynolds	.05	.02	.01
☐ 130 Wally Backman	.05	.02	.01
☐ 131 Willie McGee	.05	.02	.01
☐ 132 Terry Kennedy	.05	.02	.01
☐ 133 Garry Templeton	.05	.02	.01
☐ 134 Lloyd McClendon	.05	.02	.01
☐ 135 Daryl Boston	.05	.02	.01
☐ 136 Jay Bell	.05	.02	.01
☐ 137 Mike Pagliarulo	.05	.02	.01
☐ 138 Vince Coleman	.05	.02	.01
☐ 139 Brett Butler	.10	.05	.01
☐ 140 Von Hayes	.05	.02	.01
☐ 141 Ramon Martinez	.15	.07	.02
☐ 142 Jack Armstrong	.05	.02	.01
☐ 143 Franklin Stubbs	.05	.02	.01
☐ 144 Checklist Card	.05	.02	.01

1990 Donruss Learning Series

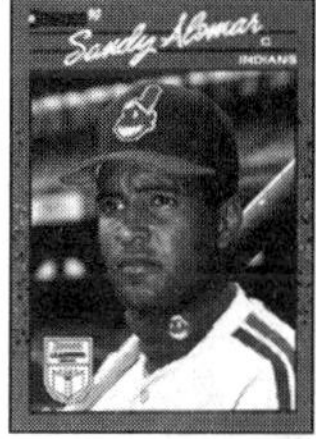

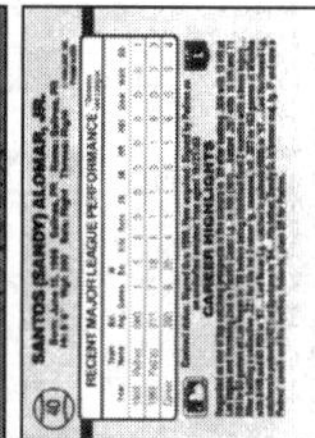

The 1990 Donruss Learning Series consists of 55 standard-size cards that served as part of an educational packet for elementary and middle school students. The cards were issued in two formats. Grades Three and Four received the cards, a historical timeline that relates events in baseball to major historical events, additional Donruss cards from wax packs, and a teacher's guide that focused on several academic subjects. Grades 5 through 8 received the cards, a teacher's guide designed for older students, and a 14-minute video shot at Chicago's Wrigley Field. The fronts feature color head shots of the players and bright red borders. The horizontally oriented backs are amber and present biography, statistics, and career highlights.

	MINT	NRMT	EXC
COMPLETE SET (55)	25.00	11.00	3.10
COMMON CARD (1-55)	.10	.05	.01
☐ 1 George Brett DK	2.50	1.10	.30
☐ 2 Kevin Mitchell	.25	.11	.03
☐ 3 Andy Van Slyke	.25	.11	.03
☐ 4 Benito Santiago	.10	.05	.01
☐ 5 Gary Carter	.25	.11	.03
☐ 6 Jose Canseco	1.00	.45	.12
☐ 7 Rickey Henderson	.75	.35	.09
☐ 8 Ken Griffey Jr.	6.00	2.70	.75
☐ 9 Ozzie Smith	2.50	1.10	.30
☐ 10 Dwight Gooden	.25	.11	.03
☐ 11 Ryne Sandberg DK	2.50	1.10	.30
☐ 12 Don Mattingly	3.00	1.35	.35
☐ 13 Ozzie Guillen	.10	.05	.01
☐ 14 Dave Righetti	.10	.05	.01
☐ 15 Rick Dempsey	.10	.05	.01
☐ 16 Tom Herr	.10	.05	.01
☐ 17 Julio Franco	.25	.11	.03
☐ 18 Von Hayes	.10	.05	.01
☐ 19 Cal Ripken	5.00	2.20	.60
☐ 20 Alan Trammell	.75	.35	.09
☐ 21 Wade Boggs	1.00	.45	.12
☐ 22 Glenn Davis	.10	.05	.01
☐ 23 Will Clark	1.25	.55	.16
☐ 24 Nolan Ryan	6.00	2.70	.75
☐ 25 George Bell	.10	.05	.01
☐ 26 Cecil Fielder	.75	.35	.09
☐ 27 Gregg Olson	.10	.05	.01
☐ 28 Tim Wallach	.10	.05	.01
☐ 29 Ron Darling	.10	.05	.01
☐ 30 Kelly Gruber	.10	.05	.01
☐ 31 Shawn Boskie	.10	.05	.01
☐ 32 Mike Greenwell	.10	.05	.01
☐ 33 Dave Parker	.25	.11	.03
☐ 34 Joe Magrane	.10	.05	.01
☐ 35 Dave Stewart	.25	.11	.03
☐ 36 Kent Hrbek	.25	.11	.03
☐ 37 Robin Yount	1.00	.45	.12
☐ 38 Bo Jackson	.75	.35	.09
☐ 39 Fernando Valenzuela	.25	.11	.03
☐ 40 Sandy Alomar Jr.	.50	.23	.06
☐ 41 Lance Parrish	.25	.11	.03
☐ 42 Candy Maldonado	.10	.05	.01
☐ 43 Mike LaValliere	.10	.05	.01
☐ 44 Jim Abbott	.10	.05	.01
☐ 45 Edgar Martinez	1.00	.45	.12
☐ 46 Kirby Puckett	2.50	1.10	.30
☐ 47 Delino DeShields	.50	.23	.06
☐ 48 Tony Gwynn	3.00	1.35	.35
☐ 49 Carlton Fisk	1.00	.45	.12
☐ 50 Mike Scott	.10	.05	.01
☐ 51 Barry Larkin	1.25	.55	.16
☐ 52 Andre Dawson	.75	.35	.09
☐ 53 Tom Glavine	1.50	.70	.19
☐ 54 Tom Browning	.10	.05	.01
☐ 55 Checklist Card	.10	.05	.01

1990 Donruss Super DK's

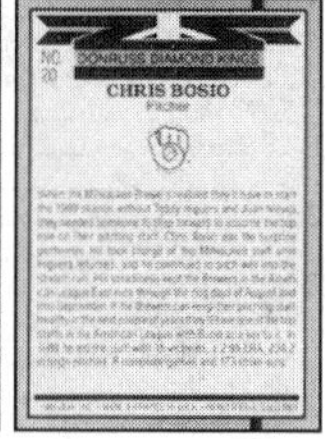

This 26-player card set was available through a mail-in offer detailed on the wax packs. The set was sent in return for 10.00 and three wrappers plus 2.00 postage and handling. The set features the popular Diamond King subseries in large (approximately 4 7/8" by 6 13/16") form. Dick Perez of Perez-Steele Galleries did another outstanding job on the artwork. The cards are essentially a large version of the Donruss regular issue Diamond Kings. There is also a jumbo sized Ryan King of Kings card. Although not listed with the regular set; it is heavily sought after by Ryan collectors.

	MINT	NRMT	EXC
COMPLETE SET (26)	12.00	5.50	1.50
COMMON CARD (1-26)	.50	.23	.06
☐ 1 Bo Jackson	.75	.35	.09
☐ 2 Steve Sax	.50	.23	.06
☐ 3 Ruben Sierra	.75	.35	.09
☐ 4 Ken Griffey Jr.	6.00	2.70	.75
☐ 5 Mickey Tettleton	.50	.23	.06
☐ 6 Dave Stewart	.75	.35	.09
☐ 7 Jim Deshaies	.50	.23	.06
☐ 8 John Smoltz	1.50	.70	.19
☐ 9 Mike Bielecki	.50	.23	.06
☐ 10 Brian Downing	.50	.23	.06
☐ 11 Kevin Mitchell	.75	.35	.09
☐ 12 Kelly Gruber	.50	.23	.06
☐ 13 Joe Magrane	.50	.23	.06
☐ 14 John Franco	.50	.23	.06
☐ 15 Ozzie Guillen	.50	.23	.06
☐ 16 Lou Whitaker	.75	.35	.09
☐ 17 John Smiley	.50	.23	.06
☐ 18 Howard Johnson	.50	.23	.06
☐ 19 Willie Randolph	.75	.35	.09
☐ 20 Chris Bosio	.50	.23	.06
☐ 21 Tommy Herr	.50	.23	.06
☐ 22 Dan Gladden	.50	.23	.06
☐ 23 Ellis Burks	1.00	.45	.12
☐ 24 Pete O'Brien	.50	.23	.06
☐ 25 Bryn Smith	.50	.23	.06
☐ 26 Ed Whitson	.50	.23	.06
☐ NNO Nolan Ryan King of Kings	12.00	5.50	1.50

1991 Donruss Previews

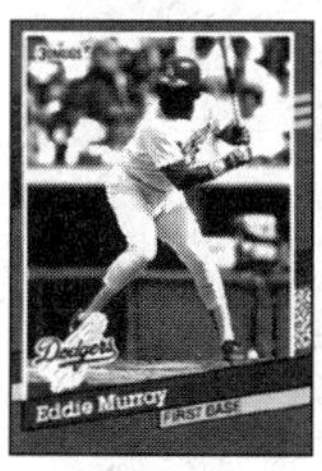

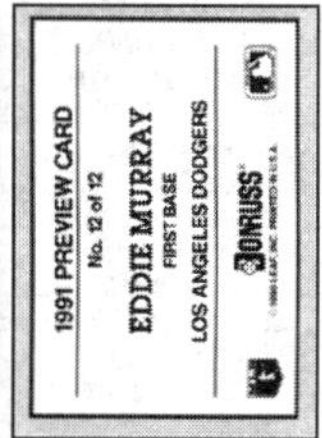

This 12-card standard-size set was issued by Donruss for hobby dealers as examples of what the 1991 Donruss cards would look like. This cards have the 1991 Donruss design on the front; the back merely says 1991 Preview card and identifies the player and the team.

	MINT	NRMT	EXC
COMPLETE SET (12)	400.00	180.00	50.00
COMMON CARD (1-12)	5.00	2.20	.60
☐ 1 Dave Justice	20.00	9.00	2.50
☐ 2 Doug Drabek	8.00	3.60	1.00
☐ 3 Scott Chiamparino	5.00	2.20	.60
☐ 4 Ken Griffey Jr.	125.00	55.00	15.50
☐ 5 Bob Welch	8.00	3.60	1.00
☐ 6 Tino Martinez	10.00	4.50	1.25
☐ 7 Nolan Ryan	125.00	55.00	15.50
☐ 8 Dwight Gooden	8.00	3.60	1.00
☐ 9 Ryne Sandberg	60.00	27.00	7.50
☐ 10 Barry Bonds	40.00	18.00	5.00
☐ 11 Jose Canseco	25.00	11.00	3.10
☐ 12 Eddie Murray	40.00	18.00	5.00

1991 Donruss

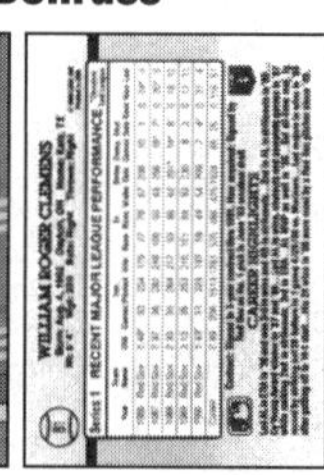

The 1991 Donruss set was issued in two series of 386 and 384 for a total of 770 standard-size cards. This set marked the first time Donruss issued cards in multiple series. The second series was issued approximately three months after the first series was issued. Cards were issued in wax packs and factory sets. As a separate promotion, wax packs were also given away with six and 12-packs of Coke and Diet Coke. First series cards feature blue borders and second series green borders with some stripes and the players name in white against a red background. Subsets include Diamond Kings (1-27), Rated Rookies (28-47/413-432), AL All-Stars (48-56), MVP's (387-412) and NL All-Stars (433-441). There were also special cards to honor the award winners and the heroes of the World Series. Rookie Cards in the set include Jeff Conine and Brian McRae. On cards 60, 70, 127, 182, 239, 294, 355, 368, and 377, the border stripes are red and yellow.

	MINT	NRMT	EXC
COMPLETE SET (770)	8.00	3.60	1.00
COMP.FACT.w/LEAF PREV	10.00	4.50	1.25
COMP.FACT.w/STUDIO PREV	10.00	4.50	1.25
COMMON CARD (1-770)	.05	.02	.01
☐ 1 Dave Stieb DK	.05	.02	.01
☐ 2 Craig Biggio DK	.15	.07	.02
☐ 3 Cecil Fielder DK	.10	.05	.01
☐ 4 Barry Bonds DK	.15	.07	.02
☐ 5 Barry Larkin DK	.15	.07	.02
☐ 6 Dave Parker DK	.10	.05	.01
☐ 7 Len Dykstra DK	.10	.05	.01
☐ 8 Bobby Thigpen DK	.05	.02	.01
☐ 9 Roger Clemens DK	.15	.07	.02
☐ 10 Ron Gant DK UER (No trademark on team logo on back)	.10	.05	.01
☐ 11 Delino DeShields DK	.05	.02	.01
☐ 12 Roberto Alomar DK UER (No trademark on team logo on back)	.15	.07	.02
☐ 13 Sandy Alomar Jr. DK	.10	.05	.01
☐ 14 Ryne Sandberg DK UER (Was DK in '85, not '83 as shown)	.15	.07	.02
☐ 15 Ramon Martinez DK	.15	.07	.02
☐ 16 Edgar Martinez DK	.10	.05	.01
☐ 17 Dave Magadan DK	.05	.02	.01
☐ 18 Matt Williams DK	.15	.07	.02
☐ 19 Rafael Palmeiro DK UER (No trademark on team logo on back)	.15	.07	.02
☐ 20 Bob Welch DK	.05	.02	.01
☐ 21 Dave Righetti DK	.05	.02	.01
☐ 22 Brian Harper DK	.05	.02	.01
☐ 23 Gregg Olson DK	.05	.02	.01
☐ 24 Kurt Stillwell DK	.05	.02	.01
☐ 25 Pedro Guerrero DK UER (No trademark on team logo on back)	.05	.02	.01
☐ 26 Chuck Finley DK UER (No trademark on team logo on back)	.05	.02	.01
☐ 27 DK Checklist 1-27	.05	.02	.01
☐ 28 Tino Martinez RR	.15	.07	.02
☐ 29 Mark Lewis RR	.05	.02	.01
☐ 30 Bernard Gilkey RR	.10	.05	.01
☐ 31 Hensley Meulens RR	.05	.02	.01
☐ 32 Derek Bell RR	.15	.07	.02
☐ 33 Jose Offerman RR	.05	.02	.01
☐ 34 Terry Bross RR	.05	.02	.01
☐ 35 Leo Gomez RR	.05	.02	.01
☐ 36 Derrick May RR	.05	.02	.01
☐ 37 Kevin Morton RR	.05	.02	.01
☐ 38 Moises Alou RR	.15	.07	.02
☐ 39 Julio Valera RR	.05	.02	.01
☐ 40 Milt Cuyler RR	.05	.02	.01
☐ 41 Phil Plantier RR	.10	.05	.01
☐ 42 Scott Chiamparino RR	.05	.02	.01
☐ 43 Ray Lankford RR	.15	.07	.02
☐ 44 Mickey Morandini RR	.05	.02	.01
☐ 45 Dave Hansen RR	.05	.02	.01
☐ 46 Kevin Belcher RR	.05	.02	.01
☐ 47 Darrin Fletcher RR	.05	.02	.01
☐ 48 Steve Sax AS	.05	.02	.01
☐ 49 Ken Griffey Jr. AS	.75	.35	.09
☐ 50A Jose Canseco AS ERR (Team in stat box should be AL, not A's)	.15	.07	.02
☐ 50B Jose Canseco AS COR	.75	.35	.09
☐ 51 Sandy Alomar Jr. AS	.10	.05	.01
☐ 52 Cal Ripken AS	.40	.18	.05
☐ 53 Rickey Henderson AS	.15	.07	.02
☐ 54 Bob Welch AS	.05	.02	.01
☐ 55 Wade Boggs AS	.15	.07	.02
☐ 56 Mark McGwire AS	.15	.07	.02
☐ 57A Jack McDowell ERR (Career stats do not include 1990)	.15	.07	.02
☐ 57B Jack McDowell COR (Career stats do not include 1990)	.25	.11	.03
☐ 58 Jose Lind	.05	.02	.01
☐ 59 Alex Fernandez	.15	.07	.02
☐ 60 Pat Combs	.05	.02	.01
☐ 61 Mike Walker	.05	.02	.01
☐ 62 Juan Samuel	.05	.02	.01
☐ 63 Mike Blowers UER (Last line has aseball, not baseball)	.05	.02	.01
☐ 64 Mark Guthrie	.05	.02	.01
☐ 65 Mark Salas	.05	.02	.01
☐ 66 Tim Jones	.05	.02	.01
☐ 67 Tim Leary	.05	.02	.01
☐ 68 Andres Galarraga	.15	.07	.02
☐ 69 Bob Milacki	.05	.02	.01
☐ 70 Tim Belcher	.05	.02	.01
☐ 71 Todd Zeile	.10	.05	.01
☐ 72 Jerome Walton	.05	.02	.01
☐ 73 Kevin Seitzer	.05	.02	.01
☐ 74 Jerald Clark	.05	.02	.01
☐ 75 John Smoltz UER (Born in Detroit, not Warren)	.15	.07	.02
☐ 76 Mike Henneman	.05	.02	.01
☐ 77 Ken Griffey Jr.	1.50	.70	.19
☐ 78 Jim Abbott	.10	.05	.01
☐ 79 Gregg Jefferies	.10	.05	.01
☐ 80 Kevin Reimer	.05	.02	.01
☐ 81 Roger Clemens	.20	.09	.03
☐ 82 Mike Fitzgerald	.05	.02	.01
☐ 83 Bruce Hurst UER (Middle name is Lee, not Vee)	.05	.02	.01
☐ 84 Eric Davis	.10	.05	.01
☐ 85 Paul Molitor	.20	.09	.03
☐ 86 Will Clark	.15	.07	.02
☐ 87 Mike Bielecki	.05	.02	.01
☐ 88 Bret Saberhagen	.10	.05	.01
☐ 89 Nolan Ryan	.75	.35	.09
☐ 90 Bobby Thigpen	.05	.02	.01
☐ 91 Dickie Thon	.05	.02	.01
☐ 92 Duane Ward	.05	.02	.01
☐ 93 Luis Polonia	.05	.02	.01
☐ 94 Terry Kennedy	.05	.02	.01
☐ 95 Kent Hrbek	.10	.05	.01
☐ 96 Danny Jackson	.05	.02	.01
☐ 97 Sid Fernandez	.05	.02	.01
☐ 98 Jimmy Key	.10	.05	.01
☐ 99 Franklin Stubbs	.05	.02	.01
☐ 100 Checklist 28-103	.05	.02	.01
☐ 101 R.J. Reynolds	.05	.02	.01
☐ 102 Dave Stewart	.10	.05	.01
☐ 103 Dan Pasqua	.05	.02	.01
☐ 104 Dan Plesac	.05	.02	.01
☐ 105 Mark McGwire	.30	.14	.04
☐ 106 John Farrell	.05	.02	.01
☐ 107 Don Mattingly	.50	.23	.06
☐ 108 Carlton Fisk	.15	.07	.02
☐ 109 Ken Oberkfell	.05	.02	.01
☐ 110 Darrel Akerfelds	.05	.02	.01
☐ 111 Gregg Olson	.05	.02	.01
☐ 112 Mike Scioscia	.05	.02	.01
☐ 113 Bryn Smith	.05	.02	.01
☐ 114 Bob Geren	.05	.02	.01
☐ 115 Tom Candiotti	.05	.02	.01
☐ 116 Kevin Tapani	.05	.02	.01
☐ 117 Jeff Treadway	.05	.02	.01
☐ 118 Alan Trammell	.10	.05	.01
☐ 119 Pete O'Brien (Blue shading goes through stats)	.05	.02	.01
☐ 120 Joel Skinner	.05	.02	.01
☐ 121 Mike LaValliere	.05	.02	.01
☐ 122 Dwight Evans	.10	.05	.01
☐ 123 Jody Reed	.05	.02	.01
☐ 124 Lee Guetterman	.05	.02	.01
☐ 125 Tim Burke	.05	.02	.01
☐ 126 Dave Johnson	.05	.02	.01
☐ 127 Fernando Valenzuela (Lower large stripe in yellow instead of blue) UER	.10	.05	.01
☐ 128 Jose DeLeon	.05	.02	.01
☐ 129 Andre Dawson	.10	.05	.01
☐ 130 Gerald Perry	.05	.02	.01
☐ 131 Greg W. Harris	.05	.02	.01
☐ 132 Tom Glavine	.15	.07	.02
☐ 133 Lance McCullers	.05	.02	.01
☐ 134 Randy Johnson	.15	.07	.02
☐ 135 Lance Parrish UER (Born in McKeesport, not Clairton)	.05	.02	.01
☐ 136 Mackey Sasser	.05	.02	.01

☐ 137 Geno Petralli	.05	.02	.01
☐ 138 Dennis Lamp	.05	.02	.01
☐ 139 Dennis Martinez	.10	.05	.01
☐ 140 Mike Pagliarulo	.05	.02	.01
☐ 141 Hal Morris	.05	.02	.01
☐ 142 Dave Parker	.10	.05	.01
☐ 143 Brett Butler	.10	.05	.01
☐ 144 Paul Assenmacher	.05	.02	.01
☐ 145 Mark Gubicza	.05	.02	.01
☐ 146 Charlie Hough	.05	.02	.01
☐ 147 Sammy Sosa	.25	.11	.03
☐ 148 Randy Ready	.05	.02	.01
☐ 149 Kelly Gruber	.05	.02	.01
☐ 150 Devon White	.10	.05	.01
☐ 151 Gary Carter	.10	.05	.01
☐ 152 Gene Larkin	.05	.02	.01
☐ 153 Chris Sabo	.05	.02	.01
☐ 154 David Cone	.10	.05	.01
☐ 155 Todd Stottlemyre	.05	.02	.01
☐ 156 Glenn Wilson	.05	.02	.01
☐ 157 Bob Walk	.05	.02	.01
☐ 158 Mike Gallego	.05	.02	.01
☐ 159 Greg Hibbard	.05	.02	.01
☐ 160 Chris Bosio	.05	.02	.01
☐ 161 Mike Moore	.05	.02	.01
☐ 162 Jerry Browne UER (Born Christiansted, should be St. Croix)	.05	.02	.01
☐ 163 Steve Sax UER (No asterisk next to his 1989 At Bats)	.05	.02	.01
☐ 164 Melido Perez	.05	.02	.01
☐ 165 Danny Darwin	.05	.02	.01
☐ 166 Roger McDowell	.05	.02	.01
☐ 167 Bill Ripken	.05	.02	.01
☐ 168 Mike Sharperson	.05	.02	.01
☐ 169 Lee Smith	.10	.05	.01
☐ 170 Matt Nokes	.05	.02	.01
☐ 171 Jesse Orosco	.05	.02	.01
☐ 172 Rick Aguilera	.10	.05	.01
☐ 173 Jim Presley	.05	.02	.01
☐ 174 Lou Whitaker	.10	.05	.01
☐ 175 Harold Reynolds	.05	.02	.01
☐ 176 Brook Jacoby	.05	.02	.01
☐ 177 Wally Backman	.05	.02	.01
☐ 178 Wade Boggs	.15	.07	.02
☐ 179 Chuck Cary (Comma after DOB, not on other cards)	.05	.02	.01
☐ 180 Tom Foley	.05	.02	.01
☐ 181 Pete Harnisch	.05	.02	.01
☐ 182 Mike Morgan	.05	.02	.01
☐ 183 Bob Tewksbury	.05	.02	.01
☐ 184 Joe Girardi	.10	.05	.01
☐ 185 Storm Davis	.05	.02	.01
☐ 186 Ed Whitson	.05	.02	.01
☐ 187 Steve Avery UER (Born in New Jersey, should be Michigan)	.15	.07	.02
☐ 188 Lloyd Moseby	.05	.02	.01
☐ 189 Scott Bankhead	.05	.02	.01
☐ 190 Mark Langston	.10	.05	.01
☐ 191 Kevin McReynolds	.05	.02	.01
☐ 192 Julio Franco	.10	.05	.01
☐ 193 John Dopson	.05	.02	.01
☐ 194 Dennis Boyd	.05	.02	.01
☐ 195 Bip Roberts	.05	.02	.01
☐ 196 Billy Hatcher	.05	.02	.01
☐ 197 Edgar Diaz	.05	.02	.01
☐ 198 Greg Litton	.05	.02	.01
☐ 199 Mark Grace	.15	.07	.02
☐ 200 Checklist 104-179	.05	.02	.01
☐ 201 George Brett	.40	.18	.05
☐ 202 Jeff Russell	.05	.02	.01
☐ 203 Ivan Calderon	.05	.02	.01
☐ 204 Ken Howell	.05	.02	.01
☐ 205 Tom Henke	.05	.02	.01
☐ 206 Bryan Harvey	.05	.02	.01
☐ 207 Steve Bedrosian	.05	.02	.01
☐ 208 Al Newman	.05	.02	.01
☐ 209 Randy Myers	.10	.05	.01
☐ 210 Daryl Boston	.05	.02	.01
☐ 211 Manny Lee	.05	.02	.01
☐ 212 Dave Smith	.05	.02	.01
☐ 213 Don Slaught	.05	.02	.01
☐ 214 Walt Weiss	.05	.02	.01
☐ 215 Donn Pall	.05	.02	.01
☐ 216 Jaime Navarro	.05	.02	.01
☐ 217 Willie Randolph	.10	.05	.01
☐ 218 Rudy Seanez	.05	.02	.01
☐ 219 Jim Leyritz	.10	.05	.01
☐ 220 Ron Karkovice	.05	.02	.01
☐ 221 Ken Caminiti	.15	.07	.02
☐ 222 Von Hayes	.05	.02	.01
☐ 223 Cal Ripken	.75	.35	.09
☐ 224 Lenny Harris	.05	.02	.01
☐ 225 Milt Thompson	.05	.02	.01
☐ 226 Alvaro Espinoza	.05	.02	.01
☐ 227 Chris James	.05	.02	.01
☐ 228 Dan Gladden	.05	.02	.01
☐ 229 Jeff Blauser	.05	.02	.01
☐ 230 Mike Heath	.05	.02	.01
☐ 231 Omar Vizquel	.15	.07	.02
☐ 232 Doug Jones	.05	.02	.01
☐ 233 Jeff King	.10	.05	.01
☐ 234 Luis Rivera	.05	.02	.01
☐ 235 Ellis Burks	.10	.05	.01
☐ 236 Greg Cadaret	.05	.02	.01
☐ 237 Dave Martinez	.05	.02	.01
☐ 238 Mark Williamson	.05	.02	.01
☐ 239 Stan Javier	.05	.02	.01
☐ 240 Ozzie Smith	.25	.11	.03
☐ 241 Shawn Boskie	.05	.02	.01
☐ 242 Tom Gordon	.05	.02	.01
☐ 243 Tony Gwynn	.40	.18	.05
☐ 244 Tommy Gregg	.05	.02	.01
☐ 245 Jeff M. Robinson	.05	.02	.01
☐ 246 Keith Comstock	.05	.02	.01
☐ 247 Jack Howell	.05	.02	.01
☐ 248 Keith Miller	.05	.02	.01
☐ 249 Bobby Witt	.05	.02	.01
☐ 250 Rob Murphy UER (Shown as on Reds in '89 in stats, should be Red Sox)	.05	.02	.01
☐ 251 Spike Owen	.05	.02	.01
☐ 252 Garry Templeton	.05	.02	.01
☐ 253 Glenn Braggs	.05	.02	.01
☐ 254 Ron Robinson	.05	.02	.01
☐ 255 Kevin Mitchell	.10	.05	.01
☐ 256 Les Lancaster	.05	.02	.01
☐ 257 Mel Stottlemyre Jr.	.05	.02	.01
☐ 258 Kenny Rogers UER (IP listed as 171, should be 172)	.05	.02	.01
☐ 259 Lance Johnson	.10	.05	.01
☐ 260 John Kruk	.10	.05	.01
☐ 261 Fred McGriff	.15	.07	.02
☐ 262 Dick Schofield	.05	.02	.01
☐ 263 Trevor Wilson	.05	.02	.01
☐ 264 David West	.05	.02	.01
☐ 265 Scott Scudder	.05	.02	.01
☐ 266 Dwight Gooden	.10	.05	.01
☐ 267 Willie Blair	.05	.02	.01
☐ 268 Mark Portugal	.05	.02	.01
☐ 269 Doug Drabek	.05	.02	.01
☐ 270 Dennis Eckersley	.10	.05	.01
☐ 271 Eric King	.05	.02	.01
☐ 272 Robin Yount	.15	.07	.02
☐ 273 Carney Lansford	.10	.05	.01
☐ 274 Carlos Baerga	.15	.07	.02
☐ 275 Dave Righetti	.05	.02	.01
☐ 276 Scott Fletcher	.05	.02	.01
☐ 277 Eric Yelding	.05	.02	.01
☐ 278 Charlie Hayes	.05	.02	.01
☐ 279 Jeff Ballard	.05	.02	.01
☐ 280 Orel Hershiser	.10	.05	.01
☐ 281 Jose Oquendo	.05	.02	.01
☐ 282 Mike Witt	.05	.02	.01
☐ 283 Mitch Webster	.05	.02	.01
☐ 284 Greg Gagne	.05	.02	.01
☐ 285 Greg Olson	.05	.02	.01
☐ 286 Tony Phillips UER (Born 4/15, should be 4/25)	.10	.05	.01
☐ 287 Scott Bradley	.05	.02	.01
☐ 288 Cory Snyder UER (In text, led is repeated and Inglewood is misspelled as Englewood)	.05	.02	.01
☐ 289 Jay Bell UER (Born in Pensacola, not Eglin AFB)	.10	.05	.01
☐ 290 Kevin Romine	.05	.02	.01
☐ 291 Jeff D. Robinson	.05	.02	.01
☐ 292 Steve Frey UER (Bats left, should be right)	.05	.02	.01
☐ 293 Craig Worthington	.05	.02	.01
☐ 294 Tim Crews	.05	.02	.01
☐ 295 Joe Magrane	.05	.02	.01
☐ 296 Hector Villanueva	.05	.02	.01
☐ 297 Terry Shumpert	.05	.02	.01
☐ 298 Joe Carter	.10	.05	.01
☐ 299 Kent Mercker UER (IP listed as 53, should be 52)	.05	.02	.01
☐ 300 Checklist 180-255	.05	.02	.01
☐ 301 Chet Lemon	.05	.02	.01
☐ 302 Mike Schooler	.05	.02	.01
☐ 303 Dante Bichette	.15	.07	.02
☐ 304 Kevin Elster	.05	.02	.01
☐ 305 Jeff Huson	.05	.02	.01
☐ 306 Greg A. Harris	.05	.02	.01
☐ 307 Marquis Grissom UER (Middle name Deon, should be Dean)	.15	.07	.02
☐ 308 Calvin Schiraldi	.05	.02	.01
☐ 309 Mariano Duncan	.05	.02	.01
☐ 310 Bill Spiers	.05	.02	.01
☐ 311 Scott Garrelts	.05	.02	.01
☐ 312 Mitch Williams	.05	.02	.01
☐ 313 Mike Macfarlane	.05	.02	.01
☐ 314 Kevin Brown	.10	.05	.01
☐ 315 Robin Ventura	.15	.07	.02
☐ 316 Darren Daulton	.10	.05	.01
☐ 317 Pat Borders	.05	.02	.01
☐ 318 Mark Eichhorn	.05	.02	.01
☐ 319 Jeff Brantley	.05	.02	.01
☐ 320 Shane Mack	.05	.02	.01
☐ 321 Rob Dibble	.05	.02	.01
☐ 322 John Franco	.05	.02	.01
☐ 323 Junior Felix	.05	.02	.01
☐ 324 Casey Candaele	.05	.02	.01
☐ 325 Bobby Bonilla	.10	.05	.01
☐ 326 Dave Henderson	.05	.02	.01
☐ 327 Wayne Edwards	.05	.02	.01
☐ 328 Mark Knudson	.05	.02	.01
☐ 329 Terry Steinbach	.10	.05	.01
☐ 330 Colby Ward UER (No comma between city and state)	.05	.02	.01
☐ 331 Oscar Azocar	.05	.02	.01
☐ 332 Scott Radinsky	.05	.02	.01
☐ 333 Eric Anthony	.05	.02	.01
☐ 334 Steve Lake	.05	.02	.01
☐ 335 Bob Melvin	.05	.02	.01
☐ 336 Kal Daniels	.05	.02	.01
☐ 337 Tom Pagnozzi	.05	.02	.01
☐ 338 Alan Mills	.05	.02	.01
☐ 339 Steve Olin	.05	.02	.01
☐ 340 Juan Berenguer	.05	.02	.01
☐ 341 Francisco Cabrera	.05	.02	.01
☐ 342 Dave Bergman	.05	.02	.01
☐ 343 Henry Cotto	.05	.02	.01
☐ 344 Sergio Valdez	.05	.02	.01
☐ 345 Bob Patterson	.05	.02	.01
☐ 346 John Marzano	.05	.02	.01
☐ 347 Dana Kiecker	.05	.02	.01
☐ 348 Dion James	.05	.02	.01
☐ 349 Hubie Brooks	.05	.02	.01
☐ 350 Bill Landrum	.05	.02	.01
☐ 351 Bill Sampen	.05	.02	.01
☐ 352 Greg Briley	.05	.02	.01
☐ 353 Paul Gibson	.05	.02	.01
☐ 354 Dave Eiland	.05	.02	.01
☐ 355 Steve Finley	.10	.05	.01
☐ 356 Bob Boone	.10	.05	.01
☐ 357 Steve Buechele	.05	.02	.01
☐ 358 Chris Hoiles	.05	.02	.01
☐ 359 Larry Walker	.15	.07	.02
☐ 360 Frank DiPino	.05	.02	.01
☐ 361 Mark Grant	.05	.02	.01
☐ 362 Dave Magadan	.05	.02	.01
☐ 363 Robby Thompson	.05	.02	.01
☐ 364 Lonnie Smith	.05	.02	.01
☐ 365 Steve Farr	.05	.02	.01
☐ 366 Dave Valle	.05	.02	.01
☐ 367 Tim Naehring	.10	.05	.01
☐ 368 Jim Acker	.05	.02	.01
☐ 369 Jeff Reardon UER (Born in Pittsfield, not Dalton)	.10	.05	.01
☐ 370 Tim Teufel	.05	.02	.01
☐ 371 Juan Gonzalez	.75	.35	.09
☐ 372 Luis Salazar	.05	.02	.01
☐ 373 Rick Honeycutt	.05	.02	.01
☐ 374 Greg Maddux	.60	.25	.07
☐ 375 Jose Uribe UER (Middle name Elta, should be Alta)	.05	.02	.01
☐ 376 Donnie Hill	.05	.02	.01
☐ 377 Don Carman	.05	.02	.01
☐ 378 Craig Grebeck	.05	.02	.01
☐ 379 Willie Fraser	.05	.02	.01
☐ 380 Glenallen Hill	.05	.02	.01
☐ 381 Joe Oliver	.05	.02	.01
☐ 382 Randy Bush	.05	.02	.01
☐ 383 Alex Cole	.05	.02	.01
☐ 384 Norm Charlton	.05	.02	.01
☐ 385 Gene Nelson	.05	.02	.01
☐ 386 Checklist 256-331	.05	.02	.01
☐ 387 Rickey Henderson MVP	.15	.07	.02
☐ 388 Lance Parrish MVP	.05	.02	.01
☐ 389 Fred McGriff MVP	.15	.07	.02
☐ 390 Dave Parker MVP	.10	.05	.01
☐ 391 Candy Maldonado MVP	.05	.02	.01
☐ 392 Ken Griffey Jr. MVP	.75	.35	.09
☐ 393 Gregg Olson MVP	.05	.02	.01
☐ 394 Rafael Palmeiro MVP	.15	.07	.02
☐ 395 Roger Clemens MVP	.15	.07	.02
☐ 396 George Brett MVP	.20	.09	.03
☐ 397 Cecil Fielder MVP	.10	.05	.01
☐ 398 Brian Harper MVP UER (Major League Performance, should be Career)	.05	.02	.01
☐ 399 Bobby Thigpen MVP	.05	.02	.01
☐ 400 Roberto Kelly MVP UER (Second Base on front and OF on back)	.05	.02	.01
☐ 401 Danny Darwin MVP	.05	.02	.01
☐ 402 Dave Justice MVP	.10	.05	.01
☐ 403 Lee Smith MVP	.10	.05	.01
☐ 404 Ryne Sandberg MVP	.15	.07	.02
☐ 405 Eddie Murray MVP	.15	.07	.02
☐ 406 Tim Wallach MVP	.05	.02	.01
☐ 407 Kevin Mitchell MVP	.05	.02	.01
☐ 408 Darryl Strawberry MVP	.10	.05	.01
☐ 409 Joe Carter MVP	.10	.05	.01
☐ 410 Len Dykstra MVP	.10	.05	.01
☐ 411 Doug Drabek MVP	.05	.02	.01
☐ 412 Chris Sabo MVP	.05	.02	.01
☐ 413 Paul Marak RR	.05	.02	.01
☐ 414 Tim McIntosh RR	.05	.02	.01
☐ 415 Brian Barnes RR	.05	.02	.01
☐ 416 Eric Gunderson RR	.05	.02	.01
☐ 417 Mike Gardiner RR	.05	.02	.01
☐ 418 Steve Carter RR	.05	.02	.01
☐ 419 Gerald Alexander RR	.05	.02	.01
☐ 420 Rich Garces RR	.05	.02	.01
☐ 421 Chuck Knoblauch RR	.25	.11	.03
☐ 422 Scott Aldred RR	.05	.02	.01
☐ 423 Wes Chamberlain RR	.05	.02	.01
☐ 424 Lance Dickson RR	.05	.02	.01
☐ 425 Greg Colbrunn RR	.10	.05	.01
☐ 426 Rich DeLucia RR UER (Misspelled Delucia on card)	.05	.02	.01
☐ 427 Jeff Conine RR	.50	.23	.06
☐ 428 Steve Decker RR	.05	.02	.01
☐ 429 Turner Ward RR	.05	.02	.01
☐ 430 Mo Vaughn RR	.50	.23	.06
☐ 431 Steve Chitren RR	.05	.02	.01
☐ 432 Mike Benjamin RR	.05	.02	.01
☐ 433 Ryne Sandberg AS	.15	.07	.02
☐ 434 Len Dykstra AS	.10	.05	.01
☐ 435 Andre Dawson AS	.10	.05	.01
☐ 436A Mike Scioscia AS (White star by name)	.05	.02	.01
☐ 436B Mike Scioscia AS (Yellow star by name)	.05	.02	.01
☐ 437 Ozzie Smith AS	.15	.07	.02
☐ 438 Kevin Mitchell AS	.05	.02	.01
☐ 439 Jack Armstrong AS	.05	.02	.01
☐ 440 Chris Sabo AS	.05	.02	.01
☐ 441 Will Clark AS	.15	.07	.02
☐ 442 Mel Hall	.05	.02	.01
☐ 443 Mark Gardner	.05	.02	.01
☐ 444 Mike Devereaux	.05	.02	.01
☐ 445 Kirk Gibson	.10	.05	.01
☐ 446 Terry Pendleton	.10	.05	.01
☐ 447 Mike Harkey	.05	.02	.01
☐ 448 Jim Eisenreich	.10	.05	.01
☐ 449 Benito Santiago	.05	.02	.01
☐ 450 Oddibe McDowell	.05	.02	.01
☐ 451 Cecil Fielder	.10	.05	.01
☐ 452 Ken Griffey Sr.	.05	.02	.01
☐ 453 Bert Blyleven	.10	.05	.01
☐ 454 Howard Johnson	.05	.02	.01
☐ 455 Monty Fariss UER (Misspelled Farris on card)	.05	.02	.01
☐ 456 Tony Pena	.05	.02	.01
☐ 457 Tim Raines	.15	.07	.02
☐ 458 Dennis Rasmussen	.05	.02	.01
☐ 459 Luis Quinones	.05	.02	.01
☐ 460 B.J. Surhoff	.10	.05	.01
☐ 461 Ernest Riles	.05	.02	.01
☐ 462 Rick Sutcliffe	.05	.02	.01
☐ 463 Danny Tartabull	.05	.02	.01
☐ 464 Pete Incaviglia	.05	.02	.01
☐ 465 Carlos Martinez	.05	.02	.01
☐ 466 Ricky Jordan	.05	.02	.01
☐ 467 John Cerutti	.05	.02	.01
☐ 468 Dave Winfield	.15	.07	.02
☐ 469 Francisco Oliveras	.05	.02	.01
☐ 470 Roy Smith	.05	.02	.01
☐ 471 Barry Larkin	.15	.07	.02
☐ 472 Ron Darling	.05	.02	.01
☐ 473 David Wells	.05	.02	.01
☐ 474 Glenn Davis	.05	.02	.01
☐ 475 Neal Heaton	.05	.02	.01
☐ 476 Ron Hassey	.05	.02	.01
☐ 477 Frank Thomas	2.00	.90	.25
☐ 478 Greg Vaughn	.10	.05	.01
☐ 479 Todd Burns	.05	.02	.01
☐ 480 Candy Maldonado	.05	.02	.01
☐ 481 Dave LaPoint	.05	.02	.01
☐ 482 Alvin Davis	.05	.02	.01
☐ 483 Mike Scott	.05	.02	.01
☐ 484 Dale Murphy	.15	.07	.02
☐ 485 Ben McDonald	.10	.05	.01
☐ 486 Jay Howell	.05	.02	.01
☐ 487 Vince Coleman	.05	.02	.01
☐ 488 Alfredo Griffin	.05	.02	.01
☐ 489 Sandy Alomar Jr.	.10	.05	.01
☐ 490 Kirby Puckett	.40	.18	.05
☐ 491 Andres Thomas	.05	.02	.01
☐ 492 Jack Morris	.10	.05	.01
☐ 493 Matt Young	.05	.02	.01
☐ 494 Greg Myers	.05	.02	.01
☐ 495 Barry Bonds	.25	.11	.03
☐ 496 Scott Cooper UER (No BA for 1990 and career)	.05	.02	.01
☐ 497 Dan Schatzeder	.05	.02	.01
☐ 498 Jesse Barfield	.05	.02	.01
☐ 499 Jerry Goff	.05	.02	.01
☐ 500 Checklist 332-408	.05	.02	.01
☐ 501 Anthony Telford	.05	.02	.01
☐ 502 Eddie Murray	.25	.11	.03
☐ 503 Omar Olivares	.05	.02	.01
☐ 504 Ryne Sandberg	.25	.11	.03
☐ 505 Jeff Montgomery	.10	.05	.01
☐ 506 Mark Parent	.05	.02	.01
☐ 507 Ron Gant	.10	.05	.01
☐ 508 Frank Tanana	.05	.02	.01
☐ 509 Jay Buhner	.15	.07	.02
☐ 510 Max Venable	.05	.02	.01

☐ 511 Wally Whitehurst .05 .02 .01
☐ 512 Gary Pettis .05 .02 .01
☐ 513 Tom Brunansky .05 .02 .01
☐ 514 Tim Wallach .05 .02 .01
☐ 515 Craig Lefferts .05 .02 .01
☐ 516 Tim Layana .05 .02 .01
☐ 517 Darryl Hamilton .10 .05 .01
☐ 518 Rick Reuschel .05 .02 .01
☐ 519 Steve Wilson .05 .02 .01
☐ 520 Kurt Stillwell .05 .02 .01
☐ 521 Rafael Palmeiro .15 .07 .02
☐ 522 Ken Patterson .05 .02 .01
☐ 523 Len Dykstra .10 .05 .01
☐ 524 Tony Fernandez .05 .02 .01
☐ 525 Kent Anderson .05 .02 .01
☐ 526 Mark Leonard .05 .02 .01
☐ 527 Allan Anderson .05 .02 .01
☐ 528 Tom Browning .05 .02 .01
☐ 529 Frank Viola .05 .02 .01
☐ 530 John Olerud .10 .05 .01
☐ 531 Juan Agosto .05 .02 .01
☐ 532 Zane Smith .05 .02 .01
☐ 533 Scott Sanderson .05 .02 .01
☐ 534 Barry Jones .05 .02 .01
☐ 535 Mike Felder .05 .02 .01
☐ 536 Jose Canseco .15 .07 .02
☐ 537 Felix Fermin .05 .02 .01
☐ 538 Roberto Kelly .05 .02 .01
☐ 539 Brian Holman .05 .02 .01
☐ 540 Mark Davidson .05 .02 .01
☐ 541 Terry Mulholland .05 .02 .01
☐ 542 Randy Milligan .05 .02 .01
☐ 543 Jose Gonzalez .05 .02 .01
☐ 544 Craig Wilson .05 .02 .01
☐ 545 Mike Hartley .05 .02 .01
☐ 546 Greg Swindell .05 .02 .01
☐ 547 Gary Gaetti .10 .05 .01
☐ 548 Dave Justice .15 .07 .02
☐ 549 Steve Searcy .05 .02 .01
☐ 550 Erik Hanson .05 .02 .01
☐ 551 Dave Stieb .05 .02 .01
☐ 552 Andy Van Slyke .10 .05 .01
☐ 553 Mike Greenwell .05 .02 .01
☐ 554 Kevin Maas .05 .02 .01
☐ 555 Delino DeShields .05 .02 .01
☐ 556 Curt Schilling .05 .02 .01
☐ 557 Ramon Martinez .15 .07 .02
☐ 558 Pedro Guerrero .05 .02 .01
☐ 559 Dwight Smith .05 .02 .01
☐ 560 Mark Davis .05 .02 .01
☐ 561 Shawn Abner .05 .02 .01
☐ 562 Charlie Leibrandt .05 .02 .01
☐ 563 John Shelby .05 .02 .01
☐ 564 Bill Swift .05 .02 .01
☐ 565 Mike Fetters .05 .02 .01
☐ 566 Alejandro Pena .05 .02 .01
☐ 567 Ruben Sierra .10 .05 .01
☐ 568 Carlos Quintana .05 .02 .01
☐ 569 Kevin Gross .05 .02 .01
☐ 570 Derek Lilliquist .05 .02 .01
☐ 571 Jack Armstrong .05 .02 .01
☐ 572 Greg Brock .05 .02 .01
☐ 573 Mike Kingery .05 .02 .01
☐ 574 Greg Smith .05 .02 .01
☐ 575 Brian McRae .25 .11 .03
☐ 576 Jack Daugherty .05 .02 .01
☐ 577 Ozzie Guillen .05 .02 .01
☐ 578 Joe Boever .05 .02 .01
☐ 579 Luis Sojo .05 .02 .01
☐ 580 Chili Davis .10 .05 .01
☐ 581 Don Robinson .05 .02 .01
☐ 582 Brian Harper .05 .02 .01
☐ 583 Paul O'Neill .10 .05 .01
☐ 584 Bob Ojeda .05 .02 .01
☐ 585 Mookie Wilson .05 .02 .01
☐ 586 Rafael Ramirez .05 .02 .01
☐ 587 Gary Redus .05 .02 .01
☐ 588 Jamie Quirk .05 .02 .01
☐ 589 Shawn Hillegas .05 .02 .01
☐ 590 Tom Edens .05 .02 .01
☐ 591 Joe Klink .05 .02 .01
☐ 592 Charles Nagy .15 .07 .02
☐ 593 Eric Plunk .05 .02 .01
☐ 594 Tracy Jones .05 .02 .01
☐ 595 Craig Biggio .15 .07 .02
☐ 596 Jose DeJesus .05 .02 .01
☐ 597 Mickey Tettleton .10 .05 .01
☐ 598 Chris Gwynn .05 .02 .01
☐ 599 Rex Hudler .05 .02 .01
☐ 600 Checklist 409-506 .05 .02 .01
☐ 601 Jim Gott .05 .02 .01
☐ 602 Jeff Manto .05 .02 .01
☐ 603 Nelson Liriano .05 .02 .01
☐ 604 Mark Lemke .05 .02 .01
☐ 605 Clay Parker .05 .02 .01
☐ 606 Edgar Martinez .10 .05 .01
☐ 607 Mark Whiten .10 .05 .01
☐ 608 Ted Power .05 .02 .01
☐ 609 Tom Bolton .05 .02 .01
☐ 610 Tom Herr .05 .02 .01
☐ 611 Andy Hawkins UER .05 .02 .01
(Pitched No-Hitter
on 7/1, not 7/2)
☐ 612 Scott Ruskin .05 .02 .01
☐ 613 Ron Kittle .05 .02 .01
☐ 614 John Wetteland .15 .07 .02
☐ 615 Mike Perez .05 .02 .01
☐ 616 Dave Clark .05 .02 .01
☐ 617 Brent Mayne .05 .02 .01
☐ 618 Jack Clark .10 .05 .01
☐ 619 Marvin Freeman .05 .02 .01
☐ 620 Edwin Nunez .05 .02 .01
☐ 621 Russ Swan .05 .02 .01
☐ 622 Johnny Ray .05 .02 .01
☐ 623 Charlie O'Brien .05 .02 .01
☐ 624 Joe Bitker .05 .02 .01
☐ 625 Mike Marshall .05 .02 .01
☐ 626 Otis Nixon .05 .02 .01
☐ 627 Andy Benes .10 .05 .01
☐ 628 Ron Oester .05 .02 .01
☐ 629 Ted Higuera .05 .02 .01
☐ 630 Kevin Bass .05 .02 .01
☐ 631 Damon Berryhill .05 .02 .01
☐ 632 Bo Jackson .10 .05 .01
☐ 633 Brad Arnsberg .05 .02 .01
☐ 634 Jerry Willard .05 .02 .01
☐ 635 Tommy Greene .05 .02 .01
☐ 636 Bob MacDonald .05 .02 .01
☐ 637 Kirk McCaskill .05 .02 .01
☐ 638 John Burkett .10 .05 .01
☐ 639 Paul Abbott .05 .02 .01
☐ 640 Todd Benzinger .05 .02 .01
☐ 641 Todd Hundley .15 .07 .02
☐ 642 George Bell .05 .02 .01
☐ 643 Javier Ortiz .05 .02 .01
☐ 644 Sid Bream .05 .02 .01
☐ 645 Bob Welch .05 .02 .01
☐ 646 Phil Bradley .05 .02 .01
☐ 647 Bill Krueger .05 .02 .01
☐ 648 Rickey Henderson .15 .07 .02
☐ 649 Kevin Wickander .05 .02 .01
☐ 650 Steve Balboni .05 .02 .01
☐ 651 Gene Harris .05 .02 .01
☐ 652 Jim Deshaies .05 .02 .01
☐ 653 Jason Grimsley .05 .02 .01
☐ 654 Joe Orsulak .05 .02 .01
☐ 655 Jim Poole .05 .02 .01
☐ 656 Felix Jose .05 .02 .01
☐ 657 Denis Cook .05 .02 .01
☐ 658 Tom Brookens .05 .02 .01
☐ 659 Junior Ortiz .05 .02 .01
☐ 660 Jeff Parrett .05 .02 .01
☐ 661 Jerry Don Gleaton .05 .02 .01
☐ 662 Brent Knackert .05 .02 .01
☐ 663 Rance Mulliniks .05 .02 .01
☐ 664 John Smiley .05 .02 .01
☐ 665 Larry Andersen .05 .02 .01
☐ 666 Willie McGee .05 .02 .01
☐ 667 Chris Nabholz .05 .02 .01
☐ 668 Brady Anderson .15 .07 .02
☐ 669 Darren Holmes UER .05 .02 .01
(19 CG's, should be 0)
☐ 670 Ken Hill .10 .05 .01
☐ 671 Gary Varsho .05 .02 .01
☐ 672 Bill Pecota .05 .02 .01
☐ 673 Fred Lynn .05 .02 .01
☐ 674 Kevin D. Brown .05 .02 .01
☐ 675 Dan Petry .05 .02 .01
☐ 676 Mike Jackson .05 .02 .01
☐ 677 Wally Joyner .10 .05 .01
☐ 678 Danny Jackson .05 .02 .01
☐ 679 Bill Haselman .05 .02 .01
☐ 680 Mike Boddicker .05 .02 .01
☐ 681 Mel Rojas .10 .05 .01
☐ 682 Roberto Alomar .20 .09 .03
☐ 683 Dave Justice ROY .10 .05 .01
☐ 684 Chuck Crim .05 .02 .01
☐ 685 Matt Williams .15 .07 .02
☐ 686 Shawon Dunston .05 .02 .01
☐ 687 Jeff Schulz .05 .02 .01
☐ 688 John Barfield .05 .02 .01
☐ 689 Gerald Young .05 .02 .01
☐ 690 Luis Gonzalez .15 .07 .02
☐ 691 Frank Wills .05 .02 .01
☐ 692 Chuck Finley .10 .05 .01
☐ 693 Sandy Alomar Jr. ROY .10 .05 .01
☐ 694 Tim Drummond .05 .02 .01
☐ 695 Herm Winningham .05 .02 .01
☐ 696 Darryl Strawberry .10 .05 .01
☐ 697 Al Leiter .10 .05 .01
☐ 698 Karl Rhodes .05 .02 .01
☐ 699 Stan Belinda .05 .02 .01
☐ 700 Checklist 507-604 .05 .02 .01
☐ 701 Lance Blankenship .05 .02 .01
☐ 702 Willie Stargell PUZ .15 .07 .02
☐ 703 Jim Gantner .05 .02 .01
☐ 704 Reggie Harris .05 .02 .01
☐ 705 Rob Ducey .05 .02 .01
☐ 706 Tim Hulett .05 .02 .01
☐ 707 Atlee Hammaker .05 .02 .01
☐ 708 Xavier Hernandez .05 .02 .01
☐ 709 Chuck McElroy .05 .02 .01
☐ 710 John Mitchell .05 .02 .01
☐ 711 Carlos Hernandez .05 .02 .01
☐ 712 Geronimo Pena .05 .02 .01
☐ 713 Jim Neidlinger .05 .02 .01
☐ 714 John Orton .05 .02 .01
☐ 715 Terry Leach .05 .02 .01
☐ 716 Mike Stanton .05 .02 .01
☐ 717 Walt Terrell .05 .02 .01
☐ 718 Luis Aquino .05 .02 .01
☐ 719 Bud Black .05 .02 .01
(Blue Jays uniform,
but Giants logo)
☐ 720 Bob Kipper .05 .02 .01
☐ 721 Jeff Gray .05 .02 .01
☐ 722 Jose Rijo .05 .02 .01
☐ 723 Curt Young .05 .02 .01
☐ 724 Jose Vizcaino .05 .02 .01
☐ 725 Randy Tomlin .05 .02 .01
☐ 726 Junior Noboa .05 .02 .01
☐ 727 Bob Welch CY .05 .02 .01
☐ 728 Gary Ward .05 .02 .01
☐ 729 Rob Deer .05 .02 .01
(Brewers uniform,
but Tigers logo)
☐ 730 David Segui .10 .05 .01
☐ 731 Mark Carreon .05 .02 .01
☐ 732 Vicente Palacios .05 .02 .01
☐ 733 Sam Horn .05 .02 .01
☐ 734 Howard Farmer .05 .02 .01
☐ 735 Ken Dayley .05 .02 .01
(Cardinals uniform,
but Blue Jays logo)
☐ 736 Kelly Mann .05 .02 .01
☐ 737 Joe Grahe .05 .02 .01
☐ 738 Kelly Downs .05 .02 .01
☐ 739 Jimmy Kremers .05 .02 .01
☐ 740 Kevin Appier .15 .07 .02
☐ 741 Jeff Reed .05 .02 .01
☐ 742 Jose Rijo WS .05 .02 .01
☐ 743 Dave Rohde .05 .02 .01
☐ 744 Dr.Dirt/Mr.Clean .10 .05 .01
Len Dykstra
Dale Murphy
UER (No '91 Donruss
logo on card front)
☐ 745 Paul Sorrento .10 .05 .01
☐ 746 Thomas Howard .05 .02 .01
☐ 747 Matt Stark .05 .02 .01
☐ 748 Harold Baines .10 .05 .01
☐ 749 Doug Dascenzo .05 .02 .01
☐ 750 Doug Drabek CY .05 .02 .01
☐ 751 Gary Sheffield .15 .07 .02
☐ 752 Terry Lee .05 .02 .01
☐ 753 Jim Vatcher .05 .02 .01
☐ 754 Lee Stevens .05 .02 .01
☐ 755 Randy Veres .05 .02 .01
☐ 756 Bill Doran .05 .02 .01
☐ 757 Gary Wayne .05 .02 .01
☐ 758 Pedro Munoz .10 .05 .01
☐ 759 Chris Hammond .05 .02 .01
☐ 760 Checklist 605-702 .05 .02 .01
☐ 761 Rickey Henderson MVP .15 .07 .02
☐ 762 Barry Bonds MVP .15 .07 .02
☐ 763 Billy Hatcher WS .05 .02 .01
UER (Line 13, on
should be one)
☐ 764 Julio Machado .05 .02 .01
☐ 765 Jose Mesa .10 .05 .01
☐ 766 Willie Randolph WS .10 .05 .01
☐ 767 Scott Erickson .10 .05 .01
☐ 768 Travis Fryman .15 .07 .02
☐ 769 Rich Rodriguez .05 .02 .01
☐ 770 Checklist 703-770 .05 .02 .01
and BC1-BC22

1991 Donruss Bonus Cards

These bonus cards are standard size and were randomly inserted in Donruss packs and highlight outstanding player achievements, the first ten in the first series and the remaining 12 in the second series picking up in time beginning with Valenzuela's no-hitter and continuing until the end of the season.

	MINT	NRMT	EXC
COMPLETE SET (22)	1.50	.70	.19
COMMON CARD (BC1-BC22)	.05	.02	.01

☐ BC1 Mark Langston .05 .02 .01
Mike Witt
No-Hits Mariners
☐ BC2 Randy Johnson .15 .07 .02
No-Hits Tigers
☐ BC3 Nolan Ryan .40 .18 .05
No-Hits A's
☐ BC4 Dave Stewart .05 .02 .01
No-Hits Blue Jays
☐ BC5 Cecil Fielder .10 .05 .01
50 Homer Club
☐ BC6 Carlton Fisk .15 .07 .02
Record Home Run
☐ BC7 Ryne Sandberg .25 .11 .03
Sets Fielding Records
☐ BC8 Gary Carter .10 .05 .01
Breaks Catching Mark
☐ BC9 Mark McGwire .30 .14 .04
Home Run Milestone
(Back says First
Baseman, others say
only base)
☐ BC10 Bo Jackson .10 .05 .01
Four Consecutive HR's
☐ BC11 Fernando Valenzuela .10 .05 .01
No Hits Cardinals
☐ BC12A Andy Hawkins ERR 1.00 .45 .12
Pitcher
☐ BC12B Andy Hawkins COR .05 .02 .01
No Hits White Sox
☐ BC13 Melido Perez .05 .02 .01
No Hits Yankees
☐ BC14 Terry Mulholland .05 .02 .01
No Hits Giants
UER (Charlie Hayes is
called Chris Hayes)
☐ BC15 Nolan Ryan .50 .23 .06
300th Win
☐ BC16 Delino DeShields .05 .02 .01
4 Hits in Debut
☐ BC17 Cal Ripken .50 .23 .06
Errorless Games
☐ BC18 Eddie Murray .25 .11 .03
Switch Hit Homers
☐ BC19 George Brett .25 .11 .03
3 Decade Champ
☐ BC20 Bobby Thigpen .05 .02 .01
Shatters Save Mark
☐ BC21 Dave Stieb .05 .02 .01
No Hits Indians
☐ BC22 Willie McGee .05 .02 .01
NL Batting Champ

1991 Donruss Elite

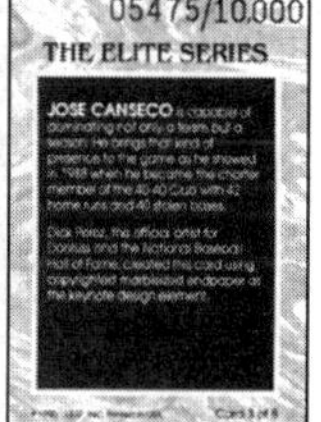

These special cards were inserted in the 1991 Donruss first and second series wax packs. Production was limited to a maximum of 10,000 cards for each card in the Elite series, and lesser production for the Sandberg Signature (5,000) and Ryan Legend (7,500) cards. This was the first time that mainstream insert cards were ever numbered allowing for verifiable proof of print runs. The regular Elite cards are photos enclosed in a bronze marble borders which surround an evenly squared photo of the players. The Sandberg Signature card has a green marble border and is signed in a blue sharpie. The Nolan Ryan Legend card is a Dick Perez drawing with silver borders. The cards are all numbered on the back, 1 out of 10,000, etc.

	MINT	NRMT	EXC
COMPLETE SET (10)	1000.00	450.00	125.00
COMMON CARD (1-8)	20.00	9.00	2.50

☐ 1 Barry Bonds 70.00 32.00 8.75
☐ 2 George Brett 120.00 55.00 15.00
☐ 3 Jose Canseco 60.00 27.00 7.50
☐ 4 Andre Dawson 40.00 18.00 5.00
☐ 5 Doug Drabek 20.00 9.00 2.50
☐ 6 Cecil Fielder 40.00 18.00 5.00
☐ 7 Rickey Henderson 40.00 18.00 5.00
☐ 8 Matt Williams 60.00 27.00 7.50
☐ L1 Nolan Ryan (Legend) 250.00 110.00 31.00
☐ S1 Ryne Sandberg 350.00 160.00 45.00
(Signature Series)

1991 Donruss Grand Slammers

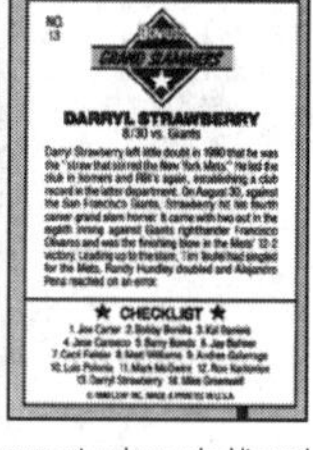

This 14-card standard-size set commemorates players who hit grand slams in 1990. The cards feature on the fronts color player photos on a computer-generated background design, enframed by white borders on a green card face crisscrossed by different color diagonal stripes. The player's name is given in a color stripe below the picture. Inside pale green borders, the back recounts grand slam homers by the player.

	MINT	NRMT	EXC
COMPLETE SET (14)	2.00	.90	.25
COMMON CARD (1-14)	.05	.02	.01
☐ 1 Joe Carter	.10	.05	.01
☐ 2 Bobby Bonilla	.10	.05	.01
☐ 3 Kal Daniels	.05	.02	.01
☐ 4 Jose Canseco	.15	.07	.02
☐ 5 Barry Bonds	.40	.18	.05
☐ 6 Jay Buhner	.15	.07	.02
☐ 7 Cecil Fielder	.10	.05	.01
☐ 8 Matt Williams	.15	.07	.02
☐ 9 Andres Galarraga	.15	.07	.02
☐ 10 Luis Polonia	.05	.02	.01
☐ 11 Mark McGwire	.50	.23	.06
☐ 12 Ron Karkovice	.05	.02	.01
☐ 13 Darryl Strawberry UER (Todd Hundley is called Randy)	.10	.05	.01
☐ 14 Mike Greenwell	.05	.02	.01

1991 Donruss Rookies

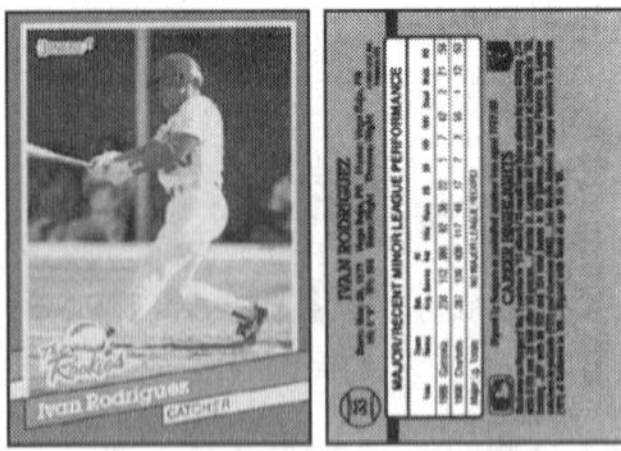

The 1991 Donruss Rookies set was issued exclusively in factory set form through hobby dealers. The cards measure the standard size and a mini puzzle featuring Hall of Famer Willie Stargell was included with the set. The fronts feature color action player photos, with white and red borders. Rookie Cards include Jeff Bagwell and Ivan Rodriguez.

	MINT	NRMT	EXC
COMPLETE FACT.SET (56)	4.00	1.80	.50
COMMON CARD (1-56)	.05	.02	.01
☐ 1 Pat Kelly	.05	.02	.01
☐ 2 Rich DeLucia	.05	.02	.01
☐ 3 Wes Chamberlain	.05	.02	.01
☐ 4 Scott Leius	.05	.02	.01
☐ 5 Darryl Kile	.10	.05	.01
☐ 6 Milt Cuyler	.05	.02	.01
☐ 7 Todd Van Poppel	.05	.02	.01
☐ 8 Ray Lankford	.10	.05	.01
☐ 9 Brian R. Hunter	.05	.02	.01
☐ 10 Tony Perezchica	.05	.02	.01
☐ 11 Ced Landrum	.05	.02	.01
☐ 12 Dave Burba	.05	.02	.01
☐ 13 Ramon Garcia	.05	.02	.01
☐ 14 Ed Sprague	.10	.05	.01
☐ 15 Warren Newson	.05	.02	.01
☐ 16 Paul Faries	.05	.02	.01
☐ 17 Luis Gonzalez	.10	.05	.01
☐ 18 Charles Nagy	.10	.05	.01
☐ 19 Chris Hammond	.05	.02	.01
☐ 20 Frank Castillo	.05	.02	.01
☐ 21 Pedro Munoz	.10	.05	.01
☐ 22 Orlando Merced	.10	.05	.01
☐ 23 Jose Melendez	.05	.02	.01
☐ 24 Kirk Dressendorfer	.05	.02	.01
☐ 25 Heathcliff Slocumb	.10	.05	.01
☐ 26 Doug Simons	.05	.02	.01
☐ 27 Mike Timlin	.05	.02	.01
☐ 28 Jeff Fassero	.15	.07	.02
☐ 29 Mark Leiter	.05	.02	.01
☐ 30 Jeff Bagwell	2.50	1.10	.30
☐ 31 Brian McRae	.10	.05	.01
☐ 32 Mark Whiten	.05	.02	.01
☐ 33 Ivan Rodriguez	1.50	.70	.19
☐ 34 Wade Taylor	.05	.02	.01
☐ 35 Darren Lewis	.05	.02	.01
☐ 36 Mo Vaughn	.50	.23	.06
☐ 37 Mike Remlinger	.05	.02	.01
☐ 38 Rick Wilkins	.05	.02	.01
☐ 39 Chuck Knoblauch	.25	.11	.03
☐ 40 Kevin Morton	.05	.02	.01
☐ 41 Carlos Rodriguez	.05	.02	.01
☐ 42 Mark Lewis	.05	.02	.01
☐ 43 Brent Mayne	.05	.02	.01
☐ 44 Chris Haney	.05	.02	.01
☐ 45 Denis Boucher	.05	.02	.01
☐ 46 Mike Gardiner	.05	.02	.01
☐ 47 Jeff Johnson	.05	.02	.01
☐ 48 Dean Palmer	.10	.05	.01
☐ 49 Chuck McElroy	.05	.02	.01
☐ 50 Chris Jones	.05	.02	.01
☐ 51 Scott Kamieniecki	.05	.02	.01
☐ 52 Al Osuna	.05	.02	.01
☐ 53 Rusty Meacham	.05	.02	.01
☐ 54 Chito Martinez	.05	.02	.01
☐ 55 Reggie Jefferson	.10	.05	.01
☐ 56 Checklist 1-56	.05	.02	.01

1991 Donruss Super DK's

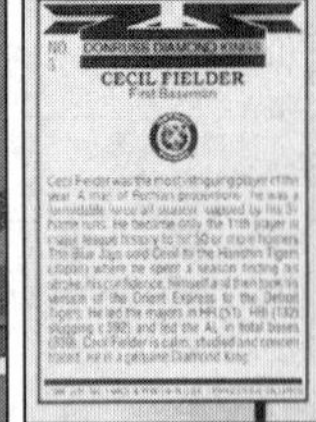

For the seventh consecutive year Donruss issued a card set featuring the players used in the current year's Diamond King subset in a larger size, approximately 5" X 7". The set again featured the art work of famed sports artist Dick Perez and was available through a postpaid mail-in offer detailed on the 1991 Donruss wax packs involving $14.00 and three wax wrappers.

	MINT	NRMT	EXC
COMPLETE SET (26)	15.00	6.75	1.85
COMMON CARD (1-26)	.50	.23	.06
☐ 1 Dave Stieb	.50	.23	.06
☐ 2 Craig Biggio	1.00	.45	.12
☐ 3 Cecil Fielder	.75	.35	.09
☐ 4 Barry Bonds	2.00	.90	.25
☐ 5 Barry Larkin	1.25	.55	.16
☐ 6 Dave Parker	.75	.35	.09
☐ 7 Len Dykstra	.75	.35	.09
☐ 8 Bobby Thigpen	.50	.23	.06
☐ 9 Roger Clemens	2.50	1.10	.30
☐ 10 Ron Gant	.75	.35	.09
☐ 11 Delino DeShields	.50	.23	.06
☐ 12 Roberto Alomar	2.00	.90	.25
☐ 13 Sandy Alomar Jr.	.75	.35	.09
☐ 14 Ryne Sandberg	2.50	1.10	.30
☐ 15 Ramon Martinez	1.00	.45	.12
☐ 16 Edgar Martinez	1.00	.45	.12
☐ 17 Dave Magadan	.50	.23	.06
☐ 18 Matt Williams	1.50	.70	.19
☐ 19 Rafael Palmeiro	1.00	.45	.12
☐ 20 Bob Welch	.50	.23	.06
☐ 21 Dave Righetti	.50	.23	.06
☐ 22 Brian Harper	.50	.23	.06
☐ 23 Gregg Olson	.50	.23	.06
☐ 24 Kurt Stillwell	.50	.23	.06
☐ 25 Pedro Guerrero	.50	.23	.06
☐ 26 Chuck Finley	.75	.35	.09

1992 Donruss Previews

This 12-card preview set was available only to Donruss dealers. The standard-size cards feature the same glossy color player photos on the fronts and player information on the backs as the regular series issue. The statistics only go through the 1990 season. Only the numbering of the cards on the back is different.

	MINT	NRMT	EXC
COMPLETE SET (12)	225.00	100.00	28.00
COMMON CARD (1-12)	5.00	2.20	.60
☐ 1 Wade Boggs	15.00	6.75	1.85
☐ 2 Barry Bonds	15.00	6.75	1.85
☐ 3 Will Clark	15.00	6.75	1.85
☐ 4 Andre Dawson	10.00	4.50	1.25
☐ 5 Dennis Eckersley	8.00	3.60	1.00
☐ 6 Robin Ventura	10.00	4.50	1.25
☐ 7 Ken Griffey Jr.	75.00	34.00	9.50
☐ 8 Kelly Gruber	5.00	2.20	.60
☐ 9 Ryan Klesko	15.00	6.75	1.85
☐ 10 Cal Ripken	60.00	27.00	7.50
☐ 11 Nolan Ryan	60.00	27.00	7.50
☐ 12 Todd Van Poppel	8.00	3.60	1.00

1992 Donruss

The 1992 Donruss set contains 784 standard-size cards issued in two separate series of 396. Cards were issued in first and second series foil wrapped packs in addition to hobby and retail factory sets. One of 21 different puzzle panels featuring Hall of Famer Rod Carew was inserted into each pack. The basic card design features glossy color player photos with white borders. Two-toned blue stripes overlay the top and bottom of the picture. Subsets include Rated Rookies (1-20, 397-421], All-Stars (21-30/422-431) and Highlights (33, 94, 154, 215, 276, 434, 495, 555, 616, 677). The only notable Rookie Card in the set features John Jaha.

	MINT	NRMT	EXC
COMPLETE SET (784)	12.00	5.50	1.50
COMPLETE HOBBY SET (788)	15.00	6.75	1.85
COMPLETE RETAIL SET (788)	25.00	11.00	3.10
COMPLETE SERIES 1 (396)	6.00	2.70	.75
COMPLETE SERIES 2 (388)	6.00	2.70	.75
COMMON CARD (1-784)	.05	.02	.01
☐ 1 Mark Wohlers RR	.15	.07	.02
☐ 2 Wil Cordero RR	.10	.05	.01
☐ 3 Kyle Abbott RR	.05	.02	.01
☐ 4 Dave Nilsson RR	.10	.05	.01
☐ 5 Kenny Lofton RR	1.00	.45	.12
☐ 6 Luis Mercedes RR	.05	.02	.01
☐ 7 Roger Salkeld RR	.05	.02	.01
☐ 8 Eddie Zosky RR	.05	.02	.01
☐ 9 Todd Van Poppel RR	.05	.02	.01
☐ 10 Frank Seminara RR	.05	.02	.01
☐ 11 Andy Ashby RR	.10	.05	.01
☐ 12 Reggie Jefferson RR	.10	.05	.01
☐ 13 Ryan Klesko RR	.50	.23	.06
☐ 14 Carlos Garcia RR	.10	.05	.01
☐ 15 John Ramos RR	.05	.02	.01
☐ 16 Eric Karros RR	.15	.07	.02
☐ 17 Patrick Lennon RR	.05	.02	.01
☐ 18 Eddie Taubensee RR	.05	.02	.01
☐ 19 Roberto Hernandez RR	.10	.05	.01
☐ 20 D.J. Dozier RR	.05	.02	.01
☐ 21 Dave Henderson AS	.05	.02	.01
☐ 22 Cal Ripken AS	.40	.18	.05
☐ 23 Wade Boggs AS	.15	.07	.02
☐ 24 Ken Griffey Jr. AS	.75	.35	.09
☐ 25 Jack Morris AS	.05	.02	.01
☐ 26 Danny Tartabull AS	.05	.02	.01
☐ 27 Cecil Fielder AS	.10	.05	.01
☐ 28 Roberto Alomar AS	.15	.07	.02
☐ 29 Sandy Alomar Jr. AS	.10	.05	.01
☐ 30 Rickey Henderson AS	.15	.07	.02
☐ 31 Ken Hill	.10	.05	.01
☐ 32 John Habyan	.05	.02	.01
☐ 33 Otis Nixon HL	.05	.02	.01
☐ 34 Tim Wallach	.05	.02	.01
☐ 35 Cal Ripken	.75	.35	.09
☐ 36 Gary Carter	.10	.05	.01
☐ 37 Juan Agosto	.05	.02	.01
☐ 38 Doug Dascenzo	.05	.02	.01
☐ 39 Kirk Gibson	.10	.05	.01
☐ 40 Benito Santiago	.05	.02	.01
☐ 41 Otis Nixon	.05	.02	.01
☐ 42 Andy Allanson	.05	.02	.01
☐ 43 Brian Holman	.05	.02	.01
☐ 44 Dick Schofield	.05	.02	.01
☐ 45 Dave Magadan	.05	.02	.01
☐ 46 Rafael Palmeiro	.15	.07	.02
☐ 47 Jody Reed	.05	.02	.01
☐ 48 Ivan Calderon	.05	.02	.01
☐ 49 Greg W. Harris	.05	.02	.01
☐ 50 Chris Sabo	.05	.02	.01
☐ 51 Paul Molitor	.20	.09	.03
☐ 52 Robby Thompson	.05	.02	.01
☐ 53 Dave Smith	.05	.02	.01
☐ 54 Mark Davis	.05	.02	.01
☐ 55 Kevin Brown	.10	.05	.01
☐ 56 Donn Pall	.05	.02	.01
☐ 57 Len Dykstra	.10	.05	.01
☐ 58 Roberto Alomar	.20	.09	.03
☐ 59 Jeff D. Robinson	.05	.02	.01
☐ 60 Willie McGee	.05	.02	.01
☐ 61 Jay Buhner	.15	.07	.02
☐ 62 Mike Pagliarulo	.05	.02	.01
☐ 63 Paul O'Neill	.10	.05	.01
☐ 64 Hubie Brooks	.05	.02	.01
☐ 65 Kelly Gruber	.05	.02	.01
☐ 66 Ken Caminiti	.15	.07	.02
☐ 67 Gary Redus	.05	.02	.01
☐ 68 Harold Baines	.10	.05	.01
☐ 69 Charlie Hough	.05	.02	.01
☐ 70 B.J. Surhoff	.10	.05	.01
☐ 71 Walt Weiss	.05	.02	.01
☐ 72 Shawn Hillegas	.05	.02	.01
☐ 73 Roberto Kelly	.05	.02	.01
☐ 74 Jeff Ballard	.05	.02	.01
☐ 75 Craig Biggio	.10	.05	.01
☐ 76 Pat Combs	.05	.02	.01
☐ 77 Jeff M. Robinson	.05	.02	.01
☐ 78 Tim Belcher	.05	.02	.01
☐ 79 Cris Carpenter	.05	.02	.01
☐ 80 Checklist 1-79	.05	.02	.01
☐ 81 Steve Avery	.10	.05	.01
☐ 82 Chris James	.05	.02	.01
☐ 83 Brian Harper	.05	.02	.01
☐ 84 Charlie Leibrandt	.05	.02	.01
☐ 85 Mickey Tettleton	.05	.02	.01
☐ 86 Pete O'Brien	.05	.02	.01
☐ 87 Danny Darwin	.05	.02	.01
☐ 88 Bob Walk	.05	.02	.01
☐ 89 Jeff Reardon	.10	.05	.01
☐ 90 Bobby Rose	.05	.02	.01
☐ 91 Danny Jackson	.05	.02	.01
☐ 92 John Morris	.05	.02	.01
☐ 93 Bud Black	.05	.02	.01
☐ 94 Tommy Greene HL	.05	.02	.01
☐ 95 Rick Aguilera	.05	.02	.01
☐ 96 Gary Gaetti	.10	.05	.01
☐ 97 David Cone	.10	.05	.01
☐ 98 John Olerud	.10	.05	.01
☐ 99 Joel Skinner	.05	.02	.01
☐ 100 Jay Bell	.10	.05	.01
☐ 101 Bob Milacki	.05	.02	.01
☐ 102 Norm Charlton	.05	.02	.01
☐ 103 Chuck Crim	.05	.02	.01
☐ 104 Terry Steinbach	.10	.05	.01
☐ 105 Juan Samuel	.05	.02	.01
☐ 106 Steve Howe	.05	.02	.01
☐ 107 Rafael Belliard	.05	.02	.01
☐ 108 Joey Cora	.10	.05	.01
☐ 109 Tommy Greene	.05	.02	.01
☐ 110 Gregg Olson	.05	.02	.01
☐ 111 Frank Tanana	.05	.02	.01
☐ 112 Lee Smith	.10	.05	.01
☐ 113 Greg A. Harris	.05	.02	.01
☐ 114 Dwayne Henry	.05	.02	.01
☐ 115 Chili Davis	.10	.05	.01
☐ 116 Kent Mercker	.05	.02	.01
☐ 117 Brian Barnes	.05	.02	.01
☐ 118 Rich DeLucia	.05	.02	.01
☐ 119 Andre Dawson	.10	.05	.01
☐ 120 Carlos Baerga	.10	.05	.01
☐ 121 Mike LaValliere	.05	.02	.01
☐ 122 Jeff Gray	.05	.02	.01
☐ 123 Bruce Hurst	.05	.02	.01
☐ 124 Alvin Davis	.05	.02	.01
☐ 125 John Candelaria	.05	.02	.01
☐ 126 Matt Nokes	.05	.02	.01
☐ 127 George Bell	.05	.02	.01
☐ 128 Bret Saberhagen	.10	.05	.01
☐ 129 Jeff Russell	.05	.02	.01
☐ 130 Jim Abbott	.05	.02	.01
☐ 131 Bill Gullickson	.05	.02	.01
☐ 132 Todd Zeile	.05	.02	.01
☐ 133 Dave Winfield	.15	.07	.02
☐ 134 Wally Whitehurst	.05	.02	.01
☐ 135 Matt Williams	.15	.07	.02
☐ 136 Tom Browning	.05	.02	.01
☐ 137 Marquis Grissom	.10	.05	.01
☐ 138 Erik Hanson	.05	.02	.01
☐ 139 Rob Dibble	.05	.02	.01
☐ 140 Don August	.05	.02	.01
☐ 141 Tom Henke	.05	.02	.01
☐ 142 Dan Pasqua	.05	.02	.01
☐ 143 George Brett	.40	.18	.05
☐ 144 Jerald Clark	.05	.02	.01
☐ 145 Robin Ventura	.10	.05	.01
☐ 146 Dale Murphy	.15	.07	.02
☐ 147 Dennis Eckersley	.10	.05	.01
☐ 148 Eric Yelding	.05	.02	.01
☐ 149 Mario Diaz	.05	.02	.01
☐ 150 Casey Candaele	.05	.02	.01
☐ 151 Steve Olin	.05	.02	.01
☐ 152 Luis Salazar	.05	.02	.01
☐ 153 Kevin Maas	.05	.02	.01
☐ 154 Nolan Ryan HL	.40	.18	.05
☐ 155 Barry Jones	.05	.02	.01
☐ 156 Chris Hoiles	.05	.02	.01
☐ 157 Bobby Ojeda	.05	.02	.01
☐ 158 Pedro Guerrero	.05	.02	.01
☐ 159 Paul Assenmacher	.05	.02	.01
☐ 160 Checklist 80-157	.05	.02	.01
☐ 161 Mike Macfarlane	.05	.02	.01
☐ 162 Craig Lefferts	.05	.02	.01
☐ 163 Brian Hunter	.05	.02	.01
☐ 164 Alan Trammell	.10	.05	.01
☐ 165 Ken Griffey Jr.	1.50	.70	.19
☐ 166 Lance Parrish	.05	.02	.01
☐ 167 Brian Downing	.05	.02	.01
☐ 168 John Barfield	.05	.02	.01
☐ 169 Jack Clark	.10	.05	.01
☐ 170 Chris Nabholz	.05	.02	.01
☐ 171 Tim Teufel	.05	.02	.01
☐ 172 Chris Hammond	.05	.02	.01
☐ 173 Robin Yount	.15	.07	.02
☐ 174 Dave Righetti	.05	.02	.01
☐ 175 Joe Girardi	.05	.02	.01
☐ 176 Mike Boddicker	.05	.02	.01
☐ 177 Dean Palmer	.10	.05	.01
☐ 178 Greg Hibbard	.05	.02	.01
☐ 179 Randy Ready	.05	.02	.01
☐ 180 Devon White	.10	.05	.01
☐ 181 Mark Eichhorn	.05	.02	.01
☐ 182 Mike Felder	.05	.02	.01
☐ 183 Joe Klink	.05	.02	.01
☐ 184 Steve Bedrosian	.05	.02	.01
☐ 185 Barry Larkin	.15	.07	.02
☐ 186 John Franco	.05	.02	.01
☐ 187 Ed Sprague	.10	.05	.01
☐ 188 Mark Portugal	.05	.02	.01
☐ 189 Jose Lind	.05	.02	.01

Card			
☐ 190 Bob Welch	.05	.02	.01
☐ 191 Alex Fernandez	.15	.07	.02
☐ 192 Gary Sheffield	.15	.07	.02
☐ 193 Rickey Henderson	.15	.07	.02
☐ 194 Rod Nichols	.05	.02	.01
☐ 195 Scott Kamieniecki	.05	.02	.01
☐ 196 Mike Flanagan	.05	.02	.01
☐ 197 Steve Finley	.10	.05	.01
☐ 198 Darren Daulton	.10	.05	.01
☐ 199 Leo Gomez	.05	.02	.01
☐ 200 Mike Morgan	.05	.02	.01
☐ 201 Bob Tewksbury	.05	.02	.01
☐ 202 Sid Bream	.05	.02	.01
☐ 203 Sandy Alomar Jr.	.10	.05	.01
☐ 204 Greg Gagne	.05	.02	.01
☐ 205 Juan Berenguer	.05	.02	.01
☐ 206 Cecil Fielder	.10	.05	.01
☐ 207 Randy Johnson	.15	.07	.02
☐ 208 Tony Pena	.05	.02	.01
☐ 209 Doug Drabek	.05	.02	.01
☐ 210 Wade Boggs	.15	.07	.02
☐ 211 Bryan Harvey	.05	.02	.01
☐ 212 Jose Vizcaino	.05	.02	.01
☐ 213 Alonzo Powell	.05	.02	.01
☐ 214 Will Clark	.15	.07	.02
☐ 215 Rickey Henderson HL	.15	.07	.02
☐ 216 Jack Morris	.10	.05	.01
☐ 217 Junior Felix	.05	.02	.01
☐ 218 Vince Coleman	.05	.02	.01
☐ 219 Jimmy Key	.10	.05	.01
☐ 220 Alex Cole	.05	.02	.01
☐ 221 Bill Landrum	.05	.02	.01
☐ 222 Randy Milligan	.05	.02	.01
☐ 223 Jose Rijo	.05	.02	.01
☐ 224 Greg Vaughn	.10	.05	.01
☐ 225 Dave Stewart	.10	.05	.01
☐ 226 Lenny Harris	.05	.02	.01
☐ 227 Scott Sanderson	.05	.02	.01
☐ 228 Jeff Blauser	.05	.02	.01
☐ 229 Ozzie Guillen	.05	.02	.01
☐ 230 John Kruk	.10	.05	.01
☐ 231 Bob Melvin	.05	.02	.01
☐ 232 Milt Cuyler	.05	.02	.01
☐ 233 Felix Jose	.05	.02	.01
☐ 234 Ellis Burks	.10	.05	.01
☐ 235 Pete Harnisch	.05	.02	.01
☐ 236 Kevin Tapani	.05	.02	.01
☐ 237 Terry Pendleton	.10	.05	.01
☐ 238 Mark Gardner	.05	.02	.01
☐ 239 Harold Reynolds	.05	.02	.01
☐ 240 Checklist 158-237	.05	.02	.01
☐ 241 Mike Harkey	.05	.02	.01
☐ 242 Felix Fermin	.05	.02	.01
☐ 243 Barry Bonds	.25	.11	.03
☐ 244 Roger Clemens	.20	.09	.03
☐ 245 Dennis Rasmussen	.05	.02	.01
☐ 246 Jose DeLeon	.05	.02	.01
☐ 247 Orel Hershiser	.10	.05	.01
☐ 248 Mel Hall	.05	.02	.01
☐ 249 Rick Wilkins	.05	.02	.01
☐ 250 Tom Gordon	.05	.02	.01
☐ 251 Kevin Reimer	.05	.02	.01
☐ 252 Luis Polonia	.05	.02	.01
☐ 253 Mike Henneman	.05	.02	.01
☐ 254 Tom Pagnozzi	.05	.02	.01
☐ 255 Chuck Finley	.05	.02	.01
☐ 256 Mackey Sasser	.05	.02	.01
☐ 257 John Burkett	.10	.05	.01
☐ 258 Hal Morris	.05	.02	.01
☐ 259 Larry Walker	.15	.07	.02
☐ 260 Billy Swift	.05	.02	.01
☐ 261 Joe Oliver	.05	.02	.01
☐ 262 Julio Machado	.05	.02	.01
☐ 263 Todd Stottlemyre	.10	.05	.01
☐ 264 Matt Merullo	.05	.02	.01
☐ 265 Brent Mayne	.05	.02	.01
☐ 266 Thomas Howard	.05	.02	.01
☐ 267 Lance Johnson	.10	.05	.01
☐ 268 Terry Mulholland	.05	.02	.01
☐ 269 Rick Honeycutt	.05	.02	.01
☐ 270 Luis Gonzalez	.10	.05	.01
☐ 271 Jose Guzman	.05	.02	.01
☐ 272 Jimmy Jones	.05	.02	.01
☐ 273 Mark Lewis	.05	.02	.01
☐ 274 Rene Gonzales	.05	.02	.01
☐ 275 Jeff Johnson	.05	.02	.01
☐ 276 Dennis Martinez HL	.05	.02	.01
☐ 277 Delino DeShields	.05	.02	.01
☐ 278 Sam Horn	.05	.02	.01
☐ 279 Kevin Gross	.05	.02	.01
☐ 280 Jose Oquendo	.05	.02	.01
☐ 281 Mark Grace	.15	.07	.02
☐ 282 Mark Gubicza	.05	.02	.01
☐ 283 Fred McGriff	.15	.07	.02
☐ 284 Ron Gant	.10	.05	.01
☐ 285 Lou Whitaker	.10	.05	.01
☐ 286 Edgar Martinez	.10	.05	.01
☐ 287 Ron Tingley	.05	.02	.01
☐ 288 Kevin McReynolds	.05	.02	.01
☐ 289 Ivan Rodriguez	.40	.18	.05
☐ 290 Mike Gardiner	.05	.02	.01
☐ 291 Chris Haney	.05	.02	.01
☐ 292 Darrin Jackson	.05	.02	.01
☐ 293 Bill Doran	.05	.02	.01
☐ 294 Ted Higuera	.05	.02	.01
☐ 295 Jeff Brantley	.10	.05	.01
☐ 296 Les Lancaster	.05	.02	.01
☐ 297 Jim Eisenreich	.05	.02	.01
☐ 298 Ruben Sierra	.10	.05	.01
☐ 299 Scott Radinsky	.05	.02	.01
☐ 300 Jose DeJesus	.05	.02	.01
☐ 301 Mike Timlin	.05	.02	.01
☐ 302 Luis Sojo	.05	.02	.01
☐ 303 Kelly Downs	.05	.02	.01
☐ 304 Scott Bankhead	.05	.02	.01
☐ 305 Pedro Munoz	.05	.02	.01
☐ 306 Scott Scudder	.05	.02	.01
☐ 307 Kevin Elster	.05	.02	.01
☐ 308 Duane Ward	.05	.02	.01
☐ 309 Darryl Kile	.05	.02	.01
☐ 310 Orlando Merced	.05	.02	.01
☐ 311 Dave Henderson	.05	.02	.01
☐ 312 Tim Raines	.15	.07	.02
☐ 313 Mark Lee	.05	.02	.01
☐ 314 Mike Gallego	.05	.02	.01
☐ 315 Charles Nagy	.10	.05	.01
☐ 316 Jesse Barfield	.05	.02	.01
☐ 317 Todd Frohwirth	.05	.02	.01
☐ 318 Al Osuna	.05	.02	.01
☐ 319 Darrin Fletcher	.05	.02	.01
☐ 320 Checklist 238-316	.05	.02	.01
☐ 321 David Segui	.05	.02	.01
☐ 322 Stan Javier	.05	.02	.01
☐ 323 Bryn Smith	.05	.02	.01
☐ 324 Jeff Treadway	.05	.02	.01
☐ 325 Mark Whiten	.10	.05	.01
☐ 326 Kent Hrbek	.10	.05	.01
☐ 327 Dave Justice	.15	.07	.02
☐ 328 Tony Phillips	.10	.05	.01
☐ 329 Rob Murphy	.05	.02	.01
☐ 330 Kevin Morton	.05	.02	.01
☐ 331 John Smiley	.05	.02	.01
☐ 332 Luis Rivera	.05	.02	.01
☐ 333 Wally Joyner	.10	.05	.01
☐ 334 Heathcliff Slocumb	.05	.02	.01
☐ 335 Rick Cerone	.05	.02	.01
☐ 336 Mike Remlinger	.05	.02	.01
☐ 337 Mike Moore	.05	.02	.01
☐ 338 Lloyd McClendon	.05	.02	.01
☐ 339 Al Newman	.05	.02	.01
☐ 340 Kirk McCaskill	.05	.02	.01
☐ 341 Howard Johnson	.05	.02	.01
☐ 342 Greg Myers	.05	.02	.01
☐ 343 Kal Daniels	.05	.02	.01
☐ 344 Bernie Williams	.25	.11	.03
☐ 345 Shane Mack	.05	.02	.01
☐ 346 Gary Thurman	.05	.02	.01
☐ 347 Dante Bichette	.15	.07	.02
☐ 348 Mark McGwire	.30	.14	.04
☐ 349 Travis Fryman	.15	.07	.02
☐ 350 Ray Lankford	.15	.07	.02
☐ 351 Mike Jeffcoat	.05	.02	.01
☐ 352 Jack McDowell	.10	.05	.01
☐ 353 Mitch Williams	.05	.02	.01
☐ 354 Mike Devereaux	.05	.02	.01
☐ 355 Andres Galarraga	.15	.07	.02
☐ 356 Henry Cotto	.05	.02	.01
☐ 357 Scott Bailes	.05	.02	.01
☐ 358 Jeff Bagwell	.60	.25	.07
☐ 359 Scott Leius	.05	.02	.01
☐ 360 Zane Smith	.05	.02	.01
☐ 361 Bill Pecota	.05	.02	.01
☐ 362 Tony Fernandez	.05	.02	.01
☐ 363 Glenn Braggs	.05	.02	.01
☐ 364 Bill Spiers	.05	.02	.01
☐ 365 Vicente Palacios	.05	.02	.01
☐ 366 Tim Burke	.05	.02	.01
☐ 367 Randy Tomlin	.05	.02	.01
☐ 368 Kenny Rogers	.05	.02	.01
☐ 369 Brett Butler	.10	.05	.01
☐ 370 Pat Kelly	.05	.02	.01
☐ 371 Bip Roberts	.05	.02	.01
☐ 372 Gregg Jefferies	.10	.05	.01
☐ 373 Kevin Bass	.05	.02	.01
☐ 374 Ron Karkovice	.05	.02	.01
☐ 375 Paul Gibson	.05	.02	.01
☐ 376 Bernard Gilkey	.10	.05	.01
☐ 377 Dave Gallagher	.05	.02	.01
☐ 378 Bill Wegman	.05	.02	.01
☐ 379 Pat Borders	.05	.02	.01
☐ 380 Ed Whitson	.05	.02	.01
☐ 381 Gilberto Reyes	.05	.02	.01
☐ 382 Russ Swan	.05	.02	.01
☐ 383 Andy Van Slyke	.10	.05	.01
☐ 384 Wes Chamberlain	.05	.02	.01
☐ 385 Steve Chitren	.05	.02	.01
☐ 386 Greg Olson	.05	.02	.01
☐ 387 Brian McRae	.10	.05	.01
☐ 388 Rich Rodriguez	.05	.02	.01
☐ 389 Steve Decker	.05	.02	.01
☐ 390 Chuck Knoblauch	.15	.07	.02
☐ 391 Bobby Witt	.05	.02	.01
☐ 392 Eddie Murray	.25	.11	.03
☐ 393 Juan Gonzalez	.60	.25	.07
☐ 394 Scott Ruskin	.05	.02	.01
☐ 395 Jay Howell	.05	.02	.01
☐ 396 Checklist 317-396	.05	.02	.01
☐ 397 Royce Clayton RR	.10	.05	.01
☐ 398 John Jaha RR	.20	.09	.03
☐ 399 Dan Wilson RR	.10	.05	.01
☐ 400 Archie Corbin RR	.05	.02	.01
☐ 401 Barry Manuel RR	.05	.02	.01
☐ 402 Kim Batiste RR	.05	.02	.01
☐ 403 Pat Mahomes RR	.05	.02	.01
☐ 404 Dave Fleming RR	.05	.02	.01
☐ 405 Jeff Juden RR	.05	.02	.01
☐ 406 Jim Thome RR	.75	.35	.09
☐ 407 Sam Militello RR	.05	.02	.01
☐ 408 Jeff Nelson RR	.05	.02	.01
☐ 409 Anthony Young RR	.05	.02	.01
☐ 410 Tino Martinez RR	.10	.05	.01
☐ 411 Jeff Mutis RR	.05	.02	.01
☐ 412 Rey Sanchez RR	.05	.02	.01
☐ 413 Chris Gardner RR	.05	.02	.01
☐ 414 John Vander Wal RR	.05	.02	.01
☐ 415 Reggie Sanders RR	.15	.07	.02
☐ 416 Brian Williams RR	.05	.02	.01
☐ 417 Mo Sanford RR	.05	.02	.01
☐ 418 David Weathers RR	.10	.05	.01
☐ 419 Hector Fajardo RR	.05	.02	.01
☐ 420 Steve Foster RR	.05	.02	.01
☐ 421 Lance Dickson RR	.05	.02	.01
☐ 422 Andre Dawson AS	.10	.05	.01
☐ 423 Ozzie Smith AS	.15	.07	.02
☐ 424 Chris Sabo AS	.05	.02	.01
☐ 425 Tony Gwynn AS	.20	.09	.03
☐ 426 Tom Glavine AS	.15	.07	.02
☐ 427 Bobby Bonilla AS	.10	.05	.01
☐ 428 Will Clark AS	.15	.07	.02
☐ 429 Ryne Sandberg AS	.15	.07	.02
☐ 430 Benito Santiago AS	.05	.02	.01
☐ 431 Ivan Calderon AS	.05	.02	.01
☐ 432 Ozzie Smith	.25	.11	.03
☐ 433 Tim Leary	.05	.02	.01
☐ 434 Bret Saberhagen HL	.05	.02	.01
☐ 435 Mel Rojas	.10	.05	.01
☐ 436 Ben McDonald	.05	.02	.01
☐ 437 Tim Crews	.05	.02	.01
☐ 438 Rex Hudler	.05	.02	.01
☐ 439 Chico Walker	.05	.02	.01
☐ 440 Kurt Stillwell	.05	.02	.01
☐ 441 Tony Gwynn	.40	.18	.05
☐ 442 John Smoltz	.15	.07	.02
☐ 443 Lloyd Moseby	.05	.02	.01
☐ 444 Mike Schooler	.05	.02	.01
☐ 445 Joe Grahe	.05	.02	.01
☐ 446 Dwight Gooden	.10	.05	.01
☐ 447 Oil Can Boyd	.05	.02	.01
☐ 448 John Marzano	.05	.02	.01
☐ 449 Bret Barberie	.05	.02	.01
☐ 450 Mike Maddux	.05	.02	.01
☐ 451 Jeff Reed	.05	.02	.01
☐ 452 Dale Sveum	.05	.02	.01
☐ 453 Jose Uribe	.05	.02	.01
☐ 454 Bob Scanlan	.05	.02	.01
☐ 455 Kevin Appier	.10	.05	.01
☐ 456 Jeff Huson	.05	.02	.01
☐ 457 Ken Patterson	.05	.02	.01
☐ 458 Ricky Jordan	.05	.02	.01
☐ 459 Tom Candiotti	.05	.02	.01
☐ 460 Lee Stevens	.05	.02	.01
☐ 461 Rod Beck	.25	.11	.03
☐ 462 Dave Valle	.05	.02	.01
☐ 463 Scott Erickson	.10	.05	.01
☐ 464 Chris Jones	.05	.02	.01
☐ 465 Mark Carreon	.05	.02	.01
☐ 466 Rob Ducey	.05	.02	.01
☐ 467 Jim Corsi	.05	.02	.01
☐ 468 Jeff King	.10	.05	.01
☐ 469 Curt Young	.05	.02	.01
☐ 470 Bo Jackson	.10	.05	.01
☐ 471 Chris Bosio	.05	.02	.01
☐ 472 Jamie Quirk	.05	.02	.01
☐ 473 Jesse Orosco	.05	.02	.01
☐ 474 Alvaro Espinoza	.05	.02	.01
☐ 475 Joe Orsulak	.05	.02	.01
☐ 476 Checklist 397-477	.05	.02	.01
☐ 477 Gerald Young	.05	.02	.01
☐ 478 Wally Backman	.05	.02	.01
☐ 479 Juan Bell	.05	.02	.01
☐ 480 Mike Scioscia	.05	.02	.01
☐ 481 Omar Olivares	.05	.02	.01
☐ 482 Francisco Cabrera	.05	.02	.01
☐ 483 Greg Swindell UER (Shown on Indians, but listed on Reds)	.05	.02	.01
☐ 484 Terry Leach	.05	.02	.01
☐ 485 Tommy Gregg	.05	.02	.01
☐ 486 Scott Aldred	.05	.02	.01
☐ 487 Greg Briley	.05	.02	.01
☐ 488 Phil Plantier	.10	.05	.01
☐ 489 Curtis Wilkerson	.05	.02	.01
☐ 490 Tom Brunansky	.05	.02	.01
☐ 491 Mike Fetters	.05	.02	.01
☐ 492 Frank Castillo	.10	.05	.01
☐ 493 Joe Boever	.05	.02	.01
☐ 494 Kirt Manwaring	.05	.02	.01
☐ 495 Wilson Alvarez HL	.10	.05	.01
☐ 496 Gene Larkin	.05	.02	.01
☐ 497 Gary DiSarcina	.05	.02	.01
☐ 498 Frank Viola	.05	.02	.01
☐ 499 Manuel Lee	.05	.02	.01
☐ 500 Albert Belle	.50	.23	.06
☐ 501 Stan Belinda	.05	.02	.01
☐ 502 Dwight Evans	.10	.05	.01
☐ 503 Eric Davis	.10	.05	.01
☐ 504 Darren Holmes	.05	.02	.01
☐ 505 Mike Bordick	.10	.05	.01
☐ 506 Dave Hansen	.05	.02	.01
☐ 507 Lee Guetterman	.05	.02	.01
☐ 508 Keith Mitchell	.05	.02	.01
☐ 509 Melido Perez	.05	.02	.01
☐ 510 Dickie Thon	.05	.02	.01
☐ 511 Mark Williamson	.05	.02	.01
☐ 512 Mark Salas	.05	.02	.01
☐ 513 Milt Thompson	.05	.02	.01
☐ 514 Mo Vaughn	.40	.18	.05
☐ 515 Jim Deshaies	.05	.02	.01
☐ 516 Rich Garces	.05	.02	.01
☐ 517 Lonnie Smith	.05	.02	.01
☐ 518 Spike Owen	.05	.02	.01
☐ 519 Tracy Jones	.05	.02	.01
☐ 520 Greg Maddux	.75	.35	.09
☐ 521 Carlos Martinez	.05	.02	.01
☐ 522 Neal Heaton	.05	.02	.01
☐ 523 Mike Greenwell	.05	.02	.01
☐ 524 Andy Benes	.10	.05	.01
☐ 525 Jeff Schaefer UER (Photo actually Tino Martinez)	.05	.02	.01
☐ 526 Mike Sharperson	.05	.02	.01
☐ 527 Wade Taylor	.05	.02	.01
☐ 528 Jerome Walton	.05	.02	.01
☐ 529 Storm Davis	.05	.02	.01
☐ 530 Jose Hernandez	.05	.02	.01
☐ 531 Mark Langston	.10	.05	.01
☐ 532 Rob Deer	.05	.02	.01
☐ 533 Geronimo Pena	.05	.02	.01
☐ 534 Juan Guzman	.10	.05	.01
☐ 535 Pete Schourek	.10	.05	.01
☐ 536 Todd Benzinger	.05	.02	.01
☐ 537 Billy Hatcher	.05	.02	.01
☐ 538 Tom Foley	.05	.02	.01
☐ 539 Dave Cochrane	.05	.02	.01
☐ 540 Mariano Duncan	.05	.02	.01
☐ 541 Edwin Nunez	.05	.02	.01
☐ 542 Rance Mulliniks	.05	.02	.01
☐ 543 Carlton Fisk	.15	.07	.02
☐ 544 Luis Aquino	.05	.02	.01
☐ 545 Ricky Bones	.05	.02	.01
☐ 546 Craig Grebeck	.05	.02	.01
☐ 547 Charlie Hayes	.05	.02	.01
☐ 548 Jose Canseco	.15	.07	.02
☐ 549 Andujar Cedeno	.05	.02	.01
☐ 550 Geno Petralli	.05	.02	.01
☐ 551 Javier Ortiz	.05	.02	.01
☐ 552 Rudy Seanez	.05	.02	.01
☐ 553 Rich Gedman	.05	.02	.01
☐ 554 Eric Plunk	.05	.02	.01
☐ 555 Nolan Ryan HL (With Rich Gossage)	.25	.11	.03
☐ 556 Checklist 478-555	.05	.02	.01
☐ 557 Greg Colbrunn	.05	.02	.01
☐ 558 Chito Martinez	.05	.02	.01
☐ 559 Darryl Strawberry	.10	.05	.01
☐ 560 Luis Alicea	.05	.02	.01
☐ 561 Dwight Smith	.05	.02	.01
☐ 562 Terry Shumpert	.05	.02	.01
☐ 563 Jim Vatcher	.05	.02	.01
☐ 564 Deion Sanders	.15	.07	.02
☐ 565 Walt Terrell	.05	.02	.01
☐ 566 Dave Burba	.05	.02	.01
☐ 567 Dave Howard	.05	.02	.01
☐ 568 Todd Hundley	.10	.05	.01
☐ 569 Jack Daugherty	.05	.02	.01
☐ 570 Scott Cooper	.05	.02	.01
☐ 571 Bill Sampen	.05	.02	.01
☐ 572 Jose Melendez	.05	.02	.01
☐ 573 Freddie Benavides	.05	.02	.01
☐ 574 Jim Gantner	.05	.02	.01
☐ 575 Trevor Wilson	.05	.02	.01
☐ 576 Ryne Sandberg	.25	.11	.03
☐ 577 Kevin Seitzer	.05	.02	.01
☐ 578 Gerald Alexander	.05	.02	.01
☐ 579 Mike Huff	.05	.02	.01
☐ 580 Von Hayes	.05	.02	.01
☐ 581 Derek Bell	.15	.07	.02
☐ 582 Mike Stanley	.05	.02	.01
☐ 583 Kevin Mitchell	.10	.05	.01
☐ 584 Mike Jackson	.05	.02	.01
☐ 585 Dan Gladden	.05	.02	.01
☐ 586 Ted Power UER (Wrong year given for signing with Reds)	.05	.02	.01
☐ 587 Jeff Innis	.05	.02	.01
☐ 588 Bob MacDonald	.05	.02	.01
☐ 589 Jose Tolentino	.05	.02	.01
☐ 590 Bob Patterson	.05	.02	.01
☐ 591 Scott Brosius	.05	.02	.01
☐ 592 Frank Thomas	1.50	.70	.19
☐ 593 Darryl Hamilton	.05	.02	.01
☐ 594 Kirk Dressendorfer	.05	.02	.01
☐ 595 Jeff Shaw	.05	.02	.01
☐ 596 Don Mattingly	.50	.23	.06
☐ 597 Glenn Davis	.05	.02	.01
☐ 598 Andy Mota	.05	.02	.01
☐ 599 Jason Grimsley	.05	.02	.01
☐ 600 Jimmy Poole	.05	.02	.01
☐ 601 Jim Gott	.05	.02	.01
☐ 602 Stan Royer	.05	.02	.01

□ 603 Marvin Freeman	.05	.02	.01
□ 604 Denis Boucher	.05	.02	.01
□ 605 Denny Neagle	.15	.07	.02
□ 606 Mark Lemke	.05	.02	.01
□ 607 Jerry Don Gleaton	.05	.02	.01
□ 608 Brent Knackert	.05	.02	.01
□ 609 Carlos Quintana	.05	.02	.01
□ 610 Bobby Bonilla	.10	.05	.01
□ 611 Joe Hesketh	.05	.02	.01
□ 612 Daryl Boston	.05	.02	.01
□ 613 Shawon Dunston	.05	.02	.01
□ 614 Danny Cox	.05	.02	.01
□ 615 Darren Lewis	.05	.02	.01
□ 616 Braves No-Hitter UER	.10	.05	.01
Kent Mercker			
(Misspelled Merker			
on card front)			
Alejandro Pena			
Mark Wohlers			
□ 617 Kirby Puckett	.40	.18	.05
□ 618 Franklin Stubbs	.05	.02	.01
□ 619 Chris Donnels	.05	.02	.01
□ 620 David Wells UER	.05	.02	.01
(Career Highlights			
in black not red)			
□ 621 Mike Aldrete	.05	.02	.01
□ 622 Bob Kipper	.05	.02	.01
□ 623 Anthony Telford	.05	.02	.01
□ 624 Randy Myers	.10	.05	.01
□ 625 Willie Randolph	.10	.05	.01
□ 626 Joe Slusarski	.05	.02	.01
□ 627 John Wetteland	.10	.05	.01
□ 628 Greg Cadaret	.05	.02	.01
□ 629 Tom Glavine	.15	.07	.02
□ 630 Wilson Alvarez	.15	.07	.02
□ 631 Wally Ritchie	.05	.02	.01
□ 632 Mike Mussina	.30	.14	.04
□ 633 Mark Leiter	.05	.02	.01
□ 634 Gerald Perry	.05	.02	.01
□ 635 Matt Young	.05	.02	.01
□ 636 Checklist 556-635	.05	.02	.01
□ 637 Scott Hemond	.05	.02	.01
□ 638 David West	.05	.02	.01
□ 639 Jim Clancy	.05	.02	.01
□ 640 Doug Piatt UER	.05	.02	.01
(Not born in 1955 as			
on card; incorrect info			
on How Acquired)			
□ 641 Omar Vizquel	.10	.05	.01
□ 642 Rick Sutcliffe	.05	.02	.01
□ 643 Glenallen Hill	.05	.02	.01
□ 644 Gary Varsho	.05	.02	.01
□ 645 Tony Fossas	.05	.02	.01
□ 646 Jack Howell	.05	.02	.01
□ 647 Jim Campanis	.05	.02	.01
□ 648 Chris Gwynn	.05	.02	.01
□ 649 Jim Leyritz	.05	.02	.01
□ 650 Chuck McElroy	.05	.02	.01
□ 651 Sean Berry	.10	.05	.01
□ 652 Donald Harris	.05	.02	.01
□ 653 Don Slaught	.05	.02	.01
□ 654 Rusty Meacham	.05	.02	.01
□ 655 Scott Terry	.05	.02	.01
□ 656 Ramon Martinez	.10	.05	.01
□ 657 Keith Miller	.05	.02	.01
□ 658 Ramon Garcia	.05	.02	.01
□ 659 Milt Hill	.05	.02	.01
□ 660 Steve Frey	.05	.02	.01
□ 661 Bob McClure	.05	.02	.01
□ 662 Ced Landrum	.05	.02	.01
□ 663 Doug Henry	.05	.02	.01
□ 664 Candy Maldonado	.05	.02	.01
□ 665 Carl Willis	.05	.02	.01
□ 666 Jeff Montgomery	.10	.05	.01
□ 667 Craig Shipley	.05	.02	.01
□ 668 Warren Newson	.05	.02	.01
□ 669 Mickey Morandini	.05	.02	.01
□ 670 Brook Jacoby	.05	.02	.01
□ 671 Ryan Bowen	.05	.02	.01
□ 672 Bill Krueger	.05	.02	.01
□ 673 Rob Mallicoat	.05	.02	.01
□ 674 Doug Jones	.05	.02	.01
□ 675 Scott Livingstone	.05	.02	.01
□ 676 Danny Tartabull	.05	.02	.01
□ 677 Joe Carter HL	.15	.07	.02
□ 678 Cecil Espy	.05	.02	.01
□ 679 Randy Velarde	.05	.02	.01
□ 680 Bruce Ruffin	.05	.02	.01
□ 681 Ted Wood	.05	.02	.01
□ 682 Dan Plesac	.05	.02	.01
□ 683 Eric Bullock	.05	.02	.01
□ 684 Junior Ortiz	.05	.02	.01
□ 685 Dave Hollins	.05	.02	.01
□ 686 Dennis Martinez	.10	.05	.01
□ 687 Larry Andersen	.05	.02	.01
□ 688 Doug Simons	.05	.02	.01
□ 689 Tim Spehr	.05	.02	.01
□ 690 Calvin Jones	.05	.02	.01
□ 691 Mark Guthrie	.05	.02	.01
□ 692 Alfredo Griffin	.05	.02	.01
□ 693 Joe Carter	.10	.05	.01
□ 694 Terry Mathews	.05	.02	.01
□ 695 Pascual Perez	.05	.02	.01
□ 696 Gene Nelson	.05	.02	.01
□ 697 Gerald Williams	.05	.02	.01
□ 698 Chris Cron	.05	.02	.01
□ 699 Steve Buechele	.05	.02	.01
□ 700 Paul McClellan	.05	.02	.01
□ 701 Jim Lindeman	.05	.02	.01
□ 702 Francisco Oliveras	.05	.02	.01
□ 703 Rob Maurer	.05	.02	.01
□ 704 Pat Hentgen	.15	.07	.02
□ 705 Jaime Navarro	.05	.02	.01
□ 706 Mike Magnante	.05	.02	.01
□ 707 Nolan Ryan	.75	.35	.09
□ 708 Bobby Thigpen	.05	.02	.01
□ 709 John Cerutti	.05	.02	.01
□ 710 Steve Wilson	.05	.02	.01
□ 711 Hensley Meulens	.05	.02	.01
□ 712 Rheal Cormier	.05	.02	.01
□ 713 Scott Bradley	.05	.02	.01
□ 714 Mitch Webster	.05	.02	.01
□ 715 Roger Mason	.05	.02	.01
□ 716 Checklist 636-716	.05	.02	.01
□ 717 Jeff Fassero	.10	.05	.01
□ 718 Cal Eldred	.05	.02	.01
□ 719 Sid Fernandez	.05	.02	.01
□ 720 Bob Zupcic	.05	.02	.01
□ 721 Jose Offerman	.05	.02	.01
□ 722 Cliff Brantley	.05	.02	.01
□ 723 Ron Darling	.05	.02	.01
□ 724 Dave Stieb	.05	.02	.01
□ 725 Hector Villanueva	.05	.02	.01
□ 726 Mike Hartley	.05	.02	.01
□ 727 Arthur Rhodes	.05	.02	.01
□ 728 Randy Bush	.05	.02	.01
□ 729 Steve Sax	.05	.02	.01
□ 730 Dave Otto	.05	.02	.01
□ 731 John Wehner	.05	.02	.01
□ 732 Dave Martinez	.05	.02	.01
□ 733 Ruben Amaro	.05	.02	.01
□ 734 Billy Ripken	.05	.02	.01
□ 735 Steve Farr	.05	.02	.01
□ 736 Shawn Abner	.05	.02	.01
□ 737 Gil Heredia	.05	.02	.01
□ 738 Ron Jones	.05	.02	.01
□ 739 Tony Castillo	.05	.02	.01
□ 740 Sammy Sosa	.25	.11	.03
□ 741 Julio Franco	.10	.05	.01
□ 742 Tim Naehring	.10	.05	.01
□ 743 Steve Wapnick	.05	.02	.01
□ 744 Craig Wilson	.05	.02	.01
□ 745 Darrin Chapin	.05	.02	.01
□ 746 Chris George	.05	.02	.01
□ 747 Mike Simms	.05	.02	.01
□ 748 Rosario Rodriguez	.05	.02	.01
□ 749 Skeeter Barnes	.05	.02	.01
□ 750 Roger McDowell	.05	.02	.01
□ 751 Dann Howitt	.05	.02	.01
□ 752 Paul Sorrento	.05	.02	.01
□ 753 Braulio Castillo	.05	.02	.01
□ 754 Yorkis Perez	.05	.02	.01
□ 755 Willie Fraser	.05	.02	.01
□ 756 Jeremy Hernandez	.05	.02	.01
□ 757 Curt Schilling	.05	.02	.01
□ 758 Steve Lyons	.05	.02	.01
□ 759 Dave Anderson	.05	.02	.01
□ 760 Willie Banks	.05	.02	.01
□ 761 Mark Leonard	.05	.02	.01
□ 762 Jack Armstrong	.05	.02	.01
(Listed on Indians,			
but shown on Reds)			
□ 763 Scott Servais	.05	.02	.01
□ 764 Ray Stephens	.05	.02	.01
□ 765 Junior Noboa	.05	.02	.01
□ 766 Jim Olander	.05	.02	.01
□ 767 Joe Magrane	.05	.02	.01
□ 768 Lance Blankenship	.05	.02	.01
□ 769 Mike Humphreys	.05	.02	.01
□ 770 Jarvis Brown	.05	.02	.01
□ 771 Damon Berryhill	.05	.02	.01
□ 772 Alejandro Pena	.05	.02	.01
□ 773 Jose Mesa	.10	.05	.01
□ 774 Gary Cooper	.05	.02	.01
□ 775 Carney Lansford	.10	.05	.01
□ 776 Mike Bielecki	.05	.02	.01
(Shown on Cubs,			
but listed on Braves)			
□ 777 Charlie O'Brien	.05	.02	.01
□ 778 Carlos Hernandez	.05	.02	.01
□ 779 Howard Farmer	.05	.02	.01
□ 780 Mike Stanton	.05	.02	.01
□ 781 Reggie Harris	.05	.02	.01
□ 782 Xavier Hernandez	.05	.02	.01
□ 783 Bryan Hickerson	.05	.02	.01
□ 784 Checklist 717-784	.05	.02	.01
and BC1-BC8			

1992 Donruss Bonus Cards

The 1992 Donruss Bonus Cards set contains eight standard-size. The cards are numbered on the back and checklisted below accordingly. The cards were randomly inserted in foil packs of 1992 Donruss baseball cards.

	MINT	NRMT	EXC
COMPLETE SET (8)	2.00	.90	.25
COMMON CARD (BC1-BC8)	.10	.05	.01
□ BC1 Cal Ripken MVP	.75	.35	.09
□ BC2 Terry Pendleton MVP	.10	.05	.01

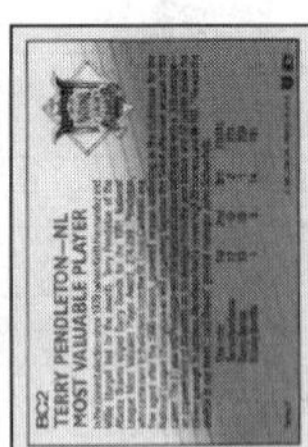

□ BC3 Roger Clemens CY	.25	.11	.03
□ BC4 Tom Glavine CY	.15	.07	.02
□ BC5 Chuck Knoblauch ROY	.15	.07	.02
□ BC6 Jeff Bagwell ROY	.60	.25	.07
□ BC7 Colorado Rockies	.50	.23	.06
□ BC8 Florida Marlins	.50	.23	.06

1992 Donruss Diamond Kings

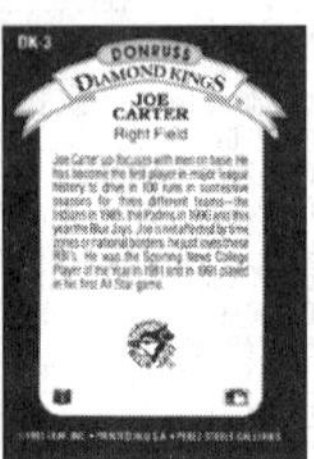

These standard-size cards were randomly inserted in 1992 Donruss I foil packs (cards 1-13 and the checklist only) and in 1992 Donruss II foil packs (cards 14-26). The fronts feature player portraits by noted sports artist Dick Perez. The words "Donruss Diamond Kings" are superimposed at the card top in a gold-trimmed blue and black banner, with the player's name in a similarly designed black stripe at the card bottom. A very limited amount of 5" by 7" cards were produced. These issues were never formally released but these cards were intended to be premiums in retail products. We are not valuing them currently since trading in these cards is very thin.

	MINT	NRMT	EXC
COMPLETE SET (27)	20.00	9.00	2.50
COMPLETE SERIES 1 (14)	16.00	7.25	2.00
COMPLETE SERIES 2 (13)	4.00	1.80	.50
COMMON CARD (DK1-DK27)	.50	.23	.06
□ DK1 Paul Molitor	1.50	.70	.19
□ DK2 Will Clark	1.00	.45	.12
□ DK3 Joe Carter	.75	.35	.09
□ DK4 Julio Franco	.75	.35	.09
□ DK5 Cal Ripken	8.00	3.60	1.00
□ DK6 Dave Justice	.75	.35	.09
□ DK7 George Bell	.75	.35	.09
□ DK8 Frank Thomas	8.00	3.60	1.00
□ DK9 Wade Boggs	1.00	.45	.12
□ DK10 Scott Sanderson	.50	.23	.06
□ DK11 Jeff Bagwell	5.00	2.20	.60
□ DK12 John Kruk	.75	.35	.09
□ DK13 Felix Jose	.50	.23	.06
□ DK14 Harold Baines	.75	.35	.09
□ DK15 Dwight Gooden	.75	.35	.09
□ DK16 Brian McRae	.75	.35	.09
□ DK17 Jay Bell	.75	.35	.09
□ DK18 Brett Butler	1.00	.45	.12
□ DK19 Hal Morris	.75	.35	.09
□ DK20 Mark Langston	.75	.35	.09
□ DK21 Scott Erickson	.75	.35	.09
□ DK22 Randy Johnson	1.25	.55	.16
□ DK23 Greg Swindell	.50	.23	.06
□ DK24 Dennis Martinez	.75	.35	.09
□ DK25 Tony Phillips	.50	.23	.06
□ DK26 Fred McGriff	1.00	.45	.12
□ DK27 Checklist 1-26 DP	.50	.23	.06
(Dick Perez)			

1992 Donruss Elite

These cards were random inserts in 1992 Donruss first and second series foil packs. Like the previous year, the cards were individually numbered of 10,000. Card fronts feature dramatic prismatic borders encasing a full color action or posed shot of the player. The numbering of the set is essentially a continuation of the series started the year before. Only 5,000 Ripken Signature Series cards were printed and only 7,500 Henderson Legends cards were printed.

	MINT	NRMT	EXC
COMPLETE SET (12)	800.00	350.00	100.00
COMMON CARD (9-18)	15.00	6.75	1.85
□ 9 Wade Boggs	25.00	11.00	3.10
□ 10 Joe Carter	25.00	11.00	3.10
□ 11 Will Clark	25.00	11.00	3.10
□ 12 Dwight Gooden	25.00	11.00	3.10
□ 13 Ken Griffey Jr.	150.00	70.00	19.00
□ 14 Tony Gwynn	60.00	27.00	7.50
□ 15 Howard Johnson	15.00	6.75	1.85
□ 16 Terry Pendleton	15.00	6.75	1.85
□ 17 Kirby Puckett	60.00	27.00	7.50
□ 18 Frank Thomas	150.00	70.00	19.00
□ L2 Rickey Henderson	50.00	22.00	6.25
(Legend Series)			
□ S2 Cal Ripken	400.00	180.00	50.00
(Signature Series)			

1992 Donruss Update

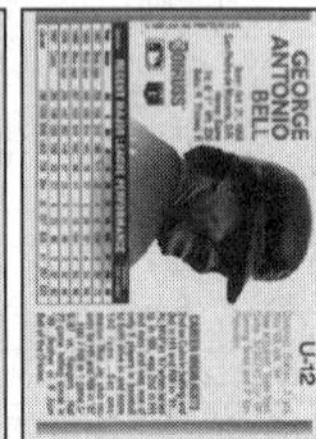

Four cards from this 22-card standard-size set were included in each retail factory set. Card design is identical to regular issue 1992 Donruss cards except for the U-prefixed numbering on back. Card numbers U1-U6 are Rated Rookie cards, while card numbers U7-U9 are Highlights cards. A tough early Kenny Lofton card, his first as a member of the Cleveland Indians, highlights this set.

	MINT	NRMT	EXC
COMPLETE SET (22)	60.00	27.00	7.50
COMMON CARD (U1-U22)	1.00	.45	.12
□ U1 Pat Listach RR	1.00	.45	.12
□ U2 Andy Stankiewicz RR	1.00	.45	.12
□ U3 Brian Jordan RR	12.00	5.50	1.50
□ U4 Dan Walters RR	1.00	.45	.12
□ U5 Chad Curtis RR	2.00	.90	.25
□ U6 Kenny Lofton RR	30.00	13.50	3.70
□ U7 Mark McGwire HL	10.00	4.50	1.25
□ U8 Eddie Murray HL	8.00	3.60	1.00
□ U9 Jeff Reardon HL	2.00	.90	.25
□ U10 Frank Viola	2.00	.90	.25
□ U11 Gary Sheffield	5.00	2.20	.60
□ U12 George Bell	2.00	.90	.25
□ U13 Rick Sutcliffe	2.00	.90	.25
□ U14 Wally Joyner	2.00	.90	.25
□ U15 Kevin Seitzer	2.00	.90	.25
□ U16 Bill Krueger	1.00	.45	.12
□ U17 Danny Tartabull	2.00	.90	.25
□ U18 Dave Winfield	4.00	1.80	.50
□ U19 Gary Carter	2.00	.90	.25
□ U20 Bobby Bonilla	2.00	.90	.25
□ U21 Cory Snyder	1.00	.45	.12
□ U22 Bill Swift	1.00	.45	.12

1992 Donruss Rookies

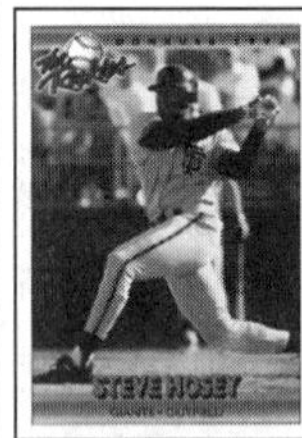

After six years of issuing "The Rookies" as a 56-card boxed set, Donruss expanded it to a 132-card standard-size set and distributed the cards exclusively in hobby and retail foil packs. The card design is the same as the 1992 Donruss regular issue except that the two-tone blue color bars have been replaced by green, as in the previous six Donruss Rookies sets. The cards are arranged in alphabetical order and numbered on the back. Rookie Cards in this set include Manny Ramirez, Shane Reynolds and Eric Young.

	MINT	NRMT	EXC
COMPLETE SET (132)	5.00	2.20	.60
COMMON CARD (1-132)	.05	.02	.01
□ 1 Kyle Abbott	.05	.02	.01
□ 2 Troy Afenir	.05	.02	.01
□ 3 Rich Amaral	.05	.02	.01
□ 4 Ruben Amaro	.05	.02	.01
□ 5 Billy Ashley	.15	.07	.02
□ 6 Pedro Astacio	.10	.05	.01
□ 7 Jim Austin	.05	.02	.01
□ 8 Robert Ayrault	.05	.02	.01
□ 9 Kevin Baez	.05	.02	.01

□ 10 Esteban Beltre	.05	.02	.01
□ 11 Brian Bohanon	.05	.02	.01
□ 12 Kent Bottenfield	.05	.02	.01
□ 13 Jeff Branson	.05	.02	.01
□ 14 Brad Brink	.05	.02	.01
□ 15 John Briscoe	.05	.02	.01
□ 16 Doug Brocail	.05	.02	.01
□ 17 Rico Brogna	.10	.05	.01
□ 18 J.T. Bruett	.05	.02	.01
□ 19 Jacob Brumfield	.05	.02	.01
□ 20 Jim Bullinger	.05	.02	.01
□ 21 Kevin Campbell	.05	.02	.01
□ 22 Pedro Castellano	.05	.02	.01
□ 23 Mike Christopher	.05	.02	.01
□ 24 Archi Cianfrocco	.05	.02	.01
□ 25 Mark Clark	.10	.05	.01
□ 26 Craig Colbert	.05	.02	.01
□ 27 Victor Cole	.05	.02	.01
□ 28 Steve Cooke	.10	.05	.01
□ 29 Tim Costo	.05	.02	.01
□ 30 Chad Curtis	.15	.07	.02
□ 31 Doug Davis	.05	.02	.01
□ 32 Gary DiSarcina	.05	.02	.01
□ 33 John Doherty	.05	.02	.01
□ 34 Mike Draper	.05	.02	.01
□ 35 Monty Fariss	.05	.02	.01
□ 36 Bien Figueroa	.05	.02	.01
□ 37 John Flaherty	.05	.02	.01
□ 38 Tim Fortugno	.05	.02	.01
□ 39 Eric Fox	.05	.02	.01
□ 40 Jeff Frye	.05	.02	.01
□ 41 Ramon Garcia	.05	.02	.01
□ 42 Brent Gates	.10	.05	.01
□ 43 Tom Goodwin	.10	.05	.01
□ 44 Buddy Groom	.05	.02	.01
□ 45 Jeff Grotewold	.05	.02	.01
□ 46 Juan Guerrero	.05	.02	.01
□ 47 Johnny Guzman	.05	.02	.01
□ 48 Shawn Hare	.05	.02	.01
□ 49 Ryan Hawblitzel	.05	.02	.01
□ 50 Bert Hefferman	.05	.02	.01
□ 51 Butch Henry	.05	.02	.01
□ 52 Cesar Hernandez	.05	.02	.01
□ 53 Vince Horsman	.05	.02	.01
□ 54 Steve Hosey	.05	.02	.01
□ 55 Pat Howell	.05	.02	.01
□ 56 Peter Hoy	.05	.02	.01
□ 57 Jonathan Hurst	.05	.02	.01
□ 58 Mark Hutton	.05	.02	.01
□ 59 Shawn Jeter	.05	.02	.01
□ 60 Joel Johnston	.05	.02	.01
□ 61 Jeff Kent	.15	.07	.02
□ 62 Kurt Knudsen	.05	.02	.01
□ 63 Kevin Koslofski	.05	.02	.01
□ 64 Danny Leon	.05	.02	.01
□ 65 Jesse Levis	.05	.02	.01
□ 66 Tom Marsh	.05	.02	.01
□ 67 Ed Martel	.05	.02	.01
□ 68 Al Martin	.15	.07	.02
□ 69 Pedro Martinez	.25	.11	.03
□ 70 Derrick May	.05	.02	.01
□ 71 Matt Maysey	.05	.02	.01
□ 72 Russ McGinnis	.05	.02	.01
□ 73 Tim McIntosh	.05	.02	.01
□ 74 Jim McNamara	.05	.02	.01
□ 75 Jeff McNeely	.05	.02	.01
□ 76 Rusty Meacham	.05	.02	.01
□ 77 Tony Menendez	.05	.02	.01
□ 78 Henry Mercedes	.05	.02	.01
□ 79 Paul Miller	.05	.02	.01
□ 80 Joe Millette	.05	.02	.01
□ 81 Blas Minor	.05	.02	.01
□ 82 Dennis Moeller	.05	.02	.01
□ 83 Raul Mondesi	.60	.25	.07
□ 84 Rob Natal	.05	.02	.01
□ 85 Troy Neel	.05	.02	.01
□ 86 David Nied	.10	.05	.01
□ 87 Jerry Nielson	.05	.02	.01
□ 88 Donovan Osborne	.10	.05	.01
□ 89 John Patterson	.05	.02	.01
□ 90 Roger Pavlik	.10	.05	.01
□ 91 Dan Peltier	.05	.02	.01
□ 92 Jim Pena	.05	.02	.01
□ 93 William Pennyfeather	.05	.02	.01
□ 94 Mike Perez	.05	.02	.01
□ 95 Hipolito Pichardo	.05	.02	.01
□ 96 Greg Pirkl	.05	.02	.01
□ 97 Harvey Pulliam	.05	.02	.01
□ 98 Manny Ramirez	2.00	.90	.25
□ 99 Pat Rapp	.10	.05	.01
□ 100 Jeff Reboulet	.05	.02	.01
□ 101 Darren Reed	.05	.02	.01
□ 102 Shane Reynolds	.30	.14	.04
□ 103 Bill Risley	.05	.02	.01
□ 104 Ben Rivera	.05	.02	.01
□ 105 Henry Rodriguez	.15	.07	.02
□ 106 Rico Rossy	.05	.02	.01
□ 107 Johnny Ruffin	.05	.02	.01
□ 108 Steve Scarsone	.05	.02	.01
□ 109 Tim Scott	.05	.02	.01
□ 110 Steve Shifflett	.05	.02	.01
□ 111 Dave Silvestri	.05	.02	.01
□ 112 Matt Stairs	.05	.02	.01
□ 113 William Suero	.05	.02	.01
□ 114 Jeff Tackett	.05	.02	.01
□ 115 Eddie Taubensee	.05	.02	.01
□ 116 Rick Trlicek	.05	.02	.01
□ 117 Scooter Tucker	.05	.02	.01
□ 118 Shane Turner	.05	.02	.01
□ 119 Julio Valera	.05	.02	.01
□ 120 Paul Wagner	.05	.02	.01
□ 121 Tim Wakefield	.15	.07	.02
□ 122 Mike Walker	.05	.02	.01
□ 123 Bruce Walton	.05	.02	.01
□ 124 Lenny Webster	.05	.02	.01
□ 125 Bob Wickman	.05	.02	.01
□ 126 Mike Williams	.05	.02	.01
□ 127 Kerry Woodson	.05	.02	.01
□ 128 Eric Young	.25	.11	.03
□ 129 Kevin Young	.05	.02	.01
□ 130 Pete Young	.05	.02	.01
□ 131 Checklist 1-66	.05	.02	.01
□ 132 Checklist 67-132	.05	.02	.01

1992 Donruss Rookies Phenoms

This 20-card standard size set features a selection young prospects. The first twelve cards were randomly inserted into 1992 Donruss The Rookies 12-card foil packs. The last eight were inserted one per 1992 Donruss Rookies 30-card jumbo pack. Each glossy card front features a black border surrounding a full color photo and gold foil type.

	MINT	NRMT	EXC
COMPLETE SET (20)	35.00	16.00	4.40
COMPLETE FOIL SET (12)	25.00	11.00	3.10
COMPLETE JUMBO SET (8)	10.00	4.50	1.25
COMMON CARD (BC1-BC12)	.50	.23	.06
COMMON CARD (BC13-BC20)	.50	.23	.06
□ BC1 Moises Alou	1.00	.45	.12
□ BC2 Bret Boone	.75	.35	.09
□ BC3 Jeff Conine	1.50	.70	.19
□ BC4 Dave Fleming	.50	.23	.06
□ BC5 Tyler Green	.50	.23	.06
□ BC6 Eric Karros	1.50	.70	.19
□ BC7 Pat Listach	.50	.23	.06
□ BC8 Kenny Lofton	8.00	3.60	1.00
□ BC9 Mike Piazza	20.00	9.00	2.50
□ BC10 Tim Salmon	5.00	2.20	.60
□ BC11 Andy Stankiewicz	.50	.23	.06
□ BC12 Dan Walters	.50	.23	.06
□ BC13 Ramon Caraballo	.50	.23	.06
□ BC14 Brian Jordan	2.50	1.10	.30
□ BC15 Ryan Klesko	4.00	1.80	.50
□ BC16 Sam Militello	.50	.23	.06
□ BC17 Frank Seminara	.50	.23	.06
□ BC18 Salomon Torres	.50	.23	.06
□ BC19 John Valentin	1.50	.70	.19
□ BC20 Wil Cordero	.75	.35	.09

1992 Donruss Coke Ryan

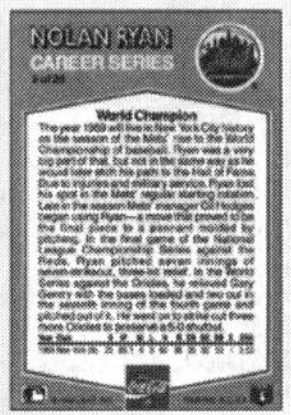

This 26-card standard-size set was produced by Donruss to commemorate each year of Ryan's professional baseball career. Both sides of the card bear the Coca-Cola logo, and four-card cello packs with one Ryan card and three regular issue 1992 Donruss cards were inserted in 12-can packs of Coca-Cola classic, caffeine-free Coca-Cola classic, diet Coke, caffeine-free diet Coke, Sprite, and diet Sprite. An offer on the back panel of specially marked Coca-Cola multi-packs (and the labels of two-liter bottles) made available boxed factory sets through a mail-in offer for 8.95 and UPC symbols from multi-pack wraps of Coca-Cola products. The promotion ran from April to June and covered nearly 90 percent of the country. The standard-size (2 1/2" by 3 1/2") cards feature on the fronts color player photos enclosed by a gold border. Blue stripes edge the pictures above and below, and in the bottom stripe appears the team name and year that the card captures. The backs are aqua and white and present season summary and statistics. The final card in the set summarizes his career and presents career statistics. The cards are numbered on the back in chronolgical order; each year Nolan is pictured with his then-current team, New York Mets (NYM), California Angels (CA), Houston Astros (HA), Texas Rangers (TR).

	MINT	NRMT	EXC
COMPLETE SET (26)	10.00	4.50	1.25
COMMON CARD (1-26)	.50	.23	.06
□ 1 Nolan Ryan 1966 NYM	.50	.23	.06
□ 2 Nolan Ryan 1968 NYM	.50	.23	.06
□ 3 Nolan Ryan 1969 NYM	.50	.23	.06
□ 4 Nolan Ryan 1970 NYM	.50	.23	.06
□ 5 Nolan Ryan 1971 NYM	.50	.23	.06
□ 6 Nolan Ryan 1972 CA	.50	.23	.06
□ 7 Nolan Ryan 1973 CA	.50	.23	.06
□ 8 Nolan Ryan 1974 CA	.50	.23	.06
□ 9 Nolan Ryan 1975 CA	.50	.23	.06
□ 10 Nolan Ryan 1976 CA	.50	.23	.06
□ 11 Nolan Ryan 1977 CA	.50	.23	.06
□ 12 Nolan Ryan 1978 CA	.50	.23	.06
□ 13 Nolan Ryan 1979 CA	.50	.23	.06
□ 14 Nolan Ryan 1980 HA	.50	.23	.06
□ 15 Nolan Ryan 1981 HA	.50	.23	.06
□ 16 Nolan Ryan 1982 HA	.50	.23	.06
□ 17 Nolan Ryan 1983 HA	.50	.23	.06
□ 18 Nolan Ryan 1984 HA	.50	.23	.06
□ 19 Nolan Ryan 1985 HA	.50	.23	.06
□ 20 Nolan Ryan 1986 HA	.50	.23	.06
□ 21 Nolan Ryan 1987 HA	.50	.23	.06
□ 22 Nolan Ryan 1988 HA	.50	.23	.06
□ 23 Nolan Ryan 1989 TR	.50	.23	.06
□ 24 Nolan Ryan 1990 TR	.50	.23	.06
□ 25 Nolan Ryan 1991 TR	.50	.23	.06
□ 26 Nolan Ryan 1992 TR	.50	.23	.06

1992 Donruss Cracker Jack I

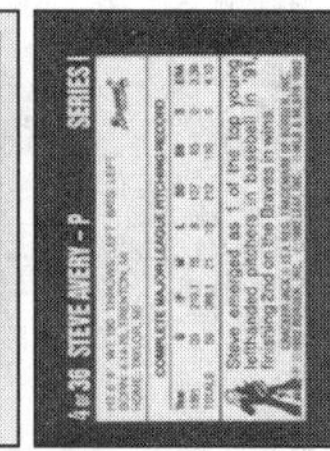

This 36-card set is the first of two series produced by Donruss for Cracker Jack, and the micro cards were protected by a paper sleeve and inserted into specially marked boxes of Cracker Jack. A side panel listed all 36 players in series I. The micro cards measure approximately 1 1/4" by 1 3/4". The front design is the same as the Donruss regular issue cards, only different color player photos are displayed. The backs, however, have a completely different design than the regular issue Donruss cards; they are horizontally oriented and present biography, major league pitching (or batting) record, and brief career summary inside navy blue borders. The cards are numbered on the back. On the paper sleeve was a mail-in offer for a mini card album with six top loading plastic pages for 4.95 per album.

	MINT	NRMT	EXC
COMPLETE SET (36)	12.00	5.50	1.50
COMMON CARD (1-36)	.05	.02	.01
□ 1 Dennis Eckersley	.10	.05	.01
□ 2 Jeff Bagwell	1.50	.70	.19
□ 3 Jim Abbott	.05	.02	.01
□ 4 Steve Avery	.40	.18	.05
□ 5 Kelly Gruber	.05	.02	.01
□ 6 Ozzie Smith	1.25	.55	.16
□ 7 Lance Dickson	.05	.02	.01
□ 8 Robin Yount	.20	.09	.03
□ 9 Brett Butler	.10	.05	.01
□ 10 Sandy Alomar Jr.	.10	.05	.01
□ 11 Travis Fryman	.40	.18	.05
□ 12 Ken Griffey Jr.	2.50	1.10	.30
□ 13 Cal Ripken	2.00	.90	.25
□ 14 Will Clark	.50	.23	.06
□ 15 Nolan Ryan	2.50	1.10	.30
□ 16 Tony Gwynn	1.25	.55	.16
□ 17 Roger Clemens	.50	.23	.06
□ 18 Wes Chamberlain	.05	.02	.01
□ 19 Barry Larkin	.50	.23	.06
□ 20 Brian McRae	.10	.05	.01
□ 21 Marquis Grissom	.10	.05	.01
□ 22 Cecil Fielder	.10	.05	.01
□ 23 Dwight Gooden	.10	.05	.01
□ 24 Chuck Knoblauch	.20	.09	.03
□ 25 Jose Canseco	.50	.23	.06
□ 26 Terry Pendleton	.10	.05	.01
□ 27 Ivan Rodriguez	1.00	.45	.12
□ 28 Ryne Sandberg	1.00	.45	.12
□ 29 Kent Hrbek	.10	.05	.01
□ 30 Ramon Martinez	.10	.05	.01
□ 31 Todd Zeile	.05	.02	.01
□ 32 Hal Morris	.05	.02	.01
□ 33 Robin Ventura	.40	.18	.05
□ 34 Doug Drabek	.05	.02	.01
□ 35 Frank Thomas	2.50	1.10	.30
□ 36 Don Mattingly	1.25	.55	.16

1992 Donruss Cracker Jack II

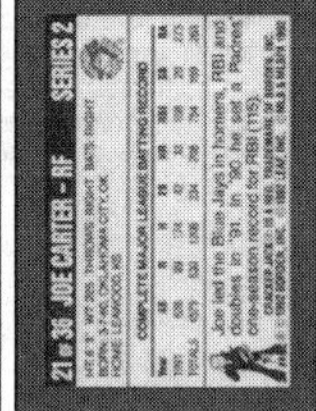

This 36-card set is the second of two series produced by Donruss for Cracker Jack. The mini cards were protected by a paper sleeve and inserted into specially marked boxes of Cracker Jacks. A side panel listed all 36 players in series II. The micro cards measure 1 1/4" by 1 3/4". The front design is the same as the Donruss regular issue cards, only different color player photos are displayed. The backs, however, have a completely different design than the regular issue Donruss cards; they are horizontally oriented and present biography, major league pitching (or batting) record, and brief career summary inside red borders. The cards are numbered on the back. On the paper sleeve was a mail-in offer for a mini card album with six top loading plastic pages for 4.95 per album.

	MINT	NRMT	EXC
COMPLETE SET (36)	7.50	3.40	.95
COMMON CARD (1-36)	.10	.05	.01
□ 1 Craig Biggio	.20	.09	.03
□ 2 Tom Glavine	.40	.18	.05
□ 3 David Justice	.40	.18	.05
□ 4 Lee Smith	.20	.09	.03
□ 5 Mark Grace	.30	.14	.04
□ 6 George Bell	.10	.05	.01
□ 7 Darryl Strawberry	.20	.09	.03
□ 8 Eric Davis	.10	.05	.01
□ 9 Ivan Calderon	.10	.05	.01
□ 10 Royce Clayton	.10	.05	.01
□ 11 Matt Williams	.30	.14	.04
□ 12 Fred McGriff	.50	.23	.06
□ 13 Len Dykstra	.20	.09	.03
□ 14 Barry Bonds	.75	.35	.09
□ 15 Reggie Sanders	.30	.14	.04
□ 16 Chris Sabo	.10	.05	.01
□ 17 Howard Johnson	.10	.05	.01
□ 18 Bobby Bonilla	.20	.09	.03
□ 19 Rickey Henderson	.40	.18	.05
□ 20 Mark Langston	.20	.09	.03
□ 21 Joe Carter	.40	.18	.05
□ 22 Paul Molitor	.50	.23	.06
□ 23 Glenallen Hill	.10	.05	.01
□ 24 Edgar Martinez	.20	.09	.03
□ 25 Gregg Olson	.10	.05	.01
□ 26 Ruben Sierra	.20	.09	.03
□ 27 Julio Franco	.20	.09	.03
□ 28 Phil Plantier	.10	.05	.01
□ 29 Wade Boggs	.40	.18	.05
□ 30 George Brett	1.00	.45	.12
□ 31 Alan Trammell	.20	.09	.03
□ 32 Kirby Puckett	1.25	.55	.16
□ 33 Scott Erickson	.10	.05	.01
□ 34 Matt Nokes	.10	.05	.01
□ 35 Danny Tartabull	.20	.09	.03
□ 36 Jack McDowell	.20	.09	.03

1992 Donruss McDonald's

This 33-card standard-size set was produced by Donruss for distribution by McDonald's Restaurants in the Toronto area. For 39 cents with the purchase of any sandwich or breakfast entree, the collector received a four-card pack featuring three cards from the MVP series and one card from the Blue Jays Gold series. A player from each MLB team is represented in the numbered 26-card MVP subset. Checklist cards were also randomly inserted throughout the foil packs. In addition, 1,000 packs included a randomly inserted prize card. By filling it out, answering the question and sending it to the address on the card, the winner received one of 1,000 numbered cards autographed by Roberto Alomar. The cards have the same design as the regular issue cards, with color action photos bordered in white and accented by blue stripes above and below the picture.

One difference is an MVP logo with the McDonald's "Golden Arches" trademark on the front. The backs present a head shot, biography, recent major league performance statistics, career highlights and the card number ("X of 26"). Again, the McDonald's "Golden Arches" trademark appears on the back alongside the other logos. One card from the six-card gold subset (of Toronto Blue Jays) was included in each 1992 Donruss McDonald's MVP four-card foil pack. The gold card fronts feature full-bleed color player photos accented by goil foil stamping. The gold cards are listed below with a "G" prefix below for reference, although a "G" prefix does not appear anywhere on the cards. The player's name appears in a dark blue bar that overlays the bottom gold foil border stripe. In a horizontal format, the backs carry biography, contract status information, recent major league performance statistics and career highlights. As with the MVP series, the McDonald's "Golden Arches" trademark adorns both sides of the card.

	MINT	NRMT	EXC
COMPLETE SET (33)	15.00	6.75	1.85
COMMON CARD (1-26)	.15	.07	.02
COMMON CARD (G1-G6)	.50	.23	.06

	MINT	NRMT	EXC
☐ 1 Cal Ripken	2.00	.90	.25
☐ 2 Frank Thomas	2.50	1.10	.30
☐ 3 George Brett	.75	.35	.09
☐ 4 Roberto Kelly	.15	.07	.02
☐ 5 Nolan Ryan	2.00	.90	.25
☐ 6 Ryne Sandberg	.75	.35	.09
☐ 7 Darryl Strawberry	.25	.11	.03
☐ 8 Len Dykstra	.25	.11	.03
☐ 9 Fred McGriff	.50	.23	.06
☐ 10 Roger Clemens	.60	.25	.07
☐ 11 Sandy Alomar Jr.	.25	.11	.03
☐ 12 Robin Yount	.50	.23	.06
☐ 13 Jose Canseco	.50	.23	.06
☐ 14 Jimmy Key	.25	.11	.03
☐ 15 Barry Larkin	.50	.23	.06
☐ 16 Dennis Martinez	.25	.11	.03
☐ 17 Andy Van Slyke	.25	.11	.03
☐ 18 Will Clark	.50	.23	.06
☐ 19 Mark Langston	.25	.11	.03
☐ 20 Cecil Fielder	.25	.11	.03
☐ 21 Kirby Puckett	1.00	.45	.12
☐ 22 Ken Griffey Jr.	2.50	1.10	.30
☐ 23 David Justice	.50	.23	.06
☐ 24 Jeff Bagwell	1.25	.55	.16
☐ 25 Howard Johnson	.15	.07	.02
☐ 26 Ozzie Smith	.75	.35	.09
☐ G1 Roberto Alomar	2.50	1.10	.30
☐ G2 Joe Carter	1.00	.45	.12
☐ G3 Kelly Gruber	.50	.23	.06
☐ G4 Jack Morris	.75	.35	.09
☐ G5 Tom Henke	.50	.23	.06
☐ G6 Devon White	.50	.23	.06
☐ NNO Checklist Card SP	.25	.11	.03

1993 Donruss Previews

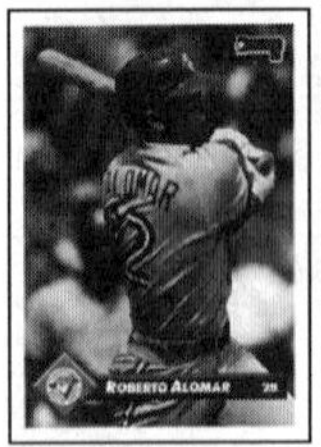

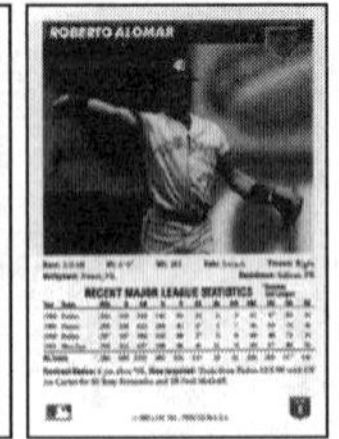

This 22-card standard-size set was issued by Donruss for hobby dealers to preview the 1993 Donruss regular issue series. The cards feature glossy color player photos with white borders on the fronts. The team logo appears in a diamond at the lower left corner, while the player's name appears in a bar that extends to the right. Both the diamond and bar are team-color coded. The top half of the back has a color close-up photo; the bottom half presents biography and recent major league statistics.

	MINT	NRMT	EXC
COMPLETE SET (22)	80.00	36.00	10.00
COMMON CARD (1-22)	1.50	.70	.19

	MINT	NRMT	EXC
☐ 1 Tom Glavine	2.00	.90	.25
☐ 2 Ryne Sandberg	6.00	2.70	.75
☐ 3 Barry Larkin	2.50	1.10	.30
☐ 4 Jeff Bagwell	8.00	3.60	1.00
☐ 5 Eric Karros	3.00	1.35	.35
☐ 6 Larry Walker	3.00	1.35	.35
☐ 7 Eddie Murray	5.00	2.20	.60
☐ 8 Darren Daulton	2.00	.90	.25
☐ 9 Andy Van Slyke	1.50	.70	.19
☐ 10 Gary Sheffield	3.00	1.35	.35
☐ 11 Will Clark	2.50	1.10	.30
☐ 12 Cal Ripken	15.00	6.75	1.85
☐ 13 Roger Clemens	2.50	1.10	.30
☐ 14 Frank Thomas	20.00	9.00	2.50
☐ 15 Cecil Fielder	2.00	.90	.25
☐ 16 George Brett	10.00	4.50	1.25
☐ 17 Robin Yount	2.50	1.10	.30
☐ 18 Don Mattingly	10.00	4.50	1.25
☐ 19 Dennis Eckersley	2.00	.90	.25
☐ 20 Ken Griffey Jr.	20.00	9.00	2.50
☐ 21 Jose Canseco	2.50	1.10	.30
☐ 22 Roberto Alomar	5.00	2.20	.60

1993 Donruss

The 792-card 1993 Donruss set was issued in two series, each with 396 standard-size cards. Cards were distributed in foil packs. The basic card fronts feature glossy color action photos with white borders. At the bottom of the picture, the team logo appears in a team color-coded diamond with the player's name in a color-coded bar extending to the right. A Rated Rookies (RR) subset , sprinkled throughout the set, spotlights 20 young prospects. There are no key Rookie Cards in this set.

	MINT	NRMT	EXC
COMPLETE SET (792)	30.00	13.50	3.70
COMPLETE SERIES 1 (396)	15.00	6.75	1.85
COMPLETE SERIES 2 (396)	15.00	6.75	1.85
COMMON CARD (1-792)	.05	.02	.01

	MINT	NRMT	EXC
☐ 1 Craig Lefferts	.05	.02	.01
☐ 2 Kent Mercker	.05	.02	.01
☐ 3 Phil Plantier	.05	.02	.01
☐ 4 Alex Arias	.05	.02	.01
☐ 5 Julio Valera	.05	.02	.01
☐ 6 Dan Wilson	.15	.07	.02
☐ 7 Frank Thomas	2.00	.90	.25
☐ 8 Eric Anthony	.05	.02	.01
☐ 9 Derek Lilliquist	.05	.02	.01
☐ 10 Rafael Bournigal	.05	.02	.01
☐ 11 Manny Alexander RR	.05	.02	.01
☐ 12 Bret Barberie	.05	.02	.01
☐ 13 Mickey Tettleton	.05	.02	.01
☐ 14 Anthony Young	.05	.02	.01
☐ 15 Tim Spehr	.05	.02	.01
☐ 16 Bob Ayrault	.05	.02	.01
☐ 17 Bill Wegman	.05	.02	.01
☐ 18 Jay Bell	.15	.07	.02
☐ 19 Rick Aguilera	.05	.02	.01
☐ 20 Todd Zeile	.05	.02	.01
☐ 21 Steve Farr	.05	.02	.01
☐ 22 Andy Benes	.15	.07	.02
☐ 23 Lance Blankenship	.05	.02	.01
☐ 24 Ted Wood	.05	.02	.01
☐ 25 Omar Vizquel	.15	.07	.02
☐ 26 Steve Avery	.15	.07	.02
☐ 27 Brian Bohanon	.05	.02	.01
☐ 28 Rick Wilkins	.05	.02	.01
☐ 29 Devon White	.05	.02	.01
☐ 30 Bobby Ayala	.15	.07	.02
☐ 31 Leo Gomez	.05	.02	.01
☐ 32 Mike Simms	.05	.02	.01
☐ 33 Ellis Burks	.15	.07	.02
☐ 34 Steve Wilson	.05	.02	.01
☐ 35 Jim Abbott	.05	.02	.01
☐ 36 Tim Wallach	.05	.02	.01
☐ 37 Wilson Alvarez	.15	.07	.02
☐ 38 Daryl Boston	.05	.02	.01
☐ 39 Sandy Alomar Jr.	.15	.07	.02
☐ 40 Mitch Williams	.05	.02	.01
☐ 41 Rico Brogna	.15	.07	.02
☐ 42 Gary Varsho	.05	.02	.01
☐ 43 Kevin Appier	.15	.07	.02
☐ 44 Eric Wedge RR	.05	.02	.01
☐ 45 Dante Bichette	.30	.14	.04
☐ 46 Jose Oquendo	.05	.02	.01
☐ 47 Mike Trombley	.05	.02	.01
☐ 48 Dan Walters	.05	.02	.01
☐ 49 Gerald Williams	.05	.02	.01
☐ 50 Bud Black	.05	.02	.01
☐ 51 Bobby Witt	.05	.02	.01
☐ 52 Mark Davis	.05	.02	.01
☐ 53 Shawn Barton	.05	.02	.01
☐ 54 Paul Assenmacher	.05	.02	.01
☐ 55 Kevin Reimer	.05	.02	.01
☐ 56 Billy Ashley RR	.05	.02	.01
☐ 57 Eddie Zosky	.05	.02	.01
☐ 58 Chris Sabo	.05	.02	.01
☐ 59 Billy Ripken	.05	.02	.01
☐ 60 Scooter Tucker	.05	.02	.01
☐ 61 Tim Wakefield RR	.15	.07	.02
☐ 62 Mitch Webster	.05	.02	.01
☐ 63 Jack Clark	.05	.02	.01
☐ 64 Mark Gardner	.05	.02	.01
☐ 65 Lee Stevens	.05	.02	.01
☐ 66 Todd Hundley	.15	.07	.02
☐ 67 Bobby Thigpen	.05	.02	.01
☐ 68 Dave Hollins	.05	.02	.01
☐ 69 Jack Armstrong	.05	.02	.01
☐ 70 Alex Cole	.05	.02	.01
☐ 71 Mark Carreon	.05	.02	.01
☐ 72 Todd Worrell	.05	.02	.01
☐ 73 Steve Shifflett	.05	.02	.01
☐ 74 Jerald Clark	.05	.02	.01
☐ 75 Paul Molitor	.40	.18	.05
☐ 76 Larry Carter	.05	.02	.01
☐ 77 Rich Rowland RR	.05	.02	.01
☐ 78 Damon Berryhill	.05	.02	.01
☐ 79 Willie Banks	.05	.02	.01
☐ 80 Hector Villanueva	.05	.02	.01
☐ 81 Mike Gallego	.05	.02	.01
☐ 82 Tim Belcher	.05	.02	.01
☐ 83 Mike Bordick	.05	.02	.01
☐ 84 Craig Biggio	.15	.07	.02
☐ 85 Lance Parrish	.05	.02	.01
☐ 86 Brett Butler	.15	.07	.02
☐ 87 Mike Timlin	.05	.02	.01
☐ 88 Brian Barnes	.05	.02	.01
☐ 89 Brady Anderson	.30	.14	.04
☐ 90 D.J. Dozier	.05	.02	.01
☐ 91 Frank Viola	.05	.02	.01
☐ 92 Darren Daulton	.15	.07	.02
☐ 93 Chad Curtis	.15	.07	.02
☐ 94 Zane Smith	.05	.02	.01
☐ 95 George Bell	.05	.02	.01
☐ 96 Rex Hudler	.05	.02	.01
☐ 97 Mark Whiten	.05	.02	.01
☐ 98 Tim Teufel	.05	.02	.01
☐ 99 Kevin Ritz	.05	.02	.01
☐ 100 Jeff Brantley	.05	.02	.01
☐ 101 Jeff Conine	.15	.07	.02
☐ 102 Vinny Castilla	.30	.14	.04
☐ 103 Greg Vaughn	.15	.07	.02
☐ 104 Steve Buechele	.05	.02	.01
☐ 105 Darren Reed	.05	.02	.01
☐ 106 Bip Roberts	.05	.02	.01
☐ 107 John Habyan	.05	.02	.01
☐ 108 Scott Servais	.05	.02	.01
☐ 109 Walt Weiss	.05	.02	.01
☐ 110 J.T. Snow RR	.30	.14	.04
☐ 111 Jay Buhner	.30	.14	.04
☐ 112 Darryl Strawberry	.15	.07	.02
☐ 113 Roger Pavlik	.15	.07	.02
☐ 114 Chris Nabholz	.05	.02	.01
☐ 115 Pat Borders	.05	.02	.01
☐ 116 Pat Howell	.05	.02	.01
☐ 117 Gregg Olson	.05	.02	.01
☐ 118 Curt Schilling	.05	.02	.01
☐ 119 Roger Clemens	.40	.18	.05
☐ 120 Victor Cole	.05	.02	.01
☐ 121 Gary DiSarcina	.05	.02	.01
☐ 122 Checklist 1-80 (Gary Carter and Kirt Manwaring	.15	.07	.02
☐ 123 Steve Sax	.05	.02	.01
☐ 124 Chuck Carr	.05	.02	.01
☐ 125 Mark Lewis	.05	.02	.01
☐ 126 Tony Gwynn	.75	.35	.09
☐ 127 Travis Fryman	.15	.07	.02
☐ 128 Dave Burba	.05	.02	.01
☐ 129 Wally Joyner	.15	.07	.02
☐ 130 John Smoltz	.30	.14	.04
☐ 131 Cal Eldred	.05	.02	.01
☐ 132 Checklist 81-159 (Roberto Alomar and Devon White)	.30	.14	.04
☐ 133 Arthur Rhodes	.05	.02	.01
☐ 134 Jeff Blauser	.05	.02	.01
☐ 135 Scott Cooper	.05	.02	.01
☐ 136 Doug Strange	.05	.02	.01
☐ 137 Luis Sojo	.05	.02	.01
☐ 138 Jeff Branson	.05	.02	.01
☐ 139 Alex Fernandez	.15	.07	.02
☐ 140 Ken Caminiti	.30	.14	.04
☐ 141 Charles Nagy	.15	.07	.02
☐ 142 Tom Candiotti	.05	.02	.01
☐ 143 Willie Greene RR	.15	.07	.02
☐ 144 John Vander Wal	.05	.02	.01
☐ 145 Kurt Knudsen	.05	.02	.01
☐ 146 John Franco	.05	.02	.01
☐ 147 Eddie Pierce	.05	.02	.01
☐ 148 Kim Batiste	.05	.02	.01
☐ 149 Darren Holmes	.05	.02	.01
☐ 150 Steve Cooke	.05	.02	.01
☐ 151 Terry Jorgensen	.05	.02	.01
☐ 152 Mark Clark	.05	.02	.01
☐ 153 Randy Velarde	.05	.02	.01
☐ 154 Greg W. Harris	.05	.02	.01
☐ 155 Kevin Campbell	.05	.02	.01
☐ 156 John Burkett	.05	.02	.01
☐ 157 Kevin Mitchell	.15	.07	.02
☐ 158 Deion Sanders	.30	.14	.04
☐ 159 Jose Canseco	.30	.14	.04
☐ 160 Jeff Hartsock	.05	.02	.01
☐ 161 Tom Quinlan	.05	.02	.01
☐ 162 Tim Pugh	.05	.02	.01
☐ 163 Glenn Davis	.05	.02	.01
☐ 164 Shane Reynolds	.30	.14	.04
☐ 165 Jody Reed	.05	.02	.01
☐ 166 Mike Sharperson	.05	.02	.01
☐ 167 Scott Lewis	.05	.02	.01
☐ 168 Dennis Martinez	.15	.07	.02
☐ 169 Scott Radinsky	.05	.02	.01
☐ 170 Dave Gallagher	.05	.02	.01
☐ 171 Jim Thome	1.00	.45	.12
☐ 172 Terry Mulholland	.05	.02	.01
☐ 173 Milt Cuyler	.05	.02	.01
☐ 174 Bob Patterson	.05	.02	.01
☐ 175 Jeff Montgomery	.15	.07	.02
☐ 176 Tim Salmon RR	.50	.23	.06
☐ 177 Franklin Stubbs	.05	.02	.01
☐ 178 Donovan Osborne	.05	.02	.01
☐ 179 Jeff Reboulet	.05	.02	.01
☐ 180 Jeremy Hernandez	.05	.02	.01
☐ 181 Charlie Hayes	.05	.02	.01
☐ 182 Matt Williams	.30	.14	.04
☐ 183 Mike Raczka	.05	.02	.01
☐ 184 Francisco Cabrera	.05	.02	.01
☐ 185 Rich DeLucia	.05	.02	.01
☐ 186 Sammy Sosa	.30	.14	.04
☐ 187 Ivan Rodriguez	.50	.23	.06
☐ 188 Bret Boone RR	.15	.07	.02
☐ 189 Juan Guzman	.15	.07	.02
☐ 190 Tom Browning	.05	.02	.01
☐ 191 Randy Milligan	.05	.02	.01
☐ 192 Steve Finley	.15	.07	.02
☐ 193 John Patterson RR	.05	.02	.01
☐ 194 Kip Gross	.05	.02	.01
☐ 195 Tony Fossas	.05	.02	.01
☐ 196 Ivan Calderon	.05	.02	.01
☐ 197 Junior Felix	.05	.02	.01
☐ 198 Pete Schourek	.15	.07	.02
☐ 199 Craig Grebeck	.05	.02	.01
☐ 200 Juan Bell	.05	.02	.01
☐ 201 Glenallen Hill	.05	.02	.01
☐ 202 Danny Jackson	.05	.02	.01
☐ 203 John Kiely	.05	.02	.01
☐ 204 Bob Tewksbury	.05	.02	.01
☐ 205 Kevin Koslofski	.05	.02	.01
☐ 206 Craig Shipley	.05	.02	.01
☐ 207 John Jaha	.30	.14	.04
☐ 208 Royce Clayton	.15	.07	.02
☐ 209 Mike Piazza RR	2.00	.90	.25
☐ 210 Ron Gant	.15	.07	.02
☐ 211 Scott Erickson	.05	.02	.01
☐ 212 Doug Dascenzo	.05	.02	.01
☐ 213 Andy Stankiewicz	.05	.02	.01
☐ 214 Geronimo Berroa	.15	.07	.02
☐ 215 Dennis Eckersley	.15	.07	.02
☐ 216 Al Osuna	.05	.02	.01
☐ 217 Tino Martinez	.15	.07	.02
☐ 218 Henry Rodriguez	.30	.14	.04
☐ 219 Ed Sprague	.15	.07	.02
☐ 220 Ken Hill	.15	.07	.02
☐ 221 Chito Martinez	.05	.02	.01
☐ 222 Bret Saberhagen	.15	.07	.02
☐ 223 Mike Greenwell	.05	.02	.01
☐ 224 Mickey Morandini	.05	.02	.01
☐ 225 Chuck Finley	.05	.02	.01
☐ 226 Denny Neagle	.15	.07	.02
☐ 227 Kirk McCaskill	.05	.02	.01
☐ 228 Rheal Cormier	.05	.02	.01
☐ 229 Paul Sorrento	.05	.02	.01
☐ 230 Darrin Jackson	.05	.02	.01
☐ 231 Rob Deer	.05	.02	.01
☐ 232 Bill Swift	.05	.02	.01
☐ 233 Kevin McReynolds	.05	.02	.01
☐ 234 Terry Pendleton	.15	.07	.02
☐ 235 Dave Nilsson	.15	.07	.02
☐ 236 Chuck McElroy	.05	.02	.01
☐ 237 Derek Parks	.05	.02	.01
☐ 238 Norm Charlton	.05	.02	.01
☐ 239 Matt Nokes	.05	.02	.01
☐ 240 Juan Guerrero	.05	.02	.01
☐ 241 Jeff Parrett	.05	.02	.01
☐ 242 Ryan Thompson RR	.05	.02	.01
☐ 243 Dave Fleming	.05	.02	.01
☐ 244 Dave Hansen	.05	.02	.01
☐ 245 Monty Fariss	.05	.02	.01
☐ 246 Archi Cianfrocco	.05	.02	.01
☐ 247 Pat Hentgen	.30	.14	.04
☐ 248 Bill Pecota	.05	.02	.01
☐ 249 Ben McDonald	.05	.02	.01
☐ 250 Cliff Brantley	.05	.02	.01
☐ 251 John Valentin	.15	.07	.02
☐ 252 Jeff King	.15	.07	.02
☐ 253 Reggie Williams	.05	.02	.01
☐ 254 Checklist 160-238 (Damon Berryhill and Alex Arias)	.05	.02	.01
☐ 255 Ozzie Guillen	.05	.02	.01
☐ 256 Mike Perez	.05	.02	.01
☐ 257 Thomas Howard	.05	.02	.01
☐ 258 Kurt Stillwell	.05	.02	.01
☐ 259 Mike Henneman	.05	.02	.01
☐ 260 Steve Decker	.05	.02	.01
☐ 261 Brent Mayne	.05	.02	.01
☐ 262 Otis Nixon	.05	.02	.01
☐ 263 Mark Kiefer	.05	.02	.01
☐ 264 Checklist 239-317	.30	.14	.04

(Don Mattingly
and Mike Bordick)
☐ 265 Richie Lewis .05 .02 .01
☐ 266 Pat Gomez .05 .02 .01
☐ 267 Scott Taylor .05 .02 .01
☐ 268 Shawon Dunston .05 .02 .01
☐ 269 Greg Myers .05 .02 .01
☐ 270 Tim Costo .05 .02 .01
☐ 271 Greg Hibbard .05 .02 .01
☐ 272 Pete Harnisch .05 .02 .01
☐ 273 Dave Mlicki .05 .02 .01
☐ 274 Orel Hershiser .15 .07 .02
☐ 275 Sean Berry RR .05 .02 .01
☐ 276 Doug Simons .05 .02 .01
☐ 277 John Doherty .05 .02 .01
☐ 278 Eddie Murray .50 .23 .06
☐ 279 Chris Haney .05 .02 .01
☐ 280 Stan Javier .05 .02 .01
☐ 281 Jaime Navarro .05 .02 .01
☐ 282 Orlando Merced .15 .07 .02
☐ 283 Kent Hrbek .15 .07 .02
☐ 284 Bernard Gilkey .15 .07 .02
☐ 285 Russ Springer .05 .02 .01
☐ 286 Mike Maddux .05 .02 .01
☐ 287 Eric Fox .05 .02 .01
☐ 288 Mark Leonard .05 .02 .01
☐ 289 Tim Leary .05 .02 .01
☐ 290 Brian Hunter .05 .02 .01
☐ 291 Donald Harris .05 .02 .01
☐ 292 Bob Scanlan .05 .02 .01
☐ 293 Turner Ward .05 .02 .01
☐ 294 Hal Morris .05 .02 .01
☐ 295 Jimmy Poole .05 .02 .01
☐ 296 Doug Jones .05 .02 .01
☐ 297 Tony Pena .05 .02 .01
☐ 298 Ramon Martinez .15 .07 .02
☐ 299 Tim Fortugno .05 .02 .01
☐ 300 Marquis Grissom .15 .07 .02
☐ 301 Lance Johnson .15 .07 .02
☐ 302 Jeff Kent .15 .07 .02
☐ 303 Reggie Jefferson .15 .07 .02
☐ 304 Wes Chamberlain .05 .02 .01
☐ 305 Shawn Hare .05 .02 .01
☐ 306 Mike LaValliere .05 .02 .01
☐ 307 Gregg Jefferies .15 .07 .02
☐ 308 Troy Neel RR .05 .02 .01
☐ 309 Pat Listach .05 .02 .01
☐ 310 Geronimo Pena .05 .02 .01
☐ 311 Pedro Munoz .05 .02 .01
☐ 312 Guillermo Velasquez .05 .02 .01
☐ 313 Roberto Kelly .05 .02 .01
☐ 314 Mike Jackson .05 .02 .01
☐ 315 Rickey Henderson .30 .14 .04
☐ 316 Mark Lemke .05 .02 .01
☐ 317 Erik Hanson .05 .02 .01
☐ 318 Derrick May .05 .02 .01
☐ 319 Geno Petralli .05 .02 .01
☐ 320 Melvin Nieves RR .30 .14 .04
☐ 321 Doug Linton .05 .02 .01
☐ 322 Rob Dibble .05 .02 .01
☐ 323 Chris Hoiles .05 .02 .01
☐ 324 Jimmy Jones .05 .02 .01
☐ 325 Dave Staton RR .05 .02 .01
☐ 326 Pedro Martinez .30 .14 .04
☐ 327 Paul Quantrill .05 .02 .01
☐ 328 Greg Colbrunn .05 .02 .01
☐ 329 Hilly Hathaway .05 .02 .01
☐ 330 Jeff Innis .05 .02 .01
☐ 331 Ron Karkovice .05 .02 .01
☐ 332 Keith Shepherd .05 .02 .01
☐ 333 Alan Embree .05 .02 .01
☐ 334 Paul Wagner .05 .02 .01
☐ 335 Dave Haas .05 .02 .01
☐ 336 Ozzie Canseco .05 .02 .01
☐ 337 Bill Sampen .05 .02 .01
☐ 338 Rich Rodriguez .05 .02 .01
☐ 339 Dean Palmer .15 .07 .02
☐ 340 Greg Litton .05 .02 .01
☐ 341 Jim Tatum RR .05 .02 .01
☐ 342 Todd Haney .05 .02 .01
☐ 343 Larry Casian .05 .02 .01
☐ 344 Ryne Sandberg .50 .23 .06
☐ 345 Sterling Hitchcock .15 .07 .02
☐ 346 Chris Hammond .05 .02 .01
☐ 347 Vince Horsman .05 .02 .01
☐ 348 Butch Henry .05 .02 .01
☐ 349 Dann Howitt .05 .02 .01
☐ 350 Roger McDowell .05 .02 .01
☐ 351 Jack Morris .15 .07 .02
☐ 352 Bill Krueger .05 .02 .01
☐ 353 Cris Colon .05 .02 .01
☐ 354 Joe Vitko .05 .02 .01
☐ 355 Willie McGee .05 .02 .01
☐ 356 Jay Baller .05 .02 .01
☐ 357 Pat Mahomes .05 .02 .01
☐ 358 Roger Mason .05 .02 .01
☐ 359 Jerry Nielsen .05 .02 .01
☐ 360 Tom Pagnozzi .05 .02 .01
☐ 361 Kevin Baez .05 .02 .01
☐ 362 Tim Scott .05 .02 .01
☐ 363 Domingo Martinez .05 .02 .01
☐ 364 Kirt Manwaring .05 .02 .01
☐ 365 Rafael Palmeiro .30 .14 .04
☐ 366 Ray Lankford .15 .07 .02
☐ 367 Tim McIntosh .05 .02 .01
☐ 368 Jessie Hollins .05 .02 .01
☐ 369 Scott Leius .05 .02 .01
☐ 370 Bill Doran .05 .02 .01
☐ 371 Sam Militello .05 .02 .01
☐ 372 Ryan Bowen .05 .02 .01
☐ 373 Dave Henderson .05 .02 .01
☐ 374 Dan Smith RR .05 .02 .01
☐ 375 Steve Reed RR .05 .02 .01
☐ 376 Jose Offerman .05 .02 .01
☐ 377 Kevin Brown .15 .07 .02
☐ 378 Darrin Fletcher .05 .02 .01
☐ 379 Duane Ward .05 .02 .01
☐ 380 Wayne Kirby RR .05 .02 .01
☐ 381 Steve Scarsone .05 .02 .01
☐ 382 Mariano Duncan .05 .02 .01
☐ 383 Ken Ryan .05 .02 .01
☐ 384 Lloyd McClendon .05 .02 .01
☐ 385 Brian Holman .05 .02 .01
☐ 386 Braulio Castillo .05 .02 .01
☐ 387 Danny Leon .05 .02 .01
☐ 388 Omar Olivares .05 .02 .01
☐ 389 Kevin Wickander .05 .02 .01
☐ 390 Fred McGriff .30 .14 .04
☐ 391 Phil Clark .05 .02 .01
☐ 392 Darren Lewis .05 .02 .01
☐ 393 Phil Hiatt .05 .02 .01
☐ 394 Mike Morgan .05 .02 .01
☐ 395 Shane Mack .05 .02 .01
☐ 396 Checklist 318-396 .15 .07 .02
(Dennis Eckersley
and Art Kusnyer CO)
☐ 397 David Segui .05 .02 .01
☐ 398 Rafael Belliard .05 .02 .01
☐ 399 Tim Naehring .05 .02 .01
☐ 400 Frank Castillo .05 .02 .01
☐ 401 Joe Grahe .05 .02 .01
☐ 402 Reggie Sanders .30 .14 .04
☐ 403 Roberto Hernandez .15 .07 .02
☐ 404 Luis Gonzalez .05 .02 .01
☐ 405 Carlos Baerga .15 .07 .02
☐ 406 Carlos Hernandez .05 .02 .01
☐ 407 Pedro Astacio RR .05 .02 .01
☐ 408 Mel Rojas .15 .07 .02
☐ 409 Scott Livingstone .05 .02 .01
☐ 410 Chico Walker .05 .02 .01
☐ 411 Brian McRae .15 .07 .02
☐ 412 Ben Rivera .05 .02 .01
☐ 413 Ricky Bones .05 .02 .01
☐ 414 Andy Van Slyke .15 .07 .02
☐ 415 Chuck Knoblauch .30 .14 .04
☐ 416 Luis Alicea .05 .02 .01
☐ 417 Bob Wickman .05 .02 .01
☐ 418 Doug Brocail .05 .02 .01
☐ 419 Scott Brosius .05 .02 .01
☐ 420 Rod Beck .15 .07 .02
☐ 421 Edgar Martinez .15 .07 .02
☐ 422 Ryan Klesko .60 .25 .07
☐ 423 Nolan Ryan 1.50 .70 .19
☐ 424 Rey Sanchez .05 .02 .01
☐ 425 Roberto Alomar .40 .18 .05
☐ 426 Barry Larkin .30 .14 .04
☐ 427 Mike Mussina .40 .18 .05
☐ 428 Jeff Bagwell .75 .35 .09
☐ 429 Mo Vaughn .50 .23 .06
☐ 430 Eric Karros .30 .14 .04
☐ 431 John Orton .05 .02 .01
☐ 432 Wil Cordero .15 .07 .02
☐ 433 Jack McDowell .15 .07 .02
☐ 434 Howard Johnson .05 .02 .01
☐ 435 Albert Belle .75 .35 .09
☐ 436 John Kruk .15 .07 .02
☐ 437 Skeeter Barnes .05 .02 .01
☐ 438 Don Slaught .05 .02 .01
☐ 439 Rusty Meacham .05 .02 .01
☐ 440 Tim Laker RR .05 .02 .01
☐ 441 Robin Yount .30 .14 .04
☐ 442 Brian Jordan .30 .14 .04
☐ 443 Kevin Tapani .05 .02 .01
☐ 444 Gary Sheffield .30 .14 .04
☐ 445 Rich Monteleone .05 .02 .01
☐ 446 Will Clark .30 .14 .04
☐ 447 Jerry Browne .05 .02 .01
☐ 448 Jeff Treadway .05 .02 .01
☐ 449 Mike Schooler .05 .02 .01
☐ 450 Mike Harkey .05 .02 .01
☐ 451 Julio Franco .15 .07 .02
☐ 452 Kevin Young RR .05 .02 .01
☐ 453 Kelly Gruber .05 .02 .01
☐ 454 Jose Rijo .05 .02 .01
☐ 455 Mike Devereaux .05 .02 .01
☐ 456 Andujar Cedeno .05 .02 .01
☐ 457 Damion Easley RR .05 .02 .01
☐ 458 Kevin Gross .05 .02 .01
☐ 459 Matt Young .05 .02 .01
☐ 460 Matt Stairs .05 .02 .01
☐ 461 Luis Polonia .05 .02 .01
☐ 462 Dwight Gooden .15 .07 .02
☐ 463 Warren Newson .05 .02 .01
☐ 464 Jose DeLeon .05 .02 .01
☐ 465 Jose Mesa .15 .07 .02
☐ 466 Danny Cox .05 .02 .01
☐ 467 Dan Gladden .05 .02 .01
☐ 468 Gerald Perry .05 .02 .01
☐ 469 Mike Boddicker .05 .02 .01
☐ 470 Jeff Gardner .05 .02 .01
☐ 471 Doug Henry .05 .02 .01
☐ 472 Mike Benjamin .05 .02 .01
☐ 473 Dan Peltier RR .05 .02 .01
☐ 474 Mike Stanton .05 .02 .01
☐ 475 John Smiley .05 .02 .01
☐ 476 Dwight Smith .05 .02 .01
☐ 477 Jim Leyritz .05 .02 .01
☐ 478 Dwayne Henry .05 .02 .01
☐ 479 Mark McGwire .60 .25 .07
☐ 480 Pete Incaviglia .05 .02 .01
☐ 481 Dave Cochrane .05 .02 .01
☐ 482 Eric Davis .15 .07 .02
☐ 483 John Olerud .05 .02 .01
☐ 484 Kent Bottenfield .05 .02 .01
☐ 485 Mark McLemore .05 .02 .01
☐ 486 Dave Magadan .05 .02 .01
☐ 487 John Marzano .05 .02 .01
☐ 488 Ruben Amaro .05 .02 .01
☐ 489 Rob Ducey .05 .02 .01
☐ 490 Stan Belinda .05 .02 .01
☐ 491 Dan Pasqua .05 .02 .01
☐ 492 Joe Magrane .05 .02 .01
☐ 493 Brook Jacoby .05 .02 .01
☐ 494 Gene Harris .05 .02 .01
☐ 495 Mark Leiter .05 .02 .01
☐ 496 Bryan Hickerson .05 .02 .01
☐ 497 Tom Gordon .05 .02 .01
☐ 498 Pete Smith .05 .02 .01
☐ 499 Chris Bosio .05 .02 .01
☐ 500 Shawn Boskie .05 .02 .01
☐ 501 Dave West .05 .02 .01
☐ 502 Milt Hill .05 .02 .01
☐ 503 Pat Kelly .05 .02 .01
☐ 504 Joe Boever .05 .02 .01
☐ 505 Terry Steinbach .15 .07 .02
☐ 506 Butch Huskey RR .30 .14 .04
☐ 507 David Valle .05 .02 .01
☐ 508 Mike Scioscia .05 .02 .01
☐ 509 Kenny Rogers .05 .02 .01
☐ 510 Moises Alou .15 .07 .02
☐ 511 David Wells .05 .02 .01
☐ 512 Mackey Sasser .05 .02 .01
☐ 513 Todd Frohwirth .05 .02 .01
☐ 514 Ricky Jordan .05 .02 .01
☐ 515 Mike Gardiner .05 .02 .01
☐ 516 Gary Redus .05 .02 .01
☐ 517 Gary Gaetti .15 .07 .02
☐ 518 Checklist .05 .02 .01
☐ 519 Carlton Fisk .30 .14 .04
☐ 520 Ozzie Smith .50 .23 .06
☐ 521 Rod Nichols .05 .02 .01
☐ 522 Benito Santiago .05 .02 .01
☐ 523 Bill Gullickson .05 .02 .01
☐ 524 Robby Thompson .05 .02 .01
☐ 525 Mike Macfarlane .05 .02 .01
☐ 526 Sid Bream .05 .02 .01
☐ 527 Darryl Hamilton .05 .02 .01
☐ 528 Checklist .05 .02 .01
☐ 529 Jeff Tackett .05 .02 .01
☐ 530 Greg Olson .05 .02 .01
☐ 531 Bob Zupcic .05 .02 .01
☐ 532 Mark Grace .30 .14 .04
☐ 533 Steve Frey .05 .02 .01
☐ 534 Dave Martinez .05 .02 .01
☐ 535 Robin Ventura .15 .07 .02
☐ 536 Casey Candaele .05 .02 .01
☐ 537 Kenny Lofton .75 .35 .09
☐ 538 Jay Howell .05 .02 .01
☐ 539 Fernando Ramsey RR .05 .02 .01
☐ 540 Larry Walker .30 .14 .04
☐ 541 Cecil Fielder .15 .07 .02
☐ 542 Lee Guetterman .05 .02 .01
☐ 543 Keith Miller .05 .02 .01
☐ 544 Len Dykstra .15 .07 .02
☐ 545 B.J. Surhoff .15 .07 .02
☐ 546 Bob Walk .05 .02 .01
☐ 547 Brian Harper .05 .02 .01
☐ 548 Lee Smith .15 .07 .02
☐ 549 Danny Tartabull .05 .02 .01
☐ 550 Frank Seminara .05 .02 .01
☐ 551 Henry Mercedes .05 .02 .01
☐ 552 Dave Righetti .05 .02 .01
☐ 553 Ken Griffey Jr. 2.00 .90 .25
☐ 554 Tom Glavine .30 .14 .04
☐ 555 Juan Gonzalez 1.00 .45 .12
☐ 556 Jim Bullinger .05 .02 .01
☐ 557 Derek Bell .15 .07 .02
☐ 558 Cesar Hernandez .05 .02 .01
☐ 559 Cal Ripken 1.50 .70 .19
☐ 560 Eddie Taubensee .05 .02 .01
☐ 561 John Flaherty .05 .02 .01
☐ 562 Todd Benzinger .05 .02 .01
☐ 563 Hubie Brooks .05 .02 .01
☐ 564 Delino DeShields .05 .02 .01
☐ 565 Tim Raines .30 .14 .04
☐ 566 Sid Fernandez .05 .02 .01
☐ 567 Steve Olin .05 .02 .01
☐ 568 Tommy Greene .05 .02 .01
☐ 569 Buddy Groom .05 .02 .01
☐ 570 Randy Tomlin .05 .02 .01
☐ 571 Hipolito Pichardo .05 .02 .01
☐ 572 Rene Arocha RR .05 .02 .01
☐ 573 Mike Fetters .05 .02 .01
☐ 574 Felix Jose .05 .02 .01
☐ 575 Gene Larkin .05 .02 .01
☐ 576 Bruce Hurst .05 .02 .01
☐ 577 Bernie Williams .40 .18 .05
☐ 578 Trevor Wilson .05 .02 .01
☐ 579 Bob Welch .05 .02 .01
☐ 580 David Justice .30 .14 .04
☐ 581 Randy Johnson .30 .14 .04
☐ 582 Jose Vizcaino .05 .02 .01
☐ 583 Jeff Huson .05 .02 .01
☐ 584 Rob Maurer RR .05 .02 .01
☐ 585 Todd Stottlemyre .15 .07 .02
☐ 586 Joe Oliver .05 .02 .01
☐ 587 Bob Milacki .05 .02 .01
☐ 588 Rob Murphy .05 .02 .01
☐ 589 Greg Pirkl RR .05 .02 .01
☐ 590 Lenny Harris .05 .02 .01
☐ 591 Luis Rivera .05 .02 .01
☐ 592 John Wetteland .15 .07 .02
☐ 593 Mark Langston .15 .07 .02
☐ 594 Bobby Bonilla .15 .07 .02
☐ 595 Esteban Beltre .05 .02 .01
☐ 596 Mike Hartley .05 .02 .01
☐ 597 Felix Fermin .05 .02 .01
☐ 598 Carlos Garcia .05 .02 .01
☐ 599 Frank Tanana .05 .02 .01
☐ 600 Pedro Guerrero .05 .02 .01
☐ 601 Terry Shumpert .05 .02 .01
☐ 602 Wally Whitehurst .05 .02 .01
☐ 603 Kevin Seitzer .05 .02 .01
☐ 604 Chris James .05 .02 .01
☐ 605 Greg Gohr RR .05 .02 .01
☐ 606 Mark Wohlers .15 .07 .02
☐ 607 Kirby Puckett .75 .35 .09
☐ 608 Greg Maddux 1.25 .55 .16
☐ 609 Don Mattingly 1.00 .45 .12
☐ 610 Greg Cadaret .05 .02 .01
☐ 611 Dave Stewart .15 .07 .02
☐ 612 Mark Portugal .05 .02 .01
☐ 613 Pete O'Brien .05 .02 .01
☐ 614 Bobby Ojeda .05 .02 .01
☐ 615 Joe Carter .15 .07 .02
☐ 616 Pete Young .05 .02 .01
☐ 617 Sam Horn .05 .02 .01
☐ 618 Vince Coleman .05 .02 .01
☐ 619 Wade Boggs .30 .14 .04
☐ 620 Todd Pratt .05 .02 .01
☐ 621 Ron Tingley .05 .02 .01
☐ 622 Doug Drabek .05 .02 .01
☐ 623 Scott Hemond .05 .02 .01
☐ 624 Tim Jones .05 .02 .01
☐ 625 Dennis Cook .05 .02 .01
☐ 626 Jose Melendez .05 .02 .01
☐ 627 Mike Munoz .05 .02 .01
☐ 628 Jim Pena .05 .02 .01
☐ 629 Gary Thurman .05 .02 .01
☐ 630 Charlie Leibrandt .05 .02 .01
☐ 631 Scott Fletcher .05 .02 .01
☐ 632 Andre Dawson .30 .14 .04
☐ 633 Greg Gagne .05 .02 .01
☐ 634 Greg Swindell .05 .02 .01
☐ 635 Kevin Maas .05 .02 .01
☐ 636 Xavier Hernandez .05 .02 .01
☐ 637 Ruben Sierra .15 .07 .02
☐ 638 Dmitri Young RR .50 .23 .06
☐ 639 Harold Reynolds .05 .02 .01
☐ 640 Tom Goodwin .05 .02 .01
☐ 641 Todd Burns .05 .02 .01
☐ 642 Jeff Fassero .15 .07 .02
☐ 643 Dave Winfield .30 .14 .04
☐ 644 Willie Randolph .15 .07 .02
☐ 645 Luis Mercedes .05 .02 .01
☐ 646 Dale Murphy .30 .14 .04
☐ 647 Danny Darwin .05 .02 .01
☐ 648 Dennis Moeller .05 .02 .01
☐ 649 Chuck Crim .05 .02 .01
☐ 650 Checklist .05 .02 .01
☐ 651 Shawn Abner .05 .02 .01
☐ 652 Tracy Woodson .05 .02 .01
☐ 653 Scott Scudder .05 .02 .01
☐ 654 Tom Lampkin .05 .02 .01
☐ 655 Alan Trammell .30 .14 .04
☐ 656 Cory Snyder .05 .02 .01
☐ 657 Chris Gwynn .05 .02 .01
☐ 658 Lonnie Smith .05 .02 .01
☐ 659 Jim Austin .05 .02 .01
☐ 660 Checklist .05 .02 .01
☐ 661 Tim Hulett .05 .02 .01
☐ 662 Marvin Freeman .05 .02 .01
☐ 663 Greg A. Harris .05 .02 .01
☐ 664 Heathcliff Slocumb .05 .02 .01
☐ 665 Mike Butcher .05 .02 .01
☐ 666 Steve Foster .05 .02 .01
☐ 667 Donn Pall .05 .02 .01
☐ 668 Darryl Kile .05 .02 .01
☐ 669 Jesse Levis .05 .02 .01
☐ 670 Jim Gott .05 .02 .01
☐ 671 Mark Hutton RR .05 .02 .01
☐ 672 Brian Drahman .05 .02 .01
☐ 673 Chad Kreuter .05 .02 .01
☐ 674 Tony Fernandez .05 .02 .01
☐ 675 Jose Lind .05 .02 .01
☐ 676 Kyle Abbott .05 .02 .01
☐ 677 Dan Plesac .05 .02 .01
☐ 678 Barry Bonds .50 .23 .06
☐ 679 Chili Davis .15 .07 .02
☐ 680 Stan Royer .05 .02 .01
☐ 681 Scott Kamieniecki .05 .02 .01

☐ 682 Carlos Martinez	.05	.02	.01
☐ 683 Mike Moore	.05	.02	.01
☐ 684 Candy Maldonado	.05	.02	.01
☐ 685 Jeff Nelson	.05	.02	.01
☐ 686 Lou Whitaker	.15	.07	.02
☐ 687 Jose Guzman	.05	.02	.01
☐ 688 Manuel Lee	.05	.02	.01
☐ 689 Bob MacDonald	.05	.02	.01
☐ 690 Scott Bankhead	.05	.02	.01
☐ 691 Alan Mills	.05	.02	.01
☐ 692 Brian Williams	.05	.02	.01
☐ 693 Tom Brunansky	.05	.02	.01
☐ 694 Lenny Webster	.05	.02	.01
☐ 695 Greg Briley	.05	.02	.01
☐ 696 Paul O'Neill	.15	.07	.02
☐ 697 Joey Cora	.15	.07	.02
☐ 698 Charlie O'Brien	.05	.02	.01
☐ 699 Junior Ortiz	.05	.02	.01
☐ 700 Ron Darling	.05	.02	.01
☐ 701 Tony Phillips	.15	.07	.02
☐ 702 William Pennyfeather	.05	.02	.01
☐ 703 Mark Gubicza	.05	.02	.01
☐ 704 Steve Hosey RR	.05	.02	.01
☐ 705 Henry Cotto	.05	.02	.01
☐ 706 David Hulse	.05	.02	.01
☐ 707 Mike Pagliarulo	.05	.02	.01
☐ 708 Dave Stieb	.05	.02	.01
☐ 709 Melido Perez	.05	.02	.01
☐ 710 Jimmy Key	.15	.07	.02
☐ 711 Jeff Russell	.05	.02	.01
☐ 712 David Cone	.15	.07	.02
☐ 713 Russ Swan	.05	.02	.01
☐ 714 Mark Guthrie	.05	.02	.01
☐ 715 Checklist	.05	.02	.01
☐ 716 Al Martin RR	.15	.07	.02
☐ 717 Randy Knorr	.05	.02	.01
☐ 718 Mike Stanley	.05	.02	.01
☐ 719 Rick Sutcliffe	.05	.02	.01
☐ 720 Terry Leach	.05	.02	.01
☐ 721 Chipper Jones RR	2.50	1.10	.30
☐ 722 Jim Eisenreich	.15	.07	.02
☐ 723 Tom Henke	.05	.02	.01
☐ 724 Jeff Frye	.05	.02	.01
☐ 725 Harold Baines	.15	.07	.02
☐ 726 Scott Sanderson	.05	.02	.01
☐ 727 Tom Foley	.05	.02	.01
☐ 728 Bryan Harvey	.05	.02	.01
☐ 729 Tom Edens	.05	.02	.01
☐ 730 Eric Young	.30	.14	.04
☐ 731 Dave Weathers	.05	.02	.01
☐ 732 Spike Owen	.05	.02	.01
☐ 733 Scott Aldred	.05	.02	.01
☐ 734 Cris Carpenter	.05	.02	.01
☐ 735 Dion James	.05	.02	.01
☐ 736 Joe Girardi	.05	.02	.01
☐ 737 Nigel Wilson RR	.05	.02	.01
☐ 738 Scott Chiamparino	.05	.02	.01
☐ 739 Jeff Reardon	.15	.07	.02
☐ 740 Willie Blair	.05	.02	.01
☐ 741 Jim Corsi	.05	.02	.01
☐ 742 Ken Patterson	.05	.02	.01
☐ 743 Andy Ashby	.15	.07	.02
☐ 744 Rob Natal	.05	.02	.01
☐ 745 Kevin Bass	.05	.02	.01
☐ 746 Freddie Benavides	.05	.02	.01
☐ 747 Chris Donnels	.05	.02	.01
☐ 748 Kerry Woodson	.05	.02	.01
☐ 749 Calvin Jones	.05	.02	.01
☐ 750 Gary Scott	.05	.02	.01
☐ 751 Joe Orsulak	.05	.02	.01
☐ 752 Armando Reynoso	.05	.02	.01
☐ 753 Monty Fariss	.05	.02	.01
☐ 754 Billy Hatcher	.05	.02	.01
☐ 755 Denis Boucher	.05	.02	.01
☐ 756 Walt Weiss	.05	.02	.01
☐ 757 Mike Fitzgerald	.05	.02	.01
☐ 758 Rudy Seanez	.05	.02	.01
☐ 759 Bret Barberie	.05	.02	.01
☐ 760 Mo Sanford	.05	.02	.01
☐ 761 Pedro Castellano	.05	.02	.01
☐ 762 Chuck Carr	.05	.02	.01
☐ 763 Steve Howe	.05	.02	.01
☐ 764 Andres Galarraga	.30	.14	.04
☐ 765 Jeff Conine	.15	.07	.02
☐ 766 Ted Power	.05	.02	.01
☐ 767 Butch Henry	.05	.02	.01
☐ 768 Steve Decker	.05	.02	.01
☐ 769 Storm Davis	.05	.02	.01
☐ 770 Vinny Castilla	.30	.14	.04
☐ 771 Junior Felix	.05	.02	.01
☐ 772 Walt Terrell	.05	.02	.01
☐ 773 Brad Ausmus	.05	.02	.01
☐ 774 Jamie McAndrew	.05	.02	.01
☐ 775 Milt Thompson	.05	.02	.01
☐ 776 Charlie Hayes	.05	.02	.01
☐ 777 Jack Armstrong	.05	.02	.01
☐ 778 Dennis Rasmussen	.05	.02	.01
☐ 779 Darren Holmes	.05	.02	.01
☐ 780 Alex Arias	.05	.02	.01
☐ 781 Randy Bush	.05	.02	.01
☐ 782 Javier Lopez RR	.50	.23	.06
☐ 783 Dante Bichette	.30	.14	.04
☐ 784 John Johnstone	.05	.02	.01
☐ 785 Rene Gonzales	.05	.02	.01
☐ 786 Alex Cole	.05	.02	.01
☐ 787 Jeromy Burnitz RR	.05	.02	.01
☐ 788 Michael Huff	.05	.02	.01
☐ 789 Anthony Telford	.05	.02	.01
☐ 790 Jerald Clark	.05	.02	.01
☐ 791 Joel Johnston	.05	.02	.01
☐ 792 David Nied RR	.05	.02	.01

1993 Donruss Diamond Kings

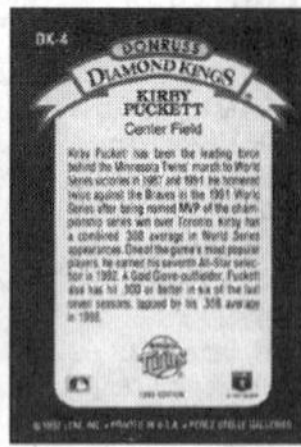

These standard-size cards, commemorating Donruss' annual selection of the games top players, were randomly inserted in 1993 Donruss packs. The first 15 cards were available in the first series of the 1993 Donruss and cards 16-31 were inserted with the second series. The cards are gold-foil stamped and feature player portraits by noted sports artist Dick Perez. Card numbers 27-28 honor the first draft picks of the new Florida Marlins and Colorado Rockies franchises. Collectors 16 years of age and younger could enter Donruss' Diamond King contest by writing an essay of 75 words or less explaining who their favorite Diamond King player was and why. Winners were awarded one of 30 framed watercolors at the National Convention, held in Chicago, July 22-25, 1993.

	MINT	NRMT	EXC
COMPLETE SET (31)	30.00	13.50	3.70
COMPLETE SERIES 1 (15)	20.00	9.00	2.50
COMPLETE SERIES 2 (16)	10.00	4.50	1.25
COMMON CARD (DK1-DK31)	.75	.35	.09
☐ DK1 Ken Griffey Jr.	12.00	5.50	1.50
☐ DK2 Ryne Sandberg	3.00	1.35	.35
☐ DK3 Roger Clemens	2.50	1.10	.30
☐ DK4 Kirby Puckett	5.00	2.20	.60
☐ DK5 Bill Swift	.75	.35	.09
☐ DK6 Larry Walker	1.50	.70	.19
☐ DK7 Juan Gonzalez	6.00	2.70	.75
☐ DK8 Wally Joyner	.75	.35	.09
☐ DK9 Andy Van Slyke	.75	.35	.09
☐ DK10 Robin Ventura	1.50	.70	.19
☐ DK11 Bip Roberts	.75	.35	.09
☐ DK12 Roberto Kelly	.75	.35	.09
☐ DK13 Carlos Baerga	.75	.35	.09
☐ DK14 Orel Hershiser	1.50	.70	.19
☐ DK15 Cecil Fielder	1.50	.70	.19
☐ DK16 Robin Yount	1.50	.70	.19
☐ DK17 Darren Daulton	1.50	.70	.19
☐ DK18 Mark McGwire	4.00	1.80	.50
☐ DK19 Tom Glavine	1.50	.70	.19
☐ DK20 Roberto Alomar	2.50	1.10	.30
☐ DK21 Gary Sheffield	2.00	.90	.25
☐ DK22 Bob Tewksbury	.75	.35	.09
☐ DK23 Brady Anderson	1.50	.70	.19
☐ DK24 Craig Biggio	1.50	.70	.19
☐ DK25 Eddie Murray	3.00	1.35	.35
☐ DK26 Luis Polonia	.75	.35	.09
☐ DK27 Nigel Wilson	.75	.35	.09
☐ DK28 David Nied	.75	.35	.09
☐ DK29 Pat Listach ROY	.75	.35	.09
☐ DK30 Eric Karros ROY	1.50	.70	.19
☐ DK31 Checklist 1-31	.75	.35	.09

1993 Donruss Elite

Cards 19-27 were random inserts in 1993 Donruss series I foil packs while cards 28-36 were inserted in series II packs. The numbering on the 1993 Elite cards follows consecutively after that of the 1992 Elite series cards, and each of the 10,000 Elite cards is serially numbered. The backs of the Elite cards also carry the serial number ("X" of 10,000) as well as the card number. The Signature Series Will Clark card was randomly inserted in 1993 Donruss foil packs; he personally autographed 5,000 cards. Featuring a Dick Perez portrait, the ten thousand Legends Series cards honor Robin Yount for his 3,000th hit achievement. The front design of the Elite cards features a cutout color player photo superimposed on a neon-colored panel framed by a gray inner border and a variegated silver metallic outer border.

	MINT	NRMT	EXC
COMPLETE SET (20)	400.00	180.00	50.00
COMMON CARD (19-36)	10.00	4.50	1.25
☐ 19 Fred McGriff	15.00	6.75	1.85
☐ 20 Ryne Sandberg	30.00	13.50	3.70
☐ 21 Eddie Murray	30.00	13.50	3.70
☐ 22 Paul Molitor	30.00	13.50	3.70
☐ 23 Barry Larkin	20.00	9.00	2.50
☐ 24 Don Mattingly	60.00	27.00	7.50
☐ 25 Dennis Eckersley	15.00	6.75	1.85
☐ 26 Roberto Alomar	25.00	11.00	3.10
☐ 27 Edgar Martinez	15.00	6.75	1.85
☐ 28 Gary Sheffield	25.00	11.00	3.10
☐ 29 Darren Daulton	15.00	6.75	1.85
☐ 30 Larry Walker	15.00	6.75	1.85
☐ 31 Barry Bonds	30.00	13.50	3.70
☐ 32 Andy Van Slyke	10.00	4.50	1.25
☐ 33 Mark McGwire	50.00	22.00	6.25
☐ 34 Cecil Fielder	15.00	6.75	1.85
☐ 35 Dave Winfield	15.00	6.75	1.85
☐ 36 Juan Gonzalez	50.00	22.00	6.25
☐ L3 Robin Yount (Legend Series)	20.00	9.00	2.50
☐ S3 Will Clark AU (Signature Series)	150.00	70.00	19.00

1993 Donruss Long Ball Leaders

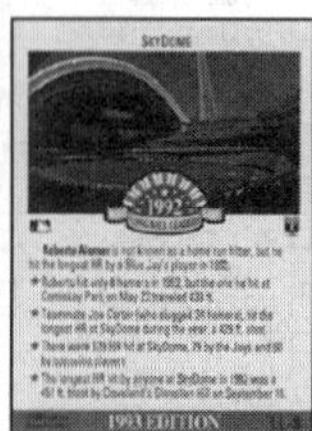

Randomly inserted in 26-card magazine distributor packs (1-9 in series I and 10-18 in series II), these standard-size cards feature some of MLB's outstanding sluggers. The fronts feature full-bleed color action player photos with a red and bright yellow stripe design across the bottom that carries the player's name and team. The Donruss Long Ball Leaders icon rests on the stripe at the lower left. The player's longest home run is printed in gold foil at the upper left.

	MINT	NRMT	EXC
COMPLETE SET (18)	60.00	27.00	7.50
COMPLETE SERIES 1 (9)	30.00	13.50	3.70
COMPLETE SERIES 2 (9)	30.00	13.50	3.70
COMMON CARD (LL1-LL18)	1.50	.70	.19
☐ LL1 Rob Deer	1.50	.70	.19
☐ LL2 Fred McGriff	2.50	1.10	.30
☐ LL3 Albert Belle	8.00	3.60	1.00
☐ LL4 Mark McGwire	6.00	2.70	.75
☐ LL5 David Justice	2.00	.90	.25
☐ LL6 Jose Canseco	2.50	1.10	.30
☐ LL7 Kent Hrbek	1.50	.70	.19
☐ LL8 Roberto Alomar	4.00	1.80	.50
☐ LL9 Ken Griffey Jr.	20.00	9.00	2.50
☐ LL10 Frank Thomas	20.00	9.00	2.50
☐ LL11 Darryl Strawberry	2.00	.90	.25
☐ LL12 Felix Jose	1.50	.70	.19
☐ LL13 Cecil Fielder	2.00	.90	.25
☐ LL14 Juan Gonzalez	10.00	4.50	1.25
☐ LL15 Ryne Sandberg	5.00	2.20	.60
☐ LL16 Gary Sheffield	3.00	1.35	.35
☐ LL17 Jeff Bagwell	8.00	3.60	1.00
☐ LL18 Larry Walker	2.50	1.10	.30

1993 Donruss MVPs

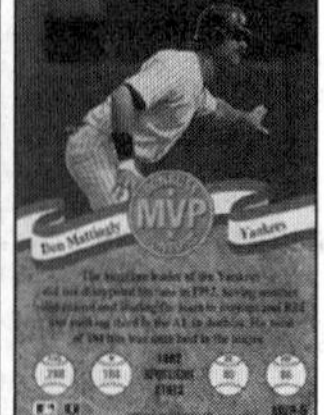

These twenty-six standard size MVP cards were issued 13 cards in each series, and they were inserted one per 23-card jumbo packs. The fronts feature full-bleed color action player photos with a red, white, and blue ribbon design across the bottom that contains the player's name and team. The Donruss MVP icon is gold-foil stamped over the ribbon.

	MINT	NRMT	EXC
COMPLETE SET (26)	30.00	13.50	3.70
COMPLETE SERIES 1 (13)	10.00	4.50	1.25
COMPLETE SERIES 2 (13)	20.00	9.00	2.50
COMMON CARD (1-26)	.50	.23	.06
☐ 1 Luis Polonia	.50	.23	.06
☐ 2 Frank Thomas	8.00	3.60	1.00
☐ 3 George Brett	3.00	1.35	.35
☐ 4 Paul Molitor	1.50	.70	.19
☐ 5 Don Mattingly	4.00	1.80	.50
☐ 6 Roberto Alomar	1.50	.70	.19
☐ 7 Terry Pendleton	.50	.23	.06
☐ 8 Eric Karros	1.00	.45	.12
☐ 9 Larry Walker	1.00	.45	.12
☐ 10 Eddie Murray	2.00	.90	.25
☐ 11 Darren Daulton	.75	.35	.09
☐ 12 Ray Lankford	.75	.35	.09
☐ 13 Will Clark	1.00	.45	.12
☐ 14 Cal Ripken	6.00	2.70	.75
☐ 15 Roger Clemens	1.50	.70	.19
☐ 16 Carlos Baerga	.50	.23	.06
☐ 17 Cecil Fielder	.75	.35	.09
☐ 18 Kirby Puckett	3.00	1.35	.35
☐ 19 Mark McGwire	2.50	1.10	.30
☐ 20 Ken Griffey Jr.	8.00	3.60	1.00
☐ 21 Juan Gonzalez	4.00	1.80	.50
☐ 22 Ryne Sandberg	2.00	.90	.25
☐ 23 Bip Roberts	.50	.23	.06
☐ 24 Jeff Bagwell	3.00	1.35	.35
☐ 25 Barry Bonds	2.00	.90	.25
☐ 26 Gary Sheffield	1.25	.55	.16

1993 Donruss Spirit of the Game

These 20 standard-size cards were randomly inserted in 1993 Donruss packs and packed approximately two per box. Cards 1-10 were first-series inserts, and cards 11-20 were second-series inserts. The fronts feature borderless glossy color action player photos. The set title, "Spirit of the Game," is stamped in gold foil script across the top or bottom of the picture.

	MINT	NRMT	EXC
COMPLETE SET (20)	20.00	9.00	2.50
COMPLETE SERIES 1 (10)	8.00	3.60	1.00
COMPLETE SERIES 2 (10)	12.00	5.50	1.50
COMMON CARD (SG1-SG20)	.50	.23	.06
☐ SG1 Mike Bordick Turning Two	.50	.23	.06
☐ SG2 Dave Justice Play at the Plate	1.00	.45	.12
☐ SG3 Roberto Alomar In There	2.00	.90	.25
☐ SG4 Dennis Eckersley Pumped	1.00	.45	.12
☐ SG5 Juan Gonzalez and Jose Canseco Dynamic Duo	4.00	1.80	.50
☐ SG6 George Bell and Frank Thomas ... Gone	2.50	1.10	.30
☐ SG7 Wade Boggs and Luis Polonia Safe or Out			
☐ SG8 Will Clark The Thrill			
☐ SG9 Bip Roberts Safe at Home	.50	.23	.06
☐ SG10 Cecil Fielder Rob Deer Mickey Tettleton Thirty 3	1.00	.45	.12
☐ SG11 Kenny Lofton Bag Bandit	4.00	1.80	.50
☐ SG12 Gary Sheffield Fred McGriff Back to Back	1.00	.45	.12
☐ SG13 Greg Gagne Barry Larkin	1.00	.45	.12
☐ SG14 Ryne Sandberg The Ball Stops Here	2.50	1.10	.30
☐ SG15 Carlos Baerga Gary Gaetti Over the Top	1.00	.45	.12
☐ SG16 Danny Tartabull At the Wall	.50	.23	.06
☐ SG17 Brady Anderson Head First	1.25	.55	.16
☐ SG18 Frank Thomas Big Hurt	10.00	4.50	1.25
☐ SG19 Kevin Gross No Hitter	.50	.23	.06
☐ SG20 Robin Yount 3,000 Hits			

1993 Donruss Elite Dominators

In a series of programs broadcast Dec. 8-13, 1993, on the Shop at Home cable network, viewers were offered the opportunity to

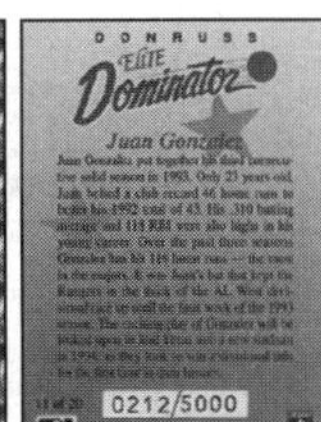

purchase a factory-sealed box of either 1993 Donruss I or II, which included one Elite Dominator card produced especially for the promotion. The set retailed for 99.00 plus 6.00 for postage and handling. Just 5,000 of each card were produced, and Nolan Ryan, Juan Gonzalez, Paul Molitor, and Don Mattingly personally signed 2,500 of their cards. The entire print run of 100,000 cards were reportedly purchased by the Shop at Home network and were to be offered periodically over the network. The standard-size Dominator cards feature on their fronts color player action shots with green prismatic foil borders. The set's title appears at the top, along with a gold foil motion-streaked baseball icon at the upper right. The player's name appears near the bottom within a red bar. The tan back is highlighted by pink stars and carries the set's name at the top, followed by the player's name and career highlights. The production number, out of a total of 5,000 produced, is shown at the bottom.

	MINT	NRMT	EXC
COMP.UNSIGNED SET (20)	1200.00	550.00	150.00
COMMON CARD (1-20)	20.00	9.00	2.50
☐ 1 Ryne Sandberg	60.00	27.00	7.50
☐ 2 Fred McGriff	40.00	18.00	5.00
☐ 3 Greg Maddux	90.00	40.00	11.00
☐ 4 Ron Gant	30.00	13.50	3.70
☐ 5 David Justice	30.00	13.50	3.70
☐ 6 Don Mattingly	75.00	34.00	9.50
☐ 7 Tim Salmon	40.00	18.00	5.00
☐ 8 Mike Piazza	100.00	45.00	12.50
☐ 9 John Olerud	20.00	9.00	2.50
☐ 10 Nolan Ryan	125.00	55.00	15.50
☐ 11 Juan Gonzalez	60.00	27.00	7.50
☐ 12 Ken Griffey Jr.	125.00	55.00	15.50
☐ 13 Frank Thomas	125.00	55.00	15.50
☐ 14 Tom Glavine	40.00	18.00	5.00
☐ 15 George Brett	60.00	27.00	7.50
☐ 16 Barry Bonds	50.00	22.00	6.25
☐ 17 Albert Belle	75.00	34.00	9.50
☐ 18 Paul Molitor	40.00	18.00	5.00
☐ 19 Cal Ripken	125.00	55.00	15.50
☐ 20 Roberto Alomar	60.00	27.00	7.50
☐ AU6 Don Mattingly AU	175.00	80.00	22.00
☐ AU10 Nolan Ryan AU	250.00	110.00	31.00
☐ AU11 Juan Gonzalez AU	125.00	55.00	15.50
☐ AU18 Paul Molitor AU	125.00	55.00	15.50

1993 Donruss Elite Supers

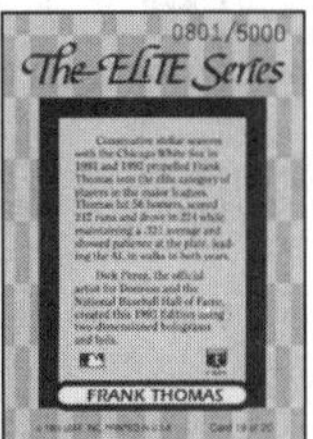

Sequentially numbered one through 5,000, these 20 oversized cards measure approximately 3 1/2" by 5" and have wide prismatic foil borders with an inner gray borders. The front displays a color player photo cutout on a brightly colored background. The subset title is written above the photo and the player's name is printed in an oval under the photo. The backs have a two-toned outer border with a navy blue inner border. On a gray background the player's profile is printed in navy blue lettering. The Elite Update set features all the players found in the regular Elite set, plus Nolan Ryan and Frank Thomas, whose cards replace numbers 19 and 20 from the earlier release, and an updated card of Barry Bonds in his Giants uniform. The backs carry the production number and the card number. Bonds in his Giants uniform. The backs carry the production number and the card number.

	MINT	NRMT	EXC
COMPLETE SET (20)	225.00	100.00	28.00
COMMON CARD (1-20)	3.00	1.35	.35
☐ 1 Fred McGriff	5.00	2.20	.60
☐ 2 Ryne Sandberg	12.00	5.50	1.50
☐ 3 Eddie Murray	12.00	5.50	1.50
☐ 4 Paul Molitor	10.00	4.50	1.25
☐ 5 Barry Larkin	5.00	2.20	.60
☐ 6 Don Mattingly	25.00	11.00	3.10
☐ 7 Dennis Eckersley	3.00	1.35	.35
☐ 8 Roberto Alomar	10.00	4.50	1.25
☐ 9 Edgar Martinez	3.00	1.35	.35
☐ 10 Gary Sheffield	10.00	4.50	1.25
☐ 11 Darren Daulton	3.00	1.35	.35
☐ 12 Larry Walker	6.00	2.70	.75
☐ 13 Barry Bonds	8.00	3.60	1.00
☐ 14 Andy Van Slyke	3.00	1.35	.35
☐ 15 Mark McGwire	15.00	6.75	1.85
☐ 16 Cecil Fielder	3.00	1.35	.35
☐ 17 Dave Winfield	5.00	2.20	.60
☐ 18 Juan Gonzalez	25.00	11.00	3.10
☐ 19 Frank Thomas	50.00	22.00	6.25
☐ 20 Nolan Ryan	40.00	18.00	5.00

1993 Donruss Masters of the Game

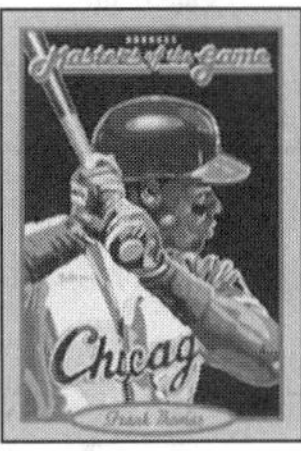

These cards were issued in individual retail re-packs, and also were included in special 18-pack boxes of 1993 Donruss second series. The cards were originally available only at retail outlets such as WalMart along with a foil pack of 1993 Donruss. These 16 postcards measure approximately 3 1/2" by 5" and feature the work of artist Dick Perez on their fronts. The color paintings are trimmed and bordered in various colors. The player's name appears within an ellipse at the bottom. The back carries the player's name and career statistics at the bottom, and the upper right corner is reserved for a stamp. A faded team logo graces the middle. A few sentences describing Perez' art technique appear vertically on the left. The MLB and MLBPA logos round out the back on the bottom.

	MINT	NRMT	EXC
COMPLETE SET (16)	60.00	27.00	7.50
COMMON CARD (1-16)	1.00	.45	.12
☐ 1 Frank Thomas	12.00	5.50	1.50
☐ 2 Nolan Ryan	10.00	4.50	1.25
☐ 3 Gary Sheffield	1.50	.70	.19
☐ 4 Fred McGriff	1.50	.70	.19
☐ 5 Ryne Sandberg	4.00	1.80	.50
☐ 6 Cal Ripken	10.00	4.50	1.25
☐ 7 Jose Canseco	1.50	.70	.19
☐ 8 Ken Griffey Jr.	12.00	5.50	1.50
☐ 9 Will Clark	1.50	.70	.19
☐ 10 Roberto Alomar	2.50	1.10	.30
☐ 11 Juan Gonzalez	6.00	2.70	.75
☐ 12 David Justice	2.00	.90	.25
☐ 13 Kirby Puckett	5.00	2.20	.60
☐ 14 Barry Bonds	2.50	1.10	.30
☐ 15 Robin Yount	1.50	.70	.19
☐ 16 Deion Sanders	2.00	.90	.25

1994 Donruss Promos

These 12 standard-size promo cards feature borderless color player action shots on their fronts. The player's name and position appear in gold foil within a team color-coded stripe near the bottom. His team logo appears within a black rectangle framed by a team color near the bottom. The set name and year, stamped in gold foil, also appear in this rectangle. Most of the backs are horizontal, and feature another borderless color player action photo. A black rectangle framed by a team color appears on one side and carries the player's name, team, uniform number, and biography. The player's 1992 stats appear within ghosted stripes near the bottom. The disclaimer "Promotional Sample" is printed diagonally across both sides of the cards. The cards are numbered on the back. Reportedly each of Leaf/Donruss' hobby accounts (roughly 3,000) received one complete 11-card promo set (including one but not both Special Edition cards) with their 1994 Donruss order form. Moreover, 42 different retail broker accounts also received five to ten complete 11-card promo sets for their presentations. From this information, it appears that approximately 3,500 11-card promo sets were printed. Each hobby account received one of two Special Edition promos, either Barry Bonds or Frank Thomas.

	MINT	NRMT	EXC
COMPLETE SET (12)	50.00	22.00	6.25
COMMON CARD (1-10)	1.00	.45	.12
☐ 1 Barry Bonds	2.50	1.10	.30
☐ 1SE Barry Bonds SP	5.00	2.20	.60
☐ 2 Darren Daulton	2.00	.90	.25
☐ 3 John Olerud	2.00	.90	.25
☐ 4 Frank Thomas	10.00	4.50	1.25
☐ 4SE Frank Thomas SP	20.00	9.00	2.50
☐ 5 Mike Piazza	6.00	2.70	.75
☐ 6 Tim Salmon	2.00	.90	.25
☐ 7 Ken Griffey Jr.	10.00	4.50	1.25
☐ 8 Fred McGriff	2.00	.90	.25
☐ 9 Don Mattingly	5.00	2.20	.60
☐ 10 Gary Sheffield	2.50	1.10	.30

1994 Donruss

The 1994 Donruss set was issued in two separate series of 330 standard-size cards for a total of 660. The fronts feature borderless color player action photos on front. The player's name and position appear in gold foil within a team color-coded stripe near the bottom. The team logo appears within a black rectangle framed by a team color near the bottom. The set name and year, stamped in gold foil, also appear in this rectangle. Most of the backs are horizontal, and feature another borderless color player action photo. A black rectangle framed by a team color appears on one side and carries the player's name, team, uniform number, and biography. The player's stats appear within ghosted stripes near the bottom. Rookie Cards include Curtis Pride and Julian Tavarez.

	MINT	NRMT	EXC
COMPLETE SET (660)	50.00	22.00	6.25
COMPLETE SERIES 1 (330)	25.00	11.00	3.10
COMPLETE SERIES 2 (330)	25.00	11.00	3.10
COMMON CARD (1-660)	.10	.05	.01
☐ 1 Nolan Ryan	3.00	1.35	.35
☐ 2 Mike Piazza	2.00	.90	.25
☐ 3 Moises Alou	.20	.09	.03
☐ 4 Ken Griffey Jr.	3.00	1.35	.35
☐ 5 Gary Sheffield	.30	.14	.04
☐ 6 Roberto Alomar	.60	.25	.07
☐ 7 John Kruk	.20	.09	.03
☐ 8 Gregg Olson	.10	.05	.01
☐ 9 Gregg Jefferies	.30	.14	.04
☐ 10 Tony Gwynn	1.25	.55	.16
☐ 11 Chad Curtis	.10	.05	.01
☐ 12 Craig Biggio	.20	.09	.03
☐ 13 John Burkett	.10	.05	.01
☐ 14 Carlos Baerga	.20	.09	.03
☐ 15 Robin Yount	.30	.14	.04
☐ 16 Dennis Eckersley	.20	.09	.03
☐ 17 Dwight Gooden	.20	.09	.03
☐ 18 Ryne Sandberg	.75	.35	.09
☐ 19 Rickey Henderson	.30	.14	.04
☐ 20 Jack McDowell	.20	.09	.03
☐ 21 Jay Bell	.20	.09	.03
☐ 22 Kevin Brown	.20	.09	.03
☐ 23 Robin Ventura	.20	.09	.03
☐ 24 Paul Molitor	.60	.25	.07
☐ 25 David Justice	.30	.14	.04
☐ 26 Rafael Palmeiro	.30	.14	.04
☐ 27 Cecil Fielder	.20	.09	.03
☐ 28 Chuck Knoblauch	.30	.14	.04
☐ 29 Dave Hollins	.10	.05	.01
☐ 30 Jimmy Key	.20	.09	.03
☐ 31 Mark Langston	.20	.09	.03
☐ 32 Darryl Kile	.10	.05	.01
☐ 33 Ruben Sierra	.20	.09	.03
☐ 34 Ron Gant	.20	.09	.03
☐ 35 Ozzie Smith	.75	.35	.09
☐ 36 Wade Boggs	.30	.14	.04
☐ 37 Marquis Grissom	.20	.09	.03
☐ 38 Will Clark	.30	.14	.04
☐ 39 Kenny Lofton	1.00	.45	.12
☐ 40 Cal Ripken	2.50	1.10	.30
☐ 41 Steve Avery	.20	.09	.03
☐ 42 Mo Vaughn	.75	.35	.09
☐ 43 Brian McRae	.20	.09	.03
☐ 44 Mickey Tettleton	.10	.05	.01
☐ 45 Barry Larkin	.30	.14	.04
☐ 46 Charlie Hayes	.10	.05	.01
☐ 47 Kevin Appier	.20	.09	.03
☐ 48 Robby Thompson	.10	.05	.01
☐ 49 Juan Gonzalez	1.50	.70	.19
☐ 50 Paul O'Neill	.20	.09	.03
☐ 51 Marcos Armas	.10	.05	.01
☐ 52 Mike Butcher	.10	.05	.01
☐ 53 Ken Caminiti	.30	.14	.04
☐ 54 Pat Borders	.10	.05	.01
☐ 55 Pedro Munoz	.10	.05	.01
☐ 56 Tim Belcher	.10	.05	.01
☐ 57 Paul Assenmacher	.10	.05	.01
☐ 58 Damon Berryhill	.10	.05	.01
☐ 59 Ricky Bones	.10	.05	.01
☐ 60 Rene Arocha	.10	.05	.01
☐ 61 Shawn Boskie	.10	.05	.01
☐ 62 Pedro Astacio	.10	.05	.01
☐ 63 Frank Bolick	.10	.05	.01
☐ 64 Bud Black	.10	.05	.01
☐ 65 Sandy Alomar Jr.	.20	.09	.03
☐ 66 Rich Amaral	.10	.05	.01
☐ 67 Luis Aquino	.10	.05	.01
☐ 68 Kevin Baez	.10	.05	.01
☐ 69 Mike Devereaux	.10	.05	.01
☐ 70 Andy Ashby	.20	.09	.03
☐ 71 Larry Andersen	.10	.05	.01
☐ 72 Steve Cooke	.10	.05	.01
☐ 73 Mario Diaz	.10	.05	.01
☐ 74 Rob Deer	.10	.05	.01
☐ 75 Bobby Ayala	.10	.05	.01
☐ 76 Freddie Benavides	.10	.05	.01
☐ 77 Stan Belinda	.10	.05	.01
☐ 78 John Doherty	.10	.05	.01
☐ 79 Willie Banks	.10	.05	.01
☐ 80 Spike Owen	.10	.05	.01
☐ 81 Mike Bordick	.10	.05	.01
☐ 82 Chili Davis	.20	.09	.03
☐ 83 Luis Gonzalez	.10	.05	.01
☐ 84 Ed Sprague	.20	.09	.03
☐ 85 Jeff Reboulet	.10	.05	.01
☐ 86 Jason Bere	.20	.09	.03
☐ 87 Mark Hutton	.10	.05	.01
☐ 88 Jeff Blauser	.10	.05	.01
☐ 89 Cal Eldred	.10	.05	.01
☐ 90 Bernard Gilkey	.20	.09	.03
☐ 91 Frank Castillo	.10	.05	.01
☐ 92 Jim Gott	.10	.05	.01
☐ 93 Greg Colbrunn	.10	.05	.01
☐ 94 Jeff Brantley	.10	.05	.01
☐ 95 Jeremy Hernandez	.10	.05	.01
☐ 96 Norm Charlton	.10	.05	.01
☐ 97 Alex Arias	.10	.05	.01
☐ 98 John Franco	.10	.05	.01
☐ 99 Chris Hoiles	.10	.05	.01
☐ 100 Brad Ausmus	.10	.05	.01
☐ 101 Wes Chamberlain	.10	.05	.01
☐ 102 Mark Dewey	.10	.05	.01
☐ 103 Benji Gil	.10	.05	.01
☐ 104 John Dopson	.10	.05	.01
☐ 105 John Smiley	.10	.05	.01
☐ 106 David Nied	.10	.05	.01
☐ 107 George Brett	1.25	.55	.16
☐ 108 Kirk Gibson	.20	.09	.03
☐ 109 Larry Casian	.10	.05	.01
☐ 110 Checklist 1-82 Ryne Sandberg	.20	.09	.03
☐ 111 Brent Gates	.10	.05	.01
☐ 112 Damion Easley	.10	.05	.01
☐ 113 Pete Harnisch	.10	.05	.01
☐ 114 Danny Cox	.10	.05	.01
☐ 115 Kevin Tapani	.10	.05	.01
☐ 116 Roberto Hernandez	.20	.09	.03
☐ 117 Domingo Jean	.10	.05	.01
☐ 118 Sid Bream	.10	.05	.01
☐ 119 Doug Henry	.10	.05	.01
☐ 120 Omar Olivares	.10	.05	.01
☐ 121 Mike Harkey	.10	.05	.01
☐ 122 Carlos Hernandez	.10	.05	.01
☐ 123 Jeff Fassero	.10	.05	.01
☐ 124 Dave Burba	.10	.05	.01
☐ 125 Wayne Kirby	.10	.05	.01
☐ 126 John Cummings	.10	.05	.01
☐ 127 Bret Barberie	.10	.05	.01
☐ 128 Todd Hundley	.20	.09	.03
☐ 129 Tim Hulett	.10	.05	.01
☐ 130 Phil Clark	.10	.05	.01
☐ 131 Danny Jackson	.10	.05	.01
☐ 132 Tom Foley	.10	.05	.01
☐ 133 Donald Harris	.10	.05	.01
☐ 134 Scott Fletcher	.10	.05	.01
☐ 135 Johnny Ruffin	.10	.05	.01
☐ 136 Jerald Clark	.10	.05	.01
☐ 137 Billy Brewer	.10	.05	.01
☐ 138 Dan Gladden	.10	.05	.01
☐ 139 Eddie Guardado	.10	.05	.01
☐ 140 Checklist 83-164 Cal Ripken	.30	.14	.04
☐ 141 Scott Hemond	.10	.05	.01
☐ 142 Steve Frey	.10	.05	.01
☐ 143 Xavier Hernandez	.10	.05	.01
☐ 144 Mark Eichhorn	.10	.05	.01
☐ 145 Ellis Burks	.20	.09	.03
☐ 146 Jim Leyritz	.10	.05	.01
☐ 147 Mark Lemke	.10	.05	.01
☐ 148 Pat Listach	.10	.05	.01
☐ 149 Donovan Osborne	.10	.05	.01
☐ 150 Glenallen Hill	.10	.05	.01
☐ 151 Orel Hershiser	.20	.09	.03
☐ 152 Darrin Fletcher	.10	.05	.01
☐ 153 Royce Clayton	.20	.09	.03
☐ 154 Derek Lilliquist	.10	.05	.01
☐ 155 Mike Felder	.10	.05	.01
☐ 156 Jeff Conine	.20	.09	.03
☐ 157 Ryan Thompson	.10	.05	.01
☐ 158 Ben McDonald	.10	.05	.01
☐ 159 Ricky Gutierrez	.10	.05	.01
☐ 160 Terry Mulholland	.10	.05	.01
☐ 161 Carlos Garcia	.10	.05	.01
☐ 162 Tom Henke	.10	.05	.01
☐ 163 Mike Greenwell	.10	.05	.01
☐ 164 Thomas Howard	.10	.05	.01
☐ 165 Joe Girardi	.10	.05	.01
☐ 166 Hubie Brooks	.10	.05	.01
☐ 167 Greg Gohr	.10	.05	.01
☐ 168 Chip Hale	.10	.05	.01

☐ 169 Rick Honeycutt .10 .05 .01
☐ 170 Hilly Hathaway .10 .05 .01
☐ 171 Todd Jones .10 .05 .01
☐ 172 Tony Fernandez .10 .05 .01
☐ 173 Bo Jackson .20 .09 .03
☐ 174 Bobby Munoz .10 .05 .01
☐ 175 Greg McMichael .10 .05 .01
☐ 176 Graeme Lloyd .10 .05 .01
☐ 177 Tom Pagnozzi .10 .05 .01
☐ 178 Derrick May .10 .05 .01
☐ 179 Pedro Martinez .30 .14 .04
☐ 180 Ken Hill .10 .05 .01
☐ 181 Bryan Hickerson .10 .05 .01
☐ 182 Jose Mesa .20 .09 .03
☐ 183 Dave Fleming .10 .05 .01
☐ 184 Henry Cotto .10 .05 .01
☐ 185 Jeff Kent .10 .05 .01
☐ 186 Mark McLemore .10 .05 .01
☐ 187 Trevor Hoffman .20 .09 .03
☐ 188 Todd Pratt .10 .05 .01
☐ 189 Blas Minor .10 .05 .01
☐ 190 Charlie Leibrandt .10 .05 .01
☐ 191 Tony Pena .10 .05 .01
☐ 192 Larry Luebbers .10 .05 .01
☐ 193 Greg W. Harris .10 .05 .01
☐ 194 David Cone .20 .09 .03
☐ 195 Bill Gullickson .10 .05 .01
☐ 196 Brian Harper .10 .05 .01
☐ 197 Steve Karsay .10 .05 .01
☐ 198 Greg Myers .10 .05 .01
☐ 199 Mark Portugal .10 .05 .01
☐ 200 Pat Hentgen .20 .09 .03
☐ 201 Mike LaValliere .10 .05 .01
☐ 202 Mike Stanley .10 .05 .01
☐ 203 Kent Mercker .10 .05 .01
☐ 204 Dave Nilsson .20 .09 .03
☐ 205 Erik Pappas .10 .05 .01
☐ 206 Mike Morgan .10 .05 .01
☐ 207 Roger McDowell .10 .05 .01
☐ 208 Mike Lansing .20 .09 .03
☐ 209 Kirt Manwaring .10 .05 .01
☐ 210 Randy Milligan .10 .05 .01
☐ 211 Erik Hanson .10 .05 .01
☐ 212 Orestes Destrade .10 .05 .01
☐ 213 Mike Maddux .10 .05 .01
☐ 214 Alan Mills .10 .05 .01
☐ 215 Tim Mauser .10 .05 .01
☐ 216 Ben Rivera .10 .05 .01
☐ 217 Don Slaught .10 .05 .01
☐ 218 Bob Patterson .10 .05 .01
☐ 219 Carlos Quintana .10 .05 .01
☐ 220 Checklist 165-247 .20 .09 .03
Tim Raines
☐ 221 Hal Morris .10 .05 .01
☐ 222 Darren Holmes .10 .05 .01
☐ 223 Chris Gwynn .10 .05 .01
☐ 224 Chad Kreuter .10 .05 .01
☐ 225 Mike Hartley .10 .05 .01
☐ 226 Scott Lydy .10 .05 .01
☐ 227 Eduardo Perez .10 .05 .01
☐ 228 Greg Swindell .10 .05 .01
☐ 229 Al Leiter .20 .09 .03
☐ 230 Scott Radinsky .10 .05 .01
☐ 231 Bob Wickman .10 .05 .01
☐ 232 Otis Nixon .10 .05 .01
☐ 233 Kevin Reimer .10 .05 .01
☐ 234 Geronimo Pena .10 .05 .01
☐ 235 Kevin Roberson .10 .05 .01
☐ 236 Jody Reed .10 .05 .01
☐ 237 Kirk Rueter .10 .05 .01
☐ 238 Willie McGee .10 .05 .01
☐ 239 Charles Nagy .20 .09 .03
☐ 240 Tim Leary .10 .05 .01
☐ 241 Carl Everett .10 .05 .01
☐ 242 Charlie O'Brien .10 .05 .01
☐ 243 Mike Pagliarulo .10 .05 .01
☐ 244 Kerry Taylor .10 .05 .01
☐ 245 Kevin Stocker .10 .05 .01
☐ 246 Joel Johnston .10 .05 .01
☐ 247 Geno Petralli .10 .05 .01
☐ 248 Jeff Russell .10 .05 .01
☐ 249 Joe Oliver .10 .05 .01
☐ 250 Roberto Mejia .10 .05 .01
☐ 251 Chris Haney .10 .05 .01
☐ 252 Bill Krueger .10 .05 .01
☐ 253 Shane Mack .10 .05 .01
☐ 254 Terry Steinbach .20 .09 .03
☐ 255 Luis Polonia .10 .05 .01
☐ 256 Eddie Taubensee .10 .05 .01
☐ 257 Dave Stewart .20 .09 .03
☐ 258 Tim Raines .30 .14 .04
☐ 259 Bernie Williams .60 .25 .07
☐ 260 John Smoltz .30 .14 .04
☐ 261 Kevin Seitzer .10 .05 .01
☐ 262 Bob Tewksbury .10 .05 .01
☐ 263 Bob Scanlan .10 .05 .01
☐ 264 Henry Rodriguez .20 .09 .03
☐ 265 Tim Scott .10 .05 .01
☐ 266 Scott Sanderson .10 .05 .01
☐ 267 Eric Plunk .10 .05 .01
☐ 268 Edgar Martinez .20 .09 .03
☐ 269 Charlie Hough .10 .05 .01
☐ 270 Joe Orsulak .10 .05 .01
☐ 271 Harold Reynolds .10 .05 .01
☐ 272 Tim Teufel .10 .05 .01
☐ 273 Bobby Thigpen .10 .05 .01
☐ 274 Randy Tomlin .10 .05 .01
☐ 275 Gary Redus .10 .05 .01
☐ 276 Ken Ryan .10 .05 .01
☐ 277 Tim Pugh .10 .05 .01
☐ 278 J. Owens .10 .05 .01
☐ 279 Phil Hiatt .10 .05 .01
☐ 280 Alan Trammell .20 .09 .03
☐ 281 Dave McCarty .10 .05 .01
☐ 282 Bob Welch .10 .05 .01
☐ 283 J.T. Snow .20 .09 .03
☐ 284 Brian Williams .10 .05 .01
☐ 285 Devon White .10 .05 .01
☐ 286 Steve Sax .10 .05 .01
☐ 287 Tony Tarasco .10 .05 .01
☐ 288 Bill Spiers .10 .05 .01
☐ 289 Allen Watson .10 .05 .01
☐ 290 Checklist 248-330 .20 .09 .03
Rickey Henderson
☐ 291 Jose Vizcaino .10 .05 .01
☐ 292 Darryl Strawberry .20 .09 .03
☐ 293 John Wetteland .20 .09 .03
☐ 294 Bill Swift .10 .05 .01
☐ 295 Jeff Treadway .10 .05 .01
☐ 296 Tino Martinez .20 .09 .03
☐ 297 Richie Lewis .10 .05 .01
☐ 298 Bret Saberhagen .20 .09 .03
☐ 299 Arthur Rhodes .10 .05 .01
☐ 300 Guillermo Velasquez .10 .05 .01
☐ 301 Milt Thompson .10 .05 .01
☐ 302 Doug Strange .10 .05 .01
☐ 303 Aaron Sele .20 .09 .03
☐ 304 Bip Roberts .10 .05 .01
☐ 305 Bruce Ruffin .10 .05 .01
☐ 306 Jose Lind .10 .05 .01
☐ 307 David Wells .10 .05 .01
☐ 308 Bobby Witt .10 .05 .01
☐ 309 Mark Wohlers .20 .09 .03
☐ 310 B.J. Surhoff .10 .05 .01
☐ 311 Mark Whiten .10 .05 .01
☐ 312 Turk Wendell .10 .05 .01
☐ 313 Raul Mondesi .30 .14 .04
☐ 314 Brian Turang .10 .05 .01
☐ 315 Chris Hammond .10 .05 .01
☐ 316 Tim Bogar .10 .05 .01
☐ 317 Brad Pennington .10 .05 .01
☐ 318 Tim Worrell .10 .05 .01
☐ 319 Mitch Williams .10 .05 .01
☐ 320 Rondell White .30 .14 .04
☐ 321 Frank Viola .10 .05 .01
☐ 322 Manny Ramirez 1.00 .45 .12
☐ 323 Gary Wayne .10 .05 .01
☐ 324 Mike Macfarlane .10 .05 .01
☐ 325 Russ Springer .10 .05 .01
☐ 326 Tim Wallach .10 .05 .01
☐ 327 Salomon Torres .10 .05 .01
☐ 328 Omar Vizquel .20 .09 .03
☐ 329 Andy Tomberlin .10 .05 .01
☐ 330 Chris Sabo .10 .05 .01
☐ 331 Mike Mussina .60 .25 .07
☐ 332 Andy Benes .20 .09 .03
☐ 333 Darren Daulton .20 .09 .03
☐ 334 Orlando Merced .20 .09 .03
☐ 335 Mark McGwire 1.00 .45 .12
☐ 336 Dave Winfield .30 .14 .04
☐ 337 Sammy Sosa .30 .14 .04
☐ 338 Eric Karros .20 .09 .03
☐ 339 Greg Vaughn .30 .14 .04
☐ 340 Don Mattingly 1.50 .70 .19
☐ 341 Frank Thomas 3.00 1.35 .35
☐ 342 Fred McGriff .30 .14 .04
☐ 343 Kirby Puckett 1.25 .55 .16
☐ 344 Roberto Kelly .10 .05 .01
☐ 345 Wally Joyner .20 .09 .03
☐ 346 Andres Galarraga .30 .14 .04
☐ 347 Bobby Bonilla .20 .09 .03
☐ 348 Benito Santiago .10 .05 .01
☐ 349 Barry Bonds .75 .35 .09
☐ 350 Delino DeShields .10 .05 .01
☐ 351 Albert Belle 1.25 .55 .16
☐ 352 Randy Johnson .30 .14 .04
☐ 353 Tim Salmon .30 .14 .04
☐ 354 John Olerud .10 .05 .01
☐ 355 Dean Palmer .20 .09 .03
☐ 356 Roger Clemens .60 .25 .07
☐ 357 Jim Abbott .10 .05 .01
☐ 358 Mark Grace .30 .14 .04
☐ 359 Ozzie Guillen .10 .05 .01
☐ 360 Lou Whitaker .20 .09 .03
☐ 361 Jose Rijo .10 .05 .01
☐ 362 Jeff Montgomery .20 .09 .03
☐ 363 Chuck Finley .10 .05 .01
☐ 364 Tom Glavine .30 .14 .04
☐ 365 Jeff Bagwell 1.25 .55 .16
☐ 366 Joe Carter .20 .09 .03
☐ 367 Ray Lankford .20 .09 .03
☐ 368 Ramon Martinez .20 .09 .03
☐ 369 Jay Buhner .30 .14 .04
☐ 370 Matt Williams .30 .14 .04
☐ 371 Larry Walker .30 .14 .04
☐ 372 Jose Canseco .30 .14 .04
☐ 373 Lenny Dykstra .20 .09 .03
☐ 374 Bryan Harvey .10 .05 .01
☐ 375 Andy Van Slyke .20 .09 .03
☐ 376 Ivan Rodriguez .75 .35 .09
☐ 377 Kevin Mitchell .20 .09 .03
☐ 378 Travis Fryman .20 .09 .03
☐ 379 Duane Ward .10 .05 .01
☐ 380 Greg Maddux 2.00 .90 .25
☐ 381 Scott Servais .10 .05 .01
☐ 382 Greg Olson .10 .05 .01
☐ 383 Rey Sanchez .10 .05 .01
☐ 384 Tom Kramer .10 .05 .01
☐ 385 David Valle .10 .05 .01
☐ 386 Eddie Murray .75 .35 .09
☐ 387 Kevin Higgins .10 .05 .01
☐ 388 Dan Wilson .20 .09 .03
☐ 389 Todd Frohwith .10 .05 .01
☐ 390 Gerald Williams .10 .05 .01
☐ 391 Hipolito Pichardo .10 .05 .01
☐ 392 Pat Meares .10 .05 .01
☐ 393 Luis Lopez .10 .05 .01
☐ 394 Ricky Jordan .10 .05 .01
☐ 395 Bob Walk .10 .05 .01
☐ 396 Sid Fernandez .10 .05 .01
☐ 397 Todd Worrell .10 .05 .01
☐ 398 Darryl Hamilton .10 .05 .01
☐ 399 Randy Myers .10 .05 .01
☐ 400 Rod Brewer .10 .05 .01
☐ 401 Lance Blankenship .10 .05 .01
☐ 402 Steve Finley .30 .14 .04
☐ 403 Phil Leftwich .10 .05 .01
☐ 404 Juan Guzman .20 .09 .03
☐ 405 Anthony Young .10 .05 .01
☐ 406 Jeff Gardner .10 .05 .01
☐ 407 Ryan Bowen .10 .05 .01
☐ 408 Fernando Valenzuela .20 .09 .03
☐ 409 David West .10 .05 .01
☐ 410 Kenny Rogers .10 .05 .01
☐ 411 Bob Zupcic .10 .05 .01
☐ 412 Eric Young .20 .09 .03
☐ 413 Bret Boone .20 .09 .03
☐ 414 Danny Tartabull .10 .05 .01
☐ 415 Bob MacDonald .10 .05 .01
☐ 416 Ron Karkovice .10 .05 .01
☐ 417 Scott Cooper .10 .05 .01
☐ 418 Dante Bichette .30 .14 .04
☐ 419 Tripp Cromer .10 .05 .01
☐ 420 Billy Ashley .10 .05 .01
☐ 421 Roger Smithberg .10 .05 .01
☐ 422 Dennis Martinez .20 .09 .03
☐ 423 Mike Blowers .10 .05 .01
☐ 424 Darren Lewis .10 .05 .01
☐ 425 Junior Ortiz .10 .05 .01
☐ 426 Butch Huskey .20 .09 .03
☐ 427 Jimmy Poole .10 .05 .01
☐ 428 Walt Weiss .10 .05 .01
☐ 429 Scott Bankhead .10 .05 .01
☐ 430 Deion Sanders .30 .14 .04
☐ 431 Scott Bullett .10 .05 .01
☐ 432 Jeff Huson .10 .05 .01
☐ 433 Tyler Green .10 .05 .01
☐ 434 Billy Hatcher .10 .05 .01
☐ 435 Bob Hamelin .10 .05 .01
☐ 436 Reggie Sanders .20 .09 .03
☐ 437 Scott Erickson .10 .05 .01
☐ 438 Steve Reed .10 .05 .01
☐ 439 Randy Velarde .10 .05 .01
☐ 440 Checklist 331-412 .30 .14 .04
(Tony Gwynn)
☐ 441 Terry Leach .10 .05 .01
☐ 442 Danny Bautista .10 .05 .01
☐ 443 Kent Hrbek .20 .09 .03
☐ 444 Rick Wilkins .10 .05 .01
☐ 445 Tony Phillips .20 .09 .03
☐ 446 Dion James .10 .05 .01
☐ 447 Joey Cora .10 .05 .01
☐ 448 Andre Dawson .20 .09 .03
☐ 449 Pedro Castellano .10 .05 .01
☐ 450 Tom Gordon .10 .05 .01
☐ 451 Rob Dibble .10 .05 .01
☐ 452 Ron Darling .10 .05 .01
☐ 453 Chipper Jones 2.50 1.10 .30
☐ 454 Joe Grahe .10 .05 .01
☐ 455 Domingo Cedeno .10 .05 .01
☐ 456 Tom Edens .10 .05 .01
☐ 457 Mitch Webster .10 .05 .01
☐ 458 Jose Bautista .10 .05 .01
☐ 459 Troy O'Leary .10 .05 .01
☐ 460 Todd Zeile .10 .05 .01
☐ 461 Sean Berry .10 .05 .01
☐ 462 Brad Holman .10 .05 .01
☐ 463 Dave Martinez .10 .05 .01
☐ 464 Mark Lewis .10 .05 .01
☐ 465 Paul Carey .10 .05 .01
☐ 466 Jack Armstrong .10 .05 .01
☐ 467 David Telgheder .10 .05 .01
☐ 468 Gene Harris .10 .05 .01
☐ 469 Danny Darwin .10 .05 .01
☐ 470 Kim Batiste .10 .05 .01
☐ 471 Tim Wakefield .10 .05 .01
☐ 472 Craig Lefferts .10 .05 .01
☐ 473 Jacob Brumfield .10 .05 .01
☐ 474 Lance Painter .10 .05 .01
☐ 475 Milt Cuyler .10 .05 .01
☐ 476 Melido Perez .10 .05 .01
☐ 477 Derek Parks .10 .05 .01
☐ 478 Gary DiSarcina .10 .05 .01
☐ 479 Steve Bedrosian .10 .05 .01
☐ 480 Eric Anthony .10 .05 .01
☐ 481 Julio Franco .20 .09 .03
☐ 482 Tommy Greene .10 .05 .01
☐ 483 Pat Kelly .10 .05 .01
☐ 484 Nate Minchey .10 .05 .01
☐ 485 William Pennyfeather .10 .05 .01
☐ 486 Harold Baines .20 .09 .03
☐ 487 Howard Johnson .10 .05 .01
☐ 488 Angel Miranda .10 .05 .01
☐ 489 Scott Sanders .10 .05 .01
☐ 490 Shawon Dunston .10 .05 .01
☐ 491 Mel Rojas .10 .05 .01
☐ 492 Jeff Nelson .10 .05 .01
☐ 493 Archi Cianfrocco .10 .05 .01
☐ 494 Al Martin .10 .05 .01
☐ 495 Mike Gallego .10 .05 .01
☐ 496 Mike Henneman .10 .05 .01
☐ 497 Armando Reynoso .10 .05 .01
☐ 498 Mickey Morandini .10 .05 .01
☐ 499 Rick Renteria .10 .05 .01
☐ 500 Rick Sutcliffe .10 .05 .01
☐ 501 Bobby Jones .20 .09 .03
☐ 502 Gary Gaetti .20 .09 .03
☐ 503 Rick Aguilera .10 .05 .01
☐ 504 Todd Stottlemyre .10 .05 .01
☐ 505 Mike Mohler .10 .05 .01
☐ 506 Mike Stanton .10 .05 .01
☐ 507 Jose Guzman .10 .05 .01
☐ 508 Kevin Rogers .10 .05 .01
☐ 509 Chuck Carr .10 .05 .01
☐ 510 Chris Jones .10 .05 .01
☐ 511 Brent Mayne .10 .05 .01
☐ 512 Greg Harris .10 .05 .01
☐ 513 Dave Henderson .10 .05 .01
☐ 514 Eric Hillman .10 .05 .01
☐ 515 Dan Peltier .10 .05 .01
☐ 516 Craig Shipley .10 .05 .01
☐ 517 John Valentin .20 .09 .03
☐ 518 Wilson Alvarez .20 .09 .03
☐ 519 Andujar Cedeno .10 .05 .01
☐ 520 Troy Neel .10 .05 .01
☐ 521 Tom Candiotti .10 .05 .01
☐ 522 Matt Mieske .10 .05 .01
☐ 523 Jim Thome .75 .35 .09
☐ 524 Lou Frazier .10 .05 .01
☐ 525 Mike Jackson .10 .05 .01
☐ 526 Pedro Martinez .20 .09 .03
☐ 527 Roger Pavlik .10 .05 .01
☐ 528 Kent Bottenfield .10 .05 .01
☐ 529 Felix Jose .10 .05 .01
☐ 530 Mark Guthrie .10 .05 .01
☐ 531 Steve Farr .10 .05 .01
☐ 532 Craig Paquette .10 .05 .01
☐ 533 Doug Jones .10 .05 .01
☐ 534 Luis Alicea .10 .05 .01
☐ 535 Cory Snyder .10 .05 .01
☐ 536 Paul Sorrento .10 .05 .01
☐ 537 Nigel Wilson .10 .05 .01
☐ 538 Jeff King .20 .09 .03
☐ 539 Willie Greene .20 .09 .03
☐ 540 Kirk McCaskill .10 .05 .01
☐ 541 Al Osuna .10 .05 .01
☐ 542 Greg Hibbard .10 .05 .01
☐ 543 Brett Butler .20 .09 .03
☐ 544 Jose Valentin .20 .09 .03
☐ 545 Wil Cordero .20 .09 .03
☐ 546 Chris Bosio .10 .05 .01
☐ 547 Jamie Moyer .10 .05 .01
☐ 548 Jim Eisenreich .10 .05 .01
☐ 549 Vinny Castilla .30 .14 .04
☐ 550 Checklist 413-494 .30 .14 .04
(Dave Winfield)
☐ 551 John Roper .10 .05 .01
☐ 552 Lance Johnson .20 .09 .03
☐ 553 Scott Kamieniecki .10 .05 .01
☐ 554 Mike Moore .10 .05 .01
☐ 555 Steve Buechele .10 .05 .01
☐ 556 Terry Pendleton .20 .09 .03
☐ 557 Todd Van Poppel .10 .05 .01
☐ 558 Rob Butler .10 .05 .01
☐ 559 Zane Smith .10 .05 .01
☐ 560 David Hulse .10 .05 .01
☐ 561 Tim Costo .10 .05 .01
☐ 562 John Habyan .10 .05 .01
☐ 563 Terry Jorgensen .10 .05 .01
☐ 564 Matt Nokes .10 .05 .01
☐ 565 Kevin McReynolds .10 .05 .01
☐ 566 Phil Plantier .10 .05 .01
☐ 567 Chris Turner .10 .05 .01
☐ 568 Carlos Delgado .30 .14 .04
☐ 569 John Jaha .20 .09 .03
☐ 570 Dwight Smith .10 .05 .01
☐ 571 John Vander Wal .10 .05 .01
☐ 572 Trevor Wilson .10 .05 .01
☐ 573 Felix Fermin .10 .05 .01
☐ 574 Marc Newfield .20 .09 .03
☐ 575 Jeromy Burnitz .10 .05 .01
☐ 576 Leo Gomez .10 .05 .01
☐ 577 Curt Schilling .10 .05 .01
☐ 578 Kevin Young .10 .05 .01
☐ 579 Jerry Spradlin .10 .05 .01
☐ 580 Curt Leskanic .10 .05 .01
☐ 581 Carl Willis .10 .05 .01
☐ 582 Alex Fernandez .20 .09 .03
☐ 583 Mark Holzemer .10 .05 .01
☐ 584 Domingo Martinez .10 .05 .01

☐ 585 Pete Smith	.10	.05	.01
☐ 586 Brian Jordan	.30	.14	.04
☐ 587 Kevin Gross	.10	.05	.01
☐ 588 J.R. Phillips	.10	.05	.01
☐ 589 Chris Nabholz	.10	.05	.01
☐ 590 Bill Wertz	.10	.05	.01
☐ 591 Derek Bell	.20	.09	.03
☐ 592 Brady Anderson	.30	.14	.04
☐ 593 Matt Turner	.10	.05	.01
☐ 594 Pete Incaviglia	.10	.05	.01
☐ 595 Greg Gagne	.10	.05	.01
☐ 596 John Flaherty	.10	.05	.01
☐ 597 Scott Livingstone	.10	.05	.01
☐ 598 Rod Bolton	.10	.05	.01
☐ 599 Mike Perez	.10	.05	.01
☐ 600 Checklist 495-577 (Roger Clemens)	.30	.14	.04
☐ 601 Tony Castillo	.10	.05	.01
☐ 602 Henry Mercedes	.10	.05	.01
☐ 603 Mike Fetters	.10	.05	.01
☐ 604 Rod Beck	.20	.09	.03
☐ 605 Damon Buford	.10	.05	.01
☐ 606 Matt Whiteside	.10	.05	.01
☐ 607 Shawn Green	.20	.09	.03
☐ 608 Midre Cummings	.10	.05	.01
☐ 609 Jeff McNeely	.10	.05	.01
☐ 610 Danny Sheaffer	.10	.05	.01
☐ 611 Paul Wagner	.10	.05	.01
☐ 612 Torey Lovullo	.10	.05	.01
☐ 613 Javier Lopez	.30	.14	.04
☐ 614 Mariano Duncan	.10	.05	.01
☐ 615 Doug Brocail	.10	.05	.01
☐ 616 Dave Hansen	.10	.05	.01
☐ 617 Ryan Klesko	.60	.25	.07
☐ 618 Eric Davis	.20	.09	.03
☐ 619 Scott Ruffcorn	.10	.05	.01
☐ 620 Mike Trombley	.10	.05	.01
☐ 621 Jaime Navarro	.10	.05	.01
☐ 622 Rheal Cormier	.10	.05	.01
☐ 623 Jose Offerman	.10	.05	.01
☐ 624 David Segui	.10	.05	.01
☐ 625 Robb Nen	.20	.09	.03
☐ 626 Dave Gallagher	.10	.05	.01
☐ 627 Julian Tavarez	.20	.09	.03
☐ 628 Chris Gomez	.10	.05	.01
☐ 629 Jeffrey Hammonds	.20	.09	.03
☐ 630 Scott Brosius	.10	.05	.01
☐ 631 Willie Blair	.10	.05	.01
☐ 632 Doug Drabek	.10	.05	.01
☐ 633 Bill Wegman	.10	.05	.01
☐ 634 Jeff McKnight	.10	.05	.01
☐ 635 Rich Rodriguez	.10	.05	.01
☐ 636 Steve Trachsel	.20	.09	.03
☐ 637 Buddy Groom	.10	.05	.01
☐ 638 Sterling Hitchcock	.20	.09	.03
☐ 639 Chuck McElroy	.10	.05	.01
☐ 640 Rene Gonzales	.10	.05	.01
☐ 641 Dan Plesac	.10	.05	.01
☐ 642 Jeff Branson	.10	.05	.01
☐ 643 Darrell Whitmore	.10	.05	.01
☐ 644 Paul Quantrill	.10	.05	.01
☐ 645 Rich Rowland	.10	.05	.01
☐ 646 Curtis Pride	.20	.09	.03
☐ 647 Erik Plantenberg	.10	.05	.01
☐ 648 Albie Lopez	.20	.09	.03
☐ 649 Rich Batchelor	.10	.05	.01
☐ 650 Lee Smith	.20	.09	.03
☐ 651 Cliff Floyd	.30	.14	.04
☐ 652 Pete Schourek	.20	.09	.03
☐ 653 Reggie Jefferson	.20	.09	.03
☐ 654 Bill Haselman	.10	.05	.01
☐ 655 Steve Hosey	.10	.05	.01
☐ 656 Mark Clark	.10	.05	.01
☐ 657 Mark Davis	.10	.05	.01
☐ 658 Dave Magadan	.10	.05	.01
☐ 659 Candy Maldonado	.10	.05	.01
☐ 660 Checklist 578-660 (Mark Langston)	.10	.05	.01

1994 Donruss Special Edition

Issued in two series of 50 cards, this 100-card standard-size set of 1994 Donruss Special Edition represents a Gold edition parallel of the best players in the game. The first 50 cards correspond to cards 1-50 in the first series, while the second 50 cards correspond to cards 331-380 in the second series. The cards were issued one per pack or two per jumbo pack. The full-bleed fronts display glossy color action photos accented by a holographic embossed foil stripe across the bottom containing the player's name and position.

	MINT	NRMT	EXC
COMPLETE SET (100)	20.00	9.00	2.50
COMPLETE SERIES 1 (50)	10.00	4.50	1.25
COMPLETE SERIES 2 (50)	10.00	4.50	1.25
COMMON CARD (1-50/331-380)	.20	.09	.03

*STARS: 1X to 2X BASIC CARDS

1994 Donruss Anniversary '84

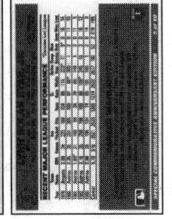

Randomly inserted in hobby foil packs at a rate of one in 12, this ten-card standard-size set reproduces selected cards from the 1984 Donruss baseball set. The cards feature white bordered color player photos on their fronts. The player's name appears in yellow lettering within a colored stripe at the bottom. The player's gold-foil team name is shown within wavy gold-foil lines near the bottom of the photo. The horizontal and white-bordered back carries the player's name and biography within a green-colored stripe across the top. A white area below contains the player's stats and, within a green panel further below, his career highlights. The cards are numbered on the back at the bottom right as "X of 10," and also carry the numbers from the original 1984 set at the upper left.

	MINT	NRMT	EXC
COMPLETE SET (10)	50.00	22.00	6.25
COMMON CARD (1-10)	2.00	.90	.25
☐ 1 Joe Carter	2.00	.90	.25
☐ 2 Robin Yount	3.50	1.55	.45
☐ 3 George Brett	6.00	2.70	.75
☐ 4 Rickey Henderson	3.50	1.55	.45
☐ 5 Nolan Ryan	15.00	6.75	1.85
☐ 6 Cal Ripken	15.00	6.75	1.85
☐ 7 Wade Boggs UER (1983 runs 10, should be 100)	3.50	1.55	.45
☐ 8 Don Mattingly	10.00	4.50	1.25
☐ 9 Ryne Sandberg	5.00	2.20	.60
☐ 10 Tony Gwynn	6.00	2.70	.75

1994 Donruss Award Winner Jumbos

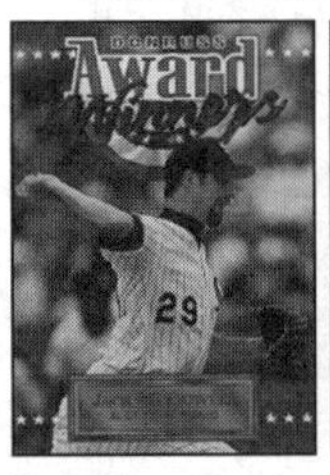

This 10-card set was issued one per jumbo foil and Canadian foil boxes and spotlights players that won various awards in 1993. Cards 1-5 were included in first series boxes and 6-10 with the second series. The cards measure approximately 3 1/2" by 5". Ten-thousand of each card were produced. Card fronts are full-bleed with a color player photo and the Award Winner logo at the top. The backs are individually numbered out of 10,000.

	MINT	NRMT	EXC
COMPLETE SET (10)	90.00	40.00	11.00
COMPLETE SERIES 1 (5)	50.00	22.00	6.25
COMPLETE SERIES 2 (5)	40.00	18.00	5.00
COMMON CARD (1-10)	3.00	1.35	.35
☐ 1 Barry Bonds MVP	8.00	3.60	1.00
☐ 2 Greg Maddux CY	20.00	9.00	2.50
☐ 3 Mike Piazza ROY	20.00	9.00	2.50
☐ 4 Barry Bonds HR King	8.00	3.60	1.00
☐ 5 Kirby Puckett AS MVP	12.00	5.50	1.50
☐ 6 Frank Thomas MVP	30.00	13.50	3.70
☐ 7 Jack McDowell CY	3.00	1.35	.35
☐ 8 Tim Salmon ROY	5.00	2.20	.60
☐ 9 Juan Gonzalez HR King	15.00	6.75	1.85
☐ 10 Paul Molitor WS MVP	6.00	2.70	.75

1994 Donruss Diamond Kings

This 30-card standard-size set was split in two series. Cards 1-14 and 29 were randomly inserted in first series packs, while cards 15-28 and 30 were inserted in second series packs. With each series, the insertion rate was one in nine. The fronts feature full-bleed player portraits by noted sports artist Dick Perez. The cards are numbered on the back with the prefix DK. Jumbo versions of these cards were inserted one per retail box.

	MINT	NRMT	EXC
COMPLETE SET (30)	50.00	22.00	6.25
COMPLETE SERIES 1 (15)	25.00	11.00	3.10
COMPLETE SERIES 2 (15)	25.00	11.00	3.10
COMMON CARD (1-30)	.50	.23	.06

*JUMBO DK's: 1X TO 2X BASIC CARDS

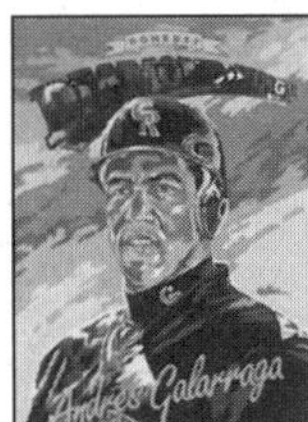
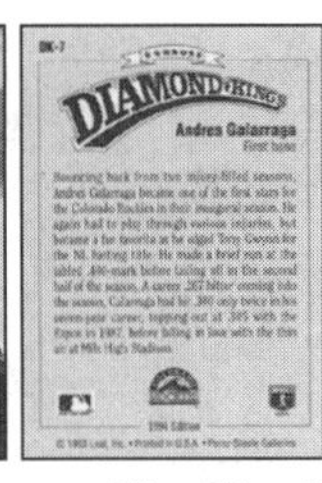

☐ 1 Barry Bonds	2.50	1.10	.30
☐ 2 Mo Vaughn	2.50	1.10	.30
☐ 3 Steve Avery	.75	.35	.09
☐ 4 Tim Salmon	1.50	.70	.19
☐ 5 Rick Wilkins	.50	.23	.06
☐ 6 Brian Harper	.50	.23	.06
☐ 7 Andres Galarraga	1.00	.45	.12
☐ 8 Albert Belle	4.00	1.80	.50
☐ 9 John Kruk	.75	.35	.09
☐ 10 Ivan Rodriguez	2.50	1.10	.30
☐ 11 Tony Gwynn	4.00	1.80	.50
☐ 12 Brian McRae	.50	.23	.06
☐ 13 Bobby Bonilla	.75	.35	.09
☐ 14 Ken Griffey Jr.	10.00	4.50	1.25
☐ 15 Mike Piazza	6.00	2.70	.75
☐ 16 Don Mattingly	5.00	2.20	.60
☐ 17 Barry Larkin	1.00	.45	.12
☐ 18 Ruben Sierra	.75	.35	.09
☐ 19 Orlando Merced	.50	.23	.06
☐ 20 Greg Vaughn	1.00	.45	.12
☐ 21 Gregg Jefferies	1.00	.45	.12
☐ 22 Cecil Fielder	.75	.35	.09
☐ 23 Moises Alou	.75	.35	.09
☐ 24 John Olerud	.75	.35	.09
☐ 25 Gary Sheffield	1.50	.70	.19
☐ 26 Mike Mussina	2.00	.90	.25
☐ 27 Jeff Bagwell	4.00	1.80	.50
☐ 28 Frank Thomas	10.00	4.50	1.25
☐ 29 Dave Winfield	1.00	.45	.12
☐ 30 Checklist	.50	.23	.06

1994 Donruss Dominators

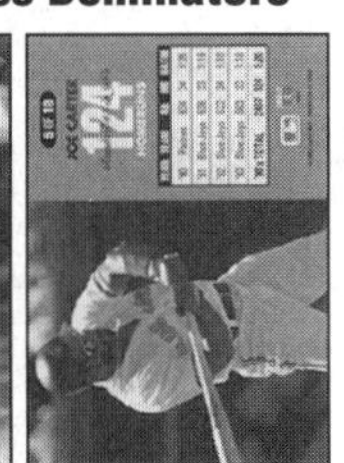

This 20-card, standard-size set was randomly inserted in all packs at a rate of one in 12. The 10 series 1 cards feature the top home run hitters of the '90s, while the 10 series 2 cards depict the decade's batting average leaders. The fronts displayed full-bleed color action shots with the set title printed along the bottom in gold and black lettering. Jumbo Dominators (3 1/2" by 5") were issued one per hobby box.

	MINT	NRMT	EXC
COMPLETE SET (20)	50.00	22.00	6.25
COMPLETE SER.1 SET (10)	20.00	9.00	2.50
COMPLETE SER.2 SET (10)	30.00	13.50	3.70
COMMON SER.1 CARD (A1-A10)	.60	.25	.07
COMMON SER.2 CARD (B1-B10)	.60	.25	.07

*JUMBOS: 1X TO 2X BASIC CARDS

☐ A1 Cecil Fielder	1.25	.55	.16
☐ A2 Barry Bonds	2.50	1.10	.30
☐ A3 Fred McGriff	1.50	.70	.19
☐ A4 Matt Williams	1.50	.70	.19
☐ A5 Joe Carter	1.25	.55	.16
☐ A6 Juan Gonzalez	5.00	2.20	.60
☐ A7 Jose Canseco	1.50	.70	.19
☐ A8 Ron Gant	1.25	.55	.16
☐ A9 Ken Griffey Jr.	10.00	4.50	1.25
☐ A10 Mark McGwire	3.00	1.35	.35
☐ B1 Tony Gwynn	4.00	1.80	.50
☐ B2 Frank Thomas	10.00	4.50	1.25
☐ B3 Paul Molitor	2.00	.90	.25
☐ B4 Edgar Martinez	1.25	.55	.16
☐ B5 Kirby Puckett	4.00	1.80	.50
☐ B6 Ken Griffey Jr.	10.00	4.50	1.25
☐ B7 Barry Bonds	2.50	1.10	.30
☐ B8 Willie McGee	.60	.25	.07
☐ B9 Lenny Dykstra	1.25	.55	.16
☐ B10 John Kruk	.60	.25	.07

1994 Donruss Elite

This 12-card set was issued in two series of six. Using a continued numbering system from previous years, cards 37-42 were randomly inserted in first series foil packs with cards 43-48 a second series offering. The cards measure the standard size. Only 10,000 of each card were produced. The color player photo inside a diamond design on the front rests on a marbleized panel framed by a red-and-white inner border and a silver foil outer border. Silver foil stripes radiate away from the edges of the picture. The player's name appears across

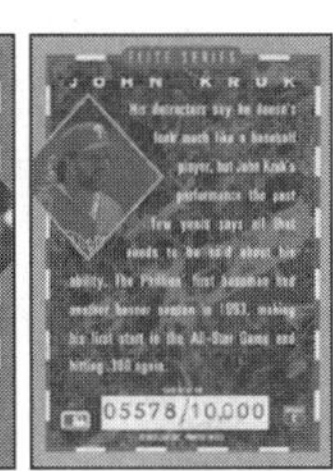

the bottom of the front. The back design is similar, but with a color head shot in a small diamond and a player profile, both resting on a marbleized panel. The bottom carries the card number, the serial number, and the production run figure.

	MINT	NRMT	EXC
COMPLETE SET (12)	200.00	90.00	25.00
COMPLETE SERIES 1 (6)	110.00	50.00	14.00
COMPLETE SERIES 2 (6)	90.00	40.00	11.00
COMMON CARD (37-48)	8.00	3.60	1.00
☐ 37 Frank Thomas	50.00	22.00	6.25
☐ 38 Tony Gwynn	20.00	9.00	2.50
☐ 39 Tim Salmon	10.00	4.50	1.25
☐ 40 Albert Belle	20.00	9.00	2.50
☐ 41 John Kruk	10.00	4.50	1.25
☐ 42 Juan Gonzalez	25.00	11.00	3.10
☐ 43 John Olerud	8.00	3.60	1.00
☐ 44 Barry Bonds	12.00	5.50	1.50
☐ 45 Ken Griffey Jr.	50.00	22.00	6.25
☐ 46 Mike Piazza	30.00	13.50	3.70
☐ 47 Jack McDowell	10.00	4.50	1.25
☐ 48 Andres Galarraga	10.00	4.50	1.25

1994 Donruss Long Ball Leaders

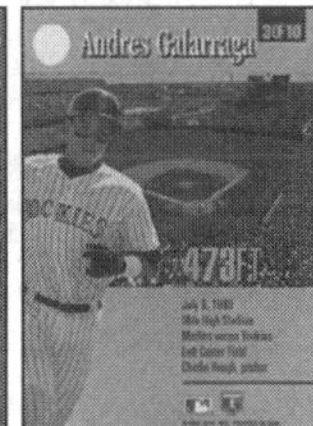

Inserted in second series hobby foil packs at a rate of one in 12, this 10-card standard-size set features some of top home run hitters and the distance of their longest home run of 1993. The card fronts have a color photo with a black right-hand border. Within the border is the Long Ball Leaders logo in silver foil. Also in silver foil at bottom, is the player's last name and the distance of the clout. Card backs contain a photo of the park with which the home run occurred as well as information such as the date, the pitcher and other particulars.

	MINT	NRMT	EXC
COMPLETE SET (10)	40.00	18.00	5.00
COMMON CARD (1-10)	1.00	.45	.12
☐ 1 Cecil Fielder	1.50	.70	.19
☐ 2 Dean Palmer	1.00	.45	.12
☐ 3 Andres Galarraga	2.50	1.10	.30
☐ 4 Bo Jackson	1.50	.70	.19
☐ 5 Ken Griffey Jr.	15.00	6.75	1.85
☐ 6 David Justice	1.00	.45	.12
☐ 7 Mike Piazza	10.00	4.50	1.25
☐ 8 Frank Thomas	15.00	6.75	1.85
☐ 9 Barry Bonds	4.00	1.80	.50
☐ 10 Juan Gonzalez	8.00	3.60	1.00

1994 Donruss MVPs

Inserted at a rate of one per first and second series jumbo pack, this 28-card standard-size set was split into two series of 14; one player for each team. The first 14 are of National League players with the latter group being American Leaguers. Full-bleed card fronts feature an action photo of the player with "MVP" in large red (American League) or blue (National) letters at the bottom. The player's name and, for Amercian League player cards only, team name are beneath the "MVP". A number of white stars stretches up the left border. The backs, which are horizontal, contain a photo, 1993 statistics, a short write-up and white stars within blue foil along the left border.

	MINT	NRMT	EXC
COMPLETE SET (28)	75.00	34.00	9.50
COMPLETE SERIES 1 (14)	15.00	6.75	1.85
COMPLETE SERIES 2 (14)	60.00	27.00	7.50
COMMON CARD (1-28)	.75	.35	.09
☐ 1 David Justice	1.50	.70	.19
☐ 2 Mark Grace	1.00	.45	.12
☐ 3 Jose Rijo	.75	.35	.09
☐ 4 Andres Galarraga	1.00	.45	.12
☐ 5 Bryan Harvey	.75	.35	.09
☐ 6 Jeff Bagwell	6.00	2.70	.75
☐ 7 Mike Piazza	10.00	4.50	1.25
☐ 8 Moises Alou	1.50	.70	.19
☐ 9 Bobby Bonilla	1.50	.70	.19
☐ 10 Len Dykstra	1.50	.70	.19
☐ 11 Jeff King	.75	.35	.09
☐ 12 Gregg Jefferies	1.50	.70	.19
☐ 13 Tony Gwynn	6.00	2.70	.75
☐ 14 Barry Bonds	4.00	1.80	.50
☐ 15 Cal Ripken Jr.	15.00	6.75	1.85
☐ 16 Mo Vaughn	4.00	1.80	.50
☐ 17 Tim Salmon	2.50	1.10	.30
☐ 18 Frank Thomas	15.00	6.75	1.85
☐ 19 Albert Belle	6.00	2.70	.75
☐ 20 Cecil Fielder	1.50	.70	.19
☐ 21 Wally Joyner	.75	.35	.09
☐ 22 Greg Vaughn	1.50	.70	.19
☐ 23 Kirby Puckett	6.00	2.70	.75
☐ 24 Don Mattingly	8.00	3.60	1.00
☐ 25 Ruben Sierra	.75	.35	.09
☐ 26 Ken Griffey Jr.	15.00	6.75	1.85
☐ 27 Juan Gonzalez	8.00	3.60	1.00
☐ 28 John Olerud	.75	.35	.09

1994 Donruss Spirit of the Game

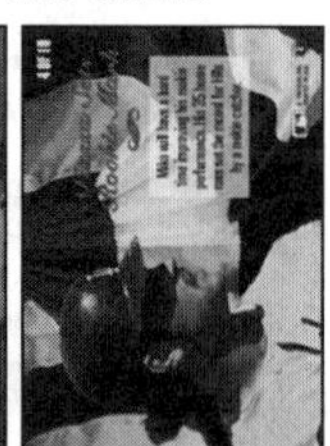

This ten card set features a selction of the games top stars. Cards 1-5 were randomly inserted in first-series magazine jumbo packs and cards 6-10 in second series magazine jumbo packs. Card fronts feature borderless, horizontal designs that have color action player photos superposed upon triple exposure sepia-toned action shots. Jumbo sized Spirit of the Game cards, individually numbered out of 10,000, were issued one per magazine jumbo box.

	MINT	NRMT	EXC
COMPLETE SET (10)	60.00	27.00	7.50
COMPLETE SERIES 1 (5)	30.00	13.50	3.70
COMPLETE SERIES 2 (5)	30.00	13.50	3.70
COMMON CARD (1-10)	1.00	.45	.12
*JUMBOS: 1X TO 2X BASIC SPIRIT OF THE GAME			
☐ 1 John Olerud	1.00	.45	.12
☐ 2 Barry Bonds	5.00	2.20	.60
☐ 3 Ken Griffey Jr.	20.00	9.00	2.50
☐ 4 Mike Piazza	12.00	5.50	1.50
☐ 5 Juan Gonzalez	10.00	4.50	1.25
☐ 6 Frank Thomas	20.00	9.00	2.50
☐ 7 Tim Salmon	3.00	1.35	.35
☐ 8 David Justice	2.00	.90	.25
☐ 9 Don Mattingly	10.00	4.50	1.25
☐ 10 Lenny Dykstra	2.00	.90	.25

1995 Donruss

The 1995 Donruss set consists of 550 standard-size cards. The first series had 330 cards while 220 cards comprised the second series. The fronts feature borderless color action player photos. A second, smaller color player photo in a homeplate shape with team color-coded borders appears in the lower left corner. The player's position in silver-foil is above this smaller photo, while his name is printed in a silver-foil bar under the photo. The borderless backs carry a color action player cutout superimposed over the team logo, along with player biography and stats for the last five years. There are no key Rookie Cards in this set.

	MINT	NRMT	EXC
COMPLETE SET (550)	40.00	18.00	5.00
COMPLETE SERIES 1 (330)	25.00	11.00	3.10
COMPLETE SERIES 2 (220)	15.00	6.75	1.85
COMMON CARD (1-550)	.10	.05	.01
☐ 1 David Justice	.30	.14	.04
☐ 2 Rene Arocha	.10	.05	.01
☐ 3 Sandy Alomar Jr.	.10	.05	.01
☐ 4 Luis Lopez	.10	.05	.01
☐ 5 Mike Piazza	2.00	.90	.25
☐ 6 Bobby Jones	.20	.09	.03
☐ 7 Damion Easley	.10	.05	.01
☐ 8 Barry Bonds	.75	.35	.09
☐ 9 Mike Mussina	.60	.25	.07
☐ 10 Kevin Seitzer	.10	.05	.01
☐ 11 John Smiley	.10	.05	.01
☐ 12 Wm.VanLandingham	.10	.05	.01
☐ 13 Ron Darling	.10	.05	.01
☐ 14 Walt Weiss	.10	.05	.01
☐ 15 Mike Lansing	.10	.05	.01
☐ 16 Allen Watson	.10	.05	.01
☐ 17 Aaron Sele	.20	.09	.03
☐ 18 Randy Johnson	.30	.14	.04
☐ 19 Dean Palmer	.20	.09	.03
☐ 20 Jeff Bagwell	1.25	.55	.16
☐ 21 Curt Schilling	.10	.05	.01
☐ 22 Darrell Whitmore	.10	.05	.01
☐ 23 Steve Trachsel	.10	.05	.01
☐ 24 Dan Wilson	.20	.09	.03
☐ 25 Steve Finley	.20	.09	.03
☐ 26 Bret Boone	.20	.09	.03
☐ 27 Charles Johnson	.20	.09	.03
☐ 28 Mike Stanton	.10	.05	.01
☐ 29 Ismael Valdes	.20	.09	.03
☐ 30 Salomon Torres	.10	.05	.01
☐ 31 Eric Anthony	.10	.05	.01
☐ 32 Spike Owen	.10	.05	.01
☐ 33 Joey Cora	.10	.05	.01
☐ 34 Robert Eenhoorn	.10	.05	.01
☐ 35 Rick White	.10	.05	.01
☐ 36 Omar Vizquel	.20	.09	.03
☐ 37 Carlos Delgado	.20	.09	.03
☐ 38 Eddie Williams	.10	.05	.01
☐ 39 Shawon Dunston	.10	.05	.01
☐ 40 Darrin Fletcher	.10	.05	.01
☐ 41 Leo Gomez	.10	.05	.01
☐ 42 Juan Gonzalez	1.50	.70	.19
☐ 43 Luis Alicea	.10	.05	.01
☐ 44 Ken Ryan	.10	.05	.01
☐ 45 Lou Whitaker	.20	.09	.03
☐ 46 Mike Blowers	.10	.05	.01
☐ 47 Willie Blair	.10	.05	.01
☐ 48 Todd Van Poppel	.10	.05	.01
☐ 49 Roberto Alomar	.60	.25	.07
☐ 50 Ozzie Smith	.75	.35	.09
☐ 51 Sterling Hitchcock	.20	.09	.03
☐ 52 Mo Vaughn	.75	.35	.09
☐ 53 Rick Aguilera	.10	.05	.01
☐ 54 Kent Mercker	.10	.05	.01
☐ 55 Don Mattingly	1.50	.70	.19
☐ 56 Bob Scanlan	.10	.05	.01
☐ 57 Wilson Alvarez	.20	.09	.03
☐ 58 Jose Mesa	.10	.05	.01
☐ 59 Scott Kamieniecki	.10	.05	.01
☐ 60 Todd Jones	.10	.05	.01
☐ 61 John Kruk	.20	.09	.03
☐ 62 Mike Stanley	.10	.05	.01
☐ 63 Tino Martinez	.20	.09	.03
☐ 64 Eddie Zambrano	.10	.05	.01
☐ 65 Todd Hundley	.20	.09	.03
☐ 66 Jamie Moyer	.10	.05	.01
☐ 67 Rich Amaral	.10	.05	.01
☐ 68 Jose Valentin	.20	.09	.03
☐ 69 Alex Gonzalez	.20	.09	.03
☐ 70 Kurt Abbott	.10	.05	.01
☐ 71 Delino DeShields	.10	.05	.01
☐ 72 Brian Anderson	.10	.05	.01
☐ 73 John Vander Wal	.10	.05	.01
☐ 74 Turner Ward	.10	.05	.01
☐ 75 Tim Raines	.30	.14	.04
☐ 76 Mark Acre	.10	.05	.01
☐ 77 Jose Offerman	.10	.05	.01
☐ 78 Jimmy Key	.20	.09	.03
☐ 79 Mark Whiten	.10	.05	.01
☐ 80 Mark Gubicza	.10	.05	.01
☐ 81 Darren Hall	.10	.05	.01
☐ 82 Travis Fryman	.20	.09	.03
☐ 83 Cal Ripken	2.50	1.10	.30
☐ 84 Geronimo Berroa	.10	.05	.01
☐ 85 Bret Barberie	.10	.05	.01
☐ 86 Andy Ashby	.20	.09	.03
☐ 87 Steve Avery	.20	.09	.03
☐ 88 Rich Becker	.10	.05	.01
☐ 89 John Valentin	.20	.09	.03
☐ 90 Glenallen Hill	.10	.05	.01
☐ 91 Carlos Garcia	.10	.05	.01
☐ 92 Dennis Martinez	.20	.09	.03
☐ 93 Pat Kelly	.10	.05	.01
☐ 94 Orlando Miller	.10	.05	.01
☐ 95 Felix Jose	.10	.05	.01
☐ 96 Mike Kingery	.10	.05	.01
☐ 97 Jeff Kent	.10	.05	.01
☐ 98 Pete Incaviglia	.10	.05	.01
☐ 99 Chad Curtis	.10	.05	.01
☐ 100 Thomas Howard	.10	.05	.01
☐ 101 Hector Carrasco	.10	.05	.01
☐ 102 Tom Pagnozzi	.10	.05	.01
☐ 103 Danny Tartabull	.10	.05	.01
☐ 104 Donnie Elliott	.10	.05	.01
☐ 105 Danny Jackson	.10	.05	.01
☐ 106 Steve Dunn	.10	.05	.01
☐ 107 Roger Salkeld	.10	.05	.01
☐ 108 Jeff King	.20	.09	.03
☐ 109 Cecil Fielder	.20	.09	.03
☐ 110 Checklist	.10	.05	.01
☐ 111 Denny Neagle	.20	.09	.03
☐ 112 Troy Neel	.10	.05	.01
☐ 113 Rod Beck	.10	.05	.01
☐ 114 Alex Rodriguez	4.00	1.80	.50
☐ 115 Joey Eischen	.10	.05	.01
☐ 116 Tom Candiotti	.10	.05	.01
☐ 117 Ray McDavid	.20	.09	.03
☐ 118 Vince Coleman	.10	.05	.01
☐ 119 Pete Harnisch	.10	.05	.01
☐ 120 David Nied	.10	.05	.01
☐ 121 Pat Rapp	.10	.05	.01
☐ 122 Sammy Sosa	.30	.14	.04
☐ 123 Steve Reed	.10	.05	.01
☐ 124 Jose Oliva	.10	.05	.01
☐ 125 Ricky Bottalico	.20	.09	.03
☐ 126 Jose DeLeon	.10	.05	.01
☐ 127 Pat Hentgen	.20	.09	.03
☐ 128 Will Clark	.30	.14	.04
☐ 129 Mark Dewey	.10	.05	.01
☐ 130 Greg Vaughn	.20	.09	.03
☐ 131 Darren Dreifort	.10	.05	.01
☐ 132 Ed Sprague	.20	.09	.03
☐ 133 Lee Smith	.20	.09	.03
☐ 134 Charles Nagy	.20	.09	.03
☐ 135 Phil Plantier	.10	.05	.01
☐ 136 Jason Jacome	.10	.05	.01
☐ 137 Jose Lima	.10	.05	.01
☐ 138 J.R. Phillips	.10	.05	.01
☐ 139 J.T. Snow	.20	.09	.03
☐ 140 Michael Huff	.10	.05	.01
☐ 141 Billy Brewer	.10	.05	.01
☐ 142 Jeromy Burnitz	.10	.05	.01
☐ 143 Ricky Bones	.10	.05	.01
☐ 144 Carlos Rodriguez	.10	.05	.01
☐ 145 Luis Gonzalez	.10	.05	.01
☐ 146 Mark Lemke	.10	.05	.01
☐ 147 Al Martin	.20	.09	.03
☐ 148 Mike Bordick	.10	.05	.01
☐ 149 Robb Nen	.10	.05	.01
☐ 150 Wil Cordero	.10	.05	.01
☐ 151 Edgar Martinez	.20	.09	.03
☐ 152 Gerald Williams	.10	.05	.01
☐ 153 Esteban Beltre	.10	.05	.01
☐ 154 Mike Moore	.10	.05	.01
☐ 155 Mark Langston	.10	.05	.01
☐ 156 Mark Clark	.10	.05	.01
☐ 157 Bobby Ayala	.10	.05	.01
☐ 158 Rick Wilkins	.10	.05	.01
☐ 159 Bobby Munoz	.10	.05	.01
☐ 160 Brett Butler CL 2000 Hits	.20	.09	.03
☐ 161 Scott Erickson	.10	.05	.01
☐ 162 Paul Molitor	.60	.25	.07
☐ 163 Jon Lieber	.10	.05	.01
☐ 164 Jason Grimsley	.10	.05	.01
☐ 165 Norberto Martin	.10	.05	.01
☐ 166 Javier Lopez	.30	.14	.04
☐ 167 Brian McRae	.20	.09	.03
☐ 168 Gary Sheffield	.30	.14	.04
☐ 169 Marcus Moore	.10	.05	.01
☐ 170 John Hudek	.10	.05	.01
☐ 171 Kelly Stinnett	.10	.05	.01
☐ 172 Chris Gomez	.10	.05	.01
☐ 173 Rey Sanchez	.10	.05	.01
☐ 174 Juan Guzman	.20	.09	.03
☐ 175 Chan Ho Park	.30	.14	.04
☐ 176 Terry Shumpert	.10	.05	.01
☐ 177 Steve Ontiveros	.10	.05	.01
☐ 178 Brad Ausmus	.10	.05	.01
☐ 179 Tim Davis	.10	.05	.01
☐ 180 Billy Ashley	.10	.05	.01
☐ 181 Vinny Castilla	.20	.09	.03
☐ 182 Bill Spiers	.10	.05	.01
☐ 183 Randy Knorr	.10	.05	.01
☐ 184 Brian Hunter	.30	.14	.04
☐ 185 Pat Meares	.10	.05	.01
☐ 186 Steve Buechele	.10	.05	.01
☐ 187 Kirt Manwaring	.10	.05	.01
☐ 188 Tim Naehring	.10	.05	.01
☐ 189 Matt Mieske	.20	.09	.03
☐ 190 Josias Manzanillo	.10	.05	.01
☐ 191 Greg McMichael	.10	.05	.01
☐ 192 Chuck Carr	.10	.05	.01
☐ 193 Midre Cummings	.10	.05	.01
☐ 194 Darryl Strawberry	.20	.09	.03
☐ 195 Greg Gagne	.10	.05	.01
☐ 196 Steve Cooke	.10	.05	.01
☐ 197 Woody Williams	.10	.05	.01
☐ 198 Ron Karkovice	.10	.05	.01
☐ 199 Phil Leftwich	.10	.05	.01
☐ 200 Jim Thome	.60	.25	.07
☐ 201 Brady Anderson	.30	.14	.04
☐ 202 Pedro Martinez	.20	.09	.03
☐ 203 Steve Karsay	.10	.05	.01
☐ 204 Reggie Sanders	.20	.09	.03
☐ 205 Bill Risley	.10	.05	.01
☐ 206 Jay Bell	.20	.09	.03
☐ 207 Kevin Brown	.20	.09	.03
☐ 208 Tim Scott	.10	.05	.01
☐ 209 Lenny Dykstra	.20	.09	.03
☐ 210 Willie Greene	.10	.05	.01
☐ 211 Jim Eisenreich	.10	.05	.01
☐ 212 Cliff Floyd	.20	.09	.03
☐ 213 Otis Nixon	.10	.05	.01
☐ 214 Eduardo Perez	.10	.05	.01
☐ 215 Manuel Lee	.10	.05	.01
☐ 216 Armando Benitez	.10	.05	.01
☐ 217 Dave McCarty	.10	.05	.01
☐ 218 Scott Livingstone	.10	.05	.01
☐ 219 Chad Kreuter	.10	.05	.01
☐ 220 Don Mattingly CL	.75	.35	.09
☐ 221 Brian Jordan	.30	.14	.04
☐ 222 Matt Whiteside	.10	.05	.01
☐ 223 Jim Edmonds	.30	.14	.04
☐ 224 Tony Gwynn	1.25	.55	.16
☐ 225 Jose Lind	.10	.05	.01
☐ 226 Marvin Freeman	.10	.05	.01
☐ 227 Ken Hill	.10	.05	.01
☐ 228 David Hulse	.10	.05	.01
☐ 229 Joe Hesketh	.10	.05	.01
☐ 230 Roberto Petagine	.10	.05	.01
☐ 231 Jeffrey Hammonds	.20	.09	.03
☐ 232 John Jaha	.20	.09	.03
☐ 233 John Burkett	.20	.09	.03
☐ 234 Hal Morris	.10	.05	.01
☐ 235 Tony Castillo	.10	.05	.01
☐ 236 Ryan Bowen	.10	.05	.01
☐ 237 Wayne Kirby	.10	.05	.01
☐ 238 Brent Mayne	.10	.05	.01
☐ 239 Jim Bullinger	.10	.05	.01
☐ 240 Mike Lieberthal	.10	.05	.01
☐ 241 Barry Larkin	.30	.14	.04
☐ 242 David Segui	.10	.05	.01
☐ 243 Jose Bautista	.10	.05	.01
☐ 244 Hector Fajardo	.10	.05	.01
☐ 245 Orel Hershiser	.20	.09	.03
☐ 246 James Mouton	.10	.05	.01
☐ 247 Scott Leius	.10	.05	.01
☐ 248 Tom Glavine	.30	.14	.04
☐ 249 Danny Bautista	.10	.05	.01
☐ 250 Jose Mercedes	.10	.05	.01
☐ 251 Marquis Grissom	.20	.09	.03
☐ 252 Charlie Hayes	.10	.05	.01
☐ 253 Ryan Klesko	.30	.14	.04
☐ 254 Vicente Palacios	.10	.05	.01
☐ 255 Matias Carrillo	.10	.05	.01
☐ 256 Gary DiSarcina	.10	.05	.01
☐ 257 Kirk Gibson	.20	.09	.03
☐ 258 Garey Ingram	.10	.05	.01
☐ 259 Alex Fernandez	.20	.09	.03
☐ 260 John Mabry	.30	.14	.04
☐ 261 Chris Howard	.10	.05	.01
☐ 262 Miguel Jimenez	.10	.05	.01
☐ 263 Heath Slocumb	.10	.05	.01
☐ 264 Albert Belle	1.25	.55	.16
☐ 265 Dave Clark	.10	.05	.01
☐ 266 Joe Orsulak	.10	.05	.01
☐ 267 Joey Hamilton	.30	.14	.04
☐ 268 Mark Portugal	.10	.05	.01
☐ 269 Kevin Tapani	.10	.05	.01
☐ 270 Sid Fernandez	.10	.05	.01
☐ 271 Steve Dreyer	.10	.05	.01
☐ 272 Denny Hocking	.10	.05	.01
☐ 273 Troy O'Leary	.10	.05	.01
☐ 274 Milt Cuyler	.10	.05	.01
☐ 275 Frank Thomas	3.00	1.35	.35
☐ 276 Jorge Fabregas	.10	.05	.01
☐ 277 Mike Gallego	.10	.05	.01
☐ 278 Mickey Morandini	.10	.05	.01
☐ 279 Roberto Hernandez	.10	.05	.01
☐ 280 Henry Rodriguez	.20	.09	.03
☐ 281 Garret Anderson	.20	.09	.03
☐ 282 Bob Wickman	.10	.05	.01
☐ 283 Gar Finnvold	.10	.05	.01
☐ 284 Paul O'Neill	.20	.09	.03
☐ 285 Royce Clayton	.10	.05	.01
☐ 286 Chuck Knoblauch	.30	.14	.04
☐ 287 Johnny Ruffin	.10	.05	.01
☐ 288 Dave Nilsson	.20	.09	.03
☐ 289 David Cone	.20	.09	.03
☐ 290 Chuck McElroy	.10	.05	.01
☐ 291 Kevin Stocker	.10	.05	.01
☐ 292 Jose Rijo	.10	.05	.01
☐ 293 Sean Berry	.10	.05	.01
☐ 294 Ozzie Guillen	.10	.05	.01
☐ 295 Chris Hoiles	.10	.05	.01
☐ 296 Kevin Foster	.10	.05	.01
☐ 297 Jeff Frye	.10	.05	.01
☐ 298 Lance Johnson	.20	.09	.03
☐ 299 Mike Kelly	.10	.05	.01
☐ 300 Ellis Burks	.20	.09	.03
☐ 301 Roberto Kelly	.10	.05	.01
☐ 302 Dante Bichette	.30	.14	.04
☐ 303 Alvaro Ezpinoza	.10	.05	.01
☐ 304 Alex Cole	.10	.05	.01
☐ 305 Rickey Henderson	.30	.14	.04
☐ 306 Dave Weathers	.10	.05	.01
☐ 307 Shane Reynolds	.20	.09	.03
☐ 308 Bobby Bonilla	.20	.09	.03
☐ 309 Junior Felix	.10	.05	.01
☐ 310 Jeff Fassero	.10	.05	.01
☐ 311 Darren Lewis	.10	.05	.01
☐ 312 John Doherty	.10	.05	.01

Card	MINT	NRMT	EXC
☐ 313 Scott Servais	.10	.05	.01
☐ 314 Rick Helling	.10	.05	.01
☐ 315 Pedro Martinez	.20	.09	.03
☐ 316 Wes Chamberlain	.10	.05	.01
☐ 317 Bryan Eversgerd	.10	.05	.01
☐ 318 Trevor Hoffman	.20	.09	.03
☐ 319 John Patterson	.10	.05	.01
☐ 320 Matt Walbeck	.10	.05	.01
☐ 321 Jeff Montgomery	.20	.09	.03
☐ 322 Mel Rojas	.10	.05	.01
☐ 323 Eddie Taubensee	.10	.05	.01
☐ 324 Ray Lankford	.20	.09	.03
☐ 325 Jose Vizcaino	.10	.05	.01
☐ 326 Carlos Baerga	.20	.09	.03
☐ 327 Jack Voigt	.10	.05	.01
☐ 328 Julio Franco	.20	.09	.03
☐ 329 Brent Gates	.10	.05	.01
☐ 330 Kirby Puckett CL	.30	.14	.04
☐ 331 Greg Maddux	2.00	.90	.25
☐ 332 Jason Bere	.10	.05	.01
☐ 333 Bill Wegman	.10	.05	.01
☐ 334 Tuffy Rhodes	.10	.05	.01
☐ 335 Kevin Young	.10	.05	.01
☐ 336 Andy Benes	.10	.05	.01
☐ 337 Pedro Astacio	.10	.05	.01
☐ 338 Reggie Jefferson	.20	.09	.03
☐ 339 Tim Belcher	.20	.09	.03
☐ 340 Ken Griffey Jr.	3.00	1.35	.35
☐ 341 Mariano Duncan	.10	.05	.01
☐ 342 Andres Galarraga	.30	.14	.04
☐ 343 Rondell White	.20	.09	.03
☐ 344 Cory Bailey	.10	.05	.01
☐ 345 Bryan Harvey	.10	.05	.01
☐ 346 John Franco	.10	.05	.01
☐ 347 Greg Swindell	.10	.05	.01
☐ 348 David West	.10	.05	.01
☐ 349 Fred McGriff	.30	.14	.04
☐ 350 Jose Canseco	.30	.14	.04
☐ 351 Orlando Merced	.10	.05	.01
☐ 352 Rheal Cormier	.10	.05	.01
☐ 353 Carlos Pulido	.10	.05	.01
☐ 354 Terry Steinbach	.20	.09	.03
☐ 355 Wade Boggs	.30	.14	.04
☐ 356 B.J. Surhoff	.20	.09	.03
☐ 357 Rafael Palmeiro	.30	.14	.04
☐ 358 Anthony Young	.10	.05	.01
☐ 359 Tom Brunansky	.10	.05	.01
☐ 360 Todd Stottlemyre	.10	.05	.01
☐ 361 Chris Turner	.10	.05	.01
☐ 362 Joe Boever	.10	.05	.01
☐ 363 Jeff Blauser	.10	.05	.01
☐ 364 Derek Bell	.20	.09	.03
☐ 365 Matt Williams	.30	.14	.04
☐ 366 Jeremy Hernandez	.10	.05	.01
☐ 367 Joe Girardi	.10	.05	.01
☐ 368 Mike Devereaux	.10	.05	.01
☐ 369 Jim Abbott	.10	.05	.01
☐ 370 Manny Ramirez	.75	.35	.09
☐ 371 Kenny Lofton	.75	.35	.09
☐ 372 Mark Smith	.10	.05	.01
☐ 373 Dave Fleming	.10	.05	.01
☐ 374 Dave Stewart	.20	.09	.03
☐ 375 Roger Pavlik	.10	.05	.01
☐ 376 Hipolito Pichardo	.10	.05	.01
☐ 377 Bill Taylor	.10	.05	.01
☐ 378 Robin Ventura	.20	.09	.03
☐ 379 Bernard Gilkey	.20	.09	.03
☐ 380 Kirby Puckett	1.25	.55	.16
☐ 381 Steve Howe	.10	.05	.01
☐ 382 Devon White	.20	.09	.03
☐ 383 Roberto Mejia	.10	.05	.01
☐ 384 Darrin Jackson	.10	.05	.01
☐ 385 Mike Morgan	.10	.05	.01
☐ 386 Rusty Meacham	.10	.05	.01
☐ 387 Bill Swift	.10	.05	.01
☐ 388 Lou Frazier	.10	.05	.01
☐ 389 Andy Van Slyke	.20	.09	.03
☐ 390 Brett Butler	.20	.09	.03
☐ 391 Bobby Witt	.10	.05	.01
☐ 392 Jeff Conine	.20	.09	.03
☐ 393 Tim Hyers	.10	.05	.01
☐ 394 Terry Pendleton	.20	.09	.03
☐ 395 Ricky Jordan	.10	.05	.01
☐ 396 Eric Plunk	.10	.05	.01
☐ 397 Melido Perez	.10	.05	.01
☐ 398 Darryl Kile	.10	.05	.01
☐ 399 Mark McLemore	.10	.05	.01
☐ 400 Greg W.Harris	.10	.05	.01
☐ 401 Jim Leyritz	.10	.05	.01
☐ 402 Doug Strange	.10	.05	.01
☐ 403 Tim Salmon	.30	.14	.04
☐ 404 Terry Mulholland	.10	.05	.01
☐ 405 Robby Thompson	.10	.05	.01
☐ 406 Ruben Sierra	.20	.09	.03
☐ 407 Tony Phillips	.20	.09	.03
☐ 408 Moises Alou	.20	.09	.03
☐ 409 Felix Fermin	.10	.05	.01
☐ 410 Pat Listach	.10	.05	.01
☐ 411 Kevin Bass	.10	.05	.01
☐ 412 Ben McDonald	.10	.05	.01
☐ 413 Scott Cooper	.10	.05	.01
☐ 414 Jody Reed	.10	.05	.01
☐ 415 Deion Sanders	.30	.14	.04
☐ 416 Ricky Gutierrez	.10	.05	.01
☐ 417 Gregg Jefferies	.20	.09	.03
☐ 418 Jack McDowell	.20	.09	.03
☐ 419 Al Leiter	.20	.09	.03
☐ 420 Tony Longmire	.10	.05	.01
☐ 421 Paul Wagner	.10	.05	.01
☐ 422 Geronimo Pena	.10	.05	.01
☐ 423 Ivan Rodriguez	.75	.35	.09
☐ 424 Kevin Gross	.10	.05	.01
☐ 425 Kirk McCaskill	.10	.05	.01
☐ 426 Greg Myers	.10	.05	.01
☐ 427 Roger Clemens	.60	.25	.07
☐ 428 Chris Hammond	.10	.05	.01
☐ 429 Randy Myers	.10	.05	.01
☐ 430 Roger Mason	.10	.05	.01
☐ 431 Bret Saberhagen	.20	.09	.03
☐ 432 Jeff Reboulet	.10	.05	.01
☐ 433 John Olerud	.10	.05	.01
☐ 434 Bill Gullickson	.10	.05	.01
☐ 435 Eddie Murray	.75	.35	.09
☐ 436 Pedro Munoz	.10	.05	.01
☐ 437 Charlie O'Brien	.10	.05	.01
☐ 438 Jeff Nelson	.10	.05	.01
☐ 439 Mike Macfarlane	.10	.05	.01
☐ 440 Don Mattingly CL 1000 RBI	.75	.35	.09
☐ 441 Derrick May	.10	.05	.01
☐ 442 John Roper	.10	.05	.01
☐ 443 Darryl Hamilton	.10	.05	.01
☐ 444 Dan Miceli	.10	.05	.01
☐ 445 Tony Eusebio	.10	.05	.01
☐ 446 Jerry Browne	.10	.05	.01
☐ 447 Wally Joyner	.20	.09	.03
☐ 448 Brian Harper	.10	.05	.01
☐ 449 Scott Fletcher	.10	.05	.01
☐ 450 Bip Roberts	.10	.05	.01
☐ 451 Pete Smith	.10	.05	.01
☐ 452 Chili Davis	.20	.09	.03
☐ 453 Dave Hollins	.10	.05	.01
☐ 454 Tony Pena	.10	.05	.01
☐ 455 Butch Henry	.10	.05	.01
☐ 456 Craig Biggio	.20	.09	.03
☐ 457 Zane Smith	.10	.05	.01
☐ 458 Ryan Thompson	.10	.05	.01
☐ 459 Mike Jackson	.10	.05	.01
☐ 460 Mark McGwire	1.00	.45	.12
☐ 461 John Smoltz	.30	.14	.04
☐ 462 Steve Scarsone	.10	.05	.01
☐ 463 Greg Colbrunn	.10	.05	.01
☐ 464 Shawn Green	.20	.09	.03
☐ 465 David Wells	.10	.05	.01
☐ 466 Jose Hernandez	.10	.05	.01
☐ 467 Chip Hale	.10	.05	.01
☐ 468 Tony Tarasco	.10	.05	.01
☐ 469 Kevin Mitchell	.20	.09	.03
☐ 470 Billy Hatcher	.10	.05	.01
☐ 471 Jay Buhner	.30	.14	.04
☐ 472 Ken Caminiti	.30	.14	.04
☐ 473 Tom Henke	.10	.05	.01
☐ 474 Todd Worrell	.10	.05	.01
☐ 475 Mark Eichhorn	.10	.05	.01
☐ 476 Bruce Ruffin	.10	.05	.01
☐ 477 Chuck Finley	.20	.09	.03
☐ 478 Marc Newfield	.20	.09	.03
☐ 479 Paul Shuey	.10	.05	.01
☐ 480 Bob Tewksbury	.10	.05	.01
☐ 481 Ramon J.Martinez	.20	.09	.03
☐ 482 Melvin Nieves	.20	.09	.03
☐ 483 Todd Zeile	.10	.05	.01
☐ 484 Benito Santiago	.10	.05	.01
☐ 485 Stan Javier	.10	.05	.01
☐ 486 Kirk Rueter	.10	.05	.01
☐ 487 Andre Dawson	.20	.09	.03
☐ 488 Eric Karros	.20	.09	.03
☐ 489 Dave Magadan	.10	.05	.01
☐ 490 Joe Carter CL 1000 RBI	.20	.09	.03
☐ 491 Randy Velarde	.10	.05	.01
☐ 492 Larry Walker	.30	.14	.04
☐ 493 Cris Carpenter	.10	.05	.01
☐ 494 Tom Gordon	.10	.05	.01
☐ 495 Dave Burba	.10	.05	.01
☐ 496 Darren Bragg	.20	.09	.03
☐ 497 Darren Daulton	.20	.09	.03
☐ 498 Don Slaught	.10	.05	.01
☐ 499 Pat Borders	.10	.05	.01
☐ 500 Lenny Harris	.10	.05	.01
☐ 501 Joe Ausanio	.10	.05	.01
☐ 502 Alan Trammell	.20	.09	.03
☐ 503 Mike Fetters	.10	.05	.01
☐ 504 Scott Ruffcorn	.10	.05	.01
☐ 505 Rich Rowland	.10	.05	.01
☐ 506 Juan Samuel	.10	.05	.01
☐ 507 Bo Jackson	.20	.09	.03
☐ 508 Jeff Branson	.10	.05	.01
☐ 509 Bernie Williams	.60	.25	.07
☐ 510 Paul Sorrento	.10	.05	.01
☐ 511 Dennis Eckersley	.20	.09	.03
☐ 512 Pat Mahomes	.10	.05	.01
☐ 513 Rusty Greer	.30	.14	.04
☐ 514 Luis Polonia	.10	.05	.01
☐ 515 Willie Banks	.10	.05	.01
☐ 516 John Wetteland	.20	.09	.03
☐ 517 Mike LaValliere	.10	.05	.01
☐ 518 Tommy Greene	.10	.05	.01
☐ 519 Mark Grace	.30	.14	.04
☐ 520 Bob Hamelin	.10	.05	.01
☐ 521 Scott Sanderson	.10	.05	.01
☐ 522 Joe Carter	.20	.09	.03
☐ 523 Jeff Brantley	.10	.05	.01
☐ 524 Andrew Lorraine	.20	.09	.03
☐ 525 Rico Brogna	.10	.05	.01
☐ 526 Shane Mack	.10	.05	.01
☐ 527 Mark Wohlers	.20	.09	.03
☐ 528 Scott Sanders	.10	.05	.01
☐ 529 Chris Bosio	.10	.05	.01
☐ 530 Andujar Cedeno	.10	.05	.01
☐ 531 Kenny Rogers	.10	.05	.01
☐ 532 Doug Drabek	.10	.05	.01
☐ 533 Curt Leskanic	.10	.05	.01
☐ 534 Craig Shipley	.10	.05	.01
☐ 535 Craig Grebeck	.10	.05	.01
☐ 536 Cal Eldred	.10	.05	.01
☐ 537 Mickey Tettleton	.10	.05	.01
☐ 538 Harold Baines	.20	.09	.03
☐ 539 Tim Wallach	.10	.05	.01
☐ 540 Damon Buford	.10	.05	.01
☐ 541 Lenny Webster	.10	.05	.01
☐ 542 Kevin Appier	.20	.09	.03
☐ 543 Raul Mondesi	.30	.14	.04
☐ 544 Eric Young	.20	.09	.03
☐ 545 Russ Davis	.10	.05	.01
☐ 546 Mike Benjamin	.10	.05	.01
☐ 547 Mike Greenwell	.10	.05	.01
☐ 548 Scott Brosius	.10	.05	.01
☐ 549 Brian Dorsett	.10	.05	.01
☐ 550 Chili Davis CL 1000 RBI	.10	.05	.01

1995 Donruss Press Proofs

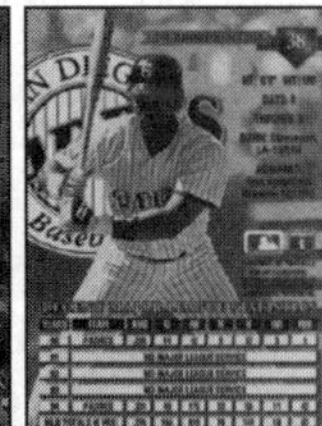

Parallel to the basic Donruss set, the Press Proofs are distinguished by the player's name, team name and Donruss logo being done in gold foil on front. The words "Press Proof are also in gold at the top. The first 2,000 cards of the production run were stamped as such and inserted at a rate of one in every 20 first and second series packs.

	MINT	NRMT	EXC
COMPLETE SET (550)	1600.00	700.00	200.00
COMPLETE SERIES 1 (330)	1000.00	450.00	125.00
COMPLETE SERIES 2 (220)	600.00	275.00	75.00
COMMON CARD (1-550)	2.50	1.10	.30

*STARS: 15X TO 30X BASIC CARDS..
*YOUNG STARS: 15X TO 25X BASIC CARDS

1995 Donruss All-Stars

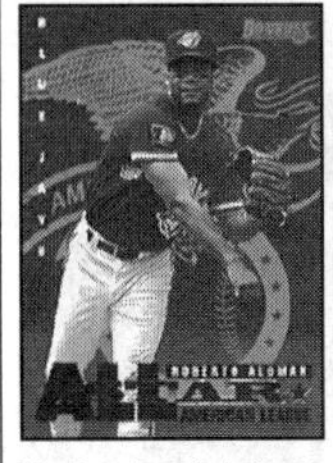

This 18-card standard-size set was randomly inserted into retail packs. The first series has the nine 1994 American League starters while the second series honored the National League starters. The fronts feature the playeris photo against a background of his league's all-star logo. The player and his team are identified on the bottom. His team is noted in the upper left corner. All of this is on a borderless card with a gray background. The horizontal backs have a player photo, a quick blurb about his starting role in the game and his performance in the 1994 All-Star game. The cards are numbered in the upper right with either an "AL-X" or an "NL-X."

	MINT	NRMT	EXC
COMPLETE SET (18)	200.00	90.00	25.00
COMPLETE SERIES 1 (9)	125.00	55.00	15.50
COMPLETE SERIES 2 (9)	75.00	34.00	9.50
COMMON CARD (AL1-AL9)	2.50	1.10	.30
COMMON CARD (NL1-NL9)	2.50	1.10	.30
☐ AL1 Jimmy Key	2.50	1.10	.30
☐ AL2 Ivan Rodriguez	10.00	4.50	1.25
☐ AL3 Frank Thomas	40.00	18.00	5.00
☐ AL4 Roberto Alomar	8.00	3.60	1.00
☐ AL5 Wade Boggs	5.00	2.20	.60
☐ AL6 Cal Ripken	35.00	16.00	4.40
☐ AL7 Joe Carter	4.00	1.80	.50
☐ AL8 Ken Griffey Jr.	40.00	18.00	5.00
☐ AL9 Kirby Puckett	15.00	6.75	1.85
☐ NL1 Greg Maddux	25.00	11.00	3.10
☐ NL2 Mike Piazza	25.00	11.00	3.10
☐ NL3 Gregg Jefferies	2.50	1.10	.30
☐ NL4 Mariano Duncan	2.50	1.10	.30
☐ NL5 Matt Williams	5.00	2.20	.60
☐ NL6 Ozzie Smith	10.00	4.50	1.25
☐ NL7 Barry Bonds	10.00	4.50	1.25
☐ NL8 Tony Gwynn	15.00	6.75	1.85
☐ NL9 David Justice	4.00	1.80	.50

1995 Donruss Bomb Squad

Randomly inserted one in every 24 retail packs and one in every 16 jumbo packs, this set features the top six home run hitters in the National and American League. These cards were only included in first series packs. Each of the six cards shows a different slugger on the either side of the card. Both the fronts and backs are horizontal and feature the player photo with a bomber as background. There are foil bombs to the left indicating how many homers the player hit in 1994. A dog tag indicates the player's position and rank among home run leaders in his league.

	MINT	NRMT	EXC
COMPLETE SET (6)	25.00	11.00	3.10
COMMON CARD (1-6)	1.50	.70	.19
☐ 1 Ken Griffey Matt Williams	8.00	3.60	1.00
☐ 2 Frank Thomas Jeff Bagwell	12.00	5.50	1.50
☐ 3 Albert Belle Barry Bonds	4.00	1.80	.50
☐ 4 Jose Canseco Fred McGriff	2.50	1.10	.30
☐ 5 Cecil Fielder Andres Galarraga	1.50	.70	.19
☐ 6 Joe Carter Kevin Mitchell	1.50	.70	.19

1995 Donruss Diamond Kings

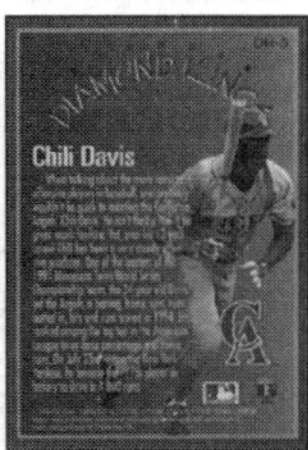

The 1995 Donruss Diamond King set consists of 29 standard-size cards that were randomly inserted in packs. The fronts feature water color player portraits by noted sports artist Dick Perez. The player's name and "Diamond Kings" are in gold foil. The backs have a dark blue border with a player photo and text. The cards are numbered on back with a DK prefix.

	MINT	NRMT	EXC
COMPLETE SET (29)	50.00	22.00	6.25
COMPLETE SERIES 1 (14)	20.00	9.00	2.50
COMPLETE SERIES 2 (15)	30.00	13.50	3.70
COMMON CARD (DK1-DK29)	1.00	.45	.12
☐ DK1 Frank Thomas	12.00	5.50	1.50
☐ DK2 Jeff Bagwell	5.00	2.20	.60
☐ DK3 Chili Davis	1.25	.55	.16
☐ DK4 Dante Bichette	1.50	.70	.19
☐ DK5 Ruben Sierra	1.00	.45	.12
☐ DK6 Jeff Conine	1.25	.55	.16
☐ DK7 Paul O'Neill	1.25	.55	.16
☐ DK8 Bobby Bonilla	1.25	.55	.16
☐ DK9 Joe Carter	1.25	.55	.16
☐ DK10 Moises Alou	1.25	.55	.16
☐ DK11 Kenny Lofton	3.00	1.35	.35
☐ DK12 Matt Williams	1.50	.70	.19
☐ DK13 Kevin Seitzer	1.00	.45	.12
☐ DK14 Sammy Sosa	2.00	.90	.25
☐ DK15 Scott Cooper	1.00	.45	.12
☐ DK16 Raul Mondesi	1.50	.70	.19
☐ DK17 Will Clark	1.50	.70	.19
☐ DK18 Lenny Dykstra	1.25	.55	.16
☐ DK19 Kirby Puckett	5.00	2.20	.60
☐ DK20 Hal Morris	1.00	.45	.12
☐ DK21 Travis Fryman	1.25	.55	.16
☐ DK22 Greg Maddux	8.00	3.60	1.00
☐ DK23 Rafael Palmeiro	1.50	.70	.19
☐ DK24 Tony Gwynn	5.00	2.20	.60
☐ DK25 David Cone	1.25	.55	.16
☐ DK26 Al Martin	1.00	.45	.12
☐ DK27 Ken Griffey Jr.	12.00	5.50	1.50

☐ DK28 Gregg Jefferies	1.25	.55	.16
☐ DK29 Checklist	1.00	.45	.12

1995 Donruss Dominators

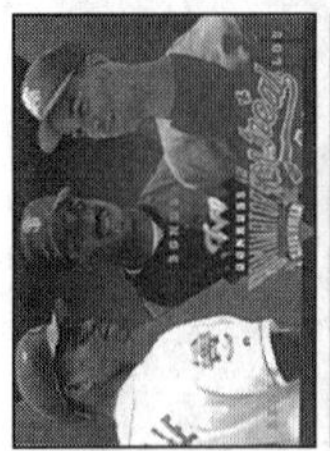

This nine-card standard-size set was randomly inserted in second series hobby packs. Each of these cards features three of the leading players at each position. The horizontal fronts have photos of all three players and identify only their last name. The words "remove protective film" cover a significant portion of the fronts as well. The backs have small action photos of the three players along with their 1994 stats. The cards are numbered in the upper right corner as "X" of 9.

	MINT	NRMT	EXC
COMPLETE SET (9)	30.00	13.50	3.70
COMMON CARD (1-9)	1.00	.45	.12
☐ 1 David Cone Mike Mussina Greg Maddux	5.00	2.20	.60
☐ 2 Ivan Rodriguez Mike Piazza Darren Daulton	4.00	1.80	.50
☐ 3 Fred McGriff Frank Thomas Jeff Bagwell	10.00	4.50	1.25
☐ 4 Roberto Alomar Carlos Baerga Craig Biggio	1.50	.70	.19
☐ 5 Robin Ventura Travis Fryman Matt Williams	1.00	.45	.12
☐ 6 Cal Ripken Barry Larkin Wil Cordero	6.00	2.70	.75
☐ 7 Albert Belle Barry Bonds Moises Alou	2.50	1.10	.30
☐ 8 Ken Griffey Kenny Lofton Marquis Grissom	8.00	3.60	1.00
☐ 9 Kirby Puckett Paul O'Neill Tony Gwynn	3.00	1.35	.35

1995 Donruss Elite

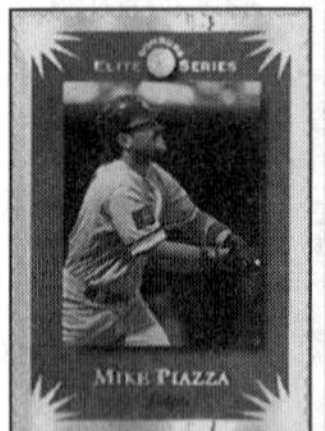

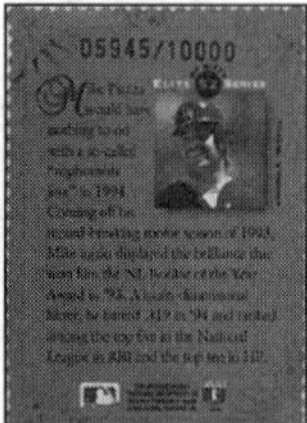

Randomly inserted one in every 210 Series 1 and 2 packs, this set consists of 12 standard-size cards that are numbered (49-60) based on where the previous year's set left off. The fronts contain an action photo surrounded by a marble border. Silver holographic foil borders the card on all four sides. Limited to 10,000, the backs are individually numbered, contain a small photo and write-up.

	MINT	NRMT	EXC
COMPLETE SET (12)	350.00	160.00	45.00
COMPLETE SERIES 1 (6)	200.00	90.00	25.00
COMPLETE SERIES 2 (6)	150.00	70.00	19.00
COMMON CARD (49-60)	8.00	3.60	1.00
☐ 49 Jeff Bagwell	25.00	11.00	3.10
☐ 50 Paul O'Neill	8.00	3.60	1.00
☐ 51 Greg Maddux	50.00	22.00	6.25
☐ 52 Mike Piazza	40.00	18.00	5.00
☐ 53 Matt Williams	10.00	4.50	1.25
☐ 54 Ken Griffey	75.00	34.00	9.50
☐ 55 Frank Thomas	75.00	34.00	9.50
☐ 56 Barry Bonds	20.00	9.00	2.50
☐ 57 Kirby Puckett	25.00	11.00	3.10
☐ 58 Fred McGriff	10.00	4.50	1.25
☐ 59 Jose Canseco	10.00	4.50	1.25
☐ 60 Albert Belle	30.00	13.50	3.70

1995 Donruss Long Ball Leaders

Inserted one in every 24 series one hobby packs, this set features eight top home run hitters. Metallic fronts have much ornamentation including a player photo, the length of the player's home run, the stadium and the date. Horizontal backs have a player photo and photo of the stadium with which the home run occurred. The back also includes all the particulars concerning the home run.

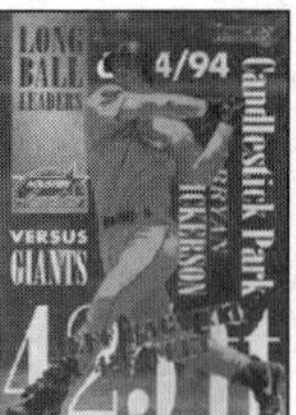

	MINT	NRMT	EXC
COMPLETE SET (8)	20.00	9.00	2.50
COMMON CARD (1-8)	1.00	.45	.12
☐ 1 Frank Thomas	8.00	3.60	1.00
☐ 2 Fred McGriff	1.50	.70	.19
☐ 3 Ken Griffey	8.00	3.60	1.00
☐ 4 Matt Williams	1.50	.70	.19
☐ 5 Mike Piazza	5.00	2.20	.60
☐ 6 Jose Canseco	1.00	.45	.12
☐ 7 Barry Bonds	2.00	.90	.25
☐ 8 Jeff Bagwell	3.00	1.35	.35

1995 Donruss Mound Marvels

This eight-card standard-size set was randomly inserted into second series magazine jumbo and retail packs. This set features eight of the leading major league starters. The horizontal fronts feature the player's photo on the left with the words "Donruss Mound Marvels" and the player's name on the right. The back features the player's photo within a circular inset along with all his 1994 stats.

	MINT	NRMT	EXC
COMPLETE SET (8)	20.00	9.00	2.50
COMMON CARD (1-8)	1.00	.45	.12
☐ 1 Greg Maddux	10.00	4.50	1.25
☐ 2 David Cone	1.50	.70	.19
☐ 3 Mike Mussina	3.00	1.35	.35
☐ 4 Bret Saberhagen	1.00	.45	.12
☐ 5 Jimmy Key	1.00	.45	.12
☐ 6 Doug Drabek	1.00	.45	.12
☐ 7 Randy Johnson	2.50	1.10	.30
☐ 8 Jason Bere	1.00	.45	.12

1995 Donruss Top of the Order

This 360-card standard-size set was distributed as a Major League Baseball Card Game. The cards were packaged in 80-card starter decks with other cards available in booster packs. The fronts carry player action photos with the player's name, team, position, and other player information needed to play the game. The green backs carry the card logo. The first 180 cards feature players in the American League with the National League represented by the second 180 cards. The cards are unnumbered and checklisted below in alphabetical order within each team. There are three levels of scarcity for these cards; common, uncommon and rare. All cards have been given either a designation of C (for common), U (for uncommon) or R (for rare).

	MINT	NRMT	EXC
COMPLETE SET (360)	600.00	275.00	75.00
COMMON CARD (1-360)	.10	.05	.01
UNCOMMON CARD (1-360)	.50	.23	.06
RARE CARD (1-360)	3.00	1.35	.35
☐ 1 Brady Anderson C	.40	.18	.05
☐ 2 Harold Baines U	1.00	.45	.12
☐ 3 Bret Barberie U	.50	.23	.06
☐ 4 Armando Benitez C	.10	.05	.01
☐ 5 Bobby Bonilla U	1.00	.45	.12
☐ 6 Scott Erickson C	.10	.05	.01
☐ 7 Leo Gomez C	.10	.05	.01
☐ 8 Curtis Goodwin R	3.00	1.35	.35
☐ 9 Jeffrey Hammonds C	.10	.05	.01
☐ 10 Chris Hoiles C	.10	.05	.01
☐ 11 Doug Jones C	.10	.05	.01
☐ 12 Ben McDonald U	.50	.23	.06
☐ 13 Mike Mussina U	3.00	1.35	.35
☐ 14 Rafael Palmeiro R	5.00	2.20	.60
☐ 15 Cal Ripken Jr. R	25.00	11.00	3.10
☐ 16 Rick Aguilera C	.10	.05	.01
☐ 17 Luis Alicea C	.10	.05	.01
☐ 18 Jose Canseco U	2.00	.90	.25
☐ 19 Roger Clemens C	.50	.23	.06
☐ 20 Mike Greenwell U	.50	.23	.06
☐ 21 Erik Hanson C	.10	.05	.01
☐ 22 Mike Macfarlane C	.10	.05	.01
☐ 23 Tim Naehring R	3.00	1.35	.35
☐ 24 Troy O'Leary U	.50	.23	.06
☐ 25 Ken Ryan C	.10	.05	.01
☐ 26 Aaron Sele C	.10	.05	.01
☐ 27 Lee Tinsley U	.50	.23	.06
☐ 28 John Valentin R	4.00	1.80	.50
☐ 29 Mo Vaughn R	7.50	3.40	.95
☐ 30 Jim Abbott C	.10	.05	.01
☐ 31 Mike Butcher C	.10	.05	.01
☐ 32 Chili Davis R	4.00	1.80	.50
☐ 33 Gary DiSarcina R	3.00	1.35	.35
☐ 34 Damion Easley C	.10	.05	.01
☐ 35 Jim Edmonds R	5.00	2.20	.60
☐ 36 Chuck Finley U	1.00	.45	.12
☐ 37 Mark Langston C	.25	.11	.03
☐ 38 Greg Myers C	.10	.05	.01
☐ 39 Spike Owen C	.10	.05	.01
☐ 40 Troy Percival R	3.00	1.35	.35
☐ 41 Tony Phillips U	1.00	.45	.12
☐ 42 Tim Salmon R	6.00	2.70	.75
☐ 43 Lee Smith R	4.00	1.80	.50
☐ 44 J.T. Snow U	.50	.23	.06
☐ 45 Jason Bere C	.10	.05	.01
☐ 46 Mike Devereaux U	.50	.23	.06
☐ 47 Ray Durham C	.50	.23	.06
☐ 48 Alex Fernandez C	.25	.11	.03
☐ 49 Ozzie Guillen R	3.00	1.35	.35
☐ 50 Roberto Hernandez C	.10	.05	.01
☐ 51 Lance Johnson U	.50	.23	.06
☐ 52 Ron Karkovice C	.10	.05	.01
☐ 53 Tim Raines U	1.00	.45	.12
☐ 54 Frank Thomas R	30.00	13.50	3.70
☐ 55 Robin Ventura U	1.00	.45	.12
☐ 56 Sandy Alomar R	4.00	1.80	.50
☐ 57 Carlos Baerga R	5.00	2.20	.60
☐ 58 Albert Belle R	15.00	6.75	1.85
☐ 59 Kenny Lofton R	8.00	3.60	1.00
☐ 60 Dennis Martinez C	.25	.11	.03
☐ 61 Jose Mesa U	1.00	.45	.12
☐ 62 Eddie Murray R	7.50	3.40	.95
☐ 63 Charles Nagy C	.25	.11	.03
☐ 64 Tony Pena C	.10	.05	.01
☐ 65 Eric Plunk R	3.00	1.35	.35
☐ 66 Manny Ramirez R	8.00	3.60	1.00
☐ 67 Paul Sorrento C	.10	.05	.01
☐ 68 Jim Thome R	6.00	2.70	.75
☐ 69 Omar Vizquel C	.25	.11	.03
☐ 70 Danny Bautista C	.10	.05	.01
☐ 71 Joe Boever C	.10	.05	.01
☐ 72 Chad Curtis C	.10	.05	.01
☐ 73 Cecil Fielder U	1.50	.70	.19
☐ 74 John Flaherty U	.50	.23	.06
☐ 75 Travis Fryman U	1.00	.45	.12
☐ 76 Kirk Gibson C	.25	.11	.03
☐ 77 Chris Gomez C	.10	.05	.01
☐ 78 Mike Henneman R	3.00	1.35	.35
☐ 79 Bob Higginson C	.75	.35	.09
☐ 80 Alan Trammell U	1.50	.70	.19
☐ 81 Lou Whitaker R	4.00	1.80	.50
☐ 82 Kevin Appier R	4.00	1.80	.50
☐ 83 Billy Brewer C	.10	.05	.01
☐ 84 Vince Coleman R	3.00	1.35	.35
☐ 85 Gary Gaetti C	.10	.05	.01
☐ 86 Greg Gagne C	.10	.05	.01
☐ 87 Tom Goodwin R	3.00	1.35	.35
☐ 88 Tom Gordon C	.10	.05	.01
☐ 89 Mark Gubicza C	.10	.05	.01
☐ 90 Bob Hamelin C	.10	.05	.01
☐ 91 Phil Hiatt C	.10	.05	.01
☐ 92 Wally Joyner R	4.00	1.80	.50
☐ 93 Brent Mayne C	.10	.05	.01
☐ 94 Jeff Montgomery C	.10	.05	.01
☐ 95 Ricky Bones C	.10	.05	.01
☐ 96 Mike Fetters C	.10	.05	.01
☐ 97 Darryl Hamilton C	.10	.05	.01
☐ 98 Pat Listach C	.10	.05	.01
☐ 99 Matt Mieske C	.10	.05	.01
☐ 100 Dave Nilsson C	.10	.05	.01
☐ 101 Joe Oliver U	.50	.23	.06
☐ 102 Kevin Seitzer U	.50	.23	.06
☐ 103 B.J. Surhoff U	.50	.23	.06
☐ 104 Jose Valentin C	.10	.05	.01
☐ 105 Greg Vaughn C	.25	.11	.03
☐ 106 Bill Wegman C	.10	.05	.01
☐ 107 Alex Cole U	.50	.23	.06
☐ 108 Marty Cordova C	.50	.23	.06
☐ 109 Chuck Knoblauch R	5.00	2.20	.60
☐ 110 Scott Leius C	.10	.05	.01
☐ 111 Pat Meares C	.10	.05	.01
☐ 112 Pedro Munoz C	.10	.05	.01
☐ 113 Kirby Puckett R	12.00	5.50	1.50
☐ 114 Scott Stahoviak C	.10	.05	.01
☐ 115 Mike Trombley C	.10	.05	.01
☐ 116 Matt Walbeck C	.10	.05	.01
☐ 117 Wade Boggs R	5.00	2.20	.60
☐ 118 David Cone U	1.00	.45	.12
☐ 119 Tony Fernandez C	.10	.05	.01
☐ 120 Don Mattingly R	15.00	6.75	1.85
☐ 121 Jack McDowell C	.25	.11	.03
☐ 122 Paul O'Neill U	1.00	.45	.12
☐ 123 Melido Perez C	.10	.05	.01
☐ 124 Luis Polonia C	.10	.05	.01
☐ 125 Ruben Sierra C	.25	.11	.03
☐ 126 Mike Stanley C	.10	.05	.01
☐ 127 Randy Velarde C	.10	.05	.01
☐ 128 John Wetteland R	4.00	1.80	.50
☐ 129 Bob Wickman C	.10	.05	.01
☐ 130 Bernie Williams C	.40	.18	.05
☐ 131 Gerald Williams C	.10	.05	.01
☐ 132 Geronimo Berroa C	.25	.11	.03
☐ 133 Mike Bordick U	.50	.23	.06
☐ 134 Scott Brosius C	.10	.05	.01
☐ 135 Dennis Eckersley C	.25	.11	.03
☐ 136 Brent Gates C	.10	.05	.01
☐ 137 Rickey Henderson U	2.00	.90	.25
☐ 138 Stan Javier C	.10	.05	.01
☐ 139 Mark McGwire R	10.00	4.50	1.25
☐ 140 Steve Ontiveros U	.50	.23	.06
☐ 141 Terry Steinbach C	.25	.11	.03
☐ 142 Todd Stottlemyre R	3.00	1.35	.35
☐ 143 Danny Tartabull C	.25	.11	.03
☐ 144 Bobby Ayala R	3.00	1.35	.35
☐ 145 Andy Benes U	1.00	.45	.12
☐ 146 Mike Blowers C	.10	.05	.01
☐ 147 Jay Buhner U	2.00	.90	.25
☐ 148 Joey Cora U	.50	.23	.06
☐ 149 Alex Diaz C	.10	.05	.01
☐ 150 Ken Griffey Jr. R	30.00	13.50	3.70
☐ 151 Randy Johnson R	6.00	2.70	.75
☐ 152 Edgar Martinez R	5.00	2.20	.60
☐ 153 Tino Martinez U	1.00	.45	.12
☐ 154 Bill Risley R	3.00	1.35	.35
☐ 155 Alex Rodriguez C	3.00	1.35	.35
☐ 156 Dan Wilson C	.25	.11	.03
☐ 157 Will Clark R	5.00	2.20	.60
☐ 158 Jeff Frye U	.50	.23	.06
☐ 159 Benji Gil C	.10	.05	.01
☐ 160 Juan Gonzalez C	1.50	.70	.19
☐ 161 Rusty Greer C	.40	.18	.05
☐ 162 Mark McLemore R	3.00	1.35	.35
☐ 163 Otis Nixon U	.50	.23	.06
☐ 164 Dean Palmer R	4.00	1.80	.50
☐ 165 Ivan Rodriguez R	7.50	3.40	.95
☐ 166 Kenny Rogers C	.10	.05	.01
☐ 167 Jeff Russell C	.10	.05	.01
☐ 168 Mickey Tettleton C	.10	.05	.01
☐ 169 Bob Tewksbury C	.10	.05	.01
☐ 170 Bobby Witt C	.10	.05	.01
☐ 171 Roberto Alomar R	8.00	3.60	1.00
☐ 172 Joe Carter R	5.00	2.20	.60
☐ 173 Alex Gonzalez C	.25	.11	.03
☐ 174 Candy Maldonado C	.10	.05	.01
☐ 175 Paul Molitor C	.60	.25	.07
☐ 176 John Olerud C	.10	.05	.01
☐ 177 Lance Parrish C	.25	.11	.03
☐ 178 Ed Sprague C	.10	.05	.01
☐ 179 Devon White C	.25	.11	.03
☐ 180 Woody Williams C	.10	.05	.01
☐ 181 Steve Avery C	.25	.11	.03
☐ 182 Jeff Blauser C	.10	.05	.01
☐ 183 Tom Glavine U	2.00	.90	.25
☐ 184 Marquis Grissom R	5.00	2.20	.60
☐ 185 Chipper Jones C	2.00	.90	.25
☐ 186 David Justice R	5.00	2.20	.60
☐ 187 Ryan Klesko U	3.00	1.35	.35
☐ 188 Mark Lemke C	.10	.05	.01
☐ 189 Javy Lopez C	.40	.18	.05
☐ 190 Greg Maddux R	20.00	9.00	2.50
☐ 191 Fred McGriff R	5.00	2.20	.60
☐ 192 Greg McMichael U	.50	.23	.06
☐ 193 John Smoltz R	6.00	2.70	.75
☐ 194 Mark Wohlers R	4.00	1.80	.50
☐ 195 Jim Bullinger U	.50	.23	.06
☐ 196 Shawon Dunston R	3.00	1.35	.35
☐ 197 Kevin Foster C	.10	.05	.01
☐ 198 Luis Gonzalez C	.10	.05	.01
☐ 199 Mark Grace R	5.00	2.20	.60
☐ 200 Brian McRae R	4.00	1.80	.50
☐ 201 Randy Myers R	3.00	1.35	.35
☐ 202 Jaime Navarro U	.50	.23	.06
☐ 203 Rey Sanchez U	.50	.23	.06
☐ 204 Scott Servais C	.10	.05	.01
☐ 205 Sammy Sosa R	6.00	2.70	.75
☐ 206 Steve Trachsel U	.50	.23	.06
☐ 207 Todd Zeile C	.10	.05	.01
☐ 208 Bret Boone R	3.00	1.35	.35
☐ 209 Jeff Branson U	.50	.23	.06
☐ 210 Jeff Brantley R	3.00	1.35	.35
☐ 211 Hector Carrasco C	.10	.05	.01
☐ 212 Ron Gant R	4.00	1.80	.50
☐ 213 Lenny Harris C	.10	.05	.01
☐ 214 Barry Larkin R	5.00	2.20	.60

☐ 215 Darren Lewis C	.10	.05	.01
☐ 216 Hal Morris C	.10	.05	.01
☐ 217 Mark Portugal C	.10	.05	.01
☐ 218 Jose Rijo U	.50	.23	.06
☐ 219 Reggie Sanders R	4.00	1.80	.50
☐ 220 Pete Schourek U	.50	.23	.06
☐ 221 John Smiley C	.10	.05	.01
☐ 222 Eddie Taubensee C	.10	.05	.01
☐ 223 David Wells C	.10	.05	.01
☐ 224 Jason Bates C	.10	.05	.01
☐ 225 Dante Bichette R	5.00	2.20	.60
☐ 226 Vinny Castilla U	1.00	.45	.12
☐ 227 Andres Galarraga R	5.00	2.20	.60
☐ 228 Joe Girardi U	.50	.23	.06
☐ 229 Mike Kingery C	.10	.05	.01
☐ 230 Steve Reed R	3.00	1.35	.35
☐ 231 Bruce Ruffin U	.50	.23	.06
☐ 232 Bret Saberhagen U	1.00	.45	.12
☐ 233 Bill Swift C	.10	.05	.01
☐ 234 Larry Walker R	4.00	1.80	.50
☐ 235 Walt Weiss C	.10	.05	.01
☐ 236 Eric Young C	.25	.11	.03
☐ 237 Kurt Abbott C	.10	.05	.01
☐ 238 John Burkett C	.10	.05	.01
☐ 239 Chuck Carr C	.10	.05	.01
☐ 240 Greg Colbrunn C	.10	.05	.01
☐ 241 Jeff Conine R	4.00	1.80	.50
☐ 242 Andre Dawson C	.25	.11	.03
☐ 243 Chris Hammond R	3.00	1.35	.35
☐ 244 Charles Johnson C	.25	.11	.03
☐ 245 Robb Nen C	.25	.11	.03
☐ 246 Terry Pendleton U	1.00	.45	.12
☐ 247 Gary Sheffield R	5.00	2.20	.60
☐ 248 Quilvio Veras C	.10	.05	.01
☐ 249 Jeff Bagwell U	6.00	2.70	.75
☐ 250 Derek Bell R	4.00	1.80	.50
☐ 251 Craig Biggio U	1.00	.45	.12
☐ 252 Doug Drabek C	.10	.05	.01
☐ 253 Tony Eusebio U	.50	.23	.06
☐ 254 John Hudek C	.10	.05	.01
☐ 255 Brian Hunter U	2.00	.90	.25
☐ 256 Todd Jones R	3.00	1.35	.35
☐ 257 Dave Magadan U	.50	.23	.06
☐ 258 Orlando Miller C	.10	.05	.01
☐ 259 James Mouton C	.10	.05	.01
☐ 260 Shane Reynolds C	.25	.11	.03
☐ 261 Greg Swindell C	.10	.05	.01
☐ 262 Billy Ashley C	.10	.05	.01
☐ 263 Tom Candiotti U	.50	.23	.06
☐ 264 Delino DeShields C	.10	.05	.01
☐ 265 Eric Karros R	4.00	1.80	.50
☐ 266 Roberto Kelly C	.10	.05	.01
☐ 267 Ramon Martinez C	.25	.11	.03
☐ 268 Raul Mondesi R	5.00	2.20	.60
☐ 269 Hideo Nomo R	15.00	6.75	1.85
☐ 270 Jose Offerman U	.50	.23	.06
☐ 271 Mike Piazza R	20.00	9.00	2.50
☐ 272 Kevin Tapani C	.10	.05	.01
☐ 273 Ismael Valdes U	1.00	.45	.12
☐ 274 Tim Wallach C	.10	.05	.01
☐ 275 Todd Worrell R	3.00	1.35	.35
☐ 276 Moises Alou R	4.00	1.80	.50
☐ 277 Sean Berry U	.50	.23	.06
☐ 278 Wil Cordero U	.50	.23	.06
☐ 279 Jeff Fassero C	.10	.05	.01
☐ 280 Darrin Fletcher C	.10	.05	.01
☐ 281 Mike Lansing C	.10	.05	.01
☐ 282 Pedro Martinez R	4.00	1.80	.50
☐ 283 Carlos Perez U	.50	.23	.06
☐ 284 Mel Rojas U	.50	.23	.06
☐ 285 Tim Scott R	3.00	1.35	.35
☐ 286 David Segui U	.50	.23	.06
☐ 287 Tony Tarasco U	.50	.23	.06
☐ 288 Rondell White C	.25	.11	.03
☐ 289 Rico Brogna C	.10	.05	.01
☐ 290 Brett Butler C	.25	.11	.03
☐ 291 John Franco C	.10	.05	.01
☐ 292 Pete Harnisch C	.10	.05	.01
☐ 293 Todd Hundley C	.25	.11	.03
☐ 294 Bobby Jones C	.10	.05	.01
☐ 295 Jeff Kent C	.10	.05	.01
☐ 296 Joe Orsulak U	.50	.23	.06
☐ 297 Ryan Thompson U	.50	.23	.06
☐ 298 Jose Vizcaino C	.10	.05	.01
☐ 299 Ricky Bottalico U	1.00	.45	.12
☐ 300 Darren Daulton C	.25	.11	.03
☐ 301 Mariano Duncan U	.50	.23	.06
☐ 302 Lenny Dykstra U	1.00	.45	.12
☐ 303 Jim Eisenreich U	.50	.23	.06
☐ 304 Tyler Green U	.50	.23	.06
☐ 305 Charlie Hayes U	.50	.23	.06
☐ 306 Dave Hollins C	.10	.05	.01
☐ 307 Gregg Jefferies C	.25	.11	.03
☐ 308 Mickey Morandini U	.50	.23	.06
☐ 309 Curt Schilling R	3.00	1.35	.35
☐ 310 Heathcliff Slocumb U	.50	.23	.06
☐ 311 Kevin Stocker C	.10	.05	.01
☐ 312 Jay Bell C	.10	.05	.01
☐ 313 Jacob Brumfield C	.10	.05	.01
☐ 314 Dave Clark U	.50	.23	.06
☐ 315 Carlos Garcia C	.10	.05	.01
☐ 316 Mark Johnson C	.10	.05	.01
☐ 317 Jeff King C	.10	.05	.01
☐ 318 Nelson Liriano U	.50	.23	.06
☐ 319 Al Martin U	.50	.23	.06
☐ 320 Orlando Merced U	.50	.23	.06
☐ 321 Dan Miceli U	.50	.23	.06
☐ 322 Denny Neagle C	.25	.11	.03
☐ 323 Mark Parent C	.10	.05	.01
☐ 324 Dan Plesac R	3.00	1.35	.35
☐ 325 Scott Cooper C	.10	.05	.01
☐ 326 Bernard Gilkey R	4.00	1.80	.50
☐ 327 Tom Henke R	3.00	1.35	.35
☐ 328 Ken Hill C	.10	.05	.01
☐ 329 Danny Jackson C	.10	.05	.01
☐ 330 Brian Jordan R	5.00	2.20	.60
☐ 331 Ray Lankford U	1.00	.45	.12
☐ 332 John Mabry U	1.00	.45	.12
☐ 333 Jose Oquendo C	.10	.05	.01
☐ 334 Tom Pagnozzi C	.10	.05	.01
☐ 335 Ozzie Smith U	4.00	1.80	.50
☐ 336 Andy Ashby U	.50	.23	.06
☐ 337 Brad Ausmus U	.50	.23	.06
☐ 338 Ken Caminiti U	2.00	.90	.25
☐ 339 Andujar Cedeno C	.10	.05	.01
☐ 340 Steve Finley R	4.00	1.80	.50
☐ 341 Tony Gwynn R	15.00	6.75	1.85
☐ 342 Joey Hamilton C	.40	.18	.05
☐ 343 Trevor Hoffman C	.25	.11	.03
☐ 344 Jody Reed C	.10	.05	.01
☐ 345 Bip Roberts R	3.00	1.35	.35
☐ 346 Eddie Williams C	.10	.05	.01
☐ 347 Rod Beck U	.50	.23	.06
☐ 348 Mike Benjamin U	.50	.23	.06
☐ 349 Barry Bonds R	8.00	3.60	1.00
☐ 350 Royce Clayton C	.10	.05	.01
☐ 351 Glenallen Hill C	.10	.05	.01
☐ 352 Kirt Manwaring C	.10	.05	.01
☐ 353 Terry Mulholland C	.10	.05	.01
☐ 354 John Patterson C	.10	.05	.01
☐ 355 J.R. Phillips C	.10	.05	.01
☐ 356 Deion Sanders R	5.00	2.20	.60
☐ 357 Steve Scarsone U	.50	.23	.06
☐ 358 Robby Thompson C	.10	.05	.01
☐ 359 William VanLandingham C	.10	.05	.01
☐ 360 Matt Williams R	5.00	2.20	.60

1996 Donruss Samples

This 8-card standard-size set was issued to preview the 1996 Donruss series. The fronts feature full-bleed color action photos. The player's number, position, team name and team logo are printed on a silver foil square at the bottom center. The horizontal backs carry a second color photo, biography, and career statistics. The disclaimer "PROMOTIONAL SAMPLE" is stamped diagonally across both sides of the cards.

	MINT	NRMT	EXC
COMPLETE SET (8)	12.00	5.50	1.50
COMMON CARD (1-8)	.50	.23	.06
☐ 1 Frank Thomas	3.00	1.35	.35
☐ 2 Barry Bonds	.50	.23	.06
☐ 3 Hideo Nomo	1.50	.70	.19
☐ 4 Ken Griffey Jr.	3.00	1.35	.35
☐ 5 Cal Ripken	2.50	1.10	.30
☐ 6 Manny Ramirez	1.00	.45	.12
☐ 7 Mike Piazza	2.00	.90	.25
☐ 8 Greg Maddux	2.00	.90	.25

1996 Donruss

The 1996 Donruss set was issued in two series of 330 and 220 cards respectively, for a total of 550. The 12-card packs had a suggested retail price of $1.79. The full-bleed fronts feature full-color action photos. The player's name is in white ink in the upper right. The Donruss logo, team name and team logo as well as uniform number and position are located in the bottom middle set against a silver foil background. The horizontal backs feature season and career stats, text, vital stats and another photo. There are no notable Rookie Cards in this set.

	MINT	NRMT	EXC
COMPLETE SET (550)	40.00	18.00	5.00
COMPLETE SERIES 1 (330)	25.00	11.00	3.10
COMPLETE SERIES 2 (220)	15.00	6.75	1.85
COMMON CARD (1-550)	.10	.05	.01
☐ 1 Frank Thomas	3.00	1.35	.35
☐ 2 Jason Bates	.10	.05	.01
☐ 3 Steve Sparks	.10	.05	.01
☐ 4 Scott Servais	.10	.05	.01
☐ 5 Angelo Encarnacion	.10	.05	.01
☐ 6 Scott Sanders	.10	.05	.01
☐ 7 Billy Ashley	.10	.05	.01
☐ 8 Alex Rodriguez	3.00	1.35	.35
☐ 9 Sean Bergman	.10	.05	.01
☐ 10 Brad Radke	.10	.05	.01
☐ 11 Andy Van Slyke	.25	.11	.03
☐ 12 Joe Girardi	.10	.05	.01
☐ 13 Mark Grudzielanek	.25	.11	.03
☐ 14 Rick Aguilera	.10	.05	.01
☐ 15 Randy Veres	.10	.05	.01
☐ 16 Tim Bogar	.10	.05	.01
☐ 17 Dave Veres	.10	.05	.01
☐ 18 Kevin Stocker	.10	.05	.01
☐ 19 Marquis Grissom	.25	.11	.03
☐ 20 Will Clark	.50	.23	.06
☐ 21 Jay Bell	.25	.11	.03
☐ 22 Allen Battle	.10	.05	.01
☐ 23 Frank Rodriguez	.25	.11	.03
☐ 24 Terry Steinbach	.25	.11	.03
☐ 25 Gerald Williams	.10	.05	.01
☐ 26 Sid Roberson	.10	.05	.01
☐ 27 Greg Zaun	.10	.05	.01
☐ 28 Ozzie Timmons	.10	.05	.01
☐ 29 Vaughn Eshelman	.10	.05	.01
☐ 30 Ed Sprague	.25	.11	.03
☐ 31 Gary DiSarcina	.10	.05	.01
☐ 32 Joe Boever	.10	.05	.01
☐ 33 Steve Avery	.25	.11	.03
☐ 34 Brad Ausmus	.10	.05	.01
☐ 35 Kirt Manwaring	.10	.05	.01
☐ 36 Gary Sheffield	.50	.23	.06
☐ 37 Jason Bere	.10	.05	.01
☐ 38 Jeff Manto	.10	.05	.01
☐ 39 David Cone	.25	.11	.03
☐ 40 Manny Ramirez	.75	.35	.09
☐ 41 Sandy Alomar Jr.	.10	.05	.01
☐ 42 Curtis Goodwin	.10	.05	.01
☐ 43 Tino Martinez	.25	.11	.03
☐ 44 Woody Williams	.10	.05	.01
☐ 45 Dean Palmer	.50	.23	.06
☐ 46 Hipolito Pichardo	.10	.05	.01
☐ 47 Jason Giambi	.50	.23	.06
☐ 48 Lance Johnson	.25	.11	.03
☐ 49 Bernard Gilkey	.25	.11	.03
☐ 50 Kirby Puckett	1.25	.55	.16
☐ 51 Tony Fernandez	.10	.05	.01
☐ 52 Alex Gonzalez	.10	.05	.01
☐ 53 Bret Saberhagen	.10	.05	.01
☐ 54 Lyle Mouton	.10	.05	.01
☐ 55 Brian McRae	.10	.05	.01
☐ 56 Mark Gubicza	.10	.05	.01
☐ 57 Sergio Valdez	.10	.05	.01
☐ 58 Darrin Fletcher	.10	.05	.01
☐ 59 Steve Parris	.10	.05	.01
☐ 60 Johnny Damon	.25	.11	.03
☐ 61 Rickey Henderson	.50	.23	.06
☐ 62 Darrell Whitmore	.10	.05	.01
☐ 63 Roberto Petagine	.10	.05	.01
☐ 64 Trenidad Hubbard	.10	.05	.01
☐ 65 Heathcliff Slocumb	.10	.05	.01
☐ 66 Steve Finley	.25	.11	.03
☐ 67 Mariano Rivera	.25	.11	.03
☐ 68 Brian L.Hunter	.25	.11	.03
☐ 69 Jamie Moyer	.10	.05	.01
☐ 70 Ellis Burks	.25	.11	.03
☐ 71 Pat Kelly	.10	.05	.01
☐ 72 Mickey Tettleton	.25	.11	.03
☐ 73 Garret Anderson	.25	.11	.03
☐ 74 Andy Pettitte	1.00	.45	.12
☐ 75 Glenallen Hill	.25	.11	.03
☐ 76 Brent Gates	.10	.05	.01
☐ 77 Lou Whitaker	.25	.11	.03
☐ 78 David Segui	.10	.05	.01
☐ 79 Dan Wilson	.10	.05	.01
☐ 80 Pat Listach	.10	.05	.01
☐ 81 Jeff Bagwell	1.25	.55	.16
☐ 82 Ben McDonald	.10	.05	.01
☐ 83 John Valentin	.25	.11	.03
☐ 84 John Jaha	.25	.11	.03
☐ 85 Pete Schourek	.25	.11	.03
☐ 86 Bryce Florie	.10	.05	.01
☐ 87 Brian Jordan	.25	.11	.03
☐ 88 Ron Karkovice	.10	.05	.01
☐ 89 Al Leiter	.10	.05	.01
☐ 90 Tony Longmire	.10	.05	.01
☐ 91 Nelson Liriano	.10	.05	.01
☐ 92 David Bell	.10	.05	.01
☐ 93 Kevin Gross	.10	.05	.01
☐ 94 Tom Candiotti	.10	.05	.01
☐ 95 Dave Martinez	.10	.05	.01
☐ 96 Greg Myers	.10	.05	.01
☐ 97 Rheal Cormier	.10	.05	.01
☐ 98 Chris Hammond	.10	.05	.01
☐ 99 Randy Myers	.10	.05	.01
☐ 100 Bill Pulsipher	.25	.11	.03
☐ 101 Jason Isringhausen	.50	.23	.06
☐ 102 Dave Stevens	.10	.05	.01
☐ 103 Roberto Alomar	.60	.25	.07
☐ 104 Bob Higginson	.50	.23	.06
☐ 105 Eddie Murray	.75	.35	.09
☐ 106 Matt Walbeck	.10	.05	.01
☐ 107 Mark Wohlers	.25	.11	.03
☐ 108 Jeff Nelson	.10	.05	.01
☐ 109 Tom Goodwin	.10	.05	.01
☐ 110 Cal Ripken CL	1.25	.55	.16
☐ 111 Rey Sanchez	.10	.05	.01
☐ 112 Hector Carrasco	.10	.05	.01
☐ 113 B.J. Surhoff	.10	.05	.01
☐ 114 Dan Miceli	.10	.05	.01
☐ 115 Dean Hartgraves	.10	.05	.01
☐ 116 John Burkett	.10	.05	.01
☐ 117 Gary Gaetti	.25	.11	.03
☐ 118 Ricky Bones	.10	.05	.01
☐ 119 Mike Macfarlane	.10	.05	.01
☐ 120 Bip Roberts	.10	.05	.01
☐ 121 Dave Mlicki	.10	.05	.01
☐ 122 Chili Davis	.10	.05	.01
☐ 123 Mark Whiten	.10	.05	.01
☐ 124 Herbert Perry	.10	.05	.01
☐ 125 Butch Henry	.10	.05	.01
☐ 126 Derek Bell	.25	.11	.03
☐ 127 Al Martin	.10	.05	.01
☐ 128 John Franco	.10	.05	.01
☐ 129 W. VanLandingham	.10	.05	.01
☐ 130 Mike Bordick	.25	.11	.03
☐ 131 Mike Mordecai	.10	.05	.01
☐ 132 Robby Thompson	.10	.05	.01
☐ 133 Greg Colbrunn	.10	.05	.01
☐ 134 Domingo Cedeno	.10	.05	.01
☐ 135 Chad Curtis	.10	.05	.01
☐ 136 Jose Hernandez	.10	.05	.01
☐ 137 Scott Klingenbeck	.10	.05	.01
☐ 138 Ryan Klesko	.50	.23	.06
☐ 139 John Smiley	.10	.05	.01
☐ 140 Charlie Hayes	.10	.05	.01
☐ 141 Jay Buhner	.50	.23	.06
☐ 142 Doug Drabek	.10	.05	.01
☐ 143 Roger Pavlik	.10	.05	.01
☐ 144 Todd Worrell	.25	.11	.03
☐ 145 Cal Ripken	2.50	1.10	.30
☐ 146 Steve Reed	.10	.05	.01
☐ 147 Chuck Finley	.10	.05	.01
☐ 148 Mike Blowers	.10	.05	.01
☐ 149 Orel Hershiser	.25	.11	.03
☐ 150 Allen Watson	.10	.05	.01
☐ 151 Ramon Martinez	.25	.11	.03
☐ 152 Melvin Nieves	.25	.11	.03
☐ 153 Tripp Cromer	.10	.05	.01
☐ 154 Yorkis Perez	.10	.05	.01
☐ 155 Stan Javier	.10	.05	.01
☐ 156 Mel Rojas	.25	.11	.03
☐ 157 Aaron Sele	.10	.05	.01
☐ 158 Eric Karros	.25	.11	.03
☐ 159 Robb Nen	.10	.05	.01
☐ 160 Raul Mondesi	.50	.23	.06
☐ 161 John Wetteland	.25	.11	.03
☐ 162 Tim Scott	.10	.05	.01
☐ 163 Kenny Rogers	.10	.05	.01
☐ 164 Melvin Bunch	.10	.05	.01
☐ 165 Rod Beck	.25	.11	.03
☐ 166 Andy Benes	.10	.05	.01
☐ 167 Lenny Dykstra	.25	.11	.03
☐ 168 Orlando Merced	.25	.11	.03
☐ 169 Tomas Perez	.25	.11	.03
☐ 170 Xavier Hernandez	.10	.05	.01
☐ 171 Ruben Sierra	.10	.05	.01
☐ 172 Alan Trammell	.25	.11	.03
☐ 173 Mike Fetters	.10	.05	.01
☐ 174 Wilson Alvarez	.50	.23	.06
☐ 175 Erik Hanson	.10	.05	.01
☐ 176 Travis Fryman	.25	.11	.03
☐ 177 Jim Abbott	.50	.23	.06
☐ 178 Bret Boone	.10	.05	.01
☐ 179 Sterling Hitchcock	.10	.05	.01
☐ 180 Pat Mahomes	.10	.05	.01
☐ 181 Mark Acre	.10	.05	.01
☐ 182 Charles Nagy	.25	.11	.03
☐ 183 Rusty Greer	.50	.23	.06
☐ 184 Mike Stanley	.10	.05	.01
☐ 185 Jim Bullinger	.10	.05	.01
☐ 186 Shane Andrews	.10	.05	.01
☐ 187 Brian Keyser	.10	.05	.01
☐ 188 Tyler Green	.10	.05	.01
☐ 189 Mark Grace	.50	.23	.06
☐ 190 Bob Hamelin	.10	.05	.01
☐ 191 Luis Ortiz	.10	.05	.01
☐ 192 Joe Carter	.25	.11	.03
☐ 193 Eddie Taubensee	.10	.05	.01
☐ 194 Brian Anderson	.10	.05	.01
☐ 195 Edgardo Alfonzo	.25	.11	.03
☐ 196 Pedro Munoz	.10	.05	.01
☐ 197 David Justice	.50	.23	.06
☐ 198 Trevor Hoffman	.25	.11	.03
☐ 199 Bobby Ayala	.10	.05	.01
☐ 200 Tony Eusebio	.10	.05	.01
☐ 201 Jeff Russell	.10	.05	.01
☐ 202 Mike Hampton	.10	.05	.01
☐ 203 Walt Weiss	.10	.05	.01
☐ 204 Joey Hamilton	.25	.11	.03
☐ 205 Roberto Hernandez	.25	.11	.03
☐ 206 Greg Vaughn	.50	.23	.06
☐ 207 Felipe Lira	.10	.05	.01
☐ 208 Harold Baines	.25	.11	.03

Card			
☐ 209 Tim Wallach	.10	.05	.01
☐ 210 Manny Alexander	.10	.05	.01
☐ 211 Tim Laker	.10	.05	.01
☐ 212 Chris Haney	.10	.05	.01
☐ 213 Brian Maxcy	.10	.05	.01
☐ 214 Eric Young	.25	.11	.03
☐ 215 Darryl Strawberry	.25	.11	.03
☐ 216 Barry Bonds	.75	.35	.09
☐ 217 Tim Naehring	.25	.11	.03
☐ 218 Scott Brosius	.25	.11	.03
☐ 219 Reggie Sanders	.25	.11	.03
☐ 220 Eddie Murray CL	.50	.23	.06
☐ 221 Luis Alicea	.10	.05	.01
☐ 222 Albert Belle	1.25	.55	.16
☐ 223 Benji Gil	.10	.05	.01
☐ 224 Dante Bichette	.50	.23	.06
☐ 225 Bobby Bonilla	.25	.11	.03
☐ 226 Todd Stottlemyre	.10	.05	.01
☐ 227 Jim Edmonds	.25	.11	.03
☐ 228 Todd Jones	.10	.05	.01
☐ 229 Shawn Green	.50	.23	.06
☐ 230 Javier Lopez	.50	.23	.06
☐ 231 Ariel Prieto	.10	.05	.01
☐ 232 Tony Phillips	.25	.11	.03
☐ 233 James Mouton	.10	.05	.01
☐ 234 Jose Oquendo	.10	.05	.01
☐ 235 Royce Clayton	.10	.05	.01
☐ 236 Chuck Carr	.10	.05	.01
☐ 237 Doug Jones	.10	.05	.01
☐ 238 Mark McLemore	.10	.05	.01
☐ 239 Bill Swift	.10	.05	.01
☐ 240 Scott Leius	.10	.05	.01
☐ 241 Russ Davis	.10	.05	.01
☐ 242 Ray Durham	.50	.23	.06
☐ 243 Matt Mieske	.10	.05	.01
☐ 244 Brent Mayne	.10	.05	.01
☐ 245 Thomas Howard	.10	.05	.01
☐ 246 Troy O'Leary	.25	.11	.03
☐ 247 Jacob Brumfield	.10	.05	.01
☐ 248 Mickey Morandini	.10	.05	.01
☐ 249 Todd Hundley	.25	.11	.03
☐ 250 Chris Bosio	.10	.05	.01
☐ 251 Omar Vizquel	.25	.11	.03
☐ 252 Mike Lansing	.10	.05	.01
☐ 253 John Mabry	.25	.11	.03
☐ 254 Mike Perez	.10	.05	.01
☐ 255 Delino DeShields	.10	.05	.01
☐ 256 Wil Cordero	.10	.05	.01
☐ 257 Mike James	.10	.05	.01
☐ 258 Todd Van Poppel	.10	.05	.01
☐ 259 Joey Cora	.10	.05	.01
☐ 260 Andre Dawson	.25	.11	.03
☐ 261 Jerry DiPoto	.10	.05	.01
☐ 262 Rick Krivda	.10	.05	.01
☐ 263 Glenn Dishman	.25	.11	.03
☐ 264 Mike Mimbs	.10	.05	.01
☐ 265 John Ericks	.10	.05	.01
☐ 266 Jose Canseco	.50	.23	.06
☐ 267 Jeff Branson	.10	.05	.01
☐ 268 Curt Leskanic	.10	.05	.01
☐ 269 Jon Nunnally	.10	.05	.01
☐ 270 Scott Stahoviak	.10	.05	.01
☐ 271 Jeff Montgomery	.10	.05	.01
☐ 272 Hal Morris	.10	.05	.01
☐ 273 Esteban Loaiza	.10	.05	.01
☐ 274 Rico Brogna	.10	.05	.01
☐ 275 Dave Winfield	.50	.23	.06
☐ 276 J.R. Phillips	.10	.05	.01
☐ 277 Todd Zeile	.10	.05	.01
☐ 278 Tom Pagnozzi	.10	.05	.01
☐ 279 Mark Lemke	.10	.05	.01
☐ 280 Dave Magadan	.10	.05	.01
☐ 281 Greg McMichael	.10	.05	.01
☐ 282 Mike Morgan	.10	.05	.01
☐ 283 Moises Alou	.25	.11	.03
☐ 284 Dennis Martinez	.25	.11	.03
☐ 285 Jeff Kent	.10	.05	.01
☐ 286 Mark Johnson	.10	.05	.01
☐ 287 Darren Lewis	.10	.05	.01
☐ 288 Brad Clontz	.10	.05	.01
☐ 289 Chad Fonville	.10	.05	.01
☐ 290 Paul Sorrento	.10	.05	.01
☐ 291 Lee Smith	.25	.11	.03
☐ 292 Tom Glavine	.50	.23	.06
☐ 293 Antonio Osuna	.10	.05	.01
☐ 294 Kevin Foster	.10	.05	.01
☐ 295 Sandy Martinez	.10	.05	.01
☐ 296 Mark Leiter	.10	.05	.01
☐ 297 Julian Tavarez	.10	.05	.01
☐ 298 Mike Kelly	.10	.05	.01
☐ 299 Joe Oliver	.10	.05	.01
☐ 300 John Flaherty	.10	.05	.01
☐ 301 Don Mattingly	1.50	.70	.19
☐ 302 Pat Meares	.10	.05	.01
☐ 303 John Doherty	.10	.05	.01
☐ 304 Joe Vitiello	.10	.05	.01
☐ 305 Vinny Castilla	.25	.11	.03
☐ 306 Jeff Brantley	.10	.05	.01
☐ 307 Mike Greenwell	.10	.05	.01
☐ 308 Midre Cummings	.10	.05	.01
☐ 309 Curt Schilling	.10	.05	.01
☐ 310 Ken Caminiti	.50	.23	.06
☐ 311 Scott Erickson	.10	.05	.01
☐ 312 Carl Everett	.10	.05	.01
☐ 313 Charles Johnson	.25	.11	.03
☐ 314 Alex Diaz	.10	.05	.01
☐ 315 Jose Mesa	.10	.05	.01
☐ 316 Mark Carreon	.10	.05	.01
☐ 317 Carlos Perez	.10	.05	.01
☐ 318 Ismael Valdes	.25	.11	.03
☐ 319 Frank Castillo	.10	.05	.01
☐ 320 Tom Henke	.25	.11	.03
☐ 321 Spike Owen	.10	.05	.01
☐ 322 Joe Orsulak	.10	.05	.01
☐ 323 Paul Menhart	.10	.05	.01
☐ 324 Pedro Borbon	.10	.05	.01
☐ 325 Paul Molitor CL	.50	.23	.06
☐ 326 Jeff Cirillo	.10	.05	.01
☐ 327 Edwin Hurtado	.10	.05	.01
☐ 328 Orlando Miller	.10	.05	.01
☐ 329 Steve Ontiveros	.10	.05	.01
☐ 330 Kirby Puckett CL	.50	.23	.06
☐ 331 Scott Bullett	.10	.05	.01
☐ 332 Andres Galarraga	.50	.23	.06
☐ 333 Cal Eldred	.10	.05	.01
☐ 334 Sammy Sosa	.50	.23	.06
☐ 335 Don Slaught	.10	.05	.01
☐ 336 Jody Reed	.10	.05	.01
☐ 337 Roger Cedeno	.25	.11	.03
☐ 338 Ken Griffey Jr.	3.00	1.35	.35
☐ 339 Todd Hollandsworth	.25	.11	.03
☐ 340 Mike Trombley	.10	.05	.01
☐ 341 Gregg Jefferies	.50	.23	.06
☐ 342 Larry Walker	.50	.23	.06
☐ 343 Pedro Martinez	.25	.11	.03
☐ 344 Dwayne Hosey	.10	.05	.01
☐ 345 Terry Pendleton	.25	.11	.03
☐ 346 Pete Harnisch	.10	.05	.01
☐ 347 Tony Castillo	.10	.05	.01
☐ 348 Paul Quantrill	.10	.05	.01
☐ 349 Fred McGriff	.50	.23	.06
☐ 350 Ivan Rodriguez	.75	.35	.09
☐ 351 Butch Huskey	.25	.11	.03
☐ 352 Ozzie Smith	.75	.35	.09
☐ 353 Marty Cordova	.25	.11	.03
☐ 354 John Wasdin	.10	.05	.01
☐ 355 Wade Boggs	.50	.23	.06
☐ 356 Dave Nilsson	.25	.11	.03
☐ 357 Rafael Palmeiro	.50	.23	.06
☐ 358 Luis Gonzalez	.10	.05	.01
☐ 359 Reggie Jefferson	.10	.05	.01
☐ 360 Carlos Delgado	.25	.11	.03
☐ 361 Orlando Palmeiro	.10	.05	.01
☐ 362 Chris Gomez	.10	.05	.01
☐ 363 John Smoltz	.50	.23	.06
☐ 364 Marc Newfield	.25	.11	.03
☐ 365 Matt Williams	.50	.23	.06
☐ 366 Jesus Tavarez	.10	.05	.01
☐ 367 Bruce Ruffin	.10	.05	.01
☐ 368 Sean Berry	.10	.05	.01
☐ 369 Randy Velarde	.10	.05	.01
☐ 370 Tony Pena	.10	.05	.01
☐ 371 Jim Thome	.60	.25	.07
☐ 372 Jeffrey Hammonds	.25	.11	.03
☐ 373 Bob Wolcott	.10	.05	.01
☐ 374 Juan Guzman	.10	.05	.01
☐ 375 Juan Gonzalez	1.50	.70	.19
☐ 376 Michael Tucker	.25	.11	.03
☐ 377 Doug Johns	.10	.05	.01
☐ 378 Mike Cameron	1.00	.45	.12
☐ 379 Ray Lankford	.25	.11	.03
☐ 380 Jose Parra	.10	.05	.01
☐ 381 Jimmy Key	.25	.11	.03
☐ 382 John Olerud	.10	.05	.01
☐ 383 Kevin Ritz	.10	.05	.01
☐ 384 Tim Raines	.50	.23	.06
☐ 385 Rich Amaral	.10	.05	.01
☐ 386 Keith Lockhart	.10	.05	.01
☐ 387 Steve Scarsone	.10	.05	.01
☐ 388 Cliff Floyd	.10	.05	.01
☐ 389 Rich Aude	.10	.05	.01
☐ 390 Hideo Nomo	.75	.35	.09
☐ 391 Geronimo Berroa	.25	.11	.03
☐ 392 Pat Rapp	.10	.05	.01
☐ 393 Dustin Hermanson	.25	.11	.03
☐ 394 Greg Maddux	2.00	.90	.25
☐ 395 Darren Daulton	.25	.11	.03
☐ 396 Kenny Lofton	.75	.35	.09
☐ 397 Ruben Rivera	.60	.25	.07
☐ 398 Billy Wagner	.50	.23	.06
☐ 399 Kevin Brown	.25	.11	.03
☐ 400 Mike Kingery	.10	.05	.01
☐ 401 Bernie Williams	.60	.25	.07
☐ 402 Otis Nixon	.10	.05	.01
☐ 403 Damion Easley	.10	.05	.01
☐ 404 Paul O'Neill	.10	.05	.01
☐ 405 Deion Sanders	.50	.23	.06
☐ 406 Dennis Eckersley	.25	.11	.03
☐ 407 Tony Clark	.60	.25	.07
☐ 408 Rondell White	.25	.11	.03
☐ 409 Luis Sojo	.10	.05	.01
☐ 410 David Hulse	.10	.05	.01
☐ 411 Shane Reynolds	.10	.05	.01
☐ 412 Chris Hoiles	.10	.05	.01
☐ 413 Lee Tinsley	.10	.05	.01
☐ 414 Scott Karl	.10	.05	.01
☐ 415 Ron Gant	.25	.11	.03
☐ 416 Brian Johnson	.10	.05	.01
☐ 417 Jose Oliva	.10	.05	.01
☐ 418 Jack McDowell	.50	.23	.06
☐ 419 Paul Molitor	.60	.25	.07
☐ 420 Ricky Bottalico	.10	.05	.01
☐ 421 Paul Wagner	.10	.05	.01
☐ 422 Terry Bradshaw	.10	.05	.01
☐ 423 Bob Tewksbury	.10	.05	.01
☐ 424 Mike Piazza	2.00	.90	.25
☐ 425 Luis Andujar	.25	.11	.03
☐ 426 Mark Langston	.10	.05	.01
☐ 427 Stan Belinda	.10	.05	.01
☐ 428 Kurt Abbott	.10	.05	.01
☐ 429 Shawon Dunston	.10	.05	.01
☐ 430 Bobby Jones	.10	.05	.01
☐ 431 Jose Vizcaino	.10	.05	.01
☐ 432 Matt Lawton	.10	.05	.01
☐ 433 Pat Hentgen	.25	.11	.03
☐ 434 Cecil Fielder	.25	.11	.03
☐ 435 Carlos Baerga	.25	.11	.03
☐ 436 Rich Becker	.25	.11	.03
☐ 437 Chipper Jones	2.00	.90	.25
☐ 438 Bill Risley	.10	.05	.01
☐ 439 Kevin Appier	.25	.11	.03
☐ 440 Wade Boggs CL 2500 Career Hits 8/23/95	.50	.23	.06
☐ 441 Jaime Navarro	.10	.05	.01
☐ 442 Barry Larkin	.50	.23	.06
☐ 443 Jose Valentin	.10	.05	.01
☐ 444 Bryan Rekar	.10	.05	.01
☐ 445 Rick Wilkins	.10	.05	.01
☐ 446 Quilvio Veras	.10	.05	.01
☐ 447 Greg Gagne	.10	.05	.01
☐ 448 Mark Kiefer	.10	.05	.01
☐ 449 Bobby Witt	.10	.05	.01
☐ 450 Andy Ashby	.10	.05	.01
☐ 451 Alex Ochoa	.25	.11	.03
☐ 452 Jorge Fabregas	.10	.05	.01
☐ 453 Gene Schall	.10	.05	.01
☐ 454 Ken Hill	.10	.05	.01
☐ 455 Tony Tarasco	.10	.05	.01
☐ 456 Donnie Wall	.10	.05	.01
☐ 457 Carlos Garcia	.10	.05	.01
☐ 458 Ryan Thompson	.10	.05	.01
☐ 459 Marvin Benard	.10	.05	.01
☐ 460 Jose Herrera	.10	.05	.01
☐ 461 Jeff Blauser	.10	.05	.01
☐ 462 Chris Hook	.10	.05	.01
☐ 463 Jeff Conine	.25	.11	.03
☐ 464 Devon White	.10	.05	.01
☐ 465 Danny Bautista	.10	.05	.01
☐ 466 Steve Trachsel	.10	.05	.01
☐ 467 C.J. Nitkowski	.10	.05	.01
☐ 468 Mike Devereaux	.10	.05	.01
☐ 469 David Wells	.10	.05	.01
☐ 470 Jim Eisenreich	.10	.05	.01
☐ 471 Edgar Martinez	.25	.11	.03
☐ 472 Craig Biggio	.25	.11	.03
☐ 473 Jeff Frye	.10	.05	.01
☐ 474 Karim Garcia	.60	.25	.07
☐ 475 Jimmy Haynes	.10	.05	.01
☐ 476 Darren Holmes	.10	.05	.01
☐ 477 Tim Salmon	.50	.23	.06
☐ 478 Randy Johnson	.50	.23	.06
☐ 479 Eric Plunk	.10	.05	.01
☐ 480 Scott Cooper	.10	.05	.01
☐ 481 Chan Ho Park	.50	.23	.06
☐ 482 Ray McDavid	.10	.05	.01
☐ 483 Mark Petkovsek	.10	.05	.01
☐ 484 Greg Swindell	.10	.05	.01
☐ 485 George Williams	.10	.05	.01
☐ 486 Yamil Benitez	.25	.11	.03
☐ 487 Tim Wakefield	.10	.05	.01
☐ 488 Kevin Tapani	.10	.05	.01
☐ 489 Derrick May	.10	.05	.01
☐ 490 Ken Griffey Jr. CL 1000 Career Hits 8/16/95	1.50	.70	.19
☐ 491 Derek Jeter	2.00	.90	.25
☐ 492 Jeff Fassero	.10	.05	.01
☐ 493 Benito Santiago	.10	.05	.01
☐ 494 Tom Gordon	.10	.05	.01
☐ 495 Jamie Brewington	.10	.05	.01
☐ 496 Vince Coleman	.10	.05	.01
☐ 497 Kevin Jordan	.10	.05	.01
☐ 498 Jeff King	.25	.11	.03
☐ 499 Mike Simms	.10	.05	.01
☐ 500 Jose Rijo	.10	.05	.01
☐ 501 Denny Neagle	.25	.11	.03
☐ 502 Jose Lima	.10	.05	.01
☐ 503 Kevin Seitzer	.10	.05	.01
☐ 504 Alex Fernandez	.25	.11	.03
☐ 505 Mo Vaughn	.75	.35	.09
☐ 506 Phil Nevin	.10	.05	.01
☐ 507 J.T. Snow	.25	.11	.03
☐ 508 Andujar Cedeno	.10	.05	.01
☐ 509 Ozzie Guillen	.10	.05	.01
☐ 510 Mark Clark	.10	.05	.01
☐ 511 Mark McGwire	1.00	.45	.12
☐ 512 Jeff Reboulet	.10	.05	.01
☐ 513 Armando Benitez	.10	.05	.01
☐ 514 LaTroy Hawkins	.10	.05	.01
☐ 515 Brett Butler	.10	.05	.01
☐ 516 Tavo Alvarez	.10	.05	.01
☐ 517 Chris Snopek	.10	.05	.01
☐ 518 Mike Mussina	.60	.25	.07
☐ 519 Darryl Kile	.10	.05	.01
☐ 520 Wally Joyner	.10	.05	.01
☐ 521 Willie McGee	.10	.05	.01
☐ 522 Kent Mercker	.10	.05	.01
☐ 523 Mike Jackson	.10	.05	.01
☐ 524 Troy Percival	.10	.05	.01
☐ 525 Tony Gwynn	1.25	.55	.16
☐ 526 Ron Coomer	.10	.05	.01
☐ 527 Darryl Hamilton	.10	.05	.01
☐ 528 Phil Plantier	.10	.05	.01
☐ 529 Norm Charlton	.10	.05	.01
☐ 530 Craig Paquette	.10	.05	.01
☐ 531 Dave Burba	.10	.05	.01
☐ 532 Mike Henneman	.10	.05	.01
☐ 533 Terrell Wade	.25	.11	.03
☐ 534 Eddie Williams	.10	.05	.01
☐ 535 Robin Ventura	.25	.11	.03
☐ 536 Chuck Knoblauch	.50	.23	.06
☐ 537 Les Norman	.10	.05	.01
☐ 538 Brady Anderson	.50	.23	.06
☐ 539 Roger Clemens	.60	.25	.07
☐ 540 Mark Portugal	.10	.05	.01
☐ 541 Mike Matheny	.10	.05	.01
☐ 542 Jeff Parrett	.10	.05	.01
☐ 543 Roberto Kelly	.10	.05	.01
☐ 544 Damon Buford	.10	.05	.01
☐ 545 Chad Ogea	.10	.05	.01
☐ 546 Jose Offerman	.10	.05	.01
☐ 547 Brian Barber	.10	.05	.01
☐ 548 Danny Tartabull	.10	.05	.01
☐ 549 Duane Singleton	.10	.05	.01
☐ 550 Tony Gwynn CL 1000 Career Runs 5/7/95	.60	.25	.07

1996 Donruss Press Proofs

Randomly inserted at a rate of one in 10 first and second series packs, these cards are parallel to the regular Donruss issue. Even though they are not sequentially numbered, production on these cards were limited to 2,000 cards. Each card is noted as being a Press Proof in gold foil on the front.

	MINT	NRMT	EXC
COMPLETE SET (550)	2000.00	900.00	250.00
COMPLETE SERIES 1 (330)	1200.00	550.00	150.00
COMPLETE SERIES 2 (220)	800.00	350.00	100.00
COMMON CARD (1-550)	2.00	.90	.25

*STARS: 12.5X TO 25X BASIC CARDS
*YOUNG STARS: 7.5X TO 15X BASIC CARDS

1996 Donruss Diamond Kings

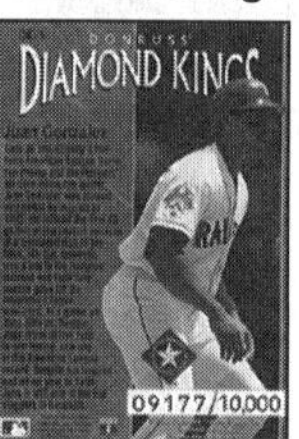

These 31 standard-size cards were randomly inserted into packs and issued in two series of 14 and 17 cards. They were inserted at a ratio of approximately one every 60 packs. The cards are sequentially numbered in the back lower right as "X" of 10,000. The fronts feature player portraits by noted sports artist Dick Perez. These cards are gold-foil stamped and the portraits are surrounded by gold-foil borders. The backs feature text about the player as well as a player photo. The cards are numbered on the back with a "DK" prefix.

	MINT	NRMT	EXC
COMPLETE SET (31)	300.00	135.00	38.00
COMPLETE SERIES 1 (14)	150.00	70.00	19.00
COMPLETE SERIES 2 (17)	150.00	70.00	19.00
COMMON CARD (1-31)	4.00	1.80	.50
☐ 1 Frank Thomas	50.00	22.00	6.25
☐ 2 Mo Vaughn	12.00	5.50	1.50
☐ 3 Manny Ramirez	12.00	5.50	1.50
☐ 4 Mark McGwire	15.00	6.75	1.85
☐ 5 Juan Gonzalez	25.00	11.00	3.10
☐ 6 Roberto Alomar	10.00	4.50	1.25
☐ 7 Tim Salmon	6.00	2.70	.75
☐ 8 Barry Bonds	12.00	5.50	1.50
☐ 9 Tony Gwynn	20.00	9.00	2.50
☐ 10 Reggie Sanders	5.00	2.20	.60
☐ 11 Larry Walker	6.00	2.70	.75
☐ 12 Pedro Martinez	5.00	2.20	.60
☐ 13 Jeff King	4.00	1.80	.50
☐ 14 Mark Grace	6.00	2.70	.75
☐ 15 Greg Maddux	25.00	11.00	3.10
☐ 16 Don Mattingly	20.00	9.00	2.50
☐ 17 Gregg Jefferies	4.00	1.80	.50
☐ 18 Chad Curtis	4.00	1.80	.50
☐ 19 Jason Isringhausen	4.00	1.80	.50
☐ 20 B.J. Surhoff	4.00	1.80	.50
☐ 21 Jeff Conine	5.00	2.20	.60
☐ 22 Kirby Puckett	20.00	9.00	2.50
☐ 23 Derek Bell	4.00	1.80	.50
☐ 24 Wally Joyner	4.00	1.80	.50
☐ 25 Brian Jordan	5.00	2.20	.60
☐ 26 Edgar Martinez	5.00	2.20	.60
☐ 27 Hideo Nomo	10.00	4.50	1.25
☐ 28 Mike Mussina	8.00	3.60	1.00

☐ 29 Eddie Murray	10.00	4.50	1.25
☐ 30 Cal Ripken	30.00	13.50	3.70
☐ 31 Checklist	4.00	1.80	.50

1996 Donruss Elite

Randomly inserted approximately one in every 75 packs, this 12-card standard-size set is continuously numbered (61-72) from the previous year. The fronts contain an action photo surrounded by a silver border. Limited to 10,000 and sequentially numbered, the backs contain a small photo and write up.

	MINT	NRMT	EXC
COMPLETE SET (12)	300.00	135.00	38.00
COMPLETE SERIES 1 (6)	150.00	70.00	19.00
COMPLETE SERIES 2 (6)	150.00	70.00	19.00
COMMON CARD (61-72)	8.00	3.60	1.00
☐ 61 Cal Ripken	60.00	27.00	7.50
☐ 62 Hideo Nomo	25.00	11.00	3.10
☐ 63 Reggie Sanders	8.00	3.60	1.00
☐ 64 Mo Vaughn	20.00	9.00	2.50
☐ 65 Tim Salmon	10.00	4.50	1.25
☐ 66 Chipper Jones	50.00	22.00	6.25
☐ 67 Manny Ramirez	12.00	5.50	1.50
☐ 68 Greg Maddux	30.00	13.50	3.70
☐ 69 Frank Thomas	50.00	22.00	6.25
☐ 70 Ken Griffey Jr.	50.00	22.00	6.25
☐ 71 Dante Bichette	10.00	4.50	1.25
☐ 72 Tony Gwynn	20.00	9.00	2.50

1996 Donruss Freeze Frame

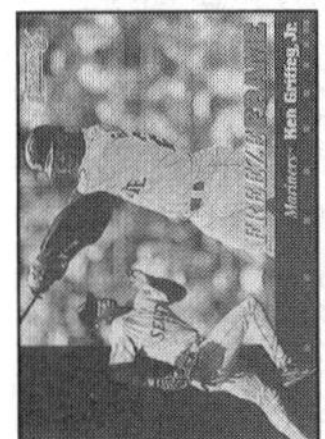

Randomly inserted in second series packs at a rate of one in 60, this 8-card standard-size set features the top hitters and pitchers in baseball. Just 5,000 of each card were produced and sequentially numbered. In a horizontal format with round corners, the fronts display a crosshatched color player photo that is bordered on the left and bottom by thick black borders. A second color player cutout is superposed on the photo. The backs have three small color photos, '95 season highlights, and a brief note.

	MINT	NRMT	EXC
COMPLETE SET (8)	200.00	90.00	25.00
COMMON CARD (1-8)	10.00	4.50	1.25
☐ 1 Frank Thomas	40.00	18.00	5.00
☐ 2 Ken Griffey Jr.	40.00	18.00	5.00
☐ 3 Cal Ripken	30.00	13.50	3.70
☐ 4 Hideo Nomo	10.00	4.50	1.25
☐ 5 Greg Maddux	25.00	11.00	3.10
☐ 6 Albert Belle	15.00	6.75	1.85
☐ 7 Chipper Jones	25.00	11.00	3.10
☐ 8 Mike Piazza	25.00	11.00	3.10

1996 Donruss Hit List

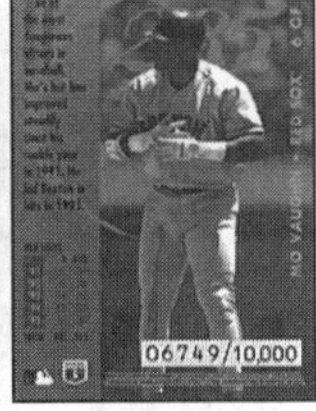

This 16-card standard-size set was randomly inserted at a rate of one in every 60 packs and salutes the most consistent hitters in the game. The cards are sequentially numbered out of 10,000. The fronts feature full-color shots set against a silver-foil background that is complemented by a team color duotone and features a gold foil team logo and "Hit List" logo. The backs have a color action photo as well as having year-by-year and career hit and batting average stats.

	MINT	NRMT	EXC
COMPLETE SET (16)	120.00	55.00	15.00
COMPLETE SERIES 1 (8)	60.00	27.00	7.50
COMPLETE SERIES 2 (8)	60.00	27.00	7.50
COMMON CARD (1-16)	3.00	1.35	.35
☐ 1 Tony Gwynn	12.00	5.50	1.50
☐ 2 Ken Griffey Jr.	30.00	13.50	3.70
☐ 3 Will Clark	6.00	2.70	.75
☐ 4 Mike Piazza	20.00	9.00	2.50
☐ 5 Carlos Baerga	3.00	1.35	.35
☐ 6 Mo Vaughn	8.00	3.60	1.00
☐ 7 Mark Grace	6.00	2.70	.75
☐ 8 Kirby Puckett	12.00	5.50	1.50
☐ 9 Frank Thomas	30.00	13.50	3.70
☐ 10 Barry Bonds	8.00	3.60	1.00
☐ 11 Jeff Bagwell	12.00	5.50	1.50
☐ 12 Edgar Martinez	4.00	1.80	.50
☐ 13 Tim Salmon	6.00	2.70	.75
☐ 14 Wade Boggs	6.00	2.70	.75
☐ 15 Don Mattingly	15.00	6.75	1.85
☐ 16 Eddie Murray	8.00	3.60	1.00

1996 Donruss Long Ball Leaders

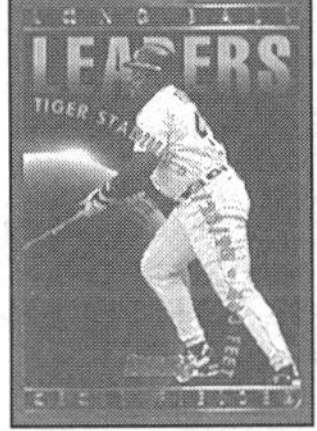

This eight-card standard-size set was randomly inserted into series one retail packs. They were inserted at a rate of approximately one in every 96 packs. The cards are sequentially numbered out of 5,000. The set highlights eight top sluggers and their farthest home run distance of 1995. The fronts feature a player photo set against a silver-foil background. The words "Long Ball Leaders" are on the top of the card while the stadium, date and distance of the blast are in the middle. The player's name is at the bottom. The back has a player photo and information about the game in which the mighty clout occurred.

	MINT	NRMT	EXC
COMPLETE SET (8)	200.00	90.00	25.00
COMMON CARD (1-8)	8.00	3.60	1.00
☐ 1 Barry Bonds	20.00	9.00	2.50
☐ 2 Ryan Klesko	12.00	5.50	1.50
☐ 3 Mark McGwire	25.00	11.00	3.10
☐ 4 Raul Mondesi	10.00	4.50	1.25
☐ 5 Cecil Fielder	8.00	3.60	1.00
☐ 6 Ken Griffey Jr.	80.00	36.00	10.00
☐ 7 Larry Walker	8.00	3.60	1.00
☐ 8 Frank Thomas	80.00	36.00	10.00

1996 Donruss Power Alley

This ten-card standard-size set was randomly inserted into series one hobby packs. They were inserted at a rate of approximately one in every 92 packs. These cards are all sequentially numbered out of 5,000. These cards feature a player photo set against a diamond design and team holographic background. The horizontal backs feature a player photo, some text and the player's 1995 power statistics.

	MINT	NRMT	EXC
COMPLETE SET (10)	150.00	70.00	19.00
COMMON CARD (1-10)	5.00	2.20	.60
☐ 1 Frank Thomas	50.00	22.00	6.25
☐ 2 Barry Bonds	12.00	5.50	1.50
☐ 3 Reggie Sanders	5.00	2.20	.60
☐ 4 Albert Belle	20.00	9.00	2.50
☐ 5 Tim Salmon	6.00	2.70	.75
☐ 6 Dante Bichette	6.00	2.70	.75
☐ 7 Mo Vaughn	12.00	5.50	1.50
☐ 8 Jim Edmonds	5.00	2.20	.60
☐ 9 Manny Ramirez	12.00	5.50	1.50
☐ 10 Ken Griffey Jr.	50.00	22.00	6.25

1996 Donruss Power Alley Die Cuts

These 10 scarce cards parallel the more common Power Alley inserts. The difference is the diecut design on the card edges. Only 500 of each card was printed and each is individually numbered on back.

	MINT	NRMT	EXC
COMPLETE SET (10)	1000.00	450.00	125.00
COMMON CARD (1-10)	30.00	13.50	3.70

*DIE CUTS: 3X TO 6X BASIC CARDS..

1996 Donruss Pure Power

Randomly inserted in retail and magazine packs only at a rate of one in eight, this eight-card set features color action player photos of eight of the most powerful players in Major League baseball.

	MINT	NRMT	EXC
COMPLETE SET (8)	175.00	80.00	22.00
COMMON CARD (1-8)	8.00	3.60	1.00
☐ 1 Raul Mondesi	8.00	3.60	1.00
☐ 2 Barry Bonds	15.00	6.75	1.85
☐ 3 Albert Belle	25.00	11.00	3.10
☐ 4 Frank Thomas	60.00	27.00	7.50
☐ 5 Mike Piazza	40.00	18.00	5.00
☐ 6 Dante Bichette	8.00	3.60	1.00
☐ 7 Manny Ramirez	15.00	6.75	1.85
☐ 8 Mo Vaughn	15.00	6.75	1.85

1996 Donruss Round Trippers

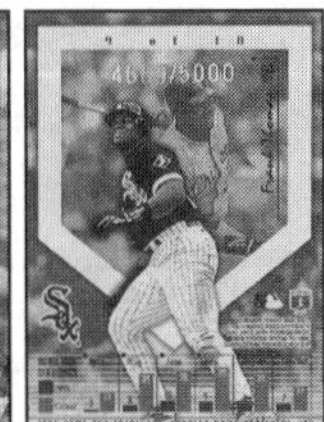

Randomly inserted in second series hobby packs at a rate of one in 55, this 10-card standard-size set honors ten of Baseball's top homerun hitters. Just 5,000 of each card were produced and consecutively numbered. On a sepia-tone background with a home plate icon carrying the 1995 season home run total, the fronts superpose a color player cutout. The player's name and "Round Trippers" are bronze foil stamped at the bottom. The backs have a similar design and present 1995 and career home run statistics by a bar graph.

	MINT	NRMT	EXC
COMPLETE SET (10)	175.00	80.00	22.00
COMMON CARD (1-10)	5.00	2.20	.60
☐ 1 Albert Belle	15.00	6.75	1.85
☐ 2 Barry Bonds	10.00	4.50	1.25
☐ 3 Jeff Bagwell	12.00	5.50	1.50
☐ 4 Tim Salmon	5.00	2.20	.60
☐ 5 Mo Vaughn	10.00	4.50	1.25
☐ 6 Ken Griffey Jr.	40.00	18.00	5.00
☐ 7 Mike Piazza	25.00	11.00	3.10
☐ 8 Cal Ripken	30.00	13.50	3.70
☐ 9 Frank Thomas	40.00	18.00	5.00
☐ 10 Dante Bichette	5.00	2.20	.60

1996 Donruss Showdown

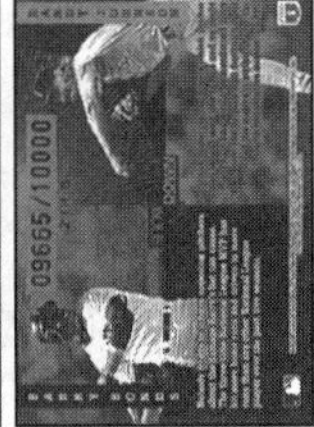

This eight-card standard-size set was randomly inserted in series one packs. These cards feature one top hitter and one top pitcher from each league. The cards are sequentially numbered out of 10,000. The horizontal fronts feature gold foil stamping and have the words "Show Down" in the middle. The backs feature color player photos as well as some text about their accomplishments.

	MINT	NRMT	EXC
COMPLETE SET (8)	150.00	70.00	19.00
COMMON CARD (1-8)	4.00	1.80	.50
☐ 1 Frank Thomas Hideo Nomo	40.00	18.00	5.00
☐ 2 Barry Bonds Randy Johnson	12.00	5.50	1.50
☐ 3 Greg Maddux Ken Griffey Jr.	50.00	22.00	6.25
☐ 4 Roger Clemens Tony Gwynn	15.00	6.75	1.85
☐ 5 Mike Piazza Mike Mussina	25.00	11.00	3.10
☐ 6 Cal Ripken Pedro J.Martinez	25.00	11.00	3.10
☐ 7 Tim Wakefield Matt Williams	4.00	1.80	.50
☐ 8 Manny Ramirez Carlos Perez	8.00	3.60	1.00

1997 Donruss

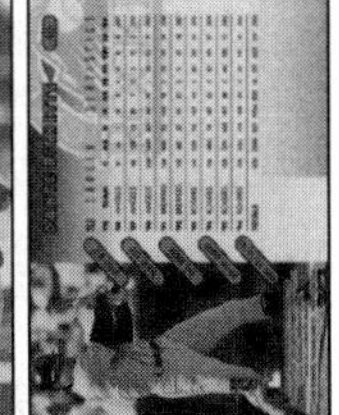

The 1997 Donruss first series totals 270 cards. The 10-card packs have a suggested retail price of $1.99 each. The card fronts feature color action player photos while the backs carry another color player photo with player information and career statistics.

	MINT	NRMT	EXC
COMPLETE SET (270)	25.00	11.00	3.10
COMMON CARD (1-270)	.10	.05	.01
☐ 1 Juan Gonzalez	1.50	.70	.19
☐ 2 Jim Edmonds	.25	.11	.03
☐ 3 Tony Gwynn	1.25	.55	.16
☐ 4 Andres Galarraga	.40	.18	.05
☐ 5 Joe Carter	.25	.11	.03
☐ 6 Raul Mondesi	.40	.18	.05
☐ 7 Greg Maddux	2.00	.90	.25
☐ 8 Travis Fryman	.25	.11	.03
☐ 9 Brian Jordan	.25	.11	.03
☐ 10 Henry Rodriguez	.25	.11	.03
☐ 11 Manny Ramirez	.75	.35	.09
☐ 12 Mark McGwire	1.00	.45	.12
☐ 13 Marc Newfield	.10	.05	.01
☐ 14 Craig Biggio	.25	.11	.03
☐ 15 Sammy Sosa	.50	.23	.06
☐ 16 Brady Anderson	.25	.11	.03
☐ 17 Wade Boggs	.40	.18	.05
☐ 18 Charles Johnson	.10	.05	.01
☐ 19 Matt Williams	.40	.18	.05
☐ 20 Denny Neagle	.10	.05	.01
☐ 21 Ken Griffey Jr.	3.00	1.35	.35
☐ 22 Robin Ventura	.25	.11	.03
☐ 23 Barry Larkin	.40	.18	.05
☐ 24 Todd Zeile	.10	.05	.01
☐ 25 Chuck Knoblauch	.50	.23	.06
☐ 26 Todd Hundley	.25	.11	.03
☐ 27 Roger Clemens	.60	.25	.07
☐ 28 Michael Tucker	.10	.05	.01
☐ 29 Rondell White	.10	.05	.01
☐ 30 Osvaldo Fernandez	.10	.05	.01
☐ 31 Ivan Rodriguez	.75	.35	.09
☐ 32 Alex Fernandez	.25	.11	.03
☐ 33 Jason Isringhausen	.25	.11	.03
☐ 34 Chipper Jones	2.00	.90	.25
☐ 35 Paul O'Neill	.10	.05	.01
☐ 36 Hideo Nomo	.75	.35	.09
☐ 37 Roberto Alomar	.60	.25	.07
☐ 38 Derek Bell	.25	.11	.03
☐ 39 Paul Molitor	.60	.25	.07
☐ 40 Andy Benes	.10	.05	.01
☐ 41 Steve Trachsel	.10	.05	.01
☐ 42 J.T. Snow	.10	.05	.01
☐ 43 Jason Kendall	.25	.11	.03
☐ 44 Alex Rodriguez	3.00	1.35	.35
☐ 45 Joey Hamilton	.25	.11	.03
☐ 46 Carlos Delgado	.25	.11	.03
☐ 47 Jason Giambi	.25	.11	.03
☐ 48 Larry Walker	.25	.11	.03
☐ 49 Derek Jeter	2.00	.90	.25
☐ 50 Kenny Lofton	.75	.35	.09
☐ 51 Devon White	.10	.05	.01
☐ 52 Matt Mieske	.10	.05	.01
☐ 53 Melvin Nieves	.10	.05	.01
☐ 54 Jose Canseco	.40	.18	.05
☐ 55 Tino Martinez	.25	.11	.03
☐ 56 Rafael Palmeiro	.40	.18	.05
☐ 57 Edgardo Alfonzo	.10	.05	.01
☐ 58 Jay Buhner	.40	.18	.05
☐ 59 Shane Reynolds	.10	.05	.01
☐ 60 Steve Finley	.10	.05	.01

Card	MINT	NRMT	EXC
☐ 61 Bobby Higginson	.25	.11	.03
☐ 62 Dean Palmer	.10	.05	.01
☐ 63 Terry Pendleton	.10	.05	.01
☐ 64 Marquis Grissom	.25	.11	.03
☐ 65 Mike Stanley	.10	.05	.01
☐ 66 Moises Alou	.25	.11	.03
☐ 67 Ray Lankford	.25	.11	.03
☐ 68 Marty Cordova	.25	.11	.03
☐ 69 John Olerud	.10	.05	.01
☐ 70 David Cone	.25	.11	.03
☐ 71 Benito Santiago	.10	.05	.01
☐ 72 Ryne Sandberg	.75	.35	.09
☐ 73 Rickey Henderson	.40	.18	.05
☐ 74 Roger Cedeno	.10	.05	.01
☐ 75 Wilson Alvarez	.10	.05	.01
☐ 76 Tim Salmon	.40	.18	.05
☐ 77 Orlando Merced	.10	.05	.01
☐ 78 Vinny Castilla	.25	.11	.03
☐ 79 Ismael Valdes	.25	.11	.03
☐ 80 Dante Bichette	.40	.18	.05
☐ 81 Kevin Brown	.25	.11	.03
☐ 82 Andy Pettitte	.75	.35	.09
☐ 83 Scott Stahoviak	.10	.05	.01
☐ 84 Mickey Tettleton	.10	.05	.01
☐ 85 Jack McDowell	.10	.05	.01
☐ 86 Tom Glavine	.40	.18	.05
☐ 87 Gregg Jefferies	.10	.05	.01
☐ 88 Chili Davis	.10	.05	.01
☐ 89 Randy Johnson	.50	.23	.06
☐ 90 John Mabry	.10	.05	.01
☐ 91 Billy Wagner	.25	.11	.03
☐ 92 Jeff Cirillo	.10	.05	.01
☐ 93 Trevor Hoffman	.10	.05	.01
☐ 94 Juan Guzman	.10	.05	.01
☐ 95 Geronimo Berroa	.10	.05	.01
☐ 96 Bernard Gilkey	.10	.05	.01
☐ 97 Danny Tartabull	.10	.05	.01
☐ 98 Johnny Damon	.10	.05	.01
☐ 99 Charlie Hayes	.10	.05	.01
☐ 100 Reggie Sanders	.25	.11	.03
☐ 101 Robby Thompson	.10	.05	.01
☐ 102 Bobby Bonilla	.25	.11	.03
☐ 103 Reggie Jefferson	.10	.05	.01
☐ 104 John Smoltz	.50	.23	.06
☐ 105 Jim Thome	.10	.05	.01
☐ 106 Ruben Rivera	.40	.18	.05
☐ 107 Darren Oliver	.10	.05	.01
☐ 108 Mo Vaughn	.75	.35	.09
☐ 109 Roger Pavlik	.10	.05	.01
☐ 110 Terry Steinbach	.10	.05	.01
☐ 111 Jermaine Dye	.50	.23	.06
☐ 112 Mark Grudzielanek	.10	.05	.01
☐ 113 Rick Aguilera	.10	.05	.01
☐ 114 Jamey Wright	.25	.11	.03
☐ 115 Eddie Murray	.75	.35	.09
☐ 116 Brian L. Hunter	.10	.05	.01
☐ 117 Hal Morris	.10	.05	.01
☐ 118 Tom Pagnozzi	.10	.05	.01
☐ 119 Mike Mussina	.60	.25	.07
☐ 120 Mark Grace	.40	.18	.05
☐ 121 Cal Ripken	2.50	1.10	.30
☐ 122 Tom Goodwin	.10	.05	.01
☐ 123 Paul Sorrento	.10	.05	.01
☐ 124 Jay Bell	.10	.05	.01
☐ 125 Todd Hollandsworth	.25	.11	.03
☐ 126 Edgar Martinez	.25	.11	.03
☐ 127 George Arias	.10	.05	.01
☐ 128 Greg Vaughn	.10	.05	.01
☐ 129 Roberto Hernandez	.10	.05	.01
☐ 130 Delino DeShields	.10	.05	.01
☐ 131 Bill Pulsipher	.10	.05	.01
☐ 132 Joey Cora	.10	.05	.01
☐ 133 Mariano Rivera	.25	.11	.03
☐ 134 Mike Piazza	2.00	.90	.25
☐ 135 Carlos Baerga	.25	.11	.03
☐ 136 Jose Mesa	.10	.05	.01
☐ 137 Will Clark	.40	.18	.05
☐ 138 Frank Thomas	3.00	1.35	.35
☐ 139 John Wetteland	.25	.11	.03
☐ 140 Shawn Estes	.10	.05	.01
☐ 141 Garret Anderson	.10	.05	.01
☐ 142 Andre Dawson	.25	.11	.03
☐ 143 Eddie Taubensee	.10	.05	.01
☐ 144 Ryan Klesko	.50	.23	.06
☐ 145 Rocky Coppinger	.25	.11	.03
☐ 146 Jeff Bagwell	1.25	.55	.16
☐ 147 Donovan Osborne	.10	.05	.01
☐ 148 Greg Myers	.10	.05	.01
☐ 149 Brant Brown	.10	.05	.01
☐ 150 Kevin Elster	.10	.05	.01
☐ 151 Bob Wells	.10	.05	.01
☐ 152 Wally Joyner	.10	.05	.01
☐ 153 Rico Brogna	.10	.05	.01
☐ 154 Dwight Gooden	.25	.11	.03
☐ 155 Jermaine Allensworth	.25	.11	.03
☐ 156 Ray Durham	.10	.05	.01
☐ 157 Cecil Fielder	.25	.11	.03
☐ 158 John Burkett	.10	.05	.01
☐ 159 Gary Sheffield	.50	.23	.06
☐ 160 Albert Belle	1.25	.55	.16
☐ 161 Tomas Perez	.10	.05	.01
☐ 162 David Doster	.10	.05	.01
☐ 163 John Valentin	.10	.05	.01
☐ 164 Danny Graves	.10	.05	.01
☐ 165 Jose Paniagua	.10	.05	.01
☐ 166 Brian Giles	.10	.05	.01
☐ 167 Barry Bonds	.75	.35	.09
☐ 168 Sterling Hitchcock	.10	.05	.01
☐ 169 Bernie Williams	.60	.25	.07
☐ 170 Fred McGriff	.40	.18	.05
☐ 171 George Williams	.10	.05	.01
☐ 172 Amaury Telemaco	.10	.05	.01
☐ 173 Ken Caminiti	.50	.23	.06
☐ 174 Ron Gant	.25	.11	.03
☐ 175 Dave Justice	.25	.11	.03
☐ 176 James Baldwin	.10	.05	.01
☐ 177 Pat Hentgen	.25	.11	.03
☐ 178 Ben McDonald	.10	.05	.01
☐ 179 Tim Naehring	.10	.05	.01
☐ 180 Jim Eisenreich	.10	.05	.01
☐ 181 Ken Hill	.10	.05	.01
☐ 182 Paul Wilson	.25	.11	.03
☐ 183 Marvin Benard	.10	.05	.01
☐ 184 Alan Benes	.25	.11	.03
☐ 185 Ellis Burks	.25	.11	.03
☐ 186 Scott Servais	.10	.05	.01
☐ 187 David Segui	.10	.05	.01
☐ 188 Scott Brosius	.10	.05	.01
☐ 189 Jose Offerman	.10	.05	.01
☐ 190 Eric Davis	.10	.05	.01
☐ 191 Brett Butler	.10	.05	.01
☐ 192 Curtis Pride	.10	.05	.01
☐ 193 Yamil Benitez	.10	.05	.01
☐ 194 Chan Ho Park	.40	.18	.05
☐ 195 Bret Boone	.10	.05	.01
☐ 196 Omar Vizquel	.25	.11	.03
☐ 197 Orlando Miller	.10	.05	.01
☐ 198 Ramon Martinez	.25	.11	.03
☐ 199 Harold Baines	.10	.05	.01
☐ 200 Eric Young	.25	.11	.03
☐ 201 Fernando Vina	.10	.05	.01
☐ 202 Alex Gonzalez	.10	.05	.01
☐ 203 Fernando Valenzuela	.25	.11	.03
☐ 204 Steve Avery	.10	.05	.01
☐ 205 Ernie Young	.10	.05	.01
☐ 206 Kevin Appier	.25	.11	.03
☐ 207 Randy Myers	.10	.05	.01
☐ 208 Jeff Suppan	.25	.11	.03
☐ 209 James Mouton	.10	.05	.01
☐ 210 Russ Davis	.10	.05	.01
☐ 211 Al Martin	.10	.05	.01
☐ 212 Troy Percival	.10	.05	.01
☐ 213 Al Leiter	.10	.05	.01
☐ 214 Dennis Eckersley	.25	.11	.03
☐ 215 Mark Johnson	.10	.05	.01
☐ 216 Eric Karros	.25	.11	.03
☐ 217 Royce Clayton	.10	.05	.01
☐ 218 Tony Phillips	.10	.05	.01
☐ 219 Tim Wakefield	.10	.05	.01
☐ 220 Alan Trammell	.25	.11	.03
☐ 221 Eduardo Perez	.10	.05	.01
☐ 222 Butch Huskey	.10	.05	.01
☐ 223 Tim Belcher	.10	.05	.01
☐ 224 Jamie Moyer	.10	.05	.01
☐ 225 F.P. Santangelo	.10	.05	.01
☐ 226 Rusty Greer	.25	.11	.03
☐ 227 Jeff Brantley	.10	.05	.01
☐ 228 Mark Langston	.10	.05	.01
☐ 229 Ray Montgomery	.10	.05	.01
☐ 230 Rich Becker	.10	.05	.01
☐ 231 Ozzie Smith	.75	.35	.09
☐ 232 Rey Ordonez	.40	.18	.05
☐ 233 Ricky Otero	.10	.05	.01
☐ 234 Mike Cameron	.50	.23	.06
☐ 235 Mike Sweeney	.25	.11	.03
☐ 236 Mark Lewis	.10	.05	.01
☐ 237 Luis Gonzalez	.10	.05	.01
☐ 238 Marcus Jensen	.10	.05	.01
☐ 239 Ed Sprague	.10	.05	.01
☐ 240 Jose Valentin	.10	.05	.01
☐ 241 Jeff Frye	.10	.05	.01
☐ 242 Charles Nagy	.25	.11	.03
☐ 243 Carlos Garcia	.10	.05	.01
☐ 244 Mike Hampton	.10	.05	.01
☐ 245 B.J. Surhoff	.10	.05	.01
☐ 246 Wilton Guerrero	.50	.23	.06
☐ 247 Frank Rodriguez	.10	.05	.01
☐ 248 Gary Gaetti	.10	.05	.01
☐ 249 Lance Johnson	.10	.05	.01
☐ 250 Darren Bragg	.10	.05	.01
☐ 251 Darryl Hamilton	.10	.05	.01
☐ 252 John Jaha	.25	.11	.03
☐ 253 Craig Paquette	.10	.05	.01
☐ 254 Jaime Navarro	.10	.05	.01
☐ 255 Shawon Dunston	.10	.05	.01
☐ 256 Mark Loretta	.10	.05	.01
☐ 257 Tim Belk	.10	.05	.01
☐ 258 Jeff Darwin	.10	.05	.01
☐ 259 Ruben Sierra	.10	.05	.01
☐ 260 Chuck Finley	.10	.05	.01
☐ 261 Darryl Strawberry	.25	.11	.03
☐ 262 Shannon Stewart	.10	.05	.01
☐ 263 Pedro Martinez	.25	.11	.03
☐ 264 Neifi Perez	.25	.11	.03
☐ 265 Jeff Conine	.25	.11	.03
☐ 266 Orel Hershiser	.25	.11	.03
☐ 267 Eddie Murray CL	.40	.18	.05
☐ 268 Paul Molitor CL	.40	.18	.05
☐ 269 Barry Bonds CL	.40	.18	.05
☐ 270 Mark McGwire CL	.40	.18	.05

1997 Donruss Press Proofs

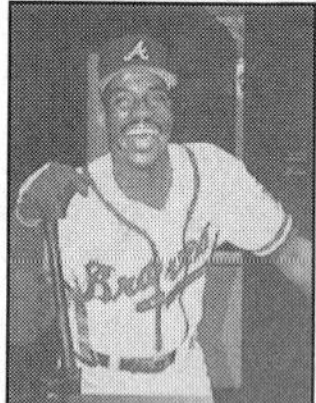
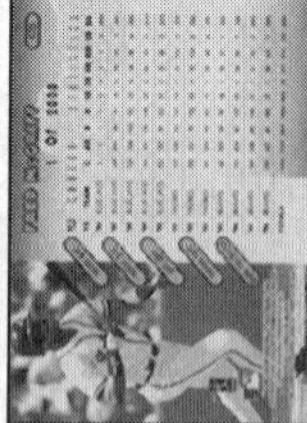

Randomly inserted in packs, this 270-card silver foil set parallels the regular 1997 Donruss set. The silver foil stamped words, "Press Proof" down the right distinguishes it from the regular set.

	MINT	NRMT	EXC
COMPLETE SET (270)	1000.00	450.00	125.00
COMMON CARD (1-270)	2.00	.90	.25
*STARS: 7.5X TO 15X BASIC CARDS			
*YOUNG STARS: 6X TO 12X BASIC CARDS			
☐ 1 Juan Gonzalez	25.00	11.00	3.10
☐ 7 Greg Maddux	30.00	13.50	3.70
☐ 21 Ken Griffey Jr.	50.00	22.00	6.25
☐ 34 Chipper Jones	30.00	13.50	3.70
☐ 44 Alex Rodriguez	50.00	22.00	6.25
☐ 49 Derek Jeter	30.00	13.50	3.70
☐ 121 Cal Ripken	40.00	18.00	5.00
☐ 134 Mike Piazza	30.00	13.50	3.70
☐ 138 Frank Thomas	50.00	22.00	6.25
☐ 160 Albert Belle	20.00	9.00	2.50

1997 Donruss Press Proofs Gold

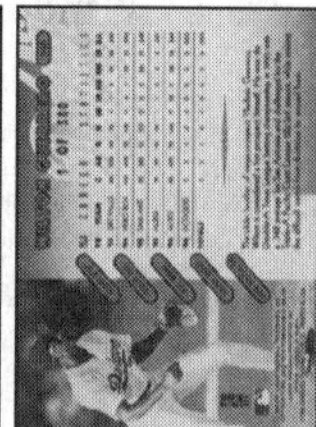

Randomly inserted in packs, this 270-card set is a die-cut parallel rendition of the regular Press Proofs set. Gold foil stamping further distinguishes it from the regular set.

	MINT	NRMT	EXC
COMPLETE SET (270)	3500.00	1600.00	450.00
COMMON CARD (1-270)	6.00	2.70	.75
*STARS: 25X TO 50X BASIC CARDS..			

1997 Donruss Armed and Dangerous

Randomly inserted in hobby packs only, this 15-card set features the League's hottest arms in the game. The fronts carry color action player photos with foil printing. The backs display player information and a color player head portrait at the end of a ribbon representing a medal. Only 5,000 of this set were produced and are sequentially numbered.

	MINT	NRMT	EXC
COMPLETE SET (15)	150.00	70.00	19.00
COMMON CARD (1-15)	5.00	2.20	.60
☐ 1 Ken Griffey Jr.	30.00	13.50	3.70
☐ 2 Raul Mondesi	5.00	2.20	.60
☐ 3 Chipper Jones	20.00	9.00	2.50
☐ 4 Ivan Rodriguez	6.00	2.70	.75
☐ 5 Randy Johnson	5.00	2.20	.60
☐ 6 Alex Rodriguez	30.00	13.50	3.70
☐ 7 Larry Walker	5.00	2.20	.60
☐ 8 Cal Ripken	25.00	11.00	3.10
☐ 9 Kenny Lofton	8.00	3.60	1.00
☐ 10 Barry Bonds	8.00	3.60	1.00
☐ 11 Derek Jeter	20.00	9.00	2.50
☐ 12 Charles Johnson	5.00	2.20	.60
☐ 13 Greg Maddux	20.00	9.00	2.50
☐ 14 Roberto Alomar	6.00	2.70	.75
☐ 15 Barry Larkin	5.00	2.20	.60

1997 Donruss Diamond Kings

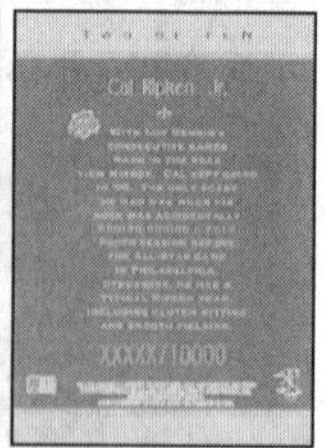

Randomly inserted in all first series packs, this 10-card set commemorates the 15th anniversary of the annual art cards in Donruss baseball sets. Only 10,000 sets were produced each of which is sequentially numbered. Ten cards were printed with the number 1,982 representing the year the insert began and could be redeemed for an original piece of artwork by Diamond Kings artist Dan Gardiner. This was the first year Gardiner painted the Diamond King series.

	MINT	NRMT	EXC
COMPLETE SET (10)	180.00	80.00	22.00
COMMON CARD (1-10)	4.00	1.80	.50
☐ 1 Ken Griffey Jr.	40.00	18.00	5.00
☐ 2 Cal Ripken	30.00	13.50	3.70
☐ 3 Mo Vaughn	12.00	5.50	1.50
☐ 4 Chuck Knoblauch	6.00	2.70	.75
☐ 5 Jeff Bagwell	15.00	6.75	1.85
☐ 6 Henry Rodriguez	4.00	1.80	.50
☐ 7 Mike Piazza	25.00	11.00	3.10
☐ 8 Ivan Rodriguez	10.00	4.50	1.25
☐ 9 Frank Thomas	40.00	18.00	5.00
☐ 10 Chipper Jones	25.00	11.00	3.10

1997 Donruss Diamond Kings Canvas

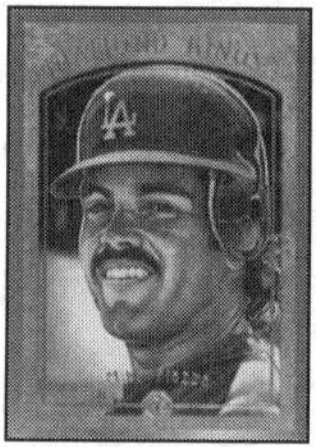
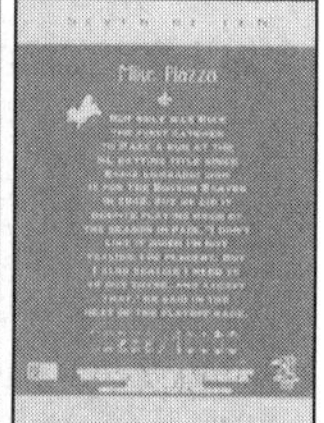

Parallel to the regular insert set, this 10-card set was printed on actual canvas stock and represents the first 500 of each Diamond King card printed.

	MINT	NRMT	EXC
COMPLETE SET (10)	900.00	400.00	110.00
COMMON CARD (1-10)	30.00	13.50	3.70
*CANVAS: 5X DIAMOND KINGS			

1997 Donruss Elite Inserts

Randomly inserted in all first series packs, this 12-card set honors perennial all-star players of the League. The fronts feature Micro-etched color action player photos, while the backs carry player information. Only 2,500 of this set were produced and are sequentially numbered.

	MINT	NRMT	EXC
COMPLETE SET (12)	600.00	275.00	75.00
COMMON CARD (1-12)	15.00	6.75	1.85
☐ 1 Frank Thomas	100.00	45.00	12.50
☐ 2 Paul Molitor	20.00	9.00	2.50
☐ 3 Sammy Sosa	15.00	6.75	1.85
☐ 4 Barry Bonds	25.00	11.00	3.10
☐ 5 Chipper Jones	60.00	27.00	7.50
☐ 6 Alex Rodriguez	100.00	45.00	12.50
☐ 7 Ken Griffey Jr.	100.00	45.00	12.50
☐ 8 Jeff Bagwell	40.00	18.00	5.00
☐ 9 Cal Ripken	80.00	36.00	10.00
☐ 10 Mo Vaughn	25.00	11.00	3.10
☐ 11 Mike Piazza	60.00	27.00	7.50
☐ 12 Juan Gonzalez UER name mispelled as Gonzales	50.00	22.00	6.25

1997 Donruss Longball Leaders

Randomly inserted in first series retail packs only, this 15-card set honors the league's most fearsome long-ball hitters. The fronts feature color action player photos and foil stamping. The backs carry player information.

	MINT	NRMT	EXC
COMPLETE SET (15)	160.00	70.00	20.00
COMMON CARD (1-15)	3.00	1.35	.35
☐ 1 Frank Thomas	40.00	18.00	5.00
☐ 2 Albert Belle	15.00	6.75	1.85
☐ 3 Mo Vaughn	10.00	4.50	1.25
☐ 4 Brady Anderson	4.00	1.80	.50
☐ 5 Greg Vaughn	3.00	1.35	.35
☐ 6 Ken Griffey Jr.	40.00	18.00	5.00
☐ 7 Jay Buhner	5.00	2.20	.60
☐ 8 Juan Gonzalez	20.00	9.00	2.50
☐ 9 Mike Piazza	25.00	11.00	3.10
☐ 10 Jeff Bagwell	15.00	6.75	1.85
☐ 11 Sammy Sosa	6.00	2.70	.75
☐ 12 Mark McGwire	12.00	5.50	1.50
☐ 13 Cecil Fielder	4.00	1.80	.50
☐ 14 Ryan Klesko	6.00	2.70	.75
☐ 15 Jose Canseco	5.00	2.20	.60

1997 Donruss Rated Rookies

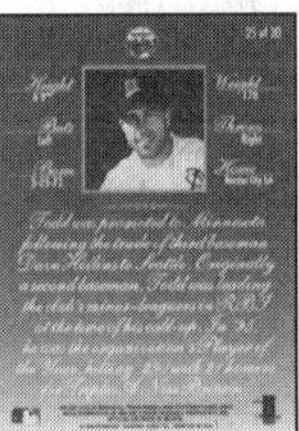

Randomly inserted in all first series packs, this 30-card set honors the top rookie prospects as chosen by Donruss to be the most likely to succeed. The fronts feature color action player photos and silver foil printing. The backs carry a player portrait and player information.

	MINT	NRMT	EXC
COMPLETE SET (30)	60.00	27.00	7.50
COMMON CARD (1-30)	1.00	.45	.12
☐ 1 Jason Thompson	1.00	.45	.12
☐ 2 LaTroy Hawkins	1.00	.45	.12
☐ 3 Scott Rolen	8.00	3.60	1.00
☐ 4 Trey Beamon	1.00	.45	.12
☐ 5 Kimera Bartee	1.00	.45	.12
☐ 6 Nerio Rodriguez	2.50	1.10	.30
☐ 7 Jeff D'Amico	1.50	.70	.19
☐ 8 Quinton McCracken	1.00	.45	.12
☐ 9 John Wasdin	1.00	.45	.12
☐ 10 Robin Jennings	1.00	.45	.12
☐ 11 Steve Gibralter	1.00	.45	.12
☐ 12 Tyler Houston	1.00	.45	.12
☐ 13 Tony Clark	2.50	1.10	.30
☐ 14 Ugueth Urbina	1.00	.45	.12
☐ 15 Karim Garcia	3.00	1.35	.35
☐ 16 Raul Casanova	1.00	.45	.12
☐ 17 Brooks Kieschnick	1.50	.70	.19
☐ 18 Luis Castillo	2.50	1.10	.30
☐ 19 Edgar Renteria	2.50	1.10	.30
☐ 20 Andruw Jones	20.00	9.00	2.50
☐ 21 Chad Mottola	1.00	.45	.12
☐ 22 Mac Suzuki	1.00	.45	.12
☐ 23 Justin Thompson	1.50	.70	.19
☐ 24 Darin Erstad	10.00	4.50	1.25
☐ 25 Todd Walker	8.00	3.60	1.00
☐ 26 Todd Greene	1.00	.45	.12
☐ 27 Vladimir Guerrero	12.00	5.50	1.50
☐ 28 Darren Dreifort	1.00	.45	.12
☐ 29 John Burke	1.00	.45	.12
☐ 30 Damon Mashore	1.00	.45	.12

1997 Donruss Rocket Launchers

Randomly inserted in first series magazine packs only, this 15-card set honers baseball's top power hitters. The fronts feature color player photos, while the backs carry player information. Only 5,000 of this set were produced and are sequentially numbered.

	MINT	NRMT	EXC
COMPLETE SET (15)	150.00	70.00	19.00
COMMON CARD (1-15)	4.00	1.80	.50
☐ 1 Frank Thomas	40.00	18.00	5.00
☐ 2 Albert Belle	15.00	6.75	1.85
☐ 3 Chipper Jones	25.00	11.00	3.10
☐ 4 Mike Piazza	25.00	11.00	3.10
☐ 5 Mo Vaughn	10.00	4.50	1.25
☐ 6 Juan Gonzalez	20.00	9.00	2.50
☐ 7 Fred McGriff	5.00	2.20	.60
☐ 8 Jeff Bagwell	15.00	6.75	1.85
☐ 9 Matt Williams	5.00	2.20	.60
☐ 10 Gary Sheffield	6.00	2.70	.75
☐ 11 Barry Bonds	10.00	4.50	1.25
☐ 12 Manny Ramirez	10.00	4.50	1.25
☐ 13 Henry Rodriguez	4.00	1.80	.50
☐ 14 Jason Giambi	4.00	1.80	.50
☐ 15 Cal Ripken	30.00	13.50	3.70

1997 Donruss Elite

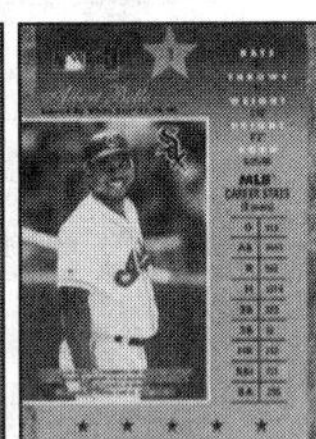

The 1997 Donruss Elite set was issued in one series totalling 150 cards. The product was distributed exclusively to hobby dealers. Each foil-wrapped pack contained eight cards and carried a suggested retail price of $3.49. Player selection was limited to the top stars (plus three player checklist cards) and card design is very similar to the Donruss Elite hockey set that was released one year earlier. Basic card fronts feature a color player photo encased by a thick silver and marble border. Backs contain another color photo and player information. Strangely enough, the backs only provide career statistics neglecting statistics from the previous season. The cards were released around February, 1997.

	MINT	NRMT	EXC
COMPLETE SET (150)	40.00	18.00	5.00
COMMON CARD (1-150)	.15	.07	.02
☐ 1 Juan Gonzalez	2.00	.90	.25
☐ 2 Alex Rodriguez	4.00	1.80	.50
☐ 3 Frank Thomas	4.00	1.80	.50
☐ 4 Greg Maddux	2.50	1.10	.30
☐ 5 Ken Griffey Jr.	4.00	1.80	.50
☐ 6 Cal Ripken	3.00	1.35	.35
☐ 7 Mike Piazza	2.50	1.10	.30
☐ 8 Chipper Jones	2.50	1.10	.30
☐ 9 Albert Belle	1.50	.70	.19
☐ 10 Andruw Jones	4.00	1.80	.50
☐ 11 Vladimir Guerrero	2.50	1.10	.30
☐ 12 Mo Vaughn UER front Gonzales	1.00	.45	.12
☐ 13 Ivan Rodriguez	1.00	.45	.12
☐ 14 Andy Pettitte	1.00	.45	.12
☐ 15 Tony Gwynn	1.50	.70	.19
☐ 16 Barry Bonds	1.00	.45	.12
☐ 17 Jeff Bagwell	1.50	.70	.19
☐ 18 Manny Ramirez	1.00	.45	.12
☐ 19 Kenny Lofton	1.00	.45	.12
☐ 20 Roberto Alomar	.75	.35	.09
☐ 21 Mark McGwire	1.25	.55	.16
☐ 22 Ryan Klesko	.60	.25	.07
☐ 23 Tim Salmon	.50	.23	.06
☐ 24 Derek Jeter	2.50	1.10	.30
☐ 25 Eddie Murray	1.00	.45	.12
☐ 26 Jermaine Dye	.60	.25	.07
☐ 27 Ruben Rivera	.50	.23	.06
☐ 28 Jim Edmonds	.30	.14	.04
☐ 29 Mike Mussina	.75	.35	.09
☐ 30 Randy Johnson	.60	.25	.07
☐ 31 Sammy Sosa	.60	.25	.07
☐ 32 Hideo Nomo	1.00	.45	.12
☐ 33 Chuck Knoblauch	.60	.25	.07
☐ 34 Paul Molitor	.75	.35	.09
☐ 35 Rafael Palmeiro	.50	.23	.06
☐ 36 Brady Anderson	.30	.14	.04
☐ 37 Will Clark	.50	.23	.06
☐ 38 Craig Biggio	.30	.14	.04
☐ 39 Jason Giambi	.30	.14	.04
☐ 40 Roger Clemens	.75	.35	.09
☐ 41 Jay Buhner	.50	.23	.06
☐ 42 Edgar Martinez	.30	.14	.04
☐ 43 Gary Sheffield	.60	.25	.07
☐ 44 Fred McGriff	.50	.23	.06
☐ 45 Bobby Bonilla	.30	.14	.04
☐ 46 Tom Glavine	.50	.23	.06
☐ 47 Wade Boggs	.50	.23	.06
☐ 48 Jeff Conine	.30	.14	.04
☐ 49 John Smoltz	.60	.25	.07
☐ 50 Jim Thome	.75	.35	.09
☐ 51 Billy Wagner	.30	.14	.04
☐ 52 Jose Canseco	.50	.23	.06
☐ 53 Javy Lopez	.30	.14	.04
☐ 54 Cecil Fielder	.30	.14	.04
☐ 55 Garret Anderson	.15	.07	.02
☐ 56 Alex Ochoa	.15	.07	.02
☐ 57 Scott Rolen	1.50	.70	.19
☐ 58 Darin Erstad	2.00	.90	.25
☐ 59 Rey Ordonez	.50	.23	.06
☐ 60 Dante Bichette	.50	.23	.06
☐ 61 Joe Carter	.30	.14	.04
☐ 62 Moises Alou	.30	.14	.04
☐ 63 Jason Isringhausen	.30	.14	.04
☐ 64 Karim Garcia	.60	.25	.07
☐ 65 Brian Jordan	.30	.14	.04
☐ 66 Ruben Sierra	.15	.07	.02
☐ 67 Todd Hollandsworth	.30	.14	.04
☐ 68 Paul Wilson	.30	.14	.04
☐ 69 Ernie Young	.15	.07	.02
☐ 70 Ryne Sandberg	1.00	.45	.12
☐ 71 Raul Mondesi	.50	.23	.06
☐ 72 George Arias	.15	.07	.02
☐ 73 Ray Durham	.15	.07	.02
☐ 74 Dean Palmer	.15	.07	.02
☐ 75 Shawn Green	.15	.07	.02
☐ 76 Eric Young	.30	.14	.04
☐ 77 Jason Kendall	.30	.14	.04
☐ 78 Greg Vaughn	.15	.07	.02
☐ 79 Terrell Wade	.15	.07	.02
☐ 80 Bill Pulsipher	.15	.07	.02
☐ 81 Bobby Higginson	.30	.14	.04
☐ 82 Mark Grudzielanek	.15	.07	.02
☐ 83 Ken Caminiti	.60	.25	.07
☐ 84 Todd Greene	.15	.07	.02
☐ 85 Carlos Delgado	.30	.14	.04
☐ 86 Mark Grace	.50	.23	.06
☐ 87 Rondell White	.15	.07	.02
☐ 88 Barry Larkin	.50	.23	.06
☐ 89 J.T. Snow	.15	.07	.02
☐ 90 Alex Gonzalez	.15	.07	.02
☐ 91 Raul Casanova	.15	.07	.02
☐ 92 Marc Newfield	.15	.07	.02
☐ 93 Jermaine Allensworth	.30	.14	.04
☐ 94 John Mabry	.15	.07	.02
☐ 95 Kirby Puckett	1.50	.70	.19
☐ 96 Travis Fryman	.30	.14	.04
☐ 97 Kevin Brown	.30	.14	.04
☐ 98 Andres Galarraga	.50	.23	.06
☐ 99 Marty Cordova	.30	.14	.04
☐ 100 Henry Rodriguez	.30	.14	.04
☐ 101 Sterling Hitchcock	.15	.07	.02
☐ 102 Trey Beamon	.15	.07	.02
☐ 103 Brett Butler	.15	.07	.02
☐ 104 Rickey Henderson	.50	.23	.06
☐ 105 Tino Martinez	.30	.14	.04
☐ 106 Kevin Appier	.30	.14	.04
☐ 107 Brian Hunter	.15	.07	.02
☐ 108 Eric Karros	.30	.14	.04
☐ 109 Andre Dawson	.30	.14	.04
☐ 110 Darryl Strawberry	.30	.14	.04
☐ 111 James Baldwin	.15	.07	.02
☐ 112 Chad Mottola	.15	.07	.02
☐ 113 Dave Nilsson	.15	.07	.02
☐ 114 Carlos Baerga	.30	.14	.04
☐ 115 Chan Ho Park	.50	.23	.06
☐ 116 John Jaha	.30	.14	.04
☐ 117 Alan Benes	.30	.14	.04
☐ 118 Mariano Rivera	.30	.14	.04
☐ 119 Ellis Burks	.30	.14	.04
☐ 120 Tony Clark	.50	.23	.06
☐ 121 Todd Walker	1.50	.70	.19
☐ 122 Dwight Gooden	.30	.14	.04
☐ 123 Ugueth Urbina	.15	.07	.02
☐ 124 David Cone	.30	.14	.04
☐ 125 Ozzie Smith	1.00	.45	.12
☐ 126 Kimera Bartee	.15	.07	.02
☐ 127 Rusty Greer	.30	.14	.04
☐ 128 Pat Hentgen	.30	.14	.04
☐ 129 Charles Johnson	.15	.07	.02
☐ 130 Quinton McCracken	.15	.07	.02
☐ 131 Troy Percival	.15	.07	.02
☐ 132 Shane Reynolds	.15	.07	.02
☐ 133 Charles Nagy	.30	.14	.04
☐ 134 Tom Goodwin	.15	.07	.02
☐ 135 Ron Gant	.30	.14	.04
☐ 136 Dan Wilson	.15	.07	.02
☐ 137 Matt Williams	.50	.23	.06
☐ 138 LaTroy Hawkins	.15	.07	.02
☐ 139 Kevin Seitzer	.15	.07	.02
☐ 140 Michael Tucker	.15	.07	.02
☐ 141 Todd Hundley	.30	.14	.04
☐ 142 Alex Fernandez	.30	.14	.04
☐ 143 Marquis Grissom	.30	.14	.04
☐ 144 Steve Finley	.15	.07	.02
☐ 145 Curtis Pride	.15	.07	.02
☐ 146 Derek Bell	.30	.14	.04
☐ 147 Butch Huskey	.15	.07	.02
☐ 148 Dwight Gooden Checklist (1-75)	.30	.14	.04
☐ 149 Al Leiter Checklist (76-150)	.15	.07	.02
☐ 150 Hideo Nomo Checklist (inserts)	.50	.23	.06

1997 Donruss Elite Gold Stars

Randomly seeded into one in every nine packs, cards from this set parallel the 150-card base issue. The distinctive gold foil fronts easily differentiate them from their silver-foiled base-issue brethren. The following cards were erroneously printed with a silver (rather than gold) logo on front: 6, 15, 25, 32, 42, 47, 57, 60, 69 and 70. Corrected gold logo versions of these cards do exist, but are in far shorter supply and exact values are not known at this time. The set is considered complete with the erroneous silver logo cards.

	MINT	NRMT	EXC
COMPLETE SET (150)	1200.00	550.00	150.00
COMMON CARD (1-150)	2.50	1.10	.30
*STARS: 8X TO 20X BASIC CARDS			
☐ 1 Juan Gonzalez	40.00	18.00	5.00
☐ 2 Alex Rodriguez	80.00	36.00	10.00
☐ 3 Frank Thomas	80.00	36.00	10.00
☐ 4 Greg Maddux	50.00	22.00	6.25
☐ 5 Ken Griffey Jr.	80.00	36.00	10.00
☐ 6 Cal Ripken ERR Silver logo on front	60.00	27.00	7.50
☐ 7 Mike Piazza	50.00	22.00	6.25
☐ 8 Chipper Jones	50.00	22.00	6.25
☐ 9 Albert Belle	30.00	13.50	3.70
☐ 10 Andruw Jones	80.00	36.00	10.00
☐ 11 Vladimir Guerrero	50.00	22.00	6.25
☐ 15 Tony Gwynn ERR Silver logo on front	30.00	13.50	3.70
☐ 17 Jeff Bagwell	30.00	13.50	3.70
☐ 24 Derek Jeter	50.00	22.00	6.25
☐ 57 Scott Rolen ERR Silver logo on front	30.00	13.50	3.70
☐ 95 Kirby Puckett	30.00	13.50	3.70
☐ 121 Todd Walker	30.00	13.50	3.70

1997 Donruss Elite Leather and Lumber

This ten-card insert set features color action veteran player photos printed on two unique materials. The fronts display a player image on real wood card stock with the end of a baseball bat as background. The backs carry same player photo printed on genuine leather card stock with a baseball and glove as background. Only 500 of each card was produced and are sequentially numbered.

	MINT	NRMT	EXC
COMPLETE SET (10)	1000.00	450.00	125.00
COMMON CARD (1-10)	30.00	13.50	3.70
☐ 1 Ken Griffey Jr.	200.00	90.00	25.00
☐ 2 Alex Rodriguez	200.00	90.00	25.00
☐ 3 Frank Thomas	200.00	90.00	25.00
☐ 4 Chipper Jones	125.00	55.00	15.50
☐ 5 Ivan Rodriguez	50.00	22.00	6.25
☐ 6 Cal Ripken	150.00	70.00	19.00
☐ 7 Barry Bonds	50.00	22.00	6.25
☐ 8 Chuck Knoblauch	30.00	13.50	3.70
☐ 9 Manny Ramirez	50.00	22.00	6.25
☐ 10 Mark McGwire	60.00	27.00	7.50

1997 Donruss Elite Passing the Torch

This 12-card insert set features eight players on four double-sided cards. A color portrait of a superstar veteran is displayed on one side with a gold foil background, and a portrait of a rising young star is printed on the flipside. Each of the eight players also has his own card to round out the 12-card set. Only 1500 of this set were produced and are sequentially numbered.

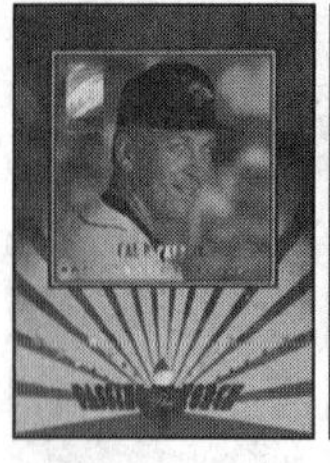

	MINT	NRMT	EXC
COMPLETE SET (12)	600.00	275.00	75.00
COMMON CARD (1-12)	25.00	11.00	3.10
☐ 1 Cal Ripken	80.00	36.00	10.00
☐ 2 Alex Rodriguez	100.00	45.00	12.50
☐ 3 Cal Ripken Alex Rodriguez	120.00	55.00	15.00
☐ 4 Kirby Puckett	60.00	27.00	7.50
☐ 5 Andruw Jones	100.00	45.00	12.50
☐ 6 Kirby Puckett Andruw Jones	100.00	45.00	12.50
☐ 7 Cecil Fielder	25.00	11.00	3.10
☐ 8 Frank Thomas	100.00	45.00	12.50
☐ 9 Cecil Fielder Frank Thomas	100.00	45.00	12.50
☐ 10 Ozzie Smith	40.00	18.00	5.00
☐ 11 Derek Jeter	60.00	27.00	7.50
☐ 12 Ozzie Smith Derek Jeter	80.00	36.00	10.00

1997 Donruss Elite Passing the Torch Autographs

This 12-card set consists of the first 150 sets of the regular "Passing the Torch" set with each card displaying an authentic player autograph. The set features a double front design which captures eight of the league's top superstars, alternating one of four different megastars on the flipside. An individual card for each of the eight players rounds out the set. Each set is sequentially numbered to 150.

	MINT	NRMT	EXC
COMPLETE SET (12)	5000.00	2200.00	600.00
COMMON CARD (1-12)	125.00	55.00	15.50
☐ 1 Cal Ripken	500.00	220.00	60.00
☐ 2 Alex Rodriguez	500.00	220.00	60.00
☐ 3 Cal Ripken Alex Rodriguez	1200.00	550.00	150.00
☐ 4 Kirby Puckett	400.00	180.00	50.00
☐ 5 Andruw Jones	400.00	180.00	50.00
☐ 6 Kirby Puckett Andruw Jones	800.00	350.00	100.00
☐ 7 Cecil Fielder	125.00	55.00	15.50
☐ 8 Frank Thomas	500.00	220.00	60.00
☐ 9 Cecil Fielder Frank Thomas	600.00	275.00	75.00
☐ 10 Ozzie Smith	250.00	110.00	31.00
☐ 11 Derek Jeter	300.00	135.00	38.00
☐ 12 Ozzie Smith Derek Jeter	500.00	220.00	60.00

1997 Donruss Elite Turn of the Century

This 20-card set showcases the stars of the next millennium and features a color player image on a silver-and-black background. The backs display another player photo with a short paragraph about the player. Only 3,500 of this set were produced and are sequentially numbered.

	MINT	NRMT	EXC
COMPLETE SET (20)	200.00	90.00	25.00
COMMON CARD (1-20)	4.00	1.80	.50
☐ 1 Alex Rodriguez	40.00	18.00	5.00
☐ 2 Andruw Jones	40.00	18.00	5.00
☐ 3 Chipper Jones	25.00	11.00	3.10
☐ 4 Todd Walker	15.00	6.75	1.85
☐ 5 Scott Rolen	15.00	6.75	1.85
☐ 6 Trey Beamon	4.00	1.80	.50
☐ 7 Derek Jeter	25.00	11.00	3.10
☐ 8 Darin Erstad	20.00	9.00	2.50
☐ 9 Tony Clark	10.00	4.50	1.25
☐ 10 Todd Greene	4.00	1.80	.50
☐ 11 Jason Giambi	5.00	2.20	.60
☐ 12 Justin Thompson	5.00	2.20	.60
☐ 13 Ernie Young	4.00	1.80	.50
☐ 14 Jason Kendall	5.00	2.20	.60
☐ 15 Alex Ochoa	4.00	1.80	.50
☐ 16 Brooks Kieschnick	5.00	2.20	.60
☐ 17 Bobby Higginson	5.00	2.20	.60
☐ 18 Ruben Rivera	6.00	2.70	.75
☐ 19 Chan Ho Park	6.00	2.70	.75
☐ 20 Chad Mottola	4.00	1.80	.50
☐ P5 Scott Rolen Promo	5.00	2.20	.60
☐ P7 Derek Jeter Promo	8.00	3.60	1.00

1997 Donruss Elite Turn of the Century Die Cuts

This 20-card set consists of the first 500 of the regular "Turn of the Century" sets which feature an exterior die-cut design. Each set is sequentially numbered to 500.

	MINT	NRMT	EXC
COMPLETE SET (20)	600.00	275.00	75.00
COMMON CARD (1-20)	15.00	6.75	1.85

*STARS: 1.5X TO 3X BASIC CARDS ..

1997 Donruss Ripken The Only Way I Know

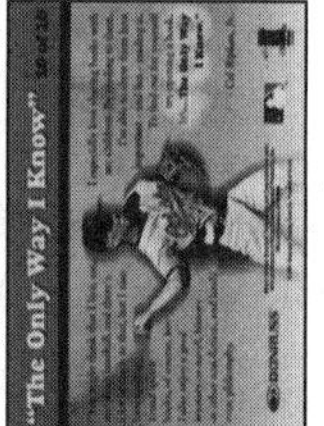

This one standard-size card, numbered 10 of 10, was only issued in copies of Cal Ripken's autobiography, "The Only Way I Know". Ripken autographed 2,131 of these cards and they were randomly inserted into the books. Cards numbered 1-9 were to be issued as an insert in the 1997 Donruss Update set.

	MINT	NRMT	EXC
COMPLETE SET (1)	5.00	2.20	.60
COMMON CARD	5.00	2.20	.60
☐ 10 Cal Ripken The Only Way I Know	5.00	2.20	.60

1953-55 Dormand PC748

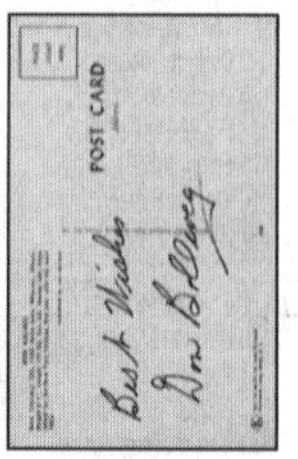

One of the most attractive and popular postcards ever issued are the full color postcards of Louis Dormand, which were issued as premiums by the Mason Candy Company. The cards are numbered on the reverse in the line which seperates the address portion from the message portion of the postcards. Two variations of the McDougald, Collins and Sain exist. Rizzuto and Mantle also exist in a 6" by 9" postcard, and a 9" by 12" postcard also exists. The Hodges card is quite scarce.

	NRMT	VG-E	GOOD
COMPLETE SET (45)	2750.00	1250.00	350.00
COMMON CARD (1-45)	20.00	9.00	2.50

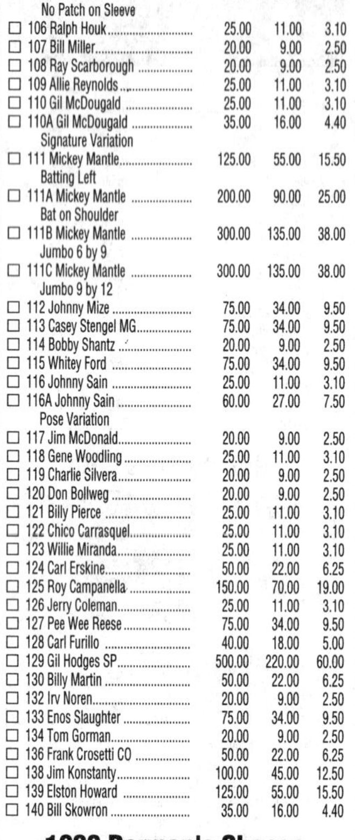

	NRMT	VG-E	GOOD
☐ 101 Phil Rizzuto	50.00	22.00	6.25
☐ 101A Phil Rizzuto Jumbo 6 by 9	125.00	55.00	15.50
☐ 102 Yogi Berra	75.00	34.00	9.50
☐ 103 Ed Lopat	25.00	11.00	3.10
☐ 104 Hank Bauer	35.00	16.00	4.40
☐ 105 Joe Collins Patch on Sleeve	20.00	9.00	2.50
☐ 105A Joe Collins No Patch on Sleeve	35.00	16.00	4.40
☐ 106 Ralph Houk	25.00	11.00	3.10
☐ 107 Bill Miller	20.00	9.00	2.50
☐ 108 Ray Scarborough	20.00	9.00	2.50
☐ 109 Allie Reynolds	25.00	11.00	3.10
☐ 110 Gil McDougald	25.00	11.00	3.10
☐ 110A Gil McDougald Signature Variation	35.00	16.00	4.40
☐ 111 Mickey Mantle Batting Left	125.00	55.00	15.50
☐ 111A Mickey Mantle Bat on Shoulder	200.00	90.00	25.00
☐ 111B Mickey Mantle Jumbo 6 by 9	300.00	135.00	38.00
☐ 111C Mickey Mantle Jumbo 9 by 12	300.00	135.00	38.00
☐ 112 Johnny Mize	75.00	34.00	9.50
☐ 113 Casey Stengel MG	75.00	34.00	9.50
☐ 114 Bobby Shantz	20.00	9.00	2.50
☐ 115 Whitey Ford	75.00	34.00	9.50
☐ 116 Johnny Sain	25.00	11.00	3.10
☐ 116A Johnny Sain Pose Variation	60.00	27.00	7.50
☐ 117 Jim McDonald	20.00	9.00	2.50
☐ 118 Gene Woodling	25.00	11.00	3.10
☐ 119 Charlie Silvera	20.00	9.00	2.50
☐ 120 Don Bollweg	20.00	9.00	2.50
☐ 121 Billy Pierce	25.00	11.00	3.10
☐ 122 Chico Carrasquel	25.00	11.00	3.10
☐ 123 Willie Miranda	25.00	11.00	3.10
☐ 124 Carl Erskine	50.00	22.00	6.25
☐ 125 Roy Campanella	150.00	70.00	19.00
☐ 126 Jerry Coleman	25.00	11.00	3.10
☐ 127 Pee Wee Reese	75.00	34.00	9.50
☐ 128 Carl Furillo	40.00	18.00	5.00
☐ 129 Gil Hodges SP	500.00	220.00	60.00
☐ 130 Billy Martin	50.00	22.00	6.25
☐ 132 Irv Noren	20.00	9.00	2.50
☐ 133 Enos Slaughter	75.00	34.00	9.50
☐ 134 Tom Gorman	20.00	9.00	2.50
☐ 136 Frank Crosetti CO	50.00	22.00	6.25
☐ 138 Jim Konstanty	100.00	45.00	12.50
☐ 139 Elston Howard	125.00	55.00	15.50
☐ 140 Bill Skowron	35.00	16.00	4.40

1986 Dorman's Cheese

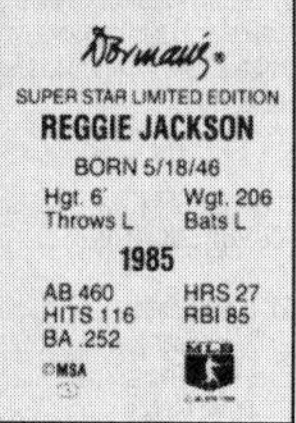

This 20-card set was issued in panels of two cards. The individual cards measure approximately 1 1/2" by 2" whereas the panels measure 3" by 2". Team logos have been removed from the photos as these cards were not licensed by Major League Baseball (team owners). The backs contain a minimum of information.

	MINT	NRMT	EXC
COMPLETE PANEL SET	18.00	8.00	2.20
COMPLETE SET	15.00	6.75	1.85
COMMON PAIR	.25	.11	.03
☐ 1 George Brett	2.50	1.10	.30
☐ 2 Jack Morris	.50	.23	.06
☐ 3 Gary Carter	.50	.23	.06
☐ 4 Cal Ripken	5.00	2.20	.60
☐ 5 Dwight Gooden	.75	.35	.09
☐ 6 Kent Hrbek	.25	.11	.03
☐ 7 Rickey Henderson	1.00	.45	.12
☐ 8 Mike Schmidt	1.50	.70	.19
☐ 9 Keith Hernandez	.50	.23	.06
☐ 10 Dale Murphy	.75	.35	.09
☐ 11 Reggie Jackson	1.50	.70	.19
☐ 12 Eddie Murray	1.50	.70	.19
☐ 13 Don Mattingly	3.00	1.35	.35
☐ 14 Ryne Sandberg	2.50	1.10	.30
☐ 15 Willie McGee	.50	.23	.06
☐ 16 Robin Yount	.75	.35	.09
☐ 17 Rick Sutcliffe	.25	.11	.03
☐ 18 Wade Boggs	1.00	.45	.12
☐ 19 Dave Winfield	1.00	.45	.12
☐ 20 Jim Rice	.50	.23	.06

1941 Double Play R330

The cards in this 75-card set measure approximately 2 1/2" by 3 1/8" was a blank-backed issue distributed by Gum Products. It consists of 75 numbered cards (two consecutive numbers per card), each

depicting two players in sepia tone photographs. Cards 81-100 contain action poses, and the last 50 numbers of the set are slightly harder to find. Cards that have been cut in half to form "singles" have a greatly reduced value. These cards have a value from five to ten percent of the uncut strips and are very difficult to sell. The player on the left has an odd number and the other player has an even number. We are using only the odd numbers to identify these panels.

	EX-MT	VG-E	GOOD
COMPLETE SET (150)	5000.00	2200.00	600.00
COMMON PAIRS (1-100)	25.00	11.00	3.10
COMMON PAIRS (101-150)	30.00	13.50	3.70
WRAPPER (1-CENT)	500.00	220.00	60.00
☐ 1 Larry French Vance Page	60.00	27.00	7.50
☐ 3 Billy Herman Stan Hack	45.00	20.00	5.50
☐ 5 Lonny Frey Johnny VanderMeer	35.00	16.00	4.40
☐ 7 Paul Derringer Bucky Walters	35.00	16.00	4.40
☐ 9 Frank McCormick Billy Werber	25.00	11.00	3.10
☐ 11 Johnny Ripple Ernie Lombardi	45.00	20.00	5.50
☐ 13 Alex Kampouris Whitlow Wyatt	25.00	11.00	3.10
☐ 15 Mickey Owen Paul Waner	45.00	20.00	5.50
☐ 17 Cookie Lavagetto Pete Reiser	30.00	13.50	3.70
☐ 19 James Wasdell Dolph Camilli	30.00	13.50	3.70
☐ 21 Dixie Walker Joe Medwick	45.00	20.00	5.50
☐ 23 Pee Wee Reese Kirby Higbe	200.00	90.00	25.00
☐ 25 Harry Danning Cliff Melton	25.00	11.00	3.10
☐ 27 Harry Gumbert Burgess Whitehead	25.00	11.00	3.10
☐ 29 Joe Orengo Joe Moore	25.00	11.00	3.10
☐ 31 Mel Ott Norman Young	100.00	45.00	12.50
☐ 33 Lee Handley Arky Vaughan	45.00	20.00	5.50
☐ 35 Bob Klinger Stanley Brown	25.00	11.00	3.10
☐ 37 Terry Moore Gus Mancuso	30.00	13.50	3.70
☐ 39 Johnny Mize Enos Slaughter	125.00	55.00	15.50
☐ 41 Johnny Cooney Sibby Sisti	25.00	11.00	3.10
☐ 43 Max West Carvel Rowell	25.00	11.00	3.10
☐ 45 Danny Litwhiler Merrill May	25.00	11.00	3.10
☐ 47 Frank Hayes Al Brancato	25.00	11.00	3.10
☐ 49 Bob Johnson Bill Nagel	30.00	13.50	3.70
☐ 51 Bobo Newsom Hank Greenberg	100.00	45.00	12.50
☐ 53 Barney McCosky Charlie Gehringer	75.00	34.00	9.50
☐ 55 Mike Higgins Dick Bartell	30.00	13.50	3.70
☐ 57 Ted Williams Jim Tabor	500.00	220.00	60.00
☐ 59 Joe Cronin Jimmy Foxx	200.00	90.00	25.00
☐ 61 Lefty Gomez Phil Rizzuto	250.00	110.00	31.00
☐ 63 Joe DiMaggio Charlie Keller	750.00	350.00	95.00
☐ 65 Red Rolfe Bill Dickey	100.00	45.00	12.50
☐ 67 Joe Gordon Red Ruffing	100.00	45.00	12.50
☐ 69 Mike Tresh Luke Appling	60.00	27.00	7.50
☐ 71 Moose Solters Johnny Rigney	25.00	11.00	3.10
☐ 73 Buddy Myer Ben Chapman	30.00	13.50	3.70
☐ 75 Cecil Travis George Case	30.00	13.50	3.70
☐ 77 Joe Krakauskas Bob Feller	125.00	55.00	15.50
☐ 79 Ken Keltner Hal Trosky	30.00	13.50	3.70
☐ 81 Ted Williams Joe Cronin	600.00	275.00	75.00
☐ 83 Joe Gordon	40.00	18.00	5.00

Charlie Keller			
☐ 85 Hank Greenberg	200.00	90.00	25.00
Red Ruffing			
☐ 87 Hal Trosky	30.00	13.50	3.70
George Case			
☐ 89 Mel Ott	100.00	45.00	12.50
Burgess Whitehead			
☐ 91 Harry Danning	25.00	11.00	3.10
Harry Gumbert			
☐ 93 Norman Young	25.00	11.00	3.10
Cliff Melton			
☐ 95 Jimmy Ripple	30.00	13.50	3.70
Bucky Walters			
☐ 97 Stan Hack	30.00	13.50	3.70
Bob Klinger			
☐ 99 Johnny Mize	75.00	34.00	9.50
Dan Litwhiler			
☐ 101 Dom Dallesandro	30.00	13.50	3.70
Augie Galan			
☐ 103 Bill Lee	40.00	18.00	5.00
Phil Cavarretta			
☐ 105 Lefty Grove	150.00	70.00	19.00
Bobby Doerr			
☐ 107 Frank Pytlak	60.00	27.00	7.50
Dom DiMaggio			
☐ 109 Jerry Priddy	35.00	16.00	4.40
Johnny Murphy			
☐ 111 Tommy Henrich	50.00	22.00	6.25
Marius Russo			
☐ 113 Frank Crosetti	50.00	22.00	6.25
Johnny Sturm			
☐ 115 Ival Goodman	30.00	13.50	3.70
Myron McCormick			
☐ 117 Eddie Joost	30.00	13.50	3.70
Ernie Koy			
☐ 119 Lloyd Waner	50.00	22.00	6.25
Hank Majeski			
☐ 121 Buddy Hassett	30.00	13.50	3.70
Eugene Moore			
☐ 123 Nick Etten	30.00	13.50	3.70
Johnny Rizzo			
☐ 125 Sam Chapman	30.00	13.50	3.70
Wally Moses			
☐ 127 Johnny Babich	30.00	13.50	3.70
Dick Siebert			
☐ 129 Nelson Potter	30.00	13.50	3.70
Benny McCoy			
☐ 131 Clarence Campbell	75.00	34.00	9.50
Lou Boudreau			
☐ 133 Rollie Hemsley	40.00	18.00	5.00
Mel Harder			
☐ 135 Gerald Walker	30.00	13.50	3.70
Joe Heving			
☐ 137 Johnny Rucker	30.00	13.50	3.70
Ace Adams			
☐ 139 Morris Arnovich	75.00	34.00	9.50
Carl Hubbell			
☐ 141 Lew Riggs	75.00	34.00	9.50
Leo Durocher			
☐ 143 Fred Fitzsimmons	30.00	13.50	3.70
Joe Vosmik			
☐ 145 Frank Crespi	30.00	13.50	3.70
Jim Brown			
☐ 147 Don Heffner	30.00	13.50	3.70
Harlond Clift			
☐ 149 Debs Garms	35.00	16.00	4.40
Elbie Fletcher			

1933 Doubleheader Discs PX3

These metal discs were issued by Gum, Inc. circa 1933. The player's picture, name and team are on the front whereas the back is blank. Also on the front is a "1" or a "2". The wrapper says, "Put 1 and 2 together and make a Double Header." Each disc is approximately 1 1/4" in diameter.

	EX-MT	VG-E	GOOD
COMPLETE SET (43)	1000.00	450.00	125.00
COMMON PLAYER (1-43)	15.00	6.75	1.85
☐ 1 Sparky Adams	15.00	6.75	1.85
☐ 2 Dale Alexander	15.00	6.75	1.85
☐ 3 Earl Averill	40.00	18.00	5.00
☐ 4 Dick Bartell	15.00	6.75	1.85
☐ 5 Wally Berger	20.00	9.00	2.50
☐ 6 Jim Bottomley	40.00	18.00	5.00
☐ 7 Lefty Brandt	15.00	6.75	1.85
☐ 8 Owen Carroll	15.00	6.75	1.85
☐ 9 Lefty Clark	15.00	6.75	1.85
☐ 10 Mickey Cochrane	70.00	32.00	8.75
☐ 11 Joe Cronin	50.00	22.00	6.25
☐ 12 Jimmy Dykes	20.00	9.00	2.50
☐ 13 George Earnshaw	20.00	9.00	2.50
☐ 14 Wes Ferrell	20.00	9.00	2.50
☐ 15 Neal Finn	15.00	6.75	1.85
☐ 16 Lew Fonseca	15.00	6.75	1.85
☐ 17 Jimmy Foxx	100.00	45.00	12.50
☐ 18 Frankie Frisch	50.00	22.00	6.25
☐ 19 Chick Fullis	15.00	6.75	1.85
☐ 20 Charley Gehringer	50.00	22.00	6.25
☐ 21 Goose Goslin	40.00	18.00	5.00
☐ 22 Johnny Hodapp	15.00	6.75	1.85
☐ 23 Frank Hogan	15.00	6.75	1.85
☐ 24 Si Johnson	15.00	6.75	1.85
☐ 25 Joe Judge	20.00	9.00	2.50
☐ 26 Chuck Klein	40.00	18.00	5.00
☐ 27 Al Lopez	35.00	16.00	4.40
☐ 28 Ray Lucas	15.00	6.75	1.85
☐ 29 Red Lucas	15.00	6.75	1.85
☐ 30 Ted Lyons	35.00	16.00	4.40
☐ 31 Firpo Marberry	15.00	6.75	1.85
☐ 32 Oscar Melillo	15.00	6.75	1.85
☐ 33 Lefty O'Doul	20.00	9.00	2.50
☐ 34 George Pipgras	15.00	6.75	1.85
☐ 35 Flint Rhem	15.00	6.75	1.85
☐ 36 Sam Rice	35.00	16.00	4.40
☐ 37 Muddy Ruel	15.00	6.75	1.85
☐ 38 Harry Seibold	15.00	6.75	1.85
☐ 39 Al Simmons	40.00	18.00	5.00
☐ 40 Joe Vosmik	15.00	6.75	1.85
☐ 41 Gerald Walker	15.00	6.75	1.85
☐ 42 Pinky Whitney	15.00	6.75	1.85
☐ 43 Hack Wilson	50.00	22.00	6.25

1950 Drake's

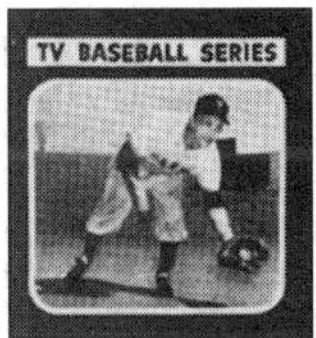

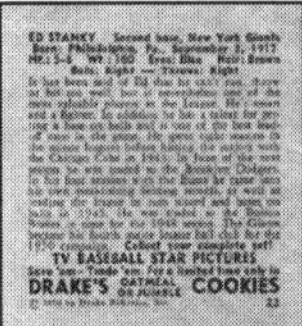

The cards in this 36-card set measure approximately 2 1/2" by 2 1/2". The 1950 Drake's Cookies set contains numbered black and white cards. The players are pictured inside a simulated television screen and the caption "TV Baseball Series" appears on the cards. The players selected for this set show a heavy representation of players from New York teams. The catalog designation for this set is D358.

	NRMT	VG-E	GOOD
COMPLETE SET (36)	7000.00	3200.00	900.00
COMMON CARD (1-36)	75.00	34.00	9.50
☐ 1 Preacher Roe	100.00	45.00	12.50
☐ 2 Clint Hartung	75.00	34.00	9.50
☐ 3 Earl Torgeson	75.00	34.00	9.50
☐ 4 Lou Brissie	75.00	34.00	9.50
☐ 5 Duke Snider	350.00	160.00	45.00
☐ 6 Roy Campanella	450.00	200.00	55.00
☐ 7 Sheldon Jones	75.00	34.00	9.50
☐ 8 Whitey Lockman	75.00	34.00	9.50
☐ 9 Bobby Thomson	100.00	45.00	12.50
☐ 10 Dick Sisler	75.00	34.00	9.50
☐ 11 Gil Hodges	200.00	90.00	25.00
☐ 12 Eddie Waitkus	75.00	34.00	9.50
☐ 13 Bobby Doerr	125.00	55.00	15.50
☐ 14 Warren Spahn	300.00	135.00	38.00
☐ 15 Buddy Kerr	75.00	34.00	9.50
☐ 16 Sid Gordon	75.00	34.00	9.50
☐ 17 Willard Marshall	75.00	34.00	9.50
☐ 18 Carl Furillo	100.00	45.00	12.50
☐ 19 Pee Wee Reese	300.00	135.00	38.00
☐ 20 Alvin Dark	100.00	45.00	12.50
☐ 21 Del Ennis	100.00	45.00	12.50
☐ 22 Ed Stanky	100.00	45.00	12.50
☐ 23 Tom Henrich	100.00	45.00	12.50
☐ 24 Yogi Berra	400.00	180.00	50.00
☐ 25 Phil Rizzuto	200.00	90.00	25.00
☐ 26 Jerry Coleman	100.00	45.00	12.50
☐ 27 Joe Page	100.00	45.00	12.50
☐ 28 Allie Reynolds	100.00	45.00	12.50
☐ 29 Ray Scarborough	75.00	34.00	9.50
☐ 30 Birdie Tebbetts	75.00	34.00	9.50
☐ 31 Maurice McDermott	75.00	34.00	9.50
☐ 32 Johnny Pesky	100.00	45.00	12.50
☐ 33 Dom DiMaggio	125.00	55.00	15.50
☐ 34 Vern Stephens	75.00	34.00	9.50
☐ 35 Bob Elliott	75.00	34.00	9.50
☐ 36 Enos Slaughter	175.00	80.00	22.00

1981 Drake's

The cards in this 33-card set measure 2 1/2" by 3 1/2". The 1981 Drake's Bakeries set contains National and American League stars. Produced in conjunction with Topps and released to the public in Drake's Cakes, this set features red frames for American League players and blue frames for National League players. A Drake's Cakes logo with the words "Big Hitters" appears on the lower front of each card. The backs are quite similar to the 1981 Topps backs but contain the Drake's logo, a different card number, and a short paragraph entitled "What Makes a Big Hitter" at the top of the card.

	NRMT	VG-E	GOOD
COMPLETE SET (33)	7.50	3.40	.95
COMMON CARD (1-33)	.05	.02	.01
☐ 1 Carl Yastrzemski	.75	.35	.09
☐ 2 Rod Carew	.75	.35	.09
☐ 3 Pete Rose	1.25	.55	.16
☐ 4 Dave Parker	.10	.05	.01
☐ 5 George Brett	2.50	1.10	.30
☐ 6 Eddie Murray	2.00	.90	.25
☐ 7 Mike Schmidt	1.25	.55	.16
☐ 8 Jim Rice	.20	.09	.03
☐ 9 Fred Lynn	.10	.05	.01
☐ 10 Reggie Jackson	.75	.35	.09
☐ 11 Steve Garvey	.25	.11	.03
☐ 12 Ken Singleton	.10	.05	.01
☐ 13 Bill Buckner	.10	.05	.01
☐ 14 Dave Winfield	1.00	.45	.12
☐ 15 Jack Clark	.10	.05	.01
☐ 16 Cecil Cooper	.10	.05	.01
☐ 17 Bob Horner	.10	.05	.01
☐ 18 George Foster	.10	.05	.01
☐ 19 Dave Kingman	.10	.05	.01
☐ 20 Cesar Cedeno	.10	.05	.01
☐ 21 Joe Charboneau	.10	.05	.01
☐ 22 George Hendrick	.05	.02	.01
☐ 23 Gary Carter	.30	.14	.04
☐ 24 Al Oliver	.10	.05	.01
☐ 25 Bruce Bochte	.05	.02	.01
☐ 26 Jerry Mumphrey	.05	.02	.01
☐ 27 Steve Kemp	.05	.02	.01
☐ 28 Bob Watson	.10	.05	.01
☐ 29 John Castino	.05	.02	.01
☐ 30 Tony Armas	.10	.05	.01
☐ 31 John Mayberry	.05	.02	.01
☐ 32 Carlton Fisk	.75	.35	.09
☐ 33 Lee Mazzilli	.05	.02	.01

1982 Drake's

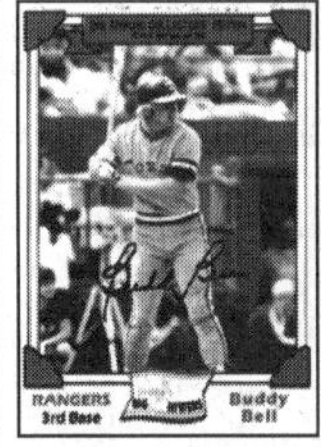

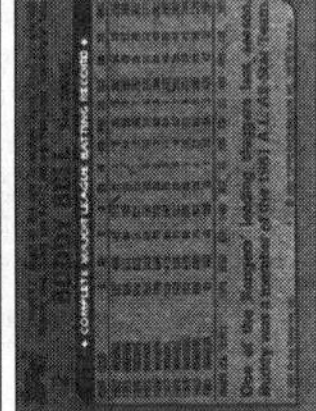

The cards in this 33-card set measure 2 1/2" by 3 1/2". The 1982 Drake's Big Hitters series cards each has the title "2nd Annual Collectors' Edition" in a ribbon design at the top of the picture area. Each color player photo has "photo mount" designs in the corners, red for the AL and green for the NL. The reverses are green and blue, the same as the regular 1982 Topps format, and the photos are larger than those of the previous year. Of the 33 hitters featured, 19 represent the National League. There are 21 returnees from the 1981 set and only one photo, that of Kennedy, is the same as that appearing in the regular Topps issue. The Drake's logo appears centered in the bottom border on the obverse. This set's card numbering is essentially in alphabetical order by the player's name.

	NRMT	VG-E	GOOD
COMPLETE SET (33)	7.50	3.40	.95
COMMON CARD (1-33)	.05	.02	.01
☐ 1 Tony Armas	.05	.02	.01
☐ 2 Buddy Bell	.10	.05	.01
☐ 3 Johnny Bench	.50	.23	.06
☐ 4 George Brett	2.00	.90	.25
☐ 5 Bill Buckner	.10	.05	.01
☐ 6 Rod Carew	.40	.18	.05
☐ 7 Gary Carter	.25	.11	.03
☐ 8 Jack Clark	.10	.05	.01
☐ 9 Cecil Cooper	.10	.05	.01
☐ 10 Jose Cruz	.05	.02	.01
☐ 11 Dwight Evans	.10	.05	.01
☐ 12 Carlton Fisk	.50	.23	.06
☐ 13 George Foster	.10	.05	.01
☐ 14 Steve Garvey	.25	.11	.03
☐ 15 Kirk Gibson	.35	.16	.04
☐ 16 Mike Hargrove	.10	.05	.01
☐ 17 George Hendrick	.05	.02	.01
☐ 18 Bob Horner	.05	.02	.01
☐ 19 Reggie Jackson	.50	.23	.06
☐ 20 Terry Kennedy	.05	.02	.01
☐ 21 Dave Kingman	.10	.05	.01
☐ 22 Greg Luzinski	.10	.05	.01
☐ 23 Bill Madlock	.05	.02	.01
☐ 24 John Mayberry	.05	.02	.01
☐ 25 Eddie Murray	1.50	.70	.19
☐ 26 Graig Nettles	.10	.05	.01
☐ 27 Jim Rice	.20	.09	.03
☐ 28 Pete Rose	1.25	.55	.16
☐ 29 Mike Schmidt	1.25	.55	.16
☐ 30 Ken Singleton	.05	.02	.01
☐ 31 Dave Winfield	.60	.25	.07
☐ 32 Butch Wynegar	.05	.02	.01
☐ 33 Richie Zisk	.05	.02	.01

1983 Drake's

The cards in this 33-card series measure 2 1/2" by 3 1/2". For the third year in a row, Drake's Cakes, in conjunction with Topps, issued a set entitled Big Hitters. The fronts appear very similar to those of the previous two years with slight variations on the framelines and player identification sections. The backs are the same as the Topps backs of this year except for the card number and the Drake's logo. This set's card numbering is essentially in alphabetical order by the player's name.

	NRMT	VG-E	GOOD
COMPLETE SET (33)	7.50	3.40	.95
COMMON CARD (1-33)	.05	.02	.01
☐ 1 Don Baylor	.10	.05	.01
☐ 2 Bill Buckner	.10	.05	.01
☐ 3 Rod Carew	.40	.18	.05
☐ 4 Gary Carter	.25	.11	.03
☐ 5 Jack Clark	.10	.05	.01
☐ 6 Cecil Cooper	.10	.05	.01
☐ 7 Dwight Evans	.10	.05	.01
☐ 8 George Foster	.10	.05	.01
☐ 9 Pedro Guerrero	.05	.02	.01
☐ 10 George Hendrick	.05	.02	.01
☐ 11 Bob Horner	.05	.02	.01
☐ 12 Reggie Jackson	.50	.23	.06
☐ 13 Steve Kemp	.05	.02	.01
☐ 14 Dave Kingman	.10	.05	.01
☐ 15 Bill Madlock	.05	.02	.01
☐ 16 Gary Matthews	.05	.02	.01
☐ 17 Hal McRae	.10	.05	.01
☐ 18 Dale Murphy	.40	.18	.05
☐ 19 Eddie Murray	1.50	.70	.19
☐ 20 Ben Oglivie	.05	.02	.01
☐ 21 Al Oliver	.10	.05	.01
☐ 22 Jim Rice	.20	.09	.03
☐ 23 Cal Ripken	4.00	1.80	.50
☐ 24 Pete Rose	1.00	.45	.12
☐ 25 Mike Schmidt	1.00	.45	.12
☐ 26 Ken Singleton	.05	.02	.01
☐ 27 Gorman Thomas	.05	.02	.01
☐ 28 Jason Thompson	.05	.02	.01
☐ 29 Mookie Wilson	.10	.05	.01
☐ 30 Willie Wilson	.05	.02	.01
☐ 31 Dave Winfield	.60	.25	.07
☐ 32 Carl Yastrzemski	.50	.23	.06
☐ 33 Robin Yount	.60	.25	.07

1984 Drake's

The cards in this 33-card set measure 2 1/2" by 3 1/2". The Fourth Annual Collectors Edition of baseball cards produced by Drake's Cakes in conjunction with Topps continued this now annual set entitled Big Hitters. As in previous years, the front contains a frameline in which the title of the set, the Drake's logo, and the player's name, his team, and position appear. The cards all feature the player in a batting action pose. While the cards fronts are different from the Topps fronts of this year, the backs differ only in the card number and the use of the Drake's logo instead of the Topps logo. This set's card numbering is essentially in alphabetical order by the player's name.

	NRMT	VG-E	GOOD
COMPLETE SET (33)	7.50	3.40	.95
COMMON CARD (1-33)	.05	.02	.01
☐ 1 Don Baylor	.10	.05	.01
☐ 2 Wade Boggs	.75	.35	.09
☐ 3 George Brett	2.00	.90	.25
☐ 4 Bill Buckner	.10	.05	.01

☐ 5 Rod Carew	.40	.18	.05
☐ 6 Gary Carter	.25	.11	.03
☐ 7 Ron Cey	.10	.05	.01
☐ 8 Cecil Cooper	.10	.05	.01
☐ 9 Andre Dawson	.30	.14	.04
☐ 10 Steve Garvey	.10	.05	.01
☐ 11 Pedro Guerrero	.10	.05	.01
☐ 12 George Hendrick	.05	.02	.01
☐ 13 Keith Hernandez	.10	.05	.01
☐ 14 Bob Horner	.05	.02	.01
☐ 15 Reggie Jackson	.50	.23	.06
☐ 16 Steve Kemp	.05	.02	.01
☐ 17 Ron Kittle	.05	.02	.01
☐ 18 Greg Luzinski	.10	.05	.01
☐ 19 Fred Lynn	.10	.05	.01
☐ 20 Bill Madlock	.05	.02	.01
☐ 21 Gary Matthews	.05	.02	.01
☐ 22 Dale Murphy	.40	.18	.05
☐ 23 Eddie Murray	1.25	.55	.16
☐ 24 Al Oliver	.10	.05	.01
☐ 25 Jim Rice	.20	.09	.03
☐ 26 Cal Ripken	4.00	1.80	.50
☐ 27 Pete Rose	1.00	.45	.12
☐ 28 Mike Schmidt	1.00	.45	.12
☐ 29 Darryl Strawberry	.50	.23	.06
☐ 30 Alan Trammell	.30	.14	.04
☐ 31 Mookie Wilson	.05	.02	.01
☐ 32 Dave Winfield	.60	.25	.07
☐ 33 Robin Yount	.50	.23	.06

1985 Drake's

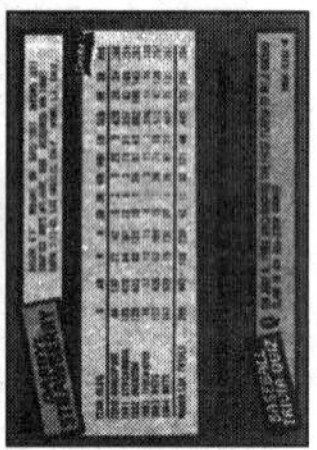

The cards in this 44-card set measure 2 1/2" by 3 1/2". The Fifth Annual Collectors Edition of baseball cards produced by Drake's Cakes in conjunction with Topps continued this apparently annual set with a new twist, for the first time, 11 pitchers were included. The "Big Hitters" are numbered 1-33 and the pitchers are numbered 34-44; each subgroup is ordered alphabetically. The cards are numbered in the upper right corner of the backs of the cards. The complete set could be obtained directly from the company by sending 2.95 with four proofs of purchase.

	NRMT	VG-E	GOOD
COMPLETE FACT. SET (44)	10.00	4.50	1.25
COMPLETE SET (44)	10.00	4.50	1.25
COMMON CARD (1-33)	.05	.02	.01
COMMON CARD (34-44)	.10	.05	.01
☐ 1 Tony Armas	.05	.02	.01
☐ 2 Harold Baines	.15	.07	.02
☐ 3 Don Baylor	.10	.05	.01
☐ 4 George Brett	1.50	.70	.19
☐ 5 Gary Carter	.25	.11	.03
☐ 6 Ron Cey	.15	.07	.02
☐ 7 Jose Cruz	.05	.02	.01
☐ 8 Alvin Davis	.05	.02	.01
☐ 9 Chili Davis	.15	.07	.02
☐ 10 Dwight Evans	.15	.07	.02
☐ 11 Steve Garvey	.25	.11	.03
☐ 12 Kirk Gibson	.35	.16	.04
☐ 13 Pedro Guerrero	.15	.07	.02
☐ 14 Tony Gwynn	2.00	.90	.25
☐ 15 Keith Hernandez	.15	.07	.02
☐ 16 Kent Hrbek	.15	.07	.02
☐ 17 Reggie Jackson	.50	.23	.06
☐ 18 Gary Matthews	.05	.02	.01
☐ 19 Don Mattingly	3.00	1.35	.35
☐ 20 Dale Murphy	.40	.18	.05
☐ 21 Eddie Murray	1.00	.45	.12
☐ 22 Dave Parker	.15	.07	.02
☐ 23 Lance Parrish	.15	.07	.02
☐ 24 Tim Raines	.15	.07	.02
☐ 25 Jim Rice	.15	.07	.02
☐ 26 Cal Ripken	3.00	1.35	.35
☐ 27 Juan Samuel	.05	.02	.01
☐ 28 Ryne Sandberg	1.50	.70	.19
☐ 29 Mike Schmidt	1.00	.45	.12
☐ 30 Darryl Strawberry	.15	.07	.02
☐ 31 Alan Trammell	.25	.11	.03
☐ 32 Dave Winfield	.60	.25	.07
☐ 33 Robin Yount	.40	.18	.05
☐ 34 Mike Boddicker	.10	.05	.01
☐ 35 Steve Carlton	.40	.18	.05
☐ 36 Dwight Gooden	1.50	.70	.19
☐ 37 Willie Hernandez	.10	.05	.01
☐ 38 Mark Langston	.25	.11	.03
☐ 39 Dan Quisenberry	.10	.05	.01
☐ 40 Dave Righetti	.10	.05	.01
☐ 41 Tom Seaver	.50	.23	.06
☐ 42 Bob Stanley	.10	.05	.01
☐ 43 Rick Sutcliffe	.10	.05	.01
☐ 44 Bruce Sutter	.10	.05	.01

1986 Drake's

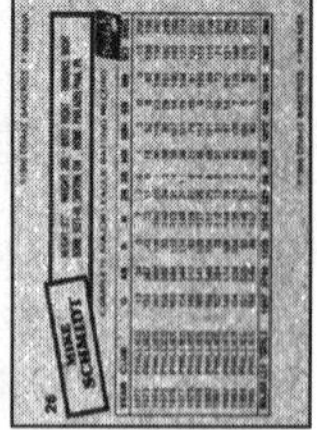

This set of 37 cards was distributed as back panels of various Drake's snack products. Each individual card measures 2 1/2" by 3 1/2". Each specially marked package features two, three, or four cards on the back. The set is easily recognized by the Drake's logo and "6th Annual Collector's Edition" at the top of the obverse. Cards are numbered on the front and the back. Cards below are coded based on the product upon which they appeared, for example, Apple Pies (AP), Cherry Pies (CP), Chocolate Donut Delites (CDD), Coffee Cake Jr. (CCJ), Creme Shortcakes (CS), Devil Dogs (DD), Fudge Brownies (FUD), Funny Bones (FB), Peanut Butter Squares (PBS), Powdered Sugar Donut Delites (PSDD), Ring Ding Jr. (RDJ), Sunny Doodles (SD), Swiss Rolls (SR), Yankee Doodles (YD), and Yodels (Y). The last nine cards are pitchers. Complete panels would be valued approximately 50 percent higher than the individual card prices listed below.

	MINT	NRMT	EXC
COMPLETE SET (37)	50.00	22.00	6.25
COMMON CARD (1-37)	.25	.11	.03
☐ 1 Gary Carter Y	.50	.23	.06
☐ 2 Dwight Evans Y	.25	.11	.03
☐ 3 Reggie Jackson SR	2.00	.90	.25
☐ 4 Dave Parker SR	.50	.23	.06
☐ 5 Rickey Henderson FB	1.50	.70	.19
☐ 6 Pedro Guerrero FB	.40	.18	.05
☐ 7 Don Mattingly YD	6.00	2.70	.75
☐ 8 Mike Marshall YD	.25	.11	.03
☐ 9 Keith Moreland YD	.25	.11	.03
☐ 10 Keith Hernandez CS	.40	.18	.05
☐ 11 Cal Ripken CS	10.00	4.50	1.25
☐ 12 Dale Murphy RDJ	.75	.35	.09
☐ 13 Jim Rice RDJ	.40	.18	.05
☐ 14 George Brett CCJ	5.00	2.20	.60
☐ 15 Tim Raines CCJ	.40	.18	.05
☐ 16 Darryl Strawberry DD	.75	.35	.09
☐ 17 Bill Buckner DD	.40	.18	.05
☐ 18 Dave Winfield AP	1.50	.70	.19
☐ 19 Ryne Sandberg AP	3.00	1.35	.35
☐ 20 Steve Balboni AP	.25	.11	.03
☐ 21 Tommy Herr AP	.25	.11	.03
☐ 22 Pete Rose CP	3.00	1.35	.35
☐ 23 Willie McGee CP	.40	.18	.05
☐ 24 Harold Baines CP	.40	.18	.05
☐ 25 Eddie Murray CP	1.50	.70	.19
☐ 26 Mike Schmidt SD/FUD	2.00	.90	.25
☐ 27 Wade Boggs SD/FUD	1.50	.70	.19
☐ 28 Kirk Gibson SD/FUD	.40	.18	.05
☐ 29 Bret Saberhagen PBS	.50	.23	.06
☐ 30 John Tudor PBS	.25	.11	.03
☐ 31 Orel Hershiser PBS	.50	.23	.06
☐ 32 Ron Guidry CDD	.40	.18	.05
☐ 33 Nolan Ryan CDD	10.00	4.50	1.25
☐ 34 Dave Stieb CDD	.25	.11	.03
☐ 35 Dwight Gooden SDD	.75	.35	.09
☐ 36 Fern.Valenzuela SDD	.40	.18	.05
☐ 37 Tom Browning SDD	.25	.11	.03

1987 Drake's

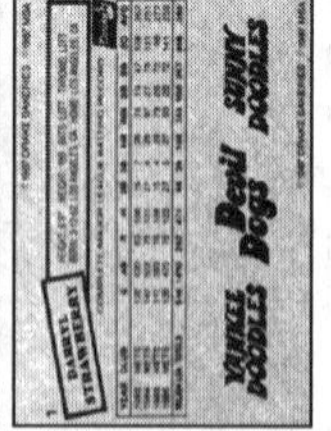

This 33-card set features 25 top hitters and eight top pitchers. Cards were printed in groups of two, three, or four on the backs of Drake's bakery products. Individual cards measure 2 1/2" by 3 1/2" and tout the 7th annual edition. Card backs feature year-by-year season statistics. The cards are numbered such that the pitchers are listed numerically last, e.g., top hitters 1-25 and pitchers 26-33). Complete panels would be valued approximately 50 percent higher than the individual card prices listed below.

	MINT	NRMT	EXC
COMPLETE SET (33)	50.00	22.00	6.25
COMMON CARD (1-33)	.25	.11	.03
☐ 1 Darryl Strawberry	.75	.35	.09
☐ 2 Wally Joyner	.60	.25	.07
☐ 3 Von Hayes	.25	.11	.03
☐ 4 Jose Canseco	3.00	1.35	.35
☐ 5 Dave Winfield	1.50	.70	.19
☐ 6 Cal Ripken	10.00	4.50	1.25
☐ 7 Keith Moreland	.25	.11	.03
☐ 8 Don Mattingly	5.00	2.20	.60
☐ 9 Willie McGee	.25	.11	.03
☐ 10 Keith Hernandez	.40	.18	.05
☐ 11 Tony Gwynn	4.00	1.80	.50
☐ 12 Rickey Henderson	1.50	.70	.19
☐ 13 Dale Murphy	.75	.35	.09
☐ 14 George Brett	4.00	1.80	.50
☐ 15 Jim Rice	.40	.18	.05
☐ 16 Wade Boggs	1.50	.70	.19
☐ 17 Kevin Bass	.25	.11	.03
☐ 18 Dave Parker	.40	.18	.05
☐ 19 Kirby Puckett	4.00	1.80	.50
☐ 20 Gary Carter	.50	.23	.06
☐ 21 Ryne Sandberg	3.00	1.35	.35
☐ 22 Harold Baines	.40	.18	.05
☐ 23 Mike Schmidt	2.00	.90	.25
☐ 24 Eddie Murray	1.50	.70	.19
☐ 25 Steve Sax	.25	.11	.03
☐ 26 Dwight Gooden	.75	.35	.09
☐ 27 Jack Morris	.40	.18	.05
☐ 28 Ron Darling	.25	.11	.03
☐ 29 Fernando Valenzuela	.40	.18	.05
☐ 30 John Tudor	.25	.11	.03
☐ 31 Roger Clemens	2.50	1.10	.30
☐ 32 Nolan Ryan	10.00	4.50	1.25
☐ 33 Mike Scott	.25	.11	.03

1988 Drake's

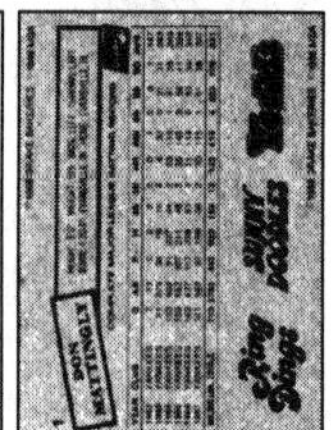

This 33-card set features 27 top hitters and six top pitchers. Cards were printed in groups of two, three, or four on the backs of Drake's bakery products. Individual cards measure approximately 2 1/2" by 3 1/2" and tout the 8th annual edition. Card backs feature year-by-year season statistics. The cards are numbered such that the pitchers are listed numerically last, e.g., top hitters 1-27 and pitchers 28-33). The product affiliations are as follows, 1-2 Ring Dings, 3-4 Devil Dogs, 5-6 Coffee Cakes, 7-9 Yankee Doodles, 10-11 Funny Bones, 12-14 Fudge Brownies, 15-18 Cherry Pies, 19-21 Sunny Doodles, 22-24 Powdered Sugar Donuts, 25-27 Chocolate Donuts, 28-29 Yodels, and 30-33 Apple Pies. Complete panels would be valued approximately 50 percent higher than the individual card prices listed below.

	MINT	NRMT	EXC
COMPLETE SET (33)	40.00	18.00	5.00
COMMON CARD (1-33)	.25	.11	.03
☐ 1 Don Mattingly	5.00	2.20	.60
☐ 2 Tim Raines	.40	.18	.05
☐ 3 Darryl Strawberry	.75	.35	.09
☐ 4 Wade Boggs	1.50	.70	.19
☐ 5 Keith Hernandez	.40	.18	.05
☐ 6 Mark McGwire	3.00	1.35	.35
☐ 7 Rickey Henderson	1.50	.70	.19
☐ 8 Mike Schmidt	2.00	.90	.25
☐ 9 Dwight Evans	.25	.11	.03
☐ 10 Gary Carter	.50	.23	.06
☐ 11 Paul Molitor	2.00	.90	.25
☐ 12 Dave Winfield	1.50	.70	.19
☐ 13 Alan Trammell	.50	.23	.06
☐ 14 Tony Gwynn	4.00	1.80	.50
☐ 15 Dale Murphy	.75	.35	.09
☐ 16 Andre Dawson	.50	.23	.06
☐ 17 Von Hayes	.25	.11	.03
☐ 18 Willie Randolph	.25	.11	.03
☐ 19 Kirby Puckett	4.00	1.80	.50
☐ 20 Juan Samuel	.25	.11	.03
☐ 21 Eddie Murray	1.50	.70	.19
☐ 22 George Bell	.25	.11	.03
☐ 23 Larry Sheets	.25	.11	.03
☐ 24 Eric Davis	.40	.18	.05
☐ 25 Cal Ripken	10.00	4.50	1.25
☐ 26 Pedro Guerrero	.25	.11	.03
☐ 27 Will Clark	2.50	1.10	.30
☐ 28 Dwight Gooden	.40	.18	.05
☐ 29 Frank Viola	.25	.11	.03
☐ 30 Roger Clemens	2.00	.90	.25
☐ 31 Rick Sutcliffe	.25	.11	.03
☐ 32 Jack Morris	.40	.18	.05
☐ 33 John Tudor	.25	.11	.03

1894 Duke Cabinets N142

These four cabinets were produced by W.H. Duke. These color cabinets measure approximately 6" X 9 1/2" and a portrait takes up almost the entire card. The player is identified on the bottom.

	EX-MT	VG-E	GOOD
COMPLETE SET (4)	7500.00	3400.00	950.00
COMMON CARD (1-4)	1500.00	700.00	190.00
☐ 1 George Davis	1500.00	700.00	190.00
☐ 2 Ed Delahanty	2500.00	1100.00	300.00
☐ 3 Billy Nash	1500.00	700.00	190.00
☐ 4 Wilbert Robinson	2500.00	1100.00	300.00

1893 Duke Talk of the Diamond N135

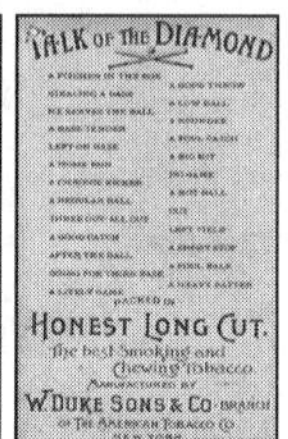

The 25 cards in Duke's Talk of the Diamond set feature a humorous situation placed alongside a baseball design. Since the reverse lists the manufacturer as a branch of the American Tobacco Company, it is thought that this set was issued about 1893. A list of the 25 titles appears on the back of each card. Most of the baseball designs are similar to those appearing in the Buchner Gold Coin set (N284).

	EX-MT	VG-E	GOOD
COMPLETE SET (25)	450.00	200.00	55.00
COMMON CARD (1-25)	20.00	9.00	2.50
☐ 1 A Good Throw	20.00	9.00	2.50
☐ 2 After the Ball	20.00	9.00	2.50
☐ 3 Lively Game	20.00	9.00	2.50
☐ 4 Three Out All Out	20.00	9.00	2.50
☐ 5 A Foul Catch	20.00	9.00	2.50
☐ 6 Left Field	20.00	9.00	2.50
☐ 7 A Base Tender	20.00	9.00	2.50
☐ 8 A Good Catch	20.00	9.00	2.50
☐ 9 A Short Stop	20.00	9.00	2.50
☐ 10 Going for Third Base	20.00	9.00	2.50
☐ 11 Home Run	20.00	9.00	2.50
☐ 12 Left on Base	20.00	9.00	2.50
☐ 13 A Foul Ball	20.00	9.00	2.50
☐ 14 A Heavy Batter	20.00	9.00	2.50
☐ 15 Stealing a Base	20.00	9.00	2.50
☐ 16 A Pitcher in the Box	20.00	9.00	2.50
☐ 17 He Serves the Ball	20.00	9.00	2.50
☐ 18 A Chronic Kicker	20.00	9.00	2.50
☐ 19 A Regular Ball	20.00	9.00	2.50
☐ 20 A Low Ball	20.00	9.00	2.50
☐ 21 A Big Hit	20.00	9.00	2.50
☐ 22 A Rounder	20.00	9.00	2.50
☐ 23 No Game	20.00	9.00	2.50
☐ 24 Out	20.00	9.00	2.50
☐ 25 A Hot Ball	20.00	9.00	2.50

1993 Duracell Power Players I

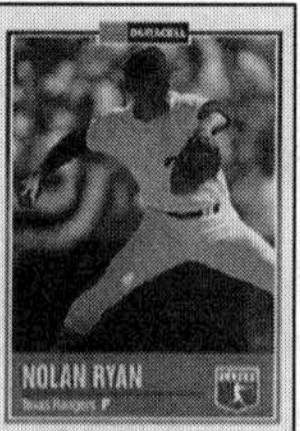

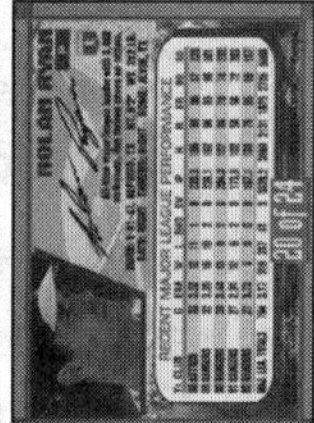

This 24-card standard-size set was divided into six packs with four cards and one Duracell Official Order Form in each pack. One pack was free with a purchase of Duracell Saver Pack or could be ordered with proof of purchase of several other Duracell products. The white-bordered color photo has a Duracell logo across the top and the player's name, team and position at the bottom edge. The horizontal back carries a close-up photo in the upper left. The player's name, autograph, biography, and recent statistics are shown superimposed over a ghosted picture of a ball park.

	MINT	NRMT	EXC
COMPLETE SET (24)	2.50	1.10	.30
COMMON CARD (1-24)	.05	.02	.01
☐ 1 Roger Clemens	.25	.11	.03
☐ 2 Frank Thomas	1.00	.45	.12
☐ 3 Andre Dawson	.15	.07	.02

☐ 4 Orel Hershiser	.10	.05	.01
☐ 5 Kirby Puckett	.50	.23	.06
☐ 6 Edgar Martinez	.10	.05	.01
☐ 7 Craig Biggio	.10	.05	.01
☐ 8 Terry Pendleton	.05	.02	.01
☐ 9 Mark McGwire	.40	.18	.05
☐ 10 Dave Stewart	.05	.02	.01
☐ 11 Ozzie Smith	.50	.23	.06
☐ 12 Doug Drabek	.05	.02	.01
☐ 13 Dwight Gooden	.10	.05	.01
☐ 14 Tony Gwynn	.50	.23	.06
☐ 15 Carlos Baerga	.50	.23	.06
☐ 16 Robin Yount	.15	.07	.02
☐ 17 Barry Bonds	.25	.11	.03
☐ 18 Bip Roberts	.05	.02	.01
☐ 19 Don Mattingly	.50	.23	.06
☐ 20 Nolan Ryan	.75	.35	.09
☐ 21 Tom Glavine	.15	.07	.02
☐ 22 Will Clark	.15	.07	.02
☐ 23 Cecil Fielder	.10	.05	.01
☐ 24 Dave Winfield	.15	.07	.02

1993 Duracell Power Players II

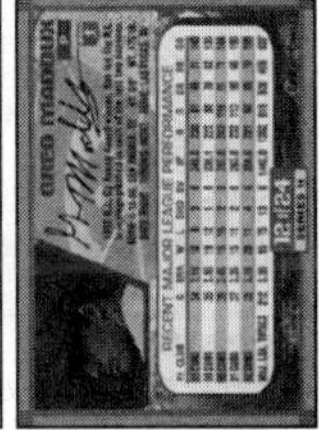

This 24-card standard-size set was divided into six packs with four cards and one Duracell Official Order Form in each pack. One pack was free with a purchase of a Duracell Saver Pack or could be ordered with proof of purchase of several other Duracell products. The white-bordered color photo has a Duracell logo across the top and the player's name, team and position at the bottom edge. The horizontal back carries a close-up photo in the upper left. The player's name, autograph, biography, and recent statistics are shown superimposed over a ghosted picture of a ballpark.

	MINT	NRMT	EXC
COMPLETE SET (24)	2.50	1.10	.30
COMMON CARD (1-24)	.05	.02	.01
☐ 1 Cal Ripken	1.00	.45	.12
☐ 2 Melido Perez	.05	.02	.01
☐ 3 John Kruk	.05	.02	.01
☐ 4 Charlie Hayes	.05	.02	.01
☐ 5 George Brett	.50	.23	.06
☐ 6 Ruben Sierra	.05	.02	.01
☐ 7 Deion Sanders	.25	.11	.03
☐ 8 Andy Van Slyke	.05	.02	.01
☐ 9 Fred McGriff	.20	.09	.03
☐ 10 Benito Santiago	.05	.02	.01
☐ 11 Charles Nagy	.10	.05	.01
☐ 12 Greg Maddux	.75	.35	.09
☐ 13 Ryne Sandberg	.50	.23	.06
☐ 14 Dennis Martinez	.05	.02	.01
☐ 15 Ken Griffey Jr.	1.25	.55	.16
☐ 16 Jim Abbott	.05	.02	.01
☐ 17 Barry Larkin	.25	.11	.03
☐ 18 Gary Sheffield	.25	.11	.03
☐ 19 Jose Canseco	.20	.09	.03
☐ 20 Jack McDowell	.05	.02	.01
☐ 21 Darryl Strawberry	.10	.05	.01
☐ 22 Delino DeShields	.05	.02	.01
☐ 23 Dennis Eckersley	.10	.05	.01
☐ 24 Paul Molitor	.20	.09	.03

1992 Dynasty Rose

Produced by Dynasty Sports Cards, this 15-card, standard-size set is aptly titled "The Hit King" and showcases Pete Rose. The white-bordered color pictures on the fronts were painted by artist Tim Seeberger. A gold foil crown and a card subtitle are printed in the wider white border below the picture. On a white background in black print, backs carry the year in a diamond icon and running narrative summarizing Rose's illustrious career.

	MINT	NRMT	EXC
COMPLETE SET (15)	10.00	4.50	1.25
COMMON CARD (1-14)	.75	.35	.09
☐ 1 Pete Rose 1963 The Rookie	.75	.35	.09
☐ 2 Pete Rose 1975 MVP	.75	.35	.09
☐ 3 Pete Rose 1976 Head First	.75	.35	.09
☐ 4 Pete Rose 1978 The Streak	.75	.35	.09
☐ 5 Pete Rose 1979 Free Agent	.75	.35	.09
☐ 6 Pete Rose 1980 Charlie Hustle	.75	.35	.09
☐ 7 Pete Rose 1981 Headed for Home	.75	.35	.09
☐ 8 Pete Rose 1983 World Series	.75	.35	.09
☐ 9 Pete Rose 1984 Trip to Canada	.75	.35	.09
☐ 10 Pete Rose 1984 Pete's Back	.75	.35	.09
☐ 11 Pete Rose 1985 4,192 Hits	.75	.35	.09
☐ 12 Pete Rose 1986 Manager	.75	.35	.09
☐ 13 Pete Rose 1991 The Teacher	.75	.35	.09
☐ 14 Pete Rose 1992 Hit King	.75	.35	.09
☐ NNO Title Card	.50	.23	.06

1914 E & S Publishing

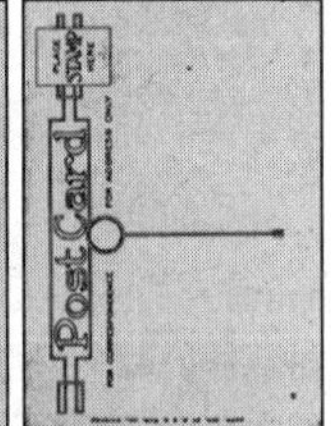

These ornate styled postcards produced by the E & S Pub. Co. of Chicago in 1914 is extremely rare. This bluetone card has a closeup head and shoulders caraciture of the player surrounded by cartoon vignettes of his career done by an obviously gifted cartoonist, possibly from one of the Chicago newspapers. The art is signed T.S. Identified players are: Joe Benz and Ty Cobb but there might be other players known. Any additions to this checklist are greatly appreciated.

	EX-MT	VG-E	GOOD
COMPLETE SET (2)	1500.00	700.00	190.00
COMMON CARD (1-2)	350.00	160.00	45.00
☐ 1 Joe Benz	350.00	160.00	45.00
☐ 2 Ty Cobb	1200.00	550.00	150.00

1911 E94

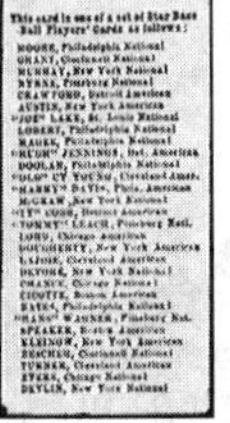

The cards in this 30-card set measure 1 1/2" by 2 3/4". The E94 format, like that of E93, consists of tinted, black and white photos on solid color backgrounds (seven colors seen; each player seen in more than one color). Issued in 1911, cards from this set may be found with advertising overstamps covering the gray print checklist on the back (begins with Moore). Some blank backs have been found, and the set is identical to M131.

	EX-MT	VG-E	GOOD
COMPLETE SET (30)	7000.00	3200.00	900.00
COMMON CARD (1-30)	100.00	45.00	12.50
☐ 1 Jimmy Austin	100.00	45.00	12.50
☐ 2 Johnny Bates	100.00	45.00	12.50
☐ 3 Bob Bescher	100.00	45.00	12.50
☐ 4 Bobby Byrne	100.00	45.00	12.50
☐ 5 Frank Chance	250.00	110.00	31.00
☐ 6 Eddie Cicotte	200.00	90.00	25.00
☐ 7 Ty Cobb	1500.00	700.00	190.00
☐ 8 Sam Crawford	250.00	110.00	31.00
☐ 9 Harry Davis	100.00	45.00	12.50
☐ 10 Art Devlin	100.00	45.00	12.50
☐ 11 Josh Devore	100.00	45.00	12.50
☐ 12 Mickey Doolan	100.00	45.00	12.50
☐ 13 Patsy Dougherty	100.00	45.00	12.50
☐ 14 Johnny Evers	250.00	110.00	31.00
☐ 15 Eddie Grant	100.00	45.00	12.50
☐ 16 Hugh Jennings	250.00	110.00	31.00
☐ 17 Red Kleinow	100.00	45.00	12.50
☐ 18 Napoleon Lajoie	500.00	220.00	60.00
☐ 19 Joe Lake	100.00	45.00	12.50
☐ 20 Tommy Leach	125.00	55.00	15.50
☐ 21 Hans Lobert	100.00	45.00	12.50
☐ 22 Harry Lord	100.00	45.00	12.50
☐ 23 Sherry Magee	100.00	45.00	12.50
☐ 24 John McGraw	300.00	135.00	38.00
☐ 25 Earl Moore	100.00	45.00	12.50
☐ 26 Red Murray	100.00	45.00	12.50
☐ 27 Tris Speaker	500.00	220.00	60.00
☐ 28 Terry Turner	100.00	45.00	12.50
☐ 29 Hans Wagner	750.00	350.00	95.00
☐ 30 Cy Young	500.00	220.00	60.00

1910 E98

The cards in this 30-card set measure 1 1/2" by 2 3/4". E98 is an anonymous set with more similarities to Standard Caramel issues than to Briggs. Most players are found with four different background colors and the brown print checklist (starts with "1. Christy Mathewson") has been alphabetized below. The set was issued in 1910.

	EX-MT	VG-E	GOOD
COMPLETE SET (30)	8500.00	3800.00	1050.00
COMMON CARD (1-30)	100.00	45.00	12.50
☐ 1 Chief Bender	300.00	135.00	38.00
☐ 2 Roger Bresnahan	300.00	135.00	38.00
☐ 3 Al Bridwell	100.00	45.00	12.50
☐ 4 Miner Brown	300.00	135.00	38.00
☐ 5 Frank Chance	350.00	160.00	45.00
☐ 6 Hal Chase	150.00	70.00	19.00
☐ 7 Fred Clarke	300.00	135.00	38.00
☐ 8 Ty Cobb	2000.00	900.00	250.00
☐ 9 Eddie Collins	350.00	160.00	45.00
☐ 10 Jack Coombs	150.00	70.00	19.00
☐ 11 Bill Dahlen	150.00	70.00	19.00
☐ 12 Harry Davis	100.00	45.00	12.50
☐ 13 Red Dooin	100.00	45.00	12.50
☐ 14 Johnny Evers	300.00	135.00	38.00
☐ 15 Russ Ford	100.00	45.00	12.50
☐ 16 Hugh Jennings	300.00	135.00	38.00
☐ 17 Johnny Kling	100.00	45.00	12.50
☐ 18 Napoleon Lajoie	400.00	180.00	50.00
☐ 19 Connie Mack	350.00	160.00	45.00
☐ 20 Christy Mathewson	500.00	220.00	60.00
☐ 21 John McGraw	350.00	160.00	45.00
☐ 22 Larry McLean	100.00	45.00	12.50
☐ 23 Chief Meyers	100.00	45.00	12.50
☐ 24 George Mullin	100.00	45.00	12.50
☐ 25 Fred Tenney	100.00	45.00	12.50
☐ 26 Joe Tinker	300.00	135.00	38.00
☐ 27 Hippo Vaughn	100.00	45.00	12.50
☐ 28 Hans Wagner	600.00	275.00	75.00
☐ 29 Ed Walsh	300.00	135.00	38.00
☐ 30 Cy Young	400.00	180.00	50.00

1910 E101

The cards in this 50-card set measure 1 1/2" by 2 3/4". The "Prominent Members of National and American Leagues" portrayed in E101 are identical to the line drawings of E92 and E105. The set was distributed about 1910. The set issuer is not mentioned anywhere on the cards. The complete set price includes all variation cards listed in the checklist below.

	EX-MT	VG-E	GOOD
COMPLETE SET (50)	8500.00	3800.00	1050.00
COMMON CARD (1-46)	100.00	45.00	12.50
☐ 1 Jack Barry	100.00	45.00	12.50
☐ 2 Harry Bemis	100.00	45.00	12.50
☐ 3A Chief Bender (white cap)	200.00	90.00	25.00
☐ 3B Chief Bender (striped cap)	200.00	90.00	25.00
☐ 4 Bill Bergen	100.00	45.00	12.50
☐ 5 Bob Bescher	100.00	45.00	12.50
☐ 6 Al Bridwell	100.00	45.00	12.50
☐ 7 Doc Casey	100.00	45.00	12.50
☐ 8 Frank Chance	250.00	110.00	31.00
☐ 9 Hal Chase	150.00	70.00	19.00
☐ 10 Ty Cobb	1800.00	800.00	220.00
☐ 11 Eddie Collins	300.00	135.00	38.00
☐ 12 Sam Crawford	200.00	90.00	25.00
☐ 13 Harry Davis	100.00	45.00	12.50
☐ 14 Art Devlin	100.00	45.00	12.50
☐ 15 Bill Donovan	100.00	45.00	12.50
☐ 16 Red Dooin	100.00	45.00	12.50
☐ 17 Mickey Doolan	100.00	45.00	12.50
☐ 18 Patsy Dougherty	100.00	45.00	12.50
☐ 19A Larry Doyle (batting)	100.00	45.00	12.50
☐ 19B Larry Doyle (throwing)	100.00	45.00	12.50
☐ 20 Johnny Evers	200.00	90.00	25.00
☐ 21 George Gibson	100.00	45.00	12.50
☐ 22 Topsy Hartsel	100.00	45.00	12.50
☐ 23 Fred Jacklitsch	100.00	45.00	12.50
☐ 24 Hugh Jennings	200.00	90.00	25.00
☐ 25 Red Kleinow	100.00	45.00	12.50
☐ 26 Otto Knabe	100.00	45.00	12.50
☐ 27 John Knight	100.00	45.00	12.50
☐ 28 Napoleon Lajoie	400.00	180.00	50.00
☐ 29 Hans Lobert	150.00	70.00	19.00
☐ 30 Sherry Magee	100.00	45.00	12.50
☐ 31 Christy Mathewson	500.00	220.00	60.00
☐ 32 John McGraw	300.00	135.00	38.00
☐ 33 Larry McLean	100.00	45.00	12.50
☐ 34A J.B. Miller (batting)	100.00	45.00	12.50
☐ 34B J.B. Miller (fielding)	100.00	45.00	12.50
☐ 35 Danny Murphy	100.00	45.00	12.50
☐ 36 Bill O'Hara	100.00	45.00	12.50
☐ 37 Germany Schaefer	100.00	45.00	12.50
☐ 38 Admiral Schlei	100.00	45.00	12.50
☐ 39 Boss Schmidt	100.00	45.00	12.50
☐ 40 Seigle (sic, Siegle)	100.00	45.00	12.50
☐ 41 Dave Shean	100.00	45.00	12.50
☐ 42 Boss Smith	100.00	45.00	12.50
☐ 43 Joe Tinker	200.00	90.00	25.00
☐ 44A Honus Wagner (batting)	600.00	275.00	75.00
☐ 44B Honus Wagner (throwing)	600.00	275.00	75.00
☐ 45 Cy Young	400.00	180.00	50.00
☐ 46 Heine Zimmerman	100.00	45.00	12.50

1910 E102

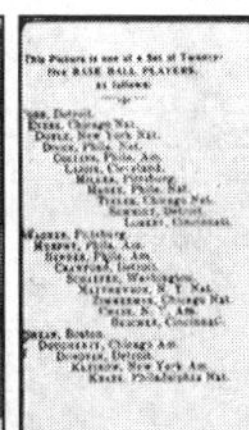

The cards in this 29-card set measure 1 1/2" by 2 3/4". The player poses in E102 are identical to those in E92. The reverse of each card carries an angled checklist (Begins with "COBB, Detroit") printed in black. Smith is not listed, and two poses exist for both Doyle and Miller. The set was issued circa 1910. The complete set price includes all variation cards listed in the checklist below.

	EX-MT	VG-E	GOOD
COMPLETE SET (29)	6000.00	2700.00	750.00
COMMON CARD	100.00	45.00	12.50
☐ 1 Chief Bender	200.00	90.00	25.00
☐ 2 Bob Bescher	100.00	45.00	12.50
☐ 3 Hal Chase	150.00	70.00	19.00
☐ 4 Ty Cobb	1800.00	800.00	220.00
☐ 5 Eddie Collins	200.00	90.00	25.00
☐ 6 Sam Crawford	200.00	90.00	25.00
☐ 7 Bill Donovan	100.00	45.00	12.50
☐ 8 Red Dooin	100.00	45.00	12.50
☐ 9 Patsy Dougherty	100.00	45.00	12.50
☐ 10A Larry Doyle (batting)	100.00	45.00	12.50
☐ 10B Larry Doyle (throwing)	100.00	45.00	12.50
☐ 11 Johnny Evers	200.00	90.00	25.00
☐ 12 Red Kleinow	100.00	45.00	12.50
☐ 13 Otto Knabe	100.00	45.00	12.50
☐ 14 Napoleon Lajoie	350.00	160.00	45.00
☐ 15 Hans Lobert	100.00	45.00	12.50
☐ 16 Sherry Magee	100.00	45.00	12.50
☐ 17 Christy Mathewson	500.00	220.00	60.00
☐ 18A J.B. Miller (batting)	100.00	45.00	12.50
☐ 18B J.B. Miller (fielding)	250.00	110.00	31.00
☐ 19 Danny Murphy	100.00	45.00	12.50
☐ 20 Germany Schaefer	100.00	45.00	12.50
☐ 21 Boss Schmidt	100.00	45.00	12.50
☐ 22 Dave Shean	100.00	45.00	12.50
☐ 23 Smith	100.00	45.00	12.50

☐ 24 Joe Tinker	200.00	90.00	25.00
☐ 25A Honus Wagner (batting)	600.00	275.00	75.00
☐ 25B Honus Wagner (throwing)	600.00	275.00	75.00
☐ 26 Heinie Zimmerman	100.00	45.00	12.50

1922 E120

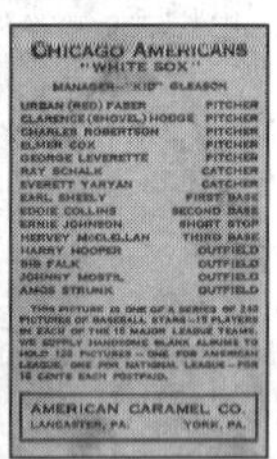

The cards in this 240-card set measure 2" by 3 1/2". The 1922 E120 set was issued by American Caramels and contains unnumbered cards which are numbered here alphabetically within team for convenience. The order of teams is alphabetically within league: Boston AL (1-15), Chicago AL (16-30), Cleveland (31-45), Detroit (46-60), New York AL (61-75), Philadelphia AL (76-90), St. Louis AL (91-105), Washington (106-120), Boston NL (121-135), Brooklyn (136-150), Chicago NL (151-165), Cincinnati (166-180), New York NL (181-195), Philadelphia NL (196-210), Pittsburgh (211-225) and St. Louis NL (226-240). This set is one of the most popular of the E card sets.

	EX-MT	VG-E	GOOD
COMPLETE SET (240)	10000.00	4500.00	1250.00
COMMON CARD (1-240)	40.00	18.00	5.00
☐ 1 George Burns	40.00	18.00	5.00
☐ 2 John Collins	40.00	18.00	5.00
☐ 3 Joe Dugan	50.00	22.00	6.25
☐ 4 Joe Harris	40.00	18.00	5.00
☐ 5 Bennie Karr	40.00	18.00	5.00
☐ 6 Harry Leibold	40.00	18.00	5.00
☐ 7 Michael Menosky	40.00	18.00	5.00
☐ 8 Elmer Myers	40.00	18.00	5.00
☐ 9 Herb Pennock	75.00	34.00	9.50
☐ 10 Clarke Pittenger	40.00	18.00	5.00
☐ 11 Derrill Pratt	40.00	18.00	5.00
☐ 12 John Quinn	50.00	22.00	6.25
☐ 13 Muddy Ruel	40.00	18.00	5.00
☐ 14 Elmer Smith	40.00	18.00	5.00
☐ 15 Al Walters	40.00	18.00	5.00
☐ 16 Eddie Collins	125.00	55.00	15.50
☐ 17 Elmer Cox	40.00	18.00	5.00
☐ 18 Urban Faber	75.00	34.00	9.50
☐ 19 Bibb Falk	40.00	18.00	5.00
☐ 20 Clarence Hodge	40.00	18.00	5.00
☐ 21 Harry Hooper	75.00	34.00	9.50
☐ 22 Ernie Johnson	40.00	18.00	5.00
☐ 23 Horace Leverette	40.00	18.00	5.00
☐ 24 Harvey McClellan	40.00	18.00	5.00
☐ 25 Johnny Mostil	40.00	18.00	5.00
☐ 26 Charles Robertson	40.00	18.00	5.00
☐ 27 Ray Schalk	75.00	34.00	9.50
☐ 28 Earl Sheely	40.00	18.00	5.00
☐ 29 Amos Strunk	40.00	18.00	5.00
☐ 30 Clarence Yaryan	40.00	18.00	5.00
☐ 31 Jim Bagby	40.00	18.00	5.00
☐ 32 Stan Coveleskie	75.00	34.00	9.50
☐ 33 Harry Gardner	40.00	18.00	5.00
☐ 34 Jack Graney	40.00	18.00	5.00
☐ 35 Charles Jamieson	40.00	18.00	5.00
☐ 36 John Mails	40.00	18.00	5.00
☐ 37 Stuffy McInnis	50.00	22.00	6.25
☐ 38 Leslie Nunamaker	40.00	18.00	5.00
☐ 39 Steve O'Neill	50.00	22.00	6.25
☐ 40 Joe Sewell	75.00	34.00	9.50
☐ 41 Allen Sothoron	40.00	18.00	5.00
☐ 42 Tris Speaker	200.00	90.00	25.00
☐ 43 George Uhle	40.00	18.00	5.00
☐ 44 Bill Wambsganss	50.00	22.00	6.25
☐ 45 Joe Wood	50.00	22.00	6.25
☐ 46 John Bassler	40.00	18.00	5.00
☐ 47 Lu Blue	40.00	18.00	5.00
☐ 48 Ty Cobb	600.00	275.00	75.00
☐ 49 Bert Cole	40.00	18.00	5.00
☐ 50 George Cutshaw	40.00	18.00	5.00
☐ 51 George Dauss	40.00	18.00	5.00
☐ 52 Howard Ehmke	50.00	22.00	6.25
☐ 53 Ira Flagstead	40.00	18.00	5.00
☐ 54 Harry Heilmann	100.00	45.00	12.50
☐ 55 Sylvester Johnson	40.00	18.00	5.00
☐ 56 Bob Jones	40.00	18.00	5.00
☐ 57 Herman Pillette	40.00	18.00	5.00
☐ 58 Emory Rigney	40.00	18.00	5.00
☐ 59 Bob Veach	40.00	18.00	5.00
☐ 60 Charles Woodall	40.00	18.00	5.00
☐ 61 Frank Baker	100.00	45.00	12.50
☐ 62 Joe Bush	50.00	22.00	6.25
☐ 63 Al DeVormer	40.00	18.00	5.00
☐ 64 Waite Hoyt	100.00	45.00	12.50
☐ 65 Sam Jones	50.00	22.00	6.25
☐ 66 Carl Mays	50.00	22.00	6.25
☐ 67 Michael McNally	40.00	18.00	5.00
☐ 68 Bob Meusel	50.00	22.00	6.25
☐ 69 Elmer Miller	40.00	18.00	5.00
☐ 70 Wally Pipp	50.00	22.00	6.25
☐ 71 Babe Ruth	800.00	350.00	100.00
☐ 72 Wallie Schang	40.00	18.00	5.00
☐ 73 Everett Scott	50.00	22.00	6.25
☐ 74 Bob Shawkey	50.00	22.00	6.25
☐ 75 Aaron Ward	40.00	18.00	5.00
☐ 76 Frank Calloway	40.00	18.00	5.00
☐ 77 Jimmy Dykes	50.00	22.00	6.25
☐ 78 Alfred Fuhrman	40.00	18.00	5.00
☐ 79 Chick Galloway	40.00	18.00	5.00
☐ 80 Bryan Harris	40.00	18.00	5.00
☐ 81 Robert Hasty	40.00	18.00	5.00
☐ 82 Joe Hauser	40.00	18.00	5.00
☐ 83 W.F.(Doc) Johnston	40.00	18.00	5.00
☐ 84 Bing Miller	40.00	18.00	5.00
☐ 85 Roy Moore	40.00	18.00	5.00
☐ 86 Roleine Naylor	40.00	18.00	5.00
☐ 87 Cy Perkins	40.00	18.00	5.00
☐ 88 Ed Rommel	50.00	22.00	6.25
☐ 89 Clarence Walker Tillie	40.00	18.00	5.00
☐ 90 Frank Welch	40.00	18.00	5.00
☐ 91 William Bayne	40.00	18.00	5.00
☐ 92 Pat Collins	40.00	18.00	5.00
☐ 93 David Danforth	40.00	18.00	5.00
☐ 94 Frank Davis	40.00	18.00	5.00
☐ 95 Francis Ellerbe	40.00	18.00	5.00
☐ 96 Walter Gerber	40.00	18.00	5.00
☐ 97 Will Jacobson	40.00	18.00	5.00
☐ 98 Marty McManus	40.00	18.00	5.00
☐ 99 Hank Severeid	40.00	18.00	5.00
☐ 100 Urban Shocker	50.00	22.00	6.25
☐ 101 Charles Shorten	40.00	18.00	5.00
☐ 102 George Sisler	125.00	55.00	15.50
☐ 103 John Tobin	40.00	18.00	5.00
☐ 104 Elam Van Gilder	40.00	18.00	5.00
☐ 105 Ken Williams	50.00	22.00	6.25
☐ 106 Henry Courtney	40.00	18.00	5.00
☐ 107 Edward Gharrity	40.00	18.00	5.00
☐ 108 Goose Goslin	100.00	45.00	12.50
☐ 109 Stanley Harris	75.00	34.00	9.50
☐ 110 Walter Johnson	200.00	90.00	25.00
☐ 111 Joe Judge	40.00	18.00	5.00
☐ 112 Clyde Milan	40.00	18.00	5.00
☐ 113 George Mogridge	40.00	18.00	5.00
☐ 114 Roger Peckinpaugh	50.00	22.00	6.25
☐ 115 Tom Phillips	40.00	18.00	5.00
☐ 116 Val Picinich	40.00	18.00	5.00
☐ 117 Sam Rice	75.00	34.00	9.50
☐ 118 Howard Shanks	40.00	18.00	5.00
☐ 119 Earl Smith	40.00	18.00	5.00
☐ 120 Tom Zachary	40.00	18.00	5.00
☐ 121 Walter Barbare	40.00	18.00	5.00
☐ 122 Norman Boeckel	40.00	18.00	5.00
☐ 123 Walton Cruise	40.00	18.00	5.00
☐ 124 Dana Fillingim	40.00	18.00	5.00
☐ 125 Horace Ford	40.00	18.00	5.00
☐ 126 Hank Gowdy	50.00	22.00	6.25
☐ 127 Walter Holke	40.00	18.00	5.00
☐ 128 Larry Kopf	40.00	18.00	5.00
☐ 129 Rube Marquard	75.00	34.00	9.50
☐ 130 Hugh McQuillan	40.00	18.00	5.00
☐ 131 Joe Oeschger	40.00	18.00	5.00
☐ 132 George O'Neil	40.00	18.00	5.00
☐ 133 Roy Powell	40.00	18.00	5.00
☐ 134 Billy Southworth	50.00	22.00	6.25
☐ 135 John Watson	40.00	18.00	5.00
☐ 136 Leon Cadore	40.00	18.00	5.00
☐ 137 Samuel Crane	40.00	18.00	5.00
☐ 138 Hank DeBerry	40.00	18.00	5.00
☐ 139 Tom Griffith	40.00	18.00	5.00
☐ 140 Burleigh Grimes	75.00	34.00	9.50
☐ 141 Bernard Hungling	40.00	18.00	5.00
☐ 142 Jimmy Johnston	40.00	18.00	5.00
☐ 143 Al Mamaux	40.00	18.00	5.00
☐ 144 Clarence Mitchell	40.00	18.00	5.00
☐ 145 Hy Myers	40.00	18.00	5.00
☐ 146 Ivan Olson	40.00	18.00	5.00
☐ 147 Dutch Reuther	50.00	22.00	6.25
☐ 148 Ray Schmandt	40.00	18.00	5.00
☐ 149 Sherrod Smith	40.00	18.00	5.00
☐ 150 Zach Wheat	75.00	34.00	9.50
☐ 151 Victor Aldridge	40.00	18.00	5.00
☐ 152 Grover Alexander	125.00	55.00	15.50
☐ 153 Tyrus Barber	40.00	18.00	5.00
☐ 154 Marty Callaghan	40.00	18.00	5.00
☐ 155 Virgil Cheeves	40.00	18.00	5.00
☐ 156 Max Flack	40.00	18.00	5.00
☐ 157 Oscar Grimes	40.00	18.00	5.00
☐ 158 Gabby Hartnett	100.00	45.00	12.50
☐ 159 Charles Hollocher	40.00	18.00	5.00
☐ 160 Percy Jones	40.00	18.00	5.00
☐ 161 Johnny Kelleher	40.00	18.00	5.00
☐ 162 Martin Krug	40.00	18.00	5.00
☐ 163 Hack Miller	40.00	18.00	5.00
☐ 164 Bob O'Farrell	50.00	22.00	6.25
☐ 165 Arnold Statz	40.00	18.00	5.00
☐ 166 Sammy Bohne	40.00	18.00	5.00
☐ 167 George Burns	40.00	18.00	5.00
☐ 168 James Caveney	40.00	18.00	5.00
☐ 169 Jake Daubert	50.00	22.00	6.25
☐ 170 Pete Donohue	40.00	18.00	5.00
☐ 171 Pat Duncan	40.00	18.00	5.00
☐ 172 John Gillespie	40.00	18.00	5.00
☐ 173 Gene Hargrave Bubbles	40.00	18.00	5.00
☐ 174 Dolph Luque	50.00	22.00	6.25
☐ 175 Cliff Markle	40.00	18.00	5.00
☐ 176 Greasy Neale	50.00	22.00	6.25
☐ 177 Ralph Pinelli	50.00	22.00	6.25
☐ 178 Eppa Rixey	75.00	34.00	9.50
☐ 179 Ed Roush	75.00	34.00	9.50
☐ 180 Ivy Wingo	40.00	18.00	5.00
☐ 181 Dave Bancroft	75.00	34.00	9.50
☐ 182 Jesse Barnes	40.00	18.00	5.00
☐ 183 Bill Cunningham	40.00	18.00	5.00
☐ 184 Phil Douglas	40.00	18.00	5.00
☐ 185 Frankie Frisch	125.00	55.00	15.50
☐ 186 Heine Groh	50.00	22.00	6.25
☐ 187 George Kelly	75.00	34.00	9.50
☐ 188 Emil Meusel	50.00	22.00	6.25
☐ 189 Art Nehf	40.00	18.00	5.00
☐ 190 John Rawlings	40.00	18.00	5.00
☐ 191 Ralph Shinners	40.00	18.00	5.00
☐ 192 Earl Smith	40.00	18.00	5.00
☐ 193 Frank Snyder	40.00	18.00	5.00
☐ 194 Fred Toney	40.00	18.00	5.00
☐ 195 Ross (Pep) Young (sic, Youngs)	75.00	34.00	9.50
☐ 196 Walter Betts	40.00	18.00	5.00
☐ 197 Art Fletcher	40.00	18.00	5.00
☐ 198 Walter Henline	40.00	18.00	5.00
☐ 199 Wilbur Hubbell	50.00	22.00	6.25
☐ 200 Lee King	40.00	18.00	5.00
☐ 201 Roy Leslie	40.00	18.00	5.00
☐ 202 Henry Meadows	40.00	18.00	5.00
☐ 203 Frank Parkinson	40.00	18.00	5.00
☐ 204 Jack Peters	40.00	18.00	5.00
☐ 205 Joseph Rapp	40.00	18.00	5.00
☐ 206 James Ring	40.00	18.00	5.00
☐ 207 Colonel Snover	40.00	18.00	5.00
☐ 208 Curtis Walker	40.00	18.00	5.00
☐ 209 Cy Williams	50.00	22.00	6.25
☐ 210 Russel Wrightstone	40.00	18.00	5.00
☐ 211 Babe Adams	50.00	22.00	6.25
☐ 212 Clyde Barnhart	40.00	18.00	5.00
☐ 213 Carlson Bigbee	40.00	18.00	5.00
☐ 214 Max Carey	75.00	34.00	9.50
☐ 215 Wilbur Cooper	40.00	18.00	5.00
☐ 216 Charles Glazner	40.00	18.00	5.00
☐ 217 Johnny Gooch	40.00	18.00	5.00
☐ 218 Charlie Grimm	50.00	22.00	6.25
☐ 219 Earl Hamilton	40.00	18.00	5.00
☐ 220 Rabbit Maranville	75.00	34.00	9.50
☐ 221 John L. Mokan	40.00	18.00	5.00
☐ 222 John Morrison	40.00	18.00	5.00
☐ 223 Walter Schmidt	40.00	18.00	5.00
☐ 224 James Tierney	40.00	18.00	5.00
☐ 225 Pie Traynor	100.00	45.00	12.50
☐ 226 Edward Ainsmith	40.00	18.00	5.00
☐ 227 Vern Clemons	40.00	18.00	5.00
☐ 228 William Doak	40.00	18.00	5.00
☐ 229 John Fournier	40.00	18.00	5.00
☐ 230 Jesse Haines	75.00	34.00	9.50
☐ 231 Cliff Heathcoate	40.00	18.00	5.00
☐ 232 Rogers Hornsby	200.00	90.00	25.00
☐ 233 John Lavan	40.00	18.00	5.00
☐ 234 Austin McHenry	40.00	18.00	5.00
☐ 235 Will Pertice	40.00	18.00	5.00
☐ 236 Joe Schultz	40.00	18.00	5.00
☐ 237 William Sherdel	40.00	18.00	5.00
☐ 238 Jack Smith	40.00	18.00	5.00
☐ 239 Milton Stock	40.00	18.00	5.00
☐ 240 George Torporcer	40.00	18.00	5.00

1921-22 E121 Series of 120

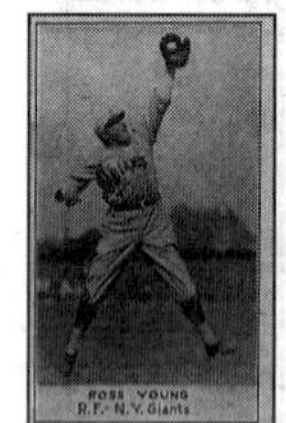

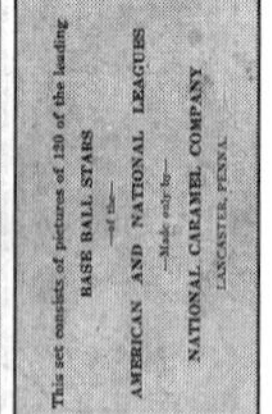

The cards in this set measure 2" by 3 1/2". Many of the photos which appear in the "Series of 80" are duplicated in the so-called "Series of 120". As noted above, the variations in titling and photos have run the known number of cards past the original statement of length and collectors should expect to encounter additions to both E121 lists in the future. The cards have been alphabetized and numbered in the checklist below. The complete set price includes all variation cards listed in the checklist below.

	EX-MT	VG-E	GOOD
COMPLETE SET (136)	10000.00	4500.00	1250.00
COMMON CARD (1-117)	30.00	13.50	3.70
☐ 1 Babe Adams	30.00	13.50	3.70
☐ 2 Grover C. Alexander	125.00	55.00	15.50
☐ 3 Jim Bagby	30.00	13.50	3.70
☐ 4 Dave Bancroft	60.00	27.00	7.50
☐ 5 Turner Barber	30.00	13.50	3.70
☐ 6A Carlson Bigbee	30.00	13.50	3.70
☐ 6B Carlson Bigbee	30.00	13.50	3.70
☐ 6C Corson L. Bigbee	30.00	13.50	3.70
☐ 6D L. Bigbee	30.00	13.50	3.70
☐ 7 Joe Bush	40.00	18.00	5.00
☐ 8 Max Carey	60.00	27.00	7.50
☐ 9 Cecil Causey	30.00	13.50	3.70
☐ 10A Ty Cobb batting	600.00	275.00	75.00
☐ 10B Ty Cobb throwing	600.00	275.00	75.00
☐ 11 Eddie Collins	75.00	34.00	9.50
☐ 12 A. Wilbur Cooper	30.00	13.50	3.70
☐ 13 Stan Coveleskie	60.00	27.00	7.50
☐ 14 Dave Danforth	30.00	13.50	3.70
☐ 15 Jake Daubert	40.00	18.00	5.00
☐ 16 George Dauss	30.00	13.50	3.70
☐ 17 Dixie Davis	30.00	13.50	3.70
☐ 18 Al DeVormer	30.00	13.50	3.70
☐ 19 William Doak	30.00	13.50	3.70
☐ 20 Phil Douglas	30.00	13.50	3.70
☐ 21 Urban Faber	60.00	27.00	7.50
☐ 22 Bib Falk	30.00	13.50	3.70
☐ 23 Chick Fewster	30.00	13.50	3.70
☐ 24 Max Flack	30.00	13.50	3.70
☐ 25 Ira Flagstead	30.00	13.50	3.70
☐ 26 Frank Frisch	100.00	45.00	12.50
☐ 27 Larry Gardner	30.00	13.50	3.70
☐ 28 Alexander Gaston	30.00	13.50	3.70
☐ 29 E.P. Gharrity	30.00	13.50	3.70
☐ 30 George Gibson	30.00	13.50	3.70
☐ 31 Whitey Glazner	30.00	13.50	3.70
☐ 32 Kid Gleason MG	30.00	13.50	3.70
☐ 33 Hank Gowdy	40.00	18.00	5.00
☐ 34 John Graney	30.00	13.50	3.70
☐ 35 Tom Griffith	30.00	13.50	3.70
☐ 36 Charlie Grimm	40.00	18.00	5.00
☐ 37 Heinie Groh	40.00	18.00	5.00
☐ 38 Jess Haines	60.00	27.00	7.50
☐ 39 Harry Harper	30.00	13.50	3.70
☐ 40A Harry Heilman	60.00	27.00	7.50
☐ 40B Harry Heilmann	60.00	27.00	7.50
☐ 41 Clarence Hodge	30.00	13.50	3.70
☐ 42A Walter Holke portrait	30.00	13.50	3.70
☐ 42B Walter Holke throwing	30.00	13.50	3.70
☐ 43 Charles Hollocher	30.00	13.50	3.70
☐ 44 Harry Hooper	60.00	27.00	7.50
☐ 45 Rogers Hornsby	125.00	55.00	15.50
☐ 46 Waite Hoyt	60.00	27.00	7.50
☐ 47 Miller Huggins MG	60.00	27.00	7.50
☐ 48 Walter Johnson	300.00	135.00	38.00
☐ 49 Joe Judge	30.00	13.50	3.70
☐ 50 George Kelly	60.00	27.00	7.50
☐ 51 Dick Kerr	40.00	18.00	5.00
☐ 52 P.J. Kilduff	30.00	13.50	3.70
☐ 53A Bill Killifer bat on shoulder	30.00	13.50	3.70
☐ 53B Bill Killifer throwing	30.00	13.50	3.70
☐ 54 John Lavan	30.00	13.50	3.70
☐ 55 Walter Mails	40.00	18.00	5.00
☐ 56 Rabbit Maranville	60.00	27.00	7.50
☐ 57 Elwood Martin	30.00	13.50	3.70
☐ 58 Carl Mays	40.00	18.00	5.00
☐ 59 John J. McGraw MG	100.00	45.00	12.50
☐ 60 Jack McInnis	40.00	18.00	5.00
☐ 61 M.J. McNally	30.00	13.50	3.70
☐ 62 Emil Meusel	40.00	18.00	5.00
☐ 63 Bob Meusel	40.00	18.00	5.00
☐ 64 Clyde Milan	30.00	13.50	3.70
☐ 65 Elmer Miller	30.00	13.50	3.70
☐ 66 Otto Miller	30.00	13.50	3.70
☐ 67 Johnny Mostil	30.00	13.50	3.70
☐ 68 Eddie Mulligan	30.00	13.50	3.70
☐ 69A Hy Myers	30.00	13.50	3.70
☐ 69B Hy Myers	30.00	13.50	3.70
☐ 70 Greasy Neale	40.00	18.00	5.00
☐ 71 Art Nehf	30.00	13.50	3.70
☐ 72 Leslie Nunamaker	30.00	13.50	3.70
☐ 73 Joe Oeschger	30.00	13.50	3.70
☐ 74 Charley O'Leary CO	30.00	13.50	3.70
☐ 75 Steve O'Neill	40.00	18.00	5.00
☐ 76 Del Pratt	30.00	13.50	3.70
☐ 77 John Rawlings	30.00	13.50	3.70
☐ 78 Sam Rice	60.00	27.00	7.50
☐ 79A Eppa J. Rixey	60.00	27.00	7.50
☐ 79B Eppa Rixey Jr.	60.00	27.00	7.50
☐ 80 Wilbert Robinson MG	60.00	27.00	7.50
☐ 81 Tom Rogers	30.00	13.50	3.70
☐ 82A Ed Rommel	40.00	18.00	5.00
☐ 82B Ed Rounnel	40.00	18.00	5.00
☐ 83 Ed Roush	60.00	27.00	7.50
☐ 84 Muddy Ruel	30.00	13.50	3.70
☐ 85 Walter Ruether	40.00	18.00	5.00
☐ 86A Babe Ruth three pictures	750.00	350.00	95.00
☐ 86B Babe Ruth three pictures	1000.00	450.00	125.00
☐ 86C Babe Ruth holding bird	750.00	350.00	95.00
☐ 86D Babe Ruth holding bird	1000.00	450.00	125.00
☐ 86E Babe Ruth holding ball in right hand	750.00	350.00	95.00

☐ 87 Bill Ryan	30.00	13.50	3.70
☐ 88A Ray Schalk catching	60.00	27.00	7.50
☐ 88B Ray Schalk bunting	60.00	27.00	7.50
☐ 89 Wally Schang	30.00	13.50	3.70
☐ 90 Ferd Schupp	30.00	13.50	3.70
☐ 91 Everett Scott	40.00	18.00	5.00
☐ 92 Joe Sewell	60.00	27.00	7.50
☐ 93 Bob Shawkey	40.00	18.00	5.00
☐ 94 Pat Shea	30.00	13.50	3.70
☐ 95 Earl Sheely	30.00	13.50	3.70
☐ 96 Urban Shocker	40.00	18.00	5.00
☐ 97A George Sisler batting	100.00	45.00	12.50
☐ 97B George Sisler throwing	100.00	45.00	12.50
☐ 98 Earl Smith	30.00	13.50	3.70
☐ 99 Elmer Smith	30.00	13.50	3.70
☐ 100 Frank Snyder	30.00	13.50	3.70
☐ 101 Bill Southworth	40.00	18.00	5.00
☐ 102A Tris Speaker large projection	125.00	55.00	15.50
☐ 102B Tris Speaker small projection	125.00	55.00	15.50
☐ 103A Milton Stock	30.00	13.50	3.70
☐ 103B Milton Stock	30.00	13.50	3.70
☐ 104 Amos Strunk	30.00	13.50	3.70
☐ 105 Zeb Terry	30.00	13.50	3.70
☐ 106 Fred Toney	30.00	13.50	3.70
☐ 107 George Toporcer	30.00	13.50	3.70
☐ 108 Bob Veach	30.00	13.50	3.70
☐ 109 Oscar Vitt	40.00	18.00	5.00
☐ 110 Curtis Walker	30.00	13.50	3.70
☐ 111 Bill Wambsganss	40.00	18.00	5.00
☐ 112 Aaron Ward	30.00	13.50	3.70
☐ 113 Zach Wheat	60.00	27.00	7.50
☐ 114A George Whitted Brooklyn	30.00	13.50	3.70
☐ 114B George Whitted Pittsburgh	30.00	13.50	3.70
☐ 115 Fred Williams	40.00	18.00	5.00
☐ 116 Ivy B. Wingo	30.00	13.50	3.70
☐ 117 Ross Young sic, Youngs	60.00	27.00	7.50

1921-22 E121 Series of 80

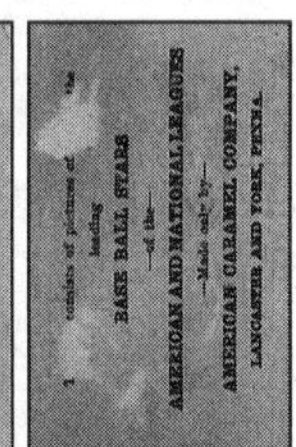

The cards in this set measure 2" by 3 1/2". The E121 sets contain many errors, misspellings and minor variations in titles and photos, which accounts for the difficulty in collecting the entire set. Many photos were taken from E135 and a fine screen is apparent on the cards. The American Caramel Co. marketed this black and white issue about 1922. Many localized advertising reverses have been found, and these cards more properly belong to the W classification than to E121. The cards have been alphabetized and numbered in the checklist below. The complete set price includes all variation cards listed in the checklist below.

	EX-MT	VG-E	GOOD
COMPLETE SET (132)	10000.00	4500.00	1250.00
COMMON CARD (1-109)	30.00	13.50	3.70
☐ 1A Grover C. Alexander	125.00	55.00	15.50
☐ 1B Grover Alexander	100.00	45.00	12.50
☐ 2 Jim Bagby	30.00	13.50	3.70
☐ 3A J. Franklin Baker	75.00	34.00	9.50
☐ 3B Frank Baker	75.00	34.00	9.50
☐ 4A Dave Bancroft batting	60.00	27.00	7.50
☐ 4B Dave Bancroft fielding	60.00	27.00	7.50
☐ 5 Ping Bodie	30.00	13.50	3.70
☐ 6 George Burns	30.00	13.50	3.70
☐ 7 Geo. J. Burns	30.00	13.50	3.70
☐ 8 Owen Bush	30.00	13.50	3.70
☐ 9A Max Carey batting	60.00	27.00	7.50
☐ 9B Max Carey hands on hips	60.00	27.00	7.50
☐ 10 Cecil Causey	30.00	13.50	3.70
☐ 11A Ty Cobb Mgr.	600.00	275.00	75.00
☐ 11B Ty Cobb Manager	600.00	275.00	75.00
☐ 12 Eddie Collins	75.00	34.00	9.50
☐ 13 Rip Collins	40.00	18.00	5.00
☐ 14 Jake Daubert	40.00	18.00	5.00
☐ 15 George Dauss	30.00	13.50	3.70
☐ 16A Charles Deal dark uniform	30.00	13.50	3.70
☐ 16B Charles Deal light uniform	30.00	13.50	3.70
☐ 17 William Doak	30.00	13.50	3.70
☐ 18 Bill Donovan	30.00	13.50	3.70
☐ 19 Phil Douglas	30.00	13.50	3.70
☐ 20A Johnny Evers Manager	60.00	27.00	7.50
☐ 20B Johnny Evers Mgr.	60.00	27.00	7.50
☐ 21A Urban Faber dark uniform	60.00	27.00	7.50
☐ 21B Urban Faber white uniform	60.00	27.00	7.50
☐ 22 Wm. Fewster	30.00	13.50	3.70
☐ 23 Eddie Foster	30.00	13.50	3.70
☐ 24 Frankie Frisch	100.00	45.00	12.50
☐ 25 Larry Gardner	30.00	13.50	3.70
☐ 26 Alexander Gaston	30.00	13.50	3.70
☐ 27 Kid Gleason MG	30.00	13.50	3.70
☐ 28 Mike Gonzalez	30.00	13.50	3.70
☐ 29 Hank Gowdy	40.00	18.00	5.00
☐ 30 John Graney	30.00	13.50	3.70
☐ 31 Tom Griffith	30.00	13.50	3.70
☐ 32 Heinie Groh	40.00	18.00	5.00
☐ 33 Harry Harper	30.00	13.50	3.70
☐ 34 Harry Heilmann	60.00	27.00	7.50
☐ 35A Walter Holke portrait	30.00	13.50	3.70
☐ 35B Walter Holke throwing	30.00	13.50	3.70
☐ 36 Charles Hollacher	30.00	13.50	3.70
☐ 37 Harry Hooper	60.00	27.00	7.50
☐ 38 Rogers Hornsby	125.00	55.00	15.50
☐ 39 Waite Hoyt	60.00	27.00	7.50
☐ 40 Miller Huggins MG	60.00	27.00	7.50
☐ 41 Baby Doll Jacobson	30.00	13.50	3.70
☐ 42 Hugh Jennings MG	60.00	27.00	7.50
☐ 43A Walter Johnson throwing	300.00	135.00	38.00
☐ 43B Walter Johnson arms at chest	300.00	135.00	38.00
☐ 44 James Johnston	30.00	13.50	3.70
☐ 45 Joe Judge	30.00	13.50	3.70
☐ 46 George Kelly	60.00	27.00	7.50
☐ 47 Dick Kerr	40.00	18.00	5.00
☐ 48 Pete Kilduff	30.00	13.50	3.70
☐ 49A Bill Killefer	30.00	13.50	3.70
☐ 49B Bill Killifer	30.00	13.50	3.70
☐ 50 John Lavan	30.00	13.50	3.70
☐ 51 Nemo Leibold	30.00	13.50	3.70
☐ 52 Duffy Lewis	30.00	13.50	3.70
☐ 53 Al Mamaux	30.00	13.50	3.70
☐ 54 Rabbit Maranville	60.00	27.00	7.50
☐ 55A Carl May (sic, Mays)	40.00	18.00	5.00
☐ 55B Carl Mays	40.00	18.00	5.00
☐ 56 John McGraw MG	100.00	45.00	12.50
☐ 57 Snuffy McInnis	40.00	18.00	5.00
☐ 58 M.J. McNally	30.00	13.50	3.70
☐ 59 Emil Muesel	40.00	18.00	5.00
☐ 60 Bob Meusel	40.00	18.00	5.00
☐ 61 Clyde Milan	30.00	13.50	3.70
☐ 62 Elmer Miller	30.00	13.50	3.70
☐ 63 Otto Miller	30.00	13.50	3.70
☐ 64 Guy Morton	30.00	13.50	3.70
☐ 65 Eddie Murphy	30.00	13.50	3.70
☐ 66 Hy Myers	30.00	13.50	3.70
☐ 67 Art Nehf	30.00	13.50	3.70
☐ 68 Steve O'Neill	30.00	13.50	3.70
☐ 69A Roger Peckinbaugh sic	40.00	18.00	5.00
☐ 69B Roger Peckinpaugh	40.00	18.00	5.00
☐ 70 Jeff Pfeffer Brooklyn	30.00	13.50	3.70
☐ 71 Jeff Pfeffer St. Louis NL	30.00	13.50	3.70
☐ 72 Wally Pipp	60.00	27.00	7.50
☐ 73 Jack Quinn	30.00	13.50	3.70
☐ 74 John Rawlings	30.00	13.50	3.70
☐ 75 Sam Rice	60.00	27.00	7.50
☐ 76 Eppa Rixey	60.00	27.00	7.50
☐ 77 Robert Roth	30.00	13.50	3.70
☐ 78 Ed Rousch	60.00	27.00	7.50
☐ 79A Babe Ruth	750.00	350.00	95.00
☐ 79B Babe Ruth	1000.00	450.00	125.00
☐ 79C George Ruth	750.00	350.00	95.00
☐ 80 Bill Ryan	30.00	13.50	3.70
☐ 81A Slim Sallee ball in hand	30.00	13.50	3.70
☐ 81B Slim Sallee no ball	30.00	13.50	3.70
☐ 82 Ray Schalk	60.00	27.00	7.50
☐ 83 Walter Schang	30.00	13.50	3.70
☐ 84A Ferd Schupp	30.00	13.50	3.70
☐ 84B Fred Schupp	30.00	13.50	3.70
☐ 85 Everett Scott	30.00	13.50	3.70
☐ 86 Hank Severeid	30.00	13.50	3.70
☐ 87 Bob Shawkey	40.00	18.00	5.00
☐ 88A Pat Shea	30.00	13.50	3.70
☐ 88B Pat Shea	30.00	13.50	3.70
☐ 89A George Sisler batting	100.00	45.00	12.50
☐ 89B George Sisler throwing	100.00	45.00	12.50
☐ 90 Earl Smith	30.00	13.50	3.70
☐ 91 Frank Snyder	30.00	13.50	3.70
☐ 92A Tris Speaker Manager	125.00	55.00	15.50
☐ 92B Tris Speaker Mgr.	125.00	55.00	15.50
☐ 93 Milton Stock	30.00	13.50	3.70
☐ 94 Amos Strunk	30.00	13.50	3.70
☐ 95 Zeb Terry	30.00	13.50	3.70
☐ 96 Chester Thomas	30.00	13.50	3.70
☐ 97A Fred Toney foot up	30.00	13.50	3.70
☐ 97B Fred Toney both feet down	30.00	13.50	3.70
☐ 98 George Tyler	30.00	13.50	3.70
☐ 99A Jim Vaughn plain uniform	30.00	13.50	3.70
☐ 99B Jim Vaughn striped uniform	30.00	13.50	3.70
☐ 100A Bob Veach arm raised	30.00	13.50	3.70
☐ 100B Bob Veach folded arms	30.00	13.50	3.70
☐ 101 Oscar Vitt	40.00	18.00	5.00
☐ 102 Bill Wambsganss	30.00	13.50	3.70
☐ 103 Aaron Ward	30.00	13.50	3.70
☐ 104 Zach Wheat	60.00	27.00	7.50
☐ 105 George Whitted	30.00	13.50	3.70
☐ 106 Fred Williams	40.00	18.00	5.00
☐ 107 Ivy Wingo	30.00	13.50	3.70
☐ 108 Joe Wood	40.00	18.00	5.00
☐ 109 Pep Young	30.00	13.50	3.70

1910 E-Unc. Orange Bordered Strip Cards

This unusual card set features black-and-white pictures surrounded by a thin orange border and measures approximately 1 5/8" by 2 5/8". These orange bordered cards apparently were part of a box of candy. Only 24 cards are checklisted below, but the box indicates that there are 144 in the whole set. Any known additions to the checklist would be welcomed.

	EX-MT	VG-E	GOOD
COMPLETE SET	3500.00	1600.00	450.00
COMMON CARD	50.00	22.00	6.25
☐ 1 Pittsburgh Pirates TP	50.00	22.00	6.25
☐ 2 Detroit Tigers TP	50.00	22.00	6.25
☐ 3 Bill Bergen	50.00	22.00	6.25
☐ 4 Bill Carrigan	50.00	22.00	6.25
☐ 5 Hal Chase	150.00	70.00	19.00
☐ 6 Fred Clarke UER (misspelled Clark)	100.00	45.00	12.50
☐ 7 Ty Cobb	1250.00	550.00	160.00
☐ 8 Sam Crawford	150.00	70.00	19.00
☐ 9 Lou Criger	50.00	22.00	6.25
☐ 10 Mickey Doolan	50.00	22.00	6.25
☐ 11 George Gibson	50.00	22.00	6.25
☐ 12 Frank LaPorte	50.00	22.00	6.25
☐ 13 Nap Lajoie	300.00	135.00	38.00
☐ 14 Harry Lord	50.00	22.00	6.25
☐ 15 Christy Mathewson	250.00	110.00	31.00
☐ 16 John McGraw MG	200.00	90.00	25.00
☐ 17 Dots Miller	50.00	22.00	6.25
☐ 18 George Mullin	50.00	22.00	6.25
☐ 19 Eddie Plank	150.00	70.00	19.00
☐ 20 Tris Speaker	250.00	110.00	31.00
☐ 21 Jake Stahl	50.00	22.00	6.25
☐ 22 Heinie Wagner	50.00	22.00	6.25
☐ 23 Honus Wagner	400.00	180.00	50.00
☐ 24 Jack Warhop	50.00	22.00	6.25

1995 Eagle Ballpark Legends

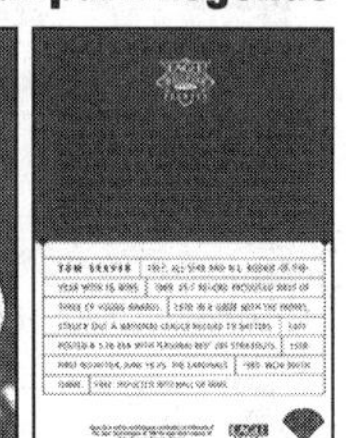

Upper Deck produced this 9-card standard-size set as part of a promotion for Eagle Ballpark Style Peanuts. The set could be obtained by sending in a cash register receipt as evidence for the purchase of 2 cans Eagle Ballpark Style Peanuts (11 oz. or larger) and $1.00 to cover shipping and handling. The fronts freature full-bleed sepia-toned player photos. The sponsor logo appears in the upper left corner, the Upper Deck logo in the lower left, and the player's name across the bottom. The backs present player profile and career highlights. Some card sets contained randomly inserted autographed Harmon Killebrew cards. These autographed cards are valued at between 20 and 30 dollars.

	MINT	NRMT	EXC
COMPLETE SET (9)	10.00	4.50	1.25
COMMON CARD (1-9)	.75	.35	.09
☐ 1 Nolan Ryan	5.00	2.20	.60
☐ 2 Reggie Jackson	2.50	1.10	.30
☐ 3 Tom Seaver	2.00	.90	.25
☐ 4 Harmon Killebrew	.75	.35	.09
☐ 5 Ted Williams	4.00	1.80	.50
☐ 6 Whitey Ford	2.00	.90	.25
☐ 7 Al Kaline	1.50	.70	.19
☐ 8 Willie Stargell	.75	.35	.09
☐ 9 Bob Gibson	.75	.35	.09

1889 Edgerton R. Williams Game

The cards measure 2 7/16" by 3 1/2" and have green tinted backs. Each card features two players on the front -- therefore 38 players in total are featured in the set. Only the cards with Baseball players are included in this checklist.

	EX-MT	VG-E	GOOD
COMPLETE SET (19)	4500.00	2000.00	550.00
COMMON CARD (1-19)	200.00	90.00	25.00
☐ 1 Cap Anson Buck Ewing	500.00	220.00	60.00
☐ 2 Dan Brouthers Arlie Latham	300.00	135.00	38.00
☐ 3 Charlie Buffington Bob Carruthers	200.00	90.00	25.00
☐ 4 Fred Carroll Hick Carpenter	200.00	90.00	25.00
☐ 5 Roger Connor Charles Comiskey	400.00	180.00	50.00
☐ 6 Pop Corkhill Jim Fogarty	200.00	90.00	25.00
☐ 7 John Clarkson Tim Keefe	400.00	180.00	50.00
☐ 8 Jerry Denny Mike Tiernan	200.00	90.00	25.00
☐ 9 Dave Foutz King Kelly	300.00	135.00	38.00
☐ 10 Pud Galvin Dave Orr	300.00	135.00	38.00
☐ 11 Jack Glasscock Tommy Tucker	250.00	110.00	31.00
☐ 12 Mike Griffin Ed McKean	200.00	90.00	25.00
☐ 13 Dummy Hoy John Reilly	250.00	110.00	31.00
☐ 14 Arthur Irwin Fred Williamson	200.00	90.00	25.00
☐ 15 Silver King John Tener	200.00	90.00	25.00
☐ 16 Al Myers Cub Stricker	200.00	90.00	25.00
☐ 17 Fred Pfeffer Jimmy Wolf	200.00	90.00	25.00
☐ 18 Toad Ramsey Gus Weyhing	200.00	90.00	25.00
☐ 19 Mickey Ward Curt Welch	200.00	90.00	25.00

1994 El Sid Pogs

Titled "Limited Edition El Sid." Blank-backed white milk cap-types. Foil on fronts; measure about 1 5/8" in diameter. No other ID markings.

	MINT	EXC	G-VG
COMPLETE SET (5)	1.00	.45	.12
COMMON CARD (1-5)	.25	.11	.03
☐ 1 Sid Fernandez 1st Major League Strikeout	.25	.11	.03
☐ 2 Sid Fernandez 200 Strikeouts Single Season	.25	.11	.03
☐ 3 Sid Fernandez 1st World Series Strikeout	.25	.11	.03
☐ 4 Sid Fernandez 1st Major League Home Run	.25	.11	.03
☐ 5 Sid Fernandez 1993	.25	.11	.03

1990 Elite Senior League

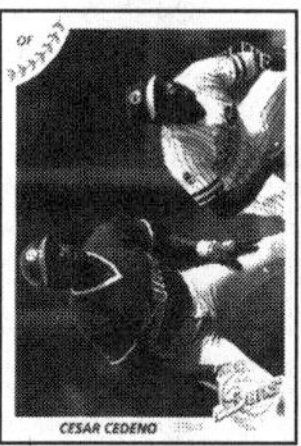

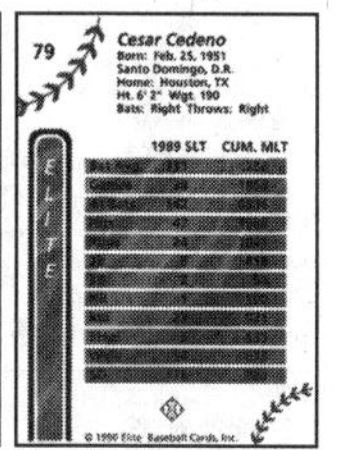

The 1990 Elite Senior Pro League Set was a 126-card standard-size set issued after the conclusion of the first Senior League season. The card stock was essentially the same type of card stock used by Upper Deck. The set featured full-color fronts and had complete Senior League stats on the back. It has been reported that there were 5,000 cases of these cards produced. Prior to the debut of the set, Elite also passed out (to prospective dealers) two promo cards for the set, Earl Weaver (numbered 120 rather than 91) and Mike Easler (numbered 1 rather than 19).

	MINT	NRMT	EXC
COMPLETE SET (126)	5.00	2.20	.60
COMMON CARD (1-126)	.05	.02	.01
☐ 1 Curt Flood COMM	.25	.11	.03
☐ 2 Bob Tolan	.05	.02	.01
☐ 3 Dick Bosman	.05	.02	.01
☐ 4 Ivan DeJesus	.05	.02	.01
☐ 5 Dock Ellis	.10	.05	.01

Card	MINT	NRMT	EXC
□ 6 Roy Howell	.05	.02	.01
□ 7 Lamar Johnson	.05	.02	.01
□ 8 Steve Kemp	.05	.02	.01
□ 9 Ken Landreaux	.05	.02	.01
□ 10 Randy Lerch	.05	.02	.01
□ 11 Jon Matlack	.05	.02	.01
□ 12 Gary Rajsich	.05	.02	.01
□ 13 Lenny Randle	.05	.02	.01
□ 14 Elias Sosa	.05	.02	.01
□ 15 Ozzie Virgil	.05	.02	.01
□ 16 Milt Wilcox	.05	.02	.01
□ 17 Steve Henderson 3X	.05	.02	.01
□ 18 Ray Burris	.05	.02	.01
□ 19 Mike Easler	.05	.02	.01
□ 20 Juan Eichelberger	.05	.02	.01
□ 21 Rollie Fingers	.50	.23	.06
□ 22 Toby Harrah	.05	.02	.01
□ 23 Randy Johnson	.05	.02	.01
□ 24 Dave Kingman	.25	.11	.03
□ 25 Lee Lacy	.05	.02	.01
□ 26 Tito Landrum	.05	.02	.01
□ 27 Paul Mirabella	.05	.02	.01
□ 28 Mickey Rivers	.10	.05	.01
□ 29 Rodney Scott	.05	.02	.01
□ 30 Tim Stoddard	.05	.02	.01
□ 31 Ron Washington	.05	.02	.01
□ 32 Jerry White	.05	.02	.01
□ 33 Dick Williams MG	.10	.05	.01
□ 34 Clete Boyer MG	.05	.02	.01
□ 35 Steve Dillard	.05	.02	.01
□ 36 Garth Iorg	.05	.02	.01
□ 37 Bruce Kison	.05	.02	.01
□ 38 Wayne Krenchicki	.05	.02	.01
□ 39 Ron LeFlore	.10	.05	.01
□ 40 Tippy Martinez	.05	.02	.01
□ 41 Omar Moreno	.05	.02	.01
□ 42 Jim Morrison	.05	.02	.01
□ 43 Graig Nettles	.15	.07	.02
□ 44 Jim Nettles	.05	.02	.01
□ 45 Wayne Nordhagen	.05	.02	.01
□ 46 Al Oliver	.15	.07	.02
□ 47 Jerry Royster	.05	.02	.01
□ 48 Sammy Stewart	.05	.02	.01
□ 49 Randy Bass	.05	.02	.01
□ 50 Vida Blue	.15	.07	.02
□ 51 Bruce Bochy	.05	.02	.01
□ 52 Doug Corbett	.05	.02	.01
□ 53 Jose Cruz	.10	.05	.01
□ 54 Jamie Easterly	.05	.02	.01
□ 55 Pete Falcone	.05	.02	.01
□ 56 Bob Galasso	.05	.02	.01
□ 57 Johnny Grubb	.05	.02	.01
□ 58 Bake McBride	.05	.02	.01
□ 59 Dyar Miller	.05	.02	.01
□ 60 Tom Paciorek	.05	.02	.01
□ 61 Ken Reitz	.05	.02	.01
□ 62 U.L. Washington	.05	.02	.01
□ 63 Alan Ashby	.05	.02	.01
□ 64 Pat Dobson	.05	.02	.01
□ 65 Doug Bird	.05	.02	.01
□ 66 Marty Castillo	.05	.02	.01
□ 67 Dan Driessen	.05	.02	.01
□ 68 Wayne Garland	.05	.02	.01
□ 69 Tim Ireland	.05	.02	.01
□ 70 Ron Jackson	.05	.02	.01
□ 71 Bobby Jones	.05	.02	.01
□ 72 Dennis Leonard	.05	.02	.01
□ 73 Rick Manning	.05	.02	.01
□ 74 Amos Otis	.10	.05	.01
□ 75 Pat Putnam	.05	.02	.01
□ 76 Eric Rasmussen	.05	.02	.01
□ 77 Paul Blair	.05	.02	.01
□ 78 Bert Campaneris	.10	.05	.01
□ 79 Cesar Cedeno	.10	.05	.01
□ 80 Ed Figueroa	.05	.02	.01
□ 81 Ross Grimsley	.05	.02	.01
□ 82 George Hendrick	.05	.02	.01
□ 83 Cliff Johnson	.05	.02	.01
□ 84 Mike Kekich	.05	.02	.01
□ 85 Rafael Landestoy	.05	.02	.01
□ 86 Larry Milbourne	.05	.02	.01
□ 87 Bobby Molinaro	.05	.02	.01
□ 88 Sid Monge	.05	.02	.01
□ 89 Rennie Stennett	.05	.02	.01
□ 90 Derrell Thomas	.05	.02	.01
□ 91 Earl Weaver MG	.50	.23	.06
□ 92 Gary Allenson	.05	.02	.01
□ 93 Pedro Borbon	.05	.02	.01
□ 94 Al Bumbry	.05	.02	.01
□ 95 Bill Campbell	.05	.02	.01
□ 96 Bernie Carbo	.05	.02	.01
□ 97 Fergie Jenkins	.50	.23	.06
□ 98 Pete LaCock	.05	.02	.01
□ 99 Bill Lee	.10	.05	.01
□ 100 Tommy McMillan	.05	.02	.01
□ 101 Joe Pittman	.05	.02	.01
□ 102 Gene Richards	.05	.02	.01
□ 103 Leon Roberts	.05	.02	.01
□ 104 Tony Scott	.05	.02	.01
□ 105 Doug Simunic	.05	.02	.01
□ 106 Rick Wise	.05	.02	.01
□ 107 Willie Aikens	.05	.02	.01
□ 108 Juan Beniquez	.05	.02	.01
□ 109 Bobby Bonds	.15	.07	.02
□ 110 Sergio Ferrer	.05	.02	.01
□ 111 Chuck Ficks	.05	.02	.01
□ 112 George Foster	.15	.07	.02
□ 113 Dave Hilton	.05	.02	.01
□ 114 Al Holland	.05	.02	.01
□ 115 Clint Hurdle	.05	.02	.01
□ 116 Bill Madlock	.15	.07	.02
□ 117 Steve Ontiveros	.05	.02	.01
□ 118 Roy Thomas	.05	.02	.01
□ 119 Luis Tiant	.15	.07	.02
□ 120 Walt Williams	.05	.02	.01
□ 121 Vida Blue	.15	.07	.02
□ 122 Bobby Bonds	.25	.11	.03
□ 123 Rollie Fingers	.50	.23	.06
□ 124 George Foster	.15	.07	.02
□ 125 Fergie Jenkins	.50	.23	.06
□ 126 Dave Kingman	.25	.11	.03

1995 Embossed

This 140-card standard-size set was issued by Topps. The cards were issued in six-card packs with five regular cards and one parallel Golden Idols card in each pack. The suggested retail price of the packs was $3 with 24 packs per box. Each case contained four boxes. Cards 97-120 are a subset dedicated to active players who have won major awards. The cards are embossed on both sides. The fronts have an embossed player photo surrounded by a gray border. In addition, the TMB (Topps Embossed) logo is in an upper corner and the playeris name at the bottom. The horizontal backs have an embossed player photo on the left, while vital statistics, seasonal and career statistics and some interesting facts about the player are on the right.

	MINT	NRMT	EXC
COMPLETE SET (140)	30.00	13.50	3.70
COMMON CARD (1-140)	.10	.05	.01
□ 1 Kenny Lofton	.75	.35	.09
□ 2 Gary Sheffield	.50	.23	.06
□ 3 Hal Morris	.25	.11	.03
□ 4 Cliff Floyd	.10	.05	.01
□ 5 Pat Hentgen	.40	.18	.05
□ 6 Tony Gwynn	1.25	.55	.16
□ 7 Jose Valentin	.10	.05	.01
□ 8 Jason Bere	.10	.05	.01
□ 9 Jeff Kent	.40	.18	.05
□ 10 John Valentin	.40	.18	.05
□ 11 Brian Anderson	.10	.05	.01
□ 12 Deion Sanders	.50	.23	.06
□ 13 Ryan Thompson	.10	.05	.01
□ 14 Ruben Sierra	.10	.05	.01
□ 15 Jay Bell	.10	.05	.01
□ 16 Chuck Carr	.10	.05	.01
□ 17 Brent Gates	.10	.05	.01
□ 18 Bret Boone	.25	.11	.03
□ 19 Paul Molitor	.60	.25	.07
□ 20 Chili Davis	.25	.11	.03
□ 21 Ryan Klesko	1.00	.45	.12
□ 22 Will Clark	.50	.23	.06
□ 23 Greg Vaughn	.10	.05	.01
□ 24 Moises Alou	.25	.11	.03
□ 25 Ray Lankford	.25	.11	.03
□ 26 Jose Rijo	.10	.05	.01
□ 27 Bobby Jones	.10	.05	.01
□ 28 Rick Wilkins	.10	.05	.01
□ 29 Cal Eldred	.10	.05	.01
□ 30 Juan Gonzalez	1.50	.70	.19
□ 31 Royce Clayton	.25	.11	.03
□ 32 Bryan Harvey	.10	.05	.01
□ 33 Dave Nilsson	.10	.05	.01
□ 34 Chris Hoiles	.25	.11	.03
□ 35 David Nied	.10	.05	.01
□ 36 Javier Lopez	.40	.18	.05
□ 37 Tim Wallach	.10	.05	.01
□ 38 Bobby Bonilla	.25	.11	.03
□ 39 Danny Tartabull	.25	.11	.03
□ 40 Andy Benes	.40	.18	.05
□ 41 Dean Palmer	.40	.18	.05
□ 42 Chris Gomez	.10	.05	.01
□ 43 Kevin Appier	.25	.11	.03
□ 44 Brady Anderson	.50	.23	.06
□ 45 Alex Fernandez	.40	.18	.05
□ 46 Roberto Kelly	.10	.05	.01
□ 47 Dave Hollins	.10	.05	.01
□ 48 Chuck Finley	.10	.05	.01
□ 49 Wade Boggs	.50	.23	.06
□ 50 Travis Fryman	.25	.11	.03
□ 51 Ken Griffey Jr.	3.00	1.35	.35
□ 52 John Olerud	.25	.11	.03
□ 53 Delino DeShields	.25	.11	.03
□ 54 Ivan Rodriguez	.75	.35	.09
□ 55 Tommy Greene	.10	.05	.01
□ 56 Tom Pagnozzi	.10	.05	.01
□ 57 Bip Roberts	.10	.05	.01
□ 58 Luis Gonzalez	.25	.11	.03
□ 59 Rey Sanchez	.10	.05	.01
□ 60 Ken Ryan	.10	.05	.01
□ 61 Darren Daulton	.25	.11	.03
□ 62 Rick Aguilera	.25	.11	.03
□ 63 Wally Joyner	.10	.05	.01
□ 64 Mike Greenwell	.10	.05	.01
□ 65 Jay Buhner	.40	.18	.05
□ 66 Craig Biggio	.40	.18	.05
□ 67 Charles Nagy	.40	.18	.05
□ 68 Devon White	.10	.05	.01
□ 69 Randy Johnson	.50	.23	.06
□ 70 Shawon Dunston	.10	.05	.01
□ 71 Kirby Puckett	1.50	.70	.19
□ 72 Paul O'Neill	.25	.11	.03
□ 73 Tino Martinez	.40	.18	.05
□ 74 Carlos Garcia	.10	.05	.01
□ 75 Ozzie Smith	.75	.35	.09
□ 76 Cecil Fielder	.40	.18	.05
□ 77 Mike Stanley	.25	.11	.03
□ 78 Lance Johnson	.25	.11	.03
□ 79 Tony Phillips	.25	.11	.03
□ 80 Bobby Munoz	.10	.05	.01
□ 81 Kevin Tapani	.10	.05	.01
□ 82 William VanLandingham	.10	.05	.01
□ 83 Dante Bichette	.40	.18	.05
□ 84 Tom Candiotti	.10	.05	.01
□ 85 Wil Cordero	.25	.11	.03
□ 86 Jeff Conine	.25	.11	.03
□ 87 Joey Hamilton	.40	.18	.05
□ 88 Mark Whiten	.10	.05	.01
□ 89 Jeff Montgomery	.25	.11	.03
□ 90 Andres Galarraga	.40	.18	.05
□ 91 Roberto Alomar	.50	.23	.06
□ 92 Orlando Merced	.10	.05	.01
□ 93 Mike Mussina	.50	.23	.06
□ 94 Pedro Martinez	.25	.11	.03
□ 95 Carlos Baerga	.25	.11	.03
□ 96 Steve Trachsel	.10	.05	.01
□ 97 Lou Whitaker	.25	.11	.03
□ 98 David Cone	.25	.11	.03
□ 99 Chuck Knoblauch	.50	.23	.06
□ 100 Frank Thomas	3.00	1.35	.35
□ 101 David Justice	.40	.18	.05
□ 102 Raul Mondesi	.60	.25	.07
□ 103 Rickey Henderson	.50	.23	.06
□ 104 Doug Drabek	.10	.05	.01
□ 105 Sandy Alomar	.25	.11	.03
□ 106 Roger Clemens	.75	.35	.09
□ 107 Mark McGwire	1.00	.45	.12
□ 108 Tim Salmon	.50	.23	.06
□ 109 Greg Maddux	1.75	.80	.22
□ 110 Mike Piazza	2.00	.90	.25
□ 111 Tom Glavine	.40	.18	.05
□ 112 Walt Weiss	.10	.05	.01
□ 113 Cal Ripken	2.50	1.10	.30
□ 114 Eddie Murray	.75	.35	.09
□ 115 Don Mattingly	1.50	.70	.19
□ 116 Ozzie Guillen	.10	.05	.01
□ 117 Bob Hamelin	.10	.05	.01
□ 118 Jeff Bagwell	1.25	.55	.16
□ 119 Eric Karros	.25	.11	.03
□ 120 Barry Bonds	.75	.35	.09
□ 121 Mickey Tettleton	.25	.11	.03
□ 122 Mark Langston	.10	.05	.01
□ 123 Robin Ventura	.25	.11	.03
□ 124 Bret Saberhagen	.10	.05	.01
□ 125 Albert Belle	1.50	.70	.19
□ 126 Rafael Palmeiro	.40	.18	.05
□ 127 Fred McGriff	.40	.18	.05
□ 128 Jimmy Key	.25	.11	.03
□ 129 Barry Larkin	.25	.11	.03
□ 130 Tim Raines	.40	.18	.05
□ 131 Len Dykstra	.25	.11	.03
□ 132 Todd Zeile	.10	.05	.01
□ 133 Joe Carter	.40	.18	.05
□ 134 Matt Williams	.40	.18	.05
□ 135 Terry Steinbach	.25	.11	.03
□ 136 Manny Ramirez	.75	.35	.09
□ 137 John Wetteland	.25	.11	.03
□ 138 Rod Beck	.25	.11	.03
□ 139 Mo Vaughn	.75	.35	.09
□ 140 Darren Lewis	.10	.05	.01

1995 Embossed Golden Idols

This 140-card parallel set was inserted one per Embossed pack. The only difference between these and the regular cards is the gold foil surrounding the front borders.

	MINT	NRMT	EXC
COMPLETE SET (140)	100.00	45.00	12.50
COMMON CARD (1-140)	.50	.23	.06

*STARS: 2.5X to 4X BASIC CARDS ...

1995 Emotion

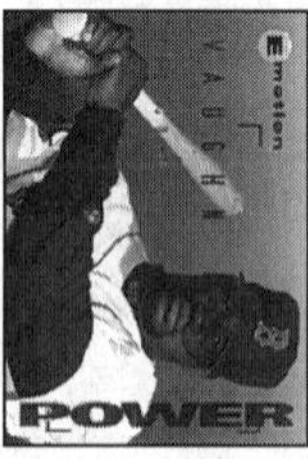

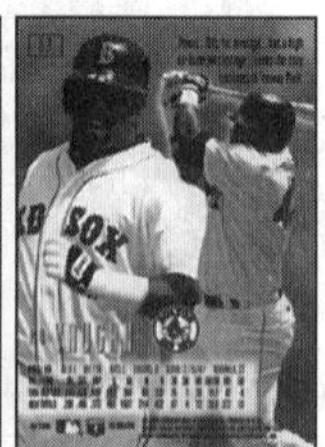

This 200-card standard-size set was produced by Fleer/SkyBox. The first-year brand has double-thick card stock with borderless fronts. Card fronts and backs are either horizontal or vertical. On the front of each player card is a theme such as Class (Cal Ripken) and Confident (Barry Bonds). The backs have two player photos, '94 stats and career numbers. The checklist is arranged alphabetically by team with AL preceding NL.

	MINT	NRMT	EXC
COMPLETE SET (200)	40.00	18.00	5.00
COMMON CARD (1-200)	.25	.11	.03
□ 1 Brady Anderson	.75	.35	.09
□ 2 Kevin Brown	.40	.18	.05
□ 3 Curtis Goodwin	.40	.18	.05
□ 4 Jeffrey Hammonds	.40	.18	.05
□ 5 Ben McDonald	.25	.11	.03
□ 6 Mike Mussina	1.00	.45	.12
□ 7 Rafael Palmeiro	.75	.35	.09
□ 8 Cal Ripken Jr.	4.00	1.80	.50
□ 9 Jose Canseco	.75	.35	.09
□ 10 Roger Clemens	1.00	.45	.12
□ 11 Vaughn Eshelman	.25	.11	.03
□ 12 Mike Greenwell	.25	.11	.03
□ 13 Erik Hanson	.25	.11	.03
□ 14 Tim Naehring	.25	.11	.03
□ 15 Aaron Sele	.40	.18	.05
□ 16 John Valentin	.40	.18	.05
□ 17 Mo Vaughn	1.25	.55	.16
□ 18 Chili Davis	.40	.18	.05
□ 19 Gary DiSarcina	.25	.11	.03
□ 20 Chuck Finley	.40	.18	.05
□ 21 Tim Salmon	.75	.35	.09
□ 22 Lee Smith	.40	.18	.05
□ 23 J.T. Snow	.40	.18	.05
□ 24 Jim Abbott	.25	.11	.03
□ 25 Jason Bere	.25	.11	.03
□ 26 Ray Durham	.40	.18	.05
□ 27 Ozzie Guillen	.25	.11	.03
□ 28 Tim Raines	.75	.35	.09
□ 29 Frank Thomas	5.00	2.20	.60
□ 30 Robin Ventura	.40	.18	.05
□ 31 Carlos Baerga	.40	.18	.05
□ 32 Albert Belle	2.00	.90	.25
□ 33 Orel Hershiser	.40	.18	.05
□ 34 Kenny Lofton	1.25	.55	.16
□ 35 Dennis Martinez	.40	.18	.05
□ 36 Eddie Murray	1.25	.55	.16
□ 37 Manny Ramirez	1.25	.55	.16
□ 38 Julian Tavarez	.25	.11	.03
□ 39 Jim Thome	1.00	.45	.12
□ 40 Dave Winfield	.75	.35	.09
□ 41 Chad Curtis	.25	.11	.03
□ 42 Cecil Fielder	.40	.18	.05
□ 43 Travis Fryman	.40	.18	.05
□ 44 Kirk Gibson	.40	.18	.05
□ 45 Bob Higginson	1.25	.55	.16
□ 46 Alan Trammell	.40	.18	.05
□ 47 Lou Whitaker	.40	.18	.05
□ 48 Kevin Appier	.40	.18	.05
□ 49 Gary Gaetti	.40	.18	.05
□ 50 Jeff Montgomery	.40	.18	.05
□ 51 Jon Nunnally	.40	.18	.05
□ 52 Ricky Bones	.25	.11	.03
□ 53 Cal Eldred	.25	.11	.03
□ 54 Joe Oliver	.25	.11	.03
□ 55 Kevin Seitzer	.25	.11	.03
□ 56 Marty Cordova	.75	.35	.09
□ 57 Chuck Knoblauch	.75	.35	.09
□ 58 Kirby Puckett	2.00	.90	.25
□ 59 Wade Boggs	.75	.35	.09
□ 60 Derek Jeter	3.00	1.35	.35
□ 61 Jimmy Key	.40	.18	.05
□ 62 Don Mattingly	2.50	1.10	.30
□ 63 Jack McDowell	.40	.18	.05
□ 64 Paul O'Neill	.40	.18	.05
□ 65 Andy Pettitte	2.00	.90	.25
□ 66 Ruben Rivera	1.50	.70	.19
□ 67 Mike Stanley	.25	.11	.03
□ 68 John Wetteland	.40	.18	.05
□ 69 Geronimo Berroa	.25	.11	.03
□ 70 Dennis Eckersley	.40	.18	.05
□ 71 Rickey Henderson	.75	.35	.09
□ 72 Mark McGwire	1.50	.70	.19
□ 73 Steve Ontiveros	.25	.11	.03
□ 74 Ruben Sierra	.40	.18	.05
□ 75 Terry Steinbach	.40	.18	.05

☐ 76 Jay Buhner	.75	.35	.09
☐ 77 Ken Griffey Jr.	5.00	2.20	.60
☐ 78 Randy Johnson	.75	.35	.09
☐ 79 Edgar Martinez	.40	.18	.05
☐ 80 Tino Martinez	.40	.18	.05
☐ 81 Marc Newfield	.40	.18	.05
☐ 82 Alex Rodriguez	6.00	2.70	.75
☐ 83 Will Clark	.75	.35	.09
☐ 84 Benji Gil	.25	.11	.03
☐ 85 Juan Gonzalez	2.50	1.10	.30
☐ 86 Rusty Greer	.75	.35	.09
☐ 87 Dean Palmer	.40	.18	.05
☐ 88 Ivan Rodriguez	1.25	.55	.16
☐ 89 Kenny Rogers	.25	.11	.03
☐ 90 Roberto Alomar	1.00	.45	.12
☐ 91 Joe Carter	.40	.18	.05
☐ 92 David Cone	.40	.18	.05
☐ 93 Alex Gonzalez	.40	.18	.05
☐ 94 Shawn Green	.40	.18	.05
☐ 95 Pat Hentgen	.40	.18	.05
☐ 96 Paul Molitor	1.00	.45	.12
☐ 97 John Olerud	.25	.11	.03
☐ 98 Devon White	.40	.18	.05
☐ 99 Steve Avery	.40	.18	.05
☐ 100 Tom Glavine	.75	.35	.09
☐ 101 Marquis Grissom	.40	.18	.05
☐ 102 Chipper Jones	3.00	1.35	.35
☐ 103 David Justice	.75	.35	.09
☐ 104 Ryan Klesko	.75	.35	.09
☐ 105 Javier Lopez	.75	.35	.09
☐ 106 Greg Maddux	3.00	1.35	.35
☐ 107 Fred McGriff	.75	.35	.09
☐ 108 John Smoltz	.75	.35	.09
☐ 109 Shawon Dunston	.25	.11	.03
☐ 110 Mark Grace	.75	.35	.09
☐ 111 Brian McRae	.40	.18	.05
☐ 112 Randy Myers	.25	.11	.03
☐ 113 Sammy Sosa	.75	.35	.09
☐ 114 Steve Trachsel	.25	.11	.03
☐ 115 Bret Boone	.40	.18	.05
☐ 116 Ron Gant	.40	.18	.05
☐ 117 Barry Larkin	.75	.35	.09
☐ 118 Deion Sanders	.75	.35	.09
☐ 119 Reggie Sanders	.40	.18	.05
☐ 120 Pete Schourek	.40	.18	.05
☐ 121 John Smiley	.25	.11	.03
☐ 122 Jason Bates	.25	.11	.03
☐ 123 Dante Bichette	.75	.35	.09
☐ 124 Vinny Castilla	.40	.18	.05
☐ 125 Andres Galarraga	.75	.35	.09
☐ 126 Larry Walker	.75	.35	.09
☐ 127 Greg Colbrunn	.25	.11	.03
☐ 128 Jeff Conine	.40	.18	.05
☐ 129 Andre Dawson	.40	.18	.05
☐ 130 Chris Hammond	.25	.11	.03
☐ 131 Charles Johnson	.40	.18	.05
☐ 132 Gary Sheffield	.75	.35	.09
☐ 133 Quilvio Veras	.25	.11	.03
☐ 134 Jeff Bagwell	2.00	.90	.25
☐ 135 Derek Bell	.40	.18	.05
☐ 136 Craig Biggio	.40	.18	.05
☐ 137 Jim Dougherty	.25	.11	.03
☐ 138 John Hudek	.25	.11	.03
☐ 139 Orlando Miller	.25	.11	.03
☐ 140 Phil Plantier	.25	.11	.03
☐ 141 Eric Karros	.40	.18	.05
☐ 142 Ramon Martinez	.40	.18	.05
☐ 143 Raul Mondesi	.75	.35	.09
☐ 144 Hideo Nomo	5.00	2.20	.60
☐ 145 Mike Piazza	3.00	1.35	.35
☐ 146 Ismael Valdes	.40	.18	.05
☐ 147 Todd Worrell	.25	.11	.03
☐ 148 Moises Alou	.40	.18	.05
☐ 149 Yamil Benitez	.75	.35	.09
☐ 150 Wil Cordero	.25	.11	.03
☐ 151 Jeff Fassero	.25	.11	.03
☐ 152 Cliff Floyd	.40	.18	.05
☐ 153 Pedro Martinez	.40	.18	.05
☐ 154 Carlos Perez	.40	.18	.05
☐ 155 Tony Tarasco	.25	.11	.03
☐ 156 Rondell White	.40	.18	.05
☐ 157 Edgardo Alfonzo	.40	.18	.05
☐ 158 Bobby Bonilla	.40	.18	.05
☐ 159 Rico Brogna	.25	.11	.03
☐ 160 Bobby Jones	.40	.18	.05
☐ 161 Bill Pulsipher	.40	.18	.05
☐ 162 Bret Saberhagen	.40	.18	.05
☐ 163 Ricky Bottalico	.40	.18	.05
☐ 164 Darren Daulton	.40	.18	.05
☐ 165 Lenny Dykstra	.40	.18	.05
☐ 166 Charlie Hayes	.25	.11	.03
☐ 167 Dave Hollins	.25	.11	.03
☐ 168 Gregg Jefferies	.40	.18	.05
☐ 169 Michael Mimbs	.40	.18	.05
☐ 170 Curt Schilling	.25	.11	.03
☐ 171 Heathcliff Slocumb	.25	.11	.03
☐ 172 Jay Bell	.40	.18	.05
☐ 173 Micah Franklin	.40	.18	.05
☐ 174 Mark Johnson	.40	.18	.05
☐ 175 Jeff King	.40	.18	.05
☐ 176 Al Martin	.40	.18	.05
☐ 177 Dan Miceli	.25	.11	.03
☐ 178 Denny Neagle	.40	.18	.05
☐ 179 Bernard Gilkey	.40	.18	.05
☐ 180 Ken Hill	.25	.11	.03
☐ 181 Brian Jordan	.75	.35	.09
☐ 182 Ray Lankford	.40	.18	.05
☐ 183 Ozzie Smith	1.25	.55	.16
☐ 184 Andy Benes	.25	.11	.03
☐ 185 Ken Caminiti	.75	.35	.09
☐ 186 Steve Finley	.40	.18	.05
☐ 187 Tony Gwynn	2.00	.90	.25
☐ 188 Joey Hamilton	.75	.35	.09
☐ 189 Melvin Nieves	.40	.18	.05
☐ 190 Scott Sanders	.25	.11	.03
☐ 191 Rod Beck	.25	.11	.03
☐ 192 Barry Bonds	1.25	.55	.16
☐ 193 Royce Clayton	.25	.11	.03
☐ 194 Glenallen Hill	.25	.11	.03
☐ 195 Darren Lewis	.25	.11	.03
☐ 196 Mark Portugal	.25	.11	.03
☐ 197 Matt Williams	.75	.35	.09
☐ 198 Checklist 1-82	.25	.11	.03
☐ 199 Checklist 83-162	.25	.11	.03
☐ 200 Checklist 163-200/Inserts	.25	.11	.03
☐ P8 Cal Ripken Promo	7.50	3.40	.95

1995 Emotion Masters

The theme of this 10-card standard-size set is the showcasing of players that come through in the clutch. Randomly inserted at a rate of one in eight packs, a player photo is superimposed over a larger photo that is ghosted in a color emblematic of that team. The player's name and the Emotion logo are at the bottom. The backs have a photo to the left and text to the right. Both sides of the card are shaded in the color scheme of the player's team.

	MINT	NRMT	EXC
COMPLETE SET (10)	75.00	34.00	9.50
COMMON CARD (1-10)	2.50	1.10	.30
☐ 1 Barry Bonds	5.00	2.20	.60
☐ 2 Juan Gonzalez	10.00	4.50	1.25
☐ 3 Ken Griffey Jr.	20.00	9.00	2.50
☐ 4 Tony Gwynn	8.00	3.60	1.00
☐ 5 Kenny Lofton	5.00	2.20	.60
☐ 6 Greg Maddux	12.00	5.50	1.50
☐ 7 Raul Mondesi	2.50	1.10	.30
☐ 8 Cal Ripken	15.00	6.75	1.85
☐ 9 Frank Thomas	20.00	9.00	2.50
☐ 10 Matt Williams	2.50	1.10	.30

1995 Emotion N-Tense

Randomly inserted at a rate of one in 37 packs, this 12-card standard-size set features fronts that have a player photo surrounded by a swirling color scheme and a large holographic "N" in the background. The backs feature a like color scheme with text and player photo.

	MINT	NRMT	EXC
COMPLETE SET (12)	200.00	90.00	25.00
COMMON CARD (1-12)	8.00	3.60	1.00
☐ 1 Jeff Bagwell	25.00	11.00	3.10
☐ 2 Albert Belle	25.00	11.00	3.10
☐ 3 Barry Bonds	15.00	6.75	1.85
☐ 4 Cecil Fielder	12.00	5.50	1.50
☐ 5 Ron Gant	8.00	3.60	1.00
☐ 6 Ken Griffey Jr.	60.00	27.00	7.50
☐ 7 Mark McGwire	18.00	8.00	2.20
☐ 8 Mike Piazza	40.00	18.00	5.00
☐ 9 Manny Ramirez	15.00	6.75	1.85
☐ 10 Frank Thomas	60.00	27.00	7.50
☐ 11 Mo Vaughn	15.00	6.75	1.85
☐ 12 Matt Williams			

1995 Emotion Ripken

This 15-card Cal Ripken standard-size set features great moments from the career of the Baltimore Orioles' great. Inserted at a rate of one in 12 packs, the moments were selected by the record-breaking shortstop. Referred to as "Timeless", an action photo of Ripken is superimposed over a silver background that includes a watch and another photo at the top. The backs elaborate on the event or events

which Cal selected. This text is superimposed over a large photo. A five-card mail-in (described on wrapper) set was also made available. The expiration was 3/1/96.

	MINT	NRMT	EXC
COMPLETE SET (10)	60.00	27.00	7.50
COMMON CARD (1-10)	6.00	2.70	.75
COMMON MAIL-IN (11-15)	8.00	3.60	1.00
☐ 1 Cal Ripken High School Pitcher	6.00	2.70	.75
☐ 2 Cal Ripken Role Model	6.00	2.70	.75
☐ 3 Cal Ripken Rookie of the Year	6.00	2.70	.75
☐ 4 Cal Ripken 1st MVP Season	6.00	2.70	.75
☐ 5 Cal Ripken 95 Consecutived Errorless Games	6.00	2.70	.75
☐ 6 Cal Ripken All-Star MVP	6.00	2.70	.75
☐ 7 Cal Ripken Conditioning	6.00	2.70	.75
☐ 8 Cal Ripken Shortstop HR Record	6.00	2.70	.75
☐ 9 Cal Ripken Literacy Work	6.00	2.70	.75
☐ 10 Cal Ripken 2000th Consecutive Game	6.00	2.70	.75
☐ 11 Cal Ripken 1995 All-Star Selection	8.00	3.60	1.00
☐ 12 Cal Ripken 35th Birthday	8.00	3.60	1.00
☐ 13 Cal Ripken Game 2,130	8.00	3.60	1.00
☐ 14 Cal Ripken Game 2,131	8.00	3.60	1.00
☐ 15 Cal Ripken 2,153 and Counting	8.00	3.60	1.00

1995 Emotion Rookies

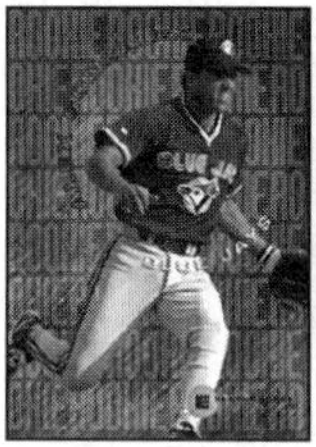

This 10-card standard-size set was inserted at a rate of one in five packs. Card fronts feature an action photo superimposed over background that is in a color consistent with that of the team's. The backs have a player photo and a write-up.

	MINT	NRMT	EXC
COMPLETE SET (10)	25.00	11.00	3.10
COMMON CARD (1-10)	1.00	.45	.12
☐ 1 Edgardo Alfonzo	1.00	.45	.12
☐ 2 Jason Bates	1.00	.45	.12
☐ 3 Marty Cordova	2.50	1.10	.30
☐ 4 Ray Durham	1.50	.70	.19
☐ 5 Alex Gonzalez	1.00	.45	.12
☐ 6 Shawn Green	1.50	.70	.19
☐ 7 Charles Johnson	1.50	.70	.19
☐ 8 Chipper Jones	10.00	4.50	1.25
☐ 9 Hideo Nomo	8.00	3.60	1.00
☐ 10 Alex Rodriguez	15.00	6.75	1.85

1996 Emotion-XL

The 1996 Emotion-XL set was issued in one series totalling 300 standard-size cards. The 7-card packs retail for $4.99 each. The fronts feature a color action player photo with either a blue, green or maroon frame and the player's name and team printed in a foil-stamped medallion. A descriptive term describing the player completes the front. The backs carry player information and statistics. The cards are grouped alphabetically by team with AL preceding NL.

	MINT	NRMT	EXC
COMPLETE SET (300)	80.00	36.00	10.00
COMMON CARD (1-300)	.25	.11	.03
☐ 1 Roberto Alomar	1.50	.70	.19
☐ 2 Brady Anderson	1.00	.45	.12
☐ 3 Bobby Bonilla	.50	.23	.06

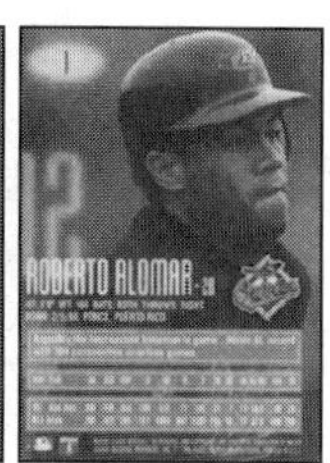

☐ 4 Jeffrey Hammonds	.25	.11	.03
☐ 5 Chris Hoiles	.25	.11	.03
☐ 6 Mike Mussina	1.50	.70	.19
☐ 7 Randy Myers	.25	.11	.03
☐ 8 Rafael Palmeiro	1.00	.45	.12
☐ 9 Cal Ripken	6.00	2.70	.75
☐ 10 B.J. Surhoff	.25	.11	.03
☐ 11 Jose Canseco	1.00	.45	.12
☐ 12 Roger Clemens	1.50	.70	.19
☐ 13 Wil Cordero	.25	.11	.03
☐ 14 Mike Greenwell	.25	.11	.03
☐ 15 Dwayne Hosey	.25	.11	.03
☐ 16 Tim Naehring	.50	.23	.06
☐ 17 Troy O'Leary	.25	.11	.03
☐ 18 Mike Stanley	.25	.11	.03
☐ 19 John Valentin	.50	.23	.06
☐ 20 Mo Vaughn	2.00	.90	.25
☐ 21 Jim Abbott	.50	.23	.06
☐ 22 Garret Anderson	1.00	.45	.12
☐ 23 George Arias	.25	.11	.03
☐ 24 Chili Davis	.25	.11	.03
☐ 25 Jim Edmonds	.50	.23	.06
☐ 26 Chuck Finley	.25	.11	.03
☐ 27 Todd Greene	.50	.23	.06
☐ 28 Mark Langston	.25	.11	.03
☐ 29 Troy Percival	.50	.23	.06
☐ 30 Tim Salmon	1.00	.45	.12
☐ 31 Lee Smith	.50	.23	.06
☐ 32 J.T. Snow	.50	.23	.06
☐ 33 Harold Baines	.50	.23	.06
☐ 34 Jason Bere	.25	.11	.03
☐ 35 Ray Durham	1.00	.45	.12
☐ 36 Alex Fernandez	.50	.23	.06
☐ 37 Ozzie Guillen	.25	.11	.03
☐ 38 Darren Lewis	.25	.11	.03
☐ 39 Lyle Mouton	.25	.11	.03
☐ 40 Tony Phillips	.50	.23	.06
☐ 41 Danny Tartabull	.25	.11	.03
☐ 42 Frank Thomas	8.00	3.60	1.00
☐ 43 Robin Ventura	.50	.23	.06
☐ 44 Sandy Alomar Jr.	.25	.11	.03
☐ 45 Carlos Baerga	.50	.23	.06
☐ 46 Albert Belle	3.00	1.35	.35
☐ 47 Julio Franco	.50	.23	.06
☐ 48 Orel Hershiser	.50	.23	.06
☐ 49 Kenny Lofton	2.00	.90	.25
☐ 50 Dennis Martinez	.50	.23	.06
☐ 51 Jack McDowell	1.00	.45	.12
☐ 52 Jose Mesa	.50	.23	.06
☐ 53 Eddie Murray	2.00	.90	.25
☐ 54 Charles Nagy	.50	.23	.06
☐ 55 Manny Ramirez	2.00	.90	.25
☐ 56 Jim Thome	1.50	.70	.19
☐ 57 Omar Vizquel	.50	.23	.06
☐ 58 Chad Curtis	.25	.11	.03
☐ 59 Cecil Fielder	.50	.23	.06
☐ 60 Travis Fryman	.50	.23	.06
☐ 61 Chris Gomez	.25	.11	.03
☐ 62 Felipe Lira	.25	.11	.03
☐ 63 Alan Trammell	.50	.23	.06
☐ 64 Kevin Appier	.50	.23	.06
☐ 65 Johnny Damon	.50	.23	.06
☐ 66 Tom Goodwin	.50	.23	.06
☐ 67 Mark Gubicza	.25	.11	.03
☐ 68 Jeff Montgomery	.25	.11	.03
☐ 69 Jon Nunnally	.25	.11	.03
☐ 70 Bip Roberts	.25	.11	.03
☐ 71 Ricky Bones	.25	.11	.03
☐ 72 Chuck Carr	.25	.11	.03
☐ 73 John Jaha	.50	.23	.06
☐ 74 Ben McDonald	.25	.11	.03
☐ 75 Matt Mieske	.25	.11	.03
☐ 76 Dave Nilsson	.50	.23	.06
☐ 77 Kevin Seitzer	.25	.11	.03
☐ 78 Greg Vaughn	1.00	.45	.12
☐ 79 Rick Aguilera	.25	.11	.03
☐ 80 Marty Cordova	.50	.23	.06
☐ 81 Roberto Kelly	.25	.11	.03
☐ 82 Chuck Knoblauch	1.00	.45	.12
☐ 83 Pat Meares	.25	.11	.03
☐ 84 Paul Molitor	1.50	.70	.19
☐ 85 Kirby Puckett	3.00	1.35	.35
☐ 86 Brad Radke	.25	.11	.03
☐ 87 Wade Boggs	1.00	.45	.12
☐ 88 David Cone	.50	.23	.06
☐ 89 Dwight Gooden	.50	.23	.06
☐ 90 Derek Jeter	5.00	2.20	.60
☐ 91 Tino Martinez	.50	.23	.06
☐ 92 Paul O'Neill	.25	.11	.03
☐ 93 Andy Pettitte	2.50	1.10	.30
☐ 94 Tim Raines	1.00	.45	.12
☐ 95 Ruben Rivera	1.50	.70	.19
☐ 96 Kenny Rogers	.25	.11	.03

☐ 97 Ruben Sierra	.25	.11	.03
☐ 98 John Wetteland	.50	.23	.06
☐ 99 Bernie Williams	1.50	.70	.19
☐ 100 Allen Battle	.25	.11	.03
☐ 101 Geronimo Berroa	.50	.23	.06
☐ 102 Brent Gates	.25	.11	.03
☐ 103 Doug Johns	.25	.11	.03
☐ 104 Mark McGwire	2.50	1.10	.30
☐ 105 Pedro Munoz	.25	.11	.03
☐ 106 Ariel Prieto	.25	.11	.03
☐ 107 Terry Steinbach	.50	.23	.06
☐ 108 Todd Van Poppel	.25	.11	.03
☐ 109 Chris Bosio	.25	.11	.03
☐ 110 Jay Buhner	1.00	.45	.12
☐ 111 Joey Cora	.25	.11	.03
☐ 112 Russ Davis	.25	.11	.03
☐ 113 Ken Griffey Jr.	8.00	3.60	1.00
☐ 114 Sterling Hitchcock	.25	.11	.03
☐ 115 Randy Johnson	1.25	.55	.16
☐ 116 Edgar Martinez	.50	.23	.06
☐ 117 Alex Rodriguez	8.00	3.60	1.00
☐ 118 Paul Sorrento	.25	.11	.03
☐ 119 Dan Wilson	.25	.11	.03
☐ 120 Will Clark	1.00	.45	.12
☐ 121 Juan Gonzalez	4.00	1.80	.50
☐ 122 Rusty Greer	1.00	.45	.12
☐ 123 Kevin Gross	.25	.11	.03
☐ 124 Ken Hill	.25	.11	.03
☐ 125 Dean Palmer	1.00	.45	.12
☐ 126 Roger Pavlik	.25	.11	.03
☐ 127 Ivan Rodriguez	2.00	.90	.25
☐ 128 Mickey Tettleton	.50	.23	.06
☐ 129 Joe Carter	.50	.23	.06
☐ 130 Carlos Delgado	.50	.23	.06
☐ 131 Alex Gonzalez	.25	.11	.03
☐ 132 Shawn Green	.25	.11	.03
☐ 133 Erik Hanson	.25	.11	.03
☐ 134 Pat Hentgen	.50	.23	.06
☐ 135 Otis Nixon	.25	.11	.03
☐ 136 John Olerud	.25	.11	.03
☐ 137 Ed Sprague	.50	.23	.06
☐ 138 Steve Avery	.50	.23	.06
☐ 139 Jermaine Dye	1.50	.70	.19
☐ 140 Tom Glavine	1.00	.45	.12
☐ 141 Marquis Grissom	.50	.23	.06
☐ 142 Chipper Jones	5.00	2.20	.60
☐ 143 David Justice	.50	.23	.06
☐ 144 Ryan Klesko	1.25	.55	.16
☐ 145 Javier Lopez	1.00	.45	.12
☐ 146 Greg Maddux	5.00	2.20	.60
☐ 147 Fred McGriff	1.00	.45	.12
☐ 148 Jason Schmidt	1.00	.45	.12
☐ 149 John Smoltz	1.25	.55	.16
☐ 150 Mark Wohlers	.50	.23	.06
☐ 151 Jim Bullinger	.25	.11	.03
☐ 152 Frank Castillo	.25	.11	.03
☐ 153 Kevin Foster	.25	.11	.03
☐ 154 Luis Gonzalez	.25	.11	.03
☐ 155 Mark Grace	1.00	.45	.12
☐ 156 Brian McRae	.25	.11	.03
☐ 157 Jaime Navarro	.25	.11	.03
☐ 158 Rey Sanchez	.25	.11	.03
☐ 159 Ryne Sandberg	2.00	.90	.25
☐ 160 Sammy Sosa	1.25	.55	.16
☐ 161 Bret Boone	.25	.11	.03
☐ 162 Jeff Brantley	.25	.11	.03
☐ 163 Vince Coleman	.25	.11	.03
☐ 164 Steve Gibralter	.25	.11	.03
☐ 165 Barry Larkin	1.00	.45	.12
☐ 166 Hal Morris	.25	.11	.03
☐ 167 Mark Portugal	.25	.11	.03
☐ 168 Reggie Sanders	.50	.23	.06
☐ 169 Pete Schourek	.25	.11	.03
☐ 170 John Smiley	.25	.11	.03
☐ 171 Jason Bates	.25	.11	.03
☐ 172 Dante Bichette	1.00	.45	.12
☐ 173 Ellis Burks	.50	.23	.06
☐ 174 Vinny Castilla	.50	.23	.06
☐ 175 Andres Galarraga	1.00	.45	.12
☐ 176 Kevin Ritz	.25	.11	.03
☐ 177 Bill Swift	.25	.11	.03
☐ 178 Larry Walker	1.00	.45	.12
☐ 179 Walt Weiss	.25	.11	.03
☐ 180 Eric Young	.50	.23	.06
☐ 181 Kurt Abbott	.25	.11	.03
☐ 182 Kevin Brown	.50	.23	.06
☐ 183 John Burkett	.25	.11	.03
☐ 184 Greg Colbrunn	.25	.11	.03
☐ 185 Jeff Conine	.50	.23	.06
☐ 186 Chris Hammond	.25	.11	.03
☐ 187 Charles Johnson	.50	.23	.06
☐ 188 Terry Pendleton	.50	.23	.06
☐ 189 Pat Rapp	.25	.11	.03
☐ 190 Gary Sheffield	1.25	.55	.16
☐ 191 Quilvio Veras	.25	.11	.03
☐ 192 Devon White	.25	.11	.03
☐ 193 Jeff Bagwell	3.00	1.35	.35
☐ 194 Derek Bell	.50	.23	.06
☐ 195 Sean Berry	.25	.11	.03
☐ 196 Craig Biggio	.50	.23	.06
☐ 197 Doug Drabek	.25	.11	.03
☐ 198 Tony Eusebio	.25	.11	.03
☐ 199 Mike Hampton	.25	.11	.03
☐ 200 Brian L.Hunter	.50	.23	.06
☐ 201 Derrick May	.25	.11	.03
☐ 202 Orlando Miller	.25	.11	.03
☐ 203 Shane Reynolds	.25	.11	.03
☐ 204 Mike Blowers	.25	.11	.03
☐ 205 Tom Candiotti	.25	.11	.03
☐ 206 Delino DeShields	.25	.11	.03
☐ 207 Greg Gagne	.25	.11	.03
☐ 208 Karim Garcia	1.50	.70	.19
☐ 209 Todd Hollandsworth	.50	.23	.06
☐ 210 Eric Karros	.50	.23	.06
☐ 211 Ramon Martinez	.50	.23	.06
☐ 212 Raul Mondesi	1.00	.45	.12
☐ 213 Hideo Nomo	2.00	.90	.25
☐ 214 Chan Ho Park	1.00	.45	.12
☐ 215 Mike Piazza	5.00	2.20	.60
☐ 216 Ismael Valdes	.50	.23	.06
☐ 217 Todd Worrell	.50	.23	.06
☐ 218 Moises Alou	.50	.23	.06
☐ 219 Yamil Benitez	.50	.23	.06
☐ 220 Jeff Fassero	.25	.11	.03
☐ 221 Darrin Fletcher	.25	.11	.03
☐ 222 Cliff Floyd	.25	.11	.03
☐ 223 Pedro Martinez	.50	.23	.06
☐ 224 Carlos Perez	.25	.11	.03
☐ 225 Mel Rojas	.25	.11	.03
☐ 226 David Segui	.25	.11	.03
☐ 227 Rondell White	.50	.23	.06
☐ 228 Rico Brogna	.25	.11	.03
☐ 229 Carl Everett	.25	.11	.03
☐ 230 John Franco	.25	.11	.03
☐ 231 Bernard Gilkey	.50	.23	.06
☐ 232 Todd Hundley	.50	.23	.06
☐ 233 Jason Isringhausen	1.00	.45	.12
☐ 234 Lance Johnson	1.00	.45	.12
☐ 235 Bobby Jones	.25	.11	.03
☐ 236 Jeff Kent	.25	.11	.03
☐ 237 Rey Ordonez	1.00	.45	.12
☐ 238 Bill Pulsipher	.50	.23	.06
☐ 239 Jose Vizcaino	.25	.11	.03
☐ 240 Paul Wilson	.50	.23	.06
☐ 241 Ricky Bottalico	.25	.11	.03
☐ 242 Darren Daulton	.50	.23	.06
☐ 243 Lenny Dykstra	.50	.23	.06
☐ 244 Jim Eisenreich	.25	.11	.03
☐ 245 Sid Fernandez	.25	.11	.03
☐ 246 Gregg Jefferies	1.00	.45	.12
☐ 247 Mickey Morandini	.25	.11	.03
☐ 248 Benito Santiago	.25	.11	.03
☐ 249 Curt Schilling	.25	.11	.03
☐ 250 Mark Whiten	.25	.11	.03
☐ 251 Todd Zeile	.50	.23	.06
☐ 252 Jay Bell	.50	.23	.06
☐ 253 Carlos Garcia	.25	.11	.03
☐ 254 Charlie Hayes	.25	.11	.03
☐ 255 Jason Kendall	1.00	.45	.12
☐ 256 Jeff King	.50	.23	.06
☐ 257 Al Martin	.25	.11	.03
☐ 258 Orlando Merced	.50	.23	.06
☐ 259 Dan Miceli	.25	.11	.03
☐ 260 Denny Neagle	.50	.23	.06
☐ 261 Alan Benes	1.00	.45	.12
☐ 262 Andy Benes	.25	.11	.03
☐ 263 Royce Clayton	.25	.11	.03
☐ 264 Dennis Eckersley	.50	.23	.06
☐ 265 Gary Gaetti	.50	.23	.06
☐ 266 Ron Gant	.50	.23	.06
☐ 267 Brian Jordan	.50	.23	.06
☐ 268 Ray Lankford	.50	.23	.06
☐ 269 John Mabry	.50	.23	.06
☐ 270 Tom Pagnozzi	.25	.11	.03
☐ 271 Ozzie Smith	2.00	.90	.25
☐ 272 Todd Stottlemyre	.25	.11	.03
☐ 273 Andy Ashby	.25	.11	.03
☐ 274 Brad Ausmus	.25	.11	.03
☐ 275 Ken Caminiti	1.00	.45	.12
☐ 276 Steve Finley	1.00	.45	.12
☐ 277 Tony Gwynn	3.00	1.35	.35
☐ 278 Joey Hamilton	.50	.23	.06
☐ 279 Rickey Henderson	1.00	.45	.12
☐ 280 Trevor Hoffman	.50	.23	.06
☐ 281 Wally Joyner	.25	.11	.03
☐ 282 Jody Reed	.25	.11	.03
☐ 283 Bob Tewksbury	.25	.11	.03
☐ 284 Fernando Valenzuela	.50	.23	.06
☐ 285 Rod Beck	.25	.11	.03
☐ 286 Barry Bonds	2.00	.90	.25
☐ 287 Mark Carreon	.25	.11	.03
☐ 288 Shawon Dunston	.25	.11	.03
☐ 289 Osvaldo Fernandez	1.00	.45	.12
☐ 290 Glenallen Hill	.25	.11	.03
☐ 291 Stan Javier	.25	.11	.03
☐ 292 Mark Leiter	.25	.11	.03
☐ 293 Kirt Manwaring	.25	.11	.03
☐ 294 Robby Thompson	.25	.11	.03
☐ 295 William VanLandingham	.25	.11	.03
☐ 296 Allen Watson	.25	.11	.03
☐ 297 Matt Williams	1.00	.45	.12
☐ 298 Checklist	.25	.11	.03
☐ 299 Checklist	.25	.11	.03
☐ 300 Checklist	.25	.11	.03
☐ P55 Manny Ramirez Promo	2.00	.90	.25

1996 Emotion-XL D-Fense

Randomly inserted in packs at a rate of one in four, this 10-card set showcases outstanding defensive players. The fronts feature a color

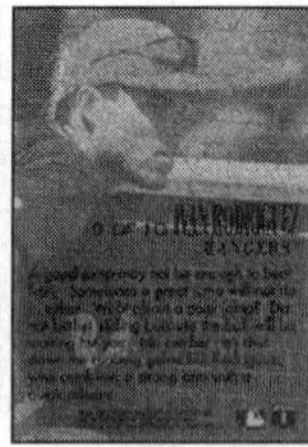

action player cut-out on a sepia portait background with silver foil print and border. The backs carry information about the player on another sepia portrait background.

	MINT	NRMT	EXC
COMPLETE SET (10)	30.00	13.50	3.70
COMMON CARD (1-10)	1.00	.45	.12
☐ 1 Roberto Alomar	2.00	.90	.25
☐ 2 Barry Bonds	2.50	1.10	.30
☐ 3 Mark Grace	1.00	.45	.12
☐ 4 Ken Griffey Jr.	10.00	4.50	1.25
☐ 5 Kenny Lofton	2.50	1.10	.30
☐ 6 Greg Maddux	6.00	2.70	.75
☐ 7 Raul Mondesi	1.00	.45	.12
☐ 8 Cal Ripken	8.00	3.60	1.00
☐ 9 Ivan Rodriguez	2.50	1.10	.30
☐ 10 Matt Williams	1.00	.45	.12

1996 Emotion-XL Legion of Boom

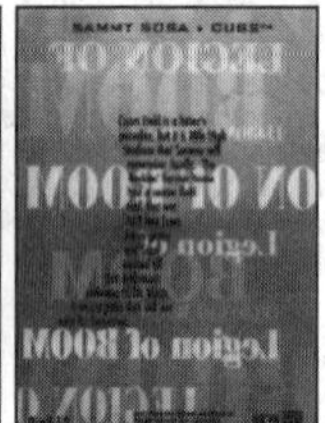

Randomly inserted in packs at a rate of one in 36, this 12-card set features the game's big hitters on cards with translucent card backs. The fronts carry a color action player cut-out with silver foil print.

	MINT	NRMT	EXC
COMPLETE SET (12)	200.00	90.00	25.00
COMMON CARD (1-12)	6.00	2.70	.75
☐ 1 Albert Belle	20.00	9.00	2.50
☐ 2 Barry Bonds	12.00	5.50	1.50
☐ 3 Juan Gonzalez	25.00	11.00	3.10
☐ 4 Ken Griffey Jr.	50.00	22.00	6.25
☐ 5 Mark McGwire	15.00	6.75	1.85
☐ 6 Mike Piazza	30.00	13.50	3.70
☐ 7 Manny Ramirez	12.00	5.50	1.50
☐ 8 Tim Salmon	6.00	2.70	.75
☐ 9 Sammy Sosa	8.00	3.60	1.00
☐ 10 Frank Thomas	50.00	22.00	6.25
☐ 11 Mo Vaughn	12.00	5.50	1.50
☐ 12 Matt Williams	6.00	2.70	.75

1996 Emotion-XL N-Tense

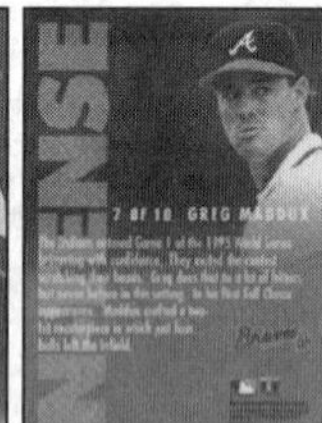

Randomly inserted in packs at a rate of one in 12, this 10-card set highlights top-clutch performers on special, front N-shaped die-cut cards. The backs carry information about the player on a player portrait background.

	MINT	NRMT	EXC
COMPLETE SET (10)	100.00	45.00	12.50
COMMON CARD (1-10)	3.00	1.35	.35
☐ 1 Albert Belle	10.00	4.50	1.25
☐ 2 Barry Bonds	6.00	2.70	.75
☐ 3 Jose Canseco	3.00	1.35	.35
☐ 4 Ken Griffey Jr.	25.00	11.00	3.10
☐ 5 Tony Gwynn	10.00	4.50	1.25
☐ 6 Randy Johnson	4.00	1.80	.50
☐ 7 Greg Maddux	15.00	6.75	1.85
☐ 8 Cal Ripken	20.00	9.00	2.50
☐ 9 Frank Thomas	25.00	11.00	3.10
☐ 10 Matt Williams	3.00	1.35	.35

1996 Emotion-XL Rare Breed

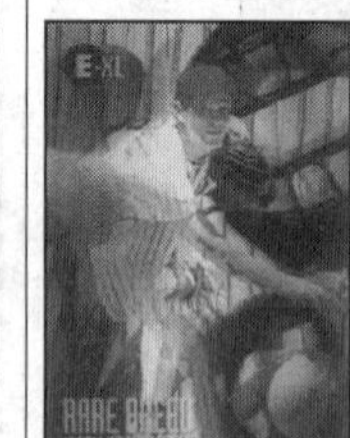

Randomly inserted in packs at a rate of one in 100, this 10-card set showcases young stars on lenticular cards. The fronts feature color action player cut-outs on a baseball graphics background. The backs carry player information over a color player portrait.

	MINT	NRMT	EXC
COMPLETE SET (10)	200.00	90.00	25.00
COMMON CARD (1-10)	6.00	2.70	.75
☐ 1 Garret Anderson	6.00	2.70	.75
☐ 2 Marty Cordova	15.00	6.75	1.85
☐ 3 Brian L.Hunter	12.00	5.50	1.50
☐ 4 Jason Isringhausen	8.00	3.60	1.00
☐ 5 Charles Johnson	8.00	3.60	1.00
☐ 6 Chipper Jones	75.00	34.00	9.50
☐ 7 Raul Mondesi	15.00	6.75	1.85
☐ 8 Hideo Nomo	30.00	13.50	3.70
☐ 9 Manny Ramirez	30.00	13.50	3.70
☐ 10 Rondell White	8.00	3.60	1.00

1969 Equitable Sports Hall of Fame*

This set consists of copies of the art work found in national magazines, especially "Sports Illustrated," honoring sports heroes that Equitable Life Assurance Society selected to be in its very own Sports Hall of Fame. The cards consists of charcoal-type drawings on white backgrounds by artists, George Loh and Robert Riger, and measure approximately 11" by 7 3/4". The cards are unnumbered and checklisted below alphabetically within the sport they played as follows: Baseball (1-18), Basketball (19-27), Bowling (28-32), Football (33-44), Golf (45-56), Hockey (57-61), Skating (62-63), Skiing (64-68), Swimming (69-72), Tennis (73-79), Track (80-86), and Yachting (87).

	NRMT	VG-E	GOOD
COMPLETE SET (87)	300.00	135.00	38.00
COMMON CARD (1-87)	2.50	1.10	.30
☐ 1 Ernie Banks	10.00	4.50	1.25
☐ 2 Roy Campanella	10.00	4.50	1.25
☐ 3 Johnny Evers	3.50	1.55	.45
☐ 4 Bob Feller	5.00	2.20	.60
☐ 5 Lou Gehrig	12.50	5.50	1.55
☐ 6 Lefty Grove	3.50	1.55	.45
☐ 7 Tom Henrich	2.50	1.10	.30
☐ 8 Carl Hubbell	4.00	1.80	.50
☐ 9 Al Kaline	6.00	2.70	.75
☐ 10 Ed Mathews	4.00	1.80	.50
☐ 11 Stan Musial	7.50	3.40	.95
☐ 12 PeeWee Reese	7.50	3.40	.95
☐ 13 Allie Reynolds	2.50	1.10	.30
☐ 14 Robin Roberts	4.00	1.80	.50
☐ 15 Brooks Robinson	6.00	2.70	.75
☐ 16 Red Ruffing	3.50	1.55	.45
☐ 17 Babe Ruth	15.00	6.75	1.85
☐ 18 Warren Spahn	4.00	1.80	.50
☐ 19 Elgin Baylor	4.00	1.80	.50
☐ 20 Wilt Chamberlain	7.50	3.40	.95
☐ 21 Bob Cousy	5.00	2.20	.60
☐ 22 Hal Grier	3.50	1.55	.45
☐ 23 George Mikan	5.00	2.20	.60
☐ 24 Bob Pettit	4.00	1.80	.50
☐ 25 Willis Reed	3.50	1.55	.45
☐ 26 Bill Russell	7.50	3.40	.95
☐ 27 Dolph Schayes	3.50	1.55	.45
☐ 28 Don Carter	3.50	1.55	.45
☐ 29 Ned Day	2.50	1.10	.30
☐ 30 Buzz Fazio	2.50	1.10	.30
☐ 31 Andy Varipapa	3.50	1.55	.45
☐ 32 Dick Weber	2.50	1.10	.30
☐ 33 Jimmy Brown	7.50	3.40	.95
☐ 34 Charlie Conerly	3.50	1.55	.45
☐ 35 Bill Dudley	2.50	1.10	.30
☐ 36 Roman Gabriel	2.50	1.10	.30
☐ 37 Red Grange	5.00	2.20	.60
☐ 38 Elroy Hirsch	3.50	1.55	.45
☐ 39 Jerry Kramer	2.50	1.10	.30
☐ 40 Vince Lombardi	6.00	2.70	.75
☐ 41 Earl Morrall	2.50	1.10	.30
☐ 42 Bronko Nagurski	4.00	1.80	.50
☐ 43 Jim Thorpe	6.00	2.70	.75
☐ 44 Alex Webster	2.50	1.10	.30
☐ 45 George Archer	2.50	1.10	.30
☐ 46 Frank Beard	2.50	1.10	.30
☐ 47 Patty Berg	2.50	1.10	.30
☐ 48 Julius Boros	2.50	1.10	.30
☐ 49 Billy Casper	3.50	1.55	.45
☐ 50 Jimmy Demaret	2.50	1.10	.30
☐ 51 Walter Hagen	4.00	1.80	.50

☐ 52 Cary Middlecoff	2.50	1.10	.30
☐ 53 Byron Nelson	7.50	3.40	.95
☐ 54 Gene Sarazen	6.00	2.70	.75
☐ 55 Sam Snead	7.50	3.40	.95
☐ 56 Ken Venturi	3.50	1.55	.45
☐ 57 Bernie Geoffrion	4.00	1.80	.50
☐ 58 Gordie Howe	7.50	3.40	.95
☐ 59 Ching Johnson	2.50	1.10	.30
☐ 60 Stan Mikita	3.50	1.55	.45
☐ 61 Maurice Richard	5.00	2.20	.60
☐ 62 Peggy Fleming	5.00	2.20	.60
☐ 63 Carol Heiss	4.00	1.80	.50
☐ 64 Dick Button	3.50	1.55	.45
☐ 65 Art Devlin	2.50	1.10	.30
☐ 66 Stein Eriksen	2.50	1.10	.30
☐ 67 P. Pitou	2.50	1.10	.30
☐ 68 Art Tokle	2.50	1.10	.30
☐ 69 Florence Chadwick	2.50	1.10	.30
☐ 70 Gertrude Ederle	2.50	1.10	.30
☐ 71 Don Schollander	3.50	1.55	.45
☐ 72 Johnny Weissmuller	4.00	1.80	.50
☐ 73 Don Budge	4.00	1.80	.50
☐ 74 Maureen Connolly	3.50	1.55	.45
☐ 75 Althea Gibson	3.50	1.55	.45
☐ 76 Billy Jean King	5.00	2.20	.60
☐ 77 Jack Kramer	3.50	1.55	.45
☐ 78 Bill Talbert	2.50	1.10	.30
☐ 79 Tony Trabert	2.50	1.10	.30
☐ 80 Glenn Cunningham	2.50	1.10	.30
☐ 81 Harrison Dillard	2.50	1.10	.30
☐ 82 Rafer Johnson	3.50	1.55	.45
☐ 83 Bob Mathias	3.50	1.55	.45
☐ 84 Jesse Owens	3.50	1.55	.45
☐ 85 Wilma Rudolph	3.50	1.55	.45
☐ 86 Frank Wycoff	2.50	1.10	.30
☐ 87 Carlton Mitchell	2.50	1.10	.30

1972 Esso Coins

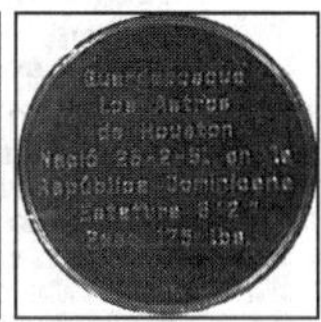

This 12-coin set measures approximately 1 1/4" in diameter and exclusively contains Spanish players. The coins are silver in color with the fronts featuring an embossed head of the player below the player's name. The backs carry in Spanish biographical and personal information. The coins are unnumbered and checklisted below in alphabetical order.

	NRMT	VG-E	GOOD
COMPLETE SET (12)	30.00	13.50	3.70
COMMON CARD (1-12)	1.00	.45	.12
☐ 1 Luis Aparicio	5.00	2.20	.60
☐ 2 Rod Carew	10.00	4.50	1.25
☐ 3 Rico Carty	1.50	.70	.19
☐ 4 Cesar Cedeno	1.50	.70	.19
☐ 5 Orlando Cepeda	4.00	1.80	.50
☐ 6 Mike Cuellar	1.50	.70	.19
☐ 7 Juan Marichal	5.00	2.20	.60
☐ 8 Felix Millan	1.00	.45	.12
☐ 9 Willie Montanez	1.00	.45	.12
☐ 10 Tony Oliva	3.00	1.35	.35
☐ 11 Tony Perez	4.00	1.80	.50
☐ 12 Manny Sanguillen	1.50	.70	.19

1949 Eureka Stamps

This set features National League players only. Apparently the promotion was not successful enough to warrant continuing on to do the American League, even though it was pre-announced in the back of the stamp album. Album is available to house the stamps. The album measures 7 1/2" by 9 1/4" whereas the individual stamps measure approximately 1 1/2" by 2". The stamps are numbered and are in full color. The album and stamp numbering is organized by teams (and alphabetically within teams), e.g., Boston Braves (3-27), Brooklyn Dodgers (28-51), Chicago Cubs (52-75), Cincinnati Reds (76-100), New York Giants (101-126), Philadelphia Phillies (127-151), Pittsburgh Pirates (152-176) and St. Louis Cardinals (177-200). At the bottom of the stamp the player's name is given in a narrow yellow strip.

	NRMT	VG-E	GOOD
COMPLETE SET (200)	1000.00	450.00	125.00
COMMON STAMP (1-200)	3.00	1.35	.35
☐ 1 Happy Chandler COMM	10.00	4.50	1.25
☐ 2 Ford Frick PRES	10.00	4.50	1.25
☐ 3 Johnny Antonelli	4.00	1.80	.50
☐ 4 Red Barrett	3.00	1.35	.35
☐ 5 Clint Conatser	3.00	1.35	.35
☐ 6 Alvin Dark	6.00	2.70	.75
☐ 7 Bob Elliott	4.00	1.80	.50
☐ 8 Glenn Elliott	3.00	1.35	.35
☐ 9 Elbie Fletcher	3.00	1.35	.35
☐ 10 Bob Hall	3.00	1.35	.35
☐ 11 Jeff Heath	3.00	1.35	.35
☐ 12 Bobby Hogue	3.00	1.35	.35
☐ 13 Tommy Holmes	4.00	1.80	.50
☐ 14 Al Lakeman	3.00	1.35	.35
☐ 15 Phil Masi	3.00	1.35	.35
☐ 16 Nelson Potter	3.00	1.35	.35
☐ 17 Pete Reiser	6.00	2.70	.75
☐ 18 Rick Rickert	3.00	1.35	.35
☐ 19 Connie Ryan	3.00	1.35	.35
☐ 20 Jim Russell	3.00	1.35	.35
☐ 21 Johnny Sain	6.00	2.70	.75
☐ 22 Bill Salkeld	3.00	1.35	.35
☐ 23 Sibby Sisti	3.00	1.35	.35
☐ 24 Billy Southworth MG	3.00	1.35	.35
☐ 25 Warren Spahn	30.00	13.50	3.70
☐ 26 Eddie Stanky	5.00	2.20	.60
☐ 27 Bill Voiselle	3.00	1.35	.35
☐ 28 Jack Banta	3.00	1.35	.35
☐ 29 Rex Barney	4.00	1.80	.50
☐ 30 Ralph Branca	6.00	2.70	.75
☐ 31 Tommy Brown	3.00	1.35	.35
☐ 32 Roy Campanella	40.00	18.00	5.00
☐ 33 Billy Cox	4.00	1.80	.50
☐ 34 Bruce Edwards	3.00	1.35	.35
☐ 35 Carl Furillo	10.00	4.50	1.25
☐ 36 Joe Hatten	3.00	1.35	.35
☐ 37 Gene Hermanski	3.00	1.35	.35
☐ 38 Gil Hodges	20.00	9.00	2.50
☐ 39 Johnny Jorgensen	3.00	1.35	.35
☐ 40 Lefty Martin	3.00	1.35	.35
☐ 41 Mike McCormick	3.00	1.35	.35
☐ 42 Eddie Miksis	3.00	1.35	.35
☐ 43 Paul Minner	3.00	1.35	.35
☐ 44 Sam Narron	3.00	1.35	.35
☐ 45 Don Newcombe	10.00	4.50	1.25
☐ 46 Jake Pitler CO	3.00	1.35	.35
☐ 47 Pee Wee Reese	30.00	13.50	3.70
☐ 48 Jackie Robinson	60.00	27.00	7.50
☐ 49 Burt Shotton MG	3.00	1.35	.35
☐ 50 Duke Snider	40.00	18.00	5.00
☐ 51 Dick Whitman	3.00	1.35	.35
☐ 52 Smoky Burgess	4.00	1.80	.50
☐ 53 Phil Cavarretta	4.00	1.80	.50
☐ 54 Bob Chipman	3.00	1.35	.35
☐ 55 Walt Dubiel	3.00	1.35	.35
☐ 56 Hank Edwards	3.00	1.35	.35
☐ 57 Frankie Gustine	3.00	1.35	.35
☐ 58 Hal Jeffcoat	3.00	1.35	.35
☐ 59 Emil Kush	3.00	1.35	.35
☐ 60 Doyle Lade	3.00	1.35	.35
☐ 61 Dutch Leonard	3.00	1.35	.35
☐ 62 Peanuts Lowrey	3.00	1.35	.35
☐ 63 Gene Mauch	5.00	2.20	.60
☐ 64 Cal McLish	3.00	1.35	.35
☐ 65 Rube Novotney	3.00	1.35	.35
☐ 66 Andy Pafko	4.00	1.80	.50
☐ 67 Bob Ramazzotti	3.00	1.35	.35
☐ 68 Herman Reich	3.00	1.35	.35
☐ 69 Bob Rush	3.00	1.35	.35
☐ 70 Johnny Schmitz	3.00	1.35	.35
☐ 71 Bob Scheffing	3.00	1.35	.35
☐ 72 Roy Smalley	4.00	1.80	.50
☐ 73 Emil Verban	3.00	1.35	.35
☐ 74 Al Walker	3.00	1.35	.35
☐ 75 Harry Walker	4.00	1.80	.50
☐ 76 Bobby Adams	3.00	1.35	.35
☐ 77 Ewell Blackwell	5.00	2.20	.60
☐ 78 Jimmy Bloodworth	3.00	1.35	.35
☐ 79 Walker Cooper	3.00	1.35	.35
☐ 80 Tony Cuccinello	3.00	1.35	.35
☐ 81 Jess Dobernick	3.00	1.35	.35
☐ 82 Eddie Erautt	3.00	1.35	.35
☐ 83 Frank Fanovich	3.00	1.35	.35
☐ 84 Howie Fox	3.00	1.35	.35
☐ 85 Grady Hatton	3.00	1.35	.35
☐ 86 Homer Howell	3.00	1.35	.35
☐ 87 Ted Kluszewski	10.00	4.50	1.25
☐ 88 Danny Litwhiler	3.00	1.35	.35
☐ 89 Everett Lively	3.00	1.35	.35
☐ 90 Lloyd Merriman	3.00	1.35	.35
☐ 91 Phil Page	3.00	1.35	.35
☐ 92 Kent Peterson	3.00	1.35	.35
☐ 93 Ken Raffensberger	3.00	1.35	.35
☐ 94 Luke Sewell CO	4.00	1.80	.50
☐ 95 Virgil Stallcup	3.00	1.35	.35
☐ 96 John Vander Meer	6.00	2.70	.75
☐ 97 Bucky Walters MG	5.00	2.20	.60
☐ 98 Herman Wehmeier	3.00	1.35	.35
☐ 99 Johnny Wyrostek	3.00	1.35	.35
☐ 100 Benny Zientara	3.00	1.35	.35
☐ 101 Hank Behrman	3.00	1.35	.35
☐ 102 Leo Durocher MG	10.00	4.50	1.25
☐ 103 Augie Galan	3.00	1.35	.35
☐ 104 Sid Gordon	3.00	1.35	.35
☐ 105 Bert Haas	3.00	1.35	.35
☐ 106 Andy Hansen	3.00	1.35	.35
☐ 107 Clint Hartung	4.00	1.80	.50
☐ 108 Kirby Higbe	3.00	1.35	.35
☐ 109 George Hausman	3.00	1.35	.35
☐ 110 Larry Jansen	4.00	1.80	.50
☐ 111 Sheldon Jones	3.00	1.35	.35
☐ 112 Monte Kennedy	3.00	1.35	.35
☐ 113 Buddy Kerr	3.00	1.35	.35
☐ 114 Dave Koslo	3.00	1.35	.35
☐ 115 Joe Lafata	3.00	1.35	.35
☐ 116 Whitey Lockman	4.00	1.80	.50
☐ 117 Jack Lohrke	3.00	1.35	.35
☐ 118 Willard Marshall	3.00	1.35	.35
☐ 119 Bill Milne	3.00	1.35	.35
☐ 120 Johnny Mize	20.00	9.00	2.50
☐ 121 Don Mueller	5.00	2.20	.60
☐ 122 Ray Mueller	3.00	1.35	.35
☐ 123 Bill Rigney	4.00	1.80	.50
☐ 124 Bobby Thomson	6.00	2.70	.75
☐ 125 Sam Webb	3.00	1.35	.35
☐ 126 Wes Westrum	4.00	1.80	.50
☐ 127 Richie Ashburn	20.00	9.00	2.50
☐ 128 Bennie Bengough CO	3.00	1.35	.35
☐ 129 Charlie Bicknell	3.00	1.35	.35
☐ 130 Buddy Blattner	3.00	1.35	.35
☐ 131 Hank Borowy	3.00	1.35	.35
☐ 132 Ralph Caballero	3.00	1.35	.35
☐ 133 Blix Donnelly	3.00	1.35	.35
☐ 134 Del Ennis	4.00	1.80	.50
☐ 135 Granville Hamner	4.00	1.80	.50
☐ 136 Ken Heintzelman	3.00	1.35	.35
☐ 137 Stan Hollmig	3.00	1.35	.35
☐ 138 Willie Jones	3.00	1.35	.35
☐ 139 Jim Konstanty	5.00	2.20	.60
☐ 140 Stan Lopata	3.00	1.35	.35
☐ 141 Jackie Mayo	3.00	1.35	.35
☐ 142 Bill Nicholson	4.00	1.80	.50
☐ 143 Robin Roberts	20.00	9.00	2.50
☐ 144 Schoolboy Rowe	5.00	2.20	.60
☐ 145 Eddie Sawyer MG	4.00	1.80	.50
☐ 146 Andy Seminick	3.00	1.35	.35
☐ 147 Ken Silvestri	3.00	1.35	.35
☐ 148 Curt Simmons	5.00	2.20	.60
☐ 149 Dick Sisler	4.00	1.80	.50
☐ 150 Ken Trinkle	3.00	1.35	.35
☐ 151 Eddie Waitkus	4.00	1.80	.50
☐ 152 Romanus Basgall	3.00	1.35	.35
☐ 153 Eddie Bockman	3.00	1.35	.35
☐ 154 Ernie Bonham	3.00	1.35	.35
☐ 155 Hugh Casey	4.00	1.80	.50
☐ 156 Pete Castiglione	3.00	1.35	.35
☐ 157 Cliff Chambers	3.00	1.35	.35
☐ 158 Murry Dickson	3.00	1.35	.35
☐ 159 Ed Fitzgerald	3.00	1.35	.35
☐ 160 Les Fleming	3.00	1.35	.35
☐ 161 Hal Gregg	3.00	1.35	.35
☐ 162 Goldie Holt	3.00	1.35	.35
☐ 163 Johnny Hopp	4.00	1.80	.50
☐ 164 Ralph Kiner	20.00	9.00	2.50
☐ 165 Vic Lombardi	3.00	1.35	.35
☐ 166 Clyde McCullough	3.00	1.35	.35
☐ 167 Bill Meyer MG	4.00	1.80	.50
☐ 168 Danny Murtaugh	4.00	1.80	.50
☐ 169 Barnacle Bill Posedel	3.00	1.35	.35
☐ 170 Elmer Riddle	3.00	1.35	.35
☐ 171 Stan Rojek	3.00	1.35	.35
☐ 172 Rip Sewell	4.00	1.80	.50
☐ 173 Eddie Stevens	3.00	1.35	.35
☐ 174 Dixie Walker	4.00	1.80	.50
☐ 175 Bill Werle	3.00	1.35	.35
☐ 176 Wally Westlake	3.00	1.35	.35
☐ 177 Bill Baker	3.00	1.35	.35
☐ 178 Al Brazle	3.00	1.35	.35
☐ 179 Harry Brecheen	4.00	1.80	.50
☐ 180 Chuck Diering	3.00	1.35	.35
☐ 181 Eddie Dyer MG	4.00	1.80	.50
☐ 182 Joe Garagiola	20.00	9.00	2.50
☐ 183 Tom Glaviano	3.00	1.35	.35
☐ 184 Jim Hearn	3.00	1.35	.35
☐ 185 Ken Johnson	3.00	1.35	.35
☐ 186 Nippy Jones	3.00	1.35	.35
☐ 187 Ed Kazak	3.00	1.35	.35
☐ 188 Lou Klein	3.00	1.35	.35
☐ 189 Marty Marion	15.00	6.75	1.85
☐ 190 George Munger	3.00	1.35	.35
☐ 191 Stan Musial	50.00	22.00	6.25
☐ 192 Spike Nelson	3.00	1.35	.35
☐ 193 Howie Pollet	3.00	1.35	.35
☐ 194 Bill Reeder	3.00	1.35	.35
☐ 195 Del Rice	3.00	1.35	.35
☐ 196 Ed Sauer	3.00	1.35	.35
☐ 197 Red Schoendienst	15.00	6.75	1.85
☐ 198 Enos Slaughter	20.00	9.00	2.50
☐ 199 Ted Wilks	3.00	1.35	.35
☐ 200 Ray Yochim	3.00	1.35	.35

1921-24 Exhibits

Although the Exhibit Supply Company issued 64 cards in 1921 and 128 cards in each of the following three years, the category of 1921-24 was created because of the large number of pictures found repeated in all four years. Each exhibit card measures 3 3/8" by 5 3/8". The cards of 1921 are characterized by ornate hand-lettered names while the cards of 1922-24 have players' names hand-written in a plainer style. Also for 1921 cards, the abbreviation used for the junior circuit is "Am.L." In contrast, cards of the 1922-24 period have the American League abbreviated "A.L." All the cards in the 1921-24 category are black and white and have blank backs; some have white borders measuring approximately 3/16" in width. There is some mislabeling of pictures, incorrect assignment of proper names and many misspellings. Some of the cards have a horizontal (HOR) orientation.

	EX-MT	VG-E	GOOD
COMPLETE SET (193)	5000.00	2200.00	600.00
COMMON CARD	20.00	9.00	2.50
☐ 1 Chas. B. Adams	25.00	11.00	3.10
☐ 2 Grover C. Alexander	50.00	22.00	6.25
☐ 3 James Bagby	20.00	9.00	2.50
☐ 4 J. Frank Baker	40.00	18.00	5.00
☐ 5 David Bancroft	35.00	16.00	4.40
☐ 6 Walter Barbare	20.00	9.00	2.50
☐ 7 Turner Barber	20.00	9.00	2.50
☐ 8 Clyde Barnhart	20.00	9.00	2.50
☐ 9 John Bassler	20.00	9.00	2.50
☐ 10 Carlson L. Bigbee	20.00	9.00	2.50
☐ 11 Ray Blades	20.00	9.00	2.50
☐ 12 Sam Bohne	20.00	9.00	2.50
☐ 13 James Bottomley	40.00	18.00	5.00
☐ 14 Geo. Burns (Cinn) portrait	20.00	9.00	2.50
☐ 15 Geo. J. Burns (New York NL)	20.00	9.00	2.50
☐ 16 George Burns (Boston AL)	20.00	9.00	2.50
☐ 17 George Burns (Cleveland)	20.00	9.00	2.50
☐ 18 Joe Bush	25.00	11.00	3.10
☐ 19 Owen Bush	20.00	9.00	2.50
☐ 20 Leon Cadore	20.00	9.00	2.50
☐ 21 Max G. Carey	40.00	18.00	5.00
☐ 22 Jim Caveney	20.00	9.00	2.50
☐ 23 Dan Clark	20.00	9.00	2.50
☐ 24 Ty R. Cobb	300.00	135.00	38.00
☐ 25 Eddie T. Collins	50.00	22.00	6.25
☐ 26 John Collins	20.00	9.00	2.50
☐ 27 Wilbur Cooper	20.00	9.00	2.50
☐ 28 Stanley Coveleskie (sic, Coveleski)	40.00	18.00	5.00
☐ 29 Walton E. Cruse (sic, Cruise)	20.00	9.00	2.50
☐ 30 George Cutshaw	20.00	9.00	2.50
☐ 31 Dave Danforth	20.00	9.00	2.50
☐ 32 Jacob E. Daubert	25.00	11.00	3.10
☐ 33 George Dauss	20.00	9.00	2.50
☐ 34 Charles A. Deal	20.00	9.00	2.50
☐ 35 Bill Doak (Brooklyn)	20.00	9.00	2.50
☐ 36 Bill Doak (St. Louis NL)	20.00	9.00	2.50
☐ 37 Joe Dugan (Boston AL)	25.00	11.00	3.10
☐ 38 Joe A. Dugan (New York AL)	25.00	11.00	3.10
☐ 39 Joe A. Dugan (Philadelphia AL)	25.00	11.00	3.10
☐ 40 Pat Duncan	20.00	9.00	2.50
☐ 41 James Dykes	25.00	11.00	3.10
☐ 42 Howard J. Ehmke (Boston AL)	25.00	11.00	3.10
☐ 43 Howard Ehmke (Detroit) (with border)	25.00	11.00	3.10
☐ 44 Wm. Evans (Umpire)	75.00	34.00	9.50
☐ 45 U.C. Red Faber	40.00	18.00	5.00
☐ 46 Bib Falk	20.00	9.00	2.50
☐ 47 Dana Fillingim	20.00	9.00	2.50
☐ 48 Ira Flagstead (Boston AL)	20.00	9.00	2.50
☐ 49 A. Fletcher	20.00	9.00	2.50
☐ 50 J.F. Fournier (Brooklyn)	20.00	9.00	2.50
☐ 51 J.F. Fournier (St. Louis NL)	20.00	9.00	2.50
☐ 52 Howard Freigau	20.00	9.00	2.50
☐ 53 Frank F. Frisch	50.00	22.00	6.25
☐ 54 C.E. Galloway	20.00	9.00	2.50
☐ 55 W.L. Gardner (Cleveland)	20.00	9.00	2.50
☐ 56 Joe Genewich	20.00	9.00	2.50
☐ 57 Wally Gerber	20.00	9.00	2.50
☐ 58 Mike Gonzales	20.00	9.00	2.50
☐ 59 H.M. "Hank" Gowdy (Boston NL)	25.00	11.00	3.10
☐ 60 H.M. "Hank" Gowdy (New York NL)	25.00	11.00	3.10

Card	EX-MT	VG-E	GOOD
☐ 61 Burleigh A. Grimes	40.00	18.00	5.00
☐ 62 Ray Grimes	20.00	9.00	2.50
☐ 63 Charles Grimm	25.00	11.00	3.10
☐ 64 Heinie Groh Cincinnati	25.00	11.00	3.10
☐ 65 Heinie Groh New York NL	25.00	11.00	3.10
☐ 66 Jesse Haines	40.00	18.00	5.00
☐ 67 Chas. L. Hartnett	40.00	18.00	5.00
☐ 68 George Harper	20.00	9.00	2.50
☐ 69 Sam Harris	20.00	9.00	2.50
☐ 70 Slim Harris	20.00	9.00	2.50
☐ 71 Clifton Heathcote	20.00	9.00	2.50
☐ 72 Harry Heilmann	50.00	22.00	6.25
☐ 73 Andy High	20.00	9.00	2.50
☐ 74 George Hildebrand UMP	25.00	11.00	3.10
☐ 75 Walter L. Holke Boston NL	20.00	9.00	2.50
☐ 76 Walter L. Holke Philadelphia NL	20.00	9.00	2.50
☐ 77 Chas.J. Hollicher sic, Hollocher	20.00	9.00	2.50
☐ 78 Rogers Hornsby	75.00	34.00	9.50
☐ 79 Wilbert Hubbell	20.00	9.00	2.50
☐ 80 Bill Jacobson	20.00	9.00	2.50
☐ 81 Charles D. Jamieson	20.00	9.00	2.50
☐ 82 E.R. Johnson	20.00	9.00	2.50
☐ 83 James H. Johnson	20.00	9.00	2.50
☐ 84 Walter P. Johnson	125.00	55.00	15.50
☐ 85 Sam P. Jones	20.00	9.00	2.50
☐ 86 Joe Judge	20.00	9.00	2.50
☐ 87 Willie Kamm	20.00	9.00	2.50
☐ 88 Tony Kaufman	20.00	9.00	2.50
☐ 89 George L. Kelly	40.00	18.00	5.00
☐ 90 Dick Kerr	25.00	11.00	3.10
☐ 91 William L. Killefer	20.00	9.00	2.50
☐ 92 Bill Klem UMP	75.00	34.00	9.50
☐ 93 Ed Konetchy	20.00	9.00	2.50
☐ 94 John "Doc" Lavan	20.00	9.00	2.50
☐ 95 Dudley Lee	20.00	9.00	2.50
☐ 96 Harry Liebold Boston AL	20.00	9.00	2.50
☐ 97 Harry Liebold Washington with border	20.00	9.00	2.50
☐ 98 Adolph Luque	25.00	11.00	3.10
☐ 99 Walter Mails	20.00	9.00	2.50
☐ 100 Geo. Maisel	20.00	9.00	2.50
☐ 101 Walt. J. Maranville	40.00	18.00	5.00
☐ 102 W.C. (Wid) Matthews	20.00	9.00	2.50
☐ 103 Carl W. Mays	25.00	11.00	3.10
☐ 104 John McGraw	50.00	22.00	6.25
☐ 105 J. Stuffy McInnis Boston AL	25.00	11.00	3.10
☐ 106 J. Stuffy McInnis Boston NL	25.00	11.00	3.10
☐ 107 Lee Meadows	20.00	9.00	2.50
☐ 108 Clyde Milan	20.00	9.00	2.50
☐ 109 Ed (Bing) Miller	20.00	9.00	2.50
☐ 110 Hack Miller	20.00	9.00	2.50
☐ 111 George Moriarty UMP	25.00	11.00	3.10
☐ 112 Johnny Morrison	20.00	9.00	2.50
☐ 113 John A. Mostil	20.00	9.00	2.50
☐ 114 Robert Meusel	25.00	11.00	3.10
☐ 115 Harry Myers	20.00	9.00	2.50
☐ 116 Rollie C. Naylor	20.00	9.00	2.50
☐ 117 A. Earl Neale	25.00	11.00	3.10
☐ 118 Arthur Nehf	25.00	11.00	3.10
☐ 119 Joe Oeschger	20.00	9.00	2.50
☐ 120 Ivan M. Olson	20.00	9.00	2.50
☐ 121 Geo. O'Neil	20.00	9.00	2.50
☐ 122 S.F."Steve" O'Neil sic, O'Neill	25.00	11.00	3.10
☐ 123 J.F. O'Neill	20.00	9.00	2.50
☐ 124 Ernest Padgett	20.00	9.00	2.50
☐ 125 Roger Peckinpaugh New York AL with border	25.00	11.00	3.10
☐ 126 Peckinpaugh Washington	25.00	11.00	3.10
☐ 127 Ralph "Cy" Perkins	20.00	9.00	2.50
☐ 128 Val Picinich Boston AL	20.00	9.00	2.50
☐ 129 Val Picinich Washington	20.00	9.00	2.50
☐ 130 Bill Piercy light background	20.00	9.00	2.50
☐ 131 Bill Piercy dark background	20.00	9.00	2.50
☐ 132 Herman Pillett	20.00	9.00	2.50
☐ 133 Wally Pipp	25.00	11.00	3.10
☐ 134 Raymond R. Powell light background	20.00	9.00	2.50
☐ 135 Raymond R. Powell dark background	20.00	9.00	2.50
☐ 136 Del Pratt Detroit	20.00	9.00	2.50
☐ 137 Derrill Pratt Boston AL	20.00	9.00	2.50
☐ 138 Joe "Goldie" Rapp	20.00	9.00	2.50
☐ 139 Walter Reuther	20.00	9.00	2.50
☐ 140 Edgar S. Rice	40.00	18.00	5.00
☐ 141 Cy Rigler UMP	25.00	11.00	3.10
☐ 142 E. E. Rigney	20.00	9.00	2.50
☐ 143 Jimmy Ring	20.00	9.00	2.50
☐ 144 Eppa Rixey	40.00	18.00	5.00
☐ 145 Chas. Robertson	20.00	9.00	2.50
☐ 146 Eddie Rommel	25.00	11.00	3.10
☐ 147 Muddy Ruel	20.00	9.00	2.50
☐ 148 George H. Babe Ruth	400.00	180.00	50.00
☐ 149 George H. Babe Ruth with border	800.00	350.00	100.00
☐ 150 J. H. Sand	20.00	9.00	2.50
☐ 151 Ray W. Schalk	40.00	18.00	5.00
☐ 152 Wallie Schang	25.00	11.00	3.10
☐ 153 Everett Scott Boston AL	25.00	11.00	3.10
☐ 154 Everett Scott New York AL	25.00	11.00	3.10
☐ 155 Harry Severeid	20.00	9.00	2.50
☐ 156 Joseph Sewell	40.00	18.00	5.00
☐ 157 H.S. Shanks photo actually Wally Schang	20.00	9.00	2.50
☐ 158 Earl Sheely	20.00	9.00	2.50
☐ 159 Urban Shocker	25.00	11.00	3.10
☐ 160 Al Simmons	50.00	22.00	6.25
☐ 161 George H. Sisler	50.00	22.00	6.25
☐ 162 Earl Smith New York NL with border	20.00	9.00	2.50
☐ 163 Earl Smith New York NL 2/3 shot	20.00	9.00	2.50
☐ 164 Elmer Smith Boston AL	20.00	9.00	2.50
☐ 165 Jack Smith	20.00	9.00	2.50
☐ 166 R.E. Smith	20.00	9.00	2.50
☐ 167 Sherrod Smith Brooklyn	20.00	9.00	2.50
☐ 168 Sherrod Smith Cleveland	20.00	9.00	2.50
☐ 169 Frank Snyder	20.00	9.00	2.50
☐ 170 Allan Sothoron	20.00	9.00	2.50
☐ 171 Tris Speaker	75.00	34.00	9.50
☐ 172 Arnold Statz	20.00	9.00	2.50
☐ 173 Casey Stengel	75.00	34.00	9.50
☐ 174 J.R. Stevenson	20.00	9.00	2.50
☐ 175 Milton Stock	20.00	9.00	2.50
☐ 176 James Tierney Boston NL	20.00	9.00	2.50
☐ 177 James Tierney Pittsburgh	20.00	9.00	2.50
☐ 178 John Tobin	20.00	9.00	2.50
☐ 179 George Toporcer	20.00	9.00	2.50
☐ 180 Robert Veach	20.00	9.00	2.50
☐ 181 Clar.(Tillie)Walker	20.00	9.00	2.50
☐ 182 Curtis Walker	20.00	9.00	2.50
☐ 183 Aaron Ward	20.00	9.00	2.50
☐ 184 Zack D. Wheat	40.00	18.00	5.00
☐ 185 Geo. B. Whitted	20.00	9.00	2.50
☐ 186 Cy Williams	20.00	9.00	2.50
☐ 187 Kenneth R. Williams	25.00	11.00	3.10
☐ 188 Ivy B. Wingo	20.00	9.00	2.50
☐ 189 Joe Wood	30.00	13.50	3.70
☐ 190 L. Woodall	20.00	9.00	2.50
☐ 191 Russell G.Wrightstone	20.00	9.00	2.50
☐ 192 Moses Yellowhorse	20.00	9.00	2.50
☐ 193 Ross Youngs	50.00	22.00	6.25

1925 Exhibits

The most dramatic change in the 1925 series from that of the preceding group was the printed legend which appeared for the first time in this printing. The subject's name, position, team and the line "(Made in U.S.A.)" appear on four separate lines in a bottom corner, enclosed in a small white box. The name of the player is printed in large capitals while the other lines are of a smaller type size. The cards are black and white, have plain backs and are unnumbered. Each exhibit card measures 3 3/8" by 5 3/8". There are 128 cards in the set and numerous misspellings exist. Note: the card marked "Robert Veach" does not picture that player, but is thought to contain a photo of Ernest Vache. A few of the cards are presented in a horizontal (HOR) format. Players are arranged below in alphabetical order by team: Boston NL 1-8, Brooklyn 9-16, Chicago 17-24, Cincinnati 25-32, New York 33-40, Philadelphia 41-48, Pittsburgh 49-56, St. Louis 57-64, Boston AL 65-72, Chicago 73-80, Cleveland 81-88, Detroit 89-96, New York 97-104, Philadelphia 105-112, St. Louis 113-120 and Washington 121-128.

	EX-MT	VG-E	GOOD
COMPLETE SET (128)	8000.00	3600.00	1000.00
COMMON CARD	50.00	22.00	6.25
☐ 1 David Bancroft	75.00	34.00	9.50
☐ 2 Jesse Barnes	50.00	22.00	6.25
☐ 3 Lawrence Benton	50.00	22.00	6.25
☐ 4 Maurice Burrus	50.00	22.00	6.25
☐ 5 Joseph Genewich	50.00	22.00	6.25
☐ 6 Frank Gibson	50.00	22.00	6.25
☐ 7 David Harris	50.00	22.00	6.25
☐ 8 George O'Neil	50.00	22.00	6.25
☐ 9 John H. Deberry	50.00	22.00	6.25
☐ 10 Art Decatur	50.00	22.00	6.25
☐ 11 Jacques F. Fournier	50.00	22.00	6.25
☐ 12 Burleigh A. Grimes	75.00	34.00	9.50
☐ 13 James H. Johnson sic, Johnston	50.00	22.00	6.25
☐ 14 Milton J. Stock	50.00	22.00	6.25
☐ 15 A.C. Dazzy Vance	75.00	34.00	9.50
☐ 16 Zack Wheat	100.00	45.00	12.50
☐ 17 Sparky Adams	50.00	22.00	6.25
☐ 18 Grover C. Alexander	150.00	70.00	19.00
☐ 19 John Brooks	50.00	22.00	6.25
☐ 20 Howard Freigau	50.00	22.00	6.25
☐ 21 Charles Grimm	60.00	27.00	7.50
☐ 22 Leo Hartnett	75.00	34.00	9.50
☐ 23 Walter Maranville	75.00	34.00	9.50
☐ 24 A.J. Weis	50.00	22.00	6.25
☐ 25 Raymond Bressler	50.00	22.00	6.25
☐ 26 Hugh M. Critz	50.00	22.00	6.25
☐ 27 Peter Donohue	50.00	22.00	6.25
☐ 28 Charles Dressen	60.00	27.00	7.50
☐ 29 John (Stuffy) McInnes (McInnis)	60.00	27.00	7.50
☐ 30 Eppa Rixey	75.00	34.00	9.50
☐ 31 Ed. Roush	100.00	45.00	12.50
☐ 32 Ivy Wingo	50.00	22.00	6.25
☐ 33 Frank Frisch	150.00	70.00	19.00
☐ 34 Heine Groh	60.00	27.00	7.50
☐ 35 Travis C. Jackson	75.00	34.00	9.50
☐ 36 Emil Meusel	50.00	22.00	6.25
☐ 37 Arthur Nehf	60.00	27.00	7.50
☐ 38 Frank Snyder	50.00	22.00	6.25
☐ 39 Wm. H. Southworth	60.00	27.00	7.50
☐ 40 William Terry	150.00	70.00	19.00
☐ 41 George Harper	50.00	22.00	6.25
☐ 42 Nelson Hawks	50.00	22.00	6.25
☐ 43 Walter Henline	50.00	22.00	6.25
☐ 44 Walter Holke	50.00	22.00	6.25
☐ 45 Wilbur Hubbell	50.00	22.00	6.25
☐ 46 John Mokan	50.00	22.00	6.25
☐ 47 John Sand	50.00	22.00	6.25
☐ 48 Fred Williams	50.00	22.00	6.25
☐ 49 Carson Bigbee	50.00	22.00	6.25
☐ 50 Max Carey	75.00	34.00	9.50
☐ 51 Hazen Cuyler	75.00	34.00	9.50
☐ 52 George Grantham	50.00	22.00	6.25
☐ 53 Ray Kremer	50.00	22.00	6.25
☐ 54 Earl Smith	50.00	22.00	6.25
☐ 55 Harold Traynor	125.00	55.00	15.50
☐ 56 Glenn Wright	50.00	22.00	6.25
☐ 57 Lester Bell HOR	50.00	22.00	6.25
☐ 58 Raymond Blates sic, Blades	50.00	22.00	6.25
☐ 59 James Bottomly sic, Bottomley	100.00	45.00	12.50
☐ 60 Max Flack	50.00	22.00	6.25
☐ 61 Rogers Hornsby	200.00	90.00	25.00
☐ 62 Clarence Mueller	50.00	22.00	6.25
☐ 63 William Sherdell	50.00	22.00	6.25
☐ 64 George Toporcer	50.00	22.00	6.25
☐ 65 Howard Ehmke	60.00	27.00	7.50
☐ 66 Ira Flagstead	50.00	22.00	6.25
☐ 67 I.Valentine Picinich	50.00	22.00	6.25
☐ 68 John Quinn	50.00	22.00	6.25
☐ 69 Charles Ruffing	100.00	45.00	12.50
☐ 70 Philip Todt	50.00	22.00	6.25
☐ 71 Robert Veach	50.00	22.00	6.25
☐ 72 William Wambsganss	50.00	22.00	6.25
☐ 73 Eddie Collins	100.00	45.00	12.50
☐ 74 Bib Falk	50.00	22.00	6.25
☐ 75 Harry Hooper	100.00	45.00	12.50
☐ 76 Willie Kamm	50.00	22.00	6.25
☐ 77 I.M. Davis	50.00	22.00	6.25
☐ 78 Ray Shalk (Schalk)	75.00	34.00	9.50
☐ 79 Earl Sheely	50.00	22.00	6.25
☐ 80 Hollis Thurston	50.00	22.00	6.25
☐ 81 Wilson Fewster	50.00	22.00	6.25
☐ 82 Charles Jamieson	50.00	22.00	6.25
☐ 83 Walter Lutzke	50.00	22.00	6.25
☐ 84 Glenn Myatt	50.00	22.00	6.25
☐ 85 Joseph Sewell	75.00	34.00	9.50
☐ 86 Sherrod Smith	50.00	22.00	6.25
☐ 87 Tristram Speaker	175.00	80.00	22.00
☐ 88 Homer Summa	50.00	22.00	6.25
☐ 89 John Bassler	50.00	22.00	6.25
☐ 90 Tyrus Cobb	800.00	350.00	100.00
☐ 91 George Dauss	50.00	22.00	6.25
☐ 92 Harry Heilmann	100.00	45.00	12.50
☐ 93 Frank O'Rourke	50.00	22.00	6.25
☐ 94 Emory Rigney	50.00	22.00	6.25
☐ 95 Al Wings(Wingo) HOR	50.00	22.00	6.25
☐ 96 Larry Woodall	50.00	22.00	6.25
☐ 97 Henry L. Gehrig	800.00	350.00	100.00
☐ 98 Robert W. Muesel sic, Meusel	60.00	27.00	7.50
☐ 99 Walter C. Pipp	100.00	45.00	12.50
☐ 100 George H. Babe Ruth	1000.00	450.00	125.00
☐ 101 Walter H. Shang sic, Schang	60.00	27.00	7.50
☐ 102 J.R. Shawkey	60.00	27.00	7.50
☐ 103 Urban J. Shocker	60.00	27.00	7.50
☐ 104 Aaron Ward	50.00	22.00	6.25
☐ 105 Max Bishop	50.00	22.00	6.25
☐ 106 James J. Dykes	60.00	27.00	7.50
☐ 107 Samuel Gray	50.00	22.00	6.25
☐ 108 Samuel Hale	50.00	22.00	6.25
☐ 109 Edmund(Bind) Miller sic, Bing	50.00	22.00	6.25
☐ 110 Ralph Perkins	50.00	22.00	6.25
☐ 111 Edwin Rommel	60.00	27.00	7.50
☐ 112 Frank Welch	50.00	22.00	6.25
☐ 113 Walter Gerber	50.00	22.00	6.25
☐ 114 William Jacobson	50.00	22.00	6.25
☐ 115 Martin McManus	50.00	22.00	6.25
☐ 116 Henry Severid sic, Severeid	50.00	22.00	6.25
☐ 117 George Sissler sic, Sisler	150.00	70.00	19.00
☐ 118 John Tobin	50.00	22.00	6.25
☐ 119 Kenneth Williams	50.00	22.00	6.25
☐ 120 Ernest Wingard	50.00	22.00	6.25
☐ 121 Oswald Bluege	50.00	22.00	6.25
☐ 122 Stanley Coveleski	75.00	34.00	9.50
☐ 123 Leon Goslin	100.00	45.00	12.50
☐ 124 Stanley Harris	75.00	34.00	9.50
☐ 125 Walter Johnson	300.00	135.00	38.00
☐ 126 Joseph Judge	60.00	27.00	7.50
☐ 127 Earl McNeely	50.00	22.00	6.25
☐ 128 Harold Ruel	50.00	22.00	6.25

1926 Exhibits

The year 1926 marked the last of the 128-card sets produced by Exhibit Supply. Of this number, 70 cards are identical to those issued in 1925 but are easily identified because of the new blue-gray color introduced in 1926. Another 21 cards use 1925 pictures but contain the line "Ex. Sup. Co., U.S.A."; these are marked with an asterisk in the checklist below. The 37 photos new to this set have an unboxed legend and carry the new company line. Bischoff is incorrectly placed with Boston, N.L. (should be A.L.); the picture of Galloway is reversed; the photos of Hunnefield and Thomas are wrongly exchanged. Each exhibit card measures 3 3/8" by 5 3/8". Players are in alphabetical order by team: Boston NL 1-8, Brooklyn 9-16, Chicago 17-24, Cincinnati 25-32, New York 33-40, Philadelphia 41-48, Pittsburgh 49-56, St. Louis 57-64, Boston AL 65-72, Chicago 73-80, Cleveland 81-88, Detroit 89-96, New York 97-104, Philadelphia 105-112, St. Louis 113-120 and Washington 121-128.

	EX-MT	VG-E	GOOD
COMPLETE SET (128)	8000.00	3600.00	1000.00
COMMON CARD	50.00	22.00	6.25
☐ 1 Lawrence Benton	50.00	22.00	6.25
☐ 2 Andrew High	50.00	22.00	6.25
☐ 3 Maurice Burrus	50.00	22.00	6.25
☐ 4 David Bancroft	75.00	34.00	9.50
☐ 5 Joseph Genewich	50.00	22.00	6.25
☐ 6 Bernie F. Neis	50.00	22.00	6.25
☐ 7 Edward Taylor	50.00	22.00	6.25
☐ 8 J. Taylor	50.00	22.00	6.25
☐ 9 John Butler	50.00	22.00	6.25
☐ 10 Jacques F. Furnier (sic, Fournier) *	50.00	22.00	6.25
☐ 11 Burleigh A.Grimes	75.00	34.00	9.50
☐ 12 Wilson Fewster	50.00	22.00	6.25
☐ 13 Douglas McWeeny	50.00	22.00	6.25
☐ 14 George O'Neil	50.00	22.00	6.25
☐ 15 Walter Maranville	75.00	34.00	9.50
☐ 16 Zach Wheat	100.00	45.00	12.50
☐ 17 Sparky Adams	50.00	22.00	6.25
☐ 18 J. Fred Blake	50.00	22.00	6.25
☐ 19 James E. Cooney	50.00	22.00	6.25
☐ 20 Howard Freigau	50.00	22.00	6.25
☐ 21 Charles Grimm	60.00	27.00	7.50
☐ 22 Leo Hartnett	75.00	34.00	9.50
☐ 23 C.E. Heathcote	50.00	22.00	6.25
☐ 24 Joseph M. Munson	50.00	22.00	6.25
☐ 25 Raymond Bressler	50.00	22.00	6.25
☐ 26 Hugh M. Critz	50.00	22.00	6.25
☐ 27 Peter Donohue	50.00	22.00	6.25
☐ 28 Charles Dressen	60.00	27.00	7.50
☐ 29 Walter C. Pipp	75.00	34.00	9.50
☐ 30 Eppa Rixey	75.00	34.00	9.50
☐ 31 Ed. Roush	100.00	45.00	12.50
☐ 32 Ivy Wingo	50.00	22.00	6.25
☐ 33 Edward S. Farrell	50.00	22.00	6.25
☐ 34 Frank Frisch	150.00	70.00	19.00
☐ 35 Frank Snyder	50.00	22.00	6.25
☐ 36 Fredrick Lindstrom (sic, Frederick) *	100.00	45.00	12.50
☐ 37 Hugh A.McQuillan	50.00	22.00	6.25
☐ 38 Emil Musel (sic, Meusel)	50.00	22.00	6.25
☐ 39 James J. Ring	50.00	22.00	6.25
☐ 40 William Terry	150.00	70.00	19.00

Card	EX-MT	VG-E	GOOD
☐ 41 John M. Bentley	50.00	22.00	6.25
☐ 42 Bernard Friberg	50.00	22.00	6.25
☐ 43 George Harper	50.00	22.00	6.25
☐ 44 Walter Henline	50.00	22.00	6.25
☐ 45 Clarence Huber	50.00	22.00	6.25
☐ 46 John Makan	50.00	22.00	6.25
(sic, Mokan)			
☐ 47 John Sand	50.00	22.00	6.25
☐ 48 Russell Wrigtstone	50.00	22.00	6.25
(sic, Wrightstone) *			
☐ 49 Carson Bigbee	50.00	22.00	6.25
☐ 50 Max Carey	75.00	34.00	9.50
☐ 51 Hazen Cuyler	75.00	34.00	9.50
☐ 52 George Grantham	50.00	22.00	6.25
☐ 53 Ray Kremer	50.00	22.00	6.25
☐ 54 Earl Smith	50.00	22.00	6.25
☐ 55 Harold Traynor	110.00	50.00	14.00
☐ 56 Glen Wright	50.00	22.00	6.25
☐ 57 Lester Bell	50.00	22.00	6.25
☐ 58 Raymond Blates	50.00	22.00	6.25
(sic, Blades)			
☐ 59 James Bottomly	100.00	45.00	12.50
(sic, Bottomley)			
☐ 60 Rogers Hornsby	175.00	80.00	22.00
☐ 61 Clarence Mueller	50.00	22.00	6.25
☐ 62 Robert O'Farrell	50.00	22.00	6.25
☐ 63 William Sherdell	50.00	22.00	6.25
☐ 64 George Torporcer	50.00	22.00	6.25
☐ 65 Ira Flagstead	50.00	22.00	6.25
☐ 66 Fred Haney	60.00	27.00	7.50
☐ 67 Ramon Herrera	50.00	22.00	6.25
☐ 68 John Quinn	50.00	22.00	6.25
☐ 69 Emory Rigney	50.00	22.00	6.25
☐ 70 Charles Ruffing	100.00	45.00	12.50
☐ 71 Philip Todt	50.00	22.00	6.25
☐ 72 Fred Wingfield	50.00	22.00	6.25
☐ 73 Ted Blankenship	50.00	22.00	6.25
☐ 74 Eddie Collins	100.00	45.00	12.50
☐ 75 Bib Falk	50.00	22.00	6.25
☐ 76 Wm. Hunnefield	50.00	22.00	6.25
(sic, Tommy Thomas)			
☐ 77 Willie Kamm	50.00	22.00	6.25
☐ 78 Ray Shalk (Schalk)	75.00	34.00	9.50
☐ 79 Earl Sheely	50.00	22.00	6.25
☐ 80 Hollis Thurston	50.00	22.00	6.25
☐ 81 Geo.H. Burns HOR	50.00	22.00	6.25
☐ 82 Walter Lutzke	50.00	22.00	6.25
☐ 83 Glenn Myatt	50.00	22.00	6.25
☐ 84 Joseph Sewell	75.00	34.00	9.50
☐ 85 Sherrod Smith	50.00	22.00	6.25
☐ 86 Tristram Speaker	175.00	80.00	22.00
☐ 87 Fred Spurgeon	50.00	22.00	6.25
☐ 88 Homer Summa	50.00	22.00	6.25
☐ 89 John Bassler	50.00	22.00	6.25
☐ 90 Lucerne Blue	50.00	22.00	6.25
(sic, Luzerne)			
☐ 91 Tyrus Cobb	750.00	350.00	95.00
☐ 92 George Dauss	50.00	22.00	6.25
☐ 93 Harry Heilmann	100.00	45.00	12.50
☐ 94 Frank O'Rourke	50.00	22.00	6.25
☐ 95 Charles Gehringer	150.00	70.00	19.00
(batting)			
☐ 96 John Warner	50.00	22.00	6.25
☐ 97 Patrick T.Collins	50.00	22.00	6.25
☐ 98 Earl B. Combs	100.00	45.00	12.50
☐ 99 Henry L. Gehrig	750.00	350.00	95.00
☐ 100 Anthony Lazzeri	75.00	34.00	9.50
☐ 101 Robert W. Muesel	60.00	27.00	7.50
(sic, Meusel)			
☐ 102 Geo. H. Babe Ruth	1000.00	450.00	125.00
☐ 103 J. R. Shawkey	60.00	27.00	7.50
☐ 104 Urban J. Shocker	60.00	27.00	7.50
☐ 105 Max Bishop	50.00	22.00	6.25
☐ 106 Joseph Galloway	50.00	22.00	6.25
☐ 107 James J. Dykes	60.00	27.00	7.50
☐ 108 Joseph Hauser	50.00	22.00	6.25
☐ 109 Edmund(Bind) Miller	50.00	22.00	6.25
(sic, Bing)			
☐ 110 Ralph Perkins	50.00	22.00	6.25
☐ 111 Edwin Rommel	60.00	27.00	7.50
☐ 112 Wm. Wambsganss	50.00	22.00	6.25
☐ 113 Wm. Hargrave	50.00	22.00	6.25
☐ 114 William Jacobson	50.00	22.00	6.25
☐ 115 Martin McManus	50.00	22.00	6.25
☐ 116 Oscar Melillo	50.00	22.00	6.25
☐ 117 Walter Gerber	50.00	22.00	6.25
☐ 118 George Sissler	150.00	70.00	19.00
(sic, Sisler)			
☐ 119 Kenneth Williams	50.00	22.00	6.25
☐ 120 Ernest Wingard	50.00	22.00	6.25
☐ 121 Oswald Bluege	50.00	22.00	6.25
☐ 122 Stanley Coveleski	75.00	34.00	9.50
☐ 123 Leon Goslin	75.00	34.00	9.50
☐ 124 Stanley Harris	75.00	34.00	9.50
☐ 125 Walter Johnson	300.00	135.00	38.00
☐ 126 Joseph Judge	50.00	22.00	6.25
☐ 127 Earl McNeely	50.00	22.00	6.25
☐ 128 Harold Ruel	50.00	22.00	6.25

1927 Exhibits

Two innovations characterize the 64-card set produced by Exhibit Supply Company for 1927. The first was a radical departure from the color scheme of previous sets marked by this year's light green hue. The second was the installation of the divided legend, whereby the

player's name (all caps) and team were set in one corner, and the lines "Ex. Sup. Co., Chgo." and "Made in U.S.A." were set in the other. All the photos employed in this set were taken from the previous issues in 1925 and 1926, although 13 players appear with new teams. The usual misspellings and incorrect labeling of names and initials occurs throughout the set. Note: Genewich and Hunnefield have a different style of print, and Myatt is missing the right side of the legend. Each card measures 3 3/8" by 5 3/8". Players are listed in alphabetical order by team: Boston NL 1-4, Brooklyn 5-8, Chicago 9-12, Cincinnati 13-16, New York 17-20, Philadelphia 21-24, Pittsburgh 25-28, St. Louis 29-32, Boston AL 33-36, Chicago 37-40, Cleveland 41-44, Detroit 45-48, New York 49-52, Philadelphia 53-56, St. Louis 57-60, Washington 61-64.

	EX-MT	VG-E	GOOD
COMPLETE SET (64)	3000.00	1350.00	375.00
COMMON CARD (1-64)	25.00	11.00	3.10
☐ 1 David Bancroft	50.00	22.00	6.25
☐ 2 Joseph Genewich	25.00	11.00	3.10
☐ 3 Andrew High	25.00	11.00	3.10
☐ 4 J. Taylor	25.00	11.00	3.10
☐ 5 John Buttler (Butler)	25.00	11.00	3.10
☐ 6 Wilson Fewster	25.00	11.00	3.10
☐ 7 Burleigh A. Grimes	50.00	22.00	6.25
☐ 8 Walter Henline	25.00	11.00	3.10
☐ 9 Sparky Adams	25.00	11.00	3.10
☐ 10 Charles Grimm	30.00	13.50	3.70
☐ 11 Leo Hartnett	50.00	22.00	6.25
☐ 12 Clifton Heathcote	25.00	11.00	3.10
☐ 13 Raymond Bressler	25.00	11.00	3.10
☐ 14 Walter C. Pipp	40.00	18.00	5.00
☐ 15 Eppa Rixey	50.00	22.00	6.25
☐ 16 Ivy Wingo	25.00	11.00	3.10
☐ 17 John M. Bentley	25.00	11.00	3.10
☐ 18 George Harper	25.00	11.00	3.10
☐ 19 Rogers Hornsby	100.00	45.00	12.50
☐ 20 Fredrick Lindstrom	50.00	22.00	6.25
☐ 21 A.R. Decatur	25.00	11.00	3.10
☐ 22 John "Stuffy" McInnes	30.00	13.50	3.70
(sic, McInnis)			
☐ 23 John Mokan	25.00	11.00	3.10
☐ 24 Russell Wrightstone	25.00	11.00	3.10
☐ 25 Hazen Cuyler	50.00	22.00	6.25
☐ 26 Ray Kremer	25.00	11.00	3.10
☐ 27 Earl Smith	25.00	11.00	3.10
☐ 28 Harold Traynor	60.00	27.00	7.50
☐ 29 Grover C. Alexander	75.00	34.00	9.50
☐ 30 James Bottomly	60.00	27.00	7.50
(sic, Bottomley)			
☐ 31 Robert O'Farrell	25.00	11.00	3.10
☐ 32 Wm. H. Southworth	30.00	13.50	3.70
☐ 33 Ira Flagstead	25.00	11.00	3.10
☐ 34 Fred Haney	25.00	11.00	3.10
☐ 35 Philip Todt	25.00	11.00	3.10
☐ 36 Fred Wingfield	25.00	11.00	3.10
☐ 37 Fred Blankenship	25.00	11.00	3.10
(sic, Ted)			
☐ 38 Wm. Hunnefield	25.00	11.00	3.10
(sic, Tommy Thomas)			
☐ 39 Willie Kamm	25.00	11.00	3.10
☐ 40 Ray Schalk	50.00	22.00	6.25
☐ 41 Geo. H. Burns HOR	25.00	11.00	3.10
☐ 42 Walter Lutzke	25.00	11.00	3.10
☐ 43 Glenn Myatt	25.00	11.00	3.10
☐ 44 Bernie Neis	25.00	11.00	3.10
☐ 45 John Bassler	25.00	11.00	3.10
☐ 46 George Daus	25.00	11.00	3.10
(sic, Dauss)			
☐ 47 Charles Gehringer	75.00	34.00	9.50
☐ 48 Harry Heilman	60.00	27.00	7.50
(sic, Heilmann)			
☐ 49 Henry L. Gehrig	400.00	180.00	50.00
☐ 50 Anthony Lazzeri	40.00	18.00	5.00
☐ 51 Robert W. Muesel	25.00	11.00	3.10
(sic, Meusel)			
☐ 52 Geo.H. Babe Ruth	600.00	275.00	75.00
☐ 53 Tyrus Cobb	400.00	180.00	50.00
☐ 54 Eddie Collins	60.00	27.00	7.50
☐ 55 William Wambsganns	25.00	11.00	3.10
sic, Wambsganss			
☐ 56 Zach Wheat	50.00	22.00	6.25
☐ 57 Wm. Hargrave	25.00	11.00	3.10
☐ 58 Kenneth Williams	30.00	13.50	3.70
☐ 59 George Sissler	75.00	34.00	9.50
sic, Sisler			
☐ 60 Ernest Wingard	25.00	11.00	3.10
☐ 61 Leon Goslin	60.00	27.00	7.50
☐ 62 Walter Johnson	175.00	80.00	22.00
☐ 63 Harold Ruel	25.00	11.00	3.10
☐ 64 Tristam Speaker	100.00	45.00	12.50
sic, Tristram			

1928 Exhibits

In contrast to the green color of the preceding year, the 64 Exhibit cards of 1928 are blue in color. Each card measures 3 3/8" by 5 3/8". They may be found with blank backs, or postcard backs containing a small premium offer clip-off in one corner. The use of the divided legend was continued, with the Roush card being unique in the set as it also cites his position. Of the 64 players in the set, 24 appear for the first time, while 12 of the holdovers show new poses. In addition, four players are shown with new team affiliations. The remaining 24 cards are identical to those issued in 1927 except for color. Once again, there is at least one mistaken identity and many misspellings and wrong names. A few of the cards are presented horizontally (HOR). Players are listed below in alphabetical order by team: Boston NL 1-4, Brooklyn 5-8, Chicago 9-12, Cincinnati 13-16, New York 17-20, Philadelphia 21-24, Pittsburgh 25-28, St. Louis 29-32, Boston AL 33-36, Chicago 37-40, Cleveland 41-44, Detroit 45-48, New York 49-52, Philadelphia 53-56, St. Louis 57-60 and Washington 61-64.

	EX-MT	VG-E	GOOD
COMPLETE SET (64)	2500.00	1100.00	300.00
COMMON CARD (1-64)	25.00	11.00	3.10
☐ 1 Edward Brown	25.00	11.00	3.10
☐ 2 Rogers Hornsby HOR	100.00	45.00	12.50
☐ 3 Robert Smith	25.00	11.00	3.10
☐ 4 J. Taylor	25.00	11.00	3.10
☐ 5 David Bancroft	50.00	22.00	6.25
☐ 6 Max G. Carey	50.00	22.00	6.25
☐ 7 Charles R. Hargraves	25.00	11.00	3.10
☐ 8 Arthur "Dazzy" Vance	50.00	22.00	6.25
☐ 9 E. English	25.00	11.00	3.10
☐ 10 Leo Hartnett	50.00	22.00	6.25
☐ 11 A.C. Root	25.00	11.00	3.10
☐ 12 L.R. (Hack) Wilson	75.00	34.00	9.50
☐ 13 Hugh M. Critz	25.00	11.00	3.10
☐ 14 Eugene Hargrave	25.00	11.00	3.10
☐ 15 Adolph Luque	30.00	13.50	3.70
☐ 16 William A. Zitzmann	25.00	11.00	3.10
☐ 17 Virgil Barnes	25.00	11.00	3.10
☐ 18 J. Francis Hogan	25.00	11.00	3.10
☐ 19 Fredrick Lindstrom	50.00	22.00	6.25
sic, Frederick			
☐ 20 Edd. Roush, Outfield	60.00	27.00	7.50
☐ 21 Fred Leach	25.00	11.00	3.10
☐ 22 James Ring	25.00	11.00	3.10
☐ 23 Henry Sand HOR	25.00	11.00	3.10
☐ 24 Fred Williams	30.00	13.50	3.70
☐ 25 Ray Kremer	25.00	11.00	3.10
☐ 26 Earl Smith	25.00	11.00	3.10
☐ 27 Paul Waner	50.00	22.00	6.25
☐ 28 Glenn Wright	25.00	11.00	3.10
☐ 29 Grover C. Alexander	75.00	34.00	9.50
no emblem			
☐ 30 Francis R. Blades	25.00	11.00	3.10
☐ 31 Frank Frisch	75.00	34.00	9.50
☐ 32 James Wilson	30.00	13.50	3.70
☐ 33 Ira Flagstead	25.00	11.00	3.10
☐ 34 Bryan "Slim" Harriss	25.00	11.00	3.10
☐ 35 Fred Hoffman	25.00	11.00	3.10
☐ 36 Philip Todt	25.00	11.00	3.10
☐ 37 Chalmer W. Cissell HOR	25.00	11.00	3.10
☐ 38 Bib Falk	25.00	11.00	3.10
☐ 39 Theodore Lyons	50.00	22.00	6.25
☐ 40 Harry McCurdy	25.00	11.00	3.10
☐ 41 Chas. Jamieson	25.00	11.00	3.10
☐ 42 Glenn Myatt	25.00	11.00	3.10
☐ 43 Joseph Sewell	50.00	22.00	6.25
☐ 44 Geo. Uhle	25.00	11.00	3.10
☐ 45 Robert Fothergill	25.00	11.00	3.10
☐ 46 Jack Tavener HOR	25.00	11.00	3.10
☐ 47 Earl G. Whitehill	25.00	11.00	3.10
☐ 48 Lawrence Woodall	25.00	11.00	3.10
☐ 49 Pat Collins	25.00	11.00	3.10
☐ 50 Lou Gehrig	400.00	180.00	50.00
☐ 51 Geo.H."Babe" Ruth	600.00	275.00	75.00
☐ 52 Urban J. Shocker	25.00	11.00	3.10
☐ 53 Gordon S. Cochrane	75.00	34.00	9.50
☐ 54 Howard Ehmke	30.00	13.50	3.70
☐ 55 Joseph Hauser	25.00	11.00	3.10
☐ 56 Al. Simmons	60.00	27.00	7.50
☐ 57 L.A. Blue	25.00	11.00	3.10
☐ 58 John Ogden	25.00	11.00	3.10
sic, Warren Ogden			
☐ 59 Walter Shang	30.00	13.50	3.70
sic, Schang			
☐ 60 Fred Schulte	25.00	11.00	3.10
☐ 61 Leon Goslin	50.00	22.00	6.25
☐ 62 Stanley Harris	50.00	22.00	6.25
☐ 63 Sam Jones	30.00	13.50	3.70
☐ 64 Harold Ruel	25.00	11.00	3.10

1929-30 Exhibits Four-in-One W463-1

The years 1929-30 marked the initial appearance of the Exhibit Company's famous "Four-In-One" design. Each of the 32 cards depict four players from one team, with a total of 128 players shown (eight from each of 16 major league teams). Each of these exhibit cards measures 3 3/8" by 5 3/8". The player's names and teams are located under each picture in dark blue or white print. All the reverses are post card style with the premium clip-off across one corner. There are 11 color combinations known for the fronts. The backs may be uncolored, red (black/red front) or yellow (blue/yellow front). The card labeled "Babe Herman" actually depicts Jesse Petty. The catalog designation is W463-1.

	EX-MT	VG-E	GOOD
COMPLETE SET (32)	2400.00	1100.00	300.00
COMMON CARD (1-32)	50.00	22.00	6.25
☐ 1 Pat Collins	75.00	34.00	9.50
Joe Dugan			
Edward Farrel			
(sic, Farrell)			
George Sisler			
☐ 2 Lance Richbourg	50.00	22.00	6.25
Fred Maguire			
Robert Smith			
George Harper			
☐ 3 D'Arcy Flowers	60.00	27.00	7.50
Arthur "Dazzy" Vance			
Nick Cullop			
Harvey Hendrick			
☐ 4 Floyd C. Herman	60.00	27.00	7.50
David Bancroft			
John H. Deberry			
Del L. Bisonette			
(sic, Bissonette)			
☐ 5 Leo Hartnett	150.00	70.00	19.00
C.E. Beck			
L.R. (Hack) Wilson			
Rogers Hornsby			
☐ 6 C.H. Root	60.00	27.00	7.50
Hazen Cuyler			
E. English			
C.J. Grimm			
☐ 7 H.M. Critz	60.00	27.00	7.50
W.C. Walker			
George L. Kelly			
V.J. Picinich			
☐ 8 E.V. Purdy	50.00	22.00	6.25
C.A. Pittenger			
C.F. Lucas			
H.E. Ford			
☐ 9 L. Benton	75.00	34.00	9.50
Melvin Ott			
William Terry			
Andrew Reese			
☐ 10 J.F. Hogan	75.00	34.00	9.50
Travis C. Jackson			
J.D. Welsh			
Fred Lindstrom			
☐ 11 Frank O'Doul	50.00	22.00	6.25
Bernard Friberg			
Fresco Thompson			
Donald Hurst			
☐ 12 Cy Williams	50.00	22.00	6.25
A. C. Whitney			
Ray Benge			
Lester L. Sweetland			
☐ 13 Earl J. Adams	60.00	27.00	7.50
R. Bartell			
Harold Traynor			
Earl Sheely			
☐ 14 Lloyd Waner	75.00	34.00	9.50
Charles R.Hargreaves			
Ray Kremer			
Paul Waner			
☐ 15 Grover C. Alexander	125.00	55.00	15.50
James Wilson			
Frank Frisch			
James Bottomly			
(sic, Bottomley)			
☐ 16 Fred G. Haney	60.00	27.00	7.50
Chas. J. Hafey			
Taylor Douthit			
Chas. M. Gilbert			
(sic, Gelbert)			
☐ 17 J.A. Heving	60.00	27.00	7.50
J. Rothrock			
Charles H. Ruffing			
R.R. (R.E.) Reeves			
☐ 18 P.J. Todt	50.00	22.00	6.25

	EX-MT	VG-E	GOOD
H. Rhyne			
W.W. Regan			
D. Taitt			
☐ 19 Chalmer W. Cissell	50.00	22.00	6.25
John W. Clancy			
John L. Kerr			
Willie Kamm			
☐ 20 Alex Metzler	50.00	22.00	6.25
Alphonse Thomas			
Carl Reynolds			
Martin G. Autrey			
(sic, Autry)			
☐ 21 L.A. Fonseca	60.00	27.00	7.50
Joe Sewell			
Carl Lind			
J. Tavener			
☐ 22 K. Holloway	60.00	27.00	7.50
Bibb A. Falk			
Luke Sewell			
Earl Averill			
☐ 23 Dale Alexander	75.00	34.00	9.50
G.F. McManus			
H.F. Rice			
C. Gehringer			
☐ 24 M.J. Shea	60.00	27.00	7.50
G.E. Uhle			
Harry E. Heilman			
(sic, Heilmann)			
C.N. Richardson			
☐ 25 Waite Hoyt	100.00	45.00	12.50
Anthony Lazzeri			
Benny Bengough			
Earl B. Coombs			
(sic, Combs)			
☐ 26 Mark Koenig	750.00	350.00	95.00
Geo.H."Babe" Ruth			
Leo Durocher			
Henry L. Gehrig			
☐ 27 Jimmy Foxx	150.00	70.00	19.00
Gordon S. Cochrane			
Robert M. Grove			
George Haas			
☐ 28 Homer Summa	50.00	22.00	6.25
James Dykes			
Samuel Hale			
Max Bishop			
☐ 29 Heine Manush	60.00	27.00	7.50
W.H. Shang			
(sic, Schang)			
S. Gray			
R. Kress			
☐ 30 Oscar Melillo	50.00	22.00	6.25
F.O. Rourke			
sic, O'Rourke			
L.A. Blue			
F. Schulte			
☐ 31 Leon Goslin	60.00	27.00	7.50
Oswald Bluege			
Harold Ruel			
Joseph Judge			
☐ 32 Sam Rice	60.00	27.00	7.50
Jack Hayes			
Sam P. Jones			
Chas. M. Myer			

1931-32 Exhibits Four-in-One W463-2

The collector should refer to the checklists when trying to determine the year of issue of any "Four-In-One" set because the checklist (showing the players as they are, appear in groups of four) and the card color will ultimately provide the right clues. Some of the colors of the previous issue -- black on green, orange, red or yellow, and blue on white -- are repeated in this series, but the 1931-32 cards are distinguishable by the combinations of players which appear. Each card measures 3 3/8" by 5 3/8". The backs contain a description of attainable "Free Prizes" for coupons. The backs also contain the clip-off premium coupon. There are numerous misspellings, as usual, in the set. The catalog designation for this set is W463-2.

	EX-MT	VG-E	GOOD
COMPLETE SET (32)	4000.00	1800.00	500.00
COMMON CARD (1-32)	90.00	40.00	11.00
☐ 1 Walter Maranville	100.00	45.00	12.50
J.T. Zachary			
Alfred Spohrer			
Randolph Moore			
☐ 2 Lance Richbourg	90.00	40.00	11.00
Fred Maguire			
Earl Sheely			
Walter Berger			
☐ 3 D'Arcy Flowers	100.00	45.00	12.50
Arthur "Dazzy" Vance			
Frank O'Doul			
Fresco Thompson			
☐ 4 Floyd C. Herman	90.00	40.00	11.00
Glenn Wright			
Jack Quinn			
Del L. Bisonette			
☐ 5 Leo Hartnett	250.00	110.00	31.00
J.R. Stevenson			
(sic, Stephenson)			
L.R.(Hack) Wilson			
Rogers Hornsby			
☐ 6 C.H. Root	100.00	45.00	12.50
Hazen Cuyler			
E. English			
C.J. Grimm			
☐ 7 Les Durocher	125.00	55.00	15.50
(sic, Leo)			
W.C. Walker			
Harry Heilmann			
Nick Cullop			
☐ 8 W. Roettger	90.00	40.00	11.00
Gooch			
C.F. Lucas			
H.E. Ford			
☐ 9 J.F. Hogan	110.00	50.00	14.00
Travis C. Jackson			
H.M. Critz			
Fred Lindstrom			
☐ 10 Robert O'Farrell	150.00	70.00	19.00
Melvin Ott			
William Terry			
Fred Fitzsimmons			
☐ 11 Chuck Klein	100.00	45.00	12.50
A.C. Whitney			
Ray Benge			
Buzz Arlett			
☐ 12 Harry McCurdy	90.00	40.00	11.00
Bernard Friberg			
Richard Bartell			
Donald Hurst			
☐ 13 Adam Comorosky	100.00	45.00	12.50
Gus Suhr			
Harold Traynor			
T.J. Thevenow			
☐ 14 Lloyd Waner	110.00	50.00	14.00
George Grantham			
Ray Kremer			
Paul Waner			
☐ 15 Earl J. Adams	125.00	55.00	15.50
James Wilson			
Frank Frisch			
James Bottomly			
(sic, Bottomley)			
☐ 16 Bill Hallahan	100.00	45.00	12.50
Chas. J. Hafey			
Taylor Douthit			
Chas. M. Gilbert			
(sic, Gelbert)			
☐ 17 Chas. Berry	90.00	40.00	11.00
J. Rothrock			
Robt. Reeves			
R.R. (R.E.) Reeves			
☐ 18 E.W. Webb	90.00	40.00	11.00
H. Rhyne			
Bill Sweeney			
D. MacFayden			
☐ 19 Luke L. Appling	110.00	50.00	14.00
Ted Lyons			
Chalmer W. Cissell			
Willie Kamm			
☐ 20 Smead Jolley	90.00	40.00	11.00
L.A. Blue			
Carl Reynolds			
Henry Tate			
☐ 21 Hunnefield	90.00	40.00	11.00
J. Goldman			
Ed Morgan			
Wes Ferrell			
☐ 22 L.A. Fonseca	100.00	45.00	12.50
B.A. Falk			
Luke Sewell			
Earl Averill			
☐ 23 Dale Alexander	110.00	50.00	14.00
G.F. McManus			
G.E. Uhle			
C. Gehringer			
☐ 24 Wallie Schang	100.00	45.00	12.50
E. Funk			
Mark Koenig			
Waite Hoyt			
☐ 25 W. Dickey	300.00	135.00	38.00
Anthony Lazzeri			
Herb Pennock			
Earl B. Coombs			
(sic, Combs)			
☐ 26 Lyn Lary	1250.00	550.00	160.00
Geo. H. Babe Ruth			
James Reese			
Henry L. Gehrig			
☐ 27 John Boley	100.00	45.00	12.50
James Dykes			
E.J. Miller			
Al Simmons			
☐ 28 Jimmy Foxx	150.00	70.00	19.00
Gordon S. Cochrane			
Robert M. Grove			
George Haas			
☐ 29 O. Melillo	100.00	45.00	12.50
F.O. Rourke			
(sic, O'Rourke)			
Leon Goslin			
F. Schulte			
☐ 30 W. Stewart	100.00	45.00	12.50
Richard Farrell			
(sic, Ferrell)			
S. Gray			
R. Kress			
☐ 31 Roy Spencer	110.00	50.00	14.00
Heine Manush			
Joe Cronin			
Fred Marberry			
☐ 32 O. Bluege	100.00	45.00	12.50
Joe Judge			
Sam Rice			
C. Myer			

1933 Exhibits Four-in-One W463-3

The physical dimensions of the cardboard sheet used by the Exhibit Supply Company in printing their card sets over the years allows the following correlation to be made when one establishes that 32 of the standard-sized cards (3 3/8" by 5 3/8") are printed per sheet. Sets of 128 cards are equal to four sheets, 64 cards to two sheets, 32 cards to one sheet and 16 cards to one-half sheet. Whether it was economics, the Depression, or simplicity of operation, something caused the company to change their set totals in a descending order since 1922 in 1933. The first of a series of 16-card sets was released. The fronts of these cards are black green, orange, red or yellow; the backs are blank. The catalog designation for this set is W463-3.

	EX-MT	VG-E	GOOD
COMPLETE SET (16)	2400.00	1100.00	300.00
COMMON CARD (1-16)	80.00	36.00	10.00
☐ 1 Lance Richbourg	80.00	36.00	10.00
Fred Maguire			
Earl Sheely			
Walter Berger			
☐ 2 Vincent Lopez (Al)	110.00	50.00	14.00
Glenn Wright			
Arthur Dazzy Vance			
Frank O'Doul			
☐ 3 J.R. Stephenson	80.00	36.00	10.00
C.J. Grimm			
E. English			
C.H. Root			
☐ 4 Taylor Douthit	100.00	45.00	12.50
George Grantham			
G. F. Lucas			
Chas. Hafey			
☐ 5 Fred Fitzsimmons	100.00	45.00	12.50
H. M. Critz			
Fred Lindstrom			
Robert O'Farrell			
☐ 6 Chuck Klein	100.00	45.00	12.50
Ray Benge			
Richard Bartell			
Donald Hurst			
☐ 7 Tom J. Thevenow	110.00	50.00	14.00
Paul Waner			
Gus Suhr			
Lloyd Waner			
☐ 8 Earl J. Adams	110.00	50.00	14.00
Frank Frisch			
Bill Halloran			
Chas. Gelbert			
☐ 9 D. MacFayden	80.00	36.00	10.00
E. W. Webb			
H. Rhyne			
Chas. Berry			
☐ 10 Charles Berry	100.00	45.00	12.50
Bob Seeds			
C.A. Blue			
Ted Lyons			
☐ 11 Wes Ferrell	100.00	45.00	12.50
Luke Sewell			
Ed Morgan			
Earl Averill			
☐ 12 Muddy Ruel	110.00	50.00	14.00
G.E. Uhle			
Jonathon Stone			
C. Gehringer			
☐ 13 George H."Babe" Ruth	1250.00	550.00	160.00
Herb Pennock			
Anthony Lazzeri			
W. Dickey			
☐ 14 Mickey Cochrane	250.00	110.00	31.00
Jimmy Foxx			
Al Simmons			
Robert M. Grove			
☐ 15 Richard Farrell	110.00	50.00	14.00
(sic, Ferrell)			
O. Melillo			
Leon Goslin			
S. Grey			
☐ 16 H. Manush	100.00	45.00	12.50
F. Marberry			
J. Judge			
Roy Spencer			

1934 Exhibits Four-in-One W463-4

The emergence of the bubble gum card producers in 1933-34 may have motivated Exhibit Supply to make a special effort to provide a "quality" set for 1934. The new 16-card series was printed in colors of blue, brown, olive green and violet -- all in softer tones than used in previous years. No less than 25 players appeared on cards for the first time, and another 16 were given entirely new poses. For the first time in the history of the Exhibit baseball series, there were no spelling errors. However, perfection is rarely attained in any endeavor, and the "bugaboo" of 1934 was the labeling of Al Lopez as Vincent Lopez (famous band leader and prognosticator). The cards have plain backs. Each card measures 3 3/8" by 5 3/8".

	EX-MT	VG-E	GOOD
COMPLETE SET (16)	1800.00	800.00	220.00
COMMON CARD (1-16)	50.00	22.00	6.25
☐ 1 Bill Urbansky	50.00	22.00	6.25
Ed Brandt			
Walter Berger			
Frank Hogan			
☐ 2 Vincent Lopez (Al)	60.00	27.00	7.50
Glenn Wright			
Sam Leslie			
Leonard Koenecke			
☐ 3 Chas. Klein	60.00	27.00	7.50
C.J. Grimm			
E. English			
Lon Warneke			
☐ 4 Botchi Lombardi	100.00	45.00	12.50
Tony Piet			
Jimmy Bottomley			
Chas. J. Hafey			
☐ 5 Blondy Ryan	150.00	70.00	19.00
Bill Terry			
Carl Hubbell			
Mel Ott			
☐ 6 Jimmy Wilson	50.00	22.00	6.25
Wesley Schulmerich			
Richard Bartell			
Donald Hurst			
☐ 7 T.J. Thevenow	100.00	45.00	12.50
Paul Waner			
Pie Traynor			
Lloyd Waner			
☐ 8 Pepper Martin	75.00	34.00	9.50
Frank Frisch			
Bill Hallahan			
John Rothrock			
☐ 9 Lefty Grove	100.00	45.00	12.50
Roy Johnson			
Bill Cissell			
Rick Ferrell			
☐ 10 Luke Appling	75.00	34.00	9.50
Al Simmons			
Evar Swanson			
George Earnshaw			
☐ 11 Wes Ferrell	60.00	27.00	7.50
Frank Pytlak			
Willie Kamm			
Earl Averill			
☐ 12 Mickey Cochrane	150.00	70.00	19.00
Goose Goslin			
Fred Marberry			
C. Gehringer			
☐ 13 Geo.H."Babe" Ruth	750.00	350.00	95.00
Vernon Gomez			
Lou Gehrig			
W. Dickey			
☐ 14 Mickey Cochrane	225.00	100.00	28.00
Jimmy Foxx			
Al Simmons			
Robert M. Grove			

☐ 15 Irving Burns 50.00 22.00 6.25
O. Melillo
Irving Hadley
Rollie Hemsley
☐ 16 Heine Manush 75.00 34.00 9.50
Alvin Crowder
Joe Cronin
Joe Kuhel

1935 Exhibits Four-in-One W463-5

The year 1935 marked the return of the 16-card Exhibit series to a simple slate blue color. Babe Ruth appears with Boston, N.L., the last time his card would be made while he was playing, after being included in every Exhibit series since 1921. Of the 64 players pictured, 17 are shown for the first time, while 11 of the returnees are graced with new poses. The infamous "Vincent Lopez" card returns with this set, and the photo purportedly showing Tony Cuccinello is really that of George Puccinello. The cards have plain backs. The cards measure 3 3/8" by 5 3/8".

	EX-MT	VG-E	GOOD
COMPLETE SET (16)	2400.00	1100.00	300.00
COMMON CARD (1-16)	50.00	22.00	6.25

☐ 1 Babe Ruth 750.00 350.00 95.00
Frank Hogan
Walter Berger
Ed Brandt
☐ 2 Van Mungo 60.00 27.00 7.50
Vincent Lopez (Al)
Dan Taylor
Tony Cuccinello
☐ 3 Chas. Klein 75.00 34.00 9.50
C.J. Grimm
Lon Warneke
Gabby Hartnett
☐ 4 Botchi Lombardi 100.00 45.00 12.50
Paul Derringer
Jimmy Bottomley
Chas. J. Hafey
☐ 5 Hughie Critz 150.00 70.00 19.00
Bill Terry
Carl Hubbell
Mel Ott
☐ 6 Jimmy Wilson 50.00 22.00 6.25
Phil Collins
John "Blondy" Ryan
Geo. Watkins
☐ 7 Paul Waner 100.00 45.00 12.50
Pie Traynor
Guy Bush
Floyd Vaughan
☐ 8 Pepper Martin 250.00 110.00 31.00
Frank Frisch
Jerome "Dizzy" Dean
Paul Dean
☐ 9 Lefty Grove 150.00 70.00 19.00
Billy Werber
Joe Cronin
Rick Ferrell
☐ 10 Al Simmons 75.00 34.00 9.50
Jimmy Dykes
Ted Lyons
Henry Bonura
☐ 11 Mel Harder 60.00 27.00 7.50
Hal Trosky
Willie Kamm
Earl Averill
☐ 12 Mickey Cochrane 125.00 55.00 15.50
Goose Goslin
Linwood Rowe
(sic, Lynwood)
C. Gehringer
☐ 13 Tony Lazzeri 600.00 275.00 75.00
Vernon Gomez
Lou Gehrig
W. Dickey
☐ 14 Slug Mahaffey 75.00 34.00 9.50
Jimmy Foxx
George Cramer
Bob Johnson
☐ 15 Irving Burns 50.00 22.00 6.25
Oscar Melillo
L.N. Newson
Rollie Hemsley
☐ 16 Buddy Meyer (Myer) 60.00 27.00 7.50
Earl Whitehill
H. Manush
Fred Schulte

1936 Exhibits Four-in-One W463-6

In 1936, the 16-card Exhibit set retained the "slate" or blue-gray color of the preceding year, but also added an olive green hue to the set. The cards are blank-backed, but for the first time since the "Four-In-One" design was introduced in 1929, a line reading "Ptd. in U.S.A." was placed in the bottom border on the obverse. The set contains 16 players making their debut in Exhibit cards, while nine holdovers have new poses. The photos of George Puccinelli was correctly identified and placed with Philadelphia, A.L. The cards measure 3 3/8" by 5 3/8".

	EX-MT	VG-E	GOOD
COMPLETE SET (16)	1500.00	700.00	190.00
COMMON CARD (1-16)	50.00	22.00	6.25

☐ 1 Bill Urbanski 50.00 22.00 6.25
Pinky Whitney
Walter Berger
Danny MacFayden
☐ 2 Van Mungo 60.00 27.00 7.50
Stan Bordagaray
Fred Lindstrom
Dutch Brandt
☐ 3 Billy Herman 75.00 34.00 9.50
Augie Galan
Lon Warneke
Gabby Hartnett
☐ 4 Botchie Lombardi 60.00 27.00 7.50
Paul Derringer
Babe Herman
Alex Kampouris
☐ 5 Gus. Mancuso 150.00 70.00 19.00
Bill Terry
Carl Hubbell
Mel Ott
☐ 6 Jimmy Wilson 50.00 22.00 6.25
Curt Davis
Dolph Camilli
Johnny Moore
☐ 7 Paul Waner 75.00 34.00 9.50
Pie Traynor
Guy Bush
Floyd Vaughan
☐ 8 Joe "Ducky" Medwick 150.00 70.00 19.00
Frank Frisch
Jerome "Dizzy" Dean
Paul Dean
☐ 9 Lefty Grove 150.00 70.00 19.00
Jimmy Foxx
Joe Cronin
Rick Ferrell
☐ 10 Luke Appling 75.00 34.00 9.50
Jimmy Dykes
Ted Lyons
Henry Bonura
☐ 11 Mel Harder 60.00 27.00 7.50
Hal Trosky
Joe Vosmik
Earl Averill
☐ 12 Mickey Cochrane 150.00 70.00 19.00
Goose Goslin
Linwood Rowe
(sic, Lynwood)
C. Gehringer
☐ 13 Tony Lazzeri 600.00 275.00 75.00
Vernon Gomez
Lou Gehrig
Red Ruffing
☐ 14 Charles Berry 50.00 22.00 6.25
Puccinelli
Frank Higgins
Bob Johnson
☐ 15 Harland Clift 50.00 22.00 6.25
Sammy West
Paul Andrews
Rollie Hemsley
☐ 16 Buddy Meyer (Myer) 50.00 22.00 6.25
Earl Whitehill
Ossie Bluege
L.N. Newsom

1937 Exhibits Four-in-One W463-7

It would appear that Exhibit Supply was merely "flip-flopping" color schemes during the three year period 1935-37. In 1935, the cards were blue-gray; in 1936, the cards were either blue-gray or green; in 1937, the cards appear in green only. As with the previous set, the name and team of each player is printed in two or three lines under his picture, the

"Ptd. in U.S.A." line appears in the bottom border (missing on some cards) and the backs are blank. The catalog designation is W463-7

	EX-MT	VG-E	GOOD
COMPLETE SET (16)	2000.00	900.00	250.00
COMMON CARD (1-16)	60.00	27.00	7.50

☐ 1 Bill Urbanski 75.00 34.00 9.50
Alfonso Lopez
Walter Berger
Danny MacFayden
☐ 2 Van Mungo 60.00 27.00 7.50
E. English
Johnny Moore
(Philadelphia NL)
Gordon Phelps
☐ 3 Billy Herman 80.00 36.00 10.00
Augie Galan
Bill Lee
Gabby Hartnett
☐ 4 Botchi Lombardi 60.00 27.00 7.50
Paul Derringer
Lew Riggs
Phil Weintraub
☐ 5 Gus Mancuso 150.00 70.00 19.00
Sam Leslie
Carl Hubbell
Mel Ott
☐ 6 Pinky Whitney 60.00 27.00 7.50
Wm. Walters
Dolph Camilli
Johnny Moore
☐ 7 Paul Waner 80.00 36.00 10.00
Gus Suhr
Cy Blanton
Floyd Vaughan
☐ 8 Joe "Duck" Medwick 200.00 90.00 25.00
Lon Warneke
Jerome "Dizzy" Dean
Stuart Martin
☐ 9 Lefty Grove 300.00 135.00 38.00
Jimmy Foxx
Joe Cronin
Dick Ferrell
☐ 10 Luke Appling 60.00 27.00 7.50
Jimmy Dykes
Vernon Kennedy
Henry Bonura
☐ 11 Bob Feller 200.00 90.00 25.00
Hal Trosky
Frank Pytlak
Earl Averill
☐ 12 Mickey Cochrane 150.00 70.00 19.00
Goose Goslin
Linwood Rowe
C. Gehringer
☐ 13 Tony Lazzeri 800.00 350.00 100.00
Vernon Gomez
Lou Gehrig
Joe DiMaggio
☐ 14 Billy Weber 60.00 27.00 7.50
(sic, Werber)
Harry Kelly
(sic, Kelley)
Wallace Moses
Bob Johnson
☐ 15 Harland Clift 60.00 27.00 7.50
Sammy West
Orval Hildebrand
Rollie Hemsley
☐ 16 Buddy Meyer (Myer) 60.00 27.00 7.50
Jonathan Stone
Joe Kuhel
L.N. Newsom

1938 Exhibits Four-in-One

The 1938 set of 16 cards demonstrated the fact that one consistent "quality" of Exhibit Supply sets is their inconsistency. For example, the card of Tony Cuccinello once again contains the photo of George Puccinelli, a mistake first made in 1935, corrected in 1936 and now made again in 1938. The set is also rife with name and spelling errors. Of the 64 players depicted, 12 are new arrivals and three are returnees with new poses. Another ten retained their 1937 photos but were designated new team affiliations. The cards have blank backs. The set was the last to employ the "Four-In-One" format. The catalog designation is W463-8. The cards measure 3 3/8" by 5 3/8".

	EX-MT	VG-E	GOOD
COMPLETE SET (16)	2400.00	1100.00	300.00
COMMON CARD (1-16)	75.00	34.00	9.50

☐ 1 Tony Cuccinello 75.00 34.00 9.50
(sic, Geo.Puccinelli)
Roy Johnson
Vince DiMaggio
Danny MacFayden
☐ 2 Van Mungo 75.00 34.00 9.50
Leo Durocher
Dolph Camilli
Gordon Phelps
☐ 3 Billy Herman 250.00 110.00 31.00
Augie Galan
Jerome "Dizzy" Dean
Gabby Hartnett
☐ 4 Dutch Lombardi 75.00 34.00 9.50
Paul Derringer
Lew Riggs
Ival Goodman
☐ 5 Hank Leiber 150.00 70.00 19.00
Jim Ripple
Carl Hubbell
Mel Ott
☐ 6 Pinky Whitney 75.00 34.00 9.50
Wm. Walters
Chas. Klein
Morris Arnovich
☐ 7 Paul Waner 100.00 45.00 12.50
Gus Suhr
Cy Blanton
Floyd Vaughan
☐ 8 Joe "Ducky" Medwick 100.00 45.00 12.50
Lon Warneke
John Mize
Stuart Martin
☐ 9 Lefty Grove 200.00 90.00 25.00
Jimmy Foxx
Joe Cronin
Joe Vosmik
☐ 10 Luke Appling 100.00 45.00 12.50
Luke Sewell
Mike Kreevich
Ted Lyons
☐ 11 Bob Feller 150.00 70.00 19.00
Hal Trosky
Odell Hale
Earl Averill
☐ 12 Hank Greenberg 150.00 70.00 19.00
Rudy York
Tom Bridges
C. Gehringer
☐ 13 W. Dickey 1000.00 450.00 125.00
Vernon Gomez
Lou Gehrig
Joe DiMaggio
☐ 14 Billy Weber 75.00 34.00 9.50
sic, Werber
Harry Kelly
sic, Kelley
Wallace Moses
Bob Johnson
☐ 15 Harland Clift 75.00 34.00 9.50
Sammy West
Beau Bell
L.N. Newsom
☐ 16 Buddy Meyer (Myer) 75.00 34.00 9.50
Jonathan Stone
Wes Ferrell
Rick Ferrell

1939-46 Exhibits Salutation

This collection of exhibit cards shares a common style: the "Personal Greeting" or "Salutation". The specific greeting varies from card to card -- "Yours truly, Best wishes, etc." -- as does the location of the exhibit identification (lower left, LL, or lower right, LR). Some players appear with different teams and there are occasional misspellings. Each card measures 3 3/8" by 5 3/8". The Bob Feller (Yours Truly), Andy Pafko (Yours Truly) and Ted Williams (Sincerely Yours) cards are relatively quite common as they were still being printed into the middle to late 1950s, i.e., basically until the end of their respective careers. The Jeff

Heath small picture variation (26B) is differentiated by measuring the distance between the top of his cap and the top edge of the card; for the small picture variation that distance is approximately 5/8" whereas it is only 3/8" for 26A. There is some doubt about whether Camilli #6B exists. The 50A Pafko does not exist, while the 50C Pafko is a very tough card since it was printed only in 1960.

	EX-MT	VG-E	GOOD
COMPLETE SET (84)	6000.00	2700.00	750.00
COMMON CARD	5.00	2.20	.60

Card	EX-MT	VG-E	GOOD
☐ 1A Luke Appling LL Sincerely Yours	25.00	11.00	3.10
☐ 1B Luke Appling LR Sincerely Yours	15.00	6.75	1.85
☐ 2 Earl Averill Very Best Wishes	5.00	2.20	.60
☐ 3 Charles "Red" Barrett Yours Truly	5.00	2.20	.60
☐ 4 Henry "Hank" Borowy Sincerely Yours	5.00	2.20	.60
☐ 5 Lou Boudreau Sincerely	8.00	3.60	1.00
☐ 6A Adolf Camilli LL Very Truly Yours	25.00	11.00	3.10
☐ 6B Adolf Camilli LR Very Truly Yours	200.00	90.00	25.00
☐ 7 Phil Cavarretta Cordially Yours	5.00	2.20	.60
☐ 8 Harland Clift Very Truly Yours	20.00	9.00	2.50
☐ 9 Tony Cuccinello Very Best Wishes	40.00	18.00	5.00
☐ 10 Dizzy Dean Sincerely	100.00	45.00	12.50
☐ 11 Paul Derringer Yours Truly	5.00	2.20	.60
☐ 12A Bill Dickey LL Cordially Yours	50.00	22.00	6.25
☐ 12B Bill Dickey LR Cordially Yours	50.00	22.00	6.25
☐ 13 Joe DiMaggio Cordially	125.00	55.00	15.50
☐ 14 Bob Elliott Truly Yours	5.00	2.20	.60
☐ 15A Bob Feller Best Wishes (portrait)	125.00	55.00	15.50
☐ 15B Bob Feller Yours Truly (pitching pose)	15.00	6.75	1.85
☐ 16 Dave Ferriss Best of Luck	5.00	2.20	.60
☐ 17 Jimmy Foxx Sincerely	200.00	90.00	25.00
☐ 18 Lou Gehrig Sincerely	2000.00	900.00	250.00
☐ 19 Charlie Gehringer Yours Truly	125.00	55.00	15.50
☐ 20 Vernon Gomez Sincerely Yours	200.00	90.00	25.00
☐ 21A Joe Gordon (Cleveland) Sincerely	25.00	11.00	3.10
☐ 21B Joe Gordon (New York) Sincerely	5.00	2.20	.60
☐ 22A Hank Greenberg Truly Yours	35.00	16.00	4.40
☐ 22B Henry Greenberg Very Truly Yours	150.00	70.00	19.00
☐ 23 Robert Grove Cordially Yours	125.00	55.00	15.50
☐ 24 Gabby Hartnett Cordially	350.00	160.00	45.00
☐ 25 Buddy Hassett Yours Truly	25.00	11.00	3.10
☐ 26A Jeff Heath Best Wishes	25.00	11.00	3.10
☐ 26B Jeff Heath (Small Picture) Best Wishes	5.00	2.20	.60
☐ 27 Kirby Higbe Sincerely	25.00	11.00	3.10
☐ 28A Tommy Holmes Sincerely Yours	200.00	90.00	25.00
☐ 28B Tommy Holmes Yours Truly	5.00	2.20	.60
☐ 29 Carl Hubbell Best Wishes	100.00	45.00	12.50
☐ 30 Bob Johnson Yours Truly	25.00	11.00	3.10
☐ 31A Charles Keller LL Best Wishes	25.00	11.00	3.10
☐ 31B Charles Keller LR Best Wishes	10.00	4.50	1.25
☐ 32 Ken Keltner Sincerly (sic)	50.00	22.00	6.25
☐ 33 Chuck Klein Yours Truly	300.00	135.00	38.00
☐ 34 Mike Kreevich Sincerely	250.00	110.00	31.00
☐ 35 Joe Kuhel Truly Yours	5.00	2.20	.60
☐ 36 Bill Lee Cordially Yours	20.00	9.00	2.50
☐ 37A Ernie Lombardi (1/2 B) Cordially	400.00	180.00	50.00
☐ 38B Ernie Lombardi Cordially Yours	10.00	4.50	1.25
☐ 39 Marty Marion Best Wishes	10.00	4.50	1.25
☐ 40 Merrill May Best Wishes	25.00	11.00	3.10
☐ 41A Frank McCormick LL Sincerely	25.00	11.00	3.10
☐ 41B Frank McCormick LR Sincerely	5.00	2.20	.60
☐ 42A George McQuinn LL Yours Truly	25.00	11.00	3.10
☐ 42B George McQuinn LR Yours Truly	5.00	2.20	.60
☐ 43 Joe Medwick Very Best Wishes	35.00	16.00	4.40
☐ 44A Johnny Mize LL Yours Truly	40.00	18.00	5.00
☐ 44B Johnny Mize LR Yours Truly	15.00	6.75	1.85
☐ 45 Hugh Mulcahy Cordially	25.00	11.00	3.10
☐ 46 Hal Newhouser Best Wishes	15.00	6.75	1.85
☐ 47 Louis (Buck) Newsom Sincerely	25.00	11.00	3.10
☐ 48 Buck Newson (sic) Very Best Wishes	300.00	135.00	38.00
☐ 49A Mel Ott LL Sincerely Yours	50.00	22.00	6.25
☐ 49B Mel Ott LR Sincerely Yours	40.00	18.00	5.00
☐ 50B Andy Pafko Yours Truly	5.00	2.20	.60
☐ 50C Andy Pafko Yours Truly (plain cap)	35.00	16.00	4.40
☐ 51 Claude Passeau Sincerely	5.00	2.20	.60
☐ 52A Howard Pollet LL Best Wishes	25.00	11.00	3.10
☐ 52B Howard Pollet LR Best Wishes	5.00	2.20	.60
☐ 53A Pete Reiser LL Truly Yours	100.00	45.00	12.50
☐ 53B Pete Reiser LR Truly Yours	8.00	3.60	1.00
☐ 54 Johnny Rizzo Sincerely Yours	500.00	220.00	60.00
☐ 55 Glenn Russell Sincerely	300.00	135.00	38.00
☐ 56 George Stirnweiss Yours Truly	5.00	2.20	.60
☐ 57 Cecil Travis Best Wishes	15.00	6.75	1.85
☐ 58 Paul Trout Truly Yours	5.00	2.20	.60
☐ 59 Johnny Vander Meer Cordially Yours	50.00	22.00	6.25
☐ 60 Arky Vaughan Best Wishes	25.00	11.00	3.10
☐ 61A Fred "Dixie" Walker (D on Hat) Yours Truly	5.00	2.20	.60
☐ 61B Fred "Dixie" Walker Cap blanked out Yours Truly	65.00	29.00	8.00
☐ 62 Bucky Walters Sincerely Yours	5.00	2.20	.60
☐ 63 Lon Warneke Very Truly Yours	20.00	9.00	2.50
☐ 64A Ted Williams (9) Sincerely	350.00	160.00	45.00
☐ 64B Ted Williams Sincerely Yours watch out for the illegal reprint; see set caption below	75.00	34.00	9.50
☐ 65 Rudy York Cordially	5.00	2.20	.60

1947-66 Exhibits

This grouping encompasses a wide time span but displays a common design. The following players have been illegally reprinted in mass quantities on a thinner-than-original cardboard which is also characterized by a dark gray back: Aaron, Ford, Fox, Hodges, Elston Howard, Mantle, Mays, Musial, Newcombe, Reese, Spahn, and Ted Williams. Each card measures 3 3/8" by 5 3/8". In the checklist below SIG refers to signature and SCR refers to script name on card. The abbreviations POR (portrait), BAT (batting), and FIE (fielding) are also used below. There are many levels of scarcity within this "set," essentially based on which year(s) the player's card was printed. The Mickey Mantle portrait card, for example, was only printed in 1966, the last year of production. Those scarce cards which were only produced one or two years are noted parenthetically below by the last two digits of the year(s) of issue. Cards which seem to be especially difficult to obtain are the ones produced only in 1966 which are the aforementioned Mantle Portrait, Ford, Kranepool, Richardson, Skowron (White Sox), Ward and Yastrzemski. Some leading exhibit experts believe that the salutation and these cards should be checklisted together because of the long printing history of some of the salutations.

	EX-MT	VG-E	GOOD
COMPLETE SET (321)	6500.00	2900.00	800.00
COMMON CARD	3.00	1.35	.35

Card	EX-MT	VG-E	GOOD
☐ 1 Hank Aaron (has been reprinted)	35.00	16.00	4.40
☐ 2A Joe Adcock SCR	5.00	2.20	.60
☐ 2B Joe Adcock SIG	5.00	2.20	.60
☐ 3 Max Alvis 66	35.00	16.00	4.40
☐ 4A Johnny Antonelli (Braves)	3.00	1.35	.35
☐ 4B Johnny Antonelli (Giants)	3.00	1.35	.35
☐ 5A Luis Aparicio POR	8.00	3.60	1.00
☐ 5B Luis Aparicio BAT 64	65.00	29.00	8.00
☐ 6 Luke Appling	8.00	3.60	1.00
☐ 7A Richie Ashburn (Phillies)	35.00	16.00	4.40
☐ 7B Ritchie Ashburn (sic, Richie)	10.00	4.50	1.25
☐ 7C Richie Ashburn (Cubs) 61	50.00	22.00	6.25
☐ 8 Bob Aspromonte 64/66	5.00	2.20	.60
☐ 9 Toby Atwell	5.00	2.20	.60
☐ 10A Ed Bailey 61 (Cincinnati cap)	10.00	4.50	1.25
☐ 10B Ed Bailey (no cap)	3.00	1.35	.35
☐ 11 Gene Baker	3.00	1.35	.35
☐ 12A Ernie Banks SCR	30.00	13.50	3.70
☐ 12B Ernie Banks SIG	15.00	6.75	1.85
☐ 12C Ernie Banks POR 64/66	30.00	13.50	3.70
☐ 13 Steve Barber 64/66	5.00	2.20	.60
☐ 14 Earl Battey 64/66	5.00	2.20	.60
☐ 15 Matt Batts	8.00	3.60	1.00
☐ 16A Hank Bauer (New York cap)	5.00	2.20	.60
☐ 16B Hank Bauer 61 (plain cap)	30.00	13.50	3.70
☐ 17 Frank Baumholtz	5.00	2.20	.60
☐ 18 Gene Bearden	3.00	1.35	.35
☐ 19 Joe Beggs 47	20.00	9.00	2.50
☐ 20A Yogi Berra	10.00	4.50	1.25
☐ 20B Larry "Yogi" Berra 64/66	35.00	16.00	4.40
☐ 21 Steve Bilko	3.00	1.35	.35
☐ 22A Ewell Blackwell (foot up)	8.00	3.60	1.00
☐ 22B Ewell Blackwell POR	3.00	1.35	.35
☐ 23A Don Blasingame (St. Louis cap)	3.00	1.35	.35
☐ 23B Don Blasingame (plain cap)	8.00	3.60	1.00
☐ 24 Ken Boyer 64/66	20.00	9.00	2.50
☐ 25 Ralph Branca	3.00	1.35	.35
☐ 26 Jackie Brandt 61	60.00	27.00	7.50
☐ 27 Harry Brecheen	3.00	1.35	.35
☐ 28 Tom Brewer 61	35.00	16.00	4.40
☐ 29 Lou Brissie	3.00	1.35	.35
☐ 30 Bill Bruton	3.00	1.35	.35
☐ 31A Lew Burdette (side view)	3.00	1.35	.35
☐ 31B Lew Burdette (facing) 64	25.00	11.00	3.10
☐ 32 Johnny Callison 64/66	6.00	2.70	.75
☐ 33 Roy Campanella	35.00	16.00	4.40
☐ 34A Chico Carrasquel (White Sox)	5.00	2.20	.60
☐ 34B Chico Carrasquel (plain cap)	15.00	6.75	1.85
☐ 35 George Case 47	20.00	9.00	2.50
☐ 36 Hugh Casey	10.00	4.50	1.25
☐ 37 Norm Cash 64/66	15.00	6.75	1.85
☐ 38A Orlando Cepeda POR 60/61	15.00	6.75	1.85
☐ 38B Orlando Cepeda BAT 64/66	15.00	6.75	1.85
☐ 39A Bob Cerv 60 (A's uniform)	5.00	2.20	.60
☐ 39B Bob Cerv 61 (plain uniform)	40.00	18.00	5.00
☐ 40 Dean Chance 64/66	5.00	2.20	.60
☐ 41 Spud Chandler 47	20.00	9.00	2.50
☐ 42 Tom Cheney 64/66	5.00	2.20	.60
☐ 43 Bubba Church	3.00	1.35	.35
☐ 44 Roberto Clemente	100.00	45.00	12.50
☐ 45A Rocky Colavito POR 61	100.00	45.00	12.50
☐ 45B Rocky Colavito BAT 64/66	25.00	11.00	3.10
☐ 46 Choo Choo Coleman 64	25.00	11.00	3.10
☐ 47 Gordy Coleman 66	35.00	16.00	4.40
☐ 48 Jerry Coleman	3.00	1.35	.35
☐ 49 Mort Cooper 47	25.00	11.00	3.10
☐ 50 Walker Cooper	3.00	1.35	.35
☐ 51 Roger Craig 64/66	10.00	4.50	1.25
☐ 52 Delmar Crandall	3.00	1.35	.35
☐ 53A Joe Cunningham POR 64/66	8.00	3.60	1.00
☐ 53B Joe Cunningham BAT 61	50.00	22.00	6.25
☐ 54 Guy Curtwright 47 (sic, Curtright)	20.00	9.00	2.50
☐ 55 Bud Daley 61	40.00	18.00	5.00
☐ 56A Alvin Dark (Boston cap)	10.00	4.50	1.25
☐ 56B Alvin Dark (New York cap)	5.00	2.20	.60
☐ 56C Alvin Dark (Cubs) 60	30.00	13.50	3.70
☐ 57 Murray Dickson	3.00	1.35	.35
☐ 58 Bob Dillinger	10.00	4.50	1.25
☐ 59 Dom DiMaggio	10.00	4.50	1.25
☐ 60 Joe Dobson	3.00	1.35	.35
☐ 61 Larry Doby	5.00	2.20	.60
☐ 62 Bobby Doerr	10.00	4.50	1.25
☐ 63A Dick Donovan (Braves, plain cap)	5.00	2.20	.60
☐ 63B Dick Donovan (White Sox)	3.00	1.35	.35
☐ 64 Walter Dropo	3.00	1.35	.35
☐ 65A Don Drysdale POR 60/61	35.00	16.00	4.40
☐ 65B Don Drysdale 64/66 POR 1/2	35.00	16.00	4.40
☐ 66 Luke Easter	5.00	2.20	.60
☐ 67 Bruce Edwards	10.00	4.50	1.25
☐ 68 Del Ennis	3.00	1.35	.35
☐ 69 Al Evans	3.00	1.35	.35
☐ 70 Walter Evers	3.00	1.35	.35
☐ 71A Ferris Fain FIE	10.00	4.50	1.25
☐ 71B Ferris Fain POR	5.00	2.20	.60
☐ 72 Dick Farrell 64/66	5.00	2.20	.60
☐ 73A Whitey Ford (has been reprinted) (no glove, throwing)	10.00	4.50	1.25
☐ 73B Whitey Ford POR 66	300.00	135.00	38.00
☐ 73C Ed "Whitey" Ford (glove on shoulder) 64/66	35.00	16.00	4.40
☐ 74 Dick Fowler	5.00	2.20	.60
☐ 75 Nelson Fox (has been reprinted)	15.00	6.75	1.85
☐ 76 Tito Francona 64/66	5.00	2.20	.60
☐ 77 Bob Friend	5.00	2.20	.60
☐ 78 Carl Furillo	20.00	9.00	2.50
☐ 79 Augie Galan	20.00	9.00	2.50
☐ 80 Jim Gentile 64/66	5.00	2.20	.60
☐ 81 Tony Gonzalez 64/66	5.00	2.20	.60
☐ 82A Billy Goodman FIE (fielding)	5.00	2.20	.60
☐ 82B Billy Goodman BAT 60/61	20.00	9.00	2.50
☐ 83 Ted Greengrass (sic, Jim)	10.00	4.50	1.25
☐ 84 Dick Groat	5.00	2.20	.60
☐ 85 Steve Gromek	10.00	4.50	1.25
☐ 86 Johnny Groth	3.00	1.35	.35
☐ 87 Orval Grove 47	20.00	9.00	2.50
☐ 88A Frank Gustine (Pirates)	5.00	2.20	.60
☐ 88B Frank Gustine(Cubs)	5.00	2.20	.60
☐ 89 Berthold Haas	20.00	9.00	2.50
☐ 90 Grady Hatton	5.00	2.20	.60
☐ 91 Jim Hegan	3.00	1.35	.35
☐ 92 Tom Henrich	5.00	2.20	.60
☐ 93 Ray Herbert 66	35.00	16.00	4.40
☐ 94 Gene Hermanski	10.00	4.50	1.25
☐ 95 Whitey Herzog 60/61	10.00	4.50	1.25
☐ 96 Kirby Higbe 47	20.00	9.00	2.50
☐ 97 Chuck Hinton 64/66	5.00	2.20	.60
☐ 98 Don Hoak 64	25.00	11.00	3.10
☐ 99A Gil Hodges (Brooklyn cap) (has been reprinted)	10.00	4.50	1.25
☐ 99B Gil Hodges (Los Angeles cap)	20.00	9.00	2.50
☐ 100 Johnny Hopp 47	20.00	9.00	2.50
☐ 101 Elston Howard (has been reprinted)	5.00	2.20	.60
☐ 102 Frank Howard 64/66	15.00	6.75	1.85
☐ 103 Ken Hubbs 64	100.00	45.00	12.50
☐ 104 Tex Hughson 47	20.00	9.00	2.50
☐ 105 Fred Hutchinson 50	10.00	4.50	1.25
☐ 106 Monte Irvin	10.00	4.50	1.25
☐ 107 Joey Jay 64/66	5.00	2.20	.60
☐ 108 Jackie Jensen 60	50.00	22.00	6.25
☐ 109 Sam Jethroe	5.00	2.20	.60
☐ 110 Bill Johnson 50	8.00	3.60	1.00
☐ 111 Walter Judnich 47	20.00	9.00	2.50
☐ 112A Al Kaline SCR (kneeling)	20.00	9.00	2.50
☐ 112B Al Kaline SIG POR	15.00	6.75	1.85
☐ 113 George Kell	10.00	4.50	1.25
☐ 114 Charley Keller	10.00	4.50	1.25
☐ 115 Alex Kellner	3.00	1.35	.35
☐ 116 Kenn Keltner (sic, Ken)	20.00	9.00	2.50
☐ 117A Harmon Killebrew	35.00	16.00	4.40

pinstripes, batting)
60/61
☐ 117B Harmon Killibrew 50.00 22.00 6.25
(sic, Killebrew)
POR 66
☐ 117C Harmon Killebrew 25.00 11.00 3.10
(throwing) 64/66
☐ 118 Ellis Kinder 5.00 2.20 .60
☐ 119 Ralph Kiner 10.00 4.50 1.25
☐ 120 Billy Klaus 60 35.00 16.00 4.40
☐ 121A Ted Kluszewski(Reds) 20.00 9.00 2.50
☐ 121B Ted Kluszewski 20.00 9.00 2.50
(Pirates)
☐ 121C Ted Kluszewski 50.00 22.00 6.25
(plain uniform) 60/61
☐ 122 Don Kolloway 50 10.00 4.50 1.25
☐ 123 Jim Konstanty 8.00 3.60 1.00
☐ 124 Sandy Koufax 64/66 100.00 45.00 12.50
☐ 125 Ed Kranepool 66 250.00 110.00 31.00
☐ 126A Tony Kubek 5.00 2.20 .60
(dark background)
☐ 126B Tony Kubek 5.00 2.20 .60
(light background)
☐ 127A Harvey Kuenn 60 10.00 4.50 1.25
(Detroit)
☐ 127B Harvey Kuenn 61 35.00 16.00 4.40
(plain uniform)
☐ 127C Harvey Kuenn 10.00 4.50 1.25
(San Francisco) 64/66
☐ 128 Whitey Kurowski 50 20.00 9.00 2.50
☐ 129 Eddie Lake 47 20.00 9.00 2.50
☐ 130 Jim Landis 64/66 5.00 2.20 .60
☐ 131 Don Larsen 5.00 2.20 .60
☐ 132A Bob Lemon 8.00 3.60 1.00
(left arm not shown)
☐ 132B Bob Lemon 65.00 29.00 8.00
(left arm extended)
☐ 133 Buddy Lewis 47 20.00 9.00 2.50
☐ 134 Johnny Lindell 50 20.00 9.00 2.50
☐ 135 Phil Linz 66 35.00 16.00 4.40
☐ 136 Don Lock 66 35.00 16.00 4.40
☐ 137 Whitey Lockman 5.00 2.20 .60
☐ 138 Johnny Logan 3.00 1.35 .35
☐ 139A Dale Long (Pirates) 3.00 1.35 .35
☐ 139B Dale Long (Cubs) 61 40.00 18.00 5.00
☐ 140 Ed Lopat 5.00 2.20 .60
☐ 141A Harry Lowery 10.00 4.50 1.25
(sic, Lowrey)
☐ 141B Harry Lowrey 5.00 2.20 .60
☐ 142 Sal Maglie 5.00 2.20 .60
☐ 143 Art Mahaffey 64/66 5.00 2.20 .60
☐ 144 Hank Majeski 3.00 1.35 .35
☐ 145 Frank Malzone 3.00 1.35 .35
☐ 146A Mickey Mantle 150.00 70.00 19.00
(batting to waist)
(white outline around
first letters in Mickey)
☐ 146B Mickey Mantle 250.00 110.00 31.00
(batting to waist)
(no white outline)
(has been reprinted)
☐ 146C Mickey Mantle 150.00 70.00 19.00
(batting full) 64/66
☐ 146D Mickey Mantle POR 600.00 275.00 75.00
66
☐ 147 Marty Marion 5.00 2.20 .60
☐ 148 Roger Maris 64/66 50.00 22.00 6.25
☐ 149 Willard Marshall 3.00 1.35 .35
☐ 150A Ed Matthews SCR 15.00 6.75 1.85
(sic, Mathews)
☐ 150B Eddie Mathews SIG 25.00 11.00 3.10
☐ 151 Ed Mayo 5.00 2.20 .60
☐ 152A Willie Mays 35.00 16.00 4.40
(New York)
(has been reprinted)
☐ 152B Willie Mays 35.00 16.00 4.40
(San Francisco)
☐ 153A Bill Mazeroski POR 10.00 4.50 1.25
60/61
☐ 153B Bill Mazeroski BAT 10.00 4.50 1.25
64/66
☐ 154 Ken McBride 64/66 5.00 2.20 .60
☐ 155A Barney McCaskey 25.00 11.00 3.10
(sic, McCosky)
☐ 155B Barney McCoskey 75.00 34.00 9.50
(sic, McCosky)
☐ 156 Lindy McDaniel 60/61 5.00 2.20 .60
☐ 157 Gil McDougald 5.00 2.20 .60
☐ 158 Albert Mele 35.00 16.00 4.40
☐ 159 Sam Mele 10.00 4.50 1.25
☐ 160A Orestes Minoso 5.00 2.20 .60
(White Sox)
☐ 160B Orestes Minoso 10.00 4.50 1.25
(Cleveland)
☐ 161 Dale Mitchell 3.00 1.35 .35
☐ 162 Wally Moon 5.00 2.20 .60
☐ 163 Don Mueller 25.00 11.00 3.10
☐ 164A Stan Musial 35.00 16.00 4.40
(three bats, kneeling)
(has been reprinted)
☐ 164B Stan Musial BAT 64 150.00 70.00 19.00
☐ 165 Charles Neal 64 25.00 11.00 3.10
☐ 166A Don Newcombe 10.00 4.50 1.25
(shaking hands)
☐ 166B Don Newcombe 5.00 2.20 .60
(Brooklyn cap)
(has been reprinted)
☐ 166C Don Newcombe 15.00 6.75 1.85
(plain cap)
☐ 167 Hal Newhouser 10.00 4.50 1.25
☐ 168 Ron Northey 47 25.00 11.00 3.10
☐ 169 Bill O'Dell 64/66 5.00 2.20 .60
☐ 170 Joe Page 50 20.00 9.00 2.50
☐ 171 Satchel Paige 100.00 45.00 12.50
☐ 172 Milt Pappas 64/66 5.00 2.20 .60
☐ 173 Camilo Pascual 64/66 5.00 2.20 .60
☐ 174 Albie Pearson 66 35.00 16.00 4.40
☐ 175 Johnny Pesky 3.00 1.35 .35
☐ 176 Gary Peters 66 35.00 16.00 4.40
☐ 177 Dave Philley 5.00 2.20 .60
☐ 178 Billy Pierce 60/61 5.00 2.20 .60
☐ 179 Jimmy Piersall 66 75.00 34.00 9.50
☐ 180 Vada Pinson 64/66 15.00 6.75 1.85
☐ 181 Bob Porterfield 5.00 2.20 .60
☐ 182 John "Boog" Powell 66 100.00 45.00 12.50
☐ 183 Vic Raschi 5.00 2.20 .60
☐ 184A Harold "Peewee" Reese 15.00 6.75 1.85
(ball visible along
bottom border)
☐ 184B Harold "Peewee" Reese 15.00 6.75 1.85
(ball not visible)
(has been reprinted)
☐ 185 Del Rice 3.00 1.35 .35
☐ 186 Bobby Richardson 66 300.00 135.00 38.00
☐ 187A Phil Rizzuto 15.00 6.75 1.85
(small photo)
☐ 187B Phil Rizzuto 10.00 4.50 1.25
(larger photo)
☐ 188A Robin Roberts SIG 10.00 4.50 1.25
☐ 188B Robin Roberts SCR 12.00 5.50 1.50
☐ 189 Brooks Robinson 35.00 16.00 4.40
☐ 190 Eddie Robinson POR 5.00 2.20 .60
☐ 191 Floyd Robinson 66 35.00 16.00 4.40
☐ 192 Frankie Robinson 35.00 16.00 4.40
64/66
☐ 193 Jackie Robinson 60.00 27.00 7.50
☐ 194 Preacher Roe 5.00 2.20 .60
☐ 195 Bob Rogers 66 35.00 16.00 4.40
(sic, Rodgers)
☐ 196 Richard Rollins 66 35.00 16.00 4.40
☐ 197 Pete Runnels 64 25.00 11.00 3.10
☐ 198 John Sain 5.00 2.20 .60
☐ 199 Ron Santo 64/66 20.00 9.00 2.50
☐ 200 Henry Sauer 5.00 2.20 .60
☐ 201A Carl Sawatski 3.00 1.35 .35
(Milwaukee cap)
☐ 201B Carl Sawatski 3.00 1.35 .35
(Philadelphia cap)
☐ 201C Carl Sawatski 61 25.00 11.00 3.10
(plain cap)
☐ 202 Johnny Schmitz 8.00 3.60 1.00
☐ 203A Red Schoendeinst 25.00 11.00 3.10
(one foot shown
catching)
(sic, Schoendienst)
☐ 203B Red Schoendeinst 35.00 16.00 4.40
(both feet shown
catching)
(sic, Schoendienst)
☐ 203C Red Schoendinst BAT 10.00 4.50 1.25
(sic, Schoendienst)
☐ 204A Herb Score 10.00 4.50 1.25
(Cleveland cap)
☐ 204B Herb Score 61 35.00 16.00 4.40
(plain cap)
☐ 205 Andy Seminick 5.00 2.20 .60
☐ 206 Rip Sewell 47 25.00 11.00 3.10
☐ 207 Norm Siebern 5.00 2.20 .60
☐ 208A Roy Sievers 51 50.00 22.00 6.25
(Browns)
☐ 208B Roy Sievers 5.00 2.20 .60
(Senators)
dark background)
☐ 208C Roy Sievers 5.00 2.20 .60
(Senators)
light background)
☐ 208D Roy Sievers 61 35.00 16.00 4.40
(plain uniform)
☐ 209 Curt Simmons 5.00 2.20 .60
☐ 210 Dick Sisler 5.00 2.20 .60
☐ 211A Bill Skowron 5.00 2.20 .60
(New York)
☐ 211B Bill "Moose" Skowron 250.00 110.00 31.00
(White Sox) 66
☐ 212 Enos Slaughter 10.00 4.50 1.25
☐ 213A Duke Snider 15.00 6.75 1.85
(Brooklyn)
☐ 213B Duke Snider 25.00 11.00 3.10
(Los Angeles)
☐ 214A Warren Spahn 10.00 4.50 1.25
(Boston)
(has been reprinted)
☐ 214B Warren Spahn 20.00 9.00 2.50
(Milwaukee)
☐ 215 Stanley Spence 20.00 9.00 2.50
☐ 216A Ed Stanky 5.00 2.20 .60
(plain uniform)
☐ 216B Ed Stanky (Giants) 5.00 2.20 .60
☐ 217A Vern Stephens 5.00 2.20 .60
(Browns)
☐ 217B Vern Stephens 8.00 3.60 1.00
(Red Sox)
☐ 218 Ed Stewart 3.00 1.35 .35
☐ 219 Snuffy Stirnweiss 25.00 11.00 3.10
☐ 220 George "Birdie" Tebbets 15.00 6.75 1.85
☐ 221A Frankie Thomas BAT 35.00 16.00 4.40
(Bob Skinner picture)
59
☐ 221B Frank Thomas (Cubs) 35.00 16.00 4.40
60/61
☐ 222 Lee Thomas 64/66 5.00 2.20 .60
☐ 223 Bobby Thomson 10.00 4.50 1.25
☐ 224A Earl Torgeson 3.00 1.35 .35
(Braves)
☐ 224B Earl Torgeson 60/61 5.00 2.20 .60
(plain uniform)
☐ 225 Gus Triandos 60/61 10.00 4.50 1.25
☐ 226 Virgil Trucks 5.00 2.20 .60
☐ 227 Johnny Vandermeer 47 50.00 22.00 6.25
☐ 228 Emil Verban 25.00 11.00 3.10
☐ 229A Mickey Vernon 3.00 1.35 .35
(throwing)
☐ 229B Mickey Vernon BAT 3.00 1.35 .35
☐ 230 Bill Voiselle 47 25.00 11.00 3.10
☐ 231 Leon Wagner 64/66 5.00 2.20 .60
☐ 232A Eddie Waitkus BAT 5.00 2.20 .60
(Cub uniform)
☐ 232B Eddie Waitkus BAT 5.00 2.20 .60
(plain uniform)
☐ 232C Eddie Waitkus POR 35.00 16.00 4.40
(Phillies uniform)
☐ 233 Dick Wakefield 5.00 2.20 .60
☐ 234 Harry Walker 50.00 22.00 6.25
☐ 235 Bucky Walters 10.00 4.50 1.25
☐ 236 Pete Ward 66 200.00 90.00 25.00
☐ 237 Herman Wehmeier 3.00 1.35 .35
☐ 238A Vic Wertz (Tigers) 3.00 1.35 .35
☐ 238B Vic Wertz(Red Sox) 5.00 2.20 .60
☐ 239 Wally Westlake 3.00 1.35 .35
☐ 240 Wes Westrum 35.00 16.00 4.40
☐ 241 Billy Williams 64/66 35.00 16.00 4.40
☐ 242 Maurice Wills 64/66 20.00 9.00 2.50
☐ 243A Gene Woodling SCR 3.00 1.35 .35
☐ 243B Gene Woodling SIG 5.00 2.20 .60
☐ 244 Taffy Wright 47 20.00 9.00 2.50
☐ 245 Carl Yastrzemski 66 300.00 135.00 38.00
☐ 246 Al Zarilla 51 10.00 4.50 1.25
☐ 247A Gus Zernial SCR 3.00 1.35 .35
☐ 247B Gus Zernial SIG 5.00 2.20 .60

1948 Exhibit Hall of Fame

This exhibit set, entitled "Baseball's Great Hall of Fame," consists of black and white photos on gray background. The pictures are framed on the sides by Greek columns and a short biography is printed at the bottom. The cards are blank backed. Twenty four of the cards were reissued in 1974 on extremely white stock. Each card measures 3 3/8" by 5 3/8".

	NRMT	VG-E	GOOD
COMPLETE SET (33)	600.00	275.00	75.00
COMMON CARD (1-32)	5.00	2.20	.60

☐ 1 G.C. Alexander 7.50 3.40 .95
☐ 2 Roger Bresnahan 5.00 2.20 .60
☐ 3 Frank Chance 6.00 2.70 .75
☐ 4 Jack Chesbro 5.00 2.20 .60
☐ 5 Fred Clarke 5.00 2.20 .60
☐ 6 Ty Cobb 75.00 34.00 9.50
☐ 7 Mickey Cochrane 7.50 3.40 .95
☐ 8 Eddie Collins 5.00 2.20 .60
☐ 9 Hugh Duffy 5.00 2.20 .60
☐ 10 Johnny Evers 5.00 2.20 .60
☐ 11 Frankie Frisch 6.00 2.70 .75
☐ 12 Lou Gehrig 75.00 34.00 9.50
☐ 13 Clark Griffith 5.00 2.20 .60
☐ 14 Robert "Lefty" Grove 7.50 3.40 .95
☐ 15 Rogers Hornsby 10.00 4.50 1.25
☐ 16 Carl Hubbell 6.00 2.70 .75
☐ 17 Hughie Jennings 5.00 2.20 .60
☐ 18 Walter Johnson 15.00 6.75 1.85
☐ 19 Willie Keeler 5.00 2.20 .60
☐ 20 Nap Lajoie 10.00 4.50 1.25
☐ 21 Connie Mack 7.50 3.40 .95
☐ 22 Christy Mathewson 15.00 6.75 1.85
☐ 23 John McGraw 10.00 4.50 1.25
☐ 24 Eddie Plank 6.00 2.70 .75
☐ 25A Babe Ruth 50.00 22.00 6.25
(swinging)
☐ 25B Babe Ruth 300.00 135.00 38.00
(bats in front)
ten bats pose
☐ 26 George Sisler 6.00 2.70 .75
☐ 27 Tris Speaker 10.00 4.50 1.25
☐ 28 Joe Tinker 5.00 2.20 .60
☐ 29 Rube Waddell 5.00 2.20 .60
☐ 30 Honus Wagner 15.00 6.75 1.85
☐ 31 Ed Walsh 5.00 2.20 .60
☐ 32 Cy Young 12.50 5.50 1.55

1948-56 Exhibits Team

The cards found listed in this classification were not a separate issue from the individual player cards of the same period but have been assembled together in the Price Guide for emphasis. Each of these 1948-1956 Exhibit team cards was issued to honor the champions of the National and American Leagues, except for 1953, when none were printed. Reprints of these popular cards are known to exist. Each card measures 3 3/8" by 5 3/8".

	NRMT	VG-E	GOOD
COMPLETE SET (16)	800.00	350.00	100.00
COMMON TEAM (1-16)	25.00	11.00	3.10

☐ 1 1948 Boston Braves 25.00 11.00 3.10
☐ 2 1948 Cleveland Indians 35.00 16.00 4.40
☐ 3 1949 Brooklyn Dodgers 50.00 22.00 6.25
☐ 4 1949 New York Yankees 50.00 22.00 6.25
☐ 5 1950 Philadelphia 35.00 16.00 4.40
Phillies
☐ 6 1950 New York Yankees 50.00 22.00 6.25
☐ 7 1951 New York Giants 35.00 16.00 4.40
☐ 8 1951 New York Yankees 25.00 11.00 3.10
☐ 9 1952 Brooklyn Dodgers 50.00 22.00 6.25
☐ 10 1952 New York Yankees 50.00 22.00 6.25
☐ 11 1954 New York Giants 50.00 22.00 6.25
☐ 12 1954 Cleveland Indians 50.00 22.00 6.25
☐ 13 1955 Brooklyn Dodgers 200.00 90.00 25.00
☐ 14 1955 New York Yankees 100.00 45.00 12.50
☐ 15 1956 Brooklyn Dodgers 300.00 135.00 38.00
☐ 16 1956 New York Yankees 100.00 45.00 12.50

1953 Exhibits Canadian

This numbered, blank-backed set depicts both major league players (reprinted from American Exhibit sets) and International League Montreal Royals. The cards (3 1/4" by 5 1/4") are slightly smaller than regular Exhibit issues and are printed on gray stock. Numbers 1-32 are found in green or wine-red color, while 33-64 are blue or reddish-brown. Cards 1-32 are numbered in a small, diamond-shaped white box at lower right; cards 33-64 have a large, hand-lettered number at upper right.

	NRMT	VG-E	GOOD
COMPLETE SET (64)	900.00	400.00	110.00
COMMON CARD (1-32)	6.00	2.70	.75
COMMON CARD (33-64)	4.00	1.80	.50

☐ 1 Preacher Roe 8.00 3.60 1.00
☐ 2 Luke Easter 6.00 2.70 .75
☐ 3 Gene Bearden 6.00 2.70 .75
☐ 4 Chico Carrasquel 6.00 2.70 .75
☐ 5 Vic Raschi 8.00 3.60 1.00
☐ 6 Monte Irvin 12.00 5.50 1.50
☐ 7 Hank Sauer 6.00 2.70 .75
☐ 8 Ralph Branca 8.00 3.60 1.00
☐ 9 Eddie Stanky 6.00 2.70 .75
☐ 10 Sam Jethroe 6.00 2.70 .75
☐ 11 Larry Doby 8.00 3.60 1.00
☐ 12 Hal Newhouser 12.00 5.50 1.50
☐ 13 Gil Hodges 20.00 9.00 2.50
☐ 14 Harry Brecheen 6.00 2.70 .75
☐ 15 Ed Lopat 10.00 4.50 1.25
☐ 16 Don Newcombe 10.00 4.50 1.25
☐ 17 Bob Feller 35.00 16.00 4.40
☐ 18 Tommy Holmes 6.00 2.70 .75
☐ 19 Jackie Robinson 75.00 34.00 9.50
☐ 20 Roy Campanella 75.00 34.00 9.50
☐ 21 Pee Wee Reese 30.00 13.50 3.70
☐ 22 Ralph Kiner 15.00 6.75 1.85
☐ 23 Dom DiMaggio 10.00 4.50 1.25
☐ 24 Bobby Doerr 12.00 5.50 1.50
☐ 25 Phil Rizzuto 25.00 11.00 3.10
☐ 26 Bob Elliott 6.00 2.70 .75
☐ 27 Tom Henrich 8.00 3.60 1.00
☐ 28 Joe DiMaggio 200.00 90.00 25.00
☐ 29 Harry Lowery 6.00 2.70 .75
☐ 30 Ted Williams 100.00 45.00 12.50
☐ 31 Bob Lemon 15.00 6.75 1.85
☐ 32 Warren Spahn 20.00 9.00 2.50
☐ 33 Don Hoak 6.00 2.70 .75
☐ 34 Bob Alexander 4.00 1.80 .50
☐ 35 John Simmons 4.00 1.80 .50
☐ 36 Steve Lembo 4.00 1.80 .50
☐ 37 Norman Larker 8.00 3.60 1.00
☐ 38 Bob Ludwick 4.00 1.80 .50
☐ 39 Walter Moryn 6.00 2.70 .75

☐ 40 Charlie Thompson	6.00	2.70	.75
☐ 41 Ed Roebuck	6.00	2.70	.75
☐ 42 Rose	4.00	1.80	.50
☐ 43 Edmundo Amoros	8.00	3.60	1.00
☐ 44 Bob Milliken	6.00	2.70	.75
☐ 45 Art Fabbro	4.00	1.80	.50
☐ 46 Forrest Jacobs	6.00	2.70	.75
☐ 47 Carmen Mauro	6.00	2.70	.75
☐ 48 Walter Fiala	6.00	2.70	.75
☐ 49 Rocky Nelson	6.00	2.70	.75
☐ 50 Tom Lasorda	50.00	22.00	6.25
☐ 51 Ronnie Lee	6.00	2.70	.75
☐ 52 Hampton Coleman	6.00	2.70	.75
☐ 53 Frank Marchio	6.00	2.70	.75
☐ 54 William Samson	6.00	2.70	.75
☐ 55 Gil Mills	6.00	2.70	.75
☐ 56 Al Ronning	6.00	2.70	.75
☐ 57 Stan Musial	60.00	27.00	7.50
☐ 58 Walker Cooper	6.00	2.70	.75
☐ 59 Mickey Vernon	8.00	3.60	1.00
☐ 60 Del Ennis	8.00	3.60	1.00
☐ 61 Walter Alston MG	30.00	13.50	3.70
☐ 62 Dick Sisler	6.00	2.70	.75
☐ 63 Billy Goodman	6.00	2.70	.75
☐ 64 Alex Kellner	6.00	2.70	.75

1960-61 Exhibits Wrigley HOF

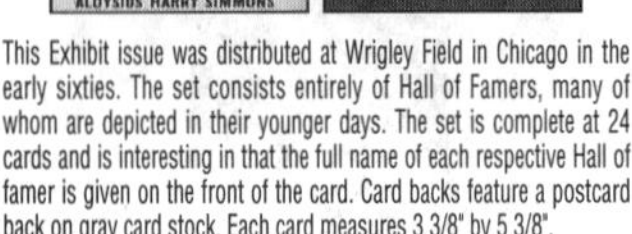

This Exhibit issue was distributed at Wrigley Field in Chicago in the early sixties. The set consists entirely of Hall of Famers, many of whom are depicted in their younger days. The set is complete at 24 cards and is interesting in that the full name of each respective Hall of famer is given on the front of the card. Card backs feature a postcard back on gray card stock. Each card measures 3 3/8" by 5 3/8".

	NRMT	VG-E	GOOD
COMPLETE SET (24)	300.00	135.00	38.00
COMMON CARD (1-24)	6.00	2.70	.75
☐ 1 Grover Cleveland Alexander	10.00	4.50	1.25
☐ 2 Adrian Constantine Anson	10.00	4.50	1.25
☐ 3 John Franklin Baker	6.00	2.70	.75
☐ 4 Roger Phillip Bresnahan	6.00	2.70	.75
☐ 5 Mordecai Peter Brown	6.00	2.70	.75
☐ 6 Frank Leroy Chance	7.50	3.40	.95
☐ 7 Tyrus Raymond Cobb	40.00	18.00	5.00
☐ 8 Edward Trowbridge Collins	7.50	3.40	.95
☐ 9 James J. Collins	6.00	2.70	.75
☐ 10 John Joseph Evers	6.00	2.70	.75
☐ 11 Henry Louis Gehrig	40.00	18.00	5.00
☐ 12 Clark C. Griffith	6.00	2.70	.75
☐ 13 Walter Perry Johnson	20.00	9.00	2.50
☐ 14 Anthony M. Lazzeri	6.00	2.70	.75
☐ 15 James Walter Vincent Maranville	6.00	2.70	.75
☐ 16 Christopher Mathewson	20.00	9.00	2.50
☐ 17 John Joseph McGraw	10.00	4.50	1.25
☐ 18 Melvin Thomass Ott	12.50	5.50	1.55
☐ 19 Herbert Jeffries Pennock	6.00	2.70	.75
☐ 20 George Herman Ruth	75.00	34.00	9.50
☐ 21 Alloysius Harry Simmons	6.00	2.70	.75
☐ 22 Tristram Speaker	12.00	5.50	1.50
☐ 23 Joseph B. Tinker	6.00	2.70	.75
☐ 24 John Peter Wagner	20.00	9.00	2.50

1962 Exhibit Stat Back

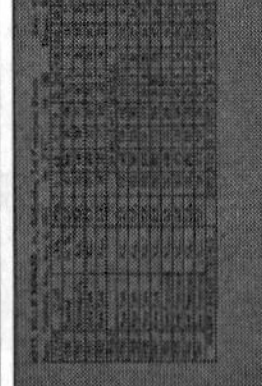

The 32-card sheet was a standard production feature of the Exhibit Supply Company, although, generally more than one sheet comprised a set. The 32-card set issued in 1962 thus amounted to one-half a normal printing, and is differentiated from other concurrent Exhibit issues by the inclusion of records, printed in black or red, on the reverse of each card. Each card measures 3 3/8" by 5 3/8". Backs printed in red ink are slightly more difficult to find but there is no difference in price.

	NRMT	VG-E	GOOD
COMPLETE SET (32)	500.00	220.00	60.00
COMMON CARD (1-32)	3.00	1.35	.35
☐ 1 Hank Aaron	35.00	16.00	4.40
☐ 2 Luis Aparicio	10.00	4.50	1.25
☐ 3 Ernie Banks	20.00	9.00	2.50
☐ 4 Larry "Yogi" Berra	30.00	13.50	3.70
☐ 5 Ken Boyer	10.00	4.50	1.25
☐ 6 Lew Burdette	5.00	2.20	.60
☐ 7 Norm Cash	10.00	4.50	1.25
☐ 8 Orlando Cepeda	10.00	4.50	1.25
☐ 9 Roberto Clemente	60.00	27.00	7.50
☐ 10 Rocky Colavito	20.00	9.00	2.50
☐ 11 Ed "Whitey" Ford	20.00	9.00	2.50
☐ 12 Nelson Fox	10.00	4.50	1.25
☐ 13 Tito Francona	3.00	1.35	.35
☐ 14 Jim Gentile	3.00	1.35	.35
☐ 15 Dick Groat	5.00	2.20	.60
☐ 16 Don Hoak	3.00	1.35	.35
☐ 17 Al Kaline	20.00	9.00	2.50
☐ 18 Harmon Killebrew	15.00	6.75	1.85
☐ 19 Sandy Koufax	50.00	22.00	6.25
☐ 20 Jim Landis	3.00	1.35	.35
☐ 21 Art Mahaffey	3.00	1.35	.35
☐ 22 Frank Malzone	3.00	1.35	.35
☐ 23 Mickey Mantle	150.00	70.00	19.00
☐ 24 Roger Maris	30.00	13.50	3.70
☐ 25 Eddie Mathews	15.00	6.75	1.85
☐ 26 Willie Mays	35.00	16.00	4.40
☐ 27 Wally Moon	3.00	1.35	.35
☐ 28 Stan Musial	35.00	16.00	4.40
☐ 29 Milt Pappas	3.00	1.35	.35
☐ 30 Vada Pinson	5.00	2.20	.60
☐ 31 Norm Siebern	3.00	1.35	.35
☐ 32 Warren Spahn	15.00	6.75	1.85

1963 Exhibit Stat Back

The 1963 Exhibit issue features 64 cards with statistics printed in red on the backs. Each card measures 3 3/8" by 5 3/8". The set is quite similar to the set of the previous year -- but this set can be distinguished by the red print on the backs and the additional year of statistics.

	NRMT	VG-E	GOOD
COMPLETE SET (64)	600.00	275.00	75.00
COMMON CARD (1-64)	3.00	1.35	.35
☐ 1 Hank Aaron	35.00	16.00	4.40
☐ 2 Luis Aparicio	10.00	4.50	1.25
☐ 3 Bob Aspromonte	3.00	1.35	.35
☐ 4 Ernie Banks	20.00	9.00	2.50
☐ 5 Steve Barber	3.00	1.35	.35
☐ 6 Earl Battey	3.00	1.35	.35
☐ 7 Larry "Yogi" Berra	30.00	13.50	3.70
☐ 8 Ken Boyer	10.00	4.50	1.25
☐ 9 Lew Burdette	5.00	2.20	.60
☐ 10 Johnny Callison	3.00	1.35	.35
☐ 11 Norm Cash	10.00	4.50	1.25
☐ 12 Orlando Cepeda	10.00	4.50	1.25
☐ 13 Dean Chance	3.00	1.35	.35
☐ 14 Tom Cheney	3.00	1.35	.35
☐ 15 Roberto Clemente	60.00	27.00	7.50
☐ 16 Rocky Colavito	10.00	4.50	1.25
☐ 17 Choo Choo Coleman	5.00	2.20	.60
☐ 18 Roger Craig	5.00	2.20	.60
☐ 19 Joe Cunningham	5.00	2.20	.60
☐ 20 Don Drysdale	15.00	6.75	1.85
☐ 21 Dick Farrell	3.00	1.35	.35
☐ 22 Ed "Whitey" Ford	20.00	9.00	2.50
☐ 23 Nelson Fox	10.00	4.50	1.25
☐ 24 Tito Francona	3.00	1.35	.35
☐ 25 Jim Gentile	3.00	1.35	.35
☐ 26 Tony Gonzales	3.00	1.35	.35
☐ 27 Dick Groat	5.00	2.20	.60
☐ 28 Ray Herbert	3.00	1.35	.35
☐ 29 Chuck Hinton	3.00	1.35	.35
☐ 30 Don Hoak	3.00	1.35	.35
☐ 31 Frank Howard	6.00	2.70	.75
☐ 32 Ken Hubbs	20.00	9.00	2.50
☐ 33 Joey Jay	3.00	1.35	.35
☐ 34 Al Kaline	20.00	9.00	2.50
☐ 35 Harmon Killebrew	15.00	6.75	1.85
☐ 36 Sandy Koufax	50.00	22.00	6.25
☐ 37 Harvey Kuenn	5.00	2.20	.60
☐ 38 Jim Landis	3.00	1.35	.35
☐ 39 Art Mahaffey	3.00	1.35	.35
☐ 40 Frank Malzone	3.00	1.35	.35
☐ 41 Mickey Mantle	150.00	70.00	19.00
☐ 42 Roger Maris	35.00	16.00	4.40
☐ 43 Eddie Mathews	15.00	6.75	1.85
☐ 44 Willie Mays	35.00	16.00	4.40
☐ 45 Bill Mazeroski	8.00	3.60	1.00
☐ 46 Ken McBride	3.00	1.35	.35
☐ 47 Wally Moon	3.00	1.35	.35
☐ 48 Stan Musial	35.00	16.00	4.40
☐ 49 Charlie Neal	5.00	2.20	.60
☐ 50 Bill O'Dell	3.00	1.35	.35
☐ 51 Milt Pappas	3.00	1.35	.35
☐ 52 Camilo Pascual	3.00	1.35	.35
☐ 53 Jim Piersall	8.00	3.60	1.00
☐ 54 Vada Pinson	8.00	3.60	1.00
☐ 55 Brooks Robinson	25.00	11.00	3.10
☐ 56 Frankie Robinson	20.00	9.00	2.50
☐ 57 Pete Runnels	3.00	1.35	.35
☐ 58 Ron Santo	8.00	3.60	1.00
☐ 59 Norm Siebern	3.00	1.35	.35
☐ 60 Warren Spahn	15.00	6.75	1.85
☐ 61 Lee Thomas	3.00	1.35	.35
☐ 62 Leon Wagner	3.00	1.35	.35
☐ 63 Billy Williams	15.00	6.75	1.85
☐ 64 Maurice Wills	10.00	4.50	1.25

1969 Expos Fud's Photography

This blank-backed set was apparently issued by Bob Solon in the Chicago area. The black-and-white cards measure approximately 3 1/2" by 3" and feature Montreal Expos players of the 1969 season. The fronts carry action player photos with a white border. The player's name appears in a white bar in the lower right corner of the photo. The words "Compliments of" are printed in the upper border, while the words "Fud's Photography" appear in the lower border. The cards are unnumbered and checklisted below in alphabetical order.

	NRMT	VG-E	GOOD
COMPLETE SET (14)	20.00	9.00	2.50
COMMON CARD (1-14)	1.25	.55	.16
☐ 1 Bob Bailey	1.50	.70	.19
☐ 2 John Bateman	1.50	.70	.19
☐ 3 Don Bosch	1.25	.55	.16
☐ 4 Jim Grant	2.00	.90	.25
☐ 5 Mack Jones	1.50	.70	.19
☐ 6 Coco Laboy	1.50	.70	.19
☐ 7 Dan McGinn	1.25	.55	.16
☐ 8 Cal McLish CO	1.25	.55	.16
☐ 9 Carl Morton	1.50	.70	.19
☐ 10 Manny Mota	2.50	1.10	.30
☐ 11 Rusty Staub	5.00	2.20	.60
☐ 12 Gary Sutherland	1.25	.55	.16
☐ 13 Mike Wegener	1.25	.55	.16
☐ 14 Floyd Wicker	1.25	.55	.16

1969 Expos Pins

These nine round pins were manufactured by Best In Sports of Montreal, measure approximately 1 1/2" in diameter and feature players from the Montreal Expos debut season in 1969. The pins have white backgrounds and carry posed color player cutouts. The player's name appears in black lettering above the photo. The pins are unnumbered and checklisted below in alphabetical order.

	NRMT	VG-E	GOOD
COMPLETE SET (9)	30.00	13.50	3.70
COMMON PIN (1-9)	2.50	1.10	.30
☐ 1 John Bateman	3.00	1.35	.35
☐ 2 Ron Brand	2.50	1.10	.30
☐ 3 Ron Fairly	4.00	1.80	.50
☐ 4 Coco Laboy	3.00	1.35	.35
☐ 5 Gene Mauch MG	4.00	1.80	.50
☐ 6 Steve Renko	2.50	1.10	.30
☐ 7 Rusty Staub	7.50	3.40	.95
☐ 8 Bill Stoneman	3.00	1.35	.35
☐ 9 Bobby Wine	2.50	1.10	.30

1970 Expos Pins

These 14 round pins measure approximately 1 1/2" in diameter and feature players from the 1970 Montreal Expos. The pins have red, white and blue backgrounds and carry circular posed color player headshots. The player's name appears in cursive black lettering below the photo. The pins are unnumbered and checklisted below in alphabetical order.

	NRMT	VG-E	GOOD
COMPLETE SET (14)	40.00	18.00	5.00
COMMON PIN (1-14)	2.50	1.10	.30
☐ 1 Expos Logo Pin	3.50	1.55	.45
☐ 2 Bob Bailey	3.50	1.55	.45
☐ 3 John Bateman	3.50	1.55	.45
☐ 4 Boots Day	2.50	1.10	.30
☐ 5 Ron Fairly	3.50	1.55	.45
☐ 6 Jim Gosger	2.50	1.10	.30
☐ 7 Ron Hunt	3.50	1.55	.45
☐ 8 Mack Jones	3.50	1.55	.45
☐ 9 Coco Laboy	3.50	1.55	.45
☐ 10 Dan McGinn	2.50	1.10	.30
☐ 11 Carl Morton	3.50	1.55	.45
☐ 12 Claude Raymond	3.50	1.55	.45
☐ 13 Rusty Staub	7.50	3.40	.95
☐ 14 Bobby Wine	2.50	1.10	.30

1970 Expos Postcards

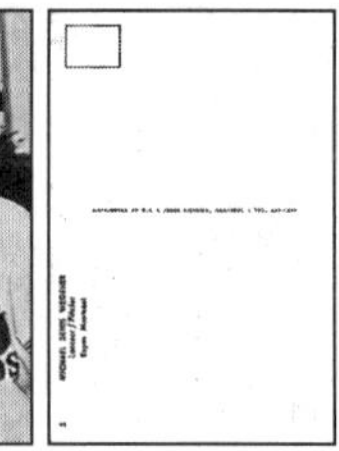

These 16 Montreal Expos postcards measure approximately 3 1/2" by 5 1/2" and feature borderless posed color player photos on their fronts. The player's facsimile autograph appears near the bottom. The backs carry the player's name and bilingual position in black ink at the upper left. The cards are numbered on the back.

	NRMT	VG-E	GOOD
COMPLETE SET (16)	20.00	9.00	2.50
COMMON CARD (1-16)	1.25	.55	.16
☐ 1 Elroy Face	3.00	1.35	.35
☐ 2 Don Shaw	1.25	.55	.16
☐ 3 Dan McGinn	1.25	.55	.16
☐ 4 Bill Stoneman	2.00	.90	.25
☐ 5 Mike Wegener	1.25	.55	.16
☐ 6 Bob Bailey	2.00	.90	.25
☐ 7 Gary Sutherland	1.25	.55	.16
☐ 8 Coco Laboy	1.50	.70	.19
☐ 9 Bobby Wine UER (Misspelled Boby on back)	1.50	.70	.19
☐ 10 Mack Jones	1.50	.70	.19
☐ 11 Rusty Staub	5.00	2.20	.60
☐ 12 Don Bosch	1.25	.55	.16
☐ 13 Larry Jaster	2.00	.90	.25
☐ 14 John Bateman	1.50	.70	.19
☐ 15 John Boccabella	1.50	.70	.19
☐ 16 Ron Brand	1.25	.55	.16

1971 Expos La Pizza Royale

Featuring members of the Montreal Expos, this set, like the Fud's set, is thought to have been issued by Bob Solon in the Chicago area. Printed on thick cardboard paper, the cards measure approximately 2 1/2" by 5". The fronts typically feature blue-tinted player photos on a dark blue background; however the set was also issued in at least three other colors: green, gold, and red. The words "La Pizza Royale" are printed in white letters above the photo, while the player's name and position in French appear under the photo. The backs are blank. The cards are unnumbered and checklisted below in alphabetical order.

	NRMT	VG-E	GOOD
COMPLETE SET (14)	25.00	11.00	3.10
COMMON CARD (1-14)	2.00	.90	.25

	NRMT	VG-E	GOOD
☐ 1 Bob Bailey	3.00	1.35	.35
☐ 2 John Boccabella	2.50	1.10	.30
☐ 3 Ron Fairly	3.50	1.55	.45
☐ 4 Jim Gosger	2.00	.90	.25
☐ 5 Coco Laboy	2.50	1.10	.30
☐ 6 Gene Mauch MG	3.00	1.35	.35
☐ 7 Rich Nye	2.00	.90	.25
☐ 8 John O'Donoghue	2.00	.90	.25
☐ 9 Adolfo Phillips	2.00	.90	.25
☐ 10 Howie Reed	2.00	.90	.25
☐ 11 Marv Staehle	2.00	.90	.25
☐ 12 Rusty Staub	7.50	3.40	.95
☐ 13 Gary Sutherland	2.00	.90	.25
☐ 14 Bobby Wine	2.50	1.10	.30

1971 Expos Pro Stars

Printed in Canada by Pro Stars Publications, these 28 blank-backed postcards measure approximately 3 1/2" by 5 1/2" and feature white-bordered color player photos. The player's name appears as a facsimile autograph across the bottom of the photo. The postcards are unnumbered and checklisted below in alphabetical order.

	NRMT	VG-E	GOOD
COMPLETE SET (28)	60.00	27.00	7.50
COMMON CARD (1-28)	2.00	.90	.25
☐ 1 Bob Bailey	3.00	1.35	.35
☐ 2 John Bateman	2.50	1.10	.30
☐ 3 John Boccabella	2.50	1.10	.30
☐ 4 Ron Brand	2.00	.90	.25
☐ 5 Boots Day	2.00	.90	.25
☐ 6 Jim Fairey	2.00	.90	.25
☐ 7 Ron Fairly	3.00	1.35	.35
☐ 8 Jim Gosger	2.00	.90	.25
☐ 9 Don Hahn	2.00	.90	.25
☐ 10 Ron Hunt	3.00	1.35	.35
☐ 11 Mack Jones	2.50	1.10	.30
☐ 12 Coco Laboy	2.50	1.10	.30
☐ 13 Mike Marshall	4.00	1.80	.50
☐ 14 Clyde Mashore	2.00	.90	.25
☐ 15 Gene Mauch MG	3.00	1.35	.35
☐ 16 Dan McGinn	2.00	.90	.25
☐ 17 Carl Morton	2.50	1.10	.30
☐ 18 John O'Donoghue	2.00	.90	.25
☐ 19 Adolfo Phillips	2.00	.90	.25
☐ 20 Claude Raymond	2.50	1.10	.30
☐ 21 Howie Reed	2.00	.90	.25
☐ 22 Steve Renko	2.00	.90	.25
☐ 23 Rusty Staub	7.50	3.40	.95
☐ 24 Bill Stoneman	3.00	1.35	.35
☐ 25 John Strohmayer	2.00	.90	.25
☐ 26 Gary Sutherland	2.00	.90	.25
☐ 27 Mike Wegener	2.00	.90	.25
☐ 28 Bobby Wine	2.50	1.10	.30

1974 Expos Weston

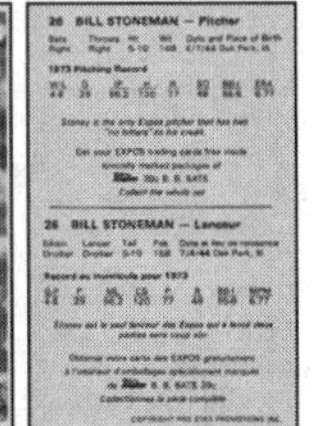

This ten-card set, featuring members of the Montreal Expos, measures approximately 3 1/2" by 5 1/2". The fronts have color player photos inside a thin white border with a facsimile autograph in black ink, and the player's name under the photo. The player's uniforms and caps have been airbrushed to remove the Expos insignia. The backs carry biography and statistics in English and French. The cards are unnumbered and checklisted below in alphabetical order.

	NRMT	VG-E	GOOD
COMPLETE SET (10)	7.50	3.40	.95
COMMON CARD (1-10)	.75	.35	.09
☐ 1 Bob Bailey	1.25	.55	.16
☐ 2 John Boccabella	1.00	.45	.12
☐ 3 Boots Day	.75	.35	.09
☐ 4 Tim Foli	1.00	.45	.12
☐ 5 Ron Hunt	1.25	.55	.16
☐ 6 Mike Jorgensen	1.00	.45	.12
☐ 7 Ernie McAnally	.75	.35	.09
☐ 8 Steve Renko	.75	.35	.09
☐ 9 Ken Singleton	2.00	.90	.25
☐ 10 Bill Stoneman	1.50	.70	.19

1976 Expos Redpath

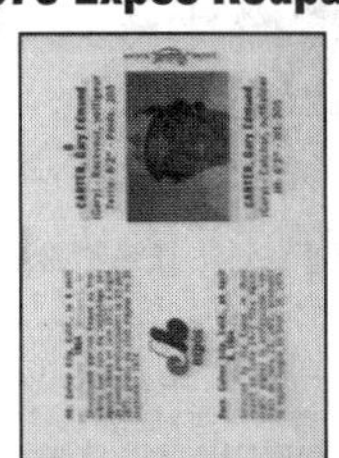

This set of 1976 Montreal Expos was issued by the Redpath Sugar company. The sheets measure approximately 3 1/4" by 10" and each sheet features four team members. The white fronts have a color, head shot of the player on the right with the player's name and position printed above the photo in French and below the photo in English. To the left of the photo is brief biography and how they were acquired by Montreal Expos written in both French and English. The players are listed below in alphabetical order.

	NRMT	VG-E	GOOD
COMMON PLAYER (1-36)	25.00	11.00	3.10
COMMON CARD (1-36)	.75	.35	.09
☐ 1 Bill Adair CO	.75	.35	.09
☐ 2 Larry Bearnarth CO	.75	.35	.09
☐ 3 Don Carrithers	.75	.35	.09
☐ 4 Gary Carter	3.00	1.35	.35
☐ 5 Larry Doby CO	1.50	.70	.19
☐ 6 Steve Dunning	.75	.35	.09
☐ 7 Jim Dwyer	.75	.35	.09
☐ 8 Tim Foli	.75	.35	.09
☐ 9 Barry Foote	.75	.35	.09
☐ 10 Pepe Frias	.75	.35	.09
☐ 11 Woodie Fryman	.75	.35	.09
☐ 12 Wayne Garrett	.75	.35	.09
☐ 13 Wayne Granger	.75	.35	.09
☐ 14 Mike Jorgensen	.75	.35	.09
☐ 15 Joe Kerrigan	.75	.35	.09
☐ 16 Clay Kirby	.75	.35	.09
☐ 17 Karl Kuehl MG	.75	.35	.09
☐ 18 Chip Lang	.75	.35	.09
☐ 19 Jim Lyttle	.75	.35	.09
☐ 20 Pete MacKanin	.75	.35	.09
☐ 21 Jose Mangual	.75	.35	.09
☐ 22 Jose Morales	.75	.35	.09
☐ 23 Dale Murray	.75	.35	.09
☐ 24 Larry Parrish	.75	.35	.09
☐ 25 Ron Piche CO	.75	.35	.09
☐ 26 Bombo Rivera	.75	.35	.09
☐ 27 Steve Rogers	1.50	.70	.19
☐ 28 Fred Scherman	.75	.35	.09
☐ 29 Don Stanhouse	.75	.35	.09
☐ 30 Chuck Taylor	.75	.35	.09
☐ 31 Andre Thornton	1.00	.45	.12
☐ 32 Del Unser	.75	.35	.09
☐ 33 Ellis Valentine	1.50	.70	.19
☐ 34 Ossie Virgil CO	1.50	.70	.19
☐ 34 Osssie Virgil CO	.75	.35	.09
☐ 35 Dan Warthen	.75	.35	.09
☐ 36 Jerry White	.75	.35	.09

1977 Expos Postcards

These 39 postcards feature all sorts of people in the Expos orginization. This was not just issued as one set, but these postcards were continually printed during the season to account for new additions.

	NRMT	VG-E	GOOD
COMPLETE SET	25.00	11.00	3.10
COMMON CARD	.75	.35	.09
☐ 1 Santo Alcala	.75	.35	.09
☐ 2 Bill Atkinson	.75	.35	.09
☐ 3 Bill Atkinson (Tree in background)	.75	.35	.09
☐ 4 Stan Bahnsen	.75	.35	.09
☐ 5 Tim Blackwell	.75	.35	.09
☐ 6 Jim Brewer CO	.75	.35	.09
☐ 7 Jackie Brown CO	.75	.35	.09
☐ 8 Gary Carter	3.50	1.55	.45
☐ 9 Dave Cash	.75	.35	.09
☐ 10 Warren Cromartie	1.00	.45	.12
☐ 11 Andre Dawson	3.50	1.55	.45
☐ 12 Andre Dawson (Wearing batting helmet)	3.50	1.55	.45
☐ 13 Barry Foote	.75	.35	.09
☐ 14 Pepe Frias	.75	.35	.09
☐ 15 Bill Gardner	.75	.35	.09
☐ 16 Wayne Garrett	.75	.35	.09
☐ 17 Gerald Hannahs	.75	.35	.09
☐ 18 Mike Jorgenson	.75	.35	.09
☐ 19 Joe Kerrigan	.75	.35	.09
☐ 20 Pete Mackanin	.75	.35	.09
☐ 21 Will McEnaney	.75	.35	.09
☐ 22 Sam Mejias	.75	.35	.09
☐ 23 Jose Morales	.75	.35	.09
☐ 24 Larry Parrish	1.00	.45	.12
☐ 25 Tony Perez	2.00	.90	.25
☐ 26 Steve Rogers	1.00	.45	.12
☐ 27 Dan Schatzeder	.75	.35	.09
☐ 28 Chris Speier	.75	.35	.09
☐ 29 Don Stanhouse	.75	.35	.09
☐ 30 Jeff Terpko	.75	.35	.09
☐ 31 Wayne Twitchell	.75	.35	.09
☐ 32 Del Unser	.75	.35	.09
☐ 33 Ellis Valentine	.75	.35	.09
☐ 34 Mickey Vernon	.75	.35	.09
☐ 35 Ozzie Virgil CO	.75	.35	.09
☐ 36 Tom Walker	.75	.35	.09
☐ 37 Dan Warthen	.75	.35	.09
☐ 38 Jerry White	.75	.35	.09
☐ 39 Dick Williams MG	1.00	.45	.12

1978 Expos Postcards

This 15-card set features a borerless front with the player's name and team in a box near the bottom. The player's position is also printed on the front in both French and English. Backs are blank. cards are aphabetically checklisted below.

	NRMT	VG-E	GOOD
COMPLETE SET (15)	15.00	6.75	1.85
COMMON CARD (1-15)	.75	.35	.09
☐ 1 Stan Bahnsen	.75	.35	.09
☐ 2 Gary Carter	2.50	1.10	.30
☐ 3 Andre Dawson	2.50	1.10	.30
☐ 4 Hal Dues	.75	.35	.09
☐ 5 Ross Grimsley	.75	.35	.09
☐ 6 Fred Holdsworth	.75	.35	.09
☐ 7 Darold Knowles	.75	.35	.09
☐ 8 Rudy May	.75	.35	.09
☐ 9 Stan Papi	.75	.35	.09
☐ 10 Larry Parrish	1.00	.45	.12
☐ 11 Bob Reece	.75	.35	.09
☐ 12 Norm Sherry CO	.75	.35	.09
☐ 13 Dan Schatzeder	.75	.35	.09
☐ 14 Chris Speier	1.00	.45	.12
☐ 15 Wayne Twitchell	.75	.35	.09

1979 Expos Postcards

These postacards feature members from the Montreal Expos organization. These postcards are blankbacked and are borderless. The only identification is the player's name and billungual player information on the bottom.

	NRMT	VG-E	GOOD
COMPLETE SET (32)	25.00	11.00	3.10
COMMON CARD (1-32)	.75	.35	.09
☐ 1 Felipe Alou CO	1.50	.70	.19
☐ 2 Stan Bahnsen	.75	.35	.09
☐ 3 Tony Bernazard	.75	.35	.09
☐ 4 Jim Brewer	.75	.35	.09
☐ 5 Dave Cash	.75	.35	.09
☐ 6 Warren Cromartie	1.00	.45	.12
☐ 7 Andre Dawson	3.00	1.35	.35
☐ 8 Duffy Dyer	.75	.35	.09
☐ 9 Woodie Fryman	.75	.35	.09
☐ 10 Mike Garman	.75	.35	.09
☐ 11 Ed Herrmann	.75	.35	.09
☐ 12 Tommy Hutton	.75	.35	.09
☐ 13 Bill Lee (With beard)	1.00	.45	.12
☐ 14 Bill Lee (Without beard)	1.00	.45	.12
☐ 15 Jim Mason	.75	.35	.09
☐ 16 Ken Macha	.75	.35	.09
☐ 17 Pat Mullin	.75	.35	.09
☐ 18 Dave Palmer	.75	.35	.09
☐ 19 Tony Perez	2.50	1.10	.30
☐ 20 Vern Rapp CO	.75	.35	.09
☐ 21 Steve Rogers	1.00	.45	.12
☐ 22 Scott Sanderson	.75	.35	.09
☐ 23 Rodney Scott (Blue background)	.75	.35	.09
☐ 24 Rodney Scott (Brown background)	.75	.35	.09
☐ 25 Norm Sherry CO	.75	.35	.09
☐ 26 Tony Solaita	.75	.35	.09
☐ 27 Elias Sosa	.75	.35	.09
☐ 28 Rusty Staub	2.00	.90	.25
☐ 29 Ellis Valentine	1.00	.45	.12
☐ 30 Ozzie Virgil CO	1.00	.45	.12
☐ 31 Jerry White	.75	.35	.09
☐ 32 Dick Williams MG	1.00	.45	.12

1980 Expos Postcards

These postcards feature members of the 1980 Montreal Expos. These postcards are similar to those issued in the three previous seasons but they have no positions on them. These are all new photos that have red and blue shoulder striping. These cards are unnumbered so we have sequenced them in alphabetical order.

	NRMT	VG-E	GOOD
COMPLETE SET (35)	15.00	6.75	1.85
COMMON CARD (1-35)	.50	.23	.06
☐ 1 Bill Almon	.50	.23	.06
☐ 2 Felipe Alou CO	1.00	.45	.12
☐ 3 Stan Bahnsen	.50	.23	.06
☐ 4 Tony Bernazard	.50	.23	.06
☐ 5 Gary Carter	2.50	1.10	.30
☐ 6 Galen Cisco CO	.50	.23	.06
☐ 7 Warren Cromartie	.75	.35	.09
☐ 8 Andre Dawson	2.00	.90	.25
☐ 9 Woodie Fryman	.50	.23	.06
☐ 10 Ross Grimsley	.50	.23	.06
☐ 11 Bill Gullickson	.75	.35	.09
☐ 12 Tommy Hutton	.50	.23	.06
☐ 13 Charlie Lea	.50	.23	.06
☐ 14 Bill Lee	.75	.35	.09
☐ 15 Ron LeFlore	.50	.23	.06
☐ 16 Ken Macha	.50	.23	.06
☐ 17 Pat Mullin CO	.50	.23	.06
☐ 18 Dale Murray	.50	.23	.06
☐ 19 Fred Norman	.50	.23	.06
☐ 20 Rowland Office	.50	.23	.06
☐ 21 David Palmer	.50	.23	.06
☐ 22 Larry Parrish	.50	.23	.06
☐ 23 Bobby Ramos	.50	.23	.06
☐ 24 Vern Rapp CO	.50	.23	.06
☐ 25 Steve Rogers	.50	.23	.06
☐ 26 Scott Sanderson	.50	.23	.06
☐ 27 Rodney Scott	.50	.23	.06
☐ 28 Norm Sherry CO	.50	.23	.06
☐ 29 Elias Sosa	.50	.23	.06
☐ 30 Chris Speier	.50	.23	.06
☐ 31 John Tamargo	.50	.23	.06
☐ 32 Ellis Valentine	.50	.23	.06
☐ 33 Ozzie Virgil CO	.50	.23	.06
☐ 34 Jerry White	.50	.23	.06
☐ 35 Dick Williams MG	1.00	.45	.12

1981 Expos Postcards

These postcards feature members of the 1981 Montreal Expos. These cards are unnumbered and we have sequenced them in alphabetical order. Many of the poses of the 1980 players were repeated. We have included only new players or players with different photos from the year before. Very early issues of Tim Raines, Jeff Reardon and Tim Wallach are included in this set.

	NRMT	VG-E	GOOD
COMPLETE SET (16)	10.00	4.50	1.25
COMMON CARD (1-16)	.50	.23	.06
☐ 1 Steve Boros CO	.50	.23	.06
☐ 2 Ray Burris	.50	.23	.06
☐ 3 Charlie Lea	.50	.23	.06
☐ 4 Bill Lee	.75	.35	.09
☐ 5 Jerry Manuel	.50	.23	.06
☐ 6 Willie Montanez	.50	.23	.06
☐ 7 Ron McLain	.50	.23	.06
☐ 8 Mike Phillips	.50	.23	.06
☐ 9 Tim Raines	5.00	2.20	.60
☐ 10 Bobby Ramos	.50	.23	.06
☐ 11 Steve Ratzer	.50	.23	.06
☐ 12 Jeff Reardon	2.50	1.10	.30
☐ 13 Steve Rogers	.50	.23	.06
☐ 14 Scott Sanderson	.50	.23	.06
☐ 15 Chris Speier	.50	.23	.06
☐ 16 Tim Wallach	1.50	.70	.19

1982 Expos Hygrade Meats

The cards in this 24-card set measure approximately 2" by 3". This series depicting the Montreal Expos was distributed by the Hygrade company in Quebec Province, Canada. Single cello-packed cards are found in packages of Hygrade smoked sausages; each has a color photo of an Expo player, with his name and uniform number in a white panel at the base of the picture. The back, printed only in French, advertises a leatherette album designed to hold a complete set of cards. The card stock is actually thick paper rather than cardboard, and the edges are rounded. The cards are unnumbered and checklisted below in alphabetical order.

	NRMT	VG-E	GOOD
COMPLETE SET (24)	40.00	18.00	5.00
COMMON CARD (1-24)	1.25	.55	.16
☐ 1 Tim Blackwell	1.25	.55	.16
☐ 2 Ray Burris	1.25	.55	.16
☐ 3 Gary Carter	10.00	4.50	1.25
☐ 4 Warren Cromartie	2.00	.90	.25
☐ 5 Andre Dawson	10.00	4.50	1.25
☐ 6 Jim Fanning MG	1.25	.55	.16
☐ 7 Terry Francona	2.00	.90	.25
☐ 8 Woodie Fryman	1.25	.55	.16
☐ 9 Bill Gullickson	2.00	.90	.25
☐ 10 Bob James	1.25	.55	.16
☐ 11 Charlie Lea	1.25	.55	.16

	NRMT	VG-E	GOOD
☐ 12 Brad Mills	1.25	.55	.16
☐ 13 John Milner	1.25	.55	.16
☐ 14 Dan Norman	1.25	.55	.16
☐ 15 Al Oliver	2.50	1.10	.30
☐ 16 Tim Raines	10.00	4.50	1.25
☐ 17 Jeff Reardon	4.00	1.80	.50
☐ 18 Steve Rogers	1.50	.70	.19
☐ 19 Scott Sanderson	1.50	.70	.19
☐ 20 Bryn Smith	1.25	.55	.16
☐ 21 Chris Speier	1.25	.55	.16
☐ 22 Frank Taveras	1.25	.55	.16
☐ 23 Tim Wallach	4.00	1.80	.50
☐ 24 Jerry White	1.25	.55	.16
☐ xx0 Leatherette Album	7.50	3.40	.95

1982 Expos Postcards

These postcards feature members of the 1982 Montreal Expos. These postcards are in the same style as used over the previous five years. The cards are unnumbered and we have sequenced them in alphabetical order.

	NRMT	VG-E	GOOD
COMPLETE SET (43)	25.00	11.00	3.10
COMMON CARD (1-43)	.50	.23	.06
☐ 1 Tim Blackwell	.50	.23	.06
☐ 2 Steve Boros CO	.50	.23	.06
☐ 3 Ray Burris	.50	.23	.06
☐ 4 Gary Carter	4.00	1.80	.50
☐ 5 Galen Cisco CO	.50	.23	.06
☐ 6 Warren Cromartie	.75	.35	.09
☐ 7 Warren Cromartie (Close-up)	.75	.35	.09
☐ 8 Andre Dawson	4.00	1.80	.50
☐ 9 Billy DeMars CO	.50	.23	.06
☐ 10 Jim Fanning MG	.50	.23	.06
☐ 11 Doug Flynn	.50	.23	.06
☐ 12 Terry Francona	1.00	.45	.12
☐ 13 Woodie Fryman	.50	.23	.06
☐ 14 Bob Gebhard CO	.50	.23	.06
☐ 15 Bill Gullickson	.50	.23	.06
☐ 16 Bob James	.50	.23	.06
☐ 17 Roy Johnson	.50	.23	.06
☐ 18 Wallace Johnson	.50	.23	.06
☐ 19 Charlie Lea	.50	.23	.06
☐ 20 Bill Lee	.75	.35	.09
☐ 21 Bryan Little	.50	.23	.06
☐ 22 Brad Mills	.50	.23	.06
☐ 23 John Milner	.50	.23	.06
☐ 24 Don Norman	.50	.23	.06
☐ 25 Al Oliver (Portrait)	1.00	.45	.12
☐ 26 Al Oliver (Bat on shoulder)	1.00	.45	.12
☐ 27 Al Oliver (Bat on shoulder under stadium roof)	1.00	.45	.12
☐ 28 Rowland Office	.50	.23	.06
☐ 29 David Palmer	.50	.23	.06
☐ 30 Mike Phillips	.50	.23	.06
☐ 31 Tim Raines	4.00	1.80	.50
☐ 32 Vern Rapp CO	.50	.23	.06
☐ 33 Jeff Reardon	2.00	.90	.25
☐ 34 Steve Rogers	.50	.23	.06
☐ 35 Scott Sanderson	.50	.23	.06
☐ 36 Dan Schatzeder	.50	.23	.06
☐ 37 Rodney Scott	.50	.23	.06
☐ 38 Bryn Smith	.50	.23	.06
☐ 39 Chris Speier	.50	.23	.06
☐ 40 Tim Wallach	3.00	1.35	.35
☐ 41 Jerry White	.50	.23	.06
☐ 42 Joel Youngblood	.50	.23	.06
☐ 43 Frank Taveras	.50	.23	.06

1982 Expos Zellers

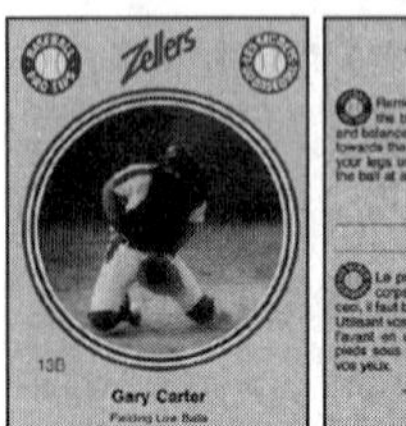

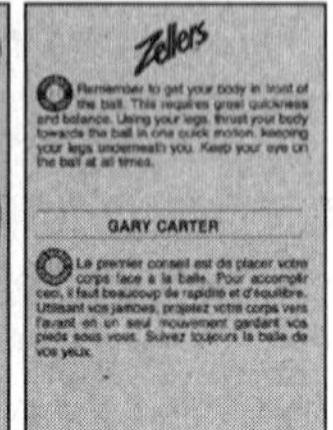

Sponsored by Zellers Department Stores and subtitled "Baseball Pro Tips," the 60 standard-size cards comprising this set were originally distributed in 20 perforated three-card panels. The yellow-bordered fronts feature circular color player action shots circumscribed by red, white, and blue lines. The player's name appears in black lettering in the yellow margin below the photo. Below his name is a description in both English and French of the action depicted. The back carries the "Pro Tip" in English and French explaining the techniques used by the player pictured on the front. The cards are numbered on the front, and each card is marked "A," "B" or "C" next to its number, which denotes its location on the original three-card panel. Eleven players and one coach of the Montreal Expos are featured, each explaining a particular facet of baseball in the three card sequences which comprise a panel. Gary Carter (5), Cromartie (2), Dawson (3) and Francona (2) are pictured on multiple panels. The prices below are for intact three-card panels.

	NRMT	VG-E	GOOD
COMPLETE SET (20)	20.00	9.00	2.50
COMMON PANEL (1-20)	.75	.35	.09
☐ 1 Gary Carter (Catching position)	1.00	.45	.12
☐ 2 Steve Rogers (Pitching stance)	.75	.35	.09
☐ 3 Tim Raines (Sliding)	2.00	.90	.25
☐ 4 Andre Dawson (Batting stance)	2.00	.90	.25
☐ 5 Terry Francona (Contact hitting)	1.00	.45	.12
☐ 6 Gary Carter (Fielding pop fouls)	1.00	.45	.12
☐ 7 Warren Cromartie (Fielding at 1B)	.75	.35	.09
☐ 8 Chris Speier (Fielding at SS)	.75	.35	.09
☐ 9 Billy DeMars CO (Signals)	.75	.35	.09
☐ 10 Andre Dawson (Batting)	2.00	.90	.25
☐ 11 Terry Francona (Outfield throws)	1.00	.45	.12
☐ 12 Woodie Fryman (Holding runner)	.75	.35	.09
☐ 13 Gary Carter (Fielding low balls)	1.00	.45	.12
☐ 14 Andre Dawson (Playing CF)	2.00	.90	.25
☐ 15 Bill Gullickson (Slurve)	1.00	.45	.12
☐ 16 Gary Carter (Catching stance)	1.00	.45	.12
☐ 17 Scott Sanderson (Fielding as a P)	1.00	.45	.12
☐ 18 Warren Cromartie (Handling bad throws)	.75	.35	.09
☐ 19 Gary Carter (Hitting stride)	1.00	.45	.12
☐ 20 Ray Burris (Holding runner)	.75	.35	.09

1983 Expos Postcards

These 25 blank-backed Expos postcards measure approximately 3 1/2" by 5 1/2" and feature posed color player photos that are borderless, except at the bottom, where a white margin carries the player's name in black lettering. The cards are unnumbered and checklisted below in alphabetical order.

	NRMT	VG-E	GOOD
COMPLETE SET (30)	30.00	13.50	3.70
COMMON CARD (1-30)	1.00	.45	.12
☐ 1 Tim Blackwell	1.00	.45	.12
☐ 2 Gary Carter	5.00	2.20	.60
☐ 3 Galen Cisco CO	1.00	.45	.12
☐ 4 Terry Crowley	1.00	.45	.12
☐ 5 Billy DeMars CO	1.00	.45	.12
☐ 6 Terry Francona	1.25	.55	.16
☐ 7 Woodie Fryman	1.25	.55	.16
☐ 8 Bill Gullickson	1.25	.55	.16
☐ 9 Bob James	1.00	.45	.12
☐ 10 Joe Kerrigan CO	1.00	.45	.12
☐ 11 Charlie Lea	1.00	.45	.12
☐ 12 Randy Lerch	1.00	.45	.12
☐ 13 Bryan Little	1.00	.45	.12
☐ 14 Ron McClain TR	1.00	.45	.12
☐ 15 Brad Mills	1.00	.45	.12
☐ 16 David Palmer	1.00	.45	.12
☐ 17 Mike Phillips	1.00	.45	.12
☐ 18 Bobby Ramos	1.00	.45	.12
☐ 19 Vern Rapp CO	1.00	.45	.12
☐ 20 Jeff Reardon	2.50	1.10	.30
☐ 21 Scott Sanderson	1.00	.45	.12
☐ 22 Dan Schatzeder	1.00	.45	.12
☐ 23 Bryn Smith	1.00	.45	.12
☐ 24 Mike Vail	1.00	.45	.12
☐ 25 Bill Virdon MG	1.25	.55	.16
☐ 26 Chris Welsh	1.00	.45	.12
☐ 27 Jerry White	1.00	.45	.12
☐ 28 Tom Wieghaus	1.00	.45	.12
☐ 29 Jim Wohlford	1.00	.45	.12
☐ 30 Mel Wright CO	1.00	.45	.12

1983 Expos Stuart

These 30 standard-size cards feature players of the Montreal Expos. The fronts carry white-bordered color player photos. The player's name and uniform number, along with the Montreal Expos' and

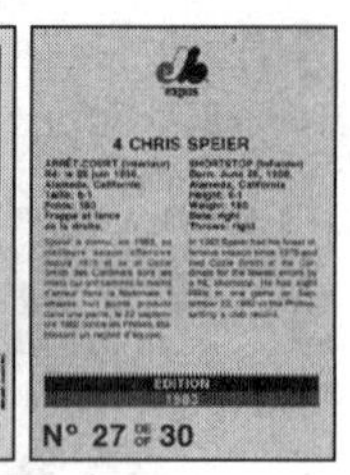

Stuart's logo, appear within the broad white margin at the bottom. The plain back carries the player's bilingual biography and career highlights and features red and blue print on off-white card stock.

	NRMT	VG-E	GOOD
COMPLETE SET (30)	10.00	4.50	1.25
COMMON CARD (1-30)	.25	.11	.03
☐ 1 Bill Virdon MG	.50	.23	.06
☐ 2 Woodie Fryman	.50	.23	.06
☐ 3 Vern Rapp CO	.25	.11	.03
☐ 4 Andre Dawson	2.00	.90	.25
☐ 5 Jeff Reardon	.50	.23	.06
☐ 6 Al Oliver	.75	.35	.09
☐ 7 Doug Flynn	.25	.11	.03
☐ 8 Gary Carter	2.00	.90	.25
☐ 9 Tim Raines	2.00	.90	.25
☐ 10 Steve Rogers	.75	.35	.09
☐ 11 Billy DeMars CO	.25	.11	.03
☐ 12 Tim Wallach	.75	.35	.09
☐ 13 Galen Cisco CO	.25	.11	.03
☐ 14 Terry Francona	.25	.11	.03
☐ 15 Bill Gullickson	.75	.35	.09
☐ 16 Ray Burris	.25	.11	.03
☐ 17 Scott Sanderson	.50	.23	.06
☐ 18 Warren Cromartie	.50	.23	.06
☐ 19 Jerry White	.25	.11	.03
☐ 20 Bobby Ramos	.25	.11	.03
☐ 21 Jim Wohlford	.25	.11	.03
☐ 22 Dan Schatzeder	.25	.11	.03
☐ 23 Charlie Lea	.25	.11	.03
☐ 24 Bryan Little UER (Misspelled Brian)	.25	.11	.03
☐ 25 Mel Wright CO	.25	.11	.03
☐ 26 Tim Blackwell	.25	.11	.03
☐ 27 Chris Speier	.25	.11	.03
☐ 28 Randy Lerch	.25	.11	.03
☐ 29 Bryn Smith	.25	.11	.03
☐ 30 Brad Mills	.25	.11	.03

1984 Expos Postcards

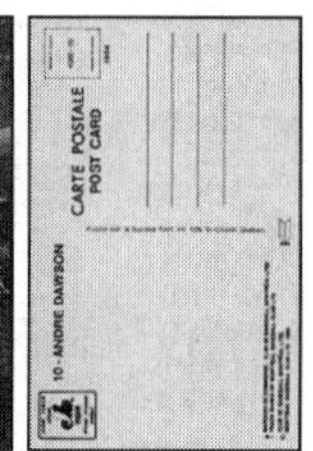

These 36 Expos postcards measure approximately 3 1/2" by 5 1/2" and feature borderless posed color player photos on their fronts. The backs carry the player's name and uniform number at the upper left. Some backs also carry the bilingual Expos' product license seal and trademarks on the left side. The rectangle for the stamp and the year of issue appear at the upper right. The postcards are unnumbered and checklisted below in alphabetical order.

	NRMT	VG-E	GOOD
COMPLETE SET (36)	35.00	16.00	4.40
COMMON CARD (1-36)	1.00	.45	.12
☐ 1 Felipe Alou CO	2.00	.90	.25
☐ 2 Fred Breining	1.00	.45	.12
☐ 3 Gary Carter	5.00	2.20	.60
☐ 4 Galen Cisco CO	1.00	.45	.12
☐ 5 Andre Dawson	5.00	2.20	.60
☐ 6 Billy DeMars CO	1.00	.45	.12
☐ 7 Miguel Dilone	1.00	.45	.12
☐ 8 Doug Flynn	1.00	.45	.12
☐ 9 Terry Francona	1.50	.70	.19
☐ 10 Mike Fuentes	1.00	.45	.12
☐ 11 Bill Gullickson	1.00	.45	.12
☐ 12 Greg A. Harris	1.00	.45	.12
☐ 13 Bob James	1.00	.45	.12
☐ 14 Roy Johnson	1.00	.45	.12
☐ 15 Joe Kerrigan CO	1.00	.45	.12
☐ 16 Charlie Lea	1.00	.45	.12
☐ 17 Bryan Little	1.00	.45	.12
☐ 18 Gary Lucas	1.00	.45	.12
☐ 19 Andy McGaffigan	1.00	.45	.12
☐ 20 Russ Nixon CO	1.00	.45	.12
☐ 21 David Palmer	1.00	.45	.12
☐ 22 Tim Raines	5.00	2.20	.60
☐ 23 Bobby Ramos	1.00	.45	.12
☐ 24 Jeff Reardon	1.50	.70	.19
☐ 25 Steve Rogers	1.00	.45	.12
☐ 26 Pete Rose	7.50	3.40	.95
☐ 27 Argenis Salazar	1.00	.45	.12
☐ 28 Dan Schatzeder	1.00	.45	.12
☐ 29 Bryn Smith	1.00	.45	.12
☐ 30 Chris Speier	1.00	.45	.12
☐ 31 Mike Stenhouse	1.00	.45	.12
☐ 32 Derrel Thomas	1.00	.45	.12
☐ 33 Mike Vail	1.00	.45	.12
☐ 34 Bill Virdon MG	1.50	.70	.19
☐ 35 Tim Wallach	2.00	.90	.25
☐ 36 Jim Wohlford	1.00	.45	.12

1984 Expos Stuart

These 40 standard-size cards feature players of the Montreal Expos. The fronts carry white-bordered color player photos framed by a red line. The player's name and uniform number, along with the Montreal Expos' and Stuart's logo, appear within the broad white margin at the bottom. The white back is also framed by a red line and carries the player's bilingual biography and career highlights. The cards are numbered on the back. The first series of 20 cards was distributed from mid-April through June; the second series was distributed in July and August. After the completion of the promotion, the remainder of the first series cards were released to a few card dealers for distribution to the hobby. This set is distinguished from the previous year by the red border around the picture on the obverse. An album was also available for holding the cards; the album is gray, white, blue, and red and contains two-pocket plastic pages.

	NRMT	VG-E	GOOD
COMPLETE SET (40)	20.00	9.00	2.50
COMMON CARD (1-20)	.25	.11	.03
COMMON CARD (21-40)	.50	.23	.06
☐ 1 Youppi (Mascot)	.50	.23	.06
☐ 2 Bill Virdon MG	.50	.23	.06
☐ 3 Billy DeMars CO	.25	.11	.03
☐ 4 Galen Cisco CO	.25	.11	.03
☐ 5 Russ Nixon CO	.25	.11	.03
☐ 6 Felipe Alou CO	.75	.35	.09
☐ 7 Dan Schatzeder	.25	.11	.03
☐ 8 Charlie Lea	.25	.11	.03
☐ 9 Roberto Ramos	.25	.11	.03
☐ 10 Bob James	.25	.11	.03
☐ 11 Andre Dawson	1.50	.70	.19
☐ 12 Gary Lucas	.25	.11	.03
☐ 13 Jeff Reardon	.50	.23	.06
☐ 14 Tim Wallach	.75	.35	.09
☐ 15 Gary Carter	1.50	.70	.19
☐ 16 Bill Gullickson	.50	.23	.06
☐ 17 Pete Rose	3.00	1.35	.35
☐ 18 Terry Francona	.25	.11	.03
☐ 19 Steve Rogers	.50	.23	.06
☐ 20 Tim Raines	1.50	.70	.19
☐ 21 Bryn Smith	.50	.23	.06
☐ 22 Greg A. Harris	.50	.23	.06
☐ 23 David Palmer	.50	.23	.06
☐ 24 Jim Wohlford	.50	.23	.06
☐ 25 Miguel Dilone	.50	.23	.06
☐ 26 Mike Stenhouse	.50	.23	.06
☐ 27 Chris Speier	.50	.23	.06
☐ 28 Derrel Thomas	.50	.23	.06
☐ 29 Doug Flynn	.50	.23	.06
☐ 30 Bryan Little	.50	.23	.06
☐ 31 Argenis Salazar	.50	.23	.06
☐ 32 Mike Fuentes	.50	.23	.06
☐ 33 Joe Kerrigan CO	.50	.23	.06
☐ 34 Andy McGaffigan	.50	.23	.06
☐ 35 Fred Breining	.50	.23	.06
☐ 36 Expo '83 All Stars: Gary Carter, Andre Dawson, Tim Raines, Steve Rogers	1.50	.70	.19
☐ 37 Co-Players of the Year: Andre Dawson, Tim Raines	1.50	.70	.19
☐ 38 Coaching Staff: Bill Virdon MG, Felipe Alou CO, Galen Cisco CO, Billy DeMars CO, Joe Kerrigan CO, Russ Nixon CO	.75	.35	.09
☐ 39 Expos Team Photo	.75	.35	.09
☐ 40 Checklist Card	.75	.35	.09
☐ xx0 Album	3.00	1.35	.35

1985 Expos Postcards

These 26 Expos postcards measure approximately 3 1/2" by 5 1/2" and feature borderless posed color player photos on their fronts. The backs carry the player's name and uniform number at the upper left.

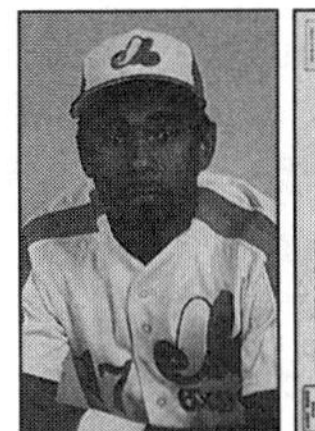

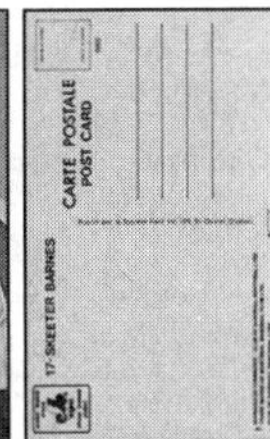

The bilingual Expos' product license seal and trademarks appear on the left side. The rectangle for the stamp and the year of issue appear at the upper right. The postcards are unnumbered and checklisted below in alphabetical order.

	NRMT	VG-E	GOOD
COMPLETE SET (26)	12.00	5.50	1.50
COMMON CARD (1-26)	.50	.23	.06
□ 1 Skeeter Barnes	.50	.23	.06
□ 2 Larry Bearnarth CO	.50	.23	.06
□ 3 Hubie Brooks	.75	.35	.09
□ 4 Tim Burke	.50	.23	.06
□ 5 Sal Butera	.50	.23	.06
□ 6 Andre Dawson	2.50	1.10	.30
□ 7 Dan Driessen	.50	.23	.06
□ 8 Mike Fitzgerald	.50	.23	.06
□ 9 Ron Hansen CO	.50	.23	.06
□ 10 Joe Hesketh	.50	.23	.06
□ 11 Vance Law	.50	.23	.06
□ 12 Mickey Mahler	.50	.23	.06
□ 13 Al Newman	.50	.23	.06
□ 14 Steve Nicosia	.50	.23	.06
□ 15 Jack O'Connor UER (Misspelled O'Conner on back)	.50	.23	.06
□ 16 David Palmer	.50	.23	.06
□ 17 Tim Raines	2.50	1.10	.30
□ 18 Rick Renick CO	.50	.23	.06
□ 19 Bert Roberge	.50	.23	.06
□ 20 Buck Rodgers MG	.50	.23	.06
□ 21 Razor Shines	.75	.35	.09
□ 22 Bryn Smith	.50	.23	.06
□ 23 Randy St. Claire	.50	.23	.06
□ 24 U.L. Washington	.50	.23	.06
□ 25 Herm Winningham	.50	.23	.06
□ 26 Youppi (Mascot)	.75	.35	.09

1986 Expos Greats TCMA

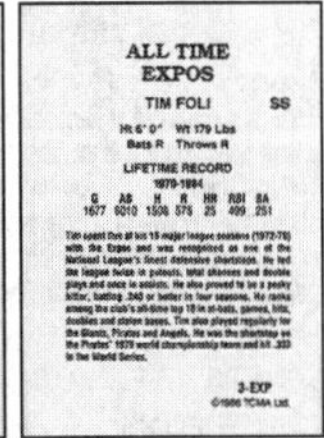

This 12-card standard-size set features some of the best Expos players from their first two decades. The fronts have player photos, their names and position. The backs have vital statistics as well as career statistics.

	MINT	NRMT	EXC
COMPLETE SET (12)	3.00	1.35	.35
COMMON CARD (1-12)	.25	.11	.03
□ 1 Ron Fairly	.50	.23	.06
□ 2 Dave Cash	.25	.11	.03
□ 3 Tim Foli	.25	.11	.03
□ 4 Bob Bailey	.25	.11	.03
□ 5 Ken Singleton	.25	.11	.03
□ 6 Ellis Valentine	.25	.11	.03
□ 7 Rusty Staub	.75	.35	.09
□ 8 John Bateman	.25	.11	.03
□ 9 Steve Rogers	.25	.11	.03
□ 10 Woodie Fryman	.25	.11	.03
□ 11 Mike Marshall	.25	.11	.03
□ 12 Jim Fanning MG	.25	.11	.03

1986 Expos Postcards

These postcards are very similar to the 85 Expos Postcards. These postcards feature no name box or fascimile autograph. The Expos logo and the player name are printed in blue. The cards are unnumbered and sequenced in alphabetical order.

	MINT	NRMT	EXC
COMPLETE SET (20)	8.00	3.60	1.00
COMMON CARD (1-20)	.50	.23	.06
□ 1 Dann Bilardello	.50	.23	.06
□ 2 Tim Burke	.50	.23	.06
□ 3 Mike Fitzgerald	.50	.23	.06
□ 4 Andres Galarraga	4.00	1.80	.50
□ 5 Joe Hesketh	.50	.23	.06
□ 6 Wayne Krenchicki	.50	.23	.06
□ 7 Ken Macha	.50	.23	.06
□ 8 Andy McGaffigan	.50	.23	.06
□ 9 Al Newman	.50	.23	.06
□ 10 Tom Nieto	.50	.23	.06
□ 11 Jeff Parrett	.50	.23	.06
□ 12 George Riley	.50	.23	.06
□ 13 Dan Schatzeder	.50	.23	.06
□ 14 Bryn Smith	.50	.23	.06
□ 15 Jason Thompson	.50	.23	.06
□ 16 Jay Tibbs	.50	.23	.06
□ 17 Tim Wallach	1.00	.45	.12
□ 18 Mitch Webster	.50	.23	.06
□ 19 Bobby Winkles CO	.50	.23	.06
□ 20 Floyd Youmans	.50	.23	.06

1986 Expos Provigo Panels

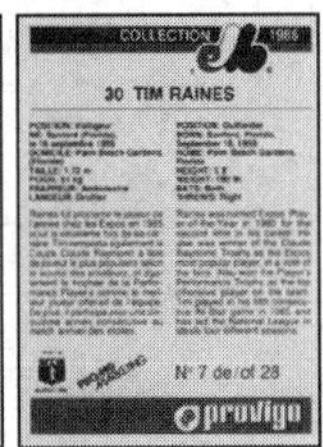

These 28 cards are found in lightly perforated panels of three (two player cards and an advertising card). The panel of three measures approximately 7 1/2" by 3 3/8", whereas each individual card measures 2 1/2" by 3 3/8". The fronts feature white-bordered color player action shots. The player's name and uniform number, along with the Provigo name and logo, appear within a yellow stripe across the bottom of the photo. The red, white, and blue Montreal Expos' logo appears at the top of the front. It also appears at the top of the white back, followed below by bilingual player biography and career highlights. An album was available to hold the cards; however in order to use the album, the cards had to be separated into individuals. The cards are attractive and the backs feature blue and red printing on a white card stock.

	MINT	NRMT	EXC
COMPLETE SET (28)	7.50	3.40	.95
COMMON CARD (1-28)	.25	.11	.03
□ 1 Hubie Brooks	.50	.23	.06
□ 2 Dann Bilardello	.25	.11	.03
□ 3 Buck Rodgers MG	.25	.11	.03
□ 4 Andy McGaffigan	.25	.11	.03
□ 5 Mitch Webster	.25	.11	.03
□ 6 Jim Wohlford	.25	.11	.03
□ 7 Tim Raines	1.00	.45	.12
□ 8 Jay Tibbs	.25	.11	.03
□ 9 Andre Dawson	.75	.35	.09
□ 10 Andres Galarraga	2.00	.90	.25
□ 11 Tim Wallach	.75	.35	.09
□ 12 Dan Schatzeder	.25	.11	.03
□ 13 Jeff Reardon	.75	.35	.09
□ 14 Coaching Staff Joe Kerrigan Bobby Winkles Larry Bearnarth	.25	.11	.03
□ 15 Jason Thompson	.25	.11	.03
□ 16 Bert Roberge	.25	.11	.03
□ 17 Tim Burke	.25	.11	.03
□ 18 Al Newman	.25	.11	.03
□ 19 Bryn Smith	.25	.11	.03
□ 20 Wayne Krenchicki	.25	.11	.03
□ 21 Joe Hesketh	.25	.11	.03
□ 22 Herm Winningham	.25	.11	.03
□ 23 Vance Law	.25	.11	.03
□ 24 Floyd Youmans	.25	.11	.03
□ 25 Jeff Parrett	.25	.11	.03
□ 26 Mike Fitzgerald	.25	.11	.03
□ 27 Youppi (Mascot)	.50	.23	.06
□ 28 Coaching Staff Rick Renick Ron Hansen Ken Macha	.25	.11	.03

1986 Expos Provigo Posters

These 12 blank-backed posters measure approximately 9" by 14 3/4", with the bottom 2 1/2" being a perforated strip carrying various Provigo coupons. The posters feature posed color photos of the Montreal Expos. These photos are borderless, except at the bottom, where a team color-coded border carries the player's name and uniform number, the Provigo and Expos logos, and the poster's number. The player's facsimile autograph appears across the photo. The backs are red and white or blue and blank.

	MINT	NRMT	EXC
COMPLETE SET (12)	15.00	6.75	1.85
COMMON CARD (1-12)	1.00	.45	.12
□ 1 Tim Raines	1.50	.70	.19
□ 2 Bryn Smith	1.00	.45	.12
□ 3 Hubie Brooks	1.50	.70	.19
□ 4 Buck Rodgers MG	1.00	.45	.12
□ 5 Mitch Webster	1.00	.45	.12
□ 6 Joe Hesketh	1.00	.45	.12
□ 7 Mike Fitzgerald	1.00	.45	.12
□ 8 Andy McGaffigan	1.00	.45	.12
□ 9 Andre Dawson	2.00	.90	.25
□ 10 Tim Wallach	2.00	.90	.25
□ 11 Jeff Reardon	2.50	1.10	.30
□ 12 Vance Law	1.00	.45	.12

1987 Expos Postcards

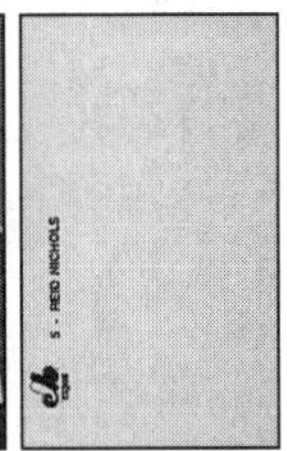

These 37 Montreal Expos postcards measure approximately 3 1/2" by 5 1/2" and feature borderless posed color player photos on their fronts. The backs are blank, except for the Expos logo and the player's name and uniform number printed in blue ink at the upper left. Otherwise, the postcards are unnumbered and so are checklisted below in alphabetical order.

	MINT	NRMT	EXC
COMPLETE SET (37)	15.00	6.75	1.85
COMMON CARD (1-37)	.50	.23	.06
□ 1 Larry Bearnarth CO	.50	.23	.06
□ 2 Hubie Brooks	.75	.35	.09
□ 3 Tim Burke	.50	.23	.06
□ 4 Casey Candaele	.50	.23	.06
□ 5 Dave Engle	.50	.23	.06
□ 6 Mike Fitzgerald	.50	.23	.06
□ 7 Tom Foley	.50	.23	.06
□ 8 Andres Galarraga	2.50	1.10	.30
□ 9 Ron Hansen CO	.50	.23	.06
□ 10 Neal Heaton	.50	.23	.06
□ 11 Joe Hesketh	.50	.23	.06
□ 12 Wallace Johnson	.50	.23	.06
□ 13 Vance Law	.50	.23	.06
□ 14 Bob McClure	.50	.23	.06
□ 15 Andy McGaffigan	.50	.23	.06
□ 16 Ken Macha	.50	.23	.06
□ 17 Jackie Moore CO	.50	.23	.06
□ 18 Reid Nichols	.50	.23	.06
□ 19 Jeff Parrett	.50	.23	.06
□ 20 Alonzo Powell	.50	.23	.06
□ 21 Tim Raines	1.50	.70	.19
□ 22 Jeff Reed	.50	.23	.06
□ 23 Luis Rivera	.50	.23	.06
□ 24 Buck Rodgers MG	.50	.23	.06
□ 25 Dan Schatzeder	.50	.23	.06
□ 26 Bob Sebra	.50	.23	.06
□ 27 Bryn Smith	.50	.23	.06
□ 28 Lary Sorensen	.50	.23	.06
□ 29 Randy St. Claire	.50	.23	.06
□ 30 John Stefero	.50	.23	.06
□ 31 Jay Tibbs	.50	.23	.06
□ 32 Tim Wallach	1.00	.45	.12
□ 33 Mitch Webster	.50	.23	.06
□ 34 Bobby Winkles CO	.50	.23	.06
□ 35 Herman Winningham	.50	.23	.06
□ 36 Floyd Youmans	.50	.23	.06
□ 37 Youppi (Mascot)	.75	.35	.09

1988 Expos Postcards

These postcards feature members of the 1988 Montreal Expos. They are similar in format to the 1987 Expos postcards. These cards are unnumbered and we have sequenced them in alphabetical order.

	MINT	NRMT	EXC
COMPLETE SET (26)	12.00	5.50	1.50
COMMON CARD (1-26)	.50	.23	.06
□ 1 Hubie Brooks	.75	.35	.09
□ 2 Tim Burke	.50	.23	.06
□ 3 Casey Candaele	.50	.23	.06
□ 4 Leonel Carrion CO	.50	.23	.06
□ 5 John Dodson	.50	.23	.06
□ 6 Mike Fitzgerald	.50	.23	.06
□ 7 Andres Galarraga	2.50	1.10	.30
□ 8 Joe Hesketh	.50	.23	.06
□ 9 Brian Holman	.50	.23	.06
□ 10 Rex Hudler	.50	.23	.06
□ 11 Tracy Jones	.50	.23	.06
□ 12 Dave Martinez	.50	.23	.06
□ 13 Dennis Martinez	1.00	.45	.12
□ 14 Graig Nettles	1.00	.45	.12
□ 15 Otis Nixon	.75	.35	.09
□ 16 Jeff Parrett	.50	.23	.06
□ 17 Pascual Perez	.50	.23	.06
□ 18 Tim Raines	1.50	.70	.19
□ 19 Luis Rivera	.50	.23	.06
□ 20 Buck Rodgers MG	.50	.23	.06
□ 21 Nelson Santovenia	.50	.23	.06
□ 22 Bryn Smith	.50	.23	.06
□ 23 Tim Wallach	1.00	.45	.12
□ 24 Mitch Webster	.50	.23	.06
□ 25 Herm Winningham	.50	.23	.06
□ 26 Floyd Youmans	.50	.23	.06

1989 Expos Postcards

These cards are very similar to the 1988 Expos Postcards. The cards are unnumbered and we have sequenced them in alphabetical order. 1995 Cy Young Winner Randy Johnson has a very early card in this set.

	MINT	NRMT	EXC
COMPLETE SET (29)	15.00	6.75	1.85
COMMON CARD (1-29)	.50	.23	.06
□ 1 Mike Aldrete	.50	.23	.06
□ 2 Larry Bearnarth CO	.50	.23	.06
□ 3 Hubie Brooks	.75	.35	.09
□ 4 Tim Burke	.50	.23	.06
□ 5 Mike Fitzgerald	.50	.23	.06
□ 6 Tom Foley	.50	.23	.06
□ 7 Steve Frey	.50	.23	.06
□ 8 Andres Galarraga	2.00	.90	.25
□ 9 Damaso Garcia	.50	.23	.06
□ 10 Brett Gideon	.50	.23	.06
□ 11 Kevin Gross	.50	.23	.06
□ 12 Ron Hansen CO	.50	.23	.06
□ 13 Gene Harris	.50	.23	.06
□ 14 Joe Hesketh	.50	.23	.06
□ 15 Randy Johnson	5.00	2.20	.60
□ 16 Rafael Landestoy CO	.50	.23	.06
□ 17 Mark Langston	1.00	.45	.12
□ 18 Ken Macha	.50	.23	.06
□ 19 Dave Martinez	.50	.23	.06
□ 20 Dennis Martinez	1.00	.45	.12
□ 21 Andy McGaffigan	.50	.23	.06
□ 22 Jackie Moore CO	.50	.23	.06
□ 23 Spike Owen	.50	.23	.06
□ 24 Tim Raines	1.50	.70	.19
□ 25 Buck Rodgers MG	.50	.23	.06
□ 26 Nelson Santovenia	.50	.23	.06
□ 27 Bryn Smith	.50	.23	.06
□ 28 Joe Sparks CO	.50	.23	.06
□ 29 Tim Wallach	1.00	.45	.12

1990 Expos Postcards

These postcards feature members of the 1990 Montreal Expos. Players featured early in their career include Delino DeShields, Marquis Grissom and Larry Walker. These cards are unnumbered are we have checklisted them in alphabetical order.

	MINT	NRMT	EXC
COMPLETE SET (37)	18.00	8.00	2.20
COMMON CARD (1-37)	.50	.23	.06
□ 1 Mike Aldrete	.50	.23	.06
□ 2 Larry Bearnarth CO	.50	.23	.06
□ 3 Dennis Boyd	.50	.23	.06
□ 4 Tim Burke	.50	.23	.06
□ 5 John Costello	.50	.23	.06
□ 6 Delino DeShields	1.25	.55	.16
□ 7 Mike Fitzgerald	.50	.23	.06
□ 8 Tom Foley	.50	.23	.06
□ 9 Steve Frey	.50	.23	.06
□ 10 Andres Galarraga	1.50	.70	.19
□ 11 Mark Gardner	.50	.23	.06
□ 12 Brett Gideon	.50	.23	.06
□ 13 Marquis Grissom	4.00	1.80	.50
□ 14 Kevin Gross	.50	.23	.06
□ 15 Drew Hall	.50	.23	.06
□ 16 Tommy Harper CO	.50	.23	.06
□ 17 Rex Hudler	.50	.23	.06
□ 18 Jeff Huson	.50	.23	.06
□ 19 Wallace Johnson	.50	.23	.06
□ 20 Rafael Landestoy CO	.50	.23	.06
□ 21 Ken Macha	.50	.23	.06
□ 22 Dave Martinez	.50	.23	.06
□ 23 Dennis Martinez	1.00	.45	.12
□ 24 Hal McRae CO	.75	.35	.09
□ 25 Otis Nixon	.75	.35	.09
□ 26 Junior Noboa	.50	.23	.06
□ 27 Spike Owen	.50	.23	.06
□ 28 Tim Raines	1.50	.70	.19
□ 29 Buck Rodgers MG	.50	.23	.06
□ 30 Tom Runnells CO	.50	.23	.06
□ 31 Bill Sampen	.50	.23	.06
□ 32 Nelson Santovenia	.50	.23	.06
□ 33 Dave Schmidt	.50	.23	.06
□ 34 Zane Smith	.50	.23	.06
□ 35 Rich Thompson	.50	.23	.06
□ 36 Larry Walker	5.00	2.20	.60
□ 37 Tim Wallach	1.00	.45	.12

1991 Expos Postcards

These postcards feature members of the 1991 Montreal Expos. They measure approximately 3 1/2" by 5 1/2" and feature borderless posed

color player photos. The player's name appears in a lower corner. These cards are unnumbered and sequenced in alphabetical order.

	MINT	NRMT	EXC
COMPLETE SET (22)	10.00	4.50	1.25
COMMON CARD (1-22)	.50	.23	.06
☐ 1 Brian Barnes	.50	.23	.06
☐ 2 Eric Bullock	.50	.23	.06
☐ 3 Ivan Calderon	.50	.23	.06
☐ 4 Mike Fitzgerald	.50	.23	.06
☐ 5 Tom Foley	.50	.23	.06
☐ 6 Steve Frey	.50	.23	.06
☐ 7 Andres Galarraga	2.00	.90	.25
☐ 8 Mark Gardner	.50	.23	.06
☐ 9 Chris Haney	.50	.23	.06
☐ 10 Ron Hassey	.50	.23	.06
☐ 11 Barry Jones	.50	.23	.06
☐ 12 Rick Mahler	.50	.23	.06
☐ 13 Dave Martinez	.50	.23	.06
☐ 14 Dennis Martinez	1.00	.45	.12
☐ 15 Chris Nabholz	.50	.23	.06
☐ 16 Junior Noboa	.50	.23	.06
☐ 17 Gilberto Reyes	.50	.23	.06
☐ 18 Mel Rojas	1.50	.70	.19
☐ 19 Tom Runnells MG	.50	.23	.06
☐ 20 Scott Ruskin	.50	.23	.06
☐ 21 Nelson Santovenia	.50	.23	.06
☐ 22 Larry Walker	2.00	.90	.25

1992 Expos Donruss Durivage

Featuring the Montreal Expos, the 26-card standard-size set was produced by Donruss for Durivage (a Canadian bread company). The fronts have posed color photos of the players without hats, framed by a gray inner border and a dark green outer border. The team logo, "Durivage" set name, and player information appear at the bottom of card front. In a horizontal format, the bilingual (English and French) backs carry biography and recent major league performance statistics, on a background of gray vertical stripes that fade to white as one moves down the card. The cards are numbered on the back, "No. X de/of 20." The complete set price does include all variations and the unnumbered checklist card.

	MINT	NRMT	EXC
COMPLETE SET (26)	60.00	27.00	7.50
COMMON CARD (1-20)	1.25	.55	.16
☐ 1 Bret Barberie	1.25	.55	.16
☐ 2A Chris Haney	2.50	1.10	.30
☐ 2B Brian Barnes	5.00	2.20	.60
☐ 3A Bill Sampen	1.50	.70	.19
☐ 3B Phil Bradley	3.00	1.35	.35
☐ 4 Ivan Calderon	1.50	.70	.19
☐ 5 Gary Carter	7.50	3.40	.95
☐ 6 Delino DeShields	6.00	2.70	.75
☐ 7 Jeff Fassero	3.00	1.35	.35
☐ 8 Darrin Fletcher	1.50	.70	.19
☐ 9 Mark Gardner	1.25	.55	.16
☐ 10 Marquis Grissom	7.50	3.40	.95
☐ 11 Ken Hill	3.00	1.35	.35
☐ 12 Dennis Martinez	3.00	1.35	.35
☐ 13 Chris Nabholz	1.25	.55	.16
☐ 14 Spike Owen	1.25	.55	.16
☐ 15A Tom Runnells MG	2.00	.90	.25
☐ 15B Felipe Alou MG	6.00	2.70	.75
☐ 16A John Vander Wal	2.50	1.10	.30
☐ 16B Matt Stairs	4.00	1.80	.50
☐ 17A Bill Landrum	1.50	.70	.19
☐ 17B Dave Wainhouse	3.00	1.35	.35
☐ 18 Larry Walker	10.00	4.50	1.25
☐ 19 Tim Wallach	3.00	1.35	.35
☐ 20 John Wetteland	3.00	1.35	.35
☐ xx0 Album	5.00	2.20	.60
☐ NNO0 Checklist Card SP	5.00	2.20	.60

1992 Expos Postcards

These postcards feature members of the 1992 Montreal Expos. They measure approximately 3 1/2" by 5 1/2" and feature borderless posed color player photos. The player's name appears in a lower corner. These postcards are unnumbered and checklisted below in alphabetical order.

	MINT	NRMT	EXC
COMPLETE SET (32)	18.00	8.00	2.20
COMMON CARD (1-32)	.50	.23	.06
☐ 1 Felipe Alou MG	1.00	.45	.12
☐ 2 Moises Alou	1.25	.55	.16
☐ 3 Pierre Arsenault ANN	.75	.35	.09
☐ 4 Bret Barberie	.50	.23	.06
☐ 5 Eric Bullock	.50	.23	.06
☐ 6 Gary Carter	2.50	1.10	.30
☐ 7 Ivan Calderon	.50	.23	.06
☐ 8 Rick Cerone	.50	.23	.06
☐ 9 Archi Cianfrocco	.50	.23	.06
☐ 10 Delino DeShields	1.00	.45	.12
☐ 11 Jeff Fassero	.75	.35	.09
☐ 12 Darrin Fletcher	.50	.23	.06
☐ 13 Tom Foley	.50	.23	.06
☐ 14 Mark Gardner	.50	.23	.06
☐ 15 Marquis Grissom	2.00	.90	.25
☐ 16 Chris Haney	.50	.23	.06
☐ 17 Tommy Harper CO	.50	.23	.06
☐ 18 Ken Hill	.75	.35	.09
☐ 19 Joe Kerrigan CO	.50	.23	.06
☐ 20 Bill Landrum	.50	.23	.06
☐ 21 Jerry Manuel CO	.50	.23	.06
☐ 22 Dennis Martinez	1.00	.45	.12
☐ 23 Chris Nabholz	.50	.23	.06
☐ 24 Spike Owen	.50	.23	.06
☐ 25 Mel Rojas	1.00	.45	.12
☐ 26 Tom Runnells MG	.50	.23	.06
☐ 27 Bill Sampen	.50	.23	.06
☐ 28 John Vander Wal	.75	.35	.09
☐ 29 Larry Walker	2.00	.90	.25
☐ 30 Tim Wallach	1.00	.45	.12
☐ 31 Jay Ward CO	.50	.23	.06
☐ 32 John Wetteland	.75	.35	.09

1993 Expos Donruss McDonald's

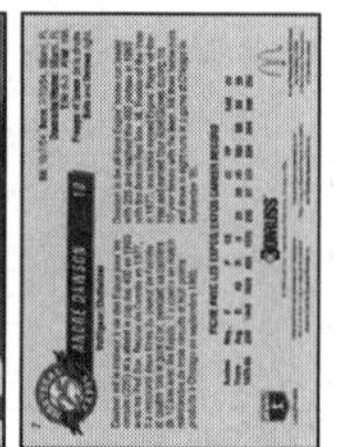

This 33-card set was produced by Donruss for McDonald's and commemorates the Montreal Expos' 25th year in baseball. The standard-size cards have fronts displaying full-bleed action pictures with the McDonald's logo at the top left. Across the bottom, the player's name and uniform number are printed on a blue stripe, with the silver-foil 25-year Expos' logo stamped to the left. The horizontal backs carry biography, statistics, and career summaries in both French and English on a beige background. The player's name and number appear near the top, printed in a dark blue stripe edged in red. The 25-year Expos' logo is displayed in the top left in red, white, and blue. The certified signed and numbered (out of 2,000) Felipe Alou card was reportedly inserted at a rate of one per case of 2,500 packs. The cards were distributed in four-card foil packs.

	MINT	NRMT	EXC
COMPLETE SET (33)	8.00	3.60	1.00
COMMON CARD (1-33)	.10	.05	.01
☐ 1 Moises Alou	.25	.11	.03
☐ 2 Andre Dawson	1.00	.45	.12
☐ 3 Delino DeShields	.75	.35	.09
☐ 4 Andres Galarraga	1.50	.70	.19
☐ 5 Marquis Grissom	1.50	.70	.19
☐ 6 Tim Raines	1.00	.45	.12
☐ 7 Larry Walker	1.50	.70	.19
☐ 8 Tim Wallach	.25	.11	.03
☐ 9 Ken Hill	.25	.11	.03
☐ 10 Dennis Martinez	.50	.23	.06
☐ 11 Jeff Reardon	.50	.23	.06
☐ 12 Gary Carter	1.50	.70	.19
☐ 13 Dave Cash	.10	.05	.01
☐ 14 Warren Cromartie	.25	.11	.03
☐ 15 Mack Jones	.10	.05	.01
☐ 16 Al Oliver	.50	.23	.06
☐ 17 Larry Parrish	.25	.11	.03
☐ 18 Rodney Scott	.10	.05	.01
☐ 19 Ken Singleton	.25	.11	.03
☐ 20 Rusty Staub	.50	.23	.06
☐ 21 Ellis Valentine	.10	.05	.01
☐ 22 Woodie Fryman	.10	.05	.01
☐ 23 Charlie Lea	.10	.05	.01
☐ 24 Bill Lee	.25	.11	.03
☐ 25 Mike Marshall	.25	.11	.03
☐ 26 Claude Raymond	.25	.11	.03
☐ 27 Steve Renko	.10	.05	.01
☐ 28 Steve Rogers	.25	.11	.03
☐ 29 Bill Stoneman	.10	.05	.01
☐ 30 Gene Mauch MG	.10	.05	.01
☐ 31 Felipe Alou MG	.25	.11	.03
☐ 32 Buck Rodgers MG	.10	.05	.01
☐ 33 Checklist 1-32	.10	.05	.01
☐ AU0 Felipe Alou AU/2000 (Certified autograph)	100.00	45.00	12.50

1993 Expos Postcards Named

These postcards are similar to the 1992 Expos postcards. They are blank-backed and we have sequenced them in alphabetical order. All these postcards have a blue background except for Wil Cordero.

	MINT	NRMT	EXC
COMPLETE SET (22)	10.00	4.50	1.25
COMMON CARD (1-22)	.50	.23	.06
☐ 1 Felipe Alou MG	1.00	.45	.12
☐ 2 Moises Alou	.75	.35	.09
☐ 3 Brian Barnes	.50	.23	.06
☐ 4 Sean Berry	.50	.23	.06
☐ 5 Frank Bolick	.50	.23	.06
☐ 6 Kent Bottenfield	.50	.23	.06
☐ 7 Greg Colbrunn	1.00	.45	.12
☐ 8 Wil Cordero	.75	.35	.09
☐ 9 Jeff Fassero	1.00	.45	.12
☐ 10 Darrin Fletcher	.50	.23	.06
☐ 11 Lou Frazier	.50	.23	.06
☐ 12 Mark Gardner	.50	.23	.06
☐ 13 Tim Johnson CO	.50	.23	.06
☐ 14 Jimmy Jones	.50	.23	.06
☐ 15 Mike Lansing	.50	.23	.06
☐ 16 Tim McIntosh	.50	.23	.06
☐ 17 Chris Nabholz	.50	.23	.06
☐ 18 Luis Pujols CO	.50	.23	.06
☐ 19 Mel Rojas	1.00	.45	.12
☐ 20 Jeff Shaw	.50	.23	.06
☐ 21 Tim Spehr	.50	.23	.06
☐ 22 Larry Walker	2.50	1.10	.30

1993 Expos Postcards

These cards have no border or player name on the front. Backs contain the Expos' logo and card number. The cards are checklisted aphabetically below.

	MINT	NRMT	EXC
COMPLETE SET (7)	5.00	2.20	.60
COMMON CARD (1-7)	.50	.23	.06
☐ 1 Moises Alou	1.00	.45	.12
☐ 2 Archi Cianfrocco	.50	.23	.06
☐ 3 Wil Cordero	.75	.35	.09
☐ 4 Delino DeShields	1.00	.45	.12
☐ 5 Dennis Martinez	1.25	.55	.16
☐ 6 Mel Rojas	.75	.35	.09
☐ 7 Larry Walker	2.00	.90	.25

1996 Expos Bookmarks

This six-card set of the Montreal Expos measures approximately 2 1/2" by 6 1/4". One side features a color player portrait with personal statistics in English and a facsimile autograph. The other side displays the same color portrait with personal statistics in French and a facsimile autograph. The cards are unnumbered and checklisted below in alphabetical order.

	MINT	NRMT	EXC
COMPLETE SET (6)	5.00	2.20	.60
COMMON CARD (1-6)	.25	.11	.03
☐ 1 Felipe Alou MG	1.00	.45	.12
☐ 2 Shane Andrews	1.00	.45	.12
☐ 3 Mark Grudzielanek	2.00	.90	.25
☐ 4 Tim Scott	.25	.11	.03
☐ 5 David Segui	1.00	.45	.12
☐ 6 Dave Veres	.25	.11	.03

1996 Expos Discs

This 24-disc set consists of six 1 5/8" perforated discs on each of four larger discs with 6 3/8" diameters. The small discs carry color action player photos with the player name, jersey number and a faded team logo on the back. The center disc in each of the large discs is the team logo.

	MINT	NRMT	EXC
COMPLETE SET (24)	5.00	2.20	.60
COMMON CARD (1-24)	.10	.05	.01
☐ 1 Felipe Alou MG	.25	.11	.03
☐ 2 Moises Alou (Batting)	.50	.23	.06
☐ 3 Moises Alou (Sliding into base)	.50	.23	.06
☐ 4 Shane Andrews	.10	.05	.01
☐ 5 Derek Aucoin	.10	.05	.01
☐ 6 Rheal Cormier	.10	.05	.01
☐ 7 Jeff Fassero	.10	.05	.01
☐ 8 Darrin Fletcher	.10	.05	.01
☐ 9 Mark Grudzielanek (Batting)	.25	.11	.03
☐ 10 Mark Grudzielanek (Fielding)	.25	.11	.03
☐ 11 Mike Lansing	.25	.11	.03
☐ 12 Pedro Martinez (With glove at mouth)	.50	.23	.06
☐ 13 Pedro Martinez (Pitching)	.50	.23	.06
☐ 14 Carlos Perez	.10	.05	.01
☐ 15 Henry Rodriguez	.25	.11	.03
☐ 16 Mel Rojas	.10	.05	.01
☐ 17 Tim Scott	.10	.05	.01
☐ 18 David Segui (Ready to catch the ball)	.25	.11	.03
☐ 19 David Segui (Catching the ball)	.25	.11	.03
☐ 20 Tim Spehr	.10	.05	.01
☐ 21 Dave Veres	.10	.05	.01
☐ 22 Rondell White (Batting)	.75	.35	.09
☐ 23 Rondell White (Running to base)	.75	.35	.09
☐ 24 Youppi(Mascot)	.25	.11	.03

1994 Extra Bases

Measuring 2 1/2" by 4 3/4", this 400 card set was issued by Fleer. Each pack contained at least one insert card. Full-bleed fronts contain a large color photo with the player's name and Extra Bases logo at the bottom. The backs are also full-bleed with a large player photo and statistics. The checklist was arranged alphabetically by team and league starting with the American League. Within each team, the player listings are alphabetical. Rookie Cards include Ray Durham and Chan Ho Park.

	MINT	NRMT	EXC
COMPLETE SET (400)	35.00	16.00	4.40
COMMON CARD (1-400)	.10	.05	.01
☐ 1 Brady Anderson	.30	.14	.04
☐ 2 Harold Baines	.20	.09	.03
☐ 3 Mike Devereaux	.10	.05	.01
☐ 4 Sid Fernandez	.10	.05	.01
☐ 5 Jeffrey Hammonds	.20	.09	.03
☐ 6 Chris Hoiles	.10	.05	.01
☐ 7 Ben McDonald	.10	.05	.01
☐ 8 Mark McLemore	.10	.05	.01
☐ 9 Mike Mussina	.30	.14	.04
☐ 10 Mike Oquist	.10	.05	.01
☐ 11 Rafael Palmeiro	.30	.14	.04
☐ 12 Cal Ripken Jr.	2.50	1.10	.30
☐ 13 Chris Sabo	.10	.05	.01
☐ 14 Lee Smith	.20	.09	.03
☐ 15 Wes Chamberlain	.10	.05	.01
☐ 16 Roger Clemens	.30	.14	.04
☐ 17 Scott Cooper	.10	.05	.01
☐ 18 Danny Darwin	.10	.05	.01
☐ 19 Andre Dawson	.20	.09	.03
☐ 20 Mike Greenwell	.10	.05	.01
☐ 21 Tim Naehring	.10	.05	.01
☐ 22 Otis Nixon	.10	.05	.01
☐ 23 Jeff Russell	.10	.05	.01
☐ 24 Ken Ryan	.10	.05	.01
☐ 25 Aaron Sele	.20	.09	.03
☐ 26 John Valentin	.20	.09	.03
☐ 27 Mo Vaughn	.75	.35	.09
☐ 28 Frank Viola	.10	.05	.01
☐ 29 Brian Anderson	.10	.05	.01
☐ 30 Chad Curtis	.10	.05	.01
☐ 31 Chili Davis	.20	.09	.03
☐ 32 Gary DiSarcina	.10	.05	.01
☐ 33 Damion Easley	.10	.05	.01
☐ 34 Jim Edmonds	.30	.14	.04
☐ 35 Chuck Finley	.10	.05	.01
☐ 36 Bo Jackson	.20	.09	.03
☐ 37 Mark Langston	.10	.05	.01
☐ 38 Harold Reynolds	.10	.05	.01

☐ 39 Tim Salmon .30 .14 .04
☐ 40 Wilson Alvarez .20 .09 .03
☐ 41 James Baldwin .30 .14 .04
☐ 42 Jason Bere .10 .05 .01
☐ 43 Joey Cora .10 .05 .01
☐ 44 Ray Durham .75 .35 .09
☐ 45 Alex Fernandez .20 .09 .03
☐ 46 Julio Franco .20 .09 .03
☐ 47 Ozzie Guillen .10 .05 .01
☐ 48 Darrin Jackson .10 .05 .01
☐ 49 Lance Johnson .20 .09 .03
☐ 50 Ron Karkovice .10 .05 .01
☐ 51 Jack McDowell .20 .09 .03
☐ 52 Tim Raines .30 .14 .04
☐ 53 Frank Thomas 3.00 1.35 .35
☐ 54 Robin Ventura .20 .09 .03
☐ 55 Sandy Alomar Jr. .20 .09 .03
☐ 56 Carlos Baerga .20 .09 .03
☐ 57 Albert Belle 1.50 .70 .19
☐ 58 Mark Clark .10 .05 .01
☐ 59 Wayne Kirby .10 .05 .01
☐ 60 Kenny Lofton 1.00 .45 .12
☐ 61 Dennis Martinez .20 .09 .03
☐ 62 Jose Mesa .20 .09 .03
☐ 63 Jack Morris .20 .09 .03
☐ 64 Eddie Murray .50 .23 .06
☐ 65 Charles Nagy .20 .09 .03
☐ 66 Manny Ramirez .75 .35 .09
☐ 67 Paul Shuey .10 .05 .01
☐ 68 Paul Sorrento .10 .05 .01
☐ 69 Jim Thome .75 .35 .09
☐ 70 Omar Vizquel .20 .09 .03
☐ 71 Eric Davis .20 .09 .03
☐ 72 John Doherty .10 .05 .01
☐ 73 Cecil Fielder .20 .09 .03
☐ 74 Travis Fryman .20 .09 .03
☐ 75 Kirk Gibson .20 .09 .03
☐ 76 Gene Harris .10 .05 .01
☐ 77 Mike Henneman .10 .05 .01
☐ 78 Mike Moore .10 .05 .01
☐ 79 Tony Phillips .20 .09 .03
☐ 80 Mickey Tettleton .10 .05 .01
☐ 81 Alan Trammell .20 .09 .03
☐ 82 Lou Whitaker .20 .09 .03
☐ 83 Kevin Appier .20 .09 .03
☐ 84 Vince Coleman .10 .05 .01
☐ 85 David Cone .20 .09 .03
☐ 86 Gary Gaetti .20 .09 .03
☐ 87 Greg Gagne .10 .05 .01
☐ 88 Tom Gordon .10 .05 .01
☐ 89 Jeff Granger .10 .05 .01
☐ 90 Bob Hamelin .10 .05 .01
☐ 91 Dave Henderson .10 .05 .01
☐ 92 Felix Jose .10 .05 .01
☐ 93 Wally Joyner .20 .09 .03
☐ 94 Jose Lind .10 .05 .01
☐ 95 Mike Macfarlane .10 .05 .01
☐ 96 Brian McRae .20 .09 .03
☐ 97 Jeff Montgomery .20 .09 .03
☐ 98 Ricky Bones .10 .05 .01
☐ 99 Jeff Bronkey .10 .05 .01
☐ 100 Alex Diaz .10 .05 .01
☐ 101 Cal Eldred .10 .05 .01
☐ 102 Darryl Hamilton .10 .05 .01
☐ 103 Brian Harper .10 .05 .01
☐ 104 John Jaha .20 .09 .03
☐ 105 Pat Listach .10 .05 .01
☐ 106 Dave Nilsson .20 .09 .03
☐ 107 Jody Reed .10 .05 .01
☐ 108 Kevin Seitzer .10 .05 .01
☐ 109 Greg Vaughn .30 .14 .04
☐ 110 Turner Ward .10 .05 .01
☐ 111 Wes Weger .10 .05 .01
☐ 112 Bill Wegman .10 .05 .01
☐ 113 Rick Aguilera .10 .05 .01
☐ 114 Rich Becker .20 .09 .03
☐ 115 Alex Cole .10 .05 .01
☐ 116 Scott Erickson .10 .05 .01
☐ 117 Kent Hrbek .20 .09 .03
☐ 118 Chuck Knoblauch .60 .25 .07
☐ 119 Scott Leius .10 .05 .01
☐ 120 Shane Mack .10 .05 .01
☐ 121 Pat Mahomes .10 .05 .01
☐ 122 Pat Meares .10 .05 .01
☐ 123 Kirby Puckett 1.25 .55 .16
☐ 124 Kevin Tapani .10 .05 .01
☐ 125 Matt Walbeck .10 .05 .01
☐ 126 Dave Winfield .30 .14 .04
☐ 127 Jim Abbott .10 .05 .01
☐ 128 Wade Boggs .30 .14 .04
☐ 129 Mike Gallego .10 .05 .01
☐ 130 Xavier Hernandez .10 .05 .01
☐ 131 Pat Kelly .10 .05 .01
☐ 132 Jimmy Key .20 .09 .03
☐ 133 Don Mattingly 1.50 .70 .19
☐ 134 Terry Mulholland .10 .05 .01
☐ 135 Matt Nokes .10 .05 .01
☐ 136 Paul O'Neill .20 .09 .03
☐ 137 Melido Perez .10 .05 .01
☐ 138 Luis Polonia .10 .05 .01
☐ 139 Mike Stanley .10 .05 .01
☐ 140 Danny Tartabull .10 .05 .01
☐ 141 Randy Velarde .10 .05 .01
☐ 142 Bernie Williams .60 .25 .07
☐ 143 Mark Acre .10 .05 .01
☐ 144 Geronimo Berroa .20 .09 .03
☐ 145 Mike Bordick .10 .05 .01
☐ 146 Scott Brosius .10 .05 .01
☐ 147 Ron Darling .10 .05 .01
☐ 148 Dennis Eckersley .20 .09 .03
☐ 149 Brent Gates .10 .05 .01
☐ 150 Rickey Henderson .30 .14 .04
☐ 151 Stan Javier .10 .05 .01
☐ 152 Steve Karsay .10 .05 .01
☐ 153 Mark McGwire 1.00 .45 .12
☐ 154 Troy Neel .10 .05 .01
☐ 155 Ruben Sierra .10 .05 .01
☐ 156 Terry Steinbach .20 .09 .03
☐ 157 Bill Taylor .10 .05 .01
☐ 158 Rich Amaral .10 .05 .01
☐ 159 Eric Anthony .10 .05 .01
☐ 160 Bobby Ayala .10 .05 .01
☐ 161 Chris Bosio .10 .05 .01
☐ 162 Jay Buhner .30 .14 .04
☐ 163 Tim Davis .10 .05 .01
☐ 164 Felix Fermin .10 .05 .01
☐ 165 Dave Fleming .10 .05 .01
☐ 166 Ken Griffey Jr. 3.00 1.35 .35
☐ 167 Reggie Jefferson .20 .09 .03
☐ 168 Randy Johnson .50 .23 .06
☐ 169 Edgar Martinez .20 .09 .03
☐ 170 Tino Martinez .20 .09 .03
☐ 171 Bill Risley .10 .05 .01
☐ 172 Roger Salkeld .10 .05 .01
☐ 173 Mac Suzuki .20 .09 .03
☐ 174 Dan Wilson .20 .09 .03
☐ 175 Kevin Brown .20 .09 .03
☐ 176 Jose Canseco .30 .14 .04
☐ 177 Will Clark .30 .14 .04
☐ 178 Juan Gonzalez 1.50 .70 .19
☐ 179 Rick Helling .10 .05 .01
☐ 180 Tom Henke .10 .05 .01
☐ 181 Chris James .10 .05 .01
☐ 182 Manuel Lee .10 .05 .01
☐ 183 Dean Palmer .20 .09 .03
☐ 184 Ivan Rodriguez .75 .35 .09
☐ 185 Kenny Rogers .10 .05 .01
☐ 186 Roberto Alomar .60 .25 .07
☐ 187 Pat Borders .10 .05 .01
☐ 188 Joe Carter .20 .09 .03
☐ 189 Carlos Delgado .30 .14 .04
☐ 190 Juan Guzman .20 .09 .03
☐ 191 Pat Hentgen .20 .09 .03
☐ 192 Paul Molitor .60 .25 .07
☐ 193 John Olerud .20 .09 .03
☐ 194 Ed Sprague .20 .09 .03
☐ 195 Dave Stewart .20 .09 .03
☐ 196 Todd Stottlemyre .10 .05 .01
☐ 197 Duane Ward .10 .05 .01
☐ 198 Devon White .10 .05 .01
☐ 199 Steve Avery .20 .09 .03
☐ 200 Jeff Blauser .10 .05 .01
☐ 201 Tom Glavine .50 .23 .06
☐ 202 David Justice .30 .14 .04
☐ 203 Mike Kelly .10 .05 .01
☐ 204 Roberto Kelly .10 .05 .01
☐ 205 Ryan Klesko .60 .25 .07
☐ 206 Mark Lemke .10 .05 .01
☐ 207 Javier Lopez .30 .14 .04
☐ 208 Greg Maddux 2.00 .90 .25
☐ 209 Fred McGriff .30 .14 .04
☐ 210 Greg McMichael .10 .05 .01
☐ 211 Kent Mercker .10 .05 .01
☐ 212 Terry Pendleton .20 .09 .03
☐ 213 John Smoltz .50 .23 .06
☐ 214 Tony Tarasco .10 .05 .01
☐ 215 Willie Banks .10 .05 .01
☐ 216 Steve Buechele .10 .05 .01
☐ 217 Shawon Dunston .10 .05 .01
☐ 218 Mark Grace .30 .14 .04
☐ 219 Brooks Kieschnick 1.00 .45 .12
☐ 220 Derrick May .10 .05 .01
☐ 221 Randy Myers .10 .05 .01
☐ 222 Karl Rhodes .10 .05 .01
☐ 223 Rey Sanchez .10 .05 .01
☐ 224 Sammy Sosa .30 .14 .04
☐ 225 Steve Trachsel .10 .05 .01
☐ 226 Rick Wilkins .10 .05 .01
☐ 227 Bret Boone .20 .09 .03
☐ 228 Jeff Brantley .10 .05 .01
☐ 229 Tom Browning .10 .05 .01
☐ 230 Hector Carrasco .10 .05 .01
☐ 231 Rob Dibble .10 .05 .01
☐ 232 Erik Hanson .10 .05 .01
☐ 233 Barry Larkin .50 .23 .06
☐ 234 Kevin Mitchell .20 .09 .03
☐ 235 Hal Morris .10 .05 .01
☐ 236 Joe Oliver .10 .05 .01
☐ 237 Jose Rijo .10 .05 .01
☐ 238 Johnny Ruffin .10 .05 .01
☐ 239 Deion Sanders .50 .23 .06
☐ 240 Reggie Sanders .20 .09 .03
☐ 241 John Smiley .10 .05 .01
☐ 242 Dante Bichette .50 .23 .06
☐ 243 Ellis Burks .20 .09 .03
☐ 244 Andres Galarraga .30 .14 .04
☐ 245 Joe Girardi .10 .05 .01
☐ 246 Greg W.Harris .10 .05 .01
☐ 247 Charlie Hayes .10 .05 .01
☐ 248 Howard Johnson .10 .05 .01
☐ 249 Roberto Mejia .10 .05 .01
☐ 250 Marcus Moore .10 .05 .01
☐ 251 David Nied .10 .05 .01
☐ 252 Armando Reynoso .10 .05 .01
☐ 253 Bruce Ruffin .10 .05 .01
☐ 254 Mark Thompson .20 .09 .03
☐ 255 Walt Weiss .10 .05 .01
☐ 256 Kurt Abbott .10 .05 .01
☐ 257 Bret Barberie .10 .05 .01
☐ 258 Chuck Carr .10 .05 .01
☐ 259 Jeff Conine .20 .09 .03
☐ 260 Chris Hammond .10 .05 .01
☐ 261 Bryan Harvey .10 .05 .01
☐ 262 Jeremy Hernandez .10 .05 .01
☐ 263 Charlie Hough .10 .05 .01
☐ 264 Dave Magadan .10 .05 .01
☐ 265 Benito Santiago .10 .05 .01
☐ 266 Gary Sheffield .50 .23 .06
☐ 267 David Weathers .10 .05 .01
☐ 268 Jeff Bagwell 1.25 .55 .16
☐ 269 Craig Biggio .20 .09 .03
☐ 270 Ken Caminiti .50 .23 .06
☐ 271 Andujar Cedeno .10 .05 .01
☐ 272 Doug Drabek .10 .05 .01
☐ 273 Steve Finley .30 .14 .04
☐ 274 Luis Gonzalez .10 .05 .01
☐ 275 Pete Harnisch .10 .05 .01
☐ 276 John Hudek .10 .05 .01
☐ 277 Darryl Kile .10 .05 .01
☐ 278 Orlando Miller .10 .05 .01
☐ 279 James Mouton .10 .05 .01
☐ 280 Shane Reynolds .20 .09 .03
☐ 281 Scott Servais .10 .05 .01
☐ 282 Greg Swindell .10 .05 .01
☐ 283 Pedro Astacio .10 .05 .01
☐ 284 Brett Butler .20 .09 .03
☐ 285 Tom Candiotti .10 .05 .01
☐ 286 Delino DeShields .10 .05 .01
☐ 287 Kevin Gross .10 .05 .01
☐ 288 Orel Hershiser .20 .09 .03
☐ 289 Eric Karros .20 .09 .03
☐ 290 Ramon Martinez .20 .09 .03
☐ 291 Raul Mondesi .75 .35 .09
☐ 292 Jose Offerman .10 .05 .01
☐ 293 Chan Ho Park 1.00 .45 .12
☐ 294 Mike Piazza 2.00 .90 .25
☐ 295 Henry Rodriguez .20 .09 .03
☐ 296 Cory Snyder .10 .05 .01
☐ 297 Tim Wallach .10 .05 .01
☐ 298 Todd Worrell .10 .05 .01
☐ 299 Moises Alou .20 .09 .03
☐ 300 Sean Berry .10 .05 .01
☐ 301 Wil Cordero .20 .09 .03
☐ 302 Joey Eischen .10 .05 .01
☐ 303 Jeff Fassero .10 .05 .01
☐ 304 Darrin Fletcher .10 .05 .01
☐ 305 Cliff Floyd .20 .09 .03
☐ 306 Marquis Grissom .20 .09 .03
☐ 307 Ken Hill .10 .05 .01
☐ 308 Mike Lansing .20 .09 .03
☐ 309 Pedro J.Martinez .30 .14 .04
☐ 310 Mel Rojas .10 .05 .01
☐ 311 Kirk Rueter .10 .05 .01
☐ 312 Larry Walker .50 .23 .06
☐ 313 John Wetteland .20 .09 .03
☐ 314 Rondell White .30 .14 .04
☐ 315 Bobby Bonilla .20 .09 .03
☐ 316 John Franco .10 .05 .01
☐ 317 Dwight Gooden .20 .09 .03
☐ 318 Todd Hundley .50 .23 .06
☐ 319 Bobby Jones .20 .09 .03
☐ 320 Jeff Kent .10 .05 .01
☐ 321 Kevin McReynolds .10 .05 .01
☐ 322 Bill Pulsipher .10 .05 .01
☐ 323 Bret Saberhagen .20 .09 .03
☐ 324 David Segui .10 .05 .01
☐ 325 Pete Smith .10 .05 .01
☐ 326 Kelly Stinnett .10 .05 .01
☐ 327 Ryan Thompson .10 .05 .01
☐ 328 Jose Vizcaino .10 .05 .01
☐ 329 Ricky Bottalico .30 .14 .04
☐ 330 Darren Daulton .20 .09 .03
☐ 331 Mariano Duncan .10 .05 .01
☐ 332 Lenny Dykstra .20 .09 .03
☐ 333 Tommy Greene .10 .05 .01
☐ 334 Billy Hatcher .10 .05 .01
☐ 335 Dave Hollins .10 .05 .01
☐ 336 Pete Incaviglia .10 .05 .01
☐ 337 Danny Jackson .10 .05 .01
☐ 338 Doug Jones .10 .05 .01
☐ 339 Ricky Jordan .10 .05 .01
☐ 340 John Kruk .20 .09 .03
☐ 341 Curt Schilling .10 .05 .01
☐ 342 Kevin Stocker .10 .05 .01
☐ 343 Jay Bell .20 .09 .03
☐ 344 Steve Cooke .10 .05 .01
☐ 345 Carlos Garcia .10 .05 .01
☐ 346 Brian Hunter .10 .05 .01
☐ 347 Jeff King .20 .09 .03
☐ 348 Al Martin .10 .05 .01
☐ 349 Orlando Merced .20 .09 .03
☐ 350 Denny Neagle .20 .09 .03
☐ 351 Don Slaught .10 .05 .01
☐ 352 Andy Van Slyke .20 .09 .03
☐ 353 Paul Wagner .10 .05 .01
☐ 354 Rick White .10 .05 .01
☐ 355 Luis Alicea .10 .05 .01
☐ 356 Rene Arocha .10 .05 .01
☐ 357 Rheal Cormier .10 .05 .01
☐ 358 Bernard Gilkey .20 .09 .03
☐ 359 Gregg Jefferies .30 .14 .04
☐ 360 Ray Lankford .20 .09 .03
☐ 361 Tom Pagnozzi .10 .05 .01
☐ 362 Mike Perez .10 .05 .01
☐ 363 Ozzie Smith .75 .35 .09
☐ 364 Bob Tewksbury .10 .05 .01
☐ 365 Mark Whiten .10 .05 .01
☐ 366 Todd Zeile .10 .05 .01
☐ 367 Andy Ashby .20 .09 .03
☐ 368 Brad Ausmus .10 .05 .01
☐ 369 Derek Bell .20 .09 .03
☐ 370 Andy Benes .20 .09 .03
☐ 371 Archi Cianfrocco .10 .05 .01
☐ 372 Tony Gwynn 1.25 .55 .16
☐ 373 Trevor Hoffman .20 .09 .03
☐ 374 Tim Hyers .10 .05 .01
☐ 375 Pedro Martinez .20 .09 .03
☐ 376 Phil Plantier .10 .05 .01
☐ 377 Bip Roberts .10 .05 .01
☐ 378 Scott Sanders .10 .05 .01
☐ 379 Dave Staton .10 .05 .01
☐ 380 Wally Whitehurst .10 .05 .01
☐ 381 Rod Beck .20 .09 .03
☐ 382 Todd Benzinger .10 .05 .01
☐ 383 Barry Bonds .75 .35 .09
☐ 384 John Burkett .10 .05 .01
☐ 385 Royce Clayton .20 .09 .03
☐ 386 Bryan Hickerson .10 .05 .01
☐ 387 Mike Jackson .10 .05 .01
☐ 388 Darren Lewis .10 .05 .01
☐ 389 Kirt Manwaring .10 .05 .01
☐ 390 Willie McGee .20 .09 .03
☐ 391 Mark Portugal .10 .05 .01
☐ 392 Bill Swift .10 .05 .01
☐ 393 Robby Thompson .10 .05 .01
☐ 394 Salomon Torres .10 .05 .01
☐ 395 Matt Williams .30 .14 .04
☐ 396 Checklist .10 .05 .01
☐ 397 Checklist .10 .05 .01
☐ 398 Checklist .10 .05 .01
☐ 399 Checklist .10 .05 .01
☐ 400 Checklist .10 .05 .01
☐ P1 Paul Molitor Promo 2.00 .90 .25

1994 Extra Bases Game Breakers

Consisting of 30 cards and randomly inserted in packs at a rate of three per eight, this set features top run producers from around the major leagues. The cards measure 2 1/2" by 4 11/16" and are horizontally designed. There are two photos on the front that bleed into one another. The back has a photo and career highlights.

	MINT	NRMT	EXC
COMPLETE SET (30)	25.00	11.00	3.10
COMMON CARD (1-30)	.25	.11	.03

☐ 1 Jeff Bagwell 2.50 1.10 .30
☐ 2 Rod Beck .25 .11 .03
☐ 3 Albert Belle 2.50 1.10 .30
☐ 4 Barry Bonds 1.25 .55 .16
☐ 5 Jose Canseco .50 .23 .06
☐ 6 Joe Carter .40 .18 .05
☐ 7 Roger Clemens .75 .35 .09
☐ 8 Darren Daulton .40 .18 .05
☐ 9 Lenny Dykstra .40 .18 .05
☐ 10 Cecil Fielder .40 .18 .05
☐ 11 Tom Glavine .60 .25 .07
☐ 12 Juan Gonzalez 2.50 1.10 .30
☐ 13 Mark Grace .50 .23 .06
☐ 14 Ken Griffey Jr. 5.00 2.20 .60
☐ 15 David Justice .40 .18 .05
☐ 16 Greg Maddux 3.00 1.35 .35
☐ 17 Don Mattingly 2.50 1.10 .30
☐ 18 Ben McDonald .25 .11 .03
☐ 19 Fred McGriff .50 .23 .06
☐ 20 Paul Molitor 1.00 .45 .12
☐ 21 John Olerud .40 .18 .05
☐ 22 Mike Piazza 3.00 1.35 .35
☐ 23 Kirby Puckett 2.00 .90 .25
☐ 24 Cal Ripken Jr. 4.00 1.80 .50
☐ 25 Tim Salmon .50 .23 .06
☐ 26 Gary Sheffield .75 .35 .09
☐ 27 Frank Thomas 5.00 2.20 .60
☐ 28 Mo Vaughn 1.00 .45 .12
☐ 29 Matt Williams .75 .35 .09
☐ 30 Dave Winfield .60 .25 .07

1994 Extra Bases Major League Hopefuls

Randomly inserted in packs at a rate of one in eight, this 10-card set features top minor league performers. Cards measure 2 1/2" by 4 11/16". Computer generated fronts contain multiple player photos. The backs have a player photo and a write-up about the player's minor league exploits.

	MINT	NRMT	EXC
COMPLETE SET (10)	10.00	4.50	1.25
COMMON CARD (1-10)	.50	.23	.06
☐ 1 James Baldwin	1.00	.45	.12
☐ 2 Ricky Bottalico	.75	.35	.09
☐ 3 Ray Durham	2.00	.90	.25
☐ 4 Joey Eischen	.50	.23	.06
☐ 5 Brooks Kieschnick	2.00	.90	.25
☐ 6 Orlando Miller	.50	.23	.06
☐ 7 Bill Pulsipher	.75	.35	.09
☐ 8 Mac Suzuki	.75	.35	.09
☐ 9 Mark Thompson	.50	.23	.06
☐ 10 Wes Weger	.50	.23	.06

1994 Extra Bases Pitchers Duel

This 10-card set measures 2 1/2" by 4 3/4". These cards were available through a wrapper offer which was good through March 31, 1995. Each card features two leading pitchers.

	MINT	NRMT	EXC
COMPLETE SET (10)	12.00	5.50	1.50
COMMON CARD (1-10)	.75	.35	.09
☐ 1 Roger Clemens Jack McDowell	3.00	1.35	.35
☐ 2 Ben McDonald Randy Johnson	3.00	1.35	.35
☐ 3 David Cone Jimmy Key	1.00	.45	.12
☐ 4 Mike Mussina Aaron Sele	2.00	.90	.25
☐ 5 Chuck Finley Wilson Alvarez	.75	.35	.09
☐ 6 Curt Schilling Steve Avery	.75	.35	.09
☐ 7 Greg Maddux Jose Rijo	3.00	1.35	.35
☐ 8 Bob Tewksbury Bret Saberhagen	.75	.35	.09
☐ 9 Tom Glavine Bill Swift	.75	.35	.09
☐ 10 Doug Drabek Orel Hershiser	.75	.35	.09

1994 Extra Bases Rookie Standouts

Randomly inserted in packs at a rate of one in four, this 20-card set features those that had potential for being top rookies in 1994. The cards measure 2 1/2" by 4 11/16". Card fronts have an action photo of the player. The background is somewhat blurred and a jagged outline appears around the player as if to allow him to stand out from the rest of the card. The backs have a player photo and text on a white background.

	MINT	NRMT	EXC
COMPLETE SET (20)	18.00	8.00	2.20
COMMON CARD (1-20)	.40	.18	.05
☐ 1 Kurt Abbott	.40	.18	.05
☐ 2 Brian Anderson	.40	.18	.05
☐ 3 Hector Carrasco	.40	.18	.05
☐ 4 Tim Davis	.40	.18	.05
☐ 5 Carlos Delgado	2.00	.90	.25
☐ 6 Cliff Floyd	.40	.18	.05
☐ 7 Bob Hamelin	.40	.18	.05
☐ 8 Jeffrey Hammonds	.50	.23	.06
☐ 9 Rick Helling	.40	.18	.05
☐ 10 Steve Karsay	.50	.23	.06
☐ 11 Ryan Klesko	.75	.35	.09
☐ 12 Javier Lopez	2.00	.90	.25
☐ 13 Raul Mondesi	2.50	1.10	.30
☐ 14 James Mouton	.40	.18	.05
☐ 15 Chan Ho Park	1.00	.45	.12
☐ 16 Manny Ramirez	4.00	1.80	.50
☐ 17 Tony Tarasco	.40	.18	.05
☐ 18 Steve Trachsel	.40	.18	.05
☐ 19 Rick White	.40	.18	.05
☐ 20 Rondell White	1.50	.70	.19

1994 Extra Bases Second Year Stars

Randomly inserted in packs at a rate of one in four, Second Year Stars takes a look at 20 top second year players and reflects on their rookie campaigns of 1993. The cards measure 2 1/2" by 4 11/16". Card fronts feature multiple photos including a large full bleed photo of the player and four smaller photos that give the appearance of being captured on film. These smaller photos run the length of the card and are on the left.

	MINT	NRMT	EXC
COMPLETE SET (20)	10.00	4.50	1.25
COMMON CARD (1-20)	.50	.23	.06
☐ 1 Bobby Ayala	.50	.23	.06
☐ 2 Jason Bere	.50	.23	.06
☐ 3 Chuck Carr	.50	.23	.06
☐ 4 Jeff Conine	.75	.35	.09
☐ 5 Steve Cooke	.50	.23	.06
☐ 6 Wil Cordero	.75	.35	.09
☐ 7 Carlos Garcia	.50	.23	.06
☐ 8 Brent Gates	.50	.23	.06
☐ 9 Trevor Hoffman	.75	.35	.09
☐ 10 Wayne Kirby	.50	.23	.06
☐ 11 Al Martin	.50	.23	.06
☐ 12 Pedro Martinez	.75	.35	.09
☐ 13 Greg McMichael	.50	.23	.06
☐ 14 Troy Neel	.50	.23	.06
☐ 15 David Nied	.50	.23	.06
☐ 16 Mike Piazza	5.00	2.20	.60
☐ 17 Kirk Rueter	.75	.35	.09
☐ 18 Tim Salmon	2.00	.90	.25
☐ 19 Aaron Sele	.75	.35	.09
☐ 20 Kevin Stocker	.50	.23	.06

1904 Fan Craze AL WG2

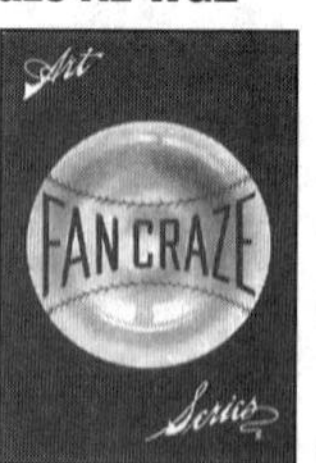

These cards were distributed as part of a baseball game produced in 1904. The cards each measure approximately 2 1/2" by 3 1/2" and have rounded corners. The card fronts show a black and white cameo photo of the player, his name, his team and the game outcome associated with that particular card. The card backs are all the same, each showing "Art Series" and "Fan Craze" in dark blue and white. This set features only players from the American League. Since the cards are unnumbered, they are listed below in alphabetical order.

	EX-MT	VG-E	GOOD
COMPLETE SET (51)	4500.00	2000.00	550.00
COMMON CARD (1-51)	75.00	34.00	9.50
☐ 1 Nick Altrock	125.00	55.00	15.50
☐ 2 Jim Barrett	75.00	34.00	9.50
☐ 3 Harry Bay	75.00	34.00	9.50
☐ 4 Chief Bender	140.00	65.00	17.50
☐ 5 Bill Bernhardt	75.00	34.00	9.50
☐ 6 Bill Bradley	75.00	34.00	9.50
☐ 7 Jack Chesbro	150.00	70.00	19.00
☐ 8 Jimmy Collins	150.00	70.00	19.00
☐ 9 Sam Crawford	150.00	70.00	19.00
☐ 10 Lou Criger	75.00	34.00	9.50
☐ 11 Lave Cross	75.00	34.00	9.50
☐ 12 Monty Cross	75.00	34.00	9.50
☐ 13 Harry Davis	75.00	34.00	9.50
☐ 14 Bill Dineen	75.00	34.00	9.50
☐ 15 Pat Donovan	75.00	34.00	9.50
☐ 16 Pat Dougherty	75.00	34.00	9.50
☐ 17 Norman Elberfeld	75.00	34.00	9.50
☐ 18 Hobe Ferris	75.00	34.00	9.50
☐ 19 Elmer Flick	140.00	65.00	17.50
☐ 20 Buck Freeman	75.00	34.00	9.50
☐ 21 Fred Glade	75.00	34.00	9.50
☐ 22 Clark Griffith	140.00	65.00	17.50
☐ 23 Charles Hickman	75.00	34.00	9.50
☐ 24 William Holmes	75.00	34.00	9.50
☐ 25 Harry Howell	75.00	34.00	9.50
☐ 26 Frank Isbell	75.00	34.00	9.50
☐ 27 Albert Jacobson	75.00	34.00	9.50
☐ 28 Ban Johnson PRES	150.00	70.00	19.00
☐ 29 Fielder Jones	75.00	34.00	9.50
☐ 30 Adrian Joss	225.00	100.00	28.00
☐ 31 Willie Keeler	225.00	100.00	28.00
☐ 32 Napoleon Lajoie	300.00	135.00	38.00
☐ 33 Connie Mack MG	225.00	100.00	28.00
☐ 34 Jimmy McAleer	75.00	34.00	9.50
☐ 35 Jim McGuire	75.00	34.00	9.50
☐ 36 Earl Moore	75.00	34.00	9.50
☐ 37 George Mullen	75.00	34.00	9.50
☐ 38 Billy Owen	75.00	34.00	9.50
☐ 39 Fred Parent	75.00	34.00	9.50
☐ 40 Case Patten	75.00	34.00	9.50
☐ 41 Eddie Plank	225.00	100.00	28.00
☐ 42 Ossie Schreckengost	75.00	34.00	9.50
☐ 43 Jake Stahl	125.00	55.00	15.50
☐ 44 Fred Stone	75.00	34.00	9.50
☐ 45 William Sudhoff	75.00	34.00	9.50
☐ 46 Roy Turner	75.00	34.00	9.50
☐ 47 Rube Waddell	150.00	70.00	19.00
☐ 48 Bob Wallace	140.00	65.00	17.50
☐ 49 G. Harris White	75.00	34.00	9.50
☐ 50 George Winters	75.00	34.00	9.50
☐ 51 Cy Young	250.00	110.00	31.00

1906 Fan Craze NL WG3

These cards were distributed as part of a baseball game produced in 1906. The cards each measure approximately 2 1/2" by 3 1/2" and have rounded corners. The card fronts show a black and white cameo photo of the player, his name, his team, and the game outcome associated with that particular card. The card backs are all the same, each showing "Art Series" and "Fan Craze" in dark blue and white. This set features only players from the National League. Since the cards are unnumbered, they are listed below in alphabetical order. The six asterisked cards do not have a game outcome at the top of the card.

	EX-MT	VG-E	GOOD
COMPLETE SET (54)	4000.00	1800.00	500.00
COMMON CARD (1-54)	75.00	34.00	9.50
☐ 1 Red Ames	75.00	34.00	9.50
☐ 2 Ginger Beaumont	75.00	34.00	9.50
☐ 3 Jake Beckley	150.00	70.00	19.00
☐ 4 Billy Bergen	75.00	34.00	9.50
☐ 5 Roger Bresnahan	125.00	55.00	15.50
☐ 6 George Brown	75.00	34.00	9.50
☐ 7 Mordacai Brown sic, Mordecai	150.00	70.00	19.00
☐ 8 Doc Casey	75.00	34.00	9.50
☐ 9 Frank Chance	150.00	70.00	19.00
☐ 10 Fred Clarke	150.00	70.00	19.00
☐ 11 Tommy Corcoran	75.00	34.00	9.50
☐ 12 Bill Dahlen	100.00	45.00	12.50
☐ 13 Mike Donlin	75.00	34.00	9.50
☐ 14 Charley Dooin	75.00	34.00	9.50
☐ 15 Mickey Doolin	75.00	34.00	9.50
☐ 16 Hugh Duffy	150.00	70.00	19.00
☐ 17 John E. Dunleavy	75.00	34.00	9.50
☐ 18 Bob Ewing	75.00	34.00	9.50
☐ 19 Chick Fraser	75.00	34.00	9.50
☐ 20 Ned Hanlon MG	75.00	34.00	9.50
☐ 21 Del Howard	75.00	34.00	9.50
☐ 22 Miller Huggins	150.00	70.00	19.00
☐ 23 Joe Kelley	150.00	70.00	19.00
☐ 24 John Kling	75.00	34.00	9.50
☐ 25 Tommy Leach	75.00	34.00	9.50
☐ 26 Harry Lumley	75.00	34.00	9.50
☐ 27 Carl Lundgren	75.00	34.00	9.50
☐ 28 Bill Maloney	75.00	34.00	9.50
☐ 29 Dan McGann	75.00	34.00	9.50
☐ 30 Joe McGinnity	150.00	70.00	19.00
☐ 31 John McGraw MG	150.00	70.00	19.00
☐ 32 Harry McIntire	75.00	34.00	9.50
☐ 33 Kid Nichols	150.00	70.00	19.00
☐ 34 Mike O'Neil	75.00	34.00	9.50
☐ 35 Orval Overall	75.00	34.00	9.50
☐ 36 Frank Pfeffer	75.00	34.00	9.50
☐ 37 Deacon Philippe	100.00	45.00	12.50
☐ 38 Charley Pittinger	75.00	34.00	9.50
☐ 39 Harry C. Pulliam PRES	75.00	34.00	9.50
☐ 40 Ed Reulbach	75.00	34.00	9.50
☐ 41 Claude Ritchey	75.00	34.00	9.50
☐ 42 Cy Seymour	75.00	34.00	9.50
☐ 43 Jim Sheckard	75.00	34.00	9.50
☐ 44 Jack Taylor	75.00	34.00	9.50
☐ 45 Dummy Taylor	75.00	34.00	9.50
☐ 46 Fred Tenney	75.00	34.00	9.50
☐ 47 Harry Theilman	75.00	34.00	9.50
☐ 48 Roy Thomas	75.00	34.00	9.50
☐ 49 Honus Wagner	400.00	180.00	50.00
☐ 50 Jake Weimer	75.00	34.00	9.50
☐ 51 Bob Wicker	75.00	34.00	9.50
☐ 52 Vic Willis	125.00	55.00	15.50
☐ 53 Lew Wiltsie	75.00	34.00	9.50
☐ 54 Irving Young	75.00	34.00	9.50

1994 FanFest Clemente

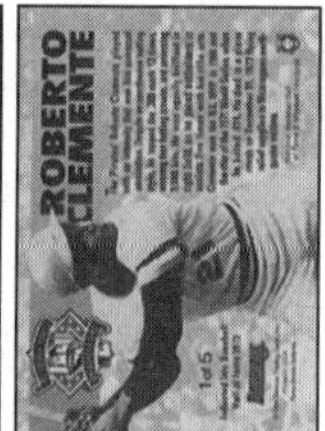

This standard-size redemption set was reportedly the brainchild of MLB's Ray Schulte, who obtained the cooperation of the five major baseball card manufacturers to each produce 15,000 special Roberto Clemente cards for the '94 All-Star FanFest in Pittsburgh, July 8-12. Each card was redeemable only at each manufacturer's booth for five wrappers of any '94 baseball product from that company. The undistributed cards were reportedly destroyed. It has been estimated that less than 10,000 of each card were distributed. All the cards are numbered on the back as "X of 5."

	MINT	NRMT	EXC
COMPLETE SET (5)	80.00	36.00	10.00
COMMON CARD (1-5)	15.00	6.75	1.85
☐ 1 Roberto Clemente Donruss Diamond King	15.00	6.75	1.85
☐ 2 Roberto Clemente 1963 Fleer Reprint	15.00	6.75	1.85
☐ 3 Roberto Clemente 1994 Pinnacle Dufex	15.00	6.75	1.85
☐ 4 Roberto Clemente 1954 Topps Archives	20.00	9.00	2.50
☐ 5 Roberto Clemente Upper Deck Electric	15.00	6.75	1.85

1995 FanFest Ryan

Five MLB licensors produced one card each as part of a wrapper redemption program featuring Nolan Ryan for All-Star FanFest in Dallas in July. Pinnacle, Ultra, and Upper Deck cards sport the design of the licensor's regular issue, while Donruss produced a special design and Topps modified Ryan's 1968 rookie card (shared with Jerry Koosman) to feature only Ryan. Again, Ray Schulte, promoter of the Pinnacle All-Star Fan Fest shows, was involved in the creation of this set. The cards are numbered on the back "X of 5."

	MINT	NRMT	EXC
COMPLETE SET (5)	40.00	18.00	5.00
COMMON CARD (1-5)	10.00	4.50	1.25
☐ 1 Nolan Ryan 1995 Upper Deck	12.00	5.50	1.50
☐ 2 Nolan Ryan 1968 Topps	10.00	4.50	1.25
☐ 3 Nolan Ryan 1995 Pinnacle	10.00	4.50	1.25
☐ 4 Nolan Ryan 1995 Ultra	12.00	5.50	1.50

☐ 5 Nolan Ryan 1995 Donruss (Special design)	10.00	4.50	1.25

1996 FanFest Carlton

These five standard-size cards marked the third straight year that a set of one player's cards were issued in conjunction with the annual All-Star Fan Fest. MLB's Ray Schulte, who originated the idea of these cards was again instrumental in arranging for the companies to issue these cards as part of a wrapper redemption program.

	MINT	NRMT	EXC
COMPLETE SET (5)	30.00	13.50	3.70
COMMON CARD (1-5)	6.00	2.70	.75
☐ 1 Steve Carlton Donruss	6.00	2.70	.75
☐ 2 Steve Carlton Fleer Ultra	6.00	2.70	.75
☐ 3 Steve Carlton Pinnacle	8.00	3.60	1.00
☐ 4 Steve Carlton 1965 Topps	8.00	3.60	1.00
☐ 5 Steve Carlton Upper Deck	6.00	2.70	.75

1913 Fatima T200

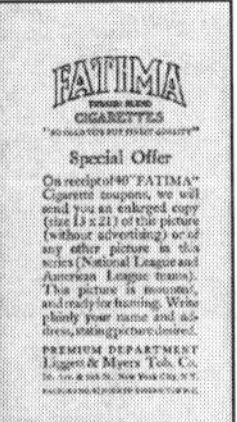

The cards in this 16-card set measure approximately 2 5/8" by 5 13/16". The 1913 Fatima Cigarettes issue contains unnumbered glossy surface team cards. Both St. Louis team cards are considered difficult to obtain. A large 13" by 21" unnumbered, heavy cardboard parallel premium issue is also known to exist and is quite scarce. These unnumbered team cards are ordered below by team alphabetical order within league.

	EX-MT	VG-E	GOOD
COMPLETE SET (16)	7000.00	3200.00	900.00
COMMON TEAM (1-16)	300.00	135.00	38.00
☐ 1 Boston AL	350.00	160.00	45.00
☐ 2 Chicago AL	350.00	160.00	45.00
☐ 3 Cleveland AL	1000.00	450.00	125.00
☐ 4 Detroit AL	750.00	350.00	95.00
☐ 5 New York AL	800.00	350.00	100.00
☐ 6 Philadelphia AL	300.00	135.00	38.00
☐ 7 St. Louis AL	600.00	275.00	75.00
☐ 8 Washington AL	400.00	180.00	50.00
☐ 9 Boston NL	400.00	180.00	50.00
☐ 10 Brooklyn NL	300.00	135.00	38.00
☐ 11 Chicago NL	350.00	160.00	45.00
☐ 12 Cincinnati NL	300.00	135.00	38.00
☐ 13 New York NL	500.00	220.00	60.00
☐ 14 Philadelphia NL	300.00	135.00	38.00
☐ 15 Pittsburg NL	400.00	180.00	50.00
☐ 16 St. Louis NL	400.00	180.00	50.00

1914 Fatima Players T222

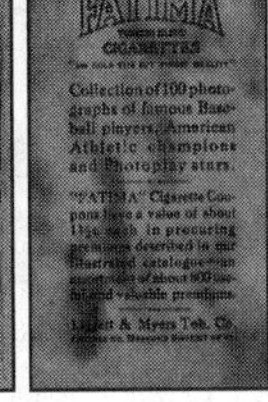

The cards in this 52-card set measure approximately 2 1/2" by 4 1/2" and are unnumbered. The cards are quite fragile on thin. brittle paper stock. The set was produced in 1914 by Liggett and Myers Tobacco Co. The players in the set have been alphabetized and numbered for reference in the checklist below.

	EX-MT	VG-E	GOOD
COMPLETE SET (52)	3500.00	1600.00	450.00
COMMON CARD	50.00	22.00	6.25
☐ 1 Grover Alexander	225.00	100.00	28.00
☐ 2 Jimmy Archer	50.00	22.00	6.25
☐ 3 James Austin	100.00	45.00	12.50
☐ 4 Jack Barry	50.00	22.00	6.25
☐ 5 George Baumgardner	50.00	22.00	6.25
☐ 6 Rube Benton	50.00	22.00	6.25
☐ 7 Roger Bresnahan	100.00	45.00	12.50
☐ 8 Mordecai Brown	100.00	45.00	12.50
☐ 9 George J. Burns	50.00	22.00	6.25
☐ 10 Joe Bush	50.00	22.00	6.25
☐ 11 George Chalmers	50.00	22.00	6.25
☐ 12 Frank Chance	150.00	70.00	19.00
☐ 13 Albert Demaree	50.00	22.00	6.25
☐ 14 Arthur Fletcher	50.00	22.00	6.25
☐ 15 Earl Hamilton	50.00	22.00	6.25
☐ 16 John Henry	100.00	45.00	12.50
☐ 17 Byron Houck	50.00	22.00	6.25
☐ 18 Miller Huggins	100.00	45.00	12.50
☐ 19 Hugh Jennings MG	100.00	45.00	12.50
☐ 20 Walter Johnson	600.00	275.00	75.00
☐ 21 Ray Keating	50.00	22.00	6.25
☐ 22 John Lapp	50.00	22.00	6.25
☐ 23 Thomas Leach	50.00	22.00	6.25
☐ 24 Nemo Leibold	50.00	22.00	6.25
☐ 25 John Frank Lelivelt	50.00	22.00	6.25
☐ 26 Hans Lobert	100.00	45.00	12.50
☐ 27 Lee Magee	50.00	22.00	6.25
☐ 28 Sherry Magee	50.00	22.00	6.25
☐ 29 Fritz Maisel	50.00	22.00	6.25
☐ 30 Rube Marquard	100.00	45.00	12.50
☐ 31 George McBride	50.00	22.00	6.25
☐ 32 Stuffy McInnis	50.00	22.00	6.25
☐ 33 Larry McLean	50.00	22.00	6.25
☐ 34 Raymond Morgan	50.00	22.00	6.25
☐ 35 Eddie Murphy	50.00	22.00	6.25
☐ 36 Red Murray	50.00	22.00	6.25
☐ 37 Rube Oldring	100.00	45.00	12.50
☐ 38 William J. Orr	50.00	22.00	6.25
☐ 39 Hub Perdue	100.00	45.00	12.50
☐ 40 Arthur Phelan	50.00	22.00	6.25
☐ 41 Ed Reulbach	100.00	45.00	12.50
☐ 42 Vic Saier	50.00	22.00	6.25
☐ 43 Slim Sallee	50.00	22.00	6.25
☐ 44 Wally Schang	50.00	22.00	6.25
☐ 45 Frank Schulte	50.00	22.00	6.25
☐ 46 Jimmy Smith	50.00	22.00	6.25
☐ 47 Amos Strunk	50.00	22.00	6.25
☐ 48 Bill Sweeney	50.00	22.00	6.25
☐ 49 Lefty Tyler	100.00	45.00	12.50
☐ 50 Oscar Vitt	50.00	22.00	6.25
☐ 51 Ivy Wingo	50.00	22.00	6.25
☐ 52 Heinie Zimmerman	50.00	22.00	6.25

1982 FBI Discs

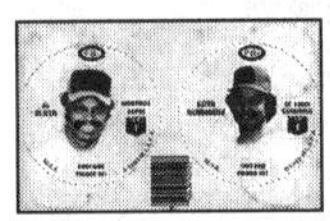

These discs were issued in Canada. These blank-backed circular white cutouts from the perforated bottoms of boxes of various FBI Foods' Bantam drinks measure approximately 2 7/8" in diameter and display black-and-white player head shots. Two players were featured on each box bottom. The player's name appears to the left of his photo; his team's name appears to the right. The cards are unnumbered and checklisted below in alphabetical order. There should be more players in this set, as the set is supposed to contain 32 players; therefore, all additions are appreciated.

	NRMT	VG-E	GOOD
COMPLETE SET (26)	750.00	350.00	95.00
COMMON DISC (1-26)	12.00	5.50	1.50
☐ 1 Vida Blue	20.00	9.00	2.50
☐ 2 Rod Carew	75.00	34.00	9.50
☐ 3 Steve Carlton	75.00	34.00	9.50
☐ 4 Gary Carter	75.00	34.00	9.50
☐ 5 Warren Cromartie	12.00	5.50	1.50
☐ 6 Andre Dawson	75.00	34.00	9.50
☐ 7 Steve Garvey	50.00	22.00	6.25
☐ 8 Rich Gossage	25.00	11.00	3.10
☐ 9 Bill Gullickson	12.00	5.50	1.50
☐ 10 Steve Henderson	12.00	5.50	1.50
☐ 11 Keith Hernandez	20.00	9.00	2.50
☐ 12 John Mayberry	12.00	5.50	1.50
☐ 13 Al Oliver	20.00	9.00	2.50
☐ 14 Dave Parker	20.00	9.00	2.50
☐ 15 Tim Raines	20.00	9.00	2.50
☐ 16 Jim Rice	20.00	9.00	2.50
☐ 17 Steve Rogers	12.00	5.50	1.50
☐ 18 Pete Rose	100.00	45.00	12.50
☐ 19 Nolan Ryan	200.00	90.00	25.00
☐ 20 Mike Schmidt	100.00	45.00	12.50
☐ 21 Tom Seaver	75.00	34.00	9.50
☐ 22 Ken Singleton	12.00	5.50	1.50
☐ 23 Dave Stieb	12.00	5.50	1.50
☐ 24 Bruce Sutter	12.00	5.50	1.50
☐ 25 Ellis Valentine	12.00	5.50	1.50
☐ 26 Dave Winfield	75.00	34.00	9.50

1985 Feg Murray's Cartoon Greats

This postcard set features the work of cartoonist Feg Murray. These cards feature reproductions of some of Murray's best works.

	NRMT	VG-E	GOOD
COMPLETE SET (20)	8.00	3.60	1.00
COMMON CARD (1-20)	.25	.11	.03
☐ 1 Feg Murray	.25	.11	.03
☐ 2 Ty Cobb Famous Guys Who Golf	1.00	.45	.12
☐ 3 Dizzy Dean Dizzy is Right	.75	.35	.09
☐ 4 Bill Dickey The Champions' Backstop	.50	.23	.06
☐ 5 Jimmy Foxx Home Run James	.75	.35	.09
☐ 6 Frank Fritsch Can Frankie Turn the Trick?	.50	.23	.06
☐ 7 Lou Gehrig The Man of the Hour	1.00	.45	.12
☐ 8 Charles Gehringer The Michigan Marvel	.75	.35	.09
☐ 9 Lefty Grove Oh, What a Relief!	.75	.35	.09
☐ 10 Gabby Hartnett The Great Gabbo	.50	.23	.06
☐ 11 Waite Hoyt Wait a Minute!	.50	.23	.06
☐ 12 Carl Hubbell Hubbell, Hubbell, Toil and Trouble	.75	.35	.09
☐ 13 John McGraw Came the Jawn	.75	.35	.09
☐ 14 Mel Ott The Pride of Louisiana	.75	.35	.09
☐ 15 Babe Ruth The Million-Dollar Baby	1.50	.70	.19
☐ 16 Babe Ruth Ain't It the Ruth	1.50	.70	.19
☐ 17 Al Simmons Hitting Like a Champion	.75	.35	.09
☐ 18 Casey Stengel Casey Comes Marching Home	.75	.35	.09
☐ 19 Bill Terry Hard-Working Playing-Manager	.50	.23	.06
☐ 20 Paul Waner Potent Poison	.75	.35	.09

1984 Fifth National Convention

These eight standard-size cards were given away at the 1984 5th Annual National held at the Aspen Hotel in Parsippany, N.J. August 9-12. Cards 1-5 below feature posed black-and-white player photos with white outer borders and brown inner borders. The player's name appears in white lettering within the brown margin below the photo. Cards 6-8 feature posed color player photos framed by a purple line and with green outer borders. Purple stars appear in the photos' upper corners. The player's name appears in white lettering in the bottom green margin. All the white backs carry the logo for the Fifth Annual National. All the players pictured were supposed to sign free autographs at the show. The cards are unnumbered and checklisted below in alphabetical order within each design type.

	NRMT	VG-E	GOOD
COMPLETE SET (8)	2.50	1.10	.30
COMMON CARD (1-8)	.25	.11	.03
☐ 1 Tom Gorman UMP	.25	.11	.03
☐ 2 Bud Harrelson	.50	.23	.06
☐ 3 Gene Hermanski	.25	.11	.03
☐ 4 Ed Lopat	.25	.11	.03
☐ 5 Bobby Thomson	.75	.35	.09
☐ 6 Joe Collins	.25	.11	.03
☐ 7 Larry Doby	.75	.35	.09
☐ 8 Willard Marshall	.25	.11	.03

1984 Fifth National Convention Tickets

This 18-card set of 5th Annual National Convention Tickets measures approximately 2" by 5 1/2" and features black-and-white head photos of 1954 baseball players on an orange background. The player's name and team are printed in black below the photo. The convention was held in Parsippany, New Jersey, on August 9 through August 12 at the Aspen Hotel. The backs are blank. The tickets are checklisted below in alphabetical order.

	NRMT	VG-E	GOOD
COMPLETE SET (18)	25.00	11.00	3.10
COMMON CARD (1-18)	.50	.23	.06
☐ 1 Hank Bauer	1.00	.45	.12
☐ 2 Yogi Berra	2.00	.90	.25
☐ 3 Alvin Dark	.75	.35	.09
☐ 4 Carl Erskine	1.00	.45	.12
☐ 5 Carl Furillo	1.00	.45	.12
☐ 6 Whitey Ford	2.00	.90	.25
☐ 7 Bob Grim	.50	.23	.06
☐ 8 Gil Hodges	2.00	.90	.25
☐ 9 Whitey Lockman	.75	.35	.09
☐ 10 Sal Maglie Johnny Antonelli	.50	.23	.06
☐ 11 Mickey Mantle	7.50	3.40	.95
☐ 12 Willie Mays	5.00	2.20	.60
☐ 13 Pee Wee Reese	2.00	.90	.25
☐ 14 Allie Reynolds	1.00	.45	.12
☐ 15 Dusty Rhodes	.50	.23	.06
☐ 16 Jackie Robinson	4.00	1.80	.50
☐ 17 Duke Snider	3.00	1.35	.35
☐ 18 Hoyt Wilhelm	1.50	.70	.19

1993 Finest Promos

Topps gave 5,000 of these three-card promo standard-size sets to its dealer customers to promote the release of its 1993 Topps Baseball's Finest set. The standard-size cards have metallic finishes on their fronts and feature color player action photos. The words "Promotional Sample 1 of 5000" appears in red lettering superposed upon the player's biography on the back of the card.

	MINT	NRMT	EXC
COMPLETE SET (3)	70.00	32.00	8.75
COMMON CARD	15.00	6.75	1.85
☐ 88 Roberto Alomar	15.00	6.75	1.85
☐ 98 Don Mattingly AS	25.00	11.00	3.10
☐ 107 Nolan Ryan	50.00	22.00	6.25

1993 Finest Promo Refractors

These cards are an extremely limited parallel version of the 1993 Finest Promos set. They feature what has become the popular refractor quality that Finest products are now known for.

	MINT	NRMT	EXC
COMPLETE SET (3)	4000.00	1800.00	500.00
COMMON CARD	800.00	350.00	100.00
☐ 88 Roberto Alomar	800.00	350.00	100.00
☐ 98 Don Mattingly AS	1200.00	550.00	150.00
☐ 107 Nolan Ryan	2500.00	1100.00	300.00

1993 Finest

This 199-card standard-size single series set is widely recognized as one of the most important issues of the 1990's. The Finest brand was Topps first attempt at the super-premium card market. Production was announced at 4,000 cases and cards were distributed exclusively through hobby dealers in the fall of 1993. This was the first time in the history of the hobby that a major manufacturer publicly released production figures. Cards were issued in 7-card foil fin-wrapped packs that carried a suggested retail price of $3.99. The product was a smashing success upon release with pack prices immediately soaring well above suggested retail prices. The popularity of the product has continued to grow throughout the years as it's place in hobby lore is now well soldified. The cards have silver-blue metallic finishes on their fronts and feature color player action photos. The set's title appears at the top, and the player's name is shown at the bottom. There are no key Rookie Cards in this set.

	MINT	NRMT	EXC
COMPLETE SET (199)	250.00	110.00	31.00
COMMON CARD (1-199)	.75	.35	.09

☐ 1 David Justice	3.00	1.35	.35
☐ 2 Lou Whitaker	1.50	.70	.19
☐ 3 Bryan Harvey	.75	.35	.09
☐ 4 Carlos Garcia	.75	.35	.09
☐ 5 Sid Fernandez	.75	.35	.09
☐ 6 Brett Butler	1.50	.70	.19
☐ 7 Scott Cooper	.75	.35	.09
☐ 8 B.J. Surhoff	1.50	.70	.19
☐ 9 Steve Finley	1.50	.70	.19
☐ 10 Curt Schilling	.75	.35	.09
☐ 11 Jeff Bagwell	12.00	5.50	1.50
☐ 12 Alex Cole	.75	.35	.09
☐ 13 John Olerud	.75	.35	.09
☐ 14 John Smiley	.75	.35	.09
☐ 15 Bip Roberts	.75	.35	.09
☐ 16 Albert Belle	12.00	5.50	1.50
☐ 17 Duane Ward	.75	.35	.09
☐ 18 Alan Trammell	3.00	1.35	.35
☐ 19 Andy Benes	1.50	.70	.19
☐ 20 Reggie Sanders	3.00	1.35	.35
☐ 21 Todd Zeile	.75	.35	.09
☐ 22 Rick Aguilera	.75	.35	.09
☐ 23 Dave Hollins	.75	.35	.09
☐ 24 Jose Rijo	.75	.35	.09
☐ 25 Matt Williams	4.00	1.80	.50
☐ 26 Sandy Alomar	1.50	.70	.19
☐ 27 Alex Fernandez	1.50	.70	.19
☐ 28 Ozzie Smith	8.00	3.60	1.00
☐ 29 Ramon Martinez	1.50	.70	.19
☐ 30 Bernie Williams	6.00	2.70	.75
☐ 31 Gary Sheffield	5.00	2.20	.60
☐ 32 Eric Karros	3.00	1.35	.35
☐ 33 Frank Viola	.75	.35	.09
☐ 34 Kevin Young	.75	.35	.09
☐ 35 Ken Hill	1.50	.70	.19
☐ 36 Tony Fernandez	.75	.35	.09
☐ 37 Tim Wakefield	1.50	.70	.19
☐ 38 John Kruk	1.50	.70	.19
☐ 39 Chris Sabo	.75	.35	.09
☐ 40 Marquis Grissom	1.50	.70	.19
☐ 41 Glenn Davis	.75	.35	.09
☐ 42 Jeff Montgomery	1.50	.70	.19
☐ 43 Kenny Lofton	12.00	5.50	1.50
☐ 44 John Burkett	.75	.35	.09
☐ 45 Darryl Hamilton	.75	.35	.09
☐ 46 Jim Abbott	.75	.35	.09
☐ 47 Ivan Rodriguez	8.00	3.60	1.00
☐ 48 Eric Young	3.00	1.35	.35
☐ 49 Mitch Williams	.75	.35	.09
☐ 50 Harold Reynolds	.75	.35	.09
☐ 51 Brian Harper	.75	.35	.09
☐ 52 Rafael Palmeiro	4.00	1.80	.50
☐ 53 Bret Saberhagen	1.50	.70	.19
☐ 54 Jeff Conine	1.50	.70	.19
☐ 55 Ivan Calderon	.75	.35	.09
☐ 56 Juan Guzman	1.50	.70	.19
☐ 57 Carlos Baerga	1.50	.70	.19
☐ 58 Charles Nagy	1.50	.70	.19
☐ 59 Wally Joyner	1.50	.70	.19
☐ 60 Charlie Hayes	.75	.35	.09
☐ 61 Shane Mack	.75	.35	.09
☐ 62 Pete Harnisch	.75	.35	.09
☐ 63 George Brett	12.00	5.50	1.50
☐ 64 Lance Johnson	1.50	.70	.19
☐ 65 Ben McDonald	.75	.35	.09
☐ 66 Bobby Bonilla	1.50	.70	.19
☐ 67 Terry Steinbach	1.50	.70	.19
☐ 68 Ron Gant	1.50	.70	.19
☐ 69 Doug Jones	.75	.35	.09
☐ 70 Paul Molitor	6.00	2.70	.75
☐ 71 Brady Anderson	4.00	1.80	.50
☐ 72 Chuck Finley	.75	.35	.09
☐ 73 Mark Grace	3.00	1.35	.35
☐ 74 Mike Devereaux	.75	.35	.09
☐ 75 Tony Phillips	1.50	.70	.19
☐ 76 Chuck Knoblauch	5.00	2.20	.60
☐ 77 Tony Gwynn	12.00	5.50	1.50
☐ 78 Kevin Appier	1.50	.70	.19
☐ 79 Sammy Sosa	5.00	2.20	.60
☐ 80 Mickey Tettleton	.75	.35	.09
☐ 81 Felix Jose	.75	.35	.09
☐ 82 Mark Langston	1.50	.70	.19
☐ 83 Gregg Jefferies	1.50	.70	.19
☐ 84 Andre Dawson AS	1.50	.70	.19
☐ 85 Greg Maddux AS	20.00	9.00	2.50
☐ 86 Rickey Henderson AS	3.00	1.35	.35
☐ 87 Tom Glavine AS	4.00	1.80	.50
☐ 88 Roberto Alomar AS	6.00	2.70	.75
☐ 89 Darryl Strawberry AS	1.50	.70	.19
☐ 90 Wade Boggs AS	3.00	1.35	.35
☐ 91 Bo Jackson AS	1.50	.70	.19
☐ 92 Mark McGwire AS	10.00	4.50	1.25
☐ 93 Robin Ventura AS	1.50	.70	.19
☐ 94 Joe Carter AS	1.50	.70	.19
☐ 95 Lee Smith AS	1.50	.70	.19
☐ 96 Cal Ripken AS	25.00	11.00	3.10
☐ 97 Larry Walker AS	3.00	1.35	.35
☐ 98 Don Mattingly AS	15.00	6.75	1.85
☐ 99 Jose Canseco AS	4.00	1.80	.50
☐ 100 Dennis Eckersley AS	1.50	.70	.19
☐ 101 Terry Pendleton AS	1.50	.70	.19
☐ 102 Frank Thomas AS	30.00	13.50	3.70
☐ 103 Barry Bonds AS	8.00	3.60	1.00
☐ 104 Roger Clemens AS	6.00	2.70	.75
☐ 105 Ryne Sandberg AS	8.00	3.60	1.00
☐ 106 Fred McGriff AS	4.00	1.80	.50
☐ 107 Nolan Ryan AS	25.00	11.00	3.10
☐ 108 Will Clark AS	4.00	1.80	.50
☐ 109 Pat Listach AS	.75	.35	.09
☐ 110 Ken Griffey Jr. AS	30.00	13.50	3.70
☐ 111 Cecil Fielder AS	1.50	.70	.19
☐ 112 Kirby Puckett AS	12.00	5.50	1.50
☐ 113 Dwight Gooden AS	1.50	.70	.19
☐ 114 Barry Larkin AS	4.00	1.80	.50
☐ 115 David Cone AS	1.50	.70	.19
☐ 116 Juan Gonzalez AS	15.00	6.75	1.85
☐ 117 Kent Hrbek	1.50	.70	.19
☐ 118 Tim Wallach	.75	.35	.09
☐ 119 Craig Biggio	1.50	.70	.19
☐ 120 Roberto Kelly	.75	.35	.09
☐ 121 Gregg Olson	.75	.35	.09
☐ 122 Eddie Murray UER 122 career strikeouts should be 1224	8.00	3.60	1.00
☐ 123 Wil Cordero	1.50	.70	.19
☐ 124 Jay Buhner	4.00	1.80	.50
☐ 125 Carlton Fisk	3.00	1.35	.35
☐ 126 Eric Davis	1.50	.70	.19
☐ 127 Doug Drabek	.75	.35	.09
☐ 128 Ozzie Guillen	.75	.35	.09
☐ 129 John Wetteland	1.50	.70	.19
☐ 130 Andres Galarraga	4.00	1.80	.50
☐ 131 Ken Caminiti	4.00	1.80	.50
☐ 132 Tom Candiotti	.75	.35	.09
☐ 133 Pat Borders	.75	.35	.09
☐ 134 Kevin Brown	1.50	.70	.19
☐ 135 Travis Fryman	1.50	.70	.19
☐ 136 Kevin Mitchell	1.50	.70	.19
☐ 137 Greg Swindell	.75	.35	.09
☐ 138 Benito Santiago	.75	.35	.09
☐ 139 Reggie Jefferson	1.50	.70	.19
☐ 140 Chris Bosio	.75	.35	.09
☐ 141 Deion Sanders	4.00	1.80	.50
☐ 142 Scott Erickson	.75	.35	.09
☐ 143 Howard Johnson	.75	.35	.09
☐ 144 Orestes Destrade	.75	.35	.09
☐ 145 Jose Guzman	.75	.35	.09
☐ 146 Chad Curtis	1.50	.70	.19
☐ 147 Cal Eldred	.75	.35	.09
☐ 148 Willie Greene	1.50	.70	.19
☐ 149 Tommy Greene	.75	.35	.09
☐ 150 Erik Hanson	.75	.35	.09
☐ 151 Bob Welch	.75	.35	.09
☐ 152 John Jaha	3.00	1.35	.35
☐ 153 Harold Baines	1.50	.70	.19
☐ 154 Randy Johnson	5.00	2.20	.60
☐ 155 Al Martin	1.50	.70	.19
☐ 156 J.T. Snow	3.00	1.35	.35
☐ 157 Mike Mussina	6.00	2.70	.75
☐ 158 Ruben Sierra	1.50	.70	.19
☐ 159 Dean Palmer	1.50	.70	.19
☐ 160 Steve Avery	1.50	.70	.19
☐ 161 Julio Franco	1.50	.70	.19
☐ 162 Dave Winfield	3.00	1.35	.35
☐ 163 Tim Salmon	6.00	2.70	.75
☐ 164 Tom Henke	.75	.35	.09
☐ 165 Mo Vaughn	8.00	3.60	1.00
☐ 166 John Smoltz	5.00	2.20	.60
☐ 167 Danny Tartabull	.75	.35	.09
☐ 168 Delino DeShields	.75	.35	.09
☐ 169 Charlie Hough	.75	.35	.09
☐ 170 Paul O'Neill	1.50	.70	.19
☐ 171 Darren Daulton	1.50	.70	.19
☐ 172 Jack McDowell	1.50	.70	.19
☐ 173 Junior Felix	.75	.35	.09
☐ 174 Jimmy Key	1.50	.70	.19
☐ 175 George Bell	.75	.35	.09
☐ 176 Mike Stanton	.75	.35	.09
☐ 177 Len Dykstra	1.50	.70	.19
☐ 178 Norm Charlton	.75	.35	.09
☐ 179 Eric Anthony	.75	.35	.09
☐ 180 Rob Dibble	.75	.35	.09
☐ 181 Otis Nixon	.75	.35	.09
☐ 182 Randy Myers	1.50	.70	.19
☐ 183 Tim Raines	3.00	1.35	.35
☐ 184 Orel Hershiser	1.50	.70	.19
☐ 185 Andy Van Slyke	1.50	.70	.19
☐ 186 Mike Lansing	1.50	.70	.19
☐ 187 Ray Lankford	1.50	.70	.19
☐ 188 Mike Morgan	.75	.35	.09
☐ 189 Moises Alou	1.50	.70	.19
☐ 190 Edgar Martinez	3.00	1.35	.35
☐ 191 John Franco	.75	.35	.09
☐ 192 Robin Yount	4.00	1.80	.50
☐ 193 Bob Tewksbury	.75	.35	.09
☐ 194 Jay Bell	1.50	.70	.19
☐ 195 Luis Gonzalez	.75	.35	.09
☐ 196 Dave Fleming	.75	.35	.09
☐ 197 Mike Greenwell	.75	.35	.09
☐ 198 David Nied	.75	.35	.09
☐ 199 Mike Piazza	30.00	13.50	3.70

1993 Finest Refractors

Randomly inserted in packs at a rate of one in 18, these 199 standard-size cards are identical to the regular-issue 1993 Topps Finest except that their fronts have been laminated with a plastic diffraction grating that gives the card a colorful 3-D appearance. Because of the known production numbers, these cards are believed to have a print run of 241 of each card. Several cards are believed to be in short supply and are notated with an asterisk. Topps, however, has never publicly released any verification of shortprinted singles, but some of the singles are accepted as being tough to find due to poor regional distribution and hoarding. Due to their high value, these cards are extremely condition sensitive, with much attention paid to centering and minor scratches on the card fronts.

	MINT	NRMT	EXC
COMPLETE SET (199)	40000.00	18000.00	5000.00
COMMON CARD (1-199)	60.00	27.00	7.50
☐ 1 David Justice	250.00	110.00	31.00
☐ 2 Lou Whitaker	100.00	45.00	12.50
☐ 3 Bryan Harvey*	250.00	110.00	31.00
☐ 4 Carlos Garcia	60.00	27.00	7.50
☐ 5 Sid Fernandez	60.00	27.00	7.50
☐ 6 Brett Butler	75.00	34.00	9.50
☐ 7 Scott Cooper	60.00	27.00	7.50
☐ 8 B.J. Surhoff	75.00	34.00	9.50
☐ 9 Steve Finley	75.00	34.00	9.50
☐ 10 Curt Schilling*	300.00	135.00	38.00
☐ 11 Jeff Bagwell	1100.00	500.00	140.00
☐ 12 Alex Cole	300.00	135.00	38.00
☐ 13 John Olerud	60.00	27.00	7.50
☐ 14 John Smiley	60.00	27.00	7.50
☐ 15 Bip Roberts	60.00	27.00	7.50
☐ 16 Albert Belle	1000.00	450.00	125.00
☐ 17 Duane Ward	60.00	27.00	7.50
☐ 18 Alan Trammell	100.00	45.00	12.50
☐ 19 Andy Benes	75.00	34.00	9.50
☐ 20 Reggie Sanders	175.00	80.00	22.00
☐ 21 Todd Zeile	60.00	27.00	7.50
☐ 22 Rick Aguilera	60.00	27.00	7.50
☐ 23 Dave Hollins	60.00	27.00	7.50
☐ 24 Jose Rijo	60.00	27.00	7.50
☐ 25 Matt Williams	500.00	220.00	60.00
☐ 26 Sandy Alomar	100.00	45.00	12.50
☐ 27 Alex Fernandez	150.00	70.00	19.00
☐ 28 Ozzie Smith	325.00	145.00	40.00
☐ 29 Ramon Martinez	75.00	34.00	9.50
☐ 30 Bernie Williams	500.00	220.00	60.00
☐ 31 Gary Sheffield	500.00	220.00	60.00
☐ 32 Eric Karros	175.00	80.00	22.00
☐ 33 Frank Viola	60.00	27.00	7.50
☐ 34 Kevin Young	75.00	34.00	9.50
☐ 35 Ken Hill	75.00	34.00	9.50
☐ 36 Tony Fernandez	60.00	27.00	7.50
☐ 37 Tim Wakefield	60.00	27.00	7.50
☐ 38 John Kruk*	200.00	90.00	25.00
☐ 39 Chris Sabo*	200.00	90.00	25.00
☐ 40 Marquis Grissom*	400.00	180.00	50.00
☐ 41 Glenn Davis*	250.00	110.00	31.00
☐ 42 Jeff Montgomery	60.00	27.00	7.50
☐ 43 Kenny Lofton	500.00	220.00	60.00
☐ 44 John Burkett	60.00	27.00	7.50
☐ 45 Darryl Hamilton	60.00	27.00	7.50
☐ 46 Jim Abbott	60.00	27.00	7.50
☐ 47 Ivan Rodriguez*	800.00	350.00	100.00
☐ 48 Eric Young	125.00	55.00	15.50
☐ 49 Mitch Williams	60.00	27.00	7.50
☐ 50 Harold Reynolds	60.00	27.00	7.50
☐ 51 Brian Harper	60.00	27.00	7.50
☐ 52 Rafael Palmeiro	225.00	100.00	28.00
☐ 53 Bret Saberhagen	60.00	27.00	7.50
☐ 54 Jeff Conine	175.00	80.00	22.00
☐ 55 Ivan Calderon	60.00	27.00	7.50
☐ 56 Juan Guzman	75.00	34.00	9.50
☐ 57 Carlos Baerga	150.00	70.00	19.00
☐ 58 Charles Nagy	175.00	80.00	22.00
☐ 59 Wally Joyner	100.00	45.00	12.50
☐ 60 Charlie Hayes	60.00	27.00	7.50
☐ 61 Shane Mack	75.00	34.00	9.50
☐ 62 Pete Harnisch	60.00	27.00	7.50
☐ 63 George Brett	700.00	325.00	90.00
☐ 64 Lance Johnson	100.00	45.00	12.50
☐ 65 Ben McDonald	75.00	34.00	9.50
☐ 66 Bobby Bonilla	100.00	45.00	12.50
☐ 67 Terry Steinbach	100.00	45.00	12.50
☐ 68 Ron Gant	100.00	45.00	12.50
☐ 69 Doug Jones	60.00	27.00	7.50
☐ 70 Paul Molitor	600.00	275.00	75.00
☐ 71 Brady Anderson	300.00	135.00	38.00
☐ 72 Chuck Finley	75.00	34.00	9.50
☐ 73 Mark Grace	250.00	110.00	31.00
☐ 74 Mike Devereaux	60.00	27.00	7.50
☐ 75 Tony Phillips	90.00	40.00	11.00
☐ 76 Chuck Knoblauch	400.00	180.00	50.00
☐ 77 Tony Gwynn	700.00	325.00	90.00
☐ 78 Kevin Appier	100.00	45.00	12.50
☐ 79 Sammy Sosa*	600.00	275.00	75.00
☐ 80 Mickey Tettleton	125.00	55.00	15.50
☐ 81 Felix Jose*	200.00	90.00	25.00
☐ 82 Mark Langston	60.00	27.00	7.50
☐ 83 Gregg Jefferies	75.00	34.00	9.50
☐ 84 Andre Dawson AS*	225.00	100.00	28.00
☐ 85 Greg Maddux AS	1400.00	650.00	180.00
☐ 86 Rickey Henderson	250.00	110.00	31.00
☐ 87 Tom Glavine AS !	275.00	125.00	34.00
☐ 88 Roberto Alomar AS	600.00	275.00	75.00
☐ 89 Darryl Strawberry AS	125.00	55.00	15.50
☐ 90 Wade Boggs AS	250.00	110.00	31.00
☐ 91 Bo Jackson AS	100.00	45.00	12.50
☐ 92 Mark McGwire AS	650.00	300.00	80.00
☐ 93 Robin Ventura AS	150.00	70.00	19.00
☐ 94 Joe Carter AS	150.00	70.00	19.00
☐ 95 Lee Smith AS	75.00	34.00	9.50
☐ 96 Cal Ripken AS	2300.00	1050.00	300.00
☐ 97 Larry Walker AS	350.00	160.00	45.00
☐ 98 Don Mattingly AS	500.00	220.00	60.00
☐ 99 Jose Canseco AS !	250.00	110.00	31.00
☐ 100 Dennis Eckersley AS	100.00	45.00	12.50
☐ 101 Terry Pendleton AS	75.00	34.00	9.50
☐ 102 Frank Thomas AS	1500.00	700.00	190.00
☐ 103 Barry Bonds AS	700.00	325.00	90.00
☐ 104 Roger Clemens AS	250.00	110.00	31.00
☐ 105 Ryne Sandberg AS	300.00	135.00	38.00
☐ 106 Fred McGriff AS	300.00	135.00	38.00
☐ 107 Nolan Ryan AS !	1500.00	700.00	190.00
☐ 108 Will Clark AS	250.00	110.00	31.00
☐ 109 Pat Listach AS	60.00	27.00	7.50
☐ 110 Ken Griffey Jr. AS !	2000.00	900.00	250.00
☐ 111 Cecil Fielder AS	175.00	80.00	22.00
☐ 112 Kirby Puckett AS	400.00	180.00	50.00
☐ 113 Dwight Gooden AS	150.00	70.00	19.00
☐ 114 Barry Larkin AS	250.00	110.00	31.00
☐ 115 David Cone AS	125.00	55.00	15.50
☐ 116 Juan Gonzalez AS	1500.00	700.00	190.00
☐ 117 Kent Hrbek	60.00	27.00	7.50
☐ 118 Tim Wallach	60.00	27.00	7.50
☐ 119 Craig Biggio	150.00	70.00	19.00
☐ 120 Roberto Kelly	60.00	27.00	7.50
☐ 121 Gregg Olson	60.00	27.00	7.50
☐ 122 Eddie Murray UER 122 career strikeouts should be 1224	650.00	300.00	80.00
☐ 123 Wil Cordero	75.00	34.00	9.50
☐ 124 Jay Buhner	250.00	110.00	31.00
☐ 125 Carlton Fisk	175.00	80.00	22.00
☐ 126 Eric Davis	75.00	34.00	9.50
☐ 127 Doug Drabek	60.00	27.00	7.50
☐ 128 Ozzie Guillen	60.00	27.00	7.50
☐ 129 John Wetteland	100.00	45.00	12.50
☐ 130 Andres Galarraga	250.00	110.00	31.00
☐ 131 Ken Caminiti	275.00	125.00	34.00
☐ 132 Tom Candiotti	60.00	27.00	7.50
☐ 133 Pat Borders	60.00	27.00	7.50
☐ 134 Kevin Brown*	225.00	100.00	28.00
☐ 135 Travis Fryman	125.00	55.00	15.50
☐ 136 Kevin Mitchell	60.00	27.00	7.50
☐ 137 Greg Swindell	60.00	27.00	7.50
☐ 138 Benito Santiago	60.00	27.00	7.50
☐ 139 Reggie Jefferson	75.00	34.00	9.50
☐ 140 Chris Bosio	60.00	27.00	7.50
☐ 141 Deion Sanders	200.00	90.00	25.00
☐ 142 Scott Erickson	60.00	27.00	7.50
☐ 143 Howard Johnson	60.00	27.00	7.50
☐ 144 Orestes Destrade	60.00	27.00	7.50
☐ 145 Jose Guzman	60.00	27.00	7.50
☐ 146 Chad Curtis	60.00	27.00	7.50
☐ 147 Cal Eldred	60.00	27.00	7.50
☐ 148 Willie Greene	75.00	34.00	9.50
☐ 149 Tommy Greene	60.00	27.00	7.50
☐ 150 Erik Hanson	60.00	27.00	7.50
☐ 151 Bob Welch	60.00	27.00	7.50
☐ 152 John Jaha	100.00	45.00	12.50
☐ 153 Harold Baines	100.00	45.00	12.50
☐ 154 Randy Johnson	500.00	220.00	60.00
☐ 155 Al Martin *	125.00	55.00	15.50
☐ 156 J.T. Snow	125.00	55.00	15.50
☐ 157 Mike Mussina	400.00	180.00	50.00
☐ 158 Ruben Sierra	75.00	34.00	9.50
☐ 159 Dean Palmer	175.00	80.00	22.00
☐ 160 Steve Avery	100.00	45.00	12.50
☐ 161 Julio Franco	100.00	45.00	12.50
☐ 162 Dave Winfield	175.00	80.00	22.00
☐ 163 Tim Salmon	400.00	180.00	50.00
☐ 164 Tom Henke	60.00	27.00	7.50
☐ 165 Mo Vaughn	500.00	220.00	60.00
☐ 166 John Smoltz	350.00	160.00	45.00
☐ 167 Danny Tartabull	60.00	27.00	7.50
☐ 168 Delino DeShields	60.00	27.00	7.50
☐ 169 Charlie Hough	60.00	27.00	7.50
☐ 170 Paul O'Neill	100.00	45.00	12.50
☐ 171 Darren Daulton	75.00	34.00	9.50
☐ 172 Jack McDowell	90.00	40.00	11.00
☐ 173 Junior Felix*	200.00	90.00	25.00
☐ 174 Jimmy Key	60.00	27.00	7.50
☐ 175 George Bell	60.00	27.00	7.50
☐ 176 Mike Stanton	60.00	27.00	7.50
☐ 177 Len Dykstra	75.00	34.00	9.50
☐ 178 Norm Charlton	60.00	27.00	7.50
☐ 179 Eric Anthony	60.00	27.00	7.50
☐ 180 Rob Dibble	60.00	27.00	7.50
☐ 181 Otis Nixon	60.00	27.00	7.50
☐ 182 Randy Myers *	75.00	34.00	9.50
☐ 183 Tim Raines	75.00	34.00	9.50
☐ 184 Orel Hershiser	100.00	45.00	12.50
☐ 185 Andy Van Slyke	75.00	34.00	9.50
☐ 186 Mike Lansing	75.00	34.00	9.50
☐ 187 Ray Lankford	125.00	55.00	15.50
☐ 188 Mike Morgan	60.00	27.00	7.50
☐ 189 Moises Alou*	225.00	100.00	28.00
☐ 190 Edgar Martinez	200.00	90.00	25.00
☐ 191 John Franco	60.00	27.00	7.50
☐ 192 Robin Yount	225.00	100.00	28.00
☐ 193 Bob Tewksbury*	175.00	80.00	22.00
☐ 194 Jay Bell	75.00	34.00	9.50
☐ 195 Luis Gonzalez	60.00	27.00	7.50
☐ 196 Dave Fleming	60.00	27.00	7.50
☐ 197 Mike Greenwell	60.00	27.00	7.50
☐ 198 David Nied	60.00	27.00	7.50
☐ 199 Mike Piazza	1300.00	575.00	160.00

1993 Finest Jumbos

These oversized (approximately 4" by 6") cards were inserted one per sealed box of 1993 Topps Finest packs and feature reproductions of 33 players from that set's All-Star subset (84-116). Some hobby dealers believe because of the known production numbers that slightly less than 1,500 of each of these cards were produced.

	MINT	NRMT	EXC
COMPLETE SET (33)	500.00	220.00	60.00
COMMON CARD (84-116)	5.00	2.20	.60
☐ 84 Andre Dawson	6.00	2.70	.75
☐ 85 Greg Maddux	40.00	18.00	5.00
☐ 86 Rickey Henderson	8.00	3.60	1.00
☐ 87 Tom Glavine	8.00	3.60	1.00
☐ 88 Roberto Alomar	12.00	5.50	1.50
☐ 89 Darryl Strawberry	6.00	2.70	.75
☐ 90 Wade Boggs	8.00	3.60	1.00
☐ 91 Bo Jackson	6.00	2.70	.75
☐ 92 Mark McGwire	18.00	8.00	2.20
☐ 93 Robin Ventura	6.00	2.70	.75
☐ 94 Joe Carter	6.00	2.70	.75
☐ 95 Lee Smith	6.00	2.70	.75
☐ 96 Cal Ripken	50.00	22.00	6.25
☐ 97 Larry Walker	8.00	3.60	1.00
☐ 98 Don Mattingly	30.00	13.50	3.70
☐ 99 Jose Canseco	8.00	3.60	1.00
☐ 100 Dennis Eckersley	6.00	2.70	.75
☐ 101 Terry Pendleton	6.00	2.70	.75
☐ 102 Frank Thomas	60.00	27.00	7.50
☐ 103 Barry Bonds	15.00	6.75	1.85
☐ 104 Roger Clemens	12.00	5.50	1.50
☐ 105 Ryne Sandberg	15.00	6.75	1.85
☐ 106 Fred McGriff	8.00	3.60	1.00
☐ 107 Nolan Ryan	50.00	22.00	6.25
☐ 108 Will Clark	8.00	3.60	1.00
☐ 109 Pat Listach	5.00	2.20	.60
☐ 110 Ken Griffey Jr.	60.00	27.00	7.50
☐ 111 Cecil Fielder	6.00	2.70	.75
☐ 112 Kirby Puckett	25.00	11.00	3.10
☐ 113 Dwight Gooden	6.00	2.70	.75
☐ 114 Barry Larkin	8.00	3.60	1.00
☐ 115 David Cone	6.00	2.70	.75
☐ 116 Juan Gonzalez	30.00	13.50	3.70

1994 Finest Pre-Production

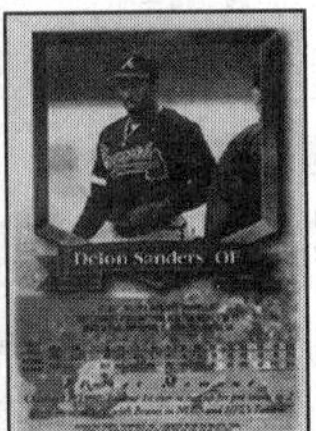

This 40-card preview standard-size set is identical in design to the basic Finest set. Cards were randomly inserted at a rate of one in 36 in second series Topps packs and three cards were issued with each Topps factory set. The card numbers on back correspond to those of the regular issue. The only way to distinguish between the preview and basic cards is "Pre-Production" in small red letters on back.

	MINT	NRMT	EXC
COMPLETE SET (40)	175.00	80.00	22.00
COMMON CARD	2.50	1.10	.30
☐ 22P Deion Sanders	5.00	2.20	.60
☐ 23P Jose Offerman	2.50	1.10	.30
☐ 26P Alex Fernandez	3.50	1.55	.45
☐ 31P Steve Finley	5.00	2.20	.60
☐ 35P Andres Galarraga	12.00	5.50	1.50
☐ 43P Reggie Sanders	3.50	1.55	.45
☐ 47P Dave Hollins	2.50	1.10	.30
☐ 52P David Cone	3.50	1.55	.45
☐ 59P Dante Bichette	12.00	5.50	1.50
☐ 61P Orlando Merced	3.50	1.55	.45
☐ 62P Brian McRae	3.50	1.55	.45
☐ 66P Mike Mussina	20.00	9.00	2.50
☐ 76P Mike Stanley	3.50	1.55	.45
☐ 78P Mark McGwire	30.00	13.50	3.70
☐ 79P Pat Listach	2.50	1.10	.30
☐ 82P Dwight Gooden	3.50	1.55	.45
☐ 84P Phil Plantier	2.50	1.10	.30
☐ 90P Jeff Russell	2.50	1.10	.30
☐ 92P Gregg Jefferies	5.00	2.20	.60
☐ 93P Jose Guzman	2.50	1.10	.30
☐ 100P John Smoltz	15.00	6.75	1.85
☐ 102P Jim Thome	25.00	11.00	3.10
☐ 121P Moises Alou	3.50	1.55	.45
☐ 125P Devon White	3.50	1.55	.45
☐ 126P Ivan Rodriguez	25.00	11.00	3.10
☐ 130P Dave Magadan	2.50	1.10	.30
☐ 136P Ozzie Smith	25.00	11.00	3.10
☐ 141P Chris Hoiles	3.50	1.55	.45
☐ 149P Jim Abbott	3.50	1.55	.45
☐ 151P Bill Swift	2.50	1.10	.30
☐ 154P Edgar Martinez	12.00	5.50	1.50
☐ 157P J.T. Snow	3.50	1.55	.45
☐ 159P Alan Trammell	3.50	1.55	.45
☐ 163P Roberto Kelly	2.50	1.10	.30
☐ 166P Scott Erickson	3.50	1.55	.45
☐ 168P Scott Cooper	2.50	1.10	.30
☐ 169P Rod Beck	3.50	1.55	.45
☐ 177P Dean Palmer	3.50	1.55	.45
☐ 182P Todd Van Poppel	2.50	1.10	.30
☐ 185P Paul Sorrento	2.50	1.10	.30

1994 Finest

The 1994 Topps Finest baseball set consists of two series of 220 cards each, for a total of 440 standard-size cards. Each series includes 40 special design Finest cards: 20 top 1993 rookies (1-20), 20 top 1994 rookies (421-440) and 40 top veterans (201-240). These glossy and metallic cards have a color photo on front with green and gold borders. A color photo on back is accompanied by statistics and a "Finest Moment" note. Some series 2 packs contained either one or two series 1 cards. The only notable Rookie Card is Chan Ho Park.

	MINT	NRMT	EXC
COMPLETE SET (440)	180.00	80.00	22.00
COMPLETE SERIES 1 (220)	90.00	40.00	11.00
COMPLETE SERIES 2 (220)	90.00	40.00	11.00
COMMON CARD (1-440)	.50	.23	.06
☐ 1 Mike Piazza FIN	8.00	3.60	1.00
☐ 2 Kevin Stocker FIN	.50	.23	.06
☐ 3 Greg McMichael FIN	.50	.23	.06
☐ 4 Jeff Conine FIN	.75	.35	.09
☐ 5 Rene Arocha FIN	.50	.23	.06
☐ 6 Aaron Sele FIN	.75	.35	.09
☐ 7 Brent Gates FIN	.50	.23	.06
☐ 8 Chuck Carr FIN	.50	.23	.06
☐ 9 Kirk Rueter FIN	.50	.23	.06
☐ 10 Mike Lansing FIN	.75	.35	.09
☐ 11 Al Martin FIN	.50	.23	.06
☐ 12 Jason Bere FIN	.75	.35	.09
☐ 13 Troy Neel FIN	.50	.23	.06
☐ 14 Armando Reynoso FIN	.50	.23	.06
☐ 15 Jeromy Burnitz FIN	.50	.23	.06
☐ 16 Rich Amaral FIN	.50	.23	.06
☐ 17 David McCarty FIN	.50	.23	.06
☐ 18 Tim Salmon FIN	2.00	.90	.25
☐ 19 Steve Cooke FIN	.50	.23	.06
☐ 20 Wil Cordero FIN	.75	.35	.09
☐ 21 Kevin Tapani	.50	.23	.06
☐ 22 Deion Sanders	1.00	.45	.12
☐ 23 Jose Offerman	.50	.23	.06
☐ 24 Mark Langston	.75	.35	.09
☐ 25 Ken Hill	.50	.23	.06
☐ 26 Alex Fernandez	.75	.35	.09
☐ 27 Jeff Blauser	.50	.23	.06
☐ 28 Royce Clayton	.75	.35	.09
☐ 29 Brad Ausmus	.50	.23	.06
☐ 30 Ryan Bowen	.50	.23	.06
☐ 31 Steve Finley	1.00	.45	.12
☐ 32 Charlie Hayes	.50	.23	.06
☐ 33 Jeff Kent	.50	.23	.06
☐ 34 Mike Henneman	.50	.23	.06
☐ 35 Andres Galarraga	1.00	.45	.12
☐ 36 Wayne Kirby	.50	.23	.06
☐ 37 Joe Oliver	.50	.23	.06
☐ 38 Terry Steinbach	.75	.35	.09
☐ 39 Ryan Thompson	.50	.23	.06
☐ 40 Luis Alicea	.50	.23	.06
☐ 41 Randy Velarde	.50	.23	.06
☐ 42 Bob Tewksbury	.50	.23	.06
☐ 43 Reggie Sanders	.75	.35	.09
☐ 44 Brian Williams	.50	.23	.06
☐ 45 Joe Orsulak	.50	.23	.06
☐ 46 Jose Lind	.50	.23	.06
☐ 47 Dave Hollins	.50	.23	.06
☐ 48 Graeme Lloyd	.50	.23	.06
☐ 49 Jim Gott	.50	.23	.06
☐ 50 Andre Dawson	.75	.35	.09
☐ 51 Steve Buechele	.50	.23	.06
☐ 52 David Cone	.75	.35	.09
☐ 53 Ricky Gutierrez	.50	.23	.06
☐ 54 Lance Johnson	.75	.35	.09
☐ 55 Tino Martinez	.75	.35	.09
☐ 56 Phil Hiatt	.50	.23	.06
☐ 57 Carlos Garcia	.50	.23	.06
☐ 58 Danny Darwin	.50	.23	.06
☐ 59 Dante Bichette	1.00	.45	.12
☐ 60 Scott Kamieniecki	.50	.23	.06
☐ 61 Orlando Merced	.75	.35	.09
☐ 62 Brian McRae	.75	.35	.09
☐ 63 Pat Kelly	.50	.23	.06
☐ 64 Tom Henke	.50	.23	.06
☐ 65 Jeff King	.75	.35	.09
☐ 66 Mike Mussina	2.50	1.10	.30
☐ 67 Tim Pugh	.50	.23	.06
☐ 68 Robby Thompson	.50	.23	.06
☐ 69 Paul O'Neill	.75	.35	.09
☐ 70 Hal Morris	.50	.23	.06
☐ 71 Ron Karkovice	.50	.23	.06
☐ 72 Joe Girardi	.50	.23	.06
☐ 73 Eduardo Perez	.50	.23	.06
☐ 74 Raul Mondesi	2.00	.90	.25
☐ 75 Mike Gallego	.50	.23	.06
☐ 76 Mike Stanley	.50	.23	.06
☐ 77 Kevin Roberson	.50	.23	.06
☐ 78 Mark McGwire	4.00	1.80	.50
☐ 79 Pat Listach	.50	.23	.06
☐ 80 Eric Davis	.75	.35	.09
☐ 81 Mike Bordick	.50	.23	.06
☐ 82 Doc Gooden	.75	.35	.09
☐ 83 Mike Moore	.50	.23	.06
☐ 84 Phil Plantier	.50	.23	.06
☐ 85 Darren Lewis	.50	.23	.06
☐ 86 Rick Wilkins	.50	.23	.06
☐ 87 Darryl Strawberry	.75	.35	.09
☐ 88 Rob Dibble	.50	.23	.06
☐ 89 Greg Vaughn	1.00	.45	.12
☐ 90 Jeff Russell	.50	.23	.06
☐ 91 Mark Lewis	.50	.23	.06
☐ 92 Gregg Jefferies	1.00	.45	.12
☐ 93 Jose Guzman	.50	.23	.06
☐ 94 Kenny Rogers	.50	.23	.06
☐ 95 Mark Lemke	.50	.23	.06
☐ 96 Mike Morgan	.50	.23	.06
☐ 97 Andujar Cedeno	.50	.23	.06
☐ 98 Orel Hershiser	.75	.35	.09
☐ 99 Greg Swindell	.50	.23	.06
☐ 100 John Smoltz	2.00	.90	.25
☐ 101 Pedro Martinez	1.00	.45	.12
☐ 102 Jim Thome	3.00	1.35	.35
☐ 103 David Segui	.50	.23	.06
☐ 104 Charles Nagy	.75	.35	.09
☐ 105 Shane Mack	.50	.23	.06
☐ 106 John Jaha	.75	.35	.09
☐ 107 Tom Candiotti	.50	.23	.06
☐ 108 David Wells	.50	.23	.06
☐ 109 Bobby Jones	.75	.35	.09
☐ 110 Bob Hamelin	.50	.23	.06
☐ 111 Bernard Gilkey	.75	.35	.09
☐ 112 Chili Davis	.75	.35	.09
☐ 113 Todd Stottlemyre	.50	.23	.06
☐ 114 Derek Bell	.75	.35	.09
☐ 115 Mark McLemore	.50	.23	.06
☐ 116 Mark Whiten	.50	.23	.06
☐ 117 Mike Devereaux	.50	.23	.06
☐ 118 Terry Pendleton	.75	.35	.09
☐ 119 Pat Meares	.50	.23	.06
☐ 120 Pete Harnisch	.50	.23	.06
☐ 121 Moises Alou	.75	.35	.09
☐ 122 Jay Buhner	1.00	.45	.12
☐ 123 Wes Chamberlain	.50	.23	.06
☐ 124 Mike Perez	.50	.23	.06
☐ 125 Devon White	.50	.23	.06
☐ 126 Ivan Rodriguez	3.00	1.35	.35
☐ 127 Don Slaught	.50	.23	.06
☐ 128 John Valentin	.75	.35	.09
☐ 129 Jaime Navarro	.50	.23	.06
☐ 130 Dave Magadan	.50	.23	.06
☐ 131 Brady Anderson	1.00	.45	.12
☐ 132 Juan Guzman	.75	.35	.09
☐ 133 John Wetteland	.75	.35	.09
☐ 134 Dave Stewart	.75	.35	.09
☐ 135 Scott Servais	.50	.23	.06
☐ 136 Ozzie Smith	3.00	1.35	.35
☐ 137 Darrin Fletcher	.50	.23	.06
☐ 138 Jose Mesa	.75	.35	.09
☐ 139 Wilson Alvarez	.75	.35	.09
☐ 140 Pete Incaviglia	.50	.23	.06
☐ 141 Chris Hoiles	.50	.23	.06
☐ 142 Darryl Hamilton	.50	.23	.06
☐ 143 Chuck Finley	.50	.23	.06
☐ 144 Archi Cianfrocco	.50	.23	.06
☐ 145 Bill Wegman	.50	.23	.06
☐ 146 Joey Cora	.50	.23	.06
☐ 147 Darrell Whitmore	.50	.23	.06
☐ 148 David Hulse	.50	.23	.06
☐ 149 Jim Abbott	.50	.23	.06
☐ 150 Curt Schilling	.50	.23	.06
☐ 151 Bill Swift	.50	.23	.06
☐ 152 Tommy Greene	.50	.23	.06
☐ 153 Roberto Mejia	.50	.23	.06
☐ 154 Edgar Martinez	.75	.35	.09
☐ 155 Roger Pavlik	.50	.23	.06
☐ 156 Randy Tomlin	.50	.23	.06
☐ 157 J.T. Snow	.75	.35	.09
☐ 158 Bob Welch	.50	.23	.06
☐ 159 Alan Trammell	.75	.35	.09
☐ 160 Ed Sprague	.75	.35	.09
☐ 161 Ben McDonald	.50	.23	.06
☐ 162 Derrick May	.50	.23	.06
☐ 163 Roberto Kelly	.50	.23	.06
☐ 164 Bryan Harvey	.50	.23	.06
☐ 165 Ron Gant	.75	.35	.09
☐ 166 Scott Erickson	.50	.23	.06
☐ 167 Anthony Young	.50	.23	.06
☐ 168 Scott Cooper	.50	.23	.06
☐ 169 Rod Beck	.75	.35	.09
☐ 170 John Franco	.50	.23	.06
☐ 171 Gary DiSarcina	.50	.23	.06
☐ 172 Dave Fleming	.50	.23	.06
☐ 173 Wade Boggs	1.00	.45	.12
☐ 174 Kevin Appier	.75	.35	.09
☐ 175 Jose Bautista	.50	.23	.06
☐ 176 Wally Joyner	.75	.35	.09
☐ 177 Dean Palmer	.75	.35	.09
☐ 178 Tony Phillips	.75	.35	.09
☐ 179 John Smiley	.50	.23	.06
☐ 180 Charlie Hough	.50	.23	.06
☐ 181 Scott Fletcher	.50	.23	.06
☐ 182 Todd Van Poppel	.50	.23	.06
☐ 183 Mike Blowers	.50	.23	.06
☐ 184 Willie McGee	.50	.23	.06
☐ 185 Paul Sorrento	.50	.23	.06
☐ 186 Eric Young	.75	.35	.09
☐ 187 Bret Barberie	.50	.23	.06
☐ 188 Manuel Lee	.50	.23	.06
☐ 189 Jeff Branson	.50	.23	.06
☐ 190 Jim Deshaies	.50	.23	.06
☐ 191 Ken Caminiti	2.00	.90	.25
☐ 192 Tim Raines	1.00	.45	.12
☐ 193 Joe Grahe	.50	.23	.06
☐ 194 Hipolito Pichardo	.50	.23	.06
☐ 195 Denny Neagle	.75	.35	.09
☐ 196 Jeff Gardner	.50	.23	.06
☐ 197 Mike Benjamin	.50	.23	.06
☐ 198 Milt Thompson	.50	.23	.06
☐ 199 Bruce Ruffin	.50	.23	.06
☐ 200 Chris Hammond UER (Back of card has Mariners; should be Marlins)	.50	.23	.06
☐ 201 Tony Gwynn FIN	5.00	2.20	.60
☐ 202 Robin Ventura FIN	.75	.35	.09
☐ 203 Frank Thomas FIN	12.00	5.50	1.50
☐ 204 Kirby Puckett FIN	5.00	2.20	.60
☐ 205 Roberto Alomar FIN	2.50	1.10	.30
☐ 206 Dennis Eckersley FIN	.75	.35	.09
☐ 207 Joe Carter FIN	.75	.35	.09
☐ 208 Albert Belle FIN	5.00	2.20	.60
☐ 209 Greg Maddux FIN	8.00	3.60	1.00
☐ 210 Ryne Sandberg FIN	3.00	1.35	.35
☐ 211 Juan Gonzalez FIN	6.00	2.70	.75
☐ 212 Jeff Bagwell FIN	5.00	2.20	.60
☐ 213 Randy Johnson FIN	2.00	.90	.25
☐ 214 Matt Williams FIN	1.00	.45	.12
☐ 215 Dave Winfield FIN	1.00	.45	.12
☐ 216 Larry Walker FIN	1.00	.45	.12
☐ 217 Roger Clemens FIN	2.50	1.10	.30
☐ 218 Kenny Lofton FIN	4.00	1.80	.50
☐ 219 Cecil Fielder FIN	.75	.35	.09
☐ 220 Darren Daulton FIN	.75	.35	.09
☐ 221 John Olerud FIN	.50	.23	.06
☐ 222 Jose Canseco FIN	1.00	.45	.12
☐ 223 Rickey Henderson FIN	1.00	.45	.12
☐ 224 Fred McGriff FIN	1.00	.45	.12
☐ 225 Gary Sheffield FIN	2.00	.90	.25
☐ 226 Jack McDowell FIN	.75	.35	.09
☐ 227 Rafael Palmeiro FIN	1.00	.45	.12
☐ 228 Travis Fryman FIN	.75	.35	.09
☐ 229 Marquis Grissom FIN	.75	.35	.09
☐ 230 Barry Bonds FIN	3.00	1.35	.35
☐ 231 Carlos Baerga FIN	.75	.35	.09
☐ 232 Ken Griffey Jr. FIN	12.00	5.50	1.50
☐ 233 David Justice FIN	1.00	.45	.12
☐ 234 Bobby Bonilla FIN	.75	.35	.09
☐ 235 Cal Ripken FIN	10.00	4.50	1.25
☐ 236 Sammy Sosa FIN	2.00	.90	.25
☐ 237 Len Dykstra FIN	.75	.35	.09
☐ 238 Will Clark FIN	1.00	.45	.12
☐ 239 Paul Molitor FIN	2.50	1.10	.30
☐ 240 Barry Larkin FIN	1.00	.45	.12
☐ 241 Bo Jackson	.75	.35	.09
☐ 242 Mitch Williams	.50	.23	.06
☐ 243 Ron Darling	.50	.23	.06
☐ 244 Darryl Kile	.50	.23	.06
☐ 245 Geronimo Berroa	.75	.35	.09
☐ 246 Gregg Olson	.50	.23	.06
☐ 247 Brian Harper	.50	.23	.06
☐ 248 Rheal Cormier	.50	.23	.06
☐ 249 Rey Sanchez	.50	.23	.06
☐ 250 Jeff Fassero	.50	.23	.06
☐ 251 Sandy Alomar	.75	.35	.09
☐ 252 Chris Bosio	.50	.23	.06
☐ 253 Andy Stankiewicz	.50	.23	.06
☐ 254 Harold Baines	.75	.35	.09
☐ 255 Andy Ashby	.75	.35	.09
☐ 256 Tyler Green	.50	.23	.06
☐ 257 Kevin Brown	.75	.35	.09
☐ 258 Mo Vaughn	3.00	1.35	.35
☐ 259 Mike Harkey	.50	.23	.06
☐ 260 Dave Henderson	.50	.23	.06
☐ 261 Kent Hrbek	.75	.35	.09
☐ 262 Darrin Jackson	.50	.23	.06

□ 263 Bob Wickman	.50	.23	.06
□ 264 Spike Owen	.50	.23	.06
□ 265 Todd Jones	.50	.23	.06
□ 266 Pat Borders	.50	.23	.06
□ 267 Tom Glavine	1.00	.45	.12
□ 268 Dave Nilsson	.75	.35	.09
□ 269 Rich Batchelor	.50	.23	.06
□ 270 Delino DeShields	.50	.23	.06
□ 271 Felix Fermin	.50	.23	.06
□ 272 Orestes Destrade	.50	.23	.06
□ 273 Mickey Morandini	.50	.23	.06
□ 274 Otis Nixon	.50	.23	.06
□ 275 Ellis Burks	.75	.35	.09
□ 276 Greg Gagne	.50	.23	.06
□ 277 John Doherty	.50	.23	.06
□ 278 Julio Franco	.75	.35	.09
□ 279 Bernie Williams	2.50	1.10	.30
□ 280 Rick Aguilera	.50	.23	.06
□ 281 Mickey Tettleton	.50	.23	.06
□ 282 David Nied	.50	.23	.06
□ 283 Johnny Ruffin	.50	.23	.06
□ 284 Dan Wilson	.75	.35	.09
□ 285 Omar Vizquel	.75	.35	.09
□ 286 Willie Banks	.50	.23	.06
□ 287 Erik Pappas	.50	.23	.06
□ 288 Cal Eldred	.50	.23	.06
□ 289 Bobby Witt	.50	.23	.06
□ 290 Luis Gonzalez	.50	.23	.06
□ 291 Greg Pirkl	.50	.23	.06
□ 292 Alex Cole	.50	.23	.06
□ 293 Ricky Bones	.50	.23	.06
□ 294 Denis Boucher	.50	.23	.06
□ 295 John Burkett	.50	.23	.06
□ 296 Steve Trachsel	.75	.35	.09
□ 297 Ricky Jordan	.50	.23	.06
□ 298 Mark Dewey	.50	.23	.06
□ 299 Jimmy Key	.75	.35	.09
□ 300 Mike Macfarlane	.50	.23	.06
□ 301 Tim Belcher	.50	.23	.06
□ 302 Carlos Reyes	.50	.23	.06
□ 303 Greg A. Harris	.50	.23	.06
□ 304 Brian Anderson	.75	.35	.09
□ 305 Terry Mulholland	.50	.23	.06
□ 306 Felix Jose	.50	.23	.06
□ 307 Darren Holmes	.50	.23	.06
□ 308 Jose Rijo	.50	.23	.06
□ 309 Paul Wagner	.50	.23	.06
□ 310 Bob Scanlan	.50	.23	.06
□ 311 Mike Jackson	.50	.23	.06
□ 312 Jose Vizcaino	.50	.23	.06
□ 313 Rob Butler	.50	.23	.06
□ 314 Kevin Seitzer	.50	.23	.06
□ 315 Geronimo Pena	.50	.23	.06
□ 316 Hector Carrasco	.50	.23	.06
□ 317 Eddie Murray	3.00	1.35	.35
□ 318 Roger Salkeld	.50	.23	.06
□ 319 Todd Hundley	.75	.35	.09
□ 320 Danny Jackson	.50	.23	.06
□ 321 Kevin Young	.50	.23	.06
□ 322 Mike Greenwell	.50	.23	.06
□ 323 Kevin Mitchell	.75	.35	.09
□ 324 Chuck Knoblauch	2.00	.90	.25
□ 325 Danny Tartabull	.50	.23	.06
□ 326 Vince Coleman	.50	.23	.06
□ 327 Marvin Freeman	.50	.23	.06
□ 328 Andy Benes	.75	.35	.09
□ 329 Mike Kelly	.50	.23	.06
□ 330 Karl Rhodes	.50	.23	.06
□ 331 Allen Watson	.50	.23	.06
□ 332 Damion Easley	.50	.23	.06
□ 333 Reggie Jefferson	.75	.35	.09
□ 334 Kevin McReynolds	.50	.23	.06
□ 335 Arthur Rhodes	.50	.23	.06
□ 336 Brian R. Hunter	.50	.23	.06
□ 337 Tom Browning	.50	.23	.06
□ 338 Pedro Munoz	.50	.23	.06
□ 339 Billy Ripken	.50	.23	.06
□ 340 Gene Harris	.50	.23	.06
□ 341 Fernando Vina	.50	.23	.06
□ 342 Sean Berry	.50	.23	.06
□ 343 Pedro Astacio	.50	.23	.06
□ 344 B.J. Surhoff	.50	.23	.06
□ 345 Doug Drabek	.50	.23	.06
□ 346 Jody Reed	.50	.23	.06
□ 347 Ray Lankford	.75	.35	.09
□ 348 Steve Farr	.50	.23	.06
□ 349 Eric Anthony	.50	.23	.06
□ 350 Pete Smith	.50	.23	.06
□ 351 Lee Smith	.75	.35	.09
□ 352 Mariano Duncan	.50	.23	.06
□ 353 Doug Strange	.50	.23	.06
□ 354 Tim Bogar	.50	.23	.06
□ 355 Dave Weathers	.50	.23	.06
□ 356 Eric Karros	.75	.35	.09
□ 357 Randy Myers	.50	.23	.06
□ 358 Chad Curtis	.50	.23	.06
□ 359 Steve Avery	.75	.35	.09
□ 360 Brian Jordan	1.00	.45	.12
□ 361 Tim Wallach	.50	.23	.06
□ 362 Pedro Martinez	1.00	.45	.12
□ 363 Bip Roberts	.50	.23	.06
□ 364 Lou Whitaker	.75	.35	.09
□ 365 Luis Polonia	.50	.23	.06
□ 366 Benny Santiago	.50	.23	.06
□ 367 Brett Butler	.75	.35	.09
□ 368 Shawon Dunston	.50	.23	.06
□ 369 Kelly Stinnett	.50	.23	.06
□ 370 Chris Turner	.50	.23	.06
□ 371 Ruben Sierra	.75	.35	.09
□ 372 Greg A. Harris	.50	.23	.06
□ 373 Xavier Hernandez	.50	.23	.06
□ 374 Howard Johnson	.50	.23	.06
□ 375 Duane Ward	.50	.23	.06
□ 376 Roberto Hernandez	.75	.35	.09
□ 377 Scott Leius	.50	.23	.06
□ 378 Dave Valle	.50	.23	.06
□ 379 Sid Fernandez	.50	.23	.06
□ 380 Doug Jones	.50	.23	.06
□ 381 Zane Smith	.50	.23	.06
□ 382 Craig Biggio	.75	.35	.09
□ 383 Rick White	.50	.23	.06
□ 384 Tom Pagnozzi	.50	.23	.06
□ 385 Chris James	.50	.23	.06
□ 386 Bret Boone	.75	.35	.09
□ 387 Jeff Montgomery	.75	.35	.09
□ 388 Chad Kreuter	.50	.23	.06
□ 389 Greg Hibbard	.50	.23	.06
□ 390 Mark Grace	1.00	.45	.12
□ 391 Phil Leftwich	.50	.23	.06
□ 392 Don Mattingly	6.00	2.70	.75
□ 393 Ozzie Guillen	.50	.23	.06
□ 394 Gary Gaetti	.75	.35	.09
□ 395 Erik Hanson	.50	.23	.06
□ 396 Scott Brosius	.50	.23	.06
□ 397 Tom Gordon	.50	.23	.06
□ 398 Bill Gullickson	.50	.23	.06
□ 399 Matt Mieske	.50	.23	.06
□ 400 Pat Hentgen	.75	.35	.09
□ 401 Walt Weiss	.50	.23	.06
□ 402 Greg Blosser	.50	.23	.06
□ 403 Stan Javier	.50	.23	.06
□ 404 Doug Henry	.50	.23	.06
□ 405 Ramon Martinez	.75	.35	.09
□ 406 Frank Viola	.50	.23	.06
□ 407 Mike Hampton	.75	.35	.09
□ 408 Andy Van Slyke	.75	.35	.09
□ 409 Bobby Ayala	.50	.23	.06
□ 410 Todd Zeile	.50	.23	.06
□ 411 Jay Bell	.75	.35	.09
□ 412 Denny Martinez	.75	.35	.09
□ 413 Mark Portugal	.50	.23	.06
□ 414 Bobby Munoz	.50	.23	.06
□ 415 Kirt Manwaring	.50	.23	.06
□ 416 John Kruk	.75	.35	.09
□ 417 Trevor Hoffman	.75	.35	.09
□ 418 Chris Sabo	.50	.23	.06
□ 419 Bret Saberhagen	.75	.35	.09
□ 420 Chris Nabholz	.50	.23	.06
□ 421 James Mouton FIN	.75	.35	.09
□ 422 Tony Tarasco FIN	.50	.23	.06
□ 423 Carlos Delgado FIN	1.00	.45	.12
□ 424 Rondell White FIN	1.00	.45	.12
□ 425 Javier Lopez FIN	1.00	.45	.12
□ 426 Chan Ho Park FIN	4.00	1.80	.50
□ 427 Cliff Floyd FIN	1.00	.45	.12
□ 428 Dave Staton FIN	.50	.23	.06
□ 429 J.R. Phillips FIN	.50	.23	.06
□ 430 Manny Ramirez FIN	4.00	1.80	.50
□ 431 Kurt Abbott FIN	.75	.35	.09
□ 432 Melvin Nieves FIN	.75	.35	.09
□ 433 Alex Gonzalez FIN	.75	.35	.09
□ 434 Rick Helling FIN	.50	.23	.06
□ 435 Danny Bautista FIN	.50	.23	.06
□ 436 Matt Walbeck FIN	.50	.23	.06
□ 437 Ryan Klesko FIN	2.50	1.10	.30
□ 438 Steve Karsay FIN	.50	.23	.06
□ 439 Salomon Torres FIN	.50	.23	.06
□ 440 Scott Ruffcorn FIN	.50	.23	.06

1994 Finest Refractors

The 1994 Topps Finest Refractors baseball set consists of two series of 220 cards each, for a total of 440 cards. These special cards were inserted at a rate of one in every nine packs. They are identical to the basic Finest card except for a more intense luster and 3-D appearance.

	MINT	NRMT	EXC
COMPLETE SET (440)	2800.00	1250.00	350.00
COMPLETE SERIES 1 (220)	1400.00	650.00	180.00
COMPLETE SERIES 2 (220)	1400.00	650.00	180.00
COMMON CARD (1-440)	3.00	1.35	.35
*STARS: 5X TO 10X BASIC CARDS			
*YOUNG STARS: 3X TO 6X BASIC CARDS			

□ 1 Mike Piazza FIN	80.00	36.00	10.00
□ 18 Tim Salmon FIN	20.00	9.00	2.50
□ 35 Andres Galarraga	15.00	6.75	1.85
□ 59 Dante Bichette	15.00	6.75	1.85
□ 66 Mike Mussina	25.00	11.00	3.10
□ 74 Raul Mondesi	20.00	9.00	2.50
□ 78 Mark McGwire	40.00	18.00	5.00
□ 100 John Smoltz	20.00	9.00	2.50
□ 102 Jim Thome	30.00	13.50	3.70
□ 122 Jay Buhner	20.00	9.00	2.50
□ 126 Ivan Rodriguez	30.00	13.50	3.70
□ 131 Brady Anderson	20.00	9.00	2.50
□ 136 Ozzie Smith	30.00	13.50	3.70
□ 173 Wade Boggs	15.00	6.75	1.85
□ 191 Ken Caminiti	20.00	9.00	2.50
□ 201 Tony Gwynn FIN	50.00	22.00	6.25
□ 203 Frank Thomas FIN	125.00	55.00	15.50
□ 204 Kirby Puckett FIN	50.00	22.00	6.25
□ 205 Roberto Alomar FIN	25.00	11.00	3.10
□ 208 Albert Belle FIN	50.00	22.00	6.25
□ 209 Greg Maddux FIN	80.00	36.00	10.00
□ 210 Ryne Sandberg FIN	30.00	13.50	3.70
□ 211 Juan Gonzalez FIN	60.00	27.00	7.50
□ 212 Jeff Bagwell FIN	50.00	22.00	6.25
□ 213 Randy Johnson FIN	20.00	9.00	2.50
□ 214 Matt Williams FIN	15.00	6.75	1.85
□ 215 Dave Winfield FIN	15.00	6.75	1.85
□ 216 Larry Walker FIN	15.00	6.75	1.85
□ 217 Roger Clemens FIN	25.00	11.00	3.10
□ 218 Kenny Lofton FIN	40.00	18.00	5.00
□ 222 Jose Canseco FIN	15.00	6.75	1.85
□ 223 Rickey Henderson FIN	15.00	6.75	1.85
□ 224 Fred McGriff FIN	15.00	6.75	1.85
□ 225 Gary Sheffield FIN	25.00	11.00	3.10
□ 227 Rafael Palmeiro FIN	15.00	6.75	1.85
□ 230 Barry Bonds FIN	40.00	18.00	5.00
□ 232 Ken Griffey Jr. FIN	125.00	55.00	15.50
□ 235 Cal Ripken FIN	100.00	45.00	12.50
□ 236 Sammy Sosa FIN	22.00	10.00	2.70
□ 238 Will Clark FIN	15.00	6.75	1.85
□ 239 Paul Molitor FIN	25.00	11.00	3.10
□ 240 Barry Larkin FIN	15.00	6.75	1.85
□ 258 Mo Vaughn	30.00	13.50	3.70
□ 267 Tom Glavine	15.00	6.75	1.85
□ 279 Bernie Williams	25.00	11.00	3.10
□ 317 Eddie Murray	30.00	13.50	3.70
□ 319 Todd Hundley	15.00	6.75	1.85
□ 324 Chuck Knoblauch	20.00	9.00	2.50
□ 392 Don Mattingly	60.00	27.00	7.50
□ 426 Chan Ho Park FIN	20.00	9.00	2.50
□ 430 Manny Ramirez FIN	40.00	18.00	5.00
□ 437 Ryan Klesko FIN	25.00	11.00	3.10

1994 Finest Jumbos

Inserted one per Finest box, this 80-card over-sized set (3 1/2" by 5") was issued in two series of 40. Each of the 80 cards is identical in design to the special "Finest" cards from the basic Finest set except for the size. The "Finest" subset was designated to showcase top rookies, prospects and veterans. The card numbering is the same as the corresponding basic issue cards. Hence, the first series comprises of cards 1-20 and 201-220. The second series is cards 221-240 and 421-440.

	MINT	NRMT	EXC
COMPLETE SET (80)	350.00	160.00	45.00
COMPLETE SERIES 1 (40)	200.00	90.00	25.00
COMPLETE SERIES 2 (40)	150.00	70.00	19.00
COMMON CARD (1-20/201-220)	1.00	.45	.12
COMMON CARD (221-240/421-440)	1.00	.45	.12
*STARS: 1.5X to 3X BASIC CARDS			

1995 Finest

Consisting of 330 standard-size cards, this set was issued in series of 220 and 110. A protective film, designed to keep the card from scratching and to maintain original gloss, covers the front. With the Finest logo at the top, a silver baseball diamond design surrounded by green (field) form the background to an action photo. Horizontally designed backs have a photo to the right with statistical information to the left. A Finest Moment, or career highlight, is also included. Rookie Cards in this set include Bobby Higginson and Hideo Nomo.

	MINT	NRMT	EXC
COMPLETE SET (330)	125.00	55.00	15.50
COMPLETE SERIES 1 (220)	80.00	36.00	10.00
COMPLETE SERIES 2 (110)	45.00	20.00	5.50
COMMON CARD (1-330)	.25	.11	.03

□ 1 Raul Mondesi	1.25	.55	.16
□ 2 Kurt Abbott	.25	.11	.03
□ 3 Chris Gomez	.25	.11	.03
□ 4 Manny Ramirez	2.50	1.10	.30
□ 5 Rondell White	.50	.23	.06
□ 6 William VanLandingham	.25	.11	.03
□ 7 Jon Lieber	.25	.11	.03
□ 8 Ryan Klesko	1.25	.55	.16
□ 9 John Hudek	.25	.11	.03
□ 10 Joey Hamilton	1.25	.55	.16
□ 11 Bob Hamelin	.25	.11	.03
□ 12 Brian Anderson	.25	.11	.03
□ 13 Mike Lieberthal	.25	.11	.03
□ 14 Rico Brogna	.25	.11	.03
□ 15 Rusty Greer	1.25	.55	.16
□ 16 Carlos Delgado	.50	.23	.06
□ 17 Jim Edmonds	1.25	.55	.16
□ 18 Steve Trachsel	.25	.11	.03
□ 19 Matt Walbeck	.25	.11	.03
□ 20 Armando Benitez	.25	.11	.03
□ 21 Steve Karsay	.25	.11	.03
□ 22 Jose Oliva	.25	.11	.03
□ 23 Cliff Floyd	.50	.23	.06
□ 24 Kevin Foster	.25	.11	.03
□ 25 Javier Lopez	1.25	.55	.16
□ 26 Jose Valentin	.50	.23	.06
□ 27 James Mouton	.25	.11	.03
□ 28 Hector Carrasco	.25	.11	.03
□ 29 Orlando Miller	.25	.11	.03
□ 30 Garret Anderson	.50	.23	.06
□ 31 Marvin Freeman	.25	.11	.03
□ 32 Brett Butler	.50	.23	.06
□ 33 Roberto Kelly	.25	.11	.03
□ 34 Rod Beck	.25	.11	.03
□ 35 Jose Rijo	.25	.11	.03
□ 36 Edgar Martinez	.50	.23	.06
□ 37 Jim Thome	2.00	.90	.25
□ 38 Rick Wilkins	.25	.11	.03
□ 39 Wally Joyner	.50	.23	.06
□ 40 Wil Cordero	.25	.11	.03
□ 41 Tommy Greene	.25	.11	.03
□ 42 Travis Fryman	.50	.23	.06
□ 43 Don Slaught	.25	.11	.03
□ 44 Brady Anderson	1.25	.55	.16
□ 45 Matt Williams	1.25	.55	.16
□ 46 Rene Arocha	.25	.11	.03
□ 47 Rickey Henderson	1.25	.55	.16
□ 48 Mike Mussina	2.00	.90	.25
□ 49 Greg McMichael	.25	.11	.03
□ 50 Jody Reed	.25	.11	.03
□ 51 Tino Martinez	.50	.23	.06
□ 52 Dave Clark	.25	.11	.03
□ 53 John Valentin	.50	.23	.06
□ 54 Bret Boone	.50	.23	.06
□ 55 Walt Weiss	.25	.11	.03
□ 56 Kenny Lofton	2.50	1.10	.30
□ 57 Scott Leius	.25	.11	.03
□ 58 Eric Karros	.50	.23	.06
□ 59 John Olerud	.25	.11	.03
□ 60 Chris Hoiles	.25	.11	.03
□ 61 Sandy Alomar Jr.	.25	.11	.03
□ 62 Tim Wallach	.25	.11	.03
□ 63 Cal Eldred	.25	.11	.03
□ 64 Tom Glavine	1.25	.55	.16
□ 65 Mark Grace	1.25	.55	.16
□ 66 Rey Sanchez	.25	.11	.03
□ 67 Bobby Ayala	.25	.11	.03
□ 68 Dante Bichette	1.25	.55	.16
□ 69 Andres Galarraga	1.25	.55	.16
□ 70 Chuck Carr	.25	.11	.03
□ 71 Bobby Witt	.25	.11	.03
□ 72 Steve Avery	.50	.23	.06
□ 73 Bobby Jones	.50	.23	.06
□ 74 Delino DeShields	.25	.11	.03
□ 75 Kevin Tapani	.25	.11	.03
□ 76 Randy Johnson	1.50	.70	.19
□ 77 David Nied	.25	.11	.03
□ 78 Pat Hentgen	.50	.23	.06
□ 79 Tim Salmon	1.25	.55	.16
□ 80 Todd Zeile	.25	.11	.03
□ 81 John Wetteland	.50	.23	.06
□ 82 Albert Belle	4.00	1.80	.50
□ 83 Ben McDonald	.25	.11	.03
□ 84 Bobby Munoz	.25	.11	.03
□ 85 Bip Roberts	.25	.11	.03
□ 86 Mo Vaughn	2.50	1.10	.30
□ 87 Chuck Finley	.50	.23	.06
□ 88 Chuck Knoblauch	1.25	.55	.16
□ 89 Frank Thomas	10.00	4.50	1.25
□ 90 Danny Tartabull	.25	.11	.03
□ 91 Dean Palmer	.50	.23	.06
□ 92 Len Dykstra	.50	.23	.06
□ 93 J.R. Phillips	.25	.11	.03
□ 94 Tom Candiotti	.25	.11	.03
□ 95 Marquis Grissom	.50	.23	.06
□ 96 Barry Larkin	1.25	.55	.16
□ 97 Bryan Harvey	.25	.11	.03
□ 98 David Justice	1.25	.55	.16
□ 99 David Cone	.50	.23	.06
□ 100 Wade Boggs	1.25	.55	.16

□ 101 Jason Bere .25 .11 .03
□ 102 Hal Morris .25 .11 .03
□ 103 Fred McGriff 1.25 .55 .16
□ 104 Bobby Bonilla .50 .23 .06
□ 105 Jay Buhner 1.25 .55 .16
□ 106 Allen Watson .25 .11 .03
□ 107 Mickey Tettleton .25 .11 .03
□ 108 Kevin Appier .50 .23 .06
□ 109 Ivan Rodriguez 2.50 1.10 .30
□ 110 Carlos Garcia .25 .11 .03
□ 111 Andy Benes .25 .11 .03
□ 112 Eddie Murray 2.50 1.10 .30
□ 113 Mike Piazza 6.00 2.70 .75
□ 114 Greg Vaughn .50 .23 .06
□ 115 Paul Molitor 2.00 .90 .25
□ 116 Terry Steinbach .50 .23 .06
□ 117 Jeff Bagwell 4.00 1.80 .50
□ 118 Ken Griffey Jr. 10.00 4.50 1.25
□ 119 Gary Sheffield 1.50 .70 .19
□ 120 Cal Ripken 8.00 3.60 1.00
□ 121 Jeff Kent .25 .11 .03
□ 122 Jay Bell .50 .23 .06
□ 123 Will Clark 1.25 .55 .16
□ 124 Cecil Fielder .50 .23 .06
□ 125 Alex Fernandez .50 .23 .06
□ 126 Don Mattingly 5.00 2.20 .60
□ 127 Reggie Sanders .50 .23 .06
□ 128 Moises Alou .50 .23 .06
□ 129 Craig Biggio .50 .23 .06
□ 130 Eddie Williams .25 .11 .03
□ 131 John Franco .25 .11 .03
□ 132 John Kruk .50 .23 .06
□ 133 Jeff King .50 .23 .06
□ 134 Royce Clayton .25 .11 .03
□ 135 Doug Drabek .25 .11 .03
□ 136 Ray Lankford .50 .23 .06
□ 137 Roberto Alomar 2.00 .90 .25
□ 138 Todd Hundley .50 .23 .06
□ 139 Alex Cole .25 .11 .03
□ 140 Shawon Dunston .25 .11 .03
□ 141 John Roper .25 .11 .03
□ 142 Mark Langston .25 .11 .03
□ 143 Tom Pagnozzi .25 .11 .03
□ 144 Wilson Alvarez .50 .23 .06
□ 145 Scott Cooper .25 .11 .03
□ 146 Kevin Mitchell .50 .23 .06
□ 147 Mark Whiten .25 .11 .03
□ 148 Jeff Conine .50 .23 .06
□ 149 Chili Davis .50 .23 .06
□ 150 Luis Gonzalez .25 .11 .03
□ 151 Juan Guzman .50 .23 .06
□ 152 Mike Greenwell .25 .11 .03
□ 153 Mike Henneman .25 .11 .03
□ 154 Rick Aguilera .25 .11 .03
□ 155 Dennis Eckersley .50 .23 .06
□ 156 Darrin Fletcher .25 .11 .03
□ 157 Darren Lewis .25 .11 .03
□ 158 Juan Gonzalez 5.00 2.20 .60
□ 159 Dave Hollins .25 .11 .03
□ 160 Jimmy Key .50 .23 .06
□ 161 Roberto Hernandez .25 .11 .03
□ 162 Randy Myers .25 .11 .03
□ 163 Joe Carter .50 .23 .06
□ 164 Darren Daulton .50 .23 .06
□ 165 Mike Macfarlane .25 .11 .03
□ 166 Bret Saberhagen .50 .23 .06
□ 167 Kirby Puckett 4.00 1.80 .50
□ 168 Lance Johnson .50 .23 .06
□ 169 Mark McGwire 3.00 1.35 .35
□ 170 Jose Canseco 1.25 .55 .16
□ 171 Mike Stanley .25 .11 .03
□ 172 Lee Smith .50 .23 .06
□ 173 Robin Ventura .50 .23 .06
□ 174 Greg Gagne .25 .11 .03
□ 175 Brian McRae .50 .23 .06
□ 176 Mike Bordick .25 .11 .03
□ 177 Rafael Palmeiro 1.25 .55 .16
□ 178 Kenny Rogers .25 .11 .03
□ 179 Chad Curtis .25 .11 .03
□ 180 Devon White .50 .23 .06
□ 181 Paul O'Neill .50 .23 .06
□ 182 Ken Caminiti 1.50 .70 .19
□ 183 Dave Nilsson .50 .23 .06
□ 184 Tim Naehring .25 .11 .03
□ 185 Roger Clemens 2.00 .90 .25
□ 186 Otis Nixon .25 .11 .03
□ 187 Tim Raines 1.25 .55 .16
□ 188 Denny Martinez .50 .23 .06
□ 189 Pedro Martinez .50 .23 .06
□ 190 Jim Abbott .25 .11 .03
□ 191 Ryan Thompson .25 .11 .03
□ 192 Barry Bonds 2.50 1.10 .30
□ 193 Joe Girardi .25 .11 .03
□ 194 Steve Finley .50 .23 .06
□ 195 John Jaha .50 .23 .06
□ 196 Tony Gwynn 4.00 1.80 .50
□ 197 Sammy Sosa 1.50 .70 .19
□ 198 John Burkett .50 .23 .06
□ 199 Carlos Baerga .50 .23 .06
□ 200 Ramon Martinez .50 .23 .06
□ 201 Aaron Sele .50 .23 .06
□ 202 Eduardo Perez .25 .11 .03
□ 203 Alan Trammell .50 .23 .06
□ 204 Orlando Merced .25 .11 .03
□ 205 Deion Sanders 1.25 .55 .16
□ 206 Robb Nen .25 .11 .03
□ 207 Jack McDowell .50 .23 .06
□ 208 Ruben Sierra .50 .23 .06
□ 209 Bernie Williams 2.00 .90 .25
□ 210 Kevin Seitzer .25 .11 .03
□ 211 Charles Nagy .50 .23 .06
□ 212 Tony Phillips .50 .23 .06
□ 213 Greg Maddux 6.00 2.70 .75
□ 214 Jeff Montgomery .50 .23 .06
□ 215 Larry Walker 1.25 .55 .16
□ 216 Andy Van Slyke .50 .23 .06
□ 217 Ozzie Smith 2.50 1.10 .30
□ 218 Geronimo Pena .25 .11 .03
□ 219 Gregg Jefferies .50 .23 .06
□ 220 Lou Whitaker .50 .23 .06
□ 221 Chipper Jones 6.00 2.70 .75
□ 222 Benji Gil .25 .11 .03
□ 223 Tony Phillips .50 .23 .06
□ 224 Trevor Wilson .25 .11 .03
□ 225 Tony Tarasco .25 .11 .03
□ 226 Roberto Petagine .25 .11 .03
□ 227 Mike Macfarlane .25 .11 .03
□ 228 Hideo Nomo UER 10.00 4.50 1.25
(In 3rd line agianst)
□ 229 Mark McLemore .25 .11 .03
□ 230 Ron Gant .50 .23 .06
□ 231 Andujar Cedeno .25 .11 .03
□ 232 Mike Mimbs .50 .23 .06
□ 233 Jim Abbott .25 .11 .03
□ 234 Ricky Bones .25 .11 .03
□ 235 Marty Cordova 1.50 .70 .19
□ 236 Mark Johnson .50 .23 .06
□ 237 Marquis Grissom .50 .23 .06
□ 238 Tom Henke .25 .11 .03
□ 239 Terry Pendleton .50 .23 .06
□ 240 John Wetteland .50 .23 .06
□ 241 Lee Smith .50 .23 .06
□ 242 Jaime Navarro .25 .11 .03
□ 243 Luis Alicea .25 .11 .03
□ 244 Scott Cooper .25 .11 .03
□ 245 Gary Gaetti .50 .23 .06
□ 246 Edgardo Alfonzo UER .50 .23 .06
(Incomplete career BA)
□ 247 Brad Clontz .25 .11 .03
□ 248 Dave Mlicki .25 .11 .03
□ 249 Dave Winfield 1.25 .55 .16
□ 250 Mark Grudzielanek 2.50 1.10 .30
□ 251 Alex Gonzalez .50 .23 .06
□ 252 Kevin Brown .50 .23 .06
□ 253 Esteban Loaiza .25 .11 .03
□ 254 Vaughn Eshelman .25 .11 .03
□ 255 Bill Swift .25 .11 .03
□ 256 Brian McRae .50 .23 .06
□ 257 Bobby Higginson 2.50 1.10 .30
□ 258 Jack McDowell .50 .23 .06
□ 259 Scott Stahoviak .25 .11 .03
□ 260 Jon Nunnally .50 .23 .06
□ 261 Charlie Hayes .25 .11 .03
□ 262 Jacob Brumfield .25 .11 .03
□ 263 Chad Curtis .25 .11 .03
□ 264 Heathcliff Slocumb .25 .11 .03
□ 265 Mark Whiten .25 .11 .03
□ 266 Mickey Tettleton .25 .11 .03
□ 267 Jose Mesa .25 .11 .03
□ 268 Doug Jones .25 .11 .03
□ 269 Trevor Hoffman .50 .23 .06
□ 270 Paul Sorrento .25 .11 .03
□ 271 Shane Andrews .25 .11 .03
□ 272 Brett Butler .50 .23 .06
□ 273 Curtis Goodwin .50 .23 .06
□ 274 Larry Walker 1.25 .55 .16
□ 275 Phil Plantier .25 .11 .03
□ 276 Ken Hill .25 .11 .03
□ 277 Vinny Castilla UER .50 .23 .06
Rockies spelled Rockie
□ 278 Billy Ashley .25 .11 .03
□ 279 Derek Jeter 6.00 2.70 .75
□ 280 Bob Tewksbury .25 .11 .03
□ 281 Jose Offerman .25 .11 .03
□ 282 Glenallen Hill .25 .11 .03
□ 283 Tony Fernandez .25 .11 .03
□ 284 Mike Devereaux .25 .11 .03
□ 285 John Burkett .50 .23 .06
□ 286 Geronimo Berroa .25 .11 .03
□ 287 Quilvio Veras .25 .11 .03
□ 288 Jason Bates .25 .11 .03
□ 289 Lee Tinsley .25 .11 .03
□ 290 Derek Bell .50 .23 .06
□ 291 Jeff Fassero .25 .11 .03
□ 292 Ray Durham .50 .23 .06
□ 293 Chad Ogea .25 .11 .03
□ 294 Bill Pulsipher .50 .23 .06
□ 295 Phil Nevin .25 .11 .03
□ 296 Carlos Perez .50 .23 .06
□ 297 Roberto Kelly .25 .11 .03
□ 298 Tim Wakefield .25 .11 .03
□ 299 Jeff Manto .25 .11 .03
□ 300 Brian Hunter 1.25 .55 .16
□ 301 C.J. Nitkowski .50 .23 .06
□ 302 Dustin Hermanson .50 .23 .06
□ 303 John Mabry 1.25 .55 .16
□ 304 Orel Hershiser .50 .23 .06
□ 305 Ron Villone .25 .11 .03
□ 306 Sean Bergman .25 .11 .03
□ 307 Tom Goodwin .25 .11 .03
□ 308 Al Reyes .25 .11 .03
□ 309 Todd Stottlemyre .25 .11 .03
□ 310 Rich Becker .25 .11 .03
□ 311 Joey Cora .25 .11 .03
□ 312 Ed Sprague .50 .23 .06
□ 313 John Smoltz UER 1.50 .70 .19
(3rd line; from spelled as form)
□ 314 Frank Castillo .25 .11 .03
□ 315 Chris Hammond .25 .11 .03
□ 316 Ismael Valdes .50 .23 .06
□ 317 Pete Harnisch .25 .11 .03
□ 318 Bernard Gilkey .50 .23 .06
□ 319 John Kruk .50 .23 .06
□ 320 Marc Newfield .50 .23 .06
□ 321 Brian Johnson .25 .11 .03
□ 322 Mark Portugal .25 .11 .03
□ 323 David Hulse .25 .11 .03
□ 324 Luis Ortiz UER .25 .11 .03
(Below spelled beloe)
□ 325 Mike Benjamin .25 .11 .03
□ 326 Brian Jordan 1.25 .55 .16
□ 327 Shawn Green .50 .23 .06
□ 328 Joe Oliver .25 .11 .03
□ 329 Felipe Lira .25 .11 .03
□ 330 Andre Dawson .50 .23 .06

1995 Finest Refractors

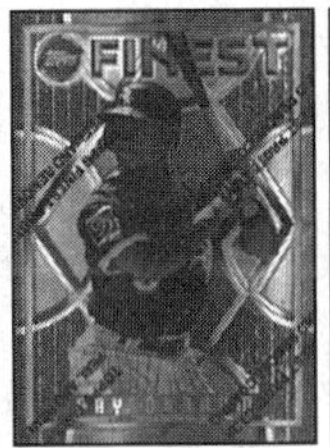
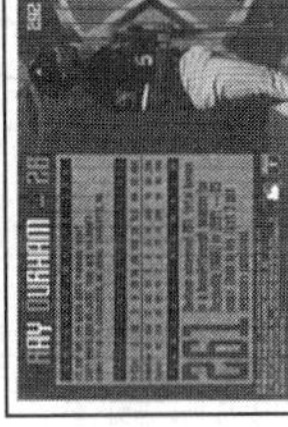

This set is a parallel to the basic Finest set, including the use of protective coating, the difference can be found in the refractive sheen. The cards were inserted at a rate of one in 12 packs.

	MINT	NRMT	EXC
COMPLETE SET (330)	4500.00	2000.00	550.00
COMPLETE SERIES 1 (220)	3500.00	1600.00	450.00
COMPLETE SERIES 2 (110)	1000.00	450.00	125.00
COMMON CARD (1-330)	10.00	4.50	1.25

*STARS: 15X TO 30X BASIC CARDS..
*YOUNG STARS: 15X TO 25X BASIC CARDS

□ 1 Raul Mondesi 40.00 18.00 5.00
□ 4 Manny Ramirez 75.00 34.00 9.50
□ 8 Ryan Klesko 50.00 22.00 6.25
□ 10 Joey Hamilton 40.00 18.00 5.00
□ 15 Rusty Greer 40.00 18.00 5.00
□ 17 Jim Edmonds 40.00 18.00 5.00
□ 37 Jim Thome 60.00 27.00 7.50
□ 44 Brady Anderson 40.00 18.00 5.00
□ 45 Matt Williams 40.00 18.00 5.00
□ 48 Mike Mussina 60.00 27.00 7.50
□ 56 Kenny Lofton 75.00 34.00 9.50
□ 64 Tom Glavine 40.00 18.00 5.00
□ 68 Dante Bichette 40.00 18.00 5.00
□ 69 Andres Galarraga 40.00 18.00 5.00
□ 76 Randy Johnson 50.00 22.00 6.25
□ 79 Tim Salmon 40.00 18.00 5.00
□ 82 Albert Belle 125.00 55.00 15.50
□ 86 Mo Vaughn 75.00 34.00 9.50
□ 88 Chuck Knoblauch 50.00 22.00 6.25
□ 89 Frank Thomas 300.00 135.00 38.00
□ 96 Barry Larkin 40.00 18.00 5.00
□ 100 Wade Boggs 40.00 18.00 5.00
□ 103 Fred McGriff 40.00 18.00 5.00
□ 105 Jay Buhner 40.00 18.00 5.00
□ 109 Ivan Rodriguez 75.00 34.00 9.50
□ 112 Eddie Murray 75.00 34.00 9.50
□ 113 Mike Piazza 175.00 80.00 22.00
□ 115 Paul Molitor 60.00 27.00 7.50
□ 117 Jeff Bagwell 125.00 55.00 15.50
□ 118 Ken Griffey Jr. 300.00 135.00 38.00
□ 119 Gary Sheffield 50.00 22.00 6.25
□ 120 Cal Ripken Jr. 250.00 110.00 31.00
□ 123 Will Clark 40.00 18.00 5.00
□ 126 Don Mattingly 150.00 70.00 19.00
□ 137 Roberto Alomar 60.00 27.00 7.50
□ 158 Juan Gonzalez 150.00 70.00 19.00
□ 167 Kirby Puckett 125.00 55.00 15.50
□ 169 Mark McGwire 100.00 45.00 12.50
□ 170 Jose Canseco 40.00 18.00 5.00
□ 177 Rafael Palmeiro 40.00 18.00 5.00
□ 182 Ken Caminiti 50.00 22.00 6.25
□ 185 Roger Clemens 50.00 22.00 6.25
□ 192 Barry Bonds 75.00 34.00 9.50
□ 196 Tony Gwynn 125.00 55.00 15.50
□ 197 Sammy Sosa 50.00 22.00 6.25
□ 209 Bernie Williams 60.00 27.00 7.50
□ 213 Greg Maddux 250.00 110.00 31.00
□ 215 Larry Walker 40.00 18.00 5.00
□ 217 Ozzie Smith 75.00 34.00 9.50
□ 221 Chipper Jones 175.00 80.00 22.00
□ 228 Hideo Nomo 135.00 60.00 17.00
□ 235 Marty Cordova 40.00 18.00 5.00
□ 249 Dave Winfield 40.00 18.00 5.00
□ 250 Mark Grudzielanek 40.00 18.00 5.00
□ 257 Bobby Higginson 40.00 18.00 5.00
□ 274 Larry Walker 40.00 18.00 5.00
□ 279 Derek Jeter 175.00 80.00 22.00
□ 300 Brian Hunter 40.00 18.00 5.00
□ 313 John Smoltz 50.00 22.00 6.25
□ 316 Ismael Valdes 40.00 18.00 5.00
□ 326 Brian Jordan 40.00 18.00 5.00

1995 Finest Flame Throwers

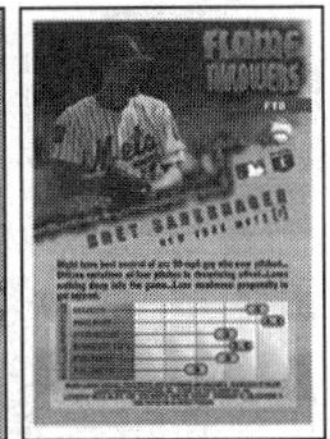

Randomly inserted in packs, this nine-card set showcases strikeout leaders who bring on the heat. With a protective coating, a player photo is superimposed over a fiery orange background. The backs have a player photo with skills ratings such as velocity.

	MINT	NRMT	EXC
COMPLETE SET (9)	75.00	34.00	9.50
COMMON CARD (1-9)	8.00	3.60	1.00

□ FT1 Jason Bere 8.00 3.60 1.00
□ FT2 Roger Clemens 20.00 9.00 2.50
□ FT3 Juan Guzman 12.00 5.50 1.50
□ FT4 John Hudek 8.00 3.60 1.00
□ FT5 Randy Johnson 20.00 9.00 2.50
□ FT6 Pedro Martinez 12.00 5.50 1.50
□ FT7 Jose Rijo 8.00 3.60 1.00
□ FT8 Bret Saberhagen 8.00 3.60 1.00
□ FT9 John Wetteland 12.00 5.50 1.50

1995 Finest Power Kings

Randomly inserted at a rate of one in 24 packs, Power Kings is an 18-card set highlighting top sluggers. With a protective coating, the fronts feature chromium technology that allows the player photo to be further enhanced as if to jump out from a blue lightning bolt background. The horizontal backs contain two small photos and power production figures.

	MINT	NRMT	EXC
COMPLETE SET (18)	200.00	90.00	25.00
COMMON CARD (1-18)	5.00	2.20	.60

□ PK1 Bob Hamelin 5.00 2.20 .60
□ PK2 Raul Mondesi 5.00 2.20 .60
□ PK3 Ryan Klesko 8.00 3.60 1.00
□ PK4 Carlos Delgado 5.00 2.20 .60
□ PK5 Manny Ramirez 12.00 5.50 1.50
□ PK6 Mike Piazza 30.00 13.50 3.70
□ PK7 Jeff Bagwell 20.00 9.00 2.50
□ PK8 Mo Vaughn 12.00 5.50 1.50
□ PK9 Frank Thomas 50.00 22.00 6.25
□ PK10 Ken Griffey Jr. 50.00 22.00 6.25
□ PK11 Albert Belle 20.00 9.00 2.50
□ PK12 Sammy Sosa 8.00 3.60 1.00
□ PK13 Dante Bichette 6.00 2.70 .75
□ PK14 Gary Sheffield 8.00 3.60 1.00
□ PK15 Matt Williams 6.00 2.70 .75
□ PK16 Fred McGriff 6.00 2.70 .75
□ PK17 Barry Bonds 12.00 5.50 1.50
□ PK18 Cecil Fielder 5.00 2.20 .60

1995 Finest Bronze

Available exclusively direct from Topps, this 6-card set features six of Baseball's hottest superstars. The fronts feature chromium metallized graphics, mounted on bronze and factory sealed in clear resin. The cards are numbered on the back "X of 6."

	MINT	NRMT	EXC
COMPLETE SET (6)	120.00	55.00	15.00
COMMON CARD (1-6)	5.00	2.20	.60

□ 1 Matt Williams	10.00	4.50	1.25
□ 2 Tony Gwynn	20.00	9.00	2.50
□ 3 Jeff Bagwell	20.00	9.00	2.50
□ 4 Ken Griffey Jr.	40.00	18.00	5.00
□ 5 Paul O'Neill	5.00	2.20	.60
□ 6 Frank Thomas	40.00	18.00	5.00

1996 Finest

The 1996 Finest set was issued in two series of 191 cards and 168 cards respectively, for a total of 359 cards. The six-card foil packs originally retailed for $5.00 each. A protective film, designed to keep the card from scratching and to maintain original gloss, covers the front. This product provides collectors with the opportunity to complete a number of sets within sets, each with a different degree of insertion. Each card is numbered twice to indicate the set count and the theme count. Series 1 set covers four distinct themes: Finest Phenoms, Finest Intimidators, Finest Gamers and Finest Sterling. Within the first three themes, some players will be common (bronze trim), some uncommon (silver) and some rare (gold). Finest Sterling consists of star players included within one of the other three themes, but featured with a new design and different photography. The breakdown for the player selection of common, uncommon and rare cards is completely random. There are 110 common, 55 uncommon (1:4 packs) and 25 rare cards (1:24 packs). Series 2 covers four distict themes also with common, uncommon and rare cards seeded at the same ratio. The four themes are: Finest Franchises which features 36 team leaders and bonafide superstars, Finest Additions which features 47 players who have switched teams in '96, Finest Prodigies which features 45 best up-and-coming players, and Finest Sterling with 39 top stars. In addition to the cards' special borders, each card will also have either "common," "uncommon", or "rare" written within the numbering box on the card backs to let collectors know which type of card they hold.

	MINT	NRMT	EXC
COMPLETE SET (359)	1500.00	700.00	190.00
COMPLETE SERIES 1 (191)	1000.00	450.00	125.00
COMPLETE SERIES 2 (168)	500.00	220.00	60.00
COMP.BRONZE SET (220)	70.00	32.00	8.75
COMP.BRONZE SER.1 (110)	30.00	13.50	3.70
COMP.BRONZE SER.2 (110)	40.00	18.00	5.00
COMMON BRONZE	.25	.11	.03
COMP.GOLD SET (48)	1200.00	550.00	150.00
COMP.GOLD SER.1 (26)	800.00	350.00	100.00
COMP.GOLD SER.2 (22)	400.00	180.00	50.00
COMMON GOLD	10.00	4.50	1.25
COMP.SILVER SET (91)	300.00	135.00	38.00
COMP.SILVER SER.1 (55)	200.00	90.00	25.00
COMP.SILVER SER.2 (36)	100.00	45.00	12.50
COMMON SILVER	2.50	1.10	.30

□ B5 Roberto Hernandez B	.25	.11	.03
□ B8 Terry Pendleton B	.50	.23	.06
□ B12 Ken Caminiti B	1.00	.45	.12
□ B15 Dan Miceli B	.25	.11	.03
□ B16 Chipper Jones B	4.00	1.80	.50
□ B17 John Wetteland B	.50	.23	.06
□ B19 Tim Naehring B	.25	.11	.03
□ B21 Eddie Murray B	1.50	.70	.19
□ B23 Kevin Appier B	.50	.23	.06
□ B24 Ken Griffey Jr. B	6.00	2.70	.75
□ B26 Brian McRae B	.50	.23	.06
□ B27 Pedro Martinez B	.50	.23	.06
□ B28 Brian Jordan B	.50	.23	.06
□ B29 Mike Fetters B	.25	.11	.03
□ B30 Carlos Delgado B	.50	.23	.06
□ B31 Shane Reynolds B	.25	.11	.03
□ B32 Terry Steinbach B	.50	.23	.06
□ B34 Mark Leiter B	.25	.11	.03
□ B36 David Segui B	.25	.11	.03
□ B40 Fred McGriff B	.75	.35	.09
□ B44 Glenallen Hill B	.25	.11	.03
□ B45 Brady Anderson B	.75	.35	.09
□ B47 Jim Thome B	1.25	.55	.16
□ B48 Frank Thomas B	6.00	2.70	.75
□ B49 Chuck Knoblauch B	.75	.35	.09
□ B50 Len Dykstra B	.50	.23	.06
□ B53 Tom Pagnozzi B	.25	.11	.03
□ B55 Ricky Bones B	.25	.11	.03
□ B56 David Justice B	.50	.23	.06
□ B57 Steve Avery B	.25	.11	.03
□ B58 Robby Thompson B	.25	.11	.03
□ B61 Tony Gwynn B	2.50	1.10	.30
□ B63 Denny Neagle B	.50	.23	.06
□ B67 Robin Ventura B	.50	.23	.06
□ B70 Kevin Seitzer B	.25	.11	.03
□ B71 Ramon Martinez B	.50	.23	.06
□ B75 Brian L.Hunter B	.50	.23	.06
□ B76 Alan Benes B	.50	.23	.06
□ B80 Ozzie Guillen B	.25	.11	.03
□ B82 Benji Gil B	.25	.11	.03
□ B85 Todd Hundley B	.50	.23	.06
□ B87 Pat Hentgen B	.50	.23	.06
□ B89 Chuck Finley B	.25	.11	.03
□ B92 Derek Jeter B	4.00	1.80	.50
□ B93 Paul O'Neill B	.50	.23	.06
□ B94 Darrin Fletcher B	.25	.11	.03
□ B96 Delino DeShields B	.25	.11	.03
□ B97 Tim Salmon B	.75	.35	.09
□ B98 John Olerud B	.25	.11	.03
□ B101 Tim Wakefield B	.25	.11	.03
□ B103 Dave Stevens B	.25	.11	.03
□ B104 Orlando Merced B	.25	.11	.03
□ B106 Jay Bell B	.25	.11	.03
□ B107 John Burkett B	.25	.11	.03
□ B108 Chris Hoiles B	.25	.11	.03
□ B110 Dave Nilsson B	.25	.11	.03
□ B111 Rod Beck B	.25	.11	.03
□ B113 Mike Piazza B	4.00	1.80	.50
□ B114 Mark Langston B	.25	.11	.03
□ B116 Rico Brogna B	.25	.11	.03
□ B118 Tom Goodwin B	.25	.11	.03
□ B119 Bryan Rekar B	.25	.11	.03
□ B120 David Cone B	.50	.23	.06
□ B122 Andy Pettitte B	2.00	.90	.25
□ B123 Chili Davis B	.50	.23	.06
□ B124 John Smoltz B	1.00	.45	.12
□ B125 Heathcliff Slocumb B	.25	.11	.03
□ B126 Dante Bichette B	.75	.35	.09
□ B128 Alex Gonzalez B	.25	.11	.03
□ B129 Jeff Montgomery B	.25	.11	.03
□ B131 Denny Martinez B	.50	.23	.06
□ B132 Mel Rojas B	.25	.11	.03
□ B133 Derek Bell B	.50	.23	.06
□ B134 Trevor Hoffman B	.25	.11	.03
□ B136 Darren Daulton B	.50	.23	.06
□ B137 Pete Schourek B	.25	.11	.03
□ B138 Phil Nevin B	.25	.11	.03
□ B139 Andres Galarraga B	.75	.35	.09
□ B140 Chad Fonville B	.25	.11	.03
□ B144 J.T. Snow B	.25	.11	.03
□ B146 Barry Bonds B	1.50	.70	.19
□ B147 Orel Hershiser B	.50	.23	.06
□ B148 Quilvio Veras B	.25	.11	.03
□ B149 Will Clark B	.75	.35	.09
□ B150 Jose Rijo B	.25	.11	.03
□ B152 Travis Fryman B	.50	.23	.06
□ B154 Alex Fernandez B	.50	.23	.06
□ B155 Wade Boggs B	.75	.35	.09
□ B156 Troy Percival B	.50	.23	.06
□ B157 Moises Alou B	.50	.23	.06
□ B158 Javy Lopez B	.50	.23	.06
□ B159 Jason Giambi B	.50	.23	.06
□ B162 Mark McGwire B	2.00	.90	.25
□ B163 Eric Karros B	.50	.23	.06
□ B166 Mickey Tettleton B	.25	.11	.03
□ B167 Barry Larkin B	.75	.35	.09
□ B169 Ruben Sierra B	.50	.23	.06
□ B170 Bill Swift B	.25	.11	.03
□ B172 Chad Curtis B	.25	.11	.03
□ B173 Dean Palmer B	.50	.23	.06
□ B175 Bobby Bonilla B	.50	.23	.06
□ B176 Greg Colbrunn B	.25	.11	.03
□ B177 Jose Mesa B	.50	.23	.06
□ B178 Mike Greenwell B	.25	.11	.03
□ B181 Doug Drabek B	.25	.11	.03
□ B183 Wilson Alvarez B	.25	.11	.03
□ B184 Marty Cordova B	.75	.35	.09
□ B185 Hal Morris B	.25	.11	.03
□ B187 Carlos Garcia B	.25	.11	.03
□ B190 Marquis Grissom B	.50	.23	.06
□ B193 Will Clark B	.75	.35	.09
□ B194 Paul Molitor B	1.25	.55	.16
□ B195 Kenny Rogers B	.25	.11	.03
□ B196 Reggie Sanders B	.50	.23	.06
□ B199 Raul Mondesi B	.75	.35	.09
□ B200 Lance Johnson B	.50	.23	.06
□ B201 Alvin Morman B	.25	.11	.03
□ B203 Jack McDowell B	.50	.23	.06
□ B204 Randy Myers B	.25	.11	.03
□ B205 Harold Baines B	.50	.23	.06
□ B206 Marty Cordova B	.75	.35	.09
□ B207 Rich Hunter B	.50	.23	.06
□ B208 Al Leiter B	.25	.11	.03
□ B209 Greg Gagne B	.25	.11	.03
□ B210 Ben McDonald B	.25	.11	.03
□ B212 Terry Adams B	.25	.11	.03
□ B213 Paul Sorrento B	.25	.11	.03
□ B214 Albert Belle B	2.50	1.10	.30
□ B215 Mike Blowers B	.25	.11	.03
□ B216 Jim Edmonds B	.50	.23	.06
□ B217 Felipe Crespo B	.25	.11	.03
□ B219 Shawon Dunston B	.25	.11	.03
□ B220 Jimmy Haynes B	.25	.11	.03
□ B221 Jose Canseco B	.75	.35	.09
□ B222 Eric Davis B	.25	.11	.03
□ B224 Tim Raines B	.50	.23	.06
□ B225 Tony Phillips B	.50	.23	.06
□ B226 Charlie Hayes B	.25	.11	.03
□ B227 Eric Owens B	.25	.11	.03
□ B228 Roberto Alomar B	1.25	.55	.16
□ B233 Kenny Lofton B	1.50	.70	.19
□ B236 Mark McGwire B	2.00	.90	.25
□ B237 Jay Buhner B	.75	.35	.09
□ B238 Craig Biggio B	.50	.23	.06
□ B240 Barry Bonds B	1.50	.70	.19
□ B244 Ron Gant B	.50	.23	.06
□ B245 Paul Wilson B	.50	.23	.06
□ B246 Todd Hollandsworth B	.75	.35	.09
□ B247 Todd Zeile B	.25	.11	.03
□ B248 David Justice B	.50	.23	.06
□ B250 Moises Alou B	.50	.23	.06
□ B251 Bob Wolcott B	.25	.11	.03
□ B252 David Wells B	.25	.11	.03
□ B253 Juan Gonzalez B	3.00	1.35	.35
□ B254 Andres Galarraga B	.75	.35	.09
□ B255 Dave Hollins B	.25	.11	.03
□ B257 Sammy Sosa B	1.00	.45	.12
□ B258 Ivan Rodriguez B	1.25	.55	.16
□ B259 Bip Roberts B	.25	.11	.03
□ B260 Tino Martinez B	.50	.23	.06
□ B262 Mike Stanley B	.25	.11	.03
□ B264 Butch Huskey B	.25	.11	.03
□ B265 Jeff Conine B	.50	.23	.06
□ B267 Mark Grace B	.75	.35	.09
□ B268 Jason Schmidt B	.50	.23	.06
□ B269 Otis Nixon B	.25	.11	.03
□ B271 Kirby Puckett B	2.50	1.10	.30
□ B273 Andy Benes B	.50	.23	.06
□ B275 Mike Piazza B	4.00	1.80	.50
□ B276 Rey Ordonez B	.75	.35	.09
□ B278 Gary Gaetti B	.25	.11	.03
□ B280 Robin Ventura B	.50	.23	.06
□ B281 Cal Ripken B	5.00	2.20	.60
□ B282 Carlos Baerga B	.50	.23	.06
□ B283 Roger Cedeno B	.25	.11	.03
□ B285 Terrell Wade B	.25	.11	.03
□ B286 Kevin Brown B	.50	.23	.06
□ B287 Rafael Palmeiro B	.75	.35	.09
□ B288 Mo Vaughn B	1.50	.70	.19
□ B292 Bob Tewksbury B	.25	.11	.03
□ B297 T.J. Mathews B	.25	.11	.03
□ B298 Manny Ramirez B	1.50	.70	.19
□ B299 Jeff Bagwell B	2.50	1.10	.30
□ B301 Wade Boggs B	.75	.35	.09
□ B303 Steve Gibralter B	.25	.11	.03
□ B304 B.J. Surhoff B	.25	.11	.03
□ B306 Royce Clayton B	.25	.11	.03
□ B307 Sal Fasano B	.25	.11	.03
□ B309 Gary Sheffield B	1.00	.45	.12
□ B310 Ken Hill B	.25	.11	.03
□ B311 Joe Girardi B	.25	.11	.03
□ B312 Matt Lawton B	.25	.11	.03
□ B314 Julio Franco B	.50	.23	.06
□ B315 Joe Carter B	.50	.23	.06
□ B316 Brooks Kieschnick B	.50	.23	.06
□ B318 Heathcliff Slocumb B	.25	.11	.03
□ B319 Barry Larkin B	.75	.35	.09
□ B320 Tony Gwynn B	2.50	1.10	.30
□ B322 Frank Thomas B	6.00	2.70	.75
□ B323 Edgar Martinez B	.75	.35	.09
□ B325 Henry Rodriguez B	.50	.23	.06
□ B326 Marvin Benard B	.25	.11	.03
□ B329 Ugueth Urbina B	.25	.11	.03
□ B331 Roger Salkeld B	.25	.11	.03
□ B332 Edgar Renteria B	.75	.35	.09
□ B333 Ryan Klesko B	1.00	.45	.12
□ B334 Ray Lankford B	.50	.23	.06
□ B336 Justin Thompson B	.50	.23	.06
□ B339 Mark Clark B	.25	.11	.03
□ B340 Ruben Rivera B	1.25	.55	.16
□ B342 Matt Williams B	.75	.35	.09
□ B343 Francisco Cordova B	.25	.11	.03
□ B344 Cecil Fielder B	.50	.23	.06
□ B348 Mark Grudzielanek B	.25	.11	.03
□ B349 Ron Coomer B	.25	.11	.03
□ B351 Rich Aurilia B	.25	.11	.03
□ B352 Jose Herrera B	.25	.11	.03
□ B356 Tony Clark B	1.25	.55	.16
□ B358 Dan Naulty B	.25	.11	.03
□ B359 Checklist B	.25	.11	.03
□ G4 Marty Cordova G	12.00	5.50	1.50
□ G6 Tony Gwynn G	40.00	18.00	5.00
□ G9 Albert Belle G	40.00	18.00	5.00
□ G18 Kirby Puckett G	40.00	18.00	5.00
□ G20 Karim Garcia G	20.00	9.00	2.50
□ G25 Cal Ripken G	80.00	36.00	10.00
□ G33 Hideo Nomo G	25.00	11.00	3.10
□ G39 Ryne Sandberg G	25.00	11.00	3.10
□ G42 Jeff Bagwell G	40.00	18.00	5.00
□ G51 Jason Isringhausen G	10.00	4.50	1.25
□ G64 Mo Vaughn G	25.00	11.00	3.10
□ G66 Dante Bichette G	12.00	5.50	1.50
□ G74 Mark McGwire G	30.00	13.50	3.70
□ G81 Kenny Lofton G	25.00	11.00	3.10
□ G83 Jim Edmonds G	10.00	4.50	1.25
□ G90 Mike Mussina G	20.00	9.00	2.50
□ G100 Jeff Conine G	10.00	4.50	1.25
□ G102 Johnny Damon G	10.00	4.50	1.25
□ G105 Barry Bonds G	25.00	11.00	3.10
□ G117 Jose Canseco G	12.00	5.50	1.50
□ G135 Ken Griffey Jr. G	100.00	45.00	12.50
□ G141 Chipper Jones G	60.00	27.00	7.50
□ G145 Greg Maddux G	60.00	27.00	7.50
□ G164 Jay Buhner G	12.00	5.50	1.50
□ G186 Frank Thomas G	100.00	45.00	12.50
□ G191 Checklist G	10.00	4.50	1.25
□ G192 Chipper Jones G	60.00	27.00	7.50
□ G197 Roberto Alomar G	20.00	9.00	2.50
□ G198 Dennis Eckersley G	10.00	4.50	1.25
□ G202 George Arias G	10.00	4.50	1.25
□ G232 Hideo Nomo G	25.00	11.00	3.10
□ G243 Chris Snopek G	10.00	4.50	1.25
□ G249 Tim Salmon G	12.00	5.50	1.50
□ G266 Matt Williams G	12.00	5.50	1.50
□ G270 Randy Johnson G	15.00	6.75	1.85
□ G279 Paul Molitor G	20.00	9.00	2.50
□ G290 Cecil Fielder G	10.00	4.50	1.25
□ G294 Livan Hernandez G	10.00	4.50	1.25
□ G300 Marty Janzen G	10.00	4.50	1.25
□ G308 Ron Gant G	10.00	4.50	1.25
□ G321 Ryan Klesko G	15.00	6.75	1.85
□ G324 Jermaine Dye G	20.00	9.00	2.50
□ G330 Jason Giambi G	12.00	5.50	1.50
□ G335 Edgar Martinez G	10.00	4.50	1.25
□ G338 Rey Ordonez G	15.00	6.75	1.85
□ G347 Sammy Sosa G	15.00	6.75	1.85
□ G354 Juan Gonzalez G	50.00	22.00	6.25
□ G355 Craig Biggio G	10.00	4.50	1.25
□ S1 Greg Maddux S UER 95 stats listed as Mariners	20.00	9.00	2.50
□ S2 Bernie Williams S	6.00	2.70	.75
□ S3 Ivan Rodriguez S	8.00	3.60	1.00
□ S7 Barry Larkin S	4.00	1.80	.50
□ S10 Ray Lankford S	3.00	1.35	.35
□ S11 Mike Piazza S	20.00	9.00	2.50
□ S13 Larry Walker S	3.00	1.35	.35
□ S14 Matt Williams S	4.00	1.80	.50
□ S22 Tim Salmon S	4.00	1.80	.50
□ S35 Edgar Martinez S	4.00	1.80	.50
□ S37 Gregg Jefferies S	3.00	1.35	.35
□ S38 Bill Pulsipher S	2.50	1.10	.30
□ S41 Shawn Green S	2.50	1.10	.30
□ S43 Jim Abbott S	2.50	1.10	.30
□ S46 Roger Clemens S	6.00	2.70	.75
□ S52 Rondell White S	3.00	1.35	.35
□ S54 Dennis Eckersley S	3.00	1.35	.35
□ S59 Hideo Nomo S	8.00	3.60	1.00
□ S60 Gary Sheffield S	5.00	2.20	.60
□ S62 Will Clark S	4.00	1.80	.50
□ S65 Bret Boone S	2.50	1.10	.30
□ S68 Rafael Palmeiro S	4.00	1.80	.50
□ S69 Carlos Baerga S	3.00	1.35	.35
□ S72 Tom Glavine S	4.00	1.80	.50
□ S73 Garret Anderson S	3.00	1.35	.35
□ S77 Randy Johnson S	5.00	2.20	.60
□ S78 Jeff King S	2.50	1.10	.30
□ S79 Kirby Puckett S	12.00	5.50	1.50
□ S84 Cecil Fielder S	3.00	1.35	.35
□ S86 Reggie Sanders S	3.00	1.35	.35
□ S88 Ryan Klesko S	5.00	2.20	.60
□ S91 John Valentin S	2.50	1.10	.30
□ S95 Manny Ramirez S	8.00	3.60	1.00
□ S99 Vinny Castilla S	3.00	1.35	.35
□ S109 Carlos Perez S	2.50	1.10	.30
□ S112 Craig Biggio S	3.00	1.35	.35
□ S115 Juan Gonzalez S	15.00	6.75	1.85
□ S121 Ray Durham S	3.00	1.35	.35
□ S127 C.J. Nitkowski S	2.50	1.10	.30
□ S130 Raul Mondesi S	4.00	1.80	.50
□ S142 Lee Smith S	3.00	1.35	.35
□ S143 Joe Carter S	3.00	1.35	.35
□ S151 Mo Vaughn S	8.00	3.60	1.00
□ S153 Frank Rodriguez S	2.50	1.10	.30
□ S160 Steve Finley S	3.00	1.35	.35
□ S161 Jeff Bagwell S	12.00	5.50	1.50
□ S165 Cal Ripken S	25.00	11.00	3.10
□ S168 Lyle Mouton S	2.50	1.10	.30
□ S171 Sammy Sosa S	5.00	2.20	.60
□ S174 John Franco S	2.50	1.10	.30
□ S179 Greg Vaughn S	3.00	1.35	.35
□ S180 Mark Wohlers S	3.00	1.35	.35
□ S182 Paul O'Neill S	3.00	1.35	.35
□ S188 Albert Belle S	12.00	5.50	1.50
□ S189 Mark Grace S	4.00	1.80	.50
□ S211 Ernie Young S	2.50	1.10	.30
□ S218 Fred McGriff S	4.00	1.80	.50
□ S223 Kimera Bartee S	2.50	1.10	.30
□ S229 Rickey Henderson S	3.00	1.35	.35
□ S230 Sterling Hitchcock S	2.50	1.10	.30
□ S231 Bernard Gilkey S	3.00	1.35	.35
□ S234 Ryne Sandberg S	8.00	3.60	1.00
□ S235 Greg Maddux S	20.00	9.00	2.50
□ S239 Todd Stottlemyre S	2.50	1.10	.30
□ S241 Jason Kendall S	6.00	2.70	.75
□ S242 Paul O'Neill S	3.00	1.35	.35
□ S256 Devon White S	2.50	1.10	.30
□ S261 Chuck Knoblauch S	4.00	1.80	.50
□ S263 Wally Joyner S	3.00	1.35	.35
□ S272 Andy Fox S	2.50	1.10	.30
□ S274 Sean Berry S	2.50	1.10	.30
□ S277 Benito Santiago S	2.50	1.10	.30
□ S284 Chad Mottola S	2.50	1.10	.30

	MINT	NRMT	EXC
☐ S289 Dante Bichette S	4.00	1.80	.50
☐ S291 Doc Gooden S	3.00	1.35	.35
☐ S293 Kevin Mitchell S	2.50	1.10	.30
☐ S295 Russ Davis S	2.50	1.10	.30
☐ S296 Chan Ho Park S	3.00	1.35	.35
☐ S302 Larry Walker S	3.00	1.35	.35
☐ S305 Ken Griffey Jr. S	30.00	13.50	3.70
☐ S313 Billy Wagner S	3.00	1.35	.35
☐ S317 Mike Grace S	4.00	1.80	.50
☐ S327 Kenny Lofton S	8.00	3.60	1.00
☐ S328 Derek Bell S	3.00	1.35	.35
☐ S337 Gary Sheffield S	5.00	2.20	.60
☐ S341 Mark Grace S	4.00	1.80	.50
☐ S345 Andres Galarraga S	4.00	1.80	.50
☐ S346 Brady Anderson S	4.00	1.80	.50
☐ S350 Derek Jeter S	15.00	6.75	1.85
☐ S353 Jay Buhner S	4.00	1.80	.50
☐ S357 Tino Martinez S	3.00	1.35	.35

1996 Finest Refractors

This 359-card set is parallel to the basic 1996 Finest set. The first 191 cards are parallel to the regular Series 1 with the second 168 cards parallel to regular Series 2. The word "refractor" is printed above the numbers on the card backs. The rate of insertion is one in 12 for a Bronze refractor (common), one in 48 for a Silver refractor (uncommon), and one in 288 for a Gold refractor (rare).

	MINT	NRMT	EXC
COMPLETE SET (359)	9400.00	4200.00	1200.00
COMPLETE SERIES 1 (191)	5800.00	2600.00	700.00
COMPLETE SERIES 2 (168)	3600.00	1600.00	450.00
COMP.BRONZE SET (220)	1400.00	650.00	180.00
COMP.BRONZE SET (110)	600.00	275.00	75.00
COMP.BRONZE SER.2 (110)	800.00	350.00	100.00
COMMON BRONZE	3.00	1.35	.35
*BRONZE STARS: 7.5X to 15 BASIC CARDS			
COMP.GOLD SET (48)	6000.00	2700.00	750.00
COMP.GOLD SER.1 (26)	4000.00	1800.00	500.00
COMP.GOLD SER.2 (22)	2000.00	900.00	250.00
COMMON GOLD	40.00	18.00	5.00
*GOLD STARS: 2.5X to 5X BASIC CARDS			
COMP.SILVER SET (91)	2000.00	900.00	250.00
COMP.SILVER SER.1 (55)	1200.00	550.00	150.00
COMP.SILVER SER.2 (36)	800.00	350.00	100.00
COMMON SILVER	10.00	4.50	1.25
*SILVER STARS: 3X to 6X BASIC CARDS			

	MINT	NRMT	EXC
☐ B12 Ken Caminiti B	12.00	5.50	1.50
☐ B16 Chipper Jones B	50.00	22.00	6.25
☐ B21 Eddie Murray B	20.00	9.00	2.50
☐ B24 Ken Griffey Jr. B	80.00	36.00	10.00
☐ B47 Jim Thome B	15.00	6.75	1.85
☐ B48 Frank Thomas B	80.00	36.00	10.00
☐ B61 Tony Gwynn B	30.00	13.50	3.70
☐ B92 Derek Jeter B	50.00	22.00	6.25
☐ B113 Mike Piazza B	50.00	22.00	6.25
☐ B122 Andy Pettitte B	20.00	9.00	2.50
☐ B124 John Smoltz B	12.00	5.50	1.50
☐ B146 Barry Bonds B	20.00	9.00	2.50
☐ B162 Mark McGwire B	25.00	11.00	3.10
☐ B194 Paul Molitor B	15.00	6.75	1.85
☐ B214 Albert Belle B	30.00	13.50	3.70
☐ B228 Roberto Alomar B	15.00	6.75	1.85
☐ B233 Kenny Lofton B	20.00	9.00	2.50
☐ B236 Mark McGwire B	25.00	11.00	3.10
☐ B240 Barry Bonds B	20.00	9.00	2.50
☐ B253 Juan Gonzalez B	40.00	18.00	5.00
☐ B257 Sammy Sosa B	12.00	5.50	1.50
☐ B258 Ivan Rodriguez B	20.00	9.00	2.50
☐ B271 Kirby Puckett B	30.00	13.50	3.70
☐ B275 Mike Piazza B	50.00	22.00	6.25
☐ B281 Cal Ripken B	60.00	27.00	7.50
☐ B288 Mo Vaughn B	20.00	9.00	2.50
☐ B298 Manny Ramirez B	20.00	9.00	2.50
☐ B299 Jeff Bagwell B	30.00	13.50	3.70
☐ B309 Gary Sheffield B	12.00	5.50	1.50
☐ B320 Tony Gwynn B	30.00	13.50	3.70
☐ B322 Frank Thomas B	80.00	36.00	10.00
☐ B333 Ryan Klesko B	12.00	5.50	1.50
☐ B340 Ruben Rivera B	12.00	5.50	1.50
☐ B356 Tony Clark B	12.00	5.50	1.50
☐ G4 Marty Cordova G	60.00	27.00	7.50
☐ G6 Tony Gwynn G	200.00	90.00	25.00
☐ G9 Albert Belle G	200.00	90.00	25.00
☐ G18 Kirby Puckett G	200.00	90.00	25.00
☐ G20 Karim Garcia G	100.00	45.00	12.50
☐ G25 Cal Ripken G	400.00	180.00	50.00
☐ G33 Hideo Nomo G	125.00	55.00	15.50
☐ G39 Ryne Sandberg G	125.00	55.00	15.50
☐ G42 Jeff Bagwell G	200.00	90.00	25.00
☐ G51 Jason Isringhausen G	50.00	22.00	6.25
☐ G64 Mo Vaughn G	125.00	55.00	15.50
☐ G66 Dante Bichette G	60.00	27.00	7.50
☐ G74 Mark McGwire G	150.00	70.00	19.00
☐ G81 Kenny Lofton G	125.00	55.00	15.50
☐ G83 Jim Edmonds G	50.00	22.00	6.25
☐ G90 Mike Mussina G	100.00	45.00	12.50
☐ G100 Jeff Conine G	50.00	22.00	6.25
☐ G102 Johnny Damon G	50.00	22.00	6.25
☐ G105 Barry Bonds G	125.00	55.00	15.50
☐ G117 Jose Canseco G	60.00	27.00	7.50
☐ G135 Ken Griffey Jr. G	500.00	220.00	60.00
☐ G141 Chipper Jones G	300.00	135.00	38.00
☐ G145 Greg Maddux G	300.00	135.00	38.00
☐ G164 Jay Buhner G	60.00	27.00	7.50
☐ G186 Frank Thomas G	500.00	220.00	60.00
☐ G191 Checklist G	40.00	18.00	5.00
☐ G192 Chipper Jones G	300.00	135.00	38.00
☐ G197 Roberto Alomar G	100.00	45.00	12.50
☐ G198 Dennis Eckersley G	50.00	22.00	6.25
☐ G202 George Arias G	40.00	18.00	5.00
☐ G232 Hideo Nomo G	125.00	55.00	15.50
☐ G243 Chris Snopek G	40.00	18.00	5.00
☐ G249 Tim Salmon G	60.00	27.00	7.50
☐ G266 Matt Williams G	60.00	27.00	7.50
☐ G270 Randy Johnson G	80.00	36.00	10.00
☐ G279 Paul Molitor G	100.00	45.00	12.50
☐ G290 Cecil Fielder G	50.00	22.00	6.25
☐ G294 Livan Hernandez G	40.00	18.00	5.00
☐ G300 Marty Janzen G	40.00	18.00	5.00
☐ G308 Ron Gant G	50.00	22.00	6.25
☐ G321 Ryan Klesko G	80.00	36.00	10.00
☐ G324 Jermaine Dye G	125.00	55.00	15.50
☐ G330 Jason Giambi G	60.00	27.00	7.50
☐ G335 Edgar Martinez G	50.00	22.00	6.25
☐ G338 Rey Ordonez G	60.00	27.00	7.50
☐ G347 Sammy Sosa G	80.00	36.00	10.00
☐ G354 Juan Gonzalez G	250.00	110.00	31.00
☐ G355 Craig Biggio G	50.00	22.00	6.25
☐ S1 Greg Maddux S UER	100.00	45.00	12.50
95 stats listed as Mariners			
☐ S2 Bernie Williams S	30.00	13.50	3.70
☐ S3 Ivan Rodriguez S	40.00	18.00	5.00
☐ S7 Barry Larkin S	20.00	9.00	2.50
☐ S11 Mike Piazza S	100.00	45.00	12.50
☐ S13 Larry Walker S	20.00	9.00	2.50
☐ S14 Matt Williams S	20.00	9.00	2.50
☐ S22 Tim Salmon S	20.00	9.00	2.50
☐ S46 Roger Clemens S	30.00	13.50	3.70
☐ S59 Hideo Nomo S	40.00	18.00	5.00
☐ S60 Gary Sheffield S	25.00	11.00	3.10
☐ S62 Will Clark S	20.00	9.00	2.50
☐ S68 Rafael Palmeiro S	20.00	9.00	2.50
☐ S72 Tom Glavine S	20.00	9.00	2.50
☐ S77 Randy Johnson S	25.00	11.00	3.10
☐ S79 Kirby Puckett S	60.00	27.00	7.50
☐ S88 Ryan Klesko S	25.00	11.00	3.10
☐ S95 Manny Ramirez S	40.00	18.00	5.00
☐ S115 Juan Gonzalez S	80.00	36.00	10.00
☐ S151 Mo Vaughn S	40.00	18.00	5.00
☐ S161 Jeff Bagwell S	60.00	27.00	7.50
☐ S165 Cal Ripken S	120.00	55.00	15.00
☐ S171 Sammy Sosa S	25.00	11.00	3.10
☐ S188 Albert Belle S	60.00	27.00	7.50
☐ S218 Fred McGriff S	20.00	9.00	2.50
☐ S234 Ryne Sandberg S	40.00	18.00	5.00
☐ S235 Greg Maddux S	100.00	45.00	12.50
☐ S241 Jason Kendall S	20.00	9.00	2.50
☐ S261 Chuck Knoblauch S	25.00	11.00	3.10
☐ S289 Dante Bichette S	20.00	9.00	2.50
☐ S302 Larry Walker S	20.00	9.00	2.50
☐ S305 Ken Griffey Jr. S	150.00	70.00	19.00
☐ S327 Kenny Lofton S	40.00	18.00	5.00
☐ S337 Gary Sheffield S	25.00	11.00	3.10
☐ S345 Andres Galarraga S	20.00	9.00	2.50
☐ S346 Brady Anderson S	20.00	9.00	2.50
☐ S350 Derek Jeter S	100.00	45.00	12.50
☐ S353 Jay Buhner S	20.00	9.00	2.50

1996 Finest Landmark

This four-card limited edition medallion set came with a Certificate of Authenticity and was produced by Topps. Only 2,000 sets were made. The fronts feature color action player photos on a gold ball and star metallic background. The backs carry player biographical and career information including batting records.

	MINT	NRMT	EXC
COMPLETE SET (4)	120.00	55.00	15.00
COMMON CARD (1-4)	12.00	5.50	1.50
☐ 1 Greg Maddux	30.00	13.50	3.70
☐ 2 Albert Belle	25.00	11.00	3.10
☐ 3 Cal Ripken	60.00	27.00	7.50
☐ 4 Eddie Murray	12.00	5.50	1.50

1997 Finest Promos

This five-card set features one promo card for each of the five themes found in the 1997 Finest Series I set. The fronts, backs, and card numbers are identical to the regular set with the exception of the words, "Promotional Sample Not for Resale" printed in red across the back. The cards are checklisted below according to their numbers in the regular set.

	MINT	NRMT	EXC
COMPLETE SET (5)	40.00	18.00	5.00
COMMON CARD	5.00	2.20	.60
☐ 1 Barry Bonds C	5.00	2.20	.60
☐ 15 Derek Jeter C	12.00	5.50	1.50
☐ 30 Mark McGwire C	10.00	4.50	1.25
☐ 143 Hideo Nomo U	15.00	6.75	1.85
☐ 159 Jeff Bagwell R	10.00	4.50	1.25

1997 Finest

The 175-card Finest I set was issued in six-card packs with a suggested retail of $5.00. The fronts feature a borderless action player photo while the backs carry player information with another player photo. The set is divided into five distinct themes: Finest Hurlers (top pitchers), Finest Blue Chips (up-and-coming future stars), Finest Power (long-ball hitters), Finest Warriors (superstar players), and Finest Masters (hottest players). All five themes have common cards (#1-100) designated with bronze trim, uncommon (#101-150) with silver trim and an insertion rate of one in four, and rare (#151-175) with gold trim and an insertion rate of one in twenty-four. The cards are numbered on the backs within the whole set and within the theme set.

	MINT	NRMT	EXC
COMPLETE SERIES 1 (175)	650.00	300.00	80.00
COMP.BRONZE SER.1 (100)	40.00	18.00	5.00
COMMON BRONZE (1-100)	.25	.11	.03
COMP.SILVER SER.1 (50)	150.00	70.00	19.00
COMMON SILVER (101-150)	1.50	.70	.19
COMP.GOLD SER.1 (25)	500.00	220.00	60.00
COMMON GOLD (151-175)	8.00	3.60	1.00

	MINT	NRMT	EXC
☐ 1 Barry Bonds B	1.25	.55	.16
☐ 2 Ryne Sandberg B	1.25	.55	.16
☐ 3 Brian Jordan B	.50	.23	.06
☐ 4 Rocky Coppinger B	.50	.23	.06
☐ 5 Dante Bichette B UER	.50	.23	.06
Card is erroneously numbered 155			
☐ 6 Al Martin B	.25	.11	.03
☐ 7 Charles Nagy B	.50	.23	.06
☐ 8 Otis Nixon B	.25	.11	.03
☐ 9 Mark Johnson B	.25	.11	.03
☐ 10 Jeff Bagwell B	2.00	.90	.25
☐ 11 Ken Hill B	.25	.11	.03
☐ 12 Willie Adams B	.25	.11	.03
☐ 13 Raul Mondesi B	.50	.23	.06
☐ 14 Reggie Sanders B	.50	.23	.06
☐ 15 Derek Jeter B	3.00	1.35	.35
☐ 16 Jermaine Dye B	.75	.35	.09
☐ 17 Edgar Renteria B	.50	.23	.06
☐ 18 Travis Fryman B	.50	.23	.06
☐ 19 Roberto Hernandez B	.25	.11	.03
☐ 20 Sammy Sosa B	.75	.35	.09
☐ 21 Garret Anderson B	.25	.11	.03
☐ 22 Rey Ordonez B	.50	.23	.06
☐ 23 Glenallen Hill B	.25	.11	.03
☐ 24 Dave Nilsson B	.25	.11	.03
☐ 25 Kevin Brown B	.50	.23	.06
☐ 26 Brian McRae B	.25	.11	.03
☐ 27 Joey Hamilton B	.50	.23	.06
☐ 28 Jamey Wright B	.50	.23	.06
☐ 29 Frank Thomas B	5.00	2.20	.60
☐ 30 Mark McGwire B	1.50	.70	.19
☐ 31 Ramon Martinez B	.50	.23	.06
☐ 32 Jaime Bluma B	.25	.11	.03
☐ 33 Frank Rodriguez B	.25	.11	.03
☐ 34 Andy Benes B	.25	.11	.03
☐ 35 Jay Buhner B	.50	.23	.06
☐ 36 Justin Thompson B	.50	.23	.06
☐ 37 Darin Erstad B	2.50	1.10	.30
☐ 38 Gregg Jefferies B	.25	.11	.03
☐ 39 Jeff D'Amico B	.50	.23	.06
☐ 40 Pedro Martinez B	.50	.23	.06
☐ 41 Nomar Garciaparra B	2.00	.90	.25
☐ 42 Jose Valentin B	.25	.11	.03
☐ 43 Pat Hentgen B	.50	.23	.06
☐ 44 Will Clark B	.50	.23	.06
☐ 45 Bernie Williams B	1.00	.45	.12
☐ 46 Luis Castillo B	.50	.23	.06
☐ 47 B.J. Surhoff B	.25	.11	.03
☐ 48 Greg Gagne B	.25	.11	.03
☐ 49 Pete Schourek B	.25	.11	.03
☐ 50 Mike Piazza B	3.00	1.35	.35
☐ 51 Dwight Gooden B	.50	.23	.06
☐ 52 Javy Lopez B	.50	.23	.06
☐ 53 Chuck Finley B	.25	.11	.03
☐ 54 James Baldwin B	.25	.11	.03
☐ 55 Jack McDowell B	.25	.11	.03
☐ 56 Royce Clayton B	.25	.11	.03
☐ 57 Carlos Delgado B	.50	.23	.06
☐ 58 Neifi Perez B	.50	.23	.06
☐ 59 Eddie Taubensee B	.25	.11	.03
☐ 60 Rafael Palmeiro B	.50	.23	.06
☐ 61 Marty Cordova B	.50	.23	.06
☐ 62 Wade Boggs B	.50	.23	.06
☐ 63 Rickey Henderson B	.50	.23	.06
☐ 64 Mike Hampton B	.25	.11	.03
☐ 65 Troy Percival B	.25	.11	.03
☐ 66 Barry Larkin B	.50	.23	.06
☐ 67 Jermaine Allensworth B	.50	.23	.06
☐ 68 Mark Clark B	.25	.11	.03
☐ 69 Mike Lansing B	.25	.11	.03
☐ 70 Mark Grudzielanek B	.25	.11	.03
☐ 71 Todd Stottlemyre B	.25	.11	.03
☐ 72 Juan Guzman B	.25	.11	.03
☐ 73 John Burkett B	.25	.11	.03
☐ 74 Wilson Alvarez B	.25	.11	.03
☐ 75 Ellis Burks B	.50	.23	.06
☐ 76 Bobby Higginson B	.50	.23	.06
☐ 77 Ricky Bottalico B	.25	.11	.03
☐ 78 Omar Vizquel B	.50	.23	.06
☐ 79 Paul Sorrento B	.25	.11	.03
☐ 80 Denny Neagle B	.25	.11	.03
☐ 81 Roger Pavlik B	.25	.11	.03
☐ 82 Mike Lieberthal B	.25	.11	.03
☐ 83 Devon White B	.25	.11	.03
☐ 84 John Olerud B	.50	.23	.06
☐ 85 Kevin Appier B	.50	.23	.06
☐ 86 Joe Girardi B	.25	.11	.03
☐ 87 Paul O'Neill B	.50	.23	.06
☐ 88 Mike Sweeney B	.50	.23	.06
☐ 89 John Smiley B	.25	.11	.03
☐ 90 Ivan Rodriguez B	1.25	.55	.16
☐ 91 Randy Myers B	.25	.11	.03
☐ 92 Bip Roberts B	.25	.11	.03
☐ 93 Jose Mesa B	.25	.11	.03
☐ 94 Paul Wilson B	.50	.23	.06
☐ 95 Mike Mussina B	1.00	.45	.12
☐ 96 Ben McDonald B	.25	.11	.03
☐ 97 John Mabry B	.25	.11	.03
☐ 98 Tom Goodwin B	.25	.11	.03
☐ 99 Edgar Martinez B	.50	.23	.06
☐ 100 Andruw Jones B	5.00	2.20	.60
☐ 101 Jose Canseco S	3.00	1.35	.35
☐ 102 Billy Wagner S	2.50	1.10	.30
☐ 103 Dante Bichette S	3.00	1.35	.35
☐ 104 Curt Schilling S	1.50	.70	.19
☐ 105 Dean Palmer S	1.50	.70	.19
☐ 106 Larry Walker S	2.50	1.10	.30
☐ 107 Bernie Williams S	5.00	2.20	.60
☐ 108 Chipper Jones S	15.00	6.75	1.85
☐ 109 Gary Sheffield S	4.00	1.80	.50
☐ 110 Randy Johnson S	4.00	1.80	.50
☐ 111 Roberto Alomar S	5.00	2.20	.60
☐ 112 Todd Walker S	10.00	4.50	1.25
☐ 113 Sandy Alomar Jr. S	1.50	.70	.19
☐ 114 John Jaha S	2.50	1.10	.30
☐ 115 Ken Caminiti S UER#'ed 135	4.00	1.80	.50
☐ 116 Ryan Klesko S	4.00	1.80	.50
☐ 117 Mariano Rivera S	2.50	1.10	.30
☐ 118 Jason Giambi S	2.50	1.10	.30
☐ 119 Lance Johnson S	1.50	.70	.19
☐ 120 Robin Ventura S	2.50	1.10	.30
☐ 121 Todd Hollandsworth S	2.50	1.10	.30
☐ 122 Johnny Damon S	1.50	.70	.19
☐ 123 William VanLandingham S	1.50	.70	.19
☐ 124 Jason Kendall S	2.50	1.10	.30
☐ 125 Vinny Castilla S	2.50	1.10	.30
☐ 126 Harold Baines S	1.50	.70	.19
☐ 127 Joe Carter S	3.00	1.35	.35
☐ 128 Craig Biggio S	2.50	1.10	.30
☐ 129 Tony Clark S	4.00	1.80	.50
☐ 130 Ron Gant S	2.50	1.10	.30
☐ 131 David Segui S	1.50	.70	.19
☐ 132 Steve Trachsel S	1.50	.70	.19
☐ 133 Scott Rolen S	10.00	4.50	1.25
☐ 134 Mike Stanley S	1.50	.70	.19
☐ 135 Cal Ripken S	20.00	9.00	2.50
☐ 136 John Smoltz S	4.00	1.80	.50
☐ 137 Bobby Jones S	1.50	.70	.19
☐ 138 Manny Ramirez S	6.00	2.70	.75
☐ 139 Ken Griffey Jr. S	25.00	11.00	3.10
☐ 140 Chuck Knoblauch S	4.00	1.80	.50
☐ 141 Mark Grace S	3.00	1.35	.35
☐ 142 Chris Snopek S	1.50	.70	.19
☐ 143 Hideo Nomo S	6.00	2.70	.75
☐ 144 Tim Salmon S	3.00	1.35	.35
☐ 145 David Cone S	2.50	1.10	.30
☐ 146 Eric Young S	2.50	1.10	.30
☐ 147 Jeff Brantley S	1.50	.70	.19
☐ 148 Jim Thome S	5.00	2.20	.60
☐ 149 Trevor Hoffman S	1.50	.70	.19
☐ 150 Juan Gonzalez S	12.00	5.50	1.50
☐ 151 Mike Piazza G	50.00	22.00	6.25
☐ 152 Ivan Rodriguez G	20.00	9.00	2.50
☐ 153 Mo Vaughn G	20.00	9.00	2.50
☐ 154 Brady Anderson G	8.00	3.60	1.00
☐ 155 Mark McGwire G	25.00	11.00	3.10
☐ 156 Rafael Palmeiro G	10.00	4.50	1.25
☐ 157 Barry Larkin G	10.00	4.50	1.25
☐ 158 Greg Maddux G	50.00	22.00	6.25
☐ 159 Jeff Bagwell G	30.00	13.50	3.70
☐ 160 Frank Thomas G	80.00	36.00	10.00
☐ 161 Ken Caminiti G	12.00	5.50	1.50
☐ 162 Andruw Jones G	80.00	36.00	10.00

☐ 163 Dennis Eckersley G	8.00	3.60	1.00
☐ 164 Jeff Conine G	8.00	3.60	1.00
☐ 165 Jim Edmonds G	8.00	3.60	1.00
☐ 166 Derek Jeter G	50.00	22.00	6.25
☐ 167 Vladimir Guerrero G	50.00	22.00	6.25
☐ 168 Sammy Sosa G	12.00	5.50	1.50
☐ 169 Tony Gwynn G	30.00	13.50	3.70
☐ 170 Andres Galarraga G	10.00	4.50	1.25
☐ 171 Todd Hundley G	8.00	3.60	1.00
☐ 172 Jay Buhner G UER#'d 164	10.00	4.50	1.25
☐ 173 Paul Molitor G	15.00	6.75	1.85
☐ 174 Kenny Lofton G	20.00	9.00	2.50
☐ 175 Barry Bonds G	20.00	9.00	2.50

1997 Finest Embossed

This 75-card set is parallel to regular set numbers 101-175. The first fifty cards feature an embossed version of cards #101-150 and have an insertion rate of one in 16. The last 25 are embossed die-cut versions of cards #151-175 with an insertion rate of one in 96 packs.

	MINT	NRMT	EXC
COMPLETE SERIES 1 (75)	1700.00	750.00	210.00
COMP.SILVER SER.1 (50)	500.00	220.00	60.00
COMMON SILVER (101-150)	5.00	2.20	.60
COMP.GOLD DC SER.1 (25)	1200.00	550.00	150.00
COMMON GOLD DC (151-175)	20.00	9.00	2.50
☐ 107 Bernie Williams S	15.00	6.75	1.85
☐ 108 Chipper Jones S	50.00	22.00	6.25
☐ 111 Roberto Alomar S	15.00	6.75	1.85
☐ 112 Todd Walker S	30.00	13.50	3.70
☐ 116 Ryan Klesko S	12.00	5.50	1.50
☐ 133 Scott Rolen S	30.00	13.50	3.70
☐ 135 Cal Ripken S	60.00	27.00	7.50
☐ 138 Manny Ramirez S	20.00	9.00	2.50
☐ 139 Ken Griffey Jr. S	80.00	36.00	10.00
☐ 143 Hideo Nomo S	20.00	9.00	2.50
☐ 148 Jim Thome S	15.00	6.75	1.85
☐ 150 Juan Gonzalez S	40.00	18.00	5.00
☐ 151 Mike Piazza G	125.00	55.00	15.50
☐ 152 Ivan Rodriguez G	50.00	22.00	6.25
☐ 153 Mo Vaughn G	50.00	22.00	6.25
☐ 155 Mark McGwire G	60.00	27.00	7.50
☐ 158 Greg Maddux G	125.00	55.00	15.50
☐ 159 Jeff Bagwell G	80.00	36.00	10.00
☐ 160 Frank Thomas G	200.00	90.00	25.00
☐ 162 Andruw Jones G	150.00	70.00	19.00
☐ 166 Derek Jeter G	125.00	55.00	15.50
☐ 167 Vladimir Guerrero G	100.00	45.00	12.50
☐ 169 Tony Gwynn G	80.00	36.00	10.00
☐ 173 Paul Molitor G	40.00	18.00	5.00
☐ 174 Kenny Lofton G	50.00	22.00	6.25
☐ 175 Barry Bonds G	50.00	22.00	6.25

1997 Finest Embossed Refractors

This 75-card set is parallel to regular set numbers 101-175 and is similar in design to the Finest Embossed parallel set with a stunning mosaic pattern. The last 25 cards are an embossed die-cut parallel version and display an extra-special hyper-plaid foil that brings each player to life. Cards #101-150 have an insertion rate of one in 192 and cards #151-175 have an insertion rate of one in 1152.

	MINT	NRMT	EXC
COMMON SILVER (101-150)	50.00	22.00	6.25
COMMON GOLD DC (151-175)	125.00	55.00	15.50
GOLD DC MINOR STARS	150.00	70.00	19.00
☐ 107 Bernie Williams S	100.00	45.00	12.50
☐ 108 Chipper Jones S	300.00	135.00	38.00
☐ 111 Roberto Alomar S	100.00	45.00	12.50
☐ 112 Todd Walker S	150.00	70.00	19.00
☐ 133 Scott Rolen S	150.00	70.00	19.00
☐ 135 Cal Ripken S	400.00	180.00	50.00
☐ 138 Manny Ramirez S	125.00	55.00	15.50
☐ 139 Ken Griffey Jr. S	500.00	220.00	60.00
☐ 143 Hideo Nomo S	125.00	55.00	15.50
☐ 148 Jim Thome S	100.00	45.00	12.50
☐ 150 Juan Gonzalez S	250.00	110.00	31.00
☐ 151 Mike Piazza G	750.00	350.00	95.00
☐ 152 Ivan Rodriguez G	300.00	135.00	38.00
☐ 153 Mo Vaughn G	300.00	135.00	38.00
☐ 155 Mark McGwire G	400.00	180.00	50.00
☐ 158 Greg Maddux G	750.00	350.00	95.00
☐ 159 Jeff Bagwell G	500.00	220.00	60.00
☐ 160 Frank Thomas G	1200.00	550.00	150.00
☐ 162 Andruw Jones G	1000.00	450.00	125.00
☐ 166 Derek Jeter G	750.00	350.00	95.00
☐ 167 Vladimir Guerrero G	600.00	275.00	75.00
☐ 169 Tony Gwynn G	500.00	220.00	60.00
☐ 173 Paul Molitor G	250.00	110.00	31.00
☐ 174 Kenny Lofton G	300.00	135.00	38.00
☐ 175 Barry Bonds G	300.00	135.00	38.00

1997 Finest Refractors

This 175-card set is parallel and similar in design to the regular set. The distinction is in the refractive quality of the card. Cards #1-100 have an insertion rate of one in 12. Cards #101-150 have an insertion rate of one in 48. Cards #151-175 have an insertion rate of one in 288.

	MINT	NRMT	EXC
COMPLETE SERIES 1 (175)	4000.00	1800.00	500.00
COMP.BRONZE SER.1 (100)	600.00	275.00	75.00
COMMON BRONZE (1-100)	3.00	1.35	.35
COMP.SILVER SET (50)	1000.00	450.00	125.00
SILVER CARD (101-150)	10.00	4.50	1.25
COMP.GOLD SET (25)	2500.00	1100.00	300.00
COMMON GOLD (151-175)	40.00	18.00	5.00
☐ 1 Barry Bonds B	20.00	9.00	2.50
☐ 2 Ryne Sandberg B	20.00	9.00	2.50
☐ 10 Jeff Bagwell B	30.00	13.50	3.70
☐ 15 Derek Jeter B	50.00	22.00	6.25
☐ 29 Frank Thomas B	80.00	36.00	10.00
☐ 30 Mark McGwire B	25.00	11.00	3.10
☐ 37 Darin Erstad B	40.00	18.00	5.00
☐ 41 Nomar Garciaparra B	30.00	13.50	3.70
☐ 50 Mike Piazza B	50.00	22.00	6.25
☐ 90 Ivan Rodriguez B	20.00	9.00	2.50
☐ 100 Andruw Jones B	80.00	36.00	10.00
☐ 108 Chipper Jones S	100.00	45.00	12.50
☐ 112 Todd Walker S	50.00	22.00	6.25
☐ 133 Scott Rolen S	50.00	22.00	6.25
☐ 135 Cal Ripken S	120.00	55.00	15.00
☐ 138 Manny Ramirez S	40.00	18.00	5.00
☐ 139 Ken Griffey Jr. S	150.00	70.00	19.00
☐ 143 Hideo Nomo S	40.00	18.00	5.00
☐ 150 Juan Gonzalez S	80.00	36.00	10.00
☐ 151 Mike Piazza G	250.00	110.00	31.00
☐ 152 Ivan Rodriguez G	100.00	45.00	12.50
☐ 153 Mo Vaughn G	100.00	45.00	12.50
☐ 155 Mark McGwire G	125.00	55.00	15.50
☐ 158 Greg Maddux G	250.00	110.00	31.00
☐ 159 Jeff Bagwell G	150.00	70.00	19.00
☐ 160 Frank Thomas G	400.00	180.00	50.00
☐ 162 Andruw Jones G	300.00	135.00	38.00
☐ 166 Derek Jeter G	250.00	110.00	31.00
☐ 167 Vladimir Guerrero G	200.00	90.00	25.00
☐ 169 Tony Gwynn G	150.00	70.00	19.00
☐ 173 Paul Molitor G	80.00	36.00	10.00
☐ 174 Kenny Lofton G	100.00	45.00	12.50
☐ 175 Barry Bonds G	100.00	45.00	12.50

1951-52 Fischer Baking Labels

One of the popular "Bread for Energy" end-labels sets, these labels are found with blue, red and yellow backgrounds. Each bread label measures 2 3/4" by 2 3/4". They were distributed mainly in the northeast section of the country and there may be an album associated with the set. These labels are unnumbered and we have sequenced them in alphabetical order. The catalog designation is D290-3.

	NRMT	VG-E	GOOD
COMPLETE SET (32)	2000.00	900.00	250.00
COMMON LABEL (1-32)	75.00	34.00	9.50
☐ 1 Vern Bickford	75.00	34.00	9.50
☐ 2 Ralph Branca	100.00	45.00	12.50
☐ 3 Harry Brecheen	75.00	34.00	9.50
☐ 4 Chico Carrasquel	75.00	34.00	9.50
☐ 5 Cliff Chambers	75.00	34.00	9.50
☐ 6 Hoot Evers	75.00	34.00	9.50
☐ 7 Ned Garver	75.00	34.00	9.50
☐ 8 Billy Goodman	75.00	34.00	9.50
☐ 9 Gil Hodges	175.00	80.00	22.00
☐ 10 Larry Jansen	75.00	34.00	9.50
☐ 11 Willie Jones	75.00	34.00	9.50
☐ 12 Eddie Joost	75.00	34.00	9.50
☐ 13 George Kell	150.00	70.00	19.00
☐ 14 Alex Kellner	75.00	34.00	9.50
☐ 15 Ted Kluszewski	125.00	55.00	15.50
☐ 16 Jim Konstanty	100.00	45.00	12.50
☐ 17 Bob Lemon	150.00	70.00	19.00
☐ 18 Cass Michaels	75.00	34.00	9.50
☐ 19 Johnny Mize	150.00	70.00	19.00
☐ 20 Irv Noren	75.00	34.00	9.50
☐ 21 Andy Pafko	75.00	34.00	9.50
☐ 22 Joe Page	100.00	45.00	12.50
☐ 23 Mel Parnell	100.00	45.00	12.50
☐ 24 Johnny Sain	125.00	55.00	15.50
☐ 25 Red Schoendienst	125.00	55.00	15.50
☐ 26 Roy Sievers	100.00	45.00	12.50
☐ 27 Roy Smalley	75.00	34.00	9.50
☐ 28 Herm Wehmeier	75.00	34.00	9.50
☐ 29 Bill Werle	75.00	34.00	9.50
☐ 30 Wes Westrum	75.00	34.00	9.50
☐ 31 Early Wynn	150.00	70.00	19.00
☐ 32 Gus Zernial	100.00	45.00	12.50

1993 Flair Promos

This 8-card standard-size set was issued to preview the design of the 1993 Flair series. These cards can be distinguished by triple zero on their backs; otherwise, they are identical to their regular issue counterparts. The cards are listed below in alphabetical order by player's last name. According to unverified reports, Fleer shredded a 5,000 count box of these cards to avoid potential difficulties with their liscening organizations.

	MINT	NRMT	EXC
COMPLETE SET (8)	350.00	160.00	45.00
COMMON CARD (1-8)	10.00	4.50	1.25
☐ 1 Will Clark	40.00	18.00	5.00
☐ 2 Darren Daulton	20.00	9.00	2.50
☐ 3 Andres Galarraga	40.00	18.00	5.00
☐ 4 Bryan Harvey	10.00	4.50	1.25
☐ 5 David Justice	30.00	13.50	3.70
☐ 6 Jody Reed	10.00	4.50	1.25
☐ 7 Nolan Ryan	200.00	90.00	25.00
☐ 8 Sammy Sosa	40.00	18.00	5.00

1993 Flair

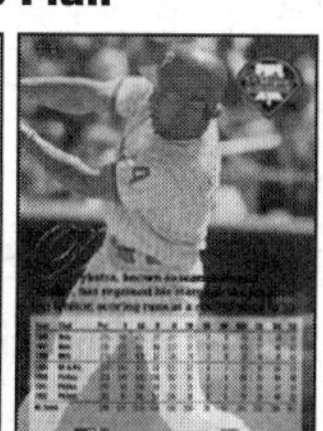

This 300-card standard-size set represents Fleer's entrance into the super-premium category of trading cards. Cards were distributed exclusively in specially encased "hardpacks". The cards are made from heavy 24 point board card stock, with an additional three points of high-gloss laminate on each side, and feature full-bleed color fronts that sport two photos of each player, one superposed upon the other. The Flair logo appears at the top and the player's name rests at the bottom, both stamped in gold foil. The cards are numbered alphabetically within teams with National League preceding American league. There are no key Rookie Cards in this set.

	MINT	NRMT	EXC
COMPLETE SET (300)	60.00	27.00	7.50
COMMON CARD (1-300)	.25	.11	.03
☐ 1 Steve Avery	.50	.23	.06
☐ 2 Jeff Blauser	.25	.11	.03
☐ 3 Ron Gant	.50	.23	.06
☐ 4 Tom Glavine	1.25	.55	.16
☐ 5 David Justice	1.25	.55	.16
☐ 6 Mark Lemke	.25	.11	.03
☐ 7 Greg Maddux	5.00	2.20	.60
☐ 8 Fred McGriff	1.25	.55	.16
☐ 9 Terry Pendleton	.50	.23	.06
☐ 10 Deion Sanders	1.25	.55	.16
☐ 11 John Smoltz	1.25	.55	.16
☐ 12 Mike Stanton	.25	.11	.03
☐ 13 Steve Buechele	.25	.11	.03
☐ 14 Mark Grace	1.25	.55	.16
☐ 15 Greg Hibbard	.25	.11	.03
☐ 16 Derrick May	.25	.11	.03
☐ 17 Chuck McElroy	.25	.11	.03
☐ 18 Mike Morgan	.25	.11	.03
☐ 19 Randy Myers	.50	.23	.06
☐ 20 Ryne Sandberg	2.00	.90	.25
☐ 21 Dwight Smith	.25	.11	.03
☐ 22 Sammy Sosa	1.25	.55	.16
☐ 23 Jose Vizcaino	.25	.11	.03
☐ 24 Tim Belcher	.25	.11	.03
☐ 25 Rob Dibble	.25	.11	.03
☐ 26 Roberto Kelly	.25	.11	.03
☐ 27 Barry Larkin	1.25	.55	.16
☐ 28 Kevin Mitchell	.50	.23	.06
☐ 29 Hal Morris	.25	.11	.03
☐ 30 Joe Oliver	.25	.11	.03
☐ 31 Jose Rijo	.25	.11	.03
☐ 32 Bip Roberts	.25	.11	.03
☐ 33 Chris Sabo	.25	.11	.03
☐ 34 Reggie Sanders	1.25	.55	.16
☐ 35 Dante Bichette	1.25	.55	.16
☐ 36 Willie Blair	.25	.11	.03
☐ 37 Jerald Clark	.25	.11	.03
☐ 38 Alex Cole	.25	.11	.03
☐ 39 Andres Galarraga	1.25	.55	.16
☐ 40 Joe Girardi	.25	.11	.03
☐ 41 Charlie Hayes	.25	.11	.03
☐ 42 Chris Jones	.25	.11	.03
☐ 43 David Nied	.25	.11	.03
☐ 44 Eric Young	1.25	.55	.16
☐ 45 Alex Arias	.25	.11	.03
☐ 46 Jack Armstrong	.25	.11	.03
☐ 47 Bret Barberie	.25	.11	.03
☐ 48 Chuck Carr	.25	.11	.03
☐ 49 Jeff Conine	.50	.23	.06
☐ 50 Orestes Destrade	.25	.11	.03
☐ 51 Chris Hammond	.25	.11	.03
☐ 52 Bryan Harvey	.25	.11	.03
☐ 53 Benito Santiago	.25	.11	.03
☐ 54 Gary Sheffield	1.25	.55	.16
☐ 55 Walt Weiss	.25	.11	.03
☐ 56 Eric Anthony	.25	.11	.03
☐ 57 Jeff Bagwell	3.00	1.35	.35
☐ 58 Craig Biggio	.50	.23	.06
☐ 59 Ken Caminiti	1.25	.55	.16
☐ 60 Andujar Cedeno	.25	.11	.03
☐ 61 Doug Drabek	.25	.11	.03
☐ 62 Steve Finley	.50	.23	.06
☐ 63 Luis Gonzalez	.25	.11	.03
☐ 64 Pete Harnisch	.25	.11	.03
☐ 65 Doug Jones	.25	.11	.03
☐ 66 Darryl Kile	.25	.11	.03
☐ 67 Greg Swindell	.25	.11	.03
☐ 68 Brett Butler	.50	.23	.06
☐ 69 Jim Gott	.25	.11	.03
☐ 70 Orel Hershiser	.50	.23	.06
☐ 71 Eric Karros	1.25	.55	.16
☐ 72 Pedro Martinez	1.25	.55	.16
☐ 73 Ramon Martinez	.50	.23	.06
☐ 74 Roger McDowell	.25	.11	.03
☐ 75 Mike Piazza	8.00	3.60	1.00
☐ 76 Jody Reed	.25	.11	.03
☐ 77 Tim Wallach	.25	.11	.03
☐ 78 Moises Alou	.50	.23	.06
☐ 79 Greg Colbrunn	.25	.11	.03
☐ 80 Wil Cordero	.50	.23	.06
☐ 81 Delino DeShields	.25	.11	.03
☐ 82 Jeff Fassero	.50	.23	.06
☐ 83 Marquis Grissom	.50	.23	.06
☐ 84 Ken Hill	.50	.23	.06
☐ 85 Mike Lansing	.50	.23	.06
☐ 86 Dennis Martinez	.50	.23	.06
☐ 87 Larry Walker	1.25	.55	.16
☐ 88 John Wetteland	.50	.23	.06
☐ 89 Bobby Bonilla	.50	.23	.06
☐ 90 Vince Coleman	.25	.11	.03
☐ 91 Dwight Gooden	.50	.23	.06
☐ 92 Todd Hundley	.50	.23	.06
☐ 93 Howard Johnson	.25	.11	.03
☐ 94 Eddie Murray	2.00	.90	.25
☐ 95 Joe Orsulak	.25	.11	.03
☐ 96 Bret Saberhagen	.50	.23	.06
☐ 97 Darren Daulton	.50	.23	.06
☐ 98 Mariano Duncan	.25	.11	.03
☐ 99 Len Dykstra	.50	.23	.06
☐ 100 Jim Eisenreich	.50	.23	.06
☐ 101 Tommy Greene	.25	.11	.03
☐ 102 Dave Hollins	.25	.11	.03
☐ 103 Pete Incaviglia	.25	.11	.03
☐ 104 Danny Jackson	.25	.11	.03
☐ 105 John Kruk	.50	.23	.06
☐ 106 Terry Mulholland	.25	.11	.03
☐ 107 Curt Schilling	.25	.11	.03
☐ 108 Mitch Williams	.25	.11	.03
☐ 109 Stan Belinda	.25	.11	.03
☐ 110 Jay Bell	.50	.23	.06
☐ 111 Steve Cooke	.25	.11	.03
☐ 112 Carlos Garcia	.25	.11	.03
☐ 113 Jeff King	.50	.23	.06
☐ 114 Al Martin	.50	.23	.06
☐ 115 Orlando Merced	.50	.23	.06
☐ 116 Don Slaught	.25	.11	.03
☐ 117 Andy Van Slyke	.50	.23	.06
☐ 118 Tim Wakefield	.50	.23	.06
☐ 119 Rene Arocha	.25	.11	.03
☐ 120 Bernard Gilkey	.50	.23	.06
☐ 121 Gregg Jefferies	.50	.23	.06
☐ 122 Ray Lankford	.50	.23	.06
☐ 123 Donovan Osborne	.25	.11	.03
☐ 124 Tom Pagnozzi	.25	.11	.03

☐ 125 Erik Pappas	.25	.11	.03
☐ 126 Geronimo Pena	.25	.11	.03
☐ 127 Lee Smith	.50	.23	.06
☐ 128 Ozzie Smith	2.00	.90	.25
☐ 129 Bob Tewksbury	.25	.11	.03
☐ 130 Mark Whiten	.25	.11	.03
☐ 131 Derek Bell	.50	.23	.06
☐ 132 Andy Benes	.50	.23	.06
☐ 133 Tony Gwynn	3.00	1.35	.35
☐ 134 Gene Harris	.25	.11	.03
☐ 135 Trevor Hoffman	1.25	.55	.16
☐ 136 Phil Plantier	.25	.11	.03
☐ 137 Rod Beck	.50	.23	.06
☐ 138 Barry Bonds	2.00	.90	.25
☐ 139 John Burkett	.25	.11	.03
☐ 140 Will Clark	1.25	.55	.16
☐ 141 Royce Clayton	.50	.23	.06
☐ 142 Mike Jackson	.25	.11	.03
☐ 143 Darren Lewis	.25	.11	.03
☐ 144 Kirt Manwaring	.25	.11	.03
☐ 145 Willie McGee	.25	.11	.03
☐ 146 Bill Swift	.25	.11	.03
☐ 147 Robby Thompson	.25	.11	.03
☐ 148 Matt Williams	1.25	.55	.16
☐ 149 Brady Anderson	1.25	.55	.16
☐ 150 Mike Devereaux	.25	.11	.03
☐ 151 Chris Hoiles	.25	.11	.03
☐ 152 Ben McDonald	.25	.11	.03
☐ 153 Mark McLemore	.25	.11	.03
☐ 154 Mike Mussina	1.50	.70	.19
☐ 155 Gregg Olson	.25	.11	.03
☐ 156 Harold Reynolds	.25	.11	.03
☐ 157 Cal Ripken UER (Back refers to his games streak going into 1992; should be 1993) Also streak is spelled steak	6.00	2.70	.75
☐ 158 Rick Sutcliffe	.25	.11	.03
☐ 159 Fernando Valenzuela	.50	.23	.06
☐ 160 Roger Clemens	1.50	.70	.19
☐ 161 Scott Cooper	.25	.11	.03
☐ 162 Andre Dawson	.50	.23	.06
☐ 163 Scott Fletcher	.25	.11	.03
☐ 164 Mike Greenwell	.25	.11	.03
☐ 165 Greg A. Harris	.25	.11	.03
☐ 166 Billy Hatcher	.25	.11	.03
☐ 167 Jeff Russell	.25	.11	.03
☐ 168 Mo Vaughn	2.00	.90	.25
☐ 169 Frank Viola	.25	.11	.03
☐ 170 Chad Curtis	.50	.23	.06
☐ 171 Chili Davis	.50	.23	.06
☐ 172 Gary DiSarcina	.25	.11	.03
☐ 173 Damion Easley	.25	.11	.03
☐ 174 Chuck Finley	.25	.11	.03
☐ 175 Mark Langston	.50	.23	.06
☐ 176 Luis Polonia	.25	.11	.03
☐ 177 Tim Salmon	2.00	.90	.25
☐ 178 Scott Sanderson	.25	.11	.03
☐ 179 J.T.Snow	1.25	.55	.16
☐ 180 Wilson Alvarez	.50	.23	.06
☐ 181 Ellis Burks	.50	.23	.06
☐ 182 Joey Cora	.50	.23	.06
☐ 183 Alex Fernandez	.50	.23	.06
☐ 184 Ozzie Guillen	.25	.11	.03
☐ 185 Roberto Hernandez	.50	.23	.06
☐ 186 Bo Jackson	.50	.23	.06
☐ 187 Lance Johnson	.50	.23	.06
☐ 188 Jack McDowell	.50	.23	.06
☐ 189 Frank Thomas	8.00	3.60	1.00
☐ 190 Robin Ventura	.50	.23	.06
☐ 191 Carlos Baerga	.50	.23	.06
☐ 192 Albert Belle	3.00	1.35	.35
☐ 193 Wayne Kirby	.25	.11	.03
☐ 194 Derek Lilliquist	.25	.11	.03
☐ 195 Kenny Lofton	3.00	1.35	.35
☐ 196 Carlos Martinez	.25	.11	.03
☐ 197 Jose Mesa	.50	.23	.06
☐ 198 Eric Plunk	.25	.11	.03
☐ 199 Paul Sorrento	.25	.11	.03
☐ 200 John Doherty	.25	.11	.03
☐ 201 Cecil Fielder	.50	.23	.06
☐ 202 Travis Fryman	.50	.23	.06
☐ 203 Kirk Gibson	.50	.23	.06
☐ 204 Mike Henneman	.25	.11	.03
☐ 205 Chad Kreuter	.25	.11	.03
☐ 206 Scott Livingstone	.25	.11	.03
☐ 207 Tony Phillips	.50	.23	.06
☐ 208 Mickey Tettleton	.25	.11	.03
☐ 209 Alan Trammell	1.25	.55	.16
☐ 210 David Wells	.25	.11	.03
☐ 211 Lou Whitaker	.50	.23	.06
☐ 212 Kevin Appier	.50	.23	.06
☐ 213 George Brett	3.00	1.35	.35
☐ 214 David Cone	.50	.23	.06
☐ 215 Tom Gordon	.25	.11	.03
☐ 216 Phil Hiatt	.25	.11	.03
☐ 217 Felix Jose	.25	.11	.03
☐ 218 Wally Joyner	.50	.23	.06
☐ 219 Jose Lind	.25	.11	.03
☐ 220 Mike Macfarlane	.25	.11	.03
☐ 221 Brian McRae	.50	.23	.06
☐ 222 Jeff Montgomery	.50	.23	.06
☐ 223 Cal Eldred	.25	.11	.03
☐ 224 Darryl Hamilton	.25	.11	.03
☐ 225 John Jaha	1.25	.55	.16
☐ 226 Pat Listach	.25	.11	.03
☐ 227 Graeme Lloyd	.25	.11	.03
☐ 228 Kevin Reimer	.25	.11	.03
☐ 229 Bill Spiers	.25	.11	.03
☐ 230 B.J.Surhoff	.50	.23	.06
☐ 231 Greg Vaughn	.50	.23	.06
☐ 232 Robin Yount	1.25	.55	.16
☐ 233 Rick Aguilera	.25	.11	.03
☐ 234 Jim Deshaies	.25	.11	.03
☐ 235 Brian Harper	.25	.11	.03
☐ 236 Kent Hrbek	.50	.23	.06
☐ 237 Chuck Knoblauch	1.25	.55	.16
☐ 238 Shane Mack	.25	.11	.03
☐ 239 David McCarty	.25	.11	.03
☐ 240 Pedro Munoz	.25	.11	.03
☐ 241 Mike Pagliarulo	.25	.11	.03
☐ 242 Kirby Puckett	3.00	1.35	.35
☐ 243 Dave Winfield	1.25	.55	.16
☐ 244 Jim Abbott	.25	.11	.03
☐ 245 Wade Boggs	1.25	.55	.16
☐ 246 Pat Kelly	.25	.11	.03
☐ 247 Jimmy Key	.50	.23	.06
☐ 248 Jim Leyritz	.25	.11	.03
☐ 249 Don Mattingly	4.00	1.80	.50
☐ 250 Matt Nokes	.25	.11	.03
☐ 251 Paul O'Neill	.50	.23	.06
☐ 252 Mike Stanley	.25	.11	.03
☐ 253 Danny Tartabull	.25	.11	.03
☐ 254 Bob Wickman	.25	.11	.03
☐ 255 Bernie Williams	1.50	.70	.19
☐ 256 Mike Bordick	.25	.11	.03
☐ 257 Dennis Eckersley	.50	.23	.06
☐ 258 Brent Gates	.50	.23	.06
☐ 259 Goose Gossage	.50	.23	.06
☐ 260 Rickey Henderson	1.25	.55	.16
☐ 261 Mark McGwire	2.50	1.10	.30
☐ 262 Ruben Sierra	.50	.23	.06
☐ 263 Terry Steinbach	.50	.23	.06
☐ 264 Bob Welch	.25	.11	.03
☐ 265 Bobby Witt	.25	.11	.03
☐ 266 Rich Amaral	.25	.11	.03
☐ 267 Chris Bosio	.25	.11	.03
☐ 268 Jay Buhner	1.25	.55	.16
☐ 269 Norm Charlton	.25	.11	.03
☐ 270 Ken Griffey Jr.	8.00	3.60	1.00
☐ 271 Erik Hanson	.25	.11	.03
☐ 272 Randy Johnson	1.25	.55	.16
☐ 273 Edgar Martinez	.50	.23	.06
☐ 274 Tino Martinez	.50	.23	.06
☐ 275 Dave Valle	.25	.11	.03
☐ 276 Omar Vizquel	.50	.23	.06
☐ 277 Kevin Brown	.50	.23	.06
☐ 278 Jose Canseco	1.25	.55	.16
☐ 279 Julio Franco	.50	.23	.06
☐ 280 Juan Gonzalez	4.00	1.80	.50
☐ 281 Tom Henke	.25	.11	.03
☐ 282 David Hulse	.25	.11	.03
☐ 283 Rafael Palmeiro	1.25	.55	.16
☐ 284 Dean Palmer	.50	.23	.06
☐ 285 Ivan Rodriguez	2.00	.90	.25
☐ 286 Nolan Ryan	6.00	2.70	.75
☐ 287 Roberto Alomar	1.50	.70	.19
☐ 288 Pat Borders	.25	.11	.03
☐ 289 Joe Carter	.50	.23	.06
☐ 290 Juan Guzman	.50	.23	.06
☐ 291 Pat Hentgen	1.25	.55	.16
☐ 292 Paul Molitor	1.50	.70	.19
☐ 293 John Olerud	.25	.11	.03
☐ 294 Ed Sprague	.50	.23	.06
☐ 295 Dave Stewart	.50	.23	.06
☐ 296 Duane Ward	.25	.11	.03
☐ 297 Devon White	.25	.11	.03
☐ 298 Checklist 1-100	.25	.11	.03
☐ 299 Checklist 101-200	.25	.11	.03
☐ 300 Checklist 201-300	.25	.11	.03

1993 Flair Wave of the Future

This 20-card standard-size limited edition insert set features a selction of top prospects. Cards were randomly seeded into1993 Flair packs. Each card is made of the same thick card stock as the regular-issue set and features full-bleed color player action photos on the fronts, with the Flair logo, player's name, and the "Wave of the Future" name and logo in gold foil, all superimposed upon an ocean breaker.

	MINT	NRMT	EXC
COMPLETE SET (20)	40.00	18.00	5.00
COMMON CARD (1-20)	1.00	.45	.12
☐ 1 Jason Bere	1.00	.45	.12
☐ 2 Jeromy Burnitz	1.00	.45	.12
☐ 3 Russ Davis	1.50	.70	.19
☐ 4 Jim Edmonds	10.00	4.50	1.25
☐ 5 Cliff Floyd	1.00	.45	.12
☐ 6 Jeffrey Hammonds	1.50	.70	.19
☐ 7 Trevor Hoffman	2.50	1.10	.30
☐ 8 Domingo Jean	1.00	.45	.12
☐ 9 David McCarty	1.00	.45	.12
☐ 10 Bobby Munoz	1.00	.45	.12
☐ 11 Brad Pennington	1.00	.45	.12
☐ 12 Mike Piazza	15.00	6.75	1.85
☐ 13 Manny Ramirez	10.00	4.50	1.25
☐ 14 John Roper	1.00	.45	.12
☐ 15 Tim Salmon	5.00	2.20	.60
☐ 16 Aaron Sele	1.50	.70	.19
☐ 17 Allen Watson	1.00	.45	.12
☐ 18 Rondell White	2.50	1.10	.30
☐ 19 Darrell Whitmore UER (Nigel Wilson back)	1.00	.45	.12
☐ 20 Nigel Wilson UER (Darrell Whitmore back)	1.00	.45	.12

1994 Flair

For the second consecutive year Fleer issued a Flair brand. The set consists of 450 full bleed cards in two series of 250 and 200. The card stock is thicker than the traditional standard card. Card fronts feature two photos with the player's name and team name at the bottom in gold foil. The first letter of the player's last name appears within a gold shield to add style to this premium brand product. The backs are horizontal with a player photo and statistics. The team logo and player's name are done in gold foil. The cards are grouped alphabetically by team within each league with AL preceding NL. Notable Rookie Cards include Chan Ho Park and Alex Rodriguez.

	MINT	NRMT	EXC
COMPLETE SET (450)	60.00	27.00	7.50
COMPLETE SERIES 1 (250)	25.00	11.00	3.10
COMPLETE SERIES 2 (200)	35.00	16.00	4.40
COMMON CARD (1-450)	.15	.07	.02
☐ 1 Harold Baines	.40	.18	.05
☐ 2 Jeffrey Hammonds	.40	.18	.05
☐ 3 Chris Hoiles	.15	.07	.02
☐ 4 Ben McDonald	.15	.07	.02
☐ 5 Mark McLemore	.15	.07	.02
☐ 6 Jamie Moyer	.15	.07	.02
☐ 7 Jim Poole	.15	.07	.02
☐ 8 Cal Ripken Jr.	4.00	1.80	.50
☐ 9 Chris Sabo	.15	.07	.02
☐ 10 Scott Bankhead	.15	.07	.02
☐ 11 Scott Cooper	.15	.07	.02
☐ 12 Danny Darwin	.15	.07	.02
☐ 13 Andre Dawson	.40	.18	.05
☐ 14 Billy Hatcher	.15	.07	.02
☐ 15 Aaron Sele	.40	.18	.05
☐ 16 John Valentin	.40	.18	.05
☐ 17 Dave Valle	.15	.07	.02
☐ 18 Mo Vaughn	1.25	.55	.16
☐ 19 Brian Anderson	.40	.18	.05
☐ 20 Gary DiSarcina	.15	.07	.02
☐ 21 Jim Edmonds	1.00	.45	.12
☐ 22 Chuck Finley	.15	.07	.02
☐ 23 Bo Jackson	.40	.18	.05
☐ 24 Mark Leiter	.15	.07	.02
☐ 25 Greg Myers	.15	.07	.02
☐ 26 Eduardo Perez	.15	.07	.02
☐ 27 Tim Salmon	.75	.35	.09
☐ 28 Wilson Alvarez	.40	.18	.05
☐ 29 Jason Bere	.40	.18	.05
☐ 30 Alex Fernandez	.40	.18	.05
☐ 31 Ozzie Guillen	.15	.07	.02
☐ 32 Joe Hall	.15	.07	.02
☐ 33 Darrin Jackson	.15	.07	.02
☐ 34 Kirk McCaskill	.15	.07	.02
☐ 35 Tim Raines	.75	.35	.09
☐ 36 Frank Thomas	5.00	2.20	.60
☐ 37 Carlos Baerga	.40	.18	.05
☐ 38 Albert Belle	2.00	.90	.25
☐ 39 Mark Clark	.15	.07	.02
☐ 40 Wayne Kirby	.15	.07	.02
☐ 41 Dennis Martinez	.40	.18	.05
☐ 42 Charles Nagy	.40	.18	.05
☐ 43 Manny Ramirez	1.50	.70	.19
☐ 44 Paul Sorrento	.15	.07	.02
☐ 45 Jim Thome	1.25	.55	.16
☐ 46 Eric Davis	.40	.18	.05
☐ 47 John Doherty	.15	.07	.02
☐ 48 Junior Felix	.15	.07	.02
☐ 49 Cecil Fielder	.40	.18	.05
☐ 50 Kirk Gibson	.40	.18	.05
☐ 51 Mike Moore	.15	.07	.02
☐ 52 Tony Phillips	.40	.18	.05
☐ 53 Alan Trammell	.40	.18	.05
☐ 54 Kevin Appier	.40	.18	.05
☐ 55 Stan Belinda	.15	.07	.02
☐ 56 Vince Coleman	.15	.07	.02
☐ 57 Greg Gagne	.15	.07	.02
☐ 58 Bob Hamelin	.15	.07	.02
☐ 59 Dave Henderson	.15	.07	.02
☐ 60 Wally Joyner	.40	.18	.05
☐ 61 Mike Macfarlane	.15	.07	.02
☐ 62 Jeff Montgomery	.40	.18	.05
☐ 63 Ricky Bones	.15	.07	.02
☐ 64 Jeff Bronkey	.15	.07	.02
☐ 65 Alex Diaz	.15	.07	.02
☐ 66 Cal Eldred	.15	.07	.02
☐ 67 Darryl Hamilton	.15	.07	.02
☐ 68 John Jaha	.40	.18	.05
☐ 69 Mark Kiefer	.15	.07	.02
☐ 70 Kevin Seitzer	.15	.07	.02
☐ 71 Turner Ward	.15	.07	.02
☐ 72 Rich Becker	.40	.18	.05
☐ 73 Scott Erickson	.15	.07	.02
☐ 74 Keith Garagozzo	.15	.07	.02
☐ 75 Kent Hrbek	.40	.18	.05
☐ 76 Scott Leius	.15	.07	.02
☐ 77 Kirby Puckett	2.00	.90	.25
☐ 78 Matt Walbeck	.15	.07	.02
☐ 79 Dave Winfield	.75	.35	.09
☐ 80 Mike Gallego	.15	.07	.02
☐ 81 Xavier Hernandez	.15	.07	.02
☐ 82 Jimmy Key	.40	.18	.05
☐ 83 Jim Leyritz	.15	.07	.02
☐ 84 Don Mattingly	2.50	1.10	.30
☐ 85 Matt Nokes	.15	.07	.02
☐ 86 Paul O'Neill	.40	.18	.05
☐ 87 Melido Perez	.15	.07	.02
☐ 88 Danny Tartabull	.15	.07	.02
☐ 89 Mike Bordick	.15	.07	.02
☐ 90 Ron Darling	.15	.07	.02
☐ 91 Dennis Eckersley	.40	.18	.05
☐ 92 Stan Javier	.15	.07	.02
☐ 93 Steve Karsay	.15	.07	.02
☐ 94 Mark McGwire	1.50	.70	.19
☐ 95 Troy Neel	.15	.07	.02
☐ 96 Terry Steinbach	.40	.18	.05
☐ 97 Bill Taylor	.15	.07	.02
☐ 98 Eric Anthony	.15	.07	.02
☐ 99 Chris Bosio	.15	.07	.02
☐ 100 Tim Davis	.15	.07	.02
☐ 101 Felix Fermin	.15	.07	.02
☐ 102 Dave Fleming	.15	.07	.02
☐ 103 Ken Griffey Jr.	5.00	2.20	.60
☐ 104 Greg Hibbard	.15	.07	.02
☐ 105 Reggie Jefferson	.40	.18	.05
☐ 106 Tino Martinez	.40	.18	.05
☐ 107 Jack Armstrong	.15	.07	.02
☐ 108 Will Clark	.75	.35	.09
☐ 109 Juan Gonzalez	2.50	1.10	.30
☐ 110 Rick Helling	.15	.07	.02
☐ 111 Tom Henke	.15	.07	.02
☐ 112 David Hulse	.15	.07	.02
☐ 113 Manuel Lee	.15	.07	.02
☐ 114 Doug Strange	.15	.07	.02
☐ 115 Roberto Alomar	1.00	.45	.12
☐ 116 Joe Carter	.40	.18	.05
☐ 117 Carlos Delgado	.75	.35	.09
☐ 118 Pat Hentgen	.40	.18	.05
☐ 119 Paul Molitor	1.00	.45	.12
☐ 120 John Olerud	.15	.07	.02
☐ 121 Dave Stewart	.40	.18	.05
☐ 122 Todd Stottlemyre	.15	.07	.02
☐ 123 Mike Timlin	.15	.07	.02
☐ 124 Jeff Blauser	.15	.07	.02
☐ 125 Tom Glavine	.75	.35	.09
☐ 126 David Justice	.75	.35	.09
☐ 127 Mike Kelly	.15	.07	.02
☐ 128 Ryan Klesko	1.00	.45	.12
☐ 129 Javier Lopez	.75	.35	.09
☐ 130 Greg Maddux	3.00	1.35	.35
☐ 131 Fred McGriff	.75	.35	.09
☐ 132 Kent Mercker	.15	.07	.02
☐ 133 Mark Wohlers	.40	.18	.05
☐ 134 Willie Banks	.15	.07	.02
☐ 135 Steve Buechele	.15	.07	.02
☐ 136 Shawon Dunston	.15	.07	.02
☐ 137 Jose Guzman	.15	.07	.02
☐ 138 Glenallen Hill	.15	.07	.02
☐ 139 Randy Myers	.15	.07	.02
☐ 140 Karl Rhodes	.15	.07	.02
☐ 141 Ryne Sandberg	1.25	.55	.16
☐ 142 Steve Trachsel	.40	.18	.05
☐ 143 Bret Boone	.40	.18	.05
☐ 144 Tom Browning	.15	.07	.02
☐ 145 Hector Carrasco	.15	.07	.02
☐ 146 Barry Larkin	.75	.35	.09
☐ 147 Hal Morris	.15	.07	.02
☐ 148 Jose Rijo	.15	.07	.02
☐ 149 Reggie Sanders	.40	.18	.05
☐ 150 John Smiley	.15	.07	.02
☐ 151 Dante Bichette	.75	.35	.09
☐ 152 Ellis Burks	.40	.18	.05
☐ 153 Joe Girardi	.15	.07	.02
☐ 154 Mike Harkey	.15	.07	.02
☐ 155 Roberto Mejia	.15	.07	.02
☐ 156 Marcus Moore	.15	.07	.02
☐ 157 Armando Reynoso	.15	.07	.02
☐ 158 Bruce Ruffin	.15	.07	.02

Card	MINT	NRMT	EXC
☐ 159 Eric Young	.40	.18	.05
☐ 160 Kurt Abbott	.40	.18	.05
☐ 161 Jeff Conine	.40	.18	.05
☐ 162 Orestes Destrade	.15	.07	.02
☐ 163 Chris Hammond	.15	.07	.02
☐ 164 Bryan Harvey	.15	.07	.02
☐ 165 Dave Magadan	.15	.07	.02
☐ 166 Gary Sheffield	.75	.35	.09
☐ 167 David Weathers	.15	.07	.02
☐ 168 Andujar Cedeno	.15	.07	.02
☐ 169 Tom Edens	.15	.07	.02
☐ 170 Luis Gonzalez	.15	.07	.02
☐ 171 Pete Harnisch	.15	.07	.02
☐ 172 Todd Jones	.15	.07	.02
☐ 173 Darryl Kile	.15	.07	.02
☐ 174 James Mouton	.40	.18	.05
☐ 175 Scott Servais	.15	.07	.02
☐ 176 Mitch Williams	.15	.07	.02
☐ 177 Pedro Astacio	.15	.07	.02
☐ 178 Orel Hershiser	.40	.18	.05
☐ 179 Raul Mondesi	.75	.35	.09
☐ 180 Jose Offerman	.15	.07	.02
☐ 181 Chan Ho Park	1.50	.70	.19
☐ 182 Mike Piazza	3.00	1.35	.35
☐ 183 Cory Snyder	.15	.07	.02
☐ 184 Tim Wallach	.15	.07	.02
☐ 185 Todd Worrell	.15	.07	.02
☐ 186 Sean Berry	.15	.07	.02
☐ 187 Wil Cordero	.40	.18	.05
☐ 188 Darrin Fletcher	.15	.07	.02
☐ 189 Cliff Floyd	.75	.35	.09
☐ 190 Marquis Grissom	.40	.18	.05
☐ 191 Rod Henderson	.15	.07	.02
☐ 192 Ken Hill	.15	.07	.02
☐ 193 Pedro Martinez	.75	.35	.09
☐ 194 Kirk Rueter	.15	.07	.02
☐ 195 Jeromy Burnitz	.15	.07	.02
☐ 196 John Franco	.15	.07	.02
☐ 197 Dwight Gooden	.40	.18	.05
☐ 198 Todd Hundley	.40	.18	.05
☐ 199 Bobby Jones	.40	.18	.05
☐ 200 Jeff Kent	.15	.07	.02
☐ 201 Mike Maddux	.15	.07	.02
☐ 202 Ryan Thompson	.15	.07	.02
☐ 203 Jose Vizcaino	.15	.07	.02
☐ 204 Darren Daulton	.40	.18	.05
☐ 205 Lenny Dykstra	.40	.18	.05
☐ 206 Jim Eisenreich	.15	.07	.02
☐ 207 Dave Hollins	.15	.07	.02
☐ 208 Danny Jackson	.15	.07	.02
☐ 209 Doug Jones	.15	.07	.02
☐ 210 Jeff Juden	.15	.07	.02
☐ 211 Ben Rivera	.15	.07	.02
☐ 212 Kevin Stocker	.15	.07	.02
☐ 213 Milt Thompson	.15	.07	.02
☐ 214 Jay Bell	.40	.18	.05
☐ 215 Steve Cooke	.15	.07	.02
☐ 216 Mark Dewey	.15	.07	.02
☐ 217 Al Martin	.15	.07	.02
☐ 218 Orlando Merced	.40	.18	.05
☐ 219 Don Slaught	.15	.07	.02
☐ 220 Zane Smith	.15	.07	.02
☐ 221 Rick White	.15	.07	.02
☐ 222 Kevin Young	.15	.07	.02
☐ 223 Rene Arocha	.15	.07	.02
☐ 224 Rheal Cormier	.15	.07	.02
☐ 225 Brian Jordan	.75	.35	.09
☐ 226 Ray Lankford	.40	.18	.05
☐ 227 Mike Perez	.15	.07	.02
☐ 228 Ozzie Smith	1.25	.55	.16
☐ 229 Mark Whiten	.15	.07	.02
☐ 230 Todd Zeile	.15	.07	.02
☐ 231 Derek Bell	.40	.18	.05
☐ 232 Archi Cianfrocco	.15	.07	.02
☐ 233 Ricky Gutierrez	.15	.07	.02
☐ 234 Trevor Hoffman	.40	.18	.05
☐ 235 Phil Plantier	.15	.07	.02
☐ 236 Dave Staton	.15	.07	.02
☐ 237 Wally Whitehurst	.15	.07	.02
☐ 238 Todd Benzinger	.15	.07	.02
☐ 239 Barry Bonds	1.25	.55	.16
☐ 240 John Burkett	.15	.07	.02
☐ 241 Royce Clayton	.40	.18	.05
☐ 242 Bryan Hickerson	.15	.07	.02
☐ 243 Mike Jackson	.15	.07	.02
☐ 244 Darren Lewis	.15	.07	.02
☐ 245 Kirt Manwaring	.15	.07	.02
☐ 246 Mark Portugal	.15	.07	.02
☐ 247 Salomon Torres	.15	.07	.02
☐ 248 Checklist	.15	.07	.02
☐ 249 Checklist	.15	.07	.02
☐ 250 Checklist	.15	.07	.02
☐ 251 Brady Anderson	.75	.35	.09
☐ 252 Mike Devereaux	.15	.07	.02
☐ 253 Sid Fernandez	.15	.07	.02
☐ 254 Leo Gomez	.15	.07	.02
☐ 255 Mike Mussina	1.00	.45	.12
☐ 256 Mike Oquist	.15	.07	.02
☐ 257 Rafael Palmeiro	.75	.35	.09
☐ 258 Lee Smith	.40	.18	.05
☐ 259 Damon Berryhill	.15	.07	.02
☐ 260 Wes Chamberlain	.15	.07	.02
☐ 261 Roger Clemens	1.00	.45	.12
☐ 262 Gar Finnvold	.15	.07	.02
☐ 263 Mike Greenwell	.15	.07	.02
☐ 264 Tim Naehring	.15	.07	.02
☐ 265 Otis Nixon	.15	.07	.02
☐ 266 Ken Ryan	.15	.07	.02
☐ 267 Chad Curtis	.15	.07	.02
☐ 268 Chili Davis	.40	.18	.05
☐ 269 Damion Easley	.15	.07	.02
☐ 270 Jorge Fabregas	.15	.07	.02
☐ 271 Mark Langston	.40	.18	.05
☐ 272 Phil Leftwich	.15	.07	.02
☐ 273 Harold Reynolds	.15	.07	.02
☐ 274 J.T. Snow	.40	.18	.05
☐ 275 Joey Cora	.15	.07	.02
☐ 276 Julio Franco	.40	.18	.05
☐ 277 Roberto Hernandez	.40	.18	.05
☐ 278 Lance Johnson	.40	.18	.05
☐ 279 Ron Karkovice	.15	.07	.02
☐ 280 Jack McDowell	.40	.18	.05
☐ 281 Robin Ventura	.40	.18	.05
☐ 282 Sandy Alomar Jr.	.40	.18	.05
☐ 283 Kenny Lofton	1.50	.70	.19
☐ 284 Jose Mesa	.40	.18	.05
☐ 285 Jack Morris	.40	.18	.05
☐ 286 Eddie Murray	1.25	.55	.16
☐ 287 Chad Ogea	.40	.18	.05
☐ 288 Eric Plunk	.15	.07	.02
☐ 289 Paul Shuey	.15	.07	.02
☐ 290 Omar Vizquel	.40	.18	.05
☐ 291 Danny Bautista	.15	.07	.02
☐ 292 Travis Fryman	.40	.18	.05
☐ 293 Greg Gohr	.15	.07	.02
☐ 294 Chris Gomez	.15	.07	.02
☐ 295 Mickey Tettleton	.15	.07	.02
☐ 296 Lou Whitaker	.40	.18	.05
☐ 297 David Cone	.40	.18	.05
☐ 298 Gary Gaetti	.40	.18	.05
☐ 299 Tom Gordon	.15	.07	.02
☐ 300 Felix Jose	.15	.07	.02
☐ 301 Jose Lind	.15	.07	.02
☐ 302 Brian McRae	.40	.18	.05
☐ 303 Mike Fetters	.15	.07	.02
☐ 304 Brian Harper	.15	.07	.02
☐ 305 Pat Listach	.15	.07	.02
☐ 306 Matt Mieske	.15	.07	.02
☐ 307 Dave Nilsson	.40	.18	.05
☐ 308 Jody Reed	.15	.07	.02
☐ 309 Greg Vaughn	.75	.35	.09
☐ 310 Bill Wegman	.15	.07	.02
☐ 311 Rick Aguilera	.15	.07	.02
☐ 312 Alex Cole	.15	.07	.02
☐ 313 Denny Hocking	.15	.07	.02
☐ 314 Chuck Knoblauch	.75	.35	.09
☐ 315 Shane Mack	.15	.07	.02
☐ 316 Pat Meares	.15	.07	.02
☐ 317 Kevin Tapani	.15	.07	.02
☐ 318 Jim Abbott	.15	.07	.02
☐ 319 Wade Boggs	.75	.35	.09
☐ 320 Sterling Hitchcock	.40	.18	.05
☐ 321 Pat Kelly	.15	.07	.02
☐ 322 Terry Mulholland	.15	.07	.02
☐ 323 Luis Polonia	.15	.07	.02
☐ 324 Mike Stanley	.15	.07	.02
☐ 325 Bob Wickman	.15	.07	.02
☐ 326 Bernie Williams	1.00	.45	.12
☐ 327 Mark Acre	.15	.07	.02
☐ 328 Geronimo Berroa	.40	.18	.05
☐ 329 Scott Brosius	.15	.07	.02
☐ 330 Brent Gates	.15	.07	.02
☐ 331 Rickey Henderson	.75	.35	.09
☐ 332 Carlos Reyes	.15	.07	.02
☐ 333 Ruben Sierra	.40	.18	.05
☐ 334 Bobby Witt	.15	.07	.02
☐ 335 Bobby Ayala	.15	.07	.02
☐ 336 Jay Buhner	.75	.35	.09
☐ 337 Randy Johnson	.75	.35	.09
☐ 338 Edgar Martinez	.40	.18	.05
☐ 339 Bill Risley	.15	.07	.02
☐ 340 Alex Rodriguez	25.00	11.00	3.10
☐ 341 Roger Salkeld	.15	.07	.02
☐ 342 Dan Wilson	.40	.18	.05
☐ 343 Kevin Brown	.40	.18	.05
☐ 344 Jose Canseco	.75	.35	.09
☐ 345 Dean Palmer	.40	.18	.05
☐ 346 Ivan Rodriguez	1.25	.55	.16
☐ 347 Kenny Rogers	.15	.07	.02
☐ 348 Pat Borders	.15	.07	.02
☐ 349 Juan Guzman	.40	.18	.05
☐ 350 Ed Sprague	.40	.18	.05
☐ 351 Devon White	.15	.07	.02
☐ 352 Steve Avery	.40	.18	.05
☐ 353 Roberto Kelly	.15	.07	.02
☐ 354 Mark Lemke	.15	.07	.02
☐ 355 Greg McMichael	.15	.07	.02
☐ 356 Terry Pendleton	.40	.18	.05
☐ 357 John Smoltz	.75	.35	.09
☐ 358 Mike Stanton	.15	.07	.02
☐ 359 Tony Tarasco	.15	.07	.02
☐ 360 Mark Grace	.75	.35	.09
☐ 361 Derrick May	.15	.07	.02
☐ 362 Rey Sanchez	.15	.07	.02
☐ 363 Sammy Sosa	.75	.35	.09
☐ 364 Rick Wilkins	.15	.07	.02
☐ 365 Jeff Brantley	.15	.07	.02
☐ 366 Tony Fernandez	.15	.07	.02
☐ 367 Chuck McElroy	.15	.07	.02
☐ 368 Kevin Mitchell	.40	.18	.05
☐ 369 John Roper	.15	.07	.02
☐ 370 Johnny Ruffin	.15	.07	.02
☐ 371 Deion Sanders	.75	.35	.09
☐ 372 Marvin Freeman	.15	.07	.02
☐ 373 Andres Galarraga	.75	.35	.09
☐ 374 Charlie Hayes	.15	.07	.02
☐ 375 Nelson Liriano	.15	.07	.02
☐ 376 David Nied	.15	.07	.02
☐ 377 Walt Weiss	.15	.07	.02
☐ 378 Bret Barberie	.15	.07	.02
☐ 379 Jerry Browne	.15	.07	.02
☐ 380 Chuck Carr	.15	.07	.02
☐ 381 Greg Colbrunn	.15	.07	.02
☐ 382 Charlie Hough	.15	.07	.02
☐ 383 Kurt Miller	.15	.07	.02
☐ 384 Benito Santiago	.15	.07	.02
☐ 385 Jeff Bagwell	2.00	.90	.25
☐ 386 Craig Biggio	.40	.18	.05
☐ 387 Ken Caminiti	.75	.35	.09
☐ 388 Doug Drabek	.15	.07	.02
☐ 389 Steve Finley	.75	.35	.09
☐ 390 John Hudek	.15	.07	.02
☐ 391 Orlando Miller	.15	.07	.02
☐ 392 Shane Reynolds	.40	.18	.05
☐ 393 Brett Butler	.40	.18	.05
☐ 394 Tom Candiotti	.15	.07	.02
☐ 395 Delino DeShields	.15	.07	.02
☐ 396 Kevin Gross	.15	.07	.02
☐ 397 Eric Karros	.40	.18	.05
☐ 398 Ramon Martinez	.40	.18	.05
☐ 399 Henry Rodriguez	.40	.18	.05
☐ 400 Moises Alou	.40	.18	.05
☐ 401 Jeff Fassero	.15	.07	.02
☐ 402 Mike Lansing	.40	.18	.05
☐ 403 Mel Rojas	.15	.07	.02
☐ 404 Larry Walker	.75	.35	.09
☐ 405 John Wetteland	.40	.18	.05
☐ 406 Gabe White	.15	.07	.02
☐ 407 Bobby Bonilla	.40	.18	.05
☐ 408 Josias Manzanillo	.15	.07	.02
☐ 409 Bret Saberhagen	.40	.18	.05
☐ 410 David Segui	.15	.07	.02
☐ 411 Mariano Duncan	.15	.07	.02
☐ 412 Tommy Greene	.15	.07	.02
☐ 413 Billy Hatcher	.15	.07	.02
☐ 414 Ricky Jordan	.15	.07	.02
☐ 415 John Kruk	.40	.18	.05
☐ 416 Bobby Munoz	.15	.07	.02
☐ 417 Curt Schilling	.15	.07	.02
☐ 418 Fernando Valenzuela	.40	.18	.05
☐ 419 David West	.15	.07	.02
☐ 420 Carlos Garcia	.15	.07	.02
☐ 421 Brian Hunter	.15	.07	.02
☐ 422 Jeff King	.40	.18	.05
☐ 423 Jon Lieber	.15	.07	.02
☐ 424 Ravelo Manzanillo	.15	.07	.02
☐ 425 Denny Neagle	.40	.18	.05
☐ 426 Andy Van Slyke	.40	.18	.05
☐ 427 Bryan Eversgerd	.15	.07	.02
☐ 428 Bernard Gilkey	.40	.18	.05
☐ 429 Gregg Jefferies	.75	.35	.09
☐ 430 Tom Pagnozzi	.15	.07	.02
☐ 431 Bob Tewksbury	.15	.07	.02
☐ 432 Allen Watson	.15	.07	.02
☐ 433 Andy Ashby	.40	.18	.05
☐ 434 Andy Benes	.40	.18	.05
☐ 435 Donnie Elliott	.15	.07	.02
☐ 436 Tony Gwynn	2.00	.90	.25
☐ 437 Joey Hamilton	1.00	.45	.12
☐ 438 Tim Hyers	.15	.07	.02
☐ 439 Luis Lopez	.15	.07	.02
☐ 440 Bip Roberts	.15	.07	.02
☐ 441 Scott Sanders	.15	.07	.02
☐ 442 Rod Beck	.40	.18	.05
☐ 443 Dave Burba	.15	.07	.02
☐ 444 Darryl Strawberry	.40	.18	.05
☐ 445 Bill Swift	.15	.07	.02
☐ 446 Robby Thompson	.15	.07	.02
☐ 447 Bill VanLandingham	.40	.18	.05
☐ 448 Matt Williams	.75	.35	.09
☐ 449 Checklist	.15	.07	.02
☐ 450 Checklist	.15	.07	.02
☐ P15 Aaron Sele Promo	1.50	.70	.19

1994 Flair Hot Gloves

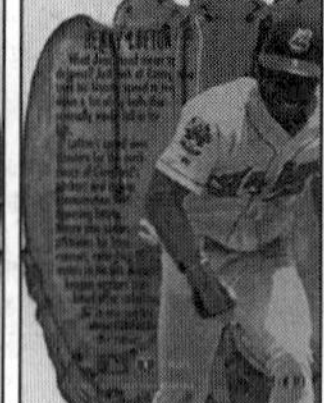

Randomly inserted in second series packs at a rate of one in 24, this set highlights 10 of the game's top players that also have outstanding defensive ability. The cards feature a special die-cut "glove" design with the player appearing within the glove. The back has a short write-up and a photo.

	MINT	NRMT	EXC
COMPLETE SET (10)	225.00	100.00	28.00
COMMON CARD (1-10)	10.00	4.50	1.25
☐ 1 Barry Bonds	20.00	9.00	2.50
☐ 2 Will Clark	10.00	4.50	1.25
☐ 3 Ken Griffey Jr.	80.00	36.00	10.00
☐ 4 Kenny Lofton	25.00	11.00	3.10
☐ 5 Greg Maddux	50.00	22.00	6.25
☐ 6 Don Mattingly	40.00	18.00	5.00
☐ 7 Kirby Puckett	30.00	13.50	3.70
☐ 8 Cal Ripken Jr.	60.00	27.00	7.50
☐ 9 Tim Salmon	15.00	6.75	1.85
☐ 10 Matt Williams	10.00	4.50	1.25

1994 Flair Hot Numbers

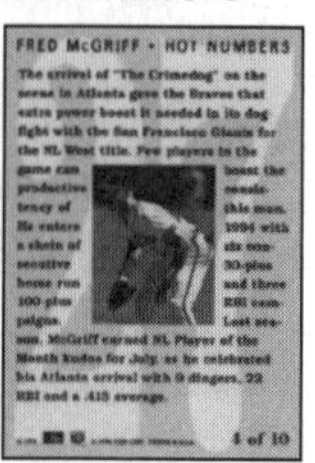

This 10-card set was randomly inserted in first series packs at a rate of one in 24. Metallic fronts feature a player photo with various numbers or statistics serving as background. The player's uniform number is part of the Hot Numbers logo at bottom left or right. The player's name is also at the bottom. The backs have a small photo centered in the middle surrounded by text highlighting achievements.

	MINT	NRMT	EXC
COMPLETE SET (10)	120.00	55.00	15.00
COMMON CARD (1-10)	2.50	1.10	.30
☐ 1 Roberto Alomar	8.00	3.60	1.00
☐ 2 Carlos Baerga	2.50	1.10	.30
☐ 3 Will Clark	6.00	2.70	.75
☐ 4 Fred McGriff	6.00	2.70	.75
☐ 5 Paul Molitor	8.00	3.60	1.00
☐ 6 John Olerud	5.00	2.20	.60
☐ 7 Mike Piazza	25.00	11.00	3.10
☐ 8 Cal Ripken Jr.	35.00	16.00	4.40
☐ 9 Ryne Sandberg	10.00	4.50	1.25
☐ 10 Frank Thomas	40.00	18.00	5.00

1994 Flair Infield Power

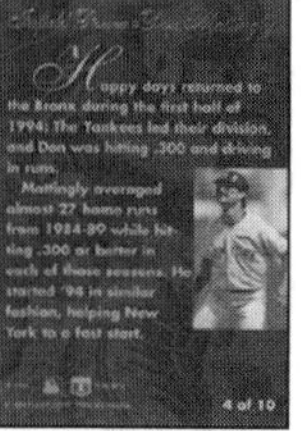

Randomly inserted in second series packs at a rate of one in five, this 10-card standard-size set spotlights major league infielders who are power hitters. Card fronts feature a horizontal format with two photos of the player. The backs contain a short write-up with emphasis on power numbers. The back also has a small photo.

	MINT	NRMT	EXC
COMPLETE SET (10)	20.00	9.00	2.50
COMMON CARD (1-10)	.50	.23	.06
☐ 1 Jeff Bagwell	3.00	1.35	.35
☐ 2 Will Clark	2.00	.90	.25
☐ 3 Darren Daulton	.50	.23	.06
☐ 4 Don Mattingly	4.00	1.80	.50
☐ 5 Fred McGriff	2.00	.90	.25
☐ 6 Rafael Palmeiro	2.00	.90	.25
☐ 7 Mike Piazza	5.00	2.20	.60
☐ 8 Cal Ripken Jr.	6.00	2.70	.75
☐ 9 Frank Thomas	8.00	3.60	1.00
☐ 10 Matt Williams	2.00	.90	.25

1994 Flair Outfield Power

This 10-card standard-size set was randomly inserted in both first and second series packs at a rate of one in five. Two photos on the front feature the player fielding and hitting. The player's name and Outfield Power serve as a dividing point between the photos. The back contains a small photo and text.

	MINT	NRMT	EXC
COMPLETE SET (10)	25.00	11.00	3.10
COMMON CARD (1-10)	.75	.35	.09
☐ 1 Albert Belle	4.00	1.80	.50
☐ 2 Barry Bonds	2.50	1.10	.30
☐ 3 Joe Carter	1.25	.55	.16
☐ 4 Lenny Dykstra	.75	.35	.09
☐ 5 Juan Gonzalez	5.00	2.20	.60

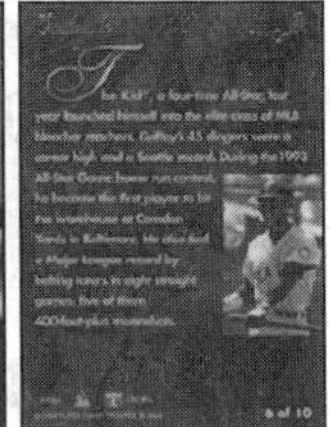

☐ 6 Ken Griffey Jr.	10.00	4.50	1.25
☐ 7 David Justice	.75	.35	.09
☐ 8 Kirby Puckett	4.00	1.80	.50
☐ 9 Tim Salmon	1.50	.70	.19
☐ 10 Dave Winfield	1.25	.55	.16

1994 Flair Wave of the Future

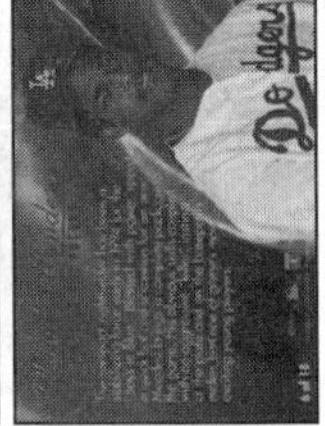

This 20-card standard-size set takes a look at potential big league stars. The cards were randomly inserted in packs at a rate of one in five -- the first 10 in series 1, the second 10 in series 2. The fronts and backs have the player superimposed over a wavy colored background. The front has the Wave of the Future logo and a paragraph or two about the player along with a photo on the back.

	MINT	NRMT	EXC
COMPLETE SET (20)	85.00	38.00	10.50
COMPLETE SER.1 SET (10)	15.00	6.75	1.85
COMPLETE SER.2 SET (10)	70.00	32.00	8.75
COMMON SER.1 CARD (A1-A10)	1.00	.45	.12
COMMON SER.2 CARD (B1-B10)	1.00	.45	.12
☐ A1 Kurt Abbott	1.50	.70	.19
☐ A2 Carlos Delgado	2.50	1.10	.30
☐ A3 Steve Karsay	1.00	.45	.12
☐ A4 Ryan Klesko	4.00	1.80	.50
☐ A5 Javier Lopez	2.50	1.10	.30
☐ A6 Raul Mondesi	3.00	1.35	.35
☐ A7 James Mouton	1.50	.70	.19
☐ A8 Chan Ho Park	4.00	1.80	.50
☐ A9 Dave Staton	1.00	.45	.12
☐ A10 Rick White	1.00	.45	.12
☐ B1 Mark Acre	1.00	.45	.12
☐ B2 Chris Gomez	1.00	.45	.12
☐ B3 Joey Hamilton	4.00	1.80	.50
☐ B4 John Hudek	1.00	.45	.12
☐ B5 Jon Lieber	1.00	.45	.12
☐ B6 Matt Mieske	1.50	.70	.19
☐ B7 Orlando Miller	1.00	.45	.12
☐ B8 Alex Rodriguez	65.00	29.00	8.00
☐ B9 Tony Tarasco	1.00	.45	.12
☐ B10 William VanLandingham	1.00	.45	.12

1995 Flair

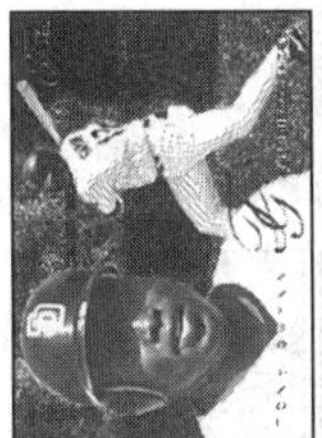

This set was issued in two series of 216 cards for a total of 432 standard-size cards. Horizontally designed fronts have a 100 percent etched foil surface containing two player photos. The backs feature a full-bleed photo with yearly statistics superimposed. The checklist is arranged alphabetically by league with AL preceding NL.

	MINT	NRMT	EXC
COMPLETE SET (432)	90.00	40.00	11.00
COMPLETE SERIES 1 (216)	50.00	22.00	6.25
COMPLETE SERIES (216)	40.00	18.00	5.00
COMMON CARD (1-432)	.25	.11	.03
☐ 1 Brady Anderson	.75	.35	.09
☐ 2 Harold Baines	.40	.18	.05
☐ 3 Leo Gomez	.25	.11	.03
☐ 4 Alan Mills	.25	.11	.03
☐ 5 Jamie Moyer	.25	.11	.03
☐ 6 Mike Mussina	1.00	.45	.12
☐ 7 Mike Oquist	.25	.11	.03
☐ 8 Arthur Rhodes	.25	.11	.03
☐ 9 Cal Ripken Jr.	4.00	1.80	.50
☐ 10 Roger Clemens	1.00	.45	.12
☐ 11 Scott Cooper	.25	.11	.03
☐ 12 Mike Greenwell	.25	.11	.03
☐ 13 Aaron Sele	.40	.18	.05
☐ 14 John Valentin	.40	.18	.05
☐ 15 Mo Vaughn	1.25	.55	.16
☐ 16 Chad Curtis	.25	.11	.03
☐ 17 Gary DiSarcina	.25	.11	.03
☐ 18 Chuck Finley	.40	.18	.05
☐ 19 Andrew Lorraine	.40	.18	.05
☐ 20 Spike Owen	.25	.11	.03
☐ 21 Tim Salmon	.75	.35	.09
☐ 22 J.T. Snow	.40	.18	.05
☐ 23 Wilson Alvarez	.40	.18	.05
☐ 24 Jason Bere	.25	.11	.03
☐ 25 Ozzie Guillen	.25	.11	.03
☐ 26 Mike LaValliere	.25	.11	.03
☐ 27 Frank Thomas	5.00	2.20	.60
☐ 28 Robin Ventura	.40	.18	.05
☐ 29 Carlos Baerga	.40	.18	.05
☐ 30 Albert Belle	2.00	.90	.25
☐ 31 Jason Grimsley	.25	.11	.03
☐ 32 Dennis Martinez	.40	.18	.05
☐ 33 Eddie Murray	1.25	.55	.16
☐ 34 Charles Nagy	.40	.18	.05
☐ 35 Manny Ramirez	1.25	.55	.16
☐ 36 Paul Sorrento	.25	.11	.03
☐ 37 John Doherty	.25	.11	.03
☐ 38 Cecil Fielder	.40	.18	.05
☐ 39 Travis Fryman	.40	.18	.05
☐ 40 Chris Gomez	.25	.11	.03
☐ 41 Tony Phillips	.40	.18	.05
☐ 42 Lou Whitaker	.40	.18	.05
☐ 43 David Cone	.40	.18	.05
☐ 44 Gary Gaetti	.40	.18	.05
☐ 45 Mark Gubicza	.25	.11	.03
☐ 46 Bob Hamelin	.25	.11	.03
☐ 47 Wally Joyner	.40	.18	.05
☐ 48 Rusty Meacham	.25	.11	.03
☐ 49 Jeff Montgomery	.40	.18	.05
☐ 50 Ricky Bones	.25	.11	.03
☐ 51 Cal Eldred	.25	.11	.03
☐ 52 Pat Listach	.25	.11	.03
☐ 53 Matt Mieske	.40	.18	.05
☐ 54 Dave Nilsson	.40	.18	.05
☐ 55 Greg Vaughn	.40	.18	.05
☐ 56 Bill Wegman	.25	.11	.03
☐ 57 Chuck Knoblauch	.75	.35	.09
☐ 58 Scott Leius	.25	.11	.03
☐ 59 Pat Mahomes	.25	.11	.03
☐ 60 Pat Meares	.25	.11	.03
☐ 61 Pedro Munoz	.25	.11	.03
☐ 62 Kirby Puckett	2.00	.90	.25
☐ 63 Wade Boggs	.75	.35	.09
☐ 64 Jimmy Key	.40	.18	.05
☐ 65 Jim Leyritz	.25	.11	.03
☐ 66 Don Mattingly	2.50	1.10	.30
☐ 67 Paul O'Neill	.40	.18	.05
☐ 68 Melido Perez	.25	.11	.03
☐ 69 Danny Tartabull	.25	.11	.03
☐ 70 John Briscoe	.25	.11	.03
☐ 71 Scott Brosius	.25	.11	.03
☐ 72 Ron Darling	.25	.11	.03
☐ 73 Brent Gates	.25	.11	.03
☐ 74 Rickey Henderson	.75	.35	.09
☐ 75 Stan Javier	.25	.11	.03
☐ 76 Mark McGwire	1.50	.70	.19
☐ 77 Todd Van Poppel	.25	.11	.03
☐ 78 Bobby Ayala	.25	.11	.03
☐ 79 Mike Blowers	.25	.11	.03
☐ 80 Jay Buhner	.75	.35	.09
☐ 81 Ken Griffey Jr.	5.00	2.20	.60
☐ 82 Randy Johnson	.75	.35	.09
☐ 83 Tino Martinez	.40	.18	.05
☐ 84 Jeff Nelson	.25	.11	.03
☐ 85 Alex Rodriguez	6.00	2.70	.75
☐ 86 Will Clark	.75	.35	.09
☐ 87 Jeff Frye	.25	.11	.03
☐ 88 Juan Gonzalez	2.50	1.10	.30
☐ 89 Rusty Greer	.75	.35	.09
☐ 90 Darren Oliver	.75	.35	.09
☐ 91 Dean Palmer	.40	.18	.05
☐ 92 Ivan Rodriguez	1.25	.55	.16
☐ 93 Matt Whiteside	.25	.11	.03
☐ 94 Roberto Alomar	1.00	.45	.12
☐ 95 Joe Carter	.40	.18	.05
☐ 96 Tony Castillo	.25	.11	.03
☐ 97 Juan Guzman	.40	.18	.05
☐ 98 Pat Hentgen	.40	.18	.05
☐ 99 Mike Huff	.25	.11	.03
☐ 100 John Olerud	.25	.11	.03
☐ 101 Woody Williams	.25	.11	.03
☐ 102 Roberto Kelly	.25	.11	.03
☐ 103 Ryan Klesko	.75	.35	.09
☐ 104 Javier Lopez	.75	.35	.09
☐ 105 Greg Maddux	3.00	1.35	.35
☐ 106 Fred McGriff	.75	.35	.09
☐ 107 Jose Oliva	.25	.11	.03
☐ 108 John Smoltz	.75	.35	.09
☐ 109 Tony Tarasco	.25	.11	.03
☐ 110 Mark Wohlers	.40	.18	.05
☐ 111 Jim Bullinger	.25	.11	.03
☐ 112 Shawon Dunston	.25	.11	.03
☐ 113 Derrick May	.25	.11	.03
☐ 114 Randy Myers	.25	.11	.03
☐ 115 Karl Rhodes	.25	.11	.03
☐ 116 Rey Sanchez	.25	.11	.03
☐ 117 Steve Trachsel	.25	.11	.03
☐ 118 Eddie Zambrano	.25	.11	.03
☐ 119 Bret Boone	.40	.18	.05
☐ 120 Brian Dorsett	.25	.11	.03
☐ 121 Hal Morris	.25	.11	.03
☐ 122 Jose Rijo	.25	.11	.03
☐ 123 John Roper	.25	.11	.03
☐ 124 Reggie Sanders	.40	.18	.05
☐ 125 Pete Schourek	.40	.18	.05
☐ 126 John Smiley	.25	.11	.03
☐ 127 Ellis Burks	.40	.18	.05
☐ 128 Vinny Castilla	.40	.18	.05
☐ 129 Marvin Freeman	.25	.11	.03
☐ 130 Andres Galarraga	.75	.35	.09
☐ 131 Mike Munoz	.25	.11	.03
☐ 132 David Nied	.25	.11	.03
☐ 133 Bruce Ruffin	.25	.11	.03
☐ 134 Walt Weiss	.25	.11	.03
☐ 135 Eric Young	.40	.18	.05
☐ 136 Greg Colbrunn	.25	.11	.03
☐ 137 Jeff Conine	.40	.18	.05
☐ 138 Jeremy Hernandez	.25	.11	.03
☐ 139 Charles Johnson	.40	.18	.05
☐ 140 Robb Nen	.25	.11	.03
☐ 141 Gary Sheffield	.75	.35	.09
☐ 142 Dave Weathers	.25	.11	.03
☐ 143 Jeff Bagwell	2.00	.90	.25
☐ 144 Craig Biggio	.40	.18	.05
☐ 145 Tony Eusebio	.25	.11	.03
☐ 146 Luis Gonzalez	.25	.11	.03
☐ 147 John Hudek	.25	.11	.03
☐ 148 Darryl Kile	.25	.11	.03
☐ 149 Dave Veres	.25	.11	.03
☐ 150 Billy Ashley	.25	.11	.03
☐ 151 Pedro Astacio	.25	.11	.03
☐ 152 Rafael Bournigal	.25	.11	.03
☐ 153 Delino DeShields	.25	.11	.03
☐ 154 Raul Mondesi	.75	.35	.09
☐ 155 Mike Piazza	3.00	1.35	.35
☐ 156 Rudy Seanez	.25	.11	.03
☐ 157 Ismael Valdes	.40	.18	.05
☐ 158 Tim Wallach	.25	.11	.03
☐ 159 Todd Worrell	.25	.11	.03
☐ 160 Moises Alou	.40	.18	.05
☐ 161 Cliff Floyd	.40	.18	.05
☐ 162 Gil Heredia	.25	.11	.03
☐ 163 Mike Lansing	.25	.11	.03
☐ 164 Pedro Martinez	.40	.18	.05
☐ 165 Kirk Rueter	.25	.11	.03
☐ 166 Tim Scott	.25	.11	.03
☐ 167 Jeff Shaw	.25	.11	.03
☐ 168 Rondell White	.40	.18	.05
☐ 169 Bobby Bonilla	.40	.18	.05
☐ 170 Rico Brogna	.25	.11	.03
☐ 171 Todd Hundley	.40	.18	.05
☐ 172 Jeff Kent	.25	.11	.03
☐ 173 Jim Lindeman	.25	.11	.03
☐ 174 Joe Orsulak	.25	.11	.03
☐ 175 Bret Saberhagen	.40	.18	.05
☐ 176 Toby Borland	.25	.11	.03
☐ 177 Darren Daulton	.40	.18	.05
☐ 178 Lenny Dykstra	.40	.18	.05
☐ 179 Jim Eisenreich	.25	.11	.03
☐ 180 Tommy Greene	.25	.11	.03
☐ 181 Tony Longmire	.25	.11	.03
☐ 182 Bobby Munoz	.25	.11	.03
☐ 183 Kevin Stocker	.25	.11	.03
☐ 184 Jay Bell	.40	.18	.05
☐ 185 Steve Cooke	.25	.11	.03
☐ 186 Ravelo Manzanillo	.25	.11	.03
☐ 187 Al Martin	.40	.18	.05
☐ 188 Denny Neagle	.40	.18	.05
☐ 189 Don Slaught	.25	.11	.03
☐ 190 Paul Wagner	.25	.11	.03
☐ 191 Rene Arocha	.25	.11	.03
☐ 192 Bernard Gilkey	.40	.18	.05
☐ 193 Jose Oquendo	.25	.11	.03
☐ 194 Tom Pagnozzi	.25	.11	.03
☐ 195 Ozzie Smith	1.25	.55	.16
☐ 196 Allen Watson	.25	.11	.03
☐ 197 Mark Whiten	.25	.11	.03
☐ 198 Andy Ashby	.40	.18	.05
☐ 199 Donnie Elliott	.25	.11	.03
☐ 200 Bryce Florie	.25	.11	.03
☐ 201 Tony Gwynn	2.00	.90	.25
☐ 202 Trevor Hoffman	.40	.18	.05
☐ 203 Brian Johnson	.25	.11	.03
☐ 204 Tim Mauser	.25	.11	.03
☐ 205 Bip Roberts	.25	.11	.03
☐ 206 Rod Beck	.25	.11	.03
☐ 207 Barry Bonds	1.25	.55	.16
☐ 208 Royce Clayton	.25	.11	.03
☐ 209 Darren Lewis	.25	.11	.03
☐ 210 Mark Portugal	.25	.11	.03
☐ 211 Kevin Rogers	.25	.11	.03
☐ 212 Wm. VanLandingham	.25	.11	.03
☐ 213 Matt Williams	.75	.35	.09
☐ 214 Checklist	.25	.11	.03
☐ 215 Checklist	.25	.11	.03
☐ 216 Checklist	.25	.11	.03
☐ 217 Bret Barberie	.25	.11	.03
☐ 218 Armando Benitez	.25	.11	.03
☐ 219 Kevin Brown	.40	.18	.05
☐ 220 Sid Fernandez	.25	.11	.03
☐ 221 Chris Hoiles	.25	.11	.03
☐ 222 Doug Jones	.25	.11	.03
☐ 223 Ben McDonald	.25	.11	.03
☐ 224 Rafael Palmeiro	.75	.35	.09
☐ 225 Andy Van Slyke	.40	.18	.05
☐ 226 Jose Canseco	.75	.35	.09
☐ 227 Vaughn Eshelman	.25	.11	.03
☐ 228 Mike Macfarlane	.25	.11	.03
☐ 229 Tim Naehring	.25	.11	.03
☐ 230 Frank Rodriguez	.40	.18	.05
☐ 231 Lee Tinsley	.25	.11	.03
☐ 232 Mark Whiten	.25	.11	.03
☐ 233 Garret Anderson	.40	.18	.05
☐ 234 Chili Davis	.40	.18	.05
☐ 235 Jim Edmonds	.75	.35	.09
☐ 236 Mark Langston	.25	.11	.03
☐ 237 Troy Percival	.25	.11	.03
☐ 238 Tony Phillips	.40	.18	.05
☐ 239 Lee Smith	.40	.18	.05
☐ 240 Jim Abbott	.25	.11	.03
☐ 241 James Baldwin	.40	.18	.05
☐ 242 Mike Devereaux	.25	.11	.03
☐ 243 Ray Durham	.40	.18	.05
☐ 244 Alex Fernandez	.40	.18	.05
☐ 245 Roberto Hernandez	.25	.11	.03
☐ 246 Lance Johnson	.40	.18	.05
☐ 247 Ron Karkovice	.25	.11	.03
☐ 248 Tim Raines	.75	.35	.09
☐ 249 Sandy Alomar Jr.	.25	.11	.03
☐ 250 Orel Hershiser	.40	.18	.05
☐ 251 Julian Tavarez	.25	.11	.03
☐ 252 Jim Thome	1.00	.45	.12
☐ 253 Omar Vizquel	.40	.18	.05
☐ 254 Dave Winfield	.75	.35	.09
☐ 255 Chad Curtis	.25	.11	.03
☐ 256 Kirk Gibson	.40	.18	.05
☐ 257 Mike Henneman	.25	.11	.03
☐ 258 Bob Higginson	1.25	.55	.16
☐ 259 Felipe Lira	.25	.11	.03
☐ 260 Rudy Pemberton	.25	.11	.03
☐ 261 Alan Trammell	.40	.18	.05
☐ 262 Kevin Appier	.40	.18	.05
☐ 263 Pat Borders	.25	.11	.03
☐ 264 Tom Gordon	.25	.11	.03
☐ 265 Jose Lind	.25	.11	.03
☐ 266 Jon Nunnally	.40	.18	.05
☐ 267 Dilson Torres	.25	.11	.03
☐ 268 Michael Tucker	.40	.18	.05
☐ 269 Jeff Cirillo	.40	.18	.05
☐ 270 Darryl Hamilton	.25	.11	.03
☐ 271 David Hulse	.25	.11	.03
☐ 272 Mark Kiefer	.25	.11	.03
☐ 273 Graeme Lloyd	.25	.11	.03
☐ 274 Joe Oliver	.25	.11	.03
☐ 275 Al Reyes	.25	.11	.03
☐ 276 Kevin Seitzer	.25	.11	.03
☐ 277 Rick Aguilera	.25	.11	.03
☐ 278 Marty Cordova	.75	.35	.09
☐ 279 Scott Erickson	.25	.11	.03
☐ 280 LaTroy Hawkins	.25	.11	.03
☐ 281 Brad Radke	.40	.18	.05
☐ 282 Kevin Tapani	.25	.11	.03
☐ 283 Tony Fernandez	.25	.11	.03
☐ 284 Sterling Hitchcock	.40	.18	.05
☐ 285 Pat Kelly	.25	.11	.03
☐ 286 Jack McDowell	.40	.18	.05
☐ 287 Andy Pettitte	2.00	.90	.25
☐ 288 Mike Stanley	.25	.11	.03
☐ 289 John Wetteland	.40	.18	.05
☐ 290 Bernie Williams	1.00	.45	.12
☐ 291 Mark Acre	.25	.11	.03
☐ 292 Geronimo Berroa	.25	.11	.03
☐ 293 Dennis Eckersley	.40	.18	.05
☐ 294 Steve Ontiveros	.25	.11	.03
☐ 295 Ruben Sierra	.40	.18	.05
☐ 296 Terry Steinbach	.40	.18	.05
☐ 297 Dave Stewart	.40	.18	.05
☐ 298 Todd Stottlemyre	.25	.11	.03
☐ 299 Darren Bragg	.40	.18	.05
☐ 300 Joey Cora	.25	.11	.03
☐ 301 Edgar Martinez	.40	.18	.05
☐ 302 Bill Risley	.25	.11	.03
☐ 303 Ron Villone	.25	.11	.03
☐ 304 Dan Wilson	.40	.18	.05
☐ 305 Benji Gil	.25	.11	.03
☐ 306 Wilson Heredia	.25	.11	.03
☐ 307 Mark McLemore	.25	.11	.03
☐ 308 Otis Nixon	.25	.11	.03
☐ 309 Kenny Rogers	.25	.11	.03
☐ 310 Jeff Russell	.25	.11	.03
☐ 311 Mickey Tettleton	.25	.11	.03
☐ 312 Bob Tewksbury	.25	.11	.03
☐ 313 David Cone	.40	.18	.05
☐ 314 Carlos Delgado	.40	.18	.05
☐ 315 Alex Gonzalez	.40	.18	.05
☐ 316 Shawn Green	.40	.18	.05
☐ 317 Paul Molitor	1.00	.45	.12
☐ 318 Ed Sprague	.40	.18	.05
☐ 319 Devon White	.40	.18	.05
☐ 320 Steve Avery	.40	.18	.05
☐ 321 Jeff Blauser	.25	.11	.03
☐ 322 Brad Clontz	.25	.11	.03

Card	MINT	NRMT	EXC
☐ 323 Tom Glavine	.75	.35	.09
☐ 324 Marquis Grissom	.40	.18	.05
☐ 325 Chipper Jones	3.00	1.35	.35
☐ 326 David Justice	.75	.35	.09
☐ 327 Mark Lemke	.25	.11	.03
☐ 328 Kent Mercker	.25	.11	.03
☐ 329 Jason Schmidt	.75	.35	.09
☐ 330 Steve Buechele	.25	.11	.03
☐ 331 Kevin Foster	.25	.11	.03
☐ 332 Mark Grace	.75	.35	.09
☐ 333 Brian McRae	.40	.18	.05
☐ 334 Sammy Sosa	.75	.35	.09
☐ 335 Ozzie Timmons	.25	.11	.03
☐ 336 Rick Wilkins	.25	.11	.03
☐ 337 Hector Carrasco	.25	.11	.03
☐ 338 Ron Gant	.40	.18	.05
☐ 339 Barry Larkin	.75	.35	.09
☐ 340 Deion Sanders	.75	.35	.09
☐ 341 Benito Santiago	.25	.11	.03
☐ 342 Roger Bailey	.25	.11	.03
☐ 343 Jason Bates	.25	.11	.03
☐ 344 Dante Bichette	.75	.35	.09
☐ 345 Joe Girardi	.25	.11	.03
☐ 346 Bill Swift	.25	.11	.03
☐ 347 Mark Thompson	.40	.18	.05
☐ 348 Larry Walker	.75	.35	.09
☐ 349 Kurt Abbott	.25	.11	.03
☐ 350 John Burkett	.40	.18	.05
☐ 351 Chuck Carr	.25	.11	.03
☐ 352 Andre Dawson	.40	.18	.05
☐ 353 Chris Hammond	.25	.11	.03
☐ 354 Charles Johnson	.40	.18	.05
☐ 355 Terry Pendleton	.40	.18	.05
☐ 356 Quilvio Veras	.25	.11	.03
☐ 357 Derek Bell	.40	.18	.05
☐ 358 Jim Dougherty	.25	.11	.03
☐ 359 Doug Drabek	.25	.11	.03
☐ 360 Todd Jones	.25	.11	.03
☐ 361 Orlando Miller	.25	.11	.03
☐ 362 James Mouton	.25	.11	.03
☐ 363 Phil Plantier	.25	.11	.03
☐ 364 Shane Reynolds	.40	.18	.05
☐ 365 Todd Hollandsworth	.75	.35	.09
☐ 366 Eric Karros	.40	.18	.05
☐ 367 Ramon Martinez	.40	.18	.05
☐ 368 Hideo Nomo	5.00	2.20	.60
☐ 369 Jose Offerman	.25	.11	.03
☐ 370 Antonio Osuna	.25	.11	.03
☐ 371 Todd Williams	.25	.11	.03
☐ 372 Shane Andrews	.25	.11	.03
☐ 373 Wil Cordero	.25	.11	.03
☐ 374 Jeff Fassero	.25	.11	.03
☐ 375 Darrin Fletcher	.25	.11	.03
☐ 376 Mark Grudzielanek	1.25	.55	.16
☐ 377 Carlos Perez	.40	.18	.05
☐ 378 Mel Rojas	.25	.11	.03
☐ 379 Tony Tarasco	.25	.11	.03
☐ 380 Edgardo Alfonzo	.40	.18	.05
☐ 381 Brett Butler	.40	.18	.05
☐ 382 Carl Everett	.25	.11	.03
☐ 383 John Franco	.25	.11	.03
☐ 384 Pete Harnisch	.25	.11	.03
☐ 385 Bobby Jones	.40	.18	.05
☐ 386 Dave Mlicki	.25	.11	.03
☐ 387 Jose Vizcaino	.25	.11	.03
☐ 388 Ricky Bottalico	.40	.18	.05
☐ 389 Tyler Green	.25	.11	.03
☐ 390 Charlie Hayes	.25	.11	.03
☐ 391 Dave Hollins	.25	.11	.03
☐ 392 Gregg Jefferies	.40	.18	.05
☐ 393 Michael Mimbs	.40	.18	.05
☐ 394 Mickey Morandini	.25	.11	.03
☐ 395 Curt Schilling	.25	.11	.03
☐ 396 Heathcliff Slocumb	.25	.11	.03
☐ 397 Jason Christiansen	.25	.11	.03
☐ 398 Midre Cummings	.25	.11	.03
☐ 399 Carlos Garcia	.25	.11	.03
☐ 400 Mark Johnson	.40	.18	.05
☐ 401 Jeff King	.40	.18	.05
☐ 402 Jon Lieber	.25	.11	.03
☐ 403 Esteban Loaiza	.25	.11	.03
☐ 404 Orlando Merced	.25	.11	.03
☐ 405 Gary Wilson	.25	.11	.03
☐ 406 Scott Cooper	.25	.11	.03
☐ 407 Tom Henke	.25	.11	.03
☐ 408 Ken Hill	.25	.11	.03
☐ 409 Danny Jackson	.25	.11	.03
☐ 410 Brian Jordan	.75	.35	.09
☐ 411 Ray Lankford	.40	.18	.05
☐ 412 John Mabry	.75	.35	.09
☐ 413 Todd Zeile	.25	.11	.03
☐ 414 Andy Benes	.25	.11	.03
☐ 415 Andres Berumen	.25	.11	.03
☐ 416 Ken Caminiti	.75	.35	.09
☐ 417 Andujar Cedeno	.25	.11	.03
☐ 418 Steve Finley	.40	.18	.05
☐ 419 Joey Hamilton	.75	.35	.09
☐ 420 Dustin Hermanson	.40	.18	.05
☐ 421 Melvin Nieves	.40	.18	.05
☐ 422 Roberto Petagine	.25	.11	.03
☐ 423 Eddie Williams	.25	.11	.03
☐ 424 Glenallen Hill	.25	.11	.03
☐ 425 Kirt Manwaring	.25	.11	.03
☐ 426 Terry Mulholland	.25	.11	.03
☐ 427 J.R. Phillips	.25	.11	.03
☐ 428 Joe Rosselli	.25	.11	.03
☐ 429 Robby Thompson	.25	.11	.03
☐ 430 Checklist	.25	.11	.03
☐ 431 Checklist	.25	.11	.03
☐ 432 Checklist	.25	.11	.03

1995 Flair Hot Gloves

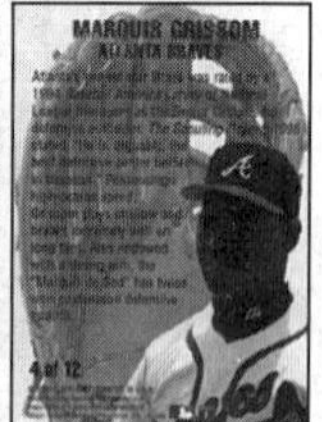

This 12-card standard-size set features players that are known for their defensive prowess. Randomly inserted in series two packs at a rate of one in 25, a player photo is superimposed over an embossed design of a bronze glove.The backs have a photo and write-up with a glove as background.

	MINT	NRMT	EXC
COMPLETE SET (12)	175.00	80.00	22.00
COMMON CARD (1-12)	5.00	2.20	.60
☐ 1 Roberto Alomar	12.00	5.50	1.50
☐ 2 Barry Bonds	15.00	6.75	1.85
☐ 3 Ken Griffey Jr.	60.00	27.00	7.50
☐ 4 Marquis Grissom	6.00	2.70	.75
☐ 5 Barry Larkin	8.00	3.60	1.00
☐ 6 Darren Lewis	5.00	2.20	.60
☐ 7 Kenny Lofton	15.00	6.75	1.85
☐ 8 Don Mattingly	30.00	13.50	3.70
☐ 9 Cal Ripken	50.00	22.00	6.25
☐ 10 Ivan Rodriguez	15.00	6.75	1.85
☐ 11 Devon White	5.00	2.20	.60
☐ 12 Matt Williams	8.00	3.60	1.00

1995 Flair Hot Numbers

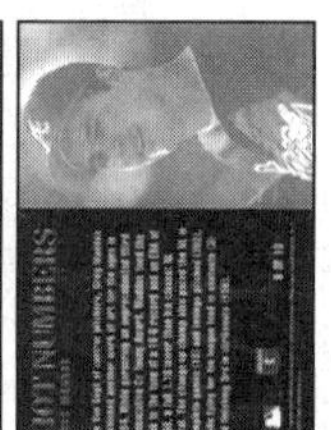

Randomly inserted in packs at a rate of one in nine, this 10-card standard-size set showcases top players. A player photo on front is superimposed over a gold background that contains player stats from 1994. Horizontal backs have a ghosted player photo to the right with highlights on the left.

	MINT	NRMT	EXC
COMPLETE SET (10)	60.00	27.00	7.50
COMMON CARD (1-10)	2.00	.90	.25
☐ 1 Jeff Bagwell	6.00	2.70	.75
☐ 2 Albert Belle	6.00	2.70	.75
☐ 3 Barry Bonds	4.00	1.80	.50
☐ 4 Ken Griffey Jr.	15.00	6.75	1.85
☐ 5 Kenny Lofton	4.00	1.80	.50
☐ 6 Greg Maddux	10.00	4.50	1.25
☐ 7 Mike Piazza	10.00	4.50	1.25
☐ 8 Cal Ripken	12.00	5.50	1.50
☐ 9 Frank Thomas	15.00	6.75	1.85
☐ 10 Matt Williams	2.00	.90	.25

1995 Flair Infield Power

Randomly inserted in second series packs at a rate of one in five, this 10-card standard-size set features sluggers that man the outfield. A player photo on front is surrounded by multiple color schemes with a horizontal back offering a player photo and highlights.

	MINT	NRMT	EXC
COMPLETE SET (10)	15.00	6.75	1.85
COMMON CARD (1-10)	.50	.23	.06
☐ 1 Jeff Bagwell	3.00	1.35	.35
☐ 2 Darren Daulton	.50	.23	.06
☐ 3 Cecil Fielder	1.00	.45	.12
☐ 4 Andres Galarraga	1.50	.70	.19
☐ 5 Fred McGriff	1.50	.70	.19
☐ 6 Rafael Palmeiro	1.50	.70	.19
☐ 7 Mike Piazza	5.00	2.20	.60
☐ 8 Frank Thomas	8.00	3.60	1.00
☐ 9 Mo Vaughn	2.00	.90	.25
☐ 10 Matt Williams	1.50	.70	.19

1995 Flair Outfield Power

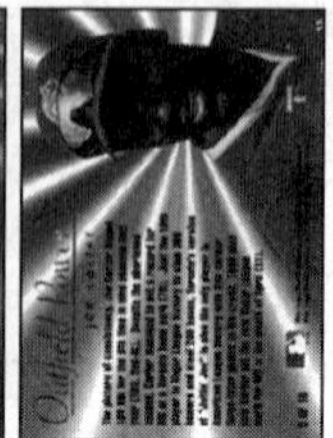

Randomly inserted in first series packs at a rate of one in six, this 10-card standard-size set features sluggers that patrol the outfield. A player photo on front is surrounded by multiple color schemes with a horizontal back offering a player photo and highlights.

	MINT	NRMT	EXC
COMPLETE SET (10)	15.00	6.75	1.85
COMMON CARD (1-10)	.50	.23	.06
☐ 1 Albert Belle	3.00	1.35	.35
☐ 2 Dante Bichette	1.00	.45	.12
☐ 3 Barry Bonds	2.00	.90	.25
☐ 4 Jose Canseco	1.00	.45	.12
☐ 5 Joe Carter	.75	.35	.09
☐ 6 Juan Gonzalez	4.00	1.80	.50
☐ 7 Ken Griffey Jr.	8.00	3.60	1.00
☐ 8 Kirby Puckett	3.00	1.35	.35
☐ 9 Gary Sheffield	1.25	.55	.16
☐ 10 Ruben Sierra	.50	.23	.06

1995 Flair Ripken

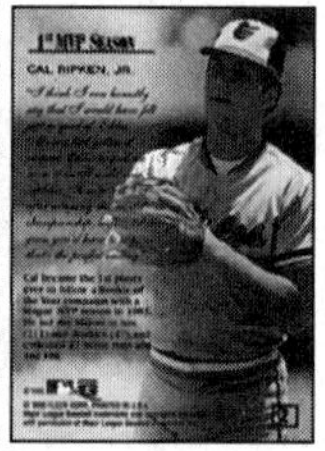

Titled "Enduring", this 10-card standard-size set is a tribute to Cal Ripken's career through the '94 season. Cards were randomly inserted in second series packs at a rate of one in 12. Full-bleed fronts have the set title in silver foil toward the bottom. The backs have a photo and a write-up on a specific achievement as selected by Cal. A five-card mail-in wrapper offer completes the set. The expiration date on this offer was March 1, 1996.

	MINT	NRMT	EXC
COMPLETE SET (10)	120.00	55.00	15.00
COMMON CARD (1-10)	12.00	5.50	1.50
COMMON MAIL-IN (11-15)	8.00	3.60	1.00
☐ 1 Cal Ripken Rookie of the Year	12.00	5.50	1.50
☐ 2 Cal Ripken 1st MVP Season	12.00	5.50	1.50
☐ 3 Cal Ripken World Series Highlight	12.00	5.50	1.50
☐ 4 Cal Ripken Family Tradition	12.00	5.50	1.50
☐ 5 Cal Ripken 8,243 Consecutive Innings	12.00	5.50	1.50
☐ 6 Cal Ripken 95 Consecutive Errorless Games	12.00	5.50	1.50
☐ 7 Cal Ripken All-Star MVP	12.00	5.50	1.50
☐ 8 Cal Ripken 1,000th RBI	12.00	5.50	1.50
☐ 9 Cal Ripken 287th Home Run	12.00	5.50	1.50
☐ 10 Cal Ripken 2,000th Consecutive Game	12.00	5.50	1.50
☐ 11 Cal Ripken Literacy	8.00	3.60	1.00
☐ 12 Cal Ripken Game 2,130	8.00	3.60	1.00
☐ 13 Cal Ripken Game 2,131	8.00	3.60	1.00
☐ 14 Cal Ripken Defensive Prowess	8.00	3.60	1.00
☐ 15 Cal Ripken 2,153 and Counting	8.00	3.60	1.00

1995 Flair Today's Spotlight

This 12-card die-cut set was randomly inserted in first series packs at a rate of one in 25 packs. The upper portion of the player photo on front has the spotlight effect as the remainder of the photo is darkened. Horizontal backs have a circular player photo to the right with text off to the left.

	MINT	NRMT	EXC
COMPLETE SET (12)	150.00	70.00	19.00
COMMON CARD (1-12)	6.00	2.70	.75
☐ 1 Jeff Bagwell	25.00	11.00	3.10
☐ 2 Jason Bere	6.00	2.70	.75
☐ 3 Cliff Floyd	6.00	2.70	.75
☐ 4 Chuck Knoblauch	10.00	4.50	1.25
☐ 5 Kenny Lofton	15.00	6.75	1.85
☐ 6 Javier Lopez	6.00	2.70	.75
☐ 7 Raul Mondesi	8.00	3.60	1.00
☐ 8 Mike Mussina	12.00	5.50	1.50
☐ 9 Mike Piazza	40.00	18.00	5.00
☐ 10 Manny Ramirez	15.00	6.75	1.85
☐ 11 Tim Salmon	8.00	3.60	1.00
☐ 12 Frank Thomas	60.00	27.00	7.50

1995 Flair Wave of the Future

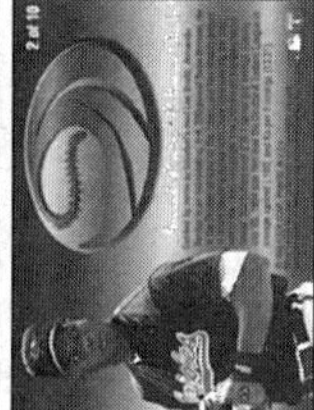

Spotlighting 10 of the game's hottest young stars, cards were randomly inseretd in second series packs at a rate of one in eight. An action photo is superimposed over primarily a solid background save for the player's name, team and same name which appear several times. The backs are horizontal with a photo and write-up.

	MINT	NRMT	EXC
COMPLETE SET (10)	25.00	11.00	3.10
COMMON CARD (1-10)	1.00	.45	.12
☐ 1 Jason Bates	1.00	.45	.12
☐ 2 Armando Benitez	1.00	.45	.12
☐ 3 Marty Cordova	3.00	1.35	.35
☐ 4 Ray Durham	2.00	.90	.25
☐ 5 Vaughn Eshelman	1.00	.45	.12
☐ 6 Carl Everett	1.00	.45	.12
☐ 7 Shawn Green	2.00	.90	.25
☐ 8 Dustin Hermanson	1.00	.45	.12
☐ 9 Chipper Jones	12.00	5.50	1.50
☐ 10 Hideo Nomo	10.00	4.50	1.25

1996 Flair

Released in July, 1996, this 400-card set was issued in one series and sold in seven-card packs at a suggested retail price of $4.99. Gold and Silver etched foil front variations exist for all cards. These color variations were printed in similar quantities and are valued equally. The fronts and backs each carry a color action player cut-out on a player portrait background with player statistics on the backs. The cards are grouped alphabetically within teams and checklisted below alphabetically according to teams for each league.

	MINT	NRMT	EXC
COMPLETE SET (400)	200.00	90.00	25.00
COMMON CARD (1-400)	.50	.23	.06

☐ 1 Roberto Alomar 2.00 .90 .25
☐ 2 Brady Anderson 1.00 .45 .12
☐ 3 Bobby Bonilla .75 .35 .09
☐ 4 Scott Erickson .50 .23 .06
☐ 5 Jeffrey Hammonds .50 .23 .06
☐ 6 Jimmy Haynes .50 .23 .06
☐ 7 Chris Hoiles .50 .23 .06
☐ 8 Kent Mercker .50 .23 .06
☐ 9 Mike Mussina 2.00 .90 .25
☐ 10 Randy Myers .50 .23 .06
☐ 11 Rafael Palmeiro 1.00 .45 .12
☐ 12 Cal Ripken 8.00 3.60 1.00
☐ 13 B.J. Surhoff .50 .23 .06
☐ 14 David Wells .50 .23 .06
☐ 15 Jose Canseco 1.00 .45 .12
☐ 16 Roger Clemens 2.00 .90 .25
☐ 17 Wil Cordero .50 .23 .06
☐ 18 Tom Gordon .50 .23 .06
☐ 19 Mike Greenwell .50 .23 .06
☐ 20 Dwayne Hosey .50 .23 .06
☐ 21 Jose Malave .50 .23 .06
☐ 22 Tim Naehring .50 .23 .06
☐ 23 Troy O'Leary .50 .23 .06
☐ 24 Aaron Sele .50 .23 .06
☐ 25 Heathcliff Slocumb .50 .23 .06
☐ 26 Mike Stanley .50 .23 .06
☐ 27 Jeff Suppan 1.00 .45 .12
☐ 28 John Valentin .75 .35 .09
☐ 29 Mo Vaughn 2.50 1.10 .30
☐ 30 Tim Wakefield .50 .23 .06
☐ 31 Jim Abbott 1.00 .45 .12
☐ 32 Garret Anderson 1.00 .45 .12
☐ 33 George Arias .50 .23 .06
☐ 34 Chili Davis .50 .23 .06
☐ 35 Gary DiSarcina .50 .23 .06
☐ 36 Jim Edmonds .75 .35 .09
☐ 37 Chuck Finley .50 .23 .06
☐ 38 Todd Greene 1.00 .45 .12
☐ 39 Mark Langston .50 .23 .06
☐ 40 Troy Percival .50 .23 .06
☐ 41 Tim Salmon 1.25 .55 .16
☐ 42 Lee Smith .75 .35 .09
☐ 43 J.T. Snow .75 .35 .09
☐ 44 Randy Velarde .50 .23 .06
☐ 45 Tim Wallach .50 .23 .06
☐ 46 Wilson Alvarez 1.00 .45 .12
☐ 47 Harold Baines 1.00 .45 .12
☐ 48 Jason Bere .50 .23 .06
☐ 49 Ray Durham 1.00 .45 .12
☐ 50 Alex Fernandez .75 .35 .09
☐ 51 Ozzie Guillen .50 .23 .06
☐ 52 Roberto Hernandez .75 .35 .09
☐ 53 Ron Karkovice .50 .23 .06
☐ 54 Darren Lewis .50 .23 .06
☐ 55 Lyle Mouton .50 .23 .06
☐ 56 Tony Phillips .75 .35 .09
☐ 57 Chris Snopek .50 .23 .06
☐ 58 Kevin Tapani .50 .23 .06
☐ 59 Danny Tartabull .50 .23 .06
☐ 60 Frank Thomas 10.00 4.50 1.25
☐ 61 Robin Ventura .75 .35 .09
☐ 62 Sandy Alomar Jr. .50 .23 .06
☐ 63 Carlos Baerga .75 .35 .09
☐ 64 Albert Belle 4.00 1.80 .50
☐ 65 Julio Franco .75 .35 .09
☐ 66 Orel Hershiser .75 .35 .09
☐ 67 Kenny Lofton 2.50 1.10 .30
☐ 68 Dennis Martinez .75 .35 .09
☐ 69 Jack McDowell 1.00 .45 .12
☐ 70 Jose Mesa .75 .35 .09
☐ 71 Eddie Murray 2.50 1.10 .30
☐ 72 Charles Nagy .75 .35 .09
☐ 73 Tony Pena .50 .23 .06
☐ 74 Manny Ramirez 2.50 1.10 .30
☐ 75 Julian Tavarez .50 .23 .06
☐ 76 Jim Thome 2.00 .90 .25
☐ 77 Omar Vizquel .75 .35 .09
☐ 78 Chad Curtis .50 .23 .06
☐ 79 Cecil Fielder .75 .35 .09
☐ 80 Travis Fryman .75 .35 .09
☐ 81 Chris Gomez .50 .23 .06
☐ 82 Bob Higginson 1.00 .45 .12
☐ 83 Mark Lewis .50 .23 .06
☐ 84 Felipe Lira .50 .23 .06
☐ 85 Alan Trammell .75 .35 .09
☐ 86 Kevin Appier .75 .35 .09
☐ 87 Johnny Damon .75 .35 .09
☐ 88 Tom Goodwin .75 .35 .09
☐ 89 Mark Gubicza .50 .23 .06
☐ 90 Bob Hamelin .50 .23 .06
☐ 91 Keith Lockhart .50 .23 .06
☐ 92 Jeff Montgomery .50 .23 .06
☐ 93 Jon Nunnally .50 .23 .06
☐ 94 Bip Roberts .50 .23 .06
☐ 95 Michael Tucker .75 .35 .09
☐ 96 Joe Vitiello .50 .23 .06
☐ 97 Ricky Bones .50 .23 .06
☐ 98 Chuck Carr .50 .23 .06
☐ 99 Jeff Cirillo .50 .23 .06
☐ 100 Mike Fetters .50 .23 .06
☐ 101 John Jaha .75 .35 .09
☐ 102 Mike Matheny .50 .23 .06
☐ 103 Ben McDonald .50 .23 .06
☐ 104 Matt Mieske .50 .23 .06
☐ 105 Dave Nilsson .75 .35 .09
☐ 106 Kevin Seitzer .50 .23 .06
☐ 107 Steve Sparks .50 .23 .06
☐ 108 Jose Valentin .50 .23 .06
☐ 109 Greg Vaughn 1.00 .45 .12
☐ 110 Rick Aguilera .50 .23 .06
☐ 111 Rich Becker .75 .35 .09
☐ 112 Marty Cordova 1.25 .55 .16
☐ 113 LaTroy Hawkins .50 .23 .06
☐ 114 Dave Hollins .50 .23 .06
☐ 115 Roberto Kelly .50 .23 .06
☐ 116 Chuck Knoblauch 1.00 .45 .12
☐ 117 Matt Lawton .50 .23 .06
☐ 118 Pat Meares .50 .23 .06
☐ 119 Paul Molitor 2.00 .90 .25
☐ 120 Kirby Puckett 4.00 1.80 .50
☐ 121 Brad Radke .50 .23 .06
☐ 122 Frank Rodriguez .75 .35 .09
☐ 123 Scott Stahoviak .50 .23 .06
☐ 124 Matt Walbeck .50 .23 .06
☐ 125 Wade Boggs 1.00 .45 .12
☐ 126 David Cone .75 .35 .09
☐ 127 Joe Girardi .50 .23 .06
☐ 128 Dwight Gooden .75 .35 .09
☐ 129 Derek Jeter 6.00 2.70 .75
☐ 130 Jimmy Key .75 .35 .09
☐ 131 Jim Leyritz .50 .23 .06
☐ 132 Tino Martinez .75 .35 .09
☐ 133 Paul O'Neill .50 .23 .06
☐ 134 Andy Pettitte 3.00 1.35 .35
☐ 135 Tim Raines 1.00 .45 .12
☐ 136 Ruben Rivera 2.00 .90 .25
☐ 137 Kenny Rogers .50 .23 .06
☐ 138 Ruben Sierra .50 .23 .06
☐ 139 John Wetteland .75 .35 .09
☐ 140 Bernie Williams 2.00 .90 .25
☐ 141 Tony Batista 1.50 .70 .19
☐ 142 Allen Battle .50 .23 .06
☐ 143 Geronimo Berroa .75 .35 .09
☐ 144 Mike Bordick .75 .35 .09
☐ 145 Scott Brosius .75 .35 .09
☐ 146 Steve Cox .50 .23 .06
☐ 147 Brent Gates .50 .23 .06
☐ 148 Jason Giambi 1.00 .45 .12
☐ 149 Doug Johns .50 .23 .06
☐ 150 Mark McGwire 3.00 1.35 .35
☐ 151 Pedro Munoz .50 .23 .06
☐ 152 Ariel Prieto .50 .23 .06
☐ 153 Terry Steinbach .75 .35 .09
☐ 154 Todd Van Poppel .50 .23 .06
☐ 155 Bobby Ayala .50 .23 .06
☐ 156 Chris Bosio .50 .23 .06
☐ 157 Jay Buhner 1.00 .45 .12
☐ 158 Joey Cora .50 .23 .06
☐ 159 Russ Davis .50 .23 .06
☐ 160 Ken Griffey Jr. 10.00 4.50 1.25
☐ 161 Sterling Hitchcock .50 .23 .06
☐ 162 Randy Johnson 1.50 .70 .19
☐ 163 Edgar Martinez .75 .35 .09
☐ 164 Alex Rodriguez 10.00 4.50 1.25
☐ 165 Paul Sorrento .50 .23 .06
☐ 166 Dan Wilson .50 .23 .06
☐ 167 Will Clark 1.00 .45 .12
☐ 168 Benji Gil .50 .23 .06
☐ 169 Juan Gonzalez 5.00 2.20 .60
☐ 170 Rusty Greer 1.00 .45 .12
☐ 171 Kevin Gross .50 .23 .06
☐ 172 Darryl Hamilton .50 .23 .06
☐ 173 Mike Henneman .50 .23 .06
☐ 174 Ken Hill .50 .23 .06
☐ 175 Mark McLemore .50 .23 .06
☐ 176 Dean Palmer 1.00 .45 .12
☐ 177 Roger Pavlik .50 .23 .06
☐ 178 Ivan Rodriguez 2.50 1.10 .30
☐ 179 Mickey Tettleton .75 .35 .09
☐ 180 Bobby Witt .50 .23 .06
☐ 181 Joe Carter .75 .35 .09
☐ 182 Felipe Crespo .50 .23 .06
☐ 183 Alex Gonzalez .50 .23 .06
☐ 184 Shawn Green .50 .23 .06
☐ 185 Juan Guzman .50 .23 .06
☐ 186 Erik Hanson .50 .23 .06
☐ 187 Pat Hentgen .75 .35 .09
☐ 188 Sandy Martinez .50 .23 .06
☐ 189 Otis Nixon .50 .23 .06
☐ 190 John Olerud .50 .23 .06
☐ 191 Paul Quantrill .50 .23 .06
☐ 192 Bill Risley .50 .23 .06
☐ 193 Ed Sprague .75 .35 .09
☐ 194 Steve Avery .50 .23 .06
☐ 195 Jeff Blauser .50 .23 .06
☐ 196 Brad Clontz .50 .23 .06
☐ 197 Jermaine Dye 2.00 .90 .25
☐ 198 Tom Glavine 1.00 .45 .12
☐ 199 Marquis Grissom .75 .35 .09
☐ 200 Chipper Jones 6.00 2.70 .75
☐ 201 David Justice .75 .35 .09
☐ 202 Ryan Klesko 1.50 .70 .19
☐ 203 Mark Lemke .50 .23 .06
☐ 204 Javier Lopez 1.00 .45 .12
☐ 205 Greg Maddux 6.00 2.70 .75
☐ 206 Fred McGriff 1.25 .55 .16
☐ 207 Greg McMichael .50 .23 .06
☐ 208 Wonderful Monds .50 .23 .06
☐ 209 Jason Schmidt 1.00 .45 .12
☐ 210 John Smoltz 1.50 .70 .19
☐ 211 Mark Wohlers .75 .35 .09
☐ 212 Jim Bullinger .50 .23 .06
☐ 213 Frank Castillo .50 .23 .06
☐ 214 Kevin Foster .50 .23 .06
☐ 215 Luis Gonzalez .50 .23 .06
☐ 216 Mark Grace 1.00 .45 .12
☐ 217 Robin Jennings .50 .23 .06
☐ 218 Doug Jones .50 .23 .06
☐ 219 Dave Magadan .50 .23 .06
☐ 220 Brian McRae .50 .23 .06
☐ 221 Jaime Navarro .50 .23 .06
☐ 222 Rey Sanchez .50 .23 .06
☐ 223 Ryne Sandberg 2.50 1.10 .30
☐ 224 Scott Servais .50 .23 .06
☐ 225 Sammy Sosa 1.50 .70 .19
☐ 226 Ozzie Timmons .50 .23 .06
☐ 227 Bret Boone .50 .23 .06
☐ 228 Jeff Branson .50 .23 .06
☐ 229 Jeff Brantley .50 .23 .06
☐ 230 Dave Burba .50 .23 .06
☐ 231 Vince Coleman .50 .23 .06
☐ 232 Steve Gibralter .50 .23 .06
☐ 233 Mike Kelly .50 .23 .06
☐ 234 Barry Larkin 1.25 .55 .16
☐ 235 Hal Morris .50 .23 .06
☐ 236 Mark Portugal .50 .23 .06
☐ 237 Jose Rijo .50 .23 .06
☐ 238 Reggie Sanders .75 .35 .09
☐ 239 Pete Schourek .75 .35 .09
☐ 240 John Smiley .50 .23 .06
☐ 241 Eddie Taubensee .50 .23 .06
☐ 242 Jason Bates .50 .23 .06
☐ 243 Dante Bichette 1.25 .55 .16
☐ 244 Ellis Burks .75 .35 .09
☐ 245 Vinny Castilla .75 .35 .09
☐ 246 Andres Galarraga 1.00 .45 .12
☐ 247 Darren Holmes .50 .23 .06
☐ 248 Curt Leskanic .50 .23 .06
☐ 249 Steve Reed .50 .23 .06
☐ 250 Kevin Rtiz .50 .23 .06
☐ 251 Bret Saberhagen .50 .23 .06
☐ 252 Bill Swift .50 .23 .06
☐ 253 Larry Walker 1.00 .45 .12
☐ 254 Walt Weiss .50 .23 .06
☐ 255 Eric Young .75 .35 .09
☐ 256 Kurt Abbott .50 .23 .06
☐ 257 Kevin Brown .75 .35 .09
☐ 258 John Burkett .50 .23 .06
☐ 259 Greg Colbrunn .50 .23 .06
☐ 260 Jeff Conine .75 .35 .09
☐ 261 Andre Dawson .75 .35 .09
☐ 262 Chris Hammond .50 .23 .06
☐ 263 Charles Johnson .75 .35 .09
☐ 264 Al Leiter .50 .23 .06
☐ 265 Robb Nen .50 .23 .06
☐ 266 Terry Pendleton .75 .35 .09
☐ 267 Pat Rapp .50 .23 .06
☐ 268 Gary Sheffield 1.50 .70 .19
☐ 269 Quilvio Veras .50 .23 .06
☐ 270 Devon White .50 .23 .06
☐ 271 Bob Abreu 1.00 .45 .12
☐ 272 Jeff Bagwell 4.00 1.80 .50
☐ 273 Derek Bell .75 .35 .09
☐ 274 Sean Berry .50 .23 .06
☐ 275 Craig Biggio .75 .35 .09
☐ 276 Doug Drabek .50 .23 .06
☐ 277 Tony Eusebio .50 .23 .06
☐ 278 Richard Hidalgo 1.00 .45 .12
☐ 279 Brian L.Hunter .75 .35 .09
☐ 280 Todd Jones .50 .23 .06
☐ 281 Derrick May .50 .23 .06
☐ 282 Orlando Miller .50 .23 .06
☐ 283 James Mouton .50 .23 .06
☐ 284 Shane Reynolds .50 .23 .06
☐ 285 Greg Swindell .50 .23 .06
☐ 286 Mike Blowers .50 .23 .06
☐ 287 Brett Butler .50 .23 .06
☐ 288 Tom Candiotti .50 .23 .06
☐ 289 Roger Cedeno .75 .35 .09
☐ 290 Delino DeShields .50 .23 .06
☐ 291 Greg Gagne .50 .23 .06
☐ 292 Karim Garcia 2.00 .90 .25
☐ 293 Todd Hollandsworth 1.25 .55 .16
☐ 294 Eric Karros .75 .35 .09
☐ 295 Ramon Martinez .75 .35 .09
☐ 296 Raul Mondesi 1.00 .45 .12
☐ 297 Hideo Nomo 2.50 1.10 .30
☐ 298 Mike Piazza 6.00 2.70 .75
☐ 299 Ismael Valdes .75 .35 .09
☐ 300 Todd Worrell .75 .35 .09
☐ 301 Moises Alou .75 .35 .09
☐ 302 Shane Andrews .50 .23 .06
☐ 303 Yamil Benitez .75 .35 .09
☐ 304 Jeff Fassero .50 .23 .06
☐ 305 Darrin Fletcher .50 .23 .06
☐ 306 Cliff Floyd .50 .23 .06
☐ 307 Mark Grudzielanek .75 .35 .09
☐ 308 Mike Lansing .50 .23 .06
☐ 309 Pedro Martinez .75 .35 .09
☐ 310 Ryan McGuire .50 .23 .06
☐ 311 Carlos Perez .50 .23 .06
☐ 312 Mel Rojas .75 .35 .09
☐ 313 David Segui .50 .23 .06
☐ 314 Rondell White .75 .35 .09
☐ 315 Edgardo Alfonzo .75 .35 .09
☐ 316 Rico Brogna .50 .23 .06
☐ 317 Carl Everett .50 .23 .06
☐ 318 John Franco .50 .23 .06
☐ 319 Bernard Gilkey .75 .35 .09
☐ 320 Todd Hundley .75 .35 .09
☐ 321 Jason Isringhausen 1.00 .45 .12
☐ 322 Lance Johnson .75 .35 .09
☐ 323 Bobby Jones .50 .23 .06
☐ 324 Jeff Kent .50 .23 .06
☐ 325 Rey Ordonez 1.00 .45 .12
☐ 326 Bill Pulsipher .75 .35 .09
☐ 327 Jose Vizcaino .50 .23 .06
☐ 328 Paul Wilson .75 .35 .09
☐ 329 Ricky Bottalico .50 .23 .06
☐ 330 Darren Daulton .75 .35 .09
☐ 331 David Doster .50 .23 .06
☐ 332 Lenny Dykstra .75 .35 .09
☐ 333 Jim Eisenreich .50 .23 .06
☐ 334 Sid Fernandez .50 .23 .06
☐ 335 Gregg Jefferies 1.00 .45 .12
☐ 336 Mickey Morandini .50 .23 .06
☐ 337 Benito Santiago .50 .23 .06
☐ 338 Curt Schilling .50 .23 .06
☐ 339 Kevin Stocker .50 .23 .06
☐ 340 David West .50 .23 .06
☐ 341 Mark Whiten .50 .23 .06
☐ 342 Todd Zeile .75 .35 .09
☐ 343 Jay Bell .75 .35 .09
☐ 344 John Ericks .50 .23 .06
☐ 345 Carlos Garcia .50 .23 .06
☐ 346 Charlie Hayes .50 .23 .06
☐ 347 Jason Kendall 1.00 .45 .12
☐ 348 Jeff King .75 .35 .09
☐ 349 Mike Kingery .50 .23 .06
☐ 350 Al Martin .50 .23 .06
☐ 351 Orlando Merced .75 .35 .09
☐ 352 Dan Miceli .50 .23 .06
☐ 353 Denny Neagle .75 .35 .09
☐ 354 Alan Benes 1.00 .45 .12
☐ 355 Andy Benes .50 .23 .06
☐ 356 Royce Clayton .50 .23 .06
☐ 357 Dennis Eckersley .75 .35 .09
☐ 358 Gary Gaetti .75 .35 .09
☐ 359 Ron Gant .75 .35 .09
☐ 360 Brian Jordan .75 .35 .09
☐ 361 Ray Lankford .75 .35 .09
☐ 362 John Mabry .75 .35 .09
☐ 363 T.J. Mathews .50 .23 .06
☐ 364 Mike Morgan .50 .23 .06
☐ 365 Donovan Osborne .50 .23 .06
☐ 366 Tom Pagnozzi .50 .23 .06
☐ 367 Ozzie Smith 2.50 1.10 .30
☐ 368 Todd Stottlemyre .50 .23 .06
☐ 369 Andy Ashby .50 .23 .06
☐ 370 Brad Ausmus .50 .23 .06
☐ 371 Ken Caminiti 1.25 .55 .16
☐ 372 Andujar Cedeno .50 .23 .06
☐ 373 Steve Finley 1.00 .45 .12
☐ 374 Tony Gwynn 4.00 1.80 .50
☐ 375 Joey Hamilton .75 .35 .09
☐ 376 Rickey Henderson 1.00 .45 .12
☐ 377 Trevor Hoffman .75 .35 .09
☐ 378 Wally Joyner .50 .23 .06
☐ 379 Marc Newfield .75 .35 .09
☐ 380 Jody Reed .50 .23 .06
☐ 381 Bob Tewksbury .50 .23 .06
☐ 382 Fernando Valenzuela .75 .35 .09
☐ 383 Rod Beck .75 .35 .09
☐ 384 Barry Bonds 2.50 1.10 .30
☐ 385 Mark Carreon .50 .23 .06
☐ 386 Shawon Dunston .50 .23 .06
☐ 387 Osvaldo Fernandez 1.00 .45 .12
☐ 388 Glenallen Hill .50 .23 .06
☐ 389 Stan Javier .50 .23 .06
☐ 390 Mark Leiter .50 .23 .06
☐ 391 Kirt Manwaring .50 .23 .06
☐ 392 Robby Thompson .50 .23 .06
☐ 393 William VanLandingham .50 .23 .06
☐ 394 Allen Watson .50 .23 .06
☐ 395 Matt Williams 1.25 .55 .16
☐ 396 Checklist (1-92) .50 .23 .06
☐ 397 Checklist (93-180) .50 .23 .06
☐ 398 Checklist (181-272) .50 .23 .06
☐ 399 Checklist (273-365) .50 .23 .06
☐ 400 Checklist (366-400/Inserts) .50 .23 .06

1996 Flair Diamond Cuts

Randomly inserted in packs at a rate of one in 20, this 12-card set showcases the game's greatest stars with rainbow holofoil and glitter coating on the card.

	MINT	NRMT	EXC
COMPLETE SET (12)	150.00	70.00	19.00
COMMON CARD (1-12)	5.00	2.20	.60
☐ 1 Jeff Bagwell	12.00	5.50	1.50
☐ 2 Albert Belle	12.00	5.50	1.50
☐ 3 Barry Bonds	8.00	3.60	1.00
☐ 4 Juan Gonzalez	15.00	6.75	1.85
☐ 5 Ken Griffey Jr.	30.00	13.50	3.70
☐ 6 Greg Maddux	20.00	9.00	2.50
☐ 7 Eddie Murray	8.00	3.60	1.00
☐ 8 Mike Piazza	20.00	9.00	2.50
☐ 9 Cal Ripken	25.00	11.00	3.10

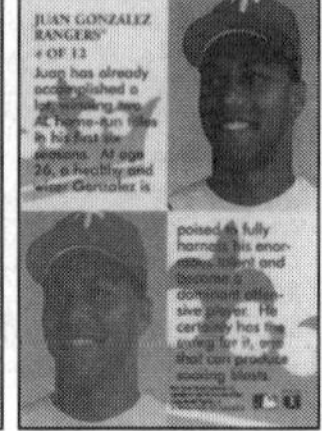

☐ 10 Frank Thomas	30.00	13.50	3.70
☐ 11 Mo Vaughn	8.00	3.60	1.00
☐ 12 Matt Williams	5.00	2.20	.60

1996 Flair Hot Gloves

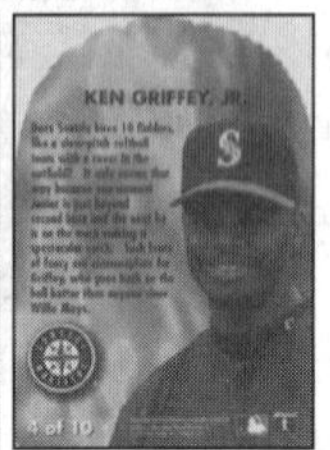

Randomly inserted in hobby packs only at a rate of one in 90, this 10-card set is printed on special, thermo-embossed die-cut cards and spotlights the best defensive players.

	MINT	NRMT	EXC
COMPLETE SET (10)	500.00	220.00	60.00
COMMON CARD (1-10)	20.00	9.00	2.50
☐ 1 Roberto Alomar	30.00	13.50	3.70
☐ 2 Barry Bonds	40.00	18.00	5.00
☐ 3 Will Clark	20.00	9.00	2.50
☐ 4 Ken Griffey Jr.	150.00	70.00	19.00
☐ 5 Kenny Lofton	40.00	18.00	5.00
☐ 6 Greg Maddux	100.00	45.00	12.50
☐ 7 Mike Piazza	100.00	45.00	12.50
☐ 8 Cal Ripken	125.00	55.00	15.50
☐ 9 Ivan Rodriguez	35.00	16.00	4.40
☐ 10 Matt Williams	20.00	9.00	2.50

1996 Flair Powerline

Randomly inserted in packs at a rate of one in 6, this 10-card set features baseball's leading power hitters. The fronts display a color action close-up player photo with a green overlay indicating his power. The backs carry a player portrait and a statement about the player's hitting power.

	MINT	NRMT	EXC
COMPLETE SET (10)	40.00	18.00	5.00
COMMON CARD (1-10)	1.25	.55	.16
☐ 1 Albert Belle	4.00	1.80	.50
☐ 2 Barry Bonds	2.50	1.10	.30
☐ 3 Juan Gonzalez	5.00	2.20	.60
☐ 4 Ken Griffey Jr.	10.00	4.50	1.25
☐ 5 Mark McGwire	3.00	1.35	.35
☐ 6 Mike Piazza	6.00	2.70	.75
☐ 7 Manny Ramirez	2.50	1.10	.30
☐ 8 Sammy Sosa	1.50	.70	.19
☐ 9 Frank Thomas	10.00	4.50	1.25
☐ 10 Matt Williams	1.25	.55	.16

1996 Flair Wave of the Future

Randomly inserted in packs at a rate of one in 72, this 20-card set highlights the top 1996 rookies and prospects on lenticular cards.

	MINT	NRMT	EXC
COMPLETE SET (20)	275.00	125.00	34.00
COMMON CARD (1-20)	10.00	4.50	1.25
☐ 1 Bob Abreu	20.00	9.00	2.50
☐ 2 George Arias	10.00	4.50	1.25
☐ 3 Tony Batista	15.00	6.75	1.85
☐ 4 Alan Benes	20.00	9.00	2.50
☐ 5 Yamil Benitez			
☐ 6 Steve Cox	10.00	4.50	1.25
☐ 7 David Doster	10.00	4.50	1.25
☐ 8 Jermaine Dye	30.00	13.50	3.70
☐ 9 Osvaldo Fernandez	10.00	4.50	1.25
☐ 10 Karim Garcia	40.00	18.00	5.00
☐ 11 Steve Gibralter	10.00	4.50	1.25
☐ 12 Todd Greene	10.00	4.50	1.25
☐ 13 Richard Hidalgo	20.00	9.00	2.50
☐ 14 Robin Jennings	10.00	4.50	1.25
☐ 15 Jason Kendall	25.00	11.00	3.10
☐ 16 Jose Malave	10.00	4.50	1.25
☐ 17 Wonderful Monds	10.00	4.50	1.25
☐ 18 Rey Ordonez	30.00	13.50	3.70
☐ 19 Ruben Rivera	30.00	13.50	3.70
☐ 20 Paul Wilson	20.00	9.00	2.50

1959 Fleer Williams

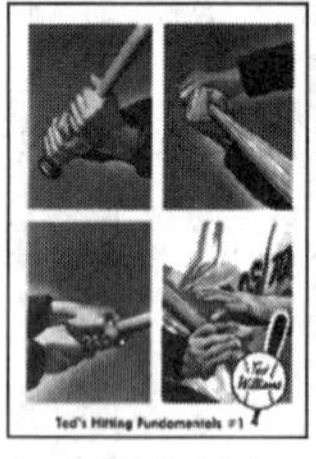
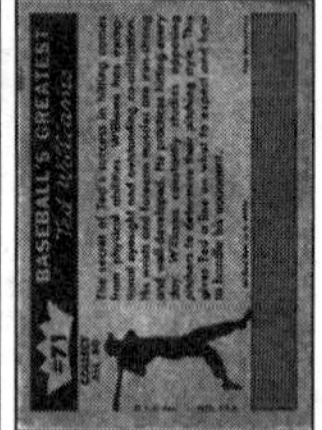

The cards in this 80-card set measure 2 1/2" by 3 1/2". The 1959 Fleer set, with a catalog designation of R418-1, portrays the life of Ted Williams. The wording of the wrapper, "Baseball's Greatest Series," has led to speculation that Fleer contemplated similar sets honoring other baseball immortals, but chose to develop instead the format of the 1960 and 1961 issues. These packs contained either six or eight cards. Card number 68, which was withdrawn early in production, is considered scarce and has even been counterfeited; the fake has a rosy coloration and a cross-hatch pattern visible over the picture area. The card numbering is arranged essentially in chronological order.

	NRMT	VG-E	GOOD
COMPLETE SET (80)	1800.00	800.00	220.00
COMMON CARD (1-80)	12.00	5.50	1.50
WRAPPER (6-CARD)	125.00	55.00	15.50
WRAPPER (8-CARD)	150.00	70.00	19.00
☐ 1 Ted Williams The Early Years Choosing up sides on the sandlots	100.00	45.00	12.50
☐ 2 Ted Wiliams Ted's Idol Babe Ruth Meeting boyhood idol Babe Ruth	100.00	45.00	12.50
☐ 3 Ted Williams Practice Makes Perfect At place practicing on the sandlots	12.00	5.50	1.50
☐ 4 Ted Williams Learns Fine Points Sliding at Herbert Hoover High	12.00	5.50	1.50
☐ 5 Ted Williams Ted's Fame Spreads At plate at Herbert Hoover High	12.00	5.50	1.50
☐ 6 Ted Williams Ted Turns Pro Portrait San Diego Padres PCL League uniform)	25.00	11.00	3.10
☐ 7 Ted Williams From Mound to Plate At plate San Diego Padres, PCL	15.00	6.75	1.85
☐ 8 Ted Williams 1937 First Full Season Making a leaping catch	15.00	6.75	1.85
☐ 9 Ted Williams Eddie Collins First Step to Majors	18.00	8.00	2.20
☐ 10 Ted Williams Gunning as Pastime Wearing hunting gear, taking aim	12.00	5.50	1.50
☐ 11 Ted Williams Jimmie Foxx First Spring Training	35.00	16.00	4.40
☐ 12 Ted Williams Burning Up Minors Pitching for Minneapolis American Association	18.00	8.00	2.20
☐ 13 Ted Williams 1939 Shows Will Stay Follow-through	15.00	6.75	1.85
☐ 14 Ted Williams Outstanding Rookie '39 Follow-through	15.00	6.75	1.85
☐ 15 Ted Williams Licks Sophomore Jinx Sliding into third base for a triple	15.00	6.75	1.85
☐ 16 Ted Williams 1941 Greatest Year Follow-through at plate	15.00	6.75	1.85
☐ 17 Ted Williams How Ted Hit .400 Youthful Williams as he looked in '41	35.00	16.00	4.40
☐ 18 Ted Williams 1941 All Star Hero Crossing plate after home run	18.00	8.00	2.20
☐ 19 Ted Williams Wins Triple Crown Crossing plate at Fenway Park	15.00	6.75	1.85
☐ 20 Ted Williams On to Naval Training In training plane at Amherst College	12.00	5.50	1.50
☐ 21 Ted Williams Honors for Williams Receiving 1942 Sporting News POY	15.00	6.75	1.85
☐ 22 Ted Williams 1944 Ted Solos In cockpit at Pensacola, FL Navy Air Station	12.00	5.50	1.50
☐ 23 Ted Williams Williams Wins Wings Wearing Naval Aviation Cadet uniform	15.00	6.75	1.85
☐ 24 Ted Williams 1945 Sharpshooter Taking Naval eye test	12.00	5.50	1.50
☐ 25 Ted Williams 1945 Ted Discharged In cockpit, giving the thumbs up	15.00	6.75	1.85
☐ 26 Ted Williams Off to Flying Start In batters box spring training, 1946	15.00	6.75	1.85
☐ 27 Ted Williams 7/9/46 One Man Show Riding blooper pitch out of park	15.00	6.75	1.85
☐ 28 Ted Williams The Williams Shift Diagram of Cleveland Indians position shift to defense Williams	12.00	5.50	1.50
☐ 29 Ted Williams Ted Hits for Cycle Close-up of follow through	18.00	8.00	2.20
☐ 30 Ted Williams Beating Williams Shift Crossing plate after home run	15.00	6.75	1.85
☐ 31 Ted Williams Sox Lose Series Sliding across plate Sept. 14, 1946	15.00	6.75	1.85
☐ 32 Ted Williams Joseph Cashman Most Valuable Player Receiving MVP Award	15.00	6.75	1.85
☐ 33 Ted Williams Another Triple Crown Famous Williams' Grip	12.00	5.50	1.50
☐ 34 Ted Williams Runs Scored Record Sliding into 2nd base in 1947 AS Game	12.00	5.50	1.50
☐ 35 Ted Williams Sox Miss Pennant Checking weight on new 36 oz. hickory bat	12.00	5.50	1.50
☐ 36 Ted Williams Banner Year for Ted Bunting down the 3rd base line	15.00	6.75	1.85
☐ 37 Ted Williams 1949 Sox Miss Again Two moods: grim and determined smiling and happy	15.00	6.75	1.85
☐ 38 Ted Williams 1949 Power Rampage Full shot of his batting follow through	15.00	6.75	1.85
☐ 39 Ted Williams Joe Cronin Eddie Collins 1950 Great Start Signing $125,000 contract	20.00	9.00	2.50
☐ 40 Ted Williams Ted Crashes into Wall Making catch in 1950 All Star game and crashing into wall	15.00	6.75	1.85
☐ 41 Ted Williams 1950 Ted Recovers Recuperating from elbow operation in hospital	12.00	5.50	1.50
☐ 42 Ted Williams Tom Yawkey Slowed by Injury	15.00	6.75	1.85
☐ 43 Ted Williams Double Play Lead Leaping high to make great catch	15.00	6.75	1.85
☐ 44 Ted Williams Back to Marines Hanging up number 9 prior to leaving for Marines	15.00	6.75	1.85
☐ 45 Ted Williams Farewell to Baseball Honored at Fenway Park prior to return to service	15.00	6.75	1.85
☐ 46 Ted Williams Ready for Combat Drawing jet pilot equipment in Willow Grove	12.00	5.50	1.50
☐ 47 Ted Williams Ted Crash Lands Jet In flying gear and jet he crash landed in	12.00	5.50	1.50
☐ 48 Ted Williams Ford Frick 1953 Ted Returns Throwing out 1st ball at All-Star Game in Cincinnati	18.00	8.00	2.20
☐ 49 Ted Williams Smash Return Giving his arm whirlpool treatment	12.00	5.50	1.50
☐ 50 Ted Williams 1954 Spring Injury Full batting pose at plate	18.00	8.00	2.20
☐ 51 Ted Williams Ted is Patched Up In first workout after fractured collar bone	12.00	5.50	1.50
☐ 52 Ted Williams 1954 Ted's Comeback Hitting a home run against Detroit	18.00	8.00	2.20
☐ 53 Ted Williams Comeback is Success Beating catcher's tag at home plate	15.00	6.75	1.85
☐ 54 Ted Williams Ted Hooks Big One With prize catch 1235 lb. black marlin	15.00	6.75	1.85
☐ 55 Ted Williams Joe Cronin Retirement "No Go" Returning from retirement	18.00	8.00	2.20
☐ 56 Ted Williams 2,000th Hit 8/11/55	15.00	6.75	1.85
☐ 57 Ted Williams 400th Homer In locker room	15.00	6.75	1.85
☐ 58 Ted Williams Williams Hits .388 Four-picture sequence of his batting swing	15.00	6.75	1.85
☐ 59 Ted Williams Hot September for Ted Full shot of follow through at plate	15.00	6.75	1.85
☐ 60 Ted Williams More Records for Ted Swinging and missing	15.00	6.75	1.85
☐ 61 Ted Williams 1957 Outfielder Warming up prior to ball game	15.00	6.75	1.85
☐ 62 Ted Williams 1958 Sixth Batting Title Slamming pitch into stands	12.00	5.50	1.50
☐ 63 Ted Williams Ted's All-Star Record Portrait and facsimile autograph	75.00	34.00	9.50
☐ 64 Ted Williams Barbara Williams Daughter and Daddy In uniform holding his daughter	12.00	5.50	1.50
☐ 65 Ted Williams 1958 August 30 Determination on face connecting with ball	15.00	6.75	1.85
☐ 66 Ted Williams 1958 Powerhouse Stance and follow through in batters box	12.00	5.50	1.50
☐ 67 Ted Williams Sam Snead Two Famous Fishermen testing fishing equipment	40.00	18.00	5.00
☐ 68 Ted Williams Bucky Harris Ted Signs for 1959 SP signing contract	1000.00	450.00	125.00
☐ 69 Ted Williams A Future Ted Williams With eager, young newcomer	15.00	6.75	1.85

Card	NRMT	VG-E	GOOD
☐ 70 Ted Williams	35.00	16.00	4.40
Jim Thorpe			
at Sportsmen's Show			
☐ 71 Ted Williams	12.00	5.50	1.50
Hitting Fund. 1			
Proper gripping of			
a baseball bat			
☐ 72 Ted Williams	12.00	5.50	1.50
Hitting Fund. 2			
Checking his swing			
☐ 73 Ted Williams	12.00	5.50	1.50
Hitting Fund. 3			
Stance and follow-through			
☐ 74 Ted Williams	12.00	5.50	1.50
Here's How			
Demonstrating in locker room			
an aspect of hitting			
☐ 75 Ted Williams	50.00	22.00	6.25
Eddie Collins			
Babe Ruth			
Williams' Value to Sox			
☐ 76 Ted Williams	12.00	5.50	1.50
On Base Record			
Awaiting intentional walk			
to first base			
☐ 77 Ted Williams	15.00	6.75	1.85
Ted Relaxes			
Displaying bonefish			
which he caught			
☐ 78 Ted Williams	15.00	6.75	1.85
Rep. Joe Martin			
Justice Earl Warren			
Honors for Williams			
Clark Griffith Memorial Award			
☐ 79 Ted Williams	25.00	11.00	3.10
Where Ted Stands			
Wielding giant eight foot bat			
when honored as modern-day Paul Bunyan			
☐ 80 Ted Williams	35.00	16.00	4.40
Ted's Goals for 1959			
Admiring his portrait			

1960 Fleer

The cards in this 79-card set measure 2 1/2" by 3 1/2". The cards from the 1960 Fleer series of Baseball Greats are sometimes mistaken for 1930s cards by collectors not familiar with this set. The cards each contain a tinted photo of a baseball immortal, and were issued in one series. There are no known scarcities, although a number 80 card (Pepper Martin reverse with either Eddie Collins or Lefty Grove obverse) exists (this is not considered part of the set). The catalog designation for 1960 Fleer is R418-2. The cards were printed on a 96-card sheet with 17 double prints. These are noted in the checklist below by DP. On the sheet the second Eddie Collins card is typically found in the number 80 position.

	NRMT	VG-E	GOOD
COMPLETE SET (79)	600.00	275.00	75.00
COMMON CARD (1-79)	4.00	1.80	.50
WRAPPER	100.00	45.00	12.50
☐ 1 Napoleon Lajoie DP	30.00	13.50	3.70
☐ 2 Christy Mathewson	15.00	6.75	1.85
☐ 3 Babe Ruth	125.00	55.00	15.50
☐ 4 Carl Hubbell	7.00	3.10	.85
☐ 5 Grover C. Alexander	7.00	3.10	.85
☐ 6 Walter Johnson DP	10.00	4.50	1.25
☐ 7 Chief Bender	4.00	1.80	.50
☐ 8 Roger Bresnahan	4.00	1.80	.50
☐ 9 Mordecai Brown	4.00	1.80	.50
☐ 10 Tris Speaker	7.00	3.10	.85
☐ 11 Arky Vaughan DP	4.00	1.80	.50
☐ 12 Zach Wheat	4.00	1.80	.50
☐ 13 George Sisler	4.00	1.80	.50
☐ 14 Connie Mack	7.00	3.10	.85
☐ 15 Clark Griffith	4.00	1.80	.50
☐ 16 Lou Boudreau DP	6.00	2.70	.75
☐ 17 Ernie Lombardi	4.00	1.80	.50
☐ 18 Heinie Manush	4.00	1.80	.50
☐ 19 Marty Marion	4.00	1.80	.50
☐ 20 Eddie Collins DP	4.00	1.80	.50
☐ 21 Rabbit Maranville DP	4.00	1.80	.50
☐ 22 Joe Medwick	4.00	1.80	.50
☐ 23 Ed Barrow	4.00	1.80	.50
☐ 24 Mickey Cochrane	6.00	2.70	.75
☐ 25 Jimmy Collins	4.00	1.80	.50
☐ 26 Bob Feller DP	15.00	6.75	1.85
☐ 27 Luke Appling	6.00	2.70	.75
☐ 28 Lou Gehrig	80.00	36.00	10.00
☐ 29 Gabby Hartnett	4.00	1.80	.50
☐ 30 Chuck Klein	4.00	1.80	.50
☐ 31 Tony Lazzeri DP	4.50	2.00	.55
☐ 32 Al Simmons	4.00	1.80	.50
☐ 33 Wilbert Robinson	4.00	1.80	.50
☐ 34 Edgar(Sam) Rice	4.00	1.80	.50
☐ 35 Herb Pennock	4.00	1.80	.50
☐ 36 Mel Ott DP	6.00	2.70	.75
☐ 37 Lefty O'Doul	4.00	1.80	.50
☐ 38 Johnny Mize	6.00	2.70	.75
☐ 39 Edmund(Bing) Miller	4.00	1.80	.50
☐ 40 Joe Tinker	4.00	1.80	.50
☐ 41 Frank Baker DP	4.00	1.80	.50
☐ 42 Ty Cobb	60.00	27.00	7.50
☐ 43 Paul Derringer	4.00	1.80	.50
☐ 44 Adrian(Cap) Anson	4.00	1.80	.50
☐ 45 Jim Bottomley	4.00	1.80	.50
☐ 46 Eddie Plank DP	4.00	1.80	.50
☐ 47 Denton(Cy) Young	10.00	4.50	1.25
☐ 48 Hack Wilson	6.00	2.70	.75
☐ 49 Edward Walsh UER	4.00	1.80	.50
(Photo actually			
Ed Walsh Jr.)			
☐ 50 Frank Chance	4.00	1.80	.50
☐ 51 Dazzy Vance DP	4.00	1.80	.50
☐ 52 Bill Terry	6.00	2.70	.75
☐ 53 Jimmy Foxx	10.00	4.50	1.25
☐ 54 Lefty Gomez	7.00	3.10	.85
☐ 55 Branch Rickey	4.00	1.80	.50
☐ 56 Ray Schalk DP	4.00	1.80	.50
☐ 57 Johnny Evers	4.00	1.80	.50
☐ 58 Charles Gehringer	6.00	2.70	.75
☐ 59 Burleigh Grimes	4.00	1.80	.50
☐ 60 Lefty Grove	7.00	3.10	.85
☐ 61 Rube Waddell DP	4.00	1.80	.50
☐ 62 John(Honus) Wagner	15.00	6.75	1.85
☐ 63 Charles(Red) Ruffing	4.00	1.80	.50
☐ 64 Kenesaw M. Landis	4.00	1.80	.50
☐ 65 Harry Heilmann	4.00	1.80	.50
☐ 66 John McGraw DP	4.00	1.80	.50
☐ 67 Hugh Jennings	4.00	1.80	.50
☐ 68 Hal Newhouser	6.00	2.70	.75
☐ 69 Waite Hoyt	4.00	1.80	.50
☐ 70 Louis(Bobo) Newsom	4.00	1.80	.50
☐ 71 Earl Averill DP	4.00	1.80	.50
☐ 72 Ted Williams	90.00	40.00	11.00
☐ 73 Warren Giles	4.00	1.80	.50
☐ 74 Ford Frick	4.00	1.80	.50
☐ 75 Hazen(Kiki) Cuyler	4.00	1.80	.50
☐ 76 Paul Waner DP	4.00	1.80	.50
☐ 77 Harold(Pie) Traynor	4.00	1.80	.50
☐ 78 Lloyd Waner	4.00	1.80	.50
☐ 79 Ralph Kiner	10.00	4.50	1.25
☐ 80A Pepper Martin SP	2000.00	900.00	250.00
(Eddie Collins			
pictured on obverse)			
☐ 80B Pepper Martin SP	1500.00	700.00	190.00
(Lefty Grove			
pictured on obverse)			

1960 Fleer Stickers

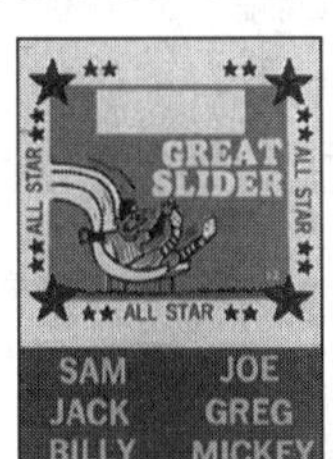

This 20-sticker set measures the standard size. The fronts feature a cartoon depicting the title of the card. The pictures are framed with red and black stars and the words "All Star" printed in blue. First names are printed below and are used to place in the blank box of each sticker to represent the person the sticker depicts. The stickers are unnumbered and checklisted below in alphabetical order.

	NRMT	VG-E	GOOD
COMPLETE SET (20)	50.00	22.00	6.25
COMMON CARD (1-20)	3.00	1.35	.35
☐ 1 Ball Boy	3.00	1.35	.35
☐ 2 The Barber	3.00	1.35	.35
☐ 3 Bat Boy	3.00	1.35	.35
☐ 4 Bench Jockey	3.00	1.35	.35
☐ 5 Bench Warmer	3.00	1.35	.35
☐ 6 Best Player	3.00	1.35	.35
☐ 7 Butter Fingers	3.00	1.35	.35
☐ 8 Coach	3.00	1.35	.35
☐ 9 Couldn't Catch a Cold	3.00	1.35	.35
☐ 10 Error King	3.00	1.35	.35
☐ 11 Foul Ball King	3.00	1.35	.35
☐ 12 Great Slider	3.00	1.35	.35
☐ 13 Great Swinger	3.00	1.35	.35
☐ 14 Home Run King	3.00	1.35	.35
☐ 15 The Knuckler	3.00	1.35	.35
☐ 16 Manager	3.00	1.35	.35
☐ 17 Slugging King	3.00	1.35	.35
☐ 18 Star Catcher	3.00	1.35	.35
☐ 19 Strikeout King	3.00	1.35	.35
☐ 20 Worst Player	3.00	1.35	.35

1961 Fleer

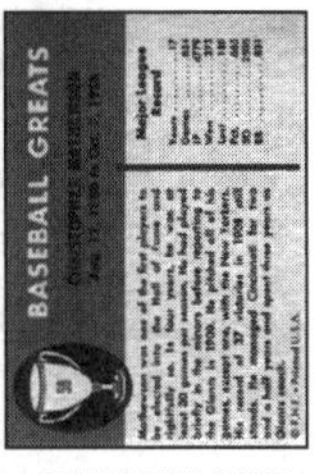

The cards in this 154-card set measure 2 1/2" by 3 1/2". In 1961, Fleer continued its Baseball Greats format by issuing this series of cards. The set was released in two distinct series, 1-88 and 89-154 (of which the latter is more difficult to obtain). The players within each series are conveniently numbered in alphabetical order. It appears that this set (the second series) continued to be issued the following year by Fleer. The catalog number for this set is F418-3. In each first series pack Fleer inserted a Major League team decal and a pennant sticker honoring past World Series winners.

	NRMT	VG-E	GOOD
COMPLETE SET (154)	1200.00	550.00	150.00
COMMON CARD (1-88)	3.00	1.35	.35
COMMON CARD (89-154)	7.00	3.10	.85
WRAPPER (5-CENT)	100.00	45.00	12.50
☐ 1 Frank Baker CL	50.00	15.00	5.00
Ty Cobb			
Zack Wheat			
☐ 2 Grover C. Alexander	6.00	2.70	.75
☐ 3 Nick Altrock	3.00	1.35	.35
☐ 4 Cap Anson	4.00	1.80	.50
☐ 5 Earl Averill	4.00	1.80	.50
☐ 6 Frank Baker	4.00	1.80	.50
☐ 7 Dave Bancroft	4.00	1.80	.50
☐ 8 Chief Bender	4.00	1.80	.50
☐ 9 Jim Bottomley	4.00	1.80	.50
☐ 10 Roger Bresnahan	4.00	1.80	.50
☐ 11 Mordecai Brown	4.00	1.80	.50
☐ 12 Max Carey	4.00	1.80	.50
☐ 13 Jack Chesbro	4.00	1.80	.50
☐ 14 Ty Cobb	50.00	22.00	6.25
☐ 15 Mickey Cochrane	4.00	1.80	.50
☐ 16 Eddie Collins	6.00	2.70	.75
☐ 17 Earle Combs	4.00	1.80	.50
☐ 18 Charles Comiskey	4.00	1.80	.50
☐ 19 Kiki Cuyler	4.00	1.80	.50
☐ 20 Paul Derringer	3.00	1.35	.35
☐ 21 Howard Ehmke	3.00	1.35	.35
☐ 22 Billy Evans	3.00	1.35	.35
☐ 23 Johnny Evers	4.00	1.80	.50
☐ 24 Urban Faber	4.00	1.80	.50
☐ 25 Bob Feller	12.00	5.50	1.50
☐ 26 Wes Ferrell	3.00	1.35	.35
☐ 27 Lew Fonseca	3.00	1.35	.35
☐ 28 Jimmy Foxx	7.00	3.10	.85
☐ 29 Ford Frick	3.00	1.35	.35
☐ 30 Frank Frisch	4.00	1.80	.50
☐ 31 Lou Gehrig	75.00	34.00	9.50
☐ 32 Charlie Gehringer	4.00	1.80	.50
☐ 33 Warren Giles	3.00	1.35	.35
☐ 34 Lefty Gomez	4.00	1.80	.50
☐ 35 Goose Goslin	4.00	1.80	.50
☐ 36 Clark Griffith	4.00	1.80	.50
☐ 37 Burleigh Grimes	4.00	1.80	.50
☐ 38 Lefty Grove	4.00	1.80	.50
☐ 39 Chick Hafey	4.00	1.80	.50
☐ 40 Jesse Haines	4.00	1.80	.50
☐ 41 Gabby Hartnett	4.00	1.80	.50
☐ 42 Harry Heilmann	4.00	1.80	.50
☐ 43 Rogers Hornsby	7.00	3.10	.85
☐ 44 Waite Hoyt	4.00	1.80	.50
☐ 45 Carl Hubbell	5.00	2.20	.60
☐ 46 Miller Huggins	4.00	1.80	.50
☐ 47 Hugh Jennings	4.00	1.80	.50
☐ 48 Ban Johnson	4.00	1.80	.50
☐ 49 Walter Johnson	12.00	5.50	1.50
☐ 50 Ralph Kiner	7.00	3.10	.85
☐ 51 Chuck Klein	4.00	1.80	.50
☐ 52 Johnny Kling	3.00	1.35	.35
☐ 53 Kenesaw M. Landis	4.00	1.80	.50
☐ 54 Tony Lazzeri	4.00	1.80	.50
☐ 55 Ernie Lombardi	4.00	1.80	.50
☐ 56 Dolf Luque	3.00	1.35	.35
☐ 57 Heinie Manush	4.00	1.80	.50
☐ 58 Marty Marion	3.00	1.35	.35
☐ 59 Christy Mathewson	12.00	5.50	1.50
☐ 60 John McGraw	4.00	1.80	.50
☐ 61 Joe Medwick	4.00	1.80	.50
☐ 62 Edmund(Bing) Miller	3.00	1.35	.35
☐ 63 Johnny Mize	4.00	1.80	.50
☐ 64 John Mostil	3.00	1.35	.35
☐ 65 Art Nehf	3.00	1.35	.35
☐ 66 Hal Newhouser	4.00	1.80	.50
☐ 67 Bobo Newsom	3.00	1.35	.35
☐ 68 Mel Ott	6.00	2.70	.75
☐ 69 Allie Reynolds	3.00	1.35	.35
☐ 70 Sam Rice	4.00	1.80	.50
☐ 71 Eppa Rixey	4.00	1.80	.50
☐ 72 Edd Roush	4.00	1.80	.50
☐ 73 Schoolboy Rowe	3.00	1.35	.35
☐ 74 Red Ruffing	4.00	1.80	.50
☐ 75 Babe Ruth	125.00	55.00	15.50
☐ 76 Joe Sewell	4.00	1.80	.50
☐ 77 Al Simmons	4.00	1.80	.50
☐ 78 George Sisler	4.00	1.80	.50
☐ 79 Tris Speaker	6.00	2.70	.75
☐ 80 Fred Toney	3.00	1.35	.35
☐ 81 Dazzy Vance	4.00	1.80	.50
☐ 82 Jim Vaughn	3.00	1.35	.35
☐ 83 Ed Walsh	4.00	1.80	.50
☐ 84 Lloyd Waner	4.00	1.80	.50
☐ 85 Paul Waner	4.00	1.80	.50
☐ 86 Zack Wheat	4.00	1.80	.50
☐ 87 Hack Wilson	4.00	1.80	.50
☐ 88 Jimmy Wilson	3.00	1.35	.35
☐ 89 George Sisler CL	60.00	18.00	6.00
Pie Traynor			
☐ 90 Babe Adams	7.00	3.10	.85
☐ 91 Dale Alexander	7.00	3.10	.85
☐ 92 Jim Bagby	7.00	3.10	.85
☐ 93 Ossie Bluege	7.00	3.10	.85
☐ 94 Lou Boudreau	10.00	4.50	1.25
☐ 95 Tom Bridges	7.00	3.10	.85
☐ 96 Donie Bush	7.00	3.10	.85
☐ 97 Dolph Camilli	7.00	3.10	.85
☐ 98 Frank Chance	10.00	4.50	1.25
☐ 99 Jimmy Collins	10.00	4.50	1.25
☐ 100 Stan Coveleskie	10.00	4.50	1.25
☐ 101 Hugh Critz	7.00	3.10	.85
☐ 102 Alvin Crowder	7.00	3.10	.85
☐ 103 Joe Dugan	7.00	3.10	.85
☐ 104 Bibb Falk	7.00	3.10	.85
☐ 105 Rick Ferrell	10.00	4.50	1.25
☐ 106 Art Fletcher	7.00	3.10	.85
☐ 107 Dennis Galehouse	7.00	3.10	.85
☐ 108 Chick Galloway	7.00	3.10	.85
☐ 109 Mule Haas	7.00	3.10	.85
☐ 110 Stan Hack	7.00	3.10	.85
☐ 111 Bump Hadley	7.00	3.10	.85
☐ 112 Billy Hamilton	10.00	4.50	1.25
☐ 113 Joe Hauser	7.00	3.10	.85
☐ 114 Babe Herman	7.00	3.10	.85
☐ 115 Travis Jackson	10.00	4.50	1.25
☐ 116 Eddie Joost	7.00	3.10	.85
☐ 117 Addie Joss	10.00	4.50	1.25
☐ 118 Joe Judge	7.00	3.10	.85
☐ 119 Joe Kuhel	7.00	3.10	.85
☐ 120 Napoleon Lajoie	18.00	8.00	2.20
☐ 121 Dutch Leonard	7.00	3.10	.85
☐ 122 Ted Lyons	10.00	4.50	1.25
☐ 123 Connie Mack	18.00	8.00	2.20
☐ 124 Rabbit Maranville	10.00	4.50	1.25
☐ 125 Fred Marberry	7.00	3.10	.85
☐ 126 Joe McGinnity	10.00	4.50	1.25
☐ 127 Oscar Melillo	7.00	3.10	.85
☐ 128 Ray Mueller	7.00	3.10	.85
☐ 129 Kid Nichols	10.00	4.50	1.25
☐ 130 Lefty O'Doul	7.00	3.10	.85
☐ 131 Bob O'Farrell	7.00	3.10	.85
☐ 132 Roger Peckinpaugh	7.00	3.10	.85
☐ 133 Herb Pennock	10.00	4.50	1.25
☐ 134 George Pipgras	7.00	3.10	.85
☐ 135 Eddie Plank	12.00	5.50	1.50
☐ 136 Ray Schalk	10.00	4.50	1.25
☐ 137 Hal Schumacher	7.00	3.10	.85
☐ 138 Luke Sewell	7.00	3.10	.85
☐ 139 Bob Shawkey	7.00	3.10	.85
☐ 140 Riggs Stephenson	7.00	3.10	.85
☐ 141 Billy Sullivan	7.00	3.10	.85
☐ 142 Bill Terry	15.00	6.75	1.85
☐ 143 Joe Tinker	10.00	4.50	1.25
☐ 144 Pie Traynor	12.00	5.50	1.50
☐ 145 Hal Trosky	7.00	3.10	.85
☐ 146 George Uhle	7.00	3.10	.85
☐ 147 Johnny VanderMeer	10.00	4.50	1.25
☐ 148 Arky Vaughan	10.00	4.50	1.25
☐ 149 Rube Waddell	10.00	4.50	1.25
☐ 150 Honus Wagner	50.00	22.00	6.25
☐ 151 Dixie Walker	7.00	3.10	.85
☐ 152 Ted Williams	125.00	55.00	15.50
☐ 153 Cy Young	40.00	18.00	5.00
☐ 154 Ross Youngs	40.00	18.00	5.00

1963 Fleer

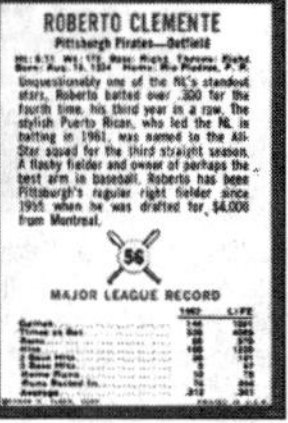

The Fleer set of current baseball players was marketed in 1963 in a gum card-style waxed wrapper package which contained a cherry cookie instead of gum. The cards were printed in sheets of 66 with the scarce card of Joe Adcock (#46) replaced by the unnumbered checklist card for the final press run. The complete set price includes the checklist card. The catalog designation for this set is R418-4. The key Rookie Card in this set is Maury Wills. The set is basically arranged numerically in alphabetical order by teams which are also in alphabetical order.

	NRMT	VG-E	GOOD
COMPLETE SET (67)	2000.00	900.00	250.00
COMMON CARD (1-66)	15.00	6.75	1.85
WRAPPER (5-CENT)	150.00	70.00	19.00

	NRMT	VG-E	GOOD
☐ 1 Steve Barber	30.00	9.00	3.00
☐ 2 Ron Hansen	15.00	6.75	1.85
☐ 3 Milt Pappas	20.00	9.00	2.50
☐ 4 Brooks Robinson	100.00	45.00	12.50
☐ 5 Willie Mays	200.00	90.00	25.00
☐ 6 Lou Clinton	15.00	6.75	1.85
☐ 7 Bill Monbouquette	15.00	6.75	1.85
☐ 8 Carl Yastrzemski	100.00	45.00	12.50
☐ 9 Ray Herbert	15.00	6.75	1.85
☐ 10 Jim Landis	15.00	6.75	1.85
☐ 11 Dick Donovan	15.00	6.75	1.85
☐ 12 Tito Francona	15.00	6.75	1.85
☐ 13 Jerry Kindall	15.00	6.75	1.85
☐ 14 Frank Lary	18.00	8.00	2.20
☐ 15 Dick Howser	18.00	8.00	2.20
☐ 16 Jerry Lumpe	15.00	6.75	1.85
☐ 17 Norm Siebern	15.00	6.75	1.85
☐ 18 Don Lee	15.00	6.75	1.85
☐ 19 Albie Pearson	18.00	8.00	2.20
☐ 20 Bob Rodgers	18.00	8.00	2.20
☐ 21 Leon Wagner	15.00	6.75	1.85
☐ 22 Jim Kaat	25.00	11.00	3.10
☐ 23 Vic Power	18.00	8.00	2.20
☐ 24 Rich Rollins	18.00	8.00	2.20
☐ 25 Bobby Richardson	30.00	13.50	3.70
☐ 26 Ralph Terry	18.00	8.00	2.20
☐ 27 Tom Cheney	15.00	6.75	1.85
☐ 28 Chuck Cottier	15.00	6.75	1.85
☐ 29 Jim Piersall	20.00	9.00	2.50
☐ 30 Dave Stenhouse	15.00	6.75	1.85
☐ 31 Glen Hobbie	15.00	6.75	1.85
☐ 32 Ron Santo	25.00	11.00	3.10
☐ 33 Gene Freese	15.00	6.75	1.85
☐ 34 Vada Pinson	20.00	9.00	2.50
☐ 35 Bob Purkey	15.00	6.75	1.85
☐ 36 Joe Amalfitano	15.00	6.75	1.85
☐ 37 Bob Aspromonte	15.00	6.75	1.85
☐ 38 Dick Farrell	15.00	6.75	1.85
☐ 39 Al Spangler	15.00	6.75	1.85
☐ 40 Tommy Davis	20.00	9.00	2.50
☐ 41 Don Drysdale	60.00	27.00	7.50
☐ 42 Sandy Koufax	200.00	90.00	25.00
☐ 43 Maury Wills	100.00	45.00	12.50
☐ 44 Frank Bolling	15.00	6.75	1.85
☐ 45 Warren Spahn	70.00	32.00	8.75
☐ 46 Joe Adcock SP	200.00	90.00	25.00
☐ 47 Roger Craig	18.00	8.00	2.20
☐ 48 Al Jackson	18.00	8.00	2.20
☐ 49 Rod Kanehl	18.00	8.00	2.20
☐ 50 Ruben Amaro	15.00	6.75	1.85
☐ 51 Johnny Callison	20.00	9.00	2.50
☐ 52 Clay Dalrymple	15.00	6.75	1.85
☐ 53 Don Demeter	15.00	6.75	1.85
☐ 54 Art Mahaffey	15.00	6.75	1.85
☐ 55 Smoky Burgess	20.00	9.00	2.50
☐ 56 Roberto Clemente	250.00	110.00	31.00
☐ 57 Roy Face	18.00	8.00	2.20
☐ 58 Vern Law	20.00	9.00	2.50
☐ 59 Bill Mazeroski	30.00	13.50	3.70
☐ 60 Ken Boyer	25.00	11.00	3.10
☐ 61 Bob Gibson	70.00	32.00	8.75
☐ 62 Gene Oliver	15.00	6.75	1.85
☐ 63 Bill White	25.00	11.00	3.10
☐ 64 Orlando Cepeda	30.00	13.50	3.70
☐ 65 Jim Davenport	15.00	6.75	1.85
☐ 66 Billy O'Dell	30.00	9.00	3.00
☐ NNO Checklist card	700.00	230.00	90.00

1966 Fleer AS Match Game

The 1966 Fleer All-Star Match Baseball Game set consists of 66 standard-size cards. The front of each card has nine rectangular boxes, one for each inning of a baseball game. These boxes are either blue (for American All Stars) or yellow (for National All Stars). In the lower right corner, a tie breaker rule is listed. When properly placed, the backs of all the cards form a composite black and white photo of Don Drysdale. The cards are numbered on the front. This is a rare instance where the set is worth much more than any individual part.

	NRMT	VG-E	GOOD
COMPLETE SET (66)	200.00	90.00	25.00
COMMON CARD (1-66)	2.50	1.10	.30

1969-72 Fleer Cloth Stickers

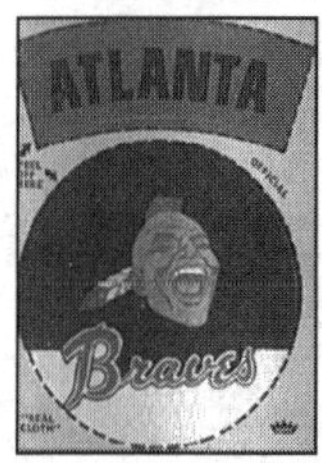

The years for these stickers are unclear so that is why the span. Any additions to the checklist are welcomed. This sticker set measures 2 1/2" by 3 1/4" and is comprised of two different types of stickers. The first group (1-24) are all the same design with the team city printed in a banner across the top and the official team logo in a circular design below. Both are designed to peel off. The second group (25-48) are of a different design with the team logo letter being the top portion and the city left off. The team name makes up the bottom section. Again, both are designed to be peeled off. The stickers are unnumbered and checklisted below in alphabetical order within each sticker type.

	NRMT	VG-E	GOOD
COMPLETE SET (48)	50.00	22.00	6.25
COMMON STICKER (1-48)	1.25	.55	.16

	NRMT	VG-E	GOOD
☐ 1 Atlanta Braves	1.25	.55	.16
☐ 2 Baltimore Orioles	1.25	.55	.16
☐ 3 Boston Red Sox	1.25	.55	.16
☐ 4 California Angels	1.25	.55	.16
☐ 5 Chicago Cubs	1.25	.55	.16
☐ 6 Chicago White Sox	1.25	.55	.16
☐ 7 Cincinnati Reds	1.25	.55	.16
☐ 8 Cleveland Indians	1.25	.55	.16
☐ 9 Detroit Tigers	1.25	.55	.16
☐ 10 Houston Astros	1.25	.55	.16
☐ 11 Kansas City Royals	1.25	.55	.16
☐ 12 Los Angeles Dodgers	1.25	.55	.16
☐ 13 Minnesota Twins	1.25	.55	.16
☐ 14 Montreal Expos	1.25	.55	.16
☐ 15 New York Mets	1.25	.55	.16
☐ 16 New York Yankees	1.25	.55	.16
☐ 17 Oakland A's	1.25	.55	.16
☐ 18 Philadelphia Phillies	1.25	.55	.16
☐ 19 Pittsburgh Pirates	1.25	.55	.16
☐ 20 St. Louis Cardinals	1.25	.55	.16
☐ 21 San Francisco Giants	1.25	.55	.16
☐ 22 Seattle Pilots	2.00	.90	.25
☐ 23 Texas Rangers	1.25	.55	.16
☐ 24 Washington Senators	1.25	.55	.16
☐ 25 Angels	1.25	.55	.16
☐ 26 Astros	1.25	.55	.16
☐ 27 Braves	1.25	.55	.16
☐ 28 Cardinals	1.25	.55	.16
☐ 29 Cubs	1.25	.55	.16
☐ 30 Dodgers	1.25	.55	.16
☐ 31 Expos	1.25	.55	.16
☐ 32 Giants	1.25	.55	.16
☐ 33 Indians	1.25	.55	.16
☐ 34 Mets	1.25	.55	.16
☐ 35 Oakland	1.25	.55	.16
☐ 36 Orioles	1.25	.55	.16
☐ 37 Phillies	1.25	.55	.16
☐ 38 Pilots	2.00	.90	.25
☐ 39 Pirates	1.25	.55	.16
☐ 40 Rangers	1.25	.55	.16
☐ 41 Reds	1.25	.55	.16
☐ 42 Red Sox	1.25	.55	.16
☐ 43 Royals	1.25	.55	.16
☐ 44 Senators	1.25	.55	.16
☐ 45 Sox	1.25	.55	.16
☐ 46 Tigers	1.25	.55	.16
☐ 47 Twins	1.25	.55	.16
☐ 48 Yankees	1.25	.55	.16

1970 Fleer World Series

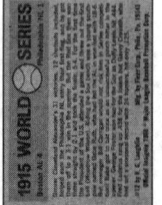

This set of 66 cards was distributed by Fleer. The cards are standard size, 2 1/2" X 3 1/2" and are in crude color on the front with light blue printing on white card stock on the back. All the years are represented except for 1904 when no World Series was played. In the list below, the winning series team is listed first. The year of the Series on the obverse is inside a white baseball. The original art for the cards in this set was drawn by sports artist R.G. Laughlin.

	NRMT	VG-E	GOOD
COMPLETE SET (66)	125.00	55.00	15.50
COMMON CARD (1-66)	1.50	.70	.19

	NRMT	VG-E	GOOD
☐ 1 1903 Red Sox/Pirates	1.50	.70	.19
☐ 2 1905 Giants/A's (Christy Mathewson)	4.00	1.80	.50
☐ 3 1906 White Sox/Cubs	1.50	.70	.19
☐ 4 1907 Cubs/Tigers	1.50	.70	.19
☐ 5 1908 Cubs/Tigers (Joe Tinker, Johnny Evers, and Frank Chance)	4.00	1.80	.50
☐ 6 1909 Pirates/Tigers (Honus Wagner and Ty Cobb)	6.00	2.70	.75
☐ 7 1910 A's/Cubs (Chief Bender and Jack Coombs)	2.50	1.10	.30
☐ 8 1911 A's/Giants (John McGraw)	2.50	1.10	.30
☐ 9 1912 Red Sox/Giants	1.50	.70	.19
☐ 10 1913 A's/Giants	1.50	.70	.19
☐ 11 1914 Braves/A's	1.50	.70	.19
☐ 12 1915 Red Sox/Phillies (Babe Ruth)	6.00	2.70	.75
☐ 13 1916 Red Sox/Dodgers (Babe Ruth)	6.00	2.70	.75
☐ 14 1917 White Sox/Giants	1.50	.70	.19
☐ 15 1918 Red Sox/Cubs	1.50	.70	.19
☐ 16 1919 Reds/White Sox	6.00	2.70	.75
☐ 17 1920 Indians/Dodgers (Stan Coveleski)	2.50	1.10	.30
☐ 18 1921 Giants/Yankees (Commissioner Landis)	1.50	.70	.19
☐ 19 1922 Giants/Yankees	1.50	.70	.19
☐ 20 1923 Yankees/Giants (Babe Ruth)	6.00	2.70	.75
☐ 21 1924 Senators/Giants (John McGraw)	2.50	1.10	.30
☐ 22 1925 Pirates/Senators (Walter Johnson)	4.00	1.80	.50
☐ 23 1926 Cardinals/Yankees (Grover C. Alexander and Tony Lazzeri)	2.50	1.10	.30
☐ 24 1927 Yankees/Pirates	1.50	.70	.19
☐ 25 1928 Yankees/Cardinals (Babe Ruth and Lou Gehrig)	6.00	2.70	.75
☐ 26 1929 A's/Cubs	1.50	.70	.19
☐ 27 1930 A's/Cardinals	1.50	.70	.19
☐ 28 1931 Cardinals/A's (Pepper Martin)	1.50	.70	.19
☐ 29 1932 Yankees/Cubs (Babe Ruth and Lou Gehrig)	6.00	2.70	.75
☐ 30 1933 Giants/Senators (Mel Ott)	2.50	1.10	.30
☐ 31 1934 Cardinals/Tigers	1.50	.70	.19
☐ 32 1935 Tigers/Cubs (Charlie Gehringer and Tommy Bridges)	2.50	1.10	.30
☐ 33 1936 Yankees/Giants	1.50	.70	.19
☐ 34 1937 Yankees/Giants (Carl Hubbell)	2.50	1.10	.30
☐ 35 1938 Yankees/Cubs (Lou Gehrig)	4.00	1.80	.50
☐ 36 1939 Yankees/Reds	1.50	.70	.19
☐ 37 1940 Reds/Tigers	1.50	.70	.19
☐ 38 1941 Yankees/Dodgers	1.50	.70	.19
☐ 39 1942 Cardinals/Yankees	1.50	.70	.19
☐ 40 1943 Yankees/Cardinals	1.50	.70	.19
☐ 41 1944 Cardinals/Browns	1.50	.70	.19
☐ 42 1945 Tigers/Cubs (Hank Greenberg)	4.00	1.80	.50
☐ 43 1946 Cardinals/Red Sox (Enos Slaughter)	2.50	1.10	.30
☐ 44 1947 Yankees/Dodgers (Al Gionfriddo)	1.50	.70	.19
☐ 45 1948 Indians/Braves	1.50	.70	.19
☐ 46 1949 Yankees/Dodgers (Allie Reynolds and Preacher Roe)	1.50	.70	.19
☐ 47 1950 Yankees/Phillies	1.50	.70	.19
☐ 48 1951 Yankees/Giants	1.50	.70	.19
☐ 49 1952 Yankees/Dodgers (Johnny Mize and Duke Snider)	4.00	1.80	.50
☐ 50 1953 Yankees/Dodgers (Carl Erskine)	1.50	.70	.19
☐ 51 1954 Giants/Indians (Johnny Antonelli)	1.50	.70	.19
☐ 52 1955 Dodgers/Yankees (Johnny Podres)	1.50	.70	.19
☐ 53 1956 Yankees/Dodgers	1.50	.70	.19
☐ 54 1957 Braves/Yankees (Lew Burdette)	1.50	.70	.19
☐ 55 1958 Yankees/Braves (Bob Turley)	1.50	.70	.19
☐ 56 1959 Dodgers/White Sox (Chuck Essegian)	1.50	.70	.19
☐ 57 1960 Pirates/Yankees	1.50	.70	.19
☐ 58 1961 Yankees/Reds (Whitey Ford)	2.50	1.10	.30
☐ 59 1962 Yankees/Giants	1.50	.70	.19
☐ 60 1963 Dodgers/Yankees (Moose Skowron)	1.50	.70	.19
☐ 61 1964 Cardinals/Yankees (Bobby Richardson)	2.50	1.10	.30
☐ 62 1965 Dodgers/Twins	1.50	.70	.19
☐ 63 1966 Orioles/Dodgers	1.50	.70	.19
☐ 64 1967 Cardinals/Red Sox	1.50	.70	.19
☐ 65 1968 Tigers/Cardinals	1.50	.70	.19
☐ 66 1969 Mets/Orioles	2.50	1.10	.30

1971 Fleer World Series

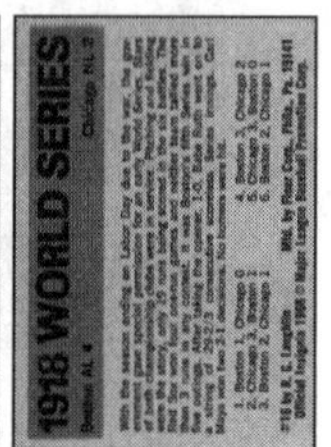

This set of 68 cards was distributed by Fleer. The cards are standard size, 2 1/2" X 3 1/2" and are in crude color on the front with brown printing on white card stock on the back. All the years since 1903 are represented in this set including 1904, when no World Series was played. That year is represented by a card explaining why there was no World Series that year. In the list below, the winning series team is listed first. The year of the Series on the obverse is inside a white square over the official World Series logo.

	NRMT	VG-E	GOOD
COMPLETE SET (68)	125.00	55.00	15.50
COMMON CARD (1-68)	1.50	.70	.19

	NRMT	VG-E	GOOD
☐ 1 1903 Red Sox/Pirates (Cy Young)	4.00	1.80	.50
☐ 2 1904 NO Series (John McGraw)	2.50	1.10	.30
☐ 3 1905 Giants/A's (Christy Mathewson, Chief Bender, and Joe McGinnity)	4.00	1.80	.50
☐ 4 1906 White Sox/Cubs	1.50	.70	.19
☐ 5 1907 Cubs/Tigers	1.50	.70	.19
☐ 6 1908 Cubs/Tigers (Ty Cobb)	5.00	2.20	.60
☐ 7 1909 Pirates/Tigers	1.50	.70	.19
☐ 8 1910 A's/Cubs (Eddie Collins)	2.50	1.10	.30
☐ 9 1911 A's/Giants (Home Run Baker)	2.50	1.10	.30
☐ 10 1912 Red Sox/Giants	1.50	.70	.19
☐ 11 1913 A's/Giants (Christy Mathewson)	4.00	1.80	.50
☐ 12 1914 Braves/A's	1.50	.70	.19
☐ 13 1915 Red Sox/Phillies (Grover Alexander)	2.50	1.10	.30
☐ 14 1916 Red Sox/Dodgers	1.50	.70	.19
☐ 15 1917 White Sox/Giants (Red Faber)	2.50	1.10	.30
☐ 16 1918 Red Sox/Cubs (Babe Ruth)	7.50	3.40	.95
☐ 17 1919 Reds/White Sox	6.00	2.70	.75
☐ 18 1920 Indians/Dodgers	1.50	.70	.19
☐ 19 1921 Giants/Yankees (Waite Hoyt)	2.50	1.10	.30
☐ 20 1922 Giants/Yankees	1.50	.70	.19
☐ 21 1923 Yankees/Giants (Herb Pennock)	2.50	1.10	.30
☐ 22 1924 Senators/Giants (Walter Johnson)	4.00	1.80	.50
☐ 23 1925 Pirates/Senators (Kiki Cuyler and Walter Johnson)	2.50	1.10	.30
☐ 24 1926 Cardinals/Yankees (Rogers Hornsby)	4.00	1.80	.50
☐ 25 1927 Yankees/Pirates	1.50	.70	.19
☐ 26 1928 Yankees/Cardinals (Lou Gehrig)	5.00	2.20	.60
☐ 27 1929 A's/Cubs	1.50	.70	.19
☐ 28 1930 A's/Cardinals (Jimmie Foxx)	4.00	1.80	.50
☐ 29 1931 Cardinals/A's (Pepper Martin)	1.50	.70	.19
☐ 30 1932 Yankees/Cubs (Babe Ruth)	7.50	3.40	.95
☐ 31 1933 Giants/Senators (Carl Hubbell)	2.50	1.10	.30
☐ 32 1934 Cardinals/Tigers	1.50	.70	.19
☐ 33 1935 Tigers/Cubs (Mickey Cochrane)	2.50	1.10	.30
☐ 34 1936 Yankees/Giants (Red Rolfe)	1.50	.70	.19
☐ 35 1937 Yankees/Giants (Tony Lazzeri)	2.50	1.10	.30
☐ 36 1938 Yankees/Cubs	1.50	.70	.19
☐ 37 1939 Yankees/Reds	1.50	.70	.19
☐ 38 1940 Reds/Tigers	1.50	.70	.19
☐ 39 1941 Yankees/Dodgers	1.50	.70	.19
☐ 40 1942 Cardinals/Yankees	1.50	.70	.19
☐ 41 1943 Yankees/Cardinals	1.50	.70	.19
☐ 42 1944 Cardinals/Browns	1.50	.70	.19
☐ 43 1945 Tigers/Cubs	4.00	1.80	.50

(Hank Greenberg)			
☐ 44 1946 Cardinals/Red Sox (Enos Slaughter)	2.50	1.10	.30
☐ 45 1947 Yankees/Dodgers	1.50	.70	.19
☐ 46 1948 Indians/Braves	1.50	.70	.19
☐ 47 1949 Yankees/Dodgers (Preacher Roe)	1.50	.70	.19
☐ 48 1950 Yankees/Phillies (Allie Reynolds)	1.50	.70	.19
☐ 49 1951 Yankees/Giants (Ed Lopat)	1.50	.70	.19
☐ 50 1952 Yankees/Dodgers (Johnny Mize)	2.50	1.10	.30
☐ 51 1953 Yankees/Dodgers	1.50	.70	.19
☐ 52 1954 Giants/Indians	1.50	.70	.19
☐ 53 1955 Dodgers/Yankees (Duke Snider)	2.50	1.10	.30
☐ 54 1956 Yankees/Dodgers	1.50	.70	.19
☐ 55 1957 Braves/Yankees	1.50	.70	.19
☐ 56 1958 Yankees/Braves (Hank Bauer)	1.50	.70	.19
☐ 57 1959 Dodgers/Wh.Sox (Duke Snider)	2.50	1.10	.30
☐ 58 1960 Pirates/Yankees	1.50	.70	.19
☐ 59 1961 Yankees/Reds (Whitey Ford)	2.50	1.10	.30
☐ 60 1962 Yankees/Giants	1.50	.70	.19
☐ 61 1963 Dodgers/Yankees	1.50	.70	.19
☐ 62 1964 Cardinals/Yankees	1.50	.70	.19
☐ 63 1965 Dodgers/Twins	1.50	.70	.19
☐ 64 1966 Orioles/Dodgers	1.50	.70	.19
☐ 65 1967 Cardinals/Red Sox	1.50	.70	.19
☐ 66 1968 Tigers/Cardinals	1.50	.70	.19
☐ 67 1969 Mets/Orioles	1.50	.70	.19
☐ 68 1970 Orioles/Reds	2.50	1.10	.30

1972 Fleer Famous Feats

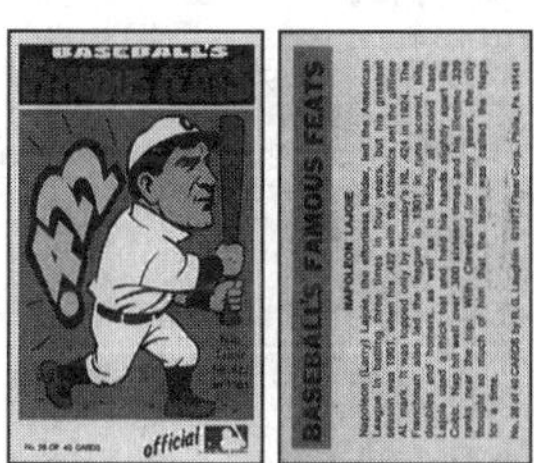

This Fleer set of 40 cards features the artwork of sports artist R.G. Laughlin. The set is titled "Baseball's Famous Feats." The cards are numbered both on the front and back. The backs are printed in light blue on white card stock. The cards measure approximately 2 1/2" by 4". This set was licensed by Major League Baseball.

	NRMT	VG-E	GOOD
COMPLETE SET (40)	40.00	18.00	5.00
COMMON CARD (1-40)	.75	.35	.09
☐ 1 Joe McGinnity	1.25	.55	.16
☐ 2 Rogers Hornsby	2.00	.90	.25
☐ 3 Christy Mathewson	2.00	.90	.25
☐ 4 Dazzy Vance	1.25	.55	.16
☐ 5 Lou Gehrig	3.00	1.35	.35
☐ 6 Jim Bottomley	1.25	.55	.16
☐ 7 Johnny Evers	1.25	.55	.16
☐ 8 Walter Johnson	2.00	.90	.25
☐ 9 Hack Wilson	1.00	.45	.12
☐ 10 Wilbert Robinson	1.25	.55	.16
☐ 11 Cy Young	1.50	.70	.19
☐ 12 Rudy York	.75	.35	.09
☐ 13 Grover C. Alexander	1.00	.45	.12
☐ 14 Fred Toney and Hippo Vaughan	.75	.35	.09
☐ 15 Ty Cobb	3.00	1.35	.35
☐ 16 Jimmie Foxx	2.00	.90	.25
☐ 17 Hub Leonard	.75	.35	.09
☐ 18 Eddie Collins	1.25	.55	.16
☐ 19 Joe Oeschger and Leon Cadore	.75	.35	.09
☐ 20 Babe Ruth	4.00	1.80	.50
☐ 21 Honus Wagner	2.00	.90	.25
☐ 22 Red Rolfe	.75	.35	.09
☐ 23 Ed Walsh	1.25	.55	.16
☐ 24 Paul Waner	1.25	.55	.16
☐ 25 Mel Ott	1.50	.70	.19
☐ 26 Eddie Plank	1.00	.45	.12
☐ 27 Sam Crawford	1.25	.55	.16
☐ 28 Napoleon Lajoie	1.50	.70	.19
☐ 29 Ed Reulbach	.75	.35	.09
☐ 30 Pinky Higgins	.75	.35	.09
☐ 31 Bill Klem	1.25	.55	.16
☐ 32 Tris Speaker	1.50	.70	.19
☐ 33 Hank Gowdy	.75	.35	.09
☐ 34 Lefty O'Doul	.75	.35	.09
☐ 35 Lloyd Waner	1.25	.55	.16
☐ 36 Chuck Klein	1.25	.55	.16
☐ 37 Deacon Phillippe	.75	.35	.09
☐ 38 Ed Delahanty	1.25	.55	.16
☐ 39 Jack Chesbro	1.25	.55	.16
☐ 40 Willie Keeler	1.00	.45	.12

1973 Fleer Wildest Days

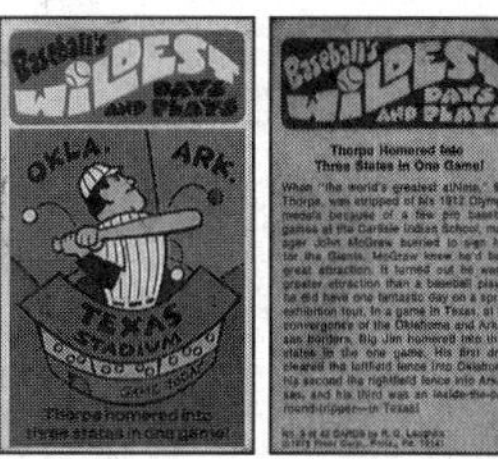

This Fleer set of 42 cards is titled "Baseball's Wildest Days and Plays" and features the artwork of sports artist R.G. Laughlin. The cards are numbered on the back. The backs are printed in dark red on white card stock. The cards measure approximately 2 1/2" by 4". This set was not licensed by Major League Baseball.

	NRMT	VG-E	GOOD
COMPLETE SET (42)	30.00	13.50	3.70
COMMON CARD (1-42)	.50	.23	.06
☐ 1 Cubs and Phillies Score 49 Runs in Game	1.00	.45	.12
☐ 2 Frank Chance Five HBP's in One Day	.75	.35	.09
☐ 3 Jim Thorpe Homered into 3 States	2.00	.90	.25
☐ 4 Eddie Gaedel Midget in Majors	1.25	.55	.16
☐ 5 Most Tied Game Ever	.50	.23	.06
☐ 6 Seven Errors in One Inning	.50	.23	.06
☐ 7 Four 20-Game Winners But No Pennant	.50	.23	.06
☐ 8 Dummy Hoy Umpires Signal Strikes	1.00	.45	.12
☐ 9 Fourteen Hits in One Inning	.50	.23	.06
☐ 10 Yankees Not Shut Out For Two Years	.50	.23	.06
☐ 11 Buck Weaver 17 Straight Fouls	1.50	.70	.19
☐ 12 George Sisler Greatest Thrill Was as a Pitcher	.75	.35	.09
☐ 13 Wrong-Way Baserunner	.50	.23	.06
☐ 14 Kiki Cuyler Sits Out Series	.75	.35	.09
☐ 15 Grounder Climbed Wall	.50	.23	.06
☐ 16 Gabby Street Washington Monument	.75	.35	.09
☐ 17 Mel Ott Ejected Twice	1.50	.70	.19
☐ 18 Shortest Pitching Career	.50	.23	.06
☐ 19 Three Homers in One Inning	.50	.23	.06
☐ 20 Bill Byron Singing Umpire	.50	.23	.06
☐ 21 Fred Clarke Walking Steal of Home	.75	.35	.09
☐ 22 Christy Mathewson 373rd Win Discovered	1.50	.70	.19
☐ 23 Hitting Through the Unglaub Arc	.50	.23	.06
☐ 24 Jim O'Rourke Catching at 52	.50	.23	.06
☐ 25 Fired for Striking Out in Series	.50	.23	.06
☐ 26 Eleven Run Inning on One Hit	.50	.23	.06
☐ 27 58 Innings in 3 Days	.50	.23	.06
☐ 28 Homer on Warm-Up Pitch	.50	.23	.06
☐ 29 Giants Win 26 Straight But Finish Fourth	.50	.23	.06
☐ 30 Player Who Stole First Base	.50	.23	.06
☐ 31 Ernie Shore Perfect Game in Relief	.75	.35	.09
☐ 32 Greatest Comeback	.50	.23	.06
☐ 33 All-Time Flash-In-The-Pan	.50	.23	.06
☐ 34 Hub Pruett Fanned Ruth 19 out of 31	1.25	.55	.16
☐ 35 Fixed Batting Race Ty Cobb Nap Lajoie	1.50	.70	.19
☐ 36 Wild-Pitch Rebound Play	.50	.23	.06
☐ 37 17 Straight Scoring Innings	.50	.23	.06
☐ 38 Wildest Opening Day	.50	.23	.06
☐ 39 Baseball's Strike One	.50	.23	.06
☐ 40 Opening Day No Hitter That Didn't Count	.50	.23	.06
☐ 41 Jimmie Foxx Six Straight Walks in One Game	1.50	.70	.19
☐ 42 Entire Team Hit and Scored in Inning	1.00	.45	.12

1974 Fleer Baseball Firsts

This Fleer set of 42 cards is titled "Baseball Firsts" and features the artwork of sports artist R.G. Laughlin. The cards are numbered on the back. The backs are printed in black on gray card stock. The cards measure approximately 2 1/2" by 4". This set was not licensed by Major League Baseball.

	NRMT	VG-E	GOOD
COMPLETE SET (42)	20.00	9.00	2.50
COMMON CARD (1-42)	.30	.14	.04
☐ 1 Slide	.60	.25	.07
☐ 2 Spring Training	.30	.14	.04
☐ 3 Bunt	.30	.14	.04
☐ 4 Catcher's Mask	.30	.14	.04
☐ 5 Lou Gehrig Four straight Homers	1.50	.70	.19
☐ 6 Radio Broadcast	.30	.14	.04
☐ 7 Numbered Uniforms	.30	.14	.04
☐ 8 Shin Guards	.30	.14	.04
☐ 9 Players Association	.30	.14	.04
☐ 10 Knuckleball	.30	.14	.04
☐ 11 Player With Glasses	.30	.14	.04
☐ 12 Baseball Cards	2.00	.90	.25
☐ 13 Standardized Rules	.30	.14	.04
☐ 14 Grand Slam	.30	.14	.04
☐ 15 Player Fined	.30	.14	.04
☐ 16 Presidential Opener	.30	.14	.04
☐ 17 Player Transaction	.30	.14	.04
☐ 18 All-Star Game	.30	.14	.04
☐ 19 Scoreboard	.30	.14	.04
☐ 20 Cork Center Ball	.30	.14	.04
☐ 21 Scorekeeping	.30	.14	.04
☐ 22 Domed Stadium	.30	.14	.04
☐ 23 Batting Helmet	.30	.14	.04
☐ 24 Fatality	.30	.14	.04
☐ 25 Unassisted Triple Play	.30	.14	.04
☐ 26 Home Run At Night	.30	.14	.04
☐ 27 Black Major Leaguer	.60	.25	.07
☐ 28 Pinch Hitter	.30	.14	.04
☐ 29 Million-Dollar World Series	.30	.14	.04
☐ 30 Tarpaulin	.30	.14	.04
☐ 31 Team Initials	.30	.14	.04
☐ 32 Pennant Playoff	.30	.14	.04
☐ 33 Glove	.30	.14	.04
☐ 34 Curve Ball	.30	.14	.04
☐ 35 Night Game	.30	.14	.04
☐ 36 Admission Charge	.30	.14	.04
☐ 37 Farm System	.30	.14	.04
☐ 38 Telecast	.30	.14	.04
☐ 39 Commissioner	.30	.14	.04
☐ 40 .400 Hitter	.30	.14	.04
☐ 41 World Series	.30	.14	.04
☐ 42 Player Into Service	.60	.25	.07

1975 Fleer Pioneers

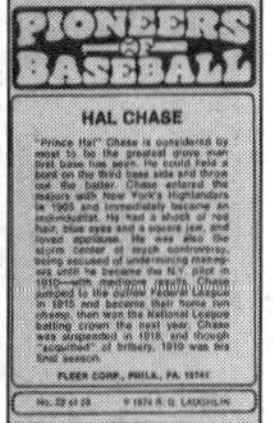

This 28-card set of brown and white sepia-toned photos of old timers is subtitled "Pioneers of Baseball. The graphics artwork was done by R.G. Laughlin. The cards measure approximately 2 1/2" X 4". The card backs are a narrative about the particular player. The cards are numbered on the back at the bottom.

	NRMT	VG-E	GOOD
COMPLETE SET (28)	15.00	6.75	1.85
COMMON CARD (1-28)	.50	.23	.06
☐ 1 Cap Anson	1.25	.55	.16
☐ 2 Harry Wright	.75	.35	.09
☐ 3 Buck Ewing	.75	.35	.09
☐ 4 Al G. Spalding	.75	.35	.09
☐ 5 Old Hoss Radbourn	.75	.35	.09
☐ 6 Dan Brouthers	.75	.35	.09
☐ 7 Roger Bresnahan	.75	.35	.09
☐ 8 Mike Kelly	.75	.35	.09
☐ 9 Ned Hanlon	.50	.23	.06
☐ 10 Ed Delahanty	.75	.35	.09
☐ 11 Pud Galvin	.75	.35	.09
☐ 12 Amos Rusie	.75	.35	.09
☐ 13 Tommy McCarthy	.75	.35	.09
☐ 14 Ty Cobb	2.00	.90	.25
☐ 15 John McGraw	.75	.35	.09
☐ 16 Home Run Baker	.75	.35	.09
☐ 17 Johnny Evers	.75	.35	.09
☐ 18 Nap Lajoie	1.00	.45	.12
☐ 19 Cy Young	1.25	.55	.16
☐ 20 Eddie Collins	.75	.35	.09
☐ 21 John Glasscock	.50	.23	.06
☐ 22 Hal Chase	.50	.23	.06
☐ 23 Mordecai Brown	.75	.35	.09
☐ 24 Jake Daubert	.50	.23	.06
☐ 25 Mike Donlin	.50	.23	.06
☐ 26 John Clarkson	.75	.35	.09
☐ 27 Buck Herzog	.50	.23	.06
☐ 28 Art Nehf	.50	.23	.06

1981 Fleer

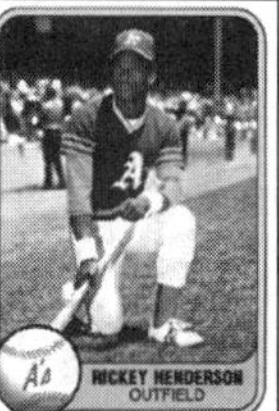

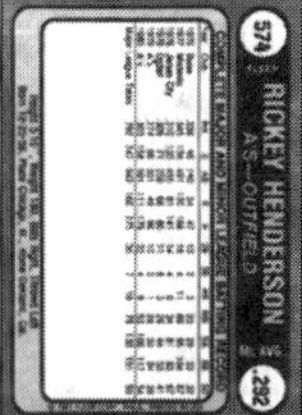

This issue of cards marks Fleer's first entry into the current player baseball card market since 1963. Cards are grouped in team order and teams are ordered based upon their standings from the 1980 season with the World Series champion Philadelphia Phillies starting off the set. Cards 638-660 feature specials and checklists. The cards of pitchers in this set erroneously show a heading (on the card backs) of "Batting Record" over their career pitching statistics. There were three distinct printings: the two following the primary run were designed to correct numerous errors. The variations caused by these multiple printings are noted in the checklist below (P1, P2, or P3). The Craig Nettles variation was corrected before the end of the first printing and thus is not included in the complete set consideration due to scarcity. Unopened packs contained 17 cards as well as a piece of gum. Unopened boxes contained 38 packs. The key Rookie Cards in this set are Danny Ainge, Harold Baines, Kirk Gibson, Jeff Reardon, and Fernando Valenzuela, whose first name was erroneously spelled Fernand on the card front.

	NRMT	VG-E	GOOD
COMPLETE SET (660)	40.00	18.00	5.00
COMMON CARD (1-660)	.10	.05	.01
☐ 1 Pete Rose UER (270 hits in '63, should be 170)	2.00	.90	.25
☐ 2 Larry Bowa	.25	.11	.03
☐ 3 Manny Trillo	.10	.05	.01
☐ 4 Bob Boone	.25	.11	.03
☐ 5 Mike Schmidt (See also 640A)	2.00	.90	.25
☐ 6 Steve Carlton P1 Golden Arm (Back "1066 Cardinals"; Number on back 6)	1.50	.70	.19
☐ 6B Steve Carlton P2 Pitcher of Year (Back "1066 Cardinals")	1.50	.70	.19
☐ 6C Steve Carlton P3 (1966 Cardinals)	1.50	.70	.19
☐ 7 Tug McGraw (See 657A)	.25	.11	.03
☐ 8 Larry Christenson	.10	.05	.01
☐ 9 Bake McBride	.10	.05	.01
☐ 10 Greg Luzinski	.25	.11	.03
☐ 11 Ron Reed	.10	.05	.01
☐ 12 Dickie Noles	.10	.05	.01
☐ 13 Keith Moreland	.25	.11	.03
☐ 14 Bob Walk	.25	.11	.03
☐ 15 Lonnie Smith	.25	.11	.03
☐ 16 Dick Ruthven	.10	.05	.01
☐ 17 Sparky Lyle	.25	.11	.03
☐ 18 Greg Gross	.10	.05	.01
☐ 19 Garry Maddox	.10	.05	.01
☐ 20 Nino Espinosa	.10	.05	.01
☐ 21 George Vukovich	.10	.05	.01
☐ 22 John Vukovich	.10	.05	.01
☐ 23 Ramon Aviles	.10	.05	.01
☐ 24A Kevin Saucier P1 (Name on back "Ken")	.10	.05	.01
☐ 24B Kevin Saucier P2 (Name on back "Ken")	.10	.05	.01
☐ 24C Kevin Saucier P3 (Name on back "Kevin")	.25	.11	.03
☐ 25 Randy Lerch	.10	.05	.01
☐ 26 Del Unser	.10	.05	.01
☐ 27 Tim McCarver	.50	.23	.06
☐ 28 George Brett	4.00	1.80	.50

(See also 655A)
☐ 29 Willie Wilson .10 .05 .01
(See also 653A)
☐ 30 Paul Splittorff .10 .05 .01
☐ 31 Dan Quisenberry .25 .11 .03
☐ 32A Amos Otis P1 .25 .11 .03
(Batting Pose;
"Outfield";
32 on back)
☐ 32B Amos Otis P2 .25 .11 .03
Series Starter
483 on back
☐ 33 Steve Busby .10 .05 .01
☐ 34 U.L. Washington .10 .05 .01
☐ 35 Dave Chalk .10 .05 .01
☐ 36 Darrell Porter .10 .05 .01
☐ 37 Marty Pattin .10 .05 .01
☐ 38 Larry Gura .10 .05 .01
☐ 39 Renie Martin .10 .05 .01
☐ 40 Rich Gale .10 .05 .01
☐ 41A Hal McRae P1 .50 .23 .06
("Royals" on front
in black letters)
☐ 41B Hal McRae P2 .25 .11 .03
("Royals" on front
in blue letters)
☐ 42 Dennis Leonard .10 .05 .01
☐ 43 Willie Aikens .10 .05 .01
☐ 44 Frank White .25 .11 .03
☐ 45 Clint Hurdle .10 .05 .01
☐ 46 John Wathan .10 .05 .01
☐ 47 Pete LaCock .10 .05 .01
☐ 48 Rance Mulliniks .10 .05 .01
☐ 49 Jeff Twitty .10 .05 .01
☐ 50 Jamie Quirk .10 .05 .01
☐ 51 Art Howe .10 .05 .01
☐ 52 Ken Forsch .10 .05 .01
☐ 53 Vern Ruhle .10 .05 .01
☐ 54 Joe Niekro .25 .11 .03
☐ 55 Frank LaCorte .10 .05 .01
☐ 56 J.R. Richard .25 .11 .03
☐ 57 Nolan Ryan 5.00 2.20 .60
☐ 58 Enos Cabell .10 .05 .01
☐ 59 Cesar Cedeno .25 .11 .03
☐ 60 Jose Cruz .25 .11 .03
☐ 61 Bill Virdon MG .10 .05 .01
☐ 62 Terry Puhl .10 .05 .01
☐ 63 Joaquin Andujar .25 .11 .03
☐ 64 Alan Ashby .10 .05 .01
☐ 65 Joe Sambito .10 .05 .01
☐ 66 Denny Walling .10 .05 .01
☐ 67 Jeff Leonard .25 .11 .03
☐ 68 Luis Pujols .10 .05 .01
☐ 69 Bruce Bochy .10 .05 .01
☐ 70 Rafael Landestoy .10 .05 .01
☐ 71 Dave Smith .25 .11 .03
☐ 72 Danny Heep .10 .05 .01
☐ 73 Julio Gonzalez .10 .05 .01
☐ 74 Craig Reynolds .10 .05 .01
☐ 75 Gary Woods .10 .05 .01
☐ 76 Dave Bergman .10 .05 .01
☐ 77 Randy Niemann .10 .05 .01
☐ 78 Joe Morgan .60 .25 .07
☐ 79 Reggie Jackson 1.25 .55 .16
(See also 650A)
☐ 80 Bucky Dent .25 .11 .03
☐ 81 Tommy John .50 .23 .06
☐ 82 Luis Tiant .25 .11 .03
☐ 83 Rick Cerone .10 .05 .01
☐ 84 Dick Howser MG .25 .11 .03
☐ 85 Lou Piniella .25 .11 .03
☐ 86 Ron Davis .10 .05 .01
☐ 87A Graig Nettles P1 10.00 4.50 1.25
ERR (Name on back
misspelled "Craig")
☐ 87B Graig Nettles P2 COR .25 .11 .03
("Graig")
☐ 88 Ron Guidry .25 .11 .03
☐ 89 Rich Gossage .50 .23 .06
☐ 90 Rudy May .10 .05 .01
☐ 91 Gaylord Perry .50 .23 .06
☐ 92 Eric Soderholm .10 .05 .01
☐ 93 Bob Watson .25 .11 .03
☐ 94 Bobby Murcer .25 .11 .03
☐ 95 Bobby Brown .10 .05 .01
☐ 96 Jim Spencer .10 .05 .01
☐ 97 Tom Underwood .10 .05 .01
☐ 98 Oscar Gamble .10 .05 .01
☐ 99 Johnny Oates .25 .11 .03
☐ 100 Fred Stanley .10 .05 .01
☐ 101 Ruppert Jones .10 .05 .01
☐ 102 Dennis Werth .10 .05 .01
☐ 103 Joe Lefebvre .10 .05 .01
☐ 104 Brian Doyle .10 .05 .01
☐ 105 Aurelio Rodriguez .10 .05 .01
☐ 106 Doug Bird .10 .05 .01
☐ 107 Mike Griffin .10 .05 .01
☐ 108 Tim Lollar .10 .05 .01
☐ 109 Willie Randolph .25 .11 .03
☐ 110 Steve Garvey .50 .23 .06
☐ 111 Reggie Smith .25 .11 .03
☐ 112 Don Sutton .50 .23 .06
☐ 113 Burt Hooton .10 .05 .01
☐ 114A Dave Lopes P1 .50 .23 .06
(Small hand on back)
☐ 114B Dave Lopes P2 .25 .11 .03
(No hand)
☐ 115 Dusty Baker .50 .23 .06
☐ 116 Tom Lasorda MG .25 .11 .03
☐ 117 Bill Russell .25 .11 .03
☐ 118 Jerry Reuss UER .25 .11 .03
("Home:" omitted)
☐ 119 Terry Forster .10 .05 .01
☐ 120A Bob Welch P1 .25 .11 .03
(Name on back
is "Bob")
☐ 120B Bob Welch P2 .50 .23 .06
(Name on back
is "Robert")
☐ 121 Don Stanhouse .10 .05 .01
☐ 122 Rick Monday .25 .11 .03
☐ 123 Derrel Thomas .10 .05 .01
☐ 124 Joe Ferguson .10 .05 .01
☐ 125 Rick Sutcliffe .25 .11 .03
☐ 126A Ron Cey P1 .50 .23 .06
(Small hand on back)
☐ 126B Ron Cey P2 .25 .11 .03
(No hand)
☐ 127 Dave Goltz .10 .05 .01
☐ 128 Jay Johnstone .25 .11 .03
☐ 129 Steve Yeager .10 .05 .01
☐ 130 Gary Weiss .10 .05 .01
☐ 131 Mike Scioscia .50 .23 .06
☐ 132 Vic Davalillo .10 .05 .01
☐ 133 Doug Rau .10 .05 .01
☐ 134 Pepe Frias .10 .05 .01
☐ 135 Mickey Hatcher .25 .11 .03
☐ 136 Steve Howe .25 .11 .03
☐ 137 Robert Castillo .10 .05 .01
☐ 138 Gary Thomasson .10 .05 .01
☐ 139 Rudy Law .10 .05 .01
☐ 140 Fernando Valenzuela 2.50 1.10 .30
UER (Misspelled
Fernand on card)
☐ 141 Manny Mota .25 .11 .03
☐ 142 Gary Carter .25 .11 .03
☐ 143 Steve Rogers .10 .05 .01
☐ 144 Warren Cromartie .10 .05 .01
☐ 145 Andre Dawson 1.50 .70 .19
☐ 146 Larry Parrish .10 .05 .01
☐ 147 Rowland Office .10 .05 .01
☐ 148 Ellis Valentine .10 .05 .01
☐ 149 Dick Williams MG .10 .05 .01
☐ 150 Bill Gullickson .50 .23 .06
☐ 151 Elias Sosa .10 .05 .01
☐ 152 John Tamargo .10 .05 .01
☐ 153 Chris Speier .10 .05 .01
☐ 154 Ron LeFlore .25 .11 .03
☐ 155 Rodney Scott .10 .05 .01
☐ 156 Stan Bahnsen .10 .05 .01
☐ 157 Bill Lee .25 .11 .03
☐ 158 Fred Norman .10 .05 .01
☐ 159 Woodie Fryman .10 .05 .01
☐ 160 David Palmer .10 .05 .01
☐ 161 Jerry White .10 .05 .01
☐ 162 Roberto Ramos .10 .05 .01
☐ 163 John D'Acquisto .10 .05 .01
☐ 164 Tommy Hutton .10 .05 .01
☐ 165 Charlie Lea .10 .05 .01
☐ 166 Scott Sanderson .10 .05 .01
☐ 167 Ken Macha .10 .05 .01
☐ 168 Tony Bernazard .10 .05 .01
☐ 169 Jim Palmer .75 .35 .09
☐ 170 Steve Stone .25 .11 .03
☐ 171 Mike Flanagan .25 .11 .03
☐ 172 Al Bumbry .25 .11 .03
☐ 173 Doug DeCinces .25 .11 .03
☐ 174 Scott McGregor .10 .05 .01
☐ 175 Mark Belanger .25 .11 .03
☐ 176 Tim Stoddard .10 .05 .01
☐ 177A Rick Dempsey P1 .50 .23 .06
(Small hand on front)
☐ 177B Rick Dempsey P2 .25 .11 .03
(No hand)
☐ 178 Earl Weaver MG .50 .23 .06
☐ 179 Tippy Martinez .10 .05 .01
☐ 180 Dennis Martinez .50 .23 .06
☐ 181 Sammy Stewart .10 .05 .01
☐ 182 Rich Dauer .10 .05 .01
☐ 183 Lee May .25 .11 .03
☐ 184 Eddie Murray 4.00 1.80 .50
☐ 185 Benny Ayala .10 .05 .01
☐ 186 John Lowenstein .10 .05 .01
☐ 187 Gary Roenicke .10 .05 .01
☐ 188 Ken Singleton .25 .11 .03
☐ 189 Dan Graham .10 .05 .01
☐ 190 Terry Crowley .10 .05 .01
☐ 191 Kiko Garcia .10 .05 .01
☐ 192 Dave Ford .10 .05 .01
☐ 193 Mark Corey .10 .05 .01
☐ 194 Lenn Sakata .10 .05 .01
☐ 195 Doug DeCinces .25 .11 .03
☐ 196 Johnny Bench 1.25 .55 .16
☐ 197 Dave Concepcion .25 .11 .03
☐ 198 Ray Knight .25 .11 .03
☐ 199 Ken Griffey .25 .11 .03
☐ 200 Tom Seaver 1.25 .55 .16
☐ 201 Dave Collins .10 .05 .01
☐ 202A George Foster P1 .25 .11 .03
Slugger
(Number on back 216)
☐ 202B George Foster P2 .25 .11 .03
Slugger
(Number on back 202)
☐ 203 Junior Kennedy .10 .05 .01
☐ 204 Frank Pastore .10 .05 .01
☐ 205 Dan Driessen .10 .05 .01
☐ 206 Hector Cruz .10 .05 .01
☐ 207 Paul Moskau .10 .05 .01
☐ 208 Charlie Leibrandt .50 .23 .06
☐ 209 Harry Spilman .10 .05 .01
☐ 210 Joe Price .10 .05 .01
☐ 211 Tom Hume .10 .05 .01
☐ 212 Joe Nolan .10 .05 .01
☐ 213 Doug Bair .10 .05 .01
☐ 214 Mario Soto .10 .05 .01
☐ 215A Bill Bonham P1 .50 .23 .06
(Small hand on back)
☐ 215B Bill Bonham P2 .10 .05 .01
(No hand)
☐ 216 George Foster .25 .11 .03
(See 202)
☐ 217 Paul Householder .10 .05 .01
☐ 218 Ron Oester .10 .05 .01
☐ 219 Sam Mejias .10 .05 .01
☐ 220 Sheldon Burnside .10 .05 .01
☐ 221 Carl Yastrzemski 1.00 .45 .12
☐ 222 Jim Rice .25 .11 .03
☐ 223 Fred Lynn .25 .11 .03
☐ 224 Carlton Fisk 1.25 .55 .16
☐ 225 Rick Burleson .10 .05 .01
☐ 226 Dennis Eckersley .75 .35 .09
☐ 227 Butch Hobson .10 .05 .01
☐ 228 Tom Burgmeier .10 .05 .01
☐ 229 Garry Hancock .10 .05 .01
☐ 230 Don Zimmer MG .10 .05 .01
☐ 231 Steve Renko .10 .05 .01
☐ 232 Dwight Evans .50 .23 .06
☐ 233 Mike Torrez .10 .05 .01
☐ 234 Bob Stanley .10 .05 .01
☐ 235 Jim Dwyer .10 .05 .01
☐ 236 Dave Stapleton .10 .05 .01
☐ 237 Glenn Hoffman .10 .05 .01
☐ 238 Jerry Remy .10 .05 .01
☐ 239 Dick Drago .10 .05 .01
☐ 240 Bill Campbell .10 .05 .01
☐ 241 Tony Perez .50 .23 .06
☐ 242 Phil Niekro .50 .23 .06
☐ 243 Dale Murphy .75 .35 .09
☐ 244 Bob Horner .25 .11 .03
☐ 245 Jeff Burroughs .10 .05 .01
☐ 246 Rick Camp .10 .05 .01
☐ 247 Bobby Cox MG .25 .11 .03
☐ 248 Bruce Benedict .10 .05 .01
☐ 249 Gene Garber .10 .05 .01
☐ 250 Jerry Royster .10 .05 .01
☐ 251A Gary Matthews P1 .50 .23 .06
(Small hand on back)
☐ 251B Gary Matthews P2 .25 .11 .03
(No hand)
☐ 252 Chris Chambliss .25 .11 .03
☐ 253 Luis Gomez .10 .05 .01
☐ 254 Bill Nahorodny .10 .05 .01
☐ 255 Doyle Alexander .10 .05 .01
☐ 256 Brian Asselstine .10 .05 .01
☐ 257 Biff Pocoroba .10 .05 .01
☐ 258 Mike Lum .10 .05 .01
☐ 259 Charlie Spikes .10 .05 .01
☐ 260 Glenn Hubbard .10 .05 .01
☐ 261 Tommy Boggs .10 .05 .01
☐ 262 Al Hrabosky .10 .05 .01
☐ 263 Rick Matula .10 .05 .01
☐ 264 Preston Hanna .10 .05 .01
☐ 265 Larry Bradford .10 .05 .01
☐ 266 Rafael Ramirez .10 .05 .01
☐ 267 Larry McWilliams .10 .05 .01
☐ 268 Rod Carew .75 .35 .09
☐ 269 Bobby Grich .25 .11 .03
☐ 270 Carney Lansford .25 .11 .03
☐ 271 Don Baylor .50 .23 .06
☐ 272 Joe Rudi .25 .11 .03
☐ 273 Dan Ford .10 .05 .01
☐ 274 Jim Fregosi MG .10 .05 .01
☐ 275 Dave Frost .10 .05 .01
☐ 276 Frank Tanana .25 .11 .03
☐ 277 Dickie Thon .25 .11 .03
☐ 278 Jason Thompson .10 .05 .01
☐ 279 Rick Miller .10 .05 .01
☐ 280 Bert Campaneris .25 .11 .03
☐ 281 Tom Donohue .10 .05 .01
☐ 282 Brian Downing .10 .05 .01
☐ 283 Fred Patek .10 .05 .01
☐ 284 Bruce Kison .10 .05 .01
☐ 285 Dave LaRoche .10 .05 .01
☐ 286 Don Aase .10 .05 .01
☐ 287 Jim Barr .10 .05 .01
☐ 288 Alfredo Martinez .10 .05 .01
☐ 289 Larry Harlow .10 .05 .01
☐ 290 Andy Hassler .10 .05 .01
☐ 291 Dave Kingman .25 .11 .03
☐ 292 Bill Buckner .25 .11 .03
☐ 293 Rick Reuschel .25 .11 .03
☐ 294 Bruce Sutter .25 .11 .03
☐ 295 Jerry Martin .10 .05 .01
☐ 296 Scot Thompson .10 .05 .01
☐ 297 Ivan DeJesus .10 .05 .01
☐ 298 Steve Dillard .10 .05 .01
☐ 299 Dick Tidrow .10 .05 .01
☐ 300 Randy Martz .10 .05 .01
☐ 301 Lenny Randle .10 .05 .01
☐ 302 Lynn McGlothen .10 .05 .01
☐ 303 Cliff Johnson .10 .05 .01
☐ 304 Tim Blackwell .10 .05 .01
☐ 305 Dennis Lamp .10 .05 .01
☐ 306 Bill Caudill .10 .05 .01
☐ 307 Carlos Lezcano .10 .05 .01
☐ 308 Jim Tracy .10 .05 .01
☐ 309 Doug Capilla UER .10 .05 .01
(Cubs on front but
Braves on back)
☐ 310 Willie Hernandez .25 .11 .03
☐ 311 Mike Vail .10 .05 .01
☐ 312 Mike Krukow .10 .05 .01
☐ 313 Barry Foote .10 .05 .01
☐ 314 Larry Biittner .10 .05 .01
☐ 315 Mike Tyson .10 .05 .01
☐ 316 Lee Mazzilli .10 .05 .01
☐ 317 John Stearns .10 .05 .01
☐ 318 Alex Trevino .10 .05 .01
☐ 319 Craig Swan .10 .05 .01
☐ 320 Frank Taveras .10 .05 .01
☐ 321 Steve Henderson .10 .05 .01
☐ 322 Neil Allen .10 .05 .01
☐ 323 Mark Bomback .10 .05 .01
☐ 324 Mike Jorgensen .10 .05 .01
☐ 325 Joe Torre MG .25 .11 .03
☐ 326 Elliott Maddox .10 .05 .01
☐ 327 Pete Falcone .10 .05 .01
☐ 328 Ray Burris .10 .05 .01
☐ 329 Claudell Washington .10 .05 .01
☐ 330 Doug Flynn .10 .05 .01
☐ 331 Joel Youngblood .10 .05 .01
☐ 332 Bill Almon .10 .05 .01
☐ 333 Tom Hausman .10 .05 .01
☐ 334 Pat Zachry .10 .05 .01
☐ 335 Jeff Reardon 1.00 .45 .12
☐ 336 Wally Backman .25 .11 .03
☐ 337 Dan Norman .10 .05 .01
☐ 338 Jerry Morales .10 .05 .01
☐ 339 Ed Farmer .10 .05 .01
☐ 340 Bob Molinaro .10 .05 .01
☐ 341 Todd Cruz .10 .05 .01
☐ 342A Britt Burns P1 .50 .23 .06
(Small hand on front)
☐ 342B Britt Burns P2 .25 .11 .03
(No hand)
☐ 343 Kevin Bell .10 .05 .01
☐ 344 Tony LaRussa MG .25 .11 .03
☐ 345 Steve Trout .10 .05 .01
☐ 346 Harold Baines 3.00 1.35 .35
☐ 347 Richard Wortham .10 .05 .01
☐ 348 Wayne Nordhagen .10 .05 .01
☐ 349 Mike Squires .10 .05 .01
☐ 350 Lamar Johnson .10 .05 .01
☐ 351 Rickey Henderson 2.00 .90 .25
(Most Stolen Bases AL)
☐ 352 Francisco Barrios .10 .05 .01
☐ 353 Thad Bosley .10 .05 .01
☐ 354 Chet Lemon .10 .05 .01
☐ 355 Bruce Kimm .10 .05 .01
☐ 356 Richard Dotson .10 .05 .01
☐ 357 Jim Morrison .10 .05 .01
☐ 358 Mike Proly .10 .05 .01
☐ 359 Greg Pryor .10 .05 .01
☐ 360 Dave Parker .25 .11 .03
☐ 361 Omar Moreno .10 .05 .01
☐ 362A Kent Tekulve P1 .25 .11 .03
(Back "1071 Waterbury"
and "1078 Pirates")
☐ 362B Kent Tekulve P2 .25 .11 .03
("1971 Waterbury" and
"1978 Pirates")
☐ 363 Willie Stargell .75 .35 .09
☐ 364 Phil Garner .25 .11 .03
☐ 365 Ed Ott .10 .05 .01
☐ 366 Don Robinson .10 .05 .01
☐ 367 Chuck Tanner MG .25 .11 .03
☐ 368 Jim Rooker .10 .05 .01
☐ 369 Dale Berra .10 .05 .01
☐ 370 Jim Bibby .10 .05 .01
☐ 371 Steve Nicosia .10 .05 .01
☐ 372 Mike Easler .10 .05 .01
☐ 373 Bill Robinson .25 .11 .03
☐ 374 Lee Lacy .10 .05 .01
☐ 375 John Candelaria .25 .11 .03
☐ 376 Manny Sanguillen .25 .11 .03
☐ 377 Rick Rhoden .10 .05 .01
☐ 378 Grant Jackson .10 .05 .01
☐ 379 Tim Foli .10 .05 .01
☐ 380 Rod Scurry .10 .05 .01
☐ 381 Bill Madlock .25 .11 .03
☐ 382A Kurt Bevacqua .25 .11 .03
P1 ERR
(P on cap backwards)
☐ 382B Kurt Bevacqua P2 .10 .05 .01
COR
☐ 383 Bert Blyleven .50 .23 .06
☐ 384 Eddie Solomon .10 .05 .01
☐ 385 Enrique Romo .10 .05 .01
☐ 386 John Milner .10 .05 .01
☐ 387 Mike Hargrove .25 .11 .03
☐ 388 Jorge Orta .10 .05 .01
☐ 389 Toby Harrah .25 .11 .03

Card	NRMT	VG-E	GOOD
□ 390 Tom Veryzer	.10	.05	.01
□ 391 Miguel Dilone	.10	.05	.01
□ 392 Dan Spillner	.10	.05	.01
□ 393 Jack Brohamer	.10	.05	.01
□ 394 Wayne Garland	.10	.05	.01
□ 395 Sid Monge	.10	.05	.01
□ 396 Rick Waits	.10	.05	.01
□ 397 Joe Charboneau	.25	.11	.03
□ 398 Gary Alexander	.10	.05	.01
□ 399 Jerry Dybzinski	.10	.05	.01
□ 400 Mike Stanton	.10	.05	.01
□ 401 Mike Paxton	.10	.05	.01
□ 402 Gary Gray	.10	.05	.01
□ 403 Rick Manning	.10	.05	.01
□ 404 Bo Diaz	.10	.05	.01
□ 405 Ron Hassey	.10	.05	.01
□ 406 Ross Grimsley	.10	.05	.01
□ 407 Victor Cruz	.10	.05	.01
□ 408 Len Barker	.10	.05	.01
□ 409 Bob Bailor	.10	.05	.01
□ 410 Otto Velez	.10	.05	.01
□ 411 Ernie Whitt	.10	.05	.01
□ 412 Jim Clancy	.10	.05	.01
□ 413 Barry Bonnell	.10	.05	.01
□ 414 Dave Stieb	.25	.11	.03
□ 415 Damaso Garcia	.10	.05	.01
□ 416 John Mayberry	.10	.05	.01
□ 417 Roy Howell	.10	.05	.01
□ 418 Danny Ainge	3.00	1.35	.35
□ 419A Jesse Jefferson P1	.10	.05	.01
(Back says Pirates)			
□ 419B Jesse Jefferson P2	.10	.05	.01
(Back says Pirates)			
□ 419C Jesse Jefferson P3	.25	.11	.03
(Back says Blue Jays)			
□ 420 Joey McLaughlin	.10	.05	.01
□ 421 Lloyd Moseby	.25	.11	.03
□ 422 Alvis Woods	.10	.05	.01
□ 423 Garth Iorg	.10	.05	.01
□ 424 Doug Ault	.10	.05	.01
□ 425 Ken Schrom	.10	.05	.01
□ 426 Mike Willis	.10	.05	.01
□ 427 Steve Braun	.10	.05	.01
□ 428 Bob Davis	.10	.05	.01
□ 429 Jerry Garvin	.10	.05	.01
□ 430 Alfredo Griffin	.10	.05	.01
□ 431 Bob Mattick MG	.10	.05	.01
□ 432 Vida Blue	.25	.11	.03
□ 433 Jack Clark	.25	.11	.03
□ 434 Willie McCovey	.75	.35	.09
□ 435 Mike Ivie	.10	.05	.01
□ 436A Darrel Evans P1 ERR	.50	.23	.06
(Name on front			
"Darrel")			
□ 436B Darrell Evans P2 COR	.50	.23	.06
(Name on front			
"Darrell")			
□ 437 Terry Whitfield	.10	.05	.01
□ 438 Rennie Stennett	.10	.05	.01
□ 439 John Montefusco	.10	.05	.01
□ 440 Jim Wohlford	.10	.05	.01
□ 441 Bill North	.10	.05	.01
□ 442 Milt May	.10	.05	.01
□ 443 Max Venable	.10	.05	.01
□ 444 Ed Whitson	.10	.05	.01
□ 445 Al Holland	.10	.05	.01
□ 446 Randy Moffitt	.10	.05	.01
□ 447 Bob Knepper	.10	.05	.01
□ 448 Gary Lavelle	.10	.05	.01
□ 449 Greg Minton	.10	.05	.01
□ 450 Johnnie LeMaster	.10	.05	.01
□ 451 Larry Herndon	.10	.05	.01
□ 452 Rich Murray	.10	.05	.01
□ 453 Joe Pettini	.10	.05	.01
□ 454 Allen Ripley	.10	.05	.01
□ 455 Dennis Littlejohn	.10	.05	.01
□ 456 Tom Griffin	.10	.05	.01
□ 457 Alan Hargesheimer	.10	.05	.01
□ 458 Joe Strain	.10	.05	.01
□ 459 Steve Kemp	.10	.05	.01
□ 460 Sparky Anderson MG	.25	.11	.03
□ 461 Alan Trammell	1.25	.55	.16
□ 462 Mark Fidrych	.50	.23	.06
□ 463 Lou Whitaker	1.00	.45	.12
□ 464 Dave Rozema	.10	.05	.01
□ 465 Milt Wilcox	.10	.05	.01
□ 466 Champ Summers	.10	.05	.01
□ 467 Lance Parrish	.25	.11	.03
□ 468 Dan Petry	.25	.11	.03
□ 469 Pat Underwood	.10	.05	.01
□ 470 Rick Peters	.10	.05	.01
□ 471 Al Cowens	.10	.05	.01
□ 472 John Wockenfuss	.10	.05	.01
□ 473 Tom Brookens	.10	.05	.01
□ 474 Richie Hebner	.10	.05	.01
□ 475 Jack Morris	.50	.23	.06
□ 476 Jim Lentine	.10	.05	.01
□ 477 Bruce Robbins	.10	.05	.01
□ 478 Mark Wagner	.10	.05	.01
□ 479 Tim Corcoran	.10	.05	.01
□ 480A Stan Papi P1	.25	.11	.03
(Front as Pitcher)			
□ 480B Stan Papi P2	.10	.05	.01
(Front as Shortstop)			
□ 481 Kirk Gibson	3.00	1.35	.35

Card	NRMT	VG-E	GOOD
□ 482 Dan Schatzeder	.10	.05	.01
□ 483A Amos Otis P1	.25	.11	.03
(See card 32)			
□ 483B Amos Otis P2	.25	.11	.03
(See card 32)			
□ 484 Dave Winfield	1.50	.70	.19
□ 485 Rollie Fingers	.50	.23	.06
□ 486 Gene Richards	.10	.05	.01
□ 487 Randy Jones	.10	.05	.01
□ 488 Ozzie Smith	4.00	1.80	.50
□ 489 Gene Tenace	.25	.11	.03
□ 490 Bill Fahey	.10	.05	.01
□ 491 John Curtis	.10	.05	.01
□ 492 Dave Cash	.10	.05	.01
□ 493A Tim Flannery P1	.25	.11	.03
(Batting right)			
□ 493B Tim Flannery P2	.10	.05	.01
(Batting left)			
□ 494 Jerry Mumphrey	.10	.05	.01
□ 495 Bob Shirley	.10	.05	.01
□ 496 Steve Mura	.10	.05	.01
□ 497 Eric Rasmussen	.10	.05	.01
□ 498 Broderick Perkins	.10	.05	.01
□ 499 Barry Evans	.10	.05	.01
□ 500 Chuck Baker	.10	.05	.01
□ 501 Luis Salazar	.10	.05	.01
□ 502 Gary Lucas	.10	.05	.01
□ 503 Mike Armstrong	.10	.05	.01
□ 504 Jerry Turner	.10	.05	.01
□ 505 Dennis Kinney	.10	.05	.01
□ 506 Willie Montanez UER	.10	.05	.01
(Misspelled Willy			
on card front)			
□ 507 Gorman Thomas	.25	.11	.03
□ 508 Ben Oglivie	.25	.11	.03
□ 509 Larry Hisle	.10	.05	.01
□ 510 Sal Bando	.25	.11	.03
□ 511 Robin Yount	1.50	.70	.19
□ 512 Mike Caldwell	.10	.05	.01
□ 513 Sixto Lezcano	.10	.05	.01
□ 514A Bill Travers P1 ERR	.25	.11	.03
("Jerry Augustine"			
with Augustine back)			
□ 514B Bill Travers P2 COR	.10	.05	.01
□ 515 Paul Molitor	2.50	1.10	.30
□ 516 Moose Haas	.10	.05	.01
□ 517 Bill Castro	.10	.05	.01
□ 518 Jim Slaton	.10	.05	.01
□ 519 Lary Sorensen	.10	.05	.01
□ 520 Bob McClure	.10	.05	.01
□ 521 Charlie Moore	.10	.05	.01
□ 522 Jim Gantner	.25	.11	.03
□ 523 Reggie Cleveland	.10	.05	.01
□ 524 Don Money	.10	.05	.01
□ 525 Bill Travers	.10	.05	.01
□ 526 Buck Martinez	.10	.05	.01
□ 527 Dick Davis	.10	.05	.01
□ 528 Ted Simmons	.25	.11	.03
□ 529 Garry Templeton	.10	.05	.01
□ 530 Ken Reitz	.10	.05	.01
□ 531 Tony Scott	.10	.05	.01
□ 532 Ken Oberkfell	.10	.05	.01
□ 533 Bob Sykes	.10	.05	.01
□ 534 Keith Smith	.10	.05	.01
□ 535 John Littlefield	.10	.05	.01
□ 536 Jim Kaat	.25	.11	.03
□ 537 Bob Forsch	.10	.05	.01
□ 538 Mike Phillips	.10	.05	.01
□ 539 Terry Landrum	.10	.05	.01
□ 540 Leon Durham	.25	.11	.03
□ 541 Terry Kennedy	.10	.05	.01
□ 542 George Hendrick	.10	.05	.01
□ 543 Dane Iorg	.10	.05	.01
□ 544 Mark Littell	.10	.05	.01
□ 545 Keith Hernandez	.25	.11	.03
□ 546 Silvio Martinez	.10	.05	.01
□ 547A Don Hood P1 ERR	.25	.11	.03
("Pete Vuckovich"			
with Vuckovich back)			
□ 547B Don Hood P2 COR	.10	.05	.01
□ 548 Bobby Bonds	.25	.11	.03
□ 549 Mike Ramsey	.10	.05	.01
□ 550 Tom Herr	.25	.11	.03
□ 551 Roy Smalley	.10	.05	.01
□ 552 Jerry Koosman	.25	.11	.03
□ 553 Ken Landreaux	.10	.05	.01
□ 554 John Castino	.10	.05	.01
□ 555 Doug Corbett	.10	.05	.01
□ 556 Bombo Rivera	.10	.05	.01
□ 557 Ron Jackson	.10	.05	.01
□ 558 Butch Wynegar	.10	.05	.01
□ 559 Hosken Powell	.10	.05	.01
□ 560 Pete Redfern	.10	.05	.01
□ 561 Roger Erickson	.10	.05	.01
□ 562 Glenn Adams	.10	.05	.01
□ 563 Rick Sofield	.10	.05	.01
□ 564 Geoff Zahn	.10	.05	.01
□ 565 Pete Mackanin	.10	.05	.01
□ 566 Mike Cubbage	.10	.05	.01
□ 567 Darrell Jackson	.10	.05	.01
□ 568 Dave Edwards	.10	.05	.01
□ 569 Rob Wilfong	.10	.05	.01
□ 570 Sal Butera	.10	.05	.01
□ 571 Jose Morales	.10	.05	.01
□ 572 Rick Langford	.10	.05	.01

Card	NRMT	VG-E	GOOD
□ 573 Mike Norris	.10	.05	.01
□ 574 Rickey Henderson	3.00	1.35	.35
□ 575 Tony Armas	.25	.11	.03
□ 576 Dave Revering	.10	.05	.01
□ 577 Jeff Newman	.10	.05	.01
□ 578 Bob Lacey	.10	.05	.01
□ 579 Brian Kingman	.10	.05	.01
□ 580 Mitchell Page	.10	.05	.01
□ 581 Billy Martin MG	.50	.23	.06
□ 582 Rob Picciolo	.10	.05	.01
□ 583 Mike Heath	.10	.05	.01
□ 584 Mickey Klutts	.10	.05	.01
□ 585 Orlando Gonzalez	.10	.05	.01
□ 586 Mike Davis	.10	.05	.01
□ 587 Wayne Gross	.10	.05	.01
□ 588 Matt Keough	.10	.05	.01
□ 589 Steve McCatty	.10	.05	.01
□ 590 Dwayne Murphy	.10	.05	.01
□ 591 Mario Guerrero	.10	.05	.01
□ 592 Dave McKay	.10	.05	.01
□ 593 Jim Essian	.10	.05	.01
□ 594 Dave Heaverlo	.10	.05	.01
□ 595 Maury Wills MG	.25	.11	.03
□ 596 Juan Beniquez	.10	.05	.01
□ 597 Rodney Craig	.10	.05	.01
□ 598 Jim Anderson	.10	.05	.01
□ 599 Floyd Bannister	.10	.05	.01
□ 600 Bruce Bochte	.10	.05	.01
□ 601 Julio Cruz	.10	.05	.01
□ 602 Ted Cox	.10	.05	.01
□ 603 Dan Meyer	.10	.05	.01
□ 604 Larry Cox	.10	.05	.01
□ 605 Bill Stein	.10	.05	.01
□ 606 Steve Garvey	.50	.23	.06
(Most Hits NL)			
□ 607 Dave Roberts	.10	.05	.01
□ 608 Leon Roberts	.10	.05	.01
□ 609 Reggie Walton	.10	.05	.01
□ 610 Dave Edler	.10	.05	.01
□ 611 Larry Milbourne	.10	.05	.01
□ 612 Kim Allen	.10	.05	.01
□ 613 Mario Mendoza	.10	.05	.01
□ 614 Tom Paciorek	.10	.05	.01
□ 615 Glenn Abbott	.10	.05	.01
□ 616 Joe Simpson	.10	.05	.01
□ 617 Mickey Rivers	.25	.11	.03
□ 618 Jim Kern	.10	.05	.01
□ 619 Jim Sundberg	.25	.11	.03
□ 620 Richie Zisk	.10	.05	.01
□ 621 Jon Matlack	.10	.05	.01
□ 622 Ferguson Jenkins	.50	.23	.06
□ 623 Pat Corrales MG	.10	.05	.01
□ 624 Ed Figueroa	.10	.05	.01
□ 625 Buddy Bell	.25	.11	.03
□ 626 Al Oliver	.25	.11	.03
□ 627 Doc Medich	.10	.05	.01
□ 628 Bump Wills	.10	.05	.01
□ 629 Rusty Staub	.25	.11	.03
□ 630 Pat Putnam	.10	.05	.01
□ 631 John Grubb	.10	.05	.01
□ 632 Danny Darwin	.25	.11	.03
□ 633 Ken Clay	.10	.05	.01
□ 634 Jim Norris	.10	.05	.01
□ 635 John Butcher	.10	.05	.01
□ 636 Dave Roberts	.10	.05	.01
□ 637 Billy Sample	.10	.05	.01
□ 638 Carl Yastrzemski	1.00	.45	.12
□ 639 Cecil Cooper	.25	.11	.03
□ 640 Mike Schmidt P1	2.00	.90	.25
(Portrait;			
"Third Base";			
number on back 5)			
□ 640B Mike Schmidt P2	2.00	.90	.25
("1980 Home Run King";			
640 on back)			
□ 641A CL: Phils/Royals P1	.25	.11	.03
41 is Hal McRae			
□ 641B CL: Phils/Royals P2	.25	.11	.03
(41 is Hal McRae,			
Double Threat)			
□ 642 CL: Astros/Yankees	.25	.11	.03
□ 643 CL: Expos/Dodgers	.25	.11	.03
□ 644A CL: Reds/Orioles P1	.25	.11	.03
(202 is George Foster;			
Joe Nolan pitcher,			
should be catcher)			
□ 644B CL: Reds/Orioles P2	.25	.11	.03
(202 is Foster Slugger;			
Joe Nolan pitcher,			
should be catcher)			
□ 645 Pete Rose	2.50	1.10	.30
Larry Bowa			
Mike Schmidt			
Triple Threat P1			
(No number on back)			
□ 645B Pete Rose	2.50	1.10	.30
Larry Bowa			
Mike Schmidt			
Triple Threat P2			
(Back numbered 645)			
□ 646 CL: Braves/Red Sox	.25	.11	.03
□ 647 CL: Cubs/Angels	.25	.11	.03
□ 648 CL: Mets/White Sox	.25	.11	.03
□ 649 CL: Indians/Pirates	.25	.11	.03
□ 650 Reggie Jackson	1.25	.55	.16

Card	NRMT	VG-E	GOOD
Mr. Baseball P1			
(Number on back 79)			
□ 650B Reggie Jackson	1.25	.55	.16
Mr. Baseball P2			
(Number on back 650)			
□ 651 CL: Giants/Blue Jays	.25	.11	.03
□ 652A CL: Tigers/Padres P1	.25	.11	.03
(483 is listed)			
□ 652B CL: Tigers/Padres P2	.25	.11	.03
(483 is deleted)			
□ 653A Willie Wilson P1	.25	.11	.03
Most Hits Most Runs			
(Number on back 29)			
□ 653B Willie Wilson P2	.25	.11	.03
Most Hits Most Runs			
(Number on back 653)			
□ 654A CL:Brewers/Cards P1	.25	.11	.03
(514 Jerry Augustine;			
547 Pete Vuckovich)			
□ 654B CL:Brewers/Cards P2	.25	.11	.03
(514 Billy Travers;			
547 Don Hood)			
□ 655 George Brett P1	4.00	1.80	.50
.390 Average			
(Number on back 28)			
□ 655B George Brett P2	4.00	1.80	.50
.390 Average			
(Number on back 655)			
□ 656 CL: Twins/Oakland A's	.25	.11	.03
□ 657A Tug McGraw P1	.25	.11	.03
Game Saver			
(Number on back 7)			
□ 657B Tug McGraw P2	.25	.11	.03
Game Saver			
(Number on back 657)			
□ 658 CL: Rangers/Mariners	.25	.11	.03
□ 659A Checklist P1	.25	.11	.03
of Special Cards			
(Last lines on front,			
Wilson Most Hits)			
□ 659B Checklist P2	.25	.11	.03
of Special Cards			
(Last lines on front,			
Otis Series Starter)			
□ 660 Steve Carlton P1	1.50	.70	.19
Golden Arm			
(Number on back 660;			
Back "1066 Cardinals")			
□ 660B Steve Carlton P2	1.50	.70	.19
Golden Arm			
("1966 Cardinals")			

1981 Fleer Sticker Cards

The stickers in this 128-sticker set measure 2 1/2" by 3 1/2". The 1981 Fleer Baseball Star Stickers consist of numbered cards with peelable, full-color sticker fronts and three unnumbered checklists. The backs of the numbered player cards are the same as the 1981 Fleer regular issue cards except for the numbers, while the checklist cards (cards 126-128 below) have sticker fronts of Jackson (1-42), Brett (43-83), and Schmidt (84-125).

	NRMT	VG-E	GOOD
COMPLETE SET (128)	45.00	20.00	5.50
COMMON CARD (1-128)	.10	.05	.01
□ 1 Steve Garvey	1.00	.45	.12
□ 2 Ron LeFlore	.20	.09	.03
□ 3 Ron Cey	.20	.09	.03
□ 4 Dave Revering	.10	.05	.01
□ 5 Tony Armas	.10	.05	.01
□ 6 Mike Norris	.10	.05	.01
□ 7 Steve Kemp	.10	.05	.01
□ 8 Bruce Bochte	.10	.05	.01
□ 9 Mike Schmidt	3.00	1.35	.35
□ 10 Scott McGregor	.10	.05	.01
□ 11 Buddy Bell	.20	.09	.03
□ 12 Carney Lansford	.20	.09	.03
□ 13 Carl Yastrzemski	2.00	.90	.25
□ 14 Ben Oglivie	.10	.05	.01
□ 15 Willie Stargell	1.00	.45	.12
□ 16 Cecil Cooper	.20	.09	.03
□ 17 Gene Richards	.10	.05	.01
□ 18 Jim Kern	.10	.05	.01
□ 19 Jerry Koosman	.20	.09	.03
□ 20 Larry Bowa	.20	.09	.03
□ 21 Kent Tekulve	.20	.09	.03
□ 22 Dan Driessen	.10	.05	.01
□ 23 Phil Niekro	1.00	.45	.12
□ 24 Dan Quisenberry	.20	.09	.03
□ 25 Dave Winfield	2.00	.90	.25
□ 26 Dave Parker	.20	.09	.03

☐ 27 Rick Langford .10 .05 .01
☐ 28 Amos Otis .20 .09 .03
☐ 29 Bill Buckner .20 .09 .03
☐ 30 Al Bumbry .10 .05 .01
☐ 31 Bake McBride .10 .05 .01
☐ 32 Mickey Rivers .20 .09 .03
☐ 33 Rick Burleson .10 .05 .01
☐ 34 Dennis Eckersley 1.50 .70 .19
☐ 35 Cesar Cedeno .20 .09 .03
☐ 36 Enos Cabell .10 .05 .01
☐ 37 Johnny Bench 2.00 .90 .25
☐ 38 Robin Yount 2.00 .90 .25
☐ 39 Mark Belanger .20 .09 .03
☐ 40 Rod Carew 1.50 .70 .19
☐ 41 George Foster .20 .09 .03
☐ 42 Lee Mazzilli .10 .05 .01
☐ 43 Pete Rose 3.00 1.35 .35
Larry Bowa
Mike Schmidt
Triple Threat
☐ 44 J.R. Richard .10 .05 .01
☐ 45 Lou Piniella .20 .09 .03
☐ 46 Ken Landreaux .10 .05 .01
☐ 47 Rollie Fingers .50 .23 .06
☐ 48 Joaquin Andujar .20 .09 .03
☐ 49 Tom Seaver 2.00 .90 .25
☐ 50 Bobby Grich .20 .09 .03
☐ 51 Jon Matlack .10 .05 .01
☐ 52 Jack Clark .20 .09 .03
☐ 53 Jim Rice .20 .09 .03
☐ 54 Rickey Henderson 5.00 2.20 .60
☐ 55 Roy Smalley .10 .05 .01
☐ 56 Mike Flanagan .10 .05 .01
☐ 57 Steve Rogers .10 .05 .01
☐ 58 Carlton Fisk 1.50 .70 .19
☐ 59 Don Sutton .30 .14 .04
☐ 60 Ken Griffey .20 .09 .03
☐ 61 Burt Hooton .10 .05 .01
☐ 62 Dusty Baker .20 .09 .03
☐ 63 Vida Blue .20 .09 .03
☐ 64 Al Oliver .20 .09 .03
☐ 65 Jim Bibby .10 .05 .01
☐ 66 Tony Perez .50 .23 .06
☐ 67 Davey Lopes .20 .09 .03
☐ 68 Bill Russell .20 .09 .03
☐ 69 Larry Parrish .10 .05 .01
☐ 70 Garry Maddox .10 .05 .01
☐ 71 Phil Garner .20 .09 .03
☐ 72 Graig Nettles .30 .14 .04
☐ 73 Gary Carter 1.00 .45 .12
☐ 74 Pete Rose 4.00 1.80 .50
☐ 75 Greg Luzinski .20 .09 .03
☐ 76 Ron Guidry .20 .09 .03
☐ 77 Gorman Thomas .10 .05 .01
☐ 78 Jose Cruz .20 .09 .03
☐ 79 Bob Boone .20 .09 .03
☐ 80 Bruce Sutter .20 .09 .03
☐ 81 Chris Chambliss .20 .09 .03
☐ 82 Paul Molitor 2.50 1.10 .30
☐ 83 Tug McGraw .20 .09 .03
☐ 84 Ferguson Jenkins .60 .25 .07
☐ 85 Steve Carlton 1.50 .70 .19
☐ 86 Miguel Dilone .10 .05 .01
☐ 87 Reggie Smith .20 .09 .03
☐ 88 Rick Cerone .10 .05 .01
☐ 89 Alan Trammell 1.00 .45 .12
☐ 90 Doug DeCinces .10 .05 .01
☐ 91 Sparky Lyle .20 .09 .03
☐ 92 Warren Cromartie .10 .05 .01
☐ 93 Rick Reuschel .20 .09 .03
☐ 94 Larry Hisle .10 .05 .01
☐ 95 Paul Splittorff .10 .05 .01
☐ 96 Manny Trillo .10 .05 .01
☐ 97 Frank White .20 .09 .03
☐ 98 Fred Lynn .20 .09 .03
☐ 99 Bob Horner .20 .09 .03
☐ 100 Omar Moreno .10 .05 .01
☐ 101 Dave Concepcion .20 .09 .03
☐ 102 Larry Gura .10 .05 .01
☐ 103 Ken Singleton .20 .09 .03
☐ 104 Steve Stone .10 .05 .01
☐ 105 Richie Zisk .10 .05 .01
☐ 106 Willie Wilson .20 .09 .03
☐ 107 Willie Randolph .20 .09 .03
☐ 108 Nolan Ryan 10.00 4.50 1.25
☐ 109 Joe Morgan 1.50 .70 .19
☐ 110 Bucky Dent .20 .09 .03
☐ 111 Dave Kingman .20 .09 .03
☐ 112 John Castino .10 .05 .01
☐ 113 Joe Rudi .10 .05 .01
☐ 114 Ed Farmer .10 .05 .01
☐ 115 Reggie Jackson 2.00 .90 .25
☐ 116 George Brett 5.00 2.20 .60
☐ 117 Eddie Murray 4.00 1.80 .50
☐ 118 Rich Gossage .30 .14 .04
☐ 119 Dale Murphy 1.50 .70 .19
☐ 120 Ted Simmons .20 .09 .03
☐ 121 Tommy John .30 .14 .04
☐ 122 Don Baylor .30 .14 .04
☐ 123 Andre Dawson 1.50 .70 .19
☐ 124 Jim Palmer 1.50 .70 .19
☐ 125 Garry Templeton .10 .05 .01
☐ 126 Reggie Jackson CL 1 1.00 .45 .12
Unnumbered
☐ 127 George Brett CL 2 3.00 1.35 .35
Unnumbered
☐ 128 Mike Schmidt CL3 2.00 .90 .25
Unnumbered

1982 Fleer

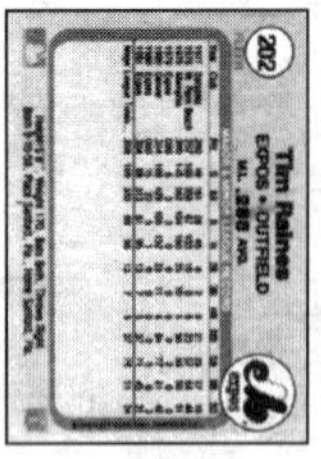

The 1982 Fleer set contains 660-card standard-size cards, of which are grouped in team order based upon standings from the previous season. Cards numbered 628 through 646 are special cards highlighting some of the stars and leaders of the 1981 season. The last 14 cards in the set (647-660) are checklist cards. The backs feature player statistics and a full-color team logo in the upper right-hand corner of each card. The complete set price below does not include any of the more valuable variation cards listed. Fleer was not allowed to insert bubble gum or other confectionary products into these packs; therefore logo stickers were included in these 15-card packs. Notable Rookie Cards in this set include Cal Ripken Jr., Lee Smith, and Dave Stewart.

	NRMT	VG-E	GOOD
COMPLETE SET (660)	70.00	32.00	8.75
COMMON CARD (1-660)	.10	.05	.01

☐ 1 Dusty Baker .40 .18 .05
☐ 2 Robert Castillo .10 .05 .01
☐ 3 Ron Cey .20 .09 .03
☐ 4 Terry Forster .10 .05 .01
☐ 5 Steve Garvey .40 .18 .05
☐ 6 Dave Goltz .10 .05 .01
☐ 7 Pedro Guerrero .20 .09 .03
☐ 8 Burt Hooton .10 .05 .01
☐ 9 Steve Howe .10 .05 .01
☐ 10 Jay Johnstone .20 .09 .03
☐ 11 Ken Landreaux .10 .05 .01
☐ 12 Dave Lopes .20 .09 .03
☐ 13 Mike A. Marshall .20 .09 .03
☐ 14 Bobby Mitchell .10 .05 .01
☐ 15 Rick Monday .10 .05 .01
☐ 16 Tom Niedenfuer .10 .05 .01
☐ 17 Ted Power .10 .05 .01
☐ 18 Jerry Reuss UER .20 .09 .03
("Home:" omitted)
☐ 19 Ron Roenicke .10 .05 .01
☐ 20 Bill Russell .20 .09 .03
☐ 21 Steve Sax .40 .18 .05
☐ 22 Mike Scioscia .20 .09 .03
☐ 23 Reggie Smith .20 .09 .03
☐ 24 Dave Stewart 1.50 .70 .19
☐ 25 Rick Sutcliffe .20 .09 .03
☐ 26 Derrel Thomas .10 .05 .01
☐ 27 Fernando Valenzuela .40 .18 .05
☐ 28 Bob Welch .20 .09 .03
☐ 29 Steve Yeager .10 .05 .01
☐ 30 Bobby Brown .10 .05 .01
☐ 31 Rick Cerone .10 .05 .01
☐ 32 Ron Davis .10 .05 .01
☐ 33 Bucky Dent .20 .09 .03
☐ 34 Barry Foote .10 .05 .01
☐ 35 George Frazier .10 .05 .01
☐ 36 Oscar Gamble .10 .05 .01
☐ 37 Rich Gossage .40 .18 .05
☐ 38 Ron Guidry .20 .09 .03
☐ 39 Reggie Jackson 1.00 .45 .12
☐ 40 Tommy John .40 .18 .05
☐ 41 Rudy May .10 .05 .01
☐ 42 Larry Milbourne .10 .05 .01
☐ 43 Jerry Mumphrey .10 .05 .01
☐ 44 Bobby Murcer .20 .09 .03
☐ 45 Gene Nelson .10 .05 .01
☐ 46 Graig Nettles .20 .09 .03
☐ 47 Johnny Oates .20 .09 .03
☐ 48 Lou Piniella .20 .09 .03
☐ 49 Willie Randolph .20 .09 .03
☐ 50 Rick Reuschel .20 .09 .03
☐ 51 Dave Revering .10 .05 .01
☐ 52 Dave Righetti .40 .18 .05
☐ 53 Aurelio Rodriguez .10 .05 .01
☐ 54 Bob Watson .20 .09 .03
☐ 55 Dennis Werth .10 .05 .01
☐ 56 Dave Winfield 1.50 .70 .19
☐ 57 Johnny Bench .75 .35 .09
☐ 58 Bruce Berenyi .10 .05 .01
☐ 59 Larry Biittner .10 .05 .01
☐ 60 Scott Brown .10 .05 .01
☐ 61 Dave Collins .10 .05 .01
☐ 62 Geoff Combe .10 .05 .01
☐ 63 Dave Concepcion .20 .09 .03
☐ 64 Dan Driessen .10 .05 .01
☐ 65 Joe Edelen .10 .05 .01
☐ 66 Reggie Foster .20 .09 .03
☐ 67 Ken Griffey .20 .09 .03
☐ 68 Paul Householder .10 .05 .01
☐ 69 Tom Hume .10 .05 .01
☐ 70 Junior Kennedy .10 .05 .01
☐ 71 Ray Knight .20 .09 .03
☐ 72 Mike LaCoss .10 .05 .01
☐ 73 Rafael Landestoy .10 .05 .01
☐ 74 Charlie Leibrandt .10 .05 .01
☐ 75 Sam Mejias .10 .05 .01
☐ 76 Paul Moskau .10 .05 .01
☐ 77 Joe Nolan .10 .05 .01
☐ 78 Mike O'Berry .10 .05 .01
☐ 79 Ron Oester .10 .05 .01
☐ 80 Frank Pastore .10 .05 .01
☐ 81 Joe Price .10 .05 .01
☐ 82 Tom Seaver .75 .35 .09
☐ 83 Mario Soto .10 .05 .01
☐ 84 Mike Vail .10 .05 .01
☐ 85 Tony Armas .10 .05 .01
☐ 86 Shooty Babitt .10 .05 .01
☐ 87 Dave Beard .10 .05 .01
☐ 88 Rick Bosetti .10 .05 .01
☐ 89 Keith Drumwright .10 .05 .01
☐ 90 Wayne Gross .10 .05 .01
☐ 91 Mike Heath .10 .05 .01
☐ 92 Rickey Henderson 2.50 1.10 .30
☐ 93 Cliff Johnson .10 .05 .01
☐ 94 Jeff Jones .10 .05 .01
☐ 95 Matt Keough .10 .05 .01
☐ 96 Brian Kingman .10 .05 .01
☐ 97 Mickey Klutts .10 .05 .01
☐ 98 Rick Langford .10 .05 .01
☐ 99 Steve McCatty .10 .05 .01
☐ 100 Dave McKay .10 .05 .01
☐ 101 Dwayne Murphy .10 .05 .01
☐ 102 Jeff Newman .10 .05 .01
☐ 103 Mike Norris .10 .05 .01
☐ 104 Bob Owchinko .10 .05 .01
☐ 105 Mitchell Page .10 .05 .01
☐ 106 Rob Picciolo .10 .05 .01
☐ 107 Jim Spencer .10 .05 .01
☐ 108 Fred Stanley .10 .05 .01
☐ 109 Tom Underwood .10 .05 .01
☐ 110 Joaquin Andujar .20 .09 .03
☐ 111 Steve Braun .10 .05 .01
☐ 112 Bob Forsch .10 .05 .01
☐ 113 George Hendrick .10 .05 .01
☐ 114 Keith Hernandez .20 .09 .03
☐ 115 Tom Herr .20 .09 .03
☐ 116 Dane Iorg .10 .05 .01
☐ 117 Jim Kaat .20 .09 .03
☐ 118 Tito Landrum .10 .05 .01
☐ 119 Sixto Lezcano .10 .05 .01
☐ 120 Mark Littell .10 .05 .01
☐ 121 John Martin .10 .05 .01
☐ 122 Silvio Martinez .10 .05 .01
☐ 123 Ken Oberkfell .10 .05 .01
☐ 124 Darrell Porter .20 .09 .03
☐ 125 Mike Ramsey .10 .05 .01
☐ 126 Orlando Sanchez .10 .05 .01
☐ 127 Bob Shirley .10 .05 .01
☐ 128 Lary Sorensen .10 .05 .01
☐ 129 Bruce Sutter .20 .09 .03
☐ 130 Bob Sykes .10 .05 .01
☐ 131 Garry Templeton .10 .05 .01
☐ 132 Gene Tenace .20 .09 .03
☐ 133 Jerry Augustine .10 .05 .01
☐ 134 Sal Bando .20 .09 .03
☐ 135 Mark Brouhard .10 .05 .01
☐ 136 Mike Caldwell .10 .05 .01
☐ 137 Reggie Cleveland .10 .05 .01
☐ 138 Cecil Cooper .20 .09 .03
☐ 139 Jamie Easterly .10 .05 .01
☐ 140 Marshall Edwards .10 .05 .01
☐ 141 Rollie Fingers .40 .18 .05
☐ 142 Jim Gantner .20 .09 .03
☐ 143 Moose Haas .10 .05 .01
☐ 144 Larry Hisle .10 .05 .01
☐ 145 Roy Howell .10 .05 .01
☐ 146 Rickey Keeton .10 .05 .01
☐ 147 Randy Lerch .10 .05 .01
☐ 148 Paul Molitor 2.00 .90 .25
☐ 149 Don Money .10 .05 .01
☐ 150 Charlie Moore .10 .05 .01
☐ 151 Ben Oglivie .20 .09 .03
☐ 152 Ted Simmons .20 .09 .03
☐ 153 Jim Slaton .10 .05 .01
☐ 154 Gorman Thomas .20 .09 .03
☐ 155 Robin Yount 1.50 .70 .19
☐ 156 Pete Vuckovich .10 .05 .01
(Should precede Yount
in the team order)
☐ 157 Benny Ayala .10 .05 .01
☐ 158 Mark Belanger .20 .09 .03
☐ 159 Al Bumbry .20 .09 .03
☐ 160 Terry Crowley .10 .05 .01
☐ 161 Rich Dauer .10 .05 .01
☐ 162 Doug DeCinces .20 .09 .03
☐ 163 Rick Dempsey .20 .09 .03
☐ 164 Jim Dwyer .10 .05 .01
☐ 165 Mike Flanagan .20 .09 .03
☐ 166 Dave Ford .10 .05 .01
☐ 167 Dan Graham .10 .05 .01
☐ 168 Wayne Krenchicki .10 .05 .01
☐ 169 John Lowenstein .10 .05 .01
☐ 170 Dennis Martinez .20 .09 .03
☐ 171 Tippy Martinez .10 .05 .01
☐ 172 Scott McGregor .10 .05 .01
☐ 173 Jose Morales .10 .05 .01
☐ 174 Eddie Murray 3.00 1.35 .35
☐ 175 Jim Palmer .60 .25 .07
☐ 176 Cal Ripken 50.00 22.00 6.25
(Fleer Ripken cards from 1982
through 1993 erroneously have 22
games played in 1981;not 23.)
☐ 177 Gary Roenicke .10 .05 .01
☐ 178 Lenn Sakata .10 .05 .01
☐ 179 Ken Singleton .20 .09 .03
☐ 180 Sammy Stewart .10 .05 .01
☐ 181 Tim Stoddard .10 .05 .01
☐ 182 Steve Stone .20 .09 .03
☐ 183 Stan Bahnsen .10 .05 .01
☐ 184 Ray Burris .10 .05 .01
☐ 185 Gary Carter .20 .09 .03
☐ 186 Warren Cromartie .10 .05 .01
☐ 187 Andre Dawson 1.00 .45 .12
☐ 188 Terry Francona .10 .05 .01
☐ 189 Woodie Fryman .10 .05 .01
☐ 190 Bill Gullickson .10 .05 .01
☐ 191 Grant Jackson .10 .05 .01
☐ 192 Wallace Johnson .10 .05 .01
☐ 193 Charlie Lea .10 .05 .01
☐ 194 Bill Lee .20 .09 .03
☐ 195 Jerry Manuel .10 .05 .01
☐ 196 Brad Mills .10 .05 .01
☐ 197 John Milner .10 .05 .01
☐ 198 Rowland Office .10 .05 .01
☐ 199 David Palmer .10 .05 .01
☐ 200 Larry Parrish .10 .05 .01
☐ 201 Mike Phillips .10 .05 .01
☐ 202 Tim Raines 1.50 .70 .19
☐ 203 Bobby Ramos .10 .05 .01
☐ 204 Jeff Reardon .40 .18 .05
☐ 205 Steve Rogers .10 .05 .01
☐ 206 Scott Sanderson .10 .05 .01
☐ 207 Rodney Scott UER .40 .18 .05
(Photo actually
Tim Raines)
☐ 208 Elias Sosa .10 .05 .01
☐ 209 Chris Speier .10 .05 .01
☐ 210 Tim Wallach .50 .23 .06
☐ 211 Jerry White .10 .05 .01
☐ 212 Alan Ashby .10 .05 .01
☐ 213 Cesar Cedeno .20 .09 .03
☐ 214 Jose Cruz .20 .09 .03
☐ 215 Kiko Garcia .10 .05 .01
☐ 216 Phil Garner .20 .09 .03
☐ 217 Danny Heep .10 .05 .01
☐ 218 Art Howe .10 .05 .01
☐ 219 Bob Knepper .10 .05 .01
☐ 220 Frank LaCorte .10 .05 .01
☐ 221 Joe Niekro .20 .09 .03
☐ 222 Joe Pittman .10 .05 .01
☐ 223 Terry Puhl .10 .05 .01
☐ 224 Luis Pujols .10 .05 .01
☐ 225 Craig Reynolds .10 .05 .01
☐ 226 J.R. Richard .20 .09 .03
☐ 227 Dave Roberts .10 .05 .01
☐ 228 Vern Ruhle .10 .05 .01
☐ 229 Nolan Ryan 5.00 2.20 .60
☐ 230 Joe Sambito .10 .05 .01
☐ 231 Tony Scott .10 .05 .01
☐ 232 Dave Smith .10 .05 .01
☐ 233 Harry Spilman .10 .05 .01
☐ 234 Don Sutton .40 .18 .05
☐ 235 Dickie Thon .10 .05 .01
☐ 236 Denny Walling .10 .05 .01
☐ 237 Gary Woods .10 .05 .01
☐ 238 Luis Aguayo .10 .05 .01
☐ 239 Ramon Aviles .10 .05 .01
☐ 240 Bob Boone .20 .09 .03
☐ 241 Larry Bowa .20 .09 .03
☐ 242 Warren Brusstar .10 .05 .01
☐ 243 Steve Carlton .75 .35 .09
☐ 244 Larry Christenson .10 .05 .01
☐ 245 Dick Davis .10 .05 .01
☐ 246 Greg Gross .10 .05 .01
☐ 247 Sparky Lyle .20 .09 .03
☐ 248 Garry Maddox .10 .05 .01
☐ 249 Gary Matthews .20 .09 .03
☐ 250 Bake McBride .10 .05 .01
☐ 251 Tug McGraw .20 .09 .03
☐ 252 Keith Moreland .10 .05 .01
☐ 253 Dickie Noles .10 .05 .01
☐ 254 Mike Proly .10 .05 .01
☐ 255 Ron Reed .10 .05 .01
☐ 256 Pete Rose 1.50 .70 .19
☐ 257 Dick Ruthven .10 .05 .01
☐ 258 Mike Schmidt 2.00 .90 .25
☐ 259 Lonnie Smith .20 .09 .03
☐ 260 Manny Trillo .10 .05 .01
☐ 261 Del Unser .10 .05 .01
☐ 262 George Vukovich .10 .05 .01
☐ 263 Tom Brookens .10 .05 .01
☐ 264 George Cappuzzello .10 .05 .01
☐ 265 Marty Castillo .10 .05 .01
☐ 266 Al Cowens .10 .05 .01
☐ 267 Kirk Gibson .75 .35 .09
☐ 268 Richie Hebner .20 .09 .03
☐ 269 Ron Jackson .10 .05 .01
☐ 270 Lynn Jones .10 .05 .01
☐ 271 Steve Kemp .10 .05 .01

Card			
☐ 272 Rick Leach	.10	.05	.01
☐ 273 Aurelio Lopez	.10	.05	.01
☐ 274 Jack Morris	.20	.09	.03
☐ 275 Kevin Saucier	.10	.05	.01
☐ 276 Lance Parrish	.40	.18	.05
☐ 277 Rick Peters	.10	.05	.01
☐ 278 Dan Petry	.10	.05	.01
☐ 279 Dave Rozema	.10	.05	.01
☐ 280 Stan Papi	.10	.05	.01
☐ 281 Dan Schatzeder	.10	.05	.01
☐ 282 Champ Summers	.10	.05	.01
☐ 283 Alan Trammell	1.00	.45	.12
☐ 284 Lou Whitaker	.40	.18	.05
☐ 285 Milt Wilcox	.10	.05	.01
☐ 286 John Wockenfuss	.10	.05	.01
☐ 287 Gary Allenson	.10	.05	.01
☐ 288 Tom Burgmeier	.10	.05	.01
☐ 289 Bill Campbell	.10	.05	.01
☐ 290 Mark Clear	.10	.05	.01
☐ 291 Steve Crawford	.10	.05	.01
☐ 292 Dennis Eckersley	.40	.18	.05
☐ 293 Dwight Evans	.40	.18	.05
☐ 294 Rich Gedman	.20	.09	.03
☐ 295 Garry Hancock	.10	.05	.01
☐ 296 Glenn Hoffman	.10	.05	.01
☐ 297 Bruce Hurst	.10	.05	.01
☐ 298 Carney Lansford	.20	.09	.03
☐ 299 Rick Miller	.10	.05	.01
☐ 300 Reid Nichols	.10	.05	.01
☐ 301 Bob Ojeda	.40	.18	.05
☐ 302 Tony Perez	.40	.18	.05
☐ 303 Chuck Rainey	.10	.05	.01
☐ 304 Jerry Remy	.10	.05	.01
☐ 305 Jim Rice	.20	.09	.03
☐ 306 Joe Rudi	.10	.05	.01
☐ 307 Bob Stanley	.10	.05	.01
☐ 308 Dave Stapleton	.10	.05	.01
☐ 309 Frank Tanana	.20	.09	.03
☐ 310 Mike Torrez	.10	.05	.01
☐ 311 John Tudor	.20	.09	.03
☐ 312 Carl Yastrzemski	.75	.35	.09
☐ 313 Buddy Bell	.20	.09	.03
☐ 314 Steve Comer	.10	.05	.01
☐ 315 Danny Darwin	.10	.05	.01
☐ 316 John Ellis	.10	.05	.01
☐ 317 John Grubb	.10	.05	.01
☐ 318 Rick Honeycutt	.10	.05	.01
☐ 319 Charlie Hough	.20	.09	.03
☐ 320 Ferguson Jenkins	.40	.18	.05
☐ 321 John Henry Johnson	.10	.05	.01
☐ 322 Jim Kern	.10	.05	.01
☐ 323 Jon Matlack	.10	.05	.01
☐ 324 Doc Medich	.10	.05	.01
☐ 325 Mario Mendoza	.10	.05	.01
☐ 326 Al Oliver	.20	.09	.03
☐ 327 Pat Putnam	.10	.05	.01
☐ 328 Mickey Rivers	.10	.05	.01
☐ 329 Leon Roberts	.10	.05	.01
☐ 330 Billy Sample	.10	.05	.01
☐ 331 Bill Stein	.10	.05	.01
☐ 332 Jim Sundberg	.20	.09	.03
☐ 333 Mark Wagner	.10	.05	.01
☐ 334 Bump Wills	.10	.05	.01
☐ 335 Bill Almon	.10	.05	.01
☐ 336 Harold Baines	.40	.18	.05
☐ 337 Ross Baumgarten	.10	.05	.01
☐ 338 Tony Bernazard	.10	.05	.01
☐ 339 Britt Burns	.10	.05	.01
☐ 340 Richard Dotson	.10	.05	.01
☐ 341 Jim Essian	.10	.05	.01
☐ 342 Ed Farmer	.10	.05	.01
☐ 343 Carlton Fisk	.75	.35	.09
☐ 344 Kevin Hickey	.10	.05	.01
☐ 345 LaMarr Hoyt	.10	.05	.01
☐ 346 Lamar Johnson	.10	.05	.01
☐ 347 Jerry Koosman	.20	.09	.03
☐ 348 Rusty Kuntz	.10	.05	.01
☐ 349 Dennis Lamp	.10	.05	.01
☐ 350 Ron LeFlore	.20	.09	.03
☐ 351 Chet Lemon	.10	.05	.01
☐ 352 Greg Luzinski	.20	.09	.03
☐ 353 Bob Molinaro	.10	.05	.01
☐ 354 Jim Morrison	.10	.05	.01
☐ 355 Wayne Nordhagen	.10	.05	.01
☐ 356 Greg Pryor	.10	.05	.01
☐ 357 Mike Squires	.10	.05	.01
☐ 358 Steve Trout	.10	.05	.01
☐ 359 Alan Bannister	.10	.05	.01
☐ 360 Len Barker	.10	.05	.01
☐ 361 Bert Blyleven	.40	.18	.05
☐ 362 Joe Charboneau	.10	.05	.01
☐ 363 John Denny	.10	.05	.01
☐ 364 Bo Diaz	.10	.05	.01
☐ 365 Miguel Dilone	.10	.05	.01
☐ 366 Jerry Dybzinski	.10	.05	.01
☐ 367 Wayne Garland	.10	.05	.01
☐ 368 Mike Hargrove	.20	.09	.03
☐ 369 Toby Harrah	.20	.09	.03
☐ 370 Ron Hassey	.10	.05	.01
☐ 371 Von Hayes	.20	.09	.03
☐ 372 Pat Kelly	.10	.05	.01
☐ 373 Duane Kuiper	.10	.05	.01
☐ 374 Rick Manning	.10	.05	.01
☐ 375 Sid Monge	.10	.05	.01
☐ 376 Jorge Orta	.10	.05	.01
☐ 377 Dave Rosello	.10	.05	.01
☐ 378 Dan Spillner	.10	.05	.01
☐ 379 Mike Stanton	.10	.05	.01
☐ 380 Andre Thornton	.10	.05	.01
☐ 381 Tom Veryzer	.10	.05	.01
☐ 382 Rick Waits	.10	.05	.01
☐ 383 Doyle Alexander	.10	.05	.01
☐ 384 Vida Blue	.20	.09	.03
☐ 385 Fred Breining	.10	.05	.01
☐ 386 Enos Cabell	.10	.05	.01
☐ 387 Jack Clark	.20	.09	.03
☐ 388 Darrell Evans	.20	.09	.03
☐ 389 Tom Griffin	.10	.05	.01
☐ 390 Larry Herndon	.10	.05	.01
☐ 391 Al Holland	.10	.05	.01
☐ 392 Gary Lavelle	.10	.05	.01
☐ 393 Johnnie LeMaster	.10	.05	.01
☐ 394 Jerry Martin	.10	.05	.01
☐ 395 Milt May	.10	.05	.01
☐ 396 Greg Minton	.10	.05	.01
☐ 397 Joe Morgan	.60	.25	.07
☐ 398 Joe Pettini	.10	.05	.01
☐ 399 Allen Ripley	.10	.05	.01
☐ 400 Billy Smith	.10	.05	.01
☐ 401 Rennie Stennett	.10	.05	.01
☐ 402 Ed Whitson	.10	.05	.01
☐ 403 Jim Wohlford	.10	.05	.01
☐ 404 Willie Aikens	.10	.05	.01
☐ 405 George Brett	3.50	1.55	.45
☐ 406 Ken Brett	.10	.05	.01
☐ 407 Dave Chalk	.10	.05	.01
☐ 408 Rich Gale	.10	.05	.01
☐ 409 Cesar Geronimo	.10	.05	.01
☐ 410 Larry Gura	.10	.05	.01
☐ 411 Clint Hurdle	.10	.05	.01
☐ 412 Mike Jones	.10	.05	.01
☐ 413 Dennis Leonard	.10	.05	.01
☐ 414 Renie Martin	.10	.05	.01
☐ 415 Lee May	.20	.09	.03
☐ 416 Hal McRae	.20	.09	.03
☐ 417 Darryl Motley	.10	.05	.01
☐ 418 Rance Mulliniks	.10	.05	.01
☐ 419 Amos Otis	.20	.09	.03
☐ 420 Ken Phelps	.10	.05	.01
☐ 421 Jamie Quirk	.10	.05	.01
☐ 422 Dan Quisenberry	.20	.09	.03
☐ 423 Paul Splittorff	.10	.05	.01
☐ 424 U.L. Washington	.10	.05	.01
☐ 425 John Wathan	.10	.05	.01
☐ 426 Frank White	.20	.09	.03
☐ 427 Willie Wilson	.20	.09	.03
☐ 428 Brian Asselstine	.10	.05	.01
☐ 429 Bruce Benedict	.10	.05	.01
☐ 430 Tommy Boggs	.10	.05	.01
☐ 431 Larry Bradford	.10	.05	.01
☐ 432 Rick Camp	.10	.05	.01
☐ 433 Chris Chambliss	.20	.09	.03
☐ 434 Gene Garber	.10	.05	.01
☐ 435 Preston Hanna	.10	.05	.01
☐ 436 Bob Horner	.20	.09	.03
☐ 437 Glenn Hubbard	.10	.05	.01
☐ 438A Al Hrabosky ERR (Height 5'1" All on reverse)	20.00	9.00	2.50
☐ 438B Al Hrabosky ERR (Height 5'1")	.40	.18	.05
☐ 438C Al Hrabosky (Height 5'10")	.20	.09	.03
☐ 439 Rufino Linares	.10	.05	.01
☐ 440 Rick Mahler	.10	.05	.01
☐ 441 Ed Miller	.10	.05	.01
☐ 442 John Montefusco	.10	.05	.01
☐ 443 Dale Murphy	.40	.18	.05
☐ 444 Phil Niekro	.40	.18	.05
☐ 445 Gaylord Perry	.40	.18	.05
☐ 446 Biff Pocoroba	.10	.05	.01
☐ 447 Rafael Ramirez	.10	.05	.01
☐ 448 Jerry Royster	.10	.05	.01
☐ 449 Claudell Washington	.10	.05	.01
☐ 450 Don Aase	.10	.05	.01
☐ 451 Don Baylor	.40	.18	.05
☐ 452 Juan Beniquez	.10	.05	.01
☐ 453 Rick Burleson	.10	.05	.01
☐ 454 Bert Campaneris	.20	.09	.03
☐ 455 Rod Carew	.75	.35	.09
☐ 456 Bob Clark	.10	.05	.01
☐ 457 Brian Downing	.10	.05	.01
☐ 458 Dan Ford	.10	.05	.01
☐ 459 Ken Forsch	.10	.05	.01
☐ 460A Dave Frost (5 mm space before ERA)	.10	.05	.01
☐ 460B Dave Frost (1 mm space)	.10	.05	.01
☐ 461 Bobby Grich	.20	.09	.03
☐ 462 Larry Harlow	.10	.05	.01
☐ 463 John Harris	.10	.05	.01
☐ 464 Andy Hassler	.10	.05	.01
☐ 465 Butch Hobson	.10	.05	.01
☐ 466 Jesse Jefferson	.10	.05	.01
☐ 467 Bruce Kison	.10	.05	.01
☐ 468 Fred Lynn	.20	.09	.03
☐ 469 Angel Moreno	.10	.05	.01
☐ 470 Ed Ott	.10	.05	.01
☐ 471 Fred Patek	.10	.05	.01
☐ 472 Steve Renko	.10	.05	.01
☐ 473 Mike Witt	.20	.09	.03
☐ 474 Geoff Zahn	.10	.05	.01
☐ 475 Gary Alexander	.10	.05	.01
☐ 476 Dale Berra	.10	.05	.01
☐ 477 Kurt Bevacqua	.10	.05	.01
☐ 478 Jim Bibby	.10	.05	.01
☐ 479 John Candelaria	.10	.05	.01
☐ 480 Victor Cruz	.10	.05	.01
☐ 481 Mike Easler	.10	.05	.01
☐ 482 Tim Foli	.10	.05	.01
☐ 483 Lee Lacy	.10	.05	.01
☐ 484 Vance Law	.10	.05	.01
☐ 485 Bill Madlock	.20	.09	.03
☐ 486 Willie Montanez	.10	.05	.01
☐ 487 Omar Moreno	.10	.05	.01
☐ 488 Steve Nicosia	.10	.05	.01
☐ 489 Dave Parker	.20	.09	.03
☐ 490 Tony Pena	.20	.09	.03
☐ 491 Pascual Perez	.10	.05	.01
☐ 492 Johnny Ray	.20	.09	.03
☐ 493 Rick Rhoden	.10	.05	.01
☐ 494 Bill Robinson	.10	.05	.01
☐ 495 Don Robinson	.10	.05	.01
☐ 496 Enrique Romo	.10	.05	.01
☐ 497 Rod Scurry	.10	.05	.01
☐ 498 Eddie Solomon	.10	.05	.01
☐ 499 Willie Stargell	.40	.18	.05
☐ 500 Kent Tekulve	.20	.09	.03
☐ 501 Jason Thompson	.10	.05	.01
☐ 502 Glenn Abbott	.10	.05	.01
☐ 503 Jim Anderson	.10	.05	.01
☐ 504 Floyd Bannister	.10	.05	.01
☐ 505 Bruce Bochte	.10	.05	.01
☐ 506 Jeff Burroughs	.10	.05	.01
☐ 507 Bryan Clark	.10	.05	.01
☐ 508 Ken Clay	.10	.05	.01
☐ 509 Julio Cruz	.10	.05	.01
☐ 510 Dick Drago	.10	.05	.01
☐ 511 Gary Gray	.10	.05	.01
☐ 512 Dan Meyer	.10	.05	.01
☐ 513 Jerry Narron	.10	.05	.01
☐ 514 Tom Paciorek	.10	.05	.01
☐ 515 Casey Parsons	.10	.05	.01
☐ 516 Lenny Randle	.10	.05	.01
☐ 517 Shane Rawley	.10	.05	.01
☐ 518 Joe Simpson	.10	.05	.01
☐ 519 Richie Zisk	.10	.05	.01
☐ 520 Neil Allen	.10	.05	.01
☐ 521 Bob Bailor	.10	.05	.01
☐ 522 Hubie Brooks	.20	.09	.03
☐ 523 Mike Cubbage	.10	.05	.01
☐ 524 Pete Falcone	.10	.05	.01
☐ 525 Doug Flynn	.10	.05	.01
☐ 526 Tom Hausman	.10	.05	.01
☐ 527 Ron Hodges	.10	.05	.01
☐ 528 Randy Jones	.10	.05	.01
☐ 529 Mike Jorgensen	.10	.05	.01
☐ 530 Dave Kingman	.20	.09	.03
☐ 531 Ed Lynch	.10	.05	.01
☐ 532 Mike G. Marshall	.10	.05	.01
☐ 533 Lee Mazzilli	.10	.05	.01
☐ 534 Dyar Miller	.10	.05	.01
☐ 535 Mike Scott	.20	.09	.03
☐ 536 Rusty Staub	.20	.09	.03
☐ 537 John Stearns	.10	.05	.01
☐ 538 Craig Swan	.10	.05	.01
☐ 539 Frank Taveras	.10	.05	.01
☐ 540 Alex Trevino	.10	.05	.01
☐ 541 Ellis Valentine	.10	.05	.01
☐ 542 Mookie Wilson	.20	.09	.03
☐ 543 Joel Youngblood	.10	.05	.01
☐ 544 Pat Zachry	.10	.05	.01
☐ 545 Glenn Adams	.10	.05	.01
☐ 546 Fernando Arroyo	.10	.05	.01
☐ 547 John Verhoeven	.10	.05	.01
☐ 548 Sal Butera	.10	.05	.01
☐ 549 John Castino	.10	.05	.01
☐ 550 Don Cooper	.10	.05	.01
☐ 551 Doug Corbett	.10	.05	.01
☐ 552 Dave Engle	.10	.05	.01
☐ 553 Roger Erickson	.10	.05	.01
☐ 554 Danny Goodwin	.10	.05	.01
☐ 555A Darrell Jackson (Black cap)	.40	.18	.05
☐ 555B Darrell Jackson (Red cap with T)	.20	.09	.03
☐ 555C Darrell Jackson (Red cap, no emblem)	3.00	1.35	.35
☐ 556 Pete Mackanin	.10	.05	.01
☐ 557 Jack O'Connor	.10	.05	.01
☐ 558 Hosken Powell	.10	.05	.01
☐ 559 Pete Redfern	.10	.05	.01
☐ 560 Roy Smalley	.10	.05	.01
☐ 561 Chuck Baker UER (Shortshop on front)	.10	.05	.01
☐ 562 Gary Ward	.10	.05	.01
☐ 563 Rob Wilfong	.10	.05	.01
☐ 564 Al Williams	.10	.05	.01
☐ 565 Butch Wynegar	.10	.05	.01
☐ 566 Randy Bass	.20	.09	.03
☐ 567 Juan Bonilla	.10	.05	.01
☐ 568 Danny Boone	.10	.05	.01
☐ 569 John Curtis	.10	.05	.01
☐ 570 Juan Eichelberger	.10	.05	.01
☐ 571 Barry Evans	.10	.05	.01
☐ 572 Tim Flannery	.10	.05	.01
☐ 573 Ruppert Jones	.10	.05	.01
☐ 574 Terry Kennedy	.10	.05	.01
☐ 575 Joe Lefebvre	.10	.05	.01
☐ 576A John Littlefield ERR (Left handed; reverse negative)	200.00	90.00	25.00
☐ 576B John Littlefield COR (Right handed)	.20	.09	.03
☐ 577 Gary Lucas	.10	.05	.01
☐ 578 Steve Mura	.10	.05	.01
☐ 579 Broderick Perkins	.10	.05	.01
☐ 580 Gene Richards	.10	.05	.01
☐ 581 Luis Salazar	.10	.05	.01
☐ 582 Ozzie Smith	3.00	1.35	.35
☐ 583 John Urrea	.10	.05	.01
☐ 584 Chris Welsh	.10	.05	.01
☐ 585 Rick Wise	.10	.05	.01
☐ 586 Doug Bird	.10	.05	.01
☐ 587 Tim Blackwell	.10	.05	.01
☐ 588 Bobby Bonds	.20	.09	.03
☐ 589 Bill Buckner	.20	.09	.03
☐ 590 Bill Caudill	.10	.05	.01
☐ 591 Hector Cruz	.10	.05	.01
☐ 592 Jody Davis	.10	.05	.01
☐ 593 Ivan DeJesus	.10	.05	.01
☐ 594 Steve Dillard	.10	.05	.01
☐ 595 Leon Durham	.20	.09	.03
☐ 596 Rawly Eastwick	.10	.05	.01
☐ 597 Steve Henderson	.10	.05	.01
☐ 598 Mike Krukow	.10	.05	.01
☐ 599 Mike Lum	.10	.05	.01
☐ 600 Randy Martz	.10	.05	.01
☐ 601 Jerry Morales	.10	.05	.01
☐ 602 Ken Reitz	.10	.05	.01
☐ 603 Lee Smith ERR (Cubs logo reversed)	6.00	2.70	.75
☐ 603B Lee Smith COR	6.00	2.70	.75
☐ 604 Dick Tidrow	.10	.05	.01
☐ 605 Jim Tracy	.10	.05	.01
☐ 606 Mike Tyson	.10	.05	.01
☐ 607 Ty Waller	.10	.05	.01
☐ 608 Danny Ainge	1.00	.45	.12
☐ 609 Jorge Bell	.75	.35	.09
☐ 610 Mark Bomback	.10	.05	.01
☐ 611 Barry Bonnell	.10	.05	.01
☐ 612 Jim Clancy	.10	.05	.01
☐ 613 Damaso Garcia	.10	.05	.01
☐ 614 Jerry Garvin	.10	.05	.01
☐ 615 Alfredo Griffin	.10	.05	.01
☐ 616 Garth Iorg	.10	.05	.01
☐ 617 Luis Leal	.10	.05	.01
☐ 618 Ken Macha	.10	.05	.01
☐ 619 John Mayberry	.10	.05	.01
☐ 620 Joey McLaughlin	.10	.05	.01
☐ 621 Lloyd Moseby	.10	.05	.01
☐ 622 Dave Stieb	.20	.09	.03
☐ 623 Jackson Todd	.10	.05	.01
☐ 624 Willie Upshaw	.10	.05	.01
☐ 625 Otto Velez	.10	.05	.01
☐ 626 Ernie Whitt	.10	.05	.01
☐ 627 Alvis Woods	.10	.05	.01
☐ 628 All Star Game Cleveland, Ohio	.20	.09	.03
☐ 629 All Star Infielders Frank White and Bucky Dent	.20	.09	.03
☐ 630 Big Red Machine Dan Driessen Dave Concepcion George Foster	.20	.09	.03
☐ 631 Bruce Sutter Top NL Relief Pitcher	.20	.09	.03
☐ 632 Steve and Carlton Steve Carlton Carlton Fisk	.50	.23	.06
☐ 633 Carl Yastrzemski 3000th Game	.60	.25	.07
☐ 634 Dynamic Duo Johnny Bench and Tom Seaver	.75	.35	.09
☐ 635 West Meets East Fernando Valenzuela and Gary Carter	.20	.09	.03
☐ 636A Fernando Valenzuela: NL SO King ("he" NL)	.40	.18	.05
☐ 636B Fernando Valenzuela: NL SO King ("the" NL)	.40	.18	.05
☐ 637 Mike Schmidt Home Run King	1.00	.45	.12
☐ 638 NL All Stars Gary Carter and Dave Parker	.20	.09	.03
☐ 639 Perfect Game UER Len Barker and Bo Diaz (Catcher actually Ron Hassey)	.20	.09	.03
☐ 640 Pete and Re-Pete Pete Rose and Son	1.00	.45	.12
☐ 641 Phillies Finest Lonnie Smith Mike Schmidt Steve Carlton	.50	.23	.06
☐ 642 Red Sox Reunion	.20	.09	.03

Fred Lynn and Dwight Evans			
☐ 643 Rickey Henderson Most Hits and Runs	1.00	.45	.12
☐ 644 Rollie Fingers Most Saves AL	.20	.09	.03
☐ 645 Tom Seaver Most 1981 Wins	.75	.35	.09
☐ 646 Yankee Powerhouse Reggie Jackson and Dave Winfield (Comma on back after outfielder)	2.00	.90	.25
☐ 646B Yankee Powerhouse Reggie Jackson and Dave Winfield (No comma)	2.00	.90	.25
☐ 647 CL: Yankees/Dodgers	.20	.09	.03
☐ 648 CL: A's/Reds	.20	.09	.03
☐ 649 CL: Cards/Brewers	.20	.09	.03
☐ 650 CL: Expos/Orioles	.20	.09	.03
☐ 651 CL: Astros/Phillies	.20	.09	.03
☐ 652 CL: Tigers/Red Sox	.20	.09	.03
☐ 653 CL: Rangers/White Sox	.20	.09	.03
☐ 654 CL: Giants/Indians	.20	.09	.03
☐ 655 CL: Royals/Braves	.20	.09	.03
☐ 656 CL: Angels/Pirates	.20	.09	.03
☐ 657 CL: Mariners/Mets	.20	.09	.03
☐ 658 CL: Padres/Twins	.20	.09	.03
☐ 659 CL: Blue Jays/Cubs	.20	.09	.03
☐ 660 Specials Checklist	.20	.09	.03

1982 Fleer Stamps

The stamps in this 242-piece set measure 1 13/16" by 2 1/2". The 1982 Fleer stamp set consists of different individual stamps issued in strips of 10 stamps each. The stamps were issued in packages with the Fleer team logo stickers. The backs are blank and an inexpensive album is available in which to place the stamps. A checklist is provided in the back of the album which lists 25 strips of 10 stamps. The checklist below lists the individual stamps plus the strip (with prefix G) to which the stamps are supposed to belong based on the album strip checklist. Complete strips have equal value to the sum of the individual stamps on the strip. Eight stamps have been doubly printed and are noted by two different strip numbers below. The numbering is essentially in team order, e.g., Los Angeles Dodgers (1-10), Cincinnati Reds (11-20), St. Louis Cardinals (21-30), Montreal Expos (31-40), Houston Astros (41-50), Philadelphia Phillies (51-60), San Francisco Giants (61-65), Atlanta Braves (66-70), Pittsburgh Pirates (71-80), New York Mets (81-90), Chicago Cubs (91-100), San Diego Padres (101-105), Combination Stamps (106-111), New York Yankees (112-121), Oakland A's (122-131), Milwaukee Brewers (132-141), Baltimore Orioles (142-151), Detroit Tigers (152-161), Boston Red Sox (162-171), Texas Rangers (172-181), Chicago White Sox (182-191), Cleveland Indians (192-201), Kansas Cit222y Royals (202-211), California Angels (212-221), Seattle Mariners (222-226), Minnesota Twins (227-231), Toronto Blue Jays (232-236) and Combination Stamps (237-242).

	NRMT	VG-E	GOOD
COMPLETE SET (242)	10.00	4.50	1.25
COMMON STAMP (1-242)	.02	.01	.01
COMMON SHEET	.25	.11	.03

☐ 1 Fern. Valenzuela G20	.50	.23	.06
☐ 2 Rick Monday G16	.02	.01	.01
☐ 3 Ron Cey G9	.05	.02	.01
☐ 4 Dusty Baker G20	.05	.02	.01
☐ 5 Burt Hooton G10	.02	.01	.01
☐ 6 Pedro Guerrero G23	.05	.02	.01
☐ 7 Jerry Reuss G12	.02	.01	.01
☐ 8 Bill Russell G7	.02	.01	.01
☐ 9 Steve Garvey G21	.08	.04	.01
☐ 10 Davey Lopes G19	.05	.02	.01
☐ 11 Tom Seaver G7	1.00	.45	.12
☐ 12 George Foster G17	.05	.02	.01
☐ 13 Frank Pastore G12	.02	.01	.01
☐ 14 Dave Collins G5	.02	.01	.01
☐ 15 Dave Concepcion G21	.05	.02	.01
☐ 16 Ken Griffey G6	.05	.02	.01
☐ 17 Johnny Bench G20	1.00	.45	.12
☐ 18 Ray Knight G16	.05	.02	.01
☐ 19 Mario Soto G9	.02	.01	.01
☐ 20 Ron Oester G19	.02	.01	.01
☐ 21 Ken Oberkfell G21	.02	.01	.01
☐ 22 Bob Forsch G4	.02	.01	.01
☐ 23 Keith Hernandez G19	.05	.02	.01
☐ 24 Dane Iorg G9	.02	.01	.01
☐ 25 George Hendrick G2	.02	.01	.01
☐ 26 Gene Tenace G24	.02	.01	.01
☐ 27 Garry Templeton G12	.02	.01	.01
☐ 28 Bruce Sutter G18	.05	.02	.01
☐ 29 Darrell Porter G14	.02	.01	.01
☐ 30 Tom Herr G3	.02	.01	.01
☐ 31 Tim Raines G11	.50	.23	.06
☐ 32 Chris Speier G13	.02	.01	.01
☐ 33 Warren Cromartie G22	.02	.01	.01
☐ 34 Larry Parrish G15	.02	.01	.01
☐ 35 Andre Dawson G10	.75	.35	.09
☐ 36 Steve Rogers G1/G25	.02	.01	.01
☐ 37 Jeff Reardon G23	.08	.04	.01
☐ 38 Rodney Scott G12	.02	.01	.01
☐ 39 Gary Carter G14	.25	.11	.03
☐ 40 Scott Sanderson G6	.02	.01	.01
☐ 41 Cesar Cedeno G7	.02	.01	.01
☐ 42 Nolan Ryan G10	4.00	1.80	.50
☐ 43 Don Sutton G24	.08	.04	.01
☐ 44 Terry Puhl G15	.02	.01	.01
☐ 45 Joe Niekro G13	.02	.01	.01
☐ 46 Tony Scott G16	.02	.01	.01
☐ 47 Joe Sambito G1	.02	.01	.01
☐ 48 Art Howe G9	.02	.01	.01
☐ 49 Bob Knepper G18	.02	.01	.01
☐ 50 Jose Cruz G22	.05	.02	.01
☐ 51 Pete Rose G16	1.50	.70	.19
☐ 52 Dick Ruthven G12	.02	.01	.01
☐ 53 Mike Schmidt G14	1.50	.70	.19
☐ 54 Steve Carlton G17	.75	.35	.09
☐ 55 Tug McGraw G4	.05	.02	.01
☐ 56 Larry Bowa G4	.05	.02	.01
☐ 57 Garry Maddox G18	.02	.01	.01
☐ 58 Gary Matthews G4	.02	.01	.01
☐ 59 Manny Trillo G15	.02	.01	.01
☐ 60 Lonnie Smith G20	.02	.01	.01
☐ 61 Vida Blue G11	.05	.02	.01
☐ 62 Milt May G12	.02	.01	.01
☐ 63 Joe Morgan G16	.50	.23	.06
☐ 64 Enos Cabell G8	.02	.01	.01
☐ 65 Jack Clark G18	.05	.02	.01
☐ 66 Claud Washington G19	.02	.01	.01
☐ 67 Gaylord Perry G16	.25	.11	.03
☐ 68 Phil Niekro G22	.25	.11	.03
☐ 69 Bob Horner G7	.02	.01	.01
☐ 70 Chris Chambliss G11	.02	.01	.01
☐ 71 Dave Parker G15	.05	.02	.01
☐ 72 Tony Pena G11	.02	.01	.01
☐ 73 Kent Tekulve G23	.02	.01	.01
☐ 74 Mike Easler G18	.02	.01	.01
☐ 75 Tim Foli G13	.02	.01	.01
☐ 76 Willie Stargell G21	.50	.23	.06
☐ 77 Bill Madlock G5	.05	.02	.01
☐ 78 Jim Bibby G14	.02	.01	.01
☐ 79 Omar Moreno G17	.02	.01	.01
☐ 80 Lee Lacy G2	.02	.01	.01
☐ 81 Hubie Brooks G24	.02	.01	.01
☐ 82 Rusty Staub G4	.05	.02	.01
☐ 83 Ellis Valentine G13	.02	.01	.01
☐ 84 Neil Allen G1	.02	.01	.01
☐ 85 Dave Kingman G9	.05	.02	.01
☐ 86 Mookie Wilson G3	.05	.02	.01
☐ 87 Doug Flynn G11	.02	.01	.01
☐ 88 Pat Zachry G8	.02	.01	.01
☐ 89 John Stearns G6	.02	.01	.01
☐ 90 Lee Mazzilli G2	.02	.01	.01
☐ 91 Ken Reitz G23	.02	.01	.01
☐ 92 Mike Krukow G11	.02	.01	.01
☐ 93 Jerry Morales G10	.02	.01	.01
☐ 94 Leon Durham G22	.02	.01	.01
☐ 95 Ivan DeJesus G2	.02	.01	.01
☐ 96 Bill Buckner G17	.05	.02	.01
☐ 97 Jim Tracy G12	.02	.01	.01
☐ 98 Steve Henderson G14	.02	.01	.01
☐ 99 Dick Tidrow G14	.02	.01	.01
☐ 100 Mike Tyson G5	.02	.01	.01
☐ 101 Ozzie Smith G12	2.00	.90	.25
☐ 102 Ruppert Jones G24	.02	.01	.01
☐ 103 Brod Perkins G10	.02	.01	.01
☐ 104 Gene Richards G15	.02	.01	.01
☐ 105 Terry Kennedy G22	.02	.01	.01
☐ 106 Jim Bibby and Willie Stargell G4	.08	.04	.01
☐ 107 Pete Rose and Larry Bowa G21	.50	.23	.06
☐ 108 Fern.Valenzuela and Warren Spahn G1/G25	.25	.11	.03
☐ 109 Pete Rose and Dave Concepcion G8	.50	.23	.06
☐ 110 Reggie Jackson and Dave Winfield G3	.75	.35	.09
☐ 111 Fernando Valenzuela and Tom Lasorda G4	.08	.04	.01
☐ 112 Reggie Jackson G6	1.00	.45	.12
☐ 113 Dave Winfield G3	.75	.35	.09
☐ 114 Lou Piniella G2	.05	.02	.01
☐ 115 Tommy John G9	.05	.02	.01
☐ 116 Rich Gossage G1/G25	.05	.02	.01
☐ 117 Ron Davis G10	.02	.01	.01
☐ 118 Rick Cerone G5	.02	.01	.01
☐ 119 Graig Nettles G8	.05	.02	.01
☐ 120 Ron Guidry G24	.05	.02	.01
☐ 121 Willie Randolph G24	.05	.02	.01
☐ 122 Dwayne Murphy G15	.02	.01	.01
☐ 123 Rickey Henderson G16	1.50	.70	.19
☐ 124 Wayne Gross G6	.02	.01	.01
☐ 125 Mike Norris G8	.02	.01	.01
☐ 126 Rick Langford G20	.02	.01	.01
☐ 127 Jim Spencer G17	.02	.01	.01
☐ 128 Tony Armas G12	.02	.01	.01
☐ 129 Matt Keough G7	.02	.01	.01
☐ 130 Jeff Jones G19	.02	.01	.01
☐ 131 Steve McCatty G3	.02	.01	.01
☐ 132 Rollie Fingers G7	.25	.11	.03
☐ 133 Jim Gantner G15	.02	.01	.01
☐ 134 Gorman Thomas G6	.02	.01	.01
☐ 135 Robin Yount G13	.75	.35	.09
☐ 136 Paul Molitor G22	1.00	.45	.12
☐ 137 Ted Simmons G10	.05	.02	.01
☐ 138 Ben Oglivie G23	.02	.01	.01
☐ 139 Moose Haas G21	.02	.01	.01
☐ 140 Cecil Cooper G24	.05	.02	.01
☐ 141 Pete Vuckovich G10	.02	.01	.01
☐ 142 Doug DeCinces G21	.02	.01	.01
☐ 143 Jim Palmer G9	.50	.23	.06
☐ 144 Steve Stone G16	.02	.01	.01
☐ 145 Mike Flanagan G19	.02	.01	.01
☐ 146 Rick Dempsey G9	.02	.01	.01
☐ 147 Al Bumbry G14	.02	.01	.01
☐ 148 Mark Belanger G8	.02	.01	.01
☐ 149 Scott McGregor G23	.02	.01	.01
☐ 150 Ken Singleton G10	.02	.01	.01
☐ 151 Eddie Murray G5	1.50	.70	.19
☐ 152 Lance Parrish G20	.08	.04	.01
☐ 153 Dave Rozema G15	.02	.01	.01
☐ 154 Champ Summers G13	.02	.01	.01
☐ 155 Alan Trammell G2	.50	.23	.06
☐ 156 Lou Whitaker G1/G25	.25	.11	.03
☐ 157 Milt Wilcox G5	.02	.01	.01
☐ 158 Kevin Saucier G24	.02	.01	.01
☐ 159 Jack Morris G14	.05	.02	.01
☐ 160 Steve Kemp G7	.02	.01	.01
☐ 161 Kirk Gibson G3	.25	.11	.03
☐ 162 Carl Yastrzemski G3	.75	.35	.09
☐ 163 Jim Rice G21	.05	.02	.01
☐ 164 Carney Lansford G15	.05	.02	.01
☐ 165 Dennis Eckersley G6	.25	.11	.03
☐ 166 Mike Torrez G5	.02	.01	.01
☐ 167 Dwight Evans G19	.05	.02	.01
☐ 168 Glenn Hoffman G18	.02	.01	.01
☐ 169 Bob Stanley G20	.02	.01	.01
☐ 170 Tony Perez G16	.08	.04	.01
☐ 171 Jerry Remy G13	.02	.01	.01
☐ 172 Buddy Bell G5	.05	.02	.01
☐ 173 Fergie Jenkins G17	.25	.11	.03
☐ 174 Mickey Rivers G9	.02	.01	.01
☐ 175 Bump Wills G2	.02	.01	.01
☐ 176 Jon Matlack G20	.02	.01	.01
☐ 177 Steve Comer G23	.02	.01	.01
☐ 178 Al Oliver G1/G25	.05	.02	.01
☐ 179 Bill Stein G3	.02	.01	.01
☐ 180 Pat Putnam G14	.02	.01	.01
☐ 181 Jim Sundberg G4	.02	.01	.01
☐ 182 Ron LeFlore G4	.05	.02	.01
☐ 183 Carlton Fisk G11	.75	.35	.09
☐ 184 Harold Baines G18	.25	.11	.03
☐ 185 Bill Almon G2	.02	.01	.01
☐ 186 Richard Dotson G9	.02	.01	.01
☐ 187 Greg Luzinski G14	.05	.02	.01
☐ 188 Mike Squires G13	.02	.01	.01
☐ 189 Britt Burns G19	.02	.01	.01
☐ 190 LaMarr Hoyt G6	.02	.01	.01
☐ 191 Chet Lemon G22	.02	.01	.01
☐ 192 Joe Charboneau G20	.02	.01	.01
☐ 193 Toby Harrah G16	.02	.01	.01
☐ 194 John Denny G22	.02	.01	.01
☐ 195 Rick Manning G8	.02	.01	.01
☐ 196 Miguel Dilone G15	.02	.01	.01
☐ 197 Bo Diaz G13	.02	.01	.01
☐ 198 Mike Hargrove G17	.05	.02	.01
☐ 199 Bert Blyleven G11	.05	.02	.01
☐ 200 Len Barker G7	.02	.01	.01
☐ 201 Andre Thornton G18	.02	.01	.01
☐ 202 George Brett G24	2.00	.90	.25
☐ 203 U.L. Washington G25	.02	.01	.01
☐ 204 Dan Quisenberry G17	.02	.01	.01
☐ 205 Larry Gura G17	.02	.01	.01
☐ 206 Willie Aikens G22	.02	.01	.01
☐ 207 Willie Wilson G21	.02	.01	.01
☐ 208 Dennis Leonard G8	.02	.01	.01
☐ 209 Frank White G6	.05	.02	.01
☐ 210 Hal McRae G23	.05	.02	.01
☐ 211 Amos Otis G18	.02	.01	.01
☐ 212 Don Aase G23	.02	.01	.01
☐ 213 Butch Hobson G6	.02	.01	.01
☐ 214 Fred Lynn G18	.05	.02	.01
☐ 215 Brian Downing G10	.02	.01	.01
☐ 216 Dan Ford G5	.02	.01	.01
☐ 217 Rod Carew G5	.75	.35	.09
☐ 218 Bobby Grich G19	.05	.02	.01
☐ 219 Rick Burleson G11	.02	.01	.01
☐ 220 Don Baylor G3	.05	.02	.01
☐ 221 Ken Forsch G17	.02	.01	.01
☐ 222 Bruce Bochte	.02	.01	.01
☐ 223 Richie Zisk	.02	.01	.01
☐ 224 Tom Paciorek	.02	.01	.01
☐ 225 Julio Cruz	.02	.01	.01
☐ 226 Jeff Burroughs	.02	.01	.01
☐ 227 Doug Corbett	.02	.01	.01
☐ 228 Roy Smalley	.02	.01	.01
☐ 229 Gary Ward	.02	.01	.01
☐ 230 John Castino	.02	.01	.01
☐ 231 Rob Wilfong	.02	.01	.01
☐ 232 Dave Stieb	.02	.01	.01
☐ 233 Otto Velez	.02	.01	.01
☐ 234 Damaso Garcia	.02	.01	.01
☐ 235 John Mayberry	.02	.01	.01
☐ 236 Alfredo Griffin	.02	.01	.01
☐ 237 Ted Williams Carl Yastrzemski	2.00	.90	.25
☐ 238 Rick Cerone Graig Nettles	.08	.04	.01
☐ 239 Buddy Bell George Brett	1.50	.70	.19
☐ 240 Steve Carlton Jim Kaat	.25	.11	.03
☐ 241 Steve Carlton Dave Parker	.25	.11	.03
☐ 242 Ron Davis Nolan Ryan	2.00	.90	.25
☐ XX Stamp Album	2.00	.90	.25

1983 Fleer

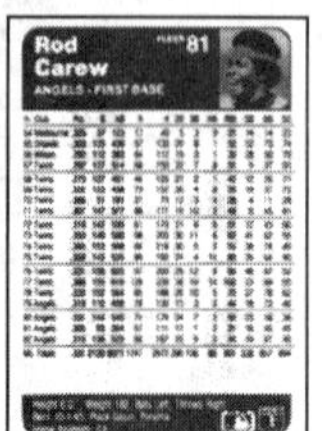

In 1983, for the third straight year, Fleer produced a baseball series of 660 standard-size cards. Of these, 1-628 are player cards, 629-646 are special cards, and 647-660 are checklist cards. The player cards are again ordered alphabetically within team and teams seeded in descending order based upon the previous season's standings. The front of each card has a colorful team logo at bottom left and the player's name and position at lower right. The reverses are done in shades of brown on white. Wax packs consisted of 15 cards plus logo stickers in a 38-pack box. Notable Rookie Cards include Wade Boggs, Tony Gwynn and Ryne Sandberg.

	NRMT	VG-E	GOOD
COMPLETE SET (660)	80.00	36.00	10.00
COMMON CARD (1-660)	.10	.05	.01

☐ 1 Joaquin Andujar	.10	.05	.01
☐ 2 Doug Bair	.10	.05	.01
☐ 3 Steve Braun	.10	.05	.01
☐ 4 Glenn Brummer	.10	.05	.01
☐ 5 Bob Forsch	.10	.05	.01
☐ 6 David Green	.10	.05	.01
☐ 7 George Hendrick	.10	.05	.01
☐ 8 Keith Hernandez	.20	.09	.03
☐ 9 Tom Herr	.20	.09	.03
☐ 10 Dane Iorg	.10	.05	.01
☐ 11 Jim Kaat	.20	.09	.03
☐ 12 Jeff Lahti	.10	.05	.01
☐ 13 Tito Landrum	.10	.05	.01
☐ 14 Dave LaPoint	.10	.05	.01
☐ 15 Willie McGee	.40	.18	.05
☐ 16 Steve Mura	.10	.05	.01
☐ 17 Ken Oberkfell	.10	.05	.01
☐ 18 Darrell Porter	.10	.05	.01
☐ 19 Mike Ramsey	.10	.05	.01
☐ 20 Gene Roof	.10	.05	.01
☐ 21 Lonnie Smith	.10	.05	.01
☐ 22 Ozzie Smith	2.00	.90	.25
☐ 23 John Stuper	.10	.05	.01
☐ 24 Bruce Sutter	.20	.09	.03
☐ 25 Gene Tenace	.20	.09	.03
☐ 26 Jerry Augustine	.10	.05	.01
☐ 27 Dwight Bernard	.10	.05	.01
☐ 28 Mark Brouhard	.10	.05	.01
☐ 29 Mike Caldwell	.10	.05	.01
☐ 30 Cecil Cooper	.20	.09	.03
☐ 31 Jamie Easterly	.10	.05	.01
☐ 32 Marshall Edwards	.10	.05	.01
☐ 33 Rollie Fingers	.40	.18	.05
☐ 34 Jim Gantner	.20	.09	.03
☐ 35 Moose Haas	.10	.05	.01
☐ 36 Roy Howell	.10	.05	.01
☐ 37 Pete Ladd	.10	.05	.01
☐ 38 Bob McClure	.10	.05	.01
☐ 39 Doc Medich	.10	.05	.01
☐ 40 Paul Molitor	1.25	.55	.16
☐ 41 Don Money	.10	.05	.01
☐ 42 Charlie Moore	.10	.05	.01
☐ 43 Ben Oglivie	.10	.05	.01
☐ 44 Ed Romero	.10	.05	.01
☐ 45 Ted Simmons	.20	.09	.03
☐ 46 Jim Slaton	.10	.05	.01
☐ 47 Don Sutton	.40	.18	.05
☐ 48 Gorman Thomas	.10	.05	.01
☐ 49 Pete Vuckovich	.10	.05	.01
☐ 50 Ned Yost	.10	.05	.01
☐ 51 Robin Yount	1.25	.55	.16
☐ 52 Benny Ayala	.10	.05	.01
☐ 53 Bob Bonner	.10	.05	.01
☐ 54 Al Bumbry	.20	.09	.03
☐ 55 Terry Crowley	.10	.05	.01
☐ 56 Storm Davis	.10	.05	.01
☐ 57 Rich Dauer	.10	.05	.01

☐ 58 Rick Dempsey UER .20 .09 .03
(Posing batting lefty)
☐ 59 Jim Dwyer .10 .05 .01
☐ 60 Mike Flanagan .20 .09 .03
☐ 61 Dan Ford .10 .05 .01
☐ 62 Glenn Gulliver .10 .05 .01
☐ 63 John Lowenstein .10 .05 .01
☐ 64 Dennis Martinez .20 .09 .03
☐ 65 Tippy Martinez .10 .05 .01
☐ 66 Scott McGregor .10 .05 .01
☐ 67 Eddie Murray 2.00 .90 .25
☐ 68 Joe Nolan .10 .05 .01
☐ 69 Jim Palmer .50 .23 .06
☐ 70 Cal Ripken 16.00 7.25 2.00
☐ 71 Gary Roenicke .10 .05 .01
☐ 72 Lenn Sakata .10 .05 .01
☐ 73 Ken Singleton .20 .09 .03
☐ 74 Sammy Stewart .10 .05 .01
☐ 75 Tim Stoddard .10 .05 .01
☐ 76 Don Aase .10 .05 .01
☐ 77 Don Baylor .40 .18 .05
☐ 78 Juan Beniquez .10 .05 .01
☐ 79 Bob Boone .20 .09 .03
☐ 80 Rick Burleson .10 .05 .01
☐ 81 Rod Carew .60 .25 .07
☐ 82 Bobby Clark .10 .05 .01
☐ 83 Doug Corbett .10 .05 .01
☐ 84 John Curtis .10 .05 .01
☐ 85 Doug DeCinces .20 .09 .03
☐ 86 Brian Downing .10 .05 .01
☐ 87 Joe Ferguson .10 .05 .01
☐ 88 Tim Foli .10 .05 .01
☐ 89 Ken Forsch .10 .05 .01
☐ 90 Dave Goltz .10 .05 .01
☐ 91 Bobby Grich .20 .09 .03
☐ 92 Andy Hassler .10 .05 .01
☐ 93 Reggie Jackson 1.00 .45 .12
☐ 94 Ron Jackson .10 .05 .01
☐ 95 Tommy John .40 .18 .05
☐ 96 Bruce Kison .10 .05 .01
☐ 97 Fred Lynn .20 .09 .03
☐ 98 Ed Ott .10 .05 .01
☐ 99 Steve Renko .10 .05 .01
☐ 100 Luis Sanchez .10 .05 .01
☐ 101 Rob Wilfong .10 .05 .01
☐ 102 Mike Witt .10 .05 .01
☐ 103 Geoff Zahn .10 .05 .01
☐ 104 Willie Aikens .10 .05 .01
☐ 105 Mike Armstrong .10 .05 .01
☐ 106 Vida Blue .20 .09 .03
☐ 107 Bud Black .20 .09 .03
☐ 108 George Brett 3.00 1.35 .35
☐ 109 Bill Castro .10 .05 .01
☐ 110 Onix Concepcion .10 .05 .01
☐ 111 Dave Frost .10 .05 .01
☐ 112 Cesar Geronimo .10 .05 .01
☐ 113 Larry Gura .10 .05 .01
☐ 114 Steve Hammond .10 .05 .01
☐ 115 Don Hood .10 .05 .01
☐ 116 Dennis Leonard .10 .05 .01
☐ 117 Jerry Martin .10 .05 .01
☐ 118 Lee May .20 .09 .03
☐ 119 Hal McRae .20 .09 .03
☐ 120 Amos Otis .20 .09 .03
☐ 121 Greg Pryor .10 .05 .01
☐ 122 Dan Quisenberry .20 .09 .03
☐ 123 Don Slaught .40 .18 .05
☐ 124 Paul Splittorff .10 .05 .01
☐ 125 U.L. Washington .10 .05 .01
☐ 126 John Wathan .10 .05 .01
☐ 127 Frank White .20 .09 .03
☐ 128 Willie Wilson .20 .09 .03
☐ 129 Steve Bedrosian UER .20 .09 .03
(Height 6'33")
☐ 130 Bruce Benedict .10 .05 .01
☐ 131 Tommy Boggs .10 .05 .01
☐ 132 Brett Butler .40 .18 .05
☐ 133 Rick Camp .10 .05 .01
☐ 134 Chris Chambliss .20 .09 .03
☐ 135 Ken Dayley .10 .05 .01
☐ 136 Gene Garber .10 .05 .01
☐ 137 Terry Harper .10 .05 .01
☐ 138 Bob Horner .10 .05 .01
☐ 139 Glenn Hubbard .10 .05 .01
☐ 140 Rufino Linares .10 .05 .01
☐ 141 Rick Mahler .10 .05 .01
☐ 142 Dale Murphy .40 .18 .05
☐ 143 Phil Niekro .40 .18 .05
☐ 144 Pascual Perez .10 .05 .01
☐ 145 Biff Pocoroba .10 .05 .01
☐ 146 Rafael Ramirez .10 .05 .01
☐ 147 Jerry Royster .10 .05 .01
☐ 148 Ken Smith .10 .05 .01
☐ 149 Bob Walk .10 .05 .01
☐ 150 Claudell Washington .10 .05 .01
☐ 151 Bob Watson .20 .09 .03
☐ 152 Larry Whisenton .10 .05 .01
☐ 153 Porfirio Altamirano .10 .05 .01
☐ 154 Marty Bystrom .10 .05 .01
☐ 155 Steve Carlton .75 .35 .09
☐ 156 Larry Christenson .10 .05 .01
☐ 157 Ivan DeJesus .10 .05 .01
☐ 158 John Denny .10 .05 .01
☐ 159 Bob Dernier .10 .05 .01
☐ 160 Bo Diaz .10 .05 .01
☐ 161 Ed Farmer .10 .05 .01
☐ 162 Greg Gross .10 .05 .01
☐ 163 Mike Krukow .10 .05 .01
☐ 164 Garry Maddox .10 .05 .01
☐ 165 Gary Matthews .20 .09 .03
☐ 166 Tug McGraw .20 .09 .03
☐ 167 Bob Molinaro .10 .05 .01
☐ 168 Sid Monge .10 .05 .01
☐ 169 Ron Reed .10 .05 .01
☐ 170 Bill Robinson .10 .05 .01
☐ 171 Pete Rose 1.25 .55 .16
☐ 172 Dick Ruthven .10 .05 .01
☐ 173 Mike Schmidt 1.50 .70 .19
☐ 174 Manny Trillo .10 .05 .01
☐ 175 Ozzie Virgil .10 .05 .01
☐ 176 George Vukovich .10 .05 .01
☐ 177 Gary Allenson .10 .05 .01
☐ 178 Luis Aponte .10 .05 .01
☐ 179 Wade Boggs 10.00 4.50 1.25
☐ 180 Tom Burgmeier .10 .05 .01
☐ 181 Mark Clear .10 .05 .01
☐ 182 Dennis Eckersley .40 .18 .05
☐ 183 Dwight Evans .20 .09 .03
☐ 184 Rich Gedman .10 .05 .01
☐ 185 Glenn Hoffman .10 .05 .01
☐ 186 Bruce Hurst .20 .09 .03
☐ 187 Carney Lansford .20 .09 .03
☐ 188 Rick Miller .10 .05 .01
☐ 189 Reid Nichols .10 .05 .01
☐ 190 Bob Ojeda .10 .05 .01
☐ 191 Tony Perez .40 .18 .05
☐ 192 Chuck Rainey .10 .05 .01
☐ 193 Jerry Remy .10 .05 .01
☐ 194 Jim Rice .20 .09 .03
☐ 195 Bob Stanley .10 .05 .01
☐ 196 Dave Stapleton .10 .05 .01
☐ 197 Mike Torrez .10 .05 .01
☐ 198 John Tudor .10 .05 .01
☐ 199 Julio Valdez .10 .05 .01
☐ 200 Carl Yastrzemski .75 .35 .09
☐ 201 Dusty Baker .20 .09 .03
☐ 202 Joe Beckwith .10 .05 .01
☐ 203 Greg Brock .10 .05 .01
☐ 204 Ron Cey .20 .09 .03
☐ 205 Terry Forster .10 .05 .01
☐ 206 Steve Garvey .40 .18 .05
☐ 207 Pedro Guerrero .20 .09 .03
☐ 208 Burt Hooton .10 .05 .01
☐ 209 Steve Howe .10 .05 .01
☐ 210 Ken Landreaux .10 .05 .01
☐ 211 Mike Marshall .10 .05 .01
☐ 212 Candy Maldonado .20 .09 .03
☐ 213 Rick Monday .10 .05 .01
☐ 214 Tom Niedenfuer .10 .05 .01
☐ 215 Jorge Orta .10 .05 .01
☐ 216 Jerry Reuss UER .20 .09 .03
("Home:" omitted)
☐ 217 Ron Roenicke .10 .05 .01
☐ 218 Vicente Romo .10 .05 .01
☐ 219 Bill Russell .20 .09 .03
☐ 220 Steve Sax .20 .09 .03
☐ 221 Mike Scioscia .20 .09 .03
☐ 222 Dave Stewart .20 .09 .03
☐ 223 Derrel Thomas .10 .05 .01
☐ 224 Fernando Valenzuela .40 .18 .05
☐ 225 Bob Welch .20 .09 .03
☐ 226 Ricky Wright .10 .05 .01
☐ 227 Steve Yeager .10 .05 .01
☐ 228 Bill Almon .10 .05 .01
☐ 229 Harold Baines .20 .09 .03
☐ 230 Salome Barojas .10 .05 .01
☐ 231 Tony Bernazard .10 .05 .01
☐ 232 Britt Burns .10 .05 .01
☐ 233 Richard Dotson .10 .05 .01
☐ 234 Ernesto Escarrega .10 .05 .01
☐ 235 Carlton Fisk .75 .35 .09
☐ 236 Jerry Hairston .10 .05 .01
☐ 237 Kevin Hickey .10 .05 .01
☐ 238 LaMarr Hoyt .20 .09 .03
☐ 239 Steve Kemp .10 .05 .01
☐ 240 Jim Kern .10 .05 .01
☐ 241 Ron Kittle .20 .09 .03
☐ 242 Jerry Koosman .20 .09 .03
☐ 243 Dennis Lamp .10 .05 .01
☐ 244 Rudy Law .10 .05 .01
☐ 245 Vance Law .10 .05 .01
☐ 246 Ron LeFlore .20 .09 .03
☐ 247 Greg Luzinski .20 .09 .03
☐ 248 Tom Paciorek .10 .05 .01
☐ 249 Aurelio Rodriguez .10 .05 .01
☐ 250 Mike Squires .10 .05 .01
☐ 251 Steve Trout .10 .05 .01
☐ 252 Jim Barr .10 .05 .01
☐ 253 Dave Bergman .10 .05 .01
☐ 254 Fred Breining .10 .05 .01
☐ 255 Bob Brenly .10 .05 .01
☐ 256 Jack Clark .20 .09 .03
☐ 257 Chili Davis .20 .09 .03
☐ 258 Darrell Evans .20 .09 .03
☐ 259 Alan Fowlkes .10 .05 .01
☐ 260 Rich Gale .10 .05 .01
☐ 261 Atlee Hammaker .10 .05 .01
☐ 262 Al Holland .10 .05 .01
☐ 263 Duane Kuiper .10 .05 .01
☐ 264 Bill Laskey .10 .05 .01
☐ 265 Gary Lavelle .10 .05 .01
☐ 266 Johnnie LeMaster .10 .05 .01
☐ 267 Renie Martin .10 .05 .01
☐ 268 Milt May .10 .05 .01
☐ 269 Greg Minton .10 .05 .01
☐ 270 Joe Morgan .40 .18 .05
☐ 271 Tom O'Malley .10 .05 .01
☐ 272 Reggie Smith .20 .09 .03
☐ 273 Guy Sularz .10 .05 .01
☐ 274 Champ Summers .10 .05 .01
☐ 275 Max Venable .10 .05 .01
☐ 276 Jim Wohlford .10 .05 .01
☐ 277 Ray Burris .10 .05 .01
☐ 278 Gary Carter .20 .09 .03
☐ 279 Warren Cromartie .10 .05 .01
☐ 280 Andre Dawson .75 .35 .09
☐ 281 Terry Francona .10 .05 .01
☐ 282 Doug Flynn .10 .05 .01
☐ 283 Woodie Fryman .10 .05 .01
☐ 284 Bill Gullickson .20 .09 .03
☐ 285 Wallace Johnson .10 .05 .01
☐ 286 Charlie Lea .10 .05 .01
☐ 287 Randy Lerch .10 .05 .01
☐ 288 Brad Mills .10 .05 .01
☐ 289 Dan Norman .10 .05 .01
☐ 290 Al Oliver .20 .09 .03
☐ 291 David Palmer .10 .05 .01
☐ 292 Tim Raines .40 .18 .05
☐ 293 Jeff Reardon .20 .09 .03
☐ 294 Steve Rogers .10 .05 .01
☐ 295 Scott Sanderson .10 .05 .01
☐ 296 Dan Schatzeder .10 .05 .01
☐ 297 Bryn Smith .10 .05 .01
☐ 298 Chris Speier .10 .05 .01
☐ 299 Tim Wallach .20 .09 .03
☐ 300 Jerry White .10 .05 .01
☐ 301 Joel Youngblood .10 .05 .01
☐ 302 Ross Baumgarten .10 .05 .01
☐ 303 Dale Berra .10 .05 .01
☐ 304 John Candelaria .10 .05 .01
☐ 305 Dick Davis .10 .05 .01
☐ 306 Mike Easler .10 .05 .01
☐ 307 Richie Hebner .20 .09 .03
☐ 308 Lee Lacy .10 .05 .01
☐ 309 Bill Madlock .20 .09 .03
☐ 310 Larry McWilliams .10 .05 .01
☐ 311 John Milner .10 .05 .01
☐ 312 Omar Moreno .10 .05 .01
☐ 313 Jim Morrison .10 .05 .01
☐ 314 Steve Nicosia .10 .05 .01
☐ 315 Dave Parker .20 .09 .03
☐ 316 Tony Pena .20 .09 .03
☐ 317 Johnny Ray .10 .05 .01
☐ 318 Rick Rhoden .10 .05 .01
☐ 319 Don Robinson .10 .05 .01
☐ 320 Enrique Romo .10 .05 .01
☐ 321 Manny Sarmiento .10 .05 .01
☐ 322 Rod Scurry .10 .05 .01
☐ 323 Jimmy Smith .10 .05 .01
☐ 324 Willie Stargell .40 .18 .05
☐ 325 Jason Thompson .10 .05 .01
☐ 326 Kent Tekulve .20 .09 .03
☐ 327A Tom Brookens .10 .05 .01
(Short .375" brown box shaded in on card back)
☐ 327B Tom Brookens .10 .05 .01
(Longer 1.25" brown box shaded in on card back)
☐ 328 Enos Cabell .10 .05 .01
☐ 329 Kirk Gibson .40 .18 .05
☐ 330 Larry Herndon .10 .05 .01
☐ 331 Mike Ivie .10 .05 .01
☐ 332 Howard Johnson .60 .25 .07
☐ 333 Lynn Jones .10 .05 .01
☐ 334 Rick Leach .10 .05 .01
☐ 335 Chet Lemon .10 .05 .01
☐ 336 Jack Morris .20 .09 .03
☐ 337 Lance Parrish .20 .09 .03
☐ 338 Larry Pashnick .10 .05 .01
☐ 339 Dan Petry .10 .05 .01
☐ 340 Dave Rozema .10 .05 .01
☐ 341 Dave Rucker .10 .05 .01
☐ 342 Elias Sosa .10 .05 .01
☐ 343 Dave Tobik .10 .05 .01
☐ 344 Alan Trammell .40 .18 .05
☐ 345 Jerry Turner .10 .05 .01
☐ 346 Jerry Ujdur .10 .05 .01
☐ 347 Pat Underwood .10 .05 .01
☐ 348 Lou Whitaker .20 .09 .03
☐ 349 Milt Wilcox .10 .05 .01
☐ 350 Glenn Wilson .20 .09 .03
☐ 351 John Wockenfuss .10 .05 .01
☐ 352 Kurt Bevacqua .10 .05 .01
☐ 353 Juan Bonilla .10 .05 .01
☐ 354 Floyd Chiffer .10 .05 .01
☐ 355 Luis DeLeon .10 .05 .01
☐ 356 Dave Dravecky .40 .18 .05
☐ 357 Dave Edwards .10 .05 .01
☐ 358 Juan Eichelberger .10 .05 .01
☐ 359 Tim Flannery .10 .05 .01
☐ 360 Tony Gwynn 20.00 9.00 2.50
☐ 361 Ruppert Jones .10 .05 .01
☐ 362 Terry Kennedy .10 .05 .01
☐ 363 Joe Lefebvre .10 .05 .01
☐ 364 Sixto Lezcano .10 .05 .01
☐ 365 Tim Lollar .10 .05 .01
☐ 366 Gary Lucas .10 .05 .01
☐ 367 John Montefusco .10 .05 .01
☐ 368 Broderick Perkins .10 .05 .01
☐ 369 Joe Pittman .10 .05 .01
☐ 370 Gene Richards .10 .05 .01
☐ 371 Luis Salazar .10 .05 .01
☐ 372 Eric Show .10 .05 .01
☐ 373 Garry Templeton .10 .05 .01
☐ 374 Chris Welsh .10 .05 .01
☐ 375 Alan Wiggins .10 .05 .01
☐ 376 Rick Cerone .10 .05 .01
☐ 377 Dave Collins .10 .05 .01
☐ 378 Roger Erickson .10 .05 .01
☐ 379 George Frazier .10 .05 .01
☐ 380 Oscar Gamble .10 .05 .01
☐ 381 Rich Gossage .40 .18 .05
☐ 382 Ken Griffey .20 .09 .03
☐ 383 Ron Guidry .20 .09 .03
☐ 384 Dave LaRoche .10 .05 .01
☐ 385 Rudy May .10 .05 .01
☐ 386 John Mayberry .10 .05 .01
☐ 387 Lee Mazzilli .10 .05 .01
☐ 388 Mike Morgan .10 .05 .01
☐ 389 Jerry Mumphrey .10 .05 .01
☐ 390 Bobby Murcer .20 .09 .03
☐ 391 Graig Nettles .20 .09 .03
☐ 392 Lou Piniella .20 .09 .03
☐ 393 Willie Randolph .20 .09 .03
☐ 394 Shane Rawley .10 .05 .01
☐ 395 Dave Righetti .20 .09 .03
☐ 396 Andre Robertson .10 .05 .01
☐ 397 Roy Smalley .10 .05 .01
☐ 398 Dave Winfield 1.25 .55 .16
☐ 399 Butch Wynegar .10 .05 .01
☐ 400 Chris Bando .10 .05 .01
☐ 401 Alan Bannister .10 .05 .01
☐ 402 Len Barker .10 .05 .01
☐ 403 Tom Brennan .10 .05 .01
☐ 404 Carmelo Castillo .10 .05 .01
☐ 405 Miguel Dilone .10 .05 .01
☐ 406 Jerry Dybzinski .10 .05 .01
☐ 407 Mike Fischlin .10 .05 .01
☐ 408 Ed Glynn UER .10 .05 .01
(Photo actually Bud Anderson)
☐ 409 Mike Hargrove .20 .09 .03
☐ 410 Toby Harrah .10 .05 .01
☐ 411 Ron Hassey .10 .05 .01
☐ 412 Von Hayes .20 .09 .03
☐ 413 Rick Manning .10 .05 .01
☐ 414 Bake McBride .10 .05 .01
☐ 415 Larry Milbourne .10 .05 .01
☐ 416 Bill Nahorodny .10 .05 .01
☐ 417 Jack Perconte .10 .05 .01
☐ 418 Lary Sorensen .10 .05 .01
☐ 419 Dan Spillner .10 .05 .01
☐ 420 Rick Sutcliffe .20 .09 .03
☐ 421 Andre Thornton .10 .05 .01
☐ 422 Rick Waits .10 .05 .01
☐ 423 Eddie Whitson .10 .05 .01
☐ 424 Jesse Barfield .20 .09 .03
☐ 425 Barry Bonnell .10 .05 .01
☐ 426 Jim Clancy .10 .05 .01
☐ 427 Damaso Garcia .10 .05 .01
☐ 428 Jerry Garvin .10 .05 .01
☐ 429 Alfredo Griffin .10 .05 .01
☐ 430 Garth Iorg .10 .05 .01
☐ 431 Roy Lee Jackson .10 .05 .01
☐ 432 Luis Leal .10 .05 .01
☐ 433 Buck Martinez .10 .05 .01
☐ 434 Joey McLaughlin .10 .05 .01
☐ 435 Lloyd Moseby .10 .05 .01
☐ 436 Rance Mulliniks .10 .05 .01
☐ 437 Dale Murray .40 .18 .05
☐ 438 Wayne Nordhagen .10 .05 .01
☐ 439 Gene Petralli .20 .09 .03
☐ 440 Hosken Powell .10 .05 .01
☐ 441 Dave Stieb .20 .09 .03
☐ 442 Willie Upshaw .10 .05 .01
☐ 443 Ernie Whitt .10 .05 .01
☐ 444 Alvis Woods .10 .05 .01
☐ 445 Alan Ashby .10 .05 .01
☐ 446 Jose Cruz .20 .09 .03
☐ 447 Kiko Garcia .10 .05 .01
☐ 448 Phil Garner .20 .09 .03
☐ 449 Danny Heep .10 .05 .01
☐ 450 Art Howe .10 .05 .01
☐ 451 Bob Knepper .10 .05 .01
☐ 452 Alan Knicely .10 .05 .01
☐ 453 Ray Knight .20 .09 .03
☐ 454 Frank LaCorte .10 .05 .01
☐ 455 Mike LaCoss .10 .05 .01
☐ 456 Randy Moffitt .10 .05 .01
☐ 457 Joe Niekro .20 .09 .03
☐ 458 Terry Puhl .10 .05 .01
☐ 459 Luis Pujols .10 .05 .01
☐ 460 Craig Reynolds .10 .05 .01
☐ 461 Bert Roberge .10 .05 .01
☐ 462 Vern Ruhle .10 .05 .01
☐ 463 Nolan Ryan 4.00 1.80 .50
☐ 464 Joe Sambito .10 .05 .01
☐ 465 Tony Scott .10 .05 .01
☐ 466 Dave Smith .10 .05 .01
☐ 467 Harry Spilman .10 .05 .01

☐ 468 Dickie Thon	.10	.05	.01
☐ 469 Denny Walling	.10	.05	.01
☐ 470 Larry Andersen	.10	.05	.01
☐ 471 Floyd Bannister	.10	.05	.01
☐ 472 Jim Beattie	.10	.05	.01
☐ 473 Bruce Bochte	.10	.05	.01
☐ 474 Manny Castillo	.10	.05	.01
☐ 475 Bill Caudill	.10	.05	.01
☐ 476 Bryan Clark	.10	.05	.01
☐ 477 Al Cowens	.10	.05	.01
☐ 478 Julio Cruz	.10	.05	.01
☐ 479 Todd Cruz	.10	.05	.01
☐ 480 Gary Gray	.10	.05	.01
☐ 481 Dave Henderson	.20	.09	.03
☐ 482 Mike Moore	.20	.09	.03
☐ 483 Gaylord Perry	.40	.18	.05
☐ 484 Dave Revering	.10	.05	.01
☐ 485 Joe Simpson	.10	.05	.01
☐ 486 Mike Stanton	.10	.05	.01
☐ 487 Rick Sweet	.10	.05	.01
☐ 488 Ed VandeBerg	.10	.05	.01
☐ 489 Richie Zisk	.10	.05	.01
☐ 490 Doug Bird	.10	.05	.01
☐ 491 Larry Bowa	.20	.09	.03
☐ 492 Bill Buckner	.20	.09	.03
☐ 493 Bill Campbell	.10	.05	.01
☐ 494 Jody Davis	.10	.05	.01
☐ 495 Leon Durham	.10	.05	.01
☐ 496 Steve Henderson	.10	.05	.01
☐ 497 Willie Hernandez	.20	.09	.03
☐ 498 Ferguson Jenkins	.40	.18	.05
☐ 499 Jay Johnstone	.20	.09	.03
☐ 500 Junior Kennedy	.10	.05	.01
☐ 501 Randy Martz	.10	.05	.01
☐ 502 Jerry Morales	.10	.05	.01
☐ 503 Keith Moreland	.10	.05	.01
☐ 504 Dickie Noles	.10	.05	.01
☐ 505 Mike Proly	.10	.05	.01
☐ 506 Allen Ripley	.10	.05	.01
☐ 507 Ryne Sandberg UER	15.00	6.75	1.85
(Should say High School			
in Spokane, Washington)			
☐ 508 Lee Smith	2.00	.90	.25
☐ 509 Pat Tabler	.10	.05	.01
☐ 510 Dick Tidrow	.10	.05	.01
☐ 511 Bump Wills	.10	.05	.01
☐ 512 Gary Woods	.10	.05	.01
☐ 513 Tony Armas	.10	.05	.01
☐ 514 Dave Beard	.10	.05	.01
☐ 515 Jeff Burroughs	.10	.05	.01
☐ 516 John D'Acquisto	.10	.05	.01
☐ 517 Wayne Gross	.10	.05	.01
☐ 518 Mike Heath	.10	.05	.01
☐ 519 Rickey Henderson UER	1.50	.70	.19
(Brock record listed			
as 120 steals)			
☐ 520 Cliff Johnson	.10	.05	.01
☐ 521 Matt Keough	.10	.05	.01
☐ 522 Brian Kingman	.10	.05	.01
☐ 523 Rick Langford	.10	.05	.01
☐ 524 Dave Lopes	.20	.09	.03
☐ 525 Steve McCatty	.10	.05	.01
☐ 526 Dave McKay	.10	.05	.01
☐ 527 Dan Meyer	.10	.05	.01
☐ 528 Dwayne Murphy	.10	.05	.01
☐ 529 Jeff Newman	.10	.05	.01
☐ 530 Mike Norris	.10	.05	.01
☐ 531 Bob Owchinko	.10	.05	.01
☐ 532 Joe Rudi	.10	.05	.01
☐ 533 Jimmy Sexton	.10	.05	.01
☐ 534 Fred Stanley	.10	.05	.01
☐ 535 Tom Underwood	.10	.05	.01
☐ 536 Neil Allen	.10	.05	.01
☐ 537 Wally Backman	.10	.05	.01
☐ 538 Bob Bailor	.10	.05	.01
☐ 539 Hubie Brooks	.20	.09	.03
☐ 540 Carlos Diaz	.10	.05	.01
☐ 541 Pete Falcone	.10	.05	.01
☐ 542 George Foster	.20	.09	.03
☐ 543 Ron Gardenhire	.10	.05	.01
☐ 544 Brian Giles	.10	.05	.01
☐ 545 Ron Hodges	.10	.05	.01
☐ 546 Randy Jones	.10	.05	.01
☐ 547 Mike Jorgensen	.10	.05	.01
☐ 548 Dave Kingman	.20	.09	.03
☐ 549 Ed Lynch	.10	.05	.01
☐ 550 Jesse Orosco	.10	.05	.01
☐ 551 Rick Ownbey	.10	.05	.01
☐ 552 Charlie Puleo	.10	.05	.01
☐ 553 Gary Rajsich	.10	.05	.01
☐ 554 Mike Scott	.20	.09	.03
☐ 555 Rusty Staub	.20	.09	.03
☐ 556 John Stearns	.10	.05	.01
☐ 557 Craig Swan	.10	.05	.01
☐ 558 Ellis Valentine	.10	.05	.01
☐ 559 Tom Veryzer	.10	.05	.01
☐ 560 Mookie Wilson	.20	.09	.03
☐ 561 Pat Zachry	.10	.05	.01
☐ 562 Buddy Bell	.20	.09	.03
☐ 563 John Butcher	.10	.05	.01
☐ 564 Steve Comer	.10	.05	.01
☐ 565 Danny Darwin	.10	.05	.01
☐ 566 Bucky Dent	.20	.09	.03
☐ 567 John Grubb	.10	.05	.01
☐ 568 Rick Honeycutt	.10	.05	.01
☐ 569 Dave Hostetler	.10	.05	.01
☐ 570 Charlie Hough	.20	.09	.03
☐ 571 Lamar Johnson	.10	.05	.01
☐ 572 Jon Matlack	.10	.05	.01
☐ 573 Paul Mirabella	.10	.05	.01
☐ 574 Larry Parrish	.10	.05	.01
☐ 575 Mike Richardt	.10	.05	.01
☐ 576 Mickey Rivers	.10	.05	.01
☐ 577 Billy Sample	.10	.05	.01
☐ 578 Dave Schmidt	.10	.05	.01
☐ 579 Bill Stein	.10	.05	.01
☐ 580 Jim Sundberg	.20	.09	.03
☐ 581 Frank Tanana	.20	.09	.03
☐ 582 Mark Wagner	.10	.05	.01
☐ 583 George Wright	.10	.05	.01
☐ 584 Johnny Bench	.75	.35	.09
☐ 585 Bruce Berenyi	.10	.05	.01
☐ 586 Larry Biittner	.10	.05	.01
☐ 587 Cesar Cedeno	.20	.09	.03
☐ 588 Dave Concepcion	.20	.09	.03
☐ 589 Dan Driessen	.10	.05	.01
☐ 590 Greg Harris	.10	.05	.01
☐ 591 Ben Hayes	.10	.05	.01
☐ 592 Paul Householder	.10	.05	.01
☐ 593 Tom Hume	.10	.05	.01
☐ 594 Wayne Krenchicki	.10	.05	.01
☐ 595 Rafael Landestoy	.10	.05	.01
☐ 596 Charlie Leibrandt	.10	.05	.01
☐ 597 Eddie Milner	.10	.05	.01
☐ 598 Ron Oester	.10	.05	.01
☐ 599 Frank Pastore	.10	.05	.01
☐ 600 Joe Price	.10	.05	.01
☐ 601 Tom Seaver	.75	.35	.09
☐ 602 Bob Shirley	.10	.05	.01
☐ 603 Mario Soto	.10	.05	.01
☐ 604 Alex Trevino	.10	.05	.01
☐ 605 Mike Vail	.10	.05	.01
☐ 606 Duane Walker	.10	.05	.01
☐ 607 Tom Brunansky	.20	.09	.03
☐ 608 Bobby Castillo	.10	.05	.01
☐ 609 John Castino	.10	.05	.01
☐ 610 Ron Davis	.10	.05	.01
☐ 611 Lenny Faedo	.10	.05	.01
☐ 612 Terry Felton	.10	.05	.01
☐ 613 Gary Gaetti	.75	.35	.09
☐ 614 Mickey Hatcher	.10	.05	.01
☐ 615 Brad Havens	.10	.05	.01
☐ 616 Kent Hrbek	.20	.09	.03
☐ 617 Randy Johnson	.10	.05	.01
☐ 618 Tim Laudner	.10	.05	.01
☐ 619 Jeff Little	.10	.05	.01
☐ 620 Bobby Mitchell	.10	.05	.01
☐ 621 Jack O'Connor	.10	.05	.01
☐ 622 John Pacella	.10	.05	.01
☐ 623 Pete Redfern	.10	.05	.01
☐ 624 Jesus Vega	.10	.05	.01
☐ 625 Frank Viola	.60	.25	.07
☐ 626 Ron Washington	.10	.05	.01
☐ 627 Gary Ward	.10	.05	.01
☐ 628 Al Williams	.10	.05	.01
☐ 629 Red Sox All-Stars	.40	.18	.05
Carl Yastrzemski			
Dennis Eckersley			
Mark Clear			
☐ 630 300 Career Wins	.20	.09	.03
Gaylord Perry			
Terry Bulling 5/6/82			
☐ 631 Pride of Venezuela	.20	.09	.03
Dave Concepcion and			
Manny Trillo			
☐ 632 All-Star Infielders	.40	.18	.05
Robin Yount and			
Buddy Bell			
☐ 633 Mr.Vet and Mr.Rookie	.75	.35	.09
Dave Winfield and			
Kent Hrbek			
☐ 634 Fountain of Youth	.60	.25	.07
Willie Stargell and			
Pete Rose			
☐ 635 Big Chiefs	.20	.09	.03
Toby Harrah and			
Andre Thornton			
☐ 636 Smith Brothers	.75	.35	.09
Ozzie Smith			
Lonnie Smith			
☐ 637 Base Stealers' Threat	.20	.09	.03
Bo Diaz and			
Gary Carter			
☐ 638 All-Star Catchers	.40	.18	.05
Carlton Fisk and			
Gary Carter			
☐ 639 The Silver Shoe	1.00	.45	.12
Rickey Henderson			
☐ 640 Home Run Threats	.40	.18	.05
Ben Oglivie and			
Reggie Jackson			
☐ 641 Two Teams Same Day	.10	.05	.01
Joel Youngblood			
August 4, 1982			
☐ 642 Last Perfect Game	.20	.09	.03
Ron Hassey and			
Len Barker			
☐ 643 Black and Blue	.20	.09	.03
Vida Blue			
☐ 644 Black and Blue	.10	.05	.01
Bud Black			
☐ 645 Speed and Power	.50	.23	.06
Reggie Jackson			
☐ 646 Speed and Power	1.00	.45	.12
Rickey Henderson			
☐ 647 CL: Cards/Brewers	.20	.09	.03
☐ 648 CL: Orioles/Angels	.20	.09	.03
☐ 649 CL: Royals/Braves	.20	.09	.03
☐ 650 CL: Phillies/Red Sox	.20	.09	.03
☐ 651 CL: Dodgers/White Sox	.20	.09	.03
☐ 652 CL: Giants/Expos	.20	.09	.03
☐ 653 CL: Pirates/Tigers	.20	.09	.03
☐ 654 CL: Padres/Yankees	.20	.09	.03
☐ 655 CL: Indians/Blue Jays	.20	.09	.03
☐ 656 CL: Astros/Mariners	.20	.09	.03
☐ 657 CL: Cubs/A's	.20	.09	.03
☐ 658 CL: Mets/Rangers	.20	.09	.03
☐ 659 CL: Reds/Twins	.20	.09	.03
☐ 660 CL: Specials/Teams	.20	.09	.03

1983 Fleer Stamps

This 288-card set features color photos of players and team logos on stamps measuring approximately 1 1/4" by 1 13/16" each. The stamps were issued on four different sheets of 72 stamps each. There are 224 player stamps and 64 team logo stamps. The team logo stamps have double and triple prints. Baseball trivia quiz questions were also included with the stamps. The stamps are unnumbered and checklisted below in alphabetical order.

	NRMT	VG-E	GOOD
COMPLETE SET (288)	10.00	4.50	1.25
COMMON CARD (1-288)	.03	.01	.01
COMMON TEAM LOGO (225-250)	.02	.01	.01
☐ 1 Willie Aikens	.03	.01	.01
☐ 2 Neil Allen	.03	.01	.01
☐ 3 Joaquin Andujar	.03	.01	.01
☐ 4 Alan Ashby	.03	.01	.01
☐ 5 Bob Bailor	.03	.01	.01
☐ 6 Harold Baines	.20	.09	.03
☐ 7 Dusty Baker	.05	.02	.01
☐ 8 Floyd Bannister	.03	.01	.01
☐ 9 Len Barker	.03	.01	.01
☐ 10 Don Baylor	.05	.02	.01
☐ 11 Dave Beard	.03	.01	.01
☐ 12 Jim Beattie	.03	.01	.01
☐ 13 Buddy Bell	.05	.02	.01
☐ 14 Johnny Bench	.75	.35	.09
☐ 15 Dale Berra	.03	.01	.01
☐ 16 Larry Biittner	.03	.01	.01
☐ 17 Vida Blue	.05	.02	.01
☐ 18 Bruce Bochte	.03	.01	.01
☐ 19 Wade Boggs	3.00	1.35	.35
☐ 20 Bob Boone	.03	.01	.01
☐ 21 Larry Bowa	.03	.01	.01
☐ 22 George Brett	2.00	.90	.25
☐ 23 Hubie Brooks	.03	.01	.01
☐ 24 Tom Brunansky	.03	.01	.01
☐ 25 Bill Buckner	.03	.01	.01
☐ 26 Al Bumbry	.03	.01	.01
☐ 27 Jeff Burroughs	.03	.01	.01
☐ 28 Enos Cabell	.03	.01	.01
☐ 29 Rod Carew	.50	.23	.06
☐ 30 Steve Carlton	.40	.18	.05
☐ 31 Gary Carter	.30	.14	.04
☐ 32 Bobby Castillo	.03	.01	.01
☐ 33 Bill Caudill	.03	.01	.01
☐ 34 Cesar Cedeno	.03	.01	.01
☐ 35 Rick Cerone	.03	.01	.01
☐ 36 Ron Cey	.05	.02	.01
☐ 37 Chris Chambliss	.03	.01	.01
☐ 38 Larry Christenson	.03	.01	.01
☐ 39 Jim Clancy	.03	.01	.01
☐ 40 Jack Clark	.05	.02	.01
☐ 41 Mark Clear	.03	.01	.01
☐ 42 Dave Concepcion	.03	.01	.01
☐ 43 Cecil Cooper	.05	.02	.01
☐ 44 Warren Cromartie	.03	.01	.01
☐ 45 Jose Cruz	.05	.02	.01
☐ 46 Danny Darwin	.05	.02	.01
☐ 47 Rich Dauer	.03	.01	.01
☐ 48 Ron Davis	.03	.01	.01
☐ 49 Andre Dawson	.50	.23	.06
☐ 50 Doug DeCinces	.03	.01	.01
☐ 51 Ivan DeJesus	.03	.01	.01
☐ 52 Luis DeLeon	.03	.01	.01
☐ 53 Bo Diaz	.03	.01	.01
☐ 54 Brian Downing	.05	.02	.01
☐ 55 Dan Driessen	.03	.01	.01
☐ 56 Leon Durham	.03	.01	.01
☐ 57 Mike Easler	.03	.01	.01
☐ 58 Dennis Eckersley	.25	.11	.03
☐ 59 Dwight Evans	.10	.05	.01
☐ 60 Rollie Fingers	.25	.11	.03
☐ 61 Carlton Fisk	.50	.23	.06
☐ 62 Mike Flanagan	.03	.01	.01
☐ 63 Bob Forsch	.03	.01	.01
☐ 64 Ken Forsch	.03	.01	.01
☐ 65 George Foster	.05	.02	.01
☐ 66 Gene Garber	.03	.01	.01
☐ 67 Damaso Garcia	.03	.01	.01
☐ 68 Phil Garner	.05	.02	.01
☐ 69 Steve Garvey	.15	.07	.02
☐ 70 Goose Gossage	.10	.05	.01
☐ 71 Ken Griffey	.05	.02	.01
☐ 72 John Grubb	.03	.01	.01
☐ 73 Ron Guidry	.05	.02	.01
☐ 74 Atlee Hammaker	.03	.01	.01
☐ 75 Mike Hargrove	.05	.02	.01
☐ 76 Toby Harrah	.03	.01	.01
☐ 77 Rickey Henderson	1.50	.70	.19
☐ 78 Keith Hernandez	.05	.02	.01
☐ 79 Larry Herndon	.03	.01	.01
☐ 80 Tom Herr	.03	.01	.01
☐ 81 Al Holland	.03	.01	.01
☐ 82 Burt Hooton	.03	.01	.01
☐ 83 Bob Horner	.03	.01	.01
☐ 84 Art Howe	.05	.02	.01
☐ 85 Steve Howe	.03	.01	.01
☐ 86 LaMarr Hoyt	.03	.01	.01
☐ 87 Kent Hrbek	.20	.09	.03
☐ 88 Tom Hume	.03	.01	.01
☐ 89 Garth Iorg	.03	.01	.01
☐ 90 Reggie Jackson	.75	.35	.09
☐ 91 Ferguson Jenkins	.25	.11	.03
☐ 92 Tommy John	.15	.07	.02
☐ 93 Ruppert Jones	.03	.01	.01
☐ 94 Steve Kemp	.03	.01	.01
☐ 95 Bruce Kison	.03	.01	.01
☐ 96 Ray Knight	.05	.02	.01
☐ 97 Jerry Koosman	.05	.02	.01
☐ 98 Duane Kuiper	.03	.01	.01
☐ 99 Ken Landreaux	.03	.01	.01
☐ 100 Carney Lansford	.03	.01	.01
☐ 101 Bill Laskey	.03	.01	.01
☐ 102 Gary Lavelle	.03	.01	.01
☐ 103 Charlie Lea	.03	.01	.01
☐ 104 Ron LeFlore	.03	.01	.01
☐ 105 Dennis Leonard	.03	.01	.01
☐ 106 Sixto Lezcano	.03	.01	.01
☐ 107 Davey Lopes	.03	.01	.01
☐ 108 John Lowenstein	.03	.01	.01
☐ 109 Greg Luzinski	.05	.02	.01
☐ 110 Fred Lynn	.10	.05	.01
☐ 111 Garry Maddox	.03	.01	.01
☐ 112 Bill Madlock	.05	.02	.01
☐ 113 Rick Manning	.03	.01	.01
☐ 114 Dennis Martinez	.05	.02	.01
☐ 115 Tippy Martinez	.03	.01	.01
☐ 116 Randy Martz	.03	.01	.01
☐ 117 Jon Matlack	.03	.01	.01
☐ 118 Gary Matthews	.05	.02	.01
☐ 119 Milt May	.03	.01	.01
☐ 120 Lee Mazzilli	.03	.01	.01
☐ 121 Bob McClure	.03	.01	.01
☐ 122 Tug McGraw	.05	.02	.01
☐ 123 Scott McGregor	.03	.01	.01
☐ 124 Hal McRae	.05	.02	.01
☐ 125 Eddie Milner	.03	.01	.01
☐ 126 Greg Minton	.03	.01	.01
☐ 127 Paul Molitor	.75	.35	.09
☐ 128 Rick Monday	.03	.01	.01
☐ 129 John Montefusco	.03	.01	.01
☐ 130 Keith Moreland	.03	.01	.01
☐ 131 Joe Morgan	.50	.23	.06
☐ 132 Jerry Mumphrey	.03	.01	.01
☐ 133 Steve Mura	.03	.01	.01
☐ 134 Dale Murphy	.40	.18	.05
☐ 135 Dwayne Murphy	.03	.01	.01
☐ 136 Eddie Murray	.50	.23	.06
☐ 137 Graig Nettles	.10	.05	.01
☐ 138 Joe Niekro	.03	.01	.01
☐ 139 Phil Niekro	.03	.01	.01
☐ 140 Ken Oberkfell	.03	.01	.01
☐ 141 Ben Oglivie	.03	.01	.01
☐ 142 Al Oliver	.03	.01	.01
☐ 143 Amos Otis	.03	.01	.01
☐ 144 Tom Paciorek	.03	.01	.01
☐ 145 Jim Palmer	.40	.18	.05
☐ 146 Dave Parker	.05	.02	.01
☐ 147 Lance Parrish	.10	.05	.01
☐ 148 Larry Parrish	.03	.01	.01
☐ 149 Tony Pena	.03	.01	.01
☐ 150 Gaylord Perry	.25	.11	.03
☐ 151 Lou Piniella	.05	.02	.01
☐ 152 Darrell Porter	.03	.01	.01
☐ 153 Hosken Powell	.03	.01	.01
☐ 154 Dan Quisenberry	.03	.01	.01
☐ 155 Tim Raines	.15	.07	.02
☐ 156 Rafael Ramirez	.03	.01	.01
☐ 157 Willie Randolph	.05	.02	.01
☐ 158 Johnny Ray	.03	.01	.01
☐ 159 Jeff Reardon	.05	.02	.01
☐ 160 Ron Reed	.03	.01	.01
☐ 161 Jerry Reuss	.03	.01	.01
☐ 162 Rick Rhoden	.03	.01	.01
☐ 163 Jim Rice	.05	.02	.01

☐ 164 Mike Richardt	.03	.01	.01
☐ 165 Cal Ripken Jr.	3.00	1.35	.35
☐ 166 Ron Roenicke	.03	.01	.01
☐ 167 Steve Rogers	.03	.01	.01
☐ 168 Pete Rose	1.00	.45	.12
☐ 169 Jerry Royster	.03	.01	.01
☐ 170 Nolan Ryan	3.00	1.35	.35
☐ 171 Manny Sarmiento	.03	.01	.01
☐ 172 Steve Sax	.03	.01	.01
☐ 173 Mike Schmidt	.75	.35	.09
☐ 174 Tom Seaver	.50	.23	.06
☐ 175 Eric Show	.03	.01	.01
☐ 176 Ted Simmons	.10	.05	.01
☐ 177 Ken Singleton	.03	.01	.01
☐ 178 Roy Smalley	.03	.01	.01
☐ 179 Lonnie Smith	.03	.01	.01
☐ 180 Ozzie Smith	1.50	.70	.19
☐ 181 Reggie Smith	.03	.01	.01
☐ 182 Mario Soto	.03	.01	.01
☐ 183 Chris Speier	.03	.01	.01
☐ 184 Dan Spillner	.03	.01	.01
☐ 185 Bob Stanley	.03	.01	.01
☐ 186 Willie Stargell	.40	.18	.05
☐ 187 Rusty Staub	.10	.05	.01
☐ 188 Dave Stieb	.03	.01	.01
☐ 189 Jim Sundberg	.03	.01	.01
☐ 190 Rick Sutcliffe	.03	.01	.01
☐ 191 Bruce Sutter	.05	.02	.01
☐ 192 Don Sutton	.25	.11	.03
☐ 193 Craig Swan	.03	.01	.01
☐ 194 Kent Tekulve	.03	.01	.01
☐ 195 Gorman Thomas	.03	.01	.01
☐ 196 Jason Thompson	.03	.01	.01
☐ 197 Dickie Thon	.03	.01	.01
☐ 198 Andre Thornton	.03	.01	.01
☐ 199 Dick Tidrow	.03	.01	.01
☐ 200 Manny Trillo	.03	.01	.01
☐ 201 John Tudor	.03	.01	.01
☐ 202 Tom Underwood	.03	.01	.01
☐ 203 Willie Upshaw	.03	.01	.01
☐ 204 Ellis Valentine	.03	.01	.01
☐ 205 Fernando Valenzuela	.30	.14	.04
☐ 206 Ed VandeBerg	.03	.01	.01
☐ 207 Pete Vuckovich	.03	.01	.01
☐ 208 Gary Ward	.03	.01	.01
☐ 209 Claudell Washington	.03	.01	.01
☐ 210 U.L. Washington	.03	.01	.01
☐ 211 Bob Watson	.05	.02	.01
☐ 212 Lou Whitaker	.20	.09	.03
☐ 213 Frank White	.03	.01	.01
☐ 214 Milt Wilcox	.03	.01	.01
☐ 215 Al Williams	.03	.01	.01
☐ 216 Bump Wills	.03	.01	.01
☐ 217 Mookie Wilson	.05	.02	.01
☐ 218 Willie Wilson	.03	.01	.01
☐ 219 Dave Winfield	.75	.35	.09
☐ 220 John Wockenfuss	.03	.01	.01
☐ 221 Carl Yastrzemski	.50	.23	.06
☐ 222 Robin Yount	.50	.23	.06
☐ 223 Pat Zachry	.03	.01	.01
☐ 224 Richie Zisk	.03	.01	.01
☐ 225 Atlanta Braves TP	.02	.01	.01
☐ 226 Baltimore Orioles DP	.02	.01	.01
☐ 227 Boston Red Sox DP	.02	.01	.01
☐ 228 California Angels TP	.02	.01	.01
☐ 229 Chicago Cubs DP	.02	.01	.01
☐ 230 Chicago White Sox TP	.02	.01	.01
☐ 231 Cincinnati Reds TP	.02	.01	.01
☐ 232 Cleveland Indians TP	.02	.01	.01
☐ 233 Detroit Tigers DP	.02	.01	.01
☐ 234 Houston Astros DP	.02	.01	.01
☐ 235 Los Angeles Dodgers TP	.02	.01	.01
☐ 236 Kansas City Royals TP	.02	.01	.01
☐ 237 Milwaukee Brewers DP	.02	.01	.01
☐ 238 Minnesota Twins TP	.02	.01	.01
☐ 239 Montreal Expos TP	.02	.01	.01
☐ 240 New York Mets DP	.02	.01	.01
☐ 241 New York Yankees DP	.02	.01	.01
☐ 242 Oakland A's DP	.02	.01	.01
☐ 243 Philadelphia Phillies TP	.02	.01	.01
☐ 244 Pittsburgh Pirates TP	.02	.01	.01
☐ 245 St. Louis Cardinals DP	.02	.01	.01
☐ 246 San Diego Padres DP	.02	.01	.01
☐ 247 San Francisco Giants TP	.02	.01	.01
☐ 248 Seattle Mariners DP	.02	.01	.01
☐ 249 Texas Rangers DP	.02	.01	.01
☐ 250 Toronto Blue Jays DP	.02	.01	.01

1983 Fleer Stickers

The stickers in this 270-sticker set measure approximately 1 13/16" by 2 1/2". The 1983 Fleer stickers set was issued in strips of ten stickers plus two team logos per strip. No album was issued for the stickers. The fronts contain player photos surrounded by a blue border with two red stars on the upper portion of a yellow frameline. While all of the players could be attained on 27 different strips, it was necessary to have 30 different strips to obtain all of the team logos. There are a few instances where the logo pictured on the front of the card relates to a different team checklisted on the back of the card. The backs of the logo stamps feature either a team checklist (CL) or poster offer (PO).

	NRMT	VG-E	GOOD
COMPLETE SET	12.50	5.50	1.55
COMMON CARD	.03	.01	.01
COMMON TEAM ISSUE	.02	.01	.01

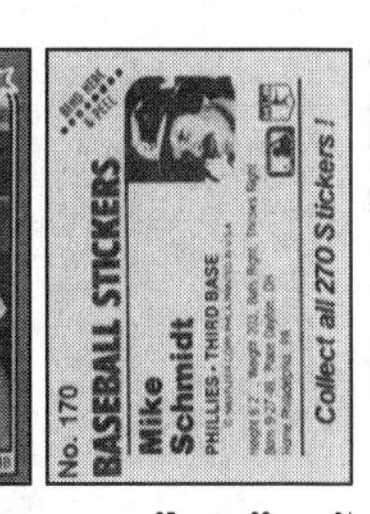

☐ 1 Bruce Sutter	.05	.02	.01
☐ 2 Willie McGee	.25	.11	.03
☐ 3 Darrell Porter	.03	.01	.01
☐ 4 Lonnie Smith	.03	.01	.01
☐ 5 Dane Iorg	.03	.01	.01
☐ 6 Keith Hernandez	.05	.02	.01
☐ 7 Joaquin Andujar	.03	.01	.01
☐ 8 Ken Oberkfell	.03	.01	.01
☐ 9 John Stuper	.03	.01	.01
☐ 10 Ozzie Smih	1.50	.70	.19
☐ 11 Bob Forsch	.03	.01	.01
☐ 12 Jim Gantner	.03	.01	.01
☐ 13 Rollie Fingers	.25	.11	.03
☐ 14 Pete Vuckovich	.03	.01	.01
☐ 15 Ben Oglivie	.03	.01	.01
☐ 16 Don Sutton	.25	.11	.03
☐ 17 Bob McClure	.03	.01	.01
☐ 18 Robin Yount	.40	.18	.05
☐ 19 Paul Molitor	.50	.23	.06
☐ 20 Gorman Thomas	.03	.01	.01
☐ 21 Mike Caldwell	.03	.01	.01
☐ 22 Ted Simmons	.05	.02	.01
☐ 23 Cecil Cooper	.05	.02	.01
☐ 24 Steve Renko	.03	.01	.01
☐ 25 Tommy John	.10	.05	.01
☐ 26 Rod Carew	.40	.18	.05
☐ 27 Bruce Kison	.03	.01	.01
☐ 28 Ken Forsch	.03	.01	.01
☐ 29 Geoff Zahn	.03	.01	.01
☐ 30 Doug DeCinces	.03	.01	.01
☐ 31 Fred Lynn	.05	.02	.01
☐ 32 Reggie Jackson	.75	.35	.09
☐ 33 Don Baylor	.05	.02	.01
☐ 34 Bob Boone	.05	.02	.01
☐ 35 Brian Downing	.03	.01	.01
☐ 36 Rich Gossage	.10	.05	.01
☐ 37 Roy Smalley	.03	.01	.01
☐ 38 Graig Nettles	.10	.05	.01
☐ 39 Dave Winfield	.50	.23	.06
☐ 40 Lee Mazzilli	.03	.01	.01
☐ 41 Jerry Mumphrey	.03	.01	.01
☐ 42 Dave Collins	.03	.01	.01
☐ 43 Rick Cerone	.03	.01	.01
☐ 44 Willie Randolph	.05	.02	.01
☐ 45 Lou Piniella	.05	.02	.01
☐ 46 Ken Griffey	.05	.02	.01
☐ 47 Ron Guidry	.05	.02	.01
☐ 48 Jack Clark	.03	.01	.01
☐ 49 Reggie Smith	.03	.01	.01
☐ 50 Atlee Hammaker	.03	.01	.01
☐ 51 Fred Breining	.03	.01	.01
☐ 52 Gary Lavelle	.03	.01	.01
☐ 53 Chili Davis	.20	.09	.03
☐ 54 Greg Minton	.03	.01	.01
☐ 55 Joe Morgan	.25	.11	.03
☐ 56 Al Holland	.03	.01	.01
☐ 57 Bill Laskey	.03	.01	.01
☐ 58 Duane Kuiper	.03	.01	.01
☐ 59 Tom Burgmeier	.03	.01	.01
☐ 60 Carl Yastrzemski	.50	.23	.06
☐ 61 Mark Clear	.03	.01	.01
☐ 62 Mike Torrez	.03	.01	.01
☐ 63 Dennis Eckersley	.25	.11	.03
☐ 64 Wade Boggs	3.00	1.35	.35
☐ 65 Bob Stanley	.03	.01	.01
☐ 66 Jim Rice	.05	.02	.01
☐ 67 Carney Lansford	.03	.01	.01
☐ 68 Jerry Remy	.03	.01	.01
☐ 69 Dwight Evans	.10	.05	.01
☐ 70 John Candelaria	.03	.01	.01
☐ 71 Bill Madlock	.05	.02	.01
☐ 72 Dave Parker	.05	.02	.01
☐ 73 Kent Tekulve	.03	.01	.01
☐ 74 Tony Pena	.03	.01	.01
☐ 75 Manny Sarmiento	.03	.01	.01
☐ 76 Johnny Ray	.03	.01	.01
☐ 77 Dale Berra	.03	.01	.01
☐ 78 Lee Lacy	.03	.01	.01
☐ 79 Jason Thompson	.03	.01	.01
☐ 80 Mike Easler	.03	.01	.01
☐ 81 Willie Stargell	.25	.11	.03
☐ 82 Rick Camp	.03	.01	.01
☐ 83 Bob Watson	.05	.02	.01
☐ 84 Bob Horner	.03	.01	.01
☐ 85 Rafael Ramirez	.03	.01	.01
☐ 86 Chris Chambliss	.03	.01	.01
☐ 87 Gene Garber	.03	.01	.01
☐ 88 Claudell Washington	.03	.01	.01
☐ 89 Steve Bedrosian	.03	.01	.01
☐ 90 Dale Murphy	.40	.18	.05
☐ 91 Phil Niekro	.25	.11	.03
☐ 92 Jerry Royster	.03	.01	.01
☐ 93 Bob Walk	.03	.01	.01
☐ 94 Frank White	.03	.01	.01
☐ 95 Dennis Leonard	.03	.01	.01
☐ 96 Vida Blue	.05	.02	.01
☐ 97 U.L. Washington	.03	.01	.01
☐ 98 George Brett	3.00	1.35	.35
☐ 99 Amos Otis	.03	.01	.01
☐ 100 Dan Quisenberry	.03	.01	.01
☐ 101 Willie Aikens	.03	.01	.01
☐ 102 Hal McRae	.03	.01	.01
☐ 103 Larry Gura	.03	.01	.01
☐ 104 Willie Wilson	.03	.01	.01
☐ 105 Damaso Garcia	.03	.01	.01
☐ 106 Hosken Powell	.03	.01	.01
☐ 107 Joey McLaughlin	.03	.01	.01
☐ 108 Jim Clancy	.03	.01	.01
☐ 109 Barry Bonnell	.03	.01	.01
☐ 110 Garth Iorg	.03	.01	.01
☐ 111 Dave Stieb	.03	.01	.01
☐ 112 Fernando Valenzuela	.10	.05	.01
☐ 113 Steve Garvey	.20	.09	.03
☐ 114 Rick Monday	.03	.01	.01
☐ 115 Burt Hooten	.03	.01	.01
☐ 116 Bill Russell	.03	.01	.01
☐ 117 Pedro Guerrero	.03	.01	.01
☐ 118 Steve Sax	.03	.01	.01
☐ 119 Steve Howe	.03	.01	.01
☐ 120 Ken Landreaux	.03	.01	.01
☐ 121 Dusty Baker	.05	.02	.01
☐ 122 Ron Cey	.05	.02	.01
☐ 123 Jerry Reuss	.03	.01	.01
☐ 124 Bump Wills	.03	.01	.01
☐ 125 Keith Moreland	.03	.01	.01
☐ 126 Dick Tidrow	.03	.01	.01
☐ 127 Bill Campbell	.03	.01	.01
☐ 128 Larry Bowa	.03	.01	.01
☐ 129 Randy Martz	.03	.01	.01
☐ 130 Ferguson Jenkins	.25	.11	.03
☐ 131 Leon Durham	.03	.01	.01
☐ 132 Bill Buckner	.05	.02	.01
☐ 133 Ron Davis	.03	.01	.01
☐ 134 Jack O'Connor	.03	.01	.01
☐ 135 Kent Hrbek	.05	.02	.01
☐ 136 Gary Ward	.03	.01	.01
☐ 137 Al Williams	.03	.01	.01
☐ 138 Tom Brunansky	.03	.01	.01
☐ 139 Bobby Castillo	.03	.01	.01
☐ 140 Dusty Baker	.10	.05	.01
Dale Murphy			
☐ 141 Nolan Ryan	2.50	1.10	.30
Alan Ashby			
☐ 142 Omar Moreno	.03	.01	.01
Lee Lacy			
sic, Lacey			
☐ 143 Al Oliver	.50	.23	.06
Pete Rose			
☐ 144 Rickey Henderson	.50	.23	.06
☐ 145 Ray Knight	.50	.23	.06
Mike Schmidt			
Pete Rose			
☐ 146 Ben Oglivie	.03	.01	.01
Hal McRae			
☐ 147 Ray Knight	.03	.01	.01
Tom Hume			
☐ 148 Buddy Bell	.25	.11	.03
Carlton Fisk			
☐ 149 Steve Kemp	.03	.01	.01
☐ 150 Rudy Law	.03	.01	.01
☐ 151 Ron LeFlore	.03	.01	.01
☐ 152 Jerry Koosman	.03	.01	.01
☐ 153 Carlton Fisk	.50	.23	.06
☐ 154 Salome Barojas	.03	.01	.01
☐ 155 Harold Baines	.05	.02	.01
☐ 156 Britt Burns	.03	.01	.01
☐ 157 Tom Paciorek	.05	.02	.01
☐ 158 Greg Luzinski	.03	.01	.01
☐ 159 LeMarr Hoyt	.03	.01	.01
☐ 160 George Wright	.03	.01	.01
☐ 161 Danny Darwin	.03	.01	.01
☐ 162 Lamar Johnson	.03	.01	.01
☐ 163 Charlie Hough	.03	.01	.01
☐ 164 Buddy Bell	.03	.01	.01
☐ 165 Jon Matlack	.03	.01	.01
☐ 166 Billy Sample	.03	.01	.01
☐ 167 Johnny Grubb	.03	.01	.01
☐ 168 Larry Parrish	.03	.01	.01
☐ 169 Ivan DeJesus	.03	.01	.01
☐ 170 Mike Schmidt	1.00	.45	.12
☐ 171 Tug McGraw	.03	.01	.01
☐ 172 Ron Reed	.03	.01	.01
☐ 173 Garry Maddox	.03	.01	.01
☐ 174 Pete Rose	1.50	.70	.19
☐ 175 Manny Trillo	.03	.01	.01
☐ 176 Steve Carlton	.75	.35	.09
☐ 177 Bo Diaz	.03	.01	.01
☐ 178 Gary Matthews	.03	.01	.01
☐ 179 Bill Caudill	.03	.01	.01
☐ 180 Ed VandeBerg	.03	.01	.01
☐ 181 Gaylord Perry	.25	.11	.03
☐ 182 Floyd Bannister	.03	.01	.01
☐ 183 Richie Zisk	.03	.01	.01
☐ 184 Al Cowens	.03	.01	.01
☐ 185 Bruce Bochte	.03	.01	.01
☐ 186 Jeff Burroughs	.03	.01	.01
☐ 187 Dave Beard	.03	.01	.01
☐ 188 Dave Lopes	.03	.01	.01
☐ 189 Dwayne Murphy	.03	.01	.01
☐ 190 Rick Langford	.03	.01	.01
☐ 191 Tom Underwood	.03	.01	.01
☐ 192 Rickey Henderson	2.00	.90	.25
☐ 193 Mike Flanagan	.03	.01	.01
☐ 194 Scott McGregor	.03	.01	.01
☐ 195 Ken Singleton	.03	.01	.01
☐ 196 Rich Dauer	.03	.01	.01
☐ 197 John Lowenstein	.03	.01	.01
☐ 198 Cal Ripken	5.00	2.20	.60
☐ 199 Dennis Martinez	.05	.02	.01
☐ 200 Jim Palmer	.50	.23	.06
☐ 201 Tippy Martinez	.03	.01	.01
☐ 202 Eddie Murray	1.00	.45	.12
☐ 203 Al Bumbry	.03	.01	.01
☐ 204 Dickie Thon	.03	.01	.01
☐ 205 Phil Garner	.03	.01	.01
☐ 206 Jose Cruz	.03	.01	.01
☐ 207 Nolan Ryan	5.00	2.20	.60
☐ 208 Ray Knight	.03	.01	.01
☐ 209 Terry Puhl	.03	.01	.01
☐ 210 Joe Niekro	.03	.01	.01
☐ 211 Art Howe	.05	.02	.01
☐ 212 Alan Ashby	.03	.01	.01
☐ 213 Tom Hume	.03	.01	.01
☐ 214 Johnny Bench	.50	.23	.06
☐ 215 Larry Biittner	.03	.01	.01
☐ 216 Mario Soto	.03	.01	.01
☐ 217 Dan Driessen	.03	.01	.01
☐ 218 Tom Seaver	.50	.23	.06
☐ 219 Dave Concepcion	.03	.01	.01
☐ 220 Wayne Krenchicki	.03	.01	.01
☐ 221 Cesar Cedeno	.03	.01	.01
☐ 222 Randy Jones	.03	.01	.01
☐ 223 Terry Kennedy	.03	.01	.01
☐ 224 Luis DeLeon	.03	.01	.01
☐ 225 Eric Show	.03	.01	.01
☐ 226 Tim Flannery	.03	.01	.01
☐ 227 Garry Templeton	.03	.01	.01
☐ 228 Tim Lollar	.03	.01	.01
☐ 229 Sixto Lezcano	.03	.01	.01
☐ 230 Bob Bailor	.03	.01	.01
☐ 231 Craig Swan	.03	.01	.01
☐ 232 Dave Kingman	.05	.02	.01
☐ 233 Mookie Wilson	.05	.02	.01
☐ 234 John Stearns	.03	.01	.01
☐ 235 Ellis Valentine	.03	.01	.01
☐ 236 Neil Allen	.03	.01	.01
☐ 237 Pat Zachry	.03	.01	.01
☐ 238 Rusty Staub	.03	.01	.01
☐ 239 George Foster	.03	.01	.01
☐ 240 Rick Sutcliffe	.03	.01	.01
☐ 241 Andre Thornton	.03	.01	.01
☐ 242 Mike Hargrove	.03	.01	.01
☐ 243 Dan Spillner	.03	.01	.01
☐ 244 Lary Sorensen	.03	.01	.01
☐ 245 Len Barker	.03	.01	.01
☐ 246 Rick Manning	.03	.01	.01
☐ 247 Toby Harrah	.03	.01	.01
☐ 248 Milt Wilcox	.03	.01	.01
☐ 249 Lou Whitaker	.05	.02	.01
☐ 250 Tom Brookens	.03	.01	.01
☐ 251 Chet Lemon	.03	.01	.01
☐ 252 Jack Morris	.05	.02	.01
☐ 253 Alan Trammell	.25	.11	.03
☐ 254 Johnny Wockenfuss	.03	.01	.01
☐ 255 Lance Parrish	.10	.05	.01
☐ 256 Larry Herndon	.03	.01	.01
☐ 257 Chris Speier	.03	.01	.01
☐ 258 Woodie Fryman	.03	.01	.01
☐ 259 Scott Sanderson	.03	.01	.01
☐ 260 Steve Rogers	.03	.01	.01
☐ 261 Warren Cromartie	.03	.01	.01
☐ 262 Gary Carter	.40	.18	.05
☐ 263 Bill Gullickson	.03	.01	.01
☐ 264 Andre Dawson	.25	.11	.03
☐ 265 Tim Raines	.10	.05	.01
☐ 266 Charlie Lea	.03	.01	.01
☐ 267 Jeff Reardon	.05	.02	.01
☐ 268 Al Oliver	.05	.02	.01
☐ 269 George Hendrick	.03	.01	.01
☐ 270 John Montefusco	.03	.01	.01
☐ NNO New York Yankees CL	.02	.01	.01
☐ NNO Kansas City Royals CL	.02	.01	.01
☐ NNO St. Louis Cardinals PO	.02	.01	.01
☐ NNO Boston Red Sox CL	.02	.01	.01
☐ NNO Boston Red Sox PO	.02	.01	.01
☐ NNO Cleveland Indians CL	.02	.01	.01
☐ NNO Toronto Blue Jays CL	.02	.01	.01
☐ NNO Montreal Expos PO	.02	.01	.01
☐ NNO Montreal Expos CL	.02	.01	.01
☐ NNO Atlanta Braves CL	.02	.01	.01
☐ NNO Atlanta Braves PO	.02	.01	.01
☐ NNO Houston Astros PO	.02	.01	.01
☐ NNO Cleveland Indians PO	.02	.01	.01
☐ NNO Seattle Mariners CL	.02	.01	.01
☐ NNO New York Mets CL	.02	.01	.01
☐ NNO Chicago Cubs CL	.02	.01	.01
☐ NNO Detroit Tigers PO	.02	.01	.01
☐ NNO Los Angeles Dodgers PO	.02	.01	.01
☐ NNO California Angels CL	.02	.01	.01
☐ NNO Toronto Blue Jays PO	.02	.01	.01
☐ NNO Baltimore Orioles PO	.02	.01	.01
☐ NNO Cincinnati Reds PO	.02	.01	.01

NNO Cincinnati Reds CL	.02	.01	.01
NNO Oakland A's CL	.02	.01	.01
NNO Seattle Mariners PO	.02	.01	.01
NNO St. Louis Cardinals CL	.02	.01	.01
NNO Detroit Tigers CL	.02	.01	.01
NNO New York Mets PO	.02	.01	.01
NNO San Diego Padres PO	.02	.01	.01
NNO San Francisco Giants PO	.02	.01	.01
NNO Pittsburgh Pirates PO	.02	.01	.01
NNO Pittsburgh Pirates CL	.02	.01	.01
NNO Minnesota Twins PO	.02	.01	.01
NNO California Angels PO	.02	.01	.01
NNO Texas Rangers CL	.02	.01	.01
NNO Philadelphia Phillies CL	.02	.01	.01
NNO Milwaukee Brewers PO	.02	.01	.01
NNO San Diego Padres CL	.02	.01	.01
NNO Milwaukee Brewers CL	.02	.01	.01
NNO Los Angeles Dodgers CL	.02	.01	.01
NNO New York Yankees PO	.02	.01	.01
NNO Minnesota Twins CL	.02	.01	.01
NNO Kansas City Royals PO	.02	.01	.01
NNO Chicago White Sox PO	.02	.01	.01
NNO Baltimore Orioles CL	.02	.01	.01
NNO Philadelphia Phillies PO	.02	.01	.01

1984 Fleer

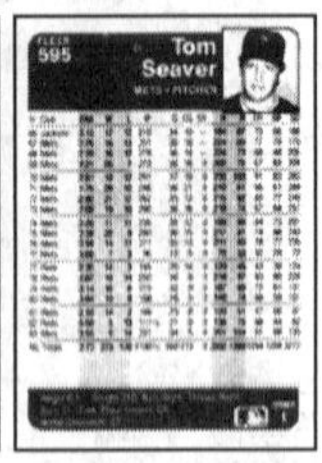

The 1984 Fleer card 660-card standard-size set featured fronts with full-color team logos along with the player's name and position and the Fleer identification. The set features many imaginative photos, several multi-player cards, and many more action shots than the 1983 card set. The backs are quite similar to the 1983 backs except that blue rather than brown ink is used. The player cards are alphabetized within team and the teams are ordered by their 1983 season finish and won-lost record. Specials (626-646) and checklist cards (647-660) make up the end of the set. Wax packs again consisted of 15 cards plus logo stickers. The key Rookie Cards in this set are Don Mattingly, Tony Phillips, Darryl Strawberry, and Andy Van Slyke.

	NRMT	VG-E	GOOD
COMPLETE SET (660)	90.00	40.00	11.00
COMMON CARD (1-660)	.15	.07	.02
1 Mike Boddicker	.15	.07	.02
2 Al Bumbry	.40	.18	.05
3 Todd Cruz	.15	.07	.02
4 Rich Dauer	.15	.07	.02
5 Storm Davis	.15	.07	.02
6 Rick Dempsey	.15	.07	.02
7 Jim Dwyer	.15	.07	.02
8 Mike Flanagan	.15	.07	.02
9 Dan Ford	.15	.07	.02
10 John Lowenstein	.15	.07	.02
11 Dennis Martinez	.40	.18	.05
12 Tippy Martinez	.15	.07	.02
13 Scott McGregor	.15	.07	.02
14 Eddie Murray	4.00	1.80	.50
15 Joe Nolan	.15	.07	.02
16 Jim Palmer	1.25	.55	.16
17 Cal Ripken	20.00	9.00	2.50
18 Gary Roenicke	.15	.07	.02
19 Lenn Sakata	.15	.07	.02
20 John Shelby	.15	.07	.02
21 Ken Singleton	.15	.07	.02
22 Sammy Stewart	.15	.07	.02
23 Tim Stoddard	.15	.07	.02
24 Marty Bystrom	.15	.07	.02
25 Steve Carlton	2.00	.90	.25
26 Ivan DeJesus	.15	.07	.02
27 John Denny	.15	.07	.02
28 Bob Dernier	.15	.07	.02
29 Bo Diaz	.15	.07	.02
30 Kiko Garcia	.15	.07	.02
31 Greg Gross	.15	.07	.02
32 Kevin Gross	.40	.18	.05
33 Von Hayes	.15	.07	.02
34 Willie Hernandez	.40	.18	.05
35 Al Holland	.15	.07	.02
36 Charles Hudson	.15	.07	.02
37 Joe Lefebvre	.15	.07	.02
38 Sixto Lezcano	.15	.07	.02
39 Garry Maddox	.15	.07	.02
40 Gary Matthews	.15	.07	.02
41 Len Matuszek	.15	.07	.02
42 Tug McGraw	.40	.18	.05
43 Joe Morgan	1.00	.45	.12
44 Tony Perez	.75	.35	.09
45 Ron Reed	.15	.07	.02
46 Pete Rose	3.00	1.35	.35
47 Juan Samuel	.75	.35	.09
48 Mike Schmidt	5.00	2.20	.60
49 Ozzie Virgil	.15	.07	.02
50 Juan Agosto	.15	.07	.02
51 Harold Baines	.40	.18	.05
52 Floyd Bannister	.15	.07	.02
53 Salome Barojas	.15	.07	.02
54 Britt Burns	.15	.07	.02
55 Julio Cruz	.15	.07	.02
56 Richard Dotson	.15	.07	.02
57 Jerry Dybzinski	.15	.07	.02
58 Carlton Fisk	2.00	.90	.25
59 Scott Fletcher	.15	.07	.02
60 Jerry Hairston	.15	.07	.02
61 Kevin Hickey	.15	.07	.02
62 Marc Hill	.15	.07	.02
63 LaMarr Hoyt	.15	.07	.02
64 Ron Kittle	.15	.07	.02
65 Jerry Koosman	.40	.18	.05
66 Dennis Lamp	.15	.07	.02
67 Rudy Law	.15	.07	.02
68 Vance Law	.15	.07	.02
69 Greg Luzinski	.40	.18	.05
70 Tom Paciorek	.15	.07	.02
71 Mike Squires	.15	.07	.02
72 Dick Tidrow	.15	.07	.02
73 Greg Walker	.40	.18	.05
74 Glenn Abbott	.15	.07	.02
75 Howard Bailey	.15	.07	.02
76 Doug Bair	.15	.07	.02
77 Juan Berenguer	.15	.07	.02
78 Tom Brookens	.40	.18	.05
79 Enos Cabell	.15	.07	.02
80 Kirk Gibson	.75	.35	.09
81 John Grubb	.15	.07	.02
82 Larry Herndon	.40	.18	.05
83 Wayne Krenchicki	.15	.07	.02
84 Rick Leach	.15	.07	.02
85 Chet Lemon	.40	.18	.05
86 Aurelio Lopez	.40	.18	.05
87 Jack Morris	.40	.18	.05
88 Lance Parrish	.40	.18	.05
89 Dan Petry	.40	.18	.05
90 Dave Rozema	.15	.07	.02
91 Alan Trammell	.75	.35	.09
92 Lou Whitaker	.40	.18	.05
93 Milt Wilcox	.15	.07	.02
94 Glenn Wilson	.40	.18	.05
95 John Wockenfuss	.15	.07	.02
96 Dusty Baker	.75	.35	.09
97 Joe Beckwith	.15	.07	.02
98 Greg Brock	.15	.07	.02
99 Jack Fimple	.15	.07	.02
100 Pedro Guerrero	.40	.18	.05
101 Rick Honeycutt	.15	.07	.02
102 Burt Hooton	.15	.07	.02
103 Steve Howe	.15	.07	.02
104 Ken Landreaux	.15	.07	.02
105 Mike Marshall	.15	.07	.02
106 Rick Monday	.15	.07	.02
107 Jose Morales	.15	.07	.02
108 Tom Niedenfuer	.15	.07	.02
109 Alejandro Pena	.40	.18	.05
110 Jerry Reuss UER ("Home:" omitted)	.15	.07	.02
111 Bill Russell	.15	.07	.02
112 Steve Sax	.40	.18	.05
113 Mike Scioscia	.15	.07	.02
114 Derrel Thomas	.15	.07	.02
115 Fernando Valenzuela	.40	.18	.05
116 Bob Welch	.15	.07	.02
117 Steve Yeager	.15	.07	.02
118 Pat Zachry	.15	.07	.02
119 Don Baylor	.75	.35	.09
120 Bert Campaneris	.40	.18	.05
121 Rick Cerone	.15	.07	.02
122 Ray Fontenot	.15	.07	.02
123 George Frazier	.15	.07	.02
124 Oscar Gamble	.15	.07	.02
125 Rich Gossage	.75	.35	.09
126 Ken Griffey	.40	.18	.05
127 Ron Guidry	.40	.18	.05
128 Jay Howell	.15	.07	.02
129 Steve Kemp	.15	.07	.02
130 Matt Keough	.15	.07	.02
131 Don Mattingly	25.00	11.00	3.10
132 John Montefusco	.15	.07	.02
133 Omar Moreno	.15	.07	.02
134 Dale Murray	.15	.07	.02
135 Graig Nettles	.40	.18	.05
136 Lou Piniella	.40	.18	.05
137 Willie Randolph	.40	.18	.05
138 Shane Rawley	.15	.07	.02
139 Dave Righetti	.40	.18	.05
140 Andre Robertson	.15	.07	.02
141 Bob Shirley	.15	.07	.02
142 Roy Smalley	.15	.07	.02
143 Dave Winfield	3.00	1.35	.35
144 Butch Wynegar	.15	.07	.02
145 Jim Acker	.15	.07	.02
146 Doyle Alexander	.15	.07	.02
147 Jesse Barfield	.40	.18	.05
148 Jorge Bell	.40	.18	.05
149 Barry Bonnell	.15	.07	.02
150 Jim Clancy	.15	.07	.02
151 Dave Collins	.15	.07	.02
152 Tony Fernandez	.75	.35	.09
153 Damaso Garcia	.15	.07	.02
154 Dave Geisel	.15	.07	.02
155 Jim Gott	.15	.07	.02
156 Alfredo Griffin	.15	.07	.02
157 Garth Iorg	.15	.07	.02
158 Roy Lee Jackson	.15	.07	.02
159 Cliff Johnson	.15	.07	.02
160 Luis Leal	.15	.07	.02
161 Buck Martinez	.15	.07	.02
162 Joey McLaughlin	.15	.07	.02
163 Randy Moffitt	.15	.07	.02
164 Lloyd Moseby	.15	.07	.02
165 Rance Mulliniks	.15	.07	.02
166 Jorge Orta	.15	.07	.02
167 Dave Stieb	.15	.07	.02
168 Willie Upshaw	.15	.07	.02
169 Ernie Whitt	.15	.07	.02
170 Len Barker	.15	.07	.02
171 Steve Bedrosian	.15	.07	.02
172 Bruce Benedict	.15	.07	.02
173 Brett Butler	.75	.35	.09
174 Rick Camp	.15	.07	.02
175 Chris Chambliss	.15	.07	.02
176 Ken Dayley	.15	.07	.02
177 Pete Falcone	.15	.07	.02
178 Terry Forster	.15	.07	.02
179 Gene Garber	.15	.07	.02
180 Terry Harper	.15	.07	.02
181 Bob Horner	.15	.07	.02
182 Glenn Hubbard	.15	.07	.02
183 Randy Johnson	.15	.07	.02
184 Craig McMurtry	.15	.07	.02
185 Donnie Moore	.15	.07	.02
186 Dale Murphy	.75	.35	.09
187 Phil Niekro	.75	.35	.09
188 Pascual Perez	.15	.07	.02
189 Biff Pocoroba	.15	.07	.02
190 Rafael Ramirez	.15	.07	.02
191 Jerry Royster	.15	.07	.02
192 Claudell Washington	.15	.07	.02
193 Bob Watson	.40	.18	.05
194 Jerry Augustine	.15	.07	.02
195 Mark Brouhard	.15	.07	.02
196 Mike Caldwell	.15	.07	.02
197 Tom Candiotti	.75	.35	.09
198 Cecil Cooper	.40	.18	.05
199 Rollie Fingers	.75	.35	.09
200 Jim Gantner	.40	.18	.05
201 Bob L. Gibson	.15	.07	.02
202 Moose Haas	.15	.07	.02
203 Roy Howell	.15	.07	.02
204 Pete Ladd	.15	.07	.02
205 Rick Manning	.15	.07	.02
206 Bob McClure	.15	.07	.02
207 Paul Molitor UER ('83 stats should say .270 BA and 608 AB)	3.00	1.35	.35
208 Don Money	.15	.07	.02
209 Charlie Moore	.15	.07	.02
210 Ben Oglivie	.15	.07	.02
211 Chuck Porter	.15	.07	.02
212 Ed Romero	.15	.07	.02
213 Ted Simmons	.40	.18	.05
214 Jim Slaton	.15	.07	.02
215 Don Sutton	.75	.35	.09
216 Tom Tellmann	.15	.07	.02
217 Pete Vuckovich	.15	.07	.02
218 Ned Yost	.15	.07	.02
219 Robin Yount	3.00	1.35	.35
220 Alan Ashby	.15	.07	.02
221 Kevin Bass	.15	.07	.02
222 Jose Cruz	.40	.18	.05
223 Bill Dawley	.15	.07	.02
224 Frank DiPino	.15	.07	.02
225 Bill Doran	.40	.18	.05
226 Phil Garner	.40	.18	.05
227 Art Howe	.15	.07	.02
228 Bob Knepper	.15	.07	.02
229 Ray Knight	.40	.18	.05
230 Frank LaCorte	.15	.07	.02
231 Mike LaCoss	.15	.07	.02
232 Mike Madden	.15	.07	.02
233 Jerry Mumphrey	.15	.07	.02
234 Joe Niekro	.40	.18	.05
235 Terry Puhl	.15	.07	.02
236 Luis Pujols	.15	.07	.02
237 Craig Reynolds	.15	.07	.02
238 Vern Ruhle	.15	.07	.02
239 Nolan Ryan	12.00	5.50	1.50
240 Mike Scott	.40	.18	.05
241 Tony Scott	.15	.07	.02
242 Dave Smith	.15	.07	.02
243 Dickie Thon	.15	.07	.02
244 Denny Walling	.15	.07	.02
245 Dale Berra	.15	.07	.02
246 Jim Bibby	.15	.07	.02
247 John Candelaria	.15	.07	.02
248 Jose DeLeon	.15	.07	.02
249 Mike Easler	.15	.07	.02
250 Cecilio Guante	.15	.07	.02
251 Richie Hebner	.15	.07	.02
252 Lee Lacy	.15	.07	.02
253 Bill Madlock	.15	.07	.02
254 Milt May	.15	.07	.02
255 Lee Mazzilli	.15	.07	.02
256 Larry McWilliams	.15	.07	.02
257 Jim Morrison	.15	.07	.02
258 Dave Parker	.40	.18	.05
259 Tony Pena	.15	.07	.02
260 Johnny Ray	.15	.07	.02
261 Rick Rhoden	.15	.07	.02
262 Don Robinson	.15	.07	.02
263 Manny Sarmiento	.15	.07	.02
264 Rod Scurry	.15	.07	.02
265 Kent Tekulve	.40	.18	.05
266 Gene Tenace	.40	.18	.05
267 Jason Thompson	.15	.07	.02
268 Lee Tunnell	.15	.07	.02
269 Marvell Wynne	.15	.07	.02
270 Ray Burris	.15	.07	.02
271 Gary Carter	.40	.18	.05
272 Warren Cromartie	.15	.07	.02
273 Andre Dawson	2.50	1.10	.30
274 Doug Flynn	.15	.07	.02
275 Terry Francona	.15	.07	.02
276 Bill Gullickson	.15	.07	.02
277 Bob James	.15	.07	.02
278 Charlie Lea	.15	.07	.02
279 Bryan Little	.15	.07	.02
280 Al Oliver	.40	.18	.05
281 Tim Raines	.75	.35	.09
282 Bobby Ramos	.15	.07	.02
283 Jeff Reardon	.40	.18	.05
284 Steve Rogers	.15	.07	.02
285 Scott Sanderson	.15	.07	.02
286 Dan Schatzeder	.15	.07	.02
287 Bryn Smith	.15	.07	.02
288 Chris Speier	.15	.07	.02
289 Manny Trillo	.15	.07	.02
290 Mike Vail	.15	.07	.02
291 Tim Wallach	.40	.18	.05
292 Chris Welsh	.15	.07	.02
293 Jim Wohlford	.15	.07	.02
294 Kurt Bevacqua	.15	.07	.02
295 Juan Bonilla	.15	.07	.02
296 Bobby Brown	.15	.07	.02
297 Luis DeLeon	.15	.07	.02
298 Dave Dravecky	.40	.18	.05
299 Tim Flannery	.15	.07	.02
300 Steve Garvey	.75	.35	.09
301 Tony Gwynn	10.00	4.50	1.25
302 Andy Hawkins	.15	.07	.02
303 Ruppert Jones	.15	.07	.02
304 Terry Kennedy	.15	.07	.02
305 Tim Lollar	.15	.07	.02
306 Gary Lucas	.15	.07	.02
307 Kevin McReynolds	.75	.35	.09
308 Sid Monge	.15	.07	.02
309 Mario Ramirez	.15	.07	.02
310 Gene Richards	.15	.07	.02
311 Luis Salazar	.15	.07	.02
312 Eric Show	.15	.07	.02
313 Elias Sosa	.15	.07	.02
314 Garry Templeton	.15	.07	.02
315 Mark Thurmond	.15	.07	.02
316 Ed Whitson	.15	.07	.02
317 Alan Wiggins	.15	.07	.02
318 Neil Allen	.15	.07	.02
319 Joaquin Andujar	.15	.07	.02
320 Steve Braun	.15	.07	.02
321 Glenn Brummer	.15	.07	.02
322 Bob Forsch	.15	.07	.02
323 David Green	.15	.07	.02
324 George Hendrick	.15	.07	.02
325 Tom Herr	.40	.18	.05
326 Dane Iorg	.15	.07	.02
327 Jeff Lahti	.15	.07	.02
328 Dave LaPoint	.15	.07	.02
329 Willie McGee	.75	.35	.09
330 Ken Oberkfell	.15	.07	.02
331 Darrell Porter	.15	.07	.02
332 Jamie Quirk	.15	.07	.02
333 Mike Ramsey	.15	.07	.02
334 Floyd Rayford	.15	.07	.02
335 Lonnie Smith	.15	.07	.02
336 Ozzie Smith	4.00	1.80	.50
337 John Stuper	.15	.07	.02
338 Bruce Sutter	.40	.18	.05
339 Andy Van Slyke UER (Batting and throwing both wrong on card back)	1.50	.70	.19
340 Dave Von Ohlen	.15	.07	.02
341 Willie Aikens	.15	.07	.02
342 Mike Armstrong	.15	.07	.02
343 Bud Black	.15	.07	.02
344 George Brett	6.00	2.70	.75
345 Onix Concepcion	.15	.07	.02
346 Keith Creel	.15	.07	.02
347 Larry Gura	.15	.07	.02
348 Don Hood	.15	.07	.02
349 Dennis Leonard	.15	.07	.02
350 Hal McRae	.40	.18	.05
351 Amos Otis	.40	.18	.05
352 Gaylord Perry	.75	.35	.09
353 Greg Pryor	.15	.07	.02
354 Dan Quisenberry	.15	.07	.02
355 Steve Renko	.15	.07	.02
356 Leon Roberts	.15	.07	.02
357 Pat Sheridan	.15	.07	.02
358 Joe Simpson	.15	.07	.02
359 Don Slaught	.40	.18	.05

□ 360 Paul Splittorff .15 .07 .02
□ 361 U.L. Washington .15 .07 .02
□ 362 John Wathan .15 .07 .02
□ 363 Frank White .40 .18 .05
□ 364 Willie Wilson .15 .07 .02
□ 365 Jim Barr .15 .07 .02
□ 366 Dave Bergman .15 .07 .02
□ 367 Fred Breining .15 .07 .02
□ 368 Bob Brenly .15 .07 .02
□ 369 Jack Clark .40 .18 .05
□ 370 Chili Davis .40 .18 .05
□ 371 Mark Davis .15 .07 .02
□ 372 Darrell Evans .40 .18 .05
□ 373 Atlee Hammaker .15 .07 .02
□ 374 Mike Krukow .15 .07 .02
□ 375 Duane Kuiper .15 .07 .02
□ 376 Bill Laskey .15 .07 .02
□ 377 Gary Lavelle .15 .07 .02
□ 378 Johnnie LeMaster .15 .07 .02
□ 379 Jeff Leonard .15 .07 .02
□ 380 Randy Lerch .15 .07 .02
□ 381 Renie Martin .15 .07 .02
□ 382 Andy McGaffigan .15 .07 .02
□ 383 Greg Minton .15 .07 .02
□ 384 Tom O'Malley .15 .07 .02
□ 385 Max Venable .15 .07 .02
□ 386 Brad Wellman .15 .07 .02
□ 387 Joel Youngblood .15 .07 .02
□ 388 Gary Allenson .15 .07 .02
□ 389 Luis Aponte .15 .07 .02
□ 390 Tony Armas .15 .07 .02
□ 391 Doug Bird .15 .07 .02
□ 392 Wade Boggs 4.00 1.80 .50
□ 393 Dennis Boyd .40 .18 .05
□ 394 Mike Brown UER P .15 .07 .02
(shown with record
of 31-104)
□ 395 Mark Clear .15 .07 .02
□ 396 Dennis Eckersley 1.25 .55 .16
□ 397 Dwight Evans .40 .18 .05
□ 398 Rich Gedman .15 .07 .02
□ 399 Glenn Hoffman .15 .07 .02
□ 400 Bruce Hurst .15 .07 .02
□ 401 John Henry Johnson .15 .07 .02
□ 402 Ed Jurak .15 .07 .02
□ 403 Rick Miller .15 .07 .02
□ 404 Jeff Newman .15 .07 .02
□ 405 Reid Nichols .15 .07 .02
□ 406 Bob Ojeda .15 .07 .02
□ 407 Jerry Remy .15 .07 .02
□ 408 Jim Rice .40 .18 .05
□ 409 Bob Stanley .15 .07 .02
□ 410 Dave Stapleton .15 .07 .02
□ 411 John Tudor .15 .07 .02
□ 412 Carl Yastrzemski 1.50 .70 .19
□ 413 Buddy Bell .40 .18 .05
□ 414 Larry Biittner .15 .07 .02
□ 415 John Butcher .15 .07 .02
□ 416 Danny Darwin .15 .07 .02
□ 417 Bucky Dent .40 .18 .05
□ 418 Dave Hostetler .15 .07 .02
□ 419 Charlie Hough .40 .18 .05
□ 420 Bobby Johnson .15 .07 .02
□ 421 Odell Jones .15 .07 .02
□ 422 Jon Matlack .15 .07 .02
□ 423 Pete O'Brien .40 .18 .05
□ 424 Larry Parrish .15 .07 .02
□ 425 Mickey Rivers .15 .07 .02
□ 426 Billy Sample .15 .07 .02
□ 427 Dave Schmidt .15 .07 .02
□ 428 Mike Smithson .15 .07 .02
□ 429 Bill Stein .15 .07 .02
□ 430 Dave Stewart .40 .18 .05
□ 431 Jim Sundberg .40 .18 .05
□ 432 Frank Tanana .40 .18 .05
□ 433 Dave Tobik .15 .07 .02
□ 434 Wayne Tolleson .15 .07 .02
□ 435 George Wright .15 .07 .02
□ 436 Bill Almon .15 .07 .02
□ 437 Keith Atherton .15 .07 .02
□ 438 Dave Beard .15 .07 .02
□ 439 Tom Burgmeier .15 .07 .02
□ 440 Jeff Burroughs .15 .07 .02
□ 441 Chris Codiroli .15 .07 .02
□ 442 Tim Conroy .15 .07 .02
□ 443 Mike Davis .15 .07 .02
□ 444 Wayne Gross .15 .07 .02
□ 445 Garry Hancock .15 .07 .02
□ 446 Mike Heath .15 .07 .02
□ 447 Rickey Henderson 3.00 1.35 .35
□ 448 Donnie Hill .15 .07 .02
□ 449 Bob Kearney .15 .07 .02
□ 450 Bill Krueger .15 .07 .02
□ 451 Rick Langford .15 .07 .02
□ 452 Carney Lansford .40 .18 .05
□ 453 Dave Lopes .40 .18 .05
□ 454 Steve McCatty .15 .07 .02
□ 455 Dan Meyer .15 .07 .02
□ 456 Dwayne Murphy .15 .07 .02
□ 457 Mike Norris .15 .07 .02
□ 458 Ricky Peters .15 .07 .02
□ 459 Tony Phillips 2.00 .90 .25
□ 460 Tom Underwood .15 .07 .02
□ 461 Mike Warren .15 .07 .02
□ 462 Johnny Bench 1.50 .70 .19
□ 463 Bruce Berenyi .15 .07 .02
□ 464 Dann Bilardello .15 .07 .02
□ 465 Cesar Cedeno .40 .18 .05
□ 466 Dave Concepcion .40 .18 .05
□ 467 Dan Driessen .15 .07 .02
□ 468 Nick Esasky .15 .07 .02
□ 469 Rich Gale .15 .07 .02
□ 470 Ben Hayes .15 .07 .02
□ 471 Paul Householder .15 .07 .02
□ 472 Tom Hume .15 .07 .02
□ 473 Alan Knicely .15 .07 .02
□ 474 Eddie Milner .15 .07 .02
□ 475 Ron Oester .15 .07 .02
□ 476 Kelly Paris .15 .07 .02
□ 477 Frank Pastore .15 .07 .02
□ 478 Ted Power .15 .07 .02
□ 479 Joe Price .15 .07 .02
□ 480 Charlie Puleo .15 .07 .02
□ 481 Gary Redus .15 .07 .02
□ 482 Bill Scherrer .15 .07 .02
□ 483 Mario Soto .15 .07 .02
□ 484 Alex Trevino .15 .07 .02
□ 485 Duane Walker .15 .07 .02
□ 486 Larry Bowa .40 .18 .05
□ 487 Warren Brusstar .15 .07 .02
□ 488 Bill Buckner .40 .18 .05
□ 489 Bill Campbell .15 .07 .02
□ 490 Ron Cey .40 .18 .05
□ 491 Jody Davis .15 .07 .02
□ 492 Leon Durham .15 .07 .02
□ 493 Mel Hall .40 .18 .05
□ 494 Ferguson Jenkins .75 .35 .09
□ 495 Jay Johnstone .40 .18 .05
□ 496 Craig Lefferts .15 .07 .02
□ 497 Carmelo Martinez .15 .07 .02
□ 498 Jerry Morales .15 .07 .02
□ 499 Keith Moreland .15 .07 .02
□ 500 Dickie Noles .15 .07 .02
□ 501 Mike Proly .15 .07 .02
□ 502 Chuck Rainey .15 .07 .02
□ 503 Dick Ruthven .15 .07 .02
□ 504 Ryne Sandberg 8.00 3.60 1.00
□ 505 Lee Smith 1.50 .70 .19
□ 506 Steve Trout .15 .07 .02
□ 507 Gary Woods .15 .07 .02
□ 508 Juan Beniquez .15 .07 .02
□ 509 Bob Boone .40 .18 .05
□ 510 Rick Burleson .15 .07 .02
□ 511 Rod Carew 1.25 .55 .16
□ 512 Bobby Clark .15 .07 .02
□ 513 John Curtis .15 .07 .02
□ 514 Doug DeCinces .15 .07 .02
□ 515 Brian Downing .15 .07 .02
□ 516 Tim Foli .15 .07 .02
□ 517 Ken Forsch .15 .07 .02
□ 518 Bobby Grich .40 .18 .05
□ 519 Andy Hassler .15 .07 .02
□ 520 Reggie Jackson 2.50 1.10 .30
□ 521 Ron Jackson .15 .07 .02
□ 522 Tommy John .75 .35 .09
□ 523 Bruce Kison .15 .07 .02
□ 524 Steve Lubratich .15 .07 .02
□ 525 Fred Lynn .40 .18 .05
□ 526 Gary Pettis .15 .07 .02
□ 527 Luis Sanchez .15 .07 .02
□ 528 Daryl Sconiers .15 .07 .02
□ 529 Ellis Valentine .15 .07 .02
□ 530 Rob Wilfong .15 .07 .02
□ 531 Mike Witt .15 .07 .02
□ 532 Geoff Zahn .15 .07 .02
□ 533 Bud Anderson .15 .07 .02
□ 534 Chris Bando .15 .07 .02
□ 535 Alan Bannister .15 .07 .02
□ 536 Bert Blyleven .40 .18 .05
□ 537 Tom Brennan .15 .07 .02
□ 538 Jamie Easterly .15 .07 .02
□ 539 Juan Eichelberger .15 .07 .02
□ 540 Jim Essian .15 .07 .02
□ 541 Mike Fischlin .15 .07 .02
□ 542 Julio Franco .75 .35 .09
□ 543 Mike Hargrove .40 .18 .05
□ 544 Toby Harrah .40 .18 .05
□ 545 Ron Hassey .15 .07 .02
□ 546 Neal Heaton .15 .07 .02
□ 547 Bake McBride .15 .07 .02
□ 548 Broderick Perkins .15 .07 .02
□ 549 Lary Sorensen .15 .07 .02
□ 550 Dan Spillner .15 .07 .02
□ 551 Rick Sutcliffe .40 .18 .05
□ 552 Pat Tabler .15 .07 .02
□ 553 Gorman Thomas .15 .07 .02
□ 554 Andre Thornton .15 .07 .02
□ 555 George Vukovich .15 .07 .02
□ 556 Darrell Brown .15 .07 .02
□ 557 Tom Brunansky .40 .18 .05
□ 558 Randy Bush .15 .07 .02
□ 559 Bobby Castillo .15 .07 .02
□ 560 John Castino .15 .07 .02
□ 561 Ron Davis .15 .07 .02
□ 562 Dave Engle .15 .07 .02
□ 563 Lenny Faedo .15 .07 .02
□ 564 Pete Filson .15 .07 .02
□ 565 Gary Gaetti .75 .35 .09
□ 566 Mickey Hatcher .15 .07 .02
□ 567 Kent Hrbek .40 .18 .05
□ 568 Rusty Kuntz .15 .07 .02
□ 569 Tim Laudner .15 .07 .02
□ 570 Rick Lysander .15 .07 .02
□ 571 Bobby Mitchell .15 .07 .02
□ 572 Ken Schrom .15 .07 .02
□ 573 Ray Smith .15 .07 .02
□ 574 Tim Teufel .15 .07 .02
□ 575 Frank Viola .75 .35 .09
□ 576 Gary Ward .15 .07 .02
□ 577 Ron Washington .15 .07 .02
□ 578 Len Whitehouse .15 .07 .02
□ 579 Al Williams .15 .07 .02
□ 580 Bob Bailor .15 .07 .02
□ 581 Mark Bradley .15 .07 .02
□ 582 Hubie Brooks .15 .07 .02
□ 583 Carlos Diaz .15 .07 .02
□ 584 George Foster .40 .18 .05
□ 585 Brian Giles .15 .07 .02
□ 586 Danny Heep .15 .07 .02
□ 587 Keith Hernandez .40 .18 .05
□ 588 Ron Hodges .15 .07 .02
□ 589 Scott Holman .15 .07 .02
□ 590 Dave Kingman .40 .18 .05
□ 591 Ed Lynch .15 .07 .02
□ 592 Jose Oquendo .40 .18 .05
□ 593 Jesse Orosco .15 .07 .02
□ 594 Junior Ortiz .15 .07 .02
□ 595 Tom Seaver 2.00 .90 .25
□ 596 Doug Sisk .15 .07 .02
□ 597 Rusty Staub .40 .18 .05
□ 598 John Stearns .15 .07 .02
□ 599 Darryl Strawberry 6.00 2.70 .75
□ 600 Craig Swan .15 .07 .02
□ 601 Walt Terrell .15 .07 .02
□ 602 Mike Torrez .15 .07 .02
□ 603 Mookie Wilson .40 .18 .05
□ 604 Jamie Allen .15 .07 .02
□ 605 Jim Beattie .15 .07 .02
□ 606 Tony Bernazard .15 .07 .02
□ 607 Manny Castillo .15 .07 .02
□ 608 Bill Caudill .15 .07 .02
□ 609 Bryan Clark .15 .07 .02
□ 610 Al Cowens .15 .07 .02
□ 611 Dave Henderson .40 .18 .05
□ 612 Steve Henderson .15 .07 .02
□ 613 Orlando Mercado .15 .07 .02
□ 614 Mike Moore .40 .18 .05
□ 615 Ricky Nelson UER .15 .07 .02
(Jamie Nelson's
stats on back)
□ 616 Spike Owen .40 .18 .05
□ 617 Pat Putnam .15 .07 .02
□ 618 Ron Roenicke .15 .07 .02
□ 619 Mike Stanton .15 .07 .02
□ 620 Bob Stoddard .15 .07 .02
□ 621 Rick Sweet .15 .07 .02
□ 622 Roy Thomas .15 .07 .02
□ 623 Ed VandeBerg .15 .07 .02
□ 624 Matt Young .15 .07 .02
□ 625 Richie Zisk .15 .07 .02
□ 626 Fred Lynn .40 .18 .05
1982 AS Game RB
□ 627 Manny Trillo .40 .18 .05
1983 AS Game RB
□ 628 Steve Garvey .75 .35 .09
NL Iron Man
□ 629 Rod Carew .75 .35 .09
AL Batting Runner-Up
□ 630 Wade Boggs 1.50 .70 .19
AL Batting Champion
□ 631 Tim Raines: Letting .75 .35 .09
Go of the Raines
□ 632 Al Oliver .40 .18 .05
Double Trouble
□ 633 Steve Sax .40 .18 .05
AS Second Base
□ 634 Dickie Thon .15 .07 .02
AS Shortstop
□ 635 Ace Firemen .40 .18 .05
Dan Quisenberry
and Tippy Martinez
□ 636 Reds Reunited .75 .35 .09
Joe Morgan
Pete Rose
Tony Perez
□ 637 Backstop Stars .40 .18 .05
Lance Parrish
Bob Boone
□ 638 George Brett and 2.00 .90 .25
Gaylord Perry
Pine Tar 7/24/83
□ 639 1983 No Hitters .40 .18 .05
Dave Righetti
Mike Warren
Bob Forsch
□ 640 Johnny Bench and 2.00 .90 .25
Carl Yastrzemski
Retiring Superstars
□ 641 Gaylord Perry .75 .35 .09
Going Out In Style
□ 642 Steve Carlton .75 .35 .09
300 Club and
Strikeout Record
□ 643 Joe Altobelli and .15 .07 .02
Paul Owens
World Series Managers
□ 644 Rick Dempsey .40 .18 .05
World Series MVP
□ 645 Mike Boddicker .15 .07 .02
WS Rookie Winner
□ 646 Scott McGregor .15 .07 .02
WS Clincher
□ 647 CL: Orioles/Royals .40 .18 .05
Joe Altobelli MG
□ 648 CL: Phillies/Giants .40 .18 .05
Paul Owens MG
□ 649 CL: White Sox/Red Sox .40 .18 .05
Tony LaRussa MG
□ 650 CL: Tigers/Rangers .40 .18 .05
Sparky Anderson MG
□ 651 CL: Dodgers/A's .40 .18 .05
Tommy Lasorda MG
□ 652 CL: Yankees/Reds .40 .18 .05
Billy Martin MG
□ 653 CL: Blue Jays/Cubs .40 .18 .05
Bobby Cox MG
□ 654 CL: Braves/Angels .40 .18 .05
Joe Torre MG
□ 655 CL: Brewers/Indians .40 .18 .05
Rene Lachemann MG
□ 656 CL: Astros/Twins .40 .18 .05
Bob Lillis MG
□ 657 CL: Pirates/Mets .40 .18 .05
Chuck Tanner MG
□ 658 CL: Expos/Mariners .40 .18 .05
Bill Virdon MG
□ 659 CL: Padres/Specials .40 .18 .05
Dick Williams MG
□ 660 CL: Cardinals/Teams .40 .18 .05
Whitey Herzog MG

1984 Fleer Update

This set was Fleer's first update set and portrayed players with their proper team for the current year and to rookies who were not in their regular issue. Like the Topps Traded sets of the time, the Fleer Update sets were distributed in factory set form through hobby dealers only. The set was quite popular with collectors, and, apparently, the print run was relatively short, as the set was quickly in short supply and exhibited a rapid and dramatic price increase. The cards are numbered on the back with a U prefix and placed in alphabetical order by player name. The key (extended) Rookie Cards in this set are Roger Clemens, John Franco, Dwight Gooden, Jimmy Key, Mark Langston, Kirby Puckett, Jose Rijo, and Bret Saberhagen. Collectors are urged to be careful if purchasing single cards of Clemens, Darling, Gooden, Puckett, Rose, or Saberhagen as these specific cards have been illegally reprinted. These fakes are blurry when compared to the real cards.

	NRMT	VG-E	GOOD
COMPLETE FACT.SET (132)	500.00	220.00	60.00
COMMON CARD (1-132)	.50	.23	.06
□ 1 Willie Aikens	.50	.23	.06
□ 2 Luis Aponte	.50	.23	.06
□ 3 Mark Bailey	.50	.23	.06
□ 4 Bob Bailor	.50	.23	.06
□ 5 Dusty Baker	1.00	.45	.12
□ 6 Steve Balboni	.50	.23	.06
□ 7 Alan Bannister	.50	.23	.06
□ 8 Marty Barrett	.75	.35	.09
□ 9 Dave Beard	.50	.23	.06
□ 10 Joe Beckwith	.50	.23	.06
□ 11 Dave Bergman	.50	.23	.06
□ 12 Tony Bernazard	.50	.23	.06
□ 13 Bruce Bochte	.50	.23	.06
□ 14 Barry Bonnell	.50	.23	.06
□ 15 Phil Bradley	.75	.35	.09
□ 16 Fred Breining	.50	.23	.06
□ 17 Mike C. Brown	.50	.23	.06
□ 18 Bill Buckner	.75	.35	.09
□ 19 Ray Burris	.50	.23	.06
□ 20 John Butcher	.50	.23	.06
□ 21 Brett Butler	2.00	.90	.25
□ 22 Enos Cabell	.50	.23	.06
□ 23 Bill Campbell	.50	.23	.06
□ 24 Bill Caudill	.50	.23	.06
□ 25 Bobby Clark	.50	.23	.06
□ 26 Bryan Clark	.50	.23	.06
□ 27 Roger Clemens	175.00	80.00	22.00
□ 28 Jaime Cocanower	.50	.23	.06
□ 29 Ron Darling	1.00	.45	.12
□ 30 Alvin Davis	.75	.35	.09
□ 31 Bob Dernier	.50	.23	.06
□ 32 Carlos Diaz	.50	.23	.06
□ 33 Mike Easler	.50	.23	.06
□ 34 Dennis Eckersley	10.00	4.50	1.25

☐ 35 Jim Essian	.50	.23	.06
☐ 36 Darrell Evans	.75	.35	.09
☐ 37 Mike Fitzgerald	.50	.23	.06
☐ 38 Tim Foli	.50	.23	.06
☐ 39 John Franco	8.00	3.60	1.00
☐ 40 George Frazier	.50	.23	.06
☐ 41 Rich Gale	.50	.23	.06
☐ 42 Barbaro Garbey	.50	.23	.06
☐ 43 Dwight Gooden	40.00	18.00	5.00
☐ 44 Rich Gossage	1.00	.45	.12
☐ 45 Wayne Gross	.50	.23	.06
☐ 46 Mark Gubicza	1.00	.45	.12
☐ 47 Jackie Gutierrez	.50	.23	.06
☐ 48 Toby Harrah	.75	.35	.09
☐ 49 Ron Hassey	.50	.23	.06
☐ 50 Richie Hebner	.50	.23	.06
☐ 51 Willie Hernandez	.75	.35	.09
☐ 52 Ed Hodge	.50	.23	.06
☐ 53 Ricky Horton	.50	.23	.06
☐ 54 Art Howe	.50	.23	.06
☐ 55 Dane Iorg	.50	.23	.06
☐ 56 Brook Jacoby	.75	.35	.09
☐ 57 Dion James	.75	.35	.09
☐ 58 Mike Jeffcoat	.50	.23	.06
☐ 59 Ruppert Jones	.50	.23	.06
☐ 60 Bob Kearney	.50	.23	.06
☐ 61 Jimmy Key	8.00	3.60	1.00
☐ 62 Dave Kingman	.75	.35	.09
☐ 63 Brad Komminsk	.50	.23	.06
☐ 64 Jerry Koosman	.75	.35	.09
☐ 65 Wayne Krenchicki	.50	.23	.06
☐ 66 Rusty Kuntz	.50	.23	.06
☐ 67 Frank LaCorte	.50	.23	.06
☐ 68 Dennis Lamp	.50	.23	.06
☐ 69 Tito Landrum	.50	.23	.06
☐ 70 Mark Langston	10.00	4.50	1.25
☐ 71 Rick Leach	.50	.23	.06
☐ 72 Craig Lefferts	.75	.35	.09
☐ 73 Gary Lucas	.50	.23	.06
☐ 74 Jerry Martin	.50	.23	.06
☐ 75 Carmelo Martinez	.50	.23	.06
☐ 76 Mike Mason	.50	.23	.06
☐ 77 Gary Matthews	.50	.23	.06
☐ 78 Andy McGaffigan	.50	.23	.06
☐ 79 Joey McLaughlin	.50	.23	.06
☐ 80 Joe Morgan	6.00	2.70	.75
☐ 81 Darryl Motley	.50	.23	.06
☐ 82 Graig Nettles	.75	.35	.09
☐ 83 Phil Niekro	2.00	.90	.25
☐ 84 Ken Oberkfell	.50	.23	.06
☐ 85 Al Oliver	.75	.35	.09
☐ 86 Jorge Orta	.50	.23	.06
☐ 87 Amos Otis	.75	.35	.09
☐ 88 Bob Owchinko	.50	.23	.06
☐ 89 Dave Parker	.75	.35	.09
☐ 90 Jack Perconte	.50	.23	.06
☐ 91 Tony Perez	3.00	1.35	.35
☐ 92 Gerald Perry	.75	.35	.09
☐ 93 Kirby Puckett	250.00	110.00	31.00
☐ 94 Shane Rawley	.50	.23	.06
☐ 95 Floyd Rayford	.50	.23	.06
☐ 96 Ron Reed	.50	.23	.06
☐ 97 R.J. Reynolds	.50	.23	.06
☐ 98 Gene Richards	.50	.23	.06
☐ 99 Jose Rijo	8.00	3.60	1.00
☐ 100 Jeff D. Robinson	.50	.23	.06
☐ 101 Ron Romanick	.50	.23	.06
☐ 102 Pete Rose	25.00	11.00	3.10
☐ 103 Bret Saberhagen	10.00	4.50	1.25
☐ 104 Scott Sanderson	.50	.23	.06
☐ 105 Dick Schofield	.75	.35	.09
☐ 106 Tom Seaver	12.00	5.50	1.50
☐ 107 Jim Slaton	.50	.23	.06
☐ 108 Mike Smithson	.50	.23	.06
☐ 109 Lary Sorensen	.50	.23	.06
☐ 110 Tim Stoddard	.50	.23	.06
☐ 111 Jeff Stone	.50	.23	.06
☐ 112 Champ Summers	.50	.23	.06
☐ 113 Jim Sundberg	.75	.35	.09
☐ 114 Rick Sutcliffe	.75	.35	.09
☐ 115 Craig Swan	.50	.23	.06
☐ 116 Derrel Thomas	.50	.23	.06
☐ 117 Gorman Thomas	.50	.23	.06
☐ 118 Alex Trevino	.50	.23	.06
☐ 119 Manny Trillo	.50	.23	.06
☐ 120 John Tudor	.50	.23	.06
☐ 121 Tom Underwood	.50	.23	.06
☐ 122 Mike Vail	.50	.23	.06
☐ 123 Tom Waddell	.50	.23	.06
☐ 124 Gary Ward	.50	.23	.06
☐ 125 Terry Whitfield	.50	.23	.06
☐ 126 Curtis Wilkerson	.50	.23	.06
☐ 127 Frank Williams	.50	.23	.06
☐ 128 Glenn Wilson	.75	.35	.09
☐ 129 John Wockenfuss	.50	.23	.06
☐ 130 Ned Yost	.50	.23	.06
☐ 131 Mike Young	.50	.23	.06
☐ 132 Checklist 1-132	.50	.23	.06

1984 Fleer Stickers

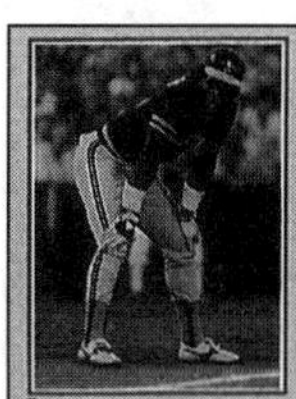

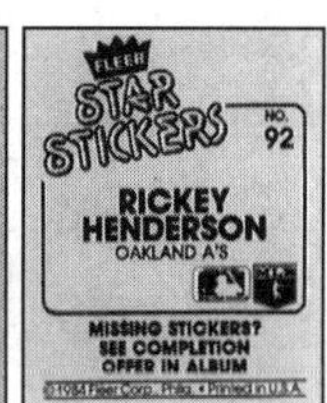

The stickers in this 126-sticker set measure approximately 1 15/16" by 2 1/2". The 1984 Fleer sticker set is a very attractive set with a beige border. Many players are featured more than once in the set due to the fact that the album issued to house the set contains league leader categories in which to place the stickers. The checklist below is ordered by categories, e.g., Game Winning RBI's (1-5), Batting Average (6-15), Home Runs (16-23), Hits (24-31), Slugging Percentage (32-39), Pinch Hits (40-43), Designated Hitter's Hits (44-47), On Base Percentage (48-55), Won/Lost Percentage (56-64), Earned Run Average (65-66), Saves (67-77), Strikeouts (78-87), Stolen Bases (88-95), Future Hall of Famers (96-103), Rookie Stars (104-113), World Series Batting (114-122) and Playoff Managers (123-126). These stickers were originally issued in packs of six for 25 cents plus a team logo.

	NRMT	VG-E	GOOD
COMPLETE SET (126)	12.00	5.50	1.50
COMMON STICKER (1-126)	.05	.02	.01
☐ 1 Dickie Thon	.05	.02	.01
☐ 2 Ken Landreaux	.05	.02	.01
☐ 3 Darrell Evans	.10	.05	.01
☐ 4 Harold Baines	.10	.05	.01
☐ 5 Dave Winfield	.30	.14	.04
☐ 6 Bill Madlock	.05	.02	.01
☐ 7 Lonnie Smith	.05	.02	.01
☐ 8 Jose Cruz	.10	.05	.01
☐ 9 George Hendrick	.05	.02	.01
☐ 10 Ray Knight	.10	.05	.01
☐ 11 Wade Boggs	.50	.23	.06
☐ 12 Rod Carew	.30	.14	.04
☐ 13 Lou Whitaker	.10	.05	.01
☐ 14 Alan Trammell	.15	.07	.02
☐ 15 Cal Ripken	2.00	.90	.25
☐ 16 Mike Schmidt	.50	.23	.06
☐ 17 Dale Murphy	.15	.07	.02
☐ 18 Andre Dawson	.15	.07	.02
☐ 19 Pedro Guerrero	.10	.05	.01
☐ 20 Jim Rice	.10	.05	.01
☐ 21 Tony Armas	.05	.02	.01
☐ 22 Ron Kittle	.05	.02	.01
☐ 23 Eddie Murray	.30	.14	.04
☐ 24 Jose Cruz	.10	.05	.01
☐ 25 Andre Dawson	.15	.07	.02
☐ 26 Rafael Ramirez	.05	.02	.01
☐ 27 Al Oliver	.10	.05	.01
☐ 28 Wade Boggs	.50	.23	.06
☐ 29 Cal Ripken	2.00	.90	.25
☐ 30 Lou Whitaker	.10	.05	.01
☐ 31 Cecil Cooper	.10	.05	.01
☐ 32 Dale Murphy	.15	.07	.02
☐ 33 Andre Dawson	.15	.07	.02
☐ 34 Pedro Guerrero	.10	.05	.01
☐ 35 Mike Schmidt	.50	.23	.06
☐ 36 George Brett	1.00	.45	.12
☐ 37 Jim Rice	.10	.05	.01
☐ 38 Eddie Murray	.40	.18	.05
☐ 39 Carlton Fisk	.40	.18	.05
☐ 40 Rusty Staub	.10	.05	.01
☐ 41 Duane Walker	.05	.02	.01
☐ 42 Steve Braun	.05	.02	.01
☐ 43 Kurt Bevacqua	.05	.02	.01
☐ 44 Hal McRae	.10	.05	.01
☐ 45 Don Baylor	.10	.05	.01
☐ 46 Ken Singleton	.05	.02	.01
☐ 47 Greg Luzinski	.10	.05	.01
☐ 48 Mike Schmidt	.50	.23	.06
☐ 49 Keith Hernandez	.10	.05	.01
☐ 50 Dale Murphy	.15	.07	.02
☐ 51 Tim Raines	.15	.07	.02
☐ 52 Wade Boggs	.50	.23	.06
☐ 53 Rickey Henderson	.40	.18	.05
☐ 54 Rod Carew	.30	.14	.04
☐ 55 Ken Singleton	.05	.02	.01
☐ 56 John Denny	.05	.02	.01
☐ 57 John Candelaria	.05	.02	.01
☐ 58 Larry McWilliams	.05	.02	.01
☐ 59 Pascual Perez	.05	.02	.01
☐ 60 Jesse Orosco	.05	.02	.01
☐ 61 Moose Haas	.05	.02	.01
☐ 62 Richard Dotson	.05	.02	.01
☐ 63 Mike Flanagan	.05	.02	.01
☐ 64 Scott McGregor	.05	.02	.01
☐ 65 Atlee Hammaker	.05	.02	.01
☐ 66 Rick Honeycutt	.05	.02	.01
☐ 67 Lee Smith	.15	.07	.02
☐ 68 Al Holland	.05	.02	.01
☐ 69 Greg Minton	.05	.02	.01
☐ 70 Bruce Sutter	.10	.05	.01
☐ 71 Jeff Reardon	.10	.05	.01
☐ 72 Frank DiPino	.05	.02	.01
☐ 73 Dan Quisenberry	.05	.02	.01
☐ 74 Bob Stanley	.05	.02	.01
☐ 75 Ron Davis	.05	.02	.01
☐ 76 Bill Caudill	.05	.02	.01
☐ 77 Peter Ladd	.05	.02	.01
☐ 78 Steve Carlton	.30	.14	.04
☐ 79 Mario Soto	.05	.02	.01
☐ 80 Larry McWilliams	.05	.02	.01
☐ 81 Fernando Valenzuela	.10	.05	.01
☐ 82 Nolan Ryan	2.00	.90	.25
☐ 83 Jack Morris	.10	.05	.01
☐ 84 Floyd Bannister	.05	.02	.01
☐ 85 Dave Stieb	.05	.02	.01
☐ 86 Dave Righetti	.05	.02	.01
☐ 87 Rick Sutcliffe	.10	.05	.01
☐ 88 Tim Raines	.15	.07	.02
☐ 89 Alan Wiggins	.05	.02	.01
☐ 90 Steve Sax	.10	.05	.01
☐ 91 Mookie Wilson	.10	.05	.01
☐ 92 Rickey Henderson	.40	.18	.05
☐ 93 Rudy Law	.05	.02	.01
☐ 94 Willie Wilson	.05	.02	.01
☐ 95 Julio Cruz	.05	.02	.01
☐ 96 Johnny Bench	.40	.18	.05
☐ 97 Carl Yastrzemski	.30	.14	.04
☐ 98 Gaylord Perry	.20	.09	.03
☐ 99 Pete Rose	.75	.35	.09
☐ 100 Joe Morgan	.20	.09	.03
☐ 101 Steve Carlton	.30	.14	.04
☐ 102 Jim Palmer	.20	.09	.03
☐ 103 Rod Carew	.40	.18	.05
☐ 104 Darryl Strawberry	.75	.35	.09
☐ 105 Craig McMurtry	.05	.02	.01
☐ 106 Mel Hall	.05	.02	.01
☐ 107 Lee Tunnell	.05	.02	.01
☐ 108 Bill Dawley	.05	.02	.01
☐ 109 Ron Kittle	.05	.02	.01
☐ 110 Mike Boddicker	.05	.02	.01
☐ 111 Julio Franco	.20	.09	.03
☐ 112 Daryl Sconiers	.05	.02	.01
☐ 113 Neal Heaton	.05	.02	.01
☐ 114 John Shelby	.05	.02	.01
☐ 115 Rick Dempsey	.05	.02	.01
☐ 116 John Lowenstein	.05	.02	.01
☐ 117 Jim Dwyer	.05	.02	.01
☐ 118 Bo Diaz	.05	.02	.01
☐ 119 Pete Rose	.75	.35	.09
☐ 120 Joe Morgan	.20	.09	.03
☐ 121 Gary Matthews	.05	.02	.01
☐ 122 Garry Maddox	.05	.02	.01
☐ 123 Paul Owens MG	.05	.02	.01
☐ 124 Tom Lasorda MG	.20	.09	.03
☐ 125 Joe Altobelli MG	.05	.02	.01
☐ 126 Tony LaRussa MG	.10	.05	.01

1985 Fleer

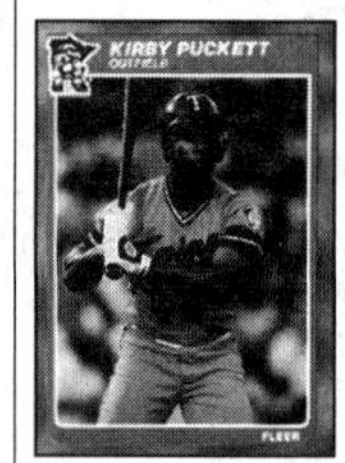

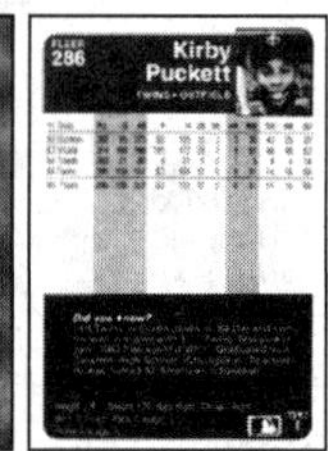

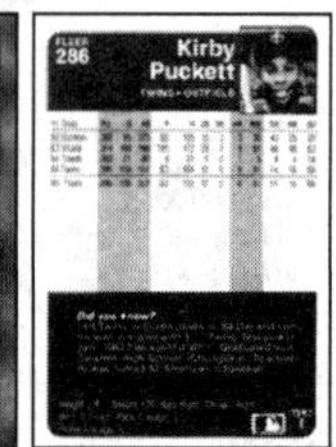

The 1985 Fleer set consists of 660 standard-size cards. Wax packs contained 15 cards plus logo stickers. Card fronts feature a full color photo, team logo along with the player's name and position. The borders enclosing the photo are color-coded to correspond to the player's team. The cards are ordered alphabetically within team. The teams are ordered based on their respective performance during the prior year. Subsets include Specials (626-643) and Major League Prospects (644-653). The black and white photo on the reverse is included for the third straight year. Notable Rookie Cards include Roger Clemens, Eric Davis, Shawon Dunston, John Franco, Dwight Gooden, Orel Hershiser, Jimmy Key, Mark Langston, Terry Pendleton, Kirby Puckett, Jose Rijo, Bret Saberhagen, and Danny Tartabull.

	NRMT	VG-E	GOOD
COMPLETE SET (660)	120.00	55.00	15.00
COMMON CARD (1-660)	.10	.05	.01
☐ 1 Doug Bair	.10	.05	.01
☐ 2 Juan Berenguer	.10	.05	.01
☐ 3 Dave Bergman	.10	.05	.01
☐ 4 Tom Brookens	.10	.05	.01
☐ 5 Marty Castillo	.10	.05	.01
☐ 6 Darrell Evans	.20	.09	.03
☐ 7 Barbaro Garbey	.10	.05	.01
☐ 8 Kirk Gibson	.20	.09	.03
☐ 9 John Grubb	.10	.05	.01
☐ 10 Willie Hernandez	.10	.05	.01
☐ 11 Larry Herndon	.10	.05	.01
☐ 12 Howard Johnson	.20	.09	.03
☐ 13 Ruppert Jones	.10	.05	.01
☐ 14 Rusty Kuntz	.10	.05	.01
☐ 15 Chet Lemon	.10	.05	.01
☐ 16 Aurelio Lopez	.10	.05	.01
☐ 17 Sid Monge	.10	.05	.01
☐ 18 Jack Morris	.20	.09	.03
☐ 19 Lance Parrish	.20	.09	.03
☐ 20 Dan Petry	.10	.05	.01
☐ 21 Dave Rozema	.10	.05	.01
☐ 22 Bill Scherrer	.10	.05	.01
☐ 23 Alan Trammell	.40	.18	.05
☐ 24 Lou Whitaker	.40	.18	.05
☐ 25 Milt Wilcox	.10	.05	.01
☐ 26 Kurt Bevacqua	.10	.05	.01
☐ 27 Greg Booker	.10	.05	.01
☐ 28 Bobby Brown	.10	.05	.01
☐ 29 Luis DeLeon	.10	.05	.01
☐ 30 Dave Dravecky	.20	.09	.03
☐ 31 Tim Flannery	.10	.05	.01
☐ 32 Steve Garvey	.40	.18	.05
☐ 33 Rich Gossage	.40	.18	.05
☐ 34 Tony Gwynn	6.00	2.70	.75
☐ 35 Greg Harris	.10	.05	.01
☐ 36 Andy Hawkins	.10	.05	.01
☐ 37 Terry Kennedy	.10	.05	.01
☐ 38 Craig Lefferts	.10	.05	.01
☐ 39 Tim Lollar	.10	.05	.01
☐ 40 Carmelo Martinez	.10	.05	.01
☐ 41 Kevin McReynolds	.20	.09	.03
☐ 42 Graig Nettles	.20	.09	.03
☐ 43 Luis Salazar	.10	.05	.01
☐ 44 Eric Show	.10	.05	.01
☐ 45 Garry Templeton	.10	.05	.01
☐ 46 Mark Thurmond	.10	.05	.01
☐ 47 Ed Whitson	.10	.05	.01
☐ 48 Alan Wiggins	.10	.05	.01
☐ 49 Rich Bordi	.10	.05	.01
☐ 50 Larry Bowa	.20	.09	.03
☐ 51 Warren Brusstar	.10	.05	.01
☐ 52 Ron Cey	.20	.09	.03
☐ 53 Henry Cotto	.10	.05	.01
☐ 54 Jody Davis	.10	.05	.01
☐ 55 Bob Dernier	.10	.05	.01
☐ 56 Leon Durham	.10	.05	.01
☐ 57 Dennis Eckersley	.40	.18	.05
☐ 58 George Frazier	.10	.05	.01
☐ 59 Richie Hebner	.10	.05	.01
☐ 60 Dave Lopes	.20	.09	.03
☐ 61 Gary Matthews	.10	.05	.01
☐ 62 Keith Moreland	.10	.05	.01
☐ 63 Rick Reuschel	.10	.05	.01
☐ 64 Dick Ruthven	.10	.05	.01
☐ 65 Ryne Sandberg	5.00	2.20	.60
☐ 66 Scott Sanderson	.10	.05	.01
☐ 67 Lee Smith	1.00	.45	.12
☐ 68 Tim Stoddard	.10	.05	.01
☐ 69 Rick Sutcliffe	.10	.05	.01
☐ 70 Steve Trout	.10	.05	.01
☐ 71 Gary Woods	.10	.05	.01
☐ 72 Wally Backman	.10	.05	.01
☐ 73 Bruce Berenyi	.10	.05	.01
☐ 74 Hubie Brooks UER (Kelvin Chapman's stats on card back)	.10	.05	.01
☐ 75 Kelvin Chapman	.10	.05	.01
☐ 76 Ron Darling	.20	.09	.03
☐ 77 Sid Fernandez	.40	.18	.05
☐ 78 Mike Fitzgerald	.10	.05	.01
☐ 79 George Foster	.20	.09	.03
☐ 80 Brent Gaff	.10	.05	.01
☐ 81 Ron Gardenhire	.10	.05	.01
☐ 82 Dwight Gooden	4.00	1.80	.50
☐ 83 Tom Gorman	.10	.05	.01
☐ 84 Danny Heep	.10	.05	.01
☐ 85 Keith Hernandez	.20	.09	.03
☐ 86 Ray Knight	.20	.09	.03
☐ 87 Ed Lynch	.10	.05	.01
☐ 88 Jose Oquendo	.10	.05	.01
☐ 89 Jesse Orosco	.10	.05	.01
☐ 90 Rafael Santana	.10	.05	.01
☐ 91 Doug Sisk	.10	.05	.01
☐ 92 Rusty Staub	.20	.09	.03
☐ 93 Darryl Strawberry	1.00	.45	.12
☐ 94 Walt Terrell	.10	.05	.01
☐ 95 Mookie Wilson	.20	.09	.03
☐ 96 Jim Acker	.10	.05	.01
☐ 97 Willie Aikens	.10	.05	.01
☐ 98 Doyle Alexander	.10	.05	.01
☐ 99 Jesse Barfield	.10	.05	.01
☐ 100 George Bell	.20	.09	.03
☐ 101 Jim Clancy	.10	.05	.01
☐ 102 Dave Collins	.10	.05	.01
☐ 103 Tony Fernandez	.20	.09	.03
☐ 104 Damaso Garcia	.10	.05	.01
☐ 105 Jim Gott	.10	.05	.01
☐ 106 Alfredo Griffin	.10	.05	.01
☐ 107 Garth Iorg	.10	.05	.01
☐ 108 Roy Lee Jackson	.10	.05	.01
☐ 109 Cliff Johnson	.10	.05	.01
☐ 110 Jimmy Key	1.00	.45	.12
☐ 111 Dennis Lamp	.10	.05	.01
☐ 112 Rick Leach	.10	.05	.01
☐ 113 Luis Leal	.10	.05	.01
☐ 114 Buck Martinez	.10	.05	.01
☐ 115 Lloyd Moseby	.10	.05	.01
☐ 116 Rance Mulliniks	.10	.05	.01
☐ 117 Dave Stieb	.20	.09	.03
☐ 118 Willie Upshaw	.10	.05	.01
☐ 119 Ernie Whitt	.10	.05	.01
☐ 120 Mike Armstrong	.10	.05	.01
☐ 121 Don Baylor	.40	.18	.05
☐ 122 Marty Bystrom	.10	.05	.01
☐ 123 Rick Cerone	.10	.05	.01
☐ 124 Joe Cowley	.10	.05	.01
☐ 125 Brian Dayett	.10	.05	.01
☐ 126 Tim Foli	.10	.05	.01
☐ 127 Ray Fontenot	.10	.05	.01
☐ 128 Ken Griffey	.20	.09	.03

☐ 129 Ron Guidry .20 .09 .03
☐ 130 Toby Harrah .10 .05 .01
☐ 131 Jay Howell .10 .05 .01
☐ 132 Steve Kemp .10 .05 .01
☐ 133 Don Mattingly 8.00 3.60 1.00
☐ 134 Bobby Meacham .10 .05 .01
☐ 135 John Montefusco .10 .05 .01
☐ 136 Omar Moreno .10 .05 .01
☐ 137 Dale Murray .10 .05 .01
☐ 138 Phil Niekro .40 .18 .05
☐ 139 Mike Pagliarulo .10 .05 .01
☐ 140 Willie Randolph .20 .09 .03
☐ 141 Dennis Rasmussen .10 .05 .01
☐ 142 Dave Righetti .20 .09 .03
☐ 143 Jose Rijo 1.00 .45 .12
☐ 144 Andre Robertson .10 .05 .01
☐ 145 Bob Shirley .10 .05 .01
☐ 146 Dave Winfield 1.50 .70 .19
☐ 147 Butch Wynegar .10 .05 .01
☐ 148 Gary Allenson .10 .05 .01
☐ 149 Tony Armas .10 .05 .01
☐ 150 Marty Barrett .10 .05 .01
☐ 151 Wade Boggs 2.50 1.10 .30
☐ 152 Dennis Boyd .10 .05 .01
☐ 153 Bill Buckner .20 .09 .03
☐ 154 Mark Clear .10 .05 .01
☐ 155 Roger Clemens 18.00 8.00 2.20
☐ 156 Steve Crawford .10 .05 .01
☐ 157 Mike Easler .10 .05 .01
☐ 158 Dwight Evans .20 .09 .03
☐ 159 Rich Gedman .10 .05 .01
☐ 160 Jackie Gutierrez .20 .09 .03
(Wade Boggs
shown on deck)
☐ 161 Bruce Hurst .10 .05 .01
☐ 162 John Henry Johnson .10 .05 .01
☐ 163 Rick Miller .10 .05 .01
☐ 164 Reid Nichols .10 .05 .01
☐ 165 Al Nipper .10 .05 .01
☐ 166 Bob Ojeda .10 .05 .01
☐ 167 Jerry Remy .10 .05 .01
☐ 168 Jim Rice .20 .09 .03
☐ 169 Bob Stanley .10 .05 .01
☐ 170 Mike Boddicker .10 .05 .01
☐ 171 Al Bumbry .10 .05 .01
☐ 172 Todd Cruz .10 .05 .01
☐ 173 Rich Dauer .10 .05 .01
☐ 174 Storm Davis .10 .05 .01
☐ 175 Rick Dempsey .10 .05 .01
☐ 176 Jim Dwyer .10 .05 .01
☐ 177 Mike Flanagan .10 .05 .01
☐ 178 Dan Ford .10 .05 .01
☐ 179 Wayne Gross .10 .05 .01
☐ 180 John Lowenstein .10 .05 .01
☐ 181 Dennis Martinez .20 .09 .03
☐ 182 Tippy Martinez .10 .05 .01
☐ 183 Scott McGregor .10 .05 .01
☐ 184 Eddie Murray 2.50 1.10 .30
☐ 185 Joe Nolan .10 .05 .01
☐ 186 Floyd Rayford .10 .05 .01
☐ 187 Cal Ripken 8.00 3.60 1.00
☐ 188 Gary Roenicke .10 .05 .01
☐ 189 Lenn Sakata .10 .05 .01
☐ 190 John Shelby .10 .05 .01
☐ 191 Ken Singleton .10 .05 .01
☐ 192 Sammy Stewart .10 .05 .01
☐ 193 Bill Swaggerty .10 .05 .01
☐ 194 Tom Underwood .10 .05 .01
☐ 195 Mike Young .10 .05 .01
☐ 196 Steve Balboni .10 .05 .01
☐ 197 Joe Beckwith .10 .05 .01
☐ 198 Bud Black .10 .05 .01
☐ 199 George Brett 4.00 1.80 .50
☐ 200 Onix Concepcion .10 .05 .01
☐ 201 Mark Gubicza .40 .18 .05
☐ 202 Larry Gura .10 .05 .01
☐ 203 Mark Huismann .10 .05 .01
☐ 204 Dane Iorg .10 .05 .01
☐ 205 Danny Jackson .10 .05 .01
☐ 206 Charlie Leibrandt .10 .05 .01
☐ 207 Hal McRae .20 .09 .03
☐ 208 Darryl Motley .10 .05 .01
☐ 209 Jorge Orta .10 .05 .01
☐ 210 Greg Pryor .10 .05 .01
☐ 211 Dan Quisenberry .20 .09 .03
☐ 212 Bret Saberhagen 1.50 .70 .19
☐ 213 Pat Sheridan .10 .05 .01
☐ 214 Don Slaught .10 .05 .01
☐ 215 U.L. Washington .10 .05 .01
☐ 216 John Wathan .10 .05 .01
☐ 217 Frank White .20 .09 .03
☐ 218 Willie Wilson .10 .05 .01
☐ 219 Neil Allen .10 .05 .01
☐ 220 Joaquin Andujar .10 .05 .01
☐ 221 Steve Braun .10 .05 .01
☐ 222 Danny Cox .10 .05 .01
☐ 223 Bob Forsch .10 .05 .01
☐ 224 David Green .10 .05 .01
☐ 225 George Hendrick .10 .05 .01
☐ 226 Tom Herr .20 .09 .03
☐ 227 Ricky Horton .10 .05 .01
☐ 228 Art Howe .10 .05 .01
☐ 229 Mike Jorgensen .10 .05 .01
☐ 230 Kurt Kepshire .10 .05 .01
☐ 231 Jeff Lahti .10 .05 .01
☐ 232 Tito Landrum .10 .05 .01
☐ 233 Dave LaPoint .10 .05 .01
☐ 234 Willie McGee .20 .09 .03
☐ 235 Tom Nieto .10 .05 .01
☐ 236 Terry Pendleton 1.50 .70 .19
☐ 237 Darrell Porter .10 .05 .01
☐ 238 Dave Rucker .10 .05 .01
☐ 239 Lonnie Smith .10 .05 .01
☐ 240 Ozzie Smith 2.50 1.10 .30
☐ 241 Bruce Sutter .20 .09 .03
☐ 242 Andy Van Slyke UER .40 .18 .05
(Bats Right,
Throws Left)
☐ 243 Dave Von Ohlen .10 .05 .01
☐ 244 Larry Andersen .10 .05 .01
☐ 245 Bill Campbell .10 .05 .01
☐ 246 Steve Carlton .75 .35 .09
☐ 247 Tim Corcoran .10 .05 .01
☐ 248 Ivan DeJesus .10 .05 .01
☐ 249 John Denny .10 .05 .01
☐ 250 Bo Diaz .10 .05 .01
☐ 251 Greg Gross .10 .05 .01
☐ 252 Kevin Gross .10 .05 .01
☐ 253 Von Hayes .10 .05 .01
☐ 254 Al Holland .10 .05 .01
☐ 255 Charles Hudson .10 .05 .01
☐ 256 Jerry Koosman .10 .05 .01
☐ 257 Joe Lefebvre .10 .05 .01
☐ 258 Sixto Lezcano .10 .05 .01
☐ 259 Garry Maddox .10 .05 .01
☐ 260 Len Matuszek .10 .05 .01
☐ 261 Tug McGraw .20 .09 .03
☐ 262 Al Oliver .20 .09 .03
☐ 263 Shane Rawley .10 .05 .01
☐ 264 Juan Samuel .10 .05 .01
☐ 265 Mike Schmidt 2.50 1.10 .30
☐ 266 Jeff Stone .10 .05 .01
☐ 267 Ozzie Virgil .10 .05 .01
☐ 268 Glenn Wilson .10 .05 .01
☐ 269 John Wockenfuss .10 .05 .01
☐ 270 Darrell Brown .10 .05 .01
☐ 271 Tom Brunansky .20 .09 .03
☐ 272 Randy Bush .10 .05 .01
☐ 273 John Butcher .10 .05 .01
☐ 274 Bobby Castillo .10 .05 .01
☐ 275 Ron Davis .10 .05 .01
☐ 276 Dave Engle .10 .05 .01
☐ 277 Pete Filson .10 .05 .01
☐ 278 Gary Gaetti .20 .09 .03
☐ 279 Mickey Hatcher .10 .05 .01
☐ 280 Ed Hodge .10 .05 .01
☐ 281 Kent Hrbek .20 .09 .03
☐ 282 Houston Jimenez .10 .05 .01
☐ 283 Tim Laudner .10 .05 .01
☐ 284 Rick Lysander .10 .05 .01
☐ 285 Dave Meier .10 .05 .01
☐ 286 Kirby Puckett 30.00 13.50 3.70
☐ 287 Pat Putnam .10 .05 .01
☐ 288 Ken Schrom .10 .05 .01
☐ 289 Mike Smithson .10 .05 .01
☐ 290 Tim Teufel .10 .05 .01
☐ 291 Frank Viola .20 .09 .03
☐ 292 Ron Washington .10 .05 .01
☐ 293 Don Aase .10 .05 .01
☐ 294 Juan Beniquez .10 .05 .01
☐ 295 Bob Boone .20 .09 .03
☐ 296 Mike C. Brown .10 .05 .01
☐ 297 Rod Carew .60 .25 .07
☐ 298 Doug Corbett .10 .05 .01
☐ 299 Doug DeCinces .10 .05 .01
☐ 300 Brian Downing .10 .05 .01
☐ 301 Ken Forsch .10 .05 .01
☐ 302 Bobby Grich .20 .09 .03
☐ 303 Reggie Jackson 1.50 .70 .19
☐ 304 Tommy John .40 .18 .05
☐ 305 Curt Kaufman .10 .05 .01
☐ 306 Bruce Kison .10 .05 .01
☐ 307 Fred Lynn .20 .09 .03
☐ 308 Gary Pettis .10 .05 .01
☐ 309 Ron Romanick .10 .05 .01
☐ 310 Luis Sanchez .10 .05 .01
☐ 311 Dick Schofield .10 .05 .01
☐ 312 Daryl Sconiers .10 .05 .01
☐ 313 Jim Slaton .10 .05 .01
☐ 314 Derrel Thomas .10 .05 .01
☐ 315 Rob Wilfong .10 .05 .01
☐ 316 Mike Witt .10 .05 .01
☐ 317 Geoff Zahn .10 .05 .01
☐ 318 Len Barker .10 .05 .01
☐ 319 Steve Bedrosian .10 .05 .01
☐ 320 Bruce Benedict .10 .05 .01
☐ 321 Rick Camp .10 .05 .01
☐ 322 Chris Chambliss .10 .05 .01
☐ 323 Jeff Dedmon .10 .05 .01
☐ 324 Terry Forster .10 .05 .01
☐ 325 Gene Garber .10 .05 .01
☐ 326 Albert Hall .10 .05 .01
☐ 327 Terry Harper .10 .05 .01
☐ 328 Bob Horner .10 .05 .01
☐ 329 Glenn Hubbard .10 .05 .01
☐ 330 Randy Johnson .10 .05 .01
☐ 331 Brad Komminsk .10 .05 .01
☐ 332 Rick Mahler .10 .05 .01
☐ 333 Craig McMurtry .10 .05 .01
☐ 334 Donnie Moore .10 .05 .01
☐ 335 Dale Murphy .40 .18 .05
☐ 336 Ken Oberkfell .10 .05 .01
☐ 337 Pascual Perez .10 .05 .01
☐ 338 Gerald Perry .10 .05 .01
☐ 339 Rafael Ramirez .10 .05 .01
☐ 340 Jerry Royster .10 .05 .01
☐ 341 Alex Trevino .10 .05 .01
☐ 342 Claudell Washington .10 .05 .01
☐ 343 Alan Ashby .10 .05 .01
☐ 344 Mark Bailey .10 .05 .01
☐ 345 Kevin Bass .10 .05 .01
☐ 346 Enos Cabell .10 .05 .01
☐ 347 Jose Cruz .20 .09 .03
☐ 348 Bill Dawley .10 .05 .01
☐ 349 Frank DiPino .10 .05 .01
☐ 350 Bill Doran .10 .05 .01
☐ 351 Phil Garner .10 .05 .01
☐ 352 Bob Knepper .10 .05 .01
☐ 353 Mike LaCoss .10 .05 .01
☐ 354 Jerry Mumphrey .10 .05 .01
☐ 355 Joe Niekro .10 .05 .01
☐ 356 Terry Puhl .10 .05 .01
☐ 357 Craig Reynolds .10 .05 .01
☐ 358 Vern Ruhle .10 .05 .01
☐ 359 Nolan Ryan 8.00 3.60 1.00
☐ 360 Joe Sambito .10 .05 .01
☐ 361 Mike Scott .10 .05 .01
☐ 362 Dave Smith .10 .05 .01
☐ 363 Julio Solano .10 .05 .01
☐ 364 Dickie Thon .10 .05 .01
☐ 365 Denny Walling .10 .05 .01
☐ 366 Dave Anderson .10 .05 .01
☐ 367 Bob Bailor .10 .05 .01
☐ 368 Greg Brock .10 .05 .01
☐ 369 Carlos Diaz .10 .05 .01
☐ 370 Pedro Guerrero .20 .09 .03
☐ 371 Orel Hershiser 2.50 1.10 .30
☐ 372 Rick Honeycutt .10 .05 .01
☐ 373 Burt Hooton .10 .05 .01
☐ 374 Ken Howell .10 .05 .01
☐ 375 Ken Landreaux .10 .05 .01
☐ 376 Candy Maldonado .10 .05 .01
☐ 377 Mike Marshall .10 .05 .01
☐ 378 Tom Niedenfuer .10 .05 .01
☐ 379 Alejandro Pena .10 .05 .01
☐ 380 Jerry Reuss UER .10 .05 .01
("Home:" omitted)
☐ 381 R.J. Reynolds .10 .05 .01
☐ 382 German Rivera .10 .05 .01
☐ 383 Bill Russell .10 .05 .01
☐ 384 Steve Sax .20 .09 .03
☐ 385 Mike Scioscia .10 .05 .01
☐ 386 Franklin Stubbs .10 .05 .01
☐ 387 Fernando Valenzuela .20 .09 .03
☐ 388 Bob Welch .10 .05 .01
☐ 389 Terry Whitfield .10 .05 .01
☐ 390 Steve Yeager .10 .05 .01
☐ 391 Pat Zachry .10 .05 .01
☐ 392 Fred Breining .10 .05 .01
☐ 393 Gary Carter .20 .09 .03
☐ 394 Andre Dawson 1.25 .55 .16
☐ 395 Miguel Dilone .10 .05 .01
☐ 396 Dan Driessen .10 .05 .01
☐ 397 Doug Flynn .10 .05 .01
☐ 398 Terry Francona .10 .05 .01
☐ 399 Bill Gullickson .10 .05 .01
☐ 400 Bob James .10 .05 .01
☐ 401 Charlie Lea .10 .05 .01
☐ 402 Bryan Little .10 .05 .01
☐ 403 Gary Lucas .10 .05 .01
☐ 404 David Palmer .10 .05 .01
☐ 405 Tim Raines .20 .09 .03
☐ 406 Mike Ramsey .10 .05 .01
☐ 407 Jeff Reardon .20 .09 .03
☐ 408 Steve Rogers .10 .05 .01
☐ 409 Dan Schatzeder .10 .05 .01
☐ 410 Bryn Smith .10 .05 .01
☐ 411 Mike Stenhouse .10 .05 .01
☐ 412 Tim Wallach .20 .09 .03
☐ 413 Jim Wohlford .10 .05 .01
☐ 414 Bill Almon .10 .05 .01
☐ 415 Keith Atherton .10 .05 .01
☐ 416 Bruce Bochte .10 .05 .01
☐ 417 Tom Burgmeier .10 .05 .01
☐ 418 Ray Burris .10 .05 .01
☐ 419 Bill Caudill .10 .05 .01
☐ 420 Chris Codiroli .10 .05 .01
☐ 421 Tim Conroy .10 .05 .01
☐ 422 Mike Davis .10 .05 .01
☐ 423 Jim Essian .10 .05 .01
☐ 424 Mike Heath .10 .05 .01
☐ 425 Rickey Henderson 1.50 .70 .19
☐ 426 Donnie Hill .10 .05 .01
☐ 427 Dave Kingman .20 .09 .03
☐ 428 Bill Krueger .10 .05 .01
☐ 429 Carney Lansford .20 .09 .03
☐ 430 Steve McCatty .10 .05 .01
☐ 431 Joe Morgan .50 .23 .06
☐ 432 Dwayne Murphy .10 .05 .01
☐ 433 Tony Phillips .40 .18 .05
☐ 434 Lary Sorensen .10 .05 .01
☐ 435 Mike Warren .10 .05 .01
☐ 436 Curt Young .10 .05 .01
☐ 437 Luis Aponte .10 .05 .01
☐ 438 Chris Bando .10 .05 .01
☐ 439 Tony Bernazard .10 .05 .01
☐ 440 Bert Blyleven .40 .18 .05
☐ 441 Brett Butler .20 .09 .03
☐ 442 Ernie Camacho .10 .05 .01
☐ 443 Joe Carter 5.00 2.20 .60
☐ 444 Carmelo Castillo .10 .05 .01
☐ 445 Jamie Easterly .10 .05 .01
☐ 446 Steve Farr .20 .09 .03
☐ 447 Mike Fischlin .10 .05 .01
☐ 448 Julio Franco .40 .18 .05
☐ 449 Mel Hall .10 .05 .01
☐ 450 Mike Hargrove .20 .09 .03
☐ 451 Neal Heaton .10 .05 .01
☐ 452 Brook Jacoby .10 .05 .01
☐ 453 Mike Jeffcoat .10 .05 .01
☐ 454 Don Schulze .10 .05 .01
☐ 455 Roy Smith .10 .05 .01
☐ 456 Pat Tabler .10 .05 .01
☐ 457 Andre Thornton .10 .05 .01
☐ 458 George Vukovich .10 .05 .01
☐ 459 Tom Waddell .10 .05 .01
☐ 460 Jerry Willard .10 .05 .01
☐ 461 Dale Berra .10 .05 .01
☐ 462 John Candelaria .10 .05 .01
☐ 463 Jose DeLeon .10 .05 .01
☐ 464 Doug Frobel .10 .05 .01
☐ 465 Cecilio Guante .10 .05 .01
☐ 466 Brian Harper .20 .09 .03
☐ 467 Lee Lacy .10 .05 .01
☐ 468 Bill Madlock .10 .05 .01
☐ 469 Lee Mazzilli .10 .05 .01
☐ 470 Larry McWilliams .10 .05 .01
☐ 471 Jim Morrison .10 .05 .01
☐ 472 Tony Pena .10 .05 .01
☐ 473 Johnny Ray .10 .05 .01
☐ 474 Rick Rhoden .10 .05 .01
☐ 475 Don Robinson .10 .05 .01
☐ 476 Rod Scurry .10 .05 .01
☐ 477 Kent Tekulve .10 .05 .01
☐ 478 Jason Thompson .10 .05 .01
☐ 479 John Tudor .10 .05 .01
☐ 480 Lee Tunnell .10 .05 .01
☐ 481 Marvell Wynne .10 .05 .01
☐ 482 Salome Barojas .10 .05 .01
☐ 483 Dave Beard .10 .05 .01
☐ 484 Jim Beattie .10 .05 .01
☐ 485 Barry Bonnell .10 .05 .01
☐ 486 Phil Bradley .20 .09 .03
☐ 487 Al Cowens .10 .05 .01
☐ 488 Alvin Davis .20 .09 .03
☐ 489 Dave Henderson .20 .09 .03
☐ 490 Steve Henderson .10 .05 .01
☐ 491 Bob Kearney .10 .05 .01
☐ 492 Mark Langston 1.25 .55 .16
☐ 493 Larry Milbourne .10 .05 .01
☐ 494 Paul Mirabella .10 .05 .01
☐ 495 Mike Moore .10 .05 .01
☐ 496 Edwin Nunez .10 .05 .01
☐ 497 Spike Owen .10 .05 .01
☐ 498 Jack Perconte .10 .05 .01
☐ 499 Ken Phelps .10 .05 .01
☐ 500 Jim Presley .20 .09 .03
☐ 501 Mike Stanton .10 .05 .01
☐ 502 Bob Stoddard .10 .05 .01
☐ 503 Gorman Thomas .10 .05 .01
☐ 504 Ed VandeBerg .10 .05 .01
☐ 505 Matt Young .10 .05 .01
☐ 506 Juan Agosto .10 .05 .01
☐ 507 Harold Baines .20 .09 .03
☐ 508 Floyd Bannister .10 .05 .01
☐ 509 Britt Burns .10 .05 .01
☐ 510 Julio Cruz .10 .05 .01
☐ 511 Richard Dotson .10 .05 .01
☐ 512 Jerry Dybzinski .10 .05 .01
☐ 513 Carlton Fisk .75 .35 .09
☐ 514 Scott Fletcher .10 .05 .01
☐ 515 Jerry Hairston .10 .05 .01
☐ 516 Marc Hill .10 .05 .01
☐ 517 LaMarr Hoyt .10 .05 .01
☐ 518 Ron Kittle .10 .05 .01
☐ 519 Rudy Law .10 .05 .01
☐ 520 Vance Law .10 .05 .01
☐ 521 Greg Luzinski .20 .09 .03
☐ 522 Gene Nelson .10 .05 .01
☐ 523 Tom Paciorek .10 .05 .01
☐ 524 Ron Reed .10 .05 .01
☐ 525 Bert Roberge .10 .05 .01
☐ 526 Tom Seaver .75 .35 .09
☐ 527 Roy Smalley .10 .05 .01
☐ 528 Dan Spillner .10 .05 .01
☐ 529 Mike Squires .10 .05 .01
☐ 530 Greg Walker .10 .05 .01
☐ 531 Cesar Cedeno .20 .09 .03
☐ 532 Dave Concepcion .20 .09 .03
☐ 533 Eric Davis 1.50 .70 .19
☐ 534 Nick Esasky .10 .05 .01
☐ 535 Tom Foley .10 .05 .01
☐ 536 John Franco UER 1.00 .45 .12
(Koufax misspelled
as Kofax on back)
☐ 537 Brad Gulden .10 .05 .01
☐ 538 Tom Hume .10 .05 .01
☐ 539 Wayne Krenchicki .10 .05 .01
☐ 540 Andy McGaffigan .10 .05 .01
☐ 541 Eddie Milner .10 .05 .01

	NRMT	VG-E	GOOD
☐ 542 Ron Oester	.10	.05	.01
☐ 543 Bob Owchinko	.10	.05	.01
☐ 544 Dave Parker	.20	.09	.03
☐ 545 Frank Pastore	.10	.05	.01
☐ 546 Tony Perez	.40	.18	.05
☐ 547 Ted Power	.10	.05	.01
☐ 548 Joe Price	.10	.05	.01
☐ 549 Gary Redus	.10	.05	.01
☐ 550 Pete Rose	2.00	.90	.25
☐ 551 Jeff Russell	.20	.09	.03
☐ 552 Mario Soto	.10	.05	.01
☐ 553 Jay Tibbs	.10	.05	.01
☐ 554 Duane Walker	.10	.05	.01
☐ 555 Alan Bannister	.10	.05	.01
☐ 556 Buddy Bell	.20	.09	.03
☐ 557 Danny Darwin	.10	.05	.01
☐ 558 Charlie Hough	.20	.09	.03
☐ 559 Bobby Jones	.10	.05	.01
☐ 560 Odell Jones	.10	.05	.01
☐ 561 Jeff Kunkel	.10	.05	.01
☐ 562 Mike Mason	.10	.05	.01
☐ 563 Pete O'Brien	.10	.05	.01
☐ 564 Larry Parrish	.10	.05	.01
☐ 565 Mickey Rivers	.10	.05	.01
☐ 566 Billy Sample	.10	.05	.01
☐ 567 Dave Schmidt	.10	.05	.01
☐ 568 Donnie Scott	.10	.05	.01
☐ 569 Dave Stewart	.20	.09	.03
☐ 570 Frank Tanana	.10	.05	.01
☐ 571 Wayne Tolleson	.10	.05	.01
☐ 572 Gary Ward	.10	.05	.01
☐ 573 Curtis Wilkerson	.10	.05	.01
☐ 574 George Wright	.10	.05	.01
☐ 575 Ned Yost	.10	.05	.01
☐ 576 Mark Brouhard	.10	.05	.01
☐ 577 Mike Caldwell	.10	.05	.01
☐ 578 Bobby Clark	.10	.05	.01
☐ 579 Jaime Cocanower	.10	.05	.01
☐ 580 Cecil Cooper	.20	.09	.03
☐ 581 Rollie Fingers	.40	.18	.05
☐ 582 Jim Gantner	.10	.05	.01
☐ 583 Moose Haas	.10	.05	.01
☐ 584 Dion James	.10	.05	.01
☐ 585 Pete Ladd	.10	.05	.01
☐ 586 Rick Manning	.10	.05	.01
☐ 587 Bob McClure	.10	.05	.01
☐ 588 Paul Molitor	2.00	.90	.25
☐ 589 Charlie Moore	.10	.05	.01
☐ 590 Ben Oglivie	.10	.05	.01
☐ 591 Chuck Porter	.10	.05	.01
☐ 592 Randy Ready	.10	.05	.01
☐ 593 Ed Romero	.10	.05	.01
☐ 594 Bill Schroeder	.10	.05	.01
☐ 595 Ray Searage	.10	.05	.01
☐ 596 Ted Simmons	.20	.09	.03
☐ 597 Jim Sundberg	.10	.05	.01
☐ 598 Don Sutton	.40	.18	.05
☐ 599 Tom Tellmann	.10	.05	.01
☐ 600 Rick Waits	.10	.05	.01
☐ 601 Robin Yount	2.00	.90	.25
☐ 602 Dusty Baker	.20	.09	.03
☐ 603 Bob Brenly	.10	.05	.01
☐ 604 Jack Clark	.20	.09	.03
☐ 605 Chili Davis	.20	.09	.03
☐ 606 Mark Davis	.10	.05	.01
☐ 607 Dan Gladden	.20	.09	.03
☐ 608 Atlee Hammaker	.10	.05	.01
☐ 609 Mike Krukow	.10	.05	.01
☐ 610 Duane Kuiper	.10	.05	.01
☐ 611 Bob Lacey	.10	.05	.01
☐ 612 Bill Laskey	.10	.05	.01
☐ 613 Gary Lavelle	.10	.05	.01
☐ 614 Johnnie LeMaster	.10	.05	.01
☐ 615 Jeff Leonard	.10	.05	.01
☐ 616 Randy Lerch	.10	.05	.01
☐ 617 Greg Minton	.10	.05	.01
☐ 618 Steve Nicosia	.10	.05	.01
☐ 619 Gene Richards	.10	.05	.01
☐ 620 Jeff D. Robinson	.10	.05	.01
☐ 621 Scot Thompson	.10	.05	.01
☐ 622 Manny Trillo	.10	.05	.01
☐ 623 Brad Wellman	.10	.05	.01
☐ 624 Frank Williams	.10	.05	.01
☐ 625 Joel Youngblood	.10	.05	.01
☐ 626 Cal Ripken IA	5.00	2.20	.60
☐ 627 Mike Schmidt IA	1.50	.70	.19
☐ 628 Giving The Signs Sparky Anderson	.20	.09	.03
☐ 629 AL Pitcher's Nightmare Dave Winfield Rickey Henderson	1.50	.70	.19
☐ 630 NL Pitcher's Nightmare Mike Schmidt Ryne Sandberg	1.50	.70	.19
☐ 631 NL All-Stars Darryl Strawberry Gary Carter Steve Garvey Ozzie Smith	.75	.35	.09
☐ 632 A-S Winning Battery Gary Carter Charlie Lea	.40	.18	.05
☐ 633 NL Pennant Clinchers Steve Garvey Rich Gossage	.40	.18	.05
☐ 634 NL Rookie Phenoms Dwight Gooden Juan Samuel	.75	.35	.09
☐ 635 Toronto's Big Guns Willie Upshaw	.10	.05	.01
☐ 636 Toronto's Big Guns Lloyd Moseby	.10	.05	.01
☐ 637 HOLLAND: Al Holland	.10	.05	.01
☐ 638 TUNNELL: Lee Tunnell	.10	.05	.01
☐ 639 500th Homer Reggie Jackson	1.00	.45	.12
☐ 640 4000th Hit Pete Rose	1.25	.55	.16
☐ 641 Father and Son Cal Ripken Jr. Cal Ripken Sr.	5.00	2.20	.60
☐ 642 Cubs: Division Champs	.20	.09	.03
☐ 643 Two Perfect Games and One No-Hitter: Mike Witt David Palmer Jack Morris	.20	.09	.03
☐ 644 Willie Lozado and Vic Mata	.10	.05	.01
☐ 645 Kelly Gruber and Randy O'Neal	.20	.09	.03
☐ 646 Jose Roman and Joel Skinner	.10	.05	.01
☐ 647 Steve Kiefer and Danny Tartabull	1.00	.45	.12
☐ 648 Rob Deer and Alejandro Sanchez	.20	.09	.03
☐ 649 Billy Hatcher and Shawon Dunston	1.00	.45	.12
☐ 650 Ron Robinson and Mike Bielecki	.10	.05	.01
☐ 651 Zane Smith and Paul Zuvella	.20	.09	.03
☐ 652 Joe Hesketh and Glenn Davis	.20	.09	.03
☐ 653 John Russell and Steve Jeltz	.10	.05	.01
☐ 654 CL: Tigers/Padres and Cubs/Mets	.20	.09	.03
☐ 655 CL: Blue Jays/Yankees and Red Sox/Orioles	.20	.09	.03
☐ 656 CL: Royals/Cardinals and Phillies/Twins	.20	.09	.03
☐ 657 CL: Angels/Braves and Astros/Dodgers	.20	.09	.03
☐ 658 CL: Expos/A's and Indians/Pirates	.20	.09	.03
☐ 659 CL: Mariners/White Sox and Reds/Rangers	.20	.09	.03
☐ 660 CL: Brewers/Giants and Special Cards	.20	.09	.03

1985 Fleer Update

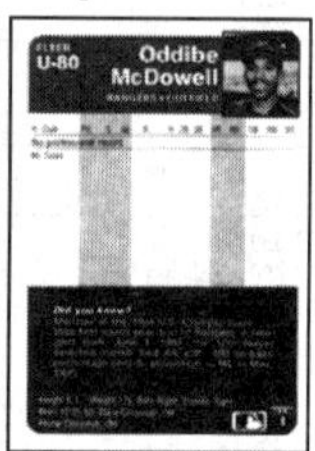

This 132-card standard-size update set was issued in factory set form exclusively through hobby dealers. Design is identical to the regular-issue 1985 Fleer cards except for the U prefixed card numbers on back. Cards are ordered alphabetically by the player's name. This set features the extended Rookie Cards of Vince Coleman, Darren Daulton, Mariano Duncan, Ozzie Guillen and Mickey Tettleton.

	NRMT	VG-E	GOOD
COMPLETE FACT.SET (132)	20.00	9.00	2.50
COMMON CARD (1-132)	.15	.07	.02

	NRMT	VG-E	GOOD
☐ 1 Don Aase	.15	.07	.02
☐ 2 Bill Almon	.15	.07	.02
☐ 3 Dusty Baker	.40	.18	.05
☐ 4 Dale Berra	.15	.07	.02
☐ 5 Karl Best	.15	.07	.02
☐ 6 Tim Birtsas	.15	.07	.02
☐ 7 Vida Blue	.40	.18	.05
☐ 8 Rich Bordi	.15	.07	.02
☐ 9 Daryl Boston	.15	.07	.02
☐ 10 Hubie Brooks	.15	.07	.02
☐ 11 Chris Brown	.15	.07	.02
☐ 12 Tom Browning	.40	.18	.05
☐ 13 Al Bumbry	.15	.07	.02
☐ 14 Tim Burke	.15	.07	.02
☐ 15 Ray Burris	.15	.07	.02
☐ 16 Jeff Burroughs	.15	.07	.02
☐ 17 Ivan Calderon	.15	.07	.02
☐ 18 Jeff Calhoun	.15	.07	.02
☐ 19 Bill Campbell	.15	.07	.02
☐ 20 Don Carman	.15	.07	.02
☐ 21 Gary Carter	.40	.18	.05
☐ 22 Bobby Castillo	.15	.07	.02
☐ 23 Bill Caudill	.15	.07	.02
☐ 24 Rick Cerone	.15	.07	.02
☐ 25 Jack Clark	.40	.18	.05
☐ 26 Pat Clements	.15	.07	.02
☐ 27 Stewart Cliburn	.15	.07	.02
☐ 28 Vince Coleman	1.00	.45	.12
☐ 29 Dave Collins	.15	.07	.02
☐ 30 Fritz Connally	.15	.07	.02
☐ 31 Henry Cotto	.15	.07	.02
☐ 32 Danny Darwin	.15	.07	.02
☐ 33 Darren Daulton	8.00	3.60	1.00
☐ 34 Jerry Davis	.15	.07	.02
☐ 35 Brian Dayett	.15	.07	.02
☐ 36 Ken Dixon	.15	.07	.02
☐ 37 Tommy Dunbar	.15	.07	.02
☐ 38 Mariano Duncan	.75	.35	.09
☐ 39 Bob Fallon	.15	.07	.02
☐ 40 Brian Fisher	.15	.07	.02
☐ 41 Mike Fitzgerald	.15	.07	.02
☐ 42 Ray Fontenot	.15	.07	.02
☐ 43 Greg Gagne	.40	.18	.05
☐ 44 Oscar Gamble	.15	.07	.02
☐ 45 Jim Gott	.15	.07	.02
☐ 46 David Green	.15	.07	.02
☐ 47 Alfredo Griffin	.15	.07	.02
☐ 48 Ozzie Guillen	1.50	.70	.19
☐ 49 Toby Harrah	.15	.07	.02
☐ 50 Ron Hassey	.15	.07	.02
☐ 51 Rickey Henderson	1.50	.70	.19
☐ 52 Steve Henderson	.15	.07	.02
☐ 53 George Hendrick	.15	.07	.02
☐ 54 Teddy Higuera	.40	.18	.05
☐ 55 Al Holland	.15	.07	.02
☐ 56 Burt Hooton	.15	.07	.02
☐ 57 Jay Howell	.15	.07	.02
☐ 58 LaMarr Hoyt	.15	.07	.02
☐ 59 Tim Hulett	.15	.07	.02
☐ 60 Bob James	.15	.07	.02
☐ 61 Cliff Johnson	.15	.07	.02
☐ 62 Howard Johnson	.40	.18	.05
☐ 63 Ruppert Jones	.15	.07	.02
☐ 64 Steve Kemp	.15	.07	.02
☐ 65 Bruce Kison	.15	.07	.02
☐ 66 Mike LaCoss	.15	.07	.02
☐ 67 Lee Lacy	.15	.07	.02
☐ 68 Dave LaPoint	.15	.07	.02
☐ 69 Gary Lavelle	.15	.07	.02
☐ 70 Vance Law	.15	.07	.02
☐ 71 Manny Lee	.15	.07	.02
☐ 72 Sixto Lezcano	.15	.07	.02
☐ 73 Tim Lollar	.15	.07	.02
☐ 74 Urbano Lugo	.15	.07	.02
☐ 75 Fred Lynn	.40	.18	.05
☐ 76 Steve Lyons	.40	.18	.05
☐ 77 Mickey Mahler	.15	.07	.02
☐ 78 Ron Mathis	.15	.07	.02
☐ 79 Len Matuszek	.15	.07	.02
☐ 80 Oddibe McDowell UER (Part of bio actually Roger's)	.40	.18	.05
☐ 81 Roger McDowell UER (Part of bio actually Oddibe's)	.40	.18	.05
☐ 82 Donnie Moore	.15	.07	.02
☐ 83 Ron Musselman	.15	.07	.02
☐ 84 Al Oliver	.40	.18	.05
☐ 85 Joe Orsulak	.40	.18	.05
☐ 86 Dan Pasqua	.40	.18	.05
☐ 87 Chris Pittaro	.15	.07	.02
☐ 88 Rick Reuschel	.15	.07	.02
☐ 89 Earnie Riles	.15	.07	.02
☐ 90 Jerry Royster	.15	.07	.02
☐ 91 Dave Rozema	.15	.07	.02
☐ 92 Dave Rucker	.15	.07	.02
☐ 93 Vern Ruhle	.15	.07	.02
☐ 94 Mark Salas	.15	.07	.02
☐ 95 Luis Salazar	.15	.07	.02
☐ 96 Joe Sambito	.15	.07	.02
☐ 97 Billy Sample	.15	.07	.02
☐ 98 Alejandro Sanchez	.15	.07	.02
☐ 99 Calvin Schiraldi	.15	.07	.02
☐ 100 Rick Schu	.15	.07	.02
☐ 101 Larry Sheets	.15	.07	.02
☐ 102 Ron Shephard	.15	.07	.02
☐ 103 Nelson Simmons	.15	.07	.02
☐ 104 Don Slaught	.15	.07	.02
☐ 105 Roy Smalley	.15	.07	.02
☐ 106 Lonnie Smith	.15	.07	.02
☐ 107 Nate Snell	.15	.07	.02
☐ 108 Lary Sorensen	.15	.07	.02
☐ 109 Chris Speier	.15	.07	.02
☐ 110 Mike Stenhouse	.15	.07	.02
☐ 111 Tim Stoddard	.15	.07	.02
☐ 112 John Stuper	.15	.07	.02
☐ 113 Jim Sundberg	.15	.07	.02
☐ 114 Bruce Sutter	.40	.18	.05
☐ 115 Don Sutton	.75	.35	.09
☐ 116 Bruce Tanner	.15	.07	.02
☐ 117 Kent Tekulve	.15	.07	.02
☐ 118 Walt Terrell	.15	.07	.02
☐ 119 Mickey Tettleton	4.00	1.80	.50
☐ 120 Rich Thompson	.15	.07	.02
☐ 121 Louis Thornton	.15	.07	.02
☐ 122 Alex Trevino	.15	.07	.02
☐ 123 John Tudor	.15	.07	.02
☐ 124 Jose Uribe	.15	.07	.02
☐ 125 Dave Valle	.15	.07	.02
☐ 126 Dave Von Ohlen	.15	.07	.02
☐ 127 Curt Wardle	.15	.07	.02
☐ 128 U.L. Washington	.15	.07	.02
☐ 129 Ed Whitson	.15	.07	.02
☐ 130 Herm Winningham	.15	.07	.02
☐ 131 Rich Yett	.15	.07	.02
☐ 132 Checklist U1-U132	.15	.07	.02

1985 Fleer Limited Edition

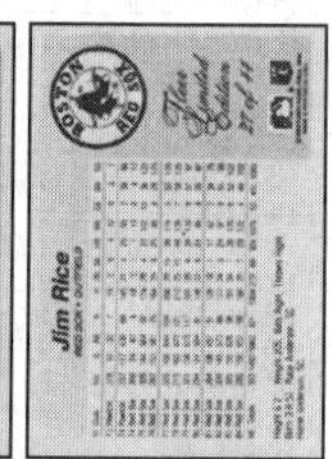

This 44-card set features standard size cards which were distributed in a colorful box as a complete set. The back of the box gives a complete checklist of the cards in the set. The cards are ordered alphabetically by the player's name. Backs of the cards are yellow and white whereas the fronts show a picture of the player inside a red banner-type border.

	NRMT	VG-E	GOOD
COMPLETE SET (44)	6.00	2.70	.75
COMMON CARD (1-44)	.05	.02	.01

	NRMT	VG-E	GOOD
☐ 1 Buddy Bell	.05	.02	.01
☐ 2 Bert Blyleven	.10	.05	.01
☐ 3 Wade Boggs	.40	.18	.05
☐ 4 George Brett	1.25	.55	.16
☐ 5 Rod Carew	.25	.11	.03
☐ 6 Steve Carlton	.25	.11	.03
☐ 7 Alvin Davis	.05	.02	.01
☐ 8 Andre Dawson	.25	.11	.03
☐ 9 Steve Garvey	.10	.05	.01
☐ 10 Rich Gossage	.10	.05	.01
☐ 11 Tony Gwynn	1.25	.55	.16
☐ 12 Keith Hernandez	.10	.05	.01
☐ 13 Kent Hrbek	.10	.05	.01
☐ 14 Reggie Jackson	.50	.23	.06
☐ 15 Dave Kingman	.10	.05	.01
☐ 16 Ron Kittle	.05	.02	.01
☐ 17 Mark Langston	.25	.11	.03
☐ 18 Jeff Leonard	.05	.02	.01
☐ 19 Bill Madlock	.05	.02	.01
☐ 20 Don Mattingly	1.50	.70	.19
☐ 21 Jack Morris	.10	.05	.01
☐ 22 Dale Murphy	.25	.11	.03
☐ 23 Eddie Murray	.60	.25	.07
☐ 24 Tony Pena	.05	.02	.01
☐ 25 Dan Quisenberry	.05	.02	.01
☐ 26 Tim Raines	.10	.05	.01
☐ 27 Jim Rice	.10	.05	.01
☐ 28 Cal Ripken	2.50	1.10	.30
☐ 29 Pete Rose	.75	.35	.09
☐ 30 Nolan Ryan	2.50	1.10	.30
☐ 31 Ryne Sandberg	1.00	.45	.12
☐ 32 Steve Sax	.05	.02	.01
☐ 33 Mike Schmidt	.50	.23	.06
☐ 34 Tom Seaver	.25	.11	.03
☐ 35 Ozzie Smith	1.00	.45	.12
☐ 36 Mario Soto	.05	.02	.01
☐ 37 Dave Stieb	.05	.02	.01
☐ 38 Darryl Strawberry	.40	.18	.05
☐ 39 Rick Sutcliffe	.05	.02	.01
☐ 40 Alan Trammell	.15	.07	.02
☐ 41 Willie Upshaw	.05	.02	.01
☐ 42 Fernando Valenzuela	.10	.05	.01
☐ 43 Dave Winfield	.25	.11	.03
☐ 44 Robin Yount	.25	.11	.03

1985 Fleer Star Stickers

The stickers in this 126-sticker set measure approximately 1 15/16" by 2 1/2". The 1985 Fleer stickers set can be housed in a Fleer sticker album. Stickers are numbered on the fronts. A distinctive feature of the set is the inclusion of stop-action (designated SA in the checklist below) photos on cards 62 through 79. These photos are actually a series of six consecutive stickers which depict a player in action through the course of an activity; e.g., Eddie Murray's swing, Tom Seaver's wind-up and Mike Schmidt fielding. The backs of these stickers are blue and similar in design to past years.

	NRMT	VG-E	GOOD
COMPLETE SET (126)	50.00	22.00	6.25
COMMON STICKER (1-126)	.10	.05	.01
☐ 1 Pete Rose	3.00	1.35	.35
☐ 2 Pete Rose	3.00	1.35	.35
☐ 3 Pete Rose	3.00	1.35	.35
☐ 4 Don Mattingly	7.50	3.40	.95
☐ 5 Dave Winfield	1.25	.55	.16
☐ 6 Wade Boggs	2.50	1.10	.30
☐ 7 Buddy Bell	.20	.09	.03
☐ 8 Tony Gwynn	6.00	2.70	.75
☐ 9 Lee Lacy	.10	.05	.01
☐ 10 Chili Davis	.20	.09	.03
☐ 11 Ryne Sandberg	4.00	1.80	.50
☐ 12 Tony Armas	.10	.05	.01
☐ 13 Jim Rice	.20	.09	.03
☐ 14 Dave Kingman	.20	.09	.03
☐ 15 Alvin Davis	.20	.09	.03
☐ 16 Gary Carter	.20	.09	.03
☐ 17 Mike Schmidt	2.50	1.10	.30
☐ 18 Dale Murphy	.30	.14	.04
☐ 19 Ron Cey	.20	.09	.03
☐ 20 Eddie Murray	1.50	.70	.19
☐ 21 Harold Baines	.20	.09	.03
☐ 22 Kirk Gibson	.20	.09	.03
☐ 23 Jim Rice	.20	.09	.03
☐ 24 Gary Matthews	.10	.05	.01
☐ 25 Keith Hernandez	.20	.09	.03
☐ 26 Gary Carter	.20	.09	.03
☐ 27 George Hendrick	.10	.05	.01
☐ 28 Tony Armas	.10	.05	.01
☐ 29 Dave Kingman	.20	.09	.03
☐ 30 Dwayne Murphy	.10	.05	.01
☐ 31 Lance Parrish	.20	.09	.03
☐ 32 Andre Thornton	.10	.05	.01
☐ 33 Dale Murphy	.30	.14	.04
☐ 34 Mike Schmidt	2.50	1.10	.30
☐ 35 Gary Carter	.20	.09	.03
☐ 36 Darryl Strawberry	.75	.35	.09
☐ 37 Don Mattingly	7.50	3.40	.95
☐ 38 Larry Parrish	.10	.05	.01
☐ 39 George Bell	.20	.09	.03
☐ 40 Dwight Evans	.20	.09	.03
☐ 41 Cal Ripken	7.50	3.40	.95
☐ 42 Tim Raines	.20	.09	.03
☐ 43 Johnny Ray	.10	.05	.01
☐ 44 Juan Samuel	.10	.05	.01
☐ 45 Ryne Sandberg	4.00	1.80	.50
☐ 46 Mike Easler	.10	.05	.01
☐ 47 Andre Thornton	.10	.05	.01
☐ 48 Dave Kingman	.20	.09	.03
☐ 49 Don Baylor	.20	.09	.03
☐ 50 Rusty Staub	.20	.09	.03
☐ 51 Steve Braun	.10	.05	.01
☐ 52 Kevin Bass	.10	.05	.01
☐ 53 Greg Gross	.10	.05	.01
☐ 54 Rickey Henderson	1.25	.55	.16
☐ 55 Dave Collins	.10	.05	.01
☐ 56 Brett Butler	.20	.09	.03
☐ 57 Gary Pettis	.10	.05	.01
☐ 58 Tim Raines	.20	.09	.03
☐ 59 Juan Samuel	.10	.05	.01
☐ 60 Alan Wiggins	.10	.05	.01
☐ 61 Lonnie Smith	.10	.05	.01
☐ 62 Eddie Murray SA	.75	.35	.09
☐ 63 Eddie Murray SA	.75	.35	.09
☐ 64 Eddie Murray SA	.75	.35	.09
☐ 65 Eddie Murray SA	.75	.35	.09
☐ 66 Eddie Murray SA	.75	.35	.09
☐ 67 Eddie Murray SA	.75	.35	.09
☐ 68 Tom Seaver SA	1.00	.45	.12
☐ 69 Tom Seaver SA	1.00	.45	.12
☐ 70 Tom Seaver SA	1.00	.45	.12
☐ 71 Tom Seaver SA	1.00	.45	.12
☐ 72 Tom Seaver SA	1.00	.45	.12
☐ 73 Tom Seaver SA	1.00	.45	.12
☐ 74 Mike Schmidt SA	1.25	.55	.16
☐ 75 Mike Schmidt SA	1.25	.55	.16
☐ 76 Mike Schmidt SA	1.25	.55	.16
☐ 77 Mike Schmidt SA	1.25	.55	.16
☐ 78 Mike Schmidt SA	1.25	.55	.16
☐ 79 Mike Schmidt SA	1.25	.55	.16
☐ 80 Mike Boddicker	.10	.05	.01
☐ 81 Bert Blyleven	.20	.09	.03
☐ 82 Jack Morris	.20	.09	.03
☐ 83 Dan Petry	.10	.05	.01
☐ 84 Frank Viola	.20	.09	.03
☐ 85 Joaquin Andujar	.10	.05	.01
☐ 86 Mario Soto	.10	.05	.01
☐ 87 Dwight Gooden	2.50	1.10	.30
☐ 88 Joe Niekro	.10	.05	.01
☐ 89 Rick Sutcliffe	.10	.05	.01
☐ 90 Mike Boddicker	.10	.05	.01
☐ 91 Dave Stieb	.10	.05	.01
☐ 92 Bert Blyleven	.20	.09	.03
☐ 93 Phil Niekro	.30	.14	.04
☐ 94 Alejandro Pena	.10	.05	.01
☐ 95 Dwight Gooden	2.50	1.10	.30
☐ 96 Orel Hershiser	2.50	1.10	.30
☐ 97 Rick Rhoden	.10	.05	.01
☐ 98 John Candelaria	.10	.05	.01
☐ 99 Dan Quisenberry	.10	.05	.01
☐ 100 Bill Caudill	.10	.05	.01
☐ 101 Willie Hernandez	.10	.05	.01
☐ 102 Dave Righetti	.20	.09	.03
☐ 103 Ron Davis	.10	.05	.01
☐ 104 Bruce Sutter	.20	.09	.03
☐ 105 Lee Smith	.30	.14	.04
☐ 106 Jesse Orosco	.10	.05	.01
☐ 107 Al Holland	.10	.05	.01
☐ 108 Goose Gossage	.20	.09	.03
☐ 109 Mark Langston	1.00	.45	.12
☐ 110 Dave Stieb	.10	.05	.01
☐ 111 Mike Witt	.10	.05	.01
☐ 112 Bert Blyleven	.20	.09	.03
☐ 113 Dwight Gooden	2.50	1.10	.30
☐ 114 Fernando Valenzuela	.20	.09	.03
☐ 115 Nolan Ryan	7.50	3.40	.95
☐ 116 Mario Soto	.10	.05	.01
☐ 117 Ron Darling	.20	.09	.03
☐ 118 Dan Gladden	.10	.05	.01
☐ 119 Jeff Stone	.10	.05	.01
☐ 120 John Franco	.50	.23	.06
☐ 121 Barbaro Garbey	.10	.05	.01
☐ 122 Kirby Puckett	12.00	5.50	1.50
☐ 123 Roger Clemens	7.50	3.40	.95
☐ 124 Bret Saberhagen	1.00	.45	.12
☐ 125 Sparky Anderson MG	.20	.09	.03
☐ 126 Dick Williams MG	.10	.05	.01

1986 Fleer

The 1986 Fleer set consists of 660-card standard-size cards. Wax packs included 15 cards plus logo stickers. Card fronts feature dark blue borders, a team logo along with the player's name and position. The player cards are alphabetized within team and the teams are ordered by their 1985 season finish and won-lost record. Subsets include Specials (626-643) and Major League Prospects (644-653). The Dennis and Tippy Martinez cards were apparently switched in the set numbering, as their adjacent numbers (279 and 280) were reversed on the Orioles checklist card. The set includes the Rookie Cards of Rick Aguilera, Jose Canseco, Darren Daulton, Len Dykstra, Cecil Fielder, Andres Galarraga, Paul O'Neill,and Mickey Tettleton.

	MINT	NRMT	EXC
COMPLETE SET (660)	60.00	27.00	7.50
COMPLETE FACT.SET (660)	70.00	32.00	8.75
COMMON CARD (1-660)	.10	.05	.01
☐ 1 Steve Balboni	.10	.05	.01
☐ 2 Joe Beckwith	.10	.05	.01
☐ 3 Buddy Biancalana	.10	.05	.01
☐ 4 Bud Black	.10	.05	.01
☐ 5 George Brett	2.00	.90	.25
☐ 6 Onix Concepcion	.10	.05	.01
☐ 7 Steve Farr	.20	.09	.03
☐ 8 Mark Gubicza	.20	.09	.03
☐ 9 Dane Iorg	.10	.05	.01
☐ 10 Danny Jackson	.10	.05	.01
☐ 11 Lynn Jones	.10	.05	.01
☐ 12 Mike Jones	.10	.05	.01
☐ 13 Charlie Leibrandt	.10	.05	.01
☐ 14 Hal McRae	.20	.09	.03
☐ 15 Omar Moreno	.10	.05	.01
☐ 16 Darryl Motley	.10	.05	.01
☐ 17 Jorge Orta	.10	.05	.01
☐ 18 Dan Quisenberry	.10	.05	.01
☐ 19 Bret Saberhagen	.30	.14	.04
☐ 20 Pat Sheridan	.10	.05	.01
☐ 21 Lonnie Smith	.10	.05	.01
☐ 22 Jim Sundberg	.10	.05	.01
☐ 23 John Wathan	.10	.05	.01
☐ 24 Frank White	.20	.09	.03
☐ 25 Willie Wilson	.10	.05	.01
☐ 26 Joaquin Andujar	.10	.05	.01
☐ 27 Steve Braun	.10	.05	.01
☐ 28 Bill Campbell	.10	.05	.01
☐ 29 Cesar Cedeno	.20	.09	.03
☐ 30 Jack Clark	.20	.09	.03
☐ 31 Vince Coleman	.30	.14	.04
☐ 32 Danny Cox	.10	.05	.01
☐ 33 Ken Dayley	.10	.05	.01
☐ 34 Ivan DeJesus	.10	.05	.01
☐ 35 Bob Forsch	.10	.05	.01
☐ 36 Brian Harper	.10	.05	.01
☐ 37 Tom Herr	.10	.05	.01
☐ 38 Ricky Horton	.10	.05	.01
☐ 39 Kurt Kepshire	.10	.05	.01
☐ 40 Jeff Lahti	.10	.05	.01
☐ 41 Tito Landrum	.10	.05	.01
☐ 42 Willie McGee	.20	.09	.03
☐ 43 Tom Nieto	.10	.05	.01
☐ 44 Terry Pendleton	.30	.14	.04
☐ 45 Darrell Porter	.20	.09	.03
☐ 46 Ozzie Smith	1.25	.55	.16
☐ 47 John Tudor	.10	.05	.01
☐ 48 Andy Van Slyke	.20	.09	.03
☐ 49 Todd Worrell	.20	.09	.03
☐ 50 Jim Acker	.10	.05	.01
☐ 51 Doyle Alexander	.10	.05	.01
☐ 52 Jesse Barfield	.10	.05	.01
☐ 53 George Bell	.20	.09	.03
☐ 54 Jeff Burroughs	.10	.05	.01
☐ 55 Bill Caudill	.10	.05	.01
☐ 56 Jim Clancy	.10	.05	.01
☐ 57 Tony Fernandez	.10	.05	.01
☐ 58 Tom Filer	.10	.05	.01
☐ 59 Damaso Garcia	.10	.05	.01
☐ 60 Tom Henke	.20	.09	.03
☐ 61 Garth Iorg	.10	.05	.01
☐ 62 Cliff Johnson	.10	.05	.01
☐ 63 Jimmy Key	.30	.14	.04
☐ 64 Dennis Lamp	.10	.05	.01
☐ 65 Gary Lavelle	.10	.05	.01
☐ 66 Buck Martinez	.10	.05	.01
☐ 67 Lloyd Moseby	.10	.05	.01
☐ 68 Rance Mulliniks	.10	.05	.01
☐ 69 Al Oliver	.20	.09	.03
☐ 70 Dave Stieb	.10	.05	.01
☐ 71 Louis Thornton	.10	.05	.01
☐ 72 Willie Upshaw	.10	.05	.01
☐ 73 Ernie Whitt	.10	.05	.01
☐ 74 Rick Aguilera	.50	.23	.06
☐ 75 Wally Backman	.10	.05	.01
☐ 76 Gary Carter	.20	.09	.03
☐ 77 Ron Darling	.10	.05	.01
☐ 78 Len Dykstra	2.00	.90	.25
☐ 79 Sid Fernandez	.20	.09	.03
☐ 80 George Foster	.20	.09	.03
☐ 81 Dwight Gooden	.60	.25	.07
☐ 82 Tom Gorman	.10	.05	.01
☐ 83 Danny Heep	.10	.05	.01
☐ 84 Keith Hernandez	.20	.09	.03
☐ 85 Howard Johnson	.20	.09	.03
☐ 86 Ray Knight	.20	.09	.03
☐ 87 Terry Leach	.10	.05	.01
☐ 88 Ed Lynch	.10	.05	.01
☐ 89 Roger McDowell	.20	.09	.03
☐ 90 Jesse Orosco	.10	.05	.01
☐ 91 Tom Paciorek	.10	.05	.01
☐ 92 Ronn Reynolds	.10	.05	.01
☐ 93 Rafael Santana	.10	.05	.01
☐ 94 Doug Sisk	.10	.05	.01
☐ 95 Rusty Staub	.20	.09	.03
☐ 96 Darryl Strawberry	.30	.14	.04
☐ 97 Mookie Wilson	.20	.09	.03
☐ 98 Neil Allen	.10	.05	.01
☐ 99 Don Baylor	.30	.14	.04
☐ 100 Dale Berra	.10	.05	.01
☐ 101 Rich Bordi	.10	.05	.01
☐ 102 Marty Bystrom	.10	.05	.01
☐ 103 Joe Cowley	.10	.05	.01
☐ 104 Brian Fisher	.10	.05	.01
☐ 105 Ken Griffey	.20	.09	.03
☐ 106 Ron Guidry	.20	.09	.03
☐ 107 Ron Hassey	.10	.05	.01
☐ 108 Rickey Henderson UER (SB Record of 120, sic)	.75	.35	.09
☐ 109 Don Mattingly	3.00	1.35	.35
☐ 110 Bobby Meacham	.10	.05	.01
☐ 111 John Montefusco	.10	.05	.01
☐ 112 Phil Niekro	.30	.14	.04
☐ 113 Mike Pagliarulo	.10	.05	.01
☐ 114 Dan Pasqua	.10	.05	.01
☐ 115 Willie Randolph	.20	.09	.03
☐ 116 Dave Righetti	.10	.05	.01
☐ 117 Andre Robertson	.10	.05	.01
☐ 118 Billy Sample	.10	.05	.01
☐ 119 Bob Shirley	.10	.05	.01
☐ 120 Ed Whitson	.10	.05	.01
☐ 121 Dave Winfield	.60	.25	.07
☐ 122 Butch Wynegar	.10	.05	.01
☐ 123 Dave Anderson	.10	.05	.01
☐ 124 Bob Bailor	.10	.05	.01
☐ 125 Greg Brock	.10	.05	.01
☐ 126 Enos Cabell	.10	.05	.01
☐ 127 Bobby Castillo	.10	.05	.01
☐ 128 Carlos Diaz	.10	.05	.01
☐ 129 Mariano Duncan	.30	.14	.04
☐ 130 Pedro Guerrero	.20	.09	.03
☐ 131 Orel Hershiser	.30	.14	.04
☐ 132 Rick Honeycutt	.10	.05	.01
☐ 133 Ken Howell	.10	.05	.01
☐ 134 Ken Landreaux	.10	.05	.01
☐ 135 Bill Madlock	.10	.05	.01
☐ 136 Candy Maldonado	.10	.05	.01
☐ 137 Mike Marshall	.10	.05	.01
☐ 138 Len Matuszek	.10	.05	.01
☐ 139 Tom Niedenfuer	.10	.05	.01
☐ 140 Alejandro Pena	.10	.05	.01
☐ 141 Jerry Reuss	.10	.05	.01
☐ 142 Bill Russell	.10	.05	.01
☐ 143 Steve Sax	.10	.05	.01
☐ 144 Mike Scioscia	.10	.05	.01
☐ 145 Fernando Valenzuela	.20	.09	.03
☐ 146 Bob Welch	.10	.05	.01
☐ 147 Terry Whitfield	.10	.05	.01
☐ 148 Juan Beniquez	.10	.05	.01
☐ 149 Bob Boone	.20	.09	.03
☐ 150 John Candelaria	.10	.05	.01
☐ 151 Rod Carew	.50	.23	.06
☐ 152 Stewart Cliburn	.10	.05	.01
☐ 153 Doug DeCinces	.10	.05	.01
☐ 154 Brian Downing	.10	.05	.01
☐ 155 Ken Forsch	.10	.05	.01
☐ 156 Craig Gerber	.10	.05	.01
☐ 157 Bobby Grich	.20	.09	.03
☐ 158 George Hendrick	.10	.05	.01
☐ 159 Al Holland	.10	.05	.01
☐ 160 Reggie Jackson	.75	.35	.09
☐ 161 Ruppert Jones	.10	.05	.01
☐ 162 Urbano Lugo	.10	.05	.01
☐ 163 Kirk McCaskill	.20	.09	.03
☐ 164 Donnie Moore	.10	.05	.01
☐ 165 Gary Pettis	.10	.05	.01
☐ 166 Ron Romanick	.10	.05	.01
☐ 167 Dick Schofield	.10	.05	.01
☐ 168 Daryl Sconiers	.10	.05	.01
☐ 169 Jim Slaton	.10	.05	.01
☐ 170 Don Sutton	.30	.14	.04
☐ 171 Mike Witt	.10	.05	.01
☐ 172 Buddy Bell	.20	.09	.03
☐ 173 Tom Browning	.10	.05	.01
☐ 174 Dave Concepcion	.20	.09	.03
☐ 175 Eric Davis	.20	.09	.03
☐ 176 Bo Diaz	.10	.05	.01
☐ 177 Nick Esasky	.10	.05	.01
☐ 178 John Franco	.30	.14	.04
☐ 179 Tom Hume	.10	.05	.01
☐ 180 Wayne Krenchicki	.10	.05	.01
☐ 181 Andy McGaffigan	.10	.05	.01
☐ 182 Eddie Milner	.10	.05	.01
☐ 183 Ron Oester	.10	.05	.01
☐ 184 Dave Parker	.20	.09	.03
☐ 185 Frank Pastore	.10	.05	.01
☐ 186 Tony Perez	.30	.14	.04
☐ 187 Ted Power	.10	.05	.01
☐ 188 Joe Price	.10	.05	.01
☐ 189 Gary Redus	.10	.05	.01
☐ 190 Ron Robinson	.10	.05	.01
☐ 191 Pete Rose	.75	.35	.09
☐ 192 Mario Soto	.10	.05	.01
☐ 193 John Stuper	.10	.05	.01
☐ 194 Jay Tibbs	.10	.05	.01
☐ 195 Dave Van Gorder	.10	.05	.01
☐ 196 Max Venable	.10	.05	.01
☐ 197 Juan Agosto	.10	.05	.01
☐ 198 Harold Baines	.20	.09	.03
☐ 199 Floyd Bannister	.10	.05	.01
☐ 200 Britt Burns	.10	.05	.01
☐ 201 Julio Cruz	.10	.05	.01
☐ 202 Joel Davis	.10	.05	.01
☐ 203 Richard Dotson	.10	.05	.01
☐ 204 Carlton Fisk	.30	.14	.04
☐ 205 Scott Fletcher	.10	.05	.01
☐ 206 Ozzie Guillen	.30	.14	.04
☐ 207 Jerry Hairston	.10	.05	.01
☐ 208 Tim Hulett	.10	.05	.01
☐ 209 Bob James	.10	.05	.01
☐ 210 Ron Kittle	.10	.05	.01
☐ 211 Rudy Law	.10	.05	.01
☐ 212 Bryan Little	.10	.05	.01
☐ 213 Gene Nelson	.10	.05	.01
☐ 214 Reid Nichols	.10	.05	.01
☐ 215 Luis Salazar	.10	.05	.01
☐ 216 Tom Seaver	.50	.23	.06
☐ 217 Dan Spillner	.10	.05	.01
☐ 218 Bruce Tanner	.10	.05	.01
☐ 219 Greg Walker	.10	.05	.01
☐ 220 Dave Wehrmeister	.10	.05	.01
☐ 221 Juan Berenguer	.10	.05	.01
☐ 222 Dave Bergman	.10	.05	.01
☐ 223 Tom Brookens	.10	.05	.01
☐ 224 Darrell Evans	.20	.09	.03
☐ 225 Barbaro Garbey	.10	.05	.01
☐ 226 Kirk Gibson	.20	.09	.03
☐ 227 John Grubb	.10	.05	.01
☐ 228 Willie Hernandez	.10	.05	.01
☐ 229 Larry Herndon	.10	.05	.01
☐ 230 Chet Lemon	.10	.05	.01
☐ 231 Aurelio Lopez	.10	.05	.01
☐ 232 Jack Morris	.20	.09	.03
☐ 233 Randy O'Neal	.10	.05	.01
☐ 234 Lance Parrish	.20	.09	.03
☐ 235 Dan Petry	.10	.05	.01
☐ 236 Alejandro Sanchez	.10	.05	.01
☐ 237 Bill Scherrer	.10	.05	.01
☐ 238 Nelson Simmons	.10	.05	.01
☐ 239 Frank Tanana	.10	.05	.01
☐ 240 Walt Terrell	.10	.05	.01
☐ 241 Alan Trammell	.30	.14	.04
☐ 242 Lou Whitaker	.20	.09	.03
☐ 243 Milt Wilcox	.10	.05	.01
☐ 244 Hubie Brooks	.10	.05	.01
☐ 245 Tim Burke	.10	.05	.01
☐ 246 Andre Dawson	.30	.14	.04
☐ 247 Mike Fitzgerald	.10	.05	.01
☐ 248 Terry Francona	.10	.05	.01
☐ 249 Bill Gullickson	.10	.05	.01
☐ 250 Joe Hesketh	.10	.05	.01
☐ 251 Bill Laskey	.10	.05	.01
☐ 252 Vance Law	.10	.05	.01
☐ 253 Charlie Lea	.10	.05	.01
☐ 254 Gary Lucas	.10	.05	.01
☐ 255 David Palmer	.10	.05	.01
☐ 256 Tim Raines	.20	.09	.03
☐ 257 Jeff Reardon	.20	.09	.03

Card			
☐ 258 Bert Roberge	.10	.05	.01
☐ 259 Dan Schatzeder	.10	.05	.01
☐ 260 Bryn Smith	.10	.05	.01
☐ 261 Randy St.Claire	.10	.05	.01
☐ 262 Scot Thompson	.10	.05	.01
☐ 263 Tim Wallach	.10	.05	.01
☐ 264 U.L. Washington	.10	.05	.01
☐ 265 Mitch Webster	.10	.05	.01
☐ 266 Herm Winningham	.10	.05	.01
☐ 267 Floyd Youmans	.10	.05	.01
☐ 268 Don Aase	.10	.05	.01
☐ 269 Mike Boddicker	.10	.05	.01
☐ 270 Rich Dauer	.10	.05	.01
☐ 271 Storm Davis	.10	.05	.01
☐ 272 Rick Dempsey	.10	.05	.01
☐ 273 Ken Dixon	.10	.05	.01
☐ 274 Jim Dwyer	.10	.05	.01
☐ 275 Mike Flanagan	.10	.05	.01
☐ 276 Wayne Gross	.10	.05	.01
☐ 277 Lee Lacy	.10	.05	.01
☐ 278 Fred Lynn	.20	.09	.03
☐ 279 Tippy Martinez	.10	.05	.01
☐ 280 Dennis Martinez	.20	.09	.03
☐ 281 Scott McGregor	.10	.05	.01
☐ 282 Eddie Murray	1.25	.55	.16
☐ 283 Floyd Rayford	.10	.05	.01
☐ 284 Cal Ripken	5.00	2.20	.60
☐ 285 Gary Roenicke	.10	.05	.01
☐ 286 Larry Sheets	.10	.05	.01
☐ 287 John Shelby	.10	.05	.01
☐ 288 Nate Snell	.10	.05	.01
☐ 289 Sammy Stewart	.10	.05	.01
☐ 290 Alan Wiggins	.10	.05	.01
☐ 291 Mike Young	.10	.05	.01
☐ 292 Alan Ashby	.10	.05	.01
☐ 293 Mark Bailey	.10	.05	.01
☐ 294 Kevin Bass	.10	.05	.01
☐ 295 Jeff Calhoun	.10	.05	.01
☐ 296 Jose Cruz	.10	.05	.01
☐ 297 Glenn Davis	.20	.09	.03
☐ 298 Bill Dawley	.10	.05	.01
☐ 299 Frank DiPino	.10	.05	.01
☐ 300 Bill Doran	.10	.05	.01
☐ 301 Phil Garner	.10	.05	.01
☐ 302 Jeff Heathcock	.10	.05	.01
☐ 303 Charlie Kerfeld	.10	.05	.01
☐ 304 Bob Knepper	.10	.05	.01
☐ 305 Ron Mathis	.10	.05	.01
☐ 306 Jerry Mumphrey	.10	.05	.01
☐ 307 Jim Pankovits	.10	.05	.01
☐ 308 Terry Puhl	.10	.05	.01
☐ 309 Craig Reynolds	.10	.05	.01
☐ 310 Nolan Ryan	5.00	2.20	.60
☐ 311 Mike Scott	.10	.05	.01
☐ 312 Dave Smith	.10	.05	.01
☐ 313 Dickie Thon	.10	.05	.01
☐ 314 Denny Walling	.10	.05	.01
☐ 315 Kurt Bevacqua	.10	.05	.01
☐ 316 Al Bumbry	.10	.05	.01
☐ 317 Jerry Davis	.10	.05	.01
☐ 318 Luis DeLeon	.10	.05	.01
☐ 319 Dave Dravecky	.20	.09	.03
☐ 320 Tim Flannery	.10	.05	.01
☐ 321 Steve Garvey	.30	.14	.04
☐ 322 Rich Gossage	.30	.14	.04
☐ 323 Tony Gwynn	2.50	1.10	.30
☐ 324 Andy Hawkins	.10	.05	.01
☐ 325 LaMarr Hoyt	.10	.05	.01
☐ 326 Roy Lee Jackson	.10	.05	.01
☐ 327 Terry Kennedy	.10	.05	.01
☐ 328 Craig Lefferts	.10	.05	.01
☐ 329 Carmelo Martinez	.10	.05	.01
☐ 330 Lance McCullers	.10	.05	.01
☐ 331 Kevin McReynolds	.20	.09	.03
☐ 332 Graig Nettles	.20	.09	.03
☐ 333 Jerry Royster	.10	.05	.01
☐ 334 Eric Show	.10	.05	.01
☐ 335 Tim Stoddard	.10	.05	.01
☐ 336 Garry Templeton	.10	.05	.01
☐ 337 Mark Thurmond	.10	.05	.01
☐ 338 Ed Wojna	.10	.05	.01
☐ 339 Tony Armas	.10	.05	.01
☐ 340 Marty Barrett	.10	.05	.01
☐ 341 Wade Boggs	1.00	.45	.12
☐ 342 Dennis Boyd	.10	.05	.01
☐ 343 Bill Buckner	.20	.09	.03
☐ 344 Mark Clear	.10	.05	.01
☐ 345 Roger Clemens	2.50	1.10	.30
☐ 346 Steve Crawford	.10	.05	.01
☐ 347 Mike Easler	.10	.05	.01
☐ 348 Dwight Evans	.20	.09	.03
☐ 349 Rich Gedman	.10	.05	.01
☐ 350 Jackie Gutierrez	.10	.05	.01
☐ 351 Glenn Hoffman	.10	.05	.01
☐ 352 Bruce Hurst	.10	.05	.01
☐ 353 Bruce Kison	.10	.05	.01
☐ 354 Tim Lollar	.10	.05	.01
☐ 355 Steve Lyons	.10	.05	.01
☐ 356 Al Nipper	.10	.05	.01
☐ 357 Bob Ojeda	.10	.05	.01
☐ 358 Jim Rice	.20	.09	.03
☐ 359 Bob Stanley	.10	.05	.01
☐ 360 Mike Trujillo	.10	.05	.01
☐ 361 Thad Bosley	.10	.05	.01
☐ 362 Warren Brusstar	.10	.05	.01
☐ 363 Ron Cey	.20	.09	.03
☐ 364 Jody Davis	.10	.05	.01
☐ 365 Bob Dernier	.10	.05	.01
☐ 366 Shawon Dunston	.20	.09	.03
☐ 367 Leon Durham	.10	.05	.01
☐ 368 Dennis Eckersley	.30	.14	.04
☐ 369 Ray Fontenot	.10	.05	.01
☐ 370 George Frazier	.10	.05	.01
☐ 371 Billy Hatcher	.20	.09	.03
☐ 372 Dave Lopes	.20	.09	.03
☐ 373 Gary Matthews	.10	.05	.01
☐ 374 Ron Meridith	.10	.05	.01
☐ 375 Keith Moreland	.10	.05	.01
☐ 376 Reggie Patterson	.10	.05	.01
☐ 377 Dick Ruthven	.10	.05	.01
☐ 378 Ryne Sandberg	2.00	.90	.25
☐ 379 Scott Sanderson	.10	.05	.01
☐ 380 Lee Smith	.30	.14	.04
☐ 381 Lary Sorensen	.10	.05	.01
☐ 382 Chris Speier	.10	.05	.01
☐ 383 Rick Sutcliffe	.10	.05	.01
☐ 384 Steve Trout	.10	.05	.01
☐ 385 Gary Woods	.10	.05	.01
☐ 386 Bert Blyleven	.30	.14	.04
☐ 387 Tom Brunansky	.10	.05	.01
☐ 388 Randy Bush	.10	.05	.01
☐ 389 John Butcher	.10	.05	.01
☐ 390 Ron Davis	.10	.05	.01
☐ 391 Dave Engle	.10	.05	.01
☐ 392 Frank Eufemia	.10	.05	.01
☐ 393 Pete Filson	.10	.05	.01
☐ 394 Gary Gaetti	.20	.09	.03
☐ 395 Greg Gagne	.20	.09	.03
☐ 396 Mickey Hatcher	.10	.05	.01
☐ 397 Kent Hrbek	.30	.14	.04
☐ 398 Tim Laudner	.10	.05	.01
☐ 399 Rick Lysander	.10	.05	.01
☐ 400 Dave Meier	.10	.05	.01
☐ 401 Kirby Puckett UER (Card has him in NL, should be AL)	5.00	2.20	.60
☐ 402 Mark Salas	.10	.05	.01
☐ 403 Ken Schrom	.10	.05	.01
☐ 404 Roy Smalley	.10	.05	.01
☐ 405 Mike Smithson	.10	.05	.01
☐ 406 Mike Stenhouse	.10	.05	.01
☐ 407 Tim Teufel	.10	.05	.01
☐ 408 Frank Viola	.20	.09	.03
☐ 409 Ron Washington	.10	.05	.01
☐ 410 Keith Atherton	.10	.05	.01
☐ 411 Dusty Baker	.20	.09	.03
☐ 412 Tim Birtsas	.10	.05	.01
☐ 413 Bruce Bochte	.10	.05	.01
☐ 414 Chris Codiroli	.10	.05	.01
☐ 415 Dave Collins	.10	.05	.01
☐ 416 Mike Davis	.10	.05	.01
☐ 417 Alfredo Griffin	.10	.05	.01
☐ 418 Mike Heath	.10	.05	.01
☐ 419 Steve Henderson	.10	.05	.01
☐ 420 Donnie Hill	.10	.05	.01
☐ 421 Jay Howell	.10	.05	.01
☐ 422 Tommy John	.30	.14	.04
☐ 423 Dave Kingman	.20	.09	.03
☐ 424 Bill Krueger	.10	.05	.01
☐ 425 Rick Langford	.10	.05	.01
☐ 426 Carney Lansford	.20	.09	.03
☐ 427 Steve McCatty	.10	.05	.01
☐ 428 Dwayne Murphy	.10	.05	.01
☐ 429 Steve Ontiveros	.20	.09	.03
☐ 430 Tony Phillips	.20	.09	.03
☐ 431 Jose Rijo	.20	.09	.03
☐ 432 Mickey Tettleton	2.00	.90	.25
☐ 433 Luis Aguayo	.10	.05	.01
☐ 434 Larry Andersen	.10	.05	.01
☐ 435 Steve Carlton	.50	.23	.06
☐ 436 Don Carman	.10	.05	.01
☐ 437 Tim Corcoran	.10	.05	.01
☐ 438 Darren Daulton	2.50	1.10	.30
☐ 439 John Denny	.10	.05	.01
☐ 440 Tom Foley	.10	.05	.01
☐ 441 Greg Gross	.10	.05	.01
☐ 442 Kevin Gross	.10	.05	.01
☐ 443 Von Hayes	.10	.05	.01
☐ 444 Charles Hudson	.10	.05	.01
☐ 445 Garry Maddox	.10	.05	.01
☐ 446 Shane Rawley	.10	.05	.01
☐ 447 Dave Rucker	.10	.05	.01
☐ 448 John Russell	.10	.05	.01
☐ 449 Juan Samuel	.10	.05	.01
☐ 450 Mike Schmidt	1.00	.45	.12
☐ 451 Rick Schu	.10	.05	.01
☐ 452 Dave Shipanoff	.10	.05	.01
☐ 453 Dave Stewart	.20	.09	.03
☐ 454 Jeff Stone	.10	.05	.01
☐ 455 Kent Tekulve	.10	.05	.01
☐ 456 Ozzie Virgil	.10	.05	.01
☐ 457 Glenn Wilson	.10	.05	.01
☐ 458 Jim Beattie	.10	.05	.01
☐ 459 Karl Best	.10	.05	.01
☐ 460 Barry Bonnell	.10	.05	.01
☐ 461 Phil Bradley	.10	.05	.01
☐ 462 Ivan Calderon	.20	.09	.03
☐ 463 Al Cowens	.10	.05	.01
☐ 464 Alvin Davis	.10	.05	.01
☐ 465 Dave Henderson	.10	.05	.01
☐ 466 Bob Kearney	.10	.05	.01
☐ 467 Mark Langston	.20	.09	.03
☐ 468 Bob Long	.10	.05	.01
☐ 469 Mike Moore	.10	.05	.01
☐ 470 Edwin Nunez	.10	.05	.01
☐ 471 Spike Owen	.10	.05	.01
☐ 472 Jack Perconte	.10	.05	.01
☐ 473 Jim Presley	.10	.05	.01
☐ 474 Donnie Scott	.10	.05	.01
☐ 475 Bill Swift	.20	.09	.03
☐ 476 Danny Tartabull	.20	.09	.03
☐ 477 Gorman Thomas	.10	.05	.01
☐ 478 Roy Thomas	.10	.05	.01
☐ 479 Ed VandeBerg	.10	.05	.01
☐ 480 Frank Wills	.10	.05	.01
☐ 481 Matt Young	.10	.05	.01
☐ 482 Ray Burris	.10	.05	.01
☐ 483 Jaime Cocanower	.10	.05	.01
☐ 484 Cecil Cooper	.20	.09	.03
☐ 485 Danny Darwin	.10	.05	.01
☐ 486 Rollie Fingers	.30	.14	.04
☐ 487 Jim Gantner	.10	.05	.01
☐ 488 Bob L. Gibson	.10	.05	.01
☐ 489 Moose Haas	.10	.05	.01
☐ 490 Teddy Higuera	.20	.09	.03
☐ 491 Paul Householder	.10	.05	.01
☐ 492 Pete Ladd	.10	.05	.01
☐ 493 Rick Manning	.10	.05	.01
☐ 494 Bob McClure	.10	.05	.01
☐ 495 Paul Molitor	1.00	.45	.12
☐ 496 Charlie Moore	.10	.05	.01
☐ 497 Ben Oglivie	.10	.05	.01
☐ 498 Randy Ready	.10	.05	.01
☐ 499 Earnie Riles	.10	.05	.01
☐ 500 Ed Romero	.10	.05	.01
☐ 501 Bill Schroeder	.10	.05	.01
☐ 502 Ray Searage	.10	.05	.01
☐ 503 Ted Simmons	.20	.09	.03
☐ 504 Pete Vuckovich	.10	.05	.01
☐ 505 Rick Waits	.10	.05	.01
☐ 506 Robin Yount	.75	.35	.09
☐ 507 Len Barker	.10	.05	.01
☐ 508 Steve Bedrosian	.10	.05	.01
☐ 509 Bruce Benedict	.10	.05	.01
☐ 510 Rick Camp	.10	.05	.01
☐ 511 Rick Cerone	.10	.05	.01
☐ 512 Chris Chambliss	.20	.09	.03
☐ 513 Jeff Dedmon	.10	.05	.01
☐ 514 Terry Forster	.10	.05	.01
☐ 515 Gene Garber	.10	.05	.01
☐ 516 Terry Harper	.10	.05	.01
☐ 517 Bob Horner	.10	.05	.01
☐ 518 Glenn Hubbard	.10	.05	.01
☐ 519 Joe Johnson	.10	.05	.01
☐ 520 Brad Komminsk	.10	.05	.01
☐ 521 Rick Mahler	.10	.05	.01
☐ 522 Dale Murphy	.30	.14	.04
☐ 523 Ken Oberkfell	.10	.05	.01
☐ 524 Pascual Perez	.10	.05	.01
☐ 525 Gerald Perry	.10	.05	.01
☐ 526 Rafael Ramirez	.10	.05	.01
☐ 527 Steve Shields	.10	.05	.01
☐ 528 Zane Smith	.10	.05	.01
☐ 529 Bruce Sutter	.20	.09	.03
☐ 530 Milt Thompson	.20	.09	.03
☐ 531 Claudell Washington	.10	.05	.01
☐ 532 Paul Zuvella	.10	.05	.01
☐ 533 Vida Blue	.20	.09	.03
☐ 534 Bob Brenly	.10	.05	.01
☐ 535 Chris Brown	.10	.05	.01
☐ 536 Chili Davis	.30	.14	.04
☐ 537 Mark Davis	.10	.05	.01
☐ 538 Rob Deer	.20	.09	.03
☐ 539 Dan Driessen	.10	.05	.01
☐ 540 Scott Garrelts	.10	.05	.01
☐ 541 Dan Gladden	.10	.05	.01
☐ 542 Jim Gott	.10	.05	.01
☐ 543 David Green	.10	.05	.01
☐ 544 Atlee Hammaker	.10	.05	.01
☐ 545 Mike Jeffcoat	.10	.05	.01
☐ 546 Mike Krukow	.10	.05	.01
☐ 547 Dave LaPoint	.10	.05	.01
☐ 548 Jeff Leonard	.10	.05	.01
☐ 549 Greg Minton	.10	.05	.01
☐ 550 Alex Trevino	.10	.05	.01
☐ 551 Manny Trillo	.10	.05	.01
☐ 552 Jose Uribe	.10	.05	.01
☐ 553 Brad Wellman	.10	.05	.01
☐ 554 Frank Williams	.10	.05	.01
☐ 555 Joel Youngblood	.10	.05	.01
☐ 556 Alan Bannister	.10	.05	.01
☐ 557 Glenn Brummer	.10	.05	.01
☐ 558 Steve Buechele	.20	.09	.03
☐ 559 Jose Guzman	.10	.05	.01
☐ 560 Toby Harrah	.10	.05	.01
☐ 561 Greg Harris	.10	.05	.01
☐ 562 Dwayne Henry	.10	.05	.01
☐ 563 Burt Hooton	.10	.05	.01
☐ 564 Charlie Hough	.20	.09	.03
☐ 565 Mike Mason	.10	.05	.01
☐ 566 Oddibe McDowell	.10	.05	.01
☐ 567 Dickie Noles	.10	.05	.01
☐ 568 Pete O'Brien	.10	.05	.01
☐ 569 Larry Parrish	.10	.05	.01
☐ 570 Dave Rozema	.10	.05	.01
☐ 571 Dave Schmidt	.10	.05	.01
☐ 572 Don Slaught	.10	.05	.01
☐ 573 Wayne Tolleson	.10	.05	.01
☐ 574 Duane Walker	.10	.05	.01
☐ 575 Gary Ward	.10	.05	.01
☐ 576 Chris Welsh	.10	.05	.01
☐ 577 Curtis Wilkerson	.10	.05	.01
☐ 578 George Wright	.10	.05	.01
☐ 579 Chris Bando	.10	.05	.01
☐ 580 Tony Bernazard	.10	.05	.01
☐ 581 Brett Butler	.20	.09	.03
☐ 582 Ernie Camacho	.10	.05	.01
☐ 583 Joe Carter	2.00	.90	.25
☐ 584 Carmen Castillo	.10	.05	.01
☐ 585 Jamie Easterly	.10	.05	.01
☐ 586 Julio Franco	.30	.14	.04
☐ 587 Mel Hall	.10	.05	.01
☐ 588 Mike Hargrove	.20	.09	.03
☐ 589 Neal Heaton	.10	.05	.01
☐ 590 Brook Jacoby	.10	.05	.01
☐ 591 Otis Nixon	.30	.14	.04
☐ 592 Jerry Reed	.10	.05	.01
☐ 593 Vern Ruhle	.10	.05	.01
☐ 594 Pat Tabler	.10	.05	.01
☐ 595 Rich Thompson	.10	.05	.01
☐ 596 Andre Thornton	.10	.05	.01
☐ 597 Dave Von Ohlen	.10	.05	.01
☐ 598 George Vukovich	.10	.05	.01
☐ 599 Tom Waddell	.10	.05	.01
☐ 600 Curt Wardle	.10	.05	.01
☐ 601 Jerry Willard	.10	.05	.01
☐ 602 Bill Almon	.10	.05	.01
☐ 603 Mike Bielecki	.10	.05	.01
☐ 604 Sid Bream	.10	.05	.01
☐ 605 Mike C. Brown	.10	.05	.01
☐ 606 Pat Clements	.10	.05	.01
☐ 607 Jose DeLeon	.10	.05	.01
☐ 608 Denny Gonzalez	.10	.05	.01
☐ 609 Cecilio Guante	.10	.05	.01
☐ 610 Steve Kemp	.10	.05	.01
☐ 611 Sammy Khalifa	.10	.05	.01
☐ 612 Lee Mazzilli	.10	.05	.01
☐ 613 Larry McWilliams	.10	.05	.01
☐ 614 Jim Morrison	.10	.05	.01
☐ 615 Joe Orsulak	.10	.05	.01
☐ 616 Tony Pena	.10	.05	.01
☐ 617 Johnny Ray	.10	.05	.01
☐ 618 Rick Reuschel	.10	.05	.01
☐ 619 R.J. Reynolds	.10	.05	.01
☐ 620 Rick Rhoden	.10	.05	.01
☐ 621 Don Robinson	.10	.05	.01
☐ 622 Jason Thompson	.10	.05	.01
☐ 623 Lee Tunnell	.10	.05	.01
☐ 624 Jim Winn	.10	.05	.01
☐ 625 Marvell Wynne	.10	.05	.01
☐ 626 Dwight Gooden IA	.30	.14	.04
☐ 627 Don Mattingly IA	1.25	.55	.16
☐ 628 4192 (Pete Rose)	.50	.23	.06
☐ 629 3000 Career Hits Rod Carew	.30	.14	.04
☐ 630 300 Career Wins Tom Seaver Phil Niekro	.30	.14	.04
☐ 631 Ouch (Don Baylor)	.20	.09	.03
☐ 632 Instant Offense Darryl Strawberry Tim Raines	.30	.14	.04
☐ 633 Shortstops Supreme Cal Ripken Alan Trammell	2.00	.90	.25
☐ 634 Boggs and 'Hero' Wade Boggs George Brett	1.25	.55	.16
☐ 635 Braves Dynamic Duo Bob Horner Dale Murphy	.20	.09	.03
☐ 636 Cardinal Ignitors Willie McGee Vince Coleman	.20	.09	.03
☐ 637 Terror on Basepaths Vince Coleman	.20	.09	.03
☐ 638 Charlie Hustle / Dr.K Pete Rose Dwight Gooden	.50	.23	.06
☐ 639 1984 and 1985 AL Batting Champs Wade Boggs Don Mattingly	1.00	.45	.12
☐ 640 NL West Sluggers Dale Murphy Steve Garvey Dave Parker	.20	.09	.03
☐ 641 Staff Aces Fernando Valenzuela Dwight Gooden	.20	.09	.03
☐ 642 Blue Jay Stoppers Jimmy Key Dave Stieb	.30	.14	.04
☐ 643 AL All-Star Backstops Carlton Fisk Rich Gedman	.20	.09	.03
☐ 644 Gene Walter and Benito Santiago	.50	.23	.06
☐ 645 Mike Woodard and Colin Ward	.10	.05	.01

Card	MINT	NRMT	EXC
☐ 646 Kal Daniels and Paul O'Neill	2.00	.90	.25
☐ 647 Andres Galarraga and Fred Toliver	5.00	2.20	.60
☐ 648 Bob Kipper and Curt Ford	.10	.05	.01
☐ 649 Jose Canseco and Eric Plunk	10.00	4.50	1.25
☐ 650 Mark McLemore and Gus Polidor	.50	.23	.06
☐ 651 Rob Woodward and Mickey Brantley	.10	.05	.01
☐ 652 Billy Joe Robidoux and Mark Funderburk	.10	.05	.01
☐ 653 Cecil Fielder and Cory Snyder	5.00	2.20	.60
☐ 654 CL: Royals/Cardinals Blue Jays/Mets	.20	.09	.03
☐ 655 CL: Yankees/Dodgers Angels/Reds UER (168 Darly Sconiers)	.20	.09	.03
☐ 656 CL: White Sox/Tigers Expos/Orioles (279 Dennis, 280 Tippy)	.20	.09	.03
☐ 657 CL: Astros/Padres Red Sox/Cubs	.20	.09	.03
☐ 658 CL: Twins/A's Phillies/Mariners	.20	.09	.03
☐ 659 CL: Brewers/Braves Giants/Rangers	.20	.09	.03
☐ 660 CL: Indians/Pirates Special Cards	.20	.09	.03

1986 Fleer All-Stars

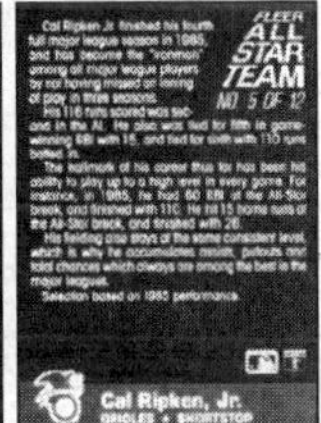

Randomly inserted in wax and cello packs, this 12-card standard-size set features top stars. The cards feature red backgrounds (American Leaguers) and blue backgrounds (National Leaguers). The 12 selections cover each position, left and right-handed starting pitchers, a reliever, and a designated hitter.

	MINT	NRMT	EXC
COMPLETE SET (12)	30.00	13.50	3.70
COMMON CARD (1-12)	.25	.11	.03
☐ 1 Don Mattingly	6.00	2.70	.75
☐ 2 Tom Herr	.25	.11	.03
☐ 3 George Brett	6.00	2.70	.75
☐ 4 Gary Carter	.35	.16	.04
☐ 5 Cal Ripken	15.00	6.75	1.85
☐ 6 Dave Parker	.35	.16	.04
☐ 7 Rickey Henderson UER (Misspelled Ricky on card back)	2.50	1.10	.30
☐ 8 Pedro Guerrero	.35	.16	.04
☐ 9 Dan Quisenberry	.25	.11	.03
☐ 10 Dwight Gooden	1.50	.70	.19
☐ 11 Gorman Thomas	.25	.11	.03
☐ 12 John Tudor	.25	.11	.03

1986 Fleer Future Hall of Famers

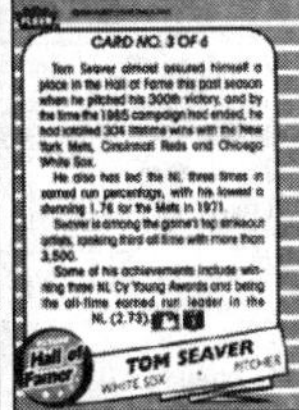

These six standard-size cards were issued one per Fleer three-packs. This set features players that Fleer predicts will be "Future Hall of Famers." The card backs describe career highlights, records, and honors won by the player.

	MINT	NRMT	EXC
COMPLETE SET (6)	18.00	8.00	2.20
COMMON CARD (1-6)	2.00	.90	.25
☐ 1 Pete Rose	3.00	1.35	.35
☐ 2 Steve Carlton	2.00	.90	.25
☐ 3 Tom Seaver	2.00	.90	.25
☐ 4 Rod Carew	2.00	.90	.25
☐ 5 Nolan Ryan	10.00	4.50	1.25
☐ 6 Reggie Jackson	2.50	1.10	.30

1986 Fleer Wax Box Cards

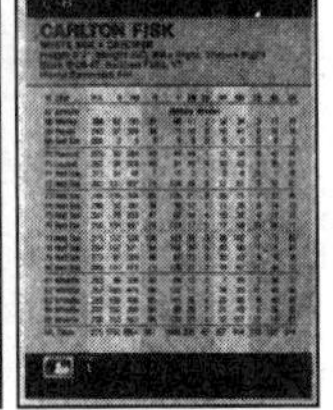

The cards in this eight-card set measure the standard size and were found on the bottom of the Fleer regular issue wax pack and cello pack boxes as four-card panel. Cards have essentially the same design as the 1986 Fleer regular issue set. These eight cards (C1 to C8) are considered a separate set in their own right and are not typically included in a complete set of the regular issue 1986 Fleer cards. The value of the panel uncut is slightly greater, perhaps by 25 percent greater, than the value of the individual cards cut up carefully.

	MINT	NRMT	EXC
COMPLETE SET (8)	5.00	2.20	.60
COMMON CARD (C1-C8)	.25	.11	.03
☐ C1 Royals Logo	.25	.11	.03
☐ C2 George Brett	2.50	1.10	.30
☐ C3 Ozzie Guillen	.50	.23	.06
☐ C4 Dale Murphy	.75	.35	.09
☐ C5 Cardinals Logo	.25	.11	.03
☐ C6 Tom Browning	.25	.11	.03
☐ C7 Gary Carter	.50	.23	.06
☐ C8 Carlton Fisk	1.00	.45	.12

1986 Fleer Update

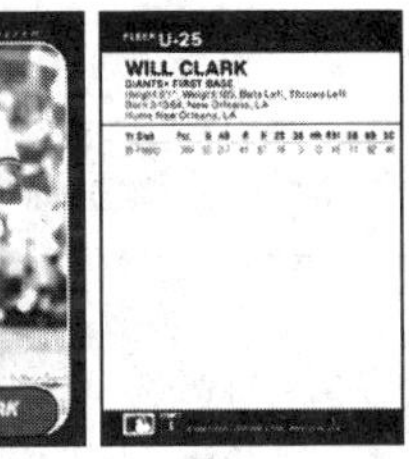

This 132-card standard-size set was distributed in factory set form through hobby dealers. In addition to the complete set of 132 cards, the box also contains 25 Team Logo Stickers.The card fronts look very similar to the 1986 Fleer regular issue. The cards are numbered (with a U prefix) alphabetically according to player's last name. The extended Rookie Cards in this set include Barry Bonds, Bobby Bonilla, Will Clark, Wally Joyner, John Kruk, Kevin Mitchell, and Ruben Sierra.

	MINT	NRMT	EXC
COMPLETE FACT.SET (132)	15.00	6.75	1.85
COMMON CARD (1-132)	.07	.03	.01
☐ 1 Mike Aldrete	.07	.03	.01
☐ 2 Andy Allanson	.07	.03	.01
☐ 3 Neil Allen	.07	.03	.01
☐ 4 Joaquin Andujar	.07	.03	.01
☐ 5 Paul Assenmacher	.07	.03	.01
☐ 6 Scott Bailes	.07	.03	.01
☐ 7 Jay Baller	.07	.03	.01
☐ 8 Scott Bankhead	.07	.03	.01
☐ 9 Bill Bathe	.07	.03	.01
☐ 10 Don Baylor	.40	.18	.05
☐ 11 Billy Beane	.07	.03	.01
☐ 12 Steve Bedrosian	.07	.03	.01
☐ 13 Juan Beniquez	.07	.03	.01
☐ 14 Barry Bonds	5.00	2.20	.60
☐ 15 Bobby Bonilla UER (Wrong birthday)	1.00	.45	.12
☐ 16 Rich Bordi	.07	.03	.01
☐ 17 Bill Campbell	.07	.03	.01
☐ 18 Tom Candiotti	.07	.03	.01
☐ 19 John Cangelosi	.07	.03	.01
☐ 20 Jose Canseco UER (Headings on back for a pitcher)	3.00	1.35	.35
☐ 21 Chuck Cary	.07	.03	.01
☐ 22 Juan Castillo	.07	.03	.01
☐ 23 Rick Cerone	.07	.03	.01
☐ 24 John Cerutti	.07	.03	.01
☐ 25 Will Clark	2.50	1.10	.30
☐ 26 Mark Clear	.07	.03	.01
☐ 27 Darnell Coles	.07	.03	.01
☐ 28 Dave Collins	.07	.03	.01
☐ 29 Tim Conroy	.07	.03	.01
☐ 30 Ed Correa	.07	.03	.01
☐ 31 Joe Cowley	.07	.03	.01
☐ 32 Bill Dawley	.07	.03	.01
☐ 33 Rob Deer	.20	.09	.03
☐ 34 John Denny	.07	.03	.01
☐ 35 Jim Deshaies	.07	.03	.01
☐ 36 Doug Drabek	.60	.25	.07
☐ 37 Mike Easler	.07	.03	.01
☐ 38 Mark Eichhorn	.07	.03	.01
☐ 39 Dave Engle	.07	.03	.01
☐ 40 Mike Fischlin	.07	.03	.01
☐ 41 Scott Fletcher	.07	.03	.01
☐ 42 Terry Forster	.07	.03	.01
☐ 43 Terry Francona	.07	.03	.01
☐ 44 Andres Galarraga	2.00	.90	.25
☐ 45 Lee Guetterman	.07	.03	.01
☐ 46 Bill Gullickson	.07	.03	.01
☐ 47 Jackie Gutierrez	.07	.03	.01
☐ 48 Moose Haas	.07	.03	.01
☐ 49 Billy Hatcher	.20	.09	.03
☐ 50 Mike Heath	.07	.03	.01
☐ 51 Guy Hoffman	.07	.03	.01
☐ 52 Tom Hume	.07	.03	.01
☐ 53 Pete Incaviglia	.40	.18	.05
☐ 54 Dane Iorg	.07	.03	.01
☐ 55 Chris James	.07	.03	.01
☐ 56 Stan Javier	.20	.09	.03
☐ 57 Tommy John	.40	.18	.05
☐ 58 Tracy Jones	.07	.03	.01
☐ 59 Wally Joyner	1.00	.45	.12
☐ 60 Wayne Krenchicki	.07	.03	.01
☐ 61 John Kruk	.75	.35	.09
☐ 62 Mike LaCoss	.07	.03	.01
☐ 63 Pete Ladd	.07	.03	.01
☐ 64 Dave LaPoint	.07	.03	.01
☐ 65 Mike LaValliere	.07	.03	.01
☐ 66 Rudy Law	.07	.03	.01
☐ 67 Dennis Leonard	.07	.03	.01
☐ 68 Steve Lombardozzi	.07	.03	.01
☐ 69 Aurelio Lopez	.07	.03	.01
☐ 70 Mickey Mahler	.07	.03	.01
☐ 71 Candy Maldonado	.07	.03	.01
☐ 72 Roger Mason	.07	.03	.01
☐ 73 Greg Mathews	.07	.03	.01
☐ 74 Andy McGaffigan	.07	.03	.01
☐ 75 Joel McKeon	.07	.03	.01
☐ 76 Kevin Mitchell	.40	.18	.05
☐ 77 Bill Mooneyham	.07	.03	.01
☐ 78 Omar Moreno	.07	.03	.01
☐ 79 Jerry Mumphrey	.07	.03	.01
☐ 80 Al Newman	.20	.09	.03
☐ 81 Phil Niekro	.40	.18	.05
☐ 82 Randy Niemann	.07	.03	.01
☐ 83 Juan Nieves	.07	.03	.01
☐ 84 Bob Ojeda	.07	.03	.01
☐ 85 Rick Ownbey	.07	.03	.01
☐ 86 Tom Paciorek	.07	.03	.01
☐ 87 David Palmer	.07	.03	.01
☐ 88 Jeff Parrett	.07	.03	.01
☐ 89 Pat Perry	.07	.03	.01
☐ 90 Dan Plesac	.07	.03	.01
☐ 91 Darrell Porter	.07	.03	.01
☐ 92 Luis Quinones	.07	.03	.01
☐ 93 Rey Quinones UER (Misspelled Quinonez)	.07	.03	.01
☐ 94 Gary Redus	.07	.03	.01
☐ 95 Jeff Reed	.07	.03	.01
☐ 96 Bip Roberts	.40	.18	.05
☐ 97 Billy Joe Robidoux	.07	.03	.01
☐ 98 Gary Roenicke	.07	.03	.01
☐ 99 Ron Roenicke	.07	.03	.01
☐ 100 Angel Salazar	.07	.03	.01
☐ 101 Joe Sambito	.07	.03	.01
☐ 102 Billy Sample	.07	.03	.01
☐ 103 Dave Schmidt	.07	.03	.01
☐ 104 Ken Schrom	.07	.03	.01
☐ 105 Ruben Sierra	1.25	.55	.16
☐ 106 Ted Simmons	.20	.09	.03
☐ 107 Sammy Stewart	.07	.03	.01
☐ 108 Kurt Stillwell	.07	.03	.01
☐ 109 Dale Sveum	.07	.03	.01
☐ 110 Tim Teufel	.07	.03	.01
☐ 111 Bob Tewksbury	.20	.09	.03
☐ 112 Andres Thomas	.07	.03	.01
☐ 113 Jason Thompson	.07	.03	.01
☐ 114 Milt Thompson	.20	.09	.03
☐ 115 Robby Thompson	.20	.09	.03
☐ 116 Jay Tibbs	.07	.03	.01
☐ 117 Fred Toliver	.07	.03	.01
☐ 118 Wayne Tolleson	.07	.03	.01
☐ 119 Alex Trevino	.07	.03	.01
☐ 120 Manny Trillo	.07	.03	.01
☐ 121 Ed VandeBerg	.07	.03	.01
☐ 122 Ozzie Virgil	.07	.03	.01
☐ 123 Tony Walker	.07	.03	.01
☐ 124 Gene Walter	.07	.03	.01
☐ 125 Duane Ward	.20	.09	.03
☐ 126 Jerry Willard	.07	.03	.01
☐ 127 Mitch Williams	.20	.09	.03
☐ 128 Reggie Williams	.07	.03	.01
☐ 129 Bobby Witt	.20	.09	.03
☐ 130 Marvell Wynne	.07	.03	.01
☐ 131 Steve Yeager	.07	.03	.01
☐ 132 Checklist 1-132	.07	.03	.01

1986 Fleer League Leaders

This 44-card standard-size set is also sometimes referred to as the Walgreen's set. Although the set was distributed through Walgreen's, there is no mention on the cards or box of that fact. The cards are easily recognizable by the fact that they contain the phrase "Fleer League Leaders" at the top of the obverse. Both sides of the cards are designed with a blue stripe on white pattern. The checklist for the set is given on the outside of the red, white, blue, and gold box in which the set was packaged.

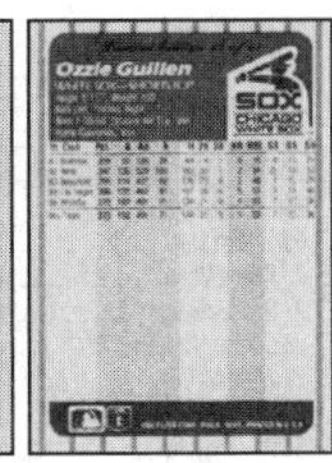

	MINT	NRMT	EXC
COMPLETE SET (44)	5.00	2.20	.60
COMMON CARD (1-44)	.05	.02	.01
☐ 1 Wade Boggs	.40	.18	.05
☐ 2 George Brett	1.25	.55	.16
☐ 3 Jose Canseco	1.50	.70	.19
☐ 4 Rod Carew	.25	.11	.03
☐ 5 Gary Carter	.10	.05	.01
☐ 6 Jack Clark	.10	.05	.01
☐ 7 Vince Coleman	.10	.05	.01
☐ 8 Jose Cruz	.05	.02	.01
☐ 9 Alvin Davis	.05	.02	.01
☐ 10 Mariano Duncan	.10	.05	.01
☐ 11 Leon Durham	.05	.02	.01
☐ 12 Carlton Fisk	.25	.11	.03
☐ 13 Julio Franco	.10	.05	.01
☐ 14 Scott Garrelts	.05	.02	.01
☐ 15 Steve Garvey	.10	.05	.01
☐ 16 Dwight Gooden	.25	.11	.03
☐ 17 Ozzie Guillen	.10	.05	.01
☐ 18 Willie Hernandez	.05	.02	.01
☐ 19 Bob Horner	.05	.02	.01
☐ 20 Kent Hrbek	.10	.05	.01
☐ 21 Charlie Leibrandt	.05	.02	.01
☐ 22 Don Mattingly	1.00	.45	.12
☐ 23 Oddibe McDowell	.05	.02	.01
☐ 24 Willie McGee	.10	.05	.01
☐ 25 Keith Moreland	.05	.02	.01
☐ 26 Lloyd Moseby	.05	.02	.01
☐ 27 Dale Murphy	.20	.09	.03
☐ 28 Phil Niekro	.20	.09	.03
☐ 29 Joe Orsulak	.05	.02	.01
☐ 30 Dave Parker	.10	.05	.01
☐ 31 Lance Parrish	.10	.05	.01
☐ 32 Kirby Puckett	1.25	.55	.16
☐ 33 Tim Raines	.10	.05	.01
☐ 34 Earnie Riles	.05	.02	.01
☐ 35 Cal Ripken	2.00	.90	.25
☐ 36 Pete Rose	.75	.35	.09
☐ 37 Bret Saberhagen	.20	.09	.03
☐ 38 Juan Samuel	.05	.02	.01
☐ 39 Ryne Sandberg	.75	.35	.09
☐ 40 Tom Seaver	.25	.11	.03
☐ 41 Lee Smith	.20	.09	.03
☐ 42 Ozzie Smith	1.00	.45	.12
☐ 43 Dave Stieb	.05	.02	.01
☐ 44 Robin Yount	.25	.11	.03

1986 Fleer Limited Edition

The 44-card boxed standard-size set was produced by Fleer for McCrory's. The cards have green and yellow borders. Card backs are printed in red and black on white card stock. The back of the original box gives a complete checklist of the players in the set. The set box also contains six logo stickers.

	MINT	NRMT	EXC
COMPLETE SET (44)	5.00	2.20	.60
COMMON CARD (1-44)	.05	.02	.01
☐ 1 Doyle Alexander	.05	.02	.01
☐ 2 Joaquin Andujar	.05	.02	.01
☐ 3 Harold Baines	.10	.05	.01
☐ 4 Wade Boggs	.30	.14	.04
☐ 5 Phil Bradley	.05	.02	.01
☐ 6 George Brett	.75	.35	.09
☐ 7 Hubie Brooks	.05	.02	.01
☐ 8 Chris Brown	.05	.02	.01
☐ 9 Tom Brunansky	.05	.02	.01
☐ 10 Gary Carter	.10	.05	.01
☐ 11 Vince Coleman	.10	.05	.01
☐ 12 Cecil Cooper	.10	.05	.01
☐ 13 Jose Cruz	.05	.02	.01
☐ 14 Mike Davis	.05	.02	.01
☐ 15 Carlton Fisk	.25	.11	.03
☐ 16 Julio Franco	.10	.05	.01
☐ 17 Damaso Garcia	.05	.02	.01
☐ 18 Rich Gedman	.05	.02	.01

	MINT	NRMT	EXC
☐ 19 Kirk Gibson	.10	.05	.01
☐ 20 Dwight Gooden	.25	.11	.03
☐ 21 Pedro Guerrero	.05	.02	.01
☐ 22 Tony Gwynn	1.00	.45	.12
☐ 23 Rickey Henderson	.25	.11	.03
☐ 24 Orel Hershiser	.25	.11	.03
☐ 25 LaMarr Hoyt	.05	.02	.01
☐ 26 Reggie Jackson	.50	.23	.06
☐ 27 Don Mattingly	1.00	.45	.12
☐ 28 Oddibe McDowell	.05	.02	.01
☐ 29 Willie McGee	.10	.05	.01
☐ 30 Paul Molitor	.50	.23	.06
☐ 31 Dale Murphy	.20	.09	.03
☐ 32 Eddie Murray	.50	.23	.06
☐ 33 Dave Parker	.10	.05	.01
☐ 34 Tony Pena	.05	.02	.01
☐ 35 Jeff Reardon	.05	.02	.01
☐ 36 Cal Ripken	2.00	.90	.25
☐ 37 Pete Rose	.75	.35	.09
☐ 38 Bret Saberhagen	.15	.07	.02
☐ 39 Juan Samuel	.05	.02	.01
☐ 40 Ryne Sandberg	.75	.35	.09
☐ 41 Mike Schmidt	.50	.23	.06
☐ 42 Lee Smith	.20	.09	.03
☐ 43 Don Sutton	.10	.05	.01
☐ 44 Lou Whitaker	.10	.05	.01

1986 Fleer Mini

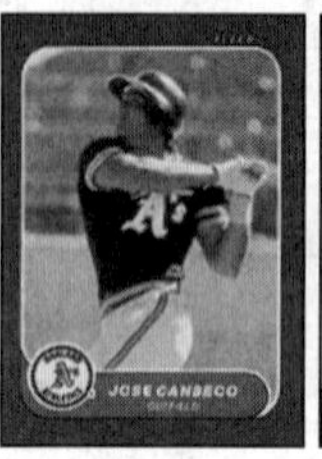

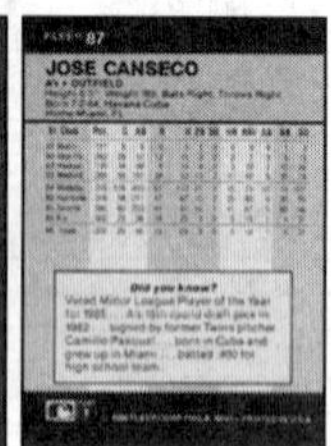

The Fleer "Classic Miniatures" set consists of 120 small cards with all new pictures of the players as compared to the 1986 Fleer regular issue. The cards are only 1 13/16" by 2 9/16", making them some of the smallest (in size) produced in recent memory. Card backs provide career year-by-year statistics. The complete set was distributed in a red, white, and silver box along with 18 logo stickers. The card numbering is done in the same team order as the 1986 Fleer regular set.

	MINT	NRMT	EXC
COMPLETE SET (120)	8.00	3.60	1.00
COMMON CARD (1-120)	.05	.02	.01
☐ 1 George Brett	1.25	.55	.16
☐ 2 Dan Quisenberry	.05	.02	.01
☐ 3 Bret Saberhagen	.15	.07	.02
☐ 4 Lonnie Smith	.05	.02	.01
☐ 5 Willie Wilson	.05	.02	.01
☐ 6 Jack Clark	.05	.02	.01
☐ 7 Vince Coleman	.10	.05	.01
☐ 8 Tom Herr	.05	.02	.01
☐ 9 Willie McGee	.10	.05	.01
☐ 10 Ozzie Smith	1.00	.45	.12
☐ 11 John Tudor	.05	.02	.01
☐ 12 Jesse Barfield	.05	.02	.01
☐ 13 George Bell	.10	.05	.01
☐ 14 Tony Fernandez	.05	.02	.01
☐ 15 Damaso Garcia	.05	.02	.01
☐ 16 Dave Stieb	.05	.02	.01
☐ 17 Gary Carter	.10	.05	.01
☐ 18 Ron Darling	.05	.02	.01
☐ 19A Dwight Gooden (R on Mets logo)	.50	.23	.06
☐ 19B Dwight Gooden (No R on Mets logo)	.50	.23	.06
☐ 20 Keith Hernandez	.10	.05	.01
☐ 21 Darryl Strawberry	.15	.07	.02
☐ 22 Ron Guidry	.10	.05	.01
☐ 23 Rickey Henderson	.50	.23	.06
☐ 24 Don Mattingly	1.25	.55	.16
☐ 25 Dave Righetti	.05	.02	.01
☐ 26 Dave Winfield	.50	.23	.06
☐ 27 Mariano Duncan	.15	.07	.02
☐ 28 Pedro Guerrero	.10	.05	.01
☐ 29 Bill Madlock	.05	.02	.01
☐ 30 Mike Marshall	.05	.02	.01
☐ 31 Fernando Valenzuela	.10	.05	.01
☐ 32 Reggie Jackson	.50	.23	.06
☐ 33 Gary Pettis	.05	.02	.01
☐ 34 Ron Romanick	.05	.02	.01
☐ 35 Don Sutton	.15	.07	.02
☐ 36 Mike Witt	.05	.02	.01
☐ 37 Buddy Bell	.10	.05	.01
☐ 38 Tom Browning	.05	.02	.01
☐ 39 Dave Parker	.10	.05	.01
☐ 40 Pete Rose	.60	.25	.07
☐ 41 Mario Soto	.05	.02	.01
☐ 42 Harold Baines	.10	.05	.01
☐ 43 Carlton Fisk	.50	.23	.06
☐ 44 Ozzie Guillen	.10	.05	.01
☐ 45 Ron Kittle	.05	.02	.01
☐ 46 Tom Seaver	.50	.23	.06
☐ 47 Kirk Gibson	.10	.05	.01
☐ 48 Jack Morris	.10	.05	.01
☐ 49 Lance Parrish	.05	.02	.01
☐ 50 Alan Trammell	.15	.07	.02
☐ 51 Lou Whitaker	.10	.05	.01
☐ 52 Hubie Brooks	.05	.02	.01
☐ 53 Andre Dawson	.40	.18	.05
☐ 54 Tim Raines	.10	.05	.01
☐ 55 Bryn Smith	.05	.02	.01
☐ 56 Tim Wallach	.05	.02	.01
☐ 57 Mike Boddicker	.05	.02	.01
☐ 58 Eddie Murray	.40	.18	.05
☐ 59 Cal Ripken	1.50	.70	.19
☐ 60 John Shelby	.05	.02	.01
☐ 61 Mike Young	.05	.02	.01
☐ 62 Jose Cruz	.05	.02	.01
☐ 63 Glenn Davis	.05	.02	.01
☐ 64 Phil Garner	.05	.02	.01
☐ 65 Nolan Ryan	2.00	.90	.25
☐ 66 Mike Scott	.05	.02	.01
☐ 67 Steve Garvey	.10	.05	.01
☐ 68 Rich Gossage	.10	.05	.01
☐ 69 Tony Gwynn	1.00	.45	.12
☐ 70 Andy Hawkins	.05	.02	.01
☐ 71 Garry Templeton	.05	.02	.01
☐ 72 Wade Boggs	.25	.11	.03
☐ 73 Roger Clemens	1.00	.45	.12
☐ 74 Dwight Evans	.10	.05	.01
☐ 75 Rich Gedman	.05	.02	.01
☐ 76 Jim Rice	.10	.05	.01
☐ 77 Shawon Dunston	.10	.05	.01
☐ 78 Leon Durham	.05	.02	.01
☐ 79 Keith Moreland	.05	.02	.01
☐ 80 Ryne Sandberg	.60	.25	.07
☐ 81 Rick Sutcliffe	.05	.02	.01
☐ 82 Bert Blyleven	.10	.05	.01
☐ 83 Tom Brunansky	.05	.02	.01
☐ 84 Kent Hrbek	.10	.05	.01
☐ 85 Kirby Puckett	1.25	.55	.16
☐ 86 Bruce Bochte	.05	.02	.01
☐ 87 Jose Canseco	.75	.35	.09
☐ 88 Mike Davis	.05	.02	.01
☐ 89 Jay Howell	.05	.02	.01
☐ 90 Dwayne Murphy	.05	.02	.01
☐ 91 Steve Carlton	.25	.11	.03
☐ 92 Von Hayes	.05	.02	.01
☐ 93 Juan Samuel	.05	.02	.01
☐ 94 Mike Schmidt	.40	.18	.05
☐ 95 Glenn Wilson	.05	.02	.01
☐ 96 Phil Bradley	.05	.02	.01
☐ 97 Alvin Davis	.05	.02	.01
☐ 98 Jim Presley	.05	.02	.01
☐ 99 Danny Tartabull	.10	.05	.01
☐ 100 Cecil Cooper	.10	.05	.01
☐ 101 Paul Molitor	.60	.25	.07
☐ 102 Ernie Riles	.05	.02	.01
☐ 103 Robin Yount	.25	.11	.03
☐ 104 Bob Horner	.05	.02	.01
☐ 105 Dale Murphy	.15	.07	.02
☐ 106 Bruce Sutter	.10	.05	.01
☐ 107 Claudell Washington	.05	.02	.01
☐ 108 Chris Brown	.05	.02	.01
☐ 109 Chili Davis	.10	.05	.01
☐ 110 Scott Garrelts	.05	.02	.01
☐ 111 Oddibe McDowell	.05	.02	.01
☐ 112 Pete O'Brien	.05	.02	.01
☐ 113 Gary Ward	.05	.02	.01
☐ 114 Brett Butler	.10	.05	.01
☐ 115 Julio Franco	.10	.05	.01
☐ 116 Brook Jacoby	.05	.02	.01
☐ 117 Mike C. Brown	.05	.02	.01
☐ 118 Joe Orsulak	.05	.02	.01
☐ 119 Tony Pena	.05	.02	.01
☐ 120 R.J. Reynolds	.05	.02	.01

1986 Fleer Sluggers/Pitchers

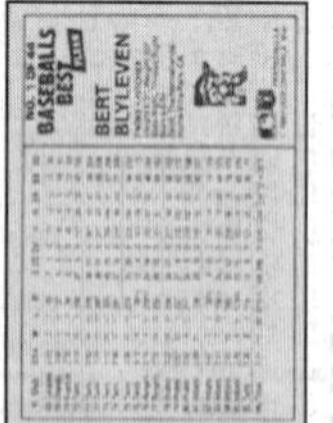

Fleer produced this 44-card boxed standard-size set although it was primarily distributed by Kress, McCrory, Newberry, T.G.Y., and other similar stores. The set features 22 sluggers and 22 pitchers and is subtitled "Baseball's Best". The set was packaged in a red, white, blue, and yellow custom box along with six logo stickers. The set checklist is given on the back of the box. The card numbering is in alphabetical order by the player's name. The Will Clark and Bobby Witt cards were the first major league cards produced of those players.

	MINT	NRMT	EXC
COMPLETE SET (44)	5.00	2.20	.60
COMMON CARD (1-44)	.05	.02	.01
☐ 1 Bert Blyleven	.10	.05	.01
☐ 2 Wade Boggs	.30	.14	.04
☐ 3 George Brett	1.00	.45	.12
☐ 4 Tom Browning	.05	.02	.01
☐ 5 Jose Canseco	1.00	.45	.12
☐ 6 Will Clark	1.50	.70	.19
☐ 7 Roger Clemens	.75	.35	.09
☐ 8 Alvin Davis	.05	.02	.01
☐ 9 Julio Franco	.10	.05	.01
☐ 10 Kirk Gibson	.10	.05	.01
☐ 11 Dwight Gooden	.25	.11	.03
☐ 12 Rich Gossage	.10	.05	.01
☐ 13 Pedro Guerrero	.05	.02	.01
☐ 14 Ron Guidry	.10	.05	.01
☐ 15 Tony Gwynn	.75	.35	.09
☐ 16 Orel Hershiser	.25	.11	.03
☐ 17 Kent Hrbek	.10	.05	.01
☐ 18 Reggie Jackson	.25	.11	.03
☐ 19 Wally Joyner	.20	.09	.03
☐ 20 Charlie Leibrandt	.05	.02	.01
☐ 21 Don Mattingly	1.00	.45	.12
☐ 22 Willie McGee	.10	.05	.01
☐ 23 Jack Morris	.10	.05	.01
☐ 24 Dale Murphy	.20	.09	.03
☐ 25 Eddie Murray	.50	.23	.06
☐ 26 Jeff Reardon	.05	.02	.01
☐ 27 Rick Reuschel	.05	.02	.01
☐ 28 Cal Ripken	2.00	.90	.25
☐ 29 Pete Rose	.50	.23	.06
☐ 30 Nolan Ryan	1.50	.70	.19
☐ 31 Bret Saberhagen	.15	.07	.02
☐ 32 Ryne Sandberg	.60	.25	.07
☐ 33 Mike Schmidt	.50	.23	.06
☐ 34 Tom Seaver	.25	.11	.03
☐ 35 Bryn Smith	.05	.02	.01
☐ 36 Mario Soto	.05	.02	.01
☐ 37 Dave Stieb	.05	.02	.01
☐ 38 Darryl Strawberry	.20	.09	.03
☐ 39 Rick Sutcliffe	.05	.02	.01
☐ 40 John Tudor	.05	.02	.01
☐ 41 Fernando Valenzuela	.10	.05	.01
☐ 42 Bobby Witt	.10	.05	.01
☐ 43 Mike Witt	.05	.02	.01
☐ 44 Robin Yount	.25	.11	.03

1986 Fleer Sluggers/Pitchers Box Cards

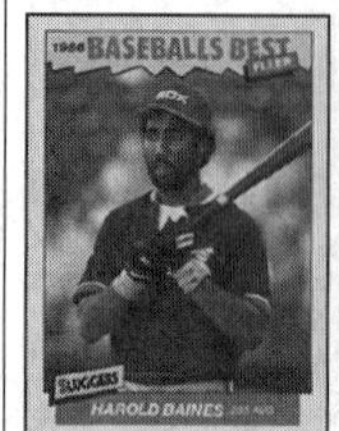

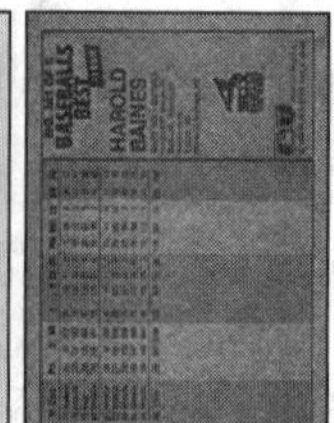

The cards in this six-card set each measure the standard size. Cards have essentially the same design as the 1986 Fleer Sluggers vs. Pitchers set of Baseball's Best. The cards were printed on the bottom of the counter display box which held 24 small boxed sets; hence theoretically these box cards are 1/24 as plentiful as the regular boxed set cards. These six cards, numbered M1 to M5 with one blank-back (unnumbered) card, are considered a separate set in their own right and are not typically included in a complete set of the 1986 Fleer Sluggers vs. Pitchers set of 44. The value of the panels uncut is slightly greater, perhaps by 25 percent greater, than the value of the individual cards cut up carefully.

	MINT	NRMT	EXC
COMPLETE SET (6)	10.00	4.50	1.25
COMMON CARD	.50	.23	.06
☐ M1 Harold Baines	.75	.35	.09
☐ M2 Steve Carlton	1.50	.70	.19
☐ M3 Gary Carter	.75	.35	.09
☐ M4 Vince Coleman	.75	.35	.09
☐ M5 Kirby Puckett	8.00	3.60	1.00
☐ NNO Team Logo (Blank back)	.50	.23	.06

1986 Fleer Sticker Cards

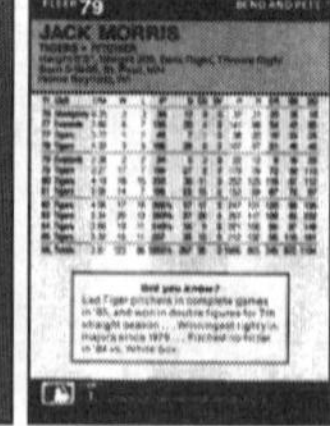

The standard-size stickers (made of card stock) 132-card set feature card photos on the front surrounded by a yellow border and a cranberry frame. The backs are printed in blue and black on white card stock. The backs contain year-by-year statistical information. They are numbered on the back in the upper left-hand corner. The card numbering is in alphabetical order by the player's name.

	MINT	NRMT	EXC
COMPLETE SET (132)	15.00	6.75	1.85
COMMON CARD (1-132)	.05	.02	.01
☐ 1 Harold Baines	.10	.05	.01
☐ 2 Jesse Barfield	.05	.02	.01
☐ 3 Don Baylor	.10	.05	.01
☐ 4 Juan Beniquez	.05	.02	.01
☐ 5 Tim Birtsas	.05	.02	.01
☐ 6 Bert Blyleven	.10	.05	.01
☐ 7 Bruce Bochte	.05	.02	.01
☐ 8 Wade Boggs	.40	.18	.05
☐ 9 Dennis Boyd	.05	.02	.01
☐ 10 Phil Bradley	.05	.02	.01
☐ 11 George Brett	1.50	.70	.19
☐ 12 Hubie Brooks	.05	.02	.01
☐ 13 Chris Brown	.05	.02	.01
☐ 14 Tom Browning	.05	.02	.01
☐ 15 Tom Brunansky	.05	.02	.01
☐ 16 Bill Buckner	.10	.05	.01
☐ 17 Britt Burns	.05	.02	.01
☐ 18 Brett Butler	.10	.05	.01
☐ 19 Jose Canseco	2.00	.90	.25
☐ 20 Rod Carew	.40	.18	.05
☐ 21 Steve Carlton	.40	.18	.05
☐ 22 Don Carman	.05	.02	.01
☐ 23 Gary Carter	.10	.05	.01
☐ 24 Jack Clark	.10	.05	.01
☐ 25 Vince Coleman	.25	.11	.03
☐ 26 Cecil Cooper	.10	.05	.01
☐ 27 Jose Cruz	.05	.02	.01
☐ 28 Ron Darling	.05	.02	.01
☐ 29 Alvin Davis	.05	.02	.01
☐ 30 Jody Davis	.05	.02	.01
☐ 31 Mike Davis	.05	.02	.01
☐ 32 Andre Dawson	.15	.07	.02
☐ 33 Mariano Duncan	.15	.07	.02
☐ 34 Shawon Dunston	.10	.05	.01
☐ 35 Leon Durham	.05	.02	.01
☐ 36 Darrell Evans	.10	.05	.01
☐ 37 Tony Fernandez	.05	.02	.01
☐ 38 Carlton Fisk	.40	.18	.05
☐ 39 John Franco	.15	.07	.02
☐ 40 Julio Franco	.10	.05	.01
☐ 41 Damaso Garcia	.05	.02	.01
☐ 42 Scott Garrelts	.05	.02	.01
☐ 43 Steve Garvey	.25	.11	.03
☐ 44 Rich Gedman	.05	.02	.01
☐ 45 Kirk Gibson	.10	.05	.01
☐ 46 Dwight Gooden	.40	.18	.05
☐ 47 Pedro Guerrero	.10	.05	.01
☐ 48 Ron Guidry	.10	.05	.01
☐ 49 Ozzie Guillen	.10	.05	.01
☐ 50 Tony Gwynn	2.00	.90	.25
☐ 51 Andy Hawkins	.05	.02	.01
☐ 52 Von Hayes	.05	.02	.01
☐ 53 Rickey Henderson	.60	.25	.07
☐ 54 Tom Henke	.05	.02	.01
☐ 55 Keith Hernandez	.10	.05	.01
☐ 56 Willie Hernandez	.05	.02	.01
☐ 57 Tommy Herr	.05	.02	.01
☐ 58 Orel Hershiser	.15	.07	.02
☐ 59 Teddy Higuera	.10	.05	.01
☐ 60 Bob Horner	.05	.02	.01
☐ 61 Charlie Hough	.05	.02	.01
☐ 62 Jay Howell	.05	.02	.01
☐ 63 LaMarr Hoyt	.05	.02	.01
☐ 64 Kent Hrbek	.10	.05	.01
☐ 65 Reggie Jackson	.60	.25	.07
☐ 66 Bob James	.05	.02	.01
☐ 67 Dave Kingman	.10	.05	.01
☐ 68 Ron Kittle	.05	.02	.01
☐ 69 Charlie Leibrandt	.05	.02	.01
☐ 70 Fred Lynn	.10	.05	.01
☐ 71 Mike Marshall	.05	.02	.01
☐ 72 Don Mattingly	2.50	1.10	.30
☐ 73 Oddibe McDowell	.05	.02	.01
☐ 74 Willie McGee	.10	.05	.01
☐ 75 Scott McGregor	.05	.02	.01
☐ 76 Paul Molitor	.60	.25	.07
☐ 77 Donnie Moore	.05	.02	.01
☐ 78 Keith Moreland	.05	.02	.01
☐ 79 Jack Morris	.10	.05	.01
☐ 80 Dale Murphy	.15	.07	.02
☐ 81 Eddie Murray	.75	.35	.09
☐ 82 Phil Niekro	.15	.07	.02
☐ 83 Joe Orsulak	.05	.02	.01
☐ 84 Dave Parker	.10	.05	.01
☐ 85 Lance Parrish	.10	.05	.01
☐ 86 Larry Parrish	.05	.02	.01
☐ 87 Tony Pena	.05	.02	.01
☐ 88 Gary Pettis	.05	.02	.01
☐ 89 Jim Presley	.05	.02	.01
☐ 90 Kirby Puckett	2.50	1.10	.30
☐ 91 Dan Quisenberry	.05	.02	.01
☐ 92 Tim Raines	.10	.05	.01
☐ 93 Johnny Ray	.05	.02	.01
☐ 94 Jeff Reardon	.10	.05	.01
☐ 95 Rick Reuschel	.05	.02	.01
☐ 96 Jim Rice	.10	.05	.01
☐ 97 Dave Righetti	.05	.02	.01
☐ 98 Earnie Riles	.05	.02	.01
☐ 99 Cal Ripken	3.00	1.35	.35
☐ 100 Ron Romanick	.05	.02	.01
☐ 101 Pete Rose	1.25	.55	.16
☐ 102 Nolan Ryan	3.00	1.35	.35

Card	MINT	NRMT	EXC
□ 103 Bret Saberhagen	.15	.07	.02
□ 104 Mark Salas	.05	.02	.01
□ 105 Juan Samuel	.05	.02	.01
□ 106 Ryne Sandberg	1.25	.55	.16
□ 107 Mike Schmidt	.75	.35	.09
□ 108 Mike Scott	.05	.02	.01
□ 109 Tom Seaver	.40	.18	.05
□ 110 Bryn Smith	.05	.02	.01
□ 111 Dave Smith	.05	.02	.01
□ 112 Lee Smith	.15	.07	.02
□ 113 Ozzie Smith	1.25	.55	.16
□ 114 Mario Soto	.05	.02	.01
□ 115 Dave Stieb	.05	.02	.01
□ 116 Darryl Strawberry	.15	.07	.02
□ 117 Bruce Sutter	.10	.05	.01
□ 118 Garry Templeton	.05	.02	.01
□ 119 Gorman Thomas	.05	.02	.01
□ 120 Andre Thornton	.05	.02	.01
□ 121 Alan Trammell	.15	.07	.02
□ 122 John Tudor	.05	.02	.01
□ 123 Fernando Valenzuela	1.00	.45	.12
□ 124 Frank Viola	.10	.05	.01
□ 125 Gary Ward	.05	.02	.01
□ 126 Lou Whitaker	.10	.05	.01
□ 127 Frank White	.10	.05	.01
□ 128 Glenn Wilson	.05	.02	.01
□ 129 Willie Wilson	.05	.02	.01
□ 130 Dave Winfield	.40	.18	.05
□ 131 Robin Yount	.40	.18	.05
□ 132 Dwight Gooden CL Dale Murphy	.25	.11	.03

1986 Fleer Stickers Wax Box Cards

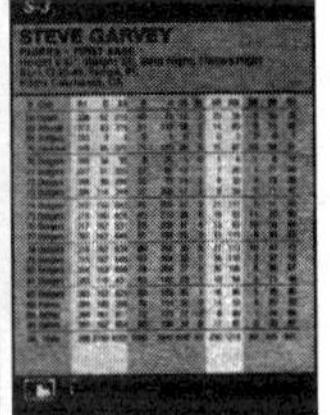

The bottoms of the Star Sticker wax boxes contained a set of four cards done in a similar format to the stickers; these cards (they are not stickers but truly cards) are numbered with the prefix S and are considered a separate set. Each individual card measures 2 1/2" by 3 1/2". The value of the panel uncut is slightly greater, perhaps by 25 percent greater, than the value of the individual cards cut up carefully.

	MINT	NRMT	EXC
COMPLETE SET (4)	4.00	1.80	.50
COMMON CARD (S1-S4)	.25	.11	.03
□ S1 Team Logo (Checklist back)	.25	.11	.03
□ S2 Wade Boggs	2.00	.90	.25
□ S3 Steve Garvey	.50	.23	.06
□ S4 Dave Winfield	1.25	.55	.16

1987 Fleer

This set consists of 660 standard-size cards. Cards were primarily issued in 17-card wax packs, rack packs and hobby and retail factory sets. Card fronts feature a distinctive light blue and white blended border encasing a color photo. Cards are again organized numerically by teams with team ordering based on the previous seasons record. The last 36 cards in the set consist of Specials (625-643), Rookie Pairs (644-653), and checklists (654-660). The key Rookie Cards in this set are Barry Bonds, Bobby Bonilla, Will Clark, Chuck Finley, Bo Jackson, Wally Joyner, John Kruk, Barry Larkin, Kevin Mitchell, Kevin Seitzer, Ruben Sierra and Devon White.

	MINT	NRMT	EXC
COMPLETE SET (660)	50.00	22.00	6.25
COMPLETE FACT.SET (672)	50.00	22.00	6.25
COMMON CARD (1-660)	.10	.05	.01

Card	MINT	NRMT	EXC
□ 1 Rick Aguilera	.25	.11	.03
□ 2 Richard Anderson	.10	.05	.01
□ 3 Wally Backman	.10	.05	.01
□ 4 Gary Carter	.25	.11	.03
□ 5 Ron Darling	.10	.05	.01
□ 6 Len Dykstra	.60	.25	.07
□ 7 Kevin Elster	.60	.25	.07
□ 8 Sid Fernandez	.10	.05	.01
□ 9 Dwight Gooden	.60	.25	.07
□ 10 Ed Hearn	.10	.05	.01
□ 11 Danny Heep	.10	.05	.01
□ 12 Keith Hernandez	.25	.11	.03
□ 13 Howard Johnson	.10	.05	.01
□ 14 Ray Knight	.25	.11	.03
□ 15 Lee Mazzilli	.10	.05	.01
□ 16 Roger McDowell	.10	.05	.01
□ 17 Kevin Mitchell	.60	.25	.07
□ 18 Randy Niemann	.10	.05	.01
□ 19 Bob Ojeda	.10	.05	.01
□ 20 Jesse Orosco	.10	.05	.01
□ 21 Rafael Santana	.10	.05	.01
□ 22 Doug Sisk	.10	.05	.01
□ 23 Darryl Strawberry	.60	.25	.07
□ 24 Tim Teufel	.10	.05	.01
□ 25 Mookie Wilson	.25	.11	.03
□ 26 Tony Armas	.10	.05	.01
□ 27 Marty Barrett	.10	.05	.01
□ 28 Don Baylor	.60	.25	.07
□ 29 Wade Boggs	.60	.25	.07
□ 30 Oil Can Boyd	.10	.05	.01
□ 31 Bill Buckner	.25	.11	.03
□ 32 Roger Clemens	1.50	.70	.19
□ 33 Steve Crawford	.10	.05	.01
□ 34 Dwight Evans	.25	.11	.03
□ 35 Rich Gedman	.10	.05	.01
□ 36 Dave Henderson	.10	.05	.01
□ 37 Bruce Hurst	.10	.05	.01
□ 38 Tim Lollar	.10	.05	.01
□ 39 Al Nipper	.10	.05	.01
□ 40 Spike Owen	.10	.05	.01
□ 41 Jim Rice	.25	.11	.03
□ 42 Ed Romero	.10	.05	.01
□ 43 Joe Sambito	.10	.05	.01
□ 44 Calvin Schiraldi	.10	.05	.01
□ 45 Tom Seaver UER Lifetime saves total 0, should be 1	.60	.25	.07
□ 46 Jeff Sellers	.10	.05	.01
□ 47 Bob Stanley	.10	.05	.01
□ 48 Sammy Stewart	.10	.05	.01
□ 49 Larry Andersen	.10	.05	.01
□ 50 Alan Ashby	.10	.05	.01
□ 51 Kevin Bass	.10	.05	.01
□ 52 Jeff Calhoun	.10	.05	.01
□ 53 Jose Cruz	.10	.05	.01
□ 54 Danny Darwin	.10	.05	.01
□ 55 Glenn Davis	.10	.05	.01
□ 56 Jim Deshaies	.10	.05	.01
□ 57 Bill Doran	.10	.05	.01
□ 58 Phil Garner	.10	.05	.01
□ 59 Billy Hatcher	.10	.05	.01
□ 60 Charlie Kerfeld	.10	.05	.01
□ 61 Bob Knepper	.10	.05	.01
□ 62 Dave Lopes	.25	.11	.03
□ 63 Aurelio Lopez	.10	.05	.01
□ 64 Jim Pankovits	.10	.05	.01
□ 65 Terry Puhl	.10	.05	.01
□ 66 Craig Reynolds	.10	.05	.01
□ 67 Nolan Ryan	3.00	1.35	.35
□ 68 Mike Scott	.10	.05	.01
□ 69 Dave Smith	.10	.05	.01
□ 70 Dickie Thon	.10	.05	.01
□ 71 Tony Walker	.10	.05	.01
□ 72 Denny Walling	.10	.05	.01
□ 73 Bob Boone	.25	.11	.03
□ 74 Rick Burleson	.10	.05	.01
□ 75 John Candelaria	.10	.05	.01
□ 76 Doug Corbett	.10	.05	.01
□ 77 Doug DeCinces	.10	.05	.01
□ 78 Brian Downing	.10	.05	.01
□ 79 Chuck Finley	.75	.35	.09
□ 80 Terry Forster	.10	.05	.01
□ 81 Bob Grich	.25	.11	.03
□ 82 George Hendrick	.10	.05	.01
□ 83 Jack Howell	.10	.05	.01
□ 84 Reggie Jackson	.60	.25	.07
□ 85 Ruppert Jones	.10	.05	.01
□ 86 Wally Joyner	1.00	.45	.12
□ 87 Gary Lucas	.10	.05	.01
□ 88 Kirk McCaskill	.10	.05	.01
□ 89 Donnie Moore	.10	.05	.01
□ 90 Gary Pettis	.10	.05	.01
□ 91 Vern Ruhle	.10	.05	.01
□ 92 Dick Schofield	.10	.05	.01
□ 93 Don Sutton	.60	.25	.07
□ 94 Rob Wilfong	.10	.05	.01
□ 95 Mike Witt	.10	.05	.01
□ 96 Doug Drabek	.75	.35	.09
□ 97 Mike Easler	.10	.05	.01
□ 98 Mike Fischlin	.10	.05	.01
□ 99 Brian Fisher	.10	.05	.01
□ 100 Ron Guidry	.25	.11	.03
□ 101 Rickey Henderson	.60	.25	.07
□ 102 Tommy John	.25	.11	.03
□ 103 Ron Kittle	.10	.05	.01
□ 104 Don Mattingly	2.00	.90	.25
□ 105 Bobby Meacham	.10	.05	.01
□ 106 Joe Niekro	.10	.05	.01
□ 107 Mike Pagliarulo	.10	.05	.01
□ 108 Dan Pasqua	.10	.05	.01
□ 109 Willie Randolph	.25	.11	.03
□ 110 Dennis Rasmussen	.10	.05	.01
□ 111 Dave Righetti	.10	.05	.01
□ 112 Gary Roenicke	.10	.05	.01
□ 113 Rod Scurry	.10	.05	.01
□ 114 Bob Shirley	.10	.05	.01
□ 115 Joel Skinner	.10	.05	.01
□ 116 Tim Stoddard	.10	.05	.01
□ 117 Bob Tewksbury	.25	.11	.03
□ 118 Wayne Tolleson	.10	.05	.01
□ 119 Claudell Washington	.10	.05	.01
□ 120 Dave Winfield	.60	.25	.07
□ 121 Steve Buechele	.10	.05	.01
□ 122 Ed Correa	.10	.05	.01
□ 123 Scott Fletcher	.10	.05	.01
□ 124 Jose Guzman	.10	.05	.01
□ 125 Toby Harrah	.10	.05	.01
□ 126 Greg Harris	.10	.05	.01
□ 127 Charlie Hough	.10	.05	.01
□ 128 Pete Incaviglia	.25	.11	.03
□ 129 Mike Mason	.10	.05	.01
□ 130 Oddibe McDowell	.10	.05	.01
□ 131 Dale Mohorcic	.10	.05	.01
□ 132 Pete O'Brien	.10	.05	.01
□ 133 Tom Paciorek	.10	.05	.01
□ 134 Larry Parrish	.10	.05	.01
□ 135 Geno Petralli	.10	.05	.01
□ 136 Darrell Porter	.10	.05	.01
□ 137 Jeff Russell	.10	.05	.01
□ 138 Ruben Sierra	2.00	.90	.25
□ 139 Don Slaught	.10	.05	.01
□ 140 Gary Ward	.10	.05	.01
□ 141 Curtis Wilkerson	.10	.05	.01
□ 142 Mitch Williams	.25	.11	.03
□ 143 Bobby Witt UER (Tulsa misspelled as Tusla; ERA should be 6.43, not .643)	.25	.11	.03
□ 144 Dave Bergman	.10	.05	.01
□ 145 Tom Brookens	.10	.05	.01
□ 146 Bill Campbell	.10	.05	.01
□ 147 Chuck Cary	.10	.05	.01
□ 148 Darnell Coles	.10	.05	.01
□ 149 Dave Collins	.10	.05	.01
□ 150 Darrell Evans	.25	.11	.03
□ 151 Kirk Gibson	.25	.11	.03
□ 152 John Grubb	.10	.05	.01
□ 153 Willie Hernandez	.10	.05	.01
□ 154 Larry Herndon	.10	.05	.01
□ 155 Eric King	.10	.05	.01
□ 156 Chet Lemon	.10	.05	.01
□ 157 Dwight Lowry	.10	.05	.01
□ 158 Jack Morris	.25	.11	.03
□ 159 Randy O'Neal	.10	.05	.01
□ 160 Lance Parrish	.25	.11	.03
□ 161 Dan Petry	.10	.05	.01
□ 162 Pat Sheridan	.10	.05	.01
□ 163 Jim Slaton	.10	.05	.01
□ 164 Frank Tanana	.10	.05	.01
□ 165 Walt Terrell	.10	.05	.01
□ 166 Mark Thurmond	.10	.05	.01
□ 167 Alan Trammell	.60	.25	.07
□ 168 Lou Whitaker	.25	.11	.03
□ 169 Luis Aguayo	.10	.05	.01
□ 170 Steve Bedrosian	.10	.05	.01
□ 171 Don Carman	.10	.05	.01
□ 172 Darren Daulton	.60	.25	.07
□ 173 Greg Gross	.10	.05	.01
□ 174 Kevin Gross	.10	.05	.01
□ 175 Von Hayes	.10	.05	.01
□ 176 Charles Hudson	.10	.05	.01
□ 177 Tom Hume	.10	.05	.01
□ 178 Steve Jeltz	.10	.05	.01
□ 179 Mike Maddux	.10	.05	.01
□ 180 Shane Rawley	.10	.05	.01
□ 181 Gary Redus	.10	.05	.01
□ 182 Ron Roenicke	.10	.05	.01
□ 183 Bruce Ruffin	.10	.05	.01
□ 184 John Russell	.10	.05	.01
□ 185 Juan Samuel	.10	.05	.01
□ 186 Dan Schatzeder	.10	.05	.01
□ 187 Mike Schmidt	.75	.35	.09
□ 188 Rick Schu	.10	.05	.01
□ 189 Jeff Stone	.10	.05	.01
□ 190 Kent Tekulve	.10	.05	.01
□ 191 Milt Thompson	.10	.05	.01
□ 192 Glenn Wilson	.10	.05	.01
□ 193 Buddy Bell	.25	.11	.03
□ 194 Tom Browning	.10	.05	.01
□ 195 Sal Butera	.10	.05	.01
□ 196 Dave Concepcion	.25	.11	.03
□ 197 Kal Daniels	.10	.05	.01
□ 198 Eric Davis	.60	.25	.07
□ 199 John Denny	.10	.05	.01
□ 200 Bo Diaz	.10	.05	.01
□ 201 Nick Esasky	.10	.05	.01
□ 202 John Franco	.25	.11	.03
□ 203 Bill Gullickson	.10	.05	.01
□ 204 Barry Larkin	6.00	2.70	.75
□ 205 Eddie Milner	.10	.05	.01
□ 206 Rob Murphy	.10	.05	.01
□ 207 Ron Oester	.10	.05	.01
□ 208 Dave Parker	.25	.11	.03
□ 209 Tony Perez	.60	.25	.07
□ 210 Ted Power	.10	.05	.01
□ 211 Joe Price	.10	.05	.01
□ 212 Ron Robinson	.10	.05	.01
□ 213 Pete Rose	.75	.35	.09
□ 214 Mario Soto	.10	.05	.01
□ 215 Kurt Stillwell	.10	.05	.01
□ 216 Max Venable	.10	.05	.01
□ 217 Chris Welsh	.10	.05	.01
□ 218 Carl Willis	.10	.05	.01
□ 219 Jesse Barfield	.10	.05	.01
□ 220 George Bell	.10	.05	.01
□ 221 Bill Caudill	.10	.05	.01
□ 222 John Cerutti	.10	.05	.01
□ 223 Jim Clancy	.10	.05	.01
□ 224 Mark Eichhorn	.10	.05	.01
□ 225 Tony Fernandez	.10	.05	.01
□ 226 Damaso Garcia	.10	.05	.01
□ 227 Kelly Gruber ERR (Wrong birth year)	.10	.05	.01
□ 228 Tom Henke	.10	.05	.01
□ 229 Garth Iorg	.10	.05	.01
□ 230 Joe Johnson	.10	.05	.01
□ 231 Cliff Johnson	.10	.05	.01
□ 232 Jimmy Key	.25	.11	.03
□ 233 Dennis Lamp	.10	.05	.01
□ 234 Rick Leach	.10	.05	.01
□ 235 Buck Martinez	.10	.05	.01
□ 236 Lloyd Moseby	.10	.05	.01
□ 237 Rance Mulliniks	.10	.05	.01
□ 238 Dave Stieb	.10	.05	.01
□ 239 Willie Upshaw	.10	.05	.01
□ 240 Ernie Whitt	.10	.05	.01
□ 241 Andy Allanson	.10	.05	.01
□ 242 Scott Bailes	.10	.05	.01
□ 243 Chris Bando	.10	.05	.01
□ 244 Tony Bernazard	.10	.05	.01
□ 245 John Butcher	.10	.05	.01
□ 246 Brett Butler	.25	.11	.03
□ 247 Ernie Camacho	.10	.05	.01
□ 248 Tom Candiotti	.10	.05	.01
□ 249 Joe Carter	.75	.35	.09
□ 250 Carmen Castillo	.10	.05	.01
□ 251 Julio Franco	.25	.11	.03
□ 252 Mel Hall	.10	.05	.01
□ 253 Brook Jacoby	.10	.05	.01
□ 254 Phil Niekro	.60	.25	.07
□ 255 Otis Nixon	.25	.11	.03
□ 256 Dickie Noles	.10	.05	.01
□ 257 Bryan Oelkers	.10	.05	.01
□ 258 Ken Schrom	.10	.05	.01
□ 259 Don Schulze	.10	.05	.01
□ 260 Cory Snyder	.10	.05	.01
□ 261 Pat Tabler	.10	.05	.01
□ 262 Andre Thornton	.10	.05	.01
□ 263 Rich Yett	.10	.05	.01
□ 264 Mike Aldrete	.25	.11	.03
□ 265 Juan Berenguer	.10	.05	.01
□ 266 Vida Blue	.25	.11	.03
□ 267 Bob Brenly	.10	.05	.01
□ 268 Chris Brown	.10	.05	.01
□ 269 Will Clark	5.00	2.20	.60
□ 270 Chili Davis	.25	.11	.03
□ 271 Mark Davis	.10	.05	.01
□ 272 Kelly Downs	.10	.05	.01
□ 273 Scott Garrelts	.10	.05	.01
□ 274 Dan Gladden	.10	.05	.01
□ 275 Mike Krukow	.10	.05	.01
□ 276 Randy Kutcher	.10	.05	.01
□ 277 Mike LaCoss	.10	.05	.01
□ 278 Jeff Leonard	.10	.05	.01
□ 279 Candy Maldonado	.10	.05	.01
□ 280 Roger Mason	.10	.05	.01
□ 281 Bob Melvin	.10	.05	.01
□ 282 Greg Minton	.10	.05	.01
□ 283 Jeff D. Robinson	.10	.05	.01
□ 284 Harry Spilman	.10	.05	.01
□ 285 Robby Thompson	.25	.11	.03
□ 286 Jose Uribe	.10	.05	.01
□ 287 Frank Williams	.10	.05	.01
□ 288 Joel Youngblood	.10	.05	.01
□ 289 Jack Clark	.25	.11	.03
□ 290 Vince Coleman	.10	.05	.01
□ 291 Tim Conroy	.10	.05	.01
□ 292 Danny Cox	.10	.05	.01
□ 293 Ken Dayley	.10	.05	.01
□ 294 Curt Ford	.10	.05	.01
□ 295 Bob Forsch	.10	.05	.01
□ 296 Tom Herr	.10	.05	.01
□ 297 Ricky Horton	.10	.05	.01
□ 298 Clint Hurdle	.10	.05	.01
□ 299 Jeff Lahti	.10	.05	.01
□ 300 Steve Lake	.10	.05	.01
□ 301 Tito Landrum	.10	.05	.01
□ 302 Mike LaValliere	.10	.05	.01
□ 303 Greg Mathews	.10	.05	.01
□ 304 Willie McGee	.10	.05	.01
□ 305 Jose Oquendo	.10	.05	.01
□ 306 Terry Pendleton	.25	.11	.03
□ 307 Pat Perry	.10	.05	.01
□ 308 Ozzie Smith	1.00	.45	.12
□ 309 Ray Soff	.10	.05	.01
□ 310 John Tudor	.10	.05	.01
□ 311 Andy Van Slyke UER (Bats R, Throws L)	.25	.11	.03
□ 312 Todd Worrell	.25	.11	.03
□ 313 Dann Bilardello	.10	.05	.01
□ 314 Hubie Brooks	.10	.05	.01
□ 315 Tim Burke	.10	.05	.01
□ 316 Andre Dawson	.60	.25	.07
□ 317 Mike Fitzgerald	.10	.05	.01

□ 318 Tom Foley .10 .05 .01
□ 319 Andres Galarraga 1.00 .45 .12
□ 320 Joe Hesketh .10 .05 .01
□ 321 Wallace Johnson .10 .05 .01
□ 322 Wayne Krenchicki .10 .05 .01
□ 323 Vance Law .10 .05 .01
□ 324 Dennis Martinez .25 .11 .03
□ 325 Bob McClure .10 .05 .01
□ 326 Andy McGaffigan .10 .05 .01
□ 327 Al Newman .10 .05 .01
□ 328 Tim Raines .25 .11 .03
□ 329 Jeff Reardon .25 .11 .03
□ 330 Luis Rivera .10 .05 .01
□ 331 Bob Sebra .10 .05 .01
□ 332 Bryn Smith .10 .05 .01
□ 333 Jay Tibbs .10 .05 .01
□ 334 Tim Wallach .10 .05 .01
□ 335 Mitch Webster .10 .05 .01
□ 336 Jim Wohlford .10 .05 .01
□ 337 Floyd Youmans .10 .05 .01
□ 338 Chris Bosio .25 .11 .03
□ 339 Glenn Braggs .10 .05 .01
□ 340 Rick Cerone .10 .05 .01
□ 341 Mark Clear .10 .05 .01
□ 342 Bryan Clutterbuck .10 .05 .01
□ 343 Cecil Cooper .25 .11 .03
□ 344 Rob Deer .10 .05 .01
□ 345 Jim Gantner .10 .05 .01
□ 346 Ted Higuera .10 .05 .01
□ 347 John Henry Johnson .10 .05 .01
□ 348 Tim Leary .10 .05 .01
□ 349 Rick Manning .10 .05 .01
□ 350 Paul Molitor .75 .35 .09
□ 351 Charlie Moore .10 .05 .01
□ 352 Juan Nieves .10 .05 .01
□ 353 Ben Oglivie .10 .05 .01
□ 354 Dan Plesac .10 .05 .01
□ 355 Ernest Riles .10 .05 .01
□ 356 Billy Joe Robidoux .10 .05 .01
□ 357 Bill Schroeder .10 .05 .01
□ 358 Dale Sveum .10 .05 .01
□ 359 Gorman Thomas .10 .05 .01
□ 360 Bill Wegman .10 .05 .01
□ 361 Robin Yount .60 .25 .07
□ 362 Steve Balboni .10 .05 .01
□ 363 Scott Bankhead .10 .05 .01
□ 364 Buddy Biancalana .10 .05 .01
□ 365 Bud Black .10 .05 .01
□ 366 George Brett 1.50 .70 .19
□ 367 Steve Farr .10 .05 .01
□ 368 Mark Gubicza .10 .05 .01
□ 369 Bo Jackson 3.00 1.35 .35
□ 370 Danny Jackson .10 .05 .01
□ 371 Mike Kingery .25 .11 .03
□ 372 Rudy Law .10 .05 .01
□ 373 Charlie Leibrandt .10 .05 .01
□ 374 Dennis Leonard .10 .05 .01
□ 375 Hal McRae .25 .11 .03
□ 376 Jorge Orta .10 .05 .01
□ 377 Jamie Quirk .10 .05 .01
□ 378 Dan Quisenberry .10 .05 .01
□ 379 Bret Saberhagen .25 .11 .03
□ 380 Angel Salazar .10 .05 .01
□ 381 Lonnie Smith .10 .05 .01
□ 382 Jim Sundberg .10 .05 .01
□ 383 Frank White .25 .11 .03
□ 384 Willie Wilson .10 .05 .01
□ 385 Joaquin Andujar .10 .05 .01
□ 386 Doug Bair .10 .05 .01
□ 387 Dusty Baker .25 .11 .03
□ 388 Bruce Bochte .10 .05 .01
□ 389 Jose Canseco 2.00 .90 .25
□ 390 Chris Codiroli .10 .05 .01
□ 391 Mike Davis .10 .05 .01
□ 392 Alfredo Griffin .10 .05 .01
□ 393 Moose Haas .10 .05 .01
□ 394 Donnie Hill .10 .05 .01
□ 395 Jay Howell .10 .05 .01
□ 396 Dave Kingman .25 .11 .03
□ 397 Carney Lansford .25 .11 .03
□ 398 Dave Leiper .10 .05 .01
□ 399 Bill Mooneyham .10 .05 .01
□ 400 Dwayne Murphy .10 .05 .01
□ 401 Steve Ontiveros .10 .05 .01
□ 402 Tony Phillips .25 .11 .03
□ 403 Eric Plunk .10 .05 .01
□ 404 Jose Rijo .10 .05 .01
□ 405 Terry Steinbach 1.00 .45 .12
□ 406 Dave Stewart .25 .11 .03
□ 407 Mickey Tettleton .25 .11 .03
□ 408 Dave Von Ohlen .10 .05 .01
□ 409 Jerry Willard .10 .05 .01
□ 410 Curt Young .10 .05 .01
□ 411 Bruce Bochy .10 .05 .01
□ 412 Dave Dravecky .25 .11 .03
□ 413 Tim Flannery .10 .05 .01
□ 414 Steve Garvey .60 .25 .07
□ 415 Rich Gossage .25 .11 .03
□ 416 Tony Gwynn 1.50 .70 .19
□ 417 Andy Hawkins .10 .05 .01
□ 418 LaMarr Hoyt .10 .05 .01
□ 419 Terry Kennedy .10 .05 .01
□ 420 John Kruk 1.00 .45 .12
□ 421 Dave LaPoint .10 .05 .01
□ 422 Craig Lefferts .10 .05 .01
□ 423 Carmelo Martinez .10 .05 .01
□ 424 Lance McCullers .10 .05 .01
□ 425 Kevin McReynolds .10 .05 .01
□ 426 Graig Nettles .25 .11 .03
□ 427 Bip Roberts .75 .35 .09
□ 428 Jerry Royster .10 .05 .01
□ 429 Benito Santiago .25 .11 .03
□ 430 Eric Show .10 .05 .01
□ 431 Bob Stoddard .10 .05 .01
□ 432 Garry Templeton .10 .05 .01
□ 433 Gene Walter .10 .05 .01
□ 434 Ed Whitson .10 .05 .01
□ 435 Marvell Wynne .10 .05 .01
□ 436 Dave Anderson .10 .05 .01
□ 437 Greg Brock .10 .05 .01
□ 438 Enos Cabell .10 .05 .01
□ 439 Mariano Duncan .10 .05 .01
□ 440 Pedro Guerrero .25 .11 .03
□ 441 Orel Hershiser .25 .11 .03
□ 442 Rick Honeycutt .10 .05 .01
□ 443 Ken Howell .10 .05 .01
□ 444 Ken Landreaux .10 .05 .01
□ 445 Bill Madlock .10 .05 .01
□ 446 Mike Marshall .10 .05 .01
□ 447 Len Matuszek .10 .05 .01
□ 448 Tom Niedenfuer .10 .05 .01
□ 449 Alejandro Pena .10 .05 .01
□ 450 Dennis Powell .10 .05 .01
□ 451 Jerry Reuss .10 .05 .01
□ 452 Bill Russell .10 .05 .01
□ 453 Steve Sax .10 .05 .01
□ 454 Mike Scioscia .10 .05 .01
□ 455 Franklin Stubbs .10 .05 .01
□ 456 Alex Trevino .10 .05 .01
□ 457 Fernando Valenzuela .25 .11 .03
□ 458 Ed VandeBerg .10 .05 .01
□ 459 Bob Welch .10 .05 .01
□ 460 Reggie Williams .10 .05 .01
□ 461 Don Aase .10 .05 .01
□ 462 Juan Beniquez .10 .05 .01
□ 463 Mike Boddicker .10 .05 .01
□ 464 Juan Bonilla .10 .05 .01
□ 465 Rich Bordi .10 .05 .01
□ 466 Storm Davis .10 .05 .01
□ 467 Rick Dempsey .25 .11 .03
□ 468 Ken Dixon .10 .05 .01
□ 469 Jim Dwyer .10 .05 .01
□ 470 Mike Flanagan .10 .05 .01
□ 471 Jackie Gutierrez .10 .05 .01
□ 472 Brad Havens .10 .05 .01
□ 473 Lee Lacy .10 .05 .01
□ 474 Fred Lynn .25 .11 .03
□ 475 Scott McGregor .10 .05 .01
□ 476 Eddie Murray 1.00 .45 .12
□ 477 Tom O'Malley .10 .05 .01
□ 478 Cal Ripken Jr. 3.00 1.35 .35
□ 479 Larry Sheets .10 .05 .01
□ 480 John Shelby .10 .05 .01
□ 481 Nate Snell .10 .05 .01
□ 482 Jim Traber .10 .05 .01
□ 483 Mike Young .10 .05 .01
□ 484 Neil Allen .10 .05 .01
□ 485 Harold Baines .25 .11 .03
□ 486 Floyd Bannister .10 .05 .01
□ 487 Daryl Boston .10 .05 .01
□ 488 Ivan Calderon .10 .05 .01
□ 489 John Cangelosi .10 .05 .01
□ 490 Steve Carlton .60 .25 .07
□ 491 Joe Cowley .10 .05 .01
□ 492 Julio Cruz .10 .05 .01
□ 493 Bill Dawley .10 .05 .01
□ 494 Jose DeLeon .10 .05 .01
□ 495 Richard Dotson .10 .05 .01
□ 496 Carlton Fisk .60 .25 .07
□ 497 Ozzie Guillen .25 .11 .03
□ 498 Jerry Hairston .10 .05 .01
□ 499 Ron Hassey .10 .05 .01
□ 500 Tim Hulett .10 .05 .01
□ 501 Bob James .10 .05 .01
□ 502 Steve Lyons .10 .05 .01
□ 503 Joel McKeon .10 .05 .01
□ 504 Gene Nelson .10 .05 .01
□ 505 Dave Schmidt .10 .05 .01
□ 506 Ray Searage .10 .05 .01
□ 507 Bobby Thigpen .25 .11 .03
□ 508 Greg Walker .10 .05 .01
□ 509 Jim Acker .10 .05 .01
□ 510 Doyle Alexander .10 .05 .01
□ 511 Paul Assenmacher .10 .05 .01
□ 512 Bruce Benedict .10 .05 .01
□ 513 Chris Chambliss .10 .05 .01
□ 514 Jeff Dedmon .10 .05 .01
□ 515 Gene Garber .10 .05 .01
□ 516 Ken Griffey .25 .11 .03
□ 517 Terry Harper .10 .05 .01
□ 518 Bob Horner .10 .05 .01
□ 519 Glenn Hubbard .10 .05 .01
□ 520 Rick Mahler .10 .05 .01
□ 521 Omar Moreno .10 .05 .01
□ 522 Dale Murphy .60 .25 .07
□ 523 Ken Oberkfell .10 .05 .01
□ 524 Ed Olwine .10 .05 .01
□ 525 David Palmer .10 .05 .01
□ 526 Rafael Ramirez .10 .05 .01
□ 527 Billy Sample .10 .05 .01
□ 528 Ted Simmons .25 .11 .03
□ 529 Zane Smith .10 .05 .01
□ 530 Bruce Sutter .10 .05 .01
□ 531 Andres Thomas .10 .05 .01
□ 532 Ozzie Virgil .10 .05 .01
□ 533 Allan Anderson .10 .05 .01
□ 534 Keith Atherton .10 .05 .01
□ 535 Billy Beane .10 .05 .01
□ 536 Bert Blyleven .25 .11 .03
□ 537 Tom Brunansky .10 .05 .01
□ 538 Randy Bush .10 .05 .01
□ 539 George Frazier .10 .05 .01
□ 540 Gary Gaetti .10 .05 .01
□ 541 Greg Gagne .10 .05 .01
□ 542 Mickey Hatcher .10 .05 .01
□ 543 Neal Heaton .10 .05 .01
□ 544 Kent Hrbek .60 .25 .07
□ 545 Roy Lee Jackson .10 .05 .01
□ 546 Tim Laudner .10 .05 .01
□ 547 Steve Lombardozzi .10 .05 .01
□ 548 Mark Portugal .25 .11 .03
□ 549 Kirby Puckett 3.00 1.35 .35
□ 550 Jeff Reed .10 .05 .01
□ 551 Mark Salas .10 .05 .01
□ 552 Roy Smalley .10 .05 .01
□ 553 Mike Smithson .10 .05 .01
□ 554 Frank Viola .10 .05 .01
□ 555 Thad Bosley .10 .05 .01
□ 556 Ron Cey .25 .11 .03
□ 557 Jody Davis .10 .05 .01
□ 558 Ron Davis .10 .05 .01
□ 559 Bob Dernier .10 .05 .01
□ 560 Frank DiPino .10 .05 .01
□ 561 Shawon Dunston UER .25 .11 .03
(Wrong birth year
listed on card back)
□ 562 Leon Durham .10 .05 .01
□ 563 Dennis Eckersley .60 .25 .07
□ 564 Terry Francona .10 .05 .01
□ 565 Dave Gumpert .10 .05 .01
□ 566 Guy Hoffman .10 .05 .01
□ 567 Ed Lynch .10 .05 .01
□ 568 Gary Matthews .10 .05 .01
□ 569 Keith Moreland .10 .05 .01
□ 570 Jamie Moyer .25 .11 .03
□ 571 Jerry Mumphrey .10 .05 .01
□ 572 Ryne Sandberg 1.00 .45 .12
□ 573 Scott Sanderson .10 .05 .01
□ 574 Lee Smith .60 .25 .07
□ 575 Chris Speier .10 .05 .01
□ 576 Rick Sutcliffe .10 .05 .01
□ 577 Manny Trillo .10 .05 .01
□ 578 Steve Trout .10 .05 .01
□ 579 Karl Best .10 .05 .01
□ 580 Scott Bradley .10 .05 .01
□ 581 Phil Bradley .10 .05 .01
□ 582 Mickey Brantley .10 .05 .01
□ 583 Mike G. Brown P .10 .05 .01
□ 584 Alvin Davis .10 .05 .01
□ 585 Lee Guetterman .10 .05 .01
□ 586 Mark Huismann .10 .05 .01
□ 587 Bob Kearney .10 .05 .01
□ 588 Pete Ladd .10 .05 .01
□ 589 Mark Langston .25 .11 .03
□ 590 Mike Moore .10 .05 .01
□ 591 Mike Morgan .10 .05 .01
□ 592 John Moses .10 .05 .01
□ 593 Ken Phelps .10 .05 .01
□ 594 Jim Presley .10 .05 .01
□ 595 Rey Quinones UER .10 .05 .01
(Quinonez on front)
□ 596 Harold Reynolds .10 .05 .01
□ 597 Billy Swift .10 .05 .01
□ 598 Danny Tartabull .25 .11 .03
□ 599 Steve Yeager .10 .05 .01
□ 600 Matt Young .10 .05 .01
□ 601 Bill Almon .10 .05 .01
□ 602 Rafael Belliard .10 .05 .01
□ 603 Mike Bielecki .10 .05 .01
□ 604 Barry Bonds 20.00 9.00 2.50
□ 605 Bobby Bonilla 2.00 .90 .25
□ 606 Sid Bream .10 .05 .01
□ 607 Mike C. Brown .10 .05 .01
□ 608 Pat Clements .10 .05 .01
□ 609 Mike Diaz .10 .05 .01
□ 610 Cecilio Guante .10 .05 .01
□ 611 Barry Jones .10 .05 .01
□ 612 Bob Kipper .10 .05 .01
□ 613 Larry McWilliams .10 .05 .01
□ 614 Jim Morrison .10 .05 .01
□ 615 Joe Orsulak .10 .05 .01
□ 616 Junior Ortiz .10 .05 .01
□ 617 Tony Pena .10 .05 .01
□ 618 Johnny Ray .10 .05 .01
□ 619 Rick Reuschel .10 .05 .01
□ 620 R.J. Reynolds .10 .05 .01
□ 621 Rick Rhoden .10 .05 .01
□ 622 Don Robinson .10 .05 .01
□ 623 Bob Walk .10 .05 .01
□ 624 Jim Winn .10 .05 .01
□ 625 Youthful Power .60 .25 .07
Pete Incaviglia
Jose Canseco
□ 626 300 Game Winners .25 .11 .03
Don Sutton
Phil Niekro
□ 627 AL Firemen .10 .05 .01
Dave Righetti
Don Aase
□ 628 Rookie All-Stars .60 .25 .07
Wally Joyner
Jose Canseco
□ 629 Magic Mets .25 .11 .03
Gary Carter
Sid Fernandez
Dwight Gooden
Keith Hernandez
Darryl Strawberry
□ 630 NL Best Righties .10 .05 .01
Mike Scott
Mike Krukow
□ 631 Sensational Southpaws .10 .05 .01
Fernando Valenzuela
John Franco
□ 632 Count'Em .10 .05 .01
Bob Horner
□ 633 AL Pitcher's Nightmare 1.00 .45 .12
Jose Canseco
Jim Rice
Kirby Puckett
□ 634 All-Star Battery .25 .11 .03
Gary Carter
Roger Clemens
□ 635 4000 Strikeouts .60 .25 .07
Steve Carlton
□ 636 Big Bats at First .60 .25 .07
Glenn Davis
Eddie Murray
□ 637 On Base .60 .25 .07
Wade Boggs
Keith Hernandez
□ 638 Sluggers Left Side .60 .25 .07
Don Mattingly
Darryl Strawberry
□ 639 Former MVP's .25 .11 .03
Dave Parker
Ryne Sandberg
□ 640 Dr. K and Super K .40 .18 .05
Dwight Gooden
Roger Clemens
□ 641 AL West Stoppers .10 .05 .01
Mike Witt
Charlie Hough
□ 642 Doubles and Triples .25 .11 .03
Juan Samuel
Tim Raines
□ 643 Outfielders with Punch .25 .11 .03
Harold Baines
Jesse Barfield
□ 644 Dave Clark and .60 .25 .07
Greg Swindell
□ 645 Ron Karkovice and .25 .11 .03
Russ Morman
□ 646 Devon White and .75 .35 .09
Willie Fraser
□ 647 Mike Stanley and .60 .25 .07
Jerry Browne
□ 648 Dave Magadan and .25 .11 .03
Phil Lombardi
□ 649 Jose Gonzalez and .10 .05 .01
Ralph Bryant
□ 650 Jimmy Jones and .10 .05 .01
Randy Asadoor
□ 651 Tracy Jones and .25 .11 .03
Marvin Freeman
□ 652 John Stefero and .75 .35 .09
Kevin Seitzer
□ 653 Rob Nelson and .10 .05 .01
Steve Fireovid
□ 654 CL: Mets/Red Sox .25 .11 .03
Astros/Angels
□ 655 CL: Yankees/Rangers .25 .11 .03
Tigers/Phillies
□ 656 CL: Reds/Blue Jays .25 .11 .03
Indians/Giants
ERR (230/231 wrong)
□ 657 CL: Cardinals/Expos .25 .11 .03
Brewers/Royals
□ 658 CL: A's/Padres .25 .11 .03
Dodgers/Orioles
□ 659 CL: White Sox/Braves .25 .11 .03
Twins/Cubs
□ 660 CL: Mariners/Pirates .25 .11 .03
Special Cards
ER (580/581 wrong)

1987 Fleer Glossy

This set parallels the regular Fleer issue. The cards were issued in a special tin which also included a glossy version of the World Series set. These 672 standard-size are differentiated only by the gloss on the front. This set was produced in fairly large quantities, although still significantly less than regular issue cards.

	MINT	NRMT	EXC
COMPLETE FACT.SET (672)	30.00	13.50	3.70
COMMON CARD (1-660)	.10	.05	.01
COMMON WORLD SERIES (WS1-WS12)	.10	.05	.01

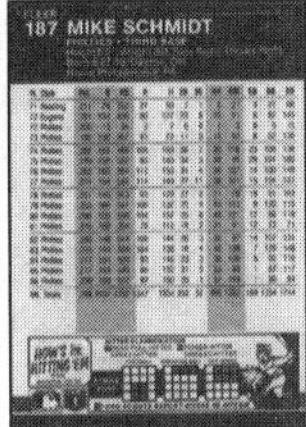

*STARS: 1X BASIC CARDS
*ROOKIES: 1X BASIC CARDS

1987 Fleer All-Stars

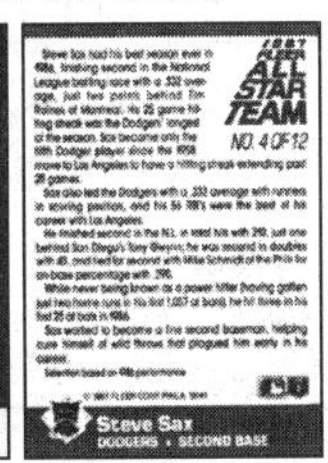

This 12-card standard-size set was distributed as an insert in packs of the Fleer regular issue. The cards are designed with a color player photo superimposed on a gray or black background with yellow stars. The player's name, team, and position are printed in orange on black or gray at the bottom of the obverse. The card backs are done predominantly in gray, red, and black and are numbered on the back in the upper right hand corner.

	MINT	NRMT	EXC
COMPLETE SET (12)	22.00	10.00	2.70
COMMON CARD (1-12)	.30	.14	.04

	MINT	NRMT	EXC
☐ 1 Don Mattingly	6.00	2.70	.75
☐ 2 Gary Carter	.50	.23	.06
☐ 3 Tony Fernandez	.30	.14	.04
☐ 4 Steve Sax	.30	.14	.04
☐ 5 Kirby Puckett	10.00	4.50	1.25
☐ 6 Mike Schmidt	2.50	1.10	.30
☐ 7 Mike Easler	.30	.14	.04
☐ 8 Todd Worrell	.30	.14	.04
☐ 9 George Bell	.30	.14	.04
☐ 10 Fernando Valenzuela	.50	.23	.06
☐ 11 Roger Clemens	5.00	2.20	.60
☐ 12 Tim Raines	.50	.23	.06

1987 Fleer Headliners

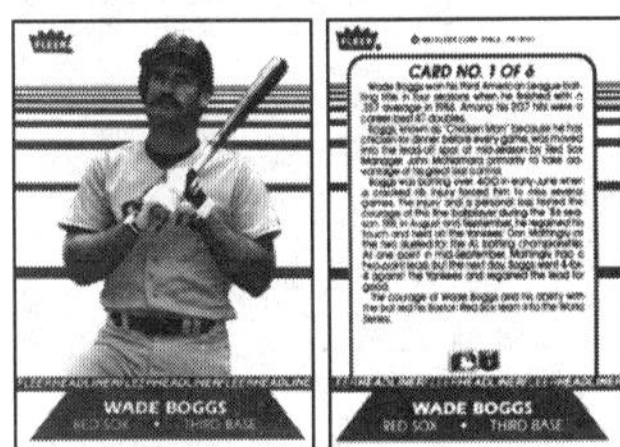

This six-card standard-size set was distributed one per rack pack as well as with three-pack wax pack rack packs. The obverse features the player photo against a beige background with irregular red stripes. The checklist below also lists each player's team affiliation. The set is sequenced in alphabetical order.

	MINT	NRMT	EXC
COMPLETE SET (6)	6.00	2.70	.75
COMMON CARD (1-6)	.50	.23	.06

	MINT	NRMT	EXC
☐ 1 Wade Boggs	1.00	.45	.12
☐ 2 Jose Canseco	3.00	1.35	.35
☐ 3 Dwight Gooden	.75	.35	.09
☐ 4 Rickey Henderson	1.00	.45	.12
☐ 5 Keith Hernandez	.50	.23	.06
☐ 6 Jim Rice	.50	.23	.06

1987 Fleer Wax Box Cards

The cards in this 16-card set measure the standard, 2 1/2" by 3 1/2". Cards have essentially the same design as the 1987 Fleer regular issue set. The cards were printed on the bottoms of the regular issue wax pack boxes. These 16 cards (C1 to C16) are considered a separate set in their own right and are not typically included in a complete set of the regular issue 1987 Fleer cards. The value of the panel uncut is slightly greater, perhaps by 25 percent greater, than the value of the individual cards cut up carefully.

	MINT	NRMT	EXC
COMPLETE SET (16)	10.00	4.50	1.25
COMMON CARDS (C1-C16)	.10	.05	.01

	MINT	NRMT	EXC
☐ C1 Mets Logo	.10	.05	.01
☐ C2 Jesse Barfield	.10	.05	.01
☐ C3 George Brett	3.00	1.35	.35
☐ C4 Dwight Gooden	.50	.23	.06
☐ C5 Boston Logo	.10	.05	.01
☐ C6 Keith Hernandez	.25	.11	.03
☐ C7 Wally Joyner	.50	.23	.06
☐ C8 Dale Murphy	.50	.23	.06
☐ C9 Astros Logo	.10	.05	.01
☐ C10 Dave Parker	.25	.11	.03
☐ C11 Kirby Puckett	2.50	1.10	.30
☐ C12 Dave Righetti	.10	.05	.01
☐ C13 Angels Logo	.10	.05	.01
☐ C14 Ryne Sandberg	2.00	.90	.25
☐ C15 Mike Schmidt	1.50	.70	.19
☐ C16 Robin Yount	.75	.35	.09

1987 Fleer World Series

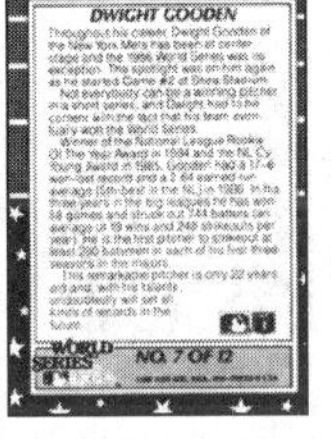

This 12-card standard-size set of features highlights of the previous year's World Series between the Mets and the Red Sox. The sets were packaged as a complete set insert with the collated sets (of the 1987 Fleer regular issue) which were sold by Fleer directly to hobby card dealers; they were not available in the general retail candy store outlets.

	MINT	NRMT	EXC
COMPLETE SET (12)	2.00	.90	.25
COMMON CARD (1-12)	.10	.05	.01

	MINT	NRMT	EXC
☐ 1 Bruce Hurst	.10	.05	.01
LH Finesse Beats Mets			
☐ 2 Keith Hernandez and	.25	.11	.03
Wade Boggs			
☐ 3 Roger Clemens HOR	1.00	.45	.12
☐ 4 Clutch Hitting	.25	.11	.03
(Gary Carter)			
☐ 5 Ron Darling	.10	.05	.01
Picks Up Slack			
☐ 6 Marty Barrett	.10	.05	.01
.433 Series BA			
☐ 7 Dwight Gooden	.50	.23	.06
☐ 8 Strategy at Work	.10	.05	.01
(Mets Conference)			
☐ 9 Dwight Evans	.25	.11	.03
Congratulated by Rich Gedman			
☐ 10 One Strike From Boston	.10	.05	.01
Victory (Dave Henderson)			
☐ 11 Series Home Run Duo	.10	.05	.01
Ray Knight			
Darryl Strawberry			
☐ 12 Ray Knight	.10	.05	.01
(Series MVP)			

1987 Fleer Update

This 132-card standard-size set was distributed exclusively in factory set form by hobby dealers. In addition to the complete set of 132 cards, the box also contained 25 Team Logo stickers. The cards look very similar to the 1987 Fleer regular issue except for the U-prefixed numbering on back. Cards are ordered alphabetically according to player's last name. The key extended Rookie Cards in this set are Ellis Burks, Mike Greenwell, Greg Maddux, Fred McGriff, Mark McGwire and Matt Williams.

	MINT	NRMT	EXC
COMPLETE FACT.SET (132)	15.00	6.75	1.85
COMMON CARD (1-132)	.05	.02	.01

	MINT	NRMT	EXC
☐ 1 Scott Bankhead	.05	.02	.01
☐ 2 Eric Bell	.05	.02	.01
☐ 3 Juan Beniquez	.05	.02	.01
☐ 4 Juan Berenguer	.05	.02	.01
☐ 5 Mike Birkbeck	.05	.02	.01
☐ 6 Randy Bockus	.05	.02	.01
☐ 7 Rod Booker	.05	.02	.01
☐ 8 Thad Bosley	.05	.02	.01
☐ 9 Greg Brock	.05	.02	.01
☐ 10 Bob Brower	.05	.02	.01
☐ 11 Chris Brown	.05	.02	.01
☐ 12 Jerry Browne	.05	.02	.01
☐ 13 Ralph Bryant	.05	.02	.01
☐ 14 DeWayne Buice	.05	.02	.01
☐ 15 Ellis Burks	1.00	.45	.12
☐ 16 Casey Candaele	.05	.02	.01
☐ 17 Steve Carlton	.20	.09	.03
☐ 18 Juan Castillo	.05	.02	.01
☐ 19 Chuck Crim	.05	.02	.01
☐ 20 Mark Davidson	.05	.02	.01
☐ 21 Mark Davis	.05	.02	.01
☐ 22 Storm Davis	.05	.02	.01
☐ 23 Bill Dawley	.05	.02	.01
☐ 24 Andre Dawson	.20	.09	.03
☐ 25 Brian Dayett	.05	.02	.01
☐ 26 Rick Dempsey	.10	.05	.01
☐ 27 Ken Dowell	.05	.02	.01
☐ 28 Dave Dravecky	.10	.05	.01
☐ 29 Mike Dunne	.05	.02	.01
☐ 30 Dennis Eckersley	.20	.09	.03
☐ 31 Cecil Fielder	.75	.35	.09
☐ 32 Brian Fisher	.05	.02	.01
☐ 33 Willie Fraser	.05	.02	.01
☐ 34 Ken Gerhart	.05	.02	.01
☐ 35 Jim Gott	.05	.02	.01
☐ 36 Dan Gladden	.05	.02	.01
☐ 37 Mike Greenwell	.20	.09	.03
☐ 38 Cecilio Guante	.05	.02	.01
☐ 39 Albert Hall	.05	.02	.01
☐ 40 Atlee Hammaker	.05	.02	.01
☐ 41 Mickey Hatcher	.05	.02	.01
☐ 42 Mike Heath	.05	.02	.01
☐ 43 Neal Heaton	.05	.02	.01
☐ 44 Mike Henneman	.20	.09	.03
☐ 45 Guy Hoffman	.05	.02	.01
☐ 46 Charles Hudson	.05	.02	.01
☐ 47 Chuck Jackson	.05	.02	.01
☐ 48 Mike Jackson	.10	.05	.01
☐ 49 Reggie Jackson	.50	.23	.06
☐ 50 Chris James	.05	.02	.01
☐ 51 Dion James	.05	.02	.01
☐ 52 Stan Javier	.05	.02	.01
☐ 53 Stan Jefferson	.05	.02	.01
☐ 54 Jimmy Jones	.05	.02	.01
☐ 55 Tracy Jones	.05	.02	.01
☐ 56 Terry Kennedy	.05	.02	.01
☐ 57 Mike Kingery	.10	.05	.01
☐ 58 Ray Knight	.10	.05	.01
☐ 59 Gene Larkin	.05	.02	.01
☐ 60 Mike LaValliere	.05	.02	.01
☐ 61 Jack Lazorko	.05	.02	.01
☐ 62 Terry Leach	.05	.02	.01
☐ 63 Rick Leach	.05	.02	.01
☐ 64 Craig Lefferts	.05	.02	.01
☐ 65 Jim Lindeman	.05	.02	.01
☐ 66 Bill Long	.05	.02	.01
☐ 67 Mike Loynd	.05	.02	.01
☐ 68 Greg Maddux	10.00	4.50	1.25
☐ 69 Bill Madlock	.05	.02	.01
☐ 70 Dave Magadan	.10	.05	.01
☐ 71 Joe Magrane	.05	.02	.01
☐ 72 Fred Manrique	.05	.02	.01
☐ 73 Mike Mason	.05	.02	.01
☐ 74 Lloyd McClendon	.05	.02	.01
☐ 75 Fred McGriff	2.00	.90	.25
☐ 76 Mark McGwire	2.00	.90	.25
☐ 77 Mark McLemore	.05	.02	.01
☐ 78 Kevin McReynolds	.05	.02	.01
☐ 79 Dave Meads	.05	.02	.01
☐ 80 Greg Minton	.05	.02	.01
☐ 81 John Mitchell	.05	.02	.01
☐ 82 Kevin Mitchell	.20	.09	.03
☐ 83 John Morris	.05	.02	.01
☐ 84 Jeff Musselman	.05	.02	.01
☐ 85 Randy Myers	.40	.18	.05
☐ 86 Gene Nelson	.05	.02	.01
☐ 87 Joe Niekro	.05	.02	.01
☐ 88 Tom Nieto	.05	.02	.01
☐ 89 Reid Nichols	.05	.02	.01
☐ 90 Matt Nokes	.10	.05	.01
☐ 91 Dickie Noles	.05	.02	.01
☐ 92 Edwin Nunez	.05	.02	.01
☐ 93 Jose Nunez	.05	.02	.01
☐ 94 Paul O'Neill	.50	.23	.06
☐ 95 Jim Paciorek	.05	.02	.01
☐ 96 Lance Parrish	.10	.05	.01
☐ 97 Bill Pecota	.05	.02	.01
☐ 98 Tony Pena	.05	.02	.01
☐ 99 Luis Polonia	.20	.09	.03
☐ 100 Randy Ready	.05	.02	.01
☐ 101 Jeff Reardon	.10	.05	.01
☐ 102 Gary Redus	.05	.02	.01
☐ 103 Rick Rhoden	.05	.02	.01
☐ 104 Wally Ritchie	.05	.02	.01
☐ 105 Jeff M. Robinson UER	.05	.02	.01
(Wrong Jeff's			
stats on back)			
☐ 106 Mark Salas	.05	.02	.01
☐ 107 Dave Schmidt	.05	.02	.01
☐ 108 Kevin Seitzer UER	.10	.05	.01
(Wrong birth year)			
☐ 109 John Shelby	.05	.02	.01
☐ 110 John Smiley	.10	.05	.01
☐ 111 Lary Sorensen	.05	.02	.01
☐ 112 Chris Speier	.05	.02	.01
☐ 113 Randy St.Claire	.05	.02	.01
☐ 114 Jim Sundberg	.05	.02	.01
☐ 115 B.J. Surhoff	.30	.14	.04
☐ 116 Greg Swindell	.20	.09	.03
☐ 117 Danny Tartabull	.10	.05	.01
☐ 118 Dorn Taylor	.05	.02	.01
☐ 119 Lee Tunnell	.05	.02	.01
☐ 120 Ed VandeBerg	.05	.02	.01
☐ 121 Andy Van Slyke	.10	.05	.01
☐ 122 Gary Ward	.05	.02	.01
☐ 123 Devon White	.20	.09	.03
☐ 124 Alan Wiggins	.05	.02	.01
☐ 125 Bill Wilkinson	.05	.02	.01
☐ 126 Jim Winn	.05	.02	.01
☐ 127 Frank Williams	.05	.02	.01
☐ 128 Ken Williams	.05	.02	.01
☐ 129 Matt Williams	4.00	1.80	.50
☐ 130 Herm Willingham	.05	.02	.01
☐ 131 Matt Young	.05	.02	.01
☐ 132 Checklist 1-132	.05	.02	.01

1987 Fleer Update Glossy

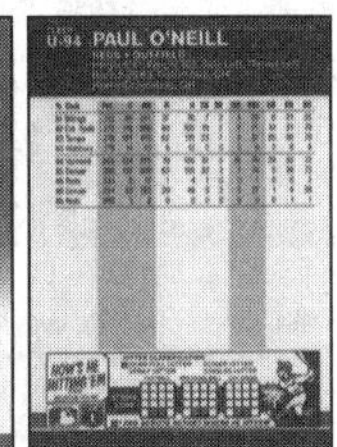

This set parallels the regular Fleer Update issue. The cards were issued in a special tin. These 132 standard-size are differentiated only by the gloss on the front. This set was produced in fairly large quantities, although still significantly less than regular issue cards.

	MINT	NRMT	EXC
COMPLETE FACT.SET (132)	10.00	4.50	1.25
COMMON CARD (1-132)	.10	.05	.01

*STARS: 1X BASIC CARDS
*ROOKIES: 1X BASIC CARDS

1987 Fleer Award Winners

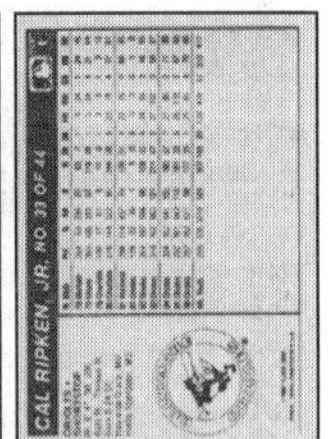

This small set of 44 standard-size cards was produced for 7-Eleven stores by Fleer. The cards feature full color fronts and yellow, white, and black backs. The card fronts are distinguished by their yellow frame around the player's full-color photo. The box for the cards describes the set as the "1987 Limited Edition Baseball's Award Winners." The checklist for the set is given on the back of the set box. The card numbering is in alphabetical order by player's name.

	MINT	NRMT	EXC
COMPLETE SET (44)	4.00	1.80	.50
COMMON CARD (1-44)	.05	.02	.01

	MINT	NRMT	EXC
☐ 1 Marty Barrett	.05	.02	.01
☐ 2 George Bell	.05	.02	.01
☐ 3 Bert Blyleven	.10	.05	.01
☐ 4 Bob Boone	.10	.05	.01
☐ 5 John Candelaria	.05	.02	.01
☐ 6 Jose Canseco	.50	.23	.06
☐ 7 Gary Carter	.10	.05	.01
☐ 8 Joe Carter	.25	.11	.03
☐ 9 Roger Clemens	.50	.23	.06
☐ 10 Cecil Cooper	.10	.05	.01
☐ 11 Eric Davis	.05	.02	.01
☐ 12 Tony Fernandez	.05	.02	.01
☐ 13 Scott Fletcher	.05	.02	.01
☐ 14 Bob Forsch	.05	.02	.01
☐ 15 Dwight Gooden	.20	.09	.03
☐ 16 Ron Guidry	.10	.05	.01
☐ 17 Ozzie Guillen	.05	.02	.01
☐ 18 Bill Gullickson	.05	.02	.01
☐ 19 Tony Gwynn	1.00	.45	.12
☐ 20 Bob Knepper	.05	.02	.01
☐ 21 Ray Knight	.05	.02	.01

	MINT	NRMT	EXC
□ 22 Mark Langston	.10	.05	.01
□ 23 Candy Maldonado	.05	.02	.01
□ 24 Don Mattingly	1.00	.45	.12
□ 25 Roger McDowell	.05	.02	.01
□ 26 Dale Murphy	.20	.09	.03
□ 27 Dave Parker	.10	.05	.01
□ 28 Lance Parrish	.10	.05	.01
□ 29 Gary Pettis	.05	.02	.01
□ 30 Kirby Puckett	1.00	.45	.12
□ 31 Johnny Ray	.05	.02	.01
□ 32 Dave Righetti	.05	.02	.01
□ 33 Cal Ripken	1.50	.70	.19
□ 34 Bret Saberhagen	.10	.05	.01
□ 35 Ryne Sandberg	.75	.35	.09
□ 36 Mike Schmidt	.50	.23	.06
□ 37 Mike Scott	.05	.02	.01
□ 38 Ozzie Smith	.75	.35	.09
□ 39 Robby Thompson	.05	.02	.01
□ 40 Fernando Valenzuela	.10	.05	.01
□ 41 Mitch Webster UER (Mike on front)	.05	.02	.01
□ 42 Frank White	.10	.05	.01
□ 43 Mike Witt	.05	.02	.01
□ 44 Todd Worrell	.05	.02	.01

1987 Fleer Baseball All-Stars

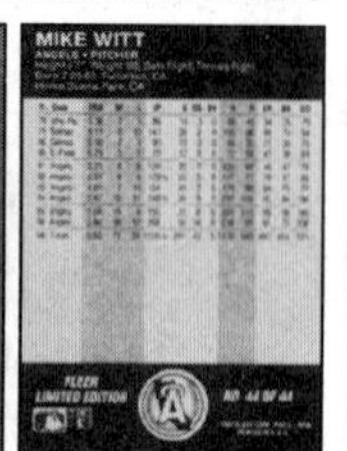

This small set of 44 standard-size cards was produced for Ben Franklin stores by Fleer. The cards feature full color fronts and red, white, and blue backs. The card fronts are easily distinguished by their white vertical stripes over a bright red background. The box for the cards proclaims "Limited Edition Baseball All-Stars" and is styled in the same manner and color scheme as the cards themselves. The checklist for the set is given on the back of the set box. The card numbering is in alphabetical order by player's name.

	MINT	NRMT	EXC
COMPLETE SET (44)	5.00	2.20	.60
COMMON CARD (1-44)	.05	.02	.01
□ 1 Harold Baines	.10	.05	.01
□ 2 Jesse Barfield	.05	.02	.01
□ 3 Wade Boggs	.30	.14	.04
□ 4 Dennis Boyd	.05	.02	.01
□ 5 Scott Bradley	.05	.02	.01
□ 6 Jose Canseco	.75	.35	.09
□ 7 Gary Carter	.10	.05	.01
□ 8 Joe Carter	.25	.11	.03
□ 9 Mark Clear	.05	.02	.01
□ 10 Roger Clemens	.50	.23	.06
□ 11 Jose Cruz	.05	.02	.01
□ 12 Chili Davis	.10	.05	.01
□ 13 Jody Davis	.05	.02	.01
□ 14 Rob Deer	.05	.02	.01
□ 15 Brian Downing	.05	.02	.01
□ 16 Sid Fernandez	.05	.02	.01
□ 17 John Franco	.10	.05	.01
□ 18 Andres Galarraga	.30	.14	.04
□ 19 Dwight Gooden	.20	.09	.03
□ 20 Tony Gwynn	1.00	.45	.12
□ 21 Charlie Hough	.05	.02	.01
□ 22 Bruce Hurst	.05	.02	.01
□ 23 Wally Joyner	.20	.09	.03
□ 24 Carney Lansford	.10	.05	.01
□ 25 Fred Lynn	.10	.05	.01
□ 26 Don Mattingly	1.00	.45	.12
□ 27 Willie McGee	.10	.05	.01
□ 28 Jack Morris	.10	.05	.01
□ 29 Dale Murphy	.20	.09	.03
□ 30 Bob Ojeda	.05	.02	.01
□ 31 Tony Pena	.05	.02	.01
□ 32 Kirby Puckett	1.00	.45	.12
□ 33 Dan Quisenberry	.05	.02	.01
□ 34 Tim Raines	.10	.05	.01
□ 35 Willie Randolph	.10	.05	.01
□ 36 Cal Ripken	2.00	.90	.25
□ 37 Pete Rose	.75	.35	.09
□ 38 Nolan Ryan	2.00	.90	.25
□ 39 Juan Samuel	.05	.02	.01
□ 40 Mike Schmidt	.50	.23	.06
□ 41 Ozzie Smith	.75	.35	.09
□ 42 Andres Thomas	.05	.02	.01
□ 43 Fernando Valenzuela	.10	.05	.01
□ 44 Mike Witt	.05	.02	.01

1987 Fleer Exciting Stars

This small 44-card boxed standard-size set was produced by Fleer for distribution by the Cumberland Farm stores. The cards feature full color fronts. The set is titled "Baseball's Exciting Stars." Each individual boxed set includes the 44 cards and six logo stickers. The checklist for the set is found on the back panel of the box. The card numbering is in alphabetical order by player's name.

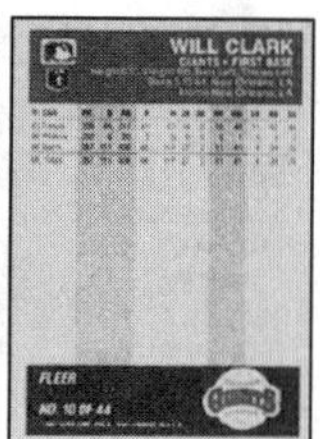

	MINT	NRMT	EXC
COMPLETE SET (44)	4.00	1.80	.50
COMMON CARD (1-44)	.05	.02	.01
□ 1 Don Aase	.05	.02	.01
□ 2 Rick Aguilera	.10	.05	.01
□ 3 Jesse Barfield	.05	.02	.01
□ 4 Wade Boggs	.30	.14	.04
□ 5 Oil Can Boyd	.05	.02	.01
□ 6 Sid Bream	.05	.02	.01
□ 7 Jose Canseco	.75	.35	.09
□ 8 Steve Carlton	.25	.11	.03
□ 9 Gary Carter	.10	.05	.01
□ 10 Will Clark	.75	.35	.09
□ 11 Roger Clemens	.60	.25	.07
□ 12 Danny Cox	.05	.02	.01
□ 13 Alvin Davis	.05	.02	.01
□ 14 Eric Davis	.05	.02	.01
□ 15 Rob Deer	.05	.02	.01
□ 16 Brian Downing	.05	.02	.01
□ 17 Gene Garber	.05	.02	.01
□ 18 Steve Garvey	.15	.07	.02
□ 19 Dwight Gooden	.15	.07	.02
□ 20 Mark Gubicza	.05	.02	.01
□ 21 Mel Hall	.05	.02	.01
□ 22 Terry Harper	.05	.02	.01
□ 23 Von Hayes	.05	.02	.01
□ 24 Rickey Henderson	.25	.11	.03
□ 25 Tom Henke	.05	.02	.01
□ 26 Willie Hernandez	.05	.02	.01
□ 27 Ted Higuera	.05	.02	.01
□ 28 Rick Honeycutt	.05	.02	.01
□ 29 Kent Hrbek	.10	.05	.01
□ 30 Wally Joyner	.15	.07	.02
□ 31 Charlie Kerfeld	.05	.02	.01
□ 32 Fred Lynn	.10	.05	.01
□ 33 Don Mattingly	1.00	.45	.12
□ 34 Tim Raines	.10	.05	.01
□ 35 Dennis Rasmussen	.05	.02	.01
□ 36 Johnny Ray	.05	.02	.01
□ 37 Jim Rice	.10	.05	.01
□ 38 Pete Rose	.75	.35	.09
□ 39 Lee Smith	.15	.07	.02
□ 40 Cory Snyder	.05	.02	.01
□ 41 Darryl Strawberry	.15	.07	.02
□ 42 Kent Tekulve	.05	.02	.01
□ 43 Willie Wilson	.05	.02	.01
□ 44 Bobby Witt	.10	.05	.01

1987 Fleer Game Winners

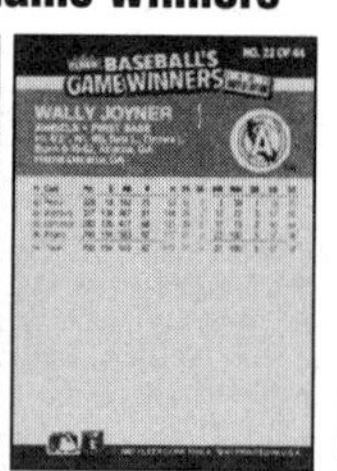

This small 44-card boxed standard-size set was produced by Fleer for distribution by several store chains, including Bi-Mart, Pay'n'Save, Mott's, M.E.Moses, and Winn's. The cards feature full color fronts. The set is titled "Baseball's Game Winners." Each individual boxed set includes the 44 cards and six logo stickers. The checklist for the set is found on the back panel of the box. The card numbering is in alphabetical order by player's name.

	MINT	NRMT	EXC
COMPLETE SET (44)	5.00	2.20	.60
COMMON CARD (1-44)	.05	.02	.01
□ 1 Harold Baines	.10	.05	.01
□ 2 Don Baylor	.10	.05	.01
□ 3 George Bell	.05	.02	.01
□ 4 Tony Bernazard	.05	.02	.01
□ 5 Wade Boggs	.30	.14	.04
□ 6 George Brett	.75	.35	.09
□ 7 Hubie Brooks	.05	.02	.01
□ 8 Jose Canseco	.75	.35	.09
□ 9 Gary Carter	.10	.05	.01
□ 10 Roger Clemens	.50	.23	.06
□ 11 Eric Davis	.05	.02	.01
□ 12 Glenn Davis	.05	.02	.01
□ 13 Shawon Dunston	.05	.02	.01
□ 14 Mark Eichhorn	.05	.02	.01
□ 15 Gary Gaetti	.05	.02	.01
□ 16 Steve Garvey	.10	.05	.01
□ 17 Kirk Gibson	.10	.05	.01
□ 18 Dwight Gooden	.20	.09	.03
□ 19 Von Hayes	.05	.02	.01
□ 20 Willie Hernandez	.05	.02	.01
□ 21 Ted Higuera	.05	.02	.01
□ 22 Wally Joyner	.20	.09	.03
□ 23 Bob Knepper	.05	.02	.01
□ 24 Mike Krukow	.05	.02	.01
□ 25 Jeff Leonard	.05	.02	.01
□ 26 Don Mattingly	1.00	.45	.12
□ 27 Kirk McCaskill	.05	.02	.01
□ 28 Kevin McReynolds	.05	.02	.01
□ 29 Jim Morrison	.05	.02	.01
□ 30 Dale Murphy	.20	.09	.03
□ 31 Pete O'Brien	.05	.02	.01
□ 32 Bob Ojeda	.05	.02	.01
□ 33 Larry Parrish	.05	.02	.01
□ 34 Ken Phelps	.05	.02	.01
□ 35 Dennis Rasmussen	.05	.02	.01
□ 36 Ernest Riles	.05	.02	.01
□ 37 Cal Ripken	2.00	.90	.25
□ 38 Ron Robinson	.05	.02	.01
□ 39 Steve Sax	.05	.02	.01
□ 40 Mike Schmidt	.50	.23	.06
□ 41 John Tudor	.05	.02	.01
□ 42 Fernando Valenzuela	.10	.05	.01
□ 43 Mike Witt	.05	.02	.01
□ 44 Curt Young	.05	.02	.01

1987 Fleer Hottest Stars

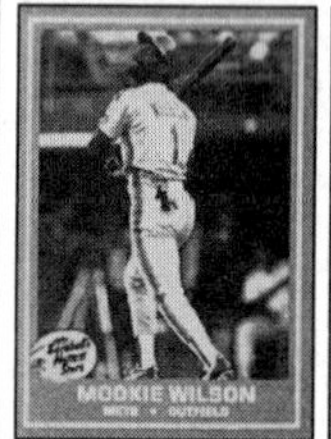

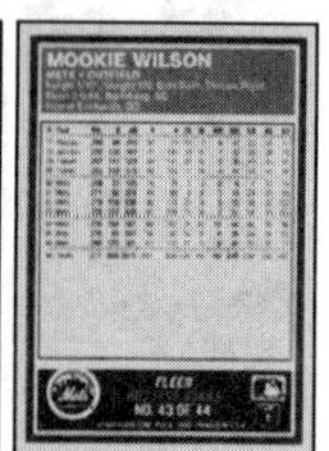

This 44-card boxed standard-size set was produced by Fleer for distribution by Revco stores all over the country. The cards feature full color fronts and red, white, and black backs. The card fronts are easily distinguished by their solid red outside borders and and white and blue inner borders framing the player's picture. The box for the cards proclaims "1987 Limited Edition Baseball's Hottest Stars" and is styled in the same manner and color scheme as the cards themselves. The checklist for the set is given on the back of the set box. The card numbering is in alphabetical order by player's name.

	MINT	NRMT	EXC
COMPLETE SET (44)	5.00	2.20	.60
COMMON CARD (1-44)	.05	.02	.01
□ 1 Joaquin Andujar	.05	.02	.01
□ 2 Harold Baines	.10	.05	.01
□ 3 Kevin Bass	.05	.02	.01
□ 4 Don Baylor	.10	.05	.01
□ 5 Barry Bonds	2.00	.90	.25
□ 6 George Brett	.75	.35	.09
□ 7 Tom Brunansky	.05	.02	.01
□ 8 Brett Butler	.10	.05	.01
□ 9 Jose Canseco	.75	.35	.09
□ 10 Roger Clemens	.60	.25	.07
□ 11 Ron Darling	.05	.02	.01
□ 12 Eric Davis	.05	.02	.01
□ 13 Andre Dawson	.20	.09	.03
□ 14 Doug DeCinces	.05	.02	.01
□ 15 Leon Durham	.05	.02	.01
□ 16 Mark Eichhorn	.05	.02	.01
□ 17 Scott Garrelts	.05	.02	.01
□ 18 Dwight Gooden	.20	.09	.03
□ 19 Dave Henderson	.05	.02	.01
□ 20 Rickey Henderson	.50	.23	.06
□ 21 Keith Hernandez	.10	.05	.01
□ 22 Ted Higuera	.05	.02	.01
□ 23 Bob Horner	.05	.02	.01
□ 24 Pete Incaviglia	.10	.05	.01
□ 25 Wally Joyner	.20	.09	.03
□ 26 Mark Langston	.05	.02	.01
□ 27 Don Mattingly UER (Pirates logo on back)	1.00	.45	.12
□ 28 Dale Murphy	.20	.09	.03
□ 29 Kirk McCaskill	.05	.02	.01
□ 30 Willie McGee	.10	.05	.01
□ 31 Dave Righetti	.05	.02	.01
□ 32 Pete Rose	.75	.35	.09
□ 33 Bruce Ruffin	.05	.02	.01
□ 34 Steve Sax	.05	.02	.01
□ 35 Mike Schmidt	.50	.23	.06
□ 36 Larry Sheets	.05	.02	.01
□ 37 Eric Show	.05	.02	.01
□ 38 Dave Smith	.05	.02	.01
□ 39 Cory Snyder	.05	.02	.01
□ 40 Frank Tanana	.05	.02	.01
□ 41 Alan Trammell	.15	.07	.02
□ 42 Reggie Williams	.05	.02	.01
□ 43 Mookie Wilson	.05	.02	.01
□ 44 Todd Worrell	.05	.02	.01

1987 Fleer League Leaders

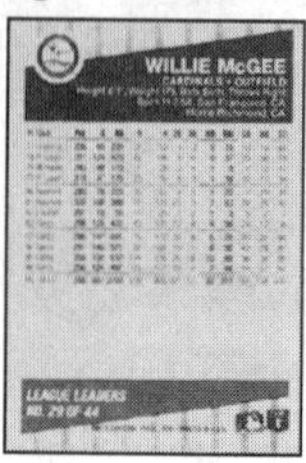

This small set of 44 standard-size cards was produced for Walgreens by Fleer. The cards feature full color fronts and red, white, and blue backs. The card fronts are easily distinguished by their light blue vertical stripes over a white background. The box for the cards proclaims a "Walgreens Exclusive" and is styled in the same manner and color scheme as the cards themselves. The checklist for the set is given on the back of the set box. The card numbering is in alphabetical order by player's name.

	MINT	NRMT	EXC
COMPLETE SET (44)	5.00	2.20	.60
COMMON CARD (1-44)	.05	.02	.01
□ 1 Jesse Barfield	.05	.02	.01
□ 2 Mike Boddicker	.05	.02	.01
□ 3 Wade Boggs	.30	.14	.04
□ 4 Phil Bradley	.05	.02	.01
□ 5 George Brett	.75	.35	.09
□ 6 Hubie Brooks	.05	.02	.01
□ 7 Chris Brown	.05	.02	.01
□ 8 Jose Canseco	.75	.35	.09
□ 9 Joe Carter	.25	.11	.03
□ 10 Roger Clemens	.60	.25	.07
□ 11 Vince Coleman	.05	.02	.01
□ 12 Joe Cowley	.05	.02	.01
□ 13 Kal Daniels	.05	.02	.01
□ 14 Glenn Davis	.05	.02	.01
□ 15 Jody Davis	.05	.02	.01
□ 16 Darrell Evans	.05	.02	.01
□ 17 Dwight Evans	.10	.05	.01
□ 18 John Franco	.10	.05	.01
□ 19 Julio Franco	.10	.05	.01
□ 20 Dwight Gooden	.20	.09	.03
□ 21 Rich Gossage	.10	.05	.01
□ 22 Tom Herr	.05	.02	.01
□ 23 Ted Higuera	.05	.02	.01
□ 24 Bob Horner	.05	.02	.01
□ 25 Pete Incaviglia	.10	.05	.01
□ 26 Wally Joyner	.20	.09	.03
□ 27 Dave Kingman	.10	.05	.01
□ 28 Don Mattingly	1.00	.45	.12
□ 29 Willie McGee	.10	.05	.01
□ 30 Donnie Moore	.05	.02	.01
□ 31 Keith Moreland	.05	.02	.01
□ 32 Eddie Murray	.50	.23	.06
□ 33 Mike Pagliarulo	.05	.02	.01
□ 34 Larry Parrish	.05	.02	.01
□ 35 Tony Pena	.05	.02	.01
□ 36 Kirby Puckett	1.00	.45	.12
□ 37 Pete Rose	.75	.35	.09
□ 38 Juan Samuel	.05	.02	.01
□ 39 Ryne Sandberg	.75	.35	.09
□ 40 Mike Schmidt	.50	.23	.06
□ 41 Darryl Strawberry	.20	.09	.03
□ 42 Greg Walker	.05	.02	.01
□ 43 Bob Welch	.05	.02	.01
□ 44 Todd Worrell	.10	.05	.01

1987 Fleer Limited Edition

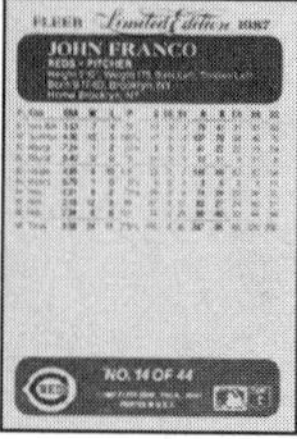

This 44-card boxed standard-size set was (mass) produced by Fleer for distribution by McCrory's and is sometimes referred to as the McCrory's set. The numerical checklist on the back of the box shows that the set is numbered alphabetically.

	MINT	NRMT	EXC
COMPLETE SET (44)	4.00	1.80	.50
COMMON CARD (1-44)	.05	.02	.01
□ 1 Floyd Bannister	.05	.02	.01
□ 2 Marty Barrett	.05	.02	.01
□ 3 Steve Bedrosian	.05	.02	.01
□ 4 George Bell	.05	.02	.01
□ 5 George Brett	1.00	.45	.12
□ 6 Jose Canseco	.60	.25	.07
□ 7 Joe Carter	.25	.11	.03
□ 8 Will Clark	.75	.35	.09

Card	MINT	NRMT	EXC
☐ 9 Roger Clemens	.60	.25	.07
☐ 10 Vince Coleman	.05	.02	.01
☐ 11 Glenn Davis	.05	.02	.01
☐ 12 Mike Davis	.05	.02	.01
☐ 13 Len Dykstra	.20	.09	.03
☐ 14 John Franco	.10	.05	.01
☐ 15 Julio Franco	.10	.05	.01
☐ 16 Steve Garvey	.10	.05	.01
☐ 17 Kirk Gibson	.10	.05	.01
☐ 18 Dwight Gooden	.20	.09	.03
☐ 19 Tony Gwynn	1.00	.45	.12
☐ 20 Keith Hernandez	.10	.05	.01
☐ 21 Teddy Higuera	.05	.02	.01
☐ 22 Kent Hrbek	.10	.05	.01
☐ 23 Wally Joyner	.20	.09	.03
☐ 24 Mike Krukow	.05	.02	.01
☐ 25 Mike Marshall	.05	.02	.01
☐ 26 Don Mattingly	1.00	.45	.12
☐ 27 Oddibe McDowell	.05	.02	.01
☐ 28 Jack Morris	.10	.05	.01
☐ 29 Lloyd Moseby	.05	.02	.01
☐ 30 Dale Murphy	.20	.09	.03
☐ 31 Eddie Murray	.60	.25	.07
☐ 32 Tony Pena	.05	.02	.01
☐ 33 Jim Presley	.05	.02	.01
☐ 34 Jeff Reardon	.05	.02	.01
☐ 35 Jim Rice	.10	.05	.01
☐ 36 Pete Rose	.75	.35	.09
☐ 37 Mike Schmidt	.50	.23	.06
☐ 38 Mike Scott	.05	.02	.01
☐ 39 Lee Smith	.15	.07	.02
☐ 40 Lonnie Smith	.05	.02	.01
☐ 41 Gary Ward	.05	.02	.01
☐ 42 Dave Winfield	.25	.11	.03
☐ 43 Todd Worrell	.05	.02	.01
☐ 44 Robin Yount	.30	.14	.04

1987 Fleer Limited Box Cards

The cards in this six-card set each measure the standard size. Cards have essentially the same design as the 1987 Fleer Limited Edition cards which were distributed by McCrory's. The cards were printed on the bottom of the counter display box which held 24 small boxed sets; hence theoretically these box cards are 1/24 as plentiful as the regular boxed set cards. These six cards, numbered C1 to C6, are considered a separate set in their own right and are not typically included in a complete set of the 1987 Fleer Limited Edition set of 44. The value of the panels uncut is slightly greater, perhaps by 25 percent greater, than the value of the individual cards cut up carefully.

	MINT	NRMT	EXC
COMPLETE SET (6)	2.00	.90	.25
COMMON CARDS (C1-C6)	.25	.11	.03
☐ C1 Ron Darling	.25	.11	.03
☐ C2 Bill Buckner	.50	.23	.06
☐ C3 John Candelaria	.25	.11	.03
☐ C4 Jack Clark	.50	.23	.06
☐ C5 Bret Saberhagen	2.00	.90	.25
☐ C6 Team Logo (Checklist back)	.25	.11	.03

1987 Fleer Mini

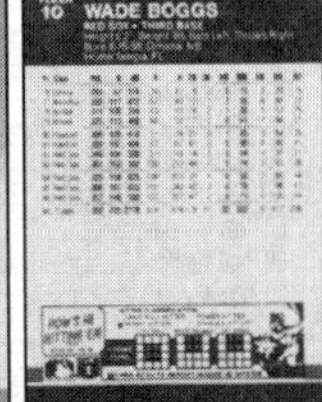

The 1987 Fleer "Classic Miniatures" set consists of 120 small cards with all new pictures of the players as compared to the 1987 Fleer regular issue. The cards are only 1 13/16" by 2 9/16", making them one of the smallest cards available. Card backs provide career year-by-year statistics. The complete set was distributed in a blue, red, white, and silver box along with 18 logo stickers. The card numbering is by alphabetical order.

	MINT	NRMT	EXC
COMPLETE SET (120)	6.00	2.70	.75
COMMON CARD (1-120)	.05	.02	.01
☐ 1 Don Aase	.05	.02	.01
☐ 2 Joaquin Andujar	.05	.02	.01
☐ 3 Harold Baines	.10	.05	.01
☐ 4 Jesse Barfield	.05	.02	.01
☐ 5 Kevin Bass	.05	.02	.01
☐ 6 Don Baylor	.10	.05	.01
☐ 7 George Bell	.05	.02	.01
☐ 8 Tony Bernazard	.05	.02	.01
☐ 9 Bert Blyleven	.10	.05	.01
☐ 10 Wade Boggs	.25	.11	.03
☐ 11 Phil Bradley	.05	.02	.01
☐ 12 Sid Bream	.05	.02	.01
☐ 13 George Brett	1.00	.45	.12
☐ 14 Hubie Brooks	.05	.02	.01
☐ 15 Chris Brown	.05	.02	.01
☐ 16 Tom Candiotti	.05	.02	.01
☐ 17 Jose Canseco	.60	.25	.07
☐ 18 Gary Carter	.10	.05	.01
☐ 19 Joe Carter	.25	.11	.03
☐ 20 Roger Clemens	.75	.35	.09
☐ 21 Vince Coleman	.05	.02	.01
☐ 22 Cecil Cooper	.10	.05	.01
☐ 23 Ron Darling	.05	.02	.01
☐ 24 Alvin Davis	.05	.02	.01
☐ 25 Chili Davis	.10	.05	.01
☐ 26 Eric Davis	.15	.07	.02
☐ 27 Glenn Davis	.05	.02	.01
☐ 28 Mike Davis	.05	.02	.01
☐ 29 Doug DeCinces	.05	.02	.01
☐ 30 Rob Deer	.05	.02	.01
☐ 31 Jim Deshaies	.05	.02	.01
☐ 32 Bo Diaz	.05	.02	.01
☐ 33 Richard Dotson	.05	.02	.01
☐ 34 Brian Downing	.05	.02	.01
☐ 35 Shawon Dunston	.05	.02	.01
☐ 36 Mark Eichhorn	.05	.02	.01
☐ 37 Dwight Evans	.10	.05	.01
☐ 38 Tony Fernandez	.05	.02	.01
☐ 39 Julio Franco	.10	.05	.01
☐ 40 Gary Gaetti	.05	.02	.01
☐ 41 Andres Galarraga	.40	.18	.05
☐ 42 Scott Garrelts	.05	.02	.01
☐ 43 Steve Garvey	.10	.05	.01
☐ 44 Kirk Gibson	.10	.05	.01
☐ 45 Dwight Gooden	.15	.07	.02
☐ 46 Ken Griffey Sr.	.10	.05	.01
☐ 47 Mark Gubicza	.05	.02	.01
☐ 48 Ozzie Guillen	.05	.02	.01
☐ 49 Bill Gullickson	.05	.02	.01
☐ 50 Tony Gwynn	1.00	.45	.12
☐ 51 Von Hayes	.05	.02	.01
☐ 52 Rickey Henderson	.50	.23	.06
☐ 53 Keith Hernandez	.10	.05	.01
☐ 54 Willie Hernandez	.05	.02	.01
☐ 55 Ted Higuera	.05	.02	.01
☐ 56 Charlie Hough	.05	.02	.01
☐ 57 Kent Hrbek	.10	.05	.01
☐ 58 Pete Incaviglia	.10	.05	.01
☐ 59 Wally Joyner	.25	.11	.03
☐ 60 Bob Knepper	.05	.02	.01
☐ 61 Mike Krukow	.05	.02	.01
☐ 62 Mark Langston	.05	.02	.01
☐ 63 Carney Lansford	.05	.02	.01
☐ 64 Jim Lindeman	.05	.02	.01
☐ 65 Bill Madlock	.05	.02	.01
☐ 66 Don Mattingly	1.00	.45	.12
☐ 67 Kirk McCaskill	.05	.02	.01
☐ 68 Lance McCullers	.05	.02	.01
☐ 69 Keith Moreland	.05	.02	.01
☐ 70 Jack Morris	.10	.05	.01
☐ 71 Jim Morrison	.05	.02	.01
☐ 72 Lloyd Moseby	.05	.02	.01
☐ 73 Jerry Mumphrey	.05	.02	.01
☐ 74 Dale Murphy	.25	.11	.03
☐ 75 Eddie Murray	.60	.25	.07
☐ 76 Pete O'Brien	.05	.02	.01
☐ 77 Bob Ojeda	.05	.02	.01
☐ 78 Jesse Orosco	.05	.02	.01
☐ 79 Dan Pasqua	.05	.02	.01
☐ 80 Dave Parker	.10	.05	.01
☐ 81 Larry Parrish	.05	.02	.01
☐ 82 Jim Presley	.05	.02	.01
☐ 83 Kirby Puckett	1.00	.45	.12
☐ 84 Dan Quisenberry	.05	.02	.01
☐ 85 Tim Raines	.10	.05	.01
☐ 86 Dennis Rasmussen	.05	.02	.01
☐ 87 Johnny Ray	.05	.02	.01
☐ 88 Jeff Reardon	.10	.05	.01
☐ 89 Jim Rice	.10	.05	.01
☐ 90 Dave Righetti	.05	.02	.01
☐ 91 Earnest Riles	.05	.02	.01
☐ 92 Cal Ripken	1.50	.70	.19
☐ 93 Ron Robinson	.05	.02	.01
☐ 94 Juan Samuel	.05	.02	.01
☐ 95 Ryne Sandberg	.60	.25	.07
☐ 96 Steve Sax	.05	.02	.01
☐ 97 Mike Schmidt	.40	.18	.05
☐ 98 Ken Schrom	.05	.02	.01
☐ 99 Mike Scott	.05	.02	.01
☐ 100 Ruben Sierra	.25	.11	.03
☐ 101 Lee Smith	.15	.07	.02
☐ 102 Ozzie Smith	.75	.35	.09
☐ 103 Cory Snyder	.05	.02	.01
☐ 104 Kent Tekulve	.05	.02	.01
☐ 105 Andres Thomas	.05	.02	.01
☐ 106 Robby Thompson	.10	.05	.01
☐ 107 Alan Trammell	.15	.07	.02
☐ 108 John Tudor	.05	.02	.01
☐ 109 Fernando Valenzuela	.10	.05	.01
☐ 110 Greg Walker	.05	.02	.01
☐ 111 Mitch Webster	.05	.02	.01
☐ 112 Lou Whitaker	.10	.05	.01
☐ 113 Frank White	.10	.05	.01
☐ 114 Reggie Williams	.05	.02	.01
☐ 115 Glenn Wilson	.05	.02	.01
☐ 116 Willie Wilson	.05	.02	.01
☐ 117 Dave Winfield	.50	.23	.06
☐ 118 Mike Witt	.05	.02	.01
☐ 119 Todd Worrell	.10	.05	.01
☐ 120 Floyd Youmans	.05	.02	.01

1987 Fleer Record Setters

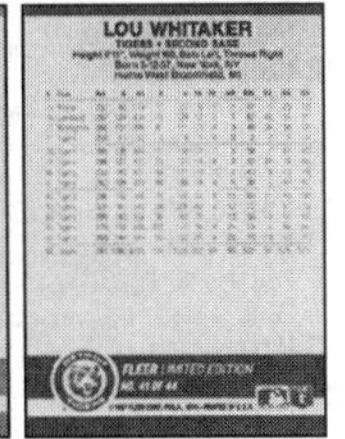

This 44-card boxed standard-size set was produced by Fleer for distribution by Eckerd's Drug Stores and is sometimes referred to as the Eckerd's set. Six team logo stickers are included in the box with the complete set. The numerical checklist on the back of the box shows that the set is numbered alphabetically.

	MINT	NRMT	EXC
COMPLETE SET (44)	4.00	1.80	.50
COMMON CARD (1-44)	.05	.02	.01
☐ 1 George Brett	.75	.35	.09
☐ 2 Chris Brown	.05	.02	.01
☐ 3 Jose Canseco UER (3 of 444 on back)	.50	.23	.06
☐ 4 Roger Clemens	.50	.23	.06
☐ 5 Alvin Davis UER (5 of 441 on back, upside down one)	.05	.02	.01
☐ 6 Shawon Dunston	.05	.02	.01
☐ 7 Tony Fernandez	.05	.02	.01
☐ 8 Carlton Fisk UER (8 of 44' on back)	.25	.11	.03
☐ 9 Gary Gaetti UER (9 of 444 on back)	.05	.02	.01
☐ 10 Gene Garber	.05	.02	.01
☐ 11 Rich Gedman	.05	.02	.01
☐ 12 Dwight Gooden	.20	.09	.03
☐ 13 Ozzie Guillen	.05	.02	.01
☐ 14 Bill Gullickson	.05	.02	.01
☐ 15 Billy Hatcher	.05	.02	.01
☐ 16 Orel Hershiser	.10	.05	.01
☐ 17 Wally Joyner	.20	.09	.03
☐ 18 Ray Knight	.05	.02	.01
☐ 19 Craig Lefferts	.05	.02	.01
☐ 20 Don Mattingly	1.00	.45	.12
☐ 21 Kevin Mitchell	.10	.05	.01
☐ 22 Lloyd Moseby	.05	.02	.01
☐ 23 Dale Murphy	.20	.09	.03
☐ 24 Eddie Murray	.50	.23	.06
☐ 25 Phil Niekro	.20	.09	.03
☐ 26 Ben Oglivie	.05	.02	.01
☐ 27 Jesse Orosco	.05	.02	.01
☐ 28 Joe Orsulak	.05	.02	.01
☐ 29 Larry Parrish	.05	.02	.01
☐ 30 Tim Raines	.10	.05	.01
☐ 31 Shane Rawley	.05	.02	.01
☐ 32 Dave Righetti	.05	.02	.01
☐ 33 Pete Rose	.75	.35	.09
☐ 34 Steve Sax	.05	.02	.01
☐ 35 Mike Schmidt	.50	.23	.06
☐ 36 Mike Scott	.05	.02	.01
☐ 37 Don Sutton	.10	.05	.01
☐ 38 Alan Trammell	.15	.07	.02
☐ 39 John Tudor	.05	.02	.01
☐ 40 Gary Ward	.05	.02	.01
☐ 41 Lou Whitaker	.10	.05	.01
☐ 42 Willie Wilson	.05	.02	.01
☐ 43 Todd Worrell	.10	.05	.01
☐ 44 Floyd Youmans	.05	.02	.01

1987 Fleer Sluggers/Pitchers

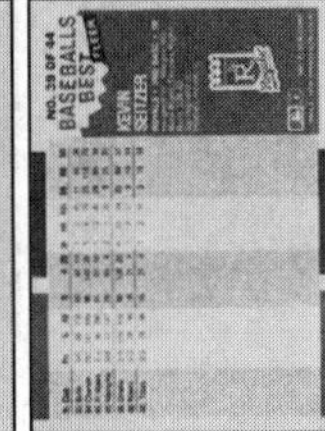

Fleer produced this 44-card boxed standard-size set although it was primarily distributed by McCrory, McLellan, Newberry, H.L.Green, T.G.Y., and other similar stores. The set features 28 sluggers and 16 pitchers and is subtitled "Baseball's Best". The set was packaged in a red, white, blue, and yellow custom box along with six logo stickers. The set checklist is given on the back of the box. The checklist on the back of the set box misspells McGwire as McGuire. The card numbering is in alphabetical order by player's name.

	MINT	NRMT	EXC
COMPLETE SET (44)	5.00	2.20	.60
COMMON CARD (1-44)	.05	.02	.01
☐ 1 Kevin Bass	.05	.02	.01
☐ 2 Jesse Barfield	.05	.02	.01
☐ 3 George Bell	.05	.02	.01
☐ 4 Wade Boggs	.30	.14	.04
☐ 5 Sid Bream	.05	.02	.01
☐ 6 George Brett	1.00	.45	.12
☐ 7 Ivan Calderon	.05	.02	.01
☐ 8 Jose Canseco	.60	.25	.07
☐ 9 Jack Clark	.10	.05	.01
☐ 10 Roger Clemens	.60	.25	.07
☐ 11 Eric Davis	.05	.02	.01
☐ 12 Andre Dawson	.25	.11	.03
☐ 13 Sid Fernandez	.05	.02	.01
☐ 14 John Franco	.10	.05	.01
☐ 15 Dwight Gooden	.20	.09	.03
☐ 16 Pedro Guerrero	.05	.02	.01
☐ 17 Tony Gwynn	1.00	.45	.12
☐ 18 Rickey Henderson	.50	.23	.06
☐ 19 Tom Henke	.05	.02	.01
☐ 20 Ted Higuera	.05	.02	.01
☐ 21 Pete Incaviglia	.10	.05	.01
☐ 22 Wally Joyner	.20	.09	.03
☐ 23 Jeff Leonard	.05	.02	.01
☐ 24 Joe Magrane	.05	.02	.01
☐ 25 Don Mattingly	1.00	.45	.12
☐ 26 Mark McGwire	1.50	.70	.19
☐ 27 Jack Morris	.10	.05	.01
☐ 28 Dale Murphy	.20	.09	.03
☐ 29 Dave Parker	.10	.05	.01
☐ 30 Ken Phelps	.05	.02	.01
☐ 31 Kirby Puckett	1.00	.45	.12
☐ 32 Tim Raines	.10	.05	.01
☐ 33 Jeff Reardon	.05	.02	.01
☐ 34 Dave Righetti	.05	.02	.01
☐ 35 Cal Ripken	2.00	.90	.25
☐ 36 Bret Saberhagen	.10	.05	.01
☐ 37 Mike Schmidt	.50	.23	.06
☐ 38 Mike Scott	.05	.02	.01
☐ 39 Kevin Seitzer	.10	.05	.01
☐ 40 Darryl Strawberry	.20	.09	.03
☐ 41 Rick Sutcliffe	.05	.02	.01
☐ 42 Pat Tabler	.05	.02	.01
☐ 43 Fernando Valenzuela	.10	.05	.01
☐ 44 Mike Witt	.05	.02	.01

1987 Fleer Sluggers/Pitchers Box Cards

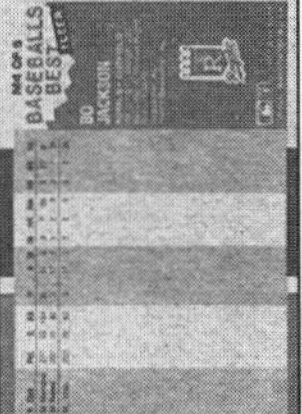

The cards in this six-card set each measure the standard size. Cards have essentially the same design as the 1987 Fleer Sluggers vs. Pitchers set of Baseball's Best. The cards were printed on the bottom of the counter display box which held 24 small boxed sets; hence theoretically these box cards are 1/24 as plentiful as the regular boxed set cards. These six cards, numbered M1 to M5 with one blank-back (unnumbered) card, are considered a separate set in their own right and are not typically included in a complete set of the 1987 Fleer Sluggers vs. Pitchers set of 44. The value of the panels uncut is slightly greater, perhaps by 25 percent greater, than the value of the individual cards cut up carefully.

	MINT	NRMT	EXC
COMPLETE SET (6)	10.00	4.50	1.25
COMMON CARD	.50	.23	.06
☐ M1 Steve Bedrosian	.50	.23	.06
☐ M2 Will Clark	6.00	2.70	.75
☐ M3 Vince Coleman	.50	.23	.06
☐ M4 Bo Jackson	3.00	1.35	.35
☐ M5 Cory Snyder	.50	.23	.06
☐ NNO Team Logo (Blank back)	.50	.23	.06

1987 Fleer Sticker Cards

These Star Stickers were distributed as a separate issue by Fleer with five star stickers and a logo sticker in each wax pack. The 132-card (sticker) set features 2 1/2" by 3 1/2" full-color fronts and even statistics on the sticker back, which is an indication that the Fleer Company understands that these stickers are rarely used as stickers but more like traditional cards. The card fronts are surrounded by a green border and the backs are printed in green and yellow on white card stock. The card numbering is in alphabetical order by player's name.

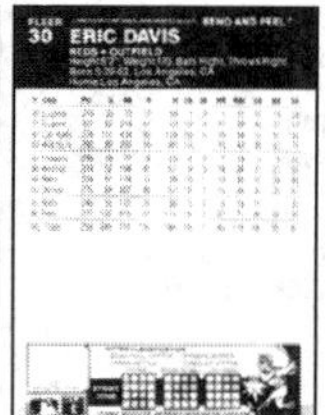

	MINT	NRMT	EXC
COMPLETE SET (132)	15.00	6.75	1.85
COMMON CARD (1-132)	.05	.02	.01
☐ 1 Don Aase	.05	.02	.01
☐ 2 Harold Baines	.10	.05	.01
☐ 3 Floyd Bannister	.05	.02	.01
☐ 4 Jesse Barfield	.05	.02	.01
☐ 5 Marty Barrett	.05	.02	.01
☐ 6 Kevin Bass	.05	.02	.01
☐ 7 Don Baylor	.10	.05	.01
☐ 8 Steve Bedrosian	.05	.02	.01
☐ 9 George Bell	.05	.02	.01
☐ 10 Bert Blyleven	.10	.05	.01
☐ 11 Mike Boddicker	.05	.02	.01
☐ 12 Wade Boggs	.40	.18	.05
☐ 13 Phil Bradley	.05	.02	.01
☐ 14 Sid Bream	.05	.02	.01
☐ 15 George Brett	1.50	.70	.19
☐ 16 Hubie Brooks	.05	.02	.01
☐ 17 Tom Brunansky	.05	.02	.01
☐ 18 Tom Candiotti	.05	.02	.01
☐ 19 Jose Canseco	1.00	.45	.12
☐ 20 Gary Carter	.10	.05	.01
☐ 21 Joe Carter	.40	.18	.05
☐ 22 Will Clark	1.50	.70	.19
☐ 23 Mark Clear	.05	.02	.01
☐ 24 Roger Clemens	1.00	.45	.12
☐ 25 Vince Coleman	.05	.02	.01
☐ 26 Jose Cruz	.05	.02	.01
☐ 27 Ron Darling	.05	.02	.01
☐ 28 Alvin Davis	.05	.02	.01
☐ 29 Chili Davis	.10	.05	.01
☐ 30 Eric Davis	.25	.11	.03
☐ 31 Glenn Davis	.05	.02	.01
☐ 32 Mike Davis	.05	.02	.01
☐ 33 Andre Dawson	.35	.16	.04
☐ 34 Doug DeCinces	.05	.02	.01
☐ 35 Brian Downing	.05	.02	.01
☐ 36 Shawon Dunston	.10	.05	.01
☐ 37 Mark Eichhorn	.05	.02	.01
☐ 38 Dwight Evans	.10	.05	.01
☐ 39 Tony Fernandez	.05	.02	.01
☐ 40 Bob Forsch	.05	.02	.01
☐ 41 John Franco	.10	.05	.01
☐ 42 Julio Franco	.10	.05	.01
☐ 43 Gary Gaetti	.05	.02	.01
☐ 44 Gene Garber	.05	.02	.01
☐ 45 Scott Garrelts	.05	.02	.01
☐ 46 Steve Garvey	.10	.05	.01
☐ 47 Kirk Gibson	.10	.05	.01
☐ 48 Dwight Gooden	.25	.11	.03
☐ 49 Ken Griffey Sr.	.10	.05	.01
☐ 50 Ozzie Guillen	.05	.02	.01
☐ 51 Bill Gullickson	.05	.02	.01
☐ 52 Tony Gwynn	1.50	.70	.19
☐ 53 Mel Hall	.05	.02	.01
☐ 54 Greg A. Harris	.05	.02	.01
☐ 55 Von Hayes	.05	.02	.01
☐ 56 Rickey Henderson	.60	.25	.07
☐ 57 Tom Henke	.05	.02	.01
☐ 58 Keith Hernandez	.10	.05	.01
☐ 59 Willie Hernandez	.05	.02	.01
☐ 60 Ted Higuera	.05	.02	.01
☐ 61 Bob Horner	.05	.02	.01
☐ 62 Charlie Hough	.05	.02	.01
☐ 63 Jay Howell	.05	.02	.01
☐ 64 Kent Hrbek	.10	.05	.01
☐ 65 Bruce Hurst	.05	.02	.01
☐ 66 Pete Incaviglia	.10	.05	.01
☐ 67 Bob James	.05	.02	.01
☐ 68 Wally Joyner	.25	.11	.03
☐ 69 Mike Krukow	.05	.02	.01
☐ 70 Mark Langston	.05	.02	.01
☐ 71 Carney Lansford	.10	.05	.01
☐ 72 Fred Lynn	.10	.05	.01
☐ 73 Bill Madlock	.05	.02	.01
☐ 74 Don Mattingly	1.50	.70	.19
☐ 75 Kirk McCaskill	.05	.02	.01
☐ 76 Lance McCullers	.05	.02	.01
☐ 77 Oddibe McDowell	.05	.02	.01
☐ 78 Paul Molitor	.60	.25	.07
☐ 79 Keith Moreland	.05	.02	.01
☐ 80 Jack Morris	.10	.05	.01
☐ 81 Jim Morrison	.05	.02	.01
☐ 82 Jerry Mumphrey	.05	.02	.01
☐ 83 Dale Murphy	.25	.11	.03
☐ 84 Eddie Murray	.75	.35	.09
☐ 85 Ben Oglivie	.05	.02	.01
☐ 86 Bob Ojeda	.05	.02	.01
☐ 87 Jesse Orosco	.05	.02	.01
☐ 88 Dave Parker	.10	.05	.01
☐ 89 Larry Parrish	.05	.02	.01
☐ 90 Tony Pena	.05	.02	.01
☐ 91 Jim Presley	.05	.02	.01
☐ 92 Kirby Puckett	1.50	.70	.19
☐ 93 Dan Quisenberry	.05	.02	.01
☐ 94 Tim Raines	.10	.05	.01
☐ 95 Dennis Rasmussen	.05	.02	.01
☐ 96 Shane Rawley	.05	.02	.01
☐ 97 Johnny Ray	.05	.02	.01
☐ 98 Jeff Reardon	.10	.05	.01
☐ 99 Jim Rice	.10	.05	.01
☐ 100 Dave Righetti	.05	.02	.01
☐ 101 Cal Ripken	3.00	1.35	.35
☐ 102 Pete Rose	1.25	.55	.16
☐ 103 Nolan Ryan	3.00	1.35	.35
☐ 104 Juan Samuel	.05	.02	.01
☐ 105 Ryne Sandberg	1.25	.55	.16
☐ 106 Steve Sax	.05	.02	.01
☐ 107 Mike Schmidt	.75	.35	.09
☐ 108 Mike Scott	.05	.02	.01
☐ 109 Dave Smith	.05	.02	.01
☐ 110 Lee Smith	.25	.11	.03
☐ 111 Lonnie Smith	.05	.02	.01
☐ 112 Ozzie Smith	1.25	.55	.16
☐ 113 Cory Snyder	.05	.02	.01
☐ 114 Darryl Strawberry	.25	.11	.03
☐ 115 Don Sutton	.10	.05	.01
☐ 116 Kent Tekulve	.05	.02	.01
☐ 117 Andres Thomas	.05	.02	.01
☐ 118 Alan Trammell	.25	.11	.03
☐ 119 John Tudor	.05	.02	.01
☐ 120 Fernando Valenzuela	.10	.05	.01
☐ 121 Bob Welch	.05	.02	.01
☐ 122 Lou Whitaker	.10	.05	.01
☐ 123 Frank White	.10	.05	.01
☐ 124 Reggie Williams	.05	.02	.01
☐ 125 Willie Wilson	.05	.02	.01
☐ 126 Dave Winfield	.40	.18	.05
☐ 127 Mike Witt	.05	.02	.01
☐ 128 Todd Worrell	.10	.05	.01
☐ 129 Curt Young	.05	.02	.01
☐ 130 Robin Yount	.40	.18	.05
☐ 131 Jose Canseco CL Don Mattingly	1.00	.45	.12
☐ 132 Bo Jackson CL Eric Davis	.30	.14	.04

1987 Fleer Stickers Wax Box Cards

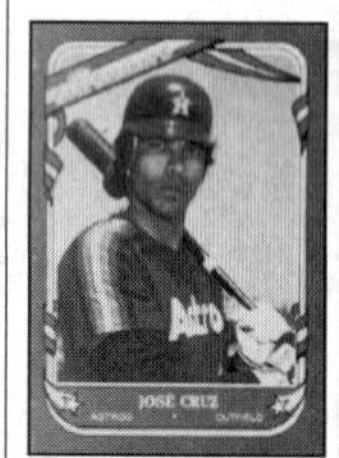

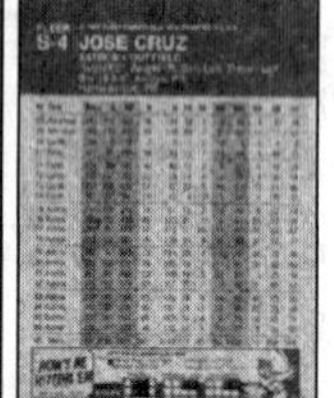

The bottoms of the Star Sticker wax boxes contained two different sets of four cards done in a similar format to the stickers; these cards (they are not stickers but truly cards) are numbered with the prefix S and are considered a separate set. The value of the panels uncut is slightly greater, perhaps by 25 percent greater, than the value of the individual cards cut up carefully. When cut properly, the individual cards measure standard size, 2 1/2" by 3 1/2".

	MINT	NRMT	EXC
COMPLETE SET (8)	5.00	2.20	.60
COMMON CARD (S1-S8)	.10	.05	.01
☐ S1 Detroit Logo	.10	.05	.01
☐ S2 Wade Boggs	1.50	.70	.19
☐ S3 Bert Blyleven	.20	.09	.03
☐ S4 Jose Cruz	.10	.05	.01
☐ S5 Glenn Davis	.10	.05	.01
☐ S6 Phillies Logo	.10	.05	.01
☐ S7 Bob Horner	.10	.05	.01
☐ S8 Don Mattingly	3.00	1.35	.35

1988 Fleer

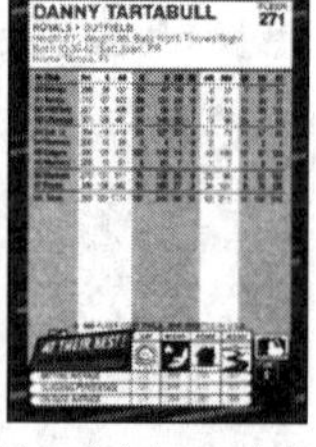

This set consists of 660 standard-size cards. Cards were primarily issued in 15-card wax packs and hobby and retail factory sets. Each wax pack contained one of 26 different "Stadium Card" stickers. Card fronts feature a distinctive white background with red and blue diagonal stripes across the card. Cards are again organized numerically by teams and team order is based upon the previous season's record. Subsets include Specials (622-640), Rookie Pairs (641-653), and checklists (654-660). Rookie Cards in this set include Jay Bell, John Burkett, Ellis Burks, Ken Caminiti, Ron Gant, Tom Glavine, Mark Grace, Gregg Jefferies, Edgar Martinez, Jack McDowell, Jeff Montgomery, and Matt Williams.

	MINT	NRMT	EXC
COMPLETE SET (660)	20.00	9.00	2.50
COMPLETE RETAIL SET (660)	20.00	9.00	2.50
COMPLETE HOBBY SET (672)	25.00	11.00	3.10
COMMON CARD (1-660)	.05	.02	.01
☐ 1 Keith Atherton	.05	.02	.01
☐ 2 Don Baylor	.30	.14	.04
☐ 3 Juan Berenguer	.05	.02	.01
☐ 4 Bert Blyleven	.15	.07	.02
☐ 5 Tom Brunansky	.05	.02	.01
☐ 6 Randy Bush	.05	.02	.01
☐ 7 Steve Carlton	.30	.14	.04
☐ 8 Mark Davidson	.05	.02	.01
☐ 9 George Frazier	.05	.02	.01
☐ 10 Gary Gaetti	.05	.02	.01
☐ 11 Greg Gagne	.05	.02	.01
☐ 12 Dan Gladden	.05	.02	.01
☐ 13 Kent Hrbek	.15	.07	.02
☐ 14 Gene Larkin	.05	.02	.01
☐ 15 Tim Laudner	.05	.02	.01
☐ 16 Steve Lombardozzi	.05	.02	.01
☐ 17 Al Newman	.05	.02	.01
☐ 18 Joe Niekro	.05	.02	.01
☐ 19 Kirby Puckett	.75	.35	.09
☐ 20 Jeff Reardon	.15	.07	.02
☐ 21A Dan Schatzeder ERR (Misspelled Schatzader on card front)	.15	.07	.02
☐ 21B Dan Schatzeder COR	.05	.02	.01
☐ 22 Roy Smalley	.05	.02	.01
☐ 23 Mike Smithson	.05	.02	.01
☐ 24 Les Straker	.05	.02	.01
☐ 25 Frank Viola	.05	.02	.01
☐ 26 Jack Clark	.15	.07	.02
☐ 27 Vince Coleman	.05	.02	.01
☐ 28 Danny Cox	.05	.02	.01
☐ 29 Bill Dawley	.05	.02	.01
☐ 30 Ken Dayley	.05	.02	.01
☐ 31 Doug DeCinces	.05	.02	.01
☐ 32 Curt Ford	.05	.02	.01
☐ 33 Bob Forsch	.05	.02	.01
☐ 34 David Green	.05	.02	.01
☐ 35 Tom Herr	.05	.02	.01
☐ 36 Ricky Horton	.05	.02	.01
☐ 37 Lance Johnson	.75	.35	.09
☐ 38 Steve Lake	.05	.02	.01
☐ 39 Jim Lindeman	.05	.02	.01
☐ 40 Joe Magrane	.05	.02	.01
☐ 41 Greg Mathews	.05	.02	.01
☐ 42 Willie McGee	.05	.02	.01
☐ 43 John Morris	.05	.02	.01
☐ 44 Jose Oquendo	.05	.02	.01
☐ 45 Tony Pena	.05	.02	.01
☐ 46 Terry Pendleton	.15	.07	.02
☐ 47 Ozzie Smith	.50	.23	.06
☐ 48 John Tudor	.05	.02	.01
☐ 49 Lee Tunnell	.05	.02	.01
☐ 50 Todd Worrell	.05	.02	.01
☐ 51 Doyle Alexander	.05	.02	.01
☐ 52 Dave Bergman	.05	.02	.01
☐ 53 Tom Brookens	.05	.02	.01
☐ 54 Darrell Evans	.15	.07	.02
☐ 55 Kirk Gibson	.15	.07	.02
☐ 56 Mike Heath	.05	.02	.01
☐ 57 Mike Henneman	.15	.07	.02
☐ 58 Willie Hernandez	.05	.02	.01
☐ 59 Larry Herndon	.05	.02	.01
☐ 60 Eric King	.05	.02	.01
☐ 61 Chet Lemon	.05	.02	.01
☐ 62 Scott Lusader	.05	.02	.01
☐ 63 Bill Madlock	.05	.02	.01
☐ 64 Jack Morris	.30	.14	.04
☐ 65 Jim Morrison	.05	.02	.01
☐ 66 Matt Nokes	.05	.02	.01
☐ 67 Dan Petry	.05	.02	.01
☐ 68A Jeff M. Robinson ERR (Stats for Jeff D. Robinson on card back, Born 12-13-60)	.30	.14	.04
☐ 68B Jeff M. Robinson COR (Born 12-14-61)	.05	.02	.01
☐ 69 Pat Sheridan	.05	.02	.01
☐ 70 Nate Snell	.05	.02	.01
☐ 71 Frank Tanana	.05	.02	.01
☐ 72 Walt Terrell	.05	.02	.01
☐ 73 Mark Thurmond	.05	.02	.01
☐ 74 Alan Trammell	.15	.07	.02
☐ 75 Lou Whitaker	.15	.07	.02
☐ 76 Mike Aldrete	.05	.02	.01
☐ 77 Bob Brenly	.05	.02	.01
☐ 78 Will Clark	.50	.23	.06
☐ 79 Chili Davis	.30	.14	.04
☐ 80 Kelly Downs	.05	.02	.01
☐ 81 Dave Dravecky	.15	.07	.02
☐ 82 Scott Garrelts	.05	.02	.01
☐ 83 Atlee Hammaker	.05	.02	.01
☐ 84 Dave Henderson	.05	.02	.01
☐ 85 Mike Krukow	.05	.02	.01
☐ 86 Mike LaCoss	.05	.02	.01
☐ 87 Craig Lefferts	.05	.02	.01
☐ 88 Jeff Leonard	.05	.02	.01
☐ 89 Candy Maldonado	.05	.02	.01
☐ 90 Eddie Milner	.05	.02	.01
☐ 91 Bob Melvin	.05	.02	.01
☐ 92 Kevin Mitchell	.15	.07	.02
☐ 93 Jon Perlman	.05	.02	.01
☐ 94 Rick Reuschel	.05	.02	.01
☐ 95 Don Robinson	.05	.02	.01
☐ 96 Chris Speier	.05	.02	.01
☐ 97 Harry Spilman	.05	.02	.01
☐ 98 Robby Thompson	.05	.02	.01
☐ 99 Jose Uribe	.05	.02	.01
☐ 100 Mark Wasinger	.05	.02	.01
☐ 101 Matt Williams	2.00	.90	.25
☐ 102 Jesse Reid	.05	.02	.01
☐ 103 George Bell	.05	.02	.01
☐ 104 Juan Beniquez	.05	.02	.01
☐ 105 John Cerutti	.05	.02	.01
☐ 106 Jim Clancy	.05	.02	.01
☐ 107 Rob Ducey	.05	.02	.01
☐ 108 Mark Eichhorn	.05	.02	.01
☐ 109 Tony Fernandez	.05	.02	.01
☐ 110 Cecil Fielder	.30	.14	.04
☐ 111 Kelly Gruber	.05	.02	.01
☐ 112 Tom Henke	.05	.02	.01
☐ 113A Garth Iorg ERR (Misspelled Iorq on card front)	.30	.14	.04
☐ 113B Garth Iorg COR	.05	.02	.01
☐ 114 Jimmy Key	.15	.07	.02
☐ 115 Rick Leach	.05	.02	.01
☐ 116 Manny Lee	.05	.02	.01
☐ 117 Nelson Liriano	.05	.02	.01
☐ 118 Fred McGriff	1.00	.45	.12
☐ 119 Lloyd Moseby	.05	.02	.01
☐ 120 Rance Mulliniks	.05	.02	.01
☐ 121 Jeff Musselman	.05	.02	.01
☐ 122 Jose Nunez	.05	.02	.01
☐ 123 Dave Stieb	.15	.07	.02
☐ 124 Willie Upshaw	.05	.02	.01
☐ 125 Duane Ward	.15	.07	.02
☐ 126 Ernie Whitt	.05	.02	.01
☐ 127 Rick Aguilera	.30	.14	.04
☐ 128 Wally Backman	.05	.02	.01
☐ 129 Mark Carreon	.30	.14	.04
☐ 130 Gary Carter	.15	.07	.02
☐ 131 David Cone	.50	.23	.06
☐ 132 Ron Darling	.05	.02	.01
☐ 133 Len Dykstra	.15	.07	.02
☐ 134 Sid Fernandez	.05	.02	.01
☐ 135 Dwight Gooden	.15	.07	.02
☐ 136 Keith Hernandez	.15	.07	.02
☐ 137 Gregg Jefferies	.75	.35	.09
☐ 138 Howard Johnson	.05	.02	.01
☐ 139 Terry Leach	.05	.02	.01
☐ 140 Barry Lyons	.05	.02	.01
☐ 141 Dave Magadan	.05	.02	.01
☐ 142 Roger McDowell	.05	.02	.01
☐ 143 Kevin McReynolds	.05	.02	.01
☐ 144 Keith A. Miller	.05	.02	.01
☐ 145 John Mitchell	.05	.02	.01
☐ 146 Randy Myers	.30	.14	.04
☐ 147 Bob Ojeda	.05	.02	.01
☐ 148 Jesse Orosco	.05	.02	.01
☐ 149 Rafael Santana	.05	.02	.01
☐ 150 Doug Sisk	.05	.02	.01
☐ 151 Darryl Strawberry	.15	.07	.02
☐ 152 Tim Teufel	.05	.02	.01
☐ 153 Gene Walter	.05	.02	.01
☐ 154 Mookie Wilson	.15	.07	.02
☐ 155 Jay Aldrich	.05	.02	.01
☐ 156 Chris Bosio	.05	.02	.01
☐ 157 Glenn Braggs	.05	.02	.01
☐ 158 Greg Brock	.05	.02	.01
☐ 159 Juan Castillo	.05	.02	.01
☐ 160 Mark Clear	.05	.02	.01
☐ 161 Cecil Cooper	.15	.07	.02
☐ 162 Chuck Crim	.05	.02	.01
☐ 163 Rob Deer	.05	.02	.01
☐ 164 Mike Felder	.05	.02	.01
☐ 165 Jim Gantner	.05	.02	.01
☐ 166 Ted Higuera	.05	.02	.01
☐ 167 Steve Kiefer	.05	.02	.01
☐ 168 Rick Manning	.05	.02	.01
☐ 169 Paul Molitor	.40	.18	.05
☐ 170 Juan Nieves	.05	.02	.01
☐ 171 Dan Plesac	.05	.02	.01
☐ 172 Earnest Riles	.05	.02	.01
☐ 173 Bill Schroeder	.05	.02	.01
☐ 174 Steve Stanicek	.05	.02	.01
☐ 175 B.J. Surhoff	.15	.07	.02
☐ 176 Dale Sveum	.05	.02	.01
☐ 177 Bill Wegman	.05	.02	.01
☐ 178 Robin Yount	.30	.14	.04
☐ 179 Hubie Brooks	.05	.02	.01
☐ 180 Tim Burke	.05	.02	.01
☐ 181 Casey Candaele	.05	.02	.01
☐ 182 Mike Fitzgerald	.05	.02	.01
☐ 183 Tom Foley	.05	.02	.01
☐ 184 Andres Galarraga	.30	.14	.04
☐ 185 Neal Heaton	.05	.02	.01
☐ 186 Wallace Johnson	.05	.02	.01
☐ 187 Vance Law	.05	.02	.01
☐ 188 Dennis Martinez	.15	.07	.02

Card			
☐ 189 Bob McClure	.05	.02	.01
☐ 190 Andy McGaffigan	.05	.02	.01
☐ 191 Reid Nichols	.05	.02	.01
☐ 192 Pascual Perez	.05	.02	.01
☐ 193 Tim Raines	.15	.07	.02
☐ 194 Jeff Reed	.05	.02	.01
☐ 195 Bob Sebra	.05	.02	.01
☐ 196 Bryn Smith	.05	.02	.01
☐ 197 Randy St.Claire	.05	.02	.01
☐ 198 Tim Wallach	.05	.02	.01
☐ 199 Mitch Webster	.05	.02	.01
☐ 200 Herm Winningham	.05	.02	.01
☐ 201 Floyd Youmans	.05	.02	.01
☐ 202 Brad Arnsberg	.05	.02	.01
☐ 203 Rick Cerone	.05	.02	.01
☐ 204 Pat Clements	.05	.02	.01
☐ 205 Henry Cotto	.05	.02	.01
☐ 206 Mike Easler	.05	.02	.01
☐ 207 Ron Guidry	.05	.02	.01
☐ 208 Bill Gullickson	.05	.02	.01
☐ 209 Rickey Henderson	.30	.14	.04
☐ 210 Charles Hudson	.05	.02	.01
☐ 211 Tommy John	.15	.07	.02
☐ 212 Roberto Kelly	.30	.14	.04
☐ 213 Ron Kittle	.05	.02	.01
☐ 214 Don Mattingly	1.00	.45	.12
☐ 215 Bobby Meacham	.05	.02	.01
☐ 216 Mike Pagliarulo	.05	.02	.01
☐ 217 Dan Pasqua	.05	.02	.01
☐ 218 Willie Randolph	.15	.07	.02
☐ 219 Rick Rhoden	.05	.02	.01
☐ 220 Dave Righetti	.15	.07	.02
☐ 221 Jerry Royster	.05	.02	.01
☐ 222 Tim Stoddard	.05	.02	.01
☐ 223 Wayne Tolleson	.05	.02	.01
☐ 224 Gary Ward	.05	.02	.01
☐ 225 Claudell Washington	.05	.02	.01
☐ 226 Dave Winfield	.30	.14	.04
☐ 227 Buddy Bell	.15	.07	.02
☐ 228 Tom Browning	.05	.02	.01
☐ 229 Dave Concepcion	.15	.07	.02
☐ 230 Kal Daniels	.05	.02	.01
☐ 231 Eric Davis	.15	.07	.02
☐ 232 Bo Diaz	.05	.02	.01
☐ 233 Nick Esasky (Has a dollar sign before '87 SB totals)	.05	.02	.01
☐ 234 John Franco	.15	.07	.02
☐ 235 Guy Hoffman	.05	.02	.01
☐ 236 Tom Hume	.05	.02	.01
☐ 237 Tracy Jones	.05	.02	.01
☐ 238 Bill Landrum	.05	.02	.01
☐ 239 Barry Larkin	.75	.35	.09
☐ 240 Terry McGriff	.05	.02	.01
☐ 241 Rob Murphy	.05	.02	.01
☐ 242 Ron Oester	.05	.02	.01
☐ 243 Dave Parker	.30	.14	.04
☐ 244 Pat Perry	.05	.02	.01
☐ 245 Ted Power	.05	.02	.01
☐ 246 Dennis Rasmussen	.05	.02	.01
☐ 247 Ron Robinson	.05	.02	.01
☐ 248 Kurt Stillwell	.05	.02	.01
☐ 249 Jeff Treadway	.05	.02	.01
☐ 250 Frank Williams	.05	.02	.01
☐ 251 Steve Balboni	.05	.02	.01
☐ 252 Bud Black	.05	.02	.01
☐ 253 Thad Bosley	.05	.02	.01
☐ 254 George Brett	.75	.35	.09
☐ 255 John Davis	.05	.02	.01
☐ 256 Steve Farr	.05	.02	.01
☐ 257 Gene Garber	.05	.02	.01
☐ 258 Jerry Don Gleaton	.05	.02	.01
☐ 259 Mark Gubicza	.05	.02	.01
☐ 260 Bo Jackson	.30	.14	.04
☐ 261 Danny Jackson	.05	.02	.01
☐ 262 Ross Jones	.05	.02	.01
☐ 263 Charlie Leibrandt	.05	.02	.01
☐ 264 Bill Pecota	.05	.02	.01
☐ 265 Melido Perez	.15	.07	.02
☐ 266 Jamie Quirk	.05	.02	.01
☐ 267 Dan Quisenberry	.05	.02	.01
☐ 268 Bret Saberhagen	.15	.07	.02
☐ 269 Angel Salazar	.05	.02	.01
☐ 270 Kevin Seitzer UER (Wrong birth year)	.15	.07	.02
☐ 271 Danny Tartabull	.05	.02	.01
☐ 272 Gary Thurman	.05	.02	.01
☐ 273 Frank White	.15	.07	.02
☐ 274 Willie Wilson	.05	.02	.01
☐ 275 Tony Bernazard	.05	.02	.01
☐ 276 Jose Canseco	.60	.25	.07
☐ 277 Mike Davis	.05	.02	.01
☐ 278 Storm Davis	.05	.02	.01
☐ 279 Dennis Eckersley	.15	.07	.02
☐ 280 Alfredo Griffin	.05	.02	.01
☐ 281 Rick Honeycutt	.05	.02	.01
☐ 282 Jay Howell	.05	.02	.01
☐ 283 Reggie Jackson	.50	.23	.06
☐ 284 Dennis Lamp	.05	.02	.01
☐ 285 Carney Lansford	.15	.07	.02
☐ 286 Mark McGwire	1.25	.55	.16
☐ 287 Dwayne Murphy	.05	.02	.01
☐ 288 Gene Nelson	.05	.02	.01
☐ 289 Steve Ontiveros	.05	.02	.01
☐ 290 Tony Phillips	.30	.14	.04
☐ 291 Eric Plunk	.05	.02	.01
☐ 292 Luis Polonia	.30	.14	.04
☐ 293 Rick Rodriguez	.05	.02	.01
☐ 294 Terry Steinbach	.30	.14	.04
☐ 295 Dave Stewart	.30	.14	.04
☐ 296 Curt Young	.05	.02	.01
☐ 297 Luis Aguayo	.05	.02	.01
☐ 298 Steve Bedrosian	.05	.02	.01
☐ 299 Jeff Calhoun	.05	.02	.01
☐ 300 Don Carman	.05	.02	.01
☐ 301 Todd Frohwirth	.05	.02	.01
☐ 302 Greg Gross	.05	.02	.01
☐ 303 Kevin Gross	.05	.02	.01
☐ 304 Von Hayes	.05	.02	.01
☐ 305 Keith Hughes	.05	.02	.01
☐ 306 Mike Jackson	.15	.07	.02
☐ 307 Chris James	.05	.02	.01
☐ 308 Steve Jeltz	.05	.02	.01
☐ 309 Mike Maddux	.05	.02	.01
☐ 310 Lance Parrish	.05	.02	.01
☐ 311 Shane Rawley	.05	.02	.01
☐ 312 Wally Ritchie	.05	.02	.01
☐ 313 Bruce Ruffin	.05	.02	.01
☐ 314 Juan Samuel	.05	.02	.01
☐ 315 Mike Schmidt	.40	.18	.05
☐ 316 Rick Schu	.05	.02	.01
☐ 317 Jeff Stone	.05	.02	.01
☐ 318 Kent Tekulve	.05	.02	.01
☐ 319 Milt Thompson	.05	.02	.01
☐ 320 Glenn Wilson	.05	.02	.01
☐ 321 Rafael Belliard	.05	.02	.01
☐ 322 Barry Bonds	1.25	.55	.16
☐ 323 Bobby Bonilla UER (Wrong birth year)	.30	.14	.04
☐ 324 Sid Bream	.05	.02	.01
☐ 325 John Cangelosi	.05	.02	.01
☐ 326 Mike Diaz	.05	.02	.01
☐ 327 Doug Drabek	.15	.07	.02
☐ 328 Mike Dunne	.05	.02	.01
☐ 329 Brian Fisher	.05	.02	.01
☐ 330 Brett Gideon	.05	.02	.01
☐ 331 Terry Harper	.05	.02	.01
☐ 332 Bob Kipper	.05	.02	.01
☐ 333 Mike LaValliere	.05	.02	.01
☐ 334 Jose Lind	.15	.07	.02
☐ 335 Junior Ortiz	.05	.02	.01
☐ 336 Vicente Palacios	.05	.02	.01
☐ 337 Bob Patterson	.05	.02	.01
☐ 338 Al Pedrique	.05	.02	.01
☐ 339 R.J. Reynolds	.05	.02	.01
☐ 340 John Smiley	.30	.14	.04
☐ 341 Andy Van Slyke UER (Wrong batting and throwing listed)	.15	.07	.02
☐ 342 Bob Walk	.05	.02	.01
☐ 343 Marty Barrett	.05	.02	.01
☐ 344 Todd Benzinger	.15	.07	.02
☐ 345 Wade Boggs	.30	.14	.04
☐ 346 Tom Bolton	.05	.02	.01
☐ 347 Oil Can Boyd	.05	.02	.01
☐ 348 Ellis Burks	1.00	.45	.12
☐ 349 Roger Clemens	.40	.18	.05
☐ 350 Steve Crawford	.05	.02	.01
☐ 351 Dwight Evans	.15	.07	.02
☐ 352 Wes Gardner	.05	.02	.01
☐ 353 Rich Gedman	.05	.02	.01
☐ 354 Mike Greenwell	.30	.14	.04
☐ 355 Sam Horn	.05	.02	.01
☐ 356 Bruce Hurst	.05	.02	.01
☐ 357 John Marzano	.05	.02	.01
☐ 358 Al Nipper	.05	.02	.01
☐ 359 Spike Owen	.05	.02	.01
☐ 360 Jody Reed	.15	.07	.02
☐ 361 Jim Rice	.30	.14	.04
☐ 362 Ed Romero	.05	.02	.01
☐ 363 Kevin Romine	.05	.02	.01
☐ 364 Joe Sambito	.05	.02	.01
☐ 365 Calvin Schiraldi	.05	.02	.01
☐ 366 Jeff Sellers	.05	.02	.01
☐ 367 Bob Stanley	.05	.02	.01
☐ 368 Scott Bankhead	.05	.02	.01
☐ 369 Phil Bradley	.05	.02	.01
☐ 370 Scott Bradley	.05	.02	.01
☐ 371 Mickey Brantley	.05	.02	.01
☐ 372 Mike Campbell	.05	.02	.01
☐ 373 Alvin Davis	.05	.02	.01
☐ 374 Lee Guetterman	.05	.02	.01
☐ 375 Dave Hengel	.05	.02	.01
☐ 376 Mike Kingery	.05	.02	.01
☐ 377 Mark Langston	.15	.07	.02
☐ 378 Edgar Martinez	1.50	.70	.19
☐ 379 Mike Moore	.05	.02	.01
☐ 380 Mike Morgan	.05	.02	.01
☐ 381 John Moses	.05	.02	.01
☐ 382 Donell Nixon	.05	.02	.01
☐ 383 Edwin Nunez	.05	.02	.01
☐ 384 Ken Phelps	.05	.02	.01
☐ 385 Jim Presley	.05	.02	.01
☐ 386 Rey Quinones	.05	.02	.01
☐ 387 Jerry Reed	.05	.02	.01
☐ 388 Harold Reynolds	.05	.02	.01
☐ 389 Dave Valle	.05	.02	.01
☐ 390 Bill Wilkinson	.05	.02	.01
☐ 391 Harold Baines	.15	.07	.02
☐ 392 Floyd Bannister	.05	.02	.01
☐ 393 Daryl Boston	.05	.02	.01
☐ 394 Ivan Calderon	.05	.02	.01
☐ 395 Jose DeLeon	.05	.02	.01
☐ 396 Richard Dotson	.05	.02	.01
☐ 397 Carlton Fisk	.30	.14	.04
☐ 398 Ozzie Guillen	.15	.07	.02
☐ 399 Ron Hassey	.05	.02	.01
☐ 400 Donnie Hill	.05	.02	.01
☐ 401 Bob James	.05	.02	.01
☐ 402 Dave LaPoint	.05	.02	.01
☐ 403 Bill Lindsey	.05	.02	.01
☐ 404 Bill Long	.05	.02	.01
☐ 405 Steve Lyons	.05	.02	.01
☐ 406 Fred Manrique	.05	.02	.01
☐ 407 Jack McDowell	.75	.35	.09
☐ 408 Gary Redus	.05	.02	.01
☐ 409 Ray Searage	.05	.02	.01
☐ 410 Bobby Thigpen	.05	.02	.01
☐ 411 Greg Walker	.05	.02	.01
☐ 412 Ken Williams	.05	.02	.01
☐ 413 Jim Winn	.05	.02	.01
☐ 414 Jody Davis	.05	.02	.01
☐ 415 Andre Dawson	.15	.07	.02
☐ 416 Brian Dayett	.05	.02	.01
☐ 417 Bob Dernier	.05	.02	.01
☐ 418 Frank DiPino	.05	.02	.01
☐ 419 Shawon Dunston	.05	.02	.01
☐ 420 Leon Durham	.05	.02	.01
☐ 421 Les Lancaster	.05	.02	.01
☐ 422 Ed Lynch	.05	.02	.01
☐ 423 Greg Maddux	2.50	1.10	.30
☐ 424 Dave Martinez	.05	.02	.01
☐ 425A Keith Moreland ERR (Photo actually Jody Davis)	1.50	.70	.19
☐ 425B Keith Moreland COR (Bat on shoulder)	.15	.07	.02
☐ 426 Jamie Moyer	.05	.02	.01
☐ 427 Jerry Mumphrey	.05	.02	.01
☐ 428 Paul Noce	.05	.02	.01
☐ 429 Rafael Palmeiro	.60	.25	.07
☐ 430 Wade Rowdon	.05	.02	.01
☐ 431 Ryne Sandberg	.50	.23	.06
☐ 432 Scott Sanderson	.05	.02	.01
☐ 433 Lee Smith	.15	.07	.02
☐ 434 Jim Sundberg	.05	.02	.01
☐ 435 Rick Sutcliffe	.05	.02	.01
☐ 436 Manny Trillo	.05	.02	.01
☐ 437 Juan Agosto	.05	.02	.01
☐ 438 Larry Andersen	.05	.02	.01
☐ 439 Alan Ashby	.05	.02	.01
☐ 440 Kevin Bass	.05	.02	.01
☐ 441 Ken Caminiti	2.00	.90	.25
☐ 442 Rocky Childress	.05	.02	.01
☐ 443 Jose Cruz	.05	.02	.01
☐ 444 Danny Darwin	.05	.02	.01
☐ 445 Glenn Davis	.05	.02	.01
☐ 446 Jim Deshaies	.05	.02	.01
☐ 447 Bill Doran	.05	.02	.01
☐ 448 Ty Gainey	.05	.02	.01
☐ 449 Billy Hatcher	.05	.02	.01
☐ 450 Jeff Heathcock	.05	.02	.01
☐ 451 Bob Knepper	.05	.02	.01
☐ 452 Rob Mallicoat	.05	.02	.01
☐ 453 Dave Meads	.05	.02	.01
☐ 454 Craig Reynolds	.05	.02	.01
☐ 455 Nolan Ryan	1.50	.70	.19
☐ 456 Mike Scott	.05	.02	.01
☐ 457 Dave Smith	.05	.02	.01
☐ 458 Denny Walling	.05	.02	.01
☐ 459 Robbie Wine	.05	.02	.01
☐ 460 Gerald Young	.05	.02	.01
☐ 461 Bob Brower	.05	.02	.01
☐ 462A Jerry Browne ERR (Photo actually Bob Brower, white player)	1.50	.70	.19
☐ 462B Jerry Browne COR (Black player)	.15	.07	.02
☐ 463 Steve Buechele	.05	.02	.01
☐ 464 Edwin Correa	.05	.02	.01
☐ 465 Cecil Espy	.05	.02	.01
☐ 466 Scott Fletcher	.05	.02	.01
☐ 467 Jose Guzman	.05	.02	.01
☐ 468 Greg Harris	.05	.02	.01
☐ 469 Charlie Hough	.15	.07	.02
☐ 470 Pete Incaviglia	.05	.02	.01
☐ 471 Paul Kilgus	.05	.02	.01
☐ 472 Mike Loynd	.05	.02	.01
☐ 473 Oddibe McDowell	.05	.02	.01
☐ 474 Dale Mohorcic	.05	.02	.01
☐ 475 Pete O'Brien	.05	.02	.01
☐ 476 Larry Parrish	.05	.02	.01
☐ 477 Geno Petralli	.05	.02	.01
☐ 478 Jeff Russell	.05	.02	.01
☐ 479 Ruben Sierra	.30	.14	.04
☐ 480 Mike Stanley	.15	.07	.02
☐ 481 Curtis Wilkerson	.05	.02	.01
☐ 482 Mitch Williams	.15	.07	.02
☐ 483 Bobby Witt	.05	.02	.01
☐ 484 Tony Armas	.05	.02	.01
☐ 485 Bob Boone	.15	.07	.02
☐ 486 Bill Buckner	.15	.07	.02
☐ 487 DeWayne Buice	.05	.02	.01
☐ 488 Brian Downing	.05	.02	.01
☐ 489 Chuck Finley	.15	.07	.02
☐ 490 Willie Fraser UER (Wrong bio stats, for George Hendrick)	.05	.02	.01
☐ 491 Jack Howell	.05	.02	.01
☐ 492 Ruppert Jones	.05	.02	.01
☐ 493 Wally Joyner	.30	.14	.04
☐ 494 Jack Lazorko	.05	.02	.01
☐ 495 Gary Lucas	.05	.02	.01
☐ 496 Kirk McCaskill	.05	.02	.01
☐ 497 Mark McLemore	.05	.02	.01
☐ 498 Darrell Miller	.05	.02	.01
☐ 499 Greg Minton	.05	.02	.01
☐ 500 Donnie Moore	.05	.02	.01
☐ 501 Gus Polidor	.05	.02	.01
☐ 502 Johnny Ray	.05	.02	.01
☐ 503 Mark Ryal	.05	.02	.01
☐ 504 Dick Schofield	.05	.02	.01
☐ 505 Don Sutton	.30	.14	.04
☐ 506 Devon White	.30	.14	.04
☐ 507 Mike Witt	.05	.02	.01
☐ 508 Dave Anderson	.05	.02	.01
☐ 509 Tim Belcher	.15	.07	.02
☐ 510 Ralph Bryant	.05	.02	.01
☐ 511 Tim Crews	.15	.07	.02
☐ 512 Mike Devereaux	.30	.14	.04
☐ 513 Mariano Duncan	.05	.02	.01
☐ 514 Pedro Guerrero	.15	.07	.02
☐ 515 Jeff Hamilton	.05	.02	.01
☐ 516 Mickey Hatcher	.05	.02	.01
☐ 517 Brad Havens	.05	.02	.01
☐ 518 Orel Hershiser	.15	.07	.02
☐ 519 Shawn Hillegas	.05	.02	.01
☐ 520 Ken Howell	.05	.02	.01
☐ 521 Tim Leary	.05	.02	.01
☐ 522 Mike Marshall	.05	.02	.01
☐ 523 Steve Sax	.05	.02	.01
☐ 524 Mike Scioscia	.05	.02	.01
☐ 525 Mike Sharperson	.05	.02	.01
☐ 526 John Shelby	.05	.02	.01
☐ 527 Franklin Stubbs	.05	.02	.01
☐ 528 Fernando Valenzuela	.15	.07	.02
☐ 529 Bob Welch	.05	.02	.01
☐ 530 Matt Young	.05	.02	.01
☐ 531 Jim Acker	.05	.02	.01
☐ 532 Paul Assenmacher	.05	.02	.01
☐ 533 Jeff Blauser	.30	.14	.04
☐ 534 Joe Boever	.05	.02	.01
☐ 535 Martin Clary	.05	.02	.01
☐ 536 Kevin Coffman	.05	.02	.01
☐ 537 Jeff Dedmon	.05	.02	.01
☐ 538 Ron Gant	1.00	.45	.12
☐ 539 Tom Glavine	2.00	.90	.25
☐ 540 Ken Griffey	.05	.02	.01
☐ 541 Albert Hall	.05	.02	.01
☐ 542 Glenn Hubbard	.05	.02	.01
☐ 543 Dion James	.05	.02	.01
☐ 544 Dale Murphy	.30	.14	.04
☐ 545 Ken Oberkfell	.05	.02	.01
☐ 546 David Palmer	.05	.02	.01
☐ 547 Gerald Perry	.05	.02	.01
☐ 548 Charlie Puleo	.05	.02	.01
☐ 549 Ted Simmons	.15	.07	.02
☐ 550 Zane Smith	.05	.02	.01
☐ 551 Andres Thomas	.05	.02	.01
☐ 552 Ozzie Virgil	.05	.02	.01
☐ 553 Don Aase	.05	.02	.01
☐ 554 Jeff Ballard	.05	.02	.01
☐ 555 Eric Bell	.05	.02	.01
☐ 556 Mike Boddicker	.05	.02	.01
☐ 557 Ken Dixon	.05	.02	.01
☐ 558 Jim Dwyer	.05	.02	.01
☐ 559 Ken Gerhart	.05	.02	.01
☐ 560 Rene Gonzales	.05	.02	.01
☐ 561 Mike Griffin	.05	.02	.01
☐ 562 John Habyan UER (Misspelled Hayban on both sides of card)	.05	.02	.01
☐ 563 Terry Kennedy	.05	.02	.01
☐ 564 Ray Knight	.15	.07	.02
☐ 565 Lee Lacy	.05	.02	.01
☐ 566 Fred Lynn	.05	.02	.01
☐ 567 Eddie Murray	.50	.23	.06
☐ 568 Tom Niedenfuer	.05	.02	.01
☐ 569 Bill Ripken	.15	.07	.02
☐ 570 Cal Ripken	1.50	.70	.19
☐ 571 Dave Schmidt	.05	.02	.01
☐ 572 Larry Sheets	.05	.02	.01
☐ 573 Pete Stanicek	.05	.02	.01
☐ 574 Mark Williamson	.05	.02	.01
☐ 575 Mike Young	.05	.02	.01
☐ 576 Shawn Abner	.05	.02	.01
☐ 577 Greg Booker	.05	.02	.01
☐ 578 Chris Brown	.05	.02	.01
☐ 579 Keith Comstock	.05	.02	.01
☐ 580 Joey Cora	.40	.18	.05
☐ 581 Mark Davis	.05	.02	.01
☐ 582 Tim Flannery (With surfboard)	.30	.14	.04
☐ 583 Goose Gossage	.30	.14	.04
☐ 584 Mark Grant	.05	.02	.01
☐ 585 Tony Gwynn	.75	.35	.09
☐ 586 Andy Hawkins	.05	.02	.01
☐ 587 Stan Jefferson	.05	.02	.01
☐ 588 Jimmy Jones	.05	.02	.01

Card	MINT	NRMT	EXC
☐ 589 John Kruk	.30	.14	.04
☐ 590 Shane Mack	.05	.02	.01
☐ 591 Carmelo Martinez	.05	.02	.01
☐ 592 Lance McCullers UER (6'11" tall)	.05	.02	.01
☐ 593 Eric Nolte	.05	.02	.01
☐ 594 Randy Ready	.05	.02	.01
☐ 595 Luis Salazar	.05	.02	.01
☐ 596 Benito Santiago	.15	.07	.02
☐ 597 Eric Show	.05	.02	.01
☐ 598 Garry Templeton	.05	.02	.01
☐ 599 Ed Whitson	.05	.02	.01
☐ 600 Scott Bailes	.05	.02	.01
☐ 601 Chris Bando	.05	.02	.01
☐ 602 Jay Bell	.40	.18	.05
☐ 603 Brett Butler	.15	.07	.02
☐ 604 Tom Candiotti	.05	.02	.01
☐ 605 Joe Carter	.30	.14	.04
☐ 606 Carmen Castillo	.05	.02	.01
☐ 607 Brian Dorsett	.05	.02	.01
☐ 608 John Farrell	.05	.02	.01
☐ 609 Julio Franco	.15	.07	.02
☐ 610 Mel Hall	.05	.02	.01
☐ 611 Tommy Hinzo	.05	.02	.01
☐ 612 Brook Jacoby	.05	.02	.01
☐ 613 Doug Jones	.15	.07	.02
☐ 614 Ken Schrom	.05	.02	.01
☐ 615 Cory Snyder	.05	.02	.01
☐ 616 Sammy Stewart	.05	.02	.01
☐ 617 Greg Swindell	.05	.02	.01
☐ 618 Pat Tabler	.05	.02	.01
☐ 619 Ed VandeBerg	.05	.02	.01
☐ 620 Eddie Williams	.15	.07	.02
☐ 621 Rich Yett	.05	.02	.01
☐ 622 Slugging Sophomores Wally Joyner Cory Snyder	.15	.07	.02
☐ 623 Dominican Dynamite George Bell Pedro Guerrero	.05	.02	.01
☐ 624 Oakland's Power Team Mark McGwire Jose Canseco	.60	.25	.07
☐ 625 Classic Relief Dave Righetti Dan Plesac	.05	.02	.01
☐ 626 All Star Righties Bret Saberhagen Mike Witt Jack Morris	.15	.07	.02
☐ 627 Game Closers John Franco Steve Bedrosian	.05	.02	.01
☐ 628 Masters/Double Play Ozzie Smith Ryne Sandberg	.50	.23	.06
☐ 629 Rookie Record Setter Mark McGwire	.60	.25	.07
☐ 630 Changing the Guard Mike Greenwell Ellis Burks Todd Benzinger	.30	.14	.04
☐ 631 NL Batting Champs Tony Gwynn Tim Raines	.30	.14	.04
☐ 632 Pitching Magic Mike Scott Orel Hershiser	.15	.07	.02
☐ 633 Big Bats at First Pat Tabler Mark McGwire	.40	.18	.05
☐ 634 Hitting King/Thief Tony Gwynn Vince Coleman	.05	.02	.01
☐ 635 Slugging Shortstops Tony Fernandez Cal Ripken Alan Trammell	.50	.23	.06
☐ 636 Tried/True Sluggers Mike Schmidt Gary Carter	.05	.02	.01
☐ 637 Crunch Time Darryl Strawberry Eric Davis	.15	.07	.02
☐ 638 AL All-Stars Matt Nokes Kirby Puckett	.30	.14	.04
☐ 639 NL All-Stars Keith Hernandez Dale Murphy	.15	.07	.02
☐ 640 The O's Brothers Billy Ripken Cal Ripken	.75	.35	.09
☐ 641 Mark Grace and Darrin Jackson	1.50	.70	.19
☐ 642 Damon Berryhill and Jeff Montgomery	.40	.18	.05
☐ 643 Felix Fermin and Jesse Reid	.05	.02	.01
☐ 644 Greg Myers and Greg Tabor	.05	.02	.01
☐ 645 Joey Meyer and Jim Eppard	.05	.02	.01
☐ 646 Adam Peterson and Randy Velarde	.15	.07	.02
☐ 647 Pete Smith and Chris Gwynn	.15	.07	.02
☐ 648 Tom Newell and Greg Jelks	.05	.02	.01
☐ 649 Mario Diaz and Clay Parker	.05	.02	.01
☐ 650 Jack Savage and Todd Simmons	.05	.02	.01
☐ 651 John Burkett and Kirt Manwaring	.30	.14	.04
☐ 652 Dave Otto and Walt Weiss	.15	.07	.02
☐ 653 Jeff King and Randell Byers	.50	.23	.06
☐ 654 CL: Twins/Cards Tigers/Giants UER (90 Bob Melvin, 91 Eddie Milner)	.15	.07	.02
☐ 655 CL: Blue Jays/Mets Brewers/Expos UER (Mets listed before Blue Jays on card)	.15	.07	.02
☐ 656 CL: Yankees/Reds Royals/A's	.15	.07	.02
☐ 657 CL: Phillies/Pirates Red Sox/Mariners	.15	.07	.02
☐ 658 CL: White Sox/Cubs Astros/Rangers	.15	.07	.02
☐ 659 CL: Angels/Dodgers Braves/Orioles	.15	.07	.02
☐ 660 CL: Padres/Indians Rookies/Specials	.15	.07	.02

1988 Fleer Glossy

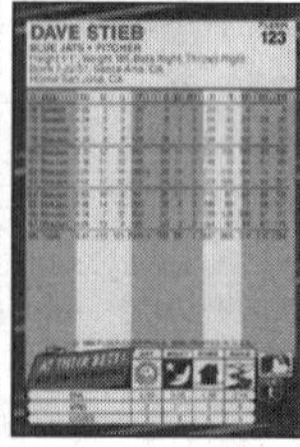

This 660 card set is a parallel to the regular Fleer issue. The cards are the same as the regular issue except for the glossy sheen on the front. The cards (along with the 12-card World Series insert set) were issued in a factory tin distributed exclusively through hobby dealers.

	MINT	NRMT	EXC
COMPLETE FACT.SET (672)	25.00	11.00	3.10
COMMON CARD (1-660)	.05	.02	.01
COMMON WORLD SERIES (WS1-WS12)	.05	.02	.01
*STARS: 2X BASIC CARDS			
*ROOKIES: 2X BASIC CARDS			

1988 Fleer All-Stars

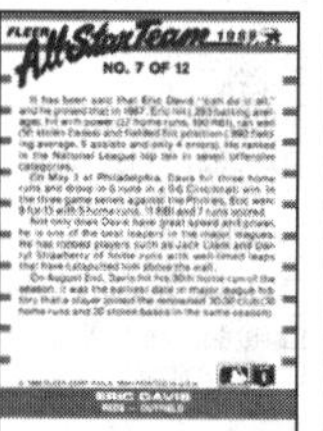

These 12 standard-size cards were inserted randomly in wax and cello packs of the 1988 Fleer set. The cards show the player silhouetted against a light green background with dark green stripes. The player's name, team, and position are printed in yellow at the bottom of the obverse. The card backs are done predominantly in green, white, and black. The players are the "best" at each position, three pitchers, eight position players, and a designated hitter.

	MINT	NRMT	EXC
COMPLETE SET (12)	6.00	2.70	.75
COMMON CARD (1-12)	.30	.14	.04
☐ 1 Matt Nokes	.30	.14	.04
☐ 2 Tom Henke	.30	.14	.04
☐ 3 Ted Higuera	.30	.14	.04
☐ 4 Roger Clemens	2.00	.90	.25
☐ 5 George Bell	.30	.14	.04
☐ 6 Andre Dawson	1.00	.45	.12
☐ 7 Eric Davis	.50	.23	.06
☐ 8 Wade Boggs	1.00	.45	.12
☐ 9 Alan Trammell	.50	.23	.06
☐ 10 Juan Samuel	.30	.14	.04
☐ 11 Jack Clark	.30	.14	.04
☐ 12 Paul Molitor	1.50	.70	.19

1988 Fleer Headliners

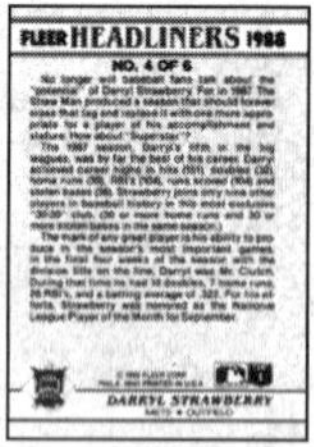

This six-card standard-size set was distributed one per rack pack. The obverse features the player photo superimposed on a gray newsprint background. The cards are printed in red, black, and white on the back describing why that particular player made headlines the previous season. The set is sequenced in alphabetical order.

	MINT	NRMT	EXC
COMPLETE SET (6)	5.00	2.20	.60
COMMON CARD (1-6)	.75	.35	.09
☐ 1 Don Mattingly	2.50	1.10	.30
☐ 2 Mark McGwire	2.50	1.10	.30
☐ 3 Jack Morris	.75	.35	.09
☐ 4 Darryl Strawberry	1.25	.55	.16
☐ 5 Dwight Gooden	1.50	.70	.19
☐ 6 Tim Raines	1.00	.45	.12

1988 Fleer Wax Box Cards

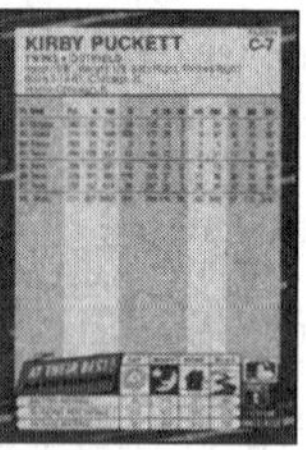

The cards in this 16-card set measure the standard size. Cards have essentially the same design as the 1988 Fleer regular issue set. The cards were printed on the bottoms of the regular issue wax pack boxes. These 16 cards (C1 to C16) are considered a separate set in their own right and are not typically included in a complete set of the regular issue 1988 Fleer cards. The value of the panel uncut is slightly greater, perhaps by 25 percent greater, than the value of the individual cards cut up carefully.

	MINT	NRMT	EXC
COMPLETE SET (16)	8.00	3.60	1.00
COMMON CARD (C1-C16)	.10	.05	.01
☐ C1 Cardinals Logo	.10	.05	.01
☐ C2 Dwight Evans	.25	.11	.03
☐ C3 Andres Galarraga	.75	.35	.09
☐ C4 Wally Joyner	.25	.11	.03
☐ C5 Twins Logo	.10	.05	.01
☐ C6 Dale Murphy	.50	.23	.06
☐ C7 Kirby Puckett	2.50	1.10	.30
☐ C8 Shane Rawley	.10	.05	.01
☐ C9 Giants Logo	.10	.05	.01
☐ C10 Ryne Sandberg	2.50	1.10	.30
☐ C11 Mike Schmidt	1.25	.55	.16
☐ C12 Kevin Seitzer	.25	.11	.03
☐ C13 Tigers Logo	.10	.05	.01
☐ C14 Dave Stewart	.25	.11	.03
☐ C15 Tim Wallach	.25	.11	.03
☐ C16 Todd Worrell	.10	.05	.01

1988 Fleer World Series

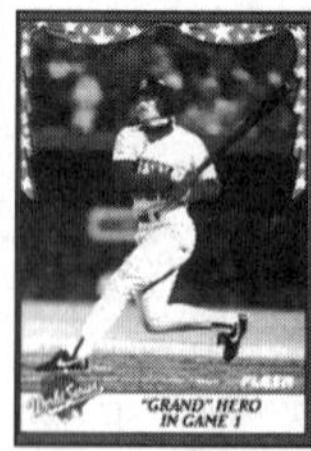

This 12-card standard-size set features highlights of the previous year's World Series between the Minnesota Twins and the St. Louis Cardinals. The sets were packaged as a complete set insert with the collated sets (of the 1988 Fleer regular issue) which were sold by Fleer directly to hobby card dealers; they were not available in the general retail candy store outlets. The set numbering is essentially in chronological order of the events from the immediate past World Series.

	MINT	NRMT	EXC
COMPLETE SET (12)	2.00	.90	.25
COMMON CARD (1-12)	.10	.05	.01
☐ 1 Dan Gladden Grand Hero Game 1	.10	.05	.01
☐ 2 Randy Bush Cardinals 'Bush' Wacked	.10	.05	.01
☐ 3 John Tudora Masterful Performance in Game 3	.10	.05	.01
☐ 4 Ozzie Smith The Wizard	.75	.35	.09
☐ 5 Todd Worrell Tony Pena Throw Smoke	.10	.05	.01
☐ 6 Vince Coleman Cardinal Attack	.10	.05	.01
☐ 7 Tom Herr Dan Driessen Herr's Wallop	.10	.05	.01
☐ 8 Kirby Puckett Kirby's Bat Comes Alive	1.00	.45	.12
☐ 9 Kent Hrbek Hrbek's Slam Forces Game 7	.25	.11	.03
☐ 10 Tom Herr Out at First	.10	.05	.01
☐ 11 Don Baylor Game 7's Play At The Plate	.25	.11	.03
☐ 12 Frank Viola Series MVP, 16 K's	.10	.05	.01

1988 Fleer Update

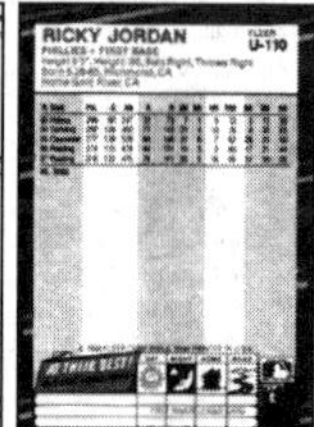

This 132-card standard-size set was distributed exclusively in factory set form in a red, white and blue, cellophane-wrapped box through hobby dealers. In addition to the complete set of 132 cards, the box also contained 25 Team Logo stickers. The cards look very similar to the 1988 Fleer regular issue except for the U-prefixed numbering on back. Cards are ordered alphabetically by player's last name. This was the first Fleer Update set to adopt the Fleer "alphabetical within team" numbering system. The key extended Rookie Cards in this set are Roberto Alomar, Craig Biggio and John Smoltz.

	MINT	NRMT	EXC
COMPLETE FACT.SET (132)	10.00	4.50	1.25
COMMON CARD (1-132)	.05	.02	.01
☐ 1 Jose Bautista	.05	.02	.01
☐ 2 Joe Orsulak	.05	.02	.01
☐ 3 Doug Sisk	.05	.02	.01
☐ 4 Craig Worthington	.05	.02	.01
☐ 5 Mike Boddicker	.05	.02	.01
☐ 6 Rick Cerone	.05	.02	.01
☐ 7 Larry Parrish	.05	.02	.01
☐ 8 Lee Smith	.10	.05	.01
☐ 9 Mike Smithson	.05	.02	.01
☐ 10 John Trautwein	.05	.02	.01
☐ 11 Sherman Corbett	.05	.02	.01
☐ 12 Chili Davis	.15	.07	.02
☐ 13 Jim Eppard	.05	.02	.01
☐ 14 Bryan Harvey	.10	.05	.01
☐ 15 John Davis	.05	.02	.01
☐ 16 Dave Gallagher	.05	.02	.01
☐ 17 Ricky Horton	.05	.02	.01
☐ 18 Dan Pasqua	.05	.02	.01
☐ 19 Melido Perez	.10	.05	.01
☐ 20 Jose Segura	.05	.02	.01
☐ 21 Andy Allanson	.05	.02	.01
☐ 22 Jon Perlman	.05	.02	.01
☐ 23 Domingo Ramos	.05	.02	.01
☐ 24 Rick Rodriguez	.05	.02	.01
☐ 25 Willie Upshaw	.05	.02	.01
☐ 26 Paul Gibson	.05	.02	.01
☐ 27 Don Heinkel	.05	.02	.01
☐ 28 Ray Knight	.10	.05	.01
☐ 29 Gary Pettis	.05	.02	.01
☐ 30 Luis Salazar	.05	.02	.01
☐ 31 Mike Macfarlane	.15	.07	.02
☐ 32 Jeff Montgomery	.15	.07	.02
☐ 33 Ted Power	.05	.02	.01
☐ 34 Israel Sanchez	.05	.02	.01
☐ 35 Kurt Stillwell	.05	.02	.01
☐ 36 Pat Tabler	.05	.02	.01
☐ 37 Don August	.05	.02	.01
☐ 38 Darryl Hamilton	.10	.05	.01
☐ 39 Jeff Leonard	.05	.02	.01
☐ 40 Joey Meyer	.05	.02	.01
☐ 41 Allan Anderson	.05	.02	.01
☐ 42 Brian Harper	.05	.02	.01
☐ 43 Tom Herr	.05	.02	.01
☐ 44 Charlie Lea	.05	.02	.01
☐ 45 John Moses (Listed as Hohn on checklist card)	.05	.02	.01
☐ 46 John Candelaria	.05	.02	.01
☐ 47 Jack Clark	.10	.05	.01
☐ 48 Richard Dotson	.05	.02	.01
☐ 49 Al Leiter	.15	.07	.02
☐ 50 Rafael Santana	.05	.02	.01
☐ 51 Don Slaught	.05	.02	.01
☐ 52 Todd Burns	.05	.02	.01
☐ 53 Dave Henderson	.05	.02	.01
☐ 54 Doug Jennings	.05	.02	.01

	MINT	NRMT	EXC
☐ 55 Dave Parker	.15	.07	.02
☐ 56 Walt Weiss	.15	.07	.02
☐ 57 Bob Welch	.05	.02	.01
☐ 58 Henry Cotto	.05	.02	.01
☐ 59 Mario Diaz UER (Listed as Marion on card front)	.05	.02	.01
☐ 60 Mike Jackson	.05	.02	.01
☐ 61 Bill Swift	.05	.02	.01
☐ 62 Jose Cecena	.05	.02	.01
☐ 63 Ray Hayward	.05	.02	.01
☐ 64 Jim Steels UER (Listed as Jim Steele on card back)	.05	.02	.01
☐ 65 Pat Borders	.10	.05	.01
☐ 66 Sil Campusano	.05	.02	.01
☐ 67 Mike Flanagan	.05	.02	.01
☐ 68 Todd Stottlemyre	.50	.23	.06
☐ 69 David Wells	.15	.07	.02
☐ 70 Jose Alvarez	.05	.02	.01
☐ 71 Paul Runge	.05	.02	.01
☐ 72 Cesar Jimenez (Card was intended for German Jiminez, it's his photo)	.05	.02	.01
☐ 73 Pete Smith	.05	.02	.01
☐ 74 John Smoltz	4.00	1.80	.50
☐ 75 Damon Berryhill	.05	.02	.01
☐ 76 Goose Gossage	.15	.07	.02
☐ 77 Mark Grace	1.50	.70	.19
☐ 78 Darrin Jackson	.05	.02	.01
☐ 79 Vance Law	.05	.02	.01
☐ 80 Jeff Pico	.05	.02	.01
☐ 81 Gary Varsho	.05	.02	.01
☐ 82 Tim Birtsas	.05	.02	.01
☐ 83 Rob Dibble	.10	.05	.01
☐ 84 Danny Jackson	.05	.02	.01
☐ 85 Paul O'Neill	.10	.05	.01
☐ 86 Jose Rijo	.05	.02	.01
☐ 87 Chris Sabo	.10	.05	.01
☐ 88 John Fishel	.05	.02	.01
☐ 89 Craig Biggio	2.00	.90	.25
☐ 90 Terry Puhl	.05	.02	.01
☐ 91 Rafael Ramirez	.05	.02	.01
☐ 92 Louie Meadows	.05	.02	.01
☐ 93 Kirk Gibson	.10	.05	.01
☐ 94 Alfredo Griffin	.05	.02	.01
☐ 95 Jay Howell	.05	.02	.01
☐ 96 Jesse Orosco	.05	.02	.01
☐ 97 Alejandro Pena	.05	.02	.01
☐ 98 Tracy Woodson	.05	.02	.01
☐ 99 John Dopson	.05	.02	.01
☐ 100 Brian Holman	.05	.02	.01
☐ 101 Rex Hudler	.05	.02	.01
☐ 102 Jeff Parrett	.05	.02	.01
☐ 103 Nelson Santovenia	.05	.02	.01
☐ 104 Kevin Elster	.15	.07	.02
☐ 105 Jeff Innis	.05	.02	.01
☐ 106 Mackey Sasser	.05	.02	.01
☐ 107 Phil Bradley	.05	.02	.01
☐ 108 Danny Clay	.05	.02	.01
☐ 109 Greg A.Harris	.05	.02	.01
☐ 110 Ricky Jordan	.10	.05	.01
☐ 111 David Palmer	.05	.02	.01
☐ 112 Jim Gott	.05	.02	.01
☐ 113 Tommy Gregg UER (Photo actually Randy Milligan)	.05	.02	.01
☐ 114 Barry Jones	.05	.02	.01
☐ 115 Randy Milligan	.05	.02	.01
☐ 116 Luis Alicea	.10	.05	.01
☐ 117 Tom Brunansky	.05	.02	.01
☐ 118 John Costello	.05	.02	.01
☐ 119 Jose DeLeon	.05	.02	.01
☐ 120 Bob Horner	.05	.02	.01
☐ 121 Scott Terry	.05	.02	.01
☐ 122 Roberto Alomar	5.00	2.20	.60
☐ 123 Dave Leiper	.05	.02	.01
☐ 124 Keith Moreland	.05	.02	.01
☐ 125 Mark Parent	.05	.02	.01
☐ 126 Dennis Rasmussen	.05	.02	.01
☐ 127 Randy Bockus	.05	.02	.01
☐ 128 Brett Butler	.10	.05	.01
☐ 129 Donell Nixon	.05	.02	.01
☐ 130 Earnest Riles	.05	.02	.01
☐ 131 Roger Samuels	.05	.02	.01
☐ 132 Checklist U1-U132	.05	.02	.01

1988 Fleer Update Glossy

This 132 card set is a parallel to the regular Fleer Update issue. Except for a glossy sheen on the front, the cards are identical to the regular Fleer issue. The cards were issued through hobby dealers in a special tin. The cards are not as plentiful as the regular Fleer update set.

	MINT	NRMT	EXC
COMPLETE FACT.SET (132)	15.00	6.75	1.85
COMMON CARD (1-132)	.10	.05	.01
*STARS: 2X BASIC CARDS			
*ROOKIES: 2X BASIC CARDS			

1988 Fleer Award Winners

This small set of 44 standard-size cards was produced for 7-Eleven stores by Fleer. The cards feature full color fronts and red, white, and blue backs. The card fronts are distinguished by the red, white, and

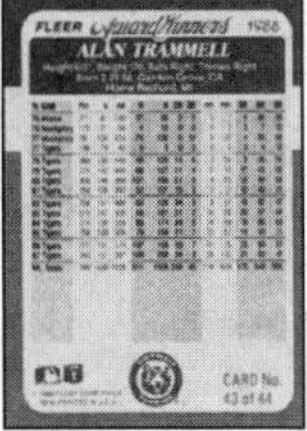

blue frame around the player's full-color photo. The box for the cards describes the set as the "1988 Limited Edition Baseball Award Winners." The checklist for the set is given on the back of the set box. The card numbering is in alphabetical order by player's name.

	MINT	NRMT	EXC
COMPLETE SET (44)	5.00	2.20	.60
COMMON CARD (1-44)	.05	.02	.01
☐ 1 Steve Bedrosian	.05	.02	.01
☐ 2 George Bell	.05	.02	.01
☐ 3 Wade Boggs	.30	.14	.04
☐ 4 Jose Canseco	.60	.25	.07
☐ 5 Will Clark	.60	.25	.07
☐ 6 Roger Clemens	.60	.25	.07
☐ 7 Kal Daniels	.05	.02	.01
☐ 8 Eric Davis	.05	.02	.01
☐ 9 Andre Dawson	.25	.11	.03
☐ 10 Mike Dunne	.05	.02	.01
☐ 11 Dwight Evans	.10	.05	.01
☐ 12 Carlton Fisk	.50	.23	.06
☐ 13 Julio Franco	.10	.05	.01
☐ 14 Dwight Gooden	.10	.05	.01
☐ 15 Pedro Guerrero	.05	.02	.01
☐ 16 Tony Gwynn	1.00	.45	.12
☐ 17 Orel Hershiser	.20	.09	.03
☐ 18 Tom Henke	.05	.02	.01
☐ 19 Ted Higuera	.05	.02	.01
☐ 20 Charlie Hough	.05	.02	.01
☐ 21 Wally Joyner	.20	.09	.03
☐ 22 Jimmy Key	.10	.05	.01
☐ 23 Don Mattingly	1.00	.45	.12
☐ 24 Mark McGwire	1.00	.45	.12
☐ 25 Paul Molitor	.50	.23	.06
☐ 26 Jack Morris	.10	.05	.01
☐ 27 Dale Murphy	.20	.09	.03
☐ 28 Terry Pendleton	.10	.05	.01
☐ 29 Kirby Puckett	1.00	.45	.12
☐ 30 Tim Raines	.10	.05	.01
☐ 31 Jeff Reardon	.05	.02	.01
☐ 32 Harold Reynolds	.10	.05	.01
☐ 33 Dave Righetti	.05	.02	.01
☐ 34 Benito Santiago	.05	.02	.01
☐ 35 Mike Schmidt	.50	.23	.06
☐ 36 Mike Scott	.05	.02	.01
☐ 37 Kevin Seitzer	.10	.05	.01
☐ 38 Larry Sheets	.05	.02	.01
☐ 39 Ozzie Smith	1.00	.45	.12
☐ 40 Darryl Strawberry	.10	.05	.01
☐ 41 Rick Sutcliffe	.05	.02	.01
☐ 42 Danny Tartabull	.05	.02	.01
☐ 43 Alan Trammell	.15	.07	.02
☐ 44 Tim Wallach	.05	.02	.01

1988 Fleer Baseball All-Stars

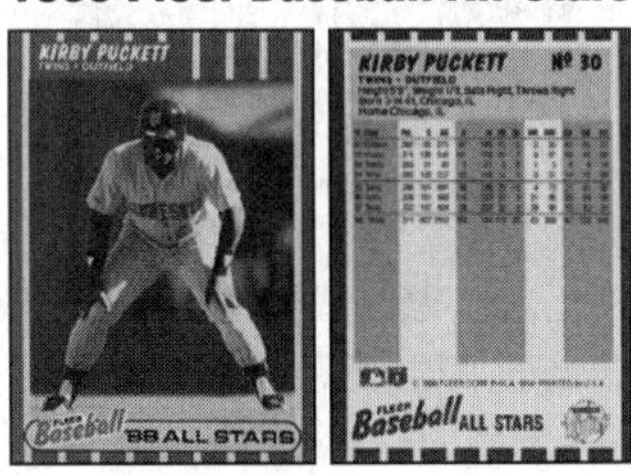

This small boxed set of 44 standard-size cards was produced exclusively for Ben Franklin Stores. The cards feature full color fronts and white and blue backs. The card fronts are distinguished by the yellow and blue striped background behind the player's full-color photo. The box for the cards describes the set as the "1988 Fleer Baseball All-Stars." The checklist for the set is given on the back of the set box. The card numbering is in alphabetical order by player's name.

	MINT	NRMT	EXC
COMPLETE SET (44)	5.00	2.20	.60
COMMON CARD (1-44)	.05	.02	.01
☐ 1 George Bell	.05	.02	.01
☐ 2 Wade Boggs	.30	.14	.04
☐ 3 Bobby Bonilla	.20	.09	.03
☐ 4 George Brett	.75	.35	.09
☐ 5 Jose Canseco	.60	.25	.07
☐ 6 Jack Clark	.10	.05	.01
☐ 7 Will Clark	.60	.25	.07
☐ 8 Roger Clemens	.60	.25	.07
☐ 9 Eric Davis	.05	.02	.01
☐ 10 Andre Dawson	.25	.11	.03
☐ 11 Julio Franco	.10	.05	.01
☐ 12 Dwight Gooden	.10	.05	.01
☐ 13 Tony Gwynn	1.00	.45	.12
☐ 14 Orel Hershiser	.20	.09	.03
☐ 15 Teddy Higuera	.05	.02	.01
☐ 16 Charlie Hough	.05	.02	.01
☐ 17 Kent Hrbek	.10	.05	.01
☐ 18 Bruce Hurst	.05	.02	.01
☐ 19 Wally Joyner	.20	.09	.03
☐ 20 Mark Langston	.05	.02	.01
☐ 21 Dave LaPoint	.05	.02	.01
☐ 22 Candy Maldonado	.05	.02	.01
☐ 23 Don Mattingly	1.00	.45	.12
☐ 24 Roger McDowell	.05	.02	.01
☐ 25 Mark McGwire	1.00	.45	.12
☐ 26 Jack Morris	.10	.05	.01
☐ 27 Dale Murphy	.20	.09	.03
☐ 28 Eddie Murray	.60	.25	.07
☐ 29 Matt Nokes	.05	.02	.01
☐ 30 Kirby Puckett	1.00	.45	.12
☐ 31 Tim Raines	.10	.05	.01
☐ 32 Willie Randolph	.10	.05	.01
☐ 33 Jeff Reardon	.05	.02	.01
☐ 34 Nolan Ryan	2.00	.90	.25
☐ 35 Juan Samuel	.05	.02	.01
☐ 36 Mike Schmidt	.50	.23	.06
☐ 37 Mike Scott	.05	.02	.01
☐ 38 Kevin Seitzer	.10	.05	.01
☐ 39 Ozzie Smith	1.00	.45	.12
☐ 40 Darryl Strawberry	.10	.05	.01
☐ 41 Rick Sutcliffe	.05	.02	.01
☐ 42 Alan Trammell	.15	.07	.02
☐ 43 Tim Wallach	.05	.02	.01
☐ 44 Dave Winfield	.25	.11	.03

1988 Fleer Baseball MVP's

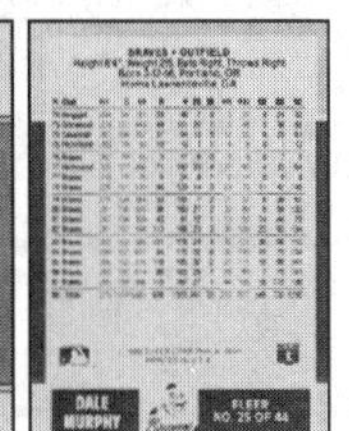

This small 44-card boxed standard-size set was produced by Fleer for distribution by the Toys'r'Us stores. The cards feature full color fronts. The set is titled "Baseball MVP." Each individual boxed set includes the 44 cards and six logo stickers. The checklist for the set is found on the back panel of the box. The card fronts have a vanilla-yellow and blue border. The box refers to Toys'r'Us but there is no mention of Toys'r'Us anywhere on the cards themselves. The card numbering is in alphabetical order by player's name.

	MINT	NRMT	EXC
COMPLETE SET (44)	5.00	2.20	.60
COMMON CARD (1-44)	.05	.02	.01
☐ 1 George Bell	.05	.02	.01
☐ 2 Wade Boggs	.30	.14	.04
☐ 3 Jose Canseco	.50	.23	.06
☐ 4 Ivan Calderon	.05	.02	.01
☐ 5 Will Clark	.60	.25	.07
☐ 6 Roger Clemens	.60	.25	.07
☐ 7 Vince Coleman	.05	.02	.01
☐ 8 Eric Davis	.05	.02	.01
☐ 9 Andre Dawson	.25	.11	.03
☐ 10 Dave Dravecky	.05	.02	.01
☐ 11 Mike Dunne	.05	.02	.01
☐ 12 Dwight Evans	.10	.05	.01
☐ 13 Sid Fernandez	.05	.02	.01
☐ 14 Tony Fernandez	.05	.02	.01
☐ 15 Julio Franco	.10	.05	.01
☐ 16 Dwight Gooden	.10	.05	.01
☐ 17 Tony Gwynn	1.00	.45	.12
☐ 18 Ted Higuera	.05	.02	.01
☐ 19 Charlie Hough	.05	.02	.01
☐ 20 Wally Joyner	.20	.09	.03
☐ 21 Mark Langston	.10	.05	.01
☐ 22 Don Mattingly	1.00	.45	.12
☐ 23 Mark McGwire	1.00	.45	.12
☐ 24 Jack Morris	.10	.05	.01
☐ 25 Dale Murphy	.20	.09	.03
☐ 26 Kirby Puckett	1.00	.45	.12
☐ 27 Tim Raines	.10	.05	.01
☐ 28 Willie Randolph	.10	.05	.01
☐ 29 Ryne Sandberg	.75	.35	.09
☐ 30 Benito Santiago	.05	.02	.01
☐ 31 Mike Schmidt	.50	.23	.06
☐ 32 Mike Scott	.05	.02	.01
☐ 33 Kevin Seitzer	.10	.05	.01
☐ 34 Larry Sheets	.05	.02	.01
☐ 35 Ozzie Smith	1.00	.45	.12
☐ 36 Dave Stewart	.10	.05	.01
☐ 37 Darryl Strawberry	.10	.05	.01
☐ 38 Rick Sutcliffe	.05	.02	.01
☐ 39 Alan Trammell	.15	.07	.02
☐ 40 Fernando Valenzuela	.10	.05	.01
☐ 41 Frank Viola	.05	.02	.01
☐ 42 Tim Wallach	.05	.02	.01
☐ 43 Dave Winfield	.50	.23	.06
☐ 44 Robin Yount	.50	.23	.06

1988 Fleer Exciting Stars

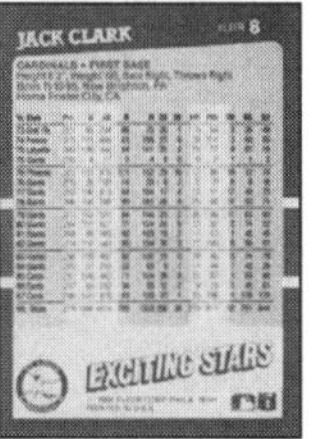

This small boxed set of 44 standard-size cards was produced exclusively for Cumberland Farm Stores. The cards feature full color fronts and red, white, and blue backs. The card fronts are distinguished by the framing of the player's full-color photo with a blue border with a red and white bar stripe across the middle. The box for the cards describes the set as the "1988 Fleer Baseball's Exciting Stars." The checklist for the set is given on the back of the set box. The card numbering is in alphabetical order by player's name.

	MINT	NRMT	EXC
COMPLETE SET (44)	5.00	2.20	.60
COMMON CARD (1-44)	.05	.02	.01
☐ 1 Harold Baines	.10	.05	.01
☐ 2 Kevin Bass	.05	.02	.01
☐ 3 George Bell	.05	.02	.01
☐ 4 Wade Boggs	.30	.14	.04
☐ 5 Mickey Brantley	.05	.02	.01
☐ 6 Sid Bream	.05	.02	.01
☐ 7 Jose Canseco	.60	.25	.07
☐ 8 Jack Clark	.10	.05	.01
☐ 9 Will Clark	.60	.25	.07
☐ 10 Roger Clemens	.60	.25	.07
☐ 11 Vince Coleman	.05	.02	.01
☐ 12 Eric Davis	.05	.02	.01
☐ 13 Andre Dawson	.25	.11	.03
☐ 14 Julio Franco	.10	.05	.01
☐ 15 Dwight Gooden	.10	.05	.01
☐ 16 Mike Greenwell	.05	.02	.01
☐ 17 Tony Gwynn	1.00	.45	.12
☐ 18 Von Hayes	.05	.02	.01
☐ 19 Tom Henke	.05	.02	.01
☐ 20 Orel Hershiser	.20	.09	.03
☐ 21 Teddy Higuera	.05	.02	.01
☐ 22 Brook Jacoby	.05	.02	.01
☐ 23 Wally Joyner	.20	.09	.03
☐ 24 Jimmy Key	.10	.05	.01
☐ 25 Don Mattingly	1.00	.45	.12
☐ 26 Mark McGwire	1.00	.45	.12
☐ 27 Jack Morris	.10	.05	.01
☐ 28 Dale Murphy	.20	.09	.03
☐ 29 Matt Nokes	.05	.02	.01
☐ 30 Kirby Puckett	1.00	.45	.12
☐ 31 Tim Raines	.10	.05	.01
☐ 32 Ryne Sandberg	.75	.35	.09
☐ 33 Benito Santiago	.05	.02	.01
☐ 34 Mike Schmidt	.50	.23	.06
☐ 35 Mike Scott	.05	.02	.01
☐ 36 Kevin Seitzer	.10	.05	.01
☐ 37 Larry Sheets	.05	.02	.01
☐ 38 Ruben Sierra	.25	.11	.03
☐ 39 Darryl Strawberry	.10	.05	.01
☐ 40 Rick Sutcliffe	.05	.02	.01
☐ 41 Danny Tartabull	.05	.02	.01
☐ 42 Alan Trammell	.15	.07	.02
☐ 43 Fernando Valenzuela	.10	.05	.01
☐ 44 Devon White	.20	.09	.03

1988 Fleer Hottest Stars

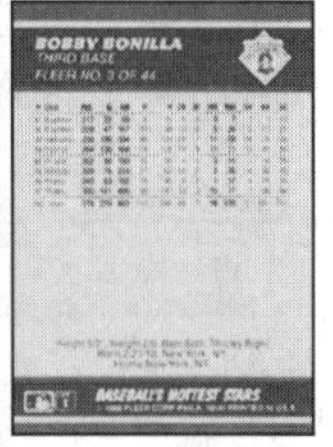

This 44-card boxed standard-size set was produced by Fleer for exclusive distribution by Revco Discount Drug stores all over the country. The cards feature full color fronts and red, white, and blue backs. The card fronts are easily distinguished by the flaming baseball in the lower right corner which says "Fleer Baseball's Hottest Stars." The player's picture is framed in red fading from orange down to yellow. The box for the cards proclaims "1988 Limited Edition Baseball's Hottest Stars" and is styled in blue, red, and yellow. The checklist for the set is given on the back of the set box. The box refers to Revco but there is no mention of Revco anywhere on the cards themselves. The card numbering is in alphabetical order by player's name.

	MINT	NRMT	EXC
COMPLETE SET (44)	5.00	2.20	.60
COMMON CARD (1-44)	.05	.02	.01

	MINT	NRMT	EXC
☐ 1 George Bell	.05	.02	.01
☐ 2 Wade Boggs	.30	.14	.04
☐ 3 Bobby Bonilla	.20	.09	.03
☐ 4 George Brett	.75	.35	.09
☐ 5 Jose Canseco	.60	.25	.07
☐ 6 Will Clark	.60	.25	.07
☐ 7 Roger Clemens	.60	.25	.07
☐ 8 Eric Davis	.05	.02	.01
☐ 9 Andre Dawson	.25	.11	.03
☐ 10 Tony Fernandez	.05	.02	.01
☐ 11 Julio Franco	.10	.05	.01
☐ 12 Gary Gaetti	.05	.02	.01
☐ 13 Dwight Gooden	.10	.05	.01
☐ 14 Mike Greenwell	.05	.02	.01
☐ 15 Tony Gwynn	1.00	.45	.12
☐ 16 Rickey Henderson	.50	.23	.06
☐ 17 Keith Hernandez	.10	.05	.01
☐ 18 Tom Herr	.05	.02	.01
☐ 19 Orel Hershiser	.20	.09	.03
☐ 20 Ted Higuera	.05	.02	.01
☐ 21 Wally Joyner	.20	.09	.03
☐ 22 Jimmy Key	.10	.05	.01
☐ 23 Mark Langston	.05	.02	.01
☐ 24 Don Mattingly	1.00	.45	.12
☐ 25 Jack McDowell	.50	.23	.06
☐ 26 Mark McGwire	1.00	.45	.12
☐ 27 Kevin Mitchell	.05	.02	.01
☐ 28 Jack Morris	.10	.05	.01
☐ 29 Dale Murphy	.20	.09	.03
☐ 30 Kirby Puckett	1.00	.45	.12
☐ 31 Tim Raines	.10	.05	.01
☐ 32 Shane Rawley	.05	.02	.01
☐ 33 Benito Santiago	.05	.02	.01
☐ 34 Mike Schmidt	.50	.23	.06
☐ 35 Mike Scott	.05	.02	.01
☐ 36 Kevin Seitzer	.10	.05	.01
☐ 37 Larry Sheets	.05	.02	.01
☐ 38 Ruben Sierra	.20	.09	.03
☐ 39 Dave Smith	.05	.02	.01
☐ 40 Ozzie Smith	1.00	.45	.12
☐ 41 Darryl Strawberry	.10	.05	.01
☐ 42 Rick Sutcliffe	.05	.02	.01
☐ 43 Pat Tabler	.05	.02	.01
☐ 44 Alan Trammell	.15	.07	.02

1988 Fleer League Leaders

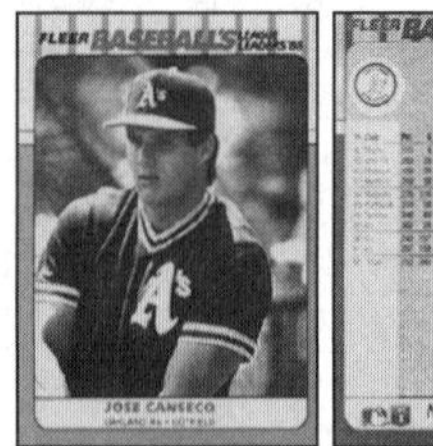
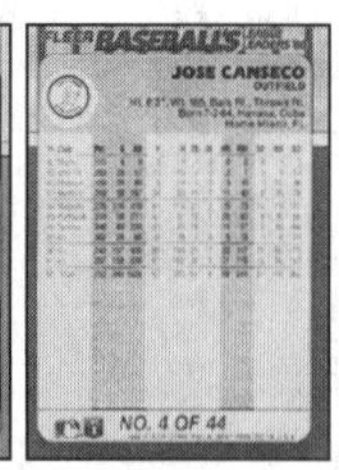

This small boxed set of 44 standard-size cards was produced exclusively for Walgreen Drug Stores. The cards feature full color fronts and pink, white, and blue backs. The card fronts are distinguished by the blue solid and striped background behind the player's full-color photo. The box for the cards describes the set as the "1988 Fleer Baseball's League Leaders." The checklist for the set is given on the back of the set box. The card numbering is in alphabetical order by player's name.

	MINT	NRMT	EXC
COMPLETE SET (44)	5.00	2.20	.60
COMMON CARD (1-44)	.05	.02	.01
☐ 1 George Bell	.05	.02	.01
☐ 2 Wade Boggs	.30	.14	.04
☐ 3 Ivan Calderon	.05	.02	.01
☐ 4 Jose Canseco	.60	.25	.07
☐ 5 Will Clark	.60	.25	.07
☐ 6 Roger Clemens	.60	.25	.07
☐ 7 Vince Coleman	.05	.02	.01
☐ 8 Eric Davis	.05	.02	.01
☐ 9 Andre Dawson	.25	.11	.03
☐ 10 Bill Doran	.05	.02	.01
☐ 11 Dwight Evans	.10	.05	.01
☐ 12 Julio Franco	.10	.05	.01
☐ 13 Gary Gaetti	.05	.02	.01
☐ 14 Andres Galarraga	.20	.09	.03
☐ 15 Dwight Gooden	.10	.05	.01
☐ 16 Tony Gwynn	1.00	.45	.12
☐ 17 Tom Henke	.05	.02	.01
☐ 18 Keith Hernandez	.10	.05	.01
☐ 19 Orel Hershiser	.20	.09	.03
☐ 20 Ted Higuera	.05	.02	.01
☐ 21 Kent Hrbek	.10	.05	.01
☐ 22 Wally Joyner	.20	.09	.03
☐ 23 Jimmy Key	.10	.05	.01
☐ 24 Mark Langston	.10	.05	.01
☐ 25 Don Mattingly	1.00	.45	.12
☐ 26 Mark McGwire	1.00	.45	.12
☐ 27 Paul Molitor	.50	.23	.06
☐ 28 Jack Morris	.10	.05	.01
☐ 29 Dale Murphy	.20	.09	.03
☐ 30 Kirby Puckett	1.00	.45	.12
☐ 31 Tim Raines	.10	.05	.01
☐ 32 Rick Reuschel	.05	.02	.01
☐ 33 Bret Saberhagen	.10	.05	.01
☐ 34 Benito Santiago	.05	.02	.01
☐ 35 Mike Schmidt	.50	.23	.06
☐ 36 Mike Scott	.05	.02	.01
☐ 37 Kevin Seitzer	.10	.05	.01
☐ 38 Larry Sheets	.05	.02	.01
☐ 39 Ruben Sierra	.20	.09	.03
☐ 40 Darryl Strawberry	.10	.05	.01
☐ 41 Rick Sutcliffe	.05	.02	.01
☐ 42 Alan Trammell	.15	.07	.02
☐ 43 Andy Van Slyke	.10	.05	.01
☐ 44 Todd Worrell	.05	.02	.01

1988 Fleer Mini

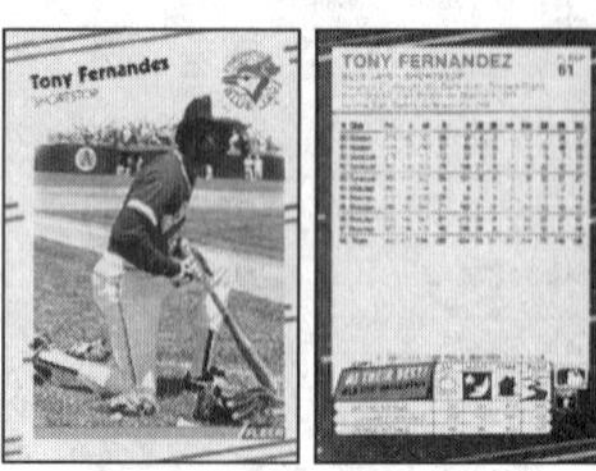

The 1988 Fleer "Classic Miniatures" set consists of 120 small cards with all new pictures of the players as compared to the 1988 Fleer regular issue. The cards are only 1 13/16" by 2 9/16", making them one of the smallest cards available. Card backs provide career year-by-year statistics. The complete set was distributed in a green, red, white, and silver box along with 18 logo stickers. The card numbering is by alphabetical team order within league and alphabetically within each team.

	MINT	NRMT	EXC
COMPLETE SET (120)	10.00	4.50	1.25
COMMON CARD (1-120)	.05	.02	.01
☐ 1 Eddie Murray	.60	.25	.07
☐ 2 Dave Schmidt	.05	.02	.01
☐ 3 Larry Sheets	.05	.02	.01
☐ 4 Wade Boggs	.25	.11	.03
☐ 5 Roger Clemens	.75	.35	.09
☐ 6 Dwight Evans	.10	.05	.01
☐ 7 Mike Greenwell	.10	.05	.01
☐ 8 Sam Horn	.05	.02	.01
☐ 9 Lee Smith	.10	.05	.01
☐ 10 Brian Downing	.05	.02	.01
☐ 11 Wally Joyner	.15	.07	.02
☐ 12 Devon White	.15	.07	.02
☐ 13 Mike Witt	.05	.02	.01
☐ 14 Ivan Calderon	.05	.02	.01
☐ 15 Ozzie Guillen	.05	.02	.01
☐ 16 Jack McDowell	.50	.23	.06
☐ 17 Kenny Williams	.05	.02	.01
☐ 18 Joe Carter	.25	.11	.03
☐ 19 Julio Franco	.10	.05	.01
☐ 20 Pat Tabler	.05	.02	.01
☐ 21 Doyle Alexander	.05	.02	.01
☐ 22 Jack Morris	.10	.05	.01
☐ 23 Matt Nokes	.05	.02	.01
☐ 24 Walt Terrell	.05	.02	.01
☐ 25 Alan Trammell	.10	.05	.01
☐ 26 Bret Saberhagen	.10	.05	.01
☐ 27 Kevin Seitzer	.10	.05	.01
☐ 28 Danny Tartabull	.05	.02	.01
☐ 29 Gary Thurman	.05	.02	.01
☐ 30 Ted Higuera	.05	.02	.01
☐ 31 Paul Molitor	.60	.25	.07
☐ 32 Dan Plesac	.05	.02	.01
☐ 33 Robin Yount	.25	.11	.03
☐ 34 Gary Gaetti	.05	.02	.01
☐ 35 Kent Hrbek	.10	.05	.01
☐ 36 Kirby Puckett	1.00	.45	.12
☐ 37 Jeff Reardon	.10	.05	.01
☐ 38 Frank Viola	.05	.02	.01
☐ 39 Jack Clark	.05	.02	.01
☐ 40 Rickey Henderson	.50	.23	.06
☐ 41 Don Mattingly	.75	.35	.09
☐ 42 Willie Randolph	.10	.05	.01
☐ 43 Dave Righetti	.05	.02	.01
☐ 44 Dave Winfield	.50	.23	.06
☐ 45 Jose Canseco	.60	.25	.07
☐ 46 Mark McGwire	1.00	.45	.12
☐ 47 Dave Parker	.10	.05	.01
☐ 48 Dave Stewart	.10	.05	.01
☐ 49 Walt Weiss	.15	.07	.02
☐ 50 Bob Welch	.05	.02	.01
☐ 51 Mickey Brantley	.05	.02	.01
☐ 52 Mark Langston	.05	.02	.01
☐ 53 Harold Reynolds	.10	.05	.01
☐ 54 Scott Fletcher	.05	.02	.01
☐ 55 Charlie Hough	.05	.02	.01
☐ 56 Pete Incaviglia	.05	.02	.01
☐ 57 Larry Parrish	.05	.02	.01
☐ 58 Ruben Sierra	.25	.11	.03
☐ 59 George Bell	.05	.02	.01
☐ 60 Mark Eichhorn	.05	.02	.01
☐ 61 Tony Fernandez	.05	.02	.01
☐ 62 Tom Henke	.05	.02	.01
☐ 63 Jimmy Key	.10	.05	.01
☐ 64 Dion James	.05	.02	.01
☐ 65 Dale Murphy	.15	.07	.02
☐ 66 Zane Smith	.05	.02	.01
☐ 67 Andre Dawson	.25	.11	.03
☐ 68 Mark Grace	1.50	.70	.19
☐ 69 Jerry Mumphrey	.05	.02	.01
☐ 70 Ryne Sandberg	1.00	.45	.12
☐ 71 Rick Sutcliffe	.05	.02	.01
☐ 72 Kal Daniels	.05	.02	.01
☐ 73 Eric Davis	.10	.05	.01
☐ 74 John Franco	.10	.05	.01
☐ 75 Ron Robinson	.05	.02	.01
☐ 76 Jeff Treadway	.05	.02	.01
☐ 77 Kevin Bass	.05	.02	.01
☐ 78 Glenn Davis	.05	.02	.01
☐ 79 Nolan Ryan	2.00	.90	.25
☐ 80 Mike Scott	.05	.02	.01
☐ 81 Dave Smith	.05	.02	.01
☐ 82 Kirk Gibson	.10	.05	.01
☐ 83 Pedro Guerrero	.05	.02	.01
☐ 84 Orel Hershiser	.20	.09	.03
☐ 85 Steve Sax	.05	.02	.01
☐ 86 Fernando Valenzuela	.10	.05	.01
☐ 87 Tim Burke	.05	.02	.01
☐ 88 Andres Galarraga	.25	.11	.03
☐ 89 Neal Heaton	.05	.02	.01
☐ 90 Tim Raines	.10	.05	.01
☐ 91 Tim Wallach	.05	.02	.01
☐ 92 Dwight Gooden	.10	.05	.01
☐ 93 Keith Hernandez	.10	.05	.01
☐ 94 Gregg Jefferies	.50	.23	.06
☐ 95 Howard Johnson	.05	.02	.01
☐ 96 Roger McDowell	.05	.02	.01
☐ 97 Darryl Strawberry	.10	.05	.01
☐ 98 Steve Bedrosian	.05	.02	.01
☐ 99 Von Hayes	.05	.02	.01
☐ 100 Shane Rawley	.05	.02	.01
☐ 101 Juan Samuel	.05	.02	.01
☐ 102 Mike Schmidt	.40	.18	.05
☐ 103 Bobby Bonilla	.25	.11	.03
☐ 104 Mike Dunne	.05	.02	.01
☐ 105 Andy Van Slyke	.10	.05	.01
☐ 106 Vince Coleman	.05	.02	.01
☐ 107 Bob Horner	.05	.02	.01
☐ 108 Willie McGee	.10	.05	.01
☐ 109 Ozzie Smith	1.00	.45	.12
☐ 110 John Tudor	.05	.02	.01
☐ 111 Todd Worrell	.05	.02	.01
☐ 112 Tony Gwynn	.75	.35	.09
☐ 113 John Kruk	.15	.07	.02
☐ 114 Lance McCullers	.05	.02	.01
☐ 115 Benito Santiago	.10	.05	.01
☐ 116 Will Clark	.60	.25	.07
☐ 117 Jeff Leonard	.05	.02	.01
☐ 118 Candy Maldonado	.05	.02	.01
☐ 119 Kirt Manwaring	.10	.05	.01
☐ 120 Don Robinson	.05	.02	.01

1988 Fleer Record Setters

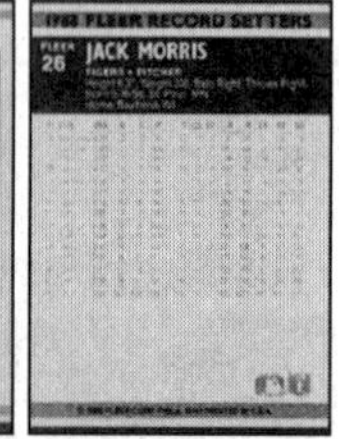

This small boxed set of 44 standard-size cards was produced exclusively for Eckerd's Drug Stores. The cards feature full color fronts and red, white, and blue backs. The card fronts are distinguished by the red and blue frame around the player's full-color photo. The box for the cards describes the set as the "1988 Baseball Record Setters." The checklist for the set is given on the back of the set box. The card numbering is in alphabetical order by player's name.

	MINT	NRMT	EXC
COMPLETE SET (44)	5.00	2.20	.60
COMMON CARD (1-44)	.05	.02	.01
☐ 1 Jesse Barfield	.05	.02	.01
☐ 2 George Bell	.05	.02	.01
☐ 3 Wade Boggs	.30	.14	.04
☐ 4 Jose Canseco	.60	.25	.07
☐ 5 Jack Clark	.10	.05	.01
☐ 6 Will Clark	.60	.25	.07
☐ 7 Roger Clemens	.60	.25	.07
☐ 8 Alvin Davis	.05	.02	.01
☐ 9 Eric Davis	.05	.02	.01
☐ 10 Andre Dawson	.25	.11	.03
☐ 11 Mike Dunne	.05	.02	.01
☐ 12 John Franco	.10	.05	.01
☐ 13 Julio Franco	.10	.05	.01
☐ 14 Dwight Gooden	.10	.05	.01
☐ 15 Mark Gubicza (Listed as Gubiczo on box checklist)	.05	.02	.01
☐ 16 Ozzie Guillen	.05	.02	.01
☐ 17 Tony Gwynn	1.00	.45	.12
☐ 18 Orel Hershiser	.20	.09	.03
☐ 19 Teddy Higuera	.05	.02	.01
☐ 20 Howard Johnson UER (Missing '87 stats on card back)	.05	.02	.01
☐ 21 Wally Joyner	.20	.09	.03
☐ 22 Jimmy Key	.10	.05	.01
☐ 23 Jeff Leonard	.05	.02	.01
☐ 24 Don Mattingly	1.00	.45	.12
☐ 25 Mark McGwire	1.00	.45	.12
☐ 26 Jack Morris	.10	.05	.01
☐ 27 Dale Murphy	.20	.09	.03
☐ 28 Larry Parrish	.05	.02	.01
☐ 29 Kirby Puckett	1.00	.45	.12
☐ 30 Tim Raines	.10	.05	.01
☐ 31 Harold Reynolds	.10	.05	.01
☐ 32 Dave Righetti	.05	.02	.01
☐ 33 Cal Ripken	2.00	.90	.25
☐ 34 Benito Santiago	.05	.02	.01
☐ 35 Mike Schmidt	.50	.23	.06
☐ 36 Mike Scott	.05	.02	.01
☐ 37 Kevin Seitzer	.10	.05	.01
☐ 38 Ozzie Smith	1.00	.45	.12
☐ 39 Darryl Strawberry	.10	.05	.01
☐ 40 Rick Sutcliffe	.05	.02	.01
☐ 41 Alan Trammell	.15	.07	.02
☐ 42 Frank Viola	.05	.02	.01
☐ 43 Mitch Williams	.05	.02	.01
☐ 44 Todd Worrell	.05	.02	.01

1988 Fleer Sluggers/Pitchers

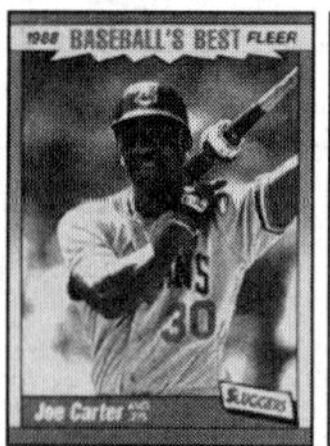

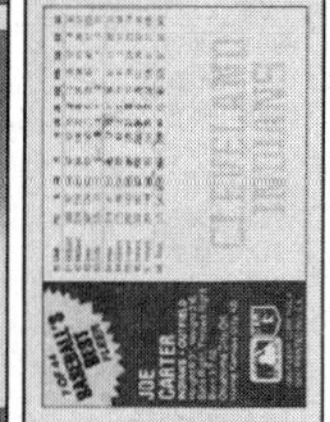

Fleer produced this 44-card boxed standard-size set although it was primarily distributed by McCrory, McLellan, J.J Newberry, H.L.Green, T.G.Y., and other similar stores. The set is subtitled "Baseball's Best". The set was packaged in a green custom box along with six logo stickers. The set checklist is given on the back of the box. The bottoms of the boxes which held the individual set boxes also contained a panel of six cards; these box bottom cards were numbered C1 through C6. The card numbering is in alphabetical order by player's name.

	MINT	NRMT	EXC
COMPLETE SET (44)	5.00	2.20	.60
COMMON CARD (1-44)	.05	.02	.01
☐ 1 George Bell	.05	.02	.01
☐ 2 Wade Boggs	.30	.14	.04
☐ 3 Bobby Bonilla	.20	.09	.03
☐ 4 Tom Brunansky	.05	.02	.01
☐ 5 Ellis Burks	.40	.18	.05
☐ 6 Jose Canseco	.60	.25	.07
☐ 7 Joe Carter	.25	.11	.03
☐ 8 Will Clark	.60	.25	.07
☐ 9 Roger Clemens	.60	.25	.07
☐ 10 Eric Davis	.05	.02	.01
☐ 11 Glenn Davis	.05	.02	.01
☐ 12 Andre Dawson	.25	.11	.03
☐ 13 Dennis Eckersley	.10	.05	.01
☐ 14 Andres Galarraga	.20	.09	.03
☐ 15 Dwight Gooden	.10	.05	.01
☐ 16 Pedro Guerrero	.05	.02	.01
☐ 17 Tony Gwynn	1.00	.45	.12
☐ 18 Orel Hershiser	.20	.09	.03
☐ 19 Ted Higuera	.05	.02	.01
☐ 20 Pete Incaviglia	.05	.02	.01
☐ 21 Danny Jackson	.05	.02	.01
☐ 22 Doug Jennings	.05	.02	.01
☐ 23 Mark Langston	.10	.05	.01
☐ 24 Dave LaPoint	.05	.02	.01
☐ 25 Mike LaValliere	.05	.02	.01
☐ 26 Don Mattingly	1.00	.45	.12
☐ 27 Mark McGwire	1.00	.45	.12
☐ 28 Dale Murphy	.20	.09	.03
☐ 29 Ken Phelps	.05	.02	.01
☐ 30 Kirby Puckett	1.00	.45	.12
☐ 31 Johnny Ray	.05	.02	.01
☐ 32 Jeff Reardon	.05	.02	.01
☐ 33 Dave Righetti	.05	.02	.01
☐ 34 Cal Ripken UER (Misspelled Ripkin on card front)	2.00	.90	.25
☐ 35 Chris Sabo	.10	.05	.01
☐ 36 Mike Schmidt	.50	.23	.06
☐ 37 Mike Scott	.05	.02	.01
☐ 38 Kevin Seitzer	.10	.05	.01
☐ 39 Dave Stewart	.10	.05	.01
☐ 40 Darryl Strawberry	.10	.05	.01
☐ 41 Greg Swindell	.05	.02	.01
☐ 42 Frank Tanana	.05	.02	.01
☐ 43 Dave Winfield	.50	.23	.06
☐ 44 Todd Worrell	.05	.02	.01

1988 Fleer Sluggers/Pitchers Box Cards

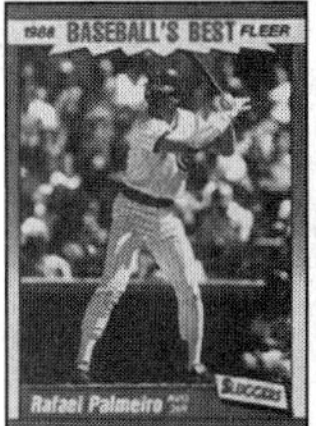

The cards in this six-card set each measure the standard size. Cards have essentially the same design as the 1988 Fleer Sluggers vs. Pitchers set of Baseball's Best. The cards were printed on the bottom of the counter display box which held 24 small boxed sets; hence theoretically these box cards are 1/24 as plentiful as the regular boxed set cards. These six cards, numbered C1 to C6 are considered a separate set in their own right and are not typically included in a complete set of the 1988 Fleer Sluggers vs. Pitchers set of 44. The value of the panels uncut is slightly greater, perhaps by 25 percent greater, than the value of the individual cards cut up carefully.

	MINT	NRMT	EXC
COMPLETE SET (6)	5.00	2.20	.60
COMMON CARDS (C1-C6)	.25	.11	.03
□ C1 Ron Darling	.25	.11	.03
□ C2 Rickey Henderson	1.50	.70	.19
□ C3 Carney Lansford	.50	.23	.06
□ C4 Rafael Palmeiro	2.50	1.10	.30
□ C5 Frank Viola	.25	.11	.03
□ C6 Twins Logo (Checklist back)	.25	.11	.03

1988 Fleer Sticker Cards

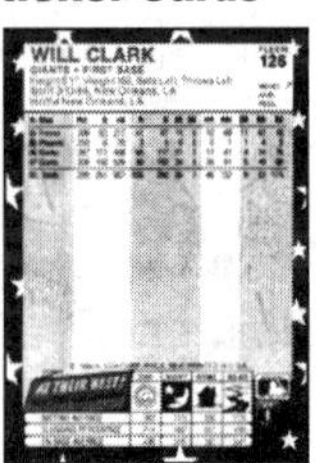

These Star Stickers were distributed as a separate issue by Fleer, with five star stickers and a logo sticker in each wax pack. The 132-card (sticker) set features 2 1/2" by 3 1/2" full-color fronts and even statistics on the sticker back, which is an indication that the Fleer Company understands that these stickers are rarely used as stickers but more like traditional cards. The card fronts are surrounded by a silver-gray border and the backs are printed in red and black on white card stock. The set numbering is in alphabetical order within team and alphabetically by team within each league.

	MINT	NRMT	EXC
COMPLETE SET (132)	15.00	6.75	1.85
COMMON CARD (1-132)	.05	.02	.01
□ 1 Mike Boddicker	.05	.02	.01
□ 2 Eddie Murray	.75	.35	.09
□ 3 Cal Ripken	3.00	1.35	.35
□ 4 Larry Sheets	.05	.02	.01
□ 5 Wade Boggs	.40	.18	.05
□ 6 Ellis Burks	.40	.18	.05
□ 7 Roger Clemens	1.00	.45	.12
□ 8 Dwight Evans	.10	.05	.01
□ 9 Mike Greenwell	.10	.05	.01
□ 10 Bruce Hurst	.05	.02	.01
□ 11 Brian Downing	.05	.02	.01
□ 12 Wally Joyner	.25	.11	.03
□ 13 Mike Witt	.05	.02	.01
□ 14 Ivan Calderon	.05	.02	.01
□ 15 Jose DeLeon	.05	.02	.01
□ 16 Ozzie Guillen	.05	.02	.01
□ 17 Bobby Thigpen	.05	.02	.01
□ 18 Joe Carter	.50	.23	.06
□ 19 Julio Franco	.10	.05	.01
□ 20 Brook Jacoby	.05	.02	.01
□ 21 Cory Snyder	.05	.02	.01
□ 22 Pat Tabler	.05	.02	.01
□ 23 Doyle Alexander	.05	.02	.01
□ 24 Kirk Gibson	.10	.05	.01
□ 25 Mike Henneman	.10	.05	.01
□ 26 Jack Morris	.25	.11	.03
□ 27 Matt Nokes	.05	.02	.01
□ 28 Walt Terrell	.05	.02	.01
□ 29 Alan Trammell	.10	.05	.01
□ 30 George Brett	1.25	.55	.16
□ 31 Charlie Leibrandt	.05	.02	.01
□ 32 Bret Saberhagen	.10	.05	.01
□ 33 Kevin Seitzer	.10	.05	.01
□ 34 Danny Tartabull	.05	.02	.01
□ 35 Frank White	.10	.05	.01
□ 36 Rob Deer	.05	.02	.01
□ 37 Ted Higuera	.05	.02	.01
□ 38 Paul Molitor	.60	.25	.07
□ 39 Dan Plesac	.05	.02	.01
□ 40 Robin Yount	.40	.18	.05
□ 41 Bert Blyleven	.10	.05	.01
□ 42 Tom Brunansky	.05	.02	.01
□ 43 Gary Gaetti	.05	.02	.01
□ 44 Kent Hrbek	.10	.05	.01
□ 45 Kirby Puckett	1.50	.70	.19
□ 46 Jeff Reardon	.10	.05	.01
□ 47 Frank Viola	.05	.02	.01
□ 48 Don Mattingly	1.50	.70	.19
□ 49 Mike Pagliarulo	.05	.02	.01
□ 50 Willie Randolph	.10	.05	.01
□ 51 Rick Rhoden	.05	.02	.01
□ 52 Dave Righetti	.05	.02	.01
□ 53 Dave Winfield	.40	.18	.05
□ 54 Jose Canseco	.25	.11	.03
□ 55 Carney Lansford	.05	.02	.01
□ 56 Mark McGwire	1.50	.70	.19
□ 57 Dave Stewart	.05	.02	.01
□ 58 Curt Young	.05	.02	.01
□ 59 Alvin Davis	.05	.02	.01
□ 60 Mark Langston	.05	.02	.01
□ 61 Ken Phelps	.05	.02	.01
□ 62 Harold Reynolds	.10	.05	.01
□ 63 Scott Fletcher	.05	.02	.01
□ 64 Charlie Hough	.05	.02	.01
□ 65 Pete Incaviglia	.05	.02	.01
□ 66 Oddibe McDowell	.05	.02	.01
□ 67 Pete O'Brien	.05	.02	.01
□ 68 Larry Parrish	.05	.02	.01
□ 69 Ruben Sierra	.25	.11	.03
□ 70 Jesse Barfield	.05	.02	.01
□ 71 George Bell	.05	.02	.01
□ 72 Tony Fernandez	.05	.02	.01
□ 73 Tom Henke	.05	.02	.01
□ 74 Jimmy Key	.10	.05	.01
□ 75 Lloyd Moseby	.05	.02	.01
□ 76 Dion James	.05	.02	.01
□ 77 Dale Murphy	.25	.11	.03
□ 78 Zane Smith	.05	.02	.01
□ 79 Andre Dawson	.10	.05	.01
□ 80 Ryne Sandberg	1.25	.55	.16
□ 81 Rick Sutcliffe	.05	.02	.01
□ 82 Kal Daniels	.05	.02	.01
□ 83 Eric Davis	.25	.11	.03
□ 84 John Franco	.10	.05	.01
□ 85 Kevin Bass	.05	.02	.01
□ 86 Glenn Davis	.05	.02	.01
□ 87 Bill Doran	.05	.02	.01
□ 88 Nolan Ryan	3.00	1.35	.35
□ 89 Mike Scott	.05	.02	.01
□ 90 Dave Smith	.05	.02	.01
□ 91 Pedro Guerrero	.05	.02	.01
□ 92 Orel Hershiser	.20	.09	.03
□ 93 Steve Sax	.05	.02	.01
□ 94 Fernando Valenzuela	.10	.05	.01
□ 95 Tim Burke	.05	.02	.01
□ 96 Andres Galarraga	.40	.18	.05
□ 97 Tim Raines	.10	.05	.01
□ 98 Tim Wallach	.05	.02	.01
□ 99 Mitch Webster	.05	.02	.01
□ 100 Ron Darling	.05	.02	.01
□ 101 Sid Fernandez	.05	.02	.01
□ 102 Dwight Gooden	.25	.11	.03
□ 103 Keith Hernandez	.10	.05	.01
□ 104 Howard Johnson	.05	.02	.01
□ 105 Roger McDowell	.05	.02	.01
□ 106 Darryl Strawberry	.10	.05	.01
□ 107 Steve Bedrosian	.05	.02	.01
□ 108 Von Hayes	.05	.02	.01
□ 109 Shane Rawley	.05	.02	.01
□ 110 Juan Samuel	.05	.02	.01
□ 111 Mike Schmidt	.75	.35	.09
□ 112 Milt Thompson	.05	.02	.01
□ 113 Sid Bream	.05	.02	.01
□ 114 Bobby Bonilla	.25	.11	.03
□ 115 Mike Dunne	.05	.02	.01
□ 116 Andy Van Slyke	.10	.05	.01
□ 117 Vince Coleman	.05	.02	.01
□ 118 Willie McGee	.10	.05	.01
□ 119 Terry Pendleton	.10	.05	.01
□ 120 Ozzie Smith	1.25	.55	.16
□ 121 John Tudor	.05	.02	.01
□ 122 Todd Worrell	.05	.02	.01
□ 123 Tony Gwynn	1.50	.70	.19
□ 124 John Kruk	.20	.09	.03
□ 125 Benito Santiago	.05	.02	.01
□ 126 Will Clark	.75	.35	.09
□ 127 Dave Dravecky	.05	.02	.01
□ 128 Jeff Leonard	.05	.02	.01
□ 129 Candy Maldonado	.05	.02	.01
□ 130 Rick Reuschel	.05	.02	.01
□ 131 Don Robinson	.05	.02	.01
□ 132 Checklist Card	.05	.02	.01

1988 Fleer Stickers Wax Box Cards

The bottoms of the Star Sticker wax boxes contained two different sets of four cards done in a similar format to the stickers; these cards (they are not stickers but truly cards) are numbered with the prefix S and are considered a separate set. The value of the panels uncut is slightly greater, perhaps by 25 percent greater, than the value of the individual cards cut up carefully.

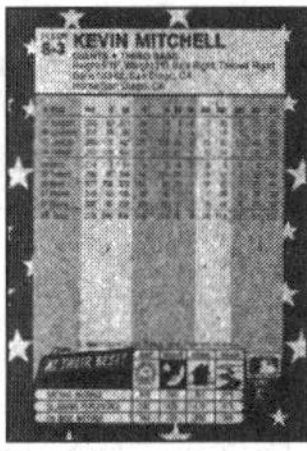

	MINT	NRMT	EXC
COMPLETE SET (8)	4.00	1.80	.50
COMMON CARD (S1-S8)	.25	.11	.03
□ S1 Don Baylor	.25	.11	.03
□ S2 Gary Carter	.50	.23	.06
□ S3 Ron Guidry	.25	.11	.03
□ S4 Rickey Henderson	1.25	.55	.16
□ S5 Kevin Mitchell	.25	.11	.03
□ S6 Mark McGwire and Eric Davis	2.00	.90	.25
□ S7 Giants Logo	.25	.11	.03
□ S8 Detroit Logo	.25	.11	.03

1988 Fleer Superstars

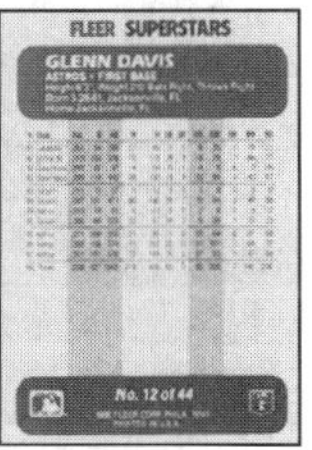

Fleer produced this 44-card boxed standard-size set although it was primarily distributed by McCrory, McLellan, J.J Newberry, H.L.Green, T.G.Y., and other similar stores. The set is subtitled "Fleer Superstars." The set was packaged in a red, white, blue, and yellow custom box along with six logo stickers. The set checklist is given on the back of the box. The bottoms of the boxes which held the individual set boxes also contained a panel of six cards; these box bottom cards were numbered C1 through C6. The card numbering is in alphabetical order by player's name.

	MINT	NRMT	EXC
COMPLETE SET (44)	5.00	2.20	.60
COMMON CARD (1-44)	.05	.02	.01
□ 1 Steve Bedrosian	.05	.02	.01
□ 2 George Bell	.05	.02	.01
□ 3 Wade Boggs	.30	.14	.04
□ 4 Barry Bonds	1.00	.45	.12
□ 5 Jose Canseco	.60	.25	.07
□ 6 Joe Carter	.25	.11	.03
□ 7 Jack Clark	.10	.05	.01
□ 8 Will Clark	.60	.25	.07
□ 9 Roger Clemens	.60	.25	.07
□ 10 Alvin Davis	.05	.02	.01
□ 11 Eric Davis	.05	.02	.01
□ 12 Glenn Davis	.05	.02	.01
□ 13 Andre Dawson	.25	.11	.03
□ 14 Dwight Gooden	.10	.05	.01
□ 15 Orel Hershiser	.20	.09	.03
□ 16 Teddy Higuera	.05	.02	.01
□ 17 Kent Hrbek	.10	.05	.01
□ 18 Wally Joyner	.20	.09	.03
□ 19 Jimmy Key	.10	.05	.01
□ 20 John Kruk	.15	.07	.02
□ 21 Jeff Leonard	.05	.02	.01
□ 22 Don Mattingly	1.00	.45	.12
□ 23 Mark McGwire	1.00	.45	.12
□ 24 Kevin McReynolds	.05	.02	.01
□ 25 Dale Murphy	.20	.09	.03
□ 26 Matt Nokes	.05	.02	.01
□ 27 Terry Pendleton	.10	.05	.01
□ 28 Kirby Puckett	1.00	.45	.12
□ 29 Tim Raines	.10	.05	.01
□ 30 Rick Rhoden	.05	.02	.01
□ 31 Cal Ripken	2.00	.90	.25
□ 32 Benito Santiago	.05	.02	.01
□ 33 Mike Schmidt	.50	.23	.06
□ 34 Mike Scott	.05	.02	.01
□ 35 Kevin Seitzer	.10	.05	.01
□ 36 Ruben Sierra	.20	.09	.03
□ 37 Cory Snyder	.05	.02	.01
□ 38 Darryl Strawberry	.10	.05	.01
□ 39 Rick Sutcliffe	.05	.02	.01
□ 40 Danny Tartabull	.05	.02	.01
□ 41 Alan Trammell	.15	.07	.02
□ 42 Kenny Williams	.05	.02	.01
□ 43 Mike Witt	.05	.02	.01
□ 44 Robin Yount	.50	.23	.06

1988 Fleer Superstars Box Cards

The cards in this six-card set each measure the standard size. Cards have essentially the same design as the 1988 Fleer Superstars set.

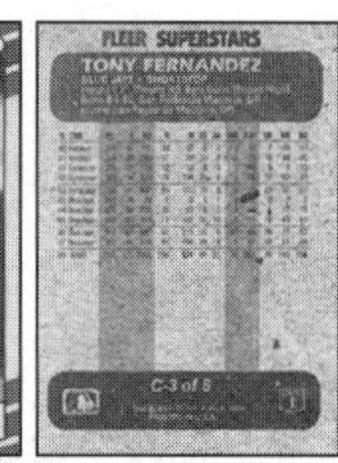

The cards were printed on the bottom of the counter display box which held 24 small boxed sets; hence theoretically these box cards are 1/24 as plentiful as the regular boxed set cards. These six cards, numbered C1 to C6 are considered a separate set in their own right and are not typically included in a complete set of the 1988 Fleer Superstars set of 44. The value of the panels uncut is slightly greater, perhaps by 25 percent greater, than the value of the individual cards cut up carefully.

	MINT	NRMT	EXC
COMPLETE SET (6)	8.00	3.60	1.00
COMMON CARD (C1-C6)	.25	.11	.03
□ C1 Pete Incaviglia	.50	.23	.06
□ C2 Rickey Henderson	2.00	.90	.25
□ C3 Tony Fernandez	.50	.23	.06
□ C4 Shane Rawley	.25	.11	.03
□ C5 Ryne Sandberg	5.00	2.20	.60
□ C6 Cardinals Logo (Checklist back)	.25	.11	.03

1988 Fleer Team Leaders

This 44-card boxed standard-size set was produced by Fleer for exclusive distribution by Kay Bee Toys and is sometimes referred to as the Fleer Kay Bee set. Six team logo stickers are included in the box with the complete set. The numerical checklist on the back of the box shows that the set is numbered alphabetically. The cards have a distinctive red border on the fronts. The Kay Bee logo is printed in the lower right corner of the obverse of each card.

	MINT	NRMT	EXC
COMPLETE SET (44)	5.00	2.20	.60
COMMON CARD (1-44)	.05	.02	.01
□ 1 George Bell	.05	.02	.01
□ 2 Wade Boggs	.30	.14	.04
□ 3 Jose Canseco	.60	.25	.07
□ 4 Will Clark	.60	.25	.07
□ 5 Roger Clemens	.60	.25	.07
□ 6 Eric Davis	.05	.02	.01
□ 7 Andre Dawson	.25	.11	.03
□ 8 Julio Franco	.10	.05	.01
□ 9 Andres Galarraga	.20	.09	.03
□ 10 Dwight Gooden	.10	.05	.01
□ 11 Tony Gwynn	1.00	.45	.12
□ 12 Tom Henke	.05	.02	.01
□ 13 Orel Hershiser	.20	.09	.03
□ 14 Kent Hrbek	.10	.05	.01
□ 15 Ted Higuera	.05	.02	.01
□ 16 Wally Joyner	.20	.09	.03
□ 17 Jimmy Key	.10	.05	.01
□ 18 Mark Langston	.05	.02	.01
□ 19 Don Mattingly	1.00	.45	.12
□ 20 Willie McGee	.10	.05	.01
□ 21 Mark McGwire	1.00	.45	.12
□ 22 Paul Molitor	.50	.23	.06
□ 23 Jack Morris	.10	.05	.01
□ 24 Dale Murphy	.20	.09	.03
□ 25 Larry Parrish	.05	.02	.01
□ 26 Kirby Puckett	1.00	.45	.12
□ 27 Tim Raines	.10	.05	.01
□ 28 Jeff Reardon	.05	.02	.01
□ 29 Dave Righetti	.05	.02	.01
□ 30 Cal Ripken	2.00	.90	.25
□ 31 Don Robinson	.05	.02	.01
□ 32 Bret Saberhagen	.10	.05	.01
□ 33 Juan Samuel	.05	.02	.01
□ 34 Mike Schmidt	.50	.23	.06
□ 35 Mike Scott	.05	.02	.01
□ 36 Kevin Seitzer	.10	.05	.01
□ 37 Dave Smith	.05	.02	.01
□ 38 Ozzie Smith	1.00	.45	.12
□ 39 Zane Smith	.05	.02	.01
□ 40 Darryl Strawberry	.10	.05	.01
□ 41 Rick Sutcliffe	.05	.02	.01
□ 42 Bobby Thigpen	.05	.02	.01
□ 43 Alan Trammell	.15	.07	.02
□ 44 Andy Van Slyke	.10	.05	.01

1989 Fleer

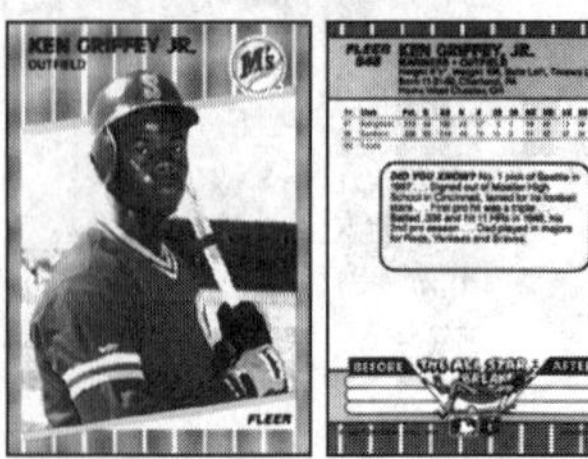

This set consists of 660 standard-size cards. Cards were primarily issued in 15-card wax packs, rack packs and hobby and retail factory sets. Card fronts feature a distinctive gray border background with white and yellow trim. Cards are again organized alphabetically within teams and teams ordered by previous season record. The last 33 cards in the set consist of Specials (628-639), Rookie Pairs (640-653), and checklists (654-660). Approximately half of the California Angels players have white rather than yellow halos. Certain Oakland A's player cards have red instead of green lines for front photo borders. Checklist cards are available either with or without positions listed for each player. Rookie Cards in this set include Sandy Alomar Jr., Brady Anderson, Dante Bichette, Craig Biggio, Ken Griffey Jr., Charlie Hayes, Ken Hill, Randy Johnson, Ramon Martinez, Hal Morris, Gary Sheffield, and John Smoltz.

	MINT	NRMT	EXC
COMPLETE SET (660)	10.00	4.50	1.25
COMPLETE RETAIL SET (660)	10.00	4.50	1.25
COMPLETE HOBBY SET (672)	12.00	5.50	1.50
COMMON CARD (1-660)	.05	.02	.01
□ 1 Don Baylor	.15	.07	.02
□ 2 Lance Blankenship	.05	.02	.01
□ 3 Todd Burns UER (Wrong birthdate; before/after All-Star stats missing)	.05	.02	.01
□ 4 Greg Cadaret UER (All-Star Break stats show 3 losses, should be 2)	.05	.02	.01
□ 5 Jose Canseco	.15	.07	.02
□ 6 Storm Davis	.05	.02	.01
□ 7 Dennis Eckersley	.10	.05	.01
□ 8 Mike Gallego	.05	.02	.01
□ 9 Ron Hassey	.05	.02	.01
□ 10 Dave Henderson	.05	.02	.01
□ 11 Rick Honeycutt	.05	.02	.01
□ 12 Glenn Hubbard	.05	.02	.01
□ 13 Stan Javier	.05	.02	.01
□ 14 Doug Jennings	.05	.02	.01
□ 15 Felix Jose	.05	.02	.01
□ 16 Carney Lansford	.10	.05	.01
□ 17 Mark McGwire	.30	.14	.04
□ 18 Gene Nelson	.05	.02	.01
□ 19 Dave Parker	.10	.05	.01
□ 20 Eric Plunk	.05	.02	.01
□ 21 Luis Polonia	.10	.05	.01
□ 22 Terry Steinbach	.10	.05	.01
□ 23 Dave Stewart	.10	.05	.01
□ 24 Walt Weiss	.05	.02	.01
□ 25 Bob Welch	.05	.02	.01
□ 26 Curt Young	.05	.02	.01
□ 27 Rick Aguilera	.15	.07	.02
□ 28 Wally Backman	.05	.02	.01
□ 29 Mark Carreon UER (After All-Star Break batting 7.14)	.05	.02	.01
□ 30 Gary Carter	.10	.05	.01
□ 31 David Cone	.15	.07	.02
□ 32 Ron Darling	.05	.02	.01
□ 33 Len Dykstra	.10	.05	.01
□ 34 Kevin Elster	.10	.05	.01
□ 35 Sid Fernandez	.05	.02	.01
□ 36 Dwight Gooden	.10	.05	.01
□ 37 Keith Hernandez	.10	.05	.01
□ 38 Gregg Jefferies	.15	.07	.02
□ 39 Howard Johnson	.05	.02	.01
□ 40 Terry Leach	.05	.02	.01
□ 41 Dave Magadan UER (Bio says 15 doubles, should be 13)	.05	.02	.01
□ 42 Bob McClure	.05	.02	.01
□ 43 Roger McDowell UER (Led Mets with 58, should be 62)	.05	.02	.01
□ 44 Kevin McReynolds	.05	.02	.01
□ 45 Keith A. Miller	.05	.02	.01
□ 46 Randy Myers	.10	.05	.01
□ 47 Bob Ojeda	.05	.02	.01
□ 48 Mackey Sasser	.05	.02	.01
□ 49 Darryl Strawberry	.10	.05	.01
□ 50 Tim Teufel	.05	.02	.01
□ 51 Dave West	.05	.02	.01
□ 52 Mookie Wilson	.10	.05	.01
□ 53 Dave Anderson	.05	.02	.01
□ 54 Tim Belcher	.05	.02	.01
□ 55 Mike Davis	.05	.02	.01
□ 56 Mike Devereaux	.05	.02	.01
□ 57 Kirk Gibson	.15	.07	.02
□ 58 Alfredo Griffin	.05	.02	.01
□ 59 Chris Gwynn	.05	.02	.01
□ 60 Jeff Hamilton	.05	.02	.01
□ 61A Danny Heep (Home: Lake Hills)	.15	.07	.02
□ 61B Danny Heep (Home: San Antonio)	.05	.02	.01
□ 62 Orel Hershiser	.10	.05	.01
□ 63 Brian Holton	.05	.02	.01
□ 64 Jay Howell	.05	.02	.01
□ 65 Tim Leary	.05	.02	.01
□ 66 Mike Marshall	.05	.02	.01
□ 67 Ramon Martinez	.25	.11	.03
□ 68 Jesse Orosco	.05	.02	.01
□ 69 Alejandro Pena	.05	.02	.01
□ 70 Steve Sax	.05	.02	.01
□ 71 Mike Scioscia	.05	.02	.01
□ 72 Mike Sharperson	.05	.02	.01
□ 73 John Shelby	.05	.02	.01
□ 74 Franklin Stubbs	.05	.02	.01
□ 75 John Tudor	.05	.02	.01
□ 76 Fernando Valenzuela	.10	.05	.01
□ 77 Tracy Woodson	.05	.02	.01
□ 78 Marty Barrett	.05	.02	.01
□ 79 Todd Benzinger	.05	.02	.01
□ 80 Mike Boddicker UER (Rochester in '76, should be '78)	.05	.02	.01
□ 81 Wade Boggs	.15	.07	.02
□ 82 Oil Can Boyd	.05	.02	.01
□ 83 Ellis Burks	.15	.07	.02
□ 84 Rick Cerone	.05	.02	.01
□ 85 Roger Clemens	.20	.09	.03
□ 86 Steve Curry	.05	.02	.01
□ 87 Dwight Evans	.10	.05	.01
□ 88 Wes Gardner	.05	.02	.01
□ 89 Rich Gedman	.05	.02	.01
□ 90 Mike Greenwell	.05	.02	.01
□ 91 Bruce Hurst	.05	.02	.01
□ 92 Dennis Lamp	.05	.02	.01
□ 93 Spike Owen	.05	.02	.01
□ 94 Larry Parrish UER (Before All-Star Break batting 1.90)	.05	.02	.01
□ 95 Carlos Quintana	.05	.02	.01
□ 96 Jody Reed	.05	.02	.01
□ 97 Jim Rice	.15	.07	.02
□ 98A Kevin Romine ERR (Photo actually Randy Kutcher batting)	.15	.07	.02
□ 98B Kevin Romine COR (Arms folded)	.05	.02	.01
□ 99 Lee Smith	.10	.05	.01
□ 100 Mike Smithson	.05	.02	.01
□ 101 Bob Stanley	.05	.02	.01
□ 102 Allan Anderson	.05	.02	.01
□ 103 Keith Atherton	.05	.02	.01
□ 104 Juan Berenguer	.05	.02	.01
□ 105 Bert Blyleven	.10	.05	.01
□ 106 Eric Bullock UER (Bats/Throws Right, should be Left)	.05	.02	.01
□ 107 Randy Bush	.05	.02	.01
□ 108 John Christensen	.05	.02	.01
□ 109 Mark Davidson	.05	.02	.01
□ 110 Gary Gaetti	.05	.02	.01
□ 111 Greg Gagne	.05	.02	.01
□ 112 Dan Gladden	.05	.02	.01
□ 113 German Gonzalez	.05	.02	.01
□ 114 Brian Harper	.05	.02	.01
□ 115 Tom Herr	.05	.02	.01
□ 116 Kent Hrbek	.10	.05	.01
□ 117 Gene Larkin	.05	.02	.01
□ 118 Tim Laudner	.05	.02	.01
□ 119 Charlie Lea	.05	.02	.01
□ 120 Steve Lombardozzi	.05	.02	.01
□ 121A John Moses (Home: Tempe)	.15	.07	.02
□ 121B John Moses (Home: Phoenix)	.05	.02	.01
□ 122 Al Newman	.05	.02	.01
□ 123 Mark Portugal	.05	.02	.01
□ 124 Kirby Puckett	.40	.18	.05
□ 125 Jeff Reardon	.10	.05	.01
□ 126 Fred Toliver	.05	.02	.01
□ 127 Frank Viola	.05	.02	.01
□ 128 Doyle Alexander	.05	.02	.01
□ 129 Dave Bergman	.05	.02	.01
□ 130A Tom Brookens ERR (Mike Heath back)	.75	.35	.09
□ 130B Tom Brookens COR	.05	.02	.01
□ 131 Paul Gibson	.05	.02	.01
□ 132A Mike Heath ERR (Tom Brookens back)	.75	.35	.09
□ 132B Mike Heath COR	.05	.02	.01
□ 133 Don Heinkel	.05	.02	.01
□ 134 Mike Henneman	.05	.02	.01
□ 135 Guillermo Hernandez	.05	.02	.01
□ 136 Eric King	.05	.02	.01
□ 137 Chet Lemon	.05	.02	.01
□ 138 Fred Lynn UER ('74, '75 stats missing)	.05	.02	.01
□ 139 Jack Morris	.10	.05	.01
□ 140 Matt Nokes	.05	.02	.01
□ 141 Gary Pettis	.05	.02	.01
□ 142 Ted Power	.05	.02	.01
□ 143 Jeff M. Robinson	.05	.02	.01
□ 144 Luis Salazar	.05	.02	.01
□ 145 Steve Searcy	.05	.02	.01
□ 146 Pat Sheridan	.05	.02	.01
□ 147 Frank Tanana	.05	.02	.01
□ 148 Alan Trammell	.10	.05	.01
□ 149 Walt Terrell	.05	.02	.01
□ 150 Jim Walewander	.05	.02	.01
□ 151 Lou Whitaker	.10	.05	.01
□ 152 Tim Birtsas	.05	.02	.01
□ 153 Tom Browning	.05	.02	.01
□ 154 Keith Brown	.05	.02	.01
□ 155 Norm Charlton	.10	.05	.01
□ 156 Dave Concepcion	.10	.05	.01
□ 157 Kal Daniels	.05	.02	.01
□ 158 Eric Davis	.10	.05	.01
□ 159 Bo Diaz	.05	.02	.01
□ 160 Rob Dibble	.10	.05	.01
□ 161 Nick Esasky	.05	.02	.01
□ 162 John Franco	.10	.05	.01
□ 163 Danny Jackson	.05	.02	.01
□ 164 Barry Larkin	.20	.09	.03
□ 165 Rob Murphy	.05	.02	.01
□ 166 Paul O'Neill	.10	.05	.01
□ 167 Jeff Reed	.05	.02	.01
□ 168 Jose Rijo	.05	.02	.01
□ 169 Ron Robinson	.05	.02	.01
□ 170 Chris Sabo	.05	.02	.01
□ 171 Candy Sierra	.05	.02	.01
□ 172 Van Snider	.05	.02	.01
□ 173A Jeff Treadway (Target registration mark above head on front in light blue)	5.00	2.20	.60
□ 173B Jeff Treadway (No target on front)	.05	.02	.01
□ 174 Frank Williams (After All-Star Break stats are jumbled)	.05	.02	.01
□ 175 Herm Winningham	.05	.02	.01
□ 176 Jim Adduci	.05	.02	.01
□ 177 Don August	.05	.02	.01
□ 178 Mike Birkbeck	.05	.02	.01
□ 179 Chris Bosio	.05	.02	.01
□ 180 Glenn Braggs	.05	.02	.01
□ 181 Greg Brock	.05	.02	.01
□ 182 Mark Clear	.05	.02	.01
□ 183 Chuck Crim	.05	.02	.01
□ 184 Rob Deer	.05	.02	.01
□ 185 Tom Filer	.05	.02	.01
□ 186 Jim Gantner	.05	.02	.01
□ 187 Darryl Hamilton	.10	.05	.01
□ 188 Ted Higuera	.05	.02	.01
□ 189 Odell Jones	.05	.02	.01
□ 190 Jeffrey Leonard	.05	.02	.01
□ 191 Joey Meyer	.05	.02	.01
□ 192 Paul Mirabella	.05	.02	.01
□ 193 Paul Molitor	.20	.09	.03
□ 194 Charlie O'Brien	.05	.02	.01
□ 195 Dan Plesac	.05	.02	.01
□ 196 Gary Sheffield	.75	.35	.09
□ 197 B.J. Surhoff	.15	.07	.02
□ 198 Dale Sveum	.05	.02	.01
□ 199 Bill Wegman	.05	.02	.01
□ 200 Robin Yount	.15	.07	.02
□ 201 Rafael Belliard	.05	.02	.01
□ 202 Barry Bonds	.40	.18	.05
□ 203 Bobby Bonilla	.15	.07	.02
□ 204 Sid Bream	.05	.02	.01
□ 205 Benny Distefano	.05	.02	.01
□ 206 Doug Drabek	.10	.05	.01
□ 207 Mike Dunne	.05	.02	.01
□ 208 Felix Fermin	.05	.02	.01
□ 209 Brian Fisher	.05	.02	.01
□ 210 Jim Gott	.05	.02	.01
□ 211 Bob Kipper	.05	.02	.01
□ 212 Dave LaPoint	.05	.02	.01
□ 213 Mike LaValliere	.05	.02	.01
□ 214 Jose Lind	.05	.02	.01
□ 215 Junior Ortiz	.05	.02	.01
□ 216 Vicente Palacios	.05	.02	.01
□ 217 Tom Prince	.05	.02	.01
□ 218 Gary Redus	.05	.02	.01
□ 219 R.J. Reynolds	.05	.02	.01
□ 220 Jeff D. Robinson	.05	.02	.01
□ 221 John Smiley	.05	.02	.01
□ 222 Andy Van Slyke	.10	.05	.01
□ 223 Bob Walk	.05	.02	.01
□ 224 Glenn Wilson	.05	.02	.01
□ 225 Jesse Barfield	.05	.02	.01
□ 226 George Bell	.05	.02	.01
□ 227 Pat Borders	.10	.05	.01
□ 228 John Cerutti	.05	.02	.01
□ 229 Jim Clancy	.05	.02	.01
□ 230 Mark Eichhorn	.05	.02	.01
□ 231 Tony Fernandez	.05	.02	.01
□ 232 Cecil Fielder	.10	.05	.01
□ 233 Mike Flanagan	.05	.02	.01
□ 234 Kelly Gruber	.05	.02	.01
□ 235 Tom Henke	.05	.02	.01
□ 236 Jimmy Key	.10	.05	.01
□ 237 Rick Leach	.05	.02	.01
□ 238 Manny Lee UER (Bio says regular shortstop, sic, Tony Fernandez)	.05	.02	.01
□ 239 Nelson Liriano	.05	.02	.01
□ 240 Fred McGriff	.20	.09	.03
□ 241 Lloyd Moseby	.05	.02	.01
□ 242 Rance Mulliniks	.05	.02	.01
□ 243 Jeff Musselman	.05	.02	.01
□ 244 Dave Stieb	.05	.02	.01
□ 245 Todd Stottlemyre	.10	.05	.01
□ 246 Duane Ward	.05	.02	.01
□ 247 David Wells	.05	.02	.01
□ 248 Ernie Whitt UER (HR total 21, should be 121)	.05	.02	.01
□ 249 Luis Aguayo	.05	.02	.01
□ 250A Neil Allen (Home: Sarasota, FL)	.75	.35	.09
□ 250B Neil Allen (Home: Syosset, NY)	.05	.02	.01
□ 251 John Candelaria	.05	.02	.01
□ 252 Jack Clark	.10	.05	.01
□ 253 Richard Dotson	.05	.02	.01
□ 254 Rickey Henderson	.15	.07	.02
□ 255 Tommy John	.10	.05	.01
□ 256 Roberto Kelly	.10	.05	.01
□ 257 Al Leiter	.10	.05	.01
□ 258 Don Mattingly	.50	.23	.06
□ 259 Dale Mohorcic	.05	.02	.01
□ 260 Hal Morris	.15	.07	.02
□ 261 Scott Nielsen	.05	.02	.01
□ 262 Mike Pagliarulo UER (Wrong birthdate)	.05	.02	.01
□ 263 Hipolito Pena	.05	.02	.01
□ 264 Ken Phelps	.05	.02	.01
□ 265 Willie Randolph	.10	.05	.01
□ 266 Rick Rhoden	.05	.02	.01
□ 267 Dave Righetti	.05	.02	.01
□ 268 Rafael Santana	.05	.02	.01
□ 269 Steve Shields	.05	.02	.01
□ 270 Joel Skinner	.05	.02	.01
□ 271 Don Slaught	.05	.02	.01
□ 272 Claudell Washington	.05	.02	.01
□ 273 Gary Ward	.05	.02	.01
□ 274 Dave Winfield	.15	.07	.02
□ 275 Luis Aquino	.05	.02	.01
□ 276 Floyd Bannister	.05	.02	.01
□ 277 George Brett	.40	.18	.05
□ 278 Bill Buckner	.10	.05	.01
□ 279 Nick Capra	.05	.02	.01
□ 280 Jose DeJesus	.05	.02	.01
□ 281 Steve Farr	.05	.02	.01
□ 282 Jerry Don Gleaton	.05	.02	.01
□ 283 Mark Gubicza	.05	.02	.01
□ 284 Tom Gordon UER (16.2 innings in '88, should be 15.2)	.10	.05	.01
□ 285 Bo Jackson	.15	.07	.02
□ 286 Charlie Leibrandt	.05	.02	.01
□ 287 Mike Macfarlane	.10	.05	.01
□ 288 Jeff Montgomery	.10	.05	.01
□ 289 Bill Pecota UER (Photo actually Brad Wellman)	.05	.02	.01
□ 290 Jamie Quirk	.05	.02	.01
□ 291 Bret Saberhagen	.10	.05	.01
□ 292 Kevin Seitzer	.05	.02	.01
□ 293 Kurt Stillwell	.05	.02	.01
□ 294 Pat Tabler	.05	.02	.01
□ 295 Danny Tartabull	.05	.02	.01
□ 296 Gary Thurman	.05	.02	.01
□ 297 Frank White	.10	.05	.01
□ 298 Willie Wilson	.05	.02	.01
□ 299 Roberto Alomar	.40	.18	.05
□ 300 Sandy Alomar Jr. UER (Wrong birthdate, says 6/16/66, should say 6/18/66)	.20	.09	.03
□ 301 Chris Brown	.05	.02	.01
□ 302 Mike Brumley UER (133 hits in '88, should be 134)	.05	.02	.01
□ 303 Mark Davis	.05	.02	.01
□ 304 Mark Grant	.05	.02	.01
□ 305 Tony Gwynn	.40	.18	.05
□ 306 Greg W. Harris	.05	.02	.01
□ 307 Andy Hawkins	.05	.02	.01
□ 308 Jimmy Jones	.05	.02	.01
□ 309 John Kruk	.10	.05	.01
□ 310 Dave Leiper	.05	.02	.01
□ 311 Carmelo Martinez	.05	.02	.01
□ 312 Lance McCullers	.05	.02	.01
□ 313 Keith Moreland	.05	.02	.01
□ 314 Dennis Rasmussen	.05	.02	.01
□ 315 Randy Ready UER (1214 games in '88, should be 114)	.05	.02	.01
□ 316 Benito Santiago	.10	.05	.01
□ 317 Eric Show	.05	.02	.01
□ 318 Todd Simmons	.05	.02	.01
□ 319 Garry Templeton	.05	.02	.01
□ 320 Dickie Thon	.05	.02	.01
□ 321 Ed Whitson	.05	.02	.01
□ 322 Marvell Wynne	.05	.02	.01

□ 323 Mike Aldrete .05 .02 .01
□ 324 Brett Butler .10 .05 .01
□ 325 Will Clark UER .20 .09 .03
(Three consecutive
100 RBI seasons)
□ 326 Kelly Downs UER .05 .02 .01
('88 stats missing)
□ 327 Dave Dravecky .10 .05 .01
□ 328 Scott Garrelts .05 .02 .01
□ 329 Atlee Hammaker .05 .02 .01
□ 330 Charlie Hayes .15 .07 .02
□ 331 Mike Krukow .05 .02 .01
□ 332 Craig Lefferts .05 .02 .01
□ 333 Candy Maldonado .05 .02 .01
□ 334 Kirt Manwaring UER .05 .02 .01
(Bats Rights)
□ 335 Bob Melvin .05 .02 .01
□ 336 Kevin Mitchell .10 .05 .01
□ 337 Donell Nixon .05 .02 .01
□ 338 Tony Perezchica .05 .02 .01
□ 339 Joe Price .05 .02 .01
□ 340 Rick Reuschel .05 .02 .01
□ 341 Earnest Riles .05 .02 .01
□ 342 Don Robinson .05 .02 .01
□ 343 Chris Speier .05 .02 .01
□ 344 Robby Thompson UER .05 .02 .01
(West Plam Beach)
□ 345 Jose Uribe .05 .02 .01
□ 346 Matt Williams .25 .11 .03
□ 347 Trevor Wilson .05 .02 .01
□ 348 Juan Agosto .05 .02 .01
□ 349 Larry Andersen .05 .02 .01
□ 350A Alan Ashby ERR 2.00 .90 .25
(Throws Rig)
□ 350B Alan Ashby COR .05 .02 .01
□ 351 Kevin Bass .05 .02 .01
□ 352 Buddy Bell .10 .05 .01
□ 353 Craig Biggio .40 .18 .05
□ 354 Danny Darwin .05 .02 .01
□ 355 Glenn Davis .05 .02 .01
□ 356 Jim Deshaies .05 .02 .01
□ 357 Bill Doran .05 .02 .01
□ 358 John Fishel .05 .02 .01
□ 359 Billy Hatcher .05 .02 .01
□ 360 Bob Knepper .05 .02 .01
□ 361 Louie Meadows UER .05 .02 .01
(Bio says 10 EBH's
and 6 SB's in '88,
should be 3 and 4)
□ 362 Dave Meads .05 .02 .01
□ 363 Jim Pankovits .05 .02 .01
□ 364 Terry Puhl .05 .02 .01
□ 365 Rafael Ramirez .05 .02 .01
□ 366 Craig Reynolds .05 .02 .01
□ 367 Mike Scott .05 .02 .01
(Card number listed
as 368 on Astros CL)
□ 368 Nolan Ryan .75 .35 .09
(Card number listed
as 367 on Astros CL)
□ 369 Dave Smith .05 .02 .01
□ 370 Gerald Young .05 .02 .01
□ 371 Hubie Brooks .05 .02 .01
□ 372 Tim Burke .05 .02 .01
□ 373 John Dopson .05 .02 .01
□ 374 Mike R. Fitzgerald .05 .02 .01
□ 375 Tom Foley .05 .02 .01
□ 376 Andres Galarraga UER .15 .07 .02
(Home: Caracus)
□ 377 Neal Heaton .05 .02 .01
□ 378 Joe Hesketh .05 .02 .01
□ 379 Brian Holman .05 .02 .01
□ 380 Rex Hudler .05 .02 .01
□ 381 Randy Johnson UER .75 .35 .09
(Innings for '85 and
'86 shown as 27 and
120, should be 27.1
and 119.2)
□ 382 Wallace Johnson .05 .02 .01
□ 383 Tracy Jones .05 .02 .01
□ 384 Dave Martinez .05 .02 .01
□ 385 Dennis Martinez .10 .05 .01
□ 386 Andy McGaffigan .05 .02 .01
□ 387 Otis Nixon .05 .02 .01
□ 388 Johnny Paredes .05 .02 .01
□ 389 Jeff Parrett .05 .02 .01
□ 390 Pascual Perez .05 .02 .01
□ 391 Tim Raines .15 .07 .02
□ 392 Luis Rivera .05 .02 .01
□ 393 Nelson Santovenia .05 .02 .01
□ 394 Bryn Smith .05 .02 .01
□ 395 Tim Wallach .05 .02 .01
□ 396 Andy Allanson UER .05 .02 .01
(1214 hits in '88,
should be 114)
□ 397 Rod Allen .05 .02 .01
□ 398 Scott Bailes .05 .02 .01
□ 399 Tom Candiotti .05 .02 .01
□ 400 Joe Carter .15 .07 .02
□ 401 Carmen Castillo UER .05 .02 .01
(After All-Star Break
batting 2.50)
□ 402 Dave Clark UER .05 .02 .01
(Card front shows
position as Rookie;
after All-Star Break
batting 3.14)
□ 403 John Farrell UER .05 .02 .01
(Typo in runs
allowed in '88)
□ 404 Julio Franco .10 .05 .01
□ 405 Don Gordon .05 .02 .01
□ 406 Mel Hall .05 .02 .01
□ 407 Brad Havens .05 .02 .01
□ 408 Brook Jacoby .05 .02 .01
□ 409 Doug Jones .05 .02 .01
□ 410 Jeff Kaiser .05 .02 .01
□ 411 Luis Medina .05 .02 .01
□ 412 Cory Snyder .05 .02 .01
□ 413 Greg Swindell .05 .02 .01
□ 414 Ron Tingley UER .05 .02 .01
(Hit HR in first ML
at-bat, should be
first AL at-bat)
□ 415 Willie Upshaw .05 .02 .01
□ 416 Ron Washington .05 .02 .01
□ 417 Rich Yett .05 .02 .01
□ 418 Damon Berryhill .05 .02 .01
□ 419 Mike Bielecki .05 .02 .01
□ 420 Doug Dascenzo .05 .02 .01
□ 421 Jody Davis UER .05 .02 .01
(Braves stats for
'88 missing)
□ 422 Andre Dawson .10 .05 .01
□ 423 Frank DiPino .05 .02 .01
□ 424 Shawon Dunston .05 .02 .01
□ 425 Rich Gossage .15 .07 .02
□ 426 Mark Grace UER .20 .09 .03
(Minor League stats
for '88 missing)
□ 427 Mike Harkey .05 .02 .01
□ 428 Darrin Jackson .05 .02 .01
□ 429 Les Lancaster .05 .02 .01
□ 430 Vance Law .05 .02 .01
□ 431 Greg Maddux .75 .35 .09
□ 432 Jamie Moyer .05 .02 .01
□ 433 Al Nipper .05 .02 .01
□ 434 Rafael Palmeiro UER .15 .07 .02
(170 hits in '88,
should be 178)
□ 435 Pat Perry .05 .02 .01
□ 436 Jeff Pico .05 .02 .01
□ 437 Ryne Sandberg .25 .11 .03
□ 438 Calvin Schiraldi .05 .02 .01
□ 439 Rick Sutcliffe .05 .02 .01
□ 440A Manny Trillo ERR 2.00 .90 .25
(Throws Rig)
□ 440B Manny Trillo COR .05 .02 .01
□ 441 Gary Varsho UER .05 .02 .01
(Wrong birthdate;
.303 should be .302;
11/28 should be 9/19)
□ 442 Mitch Webster .05 .02 .01
□ 443 Luis Alicea .05 .02 .01
□ 444 Tom Brunansky .05 .02 .01
□ 445 Vince Coleman UER .05 .02 .01
(Third straight with
83, should be fourth
straight with 81)
□ 446 John Costello UER .05 .02 .01
(Home California,
should be New York)
□ 447 Danny Cox .05 .02 .01
□ 448 Ken Dayley .05 .02 .01
□ 449 Jose DeLeon .05 .02 .01
□ 450 Curt Ford .05 .02 .01
□ 451 Pedro Guerrero .10 .05 .01
□ 452 Bob Horner .05 .02 .01
□ 453 Tim Jones .05 .02 .01
□ 454 Steve Lake .05 .02 .01
□ 455 Joe Magrane UER .05 .02 .01
(Des Moines, IO)
□ 456 Greg Mathews .05 .02 .01
□ 457 Willie McGee .05 .02 .01
□ 458 Larry McWilliams .05 .02 .01
□ 459 Jose Oquendo .05 .02 .01
□ 460 Tony Pena .05 .02 .01
□ 461 Terry Pendleton .10 .05 .01
□ 462 Steve Peters UER .05 .02 .01
(Lives in Harrah,
not Harah)
□ 463 Ozzie Smith .25 .11 .03
□ 464 Scott Terry .05 .02 .01
□ 465 Denny Walling .05 .02 .01
□ 466 Todd Worrell .05 .02 .01
□ 467 Tony Armas UER .05 .02 .01
(Before All-Star Break
batting 2.39)
□ 468 Dante Bichette .60 .25 .07
□ 469 Bob Boone .10 .05 .01
□ 470 Terry Clark .05 .02 .01
□ 471 Stew Cliburn .05 .02 .01
□ 472 Mike Cook UER .05 .02 .01
(TM near Angels logo
missing from front)
□ 473 Sherman Corbett .05 .02 .01
□ 474 Chili Davis .10 .05 .01
□ 475 Brian Downing .05 .02 .01
□ 476 Jim Eppard .05 .02 .01
□ 477 Chuck Finley .10 .05 .01
□ 478 Willie Fraser .05 .02 .01
□ 479 Bryan Harvey UER .10 .05 .01
(ML record shows 0-0,
should be 7-5)
□ 480 Jack Howell .05 .02 .01
□ 481 Wally Joyner UER .10 .05 .01
(Yorba Linda, GA)
□ 482 Jack Lazorko .05 .02 .01
□ 483 Kirk McCaskill .05 .02 .01
□ 484 Mark McLemore .05 .02 .01
□ 485 Greg Minton .05 .02 .01
□ 486 Dan Petry .05 .02 .01
□ 487 Johnny Ray .05 .02 .01
□ 488 Dick Schofield .05 .02 .01
□ 489 Devon White .10 .05 .01
□ 490 Mike Witt .05 .02 .01
□ 491 Harold Baines .10 .05 .01
□ 492 Daryl Boston .05 .02 .01
□ 493 Ivan Calderon UER .05 .02 .01
('80 stats shifted)
□ 494 Mike Diaz .05 .02 .01
□ 495 Carlton Fisk .15 .07 .02
□ 496 Dave Gallagher .05 .02 .01
□ 497 Ozzie Guillen .05 .02 .01
□ 498 Shawn Hillegas .05 .02 .01
□ 499 Lance Johnson .15 .07 .02
□ 500 Barry Jones .05 .02 .01
□ 501 Bill Long .05 .02 .01
□ 502 Steve Lyons .05 .02 .01
□ 503 Fred Manrique .05 .02 .01
□ 504 Jack McDowell .10 .05 .01
□ 505 Donn Pall .05 .02 .01
□ 506 Kelly Paris .05 .02 .01
□ 507 Dan Pasqua .05 .02 .01
□ 508 Ken Patterson .05 .02 .01
□ 509 Melido Perez .05 .02 .01
□ 510 Jerry Reuss .05 .02 .01
□ 511 Mark Salas .05 .02 .01
□ 512 Bobby Thigpen UER .05 .02 .01
('86 ERA 4.69,
should be 4.68)
□ 513 Mike Woodard .05 .02 .01
□ 514 Bob Brower .05 .02 .01
□ 515 Steve Buechele .05 .02 .01
□ 516 Jose Cecena .05 .02 .01
□ 517 Cecil Espy .05 .02 .01
□ 518 Scott Fletcher .05 .02 .01
□ 519 Cecilio Guante .05 .02 .01
('87 Yankee stats
are off-centered)
□ 520 Jose Guzman .05 .02 .01
□ 521 Ray Hayward .05 .02 .01
□ 522 Charlie Hough .10 .05 .01
□ 523 Pete Incaviglia .10 .05 .01
□ 524 Mike Jeffcoat .05 .02 .01
□ 525 Paul Kilgus .05 .02 .01
□ 526 Chad Kreuter .05 .02 .01
□ 527 Jeff Kunkel .05 .02 .01
□ 528 Oddibe McDowell .05 .02 .01
□ 529 Pete O'Brien .05 .02 .01
□ 530 Geno Petralli .05 .02 .01
□ 531 Jeff Russell .05 .02 .01
□ 532 Ruben Sierra .10 .05 .01
□ 533 Mike Stanley .05 .02 .01
□ 534A Ed VandeBerg ERR 2.00 .90 .25
(Throws Lef)
□ 534B Ed VandeBerg COR .05 .02 .01
□ 535 Curtis Wilkerson ERR .05 .02 .01
(Pitcher headings
at bottom)
□ 536 Mitch Williams .05 .02 .01
□ 537 Bobby Witt UER .05 .02 .01
('85 ERA .643,
should be 6.43)
□ 538 Steve Balboni .05 .02 .01
□ 539 Scott Bankhead .05 .02 .01
□ 540 Scott Bradley .05 .02 .01
□ 541 Mickey Brantley .05 .02 .01
□ 542 Jay Buhner .25 .11 .03
□ 543 Mike Campbell .05 .02 .01
□ 544 Darnell Coles .05 .02 .01
□ 545 Henry Cotto .05 .02 .01
□ 546 Alvin Davis .05 .02 .01
□ 547 Mario Diaz .05 .02 .01
□ 548 Ken Griffey Jr. 5.00 2.20 .60
□ 549 Erik Hanson .15 .07 .02
□ 550 Mike Jackson UER .05 .02 .01
(Lifetime ERA 3.345,
should be 3.45)
□ 551 Mark Langston .10 .05 .01
□ 552 Edgar Martinez .15 .07 .02
□ 553 Bill McGuire .05 .02 .01
□ 554 Mike Moore .05 .02 .01
□ 555 Jim Presley .05 .02 .01
□ 556 Rey Quinones .05 .02 .01
□ 557 Jerry Reed .05 .02 .01
□ 558 Harold Reynolds .05 .02 .01
□ 559 Mike Schooler .05 .02 .01
□ 560 Bill Swift .05 .02 .01
□ 561 Dave Valle .05 .02 .01
□ 562 Steve Bedrosian .05 .02 .01
□ 563 Phil Bradley .05 .02 .01
□ 564 Don Carman .05 .02 .01
□ 565 Bob Dernier .05 .02 .01
□ 566 Marvin Freeman .05 .02 .01
□ 567 Todd Frohwirth .05 .02 .01
□ 568 Greg Gross .05 .02 .01
□ 569 Kevin Gross .05 .02 .01
□ 570 Greg A. Harris .05 .02 .01
□ 571 Von Hayes .05 .02 .01
□ 572 Chris James .05 .02 .01
□ 573 Steve Jeltz .05 .02 .01
□ 574 Ron Jones UER .05 .02 .01
(Led IL in '88 with
85, should be 75)
□ 575 Ricky Jordan .10 .05 .01
□ 576 Mike Maddux .05 .02 .01
□ 577 David Palmer .05 .02 .01
□ 578 Lance Parrish .05 .02 .01
□ 579 Shane Rawley .05 .02 .01
□ 580 Bruce Ruffin .05 .02 .01
□ 581 Juan Samuel .05 .02 .01
□ 582 Mike Schmidt .20 .09 .03
□ 583 Kent Tekulve .05 .02 .01
□ 584 Milt Thompson UER .05 .02 .01
(19 hits in '88,
should be 109)
□ 585 Jose Alvarez .05 .02 .01
□ 586 Paul Assenmacher .05 .02 .01
□ 587 Bruce Benedict .05 .02 .01
□ 588 Jeff Blauser .10 .05 .01
□ 589 Terry Blocker .05 .02 .01
□ 590 Ron Gant .15 .07 .02
□ 591 Tom Glavine .25 .11 .03
□ 592 Tommy Gregg .05 .02 .01
□ 593 Albert Hall .05 .02 .01
□ 594 Dion James .05 .02 .01
□ 595 Rick Mahler .05 .02 .01
□ 596 Dale Murphy .15 .07 .02
□ 597 Gerald Perry .05 .02 .01
□ 598 Charlie Puleo .05 .02 .01
□ 599 Ted Simmons .10 .05 .01
□ 600 Pete Smith .05 .02 .01
□ 601 Zane Smith .05 .02 .01
□ 602 John Smoltz .75 .35 .09
□ 603 Bruce Sutter .05 .02 .01
□ 604 Andres Thomas .05 .02 .01
□ 605 Ozzie Virgil .05 .02 .01
□ 606 Brady Anderson .60 .25 .07
□ 607 Jeff Ballard .05 .02 .01
□ 608 Jose Bautista .05 .02 .01
□ 609 Ken Gerhart .05 .02 .01
□ 610 Terry Kennedy .05 .02 .01
□ 611 Eddie Murray .25 .11 .03
□ 612 Carl Nichols UER .05 .02 .01
(Before All-Star Break
batting 1.88)
□ 613 Tom Niedenfuer .05 .02 .01
□ 614 Joe Orsulak .05 .02 .01
□ 615 Oswald Peraza UER .05 .02 .01
(Shown as Oswaldo)
□ 616A Bill Ripken ERR 5.00 2.20 .60
(Rick Face written
on knob of bat)
□ 616B Bill Ripken 40.00 18.00 5.00
(Bat knob
whited out)
□ 616C Bill Ripken 5.00 2.20 .60
(Words on bat knob
scribbled out)
□ 616D Bill Ripken DP .15 .07 .02
(Black box covering
bat knob)
□ 617 Cal Ripken .75 .35 .09
□ 618 Dave Schmidt .05 .02 .01
□ 619 Rick Schu .05 .02 .01
□ 620 Larry Sheets .05 .02 .01
□ 621 Doug Sisk .05 .02 .01
□ 622 Pete Stanicek .05 .02 .01
□ 623 Mickey Tettleton .10 .05 .01
□ 624 Jay Tibbs .05 .02 .01
□ 625 Jim Traber .05 .02 .01
□ 626 Mark Williamson .05 .02 .01
□ 627 Craig Worthington .05 .02 .01
□ 628 Speed/Power .15 .07 .02
Jose Canseco
□ 629 Pitcher Perfect .05 .02 .01
Tom Browning
□ 630 Like Father/Like Sons .25 .11 .03
Roberto Alomar
Sandy Alomar Jr.
(Names on card listed
in wrong order) UER
□ 631 NL All Stars UER .15 .07 .02
Will Clark
Rafael Palmeiro
(Gallaraga, sic;
Clark 3 consecutive
100 RBI seasons;
third with 102 RBI's)
□ 632 Homeruns - Coast .10 .05 .01
to Coast UER
Darryl Strawberry
Will Clark (Homeruns
should be two words)
□ 633 Hot Corners - Hot .10 .05 .01
Hitters UER
Wade Boggs
Carney Lansford
(Boggs hit .366 in
'86, should be '88)

	MINT	NRMT	EXC
☐ 634 Triple A's Jose Canseco Terry Steinbach Mark McGwire	.10	.05	.01
☐ 635 Dual Heat Mark Davis Dwight Gooden	.15	.07	.02
☐ 636 NL Pitching Power UER Danny Jackson David Cone (Hersheiser, sic)	.10	.05	.01
☐ 637 Cannon Arms UER Chris Sabo Bobby Bonilla (Bobby Bonds, sic)	.10	.05	.01
☐ 638 Double Trouble UER Andres Galarraga (Misspelled Gallaraga on card back) Gerald Perry	.10	.05	.01
☐ 639 Power Center Kirby Puckett Eric Davis	.15	.07	.02
☐ 640 Steve Wilson and Cameron Drew	.05	.02	.01
☐ 641 Kevin Brown and Kevin Reimer	.15	.07	.02
☐ 642 Brad Pounders and Jerald Clark	.05	.02	.01
☐ 643 Mike Capel and Drew Hall	.05	.02	.01
☐ 644 Joe Girardi and Rolando Roomes	.15	.07	.02
☐ 645 Lenny Harris and Marty Brown	.10	.05	.01
☐ 646 Luis DeLosSantos and Jim Campbell	.05	.02	.01
☐ 647 Randy Kramer and Miguel Garcia	.05	.02	.01
☐ 648 Torey Lovullo and Robert Palacios	.05	.02	.01
☐ 649 Jim Corsi and Bob Milacki	.05	.02	.01
☐ 650 Grady Hall and Mike Rochford	.05	.02	.01
☐ 651 Terry Taylor and Vance Lovelace	.05	.02	.01
☐ 652 Ken Hill and Dennis Cook	.40	.18	.05
☐ 653 Scott Service and Shane Turner	.05	.02	.01
☐ 654 CL: Oakland/Mets Dodgers/Red Sox (10 Henderson; 68 Jess Orosco)	.05	.02	.01
☐ 655A CL: Twins/Tigers ERR Reds/Brewers (179 Boslo and Twins/Tigers positions listed)	.05	.02	.01
☐ 655B CL: Twins/Tigers COR Reds/Brewers (179 Boslo but Twins/Tigers positions not listed)	.05	.02	.01
☐ 656 CL: Pirates/Blue Jays Yankees/Royals (225 Jess Barfield)	.05	.02	.01
☐ 657 CL: Padres/Giants Astros/Expos (367/368 wrong)	.05	.02	.01
☐ 658 CL: Indians/Cubs Cardinals/Angels (449 Deleon)	.05	.02	.01
☐ 659 CL: White Sox/Rangers Mariners/Phillies	.05	.02	.01
☐ 660 CL: Braves/Orioles Specials/Checklists (632 hyphenated diff- erently and 650 Hali; 595 Rich Mahler; 619 Rich Schu)	.05	.02	.01

1989 Fleer Glossy

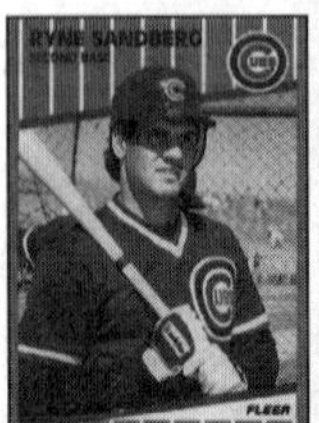

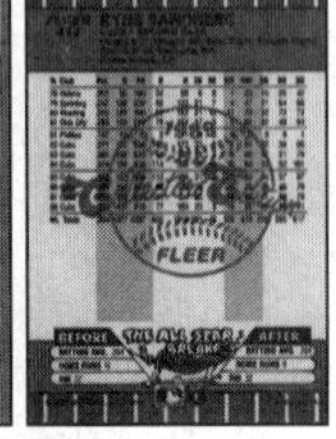

This 660 card set turned out to be the final parallel glossy issue for Fleer. These cards are identical to the regular Fleer cards except for the glossy sheen on the front. As many dealers did not order this product, this set is considerably scarcer than the regular 1989 Fleer set. Unlike the previous two seasons, the update set was not issued in Glossy form.

	MINT	NRMT	EXC
COMPLETE FACT.SET (672)	90.00	40.00	11.00
COMMON CARD (1-660)	.10	.05	.01
COMMON WORLD SERIES (WS1-WS12)	.10	.05	.01
*STARS: 6X BASIC CARDS			
*ROOKIES: 6X BASIC CARDS			

1989 Fleer All-Stars

This twelve-card standard-size subset was randomly inserted in Fleer wax and cello packs. The players selected are the 1989 Fleer Major League All-Star team. One player has been selected for each position along with a DH and three pitchers. The cards feature a distinctive green background on the card fronts. The set is sequenced in alphabetical order.

	MINT	NRMT	EXC
COMPLETE SET (12)	5.00	2.20	.60
COMMON CARD (1-12)	.25	.11	.03
☐ 1 Bobby Bonilla	.40	.18	.05
☐ 2 Jose Canseco	1.00	.45	.12
☐ 3 Will Clark	1.25	.55	.16
☐ 4 Dennis Eckersley	.40	.18	.05
☐ 5 Julio Franco	.40	.18	.05
☐ 6 Mike Greenwell	.25	.11	.03
☐ 7 Orel Hershiser	.40	.18	.05
☐ 8 Paul Molitor	1.25	.55	.16
☐ 9 Mike Scioscia	.25	.11	.03
☐ 10 Darryl Strawberry	.40	.18	.05
☐ 11 Alan Trammell	.40	.18	.05
☐ 12 Frank Viola	.25	.11	.03

1989 Fleer For The Record

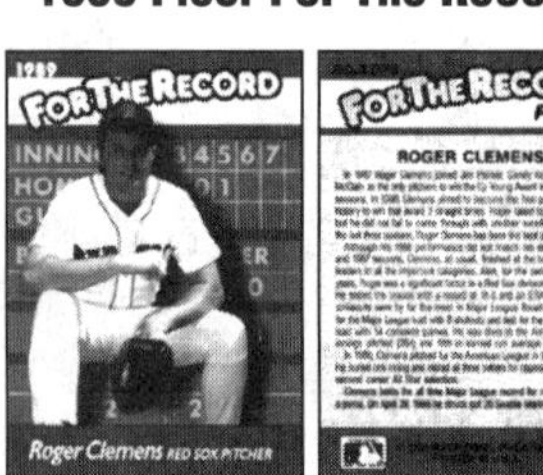

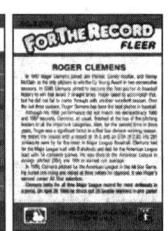

This six-card standard-size insert set was distributed one per rack pack. The set is subtitled "For The Record" and commemorates record-breaking events for those players from the previous season. The card backs are printed in red, black, and gray on white card stock. The set is sequenced in alphabetical order.

	MINT	NRMT	EXC
COMPLETE SET (6)	8.00	3.60	1.00
COMMON CARD (1-6)	.30	.14	.04
☐ 1 Wade Boggs	.75	.35	.09
☐ 2 Roger Clemens	1.25	.55	.16
☐ 3 Andres Galarraga	1.00	.45	.12
☐ 4 Kirk Gibson	.30	.14	.04
☐ 5 Greg Maddux	5.00	2.20	.60
☐ 6 Don Mattingly UER (Won batting title '83, should say '84)	3.00	1.35	.35

1989 Fleer Wax Box Cards

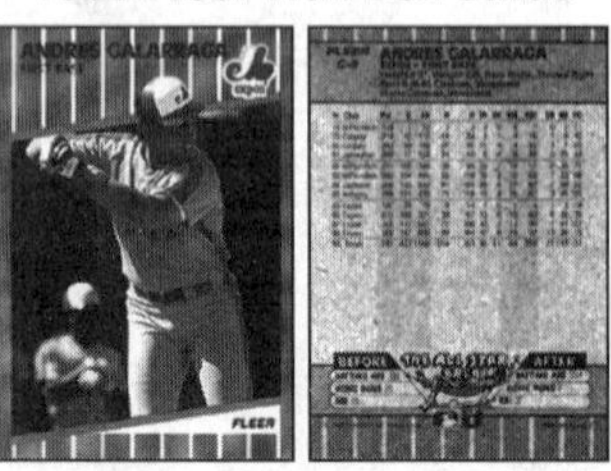

The cards in this 28-card set measure the standard 2 1/2" by 3 1/2". Cards have essentially the same design as the 1989 Fleer regular issue set. The cards were printed on the bottoms of the regular issue wax pack boxes. These 28 cards (C1 to C28) are considered a separate set in their own right and are not typically included in a complete set of the regular issue 1989 Fleer cards. The value of the panel uncut is slightly greater, perhaps by 25 percent greater, than the value of the individual cards cut up carefully. The wax box cards are further distinguished by the gray card stock used.

	MINT	NRMT	EXC
COMPLETE SET (28)	10.00	4.50	1.25
COMMON CARD (C1-C28)	.25	.11	.03
☐ C1 Mets Logo	.25	.11	.03
☐ C2 Wade Boggs	.75	.35	.09
☐ C3 George Brett	2.00	.90	.25
☐ C4 Jose Canseco UER ('88 strikeouts 121 and career strike- outs 49, should be 128 and 491)	1.00	.45	.12
☐ C5 A's Logo	.25	.11	.03
☐ C6 Will Clark	1.00	.45	.12
☐ C7 David Cone	.60	.25	.07
☐ C8 Andres Galarraga UER (Career average .289 should be .269)	.75	.35	.09
☐ C9 Dodgers Logo	.25	.11	.03
☐ C10 Kirk Gibson	.60	.25	.07
☐ C11 Mike Greenwell	.25	.11	.03
☐ C12 Tony Gwynn	2.50	1.10	.30
☐ C13 Tigers Logo	.25	.11	.03
☐ C14 Orel Hershiser	.40	.18	.05
☐ C15 Danny Jackson	.25	.11	.03
☐ C16 Wally Joyner	.40	.18	.05
☐ C17 Red Sox Logo	.25	.11	.03
☐ C18 Yankees Logo	.25	.11	.03
☐ C19 Fred McGriff UER (Career BA of .289 should be .269)	1.00	.45	.12
☐ C20 Kirby Puckett	2.50	1.10	.30
☐ C21 Chris Sabo	.25	.11	.03
☐ C22 Kevin Seitzer	.25	.11	.03
☐ C23 Pirates Logo	.25	.11	.03
☐ C24 Astros Logo	.25	.11	.03
☐ C25 Darryl Strawberry	.40	.18	.05
☐ C26 Alan Trammell	.40	.18	.05
☐ C27 Andy Van Slyke	.40	.18	.05
☐ C28 Frank Viola	.25	.11	.03

1989 Fleer World Series

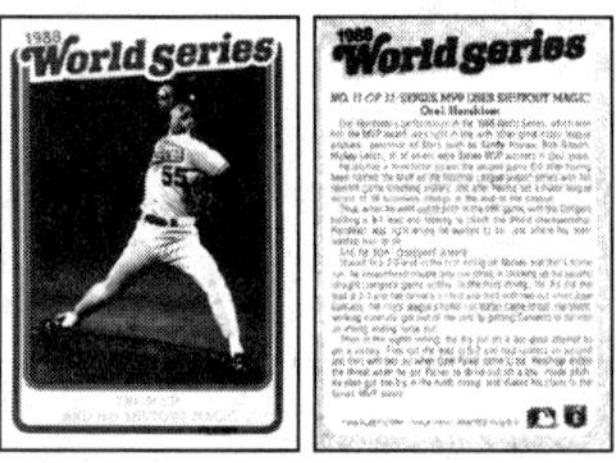

This 12-card standard-size set features highlights of the previous year's World Series between the Dodgers and the Athletics. The sets were packaged as a complete set insert with the collated sets (of the 1989 Fleer regular issue) which were sold by Fleer directly to hobby card dealers; they were not available in the general retail candy store outlets.

	MINT	NRMT	EXC
COMPLETE SET (12)	2.00	.90	.25
COMMON CARD (1-12)	.10	.05	.01
☐ 1 Mickey Hatcher Dodgers' Secret Weapon	.10	.05	.01
☐ 2 Tim Belcher Rookie Starts Series	.10	.05	.01
☐ 3 Jose Canseco Canseco Slams L.A.	.50	.23	.06
☐ 4 Mike Scioscia Dramatic Comeback	.10	.05	.01
☐ 5 Kirk Gibson Gibson Steals The Show	.50	.23	.06
☐ 6 Orel Hershiser Bulldog	.25	.11	.03
☐ 7 Mike Marshall One Swing, Three RBI's	.10	.05	.01
☐ 8 Mark McGwire Game-Winning Homer	.75	.35	.09
☐ 9 Steve Sax UER Sax's Speed Wins Game 4 (actually 42 steals in '88)	.10	.05	.01
☐ 10 Walt Weiss: Series Caps Award-Winning Year	.10	.05	.01
☐ 11 Orel Hershiser: Series MVP Uses Shutout Magic	.25	.11	.03
☐ 12 Dodger Blue, World Champs	.10	.05	.01

1989 Fleer Update

The 1989 Fleer Update set contains 132 standard-size cards. The cards were distributed exclusively in factory set form in grey and white, cellophane wrapped boxes through hobby dealers. The cards are identical in design to regular issue 1989 Fleer cards except for the U-prefixed numbering on back. The set numbering is in team order with players within teams ordered alphabetically. The set includes special cards for Nolan Ryan's 5,000th strikeout and Mike Schmidt's retirement. Rookie Cards include Kevin Appier, Joey (Albert) Belle, Deion Sanders, Greg Vaughn, Robin Ventura and Todd Zelle.

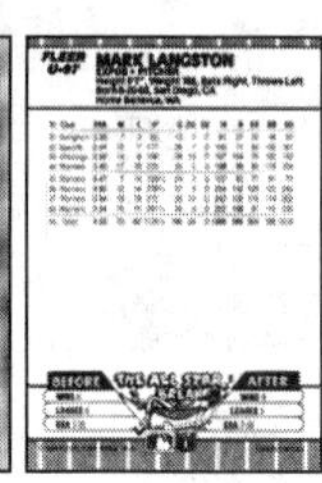

	MINT	NRMT	EXC
COMPLETE FACT.SET (132)	5.00	2.20	.60
COMMON CARD (1-132)	.05	.02	.01
☐ 1 Phil Bradley	.05	.02	.01
☐ 2 Mike Devereaux	.05	.02	.01
☐ 3 Steve Finley	.25	.11	.03
☐ 4 Kevin Hickey	.05	.02	.01
☐ 5 Brian Holton	.05	.02	.01
☐ 6 Bob Milacki	.05	.02	.01
☐ 7 Randy Milligan	.05	.02	.01
☐ 8 John Dopson	.05	.02	.01
☐ 9 Nick Esasky	.05	.02	.01
☐ 10 Rob Murphy	.05	.02	.01
☐ 11 Jim Abbott	.15	.07	.02
☐ 12 Bert Blyleven	.10	.05	.01
☐ 13 Jeff Manto	.05	.02	.01
☐ 14 Bob McClure	.05	.02	.01
☐ 15 Lance Parrish	.05	.02	.01
☐ 16 Lee Stevens	.10	.05	.01
☐ 17 Claudell Washington	.05	.02	.01
☐ 18 Mark Davis	.05	.02	.01
☐ 19 Eric King	.05	.02	.01
☐ 20 Ron Kittle	.05	.02	.01
☐ 21 Matt Merullo	.05	.02	.01
☐ 22 Steve Rosenberg	.05	.02	.01
☐ 23 Robin Ventura	.40	.18	.05
☐ 24 Keith Atherton	.05	.02	.01
☐ 25 Joey Belle	2.50	1.10	.30
☐ 26 Jerry Browne	.05	.02	.01
☐ 27 Felix Fermin	.05	.02	.01
☐ 28 Brad Komminsk	.05	.02	.01
☐ 29 Pete O'Brien	.05	.02	.01
☐ 30 Mike Brumley	.05	.02	.01
☐ 31 Tracy Jones	.05	.02	.01
☐ 32 Mike Schwabe	.05	.02	.01
☐ 33 Gary Ward	.05	.02	.01
☐ 34 Frank Williams	.05	.02	.01
☐ 35 Kevin Appier	.40	.18	.05
☐ 36 Bob Boone	.10	.05	.01
☐ 37 Luis DeLosSantos	.05	.02	.01
☐ 38 Jim Eisenreich	.10	.05	.01
☐ 39 Jaime Navarro	.15	.07	.02
☐ 40 Bill Spiers	.05	.02	.01
☐ 41 Greg Vaughn	.50	.23	.06
☐ 42 Randy Veres	.05	.02	.01
☐ 43 Wally Backman	.05	.02	.01
☐ 44 Shane Rawley	.05	.02	.01
☐ 45 Steve Balboni	.05	.02	.01
☐ 46 Jesse Barfield	.05	.02	.01
☐ 47 Alvaro Espinoza	.05	.02	.01
☐ 48 Bob Geren	.05	.02	.01
☐ 49 Mel Hall	.05	.02	.01
☐ 50 Andy Hawkins	.05	.02	.01
☐ 51 Hensley Meulens	.05	.02	.01
☐ 52 Steve Sax	.05	.02	.01
☐ 53 Deion Sanders	.75	.35	.09
☐ 54 Rickey Henderson	.15	.07	.02
☐ 55 Mike Moore	.05	.02	.01
☐ 56 Tony Phillips	.15	.07	.02
☐ 57 Greg Briley	.05	.02	.01
☐ 58 Gene Harris	.05	.02	.01
☐ 59 Randy Johnson	.75	.35	.09
☐ 60 Jeffrey Leonard	.05	.02	.01
☐ 61 Dennis Powell	.05	.02	.01
☐ 62 Omar Vizquel	.40	.18	.05
☐ 63 Kevin Brown	.15	.07	.02
☐ 64 Julio Franco	.10	.05	.01
☐ 65 Jamie Moyer	.05	.02	.01
☐ 66 Rafael Palmeiro	.15	.07	.02
☐ 67 Nolan Ryan	1.50	.70	.19
☐ 68 Francisco Cabrera	.15	.07	.02
☐ 69 Junior Felix	.05	.02	.01
☐ 70 Al Leiter	.10	.05	.01
☐ 71 Alex Sanchez	.05	.02	.01
☐ 72 Geronimo Berroa	.10	.05	.01
☐ 73 Derek Lilliquist	.05	.02	.01
☐ 74 Lonnie Smith	.05	.02	.01
☐ 75 Jeff Treadway	.05	.02	.01
☐ 76 Paul Kilgus	.05	.02	.01
☐ 77 Lloyd McClendon	.05	.02	.01
☐ 78 Scott Sanderson	.05	.02	.01
☐ 79 Dwight Smith	.10	.05	.01
☐ 80 Jerome Walton	.10	.05	.01
☐ 81 Mitch Williams	.05	.02	.01
☐ 82 Steve Wilson	.05	.02	.01
☐ 83 Todd Benzinger	.05	.02	.01
☐ 84 Ken Griffey Sr.	.05	.02	.01
☐ 85 Rick Mahler	.05	.02	.01
☐ 86 Rolando Roomes	.05	.02	.01
☐ 87 Scott Scudder	.05	.02	.01
☐ 88 Jim Clancy	.05	.02	.01

	MINT	NRMT	EXC
☐ 89 Rick Rhoden	.05	.02	.01
☐ 90 Dan Schatzeder	.05	.02	.01
☐ 91 Mike Morgan	.05	.02	.01
☐ 92 Eddie Murray	.25	.11	.03
☐ 93 Willie Randolph	.10	.05	.01
☐ 94 Ray Searage	.05	.02	.01
☐ 95 Mike Aldrete	.05	.02	.01
☐ 96 Kevin Gross	.05	.02	.01
☐ 97 Mark Langston	.10	.05	.01
☐ 98 Spike Owen	.05	.02	.01
☐ 99 Zane Smith	.05	.02	.01
☐ 100 Don Aase	.05	.02	.01
☐ 101 Barry Lyons	.05	.02	.01
☐ 102 Juan Samuel	.05	.02	.01
☐ 103 Wally Whitehurst	.05	.02	.01
☐ 104 Dennis Cook	.05	.02	.01
☐ 105 Len Dykstra	.10	.05	.01
☐ 106 Charlie Hayes	.15	.07	.02
☐ 107 Tommy Herr	.05	.02	.01
☐ 108 Ken Howell	.05	.02	.01
☐ 109 John Kruk	.10	.05	.01
☐ 110 Roger McDowell	.05	.02	.01
☐ 111 Terry Mulholland	.05	.02	.01
☐ 112 Jeff Parrett	.05	.02	.01
☐ 113 Neal Heaton	.05	.02	.01
☐ 114 Jeff King	.10	.05	.01
☐ 115 Randy Kramer	.05	.02	.01
☐ 116 Bill Landrum	.05	.02	.01
☐ 117 Cris Carpenter	.05	.02	.01
☐ 118 Frank DiPino	.05	.02	.01
☐ 119 Ken Hill	.50	.23	.06
☐ 120 Dan Quisenberry	.05	.02	.01
☐ 121 Milt Thompson	.05	.02	.01
☐ 122 Todd Zeile	.15	.07	.02
☐ 123 Jack Clark	.10	.05	.01
☐ 124 Bruce Hurst	.05	.02	.01
☐ 125 Mark Parent	.05	.02	.01
☐ 126 Bip Roberts	.10	.05	.01
☐ 127 Jeff Brantley UER (Photo actually Joe Kmak)	.05	.02	.01
☐ 128 Terry Kennedy	.05	.02	.01
☐ 129 Mike LaCoss	.05	.02	.01
☐ 130 Greg Litton	.05	.02	.01
☐ 131 Mike Schmidt	.50	.23	.06
☐ 132 Checklist 1-132	.05	.02	.01

1989 Fleer Baseball All-Stars

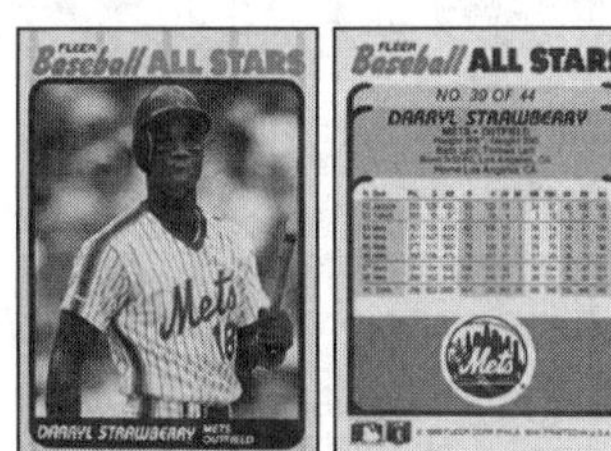

The 1989 Fleer Baseball All-Stars set contains 44 standard-size cards. The fronts are yellowish beige with salmon pinstripes; the vertically oriented backs are red, white and pink and feature career stats. The card numbering of this set is ordered alphabetically by player's name. The cards were distributed through Ben Franklin stores as a boxed set.

	MINT	NRMT	EXC
COMPLETE SET (44)	5.00	2.20	.60
COMMON CARD (1-44)	.05	.02	.01
☐ 1 Doyle Alexander	.05	.02	.01
☐ 2 George Bell	.05	.02	.01
☐ 3 Wade Boggs	.30	.14	.04
☐ 4 Bobby Bonilla	.20	.09	.03
☐ 5 Jose Canseco	.75	.35	.09
☐ 6 Will Clark	.75	.35	.09
☐ 7 Roger Clemens	.75	.35	.09
☐ 8 Vince Coleman	.05	.02	.01
☐ 9 David Cone	.40	.18	.05
☐ 10 Mark Davis	.05	.02	.01
☐ 11 Andre Dawson	.10	.05	.01
☐ 12 Dennis Eckersley	.10	.05	.01
☐ 13 Andres Galarraga	.20	.09	.03
☐ 14 Kirk Gibson	.20	.09	.03
☐ 15 Dwight Gooden	.10	.05	.01
☐ 16 Mike Greenwell	.05	.02	.01
☐ 17 Mark Gubicza	.05	.02	.01
☐ 18 Ozzie Guillen	.05	.02	.01
☐ 19 Tony Gwynn	1.00	.45	.12
☐ 20 Rickey Henderson	.50	.23	.06
☐ 21 Orel Hershiser	.20	.09	.03
☐ 22 Danny Jackson	.05	.02	.01
☐ 23 Doug Jones	.05	.02	.01
☐ 24 Ricky Jordan	.05	.02	.01
☐ 25 Bob Knepper	.05	.02	.01
☐ 26 Barry Larkin	.75	.35	.09
☐ 27 Vance Law	.05	.02	.01
☐ 28 Don Mattingly	1.00	.45	.12
☐ 29 Mark McGwire	.75	.35	.09
☐ 30 Paul Molitor	.50	.23	.06
☐ 31 Gerald Perry	.05	.02	.01
☐ 32 Kirby Puckett	1.00	.45	.12
☐ 33 Johnny Ray	.05	.02	.01
☐ 34 Harold Reynolds	.10	.05	.01
☐ 35 Cal Ripken	2.00	.90	.25
☐ 36 Don Robinson	.05	.02	.01
☐ 37 Ruben Sierra	.10	.05	.01
☐ 38 Dave Smith	.05	.02	.01
☐ 39 Darryl Strawberry	.10	.05	.01
☐ 40 Dave Stieb	.05	.02	.01
☐ 41 Alan Trammell	.10	.05	.01
☐ 42 Andy Van Slyke	.10	.05	.01
☐ 43 Frank Viola	.05	.02	.01
☐ 44 Dave Winfield	.50	.23	.06

1989 Fleer Baseball MVP's

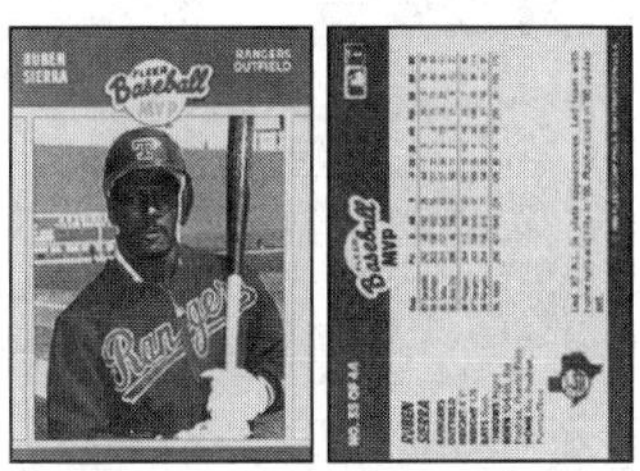

The 1989 Fleer Baseball MVP's set contains 44 standard-size cards. The fronts and backs are green and yellow. The horizontally oriented backs feature career stats. The card numbering of this set is ordered alphabetically by player's name. The cards were distributed through Toys 'R' Us stores as a boxed set.

	MINT	NRMT	EXC
COMPLETE SET (44)	6.00	2.70	.75
COMMON CARD (1-44)	.05	.02	.01
☐ 1 Steve Bedrosian	.05	.02	.01
☐ 2 George Bell	.05	.02	.01
☐ 3 Wade Boggs	.30	.14	.04
☐ 4 George Brett	.75	.35	.09
☐ 5 Hubie Brooks	.05	.02	.01
☐ 6 Jose Canseco	.60	.25	.07
☐ 7 Will Clark	.60	.25	.07
☐ 8 Roger Clemens	.60	.25	.07
☐ 9 Eric Davis	.05	.02	.01
☐ 10 Glenn Davis	.05	.02	.01
☐ 11 Andre Dawson	.10	.05	.01
☐ 12 Andres Galarraga	.20	.09	.03
☐ 13 Kirk Gibson	.20	.09	.03
☐ 14 Dwight Gooden	.10	.05	.01
☐ 15 Mark Grace	.75	.35	.09
☐ 16 Mike Greenwell	.05	.02	.01
☐ 17 Tony Gwynn	1.00	.45	.12
☐ 18 Bryan Harvey	.05	.02	.01
☐ 19 Orel Hershiser	.20	.09	.03
☐ 20 Ted Higuera	.05	.02	.01
☐ 21 Danny Jackson	.05	.02	.01
☐ 22 Mike Jackson	.05	.02	.01
☐ 23 Doug Jones	.05	.02	.01
☐ 24 Greg Maddux	2.00	.90	.25
☐ 25 Mike Marshall	.05	.02	.01
☐ 26 Don Mattingly	1.00	.45	.12
☐ 27 Fred McGriff	.60	.25	.07
☐ 28 Mark McGwire	.75	.35	.09
☐ 29 Kevin McReynolds	.05	.02	.01
☐ 30 Jack Morris	.10	.05	.01
☐ 31 Gerald Perry	.05	.02	.01
☐ 32 Kirby Puckett	1.00	.45	.12
☐ 33 Chris Sabo	.05	.02	.01
☐ 34 Mike Scott	.05	.02	.01
☐ 35 Ruben Sierra	.10	.05	.01
☐ 36 Darryl Strawberry	.10	.05	.01
☐ 37 Danny Tartabull	.05	.02	.01
☐ 38 Bobby Thigpen	.05	.02	.01
☐ 39 Alan Trammell	.10	.05	.01
☐ 40 Andy Van Slyke	.10	.05	.01
☐ 41 Frank Viola	.05	.02	.01
☐ 42 Walt Weiss	.05	.02	.01
☐ 43 Dave Winfield	.50	.23	.06
☐ 44 Todd Worrell	.05	.02	.01

1989 Fleer Exciting Stars

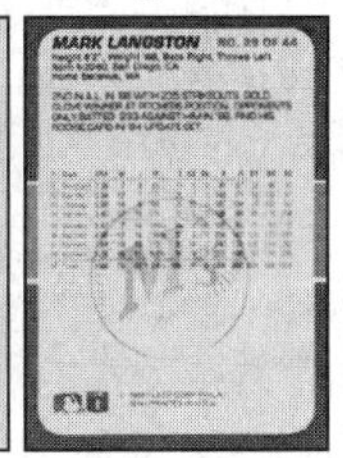

The 1989 Fleer Exciting Stars set contains 44 standard-size cards. The fronts have baby blue borders; the backs are pink and blue. The vertically oriented backs feature career stats. The card numbering of this set is ordered alphabetically by player's name. The cards were distributed as a boxed set.

	MINT	NRMT	EXC
COMPLETE SET (44)	5.00	2.20	.60
COMMON CARD (1-44)	.05	.02	.01
☐ 1 Harold Baines	.10	.05	.01
☐ 2 Wade Boggs	.30	.14	.04
☐ 3 Jose Canseco	.60	.25	.07
☐ 4 Joe Carter	.25	.11	.03
☐ 5 Will Clark	.60	.25	.07
☐ 6 Roger Clemens	.60	.25	.07
☐ 7 Vince Coleman	.05	.02	.01
☐ 8 David Cone	.40	.18	.05
☐ 9 Eric Davis	.05	.02	.01
☐ 10 Glenn Davis	.05	.02	.01
☐ 11 Andre Dawson	.10	.05	.01
☐ 12 Dwight Evans	.10	.05	.01
☐ 13 Andres Galarraga	.20	.09	.03
☐ 14 Kirk Gibson	.20	.09	.03
☐ 15 Dwight Gooden	.10	.05	.01
☐ 16 Jim Gott	.05	.02	.01
☐ 17 Mark Grace	.75	.35	.09
☐ 18 Mike Greenwell	.05	.02	.01
☐ 19 Mark Gubicza	.05	.02	.01
☐ 20 Tony Gwynn	1.00	.45	.12
☐ 21 Rickey Henderson	.50	.23	.06
☐ 22 Tom Henke	.05	.02	.01
☐ 23 Mike Henneman	.05	.02	.01
☐ 24 Orel Hershiser	.20	.09	.03
☐ 25 Danny Jackson	.05	.02	.01
☐ 26 Gregg Jefferies	.25	.11	.03
☐ 27 Ricky Jordan	.05	.02	.01
☐ 28 Wally Joyner	.10	.05	.01
☐ 29 Mark Langston	.05	.02	.01
☐ 30 Tim Leary	.05	.02	.01
☐ 31 Don Mattingly	1.00	.45	.12
☐ 32 Mark McGwire	.75	.35	.09
☐ 33 Dale Murphy	.20	.09	.03
☐ 34 Kirby Puckett	1.00	.45	.12
☐ 35 Chris Sabo	.05	.02	.01
☐ 36 Kevin Seitzer	.05	.02	.01
☐ 37 Ruben Sierra	.10	.05	.01
☐ 38 Ozzie Smith	1.00	.45	.12
☐ 39 Dave Stewart	.10	.05	.01
☐ 40 Darryl Strawberry	.10	.05	.01
☐ 41 Alan Trammell	.10	.05	.01
☐ 42 Frank Viola	.05	.02	.01
☐ 43 Dave Winfield	.30	.14	.04
☐ 44 Robin Yount	.50	.23	.06

1989 Fleer Heroes of Baseball

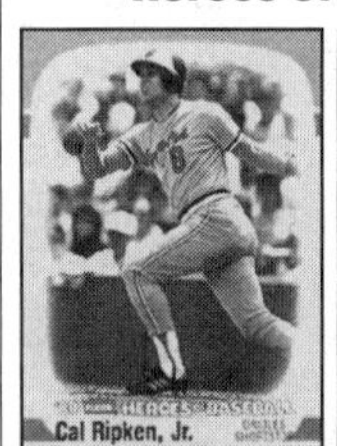

The 1989 Fleer Heroes of Baseball set contains 44 standard-size cards. The fronts and backs are red, white and blue. The vertically oriented backs feature career stats. The card numbering of this set is ordered alphabetically by player's name. The cards were distributed through Woolworth stores as a boxed set.

	MINT	NRMT	EXC
COMPLETE SET (44)	5.00	2.20	.60
COMMON CARD (1-44)	.05	.02	.01
☐ 1 George Bell	.05	.02	.01
☐ 2 Wade Boggs	.30	.14	.04
☐ 3 Barry Bonds	.75	.35	.09
☐ 4 Tom Brunansky	.05	.02	.01
☐ 5 Jose Canseco	.60	.25	.07
☐ 6 Joe Carter	.25	.11	.03
☐ 7 Will Clark	.60	.25	.07
☐ 8 Roger Clemens	.60	.25	.07
☐ 9 David Cone	.40	.18	.05
☐ 10 Eric Davis	.05	.02	.01
☐ 11 Glenn Davis	.05	.02	.01
☐ 12 Andre Dawson	.10	.05	.01
☐ 13 Dennis Eckersley	.10	.05	.01
☐ 14 John Franco	.10	.05	.01
☐ 15 Gary Gaetti	.05	.02	.01
☐ 16 Andres Galarraga	.20	.09	.03
☐ 17 Kirk Gibson	.20	.09	.03
☐ 18 Dwight Gooden	.10	.05	.01
☐ 19 Mike Greenwell	.05	.02	.01
☐ 20 Tony Gwynn	1.00	.45	.12
☐ 21 Bryan Harvey	.05	.02	.01
☐ 22 Orel Hershiser	.20	.09	.03
☐ 23 Ted Higuera	.05	.02	.01
☐ 24 Danny Jackson	.05	.02	.01
☐ 25 Ricky Jordan	.05	.02	.01
☐ 26 Don Mattingly	1.00	.45	.12
☐ 27 Fred McGriff	.60	.25	.07
☐ 28 Mark McGwire	.75	.35	.09
☐ 29 Kevin McReynolds	.05	.02	.01
☐ 30 Gerald Perry	.05	.02	.01
☐ 31 Kirby Puckett	1.00	.45	.12
☐ 32 Johnny Ray	.05	.02	.01
☐ 33 Harold Reynolds	.10	.05	.01
☐ 34 Cal Ripken	2.00	.90	.25
☐ 35 Ryne Sandberg	.75	.35	.09
☐ 36 Kevin Seitzer	.05	.02	.01
☐ 37 Ruben Sierra	.10	.05	.01
☐ 38 Darryl Strawberry	.10	.05	.01
☐ 39 Bobby Thigpen	.05	.02	.01
☐ 40 Alan Trammell	.10	.05	.01
☐ 41 Andy Van Slyke	.10	.05	.01
☐ 42 Frank Viola	.05	.02	.01
☐ 43 Dave Winfield	.50	.23	.06
☐ 44 Robin Yount	.25	.11	.03

1989 Fleer League Leaders

The 1989 Fleer League Leaders set contains 44 standard-size cards. The fronts are red and yellow; the horizontally oriented backs are light blue and red, and feature career stats. The card numbering of this set is ordered alphabetically by player's name. The cards were distributed through Woolworth stores as a boxed set.

	MINT	NRMT	EXC
COMPLETE SET (44)	5.00	2.20	.60
COMMON CARD (1-44)	.05	.02	.01
☐ 1 Allan Anderson	.05	.02	.01
☐ 2 Wade Boggs	.30	.14	.04
☐ 3 Jose Canseco	.60	.25	.07
☐ 4 Will Clark	.60	.25	.07
☐ 5 Roger Clemens	.60	.25	.07
☐ 6 Vince Coleman	.05	.02	.01
☐ 7 David Cone	.40	.18	.05
☐ 8 Kal Daniels	.05	.02	.01
☐ 9 Chili Davis	.10	.05	.01
☐ 10 Eric Davis	.05	.02	.01
☐ 11 Glenn Davis	.05	.02	.01
☐ 12 Andre Dawson	.10	.05	.01
☐ 13 John Franco	.10	.05	.01
☐ 14 Andres Galarraga	.20	.09	.03
☐ 15 Kirk Gibson	.20	.09	.03
☐ 16 Dwight Gooden	.10	.05	.01
☐ 17 Mark Grace	.75	.35	.09
☐ 18 Mike Greenwell	.05	.02	.01
☐ 19 Tony Gwynn	1.00	.45	.12
☐ 20 Orel Hershiser	.20	.09	.03
☐ 21 Pete Incaviglia	.05	.02	.01
☐ 22 Danny Jackson	.05	.02	.01
☐ 23 Gregg Jefferies	.25	.11	.03
☐ 24 Joe Magrane	.05	.02	.01
☐ 25 Don Mattingly	1.00	.45	.12
☐ 26 Fred McGriff	.60	.25	.07
☐ 27 Mark McGwire	.75	.35	.09
☐ 28 Dale Murphy	.20	.09	.03
☐ 29 Dan Plesac	.05	.02	.01
☐ 30 Kirby Puckett	1.00	.45	.12
☐ 31 Harold Reynolds	.10	.05	.01
☐ 32 Cal Ripken	2.00	.90	.25
☐ 33 Jeff M. Robinson	.05	.02	.01
☐ 34 Mike Scott	.05	.02	.01
☐ 35 Ozzie Smith	1.00	.45	.12
☐ 36 Dave Stewart	.10	.05	.01
☐ 37 Darryl Strawberry	.10	.05	.01
☐ 38 Greg Swindell	.05	.02	.01
☐ 39 Bobby Thigpen	.05	.02	.01
☐ 40 Alan Trammell	.10	.05	.01
☐ 41 Andy Van Slyke	.10	.05	.01
☐ 42 Frank Viola	.05	.02	.01
☐ 43 Dave Winfield	.50	.23	.06
☐ 44 Robin Yount	.50	.23	.06

1989 Fleer Superstars

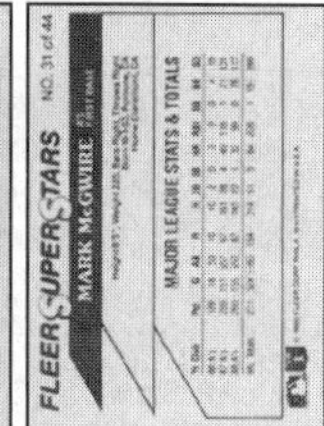

The 1989 Fleer Superstars set contains 44 standard-size cards. The fronts are red and beige; the horizontally oriented backs are yellow, and feature career stats. The card numbering of this set is ordered alphabetically by player's name. The cards were distributed as a boxed set. The back panel of the box contains the complete set checklist.

	MINT	NRMT	EXC
COMPLETE SET (44)	6.00	2.70	.75
COMMON CARD (1-44)	.05	.02	.01
☐ 1 Roberto Alomar	1.00	.45	.12
☐ 2 Harold Baines	.10	.05	.01
☐ 3 Tim Belcher	.05	.02	.01
☐ 4 Wade Boggs	.30	.14	.04
☐ 5 George Brett	.75	.35	.09
☐ 6 Jose Canseco	.60	.25	.07
☐ 7 Gary Carter	.10	.05	.01
☐ 8 Will Clark	.60	.25	.07
☐ 9 Roger Clemens	.60	.25	.07
☐ 10 Kal Daniels UER	.05	.02	.01
(Reverse negative photo on front)			
☐ 11 Eric Davis	.05	.02	.01
☐ 12 Andre Dawson	.10	.05	.01
☐ 13 Tony Fernandez	.05	.02	.01
☐ 14 Scott Fletcher	.05	.02	.01
☐ 15 Andres Galarraga	.20	.09	.03
☐ 16 Kirk Gibson	.20	.09	.03
☐ 17 Dwight Gooden	.10	.05	.01
☐ 18 Jim Gott	.05	.02	.01
☐ 19 Mark Grace	.75	.35	.09
☐ 20 Mike Greenwell	.05	.02	.01
☐ 21 Tony Gwynn	1.00	.45	.12
☐ 22 Rickey Henderson	.50	.23	.06
☐ 23 Orel Hershiser	.20	.09	.03
☐ 24 Ted Higuera	.05	.02	.01
☐ 25 Gregg Jefferies	.25	.11	.03
☐ 26 Wally Joyner	.10	.05	.01
☐ 27 Mark Langston	.05	.02	.01
☐ 28 Greg Maddux	2.00	.90	.25
☐ 29 Don Mattingly	1.00	.45	.12
☐ 30 Fred McGriff	.60	.25	.07
☐ 31 Mark McGwire	.75	.35	.09
☐ 32 Dan Plesac	.05	.02	.01
☐ 33 Kirby Puckett	1.00	.45	.12
☐ 34 Jeff Reardon	.05	.02	.01
☐ 35 Chris Sabo	.05	.02	.01
☐ 36 Mike Schmidt	.50	.23	.06
☐ 37 Mike Scott	.05	.02	.01
☐ 38 Cory Snyder	.05	.02	.01
☐ 39 Darryl Strawberry	.10	.05	.01
☐ 40 Alan Trammell	.10	.05	.01
☐ 41 Frank Viola	.05	.02	.01
☐ 42 Walt Weiss	.05	.02	.01
☐ 43 Dave Winfield	.50	.23	.06
☐ 44 Todd Worrell UER	.05	.02	.01
(Statistical headings on back for hitter)			

1990 Fleer

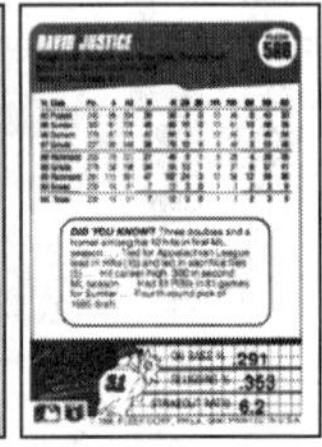

The 1990 Fleer set contains 660 standard-size cards. Cards were primarily issued in wax packs, rack packs and hobby and retail factory sets. Card fronts feature white outer borders with ribbon-like, colored inner borders. The set is again ordered numerically by teams based upon the previous season's record. Subsets include Decade Greats (621-630), Superstar Combinations (631-639), Rookie Prospects (640-653) and checklists (654-660). Rookie Cards of note include Moises Alou, Juan Gonzalez, Marquis Grissom, Dave Justice, Ben McDonald, Sammy Sosa, and Larry Walker.

	MINT	NRMT	EXC
COMPLETE SET (660)	8.00	3.60	1.00
COMPLETE RETAIL SET (660)	8.00	3.60	1.00
COMPLETE HOBBY SET (672)	10.00	4.50	1.25
COMMON CARD (1-660)	.05	.02	.01
☐ 1 Lance Blankenship	.05	.02	.01
☐ 2 Todd Burns	.05	.02	.01
☐ 3 Jose Canseco	.15	.07	.02
☐ 4 Jim Corsi	.05	.02	.01
☐ 5 Storm Davis	.05	.02	.01
☐ 6 Dennis Eckersley	.10	.05	.01
☐ 7 Mike Gallego	.05	.02	.01
☐ 8 Ron Hassey	.05	.02	.01
☐ 9 Dave Henderson	.05	.02	.01
☐ 10 Rickey Henderson	.15	.07	.02
☐ 11 Rick Honeycutt	.05	.02	.01
☐ 12 Stan Javier	.05	.02	.01
☐ 13 Felix Jose	.05	.02	.01
☐ 14 Carney Lansford	.10	.05	.01
☐ 15 Mark McGwire UER	.30	.14	.04
(1989 runs listed as 4, should be 74)			
☐ 16 Mike Moore	.05	.02	.01
☐ 17 Gene Nelson	.05	.02	.01
☐ 18 Dave Parker	.10	.05	.01
☐ 19 Tony Phillips	.15	.07	.02
☐ 20 Terry Steinbach	.10	.05	.01
☐ 21 Dave Stewart	.10	.05	.01
☐ 22 Walt Weiss	.05	.02	.01
☐ 23 Bob Welch	.05	.02	.01
☐ 24 Curt Young	.05	.02	.01
☐ 25 Paul Assenmacher	.05	.02	.01
☐ 26 Damon Berryhill	.05	.02	.01
☐ 27 Mike Bielecki	.05	.02	.01
☐ 28 Kevin Blankenship	.05	.02	.01
☐ 29 Andre Dawson	.10	.05	.01
☐ 30 Shawon Dunston	.05	.02	.01
☐ 31 Joe Girardi	.10	.05	.01
☐ 32 Mark Grace	.15	.07	.02
☐ 33 Mike Harkey	.05	.02	.01
☐ 34 Paul Kilgus	.05	.02	.01
☐ 35 Les Lancaster	.05	.02	.01
☐ 36 Vance Law	.05	.02	.01
☐ 37 Greg Maddux	.60	.25	.07
☐ 38 Lloyd McClendon	.05	.02	.01
☐ 39 Jeff Pico	.05	.02	.01
☐ 40 Ryne Sandberg	.25	.11	.03
☐ 41 Scott Sanderson	.05	.02	.01
☐ 42 Dwight Smith	.05	.02	.01
☐ 43 Rick Sutcliffe	.05	.02	.01
☐ 44 Jerome Walton	.05	.02	.01
☐ 45 Mitch Webster	.05	.02	.01
☐ 46 Curt Wilkerson	.05	.02	.01
☐ 47 Dean Wilkins	.05	.02	.01
☐ 48 Mitch Williams	.05	.02	.01
☐ 49 Steve Wilson	.05	.02	.01
☐ 50 Steve Bedrosian	.05	.02	.01
☐ 51 Mike Benjamin	.05	.02	.01
☐ 52 Jeff Brantley	.10	.05	.01
☐ 53 Brett Butler	.10	.05	.01
☐ 54 Will Clark UER	.15	.07	.02
(Did You Know says first in runs, should say tied for first)			
☐ 55 Kelly Downs	.05	.02	.01
☐ 56 Scott Garrelts	.05	.02	.01
☐ 57 Atlee Hammaker	.05	.02	.01
☐ 58 Terry Kennedy	.05	.02	.01
☐ 59 Mike LaCoss	.05	.02	.01
☐ 60 Craig Lefferts	.05	.02	.01
☐ 61 Greg Litton	.05	.02	.01
☐ 62 Candy Maldonado	.05	.02	.01
☐ 63 Kirt Manwaring UER	.05	.02	.01
(No '88 Phoenix stats as noted in box)			
☐ 64 Randy McCament	.05	.02	.01
☐ 65 Kevin Mitchell	.10	.05	.01
☐ 66 Donell Nixon	.05	.02	.01
☐ 67 Ken Oberkfell	.05	.02	.01
☐ 68 Rick Reuschel	.05	.02	.01
☐ 69 Ernest Riles	.05	.02	.01
☐ 70 Don Robinson	.05	.02	.01
☐ 71 Pat Sheridan	.05	.02	.01
☐ 72 Chris Speier	.05	.02	.01
☐ 73 Robby Thompson	.05	.02	.01
☐ 74 Jose Uribe	.05	.02	.01
☐ 75 Matt Williams	.15	.07	.02
☐ 76 George Bell	.05	.02	.01
☐ 77 Pat Borders	.05	.02	.01
☐ 78 John Cerutti	.05	.02	.01
☐ 79 Junior Felix	.05	.02	.01
☐ 80 Tony Fernandez	.05	.02	.01
☐ 81 Mike Flanagan	.05	.02	.01
☐ 82 Mauro Gozzo	.05	.02	.01
☐ 83 Kelly Gruber	.05	.02	.01
☐ 84 Tom Henke	.05	.02	.01
☐ 85 Jimmy Key	.10	.05	.01
☐ 86 Manny Lee	.05	.02	.01
☐ 87 Nelson Liriano UER	.05	.02	.01
(Should say "led the IL" instead of "led the TL")			
☐ 88 Lee Mazzilli	.05	.02	.01
☐ 89 Fred McGriff	.15	.07	.02
☐ 90 Lloyd Moseby	.05	.02	.01
☐ 91 Rance Mulliniks	.05	.02	.01
☐ 92 Alex Sanchez	.05	.02	.01
☐ 93 Dave Stieb	.05	.02	.01
☐ 94 Todd Stottlemyre	.10	.05	.01
☐ 95 Duane Ward UER	.05	.02	.01
(Double line of '87 Syracuse stats)			
☐ 96 David Wells	.05	.02	.01
☐ 97 Ernie Whitt	.05	.02	.01
☐ 98 Frank Wills	.05	.02	.01
☐ 99 Mookie Wilson	.05	.02	.01
☐ 100 Kevin Appier	.15	.07	.02
☐ 101 Luis Aquino	.05	.02	.01
☐ 102 Bob Boone	.10	.05	.01
☐ 103 George Brett	.40	.18	.05
☐ 104 Jose DeJesus	.05	.02	.01
☐ 105 Luis De Los Santos	.05	.02	.01
☐ 106 Jim Eisenreich	.05	.02	.01
☐ 107 Steve Farr	.05	.02	.01
☐ 108 Tom Gordon	.05	.02	.01
☐ 109 Mark Gubicza	.05	.02	.01
☐ 110 Bo Jackson	.10	.05	.01
☐ 111 Terry Leach	.05	.02	.01
☐ 112 Charlie Leibrandt	.05	.02	.01
☐ 113 Rick Luecken	.05	.02	.01
☐ 114 Mike Macfarlane	.05	.02	.01
☐ 115 Jeff Montgomery	.10	.05	.01
☐ 116 Bret Saberhagen	.10	.05	.01
☐ 117 Kevin Seitzer	.05	.02	.01
☐ 118 Kurt Stillwell	.05	.02	.01
☐ 119 Pat Tabler	.05	.02	.01
☐ 120 Danny Tartabull	.05	.02	.01
☐ 121 Gary Thurman	.05	.02	.01
☐ 122 Frank White	.10	.05	.01
☐ 123 Willie Wilson	.05	.02	.01
☐ 124 Matt Winters	.05	.02	.01
☐ 125 Jim Abbott	.10	.05	.01
☐ 126 Tony Armas	.05	.02	.01
☐ 127 Dante Bichette	.15	.07	.02
☐ 128 Bert Blyleven	.10	.05	.01
☐ 129 Chili Davis	.10	.05	.01
☐ 130 Brian Downing	.05	.02	.01
☐ 131 Mike Fetters	.10	.05	.01
☐ 132 Chuck Finley	.10	.05	.01
☐ 133 Willie Fraser	.05	.02	.01
☐ 134 Bryan Harvey	.05	.02	.01
☐ 135 Jack Howell	.05	.02	.01
☐ 136 Wally Joyner	.10	.05	.01
☐ 137 Jeff Manto	.05	.02	.01
☐ 138 Kirk McCaskill	.05	.02	.01
☐ 139 Bob McClure	.05	.02	.01
☐ 140 Greg Minton	.05	.02	.01
☐ 141 Lance Parrish	.05	.02	.01
☐ 142 Dan Petry	.05	.02	.01
☐ 143 Johnny Ray	.05	.02	.01
☐ 144 Dick Schofield	.05	.02	.01
☐ 145 Lee Stevens	.05	.02	.01
☐ 146 Claudell Washington	.05	.02	.01
☐ 147 Devon White	.10	.05	.01
☐ 148 Mike Witt	.05	.02	.01
☐ 149 Roberto Alomar	.25	.11	.03
☐ 150 Sandy Alomar Jr.	.15	.07	.02
☐ 151 Andy Benes	.15	.07	.02
☐ 152 Jack Clark	.10	.05	.01
☐ 153 Pat Clements	.05	.02	.01
☐ 154 Joey Cora	.10	.05	.01
☐ 155 Mark Davis	.05	.02	.01
☐ 156 Mark Grant	.05	.02	.01
☐ 157 Tony Gwynn	.40	.18	.05
☐ 158 Greg W. Harris	.05	.02	.01
☐ 159 Bruce Hurst	.05	.02	.01
☐ 160 Darrin Jackson	.05	.02	.01
☐ 161 Chris James	.05	.02	.01
☐ 162 Carmelo Martinez	.05	.02	.01
☐ 163 Mike Pagliarulo	.05	.02	.01
☐ 164 Mark Parent	.05	.02	.01
☐ 165 Dennis Rasmussen	.05	.02	.01
☐ 166 Bip Roberts	.05	.02	.01
☐ 167 Benito Santiago	.05	.02	.01
☐ 168 Calvin Schiraldi	.05	.02	.01
☐ 169 Eric Show	.05	.02	.01
☐ 170 Garry Templeton	.05	.02	.01
☐ 171 Ed Whitson	.05	.02	.01
☐ 172 Brady Anderson	.15	.07	.02
☐ 173 Jeff Ballard	.05	.02	.01
☐ 174 Phil Bradley	.05	.02	.01
☐ 175 Mike Devereaux	.05	.02	.01
☐ 176 Steve Finley	.15	.07	.02
☐ 177 Pete Harnisch	.05	.02	.01
☐ 178 Kevin Hickey	.05	.02	.01
☐ 179 Brian Holton	.05	.02	.01
☐ 180 Ben McDonald	.15	.07	.02
☐ 181 Bob Melvin	.05	.02	.01
☐ 182 Bob Milacki	.05	.02	.01
☐ 183 Randy Milligan UER	.05	.02	.01
(Double line of '87 stats)			
☐ 184 Gregg Olson	.05	.02	.01
☐ 185 Joe Orsulak	.05	.02	.01
☐ 186 Bill Ripken	.05	.02	.01
☐ 187 Cal Ripken	.75	.35	.09
☐ 188 Dave Schmidt	.05	.02	.01
☐ 189 Larry Sheets	.05	.02	.01
☐ 190 Mickey Tettleton	.10	.05	.01
☐ 191 Mark Thurmond	.05	.02	.01
☐ 192 Jay Tibbs	.05	.02	.01
☐ 193 Jim Traber	.05	.02	.01
☐ 194 Mark Williamson	.05	.02	.01
☐ 195 Craig Worthington	.05	.02	.01
☐ 196 Don Aase	.05	.02	.01
☐ 197 Blaine Beatty	.05	.02	.01
☐ 198 Mark Carreon	.05	.02	.01
☐ 199 Gary Carter	.10	.05	.01
☐ 200 David Cone	.15	.07	.02
☐ 201 Ron Darling	.05	.02	.01
☐ 202 Kevin Elster	.05	.02	.01
☐ 203 Sid Fernandez	.05	.02	.01
☐ 204 Dwight Gooden	.10	.05	.01
☐ 205 Keith Hernandez	.10	.05	.01
☐ 206 Jeff Innis	.05	.02	.01
☐ 207 Gregg Jefferies	.10	.05	.01
☐ 208 Howard Johnson	.05	.02	.01
☐ 209 Barry Lyons UER	.05	.02	.01
(Double line of '87 stats)			
☐ 210 Dave Magadan	.05	.02	.01
☐ 211 Kevin McReynolds	.05	.02	.01
☐ 212 Jeff Musselman	.05	.02	.01
☐ 213 Randy Myers	.10	.05	.01
☐ 214 Bob Ojeda	.05	.02	.01
☐ 215 Juan Samuel	.05	.02	.01
☐ 216 Mackey Sasser	.05	.02	.01
☐ 217 Darryl Strawberry	.10	.05	.01
☐ 218 Tim Teufel	.05	.02	.01
☐ 219 Frank Viola	.05	.02	.01
☐ 220 Juan Agosto	.05	.02	.01
☐ 221 Larry Andersen	.05	.02	.01
☐ 222 Eric Anthony	.10	.05	.01
☐ 223 Kevin Bass	.05	.02	.01
☐ 224 Craig Biggio	.15	.07	.02
☐ 225 Ken Caminiti	.20	.09	.03
☐ 226 Jim Clancy	.05	.02	.01
☐ 227 Danny Darwin	.05	.02	.01
☐ 228 Glenn Davis	.05	.02	.01
☐ 229 Jim Deshaies	.05	.02	.01
☐ 230 Bill Doran	.05	.02	.01
☐ 231 Bob Forsch	.05	.02	.01
☐ 232 Brian Meyer	.05	.02	.01
☐ 233 Terry Puhl	.05	.02	.01
☐ 234 Rafael Ramirez	.05	.02	.01
☐ 235 Rick Rhoden	.05	.02	.01
☐ 236 Dan Schatzeder	.05	.02	.01
☐ 237 Mike Scott	.05	.02	.01
☐ 238 Dave Smith	.05	.02	.01
☐ 239 Alex Trevino	.05	.02	.01
☐ 240 Glenn Wilson	.05	.02	.01
☐ 241 Gerald Young	.05	.02	.01
☐ 242 Tom Brunansky	.05	.02	.01
☐ 243 Cris Carpenter	.05	.02	.01
☐ 244 Alex Cole	.10	.05	.01
☐ 245 Vince Coleman	.05	.02	.01
☐ 246 John Costello	.05	.02	.01
☐ 247 Ken Dayley	.05	.02	.01
☐ 248 Jose DeLeon	.05	.02	.01
☐ 249 Frank DiPino	.05	.02	.01
☐ 250 Pedro Guerrero	.05	.02	.01
☐ 251 Ken Hill	.15	.07	.02
☐ 252 Joe Magrane	.05	.02	.01
☐ 253 Willie McGee UER	.05	.02	.01
(No decimal point before 353)			
☐ 254 John Morris	.05	.02	.01
☐ 255 Jose Oquendo	.05	.02	.01
☐ 256 Tony Pena	.05	.02	.01
☐ 257 Terry Pendleton	.10	.05	.01
☐ 258 Ted Power	.05	.02	.01
☐ 259 Dan Quisenberry	.05	.02	.01
☐ 260 Ozzie Smith	.25	.11	.03
☐ 261 Scott Terry	.05	.02	.01
☐ 262 Milt Thompson	.05	.02	.01
☐ 263 Denny Walling	.05	.02	.01
☐ 264 Todd Worrell	.05	.02	.01
☐ 265 Todd Zeile	.10	.05	.01
☐ 266 Marty Barrett	.05	.02	.01
☐ 267 Mike Boddicker	.05	.02	.01
☐ 268 Wade Boggs	.15	.07	.02
☐ 269 Ellis Burks	.15	.07	.02
☐ 270 Rick Cerone	.05	.02	.01
☐ 271 Roger Clemens	.20	.09	.03
☐ 272 John Dopson	.05	.02	.01
☐ 273 Nick Esasky	.05	.02	.01
☐ 274 Dwight Evans	.10	.05	.01
☐ 275 Wes Gardner	.05	.02	.01
☐ 276 Rich Gedman	.05	.02	.01
☐ 277 Mike Greenwell	.05	.02	.01
☐ 278 Danny Heep	.05	.02	.01
☐ 279 Eric Hetzel	.05	.02	.01
☐ 280 Dennis Lamp	.05	.02	.01
☐ 281 Rob Murphy UER	.05	.02	.01
('89 stats say Reds, should say Red Sox)			
☐ 282 Joe Price	.05	.02	.01
☐ 283 Carlos Quintana	.05	.02	.01
☐ 284 Jody Reed	.05	.02	.01
☐ 285 Luis Rivera	.05	.02	.01
☐ 286 Kevin Romine	.05	.02	.01
☐ 287 Lee Smith	.10	.05	.01
☐ 288 Mike Smithson	.05	.02	.01
☐ 289 Bob Stanley	.05	.02	.01
☐ 290 Harold Baines	.10	.05	.01
☐ 291 Kevin Brown	.15	.07	.02
☐ 292 Steve Buechele	.05	.02	.01
☐ 293 Scott Coolbaugh	.05	.02	.01
☐ 294 Jack Daugherty	.05	.02	.01
☐ 295 Cecil Espy	.05	.02	.01
☐ 296 Julio Franco	.10	.05	.01
☐ 297 Juan Gonzalez	2.00	.90	.25
☐ 298 Cecilio Guante	.05	.02	.01
☐ 299 Drew Hall	.05	.02	.01
☐ 300 Charlie Hough	.05	.02	.01
☐ 301 Pete Incaviglia	.05	.02	.01
☐ 302 Mike Jeffcoat	.05	.02	.01
☐ 303 Chad Kreuter	.05	.02	.01
☐ 304 Jeff Kunkel	.05	.02	.01
☐ 305 Rick Leach	.05	.02	.01
☐ 306 Fred Manrique	.05	.02	.01
☐ 307 Jamie Moyer	.05	.02	.01
☐ 308 Rafael Palmeiro	.15	.07	.02
☐ 309 Geno Petralli	.05	.02	.01
☐ 310 Kevin Reimer	.05	.02	.01
☐ 311 Kenny Rogers	.10	.05	.01
☐ 312 Jeff Russell	.05	.02	.01
☐ 313 Nolan Ryan	.75	.35	.09
☐ 314 Ruben Sierra	.10	.05	.01
☐ 315 Bobby Witt	.05	.02	.01
☐ 316 Chris Bosio	.05	.02	.01

☐ 317 Glenn Braggs UER .05 .02 .01
(Stats say 111 K's,
but bio says 117 K's)
☐ 318 Greg Brock .05 .02 .01
☐ 319 Chuck Crim .05 .02 .01
☐ 320 Rob Deer .05 .02 .01
☐ 321 Mike Felder .05 .02 .01
☐ 322 Tom Filer .05 .02 .01
☐ 323 Tony Fossas .05 .02 .01
☐ 324 Jim Gantner .05 .02 .01
☐ 325 Darryl Hamilton .10 .05 .01
☐ 326 Teddy Higuera .05 .02 .01
☐ 327 Mark Knudson .05 .02 .01
☐ 328 Bill Krueger UER .05 .02 .01
('86 stats missing)
☐ 329 Tim McIntosh .05 .02 .01
☐ 330 Paul Molitor .20 .09 .03
☐ 331 Jaime Navarro .05 .02 .01
☐ 332 Charlie O'Brien .05 .02 .01
☐ 333 Jeff Peterek .05 .02 .01
☐ 334 Dan Plesac .05 .02 .01
☐ 335 Jerry Reuss .05 .02 .01
☐ 336 Gary Sheffield UER .25 .11 .03
(Bio says played for
3 teams in '87, but
stats say in '88)
☐ 337 Bill Spiers .05 .02 .01
☐ 338 B.J. Surhoff .10 .05 .01
☐ 339 Greg Vaughn .15 .07 .02
☐ 340 Robin Yount .15 .07 .02
☐ 341 Hubie Brooks .05 .02 .01
☐ 342 Tim Burke .05 .02 .01
☐ 343 Mike Fitzgerald .05 .02 .01
☐ 344 Tom Foley .05 .02 .01
☐ 345 Andres Galarraga .15 .07 .02
☐ 346 Damaso Garcia .05 .02 .01
☐ 347 Marquis Grissom .50 .23 .06
☐ 348 Kevin Gross .05 .02 .01
☐ 349 Joe Hesketh .05 .02 .01
☐ 350 Jeff Huson .05 .02 .01
☐ 351 Wallace Johnson .05 .02 .01
☐ 352 Mark Langston .10 .05 .01
☐ 353A Dave Martinez 2.00 .90 .25
(Yellow on front)
☐ 353B Dave Martinez .05 .02 .01
(Red on front)
☐ 354 Dennis Martinez UER .10 .05 .01
('87 ERA is 616,
should be 6.16)
☐ 355 Andy McGaffigan .05 .02 .01
☐ 356 Otis Nixon .05 .02 .01
☐ 357 Spike Owen .05 .02 .01
☐ 358 Pascual Perez .05 .02 .01
☐ 359 Tim Raines .15 .07 .02
☐ 360 Nelson Santovenia .05 .02 .01
☐ 361 Bryn Smith .05 .02 .01
☐ 362 Zane Smith .05 .02 .01
☐ 363 Larry Walker .60 .25 .07
☐ 364 Tim Wallach .05 .02 .01
☐ 365 Rick Aguilera .10 .05 .01
☐ 366 Allan Anderson .05 .02 .01
☐ 367 Wally Backman .05 .02 .01
☐ 368 Doug Baker .05 .02 .01
☐ 369 Juan Berenguer .05 .02 .01
☐ 370 Randy Bush .05 .02 .01
☐ 371 Carmen Castillo .05 .02 .01
☐ 372 Mike Dyer .05 .02 .01
☐ 373 Gary Gaetti .10 .05 .01
☐ 374 Greg Gagne .05 .02 .01
☐ 375 Dan Gladden .05 .02 .01
☐ 376 German Gonzalez UER .05 .02 .01
(Bio says 31 saves in
'88, but stats say 30)
☐ 377 Brian Harper .05 .02 .01
☐ 378 Kent Hrbek .10 .05 .01
☐ 379 Gene Larkin .05 .02 .01
☐ 380 Tim Laudner UER .05 .02 .01
(No decimal point
before '85 BA of 238)
☐ 381 John Moses .05 .02 .01
☐ 382 Al Newman .05 .02 .01
☐ 383 Kirby Puckett .40 .18 .05
☐ 384 Shane Rawley .05 .02 .01
☐ 385 Jeff Reardon .10 .05 .01
☐ 386 Roy Smith .05 .02 .01
☐ 387 Gary Wayne .05 .02 .01
☐ 388 Dave West .05 .02 .01
☐ 389 Tim Belcher .05 .02 .01
☐ 390 Tim Crews UER .05 .02 .01
(Stats say 163 IP for
'83, but bio says 136)
☐ 391 Mike Davis .05 .02 .01
☐ 392 Rick Dempsey .05 .02 .01
☐ 393 Kirk Gibson .10 .05 .01
☐ 394 Jose Gonzalez .05 .02 .01
☐ 395 Alfredo Griffin .05 .02 .01
☐ 396 Jeff Hamilton .05 .02 .01
☐ 397 Lenny Harris .05 .02 .01
☐ 398 Mickey Hatcher .05 .02 .01
☐ 399 Orel Hershiser .10 .05 .01
☐ 400 Jay Howell .05 .02 .01
☐ 401 Mike Marshall .05 .02 .01
☐ 402 Ramon Martinez .15 .07 .02
☐ 403 Mike Morgan .05 .02 .01
☐ 404 Eddie Murray .25 .11 .03
☐ 405 Alejandro Pena .05 .02 .01
☐ 406 Willie Randolph .10 .05 .01
☐ 407 Mike Scioscia .05 .02 .01
☐ 408 Ray Searage .05 .02 .01
☐ 409 Fernando Valenzuela .10 .05 .01
☐ 410 Jose Vizcaino .15 .07 .02
☐ 411 John Wetteland .15 .07 .02
☐ 412 Jack Armstrong .05 .02 .01
☐ 413 Todd Benzinger UER .05 .02 .01
(Bio says .323 at
Pawtucket, but
stats say .321)
☐ 414 Tim Birtsas .05 .02 .01
☐ 415 Tom Browning .05 .02 .01
☐ 416 Norm Charlton .05 .02 .01
☐ 417 Eric Davis .10 .05 .01
☐ 418 Rob Dibble .05 .02 .01
☐ 419 John Franco .05 .02 .01
☐ 420 Ken Griffey Sr. .05 .02 .01
☐ 421 Chris Hammond .05 .02 .01
(No 1989 used for
"Did Not Play" stat,
actually did play for
Nashville in 1989)
☐ 422 Danny Jackson .05 .02 .01
☐ 423 Barry Larkin .15 .07 .02
☐ 424 Tim Leary .05 .02 .01
☐ 425 Rick Mahler .05 .02 .01
☐ 426 Joe Oliver .05 .02 .01
☐ 427 Paul O'Neill .10 .05 .01
☐ 428 Luis Quinones UER .05 .02 .01
('86-'88 stats are
omitted from card but
included in totals)
☐ 429 Jeff Reed .05 .02 .01
☐ 430 Jose Rijo .05 .02 .01
☐ 431 Ron Robinson .05 .02 .01
☐ 432 Rolando Roomes .05 .02 .01
☐ 433 Chris Sabo .05 .02 .01
☐ 434 Scott Scudder .05 .02 .01
☐ 435 Herm Winningham .05 .02 .01
☐ 436 Steve Balboni .05 .02 .01
☐ 437 Jesse Barfield .05 .02 .01
☐ 438 Mike Blowers .15 .07 .02
☐ 439 Tim Brookens .05 .02 .01
☐ 440 Greg Cadaret .05 .02 .01
☐ 441 Alvaro Espinoza UER .05 .02 .01
(Career games say
218, should be 219)
☐ 442 Bob Geren .05 .02 .01
☐ 443 Lee Guetterman .05 .02 .01
☐ 444 Mel Hall .05 .02 .01
☐ 445 Andy Hawkins .05 .02 .01
☐ 446 Roberto Kelly .10 .05 .01
☐ 447 Don Mattingly .50 .23 .06
☐ 448 Lance McCullers .05 .02 .01
☐ 449 Hensley Meulens .05 .02 .01
☐ 450 Dale Mohorcic .05 .02 .01
☐ 451 Clay Parker .05 .02 .01
☐ 452 Eric Plunk .05 .02 .01
☐ 453 Dave Righetti .05 .02 .01
☐ 454 Deion Sanders .20 .09 .03
☐ 455 Steve Sax .05 .02 .01
☐ 456 Don Slaught .05 .02 .01
☐ 457 Walt Terrell .05 .02 .01
☐ 458 Dave Winfield .15 .07 .02
☐ 459 Jay Bell .10 .05 .01
☐ 460 Rafael Belliard .05 .02 .01
☐ 461 Barry Bonds .25 .11 .03
☐ 462 Bobby Bonilla .10 .05 .01
☐ 463 Sid Bream .05 .02 .01
☐ 464 Benny Distefano .05 .02 .01
☐ 465 Doug Drabek .05 .02 .01
☐ 466 Jim Gott .05 .02 .01
☐ 467 Billy Hatcher UER .05 .02 .01
(.1 hits for Cubs
in 1984)
☐ 468 Neal Heaton .05 .02 .01
☐ 469 Jeff King .10 .05 .01
☐ 470 Bob Kipper .05 .02 .01
☐ 471 Randy Kramer .05 .02 .01
☐ 472 Bill Landrum .05 .02 .01
☐ 473 Mike LaValliere .05 .02 .01
☐ 474 Jose Lind .05 .02 .01
☐ 475 Junior Ortiz .05 .02 .01
☐ 476 Gary Redus .05 .02 .01
☐ 477 Rick Reed .05 .02 .01
☐ 478 R.J. Reynolds .05 .02 .01
☐ 479 Jeff D. Robinson .05 .02 .01
☐ 480 John Smiley .10 .05 .01
☐ 481 Andy Van Slyke .10 .05 .01
☐ 482 Bob Walk .05 .02 .01
☐ 483 Andy Allanson .05 .02 .01
☐ 484 Scott Bailes .05 .02 .01
☐ 485 Joey Belle UER .75 .35 .09
(Has Jay Bell
"Did You Know")
☐ 486 Bud Black .05 .02 .01
☐ 487 Jerry Browne .05 .02 .01
☐ 488 Tom Candiotti .05 .02 .01
☐ 489 Joe Carter .10 .05 .01
☐ 490 Dave Clark .05 .02 .01
(No '84 stats)
☐ 491 John Farrell .05 .02 .01
☐ 492 Felix Fermin .05 .02 .01
☐ 493 Brook Jacoby .05 .02 .01
☐ 494 Dion James .05 .02 .01
☐ 495 Doug Jones .05 .02 .01
☐ 496 Brad Komminsk .05 .02 .01
☐ 497 Rod Nichols .05 .02 .01
☐ 498 Pete O'Brien .05 .02 .01
☐ 499 Steve Olin .10 .05 .01
☐ 500 Jesse Orosco .05 .02 .01
☐ 501 Joel Skinner .05 .02 .01
☐ 502 Cory Snyder .05 .02 .01
☐ 503 Greg Swindell .05 .02 .01
☐ 504 Rich Yett .05 .02 .01
☐ 505 Scott Bankhead .05 .02 .01
☐ 506 Scott Bradley .05 .02 .01
☐ 507 Greg Briley UER .05 .02 .01
(28 SB's in bio,
but 27 in stats)
☐ 508 Jay Buhner .15 .07 .02
☐ 509 Darnell Coles .05 .02 .01
☐ 510 Keith Comstock .05 .02 .01
☐ 511 Henry Cotto .05 .02 .01
☐ 512 Alvin Davis .05 .02 .01
☐ 513 Ken Griffey Jr. 1.50 .70 .19
☐ 514 Erik Hanson .10 .05 .01
☐ 515 Gene Harris .05 .02 .01
☐ 516 Brian Holman .05 .02 .01
☐ 517 Mike Jackson .05 .02 .01
☐ 518 Randy Johnson .25 .11 .03
☐ 519 Jeffrey Leonard .05 .02 .01
☐ 520 Edgar Martinez .15 .07 .02
☐ 521 Dennis Powell .05 .02 .01
☐ 522 Jim Presley .05 .02 .01
☐ 523 Jerry Reed .05 .02 .01
☐ 524 Harold Reynolds .05 .02 .01
☐ 525 Mike Schooler .05 .02 .01
☐ 526 Bill Swift .05 .02 .01
☐ 527 Dave Valle .05 .02 .01
☐ 528 Omar Vizquel .15 .07 .02
☐ 529 Ivan Calderon .05 .02 .01
☐ 530 Carlton Fisk UER .15 .07 .02
(Bellow Falls, should
be Bellows Falls)
☐ 531 Scott Fletcher .05 .02 .01
☐ 532 Dave Gallagher .05 .02 .01
☐ 533 Ozzie Guillen .05 .02 .01
☐ 534 Greg Hibbard .05 .02 .01
☐ 535 Shawn Hillegas .05 .02 .01
☐ 536 Lance Johnson .10 .05 .01
☐ 537 Eric King .05 .02 .01
☐ 538 Ron Kittle .05 .02 .01
☐ 539 Steve Lyons .05 .02 .01
☐ 540 Carlos Martinez .05 .02 .01
☐ 541 Tom McCarthy .05 .02 .01
☐ 542 Matt Merullo .05 .02 .01
(Had 5 ML runs scored
entering '90, not 6)
☐ 543 Donn Pall UER .05 .02 .01
(Stats say pro career
began in '85,
bio says '88)
☐ 544 Dan Pasqua .05 .02 .01
☐ 545 Ken Patterson .05 .02 .01
☐ 546 Melido Perez .05 .02 .01
☐ 547 Steve Rosenberg .05 .02 .01
☐ 548 Sammy Sosa .75 .35 .09
☐ 549 Bobby Thigpen .05 .02 .01
☐ 550 Robin Ventura .15 .07 .02
☐ 551 Greg Walker .05 .02 .01
☐ 552 Don Carman .05 .02 .01
☐ 553 Pat Combs .05 .02 .01
(6 walks for Phillies
in '89 in stats,
brief bio says 4)
☐ 554 Dennis Cook .05 .02 .01
☐ 555 Darren Daulton .10 .05 .01
☐ 556 Len Dykstra .10 .05 .01
☐ 557 Curt Ford .05 .02 .01
☐ 558 Charlie Hayes .10 .05 .01
☐ 559 Von Hayes .05 .02 .01
☐ 560 Tommy Herr .05 .02 .01
☐ 561 Ken Howell .05 .02 .01
☐ 562 Steve Jeltz .05 .02 .01
☐ 563 Ron Jones .05 .02 .01
☐ 564 Ricky Jordan UER .05 .02 .01
(Duplicate line of
statistics on back)
☐ 565 John Kruk .10 .05 .01
☐ 566 Steve Lake .05 .02 .01
☐ 567 Roger McDowell .05 .02 .01
☐ 568 Terry Mulholland UER .05 .02 .01
(Did You Know refers
to Dave Magadan)
☐ 569 Dwayne Murphy .05 .02 .01
☐ 570 Jeff Parrett .05 .02 .01
☐ 571 Randy Ready .05 .02 .01
☐ 572 Bruce Ruffin .05 .02 .01
☐ 573 Dickie Thon .05 .02 .01
☐ 574 Jose Alvarez UER .05 .02 .01
('78 and '79 stats
are reversed)
☐ 575 Geronimo Berroa .10 .05 .01
☐ 576 Jeff Blauser .10 .05 .01
☐ 577 Joe Boever .05 .02 .01
☐ 578 Marty Clary UER .05 .02 .01
(No comma between
city and state)
☐ 579 Jody Davis .05 .02 .01
☐ 580 Mark Eichhorn .05 .02 .01
☐ 581 Darrell Evans .10 .05 .01
☐ 582 Ron Gant .15 .07 .02
☐ 583 Tom Glavine .15 .07 .02
☐ 584 Tommy Greene .05 .02 .01
☐ 585 Tommy Gregg .05 .02 .01
☐ 586 Dave Justice UER .50 .23 .06
(Actually had 16 2B
in Sumter in '86)
☐ 587 Mark Lemke .10 .05 .01
☐ 588 Derek Lilliquist .05 .02 .01
☐ 589 Oddibe McDowell .05 .02 .01
☐ 590 Kent Mercker ERA .10 .05 .01
(Bio says 2.75 ERA,
stats say 2.68 ERA)
☐ 591 Dale Murphy .15 .07 .02
☐ 592 Gerald Perry .05 .02 .01
☐ 593 Lonnie Smith .05 .02 .01
☐ 594 Pete Smith .05 .02 .01
☐ 595 John Smoltz .25 .11 .03
☐ 596 Mike Stanton UER .10 .05 .01
(No comma between
city and state)
☐ 597 Andres Thomas .05 .02 .01
☐ 598 Jeff Treadway .05 .02 .01
☐ 599 Doyle Alexander .05 .02 .01
☐ 600 Dave Bergman .05 .02 .01
☐ 601 Brian DuBois .05 .02 .01
☐ 602 Paul Gibson .05 .02 .01
☐ 603 Mike Heath .05 .02 .01
☐ 604 Mike Henneman .05 .02 .01
☐ 605 Guillermo Hernandez .05 .02 .01
☐ 606 Shawn Holman .05 .02 .01
☐ 607 Tracy Jones .05 .02 .01
☐ 608 Chet Lemon .05 .02 .01
☐ 609 Fred Lynn .05 .02 .01
☐ 610 Jack Morris .10 .05 .01
☐ 611 Matt Nokes .05 .02 .01
☐ 612 Gary Pettis .05 .02 .01
☐ 613 Kevin Ritz .05 .02 .01
☐ 614 Jeff M. Robinson .05 .02 .01
('88 stats are
not in line)
☐ 615 Steve Searcy .05 .02 .01
☐ 616 Frank Tanana .05 .02 .01
☐ 617 Alan Trammell .10 .05 .01
☐ 618 Gary Ward .05 .02 .01
☐ 619 Lou Whitaker .10 .05 .01
☐ 620 Frank Williams .05 .02 .01
☐ 621 George Brett '80 .20 .09 .03
COR
☐ 621A George Brett '80 1.50 .70 .19
ERR (Had 10 .390
hitting seasons)
☐ 622 Fern.Valenzuela '81 .10 .05 .01
☐ 623 Dale Murphy '82 .15 .07 .02
☐ 624A Cal Ripken '83 ERR 5.00 2.20 .60
(Misspelled Ripkin
on card back)
☐ 624B Cal Ripken '83 COR .40 .18 .05
☐ 625 Ryne Sandberg '84 .15 .07 .02
☐ 626 Don Mattingly '85 .25 .11 .03
☐ 627 Roger Clemens '86 .15 .07 .02
☐ 628 George Bell '87 .05 .02 .01
☐ 629 Jose Canseco '88 UER .15 .07 .02
(Reggie won MVP in
'83, should say '73)
☐ 630A Will Clark '89 ERR 1.00 .45 .12
(32 total bases
on card back)
☐ 630B Will Clark '89 COR .15 .07 .02
(321 total bases;
technically still
an error, listing
only 24 runs)
☐ 631 Game Savers .05 .02 .01
Mark Davis
Mitch Williams
☐ 632 Boston Igniters .15 .07 .02
Wade Boggs
Mike Greenwell
☐ 633 Starter and Stopper .05 .02 .01
Mark Gubicza
Jeff Russell
☐ 634 League's Best .25 .11 .03
Shortstops
Tony Fernandez
Cal Ripken
☐ 635 Human Dynamos .15 .07 .02
Kirby Puckett
Bo Jackson
☐ 636 300 Strikeout Club .25 .11 .03
Nolan Ryan
Mike Scott
☐ 637 The Dynamic Duo .10 .05 .01
Will Clark
Kevin Mitchell
☐ 638 AL All-Stars .30 .14 .04
Don Mattingly
Mark McGwire
☐ 639 NL East Rivals .15 .07 .02
Howard Johnson
Ryne Sandberg
☐ 640 Rudy Seanez .05 .02 .01

	MINT	NRMT	EXC
Colin Charland			
☐ 641 George Canale	.15	.07	.02
Kevin Maas UER (Canale listed as INF on front, 1B on back)			
☐ 642 Kelly Mann	.05	.02	.01
and Dave Hansen			
☐ 643 Greg Smith	.05	.02	.01
and Stu Tate			
☐ 644 Tom Drees	.05	.02	.01
and Dann Howitt			
☐ 645 Mike Roesler	.15	.07	.02
and Derrick May			
☐ 646 Scott Hemond	.05	.02	.01
and Mark Gardner			
☐ 647 John Orton	.05	.02	.01
and Scott Leius			
☐ 648 Rich Monteleone	.05	.02	.01
and Dana Williams			
☐ 649 Mike Huff	.05	.02	.01
and Steve Frey			
☐ 650 Chuck McElroy	.40	.18	.05
and Moises Alou			
☐ 651 Bobby Rose	.05	.02	.01
and Mike Hartley			
☐ 652 Matt Kinzer	.05	.02	.01
and Wayne Edwards			
☐ 653 Delino DeShields	.10	.05	.01
and Jason Grimsley			
☐ 654 CL: A's/Cubs	.05	.02	.01
Giants/Blue Jays			
☐ 655 CL: Royals/Angels	.05	.02	.01
Padres/Orioles			
☐ 656 CL: Mets/Astros	.05	.02	.01
Cards/Red Sox			
☐ 657 CL: Rangers/Brewers	.05	.02	.01
Expos/Twins			
☐ 658 CL: Dodgers/Reds	.05	.02	.01
Yankees/Pirates			
☐ 659 CL: Indians/Mariners	.05	.02	.01
White Sox/Phillies			
☐ 660A CL: Braves/Tigers	.05	.02	.01
Specials/Checklists (Checklist-660 in smaller print on card front)			
☐ 660B CL: Braves/Tigers	.05	.02	.01
Specials/Checklists (Checklist-660 in normal print on card front)			

1990 Fleer Canadian

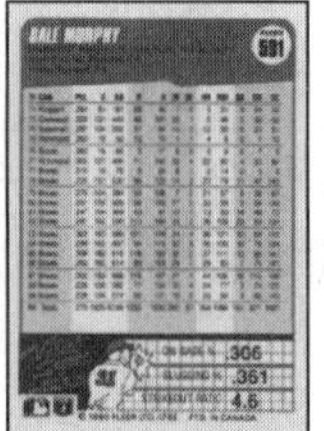

The 1990 Fleer Canadian set contains 660 standard-size cards. The cards were distributed in wax packs exclusively in Canada. The Canadian set differs from the U.S. version only in that it shows copyright "FLEER LTD./LTEE PTD. IN CANADA" on the card backs. Although these Canadian cards were undoubtedly produced in much lesser quantities compared to the U.S. issue, the fact that the versions are so similar has kept the demand down over the years.

	MINT	NRMT	EXC
COMPLETE SET (660)	75.00	34.00	9.50
COMMON CARD (1-660)	.15	.07	.02
STARS: 3X to 6X BASIC CARDS			
YOUNG STARS: 3X to 6X BASIC CARDS			

1990 Fleer All-Stars

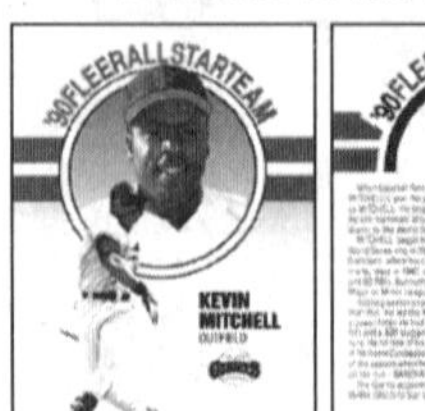

The 1990 Fleer All-Star insert set includes 12 standard-size cards. The set was randomly inserted in 33-card cellos and wax packs. The set is sequenced in alphabetical order. The fronts are white with a light gray screen and bright red stripes. The player selection for the set is Fleer's opinion of the best Major Leaguer at each position.

	MINT	NRMT	EXC
COMPLETE SET (12)	3.00	1.35	.35
COMMON CARD (1-12)	.15	.07	.02
☐ 1 Harold Baines	.30	.14	.04
☐ 2 Will Clark	.40	.18	.05
☐ 3 Mark Davis	.15	.07	.02
☐ 4 Howard Johnson UER	.15	.07	.02
(In middle of 5th line, the is misspelled th)			
☐ 5 Joe Magrane	.15	.07	.02
☐ 6 Kevin Mitchell	.30	.14	.04
☐ 7 Kirby Puckett	1.00	.45	.12
☐ 8 Cal Ripken	2.00	.90	.25
☐ 9 Ryne Sandberg	.60	.25	.07
☐ 10 Mike Scott UER	.15	.07	.02
Astros spelled Asatros on back			
☐ 11 Ruben Sierra	.30	.14	.04
☐ 12 Mickey Tettleton	.30	.14	.04

1990 Fleer League Standouts

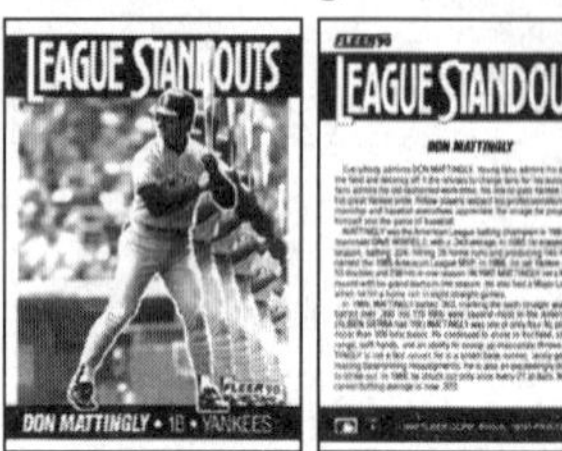

This six-card standard-size insert set was distributed one per 45-card rack pack. The set is subtitled "Standouts" and commemorates outstanding events for those players from the previous season.

	MINT	NRMT	EXC
COMPLETE SET (6)	6.00	2.70	.75
COMMON CARD (1-6)	.50	.23	.06
☐ 1 Barry Larkin	1.00	.45	.12
☐ 2 Don Mattingly	3.00	1.35	.35
☐ 3 Darryl Strawberry	.50	.23	.06
☐ 4 Jose Canseco	1.00	.45	.12
☐ 5 Wade Boggs	.75	.35	.09
☐ 6 Mark Grace UER	.75	.35	.09
(Chris Sabo misspelled as Cris)			

1990 Fleer Soaring Stars

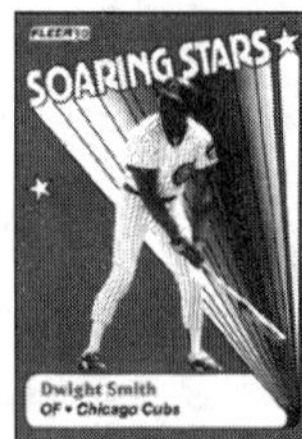

The 1990 Fleer Soaring Stars set was issued exclusively in jumbo cello packs. This 12-card, standard-size set features some of the most popular young players entering the 1990 season. The set gives the visual impression of rockets exploding in the air to honor these young players.

	MINT	NRMT	EXC
COMPLETE SET (12)	25.00	11.00	3.10
COMMON CARD (1-12)	.50	.23	.06
☐ 1 Todd Zeile	.75	.35	.09
☐ 2 Mike Stanton	.50	.23	.06
☐ 3 Larry Walker	5.00	2.20	.60
☐ 4 Robin Ventura	1.50	.70	.19
☐ 5 Scott Coolbaugh	.50	.23	.06
☐ 6 Ken Griffey Jr.	20.00	9.00	2.50
☐ 7 Tom Gordon	.50	.23	.06
☐ 8 Jerome Walton	.50	.23	.06
☐ 9 Junior Felix	.50	.23	.06
☐ 10 Jim Abbott	.75	.35	.09
☐ 11 Ricky Jordan	.50	.23	.06
☐ 12 Dwight Smith	.50	.23	.06

1990 Fleer Wax Box Cards

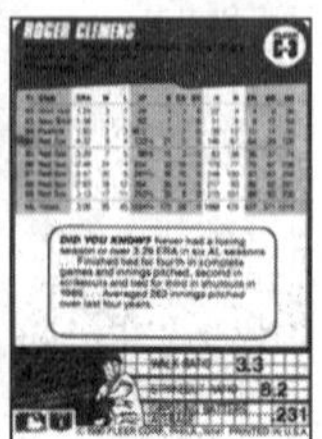

The 1990 Fleer wax box cards comprise seven different box bottoms with four cards each, for a total of 28 standard-size cards. The outer front borders are white; the inner, ribbon-like borders are different depending on the team. The vertically oriented backs are gray. The cards are numbered with a "C" prefix.

	MINT	NRMT	EXC
COMPLETE SET (28)	12.00	5.50	1.50
COMMON CARD (C1-C28)	.15	.07	.02
☐ C1 Giants Logo	.15	.07	.02
☐ C2 Tim Belcher	.15	.07	.02
☐ C3 Roger Clemens	.50	.23	.06
☐ C4 Eric Davis	.15	.07	.02
☐ C5 Glenn Davis	.15	.07	.02
☐ C6 Cubs Logo	.15	.07	.02
☐ C7 John Franco	.25	.11	.03
☐ C8 Mike Greenwell	.15	.07	.02
☐ C9 A's Logo	.15	.07	.02
☐ C10 Ken Griffey Jr.	3.00	1.35	.35
☐ C11 Pedro Guerrero	.15	.07	.02
☐ C12 Tony Gwynn	1.25	.55	.16
☐ C13 Blue Jays Logo	.15	.07	.02
☐ C14 Orel Hershiser	.25	.11	.03
☐ C15 Bo Jackson	.25	.11	.03
☐ C16 Howard Johnson	.15	.07	.02
☐ C17 Mets Logo	.15	.07	.02
☐ C18 Cardinals Logo	.15	.07	.02
☐ C19 Don Mattingly	1.50	.70	.19
☐ C20 Mark McGwire	1.00	.45	.12
☐ C21 Kevin Mitchell	.15	.07	.02
☐ C22 Kirby Puckett	1.25	.55	.16
☐ C23 Royals Logo	.15	.07	.02
☐ C24 Orioles Logo	.15	.07	.02
☐ C25 Ruben Sierra	.25	.11	.03
☐ C26 Dave Stewart	.25	.11	.03
☐ C27 Jerome Walton	.15	.07	.02
☐ C28 Robin Yount	.40	.18	.05

1990 Fleer World Series

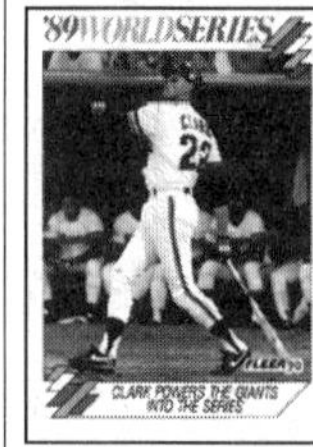

This 12-card standard-size set was issued as an insert in with the Fleer factory sets, celebrating the 1989 World Series. This set marked the fourth year that Fleer issued a special World Series set in their factory (or vend) set. The design of these cards are different from the regular Fleer issue as the photo is framed by a white border with red and blue World Series cards and the player description in black.

	MINT	NRMT	EXC
COMPLETE SET (12)	1.00	.45	.12
COMMON CARD (1-12)	.05	.02	.01
☐ 1 Mike Moore	.05	.02	.01
Final piece of puzzle			
☐ 2 Kevin Mitchell	.05	.02	.01
NL MVP			
☐ 3 Terry Steinbach	.05	.02	.01
Game Two's Crushing Blow			
☐ 4 Will Clark	.25	.11	.03
Powers Giants into Series			
☐ 5 Jose Canseco	.25	.11	.03
Canseco Crushed; WS Slump			
☐ 6 Walt Weiss	.05	.02	.01
Great Leather in the field			
☐ 7 Terry Steinbach: Game 1	.05	.02	.01
and A's Break Out on Top			
☐ 8 Dave Stewart	.05	.02	.01
Oakland's MVP			
☐ 9 Dave Parker	.10	.05	.01
Parker's Bat Produces Power			
☐ 10 Dave Parker	.25	.11	.03
Jose Canseco, Will Clark, WS record Book Game 3			
☐ 11 Rickey Henderson Swipes	.25	.11	.03
Championship Series Records			
☐ 12 Oakland A's Celebrate	.10	.05	.01
Baseball's Best in 89			

1990 Fleer Update

The 1990 Fleer Update set contains 132 standard-size cards. This set marked the seventh consecutive year Fleer issued an end of season Update set. The set was issued exclusively as a boxed set through hobby dealers. The set is checklisted alphabetically by team for each league and then alphabetically within each team. The fronts are styled the same as the 1990 Fleer regular issue set. The backs are numbered with the prefix "U" for Update. Rookie Cards in this set include Carlos Baerga, Alex Fernandez, Travis Fryman, Todd Hundley and Frank Thomas.

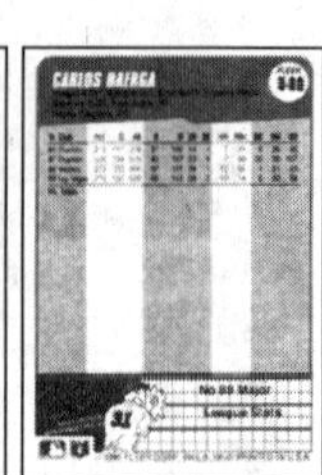

	MINT	NRMT	EXC
COMPLETE FACT.SET (132)	5.00	2.20	.60
COMMON CARD (1-132)	.05	.02	.01
☐ 1 Steve Avery	.15	.07	.02
☐ 2 Francisco Cabrera	.05	.02	.01
☐ 3 Nick Esasky	.05	.02	.01
☐ 4 Jim Kremers	.05	.02	.01
☐ 5 Greg Olson	.05	.02	.01
☐ 6 Jim Presley	.05	.02	.01
☐ 7 Shawn Boskie	.05	.02	.01
☐ 8 Joe Kraemer	.05	.02	.01
☐ 9 Luis Salazar	.05	.02	.01
☐ 10 Hector Villanueva	.05	.02	.01
☐ 11 Glenn Braggs	.05	.02	.01
☐ 12 Mariano Duncan	.05	.02	.01
☐ 13 Billy Hatcher	.05	.02	.01
☐ 14 Tim Layana	.05	.02	.01
☐ 15 Hal Morris	.10	.05	.01
☐ 16 Javier Ortiz	.05	.02	.01
☐ 17 Dave Rohde	.05	.02	.01
☐ 18 Eric Yelding	.05	.02	.01
☐ 19 Hubie Brooks	.05	.02	.01
☐ 20 Kal Daniels	.05	.02	.01
☐ 21 Dave Hansen	.05	.02	.01
☐ 22 Mike Hartley	.05	.02	.01
☐ 23 Stan Javier	.05	.02	.01
☐ 24 Jose Offerman	.10	.05	.01
☐ 25 Juan Samuel	.05	.02	.01
☐ 26 Dennis Boyd	.05	.02	.01
☐ 27 Delino DeShields	.10	.05	.01
☐ 28 Steve Frey	.05	.02	.01
☐ 29 Mark Gardner	.05	.02	.01
☐ 30 Chris Nabholz	.05	.02	.01
☐ 31 Bill Sampen	.05	.02	.01
☐ 32 Dave Schmidt	.05	.02	.01
☐ 33 Daryl Boston	.05	.02	.01
☐ 34 Chuck Carr	.15	.07	.02
☐ 35 John Franco	.05	.02	.01
☐ 36 Todd Hundley	.60	.25	.07
☐ 37 Julio Machado	.05	.02	.01
☐ 38 Alejandro Pena	.05	.02	.01
☐ 39 Darren Reed	.05	.02	.01
☐ 40 Kelvin Torve	.05	.02	.01
☐ 41 Darrel Akerfelds	.05	.02	.01
☐ 42 Jose DeJesus	.05	.02	.01
☐ 43 Dave Hollins UER	.15	.07	.02
(Misspelled Dane on card back)			
☐ 44 Carmelo Martinez	.05	.02	.01
☐ 45 Brad Moore	.05	.02	.01
☐ 46 Dale Murphy	.15	.07	.02
☐ 47 Wally Backman	.05	.02	.01
☐ 48 Stan Belinda	.05	.02	.01
☐ 49 Bob Patterson	.05	.02	.01
☐ 50 Ted Power	.05	.02	.01
☐ 51 Don Slaught	.05	.02	.01
☐ 52 Geronimo Pena	.05	.02	.01
☐ 53 Lee Smith	.10	.05	.01
☐ 54 John Tudor	.05	.02	.01
☐ 55 Joe Carter	.10	.05	.01
☐ 56 Thomas Howard	.05	.02	.01
☐ 57 Craig Lefferts	.05	.02	.01
☐ 58 Rafael Valdez	.05	.02	.01
☐ 59 Dave Anderson	.05	.02	.01
☐ 60 Kevin Bass	.05	.02	.01
☐ 61 John Burkett	.10	.05	.01
☐ 62 Gary Carter	.10	.05	.01
☐ 63 Rick Parker	.05	.02	.01
☐ 64 Trevor Wilson	.05	.02	.01
☐ 65 Chris Hoiles	.15	.07	.02
☐ 66 Tim Hulett	.05	.02	.01
☐ 67 Dave Johnson	.05	.02	.01
☐ 68 Curt Schilling	.05	.02	.01
☐ 69 David Segui	.15	.07	.02
☐ 70 Tom Brunansky	.05	.02	.01
☐ 71 Greg A. Harris	.05	.02	.01
☐ 72 Dana Kiecker	.05	.02	.01
☐ 73 Tim Naehring	.15	.07	.02
☐ 74 Tony Pena	.05	.02	.01
☐ 75 Jeff Reardon	.10	.05	.01
☐ 76 Jerry Reed	.05	.02	.01
☐ 77 Mark Eichhorn	.05	.02	.01
☐ 78 Mark Langston	.10	.05	.01
☐ 79 John Orton	.05	.02	.01
☐ 80 Luis Polonia	.05	.02	.01
☐ 81 Dave Winfield	.15	.07	.02
☐ 82 Cliff Young	.05	.02	.01
☐ 83 Wayne Edwards	.05	.02	.01
☐ 84 Alex Fernandez	.60	.25	.07
☐ 85 Craig Grebeck	.05	.02	.01
☐ 86 Scott Radinsky	.05	.02	.01
☐ 87 Frank Thomas	4.00	1.80	.50
☐ 88 Beau Allred	.05	.02	.01
☐ 89 Sandy Alomar Jr.	.15	.07	.02
☐ 90 Carlos Baerga	.30	.14	.04
☐ 91 Kevin Bearse	.05	.02	.01
☐ 92 Chris James	.05	.02	.01
☐ 93 Candy Maldonado	.05	.02	.01
☐ 94 Jeff Manto	.05	.02	.01

	MINT	NRMT	EXC
☐ 95 Cecil Fielder	.10	.05	.01
☐ 96 Travis Fryman	.40	.18	.05
☐ 97 Lloyd Moseby	.05	.02	.01
☐ 98 Edwin Nunez	.05	.02	.01
☐ 99 Tony Phillips	.15	.07	.02
☐ 100 Larry Sheets	.05	.02	.01
☐ 101 Mark Davis	.05	.02	.01
☐ 102 Storm Davis	.05	.02	.01
☐ 103 Gerald Perry	.05	.02	.01
☐ 104 Terry Shumpert	.05	.02	.01
☐ 105 Edgar Diaz	.05	.02	.01
☐ 106 Dave Parker	.10	.05	.01
☐ 107 Tim Drummond	.05	.02	.01
☐ 108 Junior Ortiz	.05	.02	.01
☐ 109 Park Pittman	.05	.02	.01
☐ 110 Kevin Tapani	.10	.05	.01
☐ 111 Oscar Azocar	.05	.02	.01
☐ 112 Jim Leyritz	.15	.07	.02
☐ 113 Kevin Maas	.05	.02	.01
☐ 114 Alan Mills	.05	.02	.01
☐ 115 Matt Nokes	.05	.02	.01
☐ 116 Pascual Perez	.05	.02	.01
☐ 117 Ozzie Canseco	.05	.02	.01
☐ 118 Scott Sanderson	.05	.02	.01
☐ 119 Tino Martinez	.15	.07	.02
☐ 120 Jeff Schaefer	.05	.02	.01
☐ 121 Matt Young	.05	.02	.01
☐ 122 Brian Bohanon	.05	.02	.01
☐ 123 Jeff Huson	.05	.02	.01
☐ 124 Ramon Manon	.05	.02	.01
☐ 125 Gary Mielke UER (Shown as Blue Jay on front)	.05	.02	.01
☐ 126 Willie Blair	.05	.02	.01
☐ 127 Glenallen Hill	.10	.05	.01
☐ 128 John Olerud UER (Listed as throwing right, should be left)	.15	.07	.02
☐ 129 Luis Sojo	.05	.02	.01
☐ 130 Mark Whiten	.15	.07	.02
☐ 131 Nolan Ryan	.75	.35	.09
☐ 132 Checklist U1-U132	.05	.02	.01

1990 Fleer Award Winners

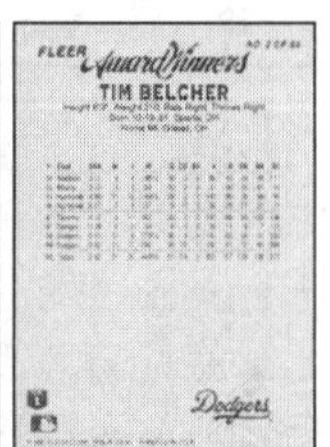

The 1990 Fleer Award Winners set was printed by Fleer for Hills stores (as well as for some 7/Eleven's) and released early in the summer of 1990. The set features a player photo within a trophy design with the player's name, team and position at the base. This 44-card standard-size set is numbered in alphabetical order, although Will Clark erroneously precedes Jack Clark. Card number 10 is listed on the box checklist as being Ron Darling, but Darling is not in the set. Consequently the numbers on the box checklist between 10 and 37 are off by one. Darryl Strawberry (38) is not listed on the box, but is included in the set. The box also includes six peel-off team logo stickers. The original suggested retail price for the set at Hills was 2.49.

	MINT	NRMT	EXC
COMPLETE SET (44)	6.00	2.70	.75
COMMON CARD (1-44)	.05	.02	.01
☐ 1 Jeff Ballard	.05	.02	.01
☐ 2 Tim Belcher	.05	.02	.01
☐ 3 Bert Blyleven	.10	.05	.01
☐ 4 Wade Boggs	.30	.14	.04
☐ 5 Bob Boone	.10	.05	.01
☐ 6 Jose Canseco	.75	.35	.09
☐ 7 Will Clark	.75	.35	.09
☐ 8 Jack Clark	.10	.05	.01
☐ 9 Vince Coleman	.05	.02	.01
☐ 10 Eric Davis	.05	.02	.01
☐ 11 Jose DeLeon	.05	.02	.01
☐ 12 Tony Fernandez	.05	.02	.01
☐ 13 Carlton Fisk	.50	.23	.06
☐ 14 Scott Garrelts	.05	.02	.01
☐ 15 Tom Gordon	.05	.02	.01
☐ 16 Ken Griffey Jr.	3.00	1.35	.35
☐ 17 Von Hayes	.05	.02	.01
☐ 18 Rickey Henderson	.50	.23	.06
☐ 19 Bo Jackson	.25	.11	.03
☐ 20 Howard Johnson	.05	.02	.01
☐ 21 Don Mattingly	1.50	.70	.19
☐ 22 Fred McGriff	.60	.25	.07
☐ 23 Kevin Mitchell	.05	.02	.01
☐ 24 Gregg Olson	.05	.02	.01
☐ 25 Gary Pettis	.05	.02	.01
☐ 26 Kirby Puckett	1.50	.70	.19
☐ 27 Harold Reynolds	.10	.05	.01
☐ 28 Jeff Russell	.05	.02	.01
☐ 29 Nolan Ryan	2.00	.90	.25
☐ 30 Bret Saberhagen	.10	.05	.01
☐ 31 Ryne Sandberg	1.50	.70	.19
☐ 32 Benito Santiago	.05	.02	.01
☐ 33 Mike Scott	.05	.02	.01
☐ 34 Ruben Sierra	.15	.07	.02
☐ 35 Lonnie Smith	.05	.02	.01
☐ 36 Ozzie Smith	1.50	.70	.19
☐ 37 Dave Stewart	.10	.05	.01
☐ 38 Darryl Strawberry	.10	.05	.01
☐ 39 Greg Swindell	.05	.02	.01
☐ 40 Andy Van Slyke	.10	.05	.01
☐ 41 Tim Wallach	.05	.02	.01
☐ 42 Jerome Walton	.05	.02	.01
☐ 43 Mitch Williams	.05	.02	.01
☐ 44 Robin Yount	.50	.23	.06

1990 Fleer Baseball All-Stars

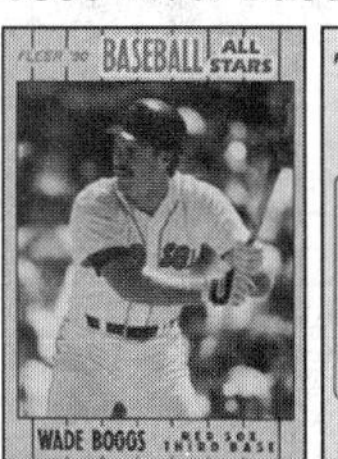

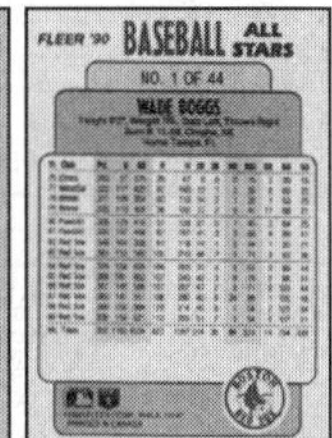

The 1990 Fleer Baseball All-Stars Set was produced by Fleer for the Ben Franklin chain and released early in the summer of 1990. This standard-size 44-card set features some of the best of today's players in alphabetical order. The design of the cards has vertical stripes on the front of the card. The set's custom box gives the set checklist on the back panel. The box also includes six peel-off team logo stickers each with a trivia quiz on back.

	MINT	NRMT	EXC
COMPLETE SET (44)	6.00	2.70	.75
COMMON CARD (1-44)	.05	.02	.01
☐ 1 Wade Boggs	.30	.14	.04
☐ 2 Bobby Bonilla	.10	.05	.01
☐ 3 Tim Burke	.05	.02	.01
☐ 4 Jose Canseco	.60	.25	.07
☐ 5 Will Clark	.60	.25	.07
☐ 6 Eric Davis	.05	.02	.01
☐ 7 Glenn Davis	.05	.02	.01
☐ 8 Julio Franco	.10	.05	.01
☐ 9 Tony Fernandez	.05	.02	.01
☐ 10 Gary Gaetti	.05	.02	.01
☐ 11 Scott Garrelts	.05	.02	.01
☐ 12 Mark Grace	.60	.25	.07
☐ 13 Mike Greenwell	.05	.02	.01
☐ 14 Ken Griffey Jr.	3.00	1.35	.35
☐ 15 Mark Gubicza	.05	.02	.01
☐ 16 Pedro Guerrero	.05	.02	.01
☐ 17 Von Hayes	.05	.02	.01
☐ 18 Orel Hershiser	.20	.09	.03
☐ 19 Bruce Hurst	.05	.02	.01
☐ 20 Bo Jackson	.25	.11	.03
☐ 21 Howard Johnson	.05	.02	.01
☐ 22 Doug Jones	.05	.02	.01
☐ 23 Barry Larkin	.60	.25	.07
☐ 24 Don Mattingly	1.50	.70	.19
☐ 25 Mark McGwire	.75	.35	.09
☐ 26 Kevin McReynolds	.05	.02	.01
☐ 27 Kevin Mitchell	.05	.02	.01
☐ 28 Dan Plesac	.05	.02	.01
☐ 29 Kirby Puckett	1.50	.70	.19
☐ 30 Cal Ripken	2.50	1.10	.30
☐ 31 Bret Saberhagen	.10	.05	.01
☐ 32 Ryne Sandberg	1.25	.55	.16
☐ 33 Steve Sax	.05	.02	.01
☐ 34 Ruben Sierra	.15	.07	.02
☐ 35 Ozzie Smith	1.25	.55	.16
☐ 36 John Smoltz	.50	.23	.06
☐ 37 Darryl Strawberry	.10	.05	.01
☐ 38 Terry Steinbach	.10	.05	.01
☐ 39 Dave Stewart	.10	.05	.01
☐ 40 Bobby Thigpen	.05	.02	.01
☐ 41 Alan Trammell	.15	.07	.02
☐ 42 Devon White	.10	.05	.01
☐ 43 Mitch Williams	.05	.02	.01
☐ 44 Robin Yount	.50	.23	.06

1990 Fleer Baseball MVP's

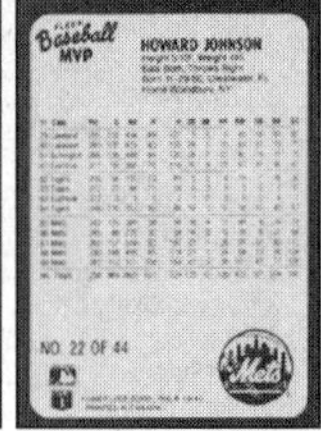

The 1990 Fleer Baseball MVP's were produced by Fleer exclusively for the Toys'R'Us chain and released early in the summer of 1990. This set has a multi-colored border, is standard size, and has 44 players arranged in alphabetical order. The set's custom box gives the set checklist on the back panel. The box also includes six peel-off team logo stickers.

	MINT	NRMT	EXC
COMPLETE SET (44)	6.00	2.70	.75
COMMON CARD (1-44)	.05	.02	.01
☐ 1 George Bell	.05	.02	.01
☐ 2 Bert Blyleven	.10	.05	.01
☐ 3 Wade Boggs	.30	.14	.04
☐ 4 Bobby Bonilla	.10	.05	.01
☐ 5 George Brett	1.50	.70	.19
☐ 6 Jose Canseco	.60	.25	.07
☐ 7 Will Clark	.60	.25	.07
☐ 8 Roger Clemens	.60	.25	.07
☐ 9 Eric Davis	.05	.02	.01
☐ 10 Glenn Davis	.05	.02	.01
☐ 11 Tony Fernandez	.05	.02	.01
☐ 12 Dwight Gooden	.10	.05	.01
☐ 13 Mike Greenwell	.05	.02	.01
☐ 14 Ken Griffey Jr.	3.00	1.35	.35
☐ 15 Pedro Guerrero	.05	.02	.01
☐ 16 Tony Gwynn	1.50	.70	.19
☐ 17 Rickey Henderson	.25	.11	.03
☐ 18 Tom Herr	.05	.02	.01
☐ 19 Orel Hershiser	.20	.09	.03
☐ 20 Kent Hrbek	.10	.05	.01
☐ 21 Bo Jackson	.25	.11	.03
☐ 22 Howard Johnson	.05	.02	.01
☐ 23 Don Mattingly	1.50	.70	.19
☐ 24 Fred McGriff	.60	.25	.07
☐ 25 Mark McGwire	.75	.35	.09
☐ 26 Kevin Mitchell	.05	.02	.01
☐ 27 Paul Molitor	.50	.23	.06
☐ 28 Dale Murphy	.20	.09	.03
☐ 29 Kirby Puckett	1.50	.70	.19
☐ 30 Tim Raines	.10	.05	.01
☐ 31 Cal Ripken	2.50	1.10	.30
☐ 32 Bret Saberhagen	.10	.05	.01
☐ 33 Ryne Sandberg	1.25	.55	.16
☐ 34 Ruben Sierra	.15	.07	.02
☐ 35 Dwight Smith	.05	.02	.01
☐ 36 Ozzie Smith	1.25	.55	.16
☐ 37 Darryl Strawberry	.10	.05	.01
☐ 38 Dave Stewart	.10	.05	.01
☐ 39 Greg Swindell	.05	.02	.01
☐ 40 Bobby Thigpen	.05	.02	.01
☐ 41 Alan Trammell	.15	.07	.02
☐ 42 Jerome Walton	.05	.02	.01
☐ 43 Mitch Williams	.05	.02	.01
☐ 44 Robin Yount	.50	.23	.06

1990 Fleer League Leaders

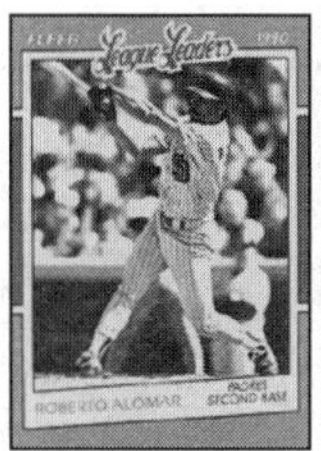

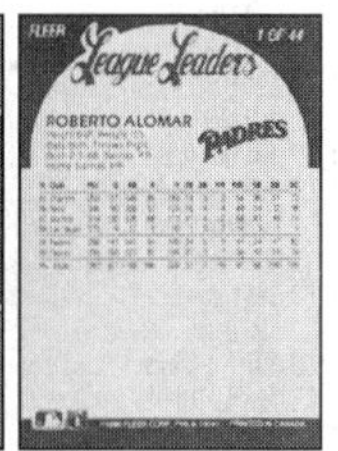

The 1990 Fleer League Leader set was issued by Fleer for Walgreen stores. This set design features solid blue borders with the players photo inset within the middle of the card. This 44-card, standard-size set is numbered in alphabetical order. The set's custom box gives the set checklist on the back panel. The box also includes six peel-off team logo stickers. The original suggested retail price for the set at Walgreen's was 2.49.

	MINT	NRMT	EXC
COMPLETE SET (44)	6.00	2.70	.75
COMMON CARD (1-44)	.05	.02	.01
☐ 1 Roberto Alomar	1.00	.45	.12
☐ 2 Tim Belcher	.05	.02	.01
☐ 3 George Bell	.05	.02	.01
☐ 4 Wade Boggs	.30	.14	.04
☐ 5 Jose Canseco	.60	.25	.07
☐ 6 Will Clark	.60	.25	.07
☐ 7 David Cone	.30	.14	.04
☐ 8 Eric Davis	.05	.02	.01
☐ 9 Glenn Davis	.05	.02	.01
☐ 10 Nick Esasky	.05	.02	.01
☐ 11 Dennis Eckersley	.15	.07	.02
☐ 12 Mark Grace	.60	.25	.07
☐ 13 Mike Greenwell	.05	.02	.01
☐ 14 Ken Griffey Jr.	3.00	1.35	.35
☐ 15 Mark Gubicza	.05	.02	.01
☐ 16 Pedro Guerrero	.05	.02	.01
☐ 17 Tony Gwynn	1.50	.70	.19
☐ 18 Rickey Henderson	.50	.23	.06
☐ 19 Bo Jackson	.25	.11	.03
☐ 20 Doug Jones	.05	.02	.01
☐ 21 Ricky Jordan	.05	.02	.01
☐ 22 Barry Larkin	.60	.25	.07
☐ 23 Don Mattingly	1.50	.70	.19
☐ 24 Fred McGriff	.60	.25	.07
☐ 25 Mark McGwire	.75	.35	.09
☐ 26 Kevin Mitchell	.05	.02	.01
☐ 27 Jack Morris	.10	.05	.01
☐ 28 Gregg Olson	.05	.02	.01
☐ 29 Dan Plesac	.05	.02	.01
☐ 30 Kirby Puckett	1.50	.70	.19
☐ 31 Nolan Ryan	2.50	1.10	.30
☐ 32 Bret Saberhagen	.05	.02	.01
☐ 33 Ryne Sandberg	1.25	.55	.16
☐ 34 Steve Sax	.05	.02	.01
☐ 35 Mike Scott	.05	.02	.01
☐ 36 Ruben Sierra	.15	.07	.02
☐ 37 Lonnie Smith	.05	.02	.01
☐ 38 Darryl Strawberry	.10	.05	.01
☐ 39 Bobby Thigpen	.05	.02	.01
☐ 40 Andy Van Slyke	.10	.05	.01
☐ 41 Tim Wallach	.05	.02	.01
☐ 42 Jerome Walton UER (Photo actually Eric Yelding)	.05	.02	.01
☐ 43 Devon White	.10	.05	.01
☐ 44 Robin Yount	.25	.11	.03

1991 Fleer

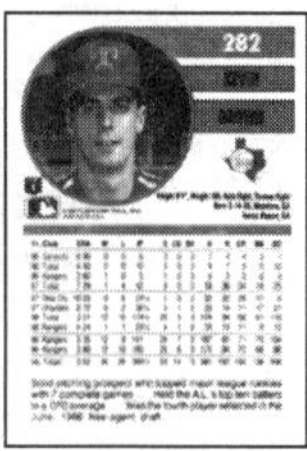

The 1991 Fleer set consists of 720 standard-size cards. Cards were primarily issued in wax packs, cello packs and factory sets. This set does not have what has been a Fleer tradition in recent years, the two-player rookie cards and there are less two-player special cards than in prior years. The design features solid yellow borders with the information in black indicating name, position, and team. The set is again ordered numerically by teams, followed by combination cards, rookie prospect pairs, and checklists. Rookie Cards in this set include Jeff Conine and Brian McRae. A number of the cards in the set can be found with photos cropped (very slightly) differently as Fleer used two separate printers in their attempt to maximize production.

	MINT	NRMT	EXC
COMPLETE SET (720)	8.00	3.60	1.00
COMPLETE RETAIL SET (732)	10.00	4.50	1.25
COMPLETE HOBBY SET (732)	10.00	4.50	1.25
COMMON CARD (1-720)	.05	.02	.01
☐ 1 Troy Afenir	.05	.02	.01
☐ 2 Harold Baines	.10	.05	.01
☐ 3 Lance Blankenship	.05	.02	.01
☐ 4 Todd Burns	.05	.02	.01
☐ 5 Jose Canseco	.15	.07	.02
☐ 6 Dennis Eckersley	.10	.05	.01
☐ 7 Mike Gallego	.05	.02	.01
☐ 8 Ron Hassey	.05	.02	.01
☐ 9 Dave Henderson	.05	.02	.01
☐ 10 Rickey Henderson	.15	.07	.02
☐ 11 Rick Honeycutt	.05	.02	.01
☐ 12 Doug Jennings	.05	.02	.01
☐ 13 Joe Klink	.05	.02	.01
☐ 14 Carney Lansford	.10	.05	.01
☐ 15 Darren Lewis	.10	.05	.01
☐ 16 Willie McGee UER (Height 6'11")	.05	.02	.01
☐ 17 Mark McGwire UER (183 extra base hits in 1987)	.30	.14	.04
☐ 18 Mike Moore	.05	.02	.01
☐ 19 Gene Nelson	.05	.02	.01
☐ 20 Dave Otto	.05	.02	.01
☐ 21 Jamie Quirk	.05	.02	.01
☐ 22 Willie Randolph	.10	.05	.01
☐ 23 Scott Sanderson	.05	.02	.01
☐ 24 Terry Steinbach	.10	.05	.01
☐ 25 Dave Stewart	.10	.05	.01
☐ 26 Walt Weiss	.05	.02	.01
☐ 27 Bob Welch	.05	.02	.01
☐ 28 Curt Young	.05	.02	.01
☐ 29 Wally Backman	.05	.02	.01
☐ 30 Stan Belinda UER (Born in Huntington, should be State College)	.05	.02	.01
☐ 31 Jay Bell	.10	.05	.01
☐ 32 Rafael Belliard	.05	.02	.01
☐ 33 Barry Bonds	.25	.11	.03
☐ 34 Bobby Bonilla	.10	.05	.01
☐ 35 Sid Bream	.05	.02	.01
☐ 36 Doug Drabek	.05	.02	.01
☐ 37 Carlos Garcia	.15	.07	.02
☐ 38 Neal Heaton	.05	.02	.01
☐ 39 Jeff King	.10	.05	.01
☐ 40 Bob Kipper	.05	.02	.01
☐ 41 Bill Landrum	.05	.02	.01
☐ 42 Mike LaValliere	.05	.02	.01
☐ 43 Jose Lind	.05	.02	.01
☐ 44 Carmelo Martinez	.05	.02	.01
☐ 45 Bob Patterson	.05	.02	.01

Card			
☐ 46 Ted Power	.05	.02	.01
☐ 47 Gary Redus	.05	.02	.01
☐ 48 R.J. Reynolds	.05	.02	.01
☐ 49 Don Slaught	.05	.02	.01
☐ 50 John Smiley	.05	.02	.01
☐ 51 Zane Smith	.05	.02	.01
☐ 52 Randy Tomlin	.05	.02	.01
☐ 53 Andy Van Slyke	.10	.05	.01
☐ 54 Bob Walk	.05	.02	.01
☐ 55 Jack Armstrong	.05	.02	.01
☐ 56 Todd Benzinger	.05	.02	.01
☐ 57 Glenn Braggs	.05	.02	.01
☐ 58 Keith Brown	.05	.02	.01
☐ 59 Tom Browning	.05	.02	.01
☐ 60 Norm Charlton	.05	.02	.01
☐ 61 Eric Davis	.10	.05	.01
☐ 62 Rob Dibble	.05	.02	.01
☐ 63 Bill Doran	.05	.02	.01
☐ 64 Mariano Duncan	.05	.02	.01
☐ 65 Chris Hammond	.05	.02	.01
☐ 66 Billy Hatcher	.05	.02	.01
☐ 67 Danny Jackson	.05	.02	.01
☐ 68 Barry Larkin	.15	.07	.02
☐ 69 Tim Layana (Black line over made in first text line)	.05	.02	.01
☐ 70 Terry Lee	.05	.02	.01
☐ 71 Rick Mahler	.05	.02	.01
☐ 72 Hal Morris	.05	.02	.01
☐ 73 Randy Myers	.10	.05	.01
☐ 74 Ron Oester	.05	.02	.01
☐ 75 Joe Oliver	.05	.02	.01
☐ 76 Paul O'Neill	.10	.05	.01
☐ 77 Luis Quinones	.05	.02	.01
☐ 78 Jeff Reed	.05	.02	.01
☐ 79 Jose Rijo	.05	.02	.01
☐ 80 Chris Sabo	.05	.02	.01
☐ 81 Scott Scudder	.05	.02	.01
☐ 82 Herm Winningham	.05	.02	.01
☐ 83 Larry Andersen	.05	.02	.01
☐ 84 Marty Barrett	.05	.02	.01
☐ 85 Mike Boddicker	.05	.02	.01
☐ 86 Wade Boggs	.15	.07	.02
☐ 87 Tom Bolton	.05	.02	.01
☐ 88 Tom Brunansky	.05	.02	.01
☐ 89 Ellis Burks	.10	.05	.01
☐ 90 Roger Clemens	.20	.09	.03
☐ 91 Scott Cooper	.05	.02	.01
☐ 92 John Dopson	.05	.02	.01
☐ 93 Dwight Evans	.10	.05	.01
☐ 94 Wes Gardner	.05	.02	.01
☐ 95 Jeff Gray	.05	.02	.01
☐ 96 Mike Greenwell	.05	.02	.01
☐ 97 Greg A. Harris	.05	.02	.01
☐ 98 Daryl Irvine	.05	.02	.01
☐ 99 Dana Kiecker	.05	.02	.01
☐ 100 Randy Kutcher	.05	.02	.01
☐ 101 Dennis Lamp	.05	.02	.01
☐ 102 Mike Marshall	.05	.02	.01
☐ 103 John Marzano	.05	.02	.01
☐ 104 Rob Murphy	.05	.02	.01
☐ 105 Tim Naehring	.10	.05	.01
☐ 106 Tony Pena	.05	.02	.01
☐ 107 Phil Plantier	.10	.05	.01
☐ 108 Carlos Quintana	.05	.02	.01
☐ 109 Jeff Reardon	.10	.05	.01
☐ 110 Jerry Reed	.05	.02	.01
☐ 111 Jody Reed	.05	.02	.01
☐ 112 Luis Rivera UER (Born 1/3/84)	.05	.02	.01
☐ 113 Kevin Romine	.05	.02	.01
☐ 114 Phil Bradley	.05	.02	.01
☐ 115 Ivan Calderon	.05	.02	.01
☐ 116 Wayne Edwards	.05	.02	.01
☐ 117 Alex Fernandez	.15	.07	.02
☐ 118 Carlton Fisk	.15	.07	.02
☐ 119 Scott Fletcher	.05	.02	.01
☐ 120 Craig Grebeck	.05	.02	.01
☐ 121 Ozzie Guillen	.05	.02	.01
☐ 122 Greg Hibbard	.05	.02	.01
☐ 123 Lance Johnson UER (Born Cincinnati, should be Lincoln Heights)	.10	.05	.01
☐ 124 Barry Jones	.05	.02	.01
☐ 125 Ron Karkovice	.05	.02	.01
☐ 126 Eric King	.05	.02	.01
☐ 127 Steve Lyons	.05	.02	.01
☐ 128 Carlos Martinez	.05	.02	.01
☐ 129 Jack McDowell UER (Stanford misspelled as Standford on back)	.10	.05	.01
☐ 130 Donn Pall (No dots over any i's in text)	.05	.02	.01
☐ 131 Dan Pasqua	.05	.02	.01
☐ 132 Ken Patterson	.05	.02	.01
☐ 133 Melido Perez	.05	.02	.01
☐ 134 Adam Peterson	.05	.02	.01
☐ 135 Scott Radinsky	.05	.02	.01
☐ 136 Sammy Sosa	.25	.11	.03
☐ 137 Bobby Thigpen	.05	.02	.01
☐ 138 Frank Thomas	2.00	.90	.25
☐ 139 Robin Ventura	.15	.07	.02
☐ 140 Daryl Boston	.05	.02	.01
☐ 141 Chuck Carr	.05	.02	.01
☐ 142 Mark Carreon	.05	.02	.01
☐ 143 David Cone	.10	.05	.01
☐ 144 Ron Darling	.05	.02	.01
☐ 145 Kevin Elster	.05	.02	.01
☐ 146 Sid Fernandez	.05	.02	.01
☐ 147 John Franco	.05	.02	.01
☐ 148 Dwight Gooden	.10	.05	.01
☐ 149 Tom Herr	.05	.02	.01
☐ 150 Todd Hundley	.15	.07	.02
☐ 151 Gregg Jefferies	.10	.05	.01
☐ 152 Howard Johnson	.05	.02	.01
☐ 153 Dave Magadan	.05	.02	.01
☐ 154 Kevin McReynolds	.05	.02	.01
☐ 155 Keith Miller UER (Text says Rochester in '87, stats say Tide-water, mixed up with other Keith Miller)	.05	.02	.01
☐ 156 Bob Ojeda	.05	.02	.01
☐ 157 Tom O'Malley	.05	.02	.01
☐ 158 Alejandro Pena	.05	.02	.01
☐ 159 Darren Reed	.05	.02	.01
☐ 160 Mackey Sasser	.05	.02	.01
☐ 161 Darryl Strawberry	.10	.05	.01
☐ 162 Tim Teufel	.05	.02	.01
☐ 163 Kelvin Torve	.05	.02	.01
☐ 164 Julio Valera	.05	.02	.01
☐ 165 Frank Viola	.05	.02	.01
☐ 166 Wally Whitehurst	.05	.02	.01
☐ 167 Jim Acker	.05	.02	.01
☐ 168 Derek Bell	.15	.07	.02
☐ 169 George Bell	.05	.02	.01
☐ 170 Willie Blair	.05	.02	.01
☐ 171 Pat Borders	.05	.02	.01
☐ 172 John Cerutti	.05	.02	.01
☐ 173 Junior Felix	.05	.02	.01
☐ 174 Tony Fernandez	.05	.02	.01
☐ 175 Kelly Gruber UER (Born in Houston, should be Bellaire)	.05	.02	.01
☐ 176 Tom Henke	.05	.02	.01
☐ 177 Glenallen Hill	.05	.02	.01
☐ 178 Jimmy Key	.10	.05	.01
☐ 179 Manny Lee	.05	.02	.01
☐ 180 Fred McGriff	.15	.07	.02
☐ 181 Rance Mulliniks	.05	.02	.01
☐ 182 Greg Myers	.05	.02	.01
☐ 183 John Olerud UER (Listed as throwing right, should be left)	.10	.05	.01
☐ 184 Luis Sojo	.05	.02	.01
☐ 185 Dave Stieb	.05	.02	.01
☐ 186 Todd Stottlemyre	.05	.02	.01
☐ 187 Duane Ward	.05	.02	.01
☐ 188 David Wells	.05	.02	.01
☐ 189 Mark Whiten	.10	.05	.01
☐ 190 Ken Williams	.05	.02	.01
☐ 191 Frank Wills	.05	.02	.01
☐ 192 Mookie Wilson	.05	.02	.01
☐ 193 Don Aase	.05	.02	.01
☐ 194 Tim Belcher UER (Born Sparta, Ohio, should say Mt. Gilead)	.05	.02	.01
☐ 195 Hubie Brooks	.05	.02	.01
☐ 196 Dennis Cook	.05	.02	.01
☐ 197 Tim Crews	.05	.02	.01
☐ 198 Kal Daniels	.05	.02	.01
☐ 199 Kirk Gibson	.10	.05	.01
☐ 200 Jim Gott	.05	.02	.01
☐ 201 Alfredo Griffin	.05	.02	.01
☐ 202 Chris Gwynn	.05	.02	.01
☐ 203 Dave Hansen	.05	.02	.01
☐ 204 Lenny Harris	.05	.02	.01
☐ 205 Mike Hartley	.05	.02	.01
☐ 206 Mickey Hatcher	.05	.02	.01
☐ 207 Carlos Hernandez	.05	.02	.01
☐ 208 Orel Hershiser	.10	.05	.01
☐ 209 Jay Howell UER (No 1982 Yankee stats)	.05	.02	.01
☐ 210 Mike Huff	.05	.02	.01
☐ 211 Stan Javier	.05	.02	.01
☐ 212 Ramon Martinez	.15	.07	.02
☐ 213 Mike Morgan	.05	.02	.01
☐ 214 Eddie Murray	.25	.11	.03
☐ 215 Jim Neidlinger	.05	.02	.01
☐ 216 Jose Offerman	.05	.02	.01
☐ 217 Jim Poole	.05	.02	.01
☐ 218 Juan Samuel	.05	.02	.01
☐ 219 Mike Scioscia	.05	.02	.01
☐ 220 Ray Searage	.05	.02	.01
☐ 221 Mike Sharperson	.05	.02	.01
☐ 222 Fernando Valenzuela	.10	.05	.01
☐ 223 Jose Vizcaino	.05	.02	.01
☐ 224 Mike Aldrete	.05	.02	.01
☐ 225 Scott Anderson	.05	.02	.01
☐ 226 Dennis Boyd	.05	.02	.01
☐ 227 Tim Burke	.05	.02	.01
☐ 228 Delino DeShields	.05	.02	.01
☐ 229 Mike Fitzgerald	.05	.02	.01
☐ 230 Tom Foley	.05	.02	.01
☐ 231 Steve Frey	.05	.02	.01
☐ 232 Andres Galarraga	.15	.07	.02
☐ 233 Mark Gardner	.05	.02	.01
☐ 234 Marquis Grissom	.15	.07	.02
☐ 235 Kevin Gross (No date given for first Expos win)	.05	.02	.01
☐ 236 Drew Hall	.05	.02	.01
☐ 237 Dave Martinez	.05	.02	.01
☐ 238 Dennis Martinez	.10	.05	.01
☐ 239 Dale Mohorcic	.05	.02	.01
☐ 240 Chris Nabholz	.05	.02	.01
☐ 241 Otis Nixon	.05	.02	.01
☐ 242 Junior Noboa	.05	.02	.01
☐ 243 Spike Owen	.05	.02	.01
☐ 244 Tim Raines	.15	.07	.02
☐ 245 Mel Rojas UER (Stats show 3.60 ERA, bio says 3.19 ERA)	.10	.05	.01
☐ 246 Scott Ruskin	.05	.02	.01
☐ 247 Bill Sampen	.05	.02	.01
☐ 248 Nelson Santovenia	.05	.02	.01
☐ 249 Dave Schmidt	.05	.02	.01
☐ 250 Larry Walker	.15	.07	.02
☐ 251 Tim Wallach	.05	.02	.01
☐ 252 Dave Anderson	.05	.02	.01
☐ 253 Kevin Bass	.05	.02	.01
☐ 254 Steve Bedrosian	.05	.02	.01
☐ 255 Jeff Brantley	.05	.02	.01
☐ 256 John Burkett	.10	.05	.01
☐ 257 Brett Butler	.10	.05	.01
☐ 258 Gary Carter	.10	.05	.01
☐ 259 Will Clark	.15	.07	.02
☐ 260 Steve Decker	.05	.02	.01
☐ 261 Kelly Downs	.05	.02	.01
☐ 262 Scott Garrelts	.05	.02	.01
☐ 263 Terry Kennedy	.05	.02	.01
☐ 264 Mike LaCoss	.05	.02	.01
☐ 265 Mark Leonard	.05	.02	.01
☐ 266 Greg Litton	.05	.02	.01
☐ 267 Kevin Mitchell	.10	.05	.01
☐ 268 Randy O'Neal	.05	.02	.01
☐ 269 Rick Parker	.05	.02	.01
☐ 270 Rick Reuschel	.05	.02	.01
☐ 271 Ernest Riles	.05	.02	.01
☐ 272 Don Robinson	.05	.02	.01
☐ 273 Robby Thompson	.05	.02	.01
☐ 274 Mark Thurmond	.05	.02	.01
☐ 275 Jose Uribe	.05	.02	.01
☐ 276 Matt Williams	.15	.07	.02
☐ 277 Trevor Wilson	.05	.02	.01
☐ 278 Gerald Alexander	.05	.02	.01
☐ 279 Brad Arnsberg	.05	.02	.01
☐ 280 Kevin Belcher	.05	.02	.01
☐ 281 Joe Bitker	.05	.02	.01
☐ 282 Kevin Brown	.10	.05	.01
☐ 283 Steve Buechele	.05	.02	.01
☐ 284 Jack Daugherty	.05	.02	.01
☐ 285 Julio Franco	.10	.05	.01
☐ 286 Juan Gonzalez	.75	.35	.09
☐ 287 Bill Haselman	.05	.02	.01
☐ 288 Charlie Hough	.05	.02	.01
☐ 289 Jeff Huson	.05	.02	.01
☐ 290 Pete Incaviglia	.05	.02	.01
☐ 291 Mike Jeffcoat	.05	.02	.01
☐ 292 Jeff Kunkel	.05	.02	.01
☐ 293 Gary Mielke	.05	.02	.01
☐ 294 Jamie Moyer	.05	.02	.01
☐ 295 Rafael Palmeiro	.15	.07	.02
☐ 296 Geno Petralli	.05	.02	.01
☐ 297 Gary Pettis	.05	.02	.01
☐ 298 Kevin Reimer	.05	.02	.01
☐ 299 Kenny Rogers	.05	.02	.01
☐ 300 Jeff Russell	.05	.02	.01
☐ 301 John Russell	.05	.02	.01
☐ 302 Nolan Ryan	.75	.35	.09
☐ 303 Ruben Sierra	.10	.05	.01
☐ 304 Bobby Witt	.05	.02	.01
☐ 305 Jim Abbott UER (Text on back states he won Sullivan Award (outstanding amateur athlete) in 1989; should be '88)	.10	.05	.01
☐ 306 Kent Anderson	.05	.02	.01
☐ 307 Dante Bichette	.15	.07	.02
☐ 308 Bert Blyleven	.10	.05	.01
☐ 309 Chili Davis	.10	.05	.01
☐ 310 Brian Downing	.05	.02	.01
☐ 311 Mark Eichhorn	.05	.02	.01
☐ 312 Mike Fetters	.05	.02	.01
☐ 313 Chuck Finley	.10	.05	.01
☐ 314 Willie Fraser	.05	.02	.01
☐ 315 Bryan Harvey	.05	.02	.01
☐ 316 Donnie Hill	.05	.02	.01
☐ 317 Wally Joyner	.10	.05	.01
☐ 318 Mark Langston	.10	.05	.01
☐ 319 Kirk McCaskill	.05	.02	.01
☐ 320 John Orton	.05	.02	.01
☐ 321 Lance Parrish	.05	.02	.01
☐ 322 Luis Polonia UER (1984 Madfison, should be Madison)	.05	.02	.01
☐ 323 Johnny Ray	.05	.02	.01
☐ 324 Bobby Rose	.05	.02	.01
☐ 325 Dick Schofield	.05	.02	.01
☐ 326 Rick Schu	.05	.02	.01
☐ 327 Lee Stevens	.05	.02	.01
☐ 328 Devon White	.10	.05	.01
☐ 329 Dave Winfield	.15	.07	.02
☐ 330 Cliff Young	.05	.02	.01
☐ 331 Dave Bergman	.05	.02	.01
☐ 332 Phil Clark	.05	.02	.01
☐ 333 Darnell Coles	.05	.02	.01
☐ 334 Milt Cuyler	.05	.02	.01
☐ 335 Cecil Fielder	.10	.05	.01
☐ 336 Travis Fryman	.15	.07	.02
☐ 337 Paul Gibson	.05	.02	.01
☐ 338 Jerry Don Gleaton	.05	.02	.01
☐ 339 Mike Heath	.05	.02	.01
☐ 340 Mike Henneman	.05	.02	.01
☐ 341 Chet Lemon	.05	.02	.01
☐ 342 Lance McCullers	.05	.02	.01
☐ 343 Jack Morris	.10	.05	.01
☐ 344 Lloyd Moseby	.05	.02	.01
☐ 345 Edwin Nunez	.05	.02	.01
☐ 346 Clay Parker	.05	.02	.01
☐ 347 Dan Petry	.05	.02	.01
☐ 348 Tony Phillips	.10	.05	.01
☐ 349 Jeff M. Robinson	.05	.02	.01
☐ 350 Mark Salas	.05	.02	.01
☐ 351 Mike Schwabe	.05	.02	.01
☐ 352 Larry Sheets	.05	.02	.01
☐ 353 John Shelby	.05	.02	.01
☐ 354 Frank Tanana	.05	.02	.01
☐ 355 Alan Trammell	.10	.05	.01
☐ 356 Gary Ward	.05	.02	.01
☐ 357 Lou Whitaker	.10	.05	.01
☐ 358 Beau Allred	.05	.02	.01
☐ 359 Sandy Alomar Jr.	.10	.05	.01
☐ 360 Carlos Baerga	.15	.07	.02
☐ 361 Kevin Bearse	.05	.02	.01
☐ 362 Tom Brookens	.05	.02	.01
☐ 363 Jerry Browne UER (No dot over i in first text line)	.05	.02	.01
☐ 364 Tom Candiotti	.05	.02	.01
☐ 365 Alex Cole	.05	.02	.01
☐ 366 John Farrell UER (Born in Neptune, should be Monmouth)	.05	.02	.01
☐ 367 Felix Fermin	.05	.02	.01
☐ 368 Keith Hernandez	.10	.05	.01
☐ 369 Brook Jacoby	.05	.02	.01
☐ 370 Chris James	.05	.02	.01
☐ 371 Dion James	.05	.02	.01
☐ 372 Doug Jones	.05	.02	.01
☐ 373 Candy Maldonado	.05	.02	.01
☐ 374 Steve Olin	.05	.02	.01
☐ 375 Jesse Orosco	.05	.02	.01
☐ 376 Rudy Seanez	.05	.02	.01
☐ 377 Joel Skinner	.05	.02	.01
☐ 378 Cory Snyder	.05	.02	.01
☐ 379 Greg Swindell	.05	.02	.01
☐ 380 Sergio Valdez	.05	.02	.01
☐ 381 Mike Walker	.05	.02	.01
☐ 382 Colby Ward	.05	.02	.01
☐ 383 Turner Ward	.05	.02	.01
☐ 384 Mitch Webster	.05	.02	.01
☐ 385 Kevin Wickander	.05	.02	.01
☐ 386 Darrel Akerfelds	.05	.02	.01
☐ 387 Joe Boever	.05	.02	.01
☐ 388 Rod Booker	.05	.02	.01
☐ 389 Sil Campusano	.05	.02	.01
☐ 390 Don Carman	.05	.02	.01
☐ 391 Wes Chamberlain	.05	.02	.01
☐ 392 Pat Combs	.05	.02	.01
☐ 393 Darren Daulton	.10	.05	.01
☐ 394 Jose DeJesus	.05	.02	.01
☐ 395A Len Dykstra Name spelled Lenny on back	.10	.05	.01
☐ 395B Len Dykstra Name spelled Len on back	.10	.05	.01
☐ 396 Jason Grimsley	.05	.02	.01
☐ 397 Charlie Hayes	.05	.02	.01
☐ 398 Von Hayes	.05	.02	.01
☐ 399 David Hollins UER (Atl-bats, should say at-bats)	.05	.02	.01
☐ 400 Ken Howell	.05	.02	.01
☐ 401 Ricky Jordan	.05	.02	.01
☐ 402 John Kruk	.10	.05	.01
☐ 403 Steve Lake	.05	.02	.01
☐ 404 Chuck Malone	.05	.02	.01
☐ 405 Roger McDowell UER (Says Phillies is saves, should say in)	.05	.02	.01
☐ 406 Chuck McElroy	.05	.02	.01
☐ 407 Mickey Morandini	.05	.02	.01
☐ 408 Terry Mulholland	.05	.02	.01
☐ 409 Dale Murphy	.15	.07	.02
☐ 410A Randy Ready ERR (No Brewers stats listed for 1983)	.05	.02	.01
☐ 410B Randy Ready COR	.05	.02	.01
☐ 411 Bruce Ruffin	.05	.02	.01
☐ 412 Dickie Thon	.05	.02	.01
☐ 413 Paul Assenmacher	.05	.02	.01
☐ 414 Damon Berryhill	.05	.02	.01
☐ 415 Mike Bielecki	.05	.02	.01
☐ 416 Shawn Boskie	.05	.02	.01
☐ 417 Dave Clark	.05	.02	.01
☐ 418 Doug Dascenzo	.05	.02	.01
☐ 419A Andre Dawson ERR (No stats for 1976)	.10	.05	.01
☐ 419B Andre Dawson COR	.10	.05	.01
☐ 420 Shawon Dunston	.05	.02	.01
☐ 421 Joe Girardi	.10	.05	.01

☐ 422 Mark Grace .15 .07 .02
☐ 423 Mike Harkey .05 .02 .01
☐ 424 Les Lancaster .05 .02 .01
☐ 425 Bill Long .05 .02 .01
☐ 426 Greg Maddux .60 .25 .07
☐ 427 Derrick May .05 .02 .01
☐ 428 Jeff Pico .05 .02 .01
☐ 429 Domingo Ramos .05 .02 .01
☐ 430 Luis Salazar .05 .02 .01
☐ 431 Ryne Sandberg .25 .11 .03
☐ 432 Dwight Smith .05 .02 .01
☐ 433 Greg Smith .05 .02 .01
☐ 434 Rick Sutcliffe .05 .02 .01
☐ 435 Gary Varsho .05 .02 .01
☐ 436 Hector Villanueva .05 .02 .01
☐ 437 Jerome Walton .05 .02 .01
☐ 438 Curtis Wilkerson .05 .02 .01
☐ 439 Mitch Williams .05 .02 .01
☐ 440 Steve Wilson .05 .02 .01
☐ 441 Marvell Wynne .05 .02 .01
☐ 442 Scott Bankhead .05 .02 .01
☐ 443 Scott Bradley .05 .02 .01
☐ 444 Greg Briley .05 .02 .01
☐ 445 Mike Brumley UER .05 .02 .01
(Text 40 SB's in 1988, stats say 41)
☐ 446 Jay Buhner .15 .07 .02
☐ 447 Dave Burba .05 .02 .01
☐ 448 Henry Cotto .05 .02 .01
☐ 449 Alvin Davis .05 .02 .01
☐ 450 Ken Griffey Jr. 1.50 .70 .19
(Bat around .300)
☐ 450A Ken Griffey Jr. 1.50 .70 .19
(Bat .300)
☐ 451 Erik Hanson .05 .02 .01
☐ 452 Gene Harris UER .05 .02 .01
(63 career runs, should be 73)
☐ 453 Brian Holman .05 .02 .01
☐ 454 Mike Jackson .05 .02 .01
☐ 455 Randy Johnson .15 .07 .02
☐ 456 Jeffrey Leonard .05 .02 .01
☐ 457 Edgar Martinez .10 .05 .01
☐ 458 Tino Martinez .15 .07 .02
☐ 459 Pete O'Brien UER .05 .02 .01
(1987 BA .266, should be .286)
☐ 460 Harold Reynolds .05 .02 .01
☐ 461 Mike Schooler .05 .02 .01
☐ 462 Bill Swift .05 .02 .01
☐ 463 David Valle .05 .02 .01
☐ 464 Omar Vizquel .15 .07 .02
☐ 465 Matt Young .05 .02 .01
☐ 466 Brady Anderson .15 .07 .02
☐ 467 Jeff Ballard UER .05 .02 .01
(Missing top of right parenthesis after Saberhagen in last text line)
☐ 468 Juan Bell .05 .02 .01
☐ 469A Mike Devereaux .10 .05 .01
(First line of text ends with six)
☐ 469B Mike Devereaux .10 .05 .01
(First line of text ends with runs)
☐ 470 Steve Finley .10 .05 .01
☐ 471 Dave Gallagher .05 .02 .01
☐ 472 Leo Gomez .05 .02 .01
☐ 473 Rene Gonzales .05 .02 .01
☐ 474 Pete Harnisch .05 .02 .01
☐ 475 Kevin Hickey .05 .02 .01
☐ 476 Chris Hoiles .05 .02 .01
☐ 477 Sam Horn .05 .02 .01
☐ 478 Tim Hulett .05 .02 .01
(Photo shows National Leaguer sliding into second base)
☐ 479 Dave Johnson .05 .02 .01
☐ 480 Ron Kittle UER .05 .02 .01
(Edmonton misspelled as Edmundton)
☐ 481 Ben McDonald .10 .05 .01
☐ 482 Bob Melvin .05 .02 .01
☐ 483 Bob Milacki .05 .02 .01
☐ 484 Randy Milligan .05 .02 .01
☐ 485 John Mitchell .05 .02 .01
☐ 486 Gregg Olson .05 .02 .01
☐ 487 Joe Orsulak .05 .02 .01
☐ 488 Joe Price .05 .02 .01
☐ 489 Bill Ripken .05 .02 .01
☐ 490 Cal Ripken .75 .35 .09
☐ 491 Curt Schilling .05 .02 .01
☐ 492 David Segui .10 .05 .01
☐ 493 Anthony Telford .05 .02 .01
☐ 494 Mickey Tettleton .10 .05 .01
☐ 495 Mark Williamson .05 .02 .01
☐ 496 Craig Worthington .05 .02 .01
☐ 497 Juan Agosto .05 .02 .01
☐ 498 Eric Anthony .05 .02 .01
☐ 499 Craig Biggio .15 .07 .02
☐ 500 Ken Caminiti UER .15 .07 .02
(Born 4/4, should be 4/21)
☐ 501 Casey Candaele .05 .02 .01
☐ 502 Andujar Cedeno .05 .02 .01
☐ 503 Danny Darwin .05 .02 .01
☐ 504 Mark Davidson .05 .02 .01
☐ 505 Glenn Davis .05 .02 .01
☐ 506 Jim Deshaies .05 .02 .01
☐ 507 Luis Gonzalez .15 .07 .02
☐ 508 Bill Gullickson .05 .02 .01
☐ 509 Xavier Hernandez .05 .02 .01
☐ 510 Brian Meyer .05 .02 .01
☐ 511 Ken Oberkfell .05 .02 .01
☐ 512 Mark Portugal .05 .02 .01
☐ 513 Rafael Ramirez .05 .02 .01
☐ 514 Karl Rhodes .05 .02 .01
☐ 515 Mike Scott .05 .02 .01
☐ 516 Mike Simms .05 .02 .01
☐ 517 Dave Smith .05 .02 .01
☐ 518 Franklin Stubbs .05 .02 .01
☐ 519 Glenn Wilson .05 .02 .01
☐ 520 Eric Yelding UER .05 .02 .01
(Text has 63 steals, stats have 64, which is correct)
☐ 521 Gerald Young .05 .02 .01
☐ 522 Shawn Abner .05 .02 .01
☐ 523 Roberto Alomar .20 .09 .03
☐ 524 Andy Benes .10 .05 .01
☐ 525 Joe Carter .10 .05 .01
☐ 526 Jack Clark .10 .05 .01
☐ 527 Joey Cora .10 .05 .01
☐ 528 Paul Faries .05 .02 .01
☐ 529 Tony Gwynn .40 .18 .05
☐ 530 Atlee Hammaker .05 .02 .01
☐ 531 Greg W. Harris .05 .02 .01
☐ 532 Thomas Howard .05 .02 .01
☐ 533 Bruce Hurst .05 .02 .01
☐ 534 Craig Lefferts .05 .02 .01
☐ 535 Derek Lilliquist .05 .02 .01
☐ 536 Fred Lynn .05 .02 .01
☐ 537 Mike Pagliarulo .05 .02 .01
☐ 538 Mark Parent .05 .02 .01
☐ 539 Dennis Rasmussen .05 .02 .01
☐ 540 Bip Roberts .05 .02 .01
☐ 541 Richard Rodriguez .05 .02 .01
☐ 542 Benito Santiago .05 .02 .01
☐ 543 Calvin Schiraldi .05 .02 .01
☐ 544 Eric Show .05 .02 .01
☐ 545 Phil Stephenson .05 .02 .01
☐ 546 Garry Templeton UER .05 .02 .01
(Born 3/24/57, should be 3/24/56)
☐ 547 Ed Whitson .05 .02 .01
☐ 548 Eddie Williams .05 .02 .01
☐ 549 Kevin Appier .15 .07 .02
☐ 550 Luis Aquino .05 .02 .01
☐ 551 Bob Boone .10 .05 .01
☐ 552 George Brett .40 .18 .05
☐ 553 Jeff Conine .50 .23 .06
☐ 554 Steve Crawford .05 .02 .01
☐ 555 Mark Davis .05 .02 .01
☐ 556 Storm Davis .05 .02 .01
☐ 557 Jim Eisenreich .10 .05 .01
☐ 558 Steve Farr .05 .02 .01
☐ 559 Tom Gordon .05 .02 .01
☐ 560 Mark Gubicza .05 .02 .01
☐ 561 Bo Jackson .10 .05 .01
☐ 562 Mike Macfarlane .05 .02 .01
☐ 563 Brian McRae .25 .11 .03
☐ 564 Jeff Montgomery .10 .05 .01
☐ 565 Bill Pecota .05 .02 .01
☐ 566 Gerald Perry .05 .02 .01
☐ 567 Bret Saberhagen .10 .05 .01
☐ 568 Jeff Schulz .05 .02 .01
☐ 569 Kevin Seitzer .05 .02 .01
☐ 570 Terry Shumpert .05 .02 .01
☐ 571 Kurt Stillwell .05 .02 .01
☐ 572 Danny Tartabull .05 .02 .01
☐ 573 Gary Thurman .05 .02 .01
☐ 574 Frank White .10 .05 .01
☐ 575 Willie Wilson .05 .02 .01
☐ 576 Chris Bosio .05 .02 .01
☐ 577 Greg Brock .05 .02 .01
☐ 578 George Canale .05 .02 .01
☐ 579 Chuck Crim .05 .02 .01
☐ 580 Rob Deer .05 .02 .01
☐ 581 Edgar Diaz .05 .02 .01
☐ 582 Tom Edens .05 .02 .01
☐ 583 Mike Felder .05 .02 .01
☐ 584 Jim Gantner .05 .02 .01
☐ 585 Darryl Hamilton .10 .05 .01
☐ 586 Ted Higuera .05 .02 .01
☐ 587 Mark Knudson .05 .02 .01
☐ 588 Bill Krueger .05 .02 .01
☐ 589 Tim McIntosh .05 .02 .01
☐ 590 Paul Mirabella .05 .02 .01
☐ 591 Paul Molitor .20 .09 .03
☐ 592 Jaime Navarro .05 .02 .01
☐ 593 Dave Parker .10 .05 .01
☐ 594 Dan Plesac .05 .02 .01
☐ 595 Ron Robinson .05 .02 .01
☐ 596 Gary Sheffield .15 .07 .02
☐ 597 Bill Spiers .05 .02 .01
☐ 598 B.J. Surhoff .10 .05 .01
☐ 599 Greg Vaughn .10 .05 .01
☐ 600 Randy Veres .05 .02 .01
☐ 601 Robin Yount .15 .07 .02
☐ 602 Rick Aguilera .10 .05 .01
☐ 603 Allan Anderson .05 .02 .01
☐ 604 Juan Berenguer .05 .02 .01
☐ 605 Randy Bush .05 .02 .01
☐ 606 Carmen Castillo .05 .02 .01
☐ 607 Tim Drummond .05 .02 .01
☐ 608 Scott Erickson .10 .05 .01
☐ 609 Gary Gaetti .10 .05 .01
☐ 610 Greg Gagne .05 .02 .01
☐ 611 Dan Gladden .05 .02 .01
☐ 612 Mark Guthrie .05 .02 .01
☐ 613 Brian Harper .05 .02 .01
☐ 614 Kent Hrbek .10 .05 .01
☐ 615 Gene Larkin .05 .02 .01
☐ 616 Terry Leach .05 .02 .01
☐ 617 Nelson Liriano .05 .02 .01
☐ 618 Shane Mack .05 .02 .01
☐ 619 John Moses .05 .02 .01
☐ 620 Pedro Munoz .10 .05 .01
☐ 621 Al Newman .05 .02 .01
☐ 622 Junior Ortiz .05 .02 .01
☐ 623 Kirby Puckett .40 .18 .05
☐ 624 Roy Smith .05 .02 .01
☐ 625 Kevin Tapani .05 .02 .01
☐ 626 Gary Wayne .05 .02 .01
☐ 627 David West .05 .02 .01
☐ 628 Cris Carpenter .05 .02 .01
☐ 629 Vince Coleman .05 .02 .01
☐ 630 Ken Dayley .05 .02 .01
☐ 631A Jose DeLeon ERR .05 .02 .01
(missing '79 Bradenton stats)
☐ 631B Jose DeLeon COR .05 .02 .01
(with '79 Bradenton stats)
☐ 632 Frank DiPino .05 .02 .01
☐ 633 Bernard Gilkey .10 .05 .01
☐ 634A Pedro Guerrero ERR .10 .05 .01
(career SB shown as "$91")
☐ 634B Pedro Guerrero COR .05 .02 .01
☐ 635 Ken Hill .10 .05 .01
☐ 636 Felix Jose .05 .02 .01
☐ 637 Ray Lankford .15 .07 .02
☐ 638 Joe Magrane .05 .02 .01
☐ 639 Tom Niedenfuer .05 .02 .01
☐ 640 Jose Oquendo .05 .02 .01
☐ 641 Tom Pagnozzi .05 .02 .01
☐ 642 Terry Pendleton .10 .05 .01
☐ 643 Mike Perez .05 .02 .01
☐ 644 Bryn Smith .05 .02 .01
☐ 645 Lee Smith .10 .05 .01
☐ 646 Ozzie Smith .25 .11 .03
☐ 647 Scott Terry .05 .02 .01
☐ 648 Bob Tewksbury .05 .02 .01
☐ 649 Milt Thompson .05 .02 .01
☐ 650 John Tudor .05 .02 .01
☐ 651 Denny Walling .05 .02 .01
☐ 652 Craig Wilson .05 .02 .01
☐ 653 Todd Worrell .05 .02 .01
☐ 654 Todd Zeile .10 .05 .01
☐ 655 Oscar Azocar .05 .02 .01
☐ 656 Steve Balboni UER .05 .02 .01
(Born 1/5/57, should be 1/16)
☐ 657 Jesse Barfield .05 .02 .01
☐ 658 Greg Cadaret .05 .02 .01
☐ 659 Chuck Cary .05 .02 .01
☐ 660 Rick Cerone .05 .02 .01
☐ 661 Dave Eiland .05 .02 .01
☐ 662 Alvaro Espinoza .05 .02 .01
☐ 663 Bob Geren .05 .02 .01
☐ 664 Lee Guetterman .05 .02 .01
☐ 665 Mel Hall .05 .02 .01
☐ 666 Andy Hawkins .05 .02 .01
☐ 667 Jimmy Jones .05 .02 .01
☐ 668 Roberto Kelly .05 .02 .01
☐ 669 Dave LaPoint UER .05 .02 .01
(No '81 Brewers stats, totals also are wrong)
☐ 670 Tim Leary .05 .02 .01
☐ 671 Jim Leyritz .10 .05 .01
☐ 672 Kevin Maas .05 .02 .01
☐ 673 Don Mattingly .50 .23 .06
☐ 674 Matt Nokes .05 .02 .01
☐ 675 Pascual Perez .05 .02 .01
☐ 676 Eric Plunk .05 .02 .01
☐ 677 Dave Righetti .05 .02 .01
☐ 678 Jeff D. Robinson .05 .02 .01
☐ 679 Steve Sax .05 .02 .01
☐ 680 Mike Witt .05 .02 .01
☐ 681 Steve Avery UER .15 .07 .02
(Born in New Jersey, should say Michigan)
☐ 682 Mike Bell .05 .02 .01
☐ 683 Jeff Blauser .05 .02 .01
☐ 684 Francisco Cabrera UER .05 .02 .01
(Born 10/16, should say 10/10)
☐ 685 Tony Castillo .05 .02 .01
☐ 686 Marty Clary UER .05 .02 .01
(Shown pitching righty, but bio has left)
☐ 687 Nick Esasky .05 .02 .01
☐ 688 Ron Gant .10 .05 .01
☐ 689 Tom Glavine .15 .07 .02
☐ 690 Mark Grant .05 .02 .01
☐ 691 Tommy Gregg .05 .02 .01
☐ 692 Dwayne Henry .05 .02 .01
☐ 693 Dave Justice .15 .07 .02
☐ 694 Jimmy Kremers .05 .02 .01
☐ 695 Charlie Leibrandt .05 .02 .01
☐ 696 Mark Lemke .05 .02 .01
☐ 697 Oddibe McDowell .05 .02 .01
☐ 698 Greg Olson .05 .02 .01
☐ 699 Jeff Parrett .05 .02 .01
☐ 700 Jim Presley .05 .02 .01
☐ 701 Victor Rosario .05 .02 .01
☐ 702 Lonnie Smith .05 .02 .01
☐ 703 Pete Smith .05 .02 .01
☐ 704 John Smoltz .15 .07 .02
☐ 705 Mike Stanton .05 .02 .01
☐ 706 Andres Thomas .05 .02 .01
☐ 707 Jeff Treadway .05 .02 .01
☐ 708 Jim Vatcher .05 .02 .01
☐ 709 Home Run Kings .15 .07 .02
Ryne Sandberg
Cecil Fielder
☐ 710 2nd Generation Stars .50 .23 .06
Barry Bonds
Ken Griffey Jr.
☐ 711 NLCS Team Leaders .15 .07 .02
Bobby Bonilla
Barry Larkin
☐ 712 Top Game Savers .05 .02 .01
Bobby Thigpen
John Franco
☐ 713 Chicago's 100 Club .10 .05 .01
Andre Dawson
Ryne Sandberg UER
(Ryno misspelled Rhino)
☐ 714 CL:A's/Pirates .05 .02 .01
Reds/Red Sox
☐ 715 CL:White Sox/Mets .05 .02 .01
Blue Jays/Dodgers
☐ 716 CL:Expos/Giants .05 .02 .01
Rangers/Angels
☐ 717 CL:Tigers/Indians .05 .02 .01
Phillies/Cubs
☐ 718 CL:Mariners/Orioles .05 .02 .01
Astros/Padres
☐ 719 CL:Royals/Brewers .05 .02 .01
Twins/Cardinals
☐ 720 CL:Yankees/Braves .05 .02 .01
Superstars/Specials

1991 Fleer All-Stars

For the sixth consecutive year Fleer issued an All-Star insert set. This year the cards were only available as random inserts in Fleer cello packs. This ten-card standard-size set is reminiscent of the 1971 Topps Greatest Moments set with two pictures on the (black-bordered) front as well as a photo on the back.

	MINT	NRMT	EXC
COMPLETE SET (10)	15.00	6.75	1.85
COMMON CARD (1-10)	.50	.23	.06
☐ 1 Ryne Sandberg	2.00	.90	.25
☐ 2 Barry Larkin	1.25	.55	.16
☐ 3 Matt Williams	1.00	.45	.12
☐ 4 Cecil Fielder	.75	.35	.09
☐ 5 Barry Bonds	2.00	.90	.25
☐ 6 Rickey Henderson	1.00	.45	.12
☐ 7 Ken Griffey Jr.	10.00	4.50	1.25
☐ 8 Jose Canseco	1.00	.45	.12
☐ 9 Benito Santiago	.50	.23	.06
☐ 10 Roger Clemens	1.50	.70	.19

1991 Fleer Pro-Visions

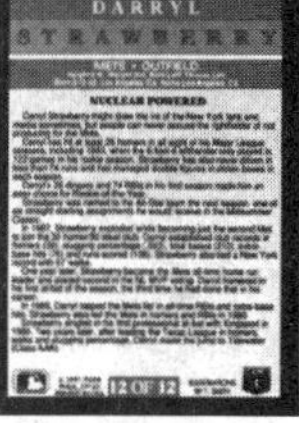

This 12-card standard-size insert set features paintings by artist Terry Smith framed by distinctive black borders on each card front. The cards were randomly inserted in wax and rack packs. An additional four-card set was issued only in 1991 Fleer factory sets. Those cards are numbered F1-F4. Unlike the 12 cards inserted in packs, these factory set cards feature white borders on front.

	MINT	NRMT	EXC
COMPLETE REG.SET (12)	4.00	1.80	.50
COMMON REG.CARD (R1-R12)	.20	.09	.03
COMP.FACTORY SET (4)	2.00	.90	.25
COMMON FACT.CARD (F1-F4)	.25	.11	.03
☐ 1 Kirby Puckett UER (.326 average, should be .328)	1.25	.55	.16
☐ 2 Will Clark UER (On tenth line, pennant misspelled pennent)	.40	.18	.05
☐ 3 Ruben Sierra UER (No apostrophe in hasn't)	.20	.09	.03
☐ 4 Mark McGwire UER (Fisk won ROY in '72, not '82)	1.00	.45	.12
☐ 5 Bo Jackson (Bio says 6', others have him at 6'1")	.30	.14	.04
☐ 6 Jose Canseco UER (Bio 6'3", 230, text has 6'4", 240)	.40	.18	.05
☐ 7 Dwight Gooden UER (2.80 ERA in Lynchburg, should be 2.50)	.30	.14	.04
☐ 8 Mike Greenwell UER (.328 BA and 87 RBI, should be .325 and 95)	.20	.09	.03
☐ 9 Roger Clemens	.60	.25	.07
☐ 10 Eric Davis	.30	.14	.04
☐ 11 Don Mattingly	1.00	.45	.12
☐ 12 Darryl Strawberry	.30	.14	.04
☐ F1 Barry Bonds	.75	.35	.09
☐ F2 Rickey Henderson	.40	.18	.05
☐ F3 Ryne Sandberg	.75	.35	.09
☐ F4 Dave Stewart	.25	.11	.03

1991 Fleer Wax Box Cards

These cards were issued on the bottom of 1991 Fleer wax boxes. This set celebrated the spate of no-hitters in 1990 and were printed on three different boxes. These standard size cards, come four to a box, three about the no-hitters and one team logo card on each box. The cards are blank backed and are numbered on the front in a subtle way. They are ordered below as they are numbered, which is by chronological order of their no-hitters. Only the player cards are listed below since there was a different team logo card on each box.

	MINT	NRMT	EXC
COMPLETE SET (9)	3.50	1.55	.45
COMMON CARD (1-9)	.15	.07	.02
☐ 1 Mark Langston and Mike Witt	.25	.11	.03
☐ 2 Randy Johnson	.50	.23	.06
☐ 3 Nolan Ryan	2.00	.90	.25
☐ 4 Dave Stewart	.25	.11	.03
☐ 5 Fernando Valenzuela	.25	.11	.03
☐ 6 Andy Hawkins	.15	.07	.02
☐ 7 Melido Perez	.15	.07	.02
☐ 8 Terry Mulholland	.15	.07	.02
☐ 9 Dave Stieb	.15	.07	.02

1991 Fleer World Series

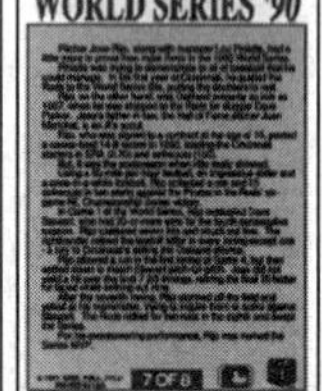

This eight-card set captures highlights from the 1990 World Series between the Cincinnati Reds and the Oakland Athletics. The set was only available as an insert with the 1991 Fleer factory sets. The standard-size cards have on the fronts color action photos, bordered in blue on a white card face. The words "World Series '90" appears in red and blue lettering above the pictures. The backs have a similar design, only with a summary of an aspect of the Series on a yellow background.

	MINT	NRMT	EXC
COMPLETE SET (8)	1.00	.45	.12
COMMON CARD (1-8)	.10	.05	.01
☐ 1 Eric Davis	.10	.05	.01
☐ 2 Billy Hatcher	.10	.05	.01
☐ 3 Jose Canseco	.50	.23	.06
☐ 4 Rickey Henderson	.50	.23	.06
☐ 5 Chris Sabo	.10	.05	.01
☐ 6 Dave Stewart	.25	.11	.03
☐ 7 Jose Rijo	.10	.05	.01
☐ 8 Reds Celebrate	.25	.11	.03

1991 Fleer Update

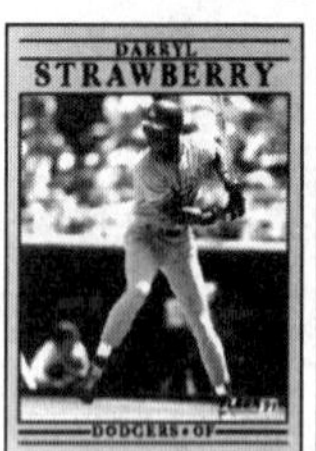

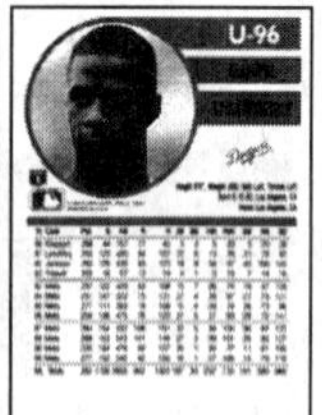

The 1991 Fleer Update set contains 132 standard-size cards. The cards were distributed exclusively in factory set form through hobby dealers. Card design is identical to regular issue 1991 Fleer cards except for the U-prefixed numbering on back. The cards are ordered alphabetically by team. The key Rookie Cards in this set are Jeff Bagwell and Ivan Rodriguez.

	MINT	NRMT	EXC
COMPLETE FACT.SET (132)	4.00	1.80	.50
COMMON CARD (1-132)	.05	.02	.01
☐ 1 Glenn Davis	.05	.02	.01
☐ 2 Dwight Evans	.10	.05	.01
☐ 3 Jose Mesa	.10	.05	.01
☐ 4 Jack Clark	.10	.05	.01
☐ 5 Danny Darwin	.05	.02	.01
☐ 6 Steve Lyons	.05	.02	.01
☐ 7 Mo Vaughn	.50	.23	.06
☐ 8 Floyd Bannister	.05	.02	.01
☐ 9 Gary Gaetti	.10	.05	.01
☐ 10 Dave Parker	.10	.05	.01
☐ 11 Joey Cora	.10	.05	.01
☐ 12 Charlie Hough	.05	.02	.01
☐ 13 Matt Merullo	.05	.02	.01
☐ 14 Warren Newson	.05	.02	.01
☐ 15 Tim Raines	.15	.07	.02
☐ 16 Albert Belle	.50	.23	.06
☐ 17 Glenallen Hill	.05	.02	.01
☐ 18 Shawn Hillegas	.05	.02	.01
☐ 19 Mark Lewis	.05	.02	.01
☐ 20 Charles Nagy	.15	.07	.02
☐ 21 Mark Whiten	.10	.05	.01
☐ 22 John Cerutti	.05	.02	.01
☐ 23 Rob Deer	.05	.02	.01
☐ 24 Mickey Tettleton	.10	.05	.01
☐ 25 Warren Cromartie	.05	.02	.01
☐ 26 Kirk Gibson	.10	.05	.01
☐ 27 David Howard	.05	.02	.01
☐ 28 Brent Mayne	.05	.02	.01
☐ 29 Dante Bichette	.15	.07	.02
☐ 30 Mark Lee	.05	.02	.01
☐ 31 Julio Machado	.05	.02	.01
☐ 32 Edwin Nunez	.05	.02	.01
☐ 33 Willie Randolph	.10	.05	.01
☐ 34 Franklin Stubbs	.05	.02	.01
☐ 35 Bill Wegman	.05	.02	.01
☐ 36 Chili Davis	.10	.05	.01
☐ 37 Chuck Knoblauch	.25	.11	.03
☐ 38 Scott Leius	.05	.02	.01
☐ 39 Jack Morris	.10	.05	.01
☐ 40 Mike Pagliarulo	.05	.02	.01
☐ 41 Lenny Webster	.05	.02	.01
☐ 42 John Habyan	.05	.02	.01
☐ 43 Steve Howe	.05	.02	.01
☐ 44 Jeff Johnson	.05	.02	.01
☐ 45 Scott Kamieniecki	.05	.02	.01
☐ 46 Pat Kelly	.10	.05	.01
☐ 47 Hensley Meulens	.05	.02	.01
☐ 48 Wade Taylor	.05	.02	.01
☐ 49 Bernie Williams	.30	.14	.04
☐ 50 Kirk Dressendorfer	.05	.02	.01
☐ 51 Ernest Riles	.05	.02	.01
☐ 52 Rich DeLucia	.05	.02	.01
☐ 53 Tracy Jones	.05	.02	.01
☐ 54 Bill Krueger	.05	.02	.01
☐ 55 Alonzo Powell	.05	.02	.01
☐ 56 Jeff Schaefer	.05	.02	.01
☐ 57 Russ Swan	.05	.02	.01
☐ 58 John Barfield	.05	.02	.01
☐ 59 Rich Gossage	.10	.05	.01
☐ 60 Jose Guzman	.05	.02	.01
☐ 61 Dean Palmer	.15	.07	.02
☐ 62 Ivan Rodriguez	1.50	.70	.19
☐ 63 Roberto Alomar	.20	.09	.03
☐ 64 Tom Candiotti	.05	.02	.01
☐ 65 Joe Carter	.10	.05	.01
☐ 66 Ed Sprague	.10	.05	.01
☐ 67 Pat Tabler	.05	.02	.01
☐ 68 Mike Timlin	.05	.02	.01
☐ 69 Devon White	.10	.05	.01
☐ 70 Rafael Belliard	.05	.02	.01
☐ 71 Juan Berenguer	.05	.02	.01
☐ 72 Sid Bream	.05	.02	.01
☐ 73 Marvin Freeman	.05	.02	.01
☐ 74 Kent Mercker	.05	.02	.01
☐ 75 Otis Nixon	.05	.02	.01
☐ 76 Terry Pendleton	.10	.05	.01
☐ 77 George Bell	.05	.02	.01
☐ 78 Danny Jackson	.05	.02	.01
☐ 79 Chuck McElroy	.05	.02	.01
☐ 80 Gary Scott	.05	.02	.01
☐ 81 Heathcliff Slocumb	.15	.07	.02
☐ 82 Dave Smith	.05	.02	.01
☐ 83 Rick Wilkins	.05	.02	.01
☐ 84 Freddie Benavides	.05	.02	.01
☐ 85 Ted Power	.05	.02	.01
☐ 86 Mo Sanford	.05	.02	.01
☐ 87 Jeff Bagwell	2.50	1.10	.30
☐ 88 Steve Finley	.10	.05	.01
☐ 89 Pete Harnisch	.05	.02	.01
☐ 90 Darryl Kile	.05	.02	.01
☐ 91 Brett Butler	.10	.05	.01
☐ 92 John Candelaria	.05	.02	.01
☐ 93 Gary Carter	.10	.05	.01
☐ 94 Kevin Gross	.05	.02	.01
☐ 95 Bob Ojeda	.05	.02	.01
☐ 96 Darryl Strawberry	.10	.05	.01
☐ 97 Ivan Calderon	.05	.02	.01
☐ 98 Ron Hassey	.05	.02	.01
☐ 99 Gilberto Reyes	.05	.02	.01
☐ 100 Hubie Brooks	.05	.02	.01
☐ 101 Rick Cerone	.05	.02	.01
☐ 102 Vince Coleman	.05	.02	.01
☐ 103 Jeff Innis	.05	.02	.01
☐ 104 Pete Schourek	.15	.07	.02
☐ 105 Andy Ashby	.15	.07	.02
☐ 106 Wally Backman	.05	.02	.01
☐ 107 Darrin Fletcher	.05	.02	.01
☐ 108 Tommy Greene	.05	.02	.01
☐ 109 John Morris	.05	.02	.01
☐ 110 Mitch Williams	.05	.02	.01
☐ 111 Lloyd McClendon	.05	.02	.01
☐ 112 Orlando Merced	.15	.07	.02
☐ 113 Vicente Palacios	.05	.02	.01
☐ 114 Gary Varsho	.05	.02	.01
☐ 115 John Wehner	.05	.02	.01
☐ 116 Rex Hudler	.05	.02	.01
☐ 117 Tim Jones	.05	.02	.01
☐ 118 Geronimo Pena	.05	.02	.01
☐ 119 Gerald Perry	.05	.02	.01
☐ 120 Larry Andersen	.05	.02	.01
☐ 121 Jerald Clark	.05	.02	.01
☐ 122 Scott Coolbaugh	.05	.02	.01
☐ 123 Tony Fernandez	.05	.02	.01
☐ 124 Darrin Jackson	.05	.02	.01
☐ 125 Fred McGriff	.15	.07	.02
☐ 126 Jose Mota	.05	.02	.01
☐ 127 Tim Teufel	.05	.02	.01
☐ 128 Bud Black	.05	.02	.01
☐ 129 Mike Felder	.05	.02	.01
☐ 130 Willie McGee	.05	.02	.01
☐ 131 Dave Righetti	.05	.02	.01
☐ 132 Checklist U1-U132	.05	.02	.01

1992 Fleer

The 1992 Fleer set contains 720 standard-size cards issued in one comprehensive series. The cards were distributed in plastic wrapped packs, 35-card cello packs, 42-card rack packs and factory sets. The card fronts shade from metallic pale green to white as one moves down the face. The team logo and player's name appear to the right of the picture, running the length of the card. The cards are ordered alphabetically within and according to teams for each league with AL preceding NL. Topical subsets feature Major League Prospects (652-680), Record Setters (681-687), League Leaders (688-697), Super Star Specials (698-707) and Pro Visions (708-713). The only notable Rookie Card features Vinny Castilla.

	MINT	NRMT	EXC
COMPLETE SET (720)	15.00	6.75	1.85
COMPLETE HOBBY SET (732)	25.00	11.00	3.10
COMPLETE RETAIL SET (732)	25.00	11.00	3.10
COMMON CARD (1-720)	.05	.02	.01
☐ 1 Brady Anderson	.15	.07	.02
☐ 2 Jose Bautista	.05	.02	.01
☐ 3 Juan Bell	.05	.02	.01
☐ 4 Glenn Davis	.05	.02	.01
☐ 5 Mike Devereaux	.05	.02	.01
☐ 6 Dwight Evans	.10	.05	.01
☐ 7 Mike Flanagan	.05	.02	.01
☐ 8 Leo Gomez	.05	.02	.01
☐ 9 Chris Hoiles	.05	.02	.01
☐ 10 Sam Horn	.05	.02	.01
☐ 11 Tim Hulett	.05	.02	.01
☐ 12 Dave Johnson	.05	.02	.01
☐ 13 Chito Martinez	.05	.02	.01
☐ 14 Ben McDonald	.05	.02	.01
☐ 15 Bob Melvin	.05	.02	.01
☐ 16 Luis Mercedes	.05	.02	.01
☐ 17 Jose Mesa	.10	.05	.01
☐ 18 Bob Milacki	.05	.02	.01
☐ 19 Randy Milligan	.05	.02	.01
☐ 20 Mike Mussina UER (Card back refers to him as Jeff)	.30	.14	.04
☐ 21 Gregg Olson	.05	.02	.01
☐ 22 Joe Orsulak	.05	.02	.01
☐ 23 Jim Poole	.05	.02	.01
☐ 24 Arthur Rhodes	.05	.02	.01
☐ 25 Billy Ripken	.05	.02	.01
☐ 26 Cal Ripken	.75	.35	.09
☐ 27 David Segui	.05	.02	.01
☐ 28 Roy Smith	.05	.02	.01
☐ 29 Anthony Telford	.05	.02	.01
☐ 30 Mark Williamson	.05	.02	.01
☐ 31 Craig Worthington	.05	.02	.01
☐ 32 Wade Boggs	.15	.07	.02
☐ 33 Tom Bolton	.05	.02	.01
☐ 34 Tom Brunansky	.05	.02	.01
☐ 35 Ellis Burks	.10	.05	.01
☐ 36 Jack Clark	.10	.05	.01
☐ 37 Roger Clemens	.20	.09	.03
☐ 38 Danny Darwin	.05	.02	.01
☐ 39 Mike Greenwell	.05	.02	.01
☐ 40 Joe Hesketh	.05	.02	.01
☐ 41 Daryl Irvine	.05	.02	.01
☐ 42 Dennis Lamp	.05	.02	.01
☐ 43 Tony Pena	.05	.02	.01
☐ 44 Phil Plantier	.10	.05	.01
☐ 45 Carlos Quintana	.05	.02	.01
☐ 46 Jeff Reardon	.10	.05	.01
☐ 47 Jody Reed	.05	.02	.01
☐ 48 Luis Rivera	.05	.02	.01
☐ 49 Mo Vaughn	.40	.18	.05
☐ 50 Jim Abbott	.05	.02	.01
☐ 51 Kyle Abbott	.05	.02	.01
☐ 52 Ruben Amaro Jr.	.05	.02	.01
☐ 53 Scott Bailes	.05	.02	.01
☐ 54 Chris Beasley	.05	.02	.01
☐ 55 Mark Eichhorn	.05	.02	.01
☐ 56 Mike Fetters	.05	.02	.01
☐ 57 Chuck Finley	.05	.02	.01
☐ 58 Gary Gaetti	.10	.05	.01
☐ 59 Dave Gallagher	.05	.02	.01
☐ 60 Donnie Hill	.05	.02	.01
☐ 61 Bryan Harvey UER (Lee Smith led the Majors with 47 saves)	.05	.02	.01
☐ 62 Wally Joyner	.10	.05	.01
☐ 63 Mark Langston	.10	.05	.01
☐ 64 Kirk McCaskill	.05	.02	.01
☐ 65 John Orton	.05	.02	.01
☐ 66 Lance Parrish	.05	.02	.01
☐ 67 Luis Polonia	.05	.02	.01
☐ 68 Bobby Rose	.05	.02	.01
☐ 69 Dick Schofield	.05	.02	.01
☐ 70 Luis Sojo	.05	.02	.01
☐ 71 Lee Stevens	.05	.02	.01
☐ 72 Dave Winfield	.15	.07	.02
☐ 73 Cliff Young	.05	.02	.01
☐ 74 Wilson Alvarez	.15	.07	.02
☐ 75 Esteban Beltre	.05	.02	.01
☐ 76 Joey Cora	.10	.05	.01
☐ 77 Brian Drahman	.05	.02	.01
☐ 78 Alex Fernandez	.15	.07	.02
☐ 79 Carlton Fisk	.15	.07	.02
☐ 80 Scott Fletcher	.05	.02	.01
☐ 81 Craig Grebeck	.05	.02	.01
☐ 82 Ozzie Guillen	.05	.02	.01
☐ 83 Greg Hibbard	.05	.02	.01
☐ 84 Charlie Hough	.05	.02	.01
☐ 85 Mike Huff	.05	.02	.01
☐ 86 Bo Jackson	.10	.05	.01
☐ 87 Lance Johnson	.10	.05	.01
☐ 88 Ron Karkovice	.05	.02	.01
☐ 89 Jack McDowell	.10	.05	.01
☐ 90 Matt Merullo	.05	.02	.01
☐ 91 Warren Newson	.05	.02	.01
☐ 92 Donn Pall UER (Called Dunn on card back)	.05	.02	.01
☐ 93 Dan Pasqua	.05	.02	.01
☐ 94 Ken Patterson	.05	.02	.01
☐ 95 Melido Perez	.05	.02	.01
☐ 96 Scott Radinsky	.05	.02	.01
☐ 97 Tim Raines	.15	.07	.02
☐ 98 Sammy Sosa	.25	.11	.03
☐ 99 Bobby Thigpen	.05	.02	.01
☐ 100 Frank Thomas	1.50	.70	.19
☐ 101 Robin Ventura	.10	.05	.01
☐ 102 Mike Aldrete	.05	.02	.01
☐ 103 Sandy Alomar Jr.	.10	.05	.01
☐ 104 Carlos Baerga	.10	.05	.01
☐ 105 Albert Belle	.50	.23	.06
☐ 106 Willie Blair	.05	.02	.01
☐ 107 Jerry Browne	.05	.02	.01
☐ 108 Alex Cole	.05	.02	.01

☐ 109 Felix Fermin .05 .02 .01
☐ 110 Glenallen Hill .05 .02 .01
☐ 111 Shawn Hillegas .05 .02 .01
☐ 112 Chris James .05 .02 .01
☐ 113 Reggie Jefferson .10 .05 .01
☐ 114 Doug Jones .05 .02 .01
☐ 115 Eric King .05 .02 .01
☐ 116 Mark Lewis .05 .02 .01
☐ 117 Carlos Martinez .05 .02 .01
☐ 118 Charles Nagy UER .10 .05 .01
(Throws right, but
card says left)
☐ 119 Rod Nichols .05 .02 .01
☐ 120 Steve Olin .05 .02 .01
☐ 121 Jesse Orosco .05 .02 .01
☐ 122 Rudy Seanez .05 .02 .01
☐ 123 Joel Skinner .05 .02 .01
☐ 124 Greg Swindell .05 .02 .01
☐ 125 Jim Thome .75 .35 .09
☐ 126 Mark Whiten .10 .05 .01
☐ 127 Scott Aldred .05 .02 .01
☐ 128 Andy Allanson .05 .02 .01
☐ 129 John Cerutti .05 .02 .01
☐ 130 Milt Cuyler .05 .02 .01
☐ 131 Mike Dalton .05 .02 .01
☐ 132 Rob Deer .05 .02 .01
☐ 133 Cecil Fielder .10 .05 .01
☐ 134 Travis Fryman .15 .07 .02
☐ 135 Dan Gakeler .05 .02 .01
☐ 136 Paul Gibson .05 .02 .01
☐ 137 Bill Gullickson .05 .02 .01
☐ 138 Mike Henneman .05 .02 .01
☐ 139 Pete Incaviglia .05 .02 .01
☐ 140 Mark Leiter .05 .02 .01
☐ 141 Scott Livingstone .05 .02 .01
☐ 142 Lloyd Moseby .05 .02 .01
☐ 143 Tony Phillips .10 .05 .01
☐ 144 Mark Salas .05 .02 .01
☐ 145 Frank Tanana .05 .02 .01
☐ 146 Walt Terrell .05 .02 .01
☐ 147 Mickey Tettleton .05 .02 .01
☐ 148 Alan Trammell .10 .05 .01
☐ 149 Lou Whitaker .10 .05 .01
☐ 150 Kevin Appier .10 .05 .01
☐ 151 Luis Aquino .05 .02 .01
☐ 152 Todd Benzinger .05 .02 .01
☐ 153 Mike Boddicker .05 .02 .01
☐ 154 George Brett .40 .18 .05
☐ 155 Storm Davis .05 .02 .01
☐ 156 Jim Eisenreich .05 .02 .01
☐ 157 Kirk Gibson .10 .05 .01
☐ 158 Tom Gordon .05 .02 .01
☐ 159 Mark Gubicza .05 .02 .01
☐ 160 David Howard .05 .02 .01
☐ 161 Mike Macfarlane .05 .02 .01
☐ 162 Brent Mayne .05 .02 .01
☐ 163 Brian McRae .10 .05 .01
☐ 164 Jeff Montgomery .10 .05 .01
☐ 165 Bill Pecota .05 .02 .01
☐ 166 Harvey Pulliam .05 .02 .01
☐ 167 Bret Saberhagen .10 .05 .01
☐ 168 Kevin Seitzer .05 .02 .01
☐ 169 Terry Shumpert .05 .02 .01
☐ 170 Kurt Stillwell .05 .02 .01
☐ 171 Danny Tartabull .05 .02 .01
☐ 172 Gary Thurman .05 .02 .01
☐ 173 Dante Bichette .15 .07 .02
☐ 174 Kevin D. Brown .05 .02 .01
☐ 175 Chuck Crim .05 .02 .01
☐ 176 Jim Gantner .05 .02 .01
☐ 177 Darryl Hamilton .05 .02 .01
☐ 178 Ted Higuera .05 .02 .01
☐ 179 Darren Holmes .05 .02 .01
☐ 180 Mark Lee .05 .02 .01
☐ 181 Julio Machado .05 .02 .01
☐ 182 Paul Molitor .20 .09 .03
☐ 183 Jaime Navarro .05 .02 .01
☐ 184 Edwin Nunez .05 .02 .01
☐ 185 Dan Plesac .05 .02 .01
☐ 186 Willie Randolph .10 .05 .01
☐ 187 Ron Robinson .05 .02 .01
☐ 188 Gary Sheffield .15 .07 .02
☐ 189 Bill Spiers .05 .02 .01
☐ 190 B.J. Surhoff .10 .05 .01
☐ 191 Dale Sveum .05 .02 .01
☐ 192 Greg Vaughn .10 .05 .01
☐ 193 Bill Wegman .05 .02 .01
☐ 194 Robin Yount .15 .07 .02
☐ 195 Rick Aguilera .05 .02 .01
☐ 196 Allan Anderson .05 .02 .01
☐ 197 Steve Bedrosian .05 .02 .01
☐ 198 Randy Bush .05 .02 .01
☐ 199 Larry Casian .05 .02 .01
☐ 200 Chili Davis .10 .05 .01
☐ 201 Scott Erickson .10 .05 .01
☐ 202 Greg Gagne .05 .02 .01
☐ 203 Dan Gladden .05 .02 .01
☐ 204 Brian Harper .05 .02 .01
☐ 205 Kent Hrbek .10 .05 .01
☐ 206 Chuck Knoblauch UER .15 .07 .02
(Career hit total
of 59 is wrong)
☐ 207 Gene Larkin .05 .02 .01
☐ 208 Terry Leach .05 .02 .01
☐ 209 Scott Leius .05 .02 .01
☐ 210 Shane Mack .05 .02 .01
☐ 211 Jack Morris .10 .05 .01
☐ 212 Pedro Munoz .05 .02 .01
☐ 213 Denny Neagle .15 .07 .02
☐ 214 Al Newman .05 .02 .01
☐ 215 Junior Ortiz .05 .02 .01
☐ 216 Mike Pagliarulo .05 .02 .01
☐ 217 Kirby Puckett .40 .18 .05
☐ 218 Paul Sorrento .05 .02 .01
☐ 219 Kevin Tapani .05 .02 .01
☐ 220 Lenny Webster .05 .02 .01
☐ 221 Jesse Barfield .05 .02 .01
☐ 222 Greg Cadaret .05 .02 .01
☐ 223 Dave Eiland .05 .02 .01
☐ 224 Alvaro Espinoza .05 .02 .01
☐ 225 Steve Farr .05 .02 .01
☐ 226 Bob Geren .05 .02 .01
☐ 227 Lee Guetterman .05 .02 .01
☐ 228 John Habyan .05 .02 .01
☐ 229 Mel Hall .05 .02 .01
☐ 230 Steve Howe .05 .02 .01
☐ 231 Mike Humphreys .05 .02 .01
☐ 232 Scott Kamieniecki .05 .02 .01
☐ 233 Pat Kelly .05 .02 .01
☐ 234 Roberto Kelly .05 .02 .01
☐ 235 Tim Leary .05 .02 .01
☐ 236 Kevin Maas .05 .02 .01
☐ 237 Don Mattingly .50 .23 .06
☐ 238 Hensley Meulens .05 .02 .01
☐ 239 Matt Nokes .05 .02 .01
☐ 240 Pascual Perez .05 .02 .01
☐ 241 Eric Plunk .05 .02 .01
☐ 242 John Ramos .05 .02 .01
☐ 243 Scott Sanderson .05 .02 .01
☐ 244 Steve Sax .05 .02 .01
☐ 245 Wade Taylor .05 .02 .01
☐ 246 Randy Velarde .05 .02 .01
☐ 247 Bernie Williams .25 .11 .03
☐ 248 Troy Afenir .05 .02 .01
☐ 249 Harold Baines .10 .05 .01
☐ 250 Lance Blankenship .05 .02 .01
☐ 251 Mike Bordick .10 .05 .01
☐ 252 Jose Canseco .15 .07 .02
☐ 253 Steve Chitren .05 .02 .01
☐ 254 Ron Darling .05 .02 .01
☐ 255 Dennis Eckersley .10 .05 .01
☐ 256 Mike Gallego .05 .02 .01
☐ 257 Dave Henderson .05 .02 .01
☐ 258 Rickey Henderson UER .15 .07 .02
(Wearing 24 on front
and 22 on back)
☐ 259 Rick Honeycutt .05 .02 .01
☐ 260 Brook Jacoby .05 .02 .01
☐ 261 Carney Lansford .10 .05 .01
☐ 262 Mark McGwire .30 .14 .04
☐ 263 Mike Moore .05 .02 .01
☐ 264 Gene Nelson .05 .02 .01
☐ 265 Jamie Quirk .05 .02 .01
☐ 266 Joe Slusarski .05 .02 .01
☐ 267 Terry Steinbach .10 .05 .01
☐ 268 Dave Stewart .10 .05 .01
☐ 269 Todd Van Poppel .05 .02 .01
☐ 270 Walt Weiss .05 .02 .01
☐ 271 Bob Welch .05 .02 .01
☐ 272 Curt Young .05 .02 .01
☐ 273 Scott Bradley .05 .02 .01
☐ 274 Greg Briley .05 .02 .01
☐ 275 Jay Buhner .15 .07 .02
☐ 276 Henry Cotto .05 .02 .01
☐ 277 Alvin Davis .05 .02 .01
☐ 278 Rich DeLucia .05 .02 .01
☐ 279 Ken Griffey Jr. 1.50 .70 .19
☐ 280 Erik Hanson .05 .02 .01
☐ 281 Brian Holman .05 .02 .01
☐ 282 Mike Jackson .05 .02 .01
☐ 283 Randy Johnson .15 .07 .02
☐ 284 Tracy Jones .05 .02 .01
☐ 285 Bill Krueger .05 .02 .01
☐ 286 Edgar Martinez .10 .05 .01
☐ 287 Tino Martinez .10 .05 .01
☐ 288 Rob Murphy .05 .02 .01
☐ 289 Pete O'Brien .05 .02 .01
☐ 290 Alonzo Powell .05 .02 .01
☐ 291 Harold Reynolds .05 .02 .01
☐ 292 Mike Schooler .05 .02 .01
☐ 293 Russ Swan .05 .02 .01
☐ 294 Bill Swift .05 .02 .01
☐ 295 Dave Valle .05 .02 .01
☐ 296 Omar Vizquel .10 .05 .01
☐ 297 Gerald Alexander .05 .02 .01
☐ 298 Brad Arnsberg .05 .02 .01
☐ 299 Kevin Brown .10 .05 .01
☐ 300 Jack Daugherty .05 .02 .01
☐ 301 Mario Diaz .05 .02 .01
☐ 302 Brian Downing .05 .02 .01
☐ 303 Julio Franco .10 .05 .01
☐ 304 Juan Gonzalez .60 .25 .07
☐ 305 Rich Gossage .10 .05 .01
☐ 306 Jose Guzman .05 .02 .01
☐ 307 Jose Hernandez .05 .02 .01
☐ 308 Jeff Huson .05 .02 .01
☐ 309 Mike Jeffcoat .05 .02 .01
☐ 310 Terry Mathews .05 .02 .01
☐ 311 Rafael Palmeiro .15 .07 .02
☐ 312 Dean Palmer .10 .05 .01
☐ 313 Geno Petralli .05 .02 .01
☐ 314 Gary Pettis .05 .02 .01
☐ 315 Kevin Reimer .05 .02 .01
☐ 316 Ivan Rodriguez .40 .18 .05
☐ 317 Kenny Rogers .05 .02 .01
☐ 318 Wayne Rosenthal .05 .02 .01
☐ 319 Jeff Russell .05 .02 .01
☐ 320 Nolan Ryan .75 .35 .09
☐ 321 Ruben Sierra .10 .05 .01
☐ 322 Jim Acker .05 .02 .01
☐ 323 Roberto Alomar .20 .09 .03
☐ 324 Derek Bell .15 .07 .02
☐ 325 Pat Borders .05 .02 .01
☐ 326 Tom Candiotti .05 .02 .01
☐ 327 Joe Carter .10 .05 .01
☐ 328 Rob Ducey .05 .02 .01
☐ 329 Kelly Gruber .05 .02 .01
☐ 330 Juan Guzman .10 .05 .01
☐ 331 Tom Henke .05 .02 .01
☐ 332 Jimmy Key .10 .05 .01
☐ 333 Manny Lee .05 .02 .01
☐ 334 Al Leiter .10 .05 .01
☐ 335 Bob MacDonald .05 .02 .01
☐ 336 Candy Maldonado .05 .02 .01
☐ 337 Rance Mulliniks .05 .02 .01
☐ 338 Greg Myers .05 .02 .01
☐ 339 John Olerud UER .10 .05 .01
(1991 BA has .256,
but text says .258)
☐ 340 Ed Sprague .10 .05 .01
☐ 341 Dave Stieb .05 .02 .01
☐ 342 Todd Stottlemyre .10 .05 .01
☐ 343 Mike Timlin .05 .02 .01
☐ 344 Duane Ward .05 .02 .01
☐ 345 David Wells .05 .02 .01
☐ 346 Devon White .10 .05 .01
☐ 347 Mookie Wilson .05 .02 .01
☐ 348 Eddie Zosky .05 .02 .01
☐ 349 Steve Avery .10 .05 .01
☐ 350 Mike Bell .05 .02 .01
☐ 351 Rafael Belliard .05 .02 .01
☐ 352 Juan Berenguer .05 .02 .01
☐ 353 Jeff Blauser .05 .02 .01
☐ 354 Sid Bream .05 .02 .01
☐ 355 Francisco Cabrera .05 .02 .01
☐ 356 Marvin Freeman .05 .02 .01
☐ 357 Ron Gant .10 .05 .01
☐ 358 Tom Glavine .15 .07 .02
☐ 359 Brian Hunter .05 .02 .01
☐ 360 Dave Justice .15 .07 .02
☐ 361 Charlie Leibrandt .05 .02 .01
☐ 362 Mark Lemke .05 .02 .01
☐ 363 Kent Mercker .05 .02 .01
☐ 364 Keith Mitchell .05 .02 .01
☐ 365 Greg Olson .05 .02 .01
☐ 366 Terry Pendleton .10 .05 .01
☐ 367 Armando Reynoso .05 .02 .01
☐ 368 Deion Sanders .15 .07 .02
☐ 369 Lonnie Smith .05 .02 .01
☐ 370 Pete Smith .05 .02 .01
☐ 371 John Smoltz .15 .07 .02
☐ 372 Mike Stanton .05 .02 .01
☐ 373 Jeff Treadway .05 .02 .01
☐ 374 Mark Wohlers .15 .07 .02
☐ 375 Paul Assenmacher .05 .02 .01
☐ 376 George Bell .05 .02 .01
☐ 377 Shawn Boskie .05 .02 .01
☐ 378 Frank Castillo .10 .05 .01
☐ 379 Andre Dawson .10 .05 .01
☐ 380 Shawon Dunston .05 .02 .01
☐ 381 Mark Grace .15 .07 .02
☐ 382 Mike Harkey .05 .02 .01
☐ 383 Danny Jackson .05 .02 .01
☐ 384 Les Lancaster .05 .02 .01
☐ 385 Ced Landrum .05 .02 .01
☐ 386 Greg Maddux .75 .35 .09
☐ 387 Derrick May .05 .02 .01
☐ 388 Chuck McElroy .05 .02 .01
☐ 389 Ryne Sandberg .25 .11 .03
☐ 390 Heathcliff Slocumb .05 .02 .01
☐ 391 Dave Smith .05 .02 .01
☐ 392 Dwight Smith .05 .02 .01
☐ 393 Rick Sutcliffe .05 .02 .01
☐ 394 Hector Villanueva .05 .02 .01
☐ 395 Chico Walker .05 .02 .01
☐ 396 Jerome Walton .05 .02 .01
☐ 397 Rick Wilkins .05 .02 .01
☐ 398 Jack Armstrong .05 .02 .01
☐ 399 Freddie Benavides .05 .02 .01
☐ 400 Glenn Braggs .05 .02 .01
☐ 401 Tom Browning .05 .02 .01
☐ 402 Norm Charlton .05 .02 .01
☐ 403 Eric Davis .10 .05 .01
☐ 404 Rob Dibble .05 .02 .01
☐ 405 Bill Doran .05 .02 .01
☐ 406 Mariano Duncan .05 .02 .01
☐ 407 Kip Gross .05 .02 .01
☐ 408 Chris Hammond .05 .02 .01
☐ 409 Billy Hatcher .05 .02 .01
☐ 410 Chris Jones .05 .02 .01
☐ 411 Barry Larkin .15 .07 .02
☐ 412 Hal Morris .05 .02 .01
☐ 413 Randy Myers .10 .05 .01
☐ 414 Joe Oliver .05 .02 .01
☐ 415 Paul O'Neill .10 .05 .01
☐ 416 Ted Power .05 .02 .01
☐ 417 Luis Quinones .05 .02 .01
☐ 418 Jeff Reed .05 .02 .01
☐ 419 Jose Rijo .05 .02 .01
☐ 420 Chris Sabo .05 .02 .01
☐ 421 Reggie Sanders .15 .07 .02
☐ 422 Scott Scudder .05 .02 .01
☐ 423 Glenn Sutko .05 .02 .01
☐ 424 Eric Anthony .05 .02 .01
☐ 425 Jeff Bagwell .60 .25 .07
☐ 426 Craig Biggio .10 .05 .01
☐ 427 Ken Caminiti .15 .07 .02
☐ 428 Casey Candaele .05 .02 .01
☐ 429 Mike Capel .05 .02 .01
☐ 430 Andujar Cedeno .05 .02 .01
☐ 431 Jim Corsi .05 .02 .01
☐ 432 Mark Davidson .05 .02 .01
☐ 433 Steve Finley .10 .05 .01
☐ 434 Luis Gonzalez .10 .05 .01
☐ 435 Pete Harnisch .05 .02 .01
☐ 436 Dwayne Henry .05 .02 .01
☐ 437 Xavier Hernandez .05 .02 .01
☐ 438 Jimmy Jones .05 .02 .01
☐ 439 Darryl Kile .05 .02 .01
☐ 440 Rob Mallicoat .05 .02 .01
☐ 441 Andy Mota .05 .02 .01
☐ 442 Al Osuna .05 .02 .01
☐ 443 Mark Portugal .05 .02 .01
☐ 444 Scott Servais .05 .02 .01
☐ 445 Mike Simms .05 .02 .01
☐ 446 Gerald Young .05 .02 .01
☐ 447 Tim Belcher .05 .02 .01
☐ 448 Brett Butler .10 .05 .01
☐ 449 John Candelaria .05 .02 .01
☐ 450 Gary Carter .10 .05 .01
☐ 451 Dennis Cook .05 .02 .01
☐ 452 Tim Crews .05 .02 .01
☐ 453 Kal Daniels .05 .02 .01
☐ 454 Jim Gott .05 .02 .01
☐ 455 Alfredo Griffin .05 .02 .01
☐ 456 Kevin Gross .05 .02 .01
☐ 457 Chris Gwynn .05 .02 .01
☐ 458 Lenny Harris .05 .02 .01
☐ 459 Orel Hershiser .10 .05 .01
☐ 460 Jay Howell .05 .02 .01
☐ 461 Stan Javier .05 .02 .01
☐ 462 Eric Karros .15 .07 .02
☐ 463 Ramon Martinez UER .10 .05 .01
(Card says bats right,
should be left)
☐ 464 Roger McDowell UER .05 .02 .01
(Wins add up to 54,
totals have 51)
☐ 465 Mike Morgan .05 .02 .01
☐ 466 Eddie Murray .25 .11 .03
☐ 467 Jose Offerman .05 .02 .01
☐ 468 Bob Ojeda .05 .02 .01
☐ 469 Juan Samuel .05 .02 .01
☐ 470 Mike Scioscia .05 .02 .01
☐ 471 Darryl Strawberry .10 .05 .01
☐ 472 Bret Barberie .05 .02 .01
☐ 473 Brian Barnes .05 .02 .01
☐ 474 Eric Bullock .05 .02 .01
☐ 475 Ivan Calderon .05 .02 .01
☐ 476 Delino DeShields .05 .02 .01
☐ 477 Jeff Fassero .10 .05 .01
☐ 478 Mike Fitzgerald .05 .02 .01
☐ 479 Steve Frey .05 .02 .01
☐ 480 Andres Galarraga .15 .07 .02
☐ 481 Mark Gardner .05 .02 .01
☐ 482 Marquis Grissom .10 .05 .01
☐ 483 Chris Haney .05 .02 .01
☐ 484 Barry Jones .05 .02 .01
☐ 485 Dave Martinez .05 .02 .01
☐ 486 Dennis Martinez .10 .05 .01
☐ 487 Chris Nabholz .05 .02 .01
☐ 488 Spike Owen .05 .02 .01
☐ 489 Gilberto Reyes .05 .02 .01
☐ 490 Mel Rojas .10 .05 .01
☐ 491 Scott Ruskin .05 .02 .01
☐ 492 Bill Sampen .05 .02 .01
☐ 493 Larry Walker .15 .07 .02
☐ 494 Tim Wallach .05 .02 .01
☐ 495 Daryl Boston .05 .02 .01
☐ 496 Hubie Brooks .05 .02 .01
☐ 497 Tim Burke .05 .02 .01
☐ 498 Mark Carreon .05 .02 .01
☐ 499 Tony Castillo .05 .02 .01
☐ 500 Vince Coleman .05 .02 .01
☐ 501 David Cone .10 .05 .01
☐ 502 Kevin Elster .05 .02 .01
☐ 503 Sid Fernandez .05 .02 .01
☐ 504 John Franco .05 .02 .01
☐ 505 Dwight Gooden .10 .05 .01
☐ 506 Todd Hundley .10 .05 .01
☐ 507 Jeff Innis .05 .02 .01
☐ 508 Gregg Jefferies .10 .05 .01
☐ 509 Howard Johnson .05 .02 .01
☐ 510 Dave Magadan .05 .02 .01
☐ 511 Terry McDaniel .05 .02 .01
☐ 512 Kevin McReynolds .05 .02 .01
☐ 513 Keith Miller .05 .02 .01
☐ 514 Charlie O'Brien .05 .02 .01
☐ 515 Mackey Sasser .05 .02 .01
☐ 516 Pete Schourek .10 .05 .01

Card	MINT	NRMT	EXC
☐ 517 Julio Valera	.05	.02	.01
☐ 518 Frank Viola	.05	.02	.01
☐ 519 Wally Whitehurst	.05	.02	.01
☐ 520 Anthony Young	.05	.02	.01
☐ 521 Andy Ashby	.10	.05	.01
☐ 522 Kim Batiste	.05	.02	.01
☐ 523 Joe Boever	.05	.02	.01
☐ 524 Wes Chamberlain	.05	.02	.01
☐ 525 Pat Combs	.05	.02	.01
☐ 526 Danny Cox	.05	.02	.01
☐ 527 Darren Daulton	.10	.05	.01
☐ 528 Jose DeJesus	.05	.02	.01
☐ 529 Len Dykstra	.10	.05	.01
☐ 530 Darrin Fletcher	.05	.02	.01
☐ 531 Tommy Greene	.05	.02	.01
☐ 532 Jason Grimsley	.05	.02	.01
☐ 533 Charlie Hayes	.05	.02	.01
☐ 534 Von Hayes	.05	.02	.01
☐ 535 Dave Hollins	.05	.02	.01
☐ 536 Ricky Jordan	.05	.02	.01
☐ 537 John Kruk	.10	.05	.01
☐ 538 Jim Lindeman	.05	.02	.01
☐ 539 Mickey Morandini	.05	.02	.01
☐ 540 Terry Mulholland	.05	.02	.01
☐ 541 Dale Murphy	.15	.07	.02
☐ 542 Randy Ready	.05	.02	.01
☐ 543 Wally Ritchie UER (Letters in data are cut off on card)	.05	.02	.01
☐ 544 Bruce Ruffin	.05	.02	.01
☐ 545 Steve Searcy	.05	.02	.01
☐ 546 Dickie Thon	.05	.02	.01
☐ 547 Mitch Williams	.05	.02	.01
☐ 548 Stan Belinda	.05	.02	.01
☐ 549 Jay Bell	.10	.05	.01
☐ 550 Barry Bonds	.25	.11	.03
☐ 551 Bobby Bonilla	.10	.05	.01
☐ 552 Steve Buechele	.05	.02	.01
☐ 553 Doug Drabek	.05	.02	.01
☐ 554 Neal Heaton	.05	.02	.01
☐ 555 Jeff King	.10	.05	.01
☐ 556 Bob Kipper	.05	.02	.01
☐ 557 Bill Landrum	.05	.02	.01
☐ 558 Mike LaValliere	.05	.02	.01
☐ 559 Jose Lind	.05	.02	.01
☐ 560 Lloyd McClendon	.05	.02	.01
☐ 561 Orlando Merced	.05	.02	.01
☐ 562 Bob Patterson	.05	.02	.01
☐ 563 Joe Redfield	.05	.02	.01
☐ 564 Gary Redus	.05	.02	.01
☐ 565 Rosario Rodriguez	.05	.02	.01
☐ 566 Don Slaught	.05	.02	.01
☐ 567 John Smiley	.05	.02	.01
☐ 568 Zane Smith	.05	.02	.01
☐ 569 Randy Tomlin	.05	.02	.01
☐ 570 Andy Van Slyke	.10	.05	.01
☐ 571 Gary Varsho	.05	.02	.01
☐ 572 Bob Walk	.05	.02	.01
☐ 573 John Wehner UER (Actually played for Carolina in 1991, not Cards)	.05	.02	.01
☐ 574 Juan Agosto	.05	.02	.01
☐ 575 Cris Carpenter	.05	.02	.01
☐ 576 Jose DeLeon	.05	.02	.01
☐ 577 Rich Gedman	.05	.02	.01
☐ 578 Bernard Gilkey	.10	.05	.01
☐ 579 Pedro Guerrero	.05	.02	.01
☐ 580 Ken Hill	.10	.05	.01
☐ 581 Rex Hudler	.05	.02	.01
☐ 582 Felix Jose	.05	.02	.01
☐ 583 Ray Lankford	.15	.07	.02
☐ 584 Omar Olivares	.05	.02	.01
☐ 585 Jose Oquendo	.05	.02	.01
☐ 586 Tom Pagnozzi	.05	.02	.01
☐ 587 Geronimo Pena	.05	.02	.01
☐ 588 Mike Perez	.05	.02	.01
☐ 589 Gerald Perry	.05	.02	.01
☐ 590 Bryn Smith	.05	.02	.01
☐ 591 Lee Smith	.10	.05	.01
☐ 592 Ozzie Smith	.25	.11	.03
☐ 593 Scott Terry	.05	.02	.01
☐ 594 Bob Tewksbury	.05	.02	.01
☐ 595 Milt Thompson	.05	.02	.01
☐ 596 Todd Zeile	.05	.02	.01
☐ 597 Larry Andersen	.05	.02	.01
☐ 598 Oscar Azocar	.05	.02	.01
☐ 599 Andy Benes	.10	.05	.01
☐ 600 Ricky Bones	.05	.02	.01
☐ 601 Jerald Clark	.05	.02	.01
☐ 602 Pat Clements	.05	.02	.01
☐ 603 Paul Faries	.05	.02	.01
☐ 604 Tony Fernandez	.05	.02	.01
☐ 605 Tony Gwynn	.40	.18	.05
☐ 606 Greg W. Harris	.05	.02	.01
☐ 607 Thomas Howard	.05	.02	.01
☐ 608 Bruce Hurst	.05	.02	.01
☐ 609 Darrin Jackson	.05	.02	.01
☐ 610 Tom Lampkin	.05	.02	.01
☐ 611 Craig Lefferts	.05	.02	.01
☐ 612 Jim Lewis	.05	.02	.01
☐ 613 Mike Maddux	.05	.02	.01
☐ 614 Fred McGriff	.15	.07	.02
☐ 615 Jose Melendez	.05	.02	.01
☐ 616 Jose Mota	.05	.02	.01
☐ 617 Dennis Rasmussen	.05	.02	.01
☐ 618 Bip Roberts	.05	.02	.01
☐ 619 Rich Rodriguez	.05	.02	.01
☐ 620 Benito Santiago	.05	.02	.01
☐ 621 Craig Shipley	.05	.02	.01
☐ 622 Tim Teufel	.05	.02	.01
☐ 623 Kevin Ward	.05	.02	.01
☐ 624 Ed Whitson	.05	.02	.01
☐ 625 Dave Anderson	.05	.02	.01
☐ 626 Kevin Bass	.05	.02	.01
☐ 627 Rod Beck	.25	.11	.03
☐ 628 Bud Black	.05	.02	.01
☐ 629 Jeff Brantley	.10	.05	.01
☐ 630 John Burkett	.10	.05	.01
☐ 631 Will Clark	.15	.07	.02
☐ 632 Royce Clayton	.10	.05	.01
☐ 633 Steve Decker	.05	.02	.01
☐ 634 Kelly Downs	.05	.02	.01
☐ 635 Mike Felder	.05	.02	.01
☐ 636 Scott Garrelts	.05	.02	.01
☐ 637 Eric Gunderson	.05	.02	.01
☐ 638 Bryan Hickerson	.05	.02	.01
☐ 639 Darren Lewis	.05	.02	.01
☐ 640 Greg Litton	.05	.02	.01
☐ 641 Kirt Manwaring	.05	.02	.01
☐ 642 Paul McClellan	.05	.02	.01
☐ 643 Willie McGee	.05	.02	.01
☐ 644 Kevin Mitchell	.10	.05	.01
☐ 645 Francisco Oliveras	.05	.02	.01
☐ 646 Mike Remlinger	.05	.02	.01
☐ 647 Dave Righetti	.05	.02	.01
☐ 648 Robby Thompson	.05	.02	.01
☐ 649 Jose Uribe	.05	.02	.01
☐ 650 Matt Williams	.15	.07	.02
☐ 651 Trevor Wilson	.05	.02	.01
☐ 652 Tom Goodwin MLP UER (Timed in 3.5, should be be timed)	.10	.05	.01
☐ 653 Terry Bross MLP	.05	.02	.01
☐ 654 Mike Christopher MLP	.05	.02	.01
☐ 655 Kenny Lofton MLP	1.00	.45	.12
☐ 656 Chris Cron MLP	.05	.02	.01
☐ 657 Willie Banks MLP	.05	.02	.01
☐ 658 Pat Rice MLP	.05	.02	.01
☐ 659A Rob Maurer MLP ERR (Name misspelled as Mauer on card front)	.75	.35	.09
☐ 659B Rob Maurer MLP COR	.10	.05	.01
☐ 660 Don Harris MLP	.05	.02	.01
☐ 661 Henry Rodriguez MLP	.15	.07	.02
☐ 662 Cliff Brantley MLP	.05	.02	.01
☐ 663 Mike Linskey MLP UER (220 pounds in data, 200 in text)	.05	.02	.01
☐ 664 Gary DiSarcina MLP	.05	.02	.01
☐ 665 Gil Heredia MLP	.05	.02	.01
☐ 666 Vinny Castilla MLP	.50	.23	.06
☐ 667 Paul Abbott MLP	.05	.02	.01
☐ 668 Monty Fariss MLP UER (Called Paul on back)	.05	.02	.01
☐ 669 Jarvis Brown MLP	.05	.02	.01
☐ 670 Wayne Kirby MLP	.05	.02	.01
☐ 671 Scott Brosius MLP	.05	.02	.01
☐ 672 Bob Hamelin MLP	.05	.02	.01
☐ 673 Joel Johnston MLP	.05	.02	.01
☐ 674 Tim Spehr MLP	.05	.02	.01
☐ 675A Jeff Gardner MLP ERR (P on front, should be SS)	.75	.35	.09
☐ 675B Jeff Gardner MLP COR	.25	.11	.03
☐ 676 Rico Rossy MLP	.05	.02	.01
☐ 677 Roberto Hernandez MLP	.10	.05	.01
☐ 678 Ted Wood MLP	.05	.02	.01
☐ 679 Cal Eldred MLP	.05	.02	.01
☐ 680 Sean Berry MLP	.10	.05	.01
☐ 681 Rickey Henderson RS	.15	.07	.02
☐ 682 Nolan Ryan RS	.40	.18	.05
☐ 683 Dennis Martinez RS	.05	.02	.01
☐ 684 Wilson Alvarez RS	.10	.05	.01
☐ 685 Joe Carter RS	.15	.07	.02
☐ 686 Dave Winfield RS	.15	.07	.02
☐ 687 David Cone RS	.10	.05	.01
☐ 688 Jose Canseco LL UER (Text on back has 42 stolen bases in '88; should be 40)	.15	.07	.02
☐ 689 Howard Johnson LL	.05	.02	.01
☐ 690 Julio Franco LL	.05	.02	.01
☐ 691 Terry Pendleton LL	.05	.02	.01
☐ 692 Cecil Fielder LL	.10	.05	.01
☐ 693 Scott Erickson LL	.05	.02	.01
☐ 694 Tom Glavine LL	.10	.05	.01
☐ 695 Dennis Martinez LL	.05	.02	.01
☐ 696 Bryan Harvey LL	.05	.02	.01
☐ 697 Lee Smith LL	.10	.05	.01
☐ 698 Super Siblings Roberto Alomar Sandy Alomar Jr.	.10	.05	.01
☐ 699 The Indispensables Bobby Bonilla Will Clark	.10	.05	.01
☐ 700 Teamwork Mark Wohlers Kent Mercker Alejandro Pena	.05	.02	.01
☐ 701 Tiger Tandems Stacy Jones Bo Jackson Gregg Olson Frank Thomas	.50	.23	.06
☐ 702 The Ignitors Paul Molitor Brett Butler	.15	.07	.02
☐ 703 Indispensables II Cal Ripken Joe Carter	.50	.23	.06
☐ 704 Power Packs Barry Larkin Kirby Puckett	.25	.11	.03
☐ 705 Today and Tomorrow Mo Vaughn Cecil Fielder	.15	.07	.02
☐ 706 Teenage Sensations Ramon Martinez Ozzie Guillen	.10	.05	.01
☐ 707 Designated Hitters Harold Baines Wade Boggs	.15	.07	.02
☐ 708 Robin Yount PV	.15	.07	.02
☐ 709 Ken Griffey Jr. PV UER (Missing quotations on back; BA has .322, but was actually .327)	.75	.35	.09
☐ 710 Nolan Ryan PV	.40	.18	.05
☐ 711 Cal Ripken PV	.40	.18	.05
☐ 712 Frank Thomas PV	.75	.35	.09
☐ 713 Dave Justice PV	.10	.05	.01
☐ 714 Checklist 1-101	.05	.02	.01
☐ 715 Checklist 102-194	.05	.02	.01
☐ 716 Checklist 195-296	.05	.02	.01
☐ 717 Checklist 297-397	.05	.02	.01
☐ 718 Checklist 398-494	.05	.02	.01
☐ 719 Checklist 495-596	.05	.02	.01
☐ 720A Checklist 597-720 ERR (659 Rob Mauer)	.05	.02	.01
☐ 720B Checklist 597-720 COR (659 Rob Maurer)	.05	.02	.01

1992 Fleer All-Stars

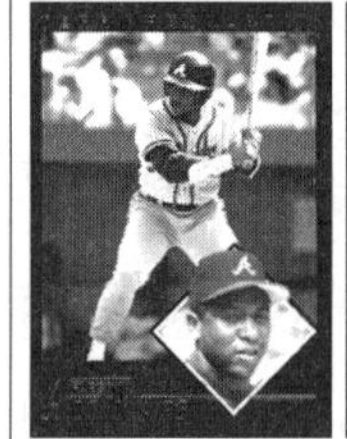

Cards from this 24-card standard-size set were randomly inserted in plastic wrap packs. Selected members of the American and National League 1991 All-Star squads comprise this set. The glossy color photos on the fronts are bordered in black and accented above and below with gold stripes and lettering. A diamond with a color head shot of the player is superimposed at the lower right corner of the picture.

	MINT	NRMT	EXC
COMPLETE SET (24)	35.00	16.00	4.40
COMMON CARD (1-24)	.50	.23	.06
☐ 1 Felix Jose	.50	.23	.06
☐ 2 Tony Gwynn	2.50	1.10	.30
☐ 3 Barry Bonds	2.00	.90	.25
☐ 4 Bobby Bonilla	.75	.35	.09
☐ 5 Mike LaValliere	.50	.23	.06
☐ 6 Tom Glavine	1.00	.45	.12
☐ 7 Ramon Martinez	.75	.35	.09
☐ 8 Lee Smith	.75	.35	.09
☐ 9 Mickey Tettleton	.50	.23	.06
☐ 10 Scott Erickson	.75	.35	.09
☐ 11 Frank Thomas	10.00	4.50	1.25
☐ 12 Danny Tartabull	.50	.23	.06
☐ 13 Will Clark	1.00	.45	.12
☐ 14 Ryne Sandberg	1.50	.70	.19
☐ 15 Terry Pendleton	.50	.23	.06
☐ 16 Barry Larkin	1.00	.45	.12
☐ 17 Rafael Palmeiro	1.00	.45	.12
☐ 18 Julio Franco	.50	.23	.06
☐ 19 Robin Ventura	.75	.35	.09
☐ 20 Cal Ripken UER (Candidte; total bases misspelled as based)	8.00	3.60	1.00
☐ 21 Joe Carter	.75	.35	.09
☐ 22 Kirby Puckett	2.50	1.10	.30
☐ 23 Ken Griffey Jr.	10.00	4.50	1.25
☐ 24 Jose Canseco	1.00	.45	.12

1992 Fleer Clemens

Roger Clemens served as a spokesperson for Fleer during 1992 and was the exclusive subject of this 15-card standard-size set. The first 12-card Clemens 'Career Highlights' subseries was randomly inserted in 1992 Fleer packs. Two-thousand signed cards were randomly inserted in wax packs and could also be won by entering a drawing. However, these cards are uncertifiable as they do not have any distinguishable marks. Moreover, a three-card Clemens subset (13-15) was available through a special mail-in offer. The glossy color photos on the fronts are bordered in black and accented with gold stripes and lettering on the top of the card. On a pale yellow background with black borders, the back has player profile and career highlights.

	MINT	NRMT	EXC
COMPLETE SET (12)	10.00	4.50	1.25
COMMON CLEMENS (1-12)	1.00	.45	.12
COMMON SEND-OFF (13-15)	1.00	.45	.12
☐ 1 Roger Clemens Quiet Storm	1.00	.45	.12
☐ 2 Roger Clemens Courted By Mets and Twins	1.00	.45	.12
☐ 3 Roger Clemens The Show	1.00	.45	.12
☐ 4 Roger Clemens Rocket Launched	1.00	.45	.12
☐ 5 Roger Clemens Time Of Trial	1.00	.45	.12
☐ 6 Roger Clemens Break Through	1.00	.45	.12
☐ 7 Roger Clemens Play It Again Roger	1.00	.45	.12
☐ 8 Roger Clemens Business As Usual	1.00	.45	.12
☐ 9 Roger Clemens Heeee's Back	1.00	.45	.12
☐ 10 Roger Clemens Blood, Sweat and Tears	1.00	.45	.12
☐ 11 Roger Clemens Prime Of Life	1.00	.45	.12
☐ 12 Roger Clemens Man For Every Season	1.00	.45	.12
☐ 13 Roger Clemens Cooperstown Bound	1.00	.45	.12
☐ 14 Roger Clemens The Heat of the Moment	1.00	.45	.12
☐ 15 Roger Clemens Final Words Q and A with 'The Rocket'	1.00	.45	.12
☐ AU0 Roger Clemens AU (Uncertified signature)	80.00	36.00	10.00
☐ NNO Roger Clemens Promo with Paul Mullan	6.00	2.70	.75

1992 Fleer Lumber Company

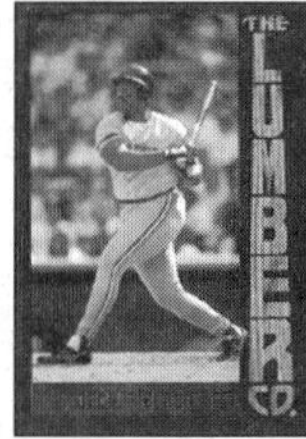

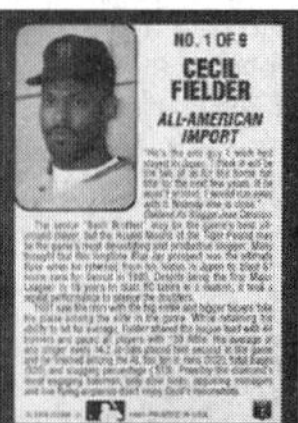

The 1992 Fleer Lumber Company standard-size set features nine outstanding hitters in Major League Baseball. This set was only available as a bonus in Fleer hobby factory sets. Inside a black glossy frame, the fronts display color action player photos, with the player's name printed in black in a gold foil bar beneath the picture. The wider right border contains the catch phrase "The Lumber Co." in the shape of a baseball bat, complete with woodgrain streaks.

	MINT	NRMT	EXC
COMPLETE SET (9)	10.00	4.50	1.25
COMMON CARD (L1-L9)	.75	.35	.09
☐ L1 Cecil Fielder	1.00	.45	.12
☐ L2 Mickey Tettleton	.75	.35	.09
☐ L3 Darryl Strawberry	1.00	.45	.12
☐ L4 Ryne Sandberg	1.50	.70	.19
☐ L5 Jose Canseco	1.25	.55	.16
☐ L6 Matt Williams UER (In 17th line, cycle is spelled cyle)	1.25	.55	.16
☐ L7 Cal Ripken	8.00	3.60	1.00
☐ L8 Barry Bonds	1.50	.70	.19
☐ L9 Ron Gant	1.00	.45	.12

1992 Fleer Rookie Sensations

Cards from the 20-card Fleer Rookie Sensations set were randomly inserted in 1992 Fleer 35-card cello packs. The cards were extremely popular upon release resulting in packs selling for levels far above suggested retail levels. The glossy color photos on the fronts have a white border on a royal blue card face. The words 'Rookie Sensations'

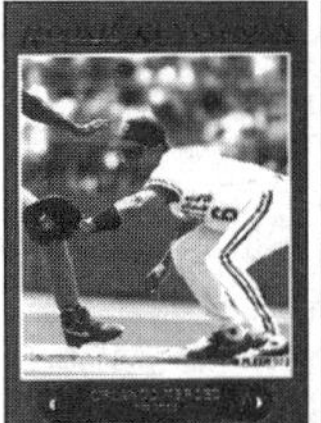

appear above the picture in gold foil lettering, while the player's name appears on a gold foil plaque beneath the picture. Through a mail-in offer for ten Fleer baseball card wrappers and 1.00 for postage and handling, Fleer offered an uncut 8 1/2" by 11" numbered promo sheet picturing ten of the 20-card set on each side in a reduced-size front-only format. The offer indicated an expiration date of July 31, 1992, or whenever the production quantity of 250,000 sheets was exhausted.

	MINT	NRMT	EXC
COMPLETE SET (20)	50.00	22.00	6.25
COMMON CARD (1-20)	1.00	.45	.12
☐ 1 Frank Thomas	30.00	13.50	3.70
☐ 2 Todd Van Poppel	1.00	.45	.12
☐ 3 Orlando Merced	1.50	.70	.19
☐ 4 Jeff Bagwell	12.00	5.50	1.50
☐ 5 Jeff Fassero	1.50	.70	.19
☐ 6 Darren Lewis	1.00	.45	.12
☐ 7 Milt Cuyler	1.00	.45	.12
☐ 8 Mike Timlin	1.00	.45	.12
☐ 9 Brian McRae	1.50	.70	.19
☐ 10 Chuck Knoblauch	4.00	1.80	.50
☐ 11 Rich DeLucia	1.00	.45	.12
☐ 12 Ivan Rodriguez	6.00	2.70	.75
☐ 13 Juan Guzman	1.50	.70	.19
☐ 14 Steve Chitren	1.00	.45	.12
☐ 15 Mark Wohlers	2.50	1.10	.30
☐ 16 Wes Chamberlain	1.00	.45	.12
☐ 17 Ray Lankford	3.00	1.35	.35
☐ 18 Chito Martinez	1.00	.45	.12
☐ 19 Phil Plantier	1.00	.45	.12
☐ 20 Scott Leius UER (Misspelled Lieus on card front)	1.00	.45	.12

1992 Fleer Smoke 'n Heat

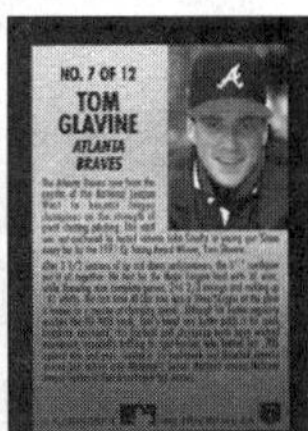

This 12-card standard-size set features outstanding major league pitchers, especially the premier fastball pitchers in both leagues. These cards were only available in Fleer's 1992 Christmas factory set. The front design features color action player photos bordered in black. The player's name appears in a gold foil bar beneath the picture, and the words "Smoke 'n Heat" are printed vertically in the wider right border.

	MINT	NRMT	EXC
COMPLETE SET (12)	10.00	4.50	1.25
COMMON CARD (S1-S12)	.50	.23	.06
☐ S1 Lee Smith	.75	.35	.09
☐ S2 Jack McDowell	.75	.35	.09
☐ S3 David Cone	.75	.35	.09
☐ S4 Roger Clemens	1.50	.70	.19
☐ S5 Nolan Ryan	6.00	2.70	.75
☐ S6 Scott Erickson	.50	.23	.06
☐ S7 Tom Glavine	1.25	.55	.16
☐ S8 Dwight Gooden	.75	.35	.09
☐ S9 Andy Benes	.75	.35	.09
☐ S10 Steve Avery	.50	.23	.06
☐ S11 Randy Johnson	1.25	.55	.16
☐ S12 Jim Abbott	.50	.23	.06

1992 Fleer Team Leaders

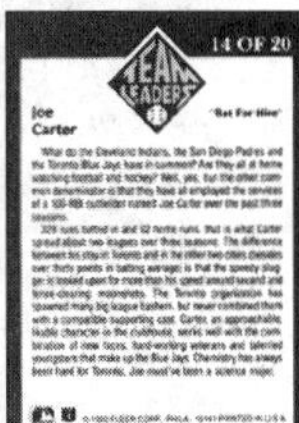

Cards from the 20-card Fleer Team Leaders set were randomly inserted in 1992 Fleer 42-card rack packs. The glossy color photos on the fronts are bordered in white and green. Two gold foil stripes below the picture intersect a diamond-shaped "Team Leaders" emblem.

	MINT	NRMT	EXC
COMPLETE SET (20)	45.00	20.00	5.50
COMMON CARD (1-20)	1.00	.45	.12
☐ 1 Don Mattingly	8.00	3.60	1.00
☐ 2 Howard Johnson	1.00	.45	.12
☐ 3 Chris Sabo UER (Where he it, should be Where he hit)	1.00	.45	.12
☐ 4 Carlton Fisk	2.00	.90	.25
☐ 5 Kirby Puckett	6.00	2.70	.75
☐ 6 Cecil Fielder	2.00	.90	.25
☐ 7 Tony Gwynn	6.00	2.70	.75
☐ 8 Will Clark	3.00	1.35	.35
☐ 9 Bobby Bonilla	2.00	.90	.25
☐ 10 Len Dykstra	2.00	.90	.25
☐ 11 Tom Glavine	3.00	1.35	.35
☐ 12 Rafael Palmeiro	3.00	1.35	.35
☐ 13 Wade Boggs	3.00	1.35	.35
☐ 14 Joe Carter	2.00	.90	.25
☐ 15 Ken Griffey Jr.	20.00	9.00	2.50
☐ 16 Darryl Strawberry	2.00	.90	.25
☐ 17 Cal Ripken	15.00	6.75	1.85
☐ 18 Danny Tartabull	1.00	.45	.12
☐ 19 Jose Canseco	3.00	1.35	.35
☐ 20 Andre Dawson	2.00	.90	.25

1992 Fleer Update

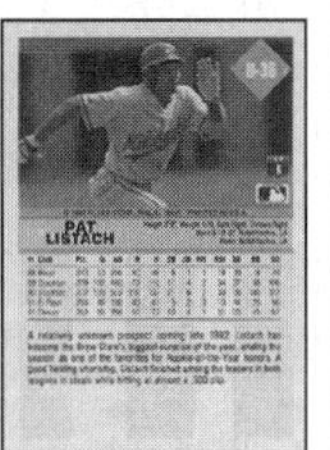

The 1992 Fleer Update set contains 132 standard-size cards. Cards were distributed exclusively in factory sets through hobby dealers. Factory sets included a four-card, black-bordered "92 Headliners" insert set for a total of 136 cards. Due to lackluster retail response for previous Fleer Update sets, wholesale orders for this product were low, resulting in a short print run. As word got out that the cards were in short supply, the secondary market prices soared not soon after release. The basic card design is identical to the regular issue 1992 Fleer cards except for the U-prefixed numbering on back. The cards are checklisted alphabetically within and according to teams for each league with AL preceding NL. Rookie Cards in this set include John Jaha, Mike Piazza, John Valentin and Eric Young. The Piazza card is widely recognized as one of the more desirable singles issued in the 1990's.

	MINT	NRMT	EXC
COMPLETE FACT.SET (136)	160.00	70.00	20.00
COMPLETE SET (132)	140.00	65.00	17.50
COMMON CARD (U1-U132)	.25	.11	.03
☐ 1 Todd Frohwirth	.25	.11	.03
☐ 2 Alan Mills	.25	.11	.03
☐ 3 Rick Sutcliffe	.25	.11	.03
☐ 4 John Valentin	2.50	1.10	.30
☐ 5 Frank Viola	.25	.11	.03
☐ 6 Bob Zupcic	.25	.11	.03
☐ 7 Mike Butcher	.25	.11	.03
☐ 8 Chad Curtis	4.00	1.80	.50
☐ 9 Damion Easley	.50	.23	.06
☐ 10 Tim Salmon	15.00	6.75	1.85
☐ 11 Julio Valera	.25	.11	.03
☐ 12 George Bell	.25	.11	.03
☐ 13 Roberto Hernandez	1.50	.70	.19
☐ 14 Shawn Jeter	.25	.11	.03
☐ 15 Thomas Howard	.25	.11	.03
☐ 16 Jesse Levis	.25	.11	.03
☐ 17 Kenny Lofton	35.00	16.00	4.40
☐ 18 Paul Sorrento	.25	.11	.03
☐ 19 Rico Brogna	.50	.23	.06
☐ 20 John Doherty	.25	.11	.03
☐ 21 Dan Gladden	.25	.11	.03
☐ 22 Buddy Groom	.25	.11	.03
☐ 23 Shawn Hare	.25	.11	.03
☐ 24 John Kiely	.25	.11	.03
☐ 25 Kurt Knudsen	.25	.11	.03
☐ 26 Gregg Jefferies	.50	.23	.06
☐ 27 Wally Joyner	.50	.23	.06
☐ 28 Kevin Koslofski	.25	.11	.03
☐ 29 Kevin McReynolds	.25	.11	.03
☐ 30 Rusty Meacham	.25	.11	.03
☐ 31 Keith Miller	.25	.11	.03
☐ 32 Hipolito Pichardo	.25	.11	.03
☐ 33 James Austin	.25	.11	.03
☐ 34 Scott Fletcher	.25	.11	.03
☐ 35 John Jaha	3.00	1.35	.35
☐ 36 Pat Listach	.50	.23	.06
☐ 37 Dave Nilsson	2.00	.90	.25
☐ 38 Kevin Seitzer	.25	.11	.03
☐ 39 Tom Edens	.25	.11	.03
☐ 40 Pat Mahomes	.25	.11	.03
☐ 41 John Smiley	.25	.11	.03
☐ 42 Charlie Hayes	.25	.11	.03
☐ 43 Sam Militello	.25	.11	.03
☐ 44 Andy Stankiewicz	.25	.11	.03
☐ 45 Danny Tartabull	.25	.11	.03
☐ 46 Bob Wickman	.25	.11	.03
☐ 47 Jerry Browne	.25	.11	.03
☐ 48 Kevin Campbell	.25	.11	.03
☐ 49 Vince Horsman	.25	.11	.03
☐ 50 Troy Neel	.25	.11	.03
☐ 51 Ruben Sierra	.50	.23	.06
☐ 52 Bruce Walton	.25	.11	.03
☐ 53 Willie Wilson	.25	.11	.03
☐ 54 Bret Boone	1.00	.45	.12
☐ 55 Dave Fleming	.25	.11	.03
☐ 56 Kevin Mitchell	.50	.23	.06
☐ 57 Jeff Nelson	.25	.11	.03
☐ 58 Shane Turner	.25	.11	.03
☐ 59 Jose Canseco	2.50	1.10	.30
☐ 60 Jeff Frye	.25	.11	.03
☐ 61 Danny Leon	.25	.11	.03
☐ 62 Roger Pavlik	1.50	.70	.19
☐ 63 David Cone	.50	.23	.06
☐ 64 Pat Hentgen	5.00	2.20	.60
☐ 65 Randy Knorr	.25	.11	.03
☐ 66 Jack Morris	.50	.23	.06
☐ 67 Dave Winfield	1.50	.70	.19
☐ 68 David Nied	.50	.23	.06
☐ 69 Otis Nixon	.25	.11	.03
☐ 70 Alejandro Pena	.25	.11	.03
☐ 71 Jeff Reardon	.50	.23	.06
☐ 72 Alex Arias	.25	.11	.03
☐ 73 Jim Bullinger	.25	.11	.03
☐ 74 Mike Morgan	.25	.11	.03
☐ 75 Rey Sanchez	.25	.11	.03
☐ 76 Bob Scanlan	.25	.11	.03
☐ 77 Sammy Sosa	4.00	1.80	.50
☐ 78 Scott Bankhead	.25	.11	.03
☐ 79 Tim Belcher	.25	.11	.03
☐ 80 Steve Foster	.25	.11	.03
☐ 81 Willie Greene	.50	.23	.06
☐ 82 Bip Roberts	.25	.11	.03
☐ 83 Scott Ruskin	.25	.11	.03
☐ 84 Greg Swindell	.25	.11	.03
☐ 85 Juan Guerrero	.25	.11	.03
☐ 86 Butch Henry	.25	.11	.03
☐ 87 Doug Jones	.25	.11	.03
☐ 88 Brian Williams	.25	.11	.03
☐ 89 Tom Candiotti	.25	.11	.03
☐ 90 Eric Davis	.50	.23	.06
☐ 91 Carlos Hernandez	.25	.11	.03
☐ 92 Mike Piazza	100.00	45.00	12.50
☐ 93 Mike Sharperson	.25	.11	.03
☐ 94 Eric Young	3.00	1.35	.35
☐ 95 Moises Alou	2.50	1.10	.30
☐ 96 Greg Colbrunn	.25	.11	.03
☐ 97 Wil Cordero	.50	.23	.06
☐ 98 Ken Hill	.50	.23	.06
☐ 99 John Vander Wal	.25	.11	.03
☐ 100 John Wetteland	.50	.23	.06
☐ 101 Bobby Bonilla	.50	.23	.06
☐ 102 Eric Hillman	.25	.11	.03
☐ 103 Pat Howell	.25	.11	.03
☐ 104 Jeff Kent	1.50	.70	.19
☐ 105 Dick Schofield	.25	.11	.03
☐ 106 Ryan Thompson	.25	.11	.03
☐ 107 Chico Walker	.25	.11	.03
☐ 108 Juan Bell	.25	.11	.03
☐ 109 Mariano Duncan	.25	.11	.03
☐ 110 Jeff Grotewold	.25	.11	.03
☐ 111 Ben Rivera	.25	.11	.03
☐ 112 Curt Schilling	.25	.11	.03
☐ 113 Victor Cole	.25	.11	.03
☐ 114 Albert Martin	1.00	.45	.12
☐ 115 Roger Mason	.25	.11	.03
☐ 116 Blas Minor	.25	.11	.03
☐ 117 Tim Wakefield	1.00	.45	.12
☐ 118 Mark Clark	.50	.23	.06
☐ 119 Rheal Cormier	.25	.11	.03
☐ 120 Donovan Osborne	.50	.23	.06
☐ 121 Todd Worrell	.25	.11	.03
☐ 122 Jeremy Hernandez	.25	.11	.03
☐ 123 Randy Myers	.50	.23	.06
☐ 124 Frank Seminara	.25	.11	.03
☐ 125 Gary Sheffield	3.00	1.35	.35
☐ 126 Dan Walters	.25	.11	.03
☐ 127 Steve Hosey	.25	.11	.03
☐ 128 Mike Jackson	.25	.11	.03
☐ 129 Jim Pena	.25	.11	.03
☐ 130 Cory Snyder	.25	.11	.03
☐ 131 Bill Swift	.25	.11	.03
☐ 132 Checklist U1-U132	.25	.11	.03

1992 Fleer Update Headliners

Each 1992 Fleer Update factory set included a four-card set of Headliner inserts. The cards are numbered separately and have a completely different design to the base cards. Each Headliner features UV coating and black borders. The set features a selection of stars that made headlines in the 1991 season. Cards are numbered on back X of 4.

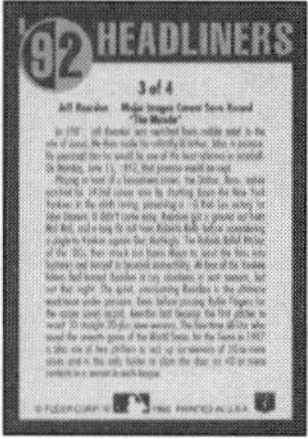

	MINT	NRMT	EXC
COMPLETE SET (4)	20.00	9.00	2.50
COMMON CARD (1-4)	1.00	.45	.12
☐ 1 Ken Griffey Jr.	15.00	6.75	1.85
☐ 2 Robin Yount	2.00	.90	.25
☐ 3 Jeff Reardon	1.00	.45	.12
☐ 4 Cecil Fielder	2.00	.90	.25

1992 Fleer Citgo The Performer

This 24-card standard-size set was produced by Fleer for 7-Eleven. During April and May at any of the 1,600 participating 7-Eleven stores, customers who purchased eight gallons or more of mid-grade or premium Citgo-brand gasoline received a packet of five trading cards. During June or while supplies last, customers who wanted additional cards could receive three trading cards of their choice per eight gallon or more fill-up by sending in a self-addressed envelope with 1.00 to cover postage and handling. The front design has color action player photos, with a metallic blue-green border that fades to white as one moves down the card face. The card front prominently features "The Performer". The team logo, player's name, and his position appear in the wider right border. The top half of the backs have close-up photos, while the bottom half carry biography and complete career statistics.

	MINT	NRMT	EXC
COMPLETE SET (24)	8.00	3.60	1.00
COMMON CARD (1-24)	.10	.05	.01
☐ 1 Nolan Ryan	1.50	.70	.19
☐ 2 Frank Thomas	1.50	.70	.19
☐ 3 Ryne Sandberg	.60	.25	.07
☐ 4 Ken Griffey Jr.	1.50	.70	.19
☐ 5 Cal Ripken	1.25	.55	.16
☐ 6 Roger Clemens	.40	.18	.05
☐ 7 Cecil Fielder	.20	.09	.03
☐ 8 Dave Justice	.20	.09	.03
☐ 9 Wade Boggs	.25	.11	.03
☐ 10 Tony Gwynn	.75	.35	.09
☐ 11 Kirby Puckett	.75	.35	.09
☐ 12 Darryl Strawberry	.20	.09	.03
☐ 13 Jose Canseco	.40	.18	.05
☐ 14 Barry Larkin	.25	.11	.03
☐ 15 Terry Pendleton	.10	.05	.01
☐ 16 Don Mattingly	.75	.35	.09
☐ 17 Rickey Henderson	.25	.11	.03
☐ 18 Ruben Sierra	.10	.05	.01
☐ 19 Jeff Bagwell	1.00	.45	.12
☐ 20 Tom Glavine	.30	.14	.04
☐ 21 Ramon Martinez	.20	.09	.03
☐ 22 Will Clark	.25	.11	.03
☐ 23 Barry Bonds	.40	.18	.05
☐ 24 Roberto Alomar	.40	.18	.05

1993 Fleer

The 720-card 1993 Fleer baseball set contains two series of 360 standard-size cards. Cards were distributed in plastic wrapped packs, cello packs, jumbo packs and rack packs. For the first time in years, Fleer did not issue a factory set. In fact, Fleer discontinued issuing factory sets from 1993-on. The card fronts show glossy color action player photos bordered in silver. A team color-coded stripe edges the left side of the picture and carries the player's name and team name. The cards are checklisted below alphabetically within and according to teams for each league with NL preceding AL. Topical subsets include League Leaders (344-348/704-708), Round Trippers (349-353/709-713), and Super Star Specials (354-357/714-717). Each series concludes with checklists (358-360/718-720). There are no key Rookie Cards in this set.

	MINT	NRMT	EXC
COMPLETE SET (720)	45.00	20.00	5.50
COMPLETE SERIES 1 (360)	22.50	10.00	2.80
COMPLETE SERIES 2 (360)	22.50	10.00	2.80
COMMON CARD (1-720)	.05	.02	.01
☐ 1 Steve Avery	.15	.07	.02
☐ 2 Sid Bream	.05	.02	.01
☐ 3 Ron Gant	.15	.07	.02
☐ 4 Tom Glavine	.30	.14	.04
☐ 5 Brian Hunter	.05	.02	.01
☐ 6 Ryan Klesko	.60	.25	.07
☐ 7 Charlie Leibrandt	.05	.02	.01
☐ 8 Kent Mercker	.05	.02	.01
☐ 9 David Nied	.05	.02	.01
☐ 10 Otis Nixon	.05	.02	.01
☐ 11 Greg Olson	.05	.02	.01
☐ 12 Terry Pendleton	.15	.07	.02
☐ 13 Deion Sanders	.30	.14	.04
☐ 14 John Smoltz	.30	.14	.04
☐ 15 Mike Stanton	.05	.02	.01
☐ 16 Mark Wohlers	.15	.07	.02
☐ 17 Paul Assenmacher	.05	.02	.01
☐ 18 Steve Buechele	.05	.02	.01
☐ 19 Shawon Dunston	.05	.02	.01
☐ 20 Mark Grace	.30	.14	.04
☐ 21 Derrick May	.05	.02	.01
☐ 22 Chuck McElroy	.05	.02	.01
☐ 23 Mike Morgan	.05	.02	.01
☐ 24 Rey Sanchez	.05	.02	.01
☐ 25 Ryne Sandberg	.50	.23	.06
☐ 26 Bob Scanlan	.05	.02	.01
☐ 27 Sammy Sosa	.30	.14	.04
☐ 28 Rick Wilkins	.05	.02	.01
☐ 29 Bobby Ayala	.15	.07	.02
☐ 30 Tim Belcher	.05	.02	.01
☐ 31 Jeff Branson	.05	.02	.01
☐ 32 Norm Charlton	.05	.02	.01
☐ 33 Steve Foster	.05	.02	.01
☐ 34 Willie Greene	.15	.07	.02
☐ 35 Chris Hammond	.05	.02	.01
☐ 36 Milt Hill	.05	.02	.01
☐ 37 Hal Morris	.05	.02	.01
☐ 38 Joe Oliver	.05	.02	.01
☐ 39 Paul O'Neill	.15	.07	.02
☐ 40 Tim Pugh	.05	.02	.01
☐ 41 Jose Rijo	.05	.02	.01
☐ 42 Bip Roberts	.05	.02	.01
☐ 43 Chris Sabo	.05	.02	.01
☐ 44 Reggie Sanders	.30	.14	.04
☐ 45 Eric Anthony	.05	.02	.01
☐ 46 Jeff Bagwell	.75	.35	.09
☐ 47 Craig Biggio	.15	.07	.02
☐ 48 Joe Boever	.05	.02	.01
☐ 49 Casey Candaele	.05	.02	.01
☐ 50 Steve Finley	.15	.07	.02
☐ 51 Luis Gonzalez	.05	.02	.01
☐ 52 Pete Harnisch	.05	.02	.01
☐ 53 Xavier Hernandez	.05	.02	.01
☐ 54 Doug Jones	.05	.02	.01
☐ 55 Eddie Taubensee	.05	.02	.01
☐ 56 Brian Williams	.05	.02	.01
☐ 57 Pedro Astacio	.05	.02	.01
☐ 58 Todd Benzinger	.05	.02	.01
☐ 59 Brett Butler	.15	.07	.02
☐ 60 Tom Candiotti	.05	.02	.01
☐ 61 Lenny Harris	.05	.02	.01
☐ 62 Carlos Hernandez	.05	.02	.01
☐ 63 Orel Hershiser	.15	.07	.02
☐ 64 Eric Karros	.30	.14	.04
☐ 65 Ramon Martinez	.15	.07	.02
☐ 66 Jose Offerman	.05	.02	.01
☐ 67 Mike Scioscia	.05	.02	.01
☐ 68 Mike Sharperson	.05	.02	.01
☐ 69 Eric Young	.30	.14	.04
☐ 70 Moises Alou	.15	.07	.02
☐ 71 Ivan Calderon	.05	.02	.01
☐ 72 Archi Cianfrocco	.05	.02	.01
☐ 73 Wil Cordero	.15	.07	.02
☐ 74 Delino DeShields	.05	.02	.01
☐ 75 Mark Gardner	.05	.02	.01
☐ 76 Ken Hill	.15	.07	.02
☐ 77 Tim Laker	.05	.02	.01
☐ 78 Chris Nabholz	.05	.02	.01
☐ 79 Mel Rojas	.15	.07	.02
☐ 80 John Vander Wal UER	.05	.02	.01
(Misspelled Vander Wall in letters on back)			
☐ 81 Larry Walker	.30	.14	.04
☐ 82 Tim Wallach	.05	.02	.01
☐ 83 John Wetteland	.15	.07	.02
☐ 84 Bobby Bonilla	.15	.07	.02
☐ 85 Daryl Boston	.05	.02	.01
☐ 86 Sid Fernandez	.05	.02	.01
☐ 87 Eric Hillman	.05	.02	.01
☐ 88 Todd Hundley	.15	.07	.02
☐ 89 Howard Johnson	.05	.02	.01
☐ 90 Jeff Kent	.15	.07	.02
☐ 91 Eddie Murray	.50	.23	.06
☐ 92 Bill Pecota	.05	.02	.01
☐ 93 Bret Saberhagen	.15	.07	.02
☐ 94 Dick Schofield	.05	.02	.01
☐ 95 Pete Schourek	.15	.07	.02
☐ 96 Anthony Young	.05	.02	.01
☐ 97 Ruben Amaro Jr.	.05	.02	.01
☐ 98 Juan Bell	.05	.02	.01
☐ 99 Wes Chamberlain	.05	.02	.01
☐ 100 Darren Daulton	.15	.07	.02
☐ 101 Mariano Duncan	.05	.02	.01
☐ 102 Mike Hartley	.05	.02	.01
☐ 103 Ricky Jordan	.05	.02	.01
☐ 104 John Kruk	.15	.07	.02
☐ 105 Mickey Morandini	.05	.02	.01
☐ 106 Terry Mulholland	.05	.02	.01
☐ 107 Ben Rivera	.05	.02	.01
☐ 108 Curt Schilling	.05	.02	.01
☐ 109 Keith Shepherd	.05	.02	.01
☐ 110 Stan Belinda	.05	.02	.01
☐ 111 Jay Bell	.15	.07	.02
☐ 112 Barry Bonds	.50	.23	.06
☐ 113 Jeff King	.15	.07	.02
☐ 114 Mike LaValliere	.05	.02	.01
☐ 115 Jose Lind	.05	.02	.01
☐ 116 Roger Mason	.05	.02	.01
☐ 117 Orlando Merced	.15	.07	.02
☐ 118 Bob Patterson	.05	.02	.01
☐ 119 Don Slaught	.05	.02	.01
☐ 120 Zane Smith	.05	.02	.01
☐ 121 Randy Tomlin	.05	.02	.01
☐ 122 Andy Van Slyke	.15	.07	.02
☐ 123 Tim Wakefield	.15	.07	.02
☐ 124 Rheal Cormier	.05	.02	.01
☐ 125 Bernard Gilkey	.15	.07	.02
☐ 126 Felix Jose	.05	.02	.01
☐ 127 Ray Lankford	.15	.07	.02
☐ 128 Bob McClure	.05	.02	.01
☐ 129 Donovan Osborne	.05	.02	.01
☐ 130 Tom Pagnozzi	.05	.02	.01
☐ 131 Geronimo Pena	.05	.02	.01
☐ 132 Mike Perez	.05	.02	.01
☐ 133 Lee Smith	.15	.07	.02
☐ 134 Bob Tewksbury	.05	.02	.01
☐ 135 Todd Worrell	.05	.02	.01
☐ 136 Todd Zeile	.05	.02	.01
☐ 137 Jerald Clark	.05	.02	.01
☐ 138 Tony Gwynn	.75	.35	.09
☐ 139 Greg W. Harris	.05	.02	.01
☐ 140 Jeremy Hernandez	.05	.02	.01
☐ 141 Darrin Jackson	.05	.02	.01
☐ 142 Mike Maddux	.05	.02	.01
☐ 143 Fred McGriff	.30	.14	.04
☐ 144 Jose Melendez	.05	.02	.01
☐ 145 Rich Rodriguez	.05	.02	.01
☐ 146 Frank Seminara	.05	.02	.01
☐ 147 Gary Sheffield	.30	.14	.04
☐ 148 Kurt Stillwell	.05	.02	.01
☐ 149 Dan Walters	.05	.02	.01
☐ 150 Rod Beck	.15	.07	.02
☐ 151 Bud Black	.05	.02	.01
☐ 152 Jeff Brantley	.05	.02	.01
☐ 153 John Burkett	.05	.02	.01
☐ 154 Will Clark	.30	.14	.04
☐ 155 Royce Clayton	.15	.07	.02
☐ 156 Mike Jackson	.05	.02	.01
☐ 157 Darren Lewis	.05	.02	.01
☐ 158 Kirt Manwaring	.05	.02	.01
☐ 159 Willie McGee	.05	.02	.01
☐ 160 Cory Snyder	.05	.02	.01
☐ 161 Bill Swift	.05	.02	.01
☐ 162 Trevor Wilson	.05	.02	.01
☐ 163 Brady Anderson	.30	.14	.04
☐ 164 Glenn Davis	.05	.02	.01
☐ 165 Mike Devereaux	.05	.02	.01
☐ 166 Todd Frohwirth	.05	.02	.01
☐ 167 Leo Gomez	.05	.02	.01
☐ 168 Chris Hoiles	.05	.02	.01
☐ 169 Ben McDonald	.05	.02	.01
☐ 170 Randy Milligan	.05	.02	.01
☐ 171 Alan Mills	.05	.02	.01
☐ 172 Mike Mussina	.40	.18	.05
☐ 173 Gregg Olson	.05	.02	.01
☐ 174 Arthur Rhodes	.05	.02	.01
☐ 175 David Segui	.05	.02	.01
☐ 176 Ellis Burks	.15	.07	.02
☐ 177 Roger Clemens	.40	.18	.05
☐ 178 Scott Cooper	.05	.02	.01
☐ 179 Danny Darwin	.05	.02	.01
☐ 180 Tony Fossas	.05	.02	.01
☐ 181 Paul Quantrill	.05	.02	.01
☐ 182 Jody Reed	.05	.02	.01
☐ 183 John Valentin	.15	.07	.02
☐ 184 Mo Vaughn	.50	.23	.06
☐ 185 Frank Viola	.05	.02	.01
☐ 186 Bob Zupcic	.05	.02	.01
☐ 187 Jim Abbott	.05	.02	.01
☐ 188 Gary DiSarcina	.05	.02	.01
☐ 189 Damion Easley	.05	.02	.01
☐ 190 Junior Felix	.05	.02	.01
☐ 191 Chuck Finley	.05	.02	.01
☐ 192 Joe Grahe	.05	.02	.01
☐ 193 Bryan Harvey	.05	.02	.01
☐ 194 Mark Langston	.15	.07	.02
☐ 195 John Orton	.05	.02	.01
☐ 196 Luis Polonia	.05	.02	.01
☐ 197 Tim Salmon	.50	.23	.06
☐ 198 Luis Sojo	.05	.02	.01
☐ 199 Wilson Alvarez	.15	.07	.02
☐ 200 George Bell	.05	.02	.01
☐ 201 Alex Fernandez	.15	.07	.02
☐ 202 Craig Grebeck	.05	.02	.01
☐ 203 Ozzie Guillen	.05	.02	.01
☐ 204 Lance Johnson	.15	.07	.02
☐ 205 Ron Karkovice	.05	.02	.01
☐ 206 Kirk McCaskill	.05	.02	.01
☐ 207 Jack McDowell	.15	.07	.02
☐ 208 Scott Radinsky	.05	.02	.01
☐ 209 Tim Raines	.30	.14	.04
☐ 210 Frank Thomas	2.00	.90	.25
☐ 211 Robin Ventura	.15	.07	.02
☐ 212 Sandy Alomar Jr.	.15	.07	.02
☐ 213 Carlos Baerga	.15	.07	.02
☐ 214 Dennis Cook	.05	.02	.01
☐ 215 Thomas Howard	.05	.02	.01
☐ 216 Mark Lewis	.05	.02	.01
☐ 217 Derek Lilliquist	.05	.02	.01
☐ 218 Kenny Lofton	.75	.35	.09
☐ 219 Charles Nagy	.15	.07	.02
☐ 220 Steve Olin	.05	.02	.01
☐ 221 Paul Sorrento	.05	.02	.01
☐ 222 Jim Thome	1.00	.45	.12
☐ 223 Mark Whiten	.05	.02	.01
☐ 224 Milt Cuyler	.05	.02	.01
☐ 225 Rob Deer	.05	.02	.01
☐ 226 John Doherty	.05	.02	.01
☐ 227 Cecil Fielder	.15	.07	.02
☐ 228 Travis Fryman	.15	.07	.02
☐ 229 Mike Henneman	.05	.02	.01
☐ 230 John Kiely UER	.05	.02	.01
(Card has batting stats of Pat Kelly)			
☐ 231 Kurt Knudsen	.05	.02	.01
☐ 232 Scott Livingstone	.05	.02	.01
☐ 233 Tony Phillips	.15	.07	.02
☐ 234 Mickey Tettleton	.05	.02	.01
☐ 235 Kevin Appier	.15	.07	.02
☐ 236 George Brett	.75	.35	.09
☐ 237 Tom Gordon	.05	.02	.01
☐ 238 Gregg Jefferies	.15	.07	.02
☐ 239 Wally Joyner	.15	.07	.02
☐ 240 Kevin Koslofski	.05	.02	.01
☐ 241 Mike Macfarlane	.05	.02	.01
☐ 242 Brian McRae	.15	.07	.02
☐ 243 Rusty Meacham	.05	.02	.01
☐ 244 Keith Miller	.05	.02	.01
☐ 245 Jeff Montgomery	.15	.07	.02
☐ 246 Hipolito Pichardo	.05	.02	.01
☐ 247 Ricky Bones	.05	.02	.01
☐ 248 Cal Eldred	.05	.02	.01
☐ 249 Mike Fetters	.05	.02	.01
☐ 250 Darryl Hamilton	.05	.02	.01
☐ 251 Doug Henry	.05	.02	.01
☐ 252 John Jaha	.30	.14	.04
☐ 253 Pat Listach	.05	.02	.01
☐ 254 Paul Molitor	.40	.18	.05
☐ 255 Jaime Navarro	.05	.02	.01
☐ 256 Kevin Seitzer	.05	.02	.01
☐ 257 B.J. Surhoff	.15	.07	.02
☐ 258 Greg Vaughn	.15	.07	.02
☐ 259 Bill Wegman	.05	.02	.01
☐ 260 Robin Yount	.30	.14	.04
☐ 261 Rick Aguilera	.05	.02	.01
☐ 262 Chili Davis	.15	.07	.02
☐ 263 Scott Erickson	.05	.02	.01
☐ 264 Greg Gagne	.05	.02	.01
☐ 265 Mark Guthrie	.05	.02	.01
☐ 266 Brian Harper	.05	.02	.01
☐ 267 Kent Hrbek	.15	.07	.02
☐ 268 Terry Jorgensen	.05	.02	.01
☐ 269 Gene Larkin	.05	.02	.01
☐ 270 Scott Leius	.05	.02	.01
☐ 271 Pat Mahomes	.05	.02	.01
☐ 272 Pedro Munoz	.05	.02	.01
☐ 273 Kirby Puckett	.75	.35	.09
☐ 274 Kevin Tapani	.05	.02	.01
☐ 275 Carl Willis	.05	.02	.01
☐ 276 Steve Farr	.05	.02	.01
☐ 277 John Habyan	.05	.02	.01
☐ 278 Mel Hall	.05	.02	.01
☐ 279 Charlie Hayes	.05	.02	.01
☐ 280 Pat Kelly	.05	.02	.01
☐ 281 Don Mattingly	1.00	.45	.12
☐ 282 Sam Militello	.05	.02	.01
☐ 283 Matt Nokes	.05	.02	.01
☐ 284 Melido Perez	.05	.02	.01
☐ 285 Andy Stankiewicz	.05	.02	.01
☐ 286 Danny Tartabull	.05	.02	.01
☐ 287 Randy Velarde	.05	.02	.01
☐ 288 Bob Wickman	.05	.02	.01
☐ 289 Bernie Williams	.40	.18	.05
☐ 290 Lance Blankenship	.05	.02	.01
☐ 291 Mike Bordick	.05	.02	.01
☐ 292 Jerry Browne	.05	.02	.01
☐ 293 Dennis Eckersley	.15	.07	.02
☐ 294 Rickey Henderson	.30	.14	.04
☐ 295 Vince Horsman	.05	.02	.01
☐ 296 Mark McGwire	.60	.25	.07
☐ 297 Jeff Parrett	.05	.02	.01
☐ 298 Ruben Sierra	.15	.07	.02
☐ 299 Terry Steinbach	.15	.07	.02
☐ 300 Walt Weiss	.05	.02	.01
☐ 301 Bob Welch	.05	.02	.01
☐ 302 Willie Wilson	.05	.02	.01
☐ 303 Bobby Witt	.05	.02	.01
☐ 304 Bret Boone	.15	.07	.02
☐ 305 Jay Buhner	.30	.14	.04
☐ 306 Dave Fleming	.05	.02	.01
☐ 307 Ken Griffey Jr.	2.00	.90	.25
☐ 308 Erik Hanson	.05	.02	.01
☐ 309 Edgar Martinez	.15	.07	.02
☐ 310 Tino Martinez	.15	.07	.02
☐ 311 Jeff Nelson	.05	.02	.01
☐ 312 Dennis Powell	.05	.02	.01
☐ 313 Mike Schooler	.05	.02	.01
☐ 314 Russ Swan	.05	.02	.01
☐ 315 Dave Valle	.05	.02	.01
☐ 316 Omar Vizquel	.15	.07	.02
☐ 317 Kevin Brown	.15	.07	.02
☐ 318 Todd Burns	.05	.02	.01
☐ 319 Jose Canseco	.30	.14	.04
☐ 320 Julio Franco	.15	.07	.02
☐ 321 Jeff Frye	.05	.02	.01
☐ 322 Juan Gonzalez	1.00	.45	.12
☐ 323 Jose Guzman	.05	.02	.01
☐ 324 Jeff Huson	.05	.02	.01
☐ 325 Dean Palmer	.15	.07	.02
☐ 326 Kevin Reimer	.05	.02	.01
☐ 327 Ivan Rodriguez	.50	.23	.06
☐ 328 Kenny Rogers	.05	.02	.01
☐ 329 Dan Smith	.05	.02	.01
☐ 330 Roberto Alomar	.40	.18	.05
☐ 331 Derek Bell	.15	.07	.02
☐ 332 Pat Borders	.05	.02	.01
☐ 333 Joe Carter	.15	.07	.02
☐ 334 Kelly Gruber	.05	.02	.01
☐ 335 Tom Henke	.05	.02	.01
☐ 336 Jimmy Key	.15	.07	.02
☐ 337 Manuel Lee	.05	.02	.01
☐ 338 Candy Maldonado	.05	.02	.01
☐ 339 John Olerud	.05	.02	.01
☐ 340 Todd Stottlemyre	.15	.07	.02
☐ 341 Duane Ward	.05	.02	.01
☐ 342 Devon White	.05	.02	.01
☐ 343 Dave Winfield	.30	.14	.04
☐ 344 Edgar Martinez LL	.15	.07	.02
☐ 345 Cecil Fielder LL	.15	.07	.02
☐ 346 Kenny Lofton LL	.30	.14	.04
☐ 347 Jack Morris LL	.05	.02	.01
☐ 348 Roger Clemens LL	.30	.14	.04
☐ 349 Fred McGriff RT	.30	.14	.04
☐ 350 Barry Bonds RT	.30	.14	.04
☐ 351 Gary Sheffield RT	.30	.14	.04
☐ 352 Darren Daulton RT	.15	.07	.02
☐ 353 Dave Hollins RT	.05	.02	.01
☐ 354 Brothers in Blue	.05	.02	.01
Pedro Martinez			
Ramon Martinez			
☐ 355 Power Packs	.75	.35	.09
Ivan Rodriguez			
Kirby Puckett			
☐ 356 Triple Threats	.30	.14	.04
Ryne Sandberg			
Gary Sheffield			
☐ 357 Infield Trifecta	.30	.14	.04
Roberto Alomar			
Chuck Knoblauch			
Carlos Baerga			
☐ 358 Checklist 1-120	.05	.02	.01
☐ 359 Checklist 121-240	.05	.02	.01
☐ 360 Checklist 241-360	.05	.02	.01
☐ 361 Rafael Belliard	.05	.02	.01
☐ 362 Damon Berryhill	.05	.02	.01
☐ 363 Mike Bielecki	.05	.02	.01
☐ 364 Jeff Blauser	.05	.02	.01
☐ 365 Francisco Cabrera	.05	.02	.01
☐ 366 Marvin Freeman	.05	.02	.01
☐ 367 David Justice	.30	.14	.04
☐ 368 Mark Lemke	.05	.02	.01
☐ 369 Alejandro Pena	.05	.02	.01
☐ 370 Jeff Reardon	.15	.07	.02
☐ 371 Lonnie Smith	.05	.02	.01
☐ 372 Pete Smith	.05	.02	.01
☐ 373 Shawn Boskie	.05	.02	.01
☐ 374 Jim Bullinger	.05	.02	.01
☐ 375 Frank Castillo	.05	.02	.01
☐ 376 Doug Dascenzo	.05	.02	.01
☐ 377 Andre Dawson	.15	.07	.02
☐ 378 Mike Harkey	.05	.02	.01
☐ 379 Greg Hibbard	.05	.02	.01
☐ 380 Greg Maddux	1.25	.55	.16
☐ 381 Ken Patterson	.05	.02	.01
☐ 382 Jeff D. Robinson	.05	.02	.01
☐ 383 Luis Salazar	.05	.02	.01
☐ 384 Dwight Smith	.05	.02	.01
☐ 385 Jose Vizcaino	.05	.02	.01
☐ 386 Scott Bankhead	.05	.02	.01
☐ 387 Tom Browning	.05	.02	.01
☐ 388 Darnell Coles	.05	.02	.01
☐ 389 Rob Dibble	.05	.02	.01
☐ 390 Bill Doran	.05	.02	.01
☐ 391 Dwayne Henry	.05	.02	.01
☐ 392 Cesar Hernandez	.05	.02	.01
☐ 393 Roberto Kelly	.05	.02	.01
☐ 394 Barry Larkin	.30	.14	.04
☐ 395 Dave Martinez	.05	.02	.01
☐ 396 Kevin Mitchell	.15	.07	.02
☐ 397 Jeff Reed	.05	.02	.01
☐ 398 Scott Ruskin	.05	.02	.01
☐ 399 Greg Swindell	.05	.02	.01
☐ 400 Dan Wilson	.15	.07	.02
☐ 401 Andy Ashby	.15	.07	.02
☐ 402 Freddie Benavides	.05	.02	.01

☐ 403 Dante Bichette .30 .14 .04
☐ 404 Willie Blair .05 .02 .01
☐ 405 Denis Boucher .05 .02 .01
☐ 406 Vinny Castilla .30 .14 .04
☐ 407 Braulio Castillo .05 .02 .01
☐ 408 Alex Cole .05 .02 .01
☐ 409 Andres Galarraga .30 .14 .04
☐ 410 Joe Girardi .05 .02 .01
☐ 411 Butch Henry .05 .02 .01
☐ 412 Darren Holmes .05 .02 .01
☐ 413 Calvin Jones .05 .02 .01
☐ 414 Steve Reed .05 .02 .01
☐ 415 Kevin Ritz .05 .02 .01
☐ 416 Jim Tatum .05 .02 .01
☐ 417 Jack Armstrong .05 .02 .01
☐ 418 Bret Barberie .05 .02 .01
☐ 419 Ryan Bowen .05 .02 .01
☐ 420 Cris Carpenter .05 .02 .01
☐ 421 Chuck Carr .05 .02 .01
☐ 422 Scott Champarino .05 .02 .01
☐ 423 Jeff Conine .15 .07 .02
☐ 424 Jim Corsi .05 .02 .01
☐ 425 Steve Decker .05 .02 .01
☐ 426 Chris Donnels .05 .02 .01
☐ 427 Monty Fariss .05 .02 .01
☐ 428 Bob Natal .05 .02 .01
☐ 429 Pat Rapp .15 .07 .02
☐ 430 Dave Weathers .05 .02 .01
☐ 431 Nigel Wilson .05 .02 .01
☐ 432 Ken Caminiti .30 .14 .04
☐ 433 Andujar Cedeno .05 .02 .01
☐ 434 Tom Edens .05 .02 .01
☐ 435 Juan Guerrero .05 .02 .01
☐ 436 Pete Incaviglia .05 .02 .01
☐ 437 Jimmy Jones .05 .02 .01
☐ 438 Darryl Kile .05 .02 .01
☐ 439 Rob Murphy .05 .02 .01
☐ 440 Al Osuna .05 .02 .01
☐ 441 Mark Portugal .05 .02 .01
☐ 442 Scott Servais .05 .02 .01
☐ 443 John Candelaria .05 .02 .01
☐ 444 Tim Crews .05 .02 .01
☐ 445 Eric Davis .15 .07 .02
☐ 446 Tom Goodwin .05 .02 .01
☐ 447 Jim Gott .05 .02 .01
☐ 448 Kevin Gross .05 .02 .01
☐ 449 Dave Hansen .05 .02 .01
☐ 450 Jay Howell .05 .02 .01
☐ 451 Roger McDowell .05 .02 .01
☐ 452 Bob Ojeda .05 .02 .01
☐ 453 Henry Rodriguez .30 .14 .04
☐ 454 Darryl Strawberry .15 .07 .02
☐ 455 Mitch Webster .05 .02 .01
☐ 456 Steve Wilson .05 .02 .01
☐ 457 Brian Barnes .05 .02 .01
☐ 458 Sean Berry .05 .02 .01
☐ 459 Jeff Fassero .15 .07 .02
☐ 460 Darrin Fletcher .05 .02 .01
☐ 461 Marquis Grissom .15 .07 .02
☐ 462 Dennis Martinez .15 .07 .02
☐ 463 Spike Owen .05 .02 .01
☐ 464 Matt Stairs .05 .02 .01
☐ 465 Sergio Valdez .05 .02 .01
☐ 466 Kevin Bass .05 .02 .01
☐ 467 Vince Coleman .05 .02 .01
☐ 468 Mark Dewey .05 .02 .01
☐ 469 Kevin Elster .05 .02 .01
☐ 470 Tony Fernandez .05 .02 .01
☐ 471 John Franco .05 .02 .01
☐ 472 Dave Gallagher .05 .02 .01
☐ 473 Paul Gibson .05 .02 .01
☐ 474 Dwight Gooden .15 .07 .02
☐ 475 Lee Guetterman .05 .02 .01
☐ 476 Jeff Innis .05 .02 .01
☐ 477 Dave Magadan .05 .02 .01
☐ 478 Charlie O'Brien .05 .02 .01
☐ 479 Willie Randolph .15 .07 .02
☐ 480 Mackey Sasser .05 .02 .01
☐ 481 Ryan Thompson .05 .02 .01
☐ 482 Chico Walker .05 .02 .01
☐ 483 Kyle Abbott .05 .02 .01
☐ 484 Bob Ayrault .05 .02 .01
☐ 485 Kim Batiste .05 .02 .01
☐ 486 Cliff Brantley .05 .02 .01
☐ 487 Jose DeLeon .05 .02 .01
☐ 488 Len Dykstra .15 .07 .02
☐ 489 Tommy Greene .05 .02 .01
☐ 490 Jeff Grotewold .05 .02 .01
☐ 491 Dave Hollins .05 .02 .01
☐ 492 Danny Jackson .05 .02 .01
☐ 493 Stan Javier .05 .02 .01
☐ 494 Tom Marsh .05 .02 .01
☐ 495 Greg Mathews .05 .02 .01
☐ 496 Dale Murphy .30 .14 .04
☐ 497 Todd Pratt .05 .02 .01
☐ 498 Mitch Williams .05 .02 .01
☐ 499 Danny Cox .05 .02 .01
☐ 500 Doug Drabek .05 .02 .01
☐ 501 Carlos Garcia .05 .02 .01
☐ 502 Lloyd McClendon .05 .02 .01
☐ 503 Denny Neagle .15 .07 .02
☐ 504 Gary Redus .05 .02 .01
☐ 505 Bob Walk .05 .02 .01
☐ 506 John Wehner .05 .02 .01
☐ 507 Luis Alicea .05 .02 .01
☐ 508 Mark Clark .05 .02 .01
☐ 509 Pedro Guerrero .05 .02 .01
☐ 510 Rex Hudler .05 .02 .01
☐ 511 Brian Jordan .30 .14 .04
☐ 512 Omar Olivares .05 .02 .01
☐ 513 Jose Oquendo .05 .02 .01
☐ 514 Gerald Perry .05 .02 .01
☐ 515 Bryn Smith .05 .02 .01
☐ 516 Craig Wilson .05 .02 .01
☐ 517 Tracy Woodson .05 .02 .01
☐ 518 Larry Andersen .05 .02 .01
☐ 519 Andy Benes .15 .07 .02
☐ 520 Jim Deshaies .05 .02 .01
☐ 521 Bruce Hurst .05 .02 .01
☐ 522 Randy Myers .15 .07 .02
☐ 523 Benito Santiago .05 .02 .01
☐ 524 Tim Scott .05 .02 .01
☐ 525 Tim Teufel .05 .02 .01
☐ 526 Mike Benjamin .05 .02 .01
☐ 527 Dave Burba .05 .02 .01
☐ 528 Craig Colbert .05 .02 .01
☐ 529 Mike Felder .05 .02 .01
☐ 530 Bryan Hickerson .05 .02 .01
☐ 531 Chris James .05 .02 .01
☐ 532 Mark Leonard .05 .02 .01
☐ 533 Greg Litton .05 .02 .01
☐ 534 Francisco Oliveras .05 .02 .01
☐ 535 John Patterson .05 .02 .01
☐ 536 Jim Pena .05 .02 .01
☐ 537 Dave Righetti .05 .02 .01
☐ 538 Robby Thompson .05 .02 .01
☐ 539 Jose Uribe .05 .02 .01
☐ 540 Matt Williams .30 .14 .04
☐ 541 Storm Davis .05 .02 .01
☐ 542 Sam Horn .05 .02 .01
☐ 543 Tim Hulett .05 .02 .01
☐ 544 Craig Lefferts .05 .02 .01
☐ 545 Chito Martinez .05 .02 .01
☐ 546 Mark McLemore .05 .02 .01
☐ 547 Luis Mercedes .05 .02 .01
☐ 548 Bob Milacki .05 .02 .01
☐ 549 Joe Orsulak .05 .02 .01
☐ 550 Billy Ripken .05 .02 .01
☐ 551 Cal Ripken Jr. 1.50 .70 .19
☐ 552 Rick Sutcliffe .05 .02 .01
☐ 553 Jeff Tackett .05 .02 .01
☐ 554 Wade Boggs .30 .14 .04
☐ 555 Tom Brunansky .05 .02 .01
☐ 556 Jack Clark .05 .02 .01
☐ 557 John Dopson .05 .02 .01
☐ 558 Mike Gardiner .05 .02 .01
☐ 559 Mike Greenwell .05 .02 .01
☐ 560 Greg A. Harris .05 .02 .01
☐ 561 Billy Hatcher .05 .02 .01
☐ 562 Joe Hesketh .05 .02 .01
☐ 563 Tony Pena .05 .02 .01
☐ 564 Phil Plantier .05 .02 .01
☐ 565 Luis Rivera .05 .02 .01
☐ 566 Herm Winningham .05 .02 .01
☐ 567 Matt Young .05 .02 .01
☐ 568 Bert Blyleven .15 .07 .02
☐ 569 Mike Butcher .05 .02 .01
☐ 570 Chuck Crim .05 .02 .01
☐ 571 Chad Curtis .15 .07 .02
☐ 572 Tim Fortugno .05 .02 .01
☐ 573 Steve Frey .05 .02 .01
☐ 574 Gary Gaetti .15 .07 .02
☐ 575 Scott Lewis .05 .02 .01
☐ 576 Lee Stevens .05 .02 .01
☐ 577 Ron Tingley .05 .02 .01
☐ 578 Julio Valera .05 .02 .01
☐ 579 Shawn Abner .05 .02 .01
☐ 580 Joey Cora .15 .07 .02
☐ 581 Chris Cron .05 .02 .01
☐ 582 Carlton Fisk .30 .14 .04
☐ 583 Roberto Hernandez .15 .07 .02
☐ 584 Charlie Hough .05 .02 .01
☐ 585 Terry Leach .05 .02 .01
☐ 586 Donn Pall .05 .02 .01
☐ 587 Dan Pasqua .05 .02 .01
☐ 588 Steve Sax .05 .02 .01
☐ 589 Bobby Thigpen .05 .02 .01
☐ 590 Albert Belle .75 .35 .09
☐ 591 Felix Fermin .05 .02 .01
☐ 592 Glenallen Hill .05 .02 .01
☐ 593 Brook Jacoby .05 .02 .01
☐ 594 Reggie Jefferson .15 .07 .02
☐ 595 Carlos Martinez .05 .02 .01
☐ 596 Jose Mesa .15 .07 .02
☐ 597 Rod Nichols .05 .02 .01
☐ 598 Junior Ortiz .05 .02 .01
☐ 599 Eric Plunk .05 .02 .01
☐ 600 Ted Power .05 .02 .01
☐ 601 Scott Scudder .05 .02 .01
☐ 602 Kevin Wickander .05 .02 .01
☐ 603 Skeeter Barnes .05 .02 .01
☐ 604 Mark Carreon .05 .02 .01
☐ 605 Dan Gladden .05 .02 .01
☐ 606 Bill Gullickson .05 .02 .01
☐ 607 Chad Kreuter .05 .02 .01
☐ 608 Mark Leiter .05 .02 .01
☐ 609 Mike Munoz .05 .02 .01
☐ 610 Rich Rowland .05 .02 .01
☐ 611 Frank Tanana .05 .02 .01
☐ 612 Walt Terrell .05 .02 .01
☐ 613 Alan Trammell .30 .14 .04
☐ 614 Lou Whitaker .15 .07 .02
☐ 615 Luis Aquino .05 .02 .01
☐ 616 Mike Boddicker .05 .02 .01
☐ 617 Jim Eisenreich .15 .07 .02
☐ 618 Mark Gubicza .05 .02 .01
☐ 619 David Howard .05 .02 .01
☐ 620 Mike Magnante .05 .02 .01
☐ 621 Brent Mayne .05 .02 .01
☐ 622 Kevin McReynolds .05 .02 .01
☐ 623 Ed Pierce .05 .02 .01
☐ 624 Bill Sampen .05 .02 .01
☐ 625 Steve Shifflett .05 .02 .01
☐ 626 Gary Thurman .05 .02 .01
☐ 627 Curtis Wilkerson .05 .02 .01
☐ 628 Chris Bosio .05 .02 .01
☐ 629 Scott Fletcher .05 .02 .01
☐ 630 Jim Gantner .05 .02 .01
☐ 631 Dave Nilsson .15 .07 .02
☐ 632 Jesse Orosco .05 .02 .01
☐ 633 Dan Plesac .05 .02 .01
☐ 634 Ron Robinson .05 .02 .01
☐ 635 Bill Spiers .05 .02 .01
☐ 636 Franklin Stubbs .05 .02 .01
☐ 637 Willie Banks .05 .02 .01
☐ 638 Randy Bush .05 .02 .01
☐ 639 Chuck Knoblauch .30 .14 .04
☐ 640 Shane Mack .05 .02 .01
☐ 641 Mike Pagliarulo .05 .02 .01
☐ 642 Jeff Reboulet .05 .02 .01
☐ 643 John Smiley .05 .02 .01
☐ 644 Mike Trombley .05 .02 .01
☐ 645 Gary Wayne .05 .02 .01
☐ 646 Lenny Webster .05 .02 .01
☐ 647 Tim Burke .05 .02 .01
☐ 648 Mike Gallego .05 .02 .01
☐ 649 Dion James .05 .02 .01
☐ 650 Jeff Johnson .05 .02 .01
☐ 651 Scott Kamieniecki .05 .02 .01
☐ 652 Kevin Maas .05 .02 .01
☐ 653 Rich Monteleone .05 .02 .01
☐ 654 Jerry Nielsen .05 .02 .01
☐ 655 Scott Sanderson .05 .02 .01
☐ 656 Mike Stanley .05 .02 .01
☐ 657 Gerald Williams .05 .02 .01
☐ 658 Curt Young .05 .02 .01
☐ 659 Harold Baines .15 .07 .02
☐ 660 Kevin Campbell .05 .02 .01
☐ 661 Ron Darling .05 .02 .01
☐ 662 Kelly Downs .05 .02 .01
☐ 663 Eric Fox .05 .02 .01
☐ 664 Dave Henderson .05 .02 .01
☐ 665 Rick Honeycutt .05 .02 .01
☐ 666 Mike Moore .05 .02 .01
☐ 667 Jamie Quirk .05 .02 .01
☐ 668 Jeff Russell .05 .02 .01
☐ 669 Dave Stewart .15 .07 .02
☐ 670 Greg Briley .05 .02 .01
☐ 671 Dave Cochrane .05 .02 .01
☐ 672 Henry Cotto .05 .02 .01
☐ 673 Rich DeLucia .05 .02 .01
☐ 674 Brian Fisher .05 .02 .01
☐ 675 Mark Grant .05 .02 .01
☐ 676 Randy Johnson .30 .14 .04
☐ 677 Tim Leary .05 .02 .01
☐ 678 Pete O'Brien .05 .02 .01
☐ 679 Lance Parrish .05 .02 .01
☐ 680 Harold Reynolds .05 .02 .01
☐ 681 Shane Turner .05 .02 .01
☐ 682 Jack Daugherty .05 .02 .01
☐ 683 David Hulse .05 .02 .01
☐ 684 Terry Mathews .05 .02 .01
☐ 685 Al Newman .05 .02 .01
☐ 686 Edwin Nunez .05 .02 .01
☐ 687 Rafael Palmeiro .30 .14 .04
☐ 688 Roger Pavlik .15 .07 .02
☐ 689 Geno Petralli .05 .02 .01
☐ 690 Nolan Ryan 1.50 .70 .19
☐ 691 David Cone .15 .07 .02
☐ 692 Alfredo Griffin .05 .02 .01
☐ 693 Juan Guzman .15 .07 .02
☐ 694 Pat Hentgen .30 .14 .04
☐ 695 Randy Knorr .05 .02 .01
☐ 696 Bob MacDonald .05 .02 .01
☐ 697 Jack Morris .15 .07 .02
☐ 698 Ed Sprague .15 .07 .02
☐ 699 Dave Stieb .05 .02 .01
☐ 700 Pat Tabler .05 .02 .01
☐ 701 Mike Timlin .05 .02 .01
☐ 702 David Wells .05 .02 .01
☐ 703 Eddie Zosky .05 .02 .01
☐ 704 Gary Sheffield LL .30 .14 .04
☐ 705 Darren Daulton LL .15 .07 .02
☐ 706 Marquis Grissom LL .15 .07 .02
☐ 707 Greg Maddux LL .60 .25 .07
☐ 708 Bill Swift LL .05 .02 .01
☐ 709 Juan Gonzalez RT .30 .14 .04
☐ 710 Mark McGwire RT .30 .14 .04
☐ 711 Cecil Fielder RT .15 .07 .02
☐ 712 Albert Belle RT .40 .18 .05
☐ 713 Joe Carter RT .15 .07 .02
☐ 714 Cecil Fielder SS .50 .23 .06
Frank Thomas
Power Brokers
☐ 715 Larry Walker SS .30 .14 .04
Darren Daulton
Unsung Heroes
☐ 716 Edgar Martinez SS .15 .07 .02
Robin Ventura
Hot Corner Hammers
☐ 717 Roger Clemens SS .30 .14 .04
Dennis Eckersley
Start to Finish
☐ 718 Checklist 361-480 .05 .02 .01
☐ 719 Checklist 481-600 .05 .02 .01
☐ 720 Checklist 601-720 .05 .02 .01

1993 Fleer All-Stars

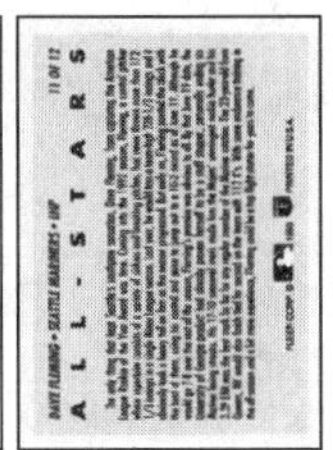

This 24-card standard-size set featuring members of the American and National league All-Star squads, was randomly inserted in wax packs. 12 American League players were seeded in series 1 packs and 12 National League players in series 2. The horizontal fronts feature a color close-up photo cut out and superposed upon a black-and-white action scene framed by white borders. The player's name and the word "All-Stars" are printed in gold foil lettering across the bottom of the picture.

	MINT	NRMT	EXC
COMPLETE SET (24)	40.00	18.00	5.00
COMPLETE SER.1 (12)	25.00	11.00	3.10
COMPLETE SER.2 (12)	15.00	6.75	1.85
COMMON CARD (AL1-AL12)	.75	.35	.09
COMMON CARD (NL1-NL12)	.75	.35	.09
☐ AL1 Frank Thomas	12.00	5.50	1.50
☐ AL2 Roberto Alomar	2.50	1.10	.30
☐ AL3 Edgar Martinez	1.50	.70	.19
☐ AL4 Pat Listach	.75	.35	.09
☐ AL5 Cecil Fielder	1.50	.70	.19
☐ AL6 Juan Gonzalez	6.00	2.70	.75
☐ AL7 Ken Griffey Jr.	12.00	5.50	1.50
☐ AL8 Joe Carter	1.50	.70	.19
☐ AL9 Kirby Puckett	5.00	2.20	.60
☐ AL10 Brian Harper	.75	.35	.09
☐ AL11 Dave Fleming	.75	.35	.09
☐ AL12 Jack McDowell	1.50	.70	.19
☐ NL1 Fred McGriff	1.50	.70	.19
☐ NL2 Delino DeShields	.75	.35	.09
☐ NL3 Gary Sheffield	2.00	.90	.25
☐ NL4 Barry Larkin	1.50	.70	.19
☐ NL5 Felix Jose	.75	.35	.09
☐ NL6 Larry Walker	1.50	.70	.19
☐ NL7 Barry Bonds	3.00	1.35	.35
☐ NL8 Andy Van Slyke	1.00	.45	.12
☐ NL9 Darren Daulton	1.00	.45	.12
☐ NL10 Greg Maddux	8.00	3.60	1.00
☐ NL11 Tom Glavine	1.50	.70	.19
☐ NL12 Lee Smith	1.00	.45	.12

1993 Fleer Glavine

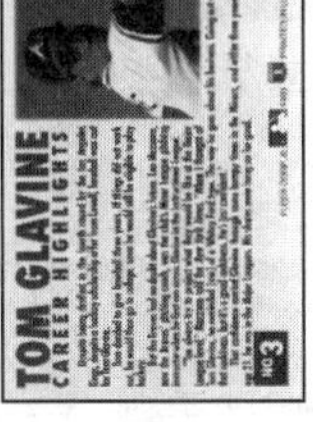

As part of the Signature Series, this 12-card standard-size set spotlights Tom Glavine. An additional three cards (13-15) were available via a mail-in offer and are generally considered to be a seperate set. The mail-in offer expired on September 30, 1993. The fronts feature glossy color action photos with white borders. The player's name and the words "Career Highlights" appear in gold foil block lettering across the bottom of the picture. The horizontal backs carry a small close-up color photo and summarize chapters of Glavine's career. The cards are numbered on the back at the lower left corner. Reportedly, a filmmaking problem during production resulted in eight variations in this 12-card insert set. Different backs appear on eight of the 12 cards. Cards 1-4 and 7-10 in wax packs feature card-back text variations from those included in the rack and jumbo magazine packs. The text differences occur in the first few words of text on the card back. No corrections were made in Series I. The correct Glavine cards appeared in Series II wax, rack, and jumbo magazine packs.

	MINT	NRMT	EXC
COMPLETE SET (12)	4.00	1.80	.50
COMMON GLAVINE (1-12)	.50	.23	.06
COMMON SEND-OFF (13-15)	2.00	.90	.25

	MINT	NRMT	EXC
☐ 1 Tom Glavine	.50	.23	.06
The Glavine family ... (Throwing to first)			
☐ 2 Tom Glavine	.50	.23	.06
High School baseball ... (Pitching, with arm behind head, shot from left side)			
☐ 3 Tom Glavine	.50	.23	.06
Despite being drafted ... (Pitching, close-up shot from left side)			
☐ 4 Tom Glavine	.50	.23	.06
Unflappable is ... (Pitching, shot from almost directly in front)			
☐ 5 Tom Glavine	.50	.23	.06
In 1989 Tom ... (Pitching, shot from right angle)			
☐ 6 Tom Glavine	.50	.23	.06
Tom Glavine had ... (Pitching, with ball below waist)			
☐ 7 Tom Glavine	.50	.23	.06
Tom Glavine's dream ... (Pitching, close-up shot with ball behind head)			
☐ 8 Tom Glavine	.50	.23	.06
After Winning ... (Pitching, shot from directly in front)			
☐ 9 Tom Glavine	.50	.23	.06
Little Leaguers ... (Pitching, just after release with left leg in air)			
☐ 10 Tom Glavine	.50	.23	.06
Will success spoil ... (Pitching, ball below waist and right leg slightly raised)			
☐ 11 Tom Glavine	.50	.23	.06
What makes Tom ... (Batting)			
☐ 12 Tom Glavine	.50	.23	.06
It was a day ... (Pitching, close-up shot wearing dark blue top)			
☐ 13 Tom Glavine	2.00	.90	.25
Send-Off 1			
☐ 14 Tom Glavine	2.00	.90	.25
Send-Off 2			
☐ 15 Tom Glavine	2.00	.90	.25
Send-Off 3			
☐ AU0 Tom Glavine AU	80.00	36.00	10.00
(Certified signature)			

1993 Fleer Golden Moments

Cards from this six-card standard-size set, featuring memorable moments from the previous season, were randomly inserted in 1993 Fleer wax packs, three each in series 1 and 2. The fronts feature glossy color action photos framed by thin aqua and white lines and a black outer border. A gold foil baseball icon appears at each corner of the picture, and the player's name and the set title "Golden Moments" appears in a gold foil bar toward the bottom of the picture. The cards are unnumbered and checklisted below in alphabetical order.

	MINT	NRMT	EXC
COMPLETE SET (6)	15.00	6.75	1.85
COMPLETE SER.1 (3)	5.00	2.20	.60
COMPLETE SER.2 (3)	10.00	4.50	1.25
COMMON SERIES 1 (A1-A3)	.50	.23	.06
COMMON SERIES 2 (B1-B3)	.50	.23	.06
☐ A1 George Brett	5.00	2.20	.60
☐ A2 Mickey Morandini	.50	.23	.06
☐ A3 Dave Winfield	1.00	.45	.12
☐ B1 Dennis Eckersley	1.00	.45	.12
☐ B2 Bip Roberts	.50	.23	.06
☐ B3 Frank Thomas and Juan Gonzalez	8.00	3.60	1.00

1993 Fleer Major League Prospects

Cards from this 36-card standard-size set, featuring a selection of prospects, were randomly inserted in wax packs, 18 each in series 1 and 2. These cards feature black-bordered color player action photos on their fronts. The player's name appears in gold foil at the top, and the set's name and logo appear in gold foil and black at the bottom. The key card in this set is Mike Piazza.

	MINT	NRMT	EXC
COMPLETE SET (36)	30.00	13.50	3.70
COMPLETE SERIES 1 (18)	20.00	9.00	2.50
COMPLETE SERIES 2 (18)	10.00	4.50	1.25
COMMON SERIES 1 (A1-A18)	.50	.23	.06
COMMON SERIES 2 (B1-B18)	.50	.23	.06
☐ A1 Melvin Nieves	1.50	.70	.19
☐ A2 Sterling Hitchcock	.50	.23	.06
☐ A3 Tim Costo	.50	.23	.06
☐ A4 Manny Alexander	.50	.23	.06
☐ A5 Alan Embree	.50	.23	.06
☐ A6 Kevin Young	.50	.23	.06
☐ A7 J.T. Snow	1.50	.70	.19
☐ A8 Russ Springer	.50	.23	.06
☐ A9 Billy Ashley	.50	.23	.06
☐ A10 Kevin Rogers	.50	.23	.06
☐ A11 Steve Hosey	.50	.23	.06
☐ A12 Eric Wedge	.50	.23	.06
☐ A13 Mike Piazza	20.00	9.00	2.50
☐ A14 Jesse Levis	.50	.23	.06
☐ A15 Rico Brogna	1.00	.45	.12
☐ A16 Alex Arias	.50	.23	.06
☐ A17 Rod Brewer	.50	.23	.06
☐ A18 Troy Neel	.50	.23	.06
☐ B1 Scooter Tucker	.50	.23	.06
☐ B2 Kerry Woodson	.50	.23	.06
☐ B3 Greg Colbrunn	1.00	.45	.12
☐ B4 Pedro Martinez	2.00	.90	.25
☐ B5 Dave Silvestri	.50	.23	.06
☐ B6 Kent Bottenfield	.50	.23	.06
☐ B7 Rafael Bournigal	.50	.23	.06
☐ B8 J.T. Bruett	.50	.23	.06
☐ B9 Dave Mlicki	.50	.23	.06
☐ B10 Paul Wagner	.50	.23	.06
☐ B11 Mike Williams	.50	.23	.06
☐ B12 Henry Mercedes	.50	.23	.06
☐ B13 Scott Taylor	.50	.23	.06
☐ B14 Dennis Moeller	.50	.23	.06
☐ B15 Javier Lopez	5.00	2.20	.60
☐ B16 Steve Cooke	.50	.23	.06
☐ B17 Pete Young	.50	.23	.06
☐ B18 Ken Ryan	.50	.23	.06

1993 Fleer Pro-Visions

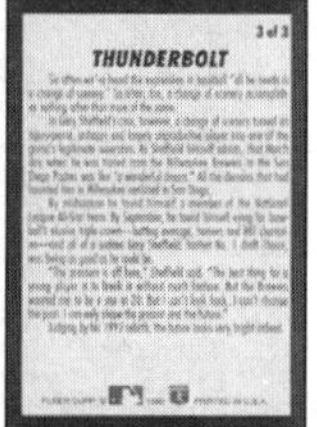

Cards from this six-card standard-size set, featuring a selection of superstars in fantasy paintings, were randomly inserted in poly packs, three each in series 1 and 2. These cards feature black-bordered fanciful color artwork of the players in action. The player's name appears in gold foil within the bottom black margin of each.

	MINT	NRMT	EXC
COMPLETE SET (6)	5.00	2.20	.60
COMPLETE SERIES 1 (3)	3.00	1.35	.35
COMPLETE SERIES 2 (3)	2.00	.90	.25
COMMON SERIES 1 (A1-A3)	.75	.35	.09
COMMON SERIES 2 (B1-B3)	.75	.35	.09
☐ A1 Roberto Alomar	2.50	1.10	.30
☐ A2 Dennis Eckersley	.75	.35	.09
☐ A3 Gary Sheffield	2.00	.90	.25
☐ B1 Andy Van Slyke	.75	.35	.09
☐ B2 Tom Glavine	1.50	.70	.19
☐ B3 Cecil Fielder	.75	.35	.09

1993 Fleer Rookie Sensations

Cards from this 20-card standard-size set, featuring a selection of 1993's top rookies, were randomly inserted in cello packs, 10 each in series 1 and 2. The cards feature blue-bordered fronts with cutout color player photos, each superposed upon a silver-colored background. The set's title and the player's name appear in gold foil in an upper corner. The key card in this set is Kenny Lofton.

	MINT	NRMT	EXC
COMPLETE SET (20)	30.00	13.50	3.70
COMPLETE SERIES 1 (10)	20.00	9.00	2.50
COMPLETE SERIES 2 (10)	10.00	4.50	1.25
COMMON CARD (RSA1-RSA10)	1.00	.45	.12
COMMON CARD (RSB1-RSB10)	1.00	.45	.12
☐ RSA1 Kenny Lofton	15.00	6.75	1.85
☐ RSA2 Cal Eldred	1.00	.45	.12
☐ RSA3 Pat Listach	1.00	.45	.12
☐ RSA4 Roberto Hernandez	1.50	.70	.19
☐ RSA5 Dave Fleming	1.00	.45	.12
☐ RSA6 Eric Karros	3.00	1.35	.35
☐ RSA7 Reggie Sanders	3.00	1.35	.35
☐ RSA8 Derrick May	1.00	.45	.12
☐ RSA9 Mike Perez	1.00	.45	.12
☐ RSA10 Donovan Osborne	1.00	.45	.12
☐ RSB1 Moises Alou	1.50	.70	.19
☐ RSB2 Pedro Astacio	1.00	.45	.12
☐ RSB3 Jim Austin	1.00	.45	.12
☐ RSB4 Chad Curtis	1.50	.70	.19
☐ RSB5 Gary DiSarcina	1.00	.45	.12
☐ RSB6 Scott Livingstone	1.00	.45	.12
☐ RSB7 Sam Militello	1.00	.45	.12
☐ RSB8 Arthur Rhodes	1.00	.45	.12
☐ RSB9 Tim Wakefield	1.50	.70	.19
☐ RSB10 Bob Zupcic	1.00	.45	.12

1993 Fleer Team Leaders

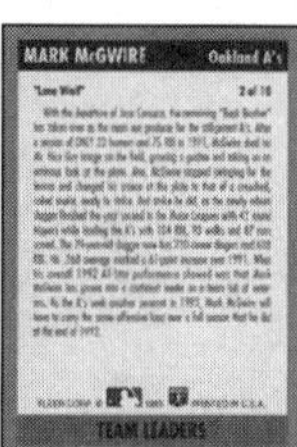

One Team Leader or Tom Glavine insert was seeded into each Fleer rack pack. Series 1 racks included 10 American League players, while series 2 racks included 10 National League players. Each of the tan-bordered standard-size cards comprising this set feature a posed color player photo on its front with a smaller cutout color action photo superposed in a lower corner. The player's name and the set's title appear vertically in gold foil along the left side within team color-coded bars.

	MINT	NRMT	EXC
COMPLETE SET (20)	70.00	32.00	8.75
COMPLETE SERIES 1 (10)	50.00	22.00	6.25
COMPLETE SERIES 2 (10)	20.00	9.00	2.50
COMMON CARD (AL1-AL10)	1.00	.45	.12
COMMON CARD (NL1-NL10)	1.00	.45	.12
☐ AL1 Kirby Puckett	8.00	3.60	1.00
☐ AL2 Mark McGwire	6.00	2.70	.75
☐ AL3 Pat Listach	1.00	.45	.12
☐ AL4 Roger Clemens	4.00	1.80	.50
☐ AL5 Frank Thomas	20.00	9.00	2.50
☐ AL6 Carlos Baerga	1.00	.45	.12
☐ AL7 Brady Anderson	2.50	1.10	.30
☐ AL8 Juan Gonzalez	10.00	4.50	1.25
☐ AL9 Roberto Alomar	4.00	1.80	.50
☐ AL10 Ken Griffey Jr.	20.00	9.00	2.50
☐ NL1 Will Clark	2.50	1.10	.30
☐ NL2 Terry Pendleton	1.00	.45	.12
☐ NL3 Ray Lankford	1.50	.70	.19
☐ NL4 Eric Karros	2.50	1.10	.30
☐ NL5 Gary Sheffield	3.00	1.35	.35
☐ NL6 Ryne Sandberg	5.00	2.20	.60
☐ NL7 Marquis Grissom	1.50	.70	.19
☐ NL8 John Kruk	1.50	.70	.19
☐ NL9 Jeff Bagwell	8.00	3.60	1.00
☐ NL10 Andy Van Slyke	1.50	.70	.19

1993 Fleer Final Edition

This 300-card standard-size set was issued exclusively in factory set form (along with ten Diamond Tribute inserts) to update and feature rookies not in the regular 1993 Fleer set. The cards are identical in design to regular issue 1993 Fleer cards except for the F-prefixed numbering. Cards are ordered alphabetically within teams with NL preceding AL. The set closes with checklist cards (298-300). The only key Rookie Card in this set features Jim Edmonds.

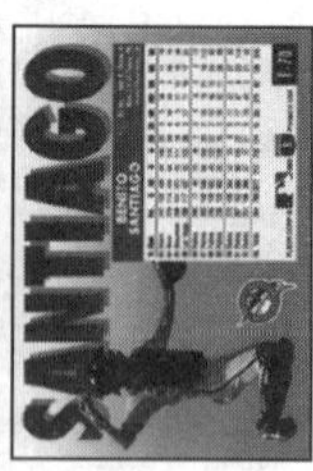

	MINT	NRMT	EXC
COMPLETE FACT.SET (310)	10.00	4.50	1.25
COMPLETE SET (300)	6.00	2.70	.75
COMMON CARD (F1-F300)	.05	.02	.01
☐ 1 Steve Bedrosian	.05	.02	.01
☐ 2 Jay Howell	.05	.02	.01
☐ 3 Greg Maddux	1.25	.55	.16
☐ 4 Greg McMichael	.15	.07	.02
☐ 5 Tony Tarasco	.15	.07	.02
☐ 6 Jose Bautista	.05	.02	.01
☐ 7 Jose Guzman	.05	.02	.01
☐ 8 Greg Hibbard	.05	.02	.01
☐ 9 Candy Maldonado	.05	.02	.01
☐ 10 Randy Myers	.15	.07	.02
☐ 11 Matt Walbeck	.05	.02	.01
☐ 12 Turk Wendell	.05	.02	.01
☐ 13 Willie Wilson	.05	.02	.01
☐ 14 Greg Cadaret	.05	.02	.01
☐ 15 Roberto Kelly	.05	.02	.01
☐ 16 Randy Milligan	.05	.02	.01
☐ 17 Kevin Mitchell	.15	.07	.02
☐ 18 Jeff Reardon	.15	.07	.02
☐ 19 John Roper	.05	.02	.01
☐ 20 John Smiley	.05	.02	.01
☐ 21 Andy Ashby	.15	.07	.02
☐ 22 Dante Bichette	.30	.14	.04
☐ 23 Willie Blair	.05	.02	.01
☐ 24 Pedro Castellano	.05	.02	.01
☐ 25 Vinny Castilla	.30	.14	.04
☐ 26 Jerald Clark	.05	.02	.01
☐ 27 Alex Cole	.05	.02	.01
☐ 28 Scott Fredrickson	.05	.02	.01
☐ 29 Jay Gainer	.05	.02	.01
☐ 30 Andres Galarraga	.30	.14	.04
☐ 31 Joe Girardi	.05	.02	.01
☐ 32 Ryan Hawblitzel	.05	.02	.01
☐ 33 Charlie Hayes	.05	.02	.01
☐ 34 Darren Holmes	.05	.02	.01
☐ 35 Chris Jones	.05	.02	.01
☐ 36 David Nied	.05	.02	.01
☐ 37 J.Owens	.15	.07	.02
☐ 38 Lance Painter	.05	.02	.01
☐ 39 Jeff Parrett	.05	.02	.01
☐ 40 Steve Reed	.05	.02	.01
☐ 41 Armando Reynoso	.05	.02	.01
☐ 42 Bruce Ruffin	.05	.02	.01
☐ 43 Danny Sheaffer	.05	.02	.01
☐ 44 Keith Shepherd	.05	.02	.01
☐ 45 Jim Tatum	.05	.02	.01
☐ 46 Gary Wayne	.05	.02	.01
☐ 47 Eric Young	.30	.14	.04
☐ 48 Luis Aquino	.05	.02	.01
☐ 49 Alex Arias	.05	.02	.01
☐ 50 Jack Armstrong	.05	.02	.01
☐ 51 Bret Barberie	.05	.02	.01
☐ 52 Geronimo Berroa	.15	.07	.02
☐ 53 Ryan Bowen	.05	.02	.01
☐ 54 Greg Briley	.05	.02	.01
☐ 55 Cris Carpenter	.05	.02	.01
☐ 56 Chuck Carr	.05	.02	.01
☐ 57 Jeff Conine	.15	.07	.02
☐ 58 Jim Corsi	.05	.02	.01
☐ 59 Orestes Destrade	.05	.02	.01
☐ 60 Junior Felix	.05	.02	.01
☐ 61 Chris Hammond	.05	.02	.01
☐ 62 Bryan Harvey	.05	.02	.01
☐ 63 Charlie Hough	.05	.02	.01
☐ 64 Joe Klink	.05	.02	.01
☐ 65 Richie Lewis UER (Refers to place of birth and residence as Illinois instead of Indiana)	.05	.02	.01
☐ 66 Mitch Lyden	.05	.02	.01
☐ 67 Bob Natal	.05	.02	.01
☐ 68 Scott Pose	.05	.02	.01
☐ 69 Rich Renteria	.05	.02	.01
☐ 70 Benito Santiago	.05	.02	.01
☐ 71 Gary Sheffield	.30	.14	.04
☐ 72 Matt Turner	.05	.02	.01
☐ 73 Walt Weiss	.05	.02	.01
☐ 74 Darrell Whitmore	.05	.02	.01
☐ 75 Nigel Wilson	.05	.02	.01
☐ 76 Kevin Bass	.05	.02	.01
☐ 77 Doug Drabek	.05	.02	.01
☐ 78 Tom Edens	.05	.02	.01
☐ 79 Chris James	.05	.02	.01
☐ 80 Greg Swindell	.05	.02	.01
☐ 81 Omar Daal	.15	.07	.02
☐ 82 Raul Mondesi	.60	.25	.07
☐ 83 Jody Reed	.05	.02	.01
☐ 84 Cory Snyder	.05	.02	.01
☐ 85 Rick Trlicek	.05	.02	.01
☐ 86 Tim Wallach	.05	.02	.01
☐ 87 Todd Worrell	.05	.02	.01
☐ 88 Tavo Alvarez	.05	.02	.01
☐ 89 Frank Bolick	.05	.02	.01
☐ 90 Kent Bottenfield	.05	.02	.01

☐ 91 Greg Colbrunn	.05	.02	.01
☐ 92 Cliff Floyd	.15	.07	.02
☐ 93 Lou Frazier	.05	.02	.01
☐ 94 Mike Gardiner	.05	.02	.01
☐ 95 Mike Lansing	.15	.07	.02
☐ 96 Bill Risley	.05	.02	.01
☐ 97 Jeff Shaw	.05	.02	.01
☐ 98 Kevin Baez	.05	.02	.01
☐ 99 Tim Bogar	.05	.02	.01
☐ 100 Jeromy Burnitz	.05	.02	.01
☐ 101 Mike Draper	.05	.02	.01
☐ 102 Darrin Jackson	.05	.02	.01
☐ 103 Mike Maddux	.05	.02	.01
☐ 104 Joe Orsulak	.05	.02	.01
☐ 105 Doug Saunders	.05	.02	.01
☐ 106 Frank Tanana	.05	.02	.01
☐ 107 Dave Telgheder	.05	.02	.01
☐ 108 Larry Andersen	.05	.02	.01
☐ 109 Jim Eisenreich	.15	.07	.02
☐ 110 Pete Incaviglia	.05	.02	.01
☐ 111 Danny Jackson	.05	.02	.01
☐ 112 David West	.05	.02	.01
☐ 113 Al Martin	.15	.07	.02
☐ 114 Blas Minor	.05	.02	.01
☐ 115 Dennis Moeller	.05	.02	.01
☐ 116 William Pennyfeather	.05	.02	.01
☐ 117 Rich Robertson	.05	.02	.01
☐ 118 Ben Shelton	.05	.02	.01
☐ 119 Lonnie Smith	.05	.02	.01
☐ 120 Freddie Toliver	.05	.02	.01
☐ 121 Paul Wagner	.05	.02	.01
☐ 122 Kevin Young	.05	.02	.01
☐ 123 Rene Arocha	.05	.02	.01
☐ 124 Gregg Jefferies	.15	.07	.02
☐ 125 Paul Kilgus	.05	.02	.01
☐ 126 Les Lancaster	.05	.02	.01
☐ 127 Joe Magrane	.05	.02	.01
☐ 128 Rob Murphy	.05	.02	.01
☐ 129 Erik Pappas	.05	.02	.01
☐ 130 Stan Royer	.05	.02	.01
☐ 131 Ozzie Smith	.50	.23	.06
☐ 132 Tom Urbani	.05	.02	.01
☐ 133 Mark Whiten	.05	.02	.01
☐ 134 Derek Bell	.15	.07	.02
☐ 135 Doug Brocail	.05	.02	.01
☐ 136 Phil Clark	.05	.02	.01
☐ 137 Mark Ettles	.05	.02	.01
☐ 138 Jeff Gardner	.05	.02	.01
☐ 139 Pat Gomez	.05	.02	.01
☐ 140 Ricky Gutierrez	.05	.02	.01
☐ 141 Gene Harris	.05	.02	.01
☐ 142 Kevin Higgins	.05	.02	.01
☐ 143 Trevor Hoffman	.30	.14	.04
☐ 144 Phil Plantier	.05	.02	.01
☐ 145 Kerry Taylor	.05	.02	.01
☐ 146 Guillermo Velasquez	.05	.02	.01
☐ 147 Wally Whitehurst	.05	.02	.01
☐ 148 Tim Worrell	.05	.02	.01
☐ 149 Todd Benzinger	.05	.02	.01
☐ 150 Barry Bonds	.50	.23	.06
☐ 151 Greg Brummett	.05	.02	.01
☐ 152 Mark Carreon	.05	.02	.01
☐ 153 Dave Martinez	.05	.02	.01
☐ 154 Jeff Reed	.05	.02	.01
☐ 155 Kevin Rogers	.05	.02	.01
☐ 156 Harold Baines	.15	.07	.02
☐ 157 Damon Buford	.05	.02	.01
☐ 158 Paul Carey	.05	.02	.01
☐ 159 Jeffrey Hammonds	.15	.07	.02
☐ 160 Jamie Moyer	.05	.02	.01
☐ 161 Sherman Obando	.05	.02	.01
☐ 162 John O'Donoghue	.05	.02	.01
☐ 163 Brad Pennington	.05	.02	.01
☐ 164 Jim Poole	.05	.02	.01
☐ 165 Harold Reynolds	.05	.02	.01
☐ 166 Fernando Valenzuela	.15	.07	.02
☐ 167 Jack Voigt	.05	.02	.01
☐ 168 Mark Williamson	.05	.02	.01
☐ 169 Scott Bankhead	.05	.02	.01
☐ 170 Greg Blosser	.05	.02	.01
☐ 171 Jim Byrd	.05	.02	.01
☐ 172 Ivan Calderon	.05	.02	.01
☐ 173 Andre Dawson	.15	.07	.02
☐ 174 Scott Fletcher	.05	.02	.01
☐ 175 Jose Melendez	.05	.02	.01
☐ 176 Carlos Quintana	.05	.02	.01
☐ 177 Jeff Russell	.05	.02	.01
☐ 178 Aaron Sele	.15	.07	.02
☐ 179 Rod Correia	.05	.02	.01
☐ 180 Chili Davis	.15	.07	.02
☐ 181 Jim Edmonds	1.50	.70	.19
☐ 182 Rene Gonzales	.05	.02	.01
☐ 183 Hilly Hathaway	.05	.02	.01
☐ 184 Torey Lovullo	.05	.02	.01
☐ 185 Greg Myers	.05	.02	.01
☐ 186 Gene Nelson	.05	.02	.01
☐ 187 Troy Percival	.15	.07	.02
☐ 188 Scott Sanderson	.05	.02	.01
☐ 189 Darryl Scott	.05	.02	.01
☐ 190 J.T. Snow	.30	.14	.04
☐ 191 Russ Springer	.05	.02	.01
☐ 192 Jason Bere	.15	.07	.02
☐ 193 Rodney Bolton	.05	.02	.01
☐ 194 Ellis Burks	.15	.07	.02
☐ 195 Bo Jackson	.15	.07	.02
☐ 196 Mike LaValliere	.05	.02	.01
☐ 197 Scott Ruffcorn	.05	.02	.01
☐ 198 Jeff Schwartz	.05	.02	.01
☐ 199 Jerry DiPoto	.05	.02	.01
☐ 200 Alvaro Espinoza	.05	.02	.01
☐ 201 Wayne Kirby	.05	.02	.01
☐ 202 Tom Kramer	.05	.02	.01
☐ 203 Jesse Levis	.05	.02	.01
☐ 204 Manny Ramirez	1.25	.55	.16
☐ 205 Jeff Treadway	.05	.02	.01
☐ 206 Bill Wertz	.05	.02	.01
☐ 207 Cliff Young	.05	.02	.01
☐ 208 Matt Young	.05	.02	.01
☐ 209 Kirk Gibson	.15	.07	.02
☐ 210 Greg Gohr	.05	.02	.01
☐ 211 Bill Krueger	.05	.02	.01
☐ 212 Bob MacDonald	.05	.02	.01
☐ 213 Mike Moore	.05	.02	.01
☐ 214 David Wells	.05	.02	.01
☐ 215 Billy Brewer	.05	.02	.01
☐ 216 David Cone	.15	.07	.02
☐ 217 Greg Gagne	.05	.02	.01
☐ 218 Mark Gardner	.05	.02	.01
☐ 219 Chris Haney	.05	.02	.01
☐ 220 Phil Hiatt	.05	.02	.01
☐ 221 Jose Lind	.05	.02	.01
☐ 222 Juan Bell	.05	.02	.01
☐ 223 Tom Brunansky	.05	.02	.01
☐ 224 Mike Ignasiak	.05	.02	.01
☐ 225 Joe Kmak	.05	.02	.01
☐ 226 Tom Lampkin	.05	.02	.01
☐ 227 Graeme Lloyd	.05	.02	.01
☐ 228 Carlos Maldonado	.05	.02	.01
☐ 229 Matt Mieske	.15	.07	.02
☐ 230 Angel Miranda	.05	.02	.01
☐ 231 Troy O'Leary	.30	.14	.04
☐ 232 Kevin Reimer	.05	.02	.01
☐ 233 Larry Casian	.05	.02	.01
☐ 234 Jim Deshaies	.05	.02	.01
☐ 235 Eddie Guardado	.05	.02	.01
☐ 236 Chip Hale	.05	.02	.01
☐ 237 Mike Maksudian	.05	.02	.01
☐ 238 David McCarty	.05	.02	.01
☐ 239 Pat Meares	.15	.07	.02
☐ 240 George Tsamis	.05	.02	.01
☐ 241 Dave Winfield	.30	.14	.04
☐ 242 Jim Abbott	.05	.02	.01
☐ 243 Wade Boggs	.30	.14	.04
☐ 244 Andy Cook	.05	.02	.01
☐ 245 Russ Davis	.15	.07	.02
☐ 246 Mike Humphreys	.05	.02	.01
☐ 247 Jimmy Key	.15	.07	.02
☐ 248 Jim Leyritz	.05	.02	.01
☐ 249 Bobby Munoz	.05	.02	.01
☐ 250 Paul O'Neill	.15	.07	.02
☐ 251 Spike Owen	.05	.02	.01
☐ 252 Dave Silvestri	.05	.02	.01
☐ 253 Marcos Armas	.05	.02	.01
☐ 254 Brent Gates	.15	.07	.02
☐ 255 Goose Gossage	.15	.07	.02
☐ 256 Scott Lydy	.05	.02	.01
☐ 257 Henry Mercedes	.05	.02	.01
☐ 258 Mike Mohler	.05	.02	.01
☐ 259 Troy Neel	.05	.02	.01
☐ 260 Edwin Nunez	.05	.02	.01
☐ 261 Craig Paquette	.05	.02	.01
☐ 262 Kevin Seitzer	.05	.02	.01
☐ 263 Rich Amaral	.05	.02	.01
☐ 264 Mike Blowers	.05	.02	.01
☐ 265 Chris Bosio	.05	.02	.01
☐ 266 Norm Charlton	.05	.02	.01
☐ 267 Jim Converse	.05	.02	.01
☐ 268 John Cummings	.05	.02	.01
☐ 269 Mike Felder	.05	.02	.01
☐ 270 Mike Hampton	.30	.14	.04
☐ 271 Bill Haselman	.05	.02	.01
☐ 272 Dwayne Henry	.05	.02	.01
☐ 273 Greg Litton	.05	.02	.01
☐ 274 Mackey Sasser	.05	.02	.01
☐ 275 Lee Tinsley	.15	.07	.02
☐ 276 David Wainhouse	.05	.02	.01
☐ 277 Jeff Bronkey	.05	.02	.01
☐ 278 Benji Gil	.15	.07	.02
☐ 279 Tom Henke	.05	.02	.01
☐ 280 Charlie Leibrandt	.05	.02	.01
☐ 281 Robb Nen	.15	.07	.02
☐ 282 Bill Ripken	.05	.02	.01
☐ 283 Jon Shave	.05	.02	.01
☐ 284 Doug Strange	.05	.02	.01
☐ 285 Matt Whiteside	.05	.02	.01
☐ 286 Scott Brow	.05	.02	.01
☐ 287 Willie Canate	.05	.02	.01
☐ 288 Tony Castillo	.05	.02	.01
☐ 289 Domingo Cedeno	.05	.02	.01
☐ 290 Darnell Coles	.05	.02	.01
☐ 291 Danny Cox	.05	.02	.01
☐ 292 Mark Eichhorn	.05	.02	.01
☐ 293 Tony Fernandez	.05	.02	.01
☐ 294 Al Leiter	.15	.07	.02
☐ 295 Paul Molitor	.40	.18	.05
☐ 296 Dave Stewart	.15	.07	.02
☐ 297 Woody Williams	.05	.02	.01
☐ 298 Checklist F1-F100	.05	.02	.01
☐ 299 Checklist F101-F200	.05	.02	.01
☐ 300 Checklist F201-F300	.05	.02	.01

1993 Fleer Final Edition Diamond Tribute

Each Fleer Final Edition factory set contained a complete 10-card set of Diamond Tribute inserts. These cards are numbered separately and feature a totally different design from the base cards. Each horizontally-designed Diamond Tribute card front features UV coating and two player images (one chest up and one full body action shot) set against the background of a blurred crowd. The set highlights a selection of top active veterans. Each card is numbered X of 10 on back.

	MINT	NRMT	EXC
COMPLETE SET (10)	4.00	1.80	.50
COMMON CARD (1-10)	.25	.11	.03
☐ 1 Wade Boggs	.50	.23	.06
☐ 2 George Brett	1.25	.55	.16
☐ 3 Andre Dawson	.50	.23	.06
☐ 4 Carlton Fisk	.50	.23	.06
☐ 5 Paul Molitor	.60	.25	.07
☐ 6 Nolan Ryan	3.00	1.35	.35
☐ 7 Lee Smith	.25	.11	.03
☐ 8 Ozzie Smith	.75	.35	.09
☐ 9 Dave Winfield	.50	.23	.06
☐ 10 Robin Yount	.50	.23	.06

1993 Fleer Atlantic

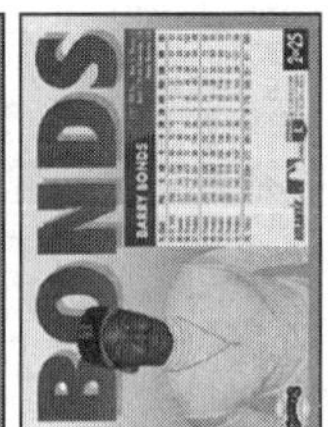

This standard-size set of 25 cards features 24 high-profile players plus a checklist and was offered free in packs of five cards with a minimum purchase of eight gallons of Atlantic gasoline. The cards were available from June 14 to July 25, 1993, at participating Atlantic retailers in New York and Pennsylvania. The action photos on the fronts are bordered in gold with the player's name, team, and position in white lettering printed on a blue stripe along the left side. The Atlantic Collector's Edition logo appears in the lower left. The horizontal back carries a color player cutout on the left side on a background that fades from white at the top to gold. The player's last name appears in bold lettering, which fades from blue to red at the top. Player statistics and biography are below. The cards are sequenced in alphabetical order. This set features one of the earliest cards picturing Barry Bonds as a member of the San Francisco Giants.

	MINT	NRMT	EXC
COMPLETE SET (25)	8.00	3.60	1.00
COMMON CARD (1-25)	.10	.05	.01
☐ 1 Roberto Alomar	.40	.18	.05
☐ 2 Barry Bonds	.40	.18	.05
☐ 3 Bobby Bonilla	.20	.09	.03
☐ 4 Will Clark	.30	.14	.04
☐ 5 Roger Clemens	.40	.18	.05
☐ 6 Darren Daulton	.20	.09	.03
☐ 7 Dennis Eckersley	.20	.09	.03
☐ 8 Cecil Fielder	.20	.09	.03
☐ 9 Tom Glavine	.30	.14	.04
☐ 10 Juan Gonzalez	1.00	.45	.12
☐ 11 Ken Griffey Jr.	2.00	.90	.25
☐ 12 John Kruk	.15	.07	.02
☐ 13 Greg Maddux	1.25	.55	.16
☐ 14 Don Mattingly	1.00	.45	.12
☐ 15 Fred McGriff	.30	.14	.04
☐ 16 Mark McGwire	.60	.25	.07
☐ 17 Terry Pendleton	.10	.05	.01
☐ 18 Kirby Puckett	.75	.35	.09
☐ 19 Cal Ripken	1.50	.70	.19
☐ 20 Nolan Ryan	1.50	.70	.19
☐ 21 Ryne Sandberg	.60	.25	.07
☐ 22 Gary Sheffield	.30	.14	.04
☐ 23 Frank Thomas	2.00	.90	.25
☐ 24 Andy Van Slyke	.20	.09	.03
☐ 25 Checklist 1-25	.10	.05	.01

1993 Fleer Fruit of the Loom

The 1993 Fleer Fruit of the Loom set consists of 66 cards measuring the standard size. Six-card packs were inserted in three-packs of Fruit of the Loom boys briefs. The cards have the same design as the

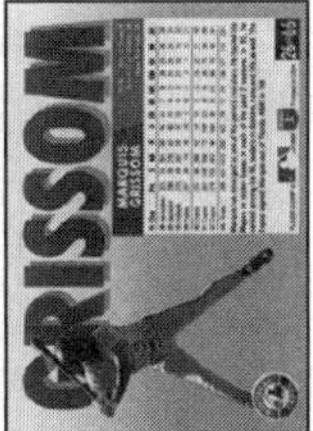

regular issue 1993 Fleer. The only exception is the Fruit of the Loom logo which appears on the front. The fronts display glossy color action player photos bordered in silver. A team color-coded stripe edges the left side of the picture and carries the player's name and team. On a background that shades from white to silver, the horizontal backs have the player's last name in team color-coded block lettering, a cut-out color player photo, and a box displaying biographical and statistical information. The cards are numbered on the back ordered alphabetically by player's name.

	MINT	NRMT	EXC
COMPLETE SET (66)	80.00	36.00	10.00
COMMON CARD (1-66)	.50	.23	.06
☐ 1 Roberto Alomar	3.00	1.35	.35
☐ 2 Brady Anderson	2.00	.90	.25
☐ 3 Jeff Bagwell	6.00	2.70	.75
☐ 4 Albert Belle	7.50	3.40	.95
☐ 5 Craig Biggio	1.00	.45	.12
☐ 6 Barry Bonds	2.50	1.10	.30
☐ 7 George Brett	6.00	2.70	.75
☐ 8 Brett Butler	1.00	.45	.12
☐ 9 Jose Canseco	1.50	.70	.19
☐ 10 Joe Carter	2.00	.90	.25
☐ 11 Will Clark	1.50	.70	.19
☐ 12 Roger Clemens	2.50	1.10	.30
☐ 13 Darren Daulton	1.00	.45	.12
☐ 14 Andre Dawson	1.00	.45	.12
☐ 15 Delino DeShields	.50	.23	.06
☐ 16 Rob Dibble	.50	.23	.06
☐ 17 Doug Drabek	.50	.23	.06
☐ 18 Dennis Eckersley	1.00	.45	.12
☐ 19 Cecil Fielder	1.00	.45	.12
☐ 20 Travis Fryman	1.00	.45	.12
☐ 21 Tom Glavine	2.00	.90	.25
☐ 22 Juan Gonzalez	7.50	3.40	.95
☐ 23 Dwight Gooden	1.00	.45	.12
☐ 24 Mark Grace	2.00	.90	.25
☐ 25 Ken Griffey Jr.	15.00	6.75	1.85
☐ 26 Marquis Grissom	1.50	.70	.19
☐ 27 Juan Guzman	.50	.23	.06
☐ 28 Tony Gwynn	5.00	2.20	.60
☐ 29 Rickey Henderson	2.00	.90	.25
☐ 30 David Justice	2.00	.90	.25
☐ 31 Eric Karros	1.25	.55	.16
☐ 32 Chuck Knoblauch	2.50	1.10	.30
☐ 33 John Kruk	1.00	.45	.12
☐ 34 Ray Lankford	1.00	.45	.12
☐ 35 Barry Larkin	1.50	.70	.19
☐ 36 Pat Listach	.50	.23	.06
☐ 37 Kenny Lofton	5.00	2.20	.60
☐ 38 Shane Mack	.50	.23	.06
☐ 39 Greg Maddux	8.00	3.60	1.00
☐ 40 Dennis Martinez	1.00	.45	.12
☐ 41 Edgar Martinez	1.00	.45	.12
☐ 42 Ramon Martinez	1.00	.45	.12
☐ 43 Don Mattingly	7.50	3.40	.95
☐ 44 Jack McDowell	1.00	.45	.12
☐ 45 Fred McGriff	1.50	.70	.19
☐ 46 Mark McGwire	5.00	2.20	.60
☐ 47 Jeff Montgomery	.50	.23	.06
☐ 48 Eddie Murray	3.00	1.35	.35
☐ 49 Charles Nagy	1.00	.45	.12
☐ 50 Tom Pagnozzi	.50	.23	.06
☐ 51 Terry Pendleton	.50	.23	.06
☐ 52 Kirby Puckett	7.50	3.40	.95
☐ 53 Jose Rijo	.50	.23	.06
☐ 54 Cal Ripken	10.00	4.50	1.25
☐ 55 Nolan Ryan	12.00	5.50	1.50
☐ 56 Ryne Sandberg	4.00	1.80	.50
☐ 57 Gary Sheffield	2.50	1.10	.30
☐ 58 Bill Swift	.50	.23	.06
☐ 59 Danny Tartabull	.50	.23	.06
☐ 60 Mickey Tettleton	.50	.23	.06
☐ 61 Frank Thomas	15.00	6.75	1.85
☐ 62 Andy Van Slyke	1.00	.45	.12
☐ 63 Robin Ventura	1.00	.45	.12
☐ 64 Larry Walker	2.00	.90	.25
☐ 65 Robin Yount	1.50	.70	.19
☐ 66 Checklist 1-66	.50	.23	.06

1994 Fleer

The 1994 Fleer baseball set consists of 720 standard-size cards. The white-bordered fronts feature color player action photos. In one corner, the player's name and position appear in a gold foil lettered arc; his team logo appears within. The backs are also white-bordered and feature a color player photo, some action, others posed. One side of the picture is ghosted and color-screened, and carries the player's name, biography, and career highlights. The bottom of the photo is also color-screened and ghosted, and carries the player's statistics. The cards are numbered on the back, grouped alphabetically within

teams, and checklisted below alphabetically according to teams for each league with AL preceding NL. The set closes with a Superstar Specials (706-713) subset. There are no key Rookie Cards in this set.

	MINT	NRMT	EXC
COMPLETE SET (720)	50.00	22.00	6.25
COMMON CARD (1-720)	.10	.05	.01
☐ 1 Brady Anderson	.50	.23	.06
☐ 2 Harold Baines	.25	.11	.03
☐ 3 Mike Devereaux	.10	.05	.01
☐ 4 Todd Frohwirth	.10	.05	.01
☐ 5 Jeffrey Hammonds	.25	.11	.03
☐ 6 Chris Hoiles	.10	.05	.01
☐ 7 Tim Hulett	.10	.05	.01
☐ 8 Ben McDonald	.10	.05	.01
☐ 9 Mark McLemore	.10	.05	.01
☐ 10 Alan Mills	.10	.05	.01
☐ 11 Jamie Moyer	.10	.05	.01
☐ 12 Mike Mussina	.60	.25	.07
☐ 13 Gregg Olson	.10	.05	.01
☐ 14 Mike Pagliarulo	.10	.05	.01
☐ 15 Brad Pennington	.10	.05	.01
☐ 16 Jim Poole	.10	.05	.01
☐ 17 Harold Reynolds	.10	.05	.01
☐ 18 Arthur Rhodes	.10	.05	.01
☐ 19 Cal Ripken Jr.	2.50	1.10	.30
☐ 20 David Segui	.10	.05	.01
☐ 21 Rick Sutcliffe	.10	.05	.01
☐ 22 Fernando Valenzuela	.25	.11	.03
☐ 23 Jack Voigt	.10	.05	.01
☐ 24 Mark Williamson	.10	.05	.01
☐ 25 Scott Bankhead	.10	.05	.01
☐ 26 Roger Clemens	.60	.25	.07
☐ 27 Scott Cooper	.10	.05	.01
☐ 28 Danny Darwin	.10	.05	.01
☐ 29 Andre Dawson	.25	.11	.03
☐ 30 Rob Deer	.10	.05	.01
☐ 31 John Dopson	.10	.05	.01
☐ 32 Scott Fletcher	.10	.05	.01
☐ 33 Mike Greenwell	.10	.05	.01
☐ 34 Greg A. Harris	.10	.05	.01
☐ 35 Billy Hatcher	.10	.05	.01
☐ 36 Bob Melvin	.10	.05	.01
☐ 37 Tony Pena	.10	.05	.01
☐ 38 Paul Quantrill	.10	.05	.01
☐ 39 Carlos Quintana	.10	.05	.01
☐ 40 Ernest Riles	.10	.05	.01
☐ 41 Jeff Russell	.10	.05	.01
☐ 42 Ken Ryan	.10	.05	.01
☐ 43 Aaron Sele	.25	.11	.03
☐ 44 John Valentin	.25	.11	.03
☐ 45 Mo Vaughn	.75	.35	.09
☐ 46 Frank Viola	.10	.05	.01
☐ 47 Bob Zupcic	.10	.05	.01
☐ 48 Mike Butcher	.10	.05	.01
☐ 49 Rod Correia	.10	.05	.01
☐ 50 Chad Curtis	.10	.05	.01
☐ 51 Chili Davis	.25	.11	.03
☐ 52 Gary DiSarcina	.10	.05	.01
☐ 53 Damion Easley	.10	.05	.01
☐ 54 Jim Edmonds	.60	.25	.07
☐ 55 Chuck Finley	.10	.05	.01
☐ 56 Steve Frey	.10	.05	.01
☐ 57 Rene Gonzales	.10	.05	.01
☐ 58 Joe Grahe	.10	.05	.01
☐ 59 Hilly Hathaway	.10	.05	.01
☐ 60 Stan Javier	.10	.05	.01
☐ 61 Mark Langston	.25	.11	.03
☐ 62 Phil Leftwich	.10	.05	.01
☐ 63 Torey Lovullo	.10	.05	.01
☐ 64 Joe Magrane	.10	.05	.01
☐ 65 Greg Myers	.10	.05	.01
☐ 66 Ken Patterson	.10	.05	.01
☐ 67 Eduardo Perez	.10	.05	.01
☐ 68 Luis Polonia	.10	.05	.01
☐ 69 Tim Salmon	.50	.23	.06
☐ 70 J.T. Snow	.25	.11	.03
☐ 71 Ron Tingley	.10	.05	.01
☐ 72 Julio Valera	.10	.05	.01
☐ 73 Wilson Alvarez	.25	.11	.03
☐ 74 Tim Belcher	.10	.05	.01
☐ 75 George Bell	.10	.05	.01
☐ 76 Jason Bere	.25	.11	.03
☐ 77 Rod Bolton	.10	.05	.01
☐ 78 Ellis Burks	.25	.11	.03
☐ 79 Joey Cora	.10	.05	.01
☐ 80 Alex Fernandez	.25	.11	.03
☐ 81 Craig Grebeck	.10	.05	.01
☐ 82 Ozzie Guillen	.10	.05	.01
☐ 83 Roberto Hernandez	.25	.11	.03
☐ 84 Bo Jackson	.25	.11	.03
☐ 85 Lance Johnson	.25	.11	.03
☐ 86 Ron Karkovice	.10	.05	.01
☐ 87 Mike LaValliere	.10	.05	.01
☐ 88 Kirk McCaskill	.10	.05	.01
☐ 89 Jack McDowell	.25	.11	.03
☐ 90 Warren Newson	.10	.05	.01
☐ 91 Dan Pasqua	.10	.05	.01
☐ 92 Scott Radinsky	.10	.05	.01
☐ 93 Tim Raines	.50	.23	.06
☐ 94 Steve Sax	.10	.05	.01
☐ 95 Jeff Schwarz	.10	.05	.01
☐ 96 Frank Thomas	3.00	1.35	.35
☐ 97 Robin Ventura	.25	.11	.03
☐ 98 Sandy Alomar Jr.	.25	.11	.03
☐ 99 Carlos Baerga	.25	.11	.03
☐ 100 Albert Belle	1.25	.55	.16
☐ 101 Mark Clark	.10	.05	.01
☐ 102 Jerry DiPoto	.10	.05	.01
☐ 103 Alvaro Espinoza	.10	.05	.01
☐ 104 Felix Fermin	.10	.05	.01
☐ 105 Jeremy Hernandez	.10	.05	.01
☐ 106 Reggie Jefferson	.25	.11	.03
☐ 107 Wayne Kirby	.10	.05	.01
☐ 108 Tom Kramer	.10	.05	.01
☐ 109 Mark Lewis	.10	.05	.01
☐ 110 Derek Lilliquist	.10	.05	.01
☐ 111 Kenny Lofton	1.00	.45	.12
☐ 112 Candy Maldonado	.10	.05	.01
☐ 113 Jose Mesa	.25	.11	.03
☐ 114 Jeff Mutis	.10	.05	.01
☐ 115 Charles Nagy	.25	.11	.03
☐ 116 Bob Ojeda	.10	.05	.01
☐ 117 Junior Ortiz	.10	.05	.01
☐ 118 Eric Plunk	.10	.05	.01
☐ 119 Manny Ramirez	1.00	.45	.12
☐ 120 Paul Sorrento	.10	.05	.01
☐ 121 Jim Thome	.75	.35	.09
☐ 122 Jeff Treadway	.10	.05	.01
☐ 123 Bill Wertz	.10	.05	.01
☐ 124 Skeeter Barnes	.10	.05	.01
☐ 125 Milt Cuyler	.10	.05	.01
☐ 126 Eric Davis	.25	.11	.03
☐ 127 John Doherty	.10	.05	.01
☐ 128 Cecil Fielder	.25	.11	.03
☐ 129 Travis Fryman	.25	.11	.03
☐ 130 Kirk Gibson	.25	.11	.03
☐ 131 Dan Gladden	.10	.05	.01
☐ 132 Greg Gohr	.10	.05	.01
☐ 133 Chris Gomez	.10	.05	.01
☐ 134 Bill Gullickson	.10	.05	.01
☐ 135 Mike Henneman	.10	.05	.01
☐ 136 Kurt Knudsen	.10	.05	.01
☐ 137 Chad Kreuter	.10	.05	.01
☐ 138 Bill Krueger	.10	.05	.01
☐ 139 Scott Livingstone	.10	.05	.01
☐ 140 Bob MacDonald	.10	.05	.01
☐ 141 Mike Moore	.10	.05	.01
☐ 142 Tony Phillips	.25	.11	.03
☐ 143 Mickey Tettleton	.10	.05	.01
☐ 144 Alan Trammell	.25	.11	.03
☐ 145 David Wells	.10	.05	.01
☐ 146 Lou Whitaker	.25	.11	.03
☐ 147 Kevin Appier	.25	.11	.03
☐ 148 Stan Belinda	.10	.05	.01
☐ 149 George Brett	1.25	.55	.16
☐ 150 Billy Brewer	.10	.05	.01
☐ 151 Hubie Brooks	.10	.05	.01
☐ 152 David Cone	.25	.11	.03
☐ 153 Gary Gaetti	.25	.11	.03
☐ 154 Greg Gagne	.10	.05	.01
☐ 155 Tom Gordon	.10	.05	.01
☐ 156 Mark Gubicza	.10	.05	.01
☐ 157 Chris Gwynn	.10	.05	.01
☐ 158 John Habyan	.10	.05	.01
☐ 159 Chris Haney	.10	.05	.01
☐ 160 Phil Hiatt	.10	.05	.01
☐ 161 Felix Jose	.10	.05	.01
☐ 162 Wally Joyner	.25	.11	.03
☐ 163 Jose Lind	.10	.05	.01
☐ 164 Mike Macfarlane	.10	.05	.01
☐ 165 Mike Magnante	.10	.05	.01
☐ 166 Brent Mayne	.10	.05	.01
☐ 167 Brian McRae	.25	.11	.03
☐ 168 Kevin McReynolds	.10	.05	.01
☐ 169 Keith Miller	.10	.05	.01
☐ 170 Jeff Montgomery	.25	.11	.03
☐ 171 Hipolito Pichardo	.10	.05	.01
☐ 172 Rico Rossy	.10	.05	.01
☐ 173 Juan Bell	.10	.05	.01
☐ 174 Ricky Bones	.10	.05	.01
☐ 175 Cal Eldred	.10	.05	.01
☐ 176 Mike Fetters	.10	.05	.01
☐ 177 Darryl Hamilton	.10	.05	.01
☐ 178 Doug Henry	.10	.05	.01
☐ 179 Mike Ignasiak	.10	.05	.01
☐ 180 John Jaha	.25	.11	.03
☐ 181 Pat Listach	.10	.05	.01
☐ 182 Graeme Lloyd	.10	.05	.01
☐ 183 Matt Mieske	.10	.05	.01
☐ 184 Angel Miranda	.10	.05	.01
☐ 185 Jaime Navarro	.10	.05	.01
☐ 186 Dave Nilsson	.25	.11	.03
☐ 187 Troy O'Leary	.10	.05	.01
☐ 188 Jesse Orosco	.10	.05	.01
☐ 189 Kevin Reimer	.10	.05	.01
☐ 190 Kevin Seitzer	.10	.05	.01
☐ 191 Bill Spiers	.10	.05	.01
☐ 192 B.J. Surhoff	.10	.05	.01
☐ 193 Dickie Thon	.10	.05	.01
☐ 194 Jose Valentin	.25	.11	.03
☐ 195 Greg Vaughn	.50	.23	.06
☐ 196 Bill Wegman	.10	.05	.01
☐ 197 Robin Yount	.50	.23	.06
☐ 198 Rick Aguilera	.10	.05	.01
☐ 199 Willie Banks	.10	.05	.01
☐ 200 Bernardo Brito	.10	.05	.01
☐ 201 Larry Casian	.10	.05	.01
☐ 202 Scott Erickson	.10	.05	.01
☐ 203 Eddie Guardado	.10	.05	.01
☐ 204 Mark Guthrie	.10	.05	.01
☐ 205 Chip Hale	.10	.05	.01
☐ 206 Brian Harper	.10	.05	.01
☐ 207 Mike Hartley	.10	.05	.01
☐ 208 Kent Hrbek	.25	.11	.03
☐ 209 Terry Jorgensen	.10	.05	.01
☐ 210 Chuck Knoblauch	.50	.23	.06
☐ 211 Gene Larkin	.10	.05	.01
☐ 212 Shane Mack	.10	.05	.01
☐ 213 David McCarty	.10	.05	.01
☐ 214 Pat Meares	.10	.05	.01
☐ 215 Pedro Munoz	.10	.05	.01
☐ 216 Derek Parks	.10	.05	.01
☐ 217 Kirby Puckett	1.25	.55	.16
☐ 218 Jeff Reboulet	.10	.05	.01
☐ 219 Kevin Tapani	.10	.05	.01
☐ 220 Mike Trombley	.10	.05	.01
☐ 221 George Tsamis	.10	.05	.01
☐ 222 Carl Willis	.10	.05	.01
☐ 223 Dave Winfield	.50	.23	.06
☐ 224 Jim Abbott	.10	.05	.01
☐ 225 Paul Assenmacher	.10	.05	.01
☐ 226 Wade Boggs	.50	.23	.06
☐ 227 Russ Davis	.25	.11	.03
☐ 228 Steve Farr	.10	.05	.01
☐ 229 Mike Gallego	.10	.05	.01
☐ 230 Paul Gibson	.10	.05	.01
☐ 231 Steve Howe	.10	.05	.01
☐ 232 Dion James	.10	.05	.01
☐ 233 Domingo Jean	.10	.05	.01
☐ 234 Scott Kamieniecki	.10	.05	.01
☐ 235 Pat Kelly	.10	.05	.01
☐ 236 Jimmy Key	.25	.11	.03
☐ 237 Jim Leyritz	.10	.05	.01
☐ 238 Kevin Maas	.10	.05	.01
☐ 239 Don Mattingly	1.50	.70	.19
☐ 240 Rich Monteleone	.10	.05	.01
☐ 241 Bobby Munoz	.10	.05	.01
☐ 242 Matt Nokes	.10	.05	.01
☐ 243 Paul O'Neill	.25	.11	.03
☐ 244 Spike Owen	.10	.05	.01
☐ 245 Melido Perez	.10	.05	.01
☐ 246 Lee Smith	.25	.11	.03
☐ 247 Mike Stanley	.10	.05	.01
☐ 248 Danny Tartabull	.10	.05	.01
☐ 249 Randy Velarde	.10	.05	.01
☐ 250 Bob Wickman	.10	.05	.01
☐ 251 Bernie Williams	.60	.25	.07
☐ 252 Mike Aldrete	.10	.05	.01
☐ 253 Marcos Armas	.10	.05	.01
☐ 254 Lance Blankenship	.10	.05	.01
☐ 255 Mike Bordick	.10	.05	.01
☐ 256 Scott Brosius	.10	.05	.01
☐ 257 Jerry Browne	.10	.05	.01
☐ 258 Ron Darling	.10	.05	.01
☐ 259 Kelly Downs	.10	.05	.01
☐ 260 Dennis Eckersley	.25	.11	.03
☐ 261 Brent Gates	.10	.05	.01
☐ 262 Goose Gossage	.25	.11	.03
☐ 263 Scott Hemond	.10	.05	.01
☐ 264 Dave Henderson	.10	.05	.01
☐ 265 Rick Honeycutt	.10	.05	.01
☐ 266 Vince Horsman	.10	.05	.01
☐ 267 Scott Lydy	.10	.05	.01
☐ 268 Mark McGwire	1.00	.45	.12
☐ 269 Mike Mohler	.10	.05	.01
☐ 270 Troy Neel	.10	.05	.01
☐ 271 Edwin Nunez	.10	.05	.01
☐ 272 Craig Paquette	.10	.05	.01
☐ 273 Ruben Sierra	.25	.11	.03
☐ 274 Terry Steinbach	.25	.11	.03
☐ 275 Todd Van Poppel	.10	.05	.01
☐ 276 Bob Welch	.10	.05	.01
☐ 277 Bobby Witt	.10	.05	.01
☐ 278 Rich Amaral	.10	.05	.01
☐ 279 Mike Blowers	.10	.05	.01
☐ 280 Bret Boone UER	.25	.11	.03
(Name spelled Brett on front)			
☐ 281 Chris Bosio	.10	.05	.01
☐ 282 Jay Buhner	.50	.23	.06
☐ 283 Norm Charlton	.10	.05	.01
☐ 284 Mike Felder	.10	.05	.01
☐ 285 Dave Fleming	.10	.05	.01
☐ 286 Ken Griffey Jr.	3.00	1.35	.35
☐ 287 Erik Hanson	.10	.05	.01
☐ 288 Bill Haselman	.10	.05	.01
☐ 289 Brad Holman	.10	.05	.01
☐ 290 Randy Johnson	.50	.23	.06
☐ 291 Tim Leary	.10	.05	.01
☐ 292 Greg Litton	.10	.05	.01
☐ 293 Dave Magadan	.10	.05	.01
☐ 294 Edgar Martinez	.25	.11	.03
☐ 295 Tino Martinez	.25	.11	.03
☐ 296 Jeff Nelson	.10	.05	.01
☐ 297 Erik Plantenberg	.10	.05	.01
☐ 298 Mackey Sasser	.10	.05	.01
☐ 299 Brian Turang	.10	.05	.01
☐ 300 Dave Valle	.10	.05	.01
☐ 301 Omar Vizquel	.25	.11	.03
☐ 302 Brian Bohanon	.10	.05	.01
☐ 303 Kevin Brown	.25	.11	.03
☐ 304 Jose Canseco UER	.50	.23	.06
(Back mentions 1991 as his 40/40 MVP season; should be '88)			
☐ 305 Mario Diaz	.10	.05	.01
☐ 306 Julio Franco	.25	.11	.03
☐ 307 Juan Gonzalez	1.50	.70	.19
☐ 308 Tom Henke	.10	.05	.01
☐ 309 David Hulse	.10	.05	.01
☐ 310 Manuel Lee	.10	.05	.01
☐ 311 Craig Lefferts	.10	.05	.01
☐ 312 Charlie Leibrandt	.10	.05	.01
☐ 313 Rafael Palmeiro	.50	.23	.06
☐ 314 Dean Palmer	.25	.11	.03
☐ 315 Roger Pavlik	.10	.05	.01
☐ 316 Dan Peltier	.10	.05	.01
☐ 317 Gene Petralli	.10	.05	.01
☐ 318 Gary Redus	.10	.05	.01
☐ 319 Ivan Rodriguez	.75	.35	.09
☐ 320 Kenny Rogers	.10	.05	.01
☐ 321 Nolan Ryan	2.50	1.10	.30
☐ 322 Doug Strange	.10	.05	.01
☐ 323 Matt Whiteside	.10	.05	.01
☐ 324 Roberto Alomar	.60	.25	.07
☐ 325 Pat Borders	.10	.05	.01
☐ 326 Joe Carter	.25	.11	.03
☐ 327 Tony Castillo	.10	.05	.01
☐ 328 Darnell Coles	.10	.05	.01
☐ 329 Danny Cox	.10	.05	.01
☐ 330 Mark Eichhorn	.10	.05	.01
☐ 331 Tony Fernandez	.10	.05	.01
☐ 332 Alfredo Griffin	.10	.05	.01
☐ 333 Juan Guzman	.25	.11	.03
☐ 334 Rickey Henderson	.50	.23	.06
☐ 335 Pat Hentgen	.25	.11	.03
☐ 336 Randy Knorr	.10	.05	.01
☐ 337 Al Leiter	.25	.11	.03
☐ 338 Paul Molitor	.60	.25	.07
☐ 339 Jack Morris	.25	.11	.03
☐ 340 John Olerud	.10	.05	.01
☐ 341 Dick Schofield	.10	.05	.01
☐ 342 Ed Sprague	.25	.11	.03
☐ 343 Dave Stewart	.25	.11	.03
☐ 344 Todd Stottlemyre	.10	.05	.01
☐ 345 Mike Timlin	.10	.05	.01
☐ 346 Duane Ward	.10	.05	.01
☐ 347 Turner Ward	.10	.05	.01
☐ 348 Devon White	.10	.05	.01
☐ 349 Woody Williams	.10	.05	.01
☐ 350 Steve Avery	.25	.11	.03
☐ 351 Steve Bedrosian	.10	.05	.01
☐ 352 Rafael Belliard	.10	.05	.01
☐ 353 Damon Berryhill	.10	.05	.01
☐ 354 Jeff Blauser	.10	.05	.01
☐ 355 Sid Bream	.10	.05	.01
☐ 356 Francisco Cabrera	.10	.05	.01
☐ 357 Marvin Freeman	.10	.05	.01
☐ 358 Ron Gant	.25	.11	.03
☐ 359 Tom Glavine	.50	.23	.06
☐ 360 Jay Howell	.10	.05	.01
☐ 361 David Justice	.50	.23	.06
☐ 362 Ryan Klesko	.60	.25	.07
☐ 363 Mark Lemke	.10	.05	.01
☐ 364 Javier Lopez	.50	.23	.06
☐ 365 Greg Maddux	2.00	.90	.25
☐ 366 Fred McGriff	.50	.23	.06
☐ 367 Greg McMichael	.10	.05	.01
☐ 368 Kent Mercker	.10	.05	.01
☐ 369 Otis Nixon	.10	.05	.01
☐ 370 Greg Olson	.10	.05	.01
☐ 371 Bill Pecota	.10	.05	.01
☐ 372 Terry Pendleton	.25	.11	.03
☐ 373 Deion Sanders	.50	.23	.06
☐ 374 Pete Smith	.10	.05	.01
☐ 375 John Smoltz	.50	.23	.06
☐ 376 Mike Stanton	.10	.05	.01
☐ 377 Tony Tarasco	.10	.05	.01
☐ 378 Mark Wohlers	.25	.11	.03
☐ 379 Jose Bautista	.10	.05	.01
☐ 380 Shawn Boskie	.10	.05	.01
☐ 381 Steve Buechele	.10	.05	.01
☐ 382 Frank Castillo	.10	.05	.01
☐ 383 Mark Grace	.50	.23	.06
☐ 384 Jose Guzman	.10	.05	.01
☐ 385 Mike Harkey	.10	.05	.01
☐ 386 Greg Hibbard	.10	.05	.01
☐ 387 Glenallen Hill	.10	.05	.01
☐ 388 Steve Lake	.10	.05	.01
☐ 389 Derrick May	.10	.05	.01
☐ 390 Chuck McElroy	.10	.05	.01
☐ 391 Mike Morgan	.10	.05	.01
☐ 392 Randy Myers	.10	.05	.01
☐ 393 Dan Plesac	.10	.05	.01
☐ 394 Kevin Roberson	.10	.05	.01
☐ 395 Rey Sanchez	.10	.05	.01
☐ 396 Ryne Sandberg	.75	.35	.09

☐ 397 Bob Scanlan .10 .05 .01
☐ 398 Dwight Smith .10 .05 .01
☐ 399 Sammy Sosa .50 .23 .06
☐ 400 Jose Vizcaino .10 .05 .01
☐ 401 Rick Wilkins .10 .05 .01
☐ 402 Willie Wilson .10 .05 .01
☐ 403 Eric Yelding .10 .05 .01
☐ 404 Bobby Ayala .10 .05 .01
☐ 405 Jeff Branson .10 .05 .01
☐ 406 Tom Browning .10 .05 .01
☐ 407 Jacob Brumfield .10 .05 .01
☐ 408 Tim Costo .10 .05 .01
☐ 409 Rob Dibble .10 .05 .01
☐ 410 Willie Greene .25 .11 .03
☐ 411 Thomas Howard .10 .05 .01
☐ 412 Roberto Kelly .10 .05 .01
☐ 413 Bill Landrum .10 .05 .01
☐ 414 Barry Larkin .50 .23 .06
☐ 415 Larry Luebbers .10 .05 .01
☐ 416 Kevin Mitchell .25 .11 .03
☐ 417 Hal Morris .10 .05 .01
☐ 418 Joe Oliver .10 .05 .01
☐ 419 Tim Pugh .10 .05 .01
☐ 420 Jeff Reardon .25 .11 .03
☐ 421 Jose Rijo .10 .05 .01
☐ 422 Bip Roberts .10 .05 .01
☐ 423 John Roper .10 .05 .01
☐ 424 Johnny Ruffin .10 .05 .01
☐ 425 Chris Sabo .10 .05 .01
☐ 426 Juan Samuel .10 .05 .01
☐ 427 Reggie Sanders .25 .11 .03
☐ 428 Scott Service .10 .05 .01
☐ 429 John Smiley .10 .05 .01
☐ 430 Jerry Spradlin .10 .05 .01
☐ 431 Kevin Wickander .10 .05 .01
☐ 432 Freddie Benavides .10 .05 .01
☐ 433 Dante Bichette .50 .23 .06
☐ 434 Willie Blair .10 .05 .01
☐ 435 Daryl Boston .10 .05 .01
☐ 436 Kent Bottenfield .10 .05 .01
☐ 437 Vinny Castilla .50 .23 .06
☐ 438 Jerald Clark .10 .05 .01
☐ 439 Alex Cole .10 .05 .01
☐ 440 Andres Galarraga .50 .23 .06
☐ 441 Joe Girardi .10 .05 .01
☐ 442 Greg W. Harris .10 .05 .01
☐ 443 Charlie Hayes .10 .05 .01
☐ 444 Darren Holmes .10 .05 .01
☐ 445 Chris Jones .10 .05 .01
☐ 446 Roberto Mejia .10 .05 .01
☐ 447 David Nied .10 .05 .01
☐ 448 J. Owens .10 .05 .01
☐ 449 Jeff Parrett .10 .05 .01
☐ 450 Steve Reed .10 .05 .01
☐ 451 Armando Reynoso .10 .05 .01
☐ 452 Bruce Ruffin .10 .05 .01
☐ 453 Mo Sanford .10 .05 .01
☐ 454 Danny Sheaffer .10 .05 .01
☐ 455 Jim Tatum .10 .05 .01
☐ 456 Gary Wayne .10 .05 .01
☐ 457 Eric Young .25 .11 .03
☐ 458 Luis Aquino .10 .05 .01
☐ 459 Alex Arias .10 .05 .01
☐ 460 Jack Armstrong .10 .05 .01
☐ 461 Bret Barberie .10 .05 .01
☐ 462 Ryan Bowen .10 .05 .01
☐ 463 Chuck Carr .10 .05 .01
☐ 464 Jeff Conine .25 .11 .03
☐ 465 Henry Cotto .10 .05 .01
☐ 466 Orestes Destrade .10 .05 .01
☐ 467 Chris Hammond .10 .05 .01
☐ 468 Bryan Harvey .10 .05 .01
☐ 469 Charlie Hough .10 .05 .01
☐ 470 Joe Klink .10 .05 .01
☐ 471 Richie Lewis .10 .05 .01
☐ 472 Bob Natal .10 .05 .01
☐ 473 Pat Rapp .10 .05 .01
☐ 474 Rich Renteria .10 .05 .01
☐ 475 Rich Rodriguez .10 .05 .01
☐ 476 Benito Santiago .10 .05 .01
☐ 477 Gary Sheffield .50 .23 .06
☐ 478 Matt Turner .10 .05 .01
☐ 479 David Weathers .10 .05 .01
☐ 480 Walt Weiss .10 .05 .01
☐ 481 Darrell Whitmore .10 .05 .01
☐ 482 Eric Anthony .10 .05 .01
☐ 483 Jeff Bagwell 1.25 .55 .16
☐ 484 Kevin Bass .10 .05 .01
☐ 485 Craig Biggio .25 .11 .03
☐ 486 Ken Caminiti .50 .23 .06
☐ 487 Andujar Cedeno .10 .05 .01
☐ 488 Chris Donnels .10 .05 .01
☐ 489 Doug Drabek .10 .05 .01
☐ 490 Steve Finley .50 .23 .06
☐ 491 Luis Gonzalez .10 .05 .01
☐ 492 Pete Harnisch .10 .05 .01
☐ 493 Xavier Hernandez .10 .05 .01
☐ 494 Doug Jones .10 .05 .01
☐ 495 Todd Jones .10 .05 .01
☐ 496 Darryl Kile .10 .05 .01
☐ 497 Al Osuna .10 .05 .01
☐ 498 Mark Portugal .10 .05 .01
☐ 499 Scott Servais .10 .05 .01
☐ 500 Greg Swindell .10 .05 .01
☐ 501 Eddie Taubensee .10 .05 .01
☐ 502 Jose Uribe .10 .05 .01
☐ 503 Brian Williams .10 .05 .01
☐ 504 Billy Ashley .10 .05 .01
☐ 505 Pedro Astacio .10 .05 .01
☐ 506 Brett Butler .25 .11 .03
☐ 507 Tom Candiotti .10 .05 .01
☐ 508 Omar Daal .10 .05 .01
☐ 509 Jim Gott .10 .05 .01
☐ 510 Kevin Gross .10 .05 .01
☐ 511 Dave Hansen .10 .05 .01
☐ 512 Carlos Hernandez .10 .05 .01
☐ 513 Orel Hershiser .25 .11 .03
☐ 514 Eric Karros .25 .11 .03
☐ 515 Pedro Martinez .50 .23 .06
☐ 516 Ramon Martinez .25 .11 .03
☐ 517 Roger McDowell .10 .05 .01
☐ 518 Raul Mondesi .50 .23 .06
☐ 519 Jose Offerman .10 .05 .01
☐ 520 Mike Piazza 2.00 .90 .25
☐ 521 Jody Reed .10 .05 .01
☐ 522 Henry Rodriguez .25 .11 .03
☐ 523 Mike Sharperson .10 .05 .01
☐ 524 Cory Snyder .10 .05 .01
☐ 525 Darryl Strawberry .25 .11 .03
☐ 526 Rick Trlicek .10 .05 .01
☐ 527 Tim Wallach .10 .05 .01
☐ 528 Mitch Webster .10 .05 .01
☐ 529 Steve Wilson .10 .05 .01
☐ 530 Todd Worrell .10 .05 .01
☐ 531 Moises Alou .25 .11 .03
☐ 532 Brian Barnes .10 .05 .01
☐ 533 Sean Berry .10 .05 .01
☐ 534 Greg Colbrunn .10 .05 .01
☐ 535 Delino DeShields .10 .05 .01
☐ 536 Jeff Fassero .10 .05 .01
☐ 537 Darrin Fletcher .10 .05 .01
☐ 538 Cliff Floyd .50 .23 .06
☐ 539 Lou Frazier .10 .05 .01
☐ 540 Marquis Grissom .25 .11 .03
☐ 541 Butch Henry .10 .05 .01
☐ 542 Ken Hill .10 .05 .01
☐ 543 Mike Lansing .25 .11 .03
☐ 544 Brian Looney .10 .05 .01
☐ 545 Dennis Martinez .25 .11 .03
☐ 546 Chris Nabholz .10 .05 .01
☐ 547 Randy Ready .10 .05 .01
☐ 548 Mel Rojas .10 .05 .01
☐ 549 Kirk Rueter .10 .05 .01
☐ 550 Tim Scott .10 .05 .01
☐ 551 Jeff Shaw .10 .05 .01
☐ 552 Tim Spehr .10 .05 .01
☐ 553 John VanderWal .10 .05 .01
☐ 554 Larry Walker .50 .23 .06
☐ 555 John Wetteland .25 .11 .03
☐ 556 Rondell White .50 .23 .06
☐ 557 Tim Bogar .10 .05 .01
☐ 558 Bobby Bonilla .25 .11 .03
☐ 559 Jeromy Burnitz .10 .05 .01
☐ 560 Sid Fernandez .10 .05 .01
☐ 561 John Franco .10 .05 .01
☐ 562 Dave Gallagher .10 .05 .01
☐ 563 Dwight Gooden .25 .11 .03
☐ 564 Eric Hillman .10 .05 .01
☐ 565 Todd Hundley .25 .11 .03
☐ 566 Jeff Innis .10 .05 .01
☐ 567 Darrin Jackson .10 .05 .01
☐ 568 Howard Johnson .10 .05 .01
☐ 569 Bobby Jones .25 .11 .03
☐ 570 Jeff Kent .10 .05 .01
☐ 571 Mike Maddux .10 .05 .01
☐ 572 Jeff McKnight .10 .05 .01
☐ 573 Eddie Murray .75 .35 .09
☐ 574 Charlie O'Brien .10 .05 .01
☐ 575 Joe Orsulak .10 .05 .01
☐ 576 Bret Saberhagen .25 .11 .03
☐ 577 Pete Schourek .25 .11 .03
☐ 578 Dave Telgheder .10 .05 .01
☐ 579 Ryan Thompson .10 .05 .01
☐ 580 Anthony Young .10 .05 .01
☐ 581 Ruben Amaro .10 .05 .01
☐ 582 Larry Andersen .10 .05 .01
☐ 583 Kim Batiste .10 .05 .01
☐ 584 Wes Chamberlain .10 .05 .01
☐ 585 Darren Daulton .25 .11 .03
☐ 586 Mariano Duncan .10 .05 .01
☐ 587 Lenny Dykstra .25 .11 .03
☐ 588 Jim Eisenreich .10 .05 .01
☐ 589 Tommy Greene .10 .05 .01
☐ 590 Dave Hollins .10 .05 .01
☐ 591 Pete Incaviglia .10 .05 .01
☐ 592 Danny Jackson .10 .05 .01
☐ 593 Ricky Jordan .10 .05 .01
☐ 594 John Kruk .25 .11 .03
☐ 595 Roger Mason .10 .05 .01
☐ 596 Mickey Morandini .10 .05 .01
☐ 597 Terry Mulholland .10 .05 .01
☐ 598 Todd Pratt .10 .05 .01
☐ 599 Ben Rivera .10 .05 .01
☐ 600 Curt Schilling .10 .05 .01
☐ 601 Kevin Stocker .10 .05 .01
☐ 602 Milt Thompson .10 .05 .01
☐ 603 David West .10 .05 .01
☐ 604 Mitch Williams .10 .05 .01
☐ 605 Jay Bell .25 .11 .03
☐ 606 Dave Clark .10 .05 .01
☐ 607 Steve Cooke .10 .05 .01
☐ 608 Tom Foley .10 .05 .01
☐ 609 Carlos Garcia .10 .05 .01
☐ 610 Joel Johnston .10 .05 .01
☐ 611 Jeff King .25 .11 .03
☐ 612 Al Martin .10 .05 .01
☐ 613 Lloyd McClendon .10 .05 .01
☐ 614 Orlando Merced .25 .11 .03
☐ 615 Blas Minor .10 .05 .01
☐ 616 Denny Neagle .25 .11 .03
☐ 617 Mark Petkovsek .10 .05 .01
☐ 618 Tom Prince .10 .05 .01
☐ 619 Don Slaught .10 .05 .01
☐ 620 Zane Smith .10 .05 .01
☐ 621 Randy Tomlin .10 .05 .01
☐ 622 Andy Van Slyke .25 .11 .03
☐ 623 Paul Wagner .10 .05 .01
☐ 624 Tim Wakefield .10 .05 .01
☐ 625 Bob Walk .10 .05 .01
☐ 626 Kevin Young .10 .05 .01
☐ 627 Luis Alicea .10 .05 .01
☐ 628 Rene Arocha .10 .05 .01
☐ 629 Rod Brewer .10 .05 .01
☐ 630 Rheal Cormier .10 .05 .01
☐ 631 Bernard Gilkey .25 .11 .03
☐ 632 Lee Guetterman .10 .05 .01
☐ 633 Gregg Jefferies .50 .23 .06
☐ 634 Brian Jordan .50 .23 .06
☐ 635 Les Lancaster .10 .05 .01
☐ 636 Ray Lankford .25 .11 .03
☐ 637 Rob Murphy .10 .05 .01
☐ 638 Omar Olivares .10 .05 .01
☐ 639 Jose Oquendo .10 .05 .01
☐ 640 Donovan Osborne .10 .05 .01
☐ 641 Tom Pagnozzi .10 .05 .01
☐ 642 Erik Pappas .10 .05 .01
☐ 643 Geronimo Pena .10 .05 .01
☐ 644 Mike Perez .10 .05 .01
☐ 645 Gerald Perry .10 .05 .01
☐ 646 Ozzie Smith .75 .35 .09
☐ 647 Bob Tewksbury .10 .05 .01
☐ 648 Allen Watson .10 .05 .01
☐ 649 Mark Whiten .10 .05 .01
☐ 650 Tracy Woodson .10 .05 .01
☐ 651 Todd Zeile .10 .05 .01
☐ 652 Andy Ashby .25 .11 .03
☐ 653 Brad Ausmus .10 .05 .01
☐ 654 Billy Bean .10 .05 .01
☐ 655 Derek Bell .25 .11 .03
☐ 656 Andy Benes .25 .11 .03
☐ 657 Doug Brocail .10 .05 .01
☐ 658 Jarvis Brown .10 .05 .01
☐ 659 Archi Cianfrocco .10 .05 .01
☐ 660 Phil Clark .10 .05 .01
☐ 661 Mark Davis .10 .05 .01
☐ 662 Jeff Gardner .10 .05 .01
☐ 663 Pat Gomez .10 .05 .01
☐ 664 Ricky Gutierrez .10 .05 .01
☐ 665 Tony Gwynn 1.25 .55 .16
☐ 666 Gene Harris .10 .05 .01
☐ 667 Kevin Higgins .10 .05 .01
☐ 668 Trevor Hoffman .25 .11 .03
☐ 669 Pedro Martinez .25 .11 .03
☐ 670 Tim Mauser .10 .05 .01
☐ 671 Melvin Nieves .25 .11 .03
☐ 672 Phil Plantier .10 .05 .01
☐ 673 Frank Seminara .10 .05 .01
☐ 674 Craig Shipley .10 .05 .01
☐ 675 Kerry Taylor .10 .05 .01
☐ 676 Tim Teufel .10 .05 .01
☐ 677 Guillermo Velasquez .10 .05 .01
☐ 678 Wally Whitehurst .10 .05 .01
☐ 679 Tim Worrell .10 .05 .01
☐ 680 Rod Beck .25 .11 .03
☐ 681 Mike Benjamin .10 .05 .01
☐ 682 Todd Benzinger .10 .05 .01
☐ 683 Bud Black .10 .05 .01
☐ 684 Barry Bonds .75 .35 .09
☐ 685 Jeff Brantley .10 .05 .01
☐ 686 Dave Burba .10 .05 .01
☐ 687 John Burkett .10 .05 .01
☐ 688 Mark Carreon .10 .05 .01
☐ 689 Will Clark .50 .23 .06
☐ 690 Royce Clayton .25 .11 .03
☐ 691 Bryan Hickerson .10 .05 .01
☐ 692 Mike Jackson .10 .05 .01
☐ 693 Darren Lewis .10 .05 .01
☐ 694 Kirt Manwaring .10 .05 .01
☐ 695 Dave Martinez .10 .05 .01
☐ 696 Willie McGee .10 .05 .01
☐ 697 John Patterson .10 .05 .01
☐ 698 Jeff Reed .10 .05 .01
☐ 699 Kevin Rogers .10 .05 .01
☐ 700 Scott Sanderson .10 .05 .01
☐ 701 Steve Scarsone .10 .05 .01
☐ 702 Billy Swift .10 .05 .01
☐ 703 Robby Thompson .10 .05 .01
☐ 704 Matt Williams .50 .23 .06
☐ 705 Trevor Wilson .10 .05 .01
☐ 706 Brave New World .50 .23 .06
Fred McGriff
Ron Gant
David Justice
☐ 707 1-2 Punch .25 .11 .03
John Olerud
Paul Molitor
☐ 708 American Heat .25 .11 .03
Mike Mussina
Jack McDowell
☐ 709 Together Again .50 .23 .06
Lou Whitaker
Alan Trammell
☐ 710 Lone Star Lumber .50 .23 .06
Rafael Palmeiro
Juan Gonzalez
☐ 711 Batmen .50 .23 .06
Brett Butler
Tony Gwynn
☐ 712 Twin Peaks .50 .23 .06
Kirby Puckett
Chuck Knoblauch
☐ 713 Back to Back .60 .25 .07
Mike Piazza
Eric Karros
☐ 714 Checklist 1 .10 .05 .01
☐ 715 Checklist 2 .10 .05 .01
☐ 716 Checklist 3 .10 .05 .01
☐ 717 Checklist 4 .10 .05 .01
☐ 718 Checklist 5 .10 .05 .01
☐ 719 Checklist 6 .10 .05 .01
☐ 720 Checklist 7 .10 .05 .01
☐ P69 Tim Salmon Promo .50 .23 .06

1994 Fleer All-Rookies

Collectors could redeem an All-Rookie Team Exchange card by mail for this nine-card set of top 1994 rookies at each position as chosen by Fleer. The expiration date to remeem this set was September 30, 1994. None of these players were in the basic 1994 Fleer set. The exchange card was randomly inserted into all pack types.

	MINT	NRMT	EXC
COMPLETE SET (9)	8.00	3.60	1.00
COMMON CARD (M1-M9)	.50	.23	.06
☐ M1 Kurt Abbott	.75	.35	.09
☐ M2 Rich Becker	.75	.35	.09
☐ M3 Carlos Delgado	4.00	1.80	.50
☐ M4 Jorge Fabregas	.50	.23	.06
☐ M5 Bob Hamelin	.50	.23	.06
☐ M6 John Hudek	.50	.23	.06
☐ M7 Tim Hyers	.50	.23	.06
☐ M8 Luis S.Lopez	.50	.23	.06
☐ M9 James Mouton	.50	.23	.06
☐ NNO Expired All-Rookie Exch.	1.50	.70	.19

1994 Fleer All-Stars

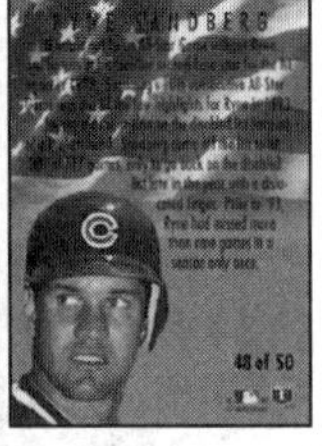

Fleer issued this 50-card standard-size set in 1994, to commemorate the All-Stars of the 1993 season. The cards were exclusively available in the Fleer wax packs at a rate of one in two. The set features 25 American League (1-25) and 25 National League (26-50) All-Stars. The full-bleed fronts feature color action player cut-out photos with an American flag background. The player's name is stamped in gold foil along the bottom edge adjacent to a 1993 All-Stars Game logo. The borderless backs carry a similar flag background with a player head shot near the bottom. The player's name and career highlights round out the back. Each league's all-stars are sequenced in alphabetical order.

	MINT	NRMT	EXC
COMPLETE SET (50)	25.00	11.00	3.10
COMMON CARD (1-50)	.25	.11	.03
☐ 1 Roberto Alomar	.75	.35	.09
☐ 2 Carlos Baerga	.25	.11	.03
☐ 3 Albert Belle	1.50	.70	.19
☐ 4 Wade Boggs	.50	.23	.06
☐ 5 Joe Carter	.40	.18	.05
☐ 6 Scott Cooper	.25	.11	.03
☐ 7 Cecil Fielder	.40	.18	.05
☐ 8 Travis Fryman	.40	.18	.05
☐ 9 Juan Gonzalez	2.00	.90	.25
☐ 10 Ken Griffey Jr.	4.00	1.80	.50

	MINT	NRMT	EXC
☐ 11 Pat Hentgen	.40	.18	.05
☐ 12 Randy Johnson	.60	.25	.07
☐ 13 Jimmy Key	.40	.18	.05
☐ 14 Mark Langston	.25	.11	.03
☐ 15 Jack McDowell	.25	.11	.03
☐ 16 Paul Molitor	.75	.35	.09
☐ 17 Jeff Montgomery	.25	.11	.03
☐ 18 Mike Mussina	.75	.35	.09
☐ 19 John Olerud	.40	.18	.05
☐ 20 Kirby Puckett	1.50	.70	.19
☐ 21 Cal Ripken	3.00	1.35	.35
☐ 22 Ivan Rodriguez	1.00	.45	.12
☐ 23 Frank Thomas	4.00	1.80	.50
☐ 24 Greg Vaughn	.25	.11	.03
☐ 25 Duane Ward	.25	.11	.03
☐ 26 Steve Avery	.25	.11	.03
☐ 27 Rod Beck	.25	.11	.03
☐ 28 Jay Bell	.25	.11	.03
☐ 29 Andy Benes	.40	.18	.05
☐ 30 Jeff Blauser	.25	.11	.03
☐ 31 Barry Bonds	1.00	.45	.12
☐ 32 Bobby Bonilla	.40	.18	.05
☐ 33 John Burkett	.25	.11	.03
☐ 34 Darren Daulton	.40	.18	.05
☐ 35 Andres Galarraga	.50	.23	.06
☐ 36 Tom Glavine	.50	.23	.06
☐ 37 Mark Grace	.50	.23	.06
☐ 38 Marquis Grissom	.40	.18	.05
☐ 39 Tony Gwynn	1.50	.70	.19
☐ 40 Bryan Harvey	.25	.11	.03
☐ 41 Dave Hollins	.25	.11	.03
☐ 42 David Justice	.40	.18	.05
☐ 43 Darryl Kile	.25	.11	.03
☐ 44 John Kruk	.25	.11	.03
☐ 45 Barry Larkin	.50	.23	.06
☐ 46 Terry Mulholland	.25	.11	.03
☐ 47 Mike Piazza	2.50	1.10	.30
☐ 48 Ryne Sandberg	1.00	.45	.12
☐ 49 Gary Sheffield	.60	.25	.07
☐ 50 John Smoltz	.60	.25	.07

1994 Fleer Award Winners

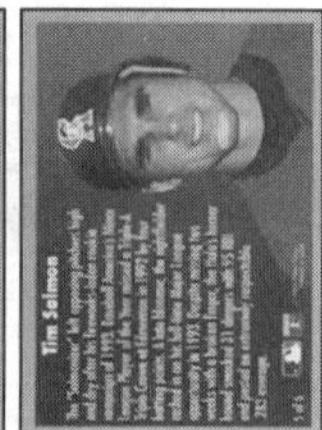

Randomly inserted in foil packs at a rate of one in 37, this six-card standard-size set spotlights six outstanding players who received awards. Inside beige borders, the horizontal fronts feature three views of the same color player photo. The words "Fleer Award Winners" and the player's name are printed in gold foil toward the bottom. The backs have a similar design to the fronts, only with one color player cutout and a season summary.

	MINT	NRMT	EXC
COMPLETE SET (6)	12.00	5.50	1.50
COMMON CARD (1-6)	.50	.23	.06
☐ 1 Frank Thomas	5.00	2.20	.60
☐ 2 Barry Bonds	1.25	.55	.16
☐ 3 Jack McDowell	.50	.23	.06
☐ 4 Greg Maddux	3.00	1.35	.35
☐ 5 Tim Salmon	.75	.35	.09
☐ 6 Mike Piazza	3.00	1.35	.35

1994 Fleer Golden Moments

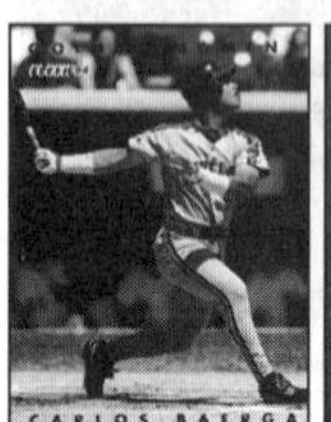

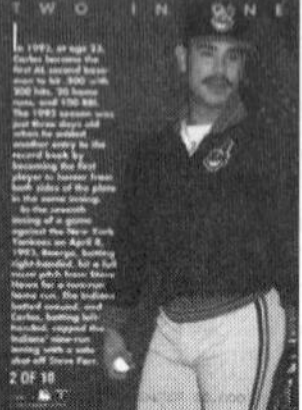

These standard-size cards were issued one per blue retail jumbo pack. The fronts feature borderless color player action photos. A shrink-wrapped package containing a jumbo set was issued one per Fleer hobby case. Jumbos were later issued for retail purposes. The production number out of a total of 10,000 appears near the bottom of the jumbos. The standard-size cards are not individually numbered.

	MINT	NRMT	EXC
COMPLETE SET (10)	40.00	18.00	5.00
COMMON CARD (1-10)	.75	.35	.09
*JUMBOS: .5X TO 1X BASIC CARDS			
☐ 1 Mark Whiten	.75	.35	.09
☐ 2 Carlos Baerga	.75	.35	.09
☐ 3 Dave Winfield	1.50	.70	.19
☐ 4 Ken Griffey Jr.	12.00	5.50	1.50
☐ 5 Bo Jackson	1.00	.45	.12
☐ 6 George Brett	5.00	2.20	.60
☐ 7 Nolan Ryan	12.00	5.50	1.50
☐ 8 Fred McGriff	1.50	.70	.19
☐ 9 Frank Thomas	12.00	5.50	1.50
☐ 10 Chris Bosio Jim Abbott Darryl Kile	.75	.35	.09

1994 Fleer League Leaders

Randomly inserted in all pack types at arate of one in 17, this 28-card set features six statistical leaders each for the American (1-6) and the National (7-12) Leagues. Inside a beige border, the fronts feature a color action player cutout superimposed on a black-and-white player photo. The player's name and the set title are gold foil stamped in the bottom border, while the player's achievement is printed vertically along the right edge of the picture. The horizontal backs have a color close-up shot on the left portion and a player summary on the right.

	MINT	NRMT	EXC
COMPLETE SET (12)	6.00	2.70	.75
COMMON CARD (1-12)	.25	.11	.03
☐ 1 John Olerud	.25	.11	.03
☐ 2 Albert Belle	2.00	.90	.25
☐ 3 Rafael Palmeiro	.50	.23	.06
☐ 4 Kenny Lofton	1.50	.70	.19
☐ 5 Jack McDowell	.50	.23	.06
☐ 6 Kevin Appier	.50	.23	.06
☐ 7 Andres Galarraga	.50	.23	.06
☐ 8 Barry Bonds	1.25	.55	.16
☐ 9 Lenny Dykstra	.50	.23	.06
☐ 10 Chuck Carr	.25	.11	.03
☐ 11 Tom Glavine UER No number on back of card	.50	.23	.06
☐ 12 Greg Maddux	3.00	1.35	.35

1994 Fleer Lumber Company

Randomly inserted in jumbo packs at a rate of one in five, this ten-card standard-size set features the best hitters in the game. The full-bleed fronts have a color action player cutout on a wood background. The player's name, team name, and the set title "Lumber Company" appear in an oval-shaped seal burned in the wood, just as one would find on a bat. On a background consisting of wooden bats laying on infield sand, the backs present a color headshot and a player profile on a ghosted panel. The cards are numbered alphabetically.

	MINT	NRMT	EXC
COMPLETE SET (10)	12.00	5.50	1.50
COMMON CARD (1-10)	.40	.18	.05
☐ 1 Albert Belle	2.00	.90	.25
☐ 2 Barry Bonds	1.25	.55	.16
☐ 3 Ron Gant	.50	.23	.06
☐ 4 Juan Gonzalez	2.50	1.10	.30
☐ 5 Ken Griffey Jr.	5.00	2.20	.60
☐ 6 David Justice	.40	.18	.05
☐ 7 Fred McGriff	.60	.25	.07
☐ 8 Rafael Palmeiro	.60	.25	.07
☐ 9 Frank Thomas	5.00	2.20	.60
☐ 10 Matt Williams	.60	.25	.07

1994 Fleer Major League Prospects

Randomly inserted in all pack types at a rate of one in six, this 35-card standard-size set showcases some of the outstanding young players in Major League Baseball. Inside beige borders, the fronts display color action photos superimposed over ghosted versions of the team logos. The set title and the player's name are gold foil stamped across the bottom of the card. On a beige background with thin blue pinstripes, the backs show a color player cutout and, on a powder blue panel, a player profile. The cards are numbered on the back "X of 35" and are sequenced in alphabetical order.

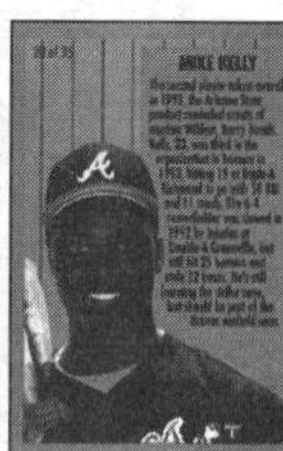

	MINT	NRMT	EXC
COMPLETE SET (35)	15.00	6.75	1.85
COMMON CARD (1-35)	.25	.11	.03
☐ 1 Kurt Abbott	.50	.23	.06
☐ 2 Brian Anderson	.25	.11	.03
☐ 3 Rich Aude	.25	.11	.03
☐ 4 Cory Bailey	.25	.11	.03
☐ 5 Danny Bautista	.25	.11	.03
☐ 6 Marty Cordova	2.00	.90	.25
☐ 7 Tripp Cromer	.25	.11	.03
☐ 8 Midre Cummings	.25	.11	.03
☐ 9 Carlos Delgado	2.50	1.10	.30
☐ 10 Steve Dreyer	.25	.11	.03
☐ 11 Steve Dunn	.25	.11	.03
☐ 12 Jeff Granger	.50	.23	.06
☐ 13 Tyrone Hill	.25	.11	.03
☐ 14 Denny Hocking	.25	.11	.03
☐ 15 John Hope	.25	.11	.03
☐ 16 Butch Huskey	.50	.23	.06
☐ 17 Miguel Jimenez	.25	.11	.03
☐ 18 Chipper Jones	10.00	4.50	1.25
☐ 19 Steve Karsay	.50	.23	.06
☐ 20 Mike Kelly	.25	.11	.03
☐ 21 Mike Lieberthal	.25	.11	.03
☐ 22 Albie Lopez	.50	.23	.06
☐ 23 Jeff McNeely	.25	.11	.03
☐ 24 Dan Miceli	.25	.11	.03
☐ 25 Nate Minchey	.25	.11	.03
☐ 26 Marc Newfield	.50	.23	.06
☐ 27 Darren Oliver	1.50	.70	.19
☐ 28 Luis Ortiz	.25	.11	.03
☐ 29 Curtis Pride	.50	.23	.06
☐ 30 Roger Salkeld	.25	.11	.03
☐ 31 Scott Sanders	.25	.11	.03
☐ 32 Dave Staton	.25	.11	.03
☐ 33 Salomon Torres	.25	.11	.03
☐ 34 Steve Trachsel	.50	.23	.06
☐ 35 Chris Turner	.25	.11	.03

1994 Fleer Pro-Visions

Randomly inserted in all pack types at a rate of one in 12, this nine-card standard-size set features on its fronts colorful artistic player caricatures with surrealistic backgrounds drawn by illustrator Wayne Still. The player's name is gold foil stamped at the lower right corner. When all nine cards are placed in order in a collector sheet, the backgrounds fit together to form a composite. The backs shade from one bright color to another and present career summaries. The cards are numbered on the back "X of 9."

	MINT	NRMT	EXC
COMPLETE SET (9)	4.00	1.80	.50
COMMON CARD (1-9)	.25	.11	.03
☐ 1 Darren Daulton	.40	.18	.05
☐ 2 John Olerud	.40	.18	.05
☐ 3 Matt Williams	.50	.23	.06
☐ 4 Carlos Baerga	.25	.11	.03
☐ 5 Ozzie Smith	1.00	.45	.12
☐ 6 Juan Gonzalez	2.00	.90	.25
☐ 7 Jack McDowell	.40	.18	.05
☐ 8 Mike Piazza	2.50	1.10	.30
☐ 9 Tony Gwynn	1.50	.70	.19

1994 Fleer Rookie Sensations

Randomly inserted in jumbo packs at a rate of one in four, this 20-card standard-size set features outstanding rookies. The fronts are "double exposed," with a player action cutout superimposed over a second photo. The team logo also appears in the team color-coded background. The set title is gold foil stamped toward the top, and the player's name is gold foil stamped on a team color-coded ribbon toward the bottom. On a white background featuring a ghosted version of the team logo, the backs have a player cutout photo and a season summary. The cards are numbered on the back "X of 20" and are sequenced in alphabetical order.

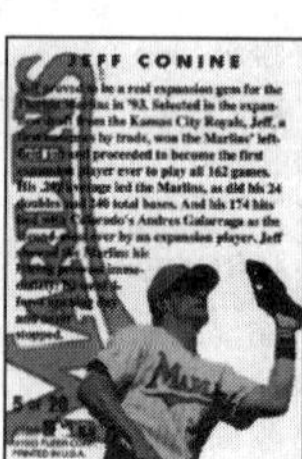

	MINT	NRMT	EXC
COMPLETE SET (20)	18.00	8.00	2.20
COMMON CARD (1-20)	.75	.35	.09
☐ 1 Rene Arocha	.75	.35	.09
☐ 2 Jason Bere	1.50	.70	.19
☐ 3 Jeromy Burnitz	1.50	.70	.19
☐ 4 Chuck Carr	.75	.35	.09
☐ 5 Jeff Conine	1.50	.70	.19
☐ 6 Steve Cooke	.75	.35	.09
☐ 7 Cliff Floyd	1.50	.70	.19
☐ 8 Jeffrey Hammonds	1.50	.70	.19
☐ 9 Wayne Kirby	.75	.35	.09
☐ 10 Mike Lansing	.75	.35	.09
☐ 11 Al Martin	1.50	.70	.19
☐ 12 Greg McMichael	.75	.35	.09
☐ 13 Troy Neel	.75	.35	.09
☐ 14 Mike Piazza	12.00	5.50	1.50
☐ 15 Armando Reynoso	.75	.35	.09
☐ 16 Kirk Rueter	.75	.35	.09
☐ 17 Tim Salmon	3.00	1.35	.35
☐ 18 Aaron Sele	1.50	.70	.19
☐ 19 J.T. Snow	1.50	.70	.19
☐ 20 Kevin Stocker	.75	.35	.09

1994 Fleer Salmon

Spotlighting American League Rookie of the Year Tim Salmon, this 15-card standard size set was issued in two forms. Cards 1-12 were randomly inserted in packs (one in eight) and 13-15 were available through a mail-in offer. Ten wrappers and 1.50 were necessary to acquire the mail-ins. The mail-in expiration date was September 30, 1994. Salmon autographed more than 2,000 of his cards. The cards feature a borderless all-foil, spectra-etched design and UV coating on both sides. The fronts feature cutout color action shots of Salmon that are superposed upon the silvery foil-and-etched design. His name appears in gold lettering near the bottom, along with the words "A.L. Rookie of the Year" in silver lettering within a gold bar. The back carries a color photo of Salmon on the right side. His name appears in ocher lettering in the upper left, followed below by career highlights in black lettering.

	MINT	NRMT	EXC
COMPLETE SET (12)	25.00	11.00	3.10
COMMON SALMON (1-12)	2.50	1.10	.30
COMMON MAIL-IN (13-15)	2.50	1.10	.30
☐ 1 Tim Salmon Watching flight of ball after hit	2.50	1.10	.30
☐ 2 Tim Salmon Trotting in to catch ball	2.50	1.10	.30
☐ 3 Tim Salmon Follow through weight on front leg	2.50	1.10	.30
☐ 4 Tim Salmon Middle of swing horizontal pose	2.50	1.10	.30
☐ 5 Tim Salmon Sliding into base	2.50	1.10	.30
☐ 6 Tim Salmon Pose swing end of bat in camera angle	2.50	1.10	.30
☐ 7 Tim Salmon Running with shades on	2.50	1.10	.30
☐ 8 Tim Salmon Bat cocked awaiting pitch	2.50	1.10	.30
☐ 9 Tim Salmon Adjusting batting gloves bat under arm	2.50	1.10	.30
☐ 10 Tim Salmon Running to base	2.50	1.10	.30
☐ 11 Tim Salmon Awaiting pitch shot from left side with catcher in view	2.50	1.10	.30
☐ 12 Tim Salmon Ready to play	2.50	1.10	.30

Card	MINT	NRMT	EXC
☐ 13 Tim Salmon Awaiting a pitch	2.50	1.10	.30
☐ 14 Tim Salmon Fielding	2.50	1.10	.30
☐ 15 Tim Salmon Running the bases	2.50	1.10	.30
☐ AU0 Tim Salmon AU (Certified autograph)	80.00	36.00	10.00

1994 Fleer Smoke 'n Heat

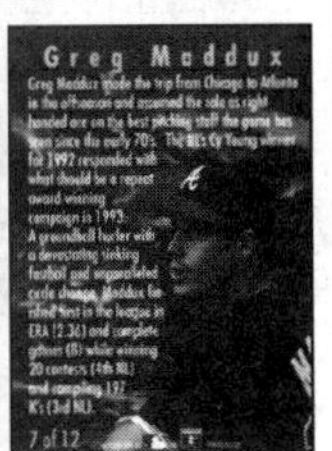

Randomly inserted in wax packs at a rate of one in 36, this 12-card standard-size set showcases the best pitchers in the game. On the fronts, color action player cutouts are superimposed on a red-and-gold fiery background that has a metallic sheen to it. The set title "Smoke 'n Heat" is printed in large block lettering. On a reddish marbleized background, the backs have another player cutout and season summary. The cards are numbered on the back "X of 12." and are sequenced in alphabetical order.

	MINT	NRMT	EXC
COMPLETE SET (12)	70.00	32.00	8.75
COMMON CARD (1-12)	2.00	.90	.25
☐ 1 Roger Clemens	6.00	2.70	.75
☐ 2 David Cone	3.00	1.35	.35
☐ 3 Juan Guzman	3.00	1.35	.35
☐ 4 Pete Harnisch	2.00	.90	.25
☐ 5 Randy Johnson	5.00	2.20	.60
☐ 6 Mark Langston	2.00	.90	.25
☐ 7 Greg Maddux	20.00	9.00	2.50
☐ 8 Mike Mussina	6.00	2.70	.75
☐ 9 Jose Rijo	2.00	.90	.25
☐ 10 Nolan Ryan	30.00	13.50	3.70
☐ 11 Curt Schilling	2.00	.90	.25
☐ 12 John Smoltz	5.00	2.20	.60

1994 Fleer Team Leaders

Randomly inserted in all pack types, this 28-card standard-size set features Fleer's selected top player from each of the 28 major league teams. The fronts feature an action player cutout superposed on a larger close-up photo with a team color-coded background, all inside beige borders. The set title, player's name, team name, and position are printed in gold foil across the bottom. On a white background with a ghosted version of the team logo, the horizontal backs carry a second color player cutout and a summary of the player's performance. The card numbering is arranged alphabetically by city according to the American (1-14) and the National (15-28) Leagues.

	MINT	NRMT	EXC
COMPLETE SET (28)	25.00	11.00	3.10
COMMON CARD (1-28)	.25	.11	.03
☐ 1 Cal Ripken	4.00	1.80	.50
☐ 2 Mo Vaughn	1.25	.55	.16
☐ 3 Tim Salmon	.75	.35	.09
☐ 4 Frank Thomas	5.00	2.20	.60
☐ 5 Carlos Baerga	.25	.11	.03
☐ 6 Cecil Fielder	.40	.18	.05
☐ 7 Brian McRae	.25	.11	.03
☐ 8 Greg Vaughn	.25	.11	.03
☐ 9 Kirby Puckett	2.00	.90	.25
☐ 10 Don Mattingly	2.50	1.10	.30
☐ 11 Mark McGwire	1.50	.70	.19
☐ 12 Ken Griffey Jr.	5.00	2.20	.60
☐ 13 Juan Gonzalez	2.50	1.10	.30
☐ 14 Paul Molitor	1.00	.45	.12
☐ 15 David Justice	.40	.18	.05
☐ 16 Ryne Sandberg	1.25	.55	.16
☐ 17 Barry Larkin	.60	.25	.07
☐ 18 Andres Galarraga	.60	.25	.07
☐ 19 Gary Sheffield	.75	.35	.09
☐ 20 Jeff Bagwell	2.00	.90	.25
☐ 21 Mike Piazza	3.00	1.35	.35
☐ 22 Marquis Grissom	.40	.18	.05
☐ 23 Bobby Bonilla	.40	.18	.05
☐ 24 Lenny Dykstra	.40	.18	.05
☐ 25 Jay Bell	.25	.11	.03
☐ 26 Gregg Jefferies	.40	.18	.05
☐ 27 Tony Gwynn	2.00	.90	.25
☐ 28 Will Clark	.60	.25	.07

1994 Fleer Update

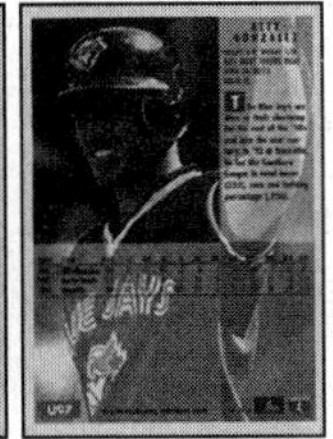

This 200-card standard-size set highlights traded players in their new uniforms and promising young rookies. The Update set was exclusively distributed in factory set form through hobby dealers. A ten card Diamond Tribute set was included in each factory set for a total of 210 cards. The cards are numbered on the back, grouped alphabetically by team by league with AL preceding NL. Key Rookie Cards include Chan Ho Park and Alex Rodriguez.

	MINT	NRMT	EXC
COMPLETE FACT.SET (210)	20.00	9.00	2.50
COMPLETE SET (200)	18.00	8.00	2.20
COMMON CARD (U1-U200)	.10	.05	.01
☐ 1 Mark Eichhorn	.10	.05	.01
☐ 2 Sid Fernandez	.10	.05	.01
☐ 3 Leo Gomez	.10	.05	.01
☐ 4 Mike Oquist	.10	.05	.01
☐ 5 Rafael Palmeiro	.40	.18	.05
☐ 6 Chris Sabo	.10	.05	.01
☐ 7 Dwight Smith	.10	.05	.01
☐ 8 Lee Smith	.25	.11	.03
☐ 9 Damon Berryhill	.10	.05	.01
☐ 10 Wes Chamberlain	.10	.05	.01
☐ 11 Gar Finnvold	.10	.05	.01
☐ 12 Chris Howard	.10	.05	.01
☐ 13 Tim Naehring	.10	.05	.01
☐ 14 Otis Nixon	.10	.05	.01
☐ 15 Brian Anderson	.25	.11	.03
☐ 16 Jorge Fabregas	.10	.05	.01
☐ 17 Rex Hudler	.10	.05	.01
☐ 18 Bo Jackson	.25	.11	.03
☐ 19 Mark Leiter	.10	.05	.01
☐ 20 Spike Owen	.10	.05	.01
☐ 21 Harold Reynolds	.10	.05	.01
☐ 22 Chris Turner	.10	.05	.01
☐ 23 Dennis Cook	.10	.05	.01
☐ 24 Jose DeLeon	.10	.05	.01
☐ 25 Julio Franco	.25	.11	.03
☐ 26 Joe Hall	.10	.05	.01
☐ 27 Darrin Jackson	.10	.05	.01
☐ 28 Dane Johnson	.10	.05	.01
☐ 29 Norberto Martin	.10	.05	.01
☐ 30 Scott Sanderson	.10	.05	.01
☐ 31 Jason Grimsley	.10	.05	.01
☐ 32 Dennis Martinez	.25	.11	.03
☐ 33 Jack Morris	.25	.11	.03
☐ 34 Eddie Murray	1.25	.55	.16
☐ 35 Chad Ogea	.25	.11	.03
☐ 36 Tony Pena	.10	.05	.01
☐ 37 Paul Shuey	.10	.05	.01
☐ 38 Omar Vizquel	.25	.11	.03
☐ 39 Danny Bautista	.10	.05	.01
☐ 40 Tim Belcher	.10	.05	.01
☐ 41 Joe Boever	.10	.05	.01
☐ 42 Storm Davis	.10	.05	.01
☐ 43 Junior Felix	.10	.05	.01
☐ 44 Mike Gardiner	.10	.05	.01
☐ 45 Buddy Groom	.10	.05	.01
☐ 46 Juan Samuel	.10	.05	.01
☐ 47 Vince Coleman	.10	.05	.01
☐ 48 Bob Hamelin	.10	.05	.01
☐ 49 Dave Henderson	.10	.05	.01
☐ 50 Rusty Meacham	.10	.05	.01
☐ 51 Terry Shumpert	.10	.05	.01
☐ 52 Jeff Bronkey	.10	.05	.01
☐ 53 Alex Diaz	.10	.05	.01
☐ 54 Brian Harper	.10	.05	.01
☐ 55 Jose Mercedes	.10	.05	.01
☐ 56 Jody Reed	.10	.05	.01
☐ 57 Bob Scanlan	.10	.05	.01
☐ 58 Turner Ward	.10	.05	.01
☐ 59 Rich Becker	.25	.11	.03
☐ 60 Alex Cole	.10	.05	.01
☐ 61 Denny Hocking	.10	.05	.01
☐ 62 Scott Leius	.10	.05	.01
☐ 63 Pat Mahomes	.10	.05	.01
☐ 64 Carlos Pulido	.10	.05	.01
☐ 65 Dave Stevens	.10	.05	.01
☐ 66 Matt Walbeck	.10	.05	.01
☐ 67 Xavier Hernandez	.10	.05	.01
☐ 68 Sterling Hitchcock	.25	.11	.03
☐ 69 Terry Mulholland	.10	.05	.01
☐ 70 Luis Polonia	.10	.05	.01
☐ 71 Gerald Williams	.10	.05	.01
☐ 72 Mark Acre	.10	.05	.01
☐ 73 Geronimo Berroa	.25	.11	.03
☐ 74 Rickey Henderson	.40	.18	.05
☐ 75 Stan Javier	.10	.05	.01
☐ 76 Steve Karsay	.10	.05	.01
☐ 77 Carlos Reyes	.10	.05	.01
☐ 78 Bill Taylor	.10	.05	.01
☐ 79 Eric Anthony	.10	.05	.01
☐ 80 Bobby Ayala	.10	.05	.01
☐ 81 Tim Davis	.10	.05	.01
☐ 82 Felix Fermin	.10	.05	.01
☐ 83 Reggie Jefferson	.25	.11	.03
☐ 84 Keith Mitchell	.10	.05	.01
☐ 85 Bill Risley	.10	.05	.01
☐ 86 Alex Rodriguez	15.00	6.75	1.85
☐ 87 Roger Salkeld	.10	.05	.01
☐ 88 Dan Wilson	.25	.11	.03
☐ 89 Cris Carpenter	.10	.05	.01
☐ 90 Will Clark	.40	.18	.05
☐ 91 Jeff Frye	.10	.05	.01
☐ 92 Rick Helling	.10	.05	.01
☐ 93 Chris James	.10	.05	.01
☐ 94 Oddibe McDowell	.10	.05	.01
☐ 95 Billy Ripken	.10	.05	.01
☐ 96 Carlos Delgado	.40	.18	.05
☐ 97 Alex Gonzalez	.25	.11	.03
☐ 98 Shawn Green	.25	.11	.03
☐ 99 Darren Hall	.10	.05	.01
☐ 100 Mike Huff	.10	.05	.01
☐ 101 Mike Kelly	.10	.05	.01
☐ 102 Roberto Kelly	.10	.05	.01
☐ 103 Charlie O'Brien	.10	.05	.01
☐ 104 Jose Oliva	.25	.11	.03
☐ 105 Gregg Olson	.10	.05	.01
☐ 106 Willie Banks	.10	.05	.01
☐ 107 Jim Bullinger	.10	.05	.01
☐ 108 Chuck Crim	.10	.05	.01
☐ 109 Shawon Dunston	.10	.05	.01
☐ 110 Karl Rhodes	.10	.05	.01
☐ 111 Steve Trachsel	.25	.11	.03
☐ 112 Anthony Young	.10	.05	.01
☐ 113 Eddie Zambrano	.10	.05	.01
☐ 114 Bret Boone	.25	.11	.03
☐ 115 Jeff Brantley	.10	.05	.01
☐ 116 Hector Carrasco	.10	.05	.01
☐ 117 Tony Fernandez	.10	.05	.01
☐ 118 Tim Fortugno	.10	.05	.01
☐ 119 Erik Hanson	.10	.05	.01
☐ 120 Chuck McElroy	.10	.05	.01
☐ 121 Deion Sanders	.40	.18	.05
☐ 122 Ellis Burks	.25	.11	.03
☐ 123 Marvin Freeman	.10	.05	.01
☐ 124 Mike Harkey	.10	.05	.01
☐ 125 Howard Johnson	.10	.05	.01
☐ 126 Mike Kingery	.10	.05	.01
☐ 127 Nelson Liriano	.10	.05	.01
☐ 128 Marcus Moore	.10	.05	.01
☐ 129 Mike Munoz	.10	.05	.01
☐ 130 Kevin Ritz	.10	.05	.01
☐ 131 Walt Weiss	.10	.05	.01
☐ 132 Kurt Abbott	.25	.11	.03
☐ 133 Jerry Browne	.10	.05	.01
☐ 134 Greg Colbrunn	.10	.05	.01
☐ 135 Jeremy Hernandez	.10	.05	.01
☐ 136 Dave Magadan	.10	.05	.01
☐ 137 Kurt Miller	.10	.05	.01
☐ 138 Robb Nen	.25	.11	.03
☐ 139 Jesus Tavarez	.10	.05	.01
☐ 140 Sid Bream	.10	.05	.01
☐ 141 Tom Edens	.10	.05	.01
☐ 142 Tony Eusebio	.10	.05	.01
☐ 143 John Hudek	.10	.05	.01
☐ 144 Brian L. Hunter	1.25	.55	.16
☐ 145 Orlando Miller	.10	.05	.01
☐ 146 James Mouton	.25	.11	.03
☐ 147 Shane Reynolds	.25	.11	.03
☐ 148 Rafael Bournigal	.10	.05	.01
☐ 149 Delino DeShields	.10	.05	.01
☐ 150 Garey Ingram	.10	.05	.01
☐ 151 Chan Ho Park	1.50	.70	.19
☐ 152 Wil Cordero	.25	.11	.03
☐ 153 Pedro Martinez	.40	.18	.05
☐ 154 Randy Milligan	.10	.05	.01
☐ 155 Lenny Webster	.10	.05	.01
☐ 156 Rico Brogna	.10	.05	.01
☐ 157 Josias Manzanillo	.10	.05	.01
☐ 158 Kevin McReynolds	.10	.05	.01
☐ 159 Mike Remlinger	.10	.05	.01
☐ 160 David Segui	.10	.05	.01
☐ 161 Pete Smith	.10	.05	.01
☐ 162 Kelly Stinnett	.10	.05	.01
☐ 163 Jose Vizcaino	.10	.05	.01
☐ 164 Billy Hatcher	.10	.05	.01
☐ 165 Doug Jones	.10	.05	.01
☐ 166 Mike Lieberthal	.10	.05	.01
☐ 167 Tony Longmire	.10	.05	.01
☐ 168 Bobby Munoz	.10	.05	.01
☐ 169 Paul Quantrill	.10	.05	.01
☐ 170 Heathcliff Slocumb	.25	.11	.03
☐ 171 Fernando Valenzuela	.25	.11	.03
☐ 172 Mark Dewey	.10	.05	.01
☐ 173 Brian R. Hunter	.10	.05	.01
☐ 174 Jon Lieber	.10	.05	.01
☐ 175 Ravelo Manzanillo	.10	.05	.01
☐ 176 Dan Miceli	.10	.05	.01
☐ 177 Rick White	.10	.05	.01
☐ 178 Bryan Eversgerd	.10	.05	.01
☐ 179 John Habyan	.10	.05	.01
☐ 180 Terry McGriff	.10	.05	.01
☐ 181 Vicente Palacios	.10	.05	.01
☐ 182 Rich Rodriguez	.10	.05	.01
☐ 183 Rick Sutcliffe	.10	.05	.01
☐ 184 Donnie Elliott	.10	.05	.01
☐ 185 Joey Hamilton	1.00	.45	.12
☐ 186 Tim Hyers	.10	.05	.01
☐ 187 Luis Lopez	.10	.05	.01
☐ 188 Ray McDavid	.25	.11	.03
☐ 189 Bip Roberts	.10	.05	.01
☐ 190 Scott Sanders	.10	.05	.01
☐ 191 Eddie Williams	.10	.05	.01
☐ 192 Steve Frey	.10	.05	.01
☐ 193 Pat Gomez	.10	.05	.01
☐ 194 Rich Monteleone	.10	.05	.01
☐ 195 Mark Portugal	.10	.05	.01
☐ 196 Darryl Strawberry	.25	.11	.03
☐ 197 Salomon Torres	.10	.05	.01
☐ 198 W.VanLandingham	.25	.11	.03
☐ 199 Checklist	.10	.05	.01
☐ 200 Checklist	.10	.05	.01

1994 Fleer Update Diamond Tribute

Each 1994 Fleer Update factory set contained a complete 10-card set of Diamond Tribute inserts. This was the third and final year that Fleer included an insert set in their factory boxed update sets. The 1994 Diamond Tribute inserts feature a player action shot cut out against a backdrop of clouds and baseballs. The selection once again focuses on the game's top veterans. Cards are numbered X of 10 on the back.

	MINT	NRMT	EXC
COMPLETE SET (10)	3.00	1.35	.35
COMMON CARD (1-10)	.25	.11	.03
☐ 1 Barry Bonds	.50	.23	.06
☐ 2 Joe Carter	.25	.11	.03
☐ 3 Will Clark	.25	.11	.03
☐ 4 Roger Clemens	.40	.18	.05
☐ 5 Tony Gwynn	.75	.35	.09
☐ 6 Don Mattingly	1.00	.45	.12
☐ 7 Fred McGriff	.25	.11	.03
☐ 8 Eddie Murray	.50	.23	.06
☐ 9 Kirby Puckett	.75	.35	.09
☐ 10 Cal Ripken	2.00	.90	.25

1994 Fleer Sunoco

These 25 standard-size cards feature white-bordered color player action shots on their fronts. The player's name and position appear in a white-lettered arc around his team's logo in one corner of the photo. The white-bordered back carries a posed color player photo that is ghosted, except for the rectangular area around the player's head. Upon the ghosted areas appear the player's name, biography, career highlights, and statistics. The cards are numbered on the back as "X of 25."

	MINT	NRMT	EXC
COMPLETE SET (25)	6.00	2.70	.75
COMMON CARD (1-25)	.10	.05	.01
☐ 1 Roberto Alomar	.40	.18	.05
☐ 2 Carlos Baerga	.40	.18	.05
☐ 3 Jeff Bagwell	.60	.25	.07
☐ 4 Jay Bell	.10	.05	.01
☐ 5 Barry Bonds	.50	.23	.06
☐ 6 Joe Carter	.20	.09	.03
☐ 7 Roger Clemens	.40	.18	.05
☐ 8 Darren Daulton	.20	.09	.03
☐ 9 Len Dykstra	.20	.09	.03
☐ 10 Cecil Fielder	.20	.09	.03
☐ 11 Tom Glavine	.25	.11	.03
☐ 12 Juan Gonzalez	.75	.35	.09
☐ 13 Ken Griffey Jr.	1.50	.70	.19
☐ 14 David Justice	.30	.14	.04
☐ 15 John Kruk	.10	.05	.01

☐ 16 Greg Maddux	1.00	.45	.12
☐ 17 Don Mattingly	.75	.35	.09
☐ 18 Jack McDowell	.20	.09	.03
☐ 19 John Olerud	.20	.09	.03
☐ 20 Mike Piazza	1.00	.45	.12
☐ 21 Kirby Puckett	.75	.35	.09
☐ 22 Tim Salmon	.25	.11	.03
☐ 23 Frank Thomas	1.50	.70	.19
☐ 24 Andy Van Slyke	.10	.05	.01
☐ 25 Checklist	.10	.05	.01

1995 Fleer

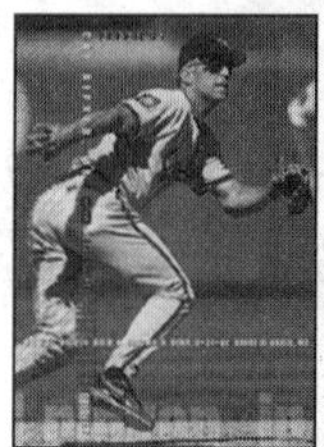

The 1995 Fleer set consists of 600 standard-size cards issued as one series. Each pack contained at least one insert card with some 'Hot Packs' containing nothing but insert cards. Full-bleed fronts have two player photos and, atypical of baseball cards fronts, biographical information such as height, weight, etc. The backgrounds are multi-colored. The backs are horizontal and contain year-by-year statistics along with a photo. There was a different design for each of baseball's six divisions. The checklist is arranged alphabetically by teams within each league with AL preceding NL. Eight card promo sets were issued to hobby dealers. These cards are extremely difficult to tell apart from the regular cards and have the same value as the regular cards. The players in this set are Marquis Grissom, David Cone, Ozzie Smith, Roger Clemens, Tim Salmon, Paul O'Neill, Juan Gonzalez and Dante Bichette.

	MINT	NRMT	EXC
COMPLETE SET (600)	50.00	22.00	6.25
COMMON CARD (1-600)	.10	.05	.01
☐ 1 Brady Anderson	.50	.23	.06
☐ 2 Harold Baines	.25	.11	.03
☐ 3 Damon Buford	.10	.05	.01
☐ 4 Mike Devereaux	.10	.05	.01
☐ 5 Mark Eichhorn	.10	.05	.01
☐ 6 Sid Fernandez	.10	.05	.01
☐ 7 Leo Gomez	.10	.05	.01
☐ 8 Jeffrey Hammonds	.25	.11	.03
☐ 9 Chris Hoiles	.10	.05	.01
☐ 10 Rick Krivda	.10	.05	.01
☐ 11 Ben McDonald	.10	.05	.01
☐ 12 Mark McLemore	.10	.05	.01
☐ 13 Alan Mills	.10	.05	.01
☐ 14 Jamie Moyer	.10	.05	.01
☐ 15 Mike Mussina	.60	.25	.07
☐ 16 Mike Oquist	.10	.05	.01
☐ 17 Rafael Palmeiro	.50	.23	.06
☐ 18 Arthur Rhodes	.10	.05	.01
☐ 19 Cal Ripken Jr.	2.50	1.10	.30
☐ 20 Chris Sabo	.10	.05	.01
☐ 21 Lee Smith	.25	.11	.03
☐ 22 Jack Voigt	.10	.05	.01
☐ 23 Damon Berryhill	.10	.05	.01
☐ 24 Tom Brunansky	.10	.05	.01
☐ 25 Wes Chamberlain	.10	.05	.01
☐ 26 Roger Clemens	.60	.25	.07
☐ 27 Scott Cooper	.10	.05	.01
☐ 28 Andre Dawson	.25	.11	.03
☐ 29 Gar Finnvold	.10	.05	.01
☐ 30 Tony Fossas	.10	.05	.01
☐ 31 Mike Greenwell	.10	.05	.01
☐ 32 Joe Hesketh	.10	.05	.01
☐ 33 Chris Howard	.10	.05	.01
☐ 34 Chris Nabholz	.10	.05	.01
☐ 35 Tim Naehring	.10	.05	.01
☐ 36 Otis Nixon	.10	.05	.01
☐ 37 Carlos Rodriguez	.10	.05	.01
☐ 38 Rich Rowland	.10	.05	.01
☐ 39 Ken Ryan	.10	.05	.01
☐ 40 Aaron Sele	.25	.11	.03
☐ 41 John Valentin	.25	.11	.03
☐ 42 Mo Vaughn	.75	.35	.09
☐ 43 Frank Viola	.10	.05	.01
☐ 44 Danny Bautista	.10	.05	.01
☐ 45 Joe Boever	.10	.05	.01
☐ 46 Milt Cuyler	.10	.05	.01
☐ 47 Storm Davis	.10	.05	.01
☐ 48 John Doherty	.10	.05	.01
☐ 49 Junior Felix	.10	.05	.01
☐ 50 Cecil Fielder	.25	.11	.03
☐ 51 Travis Fryman	.25	.11	.03
☐ 52 Mike Gardiner	.10	.05	.01
☐ 53 Kirk Gibson	.25	.11	.03
☐ 54 Chris Gomez	.10	.05	.01
☐ 55 Buddy Groom	.10	.05	.01
☐ 56 Mike Henneman	.10	.05	.01
☐ 57 Chad Kreuter	.10	.05	.01
☐ 58 Mike Moore	.10	.05	.01
☐ 59 Tony Phillips	.25	.11	.03
☐ 60 Juan Samuel	.10	.05	.01
☐ 61 Mickey Tettleton	.10	.05	.01
☐ 62 Alan Trammell	.25	.11	.03
☐ 63 David Wells	.10	.05	.01
☐ 64 Lou Whitaker	.25	.11	.03
☐ 65 Jim Abbott	.10	.05	.01
☐ 66 Joe Ausanio	.10	.05	.01
☐ 67 Wade Boggs	.50	.23	.06
☐ 68 Mike Gallego	.10	.05	.01
☐ 69 Xavier Hernandez	.10	.05	.01
☐ 70 Sterling Hitchcock	.25	.11	.03
☐ 71 Steve Howe	.10	.05	.01
☐ 72 Scott Kamieniecki	.10	.05	.01
☐ 73 Pat Kelly	.10	.05	.01
☐ 74 Jimmy Key	.25	.11	.03
☐ 75 Jim Leyritz	.10	.05	.01
☐ 76 Don Mattingly UER Photo is a reversed negative	1.50	.70	.19
☐ 77 Terry Mulholland	.10	.05	.01
☐ 78 Paul O'Neill	.25	.11	.03
☐ 79 Melido Perez	.10	.05	.01
☐ 80 Luis Polonia	.10	.05	.01
☐ 81 Mike Stanley	.10	.05	.01
☐ 82 Danny Tartabull	.10	.05	.01
☐ 83 Randy Velarde	.10	.05	.01
☐ 84 Bob Wickman	.10	.05	.01
☐ 85 Bernie Williams	.60	.25	.07
☐ 86 Gerald Williams	.10	.05	.01
☐ 87 Roberto Alomar	.60	.25	.07
☐ 88 Pat Borders	.10	.05	.01
☐ 89 Joe Carter	.25	.11	.03
☐ 90 Tony Castillo	.10	.05	.01
☐ 91 Brad Cornett	.10	.05	.01
☐ 92 Carlos Delgado	.25	.11	.03
☐ 93 Alex Gonzalez	.25	.11	.03
☐ 94 Shawn Green	.25	.11	.03
☐ 95 Juan Guzman	.25	.11	.03
☐ 96 Darren Hall	.10	.05	.01
☐ 97 Pat Hentgen	.25	.11	.03
☐ 98 Mike Huff	.10	.05	.01
☐ 99 Randy Knorr	.10	.05	.01
☐ 100 Al Leiter	.25	.11	.03
☐ 101 Paul Molitor	.60	.25	.07
☐ 102 John Olerud	.10	.05	.01
☐ 103 Dick Schofield	.10	.05	.01
☐ 104 Ed Sprague	.25	.11	.03
☐ 105 Dave Stewart	.25	.11	.03
☐ 106 Todd Stottlemyre	.10	.05	.01
☐ 107 Devon White	.25	.11	.03
☐ 108 Woody Williams	.10	.05	.01
☐ 109 Wilson Alvarez	.25	.11	.03
☐ 110 Paul Assenmacher	.10	.05	.01
☐ 111 Jason Bere	.10	.05	.01
☐ 112 Dennis Cook	.10	.05	.01
☐ 113 Joey Cora	.10	.05	.01
☐ 114 Jose DeLeon	.10	.05	.01
☐ 115 Alex Fernandez	.25	.11	.03
☐ 116 Julio Franco	.25	.11	.03
☐ 117 Craig Grebeck	.10	.05	.01
☐ 118 Ozzie Guillen	.10	.05	.01
☐ 119 Roberto Hernandez	.10	.05	.01
☐ 120 Darrin Jackson	.10	.05	.01
☐ 121 Lance Johnson	.25	.11	.03
☐ 122 Ron Karkovice	.10	.05	.01
☐ 123 Mike LaValliere	.10	.05	.01
☐ 124 Norberto Martin	.10	.05	.01
☐ 125 Kirk McCaskill	.10	.05	.01
☐ 126 Jack McDowell	.25	.11	.03
☐ 127 Tim Raines	.50	.23	.06
☐ 128 Frank Thomas	3.00	1.35	.35
☐ 129 Robin Ventura	.25	.11	.03
☐ 130 Sandy Alomar Jr.	.10	.05	.01
☐ 131 Carlos Baerga	.25	.11	.03
☐ 132 Albert Belle	1.25	.55	.16
☐ 133 Mark Clark	.10	.05	.01
☐ 134 Alvaro Espinoza	.10	.05	.01
☐ 135 Jason Grimsley	.10	.05	.01
☐ 136 Wayne Kirby	.10	.05	.01
☐ 137 Kenny Lofton	.75	.35	.09
☐ 138 Albie Lopez	.10	.05	.01
☐ 139 Dennis Martinez	.25	.11	.03
☐ 140 Jose Mesa	.10	.05	.01
☐ 141 Eddie Murray	.75	.35	.09
☐ 142 Charles Nagy	.25	.11	.03
☐ 143 Tony Pena	.10	.05	.01
☐ 144 Eric Plunk	.10	.05	.01
☐ 145 Manny Ramirez	.75	.35	.09
☐ 146 Jeff Russell	.10	.05	.01
☐ 147 Paul Shuey	.10	.05	.01
☐ 148 Paul Sorrento	.10	.05	.01
☐ 149 Jim Thome	.60	.25	.07
☐ 150 Omar Vizquel	.25	.11	.03
☐ 151 Dave Winfield	.50	.23	.06
☐ 152 Kevin Appier	.25	.11	.03
☐ 153 Billy Brewer	.10	.05	.01
☐ 154 Vince Coleman	.10	.05	.01
☐ 155 David Cone	.25	.11	.03
☐ 156 Gary Gaetti	.25	.11	.03
☐ 157 Greg Gagne	.10	.05	.01
☐ 158 Tom Gordon	.10	.05	.01
☐ 159 Mark Gubicza	.10	.05	.01
☐ 160 Bob Hamelin	.10	.05	.01
☐ 161 Dave Henderson	.10	.05	.01
☐ 162 Felix Jose	.10	.05	.01
☐ 163 Wally Joyner	.25	.11	.03
☐ 164 Jose Lind	.10	.05	.01
☐ 165 Mike Macfarlane	.10	.05	.01
☐ 166 Mike Magnante	.10	.05	.01
☐ 167 Brent Mayne	.10	.05	.01
☐ 168 Brian McRae	.25	.11	.03
☐ 169 Rusty Meacham	.10	.05	.01
☐ 170 Jeff Montgomery	.25	.11	.03
☐ 171 Hipolito Pichardo	.10	.05	.01
☐ 172 Terry Shumpert	.10	.05	.01
☐ 173 Michael Tucker	.25	.11	.03
☐ 174 Ricky Bones	.10	.05	.01
☐ 175 Jeff Cirillo	.25	.11	.03
☐ 176 Alex Diaz	.10	.05	.01
☐ 177 Cal Eldred	.10	.05	.01
☐ 178 Mike Fetters	.10	.05	.01
☐ 179 Darryl Hamilton	.10	.05	.01
☐ 180 Brian Harper	.10	.05	.01
☐ 181 John Jaha	.25	.11	.03
☐ 182 Pat Listach	.10	.05	.01
☐ 183 Graeme Lloyd	.10	.05	.01
☐ 184 Jose Mercedes	.10	.05	.01
☐ 185 Matt Mieske	.25	.11	.03
☐ 186 Dave Nilsson	.25	.11	.03
☐ 187 Jody Reed	.10	.05	.01
☐ 188 Bob Scanlan	.10	.05	.01
☐ 189 Kevin Seitzer	.10	.05	.01
☐ 190 Bill Spiers	.10	.05	.01
☐ 191 B.J. Surhoff	.25	.11	.03
☐ 192 Jose Valentin	.25	.11	.03
☐ 193 Greg Vaughn	.25	.11	.03
☐ 194 Turner Ward	.10	.05	.01
☐ 195 Bill Wegman	.10	.05	.01
☐ 196 Rick Aguilera	.10	.05	.01
☐ 197 Rich Becker	.10	.05	.01
☐ 198 Alex Cole	.10	.05	.01
☐ 199 Marty Cordova	.50	.23	.06
☐ 200 Steve Dunn	.10	.05	.01
☐ 201 Scott Erickson	.10	.05	.01
☐ 202 Mark Guthrie	.10	.05	.01
☐ 203 Chip Hale	.10	.05	.01
☐ 204 LaTroy Hawkins	.10	.05	.01
☐ 205 Denny Hocking	.10	.05	.01
☐ 206 Chuck Knoblauch	.50	.23	.06
☐ 207 Scott Leius	.10	.05	.01
☐ 208 Shane Mack	.10	.05	.01
☐ 209 Pat Mahomes	.10	.05	.01
☐ 210 Pat Meares	.10	.05	.01
☐ 211 Pedro Munoz	.10	.05	.01
☐ 212 Kirby Puckett	1.25	.55	.16
☐ 213 Jeff Reboulet	.10	.05	.01
☐ 214 Dave Stevens	.10	.05	.01
☐ 215 Kevin Tapani	.10	.05	.01
☐ 216 Matt Walbeck	.10	.05	.01
☐ 217 Carl Willis	.10	.05	.01
☐ 218 Brian Anderson	.10	.05	.01
☐ 219 Chad Curtis	.10	.05	.01
☐ 220 Chili Davis	.25	.11	.03
☐ 221 Gary DiSarcina	.10	.05	.01
☐ 222 Damion Easley	.10	.05	.01
☐ 223 Jim Edmonds	.50	.23	.06
☐ 224 Chuck Finley	.25	.11	.03
☐ 225 Joe Grahe	.10	.05	.01
☐ 226 Rex Hudler	.10	.05	.01
☐ 227 Bo Jackson	.25	.11	.03
☐ 228 Mark Langston	.10	.05	.01
☐ 229 Phil Leftwich	.10	.05	.01
☐ 230 Mark Leiter	.10	.05	.01
☐ 231 Spike Owen	.10	.05	.01
☐ 232 Bob Patterson	.10	.05	.01
☐ 233 Troy Percival	.10	.05	.01
☐ 234 Eduardo Perez	.10	.05	.01
☐ 235 Tim Salmon	.50	.23	.06
☐ 236 J.T. Snow	.25	.11	.03
☐ 237 Chris Turner	.10	.05	.01
☐ 238 Mark Acre	.10	.05	.01
☐ 239 Geronimo Berroa	.10	.05	.01
☐ 240 Mike Bordick	.10	.05	.01
☐ 241 John Briscoe	.10	.05	.01
☐ 242 Scott Brosius	.10	.05	.01
☐ 243 Ron Darling	.10	.05	.01
☐ 244 Dennis Eckersley	.25	.11	.03
☐ 245 Brent Gates	.10	.05	.01
☐ 246 Rickey Henderson	.50	.23	.06
☐ 247 Stan Javier	.10	.05	.01
☐ 248 Steve Karsay	.10	.05	.01
☐ 249 Mark McGwire	1.00	.45	.12
☐ 250 Troy Neel	.10	.05	.01
☐ 251 Steve Ontiveros	.10	.05	.01
☐ 252 Carlos Reyes	.10	.05	.01
☐ 253 Ruben Sierra	.25	.11	.03
☐ 254 Terry Steinbach	.25	.11	.03
☐ 255 Bill Taylor	.10	.05	.01
☐ 256 Todd Van Poppel	.10	.05	.01
☐ 257 Bobby Witt	.10	.05	.01
☐ 258 Rich Amaral	.10	.05	.01
☐ 259 Eric Anthony	.10	.05	.01
☐ 260 Bobby Ayala	.10	.05	.01
☐ 261 Mike Blowers	.10	.05	.01
☐ 262 Chris Bosio	.10	.05	.01
☐ 263 Jay Buhner	.50	.23	.06
☐ 264 John Cummings	.10	.05	.01
☐ 265 Tim Davis	.10	.05	.01
☐ 266 Felix Fermin	.10	.05	.01
☐ 267 Dave Fleming	.10	.05	.01
☐ 268 Goose Gossage	.25	.11	.03
☐ 269 Ken Griffey Jr.	3.00	1.35	.35
☐ 270 Reggie Jefferson	.25	.11	.03
☐ 271 Randy Johnson	.50	.23	.06
☐ 272 Edgar Martinez	.25	.11	.03
☐ 273 Tino Martinez	.25	.11	.03
☐ 274 Greg Pirkl	.10	.05	.01
☐ 275 Bill Risley	.10	.05	.01
☐ 276 Roger Salkeld	.10	.05	.01
☐ 277 Luis Sojo	.10	.05	.01
☐ 278 Mac Suzuki	.25	.11	.03
☐ 279 Dan Wilson	.25	.11	.03
☐ 280 Kevin Brown	.25	.11	.03
☐ 281 Jose Canseco	.50	.23	.06
☐ 282 Cris Carpenter	.10	.05	.01
☐ 283 Will Clark	.50	.23	.06
☐ 284 Jeff Frye	.10	.05	.01
☐ 285 Juan Gonzalez	1.50	.70	.19
☐ 286 Rick Helling	.10	.05	.01
☐ 287 Tom Henke	.10	.05	.01
☐ 288 David Hulse	.10	.05	.01
☐ 289 Chris James	.10	.05	.01
☐ 290 Manuel Lee	.10	.05	.01
☐ 291 Oddibe McDowell	.10	.05	.01
☐ 292 Dean Palmer	.25	.11	.03
☐ 293 Roger Pavlik	.10	.05	.01
☐ 294 Bill Ripken	.10	.05	.01
☐ 295 Ivan Rodriguez	.75	.35	.09
☐ 296 Kenny Rogers	.10	.05	.01
☐ 297 Doug Strange	.10	.05	.01
☐ 298 Matt Whiteside	.10	.05	.01
☐ 299 Steve Avery	.25	.11	.03
☐ 300 Steve Bedrosian	.10	.05	.01
☐ 301 Rafael Belliard	.10	.05	.01
☐ 302 Jeff Blauser	.10	.05	.01
☐ 303 Dave Gallagher	.10	.05	.01
☐ 304 Tom Glavine	.50	.23	.06
☐ 305 David Justice	.50	.23	.06
☐ 306 Mike Kelly	.10	.05	.01
☐ 307 Roberto Kelly	.10	.05	.01
☐ 308 Ryan Klesko	.50	.23	.06
☐ 309 Mark Lemke	.10	.05	.01
☐ 310 Javier Lopez	.50	.23	.06
☐ 311 Greg Maddux	2.00	.90	.25
☐ 312 Fred McGriff	.50	.23	.06
☐ 313 Greg McMichael	.10	.05	.01
☐ 314 Kent Mercker	.10	.05	.01
☐ 315 Charlie O'Brien	.10	.05	.01
☐ 316 Jose Oliva	.10	.05	.01
☐ 317 Terry Pendleton	.25	.11	.03
☐ 318 John Smoltz	.50	.23	.06
☐ 319 Mike Stanton	.10	.05	.01
☐ 320 Tony Tarasco	.10	.05	.01
☐ 321 Terrell Wade	.50	.23	.06
☐ 322 Mark Wohlers	.25	.11	.03
☐ 323 Kurt Abbott	.10	.05	.01
☐ 324 Luis Aquino	.10	.05	.01
☐ 325 Bret Barberie	.10	.05	.01
☐ 326 Ryan Bowen	.10	.05	.01
☐ 327 Jerry Browne	.10	.05	.01
☐ 328 Chuck Carr	.10	.05	.01
☐ 329 Matias Carrillo	.10	.05	.01
☐ 330 Greg Colbrunn	.10	.05	.01
☐ 331 Jeff Conine	.25	.11	.03
☐ 332 Mark Gardner	.10	.05	.01
☐ 333 Chris Hammond	.10	.05	.01
☐ 334 Bryan Harvey	.10	.05	.01
☐ 335 Richie Lewis	.10	.05	.01
☐ 336 Dave Magadan	.10	.05	.01
☐ 337 Terry Mathews	.10	.05	.01
☐ 338 Robb Nen	.10	.05	.01
☐ 339 Yorkis Perez	.10	.05	.01
☐ 340 Pat Rapp	.10	.05	.01
☐ 341 Benito Santiago	.10	.05	.01
☐ 342 Gary Sheffield	.50	.23	.06
☐ 343 Dave Weathers	.10	.05	.01
☐ 344 Moises Alou	.25	.11	.03
☐ 345 Sean Berry	.10	.05	.01
☐ 346 Wil Cordero	.10	.05	.01
☐ 347 Joey Eischen	.10	.05	.01
☐ 348 Jeff Fassero	.10	.05	.01
☐ 349 Darrin Fletcher	.10	.05	.01
☐ 350 Cliff Floyd	.25	.11	.03
☐ 351 Marquis Grissom	.25	.11	.03
☐ 352 Butch Henry	.10	.05	.01
☐ 353 Gil Heredia	.10	.05	.01
☐ 354 Ken Hill	.10	.05	.01
☐ 355 Mike Lansing	.10	.05	.01
☐ 356 Pedro Martinez	.25	.11	.03
☐ 357 Mel Rojas	.10	.05	.01
☐ 358 Kirk Rueter	.10	.05	.01
☐ 359 Tim Scott	.10	.05	.01
☐ 360 Jeff Shaw	.10	.05	.01
☐ 361 Larry Walker	.50	.23	.06
☐ 362 Lenny Webster	.10	.05	.01
☐ 363 John Wetteland	.25	.11	.03
☐ 364 Rondell White	.25	.11	.03
☐ 365 Bobby Bonilla	.25	.11	.03
☐ 366 Rico Brogna	.10	.05	.01
☐ 367 Jeromy Burnitz	.10	.05	.01
☐ 368 John Franco	.10	.05	.01
☐ 369 Dwight Gooden	.25	.11	.03
☐ 370 Todd Hundley	.25	.11	.03
☐ 371 Jason Jacome	.10	.05	.01
☐ 372 Bobby Jones	.25	.11	.03
☐ 373 Jeff Kent	.10	.05	.01
☐ 374 Jim Lindeman	.10	.05	.01

☐ 375 Josias Manzanillo .10 .05 .01
☐ 376 Roger Mason .10 .05 .01
☐ 377 Kevin McReynolds .10 .05 .01
☐ 378 Joe Orsulak .10 .05 .01
☐ 379 Bill Pulsipher .25 .11 .03
☐ 380 Bret Saberhagen .25 .11 .03
☐ 381 David Segui .10 .05 .01
☐ 382 Pete Smith .10 .05 .01
☐ 383 Kelly Stinnett .10 .05 .01
☐ 384 Ryan Thompson .10 .05 .01
☐ 385 Jose Vizcaino .10 .05 .01
☐ 386 Toby Borland .10 .05 .01
☐ 387 Ricky Bottalico .25 .11 .03
☐ 388 Darren Daulton .25 .11 .03
☐ 389 Mariano Duncan .10 .05 .01
☐ 390 Lenny Dykstra .25 .11 .03
☐ 391 Jim Eisenreich .10 .05 .01
☐ 392 Tommy Greene .10 .05 .01
☐ 393 Dave Hollins .10 .05 .01
☐ 394 Pete Incaviglia .10 .05 .01
☐ 395 Danny Jackson .10 .05 .01
☐ 396 Doug Jones .10 .05 .01
☐ 397 Ricky Jordan .10 .05 .01
☐ 398 John Kruk .25 .11 .03
☐ 399 Mike Lieberthal .10 .05 .01
☐ 400 Tony Longmire .10 .05 .01
☐ 401 Mickey Morandini .10 .05 .01
☐ 402 Bobby Munoz .10 .05 .01
☐ 403 Curt Schilling .10 .05 .01
☐ 404 Heathcliff Slocumb .10 .05 .01
☐ 405 Kevin Stocker .10 .05 .01
☐ 406 Fernando Valenzuela .25 .11 .03
☐ 407 David West .10 .05 .01
☐ 408 Willie Banks .10 .05 .01
☐ 409 Jose Bautista .10 .05 .01
☐ 410 Steve Buechele .10 .05 .01
☐ 411 Jim Bullinger .10 .05 .01
☐ 412 Chuck Crim .10 .05 .01
☐ 413 Shawon Dunston .10 .05 .01
☐ 414 Kevin Foster .10 .05 .01
☐ 415 Mark Grace .50 .23 .06
☐ 416 Jose Hernandez .10 .05 .01
☐ 417 Glenallen Hill .10 .05 .01
☐ 418 Brooks Kieschnick .50 .23 .06
☐ 419 Derrick May .10 .05 .01
☐ 420 Randy Myers .10 .05 .01
☐ 421 Dan Plesac .10 .05 .01
☐ 422 Karl Rhodes .10 .05 .01
☐ 423 Rey Sanchez .10 .05 .01
☐ 424 Sammy Sosa .50 .23 .06
☐ 425 Steve Trachsel .10 .05 .01
☐ 426 Rick Wilkins .10 .05 .01
☐ 427 Anthony Young .10 .05 .01
☐ 428 Eddie Zambrano .10 .05 .01
☐ 429 Bret Boone .25 .11 .03
☐ 430 Jeff Branson .10 .05 .01
☐ 431 Jeff Brantley .10 .05 .01
☐ 432 Hector Carrasco .10 .05 .01
☐ 433 Brian Dorsett .10 .05 .01
☐ 434 Tony Fernandez .10 .05 .01
☐ 435 Tim Fortugno .10 .05 .01
☐ 436 Erik Hanson .10 .05 .01
☐ 437 Thomas Howard .10 .05 .01
☐ 438 Kevin Jarvis .10 .05 .01
☐ 439 Barry Larkin .50 .23 .06
☐ 440 Chuck McElroy .10 .05 .01
☐ 441 Kevin Mitchell .25 .11 .03
☐ 442 Hal Morris .10 .05 .01
☐ 443 Jose Rijo .10 .05 .01
☐ 444 John Roper .10 .05 .01
☐ 445 Johnny Ruffin .10 .05 .01
☐ 446 Deion Sanders .50 .23 .06
☐ 447 Reggie Sanders .25 .11 .03
☐ 448 Pete Schourek .25 .11 .03
☐ 449 John Smiley .10 .05 .01
☐ 450 Eddie Taubensee .10 .05 .01
☐ 451 Jeff Bagwell 1.25 .55 .16
☐ 452 Kevin Bass .10 .05 .01
☐ 453 Craig Biggio .25 .11 .03
☐ 454 Ken Caminiti .50 .23 .06
☐ 455 Andujar Cedeno .10 .05 .01
☐ 456 Doug Drabek .10 .05 .01
☐ 457 Tony Eusebio .10 .05 .01
☐ 458 Mike Felder .10 .05 .01
☐ 459 Steve Finley .25 .11 .03
☐ 460 Luis Gonzalez .10 .05 .01
☐ 461 Mike Hampton .25 .11 .03
☐ 462 Pete Harnisch .10 .05 .01
☐ 463 John Hudek .10 .05 .01
☐ 464 Todd Jones .10 .05 .01
☐ 465 Darryl Kile .10 .05 .01
☐ 466 James Mouton .10 .05 .01
☐ 467 Shane Reynolds .25 .11 .03
☐ 468 Scott Servais .10 .05 .01
☐ 469 Greg Swindell .10 .05 .01
☐ 470 Dave Veres .10 .05 .01
☐ 471 Brian Williams .10 .05 .01
☐ 472 Jay Bell .25 .11 .03
☐ 473 Jacob Brumfield .10 .05 .01
☐ 474 Dave Clark .10 .05 .01
☐ 475 Steve Cooke .10 .05 .01
☐ 476 Midre Cummings .10 .05 .01
☐ 477 Mark Dewey .10 .05 .01
☐ 478 Tom Foley .10 .05 .01
☐ 479 Carlos Garcia .10 .05 .01
☐ 480 Jeff King .25 .11 .03
☐ 481 Jon Lieber .10 .05 .01
☐ 482 Ravelo Manzanillo .10 .05 .01
☐ 483 Al Martin .25 .11 .03
☐ 484 Orlando Merced .10 .05 .01
☐ 485 Danny Miceli .10 .05 .01
☐ 486 Denny Neagle .25 .11 .03
☐ 487 Lance Parrish .10 .05 .01
☐ 488 Don Slaught .10 .05 .01
☐ 489 Zane Smith .10 .05 .01
☐ 490 Andy Van Slyke .25 .11 .03
☐ 491 Paul Wagner .10 .05 .01
☐ 492 Rick White .10 .05 .01
☐ 493 Luis Alicea .10 .05 .01
☐ 494 Rene Arocha .10 .05 .01
☐ 495 Rheal Cormier .10 .05 .01
☐ 496 Bryan Eversgerd .10 .05 .01
☐ 497 Bernard Gilkey .25 .11 .03
☐ 498 John Habyan .10 .05 .01
☐ 499 Gregg Jefferies .25 .11 .03
☐ 500 Brian Jordan .50 .23 .06
☐ 501 Ray Lankford .25 .11 .03
☐ 502 John Mabry .50 .23 .06
☐ 503 Terry McGriff .10 .05 .01
☐ 504 Tom Pagnozzi .10 .05 .01
☐ 505 Vicente Palacios .10 .05 .01
☐ 506 Geronimo Pena .10 .05 .01
☐ 507 Gerald Perry .10 .05 .01
☐ 508 Rich Rodriguez .10 .05 .01
☐ 509 Ozzie Smith .75 .35 .09
☐ 510 Bob Tewksbury .10 .05 .01
☐ 511 Allen Watson .10 .05 .01
☐ 512 Mark Whiten .10 .05 .01
☐ 513 Todd Zeile .10 .05 .01
☐ 514 Dante Bichette .50 .23 .06
☐ 515 Willie Blair .10 .05 .01
☐ 516 Ellis Burks .25 .11 .03
☐ 517 Marvin Freeman .10 .05 .01
☐ 518 Andres Galarraga .50 .23 .06
☐ 519 Joe Girardi .10 .05 .01
☐ 520 Greg W. Harris .10 .05 .01
☐ 521 Charlie Hayes .10 .05 .01
☐ 522 Mike Kingery .10 .05 .01
☐ 523 Nelson Liriano .10 .05 .01
☐ 524 Mike Munoz .10 .05 .01
☐ 525 David Nied .10 .05 .01
☐ 526 Steve Reed .10 .05 .01
☐ 527 Kevin Ritz .10 .05 .01
☐ 528 Bruce Ruffin .10 .05 .01
☐ 529 John Vander Wal .10 .05 .01
☐ 530 Walt Weiss .10 .05 .01
☐ 531 Eric Young .25 .11 .03
☐ 532 Billy Ashley .10 .05 .01
☐ 533 Pedro Astacio .10 .05 .01
☐ 534 Rafael Bournigal .10 .05 .01
☐ 535 Brett Butler .25 .11 .03
☐ 536 Tom Candiotti .10 .05 .01
☐ 537 Omar Daal .10 .05 .01
☐ 538 Delino DeShields .10 .05 .01
☐ 539 Darren Dreifort .10 .05 .01
☐ 540 Kevin Gross .10 .05 .01
☐ 541 Orel Hershiser .25 .11 .03
☐ 542 Garey Ingram .10 .05 .01
☐ 543 Eric Karros .25 .11 .03
☐ 544 Ramon Martinez .25 .11 .03
☐ 545 Raul Mondesi .50 .23 .06
☐ 546 Chan Ho Park .50 .23 .06
☐ 547 Mike Piazza 2.00 .90 .25
☐ 548 Henry Rodriguez .25 .11 .03
☐ 549 Rudy Seanez .10 .05 .01
☐ 550 Ismael Valdes .25 .11 .03
☐ 551 Tim Wallach .10 .05 .01
☐ 552 Todd Worrell .10 .05 .01
☐ 553 Andy Ashby .25 .11 .03
☐ 554 Brad Ausmus .10 .05 .01
☐ 555 Derek Bell .25 .11 .03
☐ 556 Andy Benes .10 .05 .01
☐ 557 Phil Clark .10 .05 .01
☐ 558 Donnie Elliott .10 .05 .01
☐ 559 Ricky Gutierrez .10 .05 .01
☐ 560 Tony Gwynn 1.25 .55 .16
☐ 561 Joey Hamilton .50 .23 .06
☐ 562 Trevor Hoffman .25 .11 .03
☐ 563 Luis Lopez .10 .05 .01
☐ 564 Pedro A. Martinez .25 .11 .03
☐ 565 Tim Mauser .10 .05 .01
☐ 566 Phil Plantier .10 .05 .01
☐ 567 Bip Roberts .10 .05 .01
☐ 568 Scott Sanders .10 .05 .01
☐ 569 Craig Shipley .10 .05 .01
☐ 570 Jeff Tabaka .10 .05 .01
☐ 571 Eddie Williams .10 .05 .01
☐ 572 Rod Beck .10 .05 .01
☐ 573 Mike Benjamin .10 .05 .01
☐ 574 Barry Bonds .75 .35 .09
☐ 575 Dave Burba .10 .05 .01
☐ 576 John Burkett .25 .11 .03
☐ 577 Mark Carreon .10 .05 .01
☐ 578 Royce Clayton .10 .05 .01
☐ 579 Steve Frey .10 .05 .01
☐ 580 Bryan Hickerson .10 .05 .01
☐ 581 Mike Jackson .10 .05 .01
☐ 582 Darren Lewis .10 .05 .01
☐ 583 Kirt Manwaring .10 .05 .01
☐ 584 Rich Monteleone .10 .05 .01
☐ 585 John Patterson .10 .05 .01
☐ 586 J.R. Phillips .10 .05 .01
☐ 587 Mark Portugal .10 .05 .01
☐ 588 Joe Rosselli .10 .05 .01
☐ 589 Darryl Strawberry .25 .11 .03
☐ 590 Bill Swift .10 .05 .01
☐ 591 Robby Thompson .10 .05 .01
☐ 592 William VanLandingham .10 .05 .01
☐ 593 Matt Williams .50 .23 .06
☐ 594 Checklist .10 .05 .01
☐ 595 Checklist .10 .05 .01
☐ 596 Checklist .10 .05 .01
☐ 597 Checklist .10 .05 .01
☐ 598 Checklist .10 .05 .01
☐ 599 Checklist .10 .05 .01
☐ 600 Checklist .10 .05 .01

1995 Fleer All-Fleer

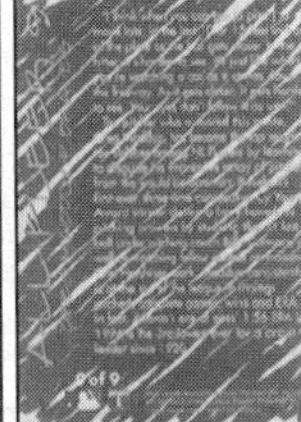

This nine-card standard-size set was available through a 1995 Fleer wrapper offer. Nine of the leading players for each position are featured in this set. The wrapper redemption offer expired on September 30, 1995. The fronts feature the player's photo covering most of the card with a small section on the right set off for the words "All Fleer 9" along with the playeris name. The backs feature player information as to why they are among the best in the game.

	MINT	NRMT	EXC
COMPLETE SET (9)	10.00	4.50	1.25
COMMON CARD (1-9)	.50	.23	.06
☐ 1 Mike Piazza	2.00	.90	.25
☐ 2 Frank Thomas	3.00	1.35	.35
☐ 3 Roberto Alomar	.60	.25	.07
☐ 4 Cal Ripken	2.50	1.10	.30
☐ 5 Matt Williams	.50	.23	.06
☐ 6 Barry Bonds	.75	.35	.09
☐ 7 Ken Griffey Jr.	3.00	1.35	.35
☐ 8 Tony Gwynn	1.00	.45	.12
☐ 9 Greg Maddux	2.00	.90	.25

1995 Fleer All-Rookies

This nine-card standard-size set was available through a Rookie Exchange redemption card randomly inserted in packs. The redemption deadline was 9/30/95. This set features players who made their major league debut in 1995. The fronts have an action photo with a grainy background. The player's name and team are in gold foil at the bottom. Horizontal backs have a player photo the left and minor league highlights to the right. The set is sequenced in alphabetical order.

	MINT	NRMT	EXC
COMPLETE SET (9)	6.00	2.70	.75
COMMON CARD (M1-M9)	.75	.35	.09
☐ M1 Edgardo Alfonzo	1.50	.70	.19
☐ M2 Jason Bates	.75	.35	.09
☐ M3 Brian Boehringer	.75	.35	.09
☐ M4 Darren Bragg	1.50	.70	.19
☐ M5 Brad Clontz	.75	.35	.09
☐ M6 Jim Dougherty	.75	.35	.09
☐ M7 Todd Hollandsworth	4.00	1.80	.50
☐ M8 Rudy Pemberton	.75	.35	.09
☐ M9 Frank Rodriguez	1.50	.70	.19
☐ NNO Expired All-Rookie Exch.	1.50	.70	.19

1995 Fleer All-Stars

Randomly inserted in all pack types at a rate of one in three, this 25-card standard-size set showcases those that participated in the 1994 mid-season classic held in Pittsburgh. Horizontally designed, the fronts contain photos of American League stars with the back protraying the National League player from the same position. On each side, the 1994 All-Star Game logo appears in gold foil as does either the A.L. or N.L. logo in silver foil.

	MINT	NRMT	EXC
COMPLETE SET (25)	12.00	5.50	1.50
COMMON CARD (1-25)	.25	.11	.03
☐ 1 Ivan Rodriguez Mike Piazza	2.00	.90	.25
☐ 2 Frank Thomas Gregg Jefferies	3.00	1.35	.35
☐ 3 Robert Alomar Mariano Duncan	.75	.35	.09
☐ 4 Wade Boggs Matt Williams	.40	.18	.05
☐ 5 Cal Ripken Jr. Ozzie Smith	2.50	1.10	.30
☐ 6 Joe Carter Barry Bonds	.75	.35	.09
☐ 7 Ken Griffey Jr. Tony Gwynn	4.00	1.80	.50
☐ 8 Kirby Puckett David Justice	1.50	.70	.19
☐ 9 Jimmy Key Greg Maddux	2.00	.90	.25
☐ 10 Chuck Knoblauch Wil Cordero	.50	.23	.06
☐ 11 Scott Cooper Ken Caminiti	.25	.11	.03
☐ 12 Will Clark Carlos Garcia	.40	.18	.05
☐ 13 Paul Molitor Jeff Bagwell	1.00	.45	.12
☐ 14 Travis Fryman Craig Biggio	.40	.18	.05
☐ 15 Mickey Tettleton Fred McGriff	.40	.18	.05
☐ 16 Kenny Lofton Moises Alou	.40	.18	.05
☐ 17 Albert Belle Marquis Grissom	1.25	.55	.16
☐ 18 Paul O'Neill Dante Bichette	.40	.18	.05
☐ 19 David Cone Ken Hill	.40	.18	.05
☐ 20 Mike Mussina Doug Drabek	.40	.18	.05
☐ 21 Randy Johnson John Hudek	.40	.18	.05
☐ 22 Pat Hentgen Danny Jackson	.40	.18	.05
☐ 23 Wilson Alvarez Rod Beck	.25	.11	.03
☐ 24 Lee Smith Randy Myers	.40	.18	.05
☐ 25 Jason Bere Doug Jones	.25	.11	.03

1995 Fleer Award Winners

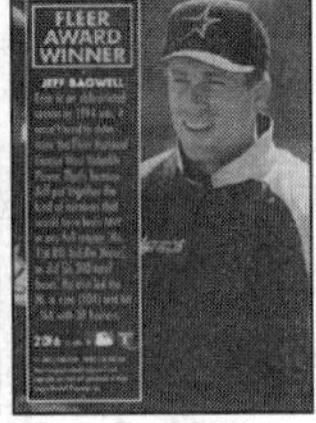

Randomly inserted in all pack types at a rate of one in 24, this six card standard-size set highlights the major award winners of 1994. Card fronts feature action photos that are full-bleed on the right border and have gold border on the left. Within the gold border are the player's name and Fleer Award Winner. The backs contain a photo with text that references 1994 accomplishments.

	MINT	NRMT	EXC
COMPLETE SET (6)	10.00	4.50	1.25
COMMON CARD (1-6)	.50	.23	.06
☐ 1 Frank Thomas	5.00	2.20	.60
☐ 2 Jeff Bagwell	2.00	.90	.25
☐ 3 David Cone	.75	.35	.09
☐ 4 Greg Maddux	3.00	1.35	.35
☐ 5 Bob Hamelin	.50	.23	.06
☐ 6 Raul Mondesi	1.00	.45	.12

1995 Fleer League Leaders

Randomly inserted in all pack types at a rate of one in 12, this 10-card standard-size set features 1994 American and National League leaders in various categories. The horizontal cards have player photos on front and back. The back also has a brief write-up concerning the accomplishment.

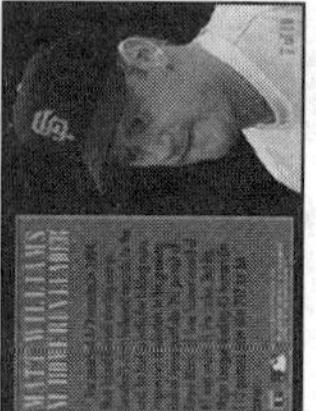

	MINT	NRMT	EXC
COMPLETE SET (10)	10.00	4.50	1.25
COMMON CARD (1-10)	.50	.23	.06
☐ 1 Paul O'Neill	.50	.23	.06
☐ 2 Ken Griffey Jr.	5.00	2.20	.60
☐ 3 Kirby Puckett	2.00	.90	.25
☐ 4 Jimmy Key	.50	.23	.06
☐ 5 Randy Johnson	.75	.35	.09
☐ 6 Tony Gwynn	2.00	.90	.25
☐ 7 Matt Williams	.50	.23	.06
☐ 8 Jeff Bagwell	2.00	.90	.25
☐ 9 Greg Maddux Ken Hill	1.50	.70	.19
☐ 10 Andy Benes	.50	.23	.06

1995 Fleer Lumber Company

Randomly inserted in retail packs at a rate of one in 24, this standard-size set highlights 10 of the game's top sluggers. Full-bleed card fronts feature an action photo with the Lumber Company logo, which includes the player's name, toward the bottom of the photo. Card backs have a player photo and woodgrain background with a write-up that highlights individual achievements. The set is sequenced in alphabetical order.

	MINT	NRMT	EXC
COMPLETE SET (10)	40.00	18.00	5.00
COMMON CARD (1-10)	1.00	.45	.12
☐ 1 Jeff Bagwell	6.00	2.70	.75
☐ 2 Albert Belle	6.00	2.70	.75
☐ 3 Barry Bonds	4.00	1.80	.50
☐ 4 Jose Canseco	3.00	1.35	.35
☐ 5 Joe Carter	2.00	.90	.25
☐ 6 Ken Griffey Jr.	15.00	6.75	1.85
☐ 7 Fred McGriff	3.00	1.35	.35
☐ 8 Kevin Mitchell	1.00	.45	.12
☐ 9 Frank Thomas	15.00	6.75	1.85
☐ 10 Matt Williams	3.00	1.35	.35

1995 Fleer Major League Prospects

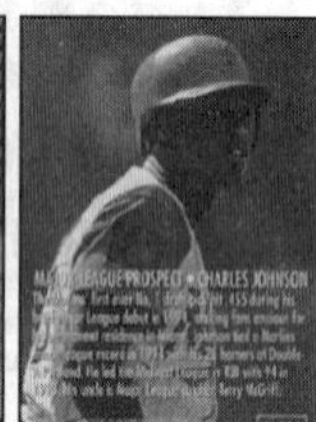

Randomly inserted in all pack types at a rate of one in six, this 10-card standard-size set spotlights major league hopefuls. Card fronts feature a player photo with the words "Major League Prospects" serving as part of the background. The player's name and team appear in silver foil at the bottom. The backs have a photo and a write-up on his minor league career. The cards are sequenced in alphabetical order.

	MINT	NRMT	EXC
COMPLETE SET (10)	12.00	5.50	1.50
COMMON CARD (1-10)	.50	.23	.06
☐ 1 Garret Anderson	.75	.35	.09
☐ 2 James Baldwin	1.25	.55	.16
☐ 3 Alan Benes	.75	.35	.09
☐ 4 Armando Benitez	.50	.23	.06
☐ 5 Ray Durham	.75	.35	.09
☐ 6 Brian L. Hunter	1.00	.45	.12
☐ 7 Derek Jeter	5.00	2.20	.60
☐ 8 Charles Johnson	.75	.35	.09
☐ 9 Orlando Miller	.75	.35	.09
☐ 10 Alex Rodriguez	8.00	3.60	1.00

1995 Fleer Pro-Visions

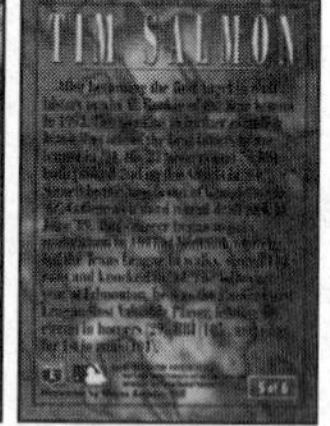

Randomly inserted in all pack types at a rate of one in nine, this six card standard-size set features top players illustrated by Wayne Anthony Still. The colorful artwork on front features the player in a surrealistic setting. The backs offer write-up on the player's previous season.

	MINT	NRMT	EXC
COMPLETE SET (6)	4.00	1.80	.50
COMMON CARD (1-6)	.50	.23	.06
☐ 1 Mike Mussina	.50	.23	.06
☐ 2 Raul Mondesi	.50	.23	.06
☐ 3 Jeff Bagwell	1.25	.55	.16
☐ 4 Greg Maddux	2.00	.90	.25
☐ 5 Tim Salmon	.50	.23	.06
☐ 6 Manny Ramirez	.75	.35	.09

1995 Fleer Rookie Sensations

Randomly inserted in 18-card packs, this 20-card standard-size set features top rookies from the 1994 season. The fronts have full-bleed color photos with the team and player's name in gold foil along the right edge. The backs also have full-bleed color photos along with player information. The set is sequenced in alphabetical order.

	MINT	NRMT	EXC
COMPLETE SET (20)	50.00	22.00	6.25
COMMON CARD (1-20)	1.00	.45	.12
☐ 1 Kurt Abbott	1.50	.70	.19
☐ 2 Rico Brogna	1.50	.70	.19
☐ 3 Hector Carrasco	1.00	.45	.12
☐ 4 Kevin Foster	1.00	.45	.12
☐ 5 Chris Gomez	1.00	.45	.12
☐ 6 Darren Hall	1.00	.45	.12
☐ 7 Bob Hamelin	1.00	.45	.12
☐ 8 Joey Hamilton	6.00	2.70	.75
☐ 9 John Hudek	1.00	.45	.12
☐ 10 Ryan Klesko	8.00	3.60	1.00
☐ 11 Javier Lopez	5.00	2.20	.60
☐ 12 Matt Mieske	1.50	.70	.19
☐ 13 Raul Mondesi	6.00	2.70	.75
☐ 14 Manny Ramirez	12.00	5.50	1.50
☐ 15 Shane Reynolds	1.50	.70	.19
☐ 16 Bill Risley	1.00	.45	.12
☐ 17 Johnny Ruffin	1.00	.45	.12
☐ 18 Steve Trachsel	1.00	.45	.12
☐ 19 William VanLandingham	1.00	.45	.12
☐ 20 Rondell White	5.00	2.20	.60

1995 Fleer Team Leaders

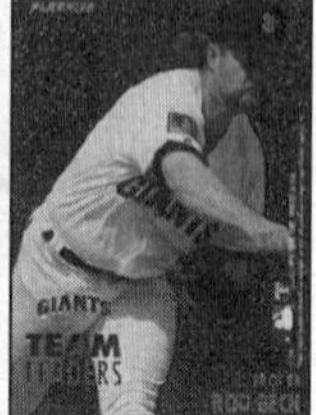

Randomly inserted in 12-card hobby packs at a rate of one in 24, this 28-card standard-size set features top players from each team. Each team is represented with card the has the team's leading hitter on one side with the leading pitcher on the other side. The team logo, "Team Leaders" and the player's name are gold foil stamped on front and back.

	MINT	NRMT	EXC
COMPLETE SET (28)	225.00	100.00	28.00
COMMON CARD (1-28)	3.00	1.35	.35
☐ 1 Cal Ripken Jr. Mike Mussina	40.00	18.00	5.00
☐ 2 Mo Vaughn Roger Clemens	12.00	5.50	1.50
☐ 3 Tim Salmon Chuck Finley	3.00	1.35	.35
☐ 4 Frank Thomas Jack McDowell	40.00	18.00	5.00
☐ 5 Albert Belle Dennis Martinez	15.00	6.75	1.85
☐ 6 Cecil Fielder Mike Moore	4.00	1.80	.50
☐ 7 Bob Hamelin David Cone	3.00	1.35	.35
☐ 8 Greg Vaughn Ricky Bones	3.00	1.35	.35
☐ 9 Kirby Puckett Rick Aguilera	15.00	6.75	1.85
☐ 10 Don Mattingly Jimmy Key	20.00	9.00	2.50
☐ 11 Ruben Sierra Dennis Eckersley	3.00	1.35	.35
☐ 12 Ken Griffey Jr. Randy Johnson	40.00	18.00	5.00
☐ 13 Jose Canseco Kenny Rogers	3.00	1.35	.35
☐ 14 Joe Carter Pat Hentgen	4.00	1.80	.50
☐ 15 David Justice Greg Maddux	25.00	11.00	3.10
☐ 16 Sammy Sosa Steve Trachsel	5.00	2.20	.60
☐ 17 Kevin Mitchell Jose Rijo	3.00	1.35	.35
☐ 18 Dante Bichette Bruce Ruffin	3.00	1.35	.35
☐ 19 Jeff Conine Robb Nen	4.00	1.80	.50
☐ 20 Jeff Bagwell Doug Drabek	15.00	6.75	1.85
☐ 21 Mike Piazza Ramon Martinez	20.00	9.00	2.50
☐ 22 Moises Alou Ken Hill	4.00	1.80	.50
☐ 23 Bobby Bonilla Bret Saberhagen	4.00	1.80	.50
☐ 24 Darren Daulton Danny Jackson	4.00	1.80	.50
☐ 25 Jay Bell Zane Smith	3.00	1.35	.35
☐ 26 Gregg Jefferies Bob Tewksbury	3.00	1.35	.35
☐ 27 Tony Gwynn Andy Benes	15.00	6.75	1.85
☐ 28 Matt Williams Rod Beck	3.00	1.35	.35

1995 Fleer Update

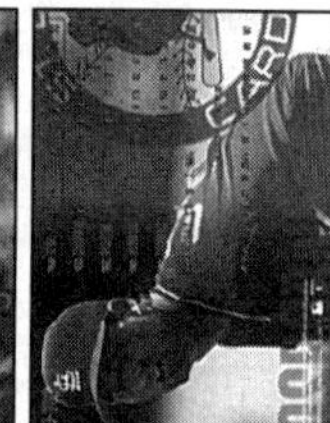

This 200-card standard-size set features many players who were either rookies in 1995 or played for new teams. These cards were issued in either 12-card packs with a suggested retail price of $1.49 or 18-card packs that had a suggested retail price of $2.29. Each Fleer Update pack included one card from several insert sets produced with this product. Hot packs featuring only these insert cards were included one every 72 packs. The full-bleed fronts have two player photos and, atypical of baseball card fronts, biographical information such as height, weight, etc. The backgrounds are multi-colored. The backs are horizontal, have yearly statistics, a photo, and are numbered with the prefix "U". The checklist is arranged alphabetically by team within each leagueis divisions. Key Rookie Cards in this set include Bobby Higginson and Hideo Nomo.

	MINT	NRMT	EXC
COMPLETE SET (200)	20.00	9.00	2.50
COMMON CARD (1-200)	.05	.02	.01
☐ 1 Manny Alexander	.05	.02	.01
☐ 2 Bret Barberie	.05	.02	.01
☐ 3 Armando Benitez	.05	.02	.01
☐ 4 Kevin Brown	.15	.07	.02
☐ 5 Doug Jones	.05	.02	.01
☐ 6 Sherman Obando	.05	.02	.01
☐ 7 Andy Van Slyke	.15	.07	.02
☐ 8 Stan Belinda	.05	.02	.01
☐ 9 Jose Canseco	.30	.14	.04
☐ 10 Vaughn Eshelman	.05	.02	.01
☐ 11 Mike Macfarlane	.05	.02	.01
☐ 12 Troy O'Leary	.05	.02	.01
☐ 13 Steve Rodriguez	.05	.02	.01
☐ 14 Lee Tinsley	.05	.02	.01
☐ 15 Tim Vanegmond	.05	.02	.01
☐ 16 Mark Whiten	.05	.02	.01
☐ 17 Sean Bergman	.05	.02	.01
☐ 18 Chad Curtis	.05	.02	.01
☐ 19 John Flaherty	.05	.02	.01
☐ 20 Bob Higginson	.50	.23	.06
☐ 21 Felipe Lira	.05	.02	.01
☐ 22 Shannon Penn	.05	.02	.01
☐ 23 Todd Steverson	.05	.02	.01
☐ 24 Sean Whiteside	.05	.02	.01
☐ 25 Tony Fernandez	.05	.02	.01
☐ 26 Jack McDowell	.15	.07	.02
☐ 27 Andy Pettitte	.75	.35	.09
☐ 28 John Wetteland	.15	.07	.02
☐ 29 David Cone	.15	.07	.02
☐ 30 Mike Timlin	.05	.02	.01
☐ 31 Duane Ward	.05	.02	.01
☐ 32 Jim Abbott	.05	.02	.01
☐ 33 James Baldwin	.15	.07	.02
☐ 34 Mike Devereaux	.05	.02	.01
☐ 35 Ray Durham	.15	.07	.02
☐ 36 Tim Fortugno	.05	.02	.01
☐ 37 Scott Ruffcorn	.05	.02	.01
☐ 38 Chris Sabo	.05	.02	.01
☐ 39 Paul Assenmacher	.05	.02	.01
☐ 40 Bud Black	.05	.02	.01
☐ 41 Orel Hershiser	.15	.07	.02
☐ 42 Julian Tavarez	.05	.02	.01
☐ 43 Dave Winfield	.30	.14	.04
☐ 44 Pat Borders	.05	.02	.01
☐ 45 Melvin Bunch	.05	.02	.01
☐ 46 Tom Goodwin	.05	.02	.01
☐ 47 Jon Nunnally	.15	.07	.02
☐ 48 Joe Randa	.05	.02	.01
☐ 49 Dilson Torres	.05	.02	.01
☐ 50 Joe Vitiello	.05	.02	.01
☐ 51 David Hulse	.05	.02	.01
☐ 52 Scott Karl	.05	.02	.01
☐ 53 Mark Kiefer	.05	.02	.01
☐ 54 Derrick May	.05	.02	.01
☐ 55 Joe Oliver	.05	.02	.01
☐ 56 Al Reyes	.05	.02	.01
☐ 57 Steve Sparks	.05	.02	.01
☐ 58 Jerald Clark	.05	.02	.01
☐ 59 Eddie Guardado	.05	.02	.01
☐ 60 Kevin Maas	.05	.02	.01
☐ 61 David McCarty	.05	.02	.01
☐ 62 Brad Radke	.15	.07	.02
☐ 63 Scott Stahoviak	.05	.02	.01
☐ 64 Garret Anderson	.15	.07	.02
☐ 65 Shawn Boskie	.05	.02	.01
☐ 66 Mike James	.05	.02	.01
☐ 67 Tony Phillips	.15	.07	.02
☐ 68 Lee Smith	.15	.07	.02
☐ 69 Mitch Williams	.05	.02	.01
☐ 70 Jim Corsi	.05	.02	.01
☐ 71 Mark Harkey	.05	.02	.01
☐ 72 Dave Stewart	.15	.07	.02
☐ 73 Todd Stottlemyre	.05	.02	.01
☐ 74 Joey Cora	.05	.02	.01
☐ 75 Chad Kreuter	.05	.02	.01
☐ 76 Jeff Nelson	.05	.02	.01
☐ 77 Alex Rodriguez	2.50	1.10	.30
☐ 78 Ron Villone	.05	.02	.01
☐ 79 Bob Wells	.05	.02	.01
☐ 80 Jose Alberro	.05	.02	.01
☐ 81 Terry Burrows	.05	.02	.01
☐ 82 Kevin Gross	.05	.02	.01
☐ 83 Wilson Heredia	.05	.02	.01
☐ 84 Mark McLemore	.05	.02	.01
☐ 85 Otis Nixon	.05	.02	.01
☐ 86 Jeff Russell	.05	.02	.01
☐ 87 Mickey Tettleton	.05	.02	.01
☐ 88 Bob Tewksbury	.05	.02	.01
☐ 89 Pedro Borbon	.05	.02	.01
☐ 90 Marquis Grissom	.15	.07	.02
☐ 91 Chipper Jones	1.25	.55	.16
☐ 92 Mike Mordecai	.05	.02	.01
☐ 93 Jason Schmidt	.30	.14	.04
☐ 94 John Burkett	.15	.07	.02
☐ 95 Andre Dawson	.15	.07	.02
☐ 96 Matt Dunbar	.05	.02	.01
☐ 97 Charles Johnson	.15	.07	.02
☐ 98 Terry Pendleton	.15	.07	.02
☐ 99 Rich Scheid	.05	.02	.01
☐ 100 Quilvio Veras	.05	.02	.01
☐ 101 Bobby Witt	.05	.02	.01
☐ 102 Eddie Zosky	.05	.02	.01
☐ 103 Shane Andrews	.05	.02	.01
☐ 104 Reid Cornelius	.05	.02	.01
☐ 105 Chad Fonville	.15	.07	.02
☐ 106 Mark Grudzielanek	.50	.23	.06
☐ 107 Roberto Kelly	.05	.02	.01
☐ 108 Carlos Perez	.15	.07	.02
☐ 109 Tony Tarasco	.05	.02	.01
☐ 110 Brett Butler	.15	.07	.02
☐ 111 Carl Everett	.05	.02	.01
☐ 112 Pete Harnisch	.05	.02	.01
☐ 113 Doug Henry	.05	.02	.01
☐ 114 Kevin Lomon	.05	.02	.01
☐ 115 Blas Minor	.05	.02	.01
☐ 116 Dave Mlicki	.05	.02	.01
☐ 117 Ricky Otero	.05	.02	.01
☐ 118 Norm Charlton	.05	.02	.01
☐ 119 Tyler Green	.05	.02	.01
☐ 120 Gene Harris	.05	.02	.01
☐ 121 Charlie Hayes	.05	.02	.01

	MINT	NRMT	EXC
□ 122 Gregg Jefferies	.15	.07	.02
□ 123 Michael Mimbs	.15	.07	.02
□ 124 Paul Quantrill	.05	.02	.01
□ 125 Frank Castillo	.05	.02	.01
□ 126 Brian McRae	.15	.07	.02
□ 127 Jaime Navarro	.05	.02	.01
□ 128 Mike Perez	.05	.02	.01
□ 129 Tanyon Sturtze	.05	.02	.01
□ 130 Ozzie Timmons	.05	.02	.01
□ 131 John Courtright	.05	.02	.01
□ 132 Ron Gant	.15	.07	.02
□ 133 Xavier Hernandez	.05	.02	.01
□ 134 Brian Hunter	.05	.02	.01
□ 135 Benito Santiago	.05	.02	.01
□ 136 Pete Smith	.05	.02	.01
□ 137 Scott Sullivan	.05	.02	.01
□ 138 Derek Bell	.15	.07	.02
□ 139 Doug Brocail	.05	.02	.01
□ 140 Ricky Gutierrez	.05	.02	.01
□ 141 Pedro Martinez	.15	.07	.02
□ 142 Orlando Miller	.05	.02	.01
□ 143 Phil Plantier	.05	.02	.01
□ 144 Craig Shipley	.05	.02	.01
□ 145 Rich Aude	.05	.02	.01
□ 146 Jason Christiansen	.05	.02	.01
□ 147 Freddy Garcia	.15	.07	.02
□ 148 Jim Gott	.05	.02	.01
□ 149 Mark Johnson	.15	.07	.02
□ 150 Esteban Loaiza	.05	.02	.01
□ 151 Dan Plesac	.05	.02	.01
□ 152 Gary Wilson	.05	.02	.01
□ 153 Allen Battle	.05	.02	.01
□ 154 Terry Bradshaw	.05	.02	.01
□ 155 Scott Cooper	.05	.02	.01
□ 156 Tripp Cromer	.05	.02	.01
□ 157 John Frascatore	.05	.02	.01
□ 158 John Habyan	.05	.02	.01
□ 159 Tom Henke	.05	.02	.01
□ 160 Ken Hill	.05	.02	.01
□ 161 Danny Jackson	.05	.02	.01
□ 162 Donovan Osborne	.05	.02	.01
□ 163 Tom Urbani	.05	.02	.01
□ 164 Roger Bailey	.05	.02	.01
□ 165 Jorge Brito	.05	.02	.01
□ 166 Vinny Castilla	.15	.07	.02
□ 167 Darren Holmes	.05	.02	.01
□ 168 Roberto Mejia	.05	.02	.01
□ 169 Bill Swift	.05	.02	.01
□ 170 Mark Thompson	.05	.02	.01
□ 171 Larry Walker	.30	.14	.04
□ 172 Greg Hansell	.05	.02	.01
□ 173 Dave Hansen	.05	.02	.01
□ 174 Carlos Hernandez	.05	.02	.01
□ 175 Hideo Nomo	2.00	.90	.25
□ 176 Jose Offerman	.05	.02	.01
□ 177 Antonio Osuna	.05	.02	.01
□ 178 Reggie Williams	.05	.02	.01
□ 179 Todd Williams	.05	.02	.01
□ 180 Andres Berumen	.05	.02	.01
□ 181 Ken Caminiti	.30	.14	.04
□ 182 Andujar Cedeno	.05	.02	.01
□ 183 Steve Finley	.15	.07	.02
□ 184 Bryce Florie	.05	.02	.01
□ 185 Dustin Hermanson	.15	.07	.02
□ 186 Ray Holbert	.05	.02	.01
□ 187 Melvin Nieves	.15	.07	.02
□ 188 Roberto Petagine	.05	.02	.01
□ 189 Jody Reed	.05	.02	.01
□ 190 Fernando Valenzuela	.15	.07	.02
□ 191 Brian Williams	.05	.02	.01
□ 192 Mark Dewey	.05	.02	.01
□ 193 Glenallen Hill	.05	.02	.01
□ 194 Chris Hook	.05	.02	.01
□ 195 Terry Mulholland	.05	.02	.01
□ 196 Steve Scarsone	.05	.02	.01
□ 197 Trevor Wilson	.05	.02	.01
□ 198 Checklist	.05	.02	.01
□ 199 Checklist	.05	.02	.01
□ 200 Checklist	.05	.02	.01

1995 Fleer Update Diamond Tribute

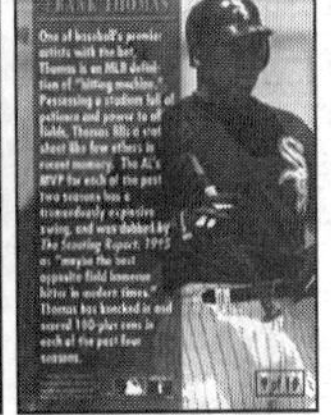

This 10-card standard-size set was inserted at a rate of one in five packs. This set features ten top players. The full-bleed fronts feature a player photo, the "Fleer 95" logo in the upper left corner, the words "Diamond Tribute" surrounding the player's team logo and the player's name on the bottom. All the words in front are in gold foil. The back is split between player information and a player photo. The cards are numbered in the lower right with an "X" of 10. The cards are sequenced in alphabetical order.

	MINT	NRMT	EXC
COMPLETE SET (10)	8.00	3.60	1.00
COMMON CARD (1-10)	.30	.14	.04
□ 1 Jeff Bagwell	1.25	.55	.16
□ 2 Albert Belle	1.25	.55	.16
□ 3 Barry Bonds	.75	.35	.09
□ 4 David Cone	.30	.14	.04
□ 5 Dennis Eckersley	.30	.14	.04
□ 6 Ken Griffey Jr.	3.00	1.35	.35
□ 7 Rickey Henderson	.30	.14	.04
□ 8 Greg Maddux	2.00	.90	.25
□ 9 Frank Thomas	3.00	1.35	.35
□ 10 Matt Williams			

1995 Fleer Update Headliners

Inserted one every three packs, this 20-card standard-size set features various major league stars. The fronts feature the playerís photo set against a newspaper headline. The word "Headliner" as well as the playerís name is printed on the bottom on the card in gold foil. The backs have some player information as well as another player photo. The cards are numbered in the lower left as "X" of 20. The cards are sequenced in alphabetical order.

	MINT	NRMT	EXC
COMPLETE SET (20)	14.00	6.25	1.75
COMMON CARD (1-20)	.25	.11	.03
□ 1 Jeff Bagwell	1.25	.55	.16
□ 2 Albert Belle	1.25	.55	.16
□ 3 Barry Bonds	.75	.35	.09
□ 4 Jose Canseco	.50	.23	.06
□ 5 Joe Carter	.40	.18	.05
□ 6 Will Clark	.50	.23	.06
□ 7 Roger Clemens	.60	.25	.07
□ 8 Lenny Dykstra	.25	.11	.03
□ 9 Cecil Fielder	.40	.18	.05
□ 10 Juan Gonzalez	1.50	.70	.19
□ 11 Ken Griffey Jr.	3.00	1.35	.35
□ 12 Kenny Lofton	.75	.35	.09
□ 13 Greg Maddux	2.00	.90	.25
□ 14 Fred McGriff	.50	.23	.06
□ 15 Mike Piazza	2.00	.90	.25
□ 16 Kirby Puckett	1.25	.55	.16
□ 17 Tim Salmon	.50	.23	.06
□ 18 Frank Thomas	3.00	1.35	.35
□ 19 Mo Vaughn	.75	.35	.09
□ 20 Matt Williams	.50	.23	.06

1995 Fleer Update Rookie Update

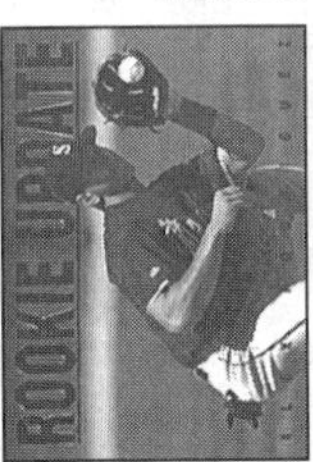

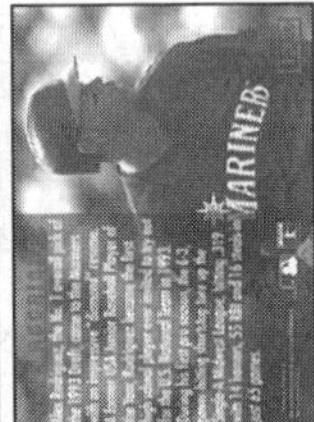

Inserted one in every four packs, this 10-card standard-size set features some of 1995's best rookies. The horizontal fronts feature the words "Rookie Update" in large letters at the top, and the "Fleer 95" logo as well as the player's name at the bottom. The rest of the card has the player's photo. To the left, the back has background information as well as a photo on the right. The cards are numbered as "X of 10". Chipper Jones and Hideo Nomo are among the players included in this set. The set is sequenced in alphabetical order.

	MINT	NRMT	EXC
COMPLETE SET (10)	15.00	6.75	1.85
COMMON CARD (1-10)	.25	.11	.03
□ 1 Shane Andrews	.25	.11	.03
□ 2 Ray Durham	.75	.35	.09
□ 3 Shawn Green	.75	.35	.09
□ 4 Charles Johnson	.75	.35	.09
□ 5 Chipper Jones	5.00	2.20	.60
□ 6 Esteban Loaiza	.25	.11	.03
□ 7 Hideo Nomo	4.00	1.80	.50
□ 8 Jon Nunnally	.25	.11	.03
□ 9 Alex Rodriguez	8.00	3.60	1.00
□ 10 Julian Tavarez	.25	.11	.03

1995 Fleer Update Smooth Leather

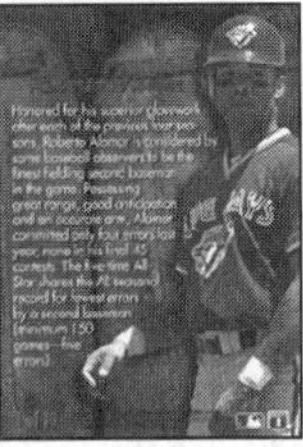

Inserted one every five packs, this 10-card standard-size set features many leading defensive wizards. The card fronts feature a player photo. Underneath the player photo, is his name along with the words "smooth leather" on the bottom. The right corner features a glove. All of this information as well as the "Fleer 95" logo is in gold print. All of this is on a card with a special leather-like coating. The back features a photo as well as fielding information. The cards are numbered in the lower left as "X of 10" and are sequenced in alphabetical order.

	MINT	NRMT	EXC
COMPLETE SET (10)	25.00	11.00	3.10
COMMON CARD (1-10)	.75	.35	.09
□ 1 Roberto Alomar	2.00	.90	.25
□ 2 Barry Bonds	2.50	1.10	.30
□ 3 Ken Griffey Jr.	10.00	4.50	1.25
□ 4 Marquis Grissom	1.00	.45	.12
□ 5 Darren Lewis	.75	.35	.09
□ 6 Kenny Lofton	2.50	1.10	.30
□ 7 Don Mattingly	5.00	2.20	.60
□ 8 Cal Ripken	8.00	3.60	1.00
□ 9 Ivan Rodriguez	2.50	1.10	.30
□ 10 Matt Williams	1.50	.70	.19

1995 Fleer Update Soaring Stars

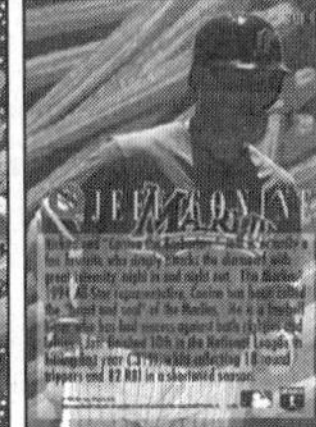

This nine-card standard-size set was inserted one every 36 packs. The fronts feature the player's photo set against a prismatic background of baseballs. The player's name, the "Soaring Stars" logo as well as a star are all printed in gold foil at the bottom. The back has a player photo, his name as well as some career information. The cards are numbered in the upper right "X of 9" and are sequenced in alphabetical order.

	MINT	NRMT	EXC
COMPLETE SET (9)	60.00	27.00	7.50
COMMON CARD (1-9)	2.50	1.10	.30
□ 1 Moises Alou UER (says .399 BA in 1994)	4.00	1.80	.50
□ 2 Jason Bere	2.50	1.10	.30
□ 3 Jeff Conine	4.00	1.80	.50
□ 4 Cliff Floyd	2.50	1.10	.30
□ 5 Pat Hentgen	4.00	1.80	.50
□ 6 Kenny Lofton	12.00	5.50	1.50
□ 7 Raul Mondesi	6.00	2.70	.75
□ 8 Mike Piazza	30.00	13.50	3.70
□ 9 Tim Salmon	6.00	2.70	.75

1996 Fleer

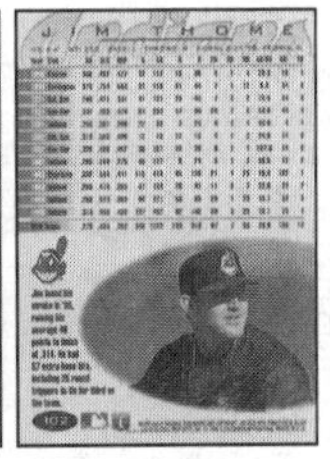

The 1996 Fleer baseball set consists of 600 standard-size cards. Cards were issued in 11-card packs with a suggested retail price of $1.49. Borderless fronts are matte-finished and have full-color action shots with the player's name, team and position stamped in gold foil. Backs contain a biography and career stats on the top and a full-color head shot with a 1995 synopsis on the bottom. The matte finish on the cards was designed so collectors could have an easier surface for cards to be autographed. Fleer included in each pack a "Thanks a Million" scratch-off game card redeemable for instant-win prizes and a chance to bat for a million-dollar prize in a Major League park. Rookie Cards in this set include Matt Lawton and Mike Sweeney.

	MINT	NRMT	EXC
COMPLETE SET (600)	70.00	32.00	8.75
COMMON CARD (1-600)	.10	.05	.01
□ 1 Manny Alexander	.10	.05	.01
□ 2 Brady Anderson	.50	.23	.06
□ 3 Harold Baines	.25	.11	.03
□ 4 Armando Benitez	.10	.05	.01
□ 5 Bobby Bonilla	.25	.11	.03
□ 6 Kevin Brown	.25	.11	.03
□ 7 Scott Erickson	.10	.05	.01
□ 8 Curtis Goodwin	.10	.05	.01
□ 9 Jeffrey Hammonds	.10	.05	.01
□ 10 Jimmy Haynes	.10	.05	.01
□ 11 Chris Hoiles	.10	.05	.01
□ 12 Doug Jones	.10	.05	.01
□ 13 Rick Krivda	.10	.05	.01
□ 14 Jeff Manto	.10	.05	.01
□ 15 Ben McDonald	.10	.05	.01
□ 16 Jamie Moyer	.10	.05	.01
□ 17 Mike Mussina	.60	.25	.07
□ 18 Jesse Orosco	.10	.05	.01
□ 19 Rafael Palmeiro	.50	.23	.06
□ 20 Cal Ripken	2.50	1.10	.30
□ 21 Rick Aguilera	.10	.05	.01
□ 22 Luis Alicea	.10	.05	.01
□ 23 Stan Belinda	.10	.05	.01
□ 24 Jose Canseco	.50	.23	.06
□ 25 Roger Clemens	.60	.25	.07
□ 26 Vaughn Eshelman	.10	.05	.01
□ 27 Mike Greenwell	.10	.05	.01
□ 28 Erik Hanson	.10	.05	.01
□ 29 Dwayne Hosey	.10	.05	.01
□ 30 Mike Macfarlane UER	.10	.05	.01
□ 31 Tim Naehring	.10	.05	.01
□ 32 Troy O'Leary	.10	.05	.01
□ 33 Aaron Sele	.10	.05	.01
□ 34 Zane Smith	.10	.05	.01
□ 35 Jeff Suppan	.50	.23	.06
□ 36 Lee Tinsley	.10	.05	.01
□ 37 John Valentin	.25	.11	.03
□ 38 Mo Vaughn	.75	.35	.09
□ 39 Tim Wakefield	.10	.05	.01
□ 40 Jim Abbott	.50	.23	.06
□ 41 Brian Anderson	.10	.05	.01
□ 42 Garret Anderson	.50	.23	.06
□ 43 Chili Davis	.10	.05	.01
□ 44 Gary DiSarcina	.10	.05	.01
□ 45 Damion Easley	.10	.05	.01
□ 46 Jim Edmonds	.25	.11	.03
□ 47 Chuck Finley	.10	.05	.01
□ 48 Todd Greene	.50	.23	.06
□ 49 Mike Harkey	.10	.05	.01
□ 50 Mike James	.10	.05	.01
□ 51 Mark Langston	.10	.05	.01
□ 52 Greg Myers	.10	.05	.01
□ 53 Orlando Palmeiro	.10	.05	.01
□ 54 Bob Patterson	.10	.05	.01
□ 55 Troy Percival	.25	.11	.03
□ 56 Tony Phillips	.25	.11	.03
□ 57 Tim Salmon	.50	.23	.06
□ 58 Lee Smith	.25	.11	.03
□ 59 J.T. Snow	.25	.11	.03
□ 60 Randy Velarde	.10	.05	.01
□ 61 Wilson Alvarez	.50	.23	.06
□ 62 Luis Andujar	.10	.05	.01
□ 63 Jason Bere	.10	.05	.01
□ 64 Ray Durham	.50	.23	.06
□ 65 Alex Fernandez	.25	.11	.03
□ 66 Ozzie Guillen	.10	.05	.01
□ 67 Roberto Hernandez	.25	.11	.03
□ 68 Lance Johnson	.25	.11	.03
□ 69 Matt Karchner	.10	.05	.01
□ 70 Ron Karkovice	.10	.05	.01
□ 71 Norberto Martin	.10	.05	.01
□ 72 Dave Martinez	.10	.05	.01
□ 73 Kirk McCaskill	.10	.05	.01
□ 74 Lyle Mouton	.10	.05	.01
□ 75 Tim Raines	.50	.23	.06
□ 76 Mike Sirotka	.10	.05	.01
□ 77 Frank Thomas	3.00	1.35	.35
□ 78 Larry Thomas	.10	.05	.01
□ 79 Robin Ventura	.25	.11	.03
□ 80 Sandy Alomar, Jr.	.10	.05	.01
□ 81 Paul Assenmacher	.10	.05	.01
□ 82 Carlos Baerga	.25	.11	.03
□ 83 Albert Belle	1.25	.55	.16
□ 84 Mark Clark	.10	.05	.01
□ 85 Alan Embree	.10	.05	.01
□ 86 Alvaro Espinoza	.10	.05	.01
□ 87 Orel Hershiser	.25	.11	.03
□ 88 Ken Hill	.10	.05	.01
□ 89 Kenny Lofton	.75	.35	.09
□ 90 Dennis Martinez	.25	.11	.03
□ 91 Jose Mesa	.25	.11	.03
□ 92 Eddie Murray	.75	.35	.09
□ 93 Charles Nagy	.25	.11	.03
□ 94 Chad Ogea	.10	.05	.01
□ 95 Tony Pena	.10	.05	.01
□ 96 Herb Perry	.10	.05	.01
□ 97 Eric Plunk	.10	.05	.01
□ 98 Jim Poole	.10	.05	.01
□ 99 Manny Ramirez	.75	.35	.09
□ 100 Paul Sorrento	.10	.05	.01
□ 101 Julian Tavarez	.10	.05	.01
□ 102 Jim Thome	.60	.25	.07

☐ 103 Omar Vizquel .25 .11 .03
☐ 104 Dave Winfield .50 .23 .06
☐ 105 Danny Bautista .10 .05 .01
☐ 106 Joe Boever .10 .05 .01
☐ 107 Chad Curtis .10 .05 .01
☐ 108 John Doherty .10 .05 .01
☐ 109 Cecil Fielder .25 .11 .03
☐ 110 John Flaherty .10 .05 .01
☐ 111 Travis Fryman .25 .11 .03
☐ 112 Chris Gomez .10 .05 .01
☐ 113 Bob Higginson .50 .23 .06
☐ 114 Mark Lewis .10 .05 .01
☐ 115 Jose Lima .10 .05 .01
☐ 116 Felipe Lira .10 .05 .01
☐ 117 Brian Maxcy .10 .05 .01
☐ 118 C.J. Nitkowski .10 .05 .01
☐ 119 Phil Plantier .10 .05 .01
☐ 120 Clint Sodowsky .10 .05 .01
☐ 121 Alan Trammell .25 .11 .03
☐ 122 Lou Whitaker .25 .11 .03
☐ 123 Kevin Appier .25 .11 .03
☐ 124 Johnny Damon .25 .11 .03
☐ 125 Gary Gaetti .25 .11 .03
☐ 126 Tom Goodwin .25 .11 .03
☐ 127 Tom Gordon .10 .05 .01
☐ 128 Mark Gubicza .10 .05 .01
☐ 129 Bob Hamelin .10 .05 .01
☐ 130 David Howard .10 .05 .01
☐ 131 Jason Jacome .10 .05 .01
☐ 132 Wally Joyner .10 .05 .01
☐ 133 Keith Lockhart .10 .05 .01
☐ 134 Brent Mayne .10 .05 .01
☐ 135 Jeff Montgomery .10 .05 .01
☐ 136 Jon Nunnally .10 .05 .01
☐ 137 Juan Samuel .10 .05 .01
☐ 138 Mike Sweeney .60 .25 .07
☐ 139 Michael Tucker .25 .11 .03
☐ 140 Joe Vitiello .10 .05 .01
☐ 141 Ricky Bones .10 .05 .01
☐ 142 Chuck Carr .10 .05 .01
☐ 143 Jeff Cirillo .10 .05 .01
☐ 144 Mike Fetters .10 .05 .01
☐ 145 Darryl Hamilton .10 .05 .01
☐ 146 David Hulse .10 .05 .01
☐ 147 John Jaha .25 .11 .03
☐ 148 Scott Karl .10 .05 .01
☐ 149 Mark Kiefer .10 .05 .01
☐ 150 Pat Listach .10 .05 .01
☐ 151 Mark Loretta .10 .05 .01
☐ 152 Mike Matheny .10 .05 .01
☐ 153 Matt Mieske .10 .05 .01
☐ 154 Dave Nilsson .25 .11 .03
☐ 155 Joe Oliver .10 .05 .01
☐ 156 Al Reyes .10 .05 .01
☐ 157 Kevin Seitzer .10 .05 .01
☐ 158 Steve Sparks .10 .05 .01
☐ 159 B.J. Surhoff .10 .05 .01
☐ 160 Jose Valentin .10 .05 .01
☐ 161 Greg Vaughn .50 .23 .06
☐ 162 Fernando Vina .10 .05 .01
☐ 163 Rich Becker .25 .11 .03
☐ 164 Ron Coomer .10 .05 .01
☐ 165 Marty Cordova .25 .11 .03
☐ 166 Chuck Knoblauch .50 .23 .06
☐ 167 Matt Lawton .10 .05 .01
☐ 168 Pat Meares .10 .05 .01
☐ 169 Paul Molitor .60 .25 .07
☐ 170 Pedro Munoz .10 .05 .01
☐ 171 Jose Parra .10 .05 .01
☐ 172 Kirby Puckett 1.25 .55 .16
☐ 173 Brad Radke .10 .05 .01
☐ 174 Jeff Reboulet .10 .05 .01
☐ 175 Rich Robertson .10 .05 .01
☐ 176 Frank Rodriguez .25 .11 .03
☐ 177 Scott Stahoviak .10 .05 .01
☐ 178 Dave Stevens .10 .05 .01
☐ 179 Matt Walbeck .10 .05 .01
☐ 180 Wade Boggs .50 .23 .06
☐ 181 David Cone .25 .11 .03
☐ 182 Tony Fernandez .10 .05 .01
☐ 183 Joe Girardi .10 .05 .01
☐ 184 Derek Jeter 2.00 .90 .25
☐ 185 Scott Kamieniecki .10 .05 .01
☐ 186 Pat Kelly .10 .05 .01
☐ 187 Jim Leyritz .10 .05 .01
☐ 188 Tino Martinez .25 .11 .03
☐ 189 Don Mattingly 1.50 .70 .19
☐ 190 Jack McDowell .50 .23 .06
☐ 191 Jeff Nelson .10 .05 .01
☐ 192 Paul O'Neill .10 .05 .01
☐ 193 Melido Perez .10 .05 .01
☐ 194 Andy Pettitte .50 .23 .06
☐ 195 Mariano Rivera .25 .11 .03
☐ 196 Ruben Sierra .10 .05 .01
☐ 197 Mike Stanley .10 .05 .01
☐ 198 Darryl Strawberry .25 .11 .03
☐ 199 John Wetteland .25 .11 .03
☐ 200 Bob Wickman .10 .05 .01
☐ 201 Bernie Williams .60 .25 .07
☐ 202 Mark Acre .10 .05 .01
☐ 203 Geronimo Berroa .25 .11 .03
☐ 204 Mike Bordick .25 .11 .03
☐ 205 Scott Brosius .25 .11 .03
☐ 206 Dennis Eckersley .25 .11 .03
☐ 207 Brent Gates .10 .05 .01
☐ 208 Jason Giambi .50 .23 .06
☐ 209 Rickey Henderson .50 .23 .06
☐ 210 Jose Herrera .10 .05 .01
☐ 211 Stan Javier .10 .05 .01
☐ 212 Doug Johns .10 .05 .01
☐ 213 Mark McGwire .50 .23 .06
☐ 214 Steve Ontiveros .10 .05 .01
☐ 215 Craig Paquette .10 .05 .01
☐ 216 Ariel Prieto .10 .05 .01
☐ 217 Carlos Reyes .10 .05 .01
☐ 218 Terry Steinbach .25 .11 .03
☐ 219 Todd Stottlemyre .10 .05 .01
☐ 220 Danny Tartabull .10 .05 .01
☐ 221 Todd Van Poppel .10 .05 .01
☐ 222 John Wasdin .10 .05 .01
☐ 223 George Williams .10 .05 .01
☐ 224 Steve Wojciechowski .10 .05 .01
☐ 225 Rich Amaral .10 .05 .01
☐ 226 Bobby Ayala .10 .05 .01
☐ 227 Tim Belcher .10 .05 .01
☐ 228 Andy Benes .10 .05 .01
☐ 229 Chris Bosio .10 .05 .01
☐ 230 Darren Bragg .10 .05 .01
☐ 231 Jay Buhner .50 .23 .06
☐ 232 Norm Charlton .10 .05 .01
☐ 233 Vince Coleman .10 .05 .01
☐ 234 Joey Cora .10 .05 .01
☐ 235 Russ Davis .10 .05 .01
☐ 236 Alex Diaz .10 .05 .01
☐ 237 Felix Fermin .10 .05 .01
☐ 238 Ken Griffey Jr. 3.00 1.35 .35
☐ 239 Sterling Hitchcock .10 .05 .01
☐ 240 Randy Johnson .50 .23 .06
☐ 241 Edgar Martinez .25 .11 .03
☐ 242 Bill Risley .10 .05 .01
☐ 243 Alex Rodriguez 3.00 1.35 .35
☐ 244 Luis Sojo .10 .05 .01
☐ 245 Dan Wilson .10 .05 .01
☐ 246 Bob Wolcott .10 .05 .01
☐ 247 Will Clark .50 .23 .06
☐ 248 Jeff Frye .10 .05 .01
☐ 249 Benji Gil .10 .05 .01
☐ 250 Juan Gonzalez 1.50 .70 .19
☐ 251 Rusty Greer .50 .23 .06
☐ 252 Kevin Gross .10 .05 .01
☐ 253 Roger McDowell .10 .05 .01
☐ 254 Mark McLemore .10 .05 .01
☐ 255 Otis Nixon .10 .05 .01
☐ 256 Luis Ortiz .10 .05 .01
☐ 257 Mike Pagliarulo .10 .05 .01
☐ 258 Dean Palmer .50 .23 .06
☐ 259 Roger Pavlik .10 .05 .01
☐ 260 Ivan Rodriguez .75 .35 .09
☐ 261 Kenny Rogers .10 .05 .01
☐ 262 Jeff Russell .10 .05 .01
☐ 263 Mickey Tettleton .25 .11 .03
☐ 264 Bob Tewksbury .10 .05 .01
☐ 265 Dave Valle .10 .05 .01
☐ 266 Matt Whiteside .10 .05 .01
☐ 267 Roberto Alomar .60 .25 .07
☐ 268 Joe Carter .25 .11 .03
☐ 269 Tony Castillo .10 .05 .01
☐ 270 Domingo Cedeno .10 .05 .01
☐ 271 Tim Crabtree UER .10 .05 .01
☐ 272 Carlos Delgado .25 .11 .03
☐ 273 Alex Gonzalez .10 .05 .01
☐ 274 Shawn Green .25 .11 .03
☐ 275 Juan Guzman .10 .05 .01
☐ 276 Pat Hentgen .25 .11 .03
☐ 277 Al Leiter .10 .05 .01
☐ 278 Sandy Martinez .10 .05 .01
☐ 279 Paul Menhart .10 .05 .01
☐ 280 John Olerud .10 .05 .01
☐ 281 Paul Quantrill .10 .05 .01
☐ 282 Ken Robinson .10 .05 .01
☐ 283 Ed Sprague .25 .11 .03
☐ 284 Mike Timlin .10 .05 .01
☐ 285 Steve Avery .25 .11 .03
☐ 286 Rafael Belliard .10 .05 .01
☐ 287 Jeff Blauser .10 .05 .01
☐ 288 Pedro Borbon .10 .05 .01
☐ 289 Brad Clontz .10 .05 .01
☐ 290 Mike Devereaux .10 .05 .01
☐ 291 Tom Glavine .50 .23 .06
☐ 292 Marquis Grissom .25 .11 .03
☐ 293 Chipper Jones 2.00 .90 .25
☐ 294 David Justice .25 .11 .03
☐ 295 Mike Kelly .10 .05 .01
☐ 296 Ryan Klesko .50 .23 .06
☐ 297 Mark Lemke .10 .05 .01
☐ 298 Javier Lopez .50 .23 .06
☐ 299 Greg Maddux 2.00 .90 .25
☐ 300 Fred McGriff .50 .23 .06
☐ 301 Greg McMichael .10 .05 .01
☐ 302 Kent Mercker .10 .05 .01
☐ 303 Mike Mordecai .10 .05 .01
☐ 304 Charlie O'Brien .10 .05 .01
☐ 305 Eduardo Perez .10 .05 .01
☐ 306 Luis Polonia .10 .05 .01
☐ 307 Jason Schmidt .50 .23 .06
☐ 308 John Smoltz .50 .23 .06
☐ 309 Terrell Wade .25 .11 .03
☐ 310 Mark Wohlers .25 .11 .03
☐ 311 Scott Bullett .10 .05 .01
☐ 312 Jim Bullinger .10 .05 .01
☐ 313 Larry Casian .10 .05 .01
☐ 314 Frank Castillo .10 .05 .01
☐ 315 Shawon Dunston .10 .05 .01
☐ 316 Kevin Foster .10 .05 .01
☐ 317 Matt Franco .10 .05 .01
☐ 318 Luis Gonzalez .10 .05 .01
☐ 319 Mark Grace .50 .23 .06
☐ 320 Jose Hernandez .10 .05 .01
☐ 321 Mike Hubbard .10 .05 .01
☐ 322 Brian McRae .10 .05 .01
☐ 323 Randy Myers .10 .05 .01
☐ 324 Jaime Navarro .10 .05 .01
☐ 325 Mark Parent .10 .05 .01
☐ 326 Mike Perez .10 .05 .01
☐ 327 Rey Sanchez .10 .05 .01
☐ 328 Ryne Sandberg .75 .35 .09
☐ 329 Scott Servais .10 .05 .01
☐ 330 Sammy Sosa .50 .23 .06
☐ 331 Ozzie Timmons .10 .05 .01
☐ 332 Steve Trachsel .10 .05 .01
☐ 333 Todd Zeile .25 .11 .03
☐ 334 Bret Boone .10 .05 .01
☐ 335 Jeff Branson .10 .05 .01
☐ 336 Jeff Brantley .10 .05 .01
☐ 337 Dave Burba .10 .05 .01
☐ 338 Hector Carrasco .10 .05 .01
☐ 339 Mariano Duncan .10 .05 .01
☐ 340 Ron Gant .25 .11 .03
☐ 341 Lenny Harris .10 .05 .01
☐ 342 Xavier Hernandez .10 .05 .01
☐ 343 Thomas Howard .10 .05 .01
☐ 344 Mike Jackson .10 .05 .01
☐ 345 Barry Larkin .50 .23 .06
☐ 346 Darren Lewis .10 .05 .01
☐ 347 Hal Morris .10 .05 .01
☐ 348 Eric Owens .10 .05 .01
☐ 349 Mark Portugal .10 .05 .01
☐ 350 Jose Rijo .10 .05 .01
☐ 351 Reggie Sanders .25 .11 .03
☐ 352 Benito Santiago .10 .05 .01
☐ 353 Pete Schourek .25 .11 .03
☐ 354 John Smiley .10 .05 .01
☐ 355 Eddie Taubensee .10 .05 .01
☐ 356 Jerome Walton .10 .05 .01
☐ 357 David Wells .10 .05 .01
☐ 358 Roger Bailey .10 .05 .01
☐ 359 Jason Bates .10 .05 .01
☐ 360 Dante Bichette .50 .23 .06
☐ 361 Ellis Burks .25 .11 .03
☐ 362 Vinny Castilla .25 .11 .03
☐ 363 Andres Galarraga .50 .23 .06
☐ 364 Darren Holmes .10 .05 .01
☐ 365 Mike Kingery .10 .05 .01
☐ 366 Curt Leskanic .10 .05 .01
☐ 367 Quinton McCracken .10 .05 .01
☐ 368 Mike Munoz .10 .05 .01
☐ 369 David Nied .10 .05 .01
☐ 370 Steve Reed .10 .05 .01
☐ 371 Bryan Rekar .10 .05 .01
☐ 372 Kevin Ritz .10 .05 .01
☐ 373 Bruce Ruffin .10 .05 .01
☐ 374 Bret Saberhagen .10 .05 .01
☐ 375 Bill Swift .10 .05 .01
☐ 376 John Vander Wal .10 .05 .01
☐ 377 Larry Walker .50 .23 .06
☐ 378 Walt Weiss .10 .05 .01
☐ 379 Eric Young .25 .11 .03
☐ 380 Kurt Abbott .10 .05 .01
☐ 381 Alex Arias .10 .05 .01
☐ 382 Jerry Browne .10 .05 .01
☐ 383 John Burkett .10 .05 .01
☐ 384 Greg Colbrunn .10 .05 .01
☐ 385 Jeff Conine .25 .11 .03
☐ 386 Andre Dawson .25 .11 .03
☐ 387 Chris Hammond .10 .05 .01
☐ 388 Charles Johnson .25 .11 .03
☐ 389 Terry Mathews .10 .05 .01
☐ 390 Robb Nen .10 .05 .01
☐ 391 Joe Orsulak .10 .05 .01
☐ 392 Terry Pendleton .25 .11 .03
☐ 393 Pat Rapp .10 .05 .01
☐ 394 Gary Sheffield .50 .23 .06
☐ 395 Jesus Tavarez .10 .05 .01
☐ 396 Marc Valdes .10 .05 .01
☐ 397 Quilvio Veras .10 .05 .01
☐ 398 Randy Veres .10 .05 .01
☐ 399 Devon White .10 .05 .01
☐ 400 Jeff Bagwell 1.25 .55 .16
☐ 401 Derek Bell .25 .11 .03
☐ 402 Craig Biggio .25 .11 .03
☐ 403 John Cangelosi .10 .05 .01
☐ 404 Jim Dougherty .10 .05 .01
☐ 405 Doug Drabek .10 .05 .01
☐ 406 Tony Eusebio .10 .05 .01
☐ 407 Ricky Gutierrez .10 .05 .01
☐ 408 Mike Hampton .10 .05 .01
☐ 409 Dean Hartgraves .10 .05 .01
☐ 410 John Hudek .10 .05 .01
☐ 411 Brian L. Hunter .10 .05 .01
☐ 412 Todd Jones .10 .05 .01
☐ 413 Darryl Kile .10 .05 .01
☐ 414 Dave Magadan .10 .05 .01
☐ 415 Derrick May .10 .05 .01
☐ 416 Orlando Miller .10 .05 .01
☐ 417 James Mouton .10 .05 .01
☐ 418 Shane Reynolds .10 .05 .01
☐ 419 Greg Swindell .10 .05 .01
☐ 420 Jeff Tabaka .10 .05 .01
☐ 421 Dave Veres .10 .05 .01
☐ 422 Billy Wagner .50 .23 .06
☐ 423 Donne Wall .10 .05 .01
☐ 424 Rick Wilkins .10 .05 .01
☐ 425 Billy Ashley .10 .05 .01
☐ 426 Mike Blowers .10 .05 .01
☐ 427 Brett Butler .10 .05 .01
☐ 428 Tom Candiotti .10 .05 .01
☐ 429 Juan Castro .10 .05 .01
☐ 430 John Cummings .10 .05 .01
☐ 431 Delino DeShields .10 .05 .01
☐ 432 Joey Eischen .10 .05 .01
☐ 433 Chad Fonville .10 .05 .01
☐ 434 Greg Gagne .10 .05 .01
☐ 435 Dave Hansen .10 .05 .01
☐ 436 Carlos Hernandez .10 .05 .01
☐ 437 Todd Hollandsworth .25 .11 .03
☐ 438 Eric Karros .25 .11 .03
☐ 439 Roberto Kelly .10 .05 .01
☐ 440 Ramon Martinez .25 .11 .03
☐ 441 Raul Mondesi .50 .23 .06
☐ 442 Hideo Nomo .75 .35 .09
☐ 443 Antonio Osuna .10 .05 .01
☐ 444 Chan Ho Park .50 .23 .06
☐ 445 Mike Piazza 2.00 .90 .25
☐ 446 Felix Rodriguez .10 .05 .01
☐ 447 Kevin Tapani .10 .05 .01
☐ 448 Ismael Valdes .10 .05 .01
☐ 449 Todd Worrell .25 .11 .03
☐ 450 Moises Alou .25 .11 .03
☐ 451 Shane Andrews .10 .05 .01
☐ 452 Yamil Benitez .25 .11 .03
☐ 453 Sean Berry .10 .05 .01
☐ 454 Wil Cordero .10 .05 .01
☐ 455 Jeff Fassero .10 .05 .01
☐ 456 Darrin Fletcher .10 .05 .01
☐ 457 Cliff Floyd .10 .05 .01
☐ 458 Mark Grudzielanek .25 .11 .03
☐ 459 Gil Heredia .10 .05 .01
☐ 460 Tim Laker .10 .05 .01
☐ 461 Mike Lansing .10 .05 .01
☐ 462 Pedro J.Martinez .25 .11 .03
☐ 463 Carlos Perez .10 .05 .01
☐ 464 Curtis Pride .10 .05 .01
☐ 465 Mel Rojas .25 .11 .03
☐ 466 Kirk Rueter .10 .05 .01
☐ 467 F.P. Santangelo .10 .05 .01
☐ 468 Tim Scott .10 .05 .01
☐ 469 David Segui .10 .05 .01
☐ 470 Tony Tarasco .10 .05 .01
☐ 471 Rondell White .25 .11 .03
☐ 472 Edgardo Alfonzo .25 .11 .03
☐ 473 Tim Bogar .10 .05 .01
☐ 474 Rico Brogna .10 .05 .01
☐ 475 Damon Buford .10 .05 .01
☐ 476 Paul Byrd .10 .05 .01
☐ 477 Carl Everett .10 .05 .01
☐ 478 John Franco .10 .05 .01
☐ 479 Todd Hundley .25 .11 .03
☐ 480 Butch Huskey .25 .11 .03
☐ 481 Jason Isringhausen .50 .23 .06
☐ 482 Bobby Jones .10 .05 .01
☐ 483 Chris Jones .10 .05 .01
☐ 484 Jeff Kent .10 .05 .01
☐ 485 Dave Mlicki .10 .05 .01
☐ 486 Robert Person .10 .05 .01
☐ 487 Bill Pulsipher .25 .11 .03
☐ 488 Kelly Stinnett .10 .05 .01
☐ 489 Ryan Thompson .10 .05 .01
☐ 490 Jose Vizcaino .10 .05 .01
☐ 491 Howard Battle .10 .05 .01
☐ 492 Toby Borland .10 .05 .01
☐ 493 Ricky Bottalico .10 .05 .01
☐ 494 Darren Daulton .25 .11 .03
☐ 495 Lenny Dykstra .25 .11 .03
☐ 496 Jim Eisenreich .10 .05 .01
☐ 497 Sid Fernandez .10 .05 .01
☐ 498 Tyler Green .10 .05 .01
☐ 499 Charlie Hayes .10 .05 .01
☐ 500 Gregg Jefferies .50 .23 .06
☐ 501 Kevin Jordan .10 .05 .01
☐ 502 Tony Longmire .10 .05 .01
☐ 503 Tom Marsh .10 .05 .01
☐ 504 Michael Mimbs .10 .05 .01
☐ 505 Mickey Morandini .10 .05 .01
☐ 506 Gene Schall .10 .05 .01
☐ 507 Curt Schilling .10 .05 .01
☐ 508 Heathcliff Slocumb .10 .05 .01
☐ 509 Kevin Stocker .10 .05 .01
☐ 510 Andy Van Slyke .25 .11 .03
☐ 511 Lenny Webster .10 .05 .01
☐ 512 Mark Whiten .10 .05 .01
☐ 513 Mike Williams .10 .05 .01
☐ 514 Jay Bell .25 .11 .03
☐ 515 Jacob Brumfield .10 .05 .01
☐ 516 Jason Christiansen .10 .05 .01
☐ 517 Dave Clark .10 .05 .01
☐ 518 Midre Cummings .10 .05 .01
☐ 519 Angelo Encarnacion .10 .05 .01
☐ 520 John Ericks .10 .05 .01
☐ 521 Carlos Garcia .10 .05 .01
☐ 522 Mark Johnson .10 .05 .01

☐ 523 Jeff King	.25	.11	.03
☐ 524 Nelson Liriano	.10	.05	.01
☐ 525 Esteban Loaiza	.10	.05	.01
☐ 526 Al Martin	.10	.05	.01
☐ 527 Orlando Merced	.25	.11	.03
☐ 528 Dan Miceli	.10	.05	.01
☐ 529 Ramon Morel	.25	.11	.03
☐ 530 Denny Neagle	.25	.11	.03
☐ 531 Steve Parris	.10	.05	.01
☐ 532 Dan Plesac	.10	.05	.01
☐ 533 Don Slaught	.10	.05	.01
☐ 534 Paul Wagner	.10	.05	.01
☐ 535 John Wehner	.10	.05	.01
☐ 536 Kevin Young	.10	.05	.01
☐ 537 Allen Battle	.10	.05	.01
☐ 538 David Bell	.10	.05	.01
☐ 539 Alan Benes	.50	.23	.06
☐ 540 Scott Cooper	.10	.05	.01
☐ 541 Tripp Cromer	.10	.05	.01
☐ 542 Tony Fossas	.10	.05	.01
☐ 543 Bernard Gilkey	.25	.11	.03
☐ 544 Tom Henke	.25	.11	.03
☐ 545 Brian Jordan	.25	.11	.03
☐ 546 Ray Lankford	.25	.11	.03
☐ 547 John Mabry	.25	.11	.03
☐ 548 T.J. Mathews	.10	.05	.01
☐ 549 Mike Morgan	.10	.05	.01
☐ 550 Jose Oliva	.10	.05	.01
☐ 551 Jose Oquendo	.10	.05	.01
☐ 552 Donovan Osborne	.10	.05	.01
☐ 553 Tom Pagnozzi	.10	.05	.01
☐ 554 Mark Petkovsek	.10	.05	.01
☐ 555 Danny Sheaffer	.10	.05	.01
☐ 556 Ozzie Smith	.75	.35	.09
☐ 557 Mark Sweeney	.10	.05	.01
☐ 558 Allen Watson	.10	.05	.01
☐ 559 Andy Ashby	.10	.05	.01
☐ 560 Brad Ausmus	.10	.05	.01
☐ 561 Willie Blair	.10	.05	.01
☐ 562 Ken Caminiti	.50	.23	.06
☐ 563 Andujar Cedeno	.10	.05	.01
☐ 564 Glenn Dishman	.10	.05	.01
☐ 565 Steve Finley	.50	.23	.06
☐ 566 Bryce Florie	.10	.05	.01
☐ 567 Tony Gwynn	1.25	.55	.16
☐ 568 Joey Hamilton	.25	.11	.03
☐ 569 Dustin Hermanson UER	.10	.05	.01
☐ 570 Trevor Hoffman	.25	.11	.03
☐ 571 Brian Johnson	.10	.05	.01
☐ 572 Marc Kroon	.10	.05	.01
☐ 573 Scott Livingstone	.10	.05	.01
☐ 574 Marc Newfield	.10	.05	.01
☐ 575 Melvin Nieves	.25	.11	.03
☐ 576 Jody Reed	.10	.05	.01
☐ 577 Bip Roberts	.10	.05	.01
☐ 578 Scott Sanders	.10	.05	.01
☐ 579 Fernando Valenzuela	.25	.11	.03
☐ 580 Eddie Williams	.10	.05	.01
☐ 581 Rod Beck	.25	.11	.03
☐ 582 Marvin Benard	.10	.05	.01
☐ 583 Barry Bonds	.75	.35	.09
☐ 584 Jamie Brewington	.10	.05	.01
☐ 585 Mark Carreon	.10	.05	.01
☐ 586 Royce Clayton	.10	.05	.01
☐ 587 Shawn Estes	.25	.11	.03
☐ 588 Glenallen Hill	.25	.11	.03
☐ 589 Mark Leiter	.10	.05	.01
☐ 590 Kirt Manwaring	.10	.05	.01
☐ 591 David McCarty	.10	.05	.01
☐ 592 Terry Mulholland	.10	.05	.01
☐ 593 John Patterson	.10	.05	.01
☐ 594 J.R. Phillips	.10	.05	.01
☐ 595 Deion Sanders	.50	.23	.06
☐ 596 Steve Scarsone	.10	.05	.01
☐ 597 Robby Thompson	.10	.05	.01
☐ 598 Sergio Valdez	.10	.05	.01
☐ 599 William Van Landingham	.10	.05	.01
☐ 600 Matt Williams	.50	.23	.06
☐ P20 Cal Ripken Promo	2.00	.90	.25

1996 Fleer Tiffany

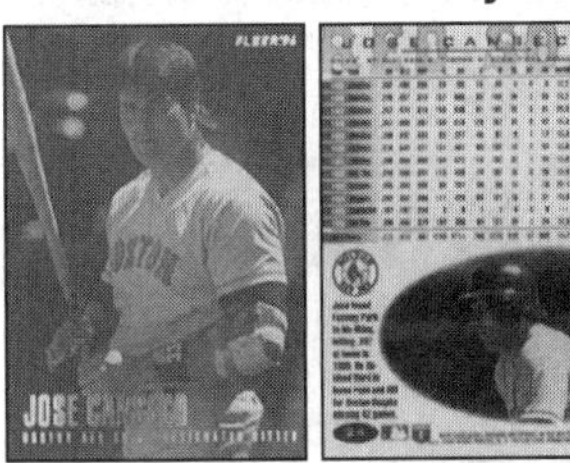

The Tiffany Collection is a 600-card parallel set that has a special UV coating that replaces the matte finish of the regular cards and silver holographic foil that takes the place of gold foil for lettering. These cards were inserted in regular packs at one card per pack.

	MINT	NRMT	EXC
COMPLETE SET (600)	250.00	110.00	31.00
COMMON CARD (1-600)	.25	.11	.03
*STARS: 2.5X to 5X BASIC CARDS			
*YOUNG STARS: 2X to 4X BASIC CARDS			

1996 Fleer Checklists

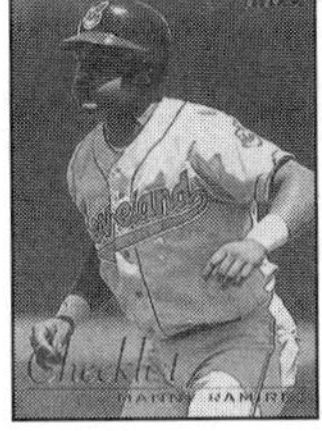

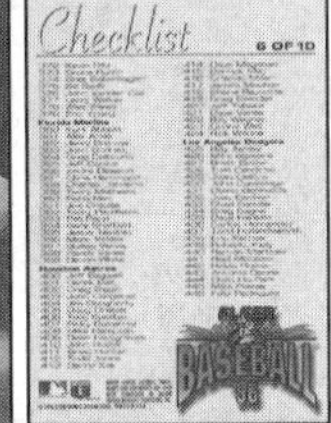

Checklist cards were seeded one per six regular packs and have glossy, borderless fronts with full-color shots of the Major League's best. "Checklist" and the player's name are stamped in gold foil. Backs list the entire rundown of '96 Fleer cards printed in black type on a white background.

	MINT	NRMT	EXC
COMPLETE SET (10)	5.00	2.20	.60
COMMON CARD (1-10)	.25	.11	.03
☐ 1 Barry Bonds	.40	.18	.05
☐ 2 Ken Griffey Jr.	1.50	.70	.19
☐ 3 Chipper Jones	1.00	.45	.12
☐ 4 Greg Maddux	1.00	.45	.12
☐ 5 Mike Piazza	1.00	.45	.12
☐ 6 Manny Ramirez	.40	.18	.05
☐ 7 Cal Ripken	1.25	.55	.16
☐ 8 Frank Thomas	1.50	.70	.19
☐ 9 Mo Vaughn	.40	.18	.05
☐ 10 Matt Williams			

1996 Fleer Golden Memories

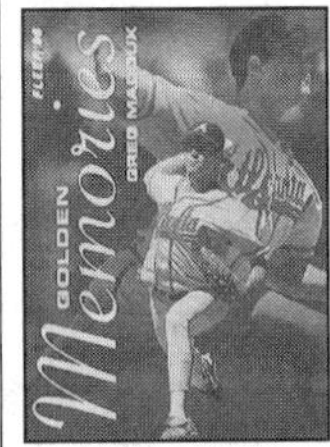

Randomly inserted at a rate of one in 10 regular packs, this 10-card standard-size set features important highlights of the 1995 season. Fronts have two action shots, one serving as a background, the other a full-color cutout. "Golden Memories" and player's name are printed vertically in white type. Backs contain a biography, player close-up and career statistics.

	MINT	NRMT	EXC
COMPLETE SET (10)	10.00	4.50	1.25
COMMON CARD (1-10)	.25	.11	.03
☐ 1 Albert Belle	2.00	.90	.25
☐ 2 Barry Bonds Sammy Sosa	1.25	.55	.16
☐ 3 Greg Maddux	3.00	1.35	.35
☐ 4 Edgar Martinez	.40	.18	.05
☐ 5 Ramon Martinez	.25	.11	.03
☐ 6 Mark McGwire	1.50	.70	.19
☐ 7 Eddie Murray	1.25	.55	.16
☐ 8 Cal Ripken	4.00	1.80	.50
☐ 9 Frank Thomas	5.00	2.20	.60
☐ 10 Alan Trammell Lou Whitaker	.40	.18	.05

1996 Fleer Lumber Company

This retail-exclusive 12-card set was inserted one in every nine packs and features RBI and HR power hitters. The fronts display a color action player cut-out on a wood background with embossed printing. The backs carry a player photo and information about the player.

	MINT	NRMT	EXC
COMPLETE SET (12)	30.00	13.50	3.70
COMMON CARD (1-12)	1.00	.45	.12
☐ 1 Albert Belle	4.00	1.80	.50
☐ 2 Dante Bichette	1.00	.45	.12
☐ 3 Barry Bonds	2.50	1.10	.30
☐ 4 Ken Griffey Jr.	10.00	4.50	1.25
☐ 5 Mark McGwire	3.00	1.35	.35
☐ 6 Mike Piazza	6.00	2.70	.75
☐ 7 Manny Ramirez	2.50	1.10	.30
☐ 8 Tim Salmon	1.00	.45	.12
☐ 9 Sammy Sosa	1.50	.70	.19
☐ 10 Frank Thomas	10.00	4.50	1.25
☐ 11 Mo Vaughn	2.50	1.10	.30
☐ 12 Matt Williams	1.00	.45	.12

1996 Fleer Postseason Glory

Randomly inserted in regular packs at a rate of one in five, this five-card standard-size set highlights great moments of the 1996 Divisional, League Championship and World Series games. Horizontal, white-bordered fronts feature a player in three full-color action cutouts with black strips on top and bottom. "Post-Season Glory" appears on top and the player's name is printed in silver hologram foil. White-bordered backs are split between a full-color player close-up and a description of his post-season play printed in white type on a black background.

	MINT	NRMT	EXC
COMPLETE SET (5)	2.00	.90	.25
COMMON CARD (1-5)	.10	.05	.01
☐ 1 Tom Glavine	.25	.11	.03
☐ 2 Ken Griffey Jr.	1.50	.70	.19
☐ 3 Orel Hershiser	.10	.05	.01
☐ 4 Randy Johnson	.25	.11	.03
☐ 5 Jim Thome	.25	.11	.03

1996 Fleer Prospects

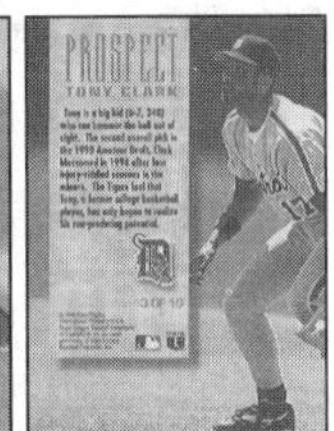

Randomly inserted at a rate of one in six regular packs, this ten-card standard-size set focuses on players moving up through the farm system. Borderless fronts have full-color head shots on one-color backgrounds. "Prospect" and the player's name are stamped in silver hologram foil. Backs feature a full-color action shot with a synopsis of talent printed in a green box.

	MINT	NRMT	EXC
COMPLETE SET (10)	5.00	2.20	.60
COMMON CARD (1-10)	.25	.11	.03
☐ 1 Yamil Benitez	.50	.23	.06
☐ 2 Roger Cedeno	.50	.23	.06
☐ 3 Tony Clark	1.50	.70	.19
☐ 4 Micah Franklin	.25	.11	.03
☐ 5 Karim Garcia	2.00	.90	.25
☐ 6 Todd Greene	.50	.23	.06
☐ 7 Alex Ochoa	.50	.23	.06
☐ 8 Ruben Rivera	1.50	.70	.19
☐ 9 Chris Snopek	.25	.11	.03
☐ 10 Shannon Stewart	.25	.11	.03

1996 Fleer Road Warriors

Randomly inserted in regular packs at a rate of one in 13, this 10-card standard-size set focuses on players who thrive on the road. Fronts feature a full-color player cutout set against a winding rural highway background. "Road Warriors" is printed in reverse type with a hazy white border and the player's name is printed in white type underneath. Backs include the player's road stats, biography and a close-up shot.

	MINT	NRMT	EXC
COMPLETE SET (10)	12.00	5.50	1.50
COMMON CARD (1-10)	.75	.35	.09
☐ 1 Derek Bell	.75	.35	.09
☐ 2 Tony Gwynn	2.00	.90	.25
☐ 3 Greg Maddux	3.00	1.35	.35
☐ 4 Mark McGwire	1.50	.70	.19
☐ 5 Mike Piazza	3.00	1.35	.35
☐ 6 Manny Ramirez	1.25	.55	.16
☐ 7 Tim Salmon	1.00	.45	.12
☐ 8 Frank Thomas	5.00	2.20	.60
☐ 9 Mo Vaughn	1.25	.55	.16
☐ 10 Matt Williams	1.00	.45	.12

1996 Fleer Rookie Sensations

Randomly inserted at a rate of one in 11 regular packs, this 15-card standard-size set highlights 1995's best rookies. Borderless, horizontal fronts have a full-color action shot and a silver hologram strip containing the player's name and team logo. Horizontal backs have full-color head shots with a player profile all printed on a white background.

	MINT	NRMT	EXC
COMPLETE SET (15)	20.00	9.00	2.50
COMMON CARD (1-15)	1.00	.45	.12
☐ 1 Garret Anderson	1.25	.55	.16
☐ 2 Marty Cordova	2.00	.90	.25
☐ 3 Johnny Damon	1.25	.55	.16
☐ 4 Ray Durham	1.50	.70	.19
☐ 5 Carl Everett	1.25	.55	.16
☐ 6 Shawn Green	1.00	.45	.12
☐ 7 Brian L.Hunter	1.25	.55	.16
☐ 8 Jason Isringhausen	1.25	.55	.16
☐ 9 Charles Johnson	1.25	.55	.16
☐ 10 Chipper Jones	10.00	4.50	1.25
☐ 11 John Mabry	1.25	.55	.16
☐ 12 Hideo Nomo	4.00	1.80	.50
☐ 13 Troy Percival	1.25	.55	.16
☐ 14 Andy Pettitte	5.00	2.20	.60
☐ 15 Quilvio Veras	1.00	.45	.12

1996 Fleer Smoke 'n Heat

Randomly inserted at a rate of one in nine regular packs, this 10-card standard-size set celebrates the pitchers with rifle arms and a high strikeout count. Fronts feature a full-color player cutout set against a red flame background. "Smoke 'n Heat" and the player's name are printed in gold type. Backs feature the pitcher's 1995 numbers, a biography and career stats along with a full-color close-up.

	MINT	NRMT	EXC
COMPLETE SET (10)	8.00	3.60	1.00
COMMON CARD (1-10)	.30	.14	.04
☐ 1 Kevin Appier	.60	.25	.07
☐ 2 Roger Clemens	1.00	.45	.12
☐ 3 David Cone	.60	.25	.07
☐ 4 Chuck Finley	.30	.14	.04
☐ 5 Randy Johnson	.75	.35	.09
☐ 6 Greg Maddux	3.00	1.35	.35
☐ 7 Pedro Martinez	.60	.25	.07
☐ 8 Hideo Nomo	1.25	.55	.16
☐ 9 John Smoltz	.75	.35	.09
☐ 10 Todd Stottlemyre	.30	.14	.04

1996 Fleer Team Leaders

This hobby-exclusive 28-card set was randomly inserted one in every nine packs and features statistical and inspirational leaders. The fronts display color action player cut-out on a foil background of the team name and logo. The backs carry a player portrait and player information.

	MINT	NRMT	EXC
COMPLETE SET (28)	80.00	36.00	10.00
COMMON CARD (1-28)	1.00	.45	.12
☐ 1 Cal Ripken	12.00	5.50	1.50
☐ 2 Mo Vaughn	4.00	1.80	.50

Card	MINT	NRMT	EXC
☐ 3 Jim Edmonds	1.50	.70	.19
☐ 4 Frank Thomas	15.00	6.75	1.85
☐ 5 Kenny Lofton	4.00	1.80	.50
☐ 6 Travis Fryman	1.50	.70	.19
☐ 7 Gary Gaetti	1.00	.45	.12
☐ 8 B.J. Surhoff	1.00	.45	.12
☐ 9 Kirby Puckett	6.00	2.70	.75
☐ 10 Don Mattingly	8.00	3.60	1.00
☐ 11 Mark McGwire	5.00	2.20	.60
☐ 12 Ken Griffey Jr.	15.00	6.75	1.85
☐ 13 Juan Gonzalez	8.00	3.60	1.00
☐ 14 Joe Carter	1.50	.70	.19
☐ 15 Greg Maddux	10.00	4.50	1.25
☐ 16 Sammy Sosa	2.50	1.10	.30
☐ 17 Barry Larkin	1.50	.70	.19
☐ 18 Dante Bichette	2.00	.90	.25
☐ 19 Jeff Conine	1.50	.70	.19
☐ 20 Jeff Bagwell	6.00	2.70	.75
☐ 21 Mike Piazza	10.00	4.50	1.25
☐ 22 Rondell White	1.50	.70	.19
☐ 23 Rico Brogna	1.00	.45	.12
☐ 24 Darren Daulton	1.50	.70	.19
☐ 25 Jeff King	1.00	.45	.12
☐ 26 Ray Lankford	1.50	.70	.19
☐ 27 Tony Gwynn	6.00	2.70	.75
☐ 28 Barry Bonds	4.00	1.80	.50

1996 Fleer Tomorrow's Legends

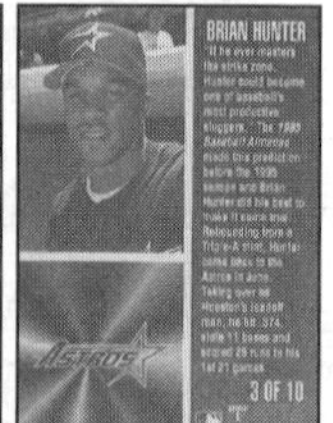

Randomly inserted in regular packs at a rate of one in 13, this 10-card set focuses on young talent with bright futures. Multicolored fronts have four panels of art that serve as a background and a full-color player cutout. "Tomorrow's Legends" and player's name are printed in white type at the bottom. Backs include the player's '95 stats, biography and a full-color close-up shot.

	MINT	NRMT	EXC
COMPLETE SET (10)	12.00	5.50	1.50
COMMON CARD (1-10)	1.00	.45	.12
☐ 1 Garret Anderson	1.00	.45	.12
☐ 2 Jim Edmonds	1.50	.70	.19
☐ 3 Brian L.Hunter	1.50	.70	.19
☐ 4 Jason Isringhausen			
☐ 5 Charles Johnson	1.50	.70	.19
☐ 6 Chipper Jones	8.00	3.60	1.00
☐ 7 Ryan Klesko			
☐ 8 Hideo Nomo	3.00	1.35	.35
☐ 9 Manny Ramirez	3.00	1.35	.35
☐ 10 Rondell White	1.50	.70	.19

1996 Fleer Zone

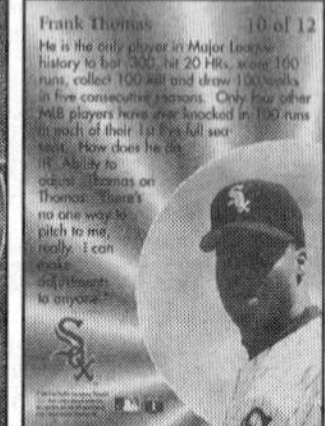

This 12-card set was randomly inserted one in every 90 packs and features "unstoppable" hitters and "unhittable" pitchers. The fronts display a color action player cut-out printed on holographic foil. The backs carry a player portrait with information as to why they were selected for this set.

	MINT	NRMT	EXC
COMPLETE SET (12)	225.00	100.00	28.00
COMMON CARD (1-12)	5.00	2.20	.60
☐ 1 Albert Belle	20.00	9.00	2.50
☐ 2 Barry Bonds	12.00	5.50	1.50
☐ 3 Ken Griffey Jr.	50.00	22.00	6.25
☐ 4 Tony Gwynn	20.00	9.00	2.50
☐ 5 Randy Johnson	8.00	3.60	1.00
☐ 6 Kenny Lofton	12.00	5.50	1.50
☐ 7 Greg Maddux	30.00	13.50	3.70
☐ 8 Edgar Martinez	5.00	2.20	.60
☐ 9 Mike Piazza	30.00	13.50	3.70
☐ 10 Frank Thomas	50.00	22.00	6.25
☐ 11 Mo Vaughn	12.00	5.50	1.50
☐ 12 Matt Williams	6.00	2.70	.75

1996 Fleer Update

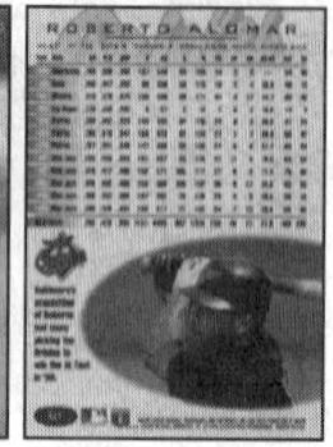

The 1996 Fleer Update set was issued in one series totalling 250 cards. The 11-card packs retail for $1.49 each. The fronts feature color action player photos. The backs carry complete player stats and a "Did you know?" fact. The cards are grouped alphabetically within teams and checklisted below alphabetically according to teams for each league with AL preceding NL. The set contains the subset: Encore (U211-U245). Notable Rookie Cards include Mike Cameron and Wilton Guerrero.

	MINT	NRMT	EXC
COMPLETE SET (250)	25.00	11.00	3.10
COMMON CARD (U1-U250)	.10	.05	.01
☐ U1 Roberto Alomar	.60	.25	.07
☐ U2 Mike Devereaux	.10	.05	.01
☐ U3 Scott McClain	.10	.05	.01
☐ U4 Roger McDowell	.10	.05	.01
☐ U5 Kent Mercker	.10	.05	.01
☐ U6 Jimmy Myers	.10	.05	.01
☐ U7 Randy Myers	.10	.05	.01
☐ U8 B.J. Surhoff	.10	.05	.01
☐ U9 Tony Tarasco	.10	.05	.01
☐ U10 David Wells	.10	.05	.01
☐ U11 Wil Cordero	.10	.05	.01
☐ U12 Tom Gordon	.10	.05	.01
☐ U13 Reggie Jefferson	.10	.05	.01
☐ U14 Jose Malave	.10	.05	.01
☐ U15 Kevin Mitchell	.10	.05	.01
☐ U16 Jamie Moyer	.10	.05	.01
☐ U17 Heathcliff Slocumb	.10	.05	.01
☐ U18 Mike Stanley	.10	.05	.01
☐ U19 George Arias	.10	.05	.01
☐ U20 Jorge Fabregas	.10	.05	.01
☐ U21 Don Slaught	.10	.05	.01
☐ U22 Randy Velarde	.10	.05	.01
☐ U23 Harold Baines	.25	.11	.03
☐ U24 Mike Cameron	1.00	.45	.12
☐ U25 Darren Lewis	.10	.05	.01
☐ U26 Tony Phillips	.25	.11	.03
☐ U27 Bill Simas	.10	.05	.01
☐ U28 Chris Snopek	.10	.05	.01
☐ U29 Kevin Tapani	.10	.05	.01
☐ U30 Danny Tartabull	.10	.05	.01
☐ U31 Julio Franco	.25	.11	.03
☐ U32 Jack McDowell	.50	.23	.06
☐ U33 Kimera Bartee	.10	.05	.01
☐ U34 Mark Lewis	.10	.05	.01
☐ U35 Melvin Nieves	.25	.11	.03
☐ U36 Mark Parent	.10	.05	.01
☐ U37 Eddie Williams	.10	.05	.01
☐ U38 Tim Belcher	.10	.05	.01
☐ U39 Sal Fasano	.10	.05	.01
☐ U40 Chris Haney	.10	.05	.01
☐ U41 Mike Macfarlane	.10	.05	.01
☐ U42 Jose Offerman	.10	.05	.01
☐ U43 Joe Randa	.10	.05	.01
☐ U44 Bip Roberts	.10	.05	.01
☐ U45 Chuck Carr	.10	.05	.01
☐ U46 Bobby Hughes	.10	.05	.01
☐ U47 Graeme Lloyd	.10	.05	.01
☐ U48 Ben McDonald	.10	.05	.01
☐ U49 Kevin Wickander	.10	.05	.01
☐ U50 Rick Aguilera	.10	.05	.01
☐ U51 Mike Durant	.10	.05	.01
☐ U52 Chip Hale	.10	.05	.01
☐ U53 LaTroy Hawkins	.10	.05	.01
☐ U54 Dave Hollins	.10	.05	.01
☐ U55 Roberto Kelly	.10	.05	.01
☐ U56 Paul Molitor	.60	.25	.07
☐ U57 Dan Naulty	.10	.05	.01
☐ U58 Mariano Duncan	.10	.05	.01
☐ U59 Andy Fox	.10	.05	.01
☐ U60 Joe Girardi	.10	.05	.01
☐ U61 Dwight Gooden	.25	.11	.03
☐ U62 Jimmy Key	.25	.11	.03
☐ U63 Matt Luke	.10	.05	.01
☐ U64 Tino Martinez	.25	.11	.03
☐ U65 Jeff Nelson	.10	.05	.01
☐ U66 Tim Raines	.50	.23	.06
☐ U67 Ruben Rivera	.60	.25	.07
☐ U68 Kenny Rogers	.10	.05	.01
☐ U69 Gerald Williams	.10	.05	.01
☐ U70 Tony Batista	.50	.23	.06
☐ U71 Allen Battle	.10	.05	.01
☐ U72 Jim Corsi	.10	.05	.01
☐ U73 Steve Cox	.10	.05	.01
☐ U74 Pedro Munoz	.10	.05	.01
☐ U75 Phil Plantier	.10	.05	.01
☐ U76 Scott Spiezio	.50	.23	.06
☐ U77 Ernie Young	.10	.05	.01
☐ U78 Russ Davis	.10	.05	.01
☐ U79 Sterling Hitchcock	.10	.05	.01
☐ U80 Edwin Hurtado	.10	.05	.01
☐ U81 Raul Ibanez	.10	.05	.01
☐ U82 Mike Jackson	.10	.05	.01
☐ U83 Ricky Jordan	.10	.05	.01
☐ U84 Paul Sorrento	.10	.05	.01
☐ U85 Doug Strange	.10	.05	.01
☐ U86 Mark Brandenberg	.10	.05	.01
☐ U87 Damon Buford	.10	.05	.01
☐ U88 Kevin Elster	.25	.11	.03
☐ U89 Darryl Hamilton	.10	.05	.01
☐ U90 Ken Hill	.25	.11	.03
☐ U91 Ed Vosberg	.10	.05	.01
☐ U92 Craig Worthington	.10	.05	.01
☐ U93 Tilson Brito	.10	.05	.01
☐ U94 Giovanni Carrara	.10	.05	.01
☐ U95 Felipe Crespo	.10	.05	.01
☐ U96 Erik Hanson	.10	.05	.01
☐ U97 Marty Janzen	.10	.05	.01
☐ U98 Otis Nixon	.10	.05	.01
☐ U99 Charlie O'Brien	.10	.05	.01
☐ U100 Robert Perez	.10	.05	.01
☐ U101 Paul Quantrill	.10	.05	.01
☐ U102 Bill Risley	.10	.05	.01
☐ U103 Juan Samuel	.10	.05	.01
☐ U104 Jermaine Dye	.60	.25	.07
☐ U105 Wonderful Monds	.10	.05	.01
☐ U106 Dwight Smith	.10	.05	.01
☐ U107 Jerome Walton	.10	.05	.01
☐ U108 Terry Adams	.10	.05	.01
☐ U109 Leo Gomez	.10	.05	.01
☐ U110 Robin Jennings	.10	.05	.01
☐ U111 Doug Jones	.10	.05	.01
☐ U112 Brooks Kieschnick	.50	.23	.06
☐ U113 Dave Magadan	.10	.05	.01
☐ U114 Jason Maxwell	.10	.05	.01
☐ U115 Rodney Myers	.10	.05	.01
☐ U116 Eric Anthony	.10	.05	.01
☐ U117 Vince Coleman	.10	.05	.01
☐ U118 Eric Davis	.25	.11	.03
☐ U119 Steve Gibralter	.10	.05	.01
☐ U120 Curtis Goodwin	.10	.05	.01
☐ U121 Willie Greene	.10	.05	.01
☐ U122 Mike Kelly	.10	.05	.01
☐ U123 Marcus Moore	.10	.05	.01
☐ U124 Chad Mottola	.10	.05	.01
☐ U125 Chris Sabo	.10	.05	.01
☐ U126 Roger Salkeld	.10	.05	.01
☐ U127 Pedro Castellano	.10	.05	.01
☐ U128 Trenidad Hubbard	.10	.05	.01
☐ U129 Jayhawk Owens	.10	.05	.01
☐ U130 Jeff Reed	.10	.05	.01
☐ U131 Kevin Brown	.25	.11	.03
☐ U132 Al Leiter	.10	.05	.01
☐ U133 Matt Mantei	.10	.05	.01
☐ U134 Dave Weathers	.10	.05	.01
☐ U135 Devon White	.10	.05	.01
☐ U136 Bob Abreu	.50	.23	.06
☐ U137 Sean Berry	.10	.05	.01
☐ U138 Doug Brocail	.10	.05	.01
☐ U139 Richard Hidalgo	.50	.23	.06
☐ U140 Alvin Morman	.10	.05	.01
☐ U141 Mike Blowers	.10	.05	.01
☐ U142 Roger Cedeno	.25	.11	.03
☐ U143 Greg Gagne	.10	.05	.01
☐ U144 Karim Garcia	.60	.25	.07
☐ U145 Wilton Guerrero	1.50	.70	.19
☐ U146 Israel Alcantara	.10	.05	.01
☐ U147 Omar Daal	.10	.05	.01
☐ U148 Ryan McGuire	.10	.05	.01
☐ U149 Sherman Obando	.10	.05	.01
☐ U150 Jose Paniagua	.10	.05	.01
☐ U151 Henry Rodriguez	.25	.11	.03
☐ U152 Andy Stankiewicz	.10	.05	.01
☐ U153 Dave Veres	.10	.05	.01
☐ U154 Juan Acevedo	.10	.05	.01
☐ U155 Mark Clark	.10	.05	.01
☐ U156 Bernard Gilkey	.25	.11	.03
☐ U157 Pete Harnisch	.10	.05	.01
☐ U158 Lance Johnson	.25	.11	.03
☐ U159 Brent Mayne	.10	.05	.01
☐ U160 Rey Ordonez	.50	.23	.06
☐ U161 Kevin Roberson	.10	.05	.01
☐ U162 Paul Wilson	.25	.11	.03
☐ U163 David Doster	.10	.05	.01
☐ U164 Mike Grace	.10	.05	.01
☐ U165 Rich Hunter	.10	.05	.01
☐ U166 Pete Incaviglia	.10	.05	.01
☐ U167 Mike Lieberthal	.10	.05	.01
☐ U168 Terry Mulholland	.10	.05	.01
☐ U169 Ken Ryan	.10	.05	.01
☐ U170 Benito Santiago	.10	.05	.01
☐ U171 Kevin Sefcik	.10	.05	.01
☐ U172 Lee Tinsley	.10	.05	.01
☐ U173 Todd Zeile	.25	.11	.03
☐ U174 Francisco Cordova	.10	.05	.01
☐ U175 Danny Darwin	.10	.05	.01
☐ U176 Charlie Hayes	.10	.05	.01
☐ U177 Jason Kendall	.50	.23	.06
☐ U178 Mike Kingery	.10	.05	.01
☐ U179 Jon Lieber	.10	.05	.01
☐ U180 Zane Smith	.10	.05	.01
☐ U181 Luis Alicea	.10	.05	.01
☐ U182 Cory Bailey	.10	.05	.01
☐ U183 Andy Benes	.10	.05	.01
☐ U184 Pat Borders	.10	.05	.01
☐ U185 Mike Busby	.10	.05	.01
☐ U186 Royce Clayton	.10	.05	.01
☐ U187 Dennis Eckersley	.25	.11	.03
☐ U188 Gary Gaetti	.25	.11	.03
☐ U189 Ron Gant	.25	.11	.03
☐ U190 Aaron Holbert	.10	.05	.01
☐ U191 Willie McGee	.10	.05	.01
☐ U192 Miguel Mejia	.10	.05	.01
☐ U193 Jeff Parrett	.10	.05	.01
☐ U194 Todd Stottlemyre	.10	.05	.01
☐ U195 Sean Bergman	.10	.05	.01
☐ U196 Archi Cianfrocco	.10	.05	.01
☐ U197 Rickey Henderson	.50	.23	.06
☐ U198 Wally Joyner	.10	.05	.01
☐ U199 Craig Shipley	.10	.05	.01
☐ U200 Bob Tewksbury	.10	.05	.01
☐ U201 Tim Worrell	.10	.05	.01
☐ U202 Rich Aurilia	.10	.05	.01
☐ U203 Doug Creek	.10	.05	.01
☐ U204 Shawon Dunston	.10	.05	.01
☐ U205 Osvaldo Fernandez	.50	.23	.06
☐ U206 Mark Gardner	.10	.05	.01
☐ U207 Stan Javier	.10	.05	.01
☐ U208 Marcus Jensen	.10	.05	.01
☐ U209 Chris Singleton	.10	.05	.01
☐ U210 Allen Watson	.10	.05	.01
☐ U211 Jeff Bagwell ENC	.60	.25	.07
☐ U212 Derek Bell ENC	.25	.11	.03
☐ U213 Albert Belle ENC	.60	.25	.07
☐ U214 Wade Boggs ENC	.50	.23	.06
☐ U215 Barry Bonds ENC	.50	.23	.06
☐ U216 Jose Canseco ENC	.50	.23	.06
☐ U217 Marty Cordova ENC	.25	.11	.03
☐ U218 Jim Edmonds ENC	.25	.11	.03
☐ U219 Cecil Fielder ENC	.25	.11	.03
☐ U220 Andres Galarraga ENC	.50	.23	.06
☐ U221 Juan Gonzalez ENC	.75	.35	.09
☐ U222 Mark Grace ENC	.50	.23	.06
☐ U223 Ken Griffey Jr. ENC	1.50	.70	.19
☐ U224 Tony Gwynn ENC	.60	.25	.07
☐ U225 Jason Isringhausen ENC	.50	.23	.06
☐ U226 Derek Jeter ENC	1.00	.45	.12
☐ U227 Randy Johnson ENC	.50	.23	.06
☐ U228 Chipper Jones ENC	1.00	.45	.12
☐ U229 Ryan Klesko ENC	.50	.23	.06
☐ U230 Barry Larkin ENC	.50	.23	.06
☐ U231 Kenny Lofton ENC	.50	.23	.06
☐ U232 Greg Maddux ENC	1.00	.45	.12
☐ U233 Raul Mondesi ENC	.50	.23	.06
☐ U234 Hideo Nomo ENC	.50	.23	.06
☐ U235 Mike Piazza ENC	1.00	.45	.12
☐ U236 Manny Ramirez ENC	.25	.11	.03
☐ U237 Cal Ripken ENC	1.25	.55	.16
☐ U238 Tim Salmon ENC	.50	.23	.06
☐ U239 Ryne Sandberg ENC	.50	.23	.06
☐ U240 Reggie Sanders ENC	.25	.11	.03
☐ U241 Gary Sheffield ENC	.50	.23	.06
☐ U242 Sammy Sosa ENC	.50	.23	.06
☐ U243 Frank Thomas ENC	1.50	.70	.19
☐ U244 Mo Vaughn ENC	.50	.23	.06
☐ U245 Matt Williams ENC	.50	.23	.06
☐ U246 Barry Bonds CL	.50	.23	.06
☐ U247 Ken Griffey Jr. CL	1.50	.70	.19
☐ U248 Rey Ordonez CL	.50	.23	.06
☐ U249 Ryne Sandberg CL	.50	.23	.06
☐ U250 Frank Thomas CL	1.50	.70	.19

1996 Fleer Update Tiffany

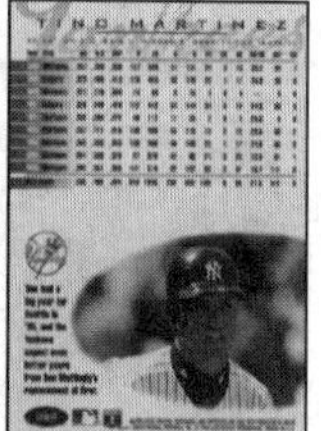

Inserted one per pack, these 250 cards parallel the basic Fleer Update cards. Unlike the basic cards, Tiffany inserts feature a layer of UV coating and a special logo on each card front.

	MINT	NRMT	EXC
COMPLETE SET (250)	125.00	55.00	15.50
COMMON CARD (U1-U250)	.25	.11	.03

*STARS: 2.5X TO 5X BASIC CARDS
*YOUNG STARS: 2X TO 4X BASIC CARDS

1996 Fleer Update Diamond Tribute

Randomly inserted in packs at a rate of one in 100, this 10-card set spotlights future Hall of Famers with holographic foils in a diamond design.

	MINT	NRMT	EXC
COMPLETE SET (10)	200.00	90.00	25.00
COMMON CARD (1-10)	6.00	2.70	.75
☐ 1 Wade Boggs	6.00	2.70	.75
☐ 2 Barry Bonds	12.00	5.50	1.50
☐ 3 Ken Griffey Jr.	50.00	22.00	6.25
☐ 4 Tony Gwynn	20.00	9.00	2.50
☐ 5 Rickey Henderson	6.00	2.70	.75
☐ 6 Greg Maddux	30.00	13.50	3.70
☐ 7 Eddie Murray	12.00	5.50	1.50
☐ 8 Cal Ripken	40.00	18.00	5.00
☐ 9 Ozzie Smith	12.00	5.50	1.50
☐ 10 Frank Thomas	50.00	22.00	6.25

1996 Fleer Update Headliners

Randomly inserted exclusively in retail packs at a rate of one in 20, cards from this 20-card set feature raised textured printing. The fronts carry color action player photos with the word "headliner" running continuously across the background.

	MINT	NRMT	EXC
COMPLETE SET (20)	50.00	22.00	6.25
COMMON CARD (1-20)	1.00	.45	.12
☐ 1 Roberto Alomar	1.50	.70	.19
☐ 2 Jeff Bagwell	3.00	1.35	.35
☐ 3 Albert Belle	3.00	1.35	.35
☐ 4 Barry Bonds	2.00	.90	.25
☐ 5 Cecil Fielder	1.00	.45	.12
☐ 6 Juan Gonzalez	4.00	1.80	.50
☐ 7 Ken Griffey Jr.	8.00	3.60	1.00
☐ 8 Tony Gwynn	3.00	1.35	.35
☐ 9 Randy Johnson	1.25	.55	.16
☐ 10 Chipper Jones	5.00	2.20	.60
☐ 11 Ryan Klesko	1.25	.55	.16
☐ 12 Kenny Lofton	2.00	.90	.25
☐ 13 Greg Maddux	5.00	2.20	.60
☐ 14 Hideo Nomo	2.00	.90	.25
☐ 15 Mike Piazza	5.00	2.20	.60
☐ 16 Manny Ramirez	2.00	.90	.25
☐ 17 Cal Ripken	6.00	2.70	.75
☐ 18 Tim Salmon	1.25	.55	.16
☐ 19 Frank Thomas	8.00	3.60	1.00
☐ 20 Matt Williams	1.25	.55	.16

1996 Fleer Update New Horizons

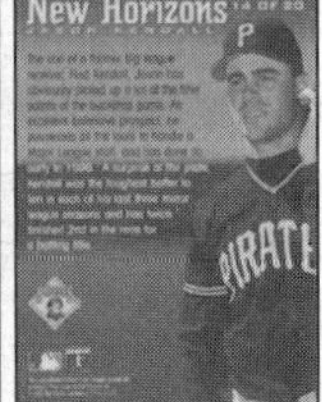

Randomly inserted in hobby packs only at a rate of one in five, this 20-card set features 1996 rookies and prospects. The fronts carry player action color photos printed on foil cards. The backs display a player portrait and information about the player.

	MINT	NRMT	EXC
COMPLETE SET (20)	15.00	6.75	1.85
COMMON CARD (1-20)	.50	.23	.06
☐ 1 Bob Abreu	1.00	.45	.12
☐ 2 George Arias	.50	.23	.06
☐ 3 Tony Batista	1.25	.55	.16
☐ 4 Steve Cox	.50	.23	.06
☐ 5 Jermaine Dye	2.00	.90	.25
☐ 6 Andy Fox	.50	.23	.06
☐ 7 Mike Grace	.50	.23	.06
☐ 8 Todd Greene	.75	.35	.09
☐ 9 Wilton Guerrero	4.00	1.80	.50
☐ 10 Richard Hidalgo	1.50	.70	.19
☐ 11 Raul Ibanez	.50	.23	.06
☐ 12 Robin Jennings	.50	.23	.06
☐ 13 Marcus Jensen	.50	.23	.06
☐ 14 Jason Kendall	2.00	.90	.25
☐ 15 Jason Maxwell	.50	.23	.06
☐ 16 Ryan McGuire	.50	.23	.06
☐ 17 Miguel Mejia	.50	.23	.06
☐ 18 Wonderful Monds	.50	.23	.06
☐ 19 Rey Ordonez	1.50	.70	.19
☐ 20 Paul Wilson	.75	.35	.09

1996 Fleer Update Smooth Leather

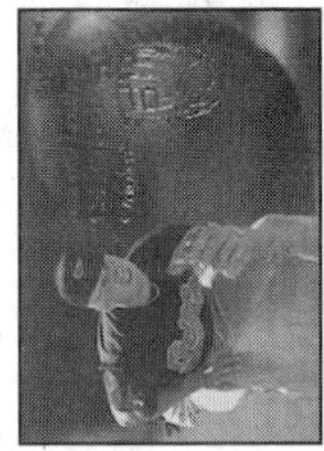

Randomly inserted in packs at a rate of one in 5, this 10-card set features ten defensive stars. The fronts display color player photos and gold foil printing. The backs carry a player portrait and information about why the player was selected for this set.

	MINT	NRMT	EXC
COMPLETE SET (10)	10.00	4.50	1.25
COMMON CARD (1-10)	.50	.23	.06
☐ 1 Roberto Alomar	.75	.35	.09
☐ 2 Barry Bonds	1.00	.45	.12
☐ 3 Will Clark	.50	.23	.06
☐ 4 Ken Griffey Jr.	4.00	1.80	.50
☐ 5 Kenny Lofton	1.00	.45	.12
☐ 6 Greg Maddux	2.50	1.10	.30
☐ 7 Raul Mondesi	.50	.23	.06
☐ 8 Rey Ordonez	.50	.23	.06
☐ 9 Cal Ripken	3.00	1.35	.35
☐ 10 Matt Williams	.50	.23	.06

1996 Fleer Update Soaring Stars

Randomly inserted in packs at a rate of one in 11, this 10-card set features 10 of the hottest young players. The fronts carry color player cut-outs on a background of soaring baseballs in etched foil. The backs display another player photo on the same background with player information.

	MINT	NRMT	EXC
COMPLETE SET (10)	30.00	13.50	3.70
COMMON CARD (1-10)	1.00	.45	.12
☐ 1 Jeff Bagwell	3.00	1.35	.35
☐ 2 Barry Bonds	2.00	.90	.25
☐ 3 Juan Gonzalez	4.00	1.80	.50
☐ 4 Ken Griffey Jr.	8.00	3.60	1.00
☐ 5 Chipper Jones	5.00	2.20	.60
☐ 6 Greg Maddux	5.00	2.20	.60
☐ 7 Mike Piazza	5.00	2.20	.60
☐ 8 Manny Ramirez	2.00	.90	.25
☐ 9 Frank Thomas	8.00	3.60	1.00
☐ 10 Matt Williams	1.00	.45	.12

1996 Fleer Braves

These 20 standard-size cards feature the same design as the regular Fleer issue, except they are UV coated, use silver foil and are numbered "x of 20". The team set packs were available at retail locations and hobby shops in 10-card packs for a suggested retail price of $1.99.

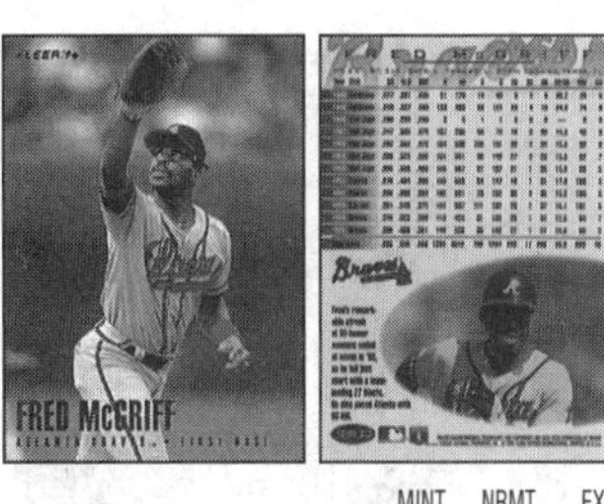

	MINT	NRMT	EXC
COMPLETE SET (20)	6.00	2.70	.75
COMMON CARD (1-20)	.10	.05	.01
☐ 1 Steve Avery	.20	.09	.03
☐ 2 Jeff Blauser	.10	.05	.01
☐ 3 Brad Clontz	.10	.05	.01
☐ 4 Tom Glavine	.50	.23	.06
☐ 5 Marquis Grissom	.20	.09	.03
☐ 6 Chipper Jones	2.00	.90	.25
☐ 7 David Justice	.30	.14	.04
☐ 8 Ryan Klesko	1.00	.45	.12
☐ 9 Mark Lemke	.10	.05	.01
☐ 10 Javier Lopez	.40	.18	.05
☐ 11 Greg Maddux	2.00	.90	.25
☐ 12 Fred McGriff	.40	.18	.05
☐ 13 Greg McMichael	.10	.05	.01
☐ 14 Eddie Perez	.10	.05	.01
☐ 15 Jason Schmidt	.30	.14	.04
☐ 16 John Smoltz	.40	.18	.05
☐ 17 Terrell Wade	.20	.09	.03
☐ 18 Mark Wohlers	.30	.14	.04
☐ 19 Logo card	.10	.05	.01
☐ 20 Checklist	.10	.05	.01

1996 Fleer Cubs

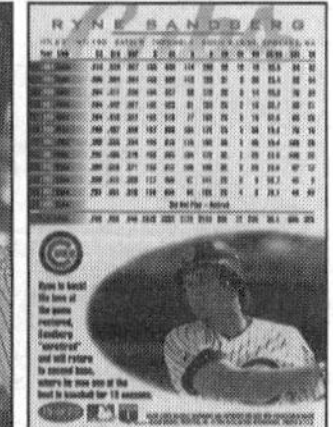

These 20 standard-size cards feature the same design as the regular Fleer issue, except they are UV coated, use silver foil and are numbered "x of 20". The team set packs were available at retail locations and hobby shops in 10-card packs for a suggested retail price of $1.99.

	MINT	NRMT	EXC
COMPLETE SET (20)	5.00	2.20	.60
COMMON CARD (1-20)	.10	.05	.01
☐ 1 Terry Adams	.10	.05	.01
☐ 2 Jim Bullinger	.10	.05	.01
☐ 3 Frank Castillo	.10	.05	.01
☐ 4 Kevin Foster	.10	.05	.01
☐ 5 Leo Gomez	.10	.05	.01
☐ 6 Luis Gonzalez	.20	.09	.03
☐ 7 Mark Grace	1.00	.45	.12
☐ 8 Jose Hernandez	.10	.05	.01
☐ 9 Robin Jennings	.10	.05	.01
☐ 10 Doug Jones	.10	.05	.01
☐ 11 Brooks Kieschnick	.30	.14	.04
☐ 12 Brian McRae	.20	.09	.03
☐ 13 Jaime Navarro	.10	.05	.01
☐ 14 Rey Sanchez	.10	.05	.01
☐ 15 Ryne Sandberg	1.50	.70	.19
☐ 16 Scott Servais	.10	.05	.01
☐ 17 Sammy Sosa	.75	.35	.09
☐ 18 Steve Trachsel	.10	.05	.01
☐ 19 Logo card	.10	.05	.01
☐ 20 Checklist	.10	.05	.01

1996 Fleer Dodgers

These 20 standard-size cards feature the same design as the regular Fleer issue, except they are UV coated, use silver foil and are numbered "x of 20". The team set packs were available at retail locations and hobby shops in 10-card packs for a suggested retail price of $1.99.

	MINT	NRMT	EXC
COMPLETE SET (20)	6.00	2.70	.75
COMMON CARD (1-20)	.15	.07	.02
☐ 1 Mike Blowers	.15	.07	.02
☐ 2 Brett Butler	.40	.18	.05
☐ 3 Tom Candiotti	.15	.07	.02
☐ 4 Roger Cedeno	.25	.11	.03
☐ 5 Delino DeShields	.15	.07	.02
☐ 6 Chad Fonville	.15	.07	.02
☐ 7 Greg Gagne	.15	.07	.02
☐ 8 Karim Garcia	.50	.23	.06
☐ 9 Todd Hollandsworth	.40	.18	.05
☐ 10 Eric Karros	.40	.18	.05
☐ 11 Ramon Martinez	.40	.18	.05
☐ 12 Raul Mondesi	.75	.35	.09
☐ 13 Hideo Nomo	2.00	.90	.25
☐ 14 Antonio Osuna	.15	.07	.02
☐ 15 Chan Ho Park	.40	.18	.05
☐ 16 Mike Piazza	2.50	1.10	.30
☐ 17 Ismael Valdes	.25	.11	.03
☐ 18 Todd Worrell	.25	.11	.03
☐ 19 Logo card	.15	.07	.02
☐ 20 Checklist	.15	.07	.02

1996 Fleer Indians

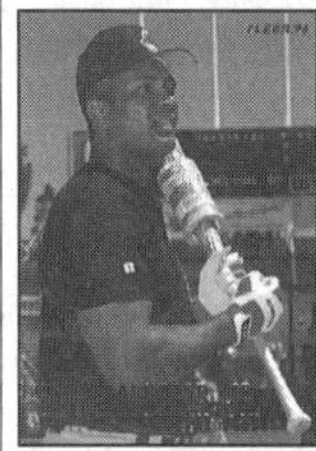
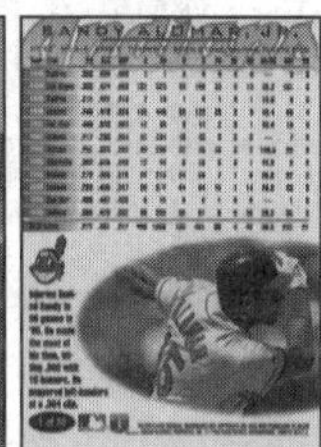

This 20-card standard-size set was issued by Fleer as a test to see how regional team issues would sell. These cards are different from the regular 1996 Fleer issues as the 10-card packs feature the Indians logo. The cards have silver-foil and are issued with UV coating and they are numbered "X" of 20. The set is sequenced in alphabetical order.

	MINT	NRMT	EXC
COMPLETE SET (20)	6.00	2.70	.75
COMMON CARD (1-20)	.10	.05	.01
☐ 1 Sandy Alomar Jr.	.25	.11	.03
☐ 2 Paul Assenmacher	.10	.05	.01
☐ 3 Carlos Baerga	.75	.35	.09
☐ 4 Albert Belle	1.50	.70	.19
☐ 5 Orel Hershiser	.25	.11	.03
☐ 6 Kenny Lofton	1.00	.45	.12
☐ 7 Dennis Martinez	.25	.11	.03
☐ 8 Jose Mesa	.25	.11	.03
☐ 9 Eddie Murray	.50	.23	.06
☐ 10 Charles Nagy	.25	.11	.03
☐ 11 Tony Pena	.10	.05	.01
☐ 12 Herb Perry	.10	.05	.01
☐ 13 Eric Plunk	.10	.05	.01
☐ 14 Jim Poole	.10	.05	.01
☐ 15 Manny Ramirez	.75	.35	.09
☐ 16 Julian Tavarez	.10	.05	.01
☐ 17 Jim Thome	1.00	.45	.12
☐ 18 Omar Vizquel	.25	.11	.03
☐ 19 Indians Logo	.10	.05	.01
☐ 20 Indians CL	.10	.05	.01

1996 Fleer Orioles

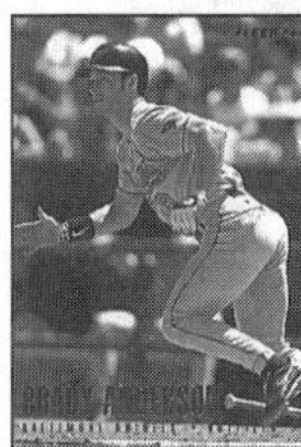

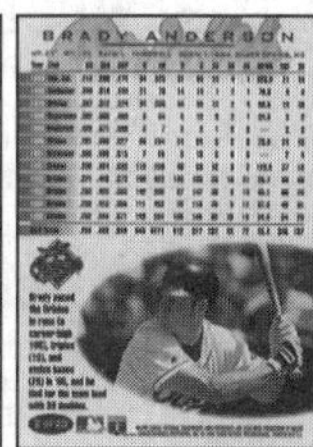

These 20 standard-size cards feature the same design as the regular Fleer issue, except they are UV coated, use silver foil and are numbered "x of 20". The team set packs were available at retail locations and hobby shops in 10-card packs for a suggested retail price of $1.99.

	MINT	NRMT	EXC
COMPLETE SET (20)	6.00	2.70	.75
COMMON CARD (1-20)	.10	.05	.01
☐ 1 Roberto Alomar	1.00	.45	.12
☐ 2 Brady Anderson	.75	.35	.09
☐ 3 Armando Benitez	.10	.05	.01
☐ 4 Bobby Bonilla	.30	.14	.04
☐ 5 Scott Erickson	.10	.05	.01
☐ 6 Jeffrey Hammonds	.10	.05	.01
☐ 7 Jimmy Haynes	.10	.05	.01
☐ 8 Chris Hoiles	.10	.05	.01

	MINT	NRMT	EXC
☐ 9 Rick Krivda	.10	.05	.01
☐ 10 Kent Mercker	.10	.05	.01
☐ 11 Mike Mussina	.75	.35	.09
☐ 12 Randy Myers	.10	.05	.01
☐ 13 Jesse Orosco	.10	.05	.01
☐ 14 Rafael Palmeiro	.50	.23	.06
☐ 15 Cal Ripken	3.00	1.35	.35
☐ 16 B.J. Surhoff	.20	.09	.03
☐ 17 Tony Tarasco	.10	.05	.01
☐ 18 David Wells	.10	.05	.01
☐ 19 Logo card	.10	.05	.01
☐ 20 Checklist	.10	.05	.01

1996 Fleer Rangers

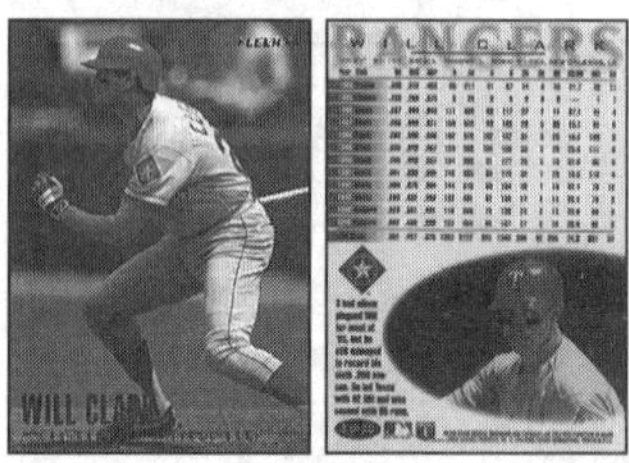

These 20 standard-size cards have the same design as the regular Fleer issue, except they are UV coated, use silver foil and are numbered "x of 20". The team set packs were available at retail locations and hobby shops in 10-card packs for a suggested price of $1.99.

	MINT	NRMT	EXC
COMPLETE SET (20)	5.00	2.20	.60
COMMON CARD (1-20)	.10	.05	.01
☐ 1 Mark Brandenburg	.10	.05	.01
☐ 2 Damon Buford	.10	.05	.01
☐ 3 Will Clark	.75	.35	.09
☐ 4 Kevin Elster	.10	.05	.01
☐ 5 Benji Gil	.10	.05	.01
☐ 6 Juan Gonzalez	1.50	.70	.19
☐ 7 Rusty Greer	.50	.23	.06
☐ 8 Kevin Gross	.10	.05	.01
☐ 9 Darryl Hamilton	.10	.05	.01
☐ 10 Ken Hill	.20	.09	.03
☐ 11 Mark McLemore	.10	.05	.01
☐ 12 Dean Palmer	.50	.23	.06
☐ 13 Roger Pavlik	.20	.09	.03
☐ 14 Ivan Rodriguez	1.00	.45	.12
☐ 15 Mickey Tettleton	.20	.09	.03
☐ 16 Dave Valle	.10	.05	.01
☐ 17 Ed Vosberg	.10	.05	.01
☐ 18 Matt Whiteside	.10	.05	.01
☐ 19 Logo card	.10	.05	.01
☐ 20 Checklist	.10	.05	.01

1996 Fleer Red Sox

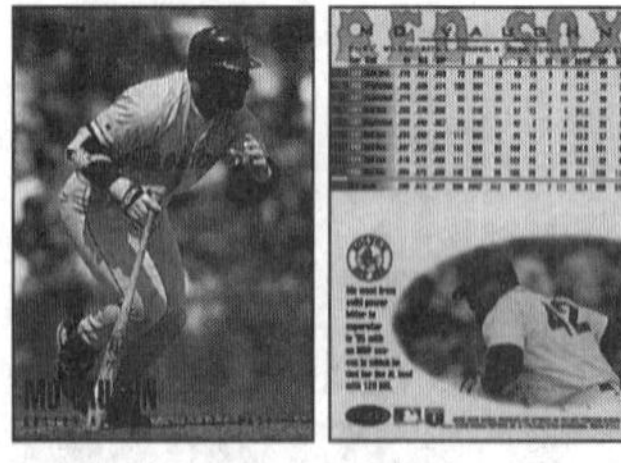

These 20 standard-size cards feature the same design as the regular Fleer issue, except they are UV coated, use silver foil and are numbered "x of 20". The team set packs were available at retail locations and hobby shops in 10-card packs for a suggested retail price of $1.99.

	MINT	NRMT	EXC
COMPLETE SET (20)	5.00	2.20	.60
COMMON CARD (1-20)	.10	.05	.01
☐ 1 Stan Belinda	.10	.05	.01
☐ 2 Jose Canseco	.50	.23	.06
☐ 3 Roger Clemens	.75	.35	.09
☐ 4 Wil Cordero	.20	.09	.03
☐ 5 Vaughn Eshelman	.10	.05	.01
☐ 6 Tom Gordon	.10	.05	.01
☐ 7 Mike Greenwell	.20	.09	.03
☐ 8 Dwayne Hosey	.10	.05	.01
☐ 9 Kevin Mitchell	.20	.09	.03
☐ 10 Tim Naehring	.20	.09	.03
☐ 11 Troy O'Leary	.10	.05	.01
☐ 12 Aaron Sele	.20	.09	.03
☐ 13 Heathcliff Slocumb	.20	.09	.03
☐ 14 Mike Stanley	.10	.05	.01
☐ 15 Jeff Suppan	.50	.23	.06
☐ 16 John Valentin	.20	.09	.03
☐ 17 Mo Vaughn	1.50	.70	.19
☐ 18 Tim Wakefield	.10	.05	.01
☐ 19 Logo card	.10	.05	.01
☐ 20 Checklist	.10	.05	.01

1996 Fleer Rockies

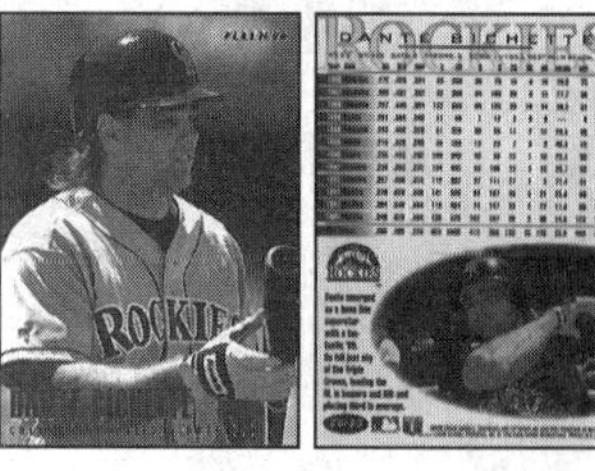

These 20 standard-size cards are same as the regular Fleer issue, except they are UV coated, they use silver foil and they are numbered "x of 20". The team set packs were available at retail locations and hobby shops in 10-card packs for a suggested price of $1.99.

	MINT	NRMT	EXC
COMPLETE SET (20)	6.00	2.70	.75
COMMON CARD (1-20)	.10	.05	.01
☐ 1 Jason Bates	.10	.05	.01
☐ 2 Dante Bichette	.75	.35	.09
☐ 3 Ellis Burks	.60	.25	.07
☐ 4 Vinny Castilla	.60	.25	.07
☐ 5 Andres Galarraga	1.00	.45	.12
☐ 6 Darren Holmes	.10	.05	.01
☐ 7 Curt Leskanic	.10	.05	.01
☐ 8 Quinton McCracken	.10	.05	.01
☐ 9 Mike Munoz	.10	.05	.01
☐ 10 Jayhawk Owens	.10	.05	.01
☐ 11 Steve Reed	.10	.05	.01
☐ 12 Kevin Ritz	.20	.09	.03
☐ 13 Bret Saberhagen	.10	.05	.01
☐ 14 Bill Swift	.10	.05	.01
☐ 15 John Vander Wal	.10	.05	.01
☐ 16 Larry Walker	1.00	.45	.12
☐ 17 Walt Weiss	.20	.09	.03
☐ 18 Eric Young	.20	.09	.03
☐ 19 Logo card	.10	.05	.01
☐ 20 Checklist	.10	.05	.01

1996 Fleer White Sox

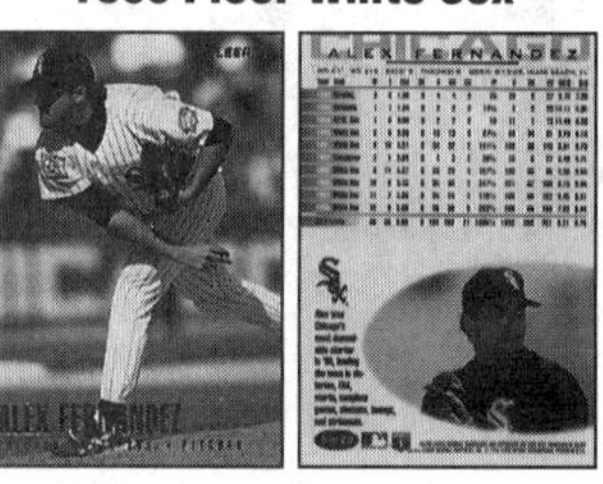

These 20 standard-size cards have the same design as the regular Fleer issue, except they are UV coated, they use silver foil and they are numbered "x of 20". The team set packs were available at retail locations and hobby shops in 10-card packs for a suggested price of $1.99.

	MINT	NRMT	EXC
COMPLETE SET (20)	6.00	2.70	.75
COMMON CARD (1-20)	.10	.05	.01
☐ 1 Wilson Alvarez	.20	.09	.03
☐ 2 Harold Baines	.20	.09	.03
☐ 3 Jason Bere	.10	.05	.01
☐ 4 Ray Durham	.30	.14	.04
☐ 5 Alex Fernandez	.40	.18	.05
☐ 6 Ozzie Guillen	.10	.05	.01
☐ 7 Roberto Hernandez	.20	.09	.03
☐ 8 Matt Karchner	.10	.05	.01
☐ 9 Ron Karkovice	.10	.05	.01
☐ 10 Darren Lewis	.10	.05	.01
☐ 11 Dave Martinez	.10	.05	.01
☐ 12 Lyle Mouton	.10	.05	.01
☐ 13 Tony Phillips	.20	.09	.03
☐ 14 Chris Snopek	.10	.05	.01
☐ 15 Kevin Tapani	.10	.05	.01
☐ 16 Danny Tartabull	.10	.05	.01
☐ 17 Frank Thomas	3.00	1.35	.35
☐ 18 Robin Ventura	.50	.23	.06
☐ 19 Logo card	.10	.05	.01
☐ 20 Checklist	.10	.05	.01

1997 Fleer

This 500-card set features color action player photos with a matte finish and gold foil printing. The backs carry another player photo with player information and career statistics. The last 10 cards (#491-500) are a Checklist subset and feature black-and-white or sepia tone photos of big-name players.

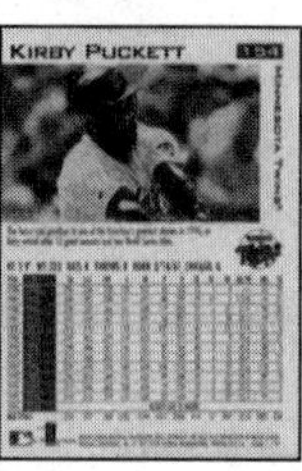

	MINT	NRMT	EXC
COMPLETE SET (500)	50.00	22.00	6.25
COMMON CARD (1-500)	.10	.05	.01
☐ 1 Roberto Alomar	.60	.25	.07
☐ 2 Brady Anderson	.25	.11	.03
☐ 3 Bobby Bonilla	.25	.11	.03
☐ 4 Rocky Coppinger	.25	.11	.03
☐ 5 Cesar Devarez	.10	.05	.01
☐ 6 Scott Erickson	.10	.05	.01
☐ 7 Jeffrey Hammonds	.10	.05	.01
☐ 8 Chris Hoiles	.10	.05	.01
☐ 9 Eddie Murray	.75	.35	.09
☐ 10 Mike Mussina	.60	.25	.07
☐ 11 Randy Myers	.10	.05	.01
☐ 12 Rafael Palmeiro	.40	.18	.05
☐ 13 Cal Ripken	2.50	1.10	.30
☐ 14 B.J. Surhoff	.10	.05	.01
☐ 15 David Wells	.10	.05	.01
☐ 16 Todd Zeile	.10	.05	.01
☐ 17 Darren Bragg	.10	.05	.01
☐ 18 Jose Canseco	.40	.18	.05
☐ 19 Roger Clemens	.60	.25	.07
☐ 20 Wil Cordero	.10	.05	.01
☐ 21 Jeff Frye	.10	.05	.01
☐ 22 Nomar Garciaparra	1.25	.55	.16
☐ 23 Tom Gordon	.10	.05	.01
☐ 24 Mike Greenwell	.10	.05	.01
☐ 25 Reggie Jefferson	.10	.05	.01
☐ 26 Jose Malave	.10	.05	.01
☐ 27 Tim Naehring	.10	.05	.01
☐ 28 Troy O'Leary	.10	.05	.01
☐ 29 Heathcliff Slocumb	.10	.05	.01
☐ 30 Mike Stanley	.10	.05	.01
☐ 31 John Valentin	.10	.05	.01
☐ 32 Mo Vaughn	.75	.35	.09
☐ 33 Tim Wakefield	.10	.05	.01
☐ 34 Garret Anderson	.10	.05	.01
☐ 35 George Arias	.10	.05	.01
☐ 36 Shawn Boskie	.10	.05	.01
☐ 37 Chili Davis	.10	.05	.01
☐ 38 Jason Dickson	.25	.11	.03
☐ 39 Gary DiSarcina	.10	.05	.01
☐ 40 Jim Edmonds	.25	.11	.03
☐ 41 Darin Erstad	1.50	.70	.19
☐ 42 Jorge Fabregas	.10	.05	.01
☐ 43 Chuck Finley	.10	.05	.01
☐ 44 Todd Greene	.10	.05	.01
☐ 45 Mike Holtz	.10	.05	.01
☐ 46 Rex Hudler	.10	.05	.01
☐ 47 Mike James	.10	.05	.01
☐ 48 Mark Langston	.10	.05	.01
☐ 49 Troy Percival	.10	.05	.01
☐ 50 Tim Salmon	.40	.18	.05
☐ 51 Jeff Schmidt	.10	.05	.01
☐ 52 J.T. Snow	.10	.05	.01
☐ 53 Randy Velarde	.10	.05	.01
☐ 54 Wilson Alvarez	.10	.05	.01
☐ 55 Harold Baines	.10	.05	.01
☐ 56 James Baldwin	.10	.05	.01
☐ 57 Jason Bere	.10	.05	.01
☐ 58 Mike Cameron	.50	.23	.06
☐ 59 Ray Durham	.10	.05	.01
☐ 60 Alex Fernandez	.25	.11	.03
☐ 61 Ozzie Guillen	.10	.05	.01
☐ 62 Roberto Hernandez	.10	.05	.01
☐ 63 Ron Karkovice	.10	.05	.01
☐ 64 Darren Lewis	.10	.05	.01
☐ 65 Dave Martinez	.10	.05	.01
☐ 66 Lyle Mouton	.10	.05	.01
☐ 67 Greg Norton	.10	.05	.01
☐ 68 Tony Phillips	.10	.05	.01
☐ 69 Chris Snopek	.10	.05	.01
☐ 70 Kevin Tapani	.10	.05	.01
☐ 71 Danny Tartabull	.10	.05	.01
☐ 72 Frank Thomas	3.00	1.35	.35
☐ 73 Robin Ventura	.25	.11	.03
☐ 74 Sandy Alomar Jr.	.10	.05	.01
☐ 75 Albert Belle	1.25	.55	.16
☐ 76 Mark Carreon	.10	.05	.01
☐ 77 Julio Franco	.10	.05	.01
☐ 78 Brian Giles	.10	.05	.01
☐ 79 Orel Hershiser	.25	.11	.03
☐ 80 Kenny Lofton	.75	.35	.09
☐ 81 Dennis Martinez	.10	.05	.01
☐ 82 Jack McDowell	.10	.05	.01
☐ 83 Jose Mesa	.10	.05	.01
☐ 84 Charles Nagy	.25	.11	.03
☐ 85 Chad Ogea	.10	.05	.01
☐ 86 Eric Plunk	.10	.05	.01
☐ 87 Manny Ramirez	.75	.35	.09
☐ 88 Kevin Seitzer	.10	.05	.01
☐ 89 Julian Tavarez	.10	.05	.01
☐ 90 Jim Thome	.60	.25	.07
☐ 91 Jose Vizcaino	.10	.05	.01
☐ 92 Omar Vizquel	.25	.11	.03
☐ 93 Brad Ausmus	.10	.05	.01
☐ 94 Kimera Bartee	.10	.05	.01
☐ 95 Raul Casanova	.10	.05	.01
☐ 96 Tony Clark	.40	.18	.05
☐ 97 John Cummings	.10	.05	.01
☐ 98 Travis Fryman	.25	.11	.03
☐ 99 Bob Higginson	.25	.11	.03
☐ 100 Mark Lewis	.10	.05	.01
☐ 101 Felipe Lira	.10	.05	.01
☐ 102 Phil Nevin	.10	.05	.01
☐ 103 Melvin Nieves	.10	.05	.01
☐ 104 Curtis Pride	.10	.05	.01
☐ 105 A.J. Sager	.10	.05	.01
☐ 106 Ruben Sierra	.10	.05	.01
☐ 107 Justin Thompson	.25	.11	.03
☐ 108 Alan Trammell	.25	.11	.03
☐ 109 Kevin Appier	.25	.11	.03
☐ 110 Tim Belcher	.10	.05	.01
☐ 111 Jaime Bluma	.10	.05	.01
☐ 112 Johnny Damon	.10	.05	.01
☐ 113 Tom Goodwin	.10	.05	.01
☐ 114 Chris Haney	.10	.05	.01
☐ 115 Keith Lockhart	.10	.05	.01
☐ 116 Mike Macfarlane	.10	.05	.01
☐ 117 Jeff Montgomery	.10	.05	.01
☐ 118 Jose Offerman	.10	.05	.01
☐ 119 Craig Paquette	.10	.05	.01
☐ 120 Joe Randa	.10	.05	.01
☐ 121 Bip Roberts	.10	.05	.01
☐ 122 Jose Rosado	.40	.18	.05
☐ 123 Mike Sweeney	.25	.11	.03
☐ 124 Michael Tucker	.10	.05	.01
☐ 125 Jeromy Burnitz	.10	.05	.01
☐ 126 Jeff Cirillo	.10	.05	.01
☐ 127 Jeff D'Amico	.25	.11	.03
☐ 128 Mike Fetters	.10	.05	.01
☐ 129 John Jaha	.25	.11	.03
☐ 130 Scott Karl	.10	.05	.01
☐ 131 Jesse Levis	.10	.05	.01
☐ 132 Mark Loretta	.10	.05	.01
☐ 133 Mike Matheny	.10	.05	.01
☐ 134 Ben McDonald	.10	.05	.01
☐ 135 Matt Mieske	.10	.05	.01
☐ 136 Marc Newfield	.10	.05	.01
☐ 137 Dave Nilsson	.10	.05	.01
☐ 138 Jose Valentin	.10	.05	.01
☐ 139 Fernando Vina	.10	.05	.01
☐ 140 Bob Wickman	.10	.05	.01
☐ 141 Gerald Williams	.10	.05	.01
☐ 142 Rick Aguilera	.10	.05	.01
☐ 143 Rich Becker	.10	.05	.01
☐ 144 Ron Coomer	.10	.05	.01
☐ 145 Marty Cordova	.25	.11	.03
☐ 146 Roberto Kelly	.10	.05	.01
☐ 147 Chuck Knoblauch	.50	.23	.06
☐ 148 Matt Lawton	.10	.05	.01
☐ 149 Pat Meares	.10	.05	.01
☐ 150 Travis Miller	.10	.05	.01
☐ 151 Paul Molitor	.60	.25	.07
☐ 152 Greg Myers	.10	.05	.01
☐ 153 Dan Naulty	.10	.05	.01
☐ 154 Kirby Puckett	1.25	.55	.16
☐ 155 Brad Radke	.10	.05	.01
☐ 156 Frank Rodriguez	.10	.05	.01
☐ 157 Scott Stahoviak	.10	.05	.01
☐ 158 Dave Stevens	.10	.05	.01
☐ 159 Matt Walbeck	.10	.05	.01
☐ 160 Todd Walker	1.25	.55	.16
☐ 161 Wade Boggs	.40	.18	.05
☐ 162 David Cone	.25	.11	.03
☐ 163 Mariano Duncan	.10	.05	.01
☐ 164 Cecil Fielder	.25	.11	.03
☐ 165 Joe Girardi	.10	.05	.01
☐ 166 Dwight Gooden	.25	.11	.03
☐ 167 Charlie Hayes	.10	.05	.01
☐ 168 Derek Jeter	2.00	.90	.25
☐ 169 Jimmy Key	.10	.05	.01
☐ 170 Jim Leyritz	.10	.05	.01
☐ 171 Tino Martinez	.25	.11	.03
☐ 172 Ramiro Mendoza	.10	.05	.01
☐ 173 Jeff Nelson	.10	.05	.01
☐ 174 Paul O'Neill	.10	.05	.01
☐ 175 Andy Pettitte	.75	.35	.09
☐ 176 Mariano Rivera	.25	.11	.03
☐ 177 Ruben Rivera	.40	.18	.05
☐ 178 Kenny Rogers	.10	.05	.01
☐ 179 Darryl Strawberry	.25	.11	.03
☐ 180 John Wetteland	.25	.11	.03
☐ 181 Bernie Williams	.60	.25	.07
☐ 182 Willie Adams	.10	.05	.01
☐ 183 Tony Batista	.40	.18	.05
☐ 184 Geronimo Berroa	.10	.05	.01
☐ 185 Mike Bordick	.10	.05	.01
☐ 186 Scott Brosius	.10	.05	.01
☐ 187 Bobby Chouinard	.10	.05	.01
☐ 188 Jim Corsi	.10	.05	.01
☐ 189 Brent Gates	.10	.05	.01
☐ 190 Jason Giambi	.25	.11	.03
☐ 191 Jose Herrera	.10	.05	.01
☐ 192 Damon Mashore	.25	.11	.03
☐ 193 Mark McGwire	1.00	.45	.12
☐ 194 Mike Mohler	.10	.05	.01
☐ 195 Scott Spiezio	.25	.11	.03
☐ 196 Terry Steinbach	.10	.05	.01
☐ 197 Bill Taylor	.10	.05	.01
☐ 198 John Wasdin	.10	.05	.01
☐ 199 Steve Wojciechowski	.10	.05	.01

☐ 200 Ernie Young .10 .05 .01
☐ 201 Rich Amaral .10 .05 .01
☐ 202 Jay Buhner .40 .18 .05
☐ 203 Norm Charlton .10 .05 .01
☐ 204 Joey Cora .10 .05 .01
☐ 205 Russ Davis .10 .05 .01
☐ 206 Ken Griffey Jr. 3.00 1.35 .35
☐ 207 Sterling Hitchcock .10 .05 .01
☐ 208 Brian Hunter .10 .05 .01
☐ 209 Raul Ibanez .10 .05 .01
☐ 210 Randy Johnson .50 .23 .06
☐ 211 Edgar Martinez .25 .11 .03
☐ 212 Jamie Moyer .10 .05 .01
☐ 213 Alex Rodriguez 3.00 1.35 .35
☐ 214 Paul Sorrento .10 .05 .01
☐ 215 Matt Wagner .10 .05 .01
☐ 216 Bob Wells .10 .05 .01
☐ 217 Dan Wilson .10 .05 .01
☐ 218 Damon Buford .10 .05 .01
☐ 219 Will Clark .40 .18 .05
☐ 220 Kevin Elster .10 .05 .01
☐ 221 Juan Gonzalez 1.50 .70 .19
☐ 222 Rusty Greer .25 .11 .03
☐ 223 Kevin Gross .10 .05 .01
☐ 224 Darryl Hamilton .10 .05 .01
☐ 225 Mike Henneman .10 .05 .01
☐ 226 Ken Hill .10 .05 .01
☐ 227 Mark McLemore .10 .05 .01
☐ 228 Darren Oliver .10 .05 .01
☐ 229 Dean Palmer .10 .05 .01
☐ 230 Roger Pavlik .10 .05 .01
☐ 231 Ivan Rodriguez .75 .35 .09
☐ 232 Mickey Tettleton .10 .05 .01
☐ 233 Bobby Witt .10 .05 .01
☐ 234 Jacob Brumfield .10 .05 .01
☐ 235 Joe Carter .25 .11 .03
☐ 236 Tim Crabtree .10 .05 .01
☐ 237 Carlos Delgado .25 .11 .03
☐ 238 Huck Flener .10 .05 .01
☐ 239 Alex Gonzalez .10 .05 .01
☐ 240 Shawn Green .10 .05 .01
☐ 241 Juan Guzman .10 .05 .01
☐ 242 Pat Hentgen .25 .11 .03
☐ 243 Marty Janzen .10 .05 .01
☐ 244 Sandy Martinez .10 .05 .01
☐ 245 Otis Nixon .10 .05 .01
☐ 246 Charlie O'Brien .10 .05 .01
☐ 247 John Olerud .10 .05 .01
☐ 248 Robert Perez .10 .05 .01
☐ 249 Ed Sprague .10 .05 .01
☐ 250 Mike Timlin .10 .05 .01
☐ 251 Steve Avery .10 .05 .01
☐ 252 Jeff Blauser .10 .05 .01
☐ 253 Brad Clontz .10 .05 .01
☐ 254 Jermaine Dye .50 .23 .06
☐ 255 Tom Glavine .40 .18 .05
☐ 256 Marquis Grissom .25 .11 .03
☐ 257 Andruw Jones 3.00 1.35 .35
☐ 258 Chipper Jones 2.00 .90 .25
☐ 259 David Justice .25 .11 .03
☐ 260 Ryan Klesko .50 .23 .06
☐ 261 Mark Lemke .10 .05 .01
☐ 262 Javier Lopez .25 .11 .03
☐ 263 Greg Maddux 2.00 .90 .25
☐ 264 Fred McGriff .40 .18 .05
☐ 265 Greg McMichael .10 .05 .01
☐ 266 Denny Neagle .10 .05 .01
☐ 267 Terry Pendleton .10 .05 .01
☐ 268 Eddie Perez .10 .05 .01
☐ 269 John Smoltz .50 .23 .06
☐ 270 Terrell Wade .10 .05 .01
☐ 271 Mark Wohlers .10 .05 .01
☐ 272 Terry Adams .10 .05 .01
☐ 273 Brant Brown .10 .05 .01
☐ 274 Leo Gomez .10 .05 .01
☐ 275 Luis Gonzalez .10 .05 .01
☐ 276 Mark Grace .40 .18 .05
☐ 277 Tyler Houston .10 .05 .01
☐ 278 Robin Jennings .10 .05 .01
☐ 279 Brooks Kieschnick .25 .11 .03
☐ 280 Brian McRae .10 .05 .01
☐ 281 Jaime Navarro .10 .05 .01
☐ 282 Ryne Sandberg .75 .35 .09
☐ 283 Scott Servais .10 .05 .01
☐ 284 Sammy Sosa .50 .23 .06
☐ 285 Dave Swartzbaugh .10 .05 .01
☐ 286 Amaury Telemaco .10 .05 .01
☐ 287 Steve Trachsel .10 .05 .01
☐ 288 Pedro Valdes .10 .05 .01
☐ 289 Turk Wendell .10 .05 .01
☐ 290 Bret Boone .10 .05 .01
☐ 291 Jeff Branson .10 .05 .01
☐ 292 Jeff Brantley .10 .05 .01
☐ 293 Eric Davis .10 .05 .01
☐ 294 Willie Greene .10 .05 .01
☐ 295 Thomas Howard .10 .05 .01
☐ 296 Barry Larkin .40 .18 .05
☐ 297 Kevin Mitchell .10 .05 .01
☐ 298 Hal Morris .10 .05 .01
☐ 299 Chad Mottola .10 .05 .01
☐ 300 Joe Oliver .10 .05 .01
☐ 301 Mark Portugal .10 .05 .01
☐ 302 Roger Salkeld .10 .05 .01
☐ 303 Reggie Sanders .25 .11 .03
☐ 304 Pete Schourek .10 .05 .01
☐ 305 John Smiley .10 .05 .01
☐ 306 Eddie Taubensee .10 .05 .01
☐ 307 Dante Bichette .40 .18 .05
☐ 308 Ellis Burks .25 .11 .03
☐ 309 Vinny Castilla .25 .11 .03
☐ 310 Andres Galarraga .40 .18 .05
☐ 311 Curt Leskanic .10 .05 .01
☐ 312 Quinton McCracken .10 .05 .01
☐ 313 Neifi Perez .25 .11 .03
☐ 314 Jeff Reed .10 .05 .01
☐ 315 Steve Reed .10 .05 .01
☐ 316 Armando Reynoso .10 .05 .01
☐ 317 Kevin Ritz .10 .05 .01
☐ 318 Bruce Ruffin .10 .05 .01
☐ 319 Larry Walker .25 .11 .03
☐ 320 Walt Weiss .10 .05 .01
☐ 321 Jamey Wright .25 .11 .03
☐ 322 Eric Young .25 .11 .03
☐ 323 Kurt Abbott .10 .05 .01
☐ 324 Alex Arias .10 .05 .01
☐ 325 Kevin Brown .25 .11 .03
☐ 326 Luis Castillo .40 .18 .05
☐ 327 Greg Colbrunn .10 .05 .01
☐ 328 Jeff Conine .25 .11 .03
☐ 329 Andre Dawson .25 .11 .03
☐ 330 Charles Johnson .10 .05 .01
☐ 331 Al Leiter .10 .05 .01
☐ 332 Ralph Milliard .10 .05 .01
☐ 333 Robb Nen .10 .05 .01
☐ 334 Pat Rapp .10 .05 .01
☐ 335 Edgar Renteria .40 .18 .05
☐ 336 Gary Sheffield .50 .23 .06
☐ 337 Devon White .10 .05 .01
☐ 338 Bob Abreu .40 .18 .05
☐ 339 Jeff Bagwell 1.25 .55 .16
☐ 340 Derek Bell .25 .11 .03
☐ 341 Sean Berry .10 .05 .01
☐ 342 Craig Biggio .25 .11 .03
☐ 343 Doug Drabek .10 .05 .01
☐ 344 Tony Eusebio .10 .05 .01
☐ 345 Ricky Gutierrez .10 .05 .01
☐ 346 Mike Hampton .10 .05 .01
☐ 347 Brian Hunter .10 .05 .01
☐ 348 Todd Jones .10 .05 .01
☐ 349 Darryl Kile .10 .05 .01
☐ 350 Derrick May .10 .05 .01
☐ 351 Orlando Miller .10 .05 .01
☐ 352 James Mouton .10 .05 .01
☐ 353 Shane Reynolds .10 .05 .01
☐ 354 Billy Wagner .25 .11 .03
☐ 355 Donne Wall .10 .05 .01
☐ 356 Mike Blowers .10 .05 .01
☐ 357 Brett Butler .10 .05 .01
☐ 358 Roger Cedeno .10 .05 .01
☐ 359 Chad Curtis .10 .05 .01
☐ 360 Delino DeShields .10 .05 .01
☐ 361 Greg Gagne .10 .05 .01
☐ 362 Karim Garcia .50 .23 .06
☐ 363 Wilton Guerrero .50 .23 .06
☐ 364 Todd Hollandsworth .25 .11 .03
☐ 365 Eric Karros .25 .11 .03
☐ 366 Ramon Martinez .25 .11 .03
☐ 367 Raul Mondesi .40 .18 .05
☐ 368 Hideo Nomo .10 .05 .01
☐ 369 Antonio Osuna .10 .05 .01
☐ 370 Chan Ho Park .40 .18 .05
☐ 371 Mike Piazza 2.00 .90 .25
☐ 372 Ismael Valdes .25 .11 .03
☐ 373 Todd Worrell .10 .05 .01
☐ 374 Moises Alou .25 .11 .03
☐ 375 Shane Andrews .10 .05 .01
☐ 376 Yamil Benitez .10 .05 .01
☐ 377 Jeff Fassero .10 .05 .01
☐ 378 Darrin Fletcher .10 .05 .01
☐ 379 Cliff Floyd .10 .05 .01
☐ 380 Mark Grudzielanek .10 .05 .01
☐ 381 Mike Lansing .10 .05 .01
☐ 382 Barry Manuel .10 .05 .01
☐ 383 Pedro Martinez .25 .11 .03
☐ 384 Henry Rodriguez .25 .11 .03
☐ 385 Mel Rojas .10 .05 .01
☐ 386 F.P. Santangelo .10 .05 .01
☐ 387 David Segui .10 .05 .01
☐ 388 Ugueth Urbina .10 .05 .01
☐ 389 Rondell White .10 .05 .01
☐ 390 Edgardo Alfonzo .10 .05 .01
☐ 391 Carlos Baerga .25 .11 .03
☐ 392 Mark Clark .10 .05 .01
☐ 393 Alvaro Espinoza .10 .05 .01
☐ 394 John Franco .10 .05 .01
☐ 395 Bernard Gilkey .10 .05 .01
☐ 396 Pete Harnisch .10 .05 .01
☐ 397 Todd Hundley .25 .11 .03
☐ 398 Butch Huskey .10 .05 .01
☐ 399 Jason Isringhausen .25 .11 .03
☐ 400 Lance Johnson .10 .05 .01
☐ 401 Bobby Jones .10 .05 .01
☐ 402 Alex Ochoa .10 .05 .01
☐ 403 Rey Ordonez .40 .18 .05
☐ 404 Robert Person .10 .05 .01
☐ 405 Paul Wilson .25 .11 .03
☐ 406 Matt Beech .10 .05 .01
☐ 407 Ron Blazier .10 .05 .01
☐ 408 Ricky Bottalico .10 .05 .01
☐ 409 Lenny Dykstra .25 .11 .03
☐ 410 Jim Eisenreich .10 .05 .01
☐ 411 Bobby Estalella .40 .18 .05
☐ 412 Mike Grace .10 .05 .01
☐ 413 Gregg Jefferies .10 .05 .01
☐ 414 Mike Lieberthal .10 .05 .01
☐ 415 Wendell Magee .25 .11 .03
☐ 416 Mickey Morandini .10 .05 .01
☐ 417 Ricky Otero .10 .05 .01
☐ 418 Scott Rolen 1.25 .55 .16
☐ 419 Ken Ryan .10 .05 .01
☐ 420 Benito Santiago .10 .05 .01
☐ 421 Curt Schilling .10 .05 .01
☐ 422 Kevin Sefcik .10 .05 .01
☐ 423 Jermaine Allensworth .25 .11 .03
☐ 424 Trey Beamon .10 .05 .01
☐ 425 Jay Bell .10 .05 .01
☐ 426 Francisco Cordova .10 .05 .01
☐ 427 Carlos Garcia .10 .05 .01
☐ 428 Mark Johnson .10 .05 .01
☐ 429 Jason Kendall .25 .11 .03
☐ 430 Jeff King .10 .05 .01
☐ 431 Jon Lieber .10 .05 .01
☐ 432 Al Martin .10 .05 .01
☐ 433 Orlando Merced .10 .05 .01
☐ 434 Ramon Morel .10 .05 .01
☐ 435 Matt Ruebel .10 .05 .01
☐ 436 Jason Schmidt .25 .11 .03
☐ 437 Marc Wilkins .10 .05 .01
☐ 438 Alan Benes .25 .11 .03
☐ 439 Andy Benes .10 .05 .01
☐ 440 Royce Clayton .10 .05 .01
☐ 441 Dennis Eckersley .25 .11 .03
☐ 442 Gary Gaetti .10 .05 .01
☐ 443 Ron Gant .25 .11 .03
☐ 444 Aaron Holbert .10 .05 .01
☐ 445 Brian Jordan .25 .11 .03
☐ 446 Ray Lankford .25 .11 .03
☐ 447 John Mabry .10 .05 .01
☐ 448 T.J. Mathews .10 .05 .01
☐ 449 Willie McGee .10 .05 .01
☐ 450 Donovan Osborne .10 .05 .01
☐ 451 Tom Pagnozzi .10 .05 .01
☐ 452 Ozzie Smith .75 .35 .09
☐ 453 Todd Stottlemyre .10 .05 .01
☐ 454 Mark Sweeney .10 .05 .01
☐ 455 Dmitri Young .25 .11 .03
☐ 456 Andy Ashby .10 .05 .01
☐ 457 Ken Caminiti .50 .23 .06
☐ 458 Archi Cianfrocco .10 .05 .01
☐ 459 Steve Finley .10 .05 .01
☐ 460 John Flaherty .10 .05 .01
☐ 461 Chris Gomez .10 .05 .01
☐ 462 Tony Gwynn 1.25 .55 .16
☐ 463 Joey Hamilton .25 .11 .03
☐ 464 Rickey Henderson .40 .18 .05
☐ 465 Trevor Hoffman .10 .05 .01
☐ 466 Brian Johnson .10 .05 .01
☐ 467 Wally Joyner .10 .05 .01
☐ 468 Jody Reed .10 .05 .01
☐ 469 Scott Sanders .10 .05 .01
☐ 470 Bob Tewksbury .10 .05 .01
☐ 471 Fernando Valenzuela .25 .11 .03
☐ 472 Greg Vaughn .10 .05 .01
☐ 473 Tim Worrell .10 .05 .01
☐ 474 Rich Aurilia .10 .05 .01
☐ 475 Rod Beck .10 .05 .01
☐ 476 Marvin Benard .10 .05 .01
☐ 477 Barry Bonds .75 .35 .09
☐ 478 Jay Canizaro .10 .05 .01
☐ 479 Shawon Dunston .10 .05 .01
☐ 480 Shawn Estes .10 .05 .01
☐ 481 Mark Gardner .10 .05 .01
☐ 482 Glenallen Hill .10 .05 .01
☐ 483 Stan Javier .10 .05 .01
☐ 484 Marcus Jensen .10 .05 .01
☐ 485 Bill Mueller .10 .05 .01
☐ 486 William VanLandingham .10 .05 .01
☐ 487 Allen Watson .10 .05 .01
☐ 488 Rick Wilkins .10 .05 .01
☐ 489 Matt Williams .40 .18 .05
☐ 490 Desi Wilson .10 .05 .01
☐ 491 Albert Belle CL .60 .25 .07
☐ 492 Ken Griffey Jr. CL 1.50 .70 .19
☐ 493 Andruw Jones CL 1.50 .70 .19
☐ 494 Chipper Jones CL 1.00 .45 .12
☐ 495 Mark McGwire CL .50 .23 .06
☐ 496 Paul Molitor CL .25 .11 .03
☐ 497 Mike Piazza CL 1.00 .45 .12
☐ 498 Cal Ripken CL 1.25 .55 .16
☐ 499 Alex Rodriguez CL 1.50 .70 .19
☐ 500 Frank Thomas CL 1.50 .70 .19

1997 Fleer Tiffany

Randomly inserted in packs at a rate of one in 20, this 500-card set is a parallel version of the regular set featuring a glossy holographic design, foil stamping, and UV coating.

	MINT	NRMT	EXC
COMPLETE SET (500)	4000.00	1800.00	500.00
COMMON CARD (1-500)	4.00	1.80	.50

*STARS: 25X TO 40X BASIC CARDS ..
*YOUNG STARS: 18X TO 30X BASIC CARDS

☐ 13 Cal Ripken 100.00 45.00 12.50
☐ 22 Nomar Garciaparra 50.00 22.00 6.25

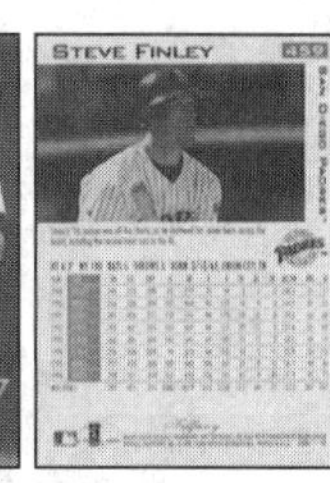

☐ 41 Darin Erstad 60.00 27.00 7.50
☐ 72 Frank Thomas 120.00 55.00 15.00
☐ 75 Albert Belle 50.00 22.00 6.25
☐ 154 Kirby Puckett 50.00 22.00 6.25
☐ 160 Todd Walker 50.00 22.00 6.25
☐ 168 Derek Jeter 75.00 34.00 9.50
☐ 206 Ken Griffey Jr. 120.00 55.00 15.00
☐ 213 Alex Rodriguez 120.00 55.00 15.00
☐ 221 Juan Gonzalez 60.00 27.00 7.50
☐ 257 Andruw Jones 120.00 55.00 15.00
☐ 258 Chipper Jones 75.00 34.00 9.50
☐ 263 Greg Maddux 75.00 34.00 9.50
☐ 339 Jeff Bagwell 50.00 22.00 6.25
☐ 371 Mike Piazza 75.00 34.00 9.50
☐ 418 Scott Rolen 50.00 22.00 6.25
☐ 462 Tony Gwynn 50.00 22.00 6.25
☐ 492 Ken Griffey Jr. CL 60.00 27.00 7.50
☐ 493 Andruw Jones CL 60.00 27.00 7.50
☐ 498 Cal Ripken CL 50.00 22.00 6.25
☐ 499 Alex Rodriguez CL 60.00 27.00 7.50
☐ 500 Frank Thomas CL 60.00 27.00 7.50

1997 Fleer Golden Memories

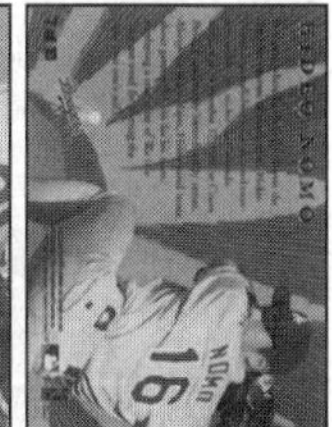

Randomly inserted in packs at a rate of one in 16, this ten-card set commemorates major achievements by individual players from the 1996 season. The fronts feature color player images on a background of the top portion of the sun and its rays. The backs carry player information.

	MINT	NRMT	EXC
COMPLETE SET (10)	15.00	6.75	1.85
COMMON CARD (1-10)	.75	.35	.09

☐ 1 Barry Bonds 1.50 .70 .19
☐ 2 Dwight Gooden .75 .35 .09
☐ 3 Todd Hundley .75 .35 .09
☐ 4 Mark McGwire 2.00 .90 .25
☐ 5 Paul Molitor 1.25 .55 .16
☐ 6 Eddie Murray 1.50 .70 .19
☐ 7 Hideo Nomo 1.50 .70 .19
☐ 8 Mike Piazza 4.00 1.80 .50
☐ 9 Cal Ripken 5.00 2.20 .60
☐ 10 Ozzie Smith 2.00 .90 .25

1997 Fleer Lumber Company

Randomly inserted exclusively in retail packs, this 18-card set features a selection of the game's top sluggers. The innovative design displays pure die-cut circular borders, simulating the effect of a cut tree.

	MINT	NRMT	EXC
COMPLETE SET (18)	180.00	80.00	22.00
COMMON CARD (1-18)	3.00	1.35	.35

☐ 1 Brady Anderson 3.00 1.35 .35
☐ 2 Jeff Bagwell 12.00 5.50 1.50
☐ 3 Albert Belle 12.00 5.50 1.50
☐ 4 Barry Bonds 8.00 3.60 1.00
☐ 5 Jay Buhner 4.00 1.80 .50
☐ 6 Ellis Burks 3.00 1.35 .35
☐ 7 Andres Galarraga 4.00 1.80 .50
☐ 8 Juan Gonzalez 15.00 6.75 1.85
☐ 9 Ken Griffey Jr. 30.00 13.50 3.70
☐ 10 Todd Hundley 3.00 1.35 .35

☐ 11 Ryan Klesko	5.00	2.20	.60
☐ 12 Mark McGwire	10.00	4.50	1.25
☐ 13 Mike Piazza	20.00	9.00	2.50
☐ 14 Alex Rodriguez	30.00	13.50	3.70
☐ 15 Gary Sheffield	5.00	2.20	.60
☐ 16 Sammy Sosa	5.00	2.20	.60
☐ 17 Frank Thomas	30.00	13.50	3.70
☐ 18 Mo Vaughn	8.00	3.60	1.00

1997 Fleer Night and Day

Randomly inserted in packs at a rate of one in 240, this ten-card set features color action player photos of superstars who excel in day games, night games, or both and are printed on lenticular 3D cards. The backs carry player information.

	MINT	NRMT	EXC
COMPLETE SET (10)	400.00	180.00	50.00
COMMON CARD (1-10)	15.00	6.75	1.85
☐ 1 Barry Bonds	20.00	9.00	2.50
☐ 2 Ellis Burks	15.00	6.75	1.85
☐ 3 Juan Gonzalez	40.00	18.00	5.00
☐ 4 Ken Griffey Jr.	80.00	36.00	10.00
☐ 5 Mark McGwire	25.00	11.00	3.10
☐ 6 Mike Piazza	50.00	22.00	6.25
☐ 7 Manny Ramirez	20.00	9.00	2.50
☐ 8 Alex Rodriguez	80.00	36.00	10.00
☐ 9 John Smoltz	15.00	6.75	1.85
☐ 10 Frank Thomas	80.00	36.00	10.00

1997 Fleer Rookie Sensations

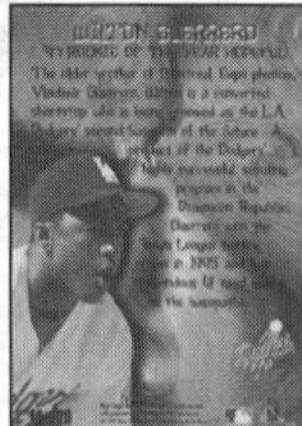

Randomly inserted in packs at a rate of one in six, this 20-card set honors the top rookies from the 1996 season and the 1997 season rookies/prospects. The fronts freature color action player images on a multi-color swirling background. The backs carry a paragraph with information about the player.

	MINT	NRMT	EXC
COMPLETE SET (20)	30.00	13.50	3.70
COMMON CARD (1-20)	.50	.23	.06
☐ 1 Jermaine Allensworth	.75	.35	.09
☐ 2 James Baldwin	.50	.23	.06
☐ 3 Alan Benes	.75	.35	.09
☐ 4 Jermaine Dye	1.25	.55	.16
☐ 5 Darin Erstad	4.00	1.80	.50
☐ 6 Todd Hollandsworth	.75	.35	.09
☐ 7 Derek Jeter	5.00	2.20	.60
☐ 8 Jason Kendall	.75	.35	.09
☐ 9 Alex Ochoa	.50	.23	.06
☐ 10 Rey Ordonez	1.00	.45	.12
☐ 11 Edgar Renteria	1.00	.45	.12
☐ 12 Bob Abreu	1.00	.45	.12
☐ 13 Nomar Garciaparra	3.00	1.35	.35
☐ 14 Wilton Guerrero	1.50	.70	.19
☐ 15 Andruw Jones	8.00	3.60	1.00
☐ 16 Wendell Magee	.75	.35	.09
☐ 17 Neifi Perez	.75	.35	.09
☐ 18 Scott Rolen	3.00	1.35	.35
☐ 19 Scott Spiezio	.75	.35	.09
☐ 20 Todd Walker	3.00	1.35	.35

1997 Fleer Team Leaders

Randomly inserted in packs at a rate of one in 28, this 28-card set honors statistical or inspirational leaders from each team on a die-cut card. The fronts feature color action player images with the player's face in the background. The backs carry a paragraph with information about the player.

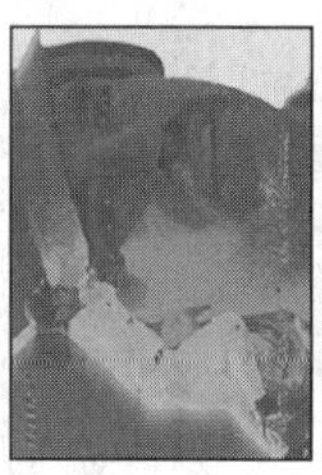

	MINT	NRMT	EXC
COMPLETE SET (28)	125.00	55.00	15.50
COMMON CARD (1-28)	1.50	.70	.19
☐ 1 Cal Ripken	15.00	6.75	1.85
☐ 2 Mo Vaughn	5.00	2.20	.60
☐ 3 Jim Edmonds	2.00	.90	.25
☐ 4 Frank Thomas	20.00	9.00	2.50
☐ 5 Albert Belle	8.00	3.60	1.00
☐ 6 Bob Higginson	2.00	.90	.25
☐ 7 Kevin Appier	2.00	.90	.25
☐ 8 John Jaha	2.00	.90	.25
☐ 9 Paul Molitor	4.00	1.80	.50
☐ 10 Andy Pettitte	5.00	2.20	.60
☐ 11 Mark McGwire	6.00	2.70	.75
☐ 12 Ken Griffey Jr.	20.00	9.00	2.50
☐ 13 Juan Gonzalez	10.00	4.50	1.25
☐ 14 Pat Hentgen	2.00	.90	.25
☐ 15 Chipper Jones	12.00	5.50	1.50
☐ 16 Mark Grace	2.50	1.10	.30
☐ 17 Barry Larkin	2.50	1.10	.30
☐ 18 Ellis Burks	2.00	.90	.25
☐ 19 Gary Sheffield	3.00	1.35	.35
☐ 20 Jeff Bagwell	8.00	3.60	1.00
☐ 21 Mike Piazza	12.00	5.50	1.50
☐ 22 Henry Rodriguez	2.00	.90	.25
☐ 23 Todd Hundley	2.00	.90	.25
☐ 24 Curt Schilling	1.50	.70	.19
☐ 25 Jeff King	1.50	.70	.19
☐ 26 Brian Jordan	2.00	.90	.25
☐ 27 Tony Gwynn	8.00	3.60	1.00
☐ 28 Barry Bonds	5.00	2.20	.60

1997 Fleer Zone

Randomly inserted in hobby packs only at a rate of one in 80, this 20-card set features color player images of some of the 1996 season's unstoppable hitters and unhittable pitchers on a holographic card. The backs carry another color photo with a paragraph about the player.

	MINT	NRMT	EXC
COMPLETE SET (20)	300.00	135.00	38.00
COMMON CARD (1-20)	4.00	1.80	.50
☐ 1 Jeff Bagwell	15.00	6.75	1.85
☐ 2 Albert Belle	15.00	6.75	1.85
☐ 3 Barry Bonds	10.00	4.50	1.25
☐ 4 Ken Caminiti	6.00	2.70	.75
☐ 5 Andres Galarraga	6.00	2.70	.75
☐ 6 Juan Gonzalez	20.00	9.00	2.50
☐ 7 Ken Griffey Jr.	40.00	18.00	5.00
☐ 8 Tony Gwynn	15.00	6.75	1.85
☐ 9 Chipper Jones	25.00	11.00	3.10
☐ 10 Greg Maddux	25.00	11.00	3.10
☐ 11 Mark McGwire	12.00	5.50	1.50
☐ 12 Dean Palmer	4.00	1.80	.50
☐ 13 Andy Pettitte	10.00	4.50	1.25
☐ 14 Mike Piazza	25.00	11.00	3.10
☐ 15 Alex Rodriguez	40.00	18.00	5.00
☐ 16 Gary Sheffield	6.00	2.70	.75
☐ 17 John Smoltz	6.00	2.70	.75
☐ 18 Frank Thomas	40.00	18.00	5.00
☐ 19 Jim Thome	8.00	3.60	1.00
☐ 20 Matt Williams	6.00	2.70	.75

1916 Fleischmann Bread D381

This 103-card set was produced by Fleischmann Breads in 1916. These unnumbered cards are arranged here for convenience in alphabetical order; cards with tabs intact are worth 50 percent more than the prices listed below. The cards measure approximately 2 3/4" by 5 1/2" (with tab) or 2 3/4" by 4 13/16" (without tab). There is also a similar set issued by Ferguson Bread which is harder to find and is distinguished by having the photo caption written on only one line rather than two as with the Fleischmann cards.

	EX-MT	VG-E	GOOD
COMPLETE SET (103)	7000.00	3200.00	900.00
COMMON CARD (1-103)	40.00	18.00	5.00
☐ 1 Babe Adams	50.00	22.00	6.25
☐ 2 Grover Alexander	175.00	80.00	22.00
☐ 3 Walt E. Alexander	40.00	18.00	5.00
☐ 4 Frank Allen	40.00	18.00	5.00
☐ 5 Fred Anderson	40.00	18.00	5.00
☐ 6 Dave Bancroft	80.00	36.00	10.00
☐ 7 Jack Barry	40.00	18.00	5.00
☐ 8 Beals Becker	40.00	18.00	5.00
☐ 9 Eddie Burns	40.00	18.00	5.00
☐ 10 George J. Burns	40.00	18.00	5.00
☐ 11 Bobby Byrne	40.00	18.00	5.00
☐ 12 Ray B. Caldwell	40.00	18.00	5.00
☐ 13 James Callahan P/MG	40.00	18.00	5.00
☐ 14 William Carrigan MG	40.00	18.00	5.00
☐ 15 Larry Cheney	40.00	18.00	5.00
☐ 16 Tom Clarke	40.00	18.00	5.00
☐ 17 Ty Cobb	1500.00	700.00	190.00
☐ 18 Ray W. Collins	40.00	18.00	5.00
☐ 19 Jack Coombs	60.00	27.00	7.50
☐ 20 A. Wilbur Cooper	40.00	18.00	5.00
☐ 21 George Cutshaw	40.00	18.00	5.00
☐ 22 Jake Daubert	50.00	22.00	6.25
☐ 23 Wheezer Dell	40.00	18.00	5.00
☐ 24 Bill Donovan	40.00	18.00	5.00
☐ 25 Larry Doyle	50.00	22.00	6.25
☐ 26 R.J. Egan	40.00	18.00	5.00
☐ 27 Johnny Evers	125.00	55.00	15.50
☐ 28 Ray Fisher	40.00	18.00	5.00
☐ 29 Harry Gardner (Sic)	40.00	18.00	5.00
☐ 30 Joe Gedeon	40.00	18.00	5.00
☐ 31 Larry Gilbert	40.00	18.00	5.00
☐ 32 Frank Gilhooley	40.00	18.00	5.00
☐ 33 Hank Gowdy	50.00	22.00	6.25
☐ 34 Sylvanus Gregg	40.00	18.00	5.00
☐ 35 Tom Griffith	40.00	18.00	5.00
☐ 36 Heinie Groh	50.00	22.00	6.25
☐ 37 Robert Harmon	40.00	18.00	5.00
☐ 38 Roy A. Hartzell	40.00	18.00	5.00
☐ 39 Claude Hendriksen	40.00	18.00	5.00
☐ 40 Olaf Hendriksen	40.00	18.00	5.00
☐ 41 Buck Herzog P/MG	40.00	18.00	5.00
☐ 42 Hugh High	40.00	18.00	5.00
☐ 43 Dick Hoblitzell	40.00	18.00	5.00
☐ 44 Herb H. Hunter	40.00	18.00	5.00
☐ 45 Harold Janvrin	40.00	18.00	5.00
☐ 46 Hugh Jennings	80.00	36.00	10.00
☐ 47 John Johnston	40.00	18.00	5.00
☐ 48 Erving Kantlehner	40.00	18.00	5.00
☐ 49 Bennie Kauff	50.00	22.00	6.25
☐ 50 Ray H. Keating	40.00	18.00	5.00
☐ 51 Wade Killefer	40.00	18.00	5.00
☐ 52 Elmer Knetzer	40.00	18.00	5.00
☐ 53 Brad W. Kocher	40.00	18.00	5.00
☐ 54 Ed Konetchy	40.00	18.00	5.00
☐ 55 Fred Lauderus (Sic)	40.00	18.00	5.00
☐ 56 Dutch Leonard	50.00	22.00	6.25
☐ 57 Duffy Lewis	50.00	22.00	6.25
☐ 58 E.H.(Slim) Love	40.00	18.00	5.00
☐ 59 Albert L. Mamaux	40.00	18.00	5.00
☐ 60 Rabbit Maranville	80.00	36.00	10.00
☐ 61 Rube Marquard	80.00	36.00	10.00
☐ 62 Christy Mathewson	350.00	160.00	45.00
☐ 63 Bill McKechnie	80.00	36.00	10.00
☐ 64 Chief Meyer (Sic)	50.00	22.00	6.25
☐ 65 Otto Miller	40.00	18.00	5.00
☐ 66 Fred Mollwitz	40.00	18.00	5.00
☐ 67 Herbie Moran	40.00	18.00	5.00
☐ 68 Mike Mowrey	40.00	18.00	5.00
☐ 69 Dan Murphy	40.00	18.00	5.00
☐ 70 Art Nehf	50.00	22.00	6.25
☐ 71 Rube Oldring	40.00	18.00	5.00
☐ 72 Oliver O'Mara	40.00	18.00	5.00
☐ 73 Dode Paskert	40.00	18.00	5.00
☐ 74 D.C.Pat Ragan	40.00	18.00	5.00
☐ 75 Wm.A. Rariden	40.00	18.00	5.00
☐ 76 Davis Robertson	40.00	18.00	5.00
☐ 77 Wm. Rodgers	40.00	18.00	5.00
☐ 78 Edw.F.Rousch (Sic)	125.00	55.00	15.50
☐ 79 Nap Rucker	50.00	22.00	6.25
☐ 80 Dick Rudolph	40.00	18.00	5.00
☐ 81 Walter Schang	50.00	22.00	6.25
☐ 82 A.J.(Rube) Schauer	40.00	18.00	5.00
☐ 83 Pete Schneider	40.00	18.00	5.00
☐ 84 Ferd M. Schupp	40.00	18.00	5.00
☐ 85 Ernie Shore	50.00	22.00	6.25
☐ 86 Red Smith	40.00	18.00	5.00
☐ 87 Fred Snodgrass	50.00	22.00	6.25
☐ 88 Tris Speaker	175.00	80.00	22.00
☐ 89 George Stallings MG	40.00	18.00	5.00
☐ 90 Casey Stengel	350.00	160.00	45.00
☐ 91 Sailor Stroud	40.00	18.00	5.00
☐ 92 Amos Strunk	40.00	18.00	5.00
☐ 93 Charles D. Thomas	40.00	18.00	5.00
☐ 94 Fred Toney	40.00	18.00	5.00
☐ 95 Walter Tragresser	40.00	18.00	5.00
☐ 96 Chas.(Jeff) Tesreau	40.00	18.00	5.00
☐ 97 Honus Wagner	350.00	160.00	45.00
☐ 98 Carl Weilman	40.00	18.00	5.00
☐ 99 Zack Wheat	80.00	36.00	10.00
☐ 100 George Whitted	40.00	18.00	5.00
☐ 101 Arthur Wilson	40.00	18.00	5.00
☐ 102 Ivy Wingo	40.00	18.00	5.00
☐ 103 Joe Wood	80.00	36.00	10.00

1991 Foul Ball

This 36-card boxed set was produced by Eclipse Enterprises and its topic is well summarized by the blurb on the box, "Baseball's Greatest Scandals, Scoundrels and Screw-ups". The cards measure the standard size and feature Gary Cohen as writer and William Cone as artist. The fronts feature color art with white borders, while the backs have extended captions on the situation portrayed by the card.

	MINT	NRMT	EXC
COMPLETE SET (36)	10.00	4.50	1.25
COMMON CARD (1-36)	.25	.11	.03
☐ 1 Foul Ball	.50	.23	.06
☐ 2 The Black Sox Scandal	1.00	.45	.12
☐ 3 The Big Cocaine Bust	.25	.11	.03
☐ 4 The Death of a Team	.25	.11	.03
☐ 5 Pete Rose Bets on Baseball	1.00	.45	.12
☐ 6 Denny McLain Takes a Fall	.25	.11	.03
☐ 7 Ty Cobb Clobbers a Fan	1.00	.45	.12
☐ 8 Juan Marichal Johnny Roseboro	.50	.23	.06
☐ 9 Phil Douglas Kenesaw M. Landis John McGraw	.25	.11	.03
☐ 10 Beer Night at the Park	.25	.11	.03
☐ 11 Disco Demolition Night	.25	.11	.03
☐ 12 Al Campanis Strikes Out	.25	.11	.03
☐ 13 Lenny Randle Frank Lucchesi	.25	.11	.03
☐ 14 George Steinbrenner Boss George Buys It	.50	.23	.06
☐ 15 The Last Stolen Base	.25	.11	.03
☐ 16 Luis Polonia Scores Twice	.25	.11	.03
☐ 17 Charlie Finley Sells Out	.25	.11	.03
☐ 18 Dave Pallone An Ump's Double Life	.25	.11	.03
☐ 19 Norm Cash The Bat Man Tells All	.25	.11	.03
☐ 20 Gaylord Perry A Professional Spitter	.50	.23	.06
☐ 21 Dock Ellis Delivers A Message	.25	.11	.03
☐ 22 A Major League Trade	.25	.11	.03
☐ 23 Ray Kroc Grabs the Mike	.25	.11	.03
☐ 24 Ted Turner Makes the Team	.25	.11	.03
☐ 25 Graig Nettles Bounces Out	.25	.11	.03
☐ 26 The Pine Tar Game	.25	.11	.03
☐ 27 Dave Winfield Gets the Bird	1.00	.45	.12
☐ 28 Pascual Perez Goes Astray	.25	.11	.03
☐ 29 Dave Stewart Gets Tricked	.25	.11	.03
☐ 30 Wade Boggs Margo Adams	1.00	.45	.12
☐ 31 Two Yankee Relievers	.25	.11	.03
☐ 32 Reggie Jackson Bar Mania	1.00	.45	.12
☐ 33 Kiteman Grounds Out	.25	.11	.03
☐ 34 Eddie Gaedel Short Career	1.00	.45	.12
☐ 35 The Flying Fan	.25	.11	.03
☐ 36 Jim Bouton Ball Four	.50	.23	.06

1887 Four Base Hits N-Unc.

The twelve known baseball cards inscribed "Four Base Hits" were catalogued in the N690 classification for two reasons: they are identical in size and format to N690-1, and two players, Mays and Roseman, have the same pictures in both sets. Although it is known that the Charles Gross Company "farmed out" some of its insert designs to other companies, "Four Base Hits" will retain this catalog number until new evidence places them elsewhere.

	EX-MT	VG-E	GOOD
COMPLETE SET	50000.00	22500.00	6200.00
COMMON CARD	4000.00	1800.00	500.00
☐ 1 Tom Dailey (sic, Daly): Chicago	4000.00	1800.00	500.00
☐ 2 John Clarkson Chicago	7500.00	3400.00	950.00
☐ 3 Pat Deasley New York	4000.00	1800.00	500.00
☐ 4 Pete Gillespie New York	4000.00	1800.00	500.00
☐ 5 Frank Hankinson Mets	4000.00	1800.00	500.00
☐ 6 Mike (King) Kelly: Boston	10000.00	4500.00	1250.00
☐ 7 Al Mays Mets	4000.00	1800.00	500.00
☐ 8 James (Chief) Roseman Mets	4000.00	1800.00	500.00
☐ 9 Marty Sullivan Chicago	4000.00	1800.00	500.00
☐ 10 George Van Haltren Chicago	4000.00	1800.00	500.00
☐ 11 John Montgomery Ward New York	7500.00	3400.00	950.00
☐ 12 Mickey Welch New York	7500.00	3400.00	950.00

1950 Four Mighty Heroes H801-6

These four cards were issued in conjuction with the release of Connie Mack's Book "My 66 Years in the Big Leagues" The players features are Mack's most memorable three personalities. The cards were also shipped in a special promotional envelope to inspire more sales of the book.

	NRMT	VG-E	GOOD
COMPLETE SET (4)	1300.00	575.00	160.00
COMMON CARD (1-4)	200.00	90.00	25.00
☐ 1 Connie Mack	250.00	110.00	31.00
☐ 2 Christy Mathewson	350.00	160.00	45.00
☐ 3 Babe Ruth	750.00	350.00	95.00
☐ 4 Rube Waddell	200.00	90.00	25.00

1980 Franchise Babe Ruth

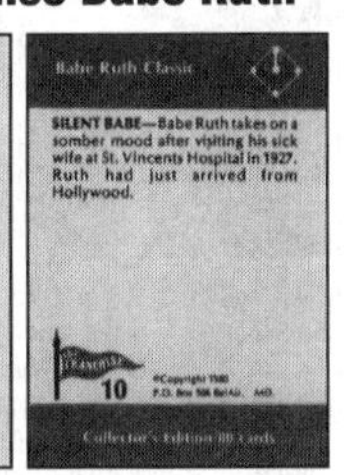

This 80-card set measures the standard size and was manufactured by the Franchise of Bel Air, Maryland. The cards present the life of Babe Ruth and include his activities both on and off the field. The fronts have black and white photos framed by white borders. The set was originally issued in complete set form and available for $8 directly from the manufacturer at the time of the issue

	NRMT	VG-E	GOOD
COMPLETE SET (80)	100.00	45.00	12.50
COMMON CARD (1-80)	1.50	.70	.19
☐ 1 Babe Ruth in Boston	1.50	.70	.19
☐ 2 Babe Ruth Youthful Babe	1.50	.70	.19
☐ 3 Babe Ruth Personal Touch	1.50	.70	.19
☐ 4 Babe Ruth Takes a Cut	1.50	.70	.19
☐ 5 Babe Ruth On Dotted Line	1.50	.70	.19
☐ 6 Babe Ruth On Stage	1.50	.70	.19
☐ 7 Babe Ruth Out of Action	1.50	.70	.19
☐ 8 Babe Ruth All Smiles	1.50	.70	.19
☐ 9 Babe Ruth Oriental Hero	1.50	.70	.19
☐ 10 Babe Ruth Silent Babe	1.50	.70	.19
☐ 11 Babe Ruth Old Times	1.50	.70	.19
☐ 12 Babe Ruth Waiting His Turn	1.50	.70	.19
☐ 13 Babe Ruth Speaking Out	1.50	.70	.19
☐ 14 Babe Ruth Shadow Slugger	1.50	.70	.19
☐ 15 Babe Ruth Youthful Ball Hawk	1.50	.70	.19
☐ 16 Babe Ruth Speed on the Bases	1.50	.70	.19
☐ 17 Babe Ruth Helping Hand	1.50	.70	.19
☐ 18 Babe Ruth in Disguise	1.50	.70	.19
☐ 19 Babe Ruth Political Boss	1.50	.70	.19
☐ 20 Babe Ruth Mail Clerk	1.50	.70	.19
☐ 21 Babe Ruth Keeping Warm	1.50	.70	.19
☐ 22 Babe Ruth Big Cut	1.50	.70	.19
☐ 23 Babe Ruth Defense, Too	1.50	.70	.19
☐ 24 Babe Ruth Playing Catch	1.50	.70	.19
☐ 25 Babe Ruth Big Swing	1.50	.70	.19
☐ 26 Babe Ruth Taking Aim	1.50	.70	.19
☐ 27 Babe Ruth Double Trouble	1.50	.70	.19
☐ 28 Babe Ruth Power Plus	1.50	.70	.19
☐ 29 Babe Ruth Running Wild	1.50	.70	.19
☐ 30 Babe Ruth Formidable Figure	1.50	.70	.19
☐ 31 Babe Ruth Effort	1.50	.70	.19
☐ 32 Babe Ruth Long Gone	1.50	.70	.19
☐ 33 Babe Ruth Up The Shaft	1.50	.70	.19
☐ 34 Babe Ruth Healthy Cut	1.50	.70	.19
☐ 35 Babe Ruth Right Choice	1.50	.70	.19
☐ 36 Babe Ruth At Rest	1.50	.70	.19
☐ 37 Babe Ruth Count It	1.50	.70	.19
☐ 38 Babe Ruth Bearded	1.50	.70	.19
☐ 39 Babe Ruth Solemn	1.50	.70	.19
☐ 40 Babe Ruth Good Cause	1.50	.70	.19
☐ 41 Babe Ruth Powder Puff	1.50	.70	.19
☐ 42 Babe Ruth He-Man Image	1.50	.70	.19
☐ 43 Babe Ruth Shedding Pounds	1.50	.70	.19
☐ 44 Babe Ruth Another Hit	1.50	.70	.19
☐ 45 Babe Ruth An Ump, Too	1.50	.70	.19
☐ 46 Babe Ruth Broken Arm	1.50	.70	.19
☐ 47 Babe Ruth New Start	1.50	.70	.19
☐ 48 Babe Ruth Diet Food	1.50	.70	.19
☐ 49 Babe Ruth Birthday Cake	1.50	.70	.19
☐ 50 Babe Ruth Good Luck	1.50	.70	.19
☐ 51 Babe Ruth Gourmet Chef	1.50	.70	.19
☐ 52 Babe Ruth Long Gone	1.50	.70	.19
☐ 53 Babe Ruth Getting Ready	1.50	.70	.19
☐ 54 Babe Ruth Thanks, Pal	1.50	.70	.19
☐ 55 Babe Ruth Called Shot	1.50	.70	.19
☐ 56 Babe Ruth On the Farm	1.50	.70	.19
☐ 57 Babe Ruth Itching to Play	1.50	.70	.19
☐ 58 Babe Ruth Big Swing	1.50	.70	.19
☐ 59 Babe Ruth Just Practice	1.50	.70	.19
☐ 60 Babe Ruth On Its Way	1.50	.70	.19
☐ 61 Babe Ruth Easy Smile	1.50	.70	.19
☐ 62 Babe Ruth In the Shade	1.50	.70	.19
☐ 63 Babe Ruth Kingly Celebration	1.50	.70	.19
☐ 64 Babe Ruth The Skipper	1.50	.70	.19
☐ 65 Babe Ruth Sandy Swing	1.50	.70	.19
☐ 66 Babe Ruth Deep Thought	1.50	.70	.19
☐ 67 Babe Ruth Bundled Up	1.50	.70	.19
☐ 68 Babe Ruth Stage Hand	1.50	.70	.19
☐ 69 Babe Ruth Mechanic, Too	1.50	.70	.19
☐ 70 Babe Ruth Serious Mood	1.50	.70	.19
☐ 71 Babe Ruth Happy Face	1.50	.70	.19
☐ 72 Babe Ruth Fashion Plate	1.50	.70	.19
☐ 73 Babe Ruth Taking a Puff	1.50	.70	.19
☐ 74 Babe Ruth Final Game as Yankee	1.50	.70	.19
☐ 75 Babe Ruth New Team	1.50	.70	.19
☐ 76 Babe Ruth Big Effort	1.50	.70	.19
☐ 77 Babe Ruth Last Game	1.50	.70	.19
☐ 78 Babe Ruth Solemn Look	1.50	.70	.19
☐ 79 Babe Ruth End is Near	1.50	.70	.19
☐ 80 Babe Ruth Farewell	1.50	.70	.19

1983 Franchise Brooks Robinson

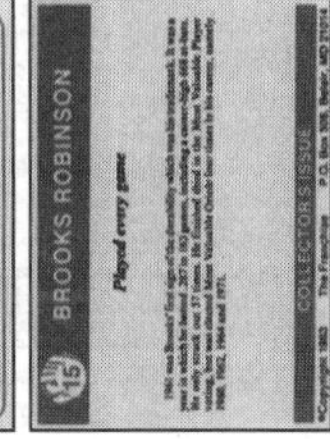

Produced by The Franchise, this 40-card standard-size set captures moments from the life and career of Brooks Robinson, the Baltimore Orioles' all-time great third baseman. On a white card face, the fronts display either posed or action black-and-white photos enclosed by an orange border stripe. Some of the front photos are horizontally oriented while others are vertically oriented. Superimposed on each card is an orange "Hall of Fame" icon. Between two orange stripes, the horizontally oriented backs feature text providing information relating to the front photo. The cards are numbered on the back in a baseball glove icon in the upper left corner.

	NRMT	VG-E	GOOD
COMPLETE SET (40)	8.00	3.60	1.00
COMMON CARD (1-40)	.25	.11	.03
☐ 1 Brooks Robinson Title Card	.50	.23	.06
☐ 2 Brooks Robinson Youngest on team	.25	.11	.03
☐ 3 Brooks Robinson All-State performer	.25	.11	.03
☐ 4 Brooks Robinson Teenager in Texas	.25	.11	.03
☐ 5 Brooks Robinson First spring training	.25	.11	.03
☐ 6 Brooks Robinson Another uniform	.25	.11	.03
☐ 7 Brooks Robinson Ron Hansen Marv Breeding Jim Gentile First solid infield	.35	.16	.04
☐ 8 Brooks Robinson Walt Dropo Celebration time	.35	.16	.04
☐ 9 Brooks Robinson Yogi Berra Instinctive baserunner	.50	.23	.06
☐ 10 Brooks Robinson Connie Robinson Wedding Day	.25	.11	.03
☐ 11 Brooks Robinson Eddie Robinson First business partner	.25	.11	.03
☐ 12 Brooks Robinson Luis Aparicio Jerry Adair Jim Gentile Second solid infield	.50	.23	.06
☐ 13 Brooks Robinson Al Kaline Two Baltimore heroes	.50	.23	.06
☐ 14 Brooks Robinson Enjoying the kids	.25	.11	.03
☐ 15 Brooks Robinson Played every game	.25	.11	.03
☐ 16 Brooks Robinson Bobby Richardson Tony Kubek Upsetting the Yankees	.35	.16	.04
☐ 17 Brooks Robinson Tom Tresh Tag out at third	.35	.16	.04
☐ 18 Brooks Robinson Jerry Adair Norm Siebern Getting net results	.35	.16	.04
☐ 19 Brooks Robinson Carl Yastrzemski Two future MVPs	.50	.23	.06
☐ 20 Brooks Robinson Rocky Marciano The original Rocky	.75	.35	.09
☐ 21 Brooks Robinson Hank Bauer Bauer's gloveman	.50	.23	.06
☐ 22 Brooks Robinson Luis Aparicio Dave Johnson Boog Powell World Series infield	.50	.23	.06
☐ 23 Brooks Robinson Boog Powell Curt Blefary Frank Robinson Orioles' power parade	.50	.23	.06
☐ 24 Brooks Robinson Hank Bauer Frank Robinson All-Star trio	.50	.23	.06
☐ 25 Brooks Robinson Frank Robinson Lethal lumber	.50	.23	.06
☐ 26 Brooks Robinson Mark Belanger Dave Johnson Boog Powell Belanger joins infield	.50	.23	.06
☐ 27 Brooks Robinson Tony Oliva Respect for Oliva	.35	.16	.04
☐ 28 Brooks Robinson Harmon Killebrew Out of Harm's way	.50	.23	.06
☐ 29 Brooks Robinson Frank Lane SCOUT Master trader	.35	.16	.04
☐ 30 Brooks Robinson Eastern Shore visit	.25	.11	.03
☐ 31 Brooks Robinson Gloves of gold	.25	.11	.03
☐ 32 Brooks Robinson Ripping the Reds	.25	.11	.03
☐ 33 Brooks Robinson Willie Stargell Rappin' with Willie	.50	.23	.06
☐ 34 Brooks Robinson Using the body	.25	.11	.03
☐ 35 Brooks Robinson Getting umps' attention	.25	.11	.03
☐ 36 Brooks Robinson Lee May Respect for teammate	.35	.16	.04
☐ 37 Brooks Robinson Doug DeCinces Touch of Class	.35	.16	.04
☐ 38 Brooks Robinson Bubble never burst	.25	.11	.03
☐ 39 Brooks Robinson Thurman Munson Honored by Yankees	.35	.16	.04
☐ 40 Brooks Robinson Harmon Killebrew Two greats at third	.50	.23	.06

1992 French's

The 1992 French's Special Edition Combo Series consists of 18 two-player cards and a title/checklist card. The cards measure the standard size. Each card features one player from the American League and one player from the National League. The cards were licensed by the MLBPA and produced by MSA (Michael Schechter Associates). Collectors could obtain the title/checklist card and three free player cards through an on-pack promotion by purchasing a 16 oz. size of French's Classic Yellow Mustard (the cards were enclosed in a plastic hangtag). Alternatively, collectors could collect all 18 player cards in the series by sending in 3.00 plus 75 cents for postage and handling along with one quality seal from the 16 oz. size of French's Classic Yellow Mustard. The released production figures were 43,000 18-card sets and 4,800,000 three-card hangtags. Both sides of the card are vertically oriented; the two color action player photos on the front are bordered in green. A white stripe with the words "Player Series" cuts across the top and intersects the French's trademark logo. Two baseball bats and a ball edge the pictures at the bottom. On a green background that features a glove, ball, bat, and home plate, the backs carry biography, player profile, and recent performance statistics for each player.

	MINT	NRMT	EXC
COMPLETE SET (19)	8.00	3.60	1.00
COMMON PAIR (1-18)	.25	.11	.03
☐ 1 Chuck Knoblauch and Jeff Bagwell	.75	.35	.09
☐ 2 Roger Clemens and Tom Glavine	.75	.35	.09
☐ 3 Julio Franco and Terry Pendleton	.25	.11	.03
☐ 4 Jose Canseco and Howard Johnson	.50	.23	.06
☐ 5 Scott Erickson and John Smiley	.25	.11	.03
☐ 6 Bryan Harvey and Lee Smith	.25	.11	.03
☐ 7 Kirby Puckett and Barry Bonds	1.00	.45	.12
☐ 8 Robin Ventura and Matt Williams	.50	.23	.06
☐ 9 Tony Pena and Tom Pagnozzi	.25	.11	.03
☐ 10 Sandy Alomar Jr. and Benito Santiago	.40	.18	.05
☐ 11 Don Mattingly and Will Clark	1.00	.45	.12
☐ 12 Roberto Alomar and Ryne Sandberg	1.00	.45	.12
☐ 13 Cal Ripken and Ozzie Smith	2.50	1.10	.30
☐ 14 Wade Boggs and Chris Sabo	.50	.23	.06
☐ 15 Ken Griffey Jr. and Dave Justice	2.00	.90	.25
☐ 16 Joe Carter and Tony Gwynn	1.00	.45	.12
☐ 17 Rickey Henderson and Darryl Strawberry	.50	.23	.06
☐ 18 Jack Morris and Steve Avery	.25	.11	.03
☐ NNO Title/Checklist Card	.25	.11	.03

1977-83 Fritsch One Year Winners

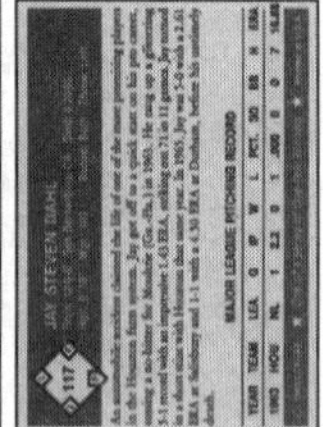

This 118-card standard-size set honors players who played roughly a season or less and were thus forgotten in baseball lore. The set was issued as three parts of one series. Cards 1-18 were issued in 1977 and feature black and white player photos, bordered in white and green. Cards 19-54 were issued in 1979 and have color player photos with white borders. Cards 55-118 were issued in 1983 and have colored photois with blue and white borders. The extended caption and Major League statistical record on the horizontally oriented backs are banded above and below by red stripes. The cards are numbered on the back in a baseball diamond in the upper left corner.

	NRMT	VG-E	GOOD
COMPLETE SET (118)	30.00	13.50	3.70
COMMON CARD (1-118)	.25	.11	.03
☐ 1 Eddie Gaedel	1.50	.70	.19
☐ 2 Chuck Connors	1.00	.45	.12
☐ 3 Joe Brovia	.25	.11	.03
☐ 4 Ross Grimsley Sr.	.25	.11	.03
☐ 5 Bob Thorpe	.25	.11	.03
☐ 6 Pete Gray	1.00	.45	.12
☐ 7 Cy Buker	.25	.11	.03
☐ 8 Ted Fritsch Sr.	.35	.16	.04
☐ 9 Ron Neccai	.35	.16	.04
☐ 10 Nino Escalera	.25	.11	.03
☐ 11 Bobo Holloman	.35	.16	.04
☐ 12 Tony Roig	.25	.11	.03
☐ 13 Paul Pettit	.35	.16	.04
☐ 14 Paul Schramka	.25	.11	.03
☐ 15 Hal Trosky Jr.	.35	.16	.04
☐ 16 Floyd Wooldridge	.25	.11	.03
☐ 17 Jim Westlake	.25	.11	.03
☐ 18 Leon Brinkopf	.25	.11	.03
☐ 19 Daryl Robertson	.25	.11	.03
☐ 20 Gerry Shoen	.25	.11	.03
☐ 21 Jim Brenneman	.25	.11	.03
☐ 22 Pat House	.25	.11	.03
☐ 23 Ken Poulsen	.25	.11	.03
☐ 24 Arlo Brunsberg	.25	.11	.03
☐ 25 Jay Hankins	.25	.11	.03
☐ 26 Chuck Nieson	.25	.11	.03
☐ 27 Dick Joyce	.25	.11	.03
☐ 28 Jim Ellis	.25	.11	.03
☐ 29 John Duffie	.25	.11	.03
☐ 30 Vern Holtgrave	.25	.11	.03
☐ 31 Bill Bethea	.25	.11	.03
☐ 32 Joe Moock	.25	.11	.03
☐ 33 John Hoffman	.25	.11	.03
☐ 34 Jorge Rubio	.25	.11	.03
☐ 35 Fred Rath	.25	.11	.03
☐ 36 Jess Hickman	.25	.11	.03
☐ 37 Tom Fisher	.25	.11	.03
☐ 38 Dick Scott	.25	.11	.03
☐ 39 Jim Hibbs	.25	.11	.03
☐ 40 Paul Gilliford	.25	.11	.03
☐ 41 Bob Botz	.25	.11	.03
☐ 42 Jack Kubiszyn	.25	.11	.03
☐ 43 Rich Rusteck	.25	.11	.03
☐ 44 Roy Gleason	.25	.11	.03
☐ 45 Glenn Vaughan	.25	.11	.03
☐ 46 Bill Graham	.25	.11	.03
☐ 47 Dennis Musgraves	.25	.11	.03
☐ 48 Ron Henry	.25	.11	.03
☐ 49 Mike Jurewicz	.25	.11	.03
☐ 50 Pidge Browne	.35	.16	.04
☐ 51 Ron Keller	.25	.11	.03
☐ 52 Doug Gallagher	.25	.11	.03
☐ 53 Dave Thies	.25	.11	.03
☐ 54 Don Eaddy	.25	.11	.03
☐ 55 Don Prince	.25	.11	.03
☐ 56 Tom Granly	.25	.11	.03
☐ 57 Roy Heiser	.25	.11	.03
☐ 58 Hank Izquierdo	.25	.11	.03
☐ 59 Rex Johnston	.25	.11	.03
☐ 60 Jack Damaska	.25	.11	.03
☐ 61 John Flavin	.25	.11	.03
☐ 62 John Glenn	.25	.11	.03
☐ 63 Stan Johnson	.25	.11	.03
☐ 64 Don Choate	.25	.11	.03
☐ 65 Bill Kern	.25	.11	.03
☐ 66 Dick Luebke	.25	.11	.03
☐ 67 Glen Clark	.25	.11	.03
☐ 68 Lamar Jacobs	.25	.11	.03
☐ 69 Rick Herrscher	.25	.11	.03
☐ 70 Jim McManus	.25	.11	.03
☐ 71 Len Church	.25	.11	.03
☐ 72 Moose Stubing	.25	.11	.03
☐ 73 Cal Emery	.25	.11	.03
☐ 74 Lee Gregory	.25	.11	.03
☐ 75 Mike Page	.25	.11	.03
☐ 76 Benny Valenzuela	.25	.11	.03
☐ 77 John Papa	.25	.11	.03
☐ 78 Jim Stump	.25	.11	.03
☐ 79 Brian McCall	.25	.11	.03
☐ 80 Al Kenders	.25	.11	.03
☐ 81 Corky Withrow	.25	.11	.03
☐ 82 Verle Tiefenthaler	.25	.11	.03
☐ 83 Dave Wissman	.25	.11	.03
☐ 84 Tom Fletcher	.25	.11	.03
☐ 85 Dale Willis	.25	.11	.03
☐ 86 Larry Foster	.25	.11	.03
☐ 87 Johnnie Seale	.25	.11	.03
☐ 88 Jim Lekew	.25	.11	.03
☐ 89 Charlie Shoemaker	.25	.11	.03
☐ 90 Don Arlich	.25	.11	.03
☐ 91 George Gerberman	.25	.11	.03
☐ 92 John Pregenger	.25	.11	.03
☐ 93 Merlin Nippert	.25	.11	.03
☐ 94 Steve Demeter	.25	.11	.03
☐ 95 John Paciorek	.35	.16	.04
☐ 96 Larry Loughlin	.25	.11	.03
☐ 97 Alan Brice	.25	.11	.03
☐ 98 Chet Boak	.25	.11	.03
☐ 99 Alan Koch	.25	.11	.03
☐ 100 Danny Thomas	.25	.11	.03
☐ 101 Elder White	.25	.11	.03
☐ 102 Jim Snyder	.25	.11	.03
☐ 103 Ted Schreiber	.25	.11	.03
☐ 104 Evans Killeen	.25	.11	.03
☐ 105 Ray Daviault	.25	.11	.03
☐ 106 Larry Foss	.25	.11	.03
☐ 107 Wayne Graham	.25	.11	.03
☐ 108 Santiago Rosario	.25	.11	.03
☐ 109 Bob Sprout	.25	.11	.03
☐ 110 Tom Hughes	.25	.11	.03
☐ 111 Em Lindbeck	.25	.11	.03
☐ 112 Ray Blemker	.25	.11	.03
☐ 113 Shaun Fitzmaurice	.25	.11	.03
☐ 114 Ron Stillwell	.25	.11	.03
☐ 115 Carl Thomas	.25	.11	.03
☐ 116 Mike DeGerick	.25	.11	.03
☐ 117 Jay Dahl	.25	.11	.03
☐ 118 Al Lary	.25	.11	.03

1988 Fritsch Baseball Card Museum

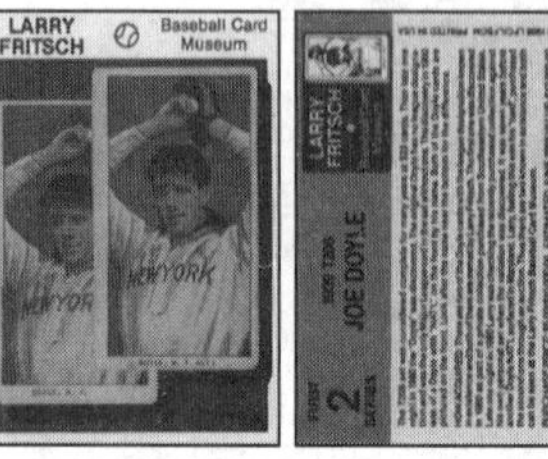

This set was issued to commemorate the opening of Larry Fritsch's Baseball Card Museum in Cooperstown, New York. This set features reprints of some of the hobby's most expensive cards.

	MINT	NRMT	EXC
COMPLETE SET (8)	8.00	3.60	1.00
COMMON CARD (1-8)	.25	.11	.03
☐ 1 Honus Wagner T206	2.50	1.10	.30
☐ 2 Joe Doyle T206 With and without NAT'L on front	.40	.18	.05
☐ 3 Ty Cobb T205	2.50	1.10	.30
☐ 4 Joe Jackson Cracker Jack	2.50	1.10	.30
☐ 5 Eddie Plank T206	1.00	.45	.12
☐ 6 Sherry Magee T206 With spellings Magie and Magee)	.40	.18	.05
☐ 7 Jim Thorpe Colgan's Chips	1.50	.70	.19
☐ 8 Baseball Card Museum Advertisement	.25	.11	.03

1928 Fro Joy

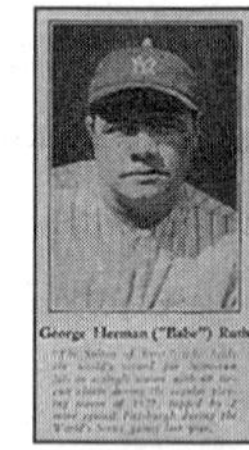

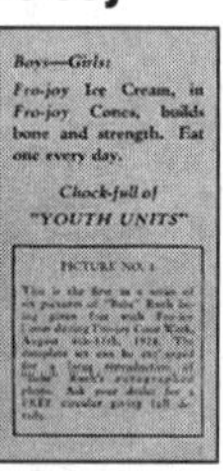

The cards in this six-card set measure approximately 2 1/16" by 4". The Fro Joy set of 1928 was designed to exploit the advertising potential of the mighty Babe Ruth. Six black and white cards explained specific baseball techniques while the reverse advertising extolled the virtues of Fro Joy ice cream and ice cream cones. Unfortunately this small set has been illegally reprinted (several times) and many of these virtually worthless fakes have been introduced into the hobby. The easiest fakes to spot are those cards (or uncut sheets) that are slightly over-sized and blue tinted; however some of the other fakes are more cleverly faithful to the original. Be very careful before purchasing Fro-Joys; obtain a qualified opinion on authenticity from an experienced dealer (preferably one who is unrelated to the dealer trying to sell you his cards). You might also show the cards (before you commit to purchase them) to an experienced printer who can advise you on the true age of the paper stock. More than one dealer has been quoted as saying that 99 percent of the Fro Joys seen are fakes.

	EX-MT	VG-E	GOOD
COMPLETE SET (6)	600.00	275.00	75.00
COMMON CARD (1-6)	100.00	45.00	12.50
☐ 1 Babe Ruth George Herman Babe Ruth	150.00	70.00	19.00
☐ 2 Babe Ruth Look Out Mr. Pitcher	100.00	45.00	12.50
☐ 3 Babe Ruth Bang The Babe Lines one out	100.00	45.00	12.50
☐ 4 Babe Ruth When the Babe Comes Out	100.00	45.00	12.50
☐ 5 Babe Ruth Babe Ruth's Grip	100.00	45.00	12.50
☐ 6 Babe Ruth Ruth is a Crack Fielder	100.00	45.00	12.50

1991 Front Row Ken Griffey Jr.

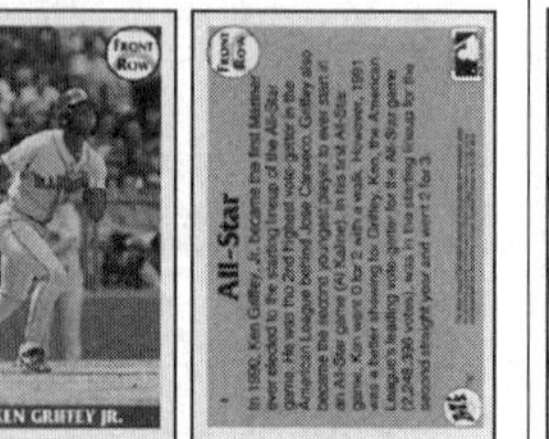

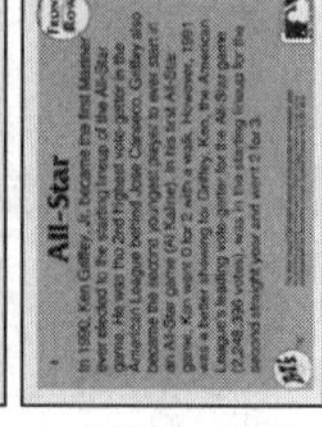

This 15-card standard-size set is composed of the ten-card insert set plus a five-card promo set. The ten-card insert set features different action shots of Ken Griffey Jr. An official certificate of authenticity included with the set gives the set serial number and production run ("X of 25,000"). These cards were randomly inserted into 1992 Front Row Baseball Draft Pick wax boxes. The standard-size cards display on the fronts color game shots bordered in white. Beneath each picture, the player's name appears in a blue stripe that intersects the team logo in the lower left corner. On a blue background, the horizontally oriented backs summarize Griffey's career. Except for a baseball icon on their backs marked with the word "Promo," the promo cards are identical with the first five cards in the insert set. The Promo cards in the checklist below have been numbered with a P suffix in order to avoid confusion. According to Front Row, 25,000 sets were produced. All these cards can be distinguished from the regular issue by their backs, which are gold-foil stamped with the "Front Row Collector's Club Charter Member" seal.

	MINT	NRMT	EXC
COMPLETE SET (15)	15.00	6.75	1.85
COMMON CARD (1-10)	1.00	.45	.12
COMMON PROMO (1P-5P)	1.00	.45	.12
☐ 1 Ken Griffey Jr. All-Star	1.00	.45	.12
☐ 1P Ken Griffey Jr. All-Star	1.00	.45	.12
☐ 2 Ken Griffey Jr. The Breakdown	1.00	.45	.12
☐ 2P Ken Griffey Jr. The Breakdown	1.00	.45	.12
☐ 3 Ken Griffey Jr. Homers	1.00	.45	.12
☐ 3P Ken Griffey Jr. Homers	1.00	.45	.12
☐ 4 Ken Griffey Jr. Gold Glove	1.00	.45	.12
☐ 4P Ken Griffey Jr. Gold Glove	1.00	.45	.12
☐ 5 Ken Griffey Jr. Drafted	1.00	.45	.12
☐ 5P Ken Griffey Jr. Drafted	1.00	.45	.12
☐ 6 Ken Griffey Jr. Up Close and Personal	1.00	.45	.12
☐ 7 Ken Griffey Jr. Background	1.00	.45	.12
☐ 8 Ken Griffey Jr. The Majors	1.00	.45	.12
☐ 9 Ken Griffey Jr. Career Highlights	1.00	.45	.12
☐ 10 Ken Griffey Jr. The American League	1.00	.45	.12

1992 Front Row ATG Holograms

These three hologram cards commemorate an outstanding season of three of baseball's all-time greats. The production run was 100,000 for each card. Measuring the standard size, the fronts feature full-bleed holograms with a cut out action player photo. The background consists of two torn edges of a sheet of paper, as if the player broke through. The set subtitle is printed vertically on the left edge, while the player's last name is printed on the right edge. With shading from dark to light red, the backs carry a color close-up photo as well as season statistics and season summary. The card serial number is printed on a Front Row holographic bar. The cards are unnumbered and checklisted below in alphabetical order.

	MINT	NRMT	EXC
COMPLETE SET (3)	5.00	2.20	.60
COMMON CARD (1-3)	1.25	.55	.16
☐ 1 Hank Aaron	2.00	.90	.25
☐ 2 Roy Campanella	1.25	.55	.16
☐ 3 Tom Seaver	2.00	.90	.25

1992 Front Row Banks

This five-card standard-size set features Hall of Famer Ernie Banks. Each set includes an official certificate of authenticity that gives the production run (25,000) and the set serial number. Banks autographed the first card in 5,000 sets that were initially offered exclusively to Front Row Collector's Club Members. Cards 1-4 carry color player photos on the fronts, while card No. 5 has a black and white photo. All pictures are bordered in white and the player's name appears in a blue stripe below each picture. On the background of a ghosted close-up photo, the horizontally oriented backs present career summary, highlights or statistics.

	MINT	NRMT	EXC
COMPLETE SET (5)	4.00	1.80	.50
COMMON CARD (1-5)	1.00	.45	.12

	MINT	NRMT	EXC
☐ 1 Ernie Banks Beginnings	1.00	.45	.12
☐ 2 Ernie Banks Complete Player	1.00	.45	.12
☐ 3 Ernie Banks Greatest Cub Ever	1.00	.45	.12
☐ 4 Ernie Banks Major League Statistics	1.00	.45	.12
☐ 5 Ernie Banks Hall of Famer	1.00	.45	.12

1992 Front Row Berra

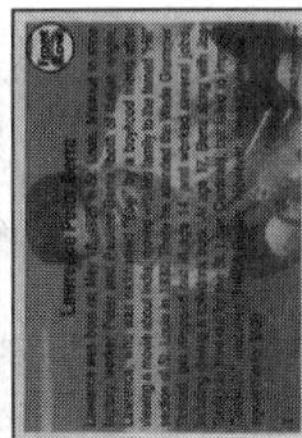

This five-card standard-size set features Hall of Famer Yogi Berra. Each set includes an official certificate of authenticity that gives the production run (25,000) and the set serial number. Berra autographed the first card in 5,000 sets that were initially offered exclusively to Front Row Collector's Club Members. Card Nos. 1 and 3 carry color player photos on the fronts, while card Nos. 2, 4 and 5 have black and white photos. All pictures are bordered in white and the player's name appears in a gray stripe below each picture. On the background of a ghosted close-up photo, the horizontal backs present biography, career summary, highlights or statistics.

	MINT	NRMT	EXC
COMPLETE SET (5)	4.00	1.80	.50
COMMON CARD (1-5)	1.00	.45	.12
☐ 1 Yogi Berra Lawrence Peter Berra	1.00	.45	.12
☐ 2 Yogi Berra Yogiisms	1.00	.45	.12
☐ 3 Yogi Berra Major League Statistics	1.00	.45	.12
☐ 4 Yogi Berra World Series Regular	1.00	.45	.12
☐ 5 Yogi Berra A Place in Cooperstown	1.00	.45	.12

1992 Front Row Brooks Robinson

This five-card standard-size set features Hall of Famer Brooks Robinson. Each set includes an official certificate of authenticity that gives the production run (25,000) and the set serial number. Robinson autographed the first card in 5,000 sets that were initially offered exclusively to Front Row Collector's Club Members. The fronts feature color player photos. All pictures are bordered in white and the player's name appears in a green stripe below each picture. On the background of a ghosted close-up photo, the horizontal backs present biography, career summary, highlights or statistics.

	MINT	NRMT	EXC
COMPLETE SET (5)	4.00	1.80	.50
COMMON CARD (1-5)	1.00	.45	.12
☐ 1 Brooks Robinson In The Field	1.00	.45	.12
☐ 2 Brooks Robinson Major League Stats	1.00	.45	.12
☐ 3 Brooks Robinson Post-Season Play	1.00	.45	.12
☐ 4 Brooks Robinson Off The Diamond	1.00	.45	.12
☐ 5 Brooks Robinson Hall of Fame	1.00	.45	.12

1992 Front Row Buck Leonard

This five-card standard-size set features Hall of Famer Buck Leonard. Each set includes an official certificate of authenticity that gives the production run (25,000) and the set serial number. Leonard autographed the first card in 5,000 sets that were initially offered exclusively to Front Row Collector's Club Members. The fronts feature black and white player photos. All pictures are bordered in white and the player's name appears in a green stripe below each picture. On the background of a ghosted close-up photo, the horizontal backs present biography, career summary, highlights or Negro League statistics.

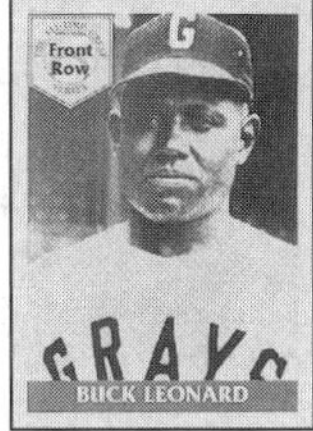

	MINT	NRMT	EXC
COMPLETE SET (5)	4.00	1.80	.50
COMMON CARD (1-5)	1.00	.45	.12
☐ 1 Buck Leonard Walter Fenner Leonard	1.00	.45	.12
☐ 2 Buck Leonard The Homestead Grays	1.00	.45	.12
☐ 3 Buck Leonard Negro League Statistics	1.00	.45	.12
☐ 4 Buck Leonard Good Enough for the Majors	1.00	.45	.12
☐ 5 Buck Leonard Honored at Cooperstown	1.00	.45	.12

1992 Front Row Dandridge

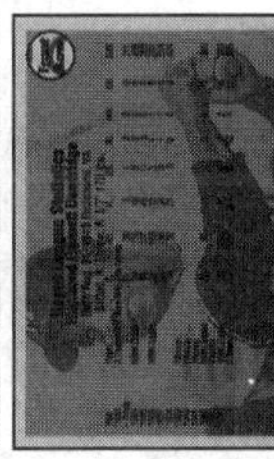

This five-card standard-size set features Hall of Famer Ray Dandridge. Each set includes an official certificate of authenticity, giving the production run (25,000) and the set serial number. Dandridge autographed the first card in 5,000 sets that were initially offered exclusively to Front Row Collector's Club Members. All the cards carry black and white photos on the fronts that are bordered in white. The player's name appears in a rust-colored stripe below each picture. On the background of a ghosted close-up photo, the horizontally oriented backs present biography, career summary, highlights or Negro League statistics.

	MINT	NRMT	EXC
COMPLETE SET (5)	4.00	1.80	.50
COMMON CARD (1-5)	1.00	.45	.12
☐ 1 Ray Dandridge The Early Years	1.00	.45	.12
☐ 2 Ray Dandridge Million Dollar Infield	1.00	.45	.12
☐ 3 Ray Dandridge Negro League Statistics	1.00	.45	.12
☐ 4 Ray Dandridge A Step Away	1.00	.45	.12
☐ 5 Ray Dandridge Raymond Emmitt Dandridge	1.00	.45	.12

1992 Front Row Ford

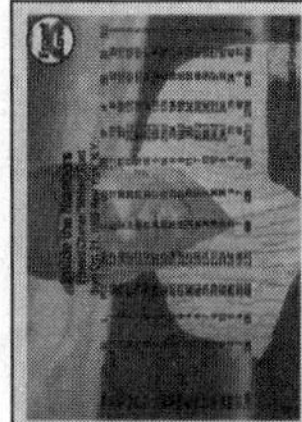

This five-card standard-size set features Hall of Famer Whitey Ford. Each set includes an official certificate of authenticity that gives the production run (25,000) and the set serial number. Ford autographed the first card in 5,000 sets that were initially offered exclusively to Front Row Collector's Club Members. The fronts feature color player photos bordered in white. The player's name appears in a black stripe below each picture. On the background of a ghosted color close-up photo, the horizontally oriented backs present biography, career summary, highlights or statistics.

	MINT	NRMT	EXC
COMPLETE SET (5)	4.00	1.80	.50
COMMON CARD (1-5)	1.00	.45	.12
☐ 1 Whitey Ford Edward Charles Ford	1.00	.45	.12
☐ 2 Whitey Ford The Chairman of the Board	1.00	.45	.12
☐ 3 Whitey Ford Accomplishments	1.00	.45	.12
☐ 4 Whitey Ford Inside the Numbers	1.00	.45	.12
☐ 5 Whitey Ford Cooperstown, NY	1.00	.45	.12

1992 Front Row Griffey Club House

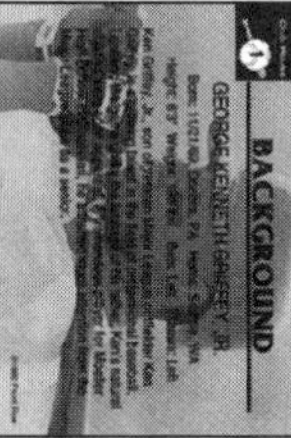

This ten-card standard-size set features full-bleed color player photos on the front. The only text on the front appears in a black square at the lower right corner, which reads "Club House Series, Ken Griffey Jr." On the background of a ghosted color close-up photo, the backs carry biography, highlights or statistics. According to Front Row, 25,000 sets were produced.

	MINT	NRMT	EXC
COMPLETE SET (10)	10.00	4.50	1.25
COMMON CARD (1-10)	1.00	.45	.12
☐ 1 Ken Griffey Jr. Background	1.00	.45	.12
☐ 2 Ken Griffey Jr. Drafted	1.00	.45	.12
☐ 3 Ken Griffey Jr. The Majors	1.00	.45	.12
☐ 4 Ken Griffey Jr. The Breakdown	1.00	.45	.12
☐ 5 Ken Griffey Jr. The American League	1.00	.45	.12
☐ 6 Ken Griffey Jr. All-Star	1.00	.45	.12
☐ 7 Ken Griffey Jr. Gold Glove	1.00	.45	.12
☐ 8 Ken Griffey Jr. Homers	1.00	.45	.12
☐ 9 Ken Griffey Jr. Career Highlights	1.00	.45	.12
☐ 10 Ken Griffey Jr. A Closer Look	1.00	.45	.12

1992 Front Row Griffey Gold

This three-card standard-size set features color player photos on the fronts bordered by 23K gold dust stamping. The player's name appears in a blue bar beneath the picture. The backs are bordered in white and have a navy blue stripe at the top and the card's subtitle in a green bar, with text relating to the subtitle on a pastel yellow panel. Each set was accompanied by a certificate of authenticity carrying the production run (20,000) and the set serial number. Front Row issued 5,000 uncut strips of the three-card set.

	MINT	NRMT	EXC
COMPLETE SET (3)	15.00	6.75	1.85
COMMON CARD (1-3)	5.00	2.20	.60
☐ 1 Ken Griffey Jr. Gold Glove	5.00	2.20	.60
☐ 2 Ken Griffey Jr. Background	5.00	2.20	.60
☐ 3 Ken Griffey Jr. Drafted	5.00	2.20	.60

1992 Front Row Griffey Holograms

This three-card hologram set features three-dimensional shots of Ken Griffey Jr. Each set includes an official certificate of authenticity giving the set serial number and production run (50,000). The hologram cards measure the standard size. Cards 1-2 have horizontally oriented backs. The white-bordered backs display color photos of Griffey along with career highlights in a blue-gray box. The cards are numbered on the back. All Seattle Mariner logos have been airbrushed off the cards as they were not licensed by the league or team.

	MINT	NRMT	EXC
COMPLETE SET (3)	6.00	2.70	.75
COMMON CARD (1-3)	2.00	.90	.25
☐ 1 Ken Griffey Jr. Making History	2.00	.90	.25
☐ 2 Ken Griffey Jr. Rewriting the Record Book	2.00	.90	.25
☐ 3 Ken Griffey Jr. Turning Up Gold	2.00	.90	.25

1992 Front Row Griffey Jr. Oversized Card

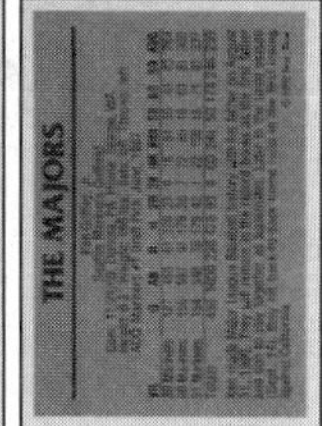

This oversized promo card measures approximately 7 1/2" X 10 1/2" and features a color action shot of Griffey at bat. The picture is bordered in white and has a black stripe across the bottom of the photo containing the player's name in white lettering. The horizontal back displays a white-bordered gray panel that carries biographical information, statistics and player information. The card is unnumbered.

	MINT	NRMT	EXC
COMPLETE SET (1)	3.00	1.35	.35
COMMON CARD	3.00	1.35	.35
☐ NNO Ken Griffey Jr.	3.00	1.35	.35

1992 Front Row Irvin

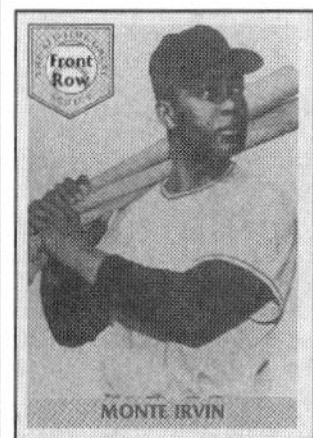

This five-card standard-size set features Hall of Famer Monte Irvin. Each set includes an official certificate of authenticity, giving the production run (25,000) and the set serial number. Irvin autographed the first card in 5,000 sets that were initially offered exclusively to Front Row Collector's Club Members. The fronts feature either black and white (cards 1-2) or color player photos (cards 3-5). All pictures are bordered in white, and the player's name appears in a gray stripe below each picture. On the background of a ghosted color close-up photo, the horizontally oriented backs present biography, career summary, highlights or statistics.

	MINT	NRMT	EXC
COMPLETE SET (5)	4.00	1.80	.50
COMMON CARD (1-5)	1.00	.45	.12
☐ 1 Monte Irvin Early Accomplishments	1.00	.45	.12
☐ 2 Monte Irvin Monte's Return	1.00	.45	.12
☐ 3 Monte Irvin The Big Leagues Past His Prime	1.00	.45	.12
☐ 4 Monte Irvin Monford Merrill Irvin	1.00	.45	.12
☐ 5 Monte Irvin A Tribute to Monte	1.00	.45	.12

1992 Front Row Seaver

This five card set feature highlights in the career of Hall of Fame pitcher Tom Seaver. Like most of the 1992 Front Row sets, this standard-size set was issued in a quantity of 25,000 sets with 5,000 of card #1 being autographed.

	MINT	NRMT	EXC
COMPLETE SET (5)	4.00	1.80	.50
COMMON CARD (1-5)	1.00	.45	.12
☐ 1 Tom Seaver	1.00	.45	.12
☐ 2 Tom Seaver	1.00	.45	.12

☐ 3 Tom Seaver	1.00	.45	.12
☐ 4 Tom Seaver	1.00	.45	.12
☐ 5 Tom Seaver	1.00	.45	.12

1992 Front Row Stargell

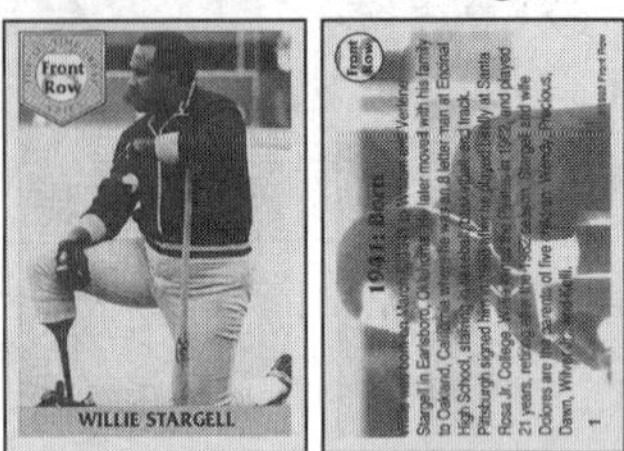

This five-card standard-size set features Hall of Famer Willie Stargell. Each set includes an official certificate of authenticity, giving the production run (25,000) and the set serial number. Stargell autographed the first card in 5,000 sets that were initially offered exclusively to Front Row Collector's Club Members. The fronts feature color player photos. All pictures are bordered in white and the player's name appears in a mustard stripe below each picture. On the background of a ghosted close-up photo, the horizontally oriented backs present biography, career summary, highlights or statistics.

	MINT	NRMT	EXC
COMPLETE SET (5)	4.00	1.80	.50
COMMON CARD (1-5)	1.00	.45	.12
☐ 1 Willie Stargell Born, 1941	1.00	.45	.12
☐ 2 Willie Stargell Comeback Player of the Year 1978	1.00	.45	.12
☐ 3 Willie Stargell 3-Time MVP, 1979	1.00	.45	.12
☐ 4 Willie Stargell An Illustrious Career, 1962-82	1.00	.45	.12
☐ 5 Willie Stargell Hall of Fame, 1988	1.00	.45	.12

1992 Front Row Thomas

This seven-card, standard-size set features on the front color player photos bordered in white. The player's name appears in white lettering in a black stripe above the picture. In a horizontal format, the backs have a second player photo as well as biography, statistics (major and minor leagues), career summary, and highlights. Each set includes an official certificate of authenticity that gives the production run (30,000) and the set serial number.

	MINT	NRMT	EXC
COMPLETE SET (7)	6.00	2.70	.75
COMMON CARD (1-7)	1.00	.45	.12
☐ 1 Frank Thomas A Good Start	1.00	.45	.12
☐ 2 Frank Thomas Multi-Talented	1.00	.45	.12
☐ 3 Frank Thomas Auburn Career Stats	1.00	.45	.12
☐ 4 Frank Thomas Accomplishments	1.00	.45	.12
☐ 5 Frank Thomas Individual Honors	1.00	.45	.12
☐ 6 Frank Thomas Minor League Stats	1.00	.45	.12
☐ 7 Frank Thomas Major League Stats	1.00	.45	.12

1992 Front Row Thomas Gold

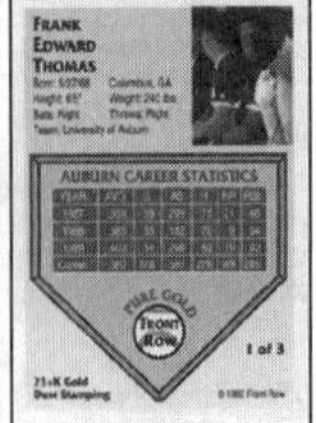

This three-card, standard-size set features color player photos on the fronts bordered by 23K gold dust stamping. The player's name appears in a green bar beneath the picture. On a mint green background bordered in white, the backs have biography, a close-up color photo, and statistics presented inside a home plate icon. Each set was accompanied by a certificate of authenticity carrying the production run (20,000) and the set serial number. Five thousand uncut strips of the three-card set were also produced. The cards are numbered on the back.

	MINT	NRMT	EXC
COMPLETE SET (3)	15.00	6.75	1.85
COMMON CARD (1-3)	5.00	2.20	.60
☐ 1 Frank Thomas Auburn Career Stats	5.00	2.20	.60
☐ 2 Frank Thomas Minor League Stats	5.00	2.20	.60
☐ 3 Frank Thomas Major League Stats	5.00	2.20	.60

1992 Front Row Tyler Green

This seven card standard-size set was among the many individual player sets issued by Front Row. Each set features highlights of Travis Green's early baseball career and includes an Official Certificate of Authenticity

	MINT	EXC	G-VG
COMMON PLAYER (1-7)	1.50	.70	.19
COMMON CARD (1-7)	.25	.11	.03
☐ 1 Tyler Green Early Success	.25	.11	.03
☐ 2 Tyler Green Wichita St. Career Statistics	.25	.11	.03
☐ 3 Tyler Green NCAA Tournament Statistics	.25	.11	.03
☐ 4 Tyler Green Honors	.25	.11	.03
☐ 5 Tyler Green Drafted	.25	.11	.03
☐ 6 Tyler Green Tyler Scott Green	.25	.11	.03
☐ 7 Tyler Green Full photo on back	.25	.11	.03

1993 Front Row Brock

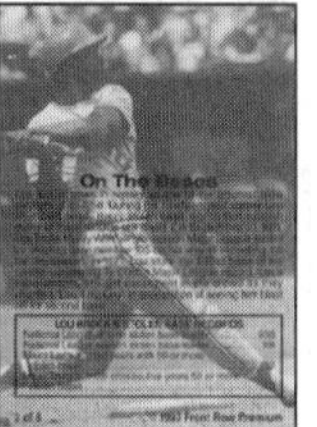

The five standard-size cards comprising this set feature borderless color photos that have the Cardinals name and logo airbrushed from Brock's uniform. His name appears in gold foil within a black bar near the bottom that merges with a black circle on the left, which contains the Front Row logo in gold foil. The set subtitle, "All Time Greats," is printed vertically in gold foil at the left edge. The backs all feature the same ghosted, full-bleed photo of Brock at bat, which provides the background for his career highlights and stats. The set comes with a certificate of authenticity that carries the serial number out of 5,000 sets produced.

	MINT	NRMT	EXC
COMPLETE SET (5)	4.00	1.80	.50
COMMON CARD (1-5)	1.00	.45	.12
☐ 1 Lou Brock Louis Clark Brock	1.00	.45	.12
☐ 2 Lou Brock On the Bases	1.00	.45	.12
☐ 3 Lou Brock At the Plate	1.00	.45	.12
☐ 4 Lou Brock In the World Series	1.00	.45	.12
☐ 5 Lou Brock In the Hall of Fame	1.00	.45	.12

1993 Front Row Fingers

Front Row issued this five-card standard-size set as part of "The Gold Collection" line. Just 5,000 sets were produced. The fronts feature full-bleed color photos. The words "The Gold Collection" are printed in gold foil along the left edge, while his name is printed in the same way on a green bar toward the bottom of the picture. Inside green borders,

the backs summarize his career on a background consisting of a ghosted action player photo. A white baseball icon at the top reads "All Time Great Series."

	MINT	NRMT	EXC
COMPLETE SET (5)	4.00	1.80	.50
COMMON CARD (1-5)	1.00	.45	.12
☐ 1 Rollie Fingers	1.00	.45	.12
☐ 2 Rollie Fingers	1.00	.45	.12
☐ 3 Rollie Fingers	1.00	.45	.12
☐ 4 Rollie Fingers	1.00	.45	.12
☐ 5 Rollie Fingers	1.00	.45	.12

1993 Front Row Griffey Jr. Gold Collection

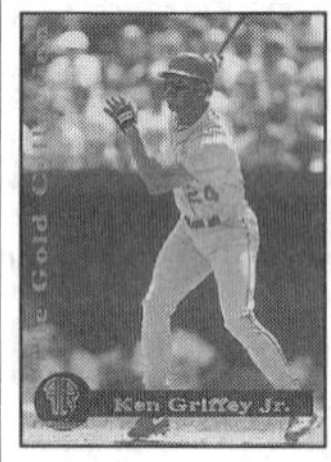

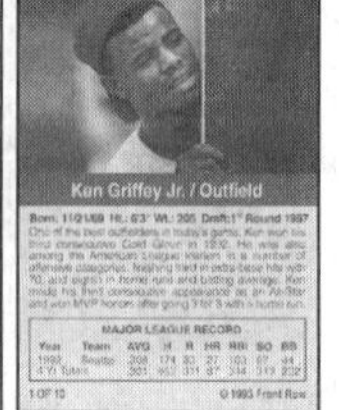

This ten-card standard-size set features borderless color action shots on its fronts. Griffey's name appears in gold foil within a black stripe near the bottom, which conjoins with the gold-foil Front Row logo within a black circle near the left edge. The words "The Gold Collection" appear vertically in gold foil on one side. The back displays another photo at the top, with his name and position within a blue stripe beneath. A biography, career highlights and stats follow below.

	MINT	NRMT	EXC
COMPLETE SET (10)	10.00	4.50	1.25
COMMON CARD (1-10)	1.00	.45	.12
☐ 1 Ken Griffey Jr.	1.00	.45	.12
☐ 2 Ken Griffey Jr.	1.00	.45	.12
☐ 3 Ken Griffey Jr.	1.00	.45	.12
☐ 4 Ken Griffey Jr.	1.00	.45	.12
☐ 5 Ken Griffey Jr.	1.00	.45	.12
☐ 6 Ken Griffey Jr.	1.00	.45	.12
☐ 7 Ken Griffey Jr.	1.00	.45	.12
☐ 8 Ken Griffey Jr.	1.00	.45	.12
☐ 9 Ken Griffey Jr.	1.00	.45	.12
☐ 10 Ken Griffey Jr.	1.00	.45	.12

1993 Front Row Palmer

This five-card Front Row Premium set spotlights former Baltimore Orioles' pitcher Jim Palmer. The cards measure the standard size and, of the sets produced only 2,000 carry an authentic autograph, which appears on the first card. The fronts display full-bleed color shots of Palmer with "All-Time Greats" printed vertically along the left edge in gold-foil lettering. Jim Palmer's name appears in gold-foil in a black bar near the bottom edge that extends from the gold foil Front Row Premium logo in the lower left. The borderless backs carry career highlights upon a ghosted action photo.

	MINT	NRMT	EXC
COMPLETE SET (5)	4.00	1.80	.50
COMMON CARD (1-5)	1.00	.45	.12
☐ 1 Jim Palmer	1.00	.45	.12
☐ 2 Jim Palmer	1.00	.45	.12
☐ 3 Jim Palmer	1.00	.45	.12
☐ 4 Jim Palmer	1.00	.45	.12
☐ 5 Jim Palmer	1.00	.45	.12

1993 Front Row Rick Ferrell

This five-card set honors the first free agent in Major League baseball (in 1928). Just 2,000 five-card sets with the first card signed were produced. Each set includes a certificate of authenticity.

	MINT	NRMT	EXC
COMPLETE SET (5)	4.00	1.80	.50
COMMON CARD (1-5)	1.00	.45	.12
☐ 1 Rick Ferrell	1.00	.45	.12
☐ 2 Rick Ferrell	1.00	.45	.12
☐ 3 Rick Ferrell	1.00	.45	.12
☐ 4 Rick Ferrell	1.00	.45	.12
☐ 5 Rick Ferrell	1.00	.45	.12

1984 Fun Foods Pins

These pins were mass marketed in early 1985 (the copyright notice on the pin backs indicate 1984) and feature 133 pins of the current stars of baseball. Each pin measures approximately 1 1/8" in diameter. There are other related "proof" type items available for this issue. The color border around the photo is coded for the player's team. On the back each pins is numbered; the player's position and a statistic are given.

	NRMT	VG-E	GOOD
COMPLETE SET (133)	15.00	6.75	1.85
COMMON PIN (1-133)	.05	.02	.01
☐ 1 Dave Winfield	.50	.23	.06
☐ 2 Lance Parrish	.10	.05	.01
☐ 3 Gary Carter	.10	.05	.01
☐ 4 Pete Rose	.50	.23	.06
☐ 5 Jim Rice	.10	.05	.01
☐ 6 George Brett	1.50	.70	.19
☐ 7 Fernando Valenzuela	.10	.05	.01
☐ 8 Darryl Strawberry	.15	.07	.02
☐ 9 Steve Garvey	.15	.07	.02
☐ 10 Rollie Fingers	.25	.11	.03
☐ 11 Mike Schmidt	1.00	.45	.12
☐ 12 Kent Tekulve	.05	.02	.01
☐ 13 Ryne Sandberg	1.25	.55	.16
☐ 14 Bruce Sutter	.10	.05	.01
☐ 15 Tom Seaver	.30	.14	.04
☐ 16 Reggie Jackson	.50	.23	.06
☐ 17 Rickey Henderson	.50	.23	.06
☐ 18 Mark Langston	.15	.07	.02
☐ 19 Jack Clark	.10	.05	.01
☐ 20 Willie Randolph	.10	.05	.01
☐ 21 Kirk Gibson	.15	.07	.02
☐ 22 Andre Dawson	.30	.14	.04
☐ 23 Dave Concepcion	.10	.05	.01
☐ 24 Tony Armas	.05	.02	.01
☐ 25 Dan Quisenberry	.05	.02	.01
☐ 26 Pedro Guerrero	.10	.05	.01
☐ 27 Dwight Gooden	.75	.35	.09
☐ 28 Tony Gwynn	1.50	.70	.19
☐ 29 Robin Yount	.30	.14	.04
☐ 30 Steve Carlton	.30	.14	.04
☐ 31 Bill Madlock	.10	.05	.01
☐ 32 Rick Sutcliffe	.10	.05	.01
☐ 33 Willie McGee	.15	.07	.02
☐ 34 Greg Luzinski	.10	.05	.01
☐ 35 Rod Carew	.40	.18	.05
☐ 36 Dave Kingman	.10	.05	.01
☐ 37 Alvin Davis	.05	.02	.01
☐ 38 Chili Davis	.10	.05	.01
☐ 39 Don Baylor	.10	.05	.01
☐ 40 Alan Trammell	.15	.07	.02
☐ 41 Tim Raines	.15	.07	.02
☐ 42 Cesar Cedeno	.05	.02	.01
☐ 43 Wade Boggs	.50	.23	.06
☐ 44 Frank White	.10	.05	.01
☐ 45 Steve Sax	.05	.02	.01
☐ 46 George Foster	.05	.02	.01
☐ 47 Terry Kennedy	.05	.02	.01
☐ 48 Cecil Cooper	.10	.05	.01
☐ 49 John Denny	.05	.02	.01
☐ 50 John Candelaria	.05	.02	.01
☐ 51 Jody Davis	.05	.02	.01
☐ 52 George Hendrick	.05	.02	.01
☐ 53 Ron Kittle	.05	.02	.01
☐ 54 Fred Lynn	.10	.05	.01
☐ 55 Carney Lansford	.05	.02	.01
☐ 56 Gorman Thomas	.05	.02	.01
☐ 57 Manny Trillo	.05	.02	.01
☐ 58 Steve Kemp	.05	.02	.01
☐ 59 Jack Morris	.10	.05	.01
☐ 60 Dan Petry	.05	.02	.01
☐ 61 Mario Soto	.05	.02	.01
☐ 62 Dwight Evans	.10	.05	.01
☐ 63 Hal McRae	.10	.05	.01
☐ 64 Mike Marshall	.05	.02	.01
☐ 65 Mookie Wilson	.10	.05	.01

Card	MINT	NRMT	EXC
☐ 66 Graig Nettles	.10	.05	.01
☐ 67 Ben Oglivie	.05	.02	.01
☐ 68 Juan Samuel	.05	.02	.01
☐ 69 Johnny Ray	.05	.02	.01
☐ 70 Gary Matthews	.10	.05	.01
☐ 71 Ozzie Smith	1.25	.55	.16
☐ 72 Carlton Fisk	.25	.11	.03
☐ 73 Doug DeCinces	.05	.02	.01
☐ 74 Joe Morgan	.25	.11	.03
☐ 75 Dave Stieb	.05	.02	.01
☐ 76 Buddy Bell	.05	.02	.01
☐ 77 Don Mattingly	1.50	.70	.19
☐ 78 Lou Whitaker	.20	.09	.03
☐ 79 Willie Hernandez	.05	.02	.01
☐ 80 Dave Parker	.10	.05	.01
☐ 81 Bob Stanley	.05	.02	.01
☐ 82 Willie Wilson	.05	.02	.01
☐ 83 Orel Hershiser	.50	.23	.06
☐ 84 Rusty Staub	.10	.05	.01
☐ 85 Goose Gossage	.15	.07	.02
☐ 86 Don Sutton	.15	.07	.02
☐ 87 Al Holland	.05	.02	.01
☐ 88 Tony Pena	.05	.02	.01
☐ 89 Ron Cey	.05	.02	.01
☐ 90 Joaquin Andujar	.05	.02	.01
☐ 91 LaMarr Hoyt	.05	.02	.01
☐ 92 Tommy John	.10	.05	.01
☐ 93 Dwayne Murphy	.05	.02	.01
☐ 94 Willie Upshaw	.05	.02	.01
☐ 95 Gary Ward	.05	.02	.01
☐ 96 Ron Guidry	.10	.05	.01
☐ 97 Chet Lemon	.05	.02	.01
☐ 98 Aurelio Lopez	.05	.02	.01
☐ 99 Tony Perez	.15	.07	.02
☐ 100 Bill Buckner	.10	.05	.01
☐ 101 Mike Hargrove	.10	.05	.01
☐ 102 Scott McGregor	.05	.02	.01
☐ 103 Dale Murphy	.20	.09	.03
☐ 104 Keith Hernandez	.10	.05	.01
☐ 105 Paul Molitor	1.00	.45	.12
☐ 106 Bert Blyleven	.10	.05	.01
☐ 107 Leon Durham	.05	.02	.01
☐ 108 Lee Smith	.15	.07	.02
☐ 109 Nolan Ryan	3.00	1.35	.35
☐ 110 Harold Baines	.10	.05	.01
☐ 111 Kent Hrbek	.10	.05	.01
☐ 112 Ron Davis	.05	.02	.01
☐ 113 George Bell	.10	.05	.01
☐ 114 Charlie Hough	.05	.02	.01
☐ 115 Phil Niekro	.25	.11	.03
☐ 116 Dave Righetti	.05	.02	.01
☐ 117 Darrell Evans	.10	.05	.01
☐ 118 Cal Ripken	3.00	1.35	.35
☐ 119 Eddie Murray	.75	.35	.09
☐ 120 Storm Davis	.05	.02	.01
☐ 121 Mike Boddicker	.05	.02	.01
☐ 122 Bob Horner	.05	.02	.01
☐ 123 Chris Chambliss	.05	.02	.01
☐ 124 Ted Simmons	.10	.05	.01
☐ 125 Andre Thornton	.05	.02	.01
☐ 126 Larry Bowa	.05	.02	.01
☐ 127 Bob Dernier	.05	.02	.01
☐ 128 Joe Niekro	.05	.02	.01
☐ 129 Jose Cruz	.10	.05	.01
☐ 130 Tom Brunansky	.05	.02	.01
☐ 131 Gary Gaetti	.15	.07	.02
☐ 132 Lloyd Moseby	.05	.02	.01
☐ 133 Frank Tanana	.10	.05	.01

1993 Fun Pack

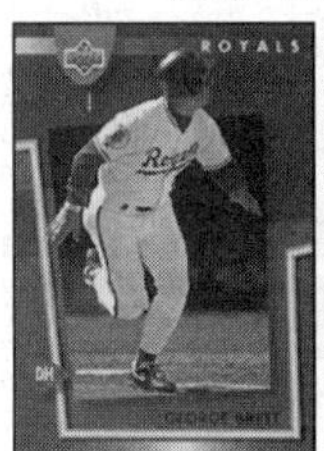

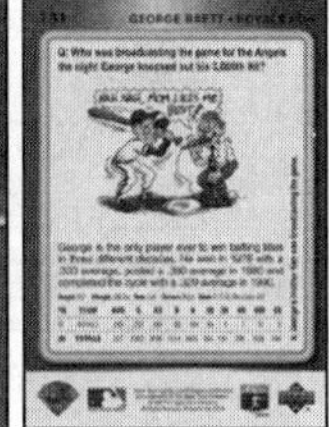

This 225-card standard-size single series set was issued by Upper Deck and targeted primarily at youngsters. Cards were distributed exclusively in hobby and retail foil fin-wrapped packs. Each card has a front that display action player photos on a bright multicolored background. The team name is printed in yellow at the top right and the player's name appears below the photo within the irregular green border. Topical subsets featured are Stars of Tomorrow (1-9), Hot Shots (10-21), Kid Stars (22-27), Upper Deck Heroes (28-36), All-Star Advice (210-215), All-Star Fold Outs (216-220), and Checklists (221-225) and randomly numbered Glow Stars. Card numbers 37-209 are arranged alphabetically according to team names, with each team subset beginning with a Glow Star card. There are no key Rookie Cards in this set.The Hot Shot subset cards were only available in retail packs or through a as a mail-in redemption promotion available in hobby packs.

	MINT	NRMT	EXC
COMPLETE SET (225)	40.00	18.00	5.00
COMMON CARD (1-225)	.05	.02	.01
☐ 1 Wil Cordero SOT	.05	.02	.01
☐ 2 Brent Gates SOT	.15	.07	.02
☐ 3 Benji Gil SOT	.15	.07	.02
☐ 4 Phil Hiatt SOT	.05	.02	.01
☐ 5 David McCarty SOT	.05	.02	.01
☐ 6 Mike Piazza SOT	2.00	.90	.25
☐ 7 Tim Salmon SOT	.50	.23	.06
☐ 8 J.T. Snow SOT	.30	.14	.04
☐ 9 Kevin Young SOT	.05	.02	.01
☐ 10 Roberto Alomar HS	.75	.35	.09
☐ 11 Barry Bonds HS	1.00	.45	.12
☐ 12 Jose Canseco HS	.30	.14	.04
☐ 13 Will Clark HS	.30	.14	.04
☐ 14 Roger Clemens HS	.75	.35	.09
☐ 15 Juan Gonzalez HS	2.00	.90	.25
☐ 16 Ken Griffey Jr. HS	4.00	1.80	.50
☐ 17 Mark McGwire HS	1.25	.55	.16
☐ 18 Nolan Ryan HS	4.00	1.80	.50
☐ 19 Ryne Sandberg HS	1.00	.45	.12
☐ 20 Gary Sheffield HS	.30	.14	.04
☐ 21 Frank Thomas HS	4.00	1.80	.50
☐ 22 Roberto Alomar KS	.30	.14	.04
☐ 23 Roger Clemens KS	.30	.14	.04
☐ 24 Ken Griffey Jr. KS	1.00	.45	.12
☐ 25 Gary Sheffield KS	.30	.14	.04
☐ 26 Nolan Ryan KS	.75	.35	.09
☐ 27 Frank Thomas KS	1.00	.45	.12
☐ 28 Reggie Jackson HERO	.30	.14	.04
☐ 29 Roger Clemens HERO	.30	.14	.04
☐ 30 Ken Griffey Jr. HERO	1.00	.45	.12
☐ 31 Bo Jackson HERO	.15	.07	.02
☐ 32 Cal Ripken Jr. HERO	.75	.35	.09
☐ 33 Nolan Ryan HERO	.75	.35	.09
☐ 34 Deion Sanders HERO	.30	.14	.04
☐ 35 Ozzie Smith HERO	.30	.14	.04
☐ 36 Frank Thomas HERO	1.00	.45	.12
☐ 37 Tim Salmon GS	.15	.07	.02
☐ 38 Chili Davis	.15	.07	.02
☐ 39 Chuck Finley	.05	.02	.01
☐ 40 Mark Langston	.15	.07	.02
☐ 41 Luis Polonia	.05	.02	.01
☐ 42 Jeff Bagwell GS	.40	.18	.05
☐ 43 Jeff Bagwell	.75	.35	.09
☐ 44 Craig Biggio	.15	.07	.02
☐ 45 Ken Caminiti	.30	.14	.04
☐ 46 Doug Drabek	.05	.02	.01
☐ 47 Steve Finley	.15	.07	.02
☐ 48 Mark McGwire GS	.30	.14	.04
☐ 49 Dennis Eckersley	.15	.07	.02
☐ 50 Rickey Henderson	.30	.14	.04
☐ 51 Mark McGwire	.60	.25	.07
☐ 52 Ruben Sierra	.15	.07	.02
☐ 53 Terry Steinbach	.15	.07	.02
☐ 54 Roberto Alomar GS	.30	.14	.04
☐ 55 Roberto Alomar	.40	.18	.05
☐ 56 Joe Carter	.15	.07	.02
☐ 57 Juan Guzman	.15	.07	.02
☐ 58 Paul Molitor	.40	.18	.05
☐ 59 Jack Morris	.15	.07	.02
☐ 60 John Olerud	.05	.02	.01
☐ 61 Tom Glavine GS	.30	.14	.04
☐ 62 Steve Avery	.15	.07	.02
☐ 63 Tom Glavine	.30	.14	.04
☐ 64 David Justice	.30	.14	.04
☐ 65 Greg Maddux	1.25	.55	.16
☐ 66 Terry Pendleton	.15	.07	.02
☐ 67 Deion Sanders	.30	.14	.04
☐ 68 John Smoltz	.30	.14	.04
☐ 69 Robin Yount GS	.30	.14	.04
☐ 70 Cal Eldred	.05	.02	.01
☐ 71 Pat Listach	.05	.02	.01
☐ 72 Greg Vaughn	.15	.07	.02
☐ 73 Robin Yount	.30	.14	.04
☐ 74 Ozzie Smith GS	.30	.14	.04
☐ 75 Gregg Jefferies	.15	.07	.02
☐ 76 Ray Lankford	.15	.07	.02
☐ 77 Lee Smith	.15	.07	.02
☐ 78 Ozzie Smith	.50	.23	.06
☐ 79 Bob Tewksbury	.05	.02	.01
☐ 80 Ryne Sandberg GS	.30	.14	.04
☐ 81 Mark Grace	.30	.14	.04
☐ 82 Mike Morgan	.05	.02	.01
☐ 83 Randy Myers	.15	.07	.02
☐ 84 Ryne Sandberg	.50	.23	.06
☐ 85 Sammy Sosa	.30	.14	.04
☐ 86 Eric Karros GS	.30	.14	.04
☐ 87 Brett Butler	.15	.07	.02
☐ 88 Orel Hershiser	.15	.07	.02
☐ 89 Eric Karros	.30	.14	.04
☐ 90 Ramon Martinez	.15	.07	.02
☐ 91 Jose Offerman	.05	.02	.01
☐ 92 Darryl Strawberry	.15	.07	.02
☐ 93 Marquis Grissom GS	.15	.07	.02
☐ 94 Delino DeShields	.05	.02	.01
☐ 95 Marquis Grissom	.15	.07	.02
☐ 96 Ken Hill	.15	.07	.02
☐ 97 Dennis Martinez	.15	.07	.02
☐ 98 Larry Walker	.30	.14	.04
☐ 99 Barry Bonds GS	.30	.14	.04
☐ 100 Barry Bonds	.50	.23	.06
☐ 101 Will Clark	.30	.14	.04
☐ 102 Bill Swift	.05	.02	.01
☐ 103 Robby Thompson	.05	.02	.01
☐ 104 Matt Williams	.30	.14	.04
☐ 105 Carlos Baerga GS	.15	.07	.02
☐ 106 Sandy Alomar Jr.	.15	.07	.02
☐ 107 Carlos Baerga	.15	.07	.02
☐ 108 Albert Belle	.75	.35	.09
☐ 109 Kenny Lofton	.75	.35	.09
☐ 110 Charles Nagy	.15	.07	.02
☐ 111 Ken Griffey Jr. GS	1.00	.45	.12
☐ 112 Jay Buhner	.30	.14	.04
☐ 113 Dave Fleming	.05	.02	.01
☐ 114 Ken Griffey Jr.	2.00	.90	.25
☐ 115 Randy Johnson	.30	.14	.04
☐ 116 Edgar Martinez	.15	.07	.02
☐ 117 Benito Santiago GS	.05	.02	.01
☐ 118 Bret Barberie	.05	.02	.01
☐ 119 Jeff Conine	.15	.07	.02
☐ 120 Brian Harvey	.05	.02	.01
☐ 121 Benito Santiago	.05	.02	.01
☐ 122 Walt Weiss	.05	.02	.01
☐ 123 Dwight Gooden GS	.15	.07	.02
☐ 124 Bobby Bonilla	.15	.07	.02
☐ 125 Tony Fernandez	.05	.02	.01
☐ 126 Dwight Gooden	.15	.07	.02
☐ 127 Howard Johnson	.05	.02	.01
☐ 128 Eddie Murray	.50	.23	.06
☐ 129 Bret Saberhagen	.15	.07	.02
☐ 130 Cal Ripken Jr. GS	.75	.35	.09
☐ 131 Brady Anderson	.30	.14	.04
☐ 132 Mike Devereaux	.05	.02	.01
☐ 133 Ben McDonald	.05	.02	.01
☐ 134 Mike Mussina	.40	.18	.05
☐ 135 Cal Ripken Jr.	1.50	.70	.19
☐ 136 Fred McGriff GS	.30	.14	.04
☐ 137 Andy Benes	.15	.07	.02
☐ 138 Tony Gwynn	.75	.35	.09
☐ 139 Fred McGriff	.30	.14	.04
☐ 140 Phil Plantier	.05	.02	.01
☐ 141 Gary Sheffield	.30	.14	.04
☐ 142 Darren Daulton GS	.15	.07	.02
☐ 143 Darren Daulton	.15	.07	.02
☐ 144 Len Dykstra	.15	.07	.02
☐ 145 Dave Hollins	.05	.02	.01
☐ 146 John Kruk	.15	.07	.02
☐ 147 Mitch Williams	.05	.02	.01
☐ 148 Andy Van Slyke GS	.05	.02	.01
☐ 149 Jay Bell	.15	.07	.02
☐ 150 Zane Smith	.05	.02	.01
☐ 151 Andy Van Slyke	.15	.07	.02
☐ 152 Tim Wakefield	.15	.07	.02
☐ 153 Juan Gonzalez GS	.30	.14	.04
☐ 154 Kevin Brown	.15	.07	.02
☐ 155 Jose Canseco	.30	.14	.04
☐ 156 Juan Gonzalez	1.00	.45	.12
☐ 157 Rafael Palmeiro	.30	.14	.04
☐ 158 Dean Palmer	.15	.07	.02
☐ 159 Ivan Rodriguez	.50	.23	.06
☐ 160 Nolan Ryan	1.50	.70	.19
☐ 161 Roger Clemens GS	.30	.14	.04
☐ 162 Roger Clemens	.40	.18	.05
☐ 163 Andre Dawson	.15	.07	.02
☐ 164 Mike Greenwell	.05	.02	.01
☐ 165 Tony Pena	.05	.02	.01
☐ 166 Frank Viola	.05	.02	.01
☐ 167 Barry Larkin GS	.30	.14	.04
☐ 168 Rob Dibble	.05	.02	.01
☐ 169 Roberto Kelly	.05	.02	.01
☐ 170 Barry Larkin	.30	.14	.04
☐ 171 Kevin Mitchell	.15	.07	.02
☐ 172 Bip Roberts	.05	.02	.01
☐ 173 Andres Galarraga GS	.30	.14	.04
☐ 174 Dante Bichette	.30	.14	.04
☐ 175 Jerald Clark	.05	.02	.01
☐ 176 Andres Galarraga	.30	.14	.04
☐ 177 Charlie Hayes	.05	.02	.01
☐ 178 David Nied	.05	.02	.01
☐ 179 David Cone GS	.15	.07	.02
☐ 180 Kevin Appier	.15	.07	.02
☐ 181 George Brett	.75	.35	.09
☐ 182 David Cone	.15	.07	.02
☐ 183 Felix Jose	.05	.02	.01
☐ 184 Wally Joyner	.15	.07	.02
☐ 185 Cecil Fielder GS	.15	.07	.02
☐ 186 Cecil Fielder	.15	.07	.02
☐ 187 Travis Fryman	.15	.07	.02
☐ 188 Tony Phillips	.15	.07	.02
☐ 189 Mickey Tettleton	.05	.02	.01
☐ 190 Lou Whitaker	.15	.07	.02
☐ 191 Kirby Puckett GS	.30	.14	.04
☐ 192 Scott Erickson	.05	.02	.01
☐ 193 Chuck Knoblauch	.30	.14	.04
☐ 194 Shane Mack	.05	.02	.01
☐ 195 Kirby Puckett	.75	.35	.09
☐ 196 Dave Winfield	.30	.14	.04
☐ 197 Frank Thomas GS	1.00	.45	.12
☐ 198 George Bell	.05	.02	.01
☐ 199 Bo Jackson	.15	.07	.02
☐ 200 Jack McDowell	.15	.07	.02
☐ 201 Tim Raines	.30	.14	.04
☐ 202 Frank Thomas	2.00	.90	.25
☐ 203 Robin Ventura	.15	.07	.02
☐ 204 Jim Abbott GS	.05	.02	.01
☐ 205 Jim Abbott	.05	.02	.01
☐ 206 Wade Boggs	.30	.14	.04
☐ 207 Jimmy Key	.15	.07	.02
☐ 208 Don Mattingly	1.00	.45	.12
☐ 209 Danny Tartabull	.05	.02	.01
☐ 210 Brett Butler ASA	.05	.02	.01
☐ 211 Tony Gwynn ASA	.40	.18	.05
☐ 212 Rickey Henderson ASA	.30	.14	.04
☐ 213 Ramon Martinez ASA	.05	.02	.01
☐ 214 Nolan Ryan ASA	.75	.35	.09
☐ 215 Ozzie Smith ASA	.30	.14	.04
☐ 216 Marquis Grissom FOLD	.15	.07	.02
☐ 217 Dean Palmer FOLD	.15	.07	.02
☐ 218 Cal Ripken Jr. FOLD	.75	.35	.09
☐ 219 Deion Sanders FOLD	.30	.14	.04
☐ 220 Darryl Strawberry FOLD	.15	.07	.02
☐ 221 David McCarty CL	.05	.02	.01
☐ 222 Barry Bonds CL	.30	.14	.04
☐ 223 Juan Gonzalez CL	.30	.14	.04
☐ 224 Ken Griffey Jr. CL	1.00	.45	.12
☐ 225 Frank Thomas CL	1.00	.45	.12
☐ NNO Hot Shots Card Expired	.30	.14	.04
☐ NNO Hot Shots Card Punched	.15	.07	.02

1993 Fun Pack All-Stars

Randomly inserted in 1993 Upper Deck Fun Packs, these nine foldouts feature combinations by position for American and National leaue All-Stars. The cards measure the standard size when closed and 2 1/2" by 7" when opened. The front of each features side-by-side color action photos of an American League and a National League player. The set's title appears above the photos within a blue stripe. The players' names appear within an irregular white stripe near the bottom. The blue-and-white back carries the rules for playing the scratch-off game and a section to keep score. The actual scratch-off lineups appear when the card is opened. The American League players and their scratch-off circles are displayed within the reddish left side of the foldout, and their National League counterparts appear within the bluish right side.

	MINT	NRMT	EXC
COMPLETE SET (9)	15.00	6.75	1.85
COMMON PAIR (AS1-AS9)	.50	.23	.06
☐ AS1 Frank Thomas Fred McGriff	5.00	2.20	.60
☐ AS2 Ivan Rodriguez Darren Daulton	1.00	.45	.12
☐ AS3 Mark McGwire Will Clark	1.00	.45	.12
☐ AS4 Roberto Alomar Ryne Sandberg	2.00	.90	.25
☐ AS5 Robin Ventura Terry Pendleton	.50	.23	.06
☐ AS6 Cal Ripken Ozzie Smith	4.00	1.80	.50
☐ AS7 Juan Gonzalez Barry Bonds	2.50	1.10	.30
☐ AS8 Ken Griffey Jr. Marquis Grissom	4.00	1.80	.50
☐ AS9 Kirby Puckett Tony Gwynn	4.00	1.80	.50

1993 Fun Pack Mascots

Randomly inserted in 1993 Upper Deck Fun Packs, these five standard-size horizontal cards feature two mascot photos on their fronts. On the left is a color photo, on the right is the hologram. These photos appear over a background that shades from yellow to orange, from right to left. The mascot's name appears vertically in white lettering within pink and purple stripes on the left edge. The words 'Mascot Madness' appear in multicolored lettering within a yellow oval near the bottom. The back is similarly designed, except the photos are replaced by the mascot's career highlights and a white stripe up the right edge carries the Major League Baseball and the MLBPA logos.

	MINT	NRMT	EXC
COMPLETE SET (5)	4.00	1.80	.50
COMMON CARD (1-5)	.75	.35	.09
☐ 1 Phillie Phanatic	1.50	.70	.19
☐ 2 Pirate Parrot	.75	.35	.09
☐ 3 Fredbird	.75	.35	.09
☐ 4 BJ Birdie	.75	.35	.09
☐ 5 Youppi	.75	.35	.09

1994 Fun Pack

Issued by Upper Deck for the second straight year, the Fun Pack set consists of 240 cards. Bright yellow and green borders surround a color player photo on the front. The backs, with much the same color scheme, are horizontal and contain a cartoon relating to the player and statistics. The following subsets are included in this set: Stars of Tomorrow (1-9), Standouts (175-192), Pro-Files (193-198), Headline Stars (199-207), What's the Call (208-216), Foldouts (217-225) and Fun Cards (226-234). Michael Jordan's baseball Rookie Card is in this set.

	MINT	NRMT	EXC
COMPLETE SET (240)	65.00	29.00	8.00
COMMON CARD (1-240)	.10	.05	.01
☐ 1 Manny Ramirez	1.00	.45	.12
☐ 2 Cliff Floyd	.50	.23	.06
☐ 3 Rondell White	.50	.23	.06
☐ 4 Carlos Delgado	.50	.23	.06
☐ 5 Chipper Jones	2.50	1.10	.30
☐ 6 Javier Lopez	.50	.23	.06
☐ 7 Ryan Klesko	.60	.25	.07
☐ 8 Steve Karsay	.10	.05	.01
☐ 9 Rich Becker	.25	.11	.03
☐ 10 Gary Sheffield	.50	.23	.06
☐ 11 Jeffrey Hammonds	.25	.11	.03
☐ 12 Roberto Alomar	.60	.25	.07
☐ 13 Brent Gates	.10	.05	.01
☐ 14 Andres Galarraga	.50	.23	.06
☐ 15 Tim Salmon	.50	.23	.06
☐ 16 Dwight Gooden	.25	.11	.03
☐ 17 Mark Grace	.50	.23	.06
☐ 18 Andy Van Slyke	.25	.11	.03
☐ 19 Juan Gonzalez	1.50	.70	.19
☐ 20 Mickey Tettleton	.10	.05	.01
☐ 21 Roger Clemens	.60	.25	.07
☐ 22 Will Clark	.50	.23	.06
☐ 23 David Justice	.50	.23	.06
☐ 24 Ken Griffey Jr.	3.00	1.35	.35
☐ 25 Barry Bonds	.75	.35	.09
☐ 26 Bill Swift	.10	.05	.01
☐ 27 Fred McGriff	.50	.23	.06
☐ 28 Randy Myers	.10	.05	.01
☐ 29 Joe Carter	.25	.11	.03
☐ 30 Nigel Wilson	.10	.05	.01
☐ 31 Mike Piazza	2.00	.90	.25
☐ 32 Dave Winfield	.50	.23	.06
☐ 33 Steve Avery	.25	.11	.03
☐ 34 Kirby Puckett	1.25	.55	.16
☐ 35 Frank Thomas	3.00	1.35	.35
☐ 36 Aaron Sele	.25	.11	.03
☐ 37 Ricky Gutierrez	.10	.05	.01
☐ 38 Curt Schilling	.10	.05	.01
☐ 39 Mike Greenwell	.10	.05	.01
☐ 40 Andy Benes	.25	.11	.03
☐ 41 Kevin Brown	.25	.11	.03
☐ 42 Mo Vaughn	.75	.35	.09
☐ 43 Dennis Eckersley	.25	.11	.03
☐ 44 Ken Hill	.10	.05	.01
☐ 45 Cecil Fielder	.25	.11	.03
☐ 46 Bobby Jones	.25	.11	.03
☐ 47 Tom Glavine	.50	.23	.06
☐ 48 Wally Joyner	.25	.11	.03
☐ 49 Ellis Burks	.25	.11	.03
☐ 50 Jason Bere	.25	.11	.03
☐ 51 Randy Johnson	.50	.23	.06
☐ 52 Darryl Kile	.10	.05	.01
☐ 53 Jeff Montgomery	.25	.11	.03
☐ 54 Alex Fernandez	.25	.11	.03
☐ 55 Kevin Appier	.25	.11	.03
☐ 56 Brian McRae	.25	.11	.03
☐ 57 John Wetteland	.25	.11	.03
☐ 58 Bob Tewksbury	.10	.05	.01
☐ 59 Todd Van Poppel	.10	.05	.01
☐ 60 Ryne Sandberg	.75	.35	.09
☐ 61 Bret Barberie	.10	.05	.01
☐ 62 Phil Plantier	.10	.05	.01
☐ 63 Chris Hoiles	.10	.05	.01
☐ 64 Tony Phillips	.25	.11	.03
☐ 65 Salomon Torres	.10	.05	.01
☐ 66 Juan Guzman	.25	.11	.03
☐ 67 Paul O'Neill	.25	.11	.03
☐ 68 Dante Bichette	.50	.23	.06
☐ 69 Lenny Dykstra	.25	.11	.03
☐ 70 Ivan Rodriguez	.75	.35	.09
☐ 71 Dean Palmer	.25	.11	.03
☐ 72 Brett Butler	.25	.11	.03
☐ 73 Rick Aguilera	.10	.05	.01
☐ 74 Robby Thompson	.10	.05	.01
☐ 75 Jim Abbott	.10	.05	.01
☐ 76 Al Martin	.10	.05	.01
☐ 77 Roberto Hernandez	.25	.11	.03
☐ 78 Jay Buhner	.50	.23	.06
☐ 79 Devon White	.10	.05	.01
☐ 80 Travis Fryman	.25	.11	.03
☐ 81 Jeromy Burnitz	.10	.05	.01
☐ 82 John Burkett	.10	.05	.01
☐ 83 Orlando Merced	.25	.11	.03
☐ 84 Jose Rijo	.10	.05	.01
☐ 85 Eddie Murray	.75	.35	.09
☐ 86 Howard Johnson	.10	.05	.01
☐ 87 Chuck Carr	.10	.05	.01
☐ 88 Pedro J. Martinez	.50	.23	.06
☐ 89 Charlie Hayes	.10	.05	.01
☐ 90 Matt Williams	.50	.23	.06
☐ 91 Steve Finley	.50	.23	.06
☐ 92 Pat Listach	.10	.05	.01
☐ 93 Sandy Alomar Jr.	.25	.11	.03
☐ 94 Delino DeShields	.10	.05	.01
☐ 95 Rod Beck	.25	.11	.03
☐ 96 Todd Zeile UER	.10	.05	.01
(Card misnumbered 97)			
☐ 97 Duane Ward UER	.10	.05	.01
(Card misnumbered 98)			
☐ 98 Darryl Hamilton	.10	.05	.01
☐ 99 John Olerud	.10	.05	.01
☐ 100 Andre Dawson	.25	.11	.03
☐ 101 Ozzie Smith	.75	.35	.09
☐ 102 Rick Wilkins	.10	.05	.01
☐ 103 Alan Trammell	.25	.11	.03
☐ 104 Jeff Blauser	.10	.05	.01
☐ 105 Bret Boone	.25	.11	.03
☐ 106 J.T. Snow	.25	.11	.03
☐ 107 Kenny Lofton	1.00	.45	.12
☐ 108 Cal Ripken Jr.	2.50	1.10	.30
☐ 109 Carlos Baerga	.25	.11	.03
☐ 110 Bip Roberts	.10	.05	.01
☐ 111 Barry Larkin	.50	.23	.06
☐ 112 Mark Langston	.25	.11	.03
☐ 113 Ozzie Guillen	.10	.05	.01
☐ 114 Chad Curtis	.10	.05	.01
☐ 115 Dave Hollins	.10	.05	.01
☐ 116 Reggie Sanders	.25	.11	.03
☐ 117 Jeff Conine	.25	.11	.03
☐ 118 Mark Whiten	.10	.05	.01
☐ 119 Tony Gwynn	1.25	.55	.16
☐ 120 John Kruk	.25	.11	.03
☐ 121 Eduardo Perez	.10	.05	.01
☐ 122 Walt Weiss	.10	.05	.01
☐ 123 Don Mattingly	1.50	.70	.19
☐ 124 Rickey Henderson	.50	.23	.06
☐ 125 Mark McGwire	1.00	.45	.12
☐ 126 Wade Boggs	.50	.23	.06
☐ 127 Bobby Bonilla	.25	.11	.03
☐ 128 Jeff King	.25	.11	.03
☐ 129 Jack McDowell	.25	.11	.03
☐ 130 Albert Belle	1.25	.55	.16
☐ 131 Greg Maddux	2.00	.90	.25
☐ 132 Dennis Martinez	.25	.11	.03
☐ 133 Jose Canseco	.50	.23	.06
☐ 134 Bryan Harvey	.10	.05	.01
☐ 135 Dave Fleming	.10	.05	.01
☐ 136 Larry Walker	.50	.23	.06
☐ 137 Ken Caminiti	.50	.23	.06
☐ 138 Doug Drabek	.10	.05	.01
☐ 139 Alex Gonzalez	.25	.11	.03
☐ 140 Darren Daulton	.25	.11	.03
☐ 141 Ruben Sierra	.25	.11	.03
☐ 142 Kirk Rueter	.10	.05	.01
☐ 143 Raul Mondesi	.50	.23	.06
☐ 144 Greg Vaughn	.50	.23	.06
☐ 145 Danny Tartabull	.10	.05	.01
☐ 146 Eric Karros	.25	.11	.03
☐ 147 Chuck Knoblauch	.50	.23	.06
☐ 148 Mike Mussina	.60	.25	.07
☐ 149 Brady Anderson	.50	.23	.06
☐ 150 Paul Molitor	.60	.25	.07
☐ 151 Bo Jackson	.25	.11	.03
☐ 152 Jeff Bagwell	1.25	.55	.16
☐ 153 Gregg Jefferies UER	.50	.23	.06
Name spelled Greg on front			
☐ 154 Rafael Palmeiro	.50	.23	.06
☐ 155 Orel Hershiser	.25	.11	.03
☐ 156 Derek Bell	.25	.11	.03
☐ 157 Jeff Kent	.10	.05	.01
☐ 158 Craig Biggio	.25	.11	.03
☐ 159 Marquis Grissom	.25	.11	.03
☐ 160 Matt Mieske	.10	.05	.01
☐ 161 Jay Bell	.25	.11	.03
☐ 162 Sammy Sosa	.50	.23	.06
☐ 163 Robin Ventura	.25	.11	.03
☐ 164 Deion Sanders	.50	.23	.06
☐ 165 Jimmy Key	.25	.11	.03
☐ 166 Cal Eldred	.10	.05	.01
☐ 167 David McCarty	.10	.05	.01
☐ 168 Carlos Garcia	.10	.05	.01
☐ 169 Willie Greene	.25	.11	.03
☐ 170 Michael Jordan	10.00	4.50	1.25
☐ 171 Roberto Mejia	.10	.05	.01
☐ 172 Phil Hiatt UER	.10	.05	.01
(Card misnumbered 72)			
☐ 173 Marc Newfield	.25	.11	.03
☐ 174 Kevin Stocker	.10	.05	.01
☐ 175 Randy Johnson STA	.50	.23	.06
☐ 176 Ivan Rodriguez STA	.50	.23	.06
☐ 177 Frank Thomas STA	1.50	.70	.19
☐ 178 Roberto Alomar STA	.50	.23	.06
☐ 179 Travis Fryman STA	.25	.11	.03
☐ 180 Cal Ripken Jr. STA	1.25	.55	.16
☐ 181 Juan Gonzalez STA	.75	.35	.09
☐ 182 Ken Griffey Jr. STA	1.50	.70	.19
☐ 183 Albert Belle STA	.60	.25	.07
☐ 184 Greg Maddux STA	1.00	.45	.12
☐ 185 Mike Piazza STA	1.00	.45	.12
☐ 186 Fred McGriff STA	.50	.23	.06
☐ 187 Robby Thompson STA	.10	.05	.01
☐ 188 Matt Williams STA	.50	.23	.06
☐ 189 Jeff Blauser STA	.10	.05	.01
☐ 190 Barry Bonds STA	.50	.23	.06
☐ 191 Lenny Dykstra STA	.10	.05	.01
☐ 192 David Justice STA	.25	.11	.03
☐ 193 Ken Griffey Jr. PF	1.50	.70	.19
☐ 194 Barry Bonds PF	.50	.23	.06
☐ 195 Frank Thomas PF	1.50	.70	.19
☐ 196 Juan Gonzalez PF	.50	.23	.06
☐ 197 Randy Johnson PF	.50	.23	.06
☐ 198 Chuck Carr PF	.10	.05	.01
☐ 199 Barry Bonds HES	1.25	.55	.16
Juan Gonzalez			
☐ 200 Ken Griffey Jr. HES	2.50	1.10	.30
Don Mattingly			
☐ 201 Roberto Alomar HES	.30	.14	.04
Carlos Baerga			
☐ 202 Dave Winfield HES	.50	.23	.06
Robin Yount			
☐ 203 Mike Piazza HES	.75	.35	.09
Tim Salmon			
☐ 204 Albert Belle HES	2.00	.90	.25
Frank Thomas			
☐ 205 Cliff Floyd HES	.30	.14	.04
Rondell White			
☐ 206 Kirby Puckett HES	1.25	.55	.16
Tony Gwynn			
☐ 207 Roger Clemens HES	1.25	.55	.16
Greg Maddux			
☐ 208 Mike Piazza WC	1.00	.45	.12
☐ 209 Jose Canseco WC	.50	.23	.06
☐ 210 Frank Thomas WC	1.50	.70	.19
☐ 211 Roberto Alomar WC	.50	.23	.06
☐ 212 Barry Bonds WC	.50	.23	.06
☐ 213 Rickey Henderson WC	.50	.23	.06
☐ 214 John Kruk WC	.10	.05	.01
☐ 215 Juan Gonzalez WC	.50	.23	.06
☐ 216 Ken Griffey Jr. WC	1.50	.70	.19
☐ 217 Roberto Alomar FOLD	.50	.23	.06
☐ 218 Craig Biggio FOLD	.25	.11	.03
☐ 219 Cal Ripken Jr. FOLD	1.25	.55	.16
☐ 220 Mike Piazza FOLD	1.00	.45	.12
☐ 221 Brent Gates FOLD	.10	.05	.01
☐ 222 Walt Weiss FOLD	.10	.05	.01
☐ 223 Bobby Bonilla FOLD	.25	.11	.03
☐ 224 Ken Griffey Jr. FOLD	1.50	.70	.19
☐ 225 Barry Bonds FOLD	.50	.23	.06
☐ 226 Barry Bonds FUN	.50	.23	.06
☐ 227 Joe Carter FUN	.25	.11	.03
☐ 228 Mike Greenwell FUN	.10	.05	.01
☐ 229 Ken Griffey Jr. FUN	1.50	.70	.19
☐ 230 John Kruk FUN	.10	.05	.01
☐ 231 Mike Piazza FUN	1.00	.45	.12
☐ 232 Kirby Puckett FUN	.50	.23	.06
☐ 233 John Smoltz FUN	.50	.23	.06
☐ 234 Rick Wilkins FUN	.10	.05	.01
☐ 235 Ken Griffey Jr.	1.50	.70	.19
Checklist 1-40			
☐ 236 Frank Thomas	1.50	.70	.19
Checklist 41-80			
☐ 237 Barry Bonds	.50	.23	.06
Checklist 81-120			
☐ 238 Mike Piazza	1.00	.45	.12
Checklist 121-160			
☐ 239 Tim Salmon	.50	.23	.06
Checklist 161-200			
☐ 240 Juan Gonzalez	.50	.23	.06
Checklist 201-240			

1976 Funky Facts

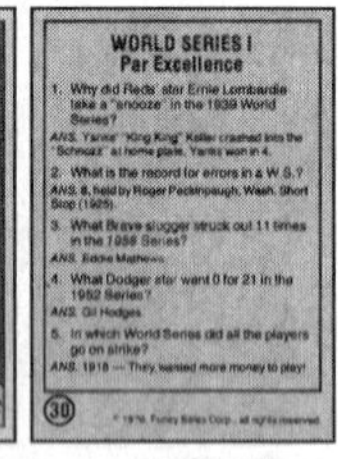

This 40-card standard-size set is subtitled "The Wierd [sic] World of Baseball". A paper insert included with the set carries a checklist on its back. Inside a white outer border and a color inner border, the fronts feature colorful cartoon drawings. A trivia question appears above each picture in a pale yellow bar. Each back shows five trivia questions and their answers. The first question repeats the question found on card fronts.

	NRMT	VG-E	GOOD
COMPLETE SET	10.00	4.50	1.25
COMMON CARD	.25	.11	.03
☐ 1 Duck	.25	.11	.03
☐ 2 In a Trance	.25	.11	.03
☐ 3 Fans vs. Players	.25	.11	.03
☐ 4 Famous Pitches	.25	.11	.03
☐ 5 Baseballeese	.25	.11	.03
☐ 6 Lilliputians	.25	.11	.03
The Small Men			
☐ 7 Nicknames	.25	.11	.03
☐ 8 Hall of Fame	.25	.11	.03
☐ 9 Team Nicknames	.25	.11	.03
☐ 10 The Good Old Days	.25	.11	.03
☐ 11 Fantastic Fans	.25	.11	.03
☐ 12 Most Valuable Players	.25	.11	.03
☐ 13 The Mound Was Green	.25	.11	.03
☐ 14 Strata Gems	.25	.11	.03
☐ 15 Raids and Wars	.25	.11	.03
☐ 16 Crime and Punishment	.25	.11	.03
☐ 17 Clowning	.25	.11	.03
☐ 18 Goofy Home Runs	.25	.11	.03
☐ 19 Traditions	.25	.11	.03
☐ 20 All in the Family	.25	.11	.03
☐ 21 World Series II	.25	.11	.03
Feet and Feats			
☐ 22 Athletes	.25	.11	.03
☐ 23 Batting Champs	.25	.11	.03
☐ 24 Double Plays	.25	.11	.03
☐ 25 The Game	.25	.11	.03
☐ 26 Supersititions	.25	.11	.03
☐ 27 On the Basepaths	.25	.11	.03
☐ 28 Fielding	.25	.11	.03
☐ 29 Weird Pitching Feats	.25	.11	.03
☐ 30 World Series I	.25	.11	.03
Par Excellence			
☐ 31 Tools of Ignorance	.25	.11	.03
Catchers			
☐ 32 Home Run Derby	.25	.11	.03
☐ 33 No Hitters	.25	.11	.03
☐ 34 Umps are Human Too	.25	.11	.03
☐ 35 The Wild Ones	.25	.11	.03
☐ 36 Batting Around	.25	.11	.03
☐ 37 Not in Shape	.25	.11	.03
☐ 38 Switch	.25	.11	.03
☐ 39 Nicknames	.25	.11	.03
Matchup			
☐ 40 International Baseball	.25	.11	.03

1888 G and B Chewing Gum Co E223

These cards measure approximately 1" by 2 1/8" and primarily feature players from the National League. This is one of the few nineteenth century issues which are not tobacco related. The set was issued by the G and B Chewing Gum Co and is the first set baseball issue released by a gum or candy company. The cards are unnumbered and we have sequenced them in alphabetical order. If more than one pose is known, we have put the number of said poses next to the player's name. The complete set price only includes one of each variation. Portrait variations are valued double of prices listed below.

	EX-MT	VG-E	GOOD
COMPLETE SET (46)	38000.00	17100.00	4800.00
COMMON CARD	750.00	350.00	95.00
☐ 1 Cap Anson	3000.00	1350.00	375.00
☐ 2 Lady Baldwin (3)	750.00	350.00	95.00
☐ 3 Steve Brady	750.00	350.00	95.00
☐ 4 Bill Brown (2)	750.00	350.00	95.00
☐ 5 Charlie Buffington	750.00	350.00	95.00
☐ 6 Oyster Burns	1000.00	450.00	125.00
☐ 7 John Clarkson	1500.00	700.00	190.00
☐ 8 John Coleman	750.00	350.00	95.00
☐ 9 Charles Comiskey	1500.00	700.00	190.00
☐ 10 Roger Connor (2)	1000.00	450.00	125.00
☐ 11 Ed Daily	750.00	350.00	95.00
☐ 12 Pat Deasley	750.00	350.00	95.00
☐ 13 Dude Esterbrook	750.00	350.00	95.00
☐ 14 Buck Ewing	1500.00	700.00	190.00
☐ 15 Charlie Ferguson	1000.00	450.00	125.00
☐ 16 Frank Flint	1000.00	450.00	125.00
☐ 17 Charles Getzein	750.00	350.00	95.00
☐ 18 Kid Gleason	1000.00	450.00	125.00
☐ 19 Frank Hankinson	750.00	350.00	95.00
☐ 20 Pete Hotaling	750.00	350.00	95.00
☐ 21 Richard Johnston	750.00	350.00	95.00
☐ 22 Tim Keefe (3)	1500.00	700.00	190.00
☐ 23 Mike Kelly (2)	1500.00	700.00	190.00
☐ 24 August Krock	750.00	350.00	95.00
☐ 25 Connie Mack	1500.00	700.00	190.00
☐ 26 George Miller	750.00	350.00	95.00
☐ 27 John Morrill	750.00	350.00	95.00
☐ 28 James Mutrie MG	750.00	350.00	95.00
☐ 29 Sam Nicoll	750.00	350.00	95.00
☐ 30 Tip O'Neill	1000.00	450.00	125.00
☐ 31 Jim O'Rourke	1500.00	700.00	190.00
☐ 32 Henry Porter	1000.00	450.00	125.00
☐ 33 Danny Richardson (2)	750.00	350.00	95.00
☐ 34 Chief Roseman	750.00	350.00	95.00
☐ 35 Jimmy Ryan (2)	1000.00	450.00	125.00
☐ 36 William J. Sowders	750.00	350.00	95.00
☐ 37 Martin J. Sullivan	750.00	350.00	95.00
☐ 38 Billy Sunday (2)	1000.00	450.00	125.00
☐ 39 Ezra Sutton	750.00	350.00	95.00
☐ 40 Mike Tiernan (2)	750.00	350.00	95.00
☐ 41 Sam Thompson	750.00	350.00	95.00
☐ 42 Lawrence Twitchell	750.00	350.00	95.00

☐ 43 George Van Haltren	750.00	350.00	95.00
☐ 44 John Montgomery Ward	1000.00	450.00	125.00
☐ 45 Curt Welch	750.00	350.00	95.00
☐ 46 Mickey Welch (2)	1500.00	700.00	190.00

1963 Gad Fun Cards

This set of 1963 Fun Cards were issued by a sports illustrator by the name of Gad from Minneapolis, Minnesota. The cards are printed on cardboard stock paper. The borderless fronts have black and white line drawings. A fun sport's fact or player career statistic is depicted in the drawing. The backs of the first six cards display numbers used to play the game explained on card #6. The other backs carry a cartoon with a joke or riddle. Copyright information is listed on the lower portion of the card.

	NRMT	VG-E	GOOD
COMPLETE SET (84)	75.00	34.00	9.50
COMMON CARD (1-84)	.50	.23	.06
☐ 1 Babe Ruth	7.50	3.40	.95
☐ 2 Lost Baseballs Fact	.50	.23	.06
☐ 3 Baseball Slang Fireman	.50	.23	.06
☐ 4 Baseball Hurling Fact	.50	.23	.06
☐ 5 Lou Gehrig	5.00	2.20	.60
☐ 6 Number Game Directions	.50	.23	.06
☐ 7 Baseball Fact Consecutive Home Runs	.50	.23	.06
☐ 8 Old Hoss Radbourne	1.00	.45	.12
☐ 9 Glen Gorbans	.50	.23	.06
☐ 10 Joe Nuxhall	.75	.35	.09
☐ 11 Ty Cobb	5.00	2.20	.60
☐ 12 Baseball Slang Jake	.50	.23	.06
☐ 13 Pop Schriver	.50	.23	.06
☐ 14 Boston Red Sox	.50	.23	.06
☐ 15 John Taylor	.50	.23	.06
☐ 16 Cincinnati Red Stockings	.50	.23	.06
☐ 17 Runs Scored in a Game	.50	.23	.06
☐ 18 Baseball Slang Duster	.50	.23	.06
☐ 19 1908 Baseball Fact	.50	.23	.06
☐ 20 Evar Swanson	.50	.23	.06
☐ 21 1929 World Series Pinch Hitters		.50	.23
.06			
☐ 22 Rogers Hornsby	2.00	.90	.25
☐ 23 Highlanders	.50	.23	.06
☐ 24 Baseball Slang Strawberry	.50	.23	.06
☐ 25 Lew Flick	.50	.23	.06
☐ 26 Cy Young	3.00	1.35	.35
☐ 27 Jim Konstanty	.50	.23	.06
☐ 28 Carl Weilman	.50	.23	.06
☐ 29 Warren Rosar	.50	.23	.06
☐ 30 Baseball Slang Rabbit Ears	.50	.23	.06
☐ 31 Graham McNamee	.50	.23	.06
☐ 32 Ty Cobb Batting Record	5.00	2.20	.60
☐ 33 Joe DiMaggio	5.00	2.20	.60
☐ 34 Babe Ruth Earnings	7.50	3.40	.95
☐ 35 Baseball Slang Chinese Homer	.50	.23	.06
☐ 36 Ed Delahanty	.50	.23	.06
☐ 37 1912 Detroit Tiger Team Strike	.50	.23	.06
☐ 38 Bobo Holloman	.50	.23	.06
☐ 39 Walter Johnson	3.00	1.35	.35
☐ 40 Sam Crawford	1.00	.45	.12
☐ 41 Lifetime Record Stolen Bases	.50	.23	.06
☐ 42 Baseball Slang Showboat	.50	.23	.06
☐ 43 Lou Gehrig 23 Bases-loaded Homers	5.00	2.20	.60
☐ 44 Yankee Stadium	.50	.23	.06
☐ 45 Nick Altrock	1.00	.45	.12
☐ 46 Moses Walker Welday Waker	1.00	.45	.12
☐ 47 Joseph Borden	.50	.23	.06
☐ 48 Baseball Slang Around the Horn"	.50	.23	.06
☐ 49 Hugh Duffy	1.00	.45	.12
☐ 50 Longest Game Baseball History	.50	.23	.06
☐ 51 Jim Scott	.50	.23	.06
☐ 52 Longest Homer in 1919	.50	.23	.06
☐ 53 Record Runs Scored in One Inning	.50	.23	.06
☐ 54 Baseball Slang Jockey	.50	.23	.06
☐ 55 Umpires in 1871	.50	.23	.06
☐ 56 Bill Phillips	.50	.23	.06
☐ 57 Eddie Collins	1.00	.45	.12
☐ 58 Milwaukee Braves	.50	.23	.06
☐ 59 Bill Wambsganss	.50	.23	.06
☐ 60 Baseball Slang Annie Oakley	.50	.23	.06
☐ 61 Bob Feller	1.00	.45	.12
☐ 62 Wally Pipp	.50	.23	.06
☐ 63 Shortest World Series Game	.50	.23	.06
☐ 64 Chicago White Sox	.50	.23	.06
☐ 65 Cleveland Indians	.50	.23	.06
☐ 66 Baseball Slang Baltimore Chop	.50	.23	.06
☐ 67 14 Pitchers Used in One Game	.50	.23	.06
☐ 68 John Sigmund	.50	.23	.06
☐ 69 Boomerang	.50	.23	.06
☐ 70 Arthur Lehmann	.50	.23	.06
☐ 71 Peter Tyler Ellis Hodgkins	.50	.23	.06
☐ 72 Archer Davidson	.50	.23	.06
☐ 73 Alex Wickham	.50	.23	.06
☐ 74 Minnesota Football Team 1949	.50	.23	.06
☐ 75 George Washington	.50	.23	.06
☐ 76 Buffalo Germans Basketball Squad	.50	.23	.06
☐ 77 Gus Simmons	.50	.23	.06
☐ 78 Tom Morris	.50	.23	.06
☐ 79 Zoe Ann Olsen	.75	.35	.09
☐ 80 Emperor of Rome Maxim	.50	.23	.06
☐ 81 Highest Football Game Score	.50	.23	.06
☐ 82 Harold Starkey	.50	.23	.06
☐ 83 A Bowling Pin	.50	.23	.06
☐ 84 Number of Bicycles in USA	.50	.23	.06

1976 Galasso Baseball's Great Hall of Fame

These 32 cards feature players considered among the all time greats. This was the first of many collector issue sets released by Renato Galasso Inc. Many of these sets were released as premiums with orders to RGI. This set is sequenced in alphabetical order.

	NRMT	VG-E	GOOD
COMPLETE SET	25.00	11.00	3.10
COMMON CARD	.25	.11	.03
☐ 1 Luke Appling	.50	.23	.06
☐ 2 Ernie Banks	1.00	.45	.12
☐ 3 Yogi Berra	1.00	.45	.12
☐ 4 Roy Campanella	1.00	.45	.12
☐ 5 Roberto Clemente	3.00	1.35	.35
☐ 6 Alvin Dark	.25	.11	.03
☐ 7 Joe DiMaggio	3.00	1.35	.35
☐ 8 Bob Feller	.75	.35	.09
☐ 9 Whitey Ford	.75	.35	.09
☐ 10 Jimmy Foxx	1.00	.45	.12
☐ 11 Lou Gehrig	3.00	1.35	.35
☐ 12 Charlie Gehringer	.50	.23	.06
☐ 13 Henry Greenberg	.50	.23	.06
☐ 14 Gabby Hartnett	.50	.23	.06
☐ 15 Carl Hubbell	.75	.35	.09
☐ 16 Al Kaline	.75	.35	.09
☐ 17 Mickey Mantle	4.00	1.80	.50
☐ 18 Willie Mays	2.00	.90	.25
☐ 19 Johnny Mize	.50	.23	.06
☐ 20 Stan Musial	1.50	.70	.19
☐ 21 Mel Ott	.50	.23	.06
☐ 22 Satchell Paige	1.50	.70	.19
☐ 23 Robin Roberts	.75	.35	.09
☐ 25 Babe Ruth	4.00	1.80	.50
☐ 26 Duke Snider	1.00	.45	.12
☐ 27 Warren Spahn	.75	.35	.09
☐ 28 Tris Speaker	.75	.35	.09
☐ 29 Honus Wagner	1.00	.45	.12
☐ 30 Ted Williams	3.00	1.35	.35
☐ 31 Rudy York	.25	.11	.03
☐ 32 Cy Young	1.00	.45	.12

1977-84 Galasso Glossy Greats

This 270-card standard-size set was issued by Renata Galasso Inc. (a hobby card dealer) and originally offered as a free bonus when ordering hand-collated Topps sets. The set may be subdivided into six series with 45 cards per series, with one series being issued per year as follows: Series 1 in 1977 featured Stars of the '50s (1-45); Series 2 in 1979 featured Stars of the '60s (46-90); Series 3 in 1980 featured Stars of the '20s (91-135); Series 4 in 1981 featured Stars of the '10s (136-180); Series 5 in 1983 featured 1933 All-Star Game (181-225); and Series 6 in 1984 featured Greatest Moments (226-270). TCMA printed the first four series and Renata Galasso Inc. the last two. The fronts display black and white player photos bordered in white. The player's name, position and team for which he played appear in the bottom white border. The backs are white, printed in red and blue ink and carry a career summary and an advertisement for Renata Galasso Inc. The backs have a red baseball in each of the upper corners with the card number in the left one.

	NRMT	VG-E	GOOD
COMPLETE SET (270)	125.00	55.00	15.50
COMMON CARD (1-270)	.10	.05	.01
☐ 1 Joe DiMaggio	3.00	1.35	.35
☐ 2 Ralph Kiner	.50	.23	.06
☐ 3 Don Larsen	.30	.14	.04
☐ 4 Robin Roberts	.50	.23	.06
☐ 5 Roy Campanella	.75	.35	.09
☐ 6 Smoky Burgess	.10	.05	.01
☐ 7 Mickey Mantle	3.00	1.35	.35
☐ 8 Willie Mays	2.00	.90	.25
☐ 9 George Kell	.50	.23	.06
☐ 10 Ted Williams	2.50	1.10	.30
☐ 11 Carl Furillo	.30	.14	.04
☐ 12 Bob Feller	.50	.23	.06
☐ 13 Casey Stengel	.75	.35	.09
☐ 14 Richie Ashburn	.50	.23	.06
☐ 15 Gil Hodges	.50	.23	.06
☐ 16 Stan Musial	2.00	.90	.25
☐ 17 Don Newcombe	.30	.14	.04
☐ 18 Jackie Jensen	.30	.14	.04
☐ 19 Lou Boudreau	.50	.23	.06
☐ 20 Jackie Robinson	2.00	.90	.25
☐ 21 Billy Goodman	.10	.05	.01
☐ 22 Satchel Paige	1.00	.45	.12
☐ 23 Hoyt Wilhelm	.50	.23	.06
☐ 24 Duke Snider	.75	.35	.09
☐ 25 Whitey Ford	1.00	.45	.12
☐ 26 Monte Irvin	.50	.23	.06
☐ 27 Hank Sauer	.10	.05	.01
☐ 28 Sal Maglie	.20	.09	.03
☐ 29 Ernie Banks	.75	.35	.09
☐ 30 Billy Pierce	.20	.09	.03
☐ 31 Pee Wee Reese	.75	.35	.09
☐ 32 Al Lopez	.50	.23	.06
☐ 33 Allie Reynolds	.20	.09	.03
☐ 34 Eddie Mathews	.50	.23	.06
☐ 35 Al Rosen	.20	.09	.03
☐ 36 Early Wynn	.50	.23	.06
☐ 37 Phil Rizzuto	.50	.23	.06
☐ 38 Warren Spahn	.50	.23	.06
☐ 39 Bobby Thomson	.30	.14	.04
☐ 40 Enos Slaughter	.50	.23	.06
☐ 41 Roberto Clemente	2.50	1.10	.30
☐ 42 Luis Aparicio	.50	.23	.06
☐ 43 Roy Sievers	.10	.05	.01
☐ 44 Hank Aaron	2.00	.90	.25
☐ 45 Mickey Vernon	.10	.05	.01
☐ 46 Lou Gehrig	3.00	1.35	.35
☐ 47 Lefty O'Doul	.20	.09	.03
☐ 48 Chuck Klein	.50	.23	.06
☐ 49 Paul Waner	.50	.23	.06
☐ 50 Mel Ott	.50	.23	.06
☐ 51 Riggs Stephenson	.20	.09	.03
☐ 52 Dizzy Dean	.50	.23	.06
☐ 53 Frank Frisch	.50	.23	.06
☐ 54 Red Ruffing	.50	.23	.06
☐ 55 Lefty Grove	.50	.23	.06
☐ 56 Heinie Manush	.50	.23	.06
☐ 57 Jimmie Foxx	.75	.35	.09
☐ 58 Al Simmons	.50	.23	.06
☐ 59 Charlie Root	.10	.05	.01
☐ 60 Goose Goslin	.50	.23	.06
☐ 61 Mickey Cochrane	.50	.23	.06
☐ 62 Gabby Hartnett	.50	.23	.06
☐ 63 Joe Medwick	.50	.23	.06
☐ 64 Ernie Lombardi	.50	.23	.06
☐ 65 Joe Cronin	.50	.23	.06
☐ 66 Pepper Martin	.20	.09	.03
☐ 67 Jim Bottomley	.50	.23	.06
☐ 68 Bill Dickey	.75	.35	.09
☐ 69 Babe Ruth	4.00	1.80	.50
☐ 70 Joe McCarthy MG	.30	.14	.04
☐ 71 Doc Cramer	.10	.05	.01
☐ 72 KiKi Cuyler	.50	.23	.06
☐ 73 Johnny Vander Meer	.30	.14	.04
☐ 74 Paul Derringer	.10	.05	.01
☐ 75 Fred Fitzsimmons	.20	.09	.03
☐ 76 Lefty Gomez	.50	.23	.06
☐ 77 Arky Vaughan	.50	.23	.06
☐ 78 Stan Hack	.10	.05	.01
☐ 79 Earl Averill	.50	.23	.06
☐ 80 Luke Appling	.50	.23	.06
☐ 81 Mel Harder	.10	.05	.01
☐ 82 Hank Greenberg	.50	.23	.06
☐ 83 Schoolboy Rowe	.10	.05	.01
☐ 84 Billy Herman	.50	.23	.06
☐ 85 Gabby Street	.10	.05	.01
☐ 86 Lloyd Waner	.40	.18	.05
☐ 87 Jocko Conlon	.30	.14	.04
☐ 88 Carl Hubbell	.75	.35	.09
☐ 89 Checklist 1	.10	.05	.01
☐ 90 Checklist 2	.10	.05	.01
☐ 91 Babe Ruth	4.00	1.80	.50
☐ 92 Rogers Hornsby	.50	.23	.06
☐ 93 Edd Roush	.40	.18	.05
☐ 94 George Sisler	.50	.23	.06
☐ 95 Harry Heilmann	.50	.23	.06
☐ 96 Tris Speaker	.75	.35	.09
☐ 97 Burleigh Grimes	.50	.23	.06
☐ 98 John McGraw	.75	.35	.09
☐ 99 Eppa Rixey	.40	.18	.05
☐ 100 Ty Cobb	3.00	1.35	.35
☐ 101 Zack Wheat	.50	.23	.06
☐ 102 Pie Traynor	.75	.35	.09
☐ 103 Max Carey	.50	.23	.06
☐ 104 Dazzy Vance	.50	.23	.06
☐ 105 Walter Johnson	1.00	.45	.12
☐ 106 Herb Pennock	.50	.23	.06
☐ 107 Joe Sewell	.50	.23	.06
☐ 108 Sam Rice	.40	.18	.05
☐ 109 Earle Combs	.50	.23	.06
☐ 110 Ted Lyons	.50	.23	.06
☐ 111 Eddie Collins	.75	.35	.09
☐ 112 Bill Terry	.50	.23	.06
☐ 113 Hack Wilson	.50	.23	.06
☐ 114 Rabbit Maranville	.40	.18	.05
☐ 115 Charlie Grimm	.20	.09	.03
☐ 116 Tony Lazzeri	.40	.18	.05
☐ 117 Waite Hoyt	.50	.23	.06
☐ 118 Stan Coveleski	.50	.23	.06
☐ 119 George Kelly	.40	.18	.05
☐ 120 Jimmie Dykes	.20	.09	.03
☐ 121 Red Faber	.40	.18	.05
☐ 122 Dave Bancroft	.40	.18	.05
☐ 123 Judge Landis COMM	.30	.14	.04
☐ 124 Branch Rickey	.30	.14	.04
☐ 125 Jesse Haines	.40	.18	.05
☐ 126 Carl Mays	.20	.09	.03
☐ 127 Fred Lindstrom	.40	.18	.05
☐ 128 Miller Huggins	.50	.23	.06
☐ 129 Sad Sam Jones	.10	.05	.01
☐ 130 Joe Judge	.20	.09	.03
☐ 131 Ross Youngs	.40	.18	.05
☐ 132 Bucky Harris	.50	.23	.06
☐ 133 Bob Meusel	.30	.14	.04
☐ 134 Billy Evans	.30	.14	.04
☐ 135 Checklist 3	.10	.05	.01
☐ 136 Ty Cobb	3.00	1.35	.35
☐ 137 Larry Lajoie	.50	.23	.06
☐ 138 Tris Speaker	.50	.23	.06
☐ 139 Heinie Groh	.10	.05	.01
☐ 140 Sam Crawford	.50	.23	.06
☐ 141 Clyde Milan	.10	.05	.01
☐ 142 Chief Bender	.50	.23	.06
☐ 143 Big Ed Walsh	.50	.23	.06
☐ 144 Walter Johnson	.75	.35	.09
☐ 145 Connie Mack MG	.50	.23	.06
☐ 146 Hal Chase	.30	.14	.04
☐ 147 Hugh Duffy	.50	.23	.06
☐ 148 Honus Wagner	.75	.35	.09
☐ 149 Tom Connolly UMP	.30	.14	.04
☐ 150 Clark Griffith	.30	.14	.04
☐ 151 Zack Wheat	.50	.23	.06
☐ 152 Christy Mathewson	.75	.35	.09
☐ 153 Grover Cleveland Alexander	.75	.35	.09
☐ 154 Joe Jackson	1.50	.70	.19
☐ 155 Home Run Baker	.50	.23	.06
☐ 156 Ed Plank	.50	.23	.06
☐ 157 Larry Doyle	.10	.05	.01
☐ 158 Rube Marquard	.50	.23	.06
☐ 159 John Evers	.50	.23	.06
☐ 160 Joe Tinker	.50	.23	.06
☐ 161 Frank Chance	.50	.23	.06
☐ 162 Wilbert Robinson MG	.30	.14	.04
☐ 163 Roger Peckinpaugh	.10	.05	.01
☐ 164 Fred Clarke	.50	.23	.06
☐ 165 Babe Ruth	4.00	1.80	.50
☐ 166 Wilbur Cooper	.10	.05	.01
☐ 167 Germany Schaefer	.20	.09	.03
☐ 168 Addie Joss	.50	.23	.06
☐ 169 Cy Young	.50	.23	.06
☐ 170 Ban Johnson PRES	.30	.14	.04
☐ 171 Joe Judge	.20	.09	.03
☐ 172 Harry Hooper	.40	.18	.05
☐ 173 Bill Klem UMP	.30	.14	.04
☐ 174 Ed Barrow MG	.30	.14	.04
☐ 175 Ed Cicotte	.30	.14	.04
☐ 176 Hughie Jennings MG	.30	.14	.04
☐ 177 Ray Schalk	.50	.23	.06
☐ 178 Nick Altrock	.30	.14	.04
☐ 179 Roger Bresnahan MG	.40	.18	.05
☐ 180 Checklist 4 The 100,000 Infield Stuffy McInnis Eddie Collins Jack Barry Frank Baker	.10	.05	.01
☐ 181 Lou Gehrig	3.00	1.35	.35
☐ 182 Eddie Collins	.50	.23	.06
☐ 183 Art Fletcher CO	.10	.05	.01
☐ 184 Jimmie Foxx	.50	.23	.06
☐ 185 Lefty Gomez	.50	.23	.06
☐ 186 Oral Hildebrand	.10	.05	.01
☐ 187 General Crowder	.10	.05	.01
☐ 188 Bill Dickey	.50	.23	.06
☐ 189 Wes Ferrell	.20	.09	.03
☐ 190 Al Simmons	.50	.23	.06
☐ 191 Tony Lazzeri	.40	.18	.05
☐ 192 Sam West	.10	.05	.01
☐ 193 Babe Ruth	4.00	1.80	.50
☐ 194 Connie Mack MG	.50	.23	.06
☐ 195 Lefty Grove	.50	.23	.06
☐ 196 Eddie Rommel	.10	.05	.01
☐ 197 Ben Chapman	.10	.05	.01
☐ 198 Joe Cronin	.50	.23	.06
☐ 199 Rick Ferrell	.40	.18	.05
☐ 200 Charlie Gehringer	.50	.23	.06
☐ 201 Jimmy Dykes	.20	.09	.03
☐ 202 Earl Averill	.50	.23	.06
☐ 203 Pepper Martin	.20	.09	.03
☐ 204 Bill Terry	.50	.23	.06
☐ 205 Pie Traynor	.50	.23	.06
☐ 206 Gabby Hartnett	.50	.23	.06

☐ 207 Frank Frisch	.50	.23	.06
☐ 208 Carl Hubbell	.50	.23	.06
☐ 209 Paul Waner	.50	.23	.06
☐ 210 Woody English	.10	.05	.01
☐ 211 Bill Hallahan	.10	.05	.01
☐ 212 Dick Bartell	.10	.05	.01
☐ 213 Bill McKechnie CO	.30	.14	.04
☐ 214 Max Carey CO	.40	.18	.05
☐ 215 John McGraw MG	.50	.23	.06
☐ 216 Jimmie Wilson	.10	.05	.01
☐ 217 Chick Hafey	.40	.18	.05
☐ 218 Chuck Klein	.50	.23	.06
☐ 219 Lefty O'Doul	.20	.09	.03
☐ 220 Wally Berger	.10	.05	.01
☐ 221 Hal Schumacher	.10	.05	.01
☐ 222 Lon Warneke	.10	.05	.01
☐ 223 Tony Cuccinello	.10	.05	.01
☐ 224 Americal League Team Photo	.10	.05	.01
☐ 225 National League Team Photo	.10	.05	.01
☐ 226 Roger Maris	.75	.35	.09
☐ 227 Babe Ruth	4.00	1.80	.50
☐ 228 Jackie Robinson	2.00	.90	.25
☐ 229 Pete Gray	.40	.18	.05
☐ 230 Ted Williams	2.50	1.10	.30
☐ 231 Hank Aaron	2.00	.90	.25
☐ 232 Mickey Mantle	3.00	1.35	.35
☐ 233 Gil Hodges	.75	.35	.09
☐ 234 Walter Johnson	.50	.23	.06
☐ 235 Joe DiMaggio	3.00	1.35	.35
☐ 236 Lou Gehrig	3.00	1.35	.35
☐ 237 Stan Musial	2.00	.90	.25
☐ 238 Mickey Cochrane	.50	.23	.06
☐ 239 Denny McLain	.20	.09	.03
☐ 240 Carl Hubbell	.50	.23	.06
☐ 241 Harvey Haddix	.10	.05	.01
☐ 242 Christy Mathewson	.50	.23	.06
☐ 243 Johnny Vander Meer	.20	.09	.03
☐ 244 Sandy Koufax	.75	.35	.09
☐ 245 Willie Mays	2.00	.90	.25
☐ 246 Don Drysdale	.50	.23	.06
☐ 247 Bobby Richardson	.20	.09	.03
☐ 248 Hoyt Wilhelm	.50	.23	.06
☐ 249 Yankee Stadium	.10	.05	.01
☐ 250 Bill Terry	.50	.23	.06
☐ 251 Roy Campanella	.75	.35	.09
☐ 252 Roberto Clemente	2.50	1.10	.30
☐ 253 Casey Stengel	.50	.23	.06
☐ 254 Ernie Banks	.75	.35	.09
☐ 255 Bobby Thomson	.30	.14	.04
☐ 256 Mel Ott	.50	.23	.06
☐ 257 Tony Oliva	.20	.09	.03
☐ 258 Satchel Paige	1.00	.45	.12
☐ 259 Joe Jackson	1.50	.70	.19
☐ 260 Larry Lajoie	.50	.23	.06
☐ 261 Bill Mazeroski	.30	.14	.04
☐ 262 Bill Wambsganss	.10	.05	.01
☐ 263 Willie McCovey	.50	.23	.06
☐ 264 Warren Spahn	.50	.23	.06
☐ 265 Lefty Gomez	.50	.23	.06
☐ 266 Dazzy Vance	.50	.23	.06
☐ 267 Sam Crawford	.50	.23	.06
☐ 268 Tris Speaker	.50	.23	.06
☐ 269 Lou Brock	.75	.35	.09
☐ 270 Cy Young	.50	.23	.06

1984 Galasso Hall of Famers Ron Lewis

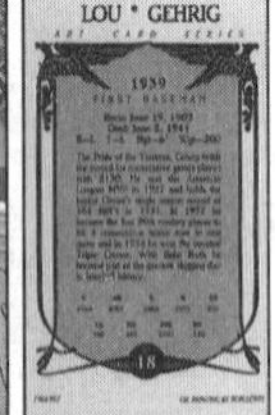

These 45 deckle edge cards measure approximately 2 3/4" by 5". The full bleed fronts have pictures of Ron Lewis oil paintings. The backs have vital statistics, a brief biography and career stats. The checklist card back says the set is numbered out of 10,000 and gives the set number. This set only covers Hall of Famers from 1936 through 1946.

	NRMT	VG-E	GOOD
COMPLETE SET (45)	15.00	6.75	1.85
COMMON CARD (1-45)	.25	.11	.03
☐ 1 Ty Cobb	2.00	.90	.25
☐ 2 Babe Ruth	2.50	1.10	.30
☐ 3 Walter Johnson	1.25	.55	.16
☐ 4 Christy Mathewson	1.00	.45	.12
☐ 5 Honus Wagner	1.25	.55	.16
☐ 6 Napoleon Lajoie	.75	.35	.09
☐ 7 Tris Speaker	.75	.35	.09
☐ 8 Cy Young	1.25	.55	.16
☐ 9 Morgan Bulkeley	.25	.11	.03
☐ 10 Ban Johnson	.25	.11	.03
☐ 11 John McGraw	.50	.23	.06
☐ 12 Connie Mack	.50	.23	.06
☐ 13 George Wright	.25	.11	.03
☐ 14 Grover Alexander	1.00	.45	.12
☐ 15 Alexander Cartwright	.25	.11	.03
☐ 16 Henry Chadwick	.25	.11	.03
☐ 17 Eddie Collins	.75	.35	.09
☐ 18 Lou Gehrig	2.00	.90	.25
☐ 19 Willie Keeler	.50	.23	.06
☐ 20 George Sisler	.50	.23	.06
☐ 21 Cap Anson	.50	.23	.06
☐ 22 Charles Comiskey	.50	.23	.06
☐ 23 Candy Cummings	.50	.23	.06
☐ 24 Buck Ewing	.50	.23	.06
☐ 25 Charlie Radbourne	.50	.23	.06
☐ 26 A.G. Spalding	.25	.11	.03
☐ 27 Rogers Hornsby	1.00	.45	.12
☐ 28 Judge Landis	.25	.11	.03
☐ 29 Roger Bresnahan	.50	.23	.06
☐ 30 Dan Brouthers	.50	.23	.06
☐ 31 Fred Clarke	.50	.23	.06
☐ 32 Jimmy Collins	.50	.23	.06
☐ 33 Ed Delahanty	.50	.23	.06
☐ 34 Hugh Duffy	.50	.23	.06
☐ 35 Hughie Jennings	.50	.23	.06
☐ 36 Mike "King" Kelly	.50	.23	.06
☐ 37 Jim O'Rouke	.50	.23	.06
☐ 38 Wilbert Robinson	.50	.23	.06
☐ 39 Jesse Burkett	.50	.23	.06
☐ 40 Frank Chance	.50	.23	.06
☐ 41 Jack Chesbro	.50	.23	.06
☐ 42 Johnny Evers	.50	.23	.06
☐ 43 Joe Tinker	.50	.23	.06
☐ 44 Eddie Plank	.50	.23	.06
☐ 45 Galasso Hall of Fame CL	.25	.11	.03

1984 Galasso Reggie Jackson

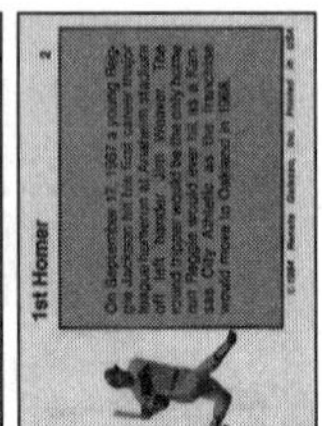

Produced by Renata Galasso, this 30-card standard-size set features color action player photos with turquoise borders. The player's first name appears in yellow script at the lower left corner. A small black-and-white cut-out photo of Jackson batting appears in the lower right corner. The horizontal backs are white and carry a pale blue box that contains career highlights. The same cut-out batting photo appears to the left of the box. The backs of card numbers 22-30 join to form a three-by-three card puzzle showing various baseball cards of Jackson against the background of his number 44 pinstriped jersey.

	NRMT	VG-E	GOOD
COMPLETE SET (30)	10.00	4.50	1.25
COMMON CARD (1-30)	.35	.16	.04
☐ 1 Reggie Jackson (Stat Card)	.35	.16	.04
☐ 2 Reggie Jackson 1st Homer	.35	.16	.04
☐ 3 Reggie Jackson Reggie Becomes a Starter	.35	.16	.04
☐ 4 Reggie Jackson 1969 An Incredible Season	.35	.16	.04
☐ 5 Reggie Jackson Honors For Reggie	.35	.16	.04
☐ 6 Reggie Jackson MVP Season	.35	.16	.04
☐ 7 Reggie Jackson The Championship Years	.35	.16	.04
☐ 8 Reggie Jackson Another Home Run Crown	.35	.16	.04
☐ 9 Reggie Jackson The Athletic Years	.35	.16	.04
☐ 10 Reggie Jackson Reggie An Oriole	.35	.16	.04
☐ 11 Reggie Jackson Free Agency	.35	.16	.04
☐ 12 Reggie Jackson Reggie A Yankee	.35	.16	.04
☐ 13 Reggie Jackson 4 Home Runs On 4 Swings	.35	.16	.04
☐ 14 Reggie Jackson A Rare Photo	.35	.16	.04
☐ 15 Reggie Jackson The Oakland Connection	.35	.16	.04
☐ 16 Reggie Jackson No 400	.35	.16	.04
☐ 17 Reggie Jackson 1980	.35	.16	.04
☐ 18 Reggie Jackson The End Of An Era	.35	.16	.04
☐ 19 Reggie Jackson Reggie An Angel	.35	.16	.04
☐ 20 Reggie Jackson 500	.35	.16	.04
☐ 21 Reggie Jackson The Future	.35	.16	.04
☐ 22 Reggie Jackson (Puzzle back; top left)	.35	.16	.04
☐ 23 Reggie Jackson (Puzzle back; middle left)	.35	.16	.04
☐ 24 Reggie Jackson (Puzzle Back) bottom left)	.35	.16	.04
☐ 25 Reggie Jackson (Puzzle back; top middle)	.35	.16	.04
☐ 26 Reggie Jackson (Puzzle back; middle middle)	.35	.16	.04
☐ 27 Reggie Jackson (Puzzle back; bottom middle)	.35	.16	.04
☐ 28 Reggie Jackson (Puzzle back; top right)	.35	.16	.04
☐ 29 Reggie Jackson (Puzzle back; middle right)	.35	.16	.04
☐ 30 Reggie Jackson (Puzzle back; bottom right)	.35	.16	.04

1920 Gassler's American Maid Bread D381-1

These cards measure approximately 2" by 3". They are unnumbered and we have sequenced them alphabetically by team which are also sequenced alphabetically.

	EX-MT	VG-E	GOOD
COMPLETE SET	1200.00	550.00	150.00
COMMON CARD	30.00	13.50	3.70
☐ 1 Kid Gleason MG	50.00	22.00	6.25
☐ 2 Harry Hooper	75.00	34.00	9.50
☐ 3 Dick Kerr	50.00	22.00	6.25
☐ 4 Amos Strunk	30.00	13.50	3.70
☐ 5 George Burns	30.00	13.50	3.70
☐ 6 W. L. Gardner	30.00	13.50	3.70
☐ 7 Rip Collins	30.00	13.50	3.70
☐ 8 Wm. Fewster	30.00	13.50	3.70
☐ 9 Harry Harper	30.00	13.50	3.70
☐ 10 Waite Hoyt	75.00	34.00	9.50
☐ 11 Miller Huggins MG	75.00	34.00	9.50
☐ 12 M.J. McNally	30.00	13.50	3.70
☐ 13 Bob Meusel	50.00	22.00	6.25
☐ 14 Walter Pipp	40.00	18.00	5.00
☐ 15 Jack Quinn	30.00	13.50	3.70
☐ 16 Robert Roth	30.00	13.50	3.70
☐ 17 Wally Schang	30.00	13.50	3.70
☐ 18 Aaron Ward	30.00	13.50	3.70
☐ 19 Wm. Jacobson	30.00	13.50	3.70
☐ 20 Clyde Milan	40.00	18.00	5.00
☐ 21 Walter Holke	30.00	13.50	3.70
☐ 22 P. J. Kilduff	30.00	13.50	3.70
☐ 23 Zach Wheat	75.00	34.00	9.50
☐ 24 Charles Deal	30.00	13.50	3.70
☐ 25 Charles Hollacher	30.00	13.50	3.70
☐ 26 Zeb Terry	30.00	13.50	3.70
☐ 27 Geo. J. Burns	30.00	13.50	3.70
☐ 28 Cecil Causey	30.00	13.50	3.70
☐ 29 Hugh Jennings MG	75.00	34.00	9.50
☐ 30 Arthur Nehf	40.00	18.00	5.00
☐ 31 John Rawlings	30.00	13.50	3.70
☐ 32 Bill Ryan	30.00	13.50	3.70
☐ 33 Pat Shea	30.00	13.50	3.70
☐ 34 Earl Smith	30.00	13.50	3.70
☐ 35 Frank Snyder	30.00	13.50	3.70
☐ 36 Jeff Pfeffer	30.00	13.50	3.70

1985 General Mills Stickers

Found in boxes of Cheerios and Honey Nut Cheerios in Canada, each General Mills sticker card features two stickers, with a National League player on the left and an American League player on the right. Each sticker pair measures approximately 3 3/4" by 2 3/8" while each individual player sticker measures 1 7/8" by 2 3/8". On a white background, the fronts feature color player portraits, with the player's name in a yellow bar under the photo. The National League player's team and position (in French and English) appear in a red bar under the photo, while the American League player's team and position (also in French and English) appear in a blue bar. The players' cap team logos have been airbrushed. The General Mills logo is printed inside a triangle in the upper left corner of each sticker. The backs are blank. The set features one player per team. The pairs are valued at the sum of the individual player values. Some players are featured with more than one partner, e.g. Gary Carter is found with either Tom Brunansky or Dave Stieb and Steve Garvey is found with either George Bell or Jim Rice. The stickers are unnumbered and checklisted below in alphabetical order by National Leaguers (1-12) and American Leaguers (13-26). The number of the sticker that each player is paired with is as follows: 1/15, 1/23, 2/16, 3/13, 3/22, 4/21, 5/26, 6/19, 7/24, 8/18, 9/14, 10/25, 11/17 and 12/20.

	NRMT	VG-E	GOOD
COMPLETE SET (26)	20.00	9.00	2.50
COMMON STICKER (1-26)	.25	.11	.03
☐ 1 Gary Carter DP	.50	.23	.06
☐ 2 Andre Dawson	1.00	.45	.12
☐ 3 Steve Garvey DP	.50	.23	.06
☐ 4 Jeff Leonard	.25	.11	.03
☐ 5 Dale Murphy	1.00	.45	.12
☐ 6 Terry Puhl	.25	.11	.03
☐ 7 Johnny Ray	.25	.11	.03
☐ 8 Ryne Sandberg	4.00	1.80	.50
☐ 9 Mike Schmidt	2.50	1.10	.30
☐ 10 Ozzie Smith	1.50	.70	.19
☐ 11 Mario Soto	.25	.11	.03
☐ 12 Fernando Valenzuela	.50	.23	.06
☐ 13 Buddy Bell	.50	.23	.06
☐ 14 George Brett	3.00	1.35	.35
☐ 15 Tom Brunansky	.25	.11	.03
☐ 16 Alvin Davis	.50	.23	.06
☐ 17 Carlton Fisk	1.25	.55	.16
☐ 18 Mike Hargrove	.50	.23	.06
☐ 19 Reggie Jackson	2.00	.90	.25
☐ 20 Dwayne Murphy	.25	.11	.03
☐ 21 Eddie Murray	1.50	.70	.19
☐ 22 Jim Rice	.50	.23	.06
☐ 23 Dave Stieb	.25	.11	.03
☐ 24 Lou Whitaker	1.00	.45	.12
☐ 25 Dave Winfield	1.25	.55	.16
☐ 26 Robin Yount	1.25	.55	.16

1986 General Mills Booklets

Printed on thin glossy stock, each of these six booklets measures approximately 15" by 3 13/16" when unfolded; each single player (and the complete booklet when folded) measures approximately 2 9/16" by 3 13/16". Each booklet features ten color player head shots, five on each side. The players' cap logos have been airbrushed. The sixth (non-player) panel is an entry for a contest to win a day with your favorite player at spring training in 1987. The player's statistics in English and French appear under each photo. The title card carries the booklet number in the top right corner. The set is sometimes referred to as the "Cheerios" set as it was inserted inside Cheerios cereal boxes; Cheerios is a product of General Mills. Booklets still in the original clear cellophane protective wrapping are worth an additional ten percent over the prices listed below.

	MINT	NRMT	EXC
COMPLETE SET (60)	200.00	90.00	25.00
COMMON CARD (1A-6J)	2.00	.90	.25
☐ 1A Wade Boggs	8.00	3.60	1.00
☐ 1B Kirk Gibson	4.00	1.80	.50
☐ 1C Rickey Henderson	8.00	3.60	1.00
☐ 1D Don Mattingly	30.00	13.50	3.70
☐ 1E Jack Morris	4.00	1.80	.50
☐ 1F Lance Parrish	2.00	.90	.25
☐ 1G Jim Rice	4.00	1.80	.50
☐ 1H Dave Righetti	2.00	.90	.25
☐ 1I Cal Ripken	50.00	22.00	6.25
☐ 1J Lou Whitaker	4.00	1.80	.50
☐ 2A Harold Baines	4.00	1.80	.50
☐ 2B Phil Bradley	2.00	.90	.25
☐ 2C George Brett	25.00	11.00	3.10
☐ 2D Carlton Fisk	8.00	3.60	1.00
☐ 2E Ozzie Guillen	4.00	1.80	.50
☐ 2F Kent Hrbek	4.00	1.80	.50
☐ 2G Reggie Jackson	10.00	4.50	1.25
☐ 2H Dan Quisenberry	2.00	.90	.25
☐ 2I Bret Saberhagen	6.00	2.70	.75
☐ 2J Frank White	2.00	.90	.25
☐ 3A Jesse Barfield	2.00	.90	.25
☐ 3B George Bell	2.00	.90	.25
☐ 3C Bill Caudill	2.00	.90	.25
☐ 3D Tony Fernandez	2.00	.90	.25
☐ 3E Damaso Garcia	2.00	.90	.25
☐ 3F Lloyd Moseby	2.00	.90	.25
☐ 3G Rance Mulliniks	2.00	.90	.25
☐ 3H Dave Stieb	2.00	.90	.25
☐ 3I Willie Upshaw	2.00	.90	.25
☐ 3J Ernie Whitt	2.00	.90	.25
☐ 4A Gary Carter	4.00	1.80	.50
☐ 4B Jack Clark	2.00	.90	.25
☐ 4C George Foster	2.00	.90	.25

☐ 4D Dwight Gooden	6.00	2.70	.75
☐ 4E Gary Matthews	2.00	.90	.25
☐ 4F Willie McGee	4.00	1.80	.50
☐ 4G Ryne Sandberg	20.00	9.00	2.50
☐ 4H Mike Schmidt	12.00	5.50	1.50
☐ 4I Lee Smith	6.00	2.70	.75
☐ 4J Ozzie Smith	15.00	6.75	1.85
☐ 5A David Concepcion	4.00	1.80	.50
☐ 5B Pedro Guerrero	2.00	.90	.25
☐ 5C Terry Kennedy	2.00	.90	.25
☐ 5D Dale Murphy	8.00	3.60	1.00
☐ 5E Graig Nettles	4.00	1.80	.50
☐ 5F Dave Parker	4.00	1.80	.50
☐ 5G Tony Perez	6.00	2.70	.75
☐ 5H Steve Sax	2.00	.90	.25
☐ 5I Bruce Sutter	2.00	.90	.25
☐ 5J Fernando Valenzuela	4.00	1.80	.50
☐ 6A Hubie Brooks	2.00	.90	.25
☐ 6B Andre Dawson	8.00	3.60	1.00
☐ 6C Mike Fitzgerald	2.00	.90	.25
☐ 6D Vance Law	2.00	.90	.25
☐ 6E Tim Raines	4.00	1.80	.50
☐ 6F Jeff Reardon	2.00	.90	.25
☐ 6G Bryn Smith	2.00	.90	.25
☐ 6H Jason Thompson	2.00	.90	.25
☐ 6I Tim Wallach	2.00	.90	.25
☐ 6J Mitch Webster	2.00	.90	.25

1987 General Mills Booklets

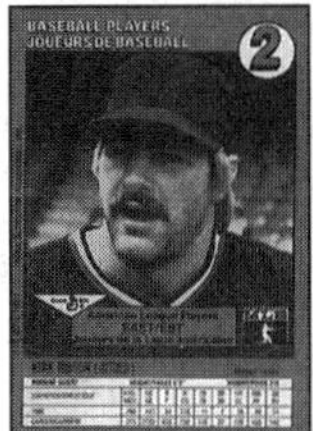

Printed on thin glossy stock, each of these six booklets measures approximately 15" by 3 3/4" when unfolded; each single player (and the complete booklet when folded) measures approximately 2 9/16" by 3 3/4". Each booklet features ten color player head shots, five on each side from a respective grouping (each division and both Canadian teams). The sixth (non-player) panel is an entry for a contest to win a day with your favorite player at Spring Training in 1988. The players' cap logos have been airbrushed. Player statistics in English and French appear under each photo. The title card carries the booklet number in the top right corner. The set is sometimes referred to as the "Cheerios" set as it was inserted inside Cheerios cereal boxes; Cheerios is a product of General Mills. Booklets still in the original clear cellophane protective wrapping are worth an additional ten percent over the prices listed below.

	MINT	NRMT	EXC
COMPLETE SET (60)	20.00	9.00	2.50
COMMON CARD (1A-6J)	.25	.11	.03
☐ 1A Jesse Barfield	.25	.11	.03
☐ 1B George Bell	.25	.11	.03
☐ 1C Tony Fernandez	.25	.11	.03
☐ 1D Kelly Gruber	.25	.11	.03
☐ 1E Tom Henke	.25	.11	.03
☐ 1F Jimmy Key	.50	.23	.06
☐ 1G Lloyd Moseby	.25	.11	.03
☐ 1H Dave Stieb	.25	.11	.03
☐ 1I Willie Upshaw	.25	.11	.03
☐ 1J Ernie Whitt	.25	.11	.03
☐ 2A Wade Boggs	.75	.35	.09
☐ 2B Roger Clemens	1.00	.45	.12
☐ 2C Kirk Gibson	.50	.23	.06
☐ 2D Rickey Henderson	.75	.35	.09
☐ 2E Don Mattingly	3.00	1.35	.35
☐ 2F Jack Morris	.50	.23	.06
☐ 2G Eddie Murray	1.00	.45	.12
☐ 2H Pat Tabler	.25	.11	.03
☐ 2I Dave Winfield	.75	.35	.09
☐ 2J Robin Yount	.75	.35	.09
☐ 3A Phil Bradley	.25	.11	.03
☐ 3B George Brett	2.00	.90	.25
☐ 3C Jose Canseco	1.00	.45	.12
☐ 3D Carlton Fisk	.75	.35	.09
☐ 3E Reggie Jackson	1.00	.45	.12
☐ 3F Wally Joyner	.50	.23	.06
☐ 3G Kirk McCaskill	.25	.11	.03
☐ 3H Larry Parrish	.25	.11	.03
☐ 3I Kirby Puckett	2.00	.90	.25
☐ 3J Dan Quisenberry	.25	.11	.03
☐ 4A Hubie Brooks	.25	.11	.03
☐ 4B Mike Fitzgerald	.25	.11	.03
☐ 4C Andres Galarraga	1.00	.45	.12
☐ 4D Vance Law	.25	.11	.03
☐ 4E Andy McGaffigan	.25	.11	.03
☐ 4F Bryn Smith	.25	.11	.03
☐ 4G Jason Thompson	.25	.11	.03
☐ 4H Tim Wallach	.25	.11	.03
☐ 4I Mitch Webster	.25	.11	.03
☐ 4J Floyd Youmans	.25	.11	.03
☐ 5A Gary Carter	.50	.23	.06
☐ 5B Dwight Gooden	.75	.35	.09
☐ 5C Keith Hernandez	.50	.23	.06
☐ 5D Willie McGee	.50	.23	.06
☐ 5E Tim Raines	.50	.23	.06
☐ 5F R.J. Reynolds	.25	.11	.03
☐ 5G Ryne Sandberg	1.50	.70	.19
☐ 5H Mike Schmidt	1.25	.55	.16
☐ 5I Ozzie Smith	1.25	.55	.16
☐ 5J Darryl Strawberry	.50	.23	.06
☐ 6A Kevin Bass	.25	.11	.03
☐ 6B Eric Davis	.50	.23	.06
☐ 6C Bill Doran	.25	.11	.03
☐ 6D Pedro Guerrero	.25	.11	.03
☐ 6E Tony Gwynn	2.50	1.10	.30
☐ 6F Dale Murphy	.75	.35	.09
☐ 6G Dave Parker	.50	.23	.06
☐ 6H Steve Sax	.25	.11	.03
☐ 6I Mike Scott	.25	.11	.03
☐ 6J Fernando Valenzuela	.50	.23	.06

1933 George C. Miller R300

The cards in this 32-card set measure 2 1/2" by 3". This set of soft tone color baseball cards issued in 1933 by the George C. Miller Company consists of 16 players from each league. The bottom portion of the reverse contained a premium offer and many cards are found with this section cut off. Cards without the coupon are considered fair to good condition at best. The Andrews card (with coupon intact) is considered scarce in relation to all other common players.

	EX-MT	VG-E	GOOD
COMPLETE SET (32)	12500.00	5600.00	1600.00
COMMON CARD (1-32)	400.00	180.00	50.00
☐ 1 Dale Alexander	400.00	180.00	50.00
☐ 2 Ivy Andrews	15000.00	6800.00	1900.00
☐ 3 Earl Averill	600.00	275.00	75.00
☐ 4 Dick Bartell	400.00	180.00	50.00
☐ 5 Wally Berger	400.00	180.00	50.00
☐ 6 Jim Bottomley	600.00	275.00	75.00
☐ 7 Joe Cronin	600.00	275.00	75.00
☐ 8 Dizzy Dean	1000.00	450.00	125.00
☐ 9 Bill Dickey	750.00	350.00	95.00
☐ 10 Jimmy Dykes	400.00	180.00	50.00
☐ 11 Wes Ferrell	400.00	180.00	50.00
☐ 12 Jimmy Foxx	1000.00	450.00	125.00
☐ 13 Frank Frisch	650.00	300.00	80.00
☐ 14 Charlie Gehringer	650.00	300.00	80.00
☐ 15 Goose Goslin	600.00	275.00	75.00
☐ 16 Charlie Grimm	400.00	180.00	50.00
☐ 17 Lefty Grove	650.00	300.00	80.00
☐ 18 Chick Hafey	600.00	275.00	75.00
☐ 19 Ray Hayworth	400.00	180.00	50.00
☐ 20 Chuck Klein	600.00	275.00	75.00
☐ 21 Rabbit Maranville	500.00	220.00	60.00
☐ 22 Oscar Melillo	400.00	180.00	50.00
☐ 23 Lefty O'Doul	400.00	180.00	50.00
☐ 24 Mel Ott	700.00	325.00	90.00
☐ 25 Carl Reynolds	400.00	180.00	50.00
☐ 26 Red Ruffing	500.00	220.00	60.00
☐ 27 Al Simmons	500.00	220.00	60.00
☐ 28 Joe Stripp	400.00	180.00	50.00
☐ 29 Bill Terry	600.00	275.00	75.00
☐ 30 Lloyd Waner	500.00	220.00	60.00
☐ 31 Paul Waner	500.00	220.00	60.00
☐ 32 Lon Warneke	400.00	180.00	50.00

1981 George Brett Promo

This promo card was distributed at the St. Louis Card Show in 1981. It commemorates his .390 season. It features an artist's rendition with a Sporting News quote on back. Just 5,000 were issued.

	NRMT	VG-E	GOOD
COMPLETE SET (1)	10.00	4.50	1.25
COMMON CARD	10.00	4.50	1.25
☐ 1 George Brett	10.00	4.50	1.25

1938-59 George Burke PC744

The Burke postcards were issued by Chicago photographer George Burke during the period from 1938 through the 1950's. Because there are hundreds known and new ones are discovered frequently, a checklist has not been provided. The reverses feature the stamped name of "Geo. Burke, his address and the city "Chicago"

	EX-MT	VG-E	GOOD
COMMON CARD (1938-48)	5.00	2.20	.60
COMMON CARD (1948-on)	2.00	.90	.25

1985 George Steinbrenner Menu

Issued in the mid 1980's these cards honored some all-time Yankee greats. These cards were issued to promote George Steinbrenner's restaurant in Tampa, Florida, spring training home of the New York Yankees. Steinbrenner has also been the Yankees owner for more than two decades.

	NRMT	VG-E	GOOD
COMPLETE SET (9)	30.00	13.50	3.70
COMMON CARD (1-9)	1.00	.45	.12
☐ 1 Yogi Berra	3.00	1.35	.35
☐ 2 Lou Gehrig	5.00	2.20	.60
☐ 3 Whitey Ford	3.00	1.35	.35
☐ 4 Elston Howard	1.00	.45	.12
☐ 5 Mickey Mantle	7.50	3.40	.95
☐ 6 Roger Maris	4.00	1.80	.50
☐ 7 Thurman Munson	2.00	.90	.25
☐ 8 Babe Ruth	7.50	3.40	.95

1906 Giants Ullman's Art Frame Series

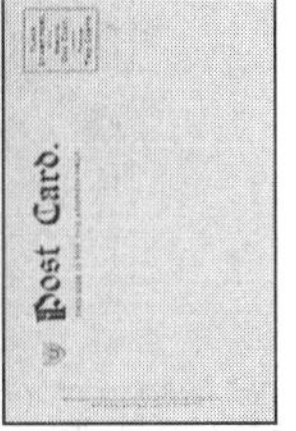

These cards, issued the year after the Giants won their first World Series, show an action view of the player or players inside a brown or green border made to resemble a picture frame. At the bottom is a gold area made to look like an identification tag for a picture containing a description of the scene and players identified. There are six known cards in the set. There are probably more cards in this set so additions to the checklist are appreciated.

	EX-MT	VG-E	GOOD
COMPLETE SET (12)	3000.00	1350.00	375.00
COMMON CARD (1-12)	200.00	90.00	25.00
☐ 1 Red Ames	250.00	110.00	31.00
☐ 2 Mike Donlin	300.00	135.00	38.00
☐ 3 George Ferguson	200.00	90.00	25.00
☐ 4 Matty Fitzgerald	200.00	90.00	25.00
☐ 5 Bill Gilbert	200.00	90.00	25.00
☐ 6 Christy Mathewson	600.00	275.00	75.00
☐ 7 Harry Mathewson	200.00	90.00	25.00
☐ 8 Dan McGann	200.00	90.00	25.00
☐ 9 Joe McGinnity	400.00	180.00	50.00
☐ 10 John McGraw MG	400.00	180.00	50.00
☐ 11 Sammy Strang Frank Bowerman	200.00	90.00	25.00
☐ 12 Hooks Wiltse	200.00	90.00	25.00

1932 Giants Schedule

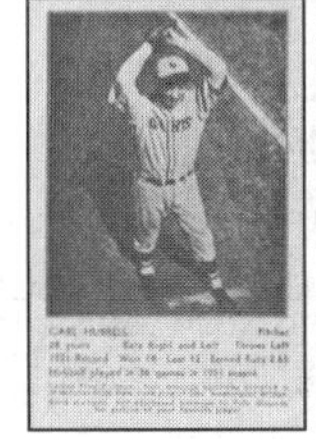

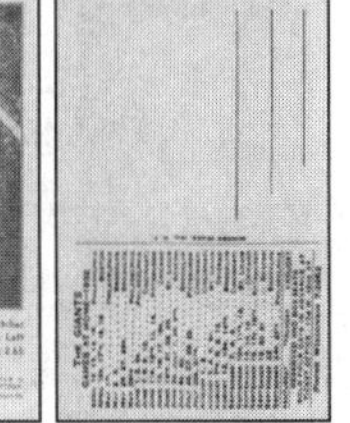

This one-card set of the 1932 New York Giants was issued in a postcard format with a black and white action photo on the front. Player information is printed in the wide bottom margin. The back displays the team's schedule.

	EX-MT	VG-E	GOOD
COMPLETE SET (1)	25.00	11.00	3.10
COMMON CARD (1)	25.00	11.00	3.10
☐ 1 Carl Hubbell	25.00	11.00	3.10

1955 Giants Golden Stamps

This 32-stamp set features color photos of the New York Giants and measures approximately 2" by 2 5/8". The stamps are designed to be placed in a 32-page album which measures approximately 8 3/8" by 10 15/16". The album contains black-and-white drawings of players with statistics and life stories. The stamps are unnumbered and listed below according to where they fall in the album.

	NRMT	VG-E	GOOD
COMPLETE SET (32)	100.00	45.00	12.50
COMMON CARD (1-32)	2.00	.90	.25
☐ 1 1954 Giants Team	7.50	3.40	.95
☐ 2 Leo Durocher	15.00	6.75	1.85

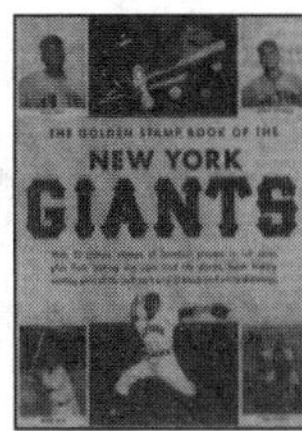

☐ 3 Johnny Antonelli	2.00	.90	.25
☐ 4 Sal Maglie	4.00	1.80	.50
☐ 5 Ruben Gomez	2.00	.90	.25
☐ 6 Hoyt Wilhelm	10.00	4.50	1.25
☐ 7 Marv Grissom	2.00	.90	.25
☐ 8 Jim Hearn	2.00	.90	.25
☐ 9 Paul Giel	2.00	.90	.25
☐ 10 Al Corwin	2.00	.90	.25
☐ 11 George Spencer	2.00	.90	.25
☐ 12 Don Liddle	2.00	.90	.25
☐ 13 Windy McCall	2.00	.90	.25
☐ 14 Al Worthington	2.00	.90	.25
☐ 15 Wes Westrum	2.00	.90	.25
☐ 16 Whitey Lockman	2.00	.90	.25
☐ 17 Dave Williams	2.00	.90	.25
☐ 18 Hank Thompson	4.00	1.80	.50
☐ 19 Alvin Dark	4.00	1.80	.50
☐ 20 Monte Irvin	10.00	4.50	1.25
☐ 21 Willie Mays	25.00	11.00	3.10
☐ 22 Don Mueller	2.00	.90	.25
☐ 23 Dusty Rhodes	2.00	.90	.25
☐ 24 Ray Katt	2.00	.90	.25
☐ 25 Joe Amalfitano	2.00	.90	.25
☐ 26 Bill Gardner	2.00	.90	.25
☐ 27 Foster Castleman	2.00	.90	.25
☐ 28 Bobby Hoffman	2.00	.90	.25
☐ 29 Bill Taylor	2.00	.90	.25
☐ 30 Manager and Coaches	4.00	1.80	.50
☐ 31 Bobby Weinstein BB	2.00	.90	.25
☐ 32 Polo Grounds	10.00	4.50	1.25

1958 Giants Armour Tabs

This set of tabs features black-and-white player photos with a facsimile autograph lithographed on tin in a figural design in orange, black, and white. The checklist may be incomplete and additions are welcome. The tabs are unnumbered and checklisted below in alphabetical order.

	NRMT	VG-E	GOOD
COMPLETE SET	20.00	9.00	2.50
COMMON CARD	10.00	4.50	1.25

1958 Giants Jay Publishing

This 12-card set of the San Francisco Giants measures approximately 5" by 7" and features black-and-white player photos in a white border. These cards were packaged 12 to a packet. The backs are blank. The cards are unnumbered and checklisted below in alphabetical order.

	NRMT	VG-E	GOOD
COMPLETE SET (12)	30.00	13.50	3.70
COMMON CARD (1-12)	2.00	.90	.25
☐ 1 John Antonelli	2.00	.90	.25
☐ 2 Curt Barclay	2.00	.90	.25
☐ 3 Paul Giel	2.00	.90	.25
☐ 4 Reuben Gomez	2.00	.90	.25
☐ 5 Willie Kirkland	2.00	.90	.25
☐ 6 Whitey Lockman	2.00	.90	.25
☐ 7 Willie Mays	10.00	4.50	1.25
☐ 8 Danny O'Connell	2.00	.90	.25
☐ 9 Hank Sauer	3.00	1.35	.35
☐ 10 Bob Schmidt	2.00	.90	.25
☐ 11 Daryl Spencer	2.00	.90	.25
☐ 12 Al Worthington	2.00	.90	.25

1958 Giants S.F. Call-Bulletin

The cards in this 25-card set measure approximately 2" by 4". The 1958 San Francisco Call-Bulletin set of unnumbered cards features black print on orange paper. These cards were given away as inserts in the San Francisco Call-Bulletin newspaper. The backs of the cards list the Giants home schedule and a radio station ad. The cards are entitled "Giant Payoff" and feature San Francisco Giant players only. The bottom part of the card (tab) could be detached as a ticket stub; hence, cards with the tab intact are worth approximately double the prices listed below. The catalog designation for this set is M126. The

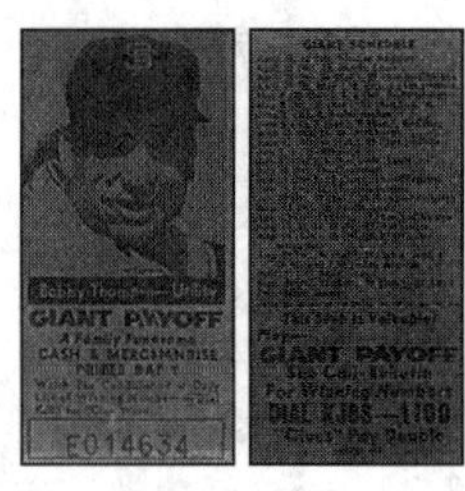

Tom Bowers card was issued in very short supply; also Bressoud, Jablonski, and Kirkland are tougher to find than the others; all of these tougher cards are indicated as SP in the checklist below.

	NRMT	VG-E	GOOD
COMPLETE SET (25)	1400.00	650.00	180.00
COMMON CARD (1-25)	10.00	4.50	1.25
☐ 1 John Antonelli	12.00	5.50	1.50
☐ 2 Curt Barclay	10.00	4.50	1.25
☐ 3 Tom Bowers SP	650.00	300.00	80.00
☐ 4 Ed Bressoud SP	125.00	55.00	15.50
☐ 5 Orlando Cepeda	50.00	22.00	6.25
☐ 6 Ray Crone	10.00	4.50	1.25
☐ 7 Jim Davenport	12.00	5.50	1.50
☐ 8 Paul Giel	25.00	11.00	3.10
☐ 9 Ruben Gomez	10.00	4.50	1.25
☐ 10 Marv Grissom	10.00	4.50	1.25
☐ 11 Ray Jablonski SP	125.00	55.00	15.50
☐ 12 Willie Kirkland SP	150.00	70.00	19.00
☐ 13 Whitey Lockman	12.00	5.50	1.50
☐ 14 Willie Mays	250.00	110.00	31.00
☐ 15 Mike McCormick	12.00	5.50	1.50
☐ 16 Stu Miller	12.00	5.50	1.50
☐ 17 Ray Monzant	10.00	4.50	1.25
☐ 18 Danny O'Connell	10.00	4.50	1.25
☐ 19 Bill Rigney MG	10.00	4.50	1.25
☐ 20 Hank Sauer	12.00	5.50	1.50
☐ 21 Bob Schmidt	10.00	4.50	1.25
☐ 22 Daryl Spencer	10.00	4.50	1.25
☐ 23 Valmy Thomas	10.00	4.50	1.25
☐ 24 Bobby Thomson	25.00	11.00	3.10
☐ 25 Al Worthington	10.00	4.50	1.25

1958-61 Giants Falstaff Beer Team Photos

This four-card set features color photos of the 1958, 1959, 1960, and 1961 San Francisco Giants teams. Each card measures approximately 6 1/4" by 9" and displays the Falstaff logo on the front. The backs carry a team promotional message.

	NRMT	VG-E	GOOD
COMPLETE SET (4)	75.00	34.00	9.50
COMMON CARD (1-4)	20.00	9.00	2.50
☐ 1 1958 Giants Team Photo	20.00	9.00	2.50
☐ 2 1959 Giants Team Photo	20.00	9.00	2.50
☐ 3 1960 Giants Team Photo	20.00	9.00	2.50
☐ 4 1961 Giants Team Photo	20.00	9.00	2.50

1960 Giants Jay Publishing

This 12-card set of the San Francisco Giants measures approximately 5" by 7" and features black-and-white player photos in a white border. These cards were packaged 12 to a packet. The backs are blank. The cards are unnumbered and checklisted below in alphabetical order.

	NRMT	VG-E	GOOD
COMPLETE SET (12)	35.00	16.00	4.40
COMMON CARD (1-12)	2.50	1.10	.30
☐ 1 John Antonelli	2.50	1.10	.30
☐ 2 Don Blasingame	2.50	1.10	.30
☐ 3 Eddie Bressoud	2.50	1.10	.30
☐ 4 Orlando Cepeda	5.00	2.20	.60
☐ 5 Jim Davenport	2.50	1.10	.30
☐ 6 Sam Jones	2.50	1.10	.30
☐ 7 Willie Kirkland	2.50	1.10	.30
☐ 8 Willie Mays	10.00	4.50	1.25
☐ 9 Willie McCovey	6.00	2.70	.75
☐ 10 Mike McCormick	2.50	1.10	.30
☐ 11 Jack Sanford	2.50	1.10	.30
☐ 12 Bob Schmidt	2.50	1.10	.30

1961 Giants Jay Publishing

This 12-card set of the San Francisco Giants measures approximately 5" by 7". The fronts feature black-and-white posed player photos with the player's and team name printed below in the white border. These cards were packaged 12 in a packet. The backs are blank. The cards are unnumbered and checklisted below in alphabetical order.

	NRMT	VG-E	GOOD
COMPLETE SET (12)	40.00	18.00	5.00
COMMON CARD (1-12)	2.50	1.10	.30
☐ 1 Felipe Alou	3.50	1.55	.45
☐ 2 Don Blasingame	2.50	1.10	.30
☐ 3 Orlando Cepeda	4.50	2.00	.55
☐ 4 Alvin Dark MG	3.00	1.35	.35
☐ 5 Jim Davenport	3.00	1.35	.35
☐ 6 Sam Jones	2.50	1.10	.30
☐ 7 Harvey Kuenn	3.50	1.55	.45
☐ 8 Juan Marichal	7.50	3.40	.95
☐ 9 Willie Mays	15.00	6.75	1.85
☐ 10 Mike McCormick	2.50	1.10	.30
☐ 11 Stu Miller	2.50	1.10	.30
☐ 12 Bob Schmidt	2.50	1.10	.30

1962 Giants Jay Publishing

This 12-card set of the San Francisco Giants measures approximately 5" by 7". The fronts feature black-and-white posed player photos with the player's and team name printed below in the white border. These cards were packaged 12 in a packet. The backs are blank. The cards are unnumbered and checklisted below in alphabetical order.

	NRMT	VG-E	GOOD
COMPLETE SET (12)	40.00	18.00	5.00
COMMON CARD (1-12)	2.50	1.10	.30
☐ 1 Felipe Alou	3.50	1.55	.45
☐ 2 Ed Bailey	2.50	1.10	.30
☐ 3 Orlando Cepeda	5.00	2.20	.60
☐ 4 Jim Davenport	3.00	1.35	.35
☐ 5 Tom Haller	2.50	1.10	.30
☐ 6 Chuck Hiller	2.50	1.10	.30
☐ 7 Harvey Kuenn	3.50	1.55	.45
☐ 8 Juan Marichal	7.50	3.40	.95
☐ 9 Willie Mays	20.00	9.00	2.50
☐ 10 Mike McCormick	2.50	1.10	.30
☐ 11 Stu Miller	2.50	1.10	.30
☐ 12 Billy Pierce	3.50	1.55	.45

1963 Giants Jay Publishing

This 12-card set of the San Francisco Giants measures approximately 5" by 7". The fronts feature black-and-white posed player photos with the player's and team name printed below in the white border. These cards were packaged 12 in a packet. The backs are blank. The cards are unnumbered and checklisted below in alphabetical order.

	NRMT	VG-E	GOOD
COMPLETE SET (12)	40.00	18.00	5.00
COMMON CARD (1-12)	2.50	1.10	.30
☐ 1 Felipe Alou	3.50	1.55	.45
☐ 2 Orlando Cepeda	5.00	2.20	.60
☐ 3 Alvin Dark MG	3.00	1.35	.35
☐ 4 Jim Davenport	3.00	1.35	.35
☐ 5 Tom Haller	2.50	1.10	.30
☐ 6 Chuck Hiller	2.50	1.10	.30
☐ 7 Willie Mays	15.00	6.75	1.85
☐ 8 Willie McCovey	5.00	2.20	.60
☐ 9 Billy O'Dell	2.50	1.10	.30
☐ 10 Jose Pagan	3.50	1.55	.45
☐ 11 Billy Pierce	3.00	1.35	.35
☐ 12 Jack Sanford	2.50	1.10	.30

1964 Giants Jay Publishing

This 12-card set of the San Francisco Giants measures approximately 5" X 7". The fronts feature black-and-white posed player photos with the player's and team name printed below in the white border. These cards were packaged 12 to a packet and originally sold for 25 cents. The backs are blank. The cards are unnumbered and checklisted below in alphabetical order.

	NRMT	VG-E	GOOD
COMPLETE SET (12)	50.00	22.00	6.25
COMMON CARD (1-12)	2.00	.90	.25
☐ 1 Orlando Cepeda	5.00	2.20	.60
☐ 2 Del Crandall	3.00	1.35	.35
☐ 3 Alvin Dark MG	3.00	1.35	.35
☐ 4 Jim Davenport	2.00	.90	.25
☐ 5 Tom Haller	2.00	.90	.25
☐ 6 Juan Marichal	10.00	4.50	1.25
☐ 7 Willie Mays	15.00	6.75	1.85
☐ 8 Willie McCovey	10.00	4.50	1.25
☐ 9 Billy O'Dell	2.00	.90	.25
☐ 10 Jose Pagan	2.00	.90	.25
☐ 11 Jack Sanford	2.00	.90	.25
☐ 12 Bob Shaw	2.00	.90	.25

1965 Giants Team Issue

These photos feature members of the 1965 San Francisco Giants. The color photos take up most of the cards with the player being identified on the bottom. The backs are blank and we have sequenced them in alphabetical order.

	NRMT	VG-E	GOOD
COMPLETE SET (10)	30.00	13.50	3.70
COMMON CARD (1-10)	2.00	.90	.25
☐ 1 Jim Davenport	2.00	.90	.25
☐ 2 Herman Franks MG	2.50	1.10	.30
☐ 3 Tom Haller	2.00	.90	.25
☐ 4 Jim Ray Hart	2.00	.90	.25
☐ 5 Juan Marichal	3.50	1.55	.45
☐ 6 Willie Mays	12.00	5.50	1.50
☐ 7 Willie McCovey	3.50	1.55	.45
☐ 8 Lindy McDaniel	2.00	.90	.25
☐ 9 Gaylord Perry	4.50	2.00	.55
☐ 10 Team Photo	5.00	2.20	.60

1970 Giants

This 12-card set is approximately 4 1/2" X 7", with the player's name and "Giants" printed on front. Cards were printed in black and white on pebbled white stock with a blank back.

	NRMT	VG-E	GOOD
COMPLETE SET (12)	30.00	13.50	3.70
COMMON CARD (1-12)	1.50	.70	.19
☐ 1 Bobby Bonds	5.00	2.20	.60
☐ 2 Dick Dietz	1.50	.70	.19
☐ 3 Charles Fox MG	1.50	.70	.19
☐ 4 Ken Henderson	1.50	.70	.19
☐ 5 Ron Hunt	2.50	1.10	.30
☐ 6 Hal Lanier	1.50	.70	.19
☐ 7 Frank Linzy	1.50	.70	.19
☐ 8 Juan Marichal	5.00	2.20	.60
☐ 9 Willie Mays	7.50	3.40	.95
☐ 10 Willie McCovey	5.00	2.20	.60
☐ 11 Gaylord Perry	5.00	2.20	.60
☐ 12 Frank Reberger	1.50	.70	.19

1970 Giants Chevrolet Bonds

This one-card set measures approximately 3" by 5 3/4" with the top half of the card containing a black-and-white photo of Giants outfielder, Bobby Bonds. The bottom white margin was where the collector could have the player sign his Giants autograph card which was issued by Chevrolet and Nor-Cal Leasing Co. The back is blank.

	NRMT	VG-E	GOOD
COMPLETE SET (1)	5.00	2.20	.60
COMMON CARD (1)	5.00	2.20	.60
☐ 1 Bobby Bonds	5.00	2.20	.60

1971 Giants Ticketron

The 1971 Ticketron San Francisco Giants set is a ten-card set featuring members of the division-winning 1971 San Francisco Giants. The set measures approximately 3 7/8" by 6" and features an attractive full-color photo framed by white borders on the front along with a facsimile autograph. The back contains an ad for Ticketron as well as the 1971 Giants home schedule. These unnumbered cards are listed in alphabetical order for convenience.

	NRMT	VG-E	GOOD
COMPLETE SET (10)	75.00	34.00	9.50
COMMON CARD (1-10)	3.00	1.35	.35
☐ 1 Bobby Bonds	9.00	4.00	1.10
☐ 2 Dick Dietz	3.00	1.35	.35
☐ 3 Charles Fox MG	3.00	1.35	.35
☐ 4 Tito Fuentes	3.00	1.35	.35
☐ 5 Ken Henderson	5.00	2.20	.60
☐ 6 Juan Marichal	15.00	6.75	1.85
☐ 7 Willie Mays	50.00	22.00	6.25
☐ 8 Willie McCovey	15.00	6.75	1.85
☐ 9 Don McMahon	3.00	1.35	.35
☐ 10 Gaylord Perry	15.00	6.75	1.85

1975 Giants

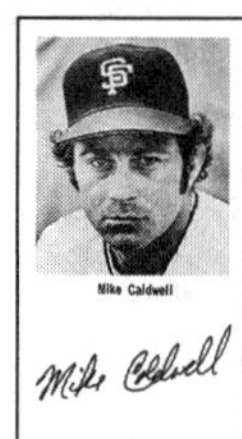

Most of the cards in this 12-card set measure approximately 3" by 5 1/2"; a few measure slightly smaller at 3" by 5". The fronts feature black-and-white portraits of members of the 1975 Giants team. The pictures are 2 1/2" by 3" and rest on a white card face accented only by the player's name printed in black below the photo and a facsimile autograph in the lower white margin. The backs are blank. The cards are unnumbered and checklisted below in alphabetical order.

	NRMT	VG-E	GOOD
COMPLETE SET (12)	10.00	4.50	1.25
COMMON CARD (1-12)	1.00	.45	.12
☐ 1 Mike Caldwell	1.25	.55	.16
☐ 2 Pete Falcone	1.00	.45	.12
☐ 3 Marc Hill	1.00	.45	.12
☐ 4 Gary Matthews	1.50	.70	.19
☐ 5 Randy Moffitt	1.00	.45	.12
☐ 6 Willie Montanez	1.00	.45	.12
☐ 7 Steve Ontiveros	1.00	.45	.12
☐ 8 Dave Rader	1.00	.45	.12
☐ 9 Derrel Thomas	1.00	.45	.12
☐ 10 Gary Thomasson	1.00	.45	.12
☐ 11 Wes Westrum MG	1.00	.45	.12
☐ 12 Charles Williams	1.00	.45	.12

1975 Giants 1951 TCMA

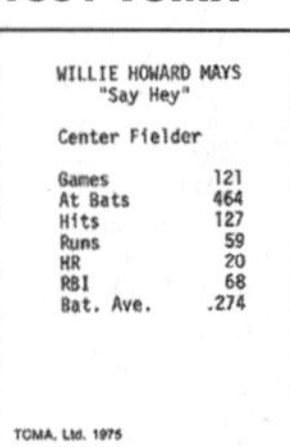
WILLIE HOWARD MAYS
"Say Hey"

Center Fielder

Games	121
At Bats	464
Hits	127
Runs	59
HR	20
RBI	68
Bat. Ave.	.274

TCMA, Ltd. 1975

This 34-card set features the 1951 New York Giants Team. The fronts display black-and-white player photos while the backs carry player statistics. The set includes two jumbo cards which measure approximately 3 1/2" by 5". The cards are unnumbered and checklisted below in alphabetical order with the jumbo cards listed last.

	NRMT	VG-E	GOOD
COMPLETE SET (34)	30.00	13.50	3.70
COMMON CARD (1-34)	.50	.23	.06
☐ 1 George Bamberger	.50	.23	.06
☐ 2 Roger Bowman	.50	.23	.06
☐ 3 Al Corwin	.50	.23	.06
☐ 4 Al Dark	1.50	.70	.19
☐ 5 Allen Gettel	.50	.23	.06
☐ 6 Clint Hartung	.50	.23	.06
☐ 7 Jim Hearn	.50	.23	.06
☐ 8 Monte Irvin	2.50	1.10	.30
☐ 9 Larry Jansen	1.00	.45	.12
☐ 10 Sheldon Jones	.50	.23	.06
☐ 11 John "Spider" Jorgensen	.50	.23	.06
☐ 12 Monte Kennedy	.50	.23	.06
☐ 13 Alex Konikowski	.50	.23	.06
☐ 14 Dave Koslo	.50	.23	.06
☐ 15 Jack Kramer	.50	.23	.06
☐ 16 Carroll "Whitey" Lockman	1.00	.45	.12
☐ 17 Jack "Lucky" Lohrke	.50	.23	.06
☐ 18 Sal Maglie	1.50	.70	.19
☐ 19 Jack Maguire	.50	.23	.06
☐ 20 Willie Mays	10.00	4.50	1.25
☐ 21 Don Mueller	1.00	.45	.12
☐ 22 Ray Noble	.50	.23	.06
☐ 23 Earl Rapp	.50	.23	.06
☐ 24 Bill Rigney	.50	.23	.06
☐ 25 George Spencer	.50	.23	.06
☐ 26 Eddie Stanky	1.00	.45	.12
☐ 27 Bobby Thomson	2.00	.90	.25
☐ 28 Hank Thompson	.50	.23	.06
☐ 29 Wes Westrum	1.00	.45	.12
☐ 30 Davey Williams	.50	.23	.06
☐ 31 Artie Wilson	.50	.23	.06
☐ 32 Sal Yvars	.50	.23	.06
☐ 33 Herman Franks CO Freddie Fitzsimmons CO Leo Durocher MG Frank Shellenback CO	1.50	.70	.19
☐ 34 Leo Durocher MG Willie Mays	5.00	2.20	.60

1977 Giants

This 25-card set measures 3 1/2" by 5" and features black-and-white close-up player photos. The pictures are framed by an orange border and set on a black card face. The player's name, position and team name appear below the picture. The backs are blank. The cards are unnumbered and checklisted below in alphabetical order.

	NRMT	VG-E	GOOD
COMPLETE SET (25)	20.00	9.00	2.50
COMMON CARD (1-25)	.75	.35	.09
☐ 1 Joe Altobelli MG	.75	.35	.09
☐ 2 Jim Barr	.75	.35	.09
☐ 3 Jack Clark	2.50	1.10	.30
☐ 4 Terry Cornutt	.75	.35	.09
☐ 5 Rob Dressler	.75	.35	.09
☐ 6 Darrell Evans	1.25	.55	.16
☐ 7 Frank Funk INS	.75	.35	.09
☐ 8 Ed Halicki	.75	.35	.09
☐ 9 Tom Haller CO	1.00	.45	.12
☐ 10 Marc Hill	.75	.35	.09
☐ 11 Skip James	.75	.35	.09
☐ 12 Bob Knepper	.75	.35	.09
☐ 13 Gary Lavelle	.75	.35	.09
☐ 14 Bill Madlock	1.50	.70	.19
☐ 15 Willie McCovey	3.00	1.35	.35
☐ 16 Randy Moffitt	.75	.35	.09
☐ 17 John Montefusco	1.00	.45	.12
☐ 18 Marty Perez	.75	.35	.09
☐ 19 Frank Riccelli	.75	.35	.09
☐ 20 Mike Sadek	.75	.35	.09
☐ 21 Hank Sauer INS	1.00	.45	.12
☐ 22 Chris Speier	1.00	.45	.12
☐ 23 Gary Thomasson	.75	.35	.09
☐ 24 Tommy Toms	.75	.35	.09
☐ 25 Bobby Winkles CO	.75	.35	.09

1979 Giants Police

The cards in this 30-card set measure approximately 2 5/8" by 4 1/8". The 1979 Police Giants set features cards numbered by the player's uniform number. This full color set features the player's photo, the Giants' logo, and the player's name, number and position on the front of the cards. A facsimile autograph in an attractive blue ink is also contained on the front. The backs, printed in orange and black, feature

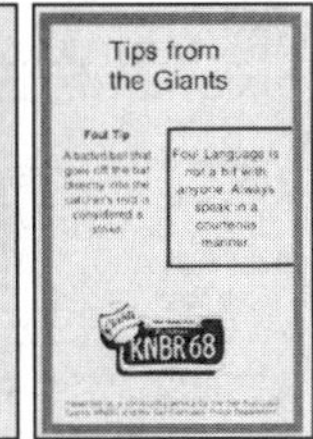

Tips from the Giants, the Giants' and sponsoring radio station, KNBR, logos and a line listing the Giants, KNBR, and the San Francisco Police Department as sponsors of the set. The 15 cards which are shown with an asterisk below were available only from the Police. The other 15 cards were given away at the ballpark on June 17, 1979. These cards look very similar to the Giants police set issued in 1980, the following year. Both sets credit Dennis Desprois photographically on each card but this (1979) set seems to have a fuzzier focus on the pictures. The sets can be distinguished on the front since this set's cards have a number sign before the player's uniform number on the front. Also on the card backs the KNBR logo is usually left justified for the cards in the 1979 set whereas the 1980 set has the KNBR logo centered on the card back.

	NRMT	VG-E	GOOD
COMPLETE SET (30)	18.00	8.00	2.20
COMMON CARD	.50	.23	.06
☐ 1 Dave Bristol MG	.50	.23	.06
☐ 2 Marc Hill	.50	.23	.06
☐ 3 Mike Sadek *	.50	.23	.06
☐ 5 Tom Haller	.50	.23	.06
☐ 6 Joe Altobelli CO *	.75	.35	.09
☐ 8 Larry Shepard CO *	.75	.35	.09
☐ 9 Heity Cruz	.50	.23	.06
☐ 10 Johnnie LeMaster	.50	.23	.06
☐ 12 Jim Davenport CO	.75	.35	.09
☐ 14 Vida Blue	1.00	.45	.12
☐ 15 Mike Ivie	.50	.23	.06
☐ 16 Roger Metzger	.50	.23	.06
☐ 17 Randy Moffitt	.50	.23	.06
☐ 18 Bill Madlock	1.00	.45	.12
☐ 21 Rob Andrews *	.50	.23	.06
☐ 22 Jack Clark *	1.50	.70	.19
☐ 25 Dave Roberts	.50	.23	.06
☐ 26 John Montefusco	.75	.35	.09
☐ 28 Ed Halicki *	.50	.23	.06
☐ 30 John Tamargo	.50	.23	.06
☐ 31 Larry Herndon	.50	.23	.06
☐ 36 Bill North *	.50	.23	.06
☐ 39 Bob Knepper *	.75	.35	.09
☐ 40 John Curtis *	.50	.23	.06
☐ 41 Darrell Evans *	1.50	.70	.19
☐ 43 Tom Griffin *	.50	.23	.06
☐ 44 Willie McCovey *	4.00	1.80	.50
☐ 45 Terry Whitfield *	.50	.23	.06
☐ 46 Gary Lavelle *	.50	.23	.06
☐ 49 Max Venable *	.50	.23	.06

1980 Giants Eureka Federal Savings

This eight-card set of the San Francisco Giants measures approximately 9 1/2" by 12" and features art work by Todd Alan Gold. Each card displays three color drawings of the same player, two action and one portrait. The backs are blank. These complimentary cards were available at all Eureka Federal Savings branches. The cards are unnumbered and checklisted below in alphabetical order.

	NRMT	VG-E	GOOD
COMPLETE SET (8)	10.00	4.50	1.25
COMMON CARD (1-8)	1.00	.45	.12
☐ 1 Al Holland	1.00	.45	.12
☐ 2 Gary Lavelle	1.00	.45	.12
☐ 3 Johnnie LeMaster	1.00	.45	.12
☐ 4 Milt May	1.00	.45	.12
☐ 5 Willie McCovey	5.00	2.20	.60
☐ 6 John Montefusco	1.00	.45	.12
☐ 7 Bill North	1.00	.45	.12
☐ 8 Rennie Stennett	1.00	.45	.12

1980 Giants Greats TCMA

This 12-card standard-size set features some great Giants from both New York and San Francisco. The fronts have red borders with the player's photo inside. The player's name is printed on the bottom. The back carries a biography.

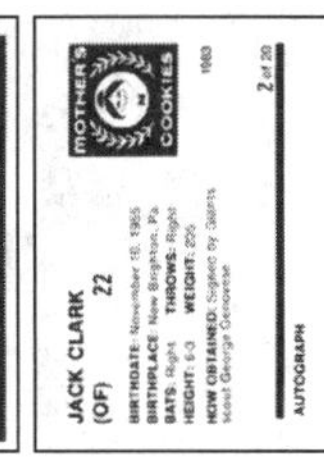

	NRMT	VG-E	GOOD
COMPLETE SET (12)	7.50	3.40	.95
COMMON CARD (1-12-)	.25	.11	.03
☐ 1 Willie Mays	2.50	1.10	.30
☐ 2 Wes Westrum	.25	.11	.03
☐ 3 Carl Hubbell	1.00	.45	.12
☐ 4 Hoyt Wilhelm	.75	.35	.09
☐ 5 Bobby Thomson	.50	.23	.06
☐ 6 Frankie Frisch	.75	.35	.09
☐ 7 Bill Terry	.75	.35	.09
☐ 8 Alvin Dark	.50	.23	.06
☐ 9 Mel Ott	1.00	.45	.12
☐ 10 Christy Mathewson	1.00	.45	.12
☐ 11 Fred Lindstrom	.50	.23	.06
☐ 12 John McGraw MG	.75	.35	.09

1980 Giants Police

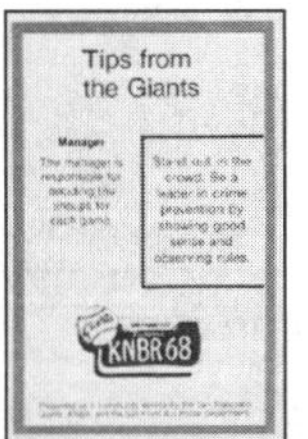

The cards in this 31-card set measure approximately 2 5/8" by 4 1/8". The 1980 Police San Francisco Giants set features cards numbered by the player's uniform number. This full color set features the player's photo, the Giants' logo, and the player's name, number and position on the front of the cards. A facsimile autograph in an attractive blue ink is also contained on the front. The backs, printed in orange and black, feature Tips from the Giants, the Giants' and sponsoring radio station, KNBR, logos and a line listing the Giants, KNBR, and the San Francisco Police Department as sponsors of the set. The sets were given away at the ballpark on May 31, 1980.

	NRMT	VG-E	GOOD
COMPLETE SET (31)	15.00	6.75	1.85
COMMON CARD	.50	.23	.06
☐ 1 Dave Bristol MG	.50	.23	.06
☐ 2 Marc Hill	.50	.23	.06
☐ 3 Mike Sadek	.50	.23	.06
☐ 5 Jim Lefebvre CO	.50	.23	.06
☐ 6 Rennie Stennett	.50	.23	.06
☐ 7 Milt May	.50	.23	.06
☐ 8 Vern Benson CO	.50	.23	.06
☐ 9 Jim Wohlford	.50	.23	.06
☐ 10 Johnnie LeMaster	.50	.23	.06
☐ 12 Jim Davenport CO	.50	.23	.06
☐ 14 Vida Blue	.75	.35	.09
☐ 15 Mike Ivie	.50	.23	.06
☐ 16 Roger Metzger	.50	.23	.06
☐ 17 Randy Moffitt	.50	.23	.06
☐ 19 Al Holland	.50	.23	.06
☐ 20 Joe Strain	.50	.23	.06
☐ 22 Jack Clark	.75	.35	.09
☐ 26 John Montefusco	.50	.23	.06
☐ 28 Ed Halicki	.50	.23	.06
☐ 31 Larry Herndon	.50	.23	.06
☐ 32 Ed Whitson	.50	.23	.06
☐ 36 Bill North	.50	.23	.06
☐ 38 Greg Minton	.50	.23	.06
☐ 39 Bob Knepper	.50	.23	.06
☐ 41 Darrell Evans	1.00	.45	.12
☐ 42 John Van Ornum	.50	.23	.06
☐ 43 Tom Griffin	.50	.23	.06
☐ 44 Willie McCovey	3.00	1.35	.35
☐ 45 Terry Whitfield	.50	.23	.06
☐ 46 Gary Lavelle	.50	.23	.06
☐ 47 Don McMahon CO	.50	.23	.06

1983 Giants Mother's

The cards in this 20-card set measure the standard size. For the first time in 30 years, Mother's Cookies issued a baseball card set. The full color set, produced by hobbyist Barry Colla, features San Francisco Giants players only. Fifteen cards were issued at the Houston Astros vs. San Francisco Giants game of August 7, 1983. Five of the cards were redeemable by sending in a coupon. The five additional cards received from redemption of the coupon were not guaranteed to be the five needed to complete the set. The fronts feature the player's photo, his name, and the Giants' logo, while the backs feature player biographies and the Mother's Cookies logo. The backs also contain a space in which to obtain the player's autograph.

	NRMT-MT	EXC	G-VG
COMPLETE SET (20)	12.00	5.50	1.50
COMMON CARD (1-20)	.50	.23	.06
☐ 1 Frank Robinson MG	2.50	1.10	.30
☐ 2 Jack Clark	1.00	.45	.12
☐ 3 Chili Davis	.75	.35	.09
☐ 4 Johnnie LeMaster	.50	.23	.06
☐ 5 Greg Minton	.50	.23	.06
☐ 6 Bob Brenly	.50	.23	.06
☐ 7 Fred Breining	.50	.23	.06
☐ 8 Jeff Leonard	.50	.23	.06
☐ 9 Darrell Evans	1.25	.55	.16
☐ 10 Tom O'Malley	.50	.23	.06
☐ 11 Duane Kuiper	.50	.23	.06
☐ 12 Mike Krukow	.50	.23	.06
☐ 13 Atlee Hammaker	.50	.23	.06
☐ 14 Gary Lavelle	.50	.23	.06
☐ 15 Bill Laskey	.50	.23	.06
☐ 16 Max Venable	.50	.23	.06
☐ 17 Joel Youngblood	.50	.23	.06
☐ 18 Dave Bergman	.50	.23	.06
☐ 19 Mike Vail	.50	.23	.06
☐ 20 Andy McGaffigan	.50	.23	.06

1984 Giants Mother's

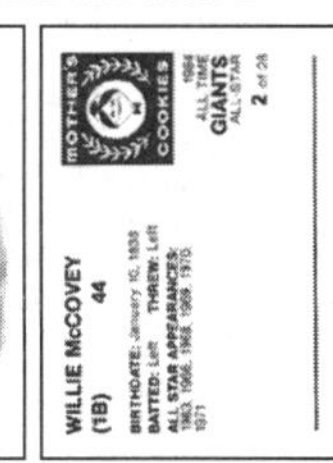

The cards in this 28-card set measure the standard-size. In 1984, the Los Angeles based Mother's Cookies Co. issued five sets of cards featuring players from major league teams. The San Francisco Giants set features previous Giant All-Star selections depicted by drawings. Similar to their 1952 and 1953 issues, the cards have rounded corners. The backs of the cards contain the Mother's Cookies logo. The cards were distributed in partial sets to fans at the respective stadiums of the teams involved. Whereas 20 cards were given to each patron, a redemption card, redeemable for eight more cards was included. Unfortunately, the eight cards received by redeeming the coupon were not necessarily the eight needed to complete a set. Hobbyist Barry Colla was involved in the production of these sets.

	NRMT-MT	EXC	G-VG
COMPLETE SET (28)	15.00	6.75	1.85
COMMON CARD (1-28)	.25	.11	.03
☐ 1 Willie Mays	5.00	2.20	.60
☐ 2 Willie McCovey	2.50	1.10	.30
☐ 3 Juan Marichal	2.00	.90	.25
☐ 4 Gaylord Perry	1.50	.70	.19
☐ 5 Tom Haller	.25	.11	.03
☐ 6 Jim Davenport	.25	.11	.03
☐ 7 Jack Clark	.75	.35	.09
☐ 8 Greg Minton	.25	.11	.03
☐ 9 Atlee Hammaker	.25	.11	.03
☐ 10 Gary Lavelle	.25	.11	.03
☐ 11 Orlando Cepeda	1.25	.55	.16
☐ 12 Bobby Bonds	.75	.35	.09
☐ 13 John Antonelli	.25	.11	.03
☐ 14 Bob Schmidt UER (Photo actually Wes Westrum)	.25	.11	.03
☐ 15 Sam Jones	.25	.11	.03
☐ 16 Mike McCormick	.25	.11	.03
☐ 17 Ed Bailey	.25	.11	.03
☐ 18 Stu Miller	.50	.23	.06
☐ 19 Felipe Alou	1.00	.45	.12
☐ 20 Jim Ray Hart	.25	.11	.03
☐ 21 Dick Dietz	.25	.11	.03
☐ 22 Chris Speier	.25	.11	.03
☐ 23 Bobby Murcer	1.00	.45	.12
☐ 24 John Montefusco	.25	.11	.03
☐ 25 Vida Blue	.75	.35	.09
☐ 26 Ed Whitson	.25	.11	.03
☐ 27 Darrell Evans	1.00	.45	.12
☐ 28 Giants Checklist Card All-Star Game Logo	.50	.23	.06

1984 Giants Postcards

This 31-card set features glossy posed color player photos of the San Francisco Giants and measures approximately 3 7/16" by 5 1/2". The

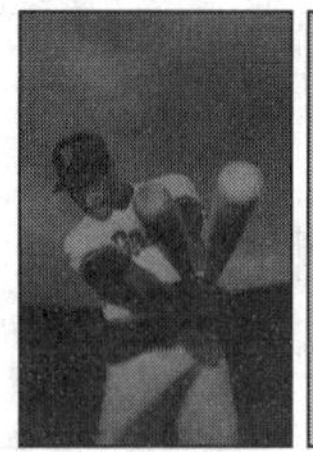
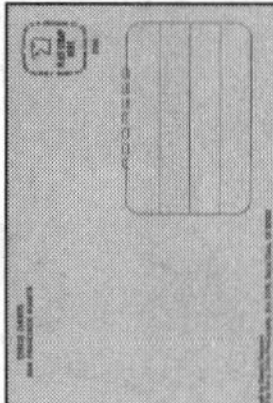

backs have a postcard format. The cards are unnumbered and checklisted below in alphabetical order.

	NRMT	VG-E	GOOD
COMPLETE SET (31)	8.00	3.60	1.00
COMMON CARD (1-31)	.25	.11	.03
☐ 1 Dusty Baker	.75	.35	.09
☐ 2 Bob Brenly	.25	.11	.03
☐ 3 Don Buford CO	.25	.11	.03
☐ 4 Jack Clark	.50	.23	.06
☐ 5 Chili Davis	.50	.23	.06
☐ 6 Mark Davis	.25	.11	.03
☐ 7 Altee Hammaker	.25	.11	.03
☐ 8 Mike Krukow	.25	.11	.03
☐ 9 Duane Kuiper	.25	.11	.03
☐ 10 Bill Laskey	.25	.11	.03
☐ 11 Gary Lavelle	.25	.11	.03
☐ 12 Johnnie LeMaster	.25	.11	.03
☐ 13 Jeff Leonard	.25	.11	.03
☐ 14 Randy Lerch	.25	.11	.03
☐ 15 Renie Martin	.25	.11	.03
☐ 16 Tom McCraw CO	.25	.11	.03
☐ 17 Greg Minton	.25	.11	.03
☐ 18 Fran Mullins	.25	.11	.03
☐ 19 Steve Nicosia	.25	.11	.03
☐ 20 Al Oliver	.75	.35	.09
☐ 21 Danny Ozark CO	.25	.11	.03
☐ 22 John Rabb	.25	.11	.03
☐ 23 Gene Richards	.25	.11	.03
☐ 24 Frank Robinson MG	1.00	.45	.12
☐ 25 Jeff Robinson	.25	.11	.03
☐ 26 Herm Starrette CO	.25	.11	.03
☐ 27 Scott Thompson	.25	.11	.03
☐ 28 Manny Trillo	.25	.11	.03
☐ 29 John Van Ornum	.25	.11	.03
☐ 30 Frank Williams	.25	.11	.03
☐ 31 Joel Youngblood	.25	.11	.03

1985 Giants Mother's

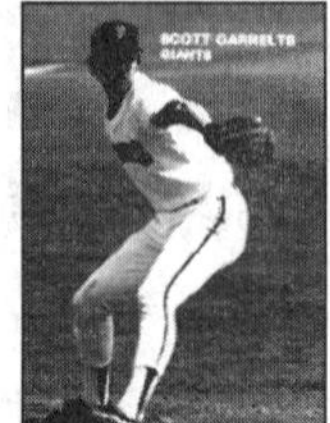

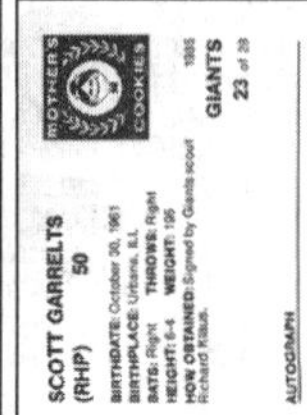

The cards in this 28-card set measure the standard size. In 1985, the Los Angeles based Mother's Cookies Co. again issued five sets of cards featuring players from major league teams. The San Francisco Giants set features current players depicted by photos on cards with rounded corners. The backs of the cards contain the Mother's Cookies logo. Cards were passed out at the stadium on June 30.

	NRMT-MT	EXC	G-VG
COMPLETE SET (28)	7.50	3.40	.95
COMMON CARD (1-28)	.25	.11	.03
☐ 1 Jim Davenport MG	.25	.11	.03
☐ 2 Chili Davis	1.00	.45	.12
☐ 3 Dan Gladden	.50	.23	.06
☐ 4 Jeff Leonard	.25	.11	.03
☐ 5 Manny Trillo	.25	.11	.03
☐ 6 Atlee Hammaker	.25	.11	.03
☐ 7 Bob Brenly	.25	.11	.03
☐ 8 Greg Minton	.25	.11	.03
☐ 9 Bill Laskey	.25	.11	.03
☐ 10 Vida Blue	.75	.35	.09
☐ 11 Mike Krukow	.25	.11	.03
☐ 12 Frank Williams	.25	.11	.03
☐ 13 Jose Uribe	.25	.11	.03
☐ 14 Johnnie LeMaster	.25	.11	.03
☐ 15 Scot Thompson	.25	.11	.03
☐ 16 Dave LaPoint	.25	.11	.03
☐ 17 David Green	.25	.11	.03
☐ 18 Chris Brown	.25	.11	.03
☐ 19 Joel Youngblood	.25	.11	.03
☐ 20 Mark Davis	.50	.23	.06
☐ 21 Jim Gott	.25	.11	.03
☐ 22 Doug Gwosdz	.25	.11	.03
☐ 23 Scott Garrelts	.25	.11	.03
☐ 24 Gary Rajsich	.25	.11	.03
☐ 25 Rob Deer	.50	.23	.06
☐ 26 Brad Wellman	.25	.11	.03
☐ 27 Giants' Coaches	.25	.11	.03
Rocky Bridges			
Chuck Hiller			
Tom McCraw			
Bob Miller			
Jack Mull			
☐ 28 Giants' Checklist	.25	.11	.03
Candlestick Park			

1985 Giants Postcards

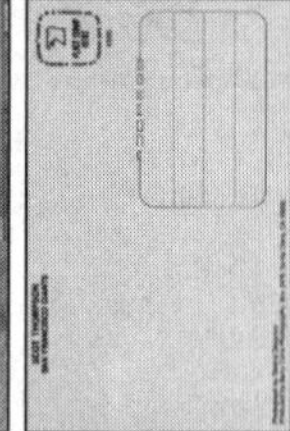

This 31-card set features glossy color player photos of the San Francisco Giants and measures approximately 3 1/2" by 5 1/2". The backs have a postcard format with the player's name printed in the upper left. The cards are unnumbered and checklisted below in alphabetical order.

	NRMT	VG-E	GOOD
COMPLETE SET (31)	8.00	3.60	1.00
COMMON CARD (1-31)	.25	.11	.03
☐ 1 Vida Blue	.50	.23	.06
☐ 2 Bob Brenly	.25	.11	.03
☐ 3 Rocky Bridges CO	.25	.11	.03
☐ 4 Chris Brown	.25	.11	.03
☐ 5 Jim Davenport MG	.25	.11	.03
☐ 6 Chili Davis	1.00	.45	.12
☐ 7 Mark Davis	.25	.11	.03
☐ 8 Rob Deer	.50	.23	.06
☐ 9 Scott Garrelts	.25	.11	.03
☐ 10 Dan Gladden	.50	.23	.06
☐ 11 Jim Gott	.25	.11	.03
☐ 12 David Green	.25	.11	.03
☐ 13 Doug Gwosdz	.25	.11	.03
☐ 14 Altee Hammaker	.25	.11	.03
☐ 15 Chuck Hiller CO	.25	.11	.03
☐ 16 Mike Krukow	.25	.11	.03
☐ 17 Dave LaPoint	.25	.11	.03
☐ 18 Bill Laskey	.25	.11	.03
☐ 19 Johnnie LeMaster	.25	.11	.03
☐ 20 Jeff Leonard	.25	.11	.03
☐ 21 Tom McCraw CO	.25	.11	.03
☐ 22 Bob Miller CO	.25	.11	.03
☐ 23 Greg Minton	.25	.11	.03
☐ 24 Jack Mull CO	.25	.11	.03
☐ 25 Gary Rajsich	.25	.11	.03
☐ 26 Scot Thompson	.25	.11	.03
☐ 27 Manny Trillo	.25	.11	.03
☐ 28 Jose Uribe	.25	.11	.03
☐ 29 Brad Wellman	.25	.11	.03
☐ 30 Frank Williams	.25	.11	.03
☐ 31 Joel Youngblood	.25	.11	.03

1986 Giants Mother's

This set consists of 28 full-color, rounded-corner cards each measuring the standard size. Starter sets (only 20 cards but also including a certificate for eight more cards) were given out at the ballpark and collectors were encouraged to trade to fill in the rest of their set. Cards were originally given out at Candlestick Park on July 13th.

	MINT	NRMT	EXC
COMPLETE SET (28)	17.50	8.00	2.20
COMMON CARD (1-28)	.25	.11	.03
☐ 1 Roger Craig MG	.50	.23	.06
☐ 2 Chili Davis	1.00	.45	.12
☐ 3 Dan Gladden	.25	.11	.03
☐ 4 Jeff Leonard	.25	.11	.03
☐ 5 Bob Brenly	.25	.11	.03
☐ 6 Atlee Hammaker	.25	.11	.03
☐ 7 Will Clark	10.00	4.50	1.25
☐ 8 Greg Minton	.25	.11	.03
☐ 9 Candy Maldonado	.25	.11	.03
☐ 10 Vida Blue	.75	.35	.09
☐ 11 Mike Krukow	.25	.11	.03
☐ 12 Bob Melvin	.25	.11	.03
☐ 13 Jose Uribe	.25	.11	.03
☐ 14 Dan Driessen	.25	.11	.03
☐ 15 Jeff D. Robinson	.25	.11	.03
☐ 16 Robby Thompson	1.00	.45	.12
☐ 17 Mike LaCoss	.25	.11	.03
☐ 18 Chris Brown	.25	.11	.03
☐ 19 Scott Garrelts	.25	.11	.03
☐ 20 Mark Davis	.50	.23	.06
☐ 21 Jim Gott	.25	.11	.03
☐ 22 Brad Wellman	.25	.11	.03
☐ 23 Roger Mason	.25	.11	.03
☐ 24 Bill Laskey	.25	.11	.03
☐ 25 Brad Gulden	.25	.11	.03
☐ 26 Joel Youngblood	.25	.11	.03
☐ 27 Juan Berenguer	.25	.11	.03
☐ 28 Checklist Card	.25	.11	.03
Bob Lillis CO			
Gordy MacKenzie CO			
Bill Fahey CO			
Norm Sherry CO			
Jose Morales CO			

1987 Giants Mother's

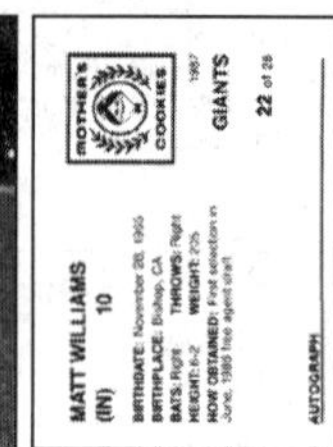

This set consists of 28 full-color, rounded-corner cards each measuring the standard size. Starter sets (only 20 cards but also including a certificate for eight more cards) were given out at the ballpark and collectors were encouraged to trade to fill in the rest of their set. Cards were originally given out at Candlestick Park on June 27th during a game against the Astros. Photos were taken by Dennis Desprois. The sets were reportedly given out free to the first 25,000 paid admissions at the game.

	MINT	NRMT	EXC
COMPLETE SET (28)	15.00	6.75	1.85
COMMON CARD (1-28)	.25	.11	.03
☐ 1 Roger Craig MG	.50	.23	.06
☐ 2 Will Clark	6.00	2.70	.75
☐ 3 Chili Davis	1.00	.45	.12
☐ 4 Bob Brenly	.25	.11	.03
☐ 5 Chris Brown	.25	.11	.03
☐ 6 Mike Krukow	.25	.11	.03
☐ 7 Candy Maldonado	.25	.11	.03
☐ 8 Jeffrey Leonard	.25	.11	.03
☐ 9 Greg Minton	.25	.11	.03
☐ 10 Robby Thompson	.75	.35	.09
☐ 11 Scott Garrelts	.25	.11	.03
☐ 12 Bob Melvin	.25	.11	.03
☐ 13 Jose Uribe	.25	.11	.03
☐ 14 Mark Davis	.50	.23	.06
☐ 15 Eddie Milner	.25	.11	.03
☐ 16 Harry Spilman	.25	.11	.03
☐ 17 Kelly Downs	.25	.11	.03
☐ 18 Chris Speier	.25	.11	.03
☐ 19 Jim Gott	.25	.11	.03
☐ 20 Joel Youngblood	.25	.11	.03
☐ 21 Mike LaCoss	.25	.11	.03
☐ 22 Matt Williams	7.50	3.40	.95
☐ 23 Roger Mason	.25	.11	.03
☐ 24 Mike Aldrete	.25	.11	.03
☐ 25 Jeff D. Robinson	.25	.11	.03
☐ 26 Mark Grant	.25	.11	.03
☐ 27 Giants' Coaches	.25	.11	.03
Don Zimmer			
Bob Lillis			
Jose Morales			
Norm Sherry			
Bill Fahey			
Gordon MacKenzie			
☐ 28 Checklist Card	.25	.11	.03
Candlestick Park			

1988 Giants Mother's

This set consists of 28 full-color, rounded-corner cards each measuring the standard size. Starter sets (only 20 cards but also including a certificate for eight more cards) were given out at the ballpark and collectors were encouraged to trade to fill in the rest of their set. Cards were originally given out at Candlestick Park on July 30th during a game. Photos were taken by Dennis Desprois. The sets were reportedly given out free to the first 35,000 paid admissions at the game.

	MINT	NRMT	EXC
COMPLETE SET (28)	10.00	4.50	1.25
COMMON CARD (1-28)	.25	.11	.03
☐ 1 Roger Craig MG	.50	.23	.06
☐ 2 Will Clark	3.00	1.35	.35
☐ 3 Kevin Mitchell	.75	.35	.09
☐ 4 Bob Brenly	.25	.11	.03
☐ 5 Mike Aldrete	.25	.11	.03
☐ 6 Mike Krukow	.25	.11	.03
☐ 7 Candy Maldonado	.25	.11	.03
☐ 8 Jeffrey Leonard	.25	.11	.03
☐ 9 Dave Dravecky	.75	.35	.09
☐ 10 Robby Thompson	.25	.11	.03
☐ 11 Scott Garrelts	.25	.11	.03
☐ 12 Bob Melvin	.25	.11	.03
☐ 13 Jose Uribe	.25	.11	.03
☐ 14 Brett Butler	1.00	.45	.12
☐ 15 Rick Reuschel	.50	.23	.06
☐ 16 Harry Spilman	.25	.11	.03
☐ 17 Kelly Downs	.25	.11	.03
☐ 18 Chris Speier	.25	.11	.03
☐ 19 Atlee Hammaker	.25	.11	.03
☐ 20 Joel Youngblood	.25	.11	.03
☐ 21 Mike LaCoss	.25	.11	.03
☐ 22 Don Robinson	.25	.11	.03
☐ 23 Mark Wasinger	.25	.11	.03
☐ 24 Craig Lefferts	.25	.11	.03
☐ 25 Phil Garner	.50	.23	.06
☐ 26 Joe Price	.25	.11	.03
☐ 27 Giants' Coaches	.50	.23	.06
Dusty Baker			
Bill Fahey			
Bob Lillis			
Jose Morales			
Gordie MacKenzie			
Norm Sherry			
☐ 28 Checklist Card	.25	.11	.03
Giants NL Champs Logo			

1989 Giants Mother's

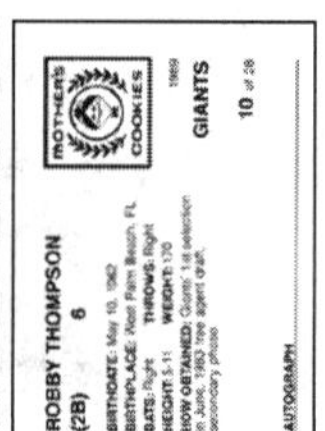

The 1989 Mother's Cookies San Francisco Giants set contains 28 standard-size cards with rounded corners. The fronts have borderless color photos, and the horizontally oriented backs have biographical information. Starter sets containing 20 of these cards were given away at a Giants home game during the 1989 season.

	MINT	NRMT	EXC
COMPLETE SET (28)	12.00	5.50	1.50
COMMON CARD (1-28)	.25	.11	.03
☐ 1 Roger Craig MG	.50	.23	.06
☐ 2 Will Clark	2.50	1.10	.30
☐ 3 Kevin Mitchell	.75	.35	.09
☐ 4 Kelly Downs	.25	.11	.03
☐ 5 Brett Butler	1.00	.45	.12
☐ 6 Mike Krukow	.25	.11	.03
☐ 7 Candy Maldonado	.25	.11	.03
☐ 8 Terry Kennedy	.25	.11	.03
☐ 9 Dave Dravecky	.75	.35	.09
☐ 10 Robby Thompson	.25	.11	.03
☐ 11 Scott Garrelts	.25	.11	.03
☐ 12 Matt Williams	4.00	1.80	.50
☐ 13 Jose Uribe	.25	.11	.03
☐ 14 Tracy Jones	.25	.11	.03
☐ 15 Rick Reuschel	.50	.23	.06
☐ 16 Ernest Riles	.25	.11	.03
☐ 17 Jeff Brantley	.75	.35	.09
☐ 18 Chris Speier	.25	.11	.03
☐ 19 Atlee Hammaker	.25	.11	.03
☐ 20 Ed Jurak	.25	.11	.03
☐ 21 Mike LaCoss	.25	.11	.03
☐ 22 Don Robinson	.25	.11	.03
☐ 23 Kirt Manwaring	.25	.11	.03
☐ 24 Craig Lefferts	.25	.11	.03
☐ 25 Donell Nixon	.25	.11	.03
☐ 26 Joe Price	.25	.11	.03
☐ 27 Rich Gossage	.75	.35	.09
☐ 28 Checklist Card	.50	.23	.06
Bill Fahey CO			
Dusty Baker CO			
Bob Lillis CO			
Wendell Kim CO			
Norm Sherry CO			

1990 Giants Mother's

The 1990 Mother's Cookies San Francisco Giants set features cards with rounded corners measuring the standard size. The cards have

full-color fronts and biographical information with no stats on the back. The Giants cards were given away at the July 29th game to the first 25,000 children 14 and under. They were distributed in 20-card random packets at the game and eight more at the redemption booths. However, both groups of cards were random and there was no guarantee of getting a complete set in the cards. The promotional idea was that the only way one could finish the set was to trade for them. The redemption certificates were to be used at the Labor Day San Francisco card show. In addition to this the Mother's A's cards were also redeemable at that show.

	MINT	NRMT	EXC
COMPLETE SET (28)	12.00	5.50	1.50
COMMON CARD (1-28)	.25	.11	.03
☐ 1 Roger Craig MG	.50	.23	.06
☐ 2 Will Clark	2.50	1.10	.30
☐ 3 Gary Carter	.50	.23	.06
☐ 4 Kelly Downs	.25	.11	.03
☐ 5 Kevin Mitchell	.75	.35	.09
☐ 6 Steve Bedrosian	.50	.23	.06
☐ 7 Brett Butler	1.00	.45	.12
☐ 8 Rick Reuschel	.50	.23	.06
☐ 9 Matt Williams	3.00	1.35	.35
☐ 10 Robby Thompson	.25	.11	.03
☐ 11 Mike LaCoss	.25	.11	.03
☐ 12 Terry Kennedy	.25	.11	.03
☐ 13 Atlee Hammaker	.25	.11	.03
☐ 14 Rick Leach	.25	.11	.03
☐ 15 Ernest Riles	.25	.11	.03
☐ 16 Scott Garrelts	.25	.11	.03
☐ 17 Jose Uribe	.25	.11	.03
☐ 18 Greg Litton	.25	.11	.03
☐ 19 Dave Anderson	.25	.11	.03
☐ 20 Don Robinson	.25	.11	.03
☐ 21 Giants Coaches Dusty Baker Bob Lillis Bill Fahey Norm Sherry Wendall Kim	.50	.23	.06
☐ 22 Bill Bathe	.25	.11	.03
☐ 23 Randy O'Neal	.25	.11	.03
☐ 24 Kevin Bass	.25	.11	.03
☐ 25 Jeff Brantley	.75	.35	.09
☐ 26 John Burkett	.75	.35	.09
☐ 27 Ernie Camacho	.25	.11	.03
☐ 28 Checklist Card	.25	.11	.03

1990 Giants Smokey

This set measures 5" by 7". These cards all contain a safety message. These cards are unnumbered so we have checklisted them below in alphabetical order.

	MINT	NRMT	EXC
COMPLETE SET (21)	12.50	5.50	1.55
COMMON CARD (1-21)	.50	.23	.06
☐ 1 Dusty Baker CO	.75	.35	.09
☐ 2 Steve Bedrosian	.75	.35	.09
☐ 3 Gary Carter	.75	.35	.09
☐ 4 Will Clark	2.50	1.10	.30
☐ 5 Roger Craig MG	.50	.23	.06
☐ 6 Kelly Downs	.50	.23	.06
☐ 7 Bill Fahey CO	.50	.23	.06
☐ 8 Scott Garrelts	.50	.23	.06
☐ 9 Atlee Hanmaker	.50	.23	.06
☐ 10 Terry Kennedy	.50	.23	.06
☐ 11 Wendell Kim CO	.50	.23	.06
☐ 12 Mike LaCoss	.50	.23	.06
☐ 13 Bob Lillis CO	.50	.23	.06
☐ 14 Greg Litton	.50	.23	.06
☐ 15 Kevin Mitchell	.75	.35	.09
☐ 16 Earnest Riles	.50	.23	.06
☐ 17 Don Robinson	.50	.23	.06
☐ 18 Norm Sherry CO	.50	.23	.06
☐ 19 Robby Thompson	.50	.23	.06
☐ 20 Jose Uribe	.50	.23	.06
☐ 21 Matt Williams	4.00	1.80	.50

1991 Giants Mother's

The 1991 Mother's Cookies San Francisco Giants set contains 28 cards with rounded corners measuring the standard size. The set includes an additional card advertising a trading card collectors album. The front design has borderless glossy color player photos from the waist up. The horizontally oriented backs are printed in red and purple, present biographical information, and have blank slots for player autographs.

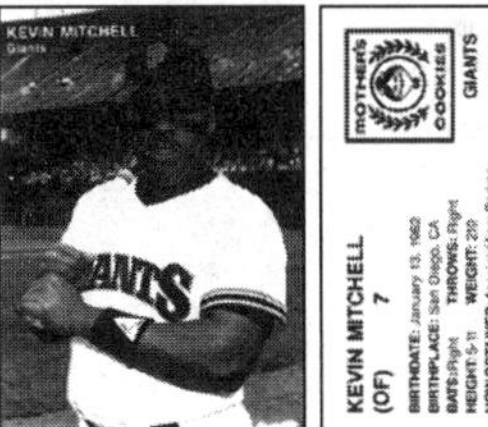

	MINT	NRMT	EXC
COMPLETE SET (28)	10.00	4.50	1.25
COMMON CARD (1-28)	.25	.11	.03
☐ 1 Roger Craig MG	.50	.23	.06
☐ 2 Will Clark	2.00	.90	.25
☐ 3 Steve Decker	.25	.11	.03
☐ 4 Kelly Downs	.25	.11	.03
☐ 5 Kevin Mitchell	.75	.35	.09
☐ 6 Willie McGee	.50	.23	.06
☐ 7 Bud Black	.25	.11	.03
☐ 8 Dave Righetti	.50	.23	.06
☐ 9 Matt Williams	2.50	1.10	.30
☐ 10 Robby Thompson	.25	.11	.03
☐ 11 Mike LaCoss	.25	.11	.03
☐ 12 Terry Kennedy	.25	.11	.03
☐ 13 Mark Leonard	.25	.11	.03
☐ 14 Rick Reuschel	.50	.23	.06
☐ 15 Mike Felder	.25	.11	.03
☐ 16 Scott Garrelts	.25	.11	.03
☐ 17 Jose Uribe	.25	.11	.03
☐ 18 Greg Litton	.25	.11	.03
☐ 19 Dave Anderson	.25	.11	.03
☐ 20 Don Robinson	.25	.11	.03
☐ 21 Mike Kingery	.25	.11	.03
☐ 22 Trevor Wilson	.25	.11	.03
☐ 23 Kirt Manwaring	.25	.11	.03
☐ 24 Kevin Bass	.25	.11	.03
☐ 25 Jeff Brantley	.75	.35	.09
☐ 26 John Burkett	.75	.35	.09
☐ 27 Giant's Coaches Dusty Baker Bill Fahey Wendell Kim Bob Lillis Norm Sherry	.50	.23	.06
☐ 28 Checklist Card Mark Letendre TR Greg Lynn TR	.25	.11	.03

1991 Giants Pacific Gas and Electric

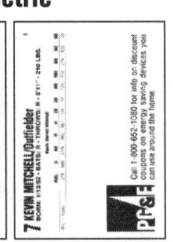

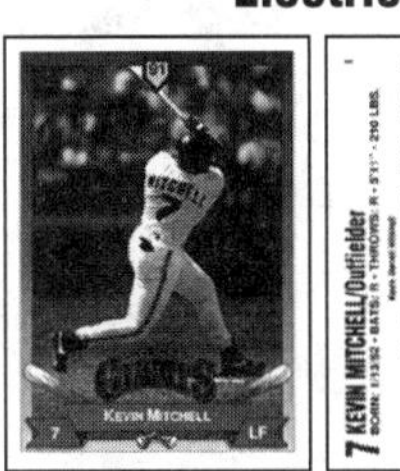

These cards were issued on six-card sheets; after perforation they measure approximately 2 1/2" by 3 1/2". One sheet was inserted in each of the first five 1991 San Francisco Giants Magazines, which were published by Woodford. The front design has color action player photos, with gray borders on a white card face. Toward the bottom of the picture are the words "San Francisco Giants," two bats, and a red banner with player information. The horizontally oriented backs are printed in black on white and include biography, Major League statistics, and various PGE (Pacific Gas and Electric) advertisements. The cards are numbered on the back in the upper right corner.

	MINT	NRMT	EXC
COMPLETE SET (30)	25.00	11.00	3.10
COMMON CARD (1-30)	.50	.23	.06
☐ 1 Kevin Mitchell	1.00	.45	.12
☐ 2 Robby Thompson	.50	.23	.06
☐ 3 John Burkett	.75	.35	.09
☐ 4 Kelly Downs	.50	.23	.06
☐ 5 Terry Kennedy	.50	.23	.06
☐ 6 Roger Craig MG	1.00	.45	.12
☐ 7 Jeff Brantley	.75	.35	.09
☐ 8 Greg Litton	.50	.23	.06
☐ 9 Trevor Wilson	.50	.23	.06
☐ 10 Kevin Bass	.75	.35	.09
☐ 11 Matt Williams	10.00	4.50	1.25
☐ 12 Jose Uribe	.50	.23	.06
☐ 13 Steve Decker	.50	.23	.06
☐ 14 Will Clark	7.50	3.40	.95
☐ 15 Dave Righetti	.75	.35	.09
☐ 16 Mike Kingery	.50	.23	.06
☐ 17 Mike LaCoss	.50	.23	.06
☐ 18 Dave Anderson	.50	.23	.06
☐ 19 Bud Black	.50	.23	.06
☐ 20 Mike Benjamin	.50	.23	.06
☐ 21 Don Robinson	.50	.23	.06
☐ 22 Mark Leonard	.50	.23	.06
☐ 23 Willie McGee	.75	.35	.09
☐ 24 Francisco Oliveras	.50	.23	.06
☐ 25 Kirt Manwaring	.50	.23	.06
☐ 26 Rick Parker	.50	.23	.06
☐ 27 Mike Remlinger	.50	.23	.06
☐ 28 Mike Felder	.50	.23	.06
☐ 29 Scott Garrelts	.50	.23	.06
☐ 30 Tony Perezchica	.50	.23	.06

1991 Giants Postcards

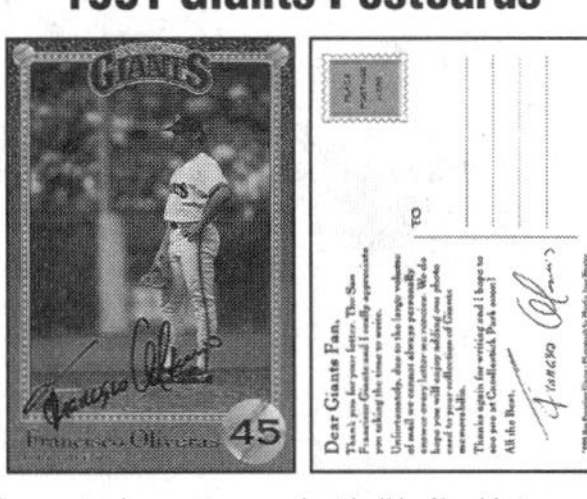

These postcards measures approximately 4" by 6" and features color player action shots on its orange and brown bordered fronts. The Giants name appears at the top, the player's name and position appear at the bottom and his uniform number appears within a baseball icon in the lower right. The white backs have a postcard format, with places for the stamp and address on the right side and a space on the left for correspondence. Many of these postcards were signed in response to fans writing in for autograph requests. The postcards are unnumbered and checklisted below in alphabetical order.

	MINT	EXC	G-VG
COMPLETE SET (2)	2.00	.90	.25
COMMON CARD	1.00	.45	.12
☐ 1 Terry Kennedy	1.00	.45	.12
☐ 2 Francisco Oliveras	1.00	.45	.12

1991 Giants S.F. Examiner

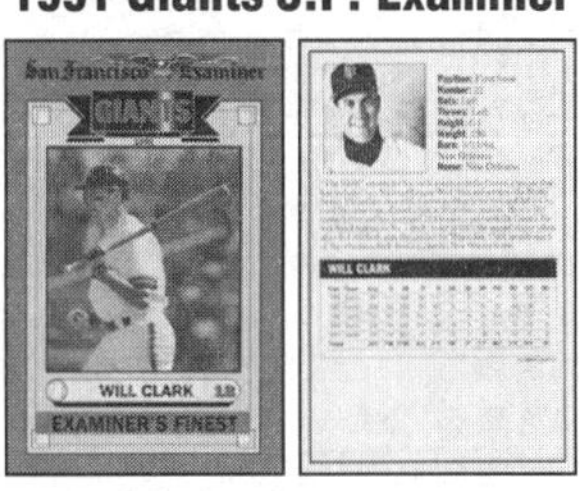

The sixteen 6" by 9" giant-sized cards in this set were issued on orange cardboard sheets measuring approximately 8 1/2" by 11" and designed for storage in a three-ring binder. The cards fronts are light gray and have color player photos enframed by thin orange border stripes. The team name appears in a black banner at the top, while the words "Examiner's Finest" appear in an orange stripe at the bottom of the card. The back has a black and white head shot, biography, career summary, and complete Major League statistics. The cards are unnumbered and checklisted below in alphabetical order.

	MINT	NRMT	EXC
COMPLETE SET (16)	30.00	13.50	3.70
COMMON CARD (1-16)	1.00	.45	.12
☐ 1 Kevin Bass	1.00	.45	.12
☐ 2 Mike Benjamin	1.00	.45	.12
☐ 3 Bud Black	1.00	.45	.12
☐ 4 Jeff Brantley	1.00	.45	.12
☐ 5 John Burkett	2.00	.90	.25
☐ 6 Will Clark	2.00	.90	.25
☐ 7 Steve Decker	1.00	.45	.12
☐ 8 Scott Garrelts	1.00	.45	.12
☐ 9 Mike LaCoss	1.00	.45	.12
☐ 10 Willie McGee	1.50	.70	.19
☐ 11 Kevin Mitchell	1.50	.70	.19
☐ 12 Dave Righetti	1.50	.70	.19
☐ 13 Don Robinson	1.00	.45	.12
☐ 14 Robby Thompson	1.00	.45	.12
☐ 15 Jose Uribe	1.00	.45	.12
☐ 16 Matt Williams	10.00	4.50	1.25

1992 Giants AT and T Team Postcards

These posccards feature team photos of the first 35 years of the San Francisco Giants. These postcards are sequenced in year order.

	MINT	EXC	G-VG
COMPLETE SET (35)	30.00	13.50	3.70
COMMON CARD (1-35)	1.00	.45	.12
☐ 1 1958 Team Photo	1.50	.70	.19
☐ 2 1959 Team Photo	1.00	.45	.12
☐ 3 1960 Team Photo	1.00	.45	.12
☐ 4 1961 Team Photo	1.00	.45	.12
☐ 5 1962 Team Photo	1.00	.45	.12
☐ 6 1963 Team Photo	1.00	.45	.12
☐ 7 1964 Team Photo	1.00	.45	.12
☐ 8 1965 Team Photo	1.50	.70	.19
☐ 9 1966 Team Photo	1.00	.45	.12
☐ 10 1967 Team Photo	1.00	.45	.12
☐ 11 1968 Team Photo	1.00	.45	.12
☐ 12 1969 Team Photo	1.00	.45	.12
☐ 13 1970 Team Photo	1.00	.45	.12
☐ 14 1971 Team Photo	1.00	.45	.12
☐ 15 1972 Team Photo	1.00	.45	.12
☐ 16 1973 Team Photo	1.00	.45	.12
☐ 17 1974 Team Photo	1.00	.45	.12
☐ 18 1975 Team Photo	1.00	.45	.12
☐ 19 1976 Team Photo	1.00	.45	.12
☐ 20 1977 Team Photo	1.00	.45	.12
☐ 21 1978 Team Photo	1.00	.45	.12
☐ 22 1979 Team Photo	1.00	.45	.12
☐ 23 1980 Team Photo	1.00	.45	.12
☐ 24 1981 Team Photo	1.00	.45	.12
☐ 25 1982 Team Photo	1.00	.45	.12
☐ 26 1983 Team Photo	1.00	.45	.12
☐ 27 1984 Team Photo	1.00	.45	.12
☐ 28 1985 Team Photo	1.00	.45	.12
☐ 29 1986 Team Photo	1.00	.45	.12
☐ 30 1987 Team Photo	1.00	.45	.12
☐ 31 1988 Team Photo	1.00	.45	.12
☐ 32 1989 Team Photo	1.50	.70	.19
☐ 33 1990 Team Photo	1.00	.45	.12
☐ 34 1991 Team Photo	1.00	.45	.12
☐ 35 1992 Team Photo	1.00	.45	.12

1992 Giants Chevron Hall of Famer Pins

This set features lapel pins of three San Francisco Giants players who are in the Baseball Hall of Fame. Each pin is attached to the bottom margin of a 2 1/2" by 5" card with a color portrait of the player in a circle framed to look like a plaque. The backs display a small black-and-white head photo with information about the player and his career. The cards are unnumbered and checklisted below in alphabetical order.

	MINT	EXC	G-VG
COMPLETE SET (3)	15.00	6.75	1.85
COMMON CARD (1-3)	3.00	1.35	.35
☐ 1 Willie Mays	10.00	4.50	1.25
☐ 2 Willie McCovey	5.00	2.20	.60
☐ 3 Gaylord Perry	3.00	1.35	.35

1992 Giants Fan Fair Fun Bucks

These "promotional buck" featured various San Francisco Giants. They are unnumbered so we have sequenced them in alphabetical order.

	MINT	EXC	G-VG
COMPLETE SET	7.50	3.40	.95
COMMON CARD	1.00	.45	.12
☐ 1 Dusty Baker	1.00	.45	.12
☐ 2 Orlando Cepeda	2.00	.90	.25
☐ 3 Willie Mays	5.00	2.20	.60

1992 Giants Mother's

The set was sponsored by Mother's Cookies and features full-bleed color player photos of the San Francisco Giants. The 28 cards in this set have rounded corners and measure the standard size. The backs, printed in purple and red, have biographical information. The set included two coupons: one featured a mail-in offer to obtain a trading card collectors album for 3.95, while the second featured a mail-in offer to obtain an additional eight trading cards.

	MINT	NRMT	EXC
COMPLETE SET (28)	10.00	4.50	1.25
COMMON CARD (1-28)	.25	.11	.03
☐ 1 Roger Craig MG	.50	.23	.06
☐ 2 Will Clark	2.00	.90	.25

	MINT	NRMT	EXC
☐ 3 Bill Swift	.25	.11	.03
☐ 4 Royce Clayton	1.00	.45	.12
☐ 5 John Burkett	.75	.35	.09
☐ 6 Willie McGee	.50	.23	.06
☐ 7 Bud Black	.25	.11	.03
☐ 8 Dave Righetti	.50	.23	.06
☐ 9 Matt Williams	2.50	1.10	.30
☐ 10 Robby Thompson	.25	.11	.03
☐ 11 Darren Lewis	.25	.11	.03
☐ 12 Mike Jackson	.25	.11	.03
☐ 13 Mark Leonard	.25	.11	.03
☐ 14 Rod Beck	1.50	.70	.19
☐ 15 Mike Felder	.25	.11	.03
☐ 16 Bryan Hickerson	.25	.11	.03
☐ 17 Jose Uribe	.25	.11	.03
☐ 18 Greg Litton	.25	.11	.03
☐ 19 Cory Snyder	.25	.11	.03
☐ 20 Jim McNamara	.25	.11	.03
☐ 21 Kelly Downs	.25	.11	.03
☐ 22 Trevor Wilson	.25	.11	.03
☐ 23 Kirt Manwaring	.25	.11	.03
☐ 24 Kevin Bass	.25	.11	.03
☐ 25 Jeff Brantley	.75	.35	.09
☐ 26 Dave Burba	.25	.11	.03
☐ 27 Chris James	.25	.11	.03
☐ 28 Checklist Card Carlos Alfonso CO Dusty Baker CO Wendell Kim CO Bob Brenly CO Bob Lillis CO	.50	.23	.06

1992 Giants Pacific Gas and Electric

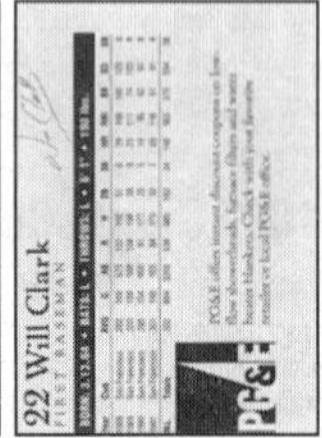

This 36-card set was sponsored by Pacific Gas and Electric and was issued in six-card perforated sheets. Each card measures approximately 2 3/4" by 3 3/4" and features on its front a brown-bordered color player action photo set off by a simulated wood picture frame. The player's name and position appear above the photo within a gold-colored banner. The Giants logo, the player's uniform number, and the year of issue all appear at the bottom. The white horizontal back carries the player's name, uniform number, position, biography, and stats. The PG and E logo along with energy use tips round out the back. The cards are unnumbered and checklisted below in alphabetical order.

	MINT	NRMT	EXC
COMPLETE SET (36)	25.00	11.00	3.10
COMMON CARD (1-36)	.50	.23	.06
☐ 1 Carlos Alfonso CO	.50	.23	.06
☐ 2 Dusty Baker CO	1.25	.55	.16
☐ 3 Kevin Bass	.50	.23	.06
☐ 4 Rod Beck	1.50	.70	.19
☐ 5 Mike Benjamin	.50	.23	.06
☐ 6 Bud Black	.50	.23	.06
☐ 7 Jeff Brantley	.75	.35	.09
☐ 8 Bob Brenly CO	.50	.23	.06
☐ 9 Dave Burba	.50	.23	.06
☐ 10 John Burkett	.50	.23	.06
☐ 11 Will Clark	3.00	1.35	.35
☐ 12 Will Clark AS	1.00	.45	.12
☐ 13 Royce Clayton	1.25	.55	.16
☐ 14 Roger Craig MG	.75	.35	.09
☐ 15 Kelly Downs	.50	.23	.06
☐ 16 Mike Felder	.50	.23	.06
☐ 17 Scott Garrelts	.50	.23	.06
☐ 18 Gil Heredia	.50	.23	.06
☐ 19 Bryan Hickerson	.50	.23	.06
☐ 20 Mike Jackson	.50	.23	.06
☐ 21 Chris James	.50	.23	.06
☐ 22 Wendell Kim CO	.50	.23	.06
☐ 23 Mark Leonard (At bat)	.50	.23	.06
☐ 24 Mark Leonard (Dropping bat)	.50	.23	.06
☐ 25 Darren Lewis	.50	.23	.06
☐ 26 Bob Lillis CO	.50	.23	.06
☐ 27 Kirt Manwaring	.50	.23	.06
☐ 28 Willie McGee	.75	.35	.09
☐ 29 Jim McNamara	.50	.23	.06
☐ 30 Dave Righetti	.75	.35	.09
☐ 31 Cory Snyder	.50	.23	.06
☐ 32 Bill Swift	.50	.23	.06
☐ 33 Robby Thompson	.50	.23	.06
☐ 34 Jose Uribe	.50	.23	.06
☐ 35 Matt Williams	6.00	2.70	.75
☐ 36 Trevor Wilson	.50	.23	.06

1993 Giants Mother's

The 1993 Mother's Cookies Giants set consists of 28 standard-size cards with rounded corners. The fronts display full-bleed color player portraits shot from the waist up. The player's name and team name appear in one of the corners. On a white background in red and purple print, the horizontal backs carry biographical information and the sponsor's logo. A blank slot for the player's autograph rounds out the back.

	MINT	NRMT	EXC
COMPLETE SET (28)	12.50	5.50	1.55
COMMON CARD (1-28)	.25	.11	.03
☐ 1 Dusty Baker MG	.50	.23	.06
☐ 2 Will Clark	2.00	.90	.25
☐ 3 Matt Williams	3.00	1.35	.35
☐ 4 Barry Bonds	3.00	1.35	.35
☐ 5 Bill Swift	.25	.11	.03
☐ 6 Royce Clayton	1.00	.45	.12
☐ 7 John Burkett	.75	.35	.09
☐ 8 Willie McGee	.50	.23	.06
☐ 9 Kirt Manwaring	.25	.11	.03
☐ 10 Dave Righetti	.50	.23	.06
☐ 11 Todd Benzinger	.25	.11	.03
☐ 12 Rod Beck	1.00	.45	.12
☐ 13 Darren Lewis	.25	.11	.03
☐ 14 Robby Thompson	.25	.11	.03
☐ 15 Mark Carreon	.25	.11	.03
☐ 16 Dave Martinez	.25	.11	.03
☐ 17 Jeff Brantley	.75	.35	.09
☐ 18 Dave Burba	.25	.11	.03
☐ 19 Mike Benjamin	.25	.11	.03
☐ 20 Mike Jackson	.25	.11	.03
☐ 21 Craig Colbert	.25	.11	.03
☐ 22 Bud Black	.25	.11	.03
☐ 23 Trevor Wilson	.25	.11	.03
☐ 24 Kevin Rogers	.25	.11	.03
☐ 25 Jeff Reed	.25	.11	.03
☐ 26 Bryan Hickerson	.25	.11	.03
☐ 27 Gino Minutelli	.25	.11	.03
☐ 28 Checklist/Coaches Dick Pole Bobby Bonds Denny Sommers Wendell Kim Bob Lillis Bob Brenly	.50	.23	.06

1993 Giants Postcards

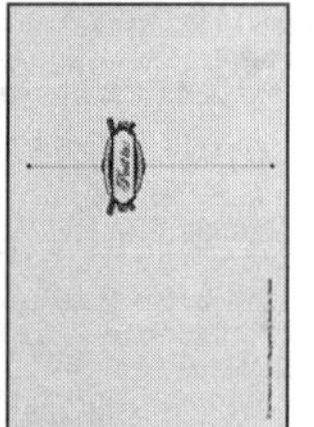

These postcards measure 4" by 6". The fronts feature black-and-white posed and action player shots. The backs are typical postcard back. The cards are unnumbered and checklisted below in alphabetical order.

	MINT	EXC	G-VG
COMPLETE SET (35)	20.00	9.00	2.50
COMMON CARD (1-35)	.50	.23	.06
☐ 1 Dusty Baker MG	1.00	.45	.12
☐ 2 Rod Beck	.50	.23	.06
☐ 3 Mike Benjamin	.50	.23	.06
☐ 4 Todd Benzinger	.50	.23	.06
☐ 5 Buddy Black	.50	.23	.06
☐ 6 Barry Bonds (Catching the ball)	2.50	1.10	.30
☐ 7 Barry Bonds (Running)	2.50	1.10	.30
☐ 8 Bobby Bonds CO	.75	.35	.09
☐ 9 Jeff Brantley	.75	.35	.09
☐ 10 Bob Brenly CO	.50	.23	.06
☐ 11 Dave Burba	.50	.23	.06
☐ 12 John Burkett	.50	.23	.06
☐ 13 Mark Carreon	.50	.23	.06
☐ 14 Will Clark (Batting)	1.50	.70	.19
☐ 15 Will Clark (Running)	1.50	.70	.19
☐ 16 Royce Clayton	1.00	.45	.12
☐ 17 Bryan Hickerson	.50	.23	.06
☐ 18 Craig Colbert	.50	.23	.06
☐ 19 Mike Jackson	.50	.23	.06
☐ 20 Wendell Kim CO	.50	.23	.06
☐ 21 Darren Lewis	.50	.23	.06
☐ 22 Bob Lillis CO	.50	.23	.06
☐ 23 Kirt Manwaring	.50	.23	.06
☐ 24 Dave Martinez	.50	.23	.06
☐ 25 Willie McGee	.75	.35	.09
☐ 26 Luis Mercedes	.50	.23	.06
☐ 27 Dick Pole CO	.50	.23	.06
☐ 28 Jeff Reed	.50	.23	.06
☐ 29 Dave Righetti	.75	.35	.09
☐ 30 Kevin Rogers	.50	.23	.06
☐ 31 Bill Swift	.50	.23	.06
☐ 32 Robby Thompson	.50	.23	.06
☐ 33 Matt Williams	2.50	1.10	.30
☐ 34 Trevor Wilson	.50	.23	.06
☐ 35 Team Photo	.75	.35	.09

1994 Giants AMC

Sponsored by AMC Theatres, these 24 blank-backed cards measure approximately 4 1/4" by 11" and feature white-bordered black-and-white player action photos. Some of the cards carry facsimile autographs across their photos. The player's name and position, as well as the AMC logo, appear in black lettering within the wide lower margin. The cards are unnumbered and checklisted below in alphabetical order.

	MINT	NRMT	EXC
COMPLETE SET (24)	25.00	11.00	3.10
COMMON CARD (1-24)	1.00	.45	.12
☐ 1 Dusty Baker MG	2.00	.90	.25
☐ 2 Rod Beck	2.50	1.10	.30
☐ 3 Mike Benjamin	1.00	.45	.12
☐ 4 Todd Benzinger	1.00	.45	.12
☐ 5 Barry Bonds	5.00	2.20	.60
☐ 6 John Burkett	1.50	.70	.19
☐ 7 Mark Carreon	1.00	.45	.12
☐ 8 Royce Clayton	1.50	.70	.19
☐ 9 Steve Frey	1.00	.45	.12
☐ 10 Mike Jackson	1.00	.45	.12
☐ 11 Darren Lewis	1.00	.45	.12
☐ 12 Kirt Manwaring	1.00	.45	.12
☐ 13 Dave Martinez	1.00	.45	.12
☐ 14 Willie McGee	1.50	.70	.19
☐ 15 Rich Monteleone	1.00	.45	.12
☐ 16 John Patterson	1.00	.45	.12
☐ 17 Mark Portugal	1.00	.45	.12
☐ 18 Jeff Reed	1.00	.45	.12
☐ 19 Kevin Rogers	1.00	.45	.12
☐ 20 Steve Scarsone	1.00	.45	.12
☐ 21 Bill Swift	1.00	.45	.12
☐ 22 Robby Thompson	1.00	.45	.12
☐ 23 Salomon Torres	1.00	.45	.12
☐ 24 Matt Williams	4.00	1.80	.50

1994 Giants Mother's

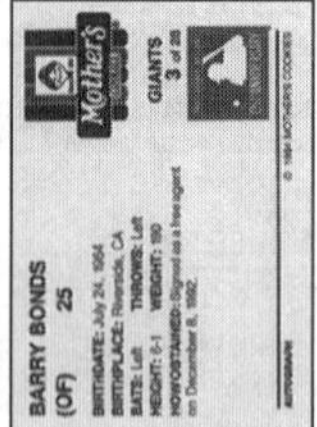

The 1994 Mother's Cookies Giants set consists of 28 standard-size cards with rounded corners. The fronts display full-bleed color player portraits shot from the waist up against a stadium background. The player's name and team name appear in one of the corners. On a white background in red and purple print, the horizontal backs carry biographical information and the sponsor's logo. A blank slot for the player's autograph rounds out the back.

	MINT	NRMT	EXC
COMPLETE SET (28)	10.00	4.50	1.25
COMMON CARD (1-28)	.25	.11	.03
☐ 1 Dusty Baker MG	.50	.23	.06
☐ 2 Robby Thompson	.25	.11	.03
☐ 3 Barry Bonds	2.50	1.10	.30
☐ 4 Royce Clayton	1.00	.45	.12
☐ 5 John Burkett	.75	.35	.09
☐ 6 Bill Swift	.25	.11	.03
☐ 7 Matt Williams	2.00	.90	.25
☐ 8 Rod Beck	1.00	.45	.12
☐ 9 Steve Scarsone	.25	.11	.03
☐ 10 Mark Portugal	.25	.11	.03
☐ 11 John Patterson	.25	.11	.03
☐ 12 Darren Lewis	.25	.11	.03
☐ 13 Kirt Manwaring	.25	.11	.03
☐ 14 Salomon Torres	.25	.11	.03
☐ 15 Willie McGee	.50	.23	.06
☐ 16 Dave Martinez	.25	.11	.03
☐ 17 Darryl Strawberry	.50	.23	.06
☐ 18 Steve Frey	.25	.11	.03
☐ 19 Rich Monteleone	.25	.11	.03
☐ 20 Todd Benzinger	.25	.11	.03
☐ 21 Jeff Reed	.25	.11	.03
☐ 22 Mike Benjamin	.25	.11	.03
☐ 23 Mike Jackson	.25	.11	.03
☐ 24 Pat Gomez	.25	.11	.03
☐ 25 Dave Burba	.25	.11	.03
☐ 26 Bryan Hickerson	.25	.11	.03
☐ 27 Mark Carreon	.25	.11	.03
☐ 28 Checklist/Coaches Bobby Bonds Bob Lillis Wendell Kim Bob Brenly Dick Pole Denny Sommers	.50	.23	.06

1994 Giants S.F. Chronicle

These three pins came attached to cards of the featured players. The brass pins carry the player's names in black lettering, except for card No. 3, which carries the player's names on their "uniforms." The cards measure approximately 2 1/2" by 5 1/8" and feature on their fronts borderless color player photos framed by a thin white line. The player's name appears in black lettering within an orange banner near the bottom. The Giants' logo is shown at the upper right. The white back carries the player's name, statistics, and career highlights. The cards and pins are unnumbered and checklisted below in alphabetical order.

	MINT	NRMT	EXC
COMPLETE SET (3)	7.50	3.40	.95
COMMON CARD (1-3)	1.00	.45	.12
☐ 1 Dusty Baker MG	2.00	.90	.25
☐ 2 Barry Bonds	5.00	2.20	.60
☐ 3 Bill Swift John Burkett	1.00	.45	.12

1994 Giants Target Bottle Caps II

Measuring approximately 1 5/8" in diameter, these eight bottle caps were issued as a perforated board measuring approximately 4 3/8" by 8". There were four rows of two caps each. The fronts feature a color player portrait. The backs carry the player's name and number. The bottle caps are unnumbered and checklisted below in alphabetical order.

	MINT	NRMT	EXC
COMPLETE SET (8)	2.50	1.10	.30
COMMON CARD (1-8)	.25	.11	.03
☐ 1 Rod Beck	.50	.23	.06
☐ 2 John Burkett	.50	.23	.06
☐ 3 Royce Clayton	.50	.23	.06
☐ 4 Dave Martinez	.25	.11	.03
☐ 5 Tony Menendez	.25	.11	.03
☐ 6 Jeff Reed	.25	.11	.03
☐ 7 Steve Scarsone	.25	.11	.03
☐ 8 Title Cap	.25	.11	.03

1994 Giants Team Issue

These nine blank-backed photo sheets measure 8" by 10" and feature on their black-and-gold-bordered fronts with black-and-white player photos of award-winning Giants. The player's name appears in white lettering at the lower left, with the award he won appearing in red lettering beneath. A description of his accomplishment appears alongside in gold-colored lettering. A facsimile autograph is printed across the photo, and baseball's 125th Anniversary logo is shown at the bottom. The sheets are unnumbered and checklisted below in alphabetical order.

	MINT	NRMT	EXC
COMPLETE SET (9)	12.00	5.50	1.50
COMMON CARD (1-9)	1.00	.45	.12
☐ 1 Dusty Baker MG (Wearing sunglasses)	1.50	.70	.19
☐ 2 Dusty Baker MG (Waving cap)	1.50	.70	.19
☐ 3 Barry Bonds (Dropping bat)	3.00	1.35	.35
☐ 4 Barry Bonds (Running)	3.00	1.35	.35
☐ 5 Barry Bonds Robby Thompson Matt Williams	2.00	.90	.25
☐ 6 Barry Bonds Kirt Manwaring Robby Thompson Matt Williams	2.00	.90	.25
☐ 7 John Burkett Bill Swift	1.00	.45	.12
☐ 8 Darren Lewis	1.00	.45	.12
☐ 9 The 1993 Giants Matt Williams Will Clark Barry Bonds Willie McGee	3.00	1.35	.35

1994 Giants U.S. Playing Cards

These 56 playing standard-size cards have rounded corners, and feature color posed and action player photos on their white-bordered fronts. The player's name and position appear near the bottom. The white and black backs carry the logos for the Giants, baseball's 125th Anniversary, MLBPA, and Bicycle Sports Collection. The set is checklisted below in playing card order by suits and assigned numbers to aces (1), jacks (11), queens (12), and kings (13).

	MINT	NRMT	EXC
COMPLETE SET (56)	4.00	1.80	.50
COMMON CARD	.05	.02	.01
☐ 1C Matt Williams	.25	.11	.03
☐ 1D Bill Swift	.05	.02	.01
☐ 1H Robby Thompson	.05	.02	.01
☐ 1S Barry Bonds	.50	.23	.06
☐ 2C John Patterson	.05	.02	.01
☐ 2D Luis Mercedes	.05	.02	.01
☐ 2H Paul Faries	.05	.02	.01
☐ 2S Salomon Torres	.05	.02	.01
☐ 3C Steve Hosey	.05	.02	.01
☐ 3D Mike Benjamin	.05	.02	.01
☐ 3H Trevor Wilson	.05	.02	.01
☐ 3S Kevin Rogers	.05	.02	.01
☐ 4C Jeff Reed	.05	.02	.01
☐ 4D Mark Carreon	.15	.07	.02
☐ 4H Steve Scarsone	.05	.02	.01
☐ 4S Todd Benzinger	.05	.02	.01
☐ 5C Mike Jackson	.05	.02	.01
☐ 5D Dave Burba	.15	.07	.02
☐ 5H Bryan Hickerson	.05	.02	.01
☐ 5S Dave Martinez	.05	.02	.01
☐ 6C Kirt Manwaring	.05	.02	.01
☐ 6D John Burkett	.05	.02	.01
☐ 6H Rod Beck	.15	.07	.02
☐ 6S Darren Lewis	.05	.02	.01
☐ 7C Royce Clayton	.15	.07	.02
☐ 7D Matt Williams	.40	.18	.05
☐ 7H Barry Bonds	.60	.25	.07
☐ 7S Willie McGee	.15	.07	.02
☐ 8C Robby Thompson	.05	.02	.01
☐ 8D Salomon Torres	.05	.02	.01
☐ 8H John Patterson	.05	.02	.01
☐ 8S Bill Swift	.05	.02	.01
☐ 9C Luis Mercedes	.05	.02	.01
☐ 9D Kevin Rogers	.05	.02	.01
☐ 9H J.R. Phillips	.05	.02	.01
☐ 9S Paul Faries	.05	.02	.01
☐ 10C Mike Benjamin	.05	.02	.01
☐ 10D Todd Benzinger	.05	.02	.01
☐ 10H Jeff Reed	.05	.02	.01
☐ 10S Trevor Wilson	.05	.02	.01
☐ 11C Mark Carreon	.15	.07	.02
☐ 11D Dave Martinez	.05	.02	.01
☐ 11H Mike Jackson	.05	.02	.01
☐ 11S Steve Scarsone	.05	.02	.01
☐ 12C Dave Burba	.05	.02	.01
☐ 12D Darren Lewis	.05	.02	.01
☐ 12H Kirt Manwaring	.05	.02	.01
☐ 12S Bryan Hickerson	.05	.02	.01
☐ 13C John Burkett	.05	.02	.01
☐ 13D Willie McGee	.15	.07	.02
☐ 13H Royce Clayton	.15	.07	.02
☐ 13S Rod Beck	.15	.07	.02
☐ NNO Featured Players	.05	.02	.01

1995 Giants Mother's

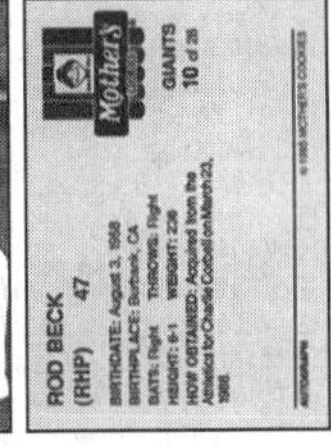

This 1995 Mother's Cookies San Francisco Giants set consists of 28 standard-size cards with rounded corners. The fronts display posed color player portraits. The player's name and team name appear in one of the top corners. The horizontal backs carry biographical information and the sponsor's logo on a white background in red and purple print. A blank slot at the bottom for the player's autograph rounds out the back.

	MINT	NRMT	EXC
COMPLETE SET (28)	10.00	4.50	1.25
COMMON CARD (1-28)	.25	.11	.03
☐ 1 Dusty Baker MG	.50	.23	.06
☐ 2 Robby Thompson	.25	.11	.03
☐ 3 Barry Bonds	2.50	1.10	.30
☐ 4 Royce Clayton	1.00	.45	.12
☐ 5 Glenallen Hill	.50	.23	.06
☐ 6 Terry Mulholland	.25	.11	.03
☐ 7 Matt Williams	2.00	.90	.25
☐ 8 Mark Portugal	.25	.11	.03
☐ 9 John Patterson	.25	.11	.03
☐ 10 Rod Beck	.75	.35	.09
☐ 11 Mark Leiter	.25	.11	.03
☐ 12 Kirt Manwaring	.25	.11	.03
☐ 13 Steve Scarsone	.25	.11	.03
☐ 14 Darren Lewis	.25	.11	.03
☐ 15 Tom Lampkin	.25	.11	.03
☐ 16 William VanLandingham	.50	.23	.06
☐ 17 Joe Rosselli	.25	.11	.03
☐ 18 Chris Hook	.25	.11	.03
☐ 19 Mark Dewey	.25	.11	.03
☐ 20 J.R. Phillips	.25	.11	.03
☐ 21 Jeff Reed	.25	.11	.03
☐ 22 Pat Gomez	.25	.11	.03
☐ 23 Mike Benjamin	.25	.11	.03
☐ 24 Trevor Wilson	.25	.11	.03
☐ 25 Dave Burba	.25	.11	.03
☐ 26 Jose Bautista	.25	.11	.03
☐ 27 Mark Carreon	.25	.11	.03
☐ 28 Coaches/Checklist Dick Pole Bobby Bonds Wendell Kim Bob Brenly Bob Lillis	.50	.23	.06

1996 Giants Mother's

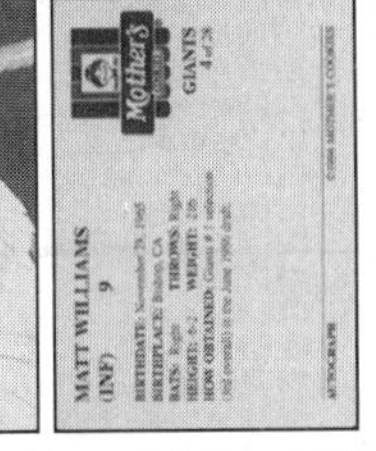

This 28-card set consists of borderless posed color player portraits in stadium settings. The player's and team's names appear in one of the top rounded corners. The backs carry biographical information and the sponsor's logo on a white background in red and purple print. A blank slot for the player's autograph rounds out the back.

	MINT	NRMT	EXC
COMPLETE SET (28)	8.00	3.60	1.00
COMMON CARD (1-28)	.25	.11	.03
☐ 1 Dusty Baker MG	.50	.23	.06
☐ 2 Barry Bonds	2.50	1.10	.30
☐ 3 Rod Beck	.50	.23	.06
☐ 4 Matt Williams	2.00	.90	.25
☐ 5 Robby Thompson	.25	.11	.03
☐ 6 Glenallen Hill	.25	.11	.03
☐ 7 Kirt Manwaring	.25	.11	.03
☐ 8 Mark Carreon	.25	.11	.03
☐ 9 Osvaldo Fernandez	1.00	.45	.12
☐ 10 J.R. Phillips	.25	.11	.03
☐ 11 Shawon Dunston	.25	.11	.03
☐ 12 Mark Leiter	.25	.11	.03
☐ 13 William VanLandingham	.50	.23	.06
☐ 14 Stan Javier	.25	.11	.03
☐ 15 Allen Watson	.25	.11	.03
☐ 16 Mel Hall	.25	.11	.03
☐ 17 Doug Creek	.25	.11	.03
☐ 18 Steve Scarsone	.25	.11	.03
☐ 19 Mark Dewey	.25	.11	.03
☐ 20 Mark Gardner	.25	.11	.03
☐ 21 David McCarty	.25	.11	.03
☐ 22 Tom Lampkin	.25	.11	.03
☐ 23 Jeff Juden	.25	.11	.03
☐ 24 Steve Decker	.25	.11	.03
☐ 25 Rich DeLucia	.25	.11	.03
☐ 26 Kim Batiste	.25	.11	.03
☐ 27 Steve Bourgeois	.25	.11	.03
☐ 28 Coaches Card CL Bob Lillis Dick Pole Bobby Bonds Jim Davenport Mike Sadek Juan Lopez Wendell Kim Carlos Alfonso	.25	.11	.03

1942 Gillette Razor Label

This label was produced by the Gillette Razor company and honors the 1941 American League and National League Champions. The narrow cardboard label measures 4 3/8" by 1 3/8". The left side has two player photos printed in blue ink, the upper head shot is of "Lefty Gomez of the New York Yankees, and below is Johnny Mize of St. Louis Cardinals. The right side also carries two player head shots in blue ink of Bucky Walters of the Cincinnati Reds, and Red Rolfe of the New York Yankees. The middle portion is printed in red, blue, and yellow and has a navy blue pennant for the American League and a red pennant for the National League. The Gillette logo is printed where the two pennants intersect.

	EX-MT	VG-E	GOOD
COMPLETE SET	50.00	22.00	6.25
COMMON CARD	50.00	22.00	6.25

1992 Gold Entertainment Ruth

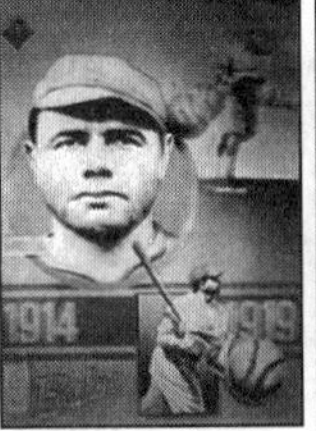

Gold Entertainment produced this five-card holographic set celebrating the life and legend of Babe Ruth, along with Lou Gehrig and Roger Maris. The artwork for these cards was created by Hollywood artists Mike Butkus and Alan Hunter. This standard-size set was sold in box cases containing 20 five-card sets (16 in silver and four in gold) and four bonus holograms (of a surprise player). The gold sets are valued at one and a half times the (silver) values listed below. The production run is reported to be 12,500 boxes, with each box carrying a numbered holographic seal. Each set features two double-sided full-bleed holograms and three full-color backs presenting biography, statistics, and quotes. The cards are numbered on the front in a diamond in the upper left corner (the cards with the color backs also carry a number on the back).

	MINT	NRMT	EXC
COMPLETE SET (5)	10.00	4.50	1.25
COMMON CARD (1-5)	2.00	.90	.25
☐ 1 Babe Ruth 1914-1919 Portrait, batting and hitting poses	2.00	.90	.25
☐ 2 Babe Ruth Lou Gehrig Two-sided hologram Ruth's stats on front Gehrig's stats on back	3.00	1.35	.35
☐ 3 Babe Ruth The Called Shot Bat extended, pointing toward outfield	2.00	.90	.25
☐ 4 Babe Ruth Roger Maris 61 in 1961 - 60 in 1927 Two-sided hologram Ruth and Maris on front	3.00	1.35	.35
☐ 5 Babe Ruth 1914-1935 Portrait and standing poses	2.00	.90	.25

1935 Gold Medal Flour R313A

The 1935 Gold Medal Flour series is complete at 12 cards. They were issued to commemorate the World Series of 1934 which featured the Detroit Tigers and the St. Louis Cardinals. Each card measures approximately 3 1/4" by 5 3/8". The cards are blank backed and unnumbered.

	EX-MT	VG-E	GOOD
COMPLETE SET (12)	500.00	220.00	60.00
COMMON CARDS (1-12)	30.00	13.50	3.70
☐ 1 Tommy Bridges	30.00	13.50	3.70
☐ 2 Mickey Cochrane	75.00	34.00	9.50
☐ 3 Dizzy Dean	125.00	55.00	15.50
☐ 4 Paul Dean	50.00	22.00	6.25
☐ 5 Frank Frisch	75.00	34.00	9.50
☐ 6 Goose Goslin	60.00	27.00	7.50
☐ 7 William Hallahan	30.00	13.50	3.70
☐ 8 Fred Marberry	30.00	13.50	3.70
☐ 9 John "Pepper" Martin	50.00	22.00	6.25
☐ 10 Joe Medwick	60.00	27.00	7.50
☐ 11 William Rogell	30.00	13.50	3.70
☐ 12 Jo-Jo White	30.00	13.50	3.70

1961 Golden Press

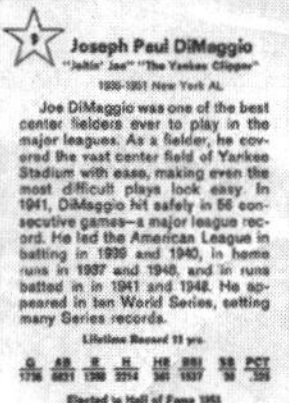

The cards in this 33-card set measure 2 1/2" by 3 1/2". The 1961 Golden Press set of full color cards features members of Baseball's Hall of Fame. The cards came in a booklet with perforations for punching the cards out of the book. The catalog designation for this set is W524. The price for the full book intact is double the complete set price listed.

	NRMT	VG-E	GOOD
COMPLETE SET (33)	125.00	55.00	15.50
COMMON CARD (1-33)	1.00	.45	.12
☐ 1 Mel Ott	4.00	1.80	.50
☐ 2 Grover C. Alexander	3.00	1.35	.35
☐ 3 Babe Ruth	40.00	18.00	5.00
☐ 4 Hank Greenberg	3.00	1.35	.35
☐ 5 Bill Terry	1.25	.55	.16
☐ 6 Carl Hubbell	1.50	.70	.19
☐ 7 Rogers Hornsby	5.00	2.20	.60
☐ 8 Dizzy Dean	7.50	3.40	.95
☐ 9 Joe DiMaggio	35.00	16.00	4.40
☐ 10 Charlie Gehringer	1.00	.45	.12
☐ 11 Gabby Hartnett	1.00	.45	.12
☐ 12 Mickey Cochrane	1.50	.70	.19
☐ 13 George Sisler	1.00	.45	.12
☐ 14 Joe Cronin	1.00	.45	.12
☐ 15 Pie Traynor	1.00	.45	.12
☐ 16 Lou Gehrig	35.00	16.00	4.40
☐ 17 Lefty Grove	3.00	1.35	.35
☐ 18 Chief Bender	1.00	.45	.12
☐ 19 Frankie Frisch	1.00	.45	.12
☐ 20 Al Simmons	1.00	.45	.12
☐ 21 Home Run Baker	1.00	.45	.12
☐ 22 Jimmy Foxx	5.00	2.20	.60
☐ 23 John McGraw	1.00	.45	.12
☐ 24 Christy Mathewson	7.50	3.40	.95
☐ 25 Ty Cobb	35.00	16.00	4.40
☐ 26 Dazzy Vance	1.00	.45	.12
☐ 27 Bill Dickey	1.50	.70	.19
☐ 28 Eddie Collins	1.50	.70	.19
☐ 29 Walter Johnson	7.50	3.40	.95
☐ 30 Tris Speaker	3.00	1.35	.35
☐ 31 Nap Lajoie	3.00	1.35	.35
☐ 32 Honus Wagner	7.50	3.40	.95
☐ 33 Cy Young	5.00	2.20	.60

1990 Good Humor Ice Cream Big League Sticks

This 26-piece set of ice cream sticks are shaped like baseball bats.They carry facsimile autographs and are individually numbered and are in alphabetical order.

	MINT	NRMT	EXC
COMPLETE SET (26)	35.00	16.00	4.40
COMMON CARD (1-26)	.25	.11	.03
☐ 1 Jim Abbott	.50	.23	.06
☐ 2 George Bell	.25	.11	.03
☐ 3 Wade Boggs	1.50	.70	.19
☐ 4 Bobby Bonilla	.50	.23	.06
☐ 5 Jose Canseco	1.50	.70	.19
☐ 6 Will Clark	1.50	.70	.19
☐ 7 Eric Davis	.50	.23	.06
☐ 8 Carlton Fisk	1.50	.70	.19
☐ 9 Kirk Gibson	.50	.23	.06
☐ 10 Dwight Gooden	.50	.23	.06
☐ 11 Ken Griffey Jr.	8.00	3.60	1.00
☐ 12 Von Hayes	.25	.11	.03
☐ 13 Don Mattingly	5.00	2.20	.60
☐ 14 Gregg Olson	.25	.11	.03
☐ 15 Kirby Puckett	4.00	1.80	.50
☐ 16 Tim Raines	.50	.23	.06
☐ 17 Nolan Ryan	6.00	2.70	.75
☐ 18 Bret Saberhagen	.25	.11	.03
☐ 19 Ryne Sandberg	5.00	2.20	.60
☐ 20 Benito Santiago	.25	.11	.03
☐ 21 Mike Scott	.25	.11	.03
☐ 22 Lonnie Smith	.25	.11	.03
☐ 23 Ozzie Smith	4.00	1.80	.50
☐ 24 Cory Snyder	.25	.11	.03
☐ 25 Alan Trammell	.75	.35	.09
☐ 26 Robin Yount	1.00	.45	.12

1888 Goodwin N162

This 50-card set issued by Goodwin was one of the major competitors to the N28 and N29 sets marketed by Allen and Ginter. It contains individuals representing 18 sports, with eight baseball players pictured. Each color card is backlisted and bears advertising for "Old Judge" and "Gypsy Queen" cigarettes on the front. The set was released to the public in 1888 and an album (catalog: A36) is associated with it as a premium issue.

	EX-MT	VG-E	GOOD
COMPLETE SET (50)	16500.00	7400.00	2100.00
COMMON BASEBALL (1-8)	700.00	325.00	90.00
COMMON BOXER	250.00	110.00	31.00
COMMON OTHERS	75.00	34.00	9.50
☐ 1 Ed Andrews: Phila.	700.00	325.00	90.00
☐ 2 Cap Anson: Chicago	3500.00	1600.00	450.00
☐ 3 Dan Brouthers: Detroit	1400.00	650.00	180.00
☐ 4 Bob Caruthers: Brooklyn	750.00	350.00	95.00
☐ 5 Fred Dunlap: Pittsburgh	700.00	325.00	90.00
☐ 6 Jack Glasscock: Indianapolis	750.00	350.00	95.00
☐ 7 Tim Keefe: New York	1400.00	650.00	180.00
☐ 8 King Kelly: Boston	2500.00	1100.00	300.00
☐ 9 Acton (Wrestler)	100.00	45.00	12.50
☐ 10 Albert (Pedestrian)	75.00	34.00	9.50
☐ 11 Beach (Oarsman)	75.00	34.00	9.50
☐ 12 Beecher (Football)	1200.00	550.00	150.00
☐ 13 Beeckman (Lawn Tennis)	100.00	45.00	12.50
☐ 14 Bogardus (Marksman)	75.00	34.00	9.50
☐ 15 Buffalo Bill Wild West Hunter	400.00	180.00	50.00
☐ 16 Daly (Billiards)	100.00	45.00	12.50
☐ 17 Jack Dempsey (Pugilist)	400.00	180.00	50.00
☐ 18 D'oro (Pool)	100.00	45.00	12.50
☐ 19 James Dwight (Lawn Tennis)	100.00	45.00	12.50
☐ 20 Fitzgerald (Pedestrian)	75.00	34.00	9.50
☐ 21 Garrison (Jockey)	75.00	34.00	9.50
☐ 22 Gaudaur (Oarsman)	75.00	34.00	9.50
☐ 23 Hanlan (Oarsman)	100.00	45.00	12.50
☐ 24 Jake Kilrain (Pugilist)	350.00	160.00	45.00
☐ 25 MacKenzie (Chess)	100.00	45.00	12.50
☐ 26 McLaughlin (Jockey)	75.00	34.00	9.50
☐ 27 Charlie Mitchell (Pugilist)	350.00	160.00	45.00
☐ 28 Muldoon (Wrestler)	100.00	45.00	12.50
☐ 29 Isaac Murphy (Jockey)	100.00	45.00	12.50
☐ 30 Myers (Runner)	75.00	34.00	9.50
☐ 31 Page (High Jumper)	75.00	34.00	9.50
☐ 32 Prince (Bicyclist)	75.00	34.00	9.50
☐ 33 Ross (Broadswordsman)	75.00	34.00	9.50
☐ 34 Rowe (Bicyclist)	75.00	34.00	9.50
☐ 35 Rowell (Pedestrian)	75.00	34.00	9.50
☐ 36 Schaefer (Billiards)	100.00	45.00	12.50
☐ 37 R.D. Sears (Lawn Tennis)	100.00	45.00	12.50
☐ 38 Sexton (Billiards)	100.00	45.00	12.50
☐ 39 Slosson (Billiards)	100.00	45.00	12.50
☐ 40 Smith (Pugilist)	250.00	110.00	31.00
☐ 41 Steinitz (Chess)	125.00	55.00	15.50
☐ 42 Stevens (Bicyclist)	75.00	34.00	9.50
☐ 43 John L. Sullivan (Pugilist)	500.00	220.00	60.00
☐ 44 Taylor (Lawn Tennis)	100.00	45.00	12.50
☐ 45 Teemer (Oarsman)	75.00	34.00	9.50
☐ 46 Vignaux (Billiards)	100.00	45.00	12.50
☐ 47 Voss (Strongest Man in the World)	75.00	34.00	9.50
☐ 48 Wood (Bicyclist)	75.00	34.00	9.50
☐ 49 Charles Wood Jockey	75.00	34.00	9.50
☐ 50 Zukertort (Chess)	100.00	45.00	12.50

1933 Goudey R319

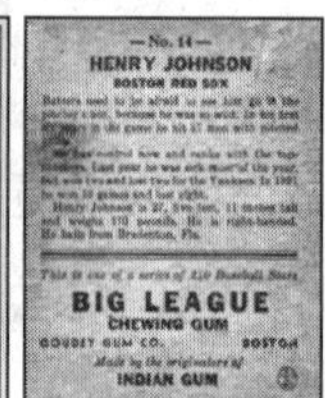

The cards in this 240-card set measure approximately 2 3/8" by 2 7/8". The 1933 Goudey set, was that company's first baseball issue. The four Babe Ruth and two Lou Gehrig cards in the set are extremely popular with collectors. Card number 106, Napoleon Lajoie, was not printed in 1933, and was circulated to a limited number of collectors in 1934 upon request (it was printed along with the 1934 Goudey cards). An album was offered to house the 1933 set. Several minor leaguers are depicted. Card number 1 (Bengough) is very rarely found in mint condition; in fact, as a general rule all the first series cards are more difficult to find in Mint condition. Players with more than one card are also sometimes differentiated below by their pose: BAT (Batting), FIELD (Fielding), PIT (Pitching), THROW (Throwing). One of the Babe Ruth cards was double printed (DP) apparently in place of the Lajoie and hence is easier to obtain than the others. Due to the scarcity of the Lajoie card, the set is considered complete at 239 cards and is priced as such below.

	EX-MT	VG-E	GOOD
COMPLETE SET (239)	40000.00	18000.00	5000.00
COMMON CARD (1-40)	60.00	27.00	7.50
COMMON CARD (41-44)	40.00	18.00	5.00
COMMON CARD (45-52)	60.00	27.00	7.50
COMMON CARD (53-240)	45.00	20.00	5.50
WRAPPER (1-CENT, BATTER)	150.00	70.00	19.00
WRAPPER (1-CENT, AD FRONT)	175.00	80.00	22.00
☐ 1 Benny Bengough	1250.00	550.00	160.00
☐ 2 Dazzy Vance	200.00	90.00	25.00
☐ 3 Hugh Critz	60.00	27.00	7.50
☐ 4 Heinie Schuble	60.00	27.00	7.50
☐ 5 Babe Herman	75.00	34.00	9.50
☐ 6 Jimmy Dykes	75.00	34.00	9.50
☐ 7 Ted Lyons	150.00	70.00	19.00
☐ 8 Roy Johnson	60.00	27.00	7.50
☐ 9 Dave Harris	60.00	27.00	7.50
☐ 10 Glenn Myatt	60.00	27.00	7.50
☐ 11 Billy Rogell	60.00	27.00	7.50
☐ 12 George Pipgras	60.00	27.00	7.50
☐ 13 Lafayette Thompson	60.00	27.00	7.50
☐ 14 Henry Johnson	60.00	27.00	7.50
☐ 15 Victor Sorrell	60.00	27.00	7.50
☐ 16 George Blaeholder	60.00	27.00	7.50
☐ 17 Watson Clark	60.00	27.00	7.50
☐ 18 Muddy Ruel	60.00	27.00	7.50
☐ 19 Bill Dickey	350.00	160.00	45.00
☐ 20 Bill Terry THROW	250.00	110.00	31.00
☐ 21 Phil Collins	60.00	27.00	7.50
☐ 22 Pie Traynor	200.00	90.00	25.00
☐ 23 Kiki Cuyler	150.00	70.00	19.00
☐ 24 Horace Ford	60.00	27.00	7.50
☐ 25 Paul Waner	150.00	70.00	19.00
☐ 26 Chalmer Cissell	60.00	27.00	7.50
☐ 27 George Connally	60.00	27.00	7.50
☐ 28 Dick Bartell	75.00	34.00	9.50
☐ 29 Jimmy Foxx	450.00	200.00	55.00
☐ 30 Frank Hogan	60.00	27.00	7.50
☐ 31 Tony Lazzeri	350.00	160.00	45.00
☐ 32 Bud Clancy	60.00	27.00	7.50
☐ 33 Ralph Kress	60.00	27.00	7.50
☐ 34 Bob O'Farrell	60.00	27.00	7.50
☐ 35 Al Simmons	350.00	160.00	45.00
☐ 36 Tommy Thevenow	60.00	27.00	7.50
☐ 37 Jimmy Wilson	60.00	27.00	7.50
☐ 38 Fred Brickell	60.00	27.00	7.50
☐ 39 Mark Koenig	75.00	34.00	9.50
☐ 40 Taylor Douthit	60.00	27.00	7.50
☐ 41 Gus Mancuso	40.00	18.00	5.00
☐ 42 Eddie Collins	125.00	55.00	15.50
☐ 43 Lew Fonseca	40.00	18.00	5.00
☐ 44 Jim Bottomley	125.00	55.00	15.50
☐ 45 Larry Benton	60.00	27.00	7.50
☐ 46 Ethan Allen	75.00	34.00	9.50
☐ 47 Heinie Manush BAT	150.00	70.00	19.00
☐ 48 Marty McManus	60.00	27.00	7.50
☐ 49 Frank Frisch	250.00	110.00	31.00
☐ 50 Ed Brandt	60.00	27.00	7.50
☐ 51 Charlie Grimm	75.00	34.00	9.50
☐ 52 Andy Cohen	60.00	27.00	7.50
☐ 53 Babe Ruth	4200.00	1900.00	525.00
☐ 54 Ray Kremer	45.00	20.00	5.50
☐ 55 Pat Malone	45.00	20.00	5.50
☐ 56 Charlie(Red) Ruffing	100.00	45.00	12.50
☐ 57 Earl Clark	45.00	20.00	5.50
☐ 58 Lefty O'Doul	75.00	34.00	9.50
☐ 59 Bing Miller	45.00	20.00	5.50
☐ 60 Waite Hoyt	100.00	45.00	12.50
☐ 61 Max Bishop	45.00	20.00	5.50
☐ 62 Pepper Martin	75.00	34.00	9.50
☐ 63 Joe Cronin BAT	125.00	55.00	15.50
☐ 64 Burleigh Grimes	100.00	45.00	12.50
☐ 65 Milt Gaston	45.00	20.00	5.50
☐ 66 George Grantham	45.00	20.00	5.50
☐ 67 Guy Bush	45.00	20.00	5.50
☐ 68 Horace Lisenbee	45.00	20.00	5.50
☐ 69 Randy Moore	45.00	20.00	5.50
☐ 70 Floyd(Pete) Scott	45.00	20.00	5.50
☐ 71 Robert J. Burke	45.00	20.00	5.50
☐ 72 Owen Carroll	45.00	20.00	5.50
☐ 73 Jess Haines	100.00	45.00	12.50
☐ 74 Eppa Rixey	100.00	45.00	12.50
☐ 75 Willie Kamm	45.00	20.00	5.50
☐ 76 Mickey Cochrane	175.00	80.00	22.00
☐ 77 Adam Comorosky	45.00	20.00	5.50
☐ 78 Jack Quinn	45.00	20.00	5.50
☐ 79 Red Faber	100.00	45.00	12.50
☐ 80 Clyde Manion	45.00	20.00	5.50
☐ 81 Sam Jones	55.00	25.00	7.00
☐ 82 Dibrell Williams	45.00	20.00	5.50
☐ 83 Pete Jablonowski	45.00	20.00	5.50
☐ 84 Glenn Spencer	45.00	20.00	5.50
☐ 85 Heinie Sand	45.00	20.00	5.50
☐ 86 Phil Todt	45.00	20.00	5.50
☐ 87 Frank O'Rourke	45.00	20.00	5.50
☐ 88 Russell Rollings	45.00	20.00	5.50
☐ 89 Tris Speaker RET	250.00	110.00	31.00
☐ 90 Jess Petty	45.00	20.00	5.50
☐ 91 Tom Zachary	55.00	25.00	7.00
☐ 92 Lou Gehrig	2500.00	1100.00	300.00
☐ 93 John Welch	45.00	20.00	5.50
☐ 94 Bill Walker	45.00	20.00	5.50
☐ 95 Alvin Crowder	45.00	20.00	5.50
☐ 96 Willis Hudlin	45.00	20.00	5.50
☐ 97 Joe Morrissey	45.00	20.00	5.50
☐ 98 Walter Berger	75.00	34.00	9.50
☐ 99 Tony Cuccinello	55.00	25.00	7.00
☐ 100 George Uhle	45.00	20.00	5.50
☐ 101 Richard Coffman	45.00	20.00	5.50
☐ 102 Travis Jackson	100.00	45.00	12.50
☐ 103 Earle Combs	100.00	45.00	12.50
☐ 104 Fred Marberry	45.00	20.00	5.50
☐ 105 Bernie Friberg	45.00	20.00	5.50
☐ 106 Napoleon Lajoie SP (Not issued until 1934)	30000.00	13500.00	3800.00
☐ 107 Heinie Manush	100.00	45.00	12.50
☐ 108 Joe Kuhel	45.00	20.00	5.50
☐ 109 Joe Cronin	125.00	55.00	15.50
☐ 110 Goose Goslin	100.00	45.00	12.50
☐ 111 Monte Weaver	45.00	20.00	5.50
☐ 112 Fred Schulte	45.00	20.00	5.50
☐ 113 Oswald Bluege	55.00	25.00	7.00
☐ 114 Luke Sewell	65.00	29.00	8.00
☐ 115 Cliff Heathcote	45.00	20.00	5.50
☐ 116 Eddie Morgan	45.00	20.00	5.50
☐ 117 Rabbit Maranville	100.00	45.00	12.50
☐ 118 Val Picinich	45.00	20.00	5.50
☐ 119 Rogers Hornsby FIELD	350.00	160.00	45.00
☐ 120 Carl Reynolds	45.00	20.00	5.50
☐ 121 Walter Stewart	45.00	20.00	5.50
☐ 122 Alvin Crowder	45.00	20.00	5.50
☐ 123 Jack Russell	45.00	20.00	5.50
☐ 124 Earl Whitehill	45.00	20.00	5.50
☐ 125 Bill Terry	250.00	110.00	31.00
☐ 126 Joe Moore	55.00	25.00	7.00
☐ 127 Mel Ott	300.00	135.00	38.00
☐ 128 Chuck Klein	150.00	70.00	19.00
☐ 129 Hal Schumacher PIT	55.00	25.00	7.00
☐ 130 Fred Fitzsimmons	55.00	25.00	7.00
☐ 131 Fred Frankhouse	45.00	20.00	5.50
☐ 132 Jim Elliott	45.00	20.00	5.50
☐ 133 Fred Lindstrom	100.00	45.00	12.50
☐ 134 Sam Rice	100.00	45.00	12.50
☐ 135 Woody English	45.00	20.00	5.50
☐ 136 Flint Rhem	45.00	20.00	5.50
☐ 137 Fred(Red) Lucas	45.00	20.00	5.50
☐ 138 Herb Pennock	100.00	45.00	12.50
☐ 139 Ben Cantwell	45.00	20.00	5.50
☐ 140 Bump Hadley	45.00	20.00	5.50
☐ 141 Ray Benge	45.00	20.00	5.50
☐ 142 Paul Richards	65.00	29.00	8.00
☐ 143 Glenn Wright	55.00	25.00	7.00
☐ 144 Babe Ruth BAT DP	3200.00	1450.00	400.00
☐ 145 Rube Walberg	45.00	20.00	5.50
☐ 146 Walter Stewart PIT	45.00	20.00	5.50
☐ 147 Leo Durocher	175.00	80.00	22.00
☐ 148 Eddie Farrell	45.00	20.00	5.50
☐ 149 Babe Ruth	4200.00	1900.00	525.00
☐ 150 Ray Kolp	45.00	20.00	5.50
☐ 151 Jake Flowers	45.00	20.00	5.50
☐ 152 Zack Taylor	45.00	20.00	5.50
☐ 153 Buddy Myer	55.00	25.00	7.00
☐ 154 Jimmy Foxx	350.00	160.00	45.00
☐ 155 Joe Judge	45.00	20.00	5.50
☐ 156 Danny MacFayden	45.00	20.00	5.50
☐ 157 Sam Byrd	45.00	20.00	5.50
☐ 158 Moe Berg	350.00	160.00	45.00
☐ 159 Oswald Bluege	55.00	25.00	7.00
☐ 160 Lou Gehrig	2500.00	1100.00	300.00
☐ 161 Al Spohrer	45.00	20.00	5.50
☐ 162 Leo Mangum	45.00	20.00	5.50
☐ 163 Luke Sewell	65.00	29.00	8.00
☐ 164 Lloyd Waner	100.00	45.00	12.50
☐ 165 Joe Sewell	100.00	45.00	12.50
☐ 166 Sam West	45.00	20.00	5.50
☐ 167 Jack Russell	45.00	20.00	5.50
☐ 168 Goose Goslin	100.00	45.00	12.50
☐ 169 Al Thomas	45.00	20.00	5.50
☐ 170 Harry McCurdy	45.00	20.00	5.50
☐ 171 Charlie Jamieson	45.00	20.00	5.50
☐ 172 Billy Hargrave	45.00	20.00	5.50
☐ 173 Roscoe Holm	45.00	20.00	5.50
☐ 174 Warren(Curly) Ogden	45.00	20.00	5.50
☐ 175 Dan Howley MG	45.00	20.00	5.50
☐ 176 John Ogden	45.00	20.00	5.50
☐ 177 Walter French	45.00	20.00	5.50
☐ 178 Jackie Warner	45.00	20.00	5.50
☐ 179 Fred Leach	45.00	20.00	5.50
☐ 180 Eddie Moore	45.00	20.00	5.50
☐ 181 Babe Ruth	4200.00	1900.00	525.00
☐ 182 Andy High	45.00	20.00	5.50
☐ 183 Rube Walberg	45.00	20.00	5.50
☐ 184 Charley Berry	55.00	25.00	7.00
☐ 185 Bob Smith	45.00	20.00	5.50
☐ 186 John Schulte	45.00	20.00	5.50
☐ 187 Heinie Manush	100.00	45.00	12.50
☐ 188 Rogers Hornsby	350.00	160.00	45.00
☐ 189 Joe Cronin	125.00	55.00	15.50
☐ 190 Fred Schulte	45.00	20.00	5.50
☐ 191 Ben Chapman	65.00	29.00	8.00
☐ 192 Walter Brown	45.00	20.00	5.50
☐ 193 Lynford Lary	45.00	20.00	5.50
☐ 194 Earl Averill	125.00	55.00	15.50
☐ 195 Evar Swanson	45.00	20.00	5.50
☐ 196 Leroy Mahaffey	45.00	20.00	5.50
☐ 197 Rick Ferrell	100.00	45.00	12.50
☐ 198 Jack Burns	45.00	20.00	5.50
☐ 199 Tom Bridges	55.00	25.00	7.00
☐ 200 Bill Hallahan	45.00	20.00	5.50
☐ 201 Ernie Orsatti	45.00	20.00	5.50
☐ 202 Gabby Hartnett	125.00	55.00	15.50
☐ 203 Lon Warneke	55.00	25.00	7.00
☐ 204 Riggs Stephenson	55.00	25.00	7.00
☐ 205 Heinie Meine	45.00	20.00	5.50
☐ 206 Gus Suhr	45.00	20.00	5.50
☐ 207 Mel Ott BAT	350.00	160.00	45.00
☐ 208 Bernie James	45.00	20.00	5.50
☐ 209 Adolfo Luque	75.00	34.00	9.50
☐ 210 Virgil Davis	45.00	20.00	5.50
☐ 211 Hack Wilson	300.00	135.00	38.00
☐ 212 Billy Urbanski	45.00	20.00	5.50
☐ 213 Earl Adams	45.00	20.00	5.50
☐ 214 John Kerr	45.00	20.00	5.50
☐ 215 Russ Van Atta	45.00	20.00	5.50
☐ 216 Vernon(Lefty) Gomez	300.00	135.00	38.00
☐ 217 Frank Crosetti	125.00	55.00	15.50
☐ 218 Wes Ferrell	55.00	25.00	7.00
☐ 219 Mule Haas UER Name spelled Hass on front	45.00	20.00	5.50
☐ 220 Lefty Grove	400.00	180.00	50.00
☐ 221 Dale Alexander	55.00	25.00	7.00
☐ 222 Charley Gehringer	250.00	110.00	31.00
☐ 223 Dizzy Dean	600.00	275.00	75.00
☐ 224 Frank Demaree	45.00	20.00	5.50
☐ 225 Bill Jurges	55.00	25.00	7.00
☐ 226 Charley Root	55.00	25.00	7.00
☐ 227 Billy Herman	125.00	55.00	15.50
☐ 228 Tony Piet	45.00	20.00	5.50
☐ 229 Floyd(Arky) Vaughan	125.00	55.00	15.50
☐ 230 Carl Hubbell PIT	200.00	90.00	25.00
☐ 231 Joe Moore FIELD	45.00	20.00	5.50
☐ 232 Lefty O'Doul	75.00	34.00	9.50
☐ 233 Johnny Vergez	45.00	20.00	5.50
☐ 234 Carl Hubbell	200.00	90.00	25.00
☐ 235 Fred Fitzsimmons	55.00	25.00	7.00
☐ 236 George Davis	45.00	20.00	5.50
☐ 237 Gus Mancuso	45.00	20.00	5.50
☐ 238 Hugh Critz	45.00	20.00	5.50
☐ 239 Leroy Parmelee	45.00	20.00	5.50
☐ 240 Hal Schumacher	125.00	55.00	15.50

1933 Goudey Canadian V353

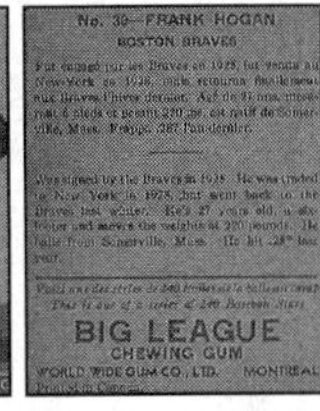

The cards in this 94-card set measure approximately 2 3/8" by 2 7/8". World Wide Gum, the Canadian subsidiary of Goudey issued this set of numbered color cards in 1933. Cards 1 to 52 contain obverses identical to the American issue, but cards 53 to 94 have a slightly different order. The fronts feature white-bordered color player drawings. The words "Big League Chewing Gum" are printed in white lettering in a red stripe near the bottom. The green ink backs are found printed in English only, or in French and English (the latter are slightly harder to find and are valued at a 25 percent premium over the prices listed below). The catalog designation for this set is V353.

	EX-MT	VG-E	GOOD
COMPLETE SET (94)	20000.00	9000.00	2500.00
COMMON CARD (1-94)	60.00	27.00	7.50

Card	EX-MT	VG-E	GOOD
☐ 1 Benny Bengough	600.00	275.00	75.00
☐ 2 Dazzy Vance	125.00	55.00	15.50
☐ 3 Hugh Critz	60.00	27.00	7.50
☐ 4 Heinie Schulbe	60.00	27.00	7.50
☐ 5 Babe Herman	90.00	40.00	11.00
☐ 6 Jimmy Dykes	75.00	34.00	9.50
☐ 7 Ted Lyons	125.00	55.00	15.50
☐ 8 Roy Johnson	60.00	27.00	7.50
☐ 9 Dave Harris	60.00	27.00	7.50
☐ 10 Glenn Myatt	60.00	27.00	7.50
☐ 11 Billy Rogell	60.00	27.00	7.50
☐ 12 George Pipgras	75.00	34.00	9.50
☐ 13 Lafayette Thompson	60.00	27.00	7.50
☐ 14 Henry Johnson	60.00	27.00	7.50
☐ 15 Victor Sorrell	60.00	27.00	7.50
☐ 16 George Blaeholder	60.00	27.00	7.50
☐ 17 Watson Clark	60.00	27.00	7.50
☐ 18 Muddy Ruel	60.00	27.00	7.50
☐ 19 Bill Dickey	350.00	160.00	45.00
☐ 20 Bill Terry	175.00	80.00	22.00
☐ 21 Phil Collins	60.00	27.00	7.50
☐ 22 Pie Traynor	150.00	70.00	19.00
☐ 23 Kiki Cuyler	125.00	55.00	15.50
☐ 24 Horace Ford	60.00	27.00	7.50
☐ 25 Paul Waner	150.00	70.00	19.00
☐ 26 Chalmer Cissell	60.00	27.00	7.50
☐ 27 George Connally	60.00	27.00	7.50
☐ 28 Dick Bartell	75.00	34.00	9.50
☐ 29 Jimmy Foxx	450.00	200.00	55.00
☐ 30 Frank Hogan	60.00	27.00	7.50
☐ 31 Tony Lazzeri	175.00	80.00	22.00
☐ 32 Bud Clancy	60.00	27.00	7.50
☐ 33 Ralph Kress	60.00	27.00	7.50
☐ 34 Bob O'Farrell	75.00	34.00	9.50
☐ 35 Al Simmons	175.00	80.00	22.00
☐ 36 Tommy Thevenow	60.00	27.00	7.50
☐ 37 Jimmy Wilson	75.00	34.00	9.50
☐ 38 Fred Bickell	60.00	27.00	7.50
☐ 39 Mark Koenig	75.00	34.00	9.50
☐ 40 Taylor Douthit	60.00	27.00	7.50
☐ 41 Gus Mancuso	60.00	27.00	7.50
☐ 42 Eddie Collins	150.00	70.00	19.00
☐ 43 Lew Fonseca	75.00	34.00	9.50
☐ 44 Jim Bottomley	125.00	55.00	15.50
☐ 45 Larry Benton	60.00	27.00	7.50
☐ 46 Ethan Allen	75.00	34.00	9.50
☐ 47 Heinie Manush	125.00	55.00	15.50
☐ 48 Marty McManus	60.00	27.00	7.50
☐ 49 Frank Frisch	150.00	70.00	19.00
☐ 50 Ed Brandt	60.00	27.00	7.50
☐ 51 Charlie Grimm	75.00	34.00	9.50
☐ 52 Andy Cohen	60.00	27.00	7.50
☐ 53 Jack Quinn	75.00	34.00	9.50
☐ 54 Urban Faber	125.00	55.00	15.50
☐ 55 Lou Gehrig	3500.00	1600.00	450.00
☐ 56 John Welch	60.00	27.00	7.50
☐ 57 Bill Walker	60.00	27.00	7.50
☐ 58 Lefty O'Doul	90.00	40.00	11.00
☐ 59 Bing Miller	75.00	34.00	9.50
☐ 60 Waite Hoyt	125.00	55.00	15.50
☐ 61 Max Bishop	75.00	34.00	9.50
☐ 62 Pepper Martin	90.00	40.00	11.00
☐ 63 Joe Cronin	150.00	70.00	19.00
☐ 64 Burleigh Grimes	125.00	55.00	15.50
☐ 65 Milt Gaston	60.00	27.00	7.50
☐ 66 George Grantham	60.00	27.00	7.50
☐ 67 Guy Bush	60.00	27.00	7.50
☐ 68 Willie Kamm	60.00	27.00	7.50
☐ 69 Mickey Cochrane	200.00	90.00	25.00
☐ 70 Adam Comorosky	60.00	27.00	7.50
☐ 71 Alvin Crowder	60.00	27.00	7.50
☐ 72 Willis Hudlin	60.00	27.00	7.50
☐ 73 Eddie Farrell	60.00	27.00	7.50
☐ 74 Leo Durocher	175.00	80.00	22.00
☐ 75 Walter Stewart	60.00	27.00	7.50
☐ 76 George Walberg	60.00	27.00	7.50
☐ 77 Glenn Wright	75.00	34.00	9.50
☐ 78 Charles(Buddy) Myer	75.00	34.00	9.50
☐ 79 James(Zack) Taylor	60.00	27.00	7.50
☐ 80 George H.(Babe)Ruth	5000.00	2200.00	600.00
☐ 81 D'Arcy(Jake) Flowers	60.00	27.00	7.50
☐ 82 Ray Kolp	60.00	27.00	7.50
☐ 83 Oswald Bluege	60.00	27.00	7.50
☐ 84 Morris (Moe) Berg	250.00	110.00	31.00
☐ 85 Jimmy Foxx	450.00	200.00	55.00
☐ 86 Sam Byrd	60.00	27.00	7.50
☐ 87 Danny MacFayden	60.00	27.00	7.50
☐ 88 Joe Judge	75.00	34.00	9.50
☐ 89 Joe Sewell	125.00	55.00	15.50
☐ 90 Lloyd Waner	125.00	55.00	15.50
☐ 91 Luke Sewell	75.00	34.00	9.50
☐ 92 Leo Mangum	60.00	27.00	7.50
☐ 93 George H.(Babe)Ruth	5000.00	2200.00	600.00
☐ 94 Al Spohrer	75.00	34.00	9.50

1934 Goudey R320

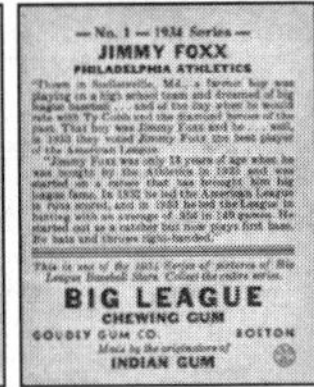

The cards in this 96-card color set measure approximately 2 3/8" by 2 7/8". Cards 1-48 are considered to be the easiest to find (although card number 1, Foxx, is very scarce in mint condition) while 73-96 are much more difficult to find. Cards of this 1934 Goudey series are slightly less abundant than cards of the 1933 Goudey set. Of the 96 cards, 84 contain a "Lou Gehrig Says" line on the front in a blue design, while 12 of the high series (80-91) contain a "Chuck Klein Says" line in a red design. These Chuck Klein cards are indicated in the checklist below by CK and are in fact the 12 National Leaguers in the high series.

	EX-MT	VG-E	GOOD
COMPLETE SET (96)	17000.00	7600.00	2100.00
COMMON CARD (1-48)	50.00	22.00	6.25
COMMON CARD (49-72)	75.00	34.00	9.50
COMMON CARD (73-96)	175.00	80.00	22.00
WRAPPER (1-CENT, WHITE)	125.00	55.00	15.50
WRAPPER (1-CENT, CLEAR)	125.00	55.00	15.50

Card	EX-MT	VG-E	GOOD
☐ 1 Jimmy Foxx	750.00	350.00	95.00
☐ 2 Mickey Cochrane	175.00	80.00	22.00
☐ 3 Charlie Grimm	60.00	27.00	7.50
☐ 4 Woody English	50.00	22.00	6.25
☐ 5 Ed Brandt	50.00	22.00	6.25
☐ 6 Dizzy Dean	600.00	275.00	75.00
☐ 7 Leo Durocher	150.00	70.00	19.00
☐ 8 Tony Piet	50.00	22.00	6.25
☐ 9 Ben Chapman	60.00	27.00	7.50
☐ 10 Chuck Klein	150.00	70.00	19.00
☐ 11 Paul Waner	125.00	55.00	15.50
☐ 12 Carl Hubbell	165.00	75.00	21.00
☐ 13 Frank Frisch	150.00	70.00	19.00
☐ 14 Willie Kamm	50.00	22.00	6.25
☐ 15 Alvin Crowder	50.00	22.00	6.25
☐ 16 Joe Kuhel	50.00	22.00	6.25
☐ 17 Hugh Critz	50.00	22.00	6.25
☐ 18 Heinie Manush	100.00	45.00	12.50
☐ 19 Lefty Grove	300.00	135.00	38.00
☐ 20 Frank Hogan	50.00	22.00	6.25
☐ 21 Bill Terry	200.00	90.00	25.00
☐ 22 Arky Vaughan	100.00	45.00	12.50
☐ 23 Charlie Gehringer	200.00	90.00	25.00
☐ 24 Ray Benge	50.00	22.00	6.25
☐ 25 Roger Cramer	60.00	27.00	7.50
☐ 26 Gerald Walker	50.00	22.00	6.25
☐ 27 Luke Appling	150.00	70.00	19.00
☐ 28 Ed Coleman	50.00	22.00	6.25
☐ 29 Larry French	50.00	22.00	6.25
☐ 30 Julius Solters	50.00	22.00	6.25
☐ 31 Buck Jordan	50.00	22.00	6.25
☐ 32 Blondy Ryan	50.00	22.00	6.25
☐ 33 Frank Hurst	50.00	22.00	6.25
☐ 34 Chick Hafey	100.00	45.00	12.50
☐ 35 Ernie Lombardi	125.00	55.00	15.50
☐ 36 Walter Betts	50.00	22.00	6.25
☐ 37 Lou Gehrig	2700.00	1200.00	350.00
☐ 38 Oral Hildebrand	50.00	22.00	6.25
☐ 39 Fred Walker	50.00	22.00	6.25
☐ 40 John Stone	50.00	22.00	6.25
☐ 41 George Earnshaw	50.00	22.00	6.25
☐ 42 John Allen	50.00	22.00	6.25
☐ 43 Dick Porter	50.00	22.00	6.25
☐ 44 Tom Bridges	60.00	27.00	7.50
☐ 45 Oscar Melillo	50.00	22.00	6.25
☐ 46 Joe Stripp	50.00	22.00	6.25
☐ 47 John Frederick	50.00	22.00	6.25
☐ 48 Tex Carleton	50.00	22.00	6.25
☐ 49 Sam Leslie	75.00	34.00	9.50
☐ 50 Walter Beck	75.00	34.00	9.50
☐ 51 Rip Collins	75.00	34.00	9.50
☐ 52 Herman Bell	75.00	34.00	9.50
☐ 53 George Watkins	75.00	34.00	9.50
☐ 54 Wesley Schulmerich	75.00	34.00	9.50
☐ 55 Ed Holley	75.00	34.00	9.50
☐ 56 Mark Koenig	90.00	40.00	11.00
☐ 57 Bill Swift	75.00	34.00	9.50
☐ 58 Earl Grace	75.00	34.00	9.50
☐ 59 Joe Mowry	75.00	34.00	9.50
☐ 60 Lynn Nelson	75.00	34.00	9.50
☐ 61 Lou Gehrig	2700.00	1200.00	350.00
☐ 62 Hank Greenberg	375.00	170.00	47.50
☐ 63 Minter Hayes	75.00	34.00	9.50
☐ 64 Frank Grube	75.00	34.00	9.50
☐ 65 Cliff Bolton	75.00	34.00	9.50
☐ 66 Mel Harder	100.00	45.00	12.50
☐ 67 Bob Weiland	75.00	34.00	9.50
☐ 68 Bob Johnson	90.00	40.00	11.00
☐ 69 John Marcum	75.00	34.00	9.50
☐ 70 Pete Fox	75.00	34.00	9.50
☐ 71 Lyle Tinning	75.00	34.00	9.50
☐ 72 Arndt Jorgens	75.00	34.00	9.50
☐ 73 Ed Wells	175.00	80.00	22.00
☐ 74 Bob Boken	175.00	80.00	22.00
☐ 75 Bill Werber	175.00	80.00	22.00
☐ 76 Hal Trosky	200.00	90.00	25.00
☐ 77 Joe Vosmik	175.00	80.00	22.00
☐ 78 Pinky Higgins	200.00	90.00	25.00
☐ 79 Ed Durham	175.00	80.00	22.00
☐ 80 Marty McManus CK	175.00	80.00	22.00
☐ 81 Bob Brown CK	175.00	80.00	22.00
☐ 82 Bill Hallahan CK	175.00	80.00	22.00
☐ 83 Jim Mooney CK	175.00	80.00	22.00
☐ 84 Paul Derringer CK	225.00	100.00	28.00
☐ 85 Adam Comorosky CK	175.00	80.00	22.00
☐ 86 Lloyd Johnson CK	175.00	80.00	22.00
☐ 87 George Darrow CK	175.00	80.00	22.00
☐ 88 Homer Peel CK	175.00	80.00	22.00
☐ 89 Linus Frey CK	175.00	80.00	22.00
☐ 90 Ki-Ki Cuyler CK	350.00	160.00	45.00
☐ 91 Dolph Camilli CK	200.00	90.00	25.00
☐ 92 Steve Larkin	175.00	80.00	22.00
☐ 93 Fred Ostermueller	175.00	80.00	22.00
☐ 94 Red Rolfe	200.00	90.00	25.00
☐ 95 Myril Hoag	175.00	80.00	22.00
☐ 96 James DeShong	300.00	135.00	38.00

1934 Goudey Canadian V354

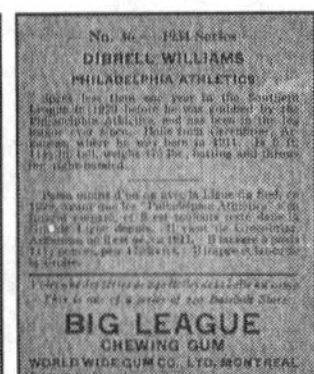

The cards in this 96-card set measure approximately 2 3/8" by 2 7/8". The 1934 Canadian Goudey set was issued by World Wide Gum Company. Cards 1 to 48 have the same format as the 1933 American Goudey issue while cards 49 to 96 have the same format as the 1934 American Goudey issue. Cards numbers 49 to 96 all have the "Lou Gehrig Says" endorsement on the front of the cards. No Chuck Klein endorsement exists as it does in the 1934 American issue. The fronts feature white-bordered color player drawings. The words "Big League Chewing Gum" are printed in white lettering within a red stripe near the bottom. The green ink backs are found printed in English only, or in French and English (the latter are slightly harder to find and are valued at a 25 percent premium over the prices listed below). The catalog designation for this set is V354.

	EX-MT	VG-E	GOOD
COMPLETE SET (96)	13000.00	5800.00	1600.00
COMMON CARD (1-96)	60.00	27.00	7.50

Card	EX-MT	VG-E	GOOD
☐ 1 Rogers Hornsby	600.00	275.00	75.00
☐ 2 Eddie Morgan	60.00	27.00	7.50
☐ 3 Val Picinich	60.00	27.00	7.50
☐ 4 Rabbit Maranville	125.00	55.00	15.50
☐ 5 Flint Rhem	60.00	27.00	7.50
☐ 6 Jim Elliott	60.00	27.00	7.50
☐ 7 Fred(Red) Lucas	60.00	27.00	7.50
☐ 8 Fred Marberry	60.00	27.00	7.50
☐ 9 Clifton Heathcote	60.00	27.00	7.50
☐ 10 Bernie Friberg	60.00	27.00	7.50
☐ 11 Woody English	60.00	27.00	7.50
☐ 12 Carl Reynolds	60.00	27.00	7.50
☐ 13 Ray Benge	60.00	27.00	7.50
☐ 14 Ben Cantwell	60.00	27.00	7.50
☐ 15 Bump Hadley	60.00	27.00	7.50
☐ 16 Herb Pennock	125.00	55.00	15.50
☐ 17 Fred Lindstrom	125.00	55.00	15.50
☐ 18 Edgar(Sam) Rice	125.00	55.00	15.50
☐ 19 Fred Frankhouse	60.00	27.00	7.50
☐ 20 Fred Fitzsimmons	75.00	34.00	9.50
☐ 21 Earle Combs	125.00	55.00	15.50
☐ 22 George Uhle	60.00	27.00	7.50
☐ 23 Richard Coffman	60.00	27.00	7.50
☐ 24 Travis Jackson	125.00	55.00	15.50
☐ 25 Robert J. Burke	60.00	27.00	7.50
☐ 26 Randy Moore	60.00	27.00	7.50
☐ 27 Heinie Sand	60.00	27.00	7.50
☐ 28 George (Babe) Ruth	5000.00	2200.00	600.00
☐ 29 Tris Speaker	300.00	135.00	38.00
☐ 30 Perce(Pat) Malone	60.00	27.00	7.50
☐ 31 Sam Jones	75.00	34.00	9.50
☐ 32 Eppa Rixey	125.00	55.00	15.50
☐ 33 Floyd (Pete) Scott	60.00	27.00	7.50
☐ 34 Pete Jablonowski	60.00	27.00	7.50
☐ 35 Clyde Manion	60.00	27.00	7.50
☐ 36 Dib Williams	60.00	27.00	7.50
☐ 37 Glenn Spencer	60.00	27.00	7.50
☐ 38 Ray Kremer	60.00	27.00	7.50
☐ 39 Phil Todt	60.00	27.00	7.50
☐ 40 Russell Rollings	60.00	27.00	7.50
☐ 41 Earl Clark	60.00	27.00	7.50
☐ 42 Jess Petty	60.00	27.00	7.50
☐ 43 Frank O'Rourke	60.00	27.00	7.50
☐ 44 Jesse Haines	125.00	55.00	15.50
☐ 45 Horace Lisenbee	60.00	27.00	7.50
☐ 46 Owen Carroll	60.00	27.00	7.50
☐ 47 Tom Zachary	75.00	34.00	9.50
☐ 48 Charlie(Red) Ruffing	150.00	70.00	19.00
☐ 49 Ray Benge	60.00	27.00	7.50
☐ 50 Woody English	60.00	27.00	7.50
☐ 51 Ben Chapman	75.00	34.00	9.50
☐ 52 Joe Kuhel	60.00	27.00	7.50
☐ 53 Bill Terry	200.00	90.00	25.00
☐ 54 Robert(Lefty) Grove	300.00	135.00	38.00
☐ 55 Jerome(Dizzy) Dean	750.00	350.00	95.00
☐ 56 Chuck Klein	150.00	70.00	19.00
☐ 57 Charley Gehringer	200.00	90.00	25.00
☐ 58 Jimmie Foxx	400.00	180.00	50.00
☐ 59 Mickey Cochrane	200.00	90.00	25.00
☐ 60 Willie Kamm	60.00	27.00	7.50
☐ 61 Charlie Grimm	75.00	34.00	9.50
☐ 62 Ed Brandt	60.00	27.00	7.50
☐ 63 Tony Piet	60.00	27.00	7.50
☐ 64 Frank Frisch	150.00	70.00	19.00
☐ 65 Alvin Crowder	60.00	27.00	7.50
☐ 66 Frank Hogan	60.00	27.00	7.50
☐ 67 Paul Waner	150.00	70.00	19.00
☐ 68 Heinie Manush	125.00	55.00	15.50
☐ 69 Leo Durocher	150.00	70.00	19.00
☐ 70 Arky Vaughan	125.00	55.00	15.50
☐ 71 Carl Hubbell	200.00	90.00	25.00
☐ 72 Hugh Critz	60.00	27.00	7.50
☐ 73 John(Blondy) Ryan	60.00	27.00	7.50
☐ 74 Doc Cramer	75.00	34.00	9.50
☐ 75 Baxter Jordan	60.00	27.00	7.50
☐ 76 Ed Coleman	60.00	27.00	7.50
☐ 77 Julius(Moose) Solters	60.00	27.00	7.50
☐ 78 Chick Hafey	125.00	55.00	15.50
☐ 79 Larry French	60.00	27.00	7.50
☐ 80 Frank(Don) Hurst	60.00	27.00	7.50
☐ 81 Gerald Walker	60.00	27.00	7.50
☐ 82 Ernie Lombardi	150.00	70.00	19.00
☐ 83 Walter(Huck) Betts	60.00	27.00	7.50
☐ 84 Luke Appling	150.00	70.00	19.00
☐ 85 John Frederick	60.00	27.00	7.50
☐ 86 Fred(Dixie) Walker	75.00	34.00	9.50
☐ 87 Tom Bridges	75.00	34.00	9.50
☐ 88 Dick Porter	60.00	27.00	7.50
☐ 89 John Stone	60.00	27.00	7.50
☐ 90 James(Tex) Carleton	60.00	27.00	7.50
☐ 91 Joe Stripp	60.00	27.00	7.50
☐ 92 Lou Gehrig	3500.00	1600.00	450.00
☐ 93 George Earnshaw	75.00	34.00	9.50
☐ 94 Oscar Melillo	60.00	27.00	7.50
☐ 95 Oral Hildebrand	60.00	27.00	7.50
☐ 96 John Allen	75.00	34.00	9.50

1934 Goudey Premiums R309-1

The most ambitious premium issue of the Goudey Gum Company was the R309-1 set of 1934. Printed on heavy cardboard, the black and white picture was embellished with a gold and frame-like border and a back stand. Each of these thick cards measures approximately 5 1/2" by 8 15/16". The Babe Ruth card seems to be more common than the other cards in this short set.

	EX-MT	VG-E	GOOD
COMPLETE SET (4)	1200.00	550.00	150.00
COMMON CARD (1-4)	250.00	110.00	31.00

Card	EX-MT	VG-E	GOOD
☐ 1 American League All-Stars of 1933	250.00	110.00	31.00
☐ 2 National League All-Stars of 1933	250.00	110.00	31.00
☐ 3 World's Champions of 1933 (New York Giants)	300.00	135.00	38.00
☐ 4 George Herman (Babe) Ruth	600.00	275.00	75.00

1935 Goudey Premiums R309-2

The 16 cards in the R309-2 Goudey Premium set are unnumbered, glossy black and white photos on thin paper stock. Teams (1-3) and individual players (4-16) are featured in this relatively scarce premium set from 1935. The ballplayer is identified by his name rendered in longhand in the "wide pen" style of later Goudey issues. This written name is not a facsimile autograph. Each card measures approximately 5 1/2" by 9".

	EX-MT	VG-E	GOOD
COMPLETE SET (16)	1500.00	700.00	190.00
COMMON TEAM (1-3)	75.00	34.00	9.50
COMMON CARD (4-16)	75.00	34.00	9.50

	EX-MT	VG-E	GOOD
☐ 1 Boston Red Sox	75.00	34.00	9.50
☐ 2 Cleveland Indians	75.00	34.00	9.50
☐ 3 Washington Senators	75.00	34.00	9.50
☐ 4 Elden Auker	75.00	34.00	9.50
☐ 5 Johnny Babich	75.00	34.00	9.50
☐ 6 Dick Bartell	75.00	34.00	9.50
☐ 7 Lester R. Bell	75.00	34.00	9.50
☐ 8 Wally Berger	75.00	34.00	9.50
☐ 9 Mickey Cochrane	175.00	80.00	22.00
☐ 10 Ervin Fox	100.00	45.00	12.50
Leon "Goose" Goslin			
Gerald Walker			
☐ 11 Vernon Gomez	125.00	55.00	15.50
☐ 12 Hank Greenberg	200.00	90.00	25.00
☐ 13 Oscar Melillo	75.00	34.00	9.50
☐ 14 Mel Ott	200.00	90.00	25.00
☐ 15 Schoolboy Rowe	75.00	34.00	9.50
☐ 16 Vito Tamulis	75.00	34.00	9.50

1935 Goudey Puzzle R321

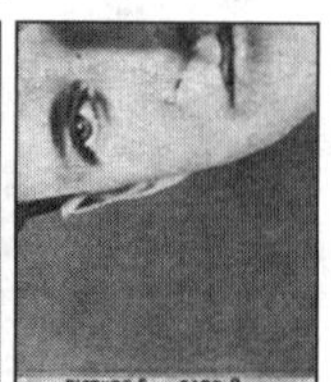

The cards in this 36-card set (the number of different front pictures) measure approximately 2 3/8" by 2 7/8". The 1935 Goudey set is sometimes called the Goudey Puzzle Set, or the Goudey 4-in-1's. There are 36 different card fronts but 114 different front/back combinations. The card number in the checklist refers to the back puzzle number, as the backs can be arranged to form a puzzle picturing a player or team. To avoid the confusion caused by two different fronts having the same back number, the rarer cards have been arbitrarily given a "1" prefix. The scarcer puzzle cards are hence all listed at the numerical end of the list below, i.e. rare puzzle 1 is listed as number 11, rare puzzle 2 is listed as 12, etc. The BLUE in the checklist refers to a card with a blue border, as most cards have a red border. The set price below includes all the cards listed. The following is the list of the puzzle back pictures: 1) Detroit Tigers; 2) Chuck Klein; 3) Frankie Frisch; 4) Mickey Cochrane; 5) Joe Cronin; 6) Jimmy Foxx; 7) Al Simmons; 8) Cleveland Indians; and 9) Washington Senators.

	EX-MT	VG-E	GOOD
COMPLETE SET (114)	13500.00	6100.00	1700.00
COMMON CARDS (1-9)	50.00	22.00	6.25
COMMON CARDS (11-17)	75.00	34.00	9.50
WRAPPER (1-CENT)	200.00	90.00	25.00

	EX-MT	VG-E	GOOD
☐ 1A Frank Frisch	150.00	70.00	19.00
Dizzy Dean			
Ernie Orsatti			
Tex Carleton			
☐ 1B Roy Mahaffey	125.00	55.00	15.50
Jimmie Foxx			
Dib Williams			
Pinky Higgins			
☐ 1C Heinie Manush	60.00	27.00	7.50
Lyn Lary			
Monte Weaver			
Bump Hadley			
☐ 1D Mickey Cochrane	125.00	55.00	15.50
Charlie Gehringer			
Tommy Bridges			
Billy Rogell			
☐ 1E Paul Waner	100.00	45.00	12.50
Guy Bush			
Waite Hoyt			
Lloyd Waner			
☐ 1F Burleigh Grimes	100.00	45.00	12.50
Chuck Klein			
Kiki Cuyler			
Woody English			
☐ 1G Sam Leslie	50.00	22.00	6.25
Lonnie Frey			
Joe Stripp			
Watson Clark			
☐ 1H Tony Piet	60.00	27.00	7.50
Adam Comorosky			
Jim Bottomley			
Sparky Adams			
☐ 1I George Earnshaw	60.00	27.00	7.50
Jimmie Dykes			
Luke Sewell			
Luke Appling			
☐ 1J Babe Ruth	1000.00	450.00	125.00
Marty McManus			
Eddie Brandt			
Rabbit Maranville			
☐ 1K Bill Terry	100.00	45.00	12.50
Hal Schumacher			
Gus Mancuso			
Travis Jackson			
☐ 1L Willie Kamm	60.00	27.00	7.50
Oral Hildebrand			
Earl Averill			
Hal Trosky			
☐ 2A Frank Frisch	150.00	70.00	19.00
Dizzy Dean			
Ernie Orsatti			
Tex Carleton			
☐ 2B Roy Mahaffey	125.00	55.00	15.50
Jimmie Foxx			
Dib Williams			
Pinky Higgins			
☐ 2C Heinie Manush	60.00	27.00	7.50
Lyn Lary			
Monte Weaver			
Bump Hadley			
☐ 2D Mickey Cochrane	125.00	55.00	15.50
Charlie Gehringer			
Tommy Bridges			
Billy Rogell			
☐ 2E Willie Kamm	60.00	27.00	7.50
Oral Hildebrand			
Earl Averill			
Hal Trosky			
☐ 2F George Earnshaw	60.00	27.00	7.50
Jimmie Dykes			
Luke Sewell			
Luke Appling			
☐ 3A Babe Ruth	1000.00	450.00	125.00
Marty McManus			
Eddie Brandt			
Rabbit Maranville			
☐ 3B Bill Terry	100.00	45.00	12.50
Hal Schumacher			
Gus Mancuso			
Travis Jackson			
☐ 3C Paul Waner	100.00	45.00	12.50
Guy Bush			
Waite Hoyt			
Lloyd Waner			
☐ 3D Burleigh Grimes	100.00	45.00	12.50
Chuck Klein			
Kiki Cuyler			
Woody English			
☐ 3E Sam Leslie	50.00	22.00	6.25
Lonnie Frey			
Joe Stripp			
Watson Clark			
☐ 3F Tony Piet	60.00	27.00	7.50
Adam Comorosky			
Jim Bottomley			
Sparky Adams			
☐ 4A Hugh Critz BLUE	100.00	45.00	12.50
Dick Bartell			
Mel Ott			
Gus Mancuso			
☐ 4B Pie Traynor BLUE	60.00	27.00	7.50
Red Lucas			
Tom Thevenow			
Glenn Wright			
☐ 4C Charlie Berry BLUE	60.00	27.00	7.50
Bobby Burke			
Red Kress			
Dazzy Vance			
☐ 4D Red Ruffing BLUE	150.00	70.00	19.00
Pat Malone			
Tony Lazzeri			
Bill Dickey			
☐ 4E Randy Moore BLUE	50.00	22.00	6.25
Shanty Hogan			
Fred Frankhouse			
Eddie Brandt			
☐ 4F Pepper Martin BLUE	50.00	22.00	6.25
Bob O'Farrell			
Sam Byrd			
Danny MacFayden			
☐ 5A Muddy Ruel	100.00	45.00	12.50
Al Simmons			
Willie Kamm			
Mickey Cochrane			
☐ 5B Willis Hudlin	60.00	27.00	7.50
George Myatt			
Adam Comorosky			
Jim Bottomley			
☐ 5C Paul Waner	100.00	45.00	12.50
Guy Bush			
Waite Hoyt			
Lloyd Waner			
☐ 5D Sam West	50.00	22.00	6.25
Oscar Melillo			
George Blaeholder			
Dick Coffman			
☐ 5E Sam Leslie	50.00	22.00	6.25
Lonnie Frey			
Joe Stripp			
Watson Clark			
☐ 5F Heine Schuble	60.00	27.00	7.50
Fred Marberry			
Goose Goslin			
General Crowder			
☐ 6A Muddy Ruel	100.00	45.00	12.50
Al Simmons			
Willie Kamm			
Mickey Cochrane			
☐ 6B Willis Hudlin	60.00	27.00	7.50
George Myatt			
Adam Comorosky			
Jim Bottomley			
☐ 6C Jimmy Wilson	50.00	22.00	6.25
Ethan Allen			
Bubba Jonnard			
Fred Brickell			
☐ 6D Sam West	50.00	22.00	6.25
Oscar Melillo			
George Blaeholder			
Dick Coffman			
☐ 6E Joe Cronin	60.00	27.00	7.50
Carl Reynolds			
Max Bishop			
Chalmer Cissell			
☐ 6F Heine Schuble	60.00	27.00	7.50
Fred Marberry			
Goose Goslin			
General Crowder			
☐ 7A Hugh Critz BLUE	100.00	45.00	12.50
Dick Bartell			
Mel Ott			
Gus Mancuso			
☐ 7B Pie Traynor BLUE	60.00	27.00	7.50
Red Lucas			
Tom Thevenow			
Glenn Wright			
☐ 7C Charlie Berry BLUE	60.00	27.00	7.50
Bobby Burke			
Red Kress			
Dazzy Vance			
☐ 7D Red Ruffing BLUE	150.00	70.00	19.00
Pat Malone			
Tom Lazzeri			
Bill Dickey			
☐ 7E Randy Moore BLUE	50.00	22.00	6.25
Shanty Hogan			
Fred Frankhouse			
Eddie Brandt			
☐ 7F Pepper Martin BLUE	50.00	22.00	6.25
Bob O'Farrell			
Sam Byrd			
Danny MacFayden			
☐ 8A Mark Koenig	50.00	22.00	6.25
Fred Fitzsimmons			
Ray Benge			
Tom Zachary			
☐ 8B Minter Hayes	60.00	27.00	7.50
Ted Lyons			
Mule Haas			
Zeke Bonura			
☐ 8C Jack Burns	50.00	22.00	6.25
Rollie Hemsley			
Frank Grube			
Bob Weiland			
☐ 8D F.Campbell	50.00	22.00	6.25
Billy Meyers			
Ival Goodman			
Alex Kampouris			
☐ 8E Jimmy DeShong	50.00	22.00	6.25
Johnny Allen			
Red Rolfe			
Dixie Walker			
☐ 8F Pete Fox	100.00	45.00	12.50
Hank Greenberg			
Gee Walker			
Schoolboy Rowe			
☐ 8G Billy Werber	60.00	27.00	7.50
Rick Ferrell			
Wes Ferrell			
Fritz Ostermueller			
☐ 8H Joe Kuhel	50.00	22.00	6.25
Earl Whitehill			
Buddy Myer			
John Stone			
☐ 8I Joe Vosmik	50.00	22.00	6.25
Bill Knickerbocker			
Mel Harder			
Lefty Stewart			
☐ 8J Bob Johnson	50.00	22.00	6.25
Ed Coleman			
Johnny Marcum			
Doc Cramer			
☐ 8K Babe Herman	60.00	27.00	7.50
Gus Suhr			
Tom Padden			
Cy Blanton			
☐ 8L Al Spohrer	50.00	22.00	6.25
Flint Rhem			
Ben Cantwell			
Larry Benton			
☐ 8M Mark Koenig	50.00	22.00	6.25
Fred Fitzsimmons			
Ray Benge			
Tom Zachary			
☐ 9B Minter Hayes	60.00	27.00	7.50
Ted Lyons			
Mule Haas			
Zeke Bonura			
☐ 9C Jack Burns	50.00	22.00	6.25
Rollie Hemsley			
Frank Grube			
Bob Weiland			
☐ 9D Bruce Campbell	50.00	22.00	6.25
Billy Meyers			
Ival Goodman			
Alex Kampouris			
☐ 9E Jimmy DeShong	50.00	22.00	6.25
Johnny Allen			
Red Rolfe			
Fred Walker			
☐ 9F Pete Fox	100.00	45.00	12.50
Hank Greenberg			
Gee Walker			
Schoolboy Rowe			
☐ 9G Billy Werber	60.00	27.00	7.50
Rick Ferrell			
Wes Ferrell			
F.Ostermueller			
☐ 9H Joe Kuhel	50.00	22.00	6.25
Earl Whitehill			
Buddy Myer			
John Stone			
☐ 9I Joe Vosmik	50.00	22.00	6.25
Bill Knickerbocker			
Mel Harder			
Lefty Stewart			
☐ 9J Bob Johnson	50.00	22.00	6.25
Ed Coleman			
Johnny Marcum			
Doc Cramer			
☐ 9K Babe Herman	60.00	27.00	7.50
Gus Suhr			
Tom Padden			
Cy Blanton			
☐ 9L Al Spohrer	50.00	22.00	6.25
Flint Rhem			
Ben Cantwell			
Larry Benton			
☐ 11E Jimmy Wilson	75.00	34.00	9.50
Johnny Allen			
Bubba Jonnard			
Fred Brickell			
☐ 11F Sam West	75.00	34.00	9.50
Oscar Melillo			
George Blaeholder			
Dick Coffman			
☐ 11G Joe Cronin	90.00	40.00	11.00
Carl Reynolds			
Max Bishop			
Chalmer Cissell			
☐ 11H Heine Schuble	90.00	40.00	11.00
Fred Marberry			
Goose Goslin			
General Crowder			
☐ 11J Muddy Ruel	150.00	70.00	19.00
Al Simmons			
Willie Kamm			
Mickey Cochrane			
☐ 11K Willis Hudlin	90.00	40.00	11.00
George Myatt			
Adam Comorosky			
Jim Bottomley			
☐ 12A Hugh Critz BLUE	150.00	70.00	19.00
Dick Bartell			
Mel Ott			
Gus Mancuso			
☐ 12B Pie Traynor BLUE	90.00	40.00	11.00
Red Lucas			
Tommy Thevenow			
Glenn Wright			
☐ 12C Charlie Berry BLUE	90.00	40.00	11.00
Bobby Burke			
Red Kress			
Dazzy Vance			
☐ 12D Red Ruffing BLUE	225.00	100.00	28.00
Pat Malone			
Tony Lazzeri			
Bill Dickey			
☐ 12E Randy Moore BLUE	75.00	34.00	9.50
Shanty Hogan			
Fred Frankhouse			
Eddie Brandt			
☐ 12F Pepper Martin BLUE	75.00	34.00	9.50
Bob O'Farrell			
Sam Byrd			
Danny MacFayden			
☐ 13A Muddy Ruel	150.00	70.00	19.00

Card	EX-MT	VG-E	GOOD
Al Simmons			
Willie Kamm			
Mickey Cochrane			
☐ 13B Willis Hudlin	90.00	40.00	11.00
George Myatt			
Adam Comorosky			
Jim Bottomley			
☐ 13C Jimmy Wilson	75.00	34.00	9.50
Johnny Allen			
Bubba Jonnard			
Fred Brickell			
☐ 13D Sam West	75.00	34.00	9.50
Oscar Melillo			
George Blaeholder			
Dick Coffman			
☐ 13E Joe Cronin	90.00	40.00	11.00
Carl Reynolds			
Max Bishop			
Chalmer Cissell			
☐ 13F Heine Schuble	90.00	40.00	11.00
Fred Marberry			
Goose Goslin			
General Crowder			
☐ 14A Babe Ruth	1500.00	700.00	190.00
Marty McManus			
Eddie Brandt			
Rabbit Maranville			
☐ 14B Bill Terry	150.00	70.00	19.00
Hal Schumacher			
Gus Mancuso			
Travis Jackson			
☐ 14C Paul Waner	150.00	70.00	19.00
Guy Bush			
Waite Hoyt			
Lloyd Waner			
☐ 14D Burleigh Grimes	150.00	70.00	19.00
Chuck Klein			
Kiki Cuyler			
Woody English			
☐ 14E Sam Leslie	75.00	34.00	9.50
Lonnie Frey			
Joe Stripp			
Watson Clark			
☐ 14F Tony Piet	90.00	40.00	11.00
Adam Comorosky			
Jim Bottomley			
Sparky Adams			
☐ 15A Babe Ruth	1500.00	700.00	190.00
Marty McManus			
Eddie Brandt			
Rabbit Maranville			
☐ 15B Bill Terry	150.00	70.00	19.00
Hal Schumacher			
Gus Mancuso			
Travis Jackson			
☐ 15C Jimmy Wilson	75.00	34.00	9.50
Johnny Allen			
Bubba Jonnard			
Fred Brickell			
☐ 15D Burleigh Grimes	150.00	70.00	19.00
Chuck Klein			
Kiki Cuyler			
Woody English			
☐ 15E Joe Cronin	90.00	40.00	11.00
Carl Reynolds			
Max Bishop			
Chalmer Cissell			
☐ 15F Tony Piet	90.00	40.00	11.00
Adam Comorosky			
Jim Bottomley			
Sparky Adams			
☐ 16A Frank Frisch	225.00	100.00	28.00
Dizzy Dean			
Ernie Orsatti			
Tex Carleton			
☐ 16B Roy Mahaffey	175.00	80.00	22.00
Jimmie Foxx			
Dib Williams			
Pinky Higgins			
☐ 16C Heinie Manush	90.00	40.00	11.00
Lyn Lary			
Monte Weaver			
Bump Hadley			
☐ 16D Mickey Cochrane	175.00	80.00	22.00
Charlie Gehringer			
Tom Bridges			
Billy Rogell			
☐ 16E Willie Kamm	90.00	40.00	11.00
Oral Hildebrand			
Earl Averill			
Hal Trosky			
☐ 16F George Earnshaw	90.00	40.00	11.00
Jimmie Dykes			
Luke Sewell			
Luke Appling			
☐ 17A Frank Frisch	225.00	100.00	28.00
Dizzy Dean			
Ernie Orsatti			
Tex Carleton			
☐ 17B Roy Mahaffey	175.00	80.00	22.00
Jimmie Foxx			
Dib Williams			
Pinky Higgins			
☐ 17C Heinie Manush	90.00	40.00	11.00
Lyn Lary			
Monte Weaver			
Bump Hadley			
☐ 17D Mickey Cochrane	175.00	80.00	22.00
Charlie Gehringer			
Tom Bridges			
Billy Rogell			
☐ 17E Willie Kamm	90.00	40.00	11.00
Oral Hildebrand			
Earl Averill			
Hal Trosky			
☐ 17F George Earnshaw	90.00	40.00	11.00
Jimmie Dykes			
Luke Sewell			
Luke Appling			

1936 Goudey B/W R322

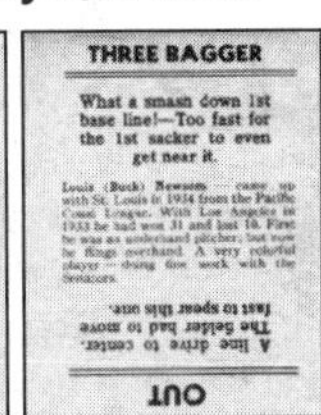

The cards in this 25-card black and white set measure approximately 2 3/8" by 2 7/8". In contrast to the color artwork of its previous sets, the 1936 Goudey set contained a simple black and white player photograph. A facsimile autograph appeared within the picture area. Each card was issued with a number of different "game situation" backs, and there may be as many as 200 different front/back combinations. This unnumbered set is checklisted and numbered below in alphabetical order for convenience.

	EX-MT	VG-E	GOOD
COMPLETE SET (25)	2000.00	900.00	250.00
COMMON CARD (1-25)	45.00	20.00	5.50
WRAPPER (1-CENT)	200.00	90.00	25.00
☐ 1 Wally Berger	60.00	27.00	7.50
☐ 2 Zeke Bonura	45.00	20.00	5.50
☐ 3 Frenchy Bordagaray	45.00	20.00	5.50
☐ 4 Bill Brubaker	45.00	20.00	5.50
☐ 5 Dolph Camilli	50.00	22.00	6.25
☐ 6 Clyde Castleman	45.00	20.00	5.50
☐ 7 Mickey Cochrane	200.00	90.00	25.00
☐ 8 Joe Coscarart	45.00	20.00	5.50
☐ 9 Frank Crosetti	75.00	34.00	9.50
☐ 10 Kiki Cuyler	90.00	40.00	11.00
☐ 11 Paul Derringer	50.00	22.00	6.25
☐ 12 Jimmy Dykes	50.00	22.00	6.25
☐ 13 Rick Ferrell	90.00	40.00	11.00
☐ 14 Lefty Gomez	175.00	80.00	22.00
☐ 15 Hank Greenberg	250.00	110.00	31.00
☐ 16 Bucky Harris	90.00	40.00	11.00
☐ 17 Rollie Hemsley	45.00	20.00	5.50
☐ 18 Pinky Higgins	50.00	22.00	6.25
☐ 19 Oral Hildebrand	45.00	20.00	5.50
☐ 20 Chuck Klein	125.00	55.00	15.50
☐ 21 Pepper Martin	75.00	34.00	9.50
☐ 22 Bobo Newsom	50.00	22.00	6.25
☐ 23 Joe Vosmik	45.00	20.00	5.50
☐ 24 Paul Waner	125.00	55.00	15.50
☐ 25 Bill Werber	45.00	20.00	5.50

1936 Goudey Wide Pens R314

The 1936 Wide Pen Premiums were issued by the Goudey Gum Company. Each card measures approximately 3 1/4" by 5 1/2". These black and white unnumbered cards could be obtained directly from a retail outlet rather than through the mail only. Some of the cards are horizontally (HOR) oriented and are so indicated. Some of the cards are portrait poses and are indicated POR in the checklist below. Four types of this card exist. Type A contains cards, mainly individual players, with "Litho USA" in the bottom border. Type B does not have the "Litho USA" marking and comes both with and without a border. Type C cards are American players on creamy paper stock with medium thickness signatures and no "Litho USA" markings. Type D consists of Canadian players from Montreal (M) or Toronto (T) on creamy stock paper with non-glossy photos. The catalog designation for this set is R314.

	EX-MT	VG-E	GOOD
COMPLETE SET (208)	7000.00	3200.00	900.00
COMMON CARD (A1-A119)	15.00	6.75	1.85
COMMON CARD (B1-B25)	40.00	18.00	5.00
COMMON CARD (C1-C25)	40.00	18.00	5.00
COMMON CARD (D1-D39)	60.00	27.00	7.50
☐ A1 Ethan Allen	20.00	9.00	2.50
☐ A2 Earl Averill	30.00	13.50	3.70
☐ A3 Dick Bartell HOR	15.00	6.75	1.85
☐ A4 Dick Bartell POR	20.00	9.00	2.50
☐ A5 Walter Berger	20.00	9.00	2.50
☐ A6 Geo. Blaeholder	15.00	6.75	1.85
☐ A7 Cy Blanton POR	15.00	6.75	1.85
☐ A8 Cliff Bolton	15.00	6.75	1.85
☐ A9 Stan Bordagaray	15.00	6.75	1.85
☐ A10 Tommy Bridges POR	20.00	9.00	2.50
☐ A11 Bill Brubaker	15.00	6.75	1.85
☐ A12 Sam Byrd	15.00	6.75	1.85
☐ A13 Dolph Camilli	20.00	9.00	2.50
☐ A14 Clydell Castleman (throwing)	15.00	6.75	1.85
☐ A15 Clydell Castleman POR	15.00	6.75	1.85
☐ A16 Phil Cavarretta HOR	30.00	13.50	3.70
☐ A17 Mickey Cochrane	25.00	11.00	3.10
☐ A18 Earle Combs HOR	30.00	13.50	3.70
☐ A19 Joe Coscarart	15.00	6.75	1.85
☐ A20 Joe Cronin	30.00	13.50	3.70
☐ A21 Frank Crosetti	30.00	13.50	3.70
☐ A22 Tony Cuccinello	15.00	6.75	1.85
☐ A23 KiKi Cuyler	30.00	13.50	3.70
☐ A24 Curt Davis	15.00	6.75	1.85
☐ A25 Virgil Davis HOR	15.00	6.75	1.85
☐ A26 Paul Derringer	20.00	9.00	2.50
☐ A27 Bill Dickey	25.00	11.00	3.10
☐ A28 Jimmy Dykes kneeling	20.00	9.00	2.50
☐ A29 Rick Ferrell HOR	30.00	13.50	3.70
☐ A30 Wes Ferrell	30.00	13.50	3.70
☐ A31 Lou Finney	15.00	6.75	1.85
☐ A32 Ervin "Pete" Fox POR	15.00	6.75	1.85
☐ A33 Tony Freitas	15.00	6.75	1.85
☐ A34 Lonnie Frey	15.00	6.75	1.85
☐ A35 Frankie Frisch	40.00	18.00	5.00
☐ A36 Augie Galan POR	15.00	6.75	1.85
☐ A37 Charles Gehringer	40.00	18.00	5.00
☐ A38 Charlie Gelbert	15.00	6.75	1.85
☐ A39 Lefty Gomez	40.00	18.00	5.00
☐ A40 Goose Goslin	30.00	13.50	3.70
☐ A41 Earl Grace	15.00	6.75	1.85
☐ A42 Hank Greenberg POR	40.00	18.00	5.00
☐ A43 Mule Haas	15.00	6.75	1.85
☐ A44 Odell Hale	15.00	6.75	1.85
☐ A45 Bill Hallahan	15.00	6.75	1.85
☐ A46 Mel Harder	20.00	9.00	2.50
☐ A47 Bucky Harris	30.00	13.50	3.70
☐ A48 Gabby Hartnett	30.00	13.50	3.70
☐ A49 Ray Hayworth	15.00	6.75	1.85
☐ A50 Rollie Hemsley	15.00	6.75	1.85
☐ A51 Babe Herman	20.00	9.00	2.50
☐ A52 Frank Higgins POR	15.00	6.75	1.85
☐ A53 Oral Hildebrand	15.00	6.75	1.85
☐ A54 Myril Hoag	15.00	6.75	1.85
☐ A55 Waite Hoyt	30.00	13.50	3.70
☐ A56 Woody Jensen	15.00	6.75	1.85
☐ A57 Bob Johnson	20.00	9.00	2.50
☐ A58 Buck Jordan	15.00	6.75	1.85
☐ A59 Alex Kampouris	15.00	6.75	1.85
☐ A60 Chuck Klein	30.00	13.50	3.70
☐ A61 Joe Kuhel	15.00	6.75	1.85
☐ A62 Lyn Lary	15.00	6.75	1.85
☐ A63 Harry Lavagetto	20.00	9.00	2.50
☐ A64 Sam Leslie	15.00	6.75	1.85
☐ A64 Freddie Lindstrom	30.00	13.50	3.70
☐ A66 Ernie Lombardi HOR	30.00	13.50	3.70
☐ A67 Al Lopez HOR	30.00	13.50	3.70
☐ A68 Dan MacFayden	15.00	6.75	1.85
☐ A69 John Marcum	15.00	6.75	1.85
☐ A70 Pepper Martin	20.00	9.00	2.50
☐ A71 Eric McNair	15.00	6.75	1.85
☐ A72 Ducky Medwick	30.00	13.50	3.70
☐ A73 Gene Moore	15.00	6.75	1.85
☐ A74 Randy Moore	15.00	6.75	1.85
☐ A75 Terry Moore	20.00	9.00	2.50
☐ A76 Edward Moriarty	15.00	6.75	1.85
☐ A77 Wally Moses POR	15.00	6.75	1.85
☐ A78 Buddy Myer	15.00	6.75	1.85
☐ A79 Buck Newsom	15.00	6.75	1.85
☐ A80 Fred Ostermueller	15.00	6.75	1.85
☐ A81 Marvin Owen	15.00	6.75	1.85
☐ A82 Tommy Padden	15.00	6.75	1.85
☐ A83 Ray Pepper	15.00	6.75	1.85
☐ A84 Tony Piet	15.00	6.75	1.85
☐ A85 Rabbit Pytlak HOR	15.00	6.75	1.85
☐ A86 Rip Radcliff	15.00	6.75	1.85
☐ A87 Bobby Reis	15.00	6.75	1.85
☐ A88 Lew Riggs	15.00	6.75	1.85
☐ A89 Bill Rogell	15.00	6.75	1.85
☐ A90 Red Rolfe	20.00	9.00	2.50
☐ A91 Schoolboy Rowe POR	20.00	9.00	2.50
☐ A92 Al Schacht	20.00	9.00	2.50
☐ A93 Luke Sewell	20.00	9.00	2.50
☐ A94 Al Simmons POR	40.00	18.00	5.00
☐ A95 John Stone	15.00	6.75	1.85
☐ A96 Gus Suhr	15.00	6.75	1.85
☐ A97 Joe Sullivan	15.00	6.75	1.85
☐ A98 Bill Swift	15.00	6.75	1.85
☐ A99 Vito Tamulis	15.00	6.75	1.85
☐ A100 Dan Taylor	15.00	6.75	1.85
☐ A101 Cecil Travis	15.00	6.75	1.85
☐ A102 Hal Trosky POR	15.00	6.75	1.85
☐ A103 Bill Urbanski	15.00	6.75	1.85
☐ A104 Russ Van Atta	15.00	6.75	1.85
☐ A105 Arky Vaughan	30.00	13.50	3.70
☐ A106 Gerald Walker	15.00	6.75	1.85
☐ A107 Buck Walters	20.00	9.00	2.50
☐ A108 Lloyd Waner	30.00	13.50	3.70
☐ A109 Paul Waner	30.00	13.50	3.70
☐ A110 Lon Warneke	15.00	6.75	1.85
☐ A111 Rabbit Warstler	15.00	6.75	1.85
☐ A112 Bill Werber	15.00	6.75	1.85
☐ A113 Jo-Jo White	15.00	6.75	1.85
☐ A114 Burgess Whitehead	15.00	6.75	1.85
☐ A115 John Whitehead POR	15.00	6.75	1.85
☐ A116 Whitlow Wyatt	15.00	6.75	1.85
☐ A117 Joe DiMaggio and Joe McCarthy MG	175.00	80.00	22.00
☐ A118 Wes Ferrell Rick Ferrell	30.00	13.50	3.70
☐ A119 Frank Pytlak Steve O'Neill	15.00	6.75	1.85
☐ B1 Mel Almada	40.00	18.00	5.00
☐ B2 Lucius Appling POR	50.00	22.00	6.25
☐ B3 Henry Bonura POR	40.00	18.00	5.00
☐ B4 Ben Chapman and Bill Werber	20.00	9.00	2.50
☐ B5 Herman Clifton	40.00	18.00	5.00
☐ B6 Roger "Doc" Cramer	40.00	18.00	5.00
☐ B7 Joe Cronin	50.00	22.00	6.25
☐ B8 Jimmy Dykes	40.00	18.00	5.00
☐ B9 Ervin "Pete" Fox	40.00	18.00	5.00
☐ B10 Jimmy Foxx	125.00	55.00	15.50
☐ B11 Hank Greenberg	75.00	34.00	9.50
☐ B12 Oral Hildebrand	40.00	18.00	5.00
☐ B13 Alex Hooks HOR	40.00	18.00	5.00
☐ B14 Willis Hudlin	40.00	18.00	5.00
☐ B15 Bill Knickerbocker	40.00	18.00	5.00
☐ B16 Heinie Manush	50.00	22.00	6.25
☐ B17 Steve O'Neill	40.00	18.00	5.00
☐ B18 Marvin Owen	40.00	18.00	5.00
☐ B19 Al Simmons	60.00	27.00	7.50
☐ B20 Lem "Moose" Solters	40.00	18.00	5.00
☐ B21 Hal Trosky (batting)	40.00	18.00	5.00
☐ B22 Joe Vosmik POR	40.00	18.00	5.00
☐ B23 Joe Vosmik(batting)	40.00	18.00	5.00
☐ B24 Joe Vosmik(fielding)	40.00	18.00	5.00
☐ B25 Earl Whitehill	40.00	18.00	5.00
☐ C1 Luke Appling batting	40.00	18.00	5.00
☐ C2 Earl Averill POR	40.00	18.00	5.00
☐ C3 Cy Blanton	40.00	18.00	5.00
☐ C4 Zeke Bonura batting	40.00	18.00	5.00
☐ C5 Tom Bridges POR	40.00	18.00	5.00
☐ C6 Joe DiMaggio	600.00	275.00	75.00
☐ C7 Bobby Doerr	40.00	18.00	5.00
☐ C8 Jimmy Dykes HOR	40.00	18.00	5.00
☐ C9 Bob Feller	75.00	34.00	9.50
☐ C10 Elbie Fletcher	40.00	18.00	5.00
☐ C11 Pete Fox (batting)	40.00	18.00	5.00
☐ C12 Gus Galan batting	40.00	18.00	5.00
☐ C13 Charles Gehringer	50.00	22.00	6.25
☐ C14 Hank Greenberg	75.00	34.00	9.50
☐ C15 Mel Harder	50.00	22.00	6.25
☐ C16 Gabby Hartnett	40.00	18.00	5.00
☐ C17 Pinky Higgins	40.00	18.00	5.00
☐ C18 Carl Hubbell	50.00	22.00	6.25
☐ C19 Wally Moses batting	40.00	18.00	5.00
☐ C20 Lou Newsom	40.00	18.00	5.00
☐ C21 Schoolboy Rowe throwing	40.00	18.00	5.00
☐ C22 Julius Solters	40.00	18.00	5.00
☐ C23 Hal Trosky	40.00	18.00	5.00
☐ C24 Joe Vosmik kneeling	40.00	18.00	5.00
☐ C25 Johnnie Whitehead throwing	40.00	18.00	5.00
☐ D1 Buddy Bates M	60.00	27.00	7.50
☐ D2 Del Bissonette M	60.00	27.00	7.50
☐ D3 Lincoln Blakely T	60.00	27.00	7.50
☐ D4 Isaac J. Boone T	60.00	27.00	7.50
☐ D5 John H. Burnett T	60.00	27.00	7.50
☐ D6 Leon Chagnon M	60.00	27.00	7.50
☐ D7 Gus Dugas M	60.00	27.00	7.50
☐ D8 Henry N. Erickson	60.00	27.00	7.50
☐ D9 Art Funk T	60.00	27.00	7.50
☐ D10 George Granger M	60.00	27.00	7.50
☐ D11 Thomas G. Heath	60.00	27.00	7.50
☐ D12 Phil Hensich M	60.00	27.00	7.50
☐ D13 LeRoy Hermann T	60.00	27.00	7.50
☐ D14 Henry Johnson M	60.00	27.00	7.50
☐ D15 Hal King M	60.00	27.00	7.50
☐ D16 Charles S. Lucas T	60.00	27.00	7.50
☐ D17 Edward S. Miller T	60.00	27.00	7.50
☐ D18 Jake F. Mooty T	60.00	27.00	7.50
☐ D19 Guy Moreau	60.00	27.00	7.50
☐ D20 George Murray T	60.00	27.00	7.50
☐ D21 Glenn Myatt M	60.00	27.00	7.50
☐ D22 Lauri Myllykangas M	60.00	27.00	7.50
☐ D23 Franci J. Nicholas T	60.00	27.00	7.50
☐ D24 Bill O'Brien	60.00	27.00	7.50
☐ D25 Thomas Oliver T	60.00	27.00	7.50
☐ D26 James Pattison T	60.00	27.00	7.50
☐ D27 Crip Polli M	60.00	27.00	7.50

☐ D28 Harlin Pool T	60.00	27.00	7.50
☐ D29 Walter Purcey T	60.00	27.00	7.50
☐ D30 Bill Rhiel M	60.00	27.00	7.50
☐ D31 Ben Sankey M	60.00	27.00	7.50
☐ D32 Leslie Scarsella T	60.00	27.00	7.50
☐ D33 Bob Seeds M	60.00	27.00	7.50
☐ D34 Frank Shaughnessy M	60.00	27.00	7.50
☐ D35 Harry Smythe M	60.00	27.00	7.50
☐ D36 Ben Tate M	60.00	27.00	7.50
☐ D37 Fresco Thompson M	60.00	27.00	7.50
☐ D38 Charles Wilson M	60.00	27.00	7.50
☐ D39 Francis Wistert HOR T	60.00	27.00	7.50

1937 Goudey Flip Movies R326

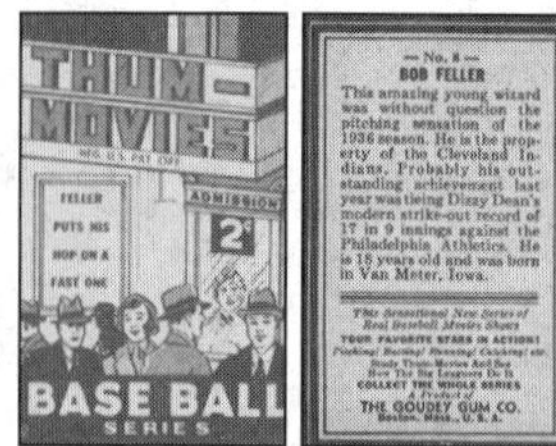

The 26 "Flip Movies" which comprise this set are a miniature version (2" by 3") of the popular penny arcade features of the period. Each movie comes in two parts, clearly labeled, and there are several cover colors as well as incorrect photos known to exist.

	EX-MT	VG-E	GOOD
COMPLETE SET (13)	1250.00	550.00	160.00
COMMON CARD (1-13)	30.00	13.50	3.70
☐ 1A John Irving Burns (Poles Two Bagger)	30.00	13.50	3.70
☐ 1B John Irving Burns (Poles Two Bagger)	30.00	13.50	3.70
☐ 2A Joe Vosmik (Triples)	30.00	13.50	3.70
☐ 2B Joe Vosmik (Triples)	30.00	13.50	3.70
☐ 3A Mel Ott (Puts It Over The Fence)	60.00	27.00	7.50
☐ 3B Mel Ott (Puts It Over The Fence)	60.00	27.00	7.50
☐ 4A Joe DiMaggio (Socks A Sizzling Long Drive)	200.00	90.00	25.00
☐ 4B Joe DiMaggio (Socks A Sizzling Long Drive)	200.00	90.00	25.00
☐ 5A Wally Moses (Leans Against A Fast Ball)	30.00	13.50	3.70
☐ 5B Wally Moses (Leans Against A Fast Ball)	30.00	13.50	3.70
☐ 6A Van Lingle Mungo (Tosses Fire-Ball)	30.00	13.50	3.70
☐ 6B Van Lingle Mungo (Tosses Fire-Ball)	30.00	13.50	3.70
☐ 7A Luke Appling (Gets Set For Double Play	50.00	22.00	6.25
☐ 7B Luke Appling (Gets Set For Double Play	50.00	22.00	6.25
☐ 8A Bob Feller (Puts His Hop On A Fast One)	60.00	27.00	7.50
☐ 8B Bob Feller (Puts His Hop On A Fast One)	60.00	27.00	7.50
☐ 9A Paul Derringer (Demonstrates Sharp Curve)	30.00	13.50	3.70
☐ 9B Paul Derringer (Demonstrates Sharp Curve)	30.00	13.50	3.70
☐ 10A Paul Waner (Big Poison Smacks A Triple)	50.00	22.00	6.25
☐ 10B Paul Waner (Big Poison Smacks A Triple)	50.00	22.00	6.25
☐ 11A Joe Medwick (Bats Hard Grounder)	50.00	22.00	6.25
☐ 11B Joe Medwick (Bats Hard Grounder)	50.00	22.00	6.25
☐ 12A James Emory Foxx (Smacks A Homer)	60.00	27.00	7.50
☐ 12B James Emory Foxx (Smacks A Homer)	60.00	27.00	7.50
☐ 13A Wally Berger (Puts One In The Bleachers)	30.00	13.50	3.70
☐ 13B Wally Berger (Puts One In The Bleachers)	30.00	13.50	3.70

1937 Goudey Knot Hole R325

The cards in this 24-card set measure approximately 2 3/8" by 2 7/8". The 1937 "Knot Hole League Game" was another of the many innovative marketing ideas of the Goudey Gum Company. Advertised as a series of 100 game cards promising "exciting" baseball action, the set actually was limited to the 24 cards listed below.

	EX-MT	VG-E	GOOD
COMPLETE SET (24)	150.00	70.00	19.00
COMMON CARD (1-24)	7.50	3.40	.95
☐ 1 Double/Foul	7.50	3.40	.95
☐ 2 Steals Home/Strike	7.50	3.40	.95
☐ 3 Ball/Out	7.50	3.40	.95
☐ 4 Strike/Ball	7.50	3.40	.95
☐ 5 Strike/Wild Pitch	7.50	3.40	.95
☐ 6 Ball/Out	7.50	3.40	.95
☐ 7 Bunt Scratch Hit/ Stolen Base	7.50	3.40	.95
☐ 8 Hit By Pitched Ball/ Out	7.50	3.40	.95
☐ 9 Foul/Ball	7.50	3.40	.95
☐ 10 Foul/Double	7.50	3.40	.95
☐ 11 Out/Ball	7.50	3.40	.95
☐ 12 Foul/Force Out	7.50	3.40	.95
☐ 13 Out/Single	7.50	3.40	.95
☐ 14 Strike/Ball	7.50	3.40	.95
☐ 15 Foul Tip/Strike	7.50	3.40	.95
☐ 16 Three Bagger/Out	10.00	4.50	1.25
☐ 17 Ball/Out	7.50	3.40	.95
☐ 18 Out/Error	7.50	3.40	.95
☐ 19 Strike/Foul	7.50	3.40	.95
☐ 20 Double Play/Out	7.50	3.40	.95
☐ 21 Home Run/Ball	7.50	3.40	.95
☐ 22 Out/Strike	7.50	3.40	.95
☐ 23 Ball/Out	7.50	3.40	.95
☐ 24 Strike/Ball	7.50	3.40	.95

1937 Goudey Thum Movies R342

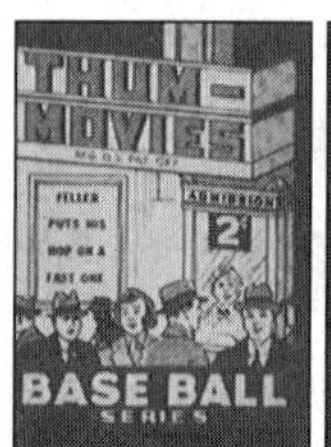

These numbered booklets are the same dimensions (2" by 3") as the R326 Flip Movies except that these are twice the thickness as they comprise both parts within a single cover. They were produced by Goudey Gum. The desirability of the set is decreased by the fact that the outside of the Thum Movie booklet does not show any picture of the player; this is in contrast to the R326 Flip Movie style which shows an inset photo of the player on the cover.

	EX-MT	VG-E	GOOD
COMPLETE SET (13)	1400.00	650.00	180.00
COMMON CARD (1-13)	75.00	34.00	9.50
☐ 1 John Irving Burns	75.00	34.00	9.50
☐ 2 Joe Vosmik	75.00	34.00	9.50
☐ 3 Mel Ott	150.00	70.00	19.00
☐ 4 Joe DiMaggio	350.00	160.00	45.00
☐ 5 Wally Moses	75.00	34.00	9.50
☐ 6 Van Lingle Mungo	75.00	34.00	9.50
☐ 7 Luke Appling	125.00	55.00	15.50
☐ 8 Bob Feller	150.00	70.00	19.00
☐ 9 Paul Derringer	75.00	34.00	9.50
☐ 10 Paul Waner	125.00	55.00	15.50
☐ 11 Joe Medwick	125.00	55.00	15.50
☐ 12 James Emory Foxx	150.00	70.00	19.00
☐ 13 Wally Berger	75.00	34.00	9.50

1938 Goudey Heads Up

The cards in this 48-card set measure approximately 2 3/8" by 2 7/8". The 1938 Goudey set is commonly referred to as the Heads-Up set, or R323 (catalog). These very popular but difficult to obtain cards came in two series of the same 24 players. The first series, numbers 241-264, is distinguished from the second series, numbers 265-288, in

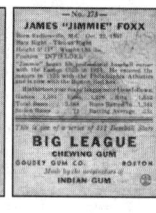

that the second contains etched cartoons and comments surrounding the player picture. Although the set starts with number 241, it is not a continuation of the 1933 Goudey set, but a separate set in its own right.

	EX-MT	VG-E	GOOD
COMPLETE SET (48)	18000.00	8100.00	2200.00
COMMON CARD (241-264)	100.00	45.00	12.50
COMMON CARD (265-288)	110.00	50.00	14.00
WRAPPER (1-CENT)	500.00	220.00	60.00
☐ 241 Charlie Gehringer	325.00	145.00	40.00
☐ 242 Pete Fox	100.00	45.00	12.50
☐ 243 Joe Kuhel	100.00	45.00	12.50
☐ 244 Frank Demaree	100.00	45.00	12.50
☐ 245 Frank Pytlak	100.00	45.00	12.50
☐ 246 Ernie Lombardi	175.00	80.00	22.00
☐ 247 Joe Vosmik	100.00	45.00	12.50
☐ 248 Dick Bartell	100.00	45.00	12.50
☐ 249 Jimmie Foxx	400.00	180.00	50.00
☐ 250 Joe DiMaggio	4500.00	2000.00	550.00
☐ 251 Bump Hadley	100.00	45.00	12.50
☐ 252 Zeke Bonura	100.00	45.00	12.50
☐ 253 Hank Greenberg	400.00	180.00	50.00
☐ 254 Van Lingle Mungo	110.00	50.00	14.00
☐ 255 Moose Solters	100.00	45.00	12.50
☐ 256 Vernon Kennedy	100.00	45.00	12.50
☐ 257 Al Lopez	175.00	80.00	22.00
☐ 258 Bobby Doerr	300.00	135.00	38.00
☐ 259 Billy Werber	100.00	45.00	12.50
☐ 260 Rudy York	110.00	50.00	14.00
☐ 261 Rip Radcliff	100.00	45.00	12.50
☐ 262 Joe Medwick	275.00	125.00	34.00
☐ 263 Marvin Owen	100.00	45.00	12.50
☐ 264 Bob Feller	650.00	300.00	80.00
☐ 265 Charlie Gehringer	350.00	160.00	45.00
☐ 266 Pete Fox	110.00	50.00	14.00
☐ 267 Joe Kuhel	110.00	50.00	14.00
☐ 268 Frank Demaree	110.00	50.00	14.00
☐ 269 Frank Pytlak	110.00	50.00	14.00
☐ 270 Ernie Lombardi	175.00	80.00	22.00
☐ 271 Joe Vosmik	110.00	50.00	14.00
☐ 272 Dick Bartell	110.00	50.00	14.00
☐ 273 Jimmie Foxx	450.00	200.00	55.00
☐ 274 Joe DiMaggio	4500.00	2000.00	550.00
☐ 275 Bump Hadley	110.00	50.00	14.00
☐ 276 Zeke Bonura	110.00	50.00	14.00
☐ 277 Hank Greenberg	450.00	200.00	55.00
☐ 278 Van Lingle Mungo	125.00	55.00	15.50
☐ 279 Moose Solters	110.00	50.00	14.00
☐ 280 Vernon Kennedy	110.00	50.00	14.00
☐ 281 Al Lopez	200.00	90.00	25.00
☐ 282 Bobby Doerr	350.00	160.00	45.00
☐ 283 Billy Werber	110.00	50.00	14.00
☐ 284 Rudy York	125.00	55.00	15.50
☐ 285 Rip Radcliff	110.00	50.00	14.00
☐ 286 Joe Medwick	300.00	135.00	38.00
☐ 287 Marvin Owen	110.00	50.00	14.00
☐ 288 Bob Feller	700.00	325.00	90.00

1939 Goudey Premiums R303A

This series of 48 paper premiums were issued in 1939 by the Goudey Company. Each premium photo measures approximately 4" by 6 3/16". This set carries the name Diamond Stars Gum on the reverse, although the National Chicle Company who produced the Diamond Stars baseball cards is in no way connected with this set. The backs contain instructions on various baseball disciplines. The color of the set is brown, not the more reddish color of sepia normally listed for this set.

	EX-MT	VG-E	GOOD
COMPLETE SET (48)	1500.00	700.00	190.00
COMMON CARD (1-48)	20.00	9.00	2.50
☐ 1 Luke Appling	30.00	13.50	3.70
☐ 2 Earl Averill	30.00	13.50	3.70
☐ 3 Wally Berger	20.00	9.00	2.50
☐ 4 Darrell Blanton	20.00	9.00	2.50
☐ 5 Zeke Bonura	20.00	9.00	2.50
☐ 6 Mace Brown	20.00	9.00	2.50
☐ 7 George Case	20.00	9.00	2.50
☐ 8 Ben Chapman	20.00	9.00	2.50
☐ 9 Joe Cronin	30.00	13.50	3.70
☐ 10 Frank Crosetti	25.00	11.00	3.10
☐ 11 Paul Derringer	25.00	11.00	3.10
☐ 12 Bill Dickey	35.00	16.00	4.40
☐ 13 Joe DiMaggio	250.00	110.00	31.00
☐ 14 Bob Feller	75.00	34.00	9.50
☐ 15 Jimmy Foxx	60.00	27.00	7.50
☐ 16 Charlie Gehringer	35.00	16.00	4.40
☐ 17 Lefty Gomez	35.00	16.00	4.40
☐ 18 Ival Goodman	20.00	9.00	2.50
☐ 19 Joe Gordon	25.00	11.00	3.10
☐ 20 Hank Greenberg	40.00	18.00	5.00
☐ 21 Buddy Hassett	20.00	9.00	2.50
☐ 22 Jeff Heath	20.00	9.00	2.50
☐ 23 Tom Henrich	25.00	11.00	3.10
☐ 24 Billy Herman	30.00	13.50	3.70
☐ 25 Frank Higgins	20.00	9.00	2.50
☐ 26 Fred Hutchinson	25.00	11.00	3.10
☐ 27 Bob Johnson	20.00	9.00	2.50
☐ 28 Ken Keltner	20.00	9.00	2.50
☐ 29 Mike Kreevich	20.00	9.00	2.50
☐ 30 Ernie Lombardi	30.00	13.50	3.70
☐ 31 Gus Mancuso	20.00	9.00	2.50
☐ 32 Eric McNair	20.00	9.00	2.50
☐ 33 Van Mungo	20.00	9.00	2.50
☐ 34 Buck Newsom	20.00	9.00	2.50
☐ 35 Mel Ott	40.00	18.00	5.00
☐ 36 Marvin Owen	20.00	9.00	2.50
☐ 37 Frankie Pytlak	20.00	9.00	2.50
☐ 38 Woody Rich	20.00	9.00	2.50
☐ 39 Charlie Root	20.00	9.00	2.50
☐ 40 Al Simmons	30.00	13.50	3.70
☐ 41 Jim Tabor	20.00	9.00	2.50
☐ 42 Cecil Travis	20.00	9.00	2.50
☐ 43 Hal Trosky	20.00	9.00	2.50
☐ 44 Arky Vaughan	30.00	13.50	3.70
☐ 45 Joe Vosmik	20.00	9.00	2.50
☐ 46 Lon Warneke	20.00	9.00	2.50
☐ 47 Ted Williams	250.00	110.00	31.00
☐ 48 Rudy York	25.00	11.00	3.10

1939 Goudey Premiums R303B

This set of 24 paper photos is slightly larger than its counterpart R303A and was also issued in 1939. Each premium photo measures approximately 4 3/4" by 7 5/16". The photos of R303A series are the same ones depicted on these cards, and the reverses contain "How to" instructions and the Diamond Stars Gum name. The photos are the same as R303A. This set comes in two distinct colors, black and sepia.

	EX-MT	VG-E	GOOD
COMPLETE SET (24)	650.00	300.00	80.00
COMMON CARD (1-24)	15.00	6.75	1.85
☐ 1 Luke Appling	25.00	11.00	3.10
☐ 2 George Case	15.00	6.75	1.85
☐ 3 Ben Chapman	15.00	6.75	1.85
☐ 4 Joe Cronin	25.00	11.00	3.10
☐ 5 Bill Dickey	30.00	13.50	3.70
☐ 6 Joe DiMaggio	200.00	90.00	25.00
☐ 7 Bob Feller	60.00	27.00	7.50
☐ 8 Jimmy Foxx	50.00	22.00	6.25
☐ 9 Lefty Gomez	30.00	13.50	3.70
☐ 10 Ival Goodman	15.00	6.75	1.85
☐ 11 Joe Gordon	20.00	9.00	2.50
☐ 12 Hank Greenberg	35.00	16.00	4.40
☐ 13 Jeff Heath	15.00	6.75	1.85
☐ 14 Billy Herman	25.00	11.00	3.10
☐ 15 Frank Higgins	15.00	6.75	1.85
☐ 16 Ken Keltner	15.00	6.75	1.85
☐ 17 Mike Kreevich	15.00	6.75	1.85
☐ 18 Ernie Lombardi	25.00	11.00	3.10
☐ 19 Gus Mancuso	15.00	6.75	1.85
☐ 20 Mel Ott	35.00	16.00	4.40
☐ 21 Al Simmons	25.00	11.00	3.10
☐ 22 Arky Vaughan	25.00	11.00	3.10
☐ 23 Joe Vosmik	15.00	6.75	1.85
☐ 24 Rudy York	20.00	9.00	2.50

1941 Goudey

The cards in this 33-card set measure 2 3/8" by 2 7/8". The 1941 Series of blank backed baseball cards was the last baseball issue marketed by Goudey before the war closed the door on that company for good. Each black and white player photo comes with four color backgrounds (blue, green, red, or yellow). Cards without numbers are probably miscut. Cards 21-25 are especially scarce in relation to the rest of the set. In fact the eight hardest to find cards in the set are, in order, 22, 24, 23, 25, 21, 27, 29 and 32. The catalog number is R324.

	EX-MT	VG-E	GOOD
COMPLETE SET (33)	2000.00	900.00	250.00
COMMON CARD (1-33)	30.00	13.50	3.70
WRAPPER (5-CENT)	200.00	90.00	25.00
☐ 1 Hugh Mulcahy	30.00	13.50	3.70
☐ 2 Harland Clift	30.00	13.50	3.70
☐ 3 Louis Chiozza	30.00	13.50	3.70
☐ 4 Warren Rosar	30.00	13.50	3.70
☐ 5 George McQuinn	30.00	13.50	3.70
☐ 6 George Dickman	30.00	13.50	3.70
☐ 7 Wayne Ambler	30.00	13.50	3.70
☐ 8 Bob Muncrief	30.00	13.50	3.70
☐ 9 Bill Dietrich	30.00	13.50	3.70
☐ 10 Taft Wright	30.00	13.50	3.70
☐ 11 Don Heffner	30.00	13.50	3.70
☐ 12 Fritz Ostermueller	30.00	13.50	3.70
☐ 13 Frank Hayes	30.00	13.50	3.70
☐ 14 John Kramer	30.00	13.50	3.70
☐ 15 Dario Lodigiani	30.00	13.50	3.70
☐ 16 George Case	30.00	13.50	3.70
☐ 17 Vito Tamulis	30.00	13.50	3.70
☐ 18 Whitlow Wyatt	30.00	13.50	3.70
☐ 19 Bill Posedel	30.00	13.50	3.70
☐ 20 Carl Hubbell	75.00	34.00	9.50
☐ 21 Harold Warstler SP	125.00	55.00	15.50
☐ 22 Joe Sullivan SP	300.00	135.00	38.00
☐ 23 Norman Young SP	200.00	90.00	25.00
☐ 24 Stanley Andrews SP	250.00	110.00	31.00
☐ 25 Morris Arnovich SP	125.00	55.00	15.50
☐ 26 Elbert Fletcher	30.00	13.50	3.70
☐ 27 Bill Crough	60.00	27.00	7.50
☐ 28 Al Todd	30.00	13.50	3.70
☐ 29 Debs Garms	50.00	22.00	6.25
☐ 30 Jim Tobin	30.00	13.50	3.70
☐ 31 Chester Ross	30.00	13.50	3.70
☐ 32 George Coffman	40.00	18.00	5.00
☐ 33 Mel Ott	125.00	55.00	15.50

1976 Great Plains Greats

This 42-card set measures approximately 2 1/2" by 3 3/4". The set was issued by the Great Plains Sports Collectors Association in conjunction with their annual show.

	NRMT	VG-E	GOOD
COMPLETE SET (42)	20.00	9.00	2.50
COMMON CARD (1-42)	.25	.11	.03
☐ 1 Bob Feller	1.50	.70	.19
☐ 2 Carl Hubbell	1.00	.45	.12
☐ 3 Jocko Conlan	.50	.23	.06
☐ 4 Hal Trosky	.25	.11	.03
☐ 5 Allie Reynolds	.25	.11	.03
☐ 6 Burleigh Grimes	.75	.35	.09
☐ 7 Jake Beckley	.50	.23	.06
☐ 8 Al Simmons	1.00	.45	.12
☐ 9 Paul Waner	1.00	.45	.12
☐ 10 Chief Bender	.75	.35	.09
☐ 11 Fred Clarke	.50	.23	.06
☐ 12 Jim Bottomley	.25	.11	.03
☐ 13 Dave Bancroft	.50	.23	.06
☐ 14 Bing Miller	.25	.11	.03
☐ 15 Walter Johnson	1.50	.70	.19
☐ 16 Grover Alexander	1.50	.70	.19
☐ 17 Bob Johnson	.25	.11	.03
☐ 18 Roger Maris	1.00	.45	.12
☐ 19 Ken Keltner	.25	.11	.03
☐ 20 Red Faber	.50	.23	.06
☐ 21 Cool Papa Bell	1.50	.70	.19
☐ 22 Yogi Berra	1.00	.45	.12
☐ 23 Fred Lindstrom	.50	.23	.06
☐ 24 Ray Schalk	.50	.23	.06
☐ 25 Lloyd Waner	.50	.23	.06
☐ 26 John Hopp	.25	.11	.03
☐ 27 Mel Harder	.25	.11	.03
☐ 28 Dutch Leonard	.25	.11	.03
☐ 29 Bob O'Farrell	.25	.11	.03
☐ 30 Cap Anson	.75	.35	.09
☐ 31 Dazzy Vance	.50	.23	.06
☐ 32 Red Schoendienst	.50	.23	.06
☐ 33 George Pipgras	.25	.11	.03
☐ 34 Harvey Kuenn	.25	.11	.03
☐ 35 Red Ruffing	.50	.23	.06
☐ 36 Roy Sievers	.25	.11	.03
☐ 37 Ken Boyer	.50	.23	.06
☐ 38 Al Smith	.25	.11	.03
☐ 39 Casey Stengel	1.00	.45	.12
☐ 40 Bob Gibson	.75	.35	.09
☐ 41 Mickey Mantle	3.00	1.35	.35
☐ 42 Denny McLain	.50	.23	.06

1988 Grenada Baseball Stamps

These stamps, featuring active major league stars as well as great retired players were issued by the Island of Grenada. Grenada, had previously gained recognition earlier in the decade as an island which had been invaded.

	MINT	NRMT	EXC
COMPLETE SET (81)	25.00	11.00	3.10
COMMON STAMP (1-81)	.05	.02	.01
☐ 1 Johnny Bench	.50	.23	.06
☐ 2 Dave Stieb	.05	.02	.01
☐ 3 Reggie Jackson	.50	.23	.06
☐ 4 Harold Baines	.10	.05	.01
☐ 5 Wade Boggs	.30	.14	.04
☐ 6 Pete O'Brien	.05	.02	.01
☐ 7 Stan Musial	1.00	.45	.12
☐ 8 Wally Joyner	.20	.09	.03
☐ 9 Grover C. Alexander	.30	.14	.04
☐ 10 Jose Cruz	.10	.05	.01
☐ 11 AL Logo	.05	.02	.01
☐ 12 Al Kaline	.40	.18	.05
☐ 13 Chuck Klein	.05	.02	.01
☐ 14 Don Mattingly	1.00	.45	.12
☐ 15 Mike Witt	.05	.02	.01
☐ 16 Mark Langston	.10	.05	.01
☐ 17 Hubie Brooks	.05	.02	.01
☐ 18 Harmon Killebrew	.40	.18	.05
☐ 19 Jackie Robinson	2.00	.90	.25
☐ 20 Dwight Gooden	.10	.05	.01
☐ 21 Brooks Robinson	.40	.18	.05
☐ 22 Nolan Ryan	2.00	.90	.25
☐ 23 Mike Schmidt	.60	.25	.07
☐ 24 Gary Gaetti	.05	.02	.01
☐ 25 Nellie Fox	.20	.09	.03
☐ 26 Tony Gwynn	.75	.35	.09
☐ 27 Dizzy Dean	.40	.18	.05
☐ 28 Luis Aparicio	.25	.11	.03
☐ 29 Paul Molitor	.40	.18	.05
☐ 30 Lou Gehrig	2.00	.90	.25
☐ 31 Jeffrey Leonard	.05	.02	.01
☐ 32 Eric Davis	.10	.05	.01
☐ 33 Pete Incaviglia	.05	.02	.01
☐ 34 Steve Rogers	.05	.02	.01
☐ 35 Ozzie Smith	.40	.18	.05
☐ 36 Randy Jones	.05	.02	.01
☐ 37 Gary Carter	.10	.05	.01
☐ 38 Hank Aaron	1.50	.70	.19
☐ 39 Gaylord Perry	.25	.11	.03
☐ 40 Ty Cobb	1.50	.70	.19
☐ 41 Andre Dawson	.10	.05	.01
☐ 42 Charlie Hough	.10	.05	.01
☐ 43 Kirby Puckett	.60	.25	.07
☐ 44 Robin Yount	.25	.11	.03
☐ 45 Don Drysdale	.40	.18	.05
☐ 46 Mickey Mantle	2.00	.90	.25
☐ 47 Roger Clemens	.25	.11	.03
☐ 48 Rod Carew	.40	.18	.05
☐ 49 Ryne Sandberg	.50	.23	.06
☐ 50 Mike Scott	.05	.02	.01
☐ 51 Tim Raines	.10	.05	.01
☐ 52 Willie Mays	1.00	.45	.12
☐ 53 Bret Saberhagen	.10	.05	.01
☐ 54 Honus Wagner	.75	.35	.09
☐ 55 George Brett	.75	.35	.09
☐ 56 Joe Carter	.20	.09	.03
☐ 57 Frank Robinson	.40	.18	.05
☐ 58 Mel Ott	.40	.18	.05
☐ 59 Benito Santiago	.05	.02	.01
☐ 60 Teddy Higuera	.05	.02	.01
☐ 61 Lloyd Moseby	.05	.02	.01
☐ 62 Bobby Bonilla	.20	.09	.03
☐ 63 Warren Spahn	.40	.18	.05
☐ 64 Ernie Banks	.50	.23	.06
☐ 65 NL Logo	.05	.02	.01
☐ 66 Julio Franco	.10	.05	.01
☐ 67 Jack Morris	.10	.05	.01
☐ 68 Fernando Valenzuela	.10	.05	.01
☐ 69 Lefty Grove	.40	.18	.05
☐ 70 Ted Williams	2.00	.90	.25
☐ 71 Darryl Strawberry	.10	.05	.01
☐ 72 Dale Murphy	.20	.09	.03
☐ 73 Roberto Clemente	2.00	.90	.25
☐ 74 Cal Ripken Jr.	2.00	.90	.25
☐ 75 Bob Feller	.40	.18	.05
☐ 76 George Bell	.05	.02	.01
☐ 77 Mark McGwire	.50	.23	.06
☐ 78 Alvin Davis	.05	.02	.01
☐ 79 Pete Rose	.75	.35	.09
☐ 80 Dan Quisenberry	.05	.02	.01
☐ 81 Babe Ruth	2.00	.90	.25

1974 Greyhound Heroes of Base Paths

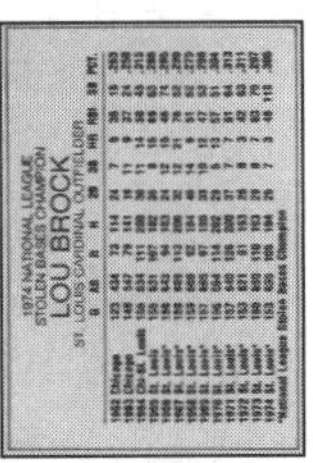

Beginning in 1965, the Greyhound Award for Stolen Bases was given to the champions in each league and the second-place finishers. The 1974 Heroes of the Base Paths pamphlet unfolds to reveal five 4" by 9" panels. The first panel is the title page and features on the back a picture of Maury Wills holding the trophy. The second and third panels have on the fronts the history of the award and major league statistics pertaining to stolen bases, while the backs have an essay on the art of base stealing. Finally, the fourth and fifth panels display six player cards; after perforation, the cards measure 4" by 3". Cards 1-4 feature the AL and NL winners and the runner-ups for each league, in that order. The player cards display a black and white head shot of the player on the left half, with player information and number of stolen bases on the right half. The backs have statistics. Both sides of the cards are framed by thin brown border stripes. Cards 5-6 display black and white player photos of past winners in the AL and NL, respectively. The cards are unnumbered.

	NRMT	VG-E	GOOD
COMPLETE SET (6)	10.00	4.50	1.25
COMMON CARD (1-6)	1.25	.55	.16
☐ 1 Bill North	1.25	.55	.16
☐ 2 Lou Brock	4.00	1.80	.50
☐ 3 Rod Carew	4.00	1.80	.50
☐ 4 Davey Lopes	1.50	.70	.19
☐ 5 American League Dagoberto Campaneris Tommy Harper Amos Otis Dave Nelson Billy North Don Buford Fred Patek Rod Carew	1.25	.55	.16
☐ 6 National League Lou Brock Maury Wills Bobby Tolan Joe Morgan Sonny Jackson Jose Cardenal Davey Lopes	1.50	.70	.19

1975 Greyhound Heroes of Base Paths

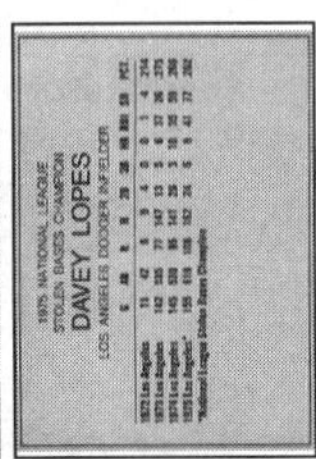

The Greyhound Award for Stolen Bases was given to the champions in each league and the second-place finishers. The 1975 Heroes of the Base Paths pamphlet unfolds to reveal five 4" by 9" panels. The first panel is the title page and features on the back a picture of Maury Wills holding the trophy. The second and third panels have on the fronts the history of the award and major league statistics pertaining to stolen bases, while backs have an essay on the art of base stealing. The fourth and fifth panels display six player cards; after perforation, cards measure approximately 4" by 3". Cards 1-4 feature the AL and NL winners and the runner-ups for each league, in that order. The player cards display a black and white head shot of the player on the left half, with player information and number of stolen bases on the right half. The backs have statistics. Both sides of the cards are framed by thin powder blue border stripes. Cards 5-6 display black and white player photos of Billy North and Davey Lopes. The cards are unnumbered.

	NRMT	VG-E	GOOD
COMPLETE SET (6)	7.50	3.40	.95
COMMON CARD (1-6)	1.00	.45	.12
☐ 1 Mickey Rivers	1.00	.45	.12
☐ 2 Davey Lopes	1.25	.55	.16
☐ 3 Claudell Washington	1.00	.45	.12
☐ 4 Joe Morgan	4.00	1.80	.50
☐ 5 Billy North	1.00	.45	.12
☐ 6 Davey Lopes	1.25	.55	.16

1976 Greyhound Heroes of Base Paths

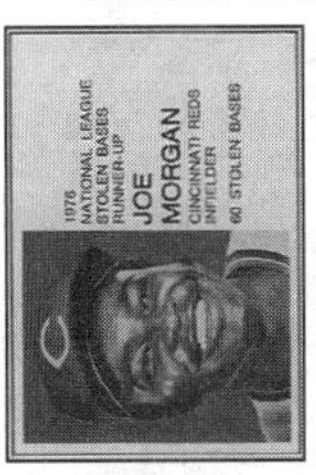
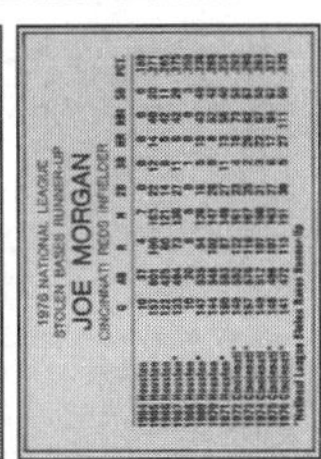

The Greyhound Award for Stolen Bases was given to the champions in each league and the second-place finishers. The 1976 Heroes of the Base Paths pamphlet unfolds to reveal five 4" by 9" panels. The first panel is the title page and features on the back a picture of Maury Wills holding the trophy. The second and third panels have on the fronts the history of the award and major league statistics pertaining to stolen bases, while the backs have an essay on the art of base stealing. The fourth and fifth panels display six player cards; after perforation, cards measure approximately 4" by 3". Cards 1-4 feature the AL and NL winners and the runner-ups for each league, in that order. The player cards display a black and white head shot of the player on the left half, with player information and number of stolen bases on the right half. The backs have statistics. Both sides of the cards are framed by thin powder reddish-brown stripes. Cards 5-6 display black and white player photos of Billy North and Davey Lopes. The cards are unnumbered.

	NRMT	VG-E	GOOD
COMPLETE SET (6)	7.50	3.40	.95
COMMON CARD (1-6)	1.00	.45	.12
☐ 1 Bill North	1.00	.45	.12
☐ 2 Davey Lopes	1.25	.55	.16
☐ 3 Ron LeFlore	1.00	.45	.12
☐ 4 Joe Morgan	4.00	1.80	.50
☐ 5 Billy North	1.00	.45	.12
☐ 6 Davey Lopes	1.25	.55	.16

1996 Griffey Nike

This one-card set was issued in conjunction with Nike's ad campaign for Ken Griffey. The front features a black-and-white image over a white background with red printing and a top and bottom blue border containing white stars and the Nike symbol. The back displays player information.

	MINT	NRMT	EXC
COMPLETE SET (1)	2.00	.90	.25
COMMON CARD (1)	2.00	.90	.25
☐ 1 Ken Griffey	2.00	.90	.25

1982 GS Gallery All-Time Greats

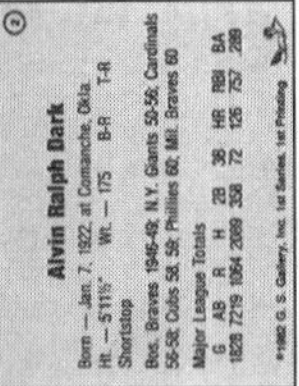

This 24-card set measure 2 1/2" by 3". Issued by long time dealer G.S. Gallery, these cards have full color pictures or drawings on the front. The backs have vital statistics and lifetime totals.

	NRMT	VG-E	GOOD
COMPLETE SET (24)	10.00	4.50	1.25
COMMON CARD (1-24)	.25	.11	.03
☐ 1 Stan Musial	2.00	.90	.25
☐ 2 Alvin Dark	.25	.11	.03
☐ 3 Harry Walker	.25	.11	.03
☐ 4 Dom DiMaggio	.50	.23	.06
☐ 5 Carl Furillo	.50	.23	.06
☐ 6 Joe DiMaggio	3.00	1.35	.35
☐ 7 Joe Adcock	.25	.11	.03
☐ 8 Lou Boudreau	.75	.35	.09
☐ 9 Ted Williams	3.00	1.35	.35
☐ 10 Phil Rizzuto	1.00	.45	.12
☐ 11 Pee Wee Reese	1.00	.45	.12
☐ 12 James Dykes	.25	.11	.03
☐ 13 Nellie Fox	.75	.35	.09
☐ 14 George Kell	.75	.35	.09
☐ 15 Ralph Kiner	.75	.35	.09
☐ 16 Roger Maris	1.00	.45	.12
☐ 17 Ted Kluszewski	.50	.23	.06
☐ 18 Wally Moon	.25	.11	.03
☐ 19 Hank Sauer	.25	.11	.03
☐ 20 Bob Thomson	.50	.23	.06
☐ 21 Mel Parnell	.25	.11	.03
☐ 22 Ewell Blackwell	.25	.11	.03
☐ 23 Richie Ashburn	1.00	.45	.12
☐ 24 Jackie Robinson	2.50	1.10	.30

1962 Guy's Potato Chip Pins

This 20-pin set measures approximately 7/8" in diameter and features a team logo on the front and a Guy's Potato Chip sponsor ad on the back. The pins are unnumbered and checklisted below according to the team's city.

	NRMT	VG-E	GOOD
COMPLETE SET (20)	80.00	36.00	10.00
COMMON CARD (1-20)	5.00	2.20	.60
☐ 1 Baltimore Orioles	5.00	2.20	.60
☐ 2 Boston Red Sox	5.00	2.20	.60
☐ 3 Chicago Cubs	5.00	2.20	.60
☐ 4 Chicago White Sox	5.00	2.20	.60
☐ 5 Cincinnati Red Legs	5.00	2.20	.60
☐ 6 Cleveland Indians	5.00	2.20	.60
☐ 7 Detroit Tigers	5.00	2.20	.60
☐ 8 Houston Colts	7.50	3.40	.95
☐ 9 Kansas City A's	6.00	2.70	.75
☐ 10 Los Angeles Angels	6.00	2.70	.75
☐ 11 Los Angeles Dodgers	5.00	2.20	.60
☐ 12 Milwaukee Braves	5.00	2.20	.60
☐ 13 Minnesota Twins	5.00	2.20	.60
☐ 14 New York Mets	7.50	3.40	.95
☐ 15 Philadelphia Phillies	5.00	2.20	.60
☐ 16 Pittsburgh Pirates	5.00	2.20	.60
☐ 17 San Francisco Giants	5.00	2.20	.60
☐ 18 St. Louis Cardinals	5.00	2.20	.60
☐ 19 Washington Nationals	6.00	2.70	.75
☐ 20 A Yankee Fan	6.00	2.70	.75

1962 H.F. Gardner Sports Stars PC768

This colorful 1960's set feature people of color stars only. The reverses can be identified by the line "Color by H.F. Gardner" at the lower left. A short biography of the subject player(s) is present on the reverse.

	NRMT	VG-E	GOOD
COMPLETE SET (5)	100.00	45.00	12.50
COMMON CARD (1-5)	5.00	2.20	.60
☐ 1 Hank Aaron Tommy Aaron	50.00	22.00	6.25
☐ 2 Billy Bruton	5.00	2.20	.60
☐ 3 Lee Maye	5.00	2.20	.60
☐ 4 Billy Williams	20.00	9.00	2.50
☐ 5 Jesse Owens	25.00	11.00	3.10

1909 H.H. Bregstone PC743

The H.H. Bregstone postcards were issued during the 1909-11 time period. They feature St. Louis Browns and St. Louis Cardinals only. The cards are sepia and black in appearance and are of consistent quality in the printing. Each cards features the line "by H.H. Bregstone, St. Louis" at the bottom of the obverse. The player's last name, his position, and his team are enumerated. The reverses features the letters AZO in the stamp area. B. Gregory of the Trolley League is probably Howie Gregory who played for the Browns that year.

	EX-MT	VG-E	GOOD
COMPLETE SET (46)	10500.00	4700.00	1300.00
COMMON CARD (1-46)	250.00	110.00	31.00
☐ 1 Bill Bailey	250.00	110.00	31.00
☐ 2 Shad Barry	250.00	110.00	31.00
☐ 3 Fred Beebe	250.00	110.00	31.00
☐ 4 Jack Bliss	250.00	110.00	31.00
☐ 5 Roger Breshnahan	500.00	220.00	60.00
☐ 6 Bobby Byrne	250.00	110.00	31.00
☐ 7 Chappy Charles	250.00	110.00	31.00
☐ 8 Frank Corridon	250.00	110.00	31.00
☐ 9 Dade Criss	250.00	110.00	31.00
☐ 10 Lou Criger	250.00	110.00	31.00
☐ 11 Joe Delahanty	250.00	110.00	31.00
☐ 12 Bill Dineen	250.00	110.00	31.00
☐ 13 Steve Evans	250.00	110.00	31.00
☐ 14 Rube Geyer	250.00	110.00	31.00
☐ 15 Billy Gilbert	250.00	110.00	31.00
☐ 16 Bert Graham	250.00	110.00	31.00
☐ 17 B. Gregory Probably Howie Gregory	250.00	110.00	31.00
☐ 18 Art Griggs	250.00	110.00	31.00
☐ 19 Bob Harmon	250.00	110.00	31.00
☐ 20 Roy Hartzell	250.00	110.00	31.00
☐ 21 Irv Higginbotham	250.00	110.00	31.00
☐ 22 Danny Hoffman	250.00	110.00	31.00
☐ 23 Harry Howell	250.00	110.00	31.00
☐ 24 Miller Huggins	400.00	180.00	50.00
☐ 25 Rudy Hulswitt	250.00	110.00	31.00
☐ 26 Johnson	250.00	110.00	31.00
☐ 27 Tom Jones	250.00	110.00	31.00
☐ 28 Ed Konetchy	250.00	110.00	31.00
☐ 29 Johnny Lush	250.00	110.00	31.00
☐ 30 Lee Magee	250.00	110.00	31.00
☐ 31 Jimmy McAleer MG	250.00	110.00	31.00
☐ 32 Rebel Oakes	250.00	110.00	31.00
☐ 33 Ham Patterson	250.00	110.00	31.00
☐ 34 Barney Pelty	250.00	110.00	31.00
☐ 35 Ed Phelps	250.00	110.00	31.00
☐ 36 Elmer Rieger	250.00	110.00	31.00
☐ 37 Charlie Rhodes	250.00	110.00	31.00
☐ 38 Slim Sallee	250.00	110.00	31.00
☐ 39 Schweitzer	250.00	110.00	31.00
☐ 40 Wib Smith	250.00	110.00	31.00
☐ 41 Jim Stephens	250.00	110.00	31.00
☐ 42 George Stone	250.00	110.00	31.00
☐ 43 Rube Waddell	400.00	180.00	50.00
☐ 44 Bobby Wallace	400.00	180.00	50.00
☐ 45 Vic Willis	400.00	180.00	50.00
☐ 46 Jim Williams	250.00	110.00	31.00

1973 Hall of Fame Picture Pack

This 20-card set measures approximately 5" by 6 3/4" and features black-and-white photos of players who are in the Baseball Hall of Fame in Cooperstown, New York. Player information and statistics are printed on the front in the bottom margin. The backs are blank. The cards are unnumbered and checklisted below in alphabetical order.

	NRMT	VG-E	GOOD
COMPLETE SET (20)	35.00	16.00	4.40
COMMON CARD (1-20)	2.00	.90	.25
☐ 1 Yogi Berra	3.00	1.35	.35
☐ 2 Roy Campanella	2.00	.90	.25
☐ 3 Ty Cobb	2.00	.90	.25
☐ 4 Joe Cronin	2.00	.90	.25
☐ 5 Dizzy Dean	2.00	.90	.25
☐ 6 Joe DiMaggio	3.00	1.35	.35
☐ 7 Bob Feller	2.00	.90	.25
☐ 8 Lou Gehrig	3.00	1.35	.35
☐ 9 Rogers Hornsby	2.00	.90	.25
☐ 10 Sandy Koufax	3.00	1.35	.35
☐ 11 Christy Mathewson	2.00	.90	.25
☐ 12 Stan Musial	3.00	1.35	.35
☐ 13 Satchel Paige	2.00	.90	.25
☐ 14 Jackie Robinson	3.00	1.35	.35
☐ 15 Babe Ruth	3.00	1.35	.35
☐ 16 Warren Spahn	2.00	.90	.25
☐ 17 Casey Stengel	2.00	.90	.25
☐ 18 Honus Wagner	2.00	.90	.25
☐ 19 Ted Williams	3.00	1.35	.35
☐ 20 Cy Young	2.00	.90	.25

1978 Halsey Hall Recalls

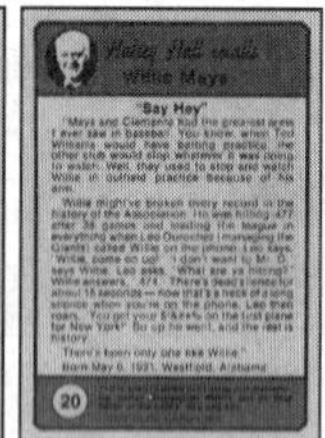

This 21-card set measures 2 1/2" by 3 3/4". The players featured were all local Minneapolis-St. Paul heroes whose exploits were remembered by local legend Halsey Hall.

	NRMT	VG-E	GOOD
COMPLETE SET (21)	14.00	6.25	1.75
COMMON CARD (1-21)	.25	.11	.03
☐ 1 Halsey Hall	.50	.23	.06
☐ 2 Ray Dandridge	1.00	.45	.12
☐ 3 Bruno Haas	.25	.11	.03
☐ 4 Fabian Gaffke	.25	.11	.03
☐ 5 George Stumpf	.25	.11	.03
☐ 6 Roy Campanella	2.00	.90	.25
☐ 7 Babe Barna	.25	.11	.03
☐ 8 Tom Sheehan	.25	.11	.03
☐ 9 Ray Moore	.25	.11	.03
☐ 10 Ted Williams	5.00	2.20	.60
☐ 11 Harley Davidson	.25	.11	.03
☐ 12 Jack Cassini	.25	.11	.03
☐ 13 Pea Ridge Day	.25	.11	.03
☐ 14 Oscar Roettger	.25	.11	.03
☐ 15 Buzz Arlett	.25	.11	.03
☐ 16 Joe Hauser	.25	.11	.03
☐ 17 Rube Benton	.25	.11	.03
☐ 18 Dave Barnhill	.25	.11	.03
☐ 19 Hoyt Wilhelm	1.00	.45	.12
☐ 20 Willie Mays	3.00	1.35	.35
☐ 21 Nicollet Park CL	.25	.11	.03

1941 Harry Hartman W711-2

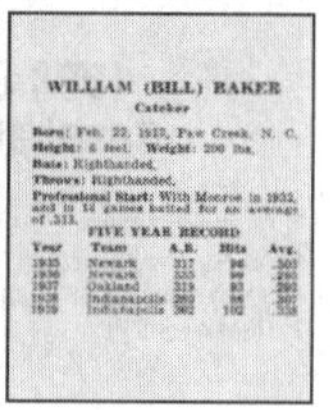

The cards in this 34-card set measure approximately 2 1/8" by 2 5/8". The W711-2 Cincinnati Reds set contains unnumbered, black and white cards and was issued in boxes which had a reverse side resembling a mailing label. This issue is sometimes called the "Harry Hartman" set. The cards are numbered below in alphabetical order by player's name with non-player cards listed at the end. The set is worth about $100 more when it is in the original mailing box.

	EX-MT	VG-E	GOOD
COMPLETE SET (34)	500.00	220.00	60.00
COMMON CARD (1-28)	15.00	6.75	1.85
COMMON CARD (29-34)	12.00	5.50	1.50
☐ 1 Morris Arnovich	15.00	6.75	1.85
☐ 2 William(Bill) Baker	15.00	6.75	1.85
☐ 3 Joseph Beggs	15.00	6.75	1.85
☐ 4 Harry Craft	18.00	8.00	2.20
☐ 5 Paul Derringer	25.00	11.00	3.10
☐ 6 Linus Frey	15.00	6.75	1.85
☐ 7 Ival Goodman	15.00	6.75	1.85
☐ 8 Hank Gowdy CO	18.00	8.00	2.20
☐ 9 Witt Guise	15.00	6.75	1.85
☐ 10 Willard Hershberger	18.00	8.00	2.20
☐ 11 John Hutchings	15.00	6.75	1.85
☐ 12 Edwin Joost	18.00	8.00	2.20
☐ 13 Ernie Lombardi	50.00	22.00	6.25
☐ 14 Frank McCormick	20.00	9.00	2.50
☐ 15 Myron McCormick	15.00	6.75	1.85
☐ 16 Bill McKechnie MG	30.00	13.50	3.70
☐ 17 Whitey Moore	15.00	6.75	1.85
☐ 18 William(Bill) Myers	15.00	6.75	1.85
☐ 19 Elmer Riddle	15.00	6.75	1.85
☐ 20 Lewis Riggs	15.00	6.75	1.85
☐ 21 James A. Ripple	15.00	6.75	1.85
☐ 22 Milburn Shoffner	15.00	6.75	1.85
☐ 23 Eugene Thompson	15.00	6.75	1.85
☐ 24 James Turner	18.00	8.00	2.20
☐ 25 John VanderMeer	30.00	13.50	3.70
☐ 26 Bucky Walters	20.00	9.00	2.50
☐ 27 Bill Werber	15.00	6.75	1.85
☐ 28 James Wilson	15.00	6.75	1.85
☐ 29 Results 1940 World Series	12.00	5.50	1.50
☐ 30 The Cincinnati Reds (Title Card)	12.00	5.50	1.50
☐ 31 The Cincinnati Reds World's Champions (Title Card)	12.00	5.50	1.50
☐ 32 Debt of Gratitude to Wm. Koehl Co.	12.00	5.50	1.50
☐ 33 Tell the World About Our Reds	12.00	5.50	1.50
☐ 34 Harry Hartman ANN	12.00	5.50	1.50

1912 Hassan Triple Folders T202

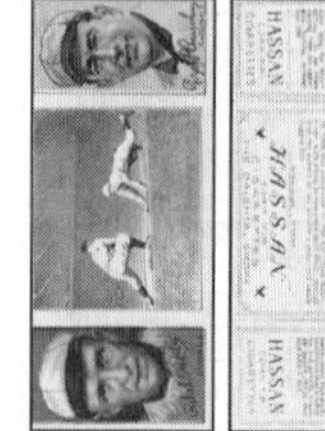

The cards in this 134-card set measure approximately 2 1/4" by 5 1/4". The 1912 T202 Hassan Triple Folder issue is perhaps the most ingenious baseball card ever issued. The two end cards of each panel are full color, T205-like individual cards whereas the black and white center panel pictures an action photo or portrait. The end cards can be folded across the center panel and stored in this manner. Seventy-six different center panels are known to exist; however, many of the center panels contain more than one combination of end cards. The center panel titles are listed below in alphabetical order while the different combinations of end cards are listed below each center panel as they appear left to right on the front of the card. A total of 132 different card fronts exist. The set price below includes all panel and player combinations listed in the checklist. Back color variations (red or black) also exist. The Birmingham's Home Run card is difficult to obtain as are other cards whose center panel exists with but one combination of end cards. The Devlin with Mathewson end panels on numbers 29A and 74C picture Devlin as a Giant. Devlin is pictured as a Rustler on 29B and 74D.

	EX-MT	VG-E	GOOD
COMPLETE SET (132)	36000.00	16200.00	4500.00
COMMON PANEL (1-76)	150.00	70.00	19.00
☐ 1A A Close Play at Home: Wallace-LaPorte	175.00	80.00	22.00
☐ 1B A Close Play at Home: Wallace-Pelty	175.00	80.00	22.00
☐ 2 A Desperate Slide: O'Leary-Cobb	1350.00	600.00	170.00
☐ 3A A Great Batsman: Barger-Bergen	150.00	70.00	19.00
☐ 3B A Great Batsman: Rucker-Bergen	150.00	70.00	19.00
☐ 4 Ambrose McConnell at Bat: Blair-Quinn	175.00	80.00	22.00
☐ 5 A Wide Throw Saves Crawford: Mullin-Stanage	200.00	90.00	25.00
☐ 6 Baker Gets His Man: Collins-Baker	350.00	160.00	45.00
☐ 7 Birmingham Gets to Third: Johnson-Street	450.00	200.00	55.00
☐ 8 Birmingham's Home Run: Birmingham-Turner	500.00	220.00	60.00
☐ 9 Bush Just Misses Austin: Moran-Magee	175.00	80.00	22.00
☐ 10A Carrigan Blocks His Man: Gaspar-McLean	150.00	70.00	19.00
☐ 10B Carrigan Blocks His Man: Wagner-Carrigan	150.00	70.00	19.00
☐ 11 Catching Him Napping: Oakes-Bresnahan	200.00	90.00	25.00
☐ 12 Caught Asleep Off First: Bresnahan-Harmon	200.00	90.00	25.00
☐ 13A Chance Beats Out a Hit: Chance-Foxen	250.00	110.00	31.00
☐ 13B Chance Beats Out a Hit: McIntire-Archer	175.00	80.00	22.00
☐ 13C Chance Beats Out a Hit: Overall-Archer	175.00	80.00	22.00
☐ 13D Chance Beats Out a Hit: Rowan-Archer	175.00	80.00	22.00
☐ 13E Chance Beats Out a Hit: Shean-Chance	250.00	110.00	31.00
☐ 14A Chase Dives into Third: Chase-Wolter	150.00	70.00	19.00
☐ 14B Chase Dives into Third: Gibson-Clarke	175.00	80.00	22.00
☐ 14C Chase Dives into Third: Phillippe-Gibson	150.00	70.00	19.00
☐ 15A Chase Gets Ball Too Late: Egan-Mitchell	150.00	70.00	19.00
☐ 15B Chase Gets Ball Too Late: Wolter-Chase	150.00	70.00	19.00
☐ 16A Chase Guarding First: Chase-Wolter	150.00	70.00	19.00
☐ 16B Chase Guarding First: Gibson-Clarke	175.00	80.00	22.00
☐ 16C Chase Guarding First: Leifield-Gibson	150.00	70.00	19.00
☐ 17 Chase Ready Squeeze Play: Paskert-Magee	175.00	80.00	22.00
☐ 18 Chase Safe at Third: Barry-Baker	200.00	90.00	25.00
☐ 19 Chief Bender Waiting: Bender-Thomas	225.00	100.00	28.00
☐ 20 Clarke Hikes for Home: Bridwell-Kling	200.00	90.00	25.00
☐ 21 Close at First: Ball-Stovall	175.00	80.00	22.00
☐ 22A Close at the Plate: Walsh-Payne	175.00	80.00	22.00
☐ 22B Close at the Plate: White-Payne	150.00	70.00	19.00
☐ 23 Close at Third (Speak- er): Wood-Speaker	350.00	160.00	45.00
☐ 24 Close at Third (Wagner): Wagner-Carrigan	175.00	80.00	22.00
☐ 25A Collins Easily Safe: Byrne-Clarke	175.00	80.00	22.00
☐ 25B Collins Easily Safe: Collins-Baker	350.00	160.00	45.00
☐ 25C Collins Easily Safe: Collins-Murphy	250.00	110.00	31.00
☐ 26 Crawford About to Smash: Stanage-Summers	200.00	90.00	25.00
☐ 27 Cree Rolls Home: Daubert-Hummell	175.00	80.00	22.00
☐ 28 Davy Jones' Great Slide: Delahanty-Jones	175.00	80.00	22.00

☐ 29A Devlin Gets His Man: Devlin (Giants)-Mathewson	300.00	135.00	38.00
☐ 29B Devlin Gets His Man: Devlin (Rustlers)-Mathewson	1000.00	450.00	125.00
☐ 29C Devlin Gets His Man: Fletcher-Mathewson	300.00	135.00	38.00
☐ 29D Devlin Gets His Man: Meyers-Mathewson	400.00	180.00	50.00
☐ 30A Donlin Out at First: Camnitz-Gibson	150.00	70.00	19.00
☐ 30B Donlin Out at First: Doyle-Merkle	150.00	70.00	19.00
☐ 30C Donlin Out at First: Leach-Wilson	150.00	70.00	19.00
☐ 30D Donlin Out at First: Magee-Dooin	150.00	70.00	19.00
☐ 30E Donlin Out at First: Phillippe-Gibson	150.00	70.00	19.00
☐ 31A Dooin Gets His Man: Dooin-Doolan	150.00	70.00	19.00
☐ 31B Dooin Gets His Man: Lobert-Dooin	150.00	70.00	19.00
☐ 31C Dooin Gets His Man: Titus-Dooin	150.00	70.00	19.00
☐ 32 Easy for Larry: Doyle-Merkle	175.00	80.00	22.00
☐ 33 Elberfeld Beats: Milan-Elberfeld	175.00	80.00	22.00
☐ 34 Elberfeld Gets His Man: Milan-Elberfeld	175.00	80.00	22.00
☐ 35 Engle in a Close Play: Speaker-Engle	250.00	110.00	31.00
☐ 36A Evers Makes Safe Slide: Archer-Evers	225.00	100.00	28.00
☐ 36B Evers Makes Safe Slide: Evers-Chance	350.00	160.00	45.00
☐ 36C Evers Makes Safe Slide: Overall-Archer	175.00	80.00	22.00
☐ 36D Evers Makes Safe Slide: Reulbach-Archer	175.00	80.00	22.00
☐ 36E Evers Makes Safe Slide: Tinker-Chance	1000.00	450.00	125.00
☐ 37 Fast Work at Third: O'Leary-Cobb	1250.00	550.00	160.00
☐ 38A Ford Putting Over Spitter: Ford-Vaughn	150.00	70.00	19.00
☐ 38B Ford Putting Over Spitter: Sweeney-Ford	150.00	70.00	19.00
☐ 39 Good Play at Third: Moriarty-Cobb	1250.00	550.00	160.00
☐ 40 Grant Gets His Man: Hoblitzel-Grant	175.00	80.00	22.00
☐ 41A Hal Chase Too Late: McIntyre-McConnell	150.00	70.00	19.00
☐ 41B Hal Chase Too Late: Suggs-McLean	150.00	70.00	19.00
☐ 42 Harry Lord at Third: Lennox-Tinker	200.00	90.00	25.00
☐ 43 Hartzell Covering: Scanlon-Dahlen	175.00	80.00	22.00
☐ 44 Hartzell Strikes Out: Groom-Gray	175.00	80.00	22.00
☐ 45 Held at Third: Tannehill-Lord	175.00	80.00	22.00
☐ 46 Jake Stahl Guarding: Cicotte-Stahl	175.00	80.00	22.00
☐ 47 Jim Delahanty at Bat: Delahanty-Jones	175.00	80.00	22.00
☐ 48A Just Before the Battle: Ames-Meyers	150.00	70.00	19.00
☐ 48B Just Before the Battle: Bresnahan-McGraw	350.00	160.00	45.00
☐ 48C Just Before the Battle: Crandall-Meyers	150.00	70.00	19.00
☐ 48D Just Before the Battle: Devore-Becker	150.00	70.00	19.00
☐ 48E Just Before the Battle: Fletcher-Mathewson	300.00	135.00	38.00
☐ 48F Just Before the Battle: Marquard-Meyers	175.00	80.00	22.00
☐ 48G Just Before the Battle: McGraw-Jennings	350.00	160.00	45.00
☐ 48H Just Before the Battle: Meyers-Mathewson	275.00	125.00	34.00
☐ 48I Just Before the Battle: Snodgrass-Murray	150.00	70.00	19.00
☐ 48J Just Before the Battle: Wiltse-Meyers	150.00	70.00	19.00
☐ 49 Knight Catches Runner: Knight-Johnson	450.00	200.00	55.00
☐ 50A Lobert Almost Caught: Bridwell-Kling	150.00	70.00	19.00
☐ 50B Lobert Almost Caught: Kling-Young	225.00	100.00	28.00
☐ 50C Lobert Almost Caught: Mattern-Kling	150.00	70.00	19.00
☐ 50D Lobert Almost Caught: Steinfeldt-Kling	150.00	70.00	19.00
☐ 51 Lobert Gets Tenney: Lobert-Dooin	175.00	80.00	22.00
☐ 52 Lord Catches His Man: Tannehill-Lord	175.00	80.00	22.00
☐ 53 McConnell Caught: Richie-Needham	175.00	80.00	22.00
☐ 54 McIntyre at Bat: McIntyre-McConnell	175.00	80.00	22.00
☐ 55 Moriarty Spiked: Willett-Stanage	175.00	80.00	22.00
☐ 56 Nearly Caught: Bates-Bescher	200.00	90.00	25.00
☐ 57 Oldring Almost Home: Lord-Oldring	175.00	80.00	22.00
☐ 58 Schaefer on First: McBride-Milan	175.00	80.00	22.00
☐ 59 Schaefer Steals Second: McBride-Griffith	200.00	90.00	25.00
☐ 60 Scoring from Second: Lord-Oldring	175.00	80.00	22.00
☐ 61A Scrambling Back: Barger-Bergen	150.00	70.00	19.00
☐ 61B Scrambling Back: Wolter-Chase	150.00	70.00	19.00
☐ 62 Speaker Almost Caught: Miller-Clarke	350.00	160.00	45.00
☐ 63 Speaker Rounding Third: Wood-Speaker	750.00	350.00	95.00
☐ 64 Speaker Scores: Speaker-Engle	400.00	180.00	50.00
☐ 65 Stahl Safe: Stovall-Austin	175.00	80.00	22.00
☐ 66 Stone About to Swing: Sheckard-Schulte	175.00	80.00	22.00
☐ 67A Sullivan Puts Up High One: Evans-Huggins	175.00	80.00	22.00
☐ 67B Sullivan Puts Up High One: Sweeney-Ford	150.00	70.00	19.00
☐ 68A Sweeney Gets Stahl: Ford-Vaughn	150.00	70.00	19.00
☐ 68B Sweeney Gets Stahl: Sweeney-Ford	150.00	70.00	19.00
☐ 69 Tenney Lands Safely: Raymond-Latham	175.00	80.00	22.00
☐ 70A The Athletic Infield: Barry-Baker	175.00	80.00	22.00
☐ 70B The Athletic Infield: Brown-Graham	150.00	70.00	19.00
☐ 70C The Athletic Infield: Hauser-Konetchy	150.00	70.00	19.00
☐ 70D The Athletic Infield: Krause-Thomas	150.00	70.00	19.00
☐ 71 The Pinch Hitter: Hoblitzel-Egan	175.00	80.00	22.00
☐ 72 The Scissors Slide: Birmingham-Turner	175.00	80.00	22.00
☐ 73A Tom Jones at Bat: Fromme-McLean	150.00	70.00	19.00
☐ 73B Tom Jones at Bat: Gaspar-McLean	150.00	70.00	19.00
☐ 74A Too Late for Devlin: Ames-Meyers	150.00	70.00	19.00
☐ 74B Too Late for Devlin: Crandall-Meyers	150.00	70.00	19.00
☐ 74C Too Late for Devlin: Devlin (Giants)-Mathewson	1000.00	450.00	125.00
☐ 74D Too Late for Devlin: Devlin (Rustlers)-Mathewson	300.00	135.00	38.00
☐ 74E Too Late for Devlin: Marquard-Meyers	175.00	80.00	22.00
☐ 74F Too Late for Devlin: Wiltse-Meyers	150.00	70.00	19.00
☐ 75A Ty Cobb Steals Third: Jennings-Cobb	2000.00	900.00	250.00
☐ 75B Ty Cobb Steals Third: Moriarty-Cobb	2000.00	900.00	250.00
☐ 75C Ty Cobb Steals Third: Stovall-Austin	1350.00	600.00	170.00
☐ 76 Wheat Strikes Out: Dahlen-Wheat	250.00	110.00	31.00

1959 Hayes Company Bauer PC750

The 1959 Hayes Company postacrd consists of but one card. The Dexter Press printed Hank Bauer card is in full color and features a facsimile autograph of Bauer at the bottom of the card.

	NRMT	VG-E	GOOD
COMPLETE SET (1)	15.00	6.75	1.85
COMMON CARD	15.00	6.75	1.85
☐ 1 Hank Bauer	15.00	6.75	1.85

1992 High 5

This 130-decal set features five players each from the 26 Major League Baseball teams. The collector could also purchase a stadium display board to display all the decals. The decals measure the standard size. The fronts are actually reusable stickers and display color action player photos. The color of the inner border varies from card to card , while the outermost border is on all cards. The pictures are accented above and on the right by a thin color stripe. The "High 5" logo and team logo appear in the upper left and lower right corners respectively. The decals are checklisted below alphabetically within and according to teams for each league as follows: Baltimore Orioles, (1-5) Boston Red Sox, (6-10) California Angels, (11-15) Chicago White Sox, (16-20) Cleveland Indians, (21-25) Detroit Tigers, (26-30) Kansas City Royals, (31-35) Milwaukee Brewers, (36-40) Minnesota Twins, (41-45) New York Yankees, (46-50) Oakland Athletics, (51-55) Seattle Mariners, (56-60) Texas Rangers, (61-65) Toronto Blue Jays, (66-70) Atlanta Braves, (71-75) Chicago Cubs, (76-80) Cincinnati Reds, (81-85) Houston Astros, (86-90) Los Angeles Dodgers, (91-95) Montreal Expos, (96-100) New York Mets, (101-105) Philadelphia Phillies, (106-110) Pittsburgh Pirates, (111-115) St. Louis Cardinals, (116-120) San Diego Padres, (121-125) and San Francisco Giants (126-130). Stickers from expansion teams Colorado Rockies and Florida Marlins were promised for 1993. However, no 1993 issued was produced.

	MINT	NRMT	EXC
COMPLETE SET (130)	75.00	34.00	9.50
COMMON CARD (1-130)	.25	.11	.03
☐ 1 Mike Deveraux	.25	.11	.03
☐ 2 Ben McDonald	.25	.11	.03
☐ 3 Gregg Olson	.25	.11	.03
☐ 4 Joe Orsulak	.25	.11	.03
☐ 5 Cal Ripken	5.00	2.20	.60
☐ 6 Wade Boggs	1.00	.45	.12
☐ 7 Roger Clemens	1.00	.45	.12
☐ 8 Phil Plantier	.25	.11	.03
☐ 9 Jeff Reardon	.50	.23	.06
☐ 10 Mo Vaughn	2.00	.90	.25
☐ 11 Jim Abbott	.50	.23	.06
☐ 12 Chuck Finley	.25	.11	.03
☐ 13 Brian Harvey	.25	.11	.03
☐ 14 Mark Langston	.25	.11	.03
☐ 15 Dave Winfield	1.00	.45	.12
☐ 16 Carlton Fisk	1.00	.45	.12
☐ 17 Jack McDowell	.75	.35	.09
☐ 18 Bobby Thigpen	.25	.11	.03
☐ 19 Frank Thomas	6.00	2.70	.75
☐ 20 Robin Ventura	.50	.23	.06
☐ 21 Steve Avery	.25	.11	.03
☐ 22 Ron Gant	.50	.23	.06
☐ 23 Tom Glavine	1.00	.45	.12
☐ 24 Dave Justice	.50	.23	.06
☐ 25 Terry Pendleton	.25	.11	.03
☐ 26 George Bell	.25	.11	.03
☐ 27 Andre Dawson	1.00	.45	.12
☐ 28 Mark Grace	2.50	1.10	.30
☐ 29 Greg Maddux	4.50	2.00	.55
☐ 30 Ryne Sandberg	3.00	1.35	.35
☐ 31 Eric Davis	.50	.23	.06
☐ 32 Barry Larkin	1.50	.70	.19
☐ 33 Hal Morris	.25	.11	.03
☐ 34 Jose Rijo	.25	.11	.03
☐ 35 Chris Sabo	.25	.11	.03
☐ 36 Jeff Bagwell	3.00	1.35	.35
☐ 37 Craig Biggio	.50	.23	.06
☐ 38 Ken Caminiti	.60	.25	.07
☐ 39 Luis Gonzalez	.25	.11	.03
☐ 40 Pete Harnisch	.25	.11	.03
☐ 41 Sandy Alomar Jr.	.50	.23	.06
☐ 42 Carlos Baerga	1.00	.45	.12
☐ 43 Albert Belle	3.00	1.35	.35
☐ 44 Alex Cole	.25	.11	.03
☐ 45 Charles Nagy	.50	.23	.06
☐ 46 Cecil Fielder	1.00	.45	.12
☐ 47 Travis Fryman	.75	.35	.09
☐ 48 Tony Phillips	.25	.11	.03
☐ 49 Alan Trammell	.50	.23	.06
☐ 50 Lou Whitaker	.50	.23	.06
☐ 51 Brett Butler	.75	.35	.09
☐ 52 Lenny Harris	.25	.11	.03
☐ 53 Ramon Martinez	.50	.23	.06
☐ 54 Eddie Murray	1.50	.70	.19
☐ 55 Darryl Strawberry	.50	.23	.06
☐ 56 Ivan Calderon	.25	.11	.03
☐ 57 Delino DeShields	.25	.11	.03
☐ 58 Marquis Grissom	.50	.23	.06
☐ 59 Dennis Martinez	.50	.23	.06
☐ 60 Larry Walker	.60	.25	.07
☐ 61 George Brett	3.00	1.35	.35
☐ 62 Jim Eisenreich	.50	.23	.06
☐ 63 Brian McRae	.50	.23	.06
☐ 64 Jeff Montgomery	.25	.11	.03
☐ 65 Bret Saberhagen	.25	.11	.03
☐ 66 Chris Bosio	.25	.11	.03
☐ 67 Paul Molitor	1.25	.55	.16
☐ 68 B.J. Surhoff	.50	.23	.06
☐ 69 Greg Vaughn	.50	.23	.06
☐ 70 Robin Yount	1.00	.45	.12
☐ 71 David Cone	.50	.23	.06
☐ 72 Dwight Gooden	.50	.23	.06
☐ 73 Gregg Jefferies	.50	.23	.06
☐ 74 Howard Johnson	.25	.11	.03
☐ 75 Kevin McReynolds	.25	.11	.03
☐ 76 Wes Chamberlain	.25	.11	.03
☐ 77 Len Dykstra	.50	.23	.06
☐ 78 John Kruk	.50	.23	.06
☐ 79 Terry Mulholland	.25	.11	.03
☐ 80 Mitch Williams	.25	.11	.03
☐ 81 Rick Aguilera	.25	.11	.03
☐ 82 Scott Erickson	.25	.11	.03
☐ 83 Kent Hrbek	.25	.11	.03
☐ 84 Kirby Puckett	4.00	1.80	.50
☐ 85 Kevin Tapani	.25	.11	.03
☐ 86 Mel Hall	.25	.11	.03
☐ 87 Roberto Kelly	.25	.11	.03
☐ 88 Kevin Maas	.25	.11	.03
☐ 89 Don Mattingly	4.00	1.80	.50
☐ 90 Steve Sax	.25	.11	.03
☐ 91 Barry Bonds	2.00	.90	.25
☐ 92 Doug Drabek	.25	.11	.03
☐ 93 John Smiley	.25	.11	.03
☐ 94 Zane Smith	.25	.11	.03
☐ 95 Andy Van Slyke	.25	.11	.03
☐ 96 Felix Jose	.25	.11	.03
☐ 97 Ray Lankford	.75	.35	.09
☐ 98 Lee Smith	.50	.23	.06
☐ 99 Ozzie Smith	3.00	1.35	.35
☐ 100 Todd Zeile	.25	.11	.03
☐ 101 Harold Baines	.25	.11	.03
☐ 102 Jose Canseco	1.50	.70	.19
☐ 103 Dennis Eckersley	.75	.35	.09
☐ 104 Dave Henderson	.25	.11	.03
☐ 105 Rickey Henderson	1.00	.45	.12
☐ 106 Jay Buhner	.75	.35	.09
☐ 107 Ken Griffey Jr.	6.00	2.70	.75
☐ 108 Randy Johnson	.60	.25	.07
☐ 109 Edgar Martinez	1.00	.45	.12
☐ 110 Harold Reynolds	.50	.23	.06
☐ 111 Julio Franco	.50	.23	.06
☐ 112 Juan Gonzalez	3.00	1.35	.35
☐ 113 Rafael Palmeiro	.75	.35	.09
☐ 114 Nolan Ryan	5.00	2.20	.60
☐ 115 Ruben Sierra	.25	.11	.03
☐ 116 Roberto Alomar	2.00	.90	.25
☐ 117 Joe Carter	.75	.35	.09
☐ 118 Kelly Gruber	.25	.11	.03
☐ 119 John Olerud	.50	.23	.06
☐ 120 Devon White	.25	.11	.03
☐ 121 Tony Fernandez	.25	.11	.03
☐ 122 Tony Gwynn	3.00	1.35	.35
☐ 123 Bruce Hurst	.25	.11	.03
☐ 124 Fred McGriff	1.00	.45	.12
☐ 125 Benito Santiago	.25	.11	.03
☐ 126 Will Clark	.75	.35	.09
☐ 127 Willie McGee	.50	.23	.06
☐ 128 Kevin Mitchell	.25	.11	.03
☐ 129 Robby Thompson	.25	.11	.03
☐ 130 Matt Williams	1.50	.70	.19

1992 High 5 Superstars

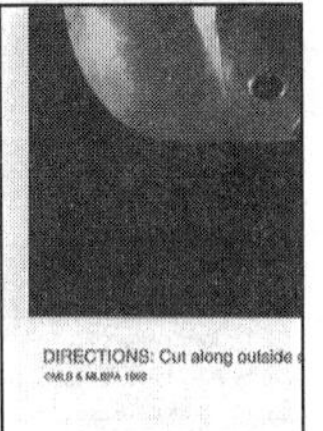
DIRECTIONS: Cut along outside

This 36-decal set features some of baseball's greatest players. Six different assortments, each featuring five player decals and one High 5 nonplayer decal, were issued (AL infielders, outfielders and pitchers as well as NL infielders, outfielders and pitchers). The decals measure the standard size. The fronts are actually reusable stickers and display color action player photos. The color of the inner border varies from decal to decal, (gradated blue, black or green) while the outermost border is white on all decals. Moreover, the pictures are accented above and on the right by a thin color stripe (red, yellow, blue or gray). The "High 5" logo and team logos appear in the upper left and lower right corners respectively. The backs of six decals combine to form six separate 5" by 7" color close-up photos of players featured on the fronts (Clark, Griffey Jr., Justice, Ryan, Strawberry and Thomas). Each of these composite pictures includes one High 5 Superstar nonplayer decal. The decals are unnumbered and checklisted below in alphabetical order.

	MINT	NRMT	EXC
COMPLETE SET (36)	40.00	18.00	5.00
COMMON CARD (1-36)	.50	.23	.06
☐ 1 Steve Avery	.50	.23	.06
☐ 2 Jeff Bagwell	2.50	1.10	.30
☐ 3 Wade Boggs	1.00	.45	.12
☐ 4 Barry Bonds	1.00	.45	.12
☐ 5 Jose Canseco	1.00	.45	.12
☐ 6 Joe Carter	.75	.35	.09
☐ 7 Will Clark	1.00	.45	.12
☐ 8 Roger Clemens	1.50	.70	.19

☐ 9 Dennis Eckersley	.75	.35	.09
☐ 10 Scott Erickson	.50	.23	.06
☐ 11 Cecil Fielder	1.00	.45	.12
☐ 12 Julio Franco	.50	.23	.06
☐ 13 Tom Glavine	1.00	.45	.12
☐ 14 Juan Gonzalez	2.50	1.10	.30
☐ 15 Dwight Gooden	.75	.35	.09
☐ 16 Ron Gant	.75	.35	.09
☐ 17 Ken Griffey Jr.	5.00	2.20	.60
☐ 18 Tony Gwynn	2.50	1.10	.30
☐ 19 Ricky Henderson	1.00	.45	.12
☐ 20 Howard Johnson	.50	.23	.06
☐ 21 Dave Justice	.75	.35	.09
☐ 22 Mark Langston	.50	.23	.06
☐ 23 Ramon Martinez	.75	.35	.09
☐ 24 Cal Ripken	4.00	1.80	.50
☐ 25 Nolan Ryan	4.00	1.80	.50
☐ 26 Ryne Sandberg	2.50	1.10	.30
☐ 27 John Smiley	.50	.23	.06
☐ 28 Darryl Strawberry	.75	.35	.09
☐ 29 Frank Thomas	5.00	2.20	.60
☐ 30 Matt Williams	1.50	.70	.19
☐ 31 High 5 Superstar (Part of Will Clark 5x7 Portrait)	.75	.35	.09
☐ 32 High 5 Superstar (Part of Ken Griffey Jr. 5x7 Portrait)	2.50	1.10	.30
☐ 33 High 5 Superstar (Part of David Justice 5x7 Portrait)	.50	.23	.06
☐ 34 High 5 Superstar (Part of Nolan Ryan 5x7 Portrait)	2.00	.90	.25
☐ 35 High 5 Superstar (Part of Darryl Strawberry 5x7 Portrait)	.50	.23	.06
☐ 36 High 5 Superstar (Part of Frank Thomas 5x7 Portrait)	2.50	1.10	.30

1958 Hires

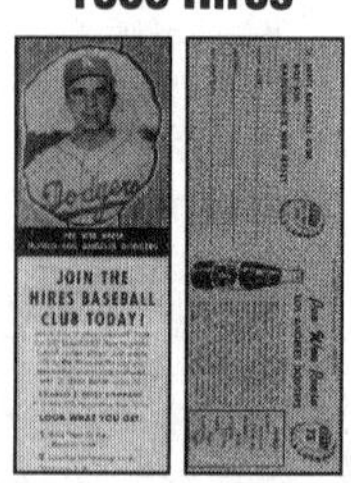

The cards in this 66-card set measure approximately 2 5/16" by 3 1/2" or 2 5/16" by 7" with tabs. The 1958 Hires Root Beer set of numbered, colored cards was issued with detachable coupons as inserts with Hires Root Beer cartons. Cards with the coupon still intact are worth 2.5 times the prices listed below. The card front picture is surrounded by a wood grain effect which makes it look like the player is seen through a knot hole. The numbering of this set is rather strange in that it begins with 10 and skips 69.

	NRMT	VG-E	GOOD
COMPLETE SET (66)	1350.00	600.00	170.00
COMMON CARD (10-76)	12.00	5.50	1.50
☐ 10 Richie Ashburn	75.00	34.00	9.50
☐ 11 Chico Carrasquel	12.00	5.50	1.50
☐ 12 Dave Philley	12.00	5.50	1.50
☐ 13 Don Newcombe	15.00	6.75	1.85
☐ 14 Wally Post	12.00	5.50	1.50
☐ 15 Rip Repulski	12.00	5.50	1.50
☐ 16 Chico Fernandez	12.00	5.50	1.50
☐ 17 Larry Doby	20.00	9.00	2.50
☐ 18 Hector Brown	12.00	5.50	1.50
☐ 19 Danny O'Connell	12.00	5.50	1.50
☐ 20 Granny Hamner	12.00	5.50	1.50
☐ 21 Dick Groat	15.00	6.75	1.85
☐ 22 Ray Narleski	12.00	5.50	1.50
☐ 23 Pee Wee Reese	75.00	34.00	9.50
☐ 24 Bob Friend	12.00	5.50	1.50
☐ 25 Willie Mays	250.00	110.00	31.00
☐ 26 Bob Nieman	12.00	5.50	1.50
☐ 27 Frank Thomas	15.00	6.75	1.85
☐ 28 Curt Simmons	15.00	6.75	1.85
☐ 29 Stan Lopata	12.00	5.50	1.50
☐ 30 Bob Skinner	12.00	5.50	1.50
☐ 31 Ron Kline	12.00	5.50	1.50
☐ 32 Willie Miranda	12.00	5.50	1.50
☐ 33 Bobby Avila	12.00	5.50	1.50
☐ 34 Clem Labine	15.00	6.75	1.85
☐ 35 Ray Jablonski	12.00	5.50	1.50
☐ 36 Bill Mazeroski	25.00	11.00	3.10
☐ 37 Billy Gardner	12.00	5.50	1.50
☐ 38 Pete Runnels	12.00	5.50	1.50
☐ 39 Jack Sanford	12.00	5.50	1.50
☐ 40 Dave Sisler	12.00	5.50	1.50
☐ 41 Don Zimmer	15.00	6.75	1.85
☐ 42 Johnny Podres	15.00	6.75	1.85
☐ 43 Dick Farrell	12.00	5.50	1.50
☐ 44 Hank Aaron	225.00	100.00	28.00
☐ 45 Bill Virdon	12.00	5.50	1.50
☐ 46 Bobby Thomson	15.00	6.75	1.85
☐ 47 Willard Nixon	12.00	5.50	1.50
☐ 48 Billy Loes	12.00	5.50	1.50
☐ 49 Hank Sauer	15.00	6.75	1.85
☐ 50 Johnny Antonelli	15.00	6.75	1.85
☐ 51 Daryl Spencer	12.00	5.50	1.50
☐ 52 Ken Lehman	12.00	5.50	1.50
☐ 53 Sammy White	12.00	5.50	1.50
☐ 54 Charley Neal	12.00	5.50	1.50
☐ 55 Don Drysdale	60.00	27.00	7.50
☐ 56 Jackie Jensen	25.00	11.00	3.10
☐ 57 Ray Katt	12.00	5.50	1.50
☐ 58 Frank Sullivan	12.00	5.50	1.50
☐ 59 Roy Face	15.00	6.75	1.85
☐ 60 Willie Jones	12.00	5.50	1.50
☐ 61 Duke Snider	75.00	34.00	9.50
☐ 62 Whitey Lockman	12.00	5.50	1.50
☐ 63 Gino Cimoli	12.00	5.50	1.50
☐ 64 Marv Grissom	12.00	5.50	1.50
☐ 65 Gene Baker	12.00	5.50	1.50
☐ 66 George Zuverink	12.00	5.50	1.50
☐ 67 Ted Kluszewski	25.00	11.00	3.10
☐ 68 Jim Busby	12.00	5.50	1.50
☐ 69 Not Issued			
☐ 70 Curt Barclay	12.00	5.50	1.50
☐ 71 Hank Foiles	12.00	5.50	1.50
☐ 72 Gene Stephens	12.00	5.50	1.50
☐ 73 Al Worthington	12.00	5.50	1.50
☐ 74 Al Walker	12.00	5.50	1.50
☐ 75 Bob Boyd	12.00	5.50	1.50
☐ 76 Al Pilarcik	12.00	5.50	1.50

1958 Hires Test

The cards in this eight-card test set measure approximately 2 5/16" by 3 1/2" or 2 5/16" by 7" with tabs. The 1958 Hires Root Beer test set features unnumbered, color cards. The card front photos are shown on a yellow or orange back ground instead of the wood grain background used in the Hires regular set. The cards contain a detachable coupon just as the regular Hires issue does. Cards were test marketed on a very limited basis in a few cities. Cards with the coupon still intact are especially tough to find and are worth triple the prices in the checklist below. The checklist below is ordered alphabetically.

	NRMT	VG-E	GOOD
COMPLETE SET (8)	1350.00	600.00	170.00
COMMON CARD (1-8)	125.00	55.00	15.50
☐ 1 Johnny Antonelli	150.00	70.00	19.00
☐ 2 Jim Busby	125.00	55.00	15.50
☐ 3 Chico Fernandez	125.00	55.00	15.50
☐ 4 Bob Friend	150.00	70.00	19.00
☐ 5 Vern Law	150.00	70.00	19.00
☐ 6 Stan Lopata	125.00	55.00	15.50
☐ 7 Willie Mays	600.00	275.00	75.00
☐ 8 Al Pilarcik	125.00	55.00	15.50

1992 Hit The Books Bookmarks

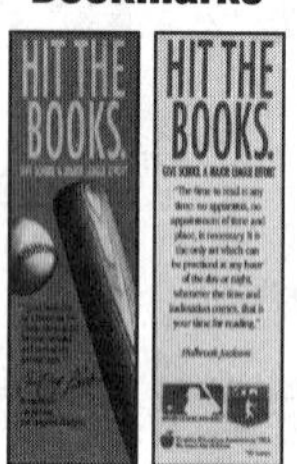

These bookmarks were produced of leading major leaguers. The purpose was to increase interest in reading and visiting local libraries. These bookmarks are unnumbered and we have sequenced them in alphabetical order.

	MINT	NRMT	EXC
COMPLETE SET (36)	50.00	22.00	6.25
COMMON CARD (1-36)	1.00	.45	.12
☐ 1 Jim Abbott	1.00	.45	.12
☐ 2 Sandy Alomar	1.50	.70	.19
☐ 3 Jay Bell	1.00	.45	.12
☐ 4 Craig Biggio	1.50	.70	.19
☐ 5 Mike Boddicker	1.00	.45	.12
☐ 6 Bobby Bonilla	1.50	.70	.19
☐ 7 George Brett	4.00	1.80	.50
☐ 8 Brett Butler	1.50	.70	.19
☐ 9 Joe Carter	2.00	.90	.25
☐ 10 Will Clark	2.50	1.10	.30
☐ 11 Colorado Rockies	1.50	.70	.19
☐ 12 Andre Dawson	2.00	.90	.25
☐ 13 Cecil Fielder	2.00	.90	.25
☐ 14 Florida Marlins	1.50	.70	.19
☐ 15 Ozzie Guillen	1.00	.45	.12
☐ 16 Tony Gwynn	4.00	1.80	.50
☐ 17 Howard Johnson	1.00	.45	.12
☐ 18 Dave Justice	1.50	.70	.19
☐ 19 Mark Langston	1.00	.45	.12
☐ 20 Barry Larkin	2.50	1.10	.30
☐ 21 Don Mattingly	4.00	1.80	.50
☐ 22 Ben McDonald	1.00	.45	.12
☐ 23 Paul Molitor	2.00	.90	.25
☐ 24 Dale Murphy	2.00	.90	.25
☐ 25 Tony Pena	1.00	.45	.12
☐ 26 Kirby Puckett	4.00	1.80	.50
☐ 27 Harold Reynolds	1.00	.45	.12
☐ 28 Cal Ripken	6.00	2.70	.75
☐ 29 Chris Sabo	1.00	.45	.12
☐ 30 Ryne Sandberg	4.00	1.80	.50
☐ 31 Mike Scioscia	1.00	.45	.12
☐ 32 Ruben Sierra	1.00	.45	.12
☐ 33 Ozzie Smith	4.00	1.80	.50
☐ 34 Dave Stewart	1.00	.45	.12
☐ 35 Andy Van Slyke	1.00	.45	.12
☐ 36 Tim Wallach	1.00	.45	.12

1989 HOF Sticker Book

Lou Gehrig, 1b

These stickers honor members of the baseball Hall of Fame. They are numbered in order of position played: First Base (1-9), Second Base (10-13), Shortstop (14-21), Third Base (22-26), Outfield (27-53), Catcher (54-58), Pitcher (59-84), Manager (85-89) and Builders (90-100).

	MINT	NRMT	EXC
COMPLETE SET (100)	12.00	5.50	1.50
COMMON STICKER (1-100)	.10	.05	.01
☐ 1 Lou Gehrig	1.00	.45	.12
☐ 2 Bill Terry	.35	.16	.04
☐ 3 Johnny Mize	.25	.11	.03
☐ 4 Willie McCovey	.25	.11	.03
☐ 5 Cap Anson	.50	.23	.06
☐ 6 Ernie Banks	.35	.16	.04
☐ 7 Dan Brouthers	.15	.07	.02
☐ 8 George Kelly	.15	.07	.02
☐ 9 Roger Connor	.15	.07	.02
☐ 10 Nap Lajoie	.35	.16	.04
☐ 11 Bobby Doerr	.15	.07	.02
☐ 12 Jackie Robinson	1.00	.45	.12
☐ 13 Frankie Frisch	.25	.11	.03
☐ 14 Honus Wagner	.50	.23	.06
☐ 15 George Wright	.15	.07	.02
☐ 16 Hughie Jennings	.15	.07	.02
☐ 17 Rabbit Maranville	.15	.07	.02
☐ 18 Luis Aparicio	.25	.11	.03
☐ 19 Joe Cronin	.25	.11	.03
☐ 20 Dave Bancroft	.15	.07	.02
☐ 21 Arky Vaughan	.15	.07	.02
☐ 22 Joe Sewell	.15	.07	.02
☐ 23 Jimmy Collins	.15	.07	.02
☐ 24 George Kell	.15	.07	.02
☐ 25 Eddie Mathews	.25	.11	.03
☐ 26 Ray Dandridge	.15	.07	.02
☐ 27 Willie Stargell	.25	.11	.03
☐ 28 Ted Williams	1.00	.45	.12
☐ 29 Billy Williams	.25	.11	.03
☐ 30 Stan Musial	.50	.23	.06
☐ 31 Ed Delahanty	.15	.07	.02
☐ 32 Monte Irvin	.15	.07	.02
☐ 33 Jesse Burkett	.15	.07	.02
☐ 34 Chick Hafey	.15	.07	.02
☐ 35 Joe Kelley	.15	.07	.02
☐ 36 Heinie Manush	.15	.07	.02
☐ 37 Ty Cobb	.75	.35	.09
☐ 38 Max Carey	.15	.07	.02
☐ 39 Joe DiMaggio	1.00	.45	.12
☐ 40 Mickey Mantle	1.00	.45	.12
☐ 41 Tris Speaker	.35	.16	.04
☐ 42 Lloyd Waner	.15	.07	.02
☐ 43 Billy Hamilton	.15	.07	.02
☐ 44 Hank Aaron	.75	.35	.09
☐ 45 Paul Waner	.25	.11	.03
☐ 46 Roberto Clemente	1.00	.45	.12
☐ 47 Babe Ruth	1.00	.45	.12
☐ 48 Chuck Klein	.15	.07	.02
☐ 49 Mel Ott	.25	.11	.03
☐ 50 Sam Crawford	.15	.07	.02
☐ 51 Willie Keeler	.15	.07	.02
☐ 52 Harry Hooper	.15	.07	.02
☐ 53 Elmer Flick	.15	.07	.02
☐ 54 Roy Campanella	.35	.16	.04
☐ 55 Roger Bresnahan	.15	.07	.02
☐ 56 Mickey Cochrane	.25	.11	.03
☐ 57 Buck Ewing	.15	.07	.02
☐ 58 Ernie Lombardi	.15	.07	.02
☐ 59 Cy Young	.50	.23	.06
☐ 60 Mordecai Brown	.15	.07	.02
☐ 61 Red Faber	.15	.07	.02
☐ 62 Bob Feller	.35	.16	.04
☐ 63 Martin Dihigo	.15	.07	.02
☐ 64 Candy Cummings	.15	.07	.02
☐ 65 Christy Mathewson	.35	.16	.04
☐ 66 Rube Marquard	.15	.07	.02
☐ 67 Herb Pennock	.15	.07	.02
☐ 68 Bob Lemon	.15	.07	.02
☐ 69 Eppa Rixey	.15	.07	.02
☐ 70 Whitey Ford	.35	.16	.04
☐ 71 Waite Hoyt	.15	.07	.02
☐ 72 Grover Alexander	.35	.16	.04
☐ 73 Dazzy Vance	.15	.07	.02
☐ 74 Lefty Grove	.25	.11	.03
☐ 75 Carl Hubbell	.25	.11	.03
☐ 76 Lefty Gomez	.15	.07	.02
☐ 77 Ed Walsh	.15	.07	.02
☐ 78 Eddie Plank	.15	.07	.02
☐ 79 Sandy Koufax	.50	.23	.06
☐ 80 Pud Galvin	.15	.07	.02
☐ 81 Hoyt Wilhelm	.15	.07	.02
☐ 82 Catfish Hunter	.15	.07	.02
☐ 83 Red Ruffing	.15	.07	.02
☐ 84 Warren Spahn	.25	.11	.03
☐ 85 Connie Mack	.25	.11	.03
☐ 86 Wilbert Robinson	.10	.05	.01
☐ 87 Joe McCarthy	.10	.05	.01
☐ 88 Bill McKechnie	.10	.05	.01
☐ 89 John McGraw	.25	.11	.03
☐ 90 Alexander Cartwright	.10	.05	.01
☐ 91 Branch Rickey	.10	.05	.01
☐ 92 Warren Giles	.10	.05	.01
☐ 93 Tom Yawkey	.10	.05	.01
☐ 94 Ed Barrow	.10	.05	.01
☐ 95 Kenesaw Landis	.10	.05	.01
☐ 96 Ban Johnson	.10	.05	.01
☐ 97 Happy Chandler	.10	.05	.01
☐ 98 Jocko Conlan	.10	.05	.01
☐ 99 Cal Hubbard	.10	.05	.01
☐ 100 Billy Evans	.10	.05	.01

1990 HOF Sticker Book

65 Willie Mays

Unlike the previous year when all the people pictured were in the Hall of Fame, this year's version features a mix of players in the Hall or players who participated in special events. These stickers are sequenced in chronological order.

	MINT	NRMT	EXC
COMPLETE SET (100)	12.00	5.50	1.50
COMMON STICKER (1-100)	.10	.05	.01
☐ 1 George Bradley	.10	.05	.01
☐ 2 Old Hoss Radbourn	.15	.07	.02
☐ 3 Guy Hecker	.10	.05	.01
☐ 4 Tim Keefe	.15	.07	.02
☐ 5 Curt Welch	.10	.05	.01
☐ 6 George Gore	.10	.05	.01
☐ 7 Tip O'Neill	.10	.05	.01
☐ 8 Hugh Duffy	.15	.07	.02
☐ 9 Cap Anson	.35	.16	.04
☐ 10 Christy Mathewson	.35	.16	.04
☐ 11 Joe McGinnity	.15	.07	.02
☐ 12 Ed Reulbach	.10	.05	.01
☐ 13 Jack Taylor	.10	.05	.01
☐ 14 Cy Young	.50	.23	.06
☐ 15 Ernie Shore	.10	.05	.01
☐ 16 Smokey Joe Wood	.10	.05	.01
☐ 17 Fred Toney Hippo Vaughn	.10	.05	.01
☐ 18 Chief Wilson	.10	.05	.01
☐ 19 Ty Cobb	.75	.35	.09
☐ 20 Fielder Jones	.10	.05	.01
☐ 21 George Stallings MG	.10	.05	.01
☐ 22 Leon Cadore Joe Oeschger	.10	.05	.01
☐ 23 George Sisler	.25	.11	.03
☐ 24 Bill Wambsganss	.10	.05	.01
☐ 25 Babe Ruth	1.00	.45	.12
☐ 26 Jim Bottomley	.15	.07	.02
☐ 27 Rogers Hornsby	.50	.23	.06
☐ 28 Walter Johnson	.50	.23	.06
☐ 29 Hack Wilson	.15	.07	.02

☐ 30 Wes Ferrell	.10	.05	.01
☐ 31 Lefty Grove	.25	.11	.03
☐ 32 Carl Hubbell	.25	.11	.03
☐ 33 Joe Sewell	.10	.05	.01
☐ 34 Johnny Frederick	.10	.05	.01
☐ 35 Rudy York	.10	.05	.01
☐ 36 Johnny Vander Meer	.10	.05	.01
☐ 37 Pinky Higgins	.10	.05	.01
☐ 38 Lou Gehrig	1.00	.45	.12
☐ 39 Joe DiMaggio	1.00	.45	.12
☐ 40 Ted Williams	1.00	.45	.12
☐ 41 Jim Tobin	.10	.05	.01
☐ 42 Hal Newhouser	.15	.07	.02
☐ 43 Cookie Lavagetto	.10	.05	.01
☐ 44 Jim Konstanty	.10	.05	.01
☐ 45 Connie Mack MG	.25	.11	.03
☐ 46 Bobby Thomson	.10	.05	.01
☐ 47 Bobo Holloman	.10	.05	.01
☐ 48 Gene Stephens	.10	.05	.01
☐ 49 Mickey Mantle	1.00	.45	.12
☐ 50 Joe Adcock	.10	.05	.01
☐ 51 Stan Musial	.50	.23	.06
☐ 52 Al Kaline	.35	.16	.04
☐ 53 Dale Long	.10	.05	.01
☐ 54 Don Larsen	.10	.05	.01
☐ 55 Dave Philley	.10	.05	.01
☐ 56 Vic Power	.10	.05	.01
☐ 57 Harvey Haddix	.10	.05	.01
☐ 58 Elroy Face	.10	.05	.01
☐ 59 Larry Sherry	.10	.05	.01
☐ 60 Casey Stengel MG	.25	.11	.03
☐ 61 Bobby Richardson	.10	.05	.01
☐ 62 Bill Mazeroski	.15	.07	.02
☐ 63 Roger Maris	.10	.05	.01
☐ 64 Bill Fischer	.10	.05	.01
☐ 65 Willie Mays	.75	.35	.09
☐ 66 Maury Wills	.10	.05	.01
☐ 67 Bert Campaneris	.10	.05	.01
☐ 68 Warren Spahn	.25	.11	.03
☐ 69 Sandy Koufax	.50	.23	.06
☐ 70 Tony Cloninger	.10	.05	.01
☐ 71 Carl Yastrzemski	.35	.16	.04
☐ 72 Denny McLain	.10	.05	.01
☐ 73 Don Drysdale	.25	.11	.03
☐ 74 Bob Gibson	.25	.11	.03
☐ 75 Frank Howard	.10	.05	.01
☐ 76 Tom Seaver	.50	.23	.06
☐ 77 Nolan Ryan	1.00	.45	.12
☐ 78 Steve Carlton	.35	.16	.04
☐ 79 Mike Marshall	.10	.05	.01
☐ 80 Nate Colbert	.10	.05	.01
☐ 81 Hank Aaron	.75	.35	.09
☐ 82 Rennie Stennett	.10	.05	.01
☐ 83 Fred Lynn	.10	.05	.01
☐ 84 Pete Rose	.50	.23	.06
☐ 85 Pedro Guerrero	.10	.05	.01
☐ 86 Lou Brock	.25	.11	.03
☐ 87 Rickey Henderson	.25	.11	.03
☐ 88 Reggie Jackson	.35	.16	.04
☐ 89 Bob Horner	.10	.05	.01
☐ 90 Don Mattingly	.35	.16	.04
☐ 91 Mark McGwire	.15	.07	.02
☐ 92 Benito Santiago	.10	.05	.01
☐ 93 George Brett	.75	.35	.09
☐ 94 Mike Schmidt	.50	.23	.06
☐ 95 Jose Canseco	.25	.11	.03
☐ 96 Andre Dawson	.15	.07	.02
☐ 97 Ron Guidry	.10	.05	.01
☐ 98 Dwight Gooden	.15	.07	.02
☐ 99 Orel Hershiser	.15	.07	.02
☐ 100 Vince Coleman	.10	.05	.01

1959 Home Run Derby

This 20-card set was produced in 1959 by American Motors to publicize a TV program. The cards are black and white and blank backed. The cards measure approximately 3 1/8" by 5 1/4". The cards are unnumbered and are ordered alphabetically below for convenience. During 1988, the 19 player cards in this set were publicly reprinted.

	NRMT	VG-E	GOOD
COMPLETE SET (20)	3000.00	1350.00	375.00
COMMON CARD (1-20)	60.00	27.00	7.50
☐ 1 Hank Aaron	450.00	200.00	55.00
☐ 2 Bob Allison	60.00	27.00	7.50
☐ 3 Ernie Banks	175.00	80.00	22.00
☐ 4 Ken Boyer	75.00	34.00	9.50
☐ 5 Bob Cerv	60.00	27.00	7.50
☐ 6 Rocky Colavito	125.00	55.00	15.50
☐ 7 Gil Hodges	125.00	55.00	15.50
☐ 8 Jackie Jensen	75.00	34.00	9.50
☐ 9 Al Kaline	175.00	80.00	22.00
☐ 10 Harmon Killebrew	175.00	80.00	22.00
☐ 11 Jim Lemon	60.00	27.00	7.50
☐ 12 Mickey Mantle	1350.00	600.00	170.00
☐ 13 Ed Mathews	175.00	80.00	22.00
☐ 14 Willie Mays	450.00	200.00	55.00
☐ 15 Wally Post	60.00	27.00	7.50
☐ 16 Frank Robinson	175.00	80.00	22.00
☐ 17 Mark Scott ANN	60.00	27.00	7.50
☐ 18 Duke Snider	200.00	90.00	25.00
☐ 19 Dick Stuart	60.00	27.00	7.50
☐ 20 Gus Triandos	60.00	27.00	7.50

1991 Homers Cookies Classics

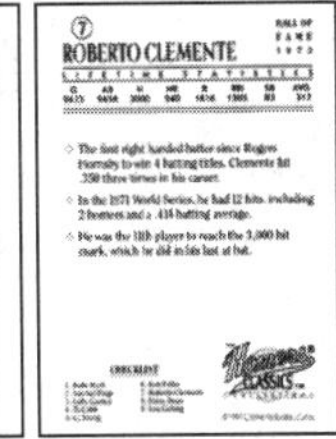

This nine-card standards-size set was sponsored by Legend Food Products in honor of Hall of Famers in baseball history. One free card was randomly inserted in each box of Homers Baseball Cookies. The cards have vintage sepia-toned player photos, with bronze borders on a white card face. The player's name appears in a bronze stripe overlaying the bottom edge of the picture. In black print on white, the back presents lifetime statistics, career highlights, and a checklist for the set.

	MINT	NRMT	EXC
COMPLETE SET (9)	9.00	4.00	1.10
COMMON CARD (1-9)	1.00	.45	.12
☐ 1 Babe Ruth	3.00	1.35	.35
☐ 2 Satchel Paige	1.50	.70	.19
☐ 3 Lefty Gomez	1.00	.45	.12
☐ 4 Ty Cobb	1.50	.70	.19
☐ 5 Cy Young	1.25	.55	.16
☐ 6 Bob Feller	1.25	.55	.16
☐ 7 Roberto Clemente	2.00	.90	.25
☐ 8 Dizzy Dean	1.25	.55	.16
☐ 9 Lou Gehrig	2.00	.90	.25

1947 Homogenized Bond *

The cards in this 48-card set measure approximately 2 1/4" by 3 1/2". The 1947 W571/D305 Homogenized Bread are sets of unnumbered cards containing 44 baseball players and four boxers. The W571 set exists in two styles. Style one is identical to the D305 set except for the back printing while style two has perforated edges and movie stars depicted on the backs. The second style of W571 cards contains only 13 cards. The four boxers in the checklist below are indicated by BOX. The checklist below is ordered alphabetically. There are 24 cards in the set which were definitely produced in greater supply. These 24 (marked by DP below) are quite a bit more common than the other 24 cards in the set.

	EX-MT	VG-E	GOOD
COMPLETE SET	900.00	400.00	110.00
COMMON CARD (1-48)	12.00	5.50	1.50
COMMON BOXER	5.00	2.20	.60
COMMON DP BASEBALL	2.00	.90	.25
COMMON DP BOXER	2.00	.90	.25
☐ 1 Rex Barney	12.00	5.50	1.50
☐ 2 Yogi Berra	175.00	80.00	22.00
☐ 3 Ewell Blackwell DP	2.00	.90	.25
☐ 4 Lou Boudreau DP	5.00	2.20	.60
☐ 5 Ralph Branca	12.00	5.50	1.50
☐ 6 Harry Brecheen DP	2.00	.90	.25
☐ 7 Primo Carnera BOX DP	2.00	.90	.25
☐ 8 Marcel Cerdan BOX	12.00	5.50	1.50
☐ 9 Dom DiMaggio	15.00	6.75	1.85
☐ 10 Joe DiMaggio	250.00	110.00	31.00
☐ 11 Bobby Doerr DP	5.00	2.20	.60
☐ 12 Bruce Edwards	12.00	5.50	1.50
☐ 13 Bob Elliott DP	2.00	.90	.25
☐ 14 Del Ennis DP	2.00	.90	.25
☐ 15 Bob Feller DP	12.00	5.50	1.50
☐ 16 Carl Furillo	20.00	9.00	2.50
☐ 17 Joe Gordon DP	2.00	.90	.25
☐ 18 Sid Gordon	12.00	5.50	1.50
☐ 19 Joe Hatten	12.00	5.50	1.50
☐ 20 Gil Hodges	75.00	34.00	9.50
☐ 21 Tommy Holmes DP	2.00	.90	.25
☐ 22 Larry Jansen	12.00	5.50	1.50
☐ 23 Sheldon Jones	12.00	5.50	1.50
☐ 24 Edwin Joost	12.00	5.50	1.50
☐ 25 Charlie Keller	15.00	6.75	1.85
☐ 26 Ken Keltner DP	2.00	.90	.25
☐ 27 Buddy Kerr	12.00	5.50	1.50
☐ 28 Ralph Kiner DP	8.00	3.60	1.00
☐ 29 Jake LaMotta BOX	12.00	5.50	1.50
☐ 30 John Lindell	12.00	5.50	1.50
☐ 31 Whitey Lockman	12.00	5.50	1.50
☐ 32 Joe Louis BOX DP	12.00	5.50	1.50
☐ 33 Willard Marshall	12.00	5.50	1.50
☐ 34 Johnny Mize DP	8.00	3.60	1.00
☐ 35 Stan Musial DP	50.00	22.00	6.25
☐ 36 Andy Pafko DP	2.00	.90	.25
☐ 37 Johnny Pesky DP	2.00	.90	.25
☐ 38 Pee Wee Reese	60.00	27.00	7.50
☐ 39 Phil Rizzuto DP	12.00	5.50	1.50
☐ 40 Aaron Robinson DP	12.00	5.50	1.50
☐ 41 Jackie Robinson DP	75.00	34.00	9.50
☐ 42 John Sain DP	5.00	2.20	.60
☐ 43 Enos Slaughter DP	8.00	3.60	1.00
☐ 44 Vern Stephens DP	2.00	.90	.25
☐ 45 Birdie Tebbetts	12.00	5.50	1.50
☐ 46 Bobby Thomson	15.00	6.75	1.85
☐ 47 Johnny VanderMeer	15.00	6.75	1.85
☐ 48 Ted Williams DP	50.00	22.00	6.25

1975 Hostess

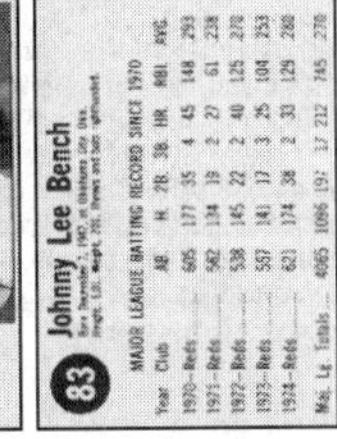

The cards in this 150-card set measure approximately 2 1/4" by 3 1/4" individually or 3 1/4" by 7 1/4" as panels of three. The 1975 Hostess set was issued in panels of three cards each on the backs of family-size packages of Hostess cakes. Card number 125, Bill Madlock, was listed correctly as an infielder and incorrectly as a pitcher. Number 11, Burt Hooton, and number 89, Doug Rader, are spelled two different ways. Some panels are more difficult to find than others as they were issued only on the backs of less popular Hostess products. These scarcer cards are shown with SP in the checklist. Although complete panel prices are not explicitly listed, they would generally have a value of 20-30 percent greater than the sum of the values of the individual players on that panel. One of the more interesting cards in the set is that of Robin Yount; Hostess issued one of the few Yount cards available in 1975, his rookie year for cards. An album to hold these cards was issued. The albums were originally intended to be given out in grocery stores. However, most seemingly were distributed through Hostess stores.

	NRMT	VG-E	GOOD
COMPLETE INDIV.SET (150)	250.00	110.00	31.00
COMMON CARD (1-150)	.50	.23	.06
☐ 1 Bob Tolan	.50	.23	.06
☐ 2 Cookie Rojas	.50	.23	.06
☐ 3 Darrell Evans	.75	.35	.09
☐ 4 Sal Bando	.75	.35	.09
☐ 5 Joe Morgan	4.00	1.80	.50
☐ 6 Mickey Lolich	.75	.35	.09
☐ 7 Don Sutton	3.00	1.35	.35
☐ 8 Bill Melton	.50	.23	.06
☐ 9 Tim Foli	.50	.23	.06
☐ 10 Joe Lahoud	.50	.23	.06
☐ 11A Burt Hooton ERR (Misspelled Bert Hooten on card	1.00	.45	.12
☐ 11B Burt Hooton COR	1.00	.45	.12
☐ 12 Paul Blair	.50	.23	.06
☐ 13 Jim Barr	.50	.23	.06
☐ 14 Toby Harrah	.75	.35	.09
☐ 15 John Milner	.50	.23	.06
☐ 16 Ken Holtzman	.50	.23	.06
☐ 17 Cesar Cedeno	.50	.23	.06
☐ 18 Dwight Evans	1.50	.70	.19
☐ 19 Willie McCovey	3.00	1.35	.35
☐ 20 Tony Oliva	1.50	.70	.19
☐ 21 Manny Sanguillen	.50	.23	.06
☐ 22 Mickey Rivers	.50	.23	.06
☐ 23 Lou Brock	3.00	1.35	.35
☐ 24 Graig Nettles UER (Craig on front)	1.50	.70	.19
☐ 25 Jim Wynn	.50	.23	.06
☐ 26 George Scott	.50	.23	.06
☐ 27 Greg Luzinski	1.00	.45	.12
☐ 28 Bert Campaneris	.75	.35	.09
☐ 29 Pete Rose	12.00	5.50	1.50
☐ 30 Buddy Bell	1.00	.45	.12
☐ 31 Gary Matthews	.75	.35	.09
☐ 32 Freddie Patek	.50	.23	.06
☐ 33 Mike Lum	.50	.23	.06
☐ 34 Ellie Rodriguez	.50	.23	.06
☐ 35 Milt May UER (Photo actually Lee May)	.50	.23	.06
☐ 36 Willie Horton	.75	.35	.09
☐ 37 Dave Winfield	20.00	9.00	2.50
☐ 38 Tom Grieve	.50	.23	.06
☐ 39 Barry Foote	.50	.23	.06
☐ 40 Joe Rudi	.50	.23	.06
☐ 41 Bake McBride	.50	.23	.06
☐ 42 Mike Cuellar	.50	.23	.06
☐ 43 Garry Maddox	.50	.23	.06
☐ 44 Carlos May	.50	.23	.06
☐ 45 Bud Harrelson	.50	.23	.06
☐ 46 Dave Chalk	.50	.23	.06
☐ 47 Dave Concepcion	1.25	.55	.16
☐ 48 Carl Yastrzemski	5.00	2.20	.60
☐ 49 Steve Garvey	2.50	1.10	.30
☐ 50 Amos Otis	.50	.23	.06
☐ 51 Rick Reuschel	.50	.23	.06
☐ 52 Rollie Fingers	3.00	1.35	.35
☐ 53 Bob Watson	1.00	.45	.12
☐ 54 John Ellis	.50	.23	.06
☐ 55 Bob Bailey	.50	.23	.06
☐ 56 Rod Carew	5.00	2.20	.60
☐ 57 Rich Hebner	.50	.23	.06
☐ 58 Nolan Ryan	40.00	18.00	5.00
☐ 59 Reggie Smith	.75	.35	.09
☐ 60 Joe Coleman	.50	.23	.06
☐ 61 Ron Cey	.75	.35	.09
☐ 62 Darrell Porter	.75	.35	.09
☐ 63 Steve Carlton	5.00	2.20	.60
☐ 64 Gene Tenace	.50	.23	.06
☐ 65 Jose Cardenal	.50	.23	.06
☐ 66 Bill Lee	.50	.23	.06
☐ 67 Dave Lopes	.75	.35	.09
☐ 68 Wilbur Wood	.50	.23	.06
☐ 69 Steve Renko	.50	.23	.06
☐ 70 Joe Torre	1.50	.70	.19
☐ 71 Ted Sizemore	.50	.23	.06
☐ 72 Bobby Grich	.75	.35	.09
☐ 73 Chris Speier	.50	.23	.06
☐ 74 Bert Blyleven	1.00	.45	.12
☐ 75 Tom Seaver	10.00	4.50	1.25
☐ 76 Nate Colbert	.50	.23	.06
☐ 77 Don Kessinger	.50	.23	.06
☐ 78 George Medich	.50	.23	.06
☐ 79 Andy Messersmith SP	.75	.35	.09
☐ 80 Robin Yount SP	30.00	13.50	3.70
☐ 81 Al Oliver SP	1.00	.45	.12
☐ 82 Bill Singer SP	.75	.35	.09
☐ 83 Johnny Bench SP	12.00	5.50	1.50
☐ 84 Gaylord Perry SP	4.00	1.80	.50
☐ 85 Dave Kingman SP	1.00	.45	.12
☐ 86 Ed Herrmann SP	.75	.35	.09
☐ 87 Ralph Garr SP	.75	.35	.09
☐ 88 Reggie Jackson SP	12.00	5.50	1.50
☐ 89A Doug Rader ERR SP (Misspelled Radar)	1.25	.55	.16
☐ 89B Doug Rader COR SP	6.00	2.70	.75
☐ 90 Elliott Maddox SP	.75	.35	.09
☐ 91 Bill Russell SP	1.25	.55	.16
☐ 92 John Mayberry SP	.75	.35	.09
☐ 93 Dave Cash SP	.75	.35	.09
☐ 94 Jeff Burroughs SP	1.00	.45	.12
☐ 95 Ted Simmons SP	1.50	.70	.19
☐ 96 Joe Decker SP	.75	.35	.09
☐ 97 Bill Buckner SP	1.00	.45	.12
☐ 98 Bobby Darwin SP	.75	.35	.09
☐ 99 Phil Niekro SP	4.00	1.80	.50
☐ 100 Jim Sundberg	.50	.23	.06
☐ 101 Greg Gross	.50	.23	.06
☐ 102 Luis Tiant	1.00	.45	.12
☐ 103 Glenn Beckert	.50	.23	.06
☐ 104 Hal McRae	1.00	.45	.12
☐ 105 Mike Jorgensen	.50	.23	.06
☐ 106 Mike Hargrove	1.00	.45	.12
☐ 107 Don Gullett	.75	.35	.09
☐ 108 Tito Fuentes	.50	.23	.06
☐ 109 John Grubb	.50	.23	.06
☐ 110 Jim Kaat	1.00	.45	.12
☐ 111 Felix Millan	.50	.23	.06
☐ 112 Don Money	.50	.23	.06
☐ 113 Rick Monday	.50	.23	.06
☐ 114 Dick Bosman	.50	.23	.06
☐ 115 Roger Metzger	.50	.23	.06
☐ 116 Fergie Jenkins	3.00	1.35	.35
☐ 117 Dusty Baker	1.00	.45	.12
☐ 118 Billy Champion SP	.75	.35	.09
☐ 119 Bob Gibson SP	5.00	2.20	.60
☐ 120 Bill Freehan SP	1.00	.45	.12
☐ 121 Cesar Geronimo	.50	.23	.06
☐ 122 Jorge Orta	.50	.23	.06
☐ 123 Cleon Jones	.50	.23	.06
☐ 124 Steve Busby	.50	.23	.06
☐ 125A Bill Madlock ERR (Pitcher)	1.50	.70	.19
☐ 125B Bill Madlock COR (Infielder)	1.50	.70	.19
☐ 126 Jim Palmer	4.00	1.80	.50
☐ 127 Tony Perez	2.50	1.10	.30
☐ 128 Larry Hisle	.50	.23	.06
☐ 129 Rusty Staub	1.00	.45	.12
☐ 130 Hank Aaron SP	20.00	9.00	2.50

	NRMT	VG-E	GOOD
☐ 131 Rennie Stennett SP	.75	.35	.09
☐ 132 Rico Petrocelli SP	.75	.35	.09
☐ 133 Mike Schmidt	15.00	6.75	1.85
☐ 134 Sparky Lyle	1.00	.45	.12
☐ 135 Willie Stargell	3.00	1.35	.35
☐ 136 Ken Henderson	.50	.23	.06
☐ 137 Willie Montanez	.50	.23	.06
☐ 138 Thurman Munson	4.00	1.80	.50
☐ 139 Richie Zisk	.50	.23	.06
☐ 140 George Hendrick	.50	.23	.06
☐ 141 Bobby Murcer	1.00	.45	.12
☐ 142 Lee May	.50	.23	.06
☐ 143 Carlton Fisk	7.50	3.40	.95
☐ 144 Brooks Robinson	5.00	2.20	.60
☐ 145 Bobby Bonds	1.50	.70	.19
☐ 146 Gary Sutherland	.50	.23	.06
☐ 147 Oscar Gamble	.50	.23	.06
☐ 148 Jim Hunter	4.00	1.80	.50
☐ 149 Tug McGraw	1.00	.45	.12
☐ 150 Dave McNally	.75	.35	.09
☐ XX Album	8.00	3.60	1.00

1975 Hostess Twinkie

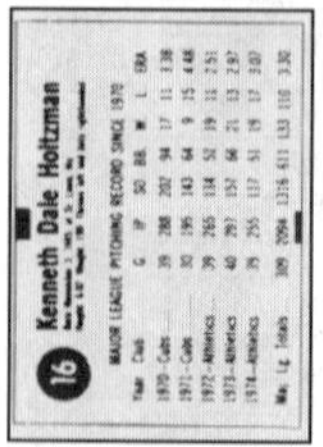

The cards in this 60-card set measure approximately 2 1/4" by 3 1/4". The 1975 Hostess Twinkie set was issued on a limited basis in the far western part of the country. The set contains the same numbers as the regular set to number 36; however, the set is skip numbered after number 36. The cards were issued as the backs for 25-cent Twinkies packs. The fronts are indistinguishable from the regular Hostess cards; however the card backs are different in that the Twinkie cards have a thick black bar in the middle of the reverse. The cards are frequently found with product stains. One of the more interesting cards in the set is that of Robin Yount; Hostess issued one of the few Yount cards available in 1975, his rookie year for cards.

	NRMT	VG-E	GOOD
COMPLETE SET (60)	125.00	55.00	15.50
COMMON CARD	1.00	.45	.12
☐ 1 Bob Tolan	1.00	.45	.12
☐ 2 Cookie Rojas	1.00	.45	.12
☐ 3 Darrell Evans	1.25	.55	.16
☐ 4 Sal Bando	1.25	.55	.16
☐ 5 Joe Morgan	6.00	2.70	.75
☐ 6 Mickey Lolich	1.50	.70	.19
☐ 7 Don Sutton	5.00	2.20	.60
☐ 8 Bill Melton	1.00	.45	.12
☐ 9 Tim Foli	1.00	.45	.12
☐ 10 Joe Lahoud	1.00	.45	.12
☐ 11 Burt Hooton UER (Misspelled Bert Hooten on card)	1.00	.45	.12
☐ 12 Paul Blair	1.00	.45	.12
☐ 13 Jim Barr	1.00	.45	.12
☐ 14 Toby Harrah	1.00	.45	.12
☐ 15 John Milner	1.00	.45	.12
☐ 16 Ken Holtzman	1.00	.45	.12
☐ 17 Cesar Cedeno	1.00	.45	.12
☐ 18 Dwight Evans	2.00	.90	.25
☐ 19 Willie McCovey	5.00	2.20	.60
☐ 20 Tony Oliva	1.50	.70	.19
☐ 21 Manny Sanguillen	1.00	.45	.12
☐ 22 Mickey Rivers	1.00	.45	.12
☐ 23 Lou Brock	6.00	2.70	.75
☐ 24 Graig Nettles UER (Craig on front)	2.00	.90	.25
☐ 25 Jim Wynn	1.00	.45	.12
☐ 26 George Scott	1.00	.45	.12
☐ 27 Greg Luzinski	1.25	.55	.16
☐ 28 Bert Campaneris	1.00	.45	.12
☐ 29 Pete Rose	15.00	6.75	1.85
☐ 30 Buddy Bell	1.50	.70	.19
☐ 31 Gary Matthews	1.00	.45	.12
☐ 32 Freddie Patek	1.00	.45	.12
☐ 33 Mike Lum	1.00	.45	.12
☐ 34 Ellie Rodriguez	1.00	.45	.12
☐ 35 Milt May UER (Lee May picture)	1.00	.45	.12
☐ 36 Willie Horton	1.00	.45	.12
☐ 40 Joe Rudi	1.00	.45	.12
☐ 43 Garry Maddox	1.00	.45	.12
☐ 46 Dave Chalk	1.00	.45	.12
☐ 49 Steve Garvey	4.00	1.80	.50
☐ 52 Rollie Fingers	5.00	2.20	.60
☐ 58 Nolan Ryan	50.00	22.00	6.25
☐ 61 Ron Cey	1.50	.70	.19
☐ 64 Gene Tenace	1.00	.45	.12
☐ 65 Jose Cardenal	1.00	.45	.12
☐ 67 Dave Lopes	1.50	.70	.19
☐ 68 Wilbur Wood	1.00	.45	.12
☐ 73 Chris Speier	1.00	.45	.12
☐ 77 Don Kessinger	1.00	.45	.12
☐ 79 Andy Messersmith	1.00	.45	.12
☐ 80 Robin Yount	35.00	16.00	4.40
☐ 82 Bill Singer	1.00	.45	.12
☐ 103 Glenn Beckert	1.00	.45	.12
☐ 110 Jim Kaat	1.50	.70	.19
☐ 112 Don Money	1.00	.45	.12
☐ 113 Rick Monday	1.00	.45	.12
☐ 122 Jorge Orta	1.00	.45	.12
☐ 125 Bill Madlock	1.50	.70	.19
☐ 130 Hank Aaron	20.00	9.00	2.50
☐ 136 Ken Henderson	1.00	.45	.12

1976 Hostess

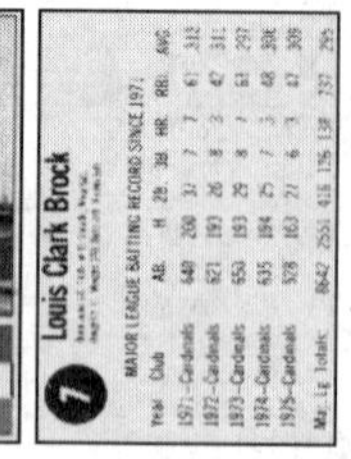

The cards in this 150-card set measure approximately 2 1/4" by 3 1/4" individually or 3 1/4" by 7 1/4" as panels of three. The 1976 Hostess set contains full-color, numbered cards issued in panels of three cards each on family-size packages of Hostess cakes. Scarcer panels (those only found on less popular Hostess products) are listed in the checklist below with SP. Complete panels of three have a value 20-30 percent more than the sum of the individual cards on the panel. Nine additional numbers (151-159) were apparently planned but never actually issued. These exist as proof cards and are quite scarce, e.g., 151 Ferguson Jenkins (even though he already appears in the set as card number 138), 152 Mike Cuellar, 153 Tom Murphy, 154 Al Cowens, 155 Barry Foote, 156 Steve Carlton, 157 Richie Zisk, 158 Ken Holtzman, and 159 Cliff Johnson. One of the more interesting cards in the set is that of Dennis Eckersley; Hostess issued one of the few Eckersley cards available in 1976, his rookie year for cards. An album to hold these cards were issued.

	NRMT	VG-E	GOOD
COMPLETE INDIV.SET (150)	250.00	110.00	31.00
COMMON CARD (1-150)	.50	.23	.06
☐ 1 Fred Lynn	1.00	.45	.12
☐ 2 Joe Morgan	4.00	1.80	.50
☐ 3 Phil Niekro	4.00	1.80	.50
☐ 4 Gaylord Perry	4.00	1.80	.50
☐ 5 Bob Watson	.75	.35	.09
☐ 6 Bill Freehan	.75	.35	.09
☐ 7 Lou Brock	4.00	1.80	.50
☐ 8 Al Fitzmorris	.50	.23	.06
☐ 9 Rennie Stennett	.50	.23	.06
☐ 10 Tony Oliva	1.50	.70	.19
☐ 11 Robin Yount	20.00	9.00	2.50
☐ 12 Rick Manning	.50	.23	.06
☐ 13 Bobby Grich	.75	.35	.09
☐ 14 Terry Forster	.50	.23	.06
☐ 15 Dave Kingman	.75	.35	.09
☐ 16 Thurman Munson	4.00	1.80	.50
☐ 17 Rick Reuschel	.50	.23	.06
☐ 18 Bobby Bonds	1.50	.70	.19
☐ 19 Steve Garvey	3.00	1.35	.35
☐ 20 Vida Blue	.75	.35	.09
☐ 21 Dave Rader	.50	.23	.06
☐ 22 Johnny Bench	7.50	3.40	.95
☐ 23 Luis Tiant	.75	.35	.09
☐ 24 Darrell Evans	.75	.35	.09
☐ 25 Larry Dierker	.75	.35	.09
☐ 26 Willie Horton	.75	.35	.09
☐ 27 John Ellis	.50	.23	.06
☐ 28 Al Cowens	.50	.23	.06
☐ 29 Jerry Reuss	.50	.23	.06
☐ 30 Reggie Smith	.75	.35	.09
☐ 31 Bobby Darwin SP	.75	.35	.09
☐ 32 Fritz Peterson SP	.75	.35	.09
☐ 33 Rod Carew SP	10.00	4.50	1.25
☐ 34 Carlos May SP	.75	.35	.09
☐ 35 Tom Seaver SP	15.00	6.75	1.85
☐ 36 Brooks Robinson SP	10.00	4.50	1.25
☐ 37 Jose Cardenal	.50	.23	.06
☐ 38 Ron Blomberg	.50	.23	.06
☐ 39 Leroy Stanton	.50	.23	.06
☐ 40 Dave Cash	.50	.23	.06
☐ 41 John Montefusco	.50	.23	.06
☐ 42 Bob Tolan	.50	.23	.06
☐ 43 Carl Morton	.50	.23	.06
☐ 44 Rick Burleson	.50	.23	.06
☐ 45 Don Gullett	.50	.23	.06
☐ 46 Vern Ruhle	.50	.23	.06
☐ 47 Cesar Cedeno	.75	.35	.09
☐ 48 Toby Harrah	.50	.23	.06
☐ 49 Willie Stargell	4.00	1.80	.50
☐ 50 Al Hrabosky	.50	.23	.06
☐ 51 Amos Otis	.50	.23	.06
☐ 52 Bud Harrelson	.50	.23	.06
☐ 53 Jim Hughes	.50	.23	.06
☐ 54 George Scott	.50	.23	.06
☐ 55 Mike Vail SP	.75	.35	.09
☐ 56 Jim Palmer SP	6.00	2.70	.75
☐ 57 Jorge Orta SP	.75	.35	.09
☐ 58 Chris Chambliss SP	1.00	.45	.12
☐ 59 Dave Chalk SP	.75	.35	.09
☐ 60 Ray Burris SP	.75	.35	.09
☐ 61 Bert Campaneris SP	1.00	.45	.12
☐ 62 Gary Carter SP	12.00	5.50	1.50
☐ 63 Ron Cey SP	1.00	.45	.12
☐ 64 Carlton Fisk SP	7.50	3.40	.95
☐ 65 Marty Perez SP	.75	.35	.09
☐ 66 Pete Rose SP	20.00	9.00	2.50
☐ 67 Roger Metzger SP	.75	.35	.09
☐ 68 Jim Sundberg SP	.75	.35	.09
☐ 69 Ron LeFlore SP	.75	.35	.09
☐ 70 Ted Sizemore SP	.75	.35	.09
☐ 71 Steve Busby SP	.75	.35	.09
☐ 72 Manny Sanguillen SP	.75	.35	.09
☐ 73 Larry Hisle SP	.75	.35	.09
☐ 74 Pete Broberg SP	.75	.35	.09
☐ 75 Boog Powell SP	1.50	.70	.19
☐ 76 Ken Singleton SP	.75	.35	.09
☐ 77 Rich Gossage SP	2.00	.90	.25
☐ 78 Jerry Grote SP	.75	.35	.09
☐ 79 Nolan Ryan SP	50.00	22.00	6.25
☐ 80 Rick Monday SP	1.00	.45	.12
☐ 81 Graig Nettles SP	1.50	.70	.19
☐ 82 Chris Speier	.50	.23	.06
☐ 83 Dave Winfield	12.00	5.50	1.50
☐ 84 Mike Schmidt	15.00	6.75	1.85
☐ 85 Buzz Capra	.50	.23	.06
☐ 86 Tony Perez	2.50	1.10	.30
☐ 87 Dwight Evans	1.50	.70	.19
☐ 88 Mike Hargrove	.75	.35	.09
☐ 89 Joe Coleman	.50	.23	.06
☐ 90 Greg Gross	.50	.23	.06
☐ 91 John Mayberry	.50	.23	.06
☐ 92 John Candelaria	.75	.35	.09
☐ 93 Bake McBride	.50	.23	.06
☐ 94 Hank Aaron	15.00	6.75	1.85
☐ 95 Buddy Bell	.75	.35	.09
☐ 96 Steve Braun	.50	.23	.06
☐ 97 Jon Matlack	.50	.23	.06
☐ 98 Lee May	.50	.23	.06
☐ 99 Wilbur Wood	.50	.23	.06
☐ 100 Bill Madlock	.75	.35	.09
☐ 101 Frank Tanana	.75	.35	.09
☐ 102 Mickey Rivers	.50	.23	.06
☐ 103 Mike Ivie	.50	.23	.06
☐ 104 Rollie Fingers	3.00	1.35	.35
☐ 105 Dave Lopes	.75	.35	.09
☐ 106 George Foster	1.00	.45	.12
☐ 107 Denny Doyle	.50	.23	.06
☐ 108 Earl Williams	.50	.23	.06
☐ 109 Tom Veryzer	.50	.23	.06
☐ 110 J.R. Richard	.75	.35	.09
☐ 111 Jeff Burroughs	.50	.23	.06
☐ 112 Al Oliver	.75	.35	.09
☐ 113 Ted Simmons	1.00	.45	.12
☐ 114 George Brett	45.00	20.00	5.50
☐ 115 Frank Duffy	.50	.23	.06
☐ 116 Bert Blyleven	1.00	.45	.12
☐ 117 Darrell Porter	.50	.23	.06
☐ 118 Don Baylor	1.00	.45	.12
☐ 119 Bucky Dent	.75	.35	.09
☐ 120 Felix Millan	.50	.23	.06
☐ 121 Mike Cuellar	.50	.23	.06
☐ 122 Gene Tenace	.50	.23	.06
☐ 123 Bobby Murcer	.75	.35	.09
☐ 124 Willie McCovey	4.00	1.80	.50
☐ 125 Greg Luzinski	.75	.35	.09
☐ 126 Larry Parrish	.50	.23	.06
☐ 127 Jim Rice	2.00	.90	.25
☐ 128 Dave Concepcion	1.00	.45	.12
☐ 129 Jim Wynn	.50	.23	.06
☐ 130 Tom Grieve	.50	.23	.06
☐ 131 Mike Cosgrove	.50	.23	.06
☐ 132 Dan Meyer	.50	.23	.06
☐ 133 Dave Parker	2.00	.90	.25
☐ 134 Don Kessinger	.50	.23	.06
☐ 135 Hal McRae	.75	.35	.09
☐ 136 Don Money	.50	.23	.06
☐ 137 Dennis Eckersley	20.00	9.00	2.50
☐ 138 Fergie Jenkins	3.00	1.35	.35
☐ 139 Mike Torrez	.50	.23	.06
☐ 140 Jerry Morales	.50	.23	.06
☐ 141 Jim Hunter	3.00	1.35	.35
☐ 142 Gary Matthews	.50	.23	.06
☐ 143 Randy Jones	.50	.23	.06
☐ 144 Mike Jorgensen	.50	.23	.06
☐ 145 Larry Bowa	.75	.35	.09
☐ 146 Reggie Jackson	12.00	5.50	1.50
☐ 147 Steve Yeager	.50	.23	.06
☐ 148 Dave May	.50	.23	.06
☐ 149 Carl Yastrzemski	6.00	2.70	.75
☐ 150 Cesar Geronimo	.50	.23	.06
☐ XX Album	8.00	3.60	1.00

1976 Hostess Twinkie

The cards in this 60-card set measure approximately 2 1/4" by 3 1/4". The 1976 Hostess Twinkies set contains the first 60 cards of the 1976 Hostess set. These cards were issued as backs on 25-cent Twinkie packages as in the 1975 Twinkies set. The fronts are indistinguishable from the regular Hostess cards; however the card backs are different in that the Twinkie cards have a thick black bar in the middle of the reverse. The cards are frequently found with product stains.

	NRMT	VG-E	GOOD
COMPLETE SET (60)	125.00	55.00	15.50
COMMON CARD (1-60)	1.00	.45	.12
☐ 1 Fred Lynn	2.00	.90	.25
☐ 2 Joe Morgan	6.00	2.70	.75
☐ 3 Phil Niekro	5.00	2.20	.60
☐ 4 Gaylord Perry	5.00	2.20	.60
☐ 5 Bob Watson	1.25	.55	.16
☐ 6 Bill Freehan	1.25	.55	.16
☐ 7 Lou Brock	5.00	2.20	.60
☐ 8 Al Fitzmorris	1.00	.45	.12
☐ 9 Rennie Stennett	1.00	.45	.12
☐ 10 Tony Oliva	2.00	.90	.25
☐ 11 Robin Yount	15.00	6.75	1.85
☐ 12 Rick Manning	1.00	.45	.12
☐ 13 Bobby Grich	1.00	.45	.12
☐ 14 Terry Forster	1.00	.45	.12
☐ 15 Dave Kingman	2.00	.90	.25
☐ 16 Thurman Munson	6.00	2.70	.75
☐ 17 Rick Reuschel	1.00	.45	.12
☐ 18 Bobby Bonds	2.00	.90	.25
☐ 19 Steve Garvey	6.00	2.70	.75
☐ 20 Vida Blue	1.50	.70	.19
☐ 21 Dave Rader	1.00	.45	.12
☐ 22 Johnny Bench	10.00	4.50	1.25
☐ 23 Luis Tiant	1.25	.55	.16
☐ 24 Darrell Evans	1.50	.70	.19
☐ 25 Larry Dierker	1.50	.70	.19
☐ 26 Willie Horton	1.50	.70	.19
☐ 27 John Ellis	1.00	.45	.12
☐ 28 Al Cowens	1.00	.45	.12
☐ 29 Jerry Reuss	1.25	.55	.16
☐ 30 Reggie Smith	1.25	.55	.16
☐ 31 Bobby Darwin	1.00	.45	.12
☐ 32 Fritz Peterson	1.00	.45	.12
☐ 33 Rod Carew	6.00	2.70	.75
☐ 34 Carlos May	1.00	.45	.12
☐ 35 Tom Seaver	10.00	4.50	1.25
☐ 36 Brooks Robinson	6.00	2.70	.75
☐ 37 Jose Cardenal	1.00	.45	.12
☐ 38 Ron Blomberg	1.00	.45	.12
☐ 39 Leroy Stanton	1.00	.45	.12
☐ 40 Dave Cash	1.00	.45	.12
☐ 41 John Montefusco	1.00	.45	.12
☐ 42 Bob Tolan	1.00	.45	.12
☐ 43 Carl Morton	1.00	.45	.12
☐ 44 Rick Burleson	1.00	.45	.12
☐ 45 Don Gullett	1.00	.45	.12
☐ 46 Vern Ruhle	1.00	.45	.12
☐ 47 Cesar Cedeno	1.00	.45	.12
☐ 48 Toby Harrah	1.00	.45	.12
☐ 49 Willie Stargell	5.00	2.20	.60
☐ 50 Al Hrabosky	1.00	.45	.12
☐ 51 Amos Otis	1.00	.45	.12
☐ 52 Bud Harrelson	1.00	.45	.12
☐ 53 Jim Hughes	1.00	.45	.12
☐ 54 George Scott	1.00	.45	.12
☐ 55 Mike Vail	1.00	.45	.12
☐ 56 Jim Palmer	5.00	2.20	.60
☐ 57 Jorge Orta	1.00	.45	.12
☐ 58 Chris Chambliss	1.50	.70	.19
☐ 59 Dave Chalk	1.00	.45	.12
☐ 60 Ray Burris	1.00	.45	.12

1977 Hostess

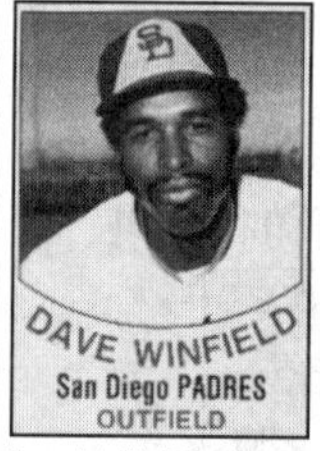

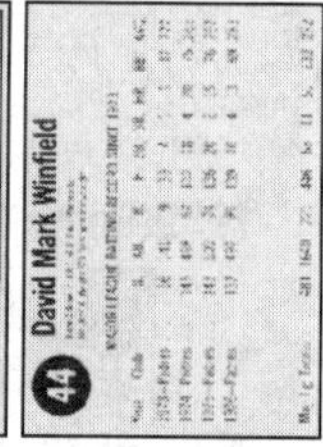

The cards in this 150-card set measure approximately 2 1/4" by 3 1/4" individually or 3 1/4" by 7 1/4" as panels of three. The 1977 Hostess set contains full-color, numbered cards issued in panels of three cards each with Hostess family-size cake products. Scarcer cards are listed in the checklist below with SP. Although complete panel prices are not explicitly listed below, they would generally have a value 20-30 percent greater than the sum of the individual players on the panel. There were ten additional cards proofed, but not produced or distributed; they are 151 Ed Kranepool, 152 Ross Grimsley, 153 Ken Brett, 154 Rowland Office, 155 Rick Wise, 156 Paul Splittorff, 157 Gerald Augustine, 158 Ken Forsch, 159 Jerry Reuss (Reuss is also number 119 in the set), and 160 Nelson Briles. There is also a complete variation set that was available one card per Twinkie package. Common cards in this Twinkie set are worth double the prices listed below, although the stars are only worth about 25 percent more. The Twinkie cards are distinguished by the thick printing bar or band printed on the card backs just below the statistics. An album to hold these cards were issued.

	NRMT	VG-E	GOOD
COMPLETE INDIV.SET (150)	250.00	110.00	31.00
COMMON CARD (1-150)	.50	.23	.06
☐ 1 Jim Palmer	4.00	1.80	.50
☐ 2 Joe Morgan	4.00	1.80	.50
☐ 3 Reggie Jackson	10.00	4.50	1.25

☐ 4 Carl Yastrzemski	6.00	2.70	.75
☐ 5 Thurman Munson	3.00	1.35	.35
☐ 6 Johnny Bench	8.00	3.60	1.00
☐ 7 Tom Seaver	8.00	3.60	1.00
☐ 8 Pete Rose	10.00	4.50	1.25
☐ 9 Rod Carew	4.00	1.80	.50
☐ 10 Luis Tiant	.75	.35	.09
☐ 11 Phil Garner	.75	.35	.09
☐ 12 Sixto Lezcano	.50	.23	.06
☐ 13 Mike Torrez	.50	.23	.06
☐ 14 Dave Lopes	.75	.35	.09
☐ 15 Doug DeCinces	.50	.23	.06
☐ 16 Jim Spencer	.50	.23	.06
☐ 17 Hal McRae	.75	.35	.09
☐ 18 Mike Hargrove	.75	.35	.09
☐ 19 Willie Montanez SP	.75	.35	.09
☐ 20 Roger Metzger SP	.75	.35	.09
☐ 21 Dwight Evans SP	1.50	.70	.19
☐ 22 Steve Rogers SP	.75	.35	.09
☐ 23 Jim Rice SP	1.00	.45	.12
☐ 24 Pete Falcone SP	.75	.35	.09
☐ 25 Greg Luzinski SP	1.50	.70	.19
☐ 26 Randy Jones SP	.75	.35	.09
☐ 27 Willie Stargell SP	5.00	2.20	.60
☐ 28 John Hiller SP	.75	.35	.09
☐ 29 Bobby Murcer SP	1.00	.45	.12
☐ 30 Rick Monday SP	.75	.35	.09
☐ 31 John Montefusco SP	.75	.35	.09
☐ 32 Lou Brock SP	5.00	2.20	.60
☐ 33 Bill North SP	.75	.35	.09
☐ 34 Robin Yount SP	20.00	9.00	2.50
☐ 35 Steve Garvey SP	6.00	2.70	.75
☐ 36 George Brett SP	35.00	16.00	4.40
☐ 37 Toby Harrah SP	.75	.35	.09
☐ 38 Jerry Royster SP	.75	.35	.09
☐ 39 Bob Watson SP	1.00	.45	.12
☐ 40 George Foster	.75	.35	.09
☐ 41 Gary Carter	4.00	1.80	.50
☐ 42 John Denny	.50	.23	.06
☐ 43 Mike Schmidt	10.00	4.50	1.25
☐ 44 Dave Winfield	10.00	4.50	1.25
☐ 45 Al Oliver	.75	.35	.09
☐ 46 Mark Fidrych	2.50	1.10	.30
☐ 47 Larry Herndon	.50	.23	.06
☐ 48 Dave Goltz	.50	.23	.06
☐ 49 Jerry Morales	.50	.23	.06
☐ 50 Ron LeFlore	.50	.23	.06
☐ 51 Fred Lynn	1.00	.45	.12
☐ 52 Vida Blue	.75	.35	.09
☐ 53 Rick Manning	.50	.23	.06
☐ 54 Bill Buckner	.75	.35	.09
☐ 55 Lee May	.50	.23	.06
☐ 56 John Mayberry	.50	.23	.06
☐ 57 Darrel Chaney	.50	.23	.06
☐ 58 Cesar Cedeno	.50	.23	.06
☐ 59 Ken Griffey	1.00	.45	.12
☐ 60 Dave Kingman	1.00	.45	.12
☐ 61 Ted Simmons	1.00	.45	.12
☐ 62 Larry Bowa	.75	.35	.09
☐ 63 Frank Tanana	.75	.35	.09
☐ 64 Jason Thompson	.50	.23	.06
☐ 65 Ken Brett	.50	.23	.06
☐ 66 Roy Smalley	.50	.23	.06
☐ 67 Ray Burris	.50	.23	.06
☐ 68 Rick Burleson	.50	.23	.06
☐ 69 Buddy Bell	.75	.35	.09
☐ 70 Don Sutton	4.00	1.80	.50
☐ 71 Mark Belanger	.50	.23	.06
☐ 72 Dennis Leonard	.50	.23	.06
☐ 73 Gaylord Perry	4.00	1.80	.50
☐ 74 Dick Ruthven	.50	.23	.06
☐ 75 Jose Cruz	.50	.23	.06
☐ 76 Cesar Geronimo	.50	.23	.06
☐ 77 Jerry Koosman	.75	.35	.09
☐ 78 Garry Templeton	.50	.23	.06
☐ 79 Jim Hunter	4.00	1.80	.50
☐ 80 John Candelaria	.50	.23	.06
☐ 81 Nolan Ryan	40.00	18.00	5.00
☐ 82 Rusty Staub	.75	.35	.09
☐ 83 Jim Barr	.50	.23	.06
☐ 84 Butch Wynegar	.50	.23	.06
☐ 85 Jose Cardenal	.50	.23	.06
☐ 86 Claudell Washington	.50	.23	.06
☐ 87 Bill Travers	.50	.23	.06
☐ 88 Rick Waits	.50	.23	.06
☐ 89 Ron Cey	.75	.35	.09
☐ 90 Al Bumbry	.50	.23	.06
☐ 91 Bucky Dent	.75	.35	.09
☐ 92 Amos Otis	.50	.23	.06
☐ 93 Tom Grieve	.50	.23	.06
☐ 94 Enos Cabell	.50	.23	.06
☐ 95 Dave Concepcion	1.00	.45	.12
☐ 96 Felix Millan	.50	.23	.06
☐ 97 Bake McBride	.50	.23	.06
☐ 98 Chris Chambliss	.75	.35	.09
☐ 99 Butch Metzger	.50	.23	.06
☐ 100 Rennie Stennett	.50	.23	.06
☐ 101 Dave Roberts	.50	.23	.06
☐ 102 Lyman Bostock	.75	.35	.09
☐ 103 Rick Reuschel	.50	.23	.06
☐ 104 Carlton Fisk	7.50	3.40	.95
☐ 105 Jim Slaton	.50	.23	.06
☐ 106 Dennis Eckersley	6.00	2.70	.75
☐ 107 Ken Singleton	.50	.23	.06
☐ 108 Ralph Garr	.50	.23	.06
☐ 109 Freddie Patek SP	.75	.35	.09
☐ 110 Jim Sundberg SP	.75	.35	.09
☐ 111 Phil Niekro SP	5.00	2.20	.60
☐ 112 J.R. Richard SP	.75	.35	.09
☐ 113 Gary Nolan SP	.75	.35	.09
☐ 114 Jon Matlack SP	.75	.35	.09
☐ 115 Keith Hernandez SP	.75	.35	.09
☐ 116 Graig Nettles SP	1.50	.70	.19
☐ 117 Steve Carlton SP	7.50	3.40	.95
☐ 118 Bill Madlock SP	1.00	.45	.12
☐ 119 Jerry Reuss SP	.75	.35	.09
☐ 120 Aurelio Rodriguez SP	.75	.35	.09
☐ 121 Dan Ford SP	.75	.35	.09
☐ 122 Ray Fosse SP	.75	.35	.09
☐ 123 George Hendrick SP	.75	.35	.09
☐ 124 Alan Ashby	.50	.23	.06
☐ 125 Joe Lis	.50	.23	.06
☐ 126 Sal Bando	.50	.23	.06
☐ 127 Richie Zisk	.50	.23	.06
☐ 128 Rich Gossage	1.00	.45	.12
☐ 129 Don Baylor	.75	.35	.09
☐ 130 Dave McKay	.50	.23	.06
☐ 131 Bob Grich	.75	.35	.09
☐ 132 Dave Pagan	.50	.23	.06
☐ 133 Dave Cash	.50	.23	.06
☐ 134 Steve Braun	.50	.23	.06
☐ 135 Dan Meyer	.50	.23	.06
☐ 136 Bill Stein	.50	.23	.06
☐ 137 Rollie Fingers	3.00	1.35	.35
☐ 138 Brian Downing	.50	.23	.06
☐ 139 Bill Singer	.50	.23	.06
☐ 140 Doyle Alexander	.50	.23	.06
☐ 141 Gene Tenace	.50	.23	.06
☐ 142 Gary Matthews	.50	.23	.06
☐ 143 Don Gullett	.50	.23	.06
☐ 144 Wayne Garland	.50	.23	.06
☐ 145 Pete Broberg	.50	.23	.06
☐ 146 Joe Rudi	.50	.23	.06
☐ 147 Glenn Abbott	.50	.23	.06
☐ 148 George Scott	.50	.23	.06
☐ 149 Bert Campaneris	.50	.23	.06
☐ 150 Andy Messersmith	.50	.23	.06
☐ XX Album	8.00	3.60	1.00

1978 Hostess

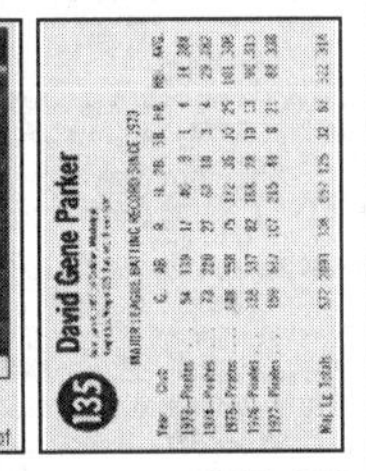

The cards in this 150-card set measure approximately 2 1/4" by 3 1/4" individually or 3 1/4" by 7 1/4" as panels of three. The 1978 Hostess set contains full-color, numbered cards issued in panels of three cards each on family packages of Hostess cake products. Scarcer cards are listed in the checklist with SP. The 1978 Hostess panels are considered by some collectors to be somewhat more difficult to obtain than Hostess panels of other years. Although complete panel prices are not explicitly listed below, they would generally have a value 20-25 percent greater than the sum of the individual players on the panel. There is additional interest in Eddie Murray number 31, since this card corresponds to his rookie year in cards. An album to hold all these cards were issued. There was an album issued for these cards. It was priced below.

	NRMT	VG-E	GOOD
COMPLETE INDIV.SET (150)	250.00	110.00	31.00
COMMON CARD (1-150)	.50	.23	.06
☐ 1 Butch Hobson	.50	.23	.06
☐ 2 George Foster	.75	.35	.09
☐ 3 Bob Forsch	.50	.23	.06
☐ 4 Tony Perez	1.50	.70	.19
☐ 5 Bruce Sutter	1.00	.45	.12
☐ 6 Hal McRae	.75	.35	.09
☐ 7 Tommy John	1.25	.55	.16
☐ 8 Greg Luzinski	.75	.35	.09
☐ 9 Enos Cabell	.50	.23	.06
☐ 10 Doug DeCinces	.50	.23	.06
☐ 11 Willie Stargell	3.00	1.35	.35
☐ 12 Ed Halicki	.50	.23	.06
☐ 13 Larry Hisle	.50	.23	.06
☐ 14 Jim Slaton	.50	.23	.06
☐ 15 Buddy Bell	.75	.35	.09
☐ 16 Earl Williams	.50	.23	.06
☐ 17 Glenn Abbott	.50	.23	.06
☐ 18 Dan Ford	.50	.23	.06
☐ 19 Gary Matthews	.50	.23	.06
☐ 20 Eric Soderholm	.50	.23	.06
☐ 21 Bump Wills	.50	.23	.06
☐ 22 Keith Hernandez	1.50	.70	.19
☐ 23 Dave Cash	.50	.23	.06
☐ 24 George Scott	.50	.23	.06
☐ 25 Ron Guidry	1.00	.45	.12
☐ 26 Dave Kingman	1.00	.45	.12
☐ 27 George Brett	30.00	13.50	3.70
☐ 28 Bob Watson SP	1.00	.45	.12
☐ 29 Bob Boone SP	1.50	.70	.19
☐ 30 Reggie Smith SP	.75	.35	.09
☐ 31 Eddie Murray SP	50.00	22.00	6.25
☐ 32 Gary Lavelle SP	.75	.35	.09
☐ 33 Rennie Stennett SP	.75	.35	.09
☐ 34 Duane Kuiper SP	.75	.35	.09
☐ 35 Sixto Lezcano SP	.75	.35	.09
☐ 36 Dave Rozema SP	.75	.35	.09
☐ 37 Butch Wynegar SP	.75	.35	.09
☐ 38 Mitchell Page SP	.75	.35	.09
☐ 39 Bill Stein SP	.75	.35	.09
☐ 40 Elliott Maddox	.50	.23	.06
☐ 41 Mike Hargrove	.75	.35	.09
☐ 42 Bobby Bonds	1.50	.70	.19
☐ 43 Garry Templeton	.50	.23	.06
☐ 44 Johnny Bench	8.00	3.60	1.00
☐ 45 Jim Rice	2.00	.90	.25
☐ 46 Bill Buckner	.75	.35	.09
☐ 47 Reggie Jackson	8.00	3.60	1.00
☐ 48 Freddie Patek	.50	.23	.06
☐ 49 Steve Carlton	4.00	1.80	.50
☐ 50 Cesar Cedeno	.50	.23	.06
☐ 51 Steve Yeager	.50	.23	.06
☐ 52 Phil Garner	.75	.35	.09
☐ 53 Lee May	.50	.23	.06
☐ 54 Darrell Evans	.75	.35	.09
☐ 55 Steve Kemp	.50	.23	.06
☐ 56 Dusty Baker	.75	.35	.09
☐ 57 Ray Fosse	.50	.23	.06
☐ 58 Manny Sanguillen	.50	.23	.06
☐ 59 Tom Johnson	.50	.23	.06
☐ 60 Lee Stanton	.50	.23	.06
☐ 61 Jeff Burroughs	.50	.23	.06
☐ 62 Bobby Grich	.75	.35	.09
☐ 63 Dave Winfield	8.00	3.60	1.00
☐ 64 Dan Driessen	.50	.23	.06
☐ 65 Ted Simmons	1.00	.45	.12
☐ 66 Jerry Remy	.50	.23	.06
☐ 67 Al Cowens	.50	.23	.06
☐ 68 Sparky Lyle	.75	.35	.09
☐ 69 Manny Trillo	.50	.23	.06
☐ 70 Don Sutton	3.00	1.35	.35
☐ 71 Larry Bowa	.75	.35	.09
☐ 72 Jose Cruz	.50	.23	.06
☐ 73 Willie McCovey	3.00	1.35	.35
☐ 74 Bert Blyleven	1.00	.45	.12
☐ 75 Ken Singleton	.50	.23	.06
☐ 76 Bill North	.50	.23	.06
☐ 77 Jason Thompson	.50	.23	.06
☐ 78 Dennis Eckersley	4.00	1.80	.50
☐ 79 Jim Sundberg	.50	.23	.06
☐ 80 Jerry Koosman	.75	.35	.09
☐ 81 Bruce Bochte	.50	.23	.06
☐ 82 George Hendrick	.50	.23	.06
☐ 83 Nolan Ryan	40.00	18.00	5.00
☐ 84 Roy Howell	.50	.23	.06
☐ 85 Roger Metzger	.50	.23	.06
☐ 86 Doc Medich	.50	.23	.06
☐ 87 Joe Morgan	4.00	1.80	.50
☐ 88 Dennis Leonard	.50	.23	.06
☐ 89 Willie Randolph	1.00	.45	.12
☐ 90 Bobby Murcer	.75	.35	.09
☐ 91 Rick Manning	.50	.23	.06
☐ 92 J.R. Richard	.50	.23	.06
☐ 93 Ron Cey	.75	.35	.09
☐ 94 Sal Bando	.50	.23	.06
☐ 95 Ron LeFlore	.50	.23	.06
☐ 96 Dave Goltz	.50	.23	.06
☐ 97 Dan Meyer	.50	.23	.06
☐ 98 Chris Chambliss	.50	.23	.06
☐ 99 Biff Pocoroba	.50	.23	.06
☐ 100 Oscar Gamble	.50	.23	.06
☐ 101 Frank Tanana	.50	.23	.06
☐ 102 Len Randle	.50	.23	.06
☐ 103 Tommy Hutton	.50	.23	.06
☐ 104 John Candelaria	.50	.23	.06
☐ 105 Jorge Orta	.50	.23	.06
☐ 106 Ken Reitz	.50	.23	.06
☐ 107 Bill Campbell	.50	.23	.06
☐ 108 Dave Concepcion	1.00	.45	.12
☐ 109 Joe Ferguson	.50	.23	.06
☐ 110 Mickey Rivers	.50	.23	.06
☐ 111 Paul Splittorff	.50	.23	.06
☐ 112 Dave Lopes	.50	.23	.06
☐ 113 Mike Schmidt	10.00	4.50	1.25
☐ 114 Joe Rudi	.50	.23	.06
☐ 115 Milt May	.50	.23	.06
☐ 116 Jim Palmer	4.00	1.80	.50
☐ 117 Bill Madlock	.75	.35	.09
☐ 118 Roy Smalley	.50	.23	.06
☐ 119 Cecil Cooper	1.00	.45	.12
☐ 120 Rick Langford	.50	.23	.06
☐ 121 Ruppert Jones	.50	.23	.06
☐ 122 Phil Niekro	3.00	1.35	.35
☐ 123 Toby Harrah	.50	.23	.06
☐ 124 Chet Lemon	.50	.23	.06
☐ 125 Gene Tenace	.50	.23	.06
☐ 126 Steve Henderson	.50	.23	.06
☐ 127 Mike Torrez	.50	.23	.06
☐ 128 Pete Rose	10.00	4.50	1.25
☐ 129 John Denny	.50	.23	.06
☐ 130 Darrell Porter	.50	.23	.06
☐ 131 Rick Reuschel	.50	.23	.06
☐ 132 Graig Nettles	.75	.35	.09
☐ 133 Garry Maddox	.50	.23	.06
☐ 134 Mike Flanagan	.50	.23	.06
☐ 135 Dave Parker	1.00	.45	.12
☐ 136 Terry Whitfield	.50	.23	.06
☐ 137 Wayne Garland	.50	.23	.06
☐ 138 Robin Yount	10.00	4.50	1.25
☐ 139 Gaylord Perry	3.00	1.35	.35
☐ 140 Rod Carew	4.00	1.80	.50
☐ 141 Wayne Gross	.50	.23	.06
☐ 142 Barry Bonnell	.50	.23	.06
☐ 143 Willie Montanez	.50	.23	.06
☐ 144 Rollie Fingers	3.00	1.35	.35
☐ 145 Lyman Bostock	.75	.35	.09
☐ 146 Gary Carter	3.00	1.35	.35
☐ 147 Ron Blomberg	.50	.23	.06
☐ 148 Bob Bailor	.50	.23	.06
☐ 149 Tom Seaver	6.00	2.70	.75
☐ 150 Thurman Munson	4.00	1.80	.50
☐ XX Album	8.00	3.60	1.00

1979 Hostess

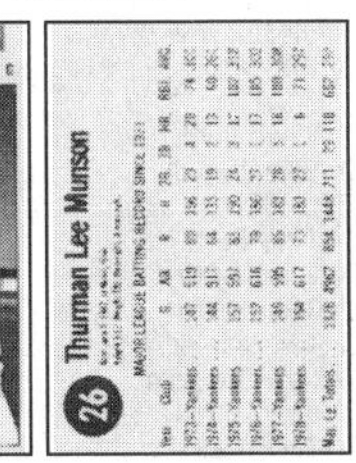

The cards in this 150-card set measure approximately 2 1/4" by 3 1/4" individually or 3 1/4" by 7 1/4" as panels of three. The 1979 Hostess set contains full color, numbered cards issued in panels of three cards each on the backs of family sized Hostess cake products. Scarcer cards are listed in the checklist below with SP. Although complete panel prices are not explicitly listed below they would generally have a value 20-25 percent greater than the sum of the individual players on the panel. The collectors who don't consider 1978 to be the most difficult Hostess to acquire, believe that 1979's are the toughest to get. The shelf life on the 1979's seemed to be slightly shorter than other years.There is additional interest in Ozzie Smith (102) since this card corresponds to his rookie year in cards. An album to hold these cards were issued.

	NRMT	VG-E	GOOD
COMPLETE INDIV.SET (150)	250.00	110.00	31.00
COMMON CARD (1-150)	.50	.23	.06
☐ 1 John Denny	.50	.23	.06
☐ 2 Jim Rice	1.50	.70	.19
☐ 3 Doug Bair	.50	.23	.06
☐ 4 Darrell Porter	.50	.23	.06
☐ 5 Ross Grimsley	.50	.23	.06
☐ 6 Bobby Murcer	.75	.35	.09
☐ 7 Lee Mazzilli	.50	.23	.06
☐ 8 Steve Garvey	2.00	.90	.25
☐ 9 Mike Schmidt	10.00	4.50	1.25
☐ 10 Terry Whitfield	.50	.23	.06
☐ 11 Jim Palmer	4.00	1.80	.50
☐ 12 Omar Moreno	.50	.23	.06
☐ 13 Duane Kuiper	.50	.23	.06
☐ 14 Mike Caldwell	.50	.23	.06
☐ 15 Steve Kemp	.50	.23	.06
☐ 16 Dave Goltz	.50	.23	.06
☐ 17 Mitchell Page	.50	.23	.06
☐ 18 Bill Stein	.50	.23	.06
☐ 19 Gene Tenace	.50	.23	.06
☐ 20 Jeff Burroughs	.50	.23	.06
☐ 21 Francisco Barrios	.50	.23	.06
☐ 22 Mike Torrez	.50	.23	.06
☐ 23 Ken Reitz	.50	.23	.06
☐ 24 Gary Carter	3.00	1.35	.35
☐ 25 Al Hrabosky	.50	.23	.06
☐ 26 Thurman Munson	4.00	1.80	.50
☐ 27 Bill Buckner	.75	.35	.09
☐ 28 Ron Cey SP	1.00	.45	.12
☐ 29 J.R. Richard SP	.75	.35	.09
☐ 30 Greg Luzinski SP	1.00	.45	.12
☐ 31 Ed Ott SP	.75	.35	.09
☐ 32 Dennis Martinez SP	3.00	1.35	.35
☐ 33 Darrell Evans SP	1.00	.45	.12
☐ 34 Ron LeFlore	.50	.23	.06
☐ 35 Rick Waits	.50	.23	.06
☐ 36 Cecil Cooper	.75	.35	.09
☐ 37 Leon Roberts	.50	.23	.06
☐ 38 Rod Carew	4.00	1.80	.50
☐ 39 John Henry Johnson	.50	.23	.06
☐ 40 Chet Lemon	.50	.23	.06
☐ 41 Craig Swan	.50	.23	.06
☐ 42 Gary Matthews	.50	.23	.06
☐ 43 Lamar Johnson	.50	.23	.06
☐ 44 Ted Simmons	.75	.35	.09
☐ 45 Ken Griffey	.75	.35	.09
☐ 46 Fred Patek	.50	.23	.06
☐ 47 Frank Tanana	.75	.35	.09
☐ 48 Goose Gossage	1.00	.45	.12
☐ 49 Burt Hooton	.50	.23	.06
☐ 50 Ellis Valentine	.50	.23	.06
☐ 51 Ken Forsch	.50	.23	.06
☐ 52 Bob Knepper	.50	.23	.06
☐ 53 Dave Parker	2.00	.90	.25

	MINT	NRMT	EXC
☐ 54 Doug DeCinces	.50	.23	.06
☐ 55 Robin Yount	10.00	4.50	1.25
☐ 56 Rusty Staub	.75	.35	.09
☐ 57 Gary Alexander	.50	.23	.06
☐ 58 Julio Cruz	.50	.23	.06
☐ 59 Matt Keough	.50	.23	.06
☐ 60 Roy Smalley	.50	.23	.06
☐ 61 Joe Morgan	4.00	1.80	.50
☐ 62 Phil Niekro	3.00	1.35	.35
☐ 63 Don Baylor	.75	.35	.09
☐ 64 Dwight Evans	.75	.35	.09
☐ 65 Tom Seaver	6.00	2.70	.75
☐ 66 George Hendrick	.50	.23	.06
☐ 67 Rick Reuschel	.50	.23	.06
☐ 68 George Brett	20.00	9.00	2.50
☐ 69 Lou Piniella	.75	.35	.09
☐ 70 Enos Cabell	.50	.23	.06
☐ 71 Steve Carlton	4.00	1.80	.50
☐ 72 Reggie Smith	.75	.35	.09
☐ 73 Rick Dempsey SP	.75	.35	.09
☐ 74 Vida Blue SP	1.00	.45	.12
☐ 75 Phil Garner SP	1.00	.45	.12
☐ 76 Rick Manning SP	.75	.35	.09
☐ 77 Mark Fidrych SP	1.00	.45	.12
☐ 78 Mario Guerrero SP	.75	.35	.09
☐ 79 Bob Stinson SP	.75	.35	.09
☐ 80 Al Oliver SP	1.00	.45	.12
☐ 81 Doug Flynn SP	.75	.35	.09
☐ 82 John Mayberry	.50	.23	.06
☐ 83 Gaylord Perry	3.00	1.35	.35
☐ 84 Joe Rudi	.50	.23	.06
☐ 85 Dave Concepcion	1.00	.45	.12
☐ 86 John Candelaria	.50	.23	.06
☐ 87 Pete Vuckovich	.50	.23	.06
☐ 88 Ivan DeJesus	.50	.23	.06
☐ 89 Ron Guidry	1.25	.55	.16
☐ 90 Hal McRae	.75	.35	.09
☐ 91 Cesar Cedeno	.50	.23	.06
☐ 92 Don Sutton	3.00	1.35	.35
☐ 93 Andre Thornton	.50	.23	.06
☐ 94 Roger Erickson	.50	.23	.06
☐ 95 Larry Hisle	.50	.23	.06
☐ 96 Jason Thompson	.50	.23	.06
☐ 97 Jim Sundberg	.50	.23	.06
☐ 98 Bob Horner	.75	.35	.09
☐ 99 Ruppert Jones	.50	.23	.06
☐ 100 Willie Montanez	.50	.23	.06
☐ 101 Nolan Ryan	40.00	18.00	5.00
☐ 102 Ozzie Smith	40.00	18.00	5.00
☐ 103 Eric Soderholm	.50	.23	.06
☐ 104 Willie Stargell	4.00	1.80	.50
☐ 105A Bob Bailor ERR (Reverse negative)	.75	.35	.09
☐ 105B Bob Bailor COR	1.50	.70	.19
☐ 106 Carlton Fisk	5.00	2.20	.60
☐ 107 George Foster	.75	.35	.09
☐ 108 Keith Hernandez	1.50	.70	.19
☐ 109 Dennis Leonard	.50	.23	.06
☐ 110 Graig Nettles	1.00	.45	.12
☐ 111 Jose Cruz	.75	.35	.09
☐ 112 Bobby Grich	.75	.35	.09
☐ 113 Bob Boone	.75	.35	.09
☐ 114 Dave Lopes	.50	.23	.06
☐ 115 Eddie Murray	20.00	9.00	2.50
☐ 116 Jack Clark	1.25	.55	.16
☐ 117 Lou Whitaker	4.00	1.80	.50
☐ 118 Miguel Dilone	.50	.23	.06
☐ 119 Sal Bando	.50	.23	.06
☐ 120 Reggie Jackson	8.00	3.60	1.00
☐ 121 Dale Murphy	8.00	3.60	1.00
☐ 122 Jon Matlack	.50	.23	.06
☐ 123 Bruce Bochte	.50	.23	.06
☐ 124 John Stearns	.50	.23	.06
☐ 125 Dave Winfield	8.00	3.60	1.00
☐ 126 Jorge Orta	.50	.23	.06
☐ 127 Garry Templeton	.50	.23	.06
☐ 128 Johnny Bench	6.00	2.70	.75
☐ 129 Butch Hobson	.50	.23	.06
☐ 130 Bruce Sutter	.75	.35	.09
☐ 131 Bucky Dent	.75	.35	.09
☐ 132 Amos Otis	.50	.23	.06
☐ 133 Bert Blyleven	1.00	.45	.12
☐ 134 Larry Bowa	.75	.35	.09
☐ 135 Ken Singleton	.50	.23	.06
☐ 136 Sixto Lezcano	.50	.23	.06
☐ 137 Roy Howell	.50	.23	.06
☐ 138 Bill Madlock	.75	.35	.09
☐ 139 Dave Revering	.50	.23	.06
☐ 140 Richie Zisk	.50	.23	.06
☐ 141 Butch Wynegar	.50	.23	.06
☐ 142 Alan Ashby	.50	.23	.06
☐ 143 Sparky Lyle	.75	.35	.09
☐ 144 Pete Rose	10.00	4.50	1.25
☐ 145 Dennis Eckersley	2.50	1.10	.30
☐ 146 Dave Kingman	1.00	.45	.12
☐ 147 Buddy Bell	.75	.35	.09
☐ 148 Mike Hargrove	.75	.35	.09
☐ 149 Jerry Koosman	.75	.35	.09
☐ 150 Toby Harrah	.50	.23	.06
☐ XX Album	8.00	3.60	1.00

1987 Hostess Stickers

This set of 30 small, full-color stickers was produced in Canada by Hostess Potato Chips and distributed in bags of potato chips. Each sticker was loosely wrapped in cellophane (to protect against potato chip stains) and measures approximately 1 3/8" by 1 3/4" with rounded corners. The backs of the stickers contain the player's name, team and position in English as well as in French. They are numbered on the front in the lower left corner. The first six cards are Blue Jays and Expos; the rest of the set consists of one player per American team.

	MINT	NRMT	EXC
COMPLETE SET (30)	40.00	18.00	5.00
COMMON STICKER (1-30)	.50	.23	.06
☐ 1 Jesse Barfield	.50	.23	.06
☐ 2 Ernie Whitt	.50	.23	.06
☐ 3 George Bell	.50	.23	.06
☐ 4 Hubie Brooks	.50	.23	.06
☐ 5 Tim Wallach	.50	.23	.06
☐ 6 Floyd Youmans	.50	.23	.06
☐ 7 Dale Murphy	1.25	.55	.16
☐ 8 Ryne Sandberg	5.00	2.20	.60
☐ 9 Eric Davis	.75	.35	.09
☐ 10 Mike Scott	.50	.23	.06
☐ 11 Fernando Valenzuela	.75	.35	.09
☐ 12 Gary Carter	.75	.35	.09
☐ 13 Mike Schmidt	4.00	1.80	.50
☐ 14 Tony Pena	.50	.23	.06
☐ 15 Ozzie Smith	5.00	2.20	.60
☐ 16 Tony Gwynn	6.00	2.70	.75
☐ 17 Mike Krukow	.50	.23	.06
☐ 18 Eddie Murray	3.00	1.35	.35
☐ 19 Wade Boggs	1.50	.70	.19
☐ 20 Wally Joyner	1.25	.55	.16
☐ 21 Harold Baines	.75	.35	.09
☐ 22 Brook Jacoby	.50	.23	.06
☐ 23 Lou Whitaker	.75	.35	.09
☐ 24 George Brett	5.00	2.20	.60
☐ 25 Robin Yount	1.50	.70	.19
☐ 26 Kirby Puckett	6.00	2.70	.75
☐ 27 Don Mattingly	6.00	2.70	.75
☐ 28 Jose Canseco	4.00	1.80	.50
☐ 29 Phil Bradley	.50	.23	.06
☐ 30 Pete O'Brien	.50	.23	.06

1993 Hostess

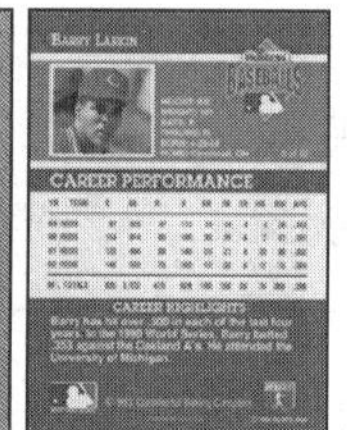

These standard-size cards were free with the purchase of packages of Hostess Baseballs, a new snack food. The frosted yellow cakes have creamy filling and were decorated with red icing to resemble the stitching of a baseball. Each two-cake snack pack contained one three-card pack and cost 85 cents, while each eight-cake family pack contained two packs and cost 2.99. The cards were issued in two series (1-16 and 17-32), the first being available nationally beginning on April 12 and the second series beginning mid-season. A checklist was included on the back of each family pack. The cards feature color action player photos inside a white inner border and an outer border consisting of blue and white diagonal pinstripes. The player's name and the team logo are on a red banner toward the bottom of the card. On blue, red, and white panels, the backs display a color head shot, biography, career performance statistics, and career highlights.

	MINT	NRMT	EXC
COMPLETE SET (32)	7.50	3.40	.95
COMMON CARD (1-32)	.10	.05	.01
☐ 1 Andy Van Slyke	.10	.05	.01
☐ 2 Ryne Sandberg	.50	.23	.06
☐ 3 Bobby Bonilla	.20	.09	.03
☐ 4 John Kruk	.20	.09	.03
☐ 5 Ray Lankford	.20	.09	.03
☐ 6 Gary Sheffield	.40	.18	.05
☐ 7 Darryl Strawberry	.20	.09	.03
☐ 8 Barry Larkin	.25	.11	.03
☐ 9 Terry Pendleton	.10	.05	.01
☐ 10 Jose Canseco	.30	.14	.04
☐ 11 Dennis Eckersley	.20	.09	.03
☐ 12 Brian McRae	.10	.05	.01
☐ 13 Frank Thomas	1.50	.70	.19
☐ 14 Roberto Alomar	.50	.23	.06
☐ 15 Carlos Baerga	.30	.14	.04
☐ 16 Cecil Fielder	.20	.09	.03
☐ 17 Will Clark	.20	.09	.03
☐ 18 Andres Galarraga	.30	.14	.04
☐ 19 Jeff Bagwell	.75	.35	.09
☐ 20 Brett Butler	.20	.09	.03
☐ 21 Benito Santiago	.10	.05	.01
☐ 22 Tom Glavine	.30	.14	.04
☐ 23 Rickey Henderson	.30	.14	.04
☐ 24 Wally Joyner	.10	.05	.01
☐ 25 Ken Griffey Jr.	1.50	.70	.19
☐ 26 Cal Ripken	1.25	.55	.16
☐ 27 Roger Clemens	.50	.23	.06
☐ 28 Don Mattingly	.75	.35	.09
☐ 29 Kirby Puckett	.75	.35	.09
☐ 30 Larry Walker	.15	.07	.02
☐ 31 Jack McDowell	.10	.05	.01
☐ 32 Pat Listach	.10	.05	.01

1990 Hottest 50 Players Stickers

Issued by Publications International, this sticker album measures 8 1/4" by 10 7/8" and includes 50 giant player stickers and 6 bonus stadium stickers. The oversized stickers measure 4 1/8 by 5 1/2" and feature glossy color action player photos inside a white border. The NL players stickers have a red stripe at the top and a blue stripe at the bottom, while the AL Rookies stickers have a blue stripe at the top and a red stripe at the bottom. The 32-page sticker album has slots for two stickers per page and presents career summary, biography, and statistics out to the side. The stickers are unnumbered and checklisted below in alphabetical order.

	MINT	NRMT	EXC
COMPLETE SET (56)	35.00	16.00	4.40
COMMON STICKER (1-56)	.25	.11	.03
☐ 1 George Bell	.25	.11	.03
☐ 2 Wade Boggs	1.00	.45	.12
☐ 3 Bobby Bonilla	.50	.23	.06
☐ 4 Jose Canseco	1.25	.55	.16
☐ 5 Joe Carter	1.25	.55	.16
☐ 6 Will Clark	1.25	.55	.16
☐ 7 Roger Clemens	1.25	.55	.16
☐ 8 Alvin Davis	.25	.11	.03
☐ 9 Eric Davis	.25	.11	.03
☐ 10 Glenn Davis	.25	.11	.03
☐ 11 Mark Davis	.25	.11	.03
☐ 12 Carlton Fisk	1.00	.45	.12
☐ 13 John Franco	.25	.11	.03
☐ 14 Gary Gaetti	.25	.11	.03
☐ 15 Andres Galarraga	1.25	.55	.16
☐ 16 Dwight Gooden	.50	.23	.06
☐ 17 Mark Grace	1.25	.55	.16
☐ 18 Pedro Guerrero	.25	.11	.03
☐ 19 Tony Gwynn	4.00	1.80	.50
☐ 20 Rickey Henderson	1.00	.45	.12
☐ 21 Orel Hershiser	.50	.23	.06
☐ 22 Bo Jackson	.50	.23	.06
☐ 23 Ricky Jordan	.25	.11	.03
☐ 24 Wally Joyner	.50	.23	.06
☐ 25 Don Mattingly	5.00	2.20	.60
☐ 26 Fred McGriff	1.25	.55	.16
☐ 27 Kevin Mitchell	.25	.11	.03
☐ 28 Paul Molitor	1.50	.70	.19
☐ 29 Dale Murphy	1.00	.45	.12
☐ 30 Eddie Murray	2.00	.90	.25
☐ 31 Kirby Puckett	4.00	1.80	.50
☐ 32 Tim Raines	.50	.23	.06
☐ 33 Harold Reynolds	.25	.11	.03
☐ 34 Cal Ripken Jr.	10.00	4.50	1.25
☐ 35 Nolan Ryan	10.00	4.50	1.25
☐ 36 Bret Saberhagen	.50	.23	.06
☐ 37 Ryne Sandberg	3.00	1.35	.35
☐ 38 Steve Sax	.25	.11	.03
☐ 39 Mike Scott	.25	.11	.03
☐ 40 Ruben Sierra	.50	.23	.06
☐ 41 Ozzie Smith	2.50	1.10	.30
☐ 42 John Smoltz	1.50	.70	.19
☐ 43 Darryl Strawberry	.50	.23	.06
☐ 44 Greg Swindell	.25	.11	.03
☐ 45 Mickey Tettleton	.50	.23	.06
☐ 46 Alan Trammell	.50	.23	.06
☐ 47 Andy Van Slyke	.50	.23	.06
☐ 48 Lou Whitaker	.50	.23	.06
☐ 49 Devon White	.50	.23	.06
☐ 50 Robin Yount	1.25	.55	.16
☐ 51 Dodger Stadium	.25	.11	.03
☐ 52 Jack Murphy Stadium	.25	.11	.03
☐ 53 Shea Stadium	.25	.11	.03
☐ 54 Three Rivers Stadium	.25	.11	.03
☐ 55 Tiger Stadium	.25	.11	.03
☐ 56 Yankee Stadium	.25	.11	.03

1990 Hottest 50 Rookies Stickers

Issued by Publications International, this sticker album measures 8 1/4" by 10 7/8" and includes 50 giant rookie stickers and 6 bonus stadium stickers. The oversized stickers measure 4 1/8 by 5 1/2" and feature glossy color action player photos inside a white border. The NL Rookie stickers have a red stripe at the top and a blue stripe at the bottom, while the AL Rookie stickers have a blue stripe at the top and a red stripe at the bottom. The 32-page sticker album has slots for two stickers per page and presents career summary, biography, and statistics out to the side. The stickers are unnumbered and checklisted below in alphabetical order.

	MINT	NRMT	EXC
COMPLETE SET (56)	20.00	9.00	2.50
COMMON STICKER (1-56)	.25	.11	.03
☐ 1 Jim Abbott	.50	.23	.06
☐ 2 Sandy Alomar Jr.	.75	.35	.09
☐ 3 Kent Anderson	.25	.11	.03
☐ 4 Eric Anthony	.25	.11	.03
☐ 5 Jeff Ballard	.25	.11	.03
☐ 6 Albert Belle	5.00	2.20	.60
☐ 7 Andy Benes	.75	.35	.09
☐ 8 Lance Blankenship	.25	.11	.03
☐ 9 Jeff Brantley	.25	.11	.03
☐ 10 Cris Carpenter	.25	.11	.03
☐ 11 Mark Carreon	.25	.11	.03
☐ 12 Dennis Cook	.25	.11	.03
☐ 13 Scott Coolbaugh	.25	.11	.03
☐ 14 Luis de los Santos	.25	.11	.03
☐ 15 Junior Felix	.25	.11	.03
☐ 16 Mark Gardner	.25	.11	.03
☐ 17 German Gonzalez	.25	.11	.03
☐ 18 Tom Gordon	.25	.11	.03
☐ 19 Ken Griffey Jr.	10.00	4.50	1.25
☐ 20 Marquis Grissom	1.00	.45	.12
☐ 21 Charlie Hayes	.25	.11	.03
☐ 22 Gregg Jefferies	.50	.23	.06
☐ 23 Randy Johnson	2.50	1.10	.30
☐ 24 Felix Jose	.25	.11	.03
☐ 25 Jeff King	.25	.11	.03
☐ 26 Randy Kramer	.25	.11	.03
☐ 27 Derek Lilliquist	.25	.11	.03
☐ 28 Greg Litton	.25	.11	.03
☐ 29 Kelly Mann	.25	.11	.03
☐ 30 Ramon Martinez	.75	.35	.09
☐ 31 Luis Medina	.25	.11	.03
☐ 32 Hal Morris	.50	.23	.06
☐ 33 Joe Oliver	.25	.11	.03
☐ 34 Gregg Olson	.25	.11	.03
☐ 35 Dean Palmer	1.00	.45	.12
☐ 36 Carlos Quintana	.25	.11	.03
☐ 37 Kevin Ritz	.50	.23	.06
☐ 38 Deion Sanders	1.50	.70	.19
☐ 39 Scott Scudder	.25	.11	.03
☐ 40 Steve Searcy	.25	.11	.03
☐ 41 Gary Sheffield	1.50	.70	.19
☐ 42 Dwight Smith	.25	.11	.03
☐ 43 Sammy Sosa	1.50	.70	.19
☐ 44 Greg Vaughn	.75	.35	.09
☐ 45 Robin Ventura	1.00	.45	.12
☐ 46 Jerome Walton	.25	.11	.03
☐ 47 Dave West	.25	.11	.03
☐ 48 John Wetteland	.75	.35	.09
☐ 49 Eric Yelding	.25	.11	.03
☐ 50 Todd Zeile	.50	.23	.06
☐ 51 Dodger Stadium	.25	.11	.03
☐ 52 Jack Murphy Stadium	.25	.11	.03
☐ 53 Shea Stadium	.25	.11	.03
☐ 54 Three Rivers Stadium	.25	.11	.03
☐ 55 Tiger Stadium	.25	.11	.03
☐ 56 Yankee Stadium	.25	.11	.03

1988 Houston Show

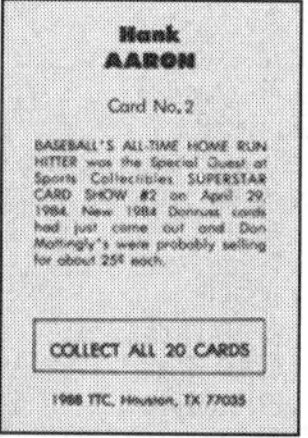

This 20-card set measures approximately 2 1/4" by 3 1/4". On a white card face, the fronts feature black-and-white player photos accented by a purple picture frame. A white star appears at each corner of the frame, and a row of purple stars edges the pictures on the left and right sides. The backs carry the player's name, the card number, a career summary, and "1988 TTC, Houston TX 77035" as a tagline.

	MINT	NRMT	EXC
COMPLETE SET (20)	30.00	13.50	3.70
COMMON CARD (1-20)	.25	.11	.03
☐ 1 Brooks Robinson	2.00	.90	.25
☐ 2 Hank Aaron	6.00	2.70	.75
☐ 3 Gaylord Perry	1.00	.45	.12
☐ 4 Stan Musial	5.00	2.20	.60
☐ 5 Willie Mays	6.00	2.70	.75
☐ 6 Ernie Banks	3.00	1.35	.35
☐ 7 Rod Carew	2.00	.90	.25
☐ 8 Duke Snider	2.00	.90	.25
☐ 9 Mickey Mantle	15.00	6.75	1.85
☐ 10 Lou Brock	2.00	.90	.25
☐ 11 Yogi Berra	2.00	.90	.25
☐ 12 Nolan Ryan	10.00	4.50	1.25
☐ 13 Roger Clemens	3.00	1.35	.35
☐ 14 Jose Cruz	.50	.23	.06

☐ 15 Gerald Young	.25	.11	.03
☐ 16 Enos Slaughter	1.50	.70	.19
☐ 17 Glenn Davis	.25	.11	.03
☐ 18 J.R. Richard	.25	.11	.03
☐ 19 Fergie Jenkins	1.50	.70	.19
☐ 20 Pete Incaviglia	.25	.11	.03

1959 Howard Photo Service PC751

The Howard Photo Service late 1950's postcard set was, until recently, thought to contain only the Bob Turley card. However, the recently discovered Willie Mays card indicates that additional cards may be found in the future. These black and white postcards were issued in New York.

	NRMT	VG-E	GOOD
COMPLETE SET (2)	50.00	22.00	6.25
COMMON CARD (1-2)	10.00	4.50	1.25
☐ 1 Willie Mays	40.00	18.00	5.00
☐ 2 Bob Turley	10.00	4.50	1.25

1993 Hoyle

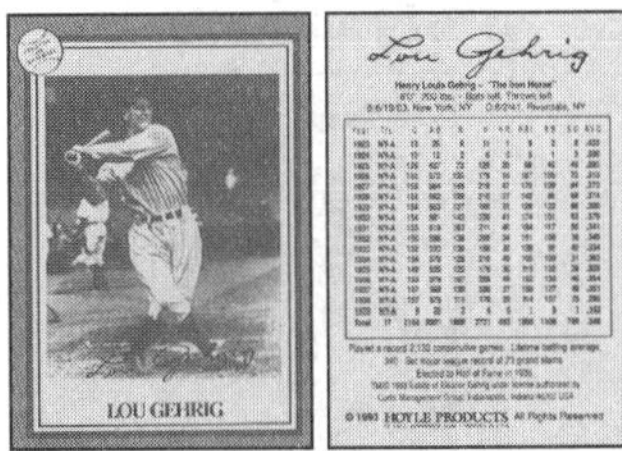

One of these nine cards was inserted in specially marked Hoyle Official Playing Card decks. The back of the card box contains a checklist for all nine cards and an opening at the bottom, where the name of the player whose card is inserted in the pack appears. The cards measure the standard size and have rounded corners. On a grey background, the fronts feature black-and-white action player photos with black and white borders. The player's name appears in a white bar under the photo, while a facsimile autograph printed on the lower portion of the photo. The backs carry a player biography and stats. The cards are unnumbered and checklisted below in alphabetical order.

	MINT	NRMT	EXC
COMPLETE SET (9)	10.00	4.50	1.25
COMMON CARD (1-9)	1.00	.45	.12
☐ 1 Ty Cobb	2.00	.90	.25
☐ 2 Dizzy Dean	1.00	.45	.12
☐ 3 Lou Gehrig	2.00	.90	.25
☐ 4 Walter Johnson	1.50	.70	.19
☐ 5 Satchel Paige	1.50	.70	.19
☐ 6 Babe Ruth	2.50	1.10	.30
☐ 7 Casey Stengel	1.00	.45	.12
☐ 8 Honus Wagner	1.50	.70	.19
☐ 9 Cy Young	1.50	.70	.19

1993 Humpty Dumpty Canadian

This 51-card set measures approximately 1 7/16" by 1 15/16" and was issued by Humpty Dumpty. The full-bleed color action photos have the player's team logo in one of the upper corners. The back carries the player's name, position, biography and statistics in both French and English. The Humpty Dumpty logo appears at the top over a navy blue border. The cards are numbered on the back.

	MINT	NRMT	EXC
COMPLETE SET (51)	35.00	16.00	4.40
COMMON CARD (1-51)	.25	.11	.03
☐ 1 Cal Ripken	4.00	1.80	.50
☐ 2 Mike Mussina	1.50	.70	.19
☐ 3 Roger Clemens	2.00	.90	.25
☐ 4 Chuck Finley	.25	.11	.03
☐ 5 Sandy Alomar Jr.	.50	.23	.06
☐ 6 Frank Thomas	5.00	2.20	.60
☐ 7 Robin Ventura	1.00	.45	.12
☐ 8 Cecil Fielder	1.00	.45	.12
☐ 9 George Brett	3.00	1.35	.35
☐ 10 Cal Eldred	.25	.11	.03
☐ 11 Kirby Puckett	2.50	1.10	.30
☐ 12 Dave Winfield	1.50	.70	.19
☐ 13 Jim Abbott	.25	.11	.03
☐ 14 Rickey Henderson	1.00	.45	.12
☐ 15 Ken Griffey Jr.	5.00	2.20	.60
☐ 16 Nolan Ryan	4.00	1.80	.50
☐ 17 Ivan Rodriguez	2.00	.90	.25
☐ 18 Paul Molitor	1.25	.55	.16
☐ 19 John Olerud	.50	.23	.06
☐ 20 Joe Carter	1.00	.45	.12
☐ 21 Jack Morris	.50	.23	.06
☐ 22 Roberto Alomar	1.50	.70	.19
☐ 23 Pat Borders	.25	.11	.03
☐ 24 Devon White	.25	.11	.03
☐ 25 Juan Guzman	.25	.11	.03
☐ 26 Steve Avery	.50	.23	.06
☐ 27 John Smoltz	1.50	.70	.19
☐ 28 Mark Grace	2.00	.90	.25
☐ 29 Jose Rijo	.25	.11	.03
☐ 30 David Nied	.25	.11	.03
☐ 31 Benito Santiago	.25	.11	.03
☐ 32 Jeff Bagwell	2.50	1.10	.30
☐ 33 Tim Wallach	.25	.11	.03
☐ 34 Eric Karros	.75	.35	.09
☐ 35 Delino DeShields	.25	.11	.03
☐ 36 Wilfredo Cordero	.25	.11	.03
☐ 37 Marquis Grissom	.50	.23	.06
☐ 38 Ken Hill	.50	.23	.06
☐ 39 Moises Alou	.50	.23	.06
☐ 40 Chris Nabholz	.25	.11	.03
☐ 41 Dennis Martinez	.50	.23	.06
☐ 42 Larry Walker	.75	.35	.09
☐ 43 Bobby Bonilla	.50	.23	.06
☐ 44 Len Dykstra	.50	.23	.06
☐ 45 Tim Wakefield	.25	.11	.03
☐ 46 Andy Van Slyke	.25	.11	.03
☐ 47 Tony Gwynn	2.50	1.10	.30
☐ 48 Fred McGriff	2.00	.90	.25
☐ 49 Barry Bonds	2.50	1.10	.30
☐ 50 Ozzie Smith	2.50	1.10	.30
☐ 51 Checklist 1-51	.25	.11	.03
☐ xx Album	5.00	2.20	.60

1987 Hygrade All-Time Greats

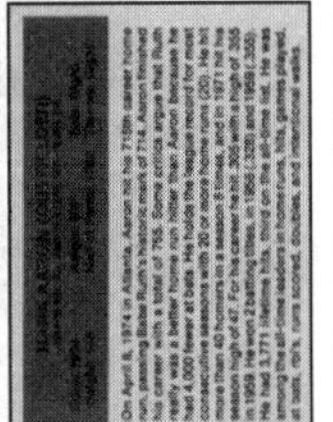

This 50-card set features some of the best players in Baseball of all time. The fronts carry a color player photo in a green border. A small gold oval in the lower left indicates the player's playing years. The backs display player information and why the player is one of the all-time greats. The cards are unnumbered and checklisted below in alphabetical order.

	MINT	NRMT	EXC
COMPLETE SET (50)	5.00	2.20	.60
COMMON CARD (1-50)	.10	.05	.01
☐ 1 Hank Aaron	1.00	.45	.12
☐ 2 Grover Alexander	.50	.23	.06
☐ 3 Luke Appling	.10	.05	.01
☐ 4 Ernie Banks	.50	.23	.06
☐ 5 Yogi Berra	.50	.23	.06
☐ 6 Three Finger Brown	.10	.05	.01
☐ 7 Roy Campanella	.50	.23	.06
☐ 8 Roberto Clemente	1.00	.45	.12
☐ 9 Ty Cobb	1.00	.45	.12
☐ 10 Mickey Cochrane	.25	.11	.03
☐ 11 Eddie Collins	.25	.11	.03
☐ 12 Sam Crawford	.25	.11	.03
☐ 13 Joe Cronin	.10	.05	.01
☐ 14 Bill Dickey	.25	.11	.03
☐ 15 Joe DiMaggio	1.00	.45	.12
☐ 16 Bob Feller	.25	.11	.03
☐ 17 Whitey Ford	.50	.23	.06
☐ 18 Jimmie Foxx	.50	.23	.06
☐ 19 Frankie Frisch	.10	.05	.01
☐ 20 Lou Gehrig	1.00	.45	.12
☐ 21 Charlie Gehringer	.10	.05	.01
☐ 22 Hank Greenberg	.50	.23	.06
☐ 23 Lefty Grove	.25	.11	.03
☐ 24 Gabby Hartnett	.10	.05	.01
☐ 25 Rogers Hornsby	.50	.23	.06
☐ 26 Carl Hubbell	.50	.23	.06
☐ 27 Walter Johnson	.75	.35	.09
☐ 28 Jim Kaat	.10	.05	.01
☐ 29 Ralph Kiner	.10	.05	.01
☐ 30 Don Larsen	.10	.05	.01
☐ 31 Mickey Mantle	1.50	.70	.19
☐ 32 Christy Mathewson	.10	.05	.01
☐ 33 Willie Mays	1.00	.45	.12
☐ 34 Stan Musial	.50	.23	.06
☐ 35 Mel Ott	.10	.05	.01
☐ 36 Brooks Robinson	.50	.23	.06
☐ 37 Jackie Robinson	1.00	.45	.12
☐ 38 Babe Ruth	1.50	.70	.19
☐ 39 Al Simmons	.10	.05	.01
☐ 40 George Sisler	.10	.05	.01
☐ 41 Duke Snider	.50	.23	.06
☐ 42 Tris Speaker	.10	.05	.01
☐ 43 Bill Terry	.10	.05	.01
☐ 44 Pie Traynor	.25	.11	.03
☐ 45 Ed Walsh	.10	.05	.01
☐ 46 Paul Waner	.25	.11	.03
☐ 47 Billy Williams	.25	.11	.03
☐ 48 Ted Williams	1.00	.45	.12
☐ 49 Maury Wills	.10	.05	.01
☐ 50 Ross Youngs	.10	.05	.01

1996 Illinois Lottery

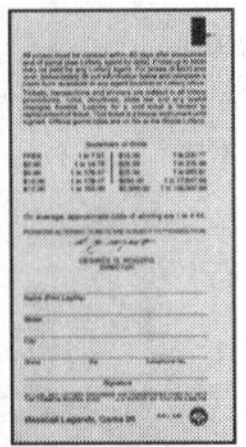

This five-card set consists of legendary Chicago Cubs and White Sox players and also included St. Louis Cardinals player, Red Schoendeinst. The cards are actually real Illinois scratch-off lottery ticket stubs and can be found scratched or unscratched. The cards are unnumbered and checklisted below in alphabetical order.

	MINT	NRMT	EXC
COMPLETE SET (5)	5.00	2.20	.60
COMMON CARD (1-5)	1.00	.45	.12
☐ 1 Ernie Banks	2.50	1.10	.30
☐ 2 Carlton Fisk	2.00	.90	.25
☐ 3 Minnie Minoso	1.00	.45	.12
☐ 4 Red Schoendeinst	1.25	.55	.16
☐ 5 Billy Williams	1.25	.55	.16

1994 Imprinted Products Pin-Cards

Made by Imprinted Products Corp., and distributed by Pinnacle Brands, these 28 pins and their accompanying cards feature American League (1-14) and National League (15-28) teams. Each pack contained one MLB team pin, one team card, and checklist. In all, 25,000 boxes were produced, with 36 single packs per box. 500 "Winner" pins were randomly inserted which could be redeemed for a free Diamond Series II set, valued at $250.00. The pins are made out of a soft bronzish metal. The pins, and their accompanying cards, are numbered on the back. The standard-size cards have on the front the team logos and the back summarize the beginnings and history of each franchise.

	MINT	NRMT	EXC
COMPLETE SET	25.00	11.00	3.10
COMMON CARD (1-28)	1.00	.45	.12
☐ 1 Baltimore Orioles	1.00	.45	.12
☐ 2 Boston Red Sox	1.00	.45	.12
☐ 3 California Angels	1.00	.45	.12
☐ 4 Chicago White Sox	1.00	.45	.12
☐ 5 Cleveland Indians	1.00	.45	.12
☐ 6 Detroit Tigers	1.00	.45	.12
☐ 7 Kansas City Royals	1.00	.45	.12
☐ 8 Milwaukee Brewers	1.00	.45	.12
☐ 9 Minnesota Twins	1.00	.45	.12
☐ 10 New York Yankees	1.00	.45	.12
☐ 11 Oakland Athletics	1.00	.45	.12
☐ 12 Seattle Mariners	1.00	.45	.12
☐ 13 Texas Rangers	1.00	.45	.12
☐ 14 Toronto Blue Jays	1.00	.45	.12
☐ 15 Atlanta Braves	1.00	.45	.12
☐ 16 Chicago Cubs	1.00	.45	.12
☐ 17 Cincinnati Reds	1.00	.45	.12
☐ 18 Colorado Rockies	1.00	.45	.12
☐ 19 Florida Marlins	1.00	.45	.12
☐ 20 Houston Astros	1.00	.45	.12
☐ 21 Los Angeles Dodgers	1.00	.45	.12
☐ 22 Montreal Expos	1.00	.45	.12
☐ 23 New York Mets	1.00	.45	.12
☐ 24 Philadelphia Phillies	1.00	.45	.12
☐ 25 Pittsburgh Pirates	1.00	.45	.12
☐ 26 St. Louis Cardinals	1.00	.45	.12
☐ 27 San Diego Padres	1.00	.45	.12
☐ 28 San Francisco Giants	1.00	.45	.12

1947 Indians Team Issue

These 26 photos measure 6" by 8 1/2". They have player photos and a facsimile autograph. All of this is framed by white borders. The backs are blank and we have sequenced these photos in alphabetical order.

	EX-MT	VG-E	GOOD
COMPLETE SET (26)	100.00	45.00	12.50
COMMON CARD (1-26)	3.00	1.35	.35
☐ 1 Don Black	3.00	1.35	.35
☐ 2 Eddie Bockman	3.00	1.35	.35
☐ 3 Lou Boudreau	10.00	4.50	1.25
☐ 4 Jack Conway	3.00	1.35	.35
☐ 5 Larry Doby	10.00	4.50	1.25
☐ 6 Hank Edwards	3.00	1.35	.35
☐ 7 Red Embree	3.00	1.35	.35
☐ 8 Bob Feller	15.00	6.75	1.85
☐ 9 Les Fleming	3.00	1.35	.35
☐ 10 Allen Gettel	3.00	1.35	.35
☐ 11 Joe Gordon	7.50	3.40	.95
☐ 12 Steve Gromek	3.00	1.35	.35
☐ 13 Mel Harder	5.00	2.20	.60
☐ 14 Jim Hegan	5.00	2.20	.60
☐ 15 Ken Keltner	5.00	2.20	.60
☐ 16 Ed Klieman	3.00	1.35	.35
☐ 17 Bob Lemon	10.00	4.50	1.25
☐ 18 Al Lopez	10.00	4.50	1.25
☐ 19 George "Catfish" Metkovich	3.00	1.35	.35
☐ 20 Dale Mitchell	5.00	2.20	.60
☐ 21 Hal Peck	3.00	1.35	.35
☐ 22 Eddie Robinson	3.00	1.35	.35
☐ 23 Hank Ruszkowksi	3.00	1.35	.35
☐ 24 Pat Seerey	3.00	1.35	.35
☐ 25 Bryan Stephens	3.00	1.35	.35
☐ 26 Les Willis	3.00	1.35	.35

1947 Indians Van Patrick PC-761

This set of 26 black and white postcards was issued in 1947 and features only Cleveland Indians. The cards were obtained by writing to Van Patrick, then the Cleveland announcer. The backs of the postcards features the name of the player on the front in a short note from Van Patrick. Two cards of Bob Feller exist; they are noted in the listings below.

	EX-MT	VG-E	GOOD
COMPLETE SET	900.00	400.00	110.00
COMMON CARD	35.00	16.00	4.40
☐ 1 Don Black	35.00	16.00	4.40
☐ 2 Eddie Bockman	35.00	16.00	4.40
☐ 3 Lou Boudreau	60.00	27.00	7.50
☐ 4 Jack Conway	35.00	16.00	4.40
☐ 5 Hank Edwards	35.00	16.00	4.40
☐ 6 Red Embree	35.00	16.00	4.40
☐ 7A Bob Feller Pitching, abode wall	75.00	34.00	9.50
☐ 7B Bob Feller Pitching, Leg up, fuzzy card back	75.00	34.00	9.50
☐ 8 Les Fleming	35.00	16.00	4.40
☐ 9 Al Gettel	35.00	16.00	4.40
☐ 10 Joe Gordon	50.00	22.00	6.25
☐ 11 Steve Gromek	35.00	16.00	4.40
☐ 12 Mel Harder	40.00	18.00	5.00
☐ 13 Jim Hegan	40.00	18.00	5.00
☐ 14 Ken Keltner	35.00	16.00	4.40
☐ 15 Eddie Klieman	35.00	16.00	4.40
☐ 16 Bob Lemon	50.00	22.00	6.25
☐ 17 Al Lopez	50.00	22.00	6.25
☐ 18 George Metkovich	35.00	16.00	4.40
☐ 19 Dale Mitchell	35.00	16.00	4.40
☐ 20 Hal Peck	35.00	16.00	4.40
☐ 21 Eddie Robinson	35.00	16.00	4.40
☐ 22 Hank Ruszowski	35.00	16.00	4.40
☐ 23 Pat Seerey	35.00	16.00	4.40
☐ 24 Bryan Stephens	35.00	16.00	4.40
☐ 25 Les Willis	35.00	16.00	4.40

1948 Indians Team Issue

This set commemorates the members of the World Champion 1948 Cleveland Indians. The black and white photos measure approximately 6 1/2" by 9" and are blank backed. We have arranged this checklist in alphabetical order.

	NRMT	VG-E	GOOD
COMPLETE SET (31)	200.00	90.00	25.00
COMMON CARD (1-31)	3.50	1.55	.45
☐ 1 Gene Bearden	5.00	2.20	.60
☐ 2 Johnny Berardino	15.00	6.75	1.85

	NRMT	VG-E	GOOD
☐ 3 Don Black	3.50	1.55	.45
☐ 4 Lou Boudreau	15.00	6.75	1.85
☐ 5 Russ Christopher	3.50	1.55	.45
☐ 6 Allie Clark	3.50	1.55	.45
☐ 7 Larry Doby	20.00	9.00	2.50
☐ 8 Hank Edwards	3.50	1.55	.45
☐ 9 Bob Feller	20.00	9.00	2.50
☐ 10 Joe Gordon	7.50	3.40	.95
☐ 11 Hank Greenberg GM In Uniform	25.00	11.00	3.10
☐ 12 Hank Greenberg GM In Street Clothes	20.00	9.00	2.50
☐ 13 Steve Gromek	3.50	1.55	.45
☐ 14 Mel Harder	5.00	2.20	.60
☐ 15 Jim Hegan	5.00	2.20	.60
☐ 16 Walt Judnich	3.50	1.55	.45
☐ 17 Ken Keltner	3.50	1.55	.45
☐ 18 Bob Kennedy	5.00	2.20	.60
☐ 19 Ed Klieman	3.50	1.55	.45
☐ 20 Bob Lemon	10.00	4.50	1.25
☐ 21 Bill McKechnie CO	7.50	3.40	.95
☐ 22 Dale Mitchell	5.00	2.20	.60
☐ 23 Bob Muncrief	3.50	1.55	.45
☐ 24 Satchel Paige	25.00	11.00	3.10
☐ 25 Hal Peck	3.50	1.55	.45
☐ 26 Eddie Robinson	3.50	1.55	.45
☐ 27 Muddy Ruel CO	3.50	1.55	.45
☐ 28 Joe Tipton	3.50	1.55	.45
☐ 29 Thurman Tucker	3.50	1.55	.45
☐ 30 Bill Veeck OWN	7.50	3.40	.95
☐ 31 Sam Zoldak	5.00	2.20	.60

1949 Indians Team Issue

These 30 photos measure approximatley 6 1/2" by 9". They feature members of the 1949 Cleveland Indians. The black and white photos are framed by white borders. The backs are blank and we have sequenced this set in alphabetical order.

	NRMT	VG-E	GOOD
COMPLETE SET (30)	175.00	80.00	22.00
COMMON CARD (1-30)	3.50	1.55	.45
☐ 1 Bob Avila	5.00	2.20	.60
☐ 2 Al Benton	3.50	1.55	.45
☐ 3 Gene Bearden	5.00	2.20	.60
☐ 4 John Berardino	10.00	4.50	1.25
☐ 5 Ray Boone	5.00	2.20	.60
☐ 6 Lou Boudreau	20.00	9.00	2.50
☐ 7 Allie Clark	3.50	1.55	.45
☐ 8 Larry Doby	20.00	9.00	2.50
☐ 9 Bob Feller	20.00	9.00	2.50
☐ 10 Mike Garcia	5.00	2.20	.60
☐ 11 Joe Gordon	7.50	3.40	.95
☐ 12 Hank Greenberg GM	20.00	9.00	2.50
☐ 13 Steve Gromek	3.50	1.55	.45
☐ 14 Jim Hegan	5.00	2.20	.60
☐ 15 Ken Keltner	3.50	1.55	.45
☐ 16 Bob Kennedy	5.00	2.20	.60
☐ 17 Bob Lemon	15.00	6.75	1.85
☐ 18 Dale Mitchell	5.00	2.20	.60
☐ 19 Satchel Paige	25.00	11.00	3.10
☐ 20 Frank Papish	3.50	1.55	.45
☐ 21 Hal Peck	3.50	1.55	.45
☐ 22 Al Rosen	7.50	3.40	.95
☐ 23 Mike Tresh	3.50	1.55	.45
☐ 24 Thurman Tucker	3.50	1.55	.45
☐ 25 Bill Veeck OWN	10.00	4.50	1.25
☐ 26 Mickey Vernon	5.00	2.20	.60
☐ 27 Early Wynn	15.00	6.75	1.85
☐ 28 Sam Zoldak	3.50	1.55	.45
☐ 29 Indians Coaches George Susce Muddy Ruel Bill McKechnie Steve O'Neill Mel Harder	5.00	2.20	.60
☐ 30 Cleveland Stadium	15.00	6.75	1.85

1950 Indians Num Num

This issue features members of the 1950 Cleveland Indians. The black and white photos measure 6 1/2" by 9". Some backs feature a redemption offer for other photos. We have checklisted the set alphabetically.

	NRMT	VG-E	GOOD
COMPLETE SET (23)	800.00	350.00	100.00
COMMON CARD (1-23)	25.00	11.00	3.10
☐ 1 Bob Avila	25.00	11.00	3.10
☐ 2 Gene Bearden	30.00	13.50	3.70
☐ 3 Al Benton	25.00	11.00	3.10
☐ 4 Ray Boone	30.00	13.50	3.70
☐ 5 Lou Boudreau	60.00	27.00	7.50
☐ 6 Allie Clark	25.00	11.00	3.10
☐ 7 Larry Doby	50.00	22.00	6.25
☐ 8 Luke Easter	40.00	18.00	5.00
☐ 9 Bob Feller	100.00	45.00	12.50
☐ 10 Mike Garcia	30.00	13.50	3.70
☐ 11 Joe Gordon	40.00	18.00	5.00
☐ 12 Steve Gromek	25.00	11.00	3.10
☐ 13 Jim Hegan	30.00	13.50	3.70
☐ 14 Bob Kennedy	30.00	13.50	3.70
☐ 15 Bob Lemon	60.00	27.00	7.50
☐ 16 Dale Mitchell	30.00	13.50	3.70
☐ 17 Ray Murray	25.00	11.00	3.10
☐ 18 Chick Pieretti	25.00	11.00	3.10
☐ 19 Al Rosen	30.00	13.50	3.70
☐ 20 Mike Tresh	30.00	13.50	3.70
☐ 21 Thurman Tucker	30.00	13.50	3.70
☐ 22 Early Wynn	60.00	27.00	7.50
☐ 23 Sam Zoldak	25.00	11.00	3.10

1950 Indians Team Issue

These 26 black and white photos measure approximately 6 1/2" by 9". They feature members of the Cleveland Indians. The photos are surrounded by a white border and have facsimile autogrpahs. The photos are unnumbered and we have sequenced them in alphabetical order.

	NRMT	VG-E	GOOD
COMPLETE SET (26)	150.00	70.00	19.00
COMMON CARD (1-26)	3.50	1.55	.45
☐ 1 Bob Avila	5.00	2.20	.60
☐ 2 Al Benton	3.50	1.55	.45
☐ 3 Ray Boone	5.00	2.20	.60
☐ 4 Lou Boudreau	12.50	5.50	1.55
☐ 5 Allie Clark	3.50	1.55	.45
☐ 6 Larry Doby	10.00	4.50	1.25
☐ 7 Luke Easter	10.00	4.50	1.25
☐ 8 Bob Feller	20.00	9.00	2.50
☐ 9 Jess Flores	3.50	1.55	.45
☐ 10 Mike Garcia	5.00	2.20	.60
☐ 11 Joe Gordon	7.50	3.40	.95
☐ 12 Hank Greenberg GM	20.00	9.00	2.50
☐ 13 Steve Gromek	3.50	1.55	.45
☐ 14 Jim Hegan	5.00	2.20	.60
☐ 15 Bob Kennedy	5.00	2.20	.60
☐ 16 Bob Lemon	12.50	5.50	1.55
☐ 17 Dale Mitchell	5.00	2.20	.60
☐ 18 Ray Murray	3.50	1.55	.45
☐ 19 Chick Pieretti	3.50	1.55	.45
☐ 20 Al Rosen	7.50	3.40	.95
☐ 21 Dick Rozek	3.50	1.55	.45
☐ 22 Ellis Ryan OWN	3.50	1.55	.45
☐ 23 Thurman Tucker	3.50	1.55	.45
☐ 24 Early Wynn	12.50	5.50	1.55
☐ 25 Sam Zoldak	3.50	1.55	.45
☐ 26 Cleveland Stadium	15.00	6.75	1.85

1952 Indians Num Num

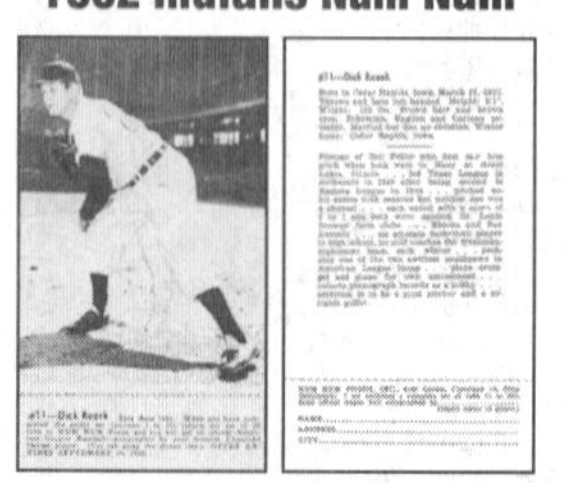

The cards in this 20-card set measure approximately 3 1/2" by 4 1/2". The 1952 Num Num Potato Chips issue features black and white, numbered cards of the Cleveland Indians. Cards came with and without coupons (tabs). The cards were issued without coupons directly by the Cleveland baseball club. When the complete set was obtained the tabs were cut off and exchanged for an autographed baseball. Card Number 16, Kennedy, is rather scarce. Cards with the tabs still intact are worth approximately double the values listed below. The catalog designation for this set is F337-2.

	NRMT	VG-E	GOOD
COMPLETE SET (20)	1000.00	450.00	125.00
COMMON CARD (1-20)	25.00	11.00	3.10
☐ 1 Lou Brissie	25.00	11.00	3.10
☐ 2 Jim Hegan	30.00	13.50	3.70
☐ 3 Birdie Tebbetts	30.00	13.50	3.70
☐ 4 Bob Lemon	50.00	22.00	6.25
☐ 5 Bob Feller	150.00	70.00	19.00
☐ 6 Early Wynn	50.00	22.00	6.25
☐ 7 Mike Garcia	30.00	13.50	3.70
☐ 8 Steve Gromek	25.00	11.00	3.10
☐ 9 Bob Chakales	25.00	11.00	3.10
☐ 10 Al Rosen	30.00	13.50	3.70
☐ 11 Dick Rozek	25.00	11.00	3.10
☐ 12 Luke Easter	30.00	13.50	3.70
☐ 13 Ray Boone	30.00	13.50	3.70
☐ 14 Bobby Avila	30.00	13.50	3.70
☐ 15 Dale Mitchell	30.00	13.50	3.70
☐ 16 Bob Kennedy SP	375.00	170.00	47.50
☐ 17 Harry Simpson	25.00	11.00	3.10
☐ 18 Larry Doby	35.00	16.00	4.40
☐ 19 Sam Jones	30.00	13.50	3.70
☐ 20 Al Lopez MG	50.00	22.00	6.25

1955 Indians Golden Stamps

This 32-stamp set features color photos of the Cleveland Indians and measures approximately 2" by 2 5/8". The stamps are designed to be placed in a 32-page album which measures approximately 8 3/8" by 10 15/16". The album contains black-and-white drawings of players with statistics and life stories. The stamps are unnumbered and listed below according to where they fall in the album.

	NRMT	VG-E	GOOD
COMPLETE SET (32)	50.00	22.00	6.25
COMMON CARD (1-32)	2.00	.90	.25
☐ 1 Al Lopez MG	6.00	2.70	.75
☐ 2 Bob Lemon	10.00	4.50	1.25
☐ 3 Early Wynn	10.00	4.50	1.25
☐ 4 Mike Garcia	3.00	1.35	.35
☐ 5 Bob Feller	15.00	6.75	1.85
☐ 6 Art Houtteman	2.00	.90	.25
☐ 7 Herb Score	4.00	1.80	.50
☐ 8 Don Mossi	3.00	1.35	.35
☐ 9 Ray Narleski	2.00	.90	.25
☐ 10 Jim Hegan	4.00	1.80	.50
☐ 11 Vic Wertz	2.00	.90	.25
☐ 12 Bobby Avila	2.00	.90	.25
☐ 13 George Strickland	2.00	.90	.25
☐ 14 Al Rosen	1.00	.45	.12
☐ 15 Larry Doby	5.00	2.20	.60
☐ 16 Ralph Kiner	5.00	2.20	.60
☐ 17 Al Smith	2.00	.90	.25
☐ 18 Wally Westlake	2.00	.90	.25
☐ 19 Hal Naragon	2.00	.90	.25
☐ 20 Hank Foiles	2.00	.90	.25
☐ 21 Hank Majeski	2.00	.90	.25
☐ 22 Bill Wight	2.00	.90	.25
☐ 23 Sam Dente	2.00	.90	.25
☐ 24 Dave Pope	2.00	.90	.25
☐ 25 Dave Philley	2.00	.90	.25
☐ 26 Dale Mitchell	3.00	1.35	.35
☐ 27 Hank Greenberg GM	15.00	6.75	1.85
☐ 28 Mel Harder CO	2.00	.90	.25
☐ 29 Ralph Kess CO	2.00	.90	.25
☐ 30 Tony Cuccinello CO	2.00	.90	.25
☐ 31 Bill Lobe CO	2.00	.90	.25
☐ 32 Cleveland Stadium	7.50	3.40	.95

1955-56 Indians Carling Black Label

This ten-card, approximately 8 1/2" by 12", set was issued by Carling Beer and celebrated members of the (then) perennial contending Cleveland Indians. These cards feature a black and white photo with the printed name of the player inserted in the photo. Underneath the photo is a joint advertisement for Carling Black Label Beer and The Cleveland Indians. The set looks like it could be easily replicated and may indeed have been reprinted. The checklist for this unnumbered set is ordered alphabetically.

	NRMT	VG-E	GOOD
COMPLETE SET (10)	100.00	45.00	12.50
COMMON CARD (1-10)	7.50	3.40	.95
☐ 1 Bob Feller	35.00	16.00	4.40
☐ 2 Mike Garcia	10.00	4.50	1.25
☐ 3 Jim Hegan	7.50	3.40	.95
☐ 4 Art Houtteman	7.50	3.40	.95
☐ 5 Ralph Kiner	7.50	3.40	.95
☐ 6 Bob Lemon	15.00	6.75	1.85
☐ 7 Al Rosen	10.00	4.50	1.25
☐ 8 Herb Score	12.00	5.50	1.50
☐ 9 Al Smith	7.50	3.40	.95
☐ 10 George Strickland	7.50	3.40	.95
☐ 11 Early Wynn	15.00	6.75	1.85

1957 Indians Sohio

The 1957 Sohio Cleveland Indians set consists of 18 perforated photos, approximately 5" by 7", in black and white with facsimile autographs on the front which were designed to be pasted into a special photo album issued by SOHIO (Standard Oil of Ohio). The set features one of the earliest Roger Maris cards which even predates his 1958 Topps rookie card. In addition, the Rocky Colavito card is popular as well as 1957 was Rocky's rookie year for cards. These unnumbered cards are listed below in alphabetical order for convenience. It has been alleged that counterfeits of this set have been recently produced.

	NRMT	VG-E	GOOD
COMPLETE SET (18)	350.00	160.00	45.00
COMMON CARD (1-18)	5.00	2.20	.60
☐ 1 Bob Avila	5.00	2.20	.60
☐ 2 Jim Busby	5.00	2.20	.60
☐ 3 Chico Carrasquel	5.00	2.20	.60
☐ 4 Rocky Colavito	75.00	34.00	9.50
☐ 5 Mike Garcia	7.50	3.40	.95
☐ 6 Jim Hegan	5.00	2.20	.60
☐ 7 Bob Lemon	35.00	16.00	4.40
☐ 8 Roger Maris	200.00	90.00	25.00
☐ 9 Don Mossi	7.50	3.40	.95
☐ 10 Ray Narleski	5.00	2.20	.60
☐ 11 Russ Nixon	5.00	2.20	.60
☐ 12 Herb Score	10.00	4.50	1.25
☐ 13 Al Smith	5.00	2.20	.60
☐ 14 George Strickland	5.00	2.20	.60
☐ 15 Bob Usher	5.00	2.20	.60
☐ 16 Vic Wertz	7.50	3.40	.95
☐ 17 Gene Woodling	7.50	3.40	.95
☐ 18 Early Wynn	35.00	16.00	4.40

1959 Indians

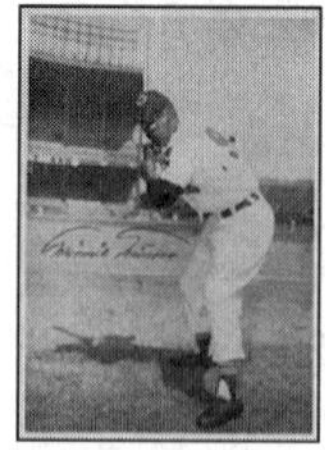

This set features black-and-white photos of the 1959 Cleveland Indians and measures approximately 6 1/2" by 9". Some of the photos have a facsimile autograph identifying the player while others have the player's name printed in a small bar in a bottom corner. The backs are blank. The cards are unnumbered and checklisted below in alphabetical order.

	NRMT	VG-E	GOOD
COMPLETE SET (20)	75.00	34.00	9.50
COMMON CARD (1-20)	3.50	1.55	.45
☐ 1 Dick Brodowski	3.50	1.55	.45
☐ 2 Rocky Colavito	10.00	4.50	1.25
☐ 3 Mike Garcia	4.00	1.80	.50
☐ 4 Joe Gordon MG	5.00	2.20	.60
☐ 5 Jim Grant	4.00	1.80	.50

	NRMT	VG-E	GOOD
☐ 6 Mel Harder CO	4.00	1.80	.50
☐ 7 Carroll Hardy	3.50	1.55	.45
☐ 8 Woodie Held	3.50	1.55	.45
☐ 9 Frank Lane GM	3.50	1.55	.45
☐ 10 Billy Martin	10.00	4.50	1.25
☐ 11 Cal McLish	3.50	1.55	.45
☐ 12 Minnie Minoso	5.00	2.20	.60
☐ 13 Hal Naragon	3.50	1.55	.45
☐ 14 Russ Nixon	3.50	1.55	.45
☐ 15 Jim Perry	4.00	1.80	.50
☐ 16 Jim Piersall	5.00	2.20	.60
☐ 17 Vic Power	4.00	1.80	.50
☐ 18 Herb Score	4.00	1.80	.50
☐ 19 George Strickland	3.50	1.55	.45
☐ 20 Ray Webster	3.50	1.55	.45

1960 Indians Jay Publishing

This 12-card set of the Cleveland Indians measures approximately 5" by 7". The fronts feature black-and-white posed player photos with the player's and team name printed below in the white border. These cards were packaged 12 to a packet and originally sold for 25 cents. The backs are blank. The cards are unnumbered and checklisted below in alphabetical order.

	NRMT	VG-E	GOOD
COMPLETE SET (12)	25.00	11.00	3.10
COMMON CARD (1-12)	2.00	.90	.25
☐ 1 Tito Francona	2.00	.90	.25
☐ 2 Jim Grant	2.00	.90	.25
☐ 3 Woody Held	2.00	.90	.25
☐ 4 Harvey Kuenn	3.00	1.35	.35
☐ 5 Barry Latman	2.00	.90	.25
☐ 6 Russ Nixon	2.00	.90	.25
☐ 7 Bubba Phillips	2.00	.90	.25
☐ 8 Jimmy Piersall	4.00	1.80	.50
☐ 9 Vic Power	3.00	1.35	.35
☐ 10 John Romano	2.00	.90	.25
☐ 11 George Strickland	2.00	.90	.25
☐ 12 John Temple	2.00	.90	.25

1962 Indians Jay Publishing

This 12-card set of the Cleveland Indians measures approximately 5" by 7". The fronts feature black-and-white posed player photos with the player's and team name printed below in the white border. These cards were packaged 12 to a packet. The backs are blank. The cards are unnumbered and checklisted below in alphabetical order.

	NRMT	VG-E	GOOD
COMPLETE SET (12)	25.00	11.00	3.10
COMMON CARD (1-12)	2.50	1.10	.30
☐ 1 Gary Bell	2.50	1.10	.30
☐ 2 Dick Donovan	2.50	1.10	.30
☐ 3 Tito Francona	3.00	1.35	.35
☐ 4 Jim Grant	3.00	1.35	.35
☐ 5 Woody Held	3.50	1.55	.45
☐ 6 Willie Kirkland	3.00	1.35	.35
☐ 7 Barry Latman	2.50	1.10	.30
☐ 8 Mel McGaha MG	2.50	1.10	.30
☐ 9 Bob Nieman	2.50	1.10	.30
☐ 10 Bubba Phillips	2.50	1.10	.30
☐ 11 Pedro Ramos	3.00	1.35	.35
☐ 12 John Romano	2.50	1.10	.30

1963 Indians Jay Publishing

This 12-card set of the Cleveland Indians measures approximately 5" by 7". The fronts feature black-and-white posed player photos with the player's and team name printed below in the white border. These cards were packaged 12 to a packet. The backs are blank. The cards are unnumbered and checklisted below in alphabetical order.

	NRMT	VG-E	GOOD
COMPLETE SET (12)	25.00	11.00	3.10
COMMON CARD (1-12)	2.00	.90	.25
☐ 1 Joe Adcock	5.00	2.20	.60
☐ 2 Gary Bell	2.00	.90	.25
☐ 3 Vic Davalillo	2.00	.90	.25
☐ 4 Mike De La Hoz	2.00	.90	.25
☐ 5 Dick Donovan	2.00	.90	.25
☐ 6 Tito Francona	3.50	1.55	.45
☐ 7 Jim Grant	3.00	1.35	.35
☐ 8 Woody Held	3.50	1.55	.45
☐ 9 Willie Kirkland	2.00	.90	.25
☐ 10 Barry Latman	2.00	.90	.25
☐ 11 John Romano	2.00	.90	.25
☐ 12 Birdie Tebbetts MG	3.00	1.35	.35

1964 Indians Jay Publishing

This 12-card set of the Cleveland Indians measures approximately 5" by 7". The fronts feature black-and-white posed player photos with the player's and team name printed below in the white border. These cards were packaged 12 to a packet. The backs are blank. The cards are unnumbered and checklisted below in alphabetical order.

	NRMT	VG-E	GOOD
COMPLETE SET (12)	25.00	11.00	3.10
COMMON CARD (1-12)	2.00	.90	.25
☐ 1 Max Alvis	3.00	1.35	.35
☐ 2 Joe Azcue	2.00	.90	.25
☐ 3 Vic Davalillo	2.00	.90	.25
☐ 4 Dick Donovan	2.00	.90	.25
☐ 5 Tito Francona	3.00	1.35	.35
☐ 6 Jim Grant	3.00	1.35	.35
☐ 7 Woody Held	3.00	1.35	.35
☐ 8 Jack Kralick	2.00	.90	.25
☐ 9 Pedro Ramos	2.00	.90	.25
☐ 10 John Romano	2.00	.90	.25
☐ 11 Al Smith	2.00	.90	.25
☐ 12 Birdie Tebbetts MG	3.50	1.55	.45

1966 Indians Team Issue

This 12-card set of theCleveland Indians measures approximately 4 7/8" by 7 1/8" and features black-and-white player photos in a white border. These cards were packaged 12 to a packet and originally sold for 25 cents. The backs are blank. The cards are unnumbered and checklisted below in alphabetical order.

	NRMT	VG-E	GOOD
COMPLETE SET (12)	30.00	13.50	3.70
COMMON CARD (1-12)	2.00	.90	.25
☐ 1 Max Alvis	2.00	.90	.25
☐ 2 Joe Azcue	2.00	.90	.25
☐ 3 Rocky Colavito	7.50	3.40	.95
☐ 4 Vic Davalillo	2.00	.90	.25
☐ 5 Chuck Hinton	2.00	.90	.25
☐ 6 Dick Howser	3.00	1.35	.35
☐ 7 Jack Kralick	2.00	.90	.25
☐ 8 Sam McDowell	3.00	1.35	.35
☐ 9 Don McMahon	2.00	.90	.25
☐ 10 Birdie Tebbetts MG	2.00	.90	.25
☐ 11 Luis Tiant	4.00	1.80	.50
☐ 12 Leon Wagner	2.00	.90	.25

1970 Indians

This 12-card set of the Cleveland Indians measures approximately 4 1/4" by 7" and features white-bordered black-and-white player photos. The player's name and team are printed in the wide top margin. The backs are blank. The cards are unnumbered and checklisted below in alphabetical order.

	NRMT	VG-E	GOOD
COMPLETE SET (12)	20.00	9.00	2.50
COMMON CARD (1-12)	1.50	.70	.19
☐ 1 Buddy Bradford	1.50	.70	.19
☐ 2 Larry Brown	1.50	.70	.19
☐ 3 Alvin Dark	2.00	.90	.25
☐ 4 Ray Fosse	2.00	.90	.25
☐ 5 Steve Hargan	1.50	.70	.19
☐ 6 Ken Harrelson	2.00	.90	.25
☐ 7 Dennis Higgins	1.50	.70	.19
☐ 8 Sam McDowell	2.00	.90	.25
☐ 9 Graig Nettles	2.50	1.10	.30
☐ 10 Vada Pinson	2.50	1.10	.30
☐ 11 Ken Suarez	1.50	.70	.19
☐ 12 Ted Uhlaender	1.50	.70	.19

1971 Indians

These 12 cards featuring members of the Cleveland Indians measure approximately 7" by 8 3/4" with the fronts having white-bordered color player photos. The player's name and team is printed in black in the white margin below the picture. The backs are blank. The cards are unnumbered and checklisted below in alphabetical order.

	NRMT	VG-E	GOOD
COMPLETE SET (12)	20.00	9.00	2.50
COMMON CARD (1-12)	1.50	.70	.19
☐ 1 Buddy Bradford	1.50	.70	.19
☐ 2 Alvin Dark MG	2.50	1.10	.30
☐ 3 Steve Dunning	1.50	.70	.19
☐ 4 Ray Fosse	2.00	.90	.25
☐ 5 Steve Hargan	1.50	.70	.19
☐ 6 Ken Harrelson	2.50	1.10	.30
☐ 7 Chuck Hinton	1.50	.70	.19
☐ 8 Ray Lamb	1.50	.70	.19
☐ 9 Sam McDowell	2.50	1.10	.30
☐ 10 Vada Pinson	2.50	1.10	.30
☐ 11 Ken Suarez	1.50	.70	.19
☐ 12 Ted Uhlaender	1.50	.70	.19

1977 Indians 1920 TCMA

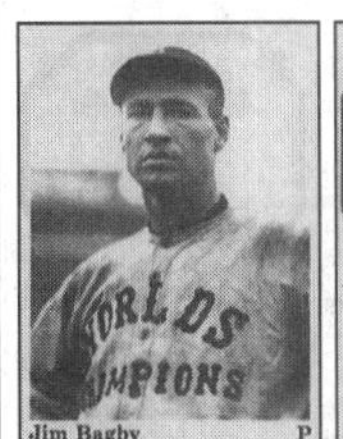

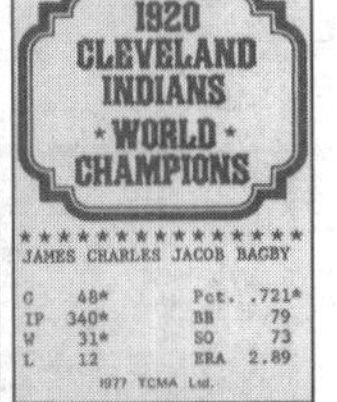

This 22-card set commemorates the 1920 World Champion Cleveland Indians. The fronts feature black-and-white player photos, while the backs display player statistics. One jumbo card measuring approximately 3 3/4" by 5" carries a story about the 1920 Cleveland Indians Team. The cards are unnumbered and checklisted below in alphabetical order with the jumbo card listed as number 22.

	NRMT	VG-E	GOOD
COMPLETE SET (22)	20.00	9.00	2.50
COMMON CARD (1-22)	.50	.23	.06
☐ 1 Jim Bagby	1.00	.45	.12
☐ 2 George Burns	.50	.23	.06
☐ 3 Ray Caldwell	.50	.23	.06
☐ 4 Ray Chapman	1.50	.70	.19
☐ 5 Stan Coleleski	2.50	1.10	.30
☐ 6 Joe Evans	.50	.23	.06
☐ 7 Larry Gardner	.50	.23	.06
☐ 8 Jack Graney	.50	.23	.06
☐ 9 Charlie Jamieson	.50	.23	.06
☐ 10 Wheeler 'Doc' Johnston	.50	.23	.06
☐ 11 Harry Lunte	.50	.23	.06
☐ 12 John 'Duster' Mails	.50	.23	.06
☐ 13 Guy Morton	.50	.23	.06
☐ 14 Les Nunamaker	.50	.23	.06
☐ 15 Steve O'Neill	1.00	.45	.12
☐ 16 Joe Sewell	2.50	1.10	.30
☐ 17 Elmer Smith	.50	.23	.06
☐ 18 Tris Speaker P/MG	5.00	2.20	.60
☐ 19 George Uhle	.50	.23	.06
☐ 20 Bill Wambsganss	1.50	.70	.19
☐ 21 Joe Wood	2.50	1.10	.30
☐ 22 Wilbert Robinson MG Tris Speaker World Series Foes	2.50	1.10	.30

1982 Indians

This issue features members of the 1982 Clevleland Indians. Since these cards are unnumbered we have sequenced them in alphabetical order.

	NRMT	VG-E	GOOD
COMPLETE SET (36)	15.00	6.75	1.85
COMMON CARD (1-36)	.50	.23	.06
☐ 1 Bud Anderson	.50	.23	.06
☐ 2 Chris Bando	.50	.23	.06
☐ 3 Alan Bannister	.50	.23	.06
☐ 4 Len Barker	.50	.23	.06
☐ 5 Bert Blyleven	1.00	.45	.12
☐ 6 John Bohnet	.50	.23	.06
☐ 7 Carmelo Castillo	.50	.23	.06
☐ 8 Joe Charboneau	.75	.35	.09
☐ 9 Rodney Craig	.50	.23	.06
☐ 10 John Denny	.50	.23	.06
☐ 11 Miguel Dilone	.50	.23	.06
☐ 12 Jerry Dybzinski	.50	.23	.06
☐ 13 Dave Garcia MG	.50	.23	.06
☐ 14 Gordy Glaser	.50	.23	.06
☐ 15 Ed Glynn	.50	.23	.06
☐ 16 Johnny Goryl CO	.50	.23	.06
☐ 17 Mike Hargrove	1.00	.45	.12
☐ 18 Toby Harrah	.50	.23	.06
☐ 19 Ron Hassey	.50	.23	.06
☐ 20 Von Hayes	.75	.35	.09
☐ 21 Neal Heaton	.50	.23	.06
☐ 22 Dennis Lewallyn	.50	.23	.06
☐ 23 Rick Manning	.50	.23	.06
☐ 24 Bake McBride	.50	.23	.06
☐ 25 Tommy McCraw CO	.50	.23	.06
☐ 26 Bill Nahorodny	.50	.23	.06
☐ 27 Karl Pagel	.50	.23	.06
☐ 28 Jack Perconte	.50	.23	.06
☐ 29 Mel Queen CO	.50	.23	.06
☐ 30 Dennis Sommers CO	.50	.23	.06
☐ 31 Lary Sorensen	.50	.23	.06
☐ 32 Dan Spillner	.50	.23	.06
☐ 33 Rick Sutcliffe	1.00	.45	.12
☐ 34 Andre Thornton	.75	.35	.09
☐ 35 Rick Waits	.50	.23	.06
☐ 36 Eddie Whitson	.50	.23	.06

1982 Indians Burger King

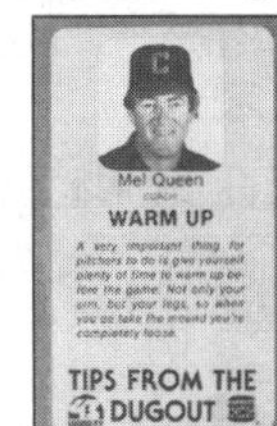

The cards in this 12-card set measure approximately 3" by 5". Tips From The Dugout is the series title of this set issued on a one card per week basis by the Burger King chain in the Cleveland area. Each card contains a black and white photo of manager Dave Garcia or coaches Goryl, McCraw, Queen and Sommers, under whom appears a paragraph explaining some aspect of inside baseball. The photo and 'Tip' are set upon a large yellow area surrounded by green borders. The cards are not numbered and are blank-backed. The logos of Burger King and WUAB-TV appear at the base of the card.

	NRMT	VG-E	GOOD
COMPLETE SET (12)	12.00	5.50	1.50
COMMON CARD (1-12)	1.00	.45	.12
☐ 1 Dave Garcia MG Be in the Game	1.00	.45	.12
☐ 2 Dave Garcia MG Sportsmanship	1.00	.45	.12
☐ 3 Johnny Goryl CO Rounding Bases	1.00	.45	.12
☐ 4 Johnny Goryl CO 3B Running	1.00	.45	.12
☐ 5 Tom McCraw CO Follow Thru	1.00	.45	.12
☐ 6 Tom McCraw CO Selecting a Bat	1.00	.45	.12
☐ 7 Tom McCraw CO Watch the Ball	1.00	.45	.12
☐ 8 Mel Queen CO Master One Pitch	1.00	.45	.12
☐ 9 Mel Queen CO Warm Up	1.00	.45	.12
☐ 10 Dennis Sommers CO Protect Fingers	1.00	.45	.12
☐ 11 Dennis Sommers CO Tagging 1st Base	1.00	.45	.12
☐ 12 Dennis Sommers CO	1.00	.45	.12

1982 Indians Team Issue

This 34-card set measures approximately 3 1/2" by 5 1/2" and features black-and-white player portraits in a white border with the player's name, position, and team name in the bottom margin. The backs are black. The cards are unnumbered and checklisted below in alphabetical order.

	MINT	NRMT	EXC
COMPLETE SET (34)	10.00	4.50	1.25
COMMON CARD (1-34)	.25	.11	.03
☐ 1 Chris Bando	.25	.11	.03
☐ 2 Alan Bannister	.25	.11	.03
☐ 3 Len Barker	.25	.11	.03
☐ 4 Bert Blyleven	1.00	.45	.12
☐ 5 John Bohnet	.25	.11	.03
☐ 6 Carmelo Castillo	.25	.11	.03
☐ 7 Joe Charboneau	.50	.23	.06
☐ 8 Rodney Craig	.25	.11	.03
☐ 9 John Denny	.25	.11	.03
☐ 10 Miguel Dilone	.25	.11	.03
☐ 11 Jerry Dybzinski	.25	.11	.03
☐ 12 Dave Garcia MG	.25	.11	.03
☐ 13 Gordy Glaser	.25	.11	.03
☐ 14 Ed Glynn	.25	.11	.03
☐ 15 Johnny Goryl CO	.25	.11	.03
☐ 16 Mike Hargrove	.50	.23	.06
☐ 17 Toby Harrah	.25	.11	.03
☐ 18 Von Hayes	1.00	.45	.12
☐ 19 Neal Heaton	.25	.11	.03
☐ 20 Ron Hassey	.25	.11	.03
☐ 21 Dennis Lewallyn	.25	.11	.03
☐ 22 Rick Manning	.25	.11	.03
☐ 23 Bake McBride	.25	.11	.03
☐ 24 Tommy McCraw CO	.25	.11	.03
☐ 25 Bill Nahorodny	.25	.11	.03
☐ 26 Jack Perconte	.25	.11	.03
☐ 27 Mel Queen CO	.25	.11	.03
☐ 28 Dennis Sommers CO	.25	.11	.03
☐ 29 Lary Sorensen	.25	.11	.03
☐ 30 Dan Spillner	.25	.11	.03
☐ 31 Rick Sutcliffe	.50	.23	.06
☐ 32 Andre Thornton	.50	.23	.06
☐ 33 Rick Waits	.25	.11	.03
☐ 34 Eddie Whitson	.25	.11	.03

1982 Indians Wheaties

The cards in this 30-card set measure approximately 2 13/16" by 4 1/8". This set of Cleveland Indians baseball players was co-produced by the Indians baseball club and Wheaties, whose respective logos appear on the front of every card. The cards were given away in groups of 10 as a promotion during games on May 30 (1-10), June 19 (11-20) and July 16, 1982 (21-30). The manager (MG), four coaches (CO), and 25 players are featured in a simple format of a color picture, player name and position. The cards are not numbered and the backs contain a Wheaties ad. The set was later sold at the Cleveland Indians gift shop. The cards are ordered below alphabetically within groups of ten as they were issued.

	NRMT	VG-E	GOOD
COMPLETE SET (30)	15.00	6.75	1.85
COMMON CARD (1-30)	.50	.23	.06
☐ 1 Bert Blyleven	1.25	.55	.16
☐ 2 Joe Charboneau	.75	.35	.09
☐ 3 Jerry Dybzinski	.50	.23	.06
☐ 4 Dave Garcia MG	.50	.23	.06
☐ 5 Toby Harrah	.75	.35	.09
☐ 6 Ron Hassey	.50	.23	.06
☐ 7 Dennis Lewallyn	.50	.23	.06
☐ 8 Rick Manning	.50	.23	.06
☐ 9 Tommy McCraw CO	.50	.23	.06
☐ 10 Rick Waits	.50	.23	.06
☐ 11 Chris Bando	.50	.23	.06
☐ 12 Len Barker	.75	.35	.09
☐ 13 Tom Brennan	.50	.23	.06
☐ 14 Rodney Craig	.50	.23	.06
☐ 15 Mike Fischlin	.50	.23	.06
☐ 16 Johnny Goryl CO	.50	.23	.06
☐ 17 Mel Queen CO	.50	.23	.06
☐ 18 Lary Sorensen	.50	.23	.06
☐ 19 Andre Thornton	1.00	.45	.12
☐ 20 Eddie Whitson	.50	.23	.06
☐ 21 Alan Bannister	.50	.23	.06
☐ 22 John Denny	.50	.23	.06
☐ 23 Miguel Dilone	.50	.23	.06
☐ 24 Mike Hargrove	1.25	.55	.16
☐ 25 Von Hayes	1.00	.45	.12
☐ 26 Bake McBride	.50	.23	.06
☐ 27 Jack Perconte	.50	.23	.06
☐ 28 Dennis Sommers CO	.50	.23	.06
☐ 29 Dan Spillner	.50	.23	.06
☐ 30 Rick Sutcliffe	1.25	.55	.16

1983 Indians Postcards

These postcards feature members of the 1983 Cleveland Indians. They are unnumbered and we have sequenced them in alphabetical order.

	NRMT	VG-E	GOOD
COMPLETE SET	10.00	4.50	1.25
COMMON CARD	.25	.11	.03
☐ 1 Bud Anderson	.25	.11	.03
☐ 2 Jay Baller	.25	.11	.03
☐ 3 Chris Bando	.25	.11	.03
☐ 4 Alan Bannister	.25	.11	.03
☐ 5 Len Barker	.25	.11	.03
☐ 6 Bert Blyleven	.75	.35	.09
☐ 7 Carmelo Castillo	.25	.11	.03
☐ 8 Wil Culmer	.25	.11	.03
☐ 9 Miguel Dilone	.25	.11	.03
☐ 10 Jerry Dybzinski	.25	.11	.03
☐ 11 Jim Essian	.25	.11	.03
☐ 12 Juan Eichelberger	.25	.11	.03
☐ 13 Mike Ferraro MG	.25	.11	.03
☐ 14 Mike Fischlin	.25	.11	.03
☐ 15 Julio Franco	2.00	.90	.25
☐ 16 Ed Glynn	.25	.11	.03
☐ 17 Mike Hargrove	.75	.35	.09
☐ 18 Toby Harrah	.25	.11	.03
☐ 19 Ron Hassey	.25	.11	.03
☐ 20 Neal Heaton	.25	.11	.03
☐ 21 Rick Manning	.25	.11	.03
☐ 22 Bake McBride	.25	.11	.03
☐ 23 Don McMahon CO	.25	.11	.03
☐ 24 Ed Napoleon CO	.25	.11	.03
☐ 25 Karl Pagel	.25	.11	.03
☐ 26 Jack Perconte	.25	.11	.03
☐ 27 Broderick Perkins	.25	.11	.03
☐ 28 Jerry Reed	.25	.11	.03
☐ 29 Kevin Rhomberg	.25	.11	.03
☐ 30 Ramon Romero	.25	.11	.03
☐ 31 Dennis Sommers CO	.25	.11	.03
☐ 32 Lary Sorensen	.25	.11	.03
☐ 33 Dan Spillner	.25	.11	.03
☐ 34 Rick Sutcliffe	.50	.23	.06
☐ 35 Andre Thornton	.75	.35	.09
☐ 36 Manny Trillo	.50	.23	.06
☐ 37 Otto Velez	.25	.11	.03
☐ 38 George Vuckovich	.25	.11	.03
☐ 39 Rick Waits	.25	.11	.03

1983 Indians Wheaties

The cards in this 32-card set measure approximately 2 13/16" by 4 1/8". The full color set of 1983 Wheaties Indians is quite similar to the Wheaties set of 1982. The backs, however, are significantly different. They contain complete career playing records of the players. The complete sets were given away at the ball park on May 15, 1983. The set was later made available at the Indians Gift Shop. The manager (MG) and several coaches (CO) are included in the set. The cards below are ordered alphabetically by the subject's name.

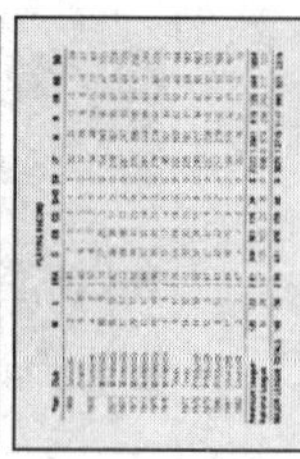

	NRMT	VG-E	GOOD
COMPLETE SET (32)	10.00	4.50	1.25
COMMON CARD (1-32)	.25	.11	.03
☐ 1 Bud Anderson	.25	.11	.03
☐ 2 Jay Baller	.25	.11	.03
☐ 3 Chris Bando	.25	.11	.03
☐ 4 Alan Bannister	.25	.11	.03
☐ 5 Len Barker	.50	.23	.06
☐ 6 Bert Blyleven	1.00	.45	.12
☐ 7 Wil Culmer	.25	.11	.03
☐ 8 Miguel Dilone	.25	.11	.03
☐ 9 Juan Eichelberger	.25	.11	.03
☐ 10 Jim Essian	.25	.11	.03
☐ 11 Mike Ferraro MG	.25	.11	.03
☐ 12 Mike Fischlin	.25	.11	.03
☐ 13 Julio Franco	2.00	.90	.25
☐ 14 Ed Glynn	.25	.11	.03
☐ 15 Johnny Goryl CO	.25	.11	.03
☐ 16 Mike Hargrove	.75	.35	.09
☐ 17 Toby Harrah	.50	.23	.06
☐ 18 Ron Hassey	.25	.11	.03
☐ 19 Neal Heaton	.25	.11	.03
☐ 20 Rick Manning	.25	.11	.03
☐ 21 Bake McBride	.25	.11	.03
☐ 22 Don McMahon CO	.25	.11	.03
☐ 23 Ed Napoleon CO	.25	.11	.03
☐ 24 Broderick Perkins	.25	.11	.03
☐ 25 Dennis Sommers CO	.25	.11	.03
☐ 26 Lary Sorensen	.25	.11	.03
☐ 27 Dan Spillner	.25	.11	.03
☐ 28 Rick Sutcliffe	1.00	.45	.12
☐ 29 Andre Thornton	.75	.35	.09
☐ 30 Manny Trillo	.50	.23	.06
☐ 31 George Vukovich	.25	.11	.03
☐ 32 Rick Waits	.25	.11	.03

1984 Indians

This 33-card set of the Cleveland Indians measures approximately 3 1/2" by 5 1/2" and features black-and-white player portraits in a white border. The player's name, position, and team are printed in the wide bottom margin. The backs are blank. The cards are unnumbered and checklisted below in alphabetical order.

	NRMT	VG-E	GOOD
COMPLETE SET (33)	10.00	4.50	1.25
COMMON CARD (1-33)	.25	.11	.03
☐ 1 Luis Aponte	.25	.11	.03
☐ 2 Chris Bando	.25	.11	.03
☐ 3 Rick Behenna	.25	.11	.03
☐ 4 Tony Bernazard	.25	.11	.03
☐ 5 Bert Blyleven	1.00	.45	.12
☐ 6 Bobby Bonds CO	.75	.35	.09
☐ 7 Brett Butler	1.50	.70	.19
☐ 8 Ernie Camacho	.25	.11	.03
☐ 9 Carmen Castillo	.25	.11	.03
☐ 10 Pat Corrales MG	.25	.11	.03
☐ 11 Jamie Easterly	.25	.11	.03
☐ 12 Mike Fischlin	.25	.11	.03
☐ 13 Julio Franco	1.50	.70	.19
☐ 14 George Frazier	.25	.11	.03
☐ 15 Johnny Goryl CO	.25	.11	.03
☐ 16 Mike Hargrove	.75	.35	.09
☐ 17 Ron Hassey	.25	.11	.03
☐ 18 Neal Heaton	.25	.11	.03
☐ 19 Brook Jacoby	.50	.23	.06
☐ 20 Mike Jeffcoat	.25	.11	.03
☐ 21 Don McMahon CO	.25	.11	.03
☐ 22 Ed Napoleon CO	.25	.11	.03
☐ 23 Otis Nixon	1.25	.55	.16
☐ 24 Broderick Perkins	.25	.11	.03
☐ 25 Kevin Rhomberg	.25	.11	.03
☐ 26 Dan Spillner	.25	.11	.03
☐ 27 Dennis Sommers	.25	.11	.03
☐ 28 Rick Sutcliffe	.50	.23	.06
☐ 29 Pat Tabler	.25	.11	.03
☐ 30 Andre Thornton	.75	.35	.09
☐ 31 George Vukovich	.25	.11	.03
☐ 32 Tom Waddell	.25	.11	.03
☐ 33 Jerry Willard	.25	.11	.03

1984 Indians Wheaties

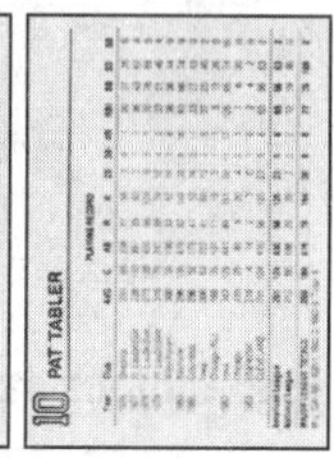

The cards in this 29-card set measure approximately 2 13/16" by 4 1/8". For the third straight year, Wheaties distributed a set of Cleveland Indians baseball cards. These over-sized cards were passed out at a Baseball Card Day at the Cleveland Stadium. Similar in appearance to the cards of the past two years, both the Indians and the Wheaties logos appear on the obverse, along with the name, team and position. Cards are numbered on the back by the player's uniform number.

	NRMT	VG-E	GOOD
COMPLETE SET (29)	10.00	4.50	1.25
COMMON CARD	.25	.11	.03
☐ 2 Brett Butler	1.25	.55	.16
☐ 4 Tony Bernazard	.25	.11	.03
☐ 8 Carmelo Castillo	.25	.11	.03
☐ 10 Pat Tabler	.25	.11	.03
☐ 13 Ernie Camacho	.25	.11	.03
☐ 14 Julio Franco	1.25	.55	.16
☐ 15 Broderick Perkins	.25	.11	.03
☐ 16 Jerry Willard	.25	.11	.03
☐ 18 Pat Corrales MG	.25	.11	.03
☐ 21 Mike Hargrove	.75	.35	.09
☐ 22 Mike Fischlin	.25	.11	.03
☐ 23 Chris Bando	.25	.11	.03
☐ 24 George Vukovich	.25	.11	.03
☐ 26 Brook Jacoby	.50	.23	.06
☐ 27 Steve Farr	.50	.23	.06
☐ 28 Bert Blyleven	1.00	.45	.12
☐ 29 Andre Thornton	.75	.35	.09
☐ 30 Joe Carter	5.00	2.20	.60
☐ 31 Steve Comer	.25	.11	.03
☐ 33 Roy Smith	.25	.11	.03
☐ 34 Mel Hall	.50	.23	.06
☐ 36 Jamie Easterly	.25	.11	.03
☐ 37 Don Schulze	.25	.11	.03
☐ 38 Luis Aponte	.25	.11	.03
☐ 44 Neal Heaton	.25	.11	.03
☐ 46 Mike Jeffcoat	.25	.11	.03
☐ 54 Tom Waddell	.25	.11	.03
☐ NNO Indians Coaches John Goryl Dennis Sommers Ed Napoleon Bobby Bonds Don McMahon	.50	.23	.06
☐ NNO Tom-E-Hawk (Mascot)	.25	.11	.03

1985 Indians

This 36-card set of the Cleveland Indians measures approximately 3 1/2" by 5 1/2" and features white-bordered, black-and-white player photos. The player's name, position and team are printed in the wide bottom margin. The backs are blank. The cards are unnumbered and checklisted below in alphabetical order.

	NRMT	VG-E	GOOD
COMPLETE SET (36)	10.00	4.50	1.25
COMMON CARD (1-36)	.25	.11	.03
☐ 1 Chris Bando	.25	.11	.03
☐ 2 Rick Behenna	.25	.11	.03
☐ 3 Butch Benton	.25	.11	.03
☐ 4 Tony Bernazard	.25	.11	.03
☐ 5 Bert Blyleven	1.00	.45	.12
☐ 6 Bobby Bonds CO	.75	.35	.09
☐ 7 Brett Butler	1.25	.55	.16
☐ 8 Ernie Camacho	.25	.11	.03
☐ 9 Joe Carter	2.50	1.10	.30
☐ 10 Carmen Castillo	.25	.11	.03
☐ 11 Pat Corrales MG	.25	.11	.03
☐ 12 Jamie Easterly	.25	.11	.03
☐ 13 Mike Fischlin	.25	.11	.03

☐ 14 Julio Franco	1.25	.55	.16
☐ 15 John Goryl CO	.25	.11	.03
☐ 16 Mel Hall	.25	.11	.03
☐ 17 Mike Hargrove	.75	.35	.09
☐ 18 Neal Heaton	.25	.11	.03
☐ 19 Brook Jacoby	.25	.11	.03
☐ 20 Mike Jeffcoat	.25	.11	.03
☐ 21 Don McMahon CO	.25	.11	.03
☐ 22 Ed Napoleon CO	.25	.11	.03
☐ 23 Otis Nixon	1.00	.45	.12
☐ 24 Geno Petralli	.25	.11	.03
☐ 25 Ramon Romero	.25	.11	.03
☐ 26 Vern Ruhle	.25	.11	.03
☐ 27 Don Schulze	.25	.11	.03
☐ 28 Jim Siwy	.25	.11	.03
☐ 29 Roy Smith	.25	.11	.03
☐ 30 Dennis Sommers	.25	.11	.03
☐ 31 Pat Tabler	.25	.11	.03
☐ 32 Andre Thornton	.75	.35	.09
☐ 33 Dave Von Ohlen	.25	.11	.03
☐ 34 George Vukovich	.25	.11	.03
☐ 35 Tom Waddell	.25	.11	.03
☐ 36 Jerry Willard	.25	.11	.03

1985 Indians Polaroid

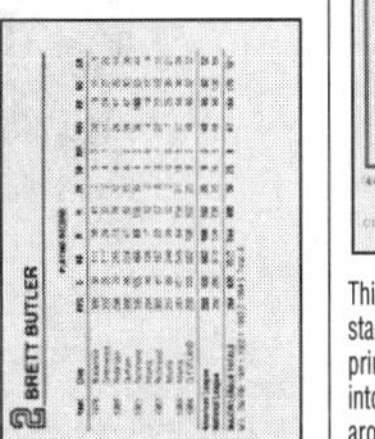

This 32-card set features cards (each measuring approximately 2 13/16" by 4 1/8") of the Cleveland Indians. The cards are unnumbered except for uniform number, as they are listed below. The set was also sponsored by J.C. Penney and was distributed at the stadium to fans in attendance on Baseball Card Day.

	NRMT	VG-E	GOOD
COMPLETE SET (32)	18.00	8.00	2.20
COMMON CARD	.50	.23	.06
☐ 2 Brett Butler	1.25	.55	.16
☐ 4 Tony Bernazard	.50	.23	.06
☐ 8 Carmen Castillo	.50	.23	.06
☐ 10 Pat Tabler	.50	.23	.06
☐ 12 Benny Ayala	.50	.23	.06
☐ 13 Ernie Camacho	.50	.23	.06
☐ 14 Julio Franco	1.25	.55	.16
☐ 16 Jerry Willard	.50	.23	.06
☐ 18 Pat Corrales MG	.50	.23	.06
☐ 20 Otis Nixon	1.50	.70	.19
☐ 21 Mike Hargrove	1.00	.45	.12
☐ 22 Mike Fischlin	.50	.23	.06
☐ 23 Chris Bando	.50	.23	.06
☐ 24 George Vukovich	.50	.23	.06
☐ 26 Brook Jacoby	.75	.35	.09
☐ 27 Mel Hall	.75	.35	.09
☐ 28 Bert Blyleven	1.25	.55	.16
☐ 29 Andre Thornton	1.25	.55	.16
☐ 30 Joe Carter	6.00	2.70	.75
☐ 32 Rick Behenna	.50	.23	.06
☐ 33 Roy Smith	.50	.23	.06
☐ 35 Jerry Reed	.50	.23	.06
☐ 36 Jamie Easterly	.50	.23	.06
☐ 38 Dave Von Ohlen	.50	.23	.06
☐ 41 Rich Thompson	.50	.23	.06
☐ 43 Bryan Clark	.50	.23	.06
☐ 44 Neal Heaton	.50	.23	.06
☐ 48 Vern Ruhle	.50	.23	.06
☐ 49 Jeff Barkley	.50	.23	.06
☐ 50 Ramon Romero	.50	.23	.06
☐ 54 Tom Waddell	.50	.23	.06
☐ NNO Coaching Staff Bobby Bonds John Goryl Don McMahon Ed Napoleon Dennis Sommers	.75	.35	.09

1986 Indians Greats TCMA

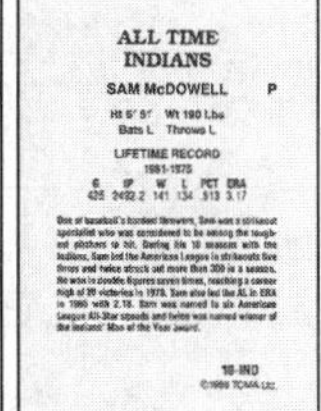

This 12-card standard-size set features some of the best all-time Cleveland Indians. The cards feature the player photo, his name and position on the front. The backs have vital statistics, a biography and career totals.

	MINT	NRMT	EXC
COMPLETE SET (12)	7.50	3.40	.95
COMMON CARD (1-12)	.25	.11	.03
☐ 1 Hal Trosky	.25	.11	.03
☐ 2 Napoleon Lajoie	1.00	.45	.12
☐ 3 Lou Boudreau	.75	.35	.09
☐ 4 Al Rosen	.25	.11	.03
☐ 5 Joe Jackson	2.00	.90	.25
☐ 6 Tris Speaker	1.25	.55	.16
☐ 7 Larry Doby	.75	.35	.09
☐ 8 Jim Hegan	.25	.11	.03
☐ 9 Cy Young	1.25	.55	.16
☐ 10 Sam McDowell	.25	.11	.03
☐ 11 Ray Narleski	.25	.11	.03
☐ 12 Al Lopez	.50	.23	.06

1986 Indians Oh Henry

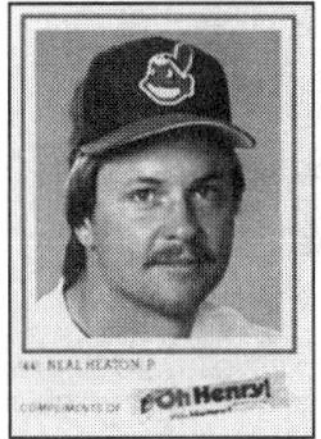

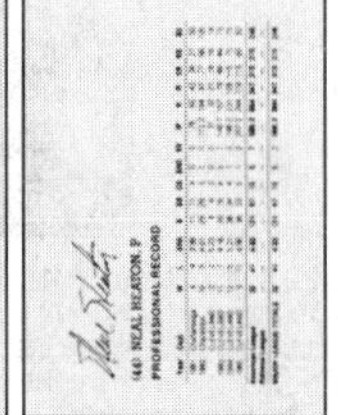

This 30-card set features Cleveland Indians and was distributed at the stadium to fans in attendance on Baseball Card Day. The cards were printed in one folded sheet which was perforated for easy separation into individual cards. The cards have white borders with a blue frame around each photo. The card backs include detailed career year-by-year statistics. The individual cards measure approximately 2 1/4" by 3 1/8" and have full-color fronts.

	MINT	NRMT	EXC
COMPLETE SET (30)	15.00	6.75	1.85
COMMON CARD	.25	.11	.03
☐ 2 Brett Butler	1.50	.70	.19
☐ 4 Tony Bernazard	.25	.11	.03
☐ 6 Andy Allanson	.25	.11	.03
☐ 7 Pat Corrales MG	.25	.11	.03
☐ 8 Carmen Castillo	.25	.11	.03
☐ 10 Pat Tabler	.25	.11	.03
☐ 13 Ernie Camacho	.25	.11	.03
☐ 14 Julio Franco	1.50	.70	.19
☐ 15 Dan Rohn	.25	.11	.03
☐ 18 Ken Schrom	.25	.11	.03
☐ 20 Otis Nixon	1.25	.55	.16
☐ 22 Fran Mullins	.25	.11	.03
☐ 23 Chris Bando	.25	.11	.03
☐ 24 Ed Williams	.25	.11	.03
☐ 26 Brook Jacoby	.50	.23	.06
☐ 27 Mel Hall	.25	.11	.03
☐ 29 Andre Thornton	1.00	.45	.12
☐ 30 Joe Carter	5.00	2.20	.60
☐ 35 Phil Niekro	2.50	1.10	.30
☐ 36 Jamie Easterly	.25	.11	.03
☐ 37 Don Schulze	.25	.11	.03
☐ 42 Rick Yett	.25	.11	.03
☐ 43 Scott Bailes	.25	.11	.03
☐ 44 Neal Heaton	.25	.11	.03
☐ 46 Jim Kern	.25	.11	.03
☐ 48 Dickie Noles	.25	.11	.03
☐ 49 Tom Candiotti	1.00	.45	.12
☐ 53 Reggie Ritter	.25	.11	.03
☐ 54 Tom Waddell	.25	.11	.03
☐ NNO Coaching Staff Jack Aker Bobby Bonds Doc Edwards John Goryl	.50	.23	.06

1987 Indians Gatorade

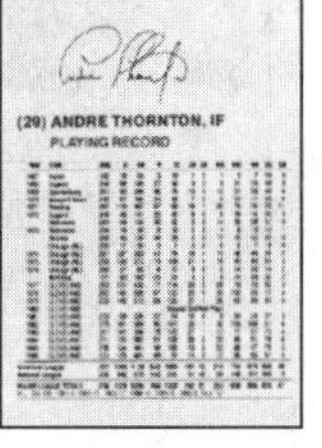

Gatorade sponsored this perforated set of 30 full-color cards of the Cleveland Indians. The cards measure approximately 2 1/8" by 3" (or 3 1/8") and feature the Gatorade logo prominently on the fronts of the cards. The cards were distributed as a tri-folded sheet (each part approximately 9 5/8" by 11 3/16") on April 25th at the stadium during the game against the Yankees. The large team photo is approximately 11 3/16" by 9 5/8". Card backs for the individual players contain year-by-year stats for that player. The cards are referenced and listed below by uniform number.

	MINT	NRMT	EXC
COMPLETE SET (30)	10.00	4.50	1.25
COMMON CARD	.25	.11	.03
☐ 2 Brett Butler	1.25	.55	.16
☐ 4 Tony Bernazard	.25	.11	.03
☐ 6 Andy Allanson	.25	.11	.03
☐ 7 Pat Corrales MG	.25	.11	.03
☐ 8 Carmen Castillo	.25	.11	.03
☐ 10 Pat Tabler	.25	.11	.03
☐ 11 Jamie Easterly	.25	.11	.03
☐ 12 Dave Clark	.25	.11	.03
☐ 13 Ernie Camacho	.25	.11	.03
☐ 14 Julio Franco	1.00	.45	.12
☐ 17 Junior Noboa	.25	.11	.03
☐ 18 Ken Schrom	.25	.11	.03
☐ 20 Otis Nixon	.50	.23	.06
☐ 21 Greg Swindell	.50	.23	.06
☐ 22 Frank Wills	.25	.11	.03
☐ 23 Chris Bando	.25	.11	.03
☐ 24 Rick Dempsey	.50	.23	.06
☐ 26 Brook Jacoby	.25	.11	.03
☐ 27 Mel Hall	.25	.11	.03
☐ 28 Cory Snyder	.50	.23	.06
☐ 29 Andre Thornton	.75	.35	.09
☐ 30 Joe Carter	4.00	1.80	.50
☐ 35 Phil Niekro	2.00	.90	.25
☐ 36 Ed VandeBerg	.25	.11	.03
☐ 42 Rich Yett	.25	.11	.03
☐ 43 Scott Bailes	.25	.11	.03
☐ 46 Doug Jones	.75	.35	.09
☐ 49 Tom Candiotti	.75	.35	.09
☐ 54 Tom Waddell	.25	.11	.03
☐ NNO Indians MG/Coaches Bobby Bonds John Goryl Pat Corrales MG Doc Edwards Jack Aker	.50	.23	.06
☐ NNO Team Photo (Large size)	3.00	1.35	.35

1988 Indians Gatorade

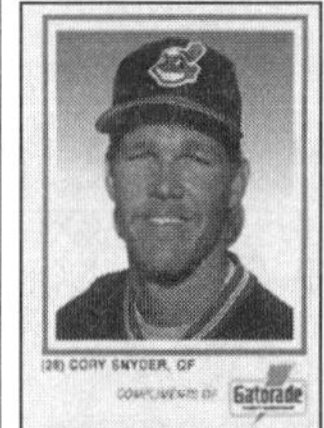

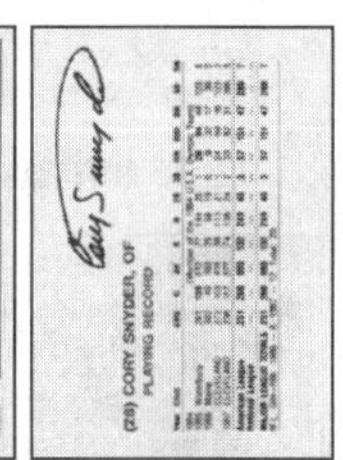

This set was distributed as 30 perforated player cards attached to a large team photo of the Cleveland Indians. The cards measure approximately 2 1/4" by 3". Card backs are oriented either horizontally or vertically. Card backs are printed in red, blue, and black on white card stock. Card backs contain a facsimile autograph of the player. Cards are not arranged on the sheet in any order. The cards are unnumbered except for uniform number, which is given on the front and back of each card. The cards are referenced and listed below by uniform number. The Gatorade logo is on the front of every card in the lower right corner.

	MINT	NRMT	EXC
COMPLETE SET (30)	8.00	3.60	1.00
COMMON CARD	.25	.11	.03
☐ 2 Tom Spencer CO	.25	.11	.03
☐ 6 Andy Allanson	.25	.11	.03
☐ 7 Luis Isaac CO	.25	.11	.03
☐ 8 Carmen Castillo	.25	.11	.03
☐ 9 Charlie Manuel CO	.25	.11	.03
☐ 10 Pat Tabler	.25	.11	.03
☐ 11 Doug Jones	.50	.23	.06
☐ 14 Julio Franco	1.00	.45	.12
☐ 15 Ron Washington	.25	.11	.03
☐ 16 Jay Bell	1.50	.70	.19
☐ 17 Bill Laskey	.25	.11	.03
☐ 20 Willie Upshaw	.25	.11	.03
☐ 21 Greg Swindell	.25	.11	.03
☐ 23 Chris Bando	.25	.11	.03
☐ 25 Dave Clark	.25	.11	.03
☐ 26 Brook Jacoby	.25	.11	.03
☐ 27 Mel Hall	.25	.11	.03
☐ 28 Cory Snyder	.25	.11	.03
☐ 30 Joe Carter	3.00	1.35	.35
☐ 31 Dan Schatzeder	.25	.11	.03
☐ 32 Doc Edwards MG	.25	.11	.03
☐ 33 Ron Kittle	.25	.11	.03
☐ 35 Mark Wiley CO	.25	.11	.03
☐ 42 Rich Yett	.25	.11	.03
☐ 43 Scott Bailes	.25	.11	.03
☐ 45 John Goryl CO	.25	.11	.03
☐ 47 Jeff Kaiser	.25	.11	.03
☐ 49 Tom Candiotti	.50	.23	.06
☐ 50 Jeff Dedmon	.25	.11	.03
☐ 52 John Farrell	.25	.11	.03
☐ NNO Team Photo (Large size)	2.50	1.10	.30

1989 Indians Team Issue

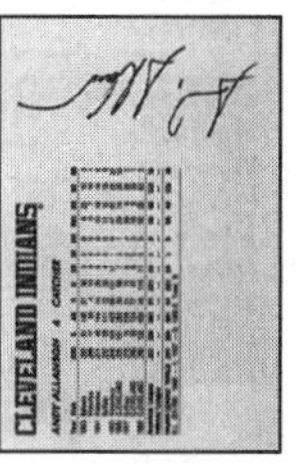

This 28-card set was available in the giftshop and was given away at the ballpark on May 13. The cards measure 2 7/8" by 4 1/4" and are printed on thin card stock. On a white card face, the fronts feature color player photos with a white inner border and red outer border. "The Tribe" logo is printed in the upper left corner, while player information is printed in the lower border. The backs carry the team name in red, while seasonal and career statistics and facsimile autograph are in blue. The cards are unnumbered and checklisted below in alphabetical order.

	MINT	NRMT	EXC
COMPLETE (28)	8.00	3.60	1.00
COMMON CARD (1-28)	.25	.11	.03
☐ 1 Luis Aguayo	.25	.11	.03
☐ 2 Andy Allanson	.25	.11	.03
☐ 3 Keith Atherton	.25	.11	.03
☐ 4 Scott Bailes	.25	.11	.03
☐ 5 Bud Black	.25	.11	.03
☐ 6 Jerry Browne	.25	.11	.03
☐ 7 Tom Candiotti	.50	.23	.06
☐ 8 Joe Carter	2.50	1.10	.30
☐ 9 Dave Clark	.25	.11	.03
☐ 10 Doc Edwards MG	.25	.11	.03
☐ 11 John Farrell	.25	.11	.03
☐ 12 Felix Fermin	.25	.11	.03
☐ 13 Brad Havens	.25	.11	.03
☐ 14 Brook Jacoby	.25	.11	.03
☐ 15 Doug Jones	.50	.23	.06
☐ 16 Pat Keedy	.25	.11	.03
☐ 17 Brad Komminsk	.25	.11	.03
☐ 18 Oddibe McDowell	.25	.11	.03
☐ 19 Luis Medina	.25	.11	.03
☐ 20 Rod Nichols	.25	.11	.03
☐ 21 Pete O'Brien	.25	.11	.03
☐ 22 Jesse Orosco	.25	.11	.03
☐ 23 Joe Skalski	.25	.11	.03
☐ 24 Joel Skinner	.25	.11	.03
☐ 25 Cory Snyder	.25	.11	.03
☐ 26 Greg Swindell	.25	.11	.03
☐ 27 Rich Yett	.25	.11	.03
☐ 28 Coaches Card Jim Davenport Luis Isaac Charlie Manuel Tom Spencer Mark Wiley	.25	.11	.03

1990 Indians Team Issue

This 46-card set was available in the giftshop for sale. The cards are unnumbered and we have checklisted them below in alphabetical order.

	MINT	NRMT	EXC
COMPLETE SET (46)	10.00	4.50	1.25
COMMON CARD (1-46)	.25	.11	.03
☐ 1 Beau Allred	.25	.11	.03
☐ 2 Sandy Alomar Jr.	.75	.35	.09
☐ 3 Carlos Baerga	.75	.35	.09
☐ 4 Kevin Bearse	.25	.11	.03
☐ 5 Joey Belle	2.50	1.10	.30
☐ 6 Bud Black	.25	.11	.03
☐ 7 Tom Brookens	.25	.11	.03
☐ 8 Jerry Browne	.25	.11	.03
☐ 9 Tom Candiotti	.50	.23	.06
☐ 10 Colin Charland	.25	.11	.03
☐ 11 Rich Dauer CO	.25	.11	.03
☐ 12 John Farrell	.25	.11	.03
☐ 13 Felix Fermin	.25	.11	.03
☐ 14 Cecilio Guante	.25	.11	.03
☐ 15 Mike Hargrove CO	.50	.23	.06
☐ 16 Keith Hernandez	.50	.23	.06
☐ 17 Luis Isaac CO	.25	.11	.03
☐ 18 Brook Jacoby	.25	.11	.03
☐ 19 Dion James	.25	.11	.03
☐ 20 Chris James	.25	.11	.03
☐ 21 Doug Jones	.50	.23	.06
☐ 22 Carl Keliipuleoli	.25	.11	.03
☐ 23 Tom Lampkin	.25	.11	.03
☐ 24 Tom Magrann	.25	.11	.03
☐ 25 Candy Maldonado	.25	.11	.03
☐ 26 Jeff Manto	.25	.11	.03
☐ 27 John McNamara MG	.25	.11	.03
☐ 28 Jose Morales CO	.25	.11	.03
☐ 29 Rod Nichols	.25	.11	.03
☐ 30 Al Nipper	.25	.11	.03
☐ 31 Steve Olin	.25	.11	.03
☐ 32 Jesse Orosco	.25	.11	.03

□ 33 Doug Robertson	.25	.11	.03
□ 34 Rudy Seanez	.25	.11	.03
□ 35 Jeff Shaw	.25	.11	.03
□ 36 Doug Sisk	.25	.11	.03
□ 37 Joe Skalksi	.25	.11	.03
□ 38 Joel Skinner	.25	.11	.03
□ 39 Cory Snyder	.25	.11	.03
□ 40 Greg Swindell	.25	.11	.03
□ 41 Sergio Valdez	.25	.11	.03
□ 42 Mike Walker	.25	.11	.03
□ 43 Mitch Webster	.25	.11	.03
□ 44 Kevin Wickander	.25	.11	.03
□ 45 Mark Wiley CO	.25	.11	.03
□ 46 Billy Williams CO	.75	.35	.09

1991 Indians Fan Club/McDonald's

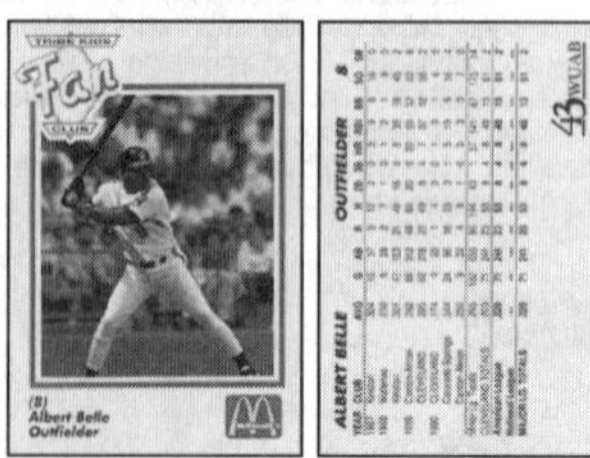

This 30-card set was sponsored by McDonald's and Channel 43 (WUAB). The cards are printed on thin card stock and measure approximately 2 7/8" by 4 1/4". On a white card face, the fronts feature a mix of posed and action color player photos that are framed by red border stripes. The "Tribe Kids Fan Club" emblem appears at the upper left corner. Player information and the sponsor logo appear in the bottom white border. The horizontally oriented backs present minor and major league statistics. The cards are unnumbered and checklisted below in alphabetical order.

	MINT	NRMT	EXC
COMPLETE SET (30)	18.00	8.00	2.20
COMMON CARD (1-30)	.50	.23	.06

□ 1 Beau Allred	.50	.23	.06
□ 2 Sandy Alomar	1.50	.70	.19
□ 3 Carlos Baerga	2.00	.90	.25
□ 4 Albert Belle	7.50	3.40	.95
□ 5 Jerry Browne	.50	.23	.06
□ 6 Tom Candiotti	.75	.35	.09
□ 7 Alex Cole	.50	.23	.06
□ 8 Bruce Egloff	.50	.23	.06
□ 9 Jose Escobar	.50	.23	.06
□ 10 Felix Fermin	.50	.23	.06
□ 11 Brook Jacoby	.50	.23	.06
□ 12 John Farrell	.50	.23	.06
□ 13 Shawn Hillegas	.50	.23	.06
□ 14 Mike Huff	.50	.23	.06
□ 15 Chris James	.50	.23	.06
□ 16 Doug Jones	.75	.35	.09
□ 17 Eric King	.50	.23	.06
□ 18 Jeff Manto	.50	.23	.06
□ 19 John McNamara MG	.50	.23	.06
□ 20 Charles Nagy	1.50	.70	.19
□ 21 Rod Nichols	.50	.23	.06
□ 22 Steve Olin	.50	.23	.06
□ 23 Jesse Orosco	.50	.23	.06
□ 24 Dave Otto	.50	.23	.06
□ 25 Joel Skinner	.50	.23	.06
□ 26 Greg Swindell	.50	.23	.06
□ 27 Mike Walker	.50	.23	.06
□ 28 Turner Ward	.50	.23	.06
□ 29 Mitch Webster	.50	.23	.06
□ 30 Coaches Card Billy Williams Jose Morales Rich Dauer Mike Hargrove Luis Isaac Mark Wiley	.75	.35	.09

1992 Indians Fan Club/McDonald's

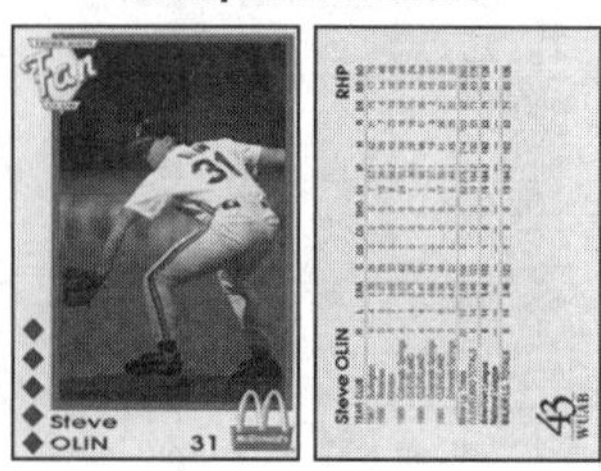

This 30-card set was sponsored by McDonald's and WUAB Channel 43. The cards are printed on thin card stock and measure approximately 2 7/8" by 4 1/4". On a white card face the fronts feature a mix of posed and action color player photos that are framed by red border stripes. The "Tribe Kids Fan Club" emblem appears at the upper left corner. Player information and the sponsor logo appear in the bottom white border. The horizontal white backs present minor and major league statistics. The cards are unnumbered and checklisted below in alphabetical order. The set was also produced as a team issue set which is distinguished by the Chief Wahoo mascot logo replacing the McDonald's logo and the removal of the WUAB references.

	MINT	NRMT	EXC
COMPLETE SET (30)	18.00	8.00	2.20
COMMON CARD (1-30)	.50	.23	.06

□ 1 Sandy Alomar Jr.	1.25	.55	.16
□ 2 Jack Armstrong	.50	.23	.06
□ 3 Brad Arnsberg	.50	.23	.06
□ 4 Carlos Baerga	.75	.35	.09
□ 5 Eric Bell	.50	.23	.06
□ 6 Albert Belle	5.00	2.20	.60
□ 7 Alex Cole	.50	.23	.06
□ 8 Dennis Cook	.50	.23	.06
□ 9 Felix Fermin	.50	.23	.06
□ 10 Mike Hargrove MG	.75	.35	.09
□ 11 Glenallen Hill	.75	.35	.09
□ 12 Thomas Howard	.50	.23	.06
□ 13 Brook Jacoby	.75	.35	.09
□ 14 Reggie Jefferson	1.00	.45	.12
□ 15 Mark Lewis	1.00	.45	.12
□ 16 Derek Lilliquist	.50	.23	.06
□ 17 Kenny Lofton	5.00	2.20	.60
□ 18 Charles Nagy	1.00	.45	.12
□ 19 Rod Nichols	.50	.23	.06
□ 20 Steve Olin	.50	.23	.06
□ 21 Junior Ortiz	.50	.23	.06
□ 22 Dave Otto	.50	.23	.06
□ 23 Tony Perezchica	.50	.23	.06
□ 24 Ted Power	.50	.23	.06
□ 25 Scott Scudder	.50	.23	.06
□ 26 Joel Skinner	.50	.23	.06
□ 27 Paul Sorrento	1.00	.45	.12
□ 28 Jim Thome	5.00	2.20	.60
□ 29 Mark Whiten	.50	.23	.06
□ 30 Coaches Card Jeff Newman Rick Adair Ken Bolek Dom Chiti Ron Clark Jose Morales Dave Nelson	.50	.23	.06

1993 Indians WUAB-TV

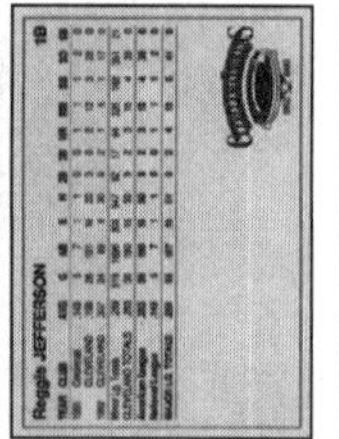

This 34-card team-issued set was available in the Indians giftshop. The WUAB Channel 43 logo appears on only one card, that of Slider, the Tribe's mascot. The cards are unnumbered and checklisted below in alphabetical order.

	MINT	NRMT	EXC
COMPLETE SET (34)	15.00	6.75	1.85
COMMON CARD (1-34)	.25	.11	.03

□ 1 Sandy Alomar Jr.	.50	.23	.06
□ 2 Carlos Baerga	.50	.23	.06
□ 3 Albert Belle	5.00	2.20	.60
□ 4 Mike Bielecki	.25	.11	.03
□ 5 Mike Christopher	.25	.11	.03
□ 6 Mark Clark	.50	.23	.06
□ 7 Dennis Cook	.25	.11	.03
□ 8 Alvaro Espinoza	.25	.11	.03
□ 9 Felix Fermin	.25	.11	.03
□ 10 Mike Hargrove MG	.25	.11	.03
□ 11 Glenallen Hill	.50	.23	.06
□ 12 Thomas Howard	.25	.11	.03
□ 13 Reggie Jefferson	.50	.23	.06
□ 14 Wayne Kirby	.25	.11	.03
□ 15 Tom Kramer	.25	.11	.03
□ 16 Mark Lewis	.50	.23	.06
□ 17 Derek Lilliquist	.25	.11	.03
□ 18 Kenny Lofton	3.00	1.35	.35
□ 19 Carlos Martinez	.25	.11	.03
□ 20 Jose Mesa	.75	.35	.09
□ 21 Jeff Mutis	.25	.11	.03
□ 22 Charles Nagy	1.00	.45	.12
□ 23 Bob Ojeda	.25	.11	.03
□ 24 Junior Ortiz	.25	.11	.03
□ 25 Eric Plunk	.25	.11	.03
□ 26 Ted Power	.25	.11	.03
□ 27 Scott Scudder	.25	.11	.03
□ 28 Joel Skinner	.25	.11	.03
□ 29 Paul Sorrento	.75	.35	.09
□ 30 Jim Thome	2.00	.90	.25
□ 31 Jeff Treadway	.25	.11	.03
□ 32 Kevin Wickander	.25	.11	.03
□ 33 The Coaching Staff Rick Adair Ken Bolke Dom Chiti Ron Clark Jose Morales Dave Nelson Jeff Newman	.25	.11	.03
□ 34 Slider (Mascot) and Liz (WUAB)	.25	.11	.03

1950-69 J.D. McCarthy PC753

One of the most prolific producers of postward postcards was J.D McCarthy on Michigan. During the 1950's and 1960's, thousands of these black and white postcards were issued. Most of the popular players of that era have been featured on the McCarthy postcards and a checklist is not provided.

	NRMT	VG-E	GOOD
COMMON PLAYER (1950'S)	3.00	1.35	.35
COMMON PLAYER (1960'S)	2.00	.90	.25

1910 J.H. Dockman All-Star Baseball E-Unc.

Produced by J.H. Dockman , Son, this unattractive issue is actually the sides of a candy package. The package measures approximately 1 7/8" by 3 3/8" and is 3/4" thick. Each package features two players, crudely drawn, one on each side. The words "All Star Baseball Package" appear on the side of the package and at the top of each player panel. The other side panel displays the words, "Candy and Gift." The end panel indicates a serial number, Dockman's name and reference to the Food and Drugs Act of 1906. A complete box is worth four times the individual value.

	EX-MT	VG-E	GOOD
COMPLETE SET (16)	1000.00	450.00	125.00
COMMON CARD (1-16)	50.00	22.00	6.25

□ 1 Henry Beckendorf	50.00	22.00	6.25
□ 2 Roger Bresnahan	100.00	45.00	12.50
□ 3 Al Burch	50.00	22.00	6.25
□ 4 Frank Chance	150.00	70.00	19.00
□ 5 Wid Conroy	50.00	22.00	6.25
□ 6 Jack Coombs	75.00	34.00	9.50
□ 7 George Gibson	50.00	22.00	6.25
□ 8 Doc Hoblitzel	50.00	22.00	6.25
□ 9 Johnny Kling	50.00	22.00	6.25
□ 10 Frank LaPorte	50.00	22.00	6.25
□ 11 Connie Mack MG	200.00	90.00	25.00
□ 12 Christy Mathewson	250.00	110.00	31.00
□ 13 Matthew McIntyre	50.00	22.00	6.25
□ 14 Jimmy Sheckard	50.00	22.00	6.25
□ 15 Al Schweitzer	50.00	22.00	6.25
□ 16 Harry Wolter	50.00	22.00	6.25

1950-54 J.J.K. Copyart Photographers

This set measures 3 1/2" by 5 1/2" and features New York Giants, Boston Braves, Philadelphia Phillies and one Brooklyn Dodger. The postcards are black and white glossy photos with no company identification on the back.

	NRMT	VG-E	GOOD
COMPLETE SET (24)	200.00	90.00	25.00
COMMON CARD (1-24)	5.00	2.20	.60

□ 1 Johnny Antonelli (2)	6.00	2.70	.75
□ 2 Sam Calderone	5.00	2.20	.60
□ 3 Del Crandall	6.00	2.70	.75
□ 4 Del Ennis	5.00	2.20	.60
□ 5 Jim Hearn (2)	5.00	2.20	.60
□ 6 Tommy Holmes	6.00	2.70	.75
□ 7 Larry Jansen	6.00	2.70	.75
□ 8 Whitey Lockman (2)	5.00	2.20	.60
□ 9 Williard Marhsall	5.00	2.20	.60
□ 10 Eddie Mathews	20.00	9.00	2.50
□ 11 Don Muellar	5.00	2.20	.60
□ 12 Danny O'Connell	5.00	2.20	.60
□ 13 Bill Rigney	6.00	2.70	.75
□ 14 Robin Roberts	15.00	6.75	1.85
□ 15 Jackie Robinson	50.00	22.00	6.25
□ 16 Hank Sauer	6.00	2.70	.75
□ 17 Red Schoendienst	15.00	6.75	1.85
□ 18 Curt Simmons	6.00	2.70	.75
□ 19 Sibby Sisti	5.00	2.20	.60
□ 20 Eddie Stanky Boston Braves	10.00	4.50	1.25
□ 21 Eddie Stanly New York Giants	10.00	4.50	1.25
□ 22 Wes Westrum	5.00	2.20	.60
□ 23 Hoyt Wilhelm	15.00	6.75	1.85
□ 24 Al Worthington	5.00	2.20	.60

1958 Jay Publishing All-Stars

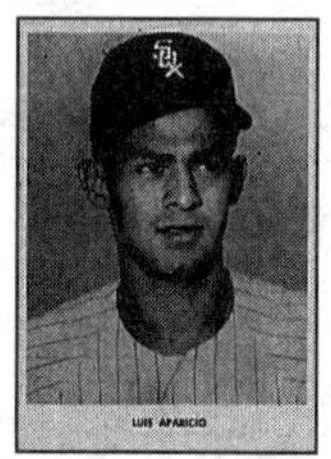

The 23 blank-backed photos comprising the 1958 Jay Publishing All-Stars set measure 5" by 7" and feature white-bordered black-and-white posed player shots. The player's name appears in black lettering within the bottom white margin. The pictures are unnumbered and checklisted below in alphabetical order.

	NRMT	VG-E	GOOD
COMPLETE SET (23)	100.00	45.00	12.50
COMMON CARD (1-23)	1.50	.70	.19

□ 1 Henry Aaron	15.00	6.75	1.85
□ 2 Luis Aparicio	6.00	2.70	.75
□ 3 Bob Cerv	1.50	.70	.19
□ 4 Delmar Crandall	1.50	.70	.19
□ 5 Whitey Ford	7.50	3.40	.95
□ 6 Nelson Fox	6.00	2.70	.75
□ 7 Bob Friend	1.50	.70	.19
□ 8 Fred Haney MG	1.50	.70	.19
□ 9 Jack Jensen	3.00	1.35	.35
□ 10 Frank Malzone	1.50	.70	.19
□ 11 Mickey Mantle	30.00	13.50	3.70
□ 12 Bill Mazeroski	5.00	2.20	.60
□ 13 Roy McMillan	1.50	.70	.19
□ 14 Stan Musial	10.00	4.50	1.25
□ 15 Bill Pierce	1.50	.70	.19
□ 16 Robin Roberts	7.50	3.40	.95
□ 17 Bob Skinner	1.50	.70	.19
□ 18 Bill Skowron	1.50	.70	.19
□ 19 Warren Spahn	7.50	3.40	.95
□ 20 Casey Stengel MG	7.50	3.40	.95
□ 21 Frank Thomas	1.50	.70	.19
□ 22 Gus Triandos	1.50	.70	.19
□ 23 Bob Turley	1.50	.70	.19

1989 Jefferies Card Collectors Co.

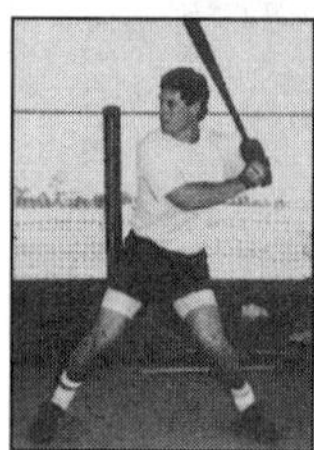

This 16-card set features borderless color photos of Gregg Jefferies from childhood to adulthood. The backs carry information about the photos.

	MINT	NRMT	EXC
COMPLETE SET (16)	4.00	1.80	.50
COMMON CARD (1-16)	.25	.11	.03

□ 1 Gregg Jefferies (At age three)	.25	.11	.03
□ 2 Gregg Jefferies (At age six)	.25	.11	.03
□ 3 Gregg Jefferies (On one knee with bat)	.25	.11	.03
□ 4 Gregg Jefferies (At age eight)	.25	.11	.03
□ 5 Gregg Jefferies (At age nine)	.25	.11	.03
□ 6 Gregg Jefferies (At age ten)	.25	.11	.03

☐ 7 Gregg Jefferies (Waiting to bat for his high school team)	.25	.11	.03
☐ 8 Gregg Jefferies (Portrait in his first tie)	.25	.11	.03
☐ 9 Gregg Jefferies (At age five)	.25	.11	.03
☐ 10 Gregg Jefferies (1985 interview)	.25	.11	.03
☐ 11 Gregg Jefferies (At age fifteen)	.25	.11	.03
☐ 12 Gregg Jefferies (In batting drill)	.25	.11	.03
☐ 13 Gregg Jefferies (At batting practice)	.25	.11	.03
☐ 14 Gregg Jefferies (Beginning his swing)	.25	.11	.03
☐ 15 Gregg Jefferies (Halfway through swing)	.25	.11	.03
☐ 16 Gregg Jefferies (Completing his swing)	.25	.11	.03

1962 Jello

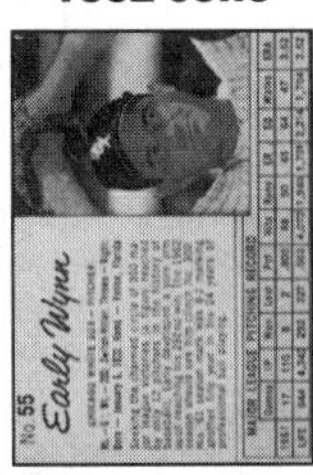

The cards in this 200-card (only 197 were ever issued) set measure 2 1/2" by 3 3/8". The 1962 Jello set has the same checklist as the Post Cereal set of the same year, but is considered by some to be a test issue. The cards are grouped numerically by team. For example: New York Yankees (1-13), Detroit (14-26), Baltimore (27-36), Cleveland (37-45), Chicago White Sox (46-55), Boston (56-64), Washington (65-73), Los Angeles Angels (74-82), Minnesota (83-91), Kansas City (92-100), Los Angeles Dodgers (101-115), Cincinnati (116-130), San Francisco (131-144), Milwaukee (145-157), St. Louis (158-168), Pittsburgh (169-181), Chicago Cubs (182-191), and Philadelphia (192-200). Although the players and numbers are identical in both sets, the Jello series has its own list of scarce and difficult cards. Numbers 29, 82 and 176 were never issued. A Jello card is easily distinguished from its counterpart in Post by the absence of the Post logo. The catalog designation for this set is F229-1.

	NRMT	VG-E	GOOD
COMPLETE SET (197)	5000.00	2200.00	600.00
COMMON CARD (1-200)	6.00	2.70	.75

	NRMT	VG-E	GOOD
☐ 1 Bill Skowron	25.00	11.00	3.10
☐ 2 Bobby Richardson	25.00	11.00	3.10
☐ 3 Cletis Boyer	12.50	5.50	1.55
☐ 4 Tony Kubek	20.00	9.00	2.50
☐ 5 Mickey Mantle	1000.00	450.00	125.00
☐ 6 Roger Maris	175.00	80.00	22.00
☐ 7 Yogi Berra	125.00	55.00	15.50
☐ 8 Elston Howard	12.50	5.50	1.55
☐ 9 Whitey Ford	75.00	34.00	9.50
☐ 10 Ralph Terry	10.00	4.50	1.25
☐ 11 John Blanchard	10.00	4.50	1.25
☐ 12 Luis Arroyo	10.00	4.50	1.25
☐ 13 Bill Stafford	15.00	6.75	1.85
☐ 14 Norm Cash	12.50	5.50	1.55
☐ 15 Jake Wood	6.00	2.70	.75
☐ 16 Steve Boros	6.00	2.70	.75
☐ 17 Chico Fernandez	6.00	2.70	.75
☐ 18 Bill Bruton	6.00	2.70	.75
☐ 19 Ken Aspromonte	6.00	2.70	.75
☐ 20 Al Kaline	60.00	27.00	7.50
☐ 21 Dick Brown	6.00	2.70	.75
☐ 22 Frank Lary	6.00	2.70	.75
☐ 23 Don Mossi	10.00	4.50	1.25
☐ 24 Phil Regan	6.00	2.70	.75
☐ 25 Charley Maxwell	6.00	2.70	.75
☐ 26 Jim Bunning	30.00	13.50	3.70
☐ 27 Jim Gentile	10.00	4.50	1.25
☐ 28 Marv Breeding	6.00	2.70	.75
☐ 29 Not issued			
☐ 30 Ron Hansen	6.00	2.70	.75
☐ 31 Jackie Brandt	25.00	11.00	3.10
☐ 32 Dick Williams	12.50	5.50	1.55
☐ 33 Gus Triandos	6.00	2.70	.75
☐ 34 Milt Pappas	6.00	2.70	.75
☐ 35 Hoyt Wilhelm	50.00	22.00	6.25
☐ 36 Chuck Estrada	6.00	2.70	.75
☐ 37 Vic Power	6.00	2.70	.75
☐ 38 Johnny Temple	6.00	2.70	.75
☐ 39 Bubba Phillips	25.00	11.00	3.10
☐ 40 Tito Francona	6.00	2.70	.75
☐ 41 Willie Kirkland	6.00	2.70	.75
☐ 42 John Romano	6.00	2.70	.75
☐ 43 Jim Perry	10.00	4.50	1.25
☐ 44 Woodie Held	6.00	2.70	.75
☐ 45 Chuck Essegian	6.00	2.70	.75
☐ 46 Roy Sievers	6.00	2.70	.75
☐ 47 Nellie Fox	35.00	16.00	4.40
☐ 48 Al Smith	6.00	2.70	.75
☐ 49 Luis Aparicio	40.00	18.00	5.00
☐ 50 Jim Landis	6.00	2.70	.75
☐ 51 Minnie Minoso	25.00	11.00	3.10
☐ 52 Andy Carey	25.00	11.00	3.10
☐ 53 Sherman Lollar	6.00	2.70	.75
☐ 54 Bill Pierce	10.00	4.50	1.25
☐ 55 Early Wynn	30.00	13.50	3.70
☐ 56 Chuck Schilling	25.00	11.00	3.10
☐ 57 Pete Runnels	10.00	4.50	1.25
☐ 58 Frank Malzone	10.00	4.50	1.25
☐ 59 Don Buddin	10.00	4.50	1.25
☐ 60 Gary Geiger	25.00	11.00	3.10
☐ 61 Carl Yastrzemski	300.00	135.00	38.00
☐ 62 Jackie Jensen	30.00	13.50	3.70
☐ 63 Jim Pagliaroni	25.00	11.00	3.10
☐ 64 Don Schwall	10.00	4.50	1.25
☐ 65 Dale Long	10.00	4.50	1.25
☐ 66 Chuck Cottier	10.00	4.50	1.25
☐ 67 Billy Klaus	25.00	11.00	3.10
☐ 68 Coot Veal	10.00	4.50	1.25
☐ 69 Marty Keough	35.00	16.00	4.40
☐ 70 Willie Tasby	35.00	16.00	4.40
☐ 71 Gene Woodling	10.00	4.50	1.25
☐ 72 Gene Green	35.00	16.00	4.40
☐ 73 Dick Donovan	10.00	4.50	1.25
☐ 74 Steve Bilko	10.00	4.50	1.25
☐ 75 Rocky Bridges	25.00	11.00	3.10
☐ 76 Eddie Yost	15.00	6.75	1.85
☐ 77 Leon Wagner	12.50	5.50	1.55
☐ 78 Albie Pearson	10.00	4.50	1.25
☐ 79 Ken Hunt	15.00	6.75	1.85
☐ 80 Earl Averill	35.00	16.00	4.40
☐ 81 Ryne Duren	12.50	5.50	1.55
☐ 82 Not issued			
☐ 83 Bob Allison	10.00	4.50	1.25
☐ 84 Billy Martin	30.00	13.50	3.70
☐ 85 Harmon Killebrew	50.00	22.00	6.25
☐ 86 Zoilo Versalles	10.00	4.50	1.25
☐ 87 Lenny Green	30.00	13.50	3.70
☐ 88 Bill Tuttle	6.00	2.70	.75
☐ 89 Jim Lemon	6.00	2.70	.75
☐ 90 Earl Battey	25.00	11.00	3.10
☐ 91 Camilo Pascual	6.00	2.70	.75
☐ 92 Norm Siebern	10.00	4.50	1.25
☐ 93 Jerry Lumpe	10.00	4.50	1.25
☐ 94 Dick Howser	12.50	5.50	1.55
☐ 95 Gene Stephens	35.00	16.00	4.40
☐ 96 Leo Posada	12.50	5.50	1.55
☐ 97 Joe Pignatano	10.00	4.50	1.25
☐ 98 Jim Archer	10.00	4.50	1.25
☐ 99 Haywood Sullivan	25.00	11.00	3.10
☐ 100 Art Ditmar	10.00	4.50	1.25
☐ 101 Gil Hodges	50.00	22.00	6.25
☐ 102 Charlie Neal	10.00	4.50	1.25
☐ 103 Daryl Spencer	10.00	4.50	1.25
☐ 104 Maury Wills	30.00	13.50	3.70
☐ 105 Tommy Davis	15.00	6.75	1.85
☐ 106 Willie Davis	15.00	6.75	1.85
☐ 107 John Roseboro	35.00	16.00	4.40
☐ 108 John Podres	15.00	6.75	1.85
☐ 109 Sandy Koufax	125.00	55.00	15.50
☐ 110 Don Drysdale	60.00	27.00	7.50
☐ 111 Larry Sherry	25.00	11.00	3.10
☐ 112 Jim Gilliam	30.00	13.50	3.70
☐ 113 Norm Larker	40.00	18.00	5.00
☐ 114 Duke Snider	75.00	34.00	9.50
☐ 115 Stan Williams	25.00	11.00	3.10
☐ 116 Gordy Coleman	75.00	34.00	9.50
☐ 117 Don Blasingame	25.00	11.00	3.10
☐ 118 Gene Freese	40.00	18.00	5.00
☐ 119 Ed Kasko	40.00	18.00	5.00
☐ 120 Gus Bell	30.00	13.50	3.70
☐ 121 Vada Pinson	15.00	6.75	1.85
☐ 122 Frank Robinson	40.00	18.00	5.00
☐ 123 Bob Purkey	10.00	4.50	1.25
☐ 124 Joey Jay	10.00	4.50	1.25
☐ 125 Jim Brosnan	10.00	4.50	1.25
☐ 126 Jim O'Toole	10.00	4.50	1.25
☐ 127 Jerry Lynch	10.00	4.50	1.25
☐ 128 Wally Post	10.00	4.50	1.25
☐ 129 Ken Hunt	10.00	4.50	1.25
☐ 130 Jerry Zimmerman	10.00	4.50	1.25
☐ 131 Willie McCovey	60.00	27.00	7.50
☐ 132 Jose Pagan	30.00	13.50	3.70
☐ 133 Felipe Alou	15.00	6.75	1.85
☐ 134 Jim Davenport	12.50	5.50	1.55
☐ 135 Harvey Kuenn	15.00	6.75	1.85
☐ 136 Orlando Cepeda	30.00	13.50	3.70
☐ 137 Ed Bailey	10.00	4.50	1.25
☐ 138 Sam Jones	10.00	4.50	1.25
☐ 139 Mike McCormick	10.00	4.50	1.25
☐ 140 Juan Marichal	75.00	34.00	9.50
☐ 141 Jack Sanford	10.00	4.50	1.25
☐ 142 Willie Mays	225.00	100.00	28.00
☐ 143 Stu Miller	60.00	27.00	7.50
☐ 144 Joe Amalfitano	10.00	4.50	1.25
☐ 145 Joe Adcock	10.00	4.50	1.25
☐ 146 Frank Bolling	6.00	2.70	.75
☐ 147 Ed Mathews	50.00	22.00	6.25
☐ 148 Roy McMillan	6.00	2.70	.75
☐ 149 Hank Aaron	200.00	90.00	25.00
☐ 150 Gino Cimoli	25.00	11.00	3.10
☐ 151 Frank Thomas	10.00	4.50	1.25
☐ 152 Joe Torre	20.00	9.00	2.50
☐ 153 Lew Burdette	12.50	5.50	1.55
☐ 154 Bob Buhl	6.00	2.70	.75
☐ 155 Carlton Willey	6.00	2.70	.75
☐ 156 Lee Maye	25.00	11.00	3.10
☐ 157 Al Spangler	35.00	16.00	4.40
☐ 158 Bill White	60.00	27.00	7.50
☐ 159 Ken Boyer	25.00	11.00	3.10
☐ 160 Joe Cunningham	10.00	4.50	1.25
☐ 161 Carl Warwick	10.00	4.50	1.25
☐ 162 Carl Sawatski	6.00	2.70	.75
☐ 163 Lindy McDaniel	6.00	2.70	.75
☐ 164 Ernie Broglio	10.00	4.50	1.25
☐ 165 Larry Jackson	6.00	2.70	.75
☐ 166 Curt Flood	30.00	13.50	3.70
☐ 167 Curt Simmons	30.00	13.50	3.70
☐ 168 Alex Grammas	25.00	11.00	3.10
☐ 169 Dick Stuart	6.00	2.70	.75
☐ 170 Bill Mazeroski	30.00	13.50	3.70
☐ 171 Don Hoak	10.00	4.50	1.25
☐ 172 Dick Groat	12.50	5.50	1.55
☐ 173 Roberto Clemente	300.00	135.00	38.00
☐ 174 Bob Skinner	25.00	11.00	3.10
☐ 175 Bill Virdon	30.00	13.50	3.70
☐ 176 Not issued			
☐ 177 Elroy Face	12.50	5.50	1.55
☐ 178 Bob Friend	6.00	2.70	.75
☐ 179 Vernon Law	30.00	13.50	3.70
☐ 180 Harvey Haddix	35.00	16.00	4.40
☐ 181 Hal Smith	25.00	11.00	3.10
☐ 182 Ed Bouchee	25.00	11.00	3.10
☐ 183 Don Zimmer	12.50	5.50	1.55
☐ 184 Ron Santo	20.00	9.00	2.50
☐ 185 Andre Rodgers	6.00	2.70	.75
☐ 186 Richie Ashburn	35.00	16.00	4.40
☐ 187 George Altman	6.00	2.70	.75
☐ 188 Ernie Banks	35.00	16.00	4.40
☐ 189 Sam Taylor	6.00	2.70	.75
☐ 190 Don Elston	6.00	2.70	.75
☐ 191 Jerry Kindall	20.00	9.00	2.50
☐ 192 Pancho Herrera	6.00	2.70	.75
☐ 193 Tony Taylor	10.00	4.50	1.25
☐ 194 Ruben Amaro	20.00	9.00	2.50
☐ 195 Don Demeter	6.00	2.70	.75
☐ 196 Bobby Gene Smith	6.00	2.70	.75
☐ 197 Clay Dalrymple	6.00	2.70	.75
☐ 198 Robin Roberts	30.00	13.50	3.70
☐ 199 Art Mahaffey	6.00	2.70	.75
☐ 200 John Buzhardt	6.00	2.70	.75

1963 Jello

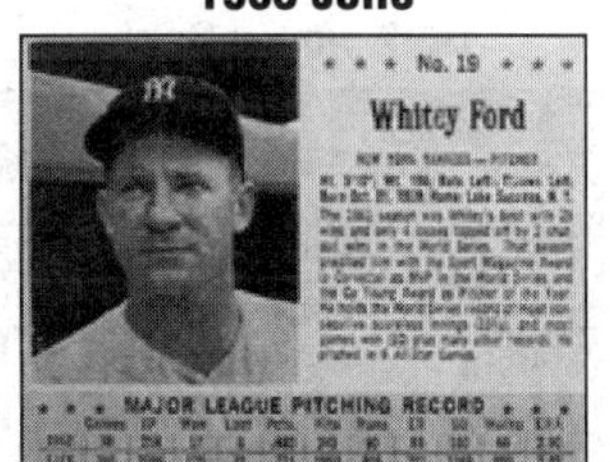

The cards in this 200-card set measure 2 1/2" by 3 3/8". The 1963 Jello set contains the same players and numbers as the Post Cereal set of the same year. The players are grouped by team with American Leaguers comprising 1-100 and National Leaguers 101-200. The ordering of teams is as follows: Minnesota (1-11), New York Yankees, Los Angeles Angels (24-34), Chicago White Sox (35-45), Detroit (46-56), Baltimore (57-66), Cleveland (67-76), Boston (77-84), Kansas City (85-92), Washington (93-100), San Francisco (101-112), Los Angeles Dodgers (113-124), Cincinnati (125-136), Pittsburgh (137-147), Milwaukee (148-157), St. Louis (158-168), Chicago Cubs (169-176), Philadelphia (177-184), Houston (185-192) and New York Mets (193-200). As in 1962, the Jello series has its own list of scarcities (many resulting from an unpopular package size). Since the Post Cereal logo was removed from the 1963 cereal set, Jello cards are primarily distinguishable by (1) smaller card size and (2) smaller print. The catalog designation is F229-2.

	NRMT	VG-E	GOOD
COMPLETE SET (200)	3250.00	1450.00	400.00
COMMON CARD (1-200)	4.00	1.80	.50

	NRMT	VG-E	GOOD
☐ 1 Vic Power	4.00	1.80	.50
☐ 2 Bernie Allen	20.00	9.00	2.50
☐ 3 Zoilo Versalles	25.00	11.00	3.10
☐ 4 Rich Rollins	4.00	1.80	.50
☐ 5 Harmon Killebrew	20.00	9.00	2.50
☐ 6 Lenny Green	25.00	11.00	3.10
☐ 7 Bob Allison	4.00	1.80	.50
☐ 8 Earl Battey	15.00	6.75	1.85
☐ 9 Camilo Pascual	6.00	2.70	.75
☐ 10 Jim Kaat	60.00	27.00	7.50
☐ 11 Jack Kralick	4.00	1.80	.50
☐ 12 Bill Skowron	25.00	11.00	3.10
☐ 13 Bobby Richardson	7.50	3.40	.95
☐ 14 Cletis Boyer	6.00	2.70	.75
☐ 15 Mickey Mantle	275.00	125.00	34.00
☐ 16 Roger Maris	100.00	45.00	12.50
☐ 17 Yogi Berra	30.00	13.50	3.70
☐ 18 Elston Howard	40.00	18.00	5.00
☐ 19 Whitey Ford	20.00	9.00	2.50
☐ 20 Ralph Terry	4.00	1.80	.50
☐ 21 John Blanchard	15.00	6.75	1.85
☐ 22 Bill Stafford	25.00	11.00	3.10
☐ 23 Tom Tresh	7.50	3.40	.95
☐ 24 Steve Bilko	4.00	1.80	.50
☐ 25 Bill Moran	4.00	1.80	.50
☐ 26 Joe Koppe	4.00	1.80	.50
☐ 27 Felix Torres	4.00	1.80	.50
☐ 28 Leon Wagner	4.00	1.80	.50
☐ 29 Albie Pearson	4.00	1.80	.50
☐ 30 Lee Thomas	4.00	1.80	.50
☐ 31 Bob Rodgers	25.00	11.00	3.10
☐ 32 Dean Chance	6.00	2.70	.75
☐ 33 Ken McBride	25.00	11.00	3.10
☐ 34 George Thomas	25.00	11.00	3.10
☐ 35 Joe Cunningham	25.00	11.00	3.10
☐ 36 Nellie Fox	10.00	4.50	1.25
☐ 37 Luis Aparicio	10.00	4.50	1.25
☐ 38 Al Smith	4.00	1.80	.50
☐ 39 Floyd Robinson	4.00	1.80	.50
☐ 40 Jim Landis	4.00	1.80	.50
☐ 41 Charlie Maxwell	4.00	1.80	.50
☐ 42 Sherman Lollar	6.00	2.70	.75
☐ 43 Early Wynn	10.00	4.50	1.25
☐ 44 Juan Pizarro	20.00	9.00	2.50
☐ 45 Ray Herbert	25.00	11.00	3.10
☐ 46 Norm Cash	7.50	3.40	.95
☐ 47 Steve Boros	30.00	13.50	3.70
☐ 48 Dick McAuliffe	6.00	2.70	.75
☐ 49 Bill Bruton	20.00	9.00	2.50
☐ 50 Rocky Colavito	7.50	3.40	.95
☐ 51 Al Kaline	20.00	9.00	2.50
☐ 52 Dick Brown	25.00	11.00	3.10
☐ 53 Jim Bunning	10.00	4.50	1.25
☐ 54 Hank Aguirre	4.00	1.80	.50
☐ 55 Frank Lary	25.00	11.00	3.10
☐ 56 Don Mossi	25.00	11.00	3.10
☐ 57 Jim Gentile	6.00	2.70	.75
☐ 58 Jackie Brandt	4.00	1.80	.50
☐ 59 Brooks Robinson	20.00	9.00	2.50
☐ 60 Ron Hansen	4.00	1.80	.50
☐ 61 Jerry Adair	50.00	22.00	6.25
☐ 62 Boog Powell	7.50	3.40	.95
☐ 63 Russ Snyder	25.00	11.00	3.10
☐ 64 Steve Barber	4.00	1.80	.50
☐ 65 Milt Pappas	25.00	11.00	3.10
☐ 66 Robin Roberts	10.00	4.50	1.25
☐ 67 Tito Francona	4.00	1.80	.50
☐ 68 Jerry Kindall	25.00	11.00	3.10
☐ 69 Woody Held	4.00	1.80	.50
☐ 70 Bubba Phillips	4.00	1.80	.50
☐ 71 Chuck Essegian	4.00	1.80	.50
☐ 72 Willie Kirkland	25.00	11.00	3.10
☐ 73 Al Luplow	4.00	1.80	.50
☐ 74 Ty Cline	50.00	22.00	6.25
☐ 75 Dick Donovan	4.00	1.80	.50
☐ 76 John Romano	4.00	1.80	.50
☐ 77 Pete Runnels	6.00	2.70	.75
☐ 78 Ed Bressoud	20.00	9.00	2.50
☐ 79 Frank Malzone	6.00	2.70	.75
☐ 80 Carl Yastrzemski	75.00	34.00	9.50
☐ 81 Gary Geiger	4.00	1.80	.50
☐ 82 Lou Clinton	20.00	9.00	2.50
☐ 83 Earl Wilson	4.00	1.80	.50
☐ 84 Bill Monbouquette	4.00	1.80	.50
☐ 85 Norm Siebern	4.00	1.80	.50
☐ 86 Jerry Lumpe	4.00	1.80	.50
☐ 87 Manny Jimenez	4.00	1.80	.50
☐ 88 Gino Cimoli	4.00	1.80	.50
☐ 89 Ed Charles	50.00	22.00	6.25
☐ 90 Ed Rakow	4.00	1.80	.50
☐ 91 Bobby Del Greco	50.00	22.00	6.25
☐ 92 Haywood Sullivan	25.00	11.00	3.10
☐ 93 Chuck Hinton	4.00	1.80	.50
☐ 94 Ken Retzer	25.00	11.00	3.10
☐ 95 Harry Bright	25.00	11.00	3.10
☐ 96 Bob Johnson	4.00	1.80	.50
☐ 97 Dave Stenhouse	20.00	9.00	2.50
☐ 98 Chuck Cottier	4.00	1.80	.50
☐ 99 Tom Cheney	4.00	1.80	.50
☐ 100 Claude Osteen	30.00	13.50	3.70
☐ 101 Orlando Cepeda	10.00	4.50	1.25
☐ 102 Chuck Hiller	20.00	9.00	2.50
☐ 103 Jose Pagan	20.00	9.00	2.50
☐ 104 Jim Davenport	4.00	1.80	.50
☐ 105 Harvey Kuenn	6.00	2.70	.75
☐ 106 Willie Mays	110.00	50.00	14.00
☐ 107 Felipe Alou	7.50	3.40	.95
☐ 108 Tom Haller	4.00	1.80	.50
☐ 109 Juan Marichal	10.00	4.50	1.25
☐ 110 Jack Sanford	4.00	1.80	.50
☐ 111 Bill O'Dell	4.00	1.80	.50
☐ 112 Willie McCovey	150.00	70.00	19.00
☐ 113 Lee Walls	20.00	9.00	2.50
☐ 114 Jim Gilliam	30.00	13.50	3.70
☐ 115 Maury Wills	7.50	3.40	.95
☐ 116 Ron Fairly	6.00	2.70	.75
☐ 117 Tommy Davis	6.00	2.70	.75
☐ 118 Duke Snider	15.00	6.75	1.85
☐ 119 Willie Davis	6.00	2.70	.75
☐ 120 John Roseboro	4.00	1.80	.50
☐ 121 Sandy Koufax	35.00	16.00	4.40
☐ 122 Stan Williams	4.00	1.80	.50
☐ 123 Don Drysdale	10.00	4.50	1.25
☐ 124 Daryl Spencer	4.00	1.80	.50
☐ 125 Gordy Coleman	4.00	1.80	.50
☐ 126 Don Blasingame	25.00	11.00	3.10
☐ 127 Leo Cardenas	4.00	1.80	.50
☐ 128 Eddie Kasko	20.00	9.00	2.50

☐ 129 Jerry Lynch	4.00	1.80	.50
☐ 130 Vada Pinson	7.50	3.40	.95
☐ 131 Frank Robinson	12.50	5.50	1.55
☐ 132 John Edwards	25.00	11.00	3.10
☐ 133 Joey Jay	4.00	1.80	.50
☐ 134 Bob Purkey	4.00	1.80	.50
☐ 135 Marty Keough	50.00	22.00	6.25
☐ 136 Jim O'Toole	25.00	11.00	3.10
☐ 137 Dick Stuart	4.00	1.80	.50
☐ 138 Bill Mazeroski	7.50	3.40	.95
☐ 139 Dick Groat	6.00	2.70	.75
☐ 140 Don Hoak	4.00	1.80	.50
☐ 141 Bob Skinner	4.00	1.80	.50
☐ 142 Bill Virdon	6.00	2.70	.75
☐ 143 Roberto Clemente	150.00	70.00	19.00
☐ 144 Smoky Burgess	6.00	2.70	.75
☐ 145 Bob Friend	4.00	1.80	.50
☐ 146 Al McBean	25.00	11.00	3.10
☐ 147 Elroy Face	6.00	2.70	.75
☐ 148 Joe Adcock	6.00	2.70	.75
☐ 149 Frank Bolling	4.00	1.80	.50
☐ 150 Roy McMillan	4.00	1.80	.50
☐ 151 Eddie Mathews	20.00	9.00	2.50
☐ 152 Hank Aaron	100.00	45.00	12.50
☐ 153 Del Crandall	25.00	11.00	3.10
☐ 154 Bob Shaw	4.00	1.80	.50
☐ 155 Lew Burdette	6.00	2.70	.75
☐ 156 Joe Torre	50.00	22.00	6.25
☐ 157 Tony Cloninger	30.00	13.50	3.70
☐ 158 Bill White	7.50	3.40	.95
☐ 159 Julian Javier	25.00	11.00	3.10
☐ 160 Ken Boyer	7.50	3.40	.95
☐ 161 Julio Gotay	25.00	11.00	3.10
☐ 162 Curt Flood	6.00	2.70	.75
☐ 163 Charlie James	50.00	22.00	6.25
☐ 164 Gene Oliver	25.00	11.00	3.10
☐ 165 Ernie Broglio	4.00	1.80	.50
☐ 166 Bob Gibson	100.00	45.00	12.50
☐ 167 Lindy McDaniel	20.00	9.00	2.50
☐ 168 Ray Washburn	4.00	1.80	.50
☐ 169 Ernie Banks	20.00	9.00	2.50
☐ 170 Ron Santo	7.50	3.40	.95
☐ 171 George Altman	4.00	1.80	.50
☐ 172 Billy Williams	75.00	34.00	9.50
☐ 173 Andre Rodgers	25.00	11.00	3.10
☐ 174 Ken Hubbs	7.50	3.40	.95
☐ 175 Don Landrum	25.00	11.00	3.10
☐ 176 Dick Bertell	25.00	11.00	3.10
☐ 177 Roy Sievers	6.00	2.70	.75
☐ 178 Tony Taylor	30.00	13.50	3.70
☐ 179 John Callison	6.00	2.70	.75
☐ 180 Don Demeter	4.00	1.80	.50
☐ 181 Tony Gonzalez	25.00	11.00	3.10
☐ 182 Wes Covington	25.00	11.00	3.10
☐ 183 Art Mahaffey	4.00	1.80	.50
☐ 184 Clay Dalrymple	4.00	1.80	.50
☐ 185 Al Spangler	4.00	1.80	.50
☐ 186 Roman Mejias	4.00	1.80	.50
☐ 187 Bob Aspromonte	30.00	13.50	3.70
☐ 188 Norm Larker	4.00	1.80	.50
☐ 189 Johnny Temple	4.00	1.80	.50
☐ 190 Carl Warwick	25.00	11.00	3.10
☐ 191 Bob Lillis	20.00	9.00	2.50
☐ 192 Dick Farrell	35.00	16.00	4.40
☐ 193 Gil Hodges	15.00	6.75	1.85
☐ 194 Marv Throneberry	6.00	2.70	.75
☐ 195 Charlie Neal	25.00	11.00	3.10
☐ 196 Frank Thomas	6.00	2.70	.75
☐ 197 Richie Ashburn	10.00	4.50	1.25
☐ 198 Felix Mantilla	20.00	9.00	2.50
☐ 199 Rod Kanehl	20.00	9.00	2.50
☐ 200 Roger Craig	35.00	16.00	4.40

1976 Jerry Jonas Promotion Cards

These eight cards were issued by Jerry Jonas Promotions as part of an attempt to secure a major league liscense. These cards were presented at the World Series meetings in 1975. These cards, featuring all time greats, were in the format of the regular 1975 Topps issue. The set is also sometimes found as an uncut sheet of all eight players.

	NRMT	VG-E	GOOD
COMPLETE SET	600.00	275.00	75.00
COMMON CARD	50.00	22.00	6.25
☐ 1 Sandy Koufax	100.00	45.00	12.50
☐ 2 Mel Ott	60.00	27.00	7.50
☐ 3 Willie Mays	150.00	70.00	19.00
☐ 4 Stan Musial	100.00	45.00	12.50
☐ 5 Rogers Hornsby	50.00	22.00	6.25
☐ 6 Honus Wagner	75.00	34.00	9.50
☐ 7 Grover Alexander	75.00	34.00	9.50
☐ 8 Robin Roberts	60.00	27.00	7.50

1991 Jimmy Dean

Michael Schechter Associates (MSA) produced this 25-card standard-size set on behalf of Jimmy Dean Sausage. These cards feature an obverse with a color player photo, enframed by yellow and red borders. Since these player photos were not expressly licensed by Major League Baseball, the team logos have been airbrushed out. In a red and white panel with yellow borders, the back has biographical information, complete major (and minor where appropriate) league statistics, and the player's facsimile autograph. The cards are

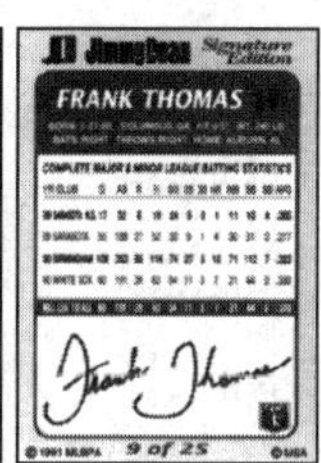

numbered on the back. During the promotion, uncut sheets were offered by the company through a mail-in offer involving Jimmy Dean proofs of purchase.

	MINT	NRMT	EXC
COMPLETE SET (25)	12.00	5.50	1.50
COMMON CARD (1-25)	.25	.11	.03
☐ 1 Will Clark	.50	.23	.06
☐ 2 Ken Griffey Jr.	3.00	1.35	.35
☐ 3 Dale Murphy	.50	.23	.06
☐ 4 Barry Bonds	.75	.35	.09
☐ 5 Darryl Strawberry	.40	.18	.05
☐ 6 Ryne Sandberg	1.25	.55	.16
☐ 7 Gary Sheffield	.60	.25	.07
☐ 8 Sandy Alomar Jr.	.40	.18	.05
☐ 9 Frank Thomas	3.00	1.35	.35
☐ 10 Barry Larkin	.50	.23	.06
☐ 11 Kirby Puckett	1.50	.70	.19
☐ 12 George Brett	1.25	.55	.16
☐ 13 Kevin Mitchell	.25	.11	.03
☐ 14 Dave Justice	.60	.25	.07
☐ 15 Cal Ripken	2.50	1.10	.30
☐ 16 Craig Biggio	.60	.25	.07
☐ 17 Rickey Henderson	.60	.25	.07
☐ 18 Roger Clemens	1.00	.45	.12
☐ 19 Jose Canseco	.50	.23	.06
☐ 20 Ozzie Smith	1.50	.70	.19
☐ 21 Cecil Fielder	.40	.18	.05
☐ 22 Dave Winfield	.50	.23	.06
☐ 23 Kevin Maas	.25	.11	.03
☐ 24 Nolan Ryan	2.50	1.10	.30
☐ 25 Dwight Gooden	.40	.18	.05

1992 Jimmy Dean

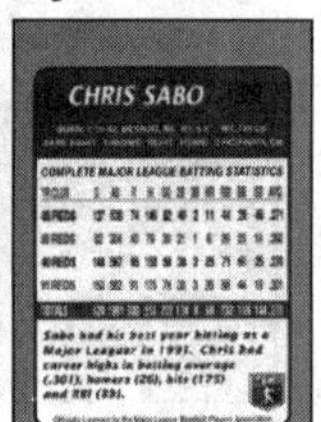

Michael Schechter Associates (MSA) produced this 18-card standard-size set for Jimmy Dean. In a cello pack, three free cards were included in any Jimmy Dean Sandwich, Flapsticks, or Links/Patties Breakfast Sausage. The fronts feature glossy color player photos with team logos airbrushed out. These pictures are bordered on the left by a black bar that includes player information printed vertically. Another bar juts out from the right at the bottom of the picture and has the company logo with the words "Jimmy Dean '92." Inside a blue border, the backs are red, white, and blue and present biography, statistics, and brief career summary.

	MINT	NRMT	EXC
COMPLETE SET (18)	8.00	3.60	1.00
COMMON CARD (1-18)	.10	.05	.01
☐ 1 Jim Abbott	.10	.05	.01
☐ 2 Barry Bonds	.50	.23	.06
☐ 3 Jeff Bagwell	1.25	.55	.16
☐ 4 Frank Thomas	2.00	.90	.25
☐ 5 Steve Avery	.25	.11	.03
☐ 6 Chris Sabo	.10	.05	.01
☐ 7 Will Clark	.50	.23	.06
☐ 8 Don Mattingly	1.00	.45	.12
☐ 9 Darryl Strawberry	.20	.09	.03
☐ 10 Roger Clemens	.50	.23	.06
☐ 11 Ken Griffey Jr.	2.00	.90	.25
☐ 12 Chuck Knoblauch	.30	.14	.04
☐ 13 Tony Gwynn	1.00	.45	.12
☐ 14 Juan Gonzalez	1.00	.45	.12
☐ 15 Cecil Fielder	.20	.09	.03
☐ 16 Bobby Bonilla	.20	.09	.03
☐ 17 Wes Chamberlain	.10	.05	.01
☐ 18 Ryne Sandberg	.75	.35	.09

1992 Jimmy Dean Living Legends

This six-card standard-size set was produced by MSA (Michael Schechter Associates) and features future candidates for the Hall of Fame. Collectors could obtain the complete set through a mail-in offer detailed on packages of Jimmy Dean Breakfast Sausage or Smoked Sausage. While supplies lasted, the sets could be obtained by sending

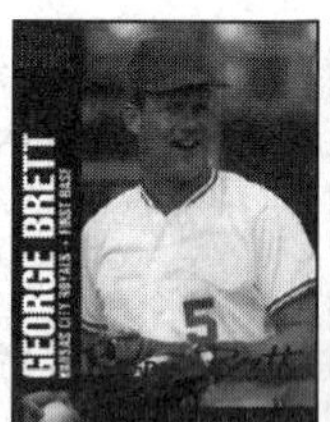

in three UPC proofs of purchase from Jimmy Dean Sausage plus 1.00 for shipping and handling. The cards feature on the fronts glossy color player photos with team logos airbrushed out. These pictures are bordered on the left by a black bar that includes player information and the words "Living Legend" in gold-foil stamping. Another black bar juts out from the right at the bottom of the picture and has "Jimmy Dean '92" also in gold foil. Finally, inscribed across each photo is the player's signature in gold foil. The backs are black, yellow, and white and carry biography, statistics, and a brief career summary. Reportedly 105,000 sets were printed.

	MINT	NRMT	EXC
COMPLETE SET (6)	15.00	6.75	1.85
COMMON CARD (1-6)	1.00	.45	.12
☐ 1 George Brett	2.50	1.10	.30
☐ 2 Carlton Fisk	1.50	.70	.19
☐ 3 Ozzie Smith	2.00	.90	.25
☐ 4 Robin Yount	1.00	.45	.12
☐ 5 Cal Ripken	5.00	2.20	.60
☐ 6 Nolan Ryan	5.00	2.20	.60

1992 Jimmy Dean Rookie Stars

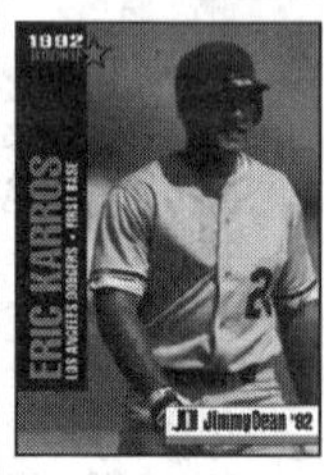

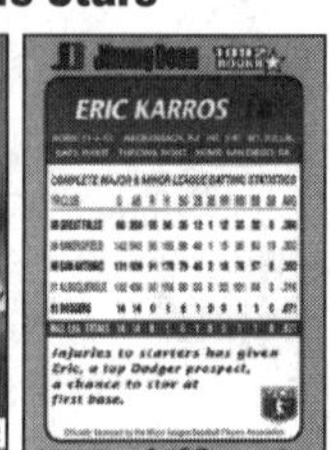

The players in this nine-card standard-size set were chosen based on actual 1992 first-half performance. Three free cards were included in specially marked packages of Jimmy Dean Sausage, Chicken Biscuits, Steak Biscuits, and MiniBurgers. The cards feature on the fronts glossy color player photos with team logos airbrushed out. These pictures are bordered on the left by a black bar that includes the player's name printed vertically in either red or blue lettering. Another bar juts out from the right at the bottom of the picture and has "Jimmy Dean '92" in black lettering. Inside light blue borders, a red and white panel displays biography, statistics, and a brief career summary. Oversized 7" by 9 3/4" versions of the cards, featuring a Rookie Star front on one side and a Living Legend front on the other, were placed at point of purchase for promotional purchases.

	MINT	NRMT	EXC
COMPLETE SET (9)	4.00	1.80	.50
COMMON CARD (1-9)	.15	.07	.02
☐ 1 Andy Stankiewicz	.15	.07	.02
☐ 2 Pat Listach	.25	.11	.03
☐ 3 Brian Jordan	1.00	.45	.12
☐ 4 Eric Karros	.75	.35	.09
☐ 5 Reggie Sanders	.75	.35	.09
☐ 6 Dave Fleming	.15	.07	.02
☐ 7 Donovan Osborne	.25	.11	.03
☐ 8 Kenny Lofton	2.00	.90	.25
☐ 9 Moises Alou	.75	.35	.09

1993 Jimmy Dean

Produced by MSA (Michael Schechter Associates) for Jimmy Dean, these 28 cards measure the standard size. Eighteen cards were distributed in packs of three inside certain packages of Jimmy Dean products. The remaining ten cards were a special issue subset that could only be obtained through redemption of UPC symbols from Jimmy Dean Roll Sausage. The fronts feature full-bleed glossy color players photos with team logos airbrushed out. In one of the card's corners, two bars (a white one and a team color-coded one) carry the Jimmy Dean logo and the player's name, respectively. On a white background with red, blue, and black print, the backs have a close-up drawing of the player as well as biographical and statistical information.

	MINT	NRMT	EXC
COMPLETE SET (28)	10.00	4.50	1.25
COMMON CARD (1-28)	.25	.11	.03
☐ 1 Frank Thomas	3.00	1.35	.35
☐ 2 Barry Larkin	.50	.23	.06
☐ 3 Cal Ripken	2.50	1.10	.30
☐ 4 Andy Van Slyke	.25	.11	.03
☐ 5 Darren Daulton	.50	.23	.06
☐ 6 Don Mattingly	1.25	.55	.16
☐ 7 Roger Clemens	.60	.25	.07
☐ 8 Juan Gonzalez	1.50	.70	.19
☐ 9 Mark Langston	.25	.11	.03
☐ 10 Barry Bonds	.75	.35	.09
☐ 11 Ken Griffey Jr.	3.00	1.35	.35
☐ 12 Cecil Fielder	.50	.23	.06
☐ 13 Kirby Puckett	1.50	.70	.19
☐ 14 Tom Glavine	.60	.25	.07
☐ 15 George Brett	1.00	.45	.12
☐ 16 Nolan Ryan	2.00	.90	.25
☐ 17 Eddie Murray	.75	.35	.09
☐ 18 Gary Sheffield	.60	.25	.07
☐ 19 Doug Drabek	.25	.11	.03
☐ 20 Ray Lankford	.50	.23	.06
☐ 21 Benito Santiago	.25	.11	.03
☐ 22 Mark McGwire	1.00	.45	.12
☐ 23 Kenny Lofton	1.25	.55	.16
☐ 24 Eric Karros	.50	.23	.06
☐ 25 Ryne Sandberg	1.00	.45	.12
☐ 26 Charlie Hayes	.25	.11	.03
☐ 27 Mike Mussina	.60	.25	.07
☐ 28 Pat Listach	.25	.11	.03

1993 Jimmy Dean Rookies

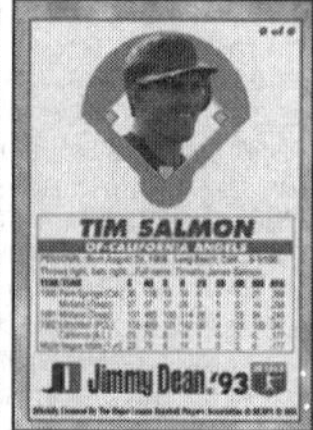

This nine-card standard-size set displays a cutout photo of the player superimposed on a gray studio background. The borderless cards carry the player's name and team on a dark gray marbleized block on the bottom. The Jimmy Dean logo and 1993 Rookies are displayed at the top left. The back carries a head shot bordered by a baseball diamond. The lower half lists the player's name, position, team, biography, and statistics. The backs are bordered in studio gray with a thin red inner border. The cards are numbered on the back following alphabetical order of the players' names.

	MINT	NRMT	EXC
COMPLETE SET (9)	6.00	2.70	.75
COMMON CARD (1-9)	.25	.11	.03
☐ 1 Rich Amaral	.25	.11	.03
☐ 2 Vinny Castilla	1.00	.45	.12
☐ 3 Jeff Conine	.50	.23	.06
☐ 4 Brent Gates	.25	.11	.03
☐ 5 Wayne Kirby	.25	.11	.03
☐ 6 Mike Lansing	.50	.23	.06
☐ 7 David Nied	.25	.11	.03
☐ 8 Mike Piazza	3.00	1.35	.35
☐ 9 Tim Salmon	1.50	.70	.19

1995 Jimmy Dean All-Time Greats

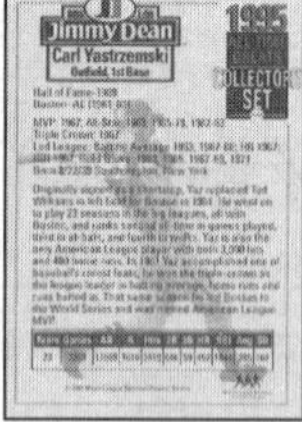

This 6-card standard-size set was cosponsored by Jimmy Dean Foods and the Major League Baseball Players Alumni Association. The cards were individually cello wrapped and inserted inside packages, and an accompanying paper insert featured coupons and a mail-in offer. (The mail-in offer was also found on boxes of Jimmy Dean Breakfast foods.) For two proofs-of-purchase plus $7.00, the collector received one autographed card featuring Billy Williams, Al Kaline, or Jim "Catfish" Hunter. Expiring December 31, 1995, the offer was limited to 12 baseball cards per original order form. The cards are checklisted below in alphabetical order.

	MINT	NRMT	EXC
COMPLETE SET (6)	5.00	2.20	.60
COMMON CARD (1-6)	1.00	.45	.12

☐ 1 Rod Carew	1.00	.45	.12
☐ 2 Jim(Catfish) Hunter	1.00	.45	.12
☐ 3 Al Kaline	1.00	.45	.12
☐ 4 Mike Schmidt	2.00	.90	.25
☐ 5 Billy Williams	1.00	.45	.12
☐ 6 Carl Yastrzemski	1.50	.70	.19
☐ NNO Jim(Catfish) Hunter AU	20.00	9.00	2.50
☐ NNO Al Kaline AU	20.00	9.00	2.50
☐ NNO Billy Williams AU	20.00	9.00	2.50

1997 Jimmy Dean

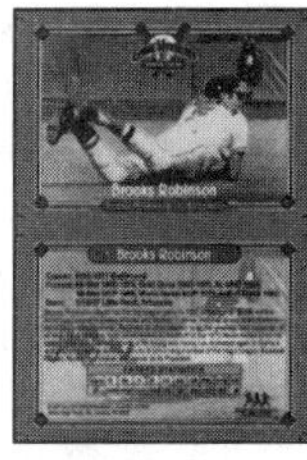

This two-card set was distributed through Jimmy Dean Products and could be obtained by sending in $12.95 and two UPCs from these products. All cards in this limited edition are autographed. The fronts feature black-and-white action player photos in a gold margin with a thin white inside border and green diamonds at the corners. The backs carry player information and career statistics. The cards are unnumbered and checklisted below in alphabetical order.

	MINT	NRMT	EXC
COMPLETE SET (2)	30.00	13.50	3.70
COMMON CARD (1-2)	15.00	6.75	1.85
☐ 1 Yogi Berra	15.00	6.75	1.85
☐ 2 Brooks Robinson	15.00	6.75	1.85

1975-76 Johnny Mize

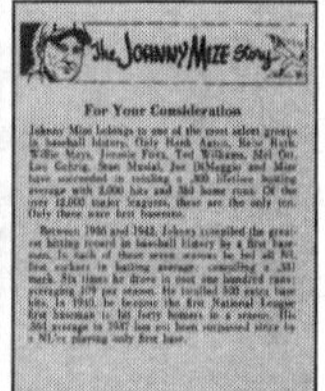

This 20-card set measures 3 1/8" by 3 3/4" and features both vertical and horizontal black-and-white photos of Johnny Mize at various stages of his life. The photos are bordered in gold and gray by a design similar to picture frame. The card title is printed below the photo in script. The backs are white and carry a variety of information. Some contain statistics, while others have quotes from other ball players or career information. The cards are unnumbered and checklisted below in alphabetical order according to either the card's title or the last name of an individual pictured with Johnny Mize.

	NRMT	VG-E	GOOD
COMPLETE SET	15.00	6.75	1.85
COMMON CARD	.75	.35	.09
☐ 1 Johnny Mize Buddy Blattner Sid Gordon Ernie Lombardi Willard Marshall	1.50	.70	.19
☐ 2 Johnny Mize Call for Phillip Morris	.75	.35	.09
☐ 3 Johnny Mize Cardinal Slugger	.75	.35	.09
☐ 4 Johnny Mize Cards' Big Stick	.75	.35	.09
☐ 5 Johnny Mize Happy Chandler COMM Bucky Harris MG	1.50	.70	.19
☐ 6 Johnny Mize Early Photo - 1913	.75	.35	.09
☐ 7 Johnny Mize 51 Homers, 1947	.75	.35	.09
☐ 8 Johnny Mize Home Run, 1952 Series	.75	.35	.09
☐ 9 Johnny Mize June 16, 1953	.75	.35	.09
☐ 10 Johnny Mize Louisville Poster 1947	.75	.35	.09
☐ 11 Johnny Mize Terry Moore	1.00	.45	.12
☐ 12 Johnny Mize NL Homer Champ 1948	.75	.35	.09
☐ 13 Johnny Mize Allie Reynolds Billy Johnson	1.00	.45	.12
☐ 14 Johnny Mize Roy Rogers	2.00	.90	.25
☐ 15 Johnny Mize Series MVP 1952	.75	.35	.09
☐ 16 Johnny Mize Enos Slaughter 1939	2.00	.90	.25
☐ 17 Johnny Mize St. Louis Star	.75	.35	.09
☐ 18 Johnny Mize The Navy - 1943	.75	.35	.09
☐ 19 Johnny Mize Vu-Master Slide	.75	.35	.09
☐ 20 Johnny Mize Gene Woodling Vic Raschi 1952	1.00	.45	.12

1910 Ju Ju Drums E286

These round "cards" have a diameter measure of 1 7/16". They were issued by Ju Ju Drums gum. The set can be dated to 1910 by the inclusion of Elmer Zacher who had his only major league season that year. These cards are unnumbered and we have sequenced them in alphabetical order.

	EX-MT	VG-E	GOOD
COMPLETE SET (43)	10000.00	4500.00	1250.00
COMMON CARD (1-43)	150.00	70.00	19.00
☐ 1 Eddie Ainsmith	150.00	70.00	19.00
☐ 2 Jimmy Austin	150.00	70.00	19.00
☐ 3 Chief Bender	400.00	180.00	50.00
☐ 4 Bruno Block	150.00	70.00	19.00
☐ 5 Jimmy Burke	150.00	70.00	19.00
☐ 6 Donie Bush	150.00	70.00	19.00
☐ 7 Frank Chance	500.00	220.00	60.00
☐ 8 Harry Cheek	150.00	70.00	19.00
☐ 9 Eddie Cicotte	300.00	135.00	38.00
☐ 10 Ty Cobb	2200.00	1000.00	275.00
☐ 11 King Cole	150.00	70.00	19.00
☐ 12 Jack Coombs	400.00	180.00	50.00
☐ 13 Bill Dahlen	150.00	70.00	19.00
☐ 14 Bert Daniels	150.00	70.00	19.00
☐ 15 George Davis	150.00	70.00	19.00
☐ 16 Larry Doyle	200.00	90.00	25.00
☐ 17 Rube Ellis	150.00	70.00	19.00
☐ 18 George Ferguson	150.00	70.00	19.00
☐ 19 Russ Ford	150.00	70.00	19.00
☐ 20 Robert Harmon	150.00	70.00	19.00
☐ 21 Robert Hyatt	150.00	70.00	19.00
☐ 22 William Killefer	150.00	70.00	19.00
☐ 23 Arthur Krueger	150.00	70.00	19.00
☐ 24 Thomas Leach	200.00	90.00	25.00
☐ 25 Christy Mathewson	850.00	375.00	105.00
☐ 26 John McGraw	500.00	220.00	60.00
☐ 27 Deacon McGuire	150.00	70.00	19.00
☐ 28 Chief Meyers	150.00	70.00	19.00
☐ 29 Roy Miller	150.00	70.00	19.00
☐ 30 George Mullin	150.00	70.00	19.00
☐ 31 Tom Needham	150.00	70.00	19.00
☐ 32 Rube Oldring	150.00	70.00	19.00
☐ 33 Barney Pelty	150.00	70.00	19.00
☐ 34 Ed Reulbach	150.00	70.00	19.00
☐ 35 John Rowan	150.00	70.00	19.00
☐ 36 David Shean	150.00	70.00	19.00
☐ 37 Tris Speaker	600.00	275.00	75.00
☐ 38 Ed Sweeney	150.00	70.00	19.00
☐ 39 Ed Walsh	400.00	180.00	50.00
☐ 40 Honus Wagner	1000.00	450.00	125.00
☐ 41 Doc White	150.00	70.00	19.00
☐ 42 Ralph Works	150.00	70.00	19.00
☐ 43 Elmer Zacher	150.00	70.00	19.00

1982 K-Mart

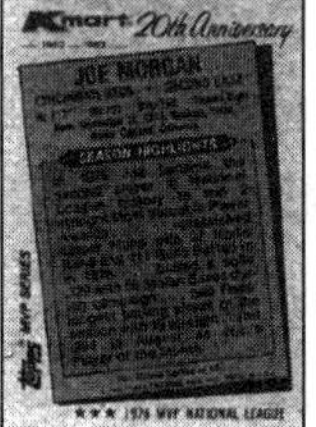

The cards in this 44-card set measure the standard size. This set was mass produced by Topps for K-Mart's 20th Anniversary Celebration and distributed in a custom box. The set features Topps cards of National and American League MVP's from 1962 through 1981. The backs highlight individual MVP winning performances. The dual National League MVP winners of 1979 and special cards commemorating the accomplishments of Drysdale (scoreless consecutive innings pitched streak), Aaron (home run record), and Rose (National League most hits lifetime record) round out the set. The 1975 Fred Lynn card is an original construction from the multi-player "Rookie Outfielders" card of Lynn of 1975. The Maury Wills card number 2, similarly, was created after the fact as Maury was not originally included in the 1962 Topps set. Topps had solved the same problem in essentially the same way in their 1975 set on card number 200.

	MINT	NRMT	EXC
COMPLETE SET (44)	2.00	.90	.25
COMMON CARD (1-44)	.05	.02	.01
☐ 1 Mickey Mantle: 62AL	.75	.35	.09
☐ 2 Maury Wills: 62NL	.10	.05	.01
☐ 3 Elston Howard: 63AL	.05	.02	.01
☐ 4 Sandy Koufax: 63NL	.25	.11	.03
☐ 5 Brooks Robinson: 64AL	.10	.05	.01
☐ 6 Ken Boyer: 64NL	.05	.02	.01
☐ 7 Zoilo Versalles: 65AL	.05	.02	.01
☐ 8 Willie Mays: 65NL	.50	.23	.06
☐ 9 Frank Robinson: 66AL	.10	.05	.01
☐ 10 Bob Clemente: 66NL	.50	.23	.06
☐ 11 Carl Yastrzemski: 67AL	.10	.05	.01
☐ 12 Orlando Cepeda: 67NL	.05	.02	.01
☐ 13 Denny McLain: 68AL	.05	.02	.01
☐ 14 Bob Gibson: 68NL	.10	.05	.01
☐ 15 Harmon Killebrew: 69AL	.10	.05	.01
☐ 16 Willie McCovey: 69NL	.10	.05	.01
☐ 17 Boog Powell: 70AL	.05	.02	.01
☐ 18 Johnny Bench: 70NL	.10	.05	.01
☐ 19 Vida Blue: 71AL	.05	.02	.01
☐ 20 Joe Torre: 71NL	.05	.02	.01
☐ 21 Rich Allen: 72AL	.05	.02	.01
☐ 22 Johnny Bench: 72NL	.10	.05	.01
☐ 23 Reggie Jackson: 73AL	.15	.07	.02
☐ 24 Pete Rose: 73NL	.25	.11	.03
☐ 25 Jeff Burroughs: 74AL	.05	.02	.01
☐ 26 Steve Garvey: 74NL	.05	.02	.01
☐ 27 Fred Lynn: 75AL	.10	.05	.01
☐ 28 Joe Morgan: 75NL	.10	.05	.01
☐ 29 Thurman Munson: 76AL	.05	.02	.01
☐ 30 Joe Morgan: 76NL	.10	.05	.01
☐ 31 Rod Carew: 77AL	.10	.05	.01
☐ 32 George Foster: 77NL	.05	.02	.01
☐ 33 Jim Rice: 78AL	.10	.05	.01
☐ 34 Dave Parker: 78NL	.10	.05	.01
☐ 35 Don Baylor: 79AL	.05	.02	.01
☐ 36 Keith Hernandez: 79NL	.10	.05	.01
☐ 37 Willie Stargell: 79NL	.10	.05	.01
☐ 38 George Brett: 80AL	.40	.18	.05
☐ 39 Mike Schmidt: 80NL	.15	.07	.02
☐ 40 Rollie Fingers: 81AL	.05	.02	.01
☐ 41 Mike Schmidt: 81NL	.15	.07	.02
☐ 42 Don Drysdale '68 HL (Scoreless innings)	.10	.05	.01
☐ 43 Hank Aaron '74 HL (Home run record)	.50	.23	.06
☐ 44 Pete Rose '81 HL (NL most hits)	.15	.07	.02

1987 K-Mart

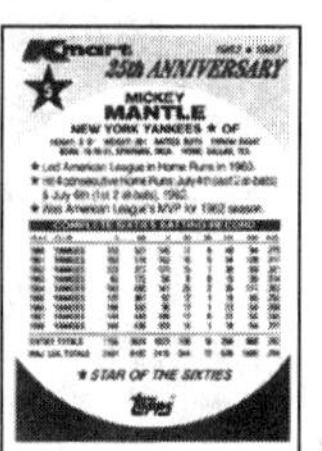

Topps produced this 33-card boxed standard-size set for K-Mart. The set celebrates K-Mart's 25th anniversary and is subtitled, "Stars of the Decades." Card fronts feature a color photo of the player oriented diagonally. Card backs provide statistics for the player's best decade. The set numbering is arranged alphabetically within decade groups: 1960s (1-11), 1970s (12-22), and 1980s (23-33).

	MINT	NRMT	EXC
COMPLETE SET (33)	4.00	1.80	.50
COMMON CARD (1-33)	.05	.02	.01
☐ 1 Hank Aaron	.75	.35	.09
☐ 2 Roberto Clemente	1.00	.45	.12
☐ 3 Bob Gibson	.15	.07	.02
☐ 4 Harmon Killebrew	.15	.07	.02
☐ 5 Mickey Mantle	1.50	.70	.19
☐ 6 Juan Marichal	.15	.07	.02
☐ 7 Roger Maris	.25	.11	.03
☐ 8 Willie Mays	.75	.35	.09
☐ 9 Brooks Robinson	.15	.07	.02
☐ 10 Frank Robinson	.15	.07	.02
☐ 11 Carl Yastrzemski	.15	.07	.02
☐ 12 Johnny Bench	.25	.11	.03
☐ 13 Lou Brock	.25	.11	.03
☐ 14 Rod Carew	.25	.11	.03
☐ 15 Steve Carlton	.25	.11	.03
☐ 16 Reggie Jackson	.40	.18	.05
☐ 17 Jim Palmer	.25	.11	.03
☐ 18 Jim Rice	.10	.05	.01
☐ 19 Pete Rose	.50	.23	.06
☐ 20 Nolan Ryan	1.50	.70	.19
☐ 21 Tom Seaver	.40	.18	.05
☐ 22 Willie Stargell	.25	.11	.03
☐ 23 Wade Boggs	.40	.18	.05
☐ 24 George Brett	.75	.35	.09
☐ 25 Gary Carter	.10	.05	.01
☐ 26 Dwight Gooden	.15	.07	.02
☐ 27 Rickey Henderson	.35	.16	.04
☐ 28 Don Mattingly	.75	.35	.09
☐ 29 Dale Murphy	.15	.07	.02
☐ 30 Eddie Murray	.35	.16	.04
☐ 31 Mike Schmidt	.50	.23	.06
☐ 32 Darryl Strawberry	.15	.07	.02
☐ 33 Fernando Valenzuela	.10	.05	.01

1988 K-Mart

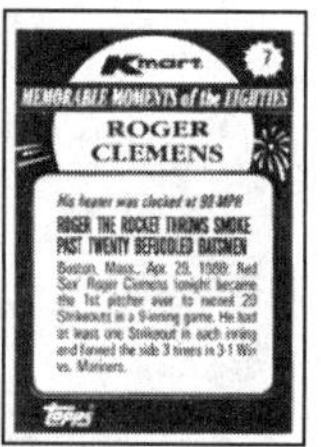

Topps produced this 33-card standard-sized boxed set exclusively for K-Mart. The set is subtitled, "Memorable Moments." Card fronts feature a color photo of the player with the K-Mart logo in lower right corner. Card backs provide details for that player's "memorable moment." The set is packaged in a bright yellow and green box with a checklist on the back panel of the box. The cards in the set were numbered by K-Mart essentially in alphabetical order.

	MINT	NRMT	EXC
COMPLETE SET (33)	4.00	1.80	.50
COMMON CARD (1-33)	.05	.02	.01
☐ 1 George Bell	.05	.02	.01
☐ 2 Wade Boggs	.30	.14	.04
☐ 3 George Brett	.75	.35	.09
☐ 4 Jose Canseco	.30	.14	.04
☐ 5 Jack Clark	.05	.02	.01
☐ 6 Will Clark	.50	.23	.06
☐ 7 Roger Clemens	.50	.23	.06
☐ 8 Vince Coleman	.05	.02	.01
☐ 9 Andre Dawson	.10	.05	.01
☐ 10 Dwight Gooden	.10	.05	.01
☐ 11 Pedro Guerrero	.05	.02	.01
☐ 12 Tony Gwynn	1.25	.55	.16
☐ 13 Rickey Henderson	.40	.18	.05
☐ 14 Keith Hernandez	.05	.02	.01
☐ 15 Don Mattingly	1.25	.55	.16
☐ 16 Mark McGwire	1.00	.45	.12
☐ 17 Paul Molitor	.40	.18	.05
☐ 18 Dale Murphy	.25	.11	.03
☐ 19 Tim Raines	.10	.05	.01
☐ 20 Dave Righetti	.05	.02	.01
☐ 21 Cal Ripken	2.00	.90	.25
☐ 22 Pete Rose	.75	.35	.09
☐ 23 Nolan Ryan	2.00	.90	.25
☐ 24 Benito Santiago	.10	.05	.01
☐ 25 Mike Schmidt	.50	.23	.06
☐ 26 Mike Scott	.05	.02	.01
☐ 27 Kevin Seitzer	.10	.05	.01
☐ 28 Ozzie Smith	1.00	.45	.12
☐ 29 Darryl Strawberry	.10	.05	.01
☐ 30 Rick Sutcliffe	.05	.02	.01
☐ 31 Fernando Valenzuela	.10	.05	.01
☐ 32 Todd Worrell	.05	.02	.01
☐ 33 Robin Yount	.25	.11	.03

1989 K-Mart

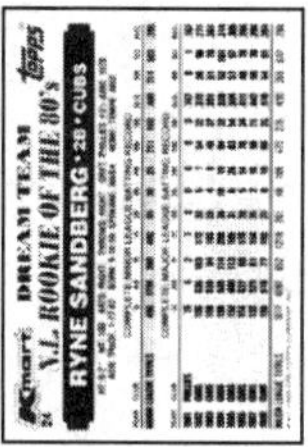

The 1989 K-Mart Dream Team set contains 33 standard-size glossy cards. The fronts are blue. The cards were distributed as a boxed set through K-Mart stores. The set features 11 major league rookies of 1988 plus 11 "American League Rookies of the '80s" and 11 "National League Rookies of the '80s". The complete subject list for the set is provided on the back panel of the custom box.

	MINT	NRMT	EXC
COMPLETE SET (33)	3.00	1.35	.35
COMMON CARD (1-33)	.05	.02	.01
☐ 1 Mark Grace	.50	.23	.06
☐ 2 Ron Gant	.25	.11	.03
☐ 3 Chris Sabo	.05	.02	.01
☐ 4 Walt Weiss	.05	.02	.01
☐ 5 Jay Buhner	.30	.14	.04
☐ 6 Cecil Espy	.05	.02	.01
☐ 7 Dave Gallagher	.05	.02	.01
☐ 8 Damon Berryhill	.05	.02	.01
☐ 9 Tim Belcher	.05	.02	.01
☐ 10 Paul Gibson	.05	.02	.01
☐ 11 Gregg Jefferies	.10	.05	.01
☐ 12 Don Mattingly	1.00	.45	.12
☐ 13 Harold Reynolds	.10	.05	.01
☐ 14 Wade Boggs	.30	.14	.04
☐ 15 Cal Ripken	2.00	.90	.25
☐ 16 Kirby Puckett	1.00	.45	.12
☐ 17 George Bell	.05	.02	.01
☐ 18 Jose Canseco	.30	.14	.04

☐ 19 Terry Steinbach	.10	.05	.01
☐ 20 Roger Clemens	.50	.23	.06
☐ 21 Mark Langston	.05	.02	.01
☐ 22 Harold Baines	.10	.05	.01
☐ 23 Will Clark	.40	.18	.05
☐ 24 Ryne Sandberg	.75	.35	.09
☐ 25 Tim Wallach	.05	.02	.01
☐ 26 Shawon Dunston	.05	.02	.01
☐ 27 Tim Raines	.10	.05	.01
☐ 28 Darryl Strawberry	.10	.05	.01
☐ 29 Tony Gwynn	1.00	.45	.12
☐ 30 Tony Pena	.05	.02	.01
☐ 31 Dwight Gooden	.10	.05	.01
☐ 32 Fernando Valenzuela	.10	.05	.01
☐ 33 Pedro Guerrero	.05	.02	.01

1990 K-Mart

The 1990 K-Mart Superstars set is a 33-card, standard-size set issued for the K-Mart chain by the Topps Company. This set was issued with a piece of gum in the custom set box.

	MINT	NRMT	EXC
COMPLETE SET (33)	4.00	1.80	.50
COMMON CARD (1-33)	.05	.02	.01
☐ 1 Will Clark	.40	.18	.05
☐ 2 Ryne Sandberg	.75	.35	.09
☐ 3 Howard Johnson	.05	.02	.01
☐ 4 Ozzie Smith	.75	.35	.09
☐ 5 Tony Gwynn	1.25	.55	.16
☐ 6 Kevin Mitchell	.05	.02	.01
☐ 7 Jerome Walton	.05	.02	.01
☐ 8 Craig Biggio	.25	.11	.03
☐ 9 Mike Scott	.05	.02	.01
☐ 10 Dwight Gooden	.10	.05	.01
☐ 11 Sid Fernandez	.05	.02	.01
☐ 12 Joe Magrane	.05	.02	.01
☐ 13 Jay Howell	.05	.02	.01
☐ 14 Mark Davis	.05	.02	.01
☐ 15 Pedro Guerrero	.05	.02	.01
☐ 16 Glenn Davis	.05	.02	.01
☐ 17 Don Mattingly	1.25	.55	.16
☐ 18 Julio Franco	.10	.05	.01
☐ 19 Wade Boggs	.25	.11	.03
☐ 20 Cal Ripken	2.00	.90	.25
☐ 21 Jose Canseco	.30	.14	.04
☐ 22 Kirby Puckett	1.25	.55	.16
☐ 23 Rickey Henderson	.25	.11	.03
☐ 24 Mickey Tettleton	.05	.02	.01
☐ 25 Nolan Ryan	2.00	.90	.25
☐ 26 Bret Saberhagen	.10	.05	.01
☐ 27 Jeff Ballard	.05	.02	.01
☐ 28 Chuck Finley	.05	.02	.01
☐ 29 Dennis Eckersley	.10	.05	.01
☐ 30 Dan Plesac	.05	.02	.01
☐ 31 Fred McGriff	.25	.11	.03
☐ 32 Mark McGwire	1.00	.45	.12
☐ 33 Tony LaRussa MG and Roger Craig MG	.05	.02	.01

1989 Kahn's Commemorative Coins

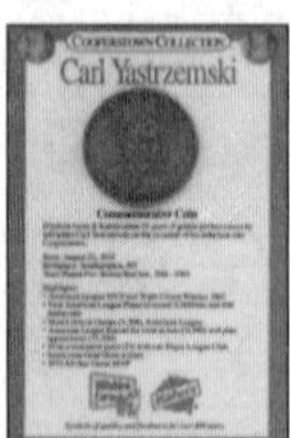

Issued in conjunction with Hillshire Farms, this two card and coin set features all-time leading hitters Carl Yastrzemski and Pete Rose. The cards measure 3 3/4" by 5 1/2" and give highlights of each player's career. The coin is attached to the card is titled "Cooperstown Collection".

	MINT	EXC	G-VG
COMPLETE SET (2)	15.00	6.75	1.85
COMMON CARD (1-2)	5.00	2.20	.60
☐ 1 Pete Rose	10.00	4.50	1.25
☐ 2 Carl Yastrzemski	5.00	2.20	.60

1955 Kahn's

The cards in this six-card set measure 3 1/4" X 4". The 1955 Kahn's Wieners set received very limited distribution. The cards were supposedly given away at an amusement park. The set portrays the players in street clothes rather than in uniform and hence are sometimes referred to as "street clothes" Kahn's. All Kahn's sets from 1955 through 1963 are black and white and contain a 1/2" tab. Cards with the tab still intact are worth approximately 50 percent more than cards without the tab. Cards feature a facsimile autograph of the player on the front. Cards are blank-backed. Only Cincinnati Redlegs players are featured.

	NRMT	VG-E	GOOD
COMPLETE SET (6)	3000.00	1350.00	375.00
COMMON CARD (1-6)	450.00	200.00	55.00
☐ 1 Gus Bell	600.00	275.00	75.00
☐ 2 Ted Kluszewski	750.00	350.00	95.00
☐ 3 Roy McMillan	450.00	200.00	55.00
☐ 4 Joe Nuxhall	500.00	220.00	60.00
☐ 5 Wally Post	450.00	200.00	55.00
☐ 6 Johnny Temple	450.00	200.00	55.00

1956 Kahn's

The cards in this 15-card set measure 3 1/4" X 4". The 1956 Kahn's set was the first set to be issued with Kahn's meat products. The cards are blank backed. The set is distinguished by the old style, short sleeve shirts on the players and the existence of backgounds (Kahn's cards of later years utilize a blank background). Cards which have the tab still intact are worth approximately 50 percent more than cards without the tab. Only Cincinnati Redlegs players are featured. The cards are listed and numbered below in alphabetical order by the subject's name. This set contains a very early Frank Robinson card.

	NRMT	VG-E	GOOD
COMPLETE SET (15)	1700.00	750.00	210.00
COMMON CARD (1-15)	80.00	36.00	10.00
☐ 1 Ed Bailey	80.00	36.00	10.00
☐ 2 Gus Bell	90.00	40.00	11.00
☐ 3 Joe Black	100.00	45.00	12.50
☐ 4 Smoky Burgess	90.00	40.00	11.00
☐ 5 Art Fowler	80.00	36.00	10.00
☐ 6 Herschel Freeman	80.00	36.00	10.00
☐ 7 Ray Jablonski	80.00	36.00	10.00
☐ 8 John Klippstein	80.00	36.00	10.00
☐ 9 Ted Kluszewski	200.00	90.00	25.00
☐ 10 Brooks Lawrence	90.00	40.00	11.00
☐ 11 Roy McMillan	90.00	40.00	11.00
☐ 12 Joe Nuxhall	90.00	40.00	11.00
☐ 13 Wally Post	90.00	40.00	11.00
☐ 14 Frank Robinson	500.00	220.00	60.00
☐ 15 Johnny Temple	90.00	40.00	11.00

1957 Kahn's

The cards in this 29-card set measure 3 1/4" by 4". The 1957 Kahn's Wieners set contains black and white, blank backed, unnumbered cards. The set features only the Cincinnati Redlegs and Pittsburgh Pirates. The cards feature a light background. Each card features a facsimile autograph of the player on the front. The Groat card exists with a "Richard Groat" autograph and also exists with the printed name "Dick Groat" on the card. The set price inlcudes both Groats. The catalog designation is F155-3. The cards are listed and numbered below in alphabetical order by the subject's name. A Bill Mazeroski card was printed during this, his Rookie Card season.

	NRMT	VG-E	GOOD
COMPLETE SET (29)	2800.00	1250.00	350.00
COMMON CARD (1-29)	60.00	27.00	7.50
☐ 1 Tom Acker	60.00	27.00	7.50
☐ 2 Ed Bailey	60.00	27.00	7.50
☐ 3 Gus Bell	75.00	34.00	9.50
☐ 4 Smoky Burgess	75.00	34.00	9.50
☐ 5 Roberto Clemente	1000.00	450.00	125.00
☐ 6 George Crowe	60.00	27.00	7.50
☐ 7 Elroy Face	90.00	40.00	11.00
☐ 8 Herschel Freeman	60.00	27.00	7.50
☐ 9 Bob Friend	75.00	34.00	9.50
☐ 10 Dick Groat	90.00	40.00	11.00
☐ 11 Richard Groat	175.00	80.00	22.00
☐ 12 Don Gross	60.00	27.00	7.50
☐ 13 Warren Hacker	60.00	27.00	7.50
☐ 14 Don Hoak	75.00	34.00	9.50
☐ 15 Hal Jeffcoat	60.00	27.00	7.50
☐ 16 Ron Kline	60.00	27.00	7.50
☐ 17 John Klippstein	60.00	27.00	7.50
☐ 18 Ted Kluszewski	175.00	80.00	22.00
☐ 19 Brooks Lawrence	75.00	34.00	9.50
☐ 20 Dale Long	60.00	27.00	7.50
☐ 21 Bill Mazeroski	200.00	90.00	25.00
☐ 22 Roy McMillan	75.00	34.00	9.50
☐ 23 Joe Nuxhall	60.00	27.00	7.50
☐ 24 Wally Post	75.00	34.00	9.50
☐ 25 Frank Robinson	400.00	180.00	50.00
☐ 26 John Temple	75.00	34.00	9.50
☐ 27 Frank Thomas	60.00	27.00	7.50
☐ 28 Bob Thurman	60.00	27.00	7.50
☐ 29 Lee Walls	60.00	27.00	7.50

1958 Kahn's

The cards in this 29-card set measure approximately 3 1/4" X 4". The 1958 Kahn's Wieners set of unnumbered, black and white cards features Cincinnati Redlegs, Philadelphia Phillies and Pittsburgh Pirates. The backs present a story for each player entitled "My Greatest Thrill in Baseball". A method of distinguishing 1958 Kahn's from 1959 Kahn's is that the word Wieners is found on the front of the 1958 but not on the front of the 1959 cards. Cards of Wally Post, Charlie Rabe and Frank Thomas are somewhat more difficult to find and are designated SP in the checklist below. The cards are listed and numbered below in alphabetical order by the subject's name.

	NRMT	VG-E	GOOD
COMPLETE SET (29)	3200.00	1450.00	400.00
COMMON CARD (1-29)	50.00	22.00	6.25
☐ 1 Ed Bailey	50.00	22.00	6.25
☐ 2 Gene Baker	50.00	22.00	6.25
☐ 3 Gus Bell	60.00	27.00	7.50
☐ 4 Smoky Burgess	60.00	27.00	7.50
☐ 5 Roberto Clemente	750.00	350.00	95.00
☐ 6 George Crowe	60.00	27.00	7.50
☐ 7 Elroy Face	75.00	34.00	9.50
☐ 8 Hank Foiles	50.00	22.00	6.25
☐ 9 Dee Fondy	50.00	22.00	6.25
☐ 10 Bob Friend	60.00	27.00	7.50
☐ 11 Dick Groat	75.00	34.00	9.50
☐ 12 Harvey Haddix	60.00	27.00	7.50
☐ 13 Don Hoak	50.00	22.00	6.25
☐ 14 Hal Jeffcoat	50.00	22.00	6.25
☐ 15 Ron Kline	50.00	22.00	6.25
☐ 16 Ted Kluszewski	125.00	55.00	15.50
☐ 17 Vernon Law	60.00	27.00	7.50
☐ 18 Brooks Lawrence	60.00	27.00	7.50
☐ 19 Bill Mazeroski	100.00	45.00	12.50
☐ 20 Roy McMillan	60.00	27.00	7.50
☐ 21 Joe Nuxhall	60.00	27.00	7.50
☐ 22 Wally Post SP	350.00	160.00	45.00
☐ 23 John Powers	50.00	22.00	6.25
☐ 24 Bob Purkey	50.00	22.00	6.25
☐ 25 Charlie Rabe SP	350.00	160.00	45.00
☐ 26 Frank Robinson	250.00	110.00	31.00
☐ 27 Bob Skinner	50.00	22.00	6.25
☐ 28 Johnny Temple	60.00	27.00	7.50
☐ 29 Frank Thomas SP	350.00	160.00	45.00

1959 Kahn's

The cards in this 38-card set measure approximately 3 1/4" X 4". The 1959 Kahn's set features members of the Cincinnati Reds, Cleveland Indians and Pittsburgh Pirates. Backs feature stories entitled "The Toughest Play I have to Make," or "The Toughest Batter I Have To Face." The Brodowski card is very scarce while Haddix, Held and McLish are considered quite difficult to obtain; these scarcities are designated SP in the checklist below. The cards are listed and numbered below in alphabetical order by the subject's name.

	NRMT	VG-E	GOOD
COMPLETE SET (38)	4500.00	2000.00	550.00
COMMON CARD (1-38)	50.00	22.00	6.25
☐ 1 Ed Bailey	50.00	22.00	6.25
☐ 2 Gary Bell	50.00	22.00	6.25
☐ 3 Gus Bell	60.00	27.00	7.50
☐ 4 Dick Brodowski SP	600.00	275.00	75.00
☐ 5 Smoky Burgess	60.00	27.00	7.50
☐ 6 Roberto Clemente	600.00	275.00	75.00
☐ 7 Rocky Colavito	125.00	55.00	15.50
☐ 8 Elroy Face	75.00	34.00	9.50
☐ 9 Bob Friend	60.00	27.00	7.50
☐ 10 Joe Gordon MG	60.00	27.00	7.50
☐ 11 Jim Grant	60.00	27.00	7.50
☐ 12 Dick Groat	75.00	34.00	9.50
☐ 13 Harvey Haddix SP (Blank back)	400.00	180.00	50.00
☐ 14 Woodie Held SP	400.00	180.00	50.00
☐ 15 Don Hoak	50.00	22.00	6.25
☐ 16 Ron Kline	50.00	22.00	6.25
☐ 17 Ted Kluszewski	125.00	55.00	15.50
☐ 18 Vernon Law	60.00	27.00	7.50
☐ 19 Jerry Lynch	50.00	22.00	6.25
☐ 20 Billy Martin	125.00	55.00	15.50
☐ 21 Bill Mazeroski	100.00	45.00	12.50
☐ 22 Cal McLish SP	400.00	180.00	50.00
☐ 23 Roy McMillan	50.00	22.00	6.25
☐ 24 Minnie Minoso	100.00	45.00	12.50
☐ 25 Russ Nixon	50.00	22.00	6.25
☐ 26 Joe Nuxhall	60.00	27.00	7.50
☐ 27 Jim Perry	75.00	34.00	9.50
☐ 28 Vada Pinson	100.00	45.00	12.50
☐ 29 Vic Power	50.00	22.00	6.25
☐ 30 Bob Purkey	50.00	22.00	6.25
☐ 31 Frank Robinson	200.00	90.00	25.00
☐ 32 Herb Score	75.00	34.00	9.50
☐ 33 Bob Skinner	50.00	22.00	6.25
☐ 34 George Strickland	50.00	22.00	6.25
☐ 35 Dick Stuart	60.00	27.00	7.50
☐ 36 Johnny Temple	50.00	22.00	6.25
☐ 37 Frank Thomas	60.00	27.00	7.50
☐ 38 George Witt	50.00	22.00	6.25

1960 Kahn's

The cards in this 42-card set measure 3 1/4" X 4". The 1960 Kahn's set features players of the Chicago Cubs, Chicago White Sox, Cincinnati Redlegs, Cleveland Indians, Pittsburgh Pirates and St. Louis Cardinals. The backs give vital player information and records through the 1959 season. Kline appears with either St. Louis or Pittsburgh. The set price includes both Kline's. The Harvey Kuenn card in this set appears with a blank back and is scarce. The cards are listed and numbered below in alphabetical order by the subject's name.

	NRMT	VG-E	GOOD
COMPLETE SET (43)	2000.00	900.00	250.00
COMMON CARD (1-42)	25.00	11.00	3.10
☐ 1 Ed Bailey	25.00	11.00	3.10
☐ 2 Gary Bell	25.00	11.00	3.10
☐ 3 Gus Bell	30.00	13.50	3.70
☐ 4 Smoky Burgess	30.00	13.50	3.70
☐ 5 Gino Cimoli	25.00	11.00	3.10
☐ 6 Roberto Clemente	400.00	180.00	50.00
☐ 7 Roy Face	30.00	13.50	3.70
☐ 8 Tito Francona	25.00	11.00	3.10
☐ 9 Bob Friend	30.00	13.50	3.70
☐ 10 Jim Grant	30.00	13.50	3.70
☐ 11 Dick Groat	40.00	18.00	5.00
☐ 12 Harvey Haddix	30.00	13.50	3.70
☐ 13 Woodie Held	25.00	11.00	3.10
☐ 14 Bill Henry	25.00	11.00	3.10
☐ 15 Don Hoak	25.00	11.00	3.10
☐ 16 Jay Hook	25.00	11.00	3.10
☐ 17 Eddie Kasko	25.00	11.00	3.10
☐ 18A Ron Kline (Pittsburgh)	50.00	22.00	6.25
☐ 18B Ron Kline (St. Louis)	50.00	22.00	6.25
☐ 19 Ted Kluszewski	60.00	27.00	7.50
☐ 20 Harvey Kuenn SP (Blank back)	350.00	160.00	45.00
☐ 21 Vernon Law	35.00	16.00	4.40
☐ 22 Brooks Lawrence	30.00	13.50	3.70
☐ 23 Jerry Lynch	25.00	11.00	3.10
☐ 24 Billy Martin	60.00	27.00	7.50
☐ 25 Bill Mazeroski	50.00	22.00	6.25
☐ 26 Cal McLish	25.00	11.00	3.10
☐ 27 Roy McMillan	25.00	11.00	3.10
☐ 28 Don Newcombe	40.00	18.00	5.00
☐ 29 Russ Nixon	30.00	13.50	3.70
☐ 30 Joe Nuxhall	30.00	13.50	3.70
☐ 31 Jim O'Toole	25.00	11.00	3.10
☐ 32 Jim Perry	30.00	13.50	3.70
☐ 33 Vada Pinson	50.00	22.00	6.25

☐ 34 Vic Power	25.00	11.00	3.10
☐ 35 Bob Purkey	25.00	11.00	3.10
☐ 36 Frank Robinson	150.00	70.00	19.00
☐ 37 Herb Score	30.00	13.50	3.70
☐ 38 Bob Skinner	25.00	11.00	3.10
☐ 39 Dick Stuart	30.00	13.50	3.70
☐ 40 Johnny Temple	30.00	13.50	3.70
☐ 41 Frank Thomas	30.00	13.50	3.70
☐ 42 Lee Walls	25.00	11.00	3.10

1961 Kahn's

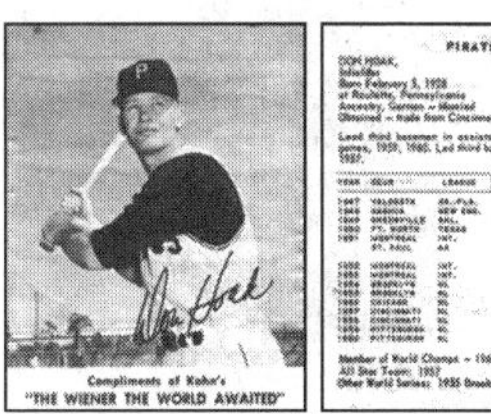

The cards in this 43-card set measure approximately 3 1/4" X 4". The 1961 Kahn's Wieners set of black and white, unnumbered cards features members of the Cincinnati Reds, Cleveland Indians and Pittsburgh Pirates. This year was the first year Kahn's made complete sets available to the public; hence they are more available, especially in the better condition grades than the Kahn's of the previous years. The backs give vital player information and year by year career statistics through 1960. The catalog designation is F155-7. The cards are listed and numbered below in alphabetical order by the subject's name.

	NRMT	VG-E	GOOD
COMPLETE SET (43)	850.00	375.00	105.00
COMMON CARD (1-43)	12.50	5.50	1.55
☐ 1 John Antonelli	12.50	5.50	1.55
☐ 2 Ed Bailey	12.50	5.50	1.55
☐ 3 Gary Bell	12.50	5.50	1.55
☐ 4 Gus Bell	15.00	6.75	1.85
☐ 5 Jim Brosnan	15.00	6.75	1.85
☐ 6 Smoky Burgess	15.00	6.75	1.85
☐ 7 Gino Cimoli	12.50	5.50	1.55
☐ 8 Roberto Clemente	300.00	135.00	38.00
☐ 9 Gordie Coleman	12.50	5.50	1.55
☐ 10 Jimmy Dykes MG	15.00	6.75	1.85
☐ 11 Roy Face	15.00	6.75	1.85
☐ 12 Tito Francona	12.50	5.50	1.55
☐ 13 Gene Freese	12.50	5.50	1.55
☐ 14 Bob Friend	15.00	6.75	1.85
☐ 15 Jim Grant	15.00	6.75	1.85
☐ 16 Dick Groat	15.00	6.75	1.85
☐ 17 Harvey Haddix	15.00	6.75	1.85
☐ 18 Woodie Held	12.50	5.50	1.55
☐ 19 Don Hoak	12.50	5.50	1.55
☐ 20 Jay Hook	12.50	5.50	1.55
☐ 21 Joey Jay	12.50	5.50	1.55
☐ 22 Eddie Kasko	12.50	5.50	1.55
☐ 23 Willie Kirkland	12.50	5.50	1.55
☐ 24 Vernon Law	15.00	6.75	1.85
☐ 25 Jerry Lynch	12.50	5.50	1.55
☐ 26 Jim Maloney	20.00	9.00	2.50
☐ 27 Bill Mazeroski	30.00	13.50	3.70
☐ 28 Wilmer Mizell	15.00	6.75	1.85
☐ 29 Rocky Nelson	12.50	5.50	1.55
☐ 30 Jim O'Toole	12.50	5.50	1.55
☐ 31 Jim Perry	15.00	6.75	1.85
☐ 32 Bubba Phillips	12.50	5.50	1.55
☐ 33 Vada Pinson	25.00	11.00	3.10
☐ 34 Wally Post	12.50	5.50	1.55
☐ 35 Vic Power	12.50	5.50	1.55
☐ 36 Bob Purkey	12.50	5.50	1.55
☐ 37 Frank Robinson	100.00	45.00	12.50
☐ 38 John Romano	12.50	5.50	1.55
☐ 39 Dick Schofield	12.50	5.50	1.55
☐ 40 Bob Skinner	12.50	5.50	1.55
☐ 41 Hal Smith	12.50	5.50	1.55
☐ 42 Dick Stuart	15.00	6.75	1.85
☐ 43 Johnny Temple	12.50	5.50	1.55

1962 Kahn's

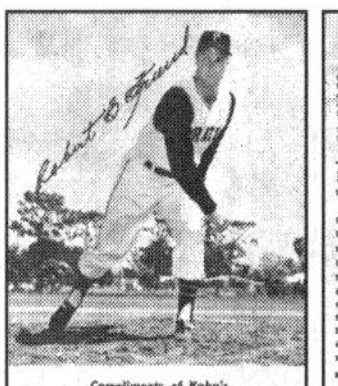

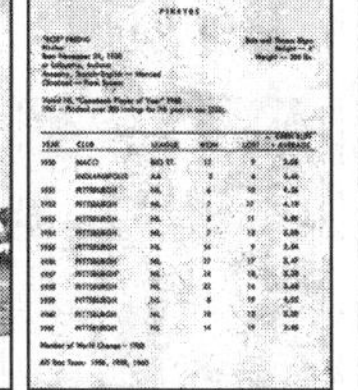

The cards in this 38-card set measure approximately 3 1/4" X 4". The 1962 Kahn's Wieners set of black and white, unnumbered cards features Cincinnati, Cleveland, Minnesota and Pittsburgh players. Card numbers 1 Bell, 33 Power and 34 Purkey exist in two different forms; these variations are listed in the checklist below. The backs of the cards contain career information. The catalog designation is F155-8. The set price below includes the set with all variation cards. The cards are listed and numbered below in alphabetical order by the subject's name.

	NRMT	VG-E	GOOD
COMPLETE SET (41)	1100.00	500.00	140.00
COMMON CARD (1-38)	10.00	4.50	1.25
☐ 1A Gary Bell (With fat man)	100.00	45.00	12.50
☐ 1B Gary Bell (No fat man)	40.00	18.00	5.00
☐ 2 Jim Brosnan	12.50	5.50	1.55
☐ 3 Smoky Burgess	12.50	5.50	1.55
☐ 4 Chico Cardenas	12.50	5.50	1.55
☐ 5 Roberto Clemente	250.00	110.00	31.00
☐ 6 Ty Cline	10.00	4.50	1.25
☐ 7 Gordon Coleman	12.50	5.50	1.55
☐ 8 Dick Donovan	10.00	4.50	1.25
☐ 9 John Edwards	10.00	4.50	1.25
☐ 10 Tito Francona	10.00	4.50	1.25
☐ 11 Gene Freese	10.00	4.50	1.25
☐ 12 Bob Friend	12.50	5.50	1.55
☐ 13 Joe Gibbon	100.00	45.00	12.50
☐ 14 Jim Grant	12.50	5.50	1.55
☐ 15 Dick Groat	15.00	6.75	1.85
☐ 16 Harvey Haddix	12.50	5.50	1.55
☐ 17 Woodie Held	10.00	4.50	1.25
☐ 18 Bill Henry	10.00	4.50	1.25
☐ 19 Don Hoak	10.00	4.50	1.25
☐ 20 Ken Hunt	10.00	4.50	1.25
☐ 21 Joey Jay	10.00	4.50	1.25
☐ 22 Eddie Kasko	10.00	4.50	1.25
☐ 23 Willie Kirkland	10.00	4.50	1.25
☐ 24 Barry Latman	10.00	4.50	1.25
☐ 25 Jerry Lynch	10.00	4.50	1.25
☐ 26 Jim Maloney	15.00	6.75	1.85
☐ 27 Bill Mazeroski	25.00	11.00	3.10
☐ 28 Jim O'Toole	10.00	4.50	1.25
☐ 29 Jim Perry	12.50	5.50	1.55
☐ 30 Bubba Phillips	10.00	4.50	1.25
☐ 31 Vada Pinson	15.00	6.75	1.85
☐ 32 Wally Post	10.00	4.50	1.25
☐ 33A Vic Power (Indians)	40.00	18.00	5.00
☐ 33B Vic Power (Twins)	100.00	45.00	12.50
☐ 34A Bob Purkey (With autograph)	40.00	18.00	5.00
☐ 34B Bob Purkey (No autograph)	100.00	45.00	12.50
☐ 35 Frank Robinson	100.00	45.00	12.50
☐ 36 John Romano	10.00	4.50	1.25
☐ 37 Dick Stuart	12.50	5.50	1.55
☐ 38 Bill Virdon	15.00	6.75	1.85

1963 Kahn's

The cards in this 30-card set measure approximately 3 1/4" X 4". The 1963 Kahn's Wieners set of black and white, unnumbered cards features players from Cincinnati, Cleveland, St. Louis, Pittsburgh and the New York Yankees. The cards feature a white border around the picture of the players. The backs contain career information. The catalog designation for this set is F155-10. The cards are listed and numbered below in alphabetical order by the subject's name.

	NRMT	VG-E	GOOD
COMPLETE SET (30)	600.00	275.00	75.00
COMMON CARD (1-30)	10.00	4.50	1.25
☐ 1 Bob Bailey	10.00	4.50	1.25
☐ 2 Don Blasingame	10.00	4.50	1.25
☐ 3 Clete Boyer	15.00	6.75	1.85
☐ 4 Smoky Burgess	12.50	5.50	1.55
☐ 5 Chico Cardenas	12.50	5.50	1.55
☐ 6 Roberto Clemente	250.00	110.00	31.00
☐ 7 Donn Clendenon	12.50	5.50	1.55
☐ 8 Gordon Coleman	12.50	5.50	1.55
☐ 9 John Edwards	10.00	4.50	1.25
☐ 10 Gene Freese	10.00	4.50	1.25
☐ 11 Bob Friend	12.50	5.50	1.55
☐ 12 Joe Gibbon	10.00	4.50	1.25
☐ 13 Dick Groat	15.00	6.75	1.85
☐ 14 Harvey Haddix	12.50	5.50	1.55
☐ 15 Elston Howard	25.00	11.00	3.10
☐ 16 Joey Jay	10.00	4.50	1.25
☐ 17 Eddie Kasko	10.00	4.50	1.25
☐ 18 Tony Kubek	30.00	13.50	3.70
☐ 19 Jerry Lynch	10.00	4.50	1.25
☐ 20 Jim Maloney	15.00	6.75	1.85
☐ 21 Bill Mazeroski	25.00	11.00	3.10
☐ 22 Joe Nuxhall	12.50	5.50	1.55
☐ 23 Jim O'Toole	10.00	4.50	1.25
☐ 24 Vada Pinson	20.00	9.00	2.50
☐ 25 Bob Purkey	10.00	4.50	1.25
☐ 26 Bobby Richardson	30.00	13.50	3.70
☐ 27 Frank Robinson	100.00	45.00	12.50
☐ 28 Bill Stafford	10.00	4.50	1.25
☐ 29 Ralph Terry	12.50	5.50	1.55
☐ 30 Bill Virdon	12.50	5.50	1.55

1964 Kahn's

The cards in this 31-card set measure 3" X 3 1/2". The 1964 Kahn's set marks the beginning of the full color cards and the elimination of the tabs which existed on previous Kahn's cards. The set of unnumbered cards contains player information through the 1963 season on the backs. The set features Cincinnati, Cleveland and Pittsburgh players. The cards are listed and numbered below in alphabetical order by the subject's name. An early card of Pete Rose highlights this set.

	NRMT	VG-E	GOOD
COMPLETE SET (31)	900.00	400.00	110.00
COMMON CARD (1-31)	10.00	4.50	1.25
☐ 1 Max Alvis	10.00	4.50	1.25
☐ 2 Bob Bailey	10.00	4.50	1.25
☐ 3 Chico Cardenas	12.50	5.50	1.55
☐ 4 Roberto Clemente	250.00	110.00	31.00
☐ 5 Donn Clendenon	12.50	5.50	1.55
☐ 6 Vic Davalillo	10.00	4.50	1.25
☐ 7 Dick Donovan	10.00	4.50	1.25
☐ 8 John Edwards	10.00	4.50	1.25
☐ 9 Bob Friend	12.50	5.50	1.55
☐ 10 Jim Grant	12.50	5.50	1.55
☐ 11 Tommy Harper	12.50	5.50	1.55
☐ 12 Woodie Held	12.50	5.50	1.55
☐ 13 Joey Jay	10.00	4.50	1.25
☐ 14 Jack Kralick	10.00	4.50	1.25
☐ 15 Jerry Lynch	10.00	4.50	1.25
☐ 16 Jim Maloney	12.50	5.50	1.55
☐ 17 Bill Mazeroski	25.00	11.00	3.10
☐ 18 Alvin McBean	10.00	4.50	1.25
☐ 19 Joe Nuxhall	12.50	5.50	1.55
☐ 20 Jim Pagliaroni	10.00	4.50	1.25
☐ 21 Vada Pinson	20.00	9.00	2.50
☐ 22 Bob Purkey	10.00	4.50	1.25
☐ 23 Pedro Ramos	10.00	4.50	1.25
☐ 24 Frank Robinson	100.00	45.00	12.50
☐ 25 John Romano	10.00	4.50	1.25
☐ 26 Pete Rose	350.00	160.00	45.00
☐ 27 John Tsitouris	10.00	4.50	1.25
☐ 28 Bob Veale	12.50	5.50	1.55
☐ 29 Bill Virdon	12.50	5.50	1.55
☐ 30 Leon Wagner	10.00	4.50	1.25
☐ 31 Fred Whitfield	10.00	4.50	1.25

1965 Kahn's

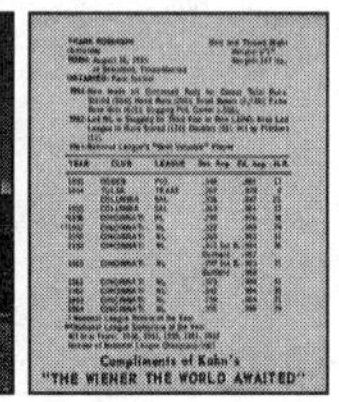

The cards in this 45-card set measure 3" X 3 1/2". The 1965 Kahn's set contains full-color, unnumbered cards. The set features Cincinnati, Cleveland, Pittsburgh and Milwaukee players. Backs contain statistical information through the 1964 season. The cards are listed and numbered below in alphabetical order by the subject's name.

	NRMT	VG-E	GOOD
COMPLETE SET (45)	1000.00	450.00	125.00
COMMON CARD (1-45)	10.00	4.50	1.25
☐ 1 Henry Aaron	150.00	70.00	19.00
☐ 2 Max Alvis	12.50	5.50	1.55
☐ 3 Joe Azcue	10.00	4.50	1.25
☐ 4 Bob Bailey	10.00	4.50	1.25
☐ 5 Frank Bolling	10.00	4.50	1.25
☐ 6 Chico Cardenas	12.50	5.50	1.55
☐ 7 Rico Carty	15.00	6.75	1.85
☐ 8 Donn Clendenon	12.50	5.50	1.55
☐ 9 Tony Cloninger	12.50	5.50	1.55
☐ 10 Gordon Coleman	10.00	4.50	1.25
☐ 11 Vic Davalillo	10.00	4.50	1.25
☐ 12 John Edwards	10.00	4.50	1.25
☐ 13 Sammy Ellis	10.00	4.50	1.25
☐ 14 Bob Friend	12.50	5.50	1.55
☐ 15 Tommy Harper	12.50	5.50	1.55
☐ 16 Chuck Hinton	10.00	4.50	1.25
☐ 17 Dick Howser	12.50	5.50	1.55
☐ 18 Joey Jay	10.00	4.50	1.25
☐ 19 Deron Johnson	12.50	5.50	1.55
☐ 20 Jack Kralick	10.00	4.50	1.25
☐ 21 Denver LeMaster	10.00	4.50	1.25
☐ 22 Jerry Lynch	10.00	4.50	1.25
☐ 23 Jim Maloney	15.00	6.75	1.85
☐ 24 Lee Maye	10.00	4.50	1.25
☐ 25 Bill Mazeroski	25.00	11.00	3.10
☐ 26 Alvin McBean	10.00	4.50	1.25
☐ 27 Bill McCool	10.00	4.50	1.25
☐ 28 Sam McDowell	15.00	6.75	1.85
☐ 29 Don McMahon	10.00	4.50	1.25
☐ 30 Denis Menke	10.00	4.50	1.25
☐ 31 Joe Nuxhall	12.50	5.50	1.55
☐ 32 Gene Oliver	10.00	4.50	1.25
☐ 33 Jim O'Toole	10.00	4.50	1.25
☐ 34 Jim Pagliaroni	10.00	4.50	1.25
☐ 35 Vada Pinson	20.00	9.00	2.50
☐ 36 Frank Robinson	100.00	45.00	12.50
☐ 37 Pete Rose	200.00	90.00	25.00
☐ 38 Willie Stargell	100.00	45.00	12.50
☐ 39 Ralph Terry	12.50	5.50	1.55
☐ 40 Luis Tiant	20.00	9.00	2.50
☐ 41 Joe Torre	25.00	11.00	3.10
☐ 42 John Tsitouris	10.00	4.50	1.25
☐ 43 Bob Veale	12.50	5.50	1.55
☐ 44 Bill Virdon	12.50	5.50	1.55
☐ 45 Leon Wagner	10.00	4.50	1.25

1966 Kahn's

The cards in this 32-card set measure 2 13/16" X 4". 1966 Kahn's full-color, unnumbered set features players from Atlanta, Cincinnati, Cleveland and Pittsburgh. The set is identified by yellow and white vertical stripes and the name Kahn's written in red across a red rose at the top. The cards contain a 1 5/16" ad in the form of a tab. Cards with the ad (tab) are worth twice as much as cards without the ad. (double the prices below) The cards are listed and numbered below in alphabetical order by the subject's name.

	NRMT	VG-E	GOOD
COMPLETE SET (32)	600.00	275.00	75.00
COMMON CARD (1-32)	8.00	3.60	1.00
☐ 1 Henry Aaron Portrait, no windbreaker under jersey	100.00	45.00	12.50
☐ 2 Felipe Alou: Braves Full pose batting screen in background	15.00	6.75	1.85
☐ 3 Max Alvis: Indians Kneeling full pose with bat no patch on jersey)	8.00	3.60	1.00
☐ 4 Bob Bailey	8.00	3.60	1.00
☐ 5 Wade Blasingame	8.00	3.60	1.00
☐ 6 Frank Bolling	8.00	3.60	1.00
☐ 7 Chico Cardenas: Reds Fielding feet at base	10.00	4.50	1.25
☐ 8 Roberto Clemente	125.00	55.00	15.50
☐ 9 Tony Cloninger: Braves Pitching foulpole in background	10.00	4.50	1.25
☐ 10 Vic Davalillo	8.00	3.60	1.00
☐ 11 John Edwards: Reds Catching	8.00	3.60	1.00
☐ 12 Sam Ellis: Reds White hat	8.00	3.60	1.00
☐ 13 Pedro Gonzalez	8.00	3.60	1.00
☐ 14 Tommy Harper: Reds Arm cocked	10.00	4.50	1.25
☐ 15 Deron Johnson: Reds Batting with batting cage in background	10.00	4.50	1.25
☐ 16 Mack Jones	8.00	3.60	1.00
☐ 17 Denver Lemaster	8.00	3.60	1.00
☐ 18 Jim Maloney: Reds Pitching white hat	10.00	4.50	1.25
☐ 19 Bill Mazeroski: Pirates Throwing	15.00	6.75	1.85
☐ 20 Bill McCool: Reds White hat	8.00	3.60	1.00
☐ 21 Sam McDowell: Indians Kneeling	10.00	4.50	1.25
☐ 22 Denis Menke: Braves White windbreaker under jersey	8.00	3.60	1.00
☐ 23 Joe Nuxhall	10.00	4.50	1.25
☐ 24 Jim Pagliaroni: Pirates Catching	8.00	3.60	1.00

	NRMT	VG-E	GOOD
☐ 25 Milt Pappas	10.00	4.50	1.25
☐ 26 Vada Pinson: Reds (Fielding ball on ground	15.00	6.75	1.85
☐ 27 Pete Rose: Reds With glove	125.00	55.00	15.50
☐ 28 Sonny Siebert: Indians Pitching signature at feet	10.00	4.50	1.25
☐ 29 Willie Stargell: Pirates Batting clouds in sky	40.00	18.00	5.00
☐ 30 Joe Torre: Braves Catching with hand on mask	20.00	9.00	2.50
☐ 31 Bob Veale: Pirates Hands at knee with glasses	10.00	4.50	1.25
☐ 32 Fred Whitfield	8.00	3.60	1.00

1967 Kahn's

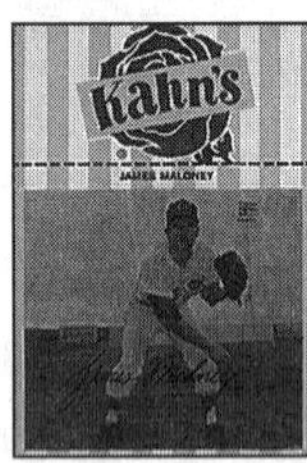

The cards in this 41-player set measure 2 13/16" X 4". The 1967 Kahn's set of full-color, unnumbered cards is almost identical in style to the 1966 issue. Different meat products had different background colors (yellow and white stripes, red and white stripes, etc.). The set features players from Atlanta, Cincinnati, Cleveland, New York Mets and Pittsburgh. Cards with the ads (see 1966 set) are worth twice as much as cards without the ad, i.e., double the prices below. The complete set price below includes all variations. The cards are listed and numbered below in alphabetical order by the subject's name.

	NRMT	VG-E	GOOD
COMPLETE SET (51)	800.00	350.00	100.00
COMMON CARD (1-41)	8.00	3.60	1.00
☐ 1A Henry Aaron: Braves (Swinging pose, batting glove, ball, and hat on ground)	100.00	45.00	12.50
☐ 1B Henry Aaron: Braves (Swinging pose, batting glove, ball, and hat on ground; Cut Along Dotted Lines printed on lower tab)	125.00	55.00	15.50
☐ 2 Gene Alley: Pirates (Portrait)	10.00	4.50	1.25
☐ 3 Felipe Alou: Braves (Full pose, bat on shoulder)	15.00	6.75	1.85
☐ 4A Matty Alou: Pirates (Portrait with bat, Matio Rojas Alou"; yellow stripes)	10.00	4.50	1.25
☐ 4B Matty Alou: Pirates (Portrait with bat Matio Rojas Alou"; red stripes)	12.50	5.50	1.55
☐ 5 Max Alvis: Indians (Fielding, hands on knees)	8.00	3.60	1.00
☐ 6A Ken Boyer (Batting righthanded; autograph at waist)	12.50	5.50	1.55
☐ 6B Ken Boyer (Batting righthanded; autograph at shoulders; Cut Along Dotted Lines printed on lower tab)	15.00	6.75	1.85
☐ 7 Chico Cardenas: Reds (Fielding hand on knee)	10.00	4.50	1.25
☐ 8 Rico Carty	10.00	4.50	1.25
☐ 9 Tony Cloninger: Braves (Pitching, no foul-pole in background)	10.00	4.50	1.25
☐ 10 Tommy Davis	10.00	4.50	1.25
☐ 11 John Edwards: Reds (Kneeling with bat)	8.00	3.60	1.00
☐ 12A Sam Ellis: Reds (All red hat)	8.00	3.60	1.00
☐ 12B Sam Ellis: Reds (All red hat; Cut Along Dotted Lines printed on lower tab)	10.00	4.50	1.25
☐ 13 Jack Fisher	8.00	3.60	1.00
☐ 14 Steve Hargan: Indians (Pitching, no clouds blue sky)	8.00	3.60	1.00
☐ 15 Tommy Harper: Reds (Fielding, glove on ground)	10.00	4.50	1.25
☐ 16A Tommy Helms (Batting righthanded; top of bat visible)	10.00	4.50	1.25
☐ 16B Tommy Helms (Batting righthanded; bat chopped above hat; Cut Along Dotted Lines printed on lower tab)	12.50	5.50	1.55
☐ 17 Deron Johnson: Reds (Batting, blue sky)	10.00	4.50	1.25
☐ 18 Ken Johnson	8.00	3.60	1.00
☐ 19 Cleon Jones	10.00	4.50	1.25
☐ 20A Ed Kranepool (Ready for throw; yellow stripes)	10.00	4.50	1.25
☐ 20B Ed Kranepool (Ready for throw; red stripes)	10.00	4.50	1.25
☐ 21A Jim Maloney: Reds (Pitching, red hat, follow thru delivery; yellow stripes)	10.00	4.50	1.25
☐ 21B Jim Maloney: Reds (Pitching, red hat, follow thru delivery; red stripes)	12.50	5.50	1.55
☐ 22 Lee May: Reds (Hands on knee)	10.00	4.50	1.25
☐ 23A Bill Mazeroski: Pirates (Portrait; autograph below waist)	20.00	9.00	2.50
☐ 23B Bill Mazeroski: Pirates (Portrait; autograph above waist; Cut Along Dotted Lines printed on lower tab)	25.00	11.00	3.10
☐ 24 Bill McCool: Reds (Red hat, left hand out)	8.00	3.60	1.00
☐ 25 Sam McDowell: Indians (Pitching, left hand under glove)	12.50	5.50	1.55
☐ 26 Denis Menke: Braves (Blue sleeves)	8.00	3.60	1.00
☐ 27 Jim Pagliaroni: Pirates (Catching no chest protector)	8.00	3.60	1.00
☐ 28 Don Pavletich	8.00	3.60	1.00
☐ 29 Tony Perez: Reds (Throwing)	40.00	18.00	5.00
☐ 30 Vada Pinson: Reds (Ready to throw)	12.50	5.50	1.55
☐ 31 Dennis Ribant	8.00	3.60	1.00
☐ 32 Pete Rose: Reds (Batting)	125.00	55.00	15.50
☐ 33 Art Shamsky: Reds	8.00	3.60	1.00
☐ 34 Bob Shaw	8.00	3.60	1.00
☐ 35 Sonny Siebert: Indians (Pitching signature at knees)	8.00	3.60	1.00
☐ 36 Willie Stargell: Pirates (Batting no clouds)	40.00	18.00	5.00
☐ 37A Joe Torre: Braves (Catching, mask on ground)	15.00	6.75	1.85
☐ 37B Joe Torre: Braves (Catching, mask on ground; Cut Along Dotted Lines printed on lower tab)	25.00	11.00	3.10
☐ 38 Bob Veale: Pirates (Portrait, hands not shown)	8.00	3.60	1.00
☐ 39 Leon Wagner: Indians (Fielding)	8.00	3.60	1.00
☐ 40A Fred Whitfield (Batting lefthanded)	8.00	3.60	1.00
☐ 40B Fred Whitfield (Batting lefthanded; Cut Along Dotted Lines printed on lower tab)	8.00	3.60	1.00
☐ 41 Woody Woodward	8.00	3.60	1.00

1968 Kahn's

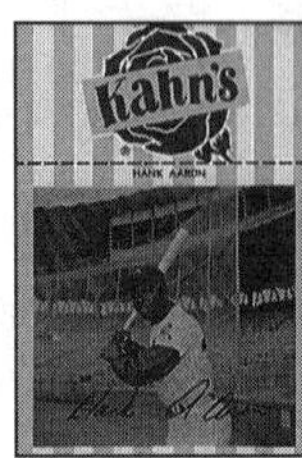

The cards in this 50-piece set contain two different sizes. The smaller of the two sizes, which contains 12 cards, is 2 13/16" X 3 1/4" with the ad tab and 2 13/16" X 1 7/8" without the ad tab. The larger size, which contains 38 cards, measures 2 13/16" X 3 7/8" with the ad tab and 2 13/16" X 2 11/16" without the ad tab. The 1968 Kahn's set of full-color, blank backed, unnumbered cards features players from Atlanta, Chicago Cubs, Chicago White Sox, Cincinnati, Cleveland, Detroit, New York Mets and Pittsburgh. In the set of 12, listed with the letter A in the checklist, Maloney exists with either yellow or yellow and green stripes at the top of the card. The large set of 38, listed with a letter B in the checklist, contains five cards which exist in two variations. The variations in this large set have either yellow or red stripes at the top of the cards, with Maloney being an exception. Maloney has either a yellow stripe or a Blue Mountain ad at the top. Cards with the ad tabs (see other Kahn's sets) are worth twice as much as cards without the ad, i.e., double the prices below. The cards are listed and numbered below in alphabetical order (within each subset) by the subject's name. The set features a card of Johnny Bench in his Rookie Card year.

	NRMT	VG-E	GOOD
COMPLETE SET (50)	1050.00	475.00	130.00
COMMON CARD	8.00	3.60	1.00
☐ A1 Hank Aaron	100.00	45.00	12.50
☐ A2 Gene Alley	10.00	4.50	1.25
☐ A3 Max Alvis	8.00	3.60	1.00
☐ A4 Clete Boyer	12.00	5.50	1.50
☐ A5 Chico Cardenas	10.00	4.50	1.25
☐ A6 Bill Freehan	12.00	5.50	1.50
☐ A7 Jim Maloney (2)	12.00	5.50	1.50
☐ A8 Lee May	12.00	5.50	1.50
☐ A9 Bill Mazeroski	20.00	9.00	2.50
☐ A10 Vada Pinson	15.00	6.75	1.85
☐ A11 Joe Torre	20.00	9.00	2.50
☐ A12 Bob Veale	10.00	4.50	1.25
☐ B1 Hank Aaron: Braves Full pose batting bat cocked	100.00	45.00	12.50
☐ B2 Tommy Agee	10.00	4.50	1.25
☐ B3 Gene Alley: Pirates Fielding, full pose	8.00	3.60	1.00
☐ B4 Felipe Alou Full pose batting, swinging player in background	15.00	6.75	1.85
☐ B5 Matty Alou: Pirates Portrait with bat Matio Alou (2)	10.00	4.50	1.25
☐ B6 Max Alvis Fielding glove on ground	8.00	3.60	1.00
☐ B7 Gerry Arrigo: Reds Pitching followthru delivery	8.00	3.60	1.00
☐ B8 John Bench	350.00	160.00	45.00
☐ B9 Clete Boyer	12.00	5.50	1.50
☐ B10 Larry Brown	8.00	3.60	1.00
☐ B11 Leo Cardenas: Reds Leaping in the air	10.00	4.50	1.25
☐ B12 Bill Freehan	12.00	5.50	1.50
☐ B13 Steve Hargan: Indians Pitching clouds in background	8.00	3.60	1.00
☐ B14 Joel Horlen White Sox Portrait	8.00	3.60	1.00
☐ B15 Tony Horton: Indians Portrait signed Anthony	8.00	3.60	1.00
☐ B16 Willie Horton	12.00	5.50	1.50
☐ B17 Ferguson Jenkins	40.00	18.00	5.00
☐ B18 Deron Johnson: Braves	10.00	4.50	1.25
☐ B19 Mack Jones: Reds	8.00	3.60	1.00
☐ B20 Bob Lee	8.00	3.60	1.00
☐ B21 Jim Maloney: Reds Red hat pitching hands up (2)	12.00	5.50	1.50
☐ B22 Lee May: Reds Batting	10.00	4.50	1.25
☐ B23 Bill Mazeroski: Pirates Fielding hands in front of body	20.00	9.00	2.50
☐ B24 Dick McAuliffe	8.00	3.60	1.00
☐ B25 Bill McCool Red hat left hand down	8.00	3.60	1.00
☐ B26 Sam McDowell: Indians Pitching left hand over glove (2)	12.00	5.50	1.50
☐ B27 Tony Perez Fielding ball in glove (2)	30.00	13.50	3.70
☐ B28 Gary Peters White Sox Portrait	8.00	3.60	1.00
☐ B29 Vada Pinson: Reds Batting	10.00	4.50	1.25
☐ B30 Chico Ruiz	8.00	3.60	1.00
☐ B31 Ron Santo: Cubs Batting follow thru (2)	25.00	11.00	3.10
☐ B32 Art Shamsky: Mets	8.00	3.60	1.00
☐ B33 Luis Tiant: Indians Hands over head	15.00	6.75	1.85
☐ B34 Joe Torre: Braves Batting	20.00	9.00	2.50
☐ B35 Bob Veale: Pirates Hands chest high	8.00	3.60	1.00
☐ B36 Leon Wagner: Indians Batting	8.00	3.60	1.00
☐ B37 Billy Williams: Cubs Bat behind back	40.00	18.00	5.00
☐ B38 Earl Wilson	8.00	3.60	1.00

1969 Kahn's

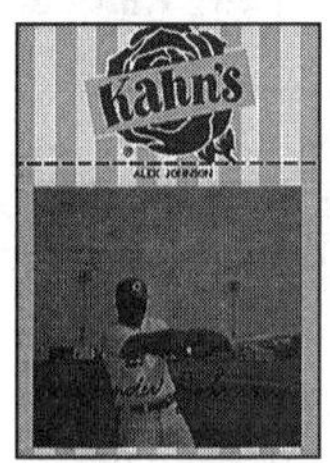

The cards in this 25-piece set contain two different sizes. The three small cards (see 1968 description) measure 2 13/16" X 3 1/4" and the 22 large cards (see 1968 description) measure 2 13/16" X 3 15/16". The 1969 Kahn's Wieners set of full-color, unnumbered cards features players from Atlanta, Chicago Cubs, Chicago White Sox, Cincinnati, Cleveland, Pittsburgh and St. Louis. The small cards have the letter A in the checklist while the large cards have the letter B in the checklist. Four of the larger cards exist in two variations (red or yellow color stripes at the top of the card). These variations are identified in the checklist below. Cards with the ad tabs (see other Kahn's sets) are worth twice as much as cards without the ad, i.e., double the prices below. The cards are listed and numbered below in alphabetical order (within each subset) by the subject's name.

	NRMT	VG-E	GOOD
COMPLETE SET (25)	450.00	200.00	55.00
COMMON CARD	8.00	3.60	1.00
☐ A1 Hank Aaron Portrait	100.00	45.00	12.50
☐ A2 Jim Maloney Pitching hands at side	10.00	4.50	1.25
☐ A3 Tony Perez Glove on	25.00	11.00	3.10
☐ B1 Hank Aaron	100.00	45.00	12.50
☐ B2 Matty Alou Batting	10.00	4.50	1.25
☐ B3 Max Alvis 69 patch	8.00	3.60	1.00
☐ B4 Gerry Arrigo Leg up	8.00	3.60	1.00
☐ B5 Steve Blass	10.00	4.50	1.25
☐ B6 Clay Carroll	8.00	3.60	1.00
☐ B7 Tony Cloninger: Reds	8.00	3.60	1.00
☐ B8 George Culver	8.00	3.60	1.00
☐ B9 Joel Horlen Pitching	10.00	4.50	1.25
☐ B10 Tony Horton Batting	10.00	4.50	1.25
☐ B11 Alex Johnson	10.00	4.50	1.25
☐ B12 Jim Maloney	10.00	4.50	1.25
☐ B13 Lee May Foot on bag (2)	10.00	4.50	1.25
☐ B14 Bill Mazeroski Hands on knees (2)	20.00	9.00	2.50
☐ B15 Sam McDowell Leg up (2)	10.00	4.50	1.25
☐ B16 Tony Perez	30.00	13.50	3.70
☐ B17 Gary Peters Pitching	8.00	3.60	1.00
☐ B18 Ron Santo Emblem (2)	20.00	9.00	2.50
☐ B19 Luis Tiant Glove at knee	15.00	6.75	1.85
☐ B20 Joe Torre: Cardinals	20.00	9.00	2.50
☐ B21 Bob Veale Hands at knees no glasses	10.00	4.50	1.25
☐ B22 Billy Williams Bat behind head	35.00	16.00	4.40

1989 Kahn's Cooperstown

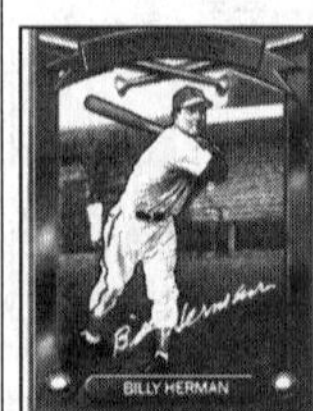

The 1989 Kahn's Cooperstown set contains 11 standard-size cards. This set is sometimes referenced as Hillshire Farms or Kahn's Cooperstown Collection. All players included in the set are members (for the most part they are recent inductees) of the Hall of Fame. The pictures are actually paintings and are surrounded by gold borders. The fronts resemble plaques and also have facsimile autographs. The cards were available from the company via a send-in offer. A set of cards was available in return for three proofs of purchase (and $1 postage and handling) from Hillshire Farms. The last card in the set is actually a coupon card for Kahn's products; this card is not even considered part of the set by some collectors. A related promotion offered two coin cards (coins laminated on cards) featuring Johnny Bench and Carl Yastrzemski. Coin cards are 5 1/2" X 3 3/4" and are blank backed.

	MINT	NRMT	EXC
COMPLETE SET (12)	5.00	2.20	.60
COMMON CARD (1-11)	.50	.23	.06
☐ 1 Cool Papa Bell	.50	.23	.06
☐ 2 Johnny Bench	1.00	.45	.12
☐ 3 Lou Brock	.75	.35	.09
☐ 4 Whitey Ford	.75	.35	.09
☐ 5 Bob Gibson	.75	.35	.09
☐ 6 Billy Herman	.50	.23	.06
☐ 7 Harmon Killebrew	.75	.35	.09
☐ 8 Eddie Mathews	.75	.35	.09
☐ 9 Brooks Robinson	1.00	.45	.12
☐ 10 Willie Stargell	1.00	.45	.12
☐ 11 Carl Yastrzemski	1.00	.45	.12
☐ 12 Coupon Card	.25	.11	.03

1887 Kalamazoo Bats N690-1

The Charles Gross Company of Philadelphia marketed this series of baseball players in 1887 in packages of tobacco with the intriguing name Kalamazoo Bats. This name involved a two-fold meaning since the word "bat" also referred to a wad of tobacco. There are 58 sepia photographs of baseball players known; most cards are blank backed although some are found with a list of premiums printed on the reverse.

	EX-MT	VG-E	GOOD
COMPLETE SET (50)	60000.00	27000.00	7500.00
COMMON PHILADELPHIA	500.00	220.00	60.00
COMMON N.Y. GIANTS	2000.00	900.00	250.00
COMMON METS	3000.00	1350.00	375.00
☐ 1 George Andrews: Phila.	500.00	220.00	60.00
☐ 2 Charlie Bastian Denny Lyons: Philadelphia	500.00	220.00	60.00
☐ 3 Louis Bierbauer: Athletics	500.00	220.00	60.00
☐ 4 Louis Bierbauer and Gallagher: Athletics	500.00	220.00	60.00
☐ 5 Charlie Buffington: Philadelphia	500.00	220.00	60.00
☐ 6 Dan Casey: Phila.	500.00	220.00	60.00
☐ 7 Jack Clements: Phila.	500.00	220.00	60.00
☐ 8 Roger Connor: New York	3000.00	1350.00	375.00
☐ 9 Larry Corcoran: New York	2000.00	900.00	250.00
☐ 10 Ed Cushman	3000.00	1350.00	375.00
☐ 11 Pat Deasley	2000.00	900.00	250.00
☐ 12 Devlin: Phila.	500.00	220.00	60.00
☐ 13 Jim Donahue: Mets	3000.00	1350.00	375.00
☐ 14 Mike Dorgan: New York	2000.00	900.00	250.00
☐ 15 Dude Esterbrooke (sic): Mets	3000.00	1350.00	375.00
☐ 16 Buck Ewing	1500.00	700.00	190.00
☐ 17 Sid Farrar: Phila.	600.00	275.00	75.00
☐ 18 Charlie Ferguson Philadelphia	500.00	220.00	60.00
☐ 19 Jim Fogarty: Phila.	500.00	220.00	60.00
☐ 20 Jim Fogarty James McGuire: Philadelphia	500.00	220.00	60.00
☐ 21 Elmer E. Foster: Mets	3000.00	1350.00	375.00
☐ 22 Gibson: Philadelphia	500.00	220.00	60.00
☐ 23 Pete Gillespie: New York	2000.00	900.00	250.00
☐ 24 Tom Gunning: Phila.	500.00	220.00	60.00
☐ 25 Art Irwin: Phila.	500.00	220.00	60.00
☐ 26 Art Irwin (Capt.) Al Maul: Philadelphia	500.00	220.00	60.00
☐ 27 Tim Keefe	1500.00	700.00	190.00
☐ 28 Ted Larkin: Athletics	500.00	220.00	60.00
☐ 29 Jack Lynch: Mets	3000.00	1350.00	375.00
☐ 30 Denny Lyons: Phila.	500.00	220.00	60.00
☐ 31 Denny Lyons Billy Taylor: Philadelphia	500.00	220.00	60.00
☐ 32 Fred Mann: Athletics	500.00	220.00	60.00
☐ 33 Charlie Mason MG	500.00	220.00	60.00
☐ 34 Bobby Mathews: Athletics	500.00	220.00	60.00
☐ 35 Al Maul: Philadelphia	500.00	220.00	60.00
☐ 36 Al Mays: Mets	3000.00	1350.00	375.00
☐ 37 Jim McGarr	500.00	220.00	60.00
☐ 38 James McGuire (one hand at chin throwing): Philadelphia	500.00	220.00	60.00
☐ 39 James McGuire (both hands at chin catching): Philadelphia	500.00	220.00	60.00
☐ 40 Jocko Milligan Henry Larkin: Athletics	500.00	220.00	60.00
☐ 41 Joe Mulvey: Phila.	500.00	220.00	60.00
☐ 42 Jack Nelson: Mets	3000.00	1350.00	375.00
☐ 43 Jim O'Rourke: New York	3000.00	1350.00	375.00
☐ 44 Dave Orr: Mets	3000.00	1350.00	375.00
☐ 45 Tom Poorman	500.00	220.00	60.00
☐ 46 Danny Richardson New York	2000.00	900.00	250.00
☐ 47 Wilbert Robinson: Athletics	1000.00	450.00	125.00
☐ 48 Wilbert Robinson Mann: Athletics	800.00	350.00	100.00
☐ 49 James (Chief) Roseman: Mets	3000.00	1350.00	375.00
☐ 50 Harry Stowe (sic Stovey) (hands at hips standing): Athletics	500.00	220.00	60.00
☐ 51 Harry Stowe (sic Stovey)(hands raised catching):Athletics	500.00	220.00	60.00
☐ 52 Harry Stowe (sic) Jocko Milligan Athletics	500.00	220.00	60.00
☐ 53 George Townsend: Athletics	500.00	220.00	60.00
☐ 54 George Townsend Jocko Milligan Athletics	500.00	220.00	60.00
☐ 55 John M. Ward	1500.00	700.00	190.00
☐ 56 Gus Weyhing	500.00	220.00	60.00
☐ 57 Pete Wood: Phila.	500.00	220.00	60.00
☐ 58 Harry Wright: Phila.-Mgr.	1750.00	800.00	220.00

1887 Kalamazoo Teams N690-2

Like the cards of set N690-1, the team cards of this set are sepia photographs and are blank-backed. There are only six teams known at the present time, and the cards themselves are slightly larger than those of the individual ballplayers in N690-1. They also appear to have been issued in 1887.

	EX-MT	VG-E	GOOD
COMPLETE SET (6)	20000.00	9000.00	2500.00
COMMON CARD (1-6)	3500.00	1600.00	450.00
☐ 1 Athletics Club	3500.00	1600.00	450.00
☐ 2 Baltimore B.B.C.	3500.00	1600.00	450.00
☐ 3 Boston B.B.C.	3500.00	1600.00	450.00
☐ 4 Detroit B.B.C.	3500.00	1600.00	450.00
☐ 5 Philadelphia B.B.C.	3500.00	1600.00	450.00
☐ 6 Pittsburg B.B.C.	3500.00	1600.00	450.00

1985 KAS Discs

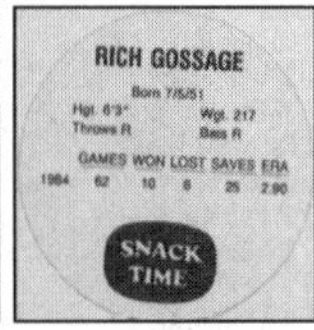

This set was apparently a test issue for the next year's more mass-produced set. Although this set is rarely seen in the secondary market, a few dealers in the mid 1980's got a small supply of this set. Typical of MSA sets all the team insignias are air-brushed out. This set was also issued in a square form.

	NRMT	VG-E	GOOD
COMPLETE SET	200.00	90.00	25.00
COMMON DISC	5.00	2.20	.60
☐ 1 Steve Carlton	15.00	6.75	1.85
☐ 2 Jack Clark	5.00	2.20	.60
☐ 3 Rich Gossage	7.50	3.40	.95
☐ 4 Tony Gwynn	25.00	11.00	3.10
☐ 5 Keith Hernandez	7.50	3.40	.95
☐ 6 Bob Horner	5.00	2.20	.60
☐ 7 Kent Hrbek	5.00	2.20	.60
☐ 8 Willie McGee	7.50	3.40	.95
☐ 9 Dan Quisenberry	5.00	2.20	.60
☐ 10 Cal Ripken	50.00	22.00	6.25
☐ 11 Ryne Sandberg	25.00	11.00	3.10
☐ 12 Mike Schmidt	20.00	9.00	2.50
☐ 13 Tom Seaver	20.00	9.00	2.50
☐ 14 Ozzie Smith	25.00	11.00	3.10
☐ 15 Rick Sutcliffe	5.00	2.20	.60
☐ 16 Bruce Sutter	5.00	2.20	.60
☐ 17 Alan Trammell	7.50	3.40	.95
☐ 18 Fernando Valenzuela	7.50	3.40	.95
☐ 19 Willie Wilson	5.00	2.20	.60
☐ 20 Dave Winfield	15.00	6.75	1.85

1986 Kay-Bee

This 33-card, standard-sized set was produced by Topps but manufactured in Northern Ireland. This boxed set retailed in Kay-Bee stores for $1.99; the checklist was listed on the back of the box. The set is subtitled "Young Superstars of Baseball" and does indeed feature many young players. The cards are numbered on the back; the set card numbering is in alphabetical order by player's name.

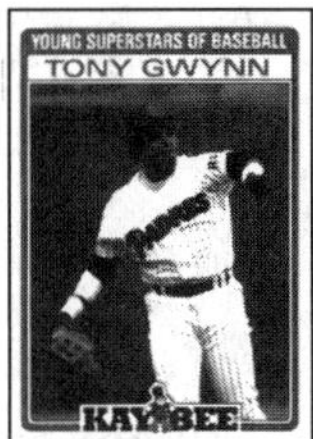

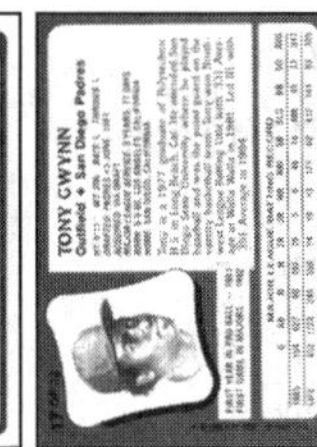

	MINT	NRMT	EXC
COMPLETE SET (33)	4.00	1.80	.50
COMMON CARD (1-33)	.10	.05	.01
☐ 1 Rick Aguilera	.15	.07	.02
☐ 2 Chris Brown	.10	.05	.01
☐ 3 Tom Browning	.10	.05	.01
☐ 4 Tom Brunansky	.10	.05	.01
☐ 5 Vince Coleman	.15	.07	.02
☐ 6 Ron Darling	.10	.05	.01
☐ 7 Alvin Davis	.10	.05	.01
☐ 8 Mariano Duncan	.25	.11	.03
☐ 9 Shawon Dunston	.15	.07	.02
☐ 10 Sid Fernandez	.10	.05	.01
☐ 11 Tony Fernandez	.10	.05	.01
☐ 12 Brian Fisher	.10	.05	.01
☐ 13 John Franco	.25	.11	.03
☐ 14 Julio Franco	.25	.11	.03
☐ 15 Dwight Gooden	.25	.11	.03
☐ 16 Ozzie Guillen	.25	.11	.03
☐ 17 Tony Gwynn	1.00	.45	.12
☐ 18 Jimmy Key	.25	.11	.03
☐ 19 Don Mattingly	1.00	.45	.12
☐ 20 Oddibe McDowell	.10	.05	.01
☐ 21 Roger McDowell	.10	.05	.01
☐ 22 Dan Pasqua	.10	.05	.01
☐ 23 Terry Pendleton	.25	.11	.03
☐ 24 Jim Presley	.10	.05	.01
☐ 25 Kirby Puckett	1.00	.45	.12
☐ 26 Earnie Riles	.10	.05	.01
☐ 27 Bret Saberhagen	.25	.11	.03
☐ 28 Mark Salas	.10	.05	.01
☐ 29 Juan Samuel	.10	.05	.01
☐ 30 Jeff Stone	.10	.05	.01
☐ 31 Darryl Strawberry	.25	.11	.03
☐ 32 Andy Van Slyke	.15	.07	.02
☐ 33 Frank Viola	.15	.07	.02

1987 Kay-Bee

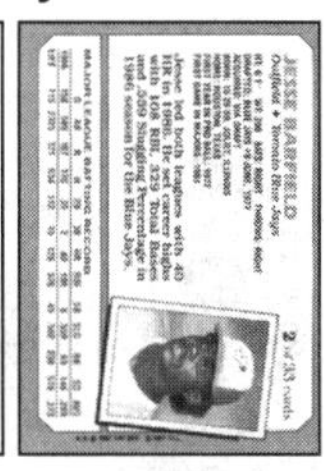

This small 33-card boxed standard-size set was produced by Topps for Kay-Bee Toy Stores. The set is subtitled "Super Stars of Baseball" and has full-color fronts. The card backs are printed in blue and black on white card stock. The checklist for the set is printed on the back panel of the yellow box. The set card numbering is alphabetical by player's name.

	MINT	NRMT	EXC
COMPLETE SET (33)	4.00	1.80	.50
COMMON CARD (1-33)	.10	.05	.01
☐ 1 Harold Baines	.15	.07	.02
☐ 2 Jesse Barfield	.10	.05	.01
☐ 3 Don Baylor	.15	.07	.02
☐ 4 Wade Boggs	.40	.18	.05
☐ 5 George Brett	.75	.35	.09
☐ 6 Hubie Brooks	.10	.05	.01
☐ 7 Jose Canseco	.60	.25	.07
☐ 8 Gary Carter	.15	.07	.02
☐ 9 Joe Carter	.25	.11	.03
☐ 10 Roger Clemens	.50	.23	.06
☐ 11 Vince Coleman	.10	.05	.01
☐ 12 Glenn Davis	.10	.05	.01
☐ 13 Dwight Gooden	.20	.09	.03
☐ 14 Pedro Guerrero	.10	.05	.01
☐ 15 Tony Gwynn	1.00	.45	.12
☐ 16 Rickey Henderson	.40	.18	.05
☐ 17 Keith Hernandez	.15	.07	.02
☐ 18 Wally Joyner	.10	.05	.01
☐ 19 Don Mattingly	1.00	.45	.12
☐ 20 Jack Morris	.15	.07	.02
☐ 21 Dale Murphy	.20	.09	.03
☐ 22 Eddie Murray	.40	.18	.05
☐ 23 Dave Parker	.15	.07	.02
☐ 24 Kirby Puckett	1.00	.45	.12
☐ 25 Tim Raines	.15	.07	.02
☐ 26 Jim Rice	.15	.07	.02
☐ 27 Dave Righetti	.10	.05	.01
☐ 28 Ryne Sandberg	.75	.35	.09
☐ 29 Mike Schmidt	.60	.25	.07
☐ 30 Mike Scott	.10	.05	.01
☐ 31 Darryl Strawberry	.20	.09	.03
☐ 32 Fernando Valenzuela	.15	.07	.02
☐ 33 Dave Winfield	.40	.18	.05

1988 Kay-Bee

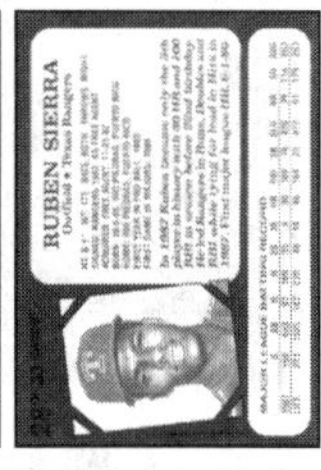

This small 33-card boxed standard-size set was produced by Topps for Kay-Bee Toy Stores. The set is subtitled "Superstars of Baseball" and have full-color fronts. The card backs are printed in blue and green on white card stock. The checklist for the set is printed on the back panel of the box. The set card numbering is alphabetical by player's name.

	MINT	NRMT	EXC
COMPLETE SET (33)	4.00	1.80	.50
COMMON CARD (1-33)	.10	.05	.01
☐ 1 George Bell	.10	.05	.01
☐ 2 Wade Boggs	.40	.18	.05
☐ 3 Jose Canseco	.40	.18	.05
☐ 4 Joe Carter	.25	.11	.03
☐ 5 Jack Clark	.10	.05	.01
☐ 6 Alvin Davis	.10	.05	.01
☐ 7 Eric Davis	.15	.07	.02
☐ 8 Andre Dawson	.30	.14	.04
☐ 9 Darrell Evans	.10	.05	.01
☐ 10 Dwight Evans	.15	.07	.02
☐ 11 Gary Gaetti	.15	.07	.02
☐ 12 Pedro Guerrero	.10	.05	.01
☐ 13 Tony Gwynn	1.00	.45	.12
☐ 14 Howard Johnson	.10	.05	.01
☐ 15 Wally Joyner	.20	.09	.03
☐ 16 Don Mattingly	1.00	.45	.12
☐ 17 Willie McGee	.10	.05	.01
☐ 18 Mark McGwire	1.00	.45	.12
☐ 19 Paul Molitor	.40	.18	.05
☐ 20 Dale Murphy	.20	.09	.03
☐ 21 Dave Parker	.15	.07	.02
☐ 22 Lance Parrish	.10	.05	.01
☐ 23 Kirby Puckett	1.00	.45	.12
☐ 24 Tim Raines	.15	.07	.02
☐ 25 Cal Ripken	1.50	.70	.19
☐ 26 Juan Samuel	.10	.05	.01
☐ 27 Mike Schmidt	.50	.23	.06
☐ 28 Ruben Sierra	.20	.09	.03
☐ 29 Darryl Strawberry	.15	.07	.02
☐ 30 Danny Tartabull	.10	.05	.01
☐ 31 Alan Trammell	.15	.07	.02
☐ 32 Tim Wallach	.10	.05	.01
☐ 33 Dave Winfield	.40	.18	.05

1989 Kay-Bee

The 1989 Kay-Bee set contains 33 standard-size glossy cards. The fronts have magenta and yellow borders. The horizontally oriented backs are brown and yellow. The cards were distributed as boxed sets through Kay-Bee toy stores. The set card numbering is alphabetical by player's name.

	MINT	NRMT	EXC
COMPLETE SET (33)	4.00	1.80	.50
COMMON CARD (1-33)	.10	.05	.01
☐ 1 Wade Boggs	.30	.14	.04
☐ 2 George Brett	.75	.35	.09
☐ 3 Jose Canseco	.30	.14	.04
☐ 4 Gary Carter	.15	.07	.02
☐ 5 Jack Clark	.10	.05	.01
☐ 6 Will Clark	.40	.18	.05
☐ 7 Roger Clemens	.50	.23	.06
☐ 8 Eric Davis	.15	.07	.02
☐ 9 Andre Dawson	.30	.14	.04
☐ 10 Dwight Evans	.10	.05	.01
☐ 11 Carlton Fisk	.40	.18	.05
☐ 12 Andres Galarraga	.30	.14	.04
☐ 13 Kirk Gibson	.20	.09	.03
☐ 14 Dwight Gooden	.15	.07	.02

☐ 15 Mike Greenwell	.10	.05	.01
☐ 16 Pedro Guerrero	.10	.05	.01
☐ 17 Tony Gwynn	.75	.35	.09
☐ 18 Rickey Henderson	.30	.14	.04
☐ 19 Orel Hershiser	.15	.07	.02
☐ 20 Don Mattingly	.75	.35	.09
☐ 21 Mark McGwire	.75	.35	.09
☐ 22 Dale Murphy	.20	.09	.03
☐ 23 Eddie Murray	.30	.14	.04
☐ 24 Kirby Puckett	.75	.35	.09
☐ 25 Tim Raines	.10	.05	.01
☐ 26 Ryne Sandberg	.60	.25	.07
☐ 27 Mike Schmidt	.40	.18	.05
☐ 28 Ozzie Smith	.75	.35	.09
☐ 29 Darryl Strawberry	.15	.07	.02
☐ 30 Alan Trammell	.15	.07	.02
☐ 31 Frank Viola	.10	.05	.01
☐ 32 Dave Winfield	.30	.14	.04
☐ 33 Robin Yount	.25	.11	.03

1990 Kay-Bee

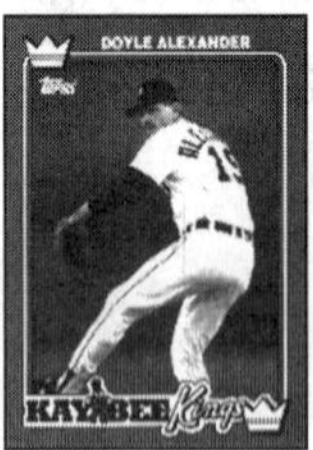

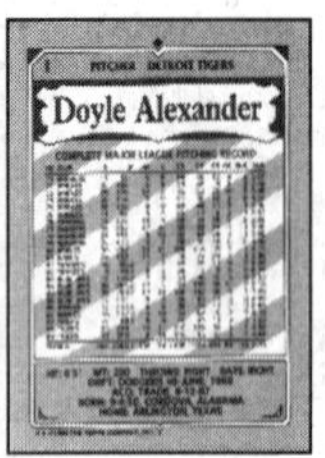

The 1990 Kay-Bee Kings of Baseball set is a standard-size 33-card set sequenced alphabetically that Topps produced for the Kay-Bee toy store chain. A solid red border inside a purple white striped box is the major design feature of this set. The set card numbering is alphabetical by player's name.

	MINT	NRMT	EXC
COMPLETE SET (33)	4.00	1.80	.50
COMMON CARD (1-33)	.10	.05	.01
☐ 1 Doyle Alexander	.10	.05	.01
☐ 2 Bert Blyleven	.10	.05	.01
☐ 3 Wade Boggs	.25	.11	.03
☐ 4 George Brett	.75	.35	.09
☐ 5 John Candelaria	.10	.05	.01
☐ 6 Gary Carter	.15	.07	.02
☐ 7 Vince Coleman	.10	.05	.01
☐ 8 Andre Dawson	.25	.11	.03
☐ 9 Dennis Eckersley	.15	.07	.02
☐ 10 Darrell Evans	.10	.05	.01
☐ 11 Dwight Evans	.15	.07	.02
☐ 12 Carlton Fisk	.30	.14	.04
☐ 13 Ken Griffey Sr.	.10	.05	.01
☐ 14 Tony Gwynn	.75	.35	.09
☐ 15 Rickey Henderson	.25	.11	.03
☐ 16 Keith Hernandez	.10	.05	.01
☐ 17 Charlie Hough	.10	.05	.01
☐ 18 Don Mattingly	.75	.35	.09
☐ 19 Jack Morris	.15	.07	.02
☐ 20 Dale Murphy	.20	.09	.03
☐ 21 Eddie Murray	.40	.18	.05
☐ 22 Dave Parker	.15	.07	.02
☐ 23 Kirby Puckett	.75	.35	.09
☐ 24 Tim Raines	.15	.07	.02
☐ 25 Rick Reuschel	.10	.05	.01
☐ 26 Jerry Reuss	.10	.05	.01
☐ 27 Jim Rice	.10	.05	.01
☐ 28 Nolan Ryan	1.50	.70	.19
☐ 29 Ozzie Smith	.75	.35	.09
☐ 30 Frank Tanana	.10	.05	.01
☐ 31 Willie Wilson	.10	.05	.01
☐ 32 Dave Winfield	.30	.14	.04
☐ 33 Robin Yount	.25	.11	.03

1970 Kellogg's

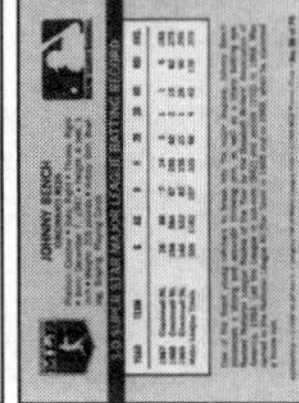

The cards in this 75-card set measure approximately 2 1/4" by 3 1/2". The 1970 Kellogg's set was Kellogg's first venture into the baseball card producing field. The design incorporates a brilliant color photo of the player set against an indistinct background, which is then covered with a layer of plastic to simulate a 3-D look. Some veteran card dealers consider cards 16-30 to be in shorter supply than the other cards in the set. The cards were individually inserted one per specially marked boxes of Kellogg's cereal. Cards still found with the wrapper intact are valued 50 percent greater than the values listed below.

	NRMT	VG-E	GOOD
COMPLETE SET (75)	225.00	100.00	28.00
COMMON CARD (1-15)	1.00	.45	.12
COMMON CARD (16-30)	1.00	.45	.12
COMMON CARD (31-75)	1.00	.45	.12
☐ 1 Ed Kranepool	1.50	.70	.19
☐ 2 Pete Rose	20.00	9.00	2.50
☐ 3 Cleon Jones	1.00	.45	.12
☐ 4 Willie McCovey	6.00	2.70	.75
☐ 5 Mel Stottlemyre	1.50	.70	.19
☐ 6 Frank Howard	1.50	.70	.19
☐ 7 Tom Seaver	15.00	6.75	1.85
☐ 8 Don Sutton	3.00	1.35	.35
☐ 9 Jim Wynn	1.00	.45	.12
☐ 10 Jim Maloney	1.00	.45	.12
☐ 11 Tommie Agee	1.00	.45	.12
☐ 12 Willie Mays	20.00	9.00	2.50
☐ 13 Juan Marichal	4.00	1.80	.50
☐ 14 Dave McNally	1.50	.70	.19
☐ 15 Frank Robinson	8.00	3.60	1.00
☐ 16 Carlos May	1.00	.45	.12
☐ 17 Bill Singer	1.00	.45	.12
☐ 18 Rick Reichardt	1.00	.45	.12
☐ 19 Boog Powell	2.00	.90	.25
☐ 20 Gaylord Perry	6.00	2.70	.75
☐ 21 Brooks Robinson	12.00	5.50	1.50
☐ 22 Luis Aparicio	6.00	2.70	.75
☐ 23 Joel Horlen	1.00	.45	.12
☐ 24 Mike Epstein	1.00	.45	.12
☐ 25 Tom Haller	1.00	.45	.12
☐ 26 Willie Crawford	1.00	.45	.12
☐ 27 Roberto Clemente	30.00	13.50	3.70
☐ 28 Matty Alou	1.00	.45	.12
☐ 29 Willie Stargell	8.00	3.60	1.00
☐ 30 Tim Cullen	1.00	.45	.12
☐ 31 Randy Hundley	1.00	.45	.12
☐ 32 Reggie Jackson	20.00	9.00	2.50
☐ 33 Rich Allen	2.00	.90	.25
☐ 34 Tim McCarver	2.00	.90	.25
☐ 35 Ray Culp	1.00	.45	.12
☐ 36 Jim Fregosi	1.00	.45	.12
☐ 37 Billy Williams	4.00	1.80	.50
☐ 38 Johnny Odom	1.00	.45	.12
☐ 39 Bert Campaneris	1.50	.70	.19
☐ 40 Ernie Banks	10.00	4.50	1.25
☐ 41 Chris Short	1.00	.45	.12
☐ 42 Ron Santo	2.00	.90	.25
☐ 43 Glenn Beckert	1.00	.45	.12
☐ 44 Lou Brock	6.00	2.70	.75
☐ 45 Larry Hisle	1.00	.45	.12
☐ 46 Reggie Smith	1.50	.70	.19
☐ 47 Rod Carew	8.00	3.60	1.00
☐ 48 Curt Flood	1.50	.70	.19
☐ 49 Jim Lonborg	1.00	.45	.12
☐ 50 Sam McDowell	1.00	.45	.12
☐ 51 Sal Bando	1.00	.45	.12
☐ 52 Al Kaline	10.00	4.50	1.25
☐ 53 Gary Nolan	1.00	.45	.12
☐ 54 Rico Petrocelli	1.50	.70	.19
☐ 55 Ollie Brown	1.00	.45	.12
☐ 56 Luis Tiant	1.50	.70	.19
☐ 57 Bill Freehan	1.50	.70	.19
☐ 58 Johnny Bench	20.00	9.00	2.50
☐ 59 Joe Pepitone	1.50	.70	.19
☐ 60 Bobby Murcer	1.50	.70	.19
☐ 61 Harmon Killebrew	8.00	3.60	1.00
☐ 62 Don Wilson	1.00	.45	.12
☐ 63 Tony Oliva	2.00	.90	.25
☐ 64 Jim Perry	1.00	.45	.12
☐ 65 Mickey Lolich	1.50	.70	.19
☐ 66 Jose Laboy	1.00	.45	.12
☐ 67 Dean Chance	1.00	.45	.12
☐ 68 Ken Harrelson	1.50	.70	.19
☐ 69 Willie Horton	1.50	.70	.19
☐ 70 Wally Bunker	1.00	.45	.12
☐ 71A Bob Gibson ERR (1959 innings pitched is blank)	6.00	2.70	.75
☐ 71B Bob Gibson COR (1959 innings is 76)	6.00	2.70	.75
☐ 72 Joe Morgan	5.00	2.20	.60
☐ 73 Denny McLain	1.50	.70	.19
☐ 74 Tommy Harper	1.00	.45	.12
☐ 75 Don Mincher	1.00	.45	.12

1971 Kellogg's

The cards in this 75-card set measure approximately 2 1/4" by 3 1/2". The 1971 set of 3-D cards marketed by the Kellogg Company is the scarcest of all that company's issues. It was distributed as single cards, one in each package of cereal, without the usual complete set mail-in offer. In addition, card dealers were unable to obtain this set in quantity, as they have in other years. All the cards are available with and without the year 1970 before XOGRAPH on the back in the lower left corner; the version without carries a slight premium for most numbers. Prices listed below are for the more common variety with the year 1970. Cards still found with the wrapper intact are valued 50 percent greater than the values listed below.

	NRMT	VG-E	GOOD
COMPLETE SET (75)	900.00	400.00	110.00
COMMON CARD (1-75)	7.00	3.10	.85
☐ 1 Wayne Simpson	7.00	3.10	.85
☐ 2 Tom Seaver	30.00	13.50	3.70
☐ 3 Jim Perry	8.00	3.60	1.00
☐ 4 Bob Robertson	7.00	3.10	.85
☐ 5 Roberto Clemente	60.00	27.00	7.50
☐ 6 Gaylord Perry	15.00	6.75	1.85
☐ 7 Felipe Alou	8.00	3.60	1.00
☐ 8 Denis Menke	7.00	3.10	.85
☐ 9A Don Kessinger No 1970 date	8.00	3.60	1.00
☐ 9B Don Kessinger ERR Dated 1970 hits 167; avg. .265	8.00	3.60	1.00
☐ 9C Don Kessinger COR Dated1970 hits 168; avg. .266	8.00	3.60	1.00
☐ 10 Willie Mays	50.00	22.00	6.25
☐ 11 Jim Hickman	7.00	3.10	.85
☐ 12 Tony Oliva	10.00	4.50	1.25
☐ 13 Manny Sanguillen	8.00	3.60	1.00
☐ 14 Frank Howard	8.00	3.60	1.00
☐ 15 Frank Robinson	25.00	11.00	3.10
☐ 16 Willie Davis	8.00	3.60	1.00
☐ 17 Lou Brock	25.00	11.00	3.10
☐ 18 Cesar Tovar	7.00	3.10	.85
☐ 19 Luis Aparicio	15.00	6.75	1.85
☐ 20 Boog Powell	10.00	4.50	1.25
☐ 21 Dick Selma	7.00	3.10	.85
☐ 22 Danny Walton	7.00	3.10	.85
☐ 23 Carl Morton	7.00	3.10	.85
☐ 24 Sonny Siebert	7.00	3.10	.85
☐ 25 Jim Merritt	7.00	3.10	.85
☐ 26 Jose Cardenal	7.00	3.10	.85
☐ 27 Don Mincher	7.00	3.10	.85
☐ 28A Clyde Wright No 1970 date team logo is Angels crest	10.00	4.50	1.25
☐ 28B Clyde Wright (No 1970 date team logo is California outline with Angels written inside	10.00	4.50	1.25
☐ 28C Clyde Wright Dated 1970 team logo is California state outline	8.00	3.60	1.00
☐ 29 Les Cain	7.00	3.10	.85
☐ 30 Danny Cater	7.00	3.10	.85
☐ 31 Don Sutton	15.00	6.75	1.85
☐ 32 Chuck Dobson	7.00	3.10	.85
☐ 33 Willie McCovey	25.00	11.00	3.10
☐ 34 Mike Epstein	7.00	3.10	.85
☐ 35 Paul Blair	7.00	3.10	.85
☐ 36A Gary Nolan No 1970 date	8.00	3.60	1.00
☐ 36B Gary Nolan Dated 1970 1970; BB 95, SO 177	8.00	3.60	1.00
☐ 36C Gary Nolan Dated 1970 1970; BB 96, SO 181	8.00	3.60	1.00
☐ 37 Sam McDowell	8.00	3.60	1.00
☐ 38 Amos Otis	8.00	3.60	1.00
☐ 39 Ray Fosse	7.00	3.10	.85
☐ 40 Mel Stottlemyre	8.00	3.60	1.00
☐ 41 Clarence Gaston	8.00	3.60	1.00
☐ 42 Dick Dietz	7.00	3.10	.85
☐ 43 Roy White	6.50	2.90	.80
☐ 44 Al Kaline	30.00	13.50	3.70
☐ 45 Carlos May	7.00	3.10	.85
☐ 46 Tommie Agee	7.00	3.10	.85
☐ 47 Tommy Harper	7.00	3.10	.85
☐ 48 Larry Dierker	7.00	3.10	.85
☐ 49 Mike Cuellar	8.00	3.60	1.00
☐ 50 Ernie Banks	30.00	13.50	3.70
☐ 51 Bob Gibson	25.00	11.00	3.10
☐ 52 Reggie Smith	8.00	3.60	1.00
☐ 53 Matty Alou	8.00	3.60	1.00
☐ 54A Alex Johnson No 1970 date team logo is Angels crest	10.00	4.50	1.25
☐ 54B Alex Johnson No 1970 date team logo is California state outline	10.00	4.50	1.25
☐ 54C Alex Johnson Dated 1970 team logo is California state outline	8.00	3.60	1.00
☐ 55 Harmon Killebrew	25.00	11.00	3.10
☐ 56 Bill Grabarkewitz	7.00	3.10	.85
☐ 57 Richie Allen	10.00	4.50	1.25
☐ 58 Tony Perez	15.00	6.75	1.85
☐ 59 Dave McNally	8.00	3.60	1.00
☐ 60 Jim Palmer	25.00	11.00	3.10
☐ 61 Billy Williams	20.00	9.00	2.50
☐ 62 Joe Torre	12.00	5.50	1.50
☐ 63 Jim Northrup	8.00	3.60	1.00
☐ 64A Jim Fregosi No 1970 date team logo is Angels crest	10.00	4.50	1.25
☐ 64B Jim Fregosi No 1970 date team logo is California state outline	10.00	4.50	1.25
☐ 64C Jim Fregosi Dated1970 1970; Hits 166, avg. .276	8.00	3.60	1.00
☐ 64D Jim Fregosi Dated1970 1970; Hits 167, avg. .278	8.00	3.60	1.00
☐ 65 Pete Rose	50.00	22.00	6.25
☐ 66A Bud Harrelson No 1970 date	8.00	3.60	1.00
☐ 66B Bud Harrelson ERR Dated 1970 1970 RBI 43	8.00	3.60	1.00
☐ 66C Bud Harrelson COR Dated 1970 1970 RBI 42	8.00	3.60	1.00
☐ 67 Tony Taylor	8.00	3.60	1.00
☐ 68 Willie Stargell	20.00	9.00	2.50
☐ 69 Tony Horton	8.00	3.60	1.00
☐ 70A Claude Osteen ERR No 1970 date card number missing	10.00	4.50	1.25
☐ 70B Claude Osteen COR No 1970 date card number present	10.00	4.50	1.25
☐ 70C Claude Osteen COR Dated 1970	8.00	3.60	1.00
☐ 71 Glenn Beckert	7.00	3.10	.85
☐ 72 Nate Colbert	7.00	3.10	.85
☐ 73A Rick Monday No 1970 date	8.00	3.60	1.00
☐ 73B Rick Monday ERR Dated 1970 1970; AB 377, avg. .289	8.00	3.60	1.00
☐ 73C Rick Monday COR Dated 1970 1970; AB 376, avg. .290	8.00	3.60	1.00
☐ 74 Tommy John	10.00	4.50	1.25
☐ 75 Chris Short	7.00	3.10	.85

1972 Kellogg's

The cards in this 54-card set measure approximately 2 1/8" by 3 1/4". The dimensions of the cards in the 1972 Kellogg's set were reduced in comparison to those of the 1971 series. In addition, the length of the set was set at 54 cards rather than the 75 of the previous year. The cards of this Kellogg's set are characterized by the diagonal bands found on the obverse. Cards still found with the wrapper intact are valued 50 percent greater than the values listed below.

	NRMT	VG-E	GOOD
COMPLETE SET (54)	75.00	34.00	9.50
COMMON CARD (1-54)	.75	.35	.09
☐ 1A Tom Seaver ERR 1970 ERA 2.85	10.00	4.50	1.25
☐ 1B Tom Seaver COR 1970 ERA 2.81	20.00	9.00	2.50
☐ 2 Amos Otis	.75	.35	.09
☐ 3A Willie Davis ERR Lifetime runs 842	1.50	.70	.19
☐ 3B Willie Davis COR Lifetime runs 841	.75	.35	.09
☐ 4 Wilbur Wood	.75	.35	.09
☐ 5 Bill Parsons	.75	.35	.09
☐ 6 Pete Rose	15.00	6.75	1.85
☐ 7A Willie McCovey ERR Lifetime HR 360	4.00	1.80	.50
☐ 7B Willie McCovey COR Lifetime HR 370	8.00	3.60	1.00
☐ 8 Ferguson Jenkins	3.00	1.35	.35
☐ 9A Vida Blue ERR Lifetime ERA 2.35	1.50	.70	.19
☐ 9B Vida Blue COR Lifetime ERA 2.31	.75	.35	.09
☐ 10 Joe Torre	1.50	.70	.19
☐ 11 Merv Rettenmund	.75	.35	.09
☐ 12 Bill Melton	.75	.35	.09
☐ 13A Jim Palmer ERR Lifetime games 170	5.00	2.20	.60
☐ 13B Jim Palmer COR Lifetime games 168	10.00	4.50	1.25
☐ 14 Doug Rader	.75	.35	.09

Card	NRMT	VG-E	GOOD
☐ 15A Dave Roberts ERR	.75	.35	.09
NL missing in bio			
☐ 15B Dave Roberts COR	1.50	.70	.19
NL in bio, line 2			
☐ 16 Bobby Murcer	1.00	.45	.12
☐ 17 Wes Parker	.75	.35	.09
☐ 18A Joe Coleman ERR	1.50	.70	.19
Lifetime BB 294			
☐ 18B Joe Coleman COR	.75	.35	.09
Lifetime BB 393			
☐ 19 Manny Sanguillen	.75	.35	.09
☐ 20 Reggie Jackson	10.00	4.50	1.25
☐ 21 Ralph Garr	.75	.35	.09
☐ 22 Jim Hunter	3.00	1.35	.35
☐ 23 Rick Wise	.75	.35	.09
☐ 24 Glenn Beckert	.75	.35	.09
☐ 25 Tony Oliva	1.50	.70	.19
☐ 26A Bob Gibson ERR	8.00	3.60	1.00
Lifetime SO 2577			
☐ 26B Bob Gibson COR	4.00	1.80	.50
Lifetime SO 2578			
☐ 27A Mike Cuellar ERR	1.50	.70	.19
1971 ERA 3.80			
☐ 27B Mike Cuellar COR	.75	.35	.09
1971 ERA 3.08			
☐ 28 Chris Speier	.75	.35	.09
☐ 29A Dave McNally ERR	1.50	.70	.19
Lifetime ERA 3.18			
☐ 29B Dave McNally COR	.75	.35	.09
Lifetime ERA 3.15			
☐ 30 Leo Cardenas	.75	.35	.09
☐ 31A Bill Freehan ERR	.75	.35	.09
Lifetime runs 497			
☐ 31B Bill Freehan COR	1.50	.70	.19
Lifetime runs 500			
☐ 32A Bud Harrelson ERR	1.50	.70	.19
Lifetime hits 634			
☐ 32B Bud Harrelson COR	.75	.35	.09
Lifetime hits 624			
☐ 33A Sam McDowell ERR	.75	.35	.09
Bio line 3 has less than 200			
☐ 33B Sam McDowell COR	1.50	.70	.19
Bio line 3 has less than 225			
☐ 34A Claude Osteen ERR	.75	.35	.09
1971 ERA 3.25			
☐ 34B Claude Osteen COR	1.50	.70	.19
1971 ERA 3.51			
☐ 35 Reggie Smith	1.00	.45	.12
☐ 36 Sonny Siebert	.75	.35	.09
☐ 37 Lee May	1.00	.45	.12
☐ 38 Mickey Lolich	1.00	.45	.12
☐ 39A Cookie Rojas ERR	1.50	.70	.19
Lifetime 2B 149			
☐ 39B Cookie Rojas COR	.75	.35	.09
Lifetime 2B 150			
☐ 40A Dick Drago ERR	1.50	.70	.19
Bio line 3 has Poyals			
☐ 40B Dick Drago COR	.75	.35	.09
Bio line 3 has Royals			
☐ 41 Nate Colbert	.75	.35	.09
☐ 42 Andy Messersmith	.75	.35	.09
☐ 43A Dave Johnson ERR	1.50	.70	.19
Lifetime AB 3110, avg. .262			
☐ 43B Dave Johnson COR	1.00	.45	.12
Lifetime AB 3113, avg. .264			
☐ 44 Steve Blass	.75	.35	.09
☐ 45 Bob Robertson	.75	.35	.09
☐ 46A Billy Williams ERR	4.00	1.80	.50
Bio has "missed only one game"			
☐ 46B Billy Williams COR	7.00	3.10	.85
Bio has that line eliminated			
☐ 47 Juan Marichal	4.00	1.80	.50
☐ 48 Lou Brock	4.00	1.80	.50
☐ 49 Roberto Clemente	20.00	9.00	2.50
☐ 50 Mel Stottlemyre	.75	.35	.09
☐ 51 Don Wilson	.75	.35	.09
☐ 52A Sal Bando ERR	.75	.35	.09
Lifetime RBI 355			
☐ 52B Sal Bando COR	1.50	.70	.19
Lifetime RBI 356			
☐ 53A Willie Stargell ERR	8.00	3.60	1.00
Lifetime 2B 197			
☐ 53B Willie Stargell COR	4.00	1.80	.50
Lifetime 2B 196			
☐ 54A Willie Mays ERR	25.00	11.00	3.10
Lifetime RBI 1855			
☐ 54B Willie Mays COR	12.50	5.50	1.55
Lifetime RBI 1856			

1972 Kellogg's ATG

The cards in this 15-card set measure 2 1/4" by 3 1/2". The 1972 All-Time Greats 3-D set was issued with Kellogg's Danish Go Rounds. The set contains two different cards of Babe Ruth. The set is a reissue of a 1970 set issued by Rold Gold Pretzels to commemorate baseball's first 100 years. The Rold Gold cards are copyrighted 1970 on the reverse and are valued at approximately double the prices listed below.

	NRMT	VG-E	GOOD
COMPLETE SET (15)	25.00	11.00	3.10
COMMON CARD (1-15)	1.00	.45	.12
☐ 1 Walter Johnson	2.00	.90	.25
☐ 2 Rogers Hornsby	1.25	.55	.16
☐ 3 John McGraw	1.25	.55	.16

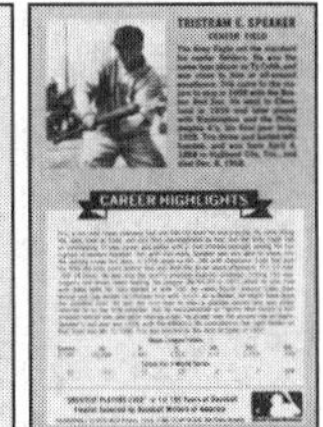

Card	NRMT	VG-E	GOOD
☐ 4 Mickey Cochrane	1.25	.55	.16
☐ 5 George Sisler	1.25	.55	.16
☐ 6 Babe Ruth	8.00	3.60	1.00
☐ 7 Lefty Grove	1.25	.55	.16
☐ 8 Pie Traynor	1.00	.45	.12
☐ 9 Honus Wagner	2.00	.90	.25
☐ 10 Eddie Collins	1.00	.45	.12
☐ 11 Tris Speaker	1.25	.55	.16
☐ 12 Cy Young	2.00	.90	.25
☐ 13 Lou Gehrig	6.00	2.70	.75
☐ 14 Babe Ruth	8.00	3.60	1.00
☐ 15 Ty Cobb	6.00	2.70	.75

1973 Kellogg's 2D

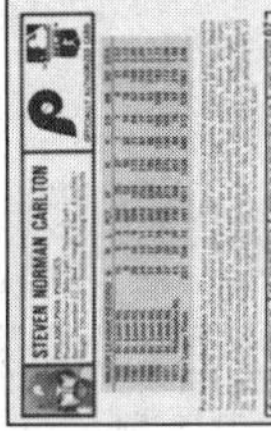

The cards in this 54-card set measure approximately 2 1/4" by 3 1/2". The 1973 Kellogg's set is the only non-3D set produced by the Kellogg Company. Apparently Kellogg's decided to have the cards produced through Visual Panographics rather than by Xograph, as in the other years. The complete set could be obtained from the company through a box-top redemption procedure. The card size is slightly larger than the previous year.

	NRMT	VG-E	GOOD
COMPLETE SET (54)	75.00	34.00	9.50
COMMON CARD (1-54)	.50	.23	.06
☐ 1 Amos Otis	.75	.35	.09
☐ 2 Ellie Rodriguez	.50	.23	.06
☐ 3 Mickey Lolich	1.00	.45	.12
☐ 4 Tony Oliva	1.00	.45	.12
☐ 5 Don Sutton	2.00	.90	.25
☐ 6 Pete Rose	15.00	6.75	1.85
☐ 7 Steve Carlton	6.00	2.70	.75
☐ 8 Bobby Bonds	1.00	.45	.12
☐ 9 Wilbur Wood	.75	.35	.09
☐ 10 Billy Williams	4.00	1.80	.50
☐ 11 Steve Blass	.50	.23	.06
☐ 12 Jon Matlack	.50	.23	.06
☐ 13 Cesar Cedeno	.75	.35	.09
☐ 14 Bob Gibson	4.00	1.80	.50
☐ 15 Sparky Lyle	1.00	.45	.12
☐ 16 Nolan Ryan	30.00	13.50	3.70
☐ 17 Jim Palmer	5.00	2.20	.60
☐ 18 Ray Fosse	.50	.23	.06
☐ 19 Bobby Murcer	.75	.35	.09
☐ 20 Jim Hunter	3.00	1.35	.35
☐ 21 Tom McCraw	.50	.23	.06
☐ 22 Reggie Jackson	8.00	3.60	1.00
☐ 23 Bill Stoneman	.50	.23	.06
☐ 24 Lou Piniella	1.00	.45	.12
☐ 25 Willie Stargell	4.00	1.80	.50
☐ 26 Dick Allen	1.00	.45	.12
☐ 27 Carlton Fisk	12.00	5.50	1.50
☐ 28 Ferguson Jenkins	3.00	1.35	.35
☐ 29 Phil Niekro	3.00	1.35	.35
☐ 30 Gary Nolan	.50	.23	.06
☐ 31 Joe Torre	1.00	.45	.12
☐ 32 Bobby Tolan	.50	.23	.06
☐ 33 Nate Colbert	.50	.23	.06
☐ 34 Joe Morgan	4.00	1.80	.50
☐ 35 Bert Blyleven	1.00	.45	.12
☐ 36 Joe Rudi	.75	.35	.09
☐ 37 Ralph Garr	.50	.23	.06
☐ 38 Gaylord Perry	3.00	1.35	.35
☐ 39 Bobby Grich	.75	.35	.09
☐ 40 Lou Brock	4.00	1.80	.50
☐ 41 Pete Broberg	.50	.23	.06
☐ 42 Manny Sanguillen	.50	.23	.06
☐ 43 Willie Davis	.75	.35	.09
☐ 44 Dave Kingman	.75	.35	.09
☐ 45 Carlos May	.50	.23	.06
☐ 46 Tom Seaver	8.00	3.60	1.00
☐ 47 Mike Cuellar	.50	.23	.06
☐ 48 Joe Coleman	.50	.23	.06
☐ 49 Claude Osteen	.50	.23	.06
☐ 50 Steve Kline	.50	.23	.06
☐ 51 Rod Carew	5.00	2.20	.60
☐ 52 Al Kaline	6.00	2.70	.75
☐ 53 Larry Dierker	.75	.35	.09
☐ 54 Ron Santo	1.00	.45	.12

1974 Kellogg's

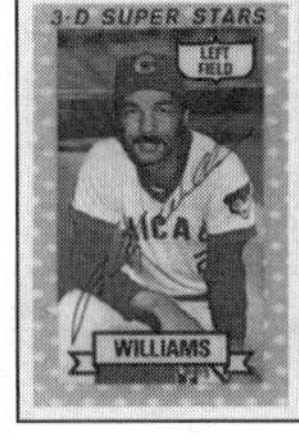

The cards in this 54-card set measure 2 1/8" by 3 1/4". In 1974 the Kellogg's set returned to its 3-D format; it also returned to the smaller-size card. Complete sets could be obtained from the company through a box-top offer. The cards are numbered on the back. Cards still found with the wrapper intact are valued 25 percent greater than the values listed below.

	NRMT	VG-E	GOOD
COMPLETE SET (54)	60.00	27.00	7.50
COMMON CARD (1-54)	.50	.23	.06
☐ 1 Bob Gibson	3.00	1.35	.35
☐ 2 Rick Monday	.50	.23	.06
☐ 3 Joe Coleman	.50	.23	.06
☐ 4 Bert Campaneris	.75	.35	.09
☐ 5 Carlton Fisk	5.00	2.20	.60
☐ 6 Jim Palmer	3.00	1.35	.35
☐ 7A Ron Santo ERR	6.00	2.70	.75
Chicago Cubs			
☐ 7B Ron Santo COR	.75	.35	.09
Chicago White Sox			
☐ 8 Nolan Ryan	25.00	11.00	3.10
☐ 9 Greg Luzinski	.75	.35	.09
☐ 10 Buddy Bell	.75	.35	.09
☐ 11 Bob Watson	.75	.35	.09
☐ 12 Bill Singer	.50	.23	.06
☐ 13 Dave May	.50	.23	.06
☐ 14 Jim Brewer	.50	.23	.06
☐ 15 Manny Sanguillen	.75	.35	.09
☐ 16 Jeff Burroughs	.75	.35	.09
☐ 17 Amos Otis	.75	.35	.09
☐ 18 Ed Goodson	.50	.23	.06
☐ 19 Nate Colbert	.50	.23	.06
☐ 20 Reggie Jackson	8.00	3.60	1.00
☐ 21 Ted Simmons	1.00	.45	.12
☐ 22 Bobby Murcer	.75	.35	.09
☐ 23 Willie Horton	.75	.35	.09
☐ 24 Orlando Cepeda	1.50	.70	.19
☐ 25 Ron Hunt	.50	.23	.06
☐ 26 Wayne Twitchell	.50	.23	.06
☐ 27 Ron Fairly	.50	.23	.06
☐ 28 Johnny Bench	6.00	2.70	.75
☐ 29 John Mayberry	.75	.35	.09
☐ 30 Rod Carew	3.00	1.35	.35
☐ 31 Ken Holtzman	.50	.23	.06
☐ 32 Billy Williams	3.00	1.35	.35
☐ 33 Dick Allen	1.50	.70	.19
☐ 34A Wilbur Wood ERR	3.00	1.35	.35
(1973 K 198)			
☐ 34B Wilbur Wood COR	.50	.23	.06
(1973 K 199)			
☐ 35 Danny Thompson	.50	.23	.06
☐ 36 Joe Morgan	3.00	1.35	.35
☐ 37 Willie Stargell	3.00	1.35	.35
☐ 38 Pete Rose	12.00	5.50	1.50
☐ 39 Bobby Bonds	1.50	.70	.19
☐ 40 Chris Speier	.50	.23	.06
☐ 41 Sparky Lyle	1.00	.45	.12
☐ 42 Cookie Rojas	.50	.23	.06
☐ 43 Tommy Davis	.75	.35	.09
☐ 44 Jim Hunter	3.00	1.35	.35
☐ 45 Willie Davis	.50	.23	.06
☐ 46 Bert Blyleven	.75	.35	.09
☐ 47 Pat Kelly	.50	.23	.06
☐ 48 Ken Singleton	.75	.35	.09
☐ 49 Manny Mota	.75	.35	.09
☐ 50 Dave Johnson	1.25	.55	.16
☐ 51 Sal Bando	.75	.35	.09
☐ 52 Tom Seaver	8.00	3.60	1.00
☐ 53 Felix Millan	.50	.23	.06
☐ 54 Ron Blomberg	.50	.23	.06

1975 Kellogg's

The cards in this 57-card set measure approximately 2 1/8" by 3 1/4". The 1975 Kellogg's 3-D set could be obtained card by card in cereal boxes or as a set from a box-top offer from the company. Card number 44, Jim Hunter, exists with the A's emblem or the Yankees emblem on the back of the card. Cards still found with the wrapper intact are valued 25 percent greater than the values listed below.

	NRMT	VG-E	GOOD
COMPLETE SET (57)	150.00	70.00	19.00
COMMON CARD (1-57)	1.00	.45	.12
☐ 1 Roy White	1.50	.70	.19
☐ 2 Ross Grimsley	1.00	.45	.12

Card	NRMT	VG-E	GOOD
☐ 3 Reggie Smith	1.50	.70	.19
☐ 4A Bob Grich ERR	1.50	.70	.19
(Bio last line begins 1973 work)			
☐ 4B Bob Grich COR	3.00	1.35	.35
(Bio last line begins because his fielding)			
☐ 5 Greg Gross	1.00	.45	.12
☐ 6 Bob Watson	1.50	.70	.19
☐ 7 Johnny Bench	10.00	4.50	1.25
☐ 8 Jeff Burroughs	1.00	.45	.12
☐ 9 Elliott Maddox	1.00	.45	.12
☐ 10 Jon Matlack	1.00	.45	.12
☐ 11 Pete Rose	20.00	9.00	2.50
☐ 12 Lee Stanton	1.00	.45	.12
☐ 13 Bake McBride	1.00	.45	.12
☐ 14 Jorge Orta	1.00	.45	.12
☐ 15 Al Oliver	1.50	.70	.19
☐ 16 John Briggs	1.00	.45	.12
☐ 17 Steve Garvey	5.00	2.20	.60
☐ 18 Brooks Robinson	7.50	3.40	.95
☐ 19 John Hiller	1.00	.45	.12
☐ 20 Lynn McGlothen	1.00	.45	.12
☐ 21 Cleon Jones	1.00	.45	.12
☐ 22 Fergie Jenkins	4.00	1.80	.50
☐ 23 Bill North	1.00	.45	.12
☐ 24 Steve Busby	1.00	.45	.12
☐ 25 Richie Zisk	1.00	.45	.12
☐ 26 Nolan Ryan	40.00	18.00	5.00
☐ 27 Joe Morgan	5.00	2.20	.60
☐ 28 Joe Rudi	1.00	.45	.12
☐ 29 Jose Cardenal	1.00	.45	.12
☐ 30 Andy Messersmith	1.00	.45	.12
☐ 31 Willie Montanez	1.00	.45	.12
☐ 32 Bill Buckner	1.50	.70	.19
☐ 33 Rod Carew	7.50	3.40	.95
☐ 34 Lou Piniella	1.50	.70	.19
☐ 35 Ralph Garr	1.00	.45	.12
☐ 36 Mike Marshall	1.00	.45	.12
☐ 37 Garry Maddox	1.00	.45	.12
☐ 38 Dwight Evans	1.50	.70	.19
☐ 39 Lou Brock	7.50	3.40	.95
☐ 40 Ken Singleton	1.00	.45	.12
☐ 41 Steve Braun	1.00	.45	.12
☐ 42 Rich Allen	2.00	.90	.25
☐ 43 John Grubb	1.00	.45	.12
☐ 44A Jim Hunter	5.00	2.20	.60
(Oakland A's team logo on back)			
☐ 44B Jim Hunter	15.00	6.75	1.85
(New York Yankees team logo on back)			
☐ 45 Gaylord Perry	4.00	1.80	.50
☐ 46 George Hendrick	1.00	.45	.12
☐ 47 Sparky Lyle	1.50	.70	.19
☐ 48 Dave Cash	1.00	.45	.12
☐ 49 Luis Tiant	1.25	.55	.16
☐ 50 Cesar Geronimo	1.00	.45	.12
☐ 51 Carl Yastrzemski	10.00	4.50	1.25
☐ 52 Ken Brett	1.00	.45	.12
☐ 53 Hal McRae	1.25	.55	.16
☐ 54 Reggie Jackson	15.00	6.75	1.85
☐ 55 Rollie Fingers	5.00	2.20	.60
☐ 56 Mike Schmidt	25.00	11.00	3.10
☐ 57 Richie Hebner	1.00	.45	.12

1976 Kellogg's

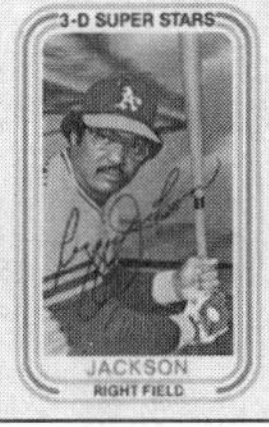

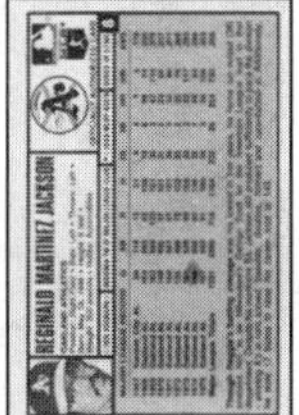

The cards in this 57-card set measure approximately 2 1/8" by 3 1/4". The 1976 Kellogg's 3-D set could be obtained card by card in cereal boxes or as a set from the company for box-tops. Card numbers 1-3 (marked in the checklist below with SP) were apparently printed apart from the other 54 and are in shorter supply. Cards still found with the wrapper intact are valued 25 percent greater than the values listed below.

	NRMT	VG-E	GOOD
COMPLETE SET (57)	75.00	34.00	9.50
COMMON CARD (1-3) SP	10.00	4.50	1.25
COMMON CARD (4-57)	.50	.23	.06

Card	NRMT	VG-E	GOOD
☐ 1 Steve Hargan SP	10.00	4.50	1.25
☐ 2 Claudell Washington SP	10.00	4.50	1.25
☐ 3 Don Gullett SP	10.00	4.50	1.25
☐ 4 Randy Jones	.50	.23	.06
☐ 5 Jim Hunter	3.00	1.35	.35
☐ 6A Clay Carroll	3.00	1.35	.35
Team logo			
Cincinnati Reds on back			
☐ 6B Clay Carroll	1.00	.45	.12
Team logo			
Chicago White Sox on back			
☐ 7 Joe Rudi	.50	.23	.06
☐ 8 Reggie Jackson	6.00	2.70	.75
☐ 9 Felix Millan	.50	.23	.06
☐ 10 Jim Rice	3.00	1.35	.35
☐ 11 Bert Blyleven	.75	.35	.09
☐ 12 Ken Singleton	.50	.23	.06
☐ 13 Don Sutton	2.50	1.10	.30
☐ 14 Joe Morgan	3.00	1.35	.35
☐ 15 Dave Parker	2.00	.90	.25
☐ 16 Dave Cash	.50	.23	.06
☐ 17 Ron LeFlore	.50	.23	.06
☐ 18 Greg Luzinski	.75	.35	.09
☐ 19 Dennis Eckersley	12.00	5.50	1.50
☐ 20 Bill Madlock	.75	.35	.09
☐ 21 George Scott	.50	.23	.06
☐ 22 Willie Stargell	3.00	1.35	.35
☐ 23 Al Hrabosky	.50	.23	.06
☐ 24 Carl Yastrzemski	6.00	2.70	.75
☐ 25A Jim Kaat	3.00	1.35	.35
Team logo			
Chicago White Sox on back			
☐ 25B Jim Kaat	1.50	.70	.19
Team logo			
Philadelphia Phillies on back			
☐ 26 Marty Perez	.50	.23	.06
☐ 27 Bob Watson	.75	.35	.09
☐ 28 Eric Soderholm	.50	.23	.06
☐ 29 Bill Lee	.50	.23	.06
☐ 30A Frank Tanana ERR	1.00	.45	.12
1975 ERA 2.63			
☐ 30B Frank Tanana COR	.75	.35	.09
1975 ERA 2.62			
☐ 31 Fred Lynn			
☐ 32A Tom Seaver ERR	7.50	3.40	.95
1967 Pct. 552			
with no decimal point)			
☐ 32B Tom Seaver COR	7.50	3.40	.95
1967 Pct. .552			
☐ 33 Steve Busby	.50	.23	.06
☐ 34 Gary Carter	4.00	1.80	.50
☐ 35 Rick Wise	.50	.23	.06
☐ 36 Johnny Bench	6.00	2.70	.75
☐ 37 Jim Palmer	3.00	1.35	.35
☐ 38 Bobby Murcer	.75	.35	.09
☐ 39 Von Joshua	.50	.23	.06
☐ 40 Lou Brock	4.00	1.80	.50
☐ 41A Mickey Rivers	2.00	.90	.25
No line in bio about Yankees			
☐ 41B Mickey Rivers	.75	.35	.09
Bio has "Yankees obtained ..."			
☐ 42 Manny Sanguillen	.50	.23	.06
☐ 43 Jerry Reuss	.50	.23	.06
☐ 44 Ken Griffey	1.00	.45	.12
☐ 45A Jorge Orta ERR	.75	.35	.09
Lifetime AB 1615			
☐ 45B Jorge Orta COR	.75	.35	.09
Lifetime AB 1616			
☐ 46 John Mayberry	.50	.23	.06
☐ 47A Vida Blue	.75	.35	.09
Bio "struck out more batters"			
☐ 47B Vida Blue	.75	.35	.09
Bio "pitched more innings"			
☐ 48 Rod Carew	4.00	1.80	.50
☐ 49A Jon Matlack ERR	.75	.35	.09
1975 ER 87			
☐ 49B Jon Matlack COR	.75	.35	.09
1975 ER 86			
☐ 50 Boog Powell	1.00	.45	.12
☐ 51A Mike Hargrove ERR	1.00	.45	.12
Lifetime AB 935			
☐ 51B Mike Hargrove COR	1.00	.45	.12
Lifetime AB 934			
☐ 52A Paul Lindblad ERR	.75	.35	.09
1975 ERA 2.43			
☐ 52B Paul Lindblad COR	.75	.35	.09
1975 ERA 2.72			
☐ 53 Thurman Munson	4.00	1.80	.50
☐ 54 Steve Garvey	2.50	1.10	.30
☐ 55 Pete Rose	12.00	5.50	1.50
☐ 56A Greg Gross ERR	.75	.35	.09
Lifetime games 334			
☐ 56B Greg Gross COR	.75	.35	.09
Lifetime games 302			
☐ 57 Ted Simmons	1.00	.45	.12

1977 Kellogg's

The cards in this 57-card set measure approximately 2 1/8" by 3 1/4". The 1977 Kellogg's series of 3-D baseball player cards could be obtained card by card from cereal boxes or by sending in box-tops and money. Each player's picture appears in miniature form on the reverse, an idea begun in 1971 and replaced in subsequent years by the use of a picture of the Kellogg's mascot. Cards still found with the wrapper intact are valued 25 percent greater than the values listed below.

	NRMT	VG-E	GOOD
COMPLETE SET (57)	50.00	22.00	6.25
COMMON CARD (1-57)	.50	.23	.06
☐ 1 George Foster	.75	.35	.09
☐ 2 Bert Campaneris	.50	.23	.06
☐ 3 Fergie Jenkins	2.50	1.10	.30
☐ 4 Dock Ellis	.50	.23	.06
☐ 5 John Montefusco	.50	.23	.06
☐ 6 George Brett	20.00	9.00	2.50
☐ 7 John Candelaria	.50	.23	.06
☐ 8 Fred Norman	.50	.23	.06
☐ 9 Bill Travers	.50	.23	.06
☐ 10 Hal McRae	.75	.35	.09
☐ 11 Doug Rau	.50	.23	.06
☐ 12 Greg Luzinski	.75	.35	.09
☐ 13 Ralph Garr	.50	.23	.06
☐ 14 Steve Garvey	2.50	1.10	.30
☐ 15 Rick Manning	.50	.23	.06
☐ 16A Lyman Bostock ERR	3.00	1.35	.35
(Dock Ellis photo			
on back)			
☐ 16B Lyman Bostock COR	.75	.35	.09
☐ 17 Randy Jones	.50	.23	.06
☐ 18 Ron Cey	.75	.35	.09
☐ 19 Dave Parker	1.25	.55	.16
☐ 20 Pete Rose	8.00	3.60	1.00
☐ 21A Wayne Garland	.50	.23	.06
(No trade to Cleve-			
land is mentioned)			
☐ 21B Wayne Garland	1.50	.70	.19
(Trade mentioned			
bio ends "now flip			
for Cleveland)			
☐ 22 Bill North	.50	.23	.06
☐ 23 Thurman Munson	2.50	1.10	.30
☐ 24 Tom Poquette	.50	.23	.06
☐ 25 Ron LeFlore	.50	.23	.06
☐ 26 Mark Fidrych	2.00	.90	.25
☐ 27 Sixto Lezcano	.50	.23	.06
☐ 28 Dave Winfield	7.50	3.40	.95
☐ 29 Jerry Koosman	.75	.35	.09
☐ 30 Mike Hargrove	.75	.35	.09
☐ 31 Willie Montanez	.50	.23	.06
☐ 32 Don Stanhouse	.50	.23	.06
☐ 33 Jay Johnstone	.50	.23	.06
☐ 34 Bake McBride	.50	.23	.06
☐ 35 Dave Kingman	.75	.35	.09
☐ 36 Fred Patek	.50	.23	.06
☐ 37 Garry Maddox	.50	.23	.06
☐ 38A Ken Reitz	.50	.23	.06
(No trade mentioned)			
☐ 38B Ken Reitz	1.50	.70	.19
(Trade mentioned)			
☐ 39 Bobby Grich	.75	.35	.09
☐ 40 Cesar Geronimo	.50	.23	.06
☐ 41 Jim Lonborg	.50	.23	.06
☐ 42 Ed Figueroa	.50	.23	.06
☐ 43 Bill Madlock	.75	.35	.09
☐ 44 Jerry Remy	.50	.23	.06
☐ 45 Frank Tanana	.75	.35	.09
☐ 46 Al Oliver	.75	.35	.09
☐ 47 Charlie Hough	.75	.35	.09
☐ 48 Lou Piniella	.75	.35	.09
☐ 49 Ken Griffey	1.50	.70	.19
☐ 50 Jose Cruz	.75	.35	.09
☐ 51 Rollie Fingers	2.50	1.10	.30
☐ 52 Chris Chambliss	.75	.35	.09
☐ 53 Rod Carew	5.00	2.20	.60
☐ 54 Andy Messersmith	.50	.23	.06
☐ 55 Mickey Rivers	.75	.35	.09
☐ 56 Butch Wynegar	.50	.23	.06
☐ 57 Steve Carlton	5.00	2.20	.60

1978 Kellogg's

The cards in this 57-card set measure 2 1/8" by 3 1/4". This 1978 3-D Kellogg's series marks the first year in which Tony the Tiger appears on the reverse of each card next to the team and MLB logos. Once again the set could be obtained as individually wrapped cards in cereal boxes or as a set via a mail-in offer. The key card in the set is Eddie Murray, as it was one of Murray's few card issues in 1978, the year of his Topps Rookie Card. Cards still found with the wrapper intact are valued 25 percent greater than the values listed below.

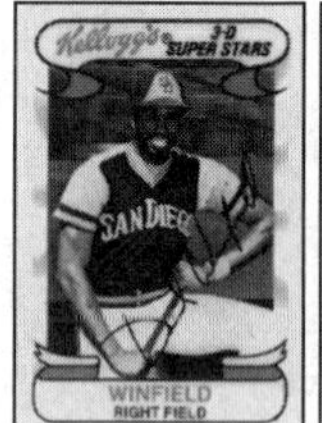

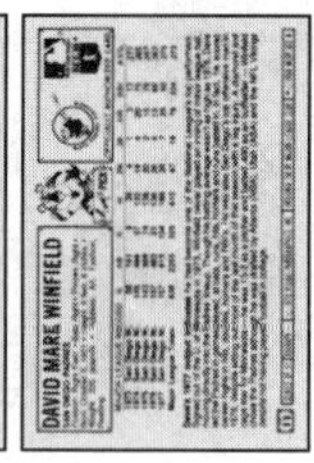

	NRMT	VG-E	GOOD
COMPLETE SET (57)	50.00	22.00	6.25
COMMON CARD (1-57)	.50	.23	.06
☐ 1 Steve Carlton	4.00	1.80	.50
☐ 2 Bucky Dent	.75	.35	.09
☐ 3 Mike Schmidt	8.00	3.60	1.00
☐ 4 Ken Griffey	1.00	.45	.12
☐ 5 Al Cowens	.50	.23	.06
☐ 6 George Brett	15.00	6.75	1.85
☐ 7 Lou Brock	3.00	1.35	.35
☐ 8 Rich Gossage	.75	.35	.09
☐ 9 Tom Johnson	.50	.23	.06
☐ 10 George Foster	.75	.35	.09
☐ 11 Dave Winfield	4.00	1.80	.50
☐ 12 Dan Meyer	.50	.23	.06
☐ 13 Chris Chambliss	.75	.35	.09
☐ 14 Paul Dade	.50	.23	.06
☐ 15 Jeff Burroughs	.50	.23	.06
☐ 16 Jose Cruz	.75	.35	.09
☐ 17 Mickey Rivers	.75	.35	.09
☐ 18 John Candelaria	.50	.23	.06
☐ 19 Ellis Valentine	.50	.23	.06
☐ 20 Hal McRae	.75	.35	.09
☐ 21 Dave Rozema	.50	.23	.06
☐ 22 Lenny Randle	.50	.23	.06
☐ 23 Willie McCovey	3.00	1.35	.35
☐ 24 Ron Cey	.75	.35	.09
☐ 25 Eddie Murray	25.00	11.00	3.10
☐ 26 Larry Bowa	.75	.35	.09
☐ 27 Tom Seaver	6.00	2.70	.75
☐ 28 Garry Maddox	.50	.23	.06
☐ 29 Rod Carew	4.00	1.80	.50
☐ 30 Thurman Munson	2.00	.90	.25
☐ 31 Garry Templeton	.75	.35	.09
☐ 32 Eric Soderholm	.50	.23	.06
☐ 33 Greg Luzinski	.75	.35	.09
☐ 34 Reggie Smith	.75	.35	.09
☐ 35 Dave Goltz	.50	.23	.06
☐ 36 Tommy John	.75	.35	.09
☐ 37 Ralph Garr	.50	.23	.06
☐ 38 Alan Bannister	.50	.23	.06
☐ 39 Bob Bailor	.50	.23	.06
☐ 40 Reggie Jackson	4.00	1.80	.50
☐ 41 Cecil Cooper	.75	.35	.09
☐ 42 Burt Hooton	.50	.23	.06
☐ 43 Sparky Lyle	.75	.35	.09
☐ 44 Steve Ontiveros	.50	.23	.06
☐ 45 Rick Reuschel	.50	.23	.06
☐ 46 Lyman Bostock	.75	.35	.09
☐ 47 Mitchell Page	.50	.23	.06
☐ 48 Bruce Sutter	1.00	.45	.12
☐ 49 Jim Rice	1.50	.70	.19
☐ 50 Ken Forsch	.50	.23	.06
☐ 51 Nolan Ryan	20.00	9.00	2.50
☐ 52 Dave Parker	1.00	.45	.12
☐ 53 Bert Blyleven	.75	.35	.09
☐ 54 Frank Tanana	.75	.35	.09
☐ 55 Ken Singleton	.50	.23	.06
☐ 56 Mike Hargrove	.75	.35	.09
☐ 57 Don Sutton	1.50	.70	.19

1979 Kellogg's

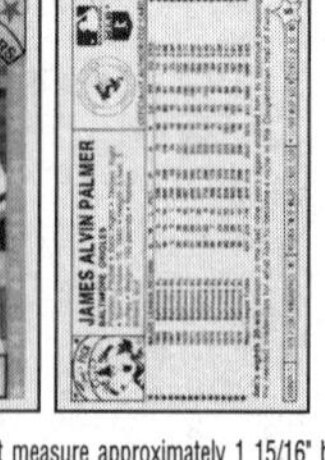

The cards in this 60-card set measure approximately 1 15/16" by 3 1/4". The 1979 edition of Kellogg's 3-D baseball cards have a 3/16" reduced width from the previous year; a nicely designed curved panel above the picture gives this set a distinctive appearance. The set contains the largest number of cards issued in a Kellogg's set since the 1971 series. Three different press runs produced numerous variations in this set. The first two printings were included in cereal boxes, while the third printing was for the complete set mail-in offer. Forty-seven cards have three variations, while thirteen cards (4, 6, 9, 15, 19, 20, 30, 33, 41, 43, 45, 51, and 54) are unchanged from the second and third printings. The three printings may be distinguished by the placement of the registered symbol by Tony the Tiger and by team logos. In the third printing, four cards (16, 18, 22, 44) show the "P" team logo (no registered symbol), and card numbers 56 and 57 omit the registered symbol by Tony. Cards still found with the wrapper intact are valued 25 percent greater than the values listed below.

	NRMT	VG-E	GOOD
COMPLETE SET (60)	30.00	13.50	3.70
COMMON CARD (1-60)	.25	.11	.03
☐ 1 Bruce Sutter	.50	.23	.06
☐ 2 Ted Simmons	.50	.23	.06
☐ 3 Ross Grimsley	.25	.11	.03
☐ 4 Wayne Nordhagen	.25	.11	.03
☐ 5 Jim Palmer	3.00	1.35	.35
☐ 6 John Henry Johnson	.25	.11	.03
☐ 7 Jason Thompson	.25	.11	.03
☐ 8 Pat Zachry	.25	.11	.03
☐ 9 Dennis Eckersley	3.00	1.35	.35
☐ 10 Paul Splittorff	.25	.11	.03
☐ 11 Ron Guidry	1.00	.45	.12
☐ 12 Jeff Burroughs	.25	.11	.03
☐ 13 Rod Carew	3.00	1.35	.35
☐ 14A Buddy Bell	1.50	.70	.19
(No trade mentioned)			
☐ 14B Buddy Bell	.50	.23	.06
(Traded to Rangers)			
☐ 15 Jim Rice	1.25	.55	.16
☐ 16 Garry Maddox	.25	.11	.03
☐ 17 Willie McCovey	2.00	.90	.25
☐ 18 Steve Carlton	3.00	1.35	.35
☐ 19 J.R. Richard	.25	.11	.03
☐ 20 Paul Molitor	8.00	3.60	1.00
☐ 21 Dave Parker	.75	.35	.09
☐ 22 Pete Rose	6.00	2.70	.75
☐ 23 Vida Blue	.50	.23	.06
☐ 24 Richie Zisk	.25	.11	.03
☐ 25 Darrell Porter	.25	.11	.03
☐ 26 Dan Driessen	.25	.11	.03
☐ 27 Geoff Zahn	.25	.11	.03
☐ 28 Phil Niekro	2.00	.90	.25
☐ 29 Tom Seaver	4.00	1.80	.50
☐ 30 Fred Lynn	.50	.23	.06
☐ 31 Bill Bonham	.25	.11	.03
☐ 32 George Foster	.50	.23	.06
☐ 33 Terry Puhl	.25	.11	.03
☐ 34 John Candelaria	.25	.11	.03
☐ 35 Bob Knepper	.25	.11	.03
☐ 36 Fred Patek	.25	.11	.03
☐ 37 Chris Chambliss	.25	.11	.03
☐ 38 Bob Forsch	.25	.11	.03
☐ 39 Ken Griffey	.50	.23	.06
☐ 40 Jack Clark	.50	.23	.06
☐ 41 Dwight Evans	.50	.23	.06
☐ 42 Lee Mazzilli	.25	.11	.03
☐ 43 Mario Guerrero	.25	.11	.03
☐ 44 Larry Bowa	.50	.23	.06
☐ 45 Carl Yastrzemski	4.00	1.80	.50
☐ 46 Reggie Jackson	4.00	1.80	.50
☐ 47 Rick Reuschel	.25	.11	.03
☐ 48 Mike Flanagan	.25	.11	.03
☐ 49 Gaylord Perry	2.00	.90	.25
☐ 50 George Brett	10.00	4.50	1.25
☐ 51 Craig Reynolds	.25	.11	.03
☐ 52 Dave Lopes	.50	.23	.06
☐ 53 Bill Almon	.25	.11	.03
☐ 54 Roy Howell	.25	.11	.03
☐ 55 Frank Tanana	.25	.11	.03
☐ 56 Doug Rau	.25	.11	.03
☐ 57 Rick Monday	.25	.11	.03
☐ 58 Jon Matlack	.25	.11	.03
☐ 59 Ron Jackson	.25	.11	.03
☐ 60 Jim Sundberg	.25	.11	.03

1980 Kellogg's

The cards in this 60-card set measure approximately 1 7/8" by 3 1/4". The 1980 Kellogg's 3-D set is quite similar to, but smaller (narrower) than, the other recent Kellogg's issues. Sets could be obtained card by card from cereal boxes or as a set from a box-top offer from the company. Cards still found with the wrapper intact are valued 25 percent greater than the values listed below.

	NRMT	VG-E	GOOD
COMPLETE SET (60)	25.00	11.00	3.10
COMMON CARD (1-60)	.25	.11	.03
☐ 1 Ross Grimsley	.25	.11	.03
☐ 2 Mike Schmidt	5.00	2.20	.60
☐ 3 Mike Flanagan	.25	.11	.03
☐ 4 Ron Guidry	.50	.23	.06
☐ 5 Bert Blyleven	.40	.18	.05
☐ 6 Dave Kingman	.35	.16	.04
☐ 7 Jeff Newman	.25	.11	.03
☐ 8 Steve Rogers	.25	.11	.03
☐ 9 George Brett	10.00	4.50	1.25
☐ 10 Bruce Sutter	.40	.18	.05
☐ 11 Gorman Thomas	.25	.11	.03
☐ 12 Darrell Porter	.25	.11	.03
☐ 13 Roy Smalley	.25	.11	.03
☐ 14 Steve Carlton	3.00	1.35	.35
☐ 15 Jim Palmer	3.00	1.35	.35

☐ 16 Bob Bailor	.25	.11	.03
☐ 17 Jason Thompson	.25	.11	.03
☐ 18 Graig Nettles	.50	.23	.06
☐ 19 Ron Cey	.50	.23	.06
☐ 20 Nolan Ryan	10.00	4.50	1.25
☐ 21 Ellis Valentine	.25	.11	.03
☐ 22 Larry Hisle	.25	.11	.03
☐ 23 Dave Parker	.75	.35	.09
☐ 24 Eddie Murray	6.00	2.70	.75
☐ 25 Willie Stargell	2.00	.90	.25
☐ 26 Reggie Jackson	4.00	1.80	.50
☐ 27 Carl Yastrzemski	3.00	1.35	.35
☐ 28 Andre Thornton	.25	.11	.03
☐ 29 Dave Lopes	.25	.11	.03
☐ 30 Ken Singleton	.25	.11	.03
☐ 31 Steve Garvey	1.50	.70	.19
☐ 32 Dave Winfield	2.00	.90	.25
☐ 33 Steve Kemp	.25	.11	.03
☐ 34 Claudell Washington	.25	.11	.03
☐ 35 Pete Rose	5.00	2.20	.60
☐ 36 Cesar Cedeno	.25	.11	.03
☐ 37 John Stearns	.25	.11	.03
☐ 38 Lee Mazzilli	.35	.16	.04
☐ 39 Larry Bowa	.35	.16	.04
☐ 40 Fred Lynn	.50	.23	.06
☐ 41 Carlton Fisk	3.00	1.35	.35
☐ 42 Vida Blue	.35	.16	.04
☐ 43 Keith Hernandez	.35	.16	.04
☐ 44 Jim Rice	1.25	.55	.16
☐ 45 Ted Simmons	.35	.16	.04
☐ 46 Chet Lemon	.25	.11	.03
☐ 47 Ferguson Jenkins	2.00	.90	.25
☐ 48 Gary Matthews	.35	.16	.04
☐ 49 Tom Seaver	4.00	1.80	.50
☐ 50 George Foster	.25	.11	.03
☐ 51 Phil Niekro	2.00	.90	.25
☐ 52 Johnny Bench	3.00	1.35	.35
☐ 53 Buddy Bell	.50	.23	.06
☐ 54 Lance Parrish	.35	.16	.04
☐ 55 Joaquin Andujar	.25	.11	.03
☐ 56 Don Baylor	.50	.23	.06
☐ 57 Jack Clark	.25	.11	.03
☐ 58 J.R. Richard	.35	.16	.04
☐ 59 Bruce Bochte	.25	.11	.03
☐ 60 Rod Carew	3.00	1.35	.35

1981 Kellogg's

The cards in this 66-card set measure 2 1/2" by 3 1/2". The 1981 Kellogg's set witnessed an increase in both the size of the card and the size of the set. For the first time, cards were not packed in cereal packages but available only by mail-in procedure. The offer for the card set was advertised on boxes of Kellogg's Corn Flakes. The cards were printed on a different stock than in previous years, presumably to prevent the cracking problem which has plagued all Kellogg's 3-D issues. At the end of the promotion, the remainder of the sets not distributed (to cereal-eaters), were "sold" into the organized hobby, thus creating a situation where the set is relatively plentiful compared to other years of Kellogg's. Cards from this set may be found without the laminated finish that creates the 3D effect.

	NRMT	VG-E	GOOD
COMPLETE SET (66)	12.00	5.50	1.50
COMMON CARD (1-66)	.10	.05	.01
☐ 1 George Foster	.20	.09	.03
☐ 2 Jim Palmer	1.00	.45	.12
☐ 3 Reggie Jackson	1.50	.70	.19
☐ 4 Al Oliver	.20	.09	.03
☐ 5 Mike Schmidt	2.00	.90	.25
☐ 6 Nolan Ryan	4.00	1.80	.50
☐ 7 Bucky Dent	.20	.09	.03
☐ 8 George Brett	3.00	1.35	.35
☐ 9 Jim Rice	.20	.09	.03
☐ 10 Steve Garvey	.30	.14	.04
☐ 11 Willie Stargell	.75	.35	.09
☐ 12 Phil Niekro	.75	.35	.09
☐ 13 Dave Parker	.20	.09	.03
☐ 14 Cesar Cedeno	.10	.05	.01
☐ 15 Don Baylor	.20	.09	.03
☐ 16 J.R. Richard	.10	.05	.01
☐ 17 Tony Perez	.50	.23	.06
☐ 18 Eddie Murray	1.50	.70	.19
☐ 19 Chet Lemon	.10	.05	.01
☐ 20 Ben Oglivie	.10	.05	.01
☐ 21 Dave Winfield	1.50	.70	.19
☐ 22 Joe Morgan	.75	.35	.09
☐ 23 Vida Blue	.20	.09	.03
☐ 24 Willie Wilson	.10	.05	.01
☐ 25 Steve Henderson	.10	.05	.01
☐ 26 Rod Carew	1.00	.45	.12
☐ 27 Garry Templeton	.10	.05	.01
☐ 28 Dave Concepcion	.20	.09	.03
☐ 29 Dave Lopes	.20	.09	.03
☐ 30 Ken Landreaux	.10	.05	.01
☐ 31 Keith Hernandez	.20	.09	.03
☐ 32 Cecil Cooper	.20	.09	.03
☐ 33 Rickey Henderson	2.00	.90	.25
☐ 34 Frank White	.20	.09	.03
☐ 35 George Hendrick	.10	.05	.01
☐ 36 Reggie Smith	.20	.09	.03
☐ 37 Tug McGraw	.10	.05	.01
☐ 38 Tom Seaver	1.50	.70	.19
☐ 39 Ken Singleton	.20	.09	.03
☐ 40 Fred Lynn	.10	.05	.01
☐ 41 Rich Gossage	.30	.14	.04
☐ 42 Terry Puhl	.10	.05	.01
☐ 43 Larry Bowa	.10	.05	.01
☐ 44 Phil Garner	.10	.05	.01
☐ 45 Ron Guidry	.15	.07	.02
☐ 46 Lee Mazzilli	.10	.05	.01
☐ 47 Dave Kingman	.20	.09	.03
☐ 48 Carl Yastrzemski	1.00	.45	.12
☐ 49 Rick Burleson	.10	.05	.01
☐ 50 Steve Carlton	1.00	.45	.12
☐ 51 Alan Trammell	.75	.35	.09
☐ 52 Tommy John	.20	.09	.03
☐ 53 Paul Molitor	2.00	.90	.25
☐ 54 Joe Charboneau	.30	.14	.04
☐ 55 Rick Langford	.10	.05	.01
☐ 56 Bruce Sutter	.20	.09	.03
☐ 57 Robin Yount	1.25	.55	.16
☐ 58 Steve Stone	.10	.05	.01
☐ 59 Larry Gura	.10	.05	.01
☐ 60 Mike Flanagan	.10	.05	.01
☐ 61 Bob Horner	.10	.05	.01
☐ 62 Bruce Bochte	.10	.05	.01
☐ 63 Pete Rose	1.50	.70	.19
☐ 64 Buddy Bell	.20	.09	.03
☐ 65 Johnny Bench	1.50	.70	.19
☐ 66 Mike Hargrove	.20	.09	.03

1982 Kellogg's

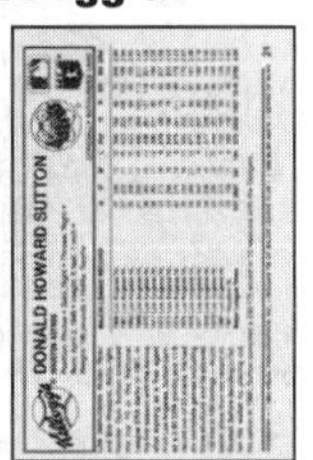

The cards in this 64-card set measure 2 1/8" by 3 1/4". The 1982 version of 3-D cards prepared for the Kellogg Company by Visual Panographics, Inc., is not only smaller in physical dimensions from the 1981 series (which was standard card size at 2 1/2" by 3 1/2") but is also two cards shorter in length (64 in '82 and 66 in '81). In addition, while retaining the policy of not inserting single cards into cereal packages and offering the sets through box-top mail-ins only, the Kellogg Company accepted box tops from four types of cereals, as opposed to only one type the previous year. Each card features a color 3-D ballplayer picture with a vertical line of white stars on each side set upon a blue background. The player's name and the word Kellogg's are printed in red on the obverse, and the card number is found on the bottom right of the reverse. Every card in the set has a statistical procedural error that was never corrected. All seasonal averages were added up and then divided by the number of seasons played.

	NRMT	VG-E	GOOD
COMPLETE SET (64)	15.00	6.75	1.85
COMMON CARD (1-64)	.15	.07	.02
☐ 1 Richie Zisk	.15	.07	.02
☐ 2 Bill Buckner	.25	.11	.03
☐ 3 George Brett	4.00	1.80	.50
☐ 4 Rickey Henderson	2.00	.90	.25
☐ 5 Jack Morris	.30	.14	.04
☐ 6 Ozzie Smith	2.50	1.10	.30
☐ 7 Rollie Fingers	.50	.23	.06
☐ 8 Tom Seaver	1.50	.70	.19
☐ 9 Fernando Valuenzuela	.50	.23	.06
☐ 10 Hubie Brooks	.15	.07	.02
☐ 11 Nolan Ryan	4.00	1.80	.50
☐ 12 Dave Winfield	1.25	.55	.16
☐ 13 Bob Horner	.25	.11	.03
☐ 14 Reggie Jackson	1.50	.70	.19
☐ 15 Burt Hooton	.15	.07	.02
☐ 16 Mike Schmidt	2.00	.90	.25
☐ 17 Bruce Sutter	.20	.09	.03
☐ 18 Pete Rose	2.00	.90	.25
☐ 19 Dave Kingman	.25	.11	.03
☐ 20 Neil Allen	.15	.07	.02
☐ 21 Don Sutton	.40	.18	.05
☐ 22 Dave Concepcion	.25	.11	.03
☐ 23 Keith Hernandez	.25	.11	.03
☐ 24 Gary Carter	.40	.18	.05
☐ 25 Carlton Fisk	1.50	.70	.19
☐ 26 Ron Guidry	.20	.09	.03
☐ 27 Steve Carlton	1.00	.45	.12
☐ 28 Robin Yount	1.50	.70	.19
☐ 29 John Castino	.15	.07	.02
☐ 30 Johnny Bench	1.00	.45	.12
☐ 31 Bob Knepper	.15	.07	.02
☐ 32 Rich Gossage	.20	.09	.03
☐ 33 Buddy Bell	.25	.11	.03
☐ 34 Art Howe	.15	.07	.02
☐ 35 Tony Armas	.15	.07	.02
☐ 36 Phil Niekro	.50	.23	.06
☐ 37 Len Barker	.15	.07	.02
☐ 38 Bob Grich	.20	.09	.03
☐ 39 Steve Kemp	.15	.07	.02
☐ 40 Kirk Gibson	.50	.23	.06
☐ 41 Carney Lansford	.15	.07	.02
☐ 42 Jim Palmer	1.00	.45	.12
☐ 43 Carl Yastrzemski	.75	.35	.09
☐ 44 Rick Burleson	.15	.07	.02
☐ 45 Dwight Evans	.25	.11	.03
☐ 46 Ron Cey	.25	.11	.03
☐ 47 Steve Garvey	.25	.11	.03
☐ 48 Dave Parker	.40	.18	.05
☐ 49 Mike Easler	.15	.07	.02
☐ 50 Dusty Baker	.25	.11	.03
☐ 51 Rod Carew	.75	.35	.09
☐ 52 Chris Chambliss	.25	.11	.03
☐ 53 Tim Raines	.40	.18	.05
☐ 54 Chet Lemon	.15	.07	.02
☐ 55 Bill Madlock	.25	.11	.03
☐ 56 George Foster	.25	.11	.03
☐ 57 Dwayne Murphy	.15	.07	.02
☐ 58 Ken Singleton	.15	.07	.02
☐ 59 Mike Norris	.15	.07	.02
☐ 60 Cecil Cooper	.25	.11	.03
☐ 61 Al Oliver	.25	.11	.03
☐ 62 Willie Wilson	.15	.07	.02
☐ 63 Vida Blue	.20	.09	.03
☐ 64 Eddie Murray	1.50	.70	.19

1983 Kellogg's

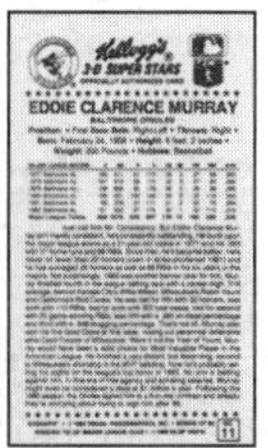

The cards in this 60-card set measure approximately 1 7/8" by 3 1/4". For the 14th year in a row, the Kellogg Company issued a card set of Major League players. The set of 3-D cards contains the photo, player's autograph, Kellogg's logo, and name and position of the player on the front of the card. The backs feature the player's team logo, career statistics, player biography, and a narrative on the player's career. Every card in the set has a statistical procedural error that was never corrected. All seasonal averages were added up and then divided by the number of seasons played.

	NRMT	VG-E	GOOD
COMPLETE SET (60)	15.00	6.75	1.85
COMMON CARD (1-60)	.15	.07	.02
☐ 1 Rod Carew	1.00	.45	.12
☐ 2 Rollie Fingers	.50	.23	.06
☐ 3 Reggie Jackson	1.50	.70	.19
☐ 4 George Brett	3.00	1.35	.35
☐ 5 Hal McRae	.30	.14	.04
☐ 6 Pete Rose	1.50	.70	.19
☐ 7 Fernando Valenzuela	.30	.14	.04
☐ 8 Rickey Henderson	1.50	.70	.19
☐ 9 Carl Yastrzemski	1.00	.45	.12
☐ 10 Rich Gossage	.30	.14	.04
☐ 11 Eddie Murray	1.25	.55	.16
☐ 12 Buddy Bell	.25	.11	.03
☐ 13 Jim Rice	.30	.14	.04
☐ 14 Robin Yount	1.50	.70	.19
☐ 15 Dave Winfield	1.00	.45	.12
☐ 16 Harold Baines	.30	.14	.04
☐ 17 Garry Templeton	.15	.07	.02
☐ 18 Bill Madlock	.30	.14	.04
☐ 19 Pete Vuckovich	.15	.07	.02
☐ 20 Pedro Guerrero	.30	.14	.04
☐ 21 Ozzie Smith	2.00	.90	.25
☐ 22 George Foster	.30	.14	.04
☐ 23 Willie Wilson	.15	.07	.02
☐ 24 Johnny Ray	.15	.07	.02
☐ 25 George Hendrick	.15	.07	.02
☐ 26 Andre Thornton	.15	.07	.02
☐ 27 Leon Durham	.15	.07	.02
☐ 28 Cecil Cooper	.15	.07	.02
☐ 29 Don Baylor	.30	.14	.04
☐ 30 Lonnie Smith	.15	.07	.02
☐ 31 Nolan Ryan	4.00	1.80	.50
☐ 32 Dan Quisenberry	.30	.14	.04
☐ 33 Len Barker	.15	.07	.02
☐ 34 Neil Allen	.15	.07	.02
☐ 35 Jack Morris	.30	.14	.04
☐ 36 Dave Stieb	.15	.07	.02
☐ 37 Bruce Sutter	.25	.11	.03
☐ 38 Jim Sundberg	.15	.07	.02
☐ 39 Jim Palmer	1.00	.45	.12
☐ 40 Lance Parrish	.25	.11	.03
☐ 41 Floyd Bannister	.15	.07	.02
☐ 42 Larry Gura	.15	.07	.02
☐ 43 Britt Burns	.15	.07	.02
☐ 44 Toby Harrah	.15	.07	.02
☐ 45 Steve Carlton	1.00	.45	.12
☐ 46 Greg Minton	.15	.07	.02
☐ 47 Gorman Thomas	.15	.07	.02
☐ 48 Jack Clark	.25	.11	.03
☐ 49 Keith Hernandez	.30	.14	.04
☐ 50 Greg Luzinski	.30	.14	.04
☐ 51 Fred Lynn	.30	.14	.04
☐ 52 Dale Murphy	.50	.23	.06
☐ 53 Kent Hrbek	.30	.14	.04
☐ 54 Bob Horner	.15	.07	.02
☐ 55 Gary Carter	.50	.23	.06
☐ 56 Carlton Fisk	1.00	.45	.12
☐ 57 Dave Concepcion	.25	.11	.03
☐ 58 Mike Schmidt	2.00	.90	.25
☐ 59 Bill Buckner	.30	.14	.04
☐ 60 Bob Grich	.30	.14	.04

1983-96 Kellogg's Cereal Boxes

Kelloggs entered the hobby with it's 1983 Fernando Valenzuela Corn Flakes box. Today, Kelloggs is probably has the biggest stable of sports spokesmen from auto racing to rodeo. We have only priced the baseball cereal boxes at this time. The prices below reflect a flat cereal box.

	NRMT	VG-E	GOOD
COMPLETE SET	350.00	160.00	45.00
COMMON BOX	20.00	9.00	2.50
☐ 1 Fernando Valenzuela (Corn Flakes)	40.00	18.00	5.00
☐ 2 Nolan Ryan (Corn Flakes)	40.00	18.00	5.00
☐ 3 1995 Colorado Rockies (Frosted Flakes)	20.00	9.00	2.50
☐ 4 Carlos Baerga (Frosted Flakes)	20.00	9.00	2.50
☐ 5 Willie Mays (Corn Flakes) Back Photo	25.00	11.00	3.10
☐ 6 Willie Mays (Rasin Bran) Back Photo	25.00	11.00	3.10
☐ 7 Roberto Clemente (Corn Flakes)	30.00	13.50	3.70
☐ 8 Yogi Berra (Corn Flakes)	25.00	11.00	3.10
☐ 9 Hank Aaron (Corn Flakes)	25.00	11.00	3.10
☐ 10 Bob Gibson (Corn Flakes)	20.00	9.00	2.50
☐ 11 Ernie Banks (Corn Flakes)	25.00	11.00	3.10
☐ 12 Steve Carlton (Corn Flakes)	20.00	9.00	2.50
☐ 13 Lou Brock (Corn Flakes)	20.00	9.00	2.50
☐ 14 Ken Griffey Jr. (Frosted Flakes)	20.00	9.00	2.50
☐ 15 Reggie Jackson (Frosted Mini-Wheats)	25.00	11.00	3.10

1991 Kellogg's 3D

Sportflics/Optigraphics produced this 15-card set for Kellogg's, and the cards measure approximately 2 1/2" by 3 5/16". The fronts have a three-dimensional image that alternates between a posed or action color shot and a head and shoulders close-up. The card face is aqua blue, with white stripes (that turn pink) and white borders. In red and dark blue print, the horizontally oriented backs have a facial drawing of the player on the left half, and career summary on the right half. The cards are numbered on the back. The cards were inserted in specially marked boxes (18 oz. and 24 oz. only) of Kellogg's Corn Flakes. In addition, the complete set and a blue display rack were available through a mail-in offer for 4.95 and two UPC symbols.

	MINT	NRMT	EXC
COMPLETE SET (15)	8.00	3.60	1.00
COMMON CARD (1-15)	.50	.23	.06
☐ 1 Gaylord Perry	.75	.35	.09
☐ 2 Hank Aaron	1.50	.70	.19
☐ 3 Willie Mays	1.50	.70	.19
☐ 4 Ernie Banks	1.25	.55	.16
☐ 5 Bob Gibson	.75	.35	.09
☐ 6 Harmon Killebrew	.75	.35	.09
☐ 7 Rollie Fingers	.75	.35	.09
☐ 8 Steve Carlton	1.00	.45	.12
☐ 9 Billy Williams	.75	.35	.09
☐ 10 Lou Brock	1.00	.45	.12
☐ 11 Yogi Berra	1.25	.55	.16
☐ 12 Warren Spahn	1.00	.45	.12
☐ 13 Boog Powell	.50	.23	.06
☐ 14 Don Baylor	.50	.23	.06
☐ 15 Ralph Kiner	.75	.35	.09

1991 Kellogg's Leyendas

This 11-card "Hispanic Legends of Baseball" set was sponsored by Kellogg's and celebrates ten Hispanic greats from Major League Baseball. The cards were inserted in boxes of Kellogg's Corn Flakes, Frosted Flakes, and Fruit Loops in selected geographic areas. The cards measure the standard size. The fronts feature color player photos bordered in white. The pictures are accented above and on the

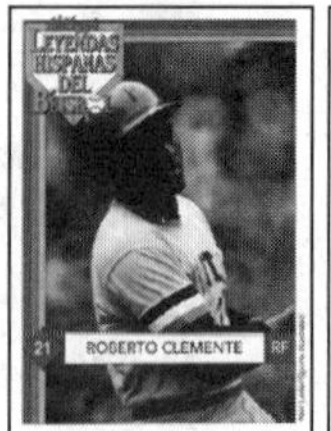

left by red, orange, and yellow border stripes. The set name appears on a home plate icon at the upper left corner, while the player's name appears in a white bar that cuts across the picture. On the bilingual (Spanish and English) backs, the biographical and statistical information are vertically oriented on the left portion, while a black and white head shot and player profile fill out the remainder of the back. The cards are unnumbered and checklisted below in alphabetical order.

	MINT	NRMT	EXC
COMPLETE SET (11)	15.00	6.75	1.85
COMMON CARD (1-10)	.50	.23	.06
☐ 1 Bert Campaneris	.75	.35	.09
☐ 2 Rod Carew	3.00	1.35	.35
☐ 3 Rico Carty	.75	.35	.09
☐ 4 Cesar Cedeno	.75	.35	.09
☐ 5 Orlando Cepeda	2.00	.90	.25
☐ 6 Roberto Clemente	12.00	5.50	1.50
☐ 7 Mike Cuellar	.75	.35	.09
☐ 8 Ed Figueroa	.50	.23	.06
☐ 9 Minnie Minoso	1.25	.55	.16
☐ 10 Manny Sanguillen	.50	.23	.06
☐ NNO Title Card	.50	.23	.06

1991 Kellogg's Stand Ups

This set was sponsored by Kellogg's in honor of six retired baseball stars as part of a promotion entitled "Baseball Greats." Six different stars are featured on the backs of (specially marked 7 oz. and 12 oz.) Kellogg's Corn Flakes boxes. Since there were two different size boxes, there are two sizes of each card, the larger is approximately 9 1/4" by 6" coming from the 12 oz. box. The color action portraits can be cut out and stood up for display, and career highlights appear to the right of the stand up. The boxes are unnumbered and checklisted below in alphabetical order. All six of these players were also included in the 15-card Kellogg's 3D Baseball Greats set. The complete set price below includes either the small or the large package cards but not both.

	MINT	NRMT	EXC
COMPLETE SET (6)	10.00	4.50	1.25
COMMON CARD (1-6)	2.00	.90	.25
☐ 1 Hank Aaron	3.50	1.55	.45
☐ 2 Ernie Banks	3.00	1.35	.35
☐ 3 Yogi Berra	3.00	1.35	.35
☐ 4 Lou Brock	2.00	.90	.25
☐ 5 Steve Carlton	2.00	.90	.25
☐ 6 Bob Gibson	2.50	1.10	.30

1992 Kellogg's All-Stars

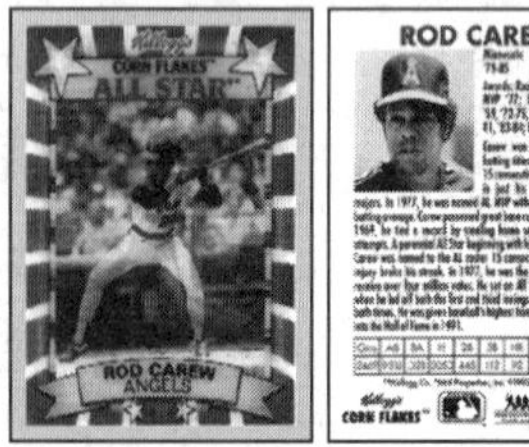

This ten-card standard-size set was produced by Optigraphics Corp. (Grand Prairie, TX) for Kellogg's and features retired baseball stars. One card was protected by a cello pack and inserted into Kellogg's cereal boxes. In the U.S., the cards were inserted in boxes of Corn Flakes, while in Canada they were inserted in Frosted Flakes and some other cereals. The complete set and a baseball display board to hold the collection were available through a mail-in offer for 4.75 and two UPC symbols from the side panel of Corn Flakes boxes (in Canada, for 7.99 and three tokens; one token was found on the side panel of each cereal box). The front of the "Double Action" cards have a three-dimensional image that alternates between two action shots and gives the impression of a batter or pitcher in motion. The pictures are bordered in red, white, and blue. The backs carry a black and white close-up photo, summary of the player's career (teams and years he played for them), awards, and career highlights. The Canadian Frosted Flakes cards are valued at two times the values listed below. The box back pictures both images of the Seaver card. While these pictures resemble the actual card, they are not standard-size or even rectangulary shaped.

	MINT	NRMT	EXC
COMPLETE SET (10)	5.00	2.20	.60
COMMON CARD (1-10)	.25	.11	.03
☐ 1 Willie Stargell	.75	.35	.09
☐ 2 Tony Perez	.50	.23	.06
☐ 3 Jim Palmer	1.00	.45	.12
☐ 4 Rod Carew	1.00	.45	.12
☐ 5 Tom Seaver	1.50	.70	.19
☐ 6 Phil Niekro	.75	.35	.09
☐ 7 Bill Madlock	.25	.11	.03
☐ 8 Jim Rice	.50	.23	.06
☐ 9 Dan Quisenberry	.25	.11	.03
☐ 10 Mike Schmidt	2.00	.90	.25

1992 Kellogg's Frosted Flakes Box Back

Some specially marked backs of Frosted Flakes show a team photo of the 1992 World Champion Toronto Blue Jays with facsimile autographs.The back is blank-backedand mesaures 7 1/2" by 11 1/8" The front features a green-bordered color team photo. All the text is billingual (French and English).

	MINT	EXC	G-VG
COMMON CARD	20.00	9.00	2.50
COMMON BOX	20.00	9.00	2.50
☐ 1 Toronto Blue Jays Team Photo (With facsimile autographs)	20.00	9.00	2.50

1994 Kellogg's Clemente

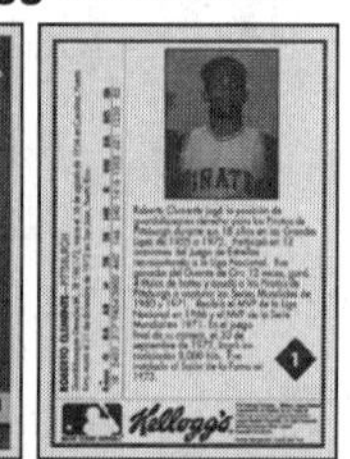

Protected by a clear plastic cello pack, these three standard-size cards were inserted into Kellogg's Corn Flakes cereal boxes in Puerto Rico, one card per box. The 18-ounce boxes commemorate the 20th anniversary of Clemente's 3,000th hit, the foundation of the Ciudad Deportiva Roberto Clemente, and his unexpected death. The fronts feature color action player photos bordered in white. The pictures are accented by green, blue and red stripes. The player's name and number are printed inside a yellow bar on the bottom of the photo. The team logo appears in the upper right corner, while the set name appears on a home plate icon at the upper left corner. On the backs, the biographical and statistical information are vertically oriented on the left portion, while a black-and-white head shot and player profile fill out the remainder. All text is in Spanish.

	MINT	NRMT	EXC
COMPLETE SET (3)	35.00	16.00	4.40
COMMON CARD (1-3)	12.00	5.50	1.50
☐ 1 Roberto Clemente Holding bat over right shoulder	12.00	5.50	1.50
☐ 2 Roberto Clemente Running, looking forward	12.00	5.50	1.50
☐ 3 Roberto Clemente Running, looking to the side	12.00	5.50	1.50

1994 Kelly Russell Studios Will Clark

This is a double matted artist's rendering which measures 14" by 11". It is accompanied by a '93 season highlights panel and baseball card panel. This issued is subtitled "The Texas Thrill." This is part of a big set: need complete set information before we price this.

	MINT	NRMT	EXC
COMPLETE SET	5.00	2.20	.60
COMMON CARD	5.00	2.20	.60
☐ 1 Will Clark	5.00	2.20	.60

1969 Kelly's Pins

This set of 20 red, white and blue pins has a very heavy emphasis on the National League and especially the midwestern city teams. The pins are unnumbered and hence are listed below in alphabetical order. The sponsor was Kelly's Potato Chips. Each pin measures approximately 1 3/16" in diameter. A black and white player photo is encircled by a blue (NL) or red (AL) band containing the player and team name as well as "Kelly's" and "ZIP".

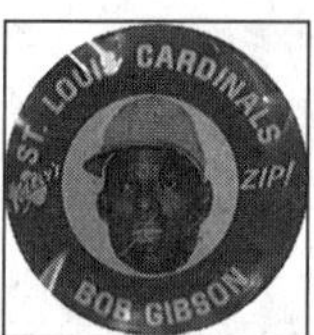

	NRMT	VG-E	GOOD
COMPLETE SET	200.00	90.00	25.00
COMMON PIN	4.00	1.80	.50
☐ 1 Luis Aparicio	12.00	5.50	1.50
☐ 2 Ernie Banks	15.00	6.75	1.85
☐ 3 Glenn Beckert	4.00	1.80	.50
☐ 4 Lou Brock	15.00	6.75	1.85
☐ 5 Curt Flood	7.50	3.40	.95
☐ 6 Bob Gibson	15.00	6.75	1.85
☐ 7 Joel Horlen	4.00	1.80	.50
☐ 8 Al Kaline	20.00	9.00	2.50
☐ 9 Don Kessinger	4.00	1.80	.50
☐ 10 Mickey Lolich	6.00	2.70	.75
☐ 11 Juan Marichal	12.00	5.50	1.50
☐ 12 Willie Mays	35.00	16.00	4.40
☐ 13 Tim McCarver	6.00	2.70	.75
☐ 14 Denny McLain	6.00	2.70	.75
☐ 15 Pete Rose	45.00	20.00	5.50
☐ 16 Ron Santo	6.00	2.70	.75
☐ 17 Joe Torre	6.00	2.70	.75
☐ 18 Pete Ward	4.00	1.80	.50
☐ 19 Billy Williams	12.00	5.50	1.50
☐ 20 Carl Yastrzemski	25.00	11.00	3.10

1888 Kimball's N184

This set of 50 color pictures of contemporary athletes was Kimball's answer to the sets produced by Allen and Ginter (N28 and N29) and Goodwin (N162). Issued in 1888, the cards are backlisted but are not numbered. The cards are listed below in alphabetical order without regard to sport. There are four baseball players in the set. An album (catalog: A42) was offered as a premium in exchange for coupons found in the tobacco packages. The baseball players are noted in the checklist below by BB after their name; boxers are noted by BOX.

	EX-MT	VG-E	GOOD
COMPLETE SET (50)	7000.00	3200.00	900.00
COMMON BASEBALL	700.00	325.00	90.00
COMMON BOXER	250.00	110.00	31.00
COMMON OTHERS	90.00	40.00	11.00
☐ 1 Wm. Beach	90.00	40.00	11.00
☐ 2 Marve Beardsley	90.00	40.00	11.00
☐ 3 Chas. P. Blatt	90.00	40.00	11.00
☐ 4 Blondin	100.00	45.00	12.50
☐ 5 Paul Boynton	90.00	40.00	11.00
☐ 6 E.A.(Ernie) Burch BB	700.00	325.00	90.00
☐ 7 Patsy Cardiff	90.00	40.00	11.00
☐ 8 Phillip Casey	90.00	40.00	11.00
☐ 9 J.C. Cockburn	90.00	40.00	11.00
☐ 10 Dell Darling BB	700.00	325.00	90.00
☐ 11 Jack Dempsey BOX	300.00	135.00	38.00
☐ 12 Della Ferrell	90.00	40.00	11.00
☐ 13 Clarence Freeman	90.00	40.00	11.00
☐ 14 Louis George	90.00	40.00	11.00
☐ 15 W.G. George	90.00	40.00	11.00
☐ 16 George W. Hamilton	100.00	45.00	12.50
☐ 17 Edward Hanlan	100.00	45.00	12.50
☐ 18 C.H. Heins	90.00	40.00	11.00
☐ 19 Hardie Henderson BB	700.00	325.00	90.00
☐ 20 Thomas H. Hume	90.00	40.00	11.00
☐ 21 J.H. Jordon	90.00	40.00	11.00
☐ 22 Johnny Kane	90.00	40.00	11.00
☐ 23 James McLaughlin	90.00	40.00	11.00
☐ 24 John McPherson	90.00	40.00	11.00
☐ 25 Joseph Morsler	90.00	40.00	11.00
☐ 26 William Muldoon	100.00	45.00	12.50
☐ 27 S. Muller	90.00	40.00	11.00
☐ 28 Isaac Murphy	100.00	45.00	12.50
☐ 29 John Murphy	90.00	40.00	11.00
☐ 30 L.E. Myers	90.00	40.00	11.00
☐ 31 Annie Oakley	300.00	135.00	38.00
☐ 32 Daniel O'Leary	90.00	40.00	11.00
☐ 33 James O'Neil BB Sic, O'Neill	750.00	350.00	95.00
☐ 34 Wm. Byrd Page	90.00	40.00	11.00
☐ 35 Axel Paulsen	90.00	40.00	11.00
☐ 36 Master Ray Perry	90.00	40.00	11.00
☐ 37 Duncan C. Ross	90.00	40.00	11.00
☐ 38 W.A. Rowe	90.00	40.00	11.00
☐ 39 Jacob Schaefer	90.00	40.00	11.00
☐ 40 M. Schloss	90.00	40.00	11.00
☐ 41 Jem Smith	90.00	40.00	11.00
☐ 42 Lillian Smith	90.00	40.00	11.00
☐ 43 Hattie Stewart	90.00	40.00	11.00
☐ 44 John L. Sullivan BOX	450.00	200.00	55.00
☐ 45 Arthur Wallace	90.00	40.00	11.00
☐ 46 Tommy Warren BOX	250.00	110.00	31.00
☐ 47 Ada Webb	90.00	40.00	11.00
☐ 48 John Wessels	90.00	40.00	11.00
☐ 49 Clarence Whistler	90.00	40.00	11.00
☐ 50 Charles Wood	90.00	40.00	11.00

1988 King-B Discs

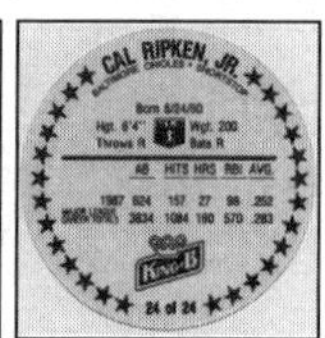

In 1988 King-B Quality Meat Products (Beef Jerky) introduced a set of 24 discs produced in conjunction with the Major League Baseball Players Association and Mike Schechter Associates. A single disc was inserted inside each specially marked package. The discs are numbered on the back and have a medium blue border on the front. Discs are approximately 2 3/8" in diameter. The disc backs contain very sparse personal or statistical information about the player and are printed in blue on white stock.

	MINT	NRMT	EXC
COMPLETE SET (24)	50.00	22.00	6.25
COMMON DISC (1-24)	1.00	.45	.12
☐ 1 Mike Schmidt	3.00	1.35	.35
☐ 2 Dale Murphy	2.00	.90	.25
☐ 3 Kirby Puckett	10.00	4.50	1.25
☐ 4 Ozzie Smith	5.00	2.20	.60
☐ 5 Tony Gwynn	8.00	3.60	1.00
☐ 6 Mark McGwire	10.00	4.50	1.25
☐ 7 George Brett	8.00	3.60	1.00
☐ 8 Darryl Strawberry	1.50	.70	.19
☐ 9 Wally Joyner	2.50	1.10	.30
☐ 10 Cory Snyder	1.00	.45	.12
☐ 11 Barry Bonds	10.00	4.50	1.25
☐ 12 Darrell Evans	1.00	.45	.12
☐ 13 Mike Scott	1.00	.45	.12
☐ 14 Andre Dawson	2.00	.90	.25
☐ 15 Don Mattingly	10.00	4.50	1.25
☐ 16 Candy Maldonado	1.00	.45	.12
☐ 17 Alvin Davis	1.00	.45	.12
☐ 18 Carlton Fisk	3.00	1.35	.35
☐ 19 Fernando Valenzuela	1.50	.70	.19
☐ 20 Roger Clemens	3.00	1.35	.35
☐ 21 Larry Parrish	1.00	.45	.12
☐ 22 Eric Davis	1.50	.70	.19
☐ 23 Paul Molitor	4.00	1.80	.50
☐ 24 Cal Ripken	12.00	5.50	1.50

1989 King-B Discs

The 1989 King-B Disc set contains 24 discs, each measuring approximately 2 3/4" in diameter. The set was prepared by MSA; there are no team logos featured on the disc. The year and lifetime statistics are featured for each player on the back of the disc. The discs were issued one per small cannister of Beef Jerky. It has been estimated that five million discs were produced for this set.

	MINT	NRMT	EXC
COMPLETE SET (24)	16.00	7.25	2.00
COMMON DISC (1-24)	.25	.11	.03
☐ 1 Kirk Gibson	.75	.35	.09
☐ 2 Eddie Murray	2.00	.90	.25
☐ 3 Wade Boggs	1.00	.45	.12
☐ 4 Mark McGwire	4.00	1.80	.50
☐ 5 Ryne Sandberg	2.50	1.10	.30
☐ 6 Ozzie Guillen	.25	.11	.03
☐ 7 Chris Sabo	.25	.11	.03
☐ 8 Joe Carter	1.00	.45	.12
☐ 9 Alan Trammell	.75	.35	.09
☐ 10 Nolan Ryan	6.00	2.70	.75
☐ 11 Bo Jackson	.75	.35	.09
☐ 12 Orel Hershiser	.50	.23	.06
☐ 13 Robin Yount	1.00	.45	.12
☐ 14 Frank Viola	.25	.11	.03
☐ 15 Darryl Strawberry	.50	.23	.06
☐ 16 Dave Winfield	1.00	.45	.12
☐ 17 Jose Canseco	1.50	.70	.19
☐ 18 Von Hayes	.25	.11	.03
☐ 19 Andy Van Slyke	.50	.23	.06
☐ 20 Pedro Guerrero	.25	.11	.03

☐ 21 Tony Gwynn	3.00	1.35	.35
☐ 22 Will Clark	1.50	.70	.19
☐ 23 Danny Jackson	.25	.11	.03
☐ 24 Pete Incaviglia	.25	.11	.03

1990 King-B Discs

The 1990 King-B Disc set contains 24 discs, each measuring approximately 2 3/4" inches in diameter. The set was prepared by MSA; there are no team logos featured on the disc. The year and lifetime statistics are featured for each player on the back of the disc. The discs were issued one per small cannister of Beef Jerky. The front design features a color head and shoulders player photo, encircled by a white-and-red inner border and a blue outer border. A banner with the words "1990 King-B" is superimposed at the bottom of the picture. In green print on blue, the back presents biography and statistics.

	MINT	NRMT	EXC
COMPLETE SET (24)	20.00	9.00	2.50
COMMON DISC (1-24)	.25	.11	.03
☐ 1 Mike Scott	.25	.11	.03
☐ 2 Kevin Mitchell	.25	.11	.03
☐ 3 Tony Gwynn	4.00	1.80	.50
☐ 4 Ozzie Smith	3.00	1.35	.35
☐ 5 Kirk Gibson	.50	.23	.06
☐ 6 Tim Raines	.25	.11	.03
☐ 7 Von Hayes	.25	.11	.03
☐ 8 Bobby Bonilla	.50	.23	.06
☐ 9 Wade Boggs	1.50	.70	.19
☐ 10 Chris Sabo	.25	.11	.03
☐ 11 Dale Murphy	1.00	.45	.12
☐ 12 Cory Snyder	.25	.11	.03
☐ 13 Fred McGriff	1.50	.70	.19
☐ 14 Don Mattingly	4.00	1.80	.50
☐ 15 Jerome Walton	.25	.11	.03
☐ 16 Ken Griffey Jr.	8.00	3.60	1.00
☐ 17 Bo Jackson	.75	.35	.09
☐ 18 Robin Yount	1.50	.70	.19
☐ 19 Rickey Henderson	1.50	.70	.19
☐ 20 Jim Abbott	.25	.11	.03
☐ 21 Kirby Puckett	4.00	1.80	.50
☐ 22 Nolan Ryan	8.00	3.60	1.00
☐ 23 Gregg Olson	.25	.11	.03
☐ 24 Lou Whitaker	.75	.35	.09

1991 King-B Discs

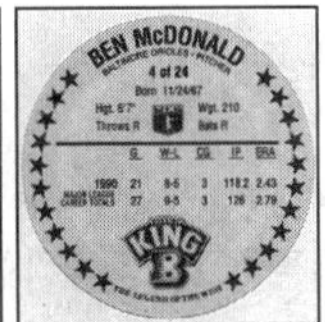

This was the fourth season that MSA issued discs as inserts in King-B meat products. These discs, which measure approximately 2 3/4" in diameter, feature leading major leaguers.

	MINT	NRMT	EXC
COMPLETE SET (24)	20.00	9.00	2.50
COMMON DISC (1-24)	.25	.11	.03
☐ 1 Willie McGee	.25	.11	.03
☐ 2 Kevin Seitzer	.25	.11	.03
☐ 3 Kevin Maas	.25	.11	.03
☐ 4 Ben McDonald	.50	.23	.06
☐ 5 Rickey Henderson	1.50	.70	.19
☐ 6 Ken Griffey Jr.	8.00	3.60	1.00
☐ 7 John Olerud	.25	.11	.03
☐ 8 Dwight Gooden	.50	.23	.06
☐ 9 Ruben Sierra	.25	.11	.03
☐ 10 Luis Polonia	.25	.11	.03
☐ 11 Wade Boggs	1.50	.70	.19
☐ 12 Ramon Martinez	1.00	.45	.12
☐ 13 Craig Biggio	1.25	.55	.16
☐ 14 Cecil Fielder	.75	.35	.09
☐ 15 Will Clark	1.50	.70	.19
☐ 16 Matt Williams	1.25	.55	.16
☐ 17 Sandy Alomar Jr.	.50	.23	.06
☐ 18 Dave Justice	1.25	.55	.16
☐ 19 Ryne Sandberg	3.00	1.35	.35
☐ 20 Benito Santiago	.25	.11	.03
☐ 21 Barry Bonds	2.00	.90	.25
☐ 22 Carlton Fisk	1.50	.70	.19
☐ 23 Kirby Puckett	4.00	1.80	.50
☐ 24 Jose Rijo	.25	.11	.03

1992 King-B Discs

These discs, which measure approximately 2 3/4" in diameter, feature top major league stars. These discs, inserted in beef jerky containers, were issued in conjunction with Michael Schecter Associates.

	MINT	NRMT	EXC
COMPLETE SET (24)	12.00	5.50	1.50
COMMON DISC (1-24)	.15	.07	.02
☐ 1 Terry Pendleton	.30	.14	.04
☐ 2 Chris Sabo	.15	.07	.02
☐ 3 Frank Thomas	3.00	1.35	.35
☐ 4 Todd Zeile	.15	.07	.02
☐ 5 Bobby Bonilla	.30	.14	.04
☐ 6 Howard Johnson	.15	.07	.02
☐ 7 Nolan Ryan	2.50	1.10	.30
☐ 8 Ken Griffey Jr.	3.00	1.35	.35
☐ 9 Roger Clemens	.75	.35	.09
☐ 10 Tony Gwynn	1.50	.70	.19
☐ 11 Steve Avery	.40	.18	.05
☐ 12 Cal Ripken	2.50	1.10	.30
☐ 13 Danny Tartabull	.15	.07	.02
☐ 14 Paul Molitor	.75	.35	.09
☐ 15 Willie McGee	.15	.07	.02
☐ 16 Wade Boggs	.60	.25	.07
☐ 17 Cecil Fielder	.30	.14	.04
☐ 18 Jack Morris	.30	.14	.04
☐ 19 Ryne Sandberg	1.25	.55	.16
☐ 20 Kirby Puckett	1.50	.70	.19
☐ 21 Craig Biggio	.40	.18	.05
☐ 22 Harold Baines	.15	.07	.02
☐ 23 Scott Erickson	.15	.07	.02
☐ 24 Joe Carter	.50	.23	.06

1993 King-B Discs

These discs marked the sixth consecutive season that Michael Schecter Associates in conjunction with King-B meat products produced a 24 disc set. This set measure approximately 2 3/4" in diameter and features major league stars.

	MINT	NRMT	EXC
COMPLETE SET (24)	5.00	2.20	.60
COMMON DISC (1-24)	.10	.05	.01
☐ 1 Barry Bonds	.25	.11	.03
☐ 2 Ken Griffey Jr.	2.00	.90	.25
☐ 3 Cal Ripken	1.50	.70	.19
☐ 4 Frank Thomas	2.00	.90	.25
☐ 5 Steve Avery	.20	.09	.03
☐ 6 Benito Santiago	.10	.05	.01
☐ 7 Luis Polonia	.10	.05	.01
☐ 8 Jose Rijo	.10	.05	.01
☐ 9 George Brett	1.00	.45	.12
☐ 10 Darren Daulton	.15	.07	.02
☐ 11 Cecil Fielder	.15	.07	.02
☐ 12 Ozzie Smith	.75	.35	.09
☐ 13 Joe Carter	.20	.09	.03
☐ 14 Dwight Gooden	.15	.07	.02
☐ 15 Tom Henke	.10	.05	.01
☐ 16 Brett Butler	.15	.07	.02
☐ 17 Nolan Ryan	1.50	.70	.19
☐ 18 Sandy Alomar	.15	.07	.02
☐ 19 Tom Glavine	.20	.09	.03
☐ 20 Rafael Palmeiro	.20	.09	.03
☐ 21 Roger Clemens	.40	.18	.05
☐ 22 Ryne Sandberg	.75	.35	.09
☐ 23 Doug Drabek	.10	.05	.01
☐ 24 Chuck Knoblauch	.30	.14	.04

1994 King-B Discs

The 1994 King-B set contains 24 round cards each measuring approximately 2 7/8" in diameter. On a white background, the fronts feature a color player portrait inside a dark purple circle that has the appearance of a disc. The player's name is printed in yellow and his team in white. All appear above the photo, while the year 1994 and the words "King B", printed on a pitcher's glove, appear under the photo. The backs present biography and statistics in purple print on white. The discs are numbered on the back.

	MINT	NRMT	EXC
COMPLETE SET (24)	5.00	2.20	.60
COMMON DISC (1-24)	.10	.05	.01
☐ 1 Fred McGriff	.25	.11	.03
☐ 2 Paul Molitor	.30	.14	.04
☐ 3 Jack McDowell	.15	.07	.02
☐ 4 Darren Daulton	.15	.07	.02
☐ 5 Wade Boggs	.30	.14	.04
☐ 6 Ken Griffey Jr.	1.00	.45	.12
☐ 7 Tim Salmon	.25	.11	.03
☐ 8 Dennis Eckersley	.15	.07	.02
☐ 9 Albert Belle	.50	.23	.06
☐ 10 Travis Fryman	.15	.07	.02
☐ 11 Chris Hoiles	.10	.05	.01
☐ 12 Kirby Puckett	.50	.23	.06
☐ 13 John Olerud	.15	.07	.02
☐ 14 Frank Thomas	1.00	.45	.12
☐ 15 Lenny Dykstra	.15	.07	.02
☐ 16 Andres Galarraga	.20	.09	.03
☐ 17 Barry Larkin	.25	.11	.03
☐ 18 Greg Maddux	.60	.25	.07
☐ 19 Mike Piazza	.60	.25	.07
☐ 20 Roberto Alomar	.30	.14	.04
☐ 21 Robin Ventura	.15	.07	.02
☐ 22 Ryne Sandberg	.40	.18	.05
☐ 23 Andy Van Slyke	.10	.05	.01
☐ 24 Barry Bonds	.25	.11	.03

1995 King-B Discs

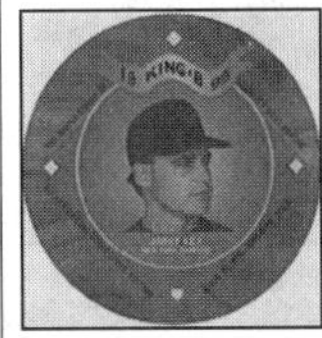

This was the eighth year that King-B, in conjunction with MSA enterprises, issued discs. The players featured are among the best in baseball. The backs have season and career stats as well as vital statistics.

	MINT	NRMT	EXC
COMPLETE SET (24)	20.00	9.00	2.50
COMMON DISC (1-24)	.15	.07	.02
☐ 1 Roberto Alomar	.75	.35	.09
☐ 2 Jeff Bagwell	1.50	.70	.19
☐ 3 Wade Boggs	.50	.23	.06
☐ 4 Barry Bonds	.75	.35	.09
☐ 5 Joe Carter	.40	.18	.05
☐ 6 Mariano Duncan	.15	.07	.02
☐ 7 Len Dykstra	.25	.11	.03
☐ 8 Andres Galarraga	.50	.23	.06
☐ 9 Matt Williams	.50	.23	.06
☐ 10 Raul Mondesi	.50	.23	.06
☐ 11 Ken Griffey Jr.	4.00	1.80	.50
☐ 12 Gregg Jefferies	.15	.07	.02
☐ 13 Fred McGriff	.50	.23	.06
☐ 14 Paul Molitor	.75	.35	.09
☐ 15 Dave Justice	.40	.18	.05
☐ 16 Mike Piazza	2.50	1.10	.30
☐ 17 Kirby Puckett	2.00	.90	.25
☐ 18 Cal Ripken	3.00	1.35	.35
☐ 19 Ivan Rodriguez	1.00	.45	.12
☐ 20 Ozzie Smith	1.00	.45	.12
☐ 21 Gary Sheffield	.60	.25	.07
☐ 22 Frank Thomas	4.00	1.80	.50
☐ 23 Greg Maddux	2.50	1.10	.30
☐ 24 Jimmy Key	.15	.07	.02

1996 King-B Discs

The 1996 King-B set consists of 24 round cards measuring approximately 2 7/8" in diameter. The fronts feature a color player photo with airbrushed uniforms. The year 1996 is on the left side, while the player's name and 9th annual Collectors edition appears on the bottom. The back has vital statistics, season and career statistics.

	MINT	NRMT	EXC
COMPLETE SET (24)	20.00	9.00	2.50
COMMON DISC (1-24)	.15	.07	.02
☐ 1 Roger Clemens	.75	.35	.09
☐ 2 Mo Vaughn	.75	.35	.09
☐ 3 Dante Bichette	.50	.23	.06
☐ 4 Jeff Bagwell	2.00	.90	.25
☐ 5 Randy Johnson	.75	.35	.09
☐ 6 Ken Griffey Jr.	3.00	1.35	.35
☐ 7 Kirby Puckett	1.50	.70	.19
☐ 8 Orel Hershiser	.25	.11	.03
☐ 9 Albert Belle	2.00	.90	.25
☐ 10 Tony Gwynn	1.50	.70	.19
☐ 11 Tom Glavine	.50	.23	.06
☐ 12 Jim Abbott	.15	.07	.02
☐ 13 Andres Galarraga	.50	.23	.06
☐ 14 Frank Thomas	4.00	1.80	.50
☐ 15 Barry Larkin	.50	.23	.06
☐ 16 Mike Piazza	2.50	1.10	.30
☐ 17 Matt Williams	.50	.23	.06
☐ 18 Greg Maddux	2.50	1.10	.30
☐ 19 Hideo Nomo	1.50	.70	.19
☐ 20 Roberto Alomar	.75	.35	.09
☐ 21 Ivan Rodriguez	1.00	.45	.12
☐ 22 Cal Ripken	3.00	1.35	.35
☐ 23 Barry Bonds	.75	.35	.09
☐ 24 Mark McGwire	1.25	.55	.16

1985 Kitty Clover Discs

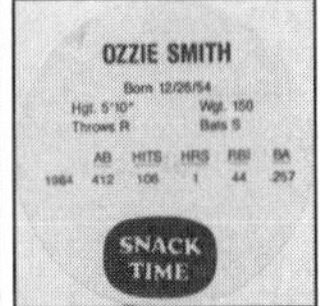

Very similar to the KAS test set, there was a Kitty Clover test set as well. The player selection is the same as the KAS test set. According to informed sources, 2000 sets were produced of this issue. The team insignias are all air-brushed out.

	NRMT	VG-E	GOOD
COMPLETE SET	700.00	325.00	90.00
COMMON DISC	15.00	6.75	1.85
☐ 1 Steve Carlton	35.00	16.00	4.40
☐ 2 Jack Clark	15.00	6.75	1.85
☐ 3 Rich Gossage	15.00	6.75	1.85
☐ 4 Tony Gwynn	75.00	34.00	9.50
☐ 5 Keith Hernandez	20.00	9.00	2.50
☐ 6 Bob Horner	15.00	6.75	1.85
☐ 7 Kent Hrbek	15.00	6.75	1.85
☐ 8 Willie McGee	20.00	9.00	2.50
☐ 9 Dan Quisenberry	15.00	6.75	1.85
☐ 10 Cal Ripken	150.00	70.00	19.00
☐ 11 Ryne Sandberg	75.00	34.00	9.50
☐ 12 Mike Schmidt	60.00	27.00	7.50
☐ 13 Tom Seaver	60.00	27.00	7.50
☐ 14 Ozzie Smith	75.00	34.00	9.50
☐ 15 Rick Sutcliffe	15.00	6.75	1.85
☐ 16 Bruce Sutter	15.00	6.75	1.85
☐ 17 Alan Trammell	17.50	8.00	2.20
☐ 18 Fernando Valenzuela	20.00	9.00	2.50
☐ 19 Willie Wilson	15.00	6.75	1.85
☐ 20 Dave Winfield	50.00	22.00	6.25

1992 Kodak Celebration Denver

Issued by Kodak to promote the Kodak Celebration of Baseball Fan Fair in Denver, August 14-16, 1992, this four-card standard-size set (plus one free admission coupon card) features Major League Baseball Players Alumni who were scheduled to appear at the show. Aside from the Jenkins card, which features a color painting of him, the fronts carry white-bordered color player action photos. The player's name and position appear in the lower right and the Kodak Celebration of Baseball logo appears in the lower left. The horizontal backs are framed by a black line and display the player's name, career highlights, and stats. The Kodak, Colorado Rockies, and MLBPA logos round out the back. The cards are unnumbered and checklisted below in alphabetical order.

	MINT	NRMT	EXC
COMPLETE SET (5)	12.00	5.50	1.50
COMMON CARD (1-5)	1.25	.55	.16
☐ 1 Orlando Cepeda	3.00	1.35	.35
☐ 2 Ferguson Jenkins Art	4.00	1.80	.50
☐ 3 Graig Nettles	2.00	.90	.25
☐ 4 Brooks Robinson	5.00	2.20	.60
☐ 5 Admission Coupon Card	1.25	.55	.16

1921 Koester's Bread World Series Issue D383

Issued in conjunction with the first all New York World Series, these cards feature members of the Giants and Yankees. The cards measure approximately 2" by 3 1/2" and are unnumbered. Therefore, we have sequenced them in alphabetical order by team. The following players are not known in the E121 issue: Ferguson, Mitchell, O'Leary, Barnes, Berry, Brown, Burkett, Cunningham and Stengel. These players sell at a premium over the other regular cards in this set.

	EX-MT	VG-E	GOOD
COMPLETE SET	3000.00	1350.00	375.00
COMMON CARD	50.00	22.00	6.25
☐ 1 Dave Bancroft	100.00	45.00	12.50
☐ 2 Jesse Barnes	50.00	22.00	6.25
☐ 3 Joe Berry	50.00	22.00	6.25
☐ 4 Eddie Brown	50.00	22.00	6.25
☐ 5 Jesse Burkett	100.00	45.00	12.50
☐ 6 George Burns	50.00	22.00	6.25
☐ 7 Red Causey	50.00	22.00	6.25
☐ 8 Bill Cunningham	50.00	22.00	6.25
☐ 9 Phil Douglas	50.00	22.00	6.25
☐ 10 Frank Frisch	100.00	45.00	12.50
☐ 11 Alex Gaston	50.00	22.00	6.25
☐ 12 Mike Gonzalez	50.00	22.00	6.25
☐ 13 Hugh Jennings CO	100.00	45.00	12.50
☐ 14 George Kelly	100.00	45.00	12.50
☐ 15 John McGraw MG	125.00	55.00	15.50
☐ 16 Irish Meusel	50.00	22.00	6.25
☐ 17 Art Nehf	75.00	34.00	9.50
☐ 18 Johnny Rawlings	50.00	22.00	6.25
☐ 19 Rosy Ryan	50.00	22.00	6.25
☐ 20 Slim Sallee	50.00	22.00	6.25
☐ 21 Red Shea	50.00	22.00	6.25
☐ 22 Earl Smith	50.00	22.00	6.25
☐ 23 Frank Snyder	50.00	22.00	6.25
☐ 24 Casey Stengel	150.00	70.00	19.00
☐ 25 Fred Toney	50.00	22.00	6.25
☐ 26 Ross Youngs	100.00	45.00	12.50
☐ 27 Frank Baker	100.00	45.00	12.50
☐ 28 Ping Bodie	50.00	22.00	6.25
☐ 29 Rip Collins	75.00	34.00	9.50
☐ 30 Al DeVormer	50.00	22.00	6.25
☐ 31 Alex Ferguson	50.00	22.00	6.25
☐ 32 Chick Fewster	50.00	22.00	6.25
☐ 33 Harry Harper	50.00	22.00	6.25
☐ 34 Chicken Hawks	50.00	22.00	6.25
☐ 35 Fred Hofmann	50.00	22.00	6.25
☐ 36 Waite Hoyt	100.00	45.00	12.50
☐ 37 Miller Huggins MG	100.00	45.00	12.50
☐ 38 Carl Mays	75.00	34.00	9.50
☐ 39 Mike McNally	50.00	22.00	6.25
☐ 40 Bob Meusel	75.00	34.00	9.50
☐ 41 Elmer Miller	50.00	22.00	6.25
☐ 42 Johnny Mitchell	50.00	22.00	6.25
☐ 43 Charlie O'Leary CO	50.00	22.00	6.25
☐ 44 Roger Peckinpaugh	75.00	34.00	9.50
☐ 45 Bill Piercy	50.00	22.00	6.25
☐ 46 Jack Quinn	75.00	34.00	9.50
☐ 47 Tom Rogers	50.00	22.00	6.25
☐ 48 Braggo Roth	50.00	22.00	6.25
☐ 49 Babe Ruth	500.00	220.00	60.00
☐ 50 Wally Schang	75.00	34.00	9.50
☐ 51 Bob Shawkey	75.00	34.00	9.50
☐ 52 Aaron Ward	50.00	22.00	6.25

1987 Kraft Foods

Specially marked boxes of 1987 Kraft Macaroni featured a pair of cards. The individual cards measure approximately 2 1/4" by 3 1/2" and are printed in color. The player's team insignia are airbrushed out as the set was only licensed by the Major League Baseball Players Association. The cards are blank backed and are numbered in the lower right corner of the card. The set is subtitled "Home Plate Heroes." The cards on the box provide a dotted blue line as a guide for accurately cutting the cards from the box. There were many different two-card panels. Panel prices are based on the sum of the individual player's values making up that particular panel.

	MINT	NRMT	EXC
COMPLETE SET (48)	30.00	13.50	3.70
COMMON CARD (1-48)	.15	.07	.02
☐ 1 Eddie Murray	1.50	.70	.19
☐ 2 Dale Murphy	1.00	.45	.12
☐ 3 Cal Ripken	4.00	1.80	.50
☐ 4 Mike Scott	.15	.07	.02
☐ 5 Jim Rice	.25	.11	.03
☐ 6 Jody Davis	.15	.07	.02
☐ 7 Wade Boggs	1.25	.55	.16
☐ 8 Ryne Sandberg	2.00	.90	.25
☐ 9 Wally Joyner	.50	.23	.06
☐ 10 Eric Davis	.25	.11	.03
☐ 11 Ozzie Guillen	.15	.07	.02
☐ 12 Tony Pena	.15	.07	.02
☐ 13 Harold Baines	.25	.11	.03
☐ 14 Johnny Ray	.15	.07	.02
☐ 15 Joe Carter	.75	.35	.09
☐ 16 Ozzie Smith	2.00	.90	.25
☐ 17 Cory Snyder	.15	.07	.02
☐ 18 Vince Coleman	.15	.07	.02
☐ 19 Kirk Gibson	.25	.11	.03
☐ 20 Steve Garvey	.50	.23	.06
☐ 21 George Brett	3.00	1.35	.35
☐ 22 John Tudor	.15	.07	.02
☐ 23 Robin Yount	1.00	.45	.12
☐ 24 Von Hayes	.15	.07	.02
☐ 25 Kent Hrbek	.15	.07	.02
☐ 26 Darryl Strawberry	.50	.23	.06
☐ 27 Kirby Puckett	2.50	1.10	.30
☐ 28 Ron Darling	.15	.07	.02
☐ 29 Don Mattingly	2.50	1.10	.30
☐ 30 Mike Schmidt	1.00	.45	.12
☐ 31 Rickey Henderson	1.25	.55	.16
☐ 32 Fernando Valenzuela	.25	.11	.03
☐ 33 Dave Winfield	1.00	.45	.12
☐ 34 Pete Rose	1.00	.45	.12
☐ 35 Jose Canseco	1.25	.55	.16
☐ 36 Glenn Davis	.15	.07	.02
☐ 37 Alvin Davis	.15	.07	.02
☐ 38 Steve Sax	.15	.07	.02
☐ 39 Pete Incaviglia	.15	.07	.02
☐ 40 Jeff Reardon	.15	.07	.02
☐ 41 Jesse Barfield	.15	.07	.02
☐ 42 Hubie Brooks	.15	.07	.02
☐ 43 George Bell	.15	.07	.02
☐ 44 Tony Gwynn	2.50	1.10	.30
☐ 45 Roger Clemens	1.50	.70	.19
☐ 46 Chili Davis	.25	.11	.03
☐ 47 Mike Witt	.15	.07	.02
☐ 48 Nolan Ryan	4.00	1.80	.50

1993 Kraft

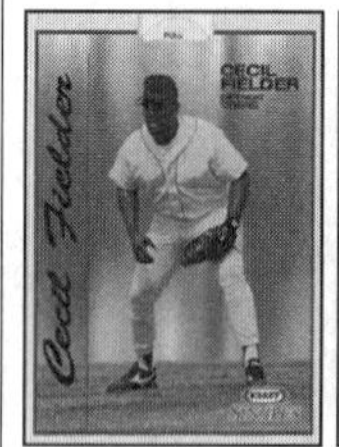

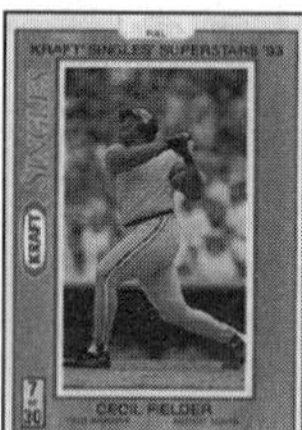

The Kraft Singles Superstars '93 Collector's series consists of 30 pop-up cards. One card was inserted in each specially marked 12-oz., 16-oz., and 3-lb. Kraft Singles package until June. Boxed sets of all the cards could be purchased through a mail-in form enclosed with each card for 1.75 plus proof-of-purchase points from Kraft Singles packages. Also a collector's album could be purchased for 4.75 plus 36 proof-of-purchase points. The standard-size cards feature a color action photo of the player in a batting stance, and these pictures are bordered by either blue (1-15) on American League cards or green (16-30) on National League cards. The backs display a color photo of the player in a fielding stance, with the player's name written in black script running along the left edge. When the pop-up tab at the top is pulled, the front photo becomes three-dimensional and pastel yellow panels are revealed, presenting tips for playing baseball at the player's position as well as the player's career highlights and statistics. The cards are numbered on the front at the lower left corner following alphabetical order by league.

	MINT	NRMT	EXC
COMPLETE SET (30)	20.00	9.00	2.50
COMMON CARD (1-30)	.30	.14	.04
☐ 1 Jim Abbott	.30	.14	.04
☐ 2 Roberto Alomar	1.00	.45	.12
☐ 3 Sandy Alomar	.50	.23	.06
☐ 4 George Brett	2.00	.90	.25
☐ 5 Roger Clemens	1.00	.45	.12
☐ 6 Dennis Eckersley	.50	.23	.06
☐ 7 Cecil Fielder	.50	.23	.06
☐ 8 Ken Griffey Jr.	5.00	2.20	.60
☐ 9 Don Mattingly	2.50	1.10	.30
☐ 10 Mark McGwire	1.50	.70	.19
☐ 11 Kirby Puckett	2.50	1.10	.30
☐ 12 Cal Ripken	5.00	2.20	.60
☐ 13 Nolan Ryan	4.00	1.80	.50
☐ 14 Robin Ventura	.50	.23	.06
☐ 15 Robin Yount	.75	.35	.09
☐ 16 Bobby Bonilla	.50	.23	.06
☐ 17 Ken Caminiti	.75	.35	.09
☐ 18 Will Clark	1.00	.45	.12
☐ 19 Darren Daulton	.50	.23	.06
☐ 20 Doug Drabek	.30	.14	.04
☐ 21 Delino DeShields	.30	.14	.04
☐ 22 Tom Glavine	.75	.35	.09
☐ 23 Tony Gwynn	2.50	1.10	.30
☐ 24 Orel Hershiser	.50	.23	.06
☐ 25 Barry Larkin	.75	.35	.09
☐ 26 Terry Pendleton	.30	.14	.04
☐ 27 Ryne Sandberg	2.00	.90	.25
☐ 28 Gary Sheffield	1.00	.45	.12
☐ 29 Lee Smith	.50	.23	.06
☐ 30 Andy Van Slyke	.30	.14	.04

1994 Kraft

The 1994 Kraft Singles Superstars set consists of 30 pop-up cards measuring approximately 2 1/2" by 3 3/8" and features "The Single Best Day" of 15 players from the American (1-15) and National (16-30) Leagues. One card was inserted in each specially marked 16-oz. and 3-lb. Kraft Singles package available in April and May. On-pack and in-store point-of-purchase mail-in offers enabled consumers to order a boxed American and/or National League 15-card set for $1.95 plus proof-of-purchase for each set. The fronts feature color action player shots bordered in blue on the AL cards and yellow on the NL cards. The player's name, position, and team appear in white lettering at one corner of the photo. The back displays another color player action shot that is perforated and cut out in such a way so that when the tab at the top is pulled, the photo becomes three-dimensional.

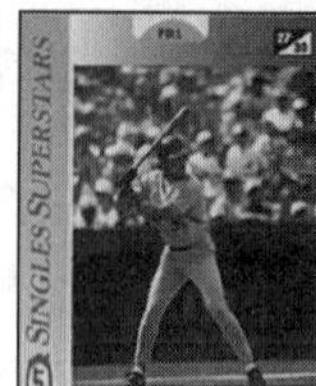

White panels are also revealed, presenting a description of the player's "Single Best Day," career highlights, and statistics. The cards are numbered on the back at the upper right, following alphabetical order by league.

	MINT	NRMT	EXC
COMPLETE SET (30)	25.00	11.00	3.10
COMMON CARD (1-30)	.30	.14	.04
☐ 1 Carlos Baerga	1.00	.45	.12
☐ 2 Dennis Eckersley	.50	.23	.06
☐ 3 Cecil Fielder	.50	.23	.06
☐ 4 Juan Gonzalez	2.50	1.10	.30
☐ 5 Ken Griffey Jr.	5.00	2.20	.60
☐ 6 Mark Langston	.30	.14	.04
☐ 7 Brian McRae	.30	.14	.04
☐ 8 Paul Molitor	1.00	.45	.12
☐ 9 Kirby Puckett	2.50	1.10	.30
☐ 10 Cal Ripken	4.00	1.80	.50
☐ 11 Danny Tartabull	.30	.14	.04
☐ 12 Frank Thomas	5.00	2.20	.60
☐ 13 Greg Vaughn	.30	.14	.04
☐ 14 Mo Vaughn	1.50	.70	.19
☐ 15 Dave Winfield	.60	.25	.07
☐ 16 Jeff Bagwell	2.50	1.10	.30
☐ 17 Barry Bonds	1.50	.70	.19
☐ 18 Bobby Bonilla	.50	.23	.06
☐ 19 Delino DeShields	.30	.14	.04
☐ 20 Lenny Dykstra	.30	.14	.04
☐ 21 Andres Galarraga	.75	.35	.09
☐ 22 Tom Glavine	.75	.35	.09
☐ 23 Mark Grace	1.00	.45	.12
☐ 24 Tony Gwynn	2.50	1.10	.30
☐ 25 David Justice	.75	.35	.09
☐ 26 Barry Larkin	1.00	.45	.12
☐ 27 Mike Piazza	3.00	1.35	.35
☐ 28 Gary Sheffield	1.00	.45	.12
☐ 29 Ozzie Smith	2.00	.90	.25
☐ 30 Andy Van Slyke	.30	.14	.04

1995 Kraft

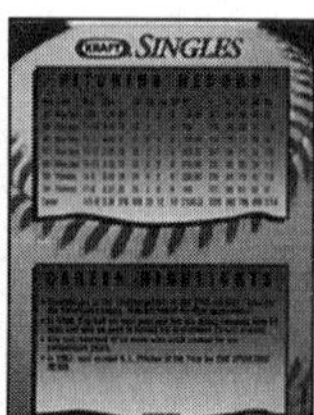

Consisting of 30 standard-size cards, the 1995 Kraft Singles Superstars Pop-up Action cards were included in specially-marked 12-ounce and 16-ounce packages of Kraft singles. One card was inserted in each package. The set could also be obtained through the mail by filling out the mail-in order form and sending in 36 Kraft Singles purchase points and $1.95 for each 15-card League set. The fronts feature full-bleed color action photos, with the player's name on a diagonal stripe cutting across the card. Against the background of a baseball, the back carries two panels, one displaying pitching (or hitting) record and the other presenting career highlights. The cards are arranged in alphabetical order within American (1-15) and National (16-30) Leagues.

	MINT	NRMT	EXC
COMPLETE SET (30)	25.00	11.00	3.10
COMMON CARD (1-30)	.25	.11	.03
☐ 1 Roberto Alomar	1.00	.45	.12
☐ 2 Joe Carter	.50	.23	.06
☐ 3 Cecil Fielder	.50	.23	.06
☐ 4 Juan Gonzalez	2.50	1.10	.30
☐ 5 Ken Griffey Jr.	5.00	2.20	.60
☐ 6 Jimmy Key	.25	.11	.03
☐ 7 Chuck Knoblauch	.75	.35	.09
☐ 8 Kenny Lofton	1.50	.70	.19
☐ 9 Mike Mussina	1.00	.45	.12
☐ 10 Paul O'Neill	.50	.23	.06
☐ 11 Kirby Puckett	2.50	1.10	.30
☐ 12 Cal Ripken	4.00	1.80	.50
☐ 13 Ivan Rodriguez	1.25	.55	.16
☐ 14 Frank Thomas	5.00	2.20	.60
☐ 15 Mo Vaughn	1.00	.45	.12
☐ 16 Moises Alou	.50	.23	.06
☐ 17 Jeff Bagwell	2.50	1.10	.30
☐ 18 Barry Bonds	1.00	.45	.12
☐ 19 Jeff Conine	.50	.23	.06
☐ 20 Len Dykstra	.50	.23	.06
☐ 21 Andres Galarraga	.75	.35	.09
☐ 22 Tony Gwynn	2.50	1.10	.30
☐ 23 Gregg Jefferies	.50	.23	.06
☐ 24 Barry Larkin	.75	.35	.09
☐ 25 Greg Maddux	3.00	1.35	.35
☐ 26 Mike Piazza	3.00	1.35	.35
☐ 27 Bret Saberhagen	.25	.11	.03
☐ 28 Ozzie Smith	2.00	.90	.25
☐ 29 Sammy Sosa	.75	.35	.09
☐ 30 Matt Williams	.75	.35	.09

1911 L1 Leathers

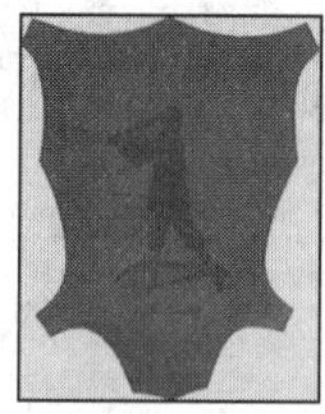

This highly prized set of baseball player pictures on a piece of leather shaped to resemble the hide of a small animal was issued during the 1911 time period. Each "leather" measures 10" by 12". While the pictures are those of the T3 Turkey Red card premium set, only the most popular players of the time are depicted. The cards are numbered at the bottom part of the leather away from the central image.

	EX-MT	VG-E	GOOD
COMPLETE SET (25)	35000.00	15800.00	4400.00
COMMON PLAYER (111-135)	650.00	300.00	80.00
☐ 111 Rube Marquard	1500.00	700.00	190.00
☐ 112 Marty O'Toole	650.00	300.00	80.00
☐ 113 Rube Benton	650.00	300.00	80.00
☐ 114 Grover C. Alexander	2000.00	900.00	250.00
☐ 115 Russ Ford	650.00	300.00	80.00
☐ 116 John McGraw MG	2000.00	900.00	250.00
☐ 117 Nap Rucker	650.00	300.00	80.00
☐ 118 Mike Mitchell	650.00	300.00	80.00
☐ 119 Chief Bender	1500.00	700.00	190.00
☐ 120 Frank Baker	1500.00	700.00	190.00
☐ 121 Napoleon Lajoie	2000.00	900.00	250.00
☐ 122 Joe Tinker	1500.00	700.00	190.00
☐ 123 Sherry Magee	650.00	300.00	80.00
☐ 124 Howie Camnitz	650.00	300.00	80.00
☐ 125 Eddie Collins	1500.00	700.00	190.00
☐ 126 Red Dooin	650.00	300.00	80.00
☐ 127 Ty Cobb	7500.00	3400.00	950.00
☐ 128 Hugh Jennings MG	1500.00	700.00	190.00
☐ 129 Roger Bresnahan	1500.00	700.00	190.00
☐ 130 Jake Stahl	650.00	300.00	80.00
☐ 131 Tris Speaker	1500.00	700.00	190.00
☐ 132 Ed Walsh	650.00	300.00	80.00
☐ 133 Christy Mathewson	3500.00	1600.00	450.00
☐ 134 Johnny Evers	1500.00	700.00	190.00
☐ 135 Walter Johnson	4500.00	2000.00	550.00

1968 Laughlin World Series

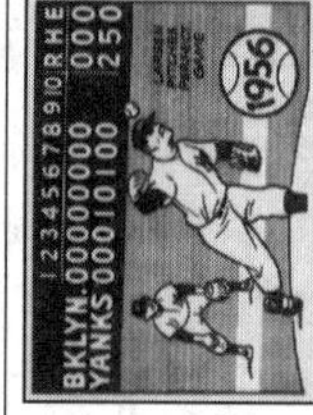

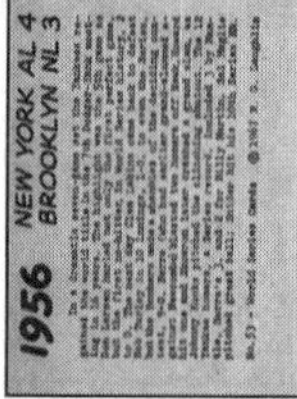

This set of 64 cards was apparently a limited test issue by sports artist R.G. Laughlin for the World Series set concept that was mass marketed by Fleer two and three years later. The cards are slightly oversized, (2 3/4" by 3 1/2") and are black and white on the front and red and white on the back. All the years are represented except for 1904 when no World Series was played. In the list below, the winning series team is listed first.

	NRMT	VG-E	GOOD
COMPLETE SET (64)	130.00	57.50	16.00
COMMON CARD (1-64)	2.00	.90	.25
☐ 1 1903 Red Sox/Pirates Deacon Phillippe	2.00	.90	.25
☐ 2 1905 Giants/A's (Christy Mathewson)	3.00	1.35	.35
☐ 3 1906 White Sox/Cubs	2.00	.90	.25
☐ 4 1907 Cubs/Tigers	2.00	.90	.25
☐ 5 1908 Cubs/Tigers (Joe Tinker Johnny Evers and Frank Chance)	4.00	1.80	.50
☐ 6 1909 Pirates/Tigers (Honus Wagner Ty Cobb)	5.00	2.20	.60
☐ 7 1910 A's/Cubs	2.00	.90	.25
☐ 8 1911 A's/Giants John McGraw MG	3.00	1.35	.35

Card	NRMT	VG-E	GOOD
☐ 9 1912 Red Sox/Giants	2.00	.90	.25
☐ 10 1913 A's/Giants	2.00	.90	.25
☐ 11 1914 Braves/A's	2.00	.90	.25
☐ 12 1915 Red Sox/Phillies	7.50	3.40	.95
(Babe Ruth)			
☐ 13 1916 Red Sox/Dodgers	7.50	3.40	.95
(Babe Ruth)			
☐ 14 1917 White Sox/Giants	2.00	.90	.25
☐ 15 1918 Red Sox/Cubs	2.00	.90	.25
☐ 16 1919 Reds/White Sox	4.00	1.80	.50
☐ 17 1920 Indians/Dodgers	2.00	.90	.25
Bill Wambsganss			
☐ 18 1921 Giants/Yankees	2.50	1.10	.30
(Waite Hoyt)			
☐ 19 1922 Giants/Yankees	2.50	1.10	.30
Frank Frisch			
Heinie Groh			
☐ 20 1923 Yankees/Giants	7.50	3.40	.95
(Babe Ruth)			
☐ 21 1924 Senators/Giants	2.00	.90	.25
☐ 22 1925 Pirates/Senators	4.00	1.80	.50
(Walter Johnson)			
☐ 23 1926 Cardinals/Yankees	3.00	1.35	.35
Grover C. Alexander			
Tony Lazzeri			
☐ 24 1927 Yankees/Pirates	2.50	1.10	.30
☐ 25 1928 Yankees/Cardinals	7.50	3.40	.95
Babe Ruth			
Lou Gehrig			
☐ 26 1929 A's/Cubs	2.00	.90	.25
☐ 27 1930 A's/Cardinals	2.00	.90	.25
☐ 28 1931 Cardinals/A's	2.50	1.10	.30
(Pepper Martin)			
☐ 29 1932 Yankees/Cubs	7.50	3.40	.95
(Babe Ruth)			
☐ 30 1933 Giants/Senators	3.00	1.35	.35
(Mel Ott)			
☐ 31 1934 Cardinals/Tigers	4.00	1.80	.50
Dizzy Dean			
Paul Dean			
☐ 32 1935 Tigers/Cubs	2.00	.90	.25
☐ 33 1936 Yankees/Giants	2.00	.90	.25
☐ 34 1937 Yankees/Giants	3.00	1.35	.35
(Carl Hubbell)			
☐ 35 1938 Yankees/Cubs	2.00	.90	.25
☐ 36 1939 Yankees/Reds	5.00	2.20	.60
(Joe DiMaggio)			
☐ 37 1940 Reds/Tigers	2.00	.90	.25
☐ 38 1941 Yankees/Dodgers	2.50	1.10	.30
(Mickey Owen)			
☐ 39 1942 Cardinals/Yankees	2.00	.90	.25
☐ 40 1943 Yankees/Cardinals	2.50	1.10	.30
Joe McCarthy MG			
☐ 41 1944 Cardinals/Browns	2.00	.90	.25
☐ 42 1945 Tigers/Cubs	3.00	1.35	.35
(Hank Greenberg)			
☐ 43 1946 Cardinals/Red Sox	3.00	1.35	.35
(Enos Slaughter)			
☐ 44 1947 Yankees/Dodgers	2.50	1.10	.30
(Al Gionfriddo)			
☐ 45 1948 Indians/Braves	3.00	1.35	.35
(Bob Feller)			
☐ 46 1949 Yankees/Dodgers	2.50	1.10	.30
Allie Reynolds			
Preacher Roe			
☐ 47 1950 Yankees/Phillies	2.00	.90	.25
☐ 48 1951 Yankees/Giants	2.00	.90	.25
☐ 49 1952 Yankees/Dodgers	3.00	1.35	.35
Johnny Mize			
Duke Snider			
☐ 50 1953 Yankees/Dodgers	3.00	1.35	.35
Casey Stengel MG			
☐ 51 1954 Giants/Indians	2.00	.90	.25
(Dusty Rhodes)			
☐ 52 1955 Dodgers/Yankees	2.50	1.10	.30
(Johnny Podres)			
☐ 53 1956 Yankees/Dodgers	2.50	1.10	.30
(Don Larsen)			
☐ 54 1957 Braves/Yankees	2.00	.90	.25
(Lew Burdette)			
☐ 55 1958 Yankees/Braves	2.00	.90	.25
(Hank Bauer)			
☐ 56 1959 Dodgers/Wh.Sox	2.00	.90	.25
(Larry Sherry)			
☐ 57 1960 Pirates/Yankees	2.50	1.10	.30
☐ 58 1961 Yankees/Reds	3.00	1.35	.35
(Whitey Ford)			
☐ 59 1962 Yankees/Giants	2.00	.90	.25
☐ 60 1963 Dodgers/Yankees	3.00	1.35	.35
(Sandy Koufax)			
☐ 61 1964 Cardinals/Yankees	7.50	3.40	.95
(Mickey Mantle)			
☐ 62 1965 Dodgers/Twins	3.00	1.35	.35
Sandy Koufax			
☐ 63 1966 Orioles/Dodgers	2.00	.90	.25
☐ 64 1967 Cardinals/Red Sox	3.00	1.35	.35
(Bob Gibson)			

1972 Laughlin Great Feats

This 51 card-set is printed on white card stock. Sports artist R.G. Laughlin is copyrighted only on the unnumbered title card but not on each card. The obverses are line drawings in black and white inside a red border. The cards measure 2 9/16" by 3 9/16". The set features "Great Feats" from baseball's past. The cards are blank backed and hence are numbered and captioned on the front. There is a variation set with a blue border and colored in flesh tones in the players pictured; this variation is a little more attractive and hence is valued a little higher. The blue-bordered variation set has larger type in the captions; in fact, the type has been reset and there are some minor wording differences. The blue-bordered set is also 1/16" wider.

	NRMT	VG-E	GOOD
COMPLETE SET (51)	45.00	20.00	5.50
COMMON CARD (1-50)	.50	.23	.06
☐ 1 Joe DiMaggio	5.00	2.20	.60
☐ 2 Walter Johnson	1.25	.55	.16
☐ 3 Rudy York	.50	.23	.06
☐ 4 Sandy Koufax	1.25	.55	.16
☐ 5 George Sisler	.75	.35	.09
☐ 6 Iron Man McGinnity	.75	.35	.09
☐ 7 Johnny VanderMeer	.50	.23	.06
☐ 8 Lou Gehrig	5.00	2.20	.60
☐ 9 Max Carey	.75	.35	.09
☐ 10 Ed Delahanty	.75	.35	.09
☐ 11 Pinky Higgins	.50	.23	.06
☐ 12 Jack Chesbro	.75	.35	.09
☐ 13 Jim Bottomley	.75	.35	.09
☐ 14 Rube Marquard	.75	.35	.09
☐ 15 Rogers Hornsby	1.00	.45	.12
☐ 16 Lefty Grove	1.00	.45	.12
☐ 17 Johnny Mize	.75	.35	.09
☐ 18 Lefty Gomez	.75	.35	.09
☐ 19 Jimmie Foxx	1.00	.45	.12
☐ 20 Casey Stengel	1.00	.45	.12
☐ 21 Dazzy Vance	.75	.35	.09
☐ 22 Jerry Lynch	.50	.23	.06
☐ 23 Hughie Jennings	.75	.35	.09
☐ 24 Stan Musial	2.00	.90	.25
☐ 25 Christy Mathewson	1.25	.55	.16
☐ 26 Elroy Face	.50	.23	.06
☐ 27 Hack Wilson	.75	.35	.09
☐ 28 Smoky Burgess	.50	.23	.06
☐ 29 Cy Young	1.25	.55	.16
☐ 30 Wilbert Robinson	.75	.35	.09
☐ 31 Wee Willie Keeler	.75	.35	.09
☐ 32 Babe Ruth	5.00	2.20	.60
☐ 33 Mickey Mantle	6.00	2.70	.75
☐ 34 Hub Leonard	.50	.23	.06
☐ 35 Ty Cobb	4.00	1.80	.50
☐ 36 Carl Hubbell	.75	.35	.09
☐ 37 Joe Oeschger and	.50	.23	.06
Leon Cadore			
☐ 38 Don Drysdale	.75	.35	.09
☐ 39 Fred Toney and	.50	.23	.06
Hippo Vaughn			
☐ 40 Joe Sewell	.75	.35	.09
☐ 41 Grover C. Alexander	1.00	.45	.12
☐ 42 Joe Adcock	.50	.23	.06
☐ 43 Eddie Collins	1.00	.45	.12
☐ 44 Bob Feller	1.25	.55	.16
☐ 45 Don Larsen	.50	.23	.06
☐ 46 Dave Philley	.50	.23	.06
☐ 47 Bill Fischer	.50	.23	.06
☐ 48 Dale Long	.50	.23	.06
☐ 49 Bill Wambsganss	.50	.23	.06
☐ 50 Roger Maris	1.50	.70	.19
☐ NNO Title Card	1.00	.45	.12

1974 Laughlin All-Star Games

This 40-card set is printed on white card stock. Sports artist R.G. Laughlin is copyrighted at the bottom of the reverse of each card. The obverses are line drawings primarily in red, light blue, black and white inside a white border. The cards measure approximately 2 11/16" by 3 3/8". The set features memorable moments from each year's All-Star Game. The cards are numbered on the back according to the last two digits of the year and captioned on the front. The backs are printed in blue on white stock. There is no card No. 45 in the set as there was no All-Star Game played in 1945 because of World War II.

	NRMT	VG-E	GOOD
COMPLETE SET (40)	35.00	16.00	4.40
COMMON CARD (33-73)	.50	.23	.06
☐ 33 Babe Ruth	6.00	2.70	.75
Homer			
☐ 34 Carl Hubbell	1.00	.45	.12
Fans Five			
☐ 35 Jimmie Foxx	1.00	.45	.12
Smashes Homer			
☐ 36 Dizzy Dean	1.00	.45	.12
Fogs 'Em			
☐ 37 Ducky Medwick	.75	.35	.09
Four Hits			
☐ 38 John VanderMeer	.60	.25	.07
No-Hit			
☐ 39 Joe DiMaggio	4.00	1.80	.50
Homers			
☐ 40 Max West's	.50	.23	.06
3-Run Shot			
☐ 41 Arky Vaughan	.75	.35	.09
Busts Two			
☐ 42 Rudy York	.60	.25	.07
2-Run Smash			
☐ 43 Bobby Doerr	.75	.35	.09
3-Run Blast			
☐ 44 Phil Cavarretta	.50	.23	.06
Reaches			
☐ 46 Ted Williams	4.00	1.80	.50
Field Day			
☐ 47 Johnny Mize	.75	.35	.09
Plants One			
☐ 48 Vic Raschi	.50	.23	.06
Pitches			
☐ 49 Jackie Robinson	3.00	1.35	.35
Scores			
☐ 50 Red Schoendienst	.75	.35	.09
Breaks			
☐ 51 Ralph Kiner	.75	.35	.09
Homers			
☐ 52 Hank Sauer	.50	.23	.06
Shot			
☐ 53 Enos Slaughter	.75	.35	.09
Hustles			
☐ 54 Al Rosen	.50	.23	.06
Hits			
☐ 55 Stan Musial	2.00	.90	.25
Homer			
☐ 56 Ken Boyer	.50	.23	.06
Super			
☐ 57 Al Kaline	1.00	.45	.12
Hits			
☐ 58 Nellie Fox	.75	.35	.09
Gets Two			
☐ 59 Frank Robinson	1.00	.45	.12
Perfect			
☐ 60 Willie Mays	3.00	1.35	.35
3-for-4			
☐ 61 Jim Bunning	.75	.35	.09
Hitless			
☐ 62 Roberto Clemente	4.00	1.80	.50
Perfect			
☐ 63 Dick Radatz	.50	.23	.06
Monster Strikeouts			
☐ 64 John Callison	.50	.23	.06
Homer			
☐ 65 Willie Stargell	.75	.35	.09
Big Day			
☐ 66 Brooks Robinson	1.00	.45	.12
Hits			
☐ 67 Fergie Jenkins	.75	.35	.09
Fans Six			
☐ 68 Tom Seaver	2.00	.90	.25
Terrific			
☐ 69 Willie McCovey	.75	.35	.09
Belts Two			
☐ 70 Carl Yatrzemski	1.00	.45	.12
Four Hits			
☐ 71 Reggie Jackson	2.00	.90	.25
Unloads			
☐ 72 Henry Aaron	3.00	1.35	.35
Hammers			
☐ 73 Bobby Bonds	.75	.35	.09
Perfect			

1974 Laughlin Old Time Black Stars

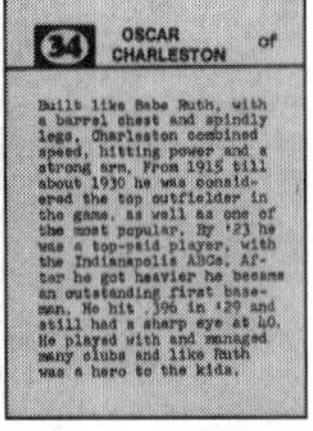

This 36-card set is printed on flat (non-glossy) white card stock. Sports artist R.G. Laughlin's work is evident but there are no copyright notices or any mention of him anywhere on any of the cards in this set. The obverses are line drawings in tan and brown. The cards measure approximately 2 5/8" by 3 1/2". The set features outstanding black players form the past. The backs are printed in brown on white stock.

	NRMT	VG-E	GOOD
COMPLETE SET (36)	50.00	22.00	6.25
COMMON CARD (1-36)	1.00	.45	.12
☐ 1 Smokey Joe Williams	3.00	1.35	.35
☐ 2 Rap Dixon	1.00	.45	.12
☐ 3 Oliver Marcelle	1.00	.45	.12
☐ 4 Bingo DeMoss	1.50	.70	.19
☐ 5 Willie Foster	1.50	.70	.19
☐ 6 John Beckwith	1.00	.45	.12
☐ 7 Floyd(Jelly) Gardner	1.00	.45	.12
☐ 8 Josh Gibson	6.00	2.70	.75
☐ 9 Jose Mendez	1.00	.45	.12
☐ 10 Pete Hill	1.00	.45	.12
☐ 11 Buck Leonard	4.00	1.80	.50
☐ 12 Jud Wilson	1.00	.45	.12
☐ 13 Willie Wells	2.00	.90	.25
☐ 14 Jimmie Lyons	1.00	.45	.12
☐ 15 Satchel Paige	6.00	2.70	.75
☐ 16 Louis Santop	1.00	.45	.12
☐ 17 Frank Grant	1.00	.45	.12
☐ 18 Christobel Torrienti	1.50	.70	.19
☐ 19 Bullet Rogan	1.50	.70	.19
☐ 20 Dave Malarcher	1.50	.70	.19
☐ 21 Spot Poles	1.00	.45	.12
☐ 22 Home Run Johnson	1.00	.45	.12
☐ 23 Charlie Grant	1.00	.45	.12
☐ 24 Cool Papa Bell	4.00	1.80	.50
☐ 25 Cannonball Dick Redding	1.00	.45	.12
☐ 26 Ray Dandridge	3.00	1.35	.35
☐ 27 Biz Mackey	2.00	.90	.25
☐ 28 Fats Jenkins	1.00	.45	.12
☐ 29 Martin Dihigo	4.00	1.80	.50
☐ 30 Mule Suttles	1.00	.45	.12
☐ 31 Bill Monroe	1.00	.45	.12
☐ 32 Dan McClellan	1.00	.45	.12
☐ 33 John Henry Lloyd	4.00	1.80	.50
☐ 34 Oscar Charleston	4.00	1.80	.50
☐ 35 Andrew(Rube) Foster	4.00	1.80	.50
☐ 36 William(Judy) Johnson	4.00	1.80	.50

1974 Laughlin Sportslang

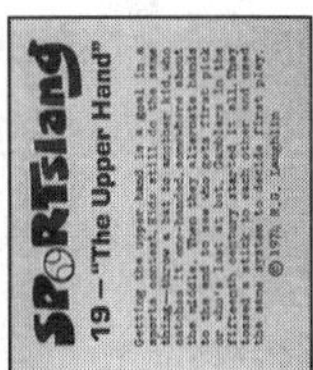

This 41-card set is printed on white card stock. Sports artist R.G. Laughlin 1974 is copyrighted at the bottom of every reverse. The obverses are drawings in red and blue on a white enamel card stock. The cards measure approximately 2 3/4" by 3 3/8". The set actually features the slang of several sports, not just baseball. The cards are numbered on the back and captioned on the front. The card back also provides an explanation of the slang term pictured on the card front.

	NRMT	VG-E	GOOD
COMPLETE SET (41)	8.00	3.60	1.00
COMMON CARD (1-41)	.25	.11	.03
☐ 1 Bull Pen	.25	.11	.03
☐ 2 Charley Horse	.25	.11	.03
☐ 3 Derby	.25	.11	.03
☐ 4 Anchor Man	.25	.11	.03
☐ 5 Mascot	.25	.11	.03
☐ 6 Annie Oakley	.35	.16	.04
☐ 7 Taxi Squad	.25	.11	.03
☐ 8 Dukes	.25	.11	.03
☐ 9 Rookie	.25	.11	.03
☐ 10 Jinx	.25	.11	.03
☐ 11 Dark Horse	.25	.11	.03
☐ 12 Hat Trick	.25	.11	.03
☐ 13 Bell Wether	.25	.11	.03
☐ 14 Love	.25	.11	.03
☐ 15 Red Dog	.25	.11	.03
☐ 16 Barnstorm	.25	.11	.03
☐ 17 Bull's Eye	.25	.11	.03
☐ 18 Rabbit Punch	.25	.11	.03
☐ 19 The Upper Hand	.25	.11	.03
☐ 20 Handi Cap	.25	.11	.03
☐ 21 Marathon	.25	.11	.03
☐ 22 Southpaw	.25	.11	.03
☐ 23 Boner	.25	.11	.03
☐ 24 Gridiron	.25	.11	.03
☐ 25 Fan	.25	.11	.03
☐ 26 Moxie	.25	.11	.03
☐ 27 Birdie	.25	.11	.03
☐ 28 Sulky	.25	.11	.03
☐ 29 Dribble	.25	.11	.03
☐ 30 Donnybrook	.25	.11	.03
☐ 31 The Real McCoy	.25	.11	.03
☐ 32 Even Stephen	.25	.11	.03
☐ 33 Chinese Homer	.25	.11	.03
☐ 34 English	.25	.11	.03
☐ 35 Garrison Finish	.25	.11	.03
☐ 36 Foot in the Bucket	.25	.11	.03
☐ 37 Steeple Chase	.25	.11	.03
☐ 38 Long Shot	.25	.11	.03

☐ 39 Nip and Tuck	.25	.11	.03
☐ 40 Battery	.25	.11	.03
☐ xx Title Card	.35	.16	.04
(Unnumbered)			

1975 Laughlin Batty Baseball

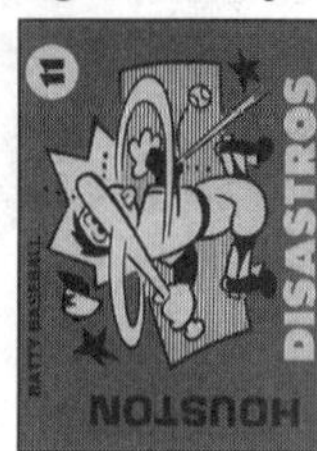

This-25 card set is printed on white card stock. Sports artist R.G. Laughlin 1975 is copyrighted on the title card. The obverses are line drawings primarily in orange, black and white. The cards measure 2 9/16" X 3 7/16". The set features a card for each team with a depiction of a fractured nickname for the team. The cards are numbered on the front. The backs are blank on white stock.

	NRMT	VG-E	GOOD
COMPLETE SET (25)	6.00	2.70	.75
COMMON CARD (1-24)	.25	.11	.03
☐ 1 Oakland Daze	.25	.11	.03
☐ 2 Boston Wet Sox	.25	.11	.03
☐ 3 Cincinnati Dreads	.25	.11	.03
☐ 4 Chicago Wide Sox	.25	.11	.03
☐ 5 Milwaukee Boozers	.25	.11	.03
☐ 6 Philadelphia Fillies	.25	.11	.03
☐ 7 Cleveland Engines	.25	.11	.03
☐ 8 New York Mitts	.25	.11	.03
☐ 9 Texas Ranchers	.25	.11	.03
☐ 10 San Francisco Gents	.25	.11	.03
☐ 11 Houston Disastros	.25	.11	.03
☐ 12 Chicago Clubs	.25	.11	.03
☐ 13 Minnesota Wins	.25	.11	.03
☐ 14 St. Louis Gardeners	.25	.11	.03
☐ 15 New York Yankers	.25	.11	.03
☐ 16 California Angles	.25	.11	.03
☐ 17 Pittsburgh Irates	.25	.11	.03
☐ 18 Los Angeles Smoggers	.25	.11	.03
☐ 19 Baltimore Oreos	.25	.11	.03
☐ 20 Montreal Expose	.25	.11	.03
☐ 21 San Diego Parties	.25	.11	.03
☐ 22 Detroit Taggers	.25	.11	.03
☐ 23 Kansas City Broils	.25	.11	.03
☐ 24 Atlanta Briefs	.25	.11	.03
☐ xx Title Card	.45	.20	.06
(Unnumbered)			

1976 Laughlin Diamond Jubilee

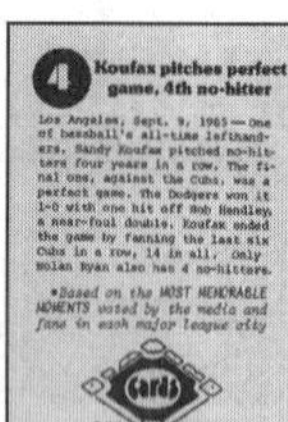

This 32-card set is printed on non-glossy white card stock. Sports artist R.Laughlin 1976 is copyrighted at the bottom of the reverse of each card. The obverses are line drawings primarily in red, blue, black and white inside a red border. The cards measure approximately 2 13/16" by 3 15/16". The set features memorable moments voted by the media and fans in each major league city. The cards are numbered on the back and captioned on the front and the back. The backs are printed in dark blue on white stock.

	NRMT	VG-E	GOOD
COMPLETE SET (32)	50.00	22.00	6.25
COMMON CARD (1-32)	.50	.23	.06
☐ 1 Nolan Ryan	8.00	3.60	1.00
☐ 2 Ernie Banks	2.00	.90	.25
☐ 3 Mickey Lolich	.50	.23	.06
☐ 4 Sandy Koufax	3.00	1.35	.35
☐ 5 Frank Robinson	2.00	.90	.25
☐ 6 Bill Mazeroski	.75	.35	.09
☐ 7 Jim Hunter	.75	.35	.09
☐ 8 Hank Aaron	5.00	2.20	.60
☐ 9 Carl Yastrzemski	2.00	.90	.25
☐ 10 Jim Bunning	.75	.35	.09
☐ 11 Brooks Robinson	2.00	.90	.25
☐ 12 John VanderMeer	.75	.35	.09
☐ 13 Harmon Killebrew	2.00	.90	.25
☐ 14 Lou Brock	2.00	.90	.25
☐ 15 Steve Busby	.50	.23	.06
☐ 16 Nate Colbert	.50	.23	.06
☐ 17 Don Larsen	.75	.35	.09
☐ 18 Willie Mays	3.00	1.35	.35
☐ 19 David Clyde	.50	.23	.06
☐ 20 Mack Jones	.50	.23	.06
☐ 21 Mike Hegan	.50	.23	.06
☐ 22 Jerry Koosman	.50	.23	.06
☐ 23 Early Wynn	.75	.35	.09
☐ 24 Nellie Fox	.75	.35	.09
☐ 25 Joe DiMaggio	6.00	2.70	.75
☐ 26 Jackie Robinson	4.00	1.80	.50
☐ 27 Ted Williams	6.00	2.70	.75
☐ 28 Lou Gehrig	6.00	2.70	.75
☐ 29 Bobby Thomson	.75	.35	.09
☐ 30 Roger Maris	1.25	.55	.16
☐ 31 Harvey Haddix	.50	.23	.06
☐ 32 Babe Ruth	7.50	3.40	.95

1976 Laughlin Indianapolis Clowns

Reece "Goose" Tatum

"Goose" played first base for the Clowns beginning in 1937 and in the winter played basketball, winding up with the Harlem Globe-trotters in 1940, where he gained national fame. Besides being a great clown, Tatum was a fine ballplayer and the Ath-letics were serious about him—but he was set with the Globetrotters. Later he got the Clowns' Birm-ingham Sam a basketball job with his Harlem Road Kings. Tatum passed away in 1966.

This 42-card set was issued to commemorate the Indianapolis Clowns, a black team that began touring in 1929 and played many games for charity. The cards measure 2 5/8" by 4 1/4". The front design has blackand-white player photos inside a white frame against a light blue card face. The team name is printed in red and white above the picture. In red courier-style print on white, the backs present extended captions. The cards are numbered on the front.

	NRMT	VG-E	GOOD
COMPLETE SET (42)	40.00	18.00	5.00
COMMON CARD (1-40)	1.00	.45	.12
☐ 1 Ed Hamman	1.50	.70	.19
Ed the Clown			
☐ 2 Dero Austin	1.00	.45	.12
☐ 3 James Williams	1.00	.45	.12
Nickname Natureboy			
☐ 4 Sam Brison	1.00	.45	.12
Nickname Birmingham			
☐ 5 Richard King	1.00	.45	.12
Nickname King Tut			
☐ 6 Syd Pollock	1.00	.45	.12
Founder			
☐ 7 Nataniel(Lefty) Small	1.00	.45	.12
☐ 8 Grant Greene	1.00	.45	.12
Nickname Double Duty			
☐ 9 Nancy Miller	1.00	.45	.12
Lady umpire			
☐ 10 Billy Vaughn	1.00	.45	.12
☐ 11 Sam Brison	1.00	.45	.12
Putout for Sam			
☐ 12 Ed Hamman	1.50	.70	.19
☐ 13 Dero Austin	1.00	.45	.12
Home delivery			
☐ 14 Steve(Nub) Anderson	1.00	.45	.12
☐ 15 Joe Cherry	1.00	.45	.12
☐ 16 Reece(Goose) Tatum	4.00	1.80	.50
☐ 17 James Williams	1.00	.45	.12
Natureboy			
☐ 18 Byron Purnell	1.00	.45	.12
☐ 19 Bat boy	1.00	.45	.12
☐ 20 Spec BeBop	1.00	.45	.12
☐ 21 Satchel Paige	5.00	2.20	.60
☐ 22 Prince Jo Henry	1.00	.45	.12
☐ 23 Ed Hamman	1.00	.45	.12
Syd Pollock			
☐ 24 Paul Casanova	1.50	.70	.19
☐ 25 Steve(Nub) Anderson	1.00	.45	.12
Nub singles			
☐ 26 Comiskey Park	1.50	.70	.19
☐ 27 Toni Stone	2.00	.90	.25
Second basewoman			
☐ 28 Dero Austin	1.00	.45	.12
Small target			
☐ 29 Sam Brison and	1.00	.45	.12
Natureboy Williams			
Calling Dr. Kildare			
☐ 30 Oscar Charleston	3.00	1.35	.35
☐ 31 Richard King	1.00	.45	.12
King Tut			
☐ 32 Ed Hamman	1.00	.45	.12
Joe Cherry			
Hal King			
Ed and prospects			
☐ 33 In style	1.00	.45	.12
Team bus			
☐ 34 Hank Aaron	5.00	2.20	.60
☐ 35 The Great Yogi	2.00	.90	.25
☐ 36 W.H.(Chauff) Wilson	1.00	.45	.12
☐ 37 Sam Brison	1.00	.45	.12
Sonny Jackson			
Doin' their thing			
☐ 38 Billy Vaughn	1.00	.45	.12
The hard way			
☐ 39 James Williams	1.00	.45	.12
1B the easy way			
☐ 40 Ed Hamman	2.00	.90	.25
Casey Stengel			
Casey and Ed			
☐ xx Title Card	1.00	.45	.12
☐ xx Baseball Laff Book	1.00	.45	.12

1977 Laughlin Erorrs

This set of 39 blank-backed cards is printed on white card stock and measures 2 5/8" by 3 3/4". Sports artist R.G. Laughlin has created illustrations for actual errors made on baseball cards over the years, a sampling of the hundreds of mistakes that found their way into print. The illustrations are bordered in green with "Erorrs" (incorrect spelling intentional) in wide white script at the top of the cards. Each card lists the year, card make and number depicted in the line drawing. The cards are unnumbered and checklisted below in chronological order.

	NRMT	VG-E	GOOD
COMPLETE SET (39)	30.00	13.50	3.70
COMMON CARD (1-39)	1.00	.45	.12
☐ 1 1933 Goudey 19	1.00	.45	.12
☐ 2 1952 Berk-Ross	1.00	.45	.12
☐ 3 1955 Bowman 48	1.00	.45	.12
☐ 4 1956 Topps 31	1.00	.45	.12
☐ 5 1956 Topps 303	1.00	.45	.12
☐ 6 1958 Topps 37	1.00	.45	.12
☐ 7 1959 Topps 274	1.00	.45	.12
☐ 8 1960 Topps 84	1.00	.45	.12
☐ 9 1961 Topps 21	1.00	.45	.12
☐ 10 1961 Topps 55	1.00	.45	.12
☐ 11 1961 Topps 99	1.00	.45	.12
☐ 12 1961 Topps 332	1.00	.45	.12
☐ 13 1961 Topps 536	1.00	.45	.12
☐ 14 1962 Post BB 104	1.00	.45	.12
☐ 15 1963 Topps 126	1.00	.45	.12
☐ 16 1964 Topps 561	1.00	.45	.12
☐ 17 1965 Topps 472	1.00	.45	.12
☐ 18 1966 Topps 36	1.00	.45	.12
☐ 19 1966 Topps 586	1.00	.45	.12
☐ 20 1967 Topps 254	1.00	.45	.12
☐ 21 1967 Topps 282	1.00	.45	.12
☐ 22 1967 Topps 449	1.00	.45	.12
☐ 23 1969 Topps 209	1.00	.45	.12
☐ 24 1969 Topps 465	1.00	.45	.12
☐ 25 1969 Topps 653	1.00	.45	.12
☐ 26 1970 Topps 282	1.00	.45	.12
☐ 27 1971 Topps Super 20	1.00	.45	.12
☐ 28 1973 Fleer 5	1.00	.45	.12
☐ 29 1973 Topps 120	1.00	.45	.12
☐ 30 1973 Topps 135	1.00	.45	.12
☐ 31 1974 Black Stars 1	1.00	.45	.12
☐ 32 1974 Fleer 20	1.00	.45	.12
☐ 33 1974 Topps 331	1.00	.45	.12
☐ 34 1974 Topps 578	1.00	.45	.12
☐ 35 1975 Hostess 35	1.00	.45	.12
☐ 36 1975 Hostess 125	1.00	.45	.12
☐ 37 1975 Topps 113	1.00	.45	.12
☐ 38 1976 Topps 210	1.00	.45	.12
☐ 39 Title card	1.00	.45	.12

1978 Laughlin Long Ago Black Stars

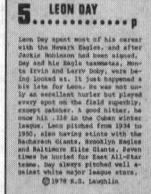

This set of 36 cards is printed on non-glossy white card stock. Sports artist R.G. Laughlin's work is evident and the reverse of each card indicates copyright by R.G. Laughlin 1978. The obverses are line drawings in light and dark green. The cards measure 2 5/8" by 3 1/2". The set features outstanding black players form the past. The cards are numbered on the back. The backs are printed in black on white stock. This is not a reissue of the similar Laughlin set from 1974 Old Time Black Stars but is actually in effect a second series with all new players.

	NRMT	VG-E	GOOD
COMPLETE SET (36)	50.00	22.00	6.25
COMMON CARD (1-36)	1.50	.70	.19
☐ 1 Ted Trent	2.00	.90	.25
☐ 2 Larry Brown	1.50	.70	.19
☐ 3 Newt Allen	3.00	1.35	.35
☐ 4 Norman Stearns	1.50	.70	.19
☐ 5 Leon Day	6.00	2.70	.75
☐ 6 Dick Lundy	1.50	.70	.19
☐ 7 Bruce Petway	2.00	.90	.25
☐ 8 Bill Drake	1.50	.70	.19
☐ 9 Chaney White	1.50	.70	.19
☐ 10 Webster McDonald	1.50	.70	.19
☐ 11 Tommy Butts	1.50	.70	.19
☐ 12 Ben Taylor	1.50	.70	.19
☐ 13 James(Joe) Greene	1.50	.70	.19
☐ 14 Dick Seay	1.50	.70	.19
☐ 15 Sammy Hughes	1.50	.70	.19
☐ 16 Ted Page	4.00	1.80	.50
☐ 17 Willie Cornelius	1.50	.70	.19
☐ 18 Pat Patterson	1.50	.70	.19
☐ 19 Frank Wickware	1.50	.70	.19
☐ 20 Albert Haywood	1.50	.70	.19
☐ 21 Bill Holland	1.50	.70	.19
☐ 22 Sol White	1.50	.70	.19
☐ 23 Chet Brewer	3.00	1.35	.35
☐ 24 Crush Holloway	1.50	.70	.19
☐ 25 George Johnson	1.50	.70	.19
☐ 26 George Scales	1.50	.70	.19
☐ 27 Dave Brown	1.50	.70	.19
☐ 28 John Donaldson	1.50	.70	.19
☐ 29 William Johnson	4.00	1.80	.50
☐ 30 Bill Yancey	3.00	1.35	.35
☐ 31 Sam Bankhead	2.00	.90	.25
☐ 32 Leroy Matlock	1.50	.70	.19
☐ 33 Quincy Troupe	2.00	.90	.25
☐ 34 Hilton Smith	3.00	1.35	.35
☐ 35 Jim Crutchfield	2.50	1.10	.30
☐ 36 Ted Radcliffe	3.00	1.35	.35

1980 Laughlin 300/400/500

This square (approximately 3 1/4" square) set of 30 players features members of the 300/400/500 club, namely 300 pitching wins, batting .400 or better, or hitting 500 homers since 1900. Cards are blank backed but are numbered on the front. The cards feature the artwork of R.G. Laughlin for the player's body connected to an out of proportion head shot stock photo. This creates an effect faintly reminiscent of the Goudey Heads Up cards.

	NRMT	VG-E	GOOD
COMPLETE SET (30)	30.00	13.50	3.70
COMMON CARD (1-30)	.60	.25	.07
☐ 1 Title Card	.60	.25	.07
☐ 2 Babe Ruth	4.00	1.80	.50
☐ 3 Walter Johnson	1.00	.45	.12
☐ 4 Ty Cobb	2.00	.90	.25
☐ 5 Christy Mathewson	1.50	.70	.19
☐ 6 Ted Williams	3.00	1.35	.35
☐ 7 Bill Terry	.60	.25	.07
☐ 8 Grover C. Alexander	.75	.35	.09
☐ 9 Napoleon Lajoie	.75	.35	.09
☐ 10 Willie Mays	1.50	.70	.19
☐ 11 Cy Young	1.00	.45	.12
☐ 12 Mel Ott	.75	.35	.09
☐ 13 Joe Jackson	2.00	.90	.25
☐ 14 Harmon Killebrew	.75	.35	.09
☐ 15 Warren Spahn	.75	.35	.09
☐ 16 Hank Aaron	2.50	1.10	.30
☐ 17 Rogers Hornsby	1.50	.70	.19
☐ 18 Mickey Mantle	4.00	1.80	.50
☐ 19 Lefty Grove	.75	.35	.09
☐ 20 Ted Williams	2.00	.90	.25
☐ 21 Jimmie Foxx	1.00	.45	.12
☐ 22 Eddie Plank	.60	.25	.07
☐ 23 Frank Robinson	.75	.35	.09
☐ 24 George Sisler	.60	.25	.07
☐ 25 Eddie Mathews	.75	.35	.09
☐ 26 Early Wynn	.60	.25	.07
☐ 27 Ernie Banks	1.00	.45	.12
☐ 28 Harry Heilmann	.60	.25	.07
☐ 29 Lou Gehrig	2.50	1.10	.30
☐ 30 Willie McCovey	.75	.35	.09

1980 Laughlin Famous Feats

This set of 40 standard-size cards is printed on white card stock. Sports artist R.G. Laughlin 1980 is copyrighted at the bottom of every obverse. The obverses are line drawings primarily in many colors. The set is subtitled "Second Series" of Famous Feats. The cards are numbered on the front. The backs are blank on white stock.

	NRMT	VG-E	GOOD
COMPLETE SET (40)	15.00	6.75	1.85
COMMON CARD (1-40)	.20	.09	.03
☐ 1 Honus Wagner	1.00	.45	.12
☐ 2 Herb Pennock	.30	.14	.04

☐ 3 Al Simmons	.30	.14	.04
☐ 4 Hack Wilson	.30	.14	.04
☐ 5 Dizzy Dean	.50	.23	.06
☐ 6 Chuck Klein	.30	.14	.04
☐ 7 Nellie Fox	.30	.14	.04
☐ 8 Lefty Grove	.50	.23	.06
☐ 9 George Sisler	.30	.14	.04
☐ 10 Lou Gehrig	1.50	.70	.19
☐ 11 Rube Waddell	.30	.14	.04
☐ 12 Max Carey	.30	.14	.04
☐ 13 Thurman Munson	.50	.23	.06
☐ 14 Mel Ott	.50	.23	.06
☐ 15 Doc White	.20	.09	.03
☐ 16 Babe Ruth	2.00	.90	.25
☐ 17 Schoolboy Rowe	.20	.09	.03
☐ 18 Jackie Robinson	1.25	.55	.16
☐ 19 Joe Medwick	.30	.14	.04
☐ 20 Casey Stengel	.75	.35	.09
☐ 21 Roberto Clemente	1.50	.70	.19
☐ 22 Christy Mathewson	.75	.35	.09
☐ 23 Jimmie Foxx	.50	.23	.06
☐ 24 Joe Jackson	1.00	.45	.12
☐ 25 Walter Johnson	.75	.35	.09
☐ 26 Tony Lazzeri	.30	.14	.04
☐ 27 Hugh Casey	.20	.09	.03
☐ 28 Ty Cobb	1.50	.70	.19
☐ 29 Stuffy McInnis	.20	.09	.03
☐ 30 Cy Young	.50	.23	.06
☐ 31 Lefty O'Doul	.20	.09	.03
☐ 32 Eddie Collins	.30	.14	.04
☐ 33 Joe McCarthy	.30	.14	.04
☐ 34 Ed Walsh	.30	.14	.04
☐ 35 George Burns	.20	.09	.03
☐ 36 Walt Dropo	.20	.09	.03
☐ 37 Connie Mack	.50	.23	.06
☐ 38 Babe Adams	.20	.09	.03
☐ 39 Rogers Hornsby	.50	.23	.06
☐ 40 Grover C. Alexander	.50	.23	.06

1913 Lawrence Semon Chance

Upon becoming the manager of the New York Yankees in 1913, cartoonist Lawrence Semon produced a postcard featuring a head and shoulder caraciture of Frank Chance. Chance's nickname at the time was "The Peerless Leader" based on his days as the Chicago Cubs manager. The postcard also reviews Chance's career as a player and manager prior to joining the Yankees.

	NRMT	VG-E	GOOD
COMPLETE SET	250.00	110.00	31.00
COMMON CARD	250.00	110.00	31.00
☐ 1 Frank Chance	250.00	110.00	31.00

1949 Leaf

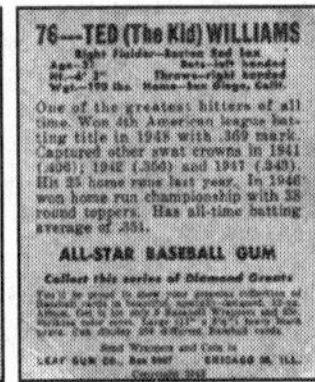

The cards in this 98-card set measure 2 3/8" by 2 7/8". The 1949 Leaf set was the first post-war baseball series issued in color. In hobby circles, it has been speculated that the set was issued in the spring of 1949. This effort was not entirely successful due to a lack of refinement which resulted in many color variations and cards out of register. In addition, the set was skip numbered from 1-168, with 49 of the 98 cards printed in limited quantities (marked with SP in the checklist). Cards 102 and 136 have variations, and cards are sometimes found with overprinted, incorrect or blank backs. The notable Rookie Cards in this set include Stan Musial, Satchel Paige, and Jackie Robinson.

	NRMT	VG-E	GOOD
COMPLETE SET (98)	25000.00	11200.00	3100.00
COMMON CARD (1-168)	25.00	11.00	3.10
WRAPPER (1-CENT)	160.00	70.00	20.00
☐ 1 Joe DiMaggio	2100.00	850.00	210.00
☐ 3 Babe Ruth	2500.00	1100.00	300.00
☐ 4 Stan Musial	850.00	375.00	105.00
☐ 5 Virgil Trucks SP	325.00	145.00	40.00
☐ 8 Satchel Paige SP	2200.00	1000.00	275.00
☐ 10 Dizzy Trout	30.00	13.50	3.70
☐ 11 Phil Rizzuto	250.00	110.00	31.00
☐ 13 Cass Michaels SP	225.00	100.00	28.00
☐ 14 Billy Johnson	30.00	13.50	3.70
☐ 17 Frank Overmire	25.00	11.00	3.10
☐ 19 Johnny Wyrostek SP	225.00	100.00	28.00
☐ 20 Hank Sauer SP	325.00	145.00	40.00
☐ 22 Al Evans	25.00	11.00	3.10
☐ 26 Sam Chapman	30.00	13.50	3.70
☐ 27 Mickey Harris	25.00	11.00	3.10
☐ 28 Jim Hegan	30.00	13.50	3.70
☐ 29 Elmer Valo	30.00	13.50	3.70
☐ 30 Billy Goodman SP	275.00	125.00	34.00
☐ 31 Lou Brissie	25.00	11.00	3.10
☐ 32 Warren Spahn	275.00	125.00	34.00
☐ 33 Peanuts Lowrey SP	225.00	100.00	28.00
☐ 36 Al Zarilla SP	225.00	100.00	28.00
☐ 38 Ted Kluszewski	150.00	70.00	19.00
☐ 39 Ewell Blackwell	55.00	25.00	7.00
☐ 42 Kent Peterson	25.00	11.00	3.10
☐ 43 Ed Stevens SP	225.00	100.00	28.00
☐ 45 Ken Keltner SP	225.00	100.00	28.00
☐ 46 Johnny Mize	100.00	45.00	12.50
☐ 47 George Vico	25.00	11.00	3.10
☐ 48 Johnny Schmitz SP	225.00	100.00	28.00
☐ 49 Del Ennis	55.00	25.00	7.00
☐ 50 Dick Wakefield	25.00	11.00	3.10
☐ 51 Al Dark SP	400.00	180.00	50.00
☐ 53 Johnny VanderMeer	40.00	18.00	5.00
☐ 54 Bobby Adams SP	225.00	100.00	28.00
☐ 55 Tommy Henrich SP	400.00	180.00	50.00
☐ 56 Larry Jansen UER (Misspelled Jensen)	30.00	13.50	3.70
☐ 57 Bob McCall	25.00	11.00	3.10
☐ 59 Luke Appling	100.00	45.00	12.50
☐ 61 Jake Early	25.00	11.00	3.10
☐ 62 Eddie Joost SP	225.00	100.00	28.00
☐ 63 Barney McCosky SP	225.00	100.00	28.00
☐ 65 Robert Elliott UER (Misspelled Elliot on card front)	40.00	18.00	5.00
☐ 66 Orval Grove SP	225.00	100.00	28.00
☐ 68 Eddie Miller SP	225.00	100.00	28.00
☐ 70 Honus Wagner CO	275.00	125.00	34.00
☐ 72 Hank Edwards	25.00	11.00	3.10
☐ 73 Pat Seerey	25.00	11.00	3.10
☐ 75 Dom DiMaggio SP	500.00	220.00	60.00
☐ 76 Ted Williams	800.00	350.00	100.00
☐ 77 Roy Smalley	25.00	11.00	3.10
☐ 78 Hoot Evers SP	225.00	100.00	28.00
☐ 79 Jackie Robinson	1000.00	450.00	125.00
☐ 81 Whitey Kurowski SP	225.00	100.00	28.00
☐ 82 Johnny Lindell	30.00	13.50	3.70
☐ 83 Bobby Doerr	100.00	45.00	12.50
☐ 84 Sid Hudson	25.00	11.00	3.10
☐ 85 Dave Philley SP	275.00	125.00	34.00
☐ 86 Ralph Weigel	25.00	11.00	3.10
☐ 88 Frank Gustine SP	225.00	100.00	28.00
☐ 91 Ralph Kiner	200.00	90.00	25.00
☐ 93 Bob Feller SP	1250.00	550.00	160.00
☐ 95 George Stirnweiss	30.00	13.50	3.70
☐ 97 Marty Marion	55.00	25.00	7.00
☐ 98 Hal Newhouser SP	500.00	220.00	60.00
☐ 102A Gene Hermansk ERR	225.00	100.00	28.00
☐ 102B Gene Hermanski COR	30.00	13.50	3.70
☐ 104 Eddie Stewart SP	225.00	100.00	28.00
☐ 106 Lou Boudreau	100.00	45.00	12.50
☐ 108 Matt Batts SP	225.00	100.00	28.00
☐ 111 Jerry Priddy	25.00	11.00	3.10
☐ 113 Dutch Leonard SP	225.00	100.00	28.00
☐ 117 Joe Gordon	30.00	13.50	3.70
☐ 120 George Kell SP	500.00	220.00	60.00
☐ 121 Johnny Pesky SP	325.00	145.00	40.00
☐ 123 Cliff Fannin SP	225.00	100.00	28.00
☐ 125 Andy Pafko	25.00	11.00	3.10
☐ 127 Enos Slaughter SP	600.00	275.00	75.00
☐ 128 Buddy Rosar	25.00	11.00	3.10
☐ 129 Kirby Higbe SP	225.00	100.00	28.00
☐ 131 Sid Gordon SP	225.00	100.00	28.00
☐ 133 Tommy Holmes SP	400.00	180.00	50.00
☐ 136A Cliff Aberson (Full sleeve)	25.00	11.00	3.10
☐ 136B Cliff Aberson (Short sleeve)	225.00	100.00	28.00
☐ 137 Harry Walker SP	275.00	125.00	34.00
☐ 138 Larry Doby SP	500.00	220.00	60.00
☐ 139 Johnny Hopp	25.00	11.00	3.10
☐ 142 Danny Murtaugh SP	325.00	145.00	40.00
☐ 143 Dick Sisler SP	225.00	100.00	28.00
☐ 144 Bob Dillinger SP	225.00	100.00	28.00
☐ 146 Pete Reiser SP	400.00	180.00	50.00
☐ 149 Hank Majeski SP	225.00	100.00	28.00
☐ 153 Floyd Baker SP	225.00	100.00	28.00
☐ 158 Harry Brecheen SP	325.00	145.00	40.00
☐ 159 Mizell Platt	25.00	11.00	3.10
☐ 160 Bob Scheffing SP	225.00	100.00	28.00
☐ 161 Vern Stephens SP	325.00	145.00	40.00
☐ 163 Fred Hutchinson SP	325.00	145.00	40.00
☐ 165 Dale Mitchell SP	325.00	145.00	40.00
☐ 168 Phil Cavarretta SP UER Name spelled Cavaretta	400.00	160.00	40.00

1949 Leaf Premiums

This set of eight large, blank-backed premiums is rather scarce. They were issued as premiums with the 1949 Leaf Gum set. The catalog designation is R401-4. The set is subtitled "Baseball's Immortals" and there is no reference anywhere on the premium to Leaf, the issuing company. These large photos measure approximately 5 1/2" x 7 3/16" and are printed on thin paper.

	NRMT	VG-E	GOOD
COMPLETE SET (8)	2250.00	1000.00	275.00
COMMON CARD (1-8)	150.00	70.00	19.00
☐ 1 Grover C. Alexander	200.00	90.00	25.00
☐ 2 Mickey Cochrane	200.00	90.00	25.00
☐ 3 Lou Gehrig	500.00	220.00	60.00
☐ 4 Walter Johnson	300.00	135.00	38.00
☐ 5 Christy Mathewson	300.00	135.00	38.00
☐ 6 John McGraw	200.00	90.00	25.00
☐ 7 Babe Ruth	750.00	350.00	95.00
☐ 8 Ed Walsh	150.00	70.00	19.00

1960 Leaf

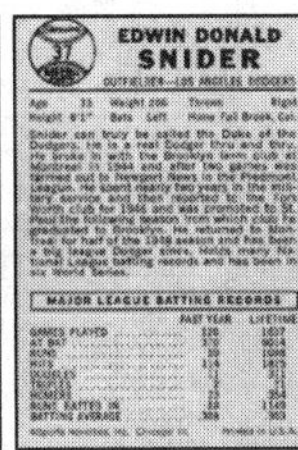

The cards in this 144-card set measure the standard size. The 1960 Leaf set was issued in a regular gum package style but with a marble instead of gum. The series was a joint production by Sports Novelties, Inc., and Leaf, two Chicago-based companies. Cards 73-144 are more difficult to find than the lower numbers. Photo variations exist (probably proof cards) for the seven cards listed with an asterisk and there is a well-known error card, number 25 showing Brooks Lawrence (in a Reds uniform) with Jim Grant's name on front, and Grant's biography and record on back. The corrected version with Grant's photo is the more difficult variety. The only notable Rookie Card in this set is Dallas Green. The complete set price below includes both versions of Jim Grant.

	NRMT	VG-E	GOOD
COMPLETE SET (145)	1750.00	800.00	220.00
COMMON CARD (1-72)	3.00	1.35	.35
COMMON CARD (73-144)	30.00	13.50	3.70
WRAPPER	50.00	22.00	6.25
☐ 1 Luis Aparicio *	24.00	6.00	3.00
☐ 2 Woody Held	3.00	1.35	.35
☐ 3 Frank Lary	5.00	2.20	.60
☐ 4 Camilo Pascual	5.00	2.20	.60
☐ 5 Pancho Herrera	3.00	1.35	.35
☐ 6 Felipe Alou	5.00	2.20	.60
☐ 7 Benjamin Daniels	3.00	1.35	.35
☐ 8 Roger Craig	5.00	2.20	.60
☐ 9 Eddie Kasko	3.00	1.35	.35
☐ 10 Bob Grim	5.00	2.20	.60
☐ 11 Jim Busby	3.00	1.35	.35
☐ 12 Ken Boyer	5.00	2.20	.60
☐ 13 Bob Boyd	3.00	1.35	.35
☐ 14 Sam Jones	5.00	2.20	.60
☐ 15 Larry Jackson	5.00	2.20	.60
☐ 16 Elroy Face	3.00	1.35	.35
☐ 17 Walt Moryn *	3.00	1.35	.35
☐ 18 Jim Gilliam	5.00	2.20	.60
☐ 19 Don Newcombe	5.00	2.20	.60
☐ 20 Glen Hobbie	3.00	1.35	.35
☐ 21 Pedro Ramos	3.00	1.35	.35
☐ 22 Ryne Duren	3.00	1.35	.35
☐ 23 Joey Jay *	5.00	2.20	.60
☐ 24 Lou Berberet	3.00	1.35	.35
☐ 25A Jim Grant ERR (Photo actually Brooks Lawrence)	15.00	6.75	1.85
☐ 25B Jim Grant COR	24.00	11.00	3.00
☐ 26 Tom Borland	3.00	1.35	.35
☐ 27 Brooks Robinson	40.00	18.00	5.00
☐ 28 Jerry Adair	3.00	1.35	.35
☐ 29 Ron Jackson	3.00	1.35	.35
☐ 30 George Strickland	3.00	1.35	.35
☐ 31 Rocky Bridges	3.00	1.35	.35
☐ 32 Bill Tuttle	3.00	1.35	.35
☐ 33 Ken Hunt	3.00	1.35	.35
☐ 34 Hal Griggs	3.00	1.35	.35
☐ 35 Jim Coates *	3.00	1.35	.35
☐ 36 Brooks Lawrence	3.00	1.35	.35
☐ 37 Duke Snider	40.00	18.00	5.00
☐ 38 Al Spangler	3.00	1.35	.35
☐ 39 Jim Owens	3.00	1.35	.35
☐ 40 Bill Virdon	3.00	1.35	.35
☐ 41 Ernie Broglio	5.00	2.20	.60
☐ 42 Andre Rodgers	3.00	1.35	.35
☐ 43 Julio Becquer	3.00	1.35	.35
☐ 44 Tony Taylor	5.00	2.20	.60
☐ 45 Jerry Lynch	5.00	2.20	.60
☐ 46 Cletis Boyer	3.00	1.35	.35
☐ 47 Jerry Lumpe	3.00	1.35	.35
☐ 48 Charlie Maxwell	5.00	2.20	.60
☐ 49 Jim Perry	5.00	2.20	.60
☐ 50 Danny McDevitt	3.00	1.35	.35
☐ 51 Juan Pizarro	3.00	1.35	.35
☐ 52 Dallas Green	10.00	4.50	1.25
☐ 53 Bob Friend	5.00	2.20	.60
☐ 54 Jack Sanford	5.00	2.20	.60
☐ 55 Jim Rivera	3.00	1.35	.35
☐ 56 Ted Wills	3.00	1.35	.35
☐ 57 Milt Pappas	5.00	2.20	.60
☐ 58 Hal Smith *	3.00	1.35	.35
☐ 59 Bobby Avila	3.00	1.35	.35
☐ 60 Clem Labine	5.00	2.20	.60
☐ 61 Norman Rehm *	3.00	1.35	.35
☐ 62 John Gabler	3.00	1.35	.35
☐ 63 John Tsitouris	3.00	1.35	.35
☐ 64 Dave Sisler	3.00	1.35	.35
☐ 65 Vic Power	5.00	2.20	.60
☐ 66 Earl Battey	3.00	1.35	.35
☐ 67 Bob Purkey	3.00	1.35	.35
☐ 68 Moe Drabowsky	5.00	2.20	.60
☐ 69 Hoyt Wilhelm	14.00	6.25	1.75
☐ 70 Humberto Robinson	3.00	1.35	.35
☐ 71 Whitey Herzog	5.00	2.20	.60
☐ 72 Dick Donovan *	3.00	1.35	.35
☐ 73 Gordon Jones	30.00	13.50	3.70
☐ 74 Joe Hicks	30.00	13.50	3.70
☐ 75 Ray Culp	40.00	18.00	5.00
☐ 76 Dick Drott	30.00	13.50	3.70
☐ 77 Bob Duliba	30.00	13.50	3.70
☐ 78 Art Ditmar	30.00	13.50	3.70
☐ 79 Steve Korcheck	30.00	13.50	3.70
☐ 80 Henry Mason	30.00	13.50	3.70
☐ 81 Harry Simpson	30.00	13.50	3.70
☐ 82 Gene Green	30.00	13.50	3.70
☐ 83 Bob Shaw	30.00	13.50	3.70
☐ 84 Howard Reed	30.00	13.50	3.70
☐ 85 Dick Stigman	30.00	13.50	3.70
☐ 86 Rip Repulski	30.00	13.50	3.70
☐ 87 Seth Morehead	30.00	13.50	3.70
☐ 88 Camilo Carreon	30.00	13.50	3.70
☐ 89 John Blanchard	40.00	18.00	5.00
☐ 90 Billy Hoeft	30.00	13.50	3.70
☐ 91 Fred Hopke	30.00	13.50	3.70
☐ 92 Joe Martin	30.00	13.50	3.70
☐ 93 Wally Shannon	30.00	13.50	3.70
☐ 94 Two Hal Smith's Hal R. Smith Hal W. Smith	40.00	18.00	5.00
☐ 95 Al Schroll	30.00	13.50	3.70
☐ 96 John Kucks	30.00	13.50	3.70
☐ 97 Tom Morgan	30.00	13.50	3.70
☐ 98 Willie Jones	30.00	13.50	3.70
☐ 99 Marshall Renfroe	30.00	13.50	3.70
☐ 100 Willie Tasby	30.00	13.50	3.70
☐ 101 Irv Noren	30.00	13.50	3.70
☐ 102 Russ Snyder	30.00	13.50	3.70
☐ 103 Bob Turley	40.00	18.00	5.00
☐ 104 Jim Woods	30.00	13.50	3.70
☐ 105 Ronnie Kline	30.00	13.50	3.70
☐ 106 Steve Bilko	30.00	13.50	3.70
☐ 107 Elmer Valo	30.00	13.50	3.70
☐ 108 Tom McAvoy	30.00	13.50	3.70
☐ 109 Stan Williams	30.00	13.50	3.70
☐ 110 Earl Averill Jr.	30.00	13.50	3.70
☐ 111 Lee Walls	30.00	13.50	3.70
☐ 112 Paul Richards MG	40.00	18.00	5.00
☐ 113 Ed Sadowski	30.00	13.50	3.70
☐ 114 Stover McIlwain	30.00	13.50	3.70
☐ 115 Chuck Tanner UER (Photo actually Ken Kuhn)	40.00	18.00	5.00
☐ 116 Lou Klimchock	30.00	13.50	3.70
☐ 117 Neil Chrisley	30.00	13.50	3.70
☐ 118 John Callison	40.00	18.00	5.00
☐ 119 Hal Smith	30.00	13.50	3.70
☐ 120 Carl Sawatski	30.00	13.50	3.70
☐ 121 Frank Leja	30.00	13.50	3.70
☐ 122 Earl Torgeson	30.00	13.50	3.70
☐ 123 Art Schult	30.00	13.50	3.70
☐ 124 Jim Brosnan	30.00	13.50	3.70
☐ 125 Sparky Anderson	60.00	27.00	7.50
☐ 126 Joe Pignatano	30.00	13.50	3.70
☐ 127 Rocky Nelson	30.00	13.50	3.70
☐ 128 Orlando Cepeda	60.00	27.00	7.50
☐ 129 Daryl Spencer	30.00	13.50	3.70
☐ 130 Ralph Lumenti	30.00	13.50	3.70
☐ 131 Sam Taylor	30.00	13.50	3.70
☐ 132 Harry Brecheen CO	40.00	18.00	5.00
☐ 133 Johnny Groth	30.00	13.50	3.70
☐ 134 Wayne Terwilliger	30.00	13.50	3.70
☐ 135 Kent Hadley	30.00	13.50	3.70
☐ 136 Faye Throneberry	30.00	13.50	3.70
☐ 137 Jack Meyer	30.00	13.50	3.70
☐ 138 Chuck Cottier	30.00	13.50	3.70
☐ 139 Joe DeMaestri	30.00	13.50	3.70
☐ 140 Gene Freese	30.00	13.50	3.70
☐ 141 Curt Flood	40.00	18.00	5.00
☐ 142 Gino Cimoli	30.00	13.50	3.70
☐ 143 Clay Dalrymple	30.00	13.50	3.70
☐ 144 Jim Bunning	70.00	17.50	7.00

1985 Leaf/Donruss

The cards in this 264-card set measure the standard size. In an effort to establish a Canadian baseball card market much as Topps' affiliate O-Pee-Chee had done, the Donruss Company in conjunction with its new parent Leaf Company issued this set to the Canadian market. The set was later released in the United States through hobby dealer channels. The cards were issued in wax packs. A piece of a large Lou Gehrig puzzle was inserted in each pack. Aside from card number

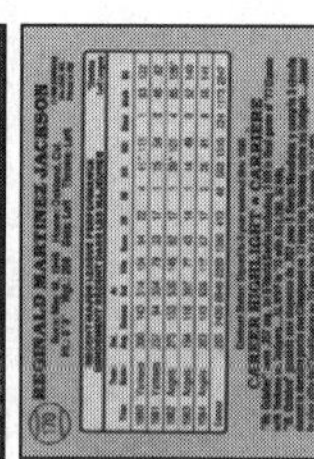

differences the cards are essentially the same as the Donruss U.S. regular issue of the cards of the same players; however the backs are in both French and English. Two cards, Dick Perez artwork of Tim Raines (252) and Dave Stieb (251), are called Canadian Greats (CG) and are not contained in the Donruss U.S. set. As in most Canadian sets, the players featured are heavily biased towards Canadian teams and those American teams closest to the Canadian border. Diamond Kings (numbers 1-26 denoted DK) and Rated Rookies (number 27 denoted RR) are included just as in the American set. Those players selected for and included as Diamond Kings do not have a regular card in the set. The player cards are numbered on the back. The checklist cards (listed at the end of the list below) are numbered one, two and three (but are not given a traditional card number); the Diamond Kings checklist card is unnumbered; and the Lou Gehrig puzzle card is mistakenly numbered 635. Key cards in this set include Roger Clemens and Dwight Gooden in their Rookie Card year.

	NRMT	VG-E	GOOD
COMPLETE SET (264)	75.00	34.00	9.50
COMMON CARD (1-263)	.05	.02	.01
1 Ryne Sandberg DK	2.50	1.10	.30
2 Doug DeCinces DK	.05	.02	.01
3 Richard Dotson DK	.05	.02	.01
4 Bert Blyleven DK	.10	.05	.01
5 Lou Whitaker DK	.25	.11	.03
6 Dan Quisenberry DK	.05	.02	.01
7 Don Mattingly DK	4.00	1.80	.50
8 Carney Lansford DK	.05	.02	.01
9 Frank Tanana DK	.05	.02	.01
10 Willie Upshaw DK	.05	.02	.01
11 Claudell Washington DK	.05	.02	.01
12 Mike Marshall DK	.05	.02	.01
13 Joaquin Andujar DK	.05	.02	.01
14 Cal Ripken DK	5.00	2.20	.60
15 Jim Rice DK	.10	.05	.01
16 Don Sutton DK	.10	.05	.01
17 Frank Viola DK	.10	.05	.01
18 Alvin Davis DK	.05	.02	.01
19 Mario Soto DK	.05	.02	.01
20 Jose Cruz DK	.05	.02	.01
21 Charlie Lea DK	.05	.02	.01
22 Jesse Orosco DK	.05	.02	.01
23 Juan Samuel DK	.05	.02	.01
24 Tony Pena DK	.05	.02	.01
25 Tony Gwynn DK	4.00	1.80	.50
26 Bob Brenly DK	.05	.02	.01
27 Steve Kiefer RR	.05	.02	.01
28 Joe Morgan	.50	.23	.06
29 Luis Leal	.05	.02	.01
30 Dan Gladden	.10	.05	.01
31 Shane Rawley	.05	.02	.01
32 Mark Clear	.05	.02	.01
33 Terry Kennedy	.05	.02	.01
34 Hal McRae	.10	.05	.01
35 Mickey Rivers	.05	.02	.01
36 Tom Brunansky	.05	.02	.01
37 LaMarr Hoyt	.05	.02	.01
38 Orel Hershiser	2.00	.90	.25
39 Chris Bando	.05	.02	.01
40 Lee Lacy	.05	.02	.01
41 Lance Parrish	.10	.05	.01
42 George Foster	.10	.05	.01
43 Kevin McReynolds	.05	.02	.01
44 Robin Yount	.75	.35	.09
45 Craig McMurtry	.05	.02	.01
46 Mike Witt	.05	.02	.01
47 Gary Redus	.05	.02	.01
48 Dennis Rasmussen	.05	.02	.01
49 Gary Woods	.05	.02	.01
50 Phil Bradley	.10	.05	.01
51 Steve Bedrosian	.05	.02	.01
52 Duane Walker	.05	.02	.01
53 Geoff Zahn	.05	.02	.01
54 Dave Stieb	.05	.02	.01
55 Pascual Perez	.05	.02	.01
56 Mark Langston	.75	.35	.09
57 Bob Dernier	.05	.02	.01
58 Joe Cowley	.05	.02	.01
59 Dan Schatzeder	.05	.02	.01
60 Ozzie Smith	2.00	.90	.25
61 Bob Knepper	.05	.02	.01
62 Keith Hernandez	.10	.05	.01
63 Rick Rhoden	.05	.02	.01
64 Alejandro Pena	.05	.02	.01
65 Damaso Garcia	.05	.02	.01
66 Chili Davis	.10	.05	.01
67 Al Oliver	.10	.05	.01
68 Alan Wiggins	.05	.02	.01
69 Darryl Motley	.05	.02	.01
70 Gary Ward	.05	.02	.01
71 John Butcher	.05	.02	.01
72 Scott McGregor	.05	.02	.01
73 Bruce Hurst	.05	.02	.01
74 Dwayne Murphy	.05	.02	.01
75 Greg Luzinski	.10	.05	.01
76 Pat Tabler	.05	.02	.01
77 Chet Lemon	.05	.02	.01
78 Jim Sundberg	.05	.02	.01
79 Wally Backman	.05	.02	.01
80 Terry Puhl	.05	.02	.01
81 Storm Davis	.05	.02	.01
82 Jim Wohlford	.05	.02	.01
83 Willie Randolph	.10	.05	.01
84 Ron Cey	.10	.05	.01
85 Jim Beattie	.05	.02	.01
86 Rafael Ramirez	.05	.02	.01
87 Cesar Cedeno	.10	.05	.01
88 Bobby Grich	.10	.05	.01
89 Jason Thompson	.05	.02	.01
90 Steve Sax	.05	.02	.01
91 Tony Fernandez	.05	.02	.01
92 Jeff Leonard	.05	.02	.01
93 Von Hayes	.05	.02	.01
94 Steve Garvey	.10	.05	.01
95 Steve Balboni	.05	.02	.01
96 Larry Parrish	.05	.02	.01
97 Tim Teufel	.05	.02	.01
98 Sammy Stewart	.05	.02	.01
99 Roger Clemens	15.00	6.75	1.85
100 Steve Kemp	.05	.02	.01
101 Tom Seaver	.75	.35	.09
102 Andre Thornton	.05	.02	.01
103 Kirk Gibson	.10	.05	.01
104 Ted Simmons	.10	.05	.01
105 David Palmer	.05	.02	.01
106 Roy Lee Jackson	.05	.02	.01
107 Kirby Puckett	15.00	6.75	1.85
108 Charlie Hough	.10	.05	.01
109 Mike Boddicker	.05	.02	.01
110 Willie Wilson	.05	.02	.01
111 Tim Lollar	.05	.02	.01
112 Tony Armas	.05	.02	.01
113 Steve Carlton	.75	.35	.09
114 Gary Lavelle	.05	.02	.01
115 Cliff Johnson	.05	.02	.01
116 Ray Burris	.05	.02	.01
117 Rudy Law	.05	.02	.01
118 Mike Scioscia	.05	.02	.01
119 Kent Tekulve UER (Telukve on back)	.05	.02	.01
120 George Vukovich	.05	.02	.01
121 Barbaro Garbey	.05	.02	.01
122 Mookie Wilson	.10	.05	.01
123 Ben Oglivie	.05	.02	.01
124 Jerry Mumphrey	.05	.02	.01
125 Willie McGee	.10	.05	.01
126 Jeff Reardon	.10	.05	.01
127 Dave Winfield	1.00	.45	.12
128 Lee Smith	.25	.11	.03
129 Ken Phelps	.05	.02	.01
130 Rick Camp	.05	.02	.01
131 Dave Concepcion	.10	.05	.01
132 Rod Carew	.75	.35	.09
133 Andre Dawson	.50	.23	.06
134 Doyle Alexander	.05	.02	.01
135 Miguel Dilone	.05	.02	.01
136 Jim Gott	.05	.02	.01
137 Eric Show	.05	.02	.01
138 Phil Niekro	.25	.11	.03
139 Rick Sutcliffe	.05	.02	.01
140 Dave Winfield Don Mattingly Two for the Title	2.00	.90	.25
141 Ken Oberkfell	.05	.02	.01
142 Jack Morris	.10	.05	.01
143 Lloyd Moseby	.05	.02	.01
144 Pete Rose	1.50	.70	.19
145 Gary Gaetti	.10	.05	.01
146 Don Baylor	.10	.05	.01
147 Bobby Meacham	.05	.02	.01
148 Frank White	.10	.05	.01
149 Mark Thurmond	.05	.02	.01
150 Dwight Evans	.10	.05	.01
151 Al Holland	.05	.02	.01
152 Joel Youngblood	.05	.02	.01
153 Rance Mulliniks	.05	.02	.01
154 Bill Caudill	.05	.02	.01
155 Carlton Fisk	1.00	.45	.12
156 Rick Honeycutt	.05	.02	.01
157 John Candelaria	.05	.02	.01
158 Alan Trammell	.25	.11	.03
159 Darryl Strawberry	.50	.23	.06
160 Aurelio Lopez	.05	.02	.01
161 Enos Cabell	.05	.02	.01
162 Dion James	.05	.02	.01
163 Bruce Sutter	.10	.05	.01
164 Razor Shines	.05	.02	.01
165 Butch Wynegar	.05	.02	.01
166 Rich Bordi	.05	.02	.01
167 Spike Owen	.05	.02	.01
168 Chris Chambliss	.05	.02	.01
169 Dave Parker	.10	.05	.01
170 Reggie Jackson	1.00	.45	.12
171 Bryn Smith	.05	.02	.01
172 Dave Collins	.05	.02	.01
173 Dave Engle	.05	.02	.01
174 Buddy Bell	.05	.02	.01
175 Mike Flanagan	.05	.02	.01
176 George Brett	3.00	1.35	.35
177 Graig Nettles	.10	.05	.01
178 Jerry Koosman	.05	.02	.01
179 Wade Boggs	2.00	.90	.25
180 Jody Davis	.05	.02	.01
181 Ernie Whitt	.05	.02	.01
182 Dave Kingman	.10	.05	.01
183 Vance Law	.05	.02	.01
184 Fernando Valenzuela	.10	.05	.01
185 Bill Madlock	.05	.02	.01
186 Brett Butler	.10	.05	.01
187 Doug Sisk	.05	.02	.01
188 Dan Petry	.05	.02	.01
189 Joe Niekro	.05	.02	.01
190 Rollie Fingers	.50	.23	.06
191 David Green	.05	.02	.01
192 Steve Rogers	.05	.02	.01
193 Ken Griffey	.10	.05	.01
194 Scott Sanderson	.05	.02	.01
195 Barry Bonnell	.05	.02	.01
196 Bruce Benedict	.05	.02	.01
197 Keith Moreland	.05	.02	.01
198 Fred Lynn	.10	.05	.01
199 Tim Wallach	.05	.02	.01
200 Kent Hrbek	.10	.05	.01
201 Pete O'Brien	.05	.02	.01
202 Bud Black	.05	.02	.01
203 Eddie Murray	2.00	.90	.25
204 Goose Gossage	.10	.05	.01
205 Mike Schmidt	1.50	.70	.19
206 Mike Easler	.05	.02	.01
207 Jack Clark	.10	.05	.01
208 Rickey Henderson	1.00	.45	.12
209 Jesse Barfield	.05	.02	.01
210 Ron Kittle	.05	.02	.01
211 Pedro Guerrero	.05	.02	.01
212 Johnny Ray	.05	.02	.01
213 Julio Franco	.10	.05	.01
214 Hubie Brooks	.05	.02	.01
215 Darrell Evans	.10	.05	.01
216 Nolan Ryan	6.00	2.70	.75
217 Jim Gantner	.05	.02	.01
218 Tim Raines	.10	.05	.01
219 Dave Righetti	.05	.02	.01
220 Gary Matthews	.05	.02	.01
221 Jack Perconte	.05	.02	.01
222 Dale Murphy	.25	.11	.03
223 Brian Downing	.05	.02	.01
224 Mickey Hatcher	.05	.02	.01
225 Lonnie Smith	.05	.02	.01
226 Jorge Orta	.05	.02	.01
227 Milt Wilcox	.05	.02	.01
228 John Denny	.05	.02	.01
229 Marty Barrett	.05	.02	.01
230 Alfredo Griffin	.05	.02	.01
231 Harold Baines	.10	.05	.01
232 Bill Russell	.10	.05	.01
233 Marvell Wynne	.05	.02	.01
234 Dwight Gooden	3.00	1.35	.35
235 Willie Hernandez	.05	.02	.01
236 Bill Gullickson	.05	.02	.01
237 Ron Guidry	.10	.05	.01
238 Leon Durham	.05	.02	.01
239 Al Cowens	.05	.02	.01
240 Bob Horner	.05	.02	.01
241 Gary Carter	.10	.05	.01
242 Glenn Hubbard	.05	.02	.01
243 Steve Trout	.05	.02	.01
244 Jay Howell	.05	.02	.01
245 Terry Francona	.05	.02	.01
246 Cecil Cooper	.10	.05	.01
247 Larry McWilliams	.05	.02	.01
248 George Bell	.05	.02	.01
249 Larry Herndon	.05	.02	.01
250 Ozzie Virgil	.05	.02	.01
251 Dave Stieb CG	.05	.02	.01
252 Tim Raines CG	.10	.05	.01
253 Ricky Horton	.05	.02	.01
254 Bill Buckner	.10	.05	.01
255 Dan Driessen	.05	.02	.01
256 Ron Darling	.05	.02	.01
257 Doug Flynn	.05	.02	.01
258 Darrell Porter	.05	.02	.01
259 George Hendrick	.05	.02	.01
260 Checklist DK 1-26 (Unnumbered)	.05	.02	.01
261 Checklist 27-106 (Unnumbered)	.05	.02	.01
262 Checklist 107-178 (Unnumbered)	.05	.02	.01
263 Checklist 179-259 (Unnumbered)	.05	.02	.01
635 Lou Gehrig Puzzle Card UER (Misnumbered)	.40	.18	.05

1986 Leaf/Donruss

This 264-card standard-size set was issued with a puzzle of Hank Aaron. Except for the numbering, the company logo and the bilingual backs, the cards are essentially the same as the Donruss U.S. regular issue cards of the same players. On a blue and black striped background, fronts feature slightly tilted color player photos. The player's name and position appear under the photo. On a light blue

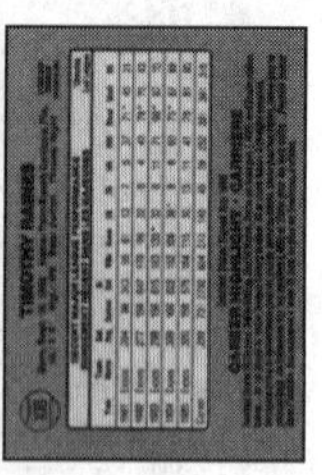

background, the horizontal backs carry player biography, statistics and career hightlights in French and English. Two cards, Dick Perez artwork of Jesse Barfield (254) and Jeff Reardon (214), are called Canadian Greats (CG) and are not contained in the Donruss U.S. set. Diamond Kings (numbers 1-26, denoted DK) and Rated Rookies (numbers 27-29, denoted RR) are included just as in the American set. The cards are numbered on the back. As in most Canadian sets, the players featured are heavily biased toward Canadian teams and those American teams closest to the Canadian border. Those players selected for and included as Diamond Kings do not have a regular card in the set. The checklist cards (listed at the end of the list below) are numbered one, two and three (but are not given a traditional card number); the Diamond Kings checklist card is also unnumbered. Two key cards in this set are Andres Galarraga and Fred McGriff, who are Rookie Cards in the 1986 Donruss set.

	MINT	NRMT	EXC
COMPLETE SET (264)	25.00	11.00	3.10
COMMON CARD (1-264)	.05	.02	.01
1 Kirk Gibson DK	.10	.05	.01
2 Goose Gossage DK	.10	.05	.01
3 Willie McGee DK	.10	.05	.01
4 George Bell DK	.05	.02	.01
5 Tony Armas DK	.05	.02	.01
6 Chili Davis DK	.10	.05	.01
7 Cecil Cooper DK	.10	.05	.01
8 Mike Boddicker DK	.05	.02	.01
9 Davey Lopes DK	.05	.02	.01
10 Bill Doran DK	.05	.02	.01
11 Bret Saberhagen DK	.25	.11	.03
12 Brett Butler DK	.10	.05	.01
13 Harold Baines DK	.10	.05	.01
14 Mike Davis DK	.05	.02	.01
15 Tony Perez DK	.25	.11	.03
16 Willie Randolph DK	.10	.05	.01
17 Bob Boone DK	.10	.05	.01
18 Orel Hershiser DK	.25	.11	.03
19 Johnny Ray DK	.05	.02	.01
20 Gary Ward DK	.05	.02	.01
21 Rick Mahler DK	.05	.02	.01
22 Phil Bradley DK	.05	.02	.01
23 Jerry Koosman DK	.10	.05	.01
24 Tom Brunansky DK	.05	.02	.01
25 Andre Dawson DK	.25	.11	.03
26 Dwight Gooden DK	.75	.35	.09
27 Andres Galarraga RR	4.00	1.80	.50
28 Fred McGriff RR	8.00	3.60	1.00
29 Dave Shipanoff RR	.05	.02	.01
30 Danny Jackson	.05	.02	.01
31 Robin Yount	.40	.18	.05
32 Mike Fitzgerald	.05	.02	.01
33 Lou Whitaker	.10	.05	.01
34 Alfredo Griffin	.05	.02	.01
35 Oil Can Boyd	.05	.02	.01
36 Ron Guidry	.10	.05	.01
37 Rickey Henderson	.50	.23	.06
38 Jack Morris	.10	.05	.01
39 Brian Downing	.05	.02	.01
40 Mike Marshall	.05	.02	.01
41 Tony Gwynn	2.00	.90	.25
42 George Brett	1.50	.70	.19
43 Jim Gantner	.05	.02	.01
44 Hubie Brooks	.05	.02	.01
45 Tony Fernandez	.05	.02	.01
46 Oddibe McDowell	.05	.02	.01
47 Ozzie Smith	1.00	.45	.12
48 Ken Griffey	.10	.05	.01
49 Jose Cruz	.05	.02	.01
50 Mariano Duncan	.25	.11	.03
51 Mike Schmidt	.75	.35	.09
52 Pat Tabler	.05	.02	.01
53 Pete Rose	.75	.35	.09
54 Frank White	.10	.05	.01
55 Carney Lansford	.05	.02	.01
56 Steve Garvey	.25	.11	.03
57 Vance Law	.05	.02	.01
58 Tony Pena	.05	.02	.01
59 Wayne Tolleson	.05	.02	.01
60 Dale Murphy	.25	.11	.03
61 LaMarr Hoyt	.05	.02	.01
62 Ryne Sandberg	1.25	.55	.16
63 Gary Carter	.10	.05	.01
64 Lee Smith	.25	.11	.03
65 Alvin Davis	.05	.02	.01
66 Edwin Nunez	.05	.02	.01
67 Kent Hrbek	.10	.05	.01
68 Dave Stieb	.05	.02	.01
69 Kirby Puckett	3.00	1.35	.35
70 Paul Molitor	.75	.35	.09
71 Glenn Hubbard	.05	.02	.01
72 Lloyd Moseby	.05	.02	.01

Card			
□ 73 Mike Smithson	.05	.02	.01
□ 74 Jeff Leonard	.05	.02	.01
□ 75 Danny Darwin	.05	.02	.01
□ 76 Kevin McReynolds	.05	.02	.01
□ 77 Bill Buckner	.10	.05	.01
□ 78 Ron Oester	.05	.02	.01
□ 79 Tommy Herr	.05	.02	.01
□ 80 Mike Pagliarulo	.05	.02	.01
□ 81 Ron Romanick	.05	.02	.01
□ 82 Brook Jacoby	.05	.02	.01
□ 83 Eddie Murray	1.00	.45	.12
□ 84 Gary Pettis	.05	.02	.01
□ 85 Chet Lemon	.05	.02	.01
□ 86 Toby Harrah	.05	.02	.01
□ 87 Mike Scioscia	.05	.02	.01
□ 88 Bert Blyleven	.10	.05	.01
□ 89 Dave Righetti	.05	.02	.01
□ 90 Bob Knepper	.05	.02	.01
□ 91 Fernando Valenzuela	.10	.05	.01
□ 92 Dave Dravecky	.10	.05	.01
□ 93 Julio Franco	.10	.05	.01
□ 94 Keith Moreland	.05	.02	.01
□ 95 Darryl Motley	.05	.02	.01
□ 96 Jack Clark	.10	.05	.01
□ 97 Tim Wallach	.05	.02	.01
□ 98 Steve Balboni	.05	.02	.01
□ 99 Storm Davis	.05	.02	.01
□ 100 Jay Howell	.05	.02	.01
□ 101 Alan Trammell	.25	.11	.03
□ 102 Willie Hernandez	.05	.02	.01
□ 103 Don Mattingly	2.00	.90	.25
□ 104 Lee Lacy	.05	.02	.01
□ 105 Pedro Guerrero	.05	.02	.01
□ 106 Willie Wilson	.05	.02	.01
□ 107 Craig Reynolds	.05	.02	.01
□ 108 Tim Raines	.10	.05	.01
□ 109 Shane Rawley	.05	.02	.01
□ 110 Larry Parrish	.05	.02	.01
□ 111 Eric Show	.05	.02	.01
□ 112 Mike Witt	.05	.02	.01
□ 113 Dennis Eckersley	.25	.11	.03
□ 114 Mike Moore	.05	.02	.01
□ 115 Vince Coleman	.10	.05	.01
□ 116 Damaso Garcia	.05	.02	.01
□ 117 Steve Carlton	.40	.18	.05
□ 118 Floyd Bannister	.05	.02	.01
□ 119 Mario Soto	.05	.02	.01
□ 120 Fred Lynn	.10	.05	.01
□ 121 Bob Horner	.05	.02	.01
□ 122 Rick Sutcliffe	.05	.02	.01
□ 123 Walt Terrell	.05	.02	.01
□ 124 Keith Hernandez	.10	.05	.01
□ 125 Dave Winfield	.50	.23	.06
□ 126 Frank Viola	.10	.05	.01
□ 127 Dwight Evans	.10	.05	.01
□ 128 Willie Upshaw	.05	.02	.01
□ 129 Andre Thornton	.05	.02	.01
□ 130 Donnie Moore	.05	.02	.01
□ 131 Darryl Strawberry	.25	.11	.03
□ 132 Nolan Ryan	3.00	1.35	.35
□ 133 Garry Templeton	.05	.02	.01
□ 134 John Tudor	.05	.02	.01
□ 135 Dave Parker	.10	.05	.01
□ 136 Larry McWilliams	.05	.02	.01
□ 137 Terry Pendleton	.25	.11	.03
□ 138 Terry Puhl	.05	.02	.01
□ 139 Bob Dernier	.05	.02	.01
□ 140 Ozzie Guillen	.25	.11	.03
□ 141 Jim Clancy	.05	.02	.01
□ 142 Cal Ripken	3.00	1.35	.35
□ 143 Mickey Hatcher	.05	.02	.01
□ 144 Dan Petry	.05	.02	.01
□ 145 Rich Gedman	.05	.02	.01
□ 146 Jim Rice	.10	.05	.01
□ 147 Butch Wynegar	.05	.02	.01
□ 148 Donnie Hill	.05	.02	.01
□ 149 Jim Sundberg	.05	.02	.01
□ 150 Joe Hesketh	.05	.02	.01
□ 151 Chris Codiroli	.05	.02	.01
□ 152 Charlie Hough	.10	.05	.01
□ 153 Herm Winningham	.05	.02	.01
□ 154 Dave Rozema	.05	.02	.01
□ 155 Don Slaught	.05	.02	.01
□ 156 Juan Beniquez	.05	.02	.01
□ 157 Ted Higuera	.05	.02	.01
□ 158 Andy Hawkins	.05	.02	.01
□ 159 Don Robinson	.05	.02	.01
□ 160 Glenn Wilson	.05	.02	.01
□ 161 Earnest Riles	.05	.02	.01
□ 162 Nick Esasky	.05	.02	.01
□ 163 Carlton Fisk	.40	.18	.05
□ 164 Claudell Washington	.05	.02	.01
□ 165 Scott McGregor	.05	.02	.01
□ 166 Nate Snell	.05	.02	.01
□ 167 Ted Simmons	.10	.05	.01
□ 168 Wade Boggs	.60	.25	.07
□ 169 Marty Barrett	.05	.02	.01
□ 170 Bud Black	.05	.02	.01
□ 171 Charlie Leibrandt	.05	.02	.01
□ 172 Charlie Lea	.05	.02	.01
□ 173 Reggie Jackson	.50	.23	.06
□ 174 Bryn Smith	.05	.02	.01
□ 175 Glenn Davis	.05	.02	.01
□ 176 Von Hayes	.05	.02	.01
□ 177 Danny Cox	.05	.02	.01
□ 178 Sammy Khalifa	.05	.02	.01
□ 179 Tom Browning	.05	.02	.01
□ 180 Scott Garrelts	.05	.02	.01
□ 181 Shawon Dunston	.10	.05	.01
□ 182 Doyle Alexander	.05	.02	.01
□ 183 Jim Presley	.05	.02	.01
□ 184 Al Cowens	.05	.02	.01
□ 185 Mark Salas	.05	.02	.01
□ 186 Tom Niedenfuer	.05	.02	.01
□ 187 Dave Henderson	.05	.02	.01
□ 188 Lonnie Smith	.05	.02	.01
□ 189 Bruce Bochte	.05	.02	.01
□ 190 Leon Durham	.05	.02	.01
□ 191 Terry Francona	.10	.05	.01
□ 192 Bruce Sutter	.10	.05	.01
□ 193 Steve Crawford	.05	.02	.01
□ 194 Bob Brenly	.05	.02	.01
□ 195 Dan Pasqua	.05	.02	.01
□ 196 Juan Samuel	.05	.02	.01
□ 197 Floyd Rayford	.05	.02	.01
□ 198 Tim Burke	.05	.02	.01
□ 199 Ben Oglivie	.05	.02	.01
□ 200 Don Carman	.05	.02	.01
□ 201 Lance Parrish	.10	.05	.01
□ 202 Terry Forster	.05	.02	.01
□ 203 Neal Heaton	.05	.02	.01
□ 204 Ivan Calderon	.05	.02	.01
□ 205 Jorge Orta	.05	.02	.01
□ 206 Tom Henke	.05	.02	.01
□ 207 Rick Reuschel	.05	.02	.01
□ 208 Dan Quisenberry	.05	.02	.01
□ 209 Pete Rose HL Ty-Breaking	1.50	.70	.19
□ 210 Floyd Youmans	.05	.02	.01
□ 211 Tom Filer	.05	.02	.01
□ 212 R.J. Reynolds	.05	.02	.01
□ 213 Gorman Thomas	.05	.02	.01
□ 214 Jeff Reardon CG	.10	.05	.01
□ 215 Chris Brown	.05	.02	.01
□ 216 Rick Aguilera	.25	.11	.03
□ 217 Ernie Whitt	.05	.02	.01
□ 218 Joe Orsulak	.05	.02	.01
□ 219 Jimmy Key	.25	.11	.03
□ 220 Atlee Hammaker	.05	.02	.01
□ 221 Ron Darling	.05	.02	.01
□ 222 Zane Smith	.05	.02	.01
□ 223 Bob Welch	.05	.02	.01
□ 224 Reid Nichols	.05	.02	.01
□ 225 Vince Coleman Willie McGee Fleet Feet	.10	.05	.01
□ 226 Mark Gubicza	.05	.02	.01
□ 227 Tim Birtsas	.05	.02	.01
□ 228 Mike Hargrove	.10	.05	.01
□ 229 Randy St. Claire	.05	.02	.01
□ 230 Larry Herndon	.05	.02	.01
□ 231 Dusty Baker	.10	.05	.01
□ 232 Mookie Wilson	.10	.05	.01
□ 233 Jeff Lahti	.05	.02	.01
□ 234 Tom Seaver	.40	.18	.05
□ 235 Mike Scott	.05	.02	.01
□ 236 Don Sutton	.25	.11	.03
□ 237 Roy Smalley	.05	.02	.01
□ 238 Bill Madlock	.05	.02	.01
□ 239 Charlie Hudson Charles on both sides	.05	.02	.01
□ 240 John Franco	.25	.11	.03
□ 241 Frank Tanana	.05	.02	.01
□ 242 Sid Fernandez	.05	.02	.01
□ 243 Phil Niekro Joe Niekro Knuckle Brothers	.10	.05	.01
□ 244 Dennis Lamp	.05	.02	.01
□ 245 Gene Nelson	.05	.02	.01
□ 246 Terry Harper	.05	.02	.01
□ 247 Vida Blue	.10	.05	.01
□ 248 Roger McDowell	.05	.02	.01
□ 249 Tony Bernazard	.05	.02	.01
□ 250 Cliff Johnson	.05	.02	.01
□ 251 Hal McRae	.10	.05	.01
□ 252 Garth Iorg	.05	.02	.01
□ 253 Mitch Webster	.05	.02	.01
□ 254 Jesse Barfield CG	.05	.02	.01
□ 255 Dan Driessen	.05	.02	.01
□ 256 Mike Brown Pirates OF	.05	.02	.01
□ 257 Ron Kittle	.05	.02	.01
□ 258 Bo Diaz	.05	.02	.01
□ 259 Hank Aaron Puzzle Card	.25	.11	.03
□ 260 Pete Rose King Of Kings	1.50	.70	.19
□ 261 Checklist DK 1-26 Unnumbered	.05	.02	.01
□ 262 Checklist 27-106 Unnumbered	.05	.02	.01
□ 263 Checklist 107-186 Unnumbered	.05	.02	.01
□ 264 Checklist 187-260 Unnumbered	.05	.02	.01

1987 Leaf/Donruss

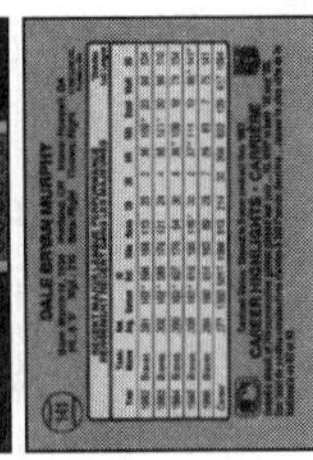

This 264-card standard-size set was issued with a puzzle of Roberto Clemente. Except for the numbering, the company logo and the bilingual backs, the cards are essentially the same as the Donruss U.S. regular issue cards of the same players. On a black background, the fronts feature color player photos with rounded corners and a thin white border. The player's name and position, and the team and manufacturer logos also appear on the front. On a golden background, the horizontal backs carry player biography, statistics and career hightlights in French and English. Two cards, Dick Perez artwork of Floyd Youmans (65) and Mark Eichhorn (173), are called Canadian Greats (CG) and are not contained in the Donruss U.S. set. Diamond Kings (numbers 1-26, denoted DK) and Rated Rookies (numbers 28-47, denoted RR) are included just as in the American set. The cards are numbered on the back. The players featured in this set are heavily biased toward Canadian teams and those American teams closest to the Canadian border. Players appearing in their Rookie Card year include Will Clark, Wally Joyner, Greg Maddux and Ruben Sierra.

	MINT	NRMT	EXC
COMPLETE SET (264)	25.00	11.00	3.10
COMMON CARD (1-264)	.05	.02	.01
□ 1 Wally Joyner DK	.25	.11	.03
□ 2 Roger Clemens DK	.50	.23	.06
□ 3 Dale Murphy DK	.25	.11	.03
□ 4 Darryl Strawberry DK	.25	.11	.03
□ 5 Ozzie Smith DK	.75	.35	.09
□ 6 Jose Canseco DK	.75	.35	.09
□ 7 Charlie Hough DK	.10	.05	.01
□ 8 Brook Jacoby DK	.05	.02	.01
□ 9 Fred Lynn DK	.10	.05	.01
□ 10 Rick Rhoden DK	.05	.02	.01
□ 11 Chris Brown DK	.05	.02	.01
□ 12 Von Hayes DK	.05	.02	.01
□ 13 Jack Morris DK	.10	.05	.01
□ 14 Kevin McReynolds DK	.05	.02	.01
□ 15 George Brett DK	.75	.35	.09
□ 16 Ted Higuera DK	.05	.02	.01
□ 17 Hubie Brooks DK	.05	.02	.01
□ 18 Mike Scott DK	.05	.02	.01
□ 19 Kirby Puckett DK	.75	.35	.09
□ 20 Dave Winfield DK	.40	.18	.05
□ 21 Lloyd Moseby DK	.05	.02	.01
□ 22 Eric Davis DK	.10	.05	.01
□ 23 Jim Presley DK	.05	.02	.01
□ 24 Keith Moreland DK	.05	.02	.01
□ 25 Greg Walker DK	.05	.02	.01
□ 26 Steve Sax DK	.05	.02	.01
□ 27 DK Checklist 1-26	.05	.02	.01
□ 28 B.J. Surhoff RR	.30	.14	.04
□ 29 Randy Myers RR	.40	.18	.05
□ 30 Ken Gerhart RR	.05	.02	.01
□ 31 Benito Santiago RR	.10	.05	.01
□ 32 Greg Swindell RR	.10	.05	.01
□ 33 Mike Birkbeck RR	.05	.02	.01
□ 34 Terry Steinbach RR	.30	.14	.04
□ 35 Bo Jackson RR	.40	.18	.05
□ 36 Greg Maddux RR	8.00	3.60	1.00
□ 37 Jim Lindeman RR	.05	.02	.01
□ 38 Devon White RR	.40	.18	.05
□ 39 Eric Bell RR	.05	.02	.01
□ 40 Will Fraser RR	.05	.02	.01
□ 41 Jerry Browne RR	.05	.02	.01
□ 42 Chris James RR	.05	.02	.01
□ 43 Rafael Palmeiro RR	1.50	.70	.19
□ 44 Pat Dodson RR	.05	.02	.01
□ 45 Duane Ward RR	.05	.02	.01
□ 46 Mark McGwire RR	5.00	2.20	.60
□ 47 Bruce Fields RR	.05	.02	.01
□ 48 Jody Davis	.05	.02	.01
□ 49 Roger McDowell	.05	.02	.01
□ 50 Jose Guzman	.05	.02	.01
□ 51 Oddibe McDowell	.05	.02	.01
□ 52 Harold Baines	.10	.05	.01
□ 53 Dave Righetti	.05	.02	.01
□ 54 Moose Haas	.05	.02	.01
□ 55 Mark Langston	.05	.02	.01
□ 56 Kirby Puckett	1.50	.70	.19
□ 57 Dwight Evans	.10	.05	.01
□ 58 Willie Randolph	.10	.05	.01
□ 59 Wally Backman	.05	.02	.01
□ 60 Bryn Smith	.05	.02	.01
□ 61 Tim Wallach	.05	.02	.01
□ 62 Joe Hesketh	.05	.02	.01
□ 63 Garry Templeton	.05	.02	.01
□ 64 Robby Thompson	.05	.02	.01
□ 65 Floyd Youmans CG	.05	.02	.01
□ 66 Ernest Riles	.05	.02	.01
□ 67 Robin Yount	.40	.18	.05
□ 68 Darryl Strawberry	.25	.11	.03
□ 69 Ernie Whitt	.05	.02	.01
□ 70 Dave Winfield	.40	.18	.05
□ 71 Paul Molitor	.60	.25	.07
□ 72 Dave Stieb	.05	.02	.01
□ 73 Tom Henke	.05	.02	.01
□ 74 Frank Viola	.10	.05	.01
□ 75 Scott Garrelts	.05	.02	.01
□ 76 Mike Boddicker	.05	.02	.01
□ 77 Keith Moreland	.05	.02	.01
□ 78 Lou Whitaker	.10	.05	.01
□ 79 Dave Parker	.10	.05	.01
□ 80 Lee Smith	.25	.11	.03
□ 81 Tom Candiotti	.05	.02	.01
□ 82 Greg A. Harris	.05	.02	.01
□ 83 Fred Lynn	.10	.05	.01
□ 84 Dwight Gooden	.25	.11	.03
□ 85 Ron Darling	.05	.02	.01
□ 86 Mike Krukow	.05	.02	.01
□ 87 Spike Owen	.05	.02	.01
□ 88 Len Dykstra	.25	.11	.03
□ 89 Rick Aguilera	.10	.05	.01
□ 90 Jim Clancy	.05	.02	.01
□ 91 Joe Johnson	.05	.02	.01
□ 92 Damaso Garcia	.05	.02	.01
□ 93 Sid Fernandez	.05	.02	.01
□ 94 Bob Ojeda	.05	.02	.01
□ 95 Ted Higuera	.05	.02	.01
□ 96 George Brett	1.25	.55	.16
□ 97 Willie Wilson	.05	.02	.01
□ 98 Cal Ripken	3.00	1.35	.35
□ 99 Kent Hrbek	.10	.05	.01
□ 100 Bert Blyleven	.10	.05	.01
□ 101 Ron Guidry	.10	.05	.01
□ 102 Andy Allanson	.05	.02	.01
□ 103 Dave Henderson	.05	.02	.01
□ 104 Kirk Gibson	.10	.05	.01
□ 105 Lloyd Moseby	.05	.02	.01
□ 106 Tony Fernandez	.05	.02	.01
□ 107 Lance Parrish	.10	.05	.01
□ 108 Ozzie Smith	.75	.35	.09
□ 109 Gary Carter	.10	.05	.01
□ 110 Eddie Murray	.60	.25	.07
□ 111 Mike Witt	.05	.02	.01
□ 112 Bobby Witt	.25	.11	.03
□ 113 Willie McGee	.10	.05	.01
□ 114 Steve Garvey	.10	.05	.01
□ 115 Glenn Davis	.05	.02	.01
□ 116 Jose Cruz	.05	.02	.01
□ 117 Ozzie Guillen	.05	.02	.01
□ 118 Alvin Davis	.05	.02	.01
□ 119 Jose Rijo	.05	.02	.01
□ 120 Bill Madlock	.05	.02	.01
□ 121 Tommy Herr	.05	.02	.01
□ 122 Mike Schmidt	.75	.35	.09
□ 123 Mike Scioscia	.05	.02	.01
□ 124 Terry Pendleton	.10	.05	.01
□ 125 Leon Durham	.05	.02	.01
□ 126 Alan Trammell	.25	.11	.03
□ 127 Jesse Barfield	.05	.02	.01
□ 128 Shawon Dunston	.05	.02	.01
□ 129 Pete Rose	.75	.35	.09
□ 130 Von Hayes	.05	.02	.01
□ 131 Julio Franco	.10	.05	.01
□ 132 Juan Samuel	.05	.02	.01
□ 133 Joe Carter	.30	.14	.04
□ 134 Brook Jacoby	.05	.02	.01
□ 135 Jack Morris	.10	.05	.01
□ 136 Bob Horner	.05	.02	.01
□ 137 Calvin Schiraldi	.05	.02	.01
□ 138 Tom Browning	.05	.02	.01
□ 139 Shane Rawley	.05	.02	.01
□ 140 Mario Soto	.05	.02	.01
□ 141 Dale Murphy	.25	.11	.03
□ 142 Hubie Brooks	.05	.02	.01
□ 143 Jeff Reardon	.10	.05	.01
□ 144 Will Clark	2.00	.90	.25
□ 145 Ed Correa	.05	.02	.01
□ 146 Glenn Wilson	.05	.02	.01
□ 147 Johnny Ray	.05	.02	.01
□ 148 Fernando Valenzuela	.10	.05	.01
□ 149 Tim Raines	.10	.05	.01
□ 150 Don Mattingly	1.50	.70	.19
□ 151 Jose Canseco	1.00	.45	.12
□ 152 Gary Pettis	.05	.02	.01
□ 153 Don Sutton	.10	.05	.01
□ 154 Jim Presley	.05	.02	.01
□ 155 Checklist 28-105	.05	.02	.01
□ 156 Dale Sveum	.05	.02	.01
□ 157 Cory Snyder	.05	.02	.01
□ 158 Jeff Sellers	.05	.02	.01
□ 159 Denny Walling	.05	.02	.01
□ 160 Danny Cox	.05	.02	.01
□ 161 Bob Forsch	.05	.02	.01
□ 162 Joaquin Andujar	.05	.02	.01
□ 163 Roberto Clemente Puzzle Card	.30	.14	.04
□ 164 Paul Assenmacher	.05	.02	.01
□ 165 Marty Barrett	.05	.02	.01
□ 166 Ray Knight	.10	.05	.01
□ 167 Rafael Santana	.05	.02	.01
□ 168 Bruce Ruffin	.05	.02	.01
□ 169 Buddy Bell	.10	.05	.01
□ 170 Kevin Mitchell	.30	.14	.04
□ 171 Ken Oberkfell	.05	.02	.01
□ 172 Gene Garber	.05	.02	.01
□ 173 Mark Eichhorn CG	.05	.02	.01
□ 174 Don Carman	.05	.02	.01
□ 175 Jesse Orosco	.05	.02	.01
□ 176 Mookie Wilson	.10	.05	.01
□ 177 Gary Ward	.05	.02	.01

☐ 178 John Franco	.10	.05	.01
☐ 179 Eric Davis	.10	.05	.01
☐ 180 Walt Terrell	.05	.02	.01
☐ 181 Phil Niekro	.25	.11	.03
☐ 182 Pat Tabler	.05	.02	.01
☐ 183 Brett Butler	.10	.05	.01
☐ 184 George Bell	.05	.02	.01
☐ 185 Pete Incaviglia	.25	.11	.03
☐ 186 Pete O'Brien	.05	.02	.01
☐ 187 Jimmy Key	.10	.05	.01
☐ 188 Frank White	.10	.05	.01
☐ 189 Mike Pagliarulo	.05	.02	.01
☐ 190 Roger Clemens	.60	.25	.07
☐ 191 Rickey Henderson	.40	.18	.05
☐ 192 Mike Easler	.05	.02	.01
☐ 193 Wade Boggs	.40	.18	.05
☐ 194 Vince Coleman	.05	.02	.01
☐ 195 Charlie Kerfeld	.05	.02	.01
☐ 196 Dickie Thon	.05	.02	.01
☐ 197 Bill Doran	.05	.02	.01
☐ 198 Alfredo Griffin	.05	.02	.01
☐ 199 Carlton Fisk	.40	.18	.05
☐ 200 Phil Bradley	.05	.02	.01
☐ 201 Reggie Jackson	.50	.23	.06
☐ 202 Bob Boone	.10	.05	.01
☐ 203 Steve Sax	.05	.02	.01
☐ 204 Tom Niedenfuer	.05	.02	.01
☐ 205 Tim Burke	.05	.02	.01
☐ 206 Floyd Youmans	.05	.02	.01
☐ 207 Jay Tibbs	.05	.02	.01
☐ 208 Chili Davis	.10	.05	.01
☐ 209 Larry Parrish	.05	.02	.01
☐ 210 John Cerutti	.05	.02	.01
☐ 211 Kevin Bass	.05	.02	.01
☐ 212 Andre Dawson	.25	.11	.03
☐ 213 Bob Sebra	.05	.02	.01
☐ 214 Kevin McReynolds	.05	.02	.01
☐ 215 Jim Morrison	.05	.02	.01
☐ 216 Candy Maldonado	.05	.02	.01
☐ 217 John Kruk	.30	.14	.04
☐ 218 Todd Worrell	.10	.05	.01
☐ 219 Barry Bonds	2.50	1.10	.30
☐ 220 Andy McGaffigan	.05	.02	.01
☐ 221 Andres Galarraga	.50	.23	.06
☐ 222 Mike Fitzgerald	.05	.02	.01
☐ 223 Kirk McCaskill	.05	.02	.01
☐ 224 Dave Smith	.05	.02	.01
☐ 225 Ruben Sierra	.50	.23	.06
☐ 226 Scott Fletcher	.05	.02	.01
☐ 227 Chet Lemon	.05	.02	.01
☐ 228 Dan Petry	.05	.02	.01
☐ 229 Mark Eichhorn	.05	.02	.01
☐ 230 Cecil Cooper	.10	.05	.01
☐ 231 Willie Upshaw	.05	.02	.01
☐ 232 Don Baylor	.10	.05	.01
☐ 233 Keith Hernandez	.10	.05	.01
☐ 234 Ryne Sandberg	1.00	.45	.12
☐ 235 Tony Gwynn	1.50	.70	.19
☐ 236 Chris Brown	.05	.02	.01
☐ 237 Pedro Guerrero	.05	.02	.01
☐ 238 Mark Gubicza	.05	.02	.01
☐ 239 Sid Bream	.05	.02	.01
☐ 240 Joe Cowley	.05	.02	.01
☐ 241 Bill Buckner	.10	.05	.01
☐ 242 John Candelaria	.05	.02	.01
☐ 243 Scott McGregor	.05	.02	.01
☐ 244 Tom Brunansky	.05	.02	.01
☐ 245 Gary Gaetti	.05	.02	.01
☐ 246 Orel Hershiser	.10	.05	.01
☐ 247 Jim Rice	.10	.05	.01
☐ 248 Oil Can Boyd	.05	.02	.01
☐ 249 Bob Knepper	.05	.02	.01
☐ 250 Danny Tartabull	.05	.02	.01
☐ 251 John Cangelosi	.05	.02	.01
☐ 252 Wally Joyner	.25	.11	.03
☐ 253 Bruce Hurst	.05	.02	.01
☐ 254 Rich Gedman	.05	.02	.01
☐ 255 Jim Deshaies	.05	.02	.01
☐ 256 Tony Pena	.05	.02	.01
☐ 257 Nolan Ryan	3.00	1.35	.35
☐ 258 Mike Scott	.05	.02	.01
☐ 259 Checklist 106-183	.05	.02	.01
☐ 260 Dennis Rasmussen	.05	.02	.01
☐ 261 Bret Saberhagen	.10	.05	.01
☐ 262 Steve Balboni	.05	.02	.01
☐ 263 Tom Seaver	.40	.18	.05
☐ 264 Checklist 184-264	.05	.02	.01

1987 Leaf Special Olympics *

This set is also known as the Candy City team as that is the logo which appears on the front of the card. This set was issued for the proceeds of the set to go to the Special Olympics. The set was in the style of the 1983 Donruss Hall of Fame Heroes set and the only additions were generic cards about various sports. The cards are standard size.

	MINT	NRMT	EXC
COMPLETE SET (18)	6.00	2.70	.75
COMMON CARD (H1-H12)	.40	.18	.05
COMMON CARD (S1-S6)	.10	.05	.01
☐ H1 Mickey Mantle	3.00	1.35	.35
☐ H2 Yogi Berra	.75	.35	.09
☐ H3 Roy Campanella	.75	.35	.09
☐ H4 Stan Musial	1.00	.45	.12

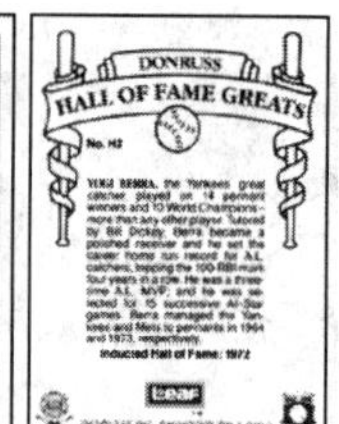

☐ H5 Ted Williams	2.00	.90	.25
☐ H6 Duke Snider	.75	.35	.09
☐ H7 Hank Aaron	2.00	.90	.25
☐ H8 Pee Wee Reese	.75	.35	.09
☐ H9 Brooks Robinson	.50	.23	.06
☐ H10 Al Kaline	.50	.23	.06
☐ H11 Willie McCovey	.40	.18	.05
☐ H12 Cool Papa Bell	.40	.18	.05
☐ S1 Basketball	.30	.14	.04
☐ S2 Softball	.10	.05	.01
☐ S3 Track And Field	.10	.05	.01
☐ S4 Soccer	.20	.09	.03
☐ S5 Gymnastics	.10	.05	.01
☐ S6 VII International Summer Games	.10	.05	.01

1988 Leaf/Donruss

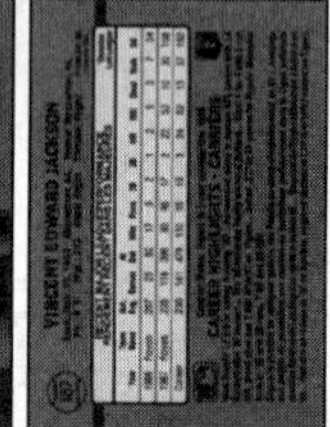

This 264-card standard-size set was issued with a puzzle of Stan Musial. Except for the numbering, the company logo and the bilingual backs, the cards are essentially the same as the Donruss U.S. regular issue cards of the same players. On a black, blue and red background, fronts feature color player photos with thin white borders. The player's name and position, and the team and manufacturer logos also appear on the front. On a light blue background, the horizontal backs carry player biography, statistics, and career hightlights in French and English. Two cards, Dick Perez artwork of George Bell (213) and Tim Wallach (255), are called Canadian Greats (CG) and are not contained in the Donruss U.S. set. Diamond Kings (numbers 1-26, denoted DK) and Rated Rookies (numbers 28-47, denoted RR) are included just as in the American set. There are also bonus cards of the the two Canadian teams' MVP's, George Bell and Tim Raines, as in the Donruss American set. The players featured are heavily biased toward Canadian teams and those American teams closest to the Canadian border. Players appearing in their Rookie Card year include Roberto Alomar, Mark Grace and Gregg Jefferies.

	MINT	NRMT	EXC
COMPLETE SET (264)	20.00	9.00	2.50
COMMON CARD (1-264)	.05	.02	.01
☐ 1 Mark McGwire DK	1.00	.45	.12
☐ 2 Tim Raines DK	.10	.05	.01
☐ 3 Benito Santiago DK	.05	.02	.01
☐ 4 Alan Trammell DK	.10	.05	.01
☐ 5 Danny Tartabull DK	.05	.02	.01
☐ 6 Ron Darling DK	.05	.02	.01
☐ 7 Paul Molitor DK	.50	.23	.06
☐ 8 Devon White DK	.25	.11	.03
☐ 9 Andre Dawson DK	.10	.05	.01
☐ 10 Julio Franco DK	.10	.05	.01
☐ 11 Scott Fletcher DK	.05	.02	.01
☐ 12 Tony Fernandez DK	.05	.02	.01
☐ 13 Shane Rawley DK	.05	.02	.01
☐ 14 Kal Daniels DK	.05	.02	.01
☐ 15 Jack Clark DK	.05	.02	.01
☐ 16 Dwight Evans DK	.10	.05	.01
☐ 17 Tommy John DK	.10	.05	.01
☐ 18 Andy Van Slyke DK	.10	.05	.01
☐ 19 Gary Gaetti DK	.10	.05	.01
☐ 20 Mark Langston DK	.05	.02	.01
☐ 21 Will Clark DK	.50	.23	.06
☐ 22 Glenn Hubbard DK	.05	.02	.01
☐ 23 Billy Hatcher DK	.05	.02	.01
☐ 24 Bob Welch DK	.05	.02	.01
☐ 25 Ivan Calderon DK	.05	.02	.01
☐ 26 Cal Ripken DK	2.00	.90	.25
☐ 27 DK Checklist 1-26	.05	.02	.01
☐ 28 Mackey Sasser RR	.05	.02	.01
☐ 29 Jeff Treadway RR	.05	.02	.01
☐ 30 Mike Campbell RR	.05	.02	.01
☐ 31 Lance Johnson RR	.30	.14	.04
☐ 32 Nelson Liriano RR	.05	.02	.01
☐ 33 Shawn Abner RR	.05	.02	.01
☐ 34 Roberto Alomar RR	2.00	.90	.25
☐ 35 Shawn Hillegas RR	.05	.02	.01
☐ 36 Joey Meyer RR	.05	.02	.01
☐ 37 Kevin Elster RR	.25	.11	.03
☐ 38 Jose Lind RR	.05	.02	.01
☐ 39 Kirt Manwaring RR	.10	.05	.01
☐ 40 Mark Grace RR	1.25	.55	.16
☐ 41 Jody Reed RR	.10	.05	.01
☐ 42 John Farrell RR	.05	.02	.01
☐ 43 Al Leiter RR	.30	.14	.04
☐ 44 Gary Thurman RR	.05	.02	.01
☐ 45 Vicente Palacios RR	.05	.02	.01
☐ 46 Eddie Williams RR	.05	.02	.01
☐ 47 Jack McDowell RR	.60	.25	.07
☐ 48 Dwight Gooden	.10	.05	.01
☐ 49 Mike Witt	.05	.02	.01
☐ 50 Wally Joyner	.25	.11	.03
☐ 51 Brook Jacoby	.05	.02	.01
☐ 52 Bert Blyleven	.10	.05	.01
☐ 53 Ted Higuera	.05	.02	.01
☐ 54 Mike Scott	.05	.02	.01
☐ 55 Jose Guzman	.05	.02	.01
☐ 56 Roger Clemens	.50	.23	.06
☐ 57 Dave Righetti	.05	.02	.01
☐ 58 Benito Santiago	.05	.02	.01
☐ 59 Ozzie Guillen	.05	.02	.01
☐ 60 Matt Nokes	.05	.02	.01
☐ 61 Fernando Valenzuela	.10	.05	.01
☐ 62 Orel Hershiser	.10	.05	.01
☐ 63 Sid Fernandez	.05	.02	.01
☐ 64 Ozzie Virgil	.05	.02	.01
☐ 65 Wade Boggs	.40	.18	.05
☐ 66 Floyd Youmans	.05	.02	.01
☐ 67 Jimmy Key	.10	.05	.01
☐ 68 Bret Saberhagen	.10	.05	.01
☐ 69 Jody Davis	.05	.02	.01
☐ 70 Shawon Dunston	.05	.02	.01
☐ 71 Julio Franco	.10	.05	.01
☐ 72 Danny Cox	.05	.02	.01
☐ 73 Jim Clancy	.05	.02	.01
☐ 74 Mark Eichhorn	.05	.02	.01
☐ 75 Scott Bradley	.05	.02	.01
☐ 76 Charlie Leibrandt	.05	.02	.01
☐ 77 Nolan Ryan	2.00	.90	.25
☐ 78 Ron Darling	.05	.02	.01
☐ 79 John Franco	.10	.05	.01
☐ 80 Dave Stieb	.05	.02	.01
☐ 81 Mike Fitzgerald	.05	.02	.01
☐ 82 Steve Bedrosian	.05	.02	.01
☐ 83 Dale Murphy	.25	.11	.03
☐ 84 Tim Burke	.05	.02	.01
☐ 85 Jack Morris	.10	.05	.01
☐ 86 Greg Walker	.05	.02	.01
☐ 87 Kevin Mitchell	.05	.02	.01
☐ 88 Doug Drabek	.05	.02	.01
☐ 89 Charlie Hough	.10	.05	.01
☐ 90 Tony Gwynn	1.00	.45	.12
☐ 91 Rick Sutcliffe	.05	.02	.01
☐ 92 Shane Rawley	.05	.02	.01
☐ 93 George Brett	.75	.35	.09
☐ 94 Frank Viola	.10	.05	.01
☐ 95 Tony Pena	.05	.02	.01
☐ 96 Jim Deshaies	.05	.02	.01
☐ 97 Mike Scioscia	.05	.02	.01
☐ 98 Rick Rhoden	.05	.02	.01
☐ 99 Terry Kennedy	.05	.02	.01
☐ 100 Cal Ripken	2.00	.90	.25
☐ 101 Pedro Guerrero	.05	.02	.01
☐ 102 Andy Van Slyke	.10	.05	.01
☐ 103 Willie McGee	.10	.05	.01
☐ 104 Mike Kingery	.05	.02	.01
☐ 105 Kevin Seitzer	.10	.05	.01
☐ 106 Robin Yount	.40	.18	.05
☐ 107 Tracy Jones	.05	.02	.01
☐ 108 Dave Magadan	.05	.02	.01
☐ 109 Mel Hall	.05	.02	.01
☐ 110 Billy Hatcher	.05	.02	.01
☐ 111 Todd Benzinger	.05	.02	.01
☐ 112 Mike LaValliere	.05	.02	.01
☐ 113 Barry Bonds	.75	.35	.09
☐ 114 Tim Raines	.10	.05	.01
☐ 115 Ozzie Smith	.60	.25	.07
☐ 116 Dave Winfield	.40	.18	.05
☐ 117 Keith Hernandez	.10	.05	.01
☐ 118 Jeffrey Leonard	.05	.02	.01
☐ 119 Larry Parrish	.05	.02	.01
☐ 120 Robby Thompson	.05	.02	.01
☐ 121 Andres Galarraga	.25	.11	.03
☐ 122 Mickey Hatcher	.05	.02	.01
☐ 123 Mark Langston	.05	.02	.01
☐ 124 Mike Schmidt	.75	.35	.09
☐ 125 Cory Snyder	.05	.02	.01
☐ 126 Andre Dawson	.10	.05	.01
☐ 127 Devon White	.25	.11	.03
☐ 128 Vince Coleman	.05	.02	.01
☐ 129 Bryn Smith	.05	.02	.01
☐ 130 Lance Parrish	.10	.05	.01
☐ 131 Willie Upshaw	.05	.02	.01
☐ 132 Pete O'Brien	.05	.02	.01
☐ 133 Tony Fernandez	.05	.02	.01
☐ 134 Billy Ripken	.05	.02	.01
☐ 135 Len Dykstra	.10	.05	.01
☐ 136 Kirk Gibson	.10	.05	.01
☐ 137 Kevin Bass	.05	.02	.01
☐ 138 Jose Canseco	.75	.35	.09
☐ 139 Kent Hrbek	.10	.05	.01
☐ 140 Lloyd Moseby	.05	.02	.01
☐ 141 Marty Barrett	.05	.02	.01
☐ 142 Carmelo Martinez	.05	.02	.01
☐ 143 Tom Foley	.05	.02	.01
☐ 144 Kirby Puckett	1.00	.45	.12
☐ 145 Rickey Henderson	.40	.18	.05
☐ 146 Juan Samuel	.05	.02	.01
☐ 147 Pete Incaviglia	.05	.02	.01
☐ 148 Greg Brock	.05	.02	.01
☐ 149 Eric Davis	.05	.02	.01
☐ 150 Kal Daniels	.05	.02	.01
☐ 151 Bob Boone	.10	.05	.01
☐ 152 John Cerutti	.05	.02	.01
☐ 153 Mike Greenwell	.05	.02	.01
☐ 154 Oddibe McDowell	.05	.02	.01
☐ 155 Scott Fletcher	.05	.02	.01
☐ 156 Gary Carter	.10	.05	.01
☐ 157 Harold Baines	.10	.05	.01
☐ 158 Greg Swindell	.05	.02	.01
☐ 159 Mark McLemore	.05	.02	.01
☐ 160 Keith Moreland	.05	.02	.01
☐ 161 Jim Gantner	.05	.02	.01
☐ 162 Willie Randolph	.10	.05	.01
☐ 163 Fred Lynn	.10	.05	.01
☐ 164 B.J. Surhoff	.10	.05	.01
☐ 165 Ken Griffey	.10	.05	.01
☐ 166 Chet Lemon	.05	.02	.01
☐ 167 Alan Trammell	.10	.05	.01
☐ 168 Paul Molitor	.50	.23	.06
☐ 169 Lou Whitaker	.10	.05	.01
☐ 170 Will Clark	.50	.23	.06
☐ 171 Dwight Evans	.10	.05	.01
☐ 172 Eddie Murray	.60	.25	.07
☐ 173 Darrell Evans	.10	.05	.01
☐ 174 Ellis Burks	.40	.18	.05
☐ 175 Ivan Calderon	.05	.02	.01
☐ 176 John Kruk	.25	.11	.03
☐ 177 Don Mattingly	1.00	.45	.12
☐ 178 Dick Schofield	.05	.02	.01
☐ 179 Bruce Hurst	.05	.02	.01
☐ 180 Ron Guidry	.10	.05	.01
☐ 181 Jack Clark	.05	.02	.01
☐ 182 Franklin Stubbs	.05	.02	.01
☐ 183 Bill Doran	.05	.02	.01
☐ 184 Joe Carter	.25	.11	.03
☐ 185 Steve Sax	.05	.02	.01
☐ 186 Glenn Davis	.05	.02	.01
☐ 187 Bo Jackson	.25	.11	.03
☐ 188 Bobby Bonilla	.25	.11	.03
☐ 189 Willie Wilson	.05	.02	.01
☐ 190 Danny Tartabull	.05	.02	.01
☐ 191 Bo Diaz	.05	.02	.01
☐ 192 Buddy Bell	.10	.05	.01
☐ 193 Tim Wallach	.05	.02	.01
☐ 194 Mark McGwire	2.00	.90	.25
☐ 195 Carney Lansford	.05	.02	.01
☐ 196 Alvin Davis	.05	.02	.01
☐ 197 Von Hayes	.05	.02	.01
☐ 198 Mitch Webster	.05	.02	.01
☐ 199 Casey Candaele	.05	.02	.01
☐ 200 Gary Gaetti	.05	.02	.01
☐ 201 Tommy Herr	.05	.02	.01
☐ 202 Wally Backman	.05	.02	.01
☐ 203 Brian Downing	.05	.02	.01
☐ 204 Rance Mulliniks	.05	.02	.01
☐ 205 Craig Reynolds	.05	.02	.01
☐ 206 Ruben Sierra	.25	.11	.03
☐ 207 Ryne Sandberg	.75	.35	.09
☐ 208 Carlton Fisk	.40	.18	.05
☐ 209 Checklist 28-107	.05	.02	.01
☐ 210 Gerald Young	.05	.02	.01
☐ 211 Tim Raines MVP (Bonus card pose)	.10	.05	.01
☐ 212 John Tudor	.05	.02	.01
☐ 213 George Bell CG	.05	.02	.01
☐ 214 George Bell MVP (Bonus card pose)	.05	.02	.01
☐ 215 Jim Rice	.10	.05	.01
☐ 216 Gerald Perry	.05	.02	.01
☐ 217 Dave Stewart	.10	.05	.01
☐ 218 Jose Uribe	.05	.02	.01
☐ 219 Rick Reuschel	.05	.02	.01
☐ 220 Darryl Strawberry	.10	.05	.01
☐ 221 Chris Brown	.05	.02	.01
☐ 222 Ted Simmons	.10	.05	.01
☐ 223 Lee Mazzilli	.05	.02	.01
☐ 224 Denny Walling	.05	.02	.01
☐ 225 Jesse Barfield	.05	.02	.01
☐ 226 Barry Larkin	.60	.25	.07
☐ 227 Harold Reynolds	.10	.05	.01
☐ 228 Kevin McReynolds	.05	.02	.01
☐ 229 Todd Worrell	.10	.05	.01
☐ 230 Tommy John	.10	.05	.01
☐ 231 Rick Aguilera	.05	.02	.01
☐ 232 Bill Madlock	.05	.02	.01
☐ 233 Roy Smalley	.05	.02	.01
☐ 234 Jeff Musselman	.05	.02	.01
☐ 235 Mike Dunne	.05	.02	.01
☐ 236 Jerry Browne	.05	.02	.01
☐ 237 Sam Horn	.05	.02	.01
☐ 238 Howard Johnson	.05	.02	.01
☐ 239 Candy Maldonado	.05	.02	.01
☐ 240 Nick Esasky	.05	.02	.01
☐ 241 Geno Petralli	.05	.02	.01
☐ 242 Herm Winningham	.05	.02	.01
☐ 243 Roger McDowell	.05	.02	.01
☐ 244 Brian Fisher	.05	.02	.01
☐ 245 John Marzano	.05	.02	.01
☐ 246 Terry Pendleton	.10	.05	.01

☐ 247 Rick Leach	.05	.02	.01
☐ 248 Pascual Perez	.05	.02	.01
☐ 249 Mookie Wilson	.10	.05	.01
☐ 250 Ernie Whitt	.05	.02	.01
☐ 251 Ron Kittle	.05	.02	.01
☐ 252 Oil Can Boyd	.05	.02	.01
☐ 253 Jim Gott	.05	.02	.01
☐ 254 George Bell	.05	.02	.01
☐ 255 Tim Wallach CG	.05	.02	.01
☐ 256 Luis Polonia	.05	.02	.01
☐ 257 Hubie Brooks	.05	.02	.01
☐ 258 Mickey Brantley	.05	.02	.01
☐ 259 Greg Jefferies	.50	.23	.06
☐ 260 Johnny Ray	.05	.02	.01
☐ 261 Checklist 108-187	.05	.02	.01
☐ 262 Dennis Martinez	.10	.05	.01
☐ 263 Stan Musial Puzzle Card	.25	.11	.03
☐ 264 Checklist 188-264	.05	.02	.01

1990 Leaf Previews

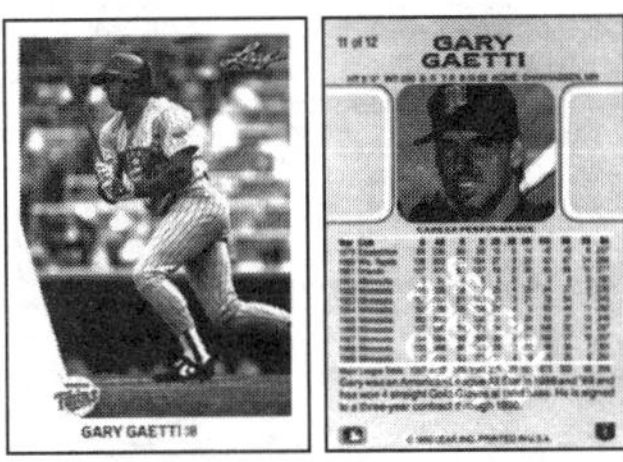

The 1990 Leaf Previews set contains standard-size cards which were mailed to dealers to announce the 1990 version of Donruss' second major set of the year marketed as an upscale alternative under their Leaf name. This 12-card set was presented in the same style as the other Leaf cards were done in except that "Special Preview" was imprinted in white on the back. The cards were released in two series of 264 and the first series was not released until mid-season.

	MINT	NRMT	EXC
COMPLETE SET (12)	450.00	200.00	55.00
COMMON CARD (1-12)	15.00	6.75	1.85
☐ 1 Steve Sax	15.00	6.75	1.85
☐ 2 Joe Carter	40.00	18.00	5.00
☐ 3 Dennis Eckersley	25.00	11.00	3.10
☐ 4 Ken Griffey Jr.	200.00	90.00	25.00
☐ 5 Barry Larkin	50.00	22.00	6.25
☐ 6 Mark Langston	15.00	6.75	1.85
☐ 7 Eric Anthony	15.00	6.75	1.85
☐ 8 Robin Ventura	40.00	18.00	5.00
☐ 9 Greg Vaughn	25.00	11.00	3.10
☐ 10 Bobby Bonilla	20.00	9.00	2.50
☐ 11 Gary Gaetti	15.00	6.75	1.85
☐ 12 Ozzie Smith	75.00	34.00	9.50

1990 Leaf

The 1990 Leaf set was the first premium set introduced by Donruss.The cards were issued in 15-card foil wrapped packs and were not available in factory sets. Each pack also contained one three-piece puzzle panel of a 63-piece Yogi Berra "Donruss Hall of Fame Diamond King" puzzle. This set, which was produced on high quality paper stock, was issued in two separate series of 264 standard-size cards each. The second series was issued approximately six weeks after the release of the first series. The cards feature full-color photos on both the front and back. Rookie Cards in the set include Carlos Baerga, Bernard Gilkey, Marquis Grissom, David Justice, Ben McDonald, Sammy Sosa, Frank Thomas and Larry Walker.

	MINT	NRMT	EXC
COMPLETE SET (528)	200.00	90.00	25.00
COMPLETE SERIES 1 (264)	80.00	36.00	10.00
COMPLETE SERIES 2 (264)	120.00	55.00	15.00
COMMON CARD (1-528)	.25	.11	.03
☐ 1 Introductory Card	.25	.11	.03
☐ 2 Mike Henneman	.25	.11	.03
☐ 3 Steve Bedrosian	.25	.11	.03
☐ 4 Mike Scott	.25	.11	.03
☐ 5 Allan Anderson	.25	.11	.03
☐ 6 Rick Sutcliffe	.25	.11	.03
☐ 7 Gregg Olson	.25	.11	.03
☐ 8 Kevin Elster	.25	.11	.03
☐ 9 Pete O'Brien	.25	.11	.03
☐ 10 Carlton Fisk	.75	.35	.09
☐ 11 Joe Magrane	.25	.11	.03
☐ 12 Roger Clemens	1.50	.70	.19
☐ 13 Tom Glavine	2.50	1.10	.30
☐ 14 Tom Gordon	.25	.11	.03
☐ 15 Todd Benzinger	.25	.11	.03
☐ 16 Hubie Brooks	.25	.11	.03
☐ 17 Roberto Kelly	.50	.23	.06
☐ 18 Barry Larkin	1.25	.55	.16
☐ 19 Mike Boddicker	.25	.11	.03
☐ 20 Roger McDowell	.25	.11	.03
☐ 21 Nolan Ryan	6.00	2.70	.75
☐ 22 John Farrell	.25	.11	.03
☐ 23 Bruce Hurst	.25	.11	.03
☐ 24 Wally Joyner	.50	.23	.06
☐ 25 Greg Maddux	18.00	8.00	2.20
☐ 26 Chris Bosio	.25	.11	.03
☐ 27 John Cerutti	.25	.11	.03
☐ 28 Tim Burke	.25	.11	.03
☐ 29 Dennis Eckersley	.50	.23	.06
☐ 30 Glenn Davis	.25	.11	.03
☐ 31 Jim Abbott	.50	.23	.06
☐ 32 Mike LaValliere	.25	.11	.03
☐ 33 Andres Thomas	.25	.11	.03
☐ 34 Lou Whitaker	.50	.23	.06
☐ 35 Alvin Davis	.25	.11	.03
☐ 36 Melido Perez	.25	.11	.03
☐ 37 Craig Biggio	1.00	.45	.12
☐ 38 Rick Aguilera	.50	.23	.06
☐ 39 Pete Harnisch	.25	.11	.03
☐ 40 David Cone	1.50	.70	.19
☐ 41 Scott Garrelts	.25	.11	.03
☐ 42 Jay Howell	.25	.11	.03
☐ 43 Eric King	.25	.11	.03
☐ 44 Pedro Guerrero	.25	.11	.03
☐ 45 Mike Bielecki	.25	.11	.03
☐ 46 Bob Boone	.50	.23	.06
☐ 47 Kevin Brown	.75	.35	.09
☐ 48 Jerry Browne	.25	.11	.03
☐ 49 Mike Scioscia	.25	.11	.03
☐ 50 Chuck Cary	.25	.11	.03
☐ 51 Wade Boggs	.75	.35	.09
☐ 52 Von Hayes	.25	.11	.03
☐ 53 Tony Fernandez	.25	.11	.03
☐ 54 Dennis Martinez	.50	.23	.06
☐ 55 Tom Candiotti	.25	.11	.03
☐ 56 Andy Benes	.75	.35	.09
☐ 57 Rob Dibble	.25	.11	.03
☐ 58 Chuck Crim	.25	.11	.03
☐ 59 John Smoltz	4.00	1.80	.50
☐ 60 Mike Heath	.25	.11	.03
☐ 61 Kevin Gross	.25	.11	.03
☐ 62 Mark McGwire	2.50	1.10	.30
☐ 63 Bert Blyleven	.50	.23	.06
☐ 64 Bob Walk	.25	.11	.03
☐ 65 Mickey Tettleton	.50	.23	.06
☐ 66 Sid Fernandez	.25	.11	.03
☐ 67 Terry Kennedy	.25	.11	.03
☐ 68 Fernando Valenzuela	.50	.23	.06
☐ 69 Don Mattingly	4.00	1.80	.50
☐ 70 Paul O'Neill	.50	.23	.06
☐ 71 Robin Yount	.75	.35	.09
☐ 72 Bret Saberhagen	.50	.23	.06
☐ 73 Geno Petralli	.25	.11	.03
☐ 74 Brook Jacoby	.25	.11	.03
☐ 75 Roberto Alomar	2.50	1.10	.30
☐ 76 Devon White	.50	.23	.06
☐ 77 Jose Lind	.25	.11	.03
☐ 78 Pat Combs	.25	.11	.03
☐ 79 Dave Stieb	.25	.11	.03
☐ 80 Tim Wallach	.25	.11	.03
☐ 81 Dave Stewart	.50	.23	.06
☐ 82 Eric Anthony	.50	.23	.06
☐ 83 Randy Bush	.25	.11	.03
☐ 84 Checklist 1-88 (Rickey Henderson)	.50	.23	.06
☐ 85 Jaime Navarro	.25	.11	.03
☐ 86 Tommy Gregg	.25	.11	.03
☐ 87 Frank Tanana	.25	.11	.03
☐ 88 Omar Vizquel	2.00	.90	.25
☐ 89 Ivan Calderon	.25	.11	.03
☐ 90 Vince Coleman	.25	.11	.03
☐ 91 Barry Bonds	2.00	.90	.25
☐ 92 Randy Milligan	.25	.11	.03
☐ 93 Frank Viola	.25	.11	.03
☐ 94 Matt Williams	2.50	1.10	.30
☐ 95 Alfredo Griffin	.25	.11	.03
☐ 96 Steve Sax	.25	.11	.03
☐ 97 Gary Gaetti	.50	.23	.06
☐ 98 Ryne Sandberg	2.00	.90	.25
☐ 99 Danny Tartabull	.25	.11	.03
☐ 100 Rafael Palmeiro	2.50	1.10	.30
☐ 101 Jesse Orosco	.25	.11	.03
☐ 102 Garry Templeton	.25	.11	.03
☐ 103 Frank DiPino	.25	.11	.03
☐ 104 Tony Pena	.25	.11	.03
☐ 105 Dickie Thon	.25	.11	.03
☐ 106 Kelly Gruber	.25	.11	.03
☐ 107 Marquis Grissom	6.00	2.70	.75
☐ 108 Jose Canseco	1.00	.45	.12
☐ 109 Mike Blowers	.75	.35	.09
☐ 110 Tom Browning	.25	.11	.03
☐ 111 Greg Vaughn	1.50	.70	.19
☐ 112 Oddibe McDowell	.25	.11	.03
☐ 113 Gary Ward	.25	.11	.03
☐ 114 Jay Buhner	2.00	.90	.25
☐ 115 Eric Show	.25	.11	.03
☐ 116 Bryan Harvey	.25	.11	.03
☐ 117 Andy Van Slyke	.50	.23	.06
☐ 118 Jeff Ballard	.25	.11	.03
☐ 119 Barry Lyons	.25	.11	.03
☐ 120 Kevin Mitchell	.50	.23	.06
☐ 121 Mike Gallego	.25	.11	.03
☐ 122 Dave Smith	.25	.11	.03
☐ 123 Kirby Puckett	3.00	1.35	.35
☐ 124 Jerome Walton	.25	.11	.03
☐ 125 Bo Jackson	.50	.23	.06
☐ 126 Harold Baines	.50	.23	.06
☐ 127 Scott Bankhead	.25	.11	.03
☐ 128 Ozzie Guillen	.25	.11	.03
☐ 129 Jose Oquendo UER (League misspelled as Legue)	.25	.11	.03
☐ 130 John Dopson	.25	.11	.03
☐ 131 Charlie Hayes	.50	.23	.06
☐ 132 Fred McGriff	1.25	.55	.16
☐ 133 Chet Lemon	.25	.11	.03
☐ 134 Gary Carter	.50	.23	.06
☐ 135 Rafael Ramirez	.25	.11	.03
☐ 136 Shane Mack	.25	.11	.03
☐ 137 Mark Grace UER (Card back has OB:L, should be B:L)	1.00	.45	.12
☐ 138 Phil Bradley	.25	.11	.03
☐ 139 Dwight Gooden	.50	.23	.06
☐ 140 Harold Reynolds	.25	.11	.03
☐ 141 Scott Fletcher	.25	.11	.03
☐ 142 Ozzie Smith	2.00	.90	.25
☐ 143 Mike Greenwell	.25	.11	.03
☐ 144 Pete Smith	.25	.11	.03
☐ 145 Mark Gubicza	.25	.11	.03
☐ 146 Chris Sabo	.25	.11	.03
☐ 147 Ramon Martinez	.75	.35	.09
☐ 148 Tim Leary	.25	.11	.03
☐ 149 Randy Myers	.50	.23	.06
☐ 150 Jody Reed	.25	.11	.03
☐ 151 Bruce Ruffin	.25	.11	.03
☐ 152 Jeff Russell	.25	.11	.03
☐ 153 Doug Jones	.25	.11	.03
☐ 154 Tony Gwynn	3.00	1.35	.35
☐ 155 Mark Langston	.50	.23	.06
☐ 156 Mitch Williams	.25	.11	.03
☐ 157 Gary Sheffield	5.00	2.20	.60
☐ 158 Tom Henke	.25	.11	.03
☐ 159 Oil Can Boyd	.25	.11	.03
☐ 160 Rickey Henderson	.75	.35	.09
☐ 161 Bill Doran	.25	.11	.03
☐ 162 Chuck Finley	.50	.23	.06
☐ 163 Jeff King	.50	.23	.06
☐ 164 Nick Esasky	.25	.11	.03
☐ 165 Cecil Fielder	.50	.23	.06
☐ 166 Dave Valle	.25	.11	.03
☐ 167 Robin Ventura	2.00	.90	.25
☐ 168 Jim Deshaies	.25	.11	.03
☐ 169 Juan Berenguer	.25	.11	.03
☐ 170 Craig Worthington	.25	.11	.03
☐ 171 Gregg Jefferies	.50	.23	.06
☐ 172 Will Clark	1.00	.45	.12
☐ 173 Kirk Gibson	.50	.23	.06
☐ 174 Checklist 89-176 (Carlton Fisk)	.75	.35	.09
☐ 175 Bobby Thigpen	.25	.11	.03
☐ 176 John Tudor	.25	.11	.03
☐ 177 Andre Dawson	.50	.23	.06
☐ 178 George Brett	3.00	1.35	.35
☐ 179 Steve Buechele	.25	.11	.03
☐ 180 Joey Belle	15.00	6.75	1.85
☐ 181 Eddie Murray	2.00	.90	.25
☐ 182 Bob Geren	.25	.11	.03
☐ 183 Rob Murphy	.25	.11	.03
☐ 184 Tom Herr	.25	.11	.03
☐ 185 George Bell	.25	.11	.03
☐ 186 Spike Owen	.25	.11	.03
☐ 187 Cory Snyder	.25	.11	.03
☐ 188 Fred Lynn	.25	.11	.03
☐ 189 Eric Davis	.50	.23	.06
☐ 190 Dave Parker	.50	.23	.06
☐ 191 Jeff Blauser	.50	.23	.06
☐ 192 Matt Nokes	.25	.11	.03
☐ 193 Delino DeShields	1.00	.45	.12
☐ 194 Scott Sanderson	.25	.11	.03
☐ 195 Lance Parrish	.25	.11	.03
☐ 196 Bobby Bonilla	.50	.23	.06
☐ 197 Cal Ripken UER (Reisterstown, should be Reisterstown)	6.00	2.70	.75
☐ 198 Kevin McReynolds	.25	.11	.03
☐ 199 Robby Thompson	.25	.11	.03
☐ 200 Tim Belcher	.25	.11	.03
☐ 201 Jesse Barfield	.25	.11	.03
☐ 202 Mariano Duncan	.25	.11	.03
☐ 203 Bill Spiers	.25	.11	.03
☐ 204 Frank White	.50	.23	.06
☐ 205 Julio Franco	.50	.23	.06
☐ 206 Greg Swindell	.25	.11	.03
☐ 207 Benito Santiago	.25	.11	.03
☐ 208 Johnny Ray	.25	.11	.03
☐ 209 Gary Redus	.25	.11	.03
☐ 210 Jeff Parrett	.25	.11	.03
☐ 211 Jimmy Key	.50	.23	.06
☐ 212 Tim Raines	.50	.23	.06
☐ 213 Carney Lansford	.50	.23	.06
☐ 214 Gerald Young	.25	.11	.03
☐ 215 Gene Larkin	.25	.11	.03
☐ 216 Dan Plesac	.25	.11	.03
☐ 217 Lonnie Smith	.25	.11	.03
☐ 218 Alan Trammell	.50	.23	.06
☐ 219 Jeffrey Leonard	.25	.11	.03
☐ 220 Sammy Sosa	8.00	3.60	1.00
☐ 221 Todd Zeile	.50	.23	.06
☐ 222 Bill Landrum	.25	.11	.03
☐ 223 Mike Devereaux	.25	.11	.03
☐ 224 Mike Marshall	.25	.11	.03
☐ 225 Jose Uribe	.25	.11	.03
☐ 226 Juan Samuel	.25	.11	.03
☐ 227 Mel Hall	.25	.11	.03
☐ 228 Kent Hrbek	.50	.23	.06
☐ 229 Shawon Dunston	.25	.11	.03
☐ 230 Kevin Seitzer	.25	.11	.03
☐ 231 Pete Incaviglia	.25	.11	.03
☐ 232 Sandy Alomar Jr.	.75	.35	.09
☐ 233 Bip Roberts	.25	.11	.03
☐ 234 Scott Terry	.25	.11	.03
☐ 235 Dwight Evans	.50	.23	.06
☐ 236 Ricky Jordan	.25	.11	.03
☐ 237 John Olerud	1.25	.55	.16
☐ 238 Zane Smith	.25	.11	.03
☐ 239 Walt Weiss	.25	.11	.03
☐ 240 Alvaro Espinoza	.25	.11	.03
☐ 241 Billy Hatcher	.25	.11	.03
☐ 242 Paul Molitor	1.50	.70	.19
☐ 243 Dale Murphy	.75	.35	.09
☐ 244 Dave Bergman	.25	.11	.03
☐ 245 Ken Griffey Jr.	25.00	11.00	3.10
☐ 246 Ed Whitson	.25	.11	.03
☐ 247 Kirk McCaskill	.25	.11	.03
☐ 248 Jay Bell	.50	.23	.06
☐ 249 Ben McDonald	1.50	.70	.19
☐ 250 Darryl Strawberry	.50	.23	.06
☐ 251 Brett Butler	.50	.23	.06
☐ 252 Terry Steinbach	.50	.23	.06
☐ 253 Ken Caminiti	2.50	1.10	.30
☐ 254 Dan Gladden	.25	.11	.03
☐ 255 Dwight Smith	.25	.11	.03
☐ 256 Kurt Stillwell	.25	.11	.03
☐ 257 Ruben Sierra	.50	.23	.06
☐ 258 Mike Schooler	.25	.11	.03
☐ 259 Lance Johnson	.50	.23	.06
☐ 260 Terry Pendleton	.50	.23	.06
☐ 261 Ellis Burks	.75	.35	.09
☐ 262 Len Dykstra	.50	.23	.06
☐ 263 Mookie Wilson	.25	.11	.03
☐ 264 Checklist 177-264 (Nolan Ryan) UER (No TM after Ranger logo)	.75	.35	.09
☐ 265 No Hit King (Nolan Ryan)	3.00	1.35	.35
☐ 266 Brian DuBois	.25	.11	.03
☐ 267 Don Robinson	.25	.11	.03
☐ 268 Glenn Wilson	.25	.11	.03
☐ 269 Kevin Tapani	.50	.23	.06
☐ 270 Marvell Wynne	.25	.11	.03
☐ 271 Billy Ripken	.25	.11	.03
☐ 272 Howard Johnson	.25	.11	.03
☐ 273 Brian Holman	.25	.11	.03
☐ 274 Dan Pasqua	.25	.11	.03
☐ 275 Ken Dayley	.25	.11	.03
☐ 276 Jeff Reardon	.50	.23	.06
☐ 277 Jim Presley	.25	.11	.03
☐ 278 Jim Eisenreich	.25	.11	.03
☐ 279 Danny Jackson	.25	.11	.03
☐ 280 Orel Hershiser	.50	.23	.06
☐ 281 Andy Hawkins	.25	.11	.03
☐ 282 Jose Rijo	.25	.11	.03
☐ 283 Luis Rivera	.25	.11	.03
☐ 284 John Kruk	.50	.23	.06
☐ 285 Jeff Huson	.25	.11	.03
☐ 286 Joel Skinner	.25	.11	.03
☐ 287 Jack Clark	.50	.23	.06
☐ 288 Chili Davis	.50	.23	.06
☐ 289 Joe Girardi	.50	.23	.06
☐ 290 B.J. Surhoff	.50	.23	.06
☐ 291 Luis Sojo	.25	.11	.03
☐ 292 Tom Foley	.25	.11	.03
☐ 293 Mike Moore	.25	.11	.03
☐ 294 Ken Oberkfell	.25	.11	.03
☐ 295 Luis Polonia	.25	.11	.03
☐ 296 Doug Drabek	.25	.11	.03
☐ 297 Dave Justice	5.00	2.20	.60
☐ 298 Paul Gibson	.25	.11	.03
☐ 299 Edgar Martinez	2.00	.90	.25
☐ 300 Frank Thomas UER (No B in front of birthdate)	85.00	38.00	10.50
☐ 301 Eric Yelding	.25	.11	.03
☐ 302 Greg Gagne	.25	.11	.03
☐ 303 Brad Komminsk	.25	.11	.03
☐ 304 Ron Darling	.25	.11	.03
☐ 305 Kevin Bass	.25	.11	.03
☐ 306 Jeff Hamilton	.25	.11	.03
☐ 307 Ron Karkovice	.25	.11	.03
☐ 308 Milt Thompson UER (Ray Lankford pictured on card back)	.75	.35	.09
☐ 309 Mike Harkey	.25	.11	.03
☐ 310 Mel Stottlemyre Jr.	.25	.11	.03
☐ 311 Kenny Rogers	.50	.23	.06

☐ 312 Mitch Webster .25 .11 .03
☐ 313 Kal Daniels .25 .11 .03
☐ 314 Matt Nokes .25 .11 .03
☐ 315 Dennis Lamp .25 .11 .03
☐ 316 Ken Howell .25 .11 .03
☐ 317 Glenallen Hill .50 .23 .06
☐ 318 Dave Martinez .25 .11 .03
☐ 319 Chris James .25 .11 .03
☐ 320 Mike Pagliarulo .25 .11 .03
☐ 321 Hal Morris .50 .23 .06
☐ 322 Rob Deer .25 .11 .03
☐ 323 Greg Olson .25 .11 .03
☐ 324 Tony Phillips .75 .35 .09
☐ 325 Larry Walker 8.00 3.60 1.00
☐ 326 Ron Hassey .25 .11 .03
☐ 327 Jack Howell .25 .11 .03
☐ 328 John Smiley .50 .23 .06
☐ 329 Steve Finley 1.00 .45 .12
☐ 330 Dave Magadan .25 .11 .03
☐ 331 Greg Litton .25 .11 .03
☐ 332 Mickey Hatcher .25 .11 .03
☐ 333 Lee Guetterman .25 .11 .03
☐ 334 Norm Charlton .25 .11 .03
☐ 335 Edgar Diaz .25 .11 .03
☐ 336 Willie Wilson .25 .11 .03
☐ 337 Bobby Witt .25 .11 .03
☐ 338 Candy Maldonado .25 .11 .03
☐ 339 Craig Lefferts .25 .11 .03
☐ 340 Dante Bichette 3.00 1.35 .35
☐ 341 Wally Backman .25 .11 .03
☐ 342 Dennis Cook .25 .11 .03
☐ 343 Pat Borders .25 .11 .03
☐ 344 Wallace Johnson .25 .11 .03
☐ 345 Willie Randolph .50 .23 .06
☐ 346 Danny Darwin .25 .11 .03
☐ 347 Al Newman .25 .11 .03
☐ 348 Mark Knudson .25 .11 .03
☐ 349 Joe Boever .25 .11 .03
☐ 350 Larry Sheets .25 .11 .03
☐ 351 Mike Jackson .25 .11 .03
☐ 352 Wayne Edwards .25 .11 .03
☐ 353 Bernard Gilkey 4.00 1.80 .50
☐ 354 Don Slaught .25 .11 .03
☐ 355 Joe Orsulak .25 .11 .03
☐ 356 John Franco .25 .11 .03
☐ 357 Jeff Brantley .50 .23 .06
☐ 358 Mike Morgan .25 .11 .03
☐ 359 Deion Sanders 3.00 1.35 .35
☐ 360 Terry Leach .25 .11 .03
☐ 361 Les Lancaster .25 .11 .03
☐ 362 Storm Davis .25 .11 .03
☐ 363 Scott Coolbaugh .25 .11 .03
☐ 364 Checklist 265-352 .75 .35 .09
(Ozzie Smith)
☐ 365 Cecilio Guante .25 .11 .03
☐ 366 Joey Cora .50 .23 .06
☐ 367 Willie McGee .25 .11 .03
☐ 368 Jerry Reed .25 .11 .03
☐ 369 Darren Daulton .50 .23 .06
☐ 370 Manny Lee .25 .11 .03
☐ 371 Mark Gardner .25 .11 .03
☐ 372 Rick Honeycutt .25 .11 .03
☐ 373 Steve Balboni .25 .11 .03
☐ 374 Jack Armstrong .25 .11 .03
☐ 375 Charlie O'Brien .25 .11 .03
☐ 376 Ron Gant 1.00 .45 .12
☐ 377 Lloyd Moseby .25 .11 .03
☐ 378 Gene Harris .25 .11 .03
☐ 379 Joe Carter .50 .23 .06
☐ 380 Scott Bailes .25 .11 .03
☐ 381 R.J. Reynolds .25 .11 .03
☐ 382 Bob Melvin .25 .11 .03
☐ 383 Tim Teufel .25 .11 .03
☐ 384 John Burkett .50 .23 .06
☐ 385 Felix Jose .25 .11 .03
☐ 386 Larry Andersen .25 .11 .03
☐ 387 David West .25 .11 .03
☐ 388 Luis Salazar .25 .11 .03
☐ 389 Mike Macfarlane .25 .11 .03
☐ 390 Charlie Hough .25 .11 .03
☐ 391 Greg Briley .25 .11 .03
☐ 392 Donn Pall .25 .11 .03
☐ 393 Bryn Smith .25 .11 .03
☐ 394 Carlos Quintana .25 .11 .03
☐ 395 Steve Lake .25 .11 .03
☐ 396 Mark Whiten .75 .35 .09
☐ 397 Edwin Nunez .25 .11 .03
☐ 398 Rick Parker .25 .11 .03
☐ 399 Mark Portugal .25 .11 .03
☐ 400 Roy Smith .25 .11 .03
☐ 401 Hector Villanueva .25 .11 .03
☐ 402 Bob Milacki .25 .11 .03
☐ 403 Alejandro Pena .25 .11 .03
☐ 404 Scott Bradley .25 .11 .03
☐ 405 Ron Kittle .25 .11 .03
☐ 406 Bob Tewksbury .25 .11 .03
☐ 407 Wes Gardner .25 .11 .03
☐ 408 Ernie Whitt .25 .11 .03
☐ 409 Terry Shumpert .25 .11 .03
☐ 410 Tim Layana .25 .11 .03
☐ 411 Chris Gwynn .25 .11 .03
☐ 412 Jeff D. Robinson .25 .11 .03
☐ 413 Scott Scudder .25 .11 .03
☐ 414 Kevin Romine .25 .11 .03
☐ 415 Jose DeJesus .25 .11 .03
☐ 416 Mike Jeffcoat .25 .11 .03
☐ 417 Rudy Seanez .25 .11 .03
☐ 418 Mike Dunne .25 .11 .03
☐ 419 Dick Schofield .25 .11 .03
☐ 420 Steve Wilson .25 .11 .03
☐ 421 Bill Krueger .25 .11 .03
☐ 422 Junior Felix .25 .11 .03
☐ 423 Drew Hall .25 .11 .03
☐ 424 Curt Young .25 .11 .03
☐ 425 Franklin Stubbs .25 .11 .03
☐ 426 Dave Winfield .75 .35 .09
☐ 427 Rick Reed .25 .11 .03
☐ 428 Charlie Leibrandt .25 .11 .03
☐ 429 Jeff M. Robinson .25 .11 .03
☐ 430 Erik Hanson .50 .23 .06
☐ 431 Barry Jones .25 .11 .03
☐ 432 Alex Trevino .25 .11 .03
☐ 433 John Moses .25 .11 .03
☐ 434 Dave Johnson .25 .11 .03
☐ 435 Mackey Sasser .25 .11 .03
☐ 436 Rick Leach .25 .11 .03
☐ 437 Lenny Harris .25 .11 .03
☐ 438 Carlos Martinez .25 .11 .03
☐ 439 Rex Hudler .25 .11 .03
☐ 440 Domingo Ramos .25 .11 .03
☐ 441 Gerald Perry .25 .11 .03
☐ 442 Jeff Russell .25 .11 .03
☐ 443 Carlos Baerga 4.00 1.80 .50
☐ 444 Checklist 353-440 .75 .35 .09
(Will Clark)
☐ 445 Stan Javier .25 .11 .03
☐ 446 Kevin Maas .50 .23 .06
☐ 447 Tom Brunansky .25 .11 .03
☐ 448 Carmelo Martinez .25 .11 .03
☐ 449 Willie Blair .25 .11 .03
☐ 450 Andres Galarraga 1.00 .45 .12
☐ 451 Bud Black .25 .11 .03
☐ 452 Greg W. Harris .25 .11 .03
☐ 453 Joe Oliver .25 .11 .03
☐ 454 Greg Brock .25 .11 .03
☐ 455 Jeff Treadway .25 .11 .03
☐ 456 Lance McCullers .25 .11 .03
☐ 457 Dave Schmidt .25 .11 .03
☐ 458 Todd Burns .25 .11 .03
☐ 459 Max Venable .25 .11 .03
☐ 460 Neal Heaton .25 .11 .03
☐ 461 Mark Williamson .25 .11 .03
☐ 462 Keith Miller .25 .11 .03
☐ 463 Mike LaCoss .25 .11 .03
☐ 464 Jose Offerman .50 .23 .06
☐ 465 Jim Leyritz .75 .35 .09
☐ 466 Glenn Braggs .25 .11 .03
☐ 467 Ron Robinson .25 .11 .03
☐ 468 Mark Davis .25 .11 .03
☐ 469 Gary Pettis .25 .11 .03
☐ 470 Keith Hernandez .50 .23 .06
☐ 471 Dennis Rasmussen .25 .11 .03
☐ 472 Mark Eichhorn .25 .11 .03
☐ 473 Ted Power .25 .11 .03
☐ 474 Terry Mulholland .25 .11 .03
☐ 475 Todd Stottlemyre .50 .23 .06
☐ 476 Jerry Goff .25 .11 .03
☐ 477 Gene Nelson .25 .11 .03
☐ 478 Rich Gedman .25 .11 .03
☐ 479 Brian Harper .25 .11 .03
☐ 480 Mike Felder .25 .11 .03
☐ 481 Steve Avery 1.50 .70 .19
☐ 482 Jack Morris .50 .23 .06
☐ 483 Randy Johnson 4.00 1.80 .50
☐ 484 Scott Radinsky .25 .11 .03
☐ 485 Jose DeLeon .25 .11 .03
☐ 486 Stan Belinda .25 .11 .03
☐ 487 Brian Holton .25 .11 .03
☐ 488 Mark Carreon .25 .11 .03
☐ 489 Trevor Wilson .25 .11 .03
☐ 490 Mike Sharperson .25 .11 .03
☐ 491 Alan Mills .25 .11 .03
☐ 492 John Candelaria .25 .11 .03
☐ 493 Paul Assenmacher .25 .11 .03
☐ 494 Steve Crawford .25 .11 .03
☐ 495 Brad Arnsberg .25 .11 .03
☐ 496 Sergio Valdez .25 .11 .03
☐ 497 Mark Parent .25 .11 .03
☐ 498 Tom Pagnozzi .25 .11 .03
☐ 499 Greg A. Harris .25 .11 .03
☐ 500 Randy Ready .25 .11 .03
☐ 501 Duane Ward .25 .11 .03
☐ 502 Nelson Santovenia .25 .11 .03
☐ 503 Joe Klink .25 .11 .03
☐ 504 Eric Plunk .25 .11 .03
☐ 505 Jeff Reed .25 .11 .03
☐ 506 Ted Higuera .25 .11 .03
☐ 507 Joe Hesketh .25 .11 .03
☐ 508 Dan Petry .25 .11 .03
☐ 509 Matt Young .25 .11 .03
☐ 510 Jerald Clark .25 .11 .03
☐ 511 John Orton .25 .11 .03
☐ 512 Scott Ruskin .25 .11 .03
☐ 513 Chris Hoiles 1.00 .45 .12
☐ 514 Daryl Boston .25 .11 .03
☐ 515 Francisco Oliveras .25 .11 .03
☐ 516 Ozzie Canseco .25 .11 .03
☐ 517 Xavier Hernandez .25 .11 .03
☐ 518 Fred Manrique .25 .11 .03
☐ 519 Shawn Boskie .25 .11 .03
☐ 520 Jeff Montgomery .50 .23 .06
☐ 521 Jack Daugherty .25 .11 .03
☐ 522 Keith Comstock .25 .11 .03
☐ 523 Greg Hibbard .25 .11 .03
☐ 524 Lee Smith .50 .23 .06
☐ 525 Dana Kiecker .25 .11 .03
☐ 526 Darrel Akerfelds .25 .11 .03
☐ 527 Greg Myers .25 .11 .03
☐ 528 Checklist 441-528 .75 .35 .09
(Ryne Sandberg)

1991 Leaf Previews

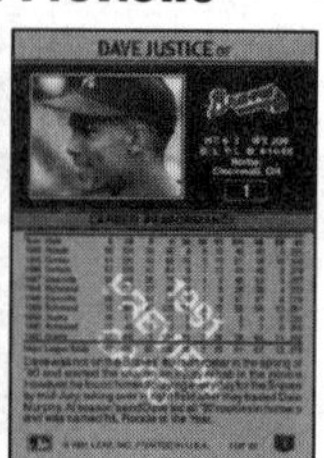

The 1991 Leaf Previews set consists of 26 standard-size cards. Cards from this set were issued as inserts (four at a time) inside specially marked 1991 Donruss hobby factory sets. The front design has color action player photos, with white and silver borders.

	MINT	NRMT	EXC
COMPLETE SET (26)	35.00	16.00	4.40
COMMON CARD (1-26)	1.00	.45	.12

☐ 1 Dave Justice 2.50 1.10 .30
☐ 2 Ryne Sandberg 5.00 2.20 .60
☐ 3 Barry Larkin 3.00 1.35 .35
☐ 4 Craig Biggio 2.00 .90 .25
☐ 5 Ramon Martinez 2.00 .90 .25
☐ 6 Tim Wallach 1.00 .45 .12
☐ 7 Dwight Gooden 1.50 .70 .19
☐ 8 Len Dykstra 1.50 .70 .19
☐ 9 Barry Bonds 5.00 2.20 .60
☐ 10 Ray Lankford 3.00 1.35 .35
☐ 11 Tony Gwynn 6.00 2.70 .75
☐ 12 Will Clark 2.00 .90 .25
☐ 13 Leo Gomez 1.00 .45 .12
☐ 14 Wade Boggs 2.00 .90 .25
☐ 15 Chuck Finley UER 1.00 .45 .12
(Position on card
back is First Base)
☐ 16 Carlton Fisk 1.50 .70 .19
☐ 17 Sandy Alomar Jr. 1.50 .70 .19
☐ 18 Cecil Fielder 1.50 .70 .19
☐ 19 Bo Jackson 1.50 .70 .19
☐ 20 Paul Molitor 2.50 1.10 .30
☐ 21 Kirby Puckett 6.00 2.70 .75
☐ 22 Don Mattingly 8.00 3.60 1.00
☐ 23 Rickey Henderson 2.00 .90 .25
☐ 24 Tino Martinez 2.00 .90 .25
☐ 25 Nolan Ryan 15.00 6.75 1.85
☐ 26 Dave Stieb 1.00 .45 .12

1991 Leaf

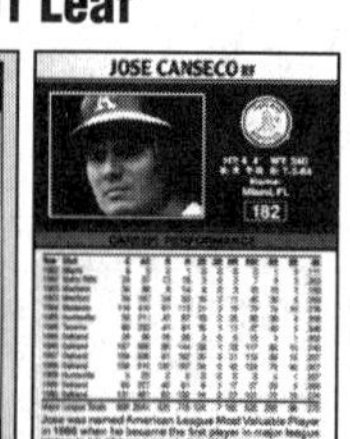

This 528-card standard size set was issued by Donruss in two separate series of 264 cards. Cards were exclusively issued in foil packs. The front design has color action player photos, with white and silver borders. A thicker stock was used for these (then) premium level cards. Rookie Cards in the set include Brian McRae and Denny Neagle.

	MINT	NRMT	EXC
COMPLETE SET (528)	15.00	6.75	1.85
COMPLETE SERIES 1 (264)	5.00	2.20	.60
COMPLETE SERIES 2 (264)	10.00	4.50	1.25
COMMON CARD (1-528)	.05	.02	.01

☐ 1 The Leaf Card .05 .02 .01
☐ 2 Kurt Stillwell .05 .02 .01
☐ 3 Bobby Witt .05 .02 .01
☐ 4 Tony Phillips .15 .07 .02
☐ 5 Scott Garrelts .05 .02 .01
☐ 6 Greg Swindell .05 .02 .01
☐ 7 Billy Ripken .05 .02 .01
☐ 8 Dave Martinez .05 .02 .01
☐ 9 Kelly Gruber .05 .02 .01
☐ 10 Juan Samuel .05 .02 .01
☐ 11 Brian Holman .05 .02 .01
☐ 12 Craig Biggio .30 .14 .04
☐ 13 Lonnie Smith .05 .02 .01
☐ 14 Ron Robinson .05 .02 .01
☐ 15 Mike LaValliere .05 .02 .01
☐ 16 Mark Davis .05 .02 .01
☐ 17 Jack Daugherty .05 .02 .01
☐ 18 Mike Henneman .05 .02 .01
☐ 19 Mike Greenwell .05 .02 .01
☐ 20 Dave Magadan .05 .02 .01
☐ 21 Mark Williamson .05 .02 .01
☐ 22 Marquis Grissom .30 .14 .04
☐ 23 Pat Borders .05 .02 .01
☐ 24 Mike Scioscia .05 .02 .01
☐ 25 Shawon Dunston .05 .02 .01
☐ 26 Randy Bush .05 .02 .01
☐ 27 John Smoltz .30 .14 .04
☐ 28 Chuck Crim .05 .02 .01
☐ 29 Don Slaught .05 .02 .01
☐ 30 Mike Macfarlane .05 .02 .01
☐ 31 Wally Joyner .15 .07 .02
☐ 32 Pat Combs .05 .02 .01
☐ 33 Tony Pena .05 .02 .01
☐ 34 Howard Johnson .05 .02 .01
☐ 35 Leo Gomez .05 .02 .01
☐ 36 Spike Owen .05 .02 .01
☐ 37 Eric Davis .15 .07 .02
☐ 38 Roberto Kelly .05 .02 .01
☐ 39 Jerome Walton .05 .02 .01
☐ 40 Shane Mack .05 .02 .01
☐ 41 Kent Mercker .05 .02 .01
☐ 42 B.J. Surhoff .15 .07 .02
☐ 43 Jerry Browne .05 .02 .01
☐ 44 Lee Smith .15 .07 .02
☐ 45 Chuck Finley .15 .07 .02
☐ 46 Terry Mulholland .05 .02 .01
☐ 47 Tom Bolton .05 .02 .01
☐ 48 Tom Herr .05 .02 .01
☐ 49 Jim Deshaies .05 .02 .01
☐ 50 Walt Weiss .05 .02 .01
☐ 51 Hal Morris .05 .02 .01
☐ 52 Lee Guetterman .05 .02 .01
☐ 53 Paul Assenmacher .05 .02 .01
☐ 54 Brian Harper .05 .02 .01
☐ 55 Paul Gibson .05 .02 .01
☐ 56 John Burkett .15 .07 .02
☐ 57 Doug Jones .05 .02 .01
☐ 58 Jose Oquendo .05 .02 .01
☐ 59 Dick Schofield .05 .02 .01
☐ 60 Dickie Thon .05 .02 .01
☐ 61 Ramon Martinez .30 .14 .04
☐ 62 Jay Buhner .30 .14 .04
☐ 63 Mark Portugal .05 .02 .01
☐ 64 Bob Welch .05 .02 .01
☐ 65 Chris Sabo .05 .02 .01
☐ 66 Chuck Cary .05 .02 .01
☐ 67 Mark Langston .15 .07 .02
☐ 68 Joe Boever .05 .02 .01
☐ 69 Jody Reed .05 .02 .01
☐ 70 Alejandro Pena .05 .02 .01
☐ 71 Jeff King .15 .07 .02
☐ 72 Tom Pagnozzi .05 .02 .01
☐ 73 Joe Oliver .05 .02 .01
☐ 74 Mike Witt .05 .02 .01
☐ 75 Hector Villanueva .05 .02 .01
☐ 76 Dan Gladden .05 .02 .01
☐ 77 Dave Justice .30 .14 .04
☐ 78 Mike Gallego .05 .02 .01
☐ 79 Tom Candiotti .05 .02 .01
☐ 80 Ozzie Smith .50 .23 .06
☐ 81 Luis Polonia .05 .02 .01
☐ 82 Randy Ready .05 .02 .01
☐ 83 Greg A. Harris .05 .02 .01
☐ 84 Checklist 1-92 .15 .07 .02
Dave Justice
☐ 85 Kevin Mitchell .15 .07 .02
☐ 86 Mark McLemore .05 .02 .01
☐ 87 Terry Steinbach .15 .07 .02
☐ 88 Tom Browning .05 .02 .01
☐ 89 Matt Nokes .05 .02 .01
☐ 90 Mike Harkey .05 .02 .01
☐ 91 Omar Vizquel .30 .14 .04
☐ 92 Dave Bergman .05 .02 .01
☐ 93 Matt Williams .30 .14 .04
☐ 94 Steve Olin .05 .02 .01
☐ 95 Craig Wilson .05 .02 .01
☐ 96 Dave Stieb .05 .02 .01
☐ 97 Ruben Sierra .15 .07 .02
☐ 98 Jay Howell .05 .02 .01
☐ 99 Scott Bradley .05 .02 .01
☐ 100 Eric Yelding .05 .02 .01
☐ 101 Rickey Henderson .30 .14 .04
☐ 102 Jeff Reed .05 .02 .01
☐ 103 Jimmy Key .15 .07 .02
☐ 104 Terry Shumpert .05 .02 .01
☐ 105 Kenny Rogers .05 .02 .01
☐ 106 Cecil Fielder .15 .07 .02
☐ 107 Robby Thompson .05 .02 .01
☐ 108 Alex Cole .05 .02 .01
☐ 109 Randy Milligan .05 .02 .01
☐ 110 Andres Galarraga .30 .14 .04
☐ 111 Bill Spiers .05 .02 .01
☐ 112 Kal Daniels .05 .02 .01
☐ 113 Henry Cotto .05 .02 .01
☐ 114 Casey Candaele .05 .02 .01
☐ 115 Jeff Blauser .05 .02 .01
☐ 116 Robin Yount .30 .14 .04
☐ 117 Ben McDonald .15 .07 .02

☐ 118 Bret Saberhagen .15 .07 .02
☐ 119 Juan Gonzalez 1.50 .70 .19
☐ 120 Lou Whitaker .15 .07 .02
☐ 121 Ellis Burks .15 .07 .02
☐ 122 Charlie O'Brien .05 .02 .01
☐ 123 John Smiley .05 .02 .01
☐ 124 Tim Burke .05 .02 .01
☐ 125 John Olerud .15 .07 .02
☐ 126 Eddie Murray .50 .23 .06
☐ 127 Greg Maddux 1.25 .55 .16
☐ 128 Kevin Tapani .05 .02 .01
☐ 129 Ron Gant .15 .07 .02
☐ 130 Jay Bell .15 .07 .02
☐ 131 Chris Hoiles .05 .02 .01
☐ 132 Tom Gordon .05 .02 .01
☐ 133 Kevin Seitzer .05 .02 .01
☐ 134 Jeff Huson .05 .02 .01
☐ 135 Jerry Don Gleaton .05 .02 .01
☐ 136 Jeff Brantley UER .05 .02 .01
(Photo actually Rick
Leach on back)
☐ 137 Felix Fermin .05 .02 .01
☐ 138 Mike Devereaux .05 .02 .01
☐ 139 Delino DeShields .05 .02 .01
☐ 140 David Wells .05 .02 .01
☐ 141 Tim Crews .05 .02 .01
☐ 142 Erik Hanson .05 .02 .01
☐ 143 Mark Davidson .05 .02 .01
☐ 144 Tommy Gregg .05 .02 .01
☐ 145 Jim Gantner .05 .02 .01
☐ 146 Jose Lind .05 .02 .01
☐ 147 Danny Tartabull .05 .02 .01
☐ 148 Geno Petralli .05 .02 .01
☐ 149 Travis Fryman .30 .14 .04
☐ 150 Tim Naehring .15 .07 .02
☐ 151 Kevin McReynolds .05 .02 .01
☐ 152 Joe Orsulak .05 .02 .01
☐ 153 Steve Frey .05 .02 .01
☐ 154 Duane Ward .05 .02 .01
☐ 155 Stan Javier .05 .02 .01
☐ 156 Damon Berryhill .05 .02 .01
☐ 157 Gene Larkin .05 .02 .01
☐ 158 Greg Olson .05 .02 .01
☐ 159 Mark Knudson .05 .02 .01
☐ 160 Carmelo Martinez .05 .02 .01
☐ 161 Storm Davis .05 .02 .01
☐ 162 Jim Abbott .15 .07 .02
☐ 163 Len Dykstra .15 .07 .02
☐ 164 Tom Brunansky .05 .02 .01
☐ 165 Dwight Gooden .15 .07 .02
☐ 166 Jose Mesa .15 .07 .02
☐ 167 Oil Can Boyd .05 .02 .01
☐ 168 Barry Larkin .30 .14 .04
☐ 169 Scott Sanderson .05 .02 .01
☐ 170 Mark Grace .30 .14 .04
☐ 171 Mark Guthrie .05 .02 .01
☐ 172 Tom Glavine .30 .14 .04
☐ 173 Gary Sheffield .30 .14 .04
☐ 174 Checklist 93-184 .30 .14 .04
Roger Clemens
☐ 175 Chris James .05 .02 .01
☐ 176 Milt Thompson .05 .02 .01
☐ 177 Donnie Hill .05 .02 .01
☐ 178 Wes Chamberlain .05 .02 .01
☐ 179 John Marzano .05 .02 .01
☐ 180 Frank Viola .05 .02 .01
☐ 181 Eric Anthony .05 .02 .01
☐ 182 Jose Canseco .30 .14 .04
☐ 183 Scott Scudder .05 .02 .01
☐ 184 Dave Eiland .05 .02 .01
☐ 185 Luis Salazar .05 .02 .01
☐ 186 Pedro Munoz .15 .07 .02
☐ 187 Steve Searcy .05 .02 .01
☐ 188 Don Robinson .05 .02 .01
☐ 189 Sandy Alomar Jr. .15 .07 .02
☐ 190 Jose DeLeon .05 .02 .01
☐ 191 John Orton .05 .02 .01
☐ 192 Darren Daulton .15 .07 .02
☐ 193 Mike Morgan .05 .02 .01
☐ 194 Greg Briley .05 .02 .01
☐ 195 Karl Rhodes .05 .02 .01
☐ 196 Harold Baines .15 .07 .02
☐ 197 Bill Doran .05 .02 .01
☐ 198 Alvaro Espinoza .05 .02 .01
☐ 199 Kirk McCaskill .05 .02 .01
☐ 200 Jose DeJesus .05 .02 .01
☐ 201 Jack Clark .15 .07 .02
☐ 202 Daryl Boston .05 .02 .01
☐ 203 Randy Tomlin .05 .02 .01
☐ 204 Pedro Guerrero .05 .02 .01
☐ 205 Billy Hatcher .05 .02 .01
☐ 206 Tim Leary .05 .02 .01
☐ 207 Ryne Sandberg .50 .23 .06
☐ 208 Kirby Puckett .75 .35 .09
☐ 209 Charlie Leibrandt .05 .02 .01
☐ 210 Rick Honeycutt .05 .02 .01
☐ 211 Joel Skinner .05 .02 .01
☐ 212 Rex Hudler .05 .02 .01
☐ 213 Bryan Harvey .05 .02 .01
☐ 214 Charlie Hayes .05 .02 .01
☐ 215 Matt Young .05 .02 .01
☐ 216 Terry Kennedy .05 .02 .01
☐ 217 Carl Nichols .05 .02 .01
☐ 218 Mike Moore .05 .02 .01
☐ 219 Paul O'Neill .15 .07 .02
☐ 220 Steve Sax .05 .02 .01
☐ 221 Shawn Boskie .05 .02 .01
☐ 222 Rich DeLucia .05 .02 .01
☐ 223 Lloyd Moseby .05 .02 .01
☐ 224 Mike Kingery .05 .02 .01
☐ 225 Carlos Baerga .30 .14 .04
☐ 226 Bryn Smith .05 .02 .01
☐ 227 Todd Stottlemyre .05 .02 .01
☐ 228 Julio Franco .15 .07 .02
☐ 229 Jim Gott .05 .02 .01
☐ 230 Mike Schooler .05 .02 .01
☐ 231 Steve Finley .15 .07 .02
☐ 232 Dave Henderson .05 .02 .01
☐ 233 Luis Quinones .05 .02 .01
☐ 234 Mark Whiten .15 .07 .02
☐ 235 Brian McRae .40 .18 .05
☐ 236 Rich Gossage .15 .07 .02
☐ 237 Rob Deer .05 .02 .01
☐ 238 Will Clark .30 .14 .04
☐ 239 Albert Belle 1.00 .45 .12
☐ 240 Bob Melvin .05 .02 .01
☐ 241 Larry Walker .30 .14 .04
☐ 242 Dante Bichette .30 .14 .04
☐ 243 Orel Hershiser .15 .07 .02
☐ 244 Pete O'Brien .05 .02 .01
☐ 245 Pete Harnisch .05 .02 .01
☐ 246 Jeff Treadway .05 .02 .01
☐ 247 Julio Machado .05 .02 .01
☐ 248 Dave Johnson .05 .02 .01
☐ 249 Kirk Gibson .15 .07 .02
☐ 250 Kevin Brown .15 .07 .02
☐ 251 Milt Cuyler .05 .02 .01
☐ 252 Jeff Reardon .15 .07 .02
☐ 253 David Cone .15 .07 .02
☐ 254 Gary Redus .05 .02 .01
☐ 255 Junior Noboa .05 .02 .01
☐ 256 Greg Myers .05 .02 .01
☐ 257 Dennis Cook .05 .02 .01
☐ 258 Joe Girardi .15 .07 .02
☐ 259 Allan Anderson .05 .02 .01
☐ 260 Paul Marak .05 .02 .01
☐ 261 Barry Bonds .50 .23 .06
☐ 262 Juan Bell .05 .02 .01
☐ 263 Russ Morman .05 .02 .01
☐ 264 Checklist 185-264 .30 .14 .04
and BC1-BC12
George Brett
☐ 265 Jerald Clark .05 .02 .01
☐ 266 Dwight Evans .15 .07 .02
☐ 267 Roberto Alomar .40 .18 .05
☐ 268 Danny Jackson .05 .02 .01
☐ 269 Brian Downing .05 .02 .01
☐ 270 John Cerutti .05 .02 .01
☐ 271 Robin Ventura .30 .14 .04
☐ 272 Gerald Perry .05 .02 .01
☐ 273 Wade Boggs .30 .14 .04
☐ 274 Dennis Martinez .15 .07 .02
☐ 275 Andy Benes .15 .07 .02
☐ 276 Tony Fossas .05 .02 .01
☐ 277 Franklin Stubbs .05 .02 .01
☐ 278 John Kruk .15 .07 .02
☐ 279 Kevin Gross .05 .02 .01
☐ 280 Von Hayes .05 .02 .01
☐ 281 Frank Thomas 4.00 1.80 .50
☐ 282 Rob Dibble .05 .02 .01
☐ 283 Mel Hall .05 .02 .01
☐ 284 Rick Mahler .05 .02 .01
☐ 285 Dennis Eckersley .15 .07 .02
☐ 286 Bernard Gilkey .15 .07 .02
☐ 287 Dan Plesac .05 .02 .01
☐ 288 Jason Grimsley .05 .02 .01
☐ 289 Mark Lewis .05 .02 .01
☐ 290 Tony Gwynn .75 .35 .09
☐ 291 Jeff Russell .05 .02 .01
☐ 292 Curt Schilling .05 .02 .01
☐ 293 Pascual Perez .05 .02 .01
☐ 294 Jack Morris .15 .07 .02
☐ 295 Hubie Brooks .05 .02 .01
☐ 296 Alex Fernandez .30 .14 .04
☐ 297 Harold Reynolds .05 .02 .01
☐ 298 Craig Worthington .05 .02 .01
☐ 299 Willie Wilson .05 .02 .01
☐ 300 Mike Maddux .05 .02 .01
☐ 301 Dave Righetti .05 .02 .01
☐ 302 Paul Molitor .40 .18 .05
☐ 303 Gary Gaetti .15 .07 .02
☐ 304 Terry Pendleton .15 .07 .02
☐ 305 Kevin Elster .05 .02 .01
☐ 306 Scott Fletcher .05 .02 .01
☐ 307 Jeff Robinson .05 .02 .01
☐ 308 Jesse Barfield .05 .02 .01
☐ 309 Mike LaCoss .05 .02 .01
☐ 310 Andy Van Slyke .15 .07 .02
☐ 311 Glenallen Hill .05 .02 .01
☐ 312 Bud Black .05 .02 .01
☐ 313 Kent Hrbek .15 .07 .02
☐ 314 Tim Teufel .05 .02 .01
☐ 315 Tony Fernandez .05 .02 .01
☐ 316 Beau Allred .05 .02 .01
☐ 317 Curtis Wilkerson .05 .02 .01
☐ 318 Bill Sampen .05 .02 .01
☐ 319 Randy Johnson .30 .14 .04
☐ 320 Mike Heath .05 .02 .01
☐ 321 Sammy Sosa .60 .25 .07
☐ 322 Mickey Tettleton .15 .07 .02
☐ 323 Jose Vizcaino .05 .02 .01
☐ 324 John Candelaria .05 .02 .01
☐ 325 Dave Howard .05 .02 .01
☐ 326 Jose Rijo .05 .02 .01
☐ 327 Todd Zeile .15 .07 .02
☐ 328 Gene Nelson .05 .02 .01
☐ 329 Dwayne Henry .05 .02 .01
☐ 330 Mike Boddicker .05 .02 .01
☐ 331 Ozzie Guillen .05 .02 .01
☐ 332 Sam Horn .05 .02 .01
☐ 333 Wally Whitehurst .05 .02 .01
☐ 334 Dave Parker .15 .07 .02
☐ 335 George Brett .75 .35 .09
☐ 336 Bobby Thigpen .05 .02 .01
☐ 337 Ed Whitson .05 .02 .01
☐ 338 Ivan Calderon .05 .02 .01
☐ 339 Mike Pagliarulo .05 .02 .01
☐ 340 Jack McDowell .15 .07 .02
☐ 341 Dana Kiecker .05 .02 .01
☐ 342 Fred McGriff .30 .14 .04
☐ 343 Mark Lee .05 .02 .01
☐ 344 Alfredo Griffin .05 .02 .01
☐ 345 Scott Bankhead .05 .02 .01
☐ 346 Darrin Jackson .05 .02 .01
☐ 347 Rafael Palmeiro .30 .14 .04
☐ 348 Steve Farr .05 .02 .01
☐ 349 Hensley Meulens .05 .02 .01
☐ 350 Danny Cox .05 .02 .01
☐ 351 Alan Trammell .15 .07 .02
☐ 352 Edwin Nunez .05 .02 .01
☐ 353 Joe Carter .15 .07 .02
☐ 354 Eric Show .05 .02 .01
☐ 355 Vance Law .05 .02 .01
☐ 356 Jeff Gray .05 .02 .01
☐ 357 Bobby Bonilla .15 .07 .02
☐ 358 Ernest Riles .05 .02 .01
☐ 359 Ron Hassey .05 .02 .01
☐ 360 Willie McGee .05 .02 .01
☐ 361 Mackey Sasser .05 .02 .01
☐ 362 Glenn Braggs .05 .02 .01
☐ 363 Mario Diaz .05 .02 .01
☐ 364 Checklist 265-356 .30 .14 .04
Barry Bonds
☐ 365 Kevin Bass .05 .02 .01
☐ 366 Pete Incaviglia .05 .02 .01
☐ 367 Luis Sojo UER .05 .02 .01
(1989 stats inter-
spersed with 1990's)
☐ 368 Lance Parrish .05 .02 .01
☐ 369 Mark Leonard .05 .02 .01
☐ 370 Heathcliff Slocumb .30 .14 .04
☐ 371 Jimmy Jones .05 .02 .01
☐ 372 Ken Griffey Jr. 3.00 1.35 .35
☐ 373 Chris Hammond .05 .02 .01
☐ 374 Chili Davis .15 .07 .02
☐ 375 Joey Cora .15 .07 .02
☐ 376 Ken Hill .15 .07 .02
☐ 377 Darryl Strawberry .15 .07 .02
☐ 378 Ron Darling .05 .02 .01
☐ 379 Sid Bream .05 .02 .01
☐ 380 Bill Swift .05 .02 .01
☐ 381 Shawn Abner .05 .02 .01
☐ 382 Eric King .05 .02 .01
☐ 383 Mickey Morandini .05 .02 .01
☐ 384 Carlton Fisk .30 .14 .04
☐ 385 Steve Lake .05 .02 .01
☐ 386 Mike Jeffcoat .05 .02 .01
☐ 387 Darren Holmes .05 .02 .01
☐ 388 Tim Wallach .05 .02 .01
☐ 389 George Bell .05 .02 .01
☐ 390 Craig Lefferts .05 .02 .01
☐ 391 Ernie Whitt .05 .02 .01
☐ 392 Felix Jose .05 .02 .01
☐ 393 Kevin Maas .05 .02 .01
☐ 394 Devon White .15 .07 .02
☐ 395 Otis Nixon .05 .02 .01
☐ 396 Chuck Knoblauch .50 .23 .06
☐ 397 Scott Coolbaugh .05 .02 .01
☐ 398 Glenn Davis .05 .02 .01
☐ 399 Manny Lee .05 .02 .01
☐ 400 Andre Dawson .15 .07 .02
☐ 401 Scott Chiamparino .05 .02 .01
☐ 402 Bill Gullickson .05 .02 .01
☐ 403 Lance Johnson .15 .07 .02
☐ 404 Juan Agosto .05 .02 .01
☐ 405 Danny Darwin .05 .02 .01
☐ 406 Barry Jones .05 .02 .01
☐ 407 Larry Andersen .05 .02 .01
☐ 408 Luis Rivera .05 .02 .01
☐ 409 Jaime Navarro .05 .02 .01
☐ 410 Roger McDowell .05 .02 .01
☐ 411 Brett Butler .15 .07 .02
☐ 412 Dale Murphy .30 .14 .04
☐ 413 Tim Raines UER .30 .14 .04
(Listed as hitting .500
in 1980, should be .050)
☐ 414 Norm Charlton .05 .02 .01
☐ 415 Greg Cadaret .05 .02 .01
☐ 416 Chris Nabholz .05 .02 .01
☐ 417 Dave Stewart .15 .07 .02
☐ 418 Rich Gedman .05 .02 .01
☐ 419 Willie Randolph .15 .07 .02
☐ 420 Mitch Williams .05 .02 .01
☐ 421 Brook Jacoby .05 .02 .01
☐ 422 Greg W. Harris .05 .02 .01
☐ 423 Nolan Ryan 1.50 .70 .19
☐ 424 Dave Rohde .05 .02 .01
☐ 425 Don Mattingly 1.00 .45 .12
☐ 426 Greg Gagne .05 .02 .01
☐ 427 Vince Coleman .05 .02 .01
☐ 428 Dan Pasqua .05 .02 .01
☐ 429 Alvin Davis .05 .02 .01
☐ 430 Cal Ripken 1.50 .70 .19
☐ 431 Jamie Quirk .05 .02 .01
☐ 432 Benito Santiago .05 .02 .01
☐ 433 Jose Uribe .05 .02 .01
☐ 434 Candy Maldonado .05 .02 .01
☐ 435 Junior Felix .05 .02 .01
☐ 436 Deion Sanders .30 .14 .04
☐ 437 John Franco .05 .02 .01
☐ 438 Greg Hibbard .05 .02 .01
☐ 439 Floyd Bannister .05 .02 .01
☐ 440 Steve Howe .05 .02 .01
☐ 441 Steve Decker .05 .02 .01
☐ 442 Vicente Palacios .05 .02 .01
☐ 443 Pat Tabler .05 .02 .01
☐ 444 Checklist 357-448 .30 .14 .04
Darryl Strawberry
☐ 445 Mike Felder .05 .02 .01
☐ 446 Al Newman .05 .02 .01
☐ 447 Chris Donnels .05 .02 .01
☐ 448 Rich Rodriguez .05 .02 .01
☐ 449 Turner Ward .05 .02 .01
☐ 450 Bob Walk .05 .02 .01
☐ 451 Gilberto Reyes .05 .02 .01
☐ 452 Mike Jackson .05 .02 .01
☐ 453 Rafael Belliard .05 .02 .01
☐ 454 Wayne Edwards .05 .02 .01
☐ 455 Andy Allanson .05 .02 .01
☐ 456 Dave Smith .05 .02 .01
☐ 457 Gary Carter .15 .07 .02
☐ 458 Warren Cromartie .05 .02 .01
☐ 459 Jack Armstrong .05 .02 .01
☐ 460 Bob Tewksbury .05 .02 .01
☐ 461 Joe Klink .05 .02 .01
☐ 462 Xavier Hernandez .05 .02 .01
☐ 463 Scott Radinsky .05 .02 .01
☐ 464 Jeff Robinson .05 .02 .01
☐ 465 Gregg Jefferies .15 .07 .02
☐ 466 Denny Neagle .60 .25 .07
☐ 467 Carmelo Martinez .05 .02 .01
☐ 468 Donn Pall .05 .02 .01
☐ 469 Bruce Hurst .05 .02 .01
☐ 470 Eric Bullock .05 .02 .01
☐ 471 Rick Aguilera .15 .07 .02
☐ 472 Charlie Hough .05 .02 .01
☐ 473 Carlos Quintana .05 .02 .01
☐ 474 Marty Barrett .05 .02 .01
☐ 475 Kevin D. Brown .05 .02 .01
☐ 476 Bobby Ojeda .05 .02 .01
☐ 477 Edgar Martinez .15 .07 .02
☐ 478 Bip Roberts .05 .02 .01
☐ 479 Mike Flanagan .05 .02 .01
☐ 480 John Habyan .05 .02 .01
☐ 481 Larry Casian .05 .02 .01
☐ 482 Wally Backman .05 .02 .01
☐ 483 Doug Dascenzo .05 .02 .01
☐ 484 Rick Dempsey .05 .02 .01
☐ 485 Ed Sprague .15 .07 .02
☐ 486 Steve Chitren .05 .02 .01
☐ 487 Mark McGwire .60 .25 .07
☐ 488 Roger Clemens .40 .18 .05
☐ 489 Orlando Merced .30 .14 .04
☐ 490 Rene Gonzales .05 .02 .01
☐ 491 Mike Stanton .05 .02 .01
☐ 492 Al Osuna .05 .02 .01
☐ 493 Rick Cerone .05 .02 .01
☐ 494 Mariano Duncan .05 .02 .01
☐ 495 Zane Smith .05 .02 .01
☐ 496 John Morris .05 .02 .01
☐ 497 Frank Tanana .05 .02 .01
☐ 498 Junior Ortiz .05 .02 .01
☐ 499 Dave Winfield .30 .14 .04
☐ 500 Gary Varsho .05 .02 .01
☐ 501 Chico Walker .05 .02 .01
☐ 502 Ken Caminiti .30 .14 .04
☐ 503 Ken Griffey Sr. .05 .02 .01
☐ 504 Randy Myers .15 .07 .02
☐ 505 Steve Bedrosian .05 .02 .01
☐ 506 Cory Snyder .05 .02 .01
☐ 507 Cris Carpenter .05 .02 .01
☐ 508 Tim Belcher .05 .02 .01
☐ 509 Jeff Hamilton .05 .02 .01
☐ 510 Steve Avery .30 .14 .04
☐ 511 Dave Valle .05 .02 .01
☐ 512 Tom Lampkin .05 .02 .01
☐ 513 Shawn Hillegas .05 .02 .01
☐ 514 Reggie Jefferson .15 .07 .02
☐ 515 Ron Karkovice .05 .02 .01
☐ 516 Doug Drabek .05 .02 .01
☐ 517 Tom Henke .05 .02 .01
☐ 518 Chris Bosio .05 .02 .01
☐ 519 Gregg Olson .05 .02 .01
☐ 520 Bob Scanlan .05 .02 .01
☐ 521 Alonzo Powell .05 .02 .01
☐ 522 Jeff Ballard .05 .02 .01
☐ 523 Ray Lankford .30 .14 .04
☐ 524 Tommy Greene .05 .02 .01
☐ 525 Mike Timlin .05 .02 .01
☐ 526 Juan Berenguer .05 .02 .01

Card	MINT	NRMT	EXC
☐ 527 Scott Erickson	.15	.07	.02
☐ 528 Checklist 449-528	.05	.02	.01
and BC13-BC26			
Sandy Alomar Jr.			

1991 Leaf Gold Rookies

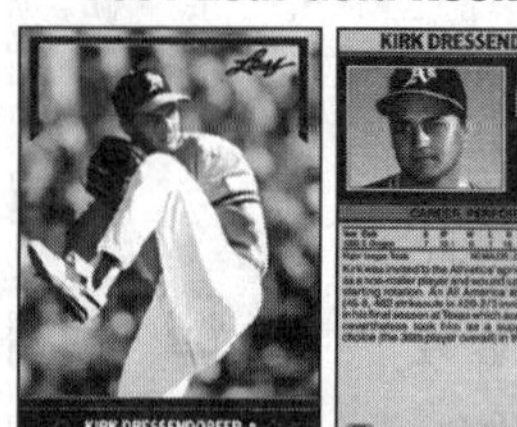

This 26-card standard size set was issued by Leaf as an insert to their 1991 Leaf regular issue.The first twelve cards were issued as random inserts in with the first series of 1991 Leaf foil packs. The rest were issued as random inserts in with the second series. The set features a selection of rookie prospects. The earliest Leaf Gold Rookie cards issued with the first series can sometimes be found with erroneous regular numbered backs 265 through 276 instead of the correct BC1 through BC12. These numbered variations are very tough to find and are valued at ten times the values listed below.

	MINT	NRMT	EXC
COMPLETE SET (26)	25.00	11.00	3.10
COMMON CARD (BC1-BC26)	.50	.23	.06
☐ BC1 Scott Leius	.50	.23	.06
☐ BC2 Luis Gonzalez	1.00	.45	.12
☐ BC3 Wil Cordero	.75	.35	.09
☐ BC4 Gary Scott	.50	.23	.06
☐ BC5 Willie Banks	.50	.23	.06
☐ BC6 Arthur Rhodes	.75	.35	.09
☐ BC7 Mo Vaughn	6.00	2.70	.75
☐ BC8 Henry Rodriguez	2.00	.90	.25
☐ BC9 Todd Van Poppel	.50	.23	.06
☐ BC10 Reggie Sanders	1.25	.55	.16
☐ BC11 Rico Brogna	.75	.35	.09
☐ BC12 Mike Mussina	3.00	1.35	.35
☐ BC13 Kirk Dressendorfer	.50	.23	.06
☐ BC14 Jeff Bagwell	6.00	2.70	.75
☐ BC15 Pete Schourek	.75	.35	.09
☐ BC16 Wade Taylor	.50	.23	.06
☐ BC17 Pat Kelly	.50	.23	.06
☐ BC18 Tim Costo	.50	.23	.06
☐ BC19 Roger Salkeld	.50	.23	.06
☐ BC20 Andujar Cedeno	.50	.23	.06
☐ BC21 Ryan Klesko UER	5.00	2.20	.60
(1990 Sumter BA .289;			
should be .368)			
☐ BC22 Mike Huff	.50	.23	.06
☐ BC23 Anthony Young	.50	.23	.06
☐ BC24 Eddie Zosky	.50	.23	.06
☐ BC25 Nolan Ryan DP UER	1.50	.70	.19
No Hitter 7			
(Word other repeated			
in 7th line)			
☐ BC26 Rickey Henderson DP	1.00	.45	.12
Record Steal			

1992 Leaf Previews

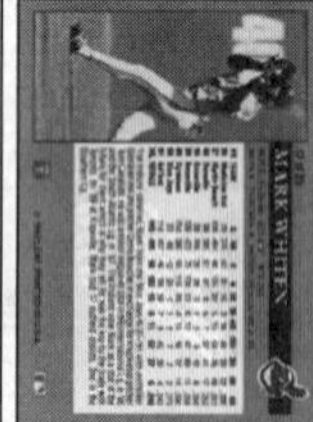

Four Leaf Preview standard-size cards were included in each 1992 Donruss hobby factory set. The cards were intended to show collectors and dealers the style of the 1992 Leaf set. The fronts carry glossy color player photos framed by silver borders.

	MINT	NRMT	EXC
COMPLETE SET (26)	60.00	27.00	7.50
COMMON CARD (1-26)	1.00	.45	.12
☐ 1 Steve Avery	1.50	.70	.19
☐ 2 Ryne Sandberg	4.00	1.80	.50
☐ 3 Chris Sabo	1.00	.45	.12
☐ 4 Jeff Bagwell	8.00	3.60	1.00
☐ 5 Darryl Strawberry	1.50	.70	.19
☐ 6 Bret Barberie	1.00	.45	.12
☐ 7 Howard Johnson	1.00	.45	.12
☐ 8 John Kruk	1.50	.70	.19
☐ 9 Andy Van Slyke	1.50	.70	.19
☐ 10 Felix Jose	1.00	.45	.12
☐ 11 Fred McGriff	2.50	1.10	.30
☐ 12 Will Clark	2.50	1.10	.30
☐ 13 Cal Ripken	10.00	4.50	1.25
☐ 14 Phil Plantier	1.00	.45	.12
☐ 15 Lee Stevens	1.00	.45	.12
☐ 16 Frank Thomas	18.00	8.00	2.20
☐ 17 Mark Whiten	1.00	.45	.12
☐ 18 Cecil Fielder	1.50	.70	.19
☐ 19 George Brett	5.00	2.20	.60
☐ 20 Robin Yount	2.50	1.10	.30
☐ 21 Scott Erickson	1.00	.45	.12
☐ 22 Don Mattingly	6.00	2.70	.75
☐ 23 Jose Canseco	2.50	1.10	.30
☐ 24 Ken Griffey Jr.	18.00	8.00	2.20
☐ 25 Nolan Ryan	10.00	4.50	1.25
☐ 26 Joe Carter	1.50	.70	.19

1992 Leaf Gold Previews

These Leaf Gold Preview cards were sent to members of the Donruss/Leaf Dealer Network who ordered 1992 Donruss Factory sets. For each set ordered, dealers received one two-card pack. These cards showed the style of the new 1992 Leaf Gold cards which would be included one per pack in the forthcoming set. The cards measure the standard size. The fronts feature color action player photos inside a gold foil picture frame and a black outer border.

	MINT	NRMT	EXC
COMPLETE SET (33)	125.00	55.00	15.50
COMMON CARD (1-33)	1.00	.45	.12
☐ 1 Steve Avery	1.50	.70	.19
☐ 2 Ryne Sandberg	10.00	4.50	1.25
☐ 3 Chris Sabo	1.00	.45	.12
☐ 4 Jeff Bagwell	12.00	5.50	1.50
☐ 5 Darryl Strawberry	1.50	.70	.19
☐ 6 Bret Barberie	1.00	.45	.12
☐ 7 Howard Johnson	1.00	.45	.12
☐ 8 John Kruk	1.00	.45	.12
☐ 9 Andy Van Slyke	1.00	.45	.12
☐ 10 Felix Jose	1.00	.45	.12
☐ 11 Fred McGriff	4.00	1.80	.50
☐ 12 Will Clark	4.00	1.80	.50
☐ 13 Cal Ripken	20.00	9.00	2.50
☐ 14 Phil Plantier	1.00	.45	.12
☐ 15 Lee Stevens	1.00	.45	.12
☐ 16 Frank Thomas	25.00	11.00	3.10
☐ 17 Mark Whiten	1.00	.45	.12
☐ 18 Cecil Fielder	1.50	.70	.19
☐ 19 George Brett	10.00	4.50	1.25
☐ 20 Robin Yount	3.00	1.35	.35
☐ 21 Scott Erickson	1.00	.45	.12
☐ 22 Don Mattingly	12.00	5.50	1.50
☐ 23 Jose Canseco	4.00	1.80	.50
☐ 24 Ken Griffey Jr.	25.00	11.00	3.10
☐ 25 Nolan Ryan	20.00	9.00	2.50
☐ 26 Joe Carter	2.50	1.10	.30
☐ 27 Deion Sanders	4.00	1.80	.50
☐ 28 Dean Palmer	1.50	.70	.19
☐ 29 Andy Benes	1.50	.70	.19
☐ 30 Gary DiSarcina	1.00	.45	.12
☐ 31 Chris Hoiles	1.00	.45	.12
☐ 32 Mark McGwire	8.00	3.60	1.00
☐ 33 Reggie Sanders	1.50	.70	.19

1992 Leaf

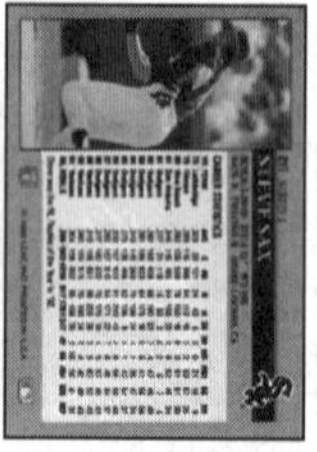

The 1992 Leaf set consists of 528 cards, issued in two separate 264-card series. Cards were distributed in first and second series 15-card foil packs. Each pack contained a selection of basic cards and one black gold parallel card. The basic card fronts feature color action player photos on a silver card face. The player's name appears in a black bar edged at the bottom by a thin red stripe. The team logo overlaps the bar at the right corner. There are no significant Rookie Cards in this set.

	MINT	NRMT	EXC
COMPLETE SET (528)	15.00	6.75	1.85
COMPLETE SERIES 1 (264)	5.00	2.20	.60
COMPLETE SERIES 2 (264)	10.00	4.50	1.25
COMMON CARD (1-528)	.05	.02	.01
☐ 1 Jim Abbott	.05	.02	.01
☐ 2 Cal Eldred	.05	.02	.01
☐ 3 Bud Black	.05	.02	.01
☐ 4 Dave Howard	.05	.02	.01
☐ 5 Luis Sojo	.05	.02	.01
☐ 6 Gary Scott	.05	.02	.01
☐ 7 Joe Oliver	.05	.02	.01
☐ 8 Chris Gardner	.05	.02	.01
☐ 9 Sandy Alomar Jr.	.10	.05	.01
☐ 10 Greg W. Harris	.05	.02	.01
☐ 11 Doug Drabek	.05	.02	.01
☐ 12 Darryl Hamilton	.05	.02	.01
☐ 13 Mike Mussina	.50	.23	.06
☐ 14 Kevin Tapani	.05	.02	.01
☐ 15 Ron Gant	.10	.05	.01
☐ 16 Mark McGwire	.50	.23	.06
☐ 17 Robin Ventura	.10	.05	.01
☐ 18 Pedro Guerrero	.05	.02	.01
☐ 19 Roger Clemens	.30	.14	.04
☐ 20 Steve Farr	.05	.02	.01
☐ 21 Frank Tanana	.05	.02	.01
☐ 22 Joe Hesketh	.05	.02	.01
☐ 23 Erik Hanson	.05	.02	.01
☐ 24 Greg Cadaret	.05	.02	.01
☐ 25 Rex Hudler	.05	.02	.01
☐ 26 Mark Grace	.25	.11	.03
☐ 27 Kelly Gruber	.05	.02	.01
☐ 28 Jeff Bagwell	1.00	.45	.12
☐ 29 Darryl Strawberry	.10	.05	.01
☐ 30 Dave Smith	.05	.02	.01
☐ 31 Kevin Appier	.10	.05	.01
☐ 32 Steve Chitren	.05	.02	.01
☐ 33 Kevin Gross	.05	.02	.01
☐ 34 Rick Aguilera	.05	.02	.01
☐ 35 Juan Guzman	.10	.05	.01
☐ 36 Joe Orsulak	.05	.02	.01
☐ 37 Tim Raines	.25	.11	.03
☐ 38 Harold Reynolds	.05	.02	.01
☐ 39 Charlie Hough	.05	.02	.01
☐ 40 Tony Phillips	.10	.05	.01
☐ 41 Nolan Ryan	1.25	.55	.16
☐ 42 Vince Coleman	.05	.02	.01
☐ 43 Andy Van Slyke	.10	.05	.01
☐ 44 Tim Burke	.05	.02	.01
☐ 45 Luis Polonia	.05	.02	.01
☐ 46 Tom Browning	.05	.02	.01
☐ 47 Willie McGee	.05	.02	.01
☐ 48 Gary DiSarcina	.05	.02	.01
☐ 49 Mark Lewis	.05	.02	.01
☐ 50 Phil Plantier	.10	.05	.01
☐ 51 Doug Dascenzo	.05	.02	.01
☐ 52 Cal Ripken	1.25	.55	.16
☐ 53 Pedro Munoz	.05	.02	.01
☐ 54 Carlos Hernandez	.05	.02	.01
☐ 55 Jerald Clark	.05	.02	.01
☐ 56 Jeff Brantley	.10	.05	.01
☐ 57 Don Mattingly	.75	.35	.09
☐ 58 Roger McDowell	.05	.02	.01
☐ 59 Steve Avery	.10	.05	.01
☐ 60 John Olerud	.10	.05	.01
☐ 61 Bill Gullickson	.05	.02	.01
☐ 62 Juan Gonzalez	1.00	.45	.12
☐ 63 Felix Jose	.05	.02	.01
☐ 64 Robin Yount	.25	.11	.03
☐ 65 Greg Briley	.05	.02	.01
☐ 66 Steve Finley	.10	.05	.01
☐ 67 Checklist 1-88	.25	.11	.03
Frank Thomas			
☐ 68 Tom Gordon	.05	.02	.01
☐ 69 Rob Dibble	.05	.02	.01
☐ 70 Glenallen Hill	.05	.02	.01
☐ 71 Calvin Jones	.05	.02	.01
☐ 72 Joe Girardi	.05	.02	.01
☐ 73 Barry Larkin	.25	.11	.03
☐ 74 Andy Benes	.10	.05	.01
☐ 75 Milt Cuyler	.05	.02	.01
☐ 76 Kevin Bass	.05	.02	.01
☐ 77 Pete Harnisch	.05	.02	.01
☐ 78 Wilson Alvarez	.25	.11	.03
☐ 79 Mike Devereaux	.05	.02	.01
☐ 80 Doug Henry	.05	.02	.01
☐ 81 Orel Hershiser	.10	.05	.01
☐ 82 Shane Mack	.05	.02	.01
☐ 83 Mike Macfarlane	.05	.02	.01
☐ 84 Thomas Howard	.05	.02	.01
☐ 85 Alex Fernandez	.25	.11	.03
☐ 86 Reggie Jefferson	.10	.05	.01
☐ 87 Leo Gomez	.05	.02	.01
☐ 88 Mel Hall	.05	.02	.01
☐ 89 Mike Greenwell	.05	.02	.01
☐ 90 Jeff Russell	.05	.02	.01
☐ 91 Steve Buechele	.05	.02	.01
☐ 92 David Cone	.10	.05	.01
☐ 93 Kevin Reimer	.05	.02	.01
☐ 94 Mark Lemke	.05	.02	.01
☐ 95 Bob Tewksbury	.05	.02	.01
☐ 96 Zane Smith	.05	.02	.01
☐ 97 Mark Eichhorn	.05	.02	.01
☐ 98 Kirby Puckett	.60	.25	.07
☐ 99 Paul O'Neill	.10	.05	.01
☐ 100 Dennis Eckersley	.10	.05	.01
☐ 101 Duane Ward	.05	.02	.01
☐ 102 Matt Nokes	.05	.02	.01
☐ 103 Mo Vaughn	.60	.25	.07
☐ 104 Pat Kelly	.05	.02	.01
☐ 105 Ron Karkovice	.05	.02	.01
☐ 106 Bill Spiers	.05	.02	.01
☐ 107 Gary Gaetti	.10	.05	.01
☐ 108 Mackey Sasser	.05	.02	.01
☐ 109 Robby Thompson	.05	.02	.01
☐ 110 Marvin Freeman	.05	.02	.01
☐ 111 Jimmy Key	.10	.05	.01
☐ 112 Dwight Gooden	.10	.05	.01
☐ 113 Charlie Leibrandt	.05	.02	.01
☐ 114 Devon White	.10	.05	.01
☐ 115 Charles Nagy	.10	.05	.01
☐ 116 Rickey Henderson	.25	.11	.03
☐ 117 Paul Assenmacher	.05	.02	.01
☐ 118 Junior Felix	.05	.02	.01
☐ 119 Julio Franco	.10	.05	.01
☐ 120 Norm Charlton	.05	.02	.01
☐ 121 Scott Servais	.05	.02	.01
☐ 122 Gerald Perry	.05	.02	.01
☐ 123 Brian McRae	.10	.05	.01
☐ 124 Don Slaught	.05	.02	.01
☐ 125 Juan Samuel	.05	.02	.01
☐ 126 Harold Baines	.10	.05	.01
☐ 127 Scott Livingstone	.05	.02	.01
☐ 128 Jay Buhner	.25	.11	.03
☐ 129 Darrin Jackson	.05	.02	.01
☐ 130 Luis Mercedes	.05	.02	.01
☐ 131 Brian Harper	.05	.02	.01
☐ 132 Howard Johnson	.05	.02	.01
☐ 133 Checklist 89-176	.25	.11	.03
Nolan Ryan			
☐ 134 Dante Bichette	.25	.11	.03
☐ 135 Dave Righetti	.05	.02	.01
☐ 136 Jeff Montgomery	.10	.05	.01
☐ 137 Joe Grahe	.05	.02	.01
☐ 138 Delino DeShields	.05	.02	.01
☐ 139 Jose Rijo	.05	.02	.01
☐ 140 Ken Caminiti	.25	.11	.03
☐ 141 Steve Olin	.05	.02	.01
☐ 142 Kurt Stillwell	.05	.02	.01
☐ 143 Jay Bell	.10	.05	.01
☐ 144 Jaime Navarro	.05	.02	.01
☐ 145 Ben McDonald	.05	.02	.01
☐ 146 Greg Gagne	.05	.02	.01
☐ 147 Jeff Blauser	.05	.02	.01
☐ 148 Carney Lansford	.10	.05	.01
☐ 149 Ozzie Guillen	.05	.02	.01
☐ 150 Milt Thompson	.05	.02	.01
☐ 151 Jeff Reardon	.10	.05	.01
☐ 152 Scott Sanderson	.05	.02	.01
☐ 153 Cecil Fielder	.10	.05	.01
☐ 154 Greg A. Harris	.05	.02	.01
☐ 155 Rich DeLucia	.05	.02	.01
☐ 156 Roberto Kelly	.05	.02	.01
☐ 157 Bryn Smith	.05	.02	.01
☐ 158 Chuck McElroy	.05	.02	.01
☐ 159 Tom Henke	.05	.02	.01
☐ 160 Luis Gonzalez	.10	.05	.01
☐ 161 Steve Wilson	.05	.02	.01
☐ 162 Shawn Boskie	.05	.02	.01
☐ 163 Mark Davis	.05	.02	.01
☐ 164 Mike Moore	.05	.02	.01
☐ 165 Mike Scioscia	.05	.02	.01
☐ 166 Scott Erickson	.10	.05	.01
☐ 167 Todd Stottlemyre	.10	.05	.01
☐ 168 Alvin Davis	.05	.02	.01
☐ 169 Greg Hibbard	.05	.02	.01
☐ 170 David Valle	.05	.02	.01
☐ 171 Dave Winfield	.25	.11	.03
☐ 172 Alan Trammell	.10	.05	.01
☐ 173 Kenny Rogers	.05	.02	.01
☐ 174 John Franco	.05	.02	.01
☐ 175 Jose Lind	.05	.02	.01
☐ 176 Pete Schourek	.10	.05	.01
☐ 177 Von Hayes	.05	.02	.01
☐ 178 Chris Hammond	.05	.02	.01
☐ 179 John Burkett	.10	.05	.01
☐ 180 Dickie Thon	.05	.02	.01
☐ 181 Joel Skinner	.05	.02	.01
☐ 182 Scott Cooper	.05	.02	.01
☐ 183 Andre Dawson	.10	.05	.01
☐ 184 Billy Ripken	.05	.02	.01
☐ 185 Kevin Mitchell	.10	.05	.01
☐ 186 Brett Butler	.10	.05	.01
☐ 187 Tony Fernandez	.05	.02	.01
☐ 188 Cory Snyder	.05	.02	.01
☐ 189 John Habyan	.05	.02	.01
☐ 190 Dennis Martinez	.10	.05	.01
☐ 191 John Smoltz	.25	.11	.03
☐ 192 Greg Myers	.05	.02	.01
☐ 193 Rob Deer	.05	.02	.01
☐ 194 Ivan Rodriguez	.60	.25	.07
☐ 195 Ray Lankford	.25	.11	.03
☐ 196 Bill Wegman	.05	.02	.01
☐ 197 Edgar Martinez	.10	.05	.01
☐ 198 Darryl Kile	.05	.02	.01
☐ 199 Checklist 177-264	.25	.11	.03
Cal Ripken			
☐ 200 Brent Mayne	.05	.02	.01
☐ 201 Larry Walker	.25	.11	.03
☐ 202 Carlos Baerga	.10	.05	.01
☐ 203 Russ Swan	.05	.02	.01
☐ 204 Mike Morgan	.05	.02	.01
☐ 205 Hal Morris	.05	.02	.01
☐ 206 Tony Gwynn	.60	.25	.07
☐ 207 Mark Leiter	.05	.02	.01

☐ 208 Kirt Manwaring	.05	.02	.01
☐ 209 Al Osuna	.05	.02	.01
☐ 210 Bobby Thigpen	.05	.02	.01
☐ 211 Chris Hoiles	.05	.02	.01
☐ 212 B.J. Surhoff	.10	.05	.01
☐ 213 Lenny Harris	.05	.02	.01
☐ 214 Scott Leius	.05	.02	.01
☐ 215 Gregg Jefferies	.10	.05	.01
☐ 216 Bruce Hurst	.05	.02	.01
☐ 217 Steve Sax	.05	.02	.01
☐ 218 Dave Otto	.05	.02	.01
☐ 219 Sam Horn	.05	.02	.01
☐ 220 Charlie Hayes	.05	.02	.01
☐ 221 Frank Viola	.05	.02	.01
☐ 222 Jose Guzman	.10	.05	.01
☐ 223 Gary Redus	.05	.02	.01
☐ 224 Dave Gallagher	.05	.02	.01
☐ 225 Dean Palmer	.10	.05	.01
☐ 226 Greg Olson	.05	.02	.01
☐ 227 Jose DeLeon	.05	.02	.01
☐ 228 Mike LaValliere	.05	.02	.01
☐ 229 Mark Langston	.10	.05	.01
☐ 230 Chuck Knoblauch	.25	.11	.03
☐ 231 Bill Doran	.05	.02	.01
☐ 232 Dave Henderson	.05	.02	.01
☐ 233 Roberto Alomar	.25	.11	.03
☐ 234 Scott Fletcher	.05	.02	.01
☐ 235 Tim Naehring	.10	.05	.01
☐ 236 Mike Gallego	.05	.02	.01
☐ 237 Lance Johnson	.10	.05	.01
☐ 238 Paul Molitor	.30	.14	.04
☐ 239 Dan Gladden	.05	.02	.01
☐ 240 Willie Randolph	.10	.05	.01
☐ 241 Will Clark	.25	.11	.03
☐ 242 Sid Bream	.05	.02	.01
☐ 243 Derek Bell	.25	.11	.03
☐ 244 Bill Pecota	.05	.02	.01
☐ 245 Terry Pendleton	.10	.05	.01
☐ 246 Randy Ready	.05	.02	.01
☐ 247 Jack Armstrong	.05	.02	.01
☐ 248 Todd Van Poppel	.05	.02	.01
☐ 249 Shawon Dunston	.05	.02	.01
☐ 250 Bobby Rose	.05	.02	.01
☐ 251 Jeff Huson	.05	.02	.01
☐ 252 Bip Roberts	.05	.02	.01
☐ 253 Doug Jones	.05	.02	.01
☐ 254 Lee Smith	.10	.05	.01
☐ 255 George Brett	.60	.25	.07
☐ 256 Randy Tomlin	.05	.02	.01
☐ 257 Todd Benzinger	.05	.02	.01
☐ 258 Dave Stewart	.10	.05	.01
☐ 259 Mark Carreon	.05	.02	.01
☐ 260 Pete O'Brien	.05	.02	.01
☐ 261 Tim Teufel	.05	.02	.01
☐ 262 Bob Milacki	.05	.02	.01
☐ 263 Mark Guthrie	.05	.02	.01
☐ 264 Darrin Fletcher	.05	.02	.01
☐ 265 Omar Vizquel	.10	.05	.01
☐ 266 Chris Bosio	.05	.02	.01
☐ 267 Jose Canseco	.25	.11	.03
☐ 268 Mike Boddicker	.05	.02	.01
☐ 269 Lance Parrish	.05	.02	.01
☐ 270 Jose Vizcaino	.05	.02	.01
☐ 271 Chris Sabo	.05	.02	.01
☐ 272 Royce Clayton	.10	.05	.01
☐ 273 Marquis Grissom	.10	.05	.01
☐ 274 Fred McGriff	.25	.11	.03
☐ 275 Barry Bonds	.40	.18	.05
☐ 276 Greg Vaughn	.10	.05	.01
☐ 277 Gregg Olson	.05	.02	.01
☐ 278 Dave Hollins	.05	.02	.01
☐ 279 Tom Glavine	.25	.11	.03
☐ 280 Bryan Hickerson UER Name spelled Brian on front	.05	.02	.01
☐ 281 Scott Radinsky	.05	.02	.01
☐ 282 Omar Olivares	.05	.02	.01
☐ 283 Ivan Calderon	.05	.02	.01
☐ 284 Kevin Maas	.05	.02	.01
☐ 285 Mickey Tettleton	.05	.02	.01
☐ 286 Wade Boggs	.25	.11	.03
☐ 287 Stan Belinda	.05	.02	.01
☐ 288 Bret Barberie	.05	.02	.01
☐ 289 Jose Oquendo	.05	.02	.01
☐ 290 Frank Castillo	.10	.05	.01
☐ 291 Dave Stieb	.05	.02	.01
☐ 292 Tommy Greene	.05	.02	.01
☐ 293 Eric Karros	.25	.11	.03
☐ 294 Greg Maddux	1.25	.55	.16
☐ 295 Jim Eisenreich	.05	.02	.01
☐ 296 Rafael Palmeiro	.25	.11	.03
☐ 297 Ramon Martinez	.10	.05	.01
☐ 298 Tim Wallach	.05	.02	.01
☐ 299 Jim Thome	1.25	.55	.16
☐ 300 Chito Martinez	.05	.02	.01
☐ 301 Mitch Williams	.05	.02	.01
☐ 302 Randy Johnson	.25	.11	.03
☐ 303 Carlton Fisk	.25	.11	.03
☐ 304 Travis Fryman	.25	.11	.03
☐ 305 Bobby Witt	.05	.02	.01
☐ 306 Dave Magadan	.05	.02	.01
☐ 307 Alex Cole	.05	.02	.01
☐ 308 Bobby Bonilla	.10	.05	.01
☐ 309 Bryan Harvey	.05	.02	.01
☐ 310 Rafael Belliard	.05	.02	.01
☐ 311 Mariano Duncan	.05	.02	.01
☐ 312 Chuck Crim	.05	.02	.01
☐ 313 John Kruk	.10	.05	.01
☐ 314 Ellis Burks	.10	.05	.01
☐ 315 Craig Biggio	.10	.05	.01
☐ 316 Glenn Davis	.05	.02	.01
☐ 317 Ryne Sandberg	.40	.18	.05
☐ 318 Mike Sharperson	.05	.02	.01
☐ 319 Rich Rodriguez	.05	.02	.01
☐ 320 Lee Guetterman	.05	.02	.01
☐ 321 Benito Santiago	.05	.02	.01
☐ 322 Jose Offerman	.05	.02	.01
☐ 323 Tony Pena	.05	.02	.01
☐ 324 Pat Borders	.05	.02	.01
☐ 325 Mike Henneman	.05	.02	.01
☐ 326 Kevin Brown	.10	.05	.01
☐ 327 Chris Nabholz	.05	.02	.01
☐ 328 Franklin Stubbs	.05	.02	.01
☐ 329 Tino Martinez	.10	.05	.01
☐ 330 Mickey Morandini	.05	.02	.01
☐ 331 Checklist 265-352 Ryne Sandberg	.25	.11	.03
☐ 332 Mark Gubicza	.05	.02	.01
☐ 333 Bill Landrum	.05	.02	.01
☐ 334 Mark Whiten	.10	.05	.01
☐ 335 Darren Daulton	.10	.05	.01
☐ 336 Rick Wilkins	.05	.02	.01
☐ 337 Brian Jordan	.60	.25	.07
☐ 338 Kevin Ward	.05	.02	.01
☐ 339 Ruben Amaro	.05	.02	.01
☐ 340 Trevor Wilson	.05	.02	.01
☐ 341 Andujar Cedeno	.05	.02	.01
☐ 342 Michael Huff	.05	.02	.01
☐ 343 Brady Anderson	.25	.11	.03
☐ 344 Craig Grebeck	.05	.02	.01
☐ 345 Bobby Ojeda	.05	.02	.01
☐ 346 Mike Pagliarulo	.05	.02	.01
☐ 347 Terry Shumpert	.05	.02	.01
☐ 348 Dann Bilardello	.05	.02	.01
☐ 349 Frank Thomas	2.50	1.10	.30
☐ 350 Albert Belle	.75	.35	.09
☐ 351 Jose Mesa	.10	.05	.01
☐ 352 Rich Monteleone	.05	.02	.01
☐ 353 Bob Walk	.05	.02	.01
☐ 354 Monty Fariss	.05	.02	.01
☐ 355 Luis Rivera	.05	.02	.01
☐ 356 Anthony Young	.05	.02	.01
☐ 357 Geno Petralli	.05	.02	.01
☐ 358 Otis Nixon	.05	.02	.01
☐ 359 Tom Pagnozzi	.05	.02	.01
☐ 360 Reggie Sanders	.25	.11	.03
☐ 361 Lee Stevens	.05	.02	.01
☐ 362 Kent Hrbek	.10	.05	.01
☐ 363 Orlando Merced	.05	.02	.01
☐ 364 Mike Bordick	.10	.05	.01
☐ 365 Dion James UER (Blue Jays logo on card back)	.05	.02	.01
☐ 366 Jack Clark	.10	.05	.01
☐ 367 Mike Stanley	.05	.02	.01
☐ 368 Randy Velarde	.05	.02	.01
☐ 369 Dan Pasqua	.05	.02	.01
☐ 370 Pat Listach	.10	.05	.01
☐ 371 Mike Fitzgerald	.05	.02	.01
☐ 372 Tom Foley	.05	.02	.01
☐ 373 Matt Williams	.25	.11	.03
☐ 374 Brian Hunter	.05	.02	.01
☐ 375 Joe Carter	.10	.05	.01
☐ 376 Bret Saberhagen	.10	.05	.01
☐ 377 Mike Stanton	.05	.02	.01
☐ 378 Hubie Brooks	.05	.02	.01
☐ 379 Eric Bell	.05	.02	.01
☐ 380 Walt Weiss	.05	.02	.01
☐ 381 Danny Jackson	.05	.02	.01
☐ 382 Manuel Lee	.05	.02	.01
☐ 383 Ruben Sierra	.10	.05	.01
☐ 384 Greg Swindell	.05	.02	.01
☐ 385 Ryan Bowen	.05	.02	.01
☐ 386 Kevin Ritz	.05	.02	.01
☐ 387 Curtis Wilkerson	.05	.02	.01
☐ 388 Gary Varsho	.05	.02	.01
☐ 389 Dave Hansen	.05	.02	.01
☐ 390 Bob Welch	.05	.02	.01
☐ 391 Lou Whitaker	.10	.05	.01
☐ 392 Ken Griffey Jr.	2.50	1.10	.30
☐ 393 Mike Maddux	.05	.02	.01
☐ 394 Arthur Rhodes	.05	.02	.01
☐ 395 Chili Davis	.10	.05	.01
☐ 396 Eddie Murray	.25	.11	.03
☐ 397 Checklist 353-440 Robin Yount	.10	.05	.01
☐ 398 Dave Cochrane	.05	.02	.01
☐ 399 Kevin Seitzer	.05	.02	.01
☐ 400 Ozzie Smith	.40	.18	.05
☐ 401 Paul Sorrento	.05	.02	.01
☐ 402 Les Lancaster	.05	.02	.01
☐ 403 Junior Noboa	.05	.02	.01
☐ 404 David Justice	.25	.11	.03
☐ 405 Andy Ashby	.10	.05	.01
☐ 406 Danny Tartabull	.05	.02	.01
☐ 407 Bill Swift	.05	.02	.01
☐ 408 Craig Lefferts	.05	.02	.01
☐ 409 Tom Candiotti	.05	.02	.01
☐ 410 Lance Blankenship	.05	.02	.01
☐ 411 Jeff Tackett	.05	.02	.01
☐ 412 Sammy Sosa	.40	.18	.05
☐ 413 Jody Reed	.05	.02	.01
☐ 414 Bruce Ruffin	.05	.02	.01
☐ 415 Gene Larkin	.05	.02	.01
☐ 416 John Vander Wal	.05	.02	.01
☐ 417 Tim Belcher	.05	.02	.01
☐ 418 Steve Frey	.05	.02	.01
☐ 419 Dick Schofield	.05	.02	.01
☐ 420 Jeff King	.10	.05	.01
☐ 421 Kim Batiste	.05	.02	.01
☐ 422 Jack McDowell	.10	.05	.01
☐ 423 Damon Berryhill	.05	.02	.01
☐ 424 Gary Wayne	.05	.02	.01
☐ 425 Jack Morris	.10	.05	.01
☐ 426 Moises Alou	.25	.11	.03
☐ 427 Mark McLemore	.05	.02	.01
☐ 428 Juan Guerrero	.05	.02	.01
☐ 429 Scott Scudder	.05	.02	.01
☐ 430 Eric Davis	.10	.05	.01
☐ 431 Joe Slusarski	.05	.02	.01
☐ 432 Todd Zeile	.05	.02	.01
☐ 433 Dwayne Henry	.05	.02	.01
☐ 434 Cliff Brantley	.05	.02	.01
☐ 435 Butch Henry	.05	.02	.01
☐ 436 Todd Worrell	.05	.02	.01
☐ 437 Bob Scanlan	.05	.02	.01
☐ 438 Wally Joyner	.10	.05	.01
☐ 439 John Flaherty	.05	.02	.01
☐ 440 Brian Downing	.05	.02	.01
☐ 441 Darren Lewis	.05	.02	.01
☐ 442 Gary Carter	.10	.05	.01
☐ 443 Wally Ritchie	.05	.02	.01
☐ 444 Chris Jones	.05	.02	.01
☐ 445 Jeff Kent	.25	.11	.03
☐ 446 Gary Sheffield	.25	.11	.03
☐ 447 Ron Darling	.05	.02	.01
☐ 448 Deion Sanders	.25	.11	.03
☐ 449 Andres Galarraga	.25	.11	.03
☐ 450 Chuck Finley	.05	.02	.01
☐ 451 Derek Lilliquist	.05	.02	.01
☐ 452 Carl Willis	.05	.02	.01
☐ 453 Wes Chamberlain	.05	.02	.01
☐ 454 Roger Mason	.05	.02	.01
☐ 455 Spike Owen	.05	.02	.01
☐ 456 Thomas Howard	.05	.02	.01
☐ 457 Dave Martinez	.05	.02	.01
☐ 458 Pete Incaviglia	.05	.02	.01
☐ 459 Keith A. Miller	.05	.02	.01
☐ 460 Mike Fetters	.05	.02	.01
☐ 461 Paul Gibson	.05	.02	.01
☐ 462 George Bell	.05	.02	.01
☐ 463 Checklist 441-528 Bobby Bonilla	.10	.05	.01
☐ 464 Terry Mulholland	.05	.02	.01
☐ 465 Storm Davis	.05	.02	.01
☐ 466 Gary Pettis	.05	.02	.01
☐ 467 Randy Bush	.05	.02	.01
☐ 468 Ken Hill	.10	.05	.01
☐ 469 Rheal Cormier	.05	.02	.01
☐ 470 Andy Stankiewicz	.05	.02	.01
☐ 471 Dave Burba	.05	.02	.01
☐ 472 Henry Cotto	.05	.02	.01
☐ 473 Dale Sveum	.05	.02	.01
☐ 474 Rich Gossage	.10	.05	.01
☐ 475 William Suero	.05	.02	.01
☐ 476 Doug Strange	.05	.02	.01
☐ 477 Bill Krueger	.05	.02	.01
☐ 478 John Wetteland	.10	.05	.01
☐ 479 Melido Perez	.05	.02	.01
☐ 480 Lonnie Smith	.05	.02	.01
☐ 481 Mike Jackson	.05	.02	.01
☐ 482 Mike Gardiner	.05	.02	.01
☐ 483 David Wells	.05	.02	.01
☐ 484 Barry Jones	.05	.02	.01
☐ 485 Scott Bankhead	.05	.02	.01
☐ 486 Terry Leach	.05	.02	.01
☐ 487 Vince Horsman	.05	.02	.01
☐ 488 Dave Eiland	.05	.02	.01
☐ 489 Alejandro Pena	.05	.02	.01
☐ 490 Julio Valera	.05	.02	.01
☐ 491 Joe Boever	.05	.02	.01
☐ 492 Paul Miller	.05	.02	.01
☐ 493 Archi Cianfrocco	.05	.02	.01
☐ 494 Dave Fleming	.05	.02	.01
☐ 495 Kyle Abbott	.05	.02	.01
☐ 496 Chad Kreuter	.05	.02	.01
☐ 497 Chris James	.05	.02	.01
☐ 498 Donnie Hill	.05	.02	.01
☐ 499 Jacob Brumfield	.05	.02	.01
☐ 500 Ricky Bones	.05	.02	.01
☐ 501 Terry Steinbach	.10	.05	.01
☐ 502 Bernard Gilkey	.10	.05	.01
☐ 503 Dennis Cook	.05	.02	.01
☐ 504 Len Dykstra	.10	.05	.01
☐ 505 Mike Bielecki	.05	.02	.01
☐ 506 Bob Kipper	.05	.02	.01
☐ 507 Jose Melendez	.05	.02	.01
☐ 508 Rick Sutcliffe	.05	.02	.01
☐ 509 Ken Patterson	.05	.02	.01
☐ 510 Andy Allanson	.05	.02	.01
☐ 511 Al Newman	.05	.02	.01
☐ 512 Mark Gardner	.05	.02	.01
☐ 513 Jeff Schaefer	.05	.02	.01
☐ 514 Jim McNamara	.05	.02	.01
☐ 515 Peter Hoy	.05	.02	.01
☐ 516 Curt Schilling	.05	.02	.01
☐ 517 Kirk McCaskill	.05	.02	.01
☐ 518 Chris Gwynn	.05	.02	.01
☐ 519 Sid Fernandez	.05	.02	.01
☐ 520 Jeff Parrett	.05	.02	.01
☐ 521 Scott Ruskin	.05	.02	.01
☐ 522 Kevin McReynolds	.05	.02	.01
☐ 523 Rick Cerone	.05	.02	.01
☐ 524 Jesse Orosco	.05	.02	.01
☐ 525 Troy Afenir	.05	.02	.01
☐ 526 John Smiley	.05	.02	.01
☐ 527 Dale Murphy	.25	.11	.03
☐ 528 Leaf Set Card	.05	.02	.01

1992 Leaf Black Gold

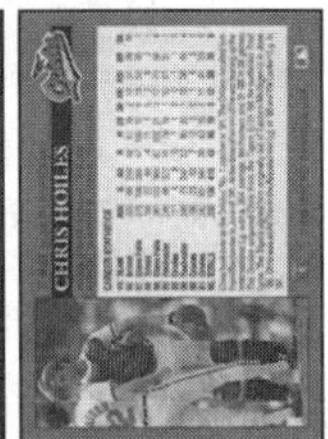

This 528-card standard-size set was issued in two 264-card series. These Black Gold cards were inserted one per foil pack. The cards are similar to the regular issue Leaf cards, except that the card face is black rather than silver and accented by a gold foil inner border. Likewise, the horizontal backs have a gold rather than a silver background. The set is noteworthy as one of the earliest parallel issues in the hobby.

	MINT	NRMT	EXC
COMPLETE SET (528)	80.00	36.00	10.00
COMPLETE SERIES 1 (264)	30.00	13.50	3.70
COMPLETE SERIES 2 (264)	50.00	22.00	6.25
COMMON CARD (1-528)	.10	.05	.01

*B.GOLD STARS: 2.5X TO 5X BASIC CARDS
*B.GOLD YOUNG STARS: 1.5X TO 3X BASIC CARDS

1992 Leaf Gold Rookies

This 24-card standard-size set honors 1992's most promising newcomers. The first 12 cards were randomly inserted in Leaf series I foil packs, while the second 12 cards were featured only in series II packs. The fronts display full-bleed color action photos highlighted by gold foil border stripes. A gold foil diamond appears at the corners of the picture frame, and the player's name appears in a black bar that extends between the bottom two diamonds. The key cards in this set are Kenny Lofton and Raul Mondesi.

	MINT	NRMT	EXC
COMPLETE SET (24)	20.00	9.00	2.50
COMPLETE SERIES 1 (12)	8.00	3.60	1.00
COMPLETE SERIES 2 (12)	12.00	5.50	1.50
COMMON CARD (BC1-BC24)	.25	.11	.03
☐ BC1 Chad Curtis	.50	.23	.06
☐ BC2 Brent Gates	.50	.23	.06
☐ BC3 Pedro Martinez	1.50	.70	.19
☐ BC4 Kenny Lofton	6.00	2.70	.75
☐ BC5 Turk Wendell	.25	.11	.03
☐ BC6 Mark Hutton	.25	.11	.03
☐ BC7 Todd Hundley	1.00	.45	.12
☐ BC8 Matt Stairs	.25	.11	.03
☐ BC9 Eddie Taubensee	.50	.23	.06
☐ BC10 David Nied	.50	.23	.06
☐ BC11 Salomon Torres	.25	.11	.03
☐ BC12 Bret Boone	.50	.23	.06
☐ BC13 Johnny Ruffin	.25	.11	.03
☐ BC14 Ed Martel	.25	.11	.03
☐ BC15 Rick Trlicek	.25	.11	.03
☐ BC16 Raul Mondesi	5.00	2.20	.60
☐ BC17 Pat Mahomes	.25	.11	.03
☐ BC18 Dan Wilson	1.00	.45	.12
☐ BC19 Donovan Osborne	.50	.23	.06
☐ BC20 Dave Silvestri	.25	.11	.03
☐ BC21 Gary DiSarcina	.25	.11	.03
☐ BC22 Denny Neagle	1.50	.70	.19
☐ BC23 Steve Hosey	.25	.11	.03
☐ BC24 John Doherty	.25	.11	.03

1993 Leaf

The 1993 Leaf baseball set consists of three series of 220, 220, and 110 standard-size cards, respectively. Cards were distributed in 14-card foil packs, jumbo packs and magazine packs. The card fronts feature color action photos that are full-bleed except at the bottom

where a diagonal black stripe (gold-foil stamped with the player's name) separates the picture from a team color-coded slate triangle. The Leaf seal embossed with gold foil is superimposed at the lower right corner. There are no key Rookie Cards in this set.

	MINT	NRMT	EXC
COMPLETE SET (550)	40.00	18.00	5.00
COMPLETE SERIES 1 (220)	18.00	8.00	2.20
COMPLETE SERIES 2 (220)	18.00	8.00	2.20
COMPLETE UPDATE (110)	5.00	2.20	.60
COMMON CARD (1-550)	.10	.05	.01
□ 1 Ben McDonald	.10	.05	.01
□ 2 Sid Fernandez	.10	.05	.01
□ 3 Juan Guzman	.20	.09	.03
□ 4 Curt Schilling	.10	.05	.01
□ 5 Ivan Rodriguez	.75	.35	.09
□ 6 Don Slaught	.10	.05	.01
□ 7 Terry Steinbach	.20	.09	.03
□ 8 Todd Zeile	.10	.05	.01
□ 9 Andy Stankiewicz	.10	.05	.01
□ 10 Tim Teufel	.10	.05	.01
□ 11 Marvin Freeman	.10	.05	.01
□ 12 Jim Austin	.10	.05	.01
□ 13 Bob Scanlan	.10	.05	.01
□ 14 Rusty Meacham	.10	.05	.01
□ 15 Casey Candaele	.10	.05	.01
□ 16 Travis Fryman	.20	.09	.03
□ 17 Jose Offerman	.10	.05	.01
□ 18 Albert Belle	1.25	.55	.16
□ 19 John Vander Wal	.10	.05	.01
□ 20 Dan Pasqua	.10	.05	.01
□ 21 Frank Viola	.10	.05	.01
□ 22 Terry Mulholland	.10	.05	.01
□ 23 Gregg Olson	.10	.05	.01
□ 24 Randy Tomlin	.10	.05	.01
□ 25 Todd Stottlemyre	.20	.09	.03
□ 26 Jose Oquendo	.10	.05	.01
□ 27 Julio Franco	.20	.09	.03
□ 28 Tony Gwynn	1.25	.55	.16
□ 29 Ruben Sierra	.20	.09	.03
□ 30 Robby Thompson	.10	.05	.01
□ 31 Jim Bullinger	.10	.05	.01
□ 32 Rick Aguilera	.10	.05	.01
□ 33 Scott Servais	.10	.05	.01
□ 34 Cal Eldred	.10	.05	.01
□ 35 Mike Piazza	3.00	1.35	.35
□ 36 Brent Mayne	.10	.05	.01
□ 37 Wil Cordero	.20	.09	.03
□ 38 Milt Cuyler	.10	.05	.01
□ 39 Howard Johnson	.10	.05	.01
□ 40 Kenny Lofton	1.25	.55	.16
□ 41 Alex Fernandez	.20	.09	.03
□ 42 Denny Neagle	.20	.09	.03
□ 43 Tony Pena	.10	.05	.01
□ 44 Bob Tewksbury	.10	.05	.01
□ 45 Glenn Davis	.10	.05	.01
□ 46 Fred McGriff	.30	.14	.04
□ 47 John Olerud	.10	.05	.01
□ 48 Steve Hosey	.10	.05	.01
□ 49 Rafael Palmeiro	.30	.14	.04
□ 50 David Justice	.30	.14	.04
□ 51 Pete Harnisch	.10	.05	.01
□ 52 Sam Militello	.10	.05	.01
□ 53 Orel Hershiser	.20	.09	.03
□ 54 Pat Mahomes	.10	.05	.01
□ 55 Greg Colbrunn	.10	.05	.01
□ 56 Greg Vaughn	.20	.09	.03
□ 57 Vince Coleman	.10	.05	.01
□ 58 Brian McRae	.20	.09	.03
□ 59 Len Dykstra	.20	.09	.03
□ 60 Dan Gladden	.10	.05	.01
□ 61 Ted Power	.10	.05	.01
□ 62 Donovan Osborne	.10	.05	.01
□ 63 Ron Karkovice	.10	.05	.01
□ 64 Frank Seminara	.10	.05	.01
□ 65 Bob Zupcic	.10	.05	.01
□ 66 Kirt Manwaring	.10	.05	.01
□ 67 Mike Devereaux	.10	.05	.01
□ 68 Mark Lemke	.10	.05	.01
□ 69 Devon White	.10	.05	.01
□ 70 Sammy Sosa	.30	.14	.04
□ 71 Pedro Astacio	.10	.05	.01
□ 72 Dennis Eckersley	.20	.09	.03
□ 73 Chris Nabholz	.10	.05	.01
□ 74 Melido Perez	.10	.05	.01
□ 75 Todd Hundley	.20	.09	.03
□ 76 Kent Hrbek	.20	.09	.03
□ 77 Mickey Morandini	.10	.05	.01
□ 78 Tim McIntosh	.10	.05	.01
□ 79 Andy Van Slyke	.20	.09	.03
□ 80 Kevin McReynolds	.10	.05	.01

□ 81 Mike Henneman	.10	.05	.01
□ 82 Greg W. Harris	.10	.05	.01
□ 83 Sandy Alomar Jr.	.20	.09	.03
□ 84 Mike Jackson	.10	.05	.01
□ 85 Ozzie Guillen	.10	.05	.01
□ 86 Jeff Blauser	.10	.05	.01
□ 87 John Valentin	.20	.09	.03
□ 88 Rey Sanchez	.10	.05	.01
□ 89 Rick Sutcliffe	.10	.05	.01
□ 90 Luis Gonzalez	.10	.05	.01
□ 91 Jeff Fassero	.20	.09	.03
□ 92 Kenny Rogers	.10	.05	.01
□ 93 Bret Saberhagen	.20	.09	.03
□ 94 Bob Welch	.10	.05	.01
□ 95 Darren Daulton	.20	.09	.03
□ 96 Mike Gallego	.10	.05	.01
□ 97 Orlando Merced	.20	.09	.03
□ 98 Chuck Knoblauch	.30	.14	.04
□ 99 Bernard Gilkey	.20	.09	.03
□ 100 Billy Ashley	.10	.05	.01
□ 101 Kevin Appier	.20	.09	.03
□ 102 Jeff Brantley	.10	.05	.01
□ 103 Bill Gullickson	.10	.05	.01
□ 104 John Smoltz	.30	.14	.04
□ 105 Paul Sorrento	.10	.05	.01
□ 106 Steve Buechele	.10	.05	.01
□ 107 Steve Sax	.10	.05	.01
□ 108 Andujar Cedeno	.10	.05	.01
□ 109 Billy Hatcher	.10	.05	.01
□ 110 Checklist	.10	.05	.01
□ 111 Alan Mills	.10	.05	.01
□ 112 John Franco	.10	.05	.01
□ 113 Jack Morris	.20	.09	.03
□ 114 Mitch Williams	.10	.05	.01
□ 115 Nolan Ryan	2.50	1.10	.30
□ 116 Jay Bell	.20	.09	.03
□ 117 Mike Bordick	.10	.05	.01
□ 118 Geronimo Pena	.10	.05	.01
□ 119 Danny Tartabull	.10	.05	.01
□ 120 Checklist	.10	.05	.01
□ 121 Steve Avery	.20	.09	.03
□ 122 Ricky Bones	.10	.05	.01
□ 123 Mike Morgan	.10	.05	.01
□ 124 Jeff Montgomery	.20	.09	.03
□ 125 Jeff Bagwell	1.25	.55	.16
□ 126 Tony Phillips	.20	.09	.03
□ 127 Lenny Harris	.10	.05	.01
□ 128 Glenallen Hill	.10	.05	.01
□ 129 Marquis Grissom	.20	.09	.03
□ 130 Gerald Williams UER (Bernie Williams picture and stats)	.10	.05	.01
□ 131 Greg A. Harris	.10	.05	.01
□ 132 Tommy Greene	.10	.05	.01
□ 133 Chris Hoiles	.10	.05	.01
□ 134 Bob Walk	.10	.05	.01
□ 135 Duane Ward	.10	.05	.01
□ 136 Tom Pagnozzi	.10	.05	.01
□ 137 Jeff Huson	.10	.05	.01
□ 138 Kurt Stillwell	.10	.05	.01
□ 139 Dave Henderson	.10	.05	.01
□ 140 Darrin Jackson	.10	.05	.01
□ 141 Frank Castillo	.10	.05	.01
□ 142 Scott Erickson	.10	.05	.01
□ 143 Darryl Kile	.10	.05	.01
□ 144 Bill Wegman	.10	.05	.01
□ 145 Steve Wilson	.10	.05	.01
□ 146 George Brett	1.25	.55	.16
□ 147 Moises Alou	.20	.09	.03
□ 148 Lou Whitaker	.20	.09	.03
□ 149 Chico Walker	.10	.05	.01
□ 150 Jerry Browne	.10	.05	.01
□ 151 Kirk McCaskill	.10	.05	.01
□ 152 Zane Smith	.10	.05	.01
□ 153 Matt Young	.10	.05	.01
□ 154 Lee Smith	.20	.09	.03
□ 155 Leo Gomez	.10	.05	.01
□ 156 Dan Walters	.10	.05	.01
□ 157 Pat Borders	.10	.05	.01
□ 158 Matt Williams	.30	.14	.04
□ 159 Dean Palmer	.20	.09	.03
□ 160 John Patterson	.10	.05	.01
□ 161 Doug Jones	.10	.05	.01
□ 162 John Habyan	.10	.05	.01
□ 163 Pedro Martinez	.30	.14	.04
□ 164 Carl Willis	.10	.05	.01
□ 165 Darrin Fletcher	.10	.05	.01
□ 166 B.J. Surhoff	.20	.09	.03
□ 167 Eddie Murray	.75	.35	.09
□ 168 Keith Miller	.10	.05	.01
□ 169 Ricky Jordan	.10	.05	.01
□ 170 Juan Gonzalez	1.50	.70	.19
□ 171 Charles Nagy	.20	.09	.03
□ 172 Mark Clark	.10	.05	.01
□ 173 Bobby Thigpen	.10	.05	.01
□ 174 Tim Scott	.10	.05	.01
□ 175 Scott Cooper	.10	.05	.01
□ 176 Royce Clayton	.20	.09	.03
□ 177 Brady Anderson	.30	.14	.04
□ 178 Sid Bream	.10	.05	.01
□ 179 Derek Bell	.20	.09	.03
□ 180 Otis Nixon	.10	.05	.01
□ 181 Kevin Gross	.10	.05	.01
□ 182 Ron Darling	.10	.05	.01
□ 183 John Wetteland	.20	.09	.03

□ 184 Mike Stanley	.10	.05	.01
□ 185 Jeff Kent	.20	.09	.03
□ 186 Brian Harper	.10	.05	.01
□ 187 Mariano Duncan	.10	.05	.01
□ 188 Robin Yount	.30	.14	.04
□ 189 Al Martin	.20	.09	.03
□ 190 Eddie Zosky	.10	.05	.01
□ 191 Mike Munoz	.10	.05	.01
□ 192 Andy Benes	.20	.09	.03
□ 193 Dennis Cook	.10	.05	.01
□ 194 Bill Swift	.10	.05	.01
□ 195 Frank Thomas	3.00	1.35	.35
□ 196 Damon Berryhill	.10	.05	.01
□ 197 Mike Greenwell	.10	.05	.01
□ 198 Mark Grace	.30	.14	.04
□ 199 Darryl Hamilton	.10	.05	.01
□ 200 Derrick May	.10	.05	.01
□ 201 Ken Hill	.20	.09	.03
□ 202 Kevin Brown	.20	.09	.03
□ 203 Dwight Gooden	.20	.09	.03
□ 204 Bobby Witt	.10	.05	.01
□ 205 Juan Bell	.10	.05	.01
□ 206 Kevin Maas	.10	.05	.01
□ 207 Jeff King	.20	.09	.03
□ 208 Scott Leius	.10	.05	.01
□ 209 Rheal Cormier	.10	.05	.01
□ 210 Darryl Strawberry	.20	.09	.03
□ 211 Tom Gordon	.10	.05	.01
□ 212 Bud Black	.10	.05	.01
□ 213 Mickey Tettleton	.10	.05	.01
□ 214 Pete Smith	.10	.05	.01
□ 215 Felix Fermin	.10	.05	.01
□ 216 Rick Wilkins	.10	.05	.01
□ 217 George Bell	.10	.05	.01
□ 218 Eric Anthony	.10	.05	.01
□ 219 Pedro Munoz	.10	.05	.01
□ 220 Checklist	.10	.05	.01
□ 221 Lance Blankenship	.10	.05	.01
□ 222 Deion Sanders	.30	.14	.04
□ 223 Craig Biggio	.20	.09	.03
□ 224 Ryne Sandberg	.75	.35	.09
□ 225 Ron Gant	.20	.09	.03
□ 226 Tom Brunansky	.10	.05	.01
□ 227 Chad Curtis	.20	.09	.03
□ 228 Joe Carter	.20	.09	.03
□ 229 Brian Jordan	.30	.14	.04
□ 230 Brett Butler	.20	.09	.03
□ 231 Frank Bolick	.10	.05	.01
□ 232 Rod Beck	.20	.09	.03
□ 233 Carlos Baerga	.20	.09	.03
□ 234 Eric Karros	.30	.14	.04
□ 235 Jack Armstrong	.10	.05	.01
□ 236 Bobby Bonilla	.20	.09	.03
□ 237 Don Mattingly	1.50	.70	.19
□ 238 Jeff Gardner	.10	.05	.01
□ 239 Dave Hollins	.10	.05	.01
□ 240 Steve Cooke	.10	.05	.01
□ 241 Jose Canseco	.30	.14	.04
□ 242 Ivan Calderon	.10	.05	.01
□ 243 Tim Belcher	.10	.05	.01
□ 244 Freddie Benavides	.10	.05	.01
□ 245 Roberto Alomar	.60	.25	.07
□ 246 Rob Deer	.10	.05	.01
□ 247 Will Clark	.30	.14	.04
□ 248 Mike Felder	.10	.05	.01
□ 249 Harold Baines	.20	.09	.03
□ 250 David Cone	.20	.09	.03
□ 251 Mark Guthrie	.10	.05	.01
□ 252 Ellis Burks	.20	.09	.03
□ 253 Jim Abbott	.10	.05	.01
□ 254 Chili Davis	.20	.09	.03
□ 255 Chris Bosio	.10	.05	.01
□ 256 Bret Barberie	.10	.05	.01
□ 257 Hal Morris	.10	.05	.01
□ 258 Dante Bichette	.30	.14	.04
□ 259 Storm Davis	.10	.05	.01
□ 260 Gary DiSarcina	.10	.05	.01
□ 261 Ken Caminiti	.30	.14	.04
□ 262 Paul Molitor	.60	.25	.07
□ 263 Joe Oliver	.10	.05	.01
□ 264 Pat Listach	.10	.05	.01
□ 265 Gregg Jefferies	.20	.09	.03
□ 266 Jose Guzman	.10	.05	.01
□ 267 Eric Davis	.20	.09	.03
□ 268 Delino DeShields	.10	.05	.01
□ 269 Barry Bonds	.75	.35	.09
□ 270 Mike Bielecki	.10	.05	.01
□ 271 Jay Buhner	.30	.14	.04
□ 272 Scott Pose	.10	.05	.01
□ 273 Tony Fernandez	.10	.05	.01
□ 274 Chito Martinez	.10	.05	.01
□ 275 Phil Plantier	.10	.05	.01
□ 276 Pete Incaviglia	.10	.05	.01
□ 277 Carlos Garcia	.10	.05	.01
□ 278 Tom Henke	.10	.05	.01
□ 279 Roger Clemens	.60	.25	.07
□ 280 Rob Dibble	.10	.05	.01
□ 281 Daryl Boston	.10	.05	.01
□ 282 Greg Gagne	.10	.05	.01
□ 283 Cecil Fielder	.20	.09	.03
□ 284 Carlton Fisk	.30	.14	.04
□ 285 Wade Boggs	.30	.14	.04
□ 286 Damion Easley	.10	.05	.01
□ 287 Norm Charlton	.10	.05	.01
□ 288 Jeff Conine	.20	.09	.03

□ 289 Roberto Kelly	.10	.05	.01
□ 290 Jerald Clark	.10	.05	.01
□ 291 Rickey Henderson	.30	.14	.04
□ 292 Chuck Finley	.10	.05	.01
□ 293 Doug Drabek	.10	.05	.01
□ 294 Dave Stewart	.20	.09	.03
□ 295 Tom Glavine	.30	.14	.04
□ 296 Jaime Navarro	.10	.05	.01
□ 297 Ray Lankford	.20	.09	.03
□ 298 Greg Hibbard	.10	.05	.01
□ 299 Jody Reed	.10	.05	.01
□ 300 Dennis Martinez	.20	.09	.03
□ 301 Dave Martinez	.10	.05	.01
□ 302 Reggie Jefferson	.20	.09	.03
□ 303 John Cummings	.10	.05	.01
□ 304 Orestes Destrade	.10	.05	.01
□ 305 Mike Maddux	.10	.05	.01
□ 306 David Segui	.10	.05	.01
□ 307 Gary Sheffield	.30	.14	.04
□ 308 Danny Jackson	.10	.05	.01
□ 309 Craig Lefferts	.10	.05	.01
□ 310 Andre Dawson	.20	.09	.03
□ 311 Barry Larkin	.30	.14	.04
□ 312 Alex Cole	.10	.05	.01
□ 313 Mark Gardner	.10	.05	.01
□ 314 Kirk Gibson	.20	.09	.03
□ 315 Shane Mack	.10	.05	.01
□ 316 Bo Jackson	.20	.09	.03
□ 317 Jimmy Key	.20	.09	.03
□ 318 Greg Myers	.10	.05	.01
□ 319 Ken Griffey Jr.	3.00	1.35	.35
□ 320 Monty Fariss	.10	.05	.01
□ 321 Kevin Mitchell	.20	.09	.03
□ 322 Andres Galarraga	.30	.14	.04
□ 323 Mark McGwire	1.00	.45	.12
□ 324 Mark Langston	.20	.09	.03
□ 325 Steve Finley	.20	.09	.03
□ 326 Greg Maddux	2.00	.90	.25
□ 327 Dave Nilsson	.20	.09	.03
□ 328 Ozzie Smith	.75	.35	.09
□ 329 Candy Maldonado	.10	.05	.01
□ 330 Checklist	.10	.05	.01
□ 331 Tim Pugh	.10	.05	.01
□ 332 Joe Girardi	.10	.05	.01
□ 333 Junior Felix	.10	.05	.01
□ 334 Greg Swindell	.10	.05	.01
□ 335 Ramon Martinez	.20	.09	.03
□ 336 Sean Berry	.10	.05	.01
□ 337 Joe Orsulak	.10	.05	.01
□ 338 Wes Chamberlain	.10	.05	.01
□ 339 Stan Belinda	.10	.05	.01
□ 340 Checklist UER (306 Luis Mercedes)	.10	.05	.01
□ 341 Bruce Hurst	.10	.05	.01
□ 342 John Burkett	.10	.05	.01
□ 343 Mike Mussina	.60	.25	.07
□ 344 Scott Fletcher	.10	.05	.01
□ 345 Rene Gonzales	.10	.05	.01
□ 346 Roberto Hernandez	.20	.09	.03
□ 347 Carlos Martinez	.10	.05	.01
□ 348 Bill Krueger	.10	.05	.01
□ 349 Felix Jose	.10	.05	.01
□ 350 John Jaha	.30	.14	.04
□ 351 Willie Banks	.10	.05	.01
□ 352 Matt Nokes	.10	.05	.01
□ 353 Kevin Seitzer	.10	.05	.01
□ 354 Erik Hanson	.10	.05	.01
□ 355 David Hulse	.10	.05	.01
□ 356 Domingo Martinez	.10	.05	.01
□ 357 Greg Olson	.10	.05	.01
□ 358 Randy Myers	.20	.09	.03
□ 359 Tom Browning	.10	.05	.01
□ 360 Charlie Hayes	.10	.05	.01
□ 361 Bryan Harvey	.10	.05	.01
□ 362 Eddie Taubensee	.10	.05	.01
□ 363 Tim Wallach	.10	.05	.01
□ 364 Mel Rojas	.20	.09	.03
□ 365 Frank Tanana	.10	.05	.01
□ 366 John Kruk	.20	.09	.03
□ 367 Tim Laker	.10	.05	.01
□ 368 Rich Rodriguez	.10	.05	.01
□ 369 Darren Lewis	.10	.05	.01
□ 370 Harold Reynolds	.10	.05	.01
□ 371 Jose Melendez	.10	.05	.01
□ 372 Joe Grahe	.10	.05	.01
□ 373 Lance Johnson	.20	.09	.03
□ 374 Jose Mesa	.20	.09	.03
□ 375 Scott Livingstone	.10	.05	.01
□ 376 Wally Joyner	.20	.09	.03
□ 377 Kevin Reimer	.10	.05	.01
□ 378 Kirby Puckett	1.25	.55	.16
□ 379 Paul O'Neill	.20	.09	.03
□ 380 Randy Johnson	.30	.14	.04
□ 381 Manuel Lee	.10	.05	.01
□ 382 Dick Schofield	.10	.05	.01
□ 383 Darren Holmes	.10	.05	.01
□ 384 Charlie Hough	.10	.05	.01
□ 385 John Orton	.10	.05	.01
□ 386 Edgar Martinez	.20	.09	.03
□ 387 Terry Pendleton	.20	.09	.03
□ 388 Dan Plesac	.10	.05	.01
□ 389 Jeff Reardon	.20	.09	.03
□ 390 David Nied	.10	.05	.01
□ 391 Dave Magadan	.10	.05	.01
□ 392 Larry Walker	.30	.14	.04

	MINT	NRMT	EXC
☐ 393 Ben Rivera	.10	.05	.01
☐ 394 Lonnie Smith	.10	.05	.01
☐ 395 Craig Shipley	.10	.05	.01
☐ 396 Willie McGee	.10	.05	.01
☐ 397 Arthur Rhodes	.10	.05	.01
☐ 398 Mike Stanton	.10	.05	.01
☐ 399 Luis Polonia	.10	.05	.01
☐ 400 Jack McDowell	.20	.09	.03
☐ 401 Mike Moore	.10	.05	.01
☐ 402 Jose Lind	.10	.05	.01
☐ 403 Bill Spiers	.10	.05	.01
☐ 404 Kevin Tapani	.10	.05	.01
☐ 405 Spike Owen	.10	.05	.01
☐ 406 Tino Martinez	.20	.09	.03
☐ 407 Charlie Leibrandt	.10	.05	.01
☐ 408 Ed Sprague	.20	.09	.03
☐ 409 Bryn Smith	.10	.05	.01
☐ 410 Benito Santiago	.10	.05	.01
☐ 411 Jose Rijo	.10	.05	.01
☐ 412 Pete O'Brien	.10	.05	.01
☐ 413 Willie Wilson	.10	.05	.01
☐ 414 Bip Roberts	.10	.05	.01
☐ 415 Eric Young	.30	.14	.04
☐ 416 Walt Weiss	.10	.05	.01
☐ 417 Milt Thompson	.10	.05	.01
☐ 418 Chris Sabo	.10	.05	.01
☐ 419 Scott Sanderson	.10	.05	.01
☐ 420 Tim Raines	.30	.14	.04
☐ 421 Alan Trammell	.30	.14	.04
☐ 422 Mike Macfarlane	.10	.05	.01
☐ 423 Dave Winfield	.30	.14	.04
☐ 424 Bob Wickman	.10	.05	.01
☐ 425 David Valle	.10	.05	.01
☐ 426 Gary Redus	.10	.05	.01
☐ 427 Turner Ward	.10	.05	.01
☐ 428 Reggie Sanders	.30	.14	.04
☐ 429 Todd Worrell	.10	.05	.01
☐ 430 Julio Valera	.10	.05	.01
☐ 431 Cal Ripken Jr.	2.50	1.10	.30
☐ 432 Mo Vaughn	.75	.35	.09
☐ 433 John Smiley	.10	.05	.01
☐ 434 Omar Vizquel	.20	.09	.03
☐ 435 Billy Ripken	.10	.05	.01
☐ 436 Cory Snyder	.10	.05	.01
☐ 437 Carlos Quintana	.10	.05	.01
☐ 438 Omar Olivares	.10	.05	.01
☐ 439 Robin Ventura	.20	.09	.03
☐ 440 Checklist	.10	.05	.01
☐ 441 Kevin Higgins	.10	.05	.01
☐ 442 Carlos Hernandez	.10	.05	.01
☐ 443 Dan Peltier	.10	.05	.01
☐ 444 Derek Lilliquist	.10	.05	.01
☐ 445 Tim Salmon	.75	.35	.09
☐ 446 Sherman Obando	.10	.05	.01
☐ 447 Pat Kelly	.10	.05	.01
☐ 448 Todd Van Poppel	.10	.05	.01
☐ 449 Mark Whiten	.10	.05	.01
☐ 450 Checklist	.10	.05	.01
☐ 451 Pat Meares	.20	.09	.03
☐ 452 Tony Tarasco	.20	.09	.03
☐ 453 Chris Gwynn	.10	.05	.01
☐ 454 Armando Reynoso	.10	.05	.01
☐ 455 Danny Darwin	.10	.05	.01
☐ 456 Willie Greene	.20	.09	.03
☐ 457 Mike Blowers	.10	.05	.01
☐ 458 Kevin Roberson	.10	.05	.01
☐ 459 Graeme Lloyd	.10	.05	.01
☐ 460 David West	.10	.05	.01
☐ 461 Joey Cora	.20	.09	.03
☐ 462 Alex Arias	.10	.05	.01
☐ 463 Chad Kreuter	.10	.05	.01
☐ 464 Mike Lansing	.20	.09	.03
☐ 465 Mike Timlin	.10	.05	.01
☐ 466 Paul Wagner	.10	.05	.01
☐ 467 Mark Portugal	.10	.05	.01
☐ 468 Jim Leyritz	.10	.05	.01
☐ 469 Ryan Klesko	1.00	.45	.12
☐ 470 Mario Diaz	.10	.05	.01
☐ 471 Guillermo Velasquez	.10	.05	.01
☐ 472 Fernando Valenzuela	.20	.09	.03
☐ 473 Raul Mondesi	1.00	.45	.12
☐ 474 Mike Pagliarulo	.10	.05	.01
☐ 475 Chris Hammond	.10	.05	.01
☐ 476 Torey Lovullo	.10	.05	.01
☐ 477 Trevor Wilson	.10	.05	.01
☐ 478 Marcos Armas	.10	.05	.01
☐ 479 Dave Gallagher	.10	.05	.01
☐ 480 Jeff Treadway	.10	.05	.01
☐ 481 Jeff Branson	.10	.05	.01
☐ 482 Dickie Thon	.10	.05	.01
☐ 483 Eduardo Perez	.10	.05	.01
☐ 484 David Wells	.10	.05	.01
☐ 485 Brian Williams	.10	.05	.01
☐ 486 Domingo Cedeno	.10	.05	.01
☐ 487 Tom Candiotti	.10	.05	.01
☐ 488 Steve Frey	.10	.05	.01
☐ 489 Greg McMichael	.20	.09	.03
☐ 490 Marc Newfield	.20	.09	.03
☐ 491 Larry Andersen	.10	.05	.01
☐ 492 Damon Buford	.10	.05	.01
☐ 493 Ricky Gutierrez	.10	.05	.01
☐ 494 Jeff Russell	.10	.05	.01
☐ 495 Vinny Castilla	.30	.14	.04
☐ 496 Wilson Alvarez	.20	.09	.03
☐ 497 Scott Bullett	.10	.05	.01
☐ 498 Larry Casian	.10	.05	.01
☐ 499 Jose Vizcaino	.10	.05	.01
☐ 500 J.T. Snow	.30	.14	.04
☐ 501 Bryan Hickerson	.10	.05	.01
☐ 502 Jeremy Hernandez	.10	.05	.01
☐ 503 Jeromy Burnitz	.10	.05	.01
☐ 504 Steve Farr	.10	.05	.01
☐ 505 J. Owens	.20	.09	.03
☐ 506 Craig Paquette	.10	.05	.01
☐ 507 Jim Eisenreich	.20	.09	.03
☐ 508 Matt Whiteside	.10	.05	.01
☐ 509 Luis Aquino	.10	.05	.01
☐ 510 Mike LaValliere	.10	.05	.01
☐ 511 Jim Gott	.10	.05	.01
☐ 512 Mark McLemore	.10	.05	.01
☐ 513 Randy Milligan	.10	.05	.01
☐ 514 Gary Gaetti	.20	.09	.03
☐ 515 Lou Frazier	.10	.05	.01
☐ 516 Rich Amaral	.10	.05	.01
☐ 517 Gene Harris	.10	.05	.01
☐ 518 Aaron Sele	.20	.09	.03
☐ 519 Mark Wohlers	.20	.09	.03
☐ 520 Scott Kamieniecki	.10	.05	.01
☐ 521 Kent Mercker	.10	.05	.01
☐ 522 Jim Deshaies	.10	.05	.01
☐ 523 Kevin Stocker	.20	.09	.03
☐ 524 Jason Bere	.20	.09	.03
☐ 525 Tim Bogar	.10	.05	.01
☐ 526 Brad Pennington	.10	.05	.01
☐ 527 Curt Leskanic	.10	.05	.01
☐ 528 Wayne Kirby	.10	.05	.01
☐ 529 Tim Costo	.10	.05	.01
☐ 530 Doug Henry	.10	.05	.01
☐ 531 Trevor Hoffman	.30	.14	.04
☐ 532 Kelly Gruber	.10	.05	.01
☐ 533 Mike Harkey	.10	.05	.01
☐ 534 John Doherty	.10	.05	.01
☐ 535 Erik Pappas	.10	.05	.01
☐ 536 Brent Gates	.20	.09	.03
☐ 537 Roger McDowell	.10	.05	.01
☐ 538 Chris Haney	.10	.05	.01
☐ 539 Blas Minor	.10	.05	.01
☐ 540 Pat Hentgen	.30	.14	.04
☐ 541 Chuck Carr	.10	.05	.01
☐ 542 Doug Strange	.10	.05	.01
☐ 543 Xavier Hernandez	.10	.05	.01
☐ 544 Paul Quantrill	.10	.05	.01
☐ 545 Anthony Young	.10	.05	.01
☐ 546 Bret Boone	.20	.09	.03
☐ 547 Dwight Smith	.10	.05	.01
☐ 548 Bobby Munoz	.10	.05	.01
☐ 549 Russ Springer	.10	.05	.01
☐ 550 Roger Pavlik	.20	.09	.03
☐ DW Dave Winfield 3000 Hits	1.00	.45	.12
☐ FT Frank Thomas AU/3500 (Certified autograph)	250.00	110.00	31.00

1993 Leaf Fasttrack

These 20 standard-size cards, featuring a selection of talented young stars, were randomly inserted into 1993 Leaf retail packs; the first ten were series I inserts, the second ten were series II inserts. The fronts feature borderless color player action photos, except in the lower right corner, where an oblique white stripe carries the motion-streaked set title.

	MINT	NRMT	EXC
COMPLETE SET (20)	100.00	45.00	12.50
COMPLETE SERIES 1 (10)	60.00	27.00	7.50
COMPLETE SERIES 2 (10)	40.00	18.00	5.00
COMMON CARD (1-20)	2.00	.90	.25
☐ 1 Frank Thomas	40.00	18.00	5.00
☐ 2 Tim Wakefield	2.00	.90	.25
☐ 3 Kenny Lofton	15.00	6.75	1.85
☐ 4 Mike Mussina	8.00	3.60	1.00
☐ 5 Juan Gonzalez	20.00	9.00	2.50
☐ 6 Chuck Knoblauch	6.00	2.70	.75
☐ 7 Eric Karros	4.00	1.80	.50
☐ 8 Ray Lankford	3.00	1.35	.35
☐ 9 Juan Guzman	2.00	.90	.25
☐ 10 Pat Listach	2.00	.90	.25
☐ 11 Carlos Baerga	2.00	.90	.25
☐ 12 Felix Jose	2.00	.90	.25
☐ 13 Steve Avery	2.00	.90	.25
☐ 14 Robin Ventura	3.00	1.35	.35
☐ 15 Ivan Rodriguez	10.00	4.50	1.25
☐ 16 Cal Eldred	2.00	.90	.25
☐ 17 Jeff Bagwell	15.00	6.75	1.85
☐ 18 David Justice	3.00	1.35	.35
☐ 19 Travis Fryman	3.00	1.35	.35
☐ 20 Marquis Grissom	3.00	1.35	.35

1993 Leaf Gold All-Stars

These 30 standard-size dual-sided cards feature members of the American and National league All-Star squads. The first 20 were inserted one per 1993 Leaf jumbo packs; the first ten were series I inserts, the second ten were series II inserts. The final ten cards were randomly inserted in 1993 Leaf Update packs. The card design features full color action photos with a diagonal stripe at the base.

	MINT	NRMT	EXC
COMPLETE REG.SET (20)	40.00	18.00	5.00
COMPLETE UPDATE SET (10)	12.00	5.50	1.50
COMMON REG.CARD (R1-R20)	.50	.23	.06
COMMON UPDATE CARD (U1-U10)	.50	.23	.06
☐ R1 Ivan Rodriguez Darren Daulton	1.00	.45	.12
☐ R2 Don Mattingly Fred McGriff	3.00	1.35	.35
☐ R3 Cecil Fielder Jeff Bagwell	3.00	1.35	.35
☐ R4 Carlos Baerga Ryne Sandberg	2.50	1.10	.30
☐ R5 Chuck Knoblauch Delino DeShields	1.00	.45	.12
☐ R6 Robin Ventura Terry Pendleton	.50	.23	.06
☐ R7 Ken Griffey Jr. Andy Van Slyke	5.00	2.20	.60
☐ R8 Joe Carter Dave Justice	1.00	.45	.12
☐ R9 Jose Canseco Tony Gwynn	3.00	1.35	.35
☐ R10 Dennis Eckersley Rob Dibble	.50	.23	.06
☐ R11 Mark McGwire Will Clark	2.00	.90	.25
☐ R12 Frank Thomas Mark Grace	5.00	2.20	.60
☐ R13 Roberto Alomar Craig Biggio	1.25	.55	.16
☐ R14 Cal Ripken Barry Larkin	5.00	2.20	.60
☐ R15 Edgar Martinez Gary Sheffield	1.00	.45	.12
☐ R16 Juan Gonzalez Barry Bonds	4.00	1.80	.50
☐ R17 Kirby Puckett Marquis Grissom	3.00	1.35	.35
☐ R18 Jim Abbott Tom Glavine	1.00	.45	.12
☐ R19 Nolan Ryan Greg Maddux	10.00	4.50	1.25
☐ R20 Roger Clemens Doug Drabek	1.00	.45	.12
☐ U1 Mark Langston Terry Mulholland	.50	.23	.06
☐ U2 Ivan Rodriguez Darren Daulton	1.00	.45	.12
☐ U3 John Olerud John Kruk	.50	.23	.06
☐ U4 Roberto Alomar Ryne Sandberg	2.50	1.10	.30
☐ U5 Wade Boggs Gary Sheffield	1.00	.45	.12
☐ U6 Cal Ripken Barry Larkin	5.00	2.20	.60
☐ U7 Kirby Puckett Bobby Bonds	3.00	1.35	.35
☐ U8 Ken Griffey Jr. Marquis Grissom	5.00	2.20	.60
☐ U9 Joe Carter David Justice	1.00	.45	.12
☐ U10 Paul Molitor Mark Grace	1.00	.45	.12

1993 Leaf Gold Rookies

These cards of promising newcomers were randomly inserted into 1993 Leaf packs; the first ten in series I, the last ten in series II, and five in the Update product. The front of each standard-size card features a borderless color player action shot. The player's name appears in white cursive lettering within a wide gray lithic stripe near the bottom, which is set off by gold-foil lines and carries the set's title in simulated bas-relief. Leaf produced jumbo (3 1/2 by 5 inch) versions for retail repacks; they are valued at approximately double the prices below.

	MINT	NRMT	EXC
COMPLETE REG.SET (20)	40.00	18.00	5.00
COMPLETE UPDATE SET (5)	20.00	9.00	2.50
COMMON REG.CARD (R1-R20)	1.00	.45	.12
COMMON UPDATE CARD (U1-U5)	.75	.35	.09

	MINT	NRMT	EXC
☐ R1 Kevin Young	1.00	.45	.12
☐ R2 Wil Cordero	1.50	.70	.19
☐ R3 Mark Kiefer	1.00	.45	.12
☐ R4 Gerald Williams	1.00	.45	.12
☐ R5 Brandon Wilson	1.00	.45	.12
☐ R6 Greg Gohr	1.00	.45	.12
☐ R7 Ryan Thompson	1.00	.45	.12
☐ R8 Tim Wakefield	1.50	.70	.19
☐ R9 Troy Neel	1.00	.45	.12
☐ R10 Tim Salmon	8.00	3.60	1.00
☐ R11 Kevin Rogers	1.00	.45	.12
☐ R12 Rod Bolton	1.00	.45	.12
☐ R13 Ken Ryan	1.00	.45	.12
☐ R14 Phil Hiatt	1.00	.45	.12
☐ R15 Rene Arocha	1.00	.45	.12
☐ R16 Nigel Wilson	1.00	.45	.12
☐ R17 J.T. Snow	1.50	.70	.19
☐ R18 Benji Gil	1.00	.45	.12
☐ R19 Chipper Jones	30.00	13.50	3.70
☐ R20 Darrell Sherman	1.00	.45	.12
☐ U1 Allen Watson	1.50	.70	.19
☐ U2 Jeffrey Hammonds	1.50	.70	.19
☐ U3 Dave McCarty	.75	.35	.09
☐ U4 Mike Piazza	20.00	9.00	2.50
☐ U5 Roberto Mejia	.75	.35	.09

1993 Leaf Heading for the Hall

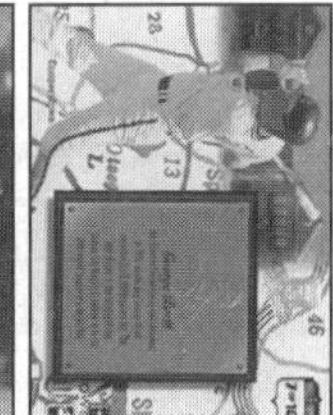

Randomly inserted into 1993 Leaf series 1 and 2 packs, this ten-card standard-size set features potential Hall of Famers. Cards 1-5 were series I inserts and cards 6-10 were series II inserts. The fronts feature borderless color player action shots, with the player's name appearing within a lithic banner near the bottom, below the set's logo.

	MINT	NRMT	EXC
COMPLETE SET (10)	30.00	13.50	3.70
COMPLETE SERIES 1 (5)	20.00	9.00	2.50
COMPLETE SERIES 2 (5)	10.00	4.50	1.25
COMMON CARD (1-10)	1.50	.70	.19
☐ 1 Nolan Ryan	12.00	5.50	1.50
☐ 2 Tony Gwynn	5.00	2.20	.60
☐ 3 Robin Yount	1.50	.70	.19
☐ 4 Eddie Murray	3.00	1.35	.35
☐ 5 Cal Ripken	12.00	5.50	1.50
☐ 6 Roger Clemens	2.50	1.10	.30
☐ 7 George Brett	5.00	2.20	.60
☐ 8 Ryne Sandberg	3.00	1.35	.35
☐ 9 Kirby Puckett	5.00	2.20	.60
☐ 10 Ozzie Smith	3.00	1.35	.35

1993 Leaf Thomas

This ten-card standard-size set spotlights Chicago White Sox slugger and Donruss/Leaf spokesperson Frank Thomas and were randomly inserted into all forms of Leaf packs. Five cards were inserted in each of the two series. The full-bleed fronts carry color action shots with "Frank" stamped in large prismatic foil letters across the bottom of the picture. Jumbo (5" by 7") versions of these cards were issued one per box of Leaf Update. The jumbos are individually numbered out of 7,500.

	MINT	NRMT	EXC
COMPLETE SET (10)	40.00	18.00	5.00
COMMON THOMAS (1-10)	5.00	2.20	.60

COMPLETE JUMBO SET (10)	60.00	27.00	7.50
*JUMBOS: 1.5X VALUE			
☐ 1 Frank Thomas Aggressive	5.00	2.20	.60
☐ 2 Frank Thomas Serious	5.00	2.20	.60
☐ 3 Frank Thomas Intense	5.00	2.20	.60
☐ 4 Frank Thomas Confident	5.00	2.20	.60
☐ 5 Frank Thomas Assertive	5.00	2.20	.60
☐ 6 Frank Thomas Power	5.00	2.20	.60
☐ 7 Frank Thomas Control	5.00	2.20	.60
☐ 8 Frank Thomas Strength	5.00	2.20	.60
☐ 9 Frank Thomas Concentration	5.00	2.20	.60
☐ 10 Frank Thomas Preparation	5.00	2.20	.60

1994 Leaf Promos

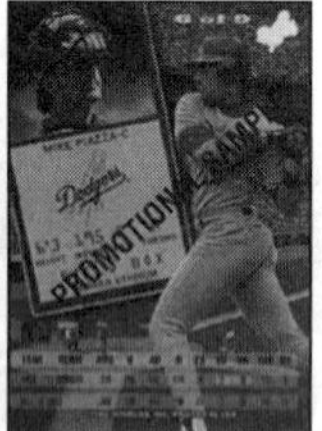

Issued to herald the release of the 1994 Leaf set, these nine promo cards measure the standard size and parallel the corresponding regular issue 1994 Leaf cards. The "Promotional Sample" disclaimer appears diagonally on the front and back. The cards are numbered on the back as "X of 9."

	MINT	NRMT	EXC
COMPLETE SET (9)	20.00	9.00	2.50
COMMON CARD (1-9)	.50	.23	.06
☐ 1 Roberto Alomar	1.25	.55	.16
☐ 2 Darren Daulton	1.00	.45	.12
☐ 3 Ken Griffey Jr.	5.00	2.20	.60
☐ 4 David Justice	.75	.35	.09
☐ 5 Don Mattingly	2.50	1.10	.30
☐ 6 Mike Piazza	3.00	1.35	.35
☐ 7 Cal Ripken	4.00	1.80	.50
☐ 8 Ryne Sandberg	2.00	.90	.25
☐ 9 Frank Thomas	5.00	2.20	.60

1994 Leaf

The 1994 Leaf baseball set consists of two series of 220 standard-size cards for a total of 440. Certain "Super Packs" contained complete insert sets. The fronts feature color action player photos, with team color-coded designs on the bottom. The player's name and the Leaf logo are foil stamped, the team name appears under the player's name. The backs carry a photo of the player's home stadium in the background with a silhouetted photo of the player in the foreground. Additionally, a headshot appears in a ticket stub-like design with biographical information, while player statistics appear on the bottom. Cards featuring players from the Texas Rangers, Cleveland Indians, Milwaukee Brewers and Houston Astros were held out of the first series in order to have up-to-date photography in each team's new uniforms. A limited number of players from the San Francisco Giants are featured in the first series because of minor modifications to the team's uniforms. Randomly inserted in hobby packs at a rate of one in 36 was a stamped version of Frank Thomas' 1990 Leaf rookie card.

	MINT	NRMT	EXC
COMPLETE SET (440)	30.00	13.50	3.70
COMPLETE SERIES 1 (220)	15.00	6.75	1.85
COMPLETE SERIES 2 (220)	15.00	6.75	1.85
COMMON CARD (1-440)	.10	.05	.01
☐ 1 Cal Ripken Jr.	2.50	1.10	.30
☐ 2 Tony Tarasco	.10	.05	.01
☐ 3 Joe Girardi	.10	.05	.01
☐ 4 Bernie Williams	.60	.25	.07
☐ 5 Chad Kreuter	.10	.05	.01
☐ 6 Troy Neel	.10	.05	.01
☐ 7 Tom Pagnozzi	.10	.05	.01
☐ 8 Kirk Rueter	.10	.05	.01
☐ 9 Chris Bosio	.10	.05	.01
☐ 10 Dwight Gooden	.25	.11	.03
☐ 11 Mariano Duncan	.10	.05	.01
☐ 12 Jay Bell	.25	.11	.03
☐ 13 Lance Johnson	.25	.11	.03
☐ 14 Richie Lewis	.10	.05	.01
☐ 15 Dave Martinez	.10	.05	.01
☐ 16 Orel Hershiser	.25	.11	.03
☐ 17 Rob Butler	.10	.05	.01
☐ 18 Glenallen Hill	.10	.05	.01
☐ 19 Chad Curtis	.10	.05	.01
☐ 20 Mike Stanton	.10	.05	.01
☐ 21 Tim Wallach	.10	.05	.01
☐ 22 Milt Thompson	.10	.05	.01
☐ 23 Kevin Young	.10	.05	.01
☐ 24 John Smiley	.10	.05	.01
☐ 25 Jeff Montgomery	.25	.11	.03
☐ 26 Robin Ventura	.25	.11	.03
☐ 27 Scott Lydy	.10	.05	.01
☐ 28 Todd Stottlemyre	.10	.05	.01
☐ 29 Mark Whiten	.10	.05	.01
☐ 30 Robby Thompson	.10	.05	.01
☐ 31 Bobby Bonilla	.25	.11	.03
☐ 32 Andy Ashby	.25	.11	.03
☐ 33 Greg Myers	.10	.05	.01
☐ 34 Billy Hatcher	.10	.05	.01
☐ 35 Brad Holman	.10	.05	.01
☐ 36 Mark McLemore	.10	.05	.01
☐ 37 Scott Sanders	.10	.05	.01
☐ 38 Jim Abbott	.10	.05	.01
☐ 39 David Wells	.10	.05	.01
☐ 40 Roberto Kelly	.10	.05	.01
☐ 41 Jeff Conine	.25	.11	.03
☐ 42 Sean Berry	.10	.05	.01
☐ 43 Mark Grace	.50	.23	.06
☐ 44 Eric Young	.25	.11	.03
☐ 45 Rick Aguilera	.10	.05	.01
☐ 46 Chipper Jones	2.50	1.10	.30
☐ 47 Mel Rojas	.10	.05	.01
☐ 48 Ryan Thompson	.10	.05	.01
☐ 49 Al Martin	.10	.05	.01
☐ 50 Cecil Fielder	.25	.11	.03
☐ 51 Pat Kelly	.10	.05	.01
☐ 52 Kevin Tapani	.10	.05	.01
☐ 53 Tim Costo	.10	.05	.01
☐ 54 Dave Hollins	.10	.05	.01
☐ 55 Kirt Manwaring	.10	.05	.01
☐ 56 Gregg Jefferies	.50	.23	.06
☐ 57 Ron Darling	.10	.05	.01
☐ 58 Bill Haselman	.10	.05	.01
☐ 59 Phil Plantier	.10	.05	.01
☐ 60 Frank Viola	.10	.05	.01
☐ 61 Todd Zeile	.10	.05	.01
☐ 62 Bret Barberie	.10	.05	.01
☐ 63 Roberto Mejia	.10	.05	.01
☐ 64 Chuck Knoblauch	.50	.23	.06
☐ 65 Jose Lind	.10	.05	.01
☐ 66 Brady Anderson	.50	.23	.06
☐ 67 Ruben Sierra	.25	.11	.03
☐ 68 Jose Vizcaino	.10	.05	.01
☐ 69 Joe Grahe	.10	.05	.01
☐ 70 Kevin Appier	.25	.11	.03
☐ 71 Wilson Alvarez	.25	.11	.03
☐ 72 Tom Candiotti	.10	.05	.01
☐ 73 John Burkett	.10	.05	.01
☐ 74 Anthony Young	.10	.05	.01
☐ 75 Scott Cooper	.10	.05	.01
☐ 76 Nigel Wilson	.10	.05	.01
☐ 77 John Valentin	.25	.11	.03
☐ 78 Dave McCarty	.10	.05	.01
☐ 79 Archi Cianfrocco	.10	.05	.01
☐ 80 Lou Whitaker	.25	.11	.03
☐ 81 Dante Bichette	.50	.23	.06
☐ 82 Mark Dewey	.10	.05	.01
☐ 83 Danny Jackson	.10	.05	.01
☐ 84 Harold Baines	.25	.11	.03
☐ 85 Todd Benzinger	.10	.05	.01
☐ 86 Damion Easley	.10	.05	.01
☐ 87 Danny Cox	.10	.05	.01
☐ 88 Jose Bautista	.10	.05	.01
☐ 89 Mike Lansing	.25	.11	.03
☐ 90 Phil Hiatt	.10	.05	.01
☐ 91 Tim Pugh	.10	.05	.01
☐ 92 Tino Martinez	.25	.11	.03
☐ 93 Raul Mondesi	.50	.23	.06
☐ 94 Greg Maddux	2.00	.90	.25
☐ 95 Al Leiter	.25	.11	.03
☐ 96 Benito Santiago	.10	.05	.01
☐ 97 Lenny Dykstra	.25	.11	.03
☐ 98 Sammy Sosa	.50	.23	.06
☐ 99 Tim Bogar	.10	.05	.01
☐ 100 Checklist	.10	.05	.01
☐ 101 Deion Sanders	.50	.23	.06
☐ 102 Bobby Witt	.10	.05	.01
☐ 103 Wil Cordero	.25	.11	.03
☐ 104 Rich Amaral	.10	.05	.01
☐ 105 Mike Mussina	.60	.25	.07
☐ 106 Reggie Sanders	.25	.11	.03
☐ 107 Ozzie Guillen	.10	.05	.01
☐ 108 Paul O'Neill	.25	.11	.03
☐ 109 Tim Salmon	.50	.23	.06
☐ 110 Rheal Cormier	.10	.05	.01
☐ 111 Billy Ashley	.10	.05	.01
☐ 112 Jeff Kent	.10	.05	.01
☐ 113 Derek Bell	.25	.11	.03
☐ 114 Danny Darwin	.10	.05	.01
☐ 115 Chip Hale	.10	.05	.01
☐ 116 Tim Raines	.50	.23	.06
☐ 117 Ed Sprague	.25	.11	.03
☐ 118 Darrin Fletcher	.10	.05	.01
☐ 119 Darren Holmes	.10	.05	.01
☐ 120 Alan Trammell	.25	.11	.03
☐ 121 Don Mattingly	1.50	.70	.19
☐ 122 Greg Gagne	.10	.05	.01
☐ 123 Jose Offerman	.10	.05	.01
☐ 124 Joe Orsulak	.10	.05	.01
☐ 125 Jack McDowell	.25	.11	.03
☐ 126 Barry Larkin	.50	.23	.06
☐ 127 Ben McDonald	.10	.05	.01
☐ 128 Mike Bordick	.10	.05	.01
☐ 129 Devon White	.10	.05	.01
☐ 130 Mike Perez	.10	.05	.01
☐ 131 Jay Buhner	.50	.23	.06
☐ 132 Phil Leftwich	.10	.05	.01
☐ 133 Tommy Greene	.10	.05	.01
☐ 134 Charlie Hayes	.10	.05	.01
☐ 135 Don Slaught	.10	.05	.01
☐ 136 Mike Gallego	.10	.05	.01
☐ 137 Dave Winfield	.50	.23	.06
☐ 138 Steve Avery	.25	.11	.03
☐ 139 Derrick May	.10	.05	.01
☐ 140 Bryan Harvey	.10	.05	.01
☐ 141 Wally Joyner	.25	.11	.03
☐ 142 Andre Dawson	.25	.11	.03
☐ 143 Andy Benes	.25	.11	.03
☐ 144 John Franco	.10	.05	.01
☐ 145 Jeff King	.25	.11	.03
☐ 146 Joe Oliver	.10	.05	.01
☐ 147 Bill Gullickson	.10	.05	.01
☐ 148 Armando Reynoso	.10	.05	.01
☐ 149 Dave Fleming	.10	.05	.01
☐ 150 Checklist	.10	.05	.01
☐ 151 Todd Van Poppel	.10	.05	.01
☐ 152 Bernard Gilkey	.25	.11	.03
☐ 153 Kevin Gross	.10	.05	.01
☐ 154 Mike Devereaux	.10	.05	.01
☐ 155 Tim Wakefield	.10	.05	.01
☐ 156 Andres Galarraga	.50	.23	.06
☐ 157 Pat Meares	.10	.05	.01
☐ 158 Jim Leyritz	.10	.05	.01
☐ 159 Mike Macfarlane	.10	.05	.01
☐ 160 Tony Phillips	.25	.11	.03
☐ 161 Brent Gates	.10	.05	.01
☐ 162 Mark Langston	.25	.11	.03
☐ 163 Allen Watson	.10	.05	.01
☐ 164 Randy Johnson	.50	.23	.06
☐ 165 Doug Brocail	.10	.05	.01
☐ 166 Rob Dibble	.10	.05	.01
☐ 167 Roberto Hernandez	.25	.11	.03
☐ 168 Felix Jose	.10	.05	.01
☐ 169 Steve Cooke	.10	.05	.01
☐ 170 Darren Daulton	.25	.11	.03
☐ 171 Eric Karros	.25	.11	.03
☐ 172 Geronimo Pena	.10	.05	.01
☐ 173 Gary DiSarcina	.10	.05	.01
☐ 174 Marquis Grissom	.25	.11	.03
☐ 175 Joey Cora	.10	.05	.01
☐ 176 Jim Eisenreich	.10	.05	.01
☐ 177 Brad Pennington	.10	.05	.01
☐ 178 Terry Steinbach	.25	.11	.03
☐ 179 Pat Borders	.10	.05	.01
☐ 180 Steve Buechele	.10	.05	.01
☐ 181 Jeff Fassero	.10	.05	.01
☐ 182 Mike Greenwell	.10	.05	.01
☐ 183 Mike Henneman	.10	.05	.01
☐ 184 Ron Karkovice	.10	.05	.01
☐ 185 Pat Hentgen	.25	.11	.03
☐ 186 Jose Guzman	.10	.05	.01
☐ 187 Brett Butler	.25	.11	.03
☐ 188 Charlie Hough	.10	.05	.01
☐ 189 Terry Pendleton	.25	.11	.03
☐ 190 Melido Perez	.10	.05	.01
☐ 191 Orestes Destrade	.10	.05	.01
☐ 192 Mike Morgan	.10	.05	.01
☐ 193 Joe Carter	.25	.11	.03
☐ 194 Jeff Blauser	.10	.05	.01
☐ 195 Chris Hoiles	.10	.05	.01
☐ 196 Ricky Gutierrez	.10	.05	.01
☐ 197 Mike Moore	.10	.05	.01
☐ 198 Carl Willis	.10	.05	.01
☐ 199 Aaron Sele	.25	.11	.03
☐ 200 Checklist	.10	.05	.01
☐ 201 Tim Naehring	.10	.05	.01
☐ 202 Scott Livingstone	.10	.05	.01
☐ 203 Luis Alicea	.10	.05	.01
☐ 204 Torey Lovullo	.10	.05	.01
☐ 205 Jim Gott	.10	.05	.01
☐ 206 Bob Wickman	.10	.05	.01
☐ 207 Greg McMichael	.10	.05	.01
☐ 208 Scott Brosius	.10	.05	.01
☐ 209 Chris Gwynn	.10	.05	.01
☐ 210 Steve Sax	.10	.05	.01
☐ 211 Dick Schofield	.10	.05	.01
☐ 212 Robb Nen	.25	.11	.03
☐ 213 Ben Rivera	.10	.05	.01
☐ 214 Vinny Castilla	.50	.23	.06
☐ 215 Jamie Moyer	.10	.05	.01
☐ 216 Wally Whitehurst	.10	.05	.01
☐ 217 Frank Castillo	.10	.05	.01
☐ 218 Mike Blowers	.10	.05	.01
☐ 219 Tim Scott	.10	.05	.01
☐ 220 Paul Wagner	.10	.05	.01
☐ 221 Jeff Bagwell	1.25	.55	.16
☐ 222 Ricky Bones	.10	.05	.01
☐ 223 Sandy Alomar Jr.	.25	.11	.03
☐ 224 Rod Beck	.25	.11	.03
☐ 225 Roberto Alomar	.60	.25	.07
☐ 226 Jack Armstrong	.10	.05	.01
☐ 227 Scott Erickson	.10	.05	.01
☐ 228 Rene Arocha	.10	.05	.01
☐ 229 Eric Anthony	.10	.05	.01
☐ 230 Jeromy Burnitz	.10	.05	.01
☐ 231 Kevin Brown	.25	.11	.03
☐ 232 Tim Belcher	.10	.05	.01
☐ 233 Bret Boone	.25	.11	.03
☐ 234 Dennis Eckersley	.25	.11	.03
☐ 235 Tom Glavine	.50	.23	.06
☐ 236 Craig Biggio	.25	.11	.03
☐ 237 Pedro Astacio	.10	.05	.01
☐ 238 Ryan Bowen	.10	.05	.01
☐ 239 Brad Ausmus	.10	.05	.01
☐ 240 Vince Coleman	.10	.05	.01
☐ 241 Jason Bere	.25	.11	.03
☐ 242 Ellis Burks	.25	.11	.03
☐ 243 Wes Chamberlain	.10	.05	.01
☐ 244 Ken Caminiti	.50	.23	.06
☐ 245 Willie Banks	.10	.05	.01
☐ 246 Sid Fernandez	.10	.05	.01
☐ 247 Carlos Baerga	.25	.11	.03
☐ 248 Carlos Garcia	.10	.05	.01
☐ 249 Jose Canseco	.50	.23	.06
☐ 250 Alex Diaz	.10	.05	.01
☐ 251 Albert Belle	1.25	.55	.16
☐ 252 Moises Alou	.25	.11	.03
☐ 253 Bobby Ayala	.10	.05	.01
☐ 254 Tony Gwynn	1.25	.55	.16
☐ 255 Roger Clemens	.60	.25	.07
☐ 256 Eric Davis	.25	.11	.03
☐ 257 Wade Boggs	.50	.23	.06
☐ 258 Chili Davis	.25	.11	.03
☐ 259 Rickey Henderson	.50	.23	.06
☐ 260 Andujar Cedeno	.10	.05	.01
☐ 261 Cris Carpenter	.10	.05	.01
☐ 262 Juan Guzman	.25	.11	.03
☐ 263 David Justice	.50	.23	.06
☐ 264 Barry Bonds	.75	.35	.09
☐ 265 Pete Incaviglia	.10	.05	.01
☐ 266 Tony Fernandez	.10	.05	.01
☐ 267 Cal Eldred	.10	.05	.01
☐ 268 Alex Fernandez	.25	.11	.03
☐ 269 Kent Hrbek	.25	.11	.03
☐ 270 Steve Farr	.10	.05	.01
☐ 271 Doug Drabek	.10	.05	.01
☐ 272 Brian Jordan	.50	.23	.06
☐ 273 Xavier Hernandez	.10	.05	.01
☐ 274 David Cone	.25	.11	.03
☐ 275 Brian Hunter	.10	.05	.01
☐ 276 Mike Harkey	.10	.05	.01
☐ 277 Delino DeShields	.10	.05	.01
☐ 278 David Hulse	.10	.05	.01
☐ 279 Mickey Tettleton	.10	.05	.01
☐ 280 Kevin McReynolds	.10	.05	.01
☐ 281 Darryl Hamilton	.10	.05	.01
☐ 282 Ken Hill	.10	.05	.01
☐ 283 Wayne Kirby	.10	.05	.01
☐ 284 Chris Hammond	.10	.05	.01
☐ 285 Mo Vaughn	.75	.35	.09
☐ 286 Ryan Klesko	.60	.25	.07
☐ 287 Rick Wilkins	.10	.05	.01
☐ 288 Bill Swift	.10	.05	.01
☐ 289 Rafael Palmeiro	.50	.23	.06
☐ 290 Brian Harper	.10	.05	.01
☐ 291 Chris Turner	.10	.05	.01
☐ 292 Luis Gonzalez	.10	.05	.01
☐ 293 Kenny Rogers	.10	.05	.01
☐ 294 Kirby Puckett	1.25	.55	.16
☐ 295 Mike Stanley	.10	.05	.01
☐ 296 Carlos Reyes	.10	.05	.01
☐ 297 Charles Nagy	.25	.11	.03
☐ 298 Reggie Jefferson	.25	.11	.03
☐ 299 Bip Roberts	.10	.05	.01
☐ 300 Darrin Jackson	.10	.05	.01
☐ 301 Mike Jackson	.10	.05	.01
☐ 302 Dave Nilsson	.25	.11	.03
☐ 303 Ramon Martinez	.25	.11	.03
☐ 304 Bobby Jones	.25	.11	.03
☐ 305 Johnny Ruffin	.10	.05	.01
☐ 306 Brian McRae	.25	.11	.03
☐ 307 Bo Jackson	.25	.11	.03
☐ 308 Dave Stewart	.25	.11	.03
☐ 309 John Smoltz	.50	.23	.06
☐ 310 Dennis Martinez	.25	.11	.03
☐ 311 Dean Palmer	.25	.11	.03
☐ 312 David Nied	.10	.05	.01
☐ 313 Eddie Murray	.75	.35	.09
☐ 314 Darryl Kile	.10	.05	.01
☐ 315 Rick Sutcliffe	.10	.05	.01
☐ 316 Shawon Dunston	.10	.05	.01
☐ 317 John Jaha	.25	.11	.03
☐ 318 Salomon Torres	.10	.05	.01
☐ 319 Gary Sheffield	.50	.23	.06
☐ 320 Curt Schilling	.10	.05	.01
☐ 321 Greg Vaughn	.50	.23	.06
☐ 322 Jay Howell	.10	.05	.01
☐ 323 Todd Hundley	.25	.11	.03

☐ 324 Chris Sabo	.10	.05	.01
☐ 325 Stan Javier	.10	.05	.01
☐ 326 Willie Greene	.25	.11	.03
☐ 327 Hipolito Pichardo	.10	.05	.01
☐ 328 Doug Strange	.10	.05	.01
☐ 329 Dan Wilson	.25	.11	.03
☐ 330 Checklist	.10	.05	.01
☐ 331 Omar Vizquel	.25	.11	.03
☐ 332 Scott Servais	.10	.05	.01
☐ 333 Bob Tewksbury	.10	.05	.01
☐ 334 Matt Williams	.50	.23	.06
☐ 335 Tom Foley	.10	.05	.01
☐ 336 Jeff Russell	.10	.05	.01
☐ 337 Scott Leius	.10	.05	.01
☐ 338 Ivan Rodriguez	.75	.35	.09
☐ 339 Kevin Seitzer	.10	.05	.01
☐ 340 Jose Rijo	.10	.05	.01
☐ 341 Eduardo Perez	.10	.05	.01
☐ 342 Kirk Gibson	.25	.11	.03
☐ 343 Randy Milligan	.10	.05	.01
☐ 344 Edgar Martinez	.25	.11	.03
☐ 345 Fred McGriff	.50	.23	.06
☐ 346 Kurt Abbott	.25	.11	.03
☐ 347 John Kruk	.25	.11	.03
☐ 348 Mike Felder	.10	.05	.01
☐ 349 Dave Staton	.10	.05	.01
☐ 350 Kenny Lofton	1.00	.45	.12
☐ 351 Graeme Lloyd	.10	.05	.01
☐ 352 David Segui	.10	.05	.01
☐ 353 Danny Tartabull	.10	.05	.01
☐ 354 Bob Welch	.10	.05	.01
☐ 355 Duane Ward	.10	.05	.01
☐ 356 Karl Rhodes	.10	.05	.01
☐ 357 Lee Smith	.25	.11	.03
☐ 358 Chris James	.10	.05	.01
☐ 359 Walt Weiss	.10	.05	.01
☐ 360 Pedro Munoz	.10	.05	.01
☐ 361 Paul Sorrento	.10	.05	.01
☐ 362 Todd Worrell	.10	.05	.01
☐ 363 Bob Hamelin	.10	.05	.01
☐ 364 Julio Franco	.25	.11	.03
☐ 365 Roberto Petagine	.25	.11	.03
☐ 366 Willie McGee	.10	.05	.01
☐ 367 Pedro Martinez	.50	.23	.06
☐ 368 Ken Griffey Jr.	3.00	1.35	.35
☐ 369 B.J. Surhoff	.10	.05	.01
☐ 370 Kevin Mitchell	.25	.11	.03
☐ 371 John Doherty	.10	.05	.01
☐ 372 Manuel Lee	.10	.05	.01
☐ 373 Terry Mulholland	.10	.05	.01
☐ 374 Zane Smith	.10	.05	.01
☐ 375 Otis Nixon	.10	.05	.01
☐ 376 Jody Reed	.10	.05	.01
☐ 377 Doug Jones	.10	.05	.01
☐ 378 John Olerud	.10	.05	.01
☐ 379 Greg Swindell	.10	.05	.01
☐ 380 Checklist	.10	.05	.01
☐ 381 Royce Clayton	.25	.11	.03
☐ 382 Jim Thome	.75	.35	.09
☐ 383 Steve Finley	.50	.23	.06
☐ 384 Ray Lankford	.25	.11	.03
☐ 385 Henry Rodriguez	.25	.11	.03
☐ 386 Dave Magadan	.10	.05	.01
☐ 387 Gary Redus	.10	.05	.01
☐ 388 Orlando Merced	.25	.11	.03
☐ 389 Tom Gordon	.10	.05	.01
☐ 390 Luis Polonia	.10	.05	.01
☐ 391 Mark McGwire	1.00	.45	.12
☐ 392 Mark Lemke	.10	.05	.01
☐ 393 Doug Henry	.10	.05	.01
☐ 394 Chuck Finley	.10	.05	.01
☐ 395 Paul Molitor	.60	.25	.07
☐ 396 Randy Myers	.10	.05	.01
☐ 397 Larry Walker	.50	.23	.06
☐ 398 Pete Harnisch	.10	.05	.01
☐ 399 Darren Lewis	.10	.05	.01
☐ 400 Frank Thomas	3.00	1.35	.35
☐ 401 Jack Morris	.25	.11	.03
☐ 402 Greg Hibbard	.10	.05	.01
☐ 403 Jeffrey Hammonds	.25	.11	.03
☐ 404 Will Clark	.50	.23	.06
☐ 405 Travis Fryman	.25	.11	.03
☐ 406 Scott Sanderson	.10	.05	.01
☐ 407 Gene Harris	.10	.05	.01
☐ 408 Chuck Carr	.10	.05	.01
☐ 409 Ozzie Smith	.75	.35	.09
☐ 410 Kent Mercker	.10	.05	.01
☐ 411 Andy Van Slyke	.25	.11	.03
☐ 412 Jimmy Key	.25	.11	.03
☐ 413 Pat Mahomes	.10	.05	.01
☐ 414 John Wetteland	.25	.11	.03
☐ 415 Todd Jones	.10	.05	.01
☐ 416 Greg Harris	.10	.05	.01
☐ 417 Kevin Stocker	.10	.05	.01
☐ 418 Juan Gonzalez	1.50	.70	.19
☐ 419 Pete Smith	.10	.05	.01
☐ 420 Pat Listach	.10	.05	.01
☐ 421 Trevor Hoffman	.25	.11	.03
☐ 422 Scott Fletcher	.10	.05	.01
☐ 423 Mark Lewis	.10	.05	.01
☐ 424 Mickey Morandini	.10	.05	.01
☐ 425 Ryne Sandberg	.75	.35	.09
☐ 426 Erik Hanson	.10	.05	.01
☐ 427 Gary Gaetti	.25	.11	.03
☐ 428 Harold Reynolds	.10	.05	.01
☐ 429 Mark Portugal	.10	.05	.01
☐ 430 David Valle	.10	.05	.01
☐ 431 Mitch Williams	.10	.05	.01
☐ 432 Howard Johnson	.10	.05	.01
☐ 433 Hal Morris	.10	.05	.01
☐ 434 Tom Henke	.10	.05	.01
☐ 435 Shane Mack	.10	.05	.01
☐ 436 Mike Piazza	2.00	.90	.25
☐ 437 Bret Saberhagen	.25	.11	.03
☐ 438 Jose Mesa	.25	.11	.03
☐ 439 Jaime Navarro	.10	.05	.01
☐ 440 Checklist	.10	.05	.01
☐ A300 Frank Thomas Leaf 5th Anniversary	4.00	1.80	.50

1994 Leaf Clean-Up Crew

Inserted in magazine jumbo packs at a rate of one in 12, this 12-card set was issued in two series of six. Full-bleed fronts contain an action photo with the Clean-Up Crew logo at bottom right and the player's name in a colored band toward bottom left. The backs contain a photo and 1993 statistics when batting fourth. The home plate area serves as background.

	MINT	NRMT	EXC
COMPLETE SET (12)	60.00	27.00	7.50
COMPLETE SERIES 1 (6)	10.00	4.50	1.25
COMPLETE SERIES 2 (6)	50.00	22.00	6.25
COMMON CARD (1-12)	3.00	1.35	.35
☐ 1 Larry Walker	6.00	2.70	.75
☐ 2 Andres Galarraga	6.00	2.70	.75
☐ 3 Dave Hollins	3.00	1.35	.35
☐ 4 Bobby Bonilla	5.00	2.20	.60
☐ 5 Cecil Fielder	5.00	2.20	.60
☐ 6 Danny Tartabull	3.00	1.35	.35
☐ 7 Juan Gonzalez	25.00	11.00	3.10
☐ 8 Joe Carter	5.00	2.20	.60
☐ 9 Fred McGriff	6.00	2.70	.75
☐ 10 Matt Williams	6.00	2.70	.75
☐ 11 Albert Belle	20.00	9.00	2.50
☐ 12 Harold Baines	3.00	1.35	.35

1994 Leaf Gamers

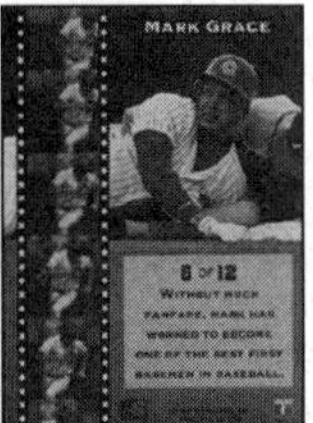

A close-up photo of the player highlights this 12-card standard-size set that was issued in two series of six. They were randomly inserted in jumbo packs at a rate of one in eight. The player's name appears at the top of the photo with the Leaf Gamers hologram logo at the bottom. The backs feature a variety of color photos including a frame by frame series resembling a film strip. There is also a small write-up.

	MINT	NRMT	EXC
COMPLETE SET (12)	150.00	70.00	19.00
COMPLETE SERIES 1 (6)	70.00	32.00	8.75
COMPLETE SERIES 2 (6)	80.00	36.00	10.00
COMMON CARD (1-12)	3.00	1.35	.35
☐ 1 Ken Griffey Jr.	40.00	18.00	5.00
☐ 2 Lenny Dykstra	3.00	1.35	.35
☐ 3 Juan Gonzalez	20.00	9.00	2.50
☐ 4 Don Mattingly	20.00	9.00	2.50
☐ 5 David Justice	3.00	1.35	.35
☐ 6 Mark Grace	5.00	2.20	.60
☐ 7 Frank Thomas	40.00	18.00	5.00
☐ 8 Barry Bonds	10.00	4.50	1.25
☐ 9 Kirby Puckett	15.00	6.75	1.85
☐ 10 Will Clark	5.00	2.20	.60
☐ 11 John Kruk	3.00	1.35	.35
☐ 12 Mike Piazza	25.00	11.00	3.10

1994 Leaf Gold Rookies

This set, which was randomly inserted in all packs at a rate of one in 18, features 20 of the hottest young stars in the majors. A color player cutout is layed over a dark brownish background that contains "94 Gold Leaf Rookie". The player's name and team appear at the bottom in silver. Horizontal backs include career highlights and two photos.

	MINT	NRMT	EXC
COMPLETE SET (20)	16.00	7.25	2.00
COMPLETE SERIES 1 (10)	12.00	5.50	1.50
COMPLETE SERIES 2 (10)	4.00	1.80	.50
COMMON CARD (1-20)	.50	.23	.06
☐ 1 Javier Lopez	2.00	.90	.25
☐ 2 Rondell White	1.25	.55	.16
☐ 3 Butch Huskey	1.00	.45	.12
☐ 4 Midre Cummings	.50	.23	.06
☐ 5 Scott Ruffcorn	.50	.23	.06
☐ 6 Manny Ramirez	5.00	2.20	.60
☐ 7 Danny Bautista	.50	.23	.06
☐ 8 Russ Davis	.50	.23	.06
☐ 9 Steve Karsay	.50	.23	.06
☐ 10 Carlos Delgado	2.00	.90	.25
☐ 11 Bob Hamelin	.50	.23	.06
☐ 12 Marcus Moore	.50	.23	.06
☐ 13 Miguel Jimenez	.50	.23	.06
☐ 14 Matt Walbeck	.50	.23	.06
☐ 15 James Mouton	1.00	.45	.12
☐ 16 Rich Becker	1.00	.45	.12
☐ 17 Brian Anderson	.50	.23	.06
☐ 18 Cliff Floyd	1.00	.45	.12
☐ 19 Steve Trachsel	1.00	.45	.12
☐ 20 Hector Carrasco	.50	.23	.06

1994 Leaf Gold Stars

Randomly inserted in all packs at a rate of one in 90, the 15 standard-size cards in this set are individually numbered and limited to 10,000 per player. The cards were issued in two series with eight cards in series one and seven in series two. The fronts are bordered by gold and have a green marble appearance with the player appearing within a diamond (outlined in gold) in the card's upper half. The player's name, gold facsimile autograph and team name appear below the photo. The backs are similar to the fronts except for 1993 highlights and the individual numbering. They are numbered "X/10,000".

	MINT	NRMT	EXC
COMPLETE SET (15)	200.00	90.00	25.00
COMPLETE SERIES 1 (8)	125.00	55.00	15.50
COMPLETE SERIES 2 (7)	75.00	34.00	9.50
COMMON CARD (1-15)	5.00	2.20	.60
☐ 1 Roberto Alomar	10.00	4.50	1.25
☐ 2 Barry Bonds	12.00	5.50	1.50
☐ 3 David Justice	5.00	2.20	.60
☐ 4 Ken Griffey Jr.	50.00	22.00	6.25
☐ 5 Lenny Dykstra	5.00	2.20	.60
☐ 6 Don Mattingly	25.00	11.00	3.10
☐ 7 Andres Galarraga	5.00	2.20	.60
☐ 8 Greg Maddux	30.00	13.50	3.70
☐ 9 Carlos Baerga	5.00	2.20	.60
☐ 10 Paul Molitor	10.00	4.50	1.25
☐ 11 Frank Thomas	50.00	22.00	6.25
☐ 12 John Olerud	5.00	2.20	.60
☐ 13 Juan Gonzalez	25.00	11.00	3.10
☐ 14 Fred McGriff	6.00	2.70	.75
☐ 15 Jack McDowell	5.00	2.20	.60

1994 Leaf MVP Contenders

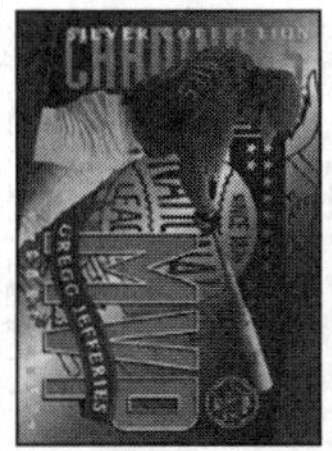
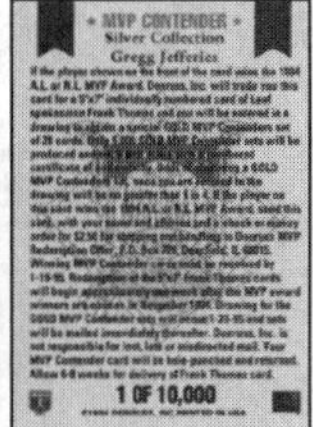

This 30-card standard-size set contains 15 players from each league who were projected to be 1994 MVP hopefuls. These unnumbered cards were randomly inserted in all second series packs at a rate of one in 36. If the player appearing on the card was named his league's MVP (Frank Thomas American League and Jeff Bagwell National League), the card could be redeemed for a 5" x 7" Frank Thomas card individually numbered out of 20,000. The backs contain all the rules and read "1 of 10,000". The expiration for redeeming Thomas and Bagwell cards was Jan. 19, 1995.

	MINT	NRMT	EXC
COMPLETE SET (30)	150.00	70.00	19.00
COMMON CARD	2.00	.90	.25
COMP.GOLD SET (30)	150.00	70.00	19.00
COMMON GOLD	2.00	.90	.25
*GOLD: .5X BASIC CARDS			

☐ A1 Carlos Baerga	2.00	.90	.25
☐ A2 Albert Belle	12.00	5.50	1.50
☐ A3 Jose Canseco	4.00	1.80	.50
☐ A4 Joe Carter	3.00	1.35	.35
☐ A5 Will Clark	4.00	1.80	.50
☐ A6 Cecil Fielder	3.00	1.35	.35
☐ A7 Juan Gonzalez	15.00	6.75	1.85
☐ A8 Ken Griffey Jr.	30.00	13.50	3.70
☐ A9 Paul Molitor	6.00	2.70	.75
☐ A10 Rafael Palmeiro	4.00	1.80	.50
☐ A11 Kirby Puckett	12.00	5.50	1.50
☐ A12 Cal Ripken Jr.	25.00	11.00	3.10
☐ A13 Frank Thomas W	30.00	13.50	3.70
☐ A14 Mo Vaughn	8.00	3.60	1.00
☐ A15 AL Bonus Card	2.00	.90	.25
☐ N1 Jeff Bagwell W	12.00	5.50	1.50
☐ N2 Dante Bichette	4.00	1.80	.50
☐ N3 Barry Bonds	8.00	3.60	1.00
☐ N4 Darren Daulton	3.00	1.35	.35
☐ N5 Andres Galarraga	4.00	1.80	.50
☐ N6 Gregg Jefferies	3.00	1.35	.35
☐ N7 David Justice	2.00	.90	.25
☐ N8 Ray Lankford	3.00	1.35	.35
☐ N9 Barry Larkin	4.00	1.80	.50
☐ N10 Fred McGriff	4.00	1.80	.50
☐ N11 Mike Piazza	20.00	9.00	2.50
☐ N12 Deion Sanders	4.00	1.80	.50
☐ N13 Gary Sheffield	5.00	2.20	.60
☐ N14 Matt Williams	4.00	1.80	.50
☐ N15 NL Bonus Card	2.00	.90	.25
☐ J400 Frank Thomas Jumbo	20.00	9.00	2.50

1994 Leaf Power Brokers

Inserted in second series retail and hobby foil packs at a rate of one in 12, this 10-card standard-size set spotlights top sluggers. Both fronts and backs are horizontal. The fronts have a small player cutout with a black background and "Power Brokers" dominating the card. Fireworks appear within "Power". The backs contain various pie charts that document the player's home run tendencies as far as home vs. away etc. There is also a small photo.

	MINT	NRMT	EXC
COMPLETE SET (10)	20.00	9.00	2.50
COMMON CARD (1-10)	.50	.23	.06
☐ 1 Frank Thomas	8.00	3.60	1.00
☐ 2 David Justice	.50	.23	.06
☐ 3 Barry Bonds	2.00	.90	.25
☐ 4 Juan Gonzalez	4.00	1.80	.50
☐ 5 Ken Griffey Jr.	8.00	3.60	1.00
☐ 6 Mike Piazza	5.00	2.20	.60
☐ 7 Cecil Fielder	.75	.35	.09
☐ 8 Fred McGriff	1.00	.45	.12
☐ 9 Joe Carter	.75	.35	.09
☐ 10 Albert Belle	3.00	1.35	.35

1994 Leaf Slideshow

Randomly inserted in first and second series packs at a rate of one in 54, these ten standard-size cards simulate mounted photographic slides, but the images of the players are actually printed on acetate. The color transparencies can be seen best when they are held up to the light. The front of each transparency is framed by a simulated white slide holder, which at its bottom bears the player's name and the game from which the photo was shot. The insert sets's title is shown in blue and merges with the blue-edged bottom. The remaining edges are black. The back, in addition to the appearance of the slide's reverse image, carries comments about the player from Frank Thomas.

	MINT	NRMT	EXC
COMPLETE SET (10)	60.00	27.00	7.50
COMPLETE SERIES 1 (5)	30.00	13.50	3.70
COMPLETE SERIES 2 (5)	30.00	13.50	3.70
COMMON CARD (1-10)	1.50	.70	.19
☐ 1 Frank Thomas	20.00	9.00	2.50
☐ 2 Mike Piazza	12.00	5.50	1.50

Card	MINT	NRMT	EXC
☐ 3 Darren Daulton	1.50	.70	.19
☐ 4 Ryne Sandberg	5.00	2.20	.60
☐ 5 Roberto Alomar	4.00	1.80	.50
☐ 6 Barry Bonds	5.00	2.20	.60
☐ 7 Juan Gonzalez	10.00	4.50	1.25
☐ 8 Tim Salmon	3.00	1.35	.35
☐ 9 Ken Griffey Jr.	20.00	9.00	2.50
☐ 10 David Justice	2.00	.90	.25

1994 Leaf Statistical Standouts

Inserted in retail and hobby foil packs at a rate of one in 12, this 10-card standard-size set features players that had significant statistical achievements in 1993. For example: Cal Ripken's home run record for a shortstop. Card fronts contain a player photo that stands out from a background that is the colors of that player's team. The back contains a photo and statistical information.

	MINT	NRMT	EXC
COMPLETE SET (10)	20.00	9.00	2.50
COMMON CARD (1-10)	.50	.23	.06
☐ 1 Frank Thomas	5.00	2.20	.60
☐ 2 Barry Bonds	1.25	.55	.16
☐ 3 Juan Gonzalez	2.50	1.10	.30
☐ 4 Mike Piazza	3.00	1.35	.35
☐ 5 Greg Maddux	3.00	1.35	.35
☐ 6 Ken Griffey Jr.	5.00	2.20	.60
☐ 7 Joe Carter	.50	.23	.06
☐ 8 Dave Winfield	.75	.35	.09
☐ 9 Tony Gwynn	2.00	.90	.25
☐ 10 Cal Ripken	4.00	1.80	.50

1995 Leaf

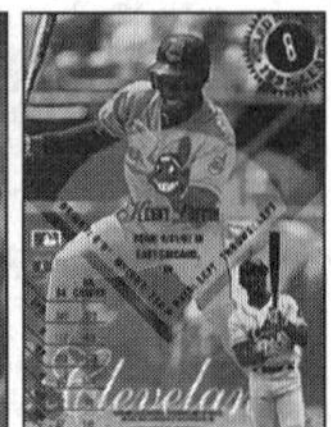

The 1995 Leaf set was issued in two series of 200 standard-size cards for a total of 400. Full-bleed fronts contain diamond-shaped player hologram in the upper left. The team name is done in silver foil up the left side. Peculiar backs contain two photos, the card number within a stamp or seal like emblem in the upper right and '94 and career stats graph toward bottom left. There are no key Rookie Cards in this set.

	MINT	NRMT	EXC
COMPLETE SET (400)	40.00	18.00	5.00
COMPLETE SERIES 1 (200)	15.00	6.75	1.85
COMPLETE SERIES 2 (200)	25.00	11.00	3.10
COMMON CARD (1-400)	.10	.05	.01
☐ 1 Frank Thomas	3.00	1.35	.35
☐ 2 Carlos Garcia	.10	.05	.01
☐ 3 Todd Hundley	.25	.11	.03
☐ 4 Damion Easley	.10	.05	.01
☐ 5 Roberto Mejia	.10	.05	.01
☐ 6 John Mabry	.50	.23	.06
☐ 7 Aaron Sele	.25	.11	.03
☐ 8 Kenny Lofton	.75	.35	.09
☐ 9 John Doherty	.10	.05	.01
☐ 10 Joe Carter	.25	.11	.03
☐ 11 Mike Lansing	.10	.05	.01
☐ 12 John Valentin	.25	.11	.03
☐ 13 Ismael Valdes	.25	.11	.03
☐ 14 Dave McCarty	.10	.05	.01
☐ 15 Melvin Nieves	.25	.11	.03
☐ 16 Bobby Jones	.25	.11	.03
☐ 17 Trevor Hoffman	.25	.11	.03
☐ 18 John Smoltz	.50	.23	.06
☐ 19 Leo Gomez	.10	.05	.01
☐ 20 Roger Pavlik	.10	.05	.01
☐ 21 Dean Palmer	.25	.11	.03
☐ 22 Rickey Henderson	.50	.23	.06
☐ 23 Eddie Taubensee	.10	.05	.01
☐ 24 Damon Buford	.10	.05	.01
☐ 25 Mark Wohlers	.25	.11	.03
☐ 26 Jim Edmonds	.50	.23	.06
☐ 27 Wilson Alvarez	.25	.11	.03
☐ 28 Matt Williams	.50	.23	.06
☐ 29 Jeff Montgomery	.25	.11	.03
☐ 30 Shawon Dunston	.10	.05	.01
☐ 31 Tom Pagnozzi	.10	.05	.01
☐ 32 Jose Lind	.10	.05	.01
☐ 33 Royce Clayton	.10	.05	.01
☐ 34 Cal Eldred	.10	.05	.01
☐ 35 Chris Gomez	.10	.05	.01
☐ 36 Henry Rodriguez	.25	.11	.03
☐ 37 Dave Fleming	.10	.05	.01
☐ 38 Jon Lieber	.10	.05	.01
☐ 39 Scott Servais	.10	.05	.01
☐ 40 Wade Boggs	.50	.23	.06
☐ 41 John Olerud	.10	.05	.01
☐ 42 Eddie Williams	.10	.05	.01
☐ 43 Paul Sorrento	.10	.05	.01
☐ 44 Ron Karkovice	.10	.05	.01
☐ 45 Kevin Foster	.10	.05	.01
☐ 46 Miguel Jimenez	.10	.05	.01
☐ 47 Reggie Sanders	.25	.11	.03
☐ 48 Rondell White	.25	.11	.03
☐ 49 Scott Leius	.10	.05	.01
☐ 50 Jose Valentin	.25	.11	.03
☐ 51 Wm. VanLandingham	.10	.05	.01
☐ 52 Denny Hocking	.10	.05	.01
☐ 53 Jeff Fassero	.10	.05	.01
☐ 54 Chris Hoiles	.10	.05	.01
☐ 55 Walt Weiss	.10	.05	.01
☐ 56 Geronimo Berroa	.10	.05	.01
☐ 57 Rich Rowland	.10	.05	.01
☐ 58 Dave Weathers	.10	.05	.01
☐ 59 Sterling Hitchcock	.25	.11	.03
☐ 60 Raul Mondesi	.50	.23	.06
☐ 61 Rusty Greer	.50	.23	.06
☐ 62 David Justice	.50	.23	.06
☐ 63 Cecil Fielder	.25	.11	.03
☐ 64 Brian Jordan	.50	.23	.06
☐ 65 Mike Lieberthal	.10	.05	.01
☐ 66 Rick Aguilera	.10	.05	.01
☐ 67 Chuck Finley	.25	.11	.03
☐ 68 Andy Ashby	.25	.11	.03
☐ 69 Alex Fernandez	.25	.11	.03
☐ 70 Ed Sprague	.25	.11	.03
☐ 71 Steve Buechele	.10	.05	.01
☐ 72 Willie Greene	.10	.05	.01
☐ 73 Dave Nilsson	.25	.11	.03
☐ 74 Bret Saberhagen	.25	.11	.03
☐ 75 Jimmy Key	.25	.11	.03
☐ 76 Darren Lewis	.10	.05	.01
☐ 77 Steve Cooke	.10	.05	.01
☐ 78 Kirk Gibson	.25	.11	.03
☐ 79 Ray Lankford	.25	.11	.03
☐ 80 Paul O'Neill	.25	.11	.03
☐ 81 Mike Bordick	.10	.05	.01
☐ 82 Wes Chamberlain	.10	.05	.01
☐ 83 Rico Brogna	.10	.05	.01
☐ 84 Kevin Appier	.25	.11	.03
☐ 85 Juan Guzman	.25	.11	.03
☐ 86 Kevin Seitzer	.10	.05	.01
☐ 87 Mickey Morandini	.10	.05	.01
☐ 88 Pedro Martinez	.25	.11	.03
☐ 89 Matt Mieske	.25	.11	.03
☐ 90 Tino Martinez	.25	.11	.03
☐ 91 Paul Shuey	.10	.05	.01
☐ 92 Bip Roberts	.10	.05	.01
☐ 93 Chili Davis	.25	.11	.03
☐ 94 Deion Sanders	.50	.23	.06
☐ 95 Darrell Whitmore	.10	.05	.01
☐ 96 Joe Orsulak	.10	.05	.01
☐ 97 Bret Boone	.25	.11	.03
☐ 98 Kent Mercker	.10	.05	.01
☐ 99 Scott Livingstone	.10	.05	.01
☐ 100 Brady Anderson	.50	.23	.06
☐ 101 James Mouton	.10	.05	.01
☐ 102 Jose Rijo	.10	.05	.01
☐ 103 Bobby Munoz	.10	.05	.01
☐ 104 Ramon Martinez	.25	.11	.03
☐ 105 Bernie Williams	.60	.25	.07
☐ 106 Troy Neel	.10	.05	.01
☐ 107 Ivan Rodriguez	.75	.35	.09
☐ 108 Salomon Torres	.10	.05	.01
☐ 109 Johnny Ruffin	.10	.05	.01
☐ 110 Darryl Kile	.10	.05	.01
☐ 111 Bobby Ayala	.10	.05	.01
☐ 112 Ron Darling	.10	.05	.01
☐ 113 Jose Lima	.10	.05	.01
☐ 114 Joey Hamilton	.50	.23	.06
☐ 115 Greg Maddux	2.00	.90	.25
☐ 116 Greg Colbrunn	.10	.05	.01
☐ 117 Ozzie Guillen	.10	.05	.01
☐ 118 Brian Anderson	.10	.05	.01
☐ 119 Jeff Bagwell	1.25	.55	.16
☐ 120 Pat Listach	.10	.05	.01
☐ 121 Sandy Alomar Jr.	.10	.05	.01
☐ 122 Jose Vizcaino	.10	.05	.01
☐ 123 Rick Helling	.10	.05	.01
☐ 124 Allen Watson	.10	.05	.01
☐ 125 Pedro Munoz	.10	.05	.01
☐ 126 Craig Biggio	.25	.11	.03
☐ 127 Kevin Stocker	.10	.05	.01
☐ 128 Wil Cordero	.10	.05	.01
☐ 129 Rafael Palmeiro	.50	.23	.06
☐ 130 Gar Finnvold	.10	.05	.01
☐ 131 Darren Hall	.10	.05	.01
☐ 132 Heath Slocumb	.10	.05	.01
☐ 133 Darrin Fletcher	.10	.05	.01
☐ 134 Cal Ripken	2.50	1.10	.30
☐ 135 Dante Bichette	.50	.23	.06
☐ 136 Don Slaught	.10	.05	.01
☐ 137 Pedro Astacio	.10	.05	.01
☐ 138 Ryan Thompson	.10	.05	.01
☐ 139 Greg Gohr	.10	.05	.01
☐ 140 Javier Lopez	.50	.23	.06
☐ 141 Lenny Dykstra	.25	.11	.03
☐ 142 Pat Rapp	.10	.05	.01
☐ 143 Mark Kiefer	.10	.05	.01
☐ 144 Greg Gagne	.10	.05	.01
☐ 145 Eduardo Perez	.10	.05	.01
☐ 146 Felix Fermin	.10	.05	.01
☐ 147 Jeff Frye	.10	.05	.01
☐ 148 Terry Steinbach	.25	.11	.03
☐ 149 Jim Eisenreich	.10	.05	.01
☐ 150 Brad Ausmus	.10	.05	.01
☐ 151 Randy Myers	.10	.05	.01
☐ 152 Rick White	.10	.05	.01
☐ 153 Mark Portugal	.10	.05	.01
☐ 154 Delino DeShields	.10	.05	.01
☐ 155 Scott Cooper	.10	.05	.01
☐ 156 Pat Hentgen	.25	.11	.03
☐ 157 Mark Gubicza	.10	.05	.01
☐ 158 Carlos Baerga	.50	.23	.06
☐ 159 Joe Girardi	.10	.05	.01
☐ 160 Rey Sanchez	.10	.05	.01
☐ 161 Todd Jones	.10	.05	.01
☐ 162 Luis Polonia	.10	.05	.01
☐ 163 Steve Trachsel	.10	.05	.01
☐ 164 Roberto Hernandez	.10	.05	.01
☐ 165 John Patterson	.10	.05	.01
☐ 166 Rene Arocha	.10	.05	.01
☐ 167 Will Clark	.50	.23	.06
☐ 168 Jim Leyritz	.10	.05	.01
☐ 169 Todd Van Poppel	.10	.05	.01
☐ 170 Robb Nen	.10	.05	.01
☐ 171 Midre Cummings	.10	.05	.01
☐ 172 Jay Buhner	.50	.23	.06
☐ 173 Kevin Tapani	.10	.05	.01
☐ 174 Mark Lemke	.10	.05	.01
☐ 175 Marcus Moore	.10	.05	.01
☐ 176 Wayne Kirby	.10	.05	.01
☐ 177 Rich Amaral	.10	.05	.01
☐ 178 Lou Whitaker	.25	.11	.03
☐ 179 Jay Bell	.25	.11	.03
☐ 180 Rick Wilkins	.10	.05	.01
☐ 181 Paul Molitor	.60	.25	.07
☐ 182 Gary Sheffield	.50	.23	.06
☐ 183 Kirby Puckett	1.25	.55	.16
☐ 184 Cliff Floyd	.25	.11	.03
☐ 185 Darren Oliver	.50	.23	.06
☐ 186 Tim Naehring	.10	.05	.01
☐ 187 John Hudek	.10	.05	.01
☐ 188 Eric Young	.25	.11	.03
☐ 189 Roger Salkeld	.10	.05	.01
☐ 190 Kirt Manwaring	.10	.05	.01
☐ 191 Kurt Abbott	.10	.05	.01
☐ 192 David Nied	.10	.05	.01
☐ 193 Todd Zeile	.10	.05	.01
☐ 194 Wally Joyner	.25	.11	.03
☐ 195 Dennis Martinez	.25	.11	.03
☐ 196 Billy Ashley	.10	.05	.01
☐ 197 Ben McDonald	.10	.05	.01
☐ 198 Bob Hamelin	.10	.05	.01
☐ 199 Chris Turner	.10	.05	.01
☐ 200 Lance Johnson	.25	.11	.03
☐ 201 Willie Banks	.10	.05	.01
☐ 202 Juan Gonzalez	1.50	.70	.19
☐ 203 Scott Sanders	.10	.05	.01
☐ 204 Scott Brosius	.10	.05	.01
☐ 205 Curt Schilling	.10	.05	.01
☐ 206 Alex Gonzalez	.25	.11	.03
☐ 207 Travis Fryman	.25	.11	.03
☐ 208 Tim Raines	.50	.23	.06
☐ 209 Steve Avery	.25	.11	.03
☐ 210 Hal Morris	.10	.05	.01
☐ 211 Ken Griffey Jr.	3.00	1.35	.35
☐ 212 Ozzie Smith	.75	.35	.09
☐ 213 Chuck Carr	.10	.05	.01
☐ 214 Ryan Klesko	.50	.23	.06
☐ 215 Robin Ventura	.25	.11	.03
☐ 216 Luis Gonzalez	.10	.05	.01
☐ 217 Ken Ryan	.10	.05	.01
☐ 218 Mike Piazza	2.00	.90	.25
☐ 219 Matt Walbeck	.10	.05	.01
☐ 220 Jeff Kent	.10	.05	.01
☐ 221 Orlando Miller	.10	.05	.01
☐ 222 Kenny Rogers	.10	.05	.01
☐ 223 J.T. Snow	.25	.11	.03
☐ 224 Alan Trammell	.25	.11	.03
☐ 225 John Franco	.10	.05	.01
☐ 226 Gerald Williams	.10	.05	.01
☐ 227 Andy Benes	.10	.05	.01
☐ 228 Dan Wilson	.25	.11	.03
☐ 229 Dave Hollins	.10	.05	.01
☐ 230 Vinny Castilla	.25	.11	.03
☐ 231 Devon White	.25	.11	.03
☐ 232 Fred McGriff	.50	.23	.06
☐ 233 Quilvio Veras	.10	.05	.01
☐ 234 Tom Candiotti	.10	.05	.01
☐ 235 Jason Bere	.10	.05	.01
☐ 236 Mark Langston	.10	.05	.01
☐ 237 Mel Rojas	.10	.05	.01
☐ 238 Chuck Knoblauch	.50	.23	.06
☐ 239 Bernard Gilkey	.25	.11	.03
☐ 240 Mark McGwire	1.00	.45	.12
☐ 241 Kirk Rueter	.10	.05	.01
☐ 242 Pat Kelly	.10	.05	.01
☐ 243 Ruben Sierra	.25	.11	.03
☐ 244 Randy Johnson	.50	.23	.06
☐ 245 Shane Reynolds	.25	.11	.03
☐ 246 Danny Tartabull	.10	.05	.01
☐ 247 Darryl Hamilton	.10	.05	.01
☐ 248 Danny Bautista	.10	.05	.01
☐ 249 Tom Gordon	.10	.05	.01
☐ 250 Tom Glavine	.50	.23	.06
☐ 251 Orlando Merced	.10	.05	.01
☐ 252 Eric Karros	.25	.11	.03
☐ 253 Benji Gil	.10	.05	.01
☐ 254 Sean Bergman	.10	.05	.01
☐ 255 Roger Clemens	.60	.25	.07
☐ 256 Roberto Alomar	.60	.25	.07
☐ 257 Benito Santiago	.10	.05	.01
☐ 258 Robby Thompson	.10	.05	.01
☐ 259 Marvin Freeman	.10	.05	.01
☐ 260 Jose Offerman	.10	.05	.01
☐ 261 Greg Vaughn	.25	.11	.03
☐ 262 David Segui	.10	.05	.01
☐ 263 Geronimo Pena	.10	.05	.01
☐ 264 Tim Salmon	.50	.23	.06
☐ 265 Eddie Murray	.75	.35	.09
☐ 266 Mariano Duncan	.10	.05	.01
☐ 267 Hideo Nomo	3.00	1.35	.35
☐ 268 Derek Bell	.25	.11	.03
☐ 269 Mo Vaughn	.75	.35	.09
☐ 270 Jeff King	.25	.11	.03
☐ 271 Edgar Martinez	.25	.11	.03
☐ 272 Sammy Sosa	.50	.23	.06
☐ 273 Scott Ruffcorn	.10	.05	.01
☐ 274 Darren Daulton	.25	.11	.03
☐ 275 John Jaha	.25	.11	.03
☐ 276 Andres Galarraga	.50	.23	.06
☐ 277 Mark Grace	.50	.23	.06
☐ 278 Mike Moore	.10	.05	.01
☐ 279 Barry Bonds	.75	.35	.09
☐ 280 Manny Ramirez	.75	.35	.09
☐ 281 Ellis Burks	.25	.11	.03
☐ 282 Greg Swindell	.10	.05	.01
☐ 283 Barry Larkin	.50	.23	.06
☐ 284 Albert Belle	1.25	.55	.16
☐ 285 Shawn Green	.25	.11	.03
☐ 286 John Roper	.10	.05	.01
☐ 287 Scott Erickson	.10	.05	.01
☐ 288 Moises Alou	.25	.11	.03
☐ 289 Mike Blowers	.10	.05	.01
☐ 290 Brent Gates	.10	.05	.01
☐ 291 Sean Berry	.10	.05	.01
☐ 292 Mike Stanley	.10	.05	.01
☐ 293 Jeff Conine	.25	.11	.03
☐ 294 Tim Wallach	.10	.05	.01
☐ 295 Bobby Bonilla	.25	.11	.03
☐ 296 Bruce Ruffin	.10	.05	.01
☐ 297 Chad Curtis	.10	.05	.01
☐ 298 Mike Greenwell	.10	.05	.01
☐ 299 Tony Gwynn	1.25	.55	.16
☐ 300 Russ Davis	.10	.05	.01
☐ 301 Danny Jackson	.10	.05	.01
☐ 302 Pete Harnisch	.10	.05	.01
☐ 303 Don Mattingly	1.50	.70	.19
☐ 304 Rheal Cormier	.10	.05	.01
☐ 305 Larry Walker	.50	.23	.06
☐ 306 Hector Carrasco	.10	.05	.01
☐ 307 Jason Jacome	.10	.05	.01
☐ 308 Phil Plantier	.10	.05	.01
☐ 309 Harold Baines	.25	.11	.03
☐ 310 Mitch Williams	.10	.05	.01
☐ 311 Charles Nagy	.25	.11	.03
☐ 312 Ken Caminiti	.50	.23	.06
☐ 313 Alex Rodriguez	4.00	1.80	.50
☐ 314 Chris Sabo	.10	.05	.01
☐ 315 Gary Gaetti	.25	.11	.03
☐ 316 Andre Dawson	.25	.11	.03
☐ 317 Mark Clark	.10	.05	.01
☐ 318 Vince Coleman	.10	.05	.01
☐ 319 Brad Clontz	.10	.05	.01
☐ 320 Steve Finley	.25	.11	.03
☐ 321 Doug Drabek	.10	.05	.01
☐ 322 Mark McLemore	.10	.05	.01
☐ 323 Stan Javier	.10	.05	.01
☐ 324 Ron Gant	.25	.11	.03
☐ 325 Charlie Hayes	.10	.05	.01
☐ 326 Carlos Delgado	.25	.11	.03
☐ 327 Ricky Bottalico	.25	.11	.03
☐ 328 Rod Beck	.10	.05	.01
☐ 329 Mark Acre	.10	.05	.01
☐ 330 Chris Bosio	.10	.05	.01
☐ 331 Tony Phillips	.25	.11	.03
☐ 332 Garret Anderson	.25	.11	.03
☐ 333 Pat Meares	.10	.05	.01
☐ 334 Todd Worrell	.10	.05	.01
☐ 335 Marquis Grissom	.25	.11	.03
☐ 336 Brent Mayne	.10	.05	.01
☐ 337 Lee Tinsley	.10	.05	.01
☐ 338 Terry Pendleton	.25	.11	.03
☐ 339 David Cone	.25	.11	.03
☐ 340 Tony Fernandez	.10	.05	.01
☐ 341 Jim Bullinger	.10	.05	.01
☐ 342 Armando Benitez	.10	.05	.01
☐ 343 John Smiley	.10	.05	.01
☐ 344 Dan Miceli	.10	.05	.01

☐ 345 Charles Johnson	.25	.11	.03
☐ 346 Lee Smith	.25	.11	.03
☐ 347 Brian McRae	.25	.11	.03
☐ 348 Jim Thome	.60	.25	.07
☐ 349 Jose Oliva	.10	.05	.01
☐ 350 Terry Mulholland	.10	.05	.01
☐ 351 Tom Henke	.10	.05	.01
☐ 352 Dennis Eckersley	.25	.11	.03
☐ 353 Sid Fernandez	.10	.05	.01
☐ 354 Paul Wagner	.10	.05	.01
☐ 355 John Dettmer	.10	.05	.01
☐ 356 John Wetteland	.25	.11	.03
☐ 357 John Burkett	.25	.11	.03
☐ 358 Marty Cordova	.50	.23	.06
☐ 359 Norm Charlton	.10	.05	.01
☐ 360 Mike Devereaux	.10	.05	.01
☐ 361 Alex Cole	.10	.05	.01
☐ 362 Brett Butler	.25	.11	.03
☐ 363 Mickey Tettleton	.10	.05	.01
☐ 364 Al Martin	.25	.11	.03
☐ 365 Tony Tarasco	.10	.05	.01
☐ 366 Pat Mahomes	.10	.05	.01
☐ 367 Gary DiSarcina	.10	.05	.01
☐ 368 Bill Swift	.10	.05	.01
☐ 369 Chipper Jones	2.00	.90	.25
☐ 370 Orel Hershiser	.25	.11	.03
☐ 371 Kevin Gross	.10	.05	.01
☐ 372 Dave Winfield	.50	.23	.06
☐ 373 Andujar Cedeno	.10	.05	.01
☐ 374 Jim Abbott	.10	.05	.01
☐ 375 Glenallen Hill	.10	.05	.01
☐ 376 Otis Nixon	.10	.05	.01
☐ 377 Roberto Kelly	.10	.05	.01
☐ 378 Chris Hammond	.10	.05	.01
☐ 379 Mike Macfarlane	.10	.05	.01
☐ 380 J.R. Phillips	.10	.05	.01
☐ 381 Luis Alicea	.10	.05	.01
☐ 382 Bret Barberie	.10	.05	.01
☐ 383 Tom Goodwin	.10	.05	.01
☐ 384 Mark Whiten	.10	.05	.01
☐ 385 Jeffrey Hammonds	.25	.11	.03
☐ 386 Omar Vizquel	.25	.11	.03
☐ 387 Mike Mussina	.60	.25	.07
☐ 388 Ricky Bones	.10	.05	.01
☐ 389 Steve Ontiveros	.10	.05	.01
☐ 390 Jeff Blauser	.10	.05	.01
☐ 391 Jose Canseco	.50	.23	.06
☐ 392 Bob Tewksbury	.10	.05	.01
☐ 393 Jacob Brumfield	.10	.05	.01
☐ 394 Doug Jones	.10	.05	.01
☐ 395 Ken Hill	.10	.05	.01
☐ 396 Pat Borders	.10	.05	.01
☐ 397 Carl Everett	.10	.05	.01
☐ 398 Gregg Jefferies	.25	.11	.03
☐ 399 Jack McDowell	.25	.11	.03
☐ 400 Denny Neagle	.25	.11	.03

1995 Leaf Checklists

Four checklist cards were randomly inserted in either series for a total of eight standard-size cards. Horizontal fronts feature a player photo from left to center with the start of the checklist to the right which continues on the back.

	MINT	NRMT	EXC
COMPLETE SET (8)	8.00	3.60	1.00
COMPLETE SERIES 1 (4)	4.00	1.80	.50
COMPLETE SERIES 2 (4)	4.00	1.80	.50
COMMON CARD (1-8)	.50	.23	.06
☐ 1 Bob Hamelin UER (Name spelled Hamlin)	.50	.23	.06
☐ 2 David Cone	.75	.35	.09
☐ 3 Frank Thomas	3.00	1.35	.35
☐ 4 Paul O'Neill	.75	.35	.09
☐ 5 Raul Mondesi	1.00	.45	.12
☐ 6 Greg Maddux	2.00	.90	.25
☐ 7 Tony Gwynn	1.25	.55	.16
☐ 8 Jeff Bagwell	1.25	.55	.16

1995 Leaf Cornerstones

Cards from this six-card standard-size set were randomly inserted in first series packs. Horizontally designed, leading first and thrid basemen from the same team are featured. The fronts have silver foil borders and team names with the team logo serving as background to the photos.The backs have a photo of either player with offensive and defensive stats.

	MINT	NRMT	EXC
COMPLETE SET (6)	10.00	4.50	1.25
COMMON CARD (1-6)	1.00	.45	.12

	MINT	NRMT	EXC
☐ 1 Frank Thomas / Robin Ventura	6.00	2.70	.75
☐ 2 Cecil Fielder / Travis Fryman	1.50	.70	.19
☐ 3 Don Mattingly / Wade Boggs	3.00	1.35	.35
☐ 4 Jeff Bagwell / Ken Caminiti	2.50	1.10	.30
☐ 5 Will Clark / Dean Palmer	1.50	.70	.19
☐ 6 J.R. Phillips / Matt Williams	1.00	.45	.12

1995 Leaf Gold Rookies

Inserted in every other first series pack, this 16-card standard-size set showcases those that were expected to have an impact in 1995. Card fronts offer two photos with various gold foil ornamentation. The backs have a large black and white photo with a smaller color photo inset at top left. The backs also contain career minor league stats.

	MINT	NRMT	EXC
COMPLETE SET (16)	6.00	2.70	.75
COMMON CARD (1-16)	.25	.11	.03
☐ 1 Alex Rodriguez	5.00	2.20	.60
☐ 2 Garret Anderson	.75	.35	.09
☐ 3 Shawn Green	.75	.35	.09
☐ 4 Armando Benitez	.25	.11	.03
☐ 5 Darren Dreifort	.25	.11	.03
☐ 6 Orlando Miller	.75	.35	.09
☐ 7 Jose Oliva	.25	.11	.03
☐ 8 Ricky Bottalico	.75	.35	.09
☐ 9 Charles Johnson	.75	.35	.09
☐ 10 Brian L.Hunter	.75	.35	.09
☐ 11 Ray McDavid	.25	.11	.03
☐ 12 Chan Ho Park	1.00	.45	.12
☐ 13 Mike Kelly	.25	.11	.03
☐ 14 Cory Bailey	.25	.11	.03
☐ 15 Alex Gonzalez	.75	.35	.09
☐ 16 Andrew Lorraine	.25	.11	.03

1995 Leaf Gold Stars

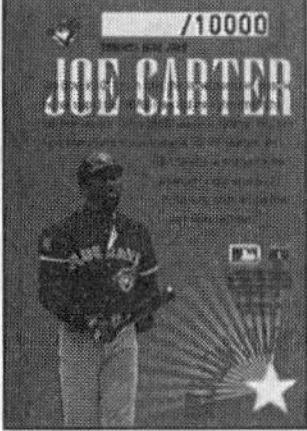

Randomly inserted in first and second series packs at a rate of one in 110, this 14-card standard-size set (eight first series, six second series) showcases some of the game's superstars.Individually numbered on back out of 10,000, the cards feature fronts that have a player photo superimposed metallic, refractive background. A die-cut star is in the lower left corner. The backs have a small player photo and brief write-up in addition to the numbering.

	MINT	NRMT	EXC
COMPLETE SET (14)	300.00	135.00	38.00
COMPLETE SERIES 1 (8)	150.00	70.00	19.00
COMPLETE SERIES 2 (6)	150.00	70.00	19.00
COMMON CARD (1-14)	8.00	3.60	1.00
☐ 1 Jeff Bagwell	20.00	9.00	2.50
☐ 2 Albert Belle	20.00	9.00	2.50
☐ 3 Tony Gwynn	20.00	9.00	2.50
☐ 4 Ken Griffey Jr.	50.00	22.00	6.25
☐ 5 Barry Bonds	12.00	5.50	1.50
☐ 6 Don Mattingly	25.00	11.00	3.10
☐ 7 Raul Mondesi	10.00	4.50	1.25
☐ 8 Joe Carter	8.00	3.60	1.00
☐ 9 Greg Maddux	35.00	16.00	4.40
☐ 10 Frank Thomas	50.00	22.00	6.25
☐ 11 Mike Piazza	30.00	13.50	3.70
☐ 12 Jose Canseco	10.00	4.50	1.25
☐ 13 Kirby Puckett	20.00	9.00	2.50
☐ 14 Matt Williams	10.00	4.50	1.25

1995 Leaf Great Gloves

This 16-card standard-size set was randomly inserted in series two packs at a rate of approximately two cards every three packs. The players featured are leading defensive players. Action photos are set against a background that includes part of a glove. The player's name and team are stamped in gold foil. The horizontal backs feature a photo set against a glove, information about the player and their 1994 defensive statistics. The cards are numbered "X" of 16 in the upper right.

	MINT	NRMT	EXC
COMPLETE SET (16)	10.00	4.50	1.25
COMMON CARD (1-16)	.25	.11	.03
☐ 1 Jeff Bagwell	1.25	.55	.16
☐ 2 Roberto Alomar	.60	.25	.07
☐ 3 Barry Bonds	.75	.35	.09
☐ 4 Wade Boggs	.50	.23	.06
☐ 5 Andres Galarraga	.50	.23	.06
☐ 6 Ken Griffey Jr.	3.00	1.35	.35
☐ 7 Marquis Grissom	.25	.11	.03
☐ 8 Kenny Lofton	.75	.35	.09
☐ 9 Barry Larkin	.50	.23	.06
☐ 10 Don Mattingly	1.50	.70	.19
☐ 11 Greg Maddux	2.00	.90	.25
☐ 12 Kirby Puckett	1.25	.55	.16
☐ 13 Ozzie Smith	.75	.35	.09
☐ 14 Cal Ripken Jr.	2.50	1.10	.30
☐ 15 Matt Williams	.50	.23	.06
☐ 16 Ivan Rodriguez	.75	.35	.09

1995 Leaf Heading for the Hall

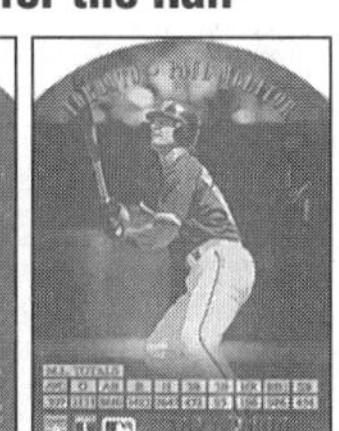

This eight-card standard-size set was randomly inserted into series two hobby packs. The cards are cut in the shape of a Hall of Fame plaque and are designed as if this were the actual information on the player's plaque in Cooperstown. The backs feature a black and white photo along with career statistics. The cards are individually numbered out of 5,000 as well.

	MINT	NRMT	EXC
COMPLETE SET (8)	300.00	135.00	38.00
COMMON CARD (1-8)	15.00	6.75	1.85
☐ 1 Frank Thomas	80.00	36.00	10.00
☐ 2 Ken Griffey Jr.	80.00	36.00	10.00
☐ 3 Jeff Bagwell	30.00	13.50	3.70
☐ 4 Barry Bonds	20.00	9.00	2.50
☐ 5 Kirby Puckett	30.00	13.50	3.70
☐ 6 Cal Ripken	60.00	27.00	7.50
☐ 7 Tony Gwynn	30.00	13.50	3.70
☐ 8 Paul Molitor	15.00	6.75	1.85

1995 Leaf Opening Day

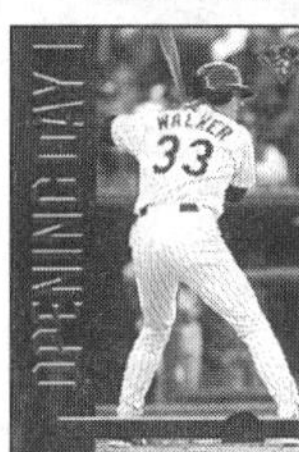
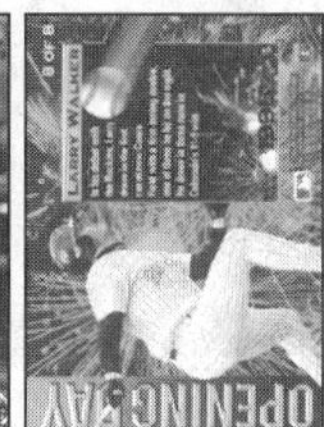

This eight-card standard-size set was available through a wrapper mail-in offer. Upon receipt of eight 1995 Leaf, Studio or Donruss wrappers, a collector received this set. Besides the wrappers, the set cost $2 in shipping and handling and the final deadline was Aug. 31, 1995. The fronts have the words "1995 Opening Day" on the left with the player's picture and name on the right. The "Leaf 95" logo is in the upper right corner. All photos were taken on opening day including shots of Larry Walker as a Colorado Rockie and Jose Canseco in his Boston Red Sox debut. The horizontal backs contain the words "Opening Day" on the left with the rest of the card dedicated to the player's photo against a background of exploding fireworks. A brief inset of the player's opening day performance is included as well. The cards are numbered "X" of 8 in the upper right corner.

	MINT	NRMT	EXC
COMPLETE SET (8)	12.00	5.50	1.50
COMMON CARD (1-8)	.40	.18	.05
☐ 1 Frank Thomas	3.00	1.35	.35
☐ 2 Jeff Bagwell	1.00	.45	.12
☐ 3 Barry Bonds	.75	.35	.09
☐ 4 Ken Griffey Jr.	3.00	1.35	.35
☐ 5 Mike Piazza	1.25	.55	.16
☐ 6 Cal Ripken	3.00	1.35	.35
☐ 7 Jose Canseco	.60	.25	.07
☐ 8 Larry Walker	.40	.18	.05

1995 Leaf Slideshow

This 16-card standard-size set was issued eight per series and randomly inserted at a rate of per box. The eight cards in the first series are numbered 1A-8A and repeated with different photos in the second series as 1B-8B. Both version carry the same value. The left side of the card front is semi-circular featuring three player translucent "slides".

	MINT	NRMT	EXC
COMPLETE SET (16)	80.00	36.00	10.00
COMPLETE SERIES 1 (8)	40.00	18.00	5.00
COMPLETE SERIES 2 (8)	40.00	18.00	5.00
COMMON CARD (1-8)	2.00	.90	.25
☐ 1A Raul Mondesi	4.00	1.80	.50
☐ 1B Raul Mondesi	4.00	1.80	.50
☐ 2A Frank Thomas	15.00	6.75	1.85
☐ 2B Frank Thomas	15.00	6.75	1.85
☐ 3A Fred McGriff	4.00	1.80	.50
☐ 3B Fred McGriff	4.00	1.80	.50
☐ 4A Cal Ripken	12.00	5.50	1.50
☐ 4B Cal Ripken	15.00	6.75	1.85
☐ 5A Jeff Bagwell	6.00	2.70	.75
☐ 5B Jeff Bagwell	6.00	2.70	.75
☐ 6A Will Clark	4.00	1.80	.50
☐ 6B Will Clark	4.00	1.80	.50
☐ 7A Matt Williams	4.00	1.80	.50
☐ 7B Matt Williams	4.00	1.80	.50
☐ 8A Ken Griffey Jr.	15.00	6.75	1.85
☐ 8B Ken Griffey Jr.	15.00	6.75	1.85

1995 Leaf Statistical Standouts

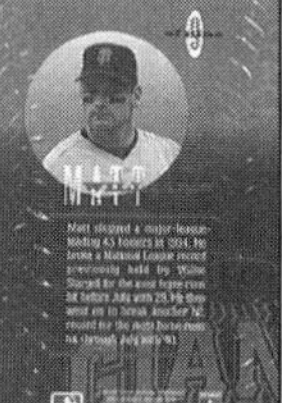

Randomly inserted in first series hobby packs at a rate of one in 70, this set features nine players who stood out from the rest statistically. The fronts contain a player photo between embossed seams or stitches of a baseball. The backs have a small circular player photo with 1994 highlights.

	MINT	NRMT	EXC
COMPLETE SET (9)	450.00	200.00	55.00
COMMON CARD (1-9)	15.00	6.75	1.85
☐ 1 Joe Carter	15.00	6.75	1.85
☐ 2 Ken Griffey Jr.	125.00	55.00	15.50
☐ 3 Don Mattingly	60.00	27.00	7.50
☐ 4 Fred McGriff	15.00	6.75	1.85
☐ 5 Paul Molitor	25.00	11.00	3.10
☐ 6 Kirby Puckett	50.00	22.00	6.25
☐ 7 Cal Ripken	100.00	45.00	12.50
☐ 8 Frank Thomas	125.00	55.00	15.50
☐ 9 Matt Williams	15.00	6.75	1.85

1995 Leaf Thomas

This six-card standard-size set was randomly inserted into series two packs. The fronts feature an action photo and have Season "X" on the bottom. The backs have a player photo, information about a specific season in Thomas' career as well as those seasonal stats.

	MINT	NRMT	EXC
COMPLETE SET (6)	25.00	11.00	3.10
COMMON CARD (1-6)	5.00	2.20	.60
☐ 1 Frank Thomas The Rookie	5.00	2.20	.60
☐ 2 Frank Thomas Sophomore Stardom	5.00	2.20	.60
☐ 3 Frank Thomas Superstar	5.00	2.20	.60
☐ 4 Frank Thomas AL MVP	5.00	2.20	.60
☐ 5 Frank Thomas Back-To-Back	5.00	2.20	.60
☐ 6 Frank Thomas The Big Hurt	5.00	2.20	.60

1995 Leaf 300 Club

Randomly inserted in first and second series mini and retail packs on a three per box basis, this set depicts all 18 players who had a career average of .300 or better entering the 1995 campaign. A large ghosted 300 serves as background to a player photo. Gold foil is at the bottom in either corner including career average in the right corner. Full-bleed backs list the 18 players and their averages to that point.

	MINT	NRMT	EXC
COMPLETE SET (18)	125.00	55.00	15.50
COMPLETE SERIES 1 (9)	50.00	22.00	6.25
COMPLETE SERIES 2 (9)	75.00	34.00	9.50
COMMON CARD (1-18)	2.00	.90	.25
☐ 1 Frank Thomas	30.00	13.50	3.70
☐ 2 Paul Molitor	6.00	2.70	.75
☐ 3 Mike Piazza	20.00	9.00	2.50
☐ 4 Moises Alou	3.00	1.35	.35
☐ 5 Mike Greenwell	2.00	.90	.25
☐ 6 Will Clark	4.00	1.80	.50
☐ 7 Hal Morris	2.00	.90	.25
☐ 8 Edgar Martinez	3.00	1.35	.35
☐ 9 Carlos Baerga	2.00	.90	.25
☐ 10 Ken Griffey Jr.	30.00	13.50	3.70
☐ 11 Wade Boggs	4.00	1.80	.50
☐ 12 Jeff Bagwell	12.00	5.50	1.50
☐ 13 Tony Gwynn	12.00	5.50	1.50
☐ 14 John Kruk	2.00	.90	.25
☐ 15 Don Mattingly	15.00	6.75	1.85
☐ 16 Mark Grace	4.00	1.80	.50
☐ 17 Kirby Puckett	12.00	5.50	1.50
☐ 18 Kenny Lofton	8.00	3.60	1.00

1996 Leaf

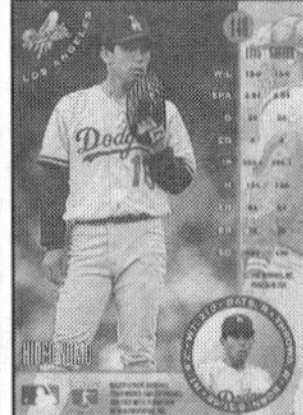

The 1996 Leaf set was issued in one series totalling 220 cards. The fronts feature color action player photos with silver foil printing and lines forming a border on the left and bottom. The backs display another player photo with 1995 season and career statistics. Card number 210 is a checklist for the insert sets and cards number 211-220 feature rookies. The fronts of these 10 cards are different in design from the first 200 with a color action player cut-out over a green-shadow background of the same picture and gold lettering. The horizontal backs carry another player cut-out on a purple-and-black background with 1995 season statistics and personal information.

	MINT	NRMT	EXC
COMPLETE SET (220)	20.00	9.00	2.50
COMMON CARD (1-220)	.10	.05	.01
☐ 1 John Smoltz	.50	.23	.06
☐ 2 Dennis Eckersley	.25	.11	.03
☐ 3 Delino DeShields	.10	.05	.01
☐ 4 Cliff Floyd	.10	.05	.01
☐ 5 Chuck Finley	.10	.05	.01
☐ 6 Cecil Fielder	.25	.11	.03
☐ 7 Tim Naehring	.10	.05	.01
☐ 8 Carlos Perez	.10	.05	.01
☐ 9 Brad Ausmus	.10	.05	.01
☐ 10 Matt Lawton	.10	.05	.01
☐ 11 Alan Trammell	.25	.11	.03
☐ 12 Steve Finley	.50	.23	.06
☐ 13 Paul O'Neill	.10	.05	.01
☐ 14 Gary Sheffield	.50	.23	.06
☐ 15 Mark McGwire	1.00	.45	.12
☐ 16 Bernie Williams	.60	.25	.07
☐ 17 Jeff Montgomery	.10	.05	.01
☐ 18 Chan Ho Park	.50	.23	.06
☐ 19 Greg Vaughn	.50	.23	.06
☐ 20 Jeff Kent	.10	.05	.01
☐ 21 Cal Ripken	2.50	1.10	.30
☐ 22 Charles Johnson	.25	.11	.03
☐ 23 Eric Karros	.25	.11	.03
☐ 24 Alex Rodriguez	3.00	1.35	.35
☐ 25 Chris Snopek	.10	.05	.01
☐ 26 Jason Isringhausen	.50	.23	.06
☐ 27 Chili Davis	.10	.05	.01
☐ 28 Chipper Jones	2.00	.90	.25
☐ 29 Bret Saberhagen	.10	.05	.01
☐ 30 Tony Clark	.60	.25	.07
☐ 31 Marty Cordova	.25	.11	.03
☐ 32 Dwayne Hosey	.10	.05	.01
☐ 33 Fred McGriff	.50	.23	.06
☐ 34 Deion Sanders	.50	.23	.06
☐ 35 Orlando Merced	.10	.05	.01
☐ 36 Brady Anderson	.50	.23	.06
☐ 37 Ray Lankford	.25	.11	.03
☐ 38 Manny Ramirez	.75	.35	.09
☐ 39 Alex Fernandez	.25	.11	.03
☐ 40 Greg Colbrunn	.10	.05	.01
☐ 41 Ken Griffey, Jr.	3.00	1.35	.35
☐ 42 Mickey Moradini	.10	.05	.01
☐ 43 Chuck Knoblauch	.50	.23	.06
☐ 44 Quinton McCracken	.10	.05	.01
☐ 45 Tim Salmon	.50	.23	.06
☐ 46 Jose Mesa	.25	.11	.03
☐ 47 Marquis Grissom	.25	.11	.03
☐ 48 Checklist	.10	.05	.01
☐ 49 Raul Mondesi	.50	.23	.06
☐ 50 Mark Grudzielanek	.25	.11	.03
☐ 51 Ray Durham	.50	.23	.06
☐ 52 Matt Williams	.50	.23	.06
☐ 53 Bob Hamelin	.10	.05	.01
☐ 54 Lenny Dykstra	.25	.11	.03
☐ 55 Jeff King	.25	.11	.03
☐ 56 LaTroy Hawkins	.10	.05	.01
☐ 57 Terry Pendleton	.10	.05	.01
☐ 58 Kevin Stocker	.10	.05	.01
☐ 59 Ozzie Timmons	.10	.05	.01
☐ 60 David Justice	.25	.11	.03
☐ 61 Ricky Bottalico	.10	.05	.01
☐ 62 Andy Ashby	.10	.05	.01
☐ 63 Larry Walker	.50	.23	.06
☐ 64 Jose Canseco	.50	.23	.06
☐ 65 Bret Boone	.10	.05	.01
☐ 66 Shawn Green	.10	.05	.01
☐ 67 Chad Curtis	.10	.05	.01
☐ 68 Travis Fryman	.25	.11	.03
☐ 69 Roger Clemens	.60	.25	.07
☐ 70 David Bell	.10	.05	.01
☐ 71 Rusty Greer	.50	.23	.06
☐ 72 Bob Higginson	.50	.23	.06
☐ 73 Joey Hamilton	.25	.11	.03
☐ 74 Kevin Seitzer	.10	.05	.01
☐ 75 Julian Tavarez	.10	.05	.01
☐ 76 Troy Percival	.10	.05	.01
☐ 77 Kirby Puckett	1.25	.55	.16
☐ 78 Barry Bonds	.75	.35	.09
☐ 79 Michael Tucker	.25	.11	.03
☐ 80 Paul Molitor	.60	.25	.07
☐ 81 Carlos Garcia	.10	.05	.01
☐ 82 Johnny Damon	.25	.11	.03
☐ 83 Mike Hampton	.10	.05	.01
☐ 84 Ariel Prieto	.10	.05	.01
☐ 85 Tony Tarasco	.10	.05	.01
☐ 86 Pete Schourek	.25	.11	.03
☐ 87 Tom Glavine	.50	.23	.06
☐ 88 Rondell White	.25	.11	.03
☐ 89 Jim Edmonds	.25	.11	.03
☐ 90 Robby Thompson	.10	.05	.01
☐ 91 Wade Boggs	.50	.23	.06
☐ 92 Pedro Martinez	.25	.11	.03
☐ 93 Gregg Jefferies	.50	.23	.06
☐ 94 Albert Belle	1.25	.55	.16
☐ 95 Benji Gil	.10	.05	.01
☐ 96 Denny Neagle	.25	.11	.03
☐ 97 Mark Langston	.10	.05	.01
☐ 98 Sandy Alomar, Jr.	.10	.05	.01
☐ 99 Tony Gwynn	1.25	.55	.16
☐ 100 Todd Hundley	.25	.11	.03
☐ 101 Dante Bichette	.50	.23	.06
☐ 102 Eddie Murray	.75	.35	.09
☐ 103 Lyle Mouton	.10	.05	.01
☐ 104 John Jaha	.25	.11	.03
☐ 105 Checklist	.10	.05	.01
☐ 106 Jon Nunnally	.10	.05	.01
☐ 107 Juan Gonzalez	1.50	.70	.19
☐ 108 Kevin Appier	.25	.11	.03
☐ 109 Brian McRae	.10	.05	.01
☐ 110 Lee Smith	.25	.11	.03
☐ 111 Tim Wakefield	.10	.05	.01
☐ 112 Sammy Sosa	.50	.23	.06
☐ 113 Jay Buhner	.50	.23	.06
☐ 114 Garret Anderson	.50	.23	.06
☐ 115 Edgar Martinez	.25	.11	.03
☐ 116 Edgardo Alfonzo	.25	.11	.03
☐ 117 Billy Ashley	.10	.05	.01
☐ 118 Joe Carter	.25	.11	.03
☐ 119 Javy Lopez	.25	.11	.03
☐ 120 Bobby Bonilla	.25	.11	.03
☐ 121 Ken Caminiti	.50	.23	.06
☐ 122 Barry Larkin	.50	.23	.06
☐ 123 Shannon Stewart	.10	.05	.01
☐ 124 Orel Hershiser	.25	.11	.03
☐ 125 Jeff Conine	.25	.11	.03
☐ 126 Mark Grace	.50	.23	.06
☐ 127 Kenny Lofton	.75	.35	.09
☐ 128 Luis Gonzalez	.10	.05	.01
☐ 129 Rico Brogna	.10	.05	.01
☐ 130 Mo Vaughn	.75	.35	.09
☐ 131 Brad Radke	.10	.05	.01
☐ 132 Jose Herrera	.10	.05	.01
☐ 133 Rick Aguilera	.10	.05	.01
☐ 134 Gary DiSarcina	.10	.05	.01
☐ 135 Andres Galarraga	.50	.23	.06
☐ 136 Carl Everett	.10	.05	.01
☐ 137 Steve Avery	.25	.11	.03
☐ 138 Vinny Castilla	.25	.11	.03
☐ 139 Dennis Martinez	.25	.11	.03
☐ 140 John Wetteland	.25	.11	.03
☐ 141 Alex Gonzalez	.10	.05	.01
☐ 142 Brian Jordan	.25	.11	.03
☐ 143 Todd Hollandsworth	.25	.11	.03
☐ 144 Terrell Wade	.25	.11	.03
☐ 145 Wilson Alvarez	.50	.23	.06
☐ 146 Reggie Sanders	.25	.11	.03
☐ 147 Will Clark	.50	.23	.06
☐ 148 Hideo Nomo	.75	.35	.09
☐ 149 J.T.Snow	.25	.11	.03
☐ 150 Frank Thomas	3.00	1.35	.35
☐ 151 Ivan Rodriguez	.75	.35	.09
☐ 152 Jay Bell	.25	.11	.03
☐ 153 Checklist	.10	.05	.01
☐ 154 David Cone	.25	.11	.03
☐ 155 Roberto Alomar	.60	.25	.07
☐ 156 Carlos Delgado	.25	.11	.03
☐ 157 Carlos Baerga	.25	.11	.03
☐ 158 Geronimo Berroa	.25	.11	.03
☐ 159 Joe Vitiello	.10	.05	.01
☐ 160 Terry Steinbach	.25	.11	.03
☐ 161 Doug Drabek	.10	.05	.01
☐ 162 David Segui	.10	.05	.01
☐ 163 Ozzie Smith	.75	.35	.09
☐ 164 Kurt Abbott	.10	.05	.01
☐ 165 Randy Johnson	.50	.23	.06
☐ 166 John Valentin	.25	.11	.03
☐ 167 Mickey Tettleton	.25	.11	.03
☐ 168 Ruben Sierra	.10	.05	.01
☐ 169 Jim Thome	.60	.25	.07
☐ 170 Mike Greenwell	.10	.05	.01
☐ 171 Quilvio Veras	.10	.05	.01
☐ 172 Robin Ventura	.25	.11	.03
☐ 173 Bill Pulsipher	.25	.11	.03
☐ 174 Rafael Palmeiro	.50	.23	.06
☐ 175 Hal Morris	.10	.05	.01
☐ 176 Ryan Klesko	.50	.23	.06
☐ 177 Eric Young	.25	.11	.03
☐ 178 Shane Andrews	.10	.05	.01
☐ 179 Brian L.Hunter	.25	.11	.03
☐ 180 Brett Butler	.10	.05	.01
☐ 181 John Olerud	.10	.05	.01
☐ 182 Moises Alou	.25	.11	.03
☐ 183 Glenallen Hill	.10	.05	.01
☐ 184 Ismael Valdes	.25	.11	.03
☐ 185 Andy Pettitte	1.00	.45	.12
☐ 186 Yamil Benitez	.25	.11	.03
☐ 187 Jason Bere	.10	.05	.01
☐ 188 Dean Palmer	.25	.11	.03
☐ 189 Jimmy Haynes	.10	.05	.01
☐ 190 Trevor Hoffman	.25	.11	.03
☐ 191 Mike Mussina	.60	.25	.07
☐ 192 Greg Maddux	2.00	.90	.25
☐ 193 Ozzie Guillen	.10	.05	.01
☐ 194 Pat Listach	.10	.05	.01
☐ 195 Derek Bell	.25	.11	.03
☐ 196 Darren Daulton	.25	.11	.03
☐ 197 John Mabry	.25	.11	.03
☐ 198 Ramon Martinez	.25	.11	.03
☐ 199 Jeff Bagwell	1.25	.55	.16
☐ 200 Mike Piazza	2.00	.90	.25
☐ 201 Al Martin	.10	.05	.01
☐ 202 Aaron Sele	.10	.05	.01
☐ 203 Ed Sprague	.25	.11	.03
☐ 204 Rod Beck	.25	.11	.03
☐ 205 Checklist	.10	.05	.01
☐ 206 Mike Lansing	.10	.05	.01
☐ 207 Craig Biggio	.25	.11	.03
☐ 208 Jeffrey Hammonds	.10	.05	.01
☐ 209 Dave Nilsson	.25	.11	.03
☐ 210 Checklist	.10	.05	.01
☐ 211 Derek Jeter	2.00	.90	.25
☐ 212 Alan Benes	.50	.23	.06
☐ 213 Jason Schmidt	.50	.23	.06
☐ 214 Alex Ochoa	.25	.11	.03
☐ 215 Ruben Rivera	.60	.25	.07
☐ 216 Roger Cedeno	.25	.11	.03
☐ 217 Jeff Suppan	.50	.23	.06
☐ 218 Billy Wagner	.50	.23	.06
☐ 219 Mark Loretta	.10	.05	.01
☐ 220 Karim Garcia	.60	.25	.07

1996 Leaf Press Proofs Bronze

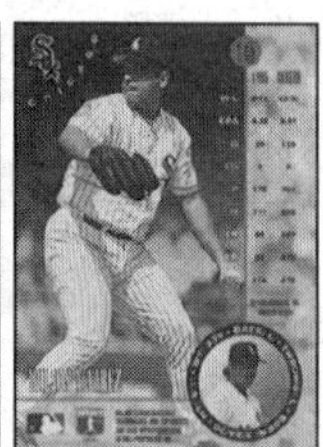

This 220-card Bronze set is parallel to the regular Leaf set and between the three types of press proofs were inserted at a rate of one in 10 packs. Similar in design to the regular set, 2,000 Bronze sets were produced and feature a special holographic foil.

	MINT	NRMT	EXC
COMPLETE SET (220)	600.00	275.00	75.00
COMMON CARD (1-220)	1.00	.45	.12

*STARS: 6X TO 12X BASIC CARDS ...
*YOUNG STARS: 5X TO 10X BASIC CARDS

1996 Leaf Press Proofs Gold

This 220-card Gold set is parallel to the regular Leaf set. Only five hundred sets were produced and they were randomly inserted into packs.

	MINT	NRMT	EXC
COMPLETE SET (220)	3000.00	1350.00	375.00
COMMON CARD (1-220)	5.00	2.20	.60

*STARS: 30X to 60X BASIC CARDS...
*YOUNG STARS: 25X to 50X BASIC CARDS

1996 Leaf Press Proofs Silver

This 220-card Silver set is also a parallel to the regular Leaf issue. One thousand sets were produced and the cards were randomly inserted into packs.

	MINT	NRMT	EXC
COMPLETE SET (220)	1200.00	550.00	150.00
COMMON CARD (1-220)	2.00	.90	.25

*STARS: 12.5X to 25X BASIC CARDS
*YOUNG STARS: 10X to 20X BASIC CARDS

1996 Leaf All-Star Game MVP Contenders

This 20 card set features possible contenders for the MVP at the 1996 All-Star Game held in Philadelphia. The cards were randomly inserted into packs. If the player on the front of the card won the MVP Award (which turned out to be Mike Piazza), the holder could send it in for a special Gold MVP Contenders set of which only 5,000 were produced.

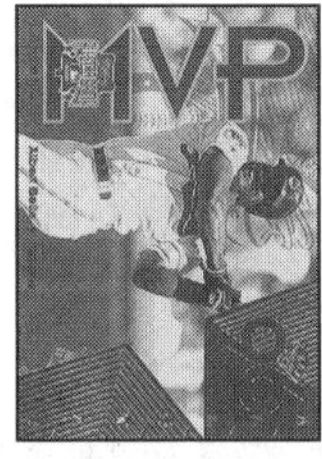

The fronts display a color action player photo. The backs carry the instructions on how to redeem the card. The expiration date for the redemption was August 15th, 1996.

	MINT	NRMT	EXC
COMPLETE SET (20	40.00	18.00	5.00
COMMON CARD (1-20)	.75	.35	.09
☐ 1 Frank Thomas	6.00	2.70	.75
☐ 2 Mike Piazza	6.00	2.70	.75
☐ 3 Sammy Sosa	1.25	.55	.16
☐ 4 Cal Ripken	5.00	2.20	.60
☐ 5 Jeff Bagwell	2.50	1.10	.30
☐ 6 Reggie Sanders	1.00	.45	.12
☐ 7 Mo Vaughn	1.50	.70	.19
☐ 8 Tony Gwynn	2.50	1.10	.30
☐ 9 Dante Bichette	1.25	.55	.16
☐ 10 Tim Salmon	1.25	.55	.16
☐ 11 Chipper Jones	4.00	1.80	.50
☐ 12 Kenny Lofton	1.50	.70	.19
☐ 13 Manny Ramirez	1.50	.70	.19
☐ 14 Barry Bonds	1.50	.70	.19
☐ 15 Raul Mondesi	1.25	.55	.16
☐ 16 Kirby Puckett	2.50	1.10	.30
☐ 17 Albert Belle	2.50	1.10	.30
☐ 18 Ken Griffey Jr.	6.00	2.70	.75
☐ 19 Greg Maddux	4.00	1.80	.50
☐ 20 Bonus Card	.75	.35	.09

1996 Leaf All-Star Game MVP Contenders Gold

This 20 card set is a parallel to the regular Leaf All-Star Gold MVP set. This set was only available if a collector sent in the winning Mike Piazza card.

	MINT	NRMT	EXC
COMPLETE SET (20)	40.00	18.00	5.00
COMMON CARD (1-20)	.75	.35	.09

*GOLD CARDS: .5X to 1X BASIC CARDS

1996 Leaf Gold Stars

Randomly inserted in hobby and retail packs at a rate of one in 200, this 15-card set honors some of the games great players on 22 karat gold trim cards. Only 2,500 cards of each player were printed and are individually numbered.

	MINT	NRMT	EXC
COMPLETE SET (15)	650.00	300.00	80.00
COMMON CARD (1-15)	12.00	5.50	1.50
☐ 1 Frank Thomas	100.00	45.00	12.50
☐ 2 Dante Bichette	15.00	6.75	1.85
☐ 3 Sammy Sosa	15.00	6.75	1.85
☐ 4 Ken Griffey Jr.	100.00	45.00	12.50
☐ 5 Mike Piazza	60.00	27.00	7.50
☐ 6 Tim Salmon	15.00	6.75	1.85
☐ 7 Hideo Nomo	25.00	11.00	3.10
☐ 8 Cal Ripken	80.00	36.00	10.00
☐ 9 Chipper Jones	60.00	27.00	7.50
☐ 10 Albert Belle	40.00	18.00	5.00
☐ 11 Tony Gwynn	40.00	18.00	5.00
☐ 12 Mo Vaughn	25.00	11.00	3.10
☐ 13 Barry Larkin	12.00	5.50	1.50
☐ 14 Manny Ramirez	25.00	11.00	3.10
☐ 15 Greg Maddux	60.00	27.00	7.50

1996 Leaf Hats Off

Randomly inserted in retail packs only at a rate of one in 72, this 8-card set was printed and embossed on a wool-like material with the feel of a Major League ball cap. Only 5,000 of each player was produced and is individually numbered.

	MINT	NRMT	EXC
COMPLETE SET (8)	200.00	90.00	25.00
COMMON CARD (1-8)	6.00	2.70	.75

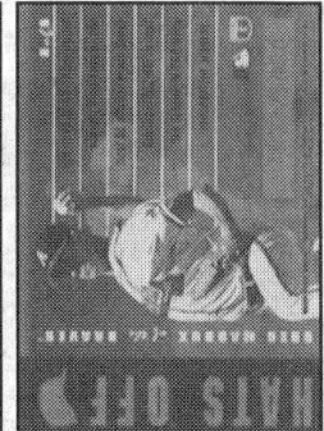

	MINT	NRMT	EXC
☐ 1 Cal Ripken	40.00	18.00	5.00
☐ 2 Barry Larkin	6.00	2.70	.75
☐ 3 Frank Thomas	50.00	22.00	6.25
☐ 4 Mo Vaughn	12.00	5.50	1.50
☐ 5 Ken Griffey Jr.	50.00	22.00	6.25
☐ 6 Hideo Nomo	12.00	5.50	1.50
☐ 7 Albert Belle	20.00	9.00	2.50
☐ 8 Greg Maddux	30.00	13.50	3.70

1996 Leaf Picture Perfect

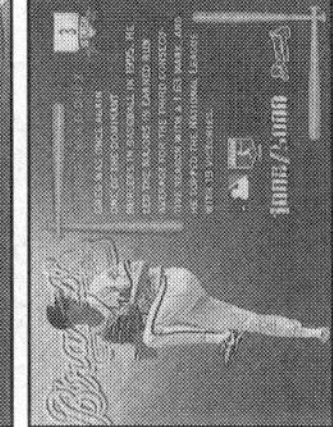

Randomly inserted in hobby (1-6) and retail (7-12) packs at a rate of one in 140, this 12-card set is printed on real wood with gold foil trim. The fronts feature a color player action framed photo. The backs carry another player photo with player information. Only 5,000 of each card were printed and are individually numbered.

	MINT	NRMT	EXC
COMPLETE SET (12)	250.00	110.00	31.00
COMMON CARD (1-12)	10.00	4.50	1.25
☐ 1 Frank Thomas	40.00	18.00	5.00
☐ 2 Cal Ripken	30.00	13.50	3.70
☐ 3 Greg Maddux	25.00	11.00	3.10
☐ 4 Manny Ramirez	10.00	4.50	1.25
☐ 5 Chipper Jones	25.00	11.00	3.10
☐ 6 Tony Gwynn	15.00	6.75	1.85
☐ 7 Ken Griffey Jr.	40.00	18.00	5.00
☐ 8 Albert Belle	15.00	6.75	1.85
☐ 9 Jeff Bagwell	15.00	6.75	1.85
☐ 10 Mike Piazza	25.00	11.00	3.10
☐ 11 Mo Vaughn	10.00	4.50	1.25
☐ 12 Barry Bonds	10.00	4.50	1.25

1996 Leaf Statistical Standouts

Randomly inserted in hobby packs only at a rate of one in 210, this 8-card set features eight players who stood out from the rest statistically. The cards were printed on a material with the feel of the leather that's between the seams or stitches of a baseball. Only 2,500 of each card was printed and is numbered individually.

	MINT	NRMT	EXC
COMPLETE SET (8)	450.00	200.00	55.00
COMMON CARD (1-8)	30.00	13.50	3.70
☐ 1 Cal Ripken	100.00	45.00	12.50
☐ 2 Tony Gwynn	50.00	22.00	6.25
☐ 3 Frank Thomas	120.00	55.00	15.00
☐ 4 Ken Griffey Jr.	120.00	55.00	15.00
☐ 5 Hideo Nomo	30.00	13.50	3.70
☐ 6 Greg Maddux	75.00	34.00	9.50
☐ 7 Albert Belle	50.00	22.00	6.25
☐ 8 Chipper Jones	75.00	34.00	9.50

1996 Leaf Thomas Greatest Hits

Randomly inserted in hobby (1-4), retail (5-7) and redemption (8) packs at a rate of one in 210, this 8-card set was printed on die-cut plastic to simulate a compact disc. The cards feature the statistical highlights of Frank Thomas. The wrapper displays the details for the special mail-in offer to obtain card number 8.

	MINT	NRMT	EXC
COMPLETE SET (8)	150.00	70.00	19.00
COMMON CARD (1-7)	25.00	11.00	3.10
COMMON EXCHANGE (8)	30.00	13.50	3.70
☐ 1 Frank Thomas 1990	25.00	11.00	3.10
☐ 2 Frank Thomas 1991	25.00	11.00	3.10
☐ 3 Frank Thomas 1992	25.00	11.00	3.10
☐ 4 Frank Thomas 1993	25.00	11.00	3.10
☐ 5 Frank Thomas 1994	25.00	11.00	3.10
☐ 6 Frank Thomas 1995	25.00	11.00	3.10
☐ 7 Frank Thomas Career	25.00	11.00	3.10
☐ 8 Frank Thomas MVP	30.00	13.50	3.70

1996 Leaf Total Bases

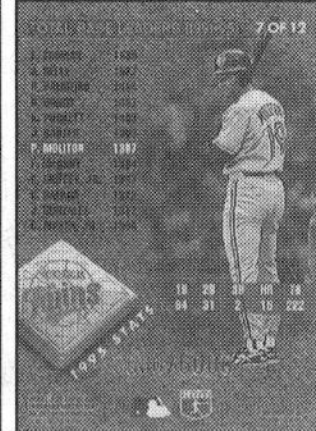

Randomly inserted in hobby packs only at a rate of one in 72, this 12-card set is printed on canvas and features the top offensive stars. Only 5,000 of each card was printed and are individually numbered. The fronts carry a color action player cut-out over a base background. The backs display another player photo and 1995 stats.

	MINT	NRMT	EXC
COMPLETE SET (12)	150.00	70.00	19.00
COMMON CARD (1-12)	3.00	1.35	.35
☐ 1 Frank Thomas	30.00	13.50	3.70
☐ 2 Albert Belle	12.00	5.50	1.50
☐ 3 Rafael Palmeiro	5.00	2.20	.60
☐ 4 Barry Bonds	8.00	3.60	1.00
☐ 5 Kirby Puckett	12.00	5.50	1.50
☐ 6 Joe Carter	4.00	1.80	.50
☐ 7 Paul Molitor	6.00	2.70	.75
☐ 8 Fred McGriff	5.00	2.20	.60
☐ 9 Ken Griffey Jr.	30.00	13.50	3.70
☐ 10 Carlos Baerga	3.00	1.35	.35
☐ 11 Juan Gonzalez	15.00	6.75	1.85
☐ 12 Cal Ripken	25.00	11.00	3.10

1994 Leaf Limited

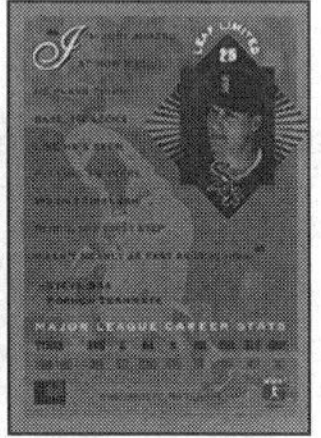

This 160-card standard-size set was issued exclusively to hobby dealers. The fronts display silver holographic Spectra Tech foiling and a silhouetted player action photo over full silver foil. The backs contain silver holographic Spectra Tech foil, two photos, and a quote about the player by well-known baseball personalities. The set is organized alphabetically within teams with AL preceding NL.

	MINT	NRMT	EXC
COMPLETE SET (160)	100.00	45.00	12.50
COMMON CARD (1-160)	.25	.11	.03
☐ 1 Jeffrey Hammonds	.50	.23	.06
☐ 2 Ben McDonald	.25	.11	.03
☐ 3 Mike Mussina	2.00	.90	.25
☐ 4 Rafael Palmeiro	1.25	.55	.16
☐ 5 Cal Ripken Jr.	8.00	3.60	1.00
☐ 6 Lee Smith	.50	.23	.06
☐ 7 Roger Clemens	2.00	.90	.25
☐ 8 Scott Cooper	.25	.11	.03
☐ 9 Andre Dawson	.50	.23	.06
☐ 10 Mike Greenwell	.25	.11	.03
☐ 11 Aaron Sele	.50	.23	.06
☐ 12 Mo Vaughn	2.50	1.10	.30
☐ 13 Brian Anderson	.50	.23	.06
☐ 14 Chad Curtis	.25	.11	.03
☐ 15 Chili Davis	.50	.23	.06
☐ 16 Gary DiSarcina	.25	.11	.03
☐ 17 Mark Langston	.50	.23	.06
☐ 18 Tim Salmon	1.50	.70	.19
☐ 19 Wilson Alvarez	.50	.23	.06
☐ 20 Jason Bere	.50	.23	.06
☐ 21 Julio Franco	.50	.23	.06
☐ 22 Jack McDowell	.50	.23	.06
☐ 23 Tim Raines	1.25	.55	.16
☐ 24 Frank Thomas	10.00	4.50	1.25
☐ 25 Robin Ventura	.50	.23	.06
☐ 26 Carlos Baerga	.50	.23	.06
☐ 27 Albert Belle	4.00	1.80	.50
☐ 28 Kenny Lofton	3.00	1.35	.35
☐ 29 Eddie Murray	2.50	1.10	.30
☐ 30 Manny Ramirez	3.00	1.35	.35
☐ 31 Cecil Fielder	.50	.23	.06
☐ 32 Travis Fryman	.50	.23	.06
☐ 33 Mickey Tettleton	.25	.11	.03
☐ 34 Alan Trammell	.50	.23	.06
☐ 35 Lou Whitaker	.50	.23	.06
☐ 36 David Cone	.50	.23	.06
☐ 37 Gary Gaetti	.50	.23	.06
☐ 38 Greg Gagne	.25	.11	.03
☐ 39 Bob Hamelin	.25	.11	.03
☐ 40 Wally Joyner	.50	.23	.06
☐ 41 Brian McRae	.50	.23	.06
☐ 42 Ricky Bones	.25	.11	.03
☐ 43 Brian Harper	.25	.11	.03
☐ 44 John Jaha	.50	.23	.06
☐ 45 Pat Listach	.25	.11	.03
☐ 46 Dave Nilsson	.50	.23	.06
☐ 47 Greg Vaughn	1.25	.55	.16
☐ 48 Kent Hrbek	.50	.23	.06
☐ 49 Chuck Knoblauch	1.25	.55	.16
☐ 50 Shane Mack	.25	.11	.03
☐ 51 Kirby Puckett	4.00	1.80	.50
☐ 52 Dave Winfield	1.25	.55	.16
☐ 53 Jim Abbott	.25	.11	.03
☐ 54 Wade Boggs	1.25	.55	.16
☐ 55 Jimmy Key	.50	.23	.06
☐ 56 Don Mattingly	5.00	2.20	.60
☐ 57 Paul O'Neill	.50	.23	.06
☐ 58 Danny Tartabull	.25	.11	.03
☐ 59 Dennis Eckersley	.50	.23	.06
☐ 60 Rickey Henderson	1.25	.55	.16
☐ 61 Mark McGwire	3.00	1.35	.35
☐ 62 Troy Neel	.25	.11	.03
☐ 63 Ruben Sierra	.50	.23	.06
☐ 64 Eric Anthony	.25	.11	.03
☐ 65 Jay Buhner	1.25	.55	.16
☐ 66 Ken Griffey Jr.	10.00	4.50	1.25
☐ 67 Randy Johnson	1.50	.70	.19
☐ 68 Edgar Martinez	.50	.23	.06
☐ 69 Tino Martinez	.50	.23	.06
☐ 70 Jose Canseco	1.25	.55	.16
☐ 71 Will Clark	1.25	.55	.16
☐ 72 Juan Gonzalez	5.00	2.20	.60
☐ 73 Dean Palmer	.50	.23	.06
☐ 74 Ivan Rodriguez	2.50	1.10	.30
☐ 75 Roberto Alomar	2.00	.90	.25
☐ 76 Joe Carter	.50	.23	.06
☐ 77 Carlos Delgado	1.25	.55	.16
☐ 78 Paul Molitor	2.00	.90	.25
☐ 79 John Olerud	.25	.11	.03
☐ 80 Devon White	.25	.11	.03
☐ 81 Steve Avery	.50	.23	.06
☐ 82 Tom Glavine	1.25	.55	.16
☐ 83 David Justice	1.25	.55	.16
☐ 84 Roberto Kelly	.25	.11	.03
☐ 85 Ryan Klesko	2.00	.90	.25
☐ 86 Javier Lopez	1.25	.55	.16
☐ 87 Greg Maddux	6.00	2.70	.75
☐ 88 Fred McGriff	1.25	.55	.16
☐ 89 Shawon Dunston	.25	.11	.03
☐ 90 Mark Grace	1.25	.55	.16
☐ 91 Derrick May	.25	.11	.03
☐ 92 Sammy Sosa	1.50	.70	.19
☐ 93 Rick Wilkins	.25	.11	.03
☐ 94 Bret Boone	.50	.23	.06
☐ 95 Barry Larkin	1.25	.55	.16
☐ 96 Kevin Mitchell	.50	.23	.06
☐ 97 Hal Morris	.25	.11	.03
☐ 98 Deion Sanders	1.25	.55	.16
☐ 99 Reggie Sanders	.50	.23	.06
☐ 100 Dante Bichette	1.25	.55	.16
☐ 101 Ellis Burks	.50	.23	.06
☐ 102 Andres Galarraga	1.25	.55	.16
☐ 103 Joe Girardi	.25	.11	.03
☐ 104 Charlie Hayes	.25	.11	.03
☐ 105 Chuck Carr	.25	.11	.03
☐ 106 Jeff Conine	.50	.23	.06
☐ 107 Bryan Harvey	.25	.11	.03
☐ 108 Benito Santiago	.25	.11	.03
☐ 109 Gary Sheffield	1.50	.70	.19
☐ 110 Jeff Bagwell	4.00	1.80	.50
☐ 111 Craig Biggio	.50	.23	.06
☐ 112 Ken Caminiti	1.25	.55	.16
☐ 113 Andujar Cedeno	.25	.11	.03
☐ 114 Doug Drabek	.25	.11	.03
☐ 115 Luis Gonzalez	.25	.11	.03
☐ 116 Brett Butler	.50	.23	.06
☐ 117 Delino DeShields	.25	.11	.03
☐ 118 Eric Karros	.50	.23	.06
☐ 119 Raul Mondesi	1.50	.70	.19

Card	MINT	NRMT	EXC
☐ 120 Mike Piazza	6.00	2.70	.75
☐ 121 Henry Rodriguez	.50	.23	.06
☐ 122 Tim Wallach	.25	.11	.03
☐ 123 Moises Alou	.50	.23	.06
☐ 124 Cliff Floyd	1.25	.55	.16
☐ 125 Marquis Grissom	.50	.23	.06
☐ 126 Ken Hill	.25	.11	.03
☐ 127 Larry Walker	1.25	.55	.16
☐ 128 John Wetteland	.50	.23	.06
☐ 129 Bobby Bonilla	.50	.23	.06
☐ 130 John Franco	.25	.11	.03
☐ 131 Jeff Kent	.25	.11	.03
☐ 132 Bret Saberhagen	.50	.23	.06
☐ 133 Ryan Thompson	.25	.11	.03
☐ 134 Darren Daulton	.50	.23	.06
☐ 135 Mariano Duncan	.25	.11	.03
☐ 136 Lenny Dykstra	.50	.23	.06
☐ 137 Danny Jackson	.25	.11	.03
☐ 138 John Kruk	.50	.23	.06
☐ 139 Jay Bell	.50	.23	.06
☐ 140 Jeff King	.50	.23	.06
☐ 141 Al Martin	.25	.11	.03
☐ 142 Orlando Merced	.50	.23	.06
☐ 143 Andy Van Slyke	.50	.23	.06
☐ 144 Bernard Gilkey	.50	.23	.06
☐ 145 Gregg Jefferies	1.25	.55	.16
☐ 146 Ray Lankford	.50	.23	.06
☐ 147 Ozzie Smith	2.50	1.10	.30
☐ 148 Mark Whiten	.25	.11	.03
☐ 149 Todd Zeile	.25	.11	.03
☐ 150 Derek Bell	.50	.23	.06
☐ 151 Andy Benes	.50	.23	.06
☐ 152 Tony Gwynn	4.00	1.80	.50
☐ 153 Phil Plantier	.25	.11	.03
☐ 154 Bip Roberts	.25	.11	.03
☐ 155 Rod Beck	.50	.23	.06
☐ 156 Barry Bonds	2.50	1.10	.30
☐ 157 John Burkett	.25	.11	.03
☐ 158 Royce Clayton	.50	.23	.06
☐ 159 Bill Swift	.25	.11	.03
☐ 160 Matt Williams	1.25	.55	.16

1994 Leaf Limited Gold All-Stars

Randomly inserted in packs at a rate of one in eight, this 18-card standard-size set features the starting players at each position in both the National and American leagues for the 1994 All-Star Game. They are identical in design to the basic Limited product except for being gold and individually numbered out of 10,000.

	MINT	NRMT	EXC
COMPLETE SET (18)	175.00	80.00	22.00
COMMON CARD (1-18)	3.00	1.35	.35
☐ 1 Frank Thomas	40.00	18.00	5.00
☐ 2 Gregg Jefferies	4.00	1.80	.50
☐ 3 Roberto Alomar	8.00	3.60	1.00
☐ 4 Mariano Duncan	3.00	1.35	.35
☐ 5 Wade Boggs	5.00	2.20	.60
☐ 6 Matt Williams	5.00	2.20	.60
☐ 7 Cal Ripken Jr.	30.00	13.50	3.70
☐ 8 Ozzie Smith	10.00	4.50	1.25
☐ 9 Kirby Puckett	15.00	6.75	1.85
☐ 10 Barry Bonds	10.00	4.50	1.25
☐ 11 Ken Griffey Jr.	40.00	18.00	5.00
☐ 12 Tony Gwynn	15.00	6.75	1.85
☐ 13 Joe Carter	4.00	1.80	.50
☐ 14 David Justice	4.00	1.80	.50
☐ 15 Ivan Rodriguez	10.00	4.50	1.25
☐ 16 Mike Piazza	25.00	11.00	3.10
☐ 17 Jimmy Key	4.00	1.80	.50
☐ 18 Greg Maddux	25.00	11.00	3.10

1994 Leaf Limited Rookies

This 80-card standard-size set was issued exclusively to hobby dealers. The set showcases top rookies and prospects of 1994. The fronts display silver holographic Spectra Tech foiling and a silhouetted player action photo over full silver foil. The word "Rookies" appears in black letters above the Leaf Limited logo at top. The backs contain silver holographic Spectra Tech foil, two photos, and a quote about the player by well-known baseball personalities. Rookie Cards in this set include Kurt Abbott, Rusty Greer, Bill VanLandingham and Ismael Valdes.

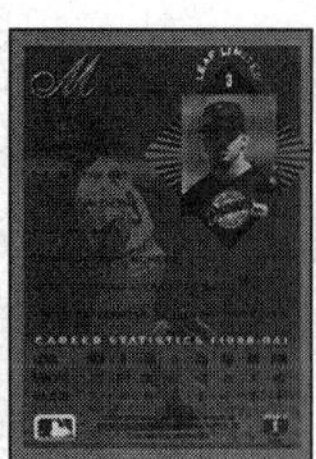

	MINT	NRMT	EXC
COMPLETE SET (80)	35.00	16.00	4.40
COMMON CARD (1-80)	.25	.11	.03
☐ 1 Charles Johnson	1.00	.45	.12
☐ 2 Rico Brogna	.25	.11	.03
☐ 3 Melvin Nieves	.50	.23	.06
☐ 4 Rich Becker	.50	.23	.06
☐ 5 Russ Davis	.50	.23	.06
☐ 6 Matt Mieske	.25	.11	.03
☐ 7 Paul Shuey	.25	.11	.03
☐ 8 Hector Carrasco	.25	.11	.03
☐ 9 J.R. Phillips	.25	.11	.03
☐ 10 Scott Ruffcorn	.25	.11	.03
☐ 11 Kurt Abbott	.50	.23	.06
☐ 12 Danny Bautista	.25	.11	.03
☐ 13 Rick White	.25	.11	.03
☐ 14 Steve Dunn	.25	.11	.03
☐ 15 Joe Ausanio	.25	.11	.03
☐ 16 Salomon Torres	.25	.11	.03
☐ 17 Ricky Bottalico	1.00	.45	.12
☐ 18 Johnny Ruffin	.25	.11	.03
☐ 19 Kevin Foster	.25	.11	.03
☐ 20 W.VanLandingham	.50	.23	.06
☐ 21 Troy O'Leary	.25	.11	.03
☐ 22 Mark Acre	.25	.11	.03
☐ 23 Norberto Martin	.25	.11	.03
☐ 24 Jason Jacome	.50	.23	.06
☐ 25 Steve Trachsel	.50	.23	.06
☐ 26 Denny Hocking	.25	.11	.03
☐ 27 Mike Lieberthal	.25	.11	.03
☐ 28 Gerald Williams	.25	.11	.03
☐ 29 John Mabry	1.25	.55	.16
☐ 30 Greg Blosser	.25	.11	.03
☐ 31 Carl Everett	.25	.11	.03
☐ 32 Steve Karsay	.25	.11	.03
☐ 33 Jose Valentin	1.25	.55	.16
☐ 34 Jon Lieber	.25	.11	.03
☐ 35 Chris Gomez	.25	.11	.03
☐ 36 Jesus Tavarez	.25	.11	.03
☐ 37 Tony Longmire	.25	.11	.03
☐ 38 Luis Lopez	.25	.11	.03
☐ 39 Matt Walbeck	.25	.11	.03
☐ 40 Rikkert Faneyte	.25	.11	.03
☐ 41 Shane Reynolds	.50	.23	.06
☐ 42 Joey Hamilton	2.00	.90	.25
☐ 43 Ismael Valdes	4.00	1.80	.50
☐ 44 Danny Miceli	.25	.11	.03
☐ 45 Darren Bragg	.50	.23	.06
☐ 46 Alex Gonzalez	.50	.23	.06
☐ 47 Rick Helling	.25	.11	.03
☐ 48 Jose Oliva	.50	.23	.06
☐ 49 Jim Edmonds	2.00	.90	.25
☐ 50 Miguel Jimenez	.25	.11	.03
☐ 51 Tony Eusebio	.25	.11	.03
☐ 52 Shawn Green	.50	.23	.06
☐ 53 Billy Ashley	.25	.11	.03
☐ 54 Rondell White	1.00	.45	.12
☐ 55 Cory Bailey	.25	.11	.03
☐ 56 Tim Davis	.25	.11	.03
☐ 57 John Hudek	.25	.11	.03
☐ 58 Darren Hall	.25	.11	.03
☐ 59 Darren Dreifort	.50	.23	.06
☐ 60 Mike Kelly	.25	.11	.03
☐ 61 Marcus Moore	.25	.11	.03
☐ 62 Garret Anderson	1.00	.45	.12
☐ 63 Brian L.Hunter	1.50	.70	.19
☐ 64 Mark Smith	.25	.11	.03
☐ 65 Garey Ingram	.25	.11	.03
☐ 66 Rusty Greer	5.00	2.20	.60
☐ 67 Marc Newfield	.50	.23	.06
☐ 68 Gar Finnvold	.25	.11	.03
☐ 69 Paul Spoljaric	.25	.11	.03
☐ 70 Ray McDavid	.50	.23	.06
☐ 71 Orlando Miller	.25	.11	.03
☐ 72 Jorge Fabregas	.25	.11	.03
☐ 73 Ray Holbert	.25	.11	.03
☐ 74 Armando Benitez	.25	.11	.03
☐ 75 Ernie Young	.75	.35	.09
☐ 76 James Mouton	.50	.23	.06
☐ 77 Robert Perez	.25	.11	.03
☐ 78 Chan Ho Park	3.00	1.35	.35
☐ 79 Roger Salkeld	.25	.11	.03
☐ 80 Tony Tarasco	.25	.11	.03

1994 Leaf Limited Rookies Phenoms

This 10-card standard-size set was randomly inserted in Leaf Limited Rookies packs at a rate of approximately of one in eight. Limited to 5,000, the set showcases top 1994 rookies. The fronts are designed much like the Limited Rookies except the card is comprised of gold foil instead of silver. Gold backs are also virtually identical to the Limited Rookies in terms of content and layout. The cards are individually numbered on back out of 5,000.

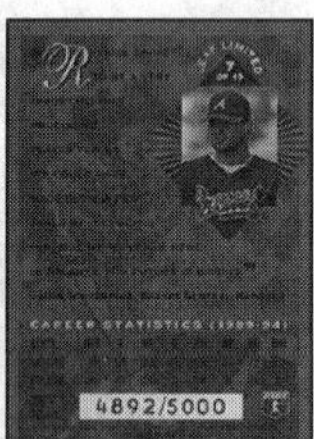

	MINT	NRMT	EXC
COMPLETE SET (10)	200.00	90.00	25.00
COMMON CARD (1-10)	8.00	3.60	1.00
☐ 1 Raul Mondesi	15.00	6.75	1.85
☐ 2 Bob Hamelin	8.00	3.60	1.00
☐ 3 Midre Cummings	8.00	3.60	1.00
☐ 4 Carlos Delgado	12.00	5.50	1.50
☐ 5 Cliff Floyd	10.00	4.50	1.25
☐ 6 Jeffrey Hammonds	8.00	3.60	1.00
☐ 7 Ryan Klesko	20.00	9.00	2.50
☐ 8 Javier Lopez	12.00	5.50	1.50
☐ 9 Manny Ramirez	30.00	13.50	3.70
☐ 10 Alex Rodriguez	100.00	45.00	12.50

1995 Leaf Limited

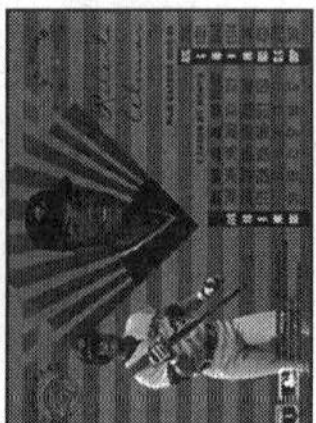

This 192 standard-size card set was issued in two series. Each series contained 96 cards. These cards were issued in six-box cases with 20 packs per box and five cards per pack. Forty-five thousand boxes of each series was produced. The fronts feature a player photo shot against a silver holographic foil background. The player is identified on the top with his team name on the right. The "Leaf Limited" logo is on the bottom of the card. The horizontal backs contain two player photos along with career stats broken down on a monthly basis. The cards are numbered in the upper right corner. Rookie Cards in this set include Bob Higginson and Hideo Nomo.

	MINT	NRMT	EXC
COMPLETE SET (192)	70.00	32.00	8.75
COMPLETE SERIES 1 (96)	35.00	16.00	4.40
COMPLETE SERIES 2 (96)	35.00	16.00	4.40
COMMON CARD (1-192)	.25	.11	.03
☐ 1 Frank Thomas	8.00	3.60	1.00
☐ 2 Geronimo Berroa	.25	.11	.03
☐ 3 Tony Phillips	.50	.23	.06
☐ 4 Roberto Alomar	2.00	.90	.25
☐ 5 Steve Avery	.50	.23	.06
☐ 6 Darryl Hamilton	.25	.11	.03
☐ 7 Scott Cooper	.25	.11	.03
☐ 8 Mark Grace	1.00	.45	.12
☐ 9 Billy Ashley	.25	.11	.03
☐ 10 Wil Cordero	.25	.11	.03
☐ 11 Barry Bonds	2.00	.90	.25
☐ 12 Kenny Lofton	2.00	.90	.25
☐ 13 Jay Buhner	1.00	.45	.12
☐ 14 Alex Rodriguez	10.00	4.50	1.25
☐ 15 Bobby Bonilla	.50	.23	.06
☐ 16 Brady Anderson	1.00	.45	.12
☐ 17 Ken Caminiti	1.00	.45	.12
☐ 18 Charlie Hayes	.25	.11	.03
☐ 19 Jay Bell	.50	.23	.06
☐ 20 Will Clark	1.00	.45	.12
☐ 21 Jose Canseco	1.00	.45	.12
☐ 22 Bret Boone	.50	.23	.06
☐ 23 Dante Bichette	1.00	.45	.12
☐ 24 Kevin Appier	.50	.23	.06
☐ 25 Chad Curtis	.25	.11	.03
☐ 26 Marty Cordova	1.00	.45	.12
☐ 27 Jason Bere	.25	.11	.03
☐ 28 Jimmy Key	.50	.23	.06
☐ 29 Rickey Henderson	1.00	.45	.12
☐ 30 Tim Salmon	1.00	.45	.12
☐ 31 Joe Carter	.50	.23	.06
☐ 32 Tom Glavine	1.00	.45	.12
☐ 33 Pat Listach	.25	.11	.03
☐ 34 Brian Jordan	1.00	.45	.12
☐ 35 Brian McRae	.50	.23	.06
☐ 36 Eric Karros	.50	.23	.06
☐ 37 Pedro Martinez	.50	.23	.06
☐ 38 Royce Clayton	.25	.11	.03
☐ 39 Eddie Murray	2.00	.90	.25
☐ 40 Randy Johnson	1.00	.45	.12
☐ 41 Jeff Conine	.50	.23	.06
☐ 42 Brett Butler	.50	.23	.06
☐ 43 Jeffrey Hammonds	.50	.23	.06
☐ 44 Andujar Cedeno	.25	.11	.03
☐ 45 Dave Hollins	.25	.11	.03
☐ 46 Jeff King	.50	.23	.06
☐ 47 Benji Gil	.25	.11	.03
☐ 48 Roger Clemens	1.50	.70	.19
☐ 49 Barry Larkin	1.00	.45	.12
☐ 50 Joe Girardi	.25	.11	.03
☐ 51 Bob Hamelin	.25	.11	.03
☐ 52 Travis Fryman	.50	.23	.06
☐ 53 Chuck Knoblauch	1.00	.45	.12
☐ 54 Ray Durham	.50	.23	.06
☐ 55 Don Mattingly	4.00	1.80	.50
☐ 56 Ruben Sierra	.50	.23	.06
☐ 57 J.T. Snow	.50	.23	.06
☐ 58 Derek Bell	.50	.23	.06
☐ 59 David Cone	.50	.23	.06
☐ 60 Marquis Grissom	.50	.23	.06
☐ 61 Kevin Seitzer	.25	.11	.03
☐ 62 Ozzie Smith	2.00	.90	.25
☐ 63 Rick Wilkins	.25	.11	.03
☐ 64 Hideo Nomo	8.00	3.60	1.00
☐ 65 Tony Tarasco	.25	.11	.03
☐ 66 Manny Ramirez	2.00	.90	.25
☐ 67 Charles Johnson	.50	.23	.06
☐ 68 Craig Biggio	.50	.23	.06
☐ 69 Bobby Jones	.50	.23	.06
☐ 70 Mike Mussina	1.50	.70	.19
☐ 71 Alex Gonzalez	.50	.23	.06
☐ 72 Gregg Jefferies	.50	.23	.06
☐ 73 Rusty Greer	1.00	.45	.12
☐ 74 Mike Greenwell	.25	.11	.03
☐ 75 Hal Morris	.25	.11	.03
☐ 76 Paul O'Neill	.50	.23	.06
☐ 77 Luis Gonzalez	.25	.11	.03
☐ 78 Chipper Jones	5.00	2.20	.60
☐ 79 Mike Piazza	5.00	2.20	.60
☐ 80 Rondell White	.50	.23	.06
☐ 81 Glenallen Hill	.25	.11	.03
☐ 82 Shawn Green	.50	.23	.06
☐ 83 Bernie Williams	1.50	.70	.19
☐ 84 Jim Thome	1.50	.70	.19
☐ 85 Terry Pendleton	.50	.23	.06
☐ 86 Rafael Palmeiro	1.00	.45	.12
☐ 87 Tony Gwynn	3.00	1.35	.35
☐ 88 Mickey Tettleton	.25	.11	.03
☐ 89 John Valentin	.50	.23	.06
☐ 90 Deion Sanders	1.00	.45	.12
☐ 91 Larry Walker	1.00	.45	.12
☐ 92 Michael Tucker	.50	.23	.06
☐ 93 Alan Trammell	.50	.23	.06
☐ 94 Tim Raines	1.00	.45	.12
☐ 95 David Justice	1.00	.45	.12
☐ 96 Tino Martinez	.50	.23	.06
☐ 97 Cal Ripken, Jr.	6.00	2.70	.75
☐ 98 Deion Sanders	1.00	.45	.12
☐ 99 Darren Daulton	.50	.23	.06
☐ 100 Paul Molitor	1.50	.70	.19
☐ 101 Randy Myers	.25	.11	.03
☐ 102 Wally Joyner	.50	.23	.06
☐ 103 Carlos Perez	.50	.23	.06
☐ 104 Brian Hunter	1.00	.45	.12
☐ 105 Wade Boggs	1.00	.45	.12
☐ 106 Bob Higginson	2.00	.90	.25
☐ 107 Jeff Kent	.25	.11	.03
☐ 108 Jose Offerman	.25	.11	.03
☐ 109 Dennis Eckersley	.50	.23	.06
☐ 110 Dave Nilsson	.50	.23	.06
☐ 111 Chuck Finley	.50	.23	.06
☐ 112 Devon White	.50	.23	.06
☐ 113 Bip Roberts	.25	.11	.03
☐ 114 Ramon Martinez	.50	.23	.06
☐ 115 Greg Maddux	5.00	2.20	.60
☐ 116 Curtis Goodwin	.50	.23	.06
☐ 117 John Jaha	.50	.23	.06
☐ 118 Ken Griffey Jr.	8.00	3.60	1.00
☐ 119 Geronimo Pena	.25	.11	.03
☐ 120 Shawon Dunston	.25	.11	.03
☐ 121 Ariel Prieto	.50	.23	.06
☐ 122 Kirby Puckett	3.00	1.35	.35
☐ 123 Carlos Baerga	.50	.23	.06
☐ 124 Todd Hundley	.50	.23	.06
☐ 125 Tim Naehring	.25	.11	.03
☐ 126 Gary Sheffield	1.00	.45	.12
☐ 127 Dean Palmer	.50	.23	.06
☐ 128 Rondell White	.50	.23	.06
☐ 129 Greg Gagne	.25	.11	.03
☐ 130 Jose Rijo	.25	.11	.03
☐ 131 Ivan Rodriguez	2.00	.90	.25
☐ 132 Jeff Bagwell	3.00	1.35	.35
☐ 133 Greg Vaughn	.50	.23	.06
☐ 134 Chili Davis	.50	.23	.06
☐ 135 Al Martin	.50	.23	.06
☐ 136 Kenny Rogers	.25	.11	.03
☐ 137 Aaron Sele	.50	.23	.06
☐ 138 Raul Mondesi	1.00	.45	.12
☐ 139 Cecil Fielder	.50	.23	.06
☐ 140 Tim Wallach	.25	.11	.03
☐ 141 Andres Galarraga	1.00	.45	.12
☐ 142 Lou Whitaker	.50	.23	.06
☐ 143 Jack McDowell	.50	.23	.06
☐ 144 Matt Williams	1.00	.45	.12
☐ 145 Ryan Klesko	1.00	.45	.12
☐ 146 Carlos Garcia	.25	.11	.03
☐ 147 Albert Belle	3.00	1.35	.35
☐ 148 Ryan Thompson	.25	.11	.03
☐ 149 Roberto Kelly	.25	.11	.03
☐ 150 Edgar Martinez	.50	.23	.06
☐ 151 Robby Thompson	.25	.11	.03
☐ 152 Mo Vaughn	2.00	.90	.25
☐ 153 Todd Zeile	.25	.11	.03
☐ 154 Harold Baines	.50	.23	.06

☐ 155 Phil Plantier	.25	.11	.03
☐ 156 Mike Stanley	.25	.11	.03
☐ 157 Ed Sprague	.50	.23	.06
☐ 158 Moises Alou	.50	.23	.06
☐ 159 Quilvio Veras	.25	.11	.03
☐ 160 Reggie Sanders	.50	.23	.06
☐ 161 Delino DeShields	.25	.11	.03
☐ 162 Rico Brogna	.25	.11	.03
☐ 163 Greg Colbrunn	.25	.11	.03
☐ 164 Steve Finley	.50	.23	.06
☐ 165 Orlando Merced	.25	.11	.03
☐ 166 Mark McGwire	2.50	1.10	.30
☐ 167 Garret Anderson	.50	.23	.06
☐ 168 Paul Sorrento	.25	.11	.03
☐ 169 Mark Langston	.25	.11	.03
☐ 170 Danny Tartabull	.25	.11	.03
☐ 171 Vinny Castilla	.50	.23	.06
☐ 172 Javier Lopez	1.00	.45	.12
☐ 173 Bret Saberhagen	.50	.23	.06
☐ 174 Eddie Williams	.25	.11	.03
☐ 175 Scott Leius	.25	.11	.03
☐ 176 Juan Gonzalez	4.00	1.80	.50
☐ 177 Gary Gaetti	.50	.23	.06
☐ 178 Jim Edmonds	1.00	.45	.12
☐ 179 John Olerud	.25	.11	.03
☐ 180 Lenny Dykstra	.50	.23	.06
☐ 181 Ray Lankford	.50	.23	.06
☐ 182 Ron Gant	.50	.23	.06
☐ 183 Doug Drabek	.25	.11	.03
☐ 184 Fred McGriff	1.00	.45	.12
☐ 185 Andy Benes	.25	.11	.03
☐ 186 Kurt Abbott	.25	.11	.03
☐ 187 Bernard Gilkey	.50	.23	.06
☐ 188 Sammy Sosa	1.00	.45	.12
☐ 189 Lee Smith	.50	.23	.06
☐ 190 Dennis Martinez	.50	.23	.06
☐ 191 Ozzie Guillen	.25	.11	.03
☐ 192 Robin Ventura	.50	.23	.06

1995 Leaf Limited Gold

These 24 standard-size quasi-parallel cards were inserted one per series one pack. Players from both series were included in this set. While using the same design as the regular issue, they are distinguished by different photos, different numbers and gold holographic foil.

	MINT	NRMT	EXC
COMPLETE SET (24)	50.00	22.00	6.25
COMMON CARD (1-24)	.50	.23	.06

☐ 1 Frank Thomas	8.00	3.60	1.00
☐ 2 Jeff Bagwell	3.00	1.35	.35
☐ 3 Raul Mondesi	1.00	.45	.12
☐ 4 Barry Bonds	2.00	.90	.25
☐ 5 Albert Belle	4.00	1.80	.50
☐ 6 Ken Griffey Jr.	8.00	3.60	1.00
☐ 7 Cal Ripken UER Name spelled Ripkin on card	6.00	2.70	.75
☐ 8 Will Clark	1.00	.45	.12
☐ 9 Jose Canseco	1.00	.45	.12
☐ 10 Larry Walker	.50	.23	.06
☐ 11 Kirby Puckett	3.00	1.35	.35
☐ 12 Don Mattingly	4.00	1.80	.50
☐ 13 Tim Salmon	1.00	.45	.12
☐ 14 Roberto Alomar	2.00	.90	.25
☐ 15 Greg Maddux	5.00	2.20	.60
☐ 16 Mike Piazza	5.00	2.20	.60
☐ 17 Matt Williams	1.00	.45	.12
☐ 18 Kenny Lofton	2.00	.90	.25
☐ 19 Alex Rodriguez UER Name spelled Rodriquez on card	10.00	4.50	1.25
☐ 20 Tony Gwynn	3.00	1.35	.35
☐ 21 Mo Vaughn	2.00	.90	.25
☐ 22 Chipper Jones	5.00	2.20	.60
☐ 23 Manny Ramirez	2.00	.90	.25
☐ 24 Deion Sanders	.50	.23	.06

1995 Leaf Limited Bat Patrol

These 24 standard-size cards were inserted one per series two pack. The fronts feature a full-bleed player photo with the player being identified on the top and the words "Bat Patrol" covering most of the middle. The horizontal backs feature another player photo as well as a year by year breakdown. The cards are numbered in the upper right corner as "X" of 24.

	MINT	NRMT	EXC
COMPLETE SET (24)	30.00	13.50	3.70
COMMON CARD (1-24)	.75	.35	.09

☐ 1 Frank Thomas	8.00	3.60	1.00
☐ 2 Tony Gwynn	3.00	1.35	.35
☐ 3 Wade Boggs	1.50	.70	.19
☐ 4 Larry Walker	1.50	.70	.19
☐ 5 Ken Griffey, Jr.	8.00	3.60	1.00
☐ 6 Jeff Bagwell	3.00	1.35	.35
☐ 7 Manny Ramirez	2.00	.90	.25
☐ 8 Mark Grace	1.50	.70	.19
☐ 9 Kenny Lofton	2.00	.90	.25
☐ 10 Mike Piazza	5.00	2.20	.60
☐ 11 Will Clark	1.50	.70	.19
☐ 12 Mo Vaughn	2.00	.90	.25
☐ 13 Carlos Baerga	.75	.35	.09
☐ 14 Rafael Palmeiro	1.50	.70	.19
☐ 15 Barry Bonds	2.00	.90	.25
☐ 16 Kirby Puckett	3.00	1.35	.35
☐ 17 Roberto Alomar	1.50	.70	.19
☐ 18 Barry Larkin	1.50	.70	.19
☐ 19 Eddie Murray	2.00	.90	.25
☐ 20 Tim Salmon	1.50	.70	.19
☐ 21 Don Mattingly	4.00	1.80	.50
☐ 22 Fred McGriff	1.50	.70	.19
☐ 23 Albert Belle	3.00	1.35	.35
☐ 24 Dante Bichette	1.50	.70	.19

1995 Leaf Limited Lumberjacks

These eight standard-size cards were randomly inserted into second series packs. The cards are individually numbered out of 5,000. The fronts feature a player photo surrounded by his name, the word "Lumberjacks" and "Handcrafted" in an semi-circular pattern. The team logo is in the background. The UV-coated horizontal backs feature a player photo against a forest background on the right along with some information on the left side. The player's career statistics are directly above the individual numbering (out of 5,000) of the card. The cards are numbered in the upper right corner.

	MINT	NRMT	EXC
COMPLETE SET (16)	600.00	275.00	75.00
COMPLETE SERIES 1 (8)	275.00	125.00	34.00
COMPLETE SERIES 2 (8)	325.00	145.00	40.00
COMMON CARD (1-16)	10.00	4.50	1.25

☐ 1 Albert Belle	40.00	18.00	5.00
☐ 2 Barry Bonds	25.00	11.00	3.10
☐ 3 Juan Gonzalez	50.00	22.00	6.25
☐ 4 Ken Griffey Jr.	100.00	45.00	12.50
☐ 5 Fred McGriff	12.00	5.50	1.50
☐ 6 Mike Piazza	50.00	22.00	6.25
☐ 7 Kirby Puckett	40.00	18.00	5.00
☐ 8 Mo Vaughn	25.00	11.00	3.10
☐ 9 Frank Thomas	100.00	45.00	12.50
☐ 10 Jeff Bagwell	40.00	18.00	5.00
☐ 11 Matt Williams	12.00	5.50	1.50
☐ 12 Jose Canseco	12.00	5.50	1.50
☐ 13 Raul Mondesi	12.00	5.50	1.50
☐ 14 Manny Ramirez	25.00	11.00	3.10
☐ 15 Cecil Fielder	10.00	4.50	1.25
☐ 16 Cal Ripken, Jr.	80.00	36.00	10.00

1996 Leaf Limited

The 1996 Leaf Limited set was issued exclusively to hobby outlets with a maximum production run of 45,000 boxes. Each box contained two smaller mini-boxes, enabling the dealer to use his imagination in the marketing of this product. The five-card packs carried a suggested retail price of $3.24. Each Master Box was sequentially- numbered via a box topper. If this number matched the 1996 year-ending stats, the collector and the dealer both had a chance to win prizes such as a Frank Thomas game-used bat, autographed batting glove, or a "Two Biggest Weapons" poster. The collector would return the winning box number to the hobby shop, and the dealer would mail it to Donruss with both receiving the same prize. The card fronts displayed color player photos with another photo and player information on the backs.

	MINT	NRMT	EXC
COMPLETE SET (90)	50.00	22.00	6.25
COMMON CARD (1-90)	.25	.11	.03

☐ 1 Ivan Rodriguez	2.00	.90	.25
☐ 2 Roger Clemens	1.50	.70	.19
☐ 3 Gary Sheffield	1.00	.45	.12
☐ 4 Tino Martinez	.50	.23	.06
☐ 5 Sammy Sosa	1.00	.45	.12
☐ 6 Reggie Sanders	.50	.23	.06
☐ 7 Ray Lankford	.50	.23	.06
☐ 8 Manny Ramirez	2.00	.90	.25
☐ 9 Jeff Bagwell	3.00	1.35	.35
☐ 10 Greg Maddux	5.00	2.20	.60
☐ 11 Ken Griffey Jr.	8.00	3.60	1.00
☐ 12 Rondell White	.50	.23	.06
☐ 13 Mike Piazza	5.00	2.20	.60
☐ 14 Marc Newfield	.50	.23	.06
☐ 15 Cal Ripken	6.00	2.70	.75
☐ 16 Carlos Delgado	.50	.23	.06
☐ 17 Tim Salmon	1.00	.45	.12
☐ 18 Andres Galarraga	1.00	.45	.12
☐ 19 Chuck Knoblauch	1.00	.45	.12
☐ 20 Matt Williams	1.00	.45	.12
☐ 21 Mark McGwire	2.50	1.10	.30
☐ 22 Ben McDonald	.25	.11	.03
☐ 23 Frank Thomas	8.00	3.60	1.00
☐ 24 Johnny Damon	.50	.23	.06
☐ 25 Gregg Jefferies	.50	.23	.06
☐ 26 Travis Fryman	.50	.23	.06
☐ 27 Chipper Jones	5.00	2.20	.60
☐ 28 David Cone	.50	.23	.06
☐ 29 Kenny Lofton	2.00	.90	.25
☐ 30 Mike Mussina	1.50	.70	.19
☐ 31 Alex Rodriguez	8.00	3.60	1.00
☐ 32 Carlos Baerga	.50	.23	.06
☐ 33 Brian Hunter	.25	.11	.03
☐ 34 Juan Gonzalez	4.00	1.80	.50
☐ 35 Bernie Williams	1.50	.70	.19
☐ 36 Wally Joyner	.25	.11	.03
☐ 37 Fred McGriff	1.00	.45	.12
☐ 38 Randy Johnson	1.00	.45	.12
☐ 39 Marty Cordova	.50	.23	.06
☐ 40 Garret Anderson	.50	.23	.06
☐ 41 Albert Belle	3.00	1.35	.35
☐ 42 Edgar Martinez	.50	.23	.06
☐ 43 Barry Larkin	1.00	.45	.12
☐ 44 Paul O'Neill	.25	.11	.03
☐ 45 Cecil Fielder	.50	.23	.06
☐ 46 Rusty Greer	1.00	.45	.12
☐ 47 Mo Vaughn	2.00	.90	.25
☐ 48 Dante Bichette	1.00	.45	.12
☐ 49 Ryan Klesko	1.00	.45	.12
☐ 50 Roberto Alomar	1.50	.70	.19
☐ 51 Raul Mondesi	1.00	.45	.12
☐ 52 Robin Ventura	.50	.23	.06
☐ 53 Tony Gwynn	3.00	1.35	.35
☐ 54 Mark Grace	1.00	.45	.12
☐ 55 Jim Thome	1.50	.70	.19
☐ 56 Jason Giambi	1.00	.45	.12
☐ 57 Tom Glavine	1.00	.45	.12
☐ 58 Jim Edmonds	.50	.23	.06
☐ 59 Pedro Martinez	.50	.23	.06
☐ 60 Charles Johnson	.50	.23	.06
☐ 61 Wade Boggs	1.00	.45	.12
☐ 62 Orlando Merced	.50	.23	.06
☐ 63 Craig Biggio	.50	.23	.06
☐ 64 Brady Anderson	1.00	.45	.12
☐ 65 Hideo Nomo	2.00	.90	.25
☐ 66 Ozzie Smith	2.00	.90	.25
☐ 67 Eddie Murray	2.00	.90	.25
☐ 68 Will Clark	1.00	.45	.12
☐ 69 Jay Buhner	1.00	.45	.12
☐ 70 Kirby Puckett	3.00	1.35	.35
☐ 71 Barry Bonds	2.00	.90	.25
☐ 72 Ray Durham	1.00	.45	.12
☐ 73 Sterling Hitchcock	.25	.11	.03
☐ 74 John Smoltz	1.00	.45	.12
☐ 75 Andre Dawson	.50	.23	.06
☐ 76 Joe Carter	.50	.23	.06
☐ 77 Ryne Sandberg	2.00	.90	.25
☐ 78 Rickey Henderson	1.00	.45	.12
☐ 79 Brian Jordan	.50	.23	.06
☐ 80 Greg Vaughn	1.00	.45	.12
☐ 81 Andy Pettitte	2.50	1.10	.30
☐ 82 Dean Palmer	1.00	.45	.12
☐ 83 Paul Molitor	1.50	.70	.19
☐ 84 Rafael Palmeiro	1.00	.45	.12
☐ 85 Henry Rodriguez	.50	.23	.06
☐ 86 Larry Walker	1.00	.45	.12
☐ 87 Ismael Valdes	.50	.23	.06
☐ 88 Derek Bell	.50	.23	.06
☐ 89 J.T. Snow	.50	.23	.06
☐ 90 Jack McDowell	1.00	.45	.12

1996 Leaf Limited Gold

Randomly inserted into one in every 11 packs, cards from this 90-card insert set parallel the regular Leaf Limited issue. Similar in design, it differs from the regular set with its gold holographic foil treatment.

	MINT	NRMT	EXC
COMPLETE SET (90)	500.00	220.00	60.00
COMMON CARD (1-90)	2.50	1.10	.30
*STARS: 5X to 10X BASIC CARDS			

1996 Leaf Limited Lumberjacks

Printed with maple stock that puts wood grains on both sides, this 10-card insert set features the league's top sluggers. The fronts carry color player photos with player information and statistics on the backs. Only 5,000 sets were produced and each card is individually numbered.

	MINT	NRMT	EXC
COMPLETE SET (10)	250.00	110.00	31.00
COMMON CARD (1-10)	10.00	4.50	1.25

☐ 1 Ken Griffey Jr.	50.00	22.00	6.25
☐ 2 Sammy Sosa	10.00	4.50	1.25
☐ 3 Cal Ripken	40.00	18.00	5.00
☐ 4 Frank Thomas	50.00	22.00	6.25
☐ 5 Alex Rodriguez	50.00	22.00	6.25
☐ 6 Mo Vaughn	12.00	5.50	1.50
☐ 7 Chipper Jones	30.00	13.50	3.70
☐ 8 Mike Piazza	30.00	13.50	3.70
☐ 9 Jeff Bagwell	20.00	9.00	2.50
☐ 10 Mark McGwire	15.00	6.75	1.85

1996 Leaf Limited Lumberjacks Black

This 10-card set is an embossed black wood version of the regular Leaf Limited Lumberjacks insert set. Only 500 sets were produced and each card is individually numbered.

	MINT	NRMT	EXC
COMPLETE SET (10)	1200.00	550.00	150.00
COMMON CARD (1-10)	50.00	22.00	6.25
*BLACK: 2.5X TO 5X BASIC CARDS			

1996 Leaf Limited Pennant Craze

This 10-card insert set features 10 superstars who have a thirst for the pennant. A special flocking technique puts the felt feel of a pennant on a die cut card. Only 2,500 sets were produced and are individually numbered.

	MINT	NRMT	EXC
COMPLETE SET (10)	550.00	250.00	70.00
COMMON CARD (1-10)	20.00	9.00	2.50

☐ 1 Juan Gonzalez	50.00	22.00	6.25
☐ 2 Cal Ripken	80.00	36.00	10.00

	MINT	NRMT	EXC
☐ 3 Frank Thomas	100.00	45.00	12.50
☐ 4 Ken Griffey Jr.	100.00	45.00	12.50
☐ 5 Albert Belle	40.00	18.00	5.00
☐ 6 Greg Maddux	60.00	27.00	7.50
☐ 7 Paul Molitor	20.00	9.00	2.50
☐ 8 Alex Rodriguez	100.00	45.00	12.50
☐ 9 Barry Bonds	25.00	11.00	3.10
☐ 10 Chipper Jones	60.00	27.00	7.50

1996 Leaf Limited Rookies

Randomly inserted in packs at a rate of one in seven, this 10-card set printed in silver holographic foil features some of the hottest rookies of the year.

	MINT	NRMT	EXC
COMPLETE SET (10)	75.00	34.00	9.50
COMMON CARD (1-10)	2.50	1.10	.30
SEMISTARS	3.00	1.35	.35
UNLISTED STARS	3.50	1.55	.45
☐ 1 Alex Ochoa	3.00	1.35	.35
☐ 2 Darin Erstad	15.00	6.75	1.85
☐ 3 Ruben Rivera	5.00	2.20	.60
☐ 4 Derek Jeter	20.00	9.00	2.50
☐ 5 Jermaine Dye	5.00	2.20	.60
☐ 6 Jason Kendall	4.00	1.80	.50
☐ 7 Mike Grace	2.50	1.10	.30
☐ 8 Andruw Jones	30.00	13.50	3.70
☐ 9 Rey Ordonez	3.50	1.55	.45
☐ 10 George Arias	2.50	1.10	.30

1996 Leaf Limited Rookies Gold

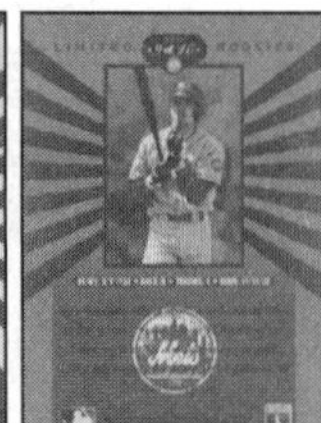

Randomly inserted with the Leaf Limited Gold set at the rate of one in 11 packs, this 10-card set is parallel to the Leaf Limited Rookies insert set. Similar in design, this set was printed in gold instead of silver holographic foil.

	MINT	NRMT	EXC
COMPLETE SET (10)	225.00	100.00	28.00
COMMON CARD (1-10)	8.00	3.60	1.00

*GOLD: 1.5X to 3X BASIC CARDS

1996 Leaf Preferred

The 1996 Leaf Preferred set was issued in one series totalling 150 cards. The 6-card packs retail for $3.49 each. Each card was printed on 20-point card stock for extra thickness and durability. The fronts feature a color action player photo and silver foil printing. The backs carry another player photo, player information and statistics. One in every ten packs contains an insert card.

	MINT	NRMT	EXC
COMPLETE SET (150)	25.00	11.00	3.10
COMMON CARD (1-150)	.10	.05	.01
☐ 1 Ken Griffey Jr.	3.00	1.35	.35
☐ 2 Rico Brogna	.10	.05	.01
☐ 3 Gregg Jefferies	.50	.23	.06
☐ 4 Reggie Sanders	.25	.11	.03
☐ 5 Manny Ramirez	.75	.35	.09
☐ 6 Shawn Green	.10	.05	.01
☐ 7 Tino Martinez	.25	.11	.03
☐ 8 Jeff Bagwell	1.25	.55	.16
☐ 9 Marc Newfield	.25	.11	.03
☐ 10 Ray Lankford	.25	.11	.03
☐ 11 Jay Bell	.10	.05	.01
☐ 12 Greg Maddux	2.00	.90	.25
☐ 13 Frank Thomas	3.00	1.35	.35
☐ 14 Travis Fryman	.25	.11	.03
☐ 15 Mark McGwire	1.00	.45	.12
☐ 16 Chuck Knoblauch	.50	.23	.06
☐ 17 Sammy Sosa	.50	.23	.06
☐ 18 Matt Williams	.50	.23	.06
☐ 19 Roger Clemens	.60	.25	.07
☐ 20 Rondell White	.25	.11	.03
☐ 21 Ivan Rodriguez	.75	.35	.09
☐ 22 Cal Ripken	2.50	1.10	.30
☐ 23 Ben McDonald	.10	.05	.01
☐ 24 Kenny Lofton	.75	.35	.09
☐ 25 Mike Piazza	2.00	.90	.25
☐ 26 David Cone	.25	.11	.03
☐ 27 Gary Sheffield	.50	.23	.06
☐ 28 Tim Salmon	.50	.23	.06
☐ 29 Andres Galarraga	.50	.23	.06
☐ 30 Johnny Damon	.25	.11	.03
☐ 31 Ozzie Smith	.75	.35	.09
☐ 32 Carlos Baerga	.25	.11	.03
☐ 33 Raul Mondesi	.50	.23	.06
☐ 34 Moises Alou	.25	.11	.03
☐ 35 Alex Rodriguez	3.00	1.35	.35
☐ 36 Mike Mussina	.60	.25	.07
☐ 37 Jason Isringhausen	.50	.23	.06
☐ 38 Barry Larkin	.50	.23	.06
☐ 39 Bernie Williams	.60	.25	.07
☐ 40 Chipper Jones	2.00	.90	.25
☐ 41 Joey Hamilton	.25	.11	.03
☐ 42 Charles Johnson	.25	.11	.03
☐ 43 Juan Gonzalez	1.50	.70	.19
☐ 44 Greg Vaughn	.50	.23	.06
☐ 45 Robin Ventura	.25	.11	.03
☐ 46 Albert Belle	1.25	.55	.16
☐ 47 Rafael Palmeiro	.50	.23	.06
☐ 48 Brian L.Hunter	.25	.11	.03
☐ 49 Mo Vaughn	.75	.35	.09
☐ 50 Paul O'Neill	.10	.05	.01
☐ 51 Mark Grace	.50	.23	.06
☐ 52 Randy Johnson	.50	.23	.06
☐ 53 Pedro Martinez	.25	.11	.03
☐ 54 Marty Cordova	.25	.11	.03
☐ 55 Garret Anderson	.50	.23	.06
☐ 56 Joe Carter	.25	.11	.03
☐ 57 Jim Thome	.60	.25	.07
☐ 58 Edgardo Alfonzo	.10	.05	.01
☐ 59 Dante Bichette	.50	.23	.06
☐ 60 Darryl Hamilton	.10	.05	.01
☐ 61 Roberto Alomar	.60	.25	.07
☐ 62 Fred McGriff	.50	.23	.06
☐ 63 Kirby Puckett	1.25	.55	.16
☐ 64 Hideo Nomo	.75	.35	.09
☐ 65 Alex Fernandez	.25	.11	.03
☐ 66 Ryan Klesko	.50	.23	.06
☐ 67 Wade Boggs	.50	.23	.06
☐ 68 Eddie Murray	.75	.35	.09
☐ 69 Eric Karros	.25	.11	.03
☐ 70 Jim Edmonds	.25	.11	.03
☐ 71 Edgar Martinez	.25	.11	.03
☐ 72 Andy Pettitte	1.00	.45	.12
☐ 73 Mark Grudzielanek	.25	.11	.03
☐ 74 Tom Glavine	.50	.23	.06
☐ 75 Ken Caminiti	.50	.23	.06
☐ 76 Will Clark	.50	.23	.06
☐ 77 Craig Biggio	.25	.11	.03
☐ 78 Brady Anderson	.50	.23	.06
☐ 79 Tony Gwynn	1.25	.55	.16
☐ 80 Larry Walker	.50	.23	.06
☐ 81 Brian Jordan	.25	.11	.03
☐ 82 Lenny Dykstra	.25	.11	.03
☐ 83 Butch Huskey	.25	.11	.03
☐ 84 Jack McDowell	.50	.23	.06
☐ 85 Cecil Fielder	.25	.11	.03
☐ 86 Jose Canseco	.50	.23	.06
☐ 87 Jason Giambi	.50	.23	.06
☐ 88 Rickey Henderson	.50	.23	.06
☐ 89 Kevin Seitzer	.10	.05	.01
☐ 90 Carlos Delgado	.25	.11	.03
☐ 91 Ryne Sandberg	.75	.35	.09
☐ 92 Dwight Gooden	.25	.11	.03
☐ 93 Michael Tucker	.25	.11	.03
☐ 94 Barry Bonds	.75	.35	.09
☐ 95 Eric Young	.25	.11	.03
☐ 96 Dean Palmer	.50	.23	.06
☐ 97 Henry Rodriguez	.25	.11	.03
☐ 98 John Mabry	.25	.11	.03
☐ 99 J.T. Snow	.25	.11	.03
☐ 100 Andre Dawson	.25	.11	.03
☐ 101 Ismael Valdes	.25	.11	.03
☐ 102 Charles Nagy	.25	.11	.03
☐ 103 Jay Buhner	.50	.23	.06
☐ 104 Derek Bell	.25	.11	.03
☐ 105 Paul Molitor	.60	.25	.07
☐ 106 Hal Morris	.10	.05	.01
☐ 107 Ray Durham	.50	.23	.06
☐ 108 Bernard Gilkey	.25	.11	.03
☐ 109 John Valentin	.25	.11	.03
☐ 110 Melvin Nieves	.25	.11	.03
☐ 111 John Smoltz	.50	.23	.06
☐ 112 Terrell Wade	.25	.11	.03
☐ 113 Chad Mottola	.10	.05	.01
☐ 114 Tony Clark	.60	.25	.07
☐ 115 John Wasdin	.10	.05	.01
☐ 116 Derek Jeter	2.00	.90	.25
☐ 117 Rey Ordonez	.50	.23	.06
☐ 118 Jason Thompson	.10	.05	.01
☐ 119 Robin Jennings	.10	.05	.01
☐ 120 Rocky Coppinger	.60	.25	.07
☐ 121 Billy Wagner	.50	.23	.06
☐ 122 Steve Gibralter	.10	.05	.01
☐ 123 Jermaine Dye	.60	.25	.07
☐ 124 Jason Kendall	.50	.23	.06
☐ 125 Mike Grace	.10	.05	.01
☐ 126 Jason Schmidt	.50	.23	.06
☐ 127 Paul Wilson	.25	.11	.03
☐ 128 Alan Benes	.50	.23	.06
☐ 129 Justin Thompson	.25	.11	.03
☐ 130 Brooks Kieschnick	.50	.23	.06
☐ 131 George Arias	.10	.05	.01
☐ 132 Osvaldo Fernandez	.25	.11	.03
☐ 133 Todd Hollandsworth	.25	.11	.03
☐ 134 Eric Owens	.10	.05	.01
☐ 135 Chan Ho Park	.50	.23	.06
☐ 136 Mark Loretta	.10	.05	.01
☐ 137 Ruben Rivera	.60	.25	.07
☐ 138 Jeff Suppan	.50	.23	.06
☐ 139 Ugueth Urbina	.10	.05	.01
☐ 140 LaTroy Hawkins	.10	.05	.01
☐ 141 Chris Snopek	.10	.05	.01
☐ 142 Edgar Renteria	.50	.23	.06
☐ 143 Raul Casanova	.25	.11	.03
☐ 144 Jose Herrera	.10	.05	.01
☐ 145 Matt Lawton	.10	.05	.01
☐ 146 Ralph Milliard	.10	.05	.01
☐ 147 Frank Thomas CL (1-64)	1.50	.70	.19
☐ 148 Jeff Bagwell CL (65-128)	.60	.25	.07
☐ 149 Ken Griffey Jr. CL (129-150/inserts)	1.50	.70	.19
☐ 150 Mike Piazza CL (inserts)	1.00	.45	.12

1996 Leaf Preferred Press Proofs

Parallel to the regular set except for gold foil printing on front, these 150 cards are each individually numbered to 500. The cards were seeded at an approximate rate of one in every 48 packs.

	MINT	NRMT	EXC
COMPLETE SET (150)	2000.00	900.00	250.00
COMMON CARD (1-150)	4.00	1.80	.50

*STARS: 30X TO 50X BASIC CARDS..
*YOUNG STARS: 25X TO 40X BASIC CARDS

1996 Leaf Preferred Staremaster

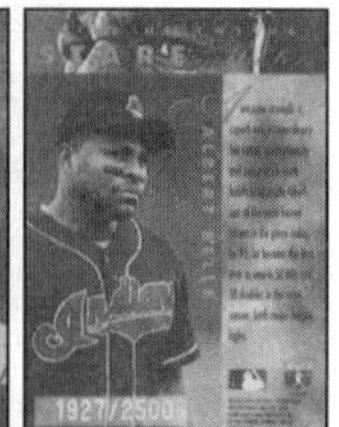

Randomly inserted at an approximate rate of one in every 144 packs, these twelve cards feature mug shots of the games most intense stares. Each card is printed on silver holographic card stock. Only 2,500 of each card was produced and are individually numbered.

	MINT	NRMT	EXC
COMPLETE SET (12)	650.00	300.00	80.00
COMMON CARD (1-12)	25.00	11.00	3.10
☐ 1 Chipper Jones	60.00	27.00	7.50
☐ 2 Alex Rodriguez	100.00	45.00	12.50
☐ 3 Derek Jeter	60.00	27.00	7.50
☐ 4 Tony Gwynn	40.00	18.00	5.00
☐ 5 Frank Thomas	100.00	45.00	12.50
☐ 6 Ken Griffey Jr.	100.00	45.00	12.50
☐ 7 Cal Ripken	80.00	36.00	10.00
☐ 8 Greg Maddux	60.00	27.00	7.50
☐ 9 Albert Belle	40.00	18.00	5.00
☐ 10 Barry Bonds	25.00	11.00	3.10
☐ 11 Jeff Bagwell	40.00	18.00	5.00
☐ 12 Mike Piazza	60.00	27.00	7.50

1996 Leaf Preferred Steel

Seeded one per pack, this all-steel, metalized set features silver framed color action player photos of the leagues most dominant players on a silver tinted background with a scriptive letter "S". The backs carry another player photo with the card logo as background and player statistics.

	MINT	NRMT	EXC
COMPLETE SET (77)	125.00	55.00	15.50
COMMON CARD (1-77)	1.00	.45	.12
☐ 1 Frank Thomas	10.00	4.50	1.25
☐ 2 Paul Molitor	2.00	.90	.25
☐ 3 Kenny Lofton	2.50	1.10	.30
☐ 4 Travis Fryman	1.25	.55	.16
☐ 5 Jeff Conine	1.25	.55	.16
☐ 6 Barry Bonds	2.50	1.10	.30
☐ 7 Gregg Jefferies	1.25	.55	.16
☐ 8 Alex Rodriguez	10.00	4.50	1.25
☐ 9 Wade Boggs	1.50	.70	.19
☐ 10 David Justice	1.00	.45	.12
☐ 11 Hideo Nomo	2.50	1.10	.30
☐ 12 Roberto Alomar	2.00	.90	.25
☐ 13 Todd Hollandsworth	1.25	.55	.16
☐ 14 Mark McGwire	3.00	1.35	.35
☐ 15 Rafael Palmeiro	1.50	.70	.19
☐ 16 Will Clark	1.50	.70	.19
☐ 17 Cal Ripken	8.00	3.60	1.00
☐ 18 Derek Bell	1.25	.55	.16
☐ 19 Gary Sheffield	1.50	.70	.19
☐ 20 Juan Gonzalez	5.00	2.20	.60
☐ 21 Garret Anderson	1.00	.45	.12
☐ 22 Mo Vaughn	2.50	1.10	.30
☐ 23 Robin Ventura	1.25	.55	.16
☐ 24 Carlos Baerga	1.25	.55	.16
☐ 25 Tim Salmon	1.50	.70	.19
☐ 26 Matt Williams	1.50	.70	.19
☐ 27 Fred McGriff	1.50	.70	.19
☐ 28 Rondell White	1.25	.55	.16
☐ 29 Ray Lankford	1.25	.55	.16
☐ 30 Lenny Dykstra	1.00	.45	.12
☐ 31 J.T. Snow	1.00	.45	.12
☐ 32 Sammy Sosa	1.50	.70	.19
☐ 33 Chipper Jones	6.00	2.70	.75
☐ 34 Bobby Bonilla	1.25	.55	.16
☐ 35 Paul Wilson	1.25	.55	.16
☐ 36 Darren Daulton	1.25	.55	.16
☐ 37 Larry Walker	1.50	.70	.19
☐ 38 Raul Mondesi	1.50	.70	.19
☐ 39 Jeff Bagwell	4.00	1.80	.50
☐ 40 Derek Jeter	6.00	2.70	.75
☐ 41 Kirby Puckett	4.00	1.80	.50
☐ 42 Jason Isringhausen	1.50	.70	.19
☐ 43 Vinny Castilla	1.25	.55	.16
☐ 44 Jim Edmonds	1.25	.55	.16
☐ 45 Ron Gant	1.25	.55	.16
☐ 46 Carlos Delgado	1.25	.55	.16
☐ 47 Jose Canseco	1.50	.70	.19
☐ 48 Tony Gwynn	4.00	1.80	.50
☐ 49 Mike Mussina	2.00	.90	.25
☐ 50 Charles Johnson	1.25	.55	.16
☐ 51 Mike Piazza	6.00	2.70	.75
☐ 52 Ken Griffey Jr.	10.00	4.50	1.25
☐ 53 Greg Maddux	6.00	2.70	.75
☐ 54 Mark Grace	1.50	.70	.19
☐ 55 Ryan Klesko	1.50	.70	.19
☐ 56 Dennis Eckersley	1.25	.55	.16
☐ 57 Rickey Henderson	1.50	.70	.19
☐ 58 Michael Tucker	1.25	.55	.16
☐ 59 Joe Carter	1.25	.55	.16
☐ 60 Randy Johnson	1.50	.70	.19
☐ 61 Brian Jordan	1.25	.55	.16
☐ 62 Shawn Green	1.00	.45	.12
☐ 63 Roger Clemens	2.00	.90	.25
☐ 64 Andres Galarraga	1.50	.70	.19
☐ 65 Johnny Damon	1.25	.55	.16
☐ 66 Ryne Sandberg	2.50	1.10	.30
☐ 67 Alan Benes	1.50	.70	.19
☐ 68 Albert Belle	4.00	1.80	.50
☐ 69 Barry Larkin	1.25	.55	.16
☐ 70 Marty Cordova	1.25	.55	.16
☐ 71 Dante Bichette	1.50	.70	.19
☐ 72 Craig Biggio	1.25	.55	.16
☐ 73 Reggie Sanders	1.25	.55	.16
☐ 74 Moises Alou	1.25	.55	.16
☐ 75 Chuck Knoblauch	1.50	.70	.19
☐ 76 Cecil Fielder	1.25	.55	.16
☐ 77 Manny Ramirez	2.50	1.10	.30

1996 Leaf Preferred Steel Gold

This 77-card parallel set is a gold rendition of the more common silver Steel inserts. The scarce gold versions are seeded at an approximate rate of one in every 24 packs.

	MINT	NRMT	EXC
COMPLETE SET (77)	1200.00	550.00	150.00
COMMON CARD (1-77)	10.00	4.50	1.25
*STARS: 5X TO 10X BASIC CARDS ...			

1996 Leaf Preferred Steel Power

This eight-card set combines a micro-etched foil card with corner interior lightening-symbol diecutting and honors eight of the top power hitters. The fronts carry a color player photo while the backs display a statement explaining why the player is included in the set along with his 1995 season hitting statistics. Only 5,000 sets were produced, and each card carries a serial number.

	MINT	NRMT	EXC
COMPLETE SET (8)	200.00	90.00	25.00
COMMON CARD (1-8)	12.00	5.50	1.50
☐ 1 Albert Belle	20.00	9.00	2.50
☐ 2 Mo Vaughn	12.00	5.50	1.50
☐ 3 Ken Griffey Jr.	50.00	22.00	6.25
☐ 4 Cal Ripken	40.00	18.00	5.00
☐ 5 Mike Piazza	30.00	13.50	3.70
☐ 6 Barry Bonds	12.00	5.50	1.50
☐ 7 Jeff Bagwell	20.00	9.00	2.50
☐ 8 Frank Thomas	50.00	22.00	6.25

1996 Leaf Signature

The 1996 Leaf Signature Set was issued in two series totalling 150 cards. The four-card packs have a suggested retail price of $9.99 each. It's interesting to note that the Extended Series was the last of the 1996 releases. In fact, it was released in January, 1997 - so late in the year that it's categorization as a 1996 issue is a bit of a stretch. Production for the Extended Series was only 40% that of the regular issue. Extended series packs actually contained a mix of both series 1 and 2 cards, thus the Extended series cards are somewhat scarcer. Card fronts feature borderless color action player photos with the card name printed in a silver foil emblem. The backs carry player information. The only notable Rookie Card is of Darin Erstad.

	MINT	NRMT	EXC
COMPLETE SET (150)	90.00	40.00	11.00
COMPLETE SERIES 1 (100)	50.00	22.00	6.25
COMPLETE SERIES 2 (50)	40.00	18.00	5.00
COMMON CARD (1-100)	.25	.11	.03
COMMON CARD (101-150)	.50	.23	.06
☐ 1 Mike Piazza	3.00	1.35	.35
☐ 2 Juan Gonzalez	2.50	1.10	.30
☐ 3 Greg Maddux	3.00	1.35	.35
☐ 4 Marc Newfield	.25	.11	.03
☐ 5 Wade Boggs	.75	.35	.09
☐ 6 Ray Lankford	.40	.18	.05
☐ 7 Frank Thomas	5.00	2.20	.60
☐ 8 Rico Brogna	.25	.11	.03
☐ 9 Tim Salmon	.60	.25	.07
☐ 10 Ken Griffey Jr.	5.00	2.20	.60
☐ 11 Manny Ramirez	1.25	.55	.16
☐ 12 Cecil Fielder	.40	.18	.05
☐ 13 Gregg Jefferies	.40	.18	.05
☐ 14 Rondell White	.40	.18	.05
☐ 15 Cal Ripken	4.00	1.80	.50
☐ 16 Alex Rodriguez	5.00	2.20	.60
☐ 17 Bernie Williams	1.00	.45	.12
☐ 18 Andres Galarraga	.60	.25	.07
☐ 19 Mike Mussina	1.00	.45	.12
☐ 20 Chuck Knoblauch	.75	.35	.09
☐ 21 Joe Carter	.40	.18	.05
☐ 22 Jeff Bagwell	2.00	.90	.25
☐ 23 Mark McGwire	1.50	.70	.19
☐ 24 Sammy Sosa	.75	.35	.09
☐ 25 Reggie Sanders	.40	.18	.05
☐ 26 Chipper Jones	3.00	1.35	.35
☐ 27 Jeff Cirillo	.25	.11	.03
☐ 28 Roger Clemens	1.00	.45	.12
☐ 29 Craig Biggio	.40	.18	.05
☐ 30 Gary Sheffield	.75	.35	.09
☐ 31 Paul O'Neill	.25	.11	.03
☐ 32 Johnny Damon	.40	.18	.05
☐ 33 Jason Isringhausen	.25	.11	.03
☐ 34 Jay Bell	.25	.11	.03
☐ 35 Henry Rodriguez	.40	.18	.05
☐ 36 Matt Williams	.60	.25	.07
☐ 37 Randy Johnson	.75	.35	.09
☐ 38 Fred McGriff	.60	.25	.07
☐ 39 Jason Giambi	.60	.25	.07
☐ 40 Ivan Rodriguez	1.25	.55	.16
☐ 41 Raul Mondesi	.60	.25	.07
☐ 42 Barry Larkin	.60	.25	.07
☐ 43 Ryan Klesko	.75	.35	.09
☐ 44 Joey Hamilton	.40	.18	.05
☐ 45 Todd Hundley	.40	.18	.05
☐ 46 Jim Edmonds	.40	.18	.05
☐ 47 Dante Bichette	.60	.25	.07
☐ 48 Roberto Alomar	1.00	.45	.12
☐ 49 Mark Grace	.60	.25	.07
☐ 50 Brady Anderson	.60	.25	.07
☐ 51 Hideo Nomo	1.25	.55	.16
☐ 52 Ozzie Smith	1.25	.55	.16
☐ 53 Robin Ventura	.40	.18	.05
☐ 54 Andy Pettitte	1.50	.70	.19
☐ 55 Kenny Lofton	1.25	.55	.16
☐ 56 John Mabry	.40	.18	.05
☐ 57 Paul Molitor	1.00	.45	.12
☐ 58 Rey Ordonez	.60	.25	.07
☐ 59 Albert Belle	2.00	.90	.25
☐ 60 Charles Johnson	.40	.18	.05
☐ 61 Edgar Martinez	.40	.18	.05
☐ 62 Derek Bell	.40	.18	.05
☐ 63 Carlos Delgado	.40	.18	.05
☐ 64 Raul Casanova	.40	.18	.05
☐ 65 Ismael Valdes	.40	.18	.05
☐ 66 J.T. Snow	.25	.11	.03
☐ 67 Derek Jeter	3.00	1.35	.35
☐ 68 Jason Kendall	.60	.25	.07
☐ 69 John Smoltz	.75	.35	.09
☐ 70 Chad Mottola	.25	.11	.03
☐ 71 Jim Thome	1.00	.45	.12
☐ 72 Will Clark	.60	.25	.07
☐ 73 Mo Vaughn	1.25	.55	.16
☐ 74 John Wasdin	.25	.11	.03
☐ 75 Rafael Palmeiro	.60	.25	.07
☐ 76 Mark Grudzielanek	.40	.18	.05
☐ 77 Larry Walker	.60	.25	.07
☐ 78 Alan Benes	.60	.25	.07
☐ 79 Michael Tucker	.40	.18	.05
☐ 80 Billy Wagner	.60	.25	.07
☐ 81 Paul Wilson	.40	.18	.05
☐ 82 Greg Vaughn	.40	.18	.05
☐ 83 Dean Palmer	.40	.18	.05
☐ 84 Ryne Sandberg	1.25	.55	.16
☐ 85 Eric Young	.40	.18	.05
☐ 86 Jay Buhner	.60	.25	.07
☐ 87 Tony Clark	1.00	.45	.12
☐ 88 Jermaine Dye	1.00	.45	.12
☐ 89 Barry Bonds	1.25	.55	.16
☐ 90 Ugueth Urbina	.25	.11	.03
☐ 91 Charles Nagy	.40	.18	.05
☐ 92 Ruben Rivera	1.00	.45	.12
☐ 93 Todd Hollandsworth	.40	.18	.05
☐ 94 Darin Erstad	5.00	2.20	.60
☐ 95 Brooks Kieschnick	.60	.25	.07
☐ 96 Edgar Renteria	.60	.25	.07
☐ 97 Lenny Dykstra	.40	.18	.05
☐ 98 Tony Gwynn	2.00	.90	.25
☐ 99 Kirby Puckett	2.00	.90	.25
☐ 100 Checklist	.25	.11	.03
☐ 101 Andruw Jones	12.00	5.50	1.50
☐ 102 Alex Ochoa	.75	.35	.09
☐ 103 David Cone	.75	.35	.09
☐ 104 Rusty Greer	.75	.35	.09
☐ 105 Jose Canseco	1.00	.45	.12
☐ 106 Ken Caminiti	1.50	.70	.19
☐ 107 Mariano Rivera	.75	.35	.09
☐ 108 Ron Gant	.75	.35	.09
☐ 109 Darryl Strawberry	.75	.35	.09
☐ 110 Vladimir Guerrero	6.00	2.70	.75
☐ 111 George Arias	.50	.23	.06
☐ 112 Jeff Conine	.75	.35	.09
☐ 113 Bobby Higginson	.75	.35	.09
☐ 114 Eric Karros	.75	.35	.09
☐ 115 Brian Hunter	.50	.23	.06
☐ 116 Eddie Murray	2.50	1.10	.30
☐ 117 Todd Walker	6.00	2.70	.75
☐ 118 Chan Ho Park	.75	.35	.09
☐ 119 John Jaha	.50	.23	.06
☐ 120 Dave Justice	.75	.35	.09
☐ 121 Makoto Suzuki	.50	.23	.06
☐ 122 Scott Rolen	4.00	1.80	.50
☐ 123 Tino Martinez	1.00	.45	.12
☐ 124 Kimera Bartee	.50	.23	.06
☐ 125 Garret Anderson	.75	.35	.09
☐ 126 Brian Jordan	.75	.35	.09
☐ 127 Andre Dawson	1.25	.55	.16
☐ 128 Javier Lopez	.75	.35	.09
☐ 129 Bill Pulsipher	.50	.23	.06
☐ 130 Dwight Gooden	.75	.35	.09
☐ 131 Al Martin	.50	.23	.06
☐ 132 Terrell Wade	.50	.23	.06
☐ 133 Steve Gibralter	.50	.23	.06
☐ 134 Tom Glavine	1.25	.55	.16
☐ 135 Kevin Appier	.75	.35	.09
☐ 136 Tim Raines	.75	.35	.09
☐ 137 Curtis Pride	.50	.23	.06
☐ 138 Todd Greene	.50	.23	.06
☐ 139 Bobby Bonilla	.75	.35	.09
☐ 140 Trey Beamon	.75	.35	.09
☐ 141 Marty Cordova	.75	.35	.09
☐ 142 Rickey Henderson	.75	.35	.09
☐ 143 Ellis Burks	.75	.35	.09
☐ 144 Dennis Eckersley	.75	.35	.09
☐ 145 Kevin Brown	.75	.35	.09
☐ 146 Carlos Baerga	.50	.23	.06
☐ 147 Brett Butler	.75	.35	.09
☐ 148 Marquis Grissom	.75	.35	.09
☐ 149 Karim Garcia	2.00	.90	.25
☐ 150 Frank Thomas CL	5.00	2.20	.60

1996 Leaf Signature Press Proofs Gold

Randomly inserted in first series packs at an approximate rate of one in 12 and second series packs at an approximate rate of one in 8, this 150-card set is parallel to the regular version. Card numbers 1-100 were seeded into first series packs and 101-150 in Extended series packs. The design is similar to the regular card with the exception of the card name being printed in a gold foil emblem and the words "Press Proof" printed in gold foil vertically down the side.

	MINT	NRMT	EXC
COMPLETE SET (150)	1200.00	550.00	150.00
COMPLETE SERIES 1 (100)	800.00	350.00	100.00
COMPLETE SERIES 2 (50)	400.00	180.00	50.00
COMMON CARD (1-100)	3.00	1.35	.35
COMMON CARD (101-150)	3.00	1.35	.35
*SER.1 STARS: 7.5X TO 15X BASIC CARDS			
*SER.1 YOUNG STARS: 6X TO 12X BASIC CARDS			
*SER.2 STARS: 4X TO 8X BASIC CARDS			
*SER.2 YOUNG STARS: 3X TO 6X BASIC CARDS			

1996 Leaf Signature Press Proofs Platinum

Randomly inserted exclusively into Extended Series packs at the rate of one in 24, this 150-card set is parallel to the regular Leaf Signature Set. Only 150 sets were produced. Unlike the multi-series base set and Gold Press Proofs, these scarce Platinum cards were issued in one comprehensive series. The cards are similar in design to the regular set with the exception of holographic platinum foil stamping. A set price has not been provided due to scarcity.

	MINT	NRMT	EXC
COMMON CARD (1-150)	10.00	4.50	1.25
*SER.1 STARS: 25X TO 50X BASIC CARDS			
*SER.1 YOUNG STARS: 20X TO 40X BASIC CARDS			
*SER.2 STARS: 12.5X TO 25X BASIC CARDS			
*SER.2 YOUNG STARS: 10X TO 20X BASIC CARDS			
☐ 1 Mike Piazza	150.00	70.00	19.00
☐ 2 Juan Gonzalez	120.00	55.00	15.00
☐ 3 Greg Maddux	150.00	70.00	19.00
☐ 7 Frank Thomas	250.00	110.00	31.00
☐ 10 Ken Griffey Jr.	250.00	110.00	31.00
☐ 15 Cal Ripken	200.00	90.00	25.00
☐ 16 Alex Rodriguez	250.00	110.00	31.00
☐ 23 Mark McGwire	75.00	34.00	9.50
☐ 26 Chipper Jones	150.00	70.00	19.00
☐ 54 Andy Pettitte	75.00	34.00	9.50
☐ 59 Albert Belle	100.00	45.00	12.50
☐ 67 Derek Jeter	120.00	55.00	15.00
☐ 94 Darin Erstad	120.00	55.00	15.00
☐ 98 Tony Gwynn	100.00	45.00	12.50
☐ 99 Kirby Puckett	100.00	45.00	12.50
☐ 101 Andruw Jones	250.00	110.00	31.00
☐ 110 Vladimir Guerrero	120.00	55.00	15.00
☐ 117 Todd Walker	120.00	55.00	15.00
☐ 122 Scott Rolen	75.00	34.00	9.50
☐ 150 Frank Thomas CL	120.00	55.00	15.00

1996 Leaf Signature Autographs

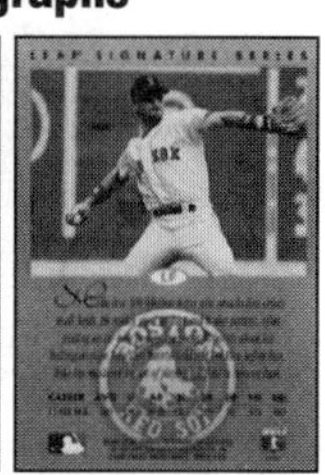

Inserted into 1996 Leaf Signature Series first series packs, these unnumbered cards were one of the first major autograph issues featured in an MLB-licensed trading card set. First series packs contained at least one autograph, with the chance of getting more. Donruss/Leaf reports that all but 10 players in the Leaf Signature Series signed close to 5,000 total autographs (3,500 bronze, 1,000 silver, 500 gold). The 10 players who signed 1,000 (700 bronze, 200 silver, 100 gold) are: Roberto Alomar, Wade Boggs, Derek Jeter, Kenny Lofton, Paul Molitor, Raul Mondesi, Manny Ramirez, Alex Rodriguez, Frank Thomas and Mo Vaughn. It's also important to note that six additional players did not submit their cards in time to be included in first series packs. Thus, their cards were thrown into Extended series packs. Those six players are as follows: Brian L.Hunter, Carlos Delgado, Phil Plantier, Jim Thome, Terrell Wade and Ernie Young. Thome signed only silver and gold foil cards, thus the Bronze set is considered complete at 251 cards. Prices below refer exclusively to Bronze versions. Blue and black ink variations have been found for Carlos Delgado, Alex Rodriguez and Michael Tucker. No consistent premiums for these variations has been tracked. Finally, an autographed jumbo silver foil version of the Frank Thomas card was distributed to dealers in March, 1997. Dealers received either this first series or the Extended Series jumbo Thomas for every Extended Series case ordered. Each Thomas jumbo is individually serial numbered to 1,500.

	MINT	NRMT	EXC
COMPLETE SET (251)	2200.00	1000.00	275.00
COMMON CARD (1-251)	4.00	1.80	.50
☐ 1 Kurt Abbott	4.00	1.80	.50
☐ 2 Juan Acevedo	4.00	1.80	.50
☐ 3 Terry Adams	4.00	1.80	.50
☐ 4 Manny Alexander	4.00	1.80	.50
☐ 5 Roberto Alomar SP	90.00	40.00	11.00
☐ 6 Moises Alou	6.00	2.70	.75
☐ 7 Wilson Alvarez	8.00	3.60	1.00
☐ 8 Garret Anderson	8.00	3.60	1.00
☐ 9 Shane Andrews	4.00	1.80	.50
☐ 10 Andy Ashby	4.00	1.80	.50
☐ 11 Pedro Astacio	4.00	1.80	.50
☐ 12 Brad Ausmus	4.00	1.80	.50
☐ 13 Bobby Ayala	4.00	1.80	.50
☐ 14 Carlos Baerga	6.00	2.70	.75
☐ 15 Harold Baines	8.00	3.60	1.00
☐ 16 Jason Bates	4.00	1.80	.50
☐ 17 Allen Battle	4.00	1.80	.50
☐ 18 Rich Becker	4.00	1.80	.50
☐ 19 David Bell	4.00	1.80	.50
☐ 20 Rafael Belliard	4.00	1.80	.50
☐ 21 Andy Benes	4.00	1.80	.50
☐ 22 Armando Benitez	4.00	1.80	.50
☐ 23 Jason Bere	4.00	1.80	.50
☐ 24 Geronimo Berroa	4.00	1.80	.50
☐ 25 Willie Blair	4.00	1.80	.50
☐ 26 Mike Blowers	4.00	1.80	.50
☐ 27 Wade Boggs SP	135.00	60.00	17.00
☐ 28 Ricky Bones	4.00	1.80	.50
☐ 29 Mike Bordick	4.00	1.80	.50
☐ 30 Toby Borland	4.00	1.80	.50
☐ 31 Ricky Bottalico	4.00	1.80	.50
☐ 32 Darren Bragg	4.00	1.80	.50
☐ 33 Jeff Branson	4.00	1.80	.50
☐ 34 Tilson Brito	4.00	1.80	.50
☐ 35 Rico Brogna	4.00	1.80	.50
☐ 36 Scott Brosius	4.00	1.80	.50
☐ 37 Damon Buford	4.00	1.80	.50
☐ 38 Mike Busby	4.00	1.80	.50
☐ 39 Tom Candiotti	4.00	1.80	.50
☐ 40 Frank Castillo	4.00	1.80	.50
☐ 41 Andujar Cedeno	4.00	1.80	.50
☐ 42 Domingo Cedeno	4.00	1.80	.50
☐ 43 Roger Cedeno	6.00	2.70	.75
☐ 44 Norm Charlton	4.00	1.80	.50
☐ 45 Jeff Cirillo	4.00	1.80	.50
☐ 46 Will Clark	15.00	6.75	1.85
☐ 47 Jeff Conine	10.00	4.50	1.25
☐ 48 Steve Cooke	4.00	1.80	.50
☐ 49 Joey Cora	4.00	1.80	.50
☐ 50 Marty Cordova	15.00	6.75	1.85
☐ 51 Rheal Cormier	4.00	1.80	.50

☐ 52 Felipe Crespo 4.00 1.80 .50
☐ 53 Chad Curtis 4.00 1.80 .50
☐ 54 Johnny Damon 10.00 4.50 1.25
☐ 55 Russ Davis 4.00 1.80 .50
☐ 56 Andre Dawson 12.00 5.50 1.50
☐ 57 Carlos Delgado 12.00 5.50 1.50
☐ 58 Doug Drabek 4.00 1.80 .50
☐ 59 Darren Dreifort 4.00 1.80 .50
☐ 60 Shawon Dunston 4.00 1.80 .50
☐ 61 Ray Durham 6.00 2.70 .75
☐ 62 Jim Edmonds 12.00 5.50 1.50
☐ 63 Joey Eischen 4.00 1.80 .50
☐ 64 Jim Eisenreich 4.00 1.80 .50
☐ 65 Sal Fasano 4.00 1.80 .50
☐ 66 Jeff Fassero 4.00 1.80 .50
☐ 67 Alex Fernandez 10.00 4.50 1.25
☐ 68 Darrin Fletcher 4.00 1.80 .50
☐ 69 Chad Fonville 4.00 1.80 .50
☐ 70 Kevin Foster 4.00 1.80 .50
☐ 71 John Franco 4.00 1.80 .50
☐ 72 Julio Franco 6.00 2.70 .75
☐ 73 Marvin Freeman 4.00 1.80 .50
☐ 74 Travis Fryman 10.00 4.50 1.25
☐ 75 Gary Gaetti 6.00 2.70 .75
☐ 76 Carlos Garcia 4.00 1.80 .50
☐ 77 Jason Giambi 12.00 5.50 1.50
☐ 78 Benji Gil 4.00 1.80 .50
☐ 79 Greg Gohr 4.00 1.80 .50
☐ 80 Chris Gomez 4.00 1.80 .50
☐ 81 Leo Gomez 4.00 1.80 .50
☐ 82 Tom Goodwin 4.00 1.80 .50
☐ 83 Mike Grace 4.00 1.80 .50
☐ 84 Mike Greenwell 4.00 1.80 .50
☐ 85 Rusty Greer 10.00 4.50 1.25
☐ 86 Mark Grudzielanek 6.00 2.70 .75
☐ 87 Mark Gubicza 4.00 1.80 .50
☐ 88 Juan Guzman 4.00 1.80 .50
☐ 89 Darryl Hamilton 4.00 1.80 .50
☐ 90 Joey Hamilton 6.00 2.70 .75
☐ 91 Chris Hammond 4.00 1.80 .50
☐ 92 Mike Hampton 4.00 1.80 .50
☐ 93 Chris Haney 4.00 1.80 .50
☐ 94 Todd Haney 4.00 1.80 .50
☐ 95 Erik Hanson 4.00 1.80 .50
☐ 96 Pete Harnisch 4.00 1.80 .50
☐ 97 LaTroy Hawkins 4.00 1.80 .50
☐ 98 Charlie Hayes 4.00 1.80 .50
☐ 99 Jimmy Haynes 4.00 1.80 .50
☐ 100 Roberto Hernandez 6.00 2.70 .75
☐ 101 Bobby Higginson 6.00 2.70 .75
☐ 102 Glenallen Hill 4.00 1.80 .50
☐ 103 Ken Hill 6.00 2.70 .75
☐ 104 Sterling Hitchcock 4.00 1.80 .50
☐ 105 Trevor Hoffman 6.00 2.70 .75
☐ 106 Dave Hollins 4.00 1.80 .50
☐ 107 Dwayne Hosey 4.00 1.80 .50
☐ 108 Thomas Howard 4.00 1.80 .50
☐ 109 Steve Howe 4.00 1.80 .50
☐ 110 John Hudek 4.00 1.80 .50
☐ 111 Rex Hudler 4.00 1.80 .50
☐ 112 Brian L. Hunter 6.00 2.70 .75
☐ 113 Butch Huskey 6.00 2.70 .75
☐ 114 Mark Hutton 4.00 1.80 .50
☐ 115 Jason Jacome 4.00 1.80 .50
☐ 116 John Jaha 6.00 2.70 .75
☐ 117 Reggie Jefferson 4.00 1.80 .50
☐ 118 Derek Jeter SP 150.00 70.00 19.00
☐ 119 Bobby Jones 4.00 1.80 .50
☐ 120 Todd Jones 4.00 1.80 .50
☐ 121 Brian Jordan 6.00 2.70 .75
☐ 122 Kevin Jordan 4.00 1.80 .50
☐ 123 Jeff Juden 4.00 1.80 .50
☐ 124 Ron Karkovice 4.00 1.80 .50
☐ 125 Roberto Kelly 4.00 1.80 .50
☐ 126 Mark Kiefer 4.00 1.80 .50
☐ 127 Brooks Kieschnick 8.00 3.60 1.00
☐ 128 Jeff King 6.00 2.70 .75
☐ 129 Mike Lansing 4.00 1.80 .50
☐ 130 Matt Lawton 4.00 1.80 .50
☐ 131 Al Leiter 4.00 1.80 .50
☐ 132 Mark Leiter 4.00 1.80 .50
☐ 133 Curtis Leskanic 4.00 1.80 .50
☐ 134 Darren Lewis 4.00 1.80 .50
☐ 135 Mark Lewis 4.00 1.80 .50
☐ 136 Felipe Lira 4.00 1.80 .50
☐ 137 Pat Listach 4.00 1.80 .50
☐ 138 Keith Lockhart 4.00 1.80 .50
☐ 139 Kenny Lofton SP 90.00 40.00 11.00
☐ 140 John Mabry 6.00 2.70 .75
☐ 141 Mike Macfarlane 4.00 1.80 .50
☐ 142 Kirt Manwaring 4.00 1.80 .50
☐ 143 Al Martin 4.00 1.80 .50
☐ 144 Norberto Martin 4.00 1.80 .50
☐ 145 Dennis Martinez 6.00 2.70 .75
☐ 146 Pedro Martinez 6.00 2.70 .75
☐ 147 Sandy Martinez 4.00 1.80 .50
☐ 148 Mike Matheny 4.00 1.80 .50
☐ 149 T.J. Mathews 4.00 1.80 .50
☐ 150 David McCarty 4.00 1.80 .50
☐ 151 Ben McDonald 4.00 1.80 .50
☐ 152 Pat Meares 4.00 1.80 .50
☐ 153 Orlando Merced 4.00 1.80 .50
☐ 154 Jose Mesa 6.00 2.70 .75
☐ 155 Matt Mieske 4.00 1.80 .50
☐ 156 Orlando Miller 4.00 1.80 .50
☐ 157 Mike Mimbs 4.00 1.80 .50
☐ 158 Paul Molitor SP 100.00 45.00 12.50
☐ 159 Raul Mondesi SP 50.00 22.00 6.25
☐ 160 Jeff Montgomery 4.00 1.80 .50
☐ 161 Mickey Morandini 4.00 1.80 .50
☐ 162 Lyle Mouton 4.00 1.80 .50
☐ 163 James Mouton 4.00 1.80 .50
☐ 164 Jamie Moyer 4.00 1.80 .50
☐ 165 Rodney Myers 4.00 1.80 .50
☐ 166 Denny Neagle 6.00 2.70 .75
☐ 167 Robb Nen 4.00 1.80 .50
☐ 168 Marc Newfield 6.00 2.70 .75
☐ 169 Dave Nilsson 6.00 2.70 .75
☐ 170 Jon Nunnally 4.00 1.80 .50
☐ 171 Chad Ogea 4.00 1.80 .50
☐ 172 Troy O'Leary 4.00 1.80 .50
☐ 173 Rey Ordonez 15.00 6.75 1.85
☐ 174 Jayhawk Owens 4.00 1.80 .50
☐ 175 Tom Pagnozzi 4.00 1.80 .50
☐ 176 Dean Palmer 8.00 3.60 1.00
☐ 177 Roger Pavlik 4.00 1.80 .50
☐ 178 Troy Percival 4.00 1.80 .50
☐ 179 Carlos Perez 4.00 1.80 .50
☐ 180 Robert Perez 4.00 1.80 .50
☐ 181 Andy Pettitte 30.00 13.50 3.70
☐ 182 Phil Plantier 4.00 1.80 .50
☐ 183 Mike Potts 4.00 1.80 .50
☐ 184 Curtis Pride 4.00 1.80 .50
☐ 185 Ariel Prieto 4.00 1.80 .50
☐ 186 Bill Pulsipher 6.00 2.70 .75
☐ 187 Brad Radke 4.00 1.80 .50
☐ 188 Manny Ramirez SP 50.00 22.00 6.25
☐ 189 Joe Randa 4.00 1.80 .50
☐ 190 Pat Rapp 4.00 1.80 .50
☐ 191 Bryan Rekar 4.00 1.80 .50
☐ 192 Shane Reynolds 4.00 1.80 .50
☐ 193 Arthur Rhodes 4.00 1.80 .50
☐ 194 Mariano Rivera 15.00 6.75 1.85
☐ 195 Alex Rodriguez SP 250.00 110.00 31.00
☐ 196 Frank Rodriguez 4.00 1.80 .50
☐ 197 Mel Rojas 4.00 1.80 .50
☐ 198 Ken Ryan 4.00 1.80 .50
☐ 199 Bret Saberhagen 4.00 1.80 .50
☐ 200 Tim Salmon 15.00 6.75 1.85
☐ 201 Rey Sanchez 4.00 1.80 .50
☐ 202 Scott Sanders 4.00 1.80 .50
☐ 203 Steve Scarsone 4.00 1.80 .50
☐ 204 Curt Schilling 4.00 1.80 .50
☐ 205 Jason Schmidt 8.00 3.60 1.00
☐ 206 David Segui 4.00 1.80 .50
☐ 207 Kevin Seitzer 4.00 1.80 .50
☐ 208 Scott Servais 4.00 1.80 .50
☐ 209 Don Slaught 4.00 1.80 .50
☐ 210 Zane Smith 4.00 1.80 .50
☐ 211 Paul Sorrento 4.00 1.80 .50
☐ 212 Scott Stahoviak 4.00 1.80 .50
☐ 213 Mike Stanley 4.00 1.80 .50
☐ 214 Terry Steinbach 4.00 1.80 .50
☐ 215 Kevin Stocker 4.00 1.80 .50
☐ 216 Jeff Suppan 10.00 4.50 1.25
☐ 217 Bill Swift 4.00 1.80 .50
☐ 218 Greg Swindell 4.00 1.80 .50
☐ 219 Kevin Tapani 4.00 1.80 .50
☐ 220 Danny Tartabull 4.00 1.80 .50
☐ 221 Julian Tavarez 4.00 1.80 .50
☐ 222 Frank Thomas SP 250.00 110.00 31.00
☐ 223 Ozzie Timmons 4.00 1.80 .50
☐ 224 Michael Tucker 6.00 2.70 .75
☐ 225 Ismael Valdes 4.00 1.80 .50
☐ 226 Jose Valentin 4.00 1.80 .50
☐ 227 Todd Van Poppel 4.00 1.80 .50
☐ 228 Mo Vaughn SP 90.00 40.00 11.00
☐ 229 Quilvio Veras 4.00 1.80 .50
☐ 230 Fernando Vina 4.00 1.80 .50
☐ 231 Joe Vitiello 4.00 1.80 .50
☐ 232 Jose Vizcaino 4.00 1.80 .50
☐ 233 Omar Vizquel 10.00 4.50 1.25
☐ 234 Terrell Wade 6.00 2.70 .75
☐ 235 Paul Wagner 4.00 1.80 .50
☐ 236 Matt Walbeck 4.00 1.80 .50
☐ 237 Jerome Walton 4.00 1.80 .50
☐ 238 Turner Ward 4.00 1.80 .50
☐ 239 Allen Watson 4.00 1.80 .50
☐ 240 David Weathers 4.00 1.80 .50
☐ 241 Walt Weiss 4.00 1.80 .50
☐ 242 Turk Wendell 4.00 1.80 .50
☐ 243 Rondell White 10.00 4.50 1.25
☐ 244 Brian Williams 4.00 1.80 .50
☐ 245 George Williams 4.00 1.80 .50
☐ 246 Paul Wilson 10.00 4.50 1.25
☐ 247 Bobby Witt 4.00 1.80 .50
☐ 248 Bob Wolcott 4.00 1.80 .50
☐ 249 Eric Young 6.00 2.70 .75
☐ 250 Ernie Young 4.00 1.80 .50
☐ 251 Greg Zaun 4.00 1.80 .50
☐ NNO F.Thomas Jumbo AU 100.00 45.00 12.50

1996 Leaf Signature Autographs Gold

Randomly inserted primarily in first series packs, this 252-card set is parallel to the regular set and is similar in design with the exception of the gold foil printing on each card front. Each player signed 500 cards, except for the SP's of which only 100 of each are signed. Jim Thome erroneously signed 514 Gold cards.

	MINT	NRMT	EXC
COMPLETE SET (252)	5500.00	2500.00	700.00
COMMON CARD (1-252)	10.00	4.50	1.25
*GOLD: 2.5X BRONZE CARDS			

☐ 223 Jim Thome SP514 80.00 36.00 10.00

1996 Leaf Signature Autographs Silver

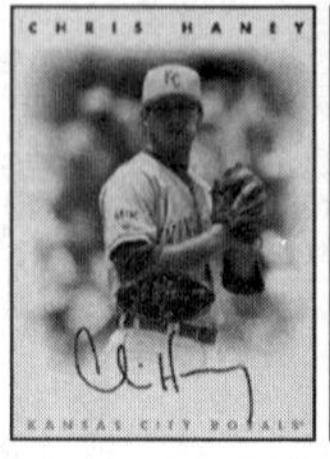

Randomly inserted primarily in first series packs, this 252-card set is parallel to the regular set and is similar in design with the exception of the silver foil printing on each card front. Each player signed 1000 silver cards, except for the SP's of which only 200 are signed. Jim Thome erroneously signed 410 Silver cards.

	MINT	NRMT	EXC
COMPLETE SET (252)	3300.00	1500.00	400.00
COMMON CARD (1-252)	6.00	2.70	.75
*SILVER: 1.5X BRONZE CARDS			

☐ 223 Jim Thome SP410 80.00 36.00 10.00

1996 Leaf Signature Extended Autographs

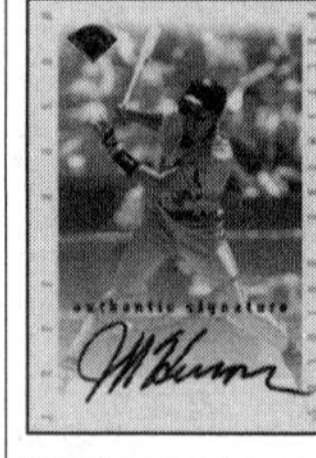

At least two autographed cards from this 217-card set were inserted in every Extended Series pack. Super Packs with four autographed cards were seeded one in every 12 packs. Most players signed 5000 cards, but short prints (500-2500 of each) do exist. On average, one in every nine packs contains a short print. All short print cards are individually noted below. By mistake, Andruw Jones, Ryan Klesko, Andy Pettitte, Kirby Puckett and Frank Thomas signed a few hundred of each of their cards in blue ink instead of black. No difference in price has been noted. Also, the Juan Gonzalez, Andruw Jones and Alex Rodriguez cards available in packs were not signed. All three cards had information on the back on how to mail them into Donruss/Leaf for an actual signed version. Middle relievers Doug Creek and Steve Parris failed to sign all 5000 of their cards. Creek submitted 1,950 cards and Parris submitted 1,800. Finally, an autographed jumbo version of the Extended Series Frank Thomas card was distributed to dealers in March, 1997. Dealers received either this card or the first series jumbo Thomas for every Extended Series case ordered. Each Extended Thomas jumbo is individually serial numbered to 1,500.

	MINT	NRMT	EXC
COMPLETE SET (217)	3000.00	1350.00	375.00
COMMON CARD (1-217)	4.00	1.80	.50

☐ 1 Scott Aldred 4.00 1.80 .50
☐ 2 Mike Aldrete 4.00 1.80 .50
☐ 3 Rich Amaral 4.00 1.80 .50
☐ 4 Alex Arias 4.00 1.80 .50
☐ 5 Paul Assenmacher 4.00 1.80 .50
☐ 6 Roger Bailey 4.00 1.80 .50
☐ 7 Erik Bennett 4.00 1.80 .50
☐ 8 Sean Bergman 4.00 1.80 .50
☐ 9 Doug Bochtler 4.00 1.80 .50
☐ 10 Tim Bogar 4.00 1.80 .50
☐ 11 Pat Borders 4.00 1.80 .50
☐ 12 Pedro Borbon 4.00 1.80 .50
☐ 13 Shawn Boskie 4.00 1.80 .50
☐ 14 Rafael Bournigal 4.00 1.80 .50
☐ 15 Mark Brandenberg 4.00 1.80 .50
☐ 16 John Briscoe 4.00 1.80 .50
☐ 17 Jorge Brito 4.00 1.80 .50
☐ 18 Doug Brocail 4.00 1.80 .50
☐ 19 Jay Buhner SP1000 50.00 22.00 6.25
☐ 20 Scott Bullett 4.00 1.80 .50
☐ 21 Dave Burba 4.00 1.80 .50
☐ 22 Ken Caminiti SP1000 60.00 27.00 7.50
☐ 23 John Cangelosi 4.00 1.80 .50
☐ 24 Cris Carpenter 4.00 1.80 .50
☐ 25 Chuck Carr 4.00 1.80 .50
☐ 26 Larry Casian 4.00 1.80 .50
☐ 27 Tony Castillo 4.00 1.80 .50
☐ 28 Jason Christiansen 4.00 1.80 .50
☐ 29 Archi Cianfrocco 4.00 1.80 .50
☐ 30 Mark Clark 4.00 1.80 .50
☐ 31 Terry Clark 4.00 1.80 .50
☐ 32 Roger Clemens SP1000 100.00 45.00 12.50
☐ 33 Jim Converse 4.00 1.80 .50
☐ 34 Dennis Cook 4.00 1.80 .50
☐ 35 Francisco Cordova 4.00 1.80 .50
☐ 36 Jim Corsi 4.00 1.80 .50
☐ 37 Tim Crabtree 4.00 1.80 .50
☐ 38 Doug Creek SP1950 10.00 4.50 1.25
☐ 39 John Cummings 4.00 1.80 .50
☐ 40 Omar Daal 4.00 1.80 .50
☐ 41 Rich DeLucia 4.00 1.80 .50
☐ 42 Mark Dewey 4.00 1.80 .50
☐ 43 Alex Diaz 4.00 1.80 .50
☐ 44 Jermaine Dye SP2500 40.00 18.00 5.00
☐ 45 Ken Edenfield 4.00 1.80 .50
☐ 46 Mark Eichhorn 4.00 1.80 .50
☐ 47 John Ericks 4.00 1.80 .50
☐ 48 Darin Erstad 50.00 22.00 6.25
☐ 49 Alvaro Espinoza 4.00 1.80 .50
☐ 50 Jorge Fabregas 4.00 1.80 .50
☐ 51 Mike Fetters 4.00 1.80 .50
☐ 52 John Flaherty 4.00 1.80 .50
☐ 53 Bryce Florie 4.00 1.80 .50
☐ 54 Tony Fossas 4.00 1.80 .50
☐ 55 Lou Frazier 4.00 1.80 .50
☐ 56 Mike Gallego 4.00 1.80 .50
☐ 57 Karim Garcia SP2500 40.00 18.00 5.00
☐ 58 Jason Giambi 15.00 6.75 1.85
☐ 59 Ed Giovanola 4.00 1.80 .50
☐ 60 Tom Glavine SP1250 50.00 22.00 6.25
☐ 61 Juan Gonzalez SP1000 150.00 70.00 19.00
☐ 62 Craig Grebeck 4.00 1.80 .50
☐ 63 Buddy Groom 4.00 1.80 .50
☐ 64 Kevin Gross 4.00 1.80 .50
☐ 65 Eddie Guardado 4.00 1.80 .50
☐ 66 Mark Guthrie 4.00 1.80 .50
☐ 67 Tony Gwynn SP1000 125.00 55.00 15.50
☐ 68 Chip Hale 4.00 1.80 .50
☐ 69 Darren Hall 4.00 1.80 .50
☐ 70 Lee Hancock 4.00 1.80 .50
☐ 71 Dave Hansen 4.00 1.80 .50
☐ 72 Bryan Harvey 4.00 1.80 .50
☐ 73 Bill Haselman 4.00 1.80 .50
☐ 74 Mike Henneman 4.00 1.80 .50
☐ 75 Doug Henry 4.00 1.80 .50
☐ 76 Gil Heredia 4.00 1.80 .50
☐ 77 Carlos Hernandez 4.00 1.80 .50
☐ 78 Jose Hernandez 4.00 1.80 .50
☐ 79 Darren Holmes 4.00 1.80 .50
☐ 80 Mark Holzemer 4.00 1.80 .50
☐ 81 Rick Honeycutt 4.00 1.80 .50
☐ 82 Chris Hook 4.00 1.80 .50
☐ 83 Chris Howard 4.00 1.80 .50
☐ 84 Jack Howell 4.00 1.80 .50
☐ 85 David Hulse 4.00 1.80 .50
☐ 86 Edwin Hurtado 4.00 1.80 .50
☐ 87 Jeff Huson 4.00 1.80 .50
☐ 88 Mike James 4.00 1.80 .50
☐ 89 Derek Jeter SP1000 140.00 65.00 17.50
☐ 90 Brian Johnson 4.00 1.80 .50
☐ 91 Randy Johnson SP1000 60.00 27.00 7.50
☐ 92 Mark Johnson 4.00 1.80 .50
☐ 93 Andruw Jones SP2000 150.00 70.00 19.00
☐ 94 Chris Jones 4.00 1.80 .50
☐ 95 Ricky Jordan 4.00 1.80 .50
☐ 96 Matt Karchner 4.00 1.80 .50
☐ 97 Scott Karl 4.00 1.80 .50
☐ 98 Jason Kendall SP2500 25.00 11.00 3.10
☐ 99 Brian Keyser 4.00 1.80 .50
☐ 100 Mike Kingery 4.00 1.80 .50
☐ 101 Wayne Kirby 4.00 1.80 .50
☐ 102 Ryan Klesko SP1000 60.00 27.00 7.50
☐ 103 Chuck Knoblauch SP1000 60.00 27.00 7.50
☐ 104 Chad Kreuter 4.00 1.80 .50
☐ 105 Tom Lampkin 4.00 1.80 .50
☐ 106 Scott Leius 4.00 1.80 .50
☐ 107 Jon Lieber 4.00 1.80 .50
☐ 108 Nelson Liriano 4.00 1.80 .50
☐ 109 Scott Livingstone 4.00 1.80 .50
☐ 110 Graeme Lloyd 4.00 1.80 .50
☐ 111 Kenny Lofton SP1000 70.00 32.00 8.75
☐ 112 Luis Lopez 4.00 1.80 .50
☐ 113 Torey Lovullo 4.00 1.80 .50
☐ 114 Greg Maddux SP500 250.00 110.00 31.00
☐ 115 Mike Maddux 4.00 1.80 .50
☐ 116 Dave Magadan 4.00 1.80 .50
☐ 117 Mike Magnante 4.00 1.80 .50
☐ 118 Joe Magrane 4.00 1.80 .50
☐ 119 Pat Mahomes 4.00 1.80 .50
☐ 120 Matt Mantei 4.00 1.80 .50
☐ 121 John Marzano 4.00 1.80 .50

☐ 122 Terry Mathews	4.00	1.80	.50
☐ 123 Chuck McElroy	4.00	1.80	.50
☐ 124 Fred McGriff SP1000	50.00	22.00	6.25
☐ 125 Mark McLemore	4.00	1.80	.50
☐ 126 Greg McMichael	4.00	1.80	.50
☐ 127 Blas Minor	4.00	1.80	.50
☐ 128 Dave Mlicki	4.00	1.80	.50
☐ 129 Mike Mohler	4.00	1.80	.50
☐ 130 Paul Molitor SP1000	75.00	34.00	9.50
☐ 131 Steve Montgomery	4.00	1.80	.50
☐ 132 Mike Mordecai	4.00	1.80	.50
☐ 133 Mike Morgan	4.00	1.80	.50
☐ 134 Mike Munoz	4.00	1.80	.50
☐ 135 Greg Myers	4.00	1.80	.50
☐ 136 Jimmy Myers	4.00	1.80	.50
☐ 137 Mike Myers	4.00	1.80	.50
☐ 138 Bob Natal	4.00	1.80	.50
☐ 139 Dan Naulty	4.00	1.80	.50
☐ 140 Jeff Nelson	4.00	1.80	.50
☐ 141 Warren Newson	4.00	1.80	.50
☐ 142 Chris Nichting	4.00	1.80	.50
☐ 143 Melvin Nieves	4.00	1.80	.50
☐ 144 Charlie O'Brien	4.00	1.80	.50
☐ 145 Alex Ochoa	15.00	6.75	1.85
☐ 146 Omar Olivares	4.00	1.80	.50
☐ 147 Joe Oliver	4.00	1.80	.50
☐ 148 Lance Painter	4.00	1.80	.50
☐ 149 Rafael Palmeiro SP2000	30.00	13.50	3.70
☐ 150 Mark Parent	4.00	1.80	.50
☐ 151 Steve Parris SP1800	15.00	6.75	1.85
☐ 152 Bob Patterson	4.00	1.80	.50
☐ 153 Tony Pena	4.00	1.80	.50
☐ 154 Eddie Perez	4.00	1.80	.50
☐ 155 Yorkis Perez	4.00	1.80	.50
☐ 156 Robert Person	4.00	1.80	.50
☐ 157 Mark Petkovsek	4.00	1.80	.50
☐ 158 Andy Pettitte SP1000	60.00	27.00	7.50
☐ 159 J.R. Phillips	4.00	1.80	.50
☐ 160 Hipolito Pichardo	4.00	1.80	.50
☐ 161 Eric Plunk	4.00	1.80	.50
☐ 162 Jimmy Poole	4.00	1.80	.50
☐ 163 Kirby Puckett SP1000	150.00	70.00	19.00
☐ 164 Paul Quantrill	4.00	1.80	.50
☐ 165 Tom Quinlan	4.00	1.80	.50
☐ 166 Jeff Reboulet	4.00	1.80	.50
☐ 167 Jeff Reed	4.00	1.80	.50
☐ 168 Steve Reed	4.00	1.80	.50
☐ 169 Carlos Reyes	4.00	1.80	.50
☐ 170 Bill Risley	4.00	1.80	.50
☐ 171 Kevin Ritz	4.00	1.80	.50
☐ 172 Kevin Roberson	4.00	1.80	.50
☐ 173 Rich Robertson	4.00	1.80	.50
☐ 174 Alex Rodriguez SP500	325.00	145.00	40.00
☐ 175 Ivan Rodriguez SP1250	75.00	34.00	9.50
☐ 176 Bruce Ruffin	4.00	1.80	.50
☐ 177 Juan Samuel	4.00	1.80	.50
☐ 178 Tim Scott	4.00	1.80	.50
☐ 179 Kevin Sefcik	4.00	1.80	.50
☐ 180 Jeff Shaw	4.00	1.80	.50
☐ 181 Danny Sheaffer	4.00	1.80	.50
☐ 182 Craig Shipley	4.00	1.80	.50
☐ 183 Dave Silvestri	4.00	1.80	.50
☐ 184 Aaron Small	4.00	1.80	.50
☐ 185 John Smoltz SP1000	60.00	27.00	7.50
☐ 186 Luis Sojo	4.00	1.80	.50
☐ 187 Sammy Sosa SP1000	60.00	27.00	7.50
☐ 188 Steve Sparks	4.00	1.80	.50
☐ 189 Tim Spehr	4.00	1.80	.50
☐ 190 Russ Springer	4.00	1.80	.50
☐ 191 Matt Stairs	4.00	1.80	.50
☐ 192 Andy Stankiewicz	4.00	1.80	.50
☐ 193 Mike Stanton	4.00	1.80	.50
☐ 194 Kelly Stinnett	4.00	1.80	.50
☐ 195 Doug Strange	4.00	1.80	.50
☐ 196 Mark Sweeney	4.00	1.80	.50
☐ 197 Jeff Tabaka	4.00	1.80	.50
☐ 198 Jesus Tavarez	4.00	1.80	.50
☐ 199 Frank Thomas SP1000	225.00	100.00	28.00
☐ 200 Larry Thomas	4.00	1.80	.50
☐ 201 Mark Thompson	4.00	1.80	.50
☐ 202 Mike Timlin	4.00	1.80	.50
☐ 203 Steve Trachsel	4.00	1.80	.50
☐ 204 Tom Urbani	4.00	1.80	.50
☐ 205 Julio Valera	4.00	1.80	.50
☐ 206 Dave Valle	4.00	1.80	.50
☐ 207 William VanLandingham	4.00	1.80	.50
☐ 208 Mo Vaughn SP1000	70.00	32.00	8.75
☐ 209 Dave Veres	4.00	1.80	.50
☐ 210 Ed Vosberg	4.00	1.80	.50
☐ 211 Don Wengert	4.00	1.80	.50
☐ 212 Matt Whiteside	4.00	1.80	.50
☐ 213 Bob Wickman	4.00	1.80	.50
☐ 214 Matt Williams SP1250	50.00	22.00	6.25
☐ 215 Mike Williams	4.00	1.80	.50
☐ 216 Woody Williams	4.00	1.80	.50
☐ 217 Craig Worthington	4.00	1.80	.50
☐ NNO F.Thomas Jumbo AU	100.00	45.00	12.50

1996 Leaf Signature Extended Autographs Century Marks

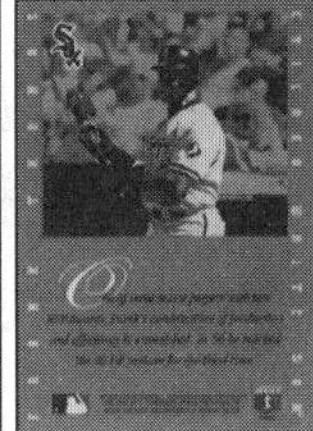

Randomly inserted exclusively into Extended Series packs, cards from this 31-card parallel set feature a selection of star and rising young prospect players taken from the more comprehensive 217-card Extended Autograph set. The cards differ by a special blue holographic foil treatment. Only 100 of each card exists. In addition, Juan Gonzalez, Derek Jeter, Andrew Jones, Rafael Palmeiro and Alex Rodriguez did not sign the cards distributed in packs. All of these players cards have information on the back on how to mail them into Leaf/Donruss to receive a signed version.

	MINT	NRMT	EXC
COMPLETE SET (31)	6000.00	2700.00	750.00
COMMON CARD (1-31)	80.00	36.00	10.00
☐ 1 Jay Buhner	125.00	55.00	15.50
☐ 2 Ken Caminiti	150.00	70.00	19.00
☐ 3 Roger Clemens	250.00	110.00	31.00
☐ 4 Jermaine Dye	125.00	55.00	15.50
☐ 5 Darin Erstad	200.00	90.00	25.00
☐ 6 Karim Garcia	125.00	55.00	15.50
☐ 7 Jason Giambi	90.00	40.00	11.00
☐ 8 Tom Glavine	125.00	55.00	15.50
☐ 9 Juan Gonzalez	350.00	160.00	45.00
☐ 10 Tony Gwynn	300.00	135.00	38.00
☐ 11 Derek Jeter	325.00	145.00	40.00
☐ 12 Randy Johnson	150.00	70.00	19.00
☐ 13 Andruw Jones	500.00	220.00	60.00
☐ 14 Jason Kendall	100.00	45.00	12.50
☐ 15 Ryan Klesko	125.00	55.00	15.50
☐ 16 Chuck Knoblauch	150.00	70.00	19.00
☐ 17 Kenny Lofton	200.00	90.00	25.00
☐ 18 Greg Maddux	500.00	220.00	60.00
☐ 19 Fred McGriff	125.00	55.00	15.50
☐ 20 Paul Molitor	150.00	70.00	19.00
☐ 21 Alex Ochoa	80.00	36.00	10.00
☐ 22 Rafael Palmeiro	125.00	55.00	15.50
☐ 23 Andy Pettitte	150.00	70.00	19.00
☐ 24 Kirby Puckett	400.00	180.00	50.00
☐ 25 Alex Rodriguez	600.00	275.00	75.00
☐ 26 Ivan Rodriguez	200.00	90.00	25.00
☐ 27 John Smoltz	150.00	70.00	19.00
☐ 28 Sammy Sosa	150.00	70.00	19.00
☐ 29 Frank Thomas	600.00	275.00	75.00
☐ 30 Mo Vaughn	200.00	90.00	25.00
☐ 31 Matt Williams	125.00	55.00	15.50

1993 Legendary Foils Promos

Dubbed the Sports Legends Series, these plaques, which measure approximately 2 5/8" by 3 3/4", feature Hall of Famers from baseball, football, basketball and hockey. They will be released at a rate of one card from each sport per month. Production was limited to 100,000 plaques for any one Hall of Famer and All-Gold Series plaques were limited to 5,000. These cards are all notated with a promo message.

	MINT	NRMT	EXC
COMPLETE SET	4.00	1.80	.50
COMMON CARD	2.00	.90	.25
☐ 1 Satchel Paige	2.00	.90	.25
☐ 2 Honus Wagner	2.00	.90	.25

1993-94 Legendary Foils

The Legendary Foils Sport Series is a monthly series featuring baseball Hall of Famers. There are two editions. One is the Gold Edition, limited to 5,000 sets, and the Colored Edition, limited to 95,000 cards per player. The cards measure approximately 3 1/2" by 5" and come in a blue and black custom designed folder. The embossed fronts carry the players portrait and a short career summary. The Gold Edition cards are shiny gold on a matte gold background, while the Color Edition cards have a blue background. The serial number also appears on the front. The backs are silver and carry Legendary Foil logos.

	MINT	NRMT	EXC
COMPLETE SET	40.00	18.00	5.00
COMMON CARD (1-12)	2.00	.90	.25
☐ 1 Roberto Clemente	6.00	2.70	.75
☐ 2 Dizzy Dean	3.00	1.35	.35
☐ 3 Lou Gehrig	6.00	2.70	.75
☐ 4 Rogers Hornsby	3.00	1.35	.35
☐ 5 Carl Hubbell	3.00	1.35	.35
☐ 6 Walter Johnson	3.00	1.35	.35
☐ 7 Tony Lazzeri	2.00	.90	.25
☐ 8 Satchel Paige	5.00	2.20	.60
☐ 9 Babe Ruth	7.50	3.40	.95
☐ 10 Casey Stengel	3.00	1.35	.35
☐ 11 Pie Traynor	3.00	1.35	.35
☐ 12 Honus Wagner	3.00	1.35	.35

1993-94 Legendary Foils Hawaii IX

This Legendary Foils card of Babe Ruth was given out at the Ninth Hawaiian Show. Just 300 cards were produced. It measures approximately 2 5/8" by 3 3/4". On a matte gold background, the embossed front carries the player's portrait inside a circle and a short career summary in shiny gold lettering underneath it. Two bats on each side frame the text, and a baseball appears above each pair of bats. The top of the card is rounded alongside the two baseballs and the top part of the circle. The words "Hawaii IX" is printed on the bottom of the front. The back is silver, carrying the Legendary Foil logo and a production number. Where the serial number appears on regular series cards, this card reads "Hawaii IX."

	MINT	NRMT	EXC
COMPLETE SET	5.00	2.20	.60
COMMON CARD	5.00	2.20	.60
☐ 1 Babe Ruth	5.00	2.20	.60

1992 Legends Sports Fingers

This three-card standard-size set was included as part of a nine-card LSM (Legends Sports Memorabilia) Athlete's Gallery insert sheet in a sports collectibles magazine bearing the same name. The fronts feature three different color photos of former baseball great Rollie Fingers playing golf. The cards are accented by a dark gray granite border above and on the left, while a silver-foil outer border frames the entire front. The Legends logo at the lower right corner rounds out the front. Inside dark gray granite borders, the back display a color head shot and advertisements for the magazine.

	MINT	NRMT	EXC
COMPLETE SET (3)	2.50	1.10	.30
COMMON CARD (1-3)	1.00	.45	.12
☐ RF1 Rollie Fingers Follow through watching drive	1.00	.45	.12
☐ RF2 Rollie Fingers Sizing up putt	1.00	.45	.12
☐ RF3 Rollie Fingers Portrait	1.00	.45	.12

1994 Legends Postcard Ryan

This postcard features Texas Ranger great Nolan Ryan. This was issued after Ryan's career finished and is a tribute to his long and fabled career which included more than 300 wins and the shattering of the exisitng strikeout record.

	MINT	NRMT	EXC
COMPLETE SET	2.00	.90	.25
COMMON CARD	2.00	.90	.25
☐ 1 Nolan Ryan	2.00	.90	.25

1993 Leon Day Commemorative Card

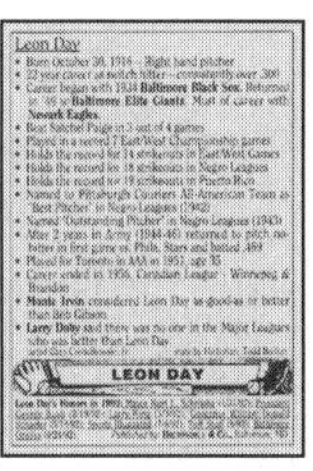

Published by Hieronimus and Co., this card measures 2 1/2" by 3 1/2" and features a portrait of Leon Day on a white background by artist Gary Cieradkowski Jr. The player's name appears in a black-and-white banner that includes drawings of a glove, bat, ball and face mask. The back is printed in black ink and carries biography and career highlights.

	MINT	NRMT	EXC
COMPLETE SET	5.00	2.20	.60
COMMON CARD	5.00	2.20	.60
☐ 1 Leon Day	5.00	2.20	.60

1992 Lime Rock Griffey Holograms

This three-card standard-size set was produced by Lime Rock and features baseball's "first family," the Griffeys. Included with each set was a serially numbered coupon that entitled the holder to a free issue of Lime Rock's Inside Trader Club Quarterly News. The sets were sold in a box and included a gold-embossed folder for displaying the cards. According to Lime Rock, 250,000 sets and 5,000 strips were produced. Moreover, 2,500 cards were personally autographed and randomly inserted. Members of Lime Rock's Inside Trader Club had the exclusive right to purchase the same cards as a strip. Also, 750 promo sets were produced and distributed at the National Sports Collectors Convention in Atlanta (the promo cards are blank backed). The cards were also produced in a gold version (reportedly 1,000 sets). Each standard-size, full-bleed hologram captures Ken Sr., Ken Jr. and Craig in game action. At the top of each front appear the words "Griffey Baseball" in the background. Also the player's autograph is inscribed across the holograms. On a pastel green background, the backs carry a color close-up photo, career summary and statistics.

	MINT	NRMT	EXC
COMPLETE SET (3)	5.00	2.20	.60
COMMON CARD (1-3)	.50	.23	.06
☐ 1 Ken Griffey Sr.	1.00	.45	.12
☐ 2 Ken Griffey Jr.	4.00	1.80	.50
☐ 3 Craig Griffey	.50	.23	.06

1991 Line Drive

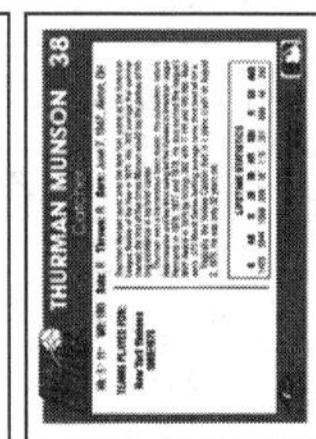

This 50-card standard-size set features notable retired players and managers. The fronts of card numbers 1-42 have color player photos with blue borders on a white card face. Card Nos. 43-50 are similar in design but have sepia-toned photos. The backs of all cards are horizontally oriented and feature biography, career highlights and lifetime statistics, all inside a red border.

	MINT	NRMT	EXC
COMPLETE SET (50)	7.50	3.40	.95
COMMON CARD (1-50)	.05	.02	.01
☐ 1 Don Drysdale	.30	.14	.04
☐ 2 Joe Torre	.20	.09	.03
☐ 3 Bob Gibson	.30	.14	.04
☐ 4 Bobby Richardson	.20	.09	.03
☐ 5 Ron Santo	.20	.09	.03
☐ 6 Eric Soderholm	.05	.02	.01
☐ 7 Yogi Berra	.50	.23	.06
☐ 8 Steve Garvey	.20	.09	.03
☐ 9 Steve Carlton	.30	.14	.04
☐ 10 Toby Harrah	.05	.02	.01
☐ 11 Luis Tiant	.15	.07	.02
☐ 12 Earl Weaver MG	.25	.11	.03

☐ 13 Bill Mazeroski	.20	.09	.03
☐ 14 Don Baylor	.15	.07	.02
☐ 15 Lew Burdette	.10	.05	.01
☐ 16 Jim Lonborg	.05	.02	.01
☐ 17 Jerry Grote	.05	.02	.01
☐ 18 Ernie Banks	.50	.23	.06
☐ 19 Doug DeCinces	.10	.05	.01
☐ 20 Jimmy Piersall	.10	.05	.01
☐ 21 Ken Holtzman	.05	.02	.01
☐ 22 Manny Mota	.05	.02	.01
☐ 23 Alvin Dark	.10	.05	.01
☐ 24 Lou Brock	.30	.14	.04
☐ 25 Ralph Houk	.05	.02	.01
☐ 26 Graig Nettles	.10	.05	.01
☐ 27 Bill White	.15	.07	.02
☐ 28 Billy Williams	.30	.14	.04
☐ 29 Willie Horton	.10	.05	.01
☐ 30 Tommie Agee	.05	.02	.01
☐ 31 Rico Petrocelli	.05	.02	.01
☐ 32 Julio Cruz	.05	.02	.01
☐ 33 Robin Roberts	.30	.14	.04
☐ 34 Dave Johnson	.05	.02	.01
☐ 35 Wilbur Wood	.05	.02	.01
☐ 36 Cesar Cedeno	.05	.02	.01
☐ 37 George Foster	.10	.05	.01
☐ 38 Thurman Munson	.30	.14	.04
☐ 39 Roberto Clemente	1.00	.45	.12
☐ 40 Eddie Mathews	.30	.14	.04
☐ 41 Harmon Killebrew	.30	.14	.04
☐ 42 Monte Irvin	.25	.11	.03
☐ 43 Bob Feller	.30	.14	.04
☐ 44 Jimmie Foxx	.25	.11	.03
☐ 45 Walter Johnson	.30	.14	.04
☐ 46 Casey Stengel	.30	.14	.04
☐ 47 Satchel Paige	.75	.35	.09
☐ 48 Ty Cobb	1.00	.45	.12
☐ 49 Mickey Cochrane	.25	.11	.03
☐ 50 Dizzy Dean	.30	.14	.04

1991 Line Drive Sandberg

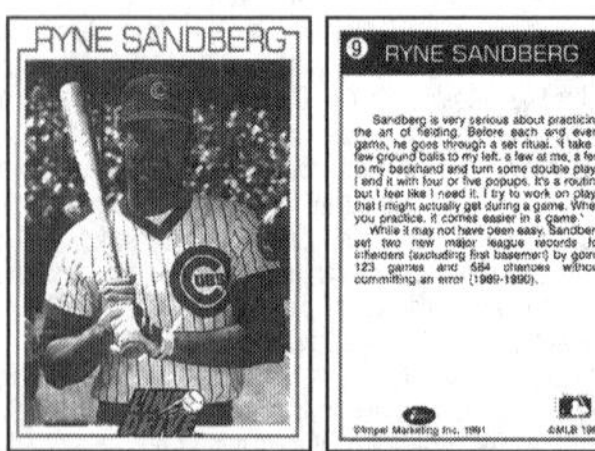

This 20-card standard-size set was sold as part of a boxed Ryne Sandberg Baseball Card Kit that included a personalized collector's album, the Ryne Sandberg Story and a free mail-in offer to receive an 8" X 10" color photo of a top baseball star. The cards feature color action photos, with blue borders on the left half of the card and red on the right half, on a white card face. In blue and red lettering, the player's name appears above the picture. In dark blue lettering and red borders, the back presents assorted information on Sandberg.

	MINT	NRMT	EXC
COMPLETE SET (20)	10.00	4.50	1.25
COMMON CARD (1-20)	.50	.23	.06
☐ 1 Ryne Sandberg Catching pop up	.50	.23	.06
☐ 2 Ryne Sandberg Running to 1st Dodger in background	.50	.23	.06
☐ 3 Ryne Sandberg Ready to release bat	.50	.23	.06
☐ 4 Ryne Sandberg Glove on ground Waiting for ball	.50	.23	.06
☐ 5 Ryne Sandberg Follow through Hands crossed Blue uniform	.50	.23	.06
☐ 6 Ryne Sandberg Blue uniform Glove at waist	.50	.23	.06
☐ 7 Ryne Sandberg Bat just below waist	.50	.23	.06
☐ 8 Ryne Sandberg Posed ready to swing	.50	.23	.06
☐ 9 Ryne Sandberg Portrait shot with moustache	.50	.23	.06
☐ 10 Ryne Sandberg Transferring ball from glove to hand	.50	.23	.06
☐ 11 Ryne Sandberg Dropping bat running to first	.50	.23	.06
☐ 12 Ryne Sandberg Running the bases	.50	.23	.06
☐ 13 Ryne Sandberg Following through end of swing White uniform	.50	.23	.06
☐ 14 Ryne Sandberg Following through end of swing Blue uniform	.50	.23	.06
☐ 15 Ryne Sandberg Leading off base	.50	.23	.06
☐ 16 Ryne Sandberg Bat behind body	.50	.23	.06
☐ 17 Ryne Sandberg Throwing	.50	.23	.06
☐ 18 Ryne Sandberg Follow through hands crossed white uniform	.50	.23	.06
☐ 19 Ryne Sandberg Glove at waist White uniform	.50	.23	.06
☐ 20 Ryne Sandberg Beginning of swing	.50	.23	.06

1973-74 Linnett Portraits

Measuring 8 1/2" by 11", these 179 charcoal drawings are facial portraits by noted sports artist Charles Linnett. The player's facsimile autograph is inscribed across the lower right corner. The backs are blank. Three portraits of players from the same team were included in each clear plastic packet. A checklist was also included in each packet, with an offer to order individual player portraits for 50 cents each. Originally, the suggested retail price was 99 cents. In later issues, the price was raised to $1.19. The portraits are unnumbered and listed alphabetically by teams as follows: Atlanta Braves (1-6), Baltimore Orioles (7-13), Boston Red Sox (14-32), California Angels (33-38), Chicago Cubs (39-46), Chicago White Sox (47-53), Cincinnati Reds (54-59), Cleveland Indians (60-67), Detroit Tigers (68-79), Houston Astros (80-86), Kansas City Royals (87-91), Los Angeles Dodgers (92-97), Milwaukee Brewers (98-103), Minnesota Twins (104-109), New York Mets (110-125), New York Yankees (126-136), Oakland A's (137-141), Philadelphia Phillies (142-147), Pittsburgh Pirates (148-153), San Diego Padres (154-156), San Francisco Giants (157-164), St. Louis Cardinals (165-171), and Texas Rangers (172-179). The Mets packages were as follows: Jon Matlack, Felix Millan and Duffy Dyer; Rusty Staub, Jerry Koosman and John Milner; and Wayne Garrett, Cleon Jones and Bud Harrelson.

	NRMT	VG-E	GOOD
COMPLETE SET	600.00	275.00	75.00
COMMON CARD	2.00	.90	.25
☐ 1 Hank Aaron	15.00	6.75	1.85
☐ 2 Darrell Evans	2.50	1.10	.30
☐ 3 Ralph Garr	2.00	.90	.25
☐ 4 Dave Johnson	2.50	1.10	.30
☐ 5 Mike Lum	2.00	.90	.25
☐ 6 Carl Morton	2.00	.90	.25
☐ 7 Mark Belanger	2.00	.90	.25
☐ 8 Paul Blair	2.00	.90	.25
☐ 9 Al Bumbry	2.00	.90	.25
☐ 10 Bobby Grich	2.50	1.10	.30
☐ 11 Lee May	2.00	.90	.25
☐ 12 Jim Palmer	7.50	3.40	.95
☐ 13 Brooks Robinson	7.50	3.40	.95
☐ 14 Luis Aparicio	4.00	1.80	.50
☐ 15 Bob Bolin	2.00	.90	.25
☐ 16 Danny Cater	2.00	.90	.25
☐ 17 Orlando Cepeda	3.00	1.35	.35
☐ 18 John Curtis	2.00	.90	.25
☐ 19 Dwight Evans	4.00	1.80	.50
☐ 20 Carlton Fisk	5.00	2.20	.60
☐ 21 Doug Griffin	2.00	.90	.25
☐ 22 Mario Guerrero	2.00	.90	.25
☐ 23 Tommy Harper	2.00	.90	.25
☐ 24 John Kennedy	2.00	.90	.25
☐ 25 Bill Lee	2.50	1.10	.30
☐ 26 Rick Miller	2.00	.90	.25
☐ 27 Bob Montgomery	2.00	.90	.25
☐ 28 Marty Pattin	2.00	.90	.25
☐ 29 Rico Petrocelli	2.00	.90	.25
☐ 30 Luis Tiant	3.00	1.35	.35
☐ 31 Bob Veale	2.00	.90	.25
☐ 32 Carl Yastrzemski	7.50	3.40	.95
☐ 33 Bob Oliver	2.00	.90	.25
☐ 34 Frank Robinson	5.00	2.20	.60
☐ 35 Nolan Ryan	25.00	11.00	3.10
☐ 36 Bill Singer	2.00	.90	.25
☐ 37 Lee Stanton	2.00	.90	.25
☐ 38 Bobby Valentine	2.00	.90	.25
☐ 39 Bill Bonham	2.00	.90	.25
☐ 40 Jose Cardenal	2.00	.90	.25
☐ 41 Don Kessinger	2.00	.90	.25
☐ 42 Bob Locker	2.00	.90	.25
☐ 43 Rick Monday	2.00	.90	.25
☐ 44 Ron Santo	3.00	1.35	.35
☐ 45 Steve Stone	2.00	.90	.25
☐ 46 Billy Williams	5.00	2.20	.60
☐ 47 Dick Allen	3.00	1.35	.35
☐ 48 Ed Herrmann	2.00	.90	.25
☐ 49 Eddie Leon	2.00	.90	.25
☐ 50 Bill Melton	2.00	.90	.25
☐ 51 Jorge Orta	2.00	.90	.25
☐ 52 Rick Reichardt	2.00	.90	.25
☐ 53 Wilbur Wood	2.00	.90	.25
☐ 54 Johnny Bench	7.50	3.40	.95
☐ 55 Cesar Geronimo	2.00	.90	.25
☐ 56 Don Gullett	2.00	.90	.25
☐ 57 Joe Morgan	5.00	2.20	.60
☐ 58 Tony Perez	3.00	1.35	.35
☐ 59 Pete Rose	15.00	6.75	1.85
☐ 60 Buddy Bell	2.50	1.10	.30
☐ 61 Chris Chambliss	2.00	.90	.25
☐ 62 John Ellis	2.00	.90	.25
☐ 63 George Hendrick	2.00	.90	.25
☐ 64 Steve Kline	2.00	.90	.25
☐ 65 Gaylord Perry	5.00	2.20	.60
☐ 66 Jim Perry	2.00	.90	.25
☐ 67 Charlie Spikes	2.00	.90	.25
☐ 68 Norm Cash	3.00	1.35	.35
☐ 69 Bill Freehan	2.50	1.10	.30
☐ 70 John Hiller	2.00	.90	.25
☐ 71 Willie Horton	2.00	.90	.25
☐ 72 Al Kaline	7.50	3.40	.95
☐ 73 Mickey Lolich	3.00	1.35	.35
☐ 74 Dick McAuliffe	2.00	.90	.25
☐ 75 Jim Northrup	2.00	.90	.25
☐ 76 Ben Oglivie	2.00	.90	.25
☐ 77 Aurelio Rodriguez	2.00	.90	.25
☐ 78 Fred Scherman	2.00	.90	.25
☐ 79 Mickey Stanley	2.00	.90	.25
☐ 80 Cesar Cedeno	2.00	.90	.25
☐ 81 Greg Gross	2.00	.90	.25
☐ 82 Roger Metzger	2.00	.90	.25
☐ 83 Jerry Reuss	2.00	.90	.25
☐ 84 Dave Roberts (P)	2.00	.90	.25
☐ 85 Bob Watson	2.00	.90	.25
☐ 86 Don Wilson	2.00	.90	.25
☐ 87 John Mayberry	2.00	.90	.25
☐ 88 Amos Otis	2.00	.90	.25
☐ 89 Fred Patek	2.00	.90	.25
☐ 90 Cookie Rojas	2.00	.90	.25
☐ 91 Paul Splittorff	2.00	.90	.25
☐ 92 Bill Buckner	2.00	.90	.25
☐ 93 Willie Crawford	2.00	.90	.25
☐ 94 Joe Ferguson	2.00	.90	.25
☐ 95 Dave Lopes	2.00	.90	.25
☐ 96 Bill Russell	2.00	.90	.25
☐ 97 Don Sutton	3.00	1.35	.35
☐ 98 John Briggs	2.00	.90	.25
☐ 99 Jim Colborn	2.00	.90	.25
☐ 100 Pedro Garcia	2.00	.90	.25
☐ 101 Dave May	2.00	.90	.25
☐ 102 Don Money	2.00	.90	.25
☐ 103 George Scott	2.00	.90	.25
☐ 104 Bert Blyleven	3.00	1.35	.35
☐ 105 Steve Braun	2.00	.90	.25
☐ 106 Steve Brye	2.00	.90	.25
☐ 107 Rod Carew	7.50	3.40	.95
☐ 108 Bobby Darwin	2.00	.90	.25
☐ 109 Danny Thompson	2.00	.90	.25
☐ 110 Duffy Dyer	2.00	.90	.25
☐ 111 Wayne Garrett	2.00	.90	.25
☐ 112 Bud Harrelson	2.00	.90	.25
☐ 113 Cleon Jones	2.00	.90	.25
☐ 114 Jerry Koosman	2.00	.90	.25
☐ 115 Teddy Martinez	2.00	.90	.25
☐ 116 Jon Matlack	2.00	.90	.25
☐ 117 Jim McAndrew	2.00	.90	.25
☐ 118 Tug McGraw	2.50	1.10	.30
☐ 119 Felix Millan	2.00	.90	.25
☐ 120 John Milner	2.00	.90	.25
☐ 121 Harry Parker	2.00	.90	.25
☐ 122 Tom Seaver	10.00	4.50	1.25
☐ 123 Rusty Staub	3.00	1.35	.35
☐ 124 George Stone	2.00	.90	.25
☐ 125 George Theodore	2.00	.90	.25
☐ 126 Bernie Allen	2.00	.90	.25
☐ 127 Felipe Alou	3.00	1.35	.35
☐ 128 Matty Alou	2.50	1.10	.30
☐ 129 Ron Blomberg	2.00	.90	.25
☐ 130 Sparky Lyle	2.50	1.10	.30
☐ 131 Gene Michael	2.00	.90	.25
☐ 132 Thurman Munson	5.00	2.20	.60
☐ 133 Bobby Murcer	3.00	1.35	.35
☐ 134 Graig Nettles	3.00	1.35	.35
☐ 135 Lou Piniella	2.50	1.10	.30
☐ 136 Mel Stottlemyre	2.00	.90	.25
☐ 137 Sal Bando	2.00	.90	.25
☐ 138 Bert Campaneris	2.50	1.10	.30
☐ 139 Rollie Fingers	5.00	2.20	.60
☐ 140 Jim Hunter	5.00	2.20	.60
☐ 141 Reggie Jackson	10.00	4.50	1.25
☐ 142 Bob Boone	2.50	1.10	.30
☐ 143 Larry Bowa	2.00	.90	.25
☐ 144 Steve Carlton	7.50	3.40	.95
☐ 145 Dave Cash	2.00	.90	.25
☐ 146 Greg Luzinski	2.50	1.10	.30
☐ 147 Willie Montanez	2.00	.90	.25
☐ 148 Ken Brett	2.00	.90	.25
☐ 149 Dave Giusti	2.00	.90	.25
☐ 150 Ed Kirkpatrick	2.00	.90	.25
☐ 151 Al Oliver	3.00	1.35	.35
☐ 152 Manny Sanguillen	2.00	.90	.25
☐ 153 Willie Stargell	7.50	3.40	.95
☐ 154 Nate Colbert	2.00	.90	.25
☐ 155 John Grubb	2.00	.90	.25
☐ 156 Dave Roberts (3B)	2.00	.90	.25
☐ 157 Bobby Bonds	3.00	1.35	.35
☐ 158 Ron Bryant	2.00	.90	.25
☐ 159 Dave Kingman	3.00	1.35	.35
☐ 160 Garry Maddox	2.00	.90	.25
☐ 161 Gary Matthews	2.00	.90	.25
☐ 162 Willie McCovey	5.00	2.20	.60
☐ 163 Sam McDowell	2.00	.90	.25
☐ 164 Chris Speier	2.00	.90	.25
☐ 165 Lou Brock	5.00	2.20	.60
☐ 166 Bernie Carbo	2.00	.90	.25
☐ 167 Bob Gibson	7.50	3.40	.95
☐ 168 Lynn McGlothen	2.00	.90	.25
☐ 169 Ted Simmons	3.00	1.35	.35
☐ 170 Reggie Smith	2.50	1.10	.30
☐ 171 Joe Torre	3.00	1.35	.35
☐ 172 Jim Bibby	2.00	.90	.25
☐ 173 Jeff Burroughs	2.00	.90	.25
☐ 174 David Clyde	2.00	.90	.25
☐ 175 Jim Fregosi	2.00	.90	.25
☐ 176 Toby Harrah	2.00	.90	.25
☐ 177 Vic Harris	2.00	.90	.25
☐ 178 Ferguson Jenkins	4.00	1.80	.50
☐ 179 Dave Nelson	2.00	.90	.25

1976 Linnett Superstars

The Linnett Superstars set contains 36 oversized cards measuring approximately 4" by 5 5/8". The cards feature black and white facial portraits of the players, with various color borders. In the corners of the portrait appear four different logos: MLB, MLBPA, team and PeeWee's. The backs have a picture and discussion of either great cars of the world or sailing ships. The cards are checklisted below according to teams as follows: Cincinnati Reds, (90-101) Boston Red Sox, (102-113) and Los Angeles Dodgers (114-125).

	NRMT	VG-E	GOOD
COMPLETE SET	125.00	55.00	15.50
COMMON CARD (90-125)	2.00	.90	.25
☐ 90 Don Gullett	2.00	.90	.25
☐ 91 Johnny Bench	7.50	3.40	.95
☐ 92 Tony Perez	5.00	2.20	.60
☐ 93 Mike Lum	2.00	.90	.25
☐ 94 Ken Griffey	4.00	1.80	.50
☐ 95 George Foster	3.00	1.35	.35
☐ 96 Joe Morgan	5.00	2.20	.60
☐ 97 Pete Rose	10.00	4.50	1.25
☐ 98 Dave Concepcion	4.00	1.80	.50
☐ 99 Cesar Geronimo	2.00	.90	.25
☐ 100 Dan Driessen	2.00	.90	.25
☐ 101 Pedro Borbon	2.00	.90	.25
☐ 102 Carl Yastrzemski	7.50	3.40	.95
☐ 103 Fred Lynn	4.00	1.80	.50
☐ 104 Dwight Evans	4.00	1.80	.50
☐ 105 Ferguson Jenkins	5.00	2.20	.60
☐ 106 Rico Petrocelli	3.00	1.35	.35
☐ 107 Denny Doyle	2.00	.90	.25
☐ 108 Luis Tiant	4.00	1.80	.50
☐ 109 Carlton Fisk	5.00	2.20	.60
☐ 110 Rick Burleson	3.00	1.35	.35
☐ 111 Bill Lee	3.00	1.35	.35
☐ 112 Rick Wise	2.00	.90	.25
☐ 113 Jim Rice	4.00	1.80	.50
☐ 114 Davey Lopes	3.00	1.35	.35
☐ 115 Steve Garvey	4.00	1.80	.50
☐ 116 Bill Russell	3.00	1.35	.35
☐ 117 Ron Cey	4.00	1.80	.50
☐ 118 Steve Yeager	2.00	.90	.25
☐ 119 Doug Rau	2.00	.90	.25
☐ 120 Don Sutton	4.00	1.80	.50
☐ 121 Joe Ferguson	2.00	.90	.25
☐ 122 Mike Marshall	2.00	.90	.25
☐ 123 Bill Buckner	2.00	.90	.25
☐ 124 Rick Rhoden	2.00	.90	.25
☐ 125 Ted Sizemore	2.00	.90	.25

1990 Little Sun Writers

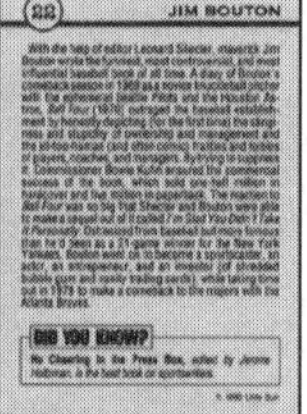

This 24-card standard-size set honors some of the more influential writers in baseball history, i.e., "major league writers." Cards measure 2 1/2" X 3 1/2" and have yellow and green borders surrounding black and white photos of the writers pictured. The writer's name is given in black lettering below the picture. The backs have brief biographies of the writers along with "Did you know" features usually about writers not in the set.

	MINT	NRMT	EXC
COMPLETE SET (24)	5.00	2.20	.60
COMMON CARD (1-24)	.25	.11	.03

☐ 1 Checklist Card	.25	.11	.03
☐ 2 Henry Chadwick	.50	.23	.06
☐ 3 Jacob C. Morse	.25	.11	.03
☐ 4 Francis C. Richter	.25	.11	.03
☐ 5 Grantland Rice	.50	.23	.06
☐ 6 Lee Allen	.25	.11	.03
☐ 7 Joe Reichler	.25	.11	.03
☐ 8 Red Smith	.50	.23	.06
☐ 9 Dick Young	.35	.16	.04
☐ 10 Jim Brosnan	.35	.16	.04
☐ 11 Charles Einstein	.35	.16	.04
☐ 12 Lawrence Ritter	.35	.16	.04
☐ 13 Roger Kahn	.50	.23	.06
☐ 14 Robert Creamer	.35	.16	.04
☐ 15 W.P. Kinsella	.50	.23	.06
☐ 16 Harold Seymour	.35	.16	.04
☐ 17 Ron Shelton	.50	.23	.06
☐ 18 Tom Clark	.25	.11	.03
☐ 19 Mark Harris	.35	.16	.04
☐ 20 John Holway	.35	.16	.04
☐ 21 Peter Golenbock	.25	.11	.03
☐ 22 Jim Bouton	.75	.35	.09
☐ 23 John Thorn	.35	.16	.04
☐ 24 Mike Shannon (Not the ex-Cardinal player)	.25	.11	.03

1887 Lone Jack N370

There are rulers and celebrities as well as baseball players in this set of sepia photographs issued by the Lone Jack Cigarette Company of Lynchburg, Va. The ballplayers are all members of the 1886 St. Louis Club which won the World Championship, and the pictures are identical to those found in set N172.

	EX-MT	VG-E	GOOD
COMPLETE SET	15000.00	6800.00	1900.00
COMMON CARD	1000.00	450.00	125.00
☐ 1 Al Bushong	1000.00	450.00	125.00
☐ 2 Bob Caruthers	1000.00	450.00	125.00
☐ 3 Charles Commiskey(sic)	2000.00	900.00	250.00
☐ 4 Dave Foutz	1000.00	450.00	125.00
☐ 5 William Gleason	1500.00	700.00	190.00
☐ 6 Nat Hudson	1000.00	450.00	125.00
☐ 7 Rudy Kimler (sic)	1000.00	450.00	125.00
☐ 8 Arlie Latham	1750.00	800.00	220.00
☐ 9 Hugh Nicol	1000.00	450.00	125.00
☐ 10 James O'Neil (sic)	1500.00	700.00	190.00
☐ 11 Bill (Yank) Robinson	1000.00	450.00	125.00
☐ 12 Chris Von Der Ahe OWN	1500.00	700.00	190.00
☐ 13 Curt Welsh (sic)	1500.00	700.00	190.00

1981 Long Beach Press Telegram

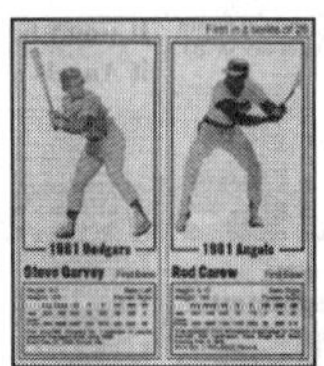

This 26-card set was distributed as a cut-out in the Long Beach Press Telegram and measures approximately 6 1/2" by 7 1/4". Each cut-out is really two cards each displaying a black-and-white player photo with player information and statistics printed below each picture.

	MINT	NRMT	EXC
COMPLETE SET (54)	40.00	18.00	5.00
COMMON CARD (1-54)	1.00	.45	.12
☐ 1 Steve Garvey Rod Carew	4.00	1.80	.50
☐ 2 Davey Lopes Bobby Grich	5.00	2.20	.60
☐ 3 Bill Russell Rick Burleson	1.50	.70	.19
☐ 4 Ron Cey Butch Hobson	1.50	.70	.19
☐ 5 Dusty Baker Don Baylor	1.50	.70	.19
☐ 6 Ken Landreaux Fred Lynn	1.00	.45	.12
☐ 7 Pedro Guerrero Dan Ford	1.00	.45	.12
☐ 8 Mike Scioscia Brian Downing	1.00	.45	.12
☐ 9 Jerry Reuss Geoff Zahn	1.50	.70	.19
☐ 10 Fernando Valenzuela Jesse Jefferson	1.00	.45	.12
☐ 11 Burt Hooton Mike Witt	1.50	.70	.19
☐ 12 Rick Sutcliffe Ken Forsch	1.50	.70	.19
☐ 13 Bob Welch Bill Travers	1.00	.45	.12
☐ 14 Bobby Castillo Andy Hassler	1.50	.70	.19
☐ 15 Steve Howe Aase	2.50	1.10	.30
☐ 16 Terry Forster Luis Sanchez	1.00	.45	.12
☐ 17 Reggie Smith Juan Beniquez	1.50	.70	.19
☐ 18 Derrel Thomas Ed Ott	1.50	.70	.19
☐ 19 Steve Yeager Tom Brunansky	1.00	.45	.12
☐ 20 Rick Monday Bert Campaneris	6.00	2.70	.75
☐ 21 Joe Ferguson Fred Patek	1.00	.45	.12
☐ 22 Jay Johnstone Juan Beniquez	1.00	.45	.12
☐ 23 Dave Goltz John D'Acquisto	1.50	.70	.19
☐ 24 Dave Stewart Steve Renko	2.50	1.10	.30
☐ 25 Pepe Frias Larry Harlow	1.00	.45	.12
☐ 26 Tom Lasorda MG Jim Fregosi MG	2.50	1.10	.30

1982 Louisville Slugger

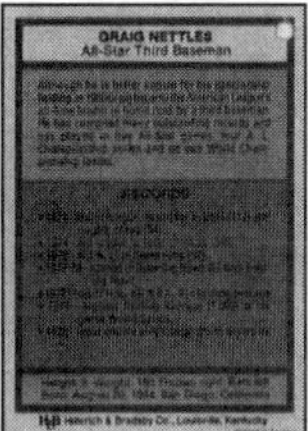

This four-card set consists of standard size tags that were attached to Louisville Slugger products. Each card has a hole in its upper left corner. The fronts feature glossy color player photos set in a lime green border design. A yellow bar within the bottom portion of the lime green border displays the Louisville Slugger brand name in red letters. A bright blue oval at the top contains the player's name. The photo is inscribed with a facsimile autograph. The backs have player profile, career highlights and biographical information divided into three sections with alternating background colors of pastel green and light blue. The player's name is at the top. All the sections are enclosed by a medium blue border. The cards are unnumbered and checklisted below in alphabetical order.

	MINT	NRMT	EXC
COMPLETE SET	5.00	2.20	.60
COMMON CARD	1.00	.45	.12
☐ 1 Steve Garvey	2.00	.90	.25
☐ 2 Pedro Guerrero	1.00	.45	.12
☐ 3 Fred Lynn	1.00	.45	.12
☐ 4 Graig Nettles	1.50	.70	.19

1910 Luxello Cigars Pins PT2

These pins feature members of both Philadelphia teams. They measure 7*' around. We have sequenced this set in alphabetical order.

	EX-MT	VG-E	GOOD
COMPLETE SET (21)	4000.00	1800.00	500.00
COMMON PIN (1-21)	200.00	90.00	25.00
☐ 1 Frank Baker	350.00	160.00	45.00
☐ 2 Jack Barry	200.00	90.00	25.00
☐ 3 John W. Bates	200.00	90.00	25.00
☐ 4 Eddie Collins	400.00	180.00	50.00
☐ 5 Jack Coombs	200.00	90.00	25.00
☐ 6 Harry Davis	200.00	90.00	25.00
☐ 7 Red Dooin	200.00	90.00	25.00
☐ 8 Mickey Doolan	200.00	90.00	25.00
☐ 9 James Dygert	200.00	90.00	25.00
☐ 10 Eddie Grant	250.00	110.00	31.00
☐ 11 William Heitmiller	200.00	90.00	25.00
☐ 12 Otto Knabe	200.00	90.00	25.00
☐ 13 Harry Krause	200.00	90.00	25.00
☐ 14 Paddy Livingston	200.00	90.00	25.00
☐ 15 George McQuillan	200.00	90.00	25.00
☐ 16 Earl Moore	200.00	90.00	25.00
☐ 17 Pat Moran	200.00	90.00	25.00
☐ 18 Danny Murphy	200.00	90.00	25.00
☐ 19 Ed Plank	350.00	160.00	45.00
☐ 20 Tully Sparks	200.00	90.00	25.00
☐ 21 John Titus	200.00	90.00	25.00

1953 MacGregor Staff

This set features black-and-white photos of players on the MacGregor Sporting Goods Advisory Staff. The cards measure approximately 8" by 9 1/8" with facsimile autographs on the fronts and blank backs. The cards are unnumbered and checklisted below in alphabetical order. The checklist may be incomplete.

	NRMT	VG-E	GOOD
COMPLETE SET	100.00	45.00	12.50
COMMON CARD	15.00	6.75	1.85
☐ 1 Ralph Kiner	25.00	11.00	3.10
☐ 2 Ted Kluszewski	20.00	9.00	2.50
☐ 3 Robin Roberts	25.00	11.00	3.10
☐ 4 Al Schoendienst	15.00	6.75	1.85
☐ 5 Warren Spahn	25.00	11.00	3.10

1960 MacGregor Staff

This 25-card set represents members of the MacGregor Sporting Goods Advisory Staff. Since the cards are unnumbered they ordered below in alphabetical order. The cards are blank backed and measure approximately 3 3/4" by 5". The photos are in black and white. The catalog designation for the set is H825-1. Cards have a facsimile autograph in white lettering on the front.

	NRMT	VG-E	GOOD
COMPLETE SET (25)	550.00	250.00	70.00
COMMON CARD (1-25)	10.00	4.50	1.25
☐ 1 Hank Aaron	125.00	55.00	15.50
☐ 2 Richie Ashburn	25.00	11.00	3.10
☐ 3 Gus Bell	12.50	5.50	1.55
☐ 4 Lou Berberet	10.00	4.50	1.25
☐ 5 Jerry Casale	10.00	4.50	1.25
☐ 6 Del Crandall	12.50	5.50	1.55
☐ 7 Art Ditmar	10.00	4.50	1.25
☐ 8 Gene Freese	10.00	4.50	1.25
☐ 9 James Gilliam	15.00	6.75	1.85
☐ 10 Ted Kluszewski	20.00	9.00	2.50
☐ 11 Jim Landis	10.00	4.50	1.25
☐ 12 Al Lopez MG	15.00	6.75	1.85
☐ 13 Willie Mays	135.00	60.00	17.00
☐ 14 Bill Mazeroski	20.00	9.00	2.50
☐ 15 Mike McCormick	12.50	5.50	1.55
☐ 16 Gil McDougald	15.00	6.75	1.85
☐ 17 Russ Nixon	10.00	4.50	1.25
☐ 18 Bill Rigney MG	10.00	4.50	1.25
☐ 19 Robin Roberts	25.00	11.00	3.10
☐ 20 Frank Robinson	40.00	18.00	5.00
☐ 21 John Roseboro	12.50	5.50	1.55
☐ 22 Red Schoendienst	20.00	9.00	2.50
☐ 23 Bill Skowron	15.00	6.75	1.85
☐ 24 Daryl Spencer	10.00	4.50	1.25
☐ 25 Johnny Temple	10.00	4.50	1.25

1965 MacGregor Staff

This ten-card set represents members of the MacGregor Sporting Goods Advisory Staff. Since the cards are unnumbered they ordered below in alphabetical order. The cards are blank backed and measure approximately 3 9/16" by 5 1/8". The photos are in black and white. The catalog designation for the set is H825-2.

	NRMT	VG-E	GOOD
COMPLETE SET (10)	350.00	160.00	45.00
COMMON CARD (1-10)	10.00	4.50	1.25
☐ 1 Roberto Clemente	150.00	70.00	19.00
☐ 2 Al Downing	10.00	4.50	1.25
☐ 3 Johnny Edwards	10.00	4.50	1.25
☐ 4 Ron Hansen	10.00	4.50	1.25
☐ 5 Deron Johnson	10.00	4.50	1.25
☐ 6 Willie Mays	125.00	55.00	15.50
☐ 7 Tony Oliva	20.00	9.00	2.50
☐ 8 Claude Osteen	10.00	4.50	1.25
☐ 9 Bobby Richardson	20.00	9.00	2.50
☐ 10 Zoilo Versalles	10.00	4.50	1.25

1989 Major League Movie

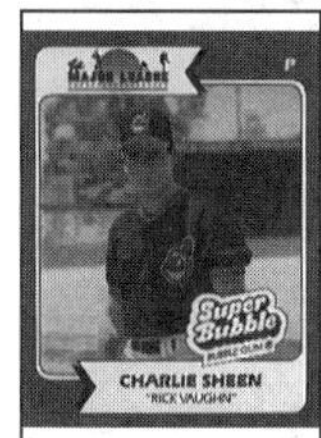

These 11 cards measure approximately 2 3/4" by 3 1/2". They were issued to promote the movie "Major League". The cards have color photos surrounded by blue borders. The actor and the role they play are noted on the bottom of the card. Their position on the imaginary Cleveland Indians is mentioned in the upper right corner. The backs are blank. We have sequenced this set in alphabetical order by actor.

	MINT	NRMT	EXC
COMPLETE SET (11)	15.00	6.75	1.85
COMMON CARD (1-11)	1.00	.45	.12
☐ 1 Tom Berenger	2.00	.90	.25
☐ 2 Corbin Bernsen	2.50	1.10	.30
☐ 3 James Gammon	1.00	.45	.12
☐ 4 Dennis Haysbert	1.00	.45	.12
☐ 5 Andy Romano	1.00	.45	.12
☐ 6 Chelcie Ross	1.00	.45	.12
☐ 7 Charlie Sheen	3.00	1.35	.35
☐ 8 Wesley Snipes	4.00	1.80	.50
☐ 9 Steve Yeager	1.50	.70	.19
☐ 10 Key Players Charlie Sheen Dennis Haysbert Tom Berenger Wesley Snipes	2.00	.90	.25
☐ 11 Team Leaders Andy Romano James Gannon Steve Yeager	1.00	.45	.12

1991 Major League Collector Pins

These gold-colored metal pins were issued by Ace Novelty and measure 1 1/8" by 1 7/8" and feature a color player photo on the fronts. The player's 1990 statistics are given on the reverse of the pin. Each pin was sold in a cardboard display package that included a '91 Score baseball card of the same player. The cards are listed below according to the checklist on the back of the cardboard display, with AL and NL teams as follows: New York Yankees (1-3), Seattle Mariners (4-7), Boston Red Sox (8-11), Minnesota Twins (12-13), Chicago White Sox (14-17), Cleveland Indians (18-19), Kansas City Royals (20-22), California Angels (23-25), Toronto Blue Jays (26-28), Baltimore Orioles (29-31), Detroit Tigers (32-34), Texas Rangers (35-37), Oakland Athletics (38-41), Milwaukee Brewers (42-43), Houston Astros (44-45), Atlanta Braves (46-47), St. Louis Cardinals (48-50), Los Angeles Dodgers (51-53), San Diego Padres (54-56), Pittsburgh Pirates (57-59), Philadelphia Phillies (60-62), San Francisco Giants (63-65), Chicago Cubs (66-69), Cincinnati Reds (70-73), New York Mets (74-77), and Montreal Expos (78-80).

	MINT	NRMT	EXC
COMPLETE SET (80)	25.00	11.00	3.10
COMMON PIN (1-80)	.10	.05	.01
☐ 1 Don Mattingly	2.50	1.10	.30
☐ 2 Kevin Maas	.10	.05	.01
☐ 3 Hensley Meulens	.10	.05	.01
☐ 4 Ken Griffey Jr.	5.00	2.20	.60
☐ 5 Ken Griffey Sr.	.25	.11	.03
☐ 6 Randy Johnson	.75	.35	.09
☐ 7 Tino Martinez	.35	.16	.04
☐ 8 Roger Clemens	.75	.35	.09
☐ 9 Wade Boggs	.50	.23	.06
☐ 10 Mo Vaughn	1.50	.70	.19
☐ 11 Ellis Burks	.25	.11	.03
☐ 12 Kirby Puckett	2.50	1.10	.30
☐ 13 Kevin Tapani	.10	.05	.01
☐ 14 Carlton Fisk	.50	.23	.06
☐ 15 Bobby Thigpen	.10	.05	.01
☐ 16 Sammy Sosa	1.00	.45	.12
☐ 17 Frank Thomas	5.00	2.20	.60
☐ 18 Sandy Alomar Jr.	.25	.11	.03
☐ 19 Mauro Gozzo	.10	.05	.01
☐ 20 Bo Jackson	.25	.11	.03
☐ 21 George Brett	3.00	1.35	.35
☐ 22 Terry Shumpert	.10	.05	.01
☐ 23 Jim Abbott	.10	.05	.01
☐ 24 Lee Stevens	.10	.05	.01

Card			
☐ 25 Mark Langston	.10	.05	.01
☐ 26 Dave Stieb	.10	.05	.01
☐ 27 John Olerud	.25	.11	.03
☐ 28 Mark Whiten	.10	.05	.01
☐ 29 Cal Ripken Jr.	4.00	1.80	.50
☐ 30 David Segui	.10	.05	.01
☐ 31 Ben McDonald	.25	.11	.03
☐ 32 Cecil Fielder	.25	.11	.03
☐ 33 Alan Trammell	.25	.11	.03
☐ 34 Travis Fryman	.35	.16	.04
☐ 35 Nolan Ryan	4.00	1.80	.50
☐ 36 Juan Gonzalez	2.50	1.10	.30
☐ 37 Scott Chiamparino	.10	.05	.01
☐ 38 Jose Canseco	.75	.35	.09
☐ 39 Mark McGwire	1.50	.70	.19
☐ 40 Rickey Henderson	1.00	.45	.12
☐ 41 Ozzie Canseco	.10	.05	.01
☐ 42 Paul Molitor	1.25	.55	.16
☐ 43 Robin Yount	.50	.23	.06
☐ 44 Eric Anthony	.10	.05	.01
☐ 45 Andujar Cedeno	.10	.05	.01
☐ 46 Dave Justice	.35	.16	.04
☐ 47 Ron Gant	.25	.11	.03
☐ 48 Todd Zeile	.10	.05	.01
☐ 49 Ozzie Smith	2.00	.90	.25
☐ 50 Ray Lankford	.35	.16	.04
☐ 51 Jose Offerman	.10	.05	.01
☐ 52 Ramon Martinez	.35	.16	.04
☐ 53 Eddie Murray	1.25	.55	.16
☐ 54 Tony Gwynn	2.00	.90	.25
☐ 55 Paul Faries	.10	.05	.01
☐ 56 Bruce Hurst	.10	.05	.01
☐ 57 Barry Bonds	1.50	.70	.19
☐ 58 Orlando Merced	.10	.05	.01
☐ 59 Doug Drabek	.10	.05	.01
☐ 60 Len Dykstra	.25	.11	.03
☐ 61 Mickey Morandini	.10	.05	.01
☐ 62 Dale Murphy	.50	.23	.06
☐ 63 Will Clark	1.00	.45	.12
☐ 64 Kevin Mitchell	.10	.05	.01
☐ 65 Matt Williams	.75	.35	.09
☐ 66 Mark Grace	1.00	.45	.12
☐ 67 Andre Dawson	.50	.23	.06
☐ 68 Ryne Sandberg	1.25	.55	.16
☐ 69 Derrick May	.10	.05	.01
☐ 70 Eric Davis	.25	.11	.03
☐ 71 Hal Morris	.10	.05	.01
☐ 72 Glenn Sutko	.10	.05	.01
☐ 73 Randy Myers	.10	.05	.01
☐ 74 Dwight Gooden	.25	.11	.03
☐ 75 Todd Hundley	.35	.16	.04
☐ 76 Dave Magadan	.10	.05	.01
☐ 77 Gregg Jefferies	.25	.11	.03
☐ 78 Delino DeShields	.10	.05	.01
☐ 79 Howard Farmer	.10	.05	.01
☐ 80 Larry Walker	.50	.23	.06

1992 Manning 1919 Black Sox Reprints

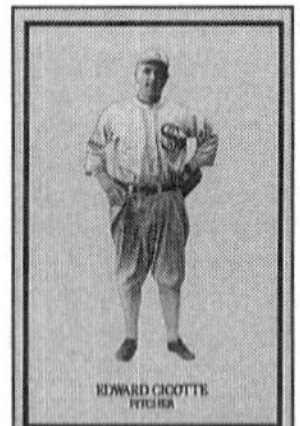

Edward Victor Cicotte
"Eddie"
Cicotte played from 1905 to 1920, compiling a lifetime pitching record of 208 wins and 149 losses, with a 2.37 earned run average. 1919 was a sensational season for Cicotte, he won 29 games and lost only 7, with an ERA of just 1.82. In the 1919 World Series he won 1 and lost 2, with a 2.92 ERA. He also committed two errors and was 0 for 8 at the plate.

Designed by TNTL Studios, (Toms River, NJ) this 26-card set measures approximately 2" by 3" and features reprinted photos of members of the 1919 White Sox team. The photos are black-and-white cut-outs against white backgrounds. Some of the cards have thin black borders but most do not. The "Shoeless Joe" Jackson card has a red border stripe and a color background that shows grass and sky. The backs of the borderless cards are blank. The backs of the other cards contain player information. The cards are unnumbered and checklisted below in alphabetical order.

	MINT	NRMT	EXC
COMPLETE SET (26)	5.00	2.20	.60
COMMON CARD (1-26)	.10	.05	.01
☐ 1 Joe Benz	.10	.05	.01
☐ 2 Eddie Cicotte	.35	.16	.04
☐ 3 Eddie Collins	.50	.23	.06
☐ 4 Shano Collins	.10	.05	.01
☐ 5 Charles Comiskey OWN	.35	.16	.04
☐ 6 Dave Danforth	.10	.05	.01
☐ 7 Red Faber	.35	.16	.04
☐ 8 Happy Felsch	.35	.16	.04
☐ 9 Chick Gandil	.25	.11	.03
☐ 10 Kid Gleason MG	.20	.09	.03
☐ 11 Joe Jackson Color background	1.00	.45	.12
☐ 12 Joe Jackson	1.00	.45	.12
☐ 13 Joe Jenkins	.10	.05	.01
☐ 14 Ted Jourdan	.10	.05	.01
☐ 15 Socks Liebold	.10	.05	.01
☐ 16 Bryd Lynn	.10	.05	.01
☐ 17 Fred McMullen	.20	.09	.03
☐ 18 Eddie Murphy	.10	.05	.01
☐ 19 Swede Risberg	.20	.09	.03
☐ 20 Pants Rowland GM	.10	.05	.01
☐ 21 Reb Russell	.10	.05	.01
☐ 22 Ray Schalk	.35	.16	.04
☐ 23 James Scott	.10	.05	.01
☐ 24 Buck Weaver	.50	.23	.06
☐ 25 Lefty Williams	.35	.16	.04
☐ 26 Mellie Wolfgang	.10	.05	.01

1995 Mantle Donor Card

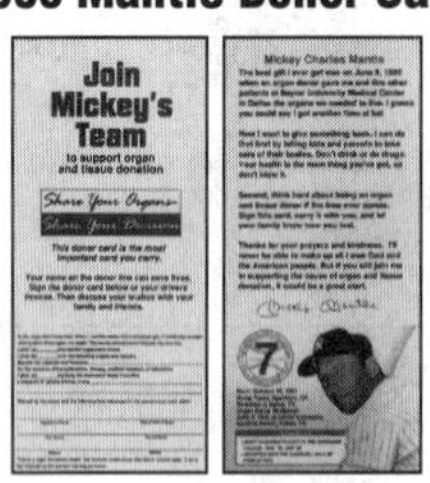

This card was issued almost immediately after Mickey Mantle received a liver tranplant on June 8, 1995. The purpose of this card was to encourage others to donate their organs to donor if it were ever needed. This card was issued by the Mickey Mantle Foundation. This card when in its original state measures 3 1/2" by 7 1/2" but part of the card could be perforated and kept as the organ donor card. That card, which feature a picture of the Mick on the front, measures 3 1/2" by 2 1/2". While we have put a nominal monetary value on this card, we prefer that the card not be traded in the secondary market, rather that it be given to people to fill out and be used if needed.

	MINT	NRMT	EXC
COMPLETE SET (1)	1.00	.45	.12
COMMON CARD (1)	1.00	.45	.12
☐ 1 Mickey Mantle	1.00	.45	.12

1923 Maple Crispette V117

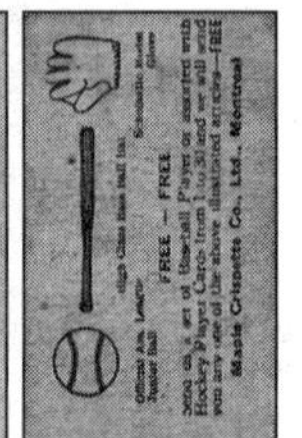

This 30-card set was produced by Maple Crispette Co. of Montreal around 1923. The cards are black and white and measure approximately 1 3/8" by 2 1/4". The card backs explain a send-in offer for a ball, bat or glove in return for 30 baseball (or hockey) cards collected. The cards are numbered on the front. The Stengel card was undoubtedly the short-printed card in the set that made the send-in offer a very difficult task to fulfill.

	EX-MT	VG-E	GOOD
COMPLETE SET (30)	12000.00	5400.00	1500.00
COMMON CARD (1-30)	40.00	18.00	5.00
☐ 1 J. Barnes	40.00	18.00	5.00
☐ 2 Pie Traynor	80.00	36.00	10.00
☐ 3 Ray Schalk	80.00	36.00	10.00
☐ 4 Eddie Collins	100.00	45.00	12.50
☐ 5 Lee Fohl MG	40.00	18.00	5.00
☐ 6 Howard Summa	40.00	18.00	5.00
☐ 7 Waite Hoyt	80.00	36.00	10.00
☐ 8 Babe Ruth	2000.00	900.00	250.00
☐ 9 Cozy Dolan CO	40.00	18.00	5.00
☐ 10 Johnny Bassler	40.00	18.00	5.00
☐ 11 George Dauss	40.00	18.00	5.00
☐ 12 Joe Sewell	80.00	36.00	10.00
☐ 13 Syl Johnson	40.00	18.00	5.00
☐ 14 Ivy Wingo	40.00	18.00	5.00
☐ 15 Casey Stengel SP	7500.00	3400.00	950.00
☐ 16 Arnold Statz	40.00	18.00	5.00
☐ 17 Emil Meusel	40.00	18.00	5.00
☐ 18 Bill Jacobson	40.00	18.00	5.00
☐ 19 Jim Bottomley	80.00	36.00	10.00
☐ 20 Sam Bohne	40.00	18.00	5.00
☐ 21 Bucky Harris	80.00	36.00	10.00
☐ 22 Ty Cobb	1000.00	450.00	125.00
☐ 23 Roger Peckinpaugh	50.00	22.00	6.25
☐ 24 Muddy Ruel	40.00	18.00	5.00
☐ 25 Bill McKechnie	80.00	36.00	10.00
☐ 26 Riggs Stephenson	50.00	22.00	6.25
☐ 27 Herb Pennock	80.00	36.00	10.00
☐ 28 Ed Roush	80.00	36.00	10.00
☐ 29 Bill Wambsganss	50.00	22.00	6.25
☐ 30 Walter Johnson	300.00	135.00	38.00

1980 Marchant Exhibits

These 32 exhibit cards, which measure the same as the original issue, was relased in 1980 and made by card dealer Paul Marchant who issued this set to honor various popular players. This set, clearly marked as reprints, are unnumbered and are sequenced in alphabetical order.

	NRMT	VG-E	GOOD
COMPLETE SET	6.00	2.70	.75
COMMON CARD (1-32)	.10	.05	.01
☐ 1 Johnny Antonelli	.10	.05	.01
☐ 2 Richie Ashburn	.35	.16	.04
☐ 3 Earl Averill	.20	.09	.03
☐ 4 Ernie Banks	.35	.16	.04
☐ 5 Ewell Blackwell	.10	.05	.01
☐ 6 Lou Brock	.35	.16	.04
☐ 7 Dean Chance	.10	.05	.01
☐ 8 Roger Craig	.10	.05	.01
☐ 9 Lou Gehrig	1.00	.45	.12
☐ 10 Gil Hodges	.35	.16	.04
☐ 11 Jackie Jensen	.10	.05	.01
☐ 12 Charlie Keller	.10	.05	.01
☐ 13 George Kell	.20	.09	.03
☐ 14 Alex Kellner	.10	.05	.01
☐ 15 Harmon Killebrew	.20	.09	.03
☐ 16 Dale Long	.10	.05	.01
☐ 17 Sal Maglie	.10	.05	.01
☐ 18 Roger Maris	.50	.23	.06
☐ 19 Willie Mays	.75	.35	.09
☐ 20 Minnie Minoso	.20	.09	.03
☐ 21 Stan Musial	.50	.23	.06
☐ 22 Billy Pierce	.10	.05	.01
☐ 23 Jim Piersall	.10	.05	.01
☐ 24 Eddie Plank	.20	.09	.03
☐ 25 Pete Reiser	.10	.05	.01
☐ 26 Brooks Robinson	.35	.16	.04
☐ 27 Pete Runnels	.10	.05	.01
☐ 28 Herb Score	.10	.05	.01
☐ 29 Warren Spahn	.35	.16	.04
☐ 30 Billy Williams	.35	.16	.04
☐ 31 1948 Indians Team	.10	.05	.01
☐ 32 1948 Braves Team	.10	.05	.01

1981 Mariners Police

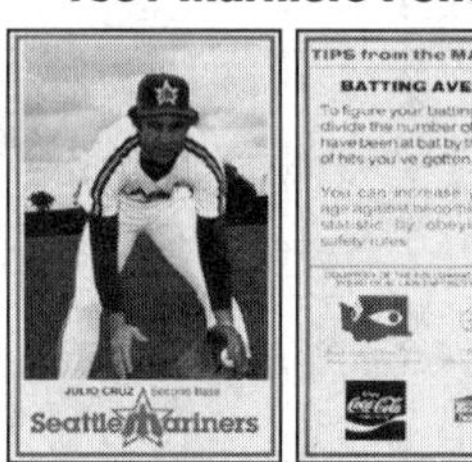

The cards in this 16-card set measure approximately 2 5/8" by 4 1/8". The full color Seattle Mariners Police set of this year was sponsored by the Washington State Crime Prevention Association, the Kiwanis Club, Coca-Cola and Ernst Home Centers. The fronts feature the player's name, his position, and the Seattle Mariners name in addition to the player's photo. The backs, in red and blue, feature Tips from the Mariners and the logos of the four sponsors of the set. The cards are numbered in the lower left corners of the backs.

	NRMT	VG-E	GOOD
COMPLETE SET (16)	7.50	3.40	.95
COMMON CARD (1-16)	.50	.23	.06
☐ 1 Jeff Burroughs	1.00	.45	.12
☐ 2 Floyd Bannister	.50	.23	.06
☐ 3 Glenn Abbott	.50	.23	.06
☐ 4 Jim Anderson	.50	.23	.06
☐ 5 Danny Meyer	.50	.23	.06
☐ 6 Julio Cruz	.50	.23	.06
☐ 7 Dave Edler	.50	.23	.06
☐ 8 Kenny Clay	.50	.23	.06
☐ 9 Lenny Randle	.50	.23	.06
☐ 10 Mike Parrott	.50	.23	.06
☐ 11 Tom Paciorek	1.00	.45	.12
☐ 12 Jerry Narron	.50	.23	.06
☐ 13 Richie Zisk	.75	.35	.09
☐ 14 Maury Wills MG	1.25	.55	.16
☐ 15 Joe Simpson	.50	.23	.06
☐ 16 Shane Rawley	.50	.23	.06

1983 Mariners Nalley's

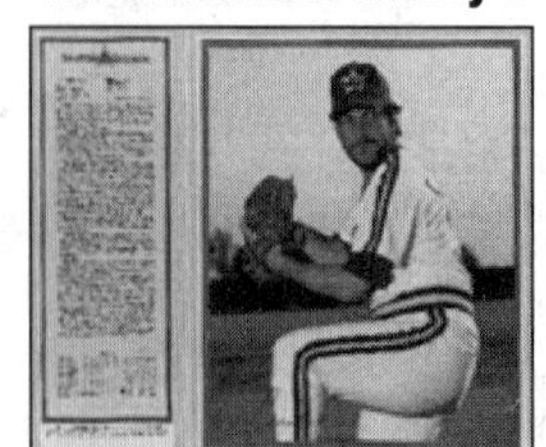

Six members of the 1983 Seattle Mariners are featured in this set. The oversized photos, approximately 8 3/4" by 10 3/4", are in full-color and take up the entire back of potato chip box. Next to the player photo is statistics and a biography. We have arranged the listing of this set in alphabetical order.

	NRMT	VG-E	GOOD
COMPLETE SET	17.50	8.00	2.20
COMMON CARD (1-6)	3.00	1.35	.35
☐ 1 Bill Caudill	3.00	1.35	.35
☐ 2 Al Cowens	3.00	1.35	.35
☐ 3 Todd Cruz	3.00	1.35	.35
☐ 4 Gaylord Perry	7.50	3.40	.95
☐ 5 Rick Sweet	3.00	1.35	.35
☐ 6 Richie Zisk	4.00	1.80	.50

1984 Mariners Mother's

The cards in this 28-card set measure the standard size. In 1984, The Los Angeles-based Mother's Cookies Co. issued five sets of cards featuring players from major league teams. The Seattle Mariners set features current players depicted by photos. Similar to their 1952 and 1953 issues, the cards have rounded corners. The backs of the cards contain the Mother's Cookies logo. The cards were distributed in partial sets to fans at the respective stadiums of the teams involved. Whereas 20 cards were given to each patron, a redemption card, redeemable for eight more cards was included. Unfortunately, the eight cards received by redeeming the coupon were not necessarily the eight needed to complete a set. Hobbyist Barry Colla was involved in the production of these sets. The key card in the set is Mark Langston, one of his earliest cards issued.

	NRMT	VG-E	GOOD
COMPLETE SET (28)	12.50	5.50	1.55
COMMON CARD (1-28)	.25	.11	.03
☐ 1 Del Crandall MG	.25	.11	.03
☐ 2 Barry Bonnell	.25	.11	.03
☐ 3 Dave Henderson	.50	.23	.06
☐ 4 Bob Kearney	.25	.11	.03
☐ 5 Mike Moore	.50	.23	.06
☐ 6 Spike Owen	.50	.23	.06
☐ 7 Gorman Thomas	.50	.23	.06
☐ 8 Ed VandeBerg	.25	.11	.03
☐ 9 Matt Young	.25	.11	.03
☐ 10 Larry Milbourne	.25	.11	.03
☐ 11 Dave Beard	.25	.11	.03
☐ 12 Jim Beattie	.25	.11	.03
☐ 13 Mark Langston	5.00	2.20	.60
☐ 14 Orlando Mercado	.25	.11	.03
☐ 15 Jack Perconte	.25	.11	.03
☐ 16 Pat Putnam	.25	.11	.03
☐ 17 Paul Mirabella	.25	.11	.03
☐ 18 Domingo Ramos	.25	.11	.03
☐ 19 Al Cowens	.25	.11	.03
☐ 20 Mike Stanton	.25	.11	.03
☐ 21 Steve Henderson	.25	.11	.03
☐ 22 Bob Stoddard	.25	.11	.03
☐ 23 Alvin Davis	1.00	.45	.12
☐ 24 Phil Bradley	.50	.23	.06
☐ 25 Roy Thomas	.25	.11	.03
☐ 26 Darnell Coles	.25	.11	.03
☐ 27 Mariners' Coaches Rick Sweet Frank Funk Ben Hines Chuck Cottier Phil Roof	.25	.11	.03
☐ 28 Mariners' Checklist Seattle Kingdome	.25	.11	.03

1985 Mariners Mother's

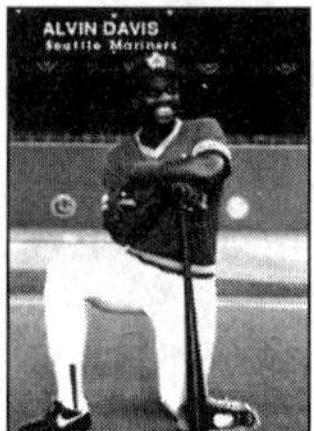

The cards in this 28-card set measure the standard size. In 1985, the Los Angeles based Mother's Cookies Co. again issued five sets of cards featuring players from major league teams. The Seattle Mariners set features current players depicted by photos on cards with rounded corners. The backs of the cards contain the Mother's Cookies logo. Cards were passed out at the stadium on August 10.

	NRMT	VG-E	GOOD
COMPLETE SET (28)	7.50	3.40	.95
COMMON CARD (1-28)	.25	.11	.03
☐ 1 Chuck Cottier MG	.25	.11	.03
☐ 2 Alvin Davis	.75	.35	.09
☐ 3 Mark Langston	2.00	.90	.25
☐ 4 Dave Henderson	.50	.23	.06

☐ 5 Ed VandeBerg	.25	.11	.03
☐ 6 Al Cowens	.25	.11	.03
☐ 7 Spike Owen	.25	.11	.03
☐ 8 Mike Moore	.25	.11	.03
☐ 9 Gorman Thomas	.50	.23	.06
☐ 10 Barry Bonnell	.25	.11	.03
☐ 11 Jack Perconte	.25	.11	.03
☐ 12 Domingo Ramos	.25	.11	.03
☐ 13 Bob Kearney	.25	.11	.03
☐ 14 Matt Young	.25	.11	.03
☐ 15 Jim Beattie	.25	.11	.03
☐ 16 Mike Stanton	.25	.11	.03
☐ 17 David Valle	.25	.11	.03
☐ 18 Ken Phelps	.25	.11	.03
☐ 19 Salome Barojas	.25	.11	.03
☐ 20 Jim Presley	.50	.23	.06
☐ 21 Phil Bradley	.50	.23	.06
☐ 22 Dave Geisel	.25	.11	.03
☐ 23 Harold Reynolds	1.25	.55	.16
☐ 24 Ed Nunez	.25	.11	.03
☐ 25 Mike Morgan	.25	.11	.03
☐ 26 Ivan Calderon	.50	.23	.06
☐ 27 Mariners' Coaches Marty Martinez Jim Mahoney Phil Roof Phil Regan Deron Johnson	.25	.11	.03
☐ 28 Checklist Card Seattle Kingdome	.25	.11	.03

1986 Mariners Greats TCMA

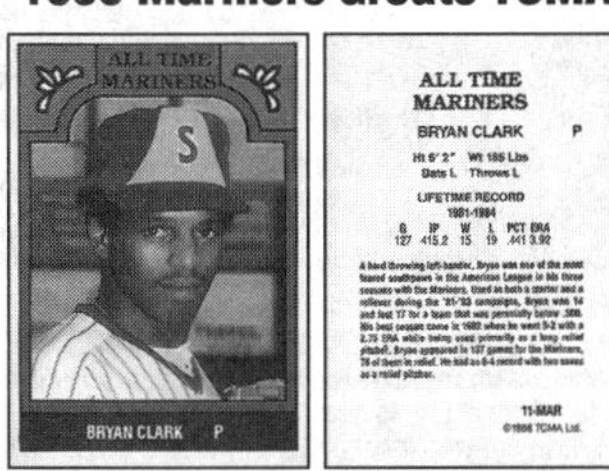

This 12-card standard-size set features some of the best players for the Mariners first decade. The front has a player photo, his name as well as his position. The back has vital statistics, a biography and career totals.

	MINT	NRMT	EXC
COMPLETE SET (12)	2.50	1.10	.30
COMMON CARD (1-12)	.25	.11	.03
☐ 1 Pat Putnam	.25	.11	.03
☐ 2 Larry Milbourne	.25	.11	.03
☐ 3 Todd Cruz	.25	.11	.03
☐ 4 Bill Stein	.25	.11	.03
☐ 5 Leon Roberts	.25	.11	.03
☐ 6 Leroy Stanton	.25	.11	.03
☐ 7 Dan Meyer	.25	.11	.03
☐ 8 Bob Stinson	.25	.11	.03
☐ 9 Glenn Abbott	.25	.11	.03
☐ 10 John Montague	.25	.11	.03
☐ 11 Bryan Clark	.25	.11	.03
☐ 12 Rene Lachemann MG	.25	.11	.03

1986 Mariners Mother's

This set consists of 28 full-color, rounded-corner cards each measuring the standard size. Starter sets (only 20 cards but also including a certificate for eight more cards) were given out at the ballpark and collectors were encouraged to trade to fill in the rest of their set. Cards were originally given out on July 27th at the Seattle Kingdome.

	MINT	NRMT	EXC
COMPLETE SET (28)	8.00	3.60	1.00
COMMON CARD (1-28)	.25	.11	.03
☐ 1 Dick Williams MG	.50	.23	.06
☐ 2 Alvin Davis	.50	.23	.06
☐ 3 Mark Langston	1.00	.45	.12
☐ 4 Dave Henderson	.50	.23	.06
☐ 5 Steve Yeager	.25	.11	.03
☐ 6 Al Cowens	.25	.11	.03
☐ 7 Jim Presley	.25	.11	.03
☐ 8 Phil Bradley	.25	.11	.03
☐ 9 Gorman Thomas	.25	.11	.03
☐ 10 Barry Bonnell	.25	.11	.03
☐ 11 Milt Wilcox	.25	.11	.03
☐ 12 Domingo Ramos	.25	.11	.03
☐ 13 Paul Mirabella	.25	.11	.03
☐ 14 Matt Young	.25	.11	.03
☐ 15 Ivan Calderon	.50	.23	.06
☐ 16 Bill Swift	.50	.23	.06
☐ 17 Pete Ladd	.25	.11	.03
☐ 18 Ken Phelps	.25	.11	.03
☐ 19 Karl Best	.25	.11	.03
☐ 20 Spike Owen	.25	.11	.03
☐ 21 Mike Moore	.25	.11	.03
☐ 22 Danny Tartabull	1.00	.45	.12
☐ 23 Bob Kearney	.25	.11	.03
☐ 24 Edwin Nunez	.25	.11	.03
☐ 25 Mike Morgan	.25	.11	.03
☐ 26 Roy Thomas	.25	.11	.03
☐ 27 Jim Beattie	.25	.11	.03
☐ 28 Checklist Card Deron Johnson CO Marty Martinez CO Phil Roof CO Phil Regan CO Ozzie Virgil CO	.25	.11	.03

1987 Mariners Mother's

This set consists of 28 full-color, rounded-corner cards each measuring the standard size. Starter sets (only 20 cards but also including a certificate for eight more cards) were given out at the ballpark and collectors were encouraged to trade to fill in the rest of their set. Cards were originally given out on August 9th at the Seattle Kingdome. Photos were taken by Barry Colla. The sets were reportedly given out free to the first 20,000 paid admissions at the game.

	MINT	NRMT	EXC
COMPLETE SET (28)	7.50	3.40	.95
COMMON CARD (1-28)	.25	.11	.03
☐ 1 Dick Williams MG	.50	.23	.06
☐ 2 Alvin Davis	.50	.23	.06
☐ 3 Mike Moore	.25	.11	.03
☐ 4 Jim Presley	.25	.11	.03
☐ 5 Mark Langston	1.00	.45	.12
☐ 6 Phil Bradley	.25	.11	.03
☐ 7 Ken Phelps	.25	.11	.03
☐ 8 Mike Morgan	.25	.11	.03
☐ 9 David Valle	.25	.11	.03
☐ 10 Harold Reynolds	.50	.23	.06
☐ 11 Edwin Nunez	.25	.11	.03
☐ 12 Bob Kearney	.25	.11	.03
☐ 13 Scott Bankhead	.25	.11	.03
☐ 14 Scott Bradley	.25	.11	.03
☐ 15 Mickey Brantley	.25	.11	.03
☐ 16 Mark Huismann	.25	.11	.03
☐ 17 Mike Kingery	.50	.23	.06
☐ 18 John Moses	.25	.11	.03
☐ 19 Donell Nixon	.25	.11	.03
☐ 20 Rey Quinones	.25	.11	.03
☐ 21 Domingo Ramos	.25	.11	.03
☐ 22 Jerry Reed	.25	.11	.03
☐ 23 Rich Renteria	.25	.11	.03
☐ 24 Rich Monteleone	.25	.11	.03
☐ 25 Mike Trujillo	.25	.11	.03
☐ 26 Bill Wilkinson	.25	.11	.03
☐ 27 John Christensen	.25	.11	.03
☐ 28 Checklist Card Billy Connors CO Frank Howard CO Bobby Tolan CO Ozzie Virgil CO Phil Roof CO	.50	.23	.06

1988 Mariners Mother's

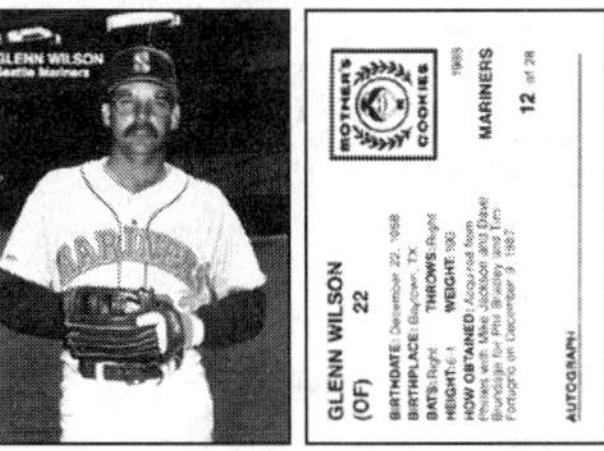

This set consists of 28 full-color, rounded-corner cards each measuring the standard size. Starter sets (only 20 cards but also including a certificate for eight more cards) were given out at the ballpark and collectors were encouraged to trade to fill in the rest of their set. Cards were originally given out on August 14th at the Seattle Kingdome. Photos were taken by Barry Colla. The sets were reportedly given out free to the first 20,000 paid admissions at the game.

	MINT	NRMT	EXC
COMPLETE SET (28)	7.50	3.40	.95
COMMON CARD (1-28)	.25	.11	.03
☐ 1 Dick Williams MG	.50	.23	.06
☐ 2 Alvin Davis	.50	.23	.06
☐ 3 Mike Moore	.25	.11	.03
☐ 4 Jim Presley	.25	.11	.03
☐ 5 Mark Langston	1.00	.45	.12
☐ 6 Henry Cotto	.25	.11	.03
☐ 7 Ken Phelps	.25	.11	.03
☐ 8 Steve Trout	.25	.11	.03
☐ 9 David Valle	.25	.11	.03
☐ 10 Harold Reynolds	.50	.23	.06
☐ 11 Edwin Nunez	.25	.11	.03
☐ 12 Glenn Wilson	.25	.11	.03
☐ 13 Scott Bankhead	.25	.11	.03
☐ 14 Scott Bradley	.25	.11	.03
☐ 15 Mickey Brantley	.25	.11	.03
☐ 16 Bruce Fields	.25	.11	.03
☐ 17 Mike Kingery	.25	.11	.03
☐ 18 Mike Campbell	.25	.11	.03
☐ 19 Mike Jackson	.50	.23	.06
☐ 20 Rey Quinones	.25	.11	.03
☐ 21 Mario Diaz	.25	.11	.03
☐ 22 Jerry Reed	.25	.11	.03
☐ 23 Rich Renteria	.25	.11	.03
☐ 24 Julio Solano	.25	.11	.03
☐ 25 Bill Swift	.25	.11	.03
☐ 26 Bill Wilkinson	.25	.11	.03
☐ 27 Mariners Coaches	.25	.11	.03
☐ 28 Checklist Card Henry Genzale EQMG Rick Griffin TR	.25	.11	.03

1989 Mariners Mother's

The 1989 Mother's Cookies Seattle Mariners set contains 28 standard-size cards with rounded corners. The fronts have borderless color photos, and the horizontally oriented backs have biographical information. Starter sets containing 20 of these cards were given away at a Mariners home game during the 1989 season. Ken Griffey Jr. has a card in his Rookie Card season in this set.

	MINT	NRMT	EXC
COMPLETE SET (28)	20.00	9.00	2.50
COMMON CARD (1-28)	.25	.11	.03
☐ 1 Jim Lefebvre MG	.50	.23	.06
☐ 2 Alvin Davis	.50	.23	.06
☐ 3 Ken Griffey Jr.	12.50	5.50	1.55
☐ 4 Jim Presley	.25	.11	.03
☐ 5 Mark Langston	.50	.23	.06
☐ 6 Henry Cotto	.25	.11	.03
☐ 7 Mickey Brantley	.25	.11	.03
☐ 8 Jeffrey Leonard	.25	.11	.03
☐ 9 Dave Valle	.25	.11	.03
☐ 10 Harold Reynolds	.50	.23	.06
☐ 11 Edgar Martinez	4.00	1.80	.50
☐ 12 Tom Niedenfuer	.25	.11	.03
☐ 13 Scott Bankhead	.25	.11	.03
☐ 14 Scott Bradley	.25	.11	.03
☐ 15 Omar Vizquel	1.50	.70	.19
☐ 16 Erik Hanson	.50	.23	.06
☐ 17 Bill Swift	.25	.11	.03
☐ 18 Mike Campbell	.25	.11	.03
☐ 19 Mike Jackson	.25	.11	.03
☐ 20 Rich Renteria	.25	.11	.03
☐ 21 Mario Diaz	.25	.11	.03
☐ 22 Jerry Reed	.25	.11	.03
☐ 23 Darnell Coles	.25	.11	.03
☐ 24 Steve Trout	.25	.11	.03
☐ 25 Mike Schooler	.25	.11	.03
☐ 26 Julio Solano	.25	.11	.03
☐ 27 Mariners Coaches Mike Paul Gene Clines Bill Plummer Bob Didier Rusty Kuntz	.25	.11	.03
☐ 28 Checklist Card Henry Genzale EQMG Rick Griffin TR	.25	.11	.03

1990 Mariners Mother's

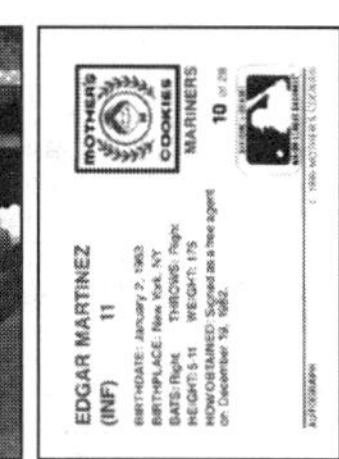

1990 Mother's Cookies Seattle Mariners set contains 28 standard-size cards with the traditional Mother's Cookies rounded corners. The cards have full-color fronts and biographical information with no stats on the back. These Mariners cards were released for the August 5th game and given to the first 25,000 people who passed through the gates. They were distributed in 20-card random packets at the game and eight more at the redemption booths. However, both groups of cards were random and there was no guarantee of getting a complete set in the cards. The promotional idea was that the only way one could finish the set was to trade for them. The redemption for eight more cards were available at the Kingdome Card Show on August 12, 1990.

	MINT	NRMT	EXC
COMPLETE SET (28)	15.00	6.75	1.85
COMMON CARD (1-28)	.25	.11	.03
☐ 1 Jim Lefebvre MG	.25	.11	.03
☐ 2 Alvin Davis	.50	.23	.06
☐ 3 Ken Griffey Jr.	7.50	3.40	.95
☐ 4 Jeffrey Leonard	.25	.11	.03
☐ 5 David Valle	.25	.11	.03
☐ 6 Harold Reynolds	.50	.23	.06
☐ 7 Jay Buhner	2.50	1.10	.30
☐ 8 Erik Hanson	.50	.23	.06
☐ 9 Henry Cotto	.25	.11	.03
☐ 10 Edgar Martinez	2.50	1.10	.30
☐ 11 Bill Swift	.25	.11	.03
☐ 12 Omar Vizquel	1.00	.45	.12
☐ 13 Randy Johnson	2.50	1.10	.30
☐ 14 Greg Briley	.25	.11	.03
☐ 15 Gene Harris	.25	.11	.03
☐ 16 Matt Young	.25	.11	.03
☐ 17 Pete O'Brien	.25	.11	.03
☐ 18 Brent Knackert	.25	.11	.03
☐ 19 Mike Jackson	.25	.11	.03
☐ 20 Brian Holman	.25	.11	.03
☐ 21 Mike Schooler	.25	.11	.03
☐ 22 Darnell Coles	.25	.11	.03
☐ 23 Keith Comstock	.25	.11	.03
☐ 24 Scott Bankhead	.25	.11	.03
☐ 25 Scott Bradley	.25	.11	.03
☐ 26 Mike Brumley	.25	.11	.03
☐ 27 Mariners Coaches Rusty Kuntz Gene Clines Bill Plummer Mike Paul Bob Didier	.25	.11	.03
☐ 28 Checklist Card Mariners Personnel Henry Genzale EQ.MG Tom Newberg ATR Rick Griffin TR	.25	.11	.03

1990 Mariners Red Apple Pin

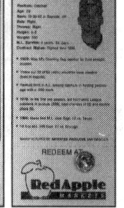

This pin features Seattle Mariner catcher Dave Valle. It was issued in conjunction with Red Apple.

	MINT	NRMT	EXC
COMPLETE SET	2.00	.90	.25
COMMON PIN	2.00	.90	.25
☐ 1 David Valle	2.00	.90	.25

1991 Mariners Country Hearth

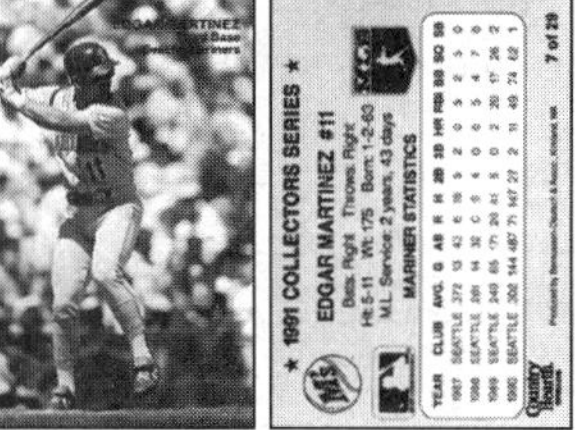

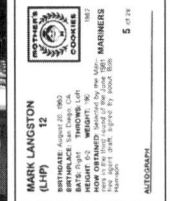

This 30-card standard-size set was sponsored and produced by the Country Hearth Breads and Langendorf Baking Company, and individual cards were inserted unprotected in specially marked loaves of Country Hearth. In addition, the cards (ten at a time) were given away to fans attending the Mariners home game at the Seattle Kingdome on August 17, 1991. The fronts have either a horizontal or vertical orientation and feature glossy color player photos with thin white borders. The player's name and team appear in small white lettering toward the top of the card face. In black print on a light gray background, the horizontally oriented backs present biography, statistics, or career highlights. According to sources, only 20,000 sets were produced, and all cards were produced in equal quantities.

	MINT	NRMT	EXC
COMPLETE SET (30)	25.00	11.00	3.10
COMMON CARD (1-29)	.50	.23	.06
☐ 1 Jim Lefebvre MG	.75	.35	.09
☐ 2 Jeff Schaefer	.50	.23	.06
☐ 3 Harold Reynolds	.75	.35	.09
☐ 4 Greg Briley	.50	.23	.06
☐ 5 Scott Bradley	.50	.23	.06
☐ 6 Dave Valle	.50	.23	.06
☐ 7 Edgar Martinez	2.50	1.10	.30
☐ 8 Pete O'Brien	.50	.23	.06
☐ 9 Omar Vizquel	1.25	.55	.16
☐ 10 Tino Martinez	2.50	1.10	.30
☐ 11 Scott Bankhead	.50	.23	.06
☐ 12 Bill Swift	.75	.35	.09
☐ 13 Jay Buhner	2.50	1.10	.30
☐ 14 Alvin Davis	.75	.35	.09
☐ 15 Ken Griffey Jr. (Ready to swing)	7.50	3.40	.95
☐ 16 Tracy Jones	.50	.23	.06
☐ 17 Brent Knackert	.50	.23	.06
☐ 18 Henry Cotto	.50	.23	.06
☐ 19 Ken Griffey Sr. (Watching ball after hit)	1.50	.70	.19
☐ 20 Keith Comstock	.50	.23	.06
☐ 21 Brian Holman	.50	.23	.06
☐ 22 Russ Swan	.50	.23	.06
☐ 23 Mike Jackson	.50	.23	.06
☐ 24 Erik Hanson	.75	.35	.09
☐ 25 Mike Schooler	.50	.23	.06
☐ 26 Randy Johnson	2.50	1.10	.30
☐ 27 Rich DeLucia	.50	.23	.06
☐ 28 Ken Griffey Jr. Ken Griffey Sr.	3.00	1.35	.35
☐ 29 Mariner Moose Mascot	.75	.35	.09
☐ NNO Title Card	1.25	.55	.16

1992 Mariners Mother's

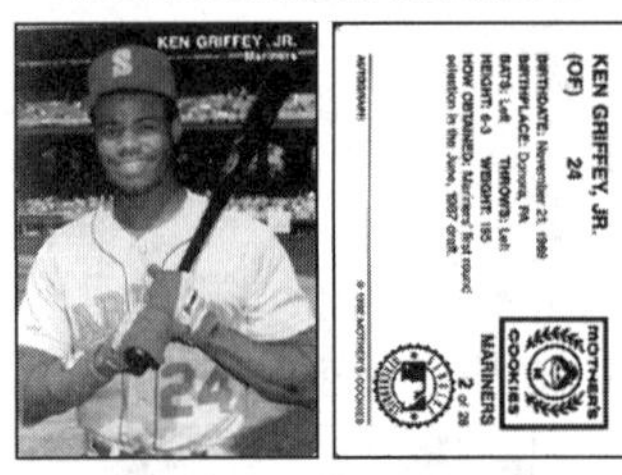

The 1992 Mother's Cookies Mariners set contains 28 cards with rounded corners measuring the standard size. The front design has borderless glossy color player photos. The player's name and team name appear in one of the upper corners. The horizontal backs are printed in red and purple, and present biography and a "how obtained" remark where appropriate. A blank slot for the player's autograph rounds out the back.

	MINT	NRMT	EXC
COMPLETE SET (28)	12.00	5.50	1.50
COMMON CARD (1-28)	.25	.11	.03
☐ 1 Bill Plummer MG	.25	.11	.03
☐ 2 Ken Griffey Jr.	6.00	2.70	.75
☐ 3 Harold Reynolds	.50	.23	.06
☐ 4 Kevin Mitchell	.50	.23	.06
☐ 5 David Valle	.25	.11	.03
☐ 6 Jay Buhner	1.50	.70	.19
☐ 7 Erik Hanson	.50	.23	.06
☐ 8 Pete O'Brien	.25	.11	.03
☐ 9 Henry Cotto	.25	.11	.03
☐ 10 Mike Schooler	.25	.11	.03
☐ 11 Tino Martinez	1.50	.70	.19
☐ 12 Dennis Powell	.25	.11	.03
☐ 13 Randy Johnson	1.50	.70	.19
☐ 14 Dave Cochrane	.25	.11	.03
☐ 15 Greg Briley	.25	.11	.03
☐ 16 Omar Vizquel	.75	.35	.09
☐ 17 Dave Fleming	.25	.11	.03
☐ 18 Matt Sinatro	.25	.11	.03
☐ 19 Jeff Nelson	.25	.11	.03
☐ 20 Edgar Martinez	1.50	.70	.19
☐ 21 Calvin Jones	.25	.11	.03
☐ 22 Russ Swan	.25	.11	.03
☐ 23 Jim Acker	.25	.11	.03
☐ 24 Jeff Schaefer	.25	.11	.03
☐ 25 Clay Parker	.25	.11	.03
☐ 26 Brian Holman	.25	.11	.03
☐ 27 Coaches Dan Warthen Russ Nixon Rusty Kuntz Marty Martinez Gene Clines Roger Hansen	.25	.11	.03
☐ 28 Checklist	.25	.11	.03

1993 Mariners Dairy Queen

Subtitled "Magic Mariner Moments," the four cards comprising this set were issued with metal pins which came attached to cardboard tabs beneath the perforated card bottoms. The cards measure approximately 2 1/2" by 3 7/8" and feature gray-bordered color action player photos on their fronts. The player's name appears in black lettering within a white bar near the bottom of the picture and the Mariners logo rests in the lower left. The player's accomplishment is displayed in a green banner across the top of the photo. The white back is framed by a thin black line and carries the player's name in black lettering above text describing his accomplishment. At the bottom are drawings of the four pins and the week of issue for each card and pin combination. The cards are numbered on the back. The white metal pins feature the player's name and number in green lettering upon a white jersey. The set's subtitle and the player's accomplishment are carried in red and green banners, respectively, across the top of the pin.

	MINT	NRMT	EXC
COMPLETE SET (4)	15.00	6.75	1.85
COMMON CARD (1-4)	1.00	.45	.12
☐ 1 Randy Johnson	3.00	1.35	.35
☐ 2 Edgar Martinez	3.00	1.35	.35
☐ 3 Chris Bosio	1.00	.45	.12
☐ 4 Ken Griffey Jr.	10.00	4.50	1.25

1993 Mariners Mother's

The 1993 Mother's Cookies Mariners set consists of 28 standard-size cards with rounded corners. The fronts display full-bleed color player portraits shot from the waist up in stadium settings. The player's name and team name appear in one of the corners. On a white background in red and purple print, the horizontal backs carry biographical information and the sponsor's logo. A blank slot for the player's autograph rounds out the back.

	MINT	NRMT	EXC
COMPLETE SET (28)	12.00	5.50	1.50
COMMON CARD (1-28)	.25	.11	.03
☐ 1 Lou Piniella MG	.75	.35	.09
☐ 2 Dave Fleming	.25	.11	.03
☐ 3 Pete O'Brien	.25	.11	.03
☐ 4 Ken Griffey Jr.	6.00	2.70	.75
☐ 5 Henry Cotto	.25	.11	.03
☐ 6 Jay Buhner	1.50	.70	.19
☐ 7 David Valle	.25	.11	.03
☐ 8 Dwayne Henry	.25	.11	.03
☐ 9 Mike Felder	.25	.11	.03
☐ 10 Norm Charlton	.50	.23	.06
☐ 11 Edgar Martinez	1.50	.70	.19
☐ 12 Erik Hanson	.50	.23	.06
☐ 13 Mike Blowers	.25	.11	.03
☐ 14 Omar Vizquel	.75	.35	.09
☐ 15 Randy Johnson	1.50	.70	.19
☐ 16 Russ Swan	.25	.11	.03
☐ 17 Tino Martinez	1.50	.70	.19
☐ 18 Rich DeLucia	.25	.11	.03
☐ 19 Jeff Nelson	.25	.11	.03
☐ 20 Chris Bosio	.25	.11	.03
☐ 21 Tim Leary	.25	.11	.03
☐ 22 Mackey Sasser	.25	.11	.03
☐ 23 Dennis Powell	.25	.11	.03
☐ 24 Mike Hampton	.75	.35	.09
☐ 25 Fernando Vina	.75	.35	.09
☐ 26 John Cummings	.25	.11	.03
☐ 27 Rich Amaral	.25	.11	.03
☐ 28 Checklist/Coaches Sam Perlozzo Sam Mejias Lee Elia Sammy Ellis John McLaren Ken Griffey Sr.	.50	.23	.06

1994 Mariners Mother's

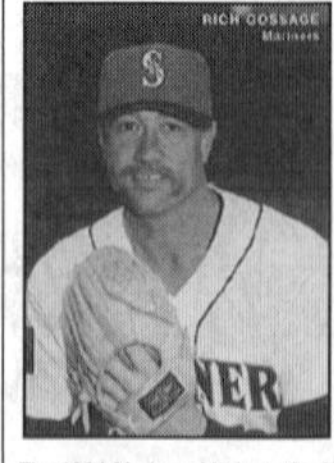

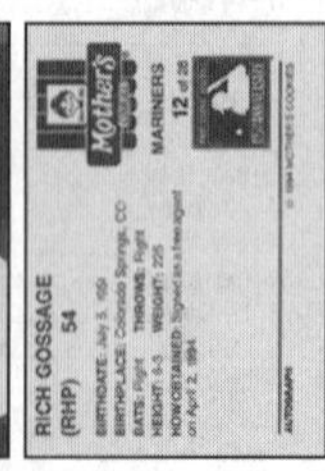

The 1994 Mariners Mother's Cookies set consists of 28 standard-size cards with rounded corners. The fronts display posed full-bleed color player portraits shot from the waist up in stadium settings. The player's name and team name appear in one of the upper corners. On a white background in red and purple print, the horizontal backs carry biographical information and the sponsor's logo. A blank slot for the player's autograph rounds out the back. The set includes a coupon with a mail-in offer to obtain a trading card collectors album for 3.95. The set had limited distribution since the original Mother's promotion night was cancelled due to the Kingdome closure and then the baseball strike.

	MINT	NRMT	EXC
COMPLETE SET (28)	17.50	8.00	2.20
COMMON CARD (1-28)	.25	.11	.03
☐ 1 Lou Piniella MG	.75	.35	.09
☐ 2 Randy Johnson	2.00	.90	.25
☐ 3 Eric Anthony	.50	.23	.06
☐ 4 Ken Griffey Jr.	6.00	2.70	.75
☐ 5 Felix Fermin	.25	.11	.03
☐ 6 Jay Buhner	2.00	.90	.25
☐ 7 Chris Bosio	.25	.11	.03
☐ 8 Reggie Jefferson	.75	.35	.09
☐ 9 Greg Hibbard	.25	.11	.03
☐ 10 Dave Fleming	.25	.11	.03
☐ 11 Rich Amaral	.25	.11	.03
☐ 12 Rich Gossage	.75	.35	.09
☐ 13 Edgar Martinez	2.00	.90	.25
☐ 14 Bobby Ayala	.25	.11	.03
☐ 15 Darren Bragg	.50	.23	.06
☐ 16 Tino Martinez	1.50	.70	.19
☐ 17 Mike Blowers	.25	.11	.03
☐ 18 John Cummings	.25	.11	.03
☐ 19 Keith Mitchell	.25	.11	.03
☐ 20 Bill Haselman	.25	.11	.03
☐ 21 Greg Pirkl	.25	.11	.03
☐ 22 Mackey Sasser	.25	.11	.03
☐ 23 Tim Davis	.25	.11	.03
☐ 24 Dan Wilson	1.25	.55	.16
☐ 25 Jeff Nelson	.25	.11	.03
☐ 26 Kevin King	.25	.11	.03
☐ 27 Torey Lovullo	.25	.11	.03
☐ 28 Checklist/Coaches Sam Perlozzo Lee Elia Sammy Ellis John McLaren Sam Mejias	.25	.11	.03

1995 Mariners Mother's

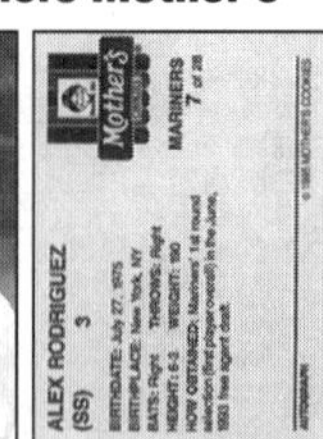

This 1995 Mother's Cookies Seattle Mariners set consists of 28 standard-size cards with rounded corners. The fronts display posed color player portraits. The player's name and team name appear in one of the top corners. The horizontal backs carry biographical information and the sponsor's logo on a white background in red and purple print. A blank slot at the bottom for the player's autograph rounds out the back.

	MINT	NRMT	EXC
COMPLETE SET (28)	17.50	8.00	2.20
COMMON CARD (1-28)	.25	.11	.03
☐ 1 Lou Piniella MG	.75	.35	.09
☐ 2 Randy Johnson	1.50	.70	.19
☐ 3 Dave Fleming	.25	.11	.03
☐ 4 Ken Griffey Jr.	5.00	2.20	.60
☐ 5 Edgar Martinez	1.50	.70	.19
☐ 6 Jay Buhner	1.00	.45	.12
☐ 7 Alex Rodriguez	7.50	3.40	.95
☐ 8 Joey Cora	.50	.23	.06
☐ 9 Tim Davis	.25	.11	.03
☐ 10 Mike Blowers	.25	.11	.03
☐ 11 Chris Bosio	.25	.11	.03
☐ 12 Dan Wilson	.75	.35	.09
☐ 13 Rich Amaral	.25	.11	.03
☐ 14 Bobby Ayala	.25	.11	.03
☐ 15 Darren Bragg	.50	.23	.06
☐ 16 Bob Wells	.25	.11	.03
☐ 17 Doug Strange	.25	.11	.03
☐ 18 Chad Kreuter	.25	.11	.03
☐ 19 Rafael Carmona	.25	.11	.03
☐ 20 Luis Sojo	.25	.11	.03
☐ 21 Tim Belcher	.50	.23	.06
☐ 22 Steve Frey	.25	.11	.03
☐ 23 Tino Martinez	1.25	.55	.16
☐ 24 Felix Fermin	.25	.11	.03
☐ 25 Jeff Nelson	.25	.11	.03
☐ 26 Alex Diaz	.25	.11	.03
☐ 27 Bill Risley	.25	.11	.03
☐ 28 Coaches/Checklist Sam Perlozzo Matt Sinatro Lee Elia Sam Mejias John McLaren Bobby Cuellar	.25	.11	.03

1995 Mariners Pacific

Produced by Pacific, this 50-card boxed standard-size set highlights the events leading up to the Seattle Mariners clinching the American League Western Division Pennant and their playoff run during the Division Series and the American League Championship Series. The set divides into game action shots (1-17) and player (and manager) cards (18-50). The fronts of all cards feature glossy, full-bleed color photos, with the caption or player's name stamped in silver foil across the bottom. The backs of the game action cards are beige and have the format of a newspaper headline and story wrapped around a small color inset photo. The backs of the player cards display a color closeup photo, 1995 stats, and a 1995 season summary.

	MINT	NRMT	EXC
COMPLETE SET (50)	15.00	6.75	1.85
COMMON CARD (1-50)	.10	.05	.01
☐ 1 Ken Griffey Jr. IA	1.50	.70	.19
☐ 2 Vince Coleman IA	.10	.05	.01
☐ 3 Luis Sojo IA	.10	.05	.01
☐ 4 Mariners win the West	.50	.23	.06
☐ 5 Randy Johnson IA	.40	.18	.05
☐ 6 Ken Griffey Jr. IA	1.50	.70	.19
☐ 7 Tino Martinez HL Edgar Martinez	.40	.18	.05
☐ 8 Edgar Martinez IA	.25	.11	.03
☐ 9 Ken Griffey Jr. IA	1.50	.70	.19
☐ 10 Thunder in the Kingdome	.25	.11	.03
☐ 11 Win ends years of futility	.25	.11	.03
☐ 12 Bob Wolcott IA	.10	.05	.01
☐ 13 Jay Buhner IA	.40	.18	.05
☐ 14 Randy Johnson IA	.40	.18	.05
☐ 15 Lou Piniella IA	.25	.11	.03
☐ 16 Joey Cora IA	.10	.05	.01
☐ 17 Dave Niehaus ANN	.25	.11	.03
☐ 18 Rich Amaral	.10	.05	.01
☐ 19 Bobby Ayala	.10	.05	.01
☐ 20 Tim Belcher	.10	.05	.01
☐ 21 Andy Benes	.40	.18	.05
☐ 22 Mike Blowers	.10	.05	.01
☐ 23 Chris Bosio	.10	.05	.01
☐ 24 Darren Bragg	.25	.11	.03
☐ 25 Jay Buhner	.75	.35	.09
☐ 26 Rafael Carmona	.10	.05	.01
☐ 27 Norm Charlton	.25	.11	.03
☐ 28 Vince Coleman	.10	.05	.01
☐ 29 Joey Cora	.25	.11	.03
☐ 30 Alex Diaz	.10	.05	.01
☐ 31 Felix Fermin	.10	.05	.01
☐ 32 Ken Griffey Jr.	3.00	1.35	.35
☐ 33 Lee Guetterman	.10	.05	.01
☐ 34 Randy Johnson	.75	.35	.09
☐ 35 Edgar Martinez	.75	.35	.09
☐ 36 Tino Martinez	.75	.35	.09
☐ 37 Jeff Nelson	.10	.05	.01
☐ 38 Warren Newson	.10	.05	.01
☐ 39 Greg Pirkl	.10	.05	.01
☐ 40 Arquimedez Pozo	.25	.11	.03
☐ 41 Bill Risley	.10	.05	.01
☐ 42 Alex Rodriguez	3.00	1.35	.35
☐ 43 Luis Sojo	.10	.05	.01
☐ 44 Doug Strange	.10	.05	.01
☐ 45 Salomon Torres	.10	.05	.01
☐ 46 Bob Wells	.10	.05	.01
☐ 47 Chris Widger	.10	.05	.01
☐ 48 Dan Wilson	.40	.18	.05

☐ 49 Bob Wolcott	.25	.11	.03
☐ 50 Lou Piniella MG	.25	.11	.03

1996 Mariners Mother's

This 28-card set consists of borderless posed color player portraits. The player's and team's names appear in one of the top rounded corners. The backs carry biographical information and the sponsor's logo on a white background in red and purple print. A blank slot for the player's autograph rounds out the back.

	MINT	NRMT	EXC
COMPLETE SET (28)	12.00	5.50	1.50
COMMON CARD (1-28)	.25	.11	.03
☐ 1 Lou Piniella MG	.75	.35	.09
☐ 2 Randy Johnson	1.00	.45	.12
☐ 3 Jay Buhner	1.00	.45	.12
☐ 4 Ken Griffey Jr.	4.00	1.80	.50
☐ 5 Ricky Jordan	.25	.11	.03
☐ 6 Rich Amaral	.25	.11	.03
☐ 7 Edgar Martinez	1.00	.45	.12
☐ 8 Joey Cora	.50	.23	.06
☐ 9 Alex Rodriguez	4.00	1.80	.50
☐ 10 Sterling Hitchcock	.50	.23	.06
☐ 11 Chris Bosio	.25	.11	.03
☐ 12 John Marzano	.25	.11	.03
☐ 13 Bob Wells	.25	.11	.03
☐ 14 Rafael Carmona	.25	.11	.03
☐ 15 Dan Wilson	.75	.35	.09
☐ 16 Norm Charlton	.50	.23	.06
☐ 17 Paul Sorrento	.50	.23	.06
☐ 18 Mike Jackson	.25	.11	.03
☐ 19 Luis Sojo	.25	.11	.03
☐ 20 Bobby Ayala	.25	.11	.03
☐ 21 Alex Diaz	.25	.11	.03
☐ 22 Doug Strange	.25	.11	.03
☐ 23 Bob Wolcott	.50	.23	.06
☐ 24 Darren Bragg	.50	.23	.06
☐ 25 Paul Menhart	.25	.11	.03
☐ 26 Edwin Hurtado	.25	.11	.03
☐ 27 Russ Davis	.50	.23	.06
☐ 28 Coaches Card CL Lee Elia John McLarren Steve Smith Mattt Sinatro Sam Mejias Bobby Cuellar	.25	.11	.03

1993 Marlins Florida Agriculture

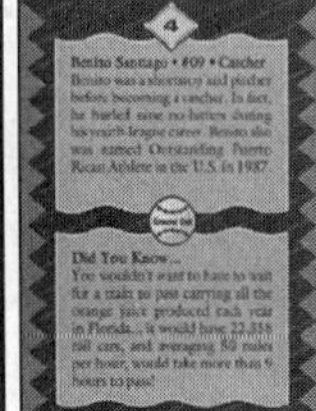

These were given out in eight-card perforated sheets at the Sunshine State Games in Tallahassee in July 1993. The sheet measures approximately 7" by 10" and features two rows of standard-size cards. Also a 8 1/12" by 11" playing-field board was included with the set for use in playing a baseball card game. The fronts feature color photos of the players posing with various fruits and vegetables. The Florida Agriculture Department's Fresh 2-U logo appears in the upper left. The backs carry player information on the upper panel and Florida agricultural statistics on the lower panel.

	MINT	NRMT	EXC
COMPLETE SET (8)	7.50	3.40	.95
COMMON CARD (1-8)	.75	.35	.09
☐ 1 Title Card	.75	.35	.09
☐ 2 Billy the Marlin (Mascot)	1.00	.45	.12
☐ 3 Ryan Bowen	.75	.35	.09
☐ 4 Benito Santiago	1.25	.55	.16
☐ 5 Richie Lewis	.75	.35	.09
☐ 6 Bret Barberie	.75	.35	.09
☐ 7 Rich Renteria	.75	.35	.09
☐ 8 Jeff Conine	3.00	1.35	.35

1993 Marlins Publix

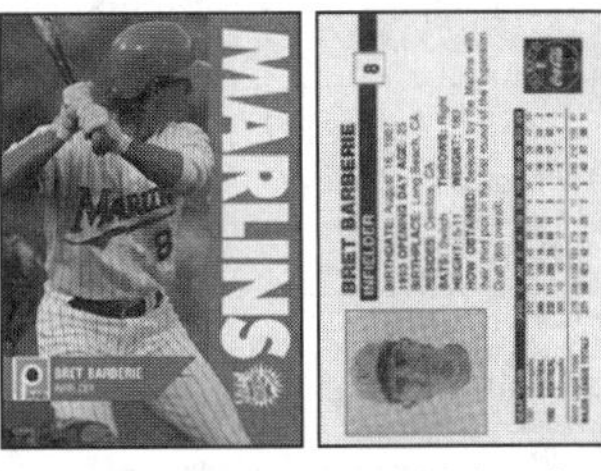

Sponsored by Coca-Cola, this 30-card standard-size inaugural season Marlins set features color player action photos on its fronts. The photos are borderless on three sides. On the right side, a teal-colored stripe carries the team name in vertical white lettering and the Marlins' inaugural season logo. The player's name and position, along with the Publix logo, appear in a teal-colored bar near the bottom of the picture. The white horizontal back carries a black-and-white head shot in the upper left. The player's name, position, uniform number, and biography are printed alongside on the right. A stat table and the Coca-Cola logo near the bottom round out the back. The cards are unnumbered and checklisted below in alphabetical order.

	MINT	NRMT	EXC
COMPLETE SET (30)	12.00	5.50	1.50
COMMON CARD (1-30)	.25	.11	.03
☐ 1 Luis Aquino	.25	.11	.03
☐ 2 Alex Arias	.25	.11	.03
☐ 3 Jack Armstrong	.25	.11	.03
☐ 4 Bret Barberie	.25	.11	.03
☐ 5 Ryan Bowen	.25	.11	.03
☐ 6 Greg Briley	.25	.11	.03
☐ 7 Chuck Carr	.25	.11	.03
☐ 8 Jeff Conine	3.00	1.35	.35
☐ 9 Henry Cotto	.25	.11	.03
☐ 10 Orestes Destrade	.25	.11	.03
☐ 11 Chris Hammond	.25	.11	.03
☐ 12 Bryan Harvey	.50	.23	.06
☐ 13 Charlie Hough	.75	.35	.09
☐ 14 Joe Klink	.25	.11	.03
☐ 15 Rene Lachemann MG	.25	.11	.03
☐ 16 Richie Lewis	.25	.11	.03
☐ 17 Bob Natal	.25	.11	.03
☐ 18 Robb Nen	1.00	.45	.12
☐ 19 Pat Rapp	.25	.11	.03
☐ 20 Rich Renteria	.25	.11	.03
☐ 21 Rich Rodriguez	.25	.11	.03
☐ 22 Benito Santiago	.75	.35	.09
☐ 23 Gary Sheffield	2.50	1.10	.30
☐ 24 Matt Turner	.25	.11	.03
☐ 25 Walt Weiss	.75	.35	.09
☐ 26 Darrell Whitmore	.25	.11	.03
☐ 27 Nigel Wilson	.25	.11	.03
☐ 28 Marcel Lachemann CO Vada Pinson CO Doug Rader CO Frank Reberger CO Cookie Rojas CO	.50	.23	.06
☐ 29 Billy the Marlin (Mascot)	.50	.23	.06
☐ 30 Coupon card	.25	.11	.03

1993 Marlins U.S. Playing Cards

This 56-card standard-size set celebrates the 1993 Inaugural Year of the Florida Marlins. The fronts of these rounded-corner cards feature full-color posed and action shots of the players while the backs have the team's teal logo on a silver background with silver pinstripes. The player's name and position appear in a teal bar at the bottom of the photo. Since this set is similar to a playing card set, the set is checklisted below as if it were a playing card deck. In the checklist C means Clubs, D means Diamonds, H means Hearts, S means Spades, and JK means Joker. The cards are checklisted in playing order by suits and numbers are assigned to Aces, (1) Jacks, (11) Queens, (12) and Kings (13). Included in the set are a Marlins' opening day player roster card and a 1993 home schedule card. The jokers, home schedule card and the opening day player roster card are unnumbered and listed at the end.

	MINT	NRMT	EXC
COMPLETE SET (56)	4.00	1.80	.50
COMMON CARD	.05	.02	.01
☐ 1C Walt Weiss	.05	.02	.01
☐ 1D Dave Magadan	.05	.02	.01
☐ 1H Benito Santiago	.15	.07	.02
☐ 1S Alex Arias	.05	.02	.01
☐ 2C Dave Magadan	.05	.02	.01
☐ 2D Jack Armstrong	.05	.02	.01
☐ 2H Walt Weiss	.05	.02	.01
☐ 2S Benito Santiago	.15	.07	.02
☐ 3C Cris Carpenter	.05	.02	.01
☐ 3D Bryan Harvey	.05	.02	.01
☐ 3H Monty Fariss	.05	.02	.01
☐ 3S Ryan Bowen	.05	.02	.01
☐ 4C Dave Magadan	.05	.02	.01
☐ 4D Richie Lewis	.05	.02	.01
☐ 4H Chris Hammond	.05	.02	.01
☐ 4S Steve Decker	.05	.02	.01
☐ 5C Bob McClure	.05	.02	.01
☐ 5D Scott Pose	.05	.02	.01
☐ 5H Joe Klink	.05	.02	.01
☐ 5S Jeff Conine	.50	.23	.06
☐ 6C Junior Felix	.05	.02	.01
☐ 6D Rich Renteria	.05	.02	.01
☐ 6H Chuck Carr	.05	.02	.01
☐ 6S Bret Barberie	.05	.02	.01
☐ 7C Walt Weiss	.05	.02	.01
☐ 7D Trevor Hoffman	.25	.11	.03
☐ 7H Alex Arias	.05	.02	.01
☐ 7S Orestes Destrade	.05	.02	.01
☐ 8C Steve Decker	.05	.02	.01
☐ 8D Jim Corsi	.05	.02	.01
☐ 8H Charlie Hough	.15	.07	.02
☐ 8S Greg Briley	.05	.02	.01
☐ 9C Jeff Conine	.50	.23	.06
☐ 9D Ryan Bowen	.05	.02	.01
☐ 9H Junior Felix	.05	.02	.01
☐ 9S Charlie Hough	.05	.02	.01
☐ 10C Bryan Harvey	.05	.02	.01
☐ 10D Orestes Destrade	.05	.02	.01
☐ 10H Jim Corsi	.05	.02	.01
☐ 10S Rob Natal	.05	.02	.01
☐ 11C Orestes Destrade	.05	.02	.01
☐ 11D Bret Barberie	.05	.02	.01
☐ 11H Jeff Conine	.50	.23	.06
☐ 11S Jack Armstrong	.05	.02	.01
☐ 12C Chris Hammond	.05	.02	.01
☐ 12D Chuck Carr	.05	.02	.01
☐ 12H Trevor Hoffman	.25	.11	.03
☐ 12S Junior Felix	.05	.02	.01
☐ 13C Monty Farris	.05	.02	.01
☐ 13D Cris Carpenter	.05	.02	.01
☐ 13H Rich Renteria	.05	.02	.01
☐ 13S Richie Lewis	.05	.02	.01
☐ JKO National League Logo	.05	.02	.01
☐ NNO 1993 Home Schedule	.05	.02	.01

1994 Mascot Mania

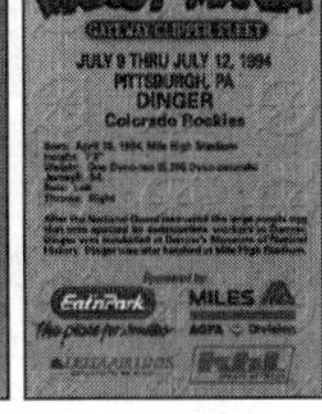

Given out in Pittsburgh during July 9 through 12, 1994, this 16-card set measures the standard size and features 16 MLB mascots. On a blue background, the fronts have color mascot photos with yellow borders. The words "1994 Mascot Mania" appear above the photo, while his name and team name are printed below. The backs carry the mascot's biography and sponsor logos. The cards are unnumbered and checklisted below in alphabetical order.

	MINT	NRMT	EXC
COMPLETE SET (16)	7.50	3.40	.95
COMMON CARD (1-16)	.50	.23	.06
☐ 1 Bernie Brewer Milwaukee Brewers	.50	.23	.06
☐ 2 Billy the Marlin Florida Marlins	.50	.23	.06
☐ 3 BJ Birdy Toronto Blue Jays	.50	.23	.06
☐ 4 Bluepper San Diego Padres	.50	.23	.06
☐ 5 Dinger Colorado Rockies	.50	.23	.06
☐ 6 Fredbird St. Louis Cardinals	.50	.23	.06
☐ 7 Homer the Brave Atlanta Braves	.50	.23	.06
☐ 8 Mariner Moose Seattle Mariners	.50	.23	.06
☐ 9 Orbit Houston Astros	.50	.23	.06
☐ 10 Oriole Bird Baltimore Orioles	.50	.23	.06
☐ 11 Phillie Phanatic Philadelphia Phillies	1.00	.45	.12
☐ 12 Pirate Parrot Pittsburgh Pirates	.50	.23	.06
☐ 13 Rally Atlanta Braves	1.00	.45	.12
☐ 14 Slider Cleveland Indians	1.00	.45	.12
☐ 15 Trunk Oakland Athletics	.50	.23	.06
☐ 16 Youppi Montreal Expos	.50	.23	.06

1989 Master Bread Discs

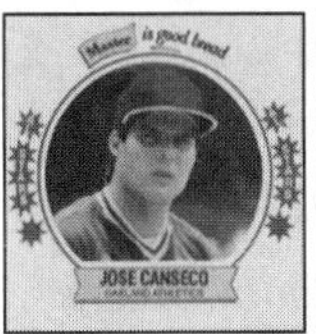

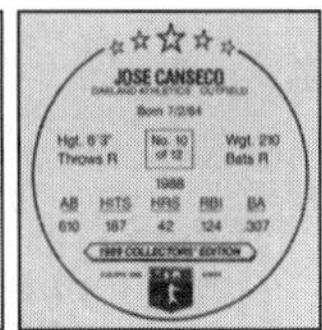

The 1989 Master Bread disc set contains 12 discs each measuring 2 3/4" in diameter. The set was produced by MSA; there are no team logos featured on the disc. The year and lifetime statistics are featured for each player on the back of the disc. The set features only American League players.

	MINT	NRMT	EXC
COMPLETE SET (12)	18.00	8.00	2.20
COMMON DISC (1-12)	.50	.23	.06
☐ 1 Frank Viola	.50	.23	.06
☐ 2 Kirby Puckett	4.00	1.80	.50
☐ 3 Gary Gaetti	.50	.23	.06
☐ 4 Alan Trammell	1.00	.45	.12
☐ 5 Wade Boggs	2.00	.90	.25
☐ 6 Don Mattingly	4.00	1.80	.50
☐ 7 Wally Joyner	1.00	.45	.12
☐ 8 Paul Molitor	2.00	.90	.25
☐ 9 George Brett	4.00	1.80	.50
☐ 10 Jose Canseco	2.00	.90	.25
☐ 11 Julio Franco	.50	.23	.06
☐ 12 Cal Ripken Jr.	8.00	3.60	1.00

1971 Mattel Mini-Records

This 18-disc set was designed to be played on a special Mattel mini-record player, which is not included in the complete set price. Each black plastic disc, approximately 2 1/2" in diameter, features a recording on one side and a color drawing of the player on the other. The picture appears on a paper disk that is glued onto the smooth unrecorded side of the mini-record. On the recorded side, the player's name and the set's subtitle appear in arcs stamped in the central portion of the mini-record. The hand-engraved player's name appears again along with a production number, copyright symbol, and the Mattel name and year of production in the ring between the central portion of the record and the grooves. The ivory discs are the ones which are double sided and are considered to be much tougher than the black discs. They were also known as "Mattel Show 'N Tell". The discs are unnumbered and checklisted below in alphabetical order.

	NRMT	VG-E	GOOD
COMPLETE SET (18)	300.00	135.00	38.00
COMMON RECOED (1-18)	10.00	4.50	1.25
☐ 1 Hank Aaron	30.00	13.50	3.70
☐ 2 Hank Aaron (Double-sided)	30.00	13.50	3.70
☐ 3 Ernie Banks	15.00	6.75	1.85
☐ 4 Ernie Banks (Double-sided)	15.00	6.75	1.85
☐ 5 Al Kaline	15.00	6.75	1.85
☐ 6 Al Kaline (Double-sided)	15.00	6.75	1.85
☐ 7 Willie Mays	30.00	13.50	3.70
☐ 8 Willie Mays (Double-sided)	30.00	13.50	3.70
☐ 9 Willie McCovey	15.00	6.75	1.85
☐ 10 Willie McCovey (Double-sided)	15.00	6.75	1.85
☐ 11 Tony Oliva	10.00	4.50	1.25
☐ 12 Tony Oliva (Double-sided)	10.00	4.50	1.25
☐ 13 Frank Robinson	15.00	6.75	1.85
☐ 14 Frank Robinson (Double-sided)	15.00	6.75	1.85
☐ 15 Tom Seaver	20.00	9.00	2.50
☐ 16 Tom Seaver (Double-sided)	20.00	9.00	2.50
☐ 17 Willie Stargell	15.00	6.75	1.85
☐ 18 Willie Stargell (Double-sided)	15.00	6.75	1.85

1992 Mattingly's #23 Restaurant

This standard-size card was sold as a fund-raiser at Don Mattingly's restaurant in Evansville, Indiana. The front features Mattingly along with two handicapped youths. The back has vital statistics, career information and some highlights.

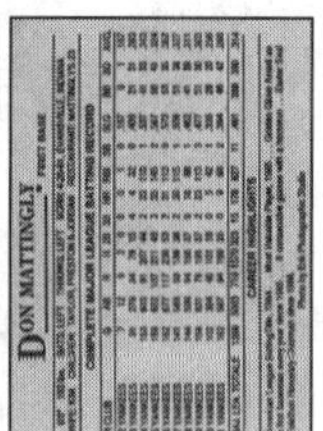

	MINT	NRMT	EXC
COMPLETE SET (1)	3.00	1.35	.35
COMMON CARD	3.00	1.35	.35
☐ 1 Don Mattingly	3.00	1.35	.35

1909-16 Max Stein/United States Publishing House PC758

These sepia-colored postcards were issued from the 1909-16 time period. The Marquard and Zimmerman cards have "United States Pub." marked on the back, leading to the theory that perhaps these two cards belong to another postcard set. The backs are quite attractive.

	EX-MT	VG-E	GOOD
COMPLETE SET (25)	7500.00	3400.00	950.00
COMMON CARD (1-25)	150.00	70.00	19.00
☐ 1 Ping Bodie	150.00	70.00	19.00
☐ 2 Frank Chance	300.00	135.00	38.00
☐ 3 Ty Cobb	1200.00	550.00	150.00
☐ 4 Johnny Evers	250.00	110.00	31.00
☐ 5 Rube Marquard	250.00	110.00	31.00
☐ 6 Christy Mathewson	600.00	275.00	75.00
☐ 7 John McGraw	350.00	160.00	45.00
☐ 8 Chief Meyers	150.00	70.00	19.00
☐ 9 Marty O'Toole	150.00	70.00	19.00
☐ 10 Frank Schulte	150.00	70.00	19.00
☐ 11 Tris Speaker	300.00	135.00	38.00
☐ 12 Jake Stahl	150.00	70.00	19.00
☐ 13 Jim Thorpe	800.00	350.00	100.00
☐ 14 Joe Tinker	250.00	110.00	31.00
☐ 15 Honus Wagner	500.00	220.00	60.00
☐ 16 Ed Walsh	300.00	135.00	38.00
☐ 17 Buck Weaver	350.00	160.00	45.00
☐ 18 Joe Wood	200.00	90.00	25.00
☐ 19 Heinie Zimmerman	150.00	70.00	19.00
☐ 20 Johnny Evers Jimmy Archer Mike Hechinger Roger Bresnahan Tom Needham	250.00	110.00	31.00
☐ 21 Doc Miller Wilbur Good Mitchell Otis Clymer Wildfire Schulte	150.00	70.00	19.00
☐ 22 Boston American Team	250.00	110.00	31.00
☐ 23 Chicago Cubs 1916	250.00	110.00	31.00
☐ 24 Cincinnati Reds 1916	300.00	135.00	38.00
☐ 25 N.Y. National Team	250.00	110.00	31.00

1895 Mayo N300

The Mayo Tobacco Works of Richmond, Va., issued this set of 48 ballplayers about 1895. The cards contain sepia portraits although some pictures appear to be black and white. There are 40 different individuals known in the set; cards 1 to 28 appear in uniform, while the last twelve (29-40) appear in street clothes. Eight of the former also appear with variations in uniform. The player's name appears within the picture area and a "Mayo's Cut Plug" ad is printed in a panel at the base of the card. Similar to the football set issued around the same time, the cards have black blank backs.

	EX-MT	VG-E	GOOD
COMPLETE SET (48)	25000.00	11200.00	3100.00
COMMON CARD (1-40)	375.00	170.00	47.50
☐ 1 Cap Anson: Chicago	2250.00	1000.00	275.00
☐ 2 Jimmy Bannon RF: Boston	375.00	170.00	47.50
☐ 3A Dan Brouthers 1B: Baltimore	750.00	350.00	95.00
☐ 3B Dan Brouthers 1B: Louisville	1000.00	450.00	125.00
☐ 4 John Clarkson P: St. Louis	750.00	350.00	95.00
☐ 5 Tommy W. Corcoran SS Brooklyn	375.00	170.00	47.50
☐ 6 Lave Cross 2B: Philadelphia	375.00	170.00	47.50
☐ 7 Hugh Duffy CF: Boston	750.00	350.00	95.00
☐ 8A Buck Ewing RF: Cincinnati	1000.00	450.00	125.00
☐ 8B Buck Ewing RF: Cleveland	1000.00	450.00	125.00
☐ 9 Dave Foutz 1B: Brooklyn	375.00	170.00	47.50
☐ 10 Charlie Ganzel C: Boston	375.00	170.00	47.50
☐ 11A Jack Glasscock SS: Pittsburgh	425.00	190.00	52.50
☐ 11B Jack Glasscock SS: Louisville	425.00	190.00	52.50
☐ 12 Mike Griffin CF: Brooklyn	375.00	170.00	47.50
☐ 13A George Haddock P: Philadelphia	375.00	170.00	47.50
☐ 13B George Haddock P: no team	375.00	170.00	47.50
☐ 14 Bill Joyce CF: Brooklyn	375.00	170.00	47.50
☐ 15 Wm.(Brickyard) Kennedy P: Brooklyn	375.00	170.00	47.50
☐ 16A Tom F. Kinslow C: Pitts.	375.00	170.00	47.50
☐ 16B Tom F. Kinslow C: no team	375.00	170.00	47.50
☐ 17 Arlie Latham 3B: Cincinnati	425.00	190.00	52.50
☐ 18 Herman Long SS: Boston	425.00	190.00	52.50
☐ 19 Tom Lovett P: Boston	375.00	170.00	47.50
☐ 20 Link Lowe 2B: Boston	425.00	190.00	52.50
☐ 21 Tommy McCarthy LF: Boston	750.00	350.00	95.00
☐ 22 Yale Murphy SS: New York	375.00	170.00	47.50
☐ 23 Billy Nash 3B: Boston	375.00	170.00	47.50
☐ 24 Kid Nicols P: Boston	750.00	350.00	95.00
☐ 25A Fred Pfeffer 2B: Louisville	375.00	170.00	47.50
☐ 25B Fred Pfeffer (Retired)	375.00	170.00	47.50
☐ 26A Amos Rusie P: New York	1200.00	550.00	150.00
☐ 26B Amos Russie (Sic) P: New York	1000.00	450.00	125.00
☐ 27 Tommy Tucker 1B: Boston	375.00	170.00	47.50
☐ 28A John Ward 2B: New York	750.00	350.00	95.00
☐ 28B John Ward (Retired)	1000.00	450.00	125.00
☐ 29 Charlie S. Abbey CF: Washington	375.00	170.00	47.50
☐ 30 Ed W. Cartwright FB: Washington	375.00	170.00	47.50
☐ 31 William F. Dahlen SS: Chicago	425.00	190.00	52.50
☐ 32 Tom P. Daly 2B: Brooklyn	375.00	170.00	47.50
☐ 33 Ed J. Delehanty LF: Phila.	1200.00	550.00	150.00
☐ 34 Bill W. Hallman 2B: Phila.	375.00	170.00	47.50
☐ 35 Billy Hamilton CF: Phila.	750.00	350.00	95.00
☐ 36 Wilbert Robinson C: Baltimore	750.00	350.00	95.00
☐ 37 James Ryan RF: Chicago	425.00	190.00	52.50
☐ 38 Billy Shindle 3B: Brooklyn	375.00	170.00	47.50
☐ 39 George J. Smith SS: Cinc.	375.00	170.00	47.50
☐ 40 Otis H. Stockdale P: Washington	375.00	170.00	47.50

1975 McCallum Cobb

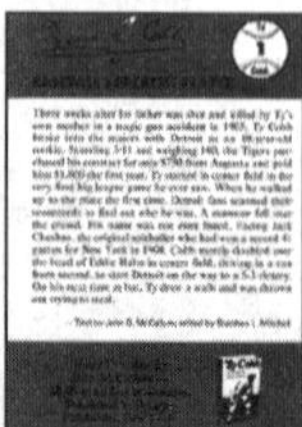

This 20-card set was produced to promote John McCallum's biography on Ty Cobb. The cards measure approximately 2 1/2" X 3 1/2" and feature on the fronts vintage black and white photos, with a hand-drawn artificial wood grain picture frame border. The title to each picture appears in a plaque below the picture. The back has a facsimile autograph and extended caption. The cards are numbered on the back in a baseball icon in the upper right corner.

	NRMT	VG-E	GOOD
COMPLETE SET (20)	20.00	9.00	2.50
COMMON CARD (1-20)	.75	.35	.09
☐ 1 Ty Breaks In	1.50	.70	.19
☐ 2 Four Inches of the Plate	.75	.35	.09
☐ 3 Slashing into Third	1.00	.45	.12
☐ 4 Inking Another Contract	.75	.35	.09
☐ 5 Captain Tyrus R. Cobb	.75	.35	.09
☐ 6 Ty with The Big Train	2.50	1.10	.30
☐ 7 The End of an Era	.75	.35	.09
☐ 8 All-Time Centerfielder	.75	.35	.09
☐ 9 Ty Could Walk 'em Down	.75	.35	.09
☐ 10 Menacing Batsman	.75	.35	.09
☐ 11 With Brother Paul	.75	.35	.09
☐ 12 Thomas Edison With Cobb	1.50	.70	.19
☐ 13 Ty Tangles with Muggsy McGraw	1.50	.70	.19
☐ 14 Author McCallum with Cy Young	1.00	.45	.12
☐ 15 Tris Speaker Joe DiMaggio and Ty Cobb	4.00	1.80	.50
☐ 16 Ted Gets a Lesson	2.00	.90	.25
☐ 17 Five for Five	.75	.35	.09
☐ 18 I have but one regret	.75	.35	.09
☐ 19 Excellence: The Cobb Standard	.75	.35	.09
☐ 20 His Favorite Photo	1.50	.70	.19

1992 MCI Ambassadors

Sponsored by MCI, the third annual Ambassadors of Baseball World Tour set consists of 16 cards. The cards were distributed by MCI to military personnel during the world tour of military bases. The standard-size cards feature white-bordered color photos of baseball stars of the past. The player's name and position, along with the set logo, appear in the bottom margin. A diagonal red stripe crosses the upper left and carries the words "Support MWR with MCI" The horizontal white back carries the player's name and position, teams he played for and the years thereof, career stats, and biography.

	MINT	NRMT	EXC
COMPLETE SET (16)	75.00	34.00	9.50
COMMON CARD (1-16)	3.00	1.35	.35
☐ 1 Earl Weaver MG	8.00	3.60	1.00
☐ 2 Steve Garvey	6.00	2.70	.75
☐ 3 Doug Flynn	4.00	1.80	.50
☐ 4 Bert Campaneris	5.00	2.20	.60
☐ 5 Bill Madlock	5.00	2.20	.60
☐ 6 Graig Nettles	5.00	2.20	.60
☐ 7 Dave Kingman	5.00	2.20	.60
☐ 8 Paul Blair	3.00	1.35	.35
☐ 9 Jeff Burroughs	3.00	1.35	.35
☐ 10 Rick Waits	3.00	1.35	.35
☐ 11 Elias Sosa	3.00	1.35	.35
☐ 12 Tug McGraw	5.00	2.20	.60
☐ 13 Ferguson Jenkins	10.00	4.50	1.25
☐ 14 Bob Feller	10.00	4.50	1.25
☐ 15 Ferguson Jenkins (Special art card)	8.00	3.60	1.00
☐ 16 Title card	3.00	1.35	.35

1993 MCI Ambassadors

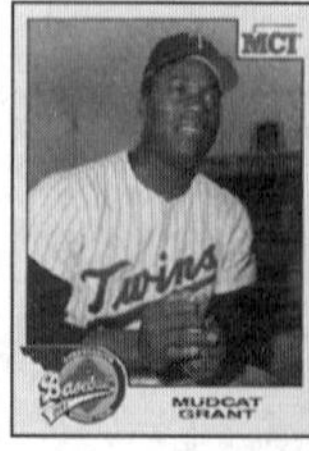

This 14-card, standard-size set was sponsored by MCI for the 1993 Ambassadors of Baseball World Tour. The cards contain a color portrait or action shot of baseball veterans with an irregular white border. The MCI logo is in the upper right and a logo of the Ambassadors of Baseball 1993 World Tour is in the lower left, with the player's name to the right. The horizontal format on the backs is printed in black on a white background. Information includes biography, statistics, and a career summary.

	MINT	NRMT	EXC
COMPLETE SET (14)	50.00	22.00	6.25
COMMON CARD (1-13)	3.00	1.35	.35
☐ 1 Vida Blue	6.00	2.70	.75
☐ 2 Paul Blair	4.00	1.80	.50
☐ 3 Mudcat Grant	4.00	1.80	.50
☐ 4 Phil Niekro	8.00	3.60	1.00
☐ 5 Bob Feller	8.00	3.60	1.00
☐ 6 Joe Charboneau	4.00	1.80	.50
☐ 7 Joe Rudi	4.00	1.80	.50
☐ 8 Catfish Hunter	8.00	3.60	1.00
☐ 9 Manny Sanguillen	4.00	1.80	.50
☐ 10 Harmon Killebrew	8.00	3.60	1.00
☐ 11 Al Oliver	6.00	2.70	.75
☐ 12 Bob Dernier	3.00	1.35	.35
☐ 13 Graig Nettles Sparky Lyle	6.00	2.70	.75
☐ NNO Title Card	3.00	1.35	.35

1994 MCI Ambassadors

The 1994 Ambassadors of Baseball 15-card standard-size set was sponsored by Major League Baseball Players Alumni and MCI. The sets were released at a few select military bases where the retired players appeared in charity games. The front design is the same as the 1993 issue, with the MCI logo at the upper right and the Ambassadors of Baseball World Tour logo at the lower left. The two tribute cards list the names of players who served during World War II.

	MINT	NRMT	EXC
COMPLETE SET (15)	35.00	16.00	4.40
COMMON CARD (1-11)	2.00	.90	.25
☐ 1 Sparky Lyle	4.00	1.80	.50
☐ 2 John Stearns	2.00	.90	.25
☐ 3 Bobby Thomson	6.00	2.70	.75
☐ 4 Jimmy Wynn	2.00	.90	.25
☐ 5 Ferguson Jenkins	8.00	3.60	1.00
☐ 6 Tug McGraw	4.00	1.80	.50
☐ 7 Paul Blair	2.00	.90	.25
☐ 8 Ron LeFlore	2.00	.90	.25
☐ 9 Manny Sanguillen	2.00	.90	.25
☐ 10 Doug Flynn	2.00	.90	.25
☐ 11 Bill North	2.00	.90	.25
☐ S1 Doug Flynn (Instructing children)	2.00	.90	.25
☐ S2 World War II Tribute Card (AL)	4.00	1.80	.50
☐ S3 World War II Tribute Card (NL)	4.00	1.80	.50
☐ S4 Manny Sanguillen (Signing autographs)	4.00	1.80	.50

1995 MCI Ambassadors

This 16-card standard-size set was sponsored by MCI, MLB, and Major League Baseball Players Alumni. Approximately 2,000 sets were produced and distributed at certain U.S. military bases where the retired players appeared in charity games. The fronts feature white-bordered color photos of baseball stars of the past. The MCI logo is at the top right with the player's name and the "Ambassadors of Baseball 1995 World Tour" logo at the bottom. The backs include the years the player was in the majors, career highlights and biography.

	MINT	NRMT	EXC
COMPLETE SET (16)	35.00	16.00	4.40
COMMON CARD (1-16)	2.00	.90	.25
☐ 1 Vida Blue	3.00	1.35	.35
☐ 2 Bert Campaneris	4.00	1.80	.50
☐ 3 Tug McGraw	3.00	1.35	.35
☐ 4 Doug Flynn	2.00	.90	.25
☐ 5 Paul Blair	2.00	.90	.25
☐ 6 Harmon Killebrew	6.00	2.70	.75
☐ 7 Sparky Lyle	3.00	1.35	.35
☐ 8 Steve Garvey	5.00	2.20	.60
☐ 9 Bert Blyleven	3.00	1.35	.35

☐ 10 Omar Moreno	2.00	.90	.25
☐ 11 Bill Lee	2.00	.90	.25
☐ 12 Maury Wills	3.00	1.35	.35
☐ 13 Dave Parker	3.00	1.35	.35
☐ 14 Luis Aparicio	6.00	2.70	.75
☐ 15 Brooks Robinson	6.00	2.70	.75
☐ 16 George Foster	4.00	1.80	.50

1991 MDA All-Stars

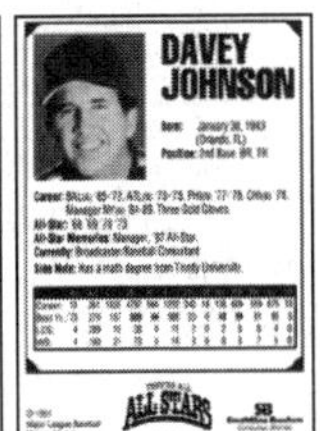

This 20-card set was produced by Smith-Kline Beecham for the Muscular Dystrophy Association. It includes 18 All-Star Alumni cards that feature retired baseball All-Stars. A vinyl album designed to house the cards was also issued. The cards measure the standard size. The front design includes white borders and a sandy background. Color action player photos are cut out and superimposed on diamonds framed by various color borders. The slogan for the set, "They're All All-Stars," appears in one of the upper corners, while the player's name appears in white lettering in a color stripe cutting across the bottom of the picture. Since the set was licensed by the Major League Baseball Players Alumni, all team logos have been airbrushed out. In black on white, the backs carry a head shot of the player (in retirement), biographical information, and statistics.

	MINT	NRMT	EXC
COMPLETE SET (20)	12.00	5.50	1.50
COMMON CARD (1-18)	.50	.23	.06
☐ 1 Steve Carlton	1.50	.70	.19
☐ 2 Ted Simmons	.50	.23	.06
☐ 3 Willie Stargell	1.25	.55	.16
☐ 4 Bill Mazeroski	.75	.35	.09
☐ 5 Ron Santo	.75	.35	.09
☐ 6 Dave Concepcion	.50	.23	.06
☐ 7 Bobby Bonds	1.00	.45	.12
☐ 8 George Foster	.50	.23	.06
☐ 9 Billy Williams	1.25	.55	.16
☐ 10 Whitey Ford	2.00	.90	.25
☐ 11 Yogi Berra	2.00	.90	.25
☐ 12 Boog Powell	.75	.35	.09
☐ 13 Davey Johnson	.50	.23	.06
☐ 14 Brooks Robinson	2.00	.90	.25
☐ 15 Jim Fregosi	.50	.23	.06
☐ 16 Harmon Killebrew	1.50	.70	.19
☐ 17 Ted Williams	4.00	1.80	.50
☐ 18 Al Kaline	1.50	.70	.19
☐ NNO MDA Fact Card Brooks Robinson Tommy	1.50	.70	.19
☐ NNO Title Card	.50	.23	.06

1992 MDA MVP

This 20-card limited edition set of alumni MVPs was sponsored by SmithKline Beecham Consumer Brands and was produced for the Muscular Dystrophy Association. The fronts feature color player photos in a white border. The backs carry a small black-and-white player head photo with player infroamtion and career statistics. The cards are designed to fit into a special white vinyl album with the set title and sponsor name printed in blue.

	MINT	NRMT	EXC
COMPLETE SET (20)	15.00	6.75	1.85
COMMON CARD (1-20)	.50	.23	.06
☐ 1 Yogi Berra	2.50	1.10	.30
☐ 2 Dick Groat	.50	.23	.06
☐ 3 Maury Wills	.75	.35	.09
☐ 4 Brooks Robinson	2.00	.90	.25
☐ 5 Orlando Cepeda	1.00	.45	.12
☐ 6 Harmon Killebrew	1.50	.70	.19
☐ 7 Boog Powell	1.00	.45	.12
☐ 8 Vida Blue	.75	.35	.09
☐ 9 Jeff Burroughs	.50	.23	.06
☐ 10 George Foster	.50	.23	.06
☐ 11 Rod Carew	2.00	.90	.25
☐ 12 Jim Rice	1.00	.45	.12
☐ 13 Don Baylor	.75	.35	.09
☐ 14 Willie Stargell	1.50	.70	.19

☐ 15 Rollie Fingers	.75	.35	.09
☐ 16 Ray Knight	.50	.23	.06
☐ 17 History Card	.50	.23	.06
☐ 18 Trivia Card	.50	.23	.06
☐ 19 Fact Sheet (Players Alumni)	.50	.23	.06
☐ 20 Harmon Killebrew Drew Fact Sheet	1.00	.45	.12

1986 Meadow Gold Blank Back

This unnumbered set of 16 full-color cards is blank backed. The cards were found (one card per package) on the flap of 1/2 gallon cartons of Meadow Gold "Double Play" ice cream. The cards are attractive but the team logos have been airbrushed away. The cards measure approximately 2 3/8" by 3 1/2." The accent colors used on the front of the cards are light blue and red. The Ripken card is supposedly a little more difficult to find.

	MINT	NRMT	EXC
COMPLETE SET (16)	45.00	20.00	5.50
COMMON CARD (1-16)	1.50	.70	.19
☐ 1 Wade Boggs	4.00	1.80	.50
☐ 2 George Brett	6.00	2.70	.75
☐ 3 Carlton Fisk	3.00	1.35	.35
☐ 4 Steve Garvey	2.00	.90	.25
☐ 5 Dwight Gooden	3.00	1.35	.35
☐ 6 Pedro Guerrero	1.50	.70	.19
☐ 7 Reggie Jackson	4.00	1.80	.50
☐ 8 Don Mattingly	6.00	2.70	.75
☐ 9 Willie McGee	2.00	.90	.25
☐ 10 Dale Murphy	3.00	1.35	.35
☐ 11 Cal Ripken	8.00	3.60	1.00
☐ 12 Pete Rose	4.00	1.80	.50
☐ 13 Ryne Sandberg	5.00	2.20	.60
☐ 14 Mike Schmidt	4.00	1.80	.50
☐ 15 Fernando Valenzuela	2.00	.90	.25
☐ 16 Dave Winfield	3.00	1.35	.35

1986 Meadow Gold Milk

These cards were printed crudely on milk cartons of various sizes of Meadow Gold milk. The cards are approximately 2 1/2" by 3 3/16" and are very similar to the Keller's Butter cards. The same art was used on the Schmidt card which is in both sets. Both Keller's and Meadow Gold are subsidiaries of Beatrice Foods. The set was licensed by Mike Schechter Associates and the Major League Baseball Players' Association. The cards are blank backed and are printed in red and brown on white waxed cardboard. Complete boxes would bring double the values listed below. Since the cards are unnumbered, they are listed below in alphabetical order.

	MINT	NRMT	EXC
COMPLETE SET (12)	50.00	22.00	6.25
COMMON CARD (1-12)	2.00	.90	.25
☐ 1 Wade Boggs	5.00	2.20	.60
☐ 2 George Brett	7.50	3.40	.95
☐ 3 Steve Carlton	3.50	1.55	.45
☐ 4 Dwight Gooden	1.50	.70	.19
☐ 5 Don Mattingly	7.50	3.40	.95
☐ 6 Willie McGee	3.00	1.35	.35
☐ 7 Dale Murphy	4.00	1.80	.50
☐ 8 Cal Ripken	12.00	5.50	1.50
☐ 9 Pete Rose	5.00	2.20	.60
☐ 10 Ryne Sandberg	7.50	3.40	.95
☐ 11 Mike Schmidt	5.00	2.20	.60
☐ 12 Fernando Valenzuela	3.00	1.35	.35

1986 Meadow Gold Stat Back

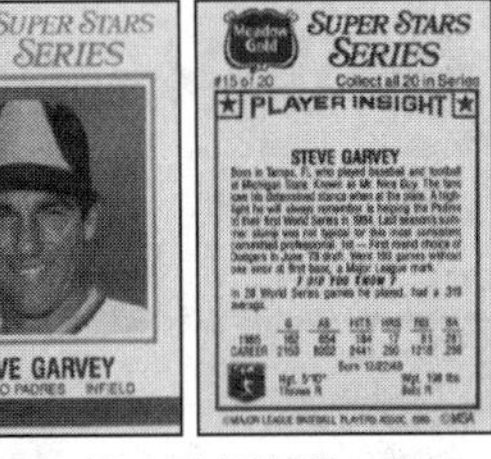

Meadow Gold produced three sets in 1986, but this was the only one with printing on the back. This full-color set contains 20 star players. The cards were distributed as two-card panels with Meadow Gold popsicles, fudgesicles and bubblegum coolers. As with the other sets, this one was only licensed by the Major League Players Association and hence the team logos have been artistically removed. The back printing is in red on white card stock. The cards measure approximately 2 9/16" by 3 1/2" and are numbered on the back. Two of the cards were misspelled by Meadow Gold as noted in the checklist below. Intact panels are valued at 50 percent more than the sum of the individual players making up the panel.

	MINT	NRMT	EXC
COMPLETE SET (20)	35.00	16.00	4.40
COMMON CARD (1-20)	1.00	.45	.12
☐ 1 George Brett	5.00	2.20	.60
☐ 2 Fernando Valenzuela	1.50	.70	.19
☐ 3 Dwight Gooden	2.00	.90	.25
☐ 4 Dale Murphy	2.00	.90	.25
☐ 5 Don Mattingly	5.00	2.20	.60
☐ 6 Reggie Jackson	2.50	1.10	.30
☐ 7 Dave Winfield	2.50	1.10	.30
☐ 8 Pete Rose	2.50	1.10	.30
☐ 9 Wade Boggs	2.00	.90	.25
☐ 10 Willie McGee	1.50	.70	.19
☐ 11 Cal Ripken ERR sic, Ripkin	6.00	2.70	.75
☐ 12 Ryne Sandberg	4.00	1.80	.50
☐ 13 Carlton Fisk	2.00	.90	.25
☐ 14 Jim Rice	1.50	.70	.19
☐ 15 Steve Garvey	1.50	.70	.19
☐ 16 Mike Schmidt	4.00	1.80	.50
☐ 17 Bruce Sutter	1.00	.45	.12
☐ 18 Pedro Guerrero	1.00	.45	.12
☐ 19 Rick Sutcliffe ERR sic, Sutcliffe	1.00	.45	.12
☐ 20 Rich Gossage	1.00	.45	.12

1911 Mecca T201

The cards in this 50-card set measure approximately 2 1/4" by 4 11/16". The 1911 Mecca Double Folder issue contains unnumbered cards. This issue was one of the first to list statistics of players portrayed on the cards. Each card portrays two players, one when the card is folded, another when the card is unfolded. The card of Dougherty and Lord is considered scarce.

	EX-MT	VG-E	GOOD
COMPLETE SET (50)	5000.00	2200.00	600.00
COMMON PAIR (1-50)	45.00	20.00	5.50
☐ 1 Frank Baker Eddie Collins	200.00	90.00	25.00
☐ 2 Jack Barry Jack Lapp	45.00	20.00	5.50
☐ 3 Bill Bergen Zach Wheat	100.00	45.00	12.50
☐ 4 Walter Blair Roy Hartzell	45.00	20.00	5.50
☐ 5 Roger Bresnahan Miller Huggins	175.00	80.00	22.00
☐ 6 Al Bridwell Christy Matthewson UER Mathewson	350.00	160.00	45.00
☐ 7 Johnny Butler Bill Abstein	45.00	20.00	5.50
☐ 8 Bobby Byrne Fred Clarke	90.00	40.00	11.00
☐ 9 Frank Chance Johnny Evers	300.00	135.00	38.00
☐ 10 Tommy Clarke Harry Gaspar	45.00	20.00	5.50
☐ 11 Ty Cobb Sam Crawford	1200.00	550.00	150.00
☐ 12 Leonard Cole Johnny Kling	45.00	20.00	5.50
☐ 13 Jack Coombs Ira Thomas	45.00	20.00	5.50
☐ 14 Jake Daubert Nap Rucker	45.00	20.00	5.50
☐ 15 Patsy Dougherty Harry Lord	300.00	135.00	38.00
☐ 16 Red Dooin John Titus	45.00	20.00	5.50
☐ 17 Tom Downey H Baker	45.00	20.00	5.50
☐ 18 Jimmy Dygert Cy Seymour	45.00	20.00	5.50
☐ 19 Kid Elberfeld George McBride UER	45.00	20.00	5.50
☐ 20 Cy Falkenberg Nap Lajoie	200.00	90.00	25.00
☐ 21 E.Fitzpatrick Ed Killian	45.00	20.00	5.50
☐ 22 Larry Gardner Tris Speaker	175.00	80.00	22.00
☐ 23 George Gibson Tommy Leach	45.00	20.00	5.50
☐ 24 Peaches Graham Al Mattern	45.00	20.00	5.50
☐ 25 Arnold Hauser Johnny Lush	45.00	20.00	5.50
☐ 26 Buck Herzog Dots Miller	45.00	20.00	5.50
☐ 27 Harry Hinchman Charles Hickman	45.00	20.00	5.50
☐ 28 Solly Hofman Mordecai Brown	100.00	45.00	12.50
☐ 29 Hugh Jennings Ed Summers	90.00	40.00	11.00
☐ 30 Otis Johnson Russ Ford	45.00	20.00	5.50
☐ 31 Tom McCarty Joe McGinnity	90.00	40.00	11.00
☐ 32 Ulysses McGlyn Jimmy Barrett	45.00	20.00	5.50
☐ 33 Larry McLean Eddie Grant	45.00	20.00	5.50
☐ 34 Fred Merkle Hooks Wiltse	45.00	20.00	5.50
☐ 35 Chief Meyers Larry Doyle	45.00	20.00	5.50
☐ 36 Earl Moore Hans Lobert	45.00	20.00	5.50
☐ 37 Fred Odwell Red Downs	45.00	20.00	5.50
☐ 38 Rube Oldring Chief Bender	100.00	45.00	12.50
☐ 39 Fred Payne Ed Walsh	90.00	40.00	11.00
☐ 40 Michael Simon Lefty Leifield	45.00	20.00	5.50
☐ 41 Charles Starr James McCabe	45.00	20.00	5.50
☐ 42 James Stephens Frank LaPorte	45.00	20.00	5.50
☐ 43 George Stovall Terry Turner	45.00	20.00	5.50
☐ 44 Gabby Street Walter Johnson	500.00	220.00	60.00
☐ 45 Ralph Stroud Bill Donovan	45.00	20.00	5.50
☐ 46 Ed Sweeney Hal Chase	45.00	20.00	5.50
☐ 47 Johny Thoney Eddie Cicotte	90.00	40.00	11.00
☐ 48 Bobby Wallace Joe Lake	90.00	40.00	11.00
☐ 49 Joseph Ward Edward Foster	45.00	20.00	5.50
☐ 50 O.Williams Sam Woodruff	45.00	20.00	5.50

1992 Megacards Ruth

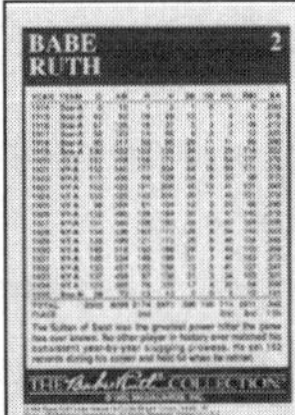

Released by Megacards, the 1992 Babe Ruth Collection consists of 165 standard-size cards, including a card for every year of his career. The cards are very similar to the Conlon sets produced in conjunction with The Sporting News. The cards were sold in both ten-card packs and 22-card blister packs. Complete sets were also available in a commemorative tin. The fronts display glossy black and white, action and portrait shots inside a white picture frame on a black card face. Captions to the pictures and the year appear in the bottom black border. The backs carry biography, statistics, highlights, or career summary. The set is arranged as follows: Babe Ruth (1-4), Year in Review (5-29), World Series (30-39), Place in History (40-70), Career Highlights (71-97), Trivia (98-104), Sultan of SWAT (105-115), The Bambino-The Man (116-142), and Being Remembered (143-163). The set concludes with checklist cards (164-165). The set could also be purchased in a special commemorative tin.

	MINT	NRMT	EXC
COMPLETE SET (165)	18.00	8.00	2.20
COMMON CARD (1-165)	.15	.07	.02
☐ 1 Babe Ruth Lifetime Pitching Statistics 1916	.35	.16	.04
☐ 2 Babe Ruth Lifetime Batting Statistics 1925	.15	.07	.02
☐ 3 Babe Ruth Lifetime-World Series Pitching 1916	.15	.07	.02
☐ 4 Babe Ruth Lifetime World Series Batting 1926	.15	.07	.02
☐ 5 Babe Ruth 22-9 Record in the Minors 1914	.15	.07	.02
☐ 6 Babe Ruth 2-1 Record First Year in Majors 1914	.15	.07	.02
☐ 7 Babe Ruth Won 17 of His Last 21 Decisions 1915	.15	.07	.02
☐ 8 Babe Ruth Led League with 1.75 ERA and 9 Shutouts 1916	.15	.07	.02
☐ 9 Babe Ruth Defeats Walter Johnson for 6th Time	.25	.11	.03

Card	MINT	NRMT	EXC
1917			
☐ 10 Babe Ruth	.15	.07	.02
Doubles as Pitcher and a Regular 1918			
☐ 11 Babe Ruth	.15	.07	.02
First Season in the Outfield 1919			
☐ 12 Babe Ruth	.15	.07	.02
Sold to Yankees for $100,000 1920			
☐ 13 Babe Ruth	.15	.07	.02
The Best Year Any Batter Ever Had 1921			
☐ 14 Babe Ruth	.15	.07	.02
Suspended for First 38 Games 1922			
☐ 15 Babe Ruth	.15	.07	.02
Wins American League MVP 1923			
☐ 16 Babe Ruth	.15	.07	.02
Wins Only Batting Title .378 1924			
☐ 17 Babe Ruth	.15	.07	.02
The Million Dollar Stomach Ache 1925			
☐ 18 Babe Ruth	.15	.07	.02
Bats .372 With a .737 SA 1926			
☐ 19 Babe Ruth	.15	.07	.02
The Best Baseball Team in History 1927			
☐ 20 Babe Ruth	.15	.07	.02
Tops 50 Home Runs 4th Time 1928			
☐ 21 Babe Ruth	.15	.07	.02
Clubs 500th Home Run 1929			
☐ 22 Babe Ruth	.15	.07	.02
Barn Barns Nine in a Week 1930			
☐ 23 Babe Ruth	.15	.07	.02
.700 Slugging Average for 9th Time 1931			
☐ 24 Babe Ruth	.15	.07	.02
Blasts Over 40 Homers for 11th Time 1932			
☐ 25 Babe Ruth	.15	.07	.02
Over 100 RBIs for 13th Time 1933			
☐ 26 Babe Ruth	.15	.07	.02
Tops 2,000 Career Walks 1934			
☐ 27 Babe Ruth	.15	.07	.02
Retires 1935			
☐ 28 Babe Ruth	.15	.07	.02
Coaches the Dodgers 1938			
☐ 29 Babe Ruth	.15	.07	.02
in Retirement 1942			
☐ 30 Babe Ruth	.15	.07	.02
Warms Bench after 18-8 Season 1915			
☐ 31 Babe Ruth	.15	.07	.02
Hurls 14 Inning Complete Game Gem 1916			
☐ 32 Babe Ruth	.15	.07	.02
Scoreless Inning Streak Soars 1918			
☐ 33 Babe Ruth	.15	.07	.02
Yankees Play in Their First World Series 1921			
☐ 34 Babe Ruth	.15	.07	.02
Goes Back to the Farm 1922			
☐ 35 Babe Ruth	.15	.07	.02
Yanks Win First World Championship 1923			
☐ 36 Babe Ruth	.15	.07	.02
Belts 4 Home Runs in Losing Cause 1926			
☐ 37 Babe Ruth	.15	.07	.02
Yanks Destroy Bucs in Four Games 1927			
☐ 38 Babe Ruth	.15	.07	.02
.625 BA and 1.375 SA 1928			
☐ 39 Babe Ruth	.15	.07	.02
Yanks Sweep Cubs 1932			
☐ 40 Babe Ruth	.15	.07	.02
Lifetime-2,056 Walks 1923			
☐ 41 Babe Ruth	.15	.07	.02
First to Fan 1,000 Times 1929			
☐ 42 Babe Ruth	.15	.07	.02
Lifetime-2,174 Runs Scored 1928			
☐ 43 Babe Ruth	.15	.07	.02
Lifetime-5,793 Total Bases 1942			
☐ 44 Babe Ruth	.15	.07	.02
Lifetime-1,356 Extra Base Hits 1928			
☐ 45 Babe Ruth	.15	.07	.02
Lifetime 714 Home Runs 1935			
☐ 46 Babe Ruth	.15	.07	.02
Lifetime 16 Grand Slams 1926			
☐ 47 Babe Ruth	.15	.07	.02
Lifetime 8.5 Home Run Percentage 1934			
☐ 48 Babe Ruth	.15	.07	.02
Lifetime Most Games 2 or More Home Runs 1927			
☐ 49 Babe Ruth	.15	.07	.02
Lifetime-11 Seasons with 40 or more HRs 1924			
☐ 50 Babe Ruth	.15	.07	.02
Lifetime-2,211 RBIs			
☐ 51 Babe Ruth	.15	.07	.02
Lifetime-.342 BA 1928			
☐ 52 Babe Ruth	.15	.07	.02
Lifetime-.690 SA 1934			
☐ 53 Babe Ruth	.15	.07	.02
Season-9 Shutouts 1916			
☐ 54 Babe Ruth	.15	.07	.02
Season-170 Walks 1930			
☐ 55 Babe Ruth	.15	.07	.02
Season-177 Runs Scored 1939			
☐ 56 Babe Ruth	.15	.07	.02
Season-.545 On-Base Percentage 1926			
☐ 57 Babe Ruth	.15	.07	.02
Season-457 Total Bases 1926			
☐ 58 Babe Ruth	.15	.07	.02
Season-119 Extra Base Hits 1947			
☐ 59 Babe Ruth	.15	.07	.02
Season 171 RBI's 1934			
☐ 60 Babe Ruth	.15	.07	.02
Season-60 Home Runs 1927			
☐ 61 Babe Ruth	.15	.07	.02
Season-11.8 Home Run Percentage 1921			
☐ 62 Babe Ruth	.15	.07	.02
Season-.847 SA 1920			
☐ 63 Babe Ruth	.15	.07	.02
World Series-3-0 Record 1915			
☐ 64 Babe Ruth	.15	.07	.02
World Series-0.87 ERA 1918			
☐ 65 Babe Ruth	.15	.07	.02
World Series-33 Walks 1928			
☐ 66 Babe Ruth	.15	.07	.02
World Series-37 Runs 1928			
☐ 67 Babe Ruth	.15	.07	.02
World Series-96 Total Bases 1923			
☐ 68 Babe Ruth	.15	.07	.02
World Series-15 Home Runs 1923			
☐ 69 Babe Ruth	.15	.07	.02
World Series-33 RBIs 1929			
☐ 70 Babe Ruth	.15	.07	.02
World Series- .744SA 1927			
☐ 71 Babe Ruth	.15	.07	.02
First Major League Victory July 11, 1914			
☐ 72 Babe Ruth	.15	.07	.02
First Major League Home Run May 6, 1915			
☐ 73 Babe Ruth	.15	.07	.02
Babe Derails Big Train 1942			
☐ 74 Babe Ruth	.15	.07	.02
Leads AL in Fielding 1928			
☐ 75 Babe Ruth	.15	.07	.02
First Home Run Record-29 1919			
☐ 76 Babe Ruth	.15	.07	.02
Becomes a Yankee 1920			
☐ 77 Babe Ruth	.15	.07	.02
First Home Run in Yankee Stadium 1923			
☐ 78 Babe Ruth	.15	.07	.02
Wins American League MVP 1923			
☐ 79 Babe Ruth	.15	.07	.02
Wins Only Batting Title 1924			
☐ 80 Babe Ruth	.15	.07	.02
Hits 3 Home Runs in Series Game October 6, 1926			
☐ 81 Babe Ruth	.75	.35	.09
Lou Gehrig Smack 107 Home Runs 1927			
☐ 82 Babe Ruth	.25	.11	.03
60th Home Run: September 30, 1927			
☐ 83 Babe Ruth	.15	.07	.02
3 Home Runs in WS Game 1928			
☐ 84 Babe Ruth	.15	.07	.02
Early Called Shots 1932			
☐ 85 Babe Ruth	.15	.07	.02
The Called Shot The Legend 1932			
☐ 86 Babe Ruth	.15	.07	.02
The Called Shot The Believers 1932			
☐ 87 Babe Ruth	.15	.07	.02
The Called Shot The Doubters 1948			
☐ 88 Babe Ruth	.15	.07	.02
The Called Shot Babe's View 1936			
☐ 89 Babe Ruth	.15	.07	.02
Slams First HR in First AS Game 1933			
☐ 90 Babe Ruth	.15	.07	.02
Last Time on the Mound 1933			
☐ 91 Babe Ruth	.15	.07	.02
Hits 700th Home Run 1934			
☐ 92 Babe Ruth	.25	.11	.03
Banzai Beibu Russu- In Japan 1934			
☐ 93 Babe Ruth	.15	.07	.02
Last Major League Homers 1935			
☐ 94 Babe Ruth	.15	.07	.02
Inaugurated Into HOF 1939			
☐ 95 Babe Ruth	.25	.11	.03
Faces Walter Johnson Again August 23, 1942			
☐ 96 Babe Ruth Day	.25	.11	.03
April 27, 1947			
☐ 97 Babe Ruth	.25	.11	.03
Farewell 1948			
☐ 98 Babe Ruth	.15	.07	.02
A Perfect Punch 1915			
☐ 99 Babe Ruth	.15	.07	.02
Yankees Best Base Thief 1920			
☐ 100 Hub Pruett	.15	.07	.02
Babe Buster 1929			
☐ 101 Babe Ruth	.15	.07	.02
Caught Stealing to End Series 1926			
☐ 102 Babe Ruth	.15	.07	.02
Never Won a Triple Crown 1926			
☐ 103 Babe Ruth	.15	.07	.02
Used a 54-Ounce Bat 1926			
☐ 104 Babe Ruth	.15	.07	.02
Bats Righty 1923			
☐ 105 Babe Ruth	.15	.07	.02
Greatness 1921			
☐ 106 Babe Ruth	.15	.07	.02
Best 1942			
☐ 107 Babe Ruth	.15	.07	.02
Outslugged Entire Teams 1923			
☐ 108 Babe Ruth	.15	.07	.02
First to Hit 30, 40 50 and 60 Home Runs 1923			
☐ 109 Babe Ruth	.15	.07	.02
The Pitkin Study 1926			
☐ 110 Babe Ruth	.15	.07	.02
First to Put the Ball into Orbit 1926			
☐ 111 Babe Ruth	.15	.07	.02
Afraid to Kill Somebody 1926			
☐ 112 Babe Ruth	.15	.07	.02
The Wonder Years 1926-1931 1927			
☐ 113 Babe Ruth	.15	.07	.02
Hit .422 with 7 HR's on Opening Days 1931			
☐ 114 Babe Ruth	.15	.07	.02
at Bat 1932			
☐ 115 Babe Ruth	.15	.07	.02
Greatest Ballplayer the Game Has Known 1942			
☐ 116 Babe Ruth	.15	.07	.02
Early Childhood			
☐ 117 Babe Ruth	.15	.07	.02
St. Mary's Industrial School 1911			
☐ 118 Babe Ruth	.15	.07	.02
Brother Matthias			
☐ 119 Babe Ruth	.15	.07	.02
Nicknames			
☐ 120 Babe Ruth	.15	.07	.02
First Wife Helen			
☐ 121 Babe's Ruth	.15	.07	.02
Second Wife Claire Ruth			
☐ 122 Babe Ruth	.35	.16	.04
Lou Gehrig Appreciation Day July 4, 1939			
☐ 123 Babe Ruth	.25	.11	.03
Friendship with Herb Pennock 1921			
☐ 124 Babe Ruth	.25	.11	.03
Miller Huggins			
☐ 125 Babe Ruth	.60	.25	.07
Ty Cobb			
☐ 126 Babe Ruth	.35	.16	.04
Walter Johnson 1942			
☐ 127 Babe Ruth	.15	.07	.02
Baseball's Greatest Drawing Card 1923			
☐ 128 Babe Ruth	.15	.07	.02
Barnstorming			
☐ 129 Babe Ruth	.15	.07	.02
Costly Confrontations 1925			
☐ 130 Babe Ruth	.15	.07	.02
He Often Played Hurt			
☐ 131 Babe Ruth	.15	.07	.02
Big Bucks 1927			
☐ 132 Babe Ruth	.15	.07	.02
Wanted to be a Manager			
☐ 133 Babe Ruth	.15	.07	.02
on the Links			
☐ 134 Babe Ruth	.15	.07	.02
in the Movies			
☐ 135 Babe Ruth	.15	.07	.02
Contributes to War Effort			
☐ 136 Babe Ruth	.15	.07	.02
Peace Negotiator			
☐ 137 Babe Ruth	.15	.07	.02
Everyone Loved the Babe			
☐ 138 Babe Ruth	.15	.07	.02
He Brought Children Joy 1929			
☐ 139 Babe Ruth	.15	.07	.02
Always Had Time for Kids			
☐ 140 Babe Ruth	.25	.11	.03
The Johnny Sylvester Story			
☐ 141 Babe Ruth	.15	.07	.02
Moving with the Great 1923			
☐ 142 Babe Ruth	.15	.07	.02
and The American Dream 1923			
☐ 143 Babe Ruth	.15	.07	.02
Remembered by Bill James 1928			
☐ 144 Babe Ruth	.15	.07	.02
Remembered by Bill James 1929			
☐ 145 Babe Ruth	.15	.07	.02
Remembered by Bill James 1920			
☐ 146 Babe Ruth	.15	.07	.02
Remembered by Mel Allen 1923			
☐ 147 Babe Ruth	.15	.07	.02
Remembered by Mel Allen 1928			
☐ 148 Babe Ruth	.15	.07	.02
Remembered by Wes Ferrell 1930			
☐ 149 Babe Ruth	.35	.16	.04
Remembered by George Bush 1948			
☐ 150 Babe Ruth	.15	.07	.02
Remembered by Ethan Allen 1948			
☐ 151 Babe Ruth	.15	.07	.02
Remembered by Daughter Dorothy 1926			
☐ 152 Babe Ruth	.15	.07	.02
Remembered by Daughter Julia 1947			
☐ 153 Babe Ruth	.15	.07	.02
Remembered by Daughter Julia 1938			
☐ 154 Babe Ruth	.15	.07	.02
Remembered by Mark Koenig 1927			
☐ 155 Babe Ruth	.15	.07	.02
Remembered by Donald Honig 1927			
☐ 156 Babe Ruth	.15	.07	.02
Remembered by Lloyd Waner and Waite Hoyt 1948			
☐ 157 Babe Ruth	.15	.07	.02
Remembered by Waite Hoyt 1938			
☐ 158 Babe Ruth	.25	.11	.03
Remembered by Bill Dickey 1938			
☐ 159 Babe Ruth	.15	.07	.02
Remembered by Bob Meusel 1922			
☐ 160 Babe Ruth	.15	.07	.02
Remembered by Jim Chapman 1941			
☐ 161 Babe Ruth	.15	.07	.02
Remembered by Christy Walsh 1926			
☐ 162 Babe Ruth	.15	.07	.02
Being Remembered Heading for Home The Babe Passes Away			
☐ 163 Babe Ruth	.15	.07	.02
Remembered by Grantland Rice 1923			
☐ 164 Checklist 1-83	.15	.07	.02
☐ 165 Checklist 84-165	.15	.07	.02

1992 Megacards Ruth Prototypes

Nine prototypes were produced to preview Megacards 1992 Babe Ruth Collection. The cards are very similar to the Conlon sets produced in conjunction with The Sporting News. The cards are standard size. These cards were clearly marked as prototypes, and the bulk of the 12,000 cards produced were included in mailings to hobby dealers. In general, some subtle differences in photos are found with some of the prototype cards.

	MINT	NRMT	EXC
COMPLETE SET (9)	25.00	11.00	3.10
COMMON CARD	3.00	1.35	.35
☐ 14 Babe Ruth	3.00	1.35	.35
Year in Review-1921 Best year any batter ever had			
☐ 31 Babe Ruth	3.00	1.35	.35
World Series-1916 Red Sox defeat Dodgers 4 games to 1			
☐ 75 Babe Ruth	3.00	1.35	.35
Place in History-1928 .342 lifetime batting average			
☐ 106 Babe Ruth	3.00	1.35	.35
Career Highlights Babe's 60th home run September 30th, 1927			
☐ 124 Babe Ruth	3.00	1.35	.35
Trivia-1926 He "did something rash"			
☐ 129 Babe Ruth	3.00	1.35	.35
Sultan of Swat-1925 First to hit 30, 40,			

50 and 60 home runs			
☐ 134 Babe Ruth	3.00	1.35	.35
Remembered-1948 by George Bush			
☐ 138 Babe Ruth	3.00	1.35	.35
Remembered-1923 by Grantland Rice			
☐ 154 Babe Ruth	3.00	1.35	.35
The Bambino-The Man			
Lou Gehrig			
Appreciation Day: July 4th, 1939			

1994 Megacards Ruthian Shots

Produced by Megacards and titled "Ruthian Shots," this five-card standard-size set was given away at card shows when the collector purchased a 1994 Conlon Collection wax box. The fronts carry full-bleed black-and-white photos of Ruth, capturing different aspects of his career and life. A white panel on the back contains a running commentary on the picture. The cards are numbered on the back in the upper right corner in a baseball icon.

	MINT	NRMT	EXC
COMPLETE SET (5)	10.00	4.50	1.25
COMMON CARD (1-5)	2.00	.90	.25
☐ 1 Babe Ruth	3.00	1.35	.35
Pitcher for the			
Boston Red Sox			
☐ 2 Babe Ruth	2.00	.90	.25
At his farm in overalls			
☐ 3 Babe Ruth	4.00	1.80	.50
Lou Gehrig			
Fishing			
☐ 4 Babe Ruth	2.00	.90	.25
Dressed in suit with			
Vote for Al Smith			
badge on lapel			
☐ 5 Babe Ruth	2.00	.90	.25
Miller Huggins MG			
Together in car			

1995 Megacards Griffey Jr. Wish List

In this 25-card standard-size set, Ken Griffey Jr. shares his personal thoughts about the game, his dreams for the future and his commitment to terminally ill and underprivileged children. The suggested retail price for each set was $9.99. The fronts feature full-bleed color action photos accented by gold foil. On a ghosted color photo, the backs present appealing stories and statistics, including a look in the future by baseball historian and statistician, Bill James. Just 100,000 sets were produced, with a percentage of all proceeds to benefit the Make-A-Wish Foundation. A sweepstakes card inside each pack entitled the collector to be entered in a chance drawing of 500 autographed collectibles (including 5 jerseys, 10 bats, 60 balls and 425 cards from this set). Also included in each set was one of three limited edition (34,000) Ken Griffey Jr. MegaCaps.

	MINT	NRMT	EXC
COMPLETE SET (25)	10.00	4.50	1.25
COMMON CARD (1-25)	.50	.23	.06
☐ 1 Introduction	.50	.23	.06
☐ 2 Ken Griffey	.50	.23	.06
Make-a-Wish Foundation			
☐ 3 Ken Griffey	.50	.23	.06
KG Wishes to play with Dad			
☐ 4 Ken Griffey	.50	.23	.06
Wishes to be the best I can be			
☐ 5 Ken Griffey	.50	.23	.06
Wishes to Make the Majors			
☐ 6 Ken Griffey	.50	.23	.06
Wishes to Play for a Winner			
☐ 7 Ken Griffey	.50	.23	.06
Wishes to Assist B.A.T.			
☐ 8 Ken Griffey	.50	.23	.06
Wishes To Improve Inner City BB			
☐ 9 Ken Griffey	.50	.23	.06
Wishes To Live for Those Around You			
☐ 10 Ken Griffey	.50	.23	.06
Wishes to be an All Around Player			
☐ 11 Ken Griffey	.50	.23	.06
Wishes to be #1 in the Draft			
☐ 12 Ken Griffey	.50	.23	.06
Wishes All-time All-Star			
☐ 13 Ken Griffey	.50	.23	.06
Wishes to Win the Gold			
☐ 14 Ken Griffey	.50	.23	.06
Wishes: Most HRs by a Father/Son Combo			
☐ 15 Ken Griffey	.50	.23	.06
Bill James explanation of Projections			
☐ 16 Ken Griffey	.50	.23	.06
Projected Career Record			
☐ 17 Ken Griffey	.50	.23	.06
Projected Career Games			
☐ 18 Ken Griffey	.50	.23	.06
Projected Career Runs			
☐ 19 Ken Griffey	.50	.23	.06
Projected Lifetime Hits			
☐ 20 Ken Griffey	.50	.23	.06
Projected Career Doubles			
☐ 21 Ken Griffey	.50	.23	.06
Projected All-Time Home Run Ranking			
☐ 22 Ken Griffey	.50	.23	.06
Projected Career RBIs			
☐ 23 Ken Griffey	.50	.23	.06
Projected Extra Base Hits			
☐ 24 Ken Griffey	.50	.23	.06
Projected Most Years			
hitting 40 or more			
☐ 25 Ken Griffey	.50	.23	.06
Projected Career Grand Slams			
☐ XX Ken Griffey AU	200.00	90.00	25.00

1995 Megacards Ruth

This 25-card standard-size set offers classic glimpses and new insights into Babe Ruth. Twenty-one cards are in black-and-white, while four cards feature computer-enhanced color (11-12, 21, 24). The suggested retail price for each set was 9.99. All card fronts carry the Babe Ruth 100th Anniversary logo in gold foil. One hundred thousand sets were produced. Each set included an official entry blank to a sweepstakes featuring the following prizes: 1 Babe Ruth autographed ball, 200 Don Mattingly autographed cards, 200 Ken Griffey Jr. autographed cards and 100 Babe Ruth 165-card sets. Also included in each set was one of three limited edition (34,000) Babe Ruth Megacaps.

	MINT	NRMT	EXC
COMPLETE SET (25)	10.00	4.50	1.25
COMMON CARD (1-25)	.40	.18	.05
☐ 1 Babe Ruth	.40	.18	.05
Baseball's Greatest Ever?			
☐ 2 Babe Ruth	.40	.18	.05
60-Home Run Club			
☐ 3 Jimmie Foxx	.75	.35	.09
Babe Ruth			
Lou Gehrig			
Al Simmons			
No Slugger Comes Close			
☐ 4 Babe Ruth	.40	.18	.05
History's Most Frequent			
Home Run Threat			
☐ 5 Babe Ruth	.40	.18	.05
Bill Dickey			
Ray Hayworth			
He Knew the Way Home			
☐ 6 Babe Ruth	1.00	.45	.12
Lou Gehrig			
He Didn't Leave Them Stranded			
☐ 7 Babe Ruth	.40	.18	.05
50-Home Run King			
☐ 8 Babe Ruth	.40	.18	.05
Long Ball Legend			
☐ 9 Lloyd Waner	.75	.35	.09
Babe Ruth			
Paul Waner			
Lou Gehrig			
.342 Plus Power			
☐ 10 Babe Ruth	.40	.18	.05
No One Hit 'em More Often			
☐ 11 Babe Ruth	.40	.18	.05
Greatest Pitching Prospect			
Color			
☐ 12 Babe Ruth	1.50	.70	.19
Lou Gehrig			
Career Year			
Color			
☐ 13 Babe Ruth	1.00	.45	.12
Don Mattingly			
Lou Gehrig			
Mr. Yankee			
☐ 14 Babe and "The Kid"	1.50	.70	.19
Babe Ruth			
Ken Griffey Jr.			
☐ 15 Babe Ruth	.40	.18	.05
Everyone Loved the Babe			
☐ 16 Babe Ruth	.40	.18	.05
Played Hurt			
☐ 17 Babe Ruth	.40	.18	.05
He Did It His Way			
☐ 18 Babe Ruth	.60	.25	.07
Miller Huggins MG			
The Rewards of Greatness			
☐ 19 Babe Ruth	.40	.18	.05
and Today's Rules			
☐ 20 Babe Ruth	.40	.18	.05
in Today's Ballparks			
☐ 21 Babe Ruth	1.50	.70	.19
Ken Griffey Jr.			
Babe and Today's Best			
Color			
☐ 22 Babe Ruth	.40	.18	.05
Vs. Today's Pitching			
☐ 23 Babe Ruth	.40	.18	.05
and Father Time			
☐ 24 Dizzy Dean	.60	.25	.07
Frankie Frisch			
Babe Ruth			
Mickey Cochrane			
Schoolboy Rowe			
How He Changed the Game			
Color			
☐ 25 Babe Ruth	.40	.18	.05
Will There Be Another Babe			

1910 Mello Mints E105

The cards in this 50-card set measure 1 1/2" by 2 3/4". The cards were manufactured by the Texas Gum Company. The cards themselves are unnumbered and the fronts are identical to these found in E92. Printed on paper, the backs are horizontally aligned and carry advertising for "Smith's Mello-Mint". The set was issued about 1910. The cards have been alphabetized and numbered in the checklist below. The complete set price includes all variation cards listed in the checklist below.

	EX-MT	VG-E	GOOD
COMPLETE SET (50)	12500.00	5600.00	1600.00
COMMON CARD (1-46)	125.00	55.00	15.50
☐ 1 Jack Barry	125.00	55.00	15.50
☐ 2 Harry Bemis	125.00	55.00	15.50
☐ 3A Chief Bender	300.00	135.00	38.00
(blue background)			
☐ 3B Chief Bender	300.00	135.00	38.00
(green background)			
☐ 4 Bill Bergen	125.00	55.00	15.50
☐ 5 Bob Bescher	125.00	55.00	15.50
☐ 6 Al Bridwell	125.00	55.00	15.50
☐ 7 Doc Casey	125.00	55.00	15.50
☐ 8 Frank Chance	350.00	160.00	45.00
☐ 9 Hal Chase	175.00	80.00	22.00
☐ 10 Ty Cobb	3000.00	1350.00	375.00
☐ 11 Eddie Collins	350.00	160.00	45.00
☐ 12 Sam Crawford	300.00	135.00	38.00
☐ 13 Harry Davis	125.00	55.00	15.50
☐ 14 Art Devlin	125.00	55.00	15.50
☐ 15 Bill Donovan	125.00	55.00	15.50
☐ 16 Red Dooin	125.00	55.00	15.50
☐ 17 Mickey Doolan	125.00	55.00	15.50
☐ 18 Patsy Dougherty	125.00	55.00	15.50
☐ 19A Larry Doyle	125.00	55.00	15.50
batting			
☐ 19B Larry Doyle	125.00	55.00	15.50
throwing			
☐ 20 Johnny Evers	300.00	135.00	38.00
☐ 21 George Gibson	125.00	55.00	15.50
☐ 22 Topsy Hartsel	125.00	55.00	15.50
☐ 23 Fred Jacklitsch	125.00	55.00	15.50
☐ 24 Hugh Jennings	300.00	135.00	38.00
☐ 25 Red Kleinow	125.00	55.00	15.50
☐ 26 Otto Knabe	125.00	55.00	15.50
☐ 27 John Knight	125.00	55.00	15.50
☐ 28 Nap Lajoie	600.00	275.00	75.00
☐ 29 Hans Lobert	125.00	55.00	15.50
☐ 30 Sherry Magee	125.00	55.00	15.50
☐ 31 Christy Mathewson	800.00	350.00	100.00
☐ 32 John McGraw MG	400.00	180.00	50.00
☐ 33 Larry McLean	125.00	55.00	15.50
☐ 34A Dots Miller	125.00	55.00	15.50
batting			
☐ 34B Dots Miller	125.00	55.00	15.50
fielding			
☐ 35 Danny Murphy	125.00	55.00	15.50
☐ 36 William O'Hara	125.00	55.00	15.50
☐ 37 Germany Schaefer	125.00	55.00	15.50
☐ 38 George Schlei	125.00	55.00	15.50
☐ 39 Charles Schmidt	125.00	55.00	15.50
☐ 40 Johnny Seigle	125.00	55.00	15.50
☐ 41 David Shean	125.00	55.00	15.50
☐ 42 Smith	125.00	55.00	15.50
☐ 43 Joe Tinker	300.00	135.00	38.00
☐ 44A Honus Wagner	1200.00	550.00	150.00
batting			
☐ 44B Honus Wagner	1200.00	550.00	150.00
throwing			
☐ 45 Cy Young	600.00	275.00	75.00
☐ 46 Heinie Zimmerman	125.00	55.00	15.50

1996 Metal Universe Promo Sheet

This set consists of one sheet picturing samples of nine cards. The front features color action player photos of nine different players each on a different metallic background. The back carries color portraits of the same players with biographical and statistical information. The words, "Promotional Sample," are stamped diagonally on both the front and back of each player's card. The cards are numbered below according to their numbers in the regular set.

	MINT	NRMT	EXC
COMPLETE SET (9)	5.00	2.20	.60
COMMON CARD	.25	.11	.03
☐ 28 Todd Greene	.25	.11	.03
☐ 67 Jon Nunnally	.25	.11	.03
☐ 81 Brad Radke	.25	.11	.03
☐ 90 Don Mattingly	1.00	.45	.12
☐ 110 Alex Rodriguez	2.00	.90	.25
☐ 116 Ivan Rodriguez	.75	.35	.09
☐ 129 Chipper Jones	1.50	.70	.19
☐ 183 Eric Karros	.50	.23	.06
☐ 216 Jeff King	.25	.11	.03

1996 Metal Universe

The Fleer Metal Universe set was issued in one series totalling 250 standard-size cards. The cards were issued in foil-wrapped packs. The theme for the set was based on intermingling fantasy comic book elements with baseball, thus each card features a player set against a wide variety of bizarre backgrounds. The cards are grouped alphabetically within teams below.

	MINT	NRMT	EXC
COMPLETE SET (250)	40.00	18.00	5.00
COMMON CARD (1-250)	.10	.05	.01
☐ 1 Roberto Alomar	.60	.25	.07
☐ 2 Brady Anderson	.50	.23	.06
☐ 3 Bobby Bonilla	.25	.11	.03
☐ 4 Chris Hoiles	.10	.05	.01
☐ 5 Ben McDonald	.10	.05	.01
☐ 6 Mike Mussina	.60	.25	.07
☐ 7 Randy Myers	.10	.05	.01
☐ 8 Rafael Palmeiro	.50	.23	.06
☐ 9 Cal Ripken	2.50	1.10	.30
☐ 10 B.J. Surhoff	.10	.05	.01
☐ 11 Luis Alicea	.10	.05	.01
☐ 12 Jose Canseco	.50	.23	.06
☐ 13 Roger Clemens	.60	.25	.07
☐ 14 Wil Cordero	.10	.05	.01
☐ 15 Tom Gordon	.10	.05	.01
☐ 16 Mike Greenwall	.10	.05	.01
☐ 17 Tim Naehring	.10	.05	.01
☐ 18 Troy O'Leary	.10	.05	.01
☐ 19 Mike Stanley	.10	.05	.01
☐ 20 John Valentin	.25	.11	.03
☐ 21 Mo Vaughn	.75	.35	.09
☐ 22 Tim Wakefield	.10	.05	.01
☐ 23 Garret Anderson	.50	.23	.06
☐ 24 Chili Davis	.10	.05	.01
☐ 25 Gary DiSarcina	.10	.05	.01
☐ 26 Jim Edmonds	.25	.11	.03
☐ 27 Chuck Finley	.10	.05	.01
☐ 28 Todd Greene	.10	.05	.01
☐ 29 Mark Langston	.10	.05	.01
☐ 30 Troy Percival	.10	.05	.01
☐ 31 Tony Phillips	.25	.11	.03
☐ 32 Tim Salmon	.50	.23	.06
☐ 33 Lee Smith	.25	.11	.03
☐ 34 J.T. Snow	.25	.11	.03
☐ 35 Ray Durham	.50	.23	.06

☐ 36 Alex Fernandez .25 .11 .03
☐ 37 Ozzie Guillen .10 .05 .01
☐ 38 Roberto Hernandez .25 .11 .03
☐ 39 Lyle Mouton .10 .05 .01
☐ 40 Frank Thomas 3.00 1.35 .35
☐ 41 Robin Ventura .25 .11 .03
☐ 42 Sandy Alomar, Jr. .10 .05 .01
☐ 43 Carlos Baerga .10 .05 .01
☐ 44 Albert Belle 1.25 .55 .16
☐ 45 Orel Hershiser .25 .11 .03
☐ 46 Kenny Lofton .75 .35 .09
☐ 47 Dennis Martinez .25 .11 .03
☐ 48 Jack McDowell .50 .23 .06
☐ 49 Jose Mesa .25 .11 .03
☐ 50 Eddie Murray .75 .35 .09
☐ 51 Charles Nagy .25 .11 .03
☐ 52 Manny Ramirez .75 .35 .09
☐ 53 Julian Tavarez .10 .05 .01
☐ 54 Jim Thome .60 .25 .07
☐ 55 Omar Vizquel .25 .11 .03
☐ 56 Chad Curtis .10 .05 .01
☐ 57 Cecil Fielder .25 .11 .03
☐ 58 John Flaherty .10 .05 .01
☐ 59 Travis Fryman .25 .11 .03
☐ 60 Chris Gomez .10 .05 .01
☐ 61 Felipe Lira .10 .05 .01
☐ 62 Kevin Appier .25 .11 .03
☐ 63 Johnny Damon .25 .11 .03
☐ 64 Tom Goodwin .10 .05 .01
☐ 65 Mark Gubicza .10 .05 .01
☐ 66 Jeff Montgomery .10 .05 .01
☐ 67 Jon Nunnally .10 .05 .01
☐ 68 Ricky Bones .10 .05 .01
☐ 69 Jeff Cirillo .10 .05 .01
☐ 70 John Jaha .25 .11 .03
☐ 71 Dave Nilsson .25 .11 .03
☐ 72 Joe Oliver .10 .05 .01
☐ 73 Kevin Seitzer .10 .05 .01
☐ 74 Greg Vaughn .50 .23 .06
☐ 75 Marty Cordova .25 .11 .03
☐ 76 Chuck Knoblauch .50 .23 .06
☐ 77 Pat Meares .10 .05 .01
☐ 78 Paul Molitor .60 .25 .07
☐ 79 Pedro Munoz .10 .05 .01
☐ 80 Kirby Puckett 1.25 .55 .16
☐ 81 Brad Radke .10 .05 .01
☐ 82 Scott Stahoviak .10 .05 .01
☐ 83 Matt Walbeck .10 .05 .01
☐ 84 Wade Boggs .50 .23 .06
☐ 85 David Cone .25 .11 .03
☐ 86 Joe Girardi .10 .05 .01
☐ 87 Derek Jeter 2.00 .90 .25
☐ 88 Jim Leyritz .10 .05 .01
☐ 89 Tino Martinez .50 .23 .06
☐ 90 Don Mattingly 1.50 .70 .19
☐ 91 Paul O'Neill .10 .05 .01
☐ 92 Andy Pettitte 1.00 .45 .12
☐ 93 Tim Raines .50 .23 .06
☐ 94 Kenny Rogers .10 .05 .01
☐ 95 Ruben Sierra .10 .05 .01
☐ 96 John Wetteland .25 .11 .03
☐ 97 Bernie Williams .60 .25 .07
☐ 98 Geronimo Berroa .25 .11 .03
☐ 99 Dennis Eckersley .50 .23 .06
☐ 100 Brent Gates .10 .05 .01
☐ 101 Mark McGwire 1.00 .45 .12
☐ 102 Steve Ontiveros .10 .05 .01
☐ 103 Terry Steinbach .25 .11 .03
☐ 104 Jay Buhner .50 .23 .06
☐ 105 Vince Coleman .10 .05 .01
☐ 106 Joey Cora .10 .05 .01
☐ 107 Ken Griffey, Jr. 3.00 1.35 .35
☐ 108 Randy Johnson .50 .23 .06
☐ 109 Edgar Martinez .25 .11 .03
☐ 110 Alex Rodriguez 3.00 1.35 .35
☐ 111 Paul Sorrento .10 .05 .01
☐ 112 Will Clark .50 .23 .06
☐ 113 Juan Gonzalez 1.50 .70 .19
☐ 114 Rusty Greer .50 .23 .06
☐ 115 Dean Palmer .50 .23 .06
☐ 116 Ivan Rodriguez .75 .35 .09
☐ 117 Mickey Tettleton .25 .11 .03
☐ 118 Joe Carter .25 .11 .03
☐ 119 Alex Gonzalez .10 .05 .01
☐ 120 Shawn Green .10 .05 .01
☐ 121 Erik Hanson .10 .05 .01
☐ 122 Pat Hentgen .25 .11 .03
☐ 123 Sandy Martinez .10 .05 .01
☐ 124 Otis Nixon .10 .05 .01
☐ 125 John Olerud .25 .11 .03
☐ 126 Steve Avery .10 .05 .01
☐ 127 Tom Glavine .50 .23 .06
☐ 128 Marquis Grissom .25 .11 .03
☐ 129 Chipper Jones 2.00 .90 .25
☐ 130 David Justice .50 .23 .06
☐ 131 Ryan Klesko .50 .23 .06
☐ 132 Mark Lemke .10 .05 .01
☐ 133 Javier Lopez .50 .23 .06
☐ 134 Greg Maddux 2.00 .90 .25
☐ 135 Fred McGriff .50 .23 .06
☐ 136 John Smoltz .50 .23 .06
☐ 137 Mark Wohlers .25 .11 .03
☐ 138 Frank Castillo .10 .05 .01
☐ 139 Shawon Dunston .10 .05 .01
☐ 140 Luis Gonzalez .10 .05 .01
☐ 141 Mark Grace .50 .23 .06
☐ 142 Brian McRae .10 .05 .01
☐ 143 Jaime Navarro .10 .05 .01
☐ 144 Rey Sanchez .10 .05 .01
☐ 145 Ryne Sandberg .75 .35 .09
☐ 146 Sammy Sosa .50 .23 .06
☐ 147 Bret Boone .10 .05 .01
☐ 148 Curtis Goodwin .10 .05 .01
☐ 149 Barry Larkin .50 .23 .06
☐ 150 Hal Morris .10 .05 .01
☐ 151 Reggie Sanders .25 .11 .03
☐ 152 Pete Schourek .25 .11 .03
☐ 153 John Smiley .10 .05 .01
☐ 154 Dante Bichette .50 .23 .06
☐ 155 Vinny Castilla .25 .11 .03
☐ 156 Andres Galarraga .50 .23 .06
☐ 157 Bret Saberhagen .10 .05 .01
☐ 158 Bill Swift .10 .05 .01
☐ 159 Larry Walker .50 .23 .06
☐ 160 Walt Weiss .10 .05 .01
☐ 161 Kurt Abbott .10 .05 .01
☐ 162 John Burkett .10 .05 .01
☐ 163 Greg Colbrunn .10 .05 .01
☐ 164 Jeff Conine .25 .11 .03
☐ 165 Chris Hammond .10 .05 .01
☐ 166 Charles Johnson .25 .11 .03
☐ 167 Al Leiter .10 .05 .01
☐ 168 Pat Rapp .10 .05 .01
☐ 169 Gary Sheffield .50 .23 .06
☐ 170 Quilvio Veras .10 .05 .01
☐ 171 Devon White .10 .05 .01
☐ 172 Jeff Bagwell 1.25 .55 .16
☐ 173 Derek Bell .25 .11 .03
☐ 174 Sean Berry .10 .05 .01
☐ 175 Craig Biggio .25 .11 .03
☐ 176 Doug Drabek .10 .05 .01
☐ 177 Tony Eusebio .10 .05 .01
☐ 178 Brian L.Hunter .25 .11 .03
☐ 179 Orlando Miller .10 .05 .01
☐ 180 Shane Reynolds .10 .05 .01
☐ 181 Mike Blowers .10 .05 .01
☐ 182 Roger Cedeno .10 .05 .01
☐ 183 Eric Karros .25 .11 .03
☐ 184 Ramon Martinez .25 .11 .03
☐ 185 Raul Mondesi .50 .23 .06
☐ 186 Hideo Nomo .75 .35 .09
☐ 187 Mike Piazza 2.00 .90 .25
☐ 188 Moises Alou .25 .11 .03
☐ 189 Yamil Benitez .25 .11 .03
☐ 190 Darrin Fletcher .10 .05 .01
☐ 191 Cliff Floyd .10 .05 .01
☐ 192 Pedro Martinez .25 .11 .03
☐ 193 Carlos Perez .10 .05 .01
☐ 194 David Segui .10 .05 .01
☐ 195 Tony Tarasco .10 .05 .01
☐ 196 Rondell White .25 .11 .03
☐ 197 Edgardo Alfonzo .25 .11 .03
☐ 198 Rico Brogna .25 .11 .03
☐ 199 Carl Everett .10 .05 .01
☐ 200 Todd Hundley .25 .11 .03
☐ 201 Jason Isringhausen .50 .23 .06
☐ 202 Lance Johnson .25 .11 .03
☐ 203 Bobby Jones .10 .05 .01
☐ 204 Jeff Kent .10 .05 .01
☐ 205 Bill Pulsipher .25 .11 .03
☐ 206 Jose Vizcaino .10 .05 .01
☐ 207 Ricky Bottalico .10 .05 .01
☐ 208 Darren Daulton .25 .11 .03
☐ 209 Lenny Dykstra .25 .11 .03
☐ 210 Jim Eisenreich .10 .05 .01
☐ 211 Gregg Jefferies .50 .23 .06
☐ 212 Mickey Morandini .10 .05 .01
☐ 213 Heathcliff Slocumb .10 .05 .01
☐ 214 Jay Bell .25 .11 .03
☐ 215 Carlos Garcia .10 .05 .01
☐ 216 Jeff King .25 .11 .03
☐ 217 Al Martin .10 .05 .01
☐ 218 Orlando Merced .25 .11 .03
☐ 219 Dan Miceli .10 .05 .01
☐ 220 Denny Neagle .25 .11 .03
☐ 221 Andy Benes .25 .11 .03
☐ 222 Royce Clayton .10 .05 .01
☐ 223 Gary Gaetti .25 .11 .03
☐ 224 Ron Gant .25 .11 .03
☐ 225 Bernard Gilkey .25 .11 .03
☐ 226 Brian Jordan .25 .11 .03
☐ 227 Ray Lankford .25 .11 .03
☐ 228 John Mabry .25 .11 .03
☐ 229 Ozzie Smith .75 .35 .09
☐ 230 Todd Stottlemyre .10 .05 .01
☐ 231 Andy Ashby .10 .05 .01
☐ 232 Brad Ausmus .10 .05 .01
☐ 233 Ken Caminiti .50 .23 .06
☐ 234 Steve Finley .50 .23 .06
☐ 235 Tony Gwynn 1.25 .55 .16
☐ 236 Joey Hamilton .25 .11 .03
☐ 237 Rickey Henderson .50 .23 .06
☐ 238 Trevor Hoffman .25 .11 .03
☐ 239 Wally Joyner .10 .05 .01
☐ 240 Rod Beck .25 .11 .03
☐ 241 Barry Bonds .75 .35 .09
☐ 242 Glenallen Hill .10 .05 .01
☐ 243 Stan Javier .10 .05 .01
☐ 244 Mark Leiter .10 .05 .01
☐ 245 Deion Sanders .50 .23 .06
☐ 246 William Van Landingham .10 .05 .01
☐ 247 Matt Williams .50 .23 .06
☐ 248 Checklist .10 .05 .01
☐ 249 Checklist .10 .05 .01
☐ 250 Checklist .10 .05 .01

1996 Metal Universe Platinum

The 1996 Fleer Metal Universe Platinum is a 250-card parallel version of the regular series and were inserted one per pack. The silver foil backgrounds differentiate these from the regular cards.

	MINT	NRMT	EXC
COMPLETE SET (250)	150.00	70.00	19.00
COMMON CARD (1-250)	.25	.11	.03

*STARS: 2X TO 4X BASIC CARDS
*YOUNG STARS: 1.5X TO 3X BASIC CARDS

1996 Metal Universe Heavy Metal

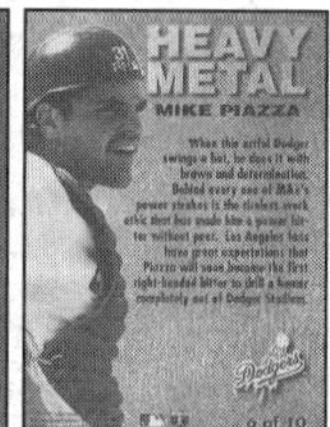

Randomly inserted in packs at a rate of one in 8 this 10-card set features the Power Hitters of Baseball. The fronts feature a color action player cut-out over a silver foil background. The backs carry a player portrait and information about the player.

	MINT	NRMT	EXC
COMPLETE SET (10)	25.00	11.00	3.10
COMMON CARD (1-10)	1.50	.70	.19

☐ 1 Albert Belle 4.00 1.80 .50
☐ 2 Barry Bonds 2.50 1.10 .30
☐ 3 Juan Gonzalez 5.00 2.20 .60
☐ 4 Ken Griffey Jr. 10.00 4.50 1.25
☐ 5 Mark McGwire 3.00 1.35 .35
☐ 6 Mike Piazza 6.00 2.70 .75
☐ 7 Sammy Sosa 1.50 .70 .19
☐ 8 Frank Thomas 10.00 4.50 1.25
☐ 9 Mo Vaughn 2.50 1.10 .30
☐ 10 Matt Williams 1.50 .70 .19

1996 Metal Universe Mining For Gold

Randomly inserted in retail packs only at a rate of one in 12, this 12-card set highlights major prospects and rookies.

	MINT	NRMT	EXC
COMPLETE SET (12)	60.00	27.00	7.50
COMMON CARD (1-12)	1.50	.70	.19

☐ 1 Yamil Benitez 4.00 1.80 .50
☐ 2 Marty Cordova 5.00 2.20 .60
☐ 3 Shawn Green 1.50 .70 .19
☐ 4 Todd Greene 4.00 1.80 .50
☐ 5 Brian Hunter 4.00 1.80 .50
☐ 6 Derek Jeter 20.00 9.00 2.50
☐ 7 Charles Johnson 4.00 1.80 .50
☐ 8 Chipper Jones 20.00 9.00 2.50
☐ 9 Hideo Nomo 10.00 4.50 1.25
☐ 10 Alex Ochoa 4.00 1.80 .50
☐ 11 Andy Pettitte 12.00 5.50 1.50
☐ 12 Quilvio Veras 1.50 .70 .19

1996 Metal Universe Mother Lode

Randomly inserted in hobby packs only at a rate of one in 12, this 12-card set features multi-tool players. The fronts carry a color action player cut-out over a silver-foil, scroll-design background. The backs display another player photo and information about the player.

	MINT	NRMT	EXC
COMPLETE SET (12)	60.00	27.00	7.50
COMMON CARD (1-12)	2.00	.90	.25

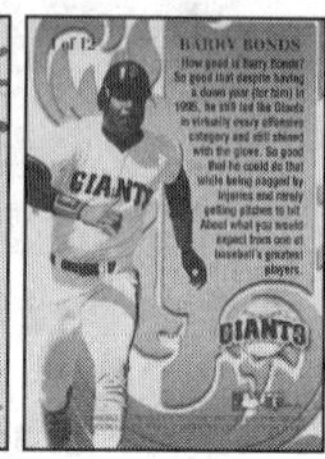

☐ 1 Barry Bonds 4.00 1.80 .50
☐ 2 Jim Edmonds 2.00 .90 .25
☐ 3 Ken Griffey Jr. 15.00 6.75 1.85
☐ 4 Kenny Lofton 4.00 1.80 .50
☐ 5 Raul Mondesi 3.00 1.35 .35
☐ 6 Rafael Palmeiro 3.00 1.35 .35
☐ 7 Manny Ramirez 4.00 1.80 .50
☐ 8 Cal Ripken 12.00 5.50 1.50
☐ 9 Tim Salmon 3.00 1.35 .35
☐ 10 Ryne Sandberg 4.00 1.80 .50
☐ 11 Frank Thomas 15.00 6.75 1.85
☐ 12 Matt Williams 3.00 1.35 .35

1996 Metal Universe Platinum Portraits

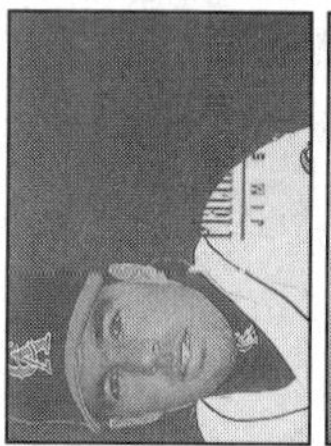

Randomly inserted in packs at a rate of one in four, this 10-card set features ten of the hottest young stars. The fronts display a player portrait on a platinum foil background. The backs carry a color action player photo and why the player is hot.

	MINT	NRMT	EXC
COMPLETE SET (10)	12.00	5.50	1.50
COMMON CARD (1-10)	.50	.23	.06

☐ 1 Garret Anderson 1.00 .45 .12
☐ 2 Marty Cordova 1.00 .45 .12
☐ 3 Jim Edmonds 1.00 .45 .12
☐ 4 Jason Isringhausen .50 .23 .06
☐ 5 Chipper Jones 5.00 2.20 .60
☐ 6 Ryan Klesko 1.50 .70 .19
☐ 7 Hideo Nomo 2.00 .90 .25
☐ 8 Carlos Perez .50 .23 .06
☐ 9 Manny Ramirez 2.00 .90 .25
☐ 10 Rondell White 1.00 .45 .12

1996 Metal Universe Titanium

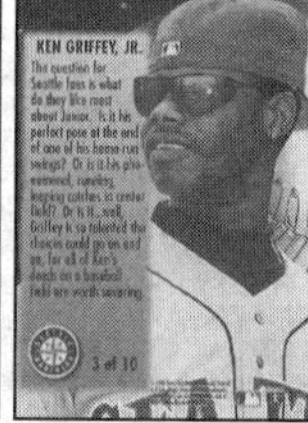

Randomly inserted in packs at a rate of one in 24, this 10-card set features ten of the fans' favorite players. The fronts feature an action color player cut-out on a foil baseball background. The backs display a player portrait and why the player is liked by the fans.

	MINT	NRMT	EXC
COMPLETE SET (10)	125.00	55.00	15.50
COMMON CARD (1-10)	3.00	1.35	.35

☐ 1 Albert Belle 10.00 4.50 1.25
☐ 2 Barry Bonds 6.00 2.70 .75
☐ 3 Ken Griffey Jr. 25.00 11.00 3.10
☐ 4 Tony Gwynn 10.00 4.50 1.25
☐ 5 Greg Maddux 15.00 6.75 1.85
☐ 6 Mike Piazza 15.00 6.75 1.85
☐ 7 Cal Ripken 20.00 9.00 2.50
☐ 8 Frank Thomas 25.00 11.00 3.10
☐ 9 Mo Vaughn 6.00 2.70 .75
☐ 10 Matt Williams 3.00 1.35 .35

1997 Metal Universe

The 1997 Metal Universe set was issued in one series totalling 250 cards and distributed in eight-card foil packs with a suggested retail price of $2.49. Printed in 100% etched foil with UV-coating, the fronts features color photos of star players on full-bleed backgrounds of

comic book art with the player's name, team, position and card logo printed near the bottom of the card. The backs carry another player photo and statistics.

	MINT	NRMT	EXC
COMPLETE SET (250)	40.00	18.00	5.00
COMMON CARD (1-250)	.10	.05	.01

	MINT	NRMT	EXC
☐ 1 Roberto Alomar	.60	.25	.07
☐ 2 Brady Anderson	.25	.11	.03
☐ 3 Rocky Coppinger	.25	.11	.03
☐ 4 Chris Hoiles	.10	.05	.01
☐ 5 Eddie Murray	.75	.35	.09
☐ 6 Mike Mussina	.60	.25	.07
☐ 7 Rafael Palmeiro	.40	.18	.05
☐ 8 Cal Ripken	2.50	1.10	.30
☐ 9 B.J. Surhoff	.10	.05	.01
☐ 10 Brant Brown	.10	.05	.01
☐ 11 Mark Grace	.40	.18	.05
☐ 12 Brian McRae	.10	.05	.01
☐ 13 Jaime Navarro	.10	.05	.01
☐ 14 Ryne Sandberg	.75	.35	.09
☐ 15 Sammy Sosa	.50	.23	.06
☐ 16 Amaury Telemaco	.10	.05	.01
☐ 17 Steve Trachsel	.10	.05	.01
☐ 18 Darren Bragg	.10	.05	.01
☐ 19 Jose Canseco	.40	.18	.05
☐ 20 Roger Clemens	.60	.25	.07
☐ 21 Nomar Garciaparra	1.25	.55	.16
☐ 22 Tom Gordon	.10	.05	.01
☐ 23 Tim Naehring	.10	.05	.01
☐ 24 Mike Stanley	.10	.05	.01
☐ 25 John Valentin	.10	.05	.01
☐ 26 Mo Vaughn	.75	.35	.09
☐ 27 Jermaine Dye	.50	.23	.06
☐ 28 Tom Glavine	.40	.18	.05
☐ 29 Marquis Grissom	.25	.11	.03
☐ 30 Andruw Jones	3.00	1.35	.35
☐ 31 Chipper Jones	2.00	.90	.25
☐ 32 Ryan Klesko	.50	.23	.06
☐ 33 Greg Maddux	2.00	.90	.25
☐ 34 Fred McGriff	.40	.18	.05
☐ 35 John Smoltz	.50	.23	.06
☐ 36 Garret Anderson	.10	.05	.01
☐ 37 George Arias	.10	.05	.01
☐ 38 Gary DiSarcina	.10	.05	.01
☐ 39 Jim Edmonds	.25	.11	.03
☐ 40 Darin Erstad	1.50	.70	.19
☐ 41 Chuck Finley	.10	.05	.01
☐ 42 Troy Percival	.10	.05	.01
☐ 43 Tim Salmon	.40	.18	.05
☐ 44 Bret Boone	.10	.05	.01
☐ 45 Jeff Brantley	.10	.05	.01
☐ 46 Eric Davis	.10	.05	.01
☐ 47 Barry Larkin	.40	.18	.05
☐ 48 Hal Morris	.10	.05	.01
☐ 49 Mark Portugal	.10	.05	.01
☐ 50 Reggie Sanders	.25	.11	.03
☐ 51 John Smiley	.10	.05	.01
☐ 52 Wilson Alvarez	.10	.05	.01
☐ 53 Harold Baines	.10	.05	.01
☐ 54 James Baldwin	.10	.05	.01
☐ 55 Albert Belle	1.25	.55	.16
☐ 56 Mike Cameron	.50	.23	.06
☐ 57 Ray Durham	.10	.05	.01
☐ 58 Alex Fernandez	.25	.11	.03
☐ 59 Roberto Hernandez	.10	.05	.01
☐ 60 Tony Phillips	.10	.05	.01
☐ 61 Frank Thomas	3.00	1.35	.35
☐ 62 Robin Ventura	.25	.11	.03
☐ 63 Jeff Cirillo	.10	.05	.01
☐ 64 Jeff D'Amico	.25	.11	.03
☐ 65 John Jaha	.25	.11	.03
☐ 66 Scott Karl	.10	.05	.01
☐ 67 Ben McDonald	.10	.05	.01
☐ 68 Marc Newfield	.10	.05	.01
☐ 69 Dave Nilsson	.10	.05	.01
☐ 70 Jose Valentin	.10	.05	.01
☐ 71 Dante Bichette	.40	.18	.05
☐ 72 Ellis Burks	.25	.11	.03
☐ 73 Vinny Castilla	.25	.11	.03
☐ 74 Andres Galarraga	.40	.18	.05
☐ 75 Kevin Ritz	.10	.05	.01
☐ 76 Larry Walker	.25	.11	.03
☐ 77 Walt Weiss	.10	.05	.01
☐ 78 Jamey Wright	.25	.11	.03
☐ 79 Eric Young	.25	.11	.03
☐ 80 Julio Franco	.10	.05	.01
☐ 81 Orel Hershiser	.25	.11	.03
☐ 82 Kenny Lofton	.75	.35	.09
☐ 83 Jack McDowell	.10	.05	.01
☐ 84 Jose Mesa	.10	.05	.01
☐ 85 Charles Nagy	.25	.11	.03
☐ 86 Manny Ramirez	.75	.35	.09
☐ 87 Jim Thome	.60	.25	.07
☐ 88 Omar Vizquel	.25	.11	.03
☐ 89 Matt Williams	.40	.18	.05
☐ 90 Kevin Appier	.25	.11	.03
☐ 91 Johnny Damon	.10	.05	.01
☐ 92 Chili Davis	.10	.05	.01
☐ 93 Tom Goodwin	.10	.05	.01
☐ 94 Keith Lockhart	.10	.05	.01
☐ 95 Jeff Montgomery	.10	.05	.01
☐ 96 Craig Paquette	.10	.05	.01
☐ 97 Jose Rosado	.40	.18	.05
☐ 98 Michael Tucker	.10	.05	.01
☐ 99 Wilton Guerrero	.50	.23	.06
☐ 100 Todd Hollandsworth	.25	.11	.03
☐ 101 Eric Karros	.25	.11	.03
☐ 102 Ramon Martinez	.25	.11	.03
☐ 103 Raul Mondesi	.40	.18	.05
☐ 104 Hideo Nomo	.75	.35	.09
☐ 105 Mike Piazza	2.00	.90	.25
☐ 106 Ismael Valdes	.25	.11	.03
☐ 107 Todd Worrell	.10	.05	.01
☐ 108 Tony Clark	.40	.18	.05
☐ 109 Travis Fryman	.25	.11	.03
☐ 110 Bob Higginson	.25	.11	.03
☐ 111 Mark Lewis	.10	.05	.01
☐ 112 Melvin Nieves	.10	.05	.01
☐ 113 Justin Thompson	.25	.11	.03
☐ 114 Wade Boggs	.40	.18	.05
☐ 115 David Cone	.25	.11	.03
☐ 116 Cecil Fielder	.25	.11	.03
☐ 117 Dwight Gooden	.25	.11	.03
☐ 118 Derek Jeter	2.00	.90	.25
☐ 119 Tino Martinez	.25	.11	.03
☐ 120 Paul O'Neill	.10	.05	.01
☐ 121 Andy Pettitte	.75	.35	.09
☐ 122 Mariano Rivera	.25	.11	.03
☐ 123 Darryl Strawberry	.25	.11	.03
☐ 124 John Wetteland	.25	.11	.03
☐ 125 Bernie Williams	.60	.25	.07
☐ 126 Tony Batista	.40	.18	.05
☐ 127 Geronimo Berroa	.10	.05	.01
☐ 128 Scott Brosius	.10	.05	.01
☐ 129 Jason Giambi	.25	.11	.03
☐ 130 Jose Herrera	.10	.05	.01
☐ 131 Mark McGwire	1.00	.45	.12
☐ 132 John Wasdin	.10	.05	.01
☐ 133 Bob Abreu	.40	.18	.05
☐ 134 Jeff Bagwell	1.25	.55	.16
☐ 135 Derek Bell	.25	.11	.03
☐ 136 Craig Biggio	.25	.11	.03
☐ 137 Brian Hunter	.10	.05	.01
☐ 138 Darryl Kile	.10	.05	.01
☐ 139 Orlando Miller	.10	.05	.01
☐ 140 Shane Reynolds	.10	.05	.01
☐ 141 Billy Wagner	.25	.11	.03
☐ 142 Donne Wall	.10	.05	.01
☐ 143 Jay Buhner	.40	.18	.05
☐ 144 Jeff Fassero	.10	.05	.01
☐ 145 Ken Griffey Jr.	3.00	1.35	.35
☐ 146 Sterling Hitchcock	.10	.05	.01
☐ 147 Randy Johnson	.50	.23	.06
☐ 148 Edgar Martinez	.25	.11	.03
☐ 149 Alex Rodriguez	3.00	1.35	.35
☐ 150 Paul Sorrento	.10	.05	.01
☐ 151 Dan Wilson	.10	.05	.01
☐ 152 Moises Alou	.25	.11	.03
☐ 153 Darrin Fletcher	.10	.05	.01
☐ 154 Cliff Floyd	.10	.05	.01
☐ 155 Mark Grudzielanek	.10	.05	.01
☐ 156 Vladimir Guerrero	2.00	.90	.25
☐ 157 Mike Lansing	.10	.05	.01
☐ 158 Pedro Martinez	.25	.11	.03
☐ 159 Henry Rodriguez	.25	.11	.03
☐ 160 Rondell White	.10	.05	.01
☐ 161 Will Clark	.40	.18	.05
☐ 162 Juan Gonzalez	1.50	.70	.19
☐ 163 Rusty Greer	.25	.11	.03
☐ 164 Ken Hill	.10	.05	.01
☐ 165 Mark McLemore	.10	.05	.01
☐ 166 Dean Palmer	.10	.05	.01
☐ 167 Roger Pavlik	.10	.05	.01
☐ 168 Ivan Rodriguez	.75	.35	.09
☐ 169 Mickey Tettleton	.10	.05	.01
☐ 170 Bobby Bonilla	.25	.11	.03
☐ 171 Kevin Brown	.25	.11	.03
☐ 172 Greg Colbrunn	.10	.05	.01
☐ 173 Jeff Conine	.25	.11	.03
☐ 174 Jim Eisenreich	.10	.05	.01
☐ 175 Charles Johnson	.10	.05	.01
☐ 176 Al Leiter	.10	.05	.01
☐ 177 Robb Nen	.10	.05	.01
☐ 178 Edgar Renteria	.40	.18	.05
☐ 179 Gary Sheffield	.50	.23	.06
☐ 180 Devon White	.10	.05	.01
☐ 181 Joe Carter	.25	.11	.03
☐ 182 Carlos Delgado	.25	.11	.03
☐ 183 Alex Gonzalez	.10	.05	.01
☐ 184 Shawn Green	.10	.05	.01
☐ 185 Juan Guzman	.10	.05	.01
☐ 186 Pat Hentgen	.25	.11	.03
☐ 187 Orlando Merced	.10	.05	.01
☐ 188 John Olerud	.10	.05	.01
☐ 189 Robert Perez	.10	.05	.01
☐ 190 Ed Sprague	.10	.05	.01
☐ 191 Mark Clark	.10	.05	.01
☐ 192 John Franco	.10	.05	.01
☐ 193 Bernard Gilkey	.10	.05	.01
☐ 194 Todd Hundley	.25	.11	.03
☐ 195 Lance Johnson	.10	.05	.01
☐ 196 Bobby Jones	.10	.05	.01
☐ 197 Alex Ochoa	.10	.05	.01
☐ 198 Rey Ordonez	.40	.18	.05
☐ 199 Paul Wilson	.25	.11	.03
☐ 200 Ricky Bottalico	.10	.05	.01
☐ 201 Gregg Jefferies	.10	.05	.01
☐ 202 Wendell Magee	.25	.11	.03
☐ 203 Mickey Morandini	.10	.05	.01
☐ 204 Ricky Otero	.10	.05	.01
☐ 205 Scott Rolen	1.25	.55	.16
☐ 206 Benito Santiago	.10	.05	.01
☐ 207 Curt Schilling	.10	.05	.01
☐ 208 Rich Becker	.10	.05	.01
☐ 209 Marty Cordova	.25	.11	.03
☐ 210 Chuck Knoblauch	.50	.23	.06
☐ 211 Pat Meares	.10	.05	.01
☐ 212 Paul Molitor	.60	.25	.07
☐ 213 Frank Rodriguez	.10	.05	.01
☐ 214 Terry Steinbach	.10	.05	.01
☐ 215 Todd Walker	1.25	.55	.16
☐ 216 Andy Ashby	.10	.05	.01
☐ 217 Ken Caminiti	.50	.23	.06
☐ 218 Steve Finley	.10	.05	.01
☐ 219 Tony Gwynn	1.25	.55	.16
☐ 220 Joey Hamilton	.25	.11	.03
☐ 221 Rickey Henderson	.40	.18	.05
☐ 222 Trevor Hoffman	.10	.05	.01
☐ 223 Wally Joyner	.10	.05	.01
☐ 224 Scott Sanders	.10	.05	.01
☐ 225 Fernando Valenzuela	.25	.11	.03
☐ 226 Greg Vaughn	.10	.05	.01
☐ 227 Alan Benes	.25	.11	.03
☐ 228 Andy Benes	.10	.05	.01
☐ 229 Dennis Eckersley	.25	.11	.03
☐ 230 Ron Gant	.25	.11	.03
☐ 231 Brian Jordan	.25	.11	.03
☐ 232 Ray Lankford	.25	.11	.03
☐ 233 John Mabry	.10	.05	.01
☐ 234 Tom Pagnozzi	.10	.05	.01
☐ 235 Todd Stottlemyre	.10	.05	.01
☐ 236 Jermaine Allensworth	.25	.11	.03
☐ 237 Francisco Cordova	.10	.05	.01
☐ 238 Jason Kendall	.25	.11	.03
☐ 239 Jeff King	.10	.05	.01
☐ 240 Al Martin	.10	.05	.01
☐ 241 Rod Beck	.10	.05	.01
☐ 242 Barry Bonds	.75	.35	.09
☐ 243 Shawn Estes	.10	.05	.01
☐ 244 Mark Gardner	.10	.05	.01
☐ 245 Glenallen Hill	.10	.05	.01
☐ 246 Bill Mueller	.10	.05	.01
☐ 247 J.T. Snow	.10	.05	.01
☐ 248 Checklist (1-107)	.10	.05	.01
☐ 249 Checklist (108-207)	.10	.05	.01
☐ 250 Checklist (208-250/inserts)	.10	.05	.01

1997 Metal Universe Blast Furnace

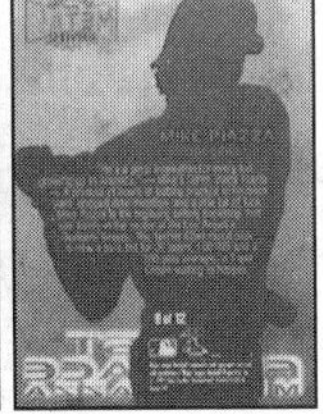

Randomly inserted in hobby packs only at a rate of one in 48, this 12-card set features color photos of some of baseball's biggest sluggers.

	MINT	NRMT	EXC
COMPLETE SET (12)	200.00	90.00	25.00
COMMON CARD (1-12)	4.00	1.80	.50

	MINT	NRMT	EXC
☐ 1 Jeff Bagwell	15.00	6.75	1.85
☐ 2 Albert Belle	15.00	6.75	1.85
☐ 3 Barry Bonds	10.00	4.50	1.25
☐ 4 Andres Galarraga	5.00	2.20	.60
☐ 5 Juan Gonzalez	20.00	9.00	2.50
☐ 6 Ken Griffey Jr.	40.00	18.00	5.00
☐ 7 Todd Hundley	4.00	1.80	.50
☐ 8 Mark McGwire	12.00	5.50	1.50
☐ 9 Mike Piazza	25.00	11.00	3.10
☐ 10 Alex Rodriguez	40.00	18.00	5.00
☐ 11 Frank Thomas	40.00	18.00	5.00
☐ 12 Mo Vaughn	10.00	4.50	1.25

1997 Metal Universe Emerald Autograph Exchange

One of six different exchange cards were randomly inserted in hobby boxes as chiptoppers (sealed inside the box, but laying on top of the packs) at a rate of one in 20 hobby boxes The exchange cards parallel

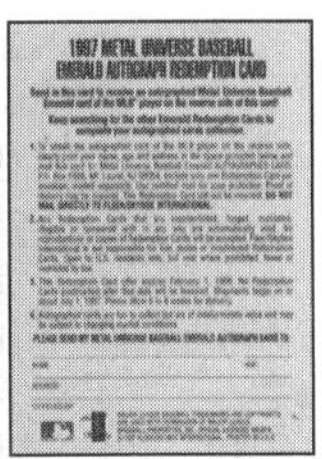
1997 METAL UNIVERSE BASEBALL
EMERALD AUTOGRAPH REDEMPTION CARD

the corresponding basic cards except for emerald foil on front. In addition, the area used for the card number on back of the regular issue card is replaced by a logo stating "certified emerald autograph". The exchange cards are unnumbered and have been assigned numbers based upon alphabetical order of each player's last name for cataloguing purposes.

	MINT	NRMT	EXC
COMPLETE SET (6)	450.00	200.00	55.00
COMMON CARD	30.00	13.50	3.70

	MINT	NRMT	EXC
☐ AU1 Darin Erstad	60.00	27.00	7.50
☐ AU2 Todd Hollandsworth	40.00	18.00	5.00
☐ AU3 Alex Ochoa	30.00	13.50	3.70
☐ AU4 Alex Rodriguez	200.00	90.00	25.00
☐ AU5 Scott Rolen	75.00	34.00	9.50
☐ AU6 Todd Walker	75.00	34.00	9.50

1997 Metal Universe Magnetic Field

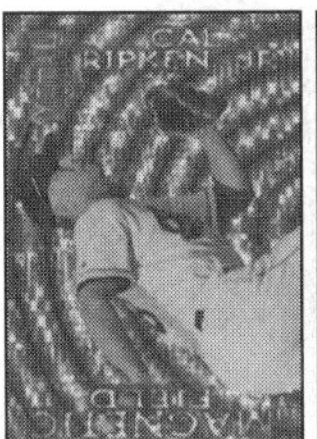

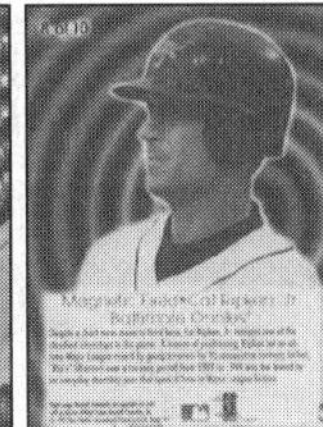

Randomly inserted in packs at a rate of one in 12, this ten-card set honors "Gold Glovers" who appear to have a special attraction to the ball. The fronts feature color player photos on refractive foil backgrounds.

	MINT	NRMT	EXC
COMPLETE SET (10)	40.00	18.00	5.00
COMMON CARD (1-10)	1.00	.45	.12

	MINT	NRMT	EXC
☐ 1 Roberto Alomar	2.50	1.10	.30
☐ 2 Jeff Bagwell	5.00	2.20	.60
☐ 3 Barry Bonds	3.00	1.35	.35
☐ 4 Ken Griffey Jr.	12.00	5.50	1.50
☐ 5 Derek Jeter	8.00	3.60	1.00
☐ 6 Kenny Lofton	3.00	1.35	.35
☐ 7 Edgar Renteria	1.00	.45	.12
☐ 8 Cal Ripken	10.00	4.50	1.25
☐ 9 Alex Rodriguez	12.00	5.50	1.50
☐ 10 Matt Williams	2.00	.90	.25

1997 Metal Universe Mining for Gold

Randomly inserted in packs at a rate of one in nine, this 10-card set features some of baseball's brightest young stars on die-cut "ingot" cards with pearlized gold coating.

	MINT	NRMT	EXC
COMPLETE SET (10)	25.00	11.00	3.10
COMMON CARD (1-10)	1.00	.45	.12

	MINT	NRMT	EXC
☐ 1 Bob Abreu	1.50	.70	.19
☐ 2 Kevin L.Brown C	1.25	.55	.16
☐ 3 Nomar Garciaparra	4.00	1.80	.50
☐ 4 Vladimir Guerrero	6.00	2.70	.75
☐ 5 Wilton Guerrero	1.50	.70	.19
☐ 6 Andruw Jones	10.00	4.50	1.25
☐ 7 Curt Lyons	1.00	.45	.12
☐ 8 Neifi Perez	1.25	.55	.16
☐ 9 Scott Rolen	4.00	1.80	.50
☐ 10 Todd Walker	4.00	1.80	.50

1997 Metal Universe Mother Lode

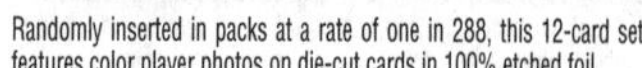

Randomly inserted in packs at a rate of one in 288, this 12-card set features color player photos on die-cut cards in 100% etched foil.

	MINT	NRMT	EXC
COMPLETE SET (12)	800.00	350.00	100.00
COMMON CARD (1-12)	20.00	9.00	2.50
☐ 1 Roberto Alomar	25.00	11.00	3.10
☐ 2 Jeff Bagwell	50.00	22.00	6.25
☐ 3 Barry Bonds	30.00	13.50	3.70
☐ 4 Ken Griffey Jr.	125.00	55.00	15.50
☐ 5 Andruw Jones	125.00	55.00	15.50
☐ 6 Chipper Jones	75.00	34.00	9.50
☐ 7 Kenny Lofton	30.00	13.50	3.70
☐ 8 Mike Piazza	75.00	34.00	9.50
☐ 9 Cal Ripken	100.00	45.00	12.50
☐ 10 Alex Rodriguez	125.00	55.00	15.50
☐ 11 Frank Thomas	125.00	55.00	15.50
☐ 12 Matt Williams	20.00	9.00	2.50

1997 Metal Universe Platinum Portraits

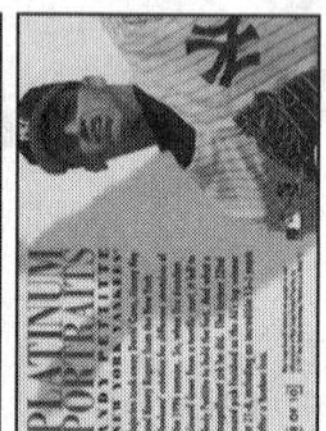

Randomly inserted in packs at a rate of one in 36, this 10-card set features color photos of some of Baseball's rising stars with backgrounds of platinum-colored etched foil.

	MINT	NRMT	EXC
COMPLETE SET (10)	80.00	36.00	10.00
COMMON CARD (1-10)	2.50	1.10	.30
☐ 1 James Baldwin	2.50	1.10	.30
☐ 2 Jermaine Dye	5.00	2.20	.60
☐ 3 Todd Hollandsworth	3.00	1.35	.35
☐ 4 Derek Jeter	20.00	9.00	2.50
☐ 5 Chipper Jones	20.00	9.00	2.50
☐ 6 Jason Kendall	3.00	1.35	.35
☐ 7 Rey Ordonez	4.00	1.80	.50
☐ 8 Andy Pettitte	8.00	3.60	1.00
☐ 9 Edgar Renteria	4.00	1.80	.50
☐ 10 Alex Rodriguez	30.00	13.50	3.70

1997 Metal Universe Titanium

Randomly inserted in packs at a rate of one in 24, this 10-card set honors some of baseball's favorite superstars. The fronts feature color player photos printed on die-cut embossed cards and sculpted on 100% etched foil.

	MINT	NRMT	EXC
COMPLETE SET (10)	100.00	45.00	12.50
COMMON CARD (1-10)	6.00	2.70	.75
☐ 1 Jeff Bagwell	8.00	3.60	1.00
☐ 2 Albert Belle	8.00	3.60	1.00
☐ 3 Ken Griffey Jr.	20.00	9.00	2.50
☐ 4 Chipper Jones	12.00	5.50	1.50
☐ 5 Greg Maddux	12.00	5.50	1.50
☐ 6 Mark McGwire	6.00	2.70	.75
☐ 7 Mike Piazza	12.00	5.50	1.50
☐ 8 Cal Ripken	15.00	6.75	1.85
☐ 9 Alex Rodriguez	20.00	9.00	2.50
☐ 10 Frank Thomas	20.00	9.00	2.50

1993 Metallic Images

As part of the Cooperstown Collection, this 20-card set came within a special collector tin and had its own individually numbered certificate of authenticity. Production was reportedly limited to 49,900 sets. The metallic cards have rounded corners and edges, measure approximately the standard size, and feature player photos, some action, others posed, reproduced on pinstriped fronts, with the player's team name above the photo. The player's name appears within an embossed banner at the bottom, which is backed by an embossed figure of a baseball diamond and crossed bats. Red, white, and blue stripes with gold stars grace each front side. The set logo appears in an upper corner. The horizontal back carries a posed player photo in the upper left and his name and position alongside to the right. Career highlights appear below. The Metallic Images and Children's Miracle Network logos at the bottom round out the back. The cards are numbered on the back in alphabetical order except for Blue and Berra. A promo card featuring Willie Mays was issued to dealers.

	MINT	NRMT	EXC
COMPLETE SET (20)	45.00	20.00	5.50
COMMON CARD (1-20)	1.50	.70	.19
☐ 1 Hank Aaron	8.00	3.60	1.00
☐ 2 Vida Blue	1.50	.70	.19
☐ 3 Yogi Berra	4.00	1.80	.50
☐ 4 Bobby Bonds	2.50	1.10	.30
☐ 5 Lou Brock	3.00	1.35	.35
☐ 6 Lew Burdette	1.50	.70	.19
☐ 7 Rod Carew	3.00	1.35	.35
☐ 8 Rocky Colavito	3.00	1.35	.35
☐ 9 George Foster	1.50	.70	.19
☐ 10 Bob Gibson	3.00	1.35	.35
☐ 11 Mickey Lolich	1.50	.70	.19
☐ 12 Willie Mays	8.00	3.60	1.00
☐ 13 Johnny Mize	3.00	1.35	.35
☐ 14 Don Newcombe	1.50	.70	.19
☐ 15 Gaylord Perry	3.00	1.35	.35
☐ 16 Boog Powell	2.50	1.10	.30
☐ 17 Bill Skowron	1.50	.70	.19
☐ 18 Warren Spahn	3.00	1.35	.35
☐ 19 Willie Stargell	3.00	1.35	.35
☐ 20 Luis Tiant	1.50	.70	.19
☐ P1 Willie Mays Promo	3.00	1.35	.35

1994 Metallic Impressions Mantle

Produced by Metallic Impressions, this 10-card standard-size set reproduces in metal the Baseball Heroes cards randomly inserted into 1994 Upper Deck second series packs. The ten cards were issued in an embossed collector's tin with an individually numbered certificate of authenticity. The fronts show photos commemorating key milestones in Mantle's career. The inserted paper backs contain career highlights and a small scrapbook-like photo. 19,950 of these sets were produced.

	MINT	NRMT	EXC
COMPLETE SET (10)	30.00	13.50	3.70
COMMON CARD (1-10)	3.00	1.35	.35
☐ 1 Mickey Mantle Header Card	3.00	1.35	.35
☐ 2 Mickey Mantle 1951 The Early Years	3.00	1.35	.35
☐ 3 Mickey Mantle 1953 Tape-Measure Home Runs	3.00	1.35	.35
☐ 4 Mickey Mantle 1956 Triple Crown Season	3.00	1.35	.35
☐ 5 Mickey Mantle 1957 Second Consecutive MVP	3.00	1.35	.35
☐ 6 Mickey Mantle 1961 Chasing the Babe	3.00	1.35	.35
☐ 7 Mickey Mantle 1964 Series Home Run Record	3.00	1.35	.35
☐ 8 Mickey Mantle 1967 500th Home Run	3.00	1.35	.35
☐ 9 Mickey Mantle 1974 Hall of Fame	3.00	1.35	.35
☐ 10 Mickey Mantle Art Card CL	3.00	1.35	.35

1995 Metallic Impressions Ripken

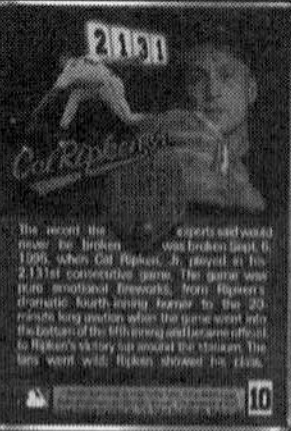

This 10-card metal-on-metal set traces Cal Ripken's career as he was just coming up from the minors to the nights he tied and broke Lou Gehrig's record. The cards are packaged in a collectors tin. Just 29,950 sets were produced and each included a Certificate of Authenticity. The fronts display color photos while the backs present commentary.

	MINT	NRMT	EXC
COMPLETE SET (10)	30.00	13.50	3.70
COMMON CARD (1-10)	3.00	1.35	.35
☐ 1 Cal Ripken	3.00	1.35	.35
☐ 2 Cal Ripken	3.00	1.35	.35
☐ 3 Cal Ripken	3.00	1.35	.35
☐ 4 Cal Ripken	3.00	1.35	.35
☐ 5 Cal Ripken	3.00	1.35	.35
☐ 6 Cal Ripken	3.00	1.35	.35
☐ 7 Cal Ripken	3.00	1.35	.35
☐ 8 Cal Ripken	3.00	1.35	.35
☐ 9 Cal Ripken	3.00	1.35	.35
☐ 10 Cal Ripken	3.00	1.35	.35

1995 Metallic Impressions Ryan

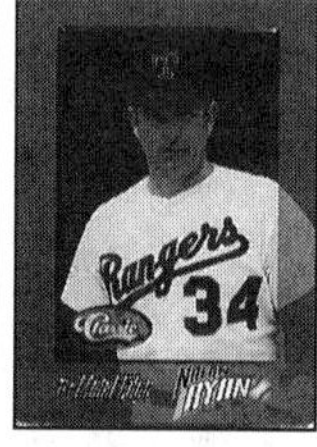

Produced by Metallic Impressions, this 10-card metal set is a retrospect of Nolan Ryan's Hall of Fame career. The cards have embossed fronts and smooth rolled edges. Each set is packaged in a collector's tin and accompanied by an individually numbered certificate of authenticity. The production run was limited to 14,950 sets.

	MINT	NRMT	EXC
COMPLETE SET (10)	30.00	13.50	3.70
COMMON CARD (1-10)	3.00	1.35	.35
☐ 1 Nolan Ryan Rangers; Portrait	3.00	1.35	.35
☐ 2 Nolan Ryan Angels; Beginning Windup	3.00	1.35	.35
☐ 3 Nolan Ryan Mets; Follow Through	3.00	1.35	.35
☐ 4 Nolan Ryan Rangers; Ball Visible	3.00	1.35	.35
☐ 5 Nolan Ryan Rangers; Uni name and no. visible	3.00	1.35	.35
☐ 6 Nolan Ryan Mets; Posed follow-through	3.00	1.35	.35
☐ 7 Nolan Ryan Astros; Pitching Motion	3.00	1.35	.35
☐ 8 Nolan Ryan Angels; Follow Through	3.00	1.35	.35
☐ 9 Nolan Ryan Astros; Portrait	3.00	1.35	.35
☐ 10 Nolan Ryan Rangers; Facing Camera	3.00	1.35	.35

1996 Metallic Impressions Griffey

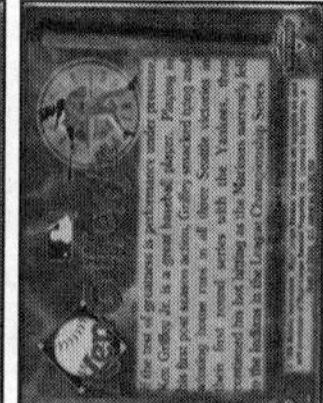

Produced by Metallic Impressions, this 10-card metal set is a retrospect of Ken Griffey, Jr. career. The cards have color action player photos on front and smooth rolled edges. Each set is packaged in a collector's tin and accompanied by an individually numbered certificate of authenticity. The production run was limited to 24,000 sets.

	MINT	NRMT	EXC
COMPLETE SET (10)	30.00	13.50	3.70
COMMON CARD (1-10)	3.00	1.35	.35
☐ 1 Ken Griffey Jr. (Portrait)	3.00	1.35	.35
☐ 2 Ken Griffey Jr. (Middle of batting swing)	3.00	1.35	.35
☐ 3 Ken Griffey Jr. (With glove)	3.00	1.35	.35
☐ 4 Ken Griffey Jr. (Fielding a hit ball)	3.00	1.35	.35
☐ 5 Ken Griffey Jr. (End of batting swing)	3.00	1.35	.35
☐ 6 Ken Griffey Jr. (Running to base)	3.00	1.35	.35
☐ 7 Ken Griffey Jr. (At bat)	3.00	1.35	.35
☐ 8 Ken Griffey Jr. (Top back view with bat)	3.00	1.35	.35
☐ 9 Ken Griffey Jr. (Catching a hit ball)	3.00	1.35	.35
☐ 10 Ken Griffey Jr. (Holding bat)	3.00	1.35	.35

1962 Mets Jay Publishing

This 12-card set of the original New York Mets measures approximately 5" X 7". The fronts feature black-and-white posed player photos with the player's and team name printed below in the white border. These cards were packaged 12 to a packet. The backs are blank. The cards are unnumbered and checklisted below in alphabetical order. A complete set in the original envelope is valued at fifty percent higher.

	NRMT	VG-E	GOOD
COMPLETE SET (12)	40.00	18.00	5.00
COMMON CARD (1-12)	2.50	1.10	.30
☐ 1 Gus Bell	3.50	1.55	.45
☐ 2 Elio Chacon	2.50	1.10	.30
☐ 3 Roger Craig	3.50	1.55	.45
☐ 4 Gil Hodges	10.00	4.50	1.25
☐ 5 Jay Hook	2.50	1.10	.30
☐ 6 Al Jackson	3.00	1.35	.35
☐ 7 Hobie Landrith	2.50	1.10	.30
☐ 8 Bob Miller	2.50	1.10	.30
☐ 9 Charlie Neal	3.00	1.35	.35
☐ 10 Casey Stengel MG	10.00	4.50	1.25
☐ 11 Frank Thomas	3.00	1.35	.35
☐ 12 Don Zimmer	3.50	1.55	.45

1963 Mets Jay Publishing

This 12-card set of the New York Mets measures approximately 5" by 7". The fronts feature black-and-white posed player photos with the player's and team name printed below in the white border. These cards were packaged 12 to a packet.The backs are blank. The cards are unnumbered and checklisted below in alphabetical order.

	NRMT	VG-E	GOOD
COMPLETE SET (12)	40.00	18.00	5.00
COMMON CARD (1-12)	2.50	1.10	.30
☐ 1 Larry Burright	2.50	1.10	.30
☐ 2 Roger Craig	3.50	1.55	.45
☐ 3 Jim Hickman	2.50	1.10	.30
☐ 4 Gil Hodges	10.00	4.50	1.25
☐ 5 Jay Hook	2.50	1.10	.30
☐ 6 Al Jackson	2.50	1.10	.30
☐ 7 Rod Kanehl	2.50	1.10	.30
☐ 8 Charlie Neal	3.50	1.55	.45
☐ 9 Duke Snider	10.00	4.50	1.25
☐ 10 Casey Stengel MG	10.00	4.50	1.25
☐ 11 Frank Thomas	3.50	1.55	.45
☐ 12 Marv Throneberry	3.50	1.55	.45

1964 Mets Jay Publishing

This 12-card set of the New York Mets measures approximately 5" by 7". The fronts feature black and white posed player photos with the player's and team name printed below in the white border. These cards were packaged 12 to an oversized envelope. The backs are blank. The cards are unnumbered and sequenced below in alphabetical order.

	NRMT	VG-E	GOOD
COMPLETE SET (12)	35.00	16.00	4.40
COMMON CARD (1-12)	2.50	1.10	.30
☐ 1 Larry Bearnarth	2.50	1.10	.30
☐ 2 Duke Carmel	2.50	1.10	.30
☐ 3 Choo Choo Coleman	2.50	1.10	.30
☐ 4 Jesse Gonder	2.50	1.10	.30
☐ 5 Tim Harkness	2.50	1.10	.30
☐ 6 Jim Hickman	3.50	1.55	.45
☐ 7 Ron Hunt	3.50	1.55	.45
☐ 8 Al Jackson	2.50	1.10	.30
☐ 9 Rod Kanehl	2.50	1.10	.30
☐ 10 Duke Snider	7.50	3.40	.95
☐ 11 Casey Stengel MG	10.00	4.50	1.25
☐ 12 Carlton Willey	2.50	1.10	.30

1965 Mets Jay Publishing

This 12-card set of New York Mets measures approximately 5" by 7". The fronts feature black and white posed player photos with the player's and team name printed below in the white border. The cards were packaged 12 to an envelope. The backs are blank and are sequenced in alphabetical order.

	NRMT	VG-E	GOOD
COMPLETE SET (12)	35.00	16.00	4.40
COMMON CARD (1-12)	2.00	.90	.25
☐ 1 Larry Bearnarth	2.00	.90	.25
☐ 2 Yogi Berra	10.00	4.50	1.25
☐ 3 Chris Cannizzaro	2.00	.90	.25
☐ 4 Galen Cisco	2.00	.90	.25
☐ 5 Jack Fisher	2.00	.90	.25
☐ 6 Jim Hickman	2.00	.90	.25
☐ 7 Ron Hunt	2.00	.90	.25
☐ 8 Al Jackson	2.00	.90	.25
☐ 9 Ed Kranepool	2.50	1.10	.30
☐ 10 Roy McMillan	2.00	.90	.25
☐ 11 Warren Spahn	7.50	3.40	.95
☐ 12 Casey Stengel MG	7.50	3.40	.95

1967 Mets Team Issue

This 12-card set of the New York Mets measures approximately 4 13/16" by 7" and features black-and-white player photos in a white border with blank backs. These cards were originally packaged 12 to a packet. The cards are unnumbered and checklisted below in alphabetical order.

	NRMT	VG-E	GOOD
COMPLETE SET (12)	25.00	11.00	3.10
COMMON CARD (1-12)	2.00	.90	.25
☐ 1 Yogi Berra CO	7.50	3.40	.95
☐ 2 Ken Boyer	5.00	2.20	.60
☐ 3 Don Cardwell	2.00	.90	.25
☐ 4 Tommy Davis	3.00	1.35	.35
☐ 5 Jack Fisher	2.00	.90	.25
☐ 6 Jerry Grote	2.00	.90	.25
☐ 7 Chuck Hiller	2.00	.90	.25
☐ 8 Cleon Jones	2.00	.90	.25
☐ 9 Ed Kranepool	2.00	.90	.25
☐ 10 Bob Shaw	2.00	.90	.25
☐ 11 Ron Swoboda	3.00	1.35	.35
☐ 12 Wes Westrum MG	2.00	.90	.25

1969 Mets Citgo

These eight 8" by 10" prints were drawn by John Wheeldon. These prints were available at Citgo for a nominal fee after a gasoline fill-up. The fronts feature a large portait pose and a smaller action pose on a colorful background. The backs have the CITGO, MLB and Mets skyline logos, the player's biography and lifetime records. There is also a picture and bio of the artist on the back. The prints are unnumbered and listed in alphabetical order.

	NRMT	VG-E	GOOD
COMPLETE SET (8)	60.00	27.00	7.50
COMMON PLAYER (8)	5.00	2.20	.60
☐ 1 Tommie Agee	5.00	2.20	.60
☐ 2 Ken Boswell	5.00	2.20	.60
☐ 3 Gary Gentry	5.00	2.20	.60
☐ 4 Jerry Grote	5.00	2.20	.60
☐ 5 Ed Kranepool	5.00	2.20	.60
☐ 6 Jerry Koosman	7.50	3.40	.95
☐ 7 Cleon Jones	5.00	2.20	.60
☐ 8 Tom Seaver	20.00	9.00	2.50

1969 Mets New York Daily News

These 9" by 12" blank-backed charcoal drawings were issued by the Daily News to celebrate the Miracle Mets. An artist named Bruce Stark drew the pictures which were put on white textured paper.Each drawing has a fascimile autograph on the lower left. The items are unnumbered and are sequenced in alphabetical order and came in a special folder which featured additional artwork.

	NRMT	VG-E	GOOD
COMPLETE SET (20)	100.00	45.00	12.50
COMMON CARD (1-20)	4.00	1.80	.50
☐ 1 Tommie Agee	4.00	1.80	.50
☐ 2 Ken Boswell	4.00	1.80	.50
☐ 3 Don Cardwell	4.00	1.80	.50
☐ 4 Donn Clendenon	5.00	2.20	.60
☐ 5 Wayne Garrett	4.00	1.80	.50
☐ 6 Gary Gentry	4.00	1.80	.50
☐ 7 Jerry Grote	5.00	2.20	.60
☐ 8 Derrel(Bud) Harrelson	7.50	3.40	.95
☐ 9 Gil Hodges MG	15.00	6.75	1.85
☐ 10 Cleon Jones	7.50	3.40	.95
☐ 11 Jerry Koosman	10.00	4.50	1.25
☐ 12 Ed Kranepool	5.00	2.20	.60
☐ 13 Jim McAndrew	4.00	1.80	.50
☐ 14 Frank(Tug) McGraw	10.00	4.50	1.25
☐ 15 Nolan Ryan	50.00	22.00	6.25
☐ 16 Tom Seaver	4.00	1.80	.50
☐ 17 Art Shamsky	4.00	1.80	.50
☐ 18 Ron Swoboda	5.00	2.20	.60
☐ 19 Ron Taylor	4.00	1.80	.50
☐ 20 Al Weis	4.00	1.80	.50

1970 Mets Transogram

The cards in this 15-card set measure 2 9/16" by 3 1/2". The 1970 Transogram Mets are a set of blank backed, unnumbered cards issued in three card panels as the backs of boxes containing small plastic statues honoring the 1969 Mets. The individual cards are the same size as the non-Met 1970 series and are numbered in the checklist according to the "series" number found on the side panels of each box. Although complete panel prices are not explicitly listed, they would generally have a value 50 percent greater than the sum of the individual players on the panel. Complete box prices would be double the sum of the listed prices.

	NRMT	VG-E	GOOD
COMPLETE INDIV. SET	350.00	160.00	45.00
COMMON CARD	4.00	1.80	.50
☐ 21A Ed Kranepool	7.50	3.40	.95
☐ 21B Al Weis	4.00	1.80	.50
☐ 21C Tom Seaver	125.00	55.00	15.50
☐ 22A Ken Boswell	4.00	1.80	.50
☐ 22B Jerry Koosman	10.00	4.50	1.25
☐ 22C Jerry Grote	5.00	2.20	.60
☐ 23A Art Shamsky	4.00	1.80	.50
☐ 23B Gary Gentry	4.00	1.80	.50
☐ 23C Tommie Agee	5.00	2.20	.60
☐ 24A Nolan Ryan	275.00	125.00	34.00
☐ 24B Tug McGraw	20.00	9.00	2.50
☐ 24C Cleon Jones	5.00	2.20	.60
☐ 25A Ron Swoboda	5.00	2.20	.60
☐ 25B Bud Harrelson	6.50	2.90	.80
☐ 25C Donn Clendenon	5.00	2.20	.60

1974 Mets Dairylea Photo Album

This set was issued in two fold-out strip booklets. each of which measures 8" by 8" in size. The inside front cover contains several small photos; the rest of the bookley contains white bordered portraits. The complete set comes in a white folder. Both the folder and booklets have the Mets logo on the front and the Dairylea trademark on the back. The books and photos are unnumbered and are sequenced the way they came in the booklet. Cards #1-13 are from the first book while #14-20 are from the second book.

	NRMT	VG-E	GOOD
COMPLETE SET (20)	100.00	45.00	12.50
COMMON PLAYER (1-20)	3.50	1.55	.45
☐ 1 Inside Front Cover	3.50	1.55	.45
☐ 2 George Theodore	3.50	1.55	.45
☐ 3 Ron Hodges	3.50	1.55	.45
☐ 4 George Stone	3.50	1.55	.45
☐ 5 Duffy Dyer	3.50	1.55	.45
☐ 6 Jack Aker	3.50	1.55	.45
☐ 7 Jim Gosger	3.50	1.55	.45
☐ 8 Bob Apodaca	3.50	1.55	.45
☐ 9 Tom Seaver	20.00	9.00	2.50
☐ 10 Bud Harrelson	5.00	2.20	.60
☐ 11 Ed Kranepool	5.00	2.20	.60
☐ 12 Rusty Staub	8.00	3.60	1.00
☐ 13 Ray Sadecki	3.50	1.55	.45
☐ 14 Front Cover Book 2	3.50	1.55	.45
☐ 15 Yogi Berra MG With Coaches	15.00	6.75	1.85
☐ 16 Ken Boswell	3.50	1.55	.45
☐ 17 Cleon Jones	3.50	1.55	.45
☐ 18 Jerry Grote	5.00	2.20	.60
☐ 19 Jerry Koosman	5.00	2.20	.60
☐ 20 Wayne Garrett	3.50	1.55	.45

1975 Mets SSPC

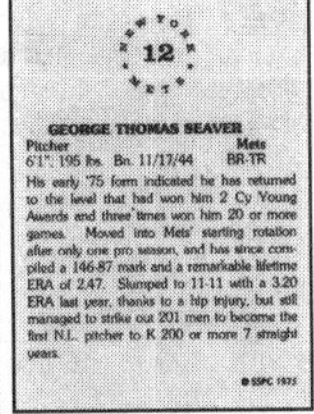

This 22-card standard-size set of New York Mets features white-bordered posed color player photos on their fronts, which are free of any other markings. The white back carries the player's name in red lettering above his blue-lettered biography and career highlights. The cards are numbered on the back within a circle formed by the player's team name. A similar set of New York Yankees was produced at the same time. The set is dated to 1975 because that year was Dave Kingman's first year as a Met and George Stone's last year.

	NRMT	VG-E	GOOD
COMPLETE SET (22)	15.00	6.75	1.85
COMMON CARD (1-22)	.50	.23	.06
☐ 1 John Milner	.50	.23	.06
☐ 2 Henry Webb	.50	.23	.06
☐ 3 Tom Hall	.50	.23	.06
☐ 4 Del Unser	.50	.23	.06
☐ 5 Wayne Garrett	.50	.23	.06
☐ 6 Jesus Alou	.75	.35	.09
☐ 7 Rusty Staub	2.00	.90	.25
☐ 8 John Stearns	.75	.35	.09
☐ 9 Dave Kingman	1.00	.45	.12
☐ 10 Ed Kranepool	.75	.35	.09
☐ 11 Cleon Jones	.75	.35	.09
☐ 12 Tom Seaver	8.00	3.60	1.00
☐ 13 George Stone	.50	.23	.06
☐ 14 Jerry Koosman	1.00	.45	.12
☐ 15 Bob Apodaca	.50	.23	.06
☐ 16 Felix Millan	.75	.35	.09
☐ 17 Gene Clines	.50	.23	.06
☐ 18 Mike Phillips	.50	.23	.06
☐ 19 Yogi Berra MG	4.00	1.80	.50
☐ 20 Joe Torre	2.00	.90	.25
☐ 21 Jon Matlack	1.00	.45	.12
☐ 22 Ricky Baldwin	.50	.23	.06

1976 Mets '63 SSPC

These 18 standard-size cards honored members of the 1963 New York Mets. These cards have color photos covering almost all of the front except for a small white border. The horizontal backs have vital statistics; a biography written as it would have been after the '63 season and career information up to that point. The cards are unnumbered and we have sequenced them in alphabetical order. These cards were inserted in the 1976 Summer edition of Collectors Quarterly.

	NRMT	VG-E	GOOD
COMPLETE SET (18)	30.00	13.50	3.70
COMMON CARD (1-18)	1.25	.55	.16
☐ 1 Ed Bauta	1.25	.55	.16
☐ 2 Duke Carmel	1.25	.55	.16
☐ 3 Joe Christopher	1.25	.55	.16
☐ 4 Choo Choo Coleman	1.50	.70	.19
☐ 5 Steve Dillon	1.25	.55	.16
☐ 6 Jesse Gonder	1.25	.55	.16
☐ 7 Pumpsie Green	1.25	.55	.16
☐ 8 Jim Hickman	1.50	.70	.19
☐ 9 Rod Kanehl	1.25	.55	.16
☐ 10 Al Moran	1.25	.55	.16
☐ 11 Grover Powell	1.25	.55	.16
☐ 12 Ted Schreiber	1.25	.55	.16
☐ 13 Norm Sherry	1.25	.55	.16
☐ 14 Dick Smith	1.25	.55	.16
☐ 15 Duke Snider	5.00	2.20	.60
☐ 16 Tracy Stallard	1.25	.55	.16
☐ 17 Casey Stengel MG	5.00	2.20	.60
☐ 18 Ernie White CO	1.25	.55	.16

1976 Mets MSA Placemats

This set of four placemats was produced by Creative Dimensions, licensed by Major League Baseball, and issued by MSA. Each placemat measures 14 1/4" by 11 1/4", has a clear matte finish, and pictures three players, each appearing in a 3" diameter circle. Player statistics and additional artwork complete the placemat. Logos have been airbrushed from the caps as is typical of all MSA products. Placemats are unnumbered and listed below in first player uniform number.

	NRMT	VG-E	GOOD
COMPLETE SET (4)	20.00	9.00	2.50
COMMON PLACEMAT (1-4)	3.00	1.35	.35
☐ 1 Bud Harrelson Tom Seaver Jerry Grote	15.00	6.75	1.85
☐ 2 Ed Kranepool Dave Kingman Joe Torre	7.50	3.40	.95
☐ 3 Bob Apodaca Felix Millan Del Unser	3.00	1.35	.35
☐ 4 Jerry Koosman Mickey Lolich Jon Matlack	5.00	2.20	.60

1978 Mets Dairylea Photo Album

This photo album was distributed at the Mets home game of May 30, 1978. This edition consists of a single booklet, 8" by 8" in size, bound on the left side. Each page contains a white-bordered, unnumbered portrait. They are listed below in the order they appear in the album.

	NRMT	VG-E	GOOD
COMPLETE SET (27)	25.00	11.00	3.10
COMMON PLAYER (1-27)	1.50	.70	.19
☐ 1 Joe Torre MG With Coaches	2.50	1.10	.30
☐ 2 Bruce Boisclair	1.50	.70	.19
☐ 3 Mike Bruhert	1.50	.70	.19
☐ 4 Mardie Cornejo	1.50	.70	.19
☐ 5 Nino Espinosa	1.50	.70	.19
☐ 6 Doug Flynn	1.50	.70	.19
☐ 7 Tim Foli	1.50	.70	.19
☐ 8 Tom Grieve	2.00	.90	.25
☐ 9 Ken Henderson	1.50	.70	.19
☐ 10 Steve Henderson	1.50	.70	.19
☐ 11 Ron Hodges	1.50	.70	.19
☐ 12 Jerry Koosman	2.50	1.10	.30
☐ 13 Ed Kranepool	2.00	.90	.25
☐ 14 Skip Lockwood	1.50	.70	.19
☐ 15 Elliott Maddox	1.50	.70	.19
☐ 16 Lee Mazzilli	2.00	.90	.25
☐ 17 Butch Metzger	1.50	.70	.19
☐ 18 Willie Montanez	1.50	.70	.19
☐ 19 Bob Myrick	1.50	.70	.19
☐ 20 Len Randle	1.50	.70	.19
☐ 21 Paul Siebert	1.50	.70	.19
☐ 22 John Stearns	1.50	.70	.19
☐ 23 Craig Swan	1.50	.70	.19
☐ 24 Bobby Valentine	2.00	.90	.25
☐ 25 Joel Youngblood	1.50	.70	.19
☐ 26 Pat Zachry	1.50	.70	.19
☐ 27 Bob Apodaca Sergio Ferrer	1.50	.70	.19

1981 Mets Magic Memory

This four card set, which measures 6 7/*' by 4 7/8" features memorable Mets teams and managers. The relevant pictures are on the card front with the backs being brown with white printing, and show statistics. Each card was individually wrapped in cellophane and distributed as a promotion at Mets home games in 1981. The cards are most commonly found with the cellophane intact and are priced accordingly below. The scheduled dates for these giveaways were July 2, July 16, July 23 and August 6. Unfortunately, due to the baseball strike of 1981 the cards were all distributed at later dates in the season.

	NRMT	VG-E	GOOD
COMPLETE SET (4)	30.00	13.50	3.70
COMMON CARD (1-4)	7.50	3.40	.95
☐ 1 1962 Mets Team Photo	7.50	3.40	.95
☐ 2 1969 Mets Team Photo	7.50	3.40	.95

☐ 3 1973 Mets Team Photo	7.50	3.40	.95
☐ 4 Famous Mets Managers	7.50	3.40	.95

1982 Mets Galasso '62

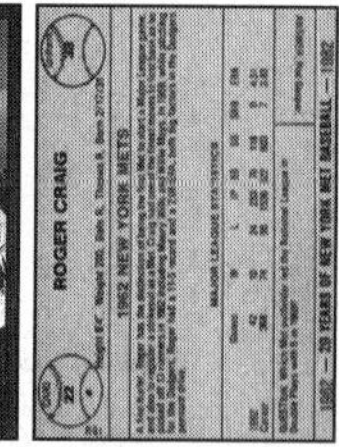

This 32-card standard-size set features posed black-and-white portraits of the 1962 New York Mets. The fronts are bordered in royal blue with the player's name and position printed in orange on the lower edge. The horizontal backs are printed in blue and orange with player biography, career highlights and statistics. A trivia question appears on the bottom, with the answer printed upside down next to it. Some sets were issued with signed Marv Throneberry cards. These signed cards add $10 to the value of the set.

	NRMT	VG-E	GOOD
COMPLETE SET (32)	10.00	4.50	1.25
COMMON CARD (1-32)	.25	.11	.03
☐ 1 Marv Throneberry	1.00	.45	.12
☐ 2 Richie Ashburn	1.50	.70	.19
☐ 3 Charlie Neal	.25	.11	.03
☐ 4 Cliff Cook	.25	.11	.03
☐ 5 Elio Chacon	.25	.11	.03
☐ 6 Chris Cannizzaro	.25	.11	.03
☐ 7 Jim Hickman	.25	.11	.03
☐ 8 Rod Kanehl	.25	.11	.03
☐ 9 Gene Woodling	.35	.16	.04
☐ 10 Gil Hodges	1.50	.70	.19
☐ 11 Al Jackson	.25	.11	.03
☐ 12 Sammy Taylor	.25	.11	.03
☐ 13 Felix Mantilla	.25	.11	.03
☐ 14 Ken MacKenzie	.25	.11	.03
☐ 15 Craig Anderson	.25	.11	.03
☐ 16 Bob Moorhead	.25	.11	.03
☐ 17 Joe Christopher	.25	.11	.03
☐ 18 Bob Miller	.25	.11	.03
☐ 19 Frank Thomas	.50	.23	.06
☐ 20 Wilmer Mizell	.25	.11	.03
☐ 21 Bill Hunter	.25	.11	.03
☐ 22 Roger Craig	.50	.23	.06
☐ 23 Jay Hook	.25	.11	.03
☐ 24 Team Photo	.50	.23	.06
☐ 25 Choo-Choo Coleman	.35	.16	.04
☐ 26 Casey Stengel MG	1.00	.45	.12
☐ 27 Cookie Lavagetto CO	.25	.11	.03
☐ 28 Solly Hemus CO	.25	.11	.03
☐ 29 Rogers Hornsby CO	1.00	.45	.12
☐ 30 Red Kress CO	.25	.11	.03
☐ 31 Red Ruffing CO	.50	.23	.06
☐ 32 George Weiss GM	.50	.23	.06

1982 Mets Photo Album

These photos were perforated on bound edge. Each blank-backed color photo would measure 7 3/4" by 8" if detached. These is a Facsmile autograph in red at lower left; the uniform number in red at upper right. The back album cover carries an ad for Sportschannel. These photos are unnumbered and we have checklisted them below in alphabetical order.

	NRMT	VG-E	GOOD
COMPLETE SET (28)	7.50	3.40	.95
COMMON CARD (1-28)	.25	.11	.03
☐ 1 Neil Allen	.25	.11	.03
☐ 2 Wally Backman	.25	.11	.03
☐ 3 Bob Bailor	.25	.11	.03
☐ 4 George Bamberger MG	.25	.11	.03
☐ 5 Hubie Brooks	.50	.23	.06
☐ 6 Pete Falcone	.25	.11	.03
☐ 7 George Foster	.75	.35	.09
☐ 8 Ron Gardenhire	.25	.11	.03
☐ 9 Tom Hausman	.25	.11	.03
☐ 10 Ron Hodges	.25	.11	.03
☐ 11 Mike Howard	.25	.11	.03
☐ 12 Randy Jones	.25	.11	.03
☐ 13 Mike Jorgensen	.25	.11	.03
☐ 14 Dave Kingman	1.00	.45	.12
☐ 15 Ed Lynch	.25	.11	.03
☐ 16 Jesse Orosco	.25	.11	.03
☐ 17 Charlie Puleo	.25	.11	.03
☐ 18 Gary Rajsich	.25	.11	.03
☐ 19 Mike Scott	.50	.23	.06
☐ 20 Rusty Staub	1.00	.45	.12
☐ 21 John Stearns	.25	.11	.03
☐ 22 Craig Swan	.25	.11	.03
☐ 23 Ellis Valentine	.25	.11	.03
☐ 24 Tom Veryzer	.25	.11	.03
☐ 25 Mookie Wilson	.75	.35	.09
☐ 26 Pat Zachry	.25	.11	.03
☐ 27 Prospects Brian J. Giles Rick Ownbey	.25	.11	.03
☐ 28 Coaches Jim Frey Bud Harrelson Frank Howard Bill Monbouquette	.50	.23	.06

1984 Mets Fan Club

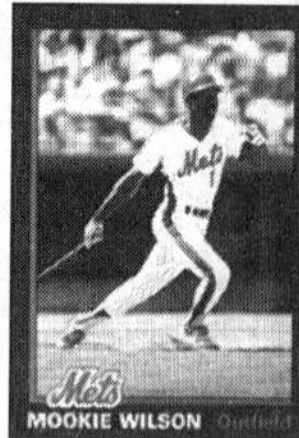

The cards in this eight-player set measure 2 1/2" by 3 1/2". The sheets were produced by Topps for the New York Mets and feature only Mets. The full sheet measures 7 1/2" by 10 1/2". Cards are together on the sheet but are perforated for those collectors who want to separate the individual player cards. The middle (ninth) card is a Mets Fan club membership card which details various promotional days at Shea Stadium on the back. The cards are numbered on the back and printed in orange and blue.

	NRMT	VG-E	GOOD
COMPLETE SET (8)	7.50	3.40	.95
COMMON CARD (1-8)	.50	.23	.06
☐ 1 Dave Johnson MG	.75	.35	.09
☐ 2 Ron Darling	1.00	.45	.12
☐ 3 George Foster	1.00	.45	.12
☐ 4 Keith Hernandez	.75	.35	.09
☐ 5 Jesse Orosco	.50	.23	.06
☐ 6 Rusty Staub	1.25	.55	.16
☐ 7 Darryl Strawberry	2.00	.90	.25
☐ 8 Mookie Wilson	.75	.35	.09
☐ NNO Membership Card	.50	.23	.06

1985 Mets Fan Club

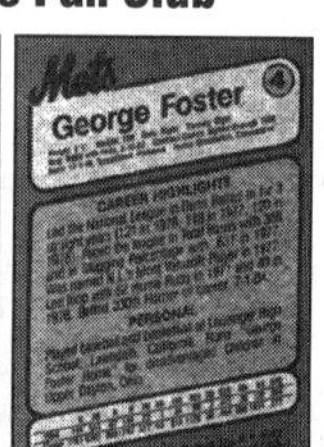

The cards in this eight-player set measure 2 1/2" by 3 1/2". The sheets were produced by Topps for the New York Mets and feature only Mets players. The full sheet measures approximately 7 1/2" by 10 1/2". Cards are together on the sheet but are perforated for those collectors who want to separate the individual player cards. The middle (ninth) card is a Mets Fan club membership card. The set was available as a membership premium for joining the Junior Mets Fan Club for 4.00. The cards are listed below in alphabetical order for convenience.

	NRMT	VG-E	GOOD
COMPLETE SET (8)	8.00	3.60	1.00
COMMON CARD (1-8)	.50	.23	.06
☐ 1 Wally Backman	.50	.23	.06
☐ 2 Bruce Berenyi	.50	.23	.06
☐ 3 Gary Carter	1.25	.55	.16
☐ 4 George Foster	1.00	.45	.12
☐ 5 Dwight Gooden	2.50	1.10	.30
☐ 6 Keith Hernandez	1.00	.45	.12
☐ 7 Doug Sisk	.50	.23	.06
☐ 8 Darryl Strawberry	1.50	.70	.19
☐ NNO Membership Card	.50	.23	.06

1985 Mets TCMA

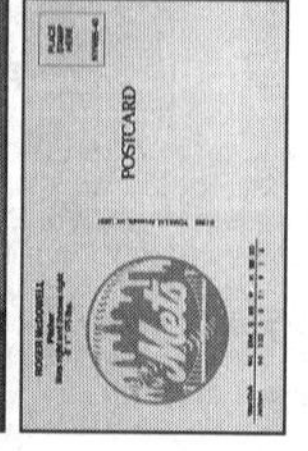

These cards measure 3 1/2" by 5 1/2". The borderless fronts consist of nothing but the photos. The postcard format backs give player identification, vital statistics and previous season stats. The cards are numbered with "NYM85-XX" in the upper right.

	NRMT	VG-E	GOOD
COMPLETE SET (40)	15.00	6.75	1.85
COMMON CARD (1-40)	.25	.11	.03
☐ 1 Davey Johnson MG	.50	.23	.06
☐ 2 Vern Hoscheit CO	.25	.11	.03
☐ 3 Bill Robinson CO	.25	.11	.03
☐ 4 Mel Stottlemyre CO	.25	.11	.03
☐ 5 Bobby Valentine CO	.25	.11	.03
☐ 6 Bruce Berenyi	.25	.11	.03
☐ 7 Jeff Bettendorf	.25	.11	.03
☐ 8 Ron Darling	.50	.23	.06
☐ 9 Sid Fernandez	.50	.23	.06
☐ 10 Brent Gaff	.25	.11	.03
☐ 11 Wes Gardner	.25	.11	.03
☐ 12 Dwight Gooden	2.00	.90	.25
☐ 13 Tom Gorman	.25	.11	.03
☐ 14 Ed Lynch	.25	.11	.03
☐ 15 Jesse Orosco	.25	.11	.03
☐ 16 Calvin Schiraldi	.25	.11	.03
☐ 17 Doug Sisk	.25	.11	.03
☐ 18 Gary Carter	1.50	.70	.19
☐ 19 John Gibbons	.25	.11	.03
☐ 20 Ronn Reynolds	.25	.11	.03
☐ 21 Wally Backman	.25	.11	.03
☐ 22 Kelvin Chapman	.25	.11	.03
☐ 23 Ron Gardenhire	.25	.11	.03
☐ 24 Keith Hernandez	1.00	.45	.12
☐ 25 Howard Johnson	.50	.23	.06
☐ 26 Ray Knight	.75	.35	.09
☐ 27 Kevin Mitchell	1.25	.55	.16
☐ 28 Terry Blocker	.25	.11	.03
☐ 29 Rafael Santana	.25	.11	.03
☐ 30 Billy Beane	.25	.11	.03
☐ 31 John Christensen	.25	.11	.03
☐ 32 Len Dykstra	2.00	.90	.25
☐ 33 George Foster	.75	.35	.09
☐ 34 Danny Heep	.25	.11	.03
☐ 35 Darryl Strawberry	1.00	.45	.12
☐ 36 Mookie Wilson	.50	.23	.06
☐ 37 Jeff Bittiger	.25	.11	.03
☐ 38 Clint Hurdle	.25	.11	.03
☐ 39 LaSchelle Tarver	.25	.11	.03
☐ 40 Roger McDowell	.75	.35	.09

1986 Mets Fan Club

The cards in this eight-player set measure 2 1/2" by 3 1/2". The sheets were produced by Topps for the New York Mets and feature only Mets. The full sheet measures approximately 7 1/2" by 10 1/2". Cards are together on the sheet but are perforated for those collectors who want to separate the individual player cards. The middle (ninth) card is a Mets Fan club membership card. The set was available as a membership premium for joining the Junior Mets Fan Club for 5.00. The cards are listed below in alphabetical order for convenience.

	MINT	NRMT	EXC
COMPLETE SET (8)	8.00	3.60	1.00
COMMON CARD (1-8)	.50	.23	.06
☐ 1 Wally Backman	.50	.23	.06
☐ 2 Gary Carter	1.25	.55	.16
☐ 3 Ron Darling	.75	.35	.09
☐ 4 Dwight Gooden	1.25	.55	.16
☐ 5 Keith Hernandez	1.00	.45	.12
☐ 6 Howard Johnson	.75	.35	.09
☐ 7 Roger McDowell	.75	.35	.09
☐ 8 Darryl Strawberry	1.00	.45	.12
☐ NNO Membership Card	.50	.23	.06

1986 Mets Greats TCMA

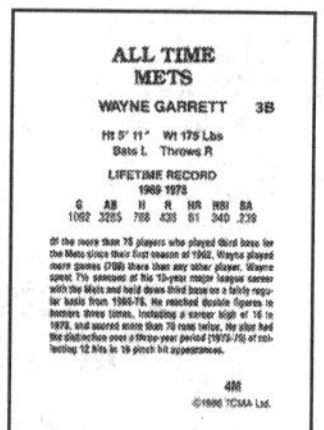

These 12 standard-size cards feature some of the best Mets from their first 25 seasons. The cards feature black-and-white player photos, his name, and position on the front. The backs have career totals, vital statistics and a biography.

	MINT	NRMT	EXC
COMPLETE SET (12)	5.00	2.20	.60
COMMON CARD (1-12)	.25	.11	.03
☐ 1 Ed Kranepool	.25	.11	.03
☐ 2 Ron Hunt	.25	.11	.03
☐ 3 Bud Harrelson	.25	.11	.03
☐ 4 Wayne Garrett	.25	.11	.03
☐ 5 Cleon Jones	.50	.23	.06
☐ 6 Tommie Agee	.25	.11	.03
☐ 7 Rusty Staub	.75	.35	.09
☐ 8 Jerry Grote	.50	.23	.06
☐ 9 Gary Gentry	.25	.11	.03
☐ 10 Jerry Koosman	.75	.35	.09
☐ 11 Tug McGraw	.75	.35	.09
☐ 12 Gil Hodges MG	1.00	.45	.12

1986 Mets TCMA

These cards measure 3 1/2" by 5 1/2". The borderless fronts consist of nothing but the photos. The postcard format backs give player identification, vital statistics and previous season stats. The cards are numbered with "NYM86-XX" in the upper right.

	MINT	NRMT	EXC
COMPLETE SET (40)	15.00	6.75	1.85
COMMON CARD (1-40)	.25	.11	.03
☐ 1 Rick Aguilera	1.00	.45	.12
☐ 2 Bruce Berenyi	.25	.11	.03
☐ 3 Ron Darling	.50	.23	.06
☐ 4 Sid Fernandez	.50	.23	.06
☐ 5 Dwight Gooden	1.50	.70	.19
☐ 6 Tom Gorman	.25	.11	.03
☐ 7 Ed Lynch	.25	.11	.03
☐ 8 Roger McDowell	.50	.23	.06
☐ 9 Randy Myers	1.00	.45	.12
☐ 10 Bob Ojeda	.25	.11	.03
☐ 11 Jesse Orosco	.25	.11	.03
☐ 12 Doug Sisk	.25	.11	.03
☐ 13 Gary Carter	1.00	.45	.12
☐ 14 John Gibbons	.25	.11	.03
☐ 15 Barry Lyons	.25	.11	.03
☐ 16 Wally Backman	.25	.11	.03
☐ 17 Ron Gardenhire	.25	.11	.03
☐ 18 Keith Hernandez	1.00	.45	.12
☐ 19 Howard Johnson	.50	.23	.06
☐ 20 Ray Knight	.75	.35	.09
☐ 21 Kevin Mitchell	1.00	.45	.12
☐ 22 Rafael Santana	.25	.11	.03
☐ 23 Tim Teufel	.25	.11	.03
☐ 24 Lenny Dykstra	1.50	.70	.19
☐ 25 George Foster	.50	.23	.06
☐ 26 Danny Heep	.25	.11	.03
☐ 27 Mel Stottlemyre CO	.25	.11	.03
☐ 28 Darryl Strawberry	.75	.35	.09
☐ 29 Mookie Wilson	.50	.23	.06
☐ 31 Randy Niemann	.25	.11	.03
☐ 32 Ed Hearn	.25	.11	.03
☐ 33 Stan Jefferson	.25	.11	.03
☐ 34 Bill Robinson CO	.25	.11	.03
☐ 35 Shawn Abner	.25	.11	.03
☐ 36 Terry Blocker	.25	.11	.03
☐ 37 Davey Johnson MG	.75	.35	.09
☐ 38 Bud Harrelson CO	.25	.11	.03
☐ 39 Vern Hoscheit CO	.25	.11	.03
☐ 40 Greg Pavlick CO	.25	.11	.03
☐ 43 Tim Corcoran	.25	.11	.03

1986 Mets World Series Champs

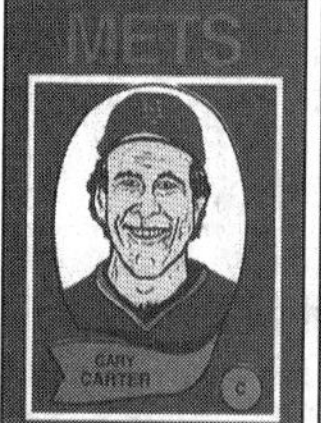

1986
WORLD SERIES
CHAMPS
BUBBLE GUMLESS CARDS
NO. 2
30 CARD SET

This 30-card limited edition set measures approximately 2 1/2" by 3 5/16" and was distributed by Jim and Dave's Sportcards. The cards were poorly cut and therefore not uniform in size. The set features the 1986 World Series champion Mets team and claims to be bubble gumless cards. This unattractive blue card front displays a head shot drawing of the player with an oval matte effect and an inner white border. The player's name is printed below the drawing on an orange banner. The player's position appears in the lower right corner printed on an orange dot. The borderless, white card backs carry a J. and D.'s logo in black ink and no player information at all. There has been some debate about the legitimacy of these cards, as many dealers believe that they should be classified the same as broder cards.

	MINT	NRMT	EXC
COMPLETE SET (30)	10.00	4.50	1.25
COMMON CARD (1-30)	.25	.11	.03
☐ 1 Keith Hernandez	1.00	.45	.12
☐ 2 Gary Carter	1.00	.45	.12
☐ 3 Wally Backman	.25	.11	.03
☐ 4 Len Dykstra	1.50	.70	.19
☐ 5 Roger McDowell	.50	.23	.06
☐ 6 Rick Aguilera	1.00	.45	.12
☐ 7 Rafael Santana	.25	.11	.03
☐ 8 Ed Hearn	.25	.11	.03
☐ 9 Doug Sisk	.25	.11	.03
☐ 10 Bruce Berenyi	.25	.11	.03
☐ 11 Darryl Strawberry	.50	.23	.06
☐ 12 Dwight Gooden	.50	.23	.06
☐ 13 Lee Mazzilli	.35	.16	.04
☐ 14 Danny Heep	.25	.11	.03
☐ 15 Howard Johnson	.35	.16	.04
☐ 16 Bob Ojeda	.35	.16	.04
☐ 17 Rick Anderson	.25	.11	.03
☐ 18 Kevin Elster	.25	.11	.03
☐ 19 Dave Magadan	.50	.23	.06
☐ 20 Randy Myers	1.00	.45	.12
☐ 21 Mookie Wilson	.35	.16	.04
☐ 22 Ron Darling	.35	.16	.04
☐ 23 Davey Johnson MG	.35	.16	.04
☐ 24 Sid Fernandez	.35	.16	.04
☐ 25 Tim Teufel	.25	.11	.03
☐ 26 Randy Niemann	.25	.11	.03
☐ 27 Jesse Orosco	.25	.11	.03
☐ 28 Kevin Mitchell	1.00	.45	.12
☐ 29 Ray Knight	.75	.35	.09
☐ 30 Checklist	.25	.11	.03

1987 Mets 1969 TCMA

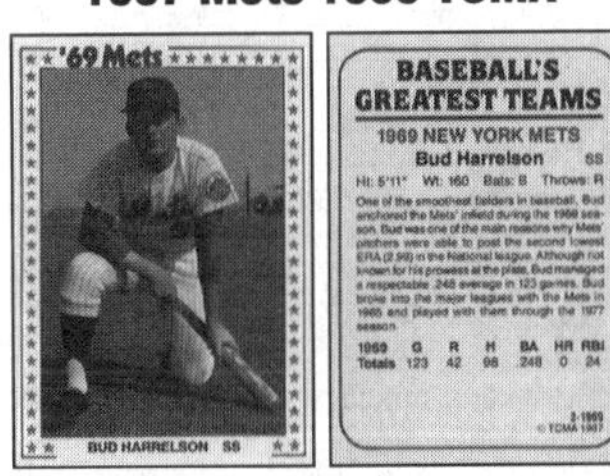

The Miracle Mets of 1969 are remembered in this standard-size set. Some of the leading players are featured with a photo, identification and position. The backs have a biography and stats from that amazing season.

	MINT	NRMT	EXC
COMPLETE SET (9)	3.00	1.35	.35
COMMON CARD (1-9)	.25	.11	.03
☐ 1 Ed Kranepool	.50	.23	.06
☐ 2 Bud Harrelson	.50	.23	.06
☐ 3 Cleon Jones Tommie Agee Ron Swoboda	.50	.23	.06
☐ 4 Jerry Koosman	.75	.35	.09
☐ 5 Gary Gentry	.25	.11	.03
☐ 6 Tug McGraw	.75	.35	.09
☐ 7 Ron Taylor	.25	.11	.03
☐ 8 Jerry Grote	.50	.23	.06
☐ 9 Ken Boswell	.25	.11	.03

1987 Mets Fan Club

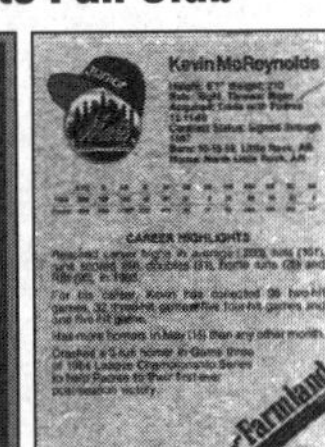

The cards in this eight-player set measure 2 1/2" by 3 1/2". The sheets were produced by Topps for the New York Mets and feature only Mets. The full sheet measures approximately 7 1/2" by 10 1/2". Cards are together on the sheet but are perforated for those collectors who want to separate the individual player cards. The cards have an outer orange border. The set was available as a membership premium for joining the Junior Mets Fan Club for 6.00. The set and club were also sponsored by Farmland Dairies Milk. The cards are unnumbered on the back although they do contain the player's uniform number on the front.

	MINT	NRMT	EXC
COMPLETE SET (9)	8.00	3.60	1.00
COMMON CARD (1-9)	.50	.23	.06
☐ 1 Gary Carter	1.25	.55	.16
☐ 2 Ron Darling	.75	.35	.09
☐ 3 Len Dykstra	2.00	.90	.25
☐ 4 Roger McDowell	.50	.23	.06
☐ 5 Kevin McReynolds	.75	.35	.09
☐ 6 Bob Ojeda	.75	.35	.09
☐ 7 Darryl Strawberry	1.25	.55	.16
☐ 8 Mookie Wilson	.75	.35	.09
☐ 9 Mets Team Card (1986 World Champs)	.50	.23	.06

1988 Mets Fan Club

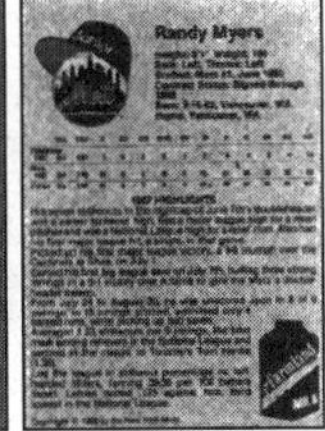

The cards in this nine-player set measure 2 1/2" by 3 1/2". The sheets were produced by Topps for the New York Mets and feature only Mets. The full sheet measures 7 1/2" by 10 1/2". Cards are together on the sheet but are perforated for those collectors who want to separate the individual player cards. The cards have an outer orange border and an inner dark blue border. The set was available as a membership premium for joining the Junior Mets Fan Club for 6.00. The set and club were also sponsored by Farmland Dairies Milk. The cards are unnumbered on the back although they do contain the player's uniform number on the front.

	MINT	NRMT	EXC
COMPLETE SET (9)	6.00	2.70	.75
COMMON CARD	.50	.23	.06
☐ 8 Gary Carter	.75	.35	.09
☐ 16 Dwight Gooden	1.00	.45	.12
☐ 17 Keith Hernandez	1.00	.45	.12
☐ 18 Darryl Strawberry	.75	.35	.09
☐ 20 Howard Johnson	.75	.35	.09
☐ 21 Kevin Elster	1.00	.45	.12
☐ 42 Roger McDowell	.50	.23	.06
☐ 48 Randy Myers	1.00	.45	.12
☐ 50 Sid Fernandez	.75	.35	.09

1988 Mets Kahn's

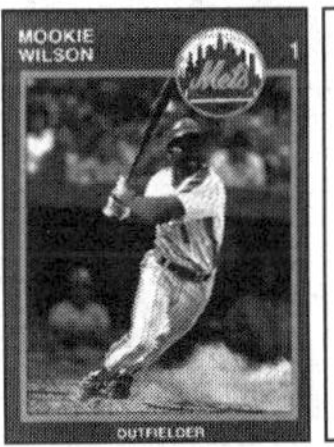

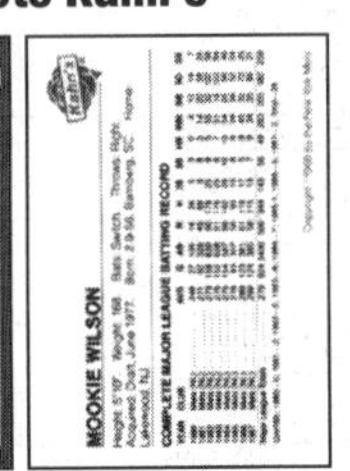

These 32-card standard-size sets were issued to the first 48,000 fans at the June 30th game between the New York Mets and the Houston Astros at Shea Stadium. The set includes 30 players, a team card, and a discount coupon card (to be redeemed at the grocery store). The cards are unnumbered except for uniform number and feature full-color photos bordered in blue and orange on the front. The Kahn's logo is printed in red in the corner of the reverse.

	MINT	NRMT	EXC
COMPLETE SET (32)	12.50	5.50	1.55
COMMON CARD	.25	.11	.03
☐ 1 Mookie Wilson	.50	.23	.06
☐ 2 Mackey Sasser	.25	.11	.03
☐ 3 Bud Harrelson CO	.50	.23	.06
☐ 4 Len Dykstra	.50	.23	.06
☐ 5 Davey Johnson MG	.50	.23	.06
☐ 6 Wally Backman	.25	.11	.03
☐ 8 Gary Carter	1.50	.70	.19
☐ 11 Tim Teufel	.25	.11	.03
☐ 12 Ron Darling	.50	.23	.06
☐ 13 Lee Mazzilli	.50	.23	.06
☐ 15 Rick Aguilera	.75	.35	.09
☐ 16 Dwight Gooden	1.50	.70	.19
☐ 17 Keith Hernandez	1.25	.55	.16
☐ 18 Darryl Strawberry	1.25	.55	.16
☐ 19 Bob Ojeda	.50	.23	.06
☐ 20 Howard Johnson	.50	.23	.06
☐ 21 Kevin Elster	1.25	.55	.16
☐ 22 Kevin McReynolds	.50	.23	.06
☐ 26 Terry Leach	.25	.11	.03
☐ 28 Bill Robinson CO	.25	.11	.03
☐ 29 Dave Magadan	.50	.23	.06
☐ 30 Mel Stottlemyre CO	.50	.23	.06
☐ 31 Gene Walter	.25	.11	.03
☐ 33 Barry Lyons	.25	.11	.03
☐ 34 Sam Perlozzo CO	.25	.11	.03
☐ 42 Roger McDowell	.50	.23	.06
☐ 44 David Cone	2.00	.90	.25
☐ 48 Randy Myers	.75	.35	.09
☐ 50 Sid Fernandez	.75	.35	.09
☐ 52 Greg Pavlick CO	.25	.11	.03
☐ NNO Team Photo Card	.50	.23	.06
☐ NNO Discount Coupon	.25	.11	.03

1989 Mets 1969 Calendar

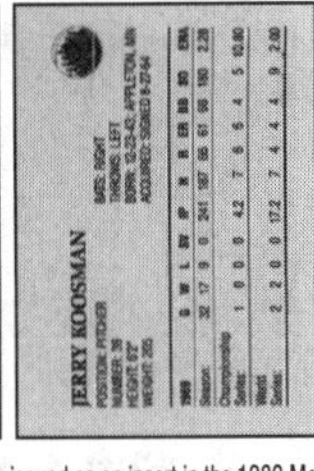

This 12-card standard size set was issued as an insert in the 1989 Met Calendar. This set features some of the most important people involved in the 1969 Miracle Met season. The cards photos are framed. The sets feature a good mix of portrait and game action photos and the backs have only the stats from 1969 on the back. The set is checklisted alphabetically below.

	MINT	NRMT	EXC
COMPLETE SET (12)	5.00	2.20	.60
COMMON CARD (1-12)	.25	.11	.03
☐ 1 Tommie Agee	.50	.23	.06
☐ 2 Donn Clendenon	.50	.23	.06
☐ 3 Wayne Garrett	.25	.11	.03
☐ 4 Jerry Grote	.50	.23	.06
☐ 5 Bud Harrelson	.50	.23	.06
☐ 6 Gil Hodges MG	1.50	.70	.19
☐ 7 Cleon Jones	.50	.23	.06
☐ 8 Jerry Koosman	.75	.35	.09
☐ 9 Ed Kranepool	.50	.23	.06
☐ 10 Tug McGraw	.75	.35	.09
☐ 11 Tom Seaver	1.50	.70	.19
☐ 12 Ron Swoboda	.50	.23	.06

1989 Mets Fan Club

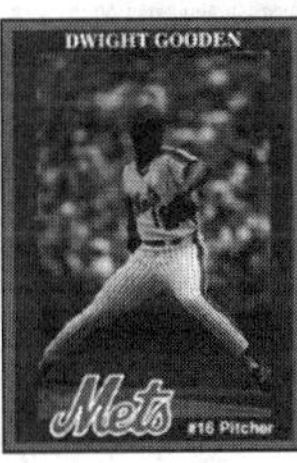

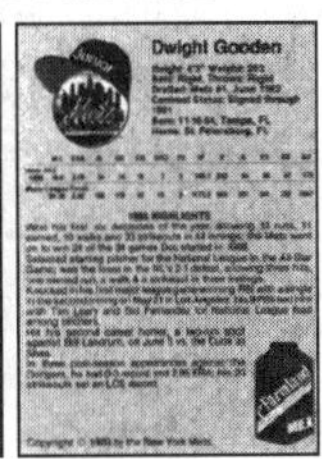

This set was produced by Topps for the Mets Fan Club as a sheet of nine cards each featuring a member of the New York Mets. The individual cards are standard size; however the set is typically traded as a sheet rather than as individual cards.

	MINT	NRMT	EXC
COMPLETE SET (9)	6.00	2.70	.75
COMMON CARD	.50	.23	.06
☐ 8 Gary Carter	1.25	.55	.16
☐ 9 Gregg Jefferies	1.50	.70	.19
☐ 16 Dwight Gooden	1.25	.55	.16
☐ 18 Darryl Strawberry	.75	.35	.09
☐ 22 Kevin McReynolds	1.00	.45	.12
☐ 25 Keith Miller	.50	.23	.06
☐ 42 Roger McDowell	.50	.23	.06
☐ 44 David Cone	1.50	.70	.19
☐ NNO Mets Team Card (Eastern Div. Champs)	.50	.23	.06

1989 Mets Kahn's

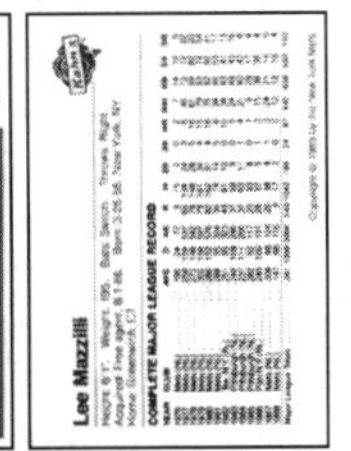

The 1989 Kahn's Mets set contains 36 (32 original and four update) standard-size cards. The fronts have color photos with Mets' colored borders (blue, orange and white). The horizontally oriented backs have career stats. The cards were available from Kahn's by sending three UPC symbols from Kahn's products and a coupon appearing in certain local newspapers. There was also a small late-season update set of Kahn's Mets showing new players who joined the Mets during the season, Jeff Innis, Keith Miller, Jeff Musselman, and Frank Viola. This "Update" subset was distributed at a different Mets Baseball Card Night game than the main set. The main set is referenced alphabetically by subject's name. The update cards are given the prefix "U" in the checklist below.

	MINT	NRMT	EXC
COMPLETE SET (36)	8.00	3.60	1.00
COMMON CARD (1-32)	.10	.05	.01
COMMON UPDATE (U1-U4)	.50	.23	.06
☐ 1 Don Aase	.10	.05	.01
☐ 2 Rick Aguilera	.50	.23	.06
☐ 3 Mark Carreon	.10	.05	.01
☐ 4 Gary Carter	1.00	.45	.12
☐ 5 David Cone	1.00	.45	.12
☐ 6 Ron Darling	.30	.14	.04
☐ 7 Kevin Elster	.30	.14	.04
☐ 8 Sid Fernandez	.50	.23	.06
☐ 9 Dwight Gooden	1.00	.45	.12
☐ 10 Bud Harrelson CO	.30	.14	.04
☐ 11 Keith Hernandez	.50	.23	.06
☐ 12 Gregg Jefferies	1.00	.45	.12
☐ 13 Davey Johnson MG	.30	.14	.04
☐ 14 Howard Johnson	.30	.14	.04
☐ 15 Barry Lyons	.10	.05	.01
☐ 16 Dave Magadan	.10	.05	.01
☐ 17 Lee Mazzilli	.30	.14	.04
☐ 18 Kevin McReynolds	.30	.14	.04
☐ 19 Randy Myers	.50	.23	.06
☐ 20 Bob Ojeda	.30	.14	.04
☐ 21 Greg Pavlick CO	.10	.05	.01
☐ 22 Sam Perlozzo CO	.10	.05	.01
☐ 23 Bill Robinson CO	.10	.05	.01
☐ 24 Juan Samuel	.10	.05	.01
☐ 25 Mackey Sasser	.10	.05	.01
☐ 26 Mel Stottlemyre CO	.30	.14	.04
☐ 27 Darryl Strawberry	.30	.14	.04
☐ 28 Tim Teufel	.10	.05	.01
☐ 29 Dave West	.10	.05	.01
☐ 30 Mookie Wilson	.30	.14	.04
☐ 31 Mets Team Photo	.30	.14	.04
☐ 32 Sponsors Card	.10	.05	.01
☐ U1 Jeff Innis	.50	.23	.06
☐ U2 Keith Miller	.50	.23	.06
☐ U3 Jeff Musselman	.50	.23	.06
☐ U4 Frank Viola	1.00	.45	.12

1990 Mets Fan Club

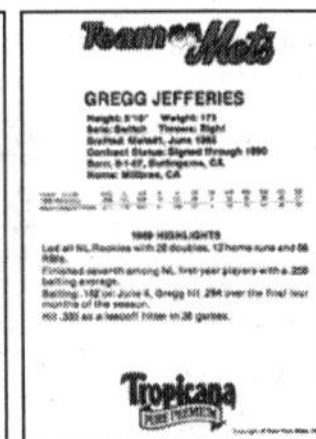

The 1990 Mets Fan Club Tropicana set was issued by the New York Mets fan club in association with the Tropicana Juice Company. For the seventh year, the Mets issued a perforated card sheet in conjunction with their fan clubs. This nine-card, standard-size set is skip-numbered and arranged by uniform numbers.

	MINT	NRMT	EXC
COMPLETE SET (9)	6.00	2.70	.75
COMMON CARD	.50	.23	.06
☐ 9 Gregg Jefferies	.75	.35	.09
☐ 16 Dwight Gooden	1.25	.55	.16
☐ 18 Darryl Strawberry	.75	.35	.09
☐ 20 Howard Johnson	.75	.35	.09
☐ 21 Kevin Elster	.75	.35	.09
☐ 25 Keith Miller	.50	.23	.06
☐ 29 Frank Viola	1.00	.45	.12
☐ 44 David Cone	1.25	.55	.16
☐ 50 Sid Fernandez	.75	.35	.09

1990 Mets Hall of Fame

This six-card set was issued by the New York Mets in conjunction with AIWA and the Wiz Home Entertainment Centers. The cards measure approximately 5" by 7" and are in the postcard type format. One set was given away to each fan attending the Mets' home game on September 9, 1990. The fronts feature borderless player photos, while the backs have brief statistics and a sponsor advertisement. The cards are unnumbered and checklisted below by year of induction.

	MINT	NRMT	EXC
COMPLETE SET	10.00	4.50	1.25
COMMON CARD (1-6)	1.00	.45	.12
☐ 1 Casey Stengel MG 1981 and Gil Hodges MG 1982	4.00	1.80	.50
☐ 2 Bud Harrelson 1986	1.00	.45	.12
☐ 3 Rusty Staub 1986	3.00	1.35	.35
☐ 4 Tom Seaver 1988	6.00	2.70	.75
☐ 5 Jerry Koosman 1989	2.00	.90	.25
☐ 6 Ed Kranepool 1990	1.00	.45	.12

1990 Mets Kahn's

The 1990 Kahn's Mets set was given away as a New York Mets stadium promotion. This standard-size set is skip-numbered by uniform number within the set and features 34 cards and two Kahn's coupon cards. Three players, Thornton, Magadan, and Mercado are

wearing different uniform numbers than listed on the front of their cards. In addition to the Shea Stadium promotion, the complete set was also available in specially marked three-packs of Kahn's Wieners.

	MINT	NRMT	EXC
COMPLETE SET (34)	7.50	3.40	.95
COMMON CARD	.25	.11	.03
☐ 1 Lou Thornton	.25	.11	.03
☐ 2 Mackey Sasser	.25	.11	.03
☐ 3 Bud Harrelson CO	.50	.23	.06
☐ 4 Mike Cubbage CO	.25	.11	.03
☐ 5 Davey Johnson MG	.50	.23	.06
☐ 6 Mike Marshall	.25	.11	.03
☐ 9 Gregg Jefferies	.50	.23	.06
☐ 10 Dave Magadan	.25	.11	.03
☐ 11 Tim Teufel	.25	.11	.03
☐ 13 Jeff Musselman	.25	.11	.03
☐ 15 Ron Darling	.50	.23	.06
☐ 16 Dwight Gooden	1.00	.45	.12
☐ 18 Darryl Strawberry	.50	.23	.06
☐ 19 Bob Ojeda	.50	.23	.06
☐ 20 Howard Johnson	.50	.23	.06
☐ 21 Kevin Elster	.50	.23	.06
☐ 22 Kevin McReynolds	.25	.11	.03
☐ 25 Keith Miller	.25	.11	.03
☐ 26 Alejandro Pena	.25	.11	.03
☐ 27 Tom O'Malley	.25	.11	.03
☐ 29 Frank Viola	.50	.23	.06
☐ 30 Mel Stottlemyre CO	.50	.23	.06
☐ 31 John Franco	.50	.23	.06
☐ 32 Doc Edwards CO	.25	.11	.03
☐ 33 Barry Lyons	.25	.11	.03
☐ 35 Orlando Mercado	.25	.11	.03
☐ 40 Jeff Innis	.25	.11	.03
☐ 44 David Cone	1.00	.45	.12
☐ 45 Mark Carreon	.25	.11	.03
☐ 47 Wally Whitehurst	.25	.11	.03
☐ 48 Julio Machado	.25	.11	.03
☐ 50 Sid Fernandez	.75	.35	.09
☐ 52 Greg Pavlick CO	.25	.11	.03
☐ NNO Team Photo	.50	.23	.06

1991 Mets Kahn's

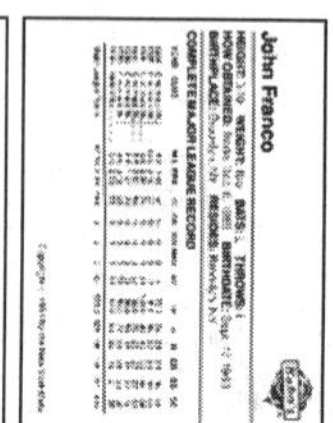

The 1991 Kahn's Mets set contains 33 cards measuring the standard size. The set is skip-numbered on the card fronts by uniform number and includes two Kahn's coupon cards. The front features color action player photos, on a white and blue pinstripe pattern. The player's name is given in an orange stripe below the picture. In a horizontal format the back presents biographical information, major league statistics, and minor league statistics where appropriate. A complete set was given away to each fan attending the New York Mets game at Shea Stadium on June 17, 1991.

	MINT	NRMT	EXC
COMPLETE SET (33)	7.50	3.40	.95
COMMON CARD	.25	.11	.03
☐ 1 Vince Coleman	.50	.23	.06
☐ 2 Mackey Sasser	.25	.11	.03
☐ 3 Bud Harrelson MG	.50	.23	.06
☐ 4 Mike Cubbage CO	.25	.11	.03
☐ 5 Charlie O'Brien	.25	.11	.03
☐ 7 Hubie Brooks	.50	.23	.06
☐ 8 Daryl Boston	.25	.11	.03
☐ 9 Gregg Jefferies	.50	.23	.06
☐ 10 Dave Magadan	.25	.11	.03
☐ 11 Tim Teufel	.25	.11	.03
☐ 13 Rick Cerone	.25	.11	.03
☐ 15 Ron Darling	.50	.23	.06
☐ 16 Dwight Gooden	1.00	.45	.12
☐ 17 David Cone	1.00	.45	.12
☐ 20 Howard Johnson	.50	.23	.06
☐ 21 Kevin Elster	.50	.23	.06
☐ 22 Kevin McReynolds	.25	.11	.03
☐ 25 Keith Miller	.25	.11	.03
☐ 26 Alejandro Pena	.25	.11	.03
☐ 28 Tom Herr	.25	.11	.03
☐ 29 Frank Viola	.50	.23	.06
☐ 30 Mel Stottlemyre CO	.50	.23	.06
☐ 31 John Franco	.50	.23	.06
☐ 32 Doc Edwards CO	.25	.11	.03
☐ 40 Jeff Innis	.25	.11	.03
☐ 43 Doug Simons	.25	.11	.03
☐ 45 Mark Carreon	.25	.11	.03
☐ 47 Wally Whitehurst	.25	.11	.03
☐ 48 Pete Schourek	.50	.23	.06
☐ 50 Sid Fernandez	.50	.23	.06
☐ 51 Tom Spencer CO	.25	.11	.03
☐ 52 Greg Pavlick CO	.25	.11	.03
☐ NNO 1991 New York Mets Team photo	.50	.23	.06

1991 Mets WIZ

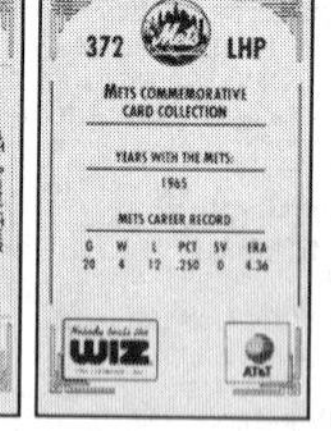

This 450-card commemorative New York Mets set was sponsored by WIZ Home Entertainment Centers and ATT. The set was issued on 30 (approximately) 10" by 9" perforated sheets (15 cards per sheet); after perforation, the cards measure approximately 2" by 3". The fronts have black and white head shots of the players on a white card face decorated with a blue picture frame design. The player's name and position are written vertically alongside the pictures. The team logo above the picture and the Wiz logo below round out the card face. In black lettering on white, the backs have the player's position, years (and stats) with the Mets, and career record. The team and sponsors' logos also appear on the back. The cards are numbered on the back and listed in alphabetical order. The set purports to show every player who ever played for the New York Mets. The set was issued in three series to be distributed at three home games during the year, e.g., the first series was issued to all fans attending the Mets home game on May 25, 1991.

	MINT	NRMT	EXC
COMPLETE SET (450)	50.00	22.00	6.25
COMMON CARD (1-439)	.10	.05	.01
☐ 1 Don Aase	.10	.05	.01
☐ 2 Tommie Agee	.30	.14	.04
☐ 3 Rick Aguilera	.50	.23	.06
☐ 4 Jack Aker	.10	.05	.01
☐ 5 Neil Allen	.10	.05	.01
☐ 6 Bill Almon	.10	.05	.01
☐ 7 Sandy Alomar Sr.	.30	.14	.04
☐ 8 Jesus Alou	.30	.14	.04
☐ 9 George Altman	.10	.05	.01
☐ 10 Luis Alvarado	.10	.05	.01
☐ 11 Craig Anderson	.10	.05	.01
☐ 12 Rick Anderson	.10	.05	.01
☐ 13 Bob Apodaca	.10	.05	.01
☐ 14 Gerry Arrigo	.10	.05	.01
☐ 15 Richie Ashburn	2.50	1.10	.30
☐ 16 Tucker Ashford	.10	.05	.01
☐ 17 Bob Aspromonte	.10	.05	.01
☐ 18 Benny Ayala	.10	.05	.01
☐ 19 Wally Backman	.10	.05	.01
☐ 20 Kevin Baez	.10	.05	.01
☐ 21 Bob Bailor	.10	.05	.01
☐ 22 Rick Baldwin	.10	.05	.01
☐ 23 Billy Baldwin	.10	.05	.01
☐ 24 Lute Barnes	.10	.05	.01
☐ 25 Ed Bauta	.10	.05	.01
☐ 26 Billy Beane	.10	.05	.01
☐ 27 Larry Bearnarth	.10	.05	.01
☐ 28 Blaine Beatty	.10	.05	.01
☐ 29 Jim Beauchamp	.10	.05	.01
☐ 30 Gus Bell	.30	.14	.04
☐ 31 Dennis Bennett	.10	.05	.01
☐ 32 Butch Benton	.10	.05	.01
☐ 33 Juan Berenguer	.10	.05	.01
☐ 34 Bruce Berenyi	.10	.05	.01
☐ 35 Dwight Bernard	.10	.05	.01
☐ 36 Yogi Berra	3.00	1.35	.35
☐ 37 Jim Bethke	.10	.05	.01
☐ 38 Mike Bishop	.10	.05	.01
☐ 39 Terry Blocker	.10	.05	.01
☐ 40 Bruce Bochy	.10	.05	.01
☐ 41 Bruce Boisclair	.10	.05	.01
☐ 42 Dan Boitano	.10	.05	.01
☐ 43 Mark Bomback	.10	.05	.01
☐ 44 Don Bosch	.10	.05	.01
☐ 45 Daryl Boston	.10	.05	.01
☐ 46 Ken Boswell	.10	.05	.01
☐ 47 Ed Bouchee	.10	.05	.01
☐ 48 Larry Bowa	.30	.14	.04
☐ 49 Ken Boyer	.50	.23	.06
☐ 50 Mark Bradley	.10	.05	.01
☐ 51 Eddie Bressoud	.10	.05	.01
☐ 52 Hubie Brooks	.30	.14	.04
☐ 53 Kevin D. Brown	.10	.05	.01
☐ 54 Leon Brown	.10	.05	.01
☐ 55 Mike Bruhert	.10	.05	.01
☐ 56 Jerry Buchek	.10	.05	.01
☐ 57 Larry Burright	.10	.05	.01
☐ 58 Ray Burris	.10	.05	.01
☐ 59 John Candelaria	.30	.14	.04
☐ 60 Chris Cannizzaro	.10	.05	.01
☐ 61 Buzz Capra	.10	.05	.01
☐ 62 Jose Cardenal	.30	.14	.04
☐ 63 Don Cardwell	.10	.05	.01
☐ 64 Duke Carmel	.10	.05	.01
☐ 65 Chuck Carr	.10	.05	.01
☐ 66 Mark Carreon	.30	.14	.04
☐ 67 Gary Carter	2.00	.90	.25
☐ 68 Elio Chacon	.10	.05	.01
☐ 69 Dean Chance	.30	.14	.04
☐ 70 Kelvin Chapman	.10	.05	.01
☐ 71 Ed Charles	.10	.05	.01
☐ 72 Rich Chiles	.10	.05	.01
☐ 73 Harry Chiti	.10	.05	.01
☐ 74 John Christensen	.10	.05	.01
☐ 75 Joe Christopher	.10	.05	.01
☐ 76 Galen Cisco	.10	.05	.01
☐ 77 Donn Clendenon	.30	.14	.04
☐ 78 Gene Clines	.10	.05	.01
☐ 79 Choo Choo Coleman	.30	.14	.04
☐ 80 Kevin Collins	.10	.05	.01
☐ 81 David Cone	2.00	.90	.25
☐ 82 Bill Connors	.10	.05	.01
☐ 83 Cliff Cook	.10	.05	.01
☐ 84 Tim Corcoran	.10	.05	.01
☐ 85 Mardie Cornejo	.10	.05	.01
☐ 86 Billy Cowan	.10	.05	.01
☐ 87 Roger Craig	.30	.14	.04
☐ 88 Jerry Cram	.10	.05	.01
☐ 89 Mike Cubbage	.10	.05	.01
☐ 90 Ron Darling	.30	.14	.04
☐ 91 Ray Daviault	.10	.05	.01
☐ 92 Tommy Davis	.30	.14	.04
☐ 93 John DeMerit	.10	.05	.01
☐ 94 Bill Denehy	.10	.05	.01
☐ 95 Jack DiLauro	.10	.05	.01
☐ 96 Carlos Diaz	.10	.05	.01
☐ 97 Mario Diaz	.10	.05	.01
☐ 98 Steve Dillon	.10	.05	.01
☐ 99 Sammy Drake	.10	.05	.01
☐ 100 Jim Dwyer	.10	.05	.01
☐ 101 Duffy Dyer	.10	.05	.01
☐ 102 Len Dykstra	1.50	.70	.19
☐ 103 Tom Edens	.10	.05	.01
☐ 104 Dave Eilers	.10	.05	.01
☐ 105 Larry Elliot	.10	.05	.01
☐ 106 Dock Ellis	.30	.14	.04
☐ 107 Kevin Elster	.30	.14	.04
☐ 108 Nino Espinosa	.10	.05	.01
☐ 109 Chuck Estrada	.10	.05	.01
☐ 110 Francisco Estrada	.10	.05	.01
☐ 111 Pete Falcone	.10	.05	.01
☐ 112 Sid Fernandez	.50	.23	.06
☐ 113 Chico Fernandez	.10	.05	.01
☐ 114 Sergio Ferrer	.10	.05	.01
☐ 115 Jack Fisher	.10	.05	.01
☐ 116 Mike Fitzgerald	.10	.05	.01
☐ 117 Shaun Fitzmaurice	.10	.05	.01
☐ 118 Gil Flores	.10	.05	.01
☐ 119 Doug Flynn	.10	.05	.01
☐ 120 Tim Foli	.10	.05	.01
☐ 121 Rich Folkers	.10	.05	.01
☐ 122 Larry Foss	.10	.05	.01
☐ 123 George Foster	.50	.23	.06
☐ 124 Leo Foster	.10	.05	.01
☐ 125 Joe Foy	.10	.05	.01
☐ 126 John Franco	.50	.23	.06
☐ 127 Jim Fregosi	.30	.14	.04
☐ 128 Bob Friend	.30	.14	.04
☐ 129 Danny Frisella	.10	.05	.01
☐ 130 Brent Gaff	.10	.05	.01
☐ 131 Bob Gallagher	.10	.05	.01
☐ 132 Ron Gardenhire	.10	.05	.01
☐ 133 Rob Gardner	.10	.05	.01
☐ 134 Wes Gardner	.10	.05	.01
☐ 135 Wayne Garrett	.10	.05	.01
☐ 136 Rod Gaspar	.10	.05	.01
☐ 137 Gary Gentry	.30	.14	.04
☐ 138 John Gibbons	.10	.05	.01
☐ 139 Bob Gibson	.10	.05	.01
☐ 140 Brian Giles	.10	.05	.01
☐ 141 Joe Ginsberg	.10	.05	.01
☐ 142 Ed Glynn	.10	.05	.01
☐ 143 Jesse Gonder	.10	.05	.01
☐ 144 Dwight Gooden	1.50	.70	.19
☐ 145 Greg Goossen	.30	.14	.04
☐ 146 Tom Gorman	.10	.05	.01
☐ 147 Jim Gosger	.10	.05	.01
☐ 148 Bill Graham	.10	.05	.01
☐ 149 Wayne Graham	.10	.05	.01
☐ 150 Dallas Green	.30	.14	.04
☐ 151 Pumpsie Green	.10	.05	.01
☐ 152 Tom Grieve	.30	.14	.04
☐ 153 Jerry Grote	.30	.14	.04
☐ 154 Joe Grzenda	.10	.05	.01
☐ 155 Don Hahn	.10	.05	.01
☐ 156 Tom Hall	.10	.05	.01
☐ 157 Jack Hamilton	.10	.05	.01
☐ 158 Ike Hampton	.10	.05	.01
☐ 159 Tim Harkness	.10	.05	.01
☐ 160 Bud Harrelson	.30	.14	.04
☐ 161 Greg A. Harris	.30	.14	.04
☐ 162 Greg Harts	.10	.05	.01
☐ 163 Andy Hassler	.10	.05	.01
☐ 164 Tom Hausman	.10	.05	.01
☐ 165 Ed Hearn	.10	.05	.01
☐ 166 Richie Hebner	.30	.14	.04
☐ 167 Danny Heep	.10	.05	.01
☐ 168 Jack Heidemann	.10	.05	.01
☐ 169 Bob Heise	.10	.05	.01
☐ 170 Ken Henderson	.10	.05	.01
☐ 171 Steve Henderson	.10	.05	.01
☐ 172 Bob Hendley	.10	.05	.01
☐ 173 Phil Hennigan	.10	.05	.01
☐ 174 Bill Hepler	.10	.05	.01
☐ 175 Ron Herbel	.10	.05	.01
☐ 176 Manny Hernandez	.10	.05	.01
☐ 177 Keith Hernandez	.75	.35	.09
☐ 178 Tommy Herr	.30	.14	.04
☐ 179 Rick Herrscher	.10	.05	.01
☐ 180 Jim Hickman	.10	.05	.01
☐ 181 Joe Hicks	.10	.05	.01
☐ 182 Chuck Hiller	.10	.05	.01
☐ 183 Dave Hillman	.10	.05	.01
☐ 184 Jerry Hinsley	.10	.05	.01
☐ 185 Gil Hodges	2.50	1.10	.30
☐ 186 Ron Hodges	.10	.05	.01
☐ 187 Scott Holman	.10	.05	.01
☐ 188 Jay Hook	.10	.05	.01
☐ 189 Mike Howard	.10	.05	.01
☐ 190 Jesse Hudson	.10	.05	.01
☐ 191 Keith Hughes	.10	.05	.01
☐ 192 Todd Hundley	2.00	.90	.25
☐ 193 Ron Hunt	.30	.14	.04
☐ 194 Willard Hunter	.10	.05	.01
☐ 195 Clint Hurdle	.10	.05	.01
☐ 196 Jeff Innis	.10	.05	.01
☐ 197 Al Jackson	.10	.05	.01
☐ 198 Roy Lee Jackson	.10	.05	.01
☐ 199 Gregg Jefferies	.75	.35	.09
☐ 200 Stan Jefferson	.10	.05	.01
☐ 201 Chris Jelic	.10	.05	.01
☐ 202 Bob D. Johnson	.10	.05	.01
☐ 203 Howard Johnson	.50	.23	.06
☐ 204 Bob W. Johnson	.10	.05	.01
☐ 205 Randy Jones	.30	.14	.04
☐ 206 Sherman Jones	.10	.05	.01
☐ 207 Cleon Jones	.30	.14	.04
☐ 208 Ross Jones	.10	.05	.01
☐ 209 Mike Jorgensen	.10	.05	.01
☐ 210 Rod Kanehl	.30	.14	.04
☐ 211 Dave Kingman	.75	.35	.09
☐ 212 Bobby Klaus	.10	.05	.01
☐ 213 Jay Kleven	.10	.05	.01
☐ 214 Lou Klimchock	.10	.05	.01
☐ 215 Ray Knight	.50	.23	.06
☐ 216 Kevin Kobel	.10	.05	.01
☐ 217 Gary Kolb	.10	.05	.01
☐ 218 Cal Koonce	.10	.05	.01
☐ 219 Jerry Koosman	.50	.23	.06
☐ 220 Ed Kranepool	.50	.23	.06
☐ 221 Gary Kroll	.10	.05	.01
☐ 222 Clem Labine	.50	.23	.06
☐ 223 Jack Lamabe	.10	.05	.01
☐ 224 Hobie Landrith	.10	.05	.01
☐ 225 Frank Lary	.30	.14	.04
☐ 226 Bill Latham	.10	.05	.01
☐ 227 Terry Leach	.10	.05	.01
☐ 228 Tim Leary	.10	.05	.01
☐ 229 John Lewis	.10	.05	.01
☐ 230 David Liddell	.10	.05	.01
☐ 231 Phil Linz	.30	.14	.04
☐ 232 Ron Locke	.10	.05	.01
☐ 233 Skip Lockwood	.10	.05	.01
☐ 234 Mickey Lolich	.50	.23	.06
☐ 235 Phil Lombardi	.10	.05	.01
☐ 236 Al Luplow	.10	.05	.01
☐ 237 Ed Lynch	.10	.05	.01
☐ 238 Barry Lyons	.10	.05	.01
☐ 239 Ken MacKenzie	.10	.05	.01
☐ 240 Julio Machado	.10	.05	.01
☐ 241 Elliott Maddox	.10	.05	.01
☐ 242 Dave Magadan	.30	.14	.04
☐ 243 Pepe Mangual	.10	.05	.01
☐ 244 Phil Mankowski	.10	.05	.01
☐ 245 Felix Mantilla	.10	.05	.01
☐ 246 Mike G. Marshall	.30	.14	.04
☐ 247 Dave Marshall	.10	.05	.01
☐ 248 Jim Marshall	.10	.05	.01
☐ 249 Mike A. Marshall	.30	.14	.04
☐ 250 J.C. Martin	.10	.05	.01
☐ 251 Jerry Martin	.10	.05	.01
☐ 252 Teddy Martinez	.10	.05	.01
☐ 253 Jon Matlack	.30	.14	.04
☐ 254 Jerry May	.10	.05	.01
☐ 255 Willie Mays	7.50	3.40	.95
☐ 256 Lee Mazzilli	.30	.14	.04
☐ 257 Jim McAndrew	.10	.05	.01
☐ 258 Bob McClure	.10	.05	.01
☐ 259 Roger McDowell	.30	.14	.04
☐ 260 Tug McGraw	.50	.23	.06
☐ 261 Jeff McKnight	.10	.05	.01
☐ 262 Roy McMillan	.30	.14	.04
☐ 263 Kevin McReynolds	.30	.14	.04
☐ 264 George Medich	.10	.05	.01

	MINT	NRMT	EXC
☐ 265 Orlando Mercado	.10	.05	.01
☐ 266 Butch Metzger	.10	.05	.01
☐ 267 Felix Millan	.30	.14	.04
☐ 268 Bob G. Miller	.10	.05	.01
☐ 269 Bob L. Miller	.10	.05	.01
☐ 270 Dyar Miller	.10	.05	.01
☐ 271 Larry Miller	.10	.05	.01
☐ 272 Keith Miller	.10	.05	.01
☐ 273 Randy Milligan	.10	.05	.01
☐ 274 John Milner	.10	.05	.01
☐ 275 John Mitchell	.10	.05	.01
☐ 276 Kevin Mitchell	.50	.23	.06
☐ 277 Wilmer Mizell	.30	.14	.04
☐ 278 Herb Moford	.10	.05	.01
☐ 279 Willie Montanez	.30	.14	.04
☐ 280 Joe Moock	.10	.05	.01
☐ 281 Tommy Moore	.10	.05	.01
☐ 282 Bob Moorhead	.10	.05	.01
☐ 283 Jerry Morales	.10	.05	.01
☐ 284 Al Moran	.10	.05	.01
☐ 285 Jose Moreno	.10	.05	.01
☐ 286 Bill Murphy	.10	.05	.01
☐ 287 Dale Murray	.50	.23	.06
☐ 288 Dennis Musgraves	.10	.05	.01
☐ 289 Jeff Musselman	.10	.05	.01
☐ 290 Randy Myers	.50	.23	.06
☐ 291 Bob Myrick	.10	.05	.01
☐ 292 Danny Napoleon	.10	.05	.01
☐ 293 Charlie Neal	.30	.14	.04
☐ 294 Randy Niemann	.10	.05	.01
☐ 295 Joe Nolan	.10	.05	.01
☐ 296 Dan Norman	.10	.05	.01
☐ 297 Ed Nunez	.10	.05	.01
☐ 298 Charlie O'Brien	.10	.05	.01
☐ 299 Tom O'Malley	.10	.05	.01
☐ 300 Bob Ojeda	.30	.14	.04
☐ 301 Jose Oquendo	.10	.05	.01
☐ 302 Jesse Orosco	.30	.14	.04
☐ 303 Junior Ortiz	.10	.05	.01
☐ 304 Brian Ostrosser	.10	.05	.01
☐ 305 Amos Otis	.30	.14	.04
☐ 306 Rick Ownbey	.10	.05	.01
☐ 307 John Pacella	.10	.05	.01
☐ 308 Tom Paciorek	.30	.14	.04
☐ 309 Harry Parker	.10	.05	.01
☐ 310 Tom Parsons	.10	.05	.01
☐ 311 Al Pedrique	.10	.05	.01
☐ 312 Brock Pemberton	.10	.05	.01
☐ 313 Alejandro Pena	.30	.14	.04
☐ 314 Bobby Pfeil	.10	.05	.01
☐ 315 Mike Phillips	.10	.05	.01
☐ 316 Jim Piersall	.50	.23	.06
☐ 317 Joe Pignatano	.10	.05	.01
☐ 318 Grover Powell	.10	.05	.01
☐ 319 Rich Puig	.10	.05	.01
☐ 320 Charlie Puleo	.10	.05	.01
☐ 321 Gary Rajsich	.10	.05	.01
☐ 322 Mario Ramirez	.10	.05	.01
☐ 323 Lenny Randle	.10	.05	.01
☐ 324 Bob Rauch	.10	.05	.01
☐ 325 Jeff Reardon	.50	.23	.06
☐ 326 Darren Reed	.10	.05	.01
☐ 327 Hal Reniff	.10	.05	.01
☐ 328 Ronn Reynolds	.10	.05	.01
☐ 329 Tom Reynolds	.10	.05	.01
☐ 330 Dennis Ribant	.10	.05	.01
☐ 331 Gordie Richardson	.10	.05	.01
☐ 332 Dave Roberts	.10	.05	.01
☐ 333 Les Rohr	.10	.05	.01
☐ 334 Luis Rosado	.10	.05	.01
☐ 335 Don Rose	.10	.05	.01
☐ 336 Don Rowe	.10	.05	.01
☐ 337 Dick Rusteck	.10	.05	.01
☐ 338 Nolan Ryan	12.50	5.50	1.55
☐ 339 Ray Sadecki	.10	.05	.01
☐ 340 Joe Sambito	.10	.05	.01
☐ 341 Amado Samuel	.10	.05	.01
☐ 342 Juan Samuel	.30	.14	.04
☐ 343 Ken Sanders	.10	.05	.01
☐ 344 Rafael Santana	.10	.05	.01
☐ 345 Mackey Sasser	.10	.05	.01
☐ 346 Mac Scarce	.10	.05	.01
☐ 347 Jim Schaffer	.10	.05	.01
☐ 348 Dan Schatzeder	.10	.05	.01
☐ 349 Calvin Schiraldi	.10	.05	.01
☐ 350 Al Schmelz	.10	.05	.01
☐ 351 Dave Schneck	.10	.05	.01
☐ 352 Ted Schreiber	.10	.05	.01
☐ 353 Don Schulze	.10	.05	.01
☐ 354 Mike Scott	.30	.14	.04
☐ 355 Ray Searage	.10	.05	.01
☐ 356 Tom Seaver	5.00	2.20	.60
☐ 357 Dick Selma	.10	.05	.01
☐ 358 Art Shamsky	.30	.14	.04
☐ 359 Bob Shaw	.30	.14	.04
☐ 360 Don Shaw	.10	.05	.01
☐ 361 Norm Sherry	.30	.14	.04
☐ 362 Craig Shipley	.10	.05	.01
☐ 363 Bart Shirley	.10	.05	.01
☐ 364 Bill Short	.10	.05	.01
☐ 365 Paul Siebert	.10	.05	.01
☐ 366 Ken Singleton	.50	.23	.06
☐ 367 Doug Sisk	.10	.05	.01
☐ 368 Bobby Gene Smith	.10	.05	.01
☐ 369 Charley Smith	.10	.05	.01
☐ 370 Dick Smith	.10	.05	.01
☐ 371 Duke Snider	3.00	1.35	.35
☐ 372 Warren Spahn	3.00	1.35	.35
☐ 373 Larry Stahl	.10	.05	.01
☐ 374 Roy Staiger	.10	.05	.01
☐ 375 Tracy Stallard	.10	.05	.01
☐ 376 Leroy Stanton	.10	.05	.01
☐ 377 Rusty Staub	.50	.23	.06
☐ 378 John Stearns	.30	.14	.04
☐ 379 John Stephenson	.10	.05	.01
☐ 380 Randy Sterling	.10	.05	.01
☐ 381 George Stone	.10	.05	.01
☐ 382 Darryl Strawberry	.75	.35	.09
☐ 383 John Strohmayer	.10	.05	.01
☐ 384 Brent Strom	.10	.05	.01
☐ 385 Dick Stuart	.30	.14	.04
☐ 386 Tom Sturdivant	.10	.05	.01
☐ 387 Bill Sudakis	.10	.05	.01
☐ 388 John Sullivan	.10	.05	.01
☐ 389 Darrell Sutherland	.10	.05	.01
☐ 390 Ron Swoboda	.30	.14	.04
☐ 391 Craig Swan	.10	.05	.01
☐ 392 Rick Sweet	.10	.05	.01
☐ 393 Pat Tabler	.10	.05	.01
☐ 394 Kevin Tapani	.50	.23	.06
☐ 395 Randy Tate	.10	.05	.01
☐ 396 Frank Taveras	.10	.05	.01
☐ 397 Chuck Taylor	.10	.05	.01
☐ 398 Ron Taylor	.10	.05	.01
☐ 399 Bob Taylor	.10	.05	.01
☐ 400 Sammy Taylor	.10	.05	.01
☐ 401 Walt Terrell	.10	.05	.01
☐ 402 Ralph Terry	.30	.14	.04
☐ 403 Tim Teufel	.10	.05	.01
☐ 404 George Theodore	.10	.05	.01
☐ 405 Frank J. Thomas	.30	.14	.04
☐ 406 Lou Thornton	.10	.05	.01
☐ 407 Marv Throneberry	.50	.23	.06
☐ 408 Dick Tidrow	.10	.05	.01
☐ 409 Rusty Tillman	.10	.05	.01
☐ 410 Jackson Todd	.10	.05	.01
☐ 411 Joe Torre	1.00	.45	.12
☐ 412 Mike Torrez	.30	.14	.04
☐ 413 Kelvin Torve	.10	.05	.01
☐ 414 Alex Trevino	.10	.05	.01
☐ 415 Wayne Twitchell	.10	.05	.01
☐ 416 Del Unser	.10	.05	.01
☐ 417 Mike Vail	.10	.05	.01
☐ 418 Bobby Valentine	.30	.14	.04
☐ 419 Ellis Valentine	.10	.05	.01
☐ 420 Julio Valera	.10	.05	.01
☐ 421 Tom Veryzer	.10	.05	.01
☐ 422 Frank Viola	.50	.23	.06
☐ 423 Bill Wakefield	.10	.05	.01
☐ 424 Gene Walter	.10	.05	.01
☐ 425 Claudell Washington	.30	.14	.04
☐ 426 Hank Webb	.10	.05	.01
☐ 427 Al Weis	.10	.05	.01
☐ 428 Dave West	.10	.05	.01
☐ 429 Wally Whitehurst	.10	.05	.01
☐ 430 Carl Willey	.10	.05	.01
☐ 431 Nick Willhite	.10	.05	.01
☐ 432 Charlie Williams	.10	.05	.01
☐ 433 Mookie Wilson	.50	.23	.06
☐ 434 Herm Winningham	.10	.05	.01
☐ 435 Gene Woodling	.30	.14	.04
☐ 436 Billy Wynne	.10	.05	.01
☐ 437 Joel Youngblood	.10	.05	.01
☐ 438 Pat Zachry	.10	.05	.01
☐ 439 Don Zimmer	.30	.14	.04
☐ NNO Checklist 1-20	.10	.05	.01
☐ NNO Checklist 41-60	.10	.05	.01
☐ NNO Checklist 81-100	.10	.05	.01
☐ NNO Checklist 121-140	.10	.05	.01
☐ NNO Checklist 161-180	.10	.05	.01
☐ NNO Checklist 201-220	.10	.05	.01
☐ NNO Checklist 241-260	.10	.05	.01
☐ NNO Checklist 281-300	.10	.05	.01
☐ NNO Checklist 321-340	.10	.05	.01
☐ NNO Checklist 361-380	.10	.05	.01
☐ NNO Checklist 401-420	.10	.05	.01

1992 Mets Kahn's

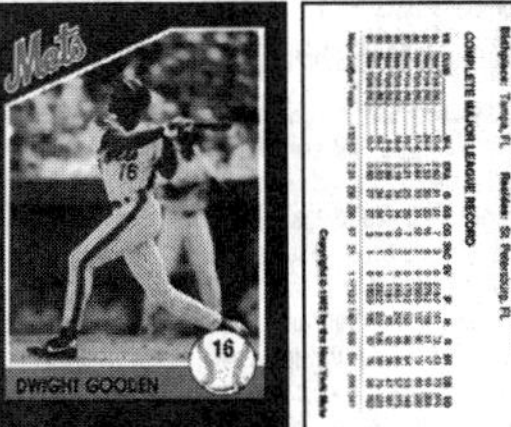

The 1992 Kahn's New York Mets set consists of 35 standard-size cards. The set included two manufacturer's coupons (one for 50 cents off Kahn's Beef Franks and another for the same amount off Kahn's Corn Dogs). The fronts feature color action player photos with a white inner border on a royal blue card face. The upper left corner of the picture is cut off to create space for the team name. An orange stripe bearing the player's name appears beneath the picture and intersects at the lower right corner a baseball with the player's uniform number. In a horizontal format, the backs carry the motto "Hardball is back," biography, and complete major league statistics. The Kahn's logo in red rounds out the back. The cards are skip-numbered by uniform number on the front and checklisted below accordingly.

	MINT	NRMT	EXC
COMPLETE SET (35)	7.50	3.40	.95
COMMON CARD	.25	.11	.03
☐ 1 Vince Coleman	.50	.23	.06
☐ 2 Mackey Sasser	.25	.11	.03
☐ 3 Junior Noboa	.25	.11	.03
☐ 4 Mike Cubbage CO	.25	.11	.03
☐ 6 Daryl Boston	.25	.11	.03
☐ 8 Dave Gallagher	.25	.11	.03
☐ 9 Todd Hundley	1.50	.70	.19
☐ 10 Jeff Torborg MG	.25	.11	.03
☐ 11 Dick Schofield	.25	.11	.03
☐ 12 Willie Randolph	.50	.23	.06
☐ 15 Kevin Elster	.50	.23	.06
☐ 16 Dwight Gooden	.50	.23	.06
☐ 17 David Cone	.50	.23	.06
☐ 18 Bret Saberhagen	.50	.23	.06
☐ 19 Anthony Young	.25	.11	.03
☐ 20 Howard Johnson	.50	.23	.06
☐ 22 Charlie O'Brien	.25	.11	.03
☐ 25 Bobby Bonilla	.50	.23	.06
☐ 26 Barry Foote CO	.25	.11	.03
☐ 27 Tom McCraw CO	.25	.11	.03
☐ 28 Dave LaRoche CO	.25	.11	.03
☐ 29 Dave Magadan	.25	.11	.03
☐ 30 Mel Stottlemyre CO	.50	.23	.06
☐ 31 John Franco	.50	.23	.06
☐ 32 Bill Pecota	.25	.11	.03
☐ 33 Eddie Murray	1.50	.70	.19
☐ 40 Jeff Innis	.25	.11	.03
☐ 44 Tim Burke	.25	.11	.03
☐ 45 Paul Gibson	.25	.11	.03
☐ 47 Wally Whitehurst	.25	.11	.03
☐ 50 Sid Fernandez	.50	.23	.06
☐ 51 John Stephenson CO	.25	.11	.03
☐ NNO Team Photo	.50	.23	.06
☐ NNO Manufacturer's Coupon Kahn's Beef Franks	.25	.11	.03
☐ NNO Manufacturer's Coupon Kahn's Corn Dogs	.25	.11	.03

1992 Mets Modell

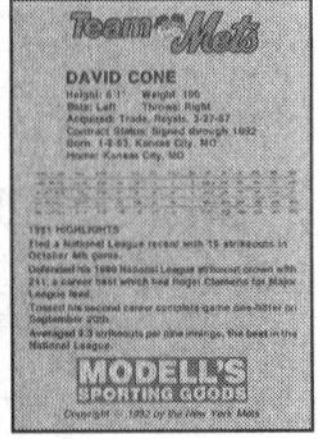

Measuring 7 1/2" by 10 1/2", this 9-card perforated sheet was sponsored by Modell's Sporting Goods and distributed as a membership benefit to Team Mets, the junior fan club. If the cards were separated, they would measure the standard size. The fronts feature white-bordered color action photos that are accented above and below by team color-coded (orange and blue) stripes. The player's name, uniform number, and position are mentioned in the bottom blue stripe. Between the Team Mets and sponsor logos, the backs present biography, statistics, and 1991 highlights. The cards are unnumbered and checklisted below in alphabetical order.

	MINT	NRMT	EXC
COMPLETE SET (9)	5.00	2.20	.60
COMMON CARD (1-9)	.40	.18	.05
☐ 1 Bobby Bonilla	.75	.35	.09
☐ 2 Vince Coleman	.40	.18	.05
☐ 3 David Cone	.75	.35	.09
☐ 4 Dwight Gooden	.75	.35	.09
☐ 5 Todd Hundley	1.00	.45	.12
☐ 6 Howard Johnson	.40	.18	.05
☐ 7 Eddie Murray	1.50	.70	.19
☐ 8 Willie Randolph	.40	.18	.05
☐ 9 Bret Saberhagen	.40	.18	.05

1993 Mets Kahn's

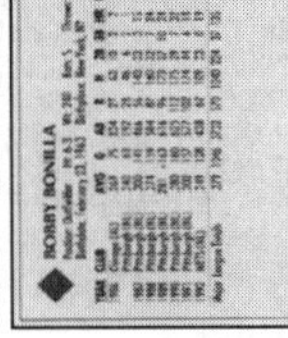

This 29-card set measures the standard size and features white-bordered color player photos on their fronts. The player's name appears in blue lettering in the upper white margin, along with his uniform number and position within orange diamonds on either side. The horizontal white backs are framed by a thin red line and carry the player's statistics. The cards are skip-numbered by uniform number on the front and checklisted below accordingly.

	MINT	NRMT	EXC
COMPLETE SET (29)	7.50	3.40	.95
COMMON CARD	.25	.11	.03
☐ 1 Tony Fernandez	.50	.23	.06
☐ 6 Joe Orsulak	.25	.11	.03
☐ 7 Jeff McKnight	.25	.11	.03
☐ 8 Dave Gallagher	.25	.11	.03
☐ 9 Todd Hundley	1.50	.70	.19
☐ 11 Vince Coleman	.50	.23	.06
☐ 12 Jeff Kent	1.00	.45	.12
☐ 16 Dwight Gooden	.75	.35	.09
☐ 18 Bret Saberhagen	.50	.23	.06
☐ 19 Anthony Young	.25	.11	.03
☐ 20 Howard Johnson	.50	.23	.06
☐ 21 Darren Reed	.25	.11	.03
☐ 22 Charlie O'Brien	.25	.11	.03
☐ 23 Tim Bogar	.25	.11	.03
☐ 25 Bobby Bonilla	.50	.23	.06
☐ 29 Frank Tanana	.50	.23	.06
☐ 31 John Franco	.50	.23	.06
☐ 33 Eddie Murray	1.50	.70	.19
☐ 34 Chico Walker	.25	.11	.03
☐ 40 Jeff Innis	.25	.11	.03
☐ 44 Ryan Thompson	.25	.11	.03
☐ 47 Mike Draper	.25	.11	.03
☐ 48 Pete Schourek	.50	.23	.06
☐ 50 Sid Fernandez	.50	.23	.06
☐ 51 Mike Maddux	.25	.11	.03
☐ NNO Team Photo	.50	.23	.06
☐ NNO Title Card	.25	.11	.03
☐ NNO Manufacturer's Coupon Kahn's Corn Dogs	.25	.11	.03
☐ NNO Manufacturer's Coupon Kahn's Hot Dogs	.25	.11	.03

1994 Mets '69 Capital Cards Postcard Promos

Licensed by Miracle of 1969 Enterprises, Inc., this boxed set of 32 postcards commemorates the 25th Anniversary of the World Championship season of the 1969 Mets. Capital Cards commissioned renowned sports artist Ron Lewis to create from oil paintings these postcards, which measure 3 1/2" by 5 1/2". Just 25,000 postcard sets were produced, with each having a unique serial number. Also 5,000 individually-numbered uncut sheets were produced. The color portraits on the fronts are white-bordered and the player's name appears in the wider bottom border. The backs have the typical postcard format and brief biographical and season statistical information in the upper left. The cards are numbered on the back and the word "PROMO" is stamped across each back.

	MINT	NRMT	EXC
COMPLETE SET (32)	20.00	9.00	2.50
COMMON CARD (1-32)	.50	.23	.06
☐ 1 Title Card	.50	.23	.06
☐ 2 Gil Hodges MG	2.00	.90	.25
☐ 3 Rube Walker CO	.50	.23	.06
☐ 4 Yogi Berra CO	2.50	1.10	.30
☐ 5 Joe Pignatano CO	.50	.23	.06
☐ 6 Ed Yost CO	.50	.23	.06
☐ 7 Tommie Agee	.75	.35	.09
☐ 8 Ken Boswell	.50	.23	.06
☐ 9 Don Cardwell	.50	.23	.06
☐ 10 Ed Charles	.50	.23	.06
☐ 11 Donn Clendenon	.75	.35	.09
☐ 12 Jack DiLauro	.50	.23	.06
☐ 13 Duffy Dyer	.50	.23	.06
☐ 14 Wayne Garrett	.50	.23	.06
☐ 15 Rod Gasper	.50	.23	.06
☐ 16 Gary Gentry	.50	.23	.06
☐ 17 Jerry Grote	.75	.35	.09
☐ 18 Bud Harrelson	.75	.35	.09
☐ 19 Cleon Jones	.75	.35	.09
☐ 20 Cal Koonce	.50	.23	.06
☐ 21 Jerry Koosman	1.00	.45	.12
☐ 22 Ed Kranepool	.75	.35	.09
☐ 23 J.C. Martin	.50	.23	.06
☐ 24 Jim McAndrew	.50	.23	.06
☐ 25 Tug McGraw	1.50	.70	.19
☐ 26 Bob Pfeil	.50	.23	.06
☐ 27 Nolan Ryan	7.50	3.40	.95
☐ 28 Tom Seaver	5.00	2.20	.60
☐ 29 Art Shamsky	.50	.23	.06
☐ 30 Ron Swoboda	.75	.35	.09
☐ 31 Ron Taylor	.50	.23	.06
☐ 32 Al Weis	.50	.23	.06

1994 Mets '69 Commemorative Sheet

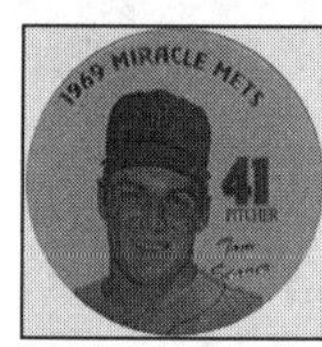

Issued in a 14 1/2" by 11 1/4" blue padded gold-stamped certificate holder, this commemorative sheet featuring 31 perforated caps was released on the 25th anniversary of the 1969 World Champion Mets. Each cap measures 1 5/8" in diameter, and the color player cutouts displayed are the same as those in the Ron Lewis postcard set. The words "1969 Miracle Mets" is gold foil-stamped at the top following the curve; likewise, the player's name is similarly impressed on the front. The backs are blank. The 31 caps are arranged on a sheet that has at its center a special 25th anniversary Mets logo. The enclosed certificate of authenticity carries the sheet serial number and total production figures (25,000). The caps are unnumbered and listed below just as they are in the postcard set, with nonplayers listed first.

	MINT	NRMT	EXC
COMPLETE SET (31)	15.00	6.75	1.85
COMMON CARD (1-31)	.25	.11	.03
☐ 1 Gil Hodges MG	1.00	.45	.12
☐ 2 Rube Walker CO	.25	.11	.03
☐ 3 Yogi Berra CO	1.00	.45	.12
☐ 4 Joe Pignatano CO	.25	.11	.03
☐ 5 Ed Yost CO	.25	.11	.03
☐ 6 Tommie Agee	.50	.23	.06
☐ 7 Ken Boswell	.25	.11	.03
☐ 8 Don Cardwell	.25	.11	.03
☐ 9 Ed Charles	.25	.11	.03
☐ 10 Donn Clendenon	.50	.23	.06
☐ 11 Jack DiLauro	.25	.11	.03
☐ 12 Duffy Dyer	.25	.11	.03
☐ 13 Wayne Garrett	.25	.11	.03
☐ 14 Rod Gaspar UER (Name misspelled Gasper on front)	.25	.11	.03
☐ 15 Gary Gentry	.25	.11	.03
☐ 16 Jerry Grote	.50	.23	.06
☐ 17 Bud Harrelson	.50	.23	.06
☐ 18 Cleon Jones	.50	.23	.06
☐ 19 Cal Koonce	.25	.11	.03
☐ 20 Jerry Koosman	.75	.35	.09
☐ 21 Ed Kranepool	.50	.23	.06
☐ 22 J.C. Martin	.25	.11	.03
☐ 23 Jim McAndrew	.25	.11	.03
☐ 24 Tug McGraw	1.00	.45	.12
☐ 25 Bobby Pfeil	.25	.11	.03
☐ 26 Nolan Ryan	5.00	2.20	.60
☐ 27 Tom Seaver	2.50	1.10	.30
☐ 28 Art Shamsky	.25	.11	.03
☐ 29 Ron Swoboda	.50	.23	.06
☐ 30- Ron Taylor	.25	.11	.03
☐ 31 Al Weis	.25	.11	.03

1994 Mets '69 Spectrum Promos

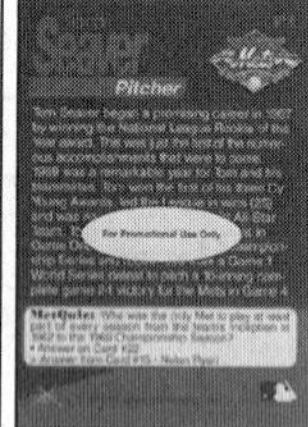

Issued to herald the commemorative 25th anniversary 1969 Miracle Mets 70-card set, these standard-size promos feature on their fronts white-bordered color photos framed by red lines. The 25th anniversary logo appears in one corner. The blue backs carry player or team season highlights. The "For Promotional Use Only" disclaimer appears within a white ellipse on the back. The cards are numbered on the back with a "P" prefix.

	MINT	NRMT	EXC
COMPLETE SET (3)	3.00	1.35	.35
COMMON CARD (P1-P3)	1.00	.45	.12
☐ P1 Tom Seaver	2.00	.90	.25
☐ P2 Jerry Koosman	1.00	.45	.12
☐ P3 Met Mania Oct. 20, 1969 (Parade showing Seaver and Koosman)	1.00	.45	.12

1994 Mets '69 Tribute

This 70-card standard-size boxed set commemorates the 1969 New York Mets championship team. Only 25,000 of these sets were

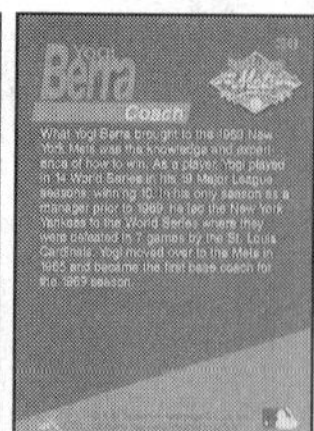

produced and each box contains a Certificate of Authenticity indicating the set number.The fronts feature color and black-and-white posed and action player photos on a white background with a thin red border. In gold foil across the top is printed "The Miracle of '69," "The '69 Countdown," or "World Champions" with the player's name at the bottom in red and blue print. The backs carry the player's name, position, career highlights, and 1969 season statistics.

	MINT	NRMT	EXC
COMPLETE SET (70)	10.00	4.50	1.25
COMMON CARD (1-69)	.10	.05	.01
☐ 1 Commemorative Card	.10	.05	.01
☐ 2 Team Photo	.20	.09	.03
☐ 3 Tom Seaver	1.50	.70	.19
☐ 4 Jerry Koosman	.35	.16	.04
☐ 5 Tommie Agee	.20	.09	.03
☐ 6 Bud Harrelson	.20	.09	.03
☐ 7 Nolan Ryan	3.00	1.35	.35
☐ 8 Jerry Grote	.20	.09	.03
☐ 9 Ron Swoboda	.20	.09	.03
☐ 10 Donn Clendenon	.20	.09	.03
☐ 11 Art Shamsky	.20	.09	.03
☐ 12 Tug McGraw	.50	.23	.06
☐ 13 Ed Kranepool	.20	.09	.03
☐ 14 Cleon Jones	.20	.09	.03
☐ 15 Ron Taylor	.10	.05	.01
☐ 16 Gary Gentry	.10	.05	.01
☐ 17 Ken Boswell	.10	.05	.01
☐ 18 Ed Charles	.10	.05	.01
☐ 19 J.C. Martin	.10	.05	.01
☐ 20 Al Weis	.10	.05	.01
☐ 21 Jack DiLauro	.10	.05	.01
☐ 22 Duffy Dyer	.10	.05	.01
☐ 23 Wayne Garrett	.10	.05	.01
☐ 24 Jim McAndrew	.10	.05	.01
☐ 25 Rod Gaspar	.10	.05	.01
☐ 26 Don Cardwell	.10	.05	.01
☐ 27 Bob Pfeil	.10	.05	.01
☐ 28 Cal Koonce	.10	.05	.01
☐ 29 Gil Hodges MG	.75	.35	.09
☐ 30 Yogi Berra CO	.75	.35	.09
☐ 31 Joe Pignatano CO	.10	.05	.01
☐ 32 Rube Walker CO	.10	.05	.01
☐ 33 Eddie Yost CO	.10	.05	.01
☐ 34 First Ever Met Game	.10	.05	.01
☐ 35 Opening Day 1969	.10	.05	.01
☐ 36 Ed Kranepool Breaks Homerun Record	.10	.05	.01
☐ 37 Jerry Koosman Sets Club Strikeout Record	.20	.09	.03
☐ 38 Donn Clendenon Mets Trade for	.10	.05	.01
☐ 39 Jerry Koosman 23 Scoreless Innings	.20	.09	.03
☐ 40 Mets Begin 7 Game Winning Streak	.10	.05	.01
☐ 41 Mets vs Division Leading Cubs	.10	.05	.01
☐ 42 Tom Seaver Near Perfect Game	.75	.35	.09
☐ 43 Mets Trail by 3 1/2 Games	.10	.05	.01
☐ 44 All-Star Break	.10	.05	.01
☐ 45 All-Star Game	.10	.05	.01
☐ 46 Mets Sweep Atlanta	.10	.05	.01
☐ 47 Mets Sweep Padres	.10	.05	.01
☐ 48 Jerry Koosman Mets Defeat Cubs Strikes Out 13	.20	.09	.03
☐ 49 Mets Defeat Cubs, 1/2 Game Back	.10	.05	.01
☐ 50 1st Place!	.10	.05	.01
☐ 51 Mets Continue 9 Game Winning Streak	.10	.05	.01
☐ 52 Tom Seaver Earns 22nd Victory	.75	.35	.09
☐ 53 Steve Carlton Strikes out 19 Mets Win	1.00	.45	.12
☐ 54 Jerry Koosman Pitches 15th Complete Game	.20	.09	.03
☐ 55 Eastern Division Champs!	.10	.05	.01
☐ 56 100th Victory	.10	.05	.01
☐ 57 Final Game, Mets Prepare for Braves	.10	.05	.01
☐ 58 N.L. Championship Series, Game 1	.10	.05	.01
☐ 59 N.L. Championship Series, Game 2	.10	.05	.01
☐ 60 N.L. Championship Series, Game 3	.10	.05	.01
☐ 61 1969 World Series, Game 1	.10	.05	.01
☐ 62 1969 World Series, Game 2	.10	.05	.01
☐ 63 1969 World Series, Game 3	.10	.05	.01
☐ 64 1969 World Series, Game 4	.10	.05	.01
☐ 65 1969 World Series, Game 5	.10	.05	.01
☐ 66 World Champions	.10	.05	.01
☐ 67 World Champions	.10	.05	.01
☐ 68 World Champions	.10	.05	.01
☐ 69 World Champions	.10	.05	.01
☐ NNO Checklist	.10	.05	.01

1994 Mets '69 Year Book

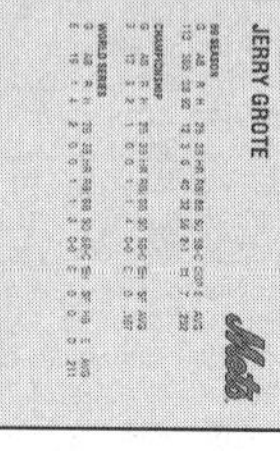

Measuring 8 1/4" by 10 7/8", this perforated sheet of nine player cards was inserted inside a reprint of the 1969 Official Year Book issued to celebrate the 25th anniversary of the World Champion Mets. If the cards were separated, they would measure 2 3/4" by 3 1/2". Inside white outer borders, the fronts feature a mix of posed and action color photos framed by an orange-and-purple inner border design. The player's name is printed in the top border, while the team logo and the uniform number are superposed over the picture. On a white background, the backs present statistics for the 1969 season, National League championship series, and the World Series. The cards are unnumbered and are checklisted below in alphabetical order.

	MINT	NRMT	EXC
COMPLETE SET (9)	2.50	1.10	.30
COMMON CARD (1-9)	.25	.11	.03
☐ 1 Ed Charles	.25	.11	.03
☐ 2 Donn Clendenon	.35	.16	.04
☐ 3 Jerry Grote	.35	.16	.04
☐ 4 Bud Harrelson	.35	.16	.04
☐ 5 Cleon Jones	.35	.16	.04
☐ 6 Jerry Koosman	.50	.23	.06
☐ 7 Art Shamsky UER (Listed as infield; should be outfield)	.25	.11	.03
☐ 8 Ron Swoboda	.35	.16	.04
☐ 9 Team Photo	.25	.11	.03

1994 Mets Team Issue

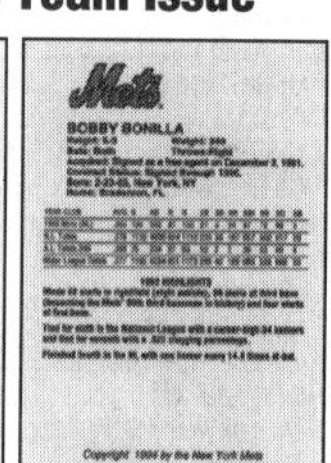

Consisting of nine cards, this 7 1/2" by 10 1/2" perforated sheet features some past and current Mets. The fronts display color action photos with a team color-coded (orange and blue) inner border and a white outer border. The player's name, uniform number, and position are printed in the lower border. In blue print on white, the backs carry biography, statistics, and either 1993 or career highlights. The cards are unnumbered and are checklisted below starting with the upper left and proceeding across and down to the lower right. The cards are also found with PruCare sponsoring on the back. There is no price differential for that set.

	MINT	NRMT	EXC
COMPLETE SET (9)	6.00	2.70	.75
COMMON CARD	.50	.23	.06
☐ 1 Bobby Bonilla	1.25	.55	.16
☐ 2 Dwight Gooden	1.25	.55	.16
☐ 3 John Franco	1.00	.45	.12
☐ 4 Jeff Kent	1.00	.45	.12
☐ 5 Kevin McReynolds	.50	.23	.06
☐ 6 Ryan Thompson	.50	.23	.06
☐ 7 Jeromy Burnitz	.75	.35	.09
☐ 8 Bud Harrelson	1.00	.45	.12
☐ 9 Mookie Wilson	1.00	.45	.12

1994 Mets Tribute Sheet '69 Spectrum

This UV-coated sheet measures 8 1/2" by 11" and pays tribute to the 1969 Miracle Mets on their 25th anniversary. Production was limited to 10,000 sheets. The blue front is a photo montage. A large photo in the middle of the sheet depicts the Mets on-field celebration upon winning the 1969 World Series. It is flanked on the right by a team photo and on the left by a shot of the Mets running onto the field to celebrate. A player photo appears in each corner: Jerry Koosman at the upper left, Tom Seaver at the upper right, Ron Swoboda at the lower left and Don Clendenon at the lower right. The 1969 Miracle Mets 25th Anniversary logo lies just below the large middle photo. The back carries a synopsis of the team's accomplishments. There were also an unspecified number of "Promo" versions produced of this sheet.

	MINT	NRMT	EXC
COMPLETE SET	5.00	2.20	.60
COMMON SHEET	5.00	2.20	.60
☐ 1 '69 Mets 25th Ann.Sheet	5.00	2.20	.60

1995 Mets Kahn's

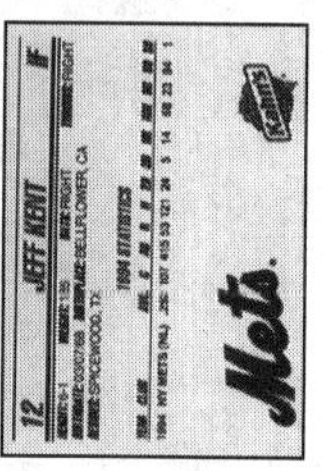

This 34-card set was sponsored by Kahn's and was issued with two manufacturer's coupons. The fronts display color player photos inside an orange picture frame. The surrounding border is gray with thin navy blue pinstripes. The player's name, number, and position are printed in team color-coded lettering in the wider bottom border. In black and red print on white, the backs present biography and 1994 statistics, as well as team and sponsor logos. The cards are unnumbered and checklisted below in alphabetical order.

	MINT	NRMT	EXC
COMPLETE SET (34)	6.00	2.70	.75
COMMON CARD (1-34)	.10	.05	.01
☐ 1 Edgardo Alfonzo	.25	.11	.03
☐ 2 Jeff Barry	.10	.05	.01
☐ 3 Tim Bogar	.10	.05	.01
☐ 4 Bobby Bonilla	.25	.11	.03
☐ 5 Rico Brogna	.50	.23	.06
☐ 6 Brett Butler	.50	.23	.06
☐ 7 Mike Cubbage CO	.10	.05	.01
☐ 8 Jerry DiPoto	.10	.05	.01
☐ 9 John Franco	.25	.11	.03
☐ 10 Dallas Green MG	.25	.11	.03
☐ 11 Eric Gunderson	.10	.05	.01
☐ 12 Pete Harnisch	.10	.05	.01
☐ 13 Doug Henry	.10	.05	.01
☐ 14 Frank Howard CO	.25	.11	.03
☐ 15 Todd Hundley	1.25	.55	.16
☐ 16 Jason Isringhausen	.50	.23	.06
☐ 17 Bobby Jones	.50	.23	.06
☐ 18 Chris Jones	.10	.05	.01
☐ 19 Jeff Kent	.50	.23	.06
☐ 20 Aaron Ledesma	.25	.11	.03
☐ 21 Tom McCraw CO	.10	.05	.01
☐ 22 Dave Mlicki	.10	.05	.01
☐ 23 Blas Minor	.10	.05	.01
☐ 24 Joe Orsulak	.10	.05	.01
☐ 25 Ricky Otero	.10	.05	.01
☐ 26 Greg Pavlick CO	.10	.05	.01
☐ 27 Bill Pulsipher	.25	.11	.03
☐ 28 Bret Saberhagen	.25	.11	.03
☐ 29 Bill Spiers	.10	.05	.01
☐ 30 Kelly Stinnett	.10	.05	.01
☐ 31 Steve Swisher CO	.10	.05	.01
☐ 32 Ryan Thompson	.10	.05	.01
☐ 33 Jose Vizcaino	.25	.11	.03
☐ 34 Bobby Wine CO	.10	.05	.01

1996 Mets Kahn's

This 34-card set was sponsored by Kahn's and issued with two manufacturer's coupons. The fronts display color player photos set on a black background with the team logo at the bottom and red and gray bars across the top. The backs carry player information and career statistics. The cards are unnumbered and checklisted below in alphabetical order.

	MINT	NRMT	EXC
COMPLETE SET (34)	12.00	5.50	1.50
COMMON CARD (1- 34)	.25	.11	.03
☐ 1 Edgardo Alfonzo	.25	.11	.03
☐ 2 Tim Bogar	.25	.11	.03
☐ 3 Rico Brogna	.75	.35	.09
☐ 4 Paul Byrd	.25	.11	.03
☐ 5 Mark Clark	.25	.11	.03
☐ 6 Mike Cubbage CO	.25	.11	.03
☐ 7 Jerry DiPoto	.25	.11	.03
☐ 8 Carl Everett	.50	.23	.06
☐ 9 John Franco	.75	.35	.09
☐ 10 Bernard Gilkey	.75	.35	.09
☐ 11 Dallas Green MG	.25	.11	.03
☐ 12 Pete Harnisch	.25	.11	.03
☐ 13 Doug Henry	.25	.11	.03
☐ 14 Frank Howard CO	.50	.23	.06
☐ 15 Todd Hundley	1.25	.55	.16
☐ 16 Butch Huskey	.25	.11	.03

☐ 17 Jason Isringhausen	.75	.35	.09
☐ 18 Lance Johnson	.75	.35	.09
☐ 19 Bobby Jones	.50	.23	.06
☐ 20 Chris Jones	.25	.11	.03
☐ 21 Brent Mayne	.25	.11	.03
☐ 22 Tom McCraw CO	.25	.11	.03
☐ 23 Dave Mlicki	.25	.11	.03
☐ 24 Alex Ochoa	1.00	.45	.12
☐ 25 Rey Ordonez	1.50	.70	.19
☐ 26 Greg Pavlick CO	.25	.11	.03
☐ 27 Robert Person	.25	.11	.03
☐ 28 Bill Pulsipher	.50	.23	.06
☐ 29 Steve Swisher	.25	.11	.03
☐ 30 Andy Tomberlin	.25	.11	.03
☐ 31 Paul Wilson	.50	.23	.06
☐ 32 Bobby Wine CO	.25	.11	.03
☐ NNO Manufacturer's Coupon Kahn's Corn Dogs	.25	.11	.03
☐ NNO Manufacturer's Coupon Kahn's Hot Dogs	.25	.11	.03

1993 Metz Baking

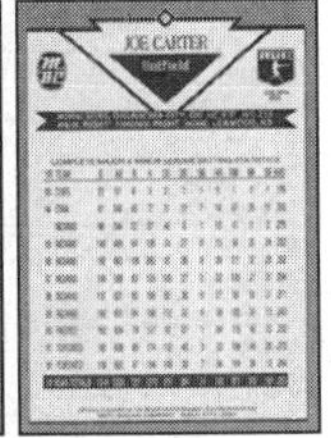

This 40-card standard-size set was produced by MSA (Michael Schechter Associates) for Metz Baking Co. The cards were issued in two series and feature on their fronts oval color drawings of the players with team names or logos airbrushed from their caps and uniforms. These drawings are bordered in red, white, and black and are displayed between two baseball bat icons. In a black banner beneath the drawing, the player's name and team appear in yellow and red, respectively. The player's position is shown within a baseball icon near the bottom of the card. In the first series, the blue fronts are edged in tan and have vertical yellow pinstripes. The second series has yellow fronts edged in red with blue pinstripes. The gray-bordered white backs all carry the same design regardless of the series. The player's name and position appear at the top. His biography appears below within a black banner, and beneath that, a stat table. The Metz and MLBPA logos in the upper corners round out the back. One card was inserted into packages of Metz products distributed in the Midwest. The cards are unnumbered and checklisted below in alphabetical order within each 20-card series.

	MINT	NRMT	EXC
COMPLETE SET (40)	5.00	2.20	.60
COMMON CARD (1-40)	.05	.02	.01
☐ 1 Wade Boggs	.20	.09	.03
☐ 2 Barry Bonds	.25	.11	.03
☐ 3 Bobby Bonilla	.10	.05	.01
☐ 4 Joe Carter	.10	.05	.01
☐ 5 Roger Clemens	.25	.11	.03
☐ 6 Doug Drabek	.05	.02	.01
☐ 7 Cecil Fielder	.10	.05	.01
☐ 8 Dwight Gooden	.10	.05	.01
☐ 9 Ken Griffey Jr.	1.00	.45	.12
☐ 10 Tony Gwynn	.50	.23	.06
☐ 11 Howard Johnson	.05	.02	.01
☐ 12 Wally Joyner	.05	.02	.01
☐ 13 Dave Justice	.10	.05	.01
☐ 14 Don Mattingly	.50	.23	.06
☐ 15 Jack McDowell	.05	.02	.01
☐ 16 Kirby Puckett	.50	.23	.06
☐ 17 Cal Ripken	.75	.35	.09
☐ 18 Ryne Sandberg	.40	.18	.05
☐ 19 Darryl Strawberry	.10	.05	.01
☐ 20 Danny Tartabull	.05	.02	.01
☐ 21 Dante Bichette	.20	.09	.03
☐ 22 Jose Canseco	.20	.09	.03
☐ 23 Will Clark	.20	.09	.03
☐ 24 Shawon Dunston	.05	.02	.01
☐ 25 Dennis Eckersley	.10	.05	.01
☐ 26 Carlton Fisk	.15	.07	.02
☐ 27 Andres Galarraga	.15	.07	.02
☐ 28 Kirk Gibson	.10	.05	.01
☐ 29 Mark Grace	.25	.11	.03
☐ 30 Rickey Henderson	.20	.09	.03
☐ 31 Kent Hrbek	.05	.02	.01
☐ 32 Barry Larkin	.20	.09	.03
☐ 33 Paul Molitor	.25	.11	.03
☐ 34 Terry Pendleton	.05	.02	.01
☐ 35 Nolan Ryan	.75	.35	.09
☐ 36 Ozzie Smith	.40	.18	.05
☐ 37 Mickey Tettleton	.05	.02	.01
☐ 38 Alan Trammell	.10	.05	.01
☐ 39 Andy Van Slyke	.05	.02	.01
☐ 40 Dave Winfield	.15	.07	.02

1971 Milk Duds

The cards in this 69-card set measure 1 13/16" by 2 5/8". The 1971 Milk Duds set contains 32 American League cards and 37 National League cards. The cards are actually numbered, but the very small number appears only on the flap of the box; nevertheless the numbers below are ordered alphabetically by player's name within league. American Leaguers are numbered 1-32 and National Leaguers 33-69. The cards are sepia toned on a tan background and were issued on the backs of five-cent boxes of Milk Duds candy. The prices listed in the checklist are for complete boxes. Cards cut from boxes are approximately one-half of the listed price. The names of three of the players in the set were misspelled and are noted in the checklist below as errors. Three of the boxes were double printed, i.e., twice as many were produced or printed compared to the other players. These double-printed players are indicated below by DP in the checklist after the player's name.

	NRMT	VG-E	GOOD
COMPLETE SET (69)	1200.00	550.00	150.00
COMMON CARD (1-69)	8.00	3.60	1.00
☐ 1 Luis Aparicio	15.00	6.75	1.85
☐ 2 Stan Bahnsen	8.00	3.60	1.00
☐ 3 Danny Cater	8.00	3.60	1.00
☐ 4 Ray Culp	8.00	3.60	1.00
☐ 5 Ray Fosse	8.00	3.60	1.00
☐ 6 Bill Freehan	15.00	6.75	1.85
☐ 7 Jim Fregosi	10.00	4.50	1.25
☐ 8 Tommy Harper	8.00	3.60	1.00
☐ 9 Frank Howard	15.00	6.75	1.85
☐ 10 Jim Hunter	25.00	11.00	3.10
☐ 11 Tommy John	12.50	5.50	1.55
☐ 12 Alex Johnson	8.00	3.60	1.00
☐ 13 Dave Johnson	10.00	4.50	1.25
☐ 14 Harmon Killebrew DP	15.00	6.75	1.85
☐ 15 Sam McDowell	10.00	4.50	1.25
☐ 16 Dave McNally	8.00	3.60	1.00
☐ 17 Bill Melton	8.00	3.60	1.00
☐ 18 Andy Messersmith	8.00	3.60	1.00
☐ 19 Thurman Munson	20.00	9.00	2.50
☐ 20 Tony Oliva	15.00	6.75	1.85
☐ 21 Jim Palmer	20.00	9.00	2.50
☐ 22 Jim Perry	10.00	4.50	1.25
☐ 23 Fritz Peterson	8.00	3.60	1.00
☐ 24 Rico Petrocelli	8.00	3.60	1.00
☐ 25 Boog Powell	10.00	4.50	1.25
☐ 26 Brooks Robinson DP	15.00	6.75	1.85
☐ 27 Frank Robinson	25.00	11.00	3.10
☐ 28 George Scott	8.00	3.60	1.00
☐ 29 Reggie Smith	10.00	4.50	1.25
☐ 30 Mel Stottlemyer ERR (sic, Stottlemyre)	10.00	4.50	1.25
☐ 31 Cesar Tovar	8.00	3.60	1.00
☐ 32 Roy White	8.00	3.60	1.00
☐ 33 Hank Aaron	50.00	22.00	6.25
☐ 34 Ernie Banks	40.00	18.00	5.00
☐ 35 Glen Beckert ERR (sic, Glenn)	8.00	3.60	1.00
☐ 36 Johnny Bench	40.00	18.00	5.00
☐ 37 Lou Brock	30.00	13.50	3.70
☐ 38 Rico Carty	10.00	4.50	1.25
☐ 39 Orlando Cepeda	10.00	4.50	1.25
☐ 40 Roberto Clemente	100.00	45.00	12.50
☐ 41 Willie Davis	8.00	3.60	1.00
☐ 42 Dick Dietz	8.00	3.60	1.00
☐ 43 Bob Gibson	15.00	6.75	1.85
☐ 44 Bill Grabarkewitz	8.00	3.60	1.00
☐ 45 Bud Harrelson	8.00	3.60	1.00
☐ 46 Jim Hickman	8.00	3.60	1.00
☐ 47 Ken Holtzman	8.00	3.60	1.00
☐ 48 Randy Hundley	15.00	6.75	1.85
☐ 49 Fergie Jenkins	15.00	6.75	1.85
☐ 50 Don Kessinger	15.00	6.75	1.85
☐ 51 Willie Mays	60.00	27.00	7.50
☐ 52 Willie McCovey	20.00	9.00	2.50
☐ 53 Dennis Menke	8.00	3.60	1.00
☐ 54 Jim Merritt	8.00	3.60	1.00
☐ 55 Felix Millan	8.00	3.60	1.00
☐ 56 Claud Osteen ERR (sic, Claude)	8.00	3.60	1.00
☐ 57 Milt Pappas (pictured in Oriole uniform)	10.00	4.50	1.25
☐ 58 Tony Perez	15.00	6.75	1.85
☐ 59 Gaylord Perry	15.00	6.75	1.85
☐ 60 Pete Rose DP	40.00	18.00	5.00
☐ 61 Manny Sanguillen	15.00	6.75	1.85
☐ 62 Ron Santo	10.00	4.50	1.25
☐ 63 Tom Seaver	25.00	11.00	3.10
☐ 64 Wayne Simpson	8.00	3.60	1.00
☐ 65 Rusty Staub	10.00	4.50	1.25
☐ 66 Bobby Tolan	8.00	3.60	1.00
☐ 67 Joe Torre	15.00	6.75	1.85
☐ 68 Luke Walker	8.00	3.60	1.00
☐ 69 Billy Williams	15.00	6.75	1.85

1993 Milk Bone Super Stars

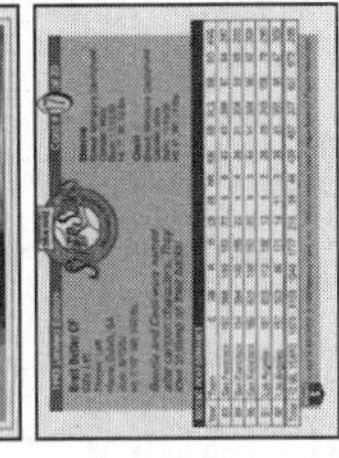

This 20-card standard-size set was featured in specially marked packages of Milk Bone Flavor Snacks and Dog Treats. Two cards were inserted in each package. Also the complete set could be obtained by sending in a mail-in form along with three Super Star Seals plus 2.50. The fronts feature a color picture of the player at home with his dog(s). At the lower left corner appears a small photo of the player in game action. The player's name and the dog's name are printed on an orange box at the lower right corner. On a pastel green panel, the horizontal backs carry player information (biography and recent performance statistics) as well as information and a player quote about the dog.

	MINT	NRMT	EXC
COMPLETE SET (20)	12.00	5.50	1.50
COMMON CARD (1-20)	.35	.16	.04
☐ 1 Paul Molitor	1.50	.70	.19
☐ 2 Tom Glavine	1.00	.45	.12
☐ 3 Barry Larkin	1.00	.45	.12
☐ 4 Mark McGwire	3.00	1.35	.35
☐ 5 Bill Swift	.35	.16	.04
☐ 6 Ken Caminiti	1.00	.45	.12
☐ 7 Will Clark	1.25	.55	.16
☐ 8 Rafael Palmeiro	1.00	.45	.12
☐ 9 Matt Young	.35	.16	.04
☐ 10 Todd Zeile	.35	.16	.04
☐ 11 Wally Joyner	.35	.16	.04
☐ 12 Cal Ripken	6.00	2.70	.75
☐ 13 Tom Foley	.35	.16	.04
☐ 14 Ben McDonald	.35	.16	.04
☐ 15 Larry Walker	1.00	.45	.12
☐ 16 Rob Dibble	.35	.16	.04
☐ 17 Brett Butler	.75	.35	.09
☐ 18 Joe Girardi	.35	.16	.04
☐ 19 Brady Anderson	1.00	.45	.12
☐ 20 Craig Biggio	.75	.35	.09

1969 Milton Bradley

These cards were distributed as part of a baseball game produced by Milton Bradley in 1969. The cards each measure approximately 2" by 3" and have square corners. The card fronts show a black and white photo of the player with his name above the photo in a white border. The game outcomes are printed on the card backs. The game was played by rolling two dice. The outcomes (two through twelve) on the back of the player's card related to the sum of the two dice. The card backs are printed in red and black on white card stock; the player's name on back and successful outcomes for the batter such as hits are printed in red. Team logos have been airbrushed from the photos in this set. The cards are typically found with perforation notches visible. Since the cards are unnumbered, they are listed below in alphabetical order. One way to tell the 1969 and 1972 Milton Bradley sets apart is that the 1969 cards all the red digits do not have a base while the 1972 red digit cards all have a base.

	NRMT	VG-E	GOOD
COMPLETE SET (296)	225.00	100.00	28.00
COMMON CARD (1-296)	.25	.11	.03
☐ 1 Hank Aaron	15.00	6.75	1.85
☐ 2 Ted Abernathy	.25	.11	.03
☐ 3 Jerry Adair	.25	.11	.03
☐ 4 Tommy Agee	.25	.11	.03
☐ 5 Bernie Allen	.25	.11	.03
☐ 6 Hank Allen	.25	.11	.03
☐ 7 Richie Allen	1.50	.70	.19
☐ 8 Gene Alley	.25	.11	.03
☐ 9 Bob Allison	.50	.23	.06
☐ 10 Felipe Alou	1.00	.45	.12
☐ 11 Jesus Alou	.25	.11	.03
☐ 12 Matty Alou	.75	.35	.09
☐ 13 Max Alvis	.25	.11	.03
☐ 14 Mike Andrews	.25	.11	.03
☐ 15 Luis Aparicio	3.00	1.35	.35
☐ 16 Jose Arcia	.25	.11	.03
☐ 17 Bob Aspromonte	.25	.11	.03
☐ 18 Joe Azcue	.25	.11	.03
☐ 19 Ernie Banks	7.50	3.40	.95
☐ 20 Steve Barber	.25	.11	.03
☐ 21 John Bateman	.25	.11	.03
☐ 22 Glenn Beckert	.25	.11	.03
☐ 23 Gary Bell	.25	.11	.03
☐ 24 Johnny Bench	12.00	5.50	1.50
☐ 25 Ken Berry	.25	.11	.03
☐ 26 Frank Bertaina	.25	.11	.03
☐ 27 Paul Blair	.25	.11	.03
☐ 28 Wade Blasingame	.25	.11	.03
☐ 29 Curt Blefary	.25	.11	.03
☐ 30 John Boccabella	.25	.11	.03
☐ 31 Bobby Bonds	3.00	1.35	.35
☐ 32 Sam Bowens	.25	.11	.03
☐ 33 Ken Boyer	1.00	.45	.12
☐ 34 Charles Bradford	.25	.11	.03
☐ 35 Darrell Brandon	.25	.11	.03
☐ 36 Jim Brewer	.25	.11	.03
☐ 37 John Briggs	.25	.11	.03
☐ 38 Nelson Briles	.25	.11	.03
☐ 39 Ed Brinkman	.25	.11	.03
☐ 40 Lou Brock	6.00	2.70	.75
☐ 41 Gates Brown	.25	.11	.03
☐ 42 Larry Brown	.25	.11	.03
☐ 43 George Brunet	.25	.11	.03
☐ 44 Jerry Buchek	.25	.11	.03
☐ 45 Don Buford	.25	.11	.03
☐ 46 Jim Bunning	3.00	1.35	.35
☐ 47 Johnny Callison	.75	.35	.09
☐ 48 Bert Campaneris	.75	.35	.09
☐ 49 Jose Cardenal	.50	.23	.06
☐ 50 Leo Cardenas	.25	.11	.03
☐ 51 Don Cardwell	.25	.11	.03
☐ 52 Rod Carew	7.50	3.40	.95
☐ 53 Paul Casanova	.25	.11	.03
☐ 54 Norm Cash	1.50	.70	.19
☐ 55 Danny Cater	.25	.11	.03
☐ 56 Orlando Cepeda	2.50	1.10	.30
☐ 57 Dean Chance	.50	.23	.06
☐ 58 Ed Charles	.25	.11	.03
☐ 59 Horace Clarke	.25	.11	.03
☐ 60 Roberto Clemente	20.00	9.00	2.50
☐ 61 Donn Clendenon	.25	.11	.03
☐ 62 Ty Cline	.25	.11	.03
☐ 63 Nate Colbert	.25	.11	.03
☐ 64 Joe Coleman	.25	.11	.03
☐ 65 Bob Cox	2.00	.90	.25
☐ 66 Mike Cuellar	.75	.35	.09
☐ 67 Ray Culp	.25	.11	.03
☐ 68 Clay Dalrymple	.25	.11	.03
☐ 69 Jim Davenport	.25	.11	.03
☐ 70 Vic Davalillo	.25	.11	.03
☐ 71 Ron Davis	.25	.11	.03
☐ 72 Tommy Davis	.75	.35	.09
☐ 73 Willie Davis	.50	.23	.06
☐ 74 Chuck Dobson	.25	.11	.03
☐ 75 John Donaldson	.25	.11	.03
☐ 76 Al Downing	.25	.11	.03
☐ 77 Moe Drabowsky	.25	.11	.03
☐ 78 Dick Ellsworth	.25	.11	.03
☐ 79 Mike Epstein	.25	.11	.03
☐ 80 Andy Etchebarren	.25	.11	.03
☐ 81 Ron Fairly	.50	.23	.06
☐ 82 Dick Farrell	.25	.11	.03
☐ 83 Curt Flood	1.00	.45	.12
☐ 84 Joe Foy	.25	.11	.03
☐ 85 Tito Francona	.25	.11	.03
☐ 86 Bill Freehan	1.00	.45	.12
☐ 87 Jim Fregosi	.75	.35	.09
☐ 88 Woodie Fryman	.25	.11	.03
☐ 89 Len Gabrielson	.25	.11	.03
☐ 90 Clarence Gaston	1.50	.70	.19
☐ 91 Jake Gibbs	.25	.11	.03
☐ 92 Russ Gibson	.25	.11	.03
☐ 93 Dave Giusti	.25	.11	.03
☐ 94 Tony Gonzalez	.25	.11	.03
☐ 95 Jim Gosger	.25	.11	.03
☐ 96 Julio Gotay	.25	.11	.03
☐ 97 Dick Green	.25	.11	.03
☐ 98 Jerry Grote	.50	.23	.06
☐ 99 Jimmie Hall	.25	.11	.03
☐ 100 Tom Haller	.25	.11	.03
☐ 101 Steve Hamilton	.25	.11	.03
☐ 102 Ron Hansen	.25	.11	.03
☐ 103 Jim Hardin	.25	.11	.03
☐ 104 Tommy Harper	.50	.23	.06
☐ 105 Bud Harrelson	.50	.23	.06
☐ 106 Ken Harrelson	1.00	.45	.12
☐ 107 Jim Ray Hart	.25	.11	.03
☐ 108 Woody Held	.25	.11	.03
☐ 109 Tommy Helms	.25	.11	.03
☐ 110 Elrod Hendricks	.25	.11	.03
☐ 111 Mike Hershberger	.25	.11	.03
☐ 112 Jack Hiatt	.25	.11	.03
☐ 113 Jim Hickman	.25	.11	.03
☐ 114 John Hiller	.25	.11	.03
☐ 115 Chuck Hinton	.25	.11	.03
☐ 116 Ken Holtzman	.50	.23	.06
☐ 117 Joel Horlen	.25	.11	.03
☐ 118 Tony Horton	.25	.11	.03
☐ 119 Willie Horton	.75	.35	.09
☐ 120 Frank Howard	1.00	.45	.12
☐ 121 Dick Howser	.50	.23	.06
☐ 122 Randy Hundley	.50	.23	.06
☐ 123 Ron Hunt	.25	.11	.03

Card			
☐ 124 Jim Hunter	4.00	1.80	.50
☐ 125 Al Jackson	.25	.11	.03
☐ 126 Larry Jackson	.50	.23	.06
☐ 127 Reggie Jackson	20.00	9.00	2.50
☐ 128 Sonny Jackson	.25	.11	.03
☐ 129 Pat Jarvis	.25	.11	.03
☐ 130 Julian Javier	.25	.11	.03
☐ 131 Ferguson Jenkins	4.00	1.80	.50
☐ 132 Manny Jimenez	.25	.11	.03
☐ 133 Tommy John	2.00	.90	.25
☐ 134 Bob Johnson	.25	.11	.03
☐ 135 Dave Johnson	1.00	.45	.12
☐ 136 Deron Johnson	.25	.11	.03
☐ 137 Lou Johnson	.25	.11	.03
☐ 138 Jay Johnstone	1.00	.45	.12
☐ 139 Cleon Jones	.50	.23	.06
☐ 140 Dalton Jones	.25	.11	.03
☐ 141 Duane Josephson	.25	.11	.03
☐ 142 Jim Kaat	2.00	.90	.25
☐ 143 Al Kaline	7.50	3.40	.95
☐ 144 Don Kessinger	.50	.23	.06
☐ 145 Harmon Killebrew	5.00	2.20	.60
☐ 146 Hal King	.25	.11	.03
☐ 147 Ed Kirkpatrick	.25	.11	.03
☐ 148 Fred Klages	.25	.11	.03
☐ 149 Ron Kline	.25	.11	.03
☐ 150 Bobby Knoop	.25	.11	.03
☐ 151 Gary Kolb	.25	.11	.03
☐ 152 Andy Kosco	.25	.11	.03
☐ 153 Ed Kranepool	.50	.23	.06
☐ 154 Lew Krausse	.25	.11	.03
☐ 155 Hal Lanier	.25	.11	.03
☐ 156 Jim LeFebvre	.25	.11	.03
☐ 157 Denny Lemaster	.25	.11	.03
☐ 158 Dave Leonhard	.25	.11	.03
☐ 159 Don Lock	.25	.11	.03
☐ 160 Mickey Lolich	1.00	.45	.12
☐ 161 Jim Lonborg	1.00	.45	.12
☐ 162 Mike Lum	.25	.11	.03
☐ 163 Sparky Lyle	2.00	.90	.25
☐ 164 Jim Maloney	.50	.23	.06
☐ 165 Juan Marichal	4.00	1.80	.50
☐ 166 J.C. Martin	.25	.11	.03
☐ 167 Marty Martinez	.25	.11	.03
☐ 168 Tom Matchick	.25	.11	.03
☐ 169 Ed Mathews	6.00	2.70	.75
☐ 170 Jerry May	.25	.11	.03
☐ 171 Lee May	.50	.23	.06
☐ 172 Lee Maye	.25	.11	.03
☐ 173 Willie Mays	15.00	6.75	1.85
☐ 174 Dal Maxvill	.25	.11	.03
☐ 175 Bill Mazeroski	2.00	.90	.25
☐ 176 Dick McAuliffe	.25	.11	.03
☐ 177 Al McBean	.25	.11	.03
☐ 178 Tim McCarver	1.50	.70	.19
☐ 179 Bill McCool	.25	.11	.03
☐ 180 Mike McCormick	.50	.23	.06
☐ 181 Willie McCovey	6.00	2.70	.75
☐ 182 Tom McCraw	.25	.11	.03
☐ 183 Lindy McDaniel	.25	.11	.03
☐ 184 Sam McDowell	.75	.35	.09
☐ 185 Orlando McFarlane	.25	.11	.03
☐ 186 Jim McGlothlin	.25	.11	.03
☐ 187 Denny McLain	1.50	.70	.19
☐ 188 Ken McMullen	.25	.11	.03
☐ 189 Dave McNally	1.00	.45	.12
☐ 190 Gerry McNertney	.25	.11	.03
☐ 191 Denis Menke	.25	.11	.03
☐ 192 Felix Millan	.25	.11	.03
☐ 193 Don Mincher	.25	.11	.03
☐ 194 Rick Monday	.50	.23	.06
☐ 195 Joe Morgan	5.00	2.20	.60
☐ 196 Bubba Morton	.25	.11	.03
☐ 197 Manny Mota	.50	.23	.06
☐ 198 Jim Nash	.25	.11	.03
☐ 199 Dave Nelson	.25	.11	.03
☐ 200 Dick Nen	.25	.11	.03
☐ 201 Phil Niekro	4.00	1.80	.50
☐ 202 Jim Northrup	.50	.23	.06
☐ 203 Rich Nye	.25	.11	.03
☐ 204 Johnny Odom	.25	.11	.03
☐ 205 Tony Oliva	2.00	.90	.25
☐ 206 Gene Oliver	.25	.11	.03
☐ 207 Phil Ortega	.25	.11	.03
☐ 208 Claude Osteen	.50	.23	.06
☐ 209 Ray Oyler	.25	.11	.03
☐ 210 Jose Pagan	.25	.11	.03
☐ 211 Jim Pagliaroni	.25	.11	.03
☐ 212 Milt Pappas	.50	.23	.06
☐ 213 Wes Parker	.25	.11	.03
☐ 214 Camilo Pascual	.25	.11	.03
☐ 215 Don Pavletich	.25	.11	.03
☐ 216 Joe Pepitone	.75	.35	.09
☐ 217 Tony Perez	2.50	1.10	.30
☐ 218 Gaylord Perry	4.00	1.80	.50
☐ 219 Jim Perry	1.00	.45	.12
☐ 220 Gary Peters	.25	.11	.03
☐ 221 Rico Petrocelli	.50	.23	.06
☐ 222 Adolpho Phillips	.25	.11	.03
☐ 223 Tom Phoebus	.25	.11	.03
☐ 224 Vada Pinson	1.50	.70	.19
☐ 225 Boog Powell	2.00	.90	.25
☐ 226 Frank Quilici	.25	.11	.03
☐ 227 Doug Rader	.25	.11	.03
☐ 228 Rich Reese	.25	.11	.03
☐ 229 Phil Regan	.25	.11	.03
☐ 230 Rick Reichardt	.25	.11	.03
☐ 231 Rick Renick	.25	.11	.03
☐ 232 Roger Repoz	.25	.11	.03
☐ 233 Dave Ricketts	.25	.11	.03
☐ 234 Bill Robinson	.25	.11	.03
☐ 235 Brooks Robinson	7.50	3.40	.95
☐ 236 Frank Robinson	7.50	3.40	.95
☐ 237 Bob Rodgers	.25	.11	.03
☐ 238 Cookie Rojas	.25	.11	.03
☐ 239 Rich Rollins	.25	.11	.03
☐ 240 Phil Roof	.25	.11	.03
☐ 241 Pete Rose	15.00	6.75	1.85
☐ 242 John Roseboro	.50	.23	.06
☐ 243 Chico Ruiz	.25	.11	.03
☐ 244 Ray Sadecki	.25	.11	.03
☐ 245 Chico Salmon	.25	.11	.03
☐ 246 Jose Santiago	.25	.11	.03
☐ 247 Ron Santo	1.50	.70	.19
☐ 248 Tom Satriano	.25	.11	.03
☐ 249 Paul Schaal	.25	.11	.03
☐ 250 Tom Seaver	12.00	5.50	1.50
☐ 251 Art Shamsky	.25	.11	.03
☐ 252 Mike Shannon	.75	.35	.09
☐ 253 Chris Short	.25	.11	.03
☐ 254 Dick Simpson	.25	.11	.03
☐ 255 Duke Sims	.25	.11	.03
☐ 256 Reggie Smith	1.00	.45	.12
☐ 257 Willie Smith	.25	.11	.03
☐ 258 Russ Snyder	.25	.11	.03
☐ 259 Al Spangler	.25	.11	.03
☐ 260 Larry Stahl	.25	.11	.03
☐ 261 Lee Stange	.25	.11	.03
☐ 262 Mickey Stanley	.25	.11	.03
☐ 263 Willie Stargell	6.00	2.70	.75
☐ 264 Rusty Staub	1.50	.70	.19
☐ 265 Mel Stottlemyre	1.00	.45	.12
☐ 266 Ed Stroud	.25	.11	.03
☐ 267 Don Sutton	4.00	1.80	.50
☐ 268 Ron Swoboda	.50	.23	.06
☐ 269 Jose Tartabull	.25	.11	.03
☐ 270 Tony Taylor	.50	.23	.06
☐ 271 Luis Tiant	1.50	.70	.19
☐ 272 Bill Tillman	.25	.11	.03
☐ 273 Bobby Tolan	.25	.11	.03
☐ 274 Jeff Torborg	.25	.11	.03
☐ 275 Joe Torre	2.50	1.10	.30
☐ 276 Cesar Tovar	.25	.11	.03
☐ 277 Dick Tracewski	.25	.11	.03
☐ 278 Tom Tresh	1.00	.45	.12
☐ 279 Ted Uhlaender	.25	.11	.03
☐ 280 Del Unser	.25	.11	.03
☐ 281 Sandy Valdespino	.25	.11	.03
☐ 282 Fred Valentine	.25	.11	.03
☐ 283 Bob Veale	.25	.11	.03
☐ 284 Zoilo Versalles	.50	.23	.06
☐ 285 Pete Ward	.25	.11	.03
☐ 286 Al Weis	.25	.11	.03
☐ 287 Don Wert	.25	.11	.03
☐ 288 Bill White	1.00	.45	.12
☐ 289 Roy White	.50	.23	.06
☐ 290 Fred Whitfield	.25	.11	.03
☐ 291 Hoyt Wilhelm	3.00	1.35	.35
☐ 292 Billy Williams	5.00	2.20	.60
☐ 293 Maury Wills	2.00	.90	.25
☐ 294 Earl Wilson	.25	.11	.03
☐ 295 Wilbur Wood	.25	.11	.03
☐ 296 Jerry Zimmerman	.25	.11	.03

1970 Milton Bradley

These cards were distributed as part of a baseball game produced by Milton Bradley in 1970. The cards each measure approximately 2 3/16" by 3 1/2" and have rounded corners. The card fronts show a black and white photo of the player with his name and vital statistics below the photo in a white border. The game outcomes are printed on the card backs. The card backs are printed in red and black on white card stock; the player's name is printed in red at the top of the card. Team logos have been airbrushed from the photos in this set. Since the cards are unnumbered, they are listed below in alphabetical order.

	NRMT	VG-E	GOOD
COMPLETE SET (28)	150.00	70.00	19.00
COMMON CARD (1-28)	.50	.23	.06
☐ 1 Hank Aaron	20.00	9.00	2.50
☐ 2 Lou Brock	7.50	3.40	.95
☐ 3 Ernie Banks	7.50	3.40	.95
☐ 4 Rod Carew	7.50	3.40	.95
☐ 5 Roberto Clemente	25.00	11.00	3.10
☐ 6 Tommy Davis	.75	.35	.09
☐ 7 Bill Freehan	.75	.35	.09
☐ 8 Jim Fregosi	.75	.35	.09
☐ 9 Tom Haller	.50	.23	.06
☐ 10 Frank Howard	1.00	.45	.12
☐ 11 Reggie Jackson	15.00	6.75	1.85
☐ 12 Harmon Killebrew	6.00	2.70	.75
☐ 13 Mickey Lolich	1.00	.45	.12
☐ 14 Juan Marichal	6.00	2.70	.75
☐ 15 Willie Mays	20.00	9.00	2.50
☐ 16 Willie McCovey	7.50	3.40	.95
☐ 17 Sam McDowell	.75	.35	.09
☐ 18 Denis Menke	.50	.23	.06
☐ 19 Don Mincher	.50	.23	.06
☐ 20 Phil Niekro	6.00	2.70	.75
☐ 21 Rico Petrocelli	.75	.35	.09
☐ 22 Boog Powell	1.50	.70	.19
☐ 23 Frank Robinson	7.50	3.40	.95
☐ 24 Pete Rose	20.00	9.00	2.50
☐ 25 Ron Santo	1.00	.45	.12
☐ 26 Tom Seaver	15.00	6.75	1.85
☐ 27 Mel Stottlemyre	.75	.35	.09
☐ 28 Tony Taylor	.50	.23	.06

1972 Milton Bradley

These cards were distributed as part of a baseball game produced by Milton Bradley in 1972. The cards each measure approximately 2" by 3" and have square corners. The card fronts show a black and white photo of the player with his name above the photo in a white border. The game outcomes are printed on the card backs. The game was played by rolling two dice. The outcomes (two through twelve) on the back of the player's card related to the sum of the two dice. The card backs are printed in red and black on white card stock; successful outcomes for the batter such as hits are printed in red. Team logos have been airbrushed from the photos in this set. The cards are typically found with perforation notches visible. Since the cards are unnumbered, they are listed below in alphabetical order.

	NRMT	VG-E	GOOD
COMPLETE SET (372)	250.00	110.00	31.00
COMMON CARD (1-372)	.25	.11	.03
☐ 1 Hank Aaron	20.00	9.00	2.50
☐ 2 Tommie Aaron	.25	.11	.03
☐ 3 Ted Abernathy	.25	.11	.03
☐ 4 Jerry Adair	.25	.11	.03
☐ 5 Tommy Agee	.25	.11	.03
☐ 6 Bernie Allen	.25	.11	.03
☐ 7 Hank Allen	.25	.11	.03
☐ 8 Richie Allen	2.00	.90	.25
☐ 9 Gene Alley	.25	.11	.03
☐ 10 Bob Allison	.50	.23	.06
☐ 11 Sandy Alomar	.25	.11	.03
☐ 12 Felipe Alou	1.00	.45	.12
☐ 13 Jesus Alou	.25	.11	.03
☐ 14 Matty Alou	.75	.35	.09
☐ 15 Max Alvis	.25	.11	.03
☐ 16 Brant Alyea	.25	.11	.03
☐ 17 Mike Andrews	.25	.11	.03
☐ 18 Luis Aparicio	4.00	1.80	.50
☐ 19 Jose Arcia	.25	.11	.03
☐ 20 Jerry Arrigo	.25	.11	.03
☐ 21 Bob Aspromonte	.25	.11	.03
☐ 22 Joe Azcue	.25	.11	.03
☐ 23 Bob Bailey	.25	.11	.03
☐ 24 Sal Bando	1.00	.45	.12
☐ 25 Ernie Banks	10.00	4.50	1.25
☐ 26 Steve Barber	.25	.11	.03
☐ 27 Bob Barton	.25	.11	.03
☐ 28 John Bateman	.25	.11	.03
☐ 29 Glenn Beckert	.25	.11	.03
☐ 30 Johnny Bench	15.00	6.75	1.85
☐ 31 Ken Berry	.25	.11	.03
☐ 32 Frank Bertaina	.25	.11	.03
☐ 33 Paul Blair	.25	.11	.03
☐ 34 Steve Blass	.25	.11	.03
☐ 35 Curt Blefary	.25	.11	.03
☐ 36 Bobby Bolin	.25	.11	.03
☐ 37 Bobby Bonds	2.00	.90	.25
☐ 38 Don Bosch	.25	.11	.03
☐ 39 Dick Bosman	.25	.11	.03
☐ 40 Dave Boswell	.25	.11	.03
☐ 41 Ken Boswell	.25	.11	.03
☐ 42 Cletis Boyer	.75	.35	.09
☐ 43 Charles Bradford	.25	.11	.03
☐ 44 Ron Brand	.25	.11	.03
☐ 45 Ken Brett	.25	.11	.03
☐ 46 Jim Brewer	.25	.11	.03
☐ 47 John Briggs	.25	.11	.03
☐ 48 Nelson Briles	.25	.11	.03
☐ 49 Ed Brinkman	.25	.11	.03
☐ 50 Jim Britton	.25	.11	.03
☐ 51 Lou Brock	8.00	3.60	1.00
☐ 52 Gates Brown	.25	.11	.03
☐ 53 Larry Brown	.25	.11	.03
☐ 54 Ollie Brown	.25	.11	.03
☐ 55 George Brunet	.25	.11	.03
☐ 56 Don Buford	.25	.11	.03
☐ 57 Wally Bunker	.25	.11	.03
☐ 58 Jim Bunning	3.00	1.35	.35
☐ 59 Bill Butler	.25	.11	.03
☐ 60 Johnny Callison	.75	.35	.09
☐ 61 Bert Campaneris	.75	.35	.09
☐ 62 Jose Cardenal	.50	.23	.06
☐ 63 Leo Cardenas	.25	.11	.03
☐ 64 Don Cardwell	.25	.11	.03
☐ 65 Rod Carew	8.00	3.60	1.00
☐ 66 Cisco Carlos	.25	.11	.03
☐ 67 Steve Carlton	10.00	4.50	1.25
☐ 68 Clay Carroll	.25	.11	.03
☐ 69 Paul Casanova	.25	.11	.03
☐ 70 Norm Cash	2.00	.90	.25
☐ 71 Danny Cater	.25	.11	.03
☐ 72 Orlando Cepeda	2.50	1.10	.30
☐ 73 Dean Chance	.50	.23	.06
☐ 74 Horace Clarke	.25	.11	.03
☐ 75 Roberto Clemente	30.00	13.50	3.70
☐ 76 Donn Clendenon	.25	.11	.03
☐ 77 Ty Cline	.25	.11	.03
☐ 78 Nate Colbert	.25	.11	.03
☐ 79 Joe Coleman	.25	.11	.03
☐ 80 Billy Conigliaro	.25	.11	.03
☐ 81 Casey Cox	.25	.11	.03
☐ 82 Mike Cuellar	.75	.35	.09
☐ 83 Ray Culp	.25	.11	.03
☐ 84 George Culver	.25	.11	.03
☐ 85 Jim Davenport	.25	.11	.03
☐ 86 Vic Davalillo	.25	.11	.03
☐ 87 Tommy Davis	.75	.35	.09
☐ 88 Willie Davis	.50	.23	.06
☐ 89 Larry Dierker	.75	.35	.09
☐ 90 Dick Dietz	.25	.11	.03
☐ 91 Chuck Dobson	.25	.11	.03
☐ 92 Pat Dobson	.25	.11	.03
☐ 93 John Donaldson	.25	.11	.03
☐ 94 Al Downing	.25	.11	.03
☐ 95 Moe Drabowsky	.25	.11	.03
☐ 96 John Edwards	.25	.11	.03
☐ 97 Thomas Egan	.25	.11	.03
☐ 98 Dick Ellsworth	.25	.11	.03
☐ 99 Mike Epstein	.25	.11	.03
☐ 100 Andy Etchebarren	.25	.11	.03
☐ 101 Ron Fairly	.75	.35	.09
☐ 102 Frank Fernandez	.25	.11	.03
☐ 103 Al Ferrara	.25	.11	.03
☐ 104 Mike Fiore	.25	.11	.03
☐ 105 Curt Flood	1.00	.45	.12
☐ 106 Joe Foy	.25	.11	.03
☐ 107 Tito Francona	.25	.11	.03
☐ 108 Bill Freehan	1.00	.45	.12
☐ 109 Jim Fregosi	.75	.35	.09
☐ 110 Woodie Fryman	.25	.11	.03
☐ 111 Vern Fuller	.25	.11	.03
☐ 112 Phil Gagliano	.25	.11	.03
☐ 113 Clarence Gaston	1.00	.45	.12
☐ 114 Jake Gibbs	.25	.11	.03
☐ 115 Russ Gibson	.25	.11	.03
☐ 116 Dave Giusti	.25	.11	.03
☐ 117 Fred Gladding	.25	.11	.03
☐ 118 Tony Gonzalez	.25	.11	.03
☐ 119 Jim Gosger	.25	.11	.03
☐ 120 Jim Grant	.25	.11	.03
☐ 121 Dick Green	.25	.11	.03
☐ 122 Tom Griffin	.25	.11	.03
☐ 123 Jerry Grote	.25	.11	.03
☐ 124 Tom Hall	.25	.11	.03
☐ 125 Tom Haller	.25	.11	.03
☐ 126 Steve Hamilton	.25	.11	.03
☐ 127 Bill Hands	.25	.11	.03
☐ 128 Jim Hannan	.25	.11	.03
☐ 129 Ron Hansen	.25	.11	.03
☐ 130 Jim Hardin	.25	.11	.03
☐ 131 Steve Hargan	.25	.11	.03
☐ 132 Tommy Harper	.50	.23	.06
☐ 133 Bud Harrelson	.50	.23	.06
☐ 134 Ken Harrelson	1.00	.45	.12
☐ 135 Jim Ray Hart	.25	.11	.03
☐ 136 Richie Hebner	.50	.23	.06
☐ 137 Mike Hedlund	.25	.11	.03
☐ 138 Tommy Helms	.25	.11	.03
☐ 139 Elrod Hendricks	.25	.11	.03
☐ 140 Ron Herbel	.25	.11	.03
☐ 141 Jackie Hernandez	.25	.11	.03
☐ 142 Mike Hershberger	.25	.11	.03
☐ 143 Jack Hiatt	.25	.11	.03
☐ 144 Dennis Higgins	.25	.11	.03
☐ 146 John Hiller	.25	.11	.03
☐ 147 Chuck Hinton	.25	.11	.03
☐ 148 Larry Hisle	.50	.23	.06
☐ 149 Ken Holtzman	.50	.23	.06
☐ 150 Joel Horlen	.25	.11	.03
☐ 151 Tony Horton	.25	.11	.03
☐ 152 Willie Horton	.75	.35	.09
☐ 153 Frank Howard	1.00	.45	.12
☐ 154 Bob Humphreys	.25	.11	.03
☐ 155 Randy Hundley	.50	.23	.06
☐ 156 Ron Hunt	.25	.11	.03
☐ 157 Jim Hunter	5.00	2.20	.60
☐ 158 Grant Jackson	.25	.11	.03
☐ 159 Reggie Jackson	15.00	6.75	1.85
☐ 160 Sonny Jackson	.25	.11	.03
☐ 161 Pat Jarvis	.25	.11	.03
☐ 162 Larry Jaster	.25	.11	.03
☐ 163 Julian Javier	.25	.11	.03
☐ 164 Ferguson Jenkins	5.00	2.20	.60
☐ 165 Tommy John	2.00	.90	.25
☐ 166 Alex Johnson	.25	.11	.03
☐ 167 Bob Johnson	.25	.11	.03
☐ 168 Dave Johnson	1.00	.45	.12
☐ 169 Deron Johnson	.25	.11	.03
☐ 170 Jay Johnstone	1.00	.45	.12
☐ 171 Cleon Jones	.25	.11	.03

Card	MINT	NRMT	EXC
☐ 172 Dalton Jones	.25	.11	.03
☐ 173 Mack Jones	.25	.11	.03
☐ 174 Rick Joseph	.25	.11	.03
☐ 175 Duane Josephson	.25	.11	.03
☐ 176 Jim Kaat	2.00	.90	.25
☐ 177 Al Kaline	10.00	4.50	1.25
☐ 178 Dick Kelley	.25	.11	.03
☐ 179 Pat Kelly	.25	.11	.03
☐ 180 Jerry Kenney	.25	.11	.03
☐ 181 Don Kessinger	.25	.11	.03
☐ 182 Harmon Killebrew	6.00	2.70	.75
☐ 183 Ed Kirkpatrick	.25	.11	.03
☐ 184 Bobby Knoop	.25	.11	.03
☐ 185 Cal Koonce	.25	.11	.03
☐ 186 Jerry Koosman	1.50	.70	.19
☐ 187 Andy Kosco	.25	.11	.03
☐ 188 Ed Kranepool	.50	.23	.06
☐ 189 Ted Kubiak	.25	.11	.03
☐ 190 Jose Laboy	.25	.11	.03
☐ 191 Joe Lahoud	.25	.11	.03
☐ 192 Bill Landis	.25	.11	.03
☐ 193 Hal Lanier	.25	.11	.03
☐ 194 Fred Lasher	.25	.11	.03
☐ 195 John Lazar	.25	.11	.03
☐ 196 Jim LeFebvre	.25	.11	.03
☐ 197 Denny Lemaster	.25	.11	.03
☐ 198 Dave Leonhard	.25	.11	.03
☐ 199 Frank Linzy	.25	.11	.03
☐ 200 Mickey Lolich	1.50	.70	.19
☐ 201 Jim Lonborg	1.00	.45	.12
☐ 202 Sparky Lyle	1.00	.45	.12
☐ 203 Jim Maloney	.50	.23	.06
☐ 204 Juan Marichal	5.00	2.20	.60
☐ 205 David Marshall	.25	.11	.03
☐ 206 J.C. Martin	.25	.11	.03
☐ 207 Marty Martinez	.25	.11	.03
☐ 208 Tom Matchick	.25	.11	.03
☐ 209 Carlos May	.25	.11	.03
☐ 210 Jerry May	.25	.11	.03
☐ 211 Lee May	.50	.23	.06
☐ 212 Lee Maye	.25	.11	.03
☐ 213 Willie Mays	20.00	9.00	2.50
☐ 214 Dal Maxvill	.25	.11	.03
☐ 215 Bill Mazeroski	2.00	.90	.25
☐ 216 Dick McAuliffe	.25	.11	.03
☐ 217 Al McBean	.25	.11	.03
☐ 218 Tim McCarver	2.00	.90	.25
☐ 219 Bill McCool	.25	.11	.03
☐ 220 Mike McCormick	.50	.23	.06
☐ 221 Willie McCovey	8.00	3.60	1.00
☐ 222 Tom McCraw	.25	.11	.03
☐ 223 Lindy McDaniel	.25	.11	.03
☐ 224 Sam McDowell	.75	.35	.09
☐ 225 Leon McFadden	.25	.11	.03
☐ 226 Dan McGinn	.25	.11	.03
☐ 227 Jim McGlothlin	.25	.11	.03
☐ 228 Tug McGraw	2.00	.90	.25
☐ 229 Denny McLain	1.50	.70	.19
☐ 230 Ken McMullen	.25	.11	.03
☐ 231 Dave McNally	1.00	.45	.12
☐ 232 Gerry McNertney	.25	.11	.03
☐ 233 Bill Melton	.25	.11	.03
☐ 234 Denis Menke	.25	.11	.03
☐ 235 Andy Messersmith	.50	.23	.06
☐ 236 Felix Millan	.25	.11	.03
☐ 237 Norm Miller	.25	.11	.03
☐ 238 Don Mincher	.25	.11	.03
☐ 239 Rick Monday	.50	.23	.06
☐ 240 Don Money	.25	.11	.03
☐ 241 Barry Moore	.25	.11	.03
☐ 242 Bob Moose	.25	.11	.03
☐ 243 Dave Morehead	.25	.11	.03
☐ 244 Joe Morgan	6.00	2.70	.75
☐ 245 Manny Mota	.50	.23	.06
☐ 246 Curt Motton	.25	.11	.03
☐ 247 Bob Murcer	1.50	.70	.19
☐ 248 Tom Murphy	.25	.11	.03
☐ 249 Ivan Murrell	.25	.11	.03
☐ 250 Jim Nash	.25	.11	.03
☐ 251 Joe Niekro	2.00	.90	.25
☐ 252 Phil Niekro	5.00	2.20	.60
☐ 253 Gary Nolan	.25	.11	.03
☐ 254 Jim Northrup	.50	.23	.06
☐ 255 Rich Nye	.25	.11	.03
☐ 256 Johnny Odom	.25	.11	.03
☐ 257 John O'Donoghue	.25	.11	.03
☐ 258 Tony Oliva	2.00	.90	.25
☐ 259 Bob Oliver	.25	.11	.03
☐ 260 Claude Osteen	.50	.23	.06
☐ 261 Ray Oyler	.25	.11	.03
☐ 262 Jose Pagan	.25	.11	.03
☐ 263 Jim Palmer	5.00	2.20	.60
☐ 264 Milt Pappas	.50	.23	.06
☐ 265 Wes Parker	.25	.11	.03
☐ 266 Freddie Patek	.50	.23	.06
☐ 267 Mike Paul	.25	.11	.03
☐ 268 Joe Pepitone	.75	.35	.09
☐ 269 Tony Perez	2.50	1.10	.30
☐ 270 Gaylord Perry	5.00	2.20	.60
☐ 271 Jim Perry	1.00	.45	.12
☐ 272 Gary Peters	.25	.11	.03
☐ 273 Rico Petrocelli	.50	.23	.06
☐ 274 Tom Phoebus	.25	.11	.03
☐ 275 Lou Piniella	2.00	.90	.25
☐ 276 Vada Pinson	1.50	.70	.19
☐ 277 Boog Powell	2.00	.90	.25
☐ 278 Jimmie Price	.25	.11	.03
☐ 279 Frank Quilici	.25	.11	.03
☐ 280 Doug Rader	.25	.11	.03
☐ 281 Ron Reed	.25	.11	.03
☐ 282 Rich Reese	.25	.11	.03
☐ 283 Phil Regan	.25	.11	.03
☐ 284 Rick Reichardt	.25	.11	.03
☐ 285 Rick Renick	.25	.11	.03
☐ 286 Roger Repoz	.25	.11	.03
☐ 287 Merv Rettenmund	.25	.11	.03
☐ 288 Dave Ricketts	.25	.11	.03
☐ 289 Juan Rios	.25	.11	.03
☐ 290 Bill Robinson	.25	.11	.03
☐ 291 Brooks Robinson	10.00	4.50	1.25
☐ 292 Frank Robinson	10.00	4.50	1.25
☐ 293 Aurelio Rodriguez	.25	.11	.03
☐ 294 Ellie Rodriguez	.25	.11	.03
☐ 295 Cookie Rojas	.25	.11	.03
☐ 296 Rich Rollins	.25	.11	.03
☐ 297 Vincente Romo	.25	.11	.03
☐ 298 Phil Roof	.25	.11	.03
☐ 299 Pete Rose	20.00	9.00	2.50
☐ 300 John Roseboro	.50	.23	.06
☐ 301 Chico Ruiz	.25	.11	.03
☐ 302 Mike Ryan	.25	.11	.03
☐ 303 Ray Sadecki	.25	.11	.03
☐ 304 Chico Salmon	.25	.11	.03
☐ 305 Manny Sanguillen	.75	.35	.09
☐ 306 Ron Santo	2.00	.90	.25
☐ 307 Tom Satriano	.25	.11	.03
☐ 308 Ted Savage	.25	.11	.03
☐ 309 Paul Schaal	.25	.11	.03
☐ 310 Dick Schofield	.25	.11	.03
☐ 311 George Scott	.50	.23	.06
☐ 312 Tom Seaver	15.00	6.75	1.85
☐ 313 Art Shamsky	.25	.11	.03
☐ 314 Mike Shannon	.75	.35	.09
☐ 315 Chris Short	.25	.11	.03
☐ 316 Duke Sims	.25	.11	.03
☐ 317 Bill Singer	.25	.11	.03
☐ 318 Reggie Smith	1.00	.45	.12
☐ 319 Willie Smith	.25	.11	.03
☐ 320 Russ Snyder	.25	.11	.03
☐ 321 Al Spangler	.25	.11	.03
☐ 322 Jim Spencer	.25	.11	.03
☐ 323 Ed Spiezio	.25	.11	.03
☐ 324 Larry Stahl	.25	.11	.03
☐ 325 Lee Stange	.25	.11	.03
☐ 326 Mickey Stanley	.25	.11	.03
☐ 327 Willie Stargell	8.00	3.60	1.00
☐ 328 Rusty Staub	2.00	.90	.25
☐ 329 Jim Stewart	.25	.11	.03
☐ 330 George Stone	.25	.11	.03
☐ 331 Bill Stoneman	.25	.11	.03
☐ 332 Mel Stottlemyre	1.00	.45	.12
☐ 333 Ed Stroud	.25	.11	.03
☐ 334 Ken Suarez	.25	.11	.03
☐ 335 Gary Sutherland	.25	.11	.03
☐ 336 Don Sutton	4.00	1.80	.50
☐ 337 Ron Swoboda	.50	.23	.06
☐ 338 Fred Talbot	.25	.11	.03
☐ 339 Jose Tartabull	.25	.11	.03
☐ 340 Ken Tatum	.25	.11	.03
☐ 341 Tony Taylor	.50	.23	.06
☐ 342 Luis Tiant	1.50	.70	.19
☐ 343 Bob Tillman	.25	.11	.03
☐ 344 Bobby Tolan	.25	.11	.03
☐ 345 Jeff Torborg	.25	.11	.03
☐ 346 Joe Torre	2.00	.90	.25
☐ 347 Cesar Tovar	.25	.11	.03
☐ 348 Tom Tresh	1.00	.45	.12
☐ 349 Ted Uhlaender	.25	.11	.03
☐ 350 Del Unser	.25	.11	.03
☐ 351 Bob Veale	.25	.11	.03
☐ 352 Zoilo Versalles	.50	.23	.06
☐ 353 Luke Walker	.25	.11	.03
☐ 354 Pete Ward	.25	.11	.03
☐ 355 Eddie Watt	.25	.11	.03
☐ 356 Ramon Webster	.25	.11	.03
☐ 357 Al Weis	.25	.11	.03
☐ 358 Don Wert	.25	.11	.03
☐ 359 Bill White	1.00	.45	.12
☐ 360 Roy White	.50	.23	.06
☐ 361 Hoyt Wilhelm	3.00	1.35	.35
☐ 362 Billy Williams	6.00	2.70	.75
☐ 363 Walt Williams	.25	.11	.03
☐ 364 Maury Wills	1.50	.70	.19
☐ 365 Don Wilson	.25	.11	.03
☐ 366 Earl Wilson	.25	.11	.03
☐ 367 Bobby Wine	.25	.11	.03
☐ 368 Rick Wise	.50	.23	.06
☐ 369 Wilbur Wood	.25	.11	.03
☐ 370 Woody Woodward	.25	.11	.03
☐ 371 Clyde Wright	.25	.11	.03
☐ 372 Jim Wynn	1.00	.45	.12

1984 Milton Bradley

The cards in this 30-card set measure the standard size. This set of full color cards was produced by Topps for the Milton Bradley Co. The set was included in a board game entitled Championship Baseball. The fronts feature portraits of the players and the name, Championship Baseball, by Milton Bradley. The backs feature the Topps logo, statistics for the past year (pitchers' cards have career statistics), and dice rolls which are part of the board game. Pitcher cards have no dice roll charts. There are 15 players from each league. These unnumbered cards are listed below in alphabetical order. The cap logos and uniforms have been air-brushed to remove all team references.

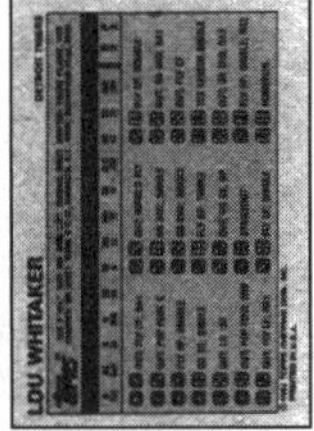

	MINT	NRMT	EXC
COMPLETE SET (30)	12.50	5.50	1.55
COMMON CARD (1-30)	.15	.07	.02
☐ 1 Wade Boggs	1.00	.45	.12
☐ 2 George Brett	3.00	1.35	.35
☐ 3 Rod Carew	.75	.35	.09
☐ 4 Steve Carlton	.75	.35	.09
☐ 5 Gary Carter	.25	.11	.03
☐ 6 Dave Concepcion	.25	.11	.03
☐ 7 Cecil Cooper	.25	.11	.03
☐ 8 Andre Dawson	.75	.35	.09
☐ 9 Carlton Fisk	1.00	.45	.12
☐ 10 Steve Garvey	.25	.11	.03
☐ 11 Pedro Guerrero	.15	.07	.02
☐ 12 Ron Guidry	.25	.11	.03
☐ 13 Rickey Henderson	1.25	.55	.16
☐ 14 Reggie Jackson	1.00	.45	.12
☐ 15 Ron Kittle	.15	.07	.02
☐ 16 Bill Madlock	.15	.07	.02
☐ 17 Dale Murphy	.75	.35	.09
☐ 18 Al Oliver	.15	.07	.02
☐ 19 Darrell Porter	.15	.07	.02
☐ 20 Cal Ripken	6.00	2.70	.75
☐ 21 Pete Rose	1.50	.70	.19
☐ 22 Steve Sax	.15	.07	.02
☐ 23 Mike Schmidt	1.50	.70	.19
☐ 24 Ted Simmons	.25	.11	.03
☐ 25 Ozzie Smith	2.00	.90	.25
☐ 26 Dave Stieb	.15	.07	.02
☐ 27 Fernando Valenzuela	.25	.11	.03
☐ 28 Lou Whitaker	.50	.23	.06
☐ 29 Dave Winfield	1.00	.45	.12
☐ 30 Robin Yount	1.00	.45	.12

1992 MJB Holographics Prototypes

The premier edition of Holoprism 1991 Rookies of the Year presented Chuck Knoblauch, the American League Rookie of the Year, and Jeff Bagwell, the National League Rookie of the Year. MJB Holographics issued a prototype card which corresponded to the first card of each set. Fronts display a holographic action image against non-game backgrounds, while the horizontally oriented backs carry color close-up photos and background information on a pastel purple panel. The cards are marked "Prototype."

	MINT	NRMT	EXC
COMPLETE SET (2)	3.00	1.35	.35
COMMON CARD	1.50	.70	.19
☐ R1 Jeff Bagwell	1.50	.70	.19
☐ R1 Chuck Knoblauch	1.50	.70	.19

1992 MJB Holographics Bagwell

The premier edition of Holoprism 1991 Rookies of the Year presented Chuck Knoblauch, the American League Rookie of the Year, and Jeff Bagwell, the National League Rookie of the Year. Each four-card holographic set was issued in a plastic "jewel box," similar to that used for storing and protecting audio compact disks. The top has a window through which the consumer can view the top card, while the back of the case displays a certificate of authenticity with the serial number of the set and the production run (250,000 sets). Also Bagwell and Knoblauch each autographed 500 cards that were randomly inserted throughout the sets. These autograph cards are rarely seen in the secondary market. Fronts display a holographic action image against non-game backgrounds, while the horizontally oriented backs carry color close-up photos and background information on a pastel purple panel.

	MINT	NRMT	EXC
COMPLETE SET (4)	1.50	.70	.19
COMMON CARD (1-4)	.40	.18	.05
☐ R1 Jeff Bagwell Batting Pose front view	.40	.18	.05
☐ R2 Jeff Bagwell Crouching posture ready to field	.40	.18	.05
☐ R3 Jeff Bagwell Follow through	.40	.18	.05
☐ R4 Jeff Bagwell Batting pose back view	.40	.18	.05

1992 MJB Holographics Knoblauch

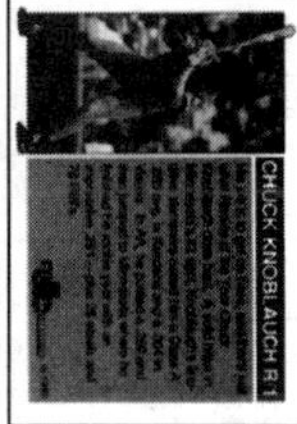

The premier edition of Holoprism 1991 Rookies of the Year presented Chuck Knoblauch, the American League Rookie of the Year, and Jeff Bagwell, the National League Rookie of the Year. Each four-card holographic set was issued in a plastic "jewel box," similar to that used for storing and protecting audio compact disks. The top has a window through which the consumer can view the top card, while the back of the case displays a certificate of authenticity with the serial number of the set and the production run (250,000 sets). Also Bagwell and Knoblauch each autographed 500 cards that were randomly inserted throughout the sets. These autograph cards are rarely seen in the secondary market. Fronts display a holographic action image against non-game backgrounds, while the horizontally oriented backs carry color close-up photos and background information on a pastel purple panel.

	MINT	NRMT	EXC
COMPLETE SET (4)	1.50	.70	.19
COMMON CARD (1-4)	.40	.18	.05
☐ R1 Chuck Knoblauch Follow through looking up	.40	.18	.05
☐ R2 Chuck Knoblauch Awaiting throw	.40	.18	.05
☐ R3 Chuck Knoblauch Follow through ready to run	.40	.18	.05
☐ R4 Chuck Knoblauch Batting pose	.40	.18	.05

1969 MLB Official Stamps

Each team is represented by nine players; hence the set consists of 216 player stamps each measuring approximately 1 3/4" by 2 7/8". There are two large albums available, one for each league. Also there are four smaller divisional albums each measuring approximately 4" by 7" and holding all the player stamps for a particular division. Stamps are unnumbered but are presented here in alphabetical order by team, Baltimore Orioles (1-9), Boston Red Sox (10-18), California Angels (19-27), Chicago White Sox (28-36), Cleveland Indians (37-45), Detroit Tigers (46-54), Kansas City Royals (55-63), Minnesota Twins (64-72), New York Yankees (73-81), Oakland A's (82-90), Seattle Pilots (91-99), Washington Senators (100-108), Atlanta Braves (109-117), Chicago Cubs (118-126), Cincinnati Reds (127-135), Houston Astros (136-144), Los Angeles Dodgers (145-153), Montreal Expos (154-162), New York Mets (163-171), Philadelphia Phillies (172-180), Pittsburgh Pirates (181-189), San Diego Padres (190-198), San Francisco Giants (199-207), and St. Louis Cardinals (208-216).

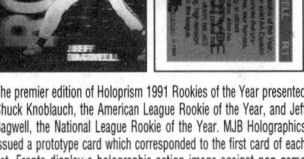

	NRMT	VG-E	GOOD
COMPLETE SET (216)	80.00	36.00	10.00
COMMON STAMP (1-216)	.20	.09	.03
☐ 1 Paul Blair	.30	.14	.04
☐ 2 Don Buford	.20	.09	.03
☐ 3 Andy Etchebarren	.20	.09	.03
☐ 4 Dave Johnson	.50	.23	.06
☐ 5 Dave McNally	.30	.14	.04
☐ 6 Tom Phoebus	.20	.09	.03
☐ 7 Boog Powell	.50	.23	.06
☐ 8 Brooks Robinson	1.50	.70	.19
☐ 9 Frank Robinson	1.50	.70	.19
☐ 10 Mike Andrews	.20	.09	.03
☐ 11 Ray Culp	.20	.09	.03
☐ 12 Dick Ellsworth	.20	.09	.03
☐ 13 Ken Harrelson	.50	.23	.06
☐ 14 Jim Lonborg	.30	.14	.04
☐ 15 Rico Petrocelli	.30	.14	.04
☐ 16 Jose Santiago	.20	.09	.03
☐ 17 George Scott	.30	.14	.04
☐ 18 Reggie Smith	.40	.18	.05
☐ 19 George Brunet	.20	.09	.03
☐ 20 Vic Davalillo	.20	.09	.03
☐ 21 Jim Fregosi	.40	.18	.05
☐ 22 Chuck Hinton	.20	.09	.03
☐ 23 Bobby Knoop	.20	.09	.03
☐ 24 Jim McGlothlin	.20	.09	.03
☐ 25 Rick Reichardt	.20	.09	.03
☐ 26 Roger Repoz	.20	.09	.03
☐ 27 Bob Rodgers	.40	.18	.05
☐ 28 Luis Aparicio	.75	.35	.09
☐ 29 Ken Berry	.20	.09	.03
☐ 30 Joe Horlen	.20	.09	.03
☐ 31 Tommy John	.75	.35	.09
☐ 32 Duane Josephson	.20	.09	.03
☐ 33 Tom McCraw	.20	.09	.03
☐ 34 Gary Peters	.30	.14	.04
☐ 35 Pete Ward	.20	.09	.03
☐ 36 Wilbur Wood	.30	.14	.04
☐ 37 Max Alvis	.20	.09	.03
☐ 38 Joe Azcue	.20	.09	.03
☐ 39 Larry Brown	.20	.09	.03
☐ 40 Jose Cardenal	.20	.09	.03
☐ 41 Tony Horton	.20	.09	.03
☐ 42 Sam McDowell	.30	.14	.04
☐ 43 Sonny Siebert	.20	.09	.03
☐ 44 Luis Tiant	.30	.14	.04
☐ 45 Zoilo Versalles	.20	.09	.03
☐ 46 Norm Cash	.40	.18	.05
☐ 47 Bill Freehan	.40	.18	.05
☐ 48 Willie Horton	.40	.18	.05
☐ 49 Al Kaline	1.50	.70	.19
☐ 50 Mickey Lolich	.40	.18	.05
☐ 51 Dick McAuliffe	.20	.09	.03
☐ 52 Denny McLain	.40	.18	.05
☐ 53 Jim Northrup	.20	.09	.03
☐ 54 Mickey Stanley	.20	.09	.03
☐ 55 Jerry Adair	.20	.09	.03
☐ 56 Wally Bunker	.20	.09	.03
☐ 57 Moe Drabowsky	.20	.09	.03
☐ 58 Joe Foy	.20	.09	.03
☐ 59 Ed Kirkpatrick	.20	.09	.03
☐ 60 Dave Morehead	.20	.09	.03
☐ 61 Roger Nelson	.20	.09	.03
☐ 62 Paul Schaal	.20	.09	.03
☐ 63 Steve Whitaker	.20	.09	.03
☐ 64 Bob Allison	.30	.14	.04
☐ 65 Rod Carew	1.50	.70	.19
☐ 66 Dean Chance	.30	.14	.04
☐ 67 Jim Kaat	.50	.23	.06
☐ 68 Harmon Killebrew	1.00	.45	.12
☐ 69 Tony Oliva	.50	.23	.06
☐ 70 John Roseboro	.20	.09	.03
☐ 71 Cesar Tovar	.20	.09	.03
☐ 72 Ted Uhlaender	.20	.09	.03
☐ 73 Horace Clarke	.20	.09	.03
☐ 74 Jake Gibbs	.20	.09	.03
☐ 75 Steve Hamilton	.20	.09	.03
☐ 76 Joe Pepitone	.30	.14	.04
☐ 77 Fritz Peterson	.20	.09	.03
☐ 78 Bill Robinson	.30	.14	.04
☐ 79 Mel Stottlemyre	.30	.14	.04
☐ 80 Tom Tresh	.40	.18	.05
☐ 81 Roy White	.30	.14	.04
☐ 82 Sal Bando	.30	.14	.04
☐ 83 Bert Campaneris	.40	.18	.05
☐ 84 Danny Cater	.20	.09	.03
☐ 85 John Donaldson	.20	.09	.03
☐ 86 Mike Hershberger	.20	.09	.03
☐ 87 Jim Hunter	1.00	.45	.12
☐ 88 Rick Monday	.30	.14	.04
☐ 89 Jim Nash	.20	.09	.03
☐ 90 John Odom	.20	.09	.03
☐ 91 Jack Aker	.20	.09	.03
☐ 92 Steve Barber	.20	.09	.03
☐ 93 Gary Bell	.20	.09	.03
☐ 94 Tommy Davis	.30	.14	.04
☐ 95 Tommy Harper	.20	.09	.03
☐ 96 Don Mincher	.20	.09	.03
☐ 97 Ray Oyler	.20	.09	.03
☐ 98 Rich Rollins	.20	.09	.03
☐ 99 Chico Salmon	.20	.09	.03
☐ 100 Bernie Allen	.20	.09	.03
☐ 101 Ed Brinkman	.20	.09	.03
☐ 102 Paul Casanova	.20	.09	.03
☐ 103 Joe Coleman Jr.	.20	.09	.03
☐ 104 Mike Epstein	.20	.09	.03
☐ 105 Frank Howard	.50	.23	.06
☐ 106 Ken McMullen	.20	.09	.03
☐ 107 Camilo Pascual	.20	.09	.03
☐ 108 Ed Stroud	.20	.09	.03
☐ 109 Hank Aaron	2.50	1.10	.30
☐ 110 Felipe Alou	.30	.14	.04
☐ 111 Bob Aspromonte	.20	.09	.03
☐ 112 Rico Carty	.30	.14	.04
☐ 113 Orlando Cepeda	.50	.23	.06
☐ 114 Pat Jarvis	.20	.09	.03
☐ 115 Felix Millan	.20	.09	.03
☐ 116 Phil Niekro	.75	.35	.09
☐ 117 Milt Pappas	.20	.09	.03
☐ 118 Ernie Banks	1.50	.70	.19
☐ 119 Glenn Beckert	.20	.09	.03
☐ 120 Bill Hands	.20	.09	.03
☐ 121 Randy Hundley	.20	.09	.03
☐ 122 Fergie Jenkins	.75	.35	.09
☐ 123 Don Kessinger	.30	.14	.04
☐ 124 Phil Regan	.20	.09	.03
☐ 125 Ron Santo	.40	.18	.05
☐ 126 Billy Williams	1.00	.45	.12
☐ 127 Johnny Bench	1.50	.70	.19
☐ 128 Tony Cloninger	.20	.09	.03
☐ 129 Tommy Helms	.20	.09	.03
☐ 130 Jim Maloney	.30	.14	.04
☐ 131 Lee May	.30	.14	.04
☐ 132 Jim Merritt	.20	.09	.03
☐ 133 Gary Nolan	.20	.09	.03
☐ 134 Tony Perez	.75	.35	.09
☐ 135 Pete Rose	2.50	1.10	.30
☐ 136 Jesus Alou	.20	.09	.03
☐ 137 Curt Blefary	.20	.09	.03
☐ 138 Larry Dierker	.20	.09	.03
☐ 139 Johnny Edwards	.20	.09	.03
☐ 140 Denis Menke	.20	.09	.03
☐ 141 Joe Morgan	.75	.35	.09
☐ 142 Doug Rader	.30	.14	.04
☐ 143 Don Wilson	.20	.09	.03
☐ 144 Jim Wynn	.30	.14	.04
☐ 145 Willie Davis	.30	.14	.04
☐ 146 Ron Fairly	.20	.09	.03
☐ 147 Len Gabrielson	.20	.09	.03
☐ 148 Tom Haller	.20	.09	.03
☐ 149 Jim LeFebvre	.20	.09	.03
☐ 150 Claude Osteen	.20	.09	.03
☐ 151 Wes Parker	.30	.14	.04
☐ 152 Bill Singer	.20	.09	.03
☐ 153 Don Sutton	.75	.35	.09
☐ 154 Bob Bailey	.20	.09	.03
☐ 155 John Bateman	.20	.09	.03
☐ 156 Ty Cline	.20	.09	.03
☐ 157 Jim Fairey	.20	.09	.03
☐ 158 Jim Grant	.20	.09	.03
☐ 159 Mack Jones	.20	.09	.03
☐ 160 Manny Mota	.30	.14	.04
☐ 161 Rusty Staub	.50	.23	.06
☐ 162 Maury Wills	.50	.23	.06
☐ 163 Tommy Agee	.20	.09	.03
☐ 164 Ed Charles	.20	.09	.03
☐ 165 Jerry Grote	.20	.09	.03
☐ 166 Bud Harrelson	.30	.14	.04
☐ 167 Cleon Jones	.20	.09	.03
☐ 168 Jerry Koosman	.40	.18	.05
☐ 169 Ed Kranepool	.20	.09	.03
☐ 170 Tom Seaver	2.00	.90	.25
☐ 171 Ron Swoboda	.20	.09	.03
☐ 172 Richie Allen	.50	.23	.06
☐ 173 Johnny Briggs	.20	.09	.03
☐ 174 Johnny Callison	.30	.14	.04
☐ 175 Woody Fryman	.20	.09	.03
☐ 176 Cookie Rojas	.20	.09	.03
☐ 177 Mike Ryan	.20	.09	.03
☐ 178 Chris Short	.20	.09	.03
☐ 179 Tony Taylor	.20	.09	.03
☐ 180 Rick Wise	.30	.14	.04
☐ 181 Gene Alley	.20	.09	.03
☐ 182 Matty Alou	.30	.14	.04
☐ 183 Jim Bunning	.75	.35	.09
☐ 184 Roberto Clemente	3.50	1.55	.45
☐ 185 Ron Davis	.20	.09	.03
☐ 186 Jerry May	.20	.09	.03
☐ 187 Bill Mazeroski	.40	.18	.05
☐ 188 Willie Stargell	1.00	.45	.12
☐ 189 Bob Veale	.20	.09	.03
☐ 190 Ollie Brown	.20	.09	.03
☐ 191 Al Ferrara	.20	.09	.03
☐ 192 Tony Gonzales	.20	.09	.03
☐ 193 Dick Kelley	.20	.09	.03
☐ 194 Bill McCool	.20	.09	.03
☐ 195 Dick Selma	.20	.09	.03
☐ 196 Tommy Sisk	.20	.09	.03
☐ 197 Ed Spiezio	.20	.09	.03
☐ 198 Larry Stahl	.20	.09	.03
☐ 199 Jim Ray Hart	.30	.14	.04
☐ 200 Ron Hunt	.20	.09	.03
☐ 201 Hal Lanier	.40	.18	.05
☐ 202 Frank Linzy	.20	.09	.03
☐ 203 Juan Marichal	1.00	.45	.12
☐ 204 Willie Mays	2.50	1.10	.30
☐ 205 Mike McCormick	.30	.14	.04
☐ 206 Willie McCovey	1.00	.45	.12
☐ 207 Gaylord Perry	.75	.35	.09
☐ 208 Nelson Briles	.20	.09	.03
☐ 209 Lou Brock	1.25	.55	.16
☐ 210 Curt Flood	.40	.18	.05
☐ 211 Bob Gibson	1.25	.55	.16
☐ 212 Julian Javier	.20	.09	.03
☐ 213 Dal Maxvill	.20	.09	.03
☐ 214 Tim McCarver	.40	.18	.05
☐ 215 Mike Shannon	.30	.14	.04
☐ 216 Joe Torre	.50	.23	.06

1970 MLB Official Stamps

These unnumbered stamps are organized below alphabetically within teams; there are 24 teams each featuring 12 player stamps. This set is much tougher to find than the set produced the year before. They are essentially the same size at 1 7/8" by 2 15/16" and as with the prior set they are not gummed on the back. Stamps are unnumbered but are presented here in alphabetical order by team, Atlanta Braves (1-12), Chicago Cubs (13-24), Cincinnati Reds (25-36), Houston Astros (37-48), Los Angeles Dodgers (49-60), Montreal Expos (61-72), New York Mets (73-84), Philadelphia Phillies (85-96), Pittsburgh Pirates (97-108), San Diego Padres (109-120), San Francisco Giants (121-132), St. Louis Cardinals (133-144), Baltimore Orioles (145-156), Boston Red Sox (157-168), California Angels (169-180), Chicago White Sox (181-192), Cleveland Indians (193-204), Detroit Tigers (205-216), Kansas City Royals (217-228), Minnesota Twins (229-240), New York Yankees (241-252), Oakland A's (253-264), Seattle Pilots (265-276) and Washington Senators (277-288).

	NRMT	VG-E	GOOD
COMPLETE SET (288)	150.00	70.00	19.00
COMMON STAMP (1-288)	.20	.09	.03
☐ 1 Hank Aaron	5.00	2.20	.60
☐ 2 Bob Aspromonte	.20	.09	.03
☐ 3 Rico Carty	.30	.14	.04
☐ 4 Orlando Cepeda	.75	.35	.09
☐ 5 Bob Didier	.20	.09	.03
☐ 6 Tony Gonzales	.20	.09	.03
☐ 7 Pat Jarvis	.20	.09	.03
☐ 8 Felix Millan	.20	.09	.03
☐ 9 Jim Nash	.20	.09	.03
☐ 10 Phil Niekro	1.50	.70	.19
☐ 11 Milt Pappas	.30	.14	.04
☐ 12 Ron Reed	.20	.09	.03
☐ 13 Ernie Banks	2.50	1.10	.30
☐ 14 Glenn Beckert	.30	.14	.04
☐ 15 Johnny Callison	.30	.14	.04
☐ 16 Bill Hands	.20	.09	.03
☐ 17 Randy Hundley	.20	.09	.03
☐ 18 Ken Holtzman	.30	.14	.04
☐ 19 Fergie Jenkins	1.50	.70	.19
☐ 20 Don Kessinger	.30	.14	.04
☐ 21 Phil Regan	.20	.09	.03
☐ 22 Ron Santo	.50	.23	.06
☐ 23 Dick Selma	.20	.09	.03
☐ 24 Billy Williams	1.50	.70	.19
☐ 25 Johnny Bench	2.50	1.10	.30
☐ 26 Tony Cloninger	.20	.09	.03
☐ 27 Wayne Granger	.20	.09	.03
☐ 28 Tommy Helms	.20	.09	.03
☐ 29 Jim Maloney	.30	.14	.04
☐ 30 Lee May	.30	.14	.04
☐ 31 Jim McGlothlin	.20	.09	.03
☐ 32 Jim Merritt	.20	.09	.03
☐ 33 Gary Nolan	.20	.09	.03
☐ 34 Tony Perez	1.00	.45	.12
☐ 35 Pete Rose	5.00	2.20	.60
☐ 36 Bobby Tolan	.30	.14	.04
☐ 37 Jesus Alou	.20	.09	.03
☐ 38 Tommy Davis	.30	.14	.04
☐ 39 Larry Dierker	.20	.09	.03
☐ 40 Johnny Edwards	.20	.09	.03
☐ 41 Fred Gladding	.20	.09	.03
☐ 42 Denver Lemaster	.20	.09	.03
☐ 43 Denis Menke	.20	.09	.03
☐ 44 Joe Morgan	1.50	.70	.19
☐ 45 Joe Pepitone	.30	.14	.04
☐ 46 Doug Rader	.20	.09	.03
☐ 47 Don Wilson	.20	.09	.03
☐ 48 Jim Wynn	.30	.14	.04
☐ 49 Willie Davis	.30	.14	.04
☐ 50 Len Gabrielson	.20	.09	.03
☐ 51 Tom Haller	.20	.09	.03
☐ 52 Jim LeFebvre	.20	.09	.03
☐ 53 Manny Mota	.30	.14	.04
☐ 54 Claude Osteen	.30	.14	.04
☐ 55 Wes Parker	.30	.14	.04
☐ 56 Bill Russell	.30	.14	.04
☐ 57 Bill Singer	.20	.09	.03
☐ 58 Ted Sizemore	.20	.09	.03
☐ 59 Don Sutton	1.50	.70	.19
☐ 60 Maury Wills	.40	.18	.05
☐ 61 Johnny Bateman	.20	.09	.03
☐ 62 Bob Bailey	.20	.09	.03
☐ 63 Ron Brand	.20	.09	.03
☐ 64 Ty Cline	.20	.09	.03
☐ 65 Ron Fairly	.20	.09	.03
☐ 66 Mack Jones	.20	.09	.03
☐ 67 Jose Laboy	.20	.09	.03
☐ 68 Claude Raymond	.20	.09	.03
☐ 69 Joe Sparma	.20	.09	.03
☐ 70 Rusty Staub	.50	.23	.06
☐ 71 Bill Stoneman	.20	.09	.03
☐ 72 Bobby Wine	.20	.09	.03
☐ 73 Tommy Agee	.20	.09	.03
☐ 74 Donn Clendenon	.20	.09	.03
☐ 75 Joe Foy	.20	.09	.03
☐ 76 Jerry Grote	.20	.09	.03
☐ 77 Bud Harrelson	.20	.09	.03
☐ 78 Cleon Jones	.20	.09	.03
☐ 79 Jerry Koosman	.40	.18	.05
☐ 80 Ed Kranepool	.20	.09	.03
☐ 81 Nolan Ryan	12.00	5.50	1.50
☐ 82 Tom Seaver	3.00	1.35	.35
☐ 83 Ron Swoboda	.30	.14	.04
☐ 84 Al Weis	.20	.09	.03
☐ 85 Johnny Briggs	.20	.09	.03
☐ 86 Jim Bunning	1.50	.70	.19
☐ 87 Curt Flood	.40	.18	.05
☐ 88 Woody Fryman	.20	.09	.03
☐ 89 Larry Hisle	.30	.14	.04
☐ 90 Joe Hoerner	.20	.09	.03
☐ 91 Grant Jackson	.20	.09	.03
☐ 92 Tim McCarver	.50	.23	.06
☐ 93 Mike Ryan	.20	.09	.03
☐ 94 Chris Short	.20	.09	.03
☐ 95 Tony Taylor	.20	.09	.03
☐ 96 Rick Wise	.30	.14	.04
☐ 97 Gene Alley	.20	.09	.03
☐ 98 Matty Alou	.30	.14	.04
☐ 99 Roberto Clemente	10.00	4.50	1.25
☐ 100 Ron Davis	.20	.09	.03
☐ 101 Richie Hebner	.20	.09	.03
☐ 102 Jerry May	.20	.09	.03
☐ 103 Bill Mazeroski	.50	.23	.06
☐ 104 Bob Moose	.20	.09	.03
☐ 105 Al Oliver	.50	.23	.06
☐ 106 Manny Sanguillen	.30	.14	.04
☐ 107 Willie Stargell	2.00	.90	.25
☐ 108 Bob Veale	.20	.09	.03
☐ 109 Ollie Brown	.20	.09	.03
☐ 110 Dave Campbell	.20	.09	.03
☐ 111 Nate Colbert	.20	.09	.03
☐ 112 Pat Dobson	.30	.14	.04
☐ 113 Al Ferrara	.20	.09	.03
☐ 114 Dick Kelley	.20	.09	.03
☐ 115 Clay Kirby	.20	.09	.03
☐ 116 Bill McCool	.20	.09	.03
☐ 117 Frank Reberger	.20	.09	.03
☐ 118 Tommie Sisk	.20	.09	.03
☐ 119 Ed Spiezio	.20	.09	.03
☐ 120 Larry Stahl	.20	.09	.03
☐ 121 Bobby Bonds	.50	.23	.06
☐ 122 Jim Davenport	.30	.14	.04
☐ 123 Dick Dietz	.20	.09	.03
☐ 124 Jim Ray Hart	.30	.14	.04
☐ 125 Ron Hunt	.20	.09	.03
☐ 126 Hal Lanier	.40	.18	.05
☐ 127 Frank Linzy	.20	.09	.03
☐ 128 Juan Marichal	1.50	.70	.19
☐ 129 Willie Mays	7.50	3.40	.95
☐ 130 Mike McCormick	.30	.14	.04
☐ 131 Willie McCovey	1.50	.70	.19
☐ 132 Gaylord Perry	1.50	.70	.19
☐ 133 Richie Allen	.50	.23	.06
☐ 134 Nelson Briles	.20	.09	.03
☐ 135 Lou Brock	2.00	.90	.25
☐ 136 Jose Cardenal	.20	.09	.03
☐ 137 Steve Carlton	2.50	1.10	.30
☐ 138 Vic Davalillo	.20	.09	.03
☐ 139 Bob Gibson	2.00	.90	.25
☐ 140 Julian Javier	.20	.09	.03
☐ 141 Dal Maxvill	.20	.09	.03
☐ 142 Cookie Rojas	.30	.14	.04
☐ 143 Mike Shannon	.30	.14	.04
☐ 144 Joe Torre	.50	.23	.06
☐ 145 Mark Belanger	.30	.14	.04
☐ 146 Paul Blair	.30	.14	.04
☐ 147 Don Buford	.20	.09	.03
☐ 148 Mike Cuellar	.30	.14	.04
☐ 149 Andy Etchebarren	.20	.09	.03
☐ 150 Dave Johnson	.50	.23	.06
☐ 151 Dave McNally	.40	.18	.05
☐ 152 Tom Phoebus	.20	.09	.03
☐ 153 Boog Powell	.50	.23	.06
☐ 154 Brooks Robinson	2.50	1.10	.30
☐ 155 Frank Robinson	2.50	1.10	.30
☐ 156 Chico Salmon	.20	.09	.03
☐ 157 Mike Andrews	.20	.09	.03
☐ 158 Ray Culp	.20	.09	.03
☐ 159 Jim Lonborg	.30	.14	.04
☐ 160 Sparky Lyle	.40	.18	.05
☐ 161 Gary Peters	.30	.14	.04
☐ 162 Rico Petrocelli	.30	.14	.04
☐ 163 Vicente Romo	.20	.09	.03
☐ 164 Tom Satriano	.20	.09	.03

☐ 165 George Scott	.30	.14	.04
☐ 166 Sonny Siebert	.20	.09	.03
☐ 167 Reggie Smith	.40	.18	.05
☐ 168 Carl Yastrzemski	2.50	1.10	.30
☐ 169 Sandy Alomar	.30	.14	.04
☐ 170 Jose Azcue	.20	.09	.03
☐ 171 Tom Egan	.20	.09	.03
☐ 172 Jim Fregosi	.40	.18	.05
☐ 173 Alex Johnson	.30	.14	.04
☐ 174 Jay Johnstone	.20	.09	.03
☐ 175 Rudy May	.20	.09	.03
☐ 176 Andy Messersmith	.30	.14	.04
☐ 177 Rick Reichardt	.20	.09	.03
☐ 178 Roger Repoz	.20	.09	.03
☐ 179 Aurelio Rodriguez	.20	.09	.03
☐ 180 Ken Tatum	.20	.09	.03
☐ 181 Luis Aparicio	1.50	.70	.19
☐ 182 Ken Berry	.20	.09	.03
☐ 183 Buddy Bradford	.20	.09	.03
☐ 184 Ron Hansen	.20	.09	.03
☐ 185 Joe Horlen	.20	.09	.03
☐ 186 Tommy John	1.00	.45	.12
☐ 187 Duane Josephson	.20	.09	.03
☐ 188 Bobby Knoop	.20	.09	.03
☐ 189 Tom McCraw	.20	.09	.03
☐ 190 Bill Melton	.20	.09	.03
☐ 191 Walt Williams	.20	.09	.03
☐ 192 Wilbur Wood	.30	.14	.04
☐ 193 Max Alvis	.20	.09	.03
☐ 194 Larry Brown	.20	.09	.03
☐ 195 Dean Chance	.20	.09	.03
☐ 196 Dick Ellsworth	.30	.14	.04
☐ 197 Vern Fuller	.20	.09	.03
☐ 198 Ken Harrelson	.50	.23	.06
☐ 199 Chuck Hinton	.20	.09	.03
☐ 200 Tony Horton	.30	.14	.04
☐ 201 Sam McDowell	.40	.18	.05
☐ 202 Vada Pinson	.50	.23	.06
☐ 203 Duke Sims	.20	.09	.03
☐ 204 Ted Uhlaender	.20	.09	.03
☐ 205 Norm Cash	.40	.18	.05
☐ 206 Bill Freehan	.40	.18	.05
☐ 207 Willie Horton	.40	.18	.05
☐ 208 Al Kaline	.20	.09	.03
☐ 209 Mike Kilkenny	.20	.09	.03
☐ 210 Mickey Lolich	.50	.23	.06
☐ 211 Dick McAuliffe	.30	.14	.04
☐ 212 Denny McLain	.50	.23	.06
☐ 213 Jim Northrup	.30	.14	.04
☐ 214 Mickey Stanley	.30	.14	.04
☐ 215 Tom Tresh	.30	.14	.04
☐ 216 Earl Wilson	.20	.09	.03
☐ 217 Jerry Adair	.20	.09	.03
☐ 218 Wally Bunker	.20	.09	.03
☐ 219 Bill Butler	.20	.09	.03
☐ 220 Moe Drabowsky	.20	.09	.03
☐ 221 Jackie Hernandez	.20	.09	.03
☐ 222 Pat Kelly	.20	.09	.03
☐ 223 Ed Kirkpatrick	.20	.09	.03
☐ 224 Dave Morehead	.20	.09	.03
☐ 225 Roger Nelson	.20	.09	.03
☐ 226 Bob Oliver	.20	.09	.03
☐ 227 Lou Piniella	.50	.23	.06
☐ 228 Paul Schaal	.20	.09	.03
☐ 229 Bob Allison	.30	.14	.04
☐ 230 Dave Boswell	.20	.09	.03
☐ 231 Leo Cardenas	.20	.09	.03
☐ 232 Rod Carew	2.50	1.10	.30
☐ 233 Jim Kaat	1.00	.45	.12
☐ 234 Harmon Killebrew	2.00	.90	.25
☐ 235 Tony Oliva	.75	.35	.09
☐ 236 Jim Perry	.30	.14	.04
☐ 237 Ron Perranoski	.30	.14	.04
☐ 238 Rich Reese	.20	.09	.03
☐ 239 Luis Tiant	.40	.18	.05
☐ 240 Cesar Tovar	.30	.14	.04
☐ 241 Jack Aker	.20	.09	.03
☐ 242 Curt Blefary	.20	.09	.03
☐ 243 Danny Cater	.20	.09	.03
☐ 244 Horace Clarke	.20	.09	.03
☐ 245 Jake Gibbs	.20	.09	.03
☐ 246 Steve Hamilton	.20	.09	.03
☐ 247 Bobby Murcer	.50	.23	.06
☐ 248 Fritz Peterson	.20	.09	.03
☐ 249 Bill Robinson	.30	.14	.04
☐ 250 Mel Stottlemyre	.40	.18	.05
☐ 251 Pete Ward	.20	.09	.03
☐ 252 Roy White	.30	.14	.04
☐ 253 Felipe Alou	.40	.18	.05
☐ 254 Sal Bando	.40	.18	.05
☐ 255 Bert Campaneris	.20	.09	.03
☐ 256 Chuck Dobson	.20	.09	.03
☐ 257 Tito Francona	.30	.14	.04
☐ 258 Dick Green	.20	.09	.03
☐ 259 Jim Hunter	1.50	.70	.19
☐ 260 Reggie Jackson	5.00	2.20	.60
☐ 261 Don Mincher	.20	.09	.03
☐ 262 Rick Monday	.30	.14	.04
☐ 263 John Odom	.20	.09	.03
☐ 264 Ray Oyler	.20	.09	.03
☐ 265 Steve Barber	.20	.09	.03
☐ 266 Bobby Bolin	.20	.09	.03
☐ 267 George Brunet	.20	.09	.03
☐ 268 Wayne Comer	.20	.09	.03
☐ 269 John Donaldson	.20	.09	.03
☐ 270 Tommy Harper	.30	.14	.04
☐ 271 Mike Hegan	.20	.09	.03
☐ 272 Mike Hershberger	.20	.09	.03
☐ 273 Steve Hovley	.20	.09	.03
☐ 274 Bob Locker	.20	.09	.03
☐ 275 Gerry McNertney	.20	.09	.03
☐ 276 Rich Rollins	.20	.09	.03
☐ 277 Bernie Allen	.20	.09	.03
☐ 278 Dick Bosman	.20	.09	.03
☐ 279 Ed Brinkman	.20	.09	.03
☐ 280 Paul Casanova	.20	.09	.03
☐ 281 Joe Coleman	.20	.09	.03
☐ 282 Mike Epstein	.20	.09	.03
☐ 283 Frank Howard	.50	.23	.06
☐ 284 Ken McMullen	.20	.09	.03
☐ 285 John Roseboro	.30	.14	.04
☐ 286 Ed Stroud	.20	.09	.03
☐ 287 Del Unser	.20	.09	.03
☐ 288 Zoilo Versalles	.30	.14	.04

1971 MLB Official Stamps

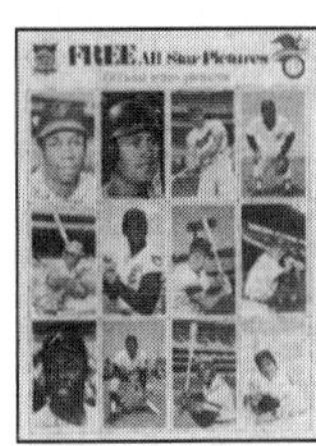

This set of stamps consists of 576 stamps contained in 24 stamp books (each containing 24 stamps) labeled Today's 1971 Team. The stamps are usually found still in the team albums. The value of each album intact with all its stamps would be the sum of the prices of all the individual player stamps inside the album. The asterisked players appear also in the All-Star album, are double printed and are more common. Stamps are unnumbered but are presented here in alphabetical order by team, Atlanta Braves (1-24), Chicago Cubs (25-48), Cincinnati Reds (49-72), Houston Astros (73-96), Los Angeles Dodgers (97-120), Montreal Expos (121-144), New York Mets (145-168), Philadelphia Phillies (169-192), Pittsburgh Pirates (193-216), San Diego Padres (217-240), San Francisco Giants (241-264), St. Louis Cardinals (265-288), Baltimore Orioles AL (289-312), Boston Red Sox (313-336), California Angels (337-360), Chicago White Sox (not included in set), Cleveland Indians (361-384), Detroit Tigers (385-408), Kansas City Royals (409-432), Milwaukee Brewers (433-456), Minnesota Twins (457-480), New York Yankees (481-504), Oakland A's (505-528), Washington Senators (529-552) and All-Stars (553-576).

	NRMT	VG-E	GOOD
COMPLETE SET (576)	150.00	70.00	19.00
COMMON STAMP	.10	.05	.01
☐ 1 Hank Aaron	3.00	1.35	.35
☐ 2 Tommy Aaron	.10	.05	.01
☐ 3 Hank Allen	.10	.05	.01
☐ 4 Clete Boyer	.25	.11	.03
☐ 5 Oscar Brown	.10	.05	.01
☐ 6 Rico Carty	.15	.07	.02
☐ 7 Orlando Cepeda	1.00	.45	.12
☐ 8 Bob Didier	.10	.05	.01
☐ 9 Ralph Garr	.15	.07	.02
☐ 10 Gil Garrido	.10	.05	.01
☐ 11 Ron Herbel	.10	.05	.01
☐ 12 Sonny Jackson	.10	.05	.01
☐ 13 Pat Jarvis	.10	.05	.01
☐ 14 Larry Jaster	.10	.05	.01
☐ 15 Hal King	.10	.05	.01
☐ 16 Mike Lum	.10	.05	.01
☐ 17 Felix Millan	.10	.05	.01
☐ 18 Jim Nash	.10	.05	.01
☐ 19 Phil Niekro	1.25	.55	.16
☐ 20 Bob Priddy	.10	.05	.01
☐ 21 Ron Reed	.10	.05	.01
☐ 22 George Stone	.10	.05	.01
☐ 23 Cecil Upshaw	.10	.05	.01
☐ 24 Hoyt Wilhelm	1.00	.45	.12
☐ 25 Ernie Banks	2.00	.90	.25
☐ 26 Glenn Beckert	.10	.05	.01
☐ 27 Danny Breeden	.10	.05	.01
☐ 28 Johnny Callison	.15	.07	.02
☐ 29 Jim Colborn	.10	.05	.01
☐ 30 Joe Decker	.10	.05	.01
☐ 31 Bill Hands	.10	.05	.01
☐ 32 Jim Hickman	.10	.05	.01
☐ 33 Ken Holtzman	.15	.07	.02
☐ 34 Randy Hundley	.10	.05	.01
☐ 35 Fergie Jenkins	1.00	.45	.12
☐ 36 Don Kessinger	.15	.07	.02
☐ 37 J.C. Martin	.10	.05	.01
☐ 38 Bob Miller	.10	.05	.01
☐ 39 Milt Pappas	.10	.05	.01
☐ 40 Joe Pepitone	.15	.07	.02
☐ 41 Juan Pizarro	.10	.05	.01
☐ 42 Paul Popovich	.10	.05	.01
☐ 43 Phil Regan	.10	.05	.01
☐ 44 Roberto Rodriguez	.10	.05	.01
☐ 45 Ken Rudolph	.10	.05	.01
☐ 46 Ron Santo	.50	.23	.06
☐ 47 Hector Torres	.10	.05	.01
☐ 48 Billy Williams	1.25	.55	.16
☐ 49 Johnny Bench	2.00	.90	.25
☐ 50 Angel Bravo	.10	.05	.01
☐ 51 Bernie Carbo	.10	.05	.01
☐ 52 Clay Carroll	.10	.05	.01
☐ 53 Darrel Chaney	.10	.05	.01
☐ 54 Ty Cline	.10	.05	.01
☐ 55 Tony Cloninger	.10	.05	.01
☐ 56 Dave Concepcion	.50	.23	.06
☐ 57 Pat Corrales	.15	.07	.02
☐ 58 Greg Garrett	.10	.05	.01
☐ 59 Wayne Granger	.10	.05	.01
☐ 60 Don Gullett	.10	.05	.01
☐ 61 Tommy Helms	.10	.05	.01
☐ 62 Lee May	.15	.07	.02
☐ 63 Jim McGlothlin	.10	.05	.01
☐ 64 Hal McRae	.10	.05	.01
☐ 65 Jim Merritt	.10	.05	.01
☐ 66 Gary Nolan	.10	.05	.01
☐ 67 Tony Perez	1.00	.45	.12
☐ 68 Pete Rose	3.00	1.35	.35
☐ 69 Wayne Simpson	.10	.05	.01
☐ 70 Jimmy Stewart	.10	.05	.01
☐ 71 Bobby Tolan	.15	.07	.02
☐ 72 Woody Woodward	.10	.05	.01
☐ 73 Jesus Alou	.10	.05	.01
☐ 74 Jack Billingham	.10	.05	.01
☐ 75 Ron Cook	.10	.05	.01
☐ 76 George Culver	.10	.05	.01
☐ 77 Larry Dierker	.10	.05	.01
☐ 78 Jack DiLauro	.10	.05	.01
☐ 79 Johnny Edwards	.10	.05	.01
☐ 80 Fred Gladding	.10	.05	.01
☐ 81 Tom Griffin	.10	.05	.01
☐ 82 Skip Guinn	.10	.05	.01
☐ 83 Jack Hiatt	.10	.05	.01
☐ 84 Denver Lemaster	.10	.05	.01
☐ 85 Marty Martinez	.10	.05	.01
☐ 86 John Mayberry	.15	.07	.02
☐ 87 Denis Menke	.10	.05	.01
☐ 88 Norm Miller	.10	.05	.01
☐ 89 Joe Morgan	1.00	.45	.12
☐ 90 Doug Rader	.10	.05	.01
☐ 91 Jim Ray	.10	.05	.01
☐ 92 Scipio Spinks	.10	.05	.01
☐ 93 Bob Watkins	.10	.05	.01
☐ 94 Bob Watson	.15	.07	.02
☐ 95 Don Wilson	.10	.05	.01
☐ 96 Jim Wynn	.25	.11	.03
☐ 97 Rich Allen	.50	.23	.06
☐ 98 Jim Brewer	.10	.05	.01
☐ 99 Bill Buckner	.50	.23	.06
☐ 100 Willie Crawford	.10	.05	.01
☐ 101 Willie Davis	.25	.11	.03
☐ 102 Al Downing	.10	.05	.01
☐ 103 Steve Garvey	1.25	.55	.16
☐ 104 Billy Grabarkewitz	.10	.05	.01
☐ 105 Tom Haller	.10	.05	.01
☐ 106 Jim LeFebvre	.10	.05	.01
☐ 107 Pete Mikkelsen	.10	.05	.01
☐ 108 Joe Moeller	.10	.05	.01
☐ 109 Manny Mota	.15	.07	.02
☐ 110 Claude Osteen	.10	.05	.01
☐ 111 Wes Parker	.15	.07	.02
☐ 112 Jose Pena	.10	.05	.01
☐ 113 Bill Russell	.25	.11	.03
☐ 114 Duke Sims	.10	.05	.01
☐ 115 Bill Singer	.10	.05	.01
☐ 116 Mike Strahler	.10	.05	.01
☐ 117 Bill Sudakis	.10	.05	.01
☐ 118 Don Sutton	1.25	.55	.16
☐ 119 Jeff Torborg	.10	.05	.01
☐ 120 Maury Wills	1.00	.45	.12
☐ 121 Bob Bailey	.10	.05	.01
☐ 122 John Bateman	.10	.05	.01
☐ 123 John Boccabella	.10	.05	.01
☐ 124 Ron Brand	.10	.05	.01
☐ 125 Boots Day	.10	.05	.01
☐ 126 Jim Fairey	.10	.05	.01
☐ 127 Ron Fairly	.15	.07	.02
☐ 128 Jim Gosger	.10	.05	.01
☐ 129 Don Hahn	.10	.05	.01
☐ 130 Ron Hunt	.10	.05	.01
☐ 131 Mack Jones	.10	.05	.01
☐ 132 Jose Laboy	.10	.05	.01
☐ 133 Mike Marshall	.15	.07	.02
☐ 134 Dan McGinn	.10	.05	.01
☐ 135 Carl Morton	.10	.05	.01
☐ 136 John O'Donoghue	.10	.05	.01
☐ 137 Adolpho Phillips	.10	.05	.01
☐ 138 Claude Raymond	.10	.05	.01
☐ 139 Steve Renko	.10	.05	.01
☐ 140 Marv Staehle	.10	.05	.01
☐ 141 Rusty Staub	.25	.11	.03
☐ 142 Bill Stoneman	.10	.05	.01
☐ 143 Gary Sutherland	.10	.05	.01
☐ 144 Bobby Wine	.10	.05	.01
☐ 145 Tommy Agee	.15	.07	.02
☐ 146 Bob Aspromonte	.10	.05	.01
☐ 147 Ken Boswell	.10	.05	.01
☐ 148 Dean Chance	.15	.07	.02
☐ 149 Donn Clendenon	.15	.07	.02
☐ 150 Duffy Dyer	.10	.05	.01
☐ 151 Dan Frisella	.10	.05	.01
☐ 152 Wayne Garrett	.10	.05	.01
☐ 153 Gary Gentry	.10	.05	.01
☐ 154 Jerry Grote	.10	.05	.01
☐ 155 Bud Harrelson	.15	.07	.02
☐ 156 Cleon Jones	.10	.05	.01
☐ 157 Jerry Koosman	.50	.23	.06
☐ 158 Ed Kranepool	.10	.05	.01
☐ 159 Dave Marshall	.10	.05	.01
☐ 160 Jim McAndrew	.10	.05	.01
☐ 161 Tug McGraw	.50	.23	.06
☐ 162 Nolan Ryan	7.50	3.40	.95
☐ 163 Ray Sadecki	.10	.05	.01
☐ 164 Tom Seaver	2.00	.90	.25
☐ 165 Art Shamsky	.10	.05	.01
☐ 166 Ron Swoboda	.10	.05	.01
☐ 167 Ron Taylor	.10	.05	.01
☐ 168 Al Weis	.10	.05	.01
☐ 169 Larry Bowa	.50	.23	.06
☐ 170 Johnny Briggs	.10	.05	.01
☐ 171 Byron Browne	.10	.05	.01
☐ 172 Jim Bunning	1.00	.45	.12
☐ 173 Billy Champion	.10	.05	.01
☐ 174 Mike Compton	.10	.05	.01
☐ 175 Denny Doyle	.10	.05	.01
☐ 176 Roger Freed	.10	.05	.01
☐ 177 Woody Fryman	.10	.05	.01
☐ 178 Oscar Gamble	.15	.07	.02
☐ 179 Terry Harmon	.10	.05	.01
☐ 180 Larry Hisle	.15	.07	.02
☐ 181 Joe Hoerner	.10	.05	.01
☐ 182 Deron Johnson	.10	.05	.01
☐ 183 Barry Lersch	.10	.05	.01
☐ 184 Tim McCarver	.50	.23	.06
☐ 185 Don Money	.10	.05	.01
☐ 186 Mike Ryan	.10	.05	.01
☐ 187 Dick Selma	.10	.05	.01
☐ 188 Chris Short	.10	.05	.01
☐ 189 Ron Stone	.10	.05	.01
☐ 190 Tony Taylor	.10	.05	.01
☐ 191 Rick Wise	.10	.05	.01
☐ 192 Billy Wilson	.10	.05	.01
☐ 193 Gene Alley	.10	.05	.01
☐ 194 Steve Blass	.10	.05	.01
☐ 195 Nelson Briles	.10	.05	.01
☐ 196 Jim Campanis	.10	.05	.01
☐ 197 Dave Cash	.10	.05	.01
☐ 198 Roberto Clemente	5.00	2.20	.60
☐ 199 Vic Davalillo	.10	.05	.01
☐ 200 Dock Ellis	.10	.05	.01
☐ 201 Jim Grant	.10	.05	.01
☐ 202 Dave Giusti	.10	.05	.01
☐ 203 Richie Hebner	.10	.05	.01
☐ 204 Jackie Hernandez	.10	.05	.01
☐ 205 Johnny Jeter	.10	.05	.01
☐ 206 Lou Marone	.10	.05	.01
☐ 207 Jose Martinez	.10	.05	.01
☐ 208 Bill Mazeroski	.50	.23	.06
☐ 209 Bob Moose	.10	.05	.01
☐ 210 Al Oliver	.50	.23	.06
☐ 211 Jose Pagan	.10	.05	.01
☐ 212 Bob Robertson	.10	.05	.01
☐ 213 Manny Sanguillen	.25	.11	.03
☐ 214 Willie Stargell	.10	.05	.01
☐ 215 Bob Veale	.10	.05	.01
☐ 216 Luke Walker	.10	.05	.01
☐ 217 Jose Arcia	.10	.05	.01
☐ 218 Bob Barton	.10	.05	.01
☐ 219 Fred Beene	.10	.05	.01
☐ 220 Ollie Brown	.10	.05	.01
☐ 221 Dave Campbell	.10	.05	.01
☐ 222 Chris Cannizzaro	.10	.05	.01
☐ 223 Nate Colbert	.10	.05	.01
☐ 224 Mike Corkins	.10	.05	.01
☐ 225 Tommy Dean	.10	.05	.01
☐ 226 Al Ferrara	.10	.05	.01
☐ 227 Rod Gaspar	.10	.05	.01
☐ 228 Clarence Gaston	.50	.23	.06
☐ 229 Enzo Hernandez	.10	.05	.01
☐ 230 Clay Kirby	.10	.05	.01
☐ 231 Don Mason	.10	.05	.01
☐ 232 Ivan Murrell	.10	.05	.01
☐ 233 Gerry Nyman	.10	.05	.01
☐ 234 Tom Phoebus	.10	.05	.01
☐ 235 Dave Roberts	.10	.05	.01
☐ 236 Gary Ross	.10	.05	.01
☐ 237 Al Santorini	.10	.05	.01
☐ 238 Al Severinsen	.10	.05	.01
☐ 239 Ron Slocum	.10	.05	.01
☐ 240 Ed Spiezio	.10	.05	.01
☐ 241 Bobby Bonds	.50	.23	.06
☐ 242 Ron Bryant	.10	.05	.01
☐ 243 Don Carrithers	.10	.05	.01
☐ 244 John Cumberland	.10	.05	.01
☐ 245 Mike Davison	.10	.05	.01
☐ 246 Dick Dietz	.10	.05	.01
☐ 247 Tito Fuentes	.10	.05	.01
☐ 248 Russ Gibson	.10	.05	.01
☐ 249 Jim Ray Hart	.10	.05	.01
☐ 250 Bob Heise	.10	.05	.01
☐ 251 Ken Henderson	.10	.05	.01
☐ 252 Steve Huntz	.10	.05	.01
☐ 253 Frank Johnson	.10	.05	.01
☐ 254 Jerry Johnson	.10	.05	.01
☐ 255 Hal Lanier	.15	.07	.02
☐ 256 Juan Marichal	1.00	.45	.12

☐ 257 Willie Mays 3.50 1.55 .45
☐ 258 Willie McCovey 1.50 .70 .19
☐ 259 Don McMahon .10 .05 .01
☐ 260 Jackie Moyer .10 .05 .01
☐ 261 Gaylord Perry 1.25 .55 .16
☐ 262 Frank Reberger .10 .05 .01
☐ 263 Rich Robertson .10 .05 .01
☐ 264 Bernie Williams .10 .05 .01
☐ 265 Matty Alou .25 .11 .03
☐ 266 Jim Beauchamp .10 .05 .01
☐ 267 Frank Bertaina .10 .05 .01
☐ 268 Lou Brock 1.50 .70 .19
☐ 269 George Brunet .10 .05 .01
☐ 270 Jose Cardenal .15 .07 .02
☐ 271 Steve Carlton 1.50 .70 .19
☐ 272 Moe Drabowsky .10 .05 .01
☐ 273 Bob Gibson 1.25 .55 .16
☐ 274 Joe Hague .10 .05 .01
☐ 275 Julian Javier .10 .05 .01
☐ 276 Leron Lee .10 .05 .01
☐ 277 Frank Linzy .10 .05 .01
☐ 278 Dal Maxvill .10 .05 .01
☐ 279 Gerry McNertney .10 .05 .01
☐ 280 Fred Norman .10 .05 .01
☐ 281 Milt Ramirez .10 .05 .01
☐ 282 Dick Schofield .10 .05 .01
☐ 283 Mike Shannon .10 .05 .01
☐ 284 Ted Sizemore .10 .05 .01
☐ 285 Bob Stinson .10 .05 .01
☐ 286 Carl Taylor .10 .05 .01
☐ 287 Joe Torre .50 .23 .06
☐ 288 Mike Torrez .15 .07 .02
☐ 289 Mark Belanger .10 .05 .01
☐ 290 Paul Blair .15 .07 .02
☐ 291 Don Buford .10 .05 .01
☐ 292 Terry Crowley .10 .05 .01
☐ 293 Mike Cuellar .15 .07 .02
☐ 294 Clay Dalrymple .10 .05 .01
☐ 295 Pat Dobson .15 .07 .02
☐ 296 Andy Etchebarren .10 .05 .01
☐ 297 Dick Hall .10 .05 .01
☐ 298 Jim Hardin .10 .05 .01
☐ 299 Elrod Hendricks .10 .05 .01
☐ 300 Grant Jackson .10 .05 .01
☐ 301 Dave Johnson .50 .23 .06
☐ 302 Dave Leonhard .10 .05 .01
☐ 303 Marcelino Lopez .10 .05 .01
☐ 304 Dave McNally .15 .07 .02
☐ 305 Curt Motton .10 .05 .01
☐ 306 Jim Palmer 1.50 .70 .19
☐ 307 Boog Powell .25 .11 .03
☐ 308 Merv Rettenmund .10 .05 .01
☐ 309 Brooks Robinson 1.50 .70 .19
☐ 310 Frank Robinson 1.25 .55 .16
☐ 311 Pete Richert .10 .05 .01
☐ 312 Chico Salmon .10 .05 .01
☐ 313 Luis Aparicio 1.00 .45 .12
☐ 314 Bobby Bolin .10 .05 .01
☐ 315 Ken Brett .10 .05 .01
☐ 316 Billy Conigliaro .15 .07 .02
☐ 317 Ray Culp .10 .05 .01
☐ 318 Mike Fiore .10 .05 .01
☐ 319 John Kennedy .10 .05 .01
☐ 320 Cal Koonce .10 .05 .01
☐ 321 Joe Lahoud .10 .05 .01
☐ 322 Bill Lee .15 .07 .02
☐ 323 Jim Lonborg .15 .07 .02
☐ 324 Sparky Lyle .50 .23 .06
☐ 325 Mike Nagy .10 .05 .01
☐ 326 Don Pavletich .10 .05 .01
☐ 327 Gary Peters .10 .05 .01
☐ 328 Rico Petrocelli .10 .05 .01
☐ 329 Vicente Romo .10 .05 .01
☐ 330 Tom Satriano .10 .05 .01
☐ 331 George Scott .25 .11 .03
☐ 332 Sonny Siebert .10 .05 .01
☐ 333 Reggie Smith .50 .23 .06
☐ 334 Jarvis Tatum .10 .05 .01
☐ 335 Ken Tatum .10 .05 .01
☐ 336 Carl Yastrzemski 2.00 .90 .25
☐ 337 Sandy Alomar .15 .07 .02
☐ 338 Jose Azcue .10 .05 .01
☐ 339 Ken Berry .10 .05 .01
☐ 340 Gene Brabender .10 .05 .01
☐ 341 Billy Cowan .10 .05 .01
☐ 342 Tony Conigliaro .50 .23 .06
☐ 343 Eddie Fisher .10 .05 .01
☐ 344 Jim Fregosi .25 .11 .03
☐ 345 Tony Gonzales .10 .05 .01
☐ 346 Alex Johnson .10 .05 .01
☐ 347 Fred Lasher .10 .05 .01
☐ 348 Jim Maloney .10 .05 .01
☐ 349 Rudy May .10 .05 .01
☐ 350 Ken McMullen .10 .05 .01
☐ 351 Andy Messersmith .15 .07 .02
☐ 352 Gerry Moses .10 .05 .01
☐ 353 Syd O'Brien .10 .05 .01
☐ 354 Mel Queen .10 .05 .01
☐ 355 Roger Repoz .10 .05 .01
☐ 356 Archie Reynolds .10 .05 .01
☐ 357 Chico Ruiz .10 .05 .01
☐ 358 Jim Spencer .10 .05 .01
☐ 359 Clyde Wright .10 .05 .01
☐ 360 Billy Wynne .10 .05 .01
☐ 361 Rick Austin .10 .05 .01
☐ 362 Buddy Bradford .10 .05 .01
☐ 363 Larry Brown .10 .05 .01
☐ 364 Lou Camilli .10 .05 .01
☐ 365 Vince Colbert .10 .05 .01
☐ 366 Ray Fosse .10 .05 .01
☐ 367 Alan Foster .10 .05 .01
☐ 368 Roy Foster .10 .05 .01
☐ 369 Rich Hand .10 .05 .01
☐ 370 Steve Hargan .10 .05 .01
☐ 371 Ken Harrelson .50 .23 .06
☐ 372 Jack Heidemann .10 .05 .01
☐ 373 Phil Hennigan .10 .05 .01
☐ 374 Dennis Higgins .10 .05 .01
☐ 375 Chuck Hinton .10 .05 .01
☐ 376 Tony Horton .10 .05 .01
☐ 377 Ray Lamb .10 .05 .01
☐ 378 Eddie Leon .10 .05 .01
☐ 379 Sam McDowell .15 .07 .02
☐ 380 Graig Nettles .50 .23 .06
☐ 381 Mike Paul .10 .05 .01
☐ 382 Vada Pinson .50 .23 .06
☐ 383 Ken Suarez .10 .05 .01
☐ 384 Ted Uhlaender .10 .05 .01
☐ 385 Eddie Brinkman .10 .05 .01
☐ 386 Gates Brown .15 .07 .02
☐ 387 Ike Brown .10 .05 .01
☐ 388 Les Cain .10 .05 .01
☐ 389 Norm Cash .50 .23 .06
☐ 390 Joe Coleman .10 .05 .01
☐ 391 Bill Freehan .25 .11 .03
☐ 392 Cesar Gutierrez .10 .05 .01
☐ 393 John Hiller .15 .07 .02
☐ 394 Willie Horton .25 .11 .03
☐ 395 Dalton Jones .10 .05 .01
☐ 396 Al Kaline 1.50 .70 .19
☐ 397 Mike Kilkenny .10 .05 .01
☐ 398 Mickey Lolich .50 .23 .06
☐ 399 Dick McAuliffe .10 .05 .01
☐ 400 Joe Niekro .50 .23 .06
☐ 401 Jim Northrup .15 .07 .02
☐ 402 Daryl Patterson .10 .05 .01
☐ 403 Jimmie Price .10 .05 .01
☐ 404 Bob Reed .10 .05 .01
☐ 405 Aurelio Rodriguez .10 .05 .01
☐ 406 Fred Scherman .10 .05 .01
☐ 407 Mickey Stanley .15 .07 .02
☐ 408 Tom Timmerman .10 .05 .01
☐ 409 Ted Abernathy .10 .05 .01
☐ 410 Wally Bunker .10 .05 .01
☐ 411 Tom Burgmeier .10 .05 .01
☐ 412 Bill Butler .10 .05 .01
☐ 413 Bruce Dal Canton .10 .05 .01
☐ 414 Dick Drago .10 .05 .01
☐ 415 Bobby Floyd .10 .05 .01
☐ 416 Gail Hopkins .10 .05 .01
☐ 417 Joe Keough .10 .05 .01
☐ 418 Ed Kirkpatrick .10 .05 .01
☐ 419 Tom Matchick .10 .05 .01
☐ 420 Jerry May .10 .05 .01
☐ 421 Aurelio Monteagudo .10 .05 .01
☐ 422 Dave Morehead .10 .05 .01
☐ 423 Bob Oliver .10 .05 .01
☐ 424 Amos Otis .15 .07 .02
☐ 425 Fred Patek .15 .07 .02
☐ 426 Lou Piniella .50 .23 .06
☐ 427 Cookie Rojas .15 .07 .02
☐ 428 Jim Rooker .10 .05 .01
☐ 429 Paul Schaal .10 .05 .01
☐ 430 Rich Severson .10 .05 .01
☐ 431 George Spriggs .10 .05 .01
☐ 432 Carl Taylor .10 .05 .01
☐ 433 Dave Baldwin .10 .05 .01
☐ 434 Ted Savage .10 .05 .01
☐ 435 Dick Ellsworth .10 .05 .01
☐ 436 John Gelnar .10 .05 .01
☐ 437 Tommy Harper .15 .07 .02
☐ 438 Mike Hegan .10 .05 .01
☐ 439 Bob Humphreys .10 .05 .01
☐ 440 Andy Kosco .10 .05 .01
☐ 441 Lew Krausse .10 .05 .01
☐ 442 Ted Kubiak .10 .05 .01
☐ 443 Skip Lockwood .10 .05 .01
☐ 444 Dave May .10 .05 .01
☐ 445 Bob Meyer .10 .05 .01
☐ 446 John Morris .10 .05 .01
☐ 447 Marty Pattin .10 .05 .01
☐ 448 Roberto Pena .10 .05 .01
☐ 449 Eduardo Rodriguez .10 .05 .01
☐ 450 Phil Roof .10 .05 .01
☐ 451 Ken Sanders .10 .05 .01
☐ 452 Russ Snyder .10 .05 .01
☐ 453 Bill Tillman .10 .05 .01
☐ 454 Bill Voss .10 .05 .01
☐ 455 Danny Walton .10 .05 .01
☐ 456 Floyd Wicker .10 .05 .01
☐ 457 Brant Alyea .10 .05 .01
☐ 458 Bert Blyleven .50 .23 .06
☐ 459 Dave Boswell .10 .05 .01
☐ 460 Leo Cardenas .10 .05 .01
☐ 461 Rod Carew 2.00 .90 .25
☐ 462 Tom Hall .10 .05 .01
☐ 463 Jim Holt .10 .05 .01
☐ 464 Jim Kaat .50 .23 .06
☐ 465 Harmon Killebrew 1.00 .45 .12
☐ 466 Charlie Manuel .10 .05 .01
☐ 467 George Mitterwald .10 .05 .01
☐ 468 Tony Oliva .50 .23 .06
☐ 469 Ron Perranoski .15 .07 .02
☐ 470 Jim Perry .15 .07 .02
☐ 471 Frank Quilici .10 .05 .01
☐ 472 Rich Reese .10 .05 .01
☐ 473 Rick Renick .10 .05 .01
☐ 474 Danny Thompson .15 .07 .02
☐ 475 Luis Tiant .25 .11 .03
☐ 476 Tom Tischinski .10 .05 .01
☐ 477 Cesar Tovar .15 .07 .02
☐ 478 Stan Williams .10 .05 .01
☐ 479 Dick Woodson .10 .05 .01
☐ 480 Bill Zepp .10 .05 .01
☐ 481 Jack Aker .10 .05 .01
☐ 482 Stan Bahnsen .10 .05 .01
☐ 483 Curt Blefary .10 .05 .01
☐ 484 Bill Burbach .10 .05 .01
☐ 485 Danny Cater .10 .05 .01
☐ 486 Horace Clarke .10 .05 .01
☐ 487 John Ellis .10 .05 .01
☐ 488 Jake Gibbs .10 .05 .01
☐ 489 Ron Hansen .10 .05 .01
☐ 490 Mike Kekich .10 .05 .01
☐ 491 Jerry Kenney .10 .05 .01
☐ 492 Ron Klimkowski .10 .05 .01
☐ 493 Steve Kline .10 .05 .01
☐ 494 Mike McCormick .10 .05 .01
☐ 495 Lindy McDaniel .10 .05 .01
☐ 496 Gene Michael .15 .07 .02
☐ 497 Thurman Munson 2.00 .90 .25
☐ 498 Bobby Murcer .50 .23 .06
☐ 499 Fritz Peterson .10 .05 .01
☐ 500 Mel Stottlemyre .50 .23 .06
☐ 501 Pete Ward .10 .05 .01
☐ 502 Gary Waslewski .10 .05 .01
☐ 503 Roy White .15 .07 .02
☐ 504 Ron Woods .10 .05 .01
☐ 505 Felipe Alou .25 .11 .03
☐ 506 Sal Bando .25 .11 .03
☐ 507 Vida Blue .50 .23 .06
☐ 508 Bert Campaneris .25 .11 .03
☐ 509 Ron Clark .10 .05 .01
☐ 510 Chuck Dobson .10 .05 .01
☐ 511 Dave Duncan .10 .05 .01
☐ 512 Frank Fernandez .10 .05 .01
☐ 513 Rollie Fingers 1.00 .45 .12
☐ 514 Dick Green .10 .05 .01
☐ 515 Steve Hovley .10 .05 .01
☐ 516 Jim Hunter 1.50 .70 .19
☐ 517 Reggie Jackson 3.00 1.35 .35
☐ 518 Marcel Lachemann .10 .05 .01
☐ 519 Paul Lindblad .10 .05 .01
☐ 520 Bob Locker .10 .05 .01
☐ 521 Don Mincher .10 .05 .01
☐ 522 Rick Monday .25 .11 .03
☐ 523 John Odom .10 .05 .01
☐ 524 Jim Roland .10 .05 .01
☐ 525 Joe Rudi .25 .11 .03
☐ 526 Diego Segui .10 .05 .01
☐ 527 Bob Stickels .10 .05 .01
☐ 528 Gene Tenace .15 .07 .02
☐ 529 Bernie Allen .10 .05 .01
☐ 530 Dick Bosman .10 .05 .01
☐ 531 Jackie Brown .10 .05 .01
☐ 532 Paul Casanova .10 .05 .01
☐ 533 Casey Cox .10 .05 .01
☐ 534 Tim Cullen .10 .05 .01
☐ 535 Mike Epstein .10 .05 .01
☐ 536 Curt Flood .50 .23 .06
☐ 537 Joe Foy .10 .05 .01
☐ 538 Jim French .10 .05 .01
☐ 539 Bill Gogolewski .10 .05 .01
☐ 540 Tom Grieve .25 .11 .03
☐ 541 Joe Grzenda .10 .05 .01
☐ 542 Frank Howard .25 .11 .03
☐ 543 Gerry Janeski .10 .05 .01
☐ 544 Darold Knowles .10 .05 .01
☐ 545 Elliott Maddox .10 .05 .01
☐ 546 Denny McLain .25 .11 .03
☐ 547 Dave Nelson .10 .05 .01
☐ 548 Horacio Pina .10 .05 .01
☐ 549 Jim Shellenback .10 .05 .01
☐ 550 Ed Stroud .10 .05 .01
☐ 551 Del Unser .10 .05 .01
☐ 552 Don Wert .10 .05 .01
☐ 553 Hank Aaron 3.00 1.35 .35
☐ 554 Luis Aparicio 1.00 .45 .12
☐ 555 Ernie Banks 2.00 .90 .25
☐ 556 Johnny Bench 2.00 .90 .25
☐ 557 Rico Carty .10 .05 .01
☐ 558 Roberto Clemente 5.00 2.20 .60
☐ 559 Bob Gibson 1.25 .55 .16
☐ 560 Willie Horton .25 .11 .03
☐ 561 Frank Howard .25 .11 .03
☐ 562 Reggie Jackson 3.00 1.35 .35
☐ 563 Fergie Jenkins 1.00 .45 .12
☐ 564 Alex Johnson .10 .05 .01
☐ 565 Al Kaline 1.50 .70 .19
☐ 566 Harmon Killebrew 1.00 .45 .12
☐ 567 Willie Mays 3.00 1.35 .35
☐ 568 Sam McDowell .15 .07 .02
☐ 569 Denny McLain .25 .11 .03
☐ 570 Boog Powell .25 .11 .03
☐ 571 Brooks Robinson 1.50 .70 .19
☐ 572 Frank Robinson 1.50 .70 .19
☐ 573 Pete Rose 3.00 1.35 .35
☐ 574 Tom Seaver 2.00 .90 .25
☐ 575 Rusty Staub .25 .11 .03
☐ 576 Carl Yastrzemski 2.00 .90 .25

1969 MLBPA Pins

This 1969 pin set of 60 was issued by the Major League Baseball Player's Association. Each pin is 7/8" in diameter. The pins are unnumbered and hence they are listed below in alphabetical order within each league, American Leaguers (1-30) and National Leaguers (31-60). This 60 pin set contains 30 pins each of National League players and American League players. The outer bands of the pins are red for American League players and blue for National League players. The pictures on the pins are black and white, head only photos. The line "c. 1969 MLBPA MFG. R.R. Winona, Minn." appears at the bottom of each pin. Many players were reprinted in 1983. The values of these players pins are therefore reduced.

	NRMT	VG-E	GOOD
COMPLETE SET	375.00	170.00	47.50
COMMON PIN (1-60)	2.00	.90	.25
☐ 1 Max Alvis Cleveland Indians	2.00	.90	.25
☐ 2 Luis Aparicio Chicago White Sox	10.00	4.50	1.25
☐ 3 George Brunet California Angels	2.00	.90	.25
☐ 4 Rod Carew Minnesota Twins	15.00	6.75	1.85
☐ 5 Dean Chance Minnesota Twins	2.50	1.10	.30
☐ 6 Bill Freehan Detroit Tigers	3.00	1.35	.35
☐ 7 Jim Fregosi California Angels	3.00	1.35	.35
☐ 8 Ken Harrelson Boston Red Sox	3.00	1.35	.35
☐ 9 Joel Horlen Chicago White Sox	2.00	.90	.25
☐ 10 Tony Horton Cleveland Indians	2.00	.90	.25
☐ 11 Willie Horton Detroit Tigers	3.00	1.35	.35
☐ 12 Frank Howard Washington Senators	3.00	1.35	.35
☐ 13 Al Kaline Detroit Tigers	12.00	5.50	1.50
☐ 14 Harmon Killebrew Minnesota Twins	12.00	5.50	1.50
☐ 15 Mickey Lolich Detroit Tigers	4.00	1.80	.50
☐ 16 Jim Lonborg Boston Red Sox	2.50	1.10	.30
☐ 17 Sam McDowell Cleveland Indians	2.50	1.10	.30
☐ 18 Denny McLain Detroit Tigers	5.00	2.20	.60
☐ 19 Rick Monday Oakland Athletics	2.50	1.10	.30
☐ 20 Tony Oliva Minnesota Twins	3.00	1.35	.35
☐ 21 Joe Pepitone New York Yankees	4.00	1.80	.50
☐ 22 Boog Powell Baltimore Orioles	5.00	2.20	.60
☐ 23 Rick Reichardt California Angels	2.00	.90	.25
☐ 24 Pete Richert Washington Senators	2.00	.90	.25
☐ 25 Brooks Robinson Baltimore Orioles	12.00	5.50	1.50
☐ 26 Frank Robinson Baltimore Orioles	15.00	6.75	1.85
☐ 27 Mel Stottlemyre New York Yankees	3.00	1.35	.35
☐ 28 Luis Tiant Cleveland Indians	4.00	1.80	.50
☐ 29 Pete Ward Chicago White Sox	2.00	.90	.25
☐ 30 Carl Yastrzemski Boston Red Sox	20.00	9.00	2.50
☐ 31 Hank Aaron Atlanta Braves	15.00	6.75	1.85
☐ 32 Felipe Alou Atlanta Braves	3.00	1.35	.35
☐ 33 Richie Allen Philadelphia Phillies	4.00	1.80	.50
☐ 34 Ernie Banks Chicago Cubs	15.00	6.75	1.85
☐ 35 Johnny Bench Cincinnati Reds	25.00	11.00	3.10
☐ 36 Lou Brock	12.00	5.50	1.50

St. Louis Cardinals			
☐ 37 Johnny Callison	2.50	1.10	.30
Philadelphia Phillies			
☐ 38 Orlando Cepeda	4.00	1.80	.50
Atlanta Braves			
☐ 39 Roberto Clemente	30.00	13.50	3.70
Pittsburgh Pirates			
☐ 40 Willie Davis	2.50	1.10	.30
Los Angeles Dodgers			
☐ 41 Don Drysdale	10.00	4.50	1.25
Los Angeles Dodgers			
☐ 42 Ron Fairly	2.50	1.10	.30
Los Angeles Dodgers			
☐ 43 Curt Flood	5.00	2.20	.60
St. Louis Cardinals			
☐ 44 Bob Gibson	12.00	5.50	1.50
St. Louis Cardinals			
☐ 45 Bud Harrelson	2.50	1.10	.30
New York Mets			
☐ 46 Jim Ray Hart	2.00	.90	.25
San Francisco Giants			
☐ 47 Tommy Helms	2.00	.90	.25
Cincinnati Reds			
☐ 48 Don Kessinger	2.50	1.10	.30
Chicago Cubs			
☐ 49 Jerry Koosman	5.00	2.20	.60
New York Mets			
☐ 50 Jim Maloney	2.50	1.10	.30
Cincinnati Reds			
☐ 51 Juan Marichal	8.00	3.60	1.00
San Francisco Giants			
☐ 52 Willie Mays	15.00	6.75	1.85
San Francisco Giants			
☐ 53 Tim McCarver	4.00	1.80	.50
St. Louis Cardinals			
☐ 54 Willie McCovey	8.00	3.60	1.00
San Francisco Giants			
☐ 55 Pete Rose	35.00	16.00	4.40
Cincinnati Reds			
☐ 56 Ron Santo	3.00	1.35	.35
Chicago Cubs			
☐ 57 Ron Swoboda	2.00	.90	.25
New York Mets			
☐ 58 Joe Torre	4.00	1.80	.50
St. Louis Cardinals			
☐ 59 Billy Williams	8.00	3.60	1.00
Chicago Cubs			
☐ 60 Jim Wynn	2.50	1.10	.30
Houston Astros			

1983 MLBPA Pins

This pin set of 36 is apparently a reprinted set and is checklisted here in order to help collectors put a fair value on the pins that they are buying, selling and trading. These are frequently mistaken for the 1969 issue after which they are patterned. There is no indication that this set was authorized by the Major League Baseball Player's Association. Each pin is 7/8" in diameter. This 36 pin set contains 18 pins each of National League players and American League players. This unnumbered set is ordered below alphabetically within league, American Leaguers (1-18) and National Leaguers (19-36). The outer bands of the pins are red for American League players and blue for National League players. The pictures on the pins are black and white, head only photos. All of the players in the set had retired before 1984 and many had retired well before 1969. The line "c 1969 MLBPA MFG. in U.S.A." appears at the bottom of each pin, i.e., no reference to Winona as with the 1969 set.

	NRMT	VG-E	GOOD
COMPLETE SET (36)	25.00	11.00	3.10
COMMON PIN (1-36)	.25	.11	.03
☐ 1 Bob Allison	.25	.11	.03
Minnesota Twins			
☐ 2 Yogi Berra	1.00	.45	.12
New York Yankees			
☐ 3 Norm Cash	.50	.23	.06
Detroit Tigers			
☐ 4 Joe DiMaggio	4.00	1.80	.50
New York Yankees			
☐ 5 Bobby Doerr	.75	.35	.09
Boston Red Sox			
☐ 6 Bob Feller	1.00	.45	.12
Cleveland Indians			
☐ 7 Whitey Ford	1.00	.45	.12
New York Yankees			
☐ 8 Nelson Fox	.75	.35	.09
Chicago White Sox			
☐ 9 Frank Howard	.25	.11	.03
Washington Senators			
☐ 10 Jim (Catfish) Hunter	.75	.35	.09
Oakland A's			
☐ 11 Al Kaline	1.00	.45	.12
Detroit Tigers			
☐ 12 Mickey Mantle	4.00	1.80	.50
New York Yankees			
☐ 13 Tony Oliva	.50	.23	.06
Minnesota Twins			
☐ 14 Satchel Paige	1.50	.70	.19
St. Louis Browns			
☐ 15 Phil Rizzuto	1.00	.45	.12
New York Yankees			
☐ 16 Brooks Robinson	1.00	.45	.12
Baltimore Orioles			
☐ 17 Bill Skowron	.50	.23	.06
New York Yankees			
☐ 18 Ted Williams	2.50	1.10	.30
Boston Red Sox			
☐ 19 Hank Aaron	2.50	1.10	.30
Atlanta Braves			
☐ 20 Roy Campanella	1.00	.45	.12
Brooklyn Dodgers			
☐ 21 Orlando Cepeda	.50	.23	.06
Atlanta Braves			
☐ 22 Roberto Clemente	3.00	1.35	.35
Pittsburgh Pirates			
☐ 23 Don Drysdale	1.00	.45	.12
Los Angeles Dodgers			
☐ 24 Sandy Koufax	2.00	.90	.25
Los Angeles Dodgers			
☐ 25 Juan Marichal	1.50	.70	.19
San Francisco Giants			
☐ 26 Eddie Mathews	1.50	.70	.19
Milwaukee Braves			
☐ 27 Willie Mays	2.50	1.10	.30
San Francisco Giants			
☐ 28 Willie McCovey	.75	.35	.09
San Francisco Giants			
☐ 29 Stan Musial	2.00	.90	.25
St. Louis Cardinals			
☐ 30 Robin Roberts	.75	.35	.09
Philadelphia Phillies			
☐ 31 Jackie Robinson	2.50	1.10	.30
Brooklyn Dodgers			
☐ 32 Ron Santo	.50	.23	.06
Chicago Cubs			
☐ 33 Duke Snider	2.00	.90	.25
Brooklyn Dodgers			
☐ 34 Warren Spahn	.75	.35	.09
Milwaukee Braves			
☐ 35 Billy Williams	.75	.35	.09
Chicago Cubs			
☐ 36 Maury Wills	.50	.23	.06
Los Angeles Dodgers			

1990 MLBPA Baseball Buttons (Pins)

These pins feature leading major league baseball players. They are sequenced by teams: Philadelphia Phillies (1-5), Los Angeles Dodgers (6-8), New York Mets (9-18), Cincinnati Reds (19-22), San Francisco Giants (23-29), Stl Louis Cardinals (30-35, 59), Pittsburgh Pirates (36-38), Houston Astros (39-45, 60), Chicago Cubs (46-54), San Diego Padres (55-58), New York Yankees (61-66, 92), Toronto Blue Jays (67), Boston Red Sox (68-73), Oakland A's (74-78, 115), Milwaukee Brewers (79-85), Detroit Tigers (86-91), California Angels (93-96), Minnesota Twins (97-100), Kansas City Royals (101-109), Baltimore Orioles (110-114, 119), Seattle Mariners (116-118, 120)

	MINT	NRMT	EXC
COMPLETE SET (120)	15.00	6.75	1.85
COMMON PIN (1-120)	.10	.05	.01
☐ 1 Tom Herr	.10	.05	.01
☐ 2 Von Hayes	.10	.05	.01
☐ 3 Ricky Jordan	.10	.05	.01
☐ 4 Dickie Thon	.10	.05	.01
☐ 5 Lenny Dykstra	.20	.09	.03
☐ 6 Kirk Gibson	.20	.09	.03
☐ 7 Fernando Valenzuela	.20	.09	.03
☐ 8 Orel Hershiser	.20	.09	.03
☐ 9 Dwight Gooden	.20	.09	.03
☐ 10 Keith Hernandez	.10	.05	.01
☐ 11 David Cone	.30	.14	.04
☐ 12 Kevin Elster	.10	.05	.01
☐ 13 Darryl Strawberry	.20	.09	.03
☐ 14 Ron Darling	.10	.05	.01
☐ 15 Kevin McReynolds	.10	.05	.01
☐ 16 Howard Johnson	.10	.05	.01
☐ 17 Gary Carter	.20	.09	.03
☐ 18 Gregg Jefferies	.20	.09	.03
☐ 19 Chris Sabo	.10	.05	.01
☐ 20 Tom Browning	.10	.05	.01
☐ 21 Barry Larkin	.50	.23	.06
☐ 22 Eric Davis	.20	.09	.03
☐ 23 Rick Reuschel	.10	.05	.01
☐ 24 Kevin Mitchell	.10	.05	.01
☐ 25 Donell Nixon	.10	.05	.01
☐ 26 Robby Thompson	.10	.05	.01
☐ 27 Brett Butler	.30	.14	.04
☐ 28 Will Clark	.75	.35	.09
☐ 29 Todd Worrell	.10	.05	.01
☐ 30 Ozzie Smith	1.25	.55	.16
☐ 31 Tom Brunansky	.10	.05	.01
☐ 32 Pedro Guerrero	.10	.05	.01
☐ 33 Willie McGee	.20	.09	.03
☐ 34 Tony Pena	.10	.05	.01
☐ 35 Vince Coleman	.10	.05	.01
☐ 36 Andy Van Slyke	.10	.05	.01
☐ 37 Barry Bonds	.75	.35	.09
☐ 38 Bobby Bonilla	.20	.09	.03
☐ 39 Alan Ashby	.10	.05	.01
☐ 40 Gerald Young	.10	.05	.01
☐ 41 Glenn Davis	.10	.05	.01
☐ 42 Ken Caminiti	.50	.23	.06
☐ 43 Mike Scott	.10	.05	.01
☐ 44 Bill Doran	.10	.05	.01
☐ 45 Kevin Bass	.10	.05	.01
☐ 46 Shawon Dunston	.10	.05	.01
☐ 47 Ryne Sandberg	1.00	.45	.12
☐ 48 Mitch Williams	.10	.05	.01
☐ 49 Greg Maddux	1.75	.80	.22
☐ 50 Jerome Walton	.10	.05	.01
☐ 51 Mark Grace	.50	.23	.06
☐ 52 Damon Berryhill	.10	.05	.01
☐ 53 Rick Sutcliffe	.10	.05	.01
☐ 54 Andre Dawson	.30	.14	.04
☐ 55 Tony Gwynn	1.25	.55	.16
☐ 56 Jack Clark	.10	.05	.01
☐ 57 Bruce Hurst	.10	.05	.01
☐ 58 Benito Santiago	.10	.05	.01
☐ 59 Jose Oquendo	.10	.05	.01
☐ 60 Terry Puhl	.10	.05	.01
☐ 61 Jesse Barfield	.10	.05	.01
☐ 62 Steve Sax	.10	.05	.01
☐ 63 Don Mattingly	1.50	.70	.19
☐ 64 Dave Winfield	.50	.23	.06
☐ 65 Don Slaught	.10	.05	.01
☐ 66 Steve Balboni	.10	.05	.01
☐ 67 George Bell	.10	.05	.01
☐ 68 Wade Boggs	.50	.23	.06
☐ 69 Roger Clemens	.50	.23	.06
☐ 70 Jim Rice	.10	.05	.01
☐ 71 Mike Greenwell	.10	.05	.01
☐ 72 Rich Gedman	.10	.05	.01
☐ 73 Carney Lansford	.10	.05	.01
☐ 74 Dave Stewart	.10	.05	.01
☐ 75 Dennis Eckersley	.20	.09	.03
☐ 76 Bob Welch	.10	.05	.01
☐ 77 Mark McGwire	1.00	.45	.12
☐ 78 Jose Canseco	.50	.23	.06
☐ 79 Paul Molitor	.75	.35	.09
☐ 80 Rob Deer	.10	.05	.01
☐ 81 Jim Gantner	.10	.05	.01
☐ 82 Robin Yount	.50	.23	.06
☐ 83 Ted Higuera	.10	.05	.01
☐ 84 B.J. Surhoff	.20	.09	.03
☐ 85 Dan Plesac	.10	.05	.01
☐ 86 Matt Nokes	.10	.05	.01
☐ 87 Chet Lemon	.10	.05	.01
☐ 88 Alan Trammell	.20	.09	.03
☐ 89 Lou Whitaker	.20	.09	.03
☐ 90 Fred Lynn	.10	.05	.01
☐ 91 Mike Heath	.10	.05	.01
☐ 92 Mel Hall	.10	.05	.01
☐ 93 Wally Joyner	.20	.09	.03
☐ 94 Lance Parrish	.20	.09	.03
☐ 95 Jim Abbott	.10	.05	.01
☐ 96 Bert Blyleven	.10	.05	.01
☐ 97 Kent Hrbek	.10	.05	.01
☐ 98 Kirby Puckett	1.50	.70	.19
☐ 99 Greg Gagne	.10	.05	.01
☐ 100 Gary Gaetti	.20	.09	.03
☐ 101 George Brett	1.50	.70	.19
☐ 102 Kevin Seitzer	.10	.05	.01
☐ 103 Charlie Leibrandt	.10	.05	.01
☐ 104 Bo Jackson	.20	.09	.03
☐ 105 Mark Gubicza	.10	.05	.01
☐ 106 Kurt Stillwell	.10	.05	.01
☐ 107 Bob Boone	.20	.09	.03
☐ 108 Frank White	.20	.09	.03
☐ 109 Willie Wilson	.10	.05	.01
☐ 110 Jeff Ballard	.10	.05	.01
☐ 111 Mickey Tettleton	.10	.05	.01
☐ 112 Cal Ripken Jr.	2.50	1.10	.30
☐ 113 Billy Ripken	.10	.05	.01
☐ 114 Gregg Olson	.10	.05	.01
☐ 115 Terry Steinbach	.20	.09	.03
☐ 116 Alvin Davis	.10	.05	.01
☐ 117 Ken Griffey Jr.	3.00	1.35	.35
☐ 118 Harold Reynolds	.20	.09	.03
☐ 119 Brady Anderson	.30	.14	.04
☐ 120 Dave Valle	.10	.05	.01

1991 MLBPA Key Chains

These key chains measure 2" by 3." A borderless color player photo appears inside a plastic case; the reverse of each picture has color logos of the team, MLB, and MLBPA. We have sequenced these unnumbered chains in alphabetical order.

	MINT	NRMT	EXC
COMPLETE SET (4)	8.00	3.60	1.00
COMMON PLAYER (1-4)	1.00	.45	.12
☐ 1 Bobby Bonilla	2.00	.90	.25
☐ 2 Kevin Maas	1.00	.45	.12
☐ 3 Mark McGwire	4.00	1.80	.50
☐ 4 Darryl Strawberry	1.50	.70	.19

1996 MLB Pins

This set consists of 37 pins that measure approximately 2 15/16" each in diameter and features color photos of Major League Baseball players. The pins are unnumbered and checklisted below in alphabetical order. Pins were only made for teams which participated in the championship series: Atlanta Braves, Baltimore Orioles, St. Louis Cardinals and New York Yankees.

	MINT	NRMT	EXC
COMPLETE SET (37)	125.00	55.00	15.50
COMMON CARD (1-37)	1.00	.45	.12
☐ 1 Roberto Alomar	7.50	3.40	.95
☐ 2 Brady Anderson	7.50	3.40	.95
☐ 3 Alan Benes	5.00	2.20	.60
☐ 4 Andy Benes	2.00	.90	.25
☐ 5 Bobby Bonilla	2.00	.90	.25
☐ 6 Pedro Borbon	1.00	.45	.12
☐ 7 Mike Devereaux	1.00	.45	.12
☐ 8 Jermaine Dye	5.00	2.20	.60
☐ 9 Dennis Eckersley	6.00	2.70	.75
☐ 10 Gary Gaetti	2.00	.90	.25
☐ 11 Ron Gant	2.00	.90	.25
☐ 12 Joe Girardi	1.00	.45	.12
☐ 13 Tony Graffanino	1.00	.45	.12
☐ 14 Marquis Grissom	2.00	.90	.25
☐ 15 Chris Hoiles	1.00	.45	.12
☐ 16 Derek Jeter	15.00	6.75	1.85
☐ 17 Brian Jordan	5.00	2.20	.60
☐ 18 Pat Kelly	1.00	.45	.12
☐ 19 Ray Lankford	2.00	.90	.25
☐ 20 Tino Martinez	2.00	.90	.25
☐ 21 Mike Mordecai	1.00	.45	.12
☐ 22 Mike Mussina	7.50	3.40	.95
☐ 23 Randy Myers	2.00	.90	.25
☐ 24 Paul O'Neill	2.00	.90	.25
☐ 25 Tom Pagnozzi	1.00	.45	.12
☐ 26 Rafael Palmeiro	4.00	1.80	.50
☐ 27 Eduardo Perez	1.00	.45	.12
☐ 28 Tim Raines	2.00	.90	.25
☐ 29 Cal Ripken	20.00	9.00	2.50
☐ 30 Ruben Rivera	5.00	2.20	.60
☐ 31 Dwight Smith	1.00	.45	.12
☐ 32 Ozzie Smith	15.00	6.75	1.85
☐ 33 Todd Stottlemyre	1.00	.45	.12
☐ 34 B.J. Surhoff	2.00	.90	.25
☐ 35 John Wetteland	2.00	.90	.25
☐ 36 Bernie Williams	7.50	3.40	.95
☐ 37 Mark Wohlers	4.00	1.80	.50

1987 M&M's Star Lineup

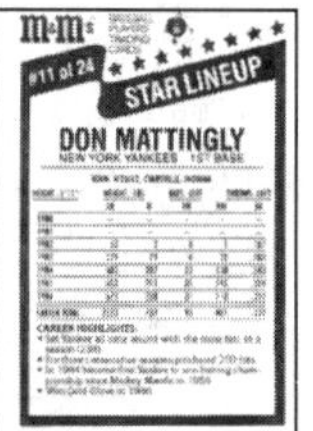

The Mars Candy Company is the sponsor of this 24-card set of cards. The cards were printed in perforated pairs. The pairs measure approximately 5" by 3 1/2" whereas the individual cards measure the standard 2 1/2" by 3 1/2". The players are shown without team logos. The cards were designed and produced by MSA, Mike Schechter Associates. The cards are numbered on the front and back. The backs show statistics for every year since 1980 even if the player was not even playing during those earlier years. The values below are for individual players; panels intact would be valued at 25 percent more than the sum of the two individual players.

	MINT	NRMT	EXC
COMPLETE PANEL SET	10.00	4.50	1.25
COMPLETE IND. SET (24)	6.00	2.70	.75
COMMON CARD (1-24)	.10	.05	.01
☐ 1 Wally Joyner	.40	.18	.05
☐ 2 Tony Pena	.10	.05	.01
☐ 3 Mike Schmidt	.75	.35	.09
☐ 4 Ryne Sandberg	1.25	.55	.16
☐ 5 Wade Boggs	.50	.23	.06
☐ 6 Jack Morris	.20	.09	.03
☐ 7 Roger Clemens	.75	.35	.09
☐ 8 Harold Baines	.10	.05	.01
☐ 9 Dale Murphy	.30	.14	.04
☐ 10 Jose Canseco	.50	.23	.06

☐ 11 Don Mattingly	1.50	.70	.19
☐ 12 Gary Carter	.20	.09	.03
☐ 13 Cal Ripken	2.50	1.10	.30
☐ 14 George Brett	1.25	.55	.16
☐ 15 Kirby Puckett	1.50	.70	.19
☐ 16 Joe Carter	.40	.18	.05
☐ 17 Mike Witt	.10	.05	.01
☐ 18 Mike Scott	.10	.05	.01
☐ 19 Fernando Valenzuela	.20	.09	.03
☐ 20 Steve Garvey	.20	.09	.03
☐ 21 Steve Sax	.10	.05	.01
☐ 22 Nolan Ryan	2.50	1.10	.30
☐ 23 Tony Gwynn	1.50	.70	.19
☐ 24 Ozzie Smith	1.25	.55	.16

1982 Montreal News

This 21-card set was cut out of the Montreal News and features various size color player photos of stars of different sports. The paper is printed in French. The cards are unnumbered and checklisted below in alphabetical order.

	MINT	NRMT	EXC
COMPLETE SET (21)	40.00	18.00	5.00
COMMON CARD (1-21)	1.00	.45	.12
☐ 1 Tracy Austin Tennis	2.00	.90	.25
☐ 2 Bjorn Borg Tennis	3.00	1.35	.35
☐ 3 Jimmy Connors Tennis	5.00	2.20	.60
☐ 4 Chris Chueden Soccer	1.00	.45	.12
☐ 5 Mario Cusson Boxing	1.00	.45	.12
☐ 6 Steve Garvey Baseball	3.00	1.35	.35
☐ 7 Rejean Houle Hockey	1.00	.45	.12
☐ 8 Mark Hunter Hockey	1.00	.45	.12
☐ 9 Frantz Mathieu Soccer	1.00	.45	.12
☐ 10 Martina Navratilova Tennis	4.00	1.80	.50
☐ 11 Wilfrid Paiement Hockey	1.00	.45	.12
☐ 12 Bob Rigby Soccer	1.00	.45	.12
☐ 13 Pete Rose Baseball	7.50	3.40	.95
☐ 14 Mike Schmidt Baseball	7.50	3.40	.95
☐ 15 Willie Stargell Baseball	3.00	1.35	.35
☐ 16 Daniel Talbot Golf	1.00	.45	.12
☐ 17 Luc Tousignant Football	1.00	.45	.12
☐ 18 Tony Towers Soccer	1.00	.45	.12
☐ 19 Thompson Usiyan Soccer	1.00	.45	.12
☐ 20 Fernando Valenzuela Baseball	2.00	.90	.25
☐ 21 Dragan Vujovic Soccer	1.00	.45	.12

1993-95 Moonlight Graham

These four standard-size cards honor Archibald Graham, who was immortalized in the movie "Field of Dreams". These cards were sold to benefit the Doc Graham scholarship funds. Each card has a different design.

	MINT	NRMT	EXC
COMPLETE SET (4)	10.00	4.50	1.25
COMMON CARD (1-4)	3.00	1.35	.35
☐ 1 Archibald Graham Life story, 1993	3.00	1.35	.35
☐ 2 Archibald Graham Field of Dreams players; 1994	3.00	1.35	.35
☐ 3 Archibald Graham 1905 World Series; 1994	3.00	1.35	.35
☐ 4 Archibald Graham Life story; 1995	3.00	1.35	.35

1991 MooTown Snackers

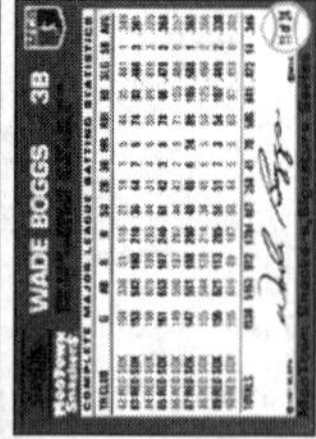

This 24-card standard-size set was sponsored by MooTown Snackers. One player card and an attached mail-in certificate (with checklist on back) were included in five-ounce packages of MooTown Snackers cheese snacks. The complete set could be purchased through the mail by sending in the mail-in certificate, three MooTown Snackers UPC codes, and 5.95. The mail-in sets did not come with the attached mail-in tab; cards with tabs are valued approximately twice the prices listed in the checklist below. The card front features a high gloss color action player photo, which is mounted diagonally on the card face. White and yellow stripes border the picture above and below. At the card top appears the company logo on a red triangle, while the words "Signature Series" appears in an aqua blue oval in the upper right corner. The player's name appears in the red triangle below the picture. The backs present statistical information in red, white, and black. On the bottom of the card a facsimile autograph and a card number round out the back.

	MINT	NRMT	EXC
COMPLETE SET (24)	25.00	11.00	3.10
COMMON CARD (1-24)	.25	.11	.03
☐ 1 Jose Canseco	.50	.23	.06
☐ 2 Kirby Puckett	3.00	1.35	.35
☐ 3 Barry Bonds	1.50	.70	.19
☐ 4 Ken Griffey Jr.	5.00	2.20	.60
☐ 5 Ryne Sandberg	2.50	1.10	.30
☐ 6 Tony Gwynn	3.00	1.35	.35
☐ 7 Kal Daniels	.25	.11	.03
☐ 8 Ozzie Smith	2.50	1.10	.30
☐ 9 Dave Justice	.50	.23	.06
☐ 10 Sandy Alomar Jr.	.50	.23	.06
☐ 11 Wade Boggs	1.00	.45	.12
☐ 12 Ozzie Guillen	.25	.11	.03
☐ 13 Dave Magadan	.25	.11	.03
☐ 14 Cal Ripken	4.00	1.80	.50
☐ 15 Don Mattingly	3.00	1.35	.35
☐ 16 Ruben Sierra	.25	.11	.03
☐ 17 Robin Yount	.50	.23	.06
☐ 18 Len Dykstra	.50	.23	.06
☐ 19 George Brett	2.50	1.10	.30
☐ 20 Lance Parrish	.25	.11	.03
☐ 21 Chris Sabo	.25	.11	.03
☐ 22 Craig Biggio	1.00	.45	.12
☐ 23 Kevin Mitchell	.25	.11	.03
☐ 24 Cecil Fielder	.50	.23	.06

1992 MooTown Snackers

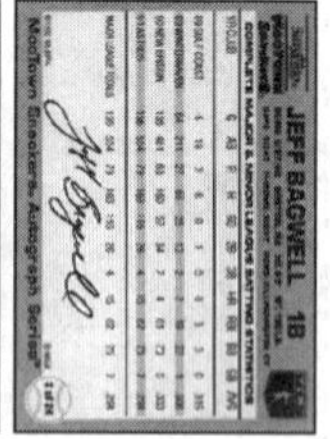

This 24-card standard-size set was produced by MSA (Michael Schechter Associates) for MooTown Snackers. The cards were inserted inside 5 ounce and 10 ounce cheese snack packages. It is reported that more than two million cards were produced. Collectors could also obtain the complete set through a mail-in offer. The cards obtained via mail did not come with the mail-in offer tabs. Cards with tabs have twice the value of the prices below. The color player photos on the fronts are bordered above and below by diagonal white and red stripes that edge a yellow border. Team logos were airbrushed out of the photos. In black print on a yellow and white background, the backs present biography, complete batting or pitching statistics, and facsimile autograph.

	MINT	NRMT	EXC
COMPLETE SET (24)	25.00	11.00	3.10
COMMON CARD (1-24)	.25	.11	.03
☐ 1 Albert Belle	2.50	1.10	.30
☐ 2 Jeff Bagwell	2.00	.90	.25
☐ 3 Jose Rijo	.25	.11	.03
☐ 4 Roger Clemens	1.00	.45	.12
☐ 5 Kevin Maas	.25	.11	.03
☐ 6 Kirby Puckett	2.50	1.10	.30
☐ 7 Ken Griffey Jr.	4.00	1.80	.50
☐ 8 Will Clark	.50	.23	.06
☐ 9 Felix Jose	.25	.11	.03
☐ 10 Cecil Fielder	.50	.23	.06
☐ 11 Darryl Strawberry	.50	.23	.06
☐ 12 John Smiley	.25	.11	.03
☐ 13 Roberto Alomar	.75	.35	.09
☐ 14 Paul Molitor	1.00	.45	.12
☐ 15 Andre Dawson	.50	.23	.06
☐ 16 Terry Mulholland	.25	.11	.03
☐ 17 Fred McGriff	.50	.23	.06
☐ 18 Dwight Gooden	.50	.23	.06
☐ 19 Rickey Henderson	1.00	.45	.12
☐ 20 Nolan Ryan	3.00	1.35	.35
☐ 21 George Brett	2.00	.90	.25
☐ 22 Tom Glavine	1.00	.45	.12
☐ 23 Cal Ripken	3.00	1.35	.35
☐ 24 Frank Thomas	4.00	1.80	.50

1909 Morton's Pennant Winner Bread Pins PB3

These are very attractive pins, approximately 1 1/4" in diameter. The set features Detroit Tigers only. Rims are styled in black and white with blue and yellow trim. The catalog designation for this set is PB3. Since the player's name is not listed explicitly on the pin, there is still one player's pin who can not be identified positively; this pin is listed last in the checklist below in the otherwise alphabetized checklist.

	EX-MT	VG-E	GOOD
COMPLETE SET (15)	3500.00	1600.00	450.00
COMMON PLAYER (1-15)	200.00	90.00	25.00
☐ 1 Donie Bush	200.00	90.00	25.00
☐ 2 Ty Cobb	1000.00	450.00	125.00
☐ 3 Sam Crawford	350.00	160.00	45.00
☐ 4 Bill Donovan	200.00	90.00	25.00
☐ 5 Hugh Jennings MG	350.00	160.00	45.00
☐ 6 Davy Jones	200.00	90.00	25.00
☐ 7 Matty McIntyre	200.00	90.00	25.00
☐ 8 George Moriarty	200.00	90.00	25.00
☐ 9 George Mullin	200.00	90.00	25.00
☐ 10 Claude Rossman	200.00	90.00	25.00
☐ 11 Herman Schaefer	250.00	110.00	31.00
☐ 12 Charles Schmidt	200.00	90.00	25.00
☐ 13 Oren Summers	200.00	90.00	25.00
☐ 14 Ed Willett	200.00	90.00	25.00
☐ 15 Unknown Player photo not recognizable	200.00	90.00	25.00

1987 Mother's McGwire

This set consists of four, full-color, rounded-corner cards each showing a different pose of A's slugging rookie Mark McGwire. Cards were originally given out at the national Card Collectors Convention in San Francisco. Later they were available through a mail-in offer involving collectors sending in two proofs-of-purchase from any Mother's Cookies products to get one free card. Photos were taken by Doug McWilliams.

	MINT	NRMT	EXC
COMPLETE SET (4)	10.00	4.50	1.25
COMMON CARD (1-4)	3.00	1.35	.35
☐ 1 Mark McGwire (Close-up shot head and shoulders)	3.00	1.35	.35
☐ 2 Mark McGwire (Waist up holding bat)	3.00	1.35	.35
☐ 3 Mark McGwire (Batting stance ready to swing)	3.00	1.35	.35
☐ 4 Mark McGwire (Home run swing follow through)	3.00	1.35	.35

1988 Mother's Will Clark

This regional set consists of four full-color, rounded-corner cards each showing a different pose of Giants' slugging first baseman Will Clark. Cards were originally found in 18 oz. packages of "Big Bags" of Mother's Cookies at stores in the Northern California area in February and March of 1988. Card backs are done in red and purple on white card stock.

	MINT	NRMT	EXC
COMPLETE SET (4)	15.00	6.75	1.85
COMMON CARD (1-4)	4.00	1.80	.50
☐ 1 Will Clark (Batting Pose Waist Up)	5.00	2.20	.60
☐ 2 Will Clark (Kneeling In On Deck Circle)	4.00	1.80	.50
☐ 3 Will Clark (Follow Through Swing)	4.00	1.80	.50
☐ 4 Will Clark (Starting Toward First Base)	5.00	2.20	.60

1988 Mother's McGwire

This regional set consists of four full-color, rounded-corner cards each showing a different pose of The Athletics' slugging first baseman Mark McGwire. Cards were originally found in 18 oz. packages of "Big Bags" of Mother's Cookies at stores in the Northern California area in February and March, 1988. Card backs are done in red and purple on white card stock.

	MINT	NRMT	EXC
COMPLETE SET (4)	10.00	4.50	1.25
COMMON CARD (1-4)	3.00	1.35	.35
☐ 1 Mark McGwire (Holding Big Bat)	3.00	1.35	.35
☐ 2 Mark McGwire (Fielding at First Base)	3.00	1.35	.35
☐ 3 Mark McGwire (Kneeling In On Deck Circle)	3.00	1.35	.35
☐ 4 Mark McGwire (Batting Pose Waist Up)	3.00	1.35	.35

1989 Mother's Canseco

The 1989 Mother's Jose Canseco set contains four standard-size cards with rounded corners. The fronts have borderless color photos, and the horizontally oriented backs have biographical information. One card was included in each specially marked box of Mother's Cookies. Since all four cards picture Jose Canseco, the pose is identified parenthetically in the checklist below in order to distinguish the card fronts.

	MINT	NRMT	EXC
COMPLETE SET (4)	8.00	3.60	1.00
COMMON CARD (1-4)	2.50	1.10	.30

☐ 1 Jose Canseco (Holding ball in hand)	2.50	1.10	.30
☐ 2 Jose Canseco (On one knee with bat)	2.50	1.10	.30
☐ 3 Jose Canseco (Swinging at pitch)	2.50	1.10	.30
☐ 4 Jose Canseco (Running toward second)	2.50	1.10	.30

1989 Mother's Will Clark

The 1989 Mother's Cookies Will Clark set contains four standard-size cards with rounded corners. The fronts have borderless color photos, and the horizontally oriented backs have biographical information. One card was included in each specially marked box of Mother's Cookies. Since all four cards picture Will Clark, the pose is identified parenthetically in the checklist below in order to distinguish the card fronts.

	MINT	NRMT	EXC
COMPLETE SET (4)	8.00	3.60	1.00
COMMON CARD (1-4)	2.50	1.10	.30
☐ 1 Will Clark (Ball in glove)	2.50	1.10	.30
☐ 2 Will Clark (Batting stance posed)	2.50	1.10	.30
☐ 3 Will Clark (Swing follow through)	2.50	1.10	.30
☐ 4 Will Clark (Starting toward first after hit still holding bat)	2.50	1.10	.30

1989 Mother's Griffey Jr.

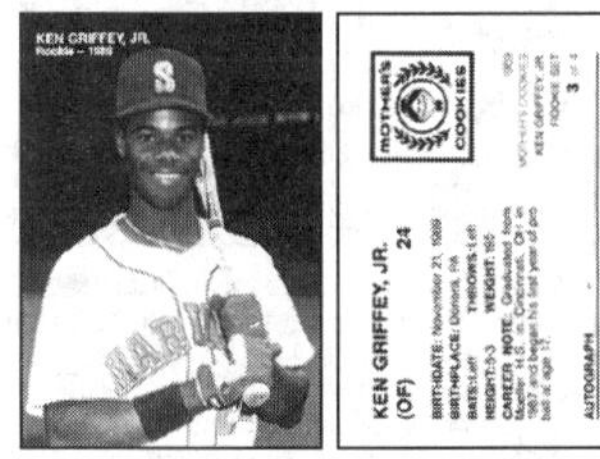

The 1989 Mother's Cookies Ken Griffey Jr. set contains four standard-size cards with rounded corners. The fronts have borderless color photos, and the horizontal backs have biographical information. One card was included in each specially marked box of Mother's Cookies. Since all four cards picture Ken Griffey Jr., the pose is identified parenthetically in the checklist below in order to distinguish the card fronts. Each card back provides a different aspect or background on Ken and his career. The photos were shot by noted sports photographer Barry Colla. It has been reported that card No. 2 is a little more difficult to find than the other cards in the set.

	MINT	NRMT	EXC
COMPLETE SET (4)	18.00	8.00	2.20
COMMON CARD (1-4)	5.00	2.20	.60
☐ 1 Ken Griffey Jr. (Arms folded)	5.00	2.20	.60
☐ 2 Ken Griffey Jr. (Baseball in hand)	6.00	2.70	.75
☐ 3 Ken Griffey Jr. (Looking straight ahead with bat)	5.00	2.20	.60
☐ 4 Ken Griffey Jr. (Looking over shoulder with bat)	5.00	2.20	.60

1989 Mother's McGwire

The 1989 Mother's Cookies Mark McGwire set contains four standard-size cards with rounded corners. The fronts have borderless color photos, and the horizontal backs have biographical information. One card was included in each specially marked box of Mother's Cookies. Since all four cards picture Mark McGwire, the pose is identified parenthetically in the checklist below in order to distinguish the card fronts.

	MINT	NRMT	EXC
COMPLETE SET (4)	8.00	3.60	1.00
COMMON CARD (1-4)	2.50	1.10	.30

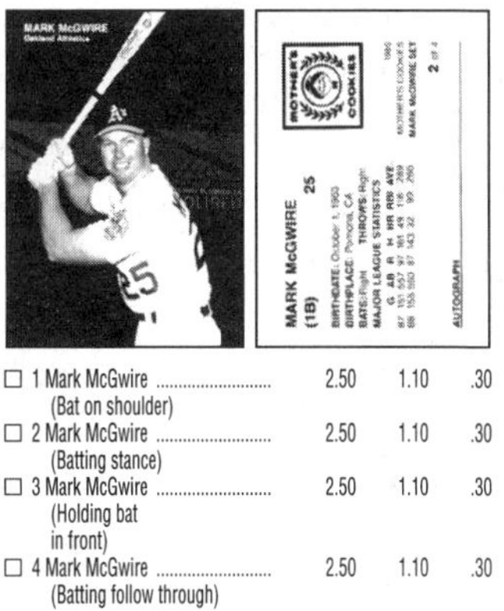

☐ 1 Mark McGwire (Bat on shoulder)	2.50	1.10	.30
☐ 2 Mark McGwire (Batting stance)	2.50	1.10	.30
☐ 3 Mark McGwire (Holding bat in front)	2.50	1.10	.30
☐ 4 Mark McGwire (Batting follow through)	2.50	1.10	.30

1990 Mother's Canseco

This is a standard Mother's Cookies set with four cards each measuring the standard size with rounded corners issued to capitalize on Jose Canseco's popularity. This four-card set features Canseco in various batting poses.

	MINT	NRMT	EXC
COMPLETE SET (4)	8.00	3.60	1.00
COMMON CARD (1-4)	2.50	1.10	.30
☐ 1 Jose Canseco (Sitting with bat over shoulders)	2.50	1.10	.30
☐ 2 Jose Canseco (Standing with bat behind shoulders)	2.50	1.10	.30
☐ 3 Jose Canseco (Batting Pose)	2.50	1.10	.30
☐ 4 Jose Canseco (Sitting on dugout steps)	2.50	1.10	.30

1990 Mother's Will Clark

This is a standard Mother's Cookies set with four cards each measuring the standard size with rounded corners issued to capitalize on Will Clark's popularity. This four-card set features Clark in various poses as indicated in the checklist below.

	MINT	NRMT	EXC
COMPLETE SET (4)	8.00	3.60	1.00
COMMON CARD (1-4)	2.50	1.10	.30
☐ 1 Will Clark (Batting pose looking over right shoulder)	2.50	1.10	.30
☐ 2 Will Clark (Holding bat on left shoulder)	2.50	1.10	.30
☐ 3 Will Clark (Holding bat ready to swing)	2.50	1.10	.30
☐ 4 Will Clark (Standing with bat behind shoulders)	2.50	1.10	.30

1990 Mother's McGwire

This is a standard Mother's Cookies set with four cards each measuring the standard size with rounded corners issued to capitalize on Mark McGwire's popularity. This four-card set features McGwire in various poses as indicated in the checklist below.

	MINT	NRMT	EXC
COMPLETE SET (4)	8.00	3.60	1.00
COMMON CARD (1-4)	2.50	1.10	.30

☐ 1 Mark McGwire (Standing with bat on right shoulder)	2.50	1.10	.30
☐ 2 Mark McGwire (Standing in dugout with bat in front)	2.50	1.10	.30
☐ 3 Mark McGwire (Fielding pose)	2.50	1.10	.30
☐ 4 Mark McGwire (Sitting on dugout steps)	2.50	1.10	.30

1990 Mother's Ryan

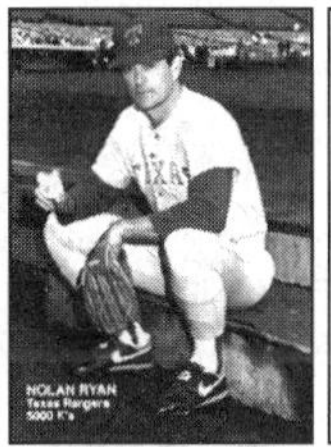

This is a typical Mother's Cookies set with four cards each measuring the standard size with rounded corners honoring Ryan's more than 5,000 strikeouts over his career. This four-card set features Ryan in various pitching poses. The second card in the set is considered tougher to find than the other three in the set. This four-card set was also issued as an unperforated strip.

	MINT	NRMT	EXC
COMPLETE SET (4)	12.50	5.50	1.55
COMMON CARD (1-4)	3.50	1.55	.45
☐ 1 Nolan Ryan (Holding ball)	3.50	1.55	.45
☐ 2 Nolan Ryan (Dugout pose)	5.00	2.20	.60
☐ 3 Nolan Ryan (Holding ball behind waist)	3.50	1.55	.45
☐ 4 Nolan Ryan (Holding ball with 5,000 K's)	3.50	1.55	.45

1990 Mother's Matt Williams

This is a standard Mother's Cookies set with four cards each measuring the standard size with rounded corners issued to capitalize on Matt Williams' popularity. This four-card set features Williams in various poses as indicated in the checklist below.

	MINT	NRMT	EXC
COMPLETE SET (4)	8.00	3.60	1.00
COMMON CARD (1-4)	2.50	1.10	.30
☐ 1 Matt Williams (Standing with bat on right shoulder)	2.50	1.10	.30
☐ 2 Matt Williams (Smiling batting pose)	2.50	1.10	.30
☐ 3 Matt Williams (Posing with glove)	2.50	1.10	.30
☐ 4 Matt Williams (Fielding pose with glove between legs)	2.50	1.10	.30

1991 Mother's Griffeys

The 1991 Mother's Cookies Father and Son set contains four cards with rounded corners measuring the standard size. The front design has borderless glossy color player photos. The horizontally oriented backs are printed in red and purple, and present biographical information as well as career notes. A blank slot for the player's autograph appears at the bottom of each card.

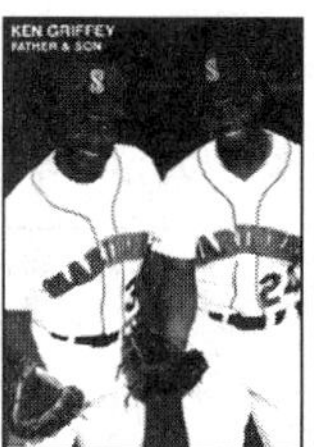
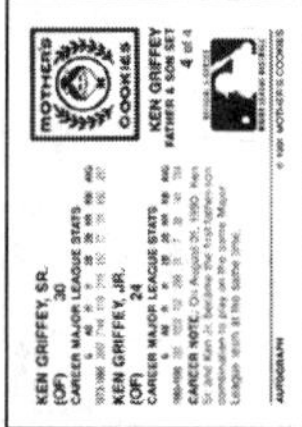

	MINT	NRMT	EXC
COMPLETE SET (4)	6.00	2.70	.75
COMMON CARD (1-4)	.75	.35	.09
☐ 1 Ken Griffey Jr. Holding bat	3.00	1.35	.35
☐ 2 Ken Griffey Sr. Holding glove	.75	.35	.09
☐ 3 Ken Griffey Sr. Ken Griffey Jr. Pose with gloves	2.00	.90	.25
☐ 4 Ken Griffey Sr. Ken Griffey Jr. Looking over shoulder	2.00	.90	.25

1991 Mother's Nolan Ryan

This four-card set was sponsored by Mother's Cookies in honor of Nolan Ryan, baseball's latest 300-game winner. One card was packaged in each box of Mother's Cookies 18-ounce family size bags of five different flavored cookies (Chocolate Chip, Cookie Parade, Oatmeal Raisin, Fudge'N Chips, and Costadas). Also collectors could purchase an uncut strip of the four cards for 7.95 with four proof-of-purchase seals, and a protective sleeve for $1. The standard-size cards have on the fronts full-bleed color posed photos with rounded corners. In red and purple print, the horizontally oriented backs have biographical information, career notes, statistics, and space for an autograph. This four-card set was also issued as an unperforated strip.

	MINT	NRMT	EXC
COMPLETE SET (4)	8.00	3.60	1.00
COMMON CARD (1-4)	2.50	1.10	.30
☐ 1 Nolan Ryan Front pose, Hand in glove	2.50	1.10	.30
☐ 2 Nolan Ryan Kneeling on one knee	2.50	1.10	.30
☐ 3 Nolan Ryan Side pose	2.50	1.10	.30
☐ 4 Nolan Ryan Front pose, Ball in hand	2.50	1.10	.30

1992 Mother's Bagwell

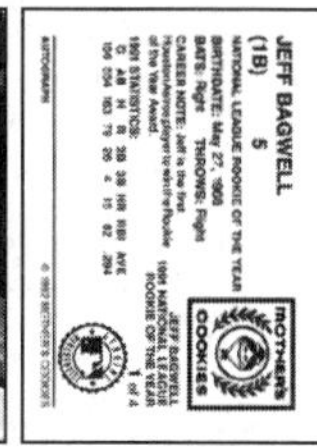

This four-card, standard-size set was sponsored by Mother's Cookies. The fronts have rounded corners and feature posed color full-bleed photos of Jeff Bagwell, the 1991 National League Rookie of the Year. The horizontally oriented backs are printed in purple and red and have biographical information, statistics, career notes, and an autograph space.

	MINT	NRMT	EXC
COMPLETE SET (4)	6.00	2.70	.75
COMMON CARD (1-4)	2.00	.90	.25
☐ 1 Jeff Bagwell (Close-up photo head and shoulders)	2.00	.90	.25
☐ 2 Jeff Bagwell (Close-up photo bat on shoulder)	2.00	.90	.25
☐ 3 Jeff Bagwell (Close-up photo from waist up)	2.00	.90	.25
☐ 4 Jeff Bagwell	2.00	.90	.25

(Close-up photo ball in glove)

1992 Mother's Knoblauch

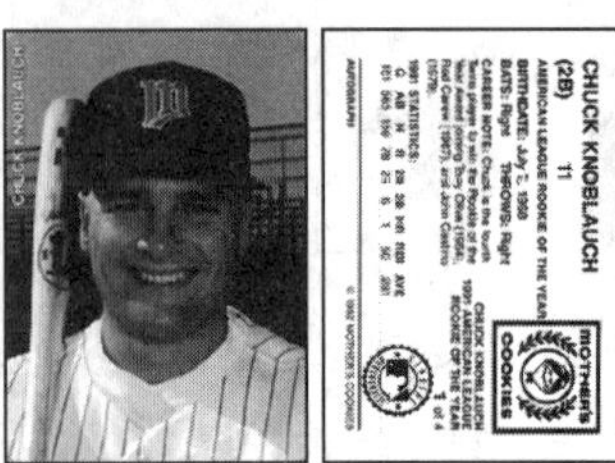

This four-card set measures the standard size and was sponsored by Mother's Cookies in honor of the 1991 American League Rookie of the Year, Chuck Knoblauch. The fronts feature borderless color photos with rounded corners. The backs are printed in red and purple and contain biographical information, career notes, and statistics.

	MINT	NRMT	EXC
COMPLETE SET (4)	6.00	2.70	.75
COMMON CARD (1-4)	2.00	.90	.25
☐ 1 Chuck Knoblauch (Close-up photo head and shoulders)	2.00	.90	.25
☐ 2 Chuck Knoblauch (Close-up photo bat on shoulder)	2.00	.90	.25
☐ 3 Chuck Knoblauch (Close-up photo from waist up)	2.00	.90	.25
☐ 4 Chuck Knoblauch (Posed action shot straddling base)	2.00	.90	.25

1992 Mother's Ryan 7 No-Hitters

The 1992 Mother's Nolan Ryan Seven No-Hitters set contains eight standard-size cards with rounded corners and glossy full-bleed color photos. Card Nos. 1-4 were included in 18-ounce Mother's Cookies family size "Big Bag" cookies. Card Nos. 5-8 were in 16-ounce packages of "sandwich" cookies. The set was also available as an uncut sheet through a mail-in offer on specially marked packages for $7.95 plus four proofs of purchase. The horizontally oriented backs are printed in red and purple and feature biographical information, career notes, highlights, and statistics for each of his no-hitters (except card No. 8).

	MINT	NRMT	EXC
COMPLETE SET (8)	12.00	5.50	1.50
COMMON CARD (1-8)	1.50	.70	.19
☐ 1 Nolan Ryan 1st No-hitter	1.50	.70	.19
☐ 2 Nolan Ryan 2nd No-hitter	1.50	.70	.19
☐ 3 Nolan Ryan 3rd No-hitter	1.50	.70	.19
☐ 4 Nolan Ryan 4th No-hitter (Holding four balls with zeroes on them)	1.50	.70	.19
☐ 5 Nolan Ryan 5th No-hitter (Astros uniform)	1.50	.70	.19
☐ 6 Nolan Ryan 6th No-hitter	1.50	.70	.19
☐ 7 Nolan Ryan 7th No-hitter	1.50	.70	.19
☐ 8 Nolan Ryan 8th No-hitter	1.50	.70	.19

1993 Mother's Ryan Farewell

This ten-card standard-size set has rounded corners and was issued by Mother's Cookies to bid farewell to Nolan Ryan. The fronts feature borderless color photos of Ryan taken at different times during his long and illustrious career. The set's logo appears in the upper left. The horizontal backs carry his biography, Ryan's stats from the team and year pictured on the front, and a place near the bottom for an autograph. The Mother's Cookies logo on the back rounds out the back. This set was also issued as a 7 5/8" by 14" sheet consisting of two rows with five cards in each row.

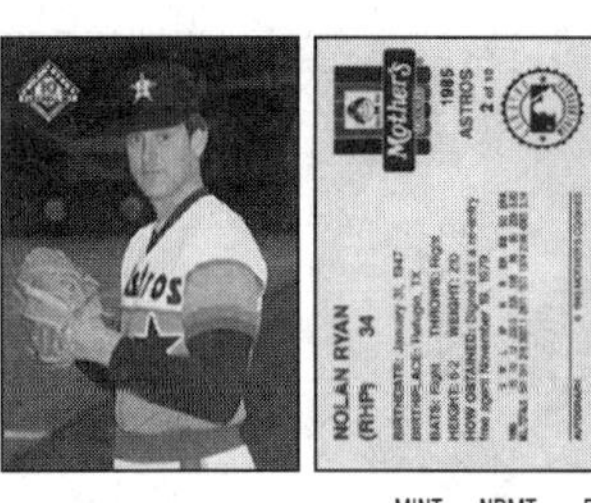

	MINT	NRMT	EXC
COMPLETE SET (10)	10.00	4.50	1.25
COMMON CARD (1-10)	1.25	.55	.16
☐ 1 Nolan Ryan 1984 Astros	1.25	.55	.16
☐ 2 Nolan Ryan 1985 Astros	1.25	.55	.16
☐ 3 Nolan Ryan 1986 Astros (Portrait painting)	1.25	.55	.16
☐ 4 Nolan Ryan 1987 Astros	1.25	.55	.16
☐ 5 Nolan Ryan 1988 Astros	1.25	.55	.16
☐ 6 Nolan Ryan 1989 Rangers	1.25	.55	.16
☐ 7 Nolan Ryan 1990 Rangers	1.25	.55	.16
☐ 8 Nolan Ryan 1991 Rangers	1.25	.55	.16
☐ 9 Nolan Ryan 1992 Rangers	1.25	.55	.16
☐ 10 Nolan Ryan 1993 Rangers	1.25	.55	.16

1994 Mother's Piazza

Issued to showcase the '93 NL ROY, these four standard-size cards have rounded corners and feature borderless posed color photos of Mike Piazza on their fronts. His name appears in white lettering in an upper corner. The white horizontal back carries his name, position, uniform number, career highlights, and statistics in red and purple lettering. A space is reserved at the bottom for an autograph. One card was included in each package of six varieties of Mother's Big Bag Cookies. The set was also issued as an uncut strip of four cards. The cards are numbered on the back as "X of 4."

	MINT	NRMT	EXC
COMPLETE SET (4)	6.00	2.70	.75
COMMON CARD (1-4)	2.00	.90	.25
☐ 1 Mike Piazza (Bat on left shoulder)	2.00	.90	.25
☐ 2 Mike Piazza (Batting pose)	2.00	.90	.25
☐ 3 Mike Piazza (Standing, posed with glove)	2.00	.90	.25
☐ 4 Mike Piazza (Crouching)	2.00	.90	.25

1994 Mother's Piazza/Salmon

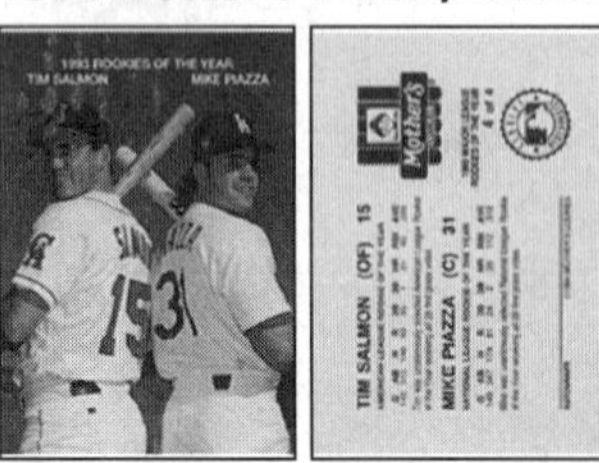

This four-card set was issued to honor Mike Piazza and Tim Salmon as the 1993 Rookies of the Year. Featuring both players on each card, these cards were packaged one per bag of Mother's Major League Double Headers. The set was also issued as an uncut strip of four cards. The individual cards measure the standard size, have rounded corners, and each features on its front a posed color photo of both Piazza and Salmon. Their names appear in white lettering above their images. The white horizontal backs carry the names, position, uniform numbers, statistics and career highlights for both players in red and purple lettering. A space is reserved at the bottom for an autograph. The cards are numbered on the back as "X of 4." Mother's Cookies also produced two chase cards, which were issued in either red or blue foil versions, and were reportedly inserted at a rate of one card per 1,000 packages of Mother's Big Bag Cookies. Less than 10,000 of the foil cards were reportedly produced. The blue card is numbered on the back "1 in a 1000 Blue", the red card "1 in 1000 Red."

	MINT	NRMT	EXC
COMPLETE SET (4)	5.00	2.20	.60
COMMON CARD (1-4)	1.50	.70	.19
☐ 1 Mike Piazza Tim Salmon (Bats on shoulders, facing front)	1.50	.70	.19
☐ 2 Mike Piazza Tim Salmon (With arms draped over each other)	1.50	.70	.19
☐ 3 Mike Piazza Tim Salmon (Shaking hands)	1.50	.70	.19
☐ 4 Mike Piazza Tim Salmon (Back to back, looking over shoulders)	1.50	.70	.19

1994 Mother's Salmon

This four-card standard size set sponsored by Mother's Cookies features Tim Salmon, the 1993 AL Rookie of the Year. One card was included in each package of six varieties of Mother's Big Bag Cookies. The borderless fronts feature color photos with his name in one of the top corners. In red and purple print, the horizonal plain white back features his name, position and uniform number at the upper left with a biography and statistics below. The cards are numbered on the back as "X of 4."

	MINT	NRMT	EXC
COMPLETE SET (4)	5.00	2.20	.60
COMMON CARD (1-4)	1.50	.70	.19
☐ 1 Tim Salmon (Bat resting on shoulder)	1.50	.70	.19
☐ 2 Tim Salmon Batting pose)	1.50	.70	.19
☐ 3 Tim Salmon (Posed by dugout)	1.50	.70	.19
☐ 4 Tim Salmon (Catching ball by wall)	1.50	.70	.19

1976 Motorola Old Timers

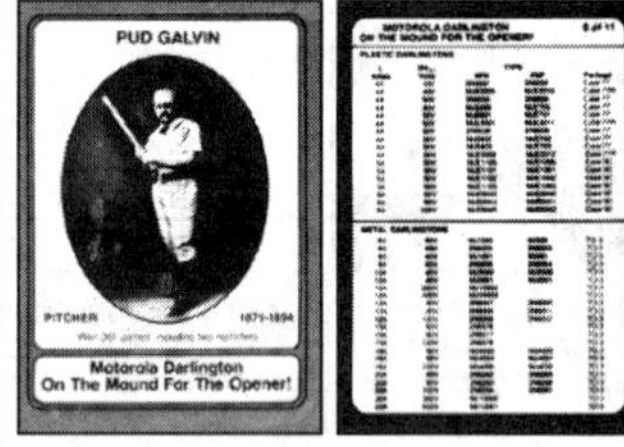

This 11-card standard-size set, issued by Motorola in 1976, honored some of Baseball's all-time greats. The front of the cards were about the player while the backs of the cards talked in technical terms about Motorola products. The cards are also made on a thin (paper-like) card stock and are very flimsy. Certain dealers have reported that there was also an edible version of these cards issued.

	NRMT	VG-E	GOOD
COMPLETE SET (11)	30.00	13.50	3.70
COMMON CARD (1-11)	1.00	.45	.12
☐ 1 Honus Wagner	5.00	2.20	.60
☐ 2 Nap Lajoie	3.00	1.35	.35
☐ 3 Ty Cobb	7.50	3.40	.95
☐ 4 William Wambsganss	1.00	.45	.12
☐ 5 Mordecai Brown	1.50	.70	.19
☐ 6 Ray Schalk	1.50	.70	.19
☐ 7 Frank Frisch	2.00	.90	.25
☐ 8 Pud Galvin	1.50	.70	.19
☐ 9 Babe Ruth	10.00	4.50	1.25
☐ 10 Grover C. Alexander	3.00	1.35	.35
☐ 11 Frank L. Chance	2.00	.90	.25

1943 MP & Co. R302-1

The 1943 MP and Co. baseball card set consists of 24 player drawings each measuring 2 11/16" by 2 1/4". This company specialized in producing strips of cards to be sold in candy stores and provided a

low quality but persistent challenge to other current sets. These unnumbered cards have been alphabetized and numbered in the checklist below. There is a variation on Foxx due to his acquisition by the Cubs from the Red Sox on June 1, 1942.

	EX-MT	VG-E	GOOD
COMPLETE SET (24)	350.00	160.00	45.00
COMMON CARD (1-24)	4.00	1.80	.50
☐ 1 Ernie Bonham	4.00	1.80	.50
☐ 2 Lou Boudreau	15.00	6.75	1.85
☐ 3 Dolph Camilli	5.00	2.20	.60
☐ 4 Mort Cooper	4.00	1.80	.50
☐ 5 Walker Cooper	4.00	1.80	.50
☐ 6 Joe Cronin	15.00	6.75	1.85
☐ 7 Hank Danning	4.00	1.80	.50
☐ 8 Bill Dickey	20.00	9.00	2.50
☐ 9 Joe DiMaggio	75.00	34.00	9.50
☐ 10 Bob Feller	25.00	11.00	3.10
☐ 11 Jimmy Foxx (Chicago Cubs)	35.00	16.00	4.40
☐ 12 Hank Greenberg	20.00	9.00	2.50
☐ 13 Stan Hack	4.00	1.80	.50
☐ 14 Tom Henrich	7.50	3.40	.95
☐ 15 Carl Hubbell	15.00	6.75	1.85
☐ 16 Joe Medwick	15.00	6.75	1.85
☐ 17 John Mize	20.00	9.00	2.50
☐ 18 Lou Novikoff	4.00	1.80	.50
☐ 19 Mel Ott	20.00	9.00	2.50
☐ 20 Pee Wee Reese	25.00	11.00	3.10
☐ 21 Pete Reiser	7.50	3.40	.95
☐ 22 Charlie Ruffing	15.00	6.75	1.85
☐ 23 Johnny Vander Meer	7.50	3.40	.95
☐ 24 Ted Williams	50.00	22.00	6.25

1949 MP & Co. R302-2

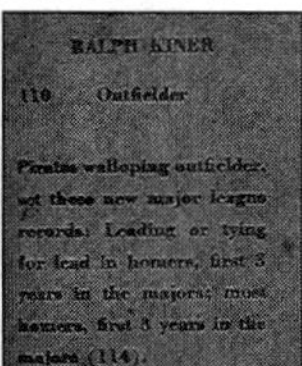

The 1949 rendition of MP and Co. was basically a re-issue of the 1943 set with different players and numbers on the back. Cards again measure approximately 2 11/16" by 2 1/4". The card fronts are even more washed out than the previous set. Card numbers 104, 118, and 120 are unknown and may be related to the two unnumbered cards found in the set. The catalog also lists this set as W523.

	NRMT	VG-E	GOOD
COMPLETE SET	250.00	110.00	31.00
COMMON CARD (100-126)	5.00	2.20	.60
☐ 100 Lou Boudreau	10.00	4.50	1.25
☐ 101 Ted Williams	50.00	22.00	6.25
☐ 102 Buddy Kerr	5.00	2.20	.60
☐ 103 Bob Feller	20.00	9.00	2.50
☐ 104 Unknown			
☐ 105 Joe DiMaggio	60.00	27.00	7.50
☐ 106 Pee Wee Reese	20.00	9.00	2.50
☐ 107 Ferris Fain	5.00	2.20	.60
☐ 108 Andy Pafko	5.00	2.20	.60
☐ 109 Del Ennis	7.50	3.40	.95
☐ 110 Ralph Kiner	10.00	4.50	1.25
☐ 111 Nippy Jones	5.00	2.20	.60
☐ 112 Del Rice	5.00	2.20	.60
☐ 113 Hank Sauer	5.00	2.20	.60
☐ 114 Gil Coan	5.00	2.20	.60
☐ 115 Eddie Joost	5.00	2.20	.60
☐ 116 Alvin Dark	7.50	3.40	.95
☐ 117 Larry Berra	20.00	9.00	2.50
☐ 118 Unknown			
☐ 119 Bob Lemon	10.00	4.50	1.25
☐ 120 Unknown			
☐ 121 Johnny Pesky	7.50	3.40	.95
☐ 122 Johnny Sain	7.50	3.40	.95
☐ 123 Hoot Evers	5.00	2.20	.60
☐ 124 Larry Doby	7.50	3.40	.95
☐ xx Tom Henrich (unnumbered)	7.50	3.40	.95
☐ xx Al Kozar (unnumbered)	5.00	2.20	.60

1992 Mr. Turkey Superstars

This 26-card set was sponsored by Mr. Turkey. One card was found on the back panel of Mr. Turkey products, such as Hardwood Smoked

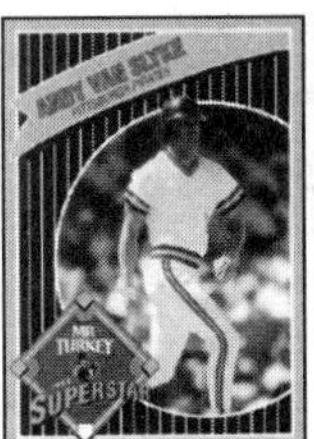

Turkey Pastrami. The standard-size player card is not perforated. On a pinstripe background whose color is team color-coded, the front design has a color action player photo cut out to fit a circular format. The extreme right portion of the circle extends off the right edge of the card. Team logos have been airbrushed out of the photos. The player's name and team name appear in a colored banner above the player photo. At the lower left corner appears the Mr. Turkey 1992 Superstar emblem, which is designed like a baseball diamond. The backs are printed in blue and carry biography and a "Let's Talk Turkey" trivia fact about the player. The cards are numbered on the back; the card numbering is actually alphabetical by player's name.

	MINT	NRMT	EXC
COMPLETE SET (26)	20.00	9.00	2.50
COMMON CARD (1-26)	.25	.11	.03
☐ 1 Jim Abbott	.25	.11	.03
☐ 2 Roberto Alomar	1.25	.55	.16
☐ 3 Sandy Alomar Jr.	.50	.23	.06
☐ 4 Craig Biggio	.50	.23	.06
☐ 5 George Brett	2.00	.90	.25
☐ 6 Will Clark	1.25	.55	.16
☐ 7 Roger Clemens	1.50	.70	.19
☐ 8 Cecil Fielder	.50	.23	.06
☐ 9 Carlton Fisk	1.00	.45	.12
☐ 10 Andres Galarraga	1.00	.45	.12
☐ 11 Dwight Gooden	.50	.23	.06
☐ 12 Ken Griffey Jr.	5.00	2.20	.60
☐ 13 Tony Gwynn	2.50	1.10	.30
☐ 14 Rickey Henderson	1.00	.45	.12
☐ 15 Dave Justice	.75	.35	.09
☐ 16 Don Mattingly	2.50	1.10	.30
☐ 17 Dale Murphy	1.00	.45	.12
☐ 18 Kirby Puckett	2.50	1.10	.30
☐ 19 Cal Ripken	4.00	1.80	.50
☐ 20 Nolan Ryan	4.00	1.80	.50
☐ 21 Chris Sabo	.25	.11	.03
☐ 22 Ryne Sandberg	2.00	.90	.25
☐ 23 Ozzie Smith	2.00	.90	.25
☐ 24 Darryl Strawberry	.50	.23	.06
☐ 25 Andy Van Slyke	.25	.11	.03
☐ 26 Robin Yount	1.00	.45	.12

1995 Mr. Turkey Baseball Greats

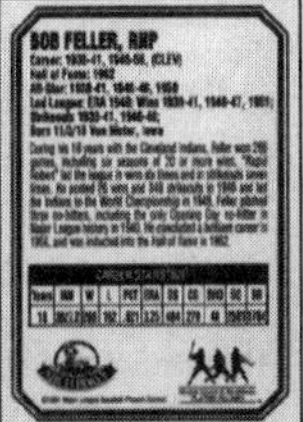

These five standard-size cards were sponsored by Mr. Turkey. On a brown background, the fronts feature sepia-toned and color action player photos. The player's name appears in a red banner on top, while the set's logo is printed in the lower right corner. All team logos have been airbrushed out of the photos. The backs carry player biography, profile and career statistics. The cards are unnumbered and checklisted below in alphabetical order.

	MINT	NRMT	EXC
COMPLETE SET (5)	8.00	3.60	1.00
COMMON CARD (1-5)	1.00	.45	.12
☐ 1 Bob Feller	2.50	1.10	.30
☐ 2 Al Kaline	2.50	1.10	.30
☐ 3 Tug McGraw	1.00	.45	.12
☐ 4 Boog Powell	1.50	.70	.19
☐ 5 Warren Spahn	2.50	1.10	.30

1924 Mrs. Sherlock's Pins PB5-4

This set of pins is subtitled "Mrs. Sherlocks Home Made Bread" at the top of each pin. Players pictured in the set are some of the legends of baseball. The pins measure approximately 7/8" in diameter and are done in black and white with a red border. Since these pins are unnumbered, they are listed below in alphabetical order.

	EX-MT	VG-E	GOOD
COMPLETE SET (10)	2500.00	1100.00	300.00
COMMON PLAYER (1-10)	60.00	27.00	7.50

	EX-MT	VG-E	GOOD
☐ 1 Grover C. Alexander	150.00	70.00	19.00
☐ 2 Ty Cobb	600.00	275.00	75.00
☐ 3 Rogers Hornsby	175.00	80.00	22.00
☐ 4 Walter Johnson	300.00	135.00	38.00
☐ 5 Rabbit Maranville	100.00	45.00	12.50
☐ 6 Paddy Moran	60.00	27.00	7.50
☐ 7 Babe Ruth	900.00	400.00	110.00
☐ 8 George Sisler	125.00	55.00	15.50
☐ 9 Tris Speaker	200.00	90.00	25.00
☐ 10 Honus Wagner	300.00	135.00	38.00

1981 MSA Mini Discs

This set of 32 discs, each measuring approximately 2 3/4" in diameter was apparently approved by the Major League Players Associations under the auspices of Mike Schecter Associates These discs are also known as the Peter Pan discs. These blank backed discs and were distributed a couple of different ways. The discs are unnumbered and are listed alphabetically.

	NRMT	VG-E	GOOD
COMPLETE SET (32)	10.00	4.50	1.25
COMMON DISC (1-32)	.10	.05	.01
☐ 1 Buddy Bell	.25	.11	.03
☐ 2 Johnny Bench	.75	.35	.09
☐ 3 Bruce Bochte	.10	.05	.01
☐ 4 George Brett	2.50	1.10	.30
☐ 5 Bill Buckner	.10	.05	.01
☐ 6 Rod Carew	.75	.35	.09
☐ 7 Steve Carlton	.75	.35	.09
☐ 8 Cesar Cedeno	.10	.05	.01
☐ 9 Jack Clark	.10	.05	.01
☐ 10 Cecil Cooper	.10	.05	.01
☐ 11 Bucky Dent	.10	.05	.01
☐ 12 Carlton Fisk	1.00	.45	.12
☐ 13 Steve Garvey	.40	.18	.05
☐ 14 Rich Gossage	.10	.05	.01
☐ 15 Mike Hargrove	.10	.05	.01
☐ 16 Keith Hernandez	.25	.11	.03
☐ 17 Bob Horner	.10	.05	.01
☐ 18 Reggie Jackson	1.25	.55	.16
☐ 19 Steve Kemp	.10	.05	.01
☐ 20 Ron LeFlore	.10	.05	.01
☐ 21 Fred Lynn	.25	.11	.03
☐ 22 Lee Mazzilli	.10	.05	.01
☐ 23 Eddie Murray	1.50	.70	.19
☐ 24 Mike Norris	.10	.05	.01
☐ 25 Dave Parker	.25	.11	.03
☐ 26 J.R. Richard	.10	.05	.01
☐ 27 Pete Rose	1.25	.55	.16
☐ 28 Mike Schmidt	1.00	.45	.12
☐ 29 Tom Seaver	.75	.35	.09
☐ 30 Roy Smalley	.10	.05	.01
☐ 31 Willie Stargell	.50	.23	.06
☐ 32 Garry Templeton	.10	.05	.01

1986 MSA Jay's Potato Chip Discs

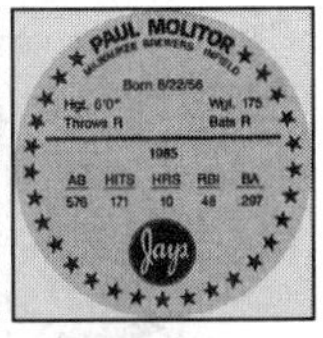

Jay's Potato Chips produced a set of 20 discs in conjunction with Mike Schechter Associates and the Major League Baseball Players Association. The discs have a bright yellow border with red and blue trim. Each disc is approximately 2 3/4" in diameter. The discs are not numbered and hence are assigned numbers below alphabetically. The disc backs contain very sparse personal or statistical information about the player. The players featured are from the Chicago Cubs, Chicago White Sox and Milwaukee Brewers.

	MINT	NRMT	EXC
COMPLETE SET (20)	20.00	9.00	2.50
COMMON DISC (1-20)	.50	.23	.06
☐ 1 Harold Baines	1.00	.45	.12
☐ 2 Cecil Cooper	.50	.23	.06
☐ 3 Jody Davis	.50	.23	.06
☐ 4 Bob Dernier	.50	.23	.06
☐ 5 Richard Dotson	.50	.23	.06
☐ 6 Shawon Dunston	1.00	.45	.12
☐ 7 Carlton Fisk	3.00	1.35	.35
☐ 8 Jim Gantner	.50	.23	.06
☐ 9 Ozzie Guillen	1.00	.45	.12
☐ 10 Teddy Higuera	.50	.23	.06
☐ 11 Ron Kittle	.50	.23	.06
☐ 12 Paul Molitor	3.00	1.35	.35
☐ 13 Keith Moreland	.50	.23	.06
☐ 14 Earnest Riles	.50	.23	.06
☐ 15 Ryne Sandberg	5.00	2.20	.60
☐ 16 Tom Seaver	3.00	1.35	.35
☐ 17 Lee Smith	1.50	.70	.19
☐ 18 Rick Sutcliffe	.50	.23	.06
☐ 19 Greg Walker	.50	.23	.06
☐ 20 Robin Yount	3.00	1.35	.35

1986 MSA Jiffy Pop Discs

Jiffy Pop Popcorn introduced a set of 20 discs produced in conjunction with the Major League Baseball Players Association and Mike Schechter Associates. A single disc was inserted inside each specially marked package. The discs are numbered on the back and have a yellow border on the front. Discs are approximately 2 3/4" in diameter. The disc backs contain very sparse personal or statistical information about the player.

	MINT	NRMT	EXC
COMPLETE SET (20)	30.00	13.50	3.70
COMMON DISC (1-20)	1.00	.45	.12
☐ 1 Jim Rice	1.50	.70	.19
☐ 2 Wade Boggs	2.50	1.10	.30
☐ 3 Lance Parrish	1.00	.45	.12
☐ 4 George Brett	4.00	1.80	.50
☐ 5 Robin Yount	2.00	.90	.25
☐ 6 Don Mattingly	5.00	2.20	.60
☐ 7 Dave Winfield	3.00	1.35	.35
☐ 8 Reggie Jackson	3.00	1.35	.35
☐ 9 Cal Ripken	6.00	2.70	.75
☐ 10 Eddie Murray	4.00	1.80	.50
☐ 11 Pete Rose	3.00	1.35	.35
☐ 12 Ryne Sandberg	4.00	1.80	.50
☐ 13 Nolan Ryan	6.00	2.70	.75
☐ 14 Fernando Valenzuela	1.50	.70	.19
☐ 15 Willie McGee	1.50	.70	.19
☐ 16 Dale Murphy	2.00	.90	.25
☐ 17 Mike Schmidt	4.00	1.80	.50
☐ 18 Steve Garvey	1.50	.70	.19
☐ 19 Gary Carter	1.50	.70	.19
☐ 20 Dwight Gooden	2.00	.90	.25

1987 MSA Iced Tea Discs

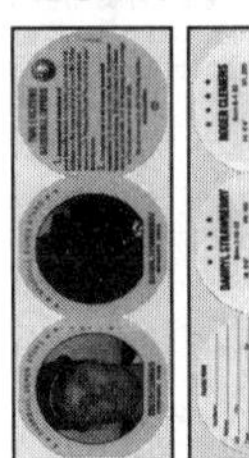

A set of 20 "Baseball Super Star" discs was produced in conjunction with the Major League Baseball Players Association and Mike Schechter Associates for various grocery chains. Sets were issued for Weis Markets, Key Foods, Our Own Tea and many others. The discs were issued as panels of three featuring two players and an offer disc. The discs have a bright yellow border on the front. Discs measure approximately 2 3/4" in diameter. Some dealers have speculated that noted hobby dealer John Broggi made the player selection for this set as well as the other iced tea disc sets. The disc backs contain very sparse personal or statistical information about the player.

	MINT	NRMT	EXC
COMPLETE SET (20)	7.50	3.40	.95
COMMON DISC (1-20)	.25	.11	.03
☐ 1 Darryl Strawberry	.50	.23	.06
☐ 2 Roger Clemens	1.00	.45	.12
☐ 3 Ron Darling	.25	.11	.03
☐ 4 Keith Hernandez	.35	.16	.04
☐ 5 Tony Pena	.25	.11	.03
☐ 6 Don Mattingly	1.50	.70	.19
☐ 7 Eric Davis	.35	.16	.04
☐ 8 Gary Carter	.35	.16	.04
☐ 9 Dave Winfield	.50	.23	.06
☐ 10 Wally Joyner	.35	.16	.04
☐ 11 Mike Schmidt	.75	.35	.09
☐ 12 Robby Thompson	.25	.11	.03
☐ 13 Wade Boggs	.50	.23	.06
☐ 14 Cal Ripken	1.50	.70	.19
☐ 15 Dale Murphy	.50	.23	.06
☐ 16 Tony Gwynn	1.00	.45	.12
☐ 17 Jose Canseco	.60	.25	.07
☐ 18 Rickey Henderson	.60	.25	.07
☐ 19 Lance Parrish	.25	.11	.03
☐ 20 Dave Righetti	.25	.11	.03

1987 MSA Jiffy Pop Discs

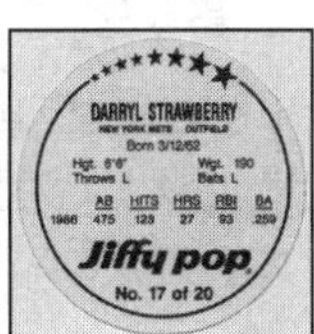

Jiffy Pop Popcorn introduced a set of 20 discs produced in conjunction with the Major League Baseball Players Association and Mike Schechter Associates. A single disc was inserted inside each specially marked package. The discs are numbered on the back and have a white border (with red stitching to resemble a baseball) on the front. Discs are approximately 2 3/4" in diameter. The disc backs contain very sparse personal or statistical information about the player.

	MINT	NRMT	EXC
COMPLETE SET (20)	30.00	13.50	3.70
COMMON DISC (1-20)	1.25	.55	.16
☐ 1 Ryne Sandberg	4.00	1.80	.50
☐ 2 Dale Murphy	2.50	1.10	.30
☐ 3 Jack Morris	1.50	.70	.19
☐ 4 Keith Hernandez	1.50	.70	.19
☐ 5 George Brett	5.00	2.20	.60
☐ 6 Don Mattingly	5.00	2.20	.60
☐ 7 Ozzie Smith	4.00	1.80	.50
☐ 8 Cal Ripken	7.50	3.40	.95
☐ 9 Dwight Gooden	1.50	.70	.19
☐ 10 Pedro Guerrero	1.25	.55	.16
☐ 11 Lou Whitaker	1.50	.70	.19
☐ 12 Roger Clemens	4.00	1.80	.50
☐ 13 Lance Parrish	1.25	.55	.16
☐ 14 Rickey Henderson	3.00	1.35	.35
☐ 15 Fernando Valenzuela	1.50	.70	.19
☐ 16 Mike Schmidt	4.00	1.80	.50
☐ 17 Darryl Strawberry	1.00	.45	.12
☐ 18 Mike Scott	1.25	.55	.16
☐ 19 Jim Rice	1.50	.70	.19
☐ 20 Wade Boggs	3.00	1.35	.35

1988 MSA Fantastic Sam's Discs

Fantastic Sam's is a national chain of family haircutters with more than 1200 locations. There are 20 numbered discs in the set each with an orange border. The set was produced in conjunction with Mike Schechter Associates. One disc was given away free each time a customer visited a participating Fantastic Sam's. Each disc is connected by a perforation to a contest disc with a scratch-off for a potential (baseball related) prize. Each disc is approximately 2 3/4" in diameter. No team logos are shown in this set.

	MINT	NRMT	EXC
COMPLETE SET (20)	6.00	2.70	.75
COMMON DISC (1-20)	.25	.11	.03
☐ 1 Kirby Puckett	2.00	.90	.25
☐ 2 George Brett	2.00	.90	.25
☐ 3 Mark McGwire	2.00	.90	.25
☐ 4 Wally Joyner	.25	.11	.03
☐ 5 Paul Molitor	1.00	.45	.12
☐ 6 Alan Trammell	.50	.23	.06
☐ 7 George Bell	.25	.11	.03
☐ 8 Wade Boggs	.50	.23	.06
☐ 9 Don Mattingly	2.00	.90	.25
☐ 10 Julio Franco	.25	.11	.03
☐ 11 Ozzie Smith	1.50	.70	.19
☐ 12 Will Clark	.75	.35	.09
☐ 13 Dale Murphy	.50	.23	.06
☐ 14 Eric Davis	.25	.11	.03
☐ 15 Andre Dawson	.50	.23	.06
☐ 16 Tim Raines	.50	.23	.06
☐ 17 Darryl Strawberry	.50	.23	.06
☐ 18 Tony Gwynn	1.50	.70	.19
☐ 19 Mike Schmidt	1.00	.45	.12
☐ 20 Pedro Guerrero	.25	.11	.03

1988 MSA Hostess Discs

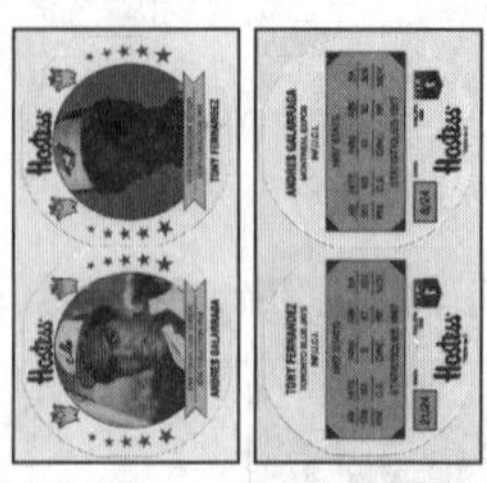

This set of 24 discs was produced by Hostess Potato Chips in conjunction with Mike Schechter Associates and the Major League Baseball Players Association. This set is one of the few disc sets to actually show the team logos. The set is subtitled Hostess Summer Doubleheaders and actually features a double disc (connected by a perforation) with a player from the Montreal Expos and a player from the Toronto Blue Jays. Each disc is approximately 2 5/8" in diameter. The discs are numbered; Montreal Expos are numbered 1-12 and Toronto Blue Jays are 13-24.

	MINT	NRMT	EXC
COMPLETE SET (24)	4.00	1.80	.50
COMMON DISC (1-24)	.10	.05	.01
☐ 1 Mitch Webster	.10	.05	.01
☐ 2 Tim Burke	.10	.05	.01
☐ 3 Tom Foley	.10	.05	.01
☐ 4 Herm Winningham	.10	.05	.01
☐ 5 Hubie Brooks	.10	.05	.01
☐ 6 Mike Fitzgerald	.10	.05	.01
☐ 7 Tim Wallach	.25	.11	.03
☐ 8 Andres Galarraga	.75	.35	.09
☐ 9 Floyd Youmans	.10	.05	.01
☐ 10 Neal Heaton	.10	.05	.01
☐ 11 Tim Raines	.25	.11	.03
☐ 12 Casey Candaele	.10	.05	.01
☐ 13 Jim Clancy	.10	.05	.01
☐ 14 Rance Mulliniks	.10	.05	.01
☐ 15 Fred McGriff	.75	.35	.09
☐ 16 Ernie Whitt	.10	.05	.01
☐ 17 Dave Stieb	.25	.11	.03
☐ 18 Mark Eichhorn	.10	.05	.01
☐ 19 Jesse Barfield	.25	.11	.03
☐ 20 Lloyd Moseby	.10	.05	.01
☐ 21 Tony Fernandez	.25	.11	.03
☐ 22 George Bell	.25	.11	.03
☐ 23 Tom Henke	.25	.11	.03
☐ 24 Jimmy Key	.25	.11	.03

1988 MSA Iced Tea Discs

A set of 20 "Baseball Super Star" discs was produced in conjunction with the Major League Baseball Players Association and Mike Schechter Associates for various grocery chains. Sets were issued for Tetley Tea, Weis Markets, Key Foods, Our Own Tea and many others. The discs were issued as panels of three featuring two players and an offer disc. The discs have a blue border on the front. Discs are approximately 2 3/4" in diameter. The disc backs contain very sparse personal or statistical information about the player.

	MINT	NRMT	EXC
COMPLETE SET (20)	8.00	3.60	1.00
COMMON DISC (1-20)	.25	.11	.03
☐ 1 Wade Boggs	.50	.23	.06
☐ 2 Ellis Burks	.50	.23	.06
☐ 3 Don Mattingly	1.50	.70	.19
☐ 4 Mark McGwire	1.50	.70	.19
☐ 5 Matt Nokes	.25	.11	.03
☐ 6 Kirby Puckett	1.50	.70	.19
☐ 7 Billy Ripken	.25	.11	.03
☐ 8 Kevin Seitzer	.35	.16	.04
☐ 9 Roger Clemens	1.00	.45	.12
☐ 10 Will Clark	.75	.35	.09
☐ 11 Vince Coleman	.25	.11	.03
☐ 12 Eric Davis	.35	.16	.04
☐ 13 Dave Magadan	.25	.11	.03
☐ 14 Dale Murphy	.50	.23	.06
☐ 15 Benito Santiago	.25	.11	.03
☐ 16 Mike Schmidt	.75	.35	.09
☐ 17 Darryl Strawberry	.35	.16	.04
☐ 18 Steve Bedrosian	.25	.11	.03
☐ 19 Dwight Gooden	.35	.16	.04
☐ 20 Fernando Valenzuela	.35	.16	.04

1988 MSA Jiffy Pop Discs

Jiffy Pop Popcorn introduced a set of 20 discs produced in conjunction with the Major League Baseball Players Association and Mike Schechter Associates. A single disc was inserted inside each specially marked package. The discs are numbered (alphabetically) on the back and have a light blue border on the front. Discs are approximately 2 3/4" in diameter. The disc backs contain very sparse personal or statistical information about the player.

	MINT	NRMT	EXC
COMPLETE SET (20)	15.00	6.75	1.85
COMMON DISC (1-20)	.75	.35	.09
☐ 1 Buddy Bell	.75	.35	.09
☐ 2 Wade Boggs	2.50	1.10	.30
☐ 3 Gary Carter	1.25	.55	.16
☐ 4 Jack Clark	.75	.35	.09
☐ 5 Will Clark	2.50	1.10	.30
☐ 6 Roger Clemens	2.50	1.10	.30
☐ 7 Vince Coleman	.75	.35	.09
☐ 8 Andre Dawson	1.25	.55	.16
☐ 9 Keith Hernandez	.75	.35	.09
☐ 10 Kent Hrbek	.75	.35	.09
☐ 11 Wally Joyner	.75	.35	.09
☐ 12 Paul Molitor	2.00	.90	.25
☐ 13 Eddie Murray	2.00	.90	.25
☐ 14 Tim Raines	1.25	.55	.16
☐ 15 Bret Saberhagen	1.25	.55	.16
☐ 16 Alan Trammell	1.25	.55	.16
☐ 17 Ozzie Virgil	.75	.35	.09
☐ 18 Tim Wallach	.75	.35	.09
☐ 19 Dave Winfield	2.00	.90	.25
☐ 20 Robin Yount	1.50	.70	.19

1989 MSA Holsum Discs

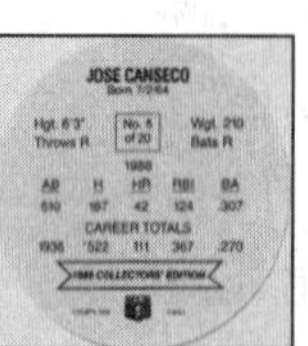

1989 Holsum Discs set is actually several sets of 20 discs issued for the following regional bakeries: Foxes Holsum (North Carolina and South Carolina), Butter Krust Bakeries (most of Pennsylvania), Phoenix Holsum (Arizona), Schafer's (Michigan) and Rainer Farms Homestyle. In Canada, Ben's Limited of Halifax distributed the discs under the Holsum/Schafer's imprint. The discs measure approximately 2 3/4" in diameter. This set was produced by MSA (Michael Schechter Associates) and like most of the MSA sets, there are no team logos on the discs. There is also an uncorrected error with Mark Grace's disc which pictures Vance Law on it.

	MINT	NRMT	EXC
COMPLETE SET (20)	12.50	5.50	1.55
COMMON DISC (1-20)	.25	.11	.03
☐ 1 Wally Joyner	.50	.23	.06
☐ 2 Wade Boggs	.75	.35	.09
☐ 3 Ozzie Smith	1.50	.70	.19
☐ 4 Don Mattingly	2.00	.90	.25
☐ 5 Jose Canseco	1.00	.45	.12
☐ 6 Tony Gwynn	1.50	.70	.19
☐ 7 Eric Davis	.25	.11	.03
☐ 8 Kirby Puckett	2.00	.90	.25
☐ 9 Kevin Seitzer	.25	.11	.03
☐ 10 Darryl Strawberry	.50	.23	.06
☐ 11 Gregg Jefferies	.50	.23	.06
☐ 12 Mark Grace UER (Photo actually Vance Law)	1.50	.70	.19
☐ 13 Matt Nokes	.25	.11	.03
☐ 14 Mark McGwire	1.50	.70	.19
☐ 15 Bobby Bonilla	.25	.11	.03
☐ 16 Roger Clemens	1.25	.55	.16
☐ 17 Frank Viola	.25	.11	.03
☐ 18 Orel Hershiser	.50	.23	.06
☐ 19 Dave Cone	.25	.11	.03
☐ 20 Kirk Gibson	.25	.11	.03

1989 MSA Iced Tea Discs

These 20 discs of MSA's Third Annual Collectors' Edition measure approximately 2 5/8" in diameter and feature on their fronts posed color player head shots within red stars on yellow backgrounds. The player's name and team appear in black lettering near the bottom. There are no team logos featured on the discs. The backs carry player biography and 1988 statistics in blue lettering. The cards are numbered on the back as "X of 20." The sets were also produced under the Tetley Teas label and inserted into their tea bag boxes.

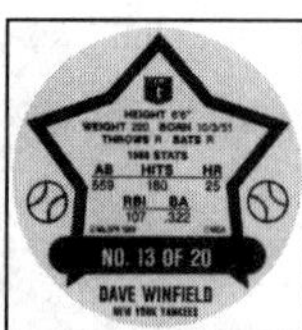

	MINT	NRMT	EXC
COMPLETE SET (20)	30.00	13.50	3.70
COMMON DISC (1-20)	1.00	.45	.12
☐ 1 Don Mattingly	7.50	3.40	.95
☐ 2 Dave Cone	1.00	.45	.12
☐ 3 Mark McGwire	6.00	2.70	.75
☐ 4 Will Clark	4.00	1.80	.50
☐ 5 Darryl Strawberry	2.00	.90	.25
☐ 6 Dwight Gooden	2.00	.90	.25
☐ 7 Wade Boggs	4.00	1.80	.50
☐ 8 Roger Clemens	5.00	2.20	.60
☐ 9 Benito Santiago	1.00	.45	.12
☐ 10 Orel Hershiser	2.00	.90	.25
☐ 11 Eric Davis	2.00	.90	.25
☐ 12 Kirby Puckett	7.50	3.40	.95
☐ 13 Dave Winfield	4.00	1.80	.50
☐ 14 Andre Dawson	3.00	1.35	.35
☐ 15 Steve Bedrosian	1.00	.45	.12
☐ 16 Cal Ripken	12.00	5.50	1.50
☐ 17 Andy Van Slyke	1.00	.45	.12
☐ 18 Jose Canseco	5.00	2.20	.60
☐ 19 Jose Oquendo	1.00	.45	.12
☐ 20 Dale Murphy	3.00	1.35	.35

1990 MSA Holsum Discs

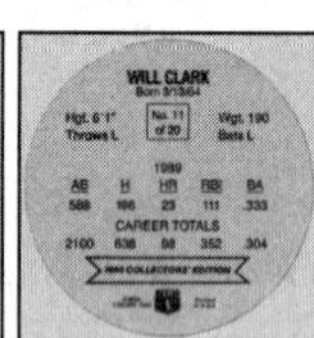

The 1990 Holsum Discs set, subtitled "Superstars," is a 20-disc set with each disc measuring approximately 2 3/4" in diameter. The front of each disc features a full color player photo with a red border. The player's name, team and position appear below the photo. The white back carries the player's name and biography at the top, followed below by 1989 and career statistics. Typical of many of the sets produced by MSA (Michael Schechter Associates), the teams' logos are airbrushed out. The discs are numbered on the back. In Canada, Ben's Limited of Halifax distributed the discs under the Holsum imprint.

	MINT	NRMT	EXC
COMPLETE SET (20)	5.00	2.20	.60
COMMON DISC (1-20)	.10	.05	.01
☐ 1 George Bell	.10	.05	.01
☐ 2 Tim Raines	.10	.05	.01
☐ 3 Tom Henke	.10	.05	.01
☐ 4 Andres Galarraga	.35	.16	.04
☐ 5 Bret Saberhagen	.10	.05	.01
☐ 6 Mark Davis	.10	.05	.01
☐ 7 Robin Yount	.35	.16	.04
☐ 8 Rickey Henderson	.60	.25	.07
☐ 9 Kevin Mitchell	.10	.05	.01
☐ 10 Howard Johnson	.10	.05	.01
☐ 11 Will Clark	.75	.35	.09
☐ 12 Orel Hershiser	.25	.11	.03
☐ 13 Fred McGriff	.75	.35	.09
☐ 14 Dave Stewart	.10	.05	.01
☐ 15 Vince Coleman	.10	.05	.01
☐ 16 Steve Sax	.10	.05	.01
☐ 17 Kirby Puckett	1.00	.45	.12
☐ 18 Tony Gwynn	1.00	.45	.12
☐ 19 Jerome Walton	.10	.05	.01
☐ 20 Gregg Olson	.10	.05	.01

1990 MSA Iced Tea Discs

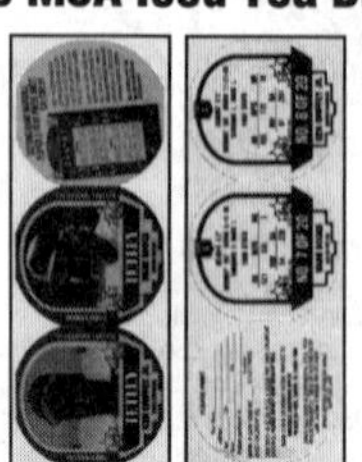

Issued in three-disc perforated strips, these 20 discs measure approximately 2 5/8" in diameter. Some of the discs have Tetley's Third Annual Collector's Edition on their fronts, while others read "Fourth Annual Collectors' Edition" and "Super Stars" on their fronts. Each strip contains two player discs and one disc for ordering a Tetley Press Sheet Calendar. Each red-bordered player disc features a color player head shot framed by a yellow line. The player's name and team name appear below the photo. The white back carries the player's name and team name at the bottom; above are the player's biography and 1989 stats. The discs are numbered on the back as "X of 20." Each disc is a tri-fold, consisting of two color player photos and a mail-in offer to receive a 15" by 25" press sheet calendar of the complete set of 20 players for only $3.50 plus four discs.

	MINT	NRMT	EXC
COMPLETE SET (20)	30.00	13.50	3.70
COMMON DISC (1-20)	1.00	.45	.12
☐ 1 Will Clark	3.00	1.35	.35
☐ 2 Howard Johnson	1.00	.45	.12
☐ 3 Chris Sabo	1.00	.45	.12
☐ 4 Jose Canseco	4.00	1.80	.50
☐ 5 Bo Jackson	1.50	.70	.19
☐ 6 Kevin Mitchell	1.00	.45	.12
☐ 7 Wade Boggs	2.00	.90	.25
☐ 8 Ken Griffey Jr.	12.00	5.50	1.50
☐ 9 George Bell	1.00	.45	.12
☐ 10 Dwight Gooden	1.50	.70	.19
☐ 11 Bobby Bonilla	1.50	.70	.19
☐ 12 Ryne Sandberg	6.00	2.70	.75
☐ 13 Kirby Puckett	6.00	2.70	.75
☐ 14 Don Mattingly	6.00	2.70	.75
☐ 15 Mark McGwire	4.00	1.80	.50
☐ 16 Frank Viola	1.00	.45	.12
☐ 17 Bret Saberhagen	1.00	.45	.12
☐ 18 Mike Greenwell	1.00	.45	.12
☐ 19 Steve Sax	1.00	.45	.12
☐ 20 Nolan Ryan	10.00	4.50	1.25

1991 MSA Holsum Discs

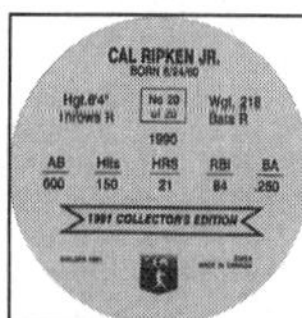

The 1991 Holsum Discs set, subtitled "Superstars" is a 20-disc set with each disc measuring approximately 2 3/4" in diameter. The discs feature on their fronts white-bordered color player head shots. The player's name, team and position appear below the photo. The white back carries the player's name and biography at the top, followed below by 1990 statistics. Typical of many of the sets produced by MSA, (Michael Schechter Associates) the teams' logos are airbrushed out. In Canada, Ben's Limited of Halifax distributed the discs under the Holsum imprint.

	MINT	NRMT	EXC
COMPLETE SET (20)	75.00	34.00	9.50
COMMON DISC (1-20)	1.50	.70	.19
☐ 1 Darryl Strawberry	2.50	1.10	.30
☐ 2 Eric Davis	2.50	1.10	.30
☐ 3 Tim Wallach	1.50	.70	.19
☐ 4 Kevin Mitchell	1.50	.70	.19
☐ 5 Tony Gwynn	15.00	6.75	1.85
☐ 6 Ryne Sandberg	12.50	5.50	1.55
☐ 7 Doug Drabek	1.50	.70	.19
☐ 8 Randy Myers	1.50	.70	.19
☐ 9 Ken Griffey Jr.	30.00	13.50	3.70
☐ 10 Alan Trammell	2.50	1.10	.30
☐ 11 Ken Griffey Sr.	2.50	1.10	.30
☐ 12 Rickey Henderson	7.50	3.40	.95
☐ 13 Roger Clemens	6.00	2.70	.75
☐ 14 Bob Welch	1.50	.70	.19
☐ 15 Kelly Gruber	1.50	.70	.19
☐ 16 Mark McGwire	10.00	4.50	1.25
☐ 17 Cecil Fielder	3.00	1.35	.35
☐ 18 Dave Stieb	1.50	.70	.19
☐ 19 Nolan Ryan	25.00	11.00	3.10
☐ 20 Cal Ripken	25.00	11.00	3.10

1992 MSA Ben's Super Hitters Discs

The 1992 Ben's Disc set is a 20-disc set, with each disc measuring approximately 2 3/4" in diameter. The set is subtitled "Super Hitters". The discs feature on their fronts white-bordered color player head shots. The player's name, team and position appear below the photo. The white back carries the player's name and biography at the top, followed below by 1991 statistics. As is typical of many of the sets produced by MSA (Michael Schechter Associates), the teams' logos are airbrushed out.

	MINT	NRMT	EXC
COMPLETE SET (20)	30.00	13.50	3.70
COMMON DISC (1-20)	1.50	.70	.19

☐ 1 Cecil Fielder	2.00	.90	.25
☐ 2 Joe Carter	2.00	.90	.25
☐ 3 Roberto Alomar	2.00	.90	.25
☐ 4 Devon White	1.50	.70	.19
☐ 5 Kelly Gruber	1.50	.70	.19
☐ 6 Cal Ripken Jr.	6.00	2.70	.75
☐ 7 Kirby Puckett	4.00	1.80	.50
☐ 8 Paul Molitor	3.00	1.35	.35
☐ 9 Julio Franco	1.50	.70	.19
☐ 10 Ken Griffey Jr.	7.50	3.40	.95
☐ 11 Frank Thomas	7.50	3.40	.95
☐ 12 Jose Canseco	3.00	1.35	.35
☐ 13 Danny Tartabull	1.50	.70	.19
☐ 14 Terry Pendleton	1.50	.70	.19
☐ 15 Tony Gwynn	4.00	1.80	.50
☐ 16 Howard Johnson	1.50	.70	.19
☐ 17 Will Clark	2.50	1.10	.30
☐ 18 Barry Bonds	3.00	1.35	.35
☐ 19 Ryne Sandberg	4.00	1.80	.50
☐ 20 Bobby Bonilla	1.50	.70	.19

1993 MSA Ben's Super Pitchers Discs

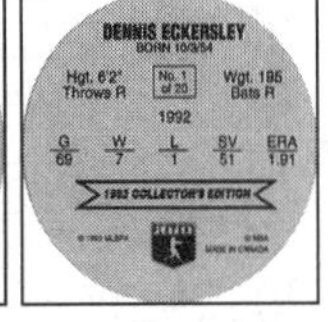

The 1993 Ben's Disc set is a 20-disc set, with each disc measuring approximately 2 3/4" in diameter. The set is subtitled "Super Pitchers". As is typical of many of the sets produced by MSA (Michael Schechter Associates), the teams' logos are airbrushed out. The discs feature white-bordered color player head shots on their fronts with the player's name, team and position appearing near the bottom. The white backs carry the player's name, biography and 1992 stats.

	MINT	NRMT	EXC
COMPLETE SET (20)	10.00	4.50	1.25
COMMON DISC (1-20)	.25	.11	.03
☐ 1 Dennis Eckersley	.75	.35	.09
☐ 2 Chris Bosio	.25	.11	.03
☐ 3 Jack Morris	.50	.23	.06
☐ 4 Greg Maddux	2.00	.90	.25
☐ 5 Dennis Martinez	.50	.23	.06
☐ 6 Tom Glavine	1.00	.45	.12
☐ 7 Doug Drabek	.25	.11	.03
☐ 8 John Smoltz	1.50	.70	.19
☐ 9 Randy Myers	.25	.11	.03
☐ 10 Jack McDowell	1.00	.45	.12
☐ 11 John Wetteland	.50	.23	.06
☐ 12 Roger Clemens	1.50	.70	.19
☐ 13 Mike Mussina	1.25	.55	.16
☐ 14 Juan Guzman	.25	.11	.03
☐ 15 Jose Rijo	.25	.11	.03
☐ 16 Tom Henke	.50	.23	.06
☐ 17 Gregg Olson	.25	.11	.03
☐ 18 Jim Abbott	.25	.11	.03
☐ 19 Jimmy Key	.25	.11	.03
☐ 20 Rheal Cormier	.25	.11	.03

1992 MTV Rock n' Jock

This three-card standard-size set was sponsored by MTV to promote the Third Annual Rock n' Jock Softball Challenge held January 11, 1992, in Los Angeles. According to the card backs, 20,000 sets were produced. The fronts feature color player photos, and each card has a different color inner border (1-brick red; 2-kelly green; 3-blue). The outer border of all cards consists of yellow, orange, and purple stars on a white background. The backs have a black and white version of the outer border of the fronts and present an advertisement for the softball challenge. There has been some debate over the years about whether or not this is a legitimate set; however an MTV PR person at the time acknowledged that the set was produced for the event by MTV.

	MINT	NRMT	EXC
COMPLETE SET (3)	5.00	2.20	.60
COMMON CARD (1-3)	.25	.11	.03
☐ 1 Hammer	.25	.11	.03
☐ 2 Frank Thomas	2.50	1.10	.30
☐ 3 Ken Griffey Jr.	2.50	1.10	.30

1985 Musial TTC

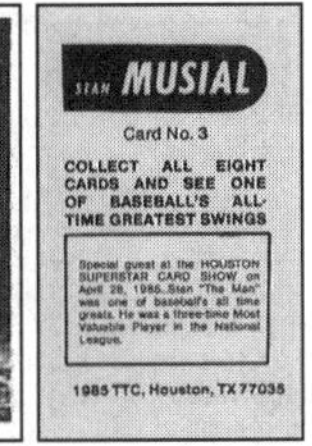

This eight-card set of Stan Musial produced by TTC of Houston, Texas, in the 1952 Bowman style, measures approximately 2 1/8" by 3 3/8". The fronts feature black-and-white photos of Stan Musial in the various stages of swinging the bat. The backs carry his name, card number, and a different career fact on each card as checklisted below.

	NRMT	VG-E	GOOD
COMPLETE SET (8)	7.50	3.40	.95
COMMON CARD (1-8)	1.00	.45	.12
☐ 1 Stan Musial Description of batting stance)	1.00	.45	.12
☐ 2 Stan Musial Batting title at age 37	1.00	.45	.12
☐ 3 Stan Musial Three-time MVP	1.00	.45	.12
☐ 4 Stan Musial (Seven batting titles	1.00	.45	.12
☐ 5 Stan Musial 3,630 career hits	1.00	.45	.12
☐ 6 Stan Musial Career information	1.00	.45	.12
☐ 7 Stan Musial Early career history	1.00	.45	.12
☐ 8 Stan Musial Hall of Fame 1969	1.00	.45	.12

1992 MVP 2 Highlights

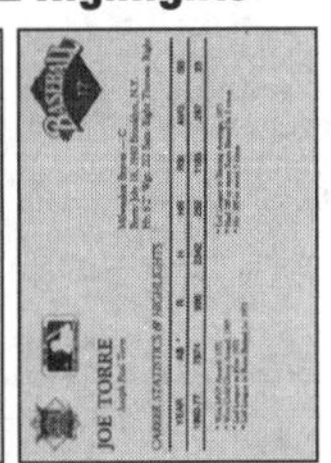

Produced by MVP Sports, this 20-card set presents an outstanding baseball player from each league for the nine positions as well as one designated hitter from each league. The cards have rounded corners and measure 2 1/2" by 3 1/2." The fronts display color player photos with a red inner border for American League and a blue inner border for National League, while the outer border of all cards is white. The team logo is superimposed at the lower right corner. On the American League cards, the horizontally oriented backs are printed on red and feature biography, career statistics, and highlights, while the National League cards are printed in blue and carry the same information. The cards are numbered in the upper right corner.

	MINT	NRMT	EXC
COMPLETE SET (20)	10.00	4.50	1.25
COMMON CARD (1-20)	.25	.11	.03
☐ 1 Willie Mays	2.00	.90	.25
☐ 2 Hank Aaron	2.00	.90	.25
☐ 3 Ted Williams	2.50	1.10	.30
☐ 4 Yogi Berra	1.00	.45	.12
☐ 5 Ernie Banks	1.00	.45	.12
☐ 6 Lou Brock	.75	.35	.09
☐ 7 Steve Carlton	1.00	.45	.12
☐ 8 Harmon Killebrew	.75	.35	.09
☐ 9 Gaylord Perry	.75	.35	.09
☐ 10 Rusty Staub	.50	.23	.06
☐ 11 Lou Boudreau	.75	.35	.09
☐ 12 Larry Doby	.50	.23	.06
☐ 13 Orlando Cepeda	.50	.23	.06
☐ 14 Bill Mazeroski	.50	.23	.06
☐ 15 Don Baylor	.50	.23	.06
☐ 16 Bill Madlock	.25	.11	.03
☐ 17 Joe Torre	.75	.35	.09
☐ 18 Boog Powell	.50	.23	.06
☐ 19 Graig Nettles	.50	.23	.06
☐ 20 Dave Johnson	.50	.23	.06

1992 MVP Game

Produced by MVP Sports, this 18-card set presents an outstanding baseball player at each position for both leagues. The cards have rounded corners and measure 2 1/4" by 3 1/2." The design but not the size is similar to that of playing cards. The backs of the American League (cards 1-9) cards are predominantly red and have the AL emblem, while the backs of the National League (cards 10-18) cards are predominantly purple and carry the NL emblem. The fronts feature a mix of (mostly color) player photos framed by two sets of thin black border stripes. One of three expressions (fly out, pick off, tag out) are

printed vertically along the left and right sides of the pictures. At the upper left and lower right corners, the player's position is given, while the team logo appears at the upper right corner. Finally, the player's name and position are printed beneath each picture. Since the cards are unnumbered, we have checklisted them below alphabetically within leagues.

	MINT	NRMT	EXC
COMPLETE SET (18)	10.00	4.50	1.25
COMMON CARD (1-18)	.25	.11	.03
☐ 1 Don Baylor	.50	.23	.06
☐ 2 Yogi Berra	1.00	.45	.12
☐ 3 Lou Boudreau	.75	.35	.09
☐ 4 Larry Doby	.50	.23	.06
☐ 5 Dave Johnson	.50	.23	.06
☐ 6 Harmon Killebrew	.75	.35	.09
☐ 7 Graig Nettles	.50	.23	.06
☐ 8 Gaylord Perry	.75	.35	.09
☐ 9 Ted Williams	2.50	1.10	.30
☐ 10 Hank Aaron	2.00	.90	.25
☐ 11 Ernie Banks	1.00	.45	.12
☐ 12 Lou Brock	.75	.35	.09
☐ 13 Steve Carlton	1.00	.45	.12
☐ 14 Orlando Cepeda	.50	.23	.06
☐ 15 Bill Madlock	.25	.11	.03
☐ 16 Willie Mays	2.00	.90	.25
☐ 17 Bill Mazeroski	.50	.23	.06
☐ 18 Joe Torre	.75	.35	.09

1889 N526 No. 7 Cigars

This set is comprised exclusively of members of the Boston Baseball Club, who are portrayed in black and white line drawings. The tobacco brand No. 7 Cigars has not yet been linked to a specific manufacturer. These cards were issued in 1889 and are similar to another series bearing Diamond S brand advertising.

	EX-MT	VG-E	GOOD
COMPLETE SET (15)	5000.00	2200.00	600.00
COMMON CARD (1-15)	300.00	135.00	38.00
☐ 1 Charles W. Bennett	300.00	135.00	38.00
☐ 2 Dennis (Dan) Brouthers	500.00	220.00	60.00
☐ 3 Tom T. Brown	300.00	135.00	38.00
☐ 4 John G. Clarkson	500.00	220.00	60.00
☐ 5 Charles W. Ganzell	300.00	135.00	38.00
☐ 6 James A. Hart	300.00	135.00	38.00
☐ 7 Richard F. Johnston	300.00	135.00	38.00
☐ 8 Mike J. (King) Kelly Captain	600.00	275.00	75.00
☐ 9 M.J. (Kid) Madden	300.00	135.00	38.00
☐ 10 William Nash	300.00	135.00	38.00
☐ 11 Jos. Quinn	300.00	135.00	38.00
☐ 12 Charles Radbourne	500.00	220.00	60.00
☐ 13 J.B. Ray (sic)	300.00	135.00	38.00
☐ 14 Hardie Richardson	300.00	135.00	38.00
☐ 15 William Sowders	300.00	135.00	38.00

1969 Nabisco Team Flakes

The cards in this 24-card set measure either 1 15/16" by 3" or 1 3/4" by 2 15/16" depending on the amount of yellow border area provided between the "cut lines." The 1969 Nabisco Team Flakes set of full color, blank-backed and unnumbered cards was issued on the backs of Team Flakes cereal boxes. The cards are numbered in the checklist below in alphabetical order. There were three different panels or box backs containing eight cards each. The cards have yellow borders and are devoid of team insignias. The catalog designation is F275-34.

	NRMT	VG-E	GOOD
COMPLETE SET (24)	600.00	275.00	75.00
COMMON CARD (1-24)	6.00	2.70	.75
☐ 1 Hank Aaron	60.00	27.00	7.50
☐ 2 Richie Allen	10.00	4.50	1.25
☐ 3 Lou Brock	35.00	16.00	4.40
☐ 4 Paul Casanova	6.00	2.70	.75
☐ 5 Roberto Clemente	100.00	45.00	12.50
☐ 6 Al Ferrara	6.00	2.70	.75
☐ 7 Bill Freehan	10.00	4.50	1.25
☐ 8 Jim Fregosi	10.00	4.50	1.25
☐ 9 Bob Gibson	35.00	16.00	4.40
☐ 10 Tony Horton	6.00	2.70	.75
☐ 11 Tommy John	15.00	6.75	1.85
☐ 12 Al Kaline	40.00	18.00	5.00
☐ 13 Jim Lonborg	6.00	2.70	.75
☐ 14 Juan Marichal	35.00	16.00	4.40
☐ 15 Willie Mays	75.00	34.00	9.50
☐ 16 Rick Monday	6.00	2.70	.75
☐ 17 Tony Oliva	15.00	6.75	1.85
☐ 18 Brooks Robinson	40.00	18.00	5.00
☐ 19 Frank Robinson	40.00	18.00	5.00
☐ 20 Pete Rose	60.00	27.00	7.50
☐ 21 Ron Santo	10.00	4.50	1.25
☐ 22 Tom Seaver	50.00	22.00	6.25
☐ 23 Rusty Staub	10.00	4.50	1.25
☐ 24 Mel Stottlemyre	6.00	2.70	.75

1992 Nabisco

This 36-card standard-size set was sponsored by Nabisco and inserted in Shreddies cereal boxes and other Nabisco products in Canada. Three collector cards were protected by a cardboard sleeve that included two Bingo game symbols and a checklist on its back. The inside of each cereal box featured a Baseball Bingo Game Board. The collector became eligible to win prizes when he completed one vertical row, which consists of two required symbols and two correctly answered trivia questions. The odd number cards are Montreal Expos, while the even number cards are Toronto Blue Jays. Each card commemorates an outstanding achievement in the history of these two baseball franchises. The fronts display a color close-up and an action portrait, and the text narrating the career highlight is neatly handwritten in both English and French. In a horizontal format, the bilingual backs carry biography, statistics (on a blue panel) and trivia questions. The team logo appears in the upper left corner, while the card number is printed in red in the upper right corner.

	MINT	NRMT	EXC
COMPLETE SET (36)	15.00	6.75	1.85
COMMON CARD (1-36)	.50	.23	.06
☐ 1 Bill Lee	.75	.35	.09
☐ 2 Cliff Johnson	.50	.23	.06
☐ 3 Ken Singleton	1.00	.45	.12
☐ 4 Al Woods	.50	.23	.06
☐ 5 Ron Hunt	.75	.35	.09
☐ 6 Barry Bonnell	.50	.23	.06
☐ 7 Tony Perez	2.00	.90	.25
☐ 8 Willie Upshaw	.50	.23	.06
☐ 9 Coco Laboy	.50	.23	.06
☐ 10 Famous Moments 1 October 5, 1985#(Blue Jays win AL East	.50	.23	.06
☐ 11 Bob Bailey	.50	.23	.06
☐ 12 Dave McKay	.50	.23	.06
☐ 13 Rodney Scott	.50	.23	.06
☐ 14 Jerry Garvin	.50	.23	.06
☐ 15 Famous Moments 2 October 11, 1981 Expos win NL East	.50	.23	.06
☐ 16 Rick Bosetti	.50	.23	.06
☐ 17 Larry Parrish	.75	.35	.09
☐ 18 Bill Singer	.50	.23	.06
☐ 19 Ron Fairly	.75	.35	.09
☐ 20 Damaso Garcia	.50	.23	.06
☐ 21 Al Oliver	.75	.35	.09
☐ 22 Famous Moments 3 September 30, 1989 Blue Jays capture Divisional Championship	.50	.23	.06
☐ 23 Claude Raymond	.50	.23	.06
☐ 24 Buck Martinez	.75	.35	.09
☐ 25 Rusty Staub	1.50	.70	.19
☐ 26 Otto Velez	.50	.23	.06
☐ 27 Mack Jones	.50	.23	.06
☐ 28 Garth Iorg	.50	.23	.06
☐ 29 Bill Stoneman	.75	.35	.09
☐ 30 Doug Ault	.50	.23	.06
☐ 31 Famous Moments 4 July 6, 1982 Expos hosts 1st AS Game played outside US	.50	.23	.06
☐ 32 Jesse Jefferson	.50	.23	.06
☐ 33 Steve Rogers	.75	.35	.09
☐ 34 Ernie Whitt	.75	.35	.09
☐ 35 John Boccabella	.50	.23	.06
☐ 36 Bob Bailor	.50	.23	.06
☐ xx Album	2.00	.90	.25

1993 Nabisco All-Star Autographs

Available by sending two proofs of purchase from specially marked Nabisco packages and 5.00, each card features an autographed color action photo of a former star on its front and comes in a special card holder along with a certificate of authenticity. Each photo is trimmed with a blue line and bordered in white. The set logo appears in the upper left and a star rests in each remaining corner. The player's name appears in white within a blue and white trimmed red rectangle at the bottom. The back has a star in each corner and is trimmed by a fine blue line. The player's name and position appear in red at the top and is followed below by the player's biography, childhood photo, and stats. Don Drysdale tragically passed away between his signing the cards and the beginning of the promotion. Nabisco honored all requests until they ran out of cards on Drysdale. The Nabisco and MLBPA logos at the bottom round out the back. The cards are unnumbered and checklisted below in alphabetical order.

	MINT	NRMT	EXC
COMPLETE SET (6)	100.00	45.00	12.50
COMMON CARD (1-6)	10.00	4.50	1.25
☐ 1 Ernie Banks	15.00	6.75	1.85
☐ 2 Don Drysdale	75.00	34.00	9.50
☐ 3 Catfish Hunter	10.00	4.50	1.25
☐ 4 Phil Niekro	10.00	4.50	1.25
☐ 5 Brooks Robinson	15.00	6.75	1.85
☐ 6 Willie Stargell	10.00	4.50	1.25

1994 Nabisco All-Star Autographs

The Nabisco Biscuit Company and the Major League Baseball Players Alumni Assocation cosponsored the "Nabisco All-Star Legends" program, which featured these four autographed baseball cards as well as All-Star appearances nationwide and free tickets to minor league baseball games. Measuring the standard size, one card could be obtained by mailing 5.00 and two proofs of purchase from Oreo, Oreo Double Stuff, Chips Ahoy, Ritz, Wheat Thins, Better Cheddars, Nabisco Grahams, and Honey Maid Grahams crackers. Each autographed card was accompanied by an MLBPAA certificate of authenticity. The fronts feature full-bleed color action photos that are accented by a thin gold picture frame. The player's autograph is inscribed in blue ink. The backs have a photo from the player's youth, career highlights, statistics, and an "All-Star Attitude" quote. The cards are unnumbered and checklisted below in alphabetical order.

	MINT	NRMT	EXC
COMPLETE SET (4)	60.00	27.00	7.50
COMMON CARD (1-4)	15.00	6.75	1.85
☐ 1 Bob Gibson AU	20.00	9.00	2.50
☐ 2 Jim Palmer AU	15.00	6.75	1.85
☐ 3 Frank Robinson AU	20.00	9.00	2.50
☐ 4 Duke Snider AU	20.00	9.00	2.50

1910 Nadja Caramel E92

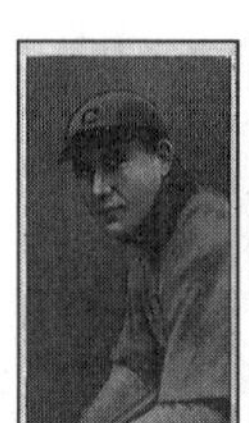

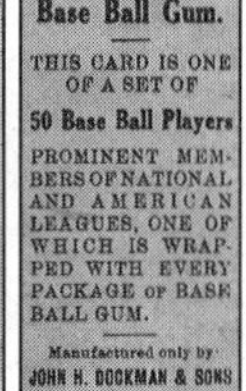

The cards in this 58-card set measure 1 1/2" by 2 3/4". This set was issued about 1910 by Dockman, Nadja, and Croft and Allen. There are four known reverses, with the "Base Ball Gum" (Dockman) back the most common, and the "Nadja" back the most difficult (Nadja backs with blue printing on the obverse belong to E104). The set contains poses identical to those in E101, E102, and E105. The ten cards marked with an asterisk are not found with Dockman back and are somewhat more difficult to find. The eight cards which are coded NADJA are available only with a Nadja back; these cards are quite scarce. Of the 40 cards which are available in all the back variations, the Croft back carries a slight premium while the Nadja back would carry double the value listed.

	EX-MT	VG-E	GOOD
COMPLETE SET (58)	10000.00	4500.00	1250.00
COMMON CARD (1-52)	75.00	34.00	9.50
☐ 1 Bill Bailey NADJA	100.00	45.00	12.50
☐ 2 Jack Barry	150.00	70.00	19.00
☐ 3 Harry Bemis	75.00	34.00	9.50
☐ 4A Chief Bender (striped cap)	300.00	135.00	38.00
☐ 4B Chief Bender (white cap)	150.00	70.00	19.00
☐ 5 Bill Bergen	75.00	34.00	9.50
☐ 6 Bob Bescher	75.00	34.00	9.50
☐ 7 Al Bridwell	75.00	34.00	9.50
☐ 8 Joe Casey	75.00	34.00	9.50
☐ 9 Frank Chance	150.00	70.00	19.00
☐ 10 Hal Chase	125.00	55.00	15.50
☐ 11 Ty Cobb	5000.00	2200.00	600.00
☐ 12 Eddie Collins	500.00	220.00	60.00
☐ 13 Sam Crawford	150.00	70.00	19.00
☐ 14 Harry Davis	75.00	34.00	9.50
☐ 15 Art Devlin	75.00	34.00	9.50
☐ 16 Bill Donovan	75.00	34.00	9.50
☐ 17 Red Dooin	150.00	70.00	19.00
☐ 18 Mickey Doolan	75.00	34.00	9.50
☐ 19 Patsy Dougherty	75.00	34.00	9.50
☐ 20A Larry Doyle (batting)	100.00	45.00	12.50
☐ 20B Larry Doyle (throwing)	100.00	45.00	12.50
☐ 21 Johnny Evers	500.00	220.00	60.00
☐ 22 George Gibson	75.00	34.00	9.50
☐ 23 Topsy Hartsel	75.00	34.00	9.50
☐ 24A Fred Hartzell NADJA (batting)	100.00	45.00	12.50
☐ 24B Fred Hartzell NADJA (fielding)	100.00	45.00	12.50
☐ 25A Harry Howell NADJA (ready to pitch)	100.00	45.00	12.50
☐ 25B Harry Howell NADJA (follow through)	100.00	45.00	12.50
☐ 26 Fred Jacklitsch	150.00	70.00	19.00
☐ 27 Hughie Jennings	150.00	70.00	19.00
☐ 28 Red Kleinow	75.00	34.00	9.50
☐ 29 Otto Knabe	150.00	70.00	19.00
☐ 30 John Knight	150.00	70.00	19.00
☐ 31 Napoleon Lajoie	300.00	135.00	38.00
☐ 32 Hans Lobert	75.00	34.00	9.50
☐ 33 Sherry Magee	75.00	34.00	9.50
☐ 34 Christy Mathewson	400.00	180.00	50.00
☐ 35 John McGraw	150.00	70.00	19.00
☐ 36 Larry McLean	75.00	34.00	9.50
☐ 37A J.B. Miller (batting)	75.00	34.00	9.50
☐ 37B J.B. Miller (fielding)	150.00	70.00	19.00
☐ 38 Danny Murphy	75.00	34.00	9.50
☐ 39 Bill O'Hara	75.00	34.00	9.50
☐ 40 Ed Phelps NADJA	100.00	45.00	12.50
☐ 41 Germany Schaefer	75.00	34.00	9.50
☐ 42 Admiral Schlei	75.00	34.00	9.50
☐ 43 Boss Schmidt	75.00	34.00	9.50
☐ 44 John Siegle	75.00	34.00	9.50
☐ 45 Dave Shean	75.00	34.00	9.50
☐ 46 Boss Schmidt	75.00	34.00	9.50
☐ 47 George Stone NADJA	100.00	45.00	12.50
☐ 48 Joe Tinker	125.00	55.00	15.50
☐ 49A Honus Wagner (batting)	500.00	220.00	60.00
☐ 49B Honus Wagner (throwing)	500.00	220.00	60.00
☐ 50 Bobby Wallace NADJA	250.00	110.00	31.00
☐ 51 Cy Young	250.00	110.00	31.00
☐ 52 Heinie Zimmerman	75.00	34.00	9.50

1910 Nadja E104

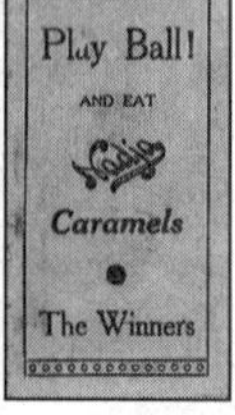

The cards in this 59-card set measure 1 1/2" by 2 3/4". The title of this set comes from the distinctive "Play Ball and eat Nadja Caramels" advertisement found on the reverse of some of the cards. The great majority of the known cards, however, are blank backed. They are grouped together because they have similar obverses and captions in blue print ("Nadja" cards with brown print captions belong to set E92). The cards are unnumbered and were issued in 1910. They have been alphabetized and numbered in the checklist below. The asterisked cards are more difficult and are referenced as Type 3. Nadja reverses are valued at three times the prices below.

	EX-MT	VG-E	GOOD
COMPLETE SET (59)	8000.00	3600.00	1000.00
COMMON CARD (1-59)	100.00	45.00	12.50
☐ 1 Bill Abstein	150.00	70.00	19.00
☐ 2 Babe Adams	100.00	45.00	12.50
☐ 3 Red Ames	150.00	70.00	19.00
☐ 4 Frank Baker	250.00	110.00	31.00
☐ 5 Jack Barry	100.00	45.00	12.50
☐ 6 Johnny Bates	150.00	70.00	19.00
☐ 7 Chief Bender	200.00	90.00	25.00
☐ 8 Kitty Bransfield	150.00	70.00	19.00
☐ 9 Al Bridwell	150.00	70.00	19.00
☐ 10 Fred Clarke	250.00	110.00	31.00
☐ 11 Eddie Collins	250.00	110.00	31.00
☐ 12 Doc Crandall	150.00	70.00	19.00
☐ 13 Sam Crawford	350.00	160.00	45.00
☐ 14 Harry Davis	100.00	45.00	12.50
☐ 15 Jim Delahanty	150.00	70.00	19.00
☐ 16 Larry Doyle	150.00	70.00	19.00
☐ 17 Jimmy Dygert	100.00	45.00	12.50
☐ 18 George Gibson	100.00	45.00	12.50
☐ 19 Eddie Grant	150.00	70.00	19.00
☐ 20 Topsy Hartsel	100.00	45.00	12.50
☐ 21 Ham Hyatt	100.00	45.00	12.50
☐ 22 Fred Jacklitsch	150.00	70.00	19.00
☐ 23 Hugh Jennings	350.00	160.00	45.00
☐ 24 Davy Jones	150.00	70.00	19.00
☐ 25 Tom Jones	150.00	70.00	19.00
☐ 26 Otto Knabe	150.00	70.00	19.00
☐ 27 Harry Krause	100.00	45.00	12.50
☐ 28 John Lapp	100.00	45.00	12.50
☐ 29 Tommy Leach	100.00	45.00	12.50
☐ 30 Sam Leever	100.00	45.00	12.50
☐ 31 Paddy Livingston	100.00	45.00	12.50
☐ 32 Bris Lord	100.00	45.00	12.50
☐ 33 Connie Mack MG	350.00	160.00	45.00
☐ 34 Nicholas Maddox	100.00	45.00	12.50
☐ 35 John McGraw	400.00	180.00	50.00
☐ 36 Matthew McIntyre	150.00	70.00	19.00
☐ 37 Dots Miller	100.00	45.00	12.50
☐ 38 Earl Moore	150.00	70.00	19.00
☐ 39 Lew Moren	150.00	70.00	19.00
☐ 40 Cy Morgan	100.00	45.00	12.50
☐ 41 George Moriarty	150.00	70.00	19.00
☐ 42 George Mullin	150.00	70.00	19.00
☐ 43 Danny Murphy	100.00	45.00	12.50
☐ 44 Red Murray	150.00	70.00	19.00
☐ 45 Simon Nicholls	150.00	70.00	19.00
☐ 46 Charlie O'Leary	150.00	70.00	19.00
☐ 47 Rube Oldring	100.00	45.00	12.50
☐ 48 Deacon Phillippe	150.00	70.00	19.00
☐ 49 Eddie Plank	250.00	110.00	31.00
☐ 50 George Schlei	150.00	70.00	19.00
☐ 51 Cy Seymour	150.00	70.00	19.00
☐ 52 Tully Sparks	150.00	70.00	19.00
☐ 53 Amos Strunk	100.00	45.00	12.50
☐ 54 Ed Summers	150.00	70.00	19.00
☐ 55 Ira Thomas	100.00	45.00	12.50
☐ 56 Honus Wagner	500.00	220.00	60.00
☐ 57 Ed Willett	150.00	70.00	19.00
☐ 58 Vic Willis	200.00	90.00	25.00
☐ 59 Chief Wilson	100.00	45.00	12.50

1967 Nassau Health Ford

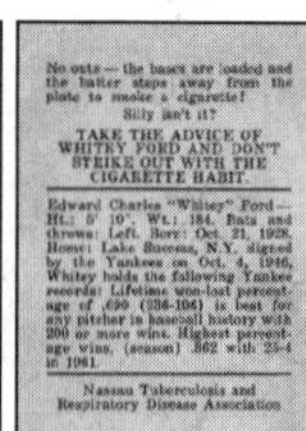

This one-card set was issued by Nassau Tuberculosis and Respiratory Disease Association and features a black-and-white photo of Whitey Ford. The back carries player information and a message about the dangers of cigarette smoking.

	NRMT	VG-E	GOOD
COMPLETE SET (1)	10.00	4.50	1.25
COMMON CARD (1)	10.00	4.50	1.25
☐ 1 Whitey Ford	10.00	4.50	1.25

1921-23 National Caramel E220

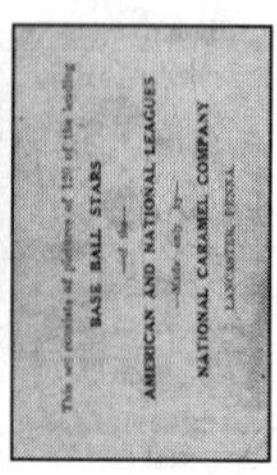

The cards in this 120-card set measure 2" by 3 1/4". There are 114 different players and six variations known for the "Baseball Stars" set marketed by the National Caramel Company. The cards are unnumbered and contain black and white photos; they are similar to set E122 but the coarse screening effect of the latter is missing. Some players appear in two poses, Burns is found with two teams, and three names are misspelled on the cards. The set was probably issued in 1922, the same year as was E122. The cards have been alphabetized and numbered in the checklist below. The complete set price includes all variation cards listed in the checklist below.

	EX-MT	VG-E	GOOD
COMPLETE SET (120)	9000.00	4000.00	1100.00
COMMON CARD (1-114)	50.00	22.00	6.25
☐ 1 Babe Adams	50.00	22.00	6.25
☐ 2 Grover C. Alexander	125.00	55.00	15.50
☐ 3 James Austin	50.00	22.00	6.25
☐ 4 Jim Bagbyk (sic, Bagby)	50.00	22.00	6.25
☐ 5 Franklin Baker	125.00	55.00	15.50
☐ 6 Dave Bancroft	75.00	34.00	9.50
☐ 7 Turner Barber	50.00	22.00	6.25
☐ 8 Geo.H. Burns Cleveland	50.00	22.00	6.25
☐ 9 Geo.J. Burns Cincinnati	50.00	22.00	6.25
☐ 10 Joe Bush	60.00	27.00	7.50
☐ 11 Leon Cadore	50.00	22.00	6.25
☐ 12 Max Carey	75.00	34.00	9.50
☐ 13 Ty Cobb	900.00	400.00	110.00
☐ 14 Eddie Collins	125.00	55.00	15.50
☐ 15 John Collins	50.00	22.00	6.25
☐ 16 Wilbur Cooper	50.00	22.00	6.25
☐ 17 Stan Coveleskie	75.00	34.00	9.50
☐ 18 Walton Cruise	50.00	22.00	6.25
☐ 19 William Cunningham	50.00	22.00	6.25
☐ 20 George Cutshaw	50.00	22.00	6.25
☐ 21 Jake Daubert	60.00	27.00	7.50
☐ 22 Chas.A. Deal	50.00	22.00	6.25
☐ 23 Bill Doak	50.00	22.00	6.25
☐ 24 Joe Dugan	60.00	27.00	7.50
☐ 25A Jimmy Dykes batting	60.00	27.00	7.50
☐ 25B Jimmy Dykes fielding	60.00	27.00	7.50
☐ 26 Red Faber	75.00	34.00	9.50
☐ 27A Chick Fewster	60.00	27.00	7.50
☐ 27B Wilson Fewster	60.00	27.00	7.50
☐ 28 Ira Flagstead	50.00	22.00	6.25
☐ 29 Art Fletcher	50.00	22.00	6.25
☐ 30 Frank Frisch	125.00	55.00	15.50
☐ 31 Larry Gardner	50.00	22.00	6.25
☐ 32 Walter Gerber	50.00	22.00	6.25
☐ 33 Charles Glazner	50.00	22.00	6.25
☐ 34 Hank Gowdy	60.00	27.00	7.50
☐ 35 J.C. Graney	50.00	22.00	6.25
☐ 36 Tommy Griffith	50.00	22.00	6.25
☐ 37 Charlie Grimm	60.00	27.00	7.50
☐ 38 Heine Groh	60.00	27.00	7.50
☐ 39 Byron Harris	50.00	22.00	6.25
☐ 40 Sam Harris	50.00	22.00	6.25
☐ 41 Harry Heilmann	100.00	45.00	12.50
☐ 42 Claude Hendrix	50.00	22.00	6.25
☐ 43 Walter Henline	50.00	22.00	6.25
☐ 44 Chas. Hollocher	50.00	22.00	6.25
☐ 45 Harry Hooper	100.00	45.00	12.50
☐ 46 Rogers Hornsby	300.00	135.00	38.00
☐ 47 Waite Hoyt	75.00	34.00	9.50
☐ 48 Wilbert Hubbell	60.00	27.00	7.50
☐ 49 Bill Jacobson	50.00	22.00	6.25
☐ 50 Walter Johnson	325.00	145.00	40.00
☐ 51 Jimmy Johnston	50.00	22.00	6.25
☐ 52 Joe Judge	50.00	22.00	6.25
☐ 53 George Kelly N.Y. Giants	75.00	34.00	9.50
☐ 54 Dick Kerr	60.00	27.00	7.50
☐ 55A Pete Kilduff bending	50.00	22.00	6.25
☐ 55B Pete Kilduff leaping	50.00	22.00	6.25
☐ 56 Larry Kopf	50.00	22.00	6.25
☐ 57 Dutch Leonard	60.00	27.00	7.50
☐ 58 Harry Liebold	50.00	22.00	6.25
☐ 59 Walter Mails	60.00	27.00	7.50
☐ 60 Walter Maranville	75.00	34.00	9.50
☐ 61 Carl Mays	60.00	27.00	7.50
☐ 62 Lee Meadows	50.00	22.00	6.25
☐ 63 Bob Meusel	60.00	27.00	7.50
☐ 64 Emil Meusel	60.00	27.00	7.50
☐ 65 Clyde Milan	50.00	22.00	6.25
☐ 66 Earl Neale	60.00	27.00	7.50
☐ 67 Robert Nehf (picture actually Arthur Nehf)	60.00	27.00	7.50
☐ 68 Bernie Neis	50.00	22.00	6.25
☐ 69 Joe Oeschger	50.00	22.00	6.25
☐ 70 Robert O'Farrell	50.00	22.00	6.25
☐ 71 Ivan Olson	50.00	22.00	6.25
☐ 72 Steve O'Neill	60.00	27.00	7.50

	EX-MT	VG-E	GOOD
☐ 73 Geo. Paskert	50.00	22.00	6.25
☐ 74 Roger Peckinpaugh	60.00	27.00	7.50
☐ 75 Herb Pennock	75.00	34.00	9.50
☐ 76 Cy Perkins	50.00	22.00	6.25
☐ 77 Scott Perry	50.00	22.00	6.25
☐ 78 Jeff Pfeffer	50.00	22.00	6.25
☐ 79 Val Picinich	50.00	22.00	6.25
☐ 80 Wally Pipp	60.00	27.00	7.50
☐ 81 Derrill Pratt	50.00	22.00	6.25
☐ 82 Goldie Rapp	50.00	22.00	6.25
☐ 83 Edgar Rice	75.00	34.00	9.50
☐ 84 Jimmy Ring	50.00	22.00	6.25
☐ 85 Eddie Roush	100.00	45.00	12.50
☐ 86 Babe Ruth	1200.00	550.00	150.00
☐ 87 Wally Schang	50.00	22.00	6.25
☐ 88 Raymond Schmandt	50.00	22.00	6.25
☐ 89 Everett Scott	60.00	27.00	7.50
☐ 90 Joe Sewell	75.00	34.00	9.50
☐ 91 Maurice Shannon	50.00	22.00	6.25
☐ 92 Bob Shawkey	60.00	27.00	7.50
☐ 93 Urban Shocker	60.00	27.00	7.50
☐ 94 George Sisler	125.00	55.00	15.50
☐ 95 Earl Smith	50.00	22.00	6.25
☐ 96 John Smith	50.00	22.00	6.25
☐ 97 Sherrod Smith	50.00	22.00	6.25
☐ 98A Frank Snyder crouching	50.00	22.00	6.25
☐ 98B Frank Snyder standing	50.00	22.00	6.25
☐ 99 Tris Speaker	150.00	70.00	19.00
☐ 100 Vernon Spencer	50.00	22.00	6.25
☐ 101 Casey Stengel	250.00	110.00	31.00
☐ 102A Milton Stock fielding	50.00	22.00	6.25
☐ 102B Milton Stock batting	50.00	22.00	6.25
☐ 103 James Vaughn	50.00	22.00	6.25
☐ 104 Robert Veach	50.00	22.00	6.25
☐ 105 Bill Wambsganss	50.00	22.00	6.25
☐ 106 Aaron Ward	50.00	22.00	6.25
☐ 107 Zach Wheat	100.00	45.00	12.50
☐ 108A George Whitted batting	50.00	22.00	6.25
☐ 108B George Whitted fielding	50.00	22.00	6.25
☐ 109 Fred C. Williams	60.00	27.00	7.50
☐ 110 Art Wilson	50.00	22.00	6.25
☐ 111 Ivy Wingo	50.00	22.00	6.25
☐ 112 Lawton Witt	50.00	22.00	6.25
☐ 113 Pep Young	50.00	22.00	6.25
☐ 114 Ross Young	100.00	45.00	12.50

1936 National Chicle Fine Pens R313

The 1936 Fine Pen Premiums were issued anonymously by the National Chicle Company. The set is complete at 120 cards. Each card measures approximately 3 1/4" by 5 3/8". The cards are blank backed, unnumbered and could be obtained directly from a retail outlet rather than through the mail only. Three types of cards exist. Cards portraying only one player are listed with the letter A in the checklist; cards which portray several players are listed with a B in the checklist; cards which feature action poses are listed with a C in the checklist. The catalog designation for this set is R313.

	EX-MT	VG-E	GOOD
COMPLETE SET (120)	2100.00	950.00	250.00
COMMON CARD (A1-A83)	15.00	6.75	1.85
COMMON CARD (B1-B14)	15.00	6.75	1.85
COMMON CARD (C1-C23)	15.00	6.75	1.85
☐ A1 Melo Almada	15.00	6.75	1.85
☐ A2 Paul Andrews	15.00	6.75	1.85
☐ A3 Elden Auker	15.00	6.75	1.85
☐ A4 Earl Averill	35.00	16.00	4.40
☐ A5 Jim Becher	15.00	6.75	1.85
☐ A6 Moe Berg	75.00	34.00	9.50
☐ A7 Walter Berger	20.00	9.00	2.50
☐ A8 Charles Berry	15.00	6.75	1.85
☐ A9 Ralph Birkhofer (sic, Birkofer)	15.00	6.75	1.85
☐ A10 Cy Blanton	15.00	6.75	1.85
☐ A11 O. Bluege	20.00	9.00	2.50
☐ A12 Cliff Bolton	15.00	6.75	1.85
☐ A13 Zeke Bonura	15.00	6.75	1.85
☐ A14 Thos. Bridges	20.00	9.00	2.50
☐ A15 Sam Byrd	15.00	6.75	1.85
☐ A16 Dolph Camilli	20.00	9.00	2.50
☐ A17 Bruce Campbell	15.00	6.75	1.85
☐ A18 Walter "Kit" Carson	15.00	6.75	1.85
☐ A19 Ben Chapman	20.00	9.00	2.50
☐ A20 Rip Collins	20.00	9.00	2.50
☐ A21 Joe Cronin	40.00	18.00	5.00
☐ A22 Frank Crosetti	25.00	11.00	3.10
☐ A23 Paul Derringer	20.00	9.00	2.50
☐ A24 Bill Dietrich	15.00	6.75	1.85
☐ A25 Carl Doyle	15.00	6.75	1.85
☐ A26 Pete Fox	15.00	6.75	1.85
☐ A27 Frankie Frisch	40.00	18.00	5.00
☐ A28 Milton Galatzer	15.00	6.75	1.85
☐ A29 Chas. Gehringer	40.00	18.00	5.00
☐ A30 Charley Gelbert	15.00	6.75	1.85
☐ A31 Jose Gomez	15.00	6.75	1.85
☐ A32 Vernon Gomez	40.00	18.00	5.00
☐ A33 Leon Goslin	35.00	16.00	4.40
☐ A34 Hank Gowdy	20.00	9.00	2.50
☐ A35 Hank Greenberg	40.00	18.00	5.00
☐ A36 Lefty Grove	40.00	18.00	5.00
☐ A37 Stan Hack	20.00	9.00	2.50
☐ A38 Odell Hale	15.00	6.75	1.85
☐ A39 Wild Bill Hallahan	15.00	6.75	1.85
☐ A40 Mel Harder	20.00	9.00	2.50
☐ A41 Stanley Bucky Harris	35.00	16.00	4.40
☐ A42 Frank Higgins	15.00	6.75	1.85
☐ A43 Oral C. Hildebrand	15.00	6.75	1.85
☐ A44 Myril Hoag	15.00	6.75	1.85
☐ A45 Rogers Hornsby	50.00	22.00	6.25
☐ A46 Waite Hoyt	35.00	16.00	4.40
☐ A47 Willis G. Hudlin(2)	15.00	6.75	1.85
☐ A48 Woody Jensen (2)	15.00	6.75	1.85
☐ A49 Wm. Knickerbocker	15.00	6.75	1.85
☐ A50 Joseph Kuhel	15.00	6.75	1.85
☐ A51 Cookie Lavagetto	20.00	9.00	2.50
☐ A52 Thornton Lee	15.00	6.75	1.85
☐ A53 Red Lucas	15.00	6.75	1.85
☐ A54 Pepper Martin	25.00	11.00	3.10
☐ A55 Joe Medwick	35.00	16.00	4.40
☐ A56 Oscar Melillo	15.00	6.75	1.85
☐ A57 Buddy Myer	15.00	6.75	1.85
☐ A58 Wallace Moses	15.00	6.75	1.85
☐ A59 V. Mungo	15.00	6.75	1.85
☐ A60 Lamar Newsom	15.00	6.75	1.85
☐ A61 Lewis(Buck) Newsom	15.00	6.75	1.85
☐ A62 Steve O'Neill	20.00	9.00	2.50
☐ A63 Tommie Padden	15.00	6.75	1.85
☐ A64 E. Babe Phillips (sic, Phelps)	15.00	6.75	1.85
☐ A65 Bill Rogel (sic, Rogell)	15.00	6.75	1.85
☐ A66 Lynn(Schoolboy) Rowe	20.00	9.00	2.50
☐ A67 Al Simmons	35.00	16.00	4.40
☐ A68 Casey Stengel MG	60.00	27.00	7.50
☐ A69 Bill Swift	15.00	6.75	1.85
☐ A70 Cecil Travis	15.00	6.75	1.85
☐ A71 Pie Traynor	35.00	16.00	4.40
☐ A72 Wm. Urbansky (sic, Urbanski)	15.00	6.75	1.85
☐ A73 Arky Vaughan	35.00	16.00	4.40
☐ A74 Joe Vosmik	15.00	6.75	1.85
☐ A75 Honus Wagner	60.00	27.00	7.50
☐ A76 Rube Walberg	20.00	9.00	2.50
☐ A77 Bill Walker	15.00	6.75	1.85
☐ A78 Gerald Walker	15.00	6.75	1.85
☐ A79 Bill Werber	15.00	6.75	1.85
☐ A80 Sam West	15.00	6.75	1.85
☐ A81 Pinkey Whitney	15.00	6.75	1.85
☐ A82 Vernon Wiltshere (sic, Wilshere)	15.00	6.75	1.85
☐ A83 Pep Young	15.00	6.75	1.85
☐ B1 Babe and his babes	15.00	6.75	1.85
☐ B2 Stan Bordagaray and Geo. Earnshaw	15.00	6.75	1.85
☐ B3 James Bucher and John Babich	15.00	6.75	1.85
☐ B4 Ben Chapman Bill Werber	15.00	6.75	1.85
☐ B5 Chicago White Sox 1936	15.00	6.75	1.85
☐ B6 Fence Busters	15.00	6.75	1.85
☐ B7 Pete Fox Al Simmons Mickey Cochrane	40.00	18.00	5.00
☐ B8 Gabby Hartnett KiKi Cuyler	40.00	18.00	5.00
☐ B9 Lefty Gomez and Red Ruffing	50.00	22.00	6.25
☐ B10 Gabby Hartnett and Lon Warneke	30.00	13.50	3.70
☐ B11 Diamond Daddies: Connie Mack John McGraw	60.00	27.00	7.50
☐ B12 Capt. Bill Myer and Chas. Dressen MG	15.00	6.75	1.85
☐ B13 Paul Waner Lloyd Waner Big Jim Weaver	35.00	16.00	4.40
☐ B14 Wes Ferrell Rick Ferrell	35.00	16.00	4.40
☐ C1 Nick Altrock and Al Schacht	20.00	9.00	2.50
☐ C2 Big Bosses Clash Dykes safe	15.00	6.75	1.85
☐ C3 Bottomley tagging Gelbert	20.00	9.00	2.50
☐ C4 Camilli catches Jurges off first	20.00	9.00	2.50
☐ C5 CCS: Radcliffe safe Harnett catching	20.00	9.00	2.50
☐ C6 CCS: L.Sewell blocks runner at plate	15.00	6.75	1.85
☐ C7 CCS: Washington safe	15.00	6.75	1.85
☐ C8 Joe DiMaggio slams it, Erickson catching	250.00	110.00	31.00
☐ C9 Double Play-McQuinn to Stine	15.00	6.75	1.85
☐ C10 Dykes catches Crosetti between 2nd and 3rd	20.00	9.00	2.50
☐ C11 Glenn uses football play at plate	15.00	6.75	1.85
☐ C12 Greenberg doubles Dickey catching	40.00	18.00	5.00
☐ C13 Hasset makes the out (sic, Hassett)	15.00	6.75	1.85
☐ C14 Lombardi says "Ugh"	35.00	16.00	4.40
☐ C15 McQuinn gets his man	15.00	6.75	1.85
☐ C16 Randy Moore hurt stealing second	15.00	6.75	1.85
☐ C17 T. Moore out at plate, Wilson catching	20.00	9.00	2.50
☐ C18 Sewell waits for ball while Clift scores	15.00	6.75	1.85
☐ C19 Talking it over	15.00	6.75	1.85
☐ C20 There she goes, CCS	15.00	6.75	1.85
☐ C21 Ump says No Cleveland vs. Detroit	15.00	6.75	1.85
☐ C22 Lloyd Waner at bat Gabby Hartnett behind plate	35.00	16.00	4.40
☐ C23 World Series 1935 Goslin out at first	35.00	16.00	4.40

1936 National Chicle Maranville Secrets R344

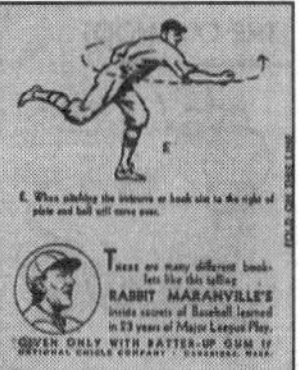

This paper set of 20 was issued in 1936 by the National Chicle Company. Each "card" measures 3 5/8" by 6". It carries the printing "Given only With Batter-Up Gum" on the back page. While the illustration shows the issue to be elongated. the papers were meant to be folded to create a four-page booklet. As the title implies. the set features instructional tips by Rabbit Maranville.

	EX-MT	VG-E	GOOD
COMPLETE SET (20)	450.00	200.00	55.00
COMMON CARD (1-20)	25.00	11.00	3.10
☐ 1 How to Pitch (the Out Shoot)	25.00	11.00	3.10
☐ 2 How to Throw (the In Shoot)	25.00	11.00	3.10
☐ 3 How to Pitch (the Drop)	25.00	11.00	3.10
☐ 4 How to Pitch (the Floater)	25.00	11.00	3.10
☐ 5 How to Run Bases	25.00	11.00	3.10
☐ 6 How to Slide	25.00	11.00	3.10
☐ 7 How to Catch Flies	25.00	11.00	3.10
☐ 8 How to Field Grounders	25.00	11.00	3.10
☐ 9 How to Tag A Man Out	25.00	11.00	3.10
☐ 10 How to Cover A Base	25.00	11.00	3.10
☐ 11 How to Bat	25.00	11.00	3.10
☐ 12 How to Steal Bases	25.00	11.00	3.10
☐ 13 How to Bunt	25.00	11.00	3.10
☐ 14 How to Coach Base Runners	25.00	11.00	3.10
☐ 15 How to Catch Behind the Bat	25.00	11.00	3.10
☐ 16 How to Throw to Bases	25.00	11.00	3.10
☐ 17 How to Signal	25.00	11.00	3.10
☐ 18 How to Umpire Balls and Strikes	25.00	11.00	3.10
☐ 19 How to Umpire Bases	25.00	11.00	3.10
☐ 20 How to Lay Out a Ball Field	25.00	11.00	3.10

1913 National Game WG5

These cards were distributed as part of a baseball game produced in 1913 as indicated by the patent date on the backs of the cards. The cards each measure approximately 2 7/16" by 3 7/16" and have rounded corners. The card fronts show a sepia photo of the player, his name, his team, and the game outcome associated with that particular card. The card backs are all the same, each showing an ornate red and white design with 'The National Game" and "Baseball" right in the middle all surrounded by a thick white outer border. Since the cards are unnumbered, they are listed below in alphabetical order. Some of the card photos are oriented horizontally (HOR). There are a number of cards without player identification. These action scenes are not explicitly listed in the checklist below and are valued as a "common" card unless a positive identification can be made of a major Hall of Famer in the action scene on the card.

	EX-MT	VG-E	GOOD
COMPLETE SET (45)	3000.00	1350.00	375.00
COMMON CARD (1-45)	30.00	13.50	3.70
COMMON ACTION CARD	15.00	6.75	1.85
☐ 1 Grover Alexander	100.00	45.00	12.50
☐ 2 Frank Baker	75.00	34.00	9.50
☐ 3 Chief Bender	75.00	34.00	9.50
☐ 4 Bob Bescher	30.00	13.50	3.70
☐ 5 Joe Birmingham	30.00	13.50	3.70
☐ 6 Roger Bresnahan	75.00	34.00	9.50
☐ 7 Nixey Callahan	30.00	13.50	3.70
☐ 8 Frank Chance	100.00	45.00	12.50
☐ 9 Hal Chase	50.00	22.00	6.25
☐ 10 Fred Clarke	75.00	34.00	9.50
☐ 11 Ty Cobb	300.00	135.00	38.00
☐ 12 Sam Crawford	75.00	34.00	9.50
☐ 13 Bill Dahlen	35.00	16.00	4.40
☐ 14 Jake Daubert	35.00	16.00	4.40
☐ 15 Red Dooin	30.00	13.50	3.70
☐ 16 Johnny Evers	100.00	45.00	12.50
☐ 17 Vean Gregg	30.00	13.50	3.70
☐ 18 Clark Griffith MG	75.00	34.00	9.50
☐ 19 Dick Hoblitzel	30.00	13.50	3.70
☐ 20 Miller Huggins HOR	100.00	45.00	12.50
☐ 21 Joe Jackson	500.00	220.00	60.00
☐ 22 Hugh Jennings MG	75.00	34.00	9.50
☐ 23 Walter Johnson	150.00	70.00	19.00
☐ 24 Ed Konetchy	30.00	13.50	3.70
☐ 25 Nap Lajoie	125.00	55.00	15.50
☐ 26 Connie Mack MG	125.00	55.00	15.50
☐ 27 Rube Marquard	75.00	34.00	9.50
☐ 28 Christy Mathewson	150.00	70.00	19.00
☐ 29 John McGraw MG	125.00	55.00	15.50
☐ 30 Larry McLean HOR	30.00	13.50	3.70
☐ 31 Chief Meyers	30.00	13.50	3.70
☐ 32 Clyde Milan	30.00	13.50	3.70
☐ 33 Marty O'Toole	30.00	13.50	3.70
☐ 34 Nap Rucker	30.00	13.50	3.70
☐ 35 Tris Speaker	125.00	55.00	15.50
☐ 36 Jake Stahl	35.00	16.00	4.40
☐ 37 George Stallings	30.00	13.50	3.70
☐ 38 George Stovall	30.00	13.50	3.70
☐ 39 Bill Sweeney	30.00	13.50	3.70
☐ 40 Joe Tinker	75.00	34.00	9.50
☐ 41 Honus Wagner	150.00	70.00	19.00
☐ 42 Ed Walsh	75.00	34.00	9.50
☐ 43 Zack Wheat	75.00	34.00	9.50
☐ 44 Joe Wood	50.00	22.00	6.25
☐ 45 Cy Young The Grand Old Man	125.00	55.00	15.50

1952 National Tea Labels

The bread labels in this set are often called "Red Borders" because of their distinctive trim. Each label measures 2 3/4" by 2 11/16". Issued with the bakery products of the National Tea Company, there are thought to be 48 different labels in the set. The six missing labels are thought to consist of two Yankees, two Indians and two Red Sox -- so that there would be exactly three representatives from each of the 16 teams. The labels are also known as the "Bread For Health" set and may have included an album. This set is the toughest of the bread label sets listed. These labels are unnumbered so we have sequenced them in alphabetical order. The catalog designation is D290-2.

	NRMT	VG-E	GOOD
COMPLETE SET (42)	3500.00	1600.00	450.00
COMMON LABEL (1-42)	100.00	45.00	12.50
☐ 1 Gene Bearden	100.00	45.00	12.50
☐ 2 Yogi Berra	350.00	160.00	45.00
☐ 3 Lou Brissie	100.00	45.00	12.50
☐ 4 Sam Chapman	100.00	45.00	12.50
☐ 5 Chuck Diering	100.00	45.00	12.50
☐ 6 Dom DiMaggio	200.00	90.00	25.00
☐ 7 Hank Edwards	100.00	45.00	12.50
☐ 8 Del Ennis	100.00	45.00	12.50
☐ 9 Ferris Fain	100.00	45.00	12.50
☐ 10 Howie Fox	100.00	45.00	12.50
☐ 11 Sid Gordon	125.00	55.00	15.50
☐ 12 Johnny Groth	100.00	45.00	12.50
☐ 13 Granny Hamner	100.00	45.00	12.50

☐ 14 Sam Jones	100.00	45.00	12.50
☐ 15 Howie Judson	100.00	45.00	12.50
☐ 16 Sherm Lollar	100.00	45.00	12.50
☐ 17 Clarence Marshall	100.00	45.00	12.50
☐ 18 Don Mueller	100.00	45.00	12.50
☐ 19 Danny Murtaugh	125.00	55.00	15.50
☐ 20 Dave Philley	100.00	45.00	12.50
☐ 21 Jerry Priddy	100.00	45.00	12.50
☐ 22 Bill Rigney	125.00	55.00	15.50
☐ 23 Robin Roberts	200.00	90.00	25.00
☐ 24 Eddie Robinson	100.00	45.00	12.50
☐ 25 Preacher Roe	150.00	70.00	19.00
☐ 26 Stan Rojek	100.00	45.00	12.50
☐ 27 Al Rosen	125.00	55.00	15.50
☐ 28 Bob Rush	100.00	45.00	12.50
☐ 29 Hank Sauer	125.00	55.00	15.50
☐ 30 Johnny Schmitz	100.00	45.00	12.50
☐ 31 Enos Slaughter	200.00	90.00	25.00
☐ 32 Duke Snider	350.00	160.00	45.00
☐ 33 Warren Spahn	300.00	135.00	38.00
☐ 34 Gerry Staley	100.00	45.00	12.50
☐ 35 Virgil Stallcup	100.00	45.00	12.50
☐ 36 George Stirnweiss	100.00	45.00	12.50
☐ 37 Earl Torgeson	100.00	45.00	12.50
☐ 38 Dizzy Trout	125.00	55.00	15.50
☐ 39 Mickey Vernon	150.00	70.00	19.00
☐ 40 Wally Westlake	100.00	45.00	12.50
☐ 41 Johnny Wyrostek	100.00	45.00	12.50
☐ 42 Eddie Yost	100.00	45.00	12.50

1995 National Packtime

This 18-card standard-size set was sponsored by MLB, MLBPA, and the six leading card companies (Donruss, Fleer, Pacific, Pinnacle, Topps, and Upper Deck). Each of the six companies produced three cards for the set, which was available only through a mail-in offer for 28 wrappers from any of the six companies listed above plus $2.00 for shipping and handling. All orders had to be postmarked by June 30, 1995; any card sets not purchased by that date were destroyed. Except for the Topps card (which has a ragged white border), all the fronts display full-bleed color action photos. The backs carry a second color photo as well as biography and statistics. The cards are numbered on the back "X of 18." An unnumbered offer card, with a checklist on its back, was found in various 1995 baseball products.

	MINT	NRMT	EXC
COMPLETE SET (18)	8.00	3.60	1.00
COMMON CARD (1-18)	.25	.11	.03
☐ 1 Frank Thomas	2.50	1.10	.30
☐ 2 Matt Williams	.50	.23	.06
☐ 3 Juan Gonzalez	1.25	.55	.16
☐ 4 Bob Hamelin	.25	.11	.03
☐ 5 Mike Piazza	1.50	.70	.19
☐ 6 Ken Griffey Jr.	2.50	1.10	.30
☐ 7 Barry Bonds	.75	.35	.09
☐ 8 Tim Salmon	.50	.23	.06
☐ 9 Jose Canseco	.50	.23	.06
☐ 10 Cal Ripken	2.00	.90	.25
☐ 11 Raul Mondesi	.50	.23	.06
☐ 12 Alex Rodriguez	2.50	1.10	.30
☐ 13 Will Clark	.50	.23	.06
☐ 14 Fred McGriff	.50	.23	.06
☐ 15 Tony Gwynn	1.25	.55	.16
☐ 16 Kenny Lofton	.75	.35	.09
☐ 17 Deion Sanders	.50	.23	.06
☐ 18 Jeff Bagwell	1.25	.55	.16

1995 National Packtime 2

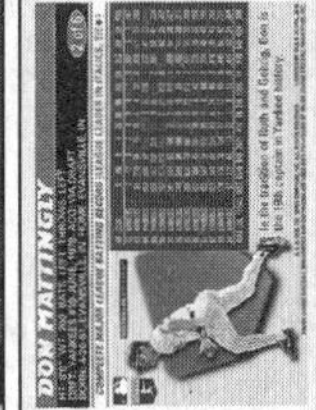

This six-card set was sponsored by MLB, MLBPA and the six leading card companies (Donruss, Fleer, Pacific, Pinnacle, Topps, and Upper Deck) who each produced one card for the set. The fronts feature borderless color action player photos, while the backs carry player information. The cards are checklisted below in alphabetical order.

	MINT	NRMT	EXC
COMPLETE SET (6)	6.00	2.70	.75
COMMON CARD (1-6)	.25	.11	.03
☐ 1 Albert Belle	1.50	.70	.19
☐ 2 Darren Daulton	.25	.11	.03
☐ 3 Randy Johnson	.50	.23	.06
☐ 4 Greg Maddux	1.50	.70	.19
☐ 5 Don Mattingly	1.50	.70	.19
☐ 6 Hideo Nomo	2.00	.90	.25

1986 Negro League Fritsch

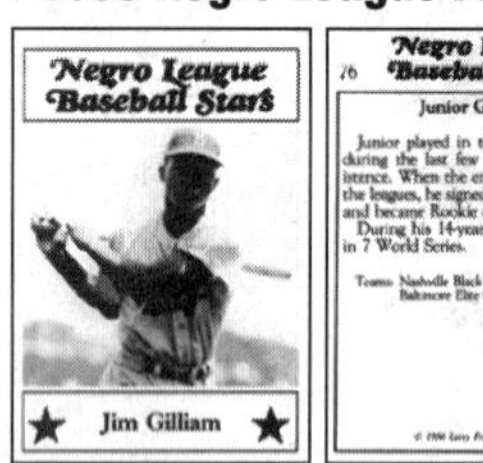

This is a 119-card standard-size set of Negro League stars. The set features black and white photos framed by the title "Negro League Baseball Stars" in red above the player's name and the player's name in red below the photo. Each card back features a brief biography of the player pictured on the front of the card. The set was produced by long time Wisconsin card hobbyist Larry Fritsch and featured most of the great players of the old Negro Leagues. An earlier version of the set was produced in 1984 by Decathlon Corporation. Each Decathlon set has a serial number; Decathlon sets are valued at double the prices listed below.

	MINT	NRMT	EXC
COMPLETE SET (119)	10.00	4.50	1.25
COMMON CARD (1-119)	.05	.02	.01
☐ 1 Buck Leonard	.50	.23	.06
☐ 2 Ted Page	.25	.11	.03
☐ 3 Cool Papa Bell	.50	.23	.06
☐ 4 Oscar Charleston Josh Gibson Ted Page Judy Johnson	.40	.18	.05
☐ 5 Judy Johnson	.40	.18	.05
☐ 6 Monte Irvin	.40	.18	.05
☐ 7 Ray Dandridge	.30	.14	.04
☐ 8 Oscar Charleston	.50	.23	.06
☐ 9 Josh Gibson	1.00	.45	.12
☐ 10 Satchel Paige	1.00	.45	.12
☐ 11 Jackie Robinson	1.00	.45	.12
☐ 12 Lorenzo(Piper) Davis	.15	.07	.02
☐ 13 Josh Johnson	.05	.02	.01
☐ 14 Lou Dials	.25	.11	.03
☐ 15 Andy Porter	.05	.02	.01
☐ 16 John Henry Lloyd	.30	.14	.04
☐ 17 Andy Watts	.05	.02	.01
☐ 18 Rube Foster	.30	.14	.04
☐ 19 Martin DiHigo	.50	.23	.06
☐ 20 Lou Dials	.25	.11	.03
☐ 21 Satchel Paige	1.00	.45	.12
☐ 22 Crush Holloway	.05	.02	.01
☐ 23 Josh Gibson	1.00	.45	.12
☐ 24 Oscar Charleston	.50	.23	.06
☐ 25 Jackie Robinson	1.00	.45	.12
☐ 26 Larry Brown	.05	.02	.01
☐ 27 Hilton Smith	.15	.07	.02
☐ 28 Moses F. Walker	.40	.18	.05
☐ 29 Jimmie Crutchfield	.25	.11	.03
☐ 30 Josh Gibson	1.00	.45	.12
☐ 31 Josh Gibson	1.00	.45	.12
☐ 32 Bullet Rogan	.20	.09	.03
☐ 33 Clint Thomas	.05	.02	.01
☐ 34 Rats Henderson	.05	.02	.01
☐ 35 Pat Scantlebury	.05	.02	.01
☐ 36 Sydney Sy Morton	.05	.02	.01
☐ 37 Larry Kimbrough	.05	.02	.01
☐ 38 Sam Jethroe	.20	.09	.03
☐ 39 Normal(Tweed) Webb	.05	.02	.01
☐ 40 Mahlon Duckett	.05	.02	.01
☐ 41 Andy Anderson	.05	.02	.01
☐ 42 Buster Haywood	.05	.02	.01
☐ 43 Bob Trice	.20	.09	.03
☐ 44 Buster Clarkson	.05	.02	.01
☐ 45 Buck O'Neil	.50	.23	.06
☐ 46 Jim Zapp	.05	.02	.01
☐ 47 Lorenzo(Piper) Davis	.20	.09	.03
☐ 48 Ed Steel	.05	.02	.01
☐ 49 Bob Boyd	.20	.09	.03
☐ 50 Marlin Carter	.05	.02	.01
☐ 51 George Giles	.05	.02	.01
☐ 52 Bill Byrd	.05	.02	.01
☐ 53 Art Pennington	.05	.02	.01
☐ 54 Max Manning	.05	.02	.01
☐ 55 Ronald Teasley	.05	.02	.01
☐ 56 Ziggy Marcell	.05	.02	.01
☐ 57 Bill Cash	.05	.02	.01
☐ 58 Joe Scott	.05	.02	.01
☐ 59 Joe Fillmore	.05	.02	.01
☐ 60 Bob Thurman	.20	.09	.03
☐ 61 Larry Kimbrough	.05	.02	.01
☐ 62 Verdell Mathis	.05	.02	.01
☐ 63 Josh Johnson	.20	.09	.03
☐ 64 Ted Radcliffe	.30	.14	.04
☐ 65 William Bobby Robinson	.15	.07	.02
☐ 66 Bingo DeMoss	.20	.09	.03
☐ 67 John Beckwith	.05	.02	.01
☐ 68 Bill Jackman	.05	.02	.01
☐ 69 Bill Drake	.05	.02	.01
☐ 70 Charlie Grant	.25	.11	.03
☐ 71 Willie Wells	.50	.23	.06
☐ 72 Jose Fernandez	.05	.02	.01
☐ 73 Isidro Fabri	.05	.02	.01
☐ 74 Frank Austin	.05	.02	.01
☐ 75 Dick Lundy	.05	.02	.01
☐ 76 Junior Gilliam	.30	.14	.04
☐ 77 John Donaldson	.05	.02	.01
☐ 78 Rap Dixon	.05	.02	.01
☐ 79 Slim Jones	.05	.02	.01
☐ 80 Sam Jones	.20	.09	.03
☐ 81 Dave Hoskins	.20	.09	.03
☐ 82 Jerry Benjamin	.05	.02	.01
☐ 83 Luke Easter	.20	.09	.03
☐ 84 Ramon Herrera	.05	.02	.01
☐ 85 Matthew Carlisle	.05	.02	.01
☐ 86 Smokey Joe Williams	.30	.14	.04
☐ 87 Marvin Williams	.05	.02	.01
☐ 88 William Yancey	.20	.09	.03
☐ 89 Monte Irvin	.50	.23	.06
☐ 90 Cool Papa Bell	.60	.25	.07
☐ 91 Biz Mackey	.40	.18	.05
☐ 92 Harry Simpson	.20	.09	.03
☐ 93 Lazerio Salazar	.05	.02	.01
☐ 94 Bill Perkins	.05	.02	.01
☐ 95 Johnny Davis	.05	.02	.01
☐ 96 Jelly Jackson	.20	.09	.03
☐ 97 Sam Bankhead	.20	.09	.03
☐ 98 Hank Thompson	.20	.09	.03
☐ 99 William Bell	.05	.02	.01
☐ 100 Cliff Bell	.05	.02	.01
☐ 101 Dave Barnhill	.05	.02	.01
☐ 102 Dan Bankhead	.20	.09	.03
☐ 103 Pepper Bassett	.05	.02	.01
☐ 104 Newt Allen	.20	.09	.03
☐ 105 George Jefferson	.05	.02	.01
☐ 106 Pat Paterson	.05	.02	.01
☐ 107 Goose Tatum	1.00	.45	.12
☐ 108 Dave Malarcher	.20	.09	.03
☐ 109 Home Run Johnson	.20	.09	.03
☐ 110 Bill Monroe	.05	.02	.01
☐ 111 Sammy Hughes	.05	.02	.01
☐ 112 Dick Redding	.20	.09	.03
☐ 113 Fats Jenkins	.05	.02	.01
☐ 114 Jimmie Lyons	.05	.02	.01
☐ 115 Mule Suttles	.20	.09	.03
☐ 116 Ted Trent	.05	.02	.01
☐ 117 George Sweatt	.05	.02	.01
☐ 118 Frank Duncan	.05	.02	.01
☐ 119 Checklist Card	.05	.02	.01

1986 Negro League Fritsch Samples

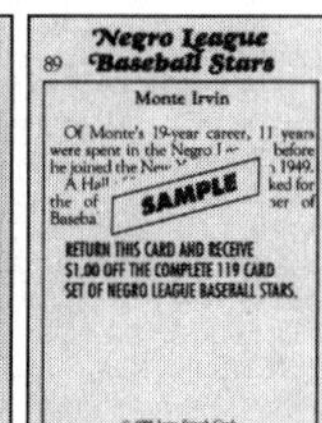

These 1986 Negro League Fritsch Samples were issued to announce the introduction of the 1986 Negro League Fritsch 119-card set. The cards measure the standard-size. The white fronts display a black-and-white player portrait with the set title appearing in red lettering above. The player's name appears below the photo also in red lettering with a red star to the left and right. The backs have blue print framed by a narrow blue line and carry a portion of the narrative to appear on the regular issue card. Stamped across the information is the word "Sample". An offer is made to return the Sample card and receive $1.50 off the complete set of 119 Negro League Baseball Stars.

	MINT	NRMT	EXC
COMPLETE SET (2)	3.00	1.35	.35
COMMON CARD	1.25	.55	.16
☐ 30 Josh Gibson	2.50	1.10	.30
☐ 89 Monte Irvin	1.25	.55	.16

1987 Negro League Phil Dixon

Produced by Phil Dixon, this 45-card set measures approximately 2 15/16" by 5". The fronts feature a mix of posed and action black-and-white player photos bordered in white. The horizontal backs carry the player's name, position, birth and death dates, and a brief career summary.

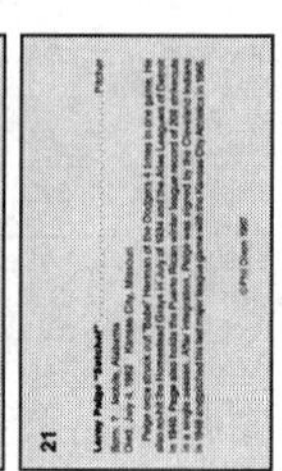

	MINT	NRMT	EXC
COMPLETE SET (45)	30.00	13.50	3.70
COMMON CARD (1-45)	.50	.23	.06
☐ 1 Samuel Hairston	.75	.35	.09
☐ 2 Elander Victor Harris (Vic)	.50	.23	.06
☐ 3 Theodore(Ted) Trent	.50	.23	.06
☐ 4 Edward Joseph Dwight (Pee Wee)	.75	.35	.09
☐ 5 Jessie Williams	.50	.23	.06
☐ 6 Josh Gibson	3.00	1.35	.35
☐ 7 Jose De La C. Mendez	.50	.23	.06
☐ 8 Joe Green	.50	.23	.06
☐ 9 Robert Boyd (The Rope)	.75	.35	.09
☐ 10 William(Plunk) Drake	.50	.23	.06
☐ 11 Alfred(Army) Cooper	.50	.23	.06
☐ 12 Charles Isam Taylor (C.I.)	.50	.23	.06
☐ 13 Dick Whitworth	.50	.23	.06
☐ 14 Tobe Smith	.50	.23	.06
☐ 15 William(Dizzy) Dismukes	.50	.23	.06
☐ 16 Richard Thomas Bayas (Subby)	.50	.23	.06
☐ 17 Hurley Allen McNair (Mack)	.50	.23	.06
☐ 18 Roy Partlow	.50	.23	.06
☐ 19 Carroll Ray Mothell (Dink)	.50	.23	.06
☐ 20 John(Buck) O'Neil	1.50	.70	.19
☐ 21 Leroy(Satchel) Paige	3.00	1.35	.35
☐ 22 Moses Fleetwood Walker	1.50	.70	.19
☐ 23 Quincy Jordan Gilmore	.50	.23	.06
☐ 24 James(Cool Papa) Bell	1.50	.70	.19
☐ 25 Andrew(Rube) Foster	1.50	.70	.19
☐ 26 George Alexander Sweatt	.50	.23	.06
☐ 27 Hilton Lee Smith	1.25	.55	.16
☐ 28 Thomas Jefferson Young (T.J.)	.50	.23	.06
☐ 29 Chet Brewer	1.00	.45	.12
☐ 30 Buck Leonard	1.50	.70	.19
☐ 31 Walter Lee Joseph (Newt)	.75	.35	.09
☐ 32 Eugene Walter Baker (Gene)	.75	.35	.09
☐ 33 Jackie Robinson	3.00	1.35	.35
☐ 34 Wilbur(Bullet) Rogan	.75	.35	.09
☐ 35 Norman(Turkey) Stearns	.50	.23	.06
☐ 36 Albert(Buster) Haywood	.50	.23	.06
☐ 37 Lorenzo(Piper) Davis	.75	.35	.09
☐ 38 Francisco Comimbre (Pancho)	.50	.23	.06
☐ 39 Bob Thurman	.75	.35	.09
☐ 40 Booker T. McDaniel (Cannonball)	.50	.23	.06
☐ 41 Newton Henry Allen (Colt)	.75	.35	.09
☐ 42 Willie Wells	1.50	.70	.19
☐ 43 Connie Johnson	1.00	.45	.12
☐ 44 George Franklin Giles	.50	.23	.06
☐ 45 Frank(Dunk) Duncan	.50	.23	.06

1988 Negro League Duquesne

This 20-card set was sponsored by the Pittsburgh Pirates with the assistance of Rob Ruck of Chatham College and Duquesne Light Company. The set celebrates Negro League Baseball by depicting major black stars who played or were involved in the negro leagues in the Pittsburgh area. The set was given away at the Pittsburgh Pirates' home game on September 10, 1988. The set was issued in a sheet with five rows of four cards each; after perforation, the cards measure the standard size. The fronts have sepia-toned player photos, with thin black borders on a white card face. A mustard-colored banner above the pictures reads "Negro League Stars." Also a mustard-colored baseball field logo appears in the lower right corner of the card face. The backs are printed in black on white and have biography as well as career summary. The Pirates' logo appears in the lower right corner.

	MINT	NRMT	EXC
COMPLETE SET (20)	27.50	12.50	3.40
COMMON CARD (1-20)	1.00	.45	.12

	MINT	NRMT	EXC
☐ 1 Andrew(Rube) Foster	2.50	1.10	.30
☐ 2 1913 Homestead Grays	1.00	.45	.12
☐ 3 Cum Posey	1.00	.45	.12
☐ 4 1926 Pittsburgh Crawfords	1.00	.45	.12
☐ 5 Gus Greenlee OWN	1.00	.45	.12
☐ 6 John Henry(Pop) Lloyd	2.50	1.10	.30
☐ 7 Oscar Charleston	2.50	1.10	.30
☐ 8 Smokey Joe Williams	1.50	.70	.19
☐ 9 William(Judy) Johnson	2.50	1.10	.30
☐ 10 Martin Dihigo	2.50	1.10	.30
☐ 11 LeRoy(Satchel) Paige	4.00	1.80	.50
☐ 12 Josh Gibson	4.00	1.80	.50
☐ 13 Sam Streeter	1.00	.45	.12
☐ 14 James(Cool Papa) Bell	3.00	1.35	.35
☐ 15 Ted Page	2.00	.90	.25
☐ 16 Walter(Buck) Leonard	2.50	1.10	.30
☐ 17 Ray(Hooks) Dandridge	2.50	1.10	.30
☐ 18 Willis Moody and Ralph(Lefty) Mellix	1.00	.45	.12
☐ 19 Harold Tinker	1.00	.45	.12
☐ 20 Monte Irvin	2.50	1.10	.30

1990 Negro League Stars

The exclusion of black and Latino players from Major League Baseball from 1889 to 1947 resulted in these same players forming their own teams and leagues, and this 36-card set pays tribute to these men. These standard size cards feature beautiful water color portraits of the players, painted by Mark Chiarello. The left side of the picture has a white border, while the bottom has a black border. The intersection of the two borders in the lower left corner is red in color. The player's name appears in the bottom black border. The backs are printed in black on white and summarize the player's career.

	MINT	NRMT	EXC
COMPLETE SET (36)	12.00	5.50	1.50
COMMON CARD (1-36)	.35	.16	.04
☐ 1 Title Card	.50	.23	.06
☐ 2 Josh Gibson	2.00	.90	.25
☐ 3 Cannonball Redding	.60	.25	.07
☐ 4 Biz Mackey	.75	.35	.09
☐ 5 Pop Lloyd	1.00	.45	.12
☐ 6 Bingo Demoss	.60	.25	.07
☐ 7 Willard Brown	.35	.16	.04
☐ 8 John Donaldson	.35	.16	.04
☐ 9 Monte Irvin	1.00	.45	.12
☐ 10 Ben Taylor	.35	.16	.04
☐ 11 Willie Wells	.75	.35	.09
☐ 12 Dave Brown	.35	.16	.04
☐ 13 Leon Day	.75	.35	.09
☐ 14 Ray Dandridge	1.00	.45	.12
☐ 15 Turkey Stearnes	.35	.16	.04
☐ 16 Rube Foster	1.00	.45	.12
☐ 17 Oliver Marcelle	.35	.16	.04
☐ 18 Judy Johnson	1.00	.45	.12
☐ 19 Christobel Torrienti	.60	.25	.07
☐ 20 Satchel Paige	2.00	.90	.25
☐ 21 Mule Suttles	.50	.23	.06
☐ 22 John Beckwith	.35	.16	.04
☐ 23 Martin Dihigo	1.00	.45	.12
☐ 24 Willie Foster	.35	.16	.04
☐ 25 Dick Lundy	.35	.16	.04
☐ 26 Buck Leonard	1.00	.45	.12
☐ 27 Smokey Joe Williams	.50	.23	.06
☐ 28 Cool Papa Bell	1.00	.45	.12
☐ 29 Bullet Rogan	.50	.23	.06
☐ 30 Newt Allen	.50	.23	.06
☐ 31 Bruce Petway	.50	.23	.06
☐ 32 Jose Mendez	.35	.16	.04
☐ 33 Louis Santop	.35	.16	.04
☐ 34 Jud Wilson	.35	.16	.04
☐ 35 Sammy T. Hughes	.35	.16	.04
☐ 36 Oscar Charleston	1.00	.45	.12

1991 Negro League Ron Lewis

This 30-card boxed set was produced by the Negro League Baseball Players Association and noted sports artist Ron Lewis and was subtitled Living Legends. Production quantities were limited to 10,000 sets, and each card of the set bears a unique serial number on the back. Also 200 uncut sheets were printed. The cards were issued in the postcard format and measure approximately 3 1/2" by 5 1/4". The front design features a full color painting of the player by Ron Lewis. The paintings are bordered in white, and the player's name appears at the bottom of the front. The backs have brief biographical information and the card number in the upper left corner. These cards were also issued in 1995 as part of a two series Negro League set. The values are about the same for either set.

	MINT	NRMT	EXC
COMPLETE SET (30)	30.00	13.50	3.70
COMMON CARD (1-30)	1.00	.45	.12
☐ 1 George Giles	1.00	.45	.12
☐ 2 Bill Cash	1.00	.45	.12
☐ 3 Bob Harvey	1.00	.45	.12
☐ 4 Lyman Bostock Sr.	1.50	.70	.19
☐ 5 Ray Dandridge	2.50	1.10	.30
☐ 6 Leon Day	2.50	1.10	.30
☐ 7 Lefty Mathis	1.00	.45	.12
☐ 8 Jimmie Crutchfield	1.50	.70	.19
☐ 9 Clyde McNeal	1.00	.45	.12
☐ 10 Bill Wright	1.00	.45	.12
☐ 11 Mahlon Duckett	1.00	.45	.12
☐ 12 Bobby Robinson	1.50	.70	.19
☐ 13 Max Manning	1.00	.45	.12
☐ 14 Armando Vazquez	1.00	.45	.12
☐ 15 Jehosie Heard	1.50	.70	.19
☐ 16 Quincy Trouppe	1.00	.45	.12
☐ 17 Wilmer Fields	1.00	.45	.12
☐ 18 Lonnie Blair	1.00	.45	.12
☐ 19 Garnett Blair	1.00	.45	.12
☐ 20 Monte Irvin	3.00	1.35	.35
☐ 21 Willie Mays	6.00	2.70	.75
☐ 22 Buck Leonard	3.50	1.55	.45
☐ 23 Frank Evans	1.00	.45	.12
☐ 24 Josh Gibson Jr.	2.00	.90	.25
☐ 25 Ted Radcliffe	1.50	.70	.19
☐ 26 Josh Johnson	1.50	.70	.19
☐ 27 Gene Benson	1.00	.45	.12
☐ 28 Lester Lockett	1.50	.70	.19
☐ 29 Bubba Hyde	1.00	.45	.12
☐ 30 Rufus Lewis	1.00	.45	.12

1992 Negro League Kraft

On August 9, 1992, at Lackawanna County Stadium, in Scranton, Pennsylvania, Eclipse Enterprises Inc. sponsored the Negro League Baseball Players Association Night. This 18-card set was created especially for this event by Eclipse artist John Clapp and given out to fans in attendance. The standard-size cards have fronts that feature watercolor portraits inside white borders. The player's name and position appear in a brick-red stripe overlaying the bottom edge of the picture. The backs carry biography and career summary between upper and lower black bars. The cards are numbered on the back. Reportedly only 11,000 of the 15,000 sets were distributed; the remainder were kept by Kraft General Foods of Glenville, Illinois.

	MINT	NRMT	EXC
COMPLETE SET (18)	15.00	6.75	1.85
COMMON CARD (1-18)	.50	.23	.06
☐ 1 Leon Day	1.50	.70	.19
☐ 2 Clinton(Casey) Jones	.50	.23	.06
☐ 3 Lester Lockett	.75	.35	.09
☐ 4 Monte Irvin	2.50	1.10	.30
☐ 5 Armando Vazquez	.50	.23	.06
☐ 6 Jimmie Crutchfield	1.00	.45	.12
☐ 7 Ted Radcliffe	1.00	.45	.12
☐ 8 Albert Haywood	.50	.23	.06
☐ 9 Artie Wilson	.75	.35	.09
☐ 10 Sam Jethroe	.75	.35	.09
☐ 11 Edsall Walker	.50	.23	.06
☐ 12 Bill Wright	.50	.23	.06
☐ 13 Jim Cohen	.50	.23	.06
☐ 14 Andy Porter	.50	.23	.06
☐ 15 Tommy Sampson	.50	.23	.06
☐ 16 Buck Leonard	3.00	1.35	.35
☐ 17 Josh Gibson	4.00	1.80	.50
☐ 18 Martinez Jackson (Reggie Jackson's father)	2.00	.90	.25

1992 Negro League Paul Lee

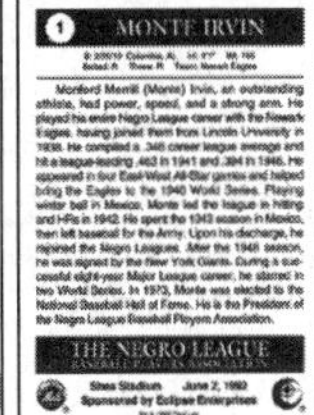

On June 2, 1992 at Shea Stadium, Eclipse Enterprises Inc. sponsored the Negro League Baseball Players Association Night. This four-card set was created especially for this event by Eclipse artist Paul Lee, and they were given out to the first 50,000 fans in attendance. Each set included an insert outlining the goals of the association. The standard-size cards feature on the fronts water color portraits inside white borders. The player's name and position appear in a brick-red stripe overlaying the bottom edge of the picture. The backs carry biography and career summary between two black bars.

	MINT	NRMT	EXC
COMPLETE SET (4)	6.00	2.70	.75
COMMON CARD (1-4)	1.50	.70	.19
☐ 1 Monte Irvin	1.50	.70	.19
☐ 2 Walter(Buck) Leonard	1.50	.70	.19
☐ 3 Josh Gibson	3.00	1.35	.35
☐ 4 Ray Dandridge	1.50	.70	.19

1992 Negro League Retort Legends I

This 100-card set was produced by R.D. Retort Enterprises of New Castle, Pennsylvania. The cards were issued in a brown box with the set name and logo stamped in gold. The production run was reported to be 10,000 individually numbered sets. Collectors who purchased the set received The Pictorial Negro League Legends Album, an 8 1/2" by 11" book containing more than 260 vintage Negro League photos, and an address list to facilitate the obtaining of autographs. The cards are "postcard" size, measuring approximately 3 1/2" by 5 1/2". The sepia-toned player photos have white borders, and player's name appears in the bottom white border. The backs carry a player profile and the serial number.

	MINT	NRMT	EXC
COMPLETE SET (100)	75.00	34.00	9.50
COMMON CARD (1-100)	.75	.35	.09
☐ 1 Otha Bailey	1.50	.70	.19
☐ 2 Harry Barnes	1.00	.45	.12
☐ 3 Gene Benson	1.00	.45	.12
☐ 4 Bill Beverly	1.00	.45	.12
☐ 5 Charlie Biot	1.00	.45	.12
☐ 6 Bob Boyd	1.50	.70	.19
☐ 7 Allen Bryant	1.00	.45	.12
☐ 8 Marlin Carter	1.00	.45	.12
☐ 9 Bill Cash	1.00	.45	.12
☐ 10 Jim Cohen	1.00	.45	.12
☐ 11 Elliot Coleman	1.00	.45	.12
☐ 12 Johnnie Cowan	1.00	.45	.12
☐ 13 Jimmie Crutchfield	1.50	.70	.19
☐ 14 Saul Davis	1.00	.45	.12
☐ 15 Piper Davis	1.50	.70	.19
☐ 16 Leon Day	2.00	.90	.25
☐ 17 Lou Dials	2.00	.90	.25
☐ 18 Mahlon Duckett	1.50	.70	.19
☐ 19 Felix Evans	1.00	.45	.12
☐ 20 Rudy Fernandez	1.00	.45	.12
☐ 21 Joe Fillmore	1.00	.45	.12
☐ 22 George Giles	1.00	.45	.12
☐ 23 Louis Gillis	1.00	.45	.12
☐ 24 Stanley Glenn	1.00	.45	.12
☐ 25 Willie Grace	1.00	.45	.12
☐ 26 Wiley Griggs	1.00	.45	.12
☐ 27 Albert Haywood	1.00	.45	.12
☐ 28 Jimmy Hill	1.00	.45	.12
☐ 29 Cowan Hyde	1.00	.45	.12
☐ 30 Monte Irvin	3.00	1.35	.35
☐ 31 Sam Jethroe	1.50	.70	.19
☐ 32 Connie Johnson	1.50	.70	.19
☐ 33 Josh Johnson	1.50	.70	.19
☐ 34 Clinton Jones	1.00	.45	.12
☐ 35 Larry Kimbrough	1.00	.45	.12
☐ 36 Clarence King	1.00	.45	.12
☐ 37 Jim LaMarque	1.00	.45	.12
☐ 38 Buck Leonard	3.00	1.35	.35
☐ 39 Max Manning	1.00	.45	.12
☐ 40 Verdell Mathis	1.00	.45	.12
☐ 41 Nath McClinic	1.00	.45	.12
☐ 42 Clinton McCord	1.00	.45	.12
☐ 43 Clyde McNeal	1.00	.45	.12
☐ 44 John Miles	1.00	.45	.12
☐ 45 Buck O'Neil	3.00	1.35	.35
☐ 46 Frank Pearson	1.00	.45	.12
☐ 47 Art Pennington	1.00	.45	.12
☐ 48 Nathaniel Peoples	1.00	.45	.12
☐ 49 Andy Porter	1.00	.45	.12
☐ 50 Ted(Double Duty) Radcliffe	1.50	.70	.19
☐ 51 Chico Renfroe	1.00	.45	.12
☐ 52 Bobby Robinson	1.50	.70	.19
☐ 53 Tommy Sampson	1.00	.45	.12
☐ 54 Joe Scott	1.00	.45	.12
☐ 55 Joe Burt Scott	1.00	.45	.12
☐ 56 Herb Simpson	1.00	.45	.12
☐ 57 Lonnie Summers	1.00	.45	.12
☐ 58 Alfred Surratt	1.00	.45	.12
☐ 59 Bob Thurman	1.50	.70	.19
☐ 60 Harold Tinker	1.00	.45	.12
☐ 61 Quincy Trouppe	1.50	.70	.19
☐ 62 Edsall Walker	1.00	.45	.12
☐ 63 Al Wilmore	1.00	.45	.12
☐ 64 Artie Wilson	1.50	.70	.19
☐ 65 Jim Zapp	1.00	.45	.12
☐ 66 Grays vs. Stars 1937	.75	.35	.09
☐ 67 Grays vs. Eagles 1943	.75	.35	.09
☐ 68 Homestead Grays 1944	.75	.35	.09
☐ 69 Grays vs. Cuban Stars 1944	.75	.35	.09
☐ 70 Grays vs. Cubans 1944	.75	.35	.09
☐ 71 Grays vs. Eagles 1945	.75	.35	.09
☐ 72 Eagles pitching staff 1941	.75	.35	.09
☐ 73 Buckeyes infield 1945	.75	.35	.09
☐ 74 Homestead Grays 1948	.75	.35	.09
☐ 75 Chicago Murderers Row 1943	.75	.35	.09
☐ 76 Indianapolis Clowns 1945	.75	.35	.09
☐ 77 East All-Stars 1937	.75	.35	.09
☐ 78 East All-Stars 1938	.75	.35	.09
☐ 79 East All-Stars 1939	.75	.35	.09
☐ 80 East All-Stars 1948	.75	.35	.09
☐ 81 West All-Stars 1948	.75	.35	.09
☐ 82 Homestead Grays 1931	.75	.35	.09
☐ 83 Homestead Grays 1938	.75	.35	.09
☐ 84 Pittsburgh Crawfords 1936	.75	.35	.09
☐ 85 K.C. Monarchs 1934	.75	.35	.09
☐ 86 K.C. Monarchs 1949	.75	.35	.09
☐ 87 Chicago American Giants 1941	.75	.35	.09
☐ 88 Chicago American Giants 1947	.75	.35	.09
☐ 89 Memphis Red Sox 1940	.75	.35	.09
☐ 90 Memphis Red Sox 1946	.75	.35	.09
☐ 91 Birmingham B.B. 1946	.75	.35	.09
☐ 92 Birmingham B.B. 1948	.75	.35	.09
☐ 93 Birmingham B.B. 1950	.75	.35	.09
☐ 94 Harlem Globetrotters 1948	.75	.35	.09
☐ 95 Cleveland Buckeyes 1947	.75	.35	.09
☐ 96 Philadelphia Stars 1944	.75	.35	.09
☐ 97 Newark Eagles 1939	.75	.35	.09
☐ 98 Baltimore Elite Giants 1949	.75	.35	.09
☐ 99 Indianapolis Clowns 1943	.75	.35	.09
☐ 100 Cincinnati Tigers 1937	.75	.35	.09

1993 Negro League Retort Legends II

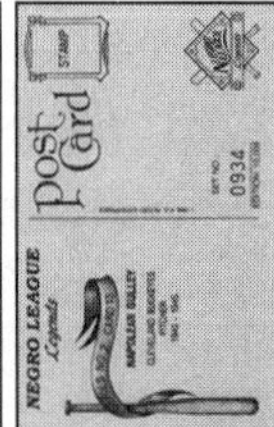

This 100-card second series of R.D. Retort Enterprises' Negro League Legends was issued in a brown box that has the set logo on the top stamped in gold foil. The cards have a postcard design, measuring approximately 3 1/2" by 5 1/2", and feature white-bordered sepia-tone player photos on their fronts. The player's (or team's) name appears in the lower margin. The back carries the player's (or team's) name on the left side, which is highlighted by a baseball bat icon. The set's logo appears at the lower right, next to the set's production number (out of 10,000).

	MINT	NRMT	EXC
COMPLETE SET (100)	75.00	34.00	9.50
COMMON CARD (1-100)	.75	.35	.09
☐ 1 Frank Barnes	1.00	.45	.12
☐ 2 John L. Bissant	1.00	.45	.12
☐ 3 Garnett E. Blair	1.00	.45	.12
☐ 4 Jim(Fire Ball) Bolden	1.00	.45	.12
☐ 5 Luther H. Branham	1.00	.45	.12
☐ 6 Sherwood(Woody) Brewer	1.00	.45	.12
☐ 7 Jimmy Dean	1.00	.45	.12
☐ 8 Frank Duncan Jr.	1.50	.70	.19
☐ 9 Wilmer(Red) Fields	1.00	.45	.12
☐ 10 Harold(Beebop) Gordon	1.00	.45	.12
☐ 11 Bill Greason	1.00	.45	.12
☐ 12 Acie(Skeet) Griggs	1.00	.45	.12
☐ 13 Napolean Gulley	1.00	.45	.12
☐ 14 Ray Haggins	1.00	.45	.12
☐ 15 Wilmer Harris	1.00	.45	.12
☐ 16 Bob Harvey	1.00	.45	.12
☐ 17 Jehosie Heard	1.50	.70	.19
☐ 18 Gordon(Hoppy) Hopkins	1.00	.45	.12
☐ 19 Herman(Doc) Horn	1.00	.45	.12
☐ 20 James(Sap) Ivory	1.00	.45	.12
☐ 21 Henry Kimbro	1.00	.45	.12
☐ 22 Milfred(Rick) Laurent	1.00	.45	.12
☐ 23 Ernest(The Kid) Long	1.00	.45	.12
☐ 24 Frank Marsh	1.00	.45	.12
☐ 25 Francis(Fran) Matthews	1.00	.45	.12
☐ 26 Jim McCurine	1.00	.45	.12
☐ 27 John Mitchell	1.00	.45	.12
☐ 28 Lee Moody	1.00	.45	.12
☐ 29 Rogers(Shape) Pierre	1.00	.45	.12
☐ 30 Nathaniel(Nat) Pollard	1.00	.45	.12

Card	MINT	NRMT	EXC
☐ 31 Merle Porter	1.00	.45	.12
☐ 32 William Powell	1.00	.45	.12
☐ 33 Ulysses A. Redd	1.00	.45	.12
☐ 34 Harry(Lefty) Rhodes	1.00	.45	.12
☐ 35 DeWitt Smallwood (Woody)	1.50	.70	.19
☐ 36 Joseph B. Spencer	1.00	.45	.12
☐ 37 Riley A. Stewart	1.00	.45	.12
☐ 38 Earl Taborn	1.00	.45	.12
☐ 39 Ron Teasley	1.00	.45	.12
☐ 40 Joe Wiley	1.00	.45	.12
☐ 41 Walter(Buck) Leonard	3.00	1.35	.35
☐ 42 Grays vs. B.E. Giants 1945	.75	.35	.09
☐ 43 Grays vs. Monarchs 1945	.75	.35	.09
☐ 44 Homestead Grays 1948	.75	.35	.09
☐ 45 Pittsburgh Crawfords 1928	.75	.35	.09
☐ 46 Pittsburgh Crawfords 1935	.75	.35	.09
☐ 47 Kansas City Monarchs 1942	.75	.35	.09
☐ 48 John(Buck) O'Neil MG William(Dizzy) Dismukes	.75	.35	.09
☐ 49 Chicago American Giants 1942	.75	.35	.09
☐ 50 Nashville Elite Giants 1935	.75	.35	.09
☐ 51 Baltimore Elite Giants 1941	.75	.35	.09
☐ 52 Birmingham Black Barons 1948	.75	.35	.09
☐ 53 Birmingham Black Barons 1959	.75	.35	.09
☐ 54 Memphis Red Sox 1954	.75	.35	.09
☐ 55 Indianapolis ABC's 1923	.75	.35	.09
☐ 56 Harlem Globetrotters 1948	.75	.35	.09
☐ 57 Harlem Globetrotters 1948	.75	.35	.09
☐ 58 Bismarck Barons 1955	.75	.35	.09
☐ 59 Culiacan 1952	.75	.35	.09
☐ 60 Santurce 1947	.75	.35	.09
☐ 61 Pittsburgh Crawfords 1928	.75	.35	.09
☐ 62 Pittsburgh Crawfords 1932	.75	.35	.09
☐ 63 Pittsburgh Crawfords 1935	.75	.35	.09
☐ 64 Homestead Grays 1937	.75	.35	.09
☐ 65 Homestead Grays 1938	.75	.35	.09
☐ 66 Homestead Grays 1940	.75	.35	.09
☐ 67 Homestead Grays 1945	.75	.35	.09
☐ 68 Homestead Grays 1948	.75	.35	.09
☐ 69 Kansas City Monarchs 1932	.75	.35	.09
☐ 70 Kansas City Monarchs 1934	.75	.35	.09
☐ 71 Kansas City Monarchs 1941	.75	.35	.09
☐ 72 Kansas City Monarchs 1946	.75	.35	.09
☐ 73 Chicago American Giants 1950	.75	.35	.09
☐ 74 Memphis Red Sox 1949	.75	.35	.09
☐ 75 Birmingham Black Barons 1946	.75	.35	.09
☐ 76 Birmingham Black Barons 1948	.75	.35	.09
☐ 77 Birmingham Black Barons 1951	.75	.35	.09
☐ 78 Birmingham Black Barons 1954	.75	.35	.09
☐ 79 St. Louis Stars 1931	.75	.35	.09
☐ 80 Newark Dodgers 1935	.75	.35	.09
☐ 81 Brooklyn Eagles 1935	.75	.35	.09
☐ 82 Newark Eagles 1946	.75	.35	.09
☐ 83 Philadelphia Stars 1939	.75	.35	.09
☐ 84 Philadelphia Stars 1946	.75	.35	.09
☐ 85 Philadelphia Stars 1949	.75	.35	.09
☐ 86 Nashville Elite Giants 1935	.75	.35	.09
☐ 87 Baltimore Elite Giants 1939	.75	.35	.09
☐ 88 Baltimore Elite Giants 1949	.75	.35	.09
☐ 89 Cleveland Buckeyes 1947	.75	.35	.09
☐ 90 Cincinnati Tigers 1936	.75	.35	.09
☐ 91 Miami Ethiopian Clowns 1940	.75	.35	.09
☐ 92 Indianapolis Clowns 1944	.75	.35	.09
☐ 93 Indianapolis Clowns 1948	.75	.35	.09
☐ 94 New York Cubans 1943	.75	.35	.09
☐ 95 Harlem Globetrotters 1948	.75	.35	.09
☐ 96 House of David 1938	1.50	.70	.19
☐ 97 E.T. Community 1926	.75	.35	.09
☐ 98 Bismarck Giants 1935	.75	.35	.09
☐ 99 American All-Stars 1945	.75	.35	.09
☐ 100 New York Stars 1949	.75	.35	.09

1995 Negro League Legends I

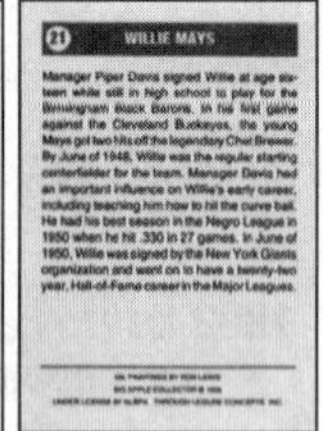

This boxed set measures the standard size and was produced by the Negro League Baseball Players Association and noted sports artist Ron Lewis. Series I and II were both issued in one box. Just 25,000 sets were produced. The white-bordered fronts feature full color player paintings by Ron Lewis. The backs carry the player's name in white letters inside a pink bar and summarize the player's career.

	MINT	NRMT	EXC
COMPLETE SET (31)	30.00	13.50	3.70
COMMON CARD (1-30)	1.00	.45	.12
☐ 1 George Giles	1.00	.45	.12
☐ 2 Bill Cash	1.00	.45	.12
☐ 3 Bob Harvey	1.00	.45	.12
☐ 4 Lyman Bostock Sr.	1.50	.70	.19
☐ 5 Ray Dandridge	2.50	1.10	.30
☐ 6 Leon Day	2.50	1.10	.30
☐ 7 Verdell Mathis	1.00	.45	.12
☐ 8 Jimmie Crutchfield	1.50	.70	.19
☐ 9 Clyde McNeal	1.00	.45	.12
☐ 10 Bill Wright	1.00	.45	.12
☐ 11 Mahlon Duckett	1.00	.45	.12
☐ 12 William (Bobby) Robinson	1.50	.70	.19
☐ 13 Max Manning	1.00	.45	.12
☐ 14 Armando Vasquez	1.00	.45	.12
☐ 15 Jehosie Heard	1.50	.70	.19
☐ 16 Quincy Trouppe	1.00	.45	.12
☐ 17 Wilmer Fields	1.00	.45	.12
☐ 18 Lonnie Blair	1.00	.45	.12
☐ 19 Garnett Blair	1.00	.45	.12
☐ 20 Monte Irvin	3.00	1.35	.35
☐ 21 Willie Mays	6.00	2.70	.75
☐ 22 Walter (Buck) Leonard	3.50	1.55	.45
☐ 23 Frank Evans	1.00	.45	.12
☐ 24 Josh Gibson Jr.	2.00	.90	.25
☐ 25 Ted Radcliffe (Double Duty)	1.50	.70	.19
☐ 26 Josh Johnson	1.50	.70	.19
☐ 27 Gene Benson	1.00	.45	.12
☐ 28 Lester Lockett	1.50	.70	.19
☐ 29 Cowan Hyde	1.00	.45	.12
☐ 30 Rufus Lewis	1.00	.45	.12
☐ NNO Checklist	1.00	.45	.12

1995 Negro League Legends II

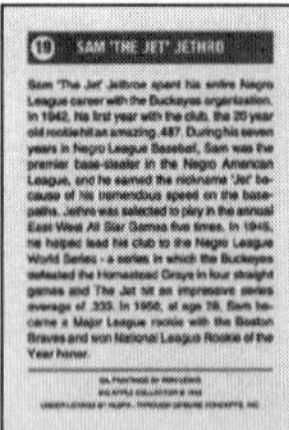

This boxed set measures the standard size and was produced by the Negro League Baseball Players Association and noted sports artist Ron Lewis. Series I and II were both issued in one box. Just 25,000 sets were produced. The white-bordered fronts feature full color player paintings by Ron Lewis. The backs carry the player's name in white letters inside a pink bar and summarize the player's career.

	MINT	NRMT	EXC
COMPLETE SET (33)	30.00	13.50	3.70
COMMON CARD (1-32)	1.00	.45	.12
☐ 1 Willie Mays Ernie Banks Hank Aaron	5.00	2.20	.60
☐ 2 Lester Lockett Lyman Bostock Sr. Bill Wright	1.00	.45	.12
☐ 3 Josh Gibson Josh Gibson Jr. Walter (Buck) Leonard	3.00	1.35	.35
☐ 4 Max Manning Monte Irvin Leon Day	2.00	.90	.25
☐ 5 Armando Vazquez Minnie Minoso Martin Dihigo	1.50	.70	.19
☐ 6 Ted Radcliffe (Double Duty)	1.50	.70	.19
☐ 7 William (Bobby) Robinson Bill Owens Norman(Turkey) Stearnes	1.00	.45	.12
☐ 8 Wilmer Fields Edsall Walker Josh Johnson	1.00	.45	.12
☐ 9 Artie Wilson Lionel Hampton	1.50	.70	.19
☐ 10 Earl Taborn	1.00	.45	.12
☐ 11 Barney Serrell (Bonnie)	1.00	.45	.12
☐ 12 Rodolfo Fernandez (Rudy)	1.00	.45	.12
☐ 13 Willie Pope	1.00	.45	.12
☐ 14 Ray Noble	1.50	.70	.19
☐ 15 Jim Cohen	1.00	.45	.12
☐ 16 Henry Kimbro	1.00	.45	.12
☐ 17 Charlie Biot	1.00	.45	.12
☐ 18 Al Wilmore	1.00	.45	.12
☐ 19 Sam Jethroe	2.00	.90	.25
☐ 20 Tommy Sampson	1.00	.45	.12
☐ 21 Charlie Rivera	1.00	.45	.12
☐ 22 Claro Duany	1.00	.45	.12
☐ 23 Russell Awkard	1.00	.45	.12
☐ 24 Art Pennington	1.00	.45	.12
☐ 25 Wilmer Harris	1.00	.45	.12
☐ 26 Napoleon Gulley	1.00	.45	.12
☐ 27 Emilio Navarro	1.00	.45	.12
☐ 28 Andy Porter	1.00	.45	.12
☐ 29 Willie Grace	1.00	.45	.12
☐ 30 Red Moore	1.00	.45	.12
☐ 31 Buck O'Neill UER (Card back says Walter "Buck" O'Niel)	3.00	1.35	.35
☐ 32 Stanley Glenn	1.00	.45	.12
☐ NNO Checklist UER (Says last name of #31 is Leonard should be O'Neill)	1.00	.45	.12

1996 Negro League Baseball Museum Kansas City

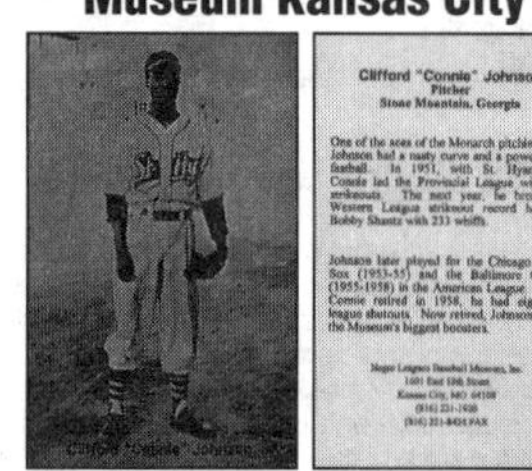

This nine-card set measures approximately 3 1/2" by 5 1/2" and features black-and-white player photos. The backs carry career information. The cards are unnumbered and checklisted below in alphabetical order.

	MINT	NRMT	EXC
COMPLETE SET (9)	10.00	4.50	1.25
COMMON CARD (1-9)	1.00	.45	.12
☐ 1 Ulysses Hollimon	1.00	.45	.12
☐ 2 Herman"Doc" Horn Jr.	1.00	.45	.12
☐ 3 Clifford"Connie" Johnson	2.00	.90	.25
☐ 4 James"Lefty" LaMarque	1.00	.45	.12
☐ 5 Henry"Pistol" Mason	1.50	.70	.19
☐ 6 Bob Motley UMP	1.00	.45	.12
☐ 7 John"Buck" O'Neil	3.00	1.35	.35
☐ 8 Jesse Rogers	1.00	.45	.12
☐ 9 Alfred"Slick" Surratt	1.00	.45	.12

1921 Neilson's V61

The 1921 Neilson's Chocolate set, titled "Big League Baseball Stars", contains 120 cards and is essentially a reproduction of the E120 set. The cards measure approximately 2" by 3 1/4". The fronts feature oval-shaped black-and-white player photos with ornamented borders. The player's name, position and team also appear on the front. The backs give information about this set and carry an ad for Neilson's chocolate. There are two versions of this set: a numbered paper issue and an unnumbered cardboard issue. Cards of the unnumbered cardboard issue are worth approximately 50 percent more than the values listed in the checklist below.

	EX-MT	VG-E	GOOD
COMPLETE SET (120)	8500.00	3800.00	1050.00
COMMON CARD (1-120)	35.00	16.00	4.40
☐ 1 George Burns	50.00	22.00	6.25
☐ 2 John Tobin	35.00	16.00	4.40
☐ 3 Tom Zachary	50.00	22.00	6.25
☐ 4 Joe Bush	50.00	22.00	6.25
☐ 5 Lu Blue	35.00	16.00	4.40
☐ 6 Tillie Walker	35.00	16.00	4.40
☐ 7 Carl Mays	50.00	22.00	6.25
☐ 8 Goose Goslin	100.00	45.00	12.50
☐ 9 Ed Rommel	50.00	22.00	6.25
☐ 10 Charles Robertson	35.00	16.00	4.40
☐ 11 Ralph Perkins	35.00	16.00	4.40
☐ 12 Joe Sewell	75.00	34.00	9.50
☐ 13 Harry Hooper	75.00	34.00	9.50
☐ 14 Red Faber	75.00	34.00	9.50
☐ 15 Bibb Falk	35.00	16.00	4.40
☐ 16 George Uhle	50.00	22.00	6.25
☐ 17 Emory Rigney	35.00	16.00	4.40
☐ 18 George Dauss	35.00	16.00	4.40
☐ 19 Herman Pillette	35.00	16.00	4.40
☐ 20 Wally Schang	50.00	22.00	6.25
☐ 21 Lawrence Woodall	35.00	16.00	4.40
☐ 22 Steve O'Neill	50.00	22.00	6.25
☐ 23 Bing Miller	35.00	16.00	4.40
☐ 24 Sylvester Johnson	35.00	16.00	4.40
☐ 25 Henry Severeid	35.00	16.00	4.40
☐ 26 Dave Danforth	35.00	16.00	4.40
☐ 27 Harry Heilmann	75.00	34.00	9.50
☐ 28 Bert Cole	35.00	16.00	4.40
☐ 29 Eddie Collins	100.00	45.00	12.50
☐ 30 Ty Cobb	1200.00	550.00	150.00
☐ 31 Bill Wambsganss	50.00	22.00	6.25
☐ 32 George Sisler	100.00	45.00	12.50
☐ 33 Bob Veach	35.00	16.00	4.40
☐ 34 Earl Sheely	35.00	16.00	4.40
☐ 35 Pat Collins	35.00	16.00	4.40
☐ 36 Frank Davis	35.00	16.00	4.40
☐ 37 Babe Ruth	1800.00	800.00	220.00
☐ 38 Bryan Harris	35.00	16.00	4.40
☐ 39 Bob Shawkey	50.00	22.00	6.25
☐ 40 Urban Shocker	50.00	22.00	6.25
☐ 41 Martin McManus	35.00	16.00	4.40
☐ 42 Clark Pittenger	35.00	16.00	4.40
☐ 43 Sam Jones	50.00	22.00	6.25
☐ 44 Waite Hoyt	100.00	45.00	12.50
☐ 45 Johnny Mostil	35.00	16.00	4.40
☐ 46 Mike Menosky	35.00	16.00	4.40
☐ 47 Walter Johnson	350.00	160.00	45.00
☐ 48 Wally Pipp	50.00	22.00	6.25
☐ 49 Walter Gerber	35.00	16.00	4.40
☐ 50 Ed Gharrity	35.00	16.00	4.40
☐ 51 Frank Ellerbe	35.00	16.00	4.40
☐ 52 Kenneth Williams	50.00	22.00	6.25
☐ 53 Joe Hauser	35.00	16.00	4.40
☐ 54 Carson Bigbee	35.00	16.00	4.40
☐ 55 Irish Meusel	35.00	16.00	4.40
☐ 56 Milton Stock	35.00	16.00	4.40
☐ 57 Wilbur Cooper	50.00	22.00	6.25
☐ 58 Tom Griffith	35.00	16.00	4.40
☐ 59 Butch Henline	35.00	16.00	4.40
☐ 60 Bubbles Hargrave	35.00	16.00	4.40
☐ 61 Russel Wrightstone	35.00	16.00	4.40
☐ 62 Frankie Frisch	100.00	45.00	12.50
☐ 63 Jack Peters	35.00	16.00	4.40
☐ 64 Walter Ruether	50.00	22.00	6.25
☐ 65 Bill Doak	35.00	16.00	4.40
☐ 66 Marty Callaghan	35.00	16.00	4.40
☐ 67 Sammy Bohne	35.00	16.00	4.40
☐ 68 Earl Hamilton	35.00	16.00	4.40
☐ 69 Grover Alexander	150.00	70.00	19.00
☐ 70 George Burns	35.00	16.00	4.40
☐ 71 Max Carey	75.00	34.00	9.50
☐ 72 Adolph Luque	50.00	22.00	6.25
☐ 73 Dave Bancroft	75.00	34.00	9.50
☐ 74 Vic Aldridge	35.00	16.00	4.40
☐ 75 Jack Smith	35.00	16.00	4.40
☐ 76 Bob O'Farrell	35.00	16.00	4.40
☐ 77 Pete Donohue	35.00	16.00	4.40
☐ 78 Babe Pinelli	35.00	16.00	4.40
☐ 79 Ed Roush	75.00	34.00	9.50
☐ 80 Norman Boeckel	35.00	16.00	4.40
☐ 81 Rogers Hornsby	250.00	110.00	31.00
☐ 82 George Toporcer	35.00	16.00	4.40
☐ 83 Ivy Wingo	35.00	16.00	4.40
☐ 84 Virgil Cheeves	35.00	16.00	4.40
☐ 85 Vern Clemons	35.00	16.00	4.40
☐ 86 Lawrence Miller	35.00	16.00	4.40
☐ 87 Johnny Kelleher	35.00	16.00	4.40
☐ 88 Heinie Groh	50.00	22.00	6.25
☐ 89 Burleigh Grimes	75.00	34.00	9.50
☐ 90 Rabbit Maranville	75.00	34.00	9.50
☐ 91 Babe Adams	50.00	22.00	6.25
☐ 92 Lee King	35.00	16.00	4.40
☐ 93 Art Nehf	50.00	22.00	6.25
☐ 94 Frank Snyder	35.00	16.00	4.40
☐ 95 Raymond Powell	35.00	16.00	4.40
☐ 96 Wilbur Hubbell	35.00	16.00	4.40
☐ 97 Leon Cadore	35.00	16.00	4.40
☐ 98 Joe Oeschger	35.00	16.00	4.40
☐ 99 Jake Daubert	35.00	16.00	4.40
☐ 100 Will Sherdel	35.00	16.00	4.40
☐ 101 Hank DeBerry	35.00	16.00	4.40
☐ 102 Johnny Lavan	35.00	16.00	4.40
☐ 103 Jesse Haines	35.00	16.00	4.40
☐ 104 Joe Rapp	35.00	16.00	4.40
☐ 105 Oscar Ray Grimes	35.00	16.00	4.40

☐ 106 Ross Youngs	75.00	34.00	9.50
☐ 107 Art Fletcher	35.00	16.00	4.40
☐ 108 Clyde Barnhart	35.00	16.00	4.40
☐ 109 Pat Duncan	35.00	16.00	4.40
☐ 110 Charlie Hollocher	35.00	16.00	4.40
☐ 111 Horace Ford	35.00	16.00	4.40
☐ 112 Bill Cunningham	35.00	16.00	4.40
☐ 113 Walter Schmidt	35.00	16.00	4.40
☐ 114 Joe Schultz	35.00	16.00	4.40
☐ 115 John Morrison	35.00	16.00	4.40
☐ 116 Jimmy Caveney	35.00	16.00	4.40
☐ 117 Zach Wheat	75.00	34.00	9.50
☐ 118 Cy Williams	50.00	22.00	6.25
☐ 119 George Kelly	75.00	34.00	9.50
☐ 120 Jimmy Ring	35.00	16.00	4.40

1984 Nestle 792

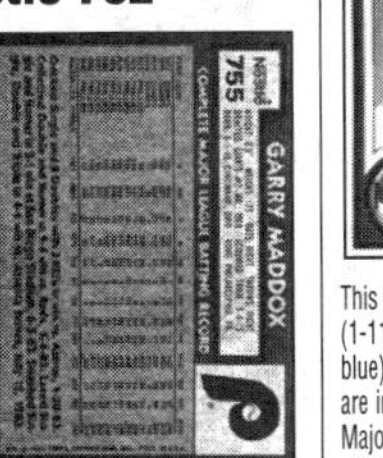

The cards in this 792-card standard-size set are extremely similar to the 1984 Topps regular issue (except for the Nestle logo instead of Topps logo on the front). In conjunction with Topps, the Nestle Company issued this set as six sheets available as a premium. The set was (as detailed on the back of the checklist card for the Nestle Dream Team cards) originally available from the Nestle Company in full sheets of 132 cards, 24" by 48", for 4.95 plus five Nestle candy wrappers per sheet. The backs are virtually identical to the Topps cards of this year, i.e., same player-number correspondence. These sheets have been cut up into individual cards and are available from a few dealers around the country. This is one of the few instances in this hobby where the complete uncut sheet is worth considerably less than the sum of the individual cards due to the expense required in having the sheet cut professionally (and precisely) into individual cards. Supposedly less than 5000 sets were printed. Since the checklist is exactly the same as that of the 1984 Topps, these Nestle cards are generally priced as a multiple of the corresponding Topps card. Individual Nestle cards are priced at up to eight times the corresponding 1984 Topps price. Please see multiplication tables below. Beware also on this set to look for fakes and forgeries. Cards billed as Nestle proofs in black and white are fakes; there are even a few counterfeits in color.

	NRMT	VG-E	GOOD
COMPLETE CUT SET (792)	425.00	190.00	52.50
COMMON CARD (1-792)	.25	.11	.03
*STARS:4X to 8X BASIC CARDS			
*ROOKIES: 3X to 6X BASIC CARDS			

1984 Nestle Dream Team

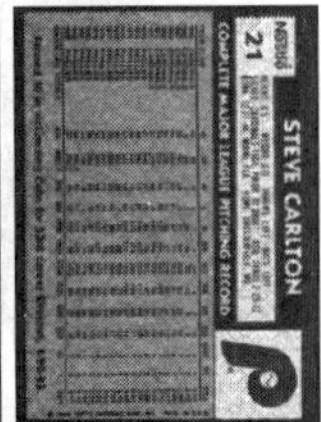

The cards in this 22-card set measure the standard size. In conjunction with Topps, the Nestle Company issued this set entitled the Dream Team. The fronts have the Nestle trademark in the upper frameline, and the backs are identical to the Topps cards of this year except for the number and the Nestle's logo. Cards 1-11 feature stars of the American League while cards 12-22 show National League stars. Each league's "Dream Team" consists of eight position players and three pitchers. The cards were included with the Nestle chocolate bars as a pack of four (three player cards and a checklist header card. This set should not be confused with the Nestle 792-card (same player-number correspondence as 1984 Topps 792) set.

	NRMT	VG-E	GOOD
COMPLETE SET (22)	25.00	11.00	3.10
COMMON CARD (1-22)	.25	.11	.03
☐ 1 Eddie Murray	2.00	.90	.25
☐ 2 Lou Whitaker	.75	.35	.09
☐ 3 George Brett	4.00	1.80	.50
☐ 4 Cal Ripken	8.00	3.60	1.00
☐ 5 Jim Rice	.75	.35	.09
☐ 6 Dave Winfield	1.00	.45	.12
☐ 7 Lloyd Moseby	.25	.11	.03
☐ 8 Lance Parrish	.50	.23	.06
☐ 9 LaMarr Hoyt	.25	.11	.03
☐ 10 Ron Guidry	.50	.23	.06
☐ 11 Dan Quisenberry	.25	.11	.03
☐ 12 Steve Garvey	.50	.23	.06
☐ 13 Johnny Ray	.25	.11	.03
☐ 14 Mike Schmidt	3.00	1.35	.35
☐ 15 Ozzie Smith	3.00	1.35	.35
☐ 16 Andre Dawson	.75	.35	.09
☐ 17 Tim Raines	.75	.35	.09
☐ 18 Dale Murphy	1.00	.45	.12
☐ 19 Tony Pena	.25	.11	.03
☐ 20 John Denny	.25	.11	.03
☐ 21 Steve Carlton	1.25	.55	.16
☐ 22 Al Holland	.25	.11	.03
☐ NNO Checklist	.25	.11	.03

1987 Nestle Dream Team

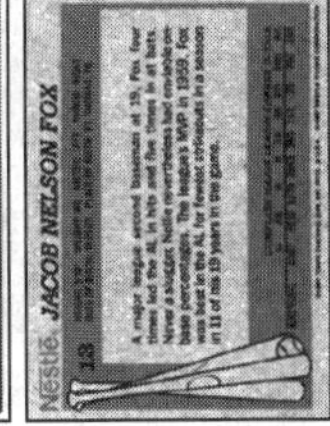

This 33-card standard-size set is, in a sense, three sets: Golden Era (1-11 gold), AL Modern Era (12-22 red), and NL Modern Era (23-33 blue). Cards have color coded borders by era. The first 11 card photos are in black and white. The Nestle set was apparently not licensed by Major League Baseball and hence the team logos are not shown in the photos. Six-packs of certain Nestle candy bars contained three cards; cards were also available through a send-in offer.

	MINT	NRMT	EXC
COMPLETE SET (33)	15.00	6.75	1.85
COMMON CARD (1-33)	.25	.11	.03
☐ 1 Lou Gehrig	1.50	.70	.19
☐ 2 Rogers Hornsby	.25	.11	.03
☐ 3 Pie Traynor	.25	.11	.03
☐ 4 Honus Wagner	1.00	.45	.12
☐ 5 Babe Ruth	2.00	.90	.25
☐ 6 Tris Speaker	.25	.11	.03
☐ 7 Ty Cobb	2.00	.90	.25
☐ 8 Mickey Cochrane	.25	.11	.03
☐ 9 Walter Johnson	1.00	.45	.12
☐ 10 Carl Hubbell	.25	.11	.03
☐ 11 Jimmy Foxx	.50	.23	.06
☐ 12 Rod Carew	.50	.23	.06
☐ 13 Nellie Fox	.25	.11	.03
☐ 14 Brooks Robinson	.50	.23	.06
☐ 15 Luis Aparicio	.25	.11	.03
☐ 16 Frank Robinson	.25	.11	.03
☐ 17 Mickey Mantle	2.50	1.10	.30
☐ 18 Ted Williams	2.00	.90	.25
☐ 19 Yogi Berra	1.00	.45	.12
☐ 20 Bob Feller	.50	.23	.06
☐ 21 Whitey Ford	.50	.23	.06
☐ 22 Harmon Killebrew	.25	.11	.03
☐ 23 Stan Musial	1.50	.70	.19
☐ 24 Jackie Robinson	2.00	.90	.25
☐ 25 Eddie Mathews	.25	.11	.03
☐ 26 Ernie Banks	.50	.23	.06
☐ 27 Roberto Clemente	2.00	.90	.25
☐ 28 Willie Mays	2.00	.90	.25
☐ 29 Hank Aaron	2.00	.90	.25
☐ 30 Johnny Bench	.50	.23	.06
☐ 31 Bob Gibson	.50	.23	.06
☐ 32 Warren Spahn	.25	.11	.03
☐ 33 Duke Snider	1.00	.45	.12
☐ NNO Checklist	.25	.11	.03

1988 Nestle

This 44-card standard-size set has yellow borders. This set was produced for Nestle by Mike Schechter Associates and was printed in Canada. The Nestle set was apparently not licensed by Major League Baseball and hence the team logos are not shown in the photos. The backs are printed in red and blue on white card stock.

	MINT	NRMT	EXC
COMPLETE SET (44)	25.00	11.00	3.10
COMMON CARD (1-44)	.25	.11	.03
☐ 1 Roger Clemens	2.00	.90	.25
☐ 2 Dale Murphy	.75	.35	.09
☐ 3 Eric Davis	.50	.23	.06
☐ 4 Gary Gaetti	.25	.11	.03
☐ 5 Ozzie Smith	2.50	1.10	.30
☐ 6 Mike Schmidt	2.00	.90	.25
☐ 7 Ozzie Guillen	.50	.23	.06
☐ 8 John Franco	.50	.23	.06
☐ 9 Andre Dawson	1.25	.55	.16
☐ 10 Mark McGwire	4.00	1.80	.50
☐ 11 Bret Saberhagen	.50	.23	.06
☐ 12 Benito Santiago	.25	.11	.03
☐ 13 Jose Uribe	.25	.11	.03
☐ 14 Will Clark	1.25	.55	.16
☐ 15 Don Mattingly	3.00	1.35	.35
☐ 16 Juan Samuel	.25	.11	.03
☐ 17 Jack Clark	.25	.11	.03
☐ 18 Darryl Strawberry	.50	.23	.06
☐ 19 Bill Doran	.25	.11	.03
☐ 20 Pete Incaviglia	.25	.11	.03
☐ 21 Dwight Gooden	.50	.23	.06
☐ 22 Willie Randolph	.25	.11	.03
☐ 23 Tim Wallach	.25	.11	.03
☐ 24 Pedro Guerrero	.25	.11	.03
☐ 25 Steve Bedrosian	.25	.11	.03
☐ 26 Gary Carter	.50	.23	.06
☐ 27 Jeff Reardon	.25	.11	.03
☐ 28 Dave Righetti	.25	.11	.03
☐ 29 Frank White	.50	.23	.06
☐ 30 Buddy Bell	.25	.11	.03
☐ 31 Tim Raines	.50	.23	.06
☐ 32 Wade Boggs	.75	.35	.09
☐ 33 Dave Winfield	1.25	.55	.16
☐ 34 George Bell	.25	.11	.03
☐ 35 Alan Trammell	.50	.23	.06
☐ 36 Joe Carter	1.25	.55	.16
☐ 37 Jose Canseco	1.25	.55	.16
☐ 38 Carlton Fisk	1.25	.55	.16
☐ 39 Kirby Puckett	3.00	1.35	.35
☐ 40 Tony Gwynn	3.00	1.35	.35
☐ 41 Matt Nokes	.25	.11	.03
☐ 42 Keith Hernandez	.50	.23	.06
☐ 43 Nolan Ryan	5.00	2.20	.60
☐ 44 Wally Joyner	.75	.35	.09

1993 Nestle Quik Bunnies

This Nestle Quik set consists of one player card and 23 bunny cards in which the bunny is portrayed in cartoons participating in various sports activities. The card measures approximately 3 13/16" by 7 5/8" and have rounded corners. The Walker card has a color player action cutout superposed over a starry sky with Walker standing over the red maple leaf of the Canadian flag. The Nestle Quik logo appears at the upper left on a yellow diagonal section. A circular headshot of Walker and the bunny at the lower left overlays a brown diagonal section showing the card number. The horizontal back has bilingual major league highlights followed by stats. The left side carries bilingual instructions on how to order a Collector Cards Binder. The cards are numbered on the front and back.

	MINT	NRMT	EXC
COMPLETE SET (24)	6.00	2.70	.75
COMMON CARD (1)	2.00	.90	.25
COMMON BUNNY (2-24)	.25	.11	.03
☐ 1 Larry Walker	2.00	.90	.25

1954 New York Journal American

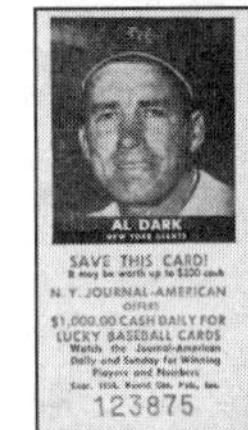

The cards in this 59-card set measure approximately 2" by 4". The 1954 New York Journal American set contains black and white, unnumbered cards issued in conjunction with the newspaper. News stands were given boxes of cards to be distributed with purchases and each card had a serial number for redemption in the contest. The set spotlights New York teams only and carries game schedules on the reverse. The cards have been assigned numbers in the listing below alphabetically within team so that Brooklyn Dodgers are 1-19, New York Giants are 20-39, and New York Yankees are 40-59. There is speculation that a 20th Dodger card may exist. The catalog designation for this set is M127.

	NRMT	VG-E	GOOD
COMPLETE SET (59)	2000.00	900.00	250.00
COMMON CARD (1-59)	12.00	5.50	1.50
☐ 1 Joe Black	20.00	9.00	2.50
☐ 2 Roy Campanella	125.00	55.00	15.50
☐ 3 Billy Cox	12.00	5.50	1.50
☐ 4 Carl Erskine	18.00	8.00	2.20
☐ 5 Carl Furillo	20.00	9.00	2.50
☐ 6 Junior Gilliam	20.00	9.00	2.50
☐ 7 Gil Hodges	60.00	27.00	7.50
☐ 8 Jim Hughes	12.00	5.50	1.50
☐ 9 Clem Labine	15.00	6.75	1.85
☐ 10 Billy Loes	12.00	5.50	1.50
☐ 11 Russ Meyer	15.00	6.75	1.85
☐ 12 Don Newcombe	20.00	9.00	2.50
☐ 13 Ervin Palica	12.00	5.50	1.50
☐ 14 Pee Wee Reese	75.00	34.00	9.50
☐ 15 Jackie Robinson	200.00	90.00	25.00
☐ 16 Preacher Roe	20.00	9.00	2.50
☐ 17 George Shuba	12.00	5.50	1.50
☐ 18 Duke Snider	125.00	55.00	15.50
☐ 19 Dick Williams	15.00	6.75	1.85
☐ 20 John Antonelli	15.00	6.75	1.85
☐ 21 Alvin Dark	14.00	6.25	1.75
☐ 22 Marv Grissom	12.00	5.50	1.50
☐ 23 Ruben Gomez	12.00	5.50	1.50
☐ 24 Jim Hearn	12.00	5.50	1.50
☐ 25 Bobby Hofman	12.00	5.50	1.50
☐ 26 Monte Irvin	40.00	18.00	5.00
☐ 27 Larry Jansen	15.00	6.75	1.85
☐ 28 Ray Katt	12.00	5.50	1.50
☐ 29 Don Liddle	12.00	5.50	1.50
☐ 30 Whitey Lockman	15.00	6.75	1.85
☐ 31 Sal Maglie	20.00	9.00	2.50
☐ 32 Willie Mays	250.00	110.00	31.00
☐ 33 Don Mueller	15.00	6.75	1.85
☐ 34 Dusty Rhodes	12.00	5.50	1.50
☐ 35 Hank Thompson	12.00	5.50	1.50
☐ 36 Wes Westrum	12.00	5.50	1.50
☐ 37 Hoyt Wilhelm	40.00	18.00	5.00
☐ 38 Davey Williams	12.00	5.50	1.50
☐ 39 Al Worthington	12.00	5.50	1.50
☐ 40 Hank Bauer	20.00	9.00	2.50
☐ 41 Yogi Berra	125.00	55.00	15.50
☐ 42 Harry Byrd	12.00	5.50	1.50
☐ 43 Andy Carey	12.00	5.50	1.50
☐ 44 Jerry Coleman	15.00	6.75	1.85
☐ 45 Joe Collins	12.00	5.50	1.50
☐ 46 Whitey Ford	75.00	34.00	9.50
☐ 47 Steve Kraly	12.00	5.50	1.50
☐ 48 Bob Kuzava	12.00	5.50	1.50
☐ 49 Frank Leja	12.00	5.50	1.50
☐ 50 Ed Lopat	18.00	8.00	2.20
☐ 51 Mickey Mantle	500.00	220.00	60.00
☐ 52 Gil McDougald	20.00	9.00	2.50
☐ 53 Bill Miller	12.00	5.50	1.50
☐ 54 Tom Morgan	12.00	5.50	1.50
☐ 55 Irv Noren	12.00	5.50	1.50
☐ 56 Allie Reynolds	18.00	8.00	2.20
☐ 57 Phil Rizzuto	60.00	27.00	7.50
☐ 58 Eddie Robinson	12.00	5.50	1.50
☐ 59 Gene Woodling	15.00	6.75	1.85

1973 New York News M138

This 22-card set features color caricatures that measure 11 1/4" X 14 3/4". The complete page featuring both players measures 22.5" by 29.5". These are printed on newsprint and are unnumbered. Cards feature Mets and Yankees players. Two cards (One Yankee and one Met) were issued every Sunday from 6/17/73 through 8/26/73 in Cartoon section centerfold. Each pair of players played the same position.

	NRMT	VG-E	GOOD
COMPLETE SET (22)	175.00	80.00	22.00
COMMON CARD (1-22)	5.00	2.20	.60
☐ 1 Yogi Berra MG	12.50	5.50	1.55
☐ 2 Ralph Houk MG	7.50	3.40	.95
☐ 3 Tom Seaver	15.00	6.75	1.85
☐ 4 Mel Stottlemyre	5.00	2.20	.60
☐ 5 Ron Blomberg	5.00	2.20	.60
☐ 6 John Milner	5.00	2.20	.60
☐ 7 Horace Clarke	5.00	2.20	.60
☐ 8 Felix Millan	5.00	2.20	.60
☐ 9 Bud Harrelson	5.00	2.20	.60
☐ 10 Gene Michael	5.00	2.20	.60
☐ 11 Jim Fregosi	7.50	3.40	.95
☐ 12 Graig Nettles	7.50	3.40	.95
☐ 13 Jerry Grote	7.50	3.40	.95
☐ 14 Thurman Munson	15.00	6.75	1.85
☐ 15 Cleon Jones	5.00	2.20	.60
☐ 16 Roy White	7.50	3.40	.95
☐ 17 Willie Mays	20.00	9.00	2.50
☐ 18 Bobby Murcer	10.00	4.50	1.25

☐ 19 Matty Alou	7.50	3.40	.95
☐ 20 Rusty Staub	10.00	4.50	1.25
☐ 21 Sparky Lyle	7.50	3.40	.95
☐ 22 Tug McGraw	7.50	3.40	.95

1974 New York News This Day in Sports

These cards are newspaper clippings of drawings by Hollreiser and are accompanied by textual description highlighting a player's unique sports feat. Cards are approximately 2" X 4 1/4". These are multisport cards and aranged in chronological order.

	NRMT	VG-E	GOOD
COMPLETE SET (40)	125.00	55.00	15.50
COMMON CARD (1-40)	2.00	.90	.25
☐ 1 Johnny Bench Yogi Berra June 2, 1972; 1951	4.00	1.80	.50
☐ 2 Byron Nelson Ben Hogan June 12, 1939	4.00	1.80	.50
☐ 3 Ted Williams June 13, 1957	5.00	2.20	.60
☐ 4 Johnny Miller June 17, 1973	2.00	.90	.25
☐ 5 Ezzard Charles Sandy Koufax June 22, 1949; 1959	3.50	1.55	.45
☐ 6 Bobby Murcer June 24, 1970	2.00	.90	.25
☐ 7 Gil Hodges Ralph Kiner June 25, 1949; 1950	3.50	1.55	.45
☐ 8 Jim Ryun June 26, 1965	2.00	.90	.25
☐ 9 Dizzy Dean July 1, 1934	2.50	1.10	.30
☐ 10 Billie Jean King Carl Hubbell July 2, 1966; 1933	2.50	1.10	.30
☐ 11 Yogi Berra July 3, 1957	3.50	1.55	.45
☐ 12 Arky Vaughan Ted Williams July 8, 1941	3.50	1.55	.45
☐ 13 Tom Seaver July 9, 1969; 1970	4.00	1.80	.50
☐ 14 Willie Stargell July 11, 1973	2.50	1.10	.30
☐ 15 Nolan Ryan July 15, 1973	10.00	4.50	1.25
☐ 16 Peter Revson July 25, 1971	2.00	.90	.25
☐ 17 Casey Stengel July 26, 1916; 1955	3.50	1.55	.45
☐ 18 Mickey Mantle Whitey Ford July 29, 1966; 1955	10.00	4.50	1.25
☐ 19 Robin Roberts Aug. 19, 1955	2.50	1.10	.30
☐ 20 Lou Gehrig Aug. 21, 1935; 1937	5.00	2.20	.60
☐ 21 Warren Spahn Roy Face Aug. 30. 1960; 1959	2.50	1.10	.30
☐ 22 George Sisler Pete Rose Sept. 4, 1920; 1973	3.50	1.55	.45
☐ 23 Sal Maglie Tommy Henrich Sept. 9, 1950; 1941	2.00	.90	.25
☐ 24 Hank Aaron Sept. 21, 1958	5.00	2.20	.60
☐ 25 Doc Blanchard Glenn Davis Sept. 30, 1944	3.50	1.55	.45
☐ 26 Dick Sisler Oct. 1, 1950	2.00	.90	.25
☐ 27 Archie Manning Oct. 4, 1969	3.50	1.55	.45
☐ 28 Pepper Martin Yogi Berra Oct. 7, 1931; 1961	3.50	1.55	.45
☐ 29 Dizzy Dean Daffy Dean Oct. 9, 1934	2.50	1.10	.30
☐ 30 Walter Johnson Oct. 11, 1925	2.50	1.10	.30
☐ 31 Harold Jackson Oct. 14, 1973	2.00	.90	.25
☐ 32 O.J. Simpson Oct. 21, 1967	5.00	2.20	.60
☐ 33 Doc Blanchard Nov. 11, 1944	2.50	1.10	.30
☐ 34 Bobby Orr Nov. 15, 1973	4.00	1.80	.50
☐ 35 Bronko Nagurski Nov. 23, 1929	2.50	1.10	.30
☐ 36 Wilt Chamberlain Dec. 6, 1963	4.00	1.80	.50
☐ 37 New York Giants Dec. 9, 1934	2.00	.90	.25
☐ 38 John Brodie Dec. 20, 1970	2.00	.90	.25
☐ 39 Roger Staubach Dec. 23, 1972	4.00	1.80	.50
☐ 40 Paul Brown Otto Graham Dec. 26, 1954	2.50	1.10	.30

1895 Newsboy N566

Newsboy Cut Plug was a tobacco brand by the National Tobacco Works of New York. The cabinet cards associated with this brand were offered as premiums in exchange for coupons or tags found in or on the packages. They were believed to have been issued around 1895. Although a number 841 has been seen, this series-which also contains actresses-has never been completely checklisted, and its exact length is not known. At this time, only 12 baseball players have been discovered. We have checklisted only the baseball players and priced them.

	EX-MT	VG-E	GOOD
COMPLETE SET (12)	6500.00	2900.00	800.00
COMMON CARD	500.00	220.00	60.00
☐ 175 Amos Rusie	1000.00	450.00	125.00
☐ 176 Michael Tiernan	500.00	220.00	60.00
☐ 177 E.D. Burke	500.00	220.00	60.00
☐ 178 J.J. Doyle	500.00	220.00	60.00
☐ 179 W.B. Fuller	500.00	220.00	60.00
☐ 180 George van Haltren	500.00	220.00	60.00
☐ 181 Dave Foutz	500.00	220.00	60.00
☐ 182 Jouett Meekin	600.00	275.00	75.00
☐ 201 W.H. (Dad) Clark (street clothes)	600.00	275.00	75.00
☐ 202 Parke Wilson (street clothes)	500.00	220.00	60.00
☐ 586 John M. Ward portrait arms folded	850.00	375.00	105.00
☐ 587 John M. Ward standing full length	850.00	375.00	105.00

1992 NewSport

This set of 30 glossy player photos was sponsored by NewSport and issued in France. The month when each card was issued is printed as a tagline on the card back. The set was also available in uncut strips. The cards measure approximately 4" by 6" and display glossy color player photos with white borders. The player's name and position appear in the top border, while the NewSport and MLB logos adorn the bottom of the card face. In French, the backs present biography, complete statistics, and career summary. The cards are unnumbered and checklisted below in alphabetical order.

	MINT	NRMT	EXC
COMPLETE SET (30)	175.00	80.00	22.00
COMMON CARD (1-30)	2.50	1.10	.30
☐ 1 Roberto Alomar	10.00	4.50	1.25
☐ 2 Wade Boggs	6.00	2.70	.75
☐ 3 George Brett	15.00	6.75	1.85
☐ 4 Will Clark	7.50	3.40	.95
☐ 5 Eric Davis	2.50	1.10	.30
☐ 6 Rob Dibble	2.50	1.10	.30
☐ 7 Doug Drabek	2.50	1.10	.30
☐ 8 Julio Franco	2.50	1.10	.30
☐ 9 Ken Griffey Jr.	40.00	18.00	5.00
☐ 10 Rickey Henderson	7.50	3.40	.95
☐ 11 Kent Hrbek	2.50	1.10	.30
☐ 12 Bo Jackson	5.00	2.20	.60
☐ 13 Howard Johnson	2.50	1.10	.30
☐ 14 Barry Larkin	7.50	3.40	.95
☐ 15 Don Mattingly	20.00	9.00	2.50
☐ 16 Fred McGriff	7.50	3.40	.95
☐ 17 Mark McGwire	12.00	5.50	1.50
☐ 18 Jack Morris	2.50	1.10	.30
☐ 19 Lloyd Moseby	2.50	1.10	.30
☐ 20 Terry Pendleton	2.50	1.10	.30
☐ 21 Cal Ripken	30.00	13.50	3.70
☐ 22 Nolan Ryan	30.00	13.50	3.70
☐ 23 Bret Saberhagen	2.50	1.10	.30
☐ 24 Ryne Sandberg	12.00	5.50	1.50
☐ 25 Benito Santiago	2.50	1.10	.30
☐ 26 Mike Scioscia	2.50	1.10	.30
☐ 27 Ozzie Smith	12.00	5.50	1.50
☐ 28 Darryl Strawberry	5.00	2.20	.60
☐ 29 Andy Van Slyke	2.50	1.10	.30
☐ 30 Frank Viola	2.50	1.10	.30

1990 Nike Mini-Posters

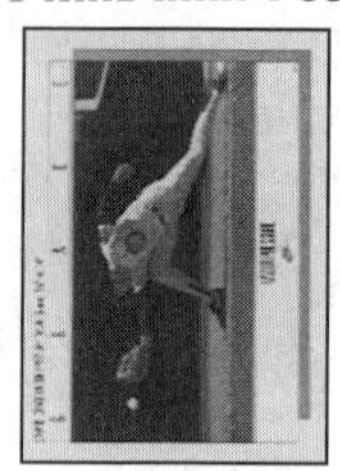

This two-card set features color action player photos and measures approximately 5" by 7". The cards are replicas of large 24" by 36" posters. The backs are blank. The cards are unnumbered and checklisted below in alphabetical order.

	MINT	EXC	G-VG
COMPLETE SET (2)	8.00	3.60	1.00
COMMON CARD (1-2)	3.00	1.35	.35
☐ 1 Mark Grace	3.00	1.35	.35
☐ 2 Kirby Puckett	5.00	2.20	.60

1994 Nintendo Griffey Jr.

This standard-size card was inserted in packages of Nintendo's video game, Ken Griffey Jr. Presents: Major League Baseball. The front features a borderless color photo of Griffey at bat. His name, team name, and position appear in white lettering within purple and blue bars near the top. His facsimile autograph in silver ink appears vertically on the left. The horizontal back features on the left side a rear view of Griffey at bat, and on the right, his 1993 season highlights. His biography and 1993 statistics are shown within a yellow stripe across the bottom. The single card is unnumbered.

	MINT	NRMT	EXC
COMPLETE SET	3.00	1.35	.35
COMMON CARD	3.00	1.35	.35
☐ 1 Ken Griffey Jr.	3.00	1.35	.35

1989 Nissen

The 1989 J.J. Nissen set contains 20 standard-size cards. The fronts have airbrushed facial photos with white and yellow borders and orange trim. The backs are white and feature career stats. The complete set price below does not include the error version of Mark Grace.

	MINT	NRMT	EXC
COMPLETE SET (20)	6.00	2.70	.75
COMMON CARD (1-20)	.10	.05	.01
☐ 1 Wally Joyner	.25	.11	.03
☐ 2 Wade Boggs	.50	.23	.06
☐ 3 Ellis Burks	1.00	.45	.12
☐ 4 Don Mattingly	2.00	.90	.25
☐ 5 Jose Canseco	.50	.23	.06
☐ 6 Mike Greenwell	.10	.05	.01
☐ 7 Eric Davis	.25	.11	.03
☐ 8 Kirby Puckett	2.00	.90	.25
☐ 9 Kevin Seitzer	.10	.05	.01
☐ 10 Darryl Strawberry	.25	.11	.03
☐ 11 Gregg Jefferies	.50	.23	.06
☐ 12A Mark Grace ERR (Photo actually Vance Law)	5.00	2.20	.60
☐ 12B Mark Grace COR	1.00	.45	.12
☐ 13 Matt Nokes	.10	.05	.01
☐ 14 Mark McGwire	2.00	.90	.25
☐ 15 Bobby Bonilla	.50	.23	.06
☐ 16 Roger Clemens	2.00	.90	.25
☐ 17 Frank Viola	.10	.05	.01
☐ 18 Orel Hershiser	.25	.11	.03
☐ 19 David Cone	.50	.23	.06
☐ 20 Ted Williams	2.50	1.10	.30

1996 NoirTech Satchel Paige

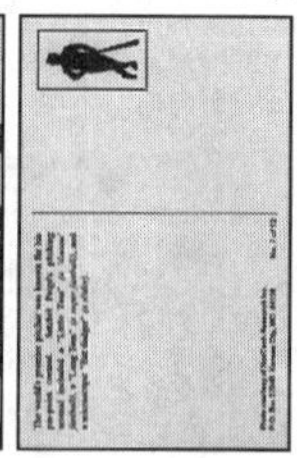

This 12-card set measures approximately 3 1/2" by 5 1/2" and features black-and-white photos of Satchel Paige. The backs carry discriptions of the front pictures in a postcard format.

	MINT	NRMT	EXC
COMPLETE SET (12)	7.50	3.40	.95
COMMON CARD (1-12)	.50	.23	.06
☐ 1 Satchel Paige Josh Gibson Cy Perkins	2.00	.90	.25
☐ 2 Satchel Paige All-Stars	.75	.35	.09
☐ 3 Satchel Paige Dizzy Dean Cecil Travis	1.00	.45	.12
☐ 4 Satchel Paige (Playing guitar)	.50	.23	.06
☐ 5 Satchel Paige (With Cessna airplane)	.50	.23	.06
☐ 6 Satchel Paige (Pitching)	.50	.23	.06
☐ 7 Satchel Paige (Ready to pitch)	.50	.23	.06
☐ 8 Satchel Paige Homespun Philosophies	.50	.23	.06
☐ 9 Satchel Paige (With his catfish catch)	.50	.23	.06
☐ 10 Satchel Paige Billie Holiday	1.50	.70	.19
☐ 11 Satchel Paige	.50	.23	.06
☐ 12 Satchel Paige Vernon Gomez	1.00	.45	.12

1953 Northland Bread Labels

This 32-label set features two players from each major league team and is one of the popular "Bread For Energy" sets. Each bread label measures 2 11/16" by 2 11/16". Although the labels are printed in black and white, the 1953 Northland Bread set includes a "Baseball Stars" album which provides additional information concerning "Baseball Immortals" and "Baseball Tips." These labels are unnumbered so we have checklisted them in alphabetical order. The amended catalog designation is D290-3A.

	NRMT	VG-E	GOOD
COMPLETE SET (32)	2000.00	900.00	250.00
COMMON LABEL (1-32)	50.00	22.00	6.25
☐ 1 Cal Abrams	50.00	22.00	6.25
☐ 2 Richie Ashburn	100.00	45.00	12.50
☐ 3 Gus Bell	60.00	27.00	7.50
☐ 4 Jim Busby	50.00	22.00	6.25
☐ 5 Clint Courtney	50.00	22.00	6.25
☐ 6 Billy Cox	50.00	22.00	6.25
☐ 7 Jim Dyck	50.00	22.00	6.25
☐ 8 Nellie Fox	100.00	45.00	12.50
☐ 9 Sid Gordon	50.00	22.00	6.25
☐ 10 Warren Hacker	50.00	22.00	6.25
☐ 11 Jim Hearn	50.00	22.00	6.25
☐ 12 Fred Hutchinson	60.00	27.00	7.50
☐ 13 Monte Irvin	100.00	45.00	12.50
☐ 14 Jackie Jensen	75.00	34.00	9.50
☐ 15 Ted Kluszewski	75.00	34.00	9.50
☐ 16 Bob Lemon	100.00	45.00	12.50
☐ 17 Mickey McDermott	50.00	22.00	6.25
☐ 18 Minnie Minoso	75.00	34.00	9.50
☐ 19 Johnny Mize	100.00	45.00	12.50
☐ 20 Mel Parnell	50.00	22.00	6.25
☐ 21 Howie Pollet	50.00	22.00	6.25
☐ 22 Jerry Priddy	50.00	22.00	6.25

Card	NRMT	VG-E	GOOD
☐ 23 Allie Reynolds	75.00	34.00	9.50
☐ 24 Preacher Roe	75.00	34.00	9.50
☐ 25 Al Rosen	60.00	27.00	7.50
☐ 26 Connie Ryan	50.00	22.00	6.25
☐ 27 Hank Sauer	50.00	22.00	6.25
☐ 28 Red Schoendienst	100.00	45.00	12.50
☐ 29 Bobby Shantz	60.00	27.00	7.50
☐ 30 Enos Slaughter	100.00	45.00	12.50
☐ 31 Warren Spahn	125.00	55.00	15.50
☐ 32 Gus Zernial	60.00	27.00	7.50

1960 Nu-Card Hi-Lites

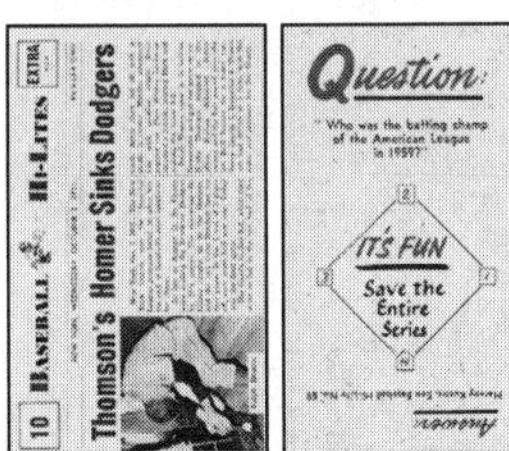

The cards in this 72-card set measure approximately 3 1/4" by 5 3/8". In 1960, the Nu-Card Company introduced its Baseball Hi-Lites set of newspaper style cards. Each card singled out an individual baseball achievement with a picture and story. The reverses contain a baseball quiz. Cards 1-18 are more valuable if found printed totally in black on the front; these are copy-righted CVC as opposed to the NCI designation found on the red and black printed fronts.

Card	NRMT	VG-E	GOOD
COMPLETE SET (72)	450.00	200.00	55.00
COMMON CARD (1-72)	3.00	1.35	.35
☐ 1 Babe Ruth Hits 3 Homers In A Series Game	40.00	18.00	5.00
☐ 2 Johnny Podres Pitching Wins Series	3.00	1.35	.35
☐ 3 Bill Bevans Pitches No-Hitter, Almost	3.00	1.35	.35
☐ 4 Box Score Devised By Reporter	3.00	1.35	.35
☐ 5 Johnny VanderMeer Pitches Two No Hitters	3.00	1.35	.35
☐ 6 Indians Take Bums	3.00	1.35	.35
☐ 7 Joe DiMaggio Comes Thru	40.00	18.00	5.00
☐ 8 Christy Mathewson Pitches Three WS Shutouts	8.00	3.60	1.00
☐ 9 Harvey Haddix Pitches 12 Perfect Innings	3.00	1.35	.35
☐ 10 Bobby Thomson Homer Sinks Dodgers	12.00	5.50	1.50
☐ 11 Carl Hubbell Strikes Out 5 A.L. Stars	8.00	3.60	1.00
☐ 12 Pickoff Ends Series	3.00	1.35	.35
☐ 13 Cards Take Series From Yanks	3.00	1.35	.35
☐ 14 Dizzy Dean Daffy Dean Win Series	8.00	3.60	1.00
☐ 15 Mickey Owen Drops Third Strike	3.00	1.35	.35
☐ 16 Babe Ruth Calls Shot	40.00	18.00	5.00
☐ 17 Fred Merkle Pulls Boner	5.00	2.20	.60
☐ 18 Don Larsen Hurls Perfect W.S. Game	8.00	3.60	1.00
☐ 19 Mickey Cochrane Bean Ball Ends Career	5.00	2.20	.60
☐ 20 Ernie Banks Belts 47 Homers Earns MVP	15.00	6.75	1.85
☐ 21 Stan Musial Hits 5 Homers in One Day	20.00	9.00	2.50
☐ 22 Mickey Mantle Hits Longest Homer	50.00	22.00	6.25
☐ 23 Roy Sievers Captures Home Run Title	3.00	1.35	.35
☐ 24 Lou Gehrig 2130 Consecutive Game Record Ends	50.00	22.00	6.25
☐ 25 Red Schoendienst Key Player Braves Pennant	5.00	2.20	.60
☐ 26 Eddie Gaedel Midget Pinch-Hits For St. Louis	5.00	2.20	.60
☐ 27 Willie Mays Makes Greatest Catch	25.00	11.00	3.10
☐ 28 Yogi Berra Homer Puts Yanks In 1st	15.00	6.75	1.85
☐ 29 Roy Campanella NL MVP	15.00	6.75	1.85
☐ 30 Bob Turley Hurls Yankees To WS Champions	3.00	1.35	.35
☐ 31 Dodgers Take Series From Sox in Six	3.00	1.35	.35
☐ 32 Carl Furillo Hero as Dodgers Beat Chicago in 3rd WS Game	3.00	1.35	.35
☐ 33 Joe Adcock Gets 4 Homers And A Double	3.00	1.35	.35
☐ 34 Bill Dickey Chosen All-Star Catcher	5.00	2.20	.60
☐ 35 Lew Burdette Beats Yanks In Three World Series Games	3.00	1.35	.35
☐ 36 Umpires Clear White Sox Bench	3.00	1.35	.35
☐ 37 PeeWee Reese Honored As Greatest Dodger SS	12.00	5.50	1.50
☐ 38 Joe DiMaggio Hits In 56 Straight	40.00	18.00	5.00
☐ 39 Ted Williams Hits .406 For Season	35.00	16.00	4.40
☐ 40 Walter Johnson Pitches 56 Straight	10.00	4.50	1.25
☐ 41 Gil Hodges Hits 4 Home Runs In Nite Game	5.00	2.20	.60
☐ 42 Hank Greenberg Returns to Tigers From Army	8.00	3.60	1.00
☐ 43 Ty Cobb Named Best Player Of All Time	25.00	11.00	3.10
☐ 44 Robin Roberts Wins 28 Games	5.00	2.20	.60
☐ 45 Phil Rizzuto Two Runs Save 1st Place	10.00	4.50	1.25
☐ 46 Tigers Beat Out Senators For Pennant	3.00	1.35	.35
☐ 47 Babe Ruth Hits 60th Home Run	40.00	18.00	5.00
☐ 48 Cy Young Honored	5.00	2.20	.60
☐ 49 Harmon Killebrew Starts Spring Training	12.00	5.50	1.50
☐ 50 Mickey Mantle Hits Longest Homer at Stadium	50.00	22.00	6.25
☐ 51 Braves Take Pennant	3.00	1.35	.35
☐ 52 Ted Williams Hero Of All-Star Game	35.00	16.00	4.40
☐ 53 Jackie Robinson Saves Dodgers For Play-off Series	35.00	16.00	4.40
☐ 54 Fred Snodgrass Muffs Fly	3.00	1.35	.35
☐ 55 Duke Snider Belts 2 Homers, Ties Record	15.00	6.75	1.85
☐ 56 Giants Win 26 Straight	3.00	1.35	.35
☐ 57 Ted Kluszewski Stars In 1st Series Win	5.00	2.20	.60
☐ 58 Mel Ott Walks 5 Times In Single Game	5.00	2.20	.60
☐ 59 Harvey Kuenn Takes A.L. Batting Title	3.00	1.35	.35
☐ 60 Bob Feller Hurls 3rd No-Hitter of Career	10.00	4.50	1.25
☐ 61 Yankees Champs Again	3.00	1.35	.35
☐ 62 Hank Aaron Bat Beats Yankees In Series	20.00	9.00	2.50
☐ 63 Warren Spahn Beats Yanks in W.S.	10.00	4.50	1.25
☐ 64 Ump's Wrong Call Helps Dodgers Beat Yanks	3.00	1.35	.35
☐ 65 Al Kaline Hits 3 Homers Two In Same Inning	12.00	5.50	1.50
☐ 66 Bob Allison Named AL ROY	3.00	1.35	.35
☐ 67 Willie McCovey Blasts Way Into Giant Lineup	10.00	4.50	1.25
☐ 68 Rocky Colavito Hits 4 Homers in One Game	15.00	6.75	1.85
☐ 69 Carl Erskine Sets Strike Out Record in World Series	3.00	1.35	.35
☐ 70 Sal Maglie Pitches No-Hit Game	3.00	1.35	.35
☐ 71 Early Wynn Victory Crushes Yanks	5.00	2.20	.60
☐ 72 Nellie Fox AL MVP	15.00	6.75	1.85

1961 Nu-Card Scoops

The cards in this 80-card set measure 2 1/2" by 3 1/2". This series depicts great moments in the history of individual ballplayers. Each card is designed as a miniature newspaper front-page, complete with data and picture. Both the number (401-480) and title are printed in red on the obverse, and the story is found on the back. An album was issued to hold the set. The set has been illegally reprinted, which has served to suppress the demand for the originals as well as the reprints.

Card	NRMT	VG-E	GOOD
COMPLETE SET (80)	250.00	110.00	31.00
COMMON CARD (401-480)	.75	.35	.09
☐ 401 Jim Gentile	1.00	.45	.12
☐ 402 Warren Spahn (No-hitter)	3.00	1.35	.35
☐ 403 Bill Mazeroski	1.50	.70	.19
☐ 404 Willie Mays: (Three triples)	12.50	5.50	1.55
☐ 405 Woodie Held	.75	.35	.09
☐ 406 Vern Law	1.00	.45	.12
☐ 407 Pete Runnels	.75	.35	.09
☐ 408 Lew Burdette (No-hitter)	1.00	.45	.12
☐ 409 Dick Stuart	.75	.35	.09
☐ 410 Don Cardwell	.75	.35	.09
☐ 411 Camilo Pascual	.75	.35	.09
☐ 412 Ed Mathews	3.00	1.35	.35
☐ 413 Dick Groat	1.00	.45	.12
☐ 414 Gene Autry OWN	5.00	2.20	.60
☐ 415 Bobby Richardson	2.00	.90	.25
☐ 416 Roger Maris	7.50	3.40	.95
☐ 417 Fred Merkle	.75	.35	.09
☐ 418 Don Larsen	1.00	.45	.12
☐ 419 Mickey Cochrane	1.50	.70	.19
☐ 420 Ernie Banks	4.00	1.80	.50
☐ 421 Stan Musial	10.00	4.50	1.25
☐ 422 Mickey Mantle (Longest homer)	30.00	13.50	3.70
☐ 423 Roy Sievers	.75	.35	.09
☐ 424 Lou Gehrig	15.00	6.75	1.85
☐ 425 Red Schoendienst	2.00	.90	.25
☐ 426 Eddie Gaedel	3.00	1.35	.35
☐ 427 Willie Mays (Greatest catch)	15.00	6.75	1.85
☐ 428 Jackie Robinson	15.00	6.75	1.85
☐ 429 Roy Campanella	7.50	3.40	.95
☐ 430 Bob Turley	.75	.35	.09
☐ 431 Larry Sherry	.75	.35	.09
☐ 432 Carl Furillo	1.00	.45	.12
☐ 433 Joe Adcock	.75	.35	.09
☐ 434 Bill Dickey	1.50	.70	.19
☐ 435 Lew Burdette 3 wins	.75	.35	.09
☐ 436 Umpire Clears Bench	.75	.35	.09
☐ 437 Pee Wee Reese	3.00	1.35	.35
☐ 438 Joe DiMaggio (56 Game Hit Streak)	15.00	6.75	1.85
☐ 439 Ted Williams (Hits .406)	15.00	6.75	1.85
☐ 440 Walter Johnson	3.00	1.35	.35
☐ 441 Gil Hodges	2.00	.90	.25
☐ 442 Hank Greenberg	3.00	1.35	.35
☐ 443 Ty Cobb	12.50	5.50	1.55
☐ 444 Robin Roberts	3.00	1.35	.35
☐ 445 Phil Rizzuto	3.00	1.35	.35
☐ 446 Hal Newhouser	3.00	1.35	.35
☐ 447 Babe Ruth 60th Homer	30.00	13.50	3.70
☐ 448 Cy Young	3.00	1.35	.35
☐ 449 Harmon Killebrew	3.00	1.35	.35
☐ 450 Mickey Mantle (Longest homer)	30.00	13.50	3.70
☐ 451 Braves Take Pennant	.75	.35	.09
☐ 452 Ted Williams (All-Star Hero)	15.00	6.75	1.85
☐ 453 Yogi Berra	7.50	3.40	.95
☐ 454 Fred Snodgrass	.75	.35	.09
☐ 455 Babe Ruth 3 Homers	25.00	11.00	3.10
☐ 456 Giants 26 Game Streak	.75	.35	.09
☐ 457 Ted Kluszewski	1.50	.70	.19
☐ 458 Mel Ott	2.00	.90	.25
☐ 459 Harvey Kuenn	1.00	.45	.12
☐ 460 Bob Feller	4.00	1.80	.50
☐ 461 Casey Stengel	3.00	1.35	.35
☐ 462 Hank Aaron	12.50	5.50	1.55
☐ 463 Spahn Beats Yanks	2.50	1.10	.30
☐ 464 Ump's Wrong Call	.75	.35	.09
☐ 465 Al Kaline	4.00	1.80	.50
☐ 466 Bob Allison	.75	.35	.09
☐ 467 Joe DiMaggio (Four Homers)	15.00	6.75	1.85
☐ 468 Rocky Colavito	3.00	1.35	.35
☐ 469 Carl Erskine	1.00	.45	.12
☐ 470 Sal Maglie	1.00	.45	.12
☐ 471 Early Wynn	2.00	.90	.25
☐ 472 Nellie Fox	2.50	1.10	.30
☐ 473 Marty Marion	1.00	.45	.12
☐ 474 Johnny Podres	1.00	.45	.12
☐ 475 Mickey Owen	.75	.35	.09
☐ 476 Dean Brothers (Dizzy and Daffy)	2.50	1.10	.30
☐ 477 Christy Mathewson	3.00	1.35	.35
☐ 478 Harvey Haddix	.75	.35	.09
☐ 479 Carl Hubbell	1.50	.70	.19
☐ 480 Bobby Thomson	1.50	.70	.19

1983 O'Connell and Son Baseball Greats

This 20-card set features drawings of major league players in circles on color backgrounds and measures approximately 4 3/4" by 6 1/4". The player's name is printed on the front as is the player's team logo. The backs are blank. The cards are unnumbered and checklisted below in alphabetical order.

Card	NRMT	VG-E	GOOD
COMPLETE SET (20)	25.00	11.00	3.10
COMMON CARD (1-20)	.25	.11	.03
☐ 1 Hank Aaron	3.00	1.35	.35
☐ 2 Johnny Bench	1.00	.45	.12
☐ 3 Yogi Berra	1.50	.70	.19
☐ 4 George Brett	2.50	1.10	.30
☐ 5 Roy Campanella	1.00	.45	.12
☐ 6 Rod Carew	1.00	.45	.12
☐ 7 Roberto Clemente	4.00	1.80	.50
☐ 8 Bob Gibson	1.00	.45	.12
☐ 9 Al Kaline	1.00	.45	.12
☐ 10 Mickey Mantle	5.00	2.20	.60
☐ 11 Joe Morgan	.50	.23	.06
☐ 12 Stan Musial	2.00	.90	.25
☐ 13 Jim Rice	.50	.23	.06
☐ 14 Frank Robinson	1.50	.70	.19
☐ 15 Pete Rose	2.00	.90	.25
☐ 16 Tom Seaver	1.00	.45	.12
☐ 17 Duke Snider	1.50	.70	.19
☐ 18 Honus Wagner	1.50	.70	.19
☐ 19 Carl Yastrzemski	1.00	.45	.12
☐ 20 Robin Yount	.25	.11	.03

1984-89 O'Connell and Son Ink

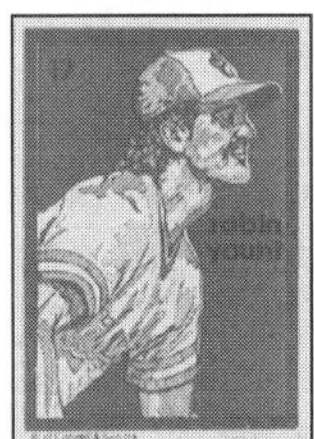

This comprises the O'Connell and Son Ink Mini-Prints. The first series set (1-36) was released at the 1984 National Convention. With the inception of The Infield Dirt in 1991, an underground hobby publication, the cards have been included free with each issue. The December 1992 issue of The Infield Dirt, issued by the producers of this set, offered the entire set for $34.95. The cards feature pen and ink or pencil drawings of major league players on color backgrounds. The player's name is printed on the front as is the card number.

Card	NRMT	VG-E	GOOD
COMPLETE SET (250)	50.00	22.00	6.25
COMMON CARD (1-250)	.10	.05	.01
☐ 1 Ted Williams	2.00	.90	.25
☐ 2 Minnie Minoso	.30	.14	.04
☐ 3 Sandy Koufax	1.00	.45	.12
☐ 4 Al Kaline	.50	.23	.06
☐ 5 Whitey Ford	.50	.23	.06
☐ 6 Wade Boggs	.50	.23	.06
☐ 7 Nolan Ryan	2.00	.90	.25
☐ 8 Greg Luzinski	.10	.05	.01
☐ 9 Cal Ripken	2.00	.90	.25
☐ 10 Carl Yastrzemski	.50	.23	.06
☐ 11 Dale Murphy	.50	.23	.06
☐ 12 Rocky Colavito	.50	.23	.06
☐ 13 George Brett	1.50	.70	.19
☐ 14 Willie McCovey	.50	.23	.06
☐ 15 Rod Carew	.50	.23	.06
☐ 16 Bob Gibson	.50	.23	.06
☐ 17 Robin Yount	.50	.23	.06
☐ 18 Steve Carlton	.50	.23	.06
☐ 19 Harmon Killebrew	.50	.23	.06
☐ 20 Willie Mays	2.00	.90	.25
☐ 21 Reggie Jackson	1.00	.45	.12
☐ 22 Eddie Mathews	.50	.23	.06
☐ 23 Eddie Murray	1.00	.45	.12
☐ 24 Johnny Bench	1.00	.45	.12
☐ 25 Mickey Mantle	2.50	1.10	.30
☐ 26 Willie Stargell	.50	.23	.06
☐ 27 Rickey Henderson	.50	.23	.06
☐ 28 Roger Maris	1.00	.45	.12

Card			
☐ 29 Darryl Strawberry	.10	.05	.01
☐ 30 Pete Rose	1.00	.45	.12
☐ 31 Jim Rice	.20	.09	.03
☐ 32 Thurman Munson	.30	.14	.04
☐ 33 Brooks Robinson	.50	.23	.06
☐ 34 Fernando Valenzuela	.20	.09	.03
☐ 35 Tony Oliva	.30	.14	.04
☐ 36 Henry Aaron	2.00	.90	.25
☐ 37 Joe Morgan	.50	.23	.06
☐ 38 Kent Hrbek	.20	.09	.03
☐ 39 Yogi Berra	.50	.23	.06
☐ 40 Stan Musial	1.50	.70	.19
☐ 41 Gary Matthews	.10	.05	.01
☐ 42 Larry Doby	.20	.09	.03
☐ 43 Steve Garvey	.20	.09	.03
☐ 44 Bob Horner	.10	.05	.01
☐ 45 Ron Guidry	.20	.09	.03
☐ 46 Ernie Banks	.50	.23	.06
☐ 47 Carlton Fisk	.50	.23	.06
☐ 48 Pee Wee Reese	.50	.23	.06
☐ 49 Bobby Shantz	.10	.05	.01
☐ 50 Joe DiMaggio	2.00	.90	.25
☐ 51 Enos Slaughter	.30	.14	.04
☐ 52 Gary Carter	.20	.09	.03
☐ 53 Bob Feller	.50	.23	.06
☐ 54 Phil Rizzuto	.50	.23	.06
☐ 55 Dave Concepcion	.20	.09	.03
☐ 56 Ron Kittle	.10	.05	.01
☐ 57 Dwight Evans	.20	.09	.03
☐ 58 Johnny Mize	.30	.14	.04
☐ 59 Richie Ashburn	.50	.23	.06
☐ 60 Roberto Clemente	2.00	.90	.25
☐ 61 Fred Lynn	.20	.09	.03
☐ 62 Billy Williams	.30	.14	.04
☐ 63 Dave Winfield	.50	.23	.06
☐ 64 Robin Roberts	.30	.14	.04
☐ 65 Billy Martin	.30	.14	.04
☐ 66 Duke Snider	.50	.23	.06
☐ 67 Luis Aparicio	.30	.14	.04
☐ 68 Mickey Vernon	.20	.09	.03
☐ 69 Mike Schmidt	.75	.35	.09
☐ 70 Frank Robinson	.50	.23	.06
☐ 71 Bill Madlock	.10	.05	.01
☐ 72 Rollie Fingers	.30	.14	.04
☐ 73 Rod Carew	.50	.23	.06
☐ 74 Carl Erskine	.10	.05	.01
☐ 75 Lou Brock	.50	.23	.06
☐ 76 Brooks Robinson	.50	.23	.06
☐ 77 Roberto Clemente	2.00	.90	.25
☐ 78 Nellie Fox	.30	.14	.04
☐ 79 Bud Harrelson	.10	.05	.01
☐ 80 Ted Williams	2.00	.90	.25
☐ 81 Walter Johnson	1.00	.45	.12
☐ 82 Cal Ripken	2.00	.90	.25
☐ 83 Lefty Grove	.50	.23	.06
☐ 84 Lou Whitaker	.20	.09	.03
☐ 85 Johnny Bench	1.00	.45	.12
☐ 86 Ty Cobb	2.00	.90	.25
☐ 87 Mike Schmidt	1.00	.45	.12
☐ 88 George Brett	1.50	.70	.19
☐ 89 Jim Bunning	.30	.14	.04
☐ 90 Babe Ruth	2.50	1.10	.30
☐ 91 Satchel Paige	.75	.35	.09
☐ 92 Warren Spahn	.30	.14	.04
☐ 93 Dale Murphy	.30	.14	.04
☐ 94 Early Wynn	.30	.14	.04
☐ 95 Reggie Jackson	1.00	.45	.12
☐ 96 Charlie Gehringer	.30	.14	.04
☐ 97 Jackie Robinson	2.00	.90	.25
☐ 98 Lou Gehrig	2.00	.90	.25
☐ 99 Hank Aaron	2.00	.90	.25
☐ 100 Mickey Mantle	2.50	1.10	.30
☐ 101 Sandy Koufax	1.00	.45	.12
☐ 102 Ryne Sandberg	.75	.35	.09
☐ 103 Don Mattingly	.75	.35	.09
☐ 104 Darryl Strawberry	.10	.05	.01
☐ 105 Tom Seaver	.50	.23	.06
☐ 106 Bil Klem	.20	.09	.03
☐ 107 Dwight Gooden	.20	.09	.03
☐ 108 Pete Rose	1.00	.45	.12
☐ 109 Elston Howard	.20	.09	.03
☐ 110 Honus Wagner	.50	.23	.06
☐ 111 Waite Hoyt	.30	.14	.04
☐ 112 Billy Bruton	.10	.05	.01
☐ 113 Gil Hodges	.50	.23	.06
☐ 114 Vic Power	.10	.05	.01
☐ 115 Al Kaline	.50	.23	.06
☐ 116 Al Lopez	.20	.09	.03
☐ 117 Rocky Bridges	.10	.05	.01
☐ 118 Junior Gilliam	.20	.09	.03
☐ 119 Christy Mathewson	.50	.23	.06
☐ 120 Hank Greenberg	.50	.23	.06
☐ 121 Eddie Mathews	.50	.23	.06
☐ 122 Van Lingle Mungo	.10	.05	.01
☐ 123 Harry "Suitcase" Simpson	.10	.05	.01
☐ 124 Carl Yastrzemski	.50	.23	.06
☐ 125 Pete Rose	1.00	.45	.12
☐ 126 Dizzy Dean	.50	.23	.06
☐ 127 Chi Chi Olivo	.10	.05	.01
☐ 128 Johnny Vander Meer	.10	.05	.01
☐ 129 Roberto Clemente	2.00	.90	.25
☐ 130 Carl Hubbell	.30	.14	.04
☐ 131 Willie Mays	2.00	.90	.25
☐ 132 Willie Stargell	.50	.23	.06
☐ 133 Sam Jethroe	.10	.05	.01
☐ 134 Pete Rose	1.00	.45	.12
☐ 135 Jackie Robinson	2.00	.90	.25
☐ 136 Yogi Berra	.50	.23	.06
☐ 137 Grover Alexander	.50	.23	.06
☐ 138 Joe Morgan	.30	.14	.04
☐ 139 Rube Foster	.30	.14	.04
☐ 140 Mickey Mantle	2.50	1.10	.30
☐ 141 Ted Williams	2.00	.90	.25
☐ 142 Jimmy Foxx	.50	.23	.06
☐ 143 Pepper Martin	.20	.09	.03
☐ 144 Henry Aaron	2.00	.90	.25
☐ 145 Vida Blue	.10	.05	.01
☐ 146 Carl Furillo	.20	.09	.03
☐ 147 Lloyd Waner	.30	.14	.04
☐ 148 Eddie Dyer	.10	.05	.01
☐ 149 Casey Stengel	.50	.23	.06
☐ 150 Mickey Mantle	2.50	1.10	.30
☐ 151 Gil Hodges	.50	.23	.06
☐ 152 Don Mossi	.10	.05	.01
☐ 153 Ron Swoboda	.10	.05	.01
☐ 154 Hoyt Wilhelm	.30	.14	.04
☐ 155 Ed Roush	.30	.14	.04
☐ 156 Mickey Lolich	.20	.09	.03
☐ 157 Jim Palmer	.10	.05	.01
☐ 158 Thurman Munson	.30	.14	.04
☐ 159 Don Zimmer	.10	.05	.01
☐ 160 Henry Aaron	2.00	.90	.25
☐ 161 Johnny Bench	.50	.23	.06
☐ 162 Orlando Cepeda	.30	.14	.04
☐ 163 Honus Wagner	.50	.23	.06
☐ 164 Tom Seaver	.50	.23	.06
☐ 165 Willie Mays	2.00	.90	.25
☐ 166 Elmer Riddle	.10	.05	.01
☐ 167 Tony Oliva	.20	.09	.03
☐ 168 Elmer Flick	.20	.09	.03
☐ 169 Curt Flood	.20	.09	.03
☐ 170 Carl Yastrzemski	.50	.23	.06
☐ 171 Charlie Keller	.20	.09	.03
☐ 172 Christy Mathewson	.50	.23	.06
☐ 173 Eddie Plank	.30	.14	.04
☐ 174 Lou Gehrig	2.00	.90	.25
☐ 175 John McGraw	.30	.14	.04
☐ 176 Mule Haas	.10	.05	.01
☐ 177 Paul Waner	.30	.14	.04
☐ 178 Steve Blass	.10	.05	.01
☐ 179 Honus Wagner	.50	.23	.06
☐ 180 Jack Barry	.10	.05	.01
☐ 181 Rocky Colavito	.50	.23	.06
☐ 182 Danny Murtaugh	.10	.05	.01
☐ 183 John Edwards	.10	.05	.01
☐ 184 Pete Rose	1.00	.45	.12
☐ 185 Roy Campanella	.50	.23	.06
☐ 186 Jerry Grote	.10	.05	.01
☐ 187 Leo Durocher	.30	.14	.04
☐ 188 Rollie Fingers	.30	.14	.04
☐ 189 Wes Parker	.10	.05	.01
☐ 190 Joe Rudi	.10	.05	.01
☐ 191 Bill Veeck	.20	.09	.03
☐ 192 Mark Fidrych	.30	.14	.04
☐ 193 George Foster	.20	.09	.03
☐ 194 Early Wynn	.30	.14	.04
☐ 195 Frank Howard	.20	.09	.03
☐ 196 Graig Nettles	.20	.09	.03
☐ 197 Juan Pizarro	.10	.05	.01
☐ 198 Jose Cruz	.10	.05	.01
☐ 199 Joe Jackson	2.00	.90	.25
☐ 200 Stan Musial	1.50	.70	.19
☐ 201 Chuck Klein	.30	.14	.04
☐ 202 Ryne Sandberg	.50	.23	.06
☐ 203 Richie Allen	.30	.14	.04
☐ 204 Bo Jackson	.10	.05	.01
☐ 205 Kevin Mitchell	.10	.05	.01
☐ 206 Al Smith Early Wynn Larry Doby	.20	.09	.03
☐ 207 Mickey Mantle	2.50	1.10	.30
☐ 208 Will Clark	.30	.14	.04
☐ 209 Cecil Fielder	.20	.09	.03
☐ 210 Bobby Richardson	.20	.09	.03
☐ 211 Nolan Ryan	2.00	.90	.25
☐ 212 Casey Stengel	.50	.23	.06
☐ 213 Ted Kluszewski	.40	.18	.05
☐ 214 Gaylord Perry	.30	.14	.04
☐ 215 Johnny Vander Meer	.10	.05	.01
☐ 216 Willie Mays	2.00	.90	.25
☐ 217 Goose Goslin	.30	.14	.04
☐ 218 Bobby Shantz	.10	.05	.01
☐ 219 Terry Pendleton	.10	.05	.01
☐ 220 Richie Ashburn	.50	.23	.06
☐ 221 Robin Yount	.50	.23	.06
☐ 222 Cal Ripken	2.00	.90	.25
☐ 223 Danny Ainge	.50	.23	.06
☐ 224 Bob Friend	.10	.05	.01
☐ 225 Orel Hershiser	.20	.09	.03
☐ 226 Wade Boggs	.50	.23	.06
☐ 227 Ballpark scene	.10	.05	.01
☐ 228 Stan Musial	1.50	.70	.19
☐ 229 Chris Short	.10	.05	.01
☐ 230 Johnny Bench	.50	.23	.06
☐ 231 Nellie Fox	.50	.23	.06
☐ 232 Ron Santo	.50	.23	.06
☐ 233 Tony Gwynn	1.25	.55	.16
☐ 234 Phil Niekro	.30	.14	.04
☐ 235 Frank Thomas	2.50	1.10	.30
☐ 236 Greg Gross	.10	.05	.01
☐ 237 Ken Griffey Jr.	2.50	1.10	.30
☐ 238 Benito Santiago	.10	.05	.01
☐ 239 Dwight Gooden	.20	.09	.03
☐ 240 Darryl Strawberry	.10	.05	.01
☐ 241 Roy Campanella	.50	.23	.06
☐ 242 Roger Clemens	.50	.23	.06
☐ 243 Kirby Puckett	1.25	.55	.16
☐ 244 Nolan Ryan	2.00	.90	.25
☐ NNO Checklist 1	.10	.05	.01
☐ NNO Checklist 3	.10	.05	.01
☐ NNO Checklist 6	.10	.05	.01
☐ NNO Checklist 5	.10	.05	.01
☐ NNO Checklist 4	.10	.05	.01
☐ NNO Checklist 2	.10	.05	.01

1937 O-Pee-Chee Batter Ups V300

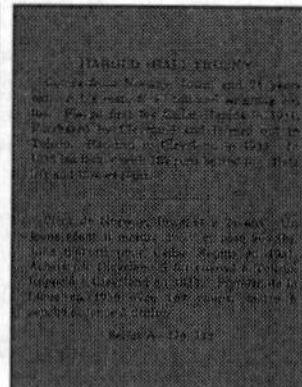

The cards in this 40-card set measure approximately 2 3/8" by 2 7/8". The fronts feature black-and-white die-cut player photos against a ballpark background with small players. The backs carry a short biography and career summary in English and French. The set is peculiar in that card numbering begins with 101. Cards without tops have greatly reduced value. The small ballplayer designs on the obverses are similar to those used on the 1934 American Goudey cards.

	EX-MT	VG-E	GOOD
COMPLETE SET (40)	8500.00	3800.00	1050.00
COMMON CARD (101-140)	60.00	27.00	7.50
☐ 101 John Lewis	60.00	27.00	7.50
☐ 102 Jack Hayes	60.00	27.00	7.50
☐ 103 Earl Averill	125.00	55.00	15.50
☐ 104 Harland Clift	60.00	27.00	7.50
☐ 105 Beau Bell	60.00	27.00	7.50
☐ 106 Jimmie Foxx	350.00	160.00	45.00
☐ 107 Hank Greenberg	275.00	125.00	34.00
☐ 108 George Selkirk	75.00	34.00	9.50
☐ 109 Wally Moses	75.00	34.00	9.50
☐ 110 Gerry Walker	60.00	27.00	7.50
☐ 111 Goose Goslin	125.00	55.00	15.50
☐ 112 Charlie Gehringer	225.00	100.00	28.00
☐ 113 Hal Trosky	60.00	27.00	7.50
☐ 114 Buddy Myer	60.00	27.00	7.50
☐ 115 Luke Appling	125.00	55.00	15.50
☐ 116 Zeke Bonura	60.00	27.00	7.50
☐ 117 Tony Lazzeri	125.00	55.00	15.50
☐ 118 Joe DiMaggio	4500.00	2000.00	550.00
☐ 119 Bill Dickey	275.00	125.00	34.00
☐ 120 Bob Feller	600.00	275.00	75.00
☐ 121 Harry Kelley	60.00	27.00	7.50
☐ 122 Johnny Allen	75.00	34.00	9.50
☐ 123 Bob Johnson	75.00	34.00	9.50
☐ 124 Joe Cronin	150.00	70.00	19.00
☐ 125 Rip Radcliff	60.00	27.00	7.50
☐ 126 Cecil Travis	75.00	34.00	9.50
☐ 127 Joe Kuhel	60.00	27.00	7.50
☐ 128 Odell Hale	60.00	27.00	7.50
☐ 129 Sam West	60.00	27.00	7.50
☐ 130 Ben Chapman	75.00	34.00	9.50
☐ 131 Monte Pearson	60.00	27.00	7.50
☐ 132 Rick Ferrell	125.00	55.00	15.50
☐ 133 Tommy Bridges	75.00	34.00	9.50
☐ 134 Schoolboy Rowe	75.00	34.00	9.50
☐ 135 Vernon Kennedy	60.00	27.00	7.50
☐ 136 Red Ruffing	150.00	70.00	19.00
☐ 137 Lefty Grove	275.00	125.00	34.00
☐ 138 Wes Ferrell	75.00	34.00	9.50
☐ 139 Buck Newsom	75.00	34.00	9.50
☐ 140 Rogers Hornsby	400.00	180.00	50.00

1965 O-Pee-Chee

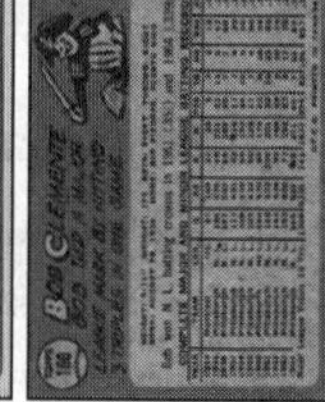

The cards in this 283-card set measure the standard size. This set is essentially the same as the regular 1965 Topps set, except that the words "Printed in Canada" appear on the bottom of the back. On a white border, the fronts feature color player photos with rounded corners. The team name appears within a pennant design below the photo. The player's name and position are also printed on the front. On a blue background, the horizontal backs carry player biography and statistics on a gray card stock. Remember the prices below apply only to the O-Pee- Chee cards -- NOT to the 1965 Topps cards which are much more plentiful.

	NRMT	VG-E	GOOD
COMPLETE SET (283)	2500.00	1100.00	300.00
COMMON CARD (1-198)	4.00	1.80	.50
COMMON CARD (199-283)	6.00	2.70	.75
☐ 1 AL Batting Leaders Tony Oliva Elston Howard Brooks Robinson	25.00	11.00	3.10
☐ 2 NL Batting Leaders Bob Clemente Hank Aaron Rico Carty	25.00	11.00	3.10
☐ 3 AL Home Run Leaders Harmon Killebrew Mickey Mantle Boog Powell	50.00	22.00	6.25
☐ 4 NL Home Run Leaders Willie Mays Billy Williams Jim Ray Hart Orlando Cepeda Johnny Callison	15.00	6.75	1.85
☐ 5 AL RBI Leaders Brooks Robinson Harmon Killebrew Mickey Mantle Dick Stuart	50.00	22.00	6.25
☐ 6 NL RBI Leaders Ken Boyer Willie Mays Ron Santo	10.00	4.50	1.25
☐ 7 AL ERA Leaders Dean Chance Joel Horlen	25.00	11.00	3.10
☐ 8 NL ERA Leaders Sandy Koufax Don Drysdale	18.00	8.00	2.20
☐ 9 AL Pitching Leaders Dean Chance Gary Peters Dave Wickersham Juan Pizarro Wally Bunker	7.50	3.40	.95
☐ 10 NL Pitching Leaders Larry Jackson Ray Sadecki Juan Marichal	7.50	3.40	.95
☐ 11 AL Strikeout Leaders Al Downing Dean Chance Camilo Pascual	7.50	3.40	.95
☐ 12 NL Strikeout Leaders Bob Veale Don Drysdale Bob Gibson	7.50	3.40	.95
☐ 13 Pedro Ramos	4.00	1.80	.50
☐ 14 Len Gabrielson	4.00	1.80	.50
☐ 15 Robin Roberts	10.00	4.50	1.25
☐ 16 Houston Rookies: Joe Morgan Sonny Jackson	75.00	34.00	9.50
☐ 17 John Romano	4.00	1.80	.50
☐ 18 Bill McCool	4.00	1.80	.50
☐ 19 Gates Brown	4.00	1.80	.50
☐ 20 Jim Bunning	10.00	4.50	1.25
☐ 21 Don Blasingame	4.00	1.80	.50
☐ 22 Charlie Smith	4.00	1.80	.50
☐ 23 Bob Tiefenauer	4.00	1.80	.50
☐ 24 Twins Team	7.50	3.40	.95
☐ 25 Al McBean	4.00	1.80	.50
☐ 26 Bob Knoop	4.00	1.80	.50
☐ 27 Dick Bertell	4.00	1.80	.50
☐ 28 Barney Schultz	4.00	1.80	.50
☐ 29 Felix Mantilla	4.00	1.80	.50
☐ 30 Jim Bouton	7.50	3.40	.95
☐ 31 Mike White	4.00	1.80	.50
☐ 32 Herman Franks MG	4.00	1.80	.50
☐ 33 Jackie Brandt	4.00	1.80	.50
☐ 34 Cal Koonce	4.00	1.80	.50
☐ 35 Ed Charles	4.00	1.80	.50
☐ 36 Bob Wine	4.00	1.80	.50
☐ 37 Fred Gladding	4.00	1.80	.50
☐ 38 Jim King	4.00	1.80	.50
☐ 39 Gerry Arrigo	4.00	1.80	.50
☐ 40 Frank Howard	6.00	2.70	.75
☐ 41 White Sox Rookies Bruce Howard Marv Staehle	4.00	1.80	.50
☐ 42 Earl Wilson	4.00	1.80	.50
☐ 43 Mike Shannon	5.00	2.20	.60
☐ 44 Wade Blasingame	4.00	1.80	.50
☐ 45 Roy McMillan	5.00	2.20	.60
☐ 46 Bob Lee	4.00	1.80	.50
☐ 47 Tommy Harper	5.00	2.20	.60
☐ 48 Claude Raymond	5.00	2.20	.60
☐ 49 Orioles Rookies Curt Blefary John Miller	6.00	2.70	.75
☐ 50 Juan Marichal	10.00	4.50	1.25
☐ 51 Bill Bryan	4.00	1.80	.50

☐ 52 Ed Roebuck 4.00 1.80 .50
☐ 53 Dick McAuliffe 5.00 2.20 .60
☐ 54 Joe Gibbon 4.00 1.80 .50
☐ 55 Tony Conigliaro 20.00 9.00 2.50
☐ 56 Ron Kline 4.00 1.80 .50
☐ 57 Cardinals Team 7.50 3.40 .95
☐ 58 Fred Talbot 4.00 1.80 .50
☐ 59 Nate Oliver 4.00 1.80 .50
☐ 60 Jim O'Toole 4.00 1.80 .50
☐ 61 Chris Cannizzaro 4.00 1.80 .50
☐ 62 Jim Kaat UER 7.50 3.40 .95
(Misspelled Katt)
☐ 63 Ty Cline 4.00 1.80 .50
☐ 64 Lou Burdette 5.00 2.20 .60
☐ 65 Tony Kubek 6.00 2.70 .75
☐ 66 Bill Rigney MG 4.00 1.80 .50
☐ 67 Harvey Haddix 5.00 2.20 .60
☐ 68 Del Crandall 5.00 2.20 .60
☐ 69 Bill Virdon 5.00 2.20 .60
☐ 70 Bill Skowron 5.00 2.20 .60
☐ 71 John O'Donoghue 4.00 1.80 .50
☐ 72 Tony Gonzalez 4.00 1.80 .50
☐ 73 Dennis Ribant 4.00 1.80 .50
☐ 74 Red Sox Rookies 15.00 6.75 1.85
Rico Petrocelli
Jerry Stephenson
☐ 75 Deron Johnson 5.00 2.20 .60
☐ 76 Sam McDowell 6.00 2.70 .75
☐ 77 Doug Camilli 4.00 1.80 .50
☐ 78 Dal Maxvill 5.00 2.20 .60
☐ 79 Checklist 1-88 10.00 4.50 1.25
☐ 80 Turk Farrell 4.00 1.80 .50
☐ 81 Don Buford 5.00 2.20 .60
☐ 82 Braves Rookies: 7.50 3.40 .95
Santos Alomar
John Braun
☐ 83 George Thomas 4.00 1.80 .50
☐ 84 Ron Herbel 4.00 1.80 .50
☐ 85 Willie Smith 4.00 1.80 .50
☐ 86 Les Narum 4.00 1.80 .50
☐ 87 Nelson Mathews 4.00 1.80 .50
☐ 88 Jack Lamabe 4.00 1.80 .50
☐ 89 Mike Hershberger 4.00 1.80 .50
☐ 90 Rich Rollins 4.00 1.80 .50
☐ 91 Cubs Team 7.50 3.40 .95
☐ 92 Dick Howser 5.00 2.20 .60
☐ 93 Jack Fisher 4.00 1.80 .50
☐ 94 Charlie Lau 4.00 1.80 .50
☐ 95 Bill Mazeroski 7.50 3.40 .95
☐ 96 Sonny Siebert 5.00 2.20 .60
☐ 97 Pedro Gonzalez 4.00 1.80 .50
☐ 98 Bob Miller 4.00 1.80 .50
☐ 99 Gil Hodges MG 10.00 4.50 1.25
☐ 100 Ken Boyer 6.00 2.70 .75
☐ 101 Fred Newman 4.00 1.80 .50
☐ 102 Steve Boros 4.00 1.80 .50
☐ 103 Harvey Kuenn 5.00 2.20 .60
☐ 104 Checklist 89-176 10.00 4.50 1.25
☐ 105 Chico Salmon 4.00 1.80 .50
☐ 106 Gene Oliver 4.00 1.80 .50
☐ 107 Phillies Rookies: 5.00 2.20 .60
Pat Corrales
Costen Shockley
☐ 108 Don Mincher 4.00 1.80 .50
☐ 109 Walt Bond 4.00 1.80 .50
☐ 110 Ron Santo 7.50 3.40 .95
☐ 111 Lee Thomas 4.00 1.80 .50
☐ 112 Derrell Griffith 4.00 1.80 .50
☐ 113 Steve Barber 4.00 1.80 .50
☐ 114 Jim Hickman 4.00 1.80 .50
☐ 115 Bobby Richardson 7.50 3.40 .95
☐ 116 Cardinals Rookies: 5.00 2.20 .60
Dave Dowling
Bob Tolan
☐ 117 Wes Stock 4.00 1.80 .50
☐ 118 Hal Lanier 4.00 1.80 .50
☐ 119 John Kennedy 4.00 1.80 .50
☐ 120 Frank Robinson 35.00 16.00 4.40
☐ 121 Gene Alley 5.00 2.20 .60
☐ 122 Bill Pleis 4.00 1.80 .50
☐ 123 Frank Thomas 5.00 2.20 .60
☐ 124 Tom Satriano 4.00 1.80 .50
☐ 125 Juan Pizarro 4.00 1.80 .50
☐ 126 Dodgers Team 7.50 3.40 .95
☐ 127 Frank Lary 4.00 1.80 .50
☐ 128 Vic Davalillo 4.00 1.80 .50
☐ 129 Bennie Daniels 4.00 1.80 .50
☐ 130 Al Kaline 35.00 16.00 4.40
☐ 131 Johnny Keane MG 4.00 1.80 .50
☐ 132 Mike Shannon WS 7.50 3.40 .95
☐ 133 Mel Stottlemyre WS 7.50 3.40 .95
☐ 134 Mickey Mantle WS 100.00 45.00 12.50
☐ 135 Ken Boyer WS 7.50 3.40 .95
☐ 136 Tim McCarver WS 7.50 3.40 .95
☐ 137 Jim Bouton WS 7.50 3.40 .95
☐ 138 Bob Gibson WS 15.00 6.75 1.85
☐ 139 World Series Summary 7.50 3.40 .95
Cards celebrate
☐ 140 Dean Chance 5.00 2.20 .60
☐ 141 Charlie James 4.00 1.80 .50
☐ 142 Bill Monbouquette 4.00 1.80 .50
☐ 143 Pirates Rookies 4.00 1.80 .50
John Gelnar
Jerry May
☐ 144 Ed Kranepool 5.00 2.20 .60
☐ 145 Luis Tiant 25.00 11.00 3.10
☐ 146 Ron Hansen 4.00 1.80 .50
☐ 147 Dennis Bennett 4.00 1.80 .50
☐ 148 Willie Kirkland 4.00 1.80 .50
☐ 149 Wayne Schurr 4.00 1.80 .50
☐ 150 Brooks Robinson 40.00 18.00 5.00
☐ 151 Athletics Team 7.50 3.40 .95
☐ 152 Phil Ortega 4.00 1.80 .50
☐ 153 Norm Cash 7.50 3.40 .95
☐ 154 Bob Humphreys 4.00 1.80 .50
☐ 155 Roger Maris 50.00 22.00 6.25
☐ 156 Bob Sadowski 4.00 1.80 .50
☐ 157 Zoilo Versalles 5.00 2.20 .60
☐ 158 Dick Sisler MG 4.00 1.80 .50
☐ 159 Jim Duffalo 4.00 1.80 .50
☐ 160 Roberto Clemente ! 175.00 80.00 22.00
☐ 161 Frank Baumann 4.00 1.80 .50
☐ 162 Russ Nixon 4.00 1.80 .50
☐ 163 John Briggs 4.00 1.80 .50
☐ 164 Al Spangler 4.00 1.80 .50
☐ 165 Dick Ellsworth 4.00 1.80 .50
☐ 166 Indians Rookies 6.00 2.70 .75
George Culver
Tommie Agee
☐ 167 Bill Wakefield 4.00 1.80 .50
☐ 168 Dick Green 5.00 2.20 .60
☐ 169 Dave Vineyard 4.00 1.80 .50
☐ 170 Hank Aaron 125.00 55.00 15.50
☐ 171 Jim Roland 4.00 1.80 .50
☐ 172 Jim Piersall 6.00 2.70 .75
☐ 173 Tigers Team 7.50 3.40 .95
☐ 174 Joe Jay 4.00 1.80 .50
☐ 175 Bob Aspromonte 4.00 1.80 .50
☐ 176 Willie McCovey 20.00 9.00 2.50
☐ 177 Pete Mikkelsen 4.00 1.80 .50
☐ 178 Dalton Jones 4.00 1.80 .50
☐ 179 Hal Woodeschick 4.00 1.80 .50
☐ 180 Bob Allison 4.00 1.80 .50
☐ 181 Senators Rookies 4.00 1.80 .50
Don Loun
Joe McCabe
☐ 182 Mike de la Hoz 4.00 1.80 .50
☐ 183 Dave Nicholson 4.00 1.80 .50
☐ 184 John Boozer 4.00 1.80 .50
☐ 185 Max Alvis 4.00 1.80 .50
☐ 186 Bill Cowan 4.00 1.80 .50
☐ 187 Casey Stengel MG 15.00 6.75 1.85
☐ 188 Sam Bowens 4.00 1.80 .50
☐ 189 Checklist 177-264 10.00 4.50 1.25
☐ 190 Bill White 6.00 2.70 .75
☐ 191 Phil Regan 5.00 2.20 .60
☐ 192 Jim Coker 4.00 1.80 .50
☐ 193 Gaylord Perry 20.00 9.00 2.50
☐ 194 Rookie Stars 5.00 2.20 .60
Bill Kelso
Rick Reichardt
☐ 195 Bob Veale 5.00 2.20 .60
☐ 196 Ron Fairly 5.00 2.20 .60
☐ 197 Diego Segui 4.00 1.80 .50
☐ 198 Smoky Burgess 5.00 2.20 .60
☐ 199 Bob Heffner 6.00 2.70 .75
☐ 200 Joe Torre 10.00 4.50 1.25
☐ 201 Twins Rookies 6.00 2.70 .75
Sandy Valdespino
Cesar Tovar
☐ 202 Leo Burke 6.00 2.70 .75
☐ 203 Dallas Green 6.00 2.70 .75
☐ 204 Russ Snyder 6.00 2.70 .75
☐ 205 Warren Spahn 35.00 16.00 4.40
☐ 206 Willie Horton 10.00 4.50 1.25
☐ 207 Pete Rose 175.00 80.00 22.00
☐ 208 Tommy John 10.00 4.50 1.25
☐ 209 Pirates Team 10.00 4.50 1.25
☐ 210 Jim Fregosi 7.50 3.40 .95
☐ 211 Steve Ridzik 6.00 2.70 .75
☐ 212 Ron Brand 6.00 2.70 .75
☐ 213 Jim Davenport 6.00 2.70 .75
☐ 214 Bob Purkey 6.00 2.70 .75
☐ 215 Pete Ward 6.00 2.70 .75
☐ 216 Al Worthington 6.00 2.70 .75
☐ 217 Walt Alston MG 10.00 4.50 1.25
☐ 218 Dick Schofield 6.00 2.70 .75
☐ 219 Bob Meyer 6.00 2.70 .75
☐ 220 Billy Williams 12.50 5.50 1.55
☐ 221 John Tsitouris 6.00 2.70 .75
☐ 222 Bob Tillman 6.00 2.70 .75
☐ 223 Dan Osinski 6.00 2.70 .75
☐ 224 Bob Chance 6.00 2.70 .75
☐ 225 Bo Belinsky 7.50 3.40 .95
☐ 226 Yankees Rookies 6.00 2.70 .75
Elvio Jimenez
Jake Gibbs
☐ 227 Bobby Klaus 6.00 2.70 .75
☐ 228 Jack Sanford 6.00 2.70 .75
☐ 229 Lou Clinton 6.00 2.70 .75
☐ 230 Ray Sadecki 6.00 2.70 .75
☐ 231 Jerry Adair 6.00 2.70 .75
☐ 232 Steve Blass 6.00 2.70 .75
☐ 233 Don Zimmer 7.50 3.40 .95
☐ 234 White Sox Team 10.00 4.50 1.25
☐ 235 Chuck Hinton 6.00 2.70 .75
☐ 236 Dennis McLain 40.00 18.00 5.00
☐ 237 Bernie Allen 6.00 2.70 .75
☐ 238 Joe Moeller 6.00 2.70 .75
☐ 239 Doc Edwards 6.00 2.70 .75
☐ 240 Bob Bruce 6.00 2.70 .75
☐ 241 Mack Jones 6.00 2.70 .75
☐ 242 George Brunet 6.00 2.70 .75
☐ 243 Reds Rookies 7.50 3.40 .95
Ted Davidson
Tommy Helms
☐ 244 Lindy McDaniel 4.00 1.80 .50
☐ 245 Joe Pepitone 7.50 3.40 .95
☐ 246 Tom Butters 6.00 2.70 .75
☐ 247 Wally Moon 7.50 3.40 .95
☐ 248 Gus Triandos 6.00 2.70 .75
☐ 249 Dave McNally 4.00 1.80 .50
☐ 250 Willie Mays 125.00 55.00 15.50
☐ 251 Billy Herman MG 7.50 3.40 .95
☐ 252 Pete Richert 6.00 2.70 .75
☐ 253 Danny Cater 6.00 2.70 .75
☐ 254 Roland Sheldon 6.00 2.70 .75
☐ 255 Camilo Pascual 7.50 3.40 .95
☐ 256 Tito Francona 6.00 2.70 .75
☐ 257 Jim Wynn 7.50 3.40 .95
☐ 258 Larry Bearnarth 6.00 2.70 .75
☐ 259 Tigers Rookies 10.00 4.50 1.25
Jim Northrup
Ray Oyler
☐ 260 Don Drysdale 25.00 11.00 3.10
☐ 261 Duke Carmel 6.00 2.70 .75
☐ 262 Bud Daley 6.00 2.70 .75
☐ 263 Marty Keough 6.00 2.70 .75
☐ 264 Bob Buhl 6.00 2.70 .75
☐ 265 Jim Pagliaroni 6.00 2.70 .75
☐ 266 Bert Campaneris 10.00 4.50 1.25
☐ 267 Senators Team 10.00 4.50 1.25
☐ 268 Ken McBride 6.00 2.70 .75
☐ 269 Frank Bolling 6.00 2.70 .75
☐ 270 Milt Pappas 4.00 1.80 .50
☐ 271 Don Wert 6.00 2.70 .75
☐ 272 Chuck Schilling 6.00 2.70 .75
☐ 273 4th Series Checklist 12.50 5.50 1.55
☐ 274 Lum Harris MG 6.00 2.70 .75
☐ 275 Dick Groat 7.50 3.40 .95
☐ 276 Hoyt Wilhelm 12.50 5.50 1.55
☐ 277 Johnny Lewis 6.00 2.70 .75
☐ 278 Ken Retzer 6.00 2.70 .75
☐ 279 Dick Tracewski 6.00 2.70 .75
☐ 280 Dick Stuart 7.50 3.40 .95
☐ 281 Bill Stafford 6.00 2.70 .75
☐ 282 Giants Rookies 40.00 18.00 5.00
Dick Estelle
Masanori Murakami
☐ 283 Fred Whitfield 7.50 3.40 .95

1966 O-Pee-Chee

The cards in this 196-card set measure 2 1/2" by 3 1/2". This set is essentially the same as the regular 1966 Topps set, except that the words "Printed in Canada" appear on the bottom of the back, and the background colors are slightly different. On a white border, the fronts feature color player photos. The team name appears within a tilted bar in the top right corner, while the player's name and position are printed inside a bar under the photo. The horizontal backs carry player biography and statistics. Remember the prices below apply only to the O-Pee- Chee cards -- NOT to the 1966 Topps cards which are much more plentiful.

	NRMT	VG-E	GOOD
COMPLETE SET (196)	1500.00	700.00	190.00
COMMON CARD (1-196)	3.00	1.35	.35

☐ 1 Willie Mays 200.00 90.00 25.00
☐ 2 Ted Abernathy 3.00 1.35 .35
☐ 3 Sam Mele MG 3.00 1.35 .35
☐ 4 Ray Culp 3.00 1.35 .35
☐ 5 Jim Fregosi 5.00 2.20 .60
☐ 6 Chuck Schilling 3.00 1.35 .35
☐ 7 Tracy Stallard 3.00 1.35 .35
☐ 8 Floyd Robinson 3.00 1.35 .35
☐ 9 Clete Boyer 5.00 2.20 .60
☐ 10 Tony Cloninger 3.00 1.35 .35
☐ 11 Senators Rookies 3.00 1.35 .35
Brant Alyea
Pete Craig
☐ 12 John Tsitouris 3.00 1.35 .35
☐ 13 Lou Johnson 3.00 1.35 .35
☐ 14 Norm Siebern 3.00 1.35 .35
☐ 15 Vern Law 5.00 2.20 .60
☐ 16 Larry Brown 3.00 1.35 .35
☐ 17 John Stephenson 3.00 1.35 .35
☐ 18 Roland Sheldon 3.00 1.35 .35
☐ 19 Giants Team 6.00 2.70 .75
☐ 20 Willie Horton 5.00 2.20 .60
☐ 21 Don Nottebart 3.00 1.35 .35
☐ 22 Joe Nossek 3.00 1.35 .35
☐ 23 Jack Sanford 3.00 1.35 .35
☐ 24 Don Kessinger 6.00 2.70 .75
☐ 25 Pete Ward 3.00 1.35 .35
☐ 26 Ray Sadecki 3.00 1.35 .35
☐ 27 Orioles Rookies 3.00 1.35 .35
Darold Knowles
Andy Etchebarren
☐ 28 Phil Niekro 25.00 11.00 3.10
☐ 29 Mike Brumley 3.00 1.35 .35
☐ 30 Pete Rose 50.00 22.00 6.25
☐ 31 Jack Cullen 3.00 1.35 .35
☐ 32 Adolfo Phillips 3.00 1.35 .35
☐ 33 Jim Pagliaroni 3.00 1.35 .35
☐ 34 Checklist 1-88 8.00 3.60 1.00
☐ 35 Ron Swoboda 6.00 2.70 .75
☐ 36 Jim Hunter 25.00 11.00 3.10
☐ 37 Billy Herman MG 5.00 2.20 .60
☐ 38 Ron Nischwitz 3.00 1.35 .35
☐ 39 Ken Henderson 3.00 1.35 .35
☐ 40 Jim Grant 3.00 1.35 .35
☐ 41 Don LeJohn 3.00 1.35 .35
☐ 42 Aubrey Gatewood 3.00 1.35 .35
☐ 43 Don Landrum 3.00 1.35 .35
☐ 44 Indians Rookies 3.00 1.35 .35
Bill Davis
Tom Kelley
☐ 45 Jim Gentile 5.00 2.20 .60
☐ 46 Howie Koplitz 3.00 1.35 .35
☐ 47 J.C. Martin 3.00 1.35 .35
☐ 48 Paul Blair 5.00 2.20 .60
☐ 49 Woody Woodward 3.00 1.35 .35
☐ 50 Mickey Mantle 300.00 135.00 38.00
☐ 51 Gordon Richardson 3.00 1.35 .35
☐ 52 Power Plus 6.00 2.70 .75
Wes Covington
Johnny Callison
☐ 53 Bob Duliba 3.00 1.35 .35
☐ 54 Jose Pagan 3.00 1.35 .35
☐ 55 Ken Harrelson 5.00 2.20 .60
☐ 56 Sandy Valdespino 3.00 1.35 .35
☐ 57 Jim Lefebvre 5.00 2.20 .60
☐ 58 Dave Wickersham 3.00 1.35 .35
☐ 59 Reds Team 6.00 2.70 .75
☐ 60 Curt Flood 6.00 2.70 .75
☐ 61 Bob Bolin 3.00 1.35 .35
☐ 62 Merritt Ranew 3.00 1.35 .35
(with sold line)
☐ 63 Jim Stewart 3.00 1.35 .35
☐ 64 Bob Bruce 3.00 1.35 .35
☐ 65 Leon Wagner 3.00 1.35 .35
☐ 66 Al Weis 3.00 1.35 .35
☐ 67 Mets Rookies 5.00 2.20 .60
Cleon Jones
Dick Selma
☐ 68 Hal Reniff 3.00 1.35 .35
☐ 69 Ken Hamlin 3.00 1.35 .35
☐ 70 Carl Yastrzemski 35.00 16.00 4.40
☐ 71 Frank Carpin 3.00 1.35 .35
☐ 72 Tony Perez 35.00 16.00 4.40
☐ 73 Jerry Zimmerman 3.00 1.35 .35
☐ 74 Don Mossi 5.00 2.20 .60
☐ 75 Tommy Davis 5.00 2.20 .60
☐ 76 Red Schoendienst MG 6.00 2.70 .75
☐ 77 Johnny Orsino 3.00 1.35 .35
☐ 78 Frank Linzy 3.00 1.35 .35
☐ 79 Joe Pepitone 5.00 2.20 .60
☐ 80 Richie Allen 7.50 3.40 .95
☐ 81 Ray Oyler 3.00 1.35 .35
☐ 82 Bob Hendley 3.00 1.35 .35
☐ 83 Albie Pearson 5.00 2.20 .60
☐ 84 Braves Rookies 3.00 1.35 .35
Jim Beauchamp
Dick Kelley
☐ 85 Eddie Fisher 3.00 1.35 .35
☐ 86 John Bateman 3.00 1.35 .35
☐ 87 Dan Napoleon 3.00 1.35 .35
☐ 88 Fred Whitfield 3.00 1.35 .35
☐ 89 Ted Davidson 3.00 1.35 .35
☐ 90 Luis Aparicio 8.00 3.60 1.00
☐ 91 Bob Uecker 25.00 11.00 3.10
(with traded line)
☐ 92 Yankees Team 15.00 6.75 1.85
☐ 93 Jim Lonborg 6.00 2.70 .75
☐ 94 Matty Alou 5.00 2.20 .60
☐ 95 Pete Richert 3.00 1.35 .35
☐ 96 Felipe Alou 6.00 2.70 .75
☐ 97 Jim Merritt 3.00 1.35 .35
☐ 98 Don Demeter 3.00 1.35 .35
☐ 99 Buc Belters 10.00 4.50 1.25
Willie Stargell
Donn Clendenon
☐ 100 Sandy Koufax 125.00 55.00 15.50
☐ 101 Checklist 89-176 8.00 3.60 1.00
☐ 102 Ed Kirkpatrick 3.00 1.35 .35
☐ 103 Dick Groat 5.00 2.20 .60
(with traded line)
☐ 104 Alex Johnson 3.00 1.35 .35
(with traded line)
☐ 105 Milt Pappas 5.00 2.20 .60
☐ 106 Rusty Staub 6.00 2.70 .75
☐ 107 A's Rookies 3.00 1.35 .35
Larry Stahl
Ron Tompkins
☐ 108 Bobby Klaus 3.00 1.35 .35
☐ 109 Ralph Terry 5.00 2.20 .60

Card	NRMT	VG-E	GOOD
☐ 110 Ernie Banks	35.00	16.00	4.40
☐ 111 Gary Peters	3.00	1.35	.35
☐ 112 Manny Mota	5.00	2.20	.60
☐ 113 Hank Aguirre	3.00	1.35	.35
☐ 114 Jim Gosger	3.00	1.35	.35
☐ 115 Bill Henry	3.00	1.35	.35
☐ 116 Walt Alston MG	6.00	2.70	.75
☐ 117 Jake Gibbs	3.00	1.35	.35
☐ 118 Mike McCormick	5.00	2.20	.60
☐ 119 Art Shamsky	3.00	1.35	.35
☐ 120 Harmon Killebrew	25.00	11.00	3.10
☐ 121 Ray Herbert	3.00	1.35	.35
☐ 122 Joe Gaines	3.00	1.35	.35
☐ 123 Pirates Rookies	3.00	1.35	.35
Frank Bork			
Jerry May			
☐ 124 Tug McGraw	6.00	2.70	.75
☐ 125 Lou Brock	25.00	11.00	3.10
☐ 126 Jim Palmer	150.00	70.00	19.00
☐ 127 Ken Berry	3.00	1.35	.35
☐ 128 Jim Landis	3.00	1.35	.35
☐ 129 Jack Kralick	3.00	1.35	.35
☐ 130 Joe Torre	7.50	3.40	.95
☐ 131 Angels Team	6.00	2.70	.75
☐ 132 Orlando Cepeda	7.50	3.40	.95
☐ 133 Don McMahon	3.00	1.35	.35
☐ 134 Wes Parker	5.00	2.20	.60
☐ 135 Dave Morehead	3.00	1.35	.35
☐ 136 Woody Held	3.00	1.35	.35
☐ 137 Pat Corrales	3.00	1.35	.35
☐ 138 Roger Repoz	3.00	1.35	.35
☐ 139 Cubs Rookies	3.00	1.35	.35
Byron Browne			
Don Young			
☐ 140 Jim Maloney	5.00	2.20	.60
☐ 141 Tom McCraw	3.00	1.35	.35
☐ 142 Don Dennis	3.00	1.35	.35
☐ 143 Jose Tartabull	5.00	2.20	.60
☐ 144 Don Schwall	3.00	1.35	.35
☐ 145 Bill Freehan	5.00	2.20	.60
☐ 146 George Altman	3.00	1.35	.35
☐ 147 Lum Harris MG	3.00	1.35	.35
☐ 148 Bob Johnson	3.00	1.35	.35
☐ 149 Dick Nen	3.00	1.35	.35
☐ 150 Rocky Colavito	15.00	6.75	1.85
☐ 151 Gary Wagner	3.00	1.35	.35
☐ 152 Frank Malzone	5.00	2.20	.60
☐ 153 Rico Carty	5.00	2.20	.60
☐ 154 Chuck Hiller	5.00	2.20	.60
☐ 155 Marcelino Lopez	3.00	1.35	.35
☐ 156 Double Play Combo	5.00	2.20	.60
Dick Schofield			
Hal Lanier			
☐ 157 Rene Lachemann	5.00	2.20	.60
☐ 158 Jim Brewer	3.00	1.35	.35
☐ 159 Chico Ruiz	3.00	1.35	.35
☐ 160 Whitey Ford	35.00	16.00	4.40
☐ 161 Jerry Lumpe	3.00	1.35	.35
☐ 162 Lee Maye	3.00	1.35	.35
☐ 163 Tito Francona	3.00	1.35	.35
☐ 164 White Sox Rookies	5.00	2.20	.60
Tommie Agee			
Marv Staehle			
☐ 165 Don Lock	3.00	1.35	.35
☐ 166 Chris Krug	3.00	1.35	.35
☐ 167 Boog Powell	10.00	4.50	1.25
☐ 168 Dan Osinski	3.00	1.35	.35
☐ 169 Duke Sims	3.00	1.35	.35
☐ 170 Cookie Rojas	5.00	2.20	.60
☐ 171 Nick Willhite	3.00	1.35	.35
☐ 172 Mets Team	7.50	3.40	.95
☐ 173 Al Spangler	3.00	1.35	.35
☐ 174 Ron Taylor	3.00	1.35	.35
☐ 175 Bert Campaneris	6.00	2.70	.75
☐ 176 Jim Davenport	3.00	1.35	.35
☐ 177 Hector Lopez	3.00	1.35	.35
☐ 178 Bob Tillman	3.00	1.35	.35
☐ 179 Cards Rookies	3.00	1.35	.35
Dennis Aust			
Bob Tolan			
☐ 180 Vada Pinson	6.00	2.70	.75
☐ 181 Al Worthington	3.00	1.35	.35
☐ 182 Jerry Lynch	3.00	1.35	.35
☐ 183 Checklist 177-264	8.00	3.60	1.00
☐ 184 Denis Menke	3.00	1.35	.35
☐ 185 Bob Buhl	5.00	2.20	.60
☐ 186 Ruben Amaro	3.00	1.35	.35
☐ 187 Chuck Dressen MG	5.00	2.20	.60
☐ 188 Al Luplow	3.00	1.35	.35
☐ 189 John Roseboro	5.00	2.20	.60
☐ 190 Jimmie Hall	3.00	1.35	.35
☐ 191 Darrell Sutherland	3.00	1.35	.35
☐ 192 Vic Power	5.00	2.20	.60
☐ 193 Dave McNally	5.00	2.20	.60
☐ 194 Senators Team	6.00	2.70	.75
☐ 195 Joe Morgan	20.00	9.00	2.50
☐ 196 Don Pavletich	5.00	2.20	.60

1967 O-Pee-Chee

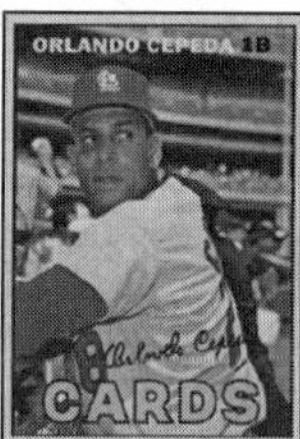

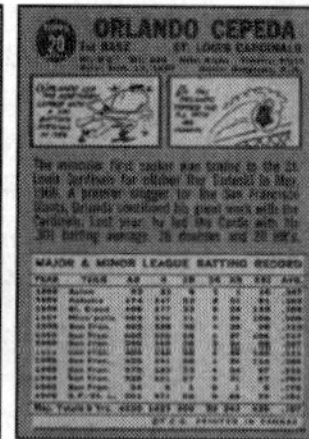

The cards in this 196-card set measure 2 1/2" by 3 1/2". This set is essentially the same as the regular 1967 Topps set, except that the words "Printed in Canada" appear on the bottom right corner of the back. On a white border, fronts feature color player photos with a thin black border. The player's name and position appear in the top part, while the team name is printed in big letters in the bottom part of the photo. On a green background, the backs carry player biography and statistics and two cartoon-like facts. Each checklist card features a small circular picture of a popular player included in that series. Remember the prices below apply only to the O-Pee-Chee cards -- NOT to the 1967 Topps cards which are much more plentiful.

	NRMT	VG-E	GOOD
COMPLETE SET (196)	1250.00	550.00	160.00
COMMON CARD (1-196)	3.00	1.35	.35
☐ 1 The Champs	25.00	11.00	3.10
Frank Robinson			
Hank Bauer			
Brooks Robinson			
☐ 2 Jack Hamilton	3.00	1.35	.35
☐ 3 Duke Sims	3.00	1.35	.35
☐ 4 Hal Lanier	3.00	1.35	.35
☐ 5 Whitey Ford	25.00	11.00	3.10
☐ 6 Dick Simpson	3.00	1.35	.35
☐ 7 Don McMahon	3.00	1.35	.35
☐ 8 Chuck Harrison	3.00	1.35	.35
☐ 9 Ron Hansen	3.00	1.35	.35
☐ 10 Matty Alou	5.00	2.20	.60
☐ 11 Barry Moore	3.00	1.35	.35
☐ 12 Dodgers Rookies	5.00	2.20	.60
Jim Campanis			
Bill Singer			
☐ 13 Joe Sparma	5.00	2.20	.60
☐ 14 Phil Linz	5.00	2.20	.60
☐ 15 Earl Battey	3.00	1.35	.35
☐ 16 Bill Hands	3.00	1.35	.35
☐ 17 Jim Gosger	3.00	1.35	.35
☐ 18 Gene Oliver	3.00	1.35	.35
☐ 19 Jim McGlothlin	3.00	1.35	.35
☐ 20 Orlando Cepeda	7.50	3.40	.95
☐ 21 Dave Bristol MG	3.00	1.35	.35
☐ 22 Gene Brabender	3.00	1.35	.35
☐ 23 Larry Elliot	3.00	1.35	.35
☐ 24 Bob Allen	3.00	1.35	.35
☐ 25 Elston Howard	6.00	2.70	.75
☐ 26 Bob Priddy	3.00	1.35	.35
(with traded line)			
☐ 27 Bob Saverine	3.00	1.35	.35
☐ 28 Barry Latman	3.00	1.35	.35
☐ 29 Tommy McCraw	3.00	1.35	.35
☐ 30 Al Kaline	20.00	9.00	2.50
☐ 31 Jim Brewer	3.00	1.35	.35
☐ 32 Bob Bailey	5.00	2.20	.60
☐ 33 Athletics Rookies	6.00	2.70	.75
Sal Bando			
Randy Schwartz			
☐ 34 Pete Cimino	3.00	1.35	.35
☐ 35 Rico Carty	5.00	2.20	.60
☐ 36 Bob Tillman	3.00	1.35	.35
☐ 37 Rick Wise	5.00	2.20	.60
☐ 38 Bob Johnson	3.00	1.35	.35
☐ 39 Curt Simmons	5.00	2.20	.60
☐ 40 Rick Reichardt	3.00	1.35	.35
☐ 41 Joe Hoerner	3.00	1.35	.35
☐ 42 Mets Team	10.00	4.50	1.25
☐ 43 Chico Salmon	3.00	1.35	.35
☐ 44 Joe Nuxhall	5.00	2.20	.60
☐ 45 Roger Maris	45.00	20.00	5.50
☐ 46 Lindy McDaniel	5.00	2.20	.60
☐ 47 Ken McMullen	3.00	1.35	.35
☐ 48 Bill Freehan	5.00	2.20	.60
☐ 49 Roy Face	5.00	2.20	.60
☐ 50 Tony Oliva	7.50	3.40	.95
☐ 51 Astros Rookies	3.00	1.35	.35
Dave Adlesh			
Wes Bales			
☐ 52 Dennis Higgins	3.00	1.35	.35
☐ 53 Clay Dalrymple	3.00	1.35	.35
☐ 54 Dick Green	3.00	1.35	.35
☐ 55 Don Drysdale	20.00	9.00	2.50
☐ 56 Jose Tartabull	5.00	2.20	.60
☐ 57 Pat Jarvis	3.00	1.35	.35
☐ 58 Paul Schaal	3.00	1.35	.35
☐ 59 Ralph Terry	5.00	2.20	.60
☐ 60 Luis Aparicio	7.50	3.40	.95
☐ 61 Gordy Coleman	3.00	1.35	.35
☐ 62 Checklist 1-109	7.50	3.40	.95
Frank Robinson			
☐ 63 Cards' Clubbers	10.00	4.50	1.25
Lou Brock			
Curt Flood			
☐ 64 Fred Valentine	3.00	1.35	.35
☐ 65 Tom Haller	5.00	2.20	.60
☐ 66 Manny Mota	5.00	2.20	.60
☐ 67 Ken Berry	3.00	1.35	.35
☐ 68 Bob Buhl	5.00	2.20	.60
☐ 69 Vic Davalillo	3.00	1.35	.35
☐ 70 Ron Santo	6.00	2.70	.75
☐ 71 Camilo Pascual	5.00	2.20	.60
☐ 72 Tigers Rookies	3.00	1.35	.35
George Korince			
(photo actually			
John Brown)			
John (Tom) Matchick			
☐ 73 Rusty Staub	6.00	2.70	.75
☐ 74 Wes Stock	3.00	1.35	.35
☐ 75 George Scott	5.00	2.20	.60
☐ 76 Jim Barbieri	3.00	1.35	.35
☐ 77 Dooley Womack	3.00	1.35	.35
☐ 78 Pat Corrales	5.00	2.20	.60
☐ 79 Bubba Morton	3.00	1.35	.35
☐ 80 Jim Maloney	5.00	2.20	.60
☐ 81 Eddie Stanky MG	5.00	2.20	.60
☐ 82 Steve Barber	3.00	1.35	.35
☐ 83 Ollie Brown	3.00	1.35	.35
☐ 84 Tommie Sisk	3.00	1.35	.35
☐ 85 Johnny Callison	5.00	2.20	.60
☐ 86 Mike McCormick	5.00	2.20	.60
(with traded line)			
☐ 87 George Altman	3.00	1.35	.35
☐ 88 Mickey Lolich	6.00	2.70	.75
☐ 89 Felix Millan	5.00	2.20	.60
☐ 90 Jim Nash	3.00	1.35	.35
☐ 91 Johnny Lewis	3.00	1.35	.35
☐ 92 Ray Washburn	3.00	1.35	.35
☐ 93 Yankees Rookies	6.00	2.70	.75
Stan Bahnsen			
Bobby Murcer			
☐ 94 Ron Fairly	5.00	2.20	.60
☐ 95 Sonny Siebert	3.00	1.35	.35
☐ 96 Art Shamsky	3.00	1.35	.35
☐ 97 Mike Cuellar	6.00	2.70	.75
☐ 98 Rich Rollins	3.00	1.35	.35
☐ 99 Lee Stange	3.00	1.35	.35
☐ 100 Frank Robinson	18.00	8.00	2.20
☐ 101 Ken Johnson	3.00	1.35	.35
☐ 102 Phillies Team	6.00	2.70	.75
☐ 103 Checklist 110-196	25.00	11.00	3.10
Mickey Mantle			
☐ 104 Minnie Rojas	3.00	1.35	.35
☐ 105 Ken Boyer	5.00	2.20	.60
☐ 106 Randy Hundley	5.00	2.20	.60
☐ 107 Joel Horlen	3.00	1.35	.35
☐ 108 Alex Johnson	5.00	2.20	.60
☐ 109 Tribe Thumpers	6.00	2.70	.75
Rocky Colavito			
Leon Wagner			
☐ 110 Jack Aker	3.00	1.35	.35
☐ 111 John Kennedy	3.00	1.35	.35
☐ 112 Dave Wickersham	3.00	1.35	.35
☐ 113 Dave Nicholson	3.00	1.35	.35
☐ 114 Jack Baldschun	3.00	1.35	.35
☐ 115 Paul Casanova	3.00	1.35	.35
☐ 116 Herman Franks MG	3.00	1.35	.35
☐ 117 Darrell Brandon	3.00	1.35	.35
☐ 118 Bernie Allen	3.00	1.35	.35
☐ 119 Wade Blasingame	3.00	1.35	.35
☐ 120 Floyd Robinson	3.00	1.35	.35
☐ 121 Ed Bressoud	3.00	1.35	.35
☐ 122 George Brunet	3.00	1.35	.35
☐ 123 Pirates Rookies	3.00	1.35	.35
Jim Price			
Luke Walker			
☐ 124 Jim Stewart	3.00	1.35	.35
☐ 125 Moe Drabowsky	5.00	2.20	.60
☐ 126 Tony Taylor	5.00	2.20	.60
☐ 127 John O'Donoghue	3.00	1.35	.35
☐ 128 Ed Spiezio	3.00	1.35	.35
☐ 129 Phil Roof	3.00	1.35	.35
☐ 130 Phil Regan	5.00	2.20	.60
☐ 131 Yankees Team	10.00	4.50	1.25
☐ 132 Ozzie Virgil	3.00	1.35	.35
☐ 133 Ron Kline	3.00	1.35	.35
☐ 134 Gates Brown	5.00	2.20	.60
☐ 135 Deron Johnson	5.00	2.20	.60
☐ 136 Carroll Sembera	3.00	1.35	.35
☐ 137 Twins Rookies	3.00	1.35	.35
Ron Clark			
Jim Ollom			
☐ 138 Dick Kelley	3.00	1.35	.35
☐ 139 Dalton Jones	3.00	1.35	.35
☐ 140 Willie Stargell	20.00	9.00	2.50
☐ 141 John Miller	3.00	1.35	.35
☐ 142 Jackie Brandt	3.00	1.35	.35
☐ 143 Sox Sockers	6.00	2.70	.75
Pete Ward			
Don Buford			
☐ 144 Bill Hepler	3.00	1.35	.35
☐ 145 Larry Brown	3.00	1.35	.35
☐ 146 Steve Carlton	100.00	45.00	12.50
☐ 147 Tom Egan	3.00	1.35	.35
☐ 148 Adolfo Phillips	3.00	1.35	.35
☐ 149 Joe Moeller	3.00	1.35	.35
☐ 150 Mickey Mantle	350.00	160.00	45.00
☐ 151 Moe Drabowsky WS	6.00	2.70	.75
☐ 152 Jim Palmer WS	10.00	4.50	1.25
☐ 153 Paul Blair WS	6.00	2.70	.75
☐ 154 Brooks Robinson WS	6.00	2.70	.75
Dave McNally			
☐ 155 World Series Summary	6.00	2.70	.75
Winners celebrate			
☐ 156 Ron Herbel	3.00	1.35	.35
☐ 157 Danny Cater	3.00	1.35	.35
☐ 158 Jimmie Coker	3.00	1.35	.35
☐ 159 Bruce Howard	3.00	1.35	.35
☐ 160 Willie Davis	5.00	2.20	.60
☐ 161 Dick Williams MG	5.00	2.20	.60
☐ 162 Billy O'Dell	3.00	1.35	.35
☐ 163 Vic Roznovsky	3.00	1.35	.35
☐ 164 Dwight Siebler	3.00	1.35	.35
☐ 165 Cleon Jones	5.00	2.20	.60
☐ 166 Eddie Mathews	20.00	9.00	2.50
☐ 167 Senators Rookies	3.00	1.35	.35
Joe Coleman			
Tim Cullen			
☐ 168 Ray Culp	3.00	1.35	.35
☐ 169 Horace Clarke	3.00	1.35	.35
☐ 170 Dick McAuliffe	5.00	2.20	.60
☐ 171 Calvin Koonce	3.00	1.35	.35
☐ 172 Bill Heath	3.00	1.35	.35
☐ 173 Cardinals Team	6.00	2.70	.75
☐ 174 Dick Radatz	3.00	1.35	.35
☐ 175 Bobby Knoop	3.00	1.35	.35
☐ 176 Sammy Ellis	3.00	1.35	.35
☐ 177 Tito Fuentes	3.00	1.35	.35
☐ 178 John Buzhardt	3.00	1.35	.35
☐ 179 Braves Rookies	3.00	1.35	.35
Charles Vaughan			
Cecil Upshaw			
☐ 180 Curt Blefary	3.00	1.35	.35
☐ 181 Terry Fox	3.00	1.35	.35
☐ 182 Ed Charles	3.00	1.35	.35
☐ 183 Jim Pagliaroni	3.00	1.35	.35
☐ 184 George Thomas	3.00	1.35	.35
☐ 185 Ken Holtzman	6.00	2.70	.75
☐ 186 Mets Maulers	6.00	2.70	.75
Ed Kranepool			
Ron Swoboda			
☐ 187 Pedro Ramos	3.00	1.35	.35
☐ 188 Ken Harrelson	5.00	2.20	.60
☐ 189 Chuck Hinton	3.00	1.35	.35
☐ 190 Turk Farrell	3.00	1.35	.35
☐ 191 Checklist 197-283	10.00	4.50	1.25
(Willie Mays)			
☐ 192 Fred Gladding	3.00	1.35	.35
☐ 193 Jose Cardenal	5.00	2.20	.60
☐ 194 Bob Allison	5.00	2.20	.60
☐ 195 Al Jackson	3.00	1.35	.35
☐ 196 Johnny Romano	5.00	2.20	.60

1967 O-Pee-Chee Paper Inserts

These posters measure approximately 5" by 7" and are very similar to the American Topps poster (paper insert) issue, except that they say "Ptd. in Canada" on the bottom. The fronts feature color player photos with thin borders. The player's name and position, team name, and the card number appear inside a circle in the lower right. A facsimile player autograph rounds out the front. The backs are blank. This Canadian version is much more difficult to find than the American version. These numbered "All-Star" inserts have fold lines which are generally not very noticeable when stored carefully. There is some confusion as to whether these posters were issued in 1967 or 1968.

	NRMT	VG-E	GOOD
COMPLETE SET (32)	250.00	110.00	31.00
COMMON CARD (1-32)	2.50	1.10	.30
☐ 1 Boog Powell	5.00	2.20	.60
☐ 2 Bert Campaneris	3.50	1.55	.45
☐ 3 Brooks Robinson	12.50	5.50	1.55
☐ 4 Tommie Agee	2.50	1.10	.30
☐ 5 Carl Yastrzemski	20.00	9.00	2.50
☐ 6 Mickey Mantle	100.00	45.00	12.50
☐ 7 Frank Howard	3.50	1.55	.45
☐ 8 Sam McDowell	3.50	1.55	.45
☐ 9 Orlando Cepeda	7.50	3.40	.95
☐ 10 Chico Cardenas	2.50	1.10	.30
☐ 11 Bob Clemente	50.00	22.00	6.25
☐ 12 Willie Mays	35.00	16.00	4.40
☐ 13 Cleon Jones	2.50	1.10	.30
☐ 14 John Callison	2.50	1.10	.30
☐ 15 Hank Aaron	35.00	16.00	4.40
☐ 16 Don Drysdale	12.50	5.50	1.55
☐ 17 Bobby Knoop	2.50	1.10	.30
☐ 18 Tony Oliva	5.00	2.20	.60
☐ 19 Frank Robinson	12.50	5.50	1.55
☐ 20 Denny McLain	5.00	2.20	.60
☐ 21 Al Kaline	12.50	5.50	1.55
☐ 22 Joe Pepitone	3.50	1.55	.45
☐ 23 Harmon Killebrew	12.50	5.50	1.55
☐ 24 Leon Wagner	2.50	1.10	.30
☐ 25 Joe Morgan	12.50	5.50	1.55
☐ 26 Ron Santo	5.00	2.20	.60

Card	NRMT	VG-E	GOOD
☐ 27 Joe Torre	5.00	2.20	.60
☐ 28 Juan Marichal	12.50	5.50	1.55
☐ 29 Matty Alou	3.50	1.55	.45
☐ 30 Felipe Alou	5.00	2.20	.60
☐ 31 Ron Hunt	2.50	1.10	.30
☐ 32 Willie McCovey	12.50	5.50	1.55

1968 O-Pee-Chee

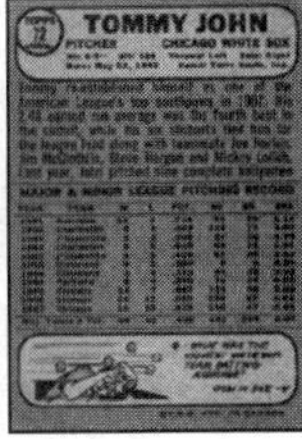

The cards in this 196-card set measure 2 1/2" by 3 1/2". This set is essentially the same as the regular 1968 Topps set, except that the words "Printed in Canada" appear on the bottom of the back and the backgrounds have a different color. The fronts feature color player photos with rounded corners. The player's name is printed under the photo, while his position and team name appear in a circle in the lower right. On a light brown background, the backs carry player biography and statistics and a cartoon-like trivia question. Each checklist card features a small circular picture of a popular player included in that series. Remember the prices below apply only to the O-Pee-Chee cards -- NOT to the 1968 Topps cards which are much more plentiful. The key card in the set is Nolan Ryan in his Rookie Card year. The first OPC cards of Hall of Famers Rod Carew and Tom Seaver also appear in this set.

Card	NRMT	VG-E	GOOD
COMPLETE SET (196)	2500.00	1100.00	300.00
COMMON CARD (1-196)	3.00	1.35	.35
☐ 1 NL Batting Leaders	35.00	16.00	4.40
Bob Clemente			
Tony Gonzalez			
Matty Alou			
☐ 2 AL Batting Leaders	15.00	6.75	1.85
Carl Yastrzemski			
Frank Robinson			
Al Kaline			
☐ 3 NL RBI Leaders	18.00	8.00	2.20
Orlando Cepeda			
Bob Clemente			
Hank Aaron			
☐ 4 AL RBI Leaders	12.50	5.50	1.55
Carl Yastrzemski			
Harmon Killebrew			
Frank Robinson			
☐ 5 NL Home Run Leaders	10.00	4.50	1.25
Hank Aaron			
Jim Wynn			
Ron Santo			
Willie McCovey			
☐ 6 AL Home Run Leaders	10.00	4.50	1.25
Carl Yastrzemski			
Harmon Killebrew			
Frank Howard			
☐ 7 NL ERA Leaders	5.00	2.20	.60
Phil Niekro			
Jim Bunning			
Chris Short			
☐ 8 AL ERA Leaders	5.00	2.20	.60
Joel Horlen			
Gary Peters			
Sonny Siebert			
☐ 9 NL Pitching Leaders	5.00	2.20	.60
Mike McCormick			
Ferguson Jenkins			
Jim Bunning			
Claude Osteen			
☐ 10 AL Pitching Leaders	5.00	2.20	.60
Jim Lonborg			
Earl Wilson			
Dean Chance			
☐ 11 NL Strikeout Leaders	6.00	2.70	.75
Jim Bunning			
Ferguson Jenkins			
Gaylord Perry			
☐ 12 AL Strikeout Leaders	5.00	2.20	.60
Jim Lonborg			
Sam McDowell			
Dean Chance			
☐ 13 Chuck Hartenstein	3.00	1.35	.35
☐ 14 Jerry McNertney	3.00	1.35	.35
☐ 15 Ron Hunt	3.00	1.35	.35
☐ 16 Indians Rookies	6.00	2.70	.75
Lou Piniella			
Richie Scheinblum			
☐ 17 Dick Hall	3.00	1.35	.35
☐ 18 Mike Hershberger	3.00	1.35	.35
☐ 19 Juan Pizarro	3.00	1.35	.35
☐ 20 Brooks Robinson	30.00	13.50	3.70
☐ 21 Ron Davis	3.00	1.35	.35
☐ 22 Pat Dobson	4.00	1.80	.50
☐ 23 Chico Cardenas	4.00	1.80	.50
☐ 24 Bobby Locke	3.00	1.35	.35
☐ 25 Julian Javier	4.00	1.80	.50
☐ 26 Darrell Brandon	3.00	1.35	.35
☐ 27 Gil Hodges MG	10.00	4.50	1.25
☐ 28 Ted Uhlaender	3.00	1.35	.35
☐ 29 Joe Verbanic	3.00	1.35	.35
☐ 30 Joe Torre	6.00	2.70	.75
☐ 31 Ed Stroud	3.00	1.35	.35
☐ 32 Joe Gibbon	3.00	1.35	.35
☐ 33 Pete Ward	3.00	1.35	.35
☐ 34 Al Ferrara	3.00	1.35	.35
☐ 35 Steve Hargan	3.00	1.35	.35
☐ 36 Pirates Rookies	4.00	1.80	.50
Bob Moose			
Bob Robertson			
☐ 37 Billy Williams	10.00	4.50	1.25
☐ 38 Tony Pierce	3.00	1.35	.35
☐ 39 Cookie Rojas	3.00	1.35	.35
☐ 40 Denny McLain	15.00	6.75	1.85
☐ 41 Julio Gotay	3.00	1.35	.35
☐ 42 Larry Haney	3.00	1.35	.35
☐ 43 Gary Bell	3.00	1.35	.35
☐ 44 Frank Kostro	3.00	1.35	.35
☐ 45 Tom Seaver	75.00	34.00	9.50
☐ 46 Dave Ricketts	3.00	1.35	.35
☐ 47 Ralph Houk MG	4.00	1.80	.50
☐ 48 Ted Davidson	3.00	1.35	.35
☐ 49 Ed Brinkman	3.00	1.35	.35
☐ 50 Willie Mays	75.00	34.00	9.50
☐ 51 Bob Locker	3.00	1.35	.35
☐ 52 Hawk Taylor	3.00	1.35	.35
☐ 53 Gene Alley	4.00	1.80	.50
☐ 54 Stan Williams	3.00	1.35	.35
☐ 55 Felipe Alou	6.00	2.70	.75
☐ 56 Orioles Rookies	3.00	1.35	.35
Dave Leonhard			
Dave May			
☐ 57 Dan Schneider	3.00	1.35	.35
☐ 58 Ed Mathews	20.00	9.00	2.50
☐ 59 Don Lock	3.00	1.35	.35
☐ 60 Ken Holtzman	4.00	1.80	.50
☐ 61 Reggie Smith	6.00	2.70	.75
☐ 62 Chuck Dobson	3.00	1.35	.35
☐ 63 Dick Kenworthy	3.00	1.35	.35
☐ 64 Jim Merritt	3.00	1.35	.35
☐ 65 John Roseboro	4.00	1.80	.50
☐ 66 Casey Cox	3.00	1.35	.35
☐ 67 Checklist 1-109	7.50	3.40	.95
Jim Kaat			
☐ 68 Ron Willis	3.00	1.35	.35
☐ 69 Tom Tresh	4.00	1.80	.50
☐ 70 Bob Veale	4.00	1.80	.50
☐ 71 Vern Fuller	3.00	1.35	.35
☐ 72 Tommy John	6.00	2.70	.75
☐ 73 Jim Ray Hart	4.00	1.80	.50
☐ 74 Milt Pappas	4.00	1.80	.50
☐ 75 Don Mincher	3.00	1.35	.35
☐ 76 Braves Rookies	4.00	1.80	.50
Jim Britton			
Ron Reed			
☐ 77 Don Wilson	4.00	1.80	.50
☐ 78 Jim Northrup	4.00	1.80	.50
☐ 79 Ted Kubiak	3.00	1.35	.35
☐ 80 Rod Carew	65.00	29.00	8.00
☐ 81 Larry Jackson	4.00	1.80	.50
☐ 82 Sam Bowens	3.00	1.35	.35
☐ 83 John Stephenson	3.00	1.35	.35
☐ 84 Bob Tolan	3.00	1.35	.35
☐ 85 Gaylord Perry	8.00	3.60	1.00
☐ 86 Willie Stargell	10.00	4.50	1.25
☐ 87 Dick Williams MG	4.00	1.80	.50
☐ 88 Phil Regan	4.00	1.80	.50
☐ 89 Jake Gibbs	3.00	1.35	.35
☐ 90 Vada Pinson	4.00	1.80	.50
☐ 91 Jim Ollom	3.00	1.35	.35
☐ 92 Ed Kranepool	4.00	1.80	.50
☐ 93 Tony Cloninger	3.00	1.35	.35
☐ 94 Lee Maye	3.00	1.35	.35
☐ 95 Bob Aspromonte	3.00	1.35	.35
☐ 96 Senators Rookies	3.00	1.35	.35
Frank Coggins			
Dick Nold			
☐ 97 Tom Phoebus	3.00	1.35	.35
☐ 98 Gary Sutherland	3.00	1.35	.35
☐ 99 Rocky Colavito	10.00	4.50	1.25
☐ 100 Bob Gibson	25.00	11.00	3.10
☐ 101 Glenn Beckert	4.00	1.80	.50
☐ 102 Jose Cardenal	4.00	1.80	.50
☐ 103 Don Sutton	8.00	3.60	1.00
☐ 104 Dick Dietz	3.00	1.35	.35
☐ 105 Al Downing	4.00	1.80	.50
☐ 106 Dalton Jones	3.00	1.35	.35
☐ 107 Checklist 110-196	6.00	2.70	.75
Juan Marichal			
☐ 108 Don Pavletich	3.00	1.35	.35
☐ 109 Bert Campaneris	4.00	1.80	.50
☐ 110 Hank Aaron	75.00	34.00	9.50
☐ 111 Rich Reese	3.00	1.35	.35
☐ 112 Woody Fryman	3.00	1.35	.35
☐ 113 Tigers Rookies	4.00	1.80	.50
Tom Matchick			
Daryl Patterson			
☐ 114 Ron Swoboda	4.00	1.80	.50
☐ 115 Sam McDowell	4.00	1.80	.50
☐ 116 Ken McMullen	3.00	1.35	.35
☐ 117 Larry Jaster	3.00	1.35	.35
☐ 118 Mark Belanger	4.00	1.80	.50
☐ 119 Ted Savage	3.00	1.35	.35
☐ 120 Mel Stottlemyre	6.00	2.70	.75
☐ 121 Jimmie Hall	3.00	1.35	.35
☐ 122 Gene Mauch MG	4.00	1.80	.50
☐ 123 Jose Santiago	3.00	1.35	.35
☐ 124 Nate Oliver	3.00	1.35	.35
☐ 125 Joel Horlen	3.00	1.35	.35
☐ 126 Bobby Etheridge	3.00	1.35	.35
☐ 127 Paul Lindblad	3.00	1.35	.35
☐ 128 Astros Rookies	3.00	1.35	.35
Tom Dukes			
Alonzo Harris			
☐ 129 Mickey Stanley	6.00	2.70	.75
☐ 130 Tony Perez	10.00	4.50	1.25
☐ 131 Frank Bertaina	3.00	1.35	.35
☐ 132 Bud Harrelson	4.00	1.80	.50
☐ 133 Fred Whitfield	3.00	1.35	.35
☐ 134 Pat Jarvis	3.00	1.35	.35
☐ 135 Paul Blair	4.00	1.80	.50
☐ 136 Randy Hundley	4.00	1.80	.50
☐ 137 Twins Team	6.00	2.70	.75
☐ 138 Ruben Amaro	3.00	1.35	.35
☐ 139 Chris Short	3.00	1.35	.35
☐ 140 Tony Conigliaro	10.00	4.50	1.25
☐ 141 Dal Maxvill	3.00	1.35	.35
☐ 142 White Sox Rookies	3.00	1.35	.35
Buddy Bradford			
Bill Voss			
☐ 143 Pete Cimino	3.00	1.35	.35
☐ 144 Joe Morgan	12.00	5.50	1.50
☐ 145 Don Drysdale	15.00	6.75	1.85
☐ 146 Sal Bando	4.00	1.80	.50
☐ 147 Frank Linzy	3.00	1.35	.35
☐ 148 Dave Bristol MG	3.00	1.35	.35
☐ 149 Bob Saverine	3.00	1.35	.35
☐ 150 Bob Clemente	100.00	45.00	12.50
☐ 151 Lou Brock WS	10.00	4.50	1.25
☐ 152 Carl Yastrzemski WS	12.50	5.50	1.55
☐ 153 Nellie Briles WS	6.00	2.70	.75
☐ 154 Bob Gibson WS	12.50	5.50	1.55
☐ 155 Jim Lonborg WS	6.00	2.70	.75
☐ 156 Rico Petrocelli WS	6.00	2.70	.75
☐ 157 World Series Game 7	6.00	2.70	.75
St. Louis wins it			
☐ 158 World Series Summary	6.00	2.70	.75
Cardinals celebrate			
☐ 159 Don Kessinger	4.00	1.80	.50
☐ 160 Earl Wilson	4.00	1.80	.50
☐ 161 Norm Miller	3.00	1.35	.35
☐ 162 Cards Rookies	4.00	1.80	.50
Hal Gilson			
Mike Torrez			
☐ 163 Gene Brabender	3.00	1.35	.35
☐ 164 Ramon Webster	3.00	1.35	.35
☐ 165 Tony Oliva	6.00	2.70	.75
☐ 166 Claude Raymond	4.00	1.80	.50
☐ 167 Elston Howard	6.00	2.70	.75
☐ 168 Dodgers Team	6.00	2.70	.75
☐ 169 Bob Bolin	3.00	1.35	.35
☐ 170 Jim Fregosi	4.00	1.80	.50
☐ 171 Don Nottebart	3.00	1.35	.35
☐ 172 Walt Williams	3.00	1.35	.35
☐ 173 John Boozer	3.00	1.35	.35
☐ 174 Bob Tillman	3.00	1.35	.35
☐ 175 Maury Wills	6.00	2.70	.75
☐ 176 Bob Allen	3.00	1.35	.35
☐ 177 Mets Rookies	1200.00	550.00	150.00
Jerry Koosman			
Nolan Ryan			
☐ 178 Don Wert	4.00	1.80	.50
☐ 179 Bill Stoneman	3.00	1.35	.35
☐ 180 Curt Flood	4.00	1.80	.50
☐ 181 Jerry Zimmerman	3.00	1.35	.35
☐ 182 Dave Giusti	3.00	1.35	.35
☐ 183 Bob Kennedy MG	4.00	1.80	.50
☐ 184 Lou Johnson	3.00	1.35	.35
☐ 185 Tom Haller	3.00	1.35	.35
☐ 186 Eddie Watt	3.00	1.35	.35
☐ 187 Sonny Jackson	3.00	1.35	.35
☐ 188 Cap Peterson	3.00	1.35	.35
☐ 189 Bill Landis	3.00	1.35	.35
☐ 190 Bill White	4.00	1.80	.50
☐ 191 Dan Frisella	3.00	1.35	.35
☐ 192 Checklist 3	10.00	4.50	1.25
Carl Yastrzemski			
☐ 193 Jack Hamilton	3.00	1.35	.35
☐ 194 Don Buford	3.00	1.35	.35
☐ 195 Joe Pepitone	4.00	1.80	.50
☐ 196 Gary Nolan	4.00	1.80	.50

1969 O-Pee-Chee

The cards in this 218-card set measure 2 1/2" by 3 1/2". This set is essentially the same as the regular 1969 Topps set, except that the words "Printed in Canada" appear on the bottom of the back and the backgrounds have a purple color. The fronts feature color player photos with rounded corners and thin black borders. The player's name and position are printed inside a circle in the top right corner, while the team name appears in the lower part of the photo. On a magenta background, the backs carry player biography and statistics. Each checklist card features a small circular picture of a popular player included in that series. Remember the prices below apply only to the O-Pee-Chee cards -- NOT to the 1969 Topps cards which are much more plentiful.

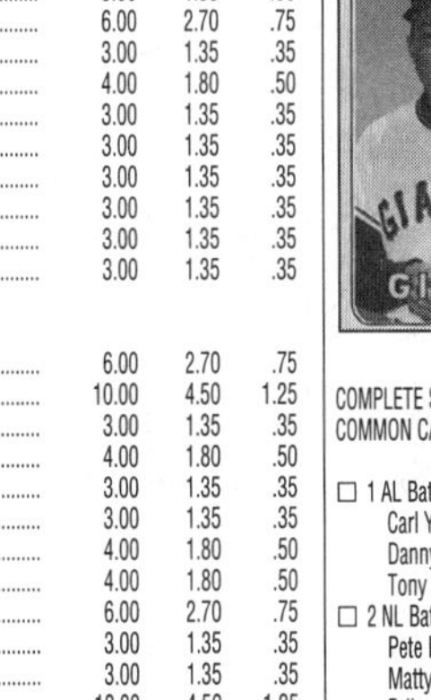

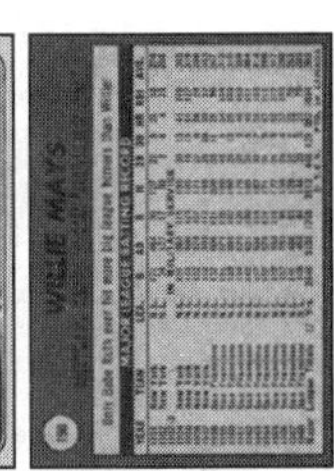

Card	NRMT	VG-E	GOOD
COMPLETE SET (218)	1000.00	450.00	125.00
COMMON CARD (1-218)	2.50	1.10	.30
☐ 1 AL Batting Leaders	15.00	6.75	1.85
Carl Yastrzemski			
Danny Cater			
Tony Oliva			
☐ 2 NL Batting Leaders	7.50	3.40	.95
Pete Rose			
Matty Alou			
Felipe Alou			
☐ 3 AL RBI Leaders	5.00	2.20	.60
Ken Harrelson			
Frank Howard			
Jim Northrup			
☐ 4 NL RBI Leaders	7.50	3.40	.95
Willie McCovey			
Ron Santo			
Billy Williams			
☐ 5 AL Home Run Leaders	5.00	2.20	.60
Frank Howard			
Willie Horton			
Ken Harrelson			
☐ 6 NL Home Run Leaders	7.50	3.40	.95
Willie McCovey			
Richie Allen			
Ernie Banks			
☐ 7 AL ERA Leaders	5.00	2.20	.60
Luis Tiant			
Sam McDowell			
Dave McNally			
☐ 8 NL ERA Leaders	7.50	3.40	.95
Bob Gibson			
Bobby Bolin			
Bob Veale			
☐ 9 AL Pitching Leaders	5.00	2.20	.60
Denny McLain			
Dave McNally			
Luis Tiant			
Mel Stottlemyre			
☐ 10 NL Pitching Leaders	7.50	3.40	.95
Juan Marichal			
Bob Gibson			
Fergie Jenkins			
☐ 11 AL Strikeout Leaders	7.50	3.40	.95
Sam McDowell			
Denny McLain			
Luis Tiant			
☐ 12 NL Strikeout Leaders	7.50	3.40	.95
Bob Gibson			
Fergie Jenkins			
Bill Singer			
☐ 13 Mickey Stanley	4.00	1.80	.50
☐ 14 Al McBean	2.50	1.10	.30
☐ 15 Boog Powell	7.50	3.40	.95
☐ 16 Giants Rookies	2.50	1.10	.30
Cesar Gutierrez			
Rich Robertson			
☐ 17 Mike Marshall	4.00	1.80	.50
☐ 18 Dick Schofield	2.50	1.10	.30
☐ 19 Ken Suarez	2.50	1.10	.30
☐ 20 Ernie Banks	20.00	9.00	2.50
☐ 21 Jose Santiago	2.50	1.10	.30
☐ 22 Jesus Alou	4.00	1.80	.50
☐ 23 Lew Krausse	2.50	1.10	.30
☐ 24 Walt Alston MG	5.00	2.20	.60
☐ 25 Roy White	4.00	1.80	.50
☐ 26 Clay Carroll	4.00	1.80	.50
☐ 27 Bernie Allen	2.50	1.10	.30
☐ 28 Mike Ryan	2.50	1.10	.30
☐ 29 Dave Morehead	2.50	1.10	.30
☐ 30 Bob Allison	4.00	1.80	.50
☐ 31 Mets Rookies	5.00	2.20	.60
Gary Gentry			
Amos Otis			
☐ 32 Sammy Ellis	2.50	1.10	.30
☐ 33 Wayne Causey	2.50	1.10	.30
☐ 34 Gary Peters	2.50	1.10	.30
☐ 35 Joe Morgan	10.00	4.50	1.25
☐ 36 Luke Walker	2.50	1.10	.30
☐ 37 Curt Motton	2.50	1.10	.30
☐ 38 Zoilo Versalles	4.00	1.80	.50
☐ 39 Dick Hughes	2.50	1.10	.30
☐ 40 Mayo Smith MG	2.50	1.10	.30
☐ 41 Bob Barton	2.50	1.10	.30
☐ 42 Tommy Harper	4.00	1.80	.50
☐ 43 Joe Niekro	4.00	1.80	.50
☐ 44 Danny Cater	2.50	1.10	.30
☐ 45 Maury Wills	5.00	2.20	.60
☐ 46 Fritz Peterson	2.50	1.10	.30
☐ 47 Paul Popovich	2.50	1.10	.30

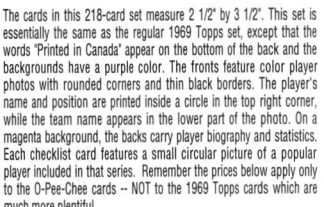

Card	NRMT	VG-E	GOOD
☐ 48 Brant Alyea	2.50	1.10	.30
☐ 49 Royals Rookies	2.50	1.10	.30
Steve Jones			
Ellie Rodriguez			
☐ 50 Roberto Clemente	75.00	34.00	9.50
(Bob on card)			
☐ 51 Woody Fryman	4.00	1.80	.50
☐ 52 Mike Andrews	2.50	1.10	.30
☐ 53 Sonny Jackson	2.50	1.10	.30
☐ 54 Cisco Carlos	2.50	1.10	.30
☐ 55 Jerry Grote	4.00	1.80	.50
☐ 56 Rich Reese	2.50	1.10	.30
☐ 57 Checklist 1-109	7.50	3.40	.95
Denny McLain			
☐ 58 Fred Gladding	2.50	1.10	.30
☐ 59 Jay Johnstone	4.00	1.80	.50
☐ 60 Nelson Briles	4.00	1.80	.50
☐ 61 Jimmie Hall	2.50	1.10	.30
☐ 62 Chico Salmon	2.50	1.10	.30
☐ 63 Jim Hickman	2.50	1.10	.30
☐ 64 Bill Monbouquette	2.50	1.10	.30
☐ 65 Willie Davis	4.00	1.80	.50
☐ 66 Orioles Rookies	2.50	1.10	.30
Mike Adamson			
Merv Rettenmund			
☐ 67 Bill Stoneman	4.00	1.80	.50
☐ 68 Dave Duncan	4.00	1.80	.50
☐ 69 Steve Hamilton	2.50	1.10	.30
☐ 70 Tommy Helms	4.00	1.80	.50
☐ 71 Steve Whitaker	2.50	1.10	.30
☐ 72 Ron Taylor	4.00	1.80	.50
☐ 73 Johnny Briggs	2.50	1.10	.30
☐ 74 Preston Gomez MG	2.50	1.10	.30
☐ 75 Luis Aparicio	7.50	3.40	.95
☐ 76 Norm Miller	2.50	1.10	.30
☐ 77 Ron Perranoski	4.00	1.80	.50
☐ 78 Tom Satriano	2.50	1.10	.30
☐ 79 Milt Pappas	4.00	1.80	.50
☐ 80 Norm Cash	5.00	2.20	.60
☐ 81 Mel Queen	2.50	1.10	.30
☐ 82 Pirates Rookies	10.00	4.50	1.25
Rich Hebner			
Al Oliver			
☐ 83 Mike Ferraro	4.00	1.80	.50
☐ 84 Bob Humphreys	2.50	1.10	.30
☐ 85 Lou Brock	20.00	9.00	2.50
☐ 86 Pete Richert	2.50	1.10	.30
☐ 87 Horace Clarke	2.50	1.10	.30
☐ 88 Rich Nye	2.50	1.10	.30
☐ 89 Russ Gibson	2.50	1.10	.30
☐ 90 Jerry Koosman	7.50	3.40	.95
☐ 91 Al Dark MG	4.00	1.80	.50
☐ 92 Jack Billingham	4.00	1.80	.50
☐ 93 Joe Foy	2.50	1.10	.30
☐ 94 Hank Aguirre	2.50	1.10	.30
☐ 95 Johnny Bench	50.00	22.00	6.25
☐ 96 Denver LeMaster	2.50	1.10	.30
☐ 97 Buddy Bradford	2.50	1.10	.30
☐ 98 Dave Giusti	2.50	1.10	.30
☐ 99 Twins Rookies	20.00	9.00	2.50
Danny Morris			
Graig Nettles			
☐ 100 Hank Aaron	60.00	27.00	7.50
☐ 101 Daryl Patterson	2.50	1.10	.30
☐ 102 Jim Davenport	2.50	1.10	.30
☐ 103 Roger Repoz	2.50	1.10	.30
☐ 104 Steve Blass	2.50	1.10	.30
☐ 105 Rick Monday	4.00	1.80	.50
☐ 106 Jim Hannan	2.50	1.10	.30
☐ 107 Checklist 110-218	7.50	3.40	.95
Bob Gibson			
☐ 108 Tony Taylor	4.00	1.80	.50
☐ 109 Jim Lonborg	4.00	1.80	.50
☐ 110 Mike Shannon	4.00	1.80	.50
☐ 111 Johnny Morris	2.50	1.10	.30
☐ 112 J.C. Martin	2.50	1.10	.30
☐ 113 Dave May	2.50	1.10	.30
☐ 114 Yankees Rookies	2.50	1.10	.30
Alan Closter			
John Cumberland			
☐ 115 Bill Hands	2.50	1.10	.30
☐ 116 Chuck Harrison	2.50	1.10	.30
☐ 117 Jim Fairey	4.00	1.80	.50
☐ 118 Stan Williams	2.50	1.10	.30
☐ 119 Doug Rader	4.00	1.80	.50
☐ 120 Pete Rose	40.00	18.00	5.00
☐ 121 Joe Grzenda	2.50	1.10	.30
☐ 122 Ron Fairly	4.00	1.80	.50
☐ 123 Wilbur Wood	4.00	1.80	.50
☐ 124 Hank Bauer MG	4.00	1.80	.50
☐ 125 Ray Sadecki	2.50	1.10	.30
☐ 126 Dick Tracewski	2.50	1.10	.30
☐ 127 Kevin Collins	2.50	1.10	.30
☐ 128 Tommie Aaron	4.00	1.80	.50
☐ 129 Bill McCool	2.50	1.10	.30
☐ 130 Carl Yastrzemski	20.00	9.00	2.50
☐ 131 Chris Cannizzaro	2.50	1.10	.30
☐ 132 Dave Baldwin	2.50	1.10	.30
☐ 133 Johnny Callison	4.00	1.80	.50
☐ 134 Jim Weaver	2.50	1.10	.30
☐ 135 Tommy Davis	4.00	1.80	.50
☐ 136 Cards Rookies	2.50	1.10	.30
Steve Huntz			
Mike Torrez			
☐ 137 Wally Bunker	2.50	1.10	.30
☐ 138 John Bateman	2.50	1.10	.30
☐ 139 Andy Kosco	2.50	1.10	.30
☐ 140 Jim Lefebvre	4.00	1.80	.50
☐ 141 Bill Dillman	2.50	1.10	.30
☐ 142 Woody Woodward	4.00	1.80	.50
☐ 143 Joe Nossek	2.50	1.10	.30
☐ 144 Bob Hendley	2.50	1.10	.30
☐ 145 Max Alvis	2.50	1.10	.30
☐ 146 Jim Perry	4.00	1.80	.50
☐ 147 Leo Durocher MG	7.50	3.40	.95
☐ 148 Lee Stange	2.50	1.10	.30
☐ 149 Ollie Brown	2.50	1.10	.30
☐ 150 Denny McLain	7.50	3.40	.95
☐ 151 Clay Dalrymple	4.00	1.80	.50
(Catching, Phillies)			
☐ 152 Tommie Sisk	2.50	1.10	.30
☐ 153 Ed Brinkman	2.50	1.10	.30
☐ 154 Jim Britton	2.50	1.10	.30
☐ 155 Pete Ward	4.00	1.80	.50
☐ 156 Houston Rookies	2.50	1.10	.30
Hal Gilson			
Leon McFadden			
☐ 157 Bob Rodgers	4.00	1.80	.50
☐ 158 Joe Gibbon	2.50	1.10	.30
☐ 159 Jerry Adair	2.50	1.10	.30
☐ 160 Vada Pinson	7.50	3.40	.95
☐ 161 John Purdin	2.50	1.10	.30
☐ 162 Bob Gibson WS	10.00	4.50	1.25
fans 17			
☐ 163 Willie Horton WS	7.50	3.40	.95
☐ 164 Tim McCarver WS	10.00	4.50	1.25
with Roger Maris			
☐ 165 Lou Brock WS	10.00	4.50	1.25
☐ 166 Al Kaline WS	10.00	4.50	1.25
☐ 167 Jim Northrup WS	7.50	3.40	.95
☐ 168 Mickey Lolich WS	10.00	4.50	1.25
Bob Gibson			
☐ 169 Tigers celebrate	7.50	3.40	.95
Dick McAuliffe			
Denny McLain			
Willie Horton			
☐ 170 Frank Howard	5.00	2.20	.60
☐ 171 Glenn Beckert	4.00	1.80	.50
☐ 172 Jerry Stephenson	2.50	1.10	.30
☐ 173 White Sox Rookies	2.50	1.10	.30
Bob Christian			
Gerry Nyman			
☐ 174 Grant Jackson	2.50	1.10	.30
☐ 175 Jim Bunning	7.50	3.40	.95
☐ 176 Joe Azcue	2.50	1.10	.30
☐ 177 Ron Reed	2.50	1.10	.30
☐ 178 Ray Oyler	4.00	1.80	.50
☐ 179 Don Pavletich	2.50	1.10	.30
☐ 180 Willie Horton	4.00	1.80	.50
☐ 181 Mel Nelson	2.50	1.10	.30
☐ 182 Bill Rigney MG	2.50	1.10	.30
☐ 183 Don Shaw	4.00	1.80	.50
☐ 184 Roberto Pena	2.50	1.10	.30
☐ 185 Tom Phoebus	2.50	1.10	.30
☐ 186 John Edwards	2.50	1.10	.30
☐ 187 Leon Wagner	2.50	1.10	.30
☐ 188 Rick Wise	4.00	1.80	.50
☐ 189 Red Sox Rookies	2.50	1.10	.30
Joe Lahoud			
John Thibodeau			
☐ 190 Willie Mays	60.00	27.00	7.50
☐ 191 Lindy McDaniel	4.00	1.80	.50
☐ 192 Jose Pagan	2.50	1.10	.30
☐ 193 Don Cardwell	2.50	1.10	.30
☐ 194 Ted Uhlaender	2.50	1.10	.30
☐ 195 John Odom	4.00	1.80	.50
☐ 196 Lum Harris MG	2.50	1.10	.30
☐ 197 Dick Selma	2.50	1.10	.30
☐ 198 Willie Smith	2.50	1.10	.30
☐ 199 Jim French	2.50	1.10	.30
☐ 200 Bob Gibson	15.00	6.75	1.85
☐ 201 Russ Snyder	2.50	1.10	.30
☐ 202 Don Wilson	4.00	1.80	.50
☐ 203 Dave Johnson	5.00	2.20	.60
☐ 204 Jack Hiatt	2.50	1.10	.30
☐ 205 Rick Reichardt	2.50	1.10	.30
☐ 206 Phillies Rookies	4.00	1.80	.50
Larry Hisle			
Barry Lersch			
☐ 207 Roy Face	4.00	1.80	.50
☐ 208 Donn Clendenon	4.00	1.80	.50
(Montreal Expos)			
☐ 209 Larry Haney UER	2.50	1.10	.30
(Reversed negative)			
☐ 210 Felix Millan	2.50	1.10	.30
☐ 211 Galen Cisco	2.50	1.10	.30
☐ 212 Tom Tresh	4.00	1.80	.50
☐ 213 Gerry Arrigo	2.50	1.10	.30
☐ 214 Checklist 3	7.50	3.40	.95
With 69T deckle CL			
on back (no player)			
☐ 215 Rico Petrocelli	4.00	1.80	.50
☐ 216 Don Sutton	8.00	3.60	1.00
☐ 217 John Donaldson	2.50	1.10	.30
☐ 218 John Roseboro	4.00	1.80	.50

1969 O-Pee-Chee Deckle

This set is very similar to the U.S. deckle version produced by Topps. The cards measure approximately 2 1/8" by 3 1/8" (slightly smaller than the American issue) and are cut with deckle edges. The fronts feature black-and-white player photos with white borders and facsimile autographs in black ink (instead of blue ink like the Topps issue). The backs are blank. The cards are unnumbered and checklisted below in alphabetical order. Remember the prices below apply only to the O-Pee-Chee Deckle cards -- NOT to the 1969 Topps Deckle cards which are much more plentiful.

	NRMT	VG-E	GOOD
COMPLETE SET (24)	200.00	90.00	25.00
COMMON CARD (1-24)	3.00	1.35	.35
☐ 1 Richie Allen	7.50	3.40	.95
☐ 2 Luis Aparicio	10.00	4.50	1.25
☐ 3 Rod Carew	15.00	6.75	1.85
☐ 4 Roberto Clemente	40.00	18.00	5.00
☐ 5 Curt Flood	3.00	1.35	.35
☐ 6 Bill Freehan	3.00	1.35	.35
☐ 7 Bob Gibson	15.00	6.75	1.85
☐ 8 Ken Harrelson	4.00	1.80	.50
☐ 9 Tommy Helms	3.00	1.35	.35
☐ 10 Tom Haller	3.00	1.35	.35
☐ 11 Willie Horton	4.00	1.80	.50
☐ 12 Frank Howard	7.50	3.40	.95
☐ 13 Willie McCovey	15.00	6.75	1.85
☐ 14 Denny McLain	7.50	3.40	.95
☐ 15 Juan Marichal	10.00	4.50	1.25
☐ 16 Willie Mays	30.00	13.50	3.70
☐ 17 Boog Powell	7.50	3.40	.95
☐ 18 Brooks Robinson	15.00	6.75	1.85
☐ 19 Ron Santo	7.50	3.40	.95
☐ 20 Rusty Staub	4.00	1.80	.50
☐ 21 Mel Stottlemyre	3.00	1.35	.35
☐ 22 Luis Tiant	3.00	1.35	.35
☐ 23 Maury Wills	4.00	1.80	.50
☐ 24 Carl Yastrzemski	15.00	6.75	1.85

1970 O-Pee-Chee

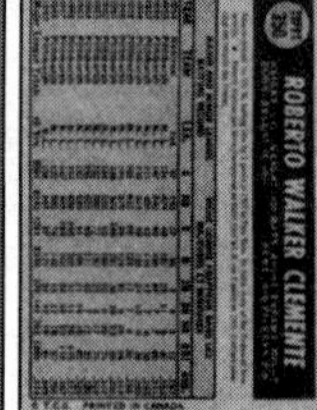

The cards in this 546-card set measure 2 1/2" by 3 1/2". This set is essentially the same as the regular 1970 Topps set, except that the words "Printed in Canada" appear on the backs and the backs are bilingual. On a gray border, the fronts feature color player photos with thin white borders. The player's name and position are printed under the photo, while the team name appears in the upper part of the picture. The horizontal backs carry player biography and statistics in French and English. The card stock is a deeper shade of yellow on the reverse for the O-Pee-Chee cards. Remember the prices below apply only to the O-Pee-Chee cards -- NOT to the 1970 Topps cards which are much more plentiful.

	NRMT	VG-E	GOOD
COMPLETE SET (546)	1500.00	700.00	190.00
COMMON CARD (1-459)	1.50	.70	.19
COMMON CARD (460-546)	2.00	.90	.25
☐ 1 New York Mets	20.00	9.00	2.50
Team Card			
☐ 2 Diego Segui	2.00	.90	.25
☐ 3 Darrel Chaney	1.50	.70	.19
☐ 4 Tom Egan	1.50	.70	.19
☐ 5 Wes Parker	2.00	.90	.25
☐ 6 Grant Jackson	1.50	.70	.19
☐ 7 Indians Rookies	1.50	.70	.19
Gary Boyd			
Russ Nagelson			
☐ 8 Jose Martinez	1.50	.70	.19
☐ 9 Checklist 1-132	12.00	5.50	1.50
☐ 10 Carl Yastrzemski	15.00	6.75	1.85
☐ 11 Nate Colbert	1.50	.70	.19
☐ 12 John Hiller	2.00	.90	.25
☐ 13 Jack Hiatt	1.50	.70	.19
☐ 14 Hank Allen	1.50	.70	.19
☐ 15 Larry Dierker	1.50	.70	.19
☐ 16 Charlie Metro MG	1.50	.70	.19
☐ 17 Hoyt Wilhelm	6.00	2.70	.75
☐ 18 Carlos May	2.00	.90	.25
☐ 19 John Boccabella	1.50	.70	.19
☐ 20 Dave McNally	2.00	.90	.25
☐ 21 A's Rookies	6.00	2.70	.75
Vida Blue			
Gene Tenace			
☐ 22 Ray Washburn	1.50	.70	.19
☐ 23 Bill Robinson	2.00	.90	.25
☐ 24 Dick Selma	1.50	.70	.19
☐ 25 Cesar Tovar	1.50	.70	.19
☐ 26 Tug McGraw	3.00	1.35	.35
☐ 27 Chuck Hinton	1.50	.70	.19
☐ 28 Billy Wilson	1.50	.70	.19
☐ 29 Sandy Alomar	2.00	.90	.25
☐ 30 Matty Alou	2.00	.90	.25
☐ 31 Marty Pattin	2.00	.90	.25
☐ 32 Harry Walker MG	1.50	.70	.19
☐ 33 Don Wert	1.50	.70	.19
☐ 34 Willie Crawford	1.50	.70	.19
☐ 35 Joel Horlen	1.50	.70	.19
☐ 36 Red Rookies	2.00	.90	.25
Danny Breeden			
Bernie Carbo			
☐ 37 Dick Drago	1.50	.70	.19
☐ 38 Mack Jones	1.50	.70	.19
☐ 39 Mike Nagy	1.50	.70	.19
☐ 40 Rich Allen	3.00	1.35	.35
☐ 41 George Lauzerique	1.50	.70	.19
☐ 42 Tito Fuentes	1.50	.70	.19
☐ 43 Jack Aker	1.50	.70	.19
☐ 44 Roberto Pena	1.50	.70	.19
☐ 45 Dave Johnson	2.50	1.10	.30
☐ 46 Ken Rudolph	1.50	.70	.19
☐ 47 Bob Miller	1.50	.70	.19
☐ 48 Gil Garrido	1.50	.70	.19
☐ 49 Tim Cullen	1.50	.70	.19
☐ 50 Tommie Agee	2.00	.90	.25
☐ 51 Bob Christian	1.50	.70	.19
☐ 52 Bruce Dal Canton	1.50	.70	.19
☐ 53 John Kennedy	1.50	.70	.19
☐ 54 Jeff Torborg	2.00	.90	.25
☐ 55 John Odom	2.00	.90	.25
☐ 56 Phillies Rookies	1.50	.70	.19
Joe Lis			
Scott Reid			
☐ 57 Pat Kelly	1.50	.70	.19
☐ 58 Dave Marshall	1.50	.70	.19
☐ 59 Dick Ellsworth	1.50	.70	.19
☐ 60 Jim Wynn	2.00	.90	.25
☐ 61 NL Batting Leaders	10.00	4.50	1.25
Pete Rose			
Bob Clemente			
Cleon Jones			
☐ 62 AL Batting Leaders	4.00	1.80	.50
Rod Carew			
Reggie Smith			
Tony Oliva			
☐ 63 NL RBI Leaders	4.00	1.80	.50
Willie McCovey			
Ron Santo			
Tony Perez			
☐ 64 AL RBI Leaders	6.00	2.70	.75
Harmon Killebrew			
Boog Powell			
Reggie Jackson			
☐ 65 NL Home Run Leaders	6.00	2.70	.75
Willie McCovey			
Hank Aaron			
Lee May			
☐ 66 AL Home Run Leaders	6.00	2.70	.75
Harmon Killebrew			
Frank Howard			
Reggie Jackson			
☐ 67 NL ERA Leaders	7.00	3.10	.85
Juan Marichal			
Steve Carlton			
Bob Gibson			
☐ 68 AL ERA Leaders	4.00	1.80	.50
Dick Bosman			
Jim Palmer			
Mike Cuellar			
☐ 69 NL Pitching Leaders	7.00	3.10	.85
Tom Seaver			
Phil Niekro			
Fergie Jenkins			
Juan Marichal			
☐ 70 AL Pitching Leaders	4.00	1.80	.50
Dennis McLain			
Mike Cuellar			
Dave Boswell			
Dave McNally			
Jim Perry			
Mel Stottlemyre			
☐ 71 NL Strikeout Leaders	4.00	1.80	.50
Fergie Jenkins			
Bob Gibson			
Bill Singer			
☐ 72 AL Strikeout Leaders	4.00	1.80	.50
Sam McDowell			
Mickey Lolich			
Andy Messersmith			
☐ 73 Wayne Granger	1.50	.70	.19
☐ 74 Angels Rookies	1.50	.70	.19
Greg Washburn			
Wally Wolf			
☐ 75 Jim Kaat	4.00	1.80	.50
☐ 76 Carl Taylor	1.50	.70	.19
☐ 77 Frank Linzy	1.50	.70	.19
☐ 78 Joe Lahoud	1.50	.70	.19
☐ 79 Clay Kirby	1.50	.70	.19

☐ 80 Don Kessinger 2.00 .90 .25
☐ 81 Dave May 1.50 .70 .19
☐ 82 Frank Fernandez 1.50 .70 .19
☐ 83 Don Cardwell 1.50 .70 .19
☐ 84 Paul Casanova 1.50 .70 .19
☐ 85 Max Alvis 1.50 .70 .19
☐ 86 Lum Harris MG 1.50 .70 .19
☐ 87 Steve Renko 2.00 .90 .25
☐ 88 Pilots Rookies 2.00 .90 .25
Miguel Fuentes
Dick Baney
☐ 89 Juan Rios 1.50 .70 .19
☐ 90 Tim McCarver 4.00 1.80 .50
☐ 91 Rich Morales 1.50 .70 .19
☐ 92 George Culver 1.50 .70 .19
☐ 93 Rick Renick 1.50 .70 .19
☐ 94 Fred Patek 2.00 .90 .25
☐ 95 Earl Wilson 2.00 .90 .25
☐ 96 Cardinals Rookies 5.00 2.20 .60
Leron Lee
Jerry Reuss
☐ 97 Joe Moeller 1.50 .70 .19
☐ 98 Gates Brown 2.00 .90 .25
☐ 99 Bobby Pfeil 1.50 .70 .19
☐ 100 Mel Stottlemyre 2.00 .90 .25
☐ 101 Bobby Floyd 1.50 .70 .19
☐ 102 Joe Rudi 2.00 .90 .25
☐ 103 Frank Reberger 1.50 .70 .19
☐ 104 Gerry Moses 1.50 .70 .19
☐ 105 Tony Gonzalez 1.50 .70 .19
☐ 106 Darold Knowles 1.50 .70 .19
☐ 107 Bobby Etheridge 1.50 .70 .19
☐ 108 Tom Burgmeier 1.50 .70 .19
☐ 109 Expos Rookies 2.00 .90 .25
Garry Jestadt
Carl Morton
☐ 110 Bob Moose 1.50 .70 .19
☐ 111 Mike Hegan 2.00 .90 .25
☐ 112 Dave Nelson 1.50 .70 .19
☐ 113 Jim Ray 1.50 .70 .19
☐ 114 Gene Michael 2.00 .90 .25
☐ 115 Alex Johnson 2.00 .90 .25
☐ 116 Sparky Lyle 3.00 1.35 .35
☐ 117 Don Young 1.50 .70 .19
☐ 118 George Mitterwald 1.50 .70 .19
☐ 119 Chuck Taylor 1.50 .70 .19
☐ 120 Sal Bando 2.00 .90 .25
☐ 121 Orioles Rookies 1.50 .70 .19
Fred Beene
Terry Crowley
☐ 122 George Stone 1.50 .70 .19
☐ 123 Don Gutteridge MG 1.50 .70 .19
☐ 124 Larry Jaster 1.50 .70 .19
☐ 125 Deron Johnson 2.00 .90 .25
☐ 126 Marty Martinez 1.50 .70 .19
☐ 127 Joe Coleman 1.50 .70 .19
☐ 128 Checklist 133-263 6.00 2.70 .75
☐ 129 Jimmie Price 1.50 .70 .19
☐ 130 Ollie Brown 1.50 .70 .19
☐ 131 Dodgers Rookies 2.00 .90 .25
Ray Lamb
Bob Stinson
☐ 132 Jim McGlothlin 1.50 .70 .19
☐ 133 Clay Carroll 1.50 .70 .19
☐ 134 Danny Walton 1.50 .70 .19
☐ 135 Dick Dietz 1.50 .70 .19
☐ 136 Steve Hargan 1.50 .70 .19
☐ 137 Art Shamsky 1.50 .70 .19
☐ 138 Joe Foy 1.50 .70 .19
☐ 139 Rich Nye 1.50 .70 .19
☐ 140 Reggie Jackson 60.00 27.00 7.50
☐ 141 Pirates Rookies 2.00 .90 .25
Dave Cash
Johnny Jeter
☐ 142 Fritz Peterson 1.50 .70 .19
☐ 143 Phil Gagliano 1.50 .70 .19
☐ 144 Ray Culp 1.50 .70 .19
☐ 145 Rico Carty 2.00 .90 .25
☐ 146 Danny Murphy 1.50 .70 .19
☐ 147 Angel Hermoso 1.50 .70 .19
☐ 148 Earl Weaver MG 6.00 2.70 .75
☐ 149 Billy Champion 1.50 .70 .19
☐ 150 Harmon Killebrew 10.00 4.50 1.25
☐ 151 Dave Roberts 1.50 .70 .19
☐ 152 Ike Brown 1.50 .70 .19
☐ 153 Gary Gentry 1.50 .70 .19
☐ 154 Senators Rookies 1.50 .70 .19
Jim Miles
Jan Dukes
☐ 155 Denis Menke 1.50 .70 .19
☐ 156 Eddie Fisher 1.50 .70 .19
☐ 157 Manny Mota 2.50 1.10 .30
☐ 158 Jerry McNertney 2.00 .90 .25
☐ 159 Tommy Helms 2.00 .90 .25
☐ 160 Phil Niekro 5.00 2.20 .60
☐ 161 Richie Scheinblum 1.50 .70 .19
☐ 162 Jerry Johnson 1.50 .70 .19
☐ 163 Syd O'Brien 1.50 .70 .19
☐ 164 Ty Cline 1.50 .70 .19
☐ 165 Ed Kirkpatrick 1.50 .70 .19
☐ 166 Al Oliver 4.00 1.80 .50
☐ 167 Bill Burbach 1.50 .70 .19
☐ 168 Dave Watkins 1.50 .70 .19
☐ 169 Tom Hall 1.50 .70 .19
☐ 170 Billy Williams 7.50 3.40 .95
☐ 171 Jim Nash 1.50 .70 .19
☐ 172 Braves Rookies 3.00 1.35 .35
Garry Hill
Ralph Garr
☐ 173 Jim Hicks 1.50 .70 .19
☐ 174 Ted Sizemore 2.00 .90 .25
☐ 175 Dick Bosman 1.50 .70 .19
☐ 176 Jim Ray Hart 2.00 .90 .25
☐ 177 Jim Northrup 2.00 .90 .25
☐ 178 Denny LeMaster 1.50 .70 .19
☐ 179 Ivan Murrell 1.50 .70 .19
☐ 180 Tommy John 4.00 1.80 .50
☐ 181 Sparky Anderson MG 6.00 2.70 .75
☐ 182 Dick Hall 1.50 .70 .19
☐ 183 Jerry Grote 2.00 .90 .25
☐ 184 Ray Fosse 2.00 .90 .25
☐ 185 Don Mincher 2.00 .90 .25
☐ 186 Rick Joseph 1.50 .70 .19
☐ 187 Mike Hedlund 1.50 .70 .19
☐ 188 Manny Sanguillen 2.00 .90 .25
☐ 189 Yankees Rookies 60.00 27.00 7.50
Thurman Munson
Dave McDonald
☐ 190 Joe Torre 3.00 1.35 .35
☐ 191 Vicente Romo 1.50 .70 .19
☐ 192 Jim Qualls 1.50 .70 .19
☐ 193 Mike Wegener 1.50 .70 .19
☐ 194 Chuck Manuel 1.50 .70 .19
☐ 195 Tom Seaver NLCS 20.00 9.00 2.50
☐ 196 Ken Boswell NLCS 3.00 1.35 .35
☐ 197 Nolan Ryan NLCS 40.00 18.00 5.00
☐ 198 Mets Celebrate 20.00 9.00 2.50
Includes Nolan Ryan
Tommie Agee
Wayne Garrett
☐ 199 Mike Cuellar ALCS 3.00 1.35 .35
☐ 200 Boog Powell ALCS 4.00 1.80 .50
☐ 201 Boog Powell ALCS 3.00 1.35 .35
Andy Etchebarren
☐ 202 AL Playoff Summary 3.00 1.35 .35
Orioles celebrate
☐ 203 Rudy May 1.50 .70 .19
☐ 204 Len Gabrielson 1.50 .70 .19
☐ 205 Bert Campaneris 2.50 1.10 .30
☐ 206 Clete Boyer 2.00 .90 .25
☐ 207 Tigers Rookies 1.50 .70 .19
Norman McRae
Bob Reed
☐ 208 Fred Gladding 1.50 .70 .19
☐ 209 Ken Suarez 1.50 .70 .19
☐ 210 Juan Marichal 7.50 3.40 .95
☐ 211 Ted Williams MG 15.00 6.75 1.85
☐ 212 Al Santorini 1.50 .70 .19
☐ 213 Andy Etchebarren 1.50 .70 .19
☐ 214 Ken Boswell 1.50 .70 .19
☐ 215 Reggie Smith 3.00 1.35 .35
☐ 216 Chuck Hartenstein 1.50 .70 .19
☐ 217 Ron Hansen 1.50 .70 .19
☐ 218 Ron Stone 1.50 .70 .19
☐ 219 Jerry Kenney 1.50 .70 .19
☐ 220 Steve Carlton 18.00 8.00 2.20
☐ 221 Ron Brand 1.50 .70 .19
☐ 222 Jim Rooker 1.50 .70 .19
☐ 223 Nate Oliver 1.50 .70 .19
☐ 224 Steve Barber 2.00 .90 .25
☐ 225 Lee May 2.50 1.10 .30
☐ 226 Ron Perranoski 2.00 .90 .25
☐ 227 Astros Rookies 2.50 1.10 .30
John Mayberry
Bob Watkins
☐ 228 Aurelio Rodriguez 2.00 .90 .25
☐ 229 Rich Robertson 1.50 .70 .19
☐ 230 Brooks Robinson 15.00 6.75 1.85
☐ 231 Luis Tiant 3.00 1.35 .35
☐ 232 Bob Didier 1.50 .70 .19
☐ 233 Lew Krausse 1.50 .70 .19
☐ 234 Tommy Dean 1.50 .70 .19
☐ 235 Mike Epstein 1.50 .70 .19
☐ 236 Bob Veale 1.50 .70 .19
☐ 237 Russ Gibson 1.50 .70 .19
☐ 238 Jose Laboy 1.50 .70 .19
☐ 239 Ken Berry 1.50 .70 .19
☐ 240 Fergie Jenkins 7.50 3.40 .95
☐ 241 Royals Rookies 1.50 .70 .19
Al Fitzmorris
Scott Northey
☐ 242 Walter Alston MG 3.00 1.35 .35
☐ 243 Joe Sparma 2.00 .90 .25
☐ 244 Checklist 264-372 6.00 2.70 .75
☐ 245 Leo Cardenas 1.50 .70 .19
☐ 246 Jim McAndrew 1.50 .70 .19
☐ 247 Lou Klimchock 1.50 .70 .19
☐ 248 Jesus Alou 1.50 .70 .19
☐ 249 Bob Locker 1.50 .70 .19
☐ 250 Willie McCovey 10.00 4.50 1.25
☐ 251 Dick Schofield 1.50 .70 .19
☐ 252 Lowell Palmer 1.50 .70 .19
☐ 253 Ron Woods 1.50 .70 .19
☐ 254 Camilo Pascual 2.00 .90 .25
☐ 255 Jim Spencer 1.50 .70 .19
☐ 256 Vic Davalillo 1.50 .70 .19
☐ 257 Dennis Higgins 1.50 .70 .19
☐ 258 Paul Popovich 1.50 .70 .19
☐ 259 Tommie Reynolds 1.50 .70 .19
☐ 260 Claude Osteen 2.00 .90 .25
☐ 261 Curt Motton 1.50 .70 .19
☐ 262 Twins Rookies 1.50 .70 .19
Jerry Morales
Jim Williams
☐ 263 Duane Josephson 2.00 .90 .25
☐ 264 Rich Hebner 2.00 .90 .25
☐ 265 Randy Hundley 1.50 .70 .19
☐ 266 Wally Bunker 1.50 .70 .19
☐ 267 Twins Rookies 1.50 .70 .19
Herman Hill
Paul Ratliff
☐ 268 Claude Raymond 1.50 .70 .19
☐ 269 Cesar Gutierrez 1.50 .70 .19
☐ 270 Chris Short 1.50 .70 .19
☐ 271 Greg Goossen 2.00 .90 .25
☐ 272 Hector Torres 1.50 .70 .19
☐ 273 Ralph Houk MG 2.00 .90 .25
☐ 274 Gerry Arrigo 1.50 .70 .19
☐ 275 Duke Sims 1.50 .70 .19
☐ 276 Ron Hunt 1.50 .70 .19
☐ 277 Paul Doyle 1.50 .70 .19
☐ 278 Tommie Aaron 2.00 .90 .25
☐ 279 Bill Lee 3.00 1.35 .35
☐ 280 Donn Clendenon 2.00 .90 .25
☐ 281 Casey Cox 1.50 .70 .19
☐ 282 Steve Huntz 1.50 .70 .19
☐ 283 Angel Bravo 1.50 .70 .19
☐ 284 Jack Baldschun 1.50 .70 .19
☐ 285 Paul Blair 2.00 .90 .25
☐ 286 Dodgers Rookies 6.00 2.70 .75
Jack Jenkins
Bill Buckner
☐ 287 Fred Talbot 1.50 .70 .19
☐ 288 Larry Hisle 2.00 .90 .25
☐ 289 Gene Brabender 1.50 .70 .19
☐ 290 Rod Carew 20.00 9.00 2.50
☐ 291 Leo Durocher MG 4.00 1.80 .50
☐ 292 Eddie Leon 1.50 .70 .19
☐ 293 Bob Bailey 2.00 .90 .25
☐ 294 Jose Azcue 1.50 .70 .19
☐ 295 Cecil Upshaw 1.50 .70 .19
☐ 296 Woody Woodward 1.50 .70 .19
☐ 297 Curt Blefary 1.50 .70 .19
☐ 298 Ken Henderson 1.50 .70 .19
☐ 299 Buddy Bradford 1.50 .70 .19
☐ 300 Tom Seaver 50.00 22.00 6.25
☐ 301 Chico Salmon 1.50 .70 .19
☐ 302 Jeff James 1.50 .70 .19
☐ 303 Brant Alyea 1.50 .70 .19
☐ 304 Bill Russell 6.00 2.70 .75
☐ 305 Don Buford WS 3.00 1.35 .35
☐ 306 Donn Clendenon WS 3.00 1.35 .35
☐ 307 Tommie Agee WS 3.00 1.35 .35
☐ 308 J.C. Martin WS 3.00 1.35 .35
☐ 309 Jerry Koosman WS 4.00 1.80 .50
☐ 310 World Series Celebration 5.00 2.20 .60
Includes Ed Kranepool
Tug McGraw
Ed Charles
☐ 311 Dick Green 1.50 .70 .19
☐ 312 Mike Torrez 2.00 .90 .25
☐ 313 Mayo Smith MG 1.50 .70 .19
☐ 314 Bill McCool 1.50 .70 .19
☐ 315 Luis Aparicio 5.00 2.20 .60
☐ 316 Skip Guinn 1.50 .70 .19
☐ 317 Red Sox Rookies 2.00 .90 .25
Billy Conigliaro
Luis Alvarado
☐ 318 Willie Smith 1.50 .70 .19
☐ 319 Clay Dalrymple 1.50 .70 .19
☐ 320 Jim Maloney 2.00 .90 .25
☐ 321 Lou Piniella 3.00 1.35 .35
☐ 322 Luke Walker 1.50 .70 .19
☐ 323 Wayne Comer 1.50 .70 .19
☐ 324 Tony Taylor 2.00 .90 .25
☐ 325 Dave Boswell 1.50 .70 .19
☐ 326 Bill Voss 1.50 .70 .19
☐ 327 Hal King 1.50 .70 .19
☐ 328 George Brunet 1.50 .70 .19
☐ 329 Chris Cannizzaro 1.50 .70 .19
☐ 330 Lou Brock 12.00 5.50 1.50
☐ 331 Chuck Dobson 1.50 .70 .19
☐ 332 Bobby Wine 2.00 .90 .25
☐ 333 Bobby Murcer 3.00 1.35 .35
☐ 334 Phil Regan 1.50 .70 .19
☐ 335 Bill Freehan 2.00 .90 .25
☐ 336 Del Unser 2.00 .90 .25
☐ 337 Mike McCormick 2.00 .90 .25
☐ 338 Paul Schaal 1.50 .70 .19
☐ 339 Johnny Edwards 1.50 .70 .19
☐ 340 Tony Conigliaro 4.00 1.80 .50
☐ 341 Bill Sudakis 1.50 .70 .19
☐ 342 Wilbur Wood 2.00 .90 .25
☐ 343 Checklist 373-459 6.00 2.70 .75
☐ 344 Marcelino Lopez 1.50 .70 .19
☐ 345 Al Ferrara 1.50 .70 .19
☐ 346 Red Schoendienst MG 3.00 1.35 .35
☐ 347 Russ Snyder 1.50 .70 .19
☐ 348 Mets Rookies 2.00 .90 .25
Mike Jorgensen
Jesse Hudson
☐ 349 Steve Hamilton 1.50 .70 .19
☐ 350 Roberto Clemente 90.00 40.00 11.00
☐ 351 Tom Murphy 1.50 .70 .19
☐ 352 Bob Barton 1.50 .70 .19
☐ 353 Stan Williams 1.50 .70 .19
☐ 354 Amos Otis 2.50 1.10 .30
☐ 355 Doug Rader 2.00 .90 .25
☐ 356 Fred Lasher 1.50 .70 .19
☐ 357 Bob Burda 1.50 .70 .19
☐ 358 Pedro Borbon 2.50 1.10 .30
☐ 359 Phil Roof 1.50 .70 .19
☐ 360 Curt Flood 3.00 1.35 .35
☐ 361 Ray Jarvis 1.50 .70 .19
☐ 362 Joe Hague 1.50 .70 .19
☐ 363 Tom Shopay 1.50 .70 .19
☐ 364 Dan McGinn 1.50 .70 .19
☐ 365 Zoilo Versalles 2.00 .90 .25
☐ 366 Barry Moore 1.50 .70 .19
☐ 367 Mike Lum 1.50 .70 .19
☐ 368 Ed Herrmann 1.50 .70 .19
☐ 369 Alan Foster 1.50 .70 .19
☐ 370 Tommy Harper 2.00 .90 .25
☐ 371 Rod Gaspar 1.50 .70 .19
☐ 372 Dave Giusti 1.50 .70 .19
☐ 373 Roy White 2.00 .90 .25
☐ 374 Tommie Sisk 1.50 .70 .19
☐ 375 Johnny Callison 2.50 1.10 .30
☐ 376 Lefty Phillips MG 1.50 .70 .19
☐ 377 Bill Butler 1.50 .70 .19
☐ 378 Jim Davenport 1.50 .70 .19
☐ 379 Tom Tischinski 1.50 .70 .19
☐ 380 Tony Perez 7.50 3.40 .95
☐ 381 Athletics Rookies 1.50 .70 .19
Bobby Brooks
Mike Olivo
☐ 382 Jack DiLauro 1.50 .70 .19
☐ 383 Mickey Stanley 2.00 .90 .25
☐ 384 Gary Neibauer 1.50 .70 .19
☐ 385 George Scott 2.00 .90 .25
☐ 386 Bill Dillman 1.50 .70 .19
☐ 387 Orioles Team 4.00 1.80 .50
☐ 388 Byron Browne 1.50 .70 .19
☐ 389 Jim Shellenback 1.50 .70 .19
☐ 390 Willie Davis 2.50 1.10 .30
☐ 391 Larry Brown 1.50 .70 .19
☐ 392 Walt Hriniak 2.00 .90 .25
☐ 393 John Gelnar 1.50 .70 .19
☐ 394 Gil Hodges MG 5.00 2.20 .60
☐ 395 Walt Williams 1.50 .70 .19
☐ 396 Steve Blass 2.00 .90 .25
☐ 397 Roger Repoz 1.50 .70 .19
☐ 398 Bill Stoneman 1.50 .70 .19
☐ 399 Yankees Team 4.00 1.80 .50
☐ 400 Denny McLain 3.00 1.35 .35
☐ 401 Giants Rookies 1.50 .70 .19
John Harrell
Bernie Williams
☐ 402 Ellie Rodriguez 1.50 .70 .19
☐ 403 Jim Bunning 4.00 1.80 .50
☐ 404 Rich Reese 1.50 .70 .19
☐ 405 Bill Hands 1.50 .70 .19
☐ 406 Mike Andrews 1.50 .70 .19
☐ 407 Bob Watson 2.50 1.10 .30
☐ 408 Paul Lindblad 1.50 .70 .19
☐ 409 Bob Tolan 1.50 .70 .19
☐ 410 Boog Powell 4.00 1.80 .50
☐ 411 Dodgers Team 4.00 1.80 .50
☐ 412 Larry Burchart 1.50 .70 .19
☐ 413 Sonny Jackson 1.50 .70 .19
☐ 414 Paul Edmondson 1.50 .70 .19
☐ 415 Julian Javier 2.00 .90 .25
☐ 416 Joe Verbanic 1.50 .70 .19
☐ 417 John Bateman 1.50 .70 .19
☐ 418 John Donaldson 1.50 .70 .19
☐ 419 Ron Taylor 2.00 .90 .25
☐ 420 Ken McMullen 2.00 .90 .25
☐ 421 Pat Dobson 2.00 .90 .25
☐ 422 Royals Team 3.00 1.35 .35
☐ 423 Jerry May 1.50 .70 .19
☐ 424 Mike Kilkenny 1.50 .70 .19
☐ 425 Bobby Bonds 6.00 2.70 .75
☐ 426 Bill Rigney MG 1.50 .70 .19
☐ 427 Fred Norman 1.50 .70 .19
☐ 428 Don Buford 1.50 .70 .19
☐ 429 Cubs Rookies 1.50 .70 .19
Randy Bobb
Jim Cosman
☐ 430 Andy Messersmith 2.00 .90 .25
☐ 431 Ron Swoboda 1.50 .70 .19
☐ 432 Checklist 460-546 6.00 2.70 .75
☐ 433 Ron Bryant 1.50 .70 .19
☐ 434 Felipe Alou 2.50 1.10 .30
☐ 435 Nelson Briles 2.00 .90 .25
☐ 436 Phillies Team 3.00 1.35 .35
☐ 437 Danny Cater 1.50 .70 .19
☐ 438 Pat Jarvis 1.50 .70 .19
☐ 439 Lee Maye 1.50 .70 .19
☐ 440 Bill Mazeroski 3.00 1.35 .35
☐ 441 John O'Donoghue 1.50 .70 .19
☐ 442 Gene Mauch MG 2.00 .90 .25
☐ 443 Al Jackson 1.50 .70 .19
☐ 444 White Sox Rookies 1.50 .70 .19
Billy Farmer
John Matias
☐ 445 Vada Pinson 3.00 1.35 .35
☐ 446 Billy Grabarkewitz 1.50 .70 .19
☐ 447 Lee Stange 1.50 .70 .19
☐ 448 Astros Team 3.00 1.35 .35
☐ 449 Jim Palmer 15.00 6.75 1.85

☐ 450 Willie McCovey AS	7.50	3.40	.95
☐ 451 Boog Powell AS	4.00	1.80	.50
☐ 452 Felix Millan AS	3.00	1.35	.35
☐ 453 Rod Carew AS	7.50	3.40	.95
☐ 454 Ron Santo AS	4.00	1.80	.50
☐ 455 Brooks Robinson AS	7.50	3.40	.95
☐ 456 Don Kessinger AS	3.50	1.55	.45
☐ 457 Rico Petrocelli AS	3.50	1.55	.45
☐ 458 Pete Rose AS	15.00	6.75	1.85
☐ 459 Reggie Jackson AS	15.00	6.75	1.85
☐ 460 Matty Alou AS	4.00	1.80	.50
☐ 461 Carl Yastrzemski AS	10.00	4.50	1.25
☐ 462 Hank Aaron AS	18.00	8.00	2.20
☐ 463 Frank Robinson AS	8.00	3.60	1.00
☐ 464 Johnny Bench AS	15.00	6.75	1.85
☐ 465 Bill Freehan AS	5.00	2.20	.60
☐ 466 Juan Marichal AS	6.00	2.70	.75
☐ 467 Denny McLain AS	5.00	2.20	.60
☐ 468 Jerry Koosman AS	5.00	2.20	.60
☐ 469 Sam McDowell AS	5.00	2.20	.60
☐ 470 Willie Stargell	12.00	5.50	1.50
☐ 471 Chris Zachary	2.00	.90	.25
☐ 472 Braves Team	4.00	1.80	.50
☐ 473 Don Bryant	2.00	.90	.25
☐ 474 Dick Kelley	2.00	.90	.25
☐ 475 Dick McAuliffe	3.00	1.35	.35
☐ 476 Don Shaw	2.00	.90	.25
☐ 477 Orioles Rookies	2.00	.90	.25
Al Severinsen			
Roger Freed			
☐ 478 Bob Heise	2.00	.90	.25
☐ 479 Dick Woodson	2.00	.90	.25
☐ 480 Glenn Beckert	2.00	.90	.25
☐ 481 Jose Tartabull	2.00	.90	.25
☐ 482 Tom Hilgendorf	2.00	.90	.25
☐ 483 Gail Hopkins	2.00	.90	.25
☐ 484 Gary Nolan	3.00	1.35	.35
☐ 485 Jay Johnstone	3.00	1.35	.35
☐ 486 Terry Harmon	2.00	.90	.25
☐ 487 Cisco Carlos	2.00	.90	.25
☐ 488 J.C. Martin	2.00	.90	.25
☐ 489 Eddie Kasko MG	2.00	.90	.25
☐ 490 Bill Singer	2.50	1.10	.30
☐ 491 Graig Nettles	7.50	3.40	.95
☐ 492 Astros Rookies	2.00	.90	.25
Keith Lampard			
Scipio Spinks			
☐ 493 Lindy McDaniel	2.50	1.10	.30
☐ 494 Larry Stahl	2.00	.90	.25
☐ 495 Dave Morehead	2.00	.90	.25
☐ 496 Steve Whitaker	2.00	.90	.25
☐ 497 Eddie Watt	2.00	.90	.25
☐ 498 Al Weis	2.00	.90	.25
☐ 499 Skip Lockwood	2.00	.90	.25
☐ 500 Hank Aaron	70.00	32.00	8.75
☐ 501 White Sox Team	4.00	1.80	.50
☐ 502 Rollie Fingers	10.00	4.50	1.25
☐ 503 Dal Maxvill	2.00	.90	.25
☐ 504 Don Pavletich	2.00	.90	.25
☐ 505 Ken Holtzman	3.00	1.35	.35
☐ 506 Ed Stroud	2.00	.90	.25
☐ 507 Pat Corrales	2.00	.90	.25
☐ 508 Joe Niekro	2.50	1.10	.30
☐ 509 Expos Team	4.00	1.80	.50
☐ 510 Tony Oliva	5.00	2.20	.60
☐ 511 Joe Hoerner	2.00	.90	.25
☐ 512 Billy Harris	2.00	.90	.25
☐ 513 Preston Gomez MG	2.00	.90	.25
☐ 514 Steve Hovley	2.00	.90	.25
☐ 515 Don Wilson	2.00	.90	.25
☐ 516 Yankees Rookies	2.00	.90	.25
John Ellis			
Jim Lyttle			
☐ 517 Joe Gibbon	2.00	.90	.25
☐ 518 Bill Melton	2.00	.90	.25
☐ 519 Don McMahon	2.00	.90	.25
☐ 520 Willie Horton	3.00	1.35	.35
☐ 521 Cal Koonce	2.00	.90	.25
☐ 522 Angels Team	4.00	1.80	.50
☐ 523 Jose Pena	2.00	.90	.25
☐ 524 Alvin Dark MG	3.00	1.35	.35
☐ 525 Jerry Adair	2.00	.90	.25
☐ 526 Ron Herbel	2.00	.90	.25
☐ 527 Don Bosch	2.00	.90	.25
☐ 528 Elrod Hendricks	3.00	1.35	.35
☐ 529 Bob Aspromonte	2.00	.90	.25
☐ 530 Bob Gibson	18.00	8.00	2.20
☐ 531 Ron Clark	2.00	.90	.25
☐ 532 Danny Murtaugh MG	3.00	1.35	.35
☐ 533 Buzz Stephen	2.00	.90	.25
☐ 534 Twins Team	4.00	1.80	.50
☐ 535 Andy Kosco	2.00	.90	.25
☐ 536 Mike Kekich	2.00	.90	.25
☐ 537 Joe Morgan	10.00	4.50	1.25
☐ 538 Bob Humphreys	2.00	.90	.25
☐ 539 Phillies Rookies	6.00	2.70	.75
Denny Doyle			
Larry Bowa			
☐ 540 Gary Peters	2.00	.90	.25
☐ 541 Bill Heath	2.00	.90	.25
☐ 542 Checklist 547-633	6.00	2.70	.75
☐ 543 Clyde Wright	2.00	.90	.25
☐ 544 Reds Team	5.00	2.20	.60
☐ 545 Ken Harrelson	3.00	1.35	.35
☐ 546 Ron Reed	3.00	1.35	.35

1971 O-Pee-Chee

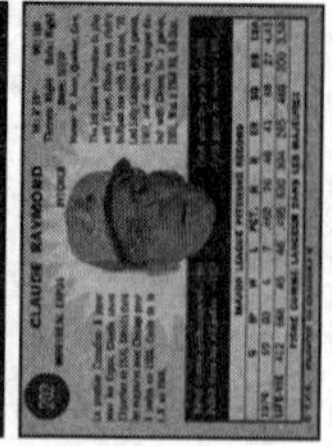

The cards in this 752-card set measure 2 1/2" by 3 1/2". The 1971 O-Pee-Chee set is a challenge to complete in "Mint" condition because the black borders are easily scratched and damaged. The O-Pee-Chee cards seem to have been cut (into individual cards) not as sharply as the Topps cards; the borders frequently appear slightly frayed. The players are also pictured in black and white on the back of the card. The next-to-last series (524-643) and the last series (644-752) are somewhat scarce. The O-Pee-Chee cards can be distinguished from Topps cards by the "Printed in Canada" on the bottom of the reverse. The reverse color is yellow instead of the green found on the backs of the 1971 Topps cards. The card backs are written in both French and English, except for cards 524-752 which were printed in English only. There are several cards which are different from the corresponding Topps card with a different pose or different team noted in bold type, i.e. "Recently Traded to ..." These changed cards are numbers 31, 32, 73, 144, 151, 161, 172, 182, 191, 202, 207, 248, 289 and 578. Remember, the prices below apply only to the 1971 O-Pee-Chee cards -- NOT Topps cards which are much more plentiful.

	NRMT	VG-E	GOOD
COMPLETE SET (752)	2750.00	1250.00	350.00
COMMON CARD (1-393)	2.00	.90	.25
COMMON CARD (394-523)	2.50	1.10	.30
COMMON CARD (524-643)	5.00	2.20	.60
COMMON CARD (644-752)	10.00	4.50	1.25
☐ 1 Orioles Team	18.00	8.00	2.20
☐ 2 Dock Ellis	2.50	1.10	.30
☐ 3 Dick McAuliffe	2.50	1.10	.30
☐ 4 Vic Davalillo	2.00	.90	.25
☐ 5 Thurman Munson	20.00	9.00	2.50
☐ 6 Ed Spiezio	2.00	.90	.25
☐ 7 Jim Holt	2.00	.90	.25
☐ 8 Mike McQueen	2.00	.90	.25
☐ 9 George Scott	2.50	1.10	.30
☐ 10 Claude Osteen	2.50	1.10	.30
☐ 11 Elliott Maddox	2.50	1.10	.30
☐ 12 Johnny Callison	2.50	1.10	.30
☐ 13 White Sox Rookies	2.00	.90	.25
Charlie Brinkman			
Dick Moloney			
☐ 14 Dave Concepcion	20.00	9.00	2.50
☐ 15 Andy Messersmith	2.50	1.10	.30
☐ 16 Ken Singleton	4.00	1.80	.50
☐ 17 Billy Sorrell	2.00	.90	.25
☐ 18 Norm Miller	2.00	.90	.25
☐ 19 Skip Pitlock	2.00	.90	.25
☐ 20 Reggie Jackson	40.00	18.00	5.00
☐ 21 Dan McGinn	2.00	.90	.25
☐ 22 Phil Roof	2.00	.90	.25
☐ 23 Oscar Gamble	2.50	1.10	.30
☐ 24 Rich Hand	2.00	.90	.25
☐ 25 Clarence Gaston	3.00	1.35	.35
☐ 26 Bert Blyleven	7.00	3.10	.85
☐ 27 Pirates Rookies	2.00	.90	.25
Fred Cambria			
Gene Clines			
☐ 28 Ron Klimkowski	2.00	.90	.25
☐ 29 Don Buford	2.00	.90	.25
☐ 30 Phil Niekro	5.00	2.20	.60
☐ 31 John Bateman	2.50	1.10	.30
(different pose)			
☐ 32 Jerry DeVanon	2.50	1.10	.30
Recently Traded To Orioles			
☐ 33 Del Unser	2.00	.90	.25
☐ 34 Sandy Vance	2.00	.90	.25
☐ 35 Lou Piniella	3.00	1.35	.35
☐ 36 Dean Chance	2.50	1.10	.30
☐ 37 Rich McKinney	2.00	.90	.25
☐ 38 Jim Colborn	2.00	.90	.25
☐ 39 Tiger Rookies	2.00	.90	.25
Lerrin LaGrow			
Gene Lamont			
☐ 40 Lee May	2.50	1.10	.30
☐ 41 Rick Austin	2.00	.90	.25
☐ 42 Boots Day	2.50	1.10	.30
☐ 43 Steve Kealey	2.00	.90	.25
☐ 44 Johnny Edwards	2.00	.90	.25
☐ 45 Jim Hunter	7.00	3.10	.85
☐ 46 Dave Campbell	2.50	1.10	.30
☐ 47 Johnny Jeter	2.00	.90	.25
☐ 48 Dave Baldwin	2.00	.90	.25
☐ 49 Don Money	2.50	1.10	.30
☐ 50 Willie McCovey	8.00	3.60	1.00
☐ 51 Steve Kline	2.00	.90	.25
☐ 52 Braves Rookies	2.00	.90	.25
Oscar Brown			
Earl Williams			
☐ 53 Paul Blair	2.50	1.10	.30
☐ 54 Checklist 1-132	6.00	2.70	.75
☐ 55 Steve Carlton	18.00	8.00	2.20
☐ 56 Duane Josephson	2.00	.90	.25
☐ 57 Von Joshua	2.00	.90	.25
☐ 58 Bill Lee	2.50	1.10	.30
☐ 59 Gene Mauch MG	2.50	1.10	.30
☐ 60 Dick Bosman	2.00	.90	.25
☐ 61 AL Batting Leaders	4.00	1.80	.50
Alex Johnson			
Carl Yastrzemski			
Tony Oliva			
☐ 62 NL Batting Leaders	3.00	1.35	.35
Rico Carty			
Joe Torre			
Manny Sanguillen			
☐ 63 AL RBI Leaders	4.00	1.80	.50
Frank Robinson			
Tony Conigliaro			
Boog Powell			
☐ 64 NL RBI Leaders	6.00	2.70	.75
Johnny Bench			
Tony Perez			
Billy Williams			
☐ 65 AL HR Leaders	4.00	1.80	.50
Frank Howard			
Harmon Killebrew			
Carl Yastrzemski			
☐ 66 NL HR Leaders	6.00	2.70	.75
Johnny Bench			
Billy Williams			
Tony Perez			
☐ 67 AL ERA Leaders	4.00	1.80	.50
Diego Segui			
Jim Palmer			
Clyde Wright			
☐ 68 NL ERA Leaders	4.00	1.80	.50
Tom Seaver			
Wayne Simpson			
Luke Walker			
☐ 69 AL Pitching Leaders	3.00	1.35	.35
Mike Cuellar			
Dave McNally			
Jim Perry			
☐ 70 NL Pitching Leaders	6.00	2.70	.75
Bob Gibson			
Gaylord Perry			
Fergie Jenkins			
☐ 71 AL Strikeout Leaders	3.00	1.35	.35
Sam McDowell			
Mickey Lolich			
Bob Johnson			
☐ 72 NL Strikeout Leaders	7.00	3.10	.85
Tom Seaver			
Bob Gibson			
Fergie Jenkins			
☐ 73 George Brunet	2.00	.90	.25
(St. Louis Cardinals)			
☐ 74 Twins Rookies	2.00	.90	.25
Pete Hamm			
Jim Nettles			
☐ 75 Gary Nolan	2.50	1.10	.30
☐ 76 Ted Savage	2.00	.90	.25
☐ 77 Mike Compton	2.00	.90	.25
☐ 78 Jim Spencer	2.00	.90	.25
☐ 79 Wade Blasingame	2.00	.90	.25
☐ 80 Bill Melton	2.00	.90	.25
☐ 81 Felix Millan	2.00	.90	.25
☐ 82 Casey Cox	2.00	.90	.25
☐ 83 Met Rookies	2.50	1.10	.30
Tim Foli			
Randy Bobb			
☐ 84 Marcel Lachemann	2.50	1.10	.30
☐ 85 Bill Grabarkewitz	2.00	.90	.25
☐ 86 Mike Kilkenny	2.00	.90	.25
☐ 87 Jack Heidemann	2.00	.90	.25
☐ 88 Hal King	2.00	.90	.25
☐ 89 Ken Brett	2.50	1.10	.30
☐ 90 Joe Pepitone	2.50	1.10	.30
☐ 91 Bob Lemon MG	3.00	1.35	.35
☐ 92 Fred Wenz	2.00	.90	.25
☐ 93 Senators Rookies	2.00	.90	.25
Norm McRae			
Denny Riddleberger			
☐ 94 Don Hahn	2.00	.90	.25
☐ 95 Luis Tiant	2.50	1.10	.30
☐ 96 Joe Hague	2.00	.90	.25
☐ 97 Floyd Wicker	2.00	.90	.25
☐ 98 Joe Decker	2.00	.90	.25
☐ 99 Mark Belanger	2.50	1.10	.30
☐ 100 Pete Rose	40.00	18.00	5.00
☐ 101 Les Cain	2.00	.90	.25
☐ 102 Astros Rookies	2.50	1.10	.30
Ken Forsch			
Larry Howard			
☐ 103 Rich Severson	2.00	.90	.25
☐ 104 Dan Frisella	2.00	.90	.25
☐ 105 Tony Conigliaro	3.00	1.35	.35
☐ 106 Tom Dukes	2.00	.90	.25
☐ 107 Roy Foster	2.00	.90	.25
☐ 108 John Cumberland	2.00	.90	.25
☐ 109 Steve Hovley	2.00	.90	.25
☐ 110 Bill Mazeroski	3.00	1.35	.35
☐ 111 Yankee Rookies	2.50	1.10	.30
Loyd Colson			
Bobby Mitchell			
☐ 112 Manny Mota	2.50	1.10	.30
☐ 113 Jerry Crider	2.00	.90	.25
☐ 114 Billy Conigliaro	2.00	.90	.25
☐ 115 Donn Clendenon	2.50	1.10	.30
☐ 116 Ken Sanders	2.00	.90	.25
☐ 117 Ted Simmons	15.00	6.75	1.85
☐ 118 Cookie Rojas	2.50	1.10	.30
☐ 119 Frank Lucchesi MG	2.00	.90	.25
☐ 120 Willie Horton	2.50	1.10	.30
☐ 121 Cubs Rookies	2.00	.90	.25
Jim Dunegan			
Roe Skidmore			
☐ 122 Eddie Watt	2.00	.90	.25
☐ 123 Checklist 133-263	6.00	2.70	.75
☐ 124 Don Gullett	3.00	1.35	.35
☐ 125 Ray Fosse	2.50	1.10	.30
☐ 126 Danny Coombs	2.00	.90	.25
☐ 127 Danny Thompson	2.00	.90	.25
☐ 128 Frank Johnson	2.00	.90	.25
☐ 129 Aurelio Monteagudo	2.00	.90	.25
☐ 130 Denis Menke	2.00	.90	.25
☐ 131 Curt Blefary	2.00	.90	.25
☐ 132 Jose Laboy	2.00	.90	.25
☐ 133 Mickey Lolich	2.50	1.10	.30
☐ 134 Jose Arcia	2.00	.90	.25
☐ 135 Rick Monday	2.50	1.10	.30
☐ 136 Duffy Dyer	2.00	.90	.25
☐ 137 Marcelino Lopez	2.00	.90	.25
☐ 138 Phillies Rookies	2.50	1.10	.30
Joe Lis			
Willie Montanez			
☐ 139 Paul Casanova	2.00	.90	.25
☐ 140 Gaylord Perry	8.00	3.60	1.00
☐ 141 Frank Quilici MG	2.00	.90	.25
☐ 142 Mack Jones	2.00	.90	.25
☐ 143 Steve Blass	2.50	1.10	.30
☐ 144 Jackie Hernandez	2.50	1.10	.30
(Pittsburgh Pirates)			
☐ 145 Bill Singer	2.50	1.10	.30
☐ 146 Ralph Houk MG	2.50	1.10	.30
☐ 147 Bob Priddy	2.00	.90	.25
☐ 148 John Mayberry	2.50	1.10	.30
☐ 149 Mike Hershberger	2.00	.90	.25
☐ 150 Sam McDowell	2.50	1.10	.30
☐ 151 Tommy Davis	3.00	1.35	.35
(Oakland A's)			
☐ 152 Angels Rookies	2.00	.90	.25
Lloyd Allen			
Winston Llenas			
☐ 153 Gary Ross	2.00	.90	.25
☐ 154 Cesar Gutierrez	2.00	.90	.25
☐ 155 Ken Henderson	2.00	.90	.25
☐ 156 Bart Johnson	2.00	.90	.25
☐ 157 Bob Bailey	2.50	1.10	.30
☐ 158 Jerry Reuss	2.50	1.10	.30
☐ 159 Jarvis Tatum	2.00	.90	.25
☐ 160 Tom Seaver	25.00	11.00	3.10
☐ 161 Ron Hunt	4.00	1.80	.50
(different pose)			
☐ 162 Jack Billingham	2.50	1.10	.30
☐ 163 Buck Martinez	2.00	.90	.25
☐ 164 Reds Rookies	2.50	1.10	.30
Frank Duffy			
Milt Wilcox			
☐ 165 Cesar Tovar	2.00	.90	.25
☐ 166 Joe Hoerner	2.00	.90	.25
☐ 167 Tom Grieve	2.50	1.10	.30
☐ 168 Bruce Dal Canton	2.00	.90	.25
☐ 169 Ed Herrmann	2.00	.90	.25
☐ 170 Mike Cuellar	2.50	1.10	.30
☐ 171 Bobby Wine	2.00	.90	.25
☐ 172 Duke Sims	2.50	1.10	.30
(Los Angeles Dodgers)			
☐ 173 Gil Garrido	2.00	.90	.25
☐ 174 Dave LaRoche	2.00	.90	.25
☐ 175 Jim Hickman	2.00	.90	.25
☐ 176 Red Sox Rookies	2.50	1.10	.30
Bob Montgomery			
Doug Griffin			
☐ 177 Hal McRae	3.00	1.35	.35
☐ 178 Dave Duncan	2.00	.90	.25
☐ 179 Mike Corkins	2.00	.90	.25
☐ 180 Al Kaline	20.00	9.00	2.50
☐ 181 Hal Lanier	2.50	1.10	.30
☐ 182 Al Downing	2.50	1.10	.30
(Los Angeles Dodgers)			
☐ 183 Gil Hodges MG	5.00	2.20	.60
☐ 184 Stan Bahnsen	2.00	.90	.25
☐ 185 Julian Javier	2.00	.90	.25
☐ 186 Bob Spence	2.00	.90	.25
☐ 187 Ted Abernathy	2.00	.90	.25
☐ 188 Dodgers Rookies	4.00	1.80	.50
Bob Valentine			
Mike Strahler			
☐ 189 George Mitterwald	2.00	.90	.25
☐ 190 Bob Tolan	2.50	1.10	.30
☐ 191 Mike Andrews	2.50	1.10	.30
(Chicago White Sox)			
☐ 192 Billy Wilson	2.00	.90	.25
☐ 193 Bob Grich	4.00	1.80	.50
☐ 194 Mike Lum	2.50	1.10	.30
☐ 195 Boog Powell ALCS	4.00	1.80	.50
☐ 196 Dave McNally ALCS	4.00	1.80	.50
☐ 197 Jim Palmer ALCS	5.00	2.20	.60
☐ 198 AL Playoff Summary	4.00	1.80	.50
Orioles Celebrate			

☐ 199 Ty Cline NLCS	4.00	1.80	.50
☐ 200 Bobby Tolan NLCS	4.00	1.80	.50
☐ 201 Ty Cline NLCS	4.00	1.80	.50
☐ 202 Claude Raymond	2.50	1.10	.30
(different pose)			
☐ 203 Larry Gura	2.50	1.10	.30
☐ 204 Brewers Rookies	2.00	.90	.25
Bernie Smith			
George Kopacz			
☐ 205 Gerry Moses	2.00	.90	.25
☐ 206 Checklist 264-393	6.00	2.70	.75
☐ 207 Alan Foster	2.50	1.10	.30
(Cleveland Indians)			
☐ 208 Billy Martin MG	4.00	1.80	.50
☐ 209 Steve Renko	2.50	1.10	.30
☐ 210 Rod Carew	20.00	9.00	2.50
☐ 211 Phil Hennigan	2.00	.90	.25
☐ 212 Rich Hebner	2.50	1.10	.30
☐ 213 Frank Baker	2.00	.90	.25
☐ 214 Al Ferrara	2.00	.90	.25
☐ 215 Diego Segui	2.00	.90	.25
☐ 216 Cardinals Rookies	2.00	.90	.25
Reggie Cleveland			
Luis Melendez			
☐ 217 Ed Stroud	2.00	.90	.25
☐ 218 Tony Cloninger	2.00	.90	.25
☐ 219 Elrod Hendricks	2.00	.90	.25
☐ 220 Ron Santo	3.00	1.35	.35
☐ 221 Dave Morehead	2.00	.90	.25
☐ 222 Bob Watson	2.50	1.10	.30
☐ 223 Cecil Upshaw	2.00	.90	.25
☐ 224 Alan Gallagher	2.00	.90	.25
☐ 225 Gary Peters	2.00	.90	.25
☐ 226 Bill Russell	2.50	1.10	.30
☐ 227 Floyd Weaver	2.00	.90	.25
☐ 228 Wayne Garrett	2.00	.90	.25
☐ 229 Jim Hannan	2.00	.90	.25
☐ 230 Willie Stargell	10.00	4.50	1.25
☐ 231 Indians Rookies	2.50	1.10	.30
Vince Colbert			
John Lowenstein			
☐ 232 John Strohmayer	2.00	.90	.25
☐ 233 Larry Bowa	3.00	1.35	.35
☐ 234 Jim Lyttle	2.00	.90	.25
☐ 235 Nate Colbert	2.50	1.10	.30
☐ 236 Bob Humphreys	2.00	.90	.25
☐ 237 Cesar Cedeno	3.00	1.35	.35
☐ 238 Chuck Dobson	2.00	.90	.25
☐ 239 Red Schoendienst MG	3.00	1.35	.35
☐ 240 Clyde Wright	2.00	.90	.25
☐ 241 Dave Nelson	2.00	.90	.25
☐ 242 Jim Ray	2.00	.90	.25
☐ 243 Carlos May	2.00	.90	.25
☐ 244 Bob Tillman	2.00	.90	.25
☐ 245 Jim Kaat	3.00	1.35	.35
☐ 246 Tony Taylor	2.00	.90	.25
☐ 247 Royals Rookies	2.50	1.10	.30
Jerry Cram			
Paul Splittorff			
☐ 248 Hoyt Wilhelm	6.00	2.70	.75
(Atlanta Braves)			
☐ 249 Chico Salmon	2.00	.90	.25
☐ 250 Johnny Bench	20.00	9.00	2.50
☐ 251 Frank Reberger	2.00	.90	.25
☐ 252 Eddie Leon	2.00	.90	.25
☐ 253 Bill Sudakis	2.00	.90	.25
☐ 254 Cal Koonce	2.00	.90	.25
☐ 255 Bob Robertson	2.50	1.10	.30
☐ 256 Tony Gonzalez	2.00	.90	.25
☐ 257 Nelson Briles	2.00	.90	.25
☐ 258 Dick Green	2.00	.90	.25
☐ 259 Dave Marshall	2.00	.90	.25
☐ 260 Tommy Harper	2.50	1.10	.30
☐ 261 Darold Knowles	2.00	.90	.25
☐ 262 Padres Rookies	2.00	.90	.25
Jim Williams			
Dave Robinson			
☐ 263 John Ellis	2.00	.90	.25
☐ 264 Joe Morgan	7.00	3.10	.85
☐ 265 Jim Northrup	2.50	1.10	.30
☐ 266 Bill Stoneman	2.50	1.10	.30
☐ 267 Rich Morales	2.00	.90	.25
☐ 268 Phillies Team	4.00	1.80	.50
☐ 269 Gail Hopkins	2.00	.90	.25
☐ 270 Rico Carty	2.50	1.10	.30
☐ 271 Bill Zepp	2.00	.90	.25
☐ 272 Tommy Helms	2.50	1.10	.30
☐ 273 Pete Richert	2.00	.90	.25
☐ 274 Ron Slocum	2.00	.90	.25
☐ 275 Vada Pinson	2.50	1.10	.30
☐ 276 Giants Rookies	8.00	3.60	1.00
Mike Davison			
George Foster			
☐ 277 Gary Waslewski	2.00	.90	.25
☐ 278 Jerry Grote	2.50	1.10	.30
☐ 279 Lefty Phillips MG	2.00	.90	.25
☐ 280 Fergie Jenkins	7.00	3.10	.85
☐ 281 Danny Walton	2.00	.90	.25
☐ 282 Jose Pagan	2.00	.90	.25
☐ 283 Dick Such	2.00	.90	.25
☐ 284 Jim Gosger	2.00	.90	.25
☐ 285 Sal Bando	2.50	1.10	.30
☐ 286 Jerry McNertney	2.00	.90	.25
☐ 287 Mike Fiore	2.00	.90	.25
☐ 288 Joe Moeller	2.00	.90	.25
☐ 289 Rusty Staub	7.50	3.40	.95
(Different pose)			
☐ 290 Tony Oliva	3.00	1.35	.35
☐ 291 George Culver	2.00	.90	.25
☐ 292 Jay Johnstone	2.50	1.10	.30
☐ 293 Pat Corrales	2.50	1.10	.30
☐ 294 Steve Dunning	2.00	.90	.25
☐ 295 Bobby Bonds	5.00	2.20	.60
☐ 296 Tom Timmermann	2.00	.90	.25
☐ 297 Johnny Briggs	2.00	.90	.25
☐ 298 Jim Nelson	2.00	.90	.25
☐ 299 Ed Kirkpatrick	2.00	.90	.25
☐ 300 Brooks Robinson	20.00	9.00	2.50
☐ 301 Earl Wilson	2.00	.90	.25
☐ 302 Phil Gagliano	2.00	.90	.25
☐ 303 Lindy McDaniel	2.50	1.10	.30
☐ 304 Ron Brand	2.00	.90	.25
☐ 305 Reggie Smith	2.50	1.10	.30
☐ 306 Jim Nash	2.00	.90	.25
☐ 307 Don Wert	2.00	.90	.25
☐ 308 Cardinals Team	4.00	1.80	.50
☐ 309 Dick Ellsworth	2.00	.90	.25
☐ 310 Tommie Agee	2.50	1.10	.30
☐ 311 Lee Stange	2.00	.90	.25
☐ 312 Harry Walker MG	2.00	.90	.25
☐ 313 Tom Hall	2.00	.90	.25
☐ 314 Jeff Torborg	2.50	1.10	.30
☐ 315 Ron Fairly	2.50	1.10	.30
☐ 316 Fred Scherman	2.00	.90	.25
☐ 317 Athletic Rookies	2.00	.90	.25
Jim Driscoll			
Angel Mangual			
☐ 318 Rudy May	2.50	1.10	.30
☐ 319 Ty Cline	2.00	.90	.25
☐ 320 Dave McNally	2.50	1.10	.30
☐ 321 Tom Matchick	2.00	.90	.25
☐ 322 Jim Beauchamp	2.00	.90	.25
☐ 323 Billy Champion	2.00	.90	.25
☐ 324 Graig Nettles	3.00	1.35	.35
☐ 325 Juan Marichal	7.00	3.10	.85
☐ 326 Richie Scheinblum	2.00	.90	.25
☐ 327 Boog Powell WS	5.00	2.20	.60
☐ 328 Don Buford WS	4.00	1.80	.50
☐ 329 Frank Robinson WS	6.00	2.70	.75
☐ 330 World Series Game 4	4.00	1.80	.50
Reds stay alive			
☐ 331 Brooks Robinson WS	7.50	3.40	.95
☐ 332 World Series Summary	4.00	1.80	.50
Orioles Celebrate			
☐ 333 Clay Kirby	2.00	.90	.25
☐ 334 Roberto Pena	2.00	.90	.25
☐ 335 Jerry Koosman	3.00	1.35	.35
☐ 336 Tigers Team	4.00	1.80	.50
☐ 337 Jesus Alou	2.00	.90	.25
☐ 338 Gene Tenace	2.50	1.10	.30
☐ 339 Wayne Simpson	2.00	.90	.25
☐ 340 Rico Petrocelli	2.50	1.10	.30
☐ 341 Steve Garvey	30.00	13.50	3.70
☐ 342 Frank Tepedino	2.00	.90	.25
☐ 343 Pirates Rookies	2.50	1.10	.30
Ed Acosta			
Milt May			
☐ 344 Ellie Rodriguez	2.00	.90	.25
☐ 345 Joel Horlen	2.00	.90	.25
☐ 346 Lum Harris MG	2.00	.90	.25
☐ 347 Ted Uhlaender	2.00	.90	.25
☐ 348 Fred Norman	2.00	.90	.25
☐ 349 Rich Reese	2.00	.90	.25
☐ 350 Billy Williams	8.00	3.60	1.00
☐ 351 Jim Shellenback	2.00	.90	.25
☐ 352 Denny Doyle	2.00	.90	.25
☐ 353 Carl Taylor	2.00	.90	.25
☐ 354 Don McMahon	2.00	.90	.25
☐ 355 Bud Harrelson	3.50	1.55	.45
☐ 356 Bob Locker	2.00	.90	.25
☐ 357 Reds Team	4.00	1.80	.50
☐ 358 Danny Cater	2.00	.90	.25
☐ 359 Ron Reed	2.00	.90	.25
☐ 360 Jim Fregosi	2.50	1.10	.30
☐ 361 Don Sutton	7.00	3.10	.85
☐ 362 Orioles Rookies	2.00	.90	.25
Mike Adamson			
Roger Freed			
☐ 363 Mike Nagy	2.00	.90	.25
☐ 364 Tommy Dean	2.00	.90	.25
☐ 365 Bob Johnson	2.00	.90	.25
☐ 366 Ron Stone	2.00	.90	.25
☐ 367 Dalton Jones	2.00	.90	.25
☐ 368 Bob Veale	2.50	1.10	.30
☐ 369 Checklist 394-523	6.00	2.70	.75
☐ 370 Joe Torre	3.00	1.35	.35
☐ 371 Jack Hiatt	2.00	.90	.25
☐ 372 Lew Krausse	2.00	.90	.25
☐ 373 Tom McCraw	2.00	.90	.25
☐ 374 Clete Boyer	2.50	1.10	.30
☐ 375 Steve Hargan	2.00	.90	.25
☐ 376 Expos Rookies	2.00	.90	.25
Clyde Mashore			
Ernie McAnally			
☐ 377 Greg Garrett	2.00	.90	.25
☐ 378 Tito Fuentes	2.50	1.10	.30
☐ 379 Wayne Granger	2.00	.90	.25
☐ 380 Ted Williams MG	12.00	5.50	1.50
☐ 381 Fred Gladding	2.00	.90	.25
☐ 382 Jake Gibbs	2.00	.90	.25
☐ 383 Rod Gaspar	2.00	.90	.25
☐ 384 Rollie Fingers	6.00	2.70	.75
☐ 385 Maury Wills	3.00	1.35	.35
☐ 386 Red Sox Team	4.00	1.80	.50
☐ 387 Ron Herbel	2.00	.90	.25
☐ 388 Al Oliver	3.00	1.35	.35
☐ 389 Ed Brinkman	2.00	.90	.25
☐ 390 Glenn Beckert	2.50	1.10	.30
☐ 391 Twins Rookies	2.50	1.10	.30
Steve Brye			
Cotton Nash			
☐ 392 Grant Jackson	2.00	.90	.25
☐ 393 Merv Rettenmund	2.50	1.10	.30
☐ 394 Clay Carroll	2.50	1.10	.30
☐ 395 Roy White	3.50	1.55	.45
☐ 396 Dick Schofield	2.50	1.10	.30
☐ 397 Alvin Dark MG	3.50	1.55	.45
☐ 398 Howie Reed	2.50	1.10	.30
☐ 399 Jim French	2.50	1.10	.30
☐ 400 Hank Aaron	75.00	34.00	9.50
☐ 401 Tom Murphy	2.50	1.10	.30
☐ 402 Dodgers Team	5.00	2.20	.60
☐ 403 Joe Coleman	2.50	1.10	.30
☐ 404 Astros Rookies	2.50	1.10	.30
Buddy Harris			
Roger Metzger			
☐ 405 Leo Cardenas	3.50	1.55	.45
☐ 406 Ray Sadecki	2.50	1.10	.30
☐ 407 Joe Rudi	3.50	1.55	.45
☐ 408 Rafael Robles	2.50	1.10	.30
☐ 409 Don Pavletich	2.50	1.10	.30
☐ 410 Ken Holtzman	3.50	1.55	.45
☐ 411 George Spriggs	2.50	1.10	.30
☐ 412 Jerry Johnson	2.50	1.10	.30
☐ 413 Pat Kelly	2.50	1.10	.30
☐ 414 Woodie Fryman	2.50	1.10	.30
☐ 415 Mike Hegan	2.50	1.10	.30
☐ 416 Gene Alley	2.50	1.10	.30
☐ 417 Dick Hall	2.50	1.10	.30
☐ 418 Adolfo Phillips	2.50	1.10	.30
☐ 419 Ron Hansen	2.50	1.10	.30
☐ 420 Jim Merritt	2.50	1.10	.30
☐ 421 John Stephenson	2.50	1.10	.30
☐ 422 Frank Bertaina	2.50	1.10	.30
☐ 423 Tigers Rookies	2.50	1.10	.30
Dennis Saunders			
Tim Marting			
☐ 424 Roberto Rodriquez	2.50	1.10	.30
☐ 425 Doug Rader	3.50	1.55	.45
☐ 426 Chris Cannizzaro	2.50	1.10	.30
☐ 427 Bernie Allen	2.50	1.10	.30
☐ 428 Jim McAndrew	2.50	1.10	.30
☐ 429 Chuck Hinton	2.50	1.10	.30
☐ 430 Wes Parker	2.50	1.10	.30
☐ 431 Tom Burgmeier	2.50	1.10	.30
☐ 432 Bob Didier	2.50	1.10	.30
☐ 433 Skip Lockwood	2.50	1.10	.30
☐ 434 Gary Sutherland	2.50	1.10	.30
☐ 435 Jose Cardenal	3.50	1.55	.45
☐ 436 Wilbur Wood	3.50	1.55	.45
☐ 437 Danny Murtaugh MG	3.50	1.55	.45
☐ 438 Mike McCormick	3.50	1.55	.45
☐ 439 Phillies Rookies	8.00	3.60	1.00
Greg Luzinski			
Scott Reid			
☐ 440 Bert Campaneris	3.50	1.55	.45
☐ 441 Milt Pappas	3.50	1.55	.45
☐ 442 Angels Team	5.00	2.20	.60
☐ 443 Rich Robertson	2.50	1.10	.30
☐ 444 Jimmie Price	2.50	1.10	.30
☐ 445 Art Shamsky	2.50	1.10	.30
☐ 446 Bobby Bolin	2.50	1.10	.30
☐ 447 Cesar Geronimo	3.50	1.55	.45
☐ 448 Dave Roberts	2.50	1.10	.30
☐ 449 Brant Alyea	2.50	1.10	.30
☐ 450 Bob Gibson	20.00	9.00	2.50
☐ 451 Joe Keough	2.50	1.10	.30
☐ 452 John Boccabella	2.50	1.10	.30
☐ 453 Terry Crowley	2.50	1.10	.30
☐ 454 Mike Paul	2.50	1.10	.30
☐ 455 Don Kessinger	3.50	1.55	.45
☐ 456 Bob Meyer	2.50	1.10	.30
☐ 457 Willie Smith	2.50	1.10	.30
☐ 458 White Sox Rookies	2.50	1.10	.30
Ron Lolich			
Dave Lemonds			
☐ 459 Jim Lefebvre	2.50	1.10	.30
☐ 460 Fritz Peterson	2.50	1.10	.30
☐ 461 Jim Ray Hart	2.50	1.10	.30
☐ 462 Senators Team	5.00	2.20	.60
☐ 463 Tom Kelley	2.50	1.10	.30
☐ 464 Aurelio Rodriguez	2.50	1.10	.30
☐ 465 Tim McCarver	4.00	1.80	.50
☐ 466 Ken Berry	2.50	1.10	.30
☐ 467 Al Santorini	2.50	1.10	.30
☐ 468 Frank Fernandez	2.50	1.10	.30
☐ 469 Bob Aspromonte	2.50	1.10	.30
☐ 470 Bob Oliver	2.50	1.10	.30
☐ 471 Tom Griffin	2.50	1.10	.30
☐ 472 Ken Rudolph	2.50	1.10	.30
☐ 473 Gary Wagner	2.50	1.10	.30
☐ 474 Jim Fairey	2.50	1.10	.30
☐ 475 Ron Perranoski	3.50	1.55	.45
☐ 476 Dal Maxvill	2.50	1.10	.30
☐ 477 Earl Weaver MG	5.00	2.20	.60
☐ 478 Bernie Carbo	2.50	1.10	.30
☐ 479 Dennis Higgins	2.50	1.10	.30
☐ 480 Manny Sanguillen	3.50	1.55	.45
☐ 481 Daryl Patterson	2.50	1.10	.30
☐ 482 Padres Team	5.00	2.20	.60
☐ 483 Gene Michael	2.50	1.10	.30
☐ 484 Don Wilson	2.50	1.10	.30
☐ 485 Ken McMullen	2.50	1.10	.30
☐ 486 Steve Huntz	2.50	1.10	.30
☐ 487 Paul Schaal	2.50	1.10	.30
☐ 488 Jerry Stephenson	2.50	1.10	.30
☐ 489 Luis Alvarado	2.50	1.10	.30
☐ 490 Deron Johnson	2.50	1.10	.30
☐ 491 Jim Hardin	2.50	1.10	.30
☐ 492 Ken Boswell	2.50	1.10	.30
☐ 493 Dave May	2.50	1.10	.30
☐ 494 Braves Rookies	3.50	1.55	.45
Ralph Garr			
Rick Kester			
☐ 495 Felipe Alou	3.50	1.55	.45
☐ 496 Woody Woodward	2.50	1.10	.30
☐ 497 Horacio Pina	2.50	1.10	.30
☐ 498 John Kennedy	2.50	1.10	.30
☐ 499 Checklist 524-643	6.00	2.70	.75
☐ 500 Jim Perry	3.50	1.55	.45
☐ 501 Andy Etchebarren	2.50	1.10	.30
☐ 502 Cubs Team	5.00	2.20	.60
☐ 503 Gates Brown	3.50	1.55	.45
☐ 504 Ken Wright	2.50	1.10	.30
☐ 505 Ollie Brown	2.50	1.10	.30
☐ 506 Bobby Knoop	2.50	1.10	.30
☐ 507 George Stone	2.50	1.10	.30
☐ 508 Roger Repoz	2.50	1.10	.30
☐ 509 Jim Grant	2.50	1.10	.30
☐ 510 Ken Harrelson	3.50	1.55	.45
☐ 511 Chris Short	4.00	1.80	.50
☐ 512 Red Sox Rookies	2.50	1.10	.30
Dick Mills			
Mike Garman			
☐ 513 Nolan Ryan	300.00	135.00	38.00
☐ 514 Ron Woods	2.50	1.10	.30
☐ 515 Carl Morton	2.50	1.10	.30
☐ 516 Ted Kubiak	2.50	1.10	.30
☐ 517 Charlie Fox MG	2.50	1.10	.30
☐ 518 Joe Grzenda	2.50	1.10	.30
☐ 519 Willie Crawford	2.50	1.10	.30
☐ 520 Tommy John	5.00	2.20	.60
☐ 521 Leron Lee	2.50	1.10	.30
☐ 522 Twins Team	5.00	2.20	.60
☐ 523 John Odom	3.50	1.55	.45
☐ 524 Mickey Stanley	6.00	2.70	.75
☐ 525 Ernie Banks	60.00	27.00	7.50
☐ 526 Ray Jarvis	5.00	2.20	.60
☐ 527 Cleon Jones	6.00	2.70	.75
☐ 528 Wally Bunker	5.00	2.20	.60
☐ 529 NL Rookie Infielders	6.00	2.70	.75
Enzo Hernandez			
Bill Buckner			
Marty Perez			
☐ 530 Carl Yastrzemski	40.00	18.00	5.00
☐ 531 Mike Torrez	6.00	2.70	.75
☐ 532 Bill Rigney MG	5.00	2.20	.60
☐ 533 Mike Ryan	5.00	2.20	.60
☐ 534 Luke Walker	5.00	2.20	.60
☐ 535 Curt Flood	7.50	3.40	.95
☐ 536 Claude Raymond	5.00	2.20	.60
☐ 537 Tom Egan	5.00	2.20	.60
☐ 538 Angel Bravo	5.00	2.20	.60
☐ 539 Larry Brown	5.00	2.20	.60
☐ 540 Larry Dierker	7.50	3.40	.95
☐ 541 Bob Burda	5.00	2.20	.60
☐ 542 Bob Miller	5.00	2.20	.60
☐ 543 Yankees Team	10.00	4.50	1.25
☐ 544 Vida Blue	10.00	4.50	1.25
☐ 545 Dick Dietz	5.00	2.20	.60
☐ 546 John Matias	5.00	2.20	.60
☐ 547 Pat Dobson	5.00	2.20	.60
☐ 548 Don Mason	5.00	2.20	.60
☐ 549 Jim Brewer	5.00	2.20	.60
☐ 550 Harmon Killebrew	30.00	13.50	3.70
☐ 551 Frank Linzy	5.00	2.20	.60
☐ 552 Buddy Bradford	5.00	2.20	.60
☐ 553 Kevin Collins	5.00	2.20	.60
☐ 554 Lowell Palmer	5.00	2.20	.60
☐ 555 Walt Williams	5.00	2.20	.60
☐ 556 Jim McGlothlin	5.00	2.20	.60
☐ 557 Tom Satriano	5.00	2.20	.60
☐ 558 Hector Torres	5.00	2.20	.60
☐ 559 AL Rookie Pitchers	5.00	2.20	.60
Terry Cox			
Bill Gogolewski			
Gary Jones			
☐ 560 Rusty Staub	7.50	3.40	.95
☐ 561 Syd O'Brien	5.00	2.20	.60
☐ 562 Dave Giusti	5.00	2.20	.60
☐ 563 Giants Team	10.00	4.50	1.25
☐ 564 Al Fitzmorris	5.00	2.20	.60
☐ 565 Jim Wynn	7.50	3.40	.95
☐ 566 Tim Cullen	5.00	2.20	.60
☐ 567 Walt Alston MG	10.00	4.50	1.25
☐ 568 Sal Campisi	5.00	2.20	.60
☐ 569 Ivan Murrell	5.00	2.20	.60
☐ 570 Jim Palmer	35.00	16.00	4.40
☐ 571 Ted Sizemore	5.00	2.20	.60
☐ 572 Jerry Kenney	5.00	2.20	.60

Card	NRMT	VG-E	GOOD
☐ 573 Ed Kranepool	7.50	3.40	.95
☐ 574 Jim Bunning	10.00	4.50	1.25
☐ 575 Bill Freehan	7.50	3.40	.95
☐ 576 Cubs Rookies	5.00	2.20	.60
Adrian Garrett			
Brock Davis			
Garry Jestadt			
☐ 577 Jim Lonborg	7.50	3.40	.95
☐ 578 Eddie Kasko	7.50	3.40	.95
(Topps 578 is			
Ron Hunt)			
☐ 579 Marty Pattin	5.00	2.20	.60
☐ 580 Tony Perez	20.00	9.00	2.50
☐ 581 Roger Nelson	5.00	2.20	.60
☐ 582 Dave Cash	7.50	3.40	.95
☐ 583 Ron Cook	5.00	2.20	.60
☐ 584 Indians Team	10.00	4.50	1.25
☐ 585 Willie Davis	7.50	3.40	.95
☐ 586 Dick Woodson	5.00	2.20	.60
☐ 587 Sonny Jackson	5.00	2.20	.60
☐ 588 Tom Bradley	5.00	2.20	.60
☐ 589 Bob Barton	5.00	2.20	.60
☐ 590 Alex Johnson	6.00	2.70	.75
☐ 591 Jackie Brown	5.00	2.20	.60
☐ 592 Randy Hundley	5.00	2.20	.60
☐ 593 Jack Aker	5.00	2.20	.60
☐ 594 Cards Rookies	7.50	3.40	.95
Bob Chlupsa			
Bob Stinson			
Al Hrabosky			
☐ 595 Dave Johnson	7.50	3.40	.95
☐ 596 Mike Jorgensen	7.50	3.40	.95
☐ 597 Ken Suarez	5.00	2.20	.60
☐ 598 Rick Wise	5.00	2.20	.60
☐ 599 Norm Cash	7.50	3.40	.95
☐ 600 Willie Mays	100.00	45.00	12.50
☐ 601 Ken Tatum	5.00	2.20	.60
☐ 602 Marty Martinez	5.00	2.20	.60
☐ 603 Pirates Team	10.00	4.50	1.25
☐ 604 John Gelnar	5.00	2.20	.60
☐ 605 Orlando Cepeda	10.00	4.50	1.25
☐ 606 Chuck Taylor	5.00	2.20	.60
☐ 607 Paul Ratliff	5.00	2.20	.60
☐ 608 Mike Wegener	5.00	2.20	.60
☐ 609 Leo Durocher MG	10.00	4.50	1.25
☐ 610 Amos Otis	7.50	3.40	.95
☐ 611 Tom Phoebus	5.00	2.20	.60
☐ 612 Indians Rookies	5.00	2.20	.60
Lou Camilli			
Ted Ford			
Steve Mingori			
☐ 613 Pedro Borbon	5.00	2.20	.60
☐ 614 Billy Cowan	5.00	2.20	.60
☐ 615 Mel Stottlemyre	7.50	3.40	.95
☐ 616 Larry Hisle	7.50	3.40	.95
☐ 617 Clay Dalrymple	5.00	2.20	.60
☐ 618 Tug McGraw	7.50	3.40	.95
☐ 619 Checklist 644-752	10.00	4.50	1.25
☐ 620 Frank Howard	7.50	3.40	.95
☐ 621 Ron Bryant	5.00	2.20	.60
☐ 622 Joe Lahoud	5.00	2.20	.60
☐ 623 Pat Jarvis	5.00	2.20	.60
☐ 624 Athletics Team	10.00	4.50	1.25
☐ 625 Lou Brock	35.00	16.00	4.40
☐ 626 Freddie Patek	7.50	3.40	.95
☐ 627 Steve Hamilton	5.00	2.20	.60
☐ 628 John Bateman	5.00	2.20	.60
☐ 629 John Hiller	7.50	3.40	.95
☐ 630 Roberto Clemente	125.00	55.00	15.50
☐ 631 Eddie Fisher	5.00	2.20	.60
☐ 632 Darrel Chaney	5.00	2.20	.60
☐ 633 AL Rookie Outfielders	5.00	2.20	.60
Bobby Brooks			
Pete Koegel			
Scott Northey			
☐ 634 Phil Regan	5.00	2.20	.60
☐ 635 Bobby Murcer	7.50	3.40	.95
☐ 636 Denny LeMaster	5.00	2.20	.60
☐ 637 Dave Bristol MG	5.00	2.20	.60
☐ 638 Stan Williams	5.00	2.20	.60
☐ 639 Tom Haller	5.00	2.20	.60
☐ 640 Frank Robinson	50.00	22.00	6.25
☐ 641 Mets Team	15.00	6.75	1.85
☐ 642 Jim Roland	5.00	2.20	.60
☐ 643 Rick Reichardt	5.00	2.20	.60
☐ 644 Jim Stewart	10.00	4.50	1.25
☐ 645 Jim Maloney	12.50	5.50	1.55
☐ 646 Bobby Floyd	10.00	4.50	1.25
☐ 647 Juan Pizarro	10.00	4.50	1.25
☐ 648 Mets Rookies	20.00	9.00	2.50
Rich Folkers			
Ted Martinez			
Jon Matlack			
☐ 649 Sparky Lyle	16.00	7.25	2.00
☐ 650 Rich Allen	40.00	18.00	5.00
☐ 651 Jerry Robertson	10.00	4.50	1.25
☐ 652 Braves Team	20.00	9.00	2.50
☐ 653 Russ Snyder	10.00	4.50	1.25
☐ 654 Don Shaw	10.00	4.50	1.25
☐ 655 Mike Epstein	10.00	4.50	1.25
☐ 656 Gerry Nyman	10.00	4.50	1.25
☐ 657 Jose Azcue	10.00	4.50	1.25
☐ 658 Paul Lindblad	10.00	4.50	1.25
☐ 659 Byron Browne	10.00	4.50	1.25
☐ 660 Ray Culp	10.00	4.50	1.25
☐ 661 Chuck Tanner MG	15.00	6.75	1.85
☐ 662 Mike Hedlund	10.00	4.50	1.25
☐ 663 Marv Staehle	10.00	4.50	1.25
☐ 664 Rookie Pitchers	15.00	6.75	1.85
Archie Reynolds			
Bob Reynolds			
Ken Reynolds			
☐ 665 Ron Swoboda	16.00	7.25	2.00
☐ 666 Gene Brabender	10.00	4.50	1.25
☐ 667 Pete Ward	10.00	4.50	1.25
☐ 668 Gary Neibauer	10.00	4.50	1.25
☐ 669 Ike Brown	10.00	4.50	1.25
☐ 670 Bill Hands	10.00	4.50	1.25
☐ 671 Bill Voss	10.00	4.50	1.25
☐ 672 Ed Crosby	10.00	4.50	1.25
☐ 673 Gerry Janeski	10.00	4.50	1.25
☐ 674 Expos Team	20.00	9.00	2.50
☐ 675 Dave Boswell	10.00	4.50	1.25
☐ 676 Tommie Reynolds	10.00	4.50	1.25
☐ 677 Jack DiLauro	10.00	4.50	1.25
☐ 678 George Thomas	10.00	4.50	1.25
☐ 679 Don O'Riley	10.00	4.50	1.25
☐ 680 Don Mincher	10.00	4.50	1.25
☐ 681 Bill Butler	10.00	4.50	1.25
☐ 682 Terry Harmon	10.00	4.50	1.25
☐ 683 Bill Burbach	10.00	4.50	1.25
☐ 684 Curt Motton	10.00	4.50	1.25
☐ 685 Moe Drabowsky	10.00	4.50	1.25
☐ 686 Chico Ruiz	10.00	4.50	1.25
☐ 687 Ron Taylor	10.00	4.50	1.25
☐ 688 Sparky Anderson MG	40.00	18.00	5.00
☐ 689 Frank Baker	10.00	4.50	1.25
☐ 690 Bob Moose	10.00	4.50	1.25
☐ 691 Bob Heise	10.00	4.50	1.25
☐ 692 AL Rookie Pitchers	10.00	4.50	1.25
Hal Haydel			
Rogelio Moret			
Wayne Twitchell			
☐ 693 Jose Pena	10.00	4.50	1.25
☐ 694 Rick Renick	10.00	4.50	1.25
☐ 695 Joe Niekro	15.00	6.75	1.85
☐ 696 Jerry Morales	10.00	4.50	1.25
☐ 697 Rickey Clark	10.00	4.50	1.25
☐ 698 Brewers Team	20.00	9.00	2.50
☐ 699 Jim Britton	10.00	4.50	1.25
☐ 700 Boog Powell	25.00	11.00	3.10
☐ 701 Bob Garibaldi	10.00	4.50	1.25
☐ 702 Milt Ramirez	10.00	4.50	1.25
☐ 703 Mike Kekich	10.00	4.50	1.25
☐ 704 J.C. Martin	10.00	4.50	1.25
☐ 705 Dick Selma	10.00	4.50	1.25
☐ 706 Joe Foy	10.00	4.50	1.25
☐ 707 Fred Lasher	10.00	4.50	1.25
☐ 708 Russ Nagelson	10.00	4.50	1.25
☐ 709 Rookie Outfielders	90.00	40.00	11.00
Dusty Baker			
Don Baylor			
Tom Paciorek			
☐ 710 Sonny Siebert	10.00	4.50	1.25
☐ 711 Larry Stahl	10.00	4.50	1.25
☐ 712 Jose Martinez	10.00	4.50	1.25
☐ 713 Mike Marshall	15.00	6.75	1.85
☐ 714 Dick Williams MG	15.00	6.75	1.85
☐ 715 Horace Clarke	10.00	4.50	1.25
☐ 716 Dave Leonhard	10.00	4.50	1.25
☐ 717 Tommie Aaron	15.00	6.75	1.85
☐ 718 Billy Wynne	10.00	4.50	1.25
☐ 719 Jerry May	10.00	4.50	1.25
☐ 720 Matty Alou	15.00	6.75	1.85
☐ 721 John Morris	10.00	4.50	1.25
☐ 722 Astros Team	20.00	9.00	2.50
☐ 723 Vicente Romo	10.00	4.50	1.25
☐ 724 Tom Tischinski	10.00	4.50	1.25
☐ 725 Gary Gentry	10.00	4.50	1.25
☐ 726 Paul Popovich	10.00	4.50	1.25
☐ 727 Ray Lamb	10.00	4.50	1.25
☐ 728 NL Rookie Outfielders	10.00	4.50	1.25
Wayne Redmond			
Keith Lampard			
Bernie Williams			
☐ 729 Dick Billings	10.00	4.50	1.25
☐ 730 Jim Rooker	10.00	4.50	1.25
☐ 731 Jim Qualls	10.00	4.50	1.25
☐ 732 Bob Reed	10.00	4.50	1.25
☐ 733 Lee Maye	10.00	4.50	1.25
☐ 734 Rob Gardner	10.00	4.50	1.25
☐ 735 Mike Shannon	12.50	5.50	1.55
☐ 736 Mel Queen	10.00	4.50	1.25
☐ 737 Preston Gomez MG	10.00	4.50	1.25
☐ 738 Russ Gibson	10.00	4.50	1.25
☐ 739 Barry Lersch	10.00	4.50	1.25
☐ 740 Luis Aparicio	25.00	11.00	3.10
☐ 741 Skip Guinn	10.00	4.50	1.25
☐ 742 Royals Team	20.00	9.00	2.50
☐ 743 John O'Donoghue	10.00	4.50	1.25
☐ 744 Chuck Manuel	10.00	4.50	1.25
☐ 745 Sandy Alomar	15.00	6.75	1.85
☐ 746 Andy Kosco	10.00	4.50	1.25
☐ 747 NL Rookie Pitchers	10.00	4.50	1.25
Al Severinsen			
Scipio Spinks			
Balor Moore			
☐ 748 John Purdin	10.00	4.50	1.25
☐ 749 Ken Szotkiewicz	10.00	4.50	1.25
☐ 750 Denny McLain	20.00	9.00	2.50
☐ 751 Al Weis	14.00	6.25	1.75
☐ 752 Dick Drago	12.00	5.50	1.50

1972 O-Pee-Chee

The cards in this 525-card set measure 2 1/2" by 3 1/2". The 1972 O-Pee-Chee set is very similar to the 1972 Topps set. On a white background, the fronts feature color player photos with multicolored frames, rounded bottom corners and the top part of the photo also rounded. The player's name and team name appear on the front. The horizontal backs carry player biography and statistics in French and English and have a different color than the 1972 Topps cards. Features appearing for the first time were "Boyhood Photos" (KP: 341-348 and 491-498) and "In Action" cards. The O-Pee-Chee cards can be distinguished from Topps cards by the "Printed in Canada" on the bottom of the back. This was the first year the cards denoted O.P.C. in the copyright line rather than T.C.G. There is one card in the set which is notably different from the corresponding Topps number on the back, No. 465 Gil Hodges, which notes his death in April of 1972. Remember, the prices below apply only to the O-Pee-Chee cards -- NOT Topps cards which are much more plentiful.

	NRMT	VG-E	GOOD
COMPLETE SET (525)	1500.00	700.00	190.00
COMMON CARD (1-263)	1.00	.45	.12
COMMON CARD (264-394)	2.00	.90	.25
COMMON CARD (395-525)	2.50	1.10	.30
☐ 1 Pirates Team	8.00	3.60	1.00
☐ 2 Ray Culp	1.00	.45	.12
☐ 3 Bob Tolan	1.00	.45	.12
☐ 4 Checklist 1-132	4.00	1.80	.50
☐ 5 John Bateman	1.00	.45	.12
☐ 6 Fred Scherman	1.00	.45	.12
☐ 7 Enzo Hernandez	1.00	.45	.12
☐ 8 Ron Swoboda	1.50	.70	.19
☐ 9 Stan Williams	1.00	.45	.12
☐ 10 Amos Otis	1.50	.70	.19
☐ 11 Bobby Valentine	1.50	.70	.19
☐ 12 Jose Cardenal	1.00	.45	.12
☐ 13 Joe Grzenda	1.00	.45	.12
☐ 14 Phillies Rookies	1.00	.45	.12
Pete Koegel			
Mike Anderson			
Wayne Twitchell			
☐ 15 Walt Williams	1.00	.45	.12
☐ 16 Mike Jorgensen	1.50	.70	.19
☐ 17 Dave Duncan	1.00	.45	.12
☐ 18 Juan Pizarro	1.00	.45	.12
☐ 19 Billy Cowan	1.00	.45	.12
☐ 20 Don Wilson	1.00	.45	.12
☐ 21 Braves Team	2.00	.90	.25
☐ 22 Rob Gardner	1.00	.45	.12
☐ 23 Ted Kubiak	1.00	.45	.12
☐ 24 Ted Ford	1.00	.45	.12
☐ 25 Bill Singer	1.00	.45	.12
☐ 26 Andy Etchebarren	1.00	.45	.12
☐ 27 Bob Johnson	1.00	.45	.12
☐ 28 Twins Rookies	1.00	.45	.12
Bob Gebhard			
Steve Brye			
Hal Haydel			
☐ 29 Bill Bonham	1.00	.45	.12
☐ 30 Rico Petrocelli	1.50	.70	.19
☐ 31 Cleon Jones	1.50	.70	.19
☐ 32 Cleon Jones IA	1.00	.45	.12
☐ 33 Billy Martin MG	4.00	1.80	.50
☐ 34 Billy Martin IA	2.00	.90	.25
☐ 35 Jerry Johnson	1.00	.45	.12
☐ 36 Jerry Johnson IA	1.00	.45	.12
☐ 37 Carl Yastrzemski	10.00	4.50	1.25
☐ 38 Carl Yastrzemski IA	6.00	2.70	.75
☐ 39 Bob Barton	1.00	.45	.12
☐ 40 Bob Barton IA	1.00	.45	.12
☐ 41 Tommy Davis	1.50	.70	.19
☐ 42 Tommy Davis IA	1.00	.45	.12
☐ 43 Rick Wise	1.50	.70	.19
☐ 44 Rick Wise IA	1.00	.45	.12
☐ 45 Glenn Beckert	1.00	.45	.12
☐ 46 Glenn Beckert IA	1.00	.45	.12
☐ 47 John Ellis	1.00	.45	.12
☐ 48 John Ellis IA	1.00	.45	.12
☐ 49 Willie Mays	30.00	13.50	3.70
☐ 50 Willie Mays IA	15.00	6.75	1.85
☐ 51 Harmon Killebrew	7.00	3.10	.85
☐ 52 Harmon Killebrew IA	3.50	1.55	.45
☐ 53 Bud Harrelson	1.50	.70	.19
☐ 54 Bud Harrelson IA	1.00	.45	.12
☐ 55 Clyde Wright	1.00	.45	.12
☐ 56 Rich Chiles	1.00	.45	.12
☐ 57 Bob Oliver	1.00	.45	.12
☐ 58 Ernie McAnally	1.00	.45	.12
☐ 59 Fred Stanley	1.00	.45	.12
☐ 60 Manny Sanguillen	1.50	.70	.19
☐ 61 Cubs Rookies	1.50	.70	.19
Burt Hooton			
Gene Hiser			
Earl Stephenson			
☐ 62 Angel Mangual	1.00	.45	.12
☐ 63 Duke Sims	1.00	.45	.12
☐ 64 Pete Broberg	1.00	.45	.12
☐ 65 Cesar Cedeno	1.50	.70	.19
☐ 66 Ray Corbin	1.00	.45	.12
☐ 67 Red Schoendienst MG	2.00	.90	.25
☐ 68 Jim York	1.00	.45	.12
☐ 69 Roger Freed	1.00	.45	.12
☐ 70 Mike Cuellar	1.50	.70	.19
☐ 71 Angels Team	2.00	.90	.25
☐ 72 Bruce Kison	1.50	.70	.19
☐ 73 Steve Huntz	1.00	.45	.12
☐ 74 Cecil Upshaw	1.00	.45	.12
☐ 75 Bert Campaneris	1.50	.70	.19
☐ 76 Don Carrithers	1.00	.45	.12
☐ 77 Ron Theobald	1.00	.45	.12
☐ 78 Steve Arlin	1.00	.45	.12
☐ 79 Red Sox Rookies	60.00	27.00	7.50
Mike Garman			
Cecil Cooper			
Carlton Fisk			
☐ 80 Tony Perez	4.00	1.80	.50
☐ 81 Mike Hedlund	1.00	.45	.12
☐ 82 Ron Woods	1.00	.45	.12
☐ 83 Dalton Jones	1.00	.45	.12
☐ 84 Vince Colbert	1.00	.45	.12
☐ 85 NL Batting Leaders	3.00	1.35	.35
Joe Torre			
Ralph Garr			
Glenn Beckert			
☐ 86 AL Batting Leaders	3.00	1.35	.35
Tony Oliva			
Bobby Murcer			
Merv Rettenmund			
☐ 87 NL RBI Leaders	5.00	2.20	.60
Joe Torre			
Willie Stargell			
Hank Aaron			
☐ 88 AL RBI Leaders	4.00	1.80	.50
Harmon Killebrew			
Frank Robinson			
Reggie Smith			
☐ 89 NL Home Run Leaders	5.00	2.20	.60
Willie Stargell			
Hank Aaron			
Lee May			
☐ 90 AL Home Run Leaders	4.00	1.80	.50
Bill Melton			
Norm Cash			
Reggie Jackson			
☐ 91 NL ERA Leaders	4.00	1.80	.50
Tom Seaver			
Dave Roberts			
(photo actually			
Danny Coombs)			
Don Wilson			
☐ 92 AL ERA Leaders	4.00	1.80	.50
Vida Blue			
Wilbur Wood			
Jim Palmer			
☐ 93 NL Pitching Leaders	5.00	2.20	.60
Fergie Jenkins			
Steve Carlton			
Al Downing			
Tom Seaver			
☐ 94 AL Pitching Leaders	3.00	1.35	.35
Mickey Lolich			
Vida Blue			
Wilbur Wood			
☐ 95 NL Strikeout Leaders	4.00	1.80	.50
Tom Seaver			
Fergie Jenkins			
Bill Stoneman			
☐ 96 AL Strikeout Leaders	3.00	1.35	.35
Mickey Lolich			
Vida Blue			
Joe Coleman			
☐ 97 Tom Kelley	1.00	.45	.12
☐ 98 Chuck Tanner MG	1.50	.70	.19
☐ 99 Ross Grimsley	1.00	.45	.12
☐ 100 Frank Robinson	10.00	4.50	1.25
☐ 101 Astros Rookies	3.00	1.35	.35
Bill Greif			
J.R. Richard			
Ray Busse			
☐ 102 Lloyd Allen	1.00	.45	.12
☐ 103 Checklist 133-263	4.00	1.80	.50
☐ 104 Toby Harrah	2.50	1.10	.30
☐ 105 Gary Gentry	1.00	.45	.12
☐ 106 Brewers Team	2.00	.90	.25
☐ 107 Jose Cruz	3.00	1.35	.35
☐ 108 Gary Waslewski	1.00	.45	.12
☐ 109 Jerry May	1.00	.45	.12
☐ 110 Ron Hunt	1.00	.45	.12
☐ 111 Jim Grant	1.00	.45	.12
☐ 112 Greg Luzinski	3.00	1.35	.35
☐ 113 Rogelio Moret	1.00	.45	.12
☐ 114 Bill Buckner	2.00	.90	.25
☐ 115 Jim Fregosi	1.50	.70	.19

☐ 116 Ed Farmer 1.00 .45 .12
☐ 117 Cleo James 1.00 .45 .12
☐ 118 Skip Lockwood 1.00 .45 .12
☐ 119 Marty Perez 1.00 .45 .12
☐ 120 Bill Freehan 1.50 .70 .19
☐ 121 Ed Sprague 1.00 .45 .12
☐ 122 Larry Biittner 1.00 .45 .12
☐ 123 Ed Acosta 1.00 .45 .12
☐ 124 Yankees Rookies 1.00 .45 .12
Alan Closter
Rusty Torres
Roger Hambright
☐ 125 Dave Cash 1.50 .70 .19
☐ 126 Bart Johnson 1.00 .45 .12
☐ 127 Duffy Dyer 1.00 .45 .12
☐ 128 Eddie Watt 1.00 .45 .12
☐ 129 Charlie Fox MG 1.00 .45 .12
☐ 130 Bob Gibson 8.00 3.60 1.00
☐ 131 Jim Nettles 1.00 .45 .12
☐ 132 Joe Morgan 6.00 2.70 .75
☐ 133 Joe Keough 1.00 .45 .12
☐ 134 Carl Morton 1.00 .45 .12
☐ 135 Vada Pinson 1.50 .70 .19
☐ 136 Darrel Chaney 1.00 .45 .12
☐ 137 Dick Williams MG 1.50 .70 .19
☐ 138 Mike Kekich 1.00 .45 .12
☐ 139 Tim McCarver 1.50 .70 .19
☐ 140 Pat Dobson 1.00 .45 .12
☐ 141 Mets Rookies 1.50 .70 .19
Buzz Capra
Leroy Stanton
Jon Matlack
☐ 142 Chris Chambliss 5.00 2.20 .60
☐ 143 Garry Jestadt 1.00 .45 .12
☐ 144 Marty Pattin 1.00 .45 .12
☐ 145 Don Kessinger 1.50 .70 .19
☐ 146 Steve Kealey 1.00 .45 .12
☐ 147 Dave Kingman 5.00 2.20 .60
☐ 148 Dick Billings 1.00 .45 .12
☐ 149 Gary Neibauer 1.00 .45 .12
☐ 150 Norm Cash 1.50 .70 .19
☐ 151 Jim Brewer 1.00 .45 .12
☐ 152 Gene Clines 1.00 .45 .12
☐ 153 Rick Auerbach 1.00 .45 .12
☐ 154 Ted Simmons 3.00 1.35 .35
☐ 155 Larry Dierker 1.00 .45 .12
☐ 156 Twins Team 2.00 .90 .25
☐ 157 Don Gullett 1.50 .70 .19
☐ 158 Jerry Kenney 1.00 .45 .12
☐ 159 John Boccabella 1.00 .45 .12
☐ 160 Andy Messersmith 1.50 .70 .19
☐ 161 Brock Davis 1.00 .45 .12
☐ 162 Brewers Rookies UER 2.00 .90 .25
Jerry Bell
Darrell Porter
Bob Reynolds
(Porter and Bell
photos switched)
☐ 163 Tug McGraw 1.50 .70 .19
☐ 164 Tug McGraw IA 1.50 .70 .19
☐ 165 Chris Speier 1.50 .70 .19
☐ 166 Chris Speier IA 1.50 .70 .19
☐ 167 Deron Johnson 1.00 .45 .12
☐ 168 Deron Johnson IA 1.00 .45 .12
☐ 169 Vida Blue 2.00 .90 .25
☐ 170 Vida Blue IA 1.50 .70 .19
☐ 171 Darrell Evans 2.00 .90 .25
☐ 172 Darrell Evans IA 1.50 .70 .19
☐ 173 Clay Kirby 1.00 .45 .12
☐ 174 Clay Kirby IA 1.00 .45 .12
☐ 175 Tom Haller 1.00 .45 .12
☐ 176 Tom Haller IA 1.00 .45 .12
☐ 177 Paul Schaal 1.00 .45 .12
☐ 178 Paul Schaal IA 1.00 .45 .12
☐ 179 Dock Ellis 1.00 .45 .12
☐ 180 Dock Ellis IA 1.00 .45 .12
☐ 181 Ed Kranepool 1.00 .45 .12
☐ 182 Ed Kranepool IA 1.00 .45 .12
☐ 183 Bill Melton 1.00 .45 .12
☐ 184 Bill Melton IA 1.00 .45 .12
☐ 185 Ron Bryant 1.00 .45 .12
☐ 186 Ron Bryant IA 1.00 .45 .12
☐ 187 Gates Brown 1.00 .45 .12
☐ 188 Frank Lucchesi MG 1.00 .45 .12
☐ 189 Gene Tenace 1.50 .70 .19
☐ 190 Dave Giusti 1.00 .45 .12
☐ 191 Jeff Burroughs 2.00 .90 .25
☐ 192 Cubs Team 2.00 .90 .25
☐ 193 Kurt Bevacqua 1.00 .45 .12
☐ 194 Fred Norman 1.00 .45 .12
☐ 195 Orlando Cepeda 3.00 1.35 .35
☐ 196 Mel Queen 1.00 .45 .12
☐ 197 Johnny Briggs 1.00 .45 .12
☐ 198 Dodgers Rookies 6.00 2.70 .75
Charlie Hough
Bob O'Brien
Mike Strahler
☐ 199 Mike Fiore 1.00 .45 .12
☐ 200 Lou Brock 8.00 3.60 1.00
☐ 201 Phil Roof 1.00 .45 .12
☐ 202 Scipio Spinks 1.00 .45 .12
☐ 203 Ron Blomberg 1.00 .45 .12
☐ 204 Tommy Helms 1.00 .45 .12
☐ 205 Dick Drago 1.00 .45 .12
☐ 206 Dal Maxvill 1.00 .45 .12
☐ 207 Tom Egan 1.00 .45 .12
☐ 208 Milt Pappas 1.50 .70 .19
☐ 209 Joe Rudi 1.50 .70 .19
☐ 210 Denny McLain 1.50 .70 .19
☐ 211 Gary Sutherland 1.00 .45 .12
☐ 212 Grant Jackson 1.00 .45 .12
☐ 213 Angels Rookies 1.00 .45 .12
Billy Parker
Art Kusnyer
Tom Silverio
☐ 214 Mike McQueen 1.00 .45 .12
☐ 215 Alex Johnson 1.00 .45 .12
☐ 216 Joe Niekro 1.50 .70 .19
☐ 217 Roger Metzger 1.00 .45 .12
☐ 218 Eddie Kasko MG 1.00 .45 .12
☐ 219 Rennie Stennett 1.50 .70 .19
☐ 220 Jim Perry 1.50 .70 .19
☐ 221 NL Playoffs 2.00 .90 .25
Bucs champs
☐ 222 Brooks Robinson ALCS 4.00 1.80 .50
☐ 223 Dave McNally WS 3.00 1.35 .35
☐ 224 Dave Johnson WS 3.00 1.35 .35
Mark Belanger
☐ 225 Manny Sanguillen WS 3.00 1.35 .35
☐ 226 Roberto Clemente WS 7.50 3.40 .95
☐ 227 Nellie Briles WS 3.00 1.35 .35
☐ 228 Frank Robinson WS 4.00 1.80 .50
Manny Sanguillen
☐ 229 Steve Blass WS 3.00 1.35 .35
☐ 230 World Series Summary 3.00 1.35 .35
Pirates celebrate
☐ 231 Casey Cox 1.00 .45 .12
☐ 232 Giants Rookies 1.00 .45 .12
Chris Arnold
Jim Barr
Dave Rader
☐ 233 Jay Johnstone 1.50 .70 .19
☐ 234 Ron Taylor 1.00 .45 .12
☐ 235 Merv Rettenmund 1.00 .45 .12
☐ 236 Jim McGlothlin 1.00 .45 .12
☐ 237 Yankees Team 2.00 .90 .25
☐ 238 Leron Lee 1.00 .45 .12
☐ 239 Tom Timmermann 1.00 .45 .12
☐ 240 Rich Allen 3.00 1.35 .35
☐ 241 Rollie Fingers 6.00 2.70 .75
☐ 242 Don Mincher 1.00 .45 .12
☐ 243 Frank Linzy 1.00 .45 .12
☐ 244 Steve Braun 1.00 .45 .12
☐ 245 Tommie Agee 1.50 .70 .19
☐ 246 Tom Burgmeier 1.00 .45 .12
☐ 247 Milt May 1.00 .45 .12
☐ 248 Tom Bradley 1.00 .45 .12
☐ 249 Harry Walker MG 1.00 .45 .12
☐ 250 Boog Powell 3.00 1.35 .35
☐ 251 Checklist 264-394 5.00 2.20 .60
☐ 252 Ken Reynolds 1.00 .45 .12
☐ 253 Sandy Alomar 1.50 .70 .19
☐ 254 Boots Day 1.00 .45 .12
☐ 255 Jim Lonborg 1.50 .70 .19
☐ 256 George Foster 3.00 1.35 .35
☐ 257 Tigers Rookies 1.00 .45 .12
Jim Foor
Tim Hosley
Paul Jata
☐ 258 Randy Hundley 1.00 .45 .12
☐ 259 Sparky Lyle 1.50 .70 .19
☐ 260 Ralph Garr 1.50 .70 .19
☐ 261 Steve Mingori 1.00 .45 .12
☐ 262 Padres Team 2.00 .90 .25
☐ 263 Felipe Alou 1.50 .70 .19
☐ 264 Tommy John 4.00 1.80 .50
☐ 265 Wes Parker 3.00 1.35 .35
☐ 266 Bobby Bolin 2.00 .90 .25
☐ 267 Dave Concepcion 4.00 1.80 .50
☐ 268 A's Rookies 2.00 .90 .25
Dwain Anderson
Chris Floethe
☐ 269 Don Hahn 2.00 .90 .25
☐ 270 Jim Palmer 8.00 3.60 1.00
☐ 271 Ken Rudolph 2.00 .90 .25
☐ 272 Mickey Rivers 4.00 1.80 .50
☐ 273 Bobby Floyd 2.00 .90 .25
☐ 274 Al Severinsen 2.00 .90 .25
☐ 275 Cesar Tovar 3.00 1.35 .35
☐ 276 Gene Mauch MG 2.00 .90 .25
☐ 277 Elliott Maddox 2.00 .90 .25
☐ 278 Dennis Higgins 2.00 .90 .25
☐ 279 Larry Brown 2.00 .90 .25
☐ 280 Willie McCovey 10.00 4.50 1.25
☐ 281 Bill Parsons 2.00 .90 .25
☐ 282 Astros Team 4.00 1.80 .50
☐ 283 Darrell Brandon 2.00 .90 .25
☐ 284 Ike Brown 2.00 .90 .25
☐ 285 Gaylord Perry 7.50 3.40 .95
☐ 286 Gene Alley 2.00 .90 .25
☐ 287 Jim Hardin 2.00 .90 .25
☐ 288 Johnny Jeter 2.00 .90 .25
☐ 289 Syd O'Brien 2.00 .90 .25
☐ 290 Sonny Siebert 2.00 .90 .25
☐ 291 Hal McRae 4.00 1.80 .50
☐ 292 Hal McRae IA 3.00 1.35 .35
☐ 293 Danny Frisella 2.00 .90 .25
☐ 294 Danny Frisella IA 2.00 .90 .25
☐ 295 Dick Dietz 2.00 .90 .25
☐ 296 Dick Dietz IA 2.00 .90 .25
☐ 297 Claude Osteen 3.00 1.35 .35
☐ 298 Claude Osteen IA 2.00 .90 .25
☐ 299 Hank Aaron 40.00 18.00 5.00
☐ 300 Hank Aaron IA 20.00 9.00 2.50
☐ 301 George Mitterwald 2.00 .90 .25
☐ 302 George Mitterwald IA 2.00 .90 .25
☐ 303 Joe Pepitone 3.00 1.35 .35
☐ 304 Joe Pepitone IA 2.00 .90 .25
☐ 305 Ken Boswell 2.00 .90 .25
☐ 306 Ken Boswell IA 2.00 .90 .25
☐ 307 Steve Renko 2.00 .90 .25
☐ 308 Steve Renko IA 2.00 .90 .25
☐ 309 Roberto Clemente 50.00 22.00 6.25
☐ 310 Roberto Clemente IA 25.00 11.00 3.10
☐ 311 Clay Carroll 2.00 .90 .25
☐ 312 Clay Carroll IA 2.00 .90 .25
☐ 313 Luis Aparicio 6.00 2.70 .75
☐ 314 Luis Aparicio IA 3.00 1.35 .35
☐ 315 Paul Splittorff 2.00 .90 .25
☐ 316 Cardinals Rookies 3.00 1.35 .35
Jim Bibby
Jorge Roque
Santiago Guzman
☐ 317 Rich Hand 2.00 .90 .25
☐ 318 Sonny Jackson 2.00 .90 .25
☐ 319 Aurelio Rodriguez 2.00 .90 .25
☐ 320 Steve Blass 3.00 1.35 .35
☐ 321 Joe Lahoud 2.00 .90 .25
☐ 322 Jose Pena 2.00 .90 .25
☐ 323 Earl Weaver MG 5.00 2.20 .60
☐ 324 Mike Ryan 2.00 .90 .25
☐ 325 Mel Stottlemyre 3.00 1.35 .35
☐ 326 Pat Kelly 2.00 .90 .25
☐ 327 Steve Stone 3.00 1.35 .35
☐ 328 Red Sox Team 4.00 1.80 .50
☐ 329 Roy Foster 2.00 .90 .25
☐ 330 Jim Hunter 6.00 2.70 .75
☐ 331 Stan Swanson 2.00 .90 .25
☐ 332 Buck Martinez 2.00 .90 .25
☐ 333 Steve Barber 2.00 .90 .25
☐ 334 Rangers Rookies 2.00 .90 .25
Bill Fahey
Jim Mason
Tom Ragland
☐ 335 Bill Hands 2.00 .90 .25
☐ 336 Marty Martinez 2.00 .90 .25
☐ 337 Mike Kilkenny 2.00 .90 .25
☐ 338 Bob Grich 4.00 1.80 .50
☐ 339 Ron Cook 2.00 .90 .25
☐ 340 Roy White 3.00 1.35 .35
☐ 341 Joe Torre KP 4.00 1.80 .50
☐ 342 Wilbur Wood KP 3.00 1.35 .35
☐ 343 Willie Stargell KP 5.00 2.20 .60
☐ 344 Dave McNally KP 3.00 1.35 .35
☐ 345 Rick Wise KP 3.00 1.35 .35
☐ 346 Jim Fregosi KP 3.00 1.35 .35
☐ 347 Tom Seaver KP 7.50 3.40 .95
☐ 348 Sal Bando KP 3.00 1.35 .35
☐ 349 Al Fitzmorris 2.00 .90 .25
☐ 350 Frank Howard 3.00 1.35 .35
☐ 351 Braves Rookies 2.00 .90 .25
Tom House
Rick Kester
Jimmy Britton
☐ 352 Dave LaRoche 2.00 .90 .25
☐ 353 Art Shamsky 2.00 .90 .25
☐ 354 Tom Murphy 2.00 .90 .25
☐ 355 Bob Watson 3.00 1.35 .35
☐ 356 Gerry Moses 2.00 .90 .25
☐ 357 Woodie Fryman 2.00 .90 .25
☐ 358 Sparky Anderson MG 4.00 1.80 .50
☐ 359 Don Pavletich 2.00 .90 .25
☐ 360 Dave Roberts 2.00 .90 .25
☐ 361 Mike Andrews 2.00 .90 .25
☐ 362 Mets Team 4.00 1.80 .50
☐ 363 Ron Klimkowski 2.00 .90 .25
☐ 364 Johnny Callison 3.00 1.35 .35
☐ 365 Dick Bosman 3.00 1.35 .35
☐ 366 Jimmy Rosario 2.00 .90 .25
☐ 367 Ron Perranoski 3.00 1.35 .35
☐ 368 Danny Thompson 2.00 .90 .25
☐ 369 Jim LeFebvre 3.00 1.35 .35
☐ 370 Don Buford 2.00 .90 .25
☐ 371 Denny LeMaster 2.00 .90 .25
☐ 372 Royals Rookies 2.00 .90 .25
Lance Clemons
Monty Montgomery
☐ 373 John Mayberry 3.00 1.35 .35
☐ 374 Jack Heidemann 2.00 .90 .25
☐ 375 Reggie Cleveland 2.00 .90 .25
☐ 376 Andy Kosco 2.00 .90 .25
☐ 377 Terry Harmon 2.00 .90 .25
☐ 378 Checklist 395-525 5.00 2.20 .60
☐ 379 Ken Berry 2.00 .90 .25
☐ 380 Earl Williams 2.00 .90 .25
☐ 381 White Sox Team 4.00 1.80 .50
☐ 382 Joe Gibbon 2.00 .90 .25
☐ 383 Brant Alyea 2.00 .90 .25
☐ 384 Dave Campbell 3.00 1.35 .35
☐ 385 Mickey Stanley 3.00 1.35 .35
☐ 386 Jim Colborn 2.00 .90 .25
☐ 387 Horace Clarke 2.00 .90 .25
☐ 388 Charlie Williams 2.00 .90 .25
☐ 389 Bill Rigney MG 2.00 .90 .25
☐ 390 Willie Davis 3.00 1.35 .35
☐ 391 Ken Sanders 2.00 .90 .25
☐ 392 Pirates Rookies 3.00 1.35 .35
Fred Cambria
Richie Zisk
☐ 393 Curt Motton 2.00 .90 .25
☐ 394 Ken Forsch 3.00 1.35 .35
☐ 395 Matty Alou 3.00 1.35 .35
☐ 396 Paul Lindblad 2.50 1.10 .30
☐ 397 Phillies Team 5.00 2.20 .60
☐ 398 Larry Hisle 3.00 1.35 .35
☐ 399 Milt Wilcox 2.50 1.10 .30
☐ 400 Tony Oliva 5.00 2.20 .60
☐ 401 Jim Nash 2.50 1.10 .30
☐ 402 Bobby Heise 2.50 1.10 .30
☐ 403 John Cumberland 2.50 1.10 .30
☐ 404 Jeff Torborg 3.00 1.35 .35
☐ 405 Ron Fairly 3.00 1.35 .35
☐ 406 George Hendrick 5.00 2.20 .60
☐ 407 Chuck Taylor 2.50 1.10 .30
☐ 408 Jim Northrup 2.50 1.10 .30
☐ 409 Frank Baker 2.50 1.10 .30
☐ 410 Fergie Jenkins 7.50 3.40 .95
☐ 411 Bob Montgomery 2.50 1.10 .30
☐ 412 Dick Kelley 2.50 1.10 .30
☐ 413 White Sox Rookies 2.50 1.10 .30
Don Eddy
Dave Lemonds
☐ 414 Bob Miller 2.50 1.10 .30
☐ 415 Cookie Rojas 3.00 1.35 .35
☐ 416 Johnny Edwards 2.50 1.10 .30
☐ 417 Tom Hall 2.50 1.10 .30
☐ 418 Tom Shopay 2.50 1.10 .30
☐ 419 Jim Spencer 2.50 1.10 .30
☐ 420 Steve Carlton 18.00 8.00 2.20
☐ 421 Ellie Rodriguez 2.50 1.10 .30
☐ 422 Ray Lamb 2.50 1.10 .30
☐ 423 Oscar Gamble 3.00 1.35 .35
☐ 424 Bill Gogolewski 2.50 1.10 .30
☐ 425 Ken Singleton 3.00 1.35 .35
☐ 426 Ken Singleton IA 2.50 1.10 .30
☐ 427 Tito Fuentes 2.50 1.10 .30
☐ 428 Tito Fuentes IA 2.50 1.10 .30
☐ 429 Bob Robertson 2.50 1.10 .30
☐ 430 Bob Robertson IA 2.50 1.10 .30
☐ 431 Clarence Gaston 5.00 2.20 .60
☐ 432 Clarence Gaston IA 3.00 1.35 .35
☐ 433 Johnny Bench 30.00 13.50 3.70
☐ 434 Johnny Bench IA 15.00 6.75 1.85
☐ 435 Reggie Jackson 30.00 13.50 3.70
☐ 436 Reggie Jackson IA 15.00 6.75 1.85
☐ 437 Maury Wills 5.00 2.20 .60
☐ 438 Maury Wills IA 3.00 1.35 .35
☐ 439 Billy Williams 6.00 2.70 .75
☐ 440 Billy Williams IA 3.00 1.35 .35
☐ 441 Thurman Munson 15.00 6.75 1.85
☐ 442 Thurman Munson IA 7.50 3.40 .95
☐ 443 Ken Henderson 2.50 1.10 .30
☐ 444 Ken Henderson IA 2.50 1.10 .30
☐ 445 Tom Seaver 30.00 13.50 3.70
☐ 446 Tom Seaver IA 15.00 6.75 1.85
☐ 447 Willie Stargell 7.50 3.40 .95
☐ 448 Willie Stargell IA 4.00 1.80 .50
☐ 449 Bob Lemon MG 4.00 1.80 .50
☐ 450 Mickey Lolich 4.00 1.80 .50
☐ 451 Tony LaRussa 5.00 2.20 .60
☐ 452 Ed Herrmann 2.50 1.10 .30
☐ 453 Barry Lersch 2.50 1.10 .30
☐ 454 A's Team 5.00 2.20 .60
☐ 455 Tommy Harper 3.00 1.35 .35
☐ 456 Mark Belanger 3.00 1.35 .35
☐ 457 Padres Rookies 2.50 1.10 .30
Darcy Fast
Derrel Thomas
Mike Ivie
☐ 458 Aurelio Monteagudo 2.50 1.10 .30
☐ 459 Rick Renick 2.50 1.10 .30
☐ 460 Al Downing 2.50 1.10 .30
☐ 461 Tim Cullen 2.50 1.10 .30
☐ 462 Rickey Clark 2.50 1.10 .30
☐ 463 Bernie Carbo 2.50 1.10 .30
☐ 464 Jim Roland 2.50 1.10 .30
☐ 465 Gil Hodges MG 15.00 6.75 1.85
(Mentions his
death on 4/2/72)
☐ 466 Norm Miller 2.50 1.10 .30
☐ 467 Steve Kline 2.50 1.10 .30
☐ 468 Richie Scheinblum 2.50 1.10 .30
☐ 469 Ron Herbel 2.50 1.10 .30
☐ 470 Ray Fosse 2.50 1.10 .30
☐ 471 Luke Walker 2.50 1.10 .30
☐ 472 Phil Gagliano 2.50 1.10 .30
☐ 473 Dan McGinn 2.50 1.10 .30
☐ 474 Orioles Rookies 18.00 8.00 2.20
Don Baylor
Roric Harrison
Johnny Oates
☐ 475 Gary Nolan 2.50 1.10 .30
☐ 476 Lee Richard 2.50 1.10 .30
☐ 477 Tom Phoebus 2.50 1.10 .30
☐ 478 Checklist 5th Series 6.00 2.70 .75
☐ 479 Don Shaw 2.50 1.10 .30
☐ 480 Lee May 3.00 1.35 .35
☐ 481 Billy Conigliaro 2.50 1.10 .30
☐ 482 Joe Hoerner 2.50 1.10 .30
☐ 483 Ken Suarez 2.50 1.10 .30

☐ 484 Lum Harris MG 2.50 1.10 .30
☐ 485 Phil Regan 2.50 1.10 .30
☐ 486 John Lowenstein 2.50 1.10 .30
☐ 487 Tigers Team 5.00 2.20 .60
☐ 488 Mike Nagy 2.50 1.10 .30
☐ 489 Expos Rookies 2.50 1.10 .30
Terry Humphrey
Keith Lampard
☐ 490 Dave McNally 3.00 1.35 .35
☐ 491 Lou Piniella KP 5.00 2.20 .60
☐ 492 Mel Stottlemyre KP 4.00 1.80 .50
☐ 493 Bob Bailey KP 4.00 1.80 .50
☐ 494 Willie Horton KP 4.00 1.80 .50
☐ 495 Bill Melton KP 3.00 1.35 .35
☐ 496 Bud Harrelson KP 4.00 1.80 .50
☐ 497 Jim Perry KP 4.00 1.80 .50
☐ 498 Brooks Robinson KP 6.00 2.70 .75
☐ 499 Vicente Romo 2.50 1.10 .30
☐ 500 Joe Torre 4.00 1.80 .50
☐ 501 Pete Hamm 2.50 1.10 .30
☐ 502 Jackie Hernandez 2.50 1.10 .30
☐ 503 Gary Peters 2.50 1.10 .30
☐ 504 Ed Spiezio 2.50 1.10 .30
☐ 505 Mike Marshall 3.00 1.35 .35
☐ 506 Indians Rookies 3.00 1.35 .35
Terry Ley
Jim Moyer
Dick Tidrow
☐ 507 Fred Gladding 2.50 1.10 .30
☐ 508 Ellie Hendricks 2.50 1.10 .30
☐ 509 Don McMahon 2.50 1.10 .30
☐ 510 Ted Williams MG 15.00 6.75 1.85
☐ 511 Tony Taylor 2.50 1.10 .30
☐ 512 Paul Popovich 2.50 1.10 .30
☐ 513 Lindy McDaniel 3.00 1.35 .35
☐ 514 Ted Sizemore 2.50 1.10 .30
☐ 515 Bert Blyleven 5.00 2.20 .60
☐ 516 Oscar Brown 2.50 1.10 .30
☐ 517 Ken Brett 3.00 1.35 .35
☐ 518 Wayne Garrett 2.50 1.10 .30
☐ 519 Ted Abernathy 2.50 1.10 .30
☐ 520 Larry Bowa 5.00 2.20 .60
☐ 521 Alan Foster 2.50 1.10 .30
☐ 522 Dodgers Team 5.00 2.20 .60
☐ 523 Chuck Dobson 2.50 1.10 .30
☐ 524 Reds Rookies 2.50 1.10 .30
Ed Armbrister
Mel Behney
☐ 525 Carlos May 3.00 1.35 .35

1973 O-Pee-Chee

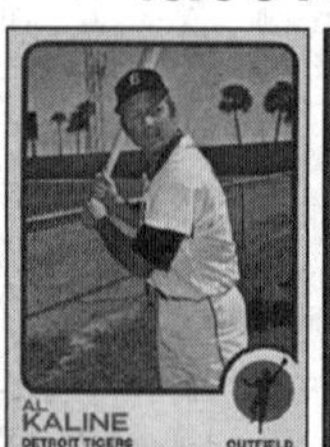

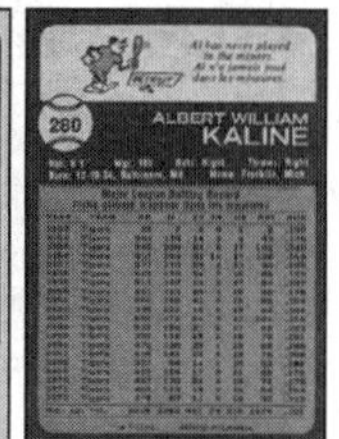

The cards in this 660-card set measure 2 1/2" by 3 1/2". This set is essentially the same as the regular 1973 Topps set, except that the words "Printed in Canada" appear on the backs and the backs are bilingual. On a white border, the fronts feature color player photos with rounded corners and thin black borders. The player's name and position and the team name are also printed on the front. An "All-Time Leaders" series (471-478) appears in this set. Kid pictures appeared again for the second year in a row (341-346). The backs carry player biography and statistics in French and English. The cards are numbered on the back. The backs appear to be more "yellow" than the Topps backs. Remember, the prices below apply only to the O-Pee-Chee cards -- NOT Topps cards which are more plentiful. Unlike the 1973 Topps set, all cards in this set were issued equally and at the same time, i.e., there were no scarce series with the O-Pee-Chee cards. Although there are no scarce series, cards 529-660 attract a slight premium. Because of the premium that high series Topps cards attract, there is a perception that O-Pee-Chee cards of the same number sequence are less available. The key card in this set is Mike Schmidt.

	NRMT	VG-E	GOOD
COMPLETE SET (660)	1000.00	450.00	125.00
COMMON CARD (1-528)	.75	.35	.09
COMMON CARD (529-660)	1.75	.80	.22

☐ 1 All-Time HR Leaders: 50.00 22.00 6.25
714 Babe Ruth
673 Hank Aaron
654 Willie Mays
☐ 2 Rich Hebner 1.00 .45 .12
☐ 3 Jim Lonborg 1.00 .45 .12
☐ 4 John Milner .75 .35 .09
☐ 5 Ed Brinkman .75 .35 .09
☐ 6 Mac Scarce .75 .35 .09
☐ 7 Texas Rangers Team 1.50 .70 .19
☐ 8 Tom Hall .75 .35 .09
☐ 9 Johnny Oates 1.00 .45 .12
☐ 10 Don Sutton 2.00 .90 .25
☐ 11 Chris Chambliss 1.25 .55 .16
☐ 12 Padres Leaders 1.00 .45 .12
Don Zimmer MG
Dave Garcia CO
Johnny Podres CO
Bob Skinner CO
Whitey Wietelmann CO
☐ 13 George Hendrick 1.00 .45 .12
☐ 14 Sonny Siebert .75 .35 .09
☐ 15 Ralph Garr 1.00 .45 .12
☐ 16 Steve Braun .75 .35 .09
☐ 17 Fred Gladding .75 .35 .09
☐ 18 Leroy Stanton .75 .35 .09
☐ 19 Tim Foli .75 .35 .09
☐ 20 Stan Bahnsen .75 .35 .09
☐ 21 Randy Hundley .75 .35 .09
☐ 22 Ted Abernathy .75 .35 .09
☐ 23 Dave Kingman 1.25 .55 .16
☐ 24 Al Santorini .75 .35 .09
☐ 25 Roy White 1.00 .45 .12
☐ 26 Pirates Team 1.50 .70 .19
☐ 27 Bill Gogolewski .75 .35 .09
☐ 28 Hal McRae 1.25 .55 .16
☐ 29 Tony Taylor 1.00 .45 .12
☐ 30 Tug McGraw 1.00 .45 .12
☐ 31 Buddy Bell 3.00 1.35 .35
☐ 32 Fred Norman .75 .35 .09
☐ 33 Jim Breazeale .75 .35 .09
☐ 34 Pat Dobson .75 .35 .09
☐ 35 Willie Davis 1.00 .45 .12
☐ 36 Steve Barber .75 .35 .09
☐ 37 Bill Robinson 1.00 .45 .12
☐ 38 Mike Epstein .75 .35 .09
☐ 39 Dave Roberts .75 .35 .09
☐ 40 Reggie Smith 1.00 .45 .12
☐ 41 Tom Walker .75 .35 .09
☐ 42 Mike Andrews .75 .35 .09
☐ 43 Randy Moffitt .75 .35 .09
☐ 44 Rick Monday 1.00 .45 .12
☐ 45 Ellie Rodriguez .75 .35 .09
(photo actually
John Felske)
☐ 46 Lindy McDaniel 1.00 .45 .12
☐ 47 Luis Melendez .75 .35 .09
☐ 48 Paul Splittorff .75 .35 .09
☐ 49 Twins Leaders 1.00 .45 .12
Frank Quilici MG
Vern Morgan CO
Bob Rodgers CO
Ralph Rowe CO
Al Worthington CO
☐ 50 Roberto Clemente 60.00 27.00 7.50
☐ 51 Chuck Seelbach .75 .35 .09
☐ 52 Denis Menke .75 .35 .09
☐ 53 Steve Dunning .75 .35 .09
☐ 54 Checklist 1-132 3.00 1.35 .35
☐ 55 Jon Matlack 1.00 .45 .12
☐ 56 Merv Rettenmund .75 .35 .09
☐ 57 Derrel Thomas .75 .35 .09
☐ 58 Mike Paul .75 .35 .09
☐ 59 Steve Yeager 2.00 .90 .25
☐ 60 Ken Holtzman 1.00 .45 .12
☐ 61 Batting Leaders 3.00 1.35 .35
Billy Williams
Rod Carew
☐ 62 Home Run Leaders 2.50 1.10 .30
Johnny Bench
Dick Allen
☐ 63 RBI Leaders 2.50 1.10 .30
Johnny Bench
Dick Allen
☐ 64 Stolen Base Leaders 2.00 .90 .25
Lou Brock
Bert Campaneris
☐ 65 ERA Leaders 2.00 .90 .25
Steve Carlton
Luis Tiant
☐ 66 Victory Leaders 2.00 .90 .25
Steve Carlton
Gaylord Perry
Wilbur Wood
☐ 67 Strikeout Leaders 35.00 16.00 4.40
Steve Carlton
Nolan Ryan
☐ 68 Leading Firemen 1.50 .70 .19
Clay Carroll
Sparky Lyle
☐ 69 Phil Gagliano .75 .35 .09
☐ 70 Milt Pappas 1.00 .45 .12
☐ 71 Johnny Briggs .75 .35 .09
☐ 72 Ron Reed .75 .35 .09
☐ 73 Ed Herrmann .75 .35 .09
☐ 74 Billy Champion .75 .35 .09
☐ 75 Vada Pinson 1.00 .45 .12
☐ 76 Doug Rader .75 .35 .09
☐ 77 Mike Torrez 1.00 .45 .12
☐ 78 Richie Scheinblum .75 .35 .09
☐ 79 Jim Willoughby .75 .35 .09
☐ 80 Tony Oliva 1.50 .70 .19
☐ 81 Chicago Cubs Leaders 2.00 .90 .25
Whitey Lockman MG
Hank Aguirre CO
Ernie Banks CO
Larry Jansen CO
Pete Reiser CO
☐ 82 Fritz Peterson .75 .35 .09
☐ 83 Leron Lee .75 .35 .09
☐ 84 Rollie Fingers 5.00 2.20 .60
☐ 85 Ted Simmons 2.00 .90 .25
☐ 86 Tom McCraw .75 .35 .09
☐ 87 Ken Boswell .75 .35 .09
☐ 88 Mickey Stanley 1.00 .45 .12
☐ 89 Jack Billingham .75 .35 .09
☐ 90 Brooks Robinson 8.00 3.60 1.00
☐ 91 Dodgers Team 1.50 .70 .19
☐ 92 Jerry Bell .75 .35 .09
☐ 93 Jesus Alou .75 .35 .09
☐ 94 Dick Billings .75 .35 .09
☐ 95 Steve Blass 1.00 .45 .12
☐ 96 Doug Griffin .75 .35 .09
☐ 97 Willie Montanez .75 .35 .09
☐ 98 Dick Woodson .75 .35 .09
☐ 99 Carl Taylor .75 .35 .09
☐ 100 Hank Aaron 35.00 16.00 4.40
☐ 101 Ken Henderson .75 .35 .09
☐ 102 Rudy May .75 .35 .09
☐ 103 Celerino Sanchez .75 .35 .09
☐ 104 Reggie Cleveland .75 .35 .09
☐ 105 Carlos May .75 .35 .09
☐ 106 Terry Humphrey .75 .35 .09
☐ 107 Phil Hennigan .75 .35 .09
☐ 108 Bill Russell 1.00 .45 .12
☐ 109 Doyle Alexander 1.00 .45 .12
☐ 110 Bob Watson 1.00 .45 .12
☐ 111 Dave Nelson .75 .35 .09
☐ 112 Gary Ross .75 .35 .09
☐ 113 Jerry Grote 1.00 .45 .12
☐ 114 Lynn McGlothen .75 .35 .09
☐ 115 Ron Santo 1.50 .70 .19
☐ 116 Yankees Leaders 1.00 .45 .12
Ralph Houk MG
Jim Hegan CO
Elston Howard CO
Dick Howser CO
Jim Turner CO
☐ 117 Ramon Hernandez .75 .35 .09
☐ 118 John Mayberry 1.00 .45 .12
☐ 119 Larry Bowa 1.00 .45 .12
☐ 120 Joe Coleman .75 .35 .09
☐ 121 Dave Rader .75 .35 .09
☐ 122 Jim Strickland .75 .35 .09
☐ 123 Sandy Alomar 1.00 .45 .12
☐ 124 Jim Hardin .75 .35 .09
☐ 125 Ron Fairly 1.00 .45 .12
☐ 126 Jim Brewer .75 .35 .09
☐ 127 Brewers Team 1.50 .70 .19
☐ 128 Ted Sizemore .75 .35 .09
☐ 129 Terry Forster 1.00 .45 .12
☐ 130 Pete Rose 18.00 8.00 2.20
☐ 131 Red Sox Leaders 1.00 .45 .12
Eddie Kasko MG
Doug Camilli CO
Don Lenhardt CO
Eddie Popowski CO
Lee Stange CO
☐ 132 Matty Alou 1.00 .45 .12
☐ 133 Dave Roberts .75 .35 .09
☐ 134 Milt Wilcox .75 .35 .09
☐ 135 Lee May 1.00 .45 .12
☐ 136 Orioles Leaders 3.00 1.35 .35
Earl Weaver MG
George Bamberger CO
Jim Frey CO
Billy Hunter CO
George Staller CO
☐ 137 Jim Beauchamp .75 .35 .09
☐ 138 Horacio Pina .75 .35 .09
☐ 139 Carmen Fanzone .75 .35 .09
☐ 140 Lou Piniella 1.25 .55 .16
☐ 141 Bruce Kison .75 .35 .09
☐ 142 Thurman Munson 6.00 2.70 .75
☐ 143 John Curtis .75 .35 .09
☐ 144 Marty Perez .75 .35 .09
☐ 145 Bobby Bonds 2.00 .90 .25
☐ 146 Woodie Fryman .75 .35 .09
☐ 147 Mike Anderson .75 .35 .09
☐ 148 Dave Goltz .75 .35 .09
☐ 149 Ron Hunt .75 .35 .09
☐ 150 Wilbur Wood 1.00 .45 .12
☐ 151 Wes Parker 1.00 .45 .12
☐ 152 Dave May .75 .35 .09
☐ 153 Al Hrabosky 1.00 .45 .12
☐ 154 Jeff Torborg 1.00 .45 .12
☐ 155 Sal Bando 1.00 .45 .12
☐ 156 Cesar Geronimo .75 .35 .09
☐ 157 Denny Riddleberger .75 .35 .09
☐ 158 Astros Team 1.50 .70 .19
☐ 159 Clarence Gaston 1.25 .55 .16
☐ 160 Jim Palmer 7.50 3.40 .95
☐ 161 Ted Martinez .75 .35 .09
☐ 162 Pete Broberg .75 .35 .09
☐ 163 Vic Davalillo .75 .35 .09
☐ 164 Monty Montgomery .75 .35 .09
☐ 165 Luis Aparicio 3.00 1.35 .35
☐ 166 Terry Harmon .75 .35 .09
☐ 167 Steve Stone 1.00 .45 .12
☐ 168 Jim Northrup 1.00 .45 .12
☐ 169 Ron Schueler .75 .35 .09
☐ 170 Harmon Killebrew 5.00 2.20 .60
☐ 171 Bernie Carbo .75 .35 .09
☐ 172 Steve Kline .75 .35 .09
☐ 173 Hal Breeden 1.00 .45 .12
☐ 174 Rich Gossage 8.00 3.60 1.00
☐ 175 Frank Robinson 7.50 3.40 .95
☐ 176 Chuck Taylor .75 .35 .09
☐ 177 Bill Plummer .75 .35 .09
☐ 178 Don Rose .75 .35 .09
☐ 179 Oakland A's Leaders 1.00 .45 .12
Dick Williams MG
Jerry Adair CO
Vern Hoscheit CO
Irv Noren CO
Wes Stock CO
☐ 180 Fergie Jenkins 5.00 2.20 .60
☐ 181 Jack Brohamer .75 .35 .09
☐ 182 Mike Caldwell 1.00 .45 .12
☐ 183 Don Buford .75 .35 .09
☐ 184 Jerry Koosman 1.00 .45 .12
☐ 185 Jim Wynn 1.00 .45 .12
☐ 186 Bill Fahey .75 .35 .09
☐ 187 Luke Walker .75 .35 .09
☐ 188 Cookie Rojas 1.00 .45 .12
☐ 189 Greg Luzinski 1.50 .70 .19
☐ 190 Bob Gibson 7.00 3.10 .85
☐ 191 Tigers Team 1.50 .70 .19
☐ 192 Pat Jarvis .75 .35 .09
☐ 193 Carlton Fisk 12.50 5.50 1.55
☐ 194 Jorge Orta .75 .35 .09
☐ 195 Clay Carroll .75 .35 .09
☐ 196 Ken McMullen .75 .35 .09
☐ 197 Ed Goodson .75 .35 .09
☐ 198 Horace Clarke .75 .35 .09
☐ 199 Bert Blyleven 2.00 .90 .25
☐ 200 Billy Williams 5.00 2.20 .60
☐ 201 George Hendrick ALCS 1.50 .70 .19
☐ 202 George Foster NLCS 1.50 .70 .19
☐ 203 Gene Tenace WS 1.50 .70 .19
☐ 204 World Series Game 2 1.50 .70 .19
A's two straight
☐ 205 Tony Perez WS 1.50 .70 .19
☐ 206 Gene Tenace WS 1.50 .70 .19
☐ 207 Blue Moon Odom WS 1.50 .70 .19
☐ 208 Johnny Bench WS 3.00 1.35 .35
☐ 209 Bert Campaneris WS 1.50 .70 .19
☐ 210 World Series Summary 1.50 .70 .19
World champions:
A's Win
☐ 211 Balor Moore .75 .35 .09
☐ 212 Joe Lahoud .75 .35 .09
☐ 213 Steve Garvey 6.00 2.70 .75
☐ 214 Steve Hamilton .75 .35 .09
☐ 215 Dusty Baker 2.00 .90 .25
☐ 216 Toby Harrah 1.00 .45 .12
☐ 217 Don Wilson .75 .35 .09
☐ 218 Aurelio Rodriguez .75 .35 .09
☐ 219 Cardinals Team 1.50 .70 .19
☐ 220 Nolan Ryan 100.00 45.00 12.50
☐ 221 Fred Kendall .75 .35 .09
☐ 222 Rob Gardner .75 .35 .09
☐ 223 Bud Harrelson 1.00 .45 .12
☐ 224 Bill Lee 1.00 .45 .12
☐ 225 Al Oliver 1.50 .70 .19
☐ 226 Ray Fosse .75 .35 .09
☐ 227 Wayne Twitchell .75 .35 .09
☐ 228 Bobby Darwin .75 .35 .09
☐ 229 Roric Harrison .75 .35 .09
☐ 230 Joe Morgan 6.00 2.70 .75
☐ 231 Bill Parsons .75 .35 .09
☐ 232 Ken Singleton 1.00 .45 .12
☐ 233 Ed Kirkpatrick .75 .35 .09
☐ 234 Bill North .75 .35 .09
☐ 235 Jim Hunter 4.00 1.80 .50
☐ 236 Tito Fuentes .75 .35 .09
☐ 237 Braves Leaders 2.50 1.10 .30
Eddie Mathews MG
Lew Burdette CO
Jim Busby CO
Roy Hartsfield CO
Ken Silvestri CO
☐ 238 Tony Muser .75 .35 .09
☐ 239 Pete Richert .75 .35 .09
☐ 240 Bobby Murcer 1.00 .45 .12
☐ 241 Dwain Anderson .75 .35 .09
☐ 242 George Culver .75 .35 .09
☐ 243 Angels Team 1.50 .70 .19
☐ 244 Ed Acosta .75 .35 .09
☐ 245 Carl Yastrzemski 10.00 4.50 1.25
☐ 246 Ken Sanders .75 .35 .09
☐ 247 Del Unser .75 .35 .09
☐ 248 Jerry Johnson .75 .35 .09
☐ 249 Larry Biittner .75 .35 .09
☐ 250 Manny Sanguillen 1.00 .45 .12
☐ 251 Roger Nelson .75 .35 .09
☐ 252 Giants Leaders 1.00 .45 .12
Charlie Fox MG
Joe Amalfitano CO
Andy Gilbert CO
Don McMahon CO
John McNamara CO
☐ 253 Mark Belanger 1.00 .45 .12
☐ 254 Bill Stoneman .75 .35 .09
☐ 255 Reggie Jackson 20.00 9.00 2.50
☐ 256 Chris Zachary .75 .35 .09
☐ 257 N.Y. Mets Leaders 4.00 1.80 .50
Yogi Berra MG
Roy McMillan CO
Joe Pignatano CO
Rube Walker CO
Eddie Yost CO
☐ 258 Tommy John 1.50 .70 .19

□ 259 Jim Holt	.75	.35	.09
□ 260 Gary Nolan	1.00	.45	.12
□ 261 Pat Kelly	.75	.35	.09
□ 262 Jack Aker	.75	.35	.09
□ 263 George Scott	1.00	.45	.12
□ 264 Checklist 133-264	3.00	1.35	.35
□ 265 Gene Michael	.75	.35	.09
□ 266 Mike Lum	.75	.35	.09
□ 267 Lloyd Allen	.75	.35	.09
□ 268 Jerry Morales	.75	.35	.09
□ 269 Tim McCarver	1.50	.70	.19
□ 270 Luis Tiant	1.00	.45	.12
□ 271 Tom Hutton	.75	.35	.09
□ 272 Ed Farmer	.75	.35	.09
□ 273 Chris Speier	.75	.35	.09
□ 274 Darold Knowles	.75	.35	.09
□ 275 Tony Perez	4.00	1.80	.50
□ 276 Joe Lovitto	.75	.35	.09
□ 277 Bob Miller	.75	.35	.09
□ 278 Orioles Team	1.50	.70	.19
□ 279 Mike Strahler	.75	.35	.09
□ 280 Al Kaline	7.00	3.10	.85
□ 281 Mike Jorgensen	.75	.35	.09
□ 282 Steve Hovley	.75	.35	.09
□ 283 Ray Sadecki	.75	.35	.09
□ 284 Glenn Borgmann	.75	.35	.09
□ 285 Don Kessinger	1.00	.45	.12
□ 286 Frank Linzy	.75	.35	.09
□ 287 Eddie Leon	.75	.35	.09
□ 288 Gary Gentry	.75	.35	.09
□ 289 Bob Oliver	.75	.35	.09
□ 290 Cesar Cedeno	1.00	.45	.12
□ 291 Rogelio Moret	.75	.35	.09
□ 292 Jose Cruz	1.00	.45	.12
□ 293 Bernie Allen	.75	.35	.09
□ 294 Steve Arlin	.75	.35	.09
□ 295 Bert Campaneris	1.00	.45	.12
□ 296 Reds Leaders	2.50	1.10	.30
Sparky Anderson MG			
Alex Grammas CO			
Ted Kluszewski CO			
George Scherger CO			
Larry Shepard CO			
□ 297 Walt Williams	.75	.35	.09
□ 298 Ron Bryant	.75	.35	.09
□ 299 Ted Ford	.75	.35	.09
□ 300 Steve Carlton	10.00	4.50	1.25
□ 301 Billy Grabarkewitz	.75	.35	.09
□ 302 Terry Crowley	.75	.35	.09
□ 303 Nelson Briles	.75	.35	.09
□ 304 Duke Sims	.75	.35	.09
□ 305 Willie Mays	40.00	18.00	5.00
□ 306 Tom Burgmeier	.75	.35	.09
□ 307 Boots Day	.75	.35	.09
□ 308 Skip Lockwood	.75	.35	.09
□ 309 Paul Popovich	.75	.35	.09
□ 310 Dick Allen	1.50	.70	.19
□ 311 Joe Decker	.75	.35	.09
□ 312 Oscar Brown	.75	.35	.09
□ 313 Jim Ray	.75	.35	.09
□ 314 Ron Swoboda	.75	.35	.09
□ 315 John Odom	.75	.35	.09
□ 316 Padres Team	1.50	.70	.19
□ 317 Danny Cater	.75	.35	.09
□ 318 Jim McGlothlin	.75	.35	.09
□ 319 Jim Spencer	.75	.35	.09
□ 320 Lou Brock	6.00	2.70	.75
□ 321 Rich Hinton	.75	.35	.09
□ 322 Garry Maddox	3.00	1.35	.35
□ 323 Tigers Leaders	2.00	.90	.25
Billy Martin MG			
Art Fowler CO			
Charlie Silvera CO			
Dick Tracewski CO			
□ 324 Al Downing	.75	.35	.09
□ 325 Boog Powell	1.50	.70	.19
□ 326 Darrell Brandon	.75	.35	.09
□ 327 John Lowenstein	.75	.35	.09
□ 328 Bill Bonham	.75	.35	.09
□ 329 Ed Kranepool	.75	.35	.09
□ 330 Rod Carew	7.50	3.40	.95
□ 331 Carl Morton	.75	.35	.09
□ 332 John Felske	.75	.35	.09
□ 333 Gene Clines	.75	.35	.09
□ 334 Freddie Patek	1.00	.45	.12
□ 335 Bob Tolan	.75	.35	.09
□ 336 Tom Bradley	.75	.35	.09
□ 337 Dave Duncan	.75	.35	.09
□ 338 Checklist 265-396	3.00	1.35	.35
□ 339 Dick Tidrow	.75	.35	.09
□ 340 Nate Colbert	.75	.35	.09
□ 341 Jim Palmer KP	1.50	.70	.19
□ 342 Sam McDowell KP	1.00	.45	.12
□ 343 Bobby Murcer KP	1.00	.45	.12
□ 344 Jim Hunter KP	1.50	.70	.19
□ 345 Chris Speier KP	1.00	.45	.12
□ 346 Gaylord Perry KP	1.50	.70	.19
□ 347 Royals Team	1.50	.70	.19
□ 348 Rennie Stennett	.75	.35	.09
□ 349 Dick McAuliffe	.75	.35	.09
□ 350 Tom Seaver	14.00	6.25	1.75
□ 351 Jimmy Stewart	.75	.35	.09
□ 352 Don Stanhouse	.75	.35	.09
□ 353 Steve Brye	.75	.35	.09
□ 354 Billy Parker	.75	.35	.09

□ 355 Mike Marshall	1.00	.45	.12
□ 356 White Sox Leaders	1.00	.45	.12
Chuck Tanner MG			
Joe Lonnett CO			
Jim Mahoney CO			
Al Monchak CO			
Johnny Sain CO			
□ 357 Ross Grimsley	.75	.35	.09
□ 358 Jim Nettles	.75	.35	.09
□ 359 Cecil Upshaw	.75	.35	.09
□ 360 Joe Rudi	1.00	.45	.12
(photo actually			
Gene Tenace)			
□ 361 Fran Healy	.75	.35	.09
□ 362 Eddie Watt	.75	.35	.09
□ 363 Jackie Hernandez	.75	.35	.09
□ 364 Rick Wise	.75	.35	.09
□ 365 Rico Petrocelli	1.00	.45	.12
□ 366 Brock Davis	.75	.35	.09
□ 367 Burt Hooton	1.00	.45	.12
□ 368 Bill Buckner	1.00	.45	.12
□ 369 Lerrin LaGrow	.75	.35	.09
□ 370 Willie Stargell	5.00	2.20	.60
□ 371 Mike Kekich	.75	.35	.09
□ 372 Oscar Gamble	1.00	.45	.12
□ 373 Clyde Wright	.75	.35	.09
□ 374 Darrell Evans	1.00	.45	.12
□ 375 Larry Dierker	.75	.35	.09
□ 376 Frank Duffy	.75	.35	.09
□ 377 Expos Leaders	.75	.35	.09
Gene Mauch MG			
Dave Bristol CO			
Larry Doby CO			
Cal McLish CO			
Jerry Zimmerman CO			
□ 378 Lenny Randle	.75	.35	.09
□ 379 Cy Acosta	.75	.35	.09
□ 380 Johnny Bench	8.00	3.60	1.00
□ 381 Vicente Romo	.75	.35	.09
□ 382 Mike Hegan	.75	.35	.09
□ 383 Diego Segui	.75	.35	.09
□ 384 Don Baylor	4.00	1.80	.50
□ 385 Jim Perry	1.00	.45	.12
□ 386 Don Money	.75	.35	.09
□ 387 Jim Barr	.75	.35	.09
□ 388 Ben Oglivie	1.00	.45	.12
□ 389 Mets Team	3.00	1.35	.35
□ 390 Mickey Lolich	1.00	.45	.12
□ 391 Lee Lacy	1.00	.45	.12
□ 392 Dick Drago	.75	.35	.09
□ 393 Jose Cardenal	.75	.35	.09
□ 394 Sparky Lyle	1.00	.45	.12
□ 395 Roger Metzger	.75	.35	.09
□ 396 Grant Jackson	.75	.35	.09
□ 397 Dave Cash	1.00	.45	.12
□ 398 Rich Hand	.75	.35	.09
□ 399 George Foster	2.00	.90	.25
□ 400 Gaylord Perry	5.00	2.20	.60
□ 401 Clyde Mashore	.75	.35	.09
□ 402 Jack Hiatt	.75	.35	.09
□ 403 Sonny Jackson	.75	.35	.09
□ 404 Chuck Brinkman	.75	.35	.09
□ 405 Cesar Tovar	.75	.35	.09
□ 406 Paul Lindblad	.75	.35	.09
□ 407 Felix Millan	.75	.35	.09
□ 408 Jim Colborn	.75	.35	.09
□ 409 Ivan Murrell	.75	.35	.09
□ 410 Willie McCovey	6.00	2.70	.75
□ 411 Ray Corbin	.75	.35	.09
□ 412 Manny Mota	1.00	.45	.12
□ 413 Tom Timmerman	.75	.35	.09
□ 414 Ken Rudolph	.75	.35	.09
□ 415 Marty Pattin	.75	.35	.09
□ 416 Paul Schaal	.75	.35	.09
□ 417 Scipio Spinks	.75	.35	.09
□ 418 Bobby Grich	1.00	.45	.12
□ 419 Casey Cox	.75	.35	.09
□ 420 Tommie Agee	.75	.35	.09
□ 421 Angels Leaders	.75	.35	.09
Bobby Winkles MG			
Tom Morgan CO			
Salty Parker CO			
Jimmie Reese CO			
John Roseboro CO			
□ 422 Bob Robertson	.75	.35	.09
□ 423 Johnny Jeter	.75	.35	.09
□ 424 Denny Doyle	.75	.35	.09
□ 425 Alex Johnson	.75	.35	.09
□ 426 Dave LaRoche	.75	.35	.09
□ 427 Rick Auerbach	.75	.35	.09
□ 428 Wayne Simpson	.75	.35	.09
□ 429 Jim Fairey	.75	.35	.09
□ 430 Vida Blue	1.50	.70	.19
□ 431 Gerry Moses	.75	.35	.09
□ 432 Dan Frisella	.75	.35	.09
□ 433 Willie Horton	1.00	.45	.12
□ 434 Giants Team	1.50	.70	.19
□ 435 Rico Carty	1.00	.45	.12
□ 436 Jim McAndrew	.75	.35	.09
□ 437 John Kennedy	.75	.35	.09
□ 438 Enzo Hernandez	.75	.35	.09
□ 439 Eddie Fisher	.75	.35	.09
□ 440 Glenn Beckert	.75	.35	.09
□ 441 Gail Hopkins	.75	.35	.09
□ 442 Dick Dietz	.75	.35	.09

□ 443 Danny Thompson	.75	.35	.09
□ 444 Ken Brett	.75	.35	.09
□ 445 Ken Berry	.75	.35	.09
□ 446 Jerry Reuss	1.00	.45	.12
□ 447 Joe Hague	.75	.35	.09
□ 448 John Hiller	1.00	.45	.12
□ 449 Indians Leaders	4.00	1.80	.50
Ken Aspromonte MG			
Rocky Colavito CO			
Joe Lutz CO			
Warren Spahn CO			
□ 450 Joe Torre	1.50	.70	.19
□ 451 John Vuckovich	.75	.35	.09
□ 452 Paul Casanova	.75	.35	.09
□ 453 Checklist 397-528	3.00	1.35	.35
□ 454 Tom Haller	.75	.35	.09
□ 455 Bill Melton	.75	.35	.09
□ 456 Dick Green	.75	.35	.09
□ 457 John Strohmayer	.75	.35	.09
□ 458 Jim Mason	.75	.35	.09
□ 459 Jimmy Howarth	.75	.35	.09
□ 460 Bill Freehan	1.00	.45	.12
□ 461 Mike Corkins	.75	.35	.09
□ 462 Ron Blomberg	.75	.35	.09
□ 463 Ken Tatum	.75	.35	.09
□ 464 Chicago Cubs Team	1.50	.70	.19
□ 465 Dave Giusti	.75	.35	.09
□ 466 Jose Arcia	.75	.35	.09
□ 467 Mike Ryan	.75	.35	.09
□ 468 Tom Griffin	.75	.35	.09
□ 469 Dan Monzon	.75	.35	.09
□ 470 Mike Cuellar	1.00	.45	.12
□ 471 Ty Cobb ATL	8.00	3.60	1.00
4191 Hits			
□ 472 Lou Gehrig ATL	14.00	6.25	1.75
23 Grand Slams			
□ 473 Hank Aaron ATL	10.00	4.50	1.25
6172 Total Bases			
□ 474 Babe Ruth ATL	18.00	8.00	2.20
2209 RBI's			
□ 475 Ty Cobb ATL	8.00	3.60	1.00
.367 Batting Average			
□ 476 Walter Johnson ATL	4.00	1.80	.50
113 Shutouts			
□ 477 Cy Young ATL	4.00	1.80	.50
511 Wins			
□ 478 Walter Johnson ATL	4.00	1.80	.50
3508 Strikeouts			
□ 479 Hal Lanier	.75	.35	.09
□ 480 Juan Marichal	5.00	2.20	.60
□ 481 White Sox Team Card	1.50	.70	.19
□ 482 Rick Reuschel	3.00	1.35	.35
□ 483 Dal Maxvill	.75	.35	.09
□ 484 Ernie McAnally	.75	.35	.09
□ 485 Norm Cash	1.00	.45	.12
□ 486 Phillies Leaders	2.00	.90	.25
Danny Ozark MG			
Carroll Beringer CO			
Billy DeMars CO			
Ray Rippelmeyer CO			
Bobby Wine CO			
□ 487 Bruce Dal Canton	.75	.35	.09
□ 488 Dave Campbell	.75	.35	.09
□ 489 Jeff Burroughs	1.00	.45	.12
□ 490 Claude Osteen	1.00	.45	.12
□ 491 Bob Montgomery	.75	.35	.09
□ 492 Pedro Borbon	.75	.35	.09
□ 493 Duffy Dyer	.75	.35	.09
□ 494 Rich Morales	.75	.35	.09
□ 495 Tommy Helms	.75	.35	.09
□ 496 Ray Lamb	.75	.35	.09
□ 497 Cardinals Leaders	3.00	1.35	.35
Red Schoendienst MG			
Vern Benson CO			
George Kissell CO			
Barney Schultz CO			
□ 498 Graig Nettles	2.50	1.10	.30
□ 499 Bob Moose	.75	.35	.09
□ 500 Oakland A's Team	1.50	.70	.19
□ 501 Larry Gura	.75	.35	.09
□ 502 Bobby Valentine	.75	.35	.09
□ 503 Phil Niekro	5.00	2.20	.60
□ 504 Earl Williams	.75	.35	.09
□ 505 Bob Bailey	.75	.35	.09
□ 506 Bart Johnson	.75	.35	.09
□ 507 Darrel Chaney	.75	.35	.09
□ 508 Gates Brown	.75	.35	.09
□ 509 Jim Nash	.75	.35	.09
□ 510 Amos Otis	1.00	.45	.12
□ 511 Sam McDowell	1.00	.45	.12
□ 512 Dalton Jones	.75	.35	.09
□ 513 Dave Marshall	.75	.35	.09
□ 514 Jerry Kenney	.75	.35	.09
□ 515 Andy Messersmith	1.00	.45	.12
□ 516 Danny Walton	.75	.35	.09
□ 517 Pirates Leaders	2.00	.90	.25
Bill Virdon MG			
Don Leppert CO			
Bill Mazeroski CO			
Dave Ricketts CO			
Mel Wright CO			
□ 518 Bob Veale	.75	.35	.09
□ 519 John Edwards	.75	.35	.09
□ 520 Mel Stottlemyre	1.00	.45	.12
□ 521 Atlanta Braves Team	1.50	.70	.19

□ 522 Leo Cardenas	.75	.35	.09
□ 523 Wayne Granger	.75	.35	.09
□ 524 Gene Tenace	1.00	.45	.12
□ 525 Jim Fregosi	1.00	.45	.12
□ 526 Ollie Brown	.75	.35	.09
□ 527 Dan McGinn	.75	.35	.09
□ 528 Paul Blair	1.00	.45	.12
□ 529 Milt May	1.75	.80	.22
□ 530 Jim Kaat	5.00	2.20	.60
□ 531 Ron Woods	1.75	.80	.22
□ 532 Steve Mingori	1.75	.80	.22
□ 533 Larry Stahl	1.75	.80	.22
□ 534 Dave Lemonds	1.75	.80	.22
□ 535 John Callison	2.50	1.10	.30
□ 536 Phillies Team	5.00	2.20	.60
□ 537 Bill Slayback	1.75	.80	.22
□ 538 Jim Ray Hart	1.75	.80	.22
□ 539 Tom Murphy	1.75	.80	.22
□ 540 Cleon Jones	1.75	.80	.22
□ 541 Bob Bolin	1.75	.80	.22
□ 542 Pat Corrales	2.50	1.10	.30
□ 543 Alan Foster	1.75	.80	.22
□ 544 Von Joshua	1.75	.80	.22
□ 545 Orlando Cepeda	5.00	2.20	.60
□ 546 Jim York	1.75	.80	.22
□ 547 Bobby Heise	1.75	.80	.22
□ 548 Don Durham	1.75	.80	.22
□ 549 Rangers Leaders	5.00	2.20	.60
Whitey Herzog MG			
Chuck Estrada CO			
Chuck Hiller CO			
Jackie Moore CO			
□ 550 Dave Johnson	2.50	1.10	.30
□ 551 Mike Kilkenny	1.75	.80	.22
□ 552 J.C. Martin	1.75	.80	.22
□ 553 Mickey Scott	1.75	.80	.22
□ 554 Dave Concepcion	5.00	2.20	.60
□ 555 Bill Hands	1.75	.80	.22
□ 556 Yankees Team	8.00	3.60	1.00
□ 557 Bernie Williams	1.75	.80	.22
□ 558 Jerry May	1.75	.80	.22
□ 559 Barry Lersch	1.75	.80	.22
□ 560 Frank Howard	3.50	1.55	.45
□ 561 Jim Geddes	1.75	.80	.22
□ 562 Wayne Garrett	1.75	.80	.22
□ 563 Larry Haney	1.75	.80	.22
□ 564 Mike Thompson	1.75	.80	.22
□ 565 Jim Hickman	1.75	.80	.22
□ 566 Lew Krausse	1.75	.80	.22
□ 567 Bob Fenwick	1.75	.80	.22
□ 568 Ray Newman	1.75	.80	.22
□ 569 Dodgers Leaders	5.00	2.20	.60
Walt Alston MG			
Red Adams CO			
Monty Basgall CO			
Jim Gilliam CO			
Tom Lasorda CO			
□ 570 Bill Singer	1.75	.80	.22
□ 571 Rusty Torres	1.75	.80	.22
□ 572 Gary Sutherland	1.75	.80	.22
□ 573 Fred Beene	1.75	.80	.22
□ 574 Bob Didier	1.75	.80	.22
□ 575 Dock Ellis	2.50	1.10	.30
□ 576 Expos Team	5.00	2.20	.60
□ 577 Eric Soderholm	1.75	.80	.22
□ 578 Ken Wright	1.75	.80	.22
□ 579 Tom Grieve	2.50	1.10	.30
□ 580 Joe Pepitone	2.50	1.10	.30
□ 581 Steve Kealey	1.75	.80	.22
□ 582 Darrell Porter	2.50	1.10	.30
□ 583 Bill Greif	1.75	.80	.22
□ 584 Chris Arnold	1.75	.80	.22
□ 585 Joe Niekro	2.50	1.10	.30
□ 586 Bill Sudakis	1.75	.80	.22
□ 587 Rich McKinney	1.75	.80	.22
□ 588 Checklist 529-660	15.00	6.75	1.85
□ 589 Ken Forsch	1.75	.80	.22
□ 590 Deron Johnson	1.75	.80	.22
□ 591 Mike Hedlund	1.75	.80	.22
□ 592 John Boccabella	1.75	.80	.22
□ 593 Royals Leaders	1.75	.80	.22
Jack McKeon MG			
Galen Cisco CO			
Harry Dunlop CO			
Charlie Lau CO			
□ 594 Vic Harris	1.75	.80	.22
□ 595 Don Gullett	2.50	1.10	.30
□ 596 Red Sox Team	5.00	2.20	.60
□ 597 Mickey Rivers	2.50	1.10	.30
□ 598 Phil Roof	1.75	.80	.22
□ 599 Ed Crosby	1.75	.80	.22
□ 600 Dave McNally	2.50	1.10	.30
□ 601 Rookie Catchers	1.50	.70	.19
Sergio Robles			
George Pena			
Rick Stelmaszek			
□ 602 Rookie Pitchers	1.50	.70	.19
Mel Behney			
Ralph Garcia			
Doug Rau			
□ 603 Rookie 3rd Basemen	1.50	.70	.19
Terry Hughes			
Bill McNulty			
Ken Reitz			
□ 604 Rookie Pitchers	1.50	.70	.19

Card	NRMT	VG-E	GOOD
Jesse Jefferson			
Dennis O'Toole			
Bob Strampe			
☐ 605 Rookie 1st Basemen	5.00	2.20	.60
Enos Cabell			
Pat Bourque			
Gonzalo Marquez			
☐ 606 Rookie Outfielders	5.00	2.20	.60
Gary Matthews			
Tom Paciorek			
Jorge Roque			
☐ 607 Rookie Shortstops	1.50	.70	.19
Pepe Frias			
Ray Busse			
Mario Guerrero			
☐ 608 Rookie Pitchers	5.00	2.20	.60
Steve Busby			
Dick Colpaert			
George Medich			
☐ 609 Rookie 2nd Basemen	6.00	2.70	.75
Larvell Blanks			
Pedro Garcia			
Dave Lopes			
☐ 610 Rookie Pitchers	5.00	2.20	.60
Jimmy Freeman			
Charlie Hough			
Hank Webb			
☐ 611 Rookie Outfielders	1.50	.70	.19
Rich Coggins			
Jim Wohlford			
Richie Zisk			
☐ 612 Rookie Pitchers	1.50	.70	.19
Steve Lawson			
Bob Reynolds			
Brent Strom			
☐ 613 Rookie Catchers	25.00	11.00	3.10
Bob Boone			
Skip Jutze			
Mike Ivie			
☐ 614 Rookie Outfielders	25.00	11.00	3.10
Al Bumbry			
Dwight Evans			
Charlie Spikes			
☐ 615 Rookie 3rd Basemen	350.00	160.00	45.00
Ron Cey			
John Hilton			
Mike Schmidt			
☐ 616 Rookie Pitchers	1.50	.70	.19
Norm Angelini			
Steve Blateric			
Mike Garman			
☐ 617 Rich Chiles	1.75	.80	.22
☐ 618 Andy Etchebarren	1.75	.80	.22
☐ 619 Billy Wilson	1.75	.80	.22
☐ 620 Tommy Harper	2.50	1.10	.30
☐ 621 Joe Ferguson	2.50	1.10	.30
☐ 622 Larry Hisle	2.50	1.10	.30
☐ 623 Steve Renko	1.75	.80	.22
☐ 624 Astros Leaders	6.00	2.70	.75
Leo Durocher MG			
Preston Gomez CO			
Grady Hatton CO			
Hub Kittle CO			
Jim Owens CO			
☐ 625 Angel Mangual	1.75	.80	.22
☐ 626 Bob Barton	1.75	.80	.22
☐ 627 Luis Alvarado	1.75	.80	.22
☐ 628 Jim Slaton	1.75	.80	.22
☐ 629 Indians Team	5.00	2.20	.60
☐ 630 Denny McLain	5.00	2.20	.60
☐ 631 Tom Matchick	1.75	.80	.22
☐ 632 Dick Selma	1.75	.80	.22
☐ 633 Ike Brown	1.75	.80	.22
☐ 634 Alan Closter	1.75	.80	.22
☐ 635 Gene Alley	2.50	1.10	.30
☐ 636 Rickey Clark	1.75	.80	.22
☐ 637 Norm Miller	1.75	.80	.22
☐ 638 Ken Reynolds	1.75	.80	.22
☐ 639 Willie Crawford	1.75	.80	.22
☐ 640 Dick Bosman	1.75	.80	.22
☐ 641 Reds Team	5.00	2.20	.60
☐ 642 Jose Laboy	1.75	.80	.22
☐ 643 Al Fitzmorris	1.75	.80	.22
☐ 644 Jack Heidemann	1.75	.80	.22
☐ 645 Bob Locker	1.75	.80	.22
☐ 646 Brewers Leaders	2.50	1.10	.30
Del Crandall MG			
Harvey Kuenn CO			
Joe Nossek CO			
Bob Shaw CO			
Jim Walton CO			
☐ 647 George Stone	1.75	.80	.22
☐ 648 Tom Egan	1.75	.80	.22
☐ 649 Rich Folkers	1.75	.80	.22
☐ 650 Felipe Alou	3.50	1.55	.45
☐ 651 Don Carrithers	1.75	.80	.22
☐ 652 Ted Kubiak	1.75	.80	.22
☐ 653 Joe Hoerner	1.75	.80	.22
☐ 654 Twins Team	5.00	2.20	.60
☐ 655 Clay Kirby	1.75	.80	.22
☐ 656 John Ellis	1.75	.80	.22
☐ 657 Bob Johnson	1.75	.80	.22
☐ 658 Elliott Maddox	1.75	.80	.22
☐ 659 Jose Pagan	1.75	.80	.22
☐ 660 Fred Scherman	4.00	1.80	.50

1973 O-Pee-Chee Blue Team Checklists

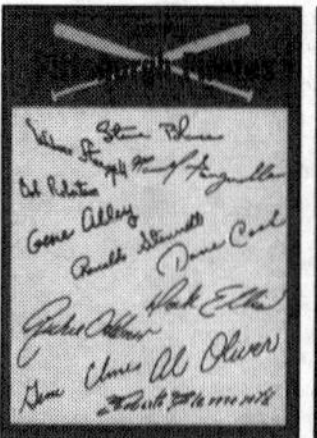

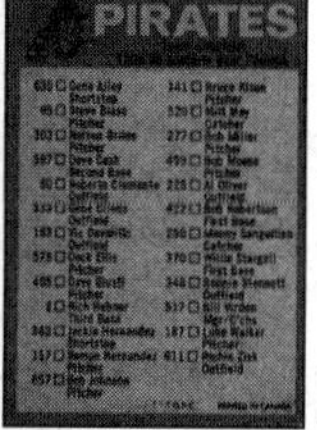

This 24-card standard-size set is somewhat difficult to find. These blue-bordered team checklist cards are very similar in design to the mass produced red trim team checklist cards issued by O-Pee-Chee the next year and obviously very similar to the Topps issue. The primary difference compared to the Topps issue is the existence of a little French language on the reverse of the O-Pee-Chee. The fronts feature facsimile autographs on a white background. On an orange background, the backs carry the team checklists. The words "Team Checklist" are printed in French and English. The cards are unnumbered and checklisted below in alphabetical order.

	NRMT	VG-E	GOOD
COMPLETE SET (24)	125.00	55.00	15.50
COMMON TEAM (1-24)	6.00	2.70	.75
☐ 1 Atlanta Braves	6.00	2.70	.75
☐ 2 Baltimore Orioles	6.00	2.70	.75
☐ 3 Boston Red Sox	6.00	2.70	.75
☐ 4 California Angels	6.00	2.70	.75
☐ 5 Chicago Cubs	6.00	2.70	.75
☐ 6 Chicago White Sox	6.00	2.70	.75
☐ 7 Cincinnati Reds	6.00	2.70	.75
☐ 8 Cleveland Indians	6.00	2.70	.75
☐ 9 Detroit Tigers	6.00	2.70	.75
☐ 10 Houston Astros	6.00	2.70	.75
☐ 11 Kansas City Royals	6.00	2.70	.75
☐ 12 Los Angeles Dodgers	6.00	2.70	.75
☐ 13 Milwaukee Brewers	6.00	2.70	.75
☐ 14 Minnesota Twins	6.00	2.70	.75
☐ 15 Montreal Expos	6.00	2.70	.75
☐ 16 New York Mets	6.00	2.70	.75
☐ 17 New York Yankees	6.00	2.70	.75
☐ 18 Oakland A's	6.00	2.70	.75
☐ 19 Philadelphia Phillies	6.00	2.70	.75
☐ 20 Pittsburgh Pirates	6.00	2.70	.75
☐ 21 San Diego Padres	6.00	2.70	.75
☐ 22 San Francisco Giants	6.00	2.70	.75
☐ 23 St. Louis Cardinals	6.00	2.70	.75
☐ 24 Texas Rangers	6.00	2.70	.75

1974 O-Pee-Chee

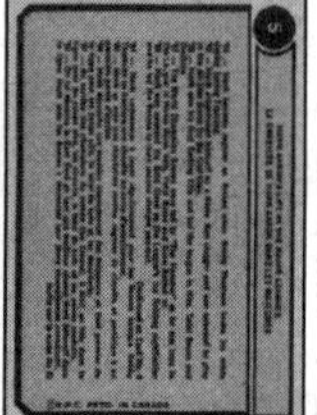

The cards in this 660-card set measure 2 1/2" by 3 1/2". The 1974 O-Pee-Chee cards are very similar to the 1974 Topps cards. Since the O-Pee-Chee cards were printed substantially later than the Topps cards, there was no "San Diego rumored moving to Washington" problem in the O-Pee-Chee set. On a white background, the fronts feature color player photos with rounded corners and blue borders. The player's name and position and the team name also appear on the front. The horizontal backs are golden yellow instead of green like the 1974 Topps and carry player biography and statistics in French and English. There are a number of obverse differences between the two sets as well; they are numbers 3, 4, 5, 6, 7, 8, 9, 99, 166 and 196. The Aaron Specials generally feature two past cards per card instead of four as in the Topps. Remember, the prices below apply only to O-Pee-Chee cards -- they are NOT prices for Topps cards as the Topps cards are generally much more available.

Card	NRMT	VG-E	GOOD
COMPLETE SET (660)	1000.00	450.00	125.00
COMMON CARD (1-660)	.50	.23	.06
☐ 1 Hank Aaron	40.00	18.00	5.00
Complete ML record			
☐ 2 Hank Aaron	8.00	3.60	1.00
Special 54-57			
Records on back			
☐ 3 Hank Aaron	12.00	5.50	1.50
Special 58-59			
☐ 4 Hank Aaron	12.00	5.50	1.50
Special 60-61			
☐ 5 Hank Aaron	12.00	5.50	1.50
Special 62-63			
☐ 6 Hank Aaron	12.00	5.50	1.50
Special 64-65			
☐ 7 Hank Aaron	12.00	5.50	1.50
Special 66-67			
☐ 8 Hank Aaron	12.00	5.50	1.50
Special 68-69			
☐ 9 Hank Aaron	12.00	5.50	1.50
Special 70-73			
Milestone homers			
☐ 10 Johnny Bench	12.00	5.50	1.50
☐ 11 Jim Bibby	.50	.23	.06
☐ 12 Dave May	.50	.23	.06
☐ 13 Tom Hilgendorf	.50	.23	.06
☐ 14 Paul Popovich	.50	.23	.06
☐ 15 Joe Torre	1.00	.45	.12
☐ 16 Orioles Team	1.00	.45	.12
☐ 17 Doug Bird	.50	.23	.06
☐ 18 Gary Thomasson	.50	.23	.06
☐ 19 Gerry Moses	.50	.23	.06
☐ 20 Nolan Ryan	75.00	34.00	9.50
☐ 21 Bob Gallagher	.50	.23	.06
☐ 22 Cy Acosta	.50	.23	.06
☐ 23 Craig Robinson	.50	.23	.06
☐ 24 John Hiller	.75	.35	.09
☐ 25 Ken Singleton	.75	.35	.09
☐ 26 Bill Campbell	.75	.35	.09
☐ 27 George Scott	.75	.35	.09
☐ 28 Manny Sanguillen	.75	.35	.09
☐ 29 Phil Niekro	3.00	1.35	.35
☐ 30 Bobby Bonds	2.00	.90	.25
☐ 31 Astros Leaders	.50	.23	.06
Preston Gomez MG			
Roger Craig CO			
Hub Kittle CO			
Grady Hatton CO			
Bob Lillis CO			
☐ 32 Johnny Grubb	.50	.23	.06
☐ 33 Don Newhauser	.50	.23	.06
☐ 34 Andy Kosco	.50	.23	.06
☐ 35 Gaylord Perry	3.00	1.35	.35
☐ 36 Cardinals Team	1.00	.45	.12
☐ 37 Dave Sells	.50	.23	.06
☐ 38 Don Kessinger	.75	.35	.09
☐ 39 Ken Suarez	.50	.23	.06
☐ 40 Jim Palmer	5.00	2.20	.60
☐ 41 Bobby Floyd	.50	.23	.06
☐ 42 Claude Osteen	.75	.35	.09
☐ 43 Jim Wynn	.75	.35	.09
☐ 44 Mel Stottlemyre	.75	.35	.09
☐ 45 Dave Johnson	.75	.35	.09
☐ 46 Pat Kelly	.50	.23	.06
☐ 47 Dick Ruthven	.50	.23	.06
☐ 48 Dick Sharon	.50	.23	.06
☐ 49 Steve Renko	.75	.35	.09
☐ 50 Rod Carew	5.00	2.20	.60
☐ 51 Bob Heise	.50	.23	.06
☐ 52 Al Oliver	1.00	.45	.12
☐ 53 Fred Kendall	.50	.23	.06
☐ 54 Elias Sosa	.50	.23	.06
☐ 55 Frank Robinson	7.50	3.40	.95
☐ 56 New York Mets Team	1.00	.45	.12
☐ 57 Darold Knowles	.50	.23	.06
☐ 58 Charlie Spikes	.50	.23	.06
☐ 59 Ross Grimsley	.50	.23	.06
☐ 60 Lou Brock	5.00	2.20	.60
☐ 61 Luis Aparicio	3.00	1.35	.35
☐ 62 Bob Locker	.50	.23	.06
☐ 63 Bill Sudakis	.50	.23	.06
☐ 64 Doug Rau	.50	.23	.06
☐ 65 Amos Otis	.75	.35	.09
☐ 66 Sparky Lyle	.75	.35	.09
☐ 67 Tommy Helms	.50	.23	.06
☐ 68 Grant Jackson	.50	.23	.06
☐ 69 Del Unser	.50	.23	.06
☐ 70 Dick Allen	1.00	.45	.12
☐ 71 Dan Frisella	.50	.23	.06
☐ 72 Aurelio Rodriguez	.50	.23	.06
☐ 73 Mike Marshall	.75	.35	.09
☐ 74 Twins Team	1.00	.45	.12
☐ 75 Jim Colborn	.50	.23	.06
☐ 76 Mickey Rivers	.75	.35	.09
☐ 77 Rich Troedson	.50	.23	.06
☐ 78 Giants Leaders	.50	.23	.06
Charlie Fox MG			
John McNamara CO			
Joe Amalfitano CO			
Andy Gilbert CO			
Don McMahon CO			
☐ 79 Gene Tenace	.75	.35	.09
☐ 80 Tom Seaver	14.00	6.25	1.75
☐ 81 Frank Duffy	.50	.23	.06
☐ 82 Dave Giusti	.50	.23	.06
☐ 83 Orlando Cepeda	1.50	.70	.19
☐ 84 Rick Wise	.50	.23	.06
☐ 85 Joe Morgan	5.00	2.20	.60
☐ 86 Joe Ferguson	.50	.23	.06
☐ 87 Fergie Jenkins	3.00	1.35	.35
☐ 88 Fred Patek	.75	.35	.09
☐ 89 Jackie Brown	.50	.23	.06
☐ 90 Bobby Murcer	1.00	.45	.12
☐ 91 Ken Forsch	.50	.23	.06
☐ 92 Paul Blair	.75	.35	.09
☐ 93 Rod Gilbreath	.50	.23	.06
☐ 94 Tigers Team	1.00	.45	.12
☐ 95 Steve Carlton	7.50	3.40	.95
☐ 96 Jerry Hairston	.50	.23	.06
☐ 97 Bob Bailey	.75	.35	.09
☐ 98 Bert Blyleven	1.00	.45	.12
☐ 99 George Theodore	1.00	.45	.12
(Topps 99 is			
Brewers Leaders)			
☐ 100 Willie Stargell	4.00	1.80	.50
☐ 101 Bobby Valentine	.75	.35	.09
☐ 102 Bill Greif	.50	.23	.06
☐ 103 Sal Bando	.75	.35	.09
☐ 104 Ron Bryant	.50	.23	.06
☐ 105 Carlton Fisk	14.00	6.25	1.75
☐ 106 Harry Parker	.50	.23	.06
☐ 107 Alex Johnson	.50	.23	.06
☐ 108 Al Hrabosky	.75	.35	.09
☐ 109 Bobby Grich	.75	.35	.09
☐ 110 Billy Williams	4.00	1.80	.50
☐ 111 Clay Carroll	.50	.23	.06
☐ 112 Dave Lopes	1.00	.45	.12
☐ 113 Dick Drago	.50	.23	.06
☐ 114 Angels Team	1.00	.45	.12
☐ 115 Willie Horton	.75	.35	.09
☐ 116 Jerry Reuss	.75	.35	.09
☐ 117 Ron Blomberg	.50	.23	.06
☐ 118 Bill Lee	.75	.35	.09
☐ 119 Phillies Leaders	.50	.23	.06
Danny Ozark MG			
Ray Rippelmeyer CO			
Bobby Wine CO			
Carroll Beringer CO			
Billy DeMars CO			
☐ 120 Wilbur Wood	.50	.23	.06
☐ 121 Larry Lintz	.50	.23	.06
☐ 122 Jim Holt	.50	.23	.06
☐ 123 Nellie Briles	.50	.23	.06
☐ 124 Bobby Coluccio	.50	.23	.06
☐ 125 Nate Colbert	.50	.23	.06
☐ 126 Checklist 1-132	2.50	1.10	.30
☐ 127 Tom Paciorek	.75	.35	.09
☐ 128 John Ellis	.50	.23	.06
☐ 129 Chris Speier	.50	.23	.06
☐ 130 Reggie Jackson	18.00	8.00	2.20
☐ 131 Bob Boone	2.00	.90	.25
☐ 132 Felix Millan	.50	.23	.06
☐ 133 David Clyde	.50	.23	.06
☐ 134 Denis Menke	.50	.23	.06
☐ 135 Roy White	.75	.35	.09
☐ 136 Rick Reuschel	1.00	.45	.12
☐ 137 Al Bumbry	.50	.23	.06
☐ 138 Eddie Brinkman	.50	.23	.06
☐ 139 Aurelio Monteagudo	.50	.23	.06
☐ 140 Darrell Evans	1.00	.45	.12
☐ 141 Pat Bourque	.50	.23	.06
☐ 142 Pedro Garcia	.50	.23	.06
☐ 143 Dick Woodson	.50	.23	.06
☐ 144 Dodgers Leaders	1.25	.55	.16
Walter Alston MG			
Tom Lasorda CO			
Jim Gilliam CO			
Red Adams CO			
Monty Basgall CO			
☐ 145 Dock Ellis	.50	.23	.06
☐ 146 Ron Fairly	.75	.35	.09
☐ 147 Bart Johnson	.50	.23	.06
☐ 148 Dave Hilton	.50	.23	.06
☐ 149 Mac Scarce	.50	.23	.06
☐ 150 John Mayberry	.75	.35	.09
☐ 151 Diego Segui	.50	.23	.06
☐ 152 Oscar Gamble	.75	.35	.09
☐ 153 Jon Matlack	.75	.35	.09
☐ 154 Astros Team	1.00	.45	.12
☐ 155 Bert Campaneris	.75	.35	.09
☐ 156 Randy Moffitt	.50	.23	.06
☐ 157 Vic Harris	.50	.23	.06
☐ 158 Jack Billingham	.50	.23	.06
☐ 159 Jim Ray Hart	.50	.23	.06
☐ 160 Brooks Robinson	7.50	3.40	.95
☐ 161 Ray Burris	.75	.35	.09
☐ 162 Bill Freehan	.75	.35	.09
☐ 163 Ken Berry	.50	.23	.06
☐ 164 Tom House	.50	.23	.06
☐ 165 Willie Davis	.75	.35	.09
☐ 166 Mickey Lolich	1.25	.55	.16
(Topps 166 is			
Royals Leaders)			
☐ 167 Luis Tiant	.75	.35	.09
☐ 168 Danny Thompson	.50	.23	.06
☐ 169 Steve Rogers	.75	.35	.09
☐ 170 Bill Melton	.50	.23	.06
☐ 171 Eduardo Rodriguez	.50	.23	.06
☐ 172 Gene Clines	.50	.23	.06
☐ 173 Randy Jones	1.00	.45	.12
☐ 174 Bill Robinson	.75	.35	.09
☐ 175 Reggie Cleveland	.50	.23	.06
☐ 176 John Lowenstein	.50	.23	.06
☐ 177 Dave Roberts	.50	.23	.06
☐ 178 Garry Maddox	.75	.35	.09
☐ 179 N.Y. Mets Leaders	2.00	.90	.25
Yogi Berra MG			
Rube Walker CO			
Eddie Yost CO			
Roy McMillan CO			
Joe Pignatano CO			
☐ 180 Ken Holtzman	.75	.35	.09
☐ 181 Cesar Geronimo	.50	.23	.06
☐ 182 Lindy McDaniel	.75	.35	.09
☐ 183 Johnny Oates	.75	.35	.09

□ 184 Rangers Team 1.00 .45 .12
□ 185 Jose Cardenal .50 .23 .06
□ 186 Fred Scherman .50 .23 .06
□ 187 Don Baylor 3.00 1.35 .35
□ 188 Rudy Meoli .50 .23 .06
□ 189 Jim Brewer .50 .23 .06
□ 190 Tony Oliva 1.00 .45 .12
□ 191 Al Fitzmorris .50 .23 .06
□ 192 Mario Guerrero .50 .23 .06
□ 193 Tom Walker .50 .23 .06
□ 194 Darrell Porter .75 .35 .09
□ 195 Carlos May .50 .23 .06
□ 196 Jim Hunter 6.00 2.70 .75
(Topps 196 is
Jim Fregosi)
□ 197 Vicente Romo .50 .23 .06
□ 198 Dave Cash .50 .23 .06
□ 199 Mike Kekich .50 .23 .06
□ 200 Cesar Cedeno .75 .35 .09
□ 201 Batting Leaders 5.00 2.20 .60
Rod Carew
Pete Rose
□ 202 Home Run Leaders 5.00 2.20 .60
Reggie Jackson
Willie Stargell
□ 203 RBI Leaders 5.00 2.20 .60
Reggie Jackson
Willie Stargell
□ 204 Stolen Base Leaders 1.25 .55 .16
Tommy Harper
Lou Brock
□ 205 Victory Leaders 1.00 .45 .12
Wilbur Wood
Ron Bryant
□ 206 ERA Leaders 5.00 2.20 .60
Jim Palmer
Tom Seaver
□ 207 Strikeout Leaders 20.00 9.00 2.50
Nolan Ryan
Tom Seaver
□ 208 Leading Firemen 1.00 .45 .12
John Hiller
Mike Marshall
□ 209 Ted Sizemore .50 .23 .06
□ 210 Bill Singer .50 .23 .06
□ 211 Chicago Cubs Team 1.00 .45 .12
□ 212 Rollie Fingers 3.00 1.35 .35
□ 213 Dave Rader .50 .23 .06
□ 214 Bill Grabarkewitz .50 .23 .06
□ 215 Al Kaline 5.00 2.20 .60
□ 216 Ray Sadecki .50 .23 .06
□ 217 Tim Foli .50 .23 .06
□ 218 John Briggs .50 .23 .06
□ 219 Doug Griffin .50 .23 .06
□ 220 Don Sutton 2.50 1.10 .30
□ 221 White Sox Leaders .75 .35 .09
Chuck Tanner MG
Jim Mahoney CO
Alex Monchak CO
Johnny Sain CO
Joe Lonnett CO
□ 222 Ramon Hernandez .50 .23 .06
□ 223 Jeff Burroughs 1.00 .45 .12
□ 224 Roger Metzger .50 .23 .06
□ 225 Paul Splittorff .50 .23 .06
□ 226 Padres Team Card 1.00 .45 .12
□ 227 Mike Lum .50 .23 .06
□ 228 Ted Kubiak .50 .23 .06
□ 229 Fritz Peterson .50 .23 .06
□ 230 Tony Perez 3.00 1.35 .35
□ 231 Dick Tidrow .50 .23 .06
□ 232 Steve Brye .50 .23 .06
□ 233 Jim Barr .50 .23 .06
□ 234 John Milner .50 .23 .06
□ 235 Dave McNally .75 .35 .09
□ 236 Cardinals Leaders 1.00 .45 .12
Red Schoendienst MG
Barney Schultz CO
George Kissell CO
Johnny Lewis CO
Vern Benson CO
□ 237 Ken Brett .50 .23 .06
□ 238 Fran Healy .75 .35 .09
□ 239 Bill Russell .75 .35 .09
□ 240 Joe Coleman .50 .23 .06
□ 241 Glenn Beckert .50 .23 .06
□ 242 Bill Gogolewski .50 .23 .06
□ 243 Bob Oliver .50 .23 .06
□ 244 Carl Morton .50 .23 .06
□ 245 Cleon Jones .50 .23 .06
□ 246 Athletics Team 1.00 .45 .12
□ 247 Rick Miller .50 .23 .06
□ 248 Tom Hall .50 .23 .06
□ 249 George Mitterwald .50 .23 .06
□ 250 Willie McCovey 6.00 2.70 .75
□ 251 Graig Nettles 2.00 .90 .25
□ 252 Dave Parker 10.00 4.50 1.25
□ 253 John Boccabella .50 .23 .06
□ 254 Stan Bahnsen .50 .23 .06
□ 255 Larry Bowa .75 .35 .09
□ 256 Tom Griffin .50 .23 .06
□ 257 Buddy Bell 1.00 .45 .12
□ 258 Jerry Morales .50 .23 .06
□ 259 Bob Reynolds .50 .23 .06
□ 260 Ted Simmons 1.50 .70 .19
□ 261 Jerry Bell .50 .23 .06
□ 262 Ed Kirkpatrick .50 .23 .06
□ 263 Checklist 133-264 2.50 1.10 .30
□ 264 Joe Rudi .75 .35 .09
□ 265 Tug McGraw 1.00 .45 .12
□ 266 Jim Northrup .75 .35 .09
□ 267 Andy Messersmith .75 .35 .09
□ 268 Tom Grieve .75 .35 .09
□ 269 Bob Johnson .50 .23 .06
□ 270 Ron Santo 1.00 .45 .12
□ 271 Bill Hands .50 .23 .06
□ 272 Paul Casanova .50 .23 .06
□ 273 Checklist 265-396 2.50 1.10 .30
□ 274 Fred Beene .50 .23 .06
□ 275 Ron Hunt .50 .23 .06
□ 276 Angels Leaders .75 .35 .09
Bobby Winkles MG
John Roseboro CO
Tom Morgan CO
Jimmie Reese CO
Salty Parker CO
□ 277 Gary Nolan .75 .35 .09
□ 278 Cookie Rojas .75 .35 .09
□ 279 Jim Crawford .50 .23 .06
□ 280 Carl Yastrzemski 6.00 2.70 .75
□ 281 Giants Team 1.00 .45 .12
□ 282 Doyle Alexander .75 .35 .09
□ 283 Mike Schmidt 60.00 27.00 7.50
□ 284 Dave Duncan .50 .23 .06
□ 285 Reggie Smith 1.00 .45 .12
□ 286 Tony Muser .50 .23 .06
□ 287 Clay Kirby .50 .23 .06
□ 288 Gorman Thomas 1.50 .70 .19
□ 289 Rick Auerbach .50 .23 .06
□ 290 Vida Blue 1.00 .45 .12
□ 291 Don Hahn .50 .23 .06
□ 292 Chuck Seelbach .50 .23 .06
□ 293 Milt May .50 .23 .06
□ 294 Steve Foucault .50 .23 .06
□ 295 Rick Monday .75 .35 .09
□ 296 Ray Corbin .50 .23 .06
□ 297 Hal Breeden .50 .23 .06
□ 298 Roric Harrison .50 .23 .06
□ 299 Gene Michael .50 .23 .06
□ 300 Pete Rose 16.00 7.25 2.00
□ 301 Bob Montgomery .50 .23 .06
□ 302 Rudy May .50 .23 .06
□ 303 George Hendrick .75 .35 .09
□ 304 Don Wilson .50 .23 .06
□ 305 Tito Fuentes .50 .23 .06
□ 306 Orioles Leaders 2.00 .90 .25
Earl Weaver MG
Jim Frey CO
George Bamberger CO
Billy Hunter CO
George Staller CO
□ 307 Luis Melendez .50 .23 .06
□ 308 Bruce Dal Canton .50 .23 .06
□ 309 Dave Roberts .50 .23 .06
□ 310 Terry Forster .75 .35 .09
□ 311 Jerry Grote .75 .35 .09
□ 312 Deron Johnson .50 .23 .06
□ 313 Barry Lersch .50 .23 .06
□ 314 Brewers Team 1.00 .45 .12
□ 315 Ron Cey 1.00 .45 .12
□ 316 Jim Perry 1.00 .45 .12
□ 317 Richie Zisk .75 .35 .09
□ 318 Jim Merritt .50 .23 .06
□ 319 Randy Hundley .50 .23 .06
□ 320 Dusty Baker 2.00 .90 .25
□ 321 Steve Braun .50 .23 .06
□ 322 Ernie McAnally .50 .23 .06
□ 323 Richie Scheinblum .50 .23 .06
□ 324 Steve Kline .50 .23 .06
□ 325 Tommy Harper .75 .35 .09
□ 326 Reds Leaders 2.50 1.10 .30
Sparky Anderson MG
Larry Shepard CO
George Scherger CO
Alex Grammas CO
Ted Kluszewski CO
□ 327 Tom Timmermann .50 .23 .06
□ 328 Skip Jutze .50 .23 .06
□ 329 Mark Belanger .75 .35 .09
□ 330 Juan Marichal 3.00 1.35 .35
□ 331 All-Star Catchers: 5.00 2.20 .60
Carlton Fisk
Johnny Bench
□ 332 All-Star 1B: 5.00 2.20 .60
Dick Allen
Hank Aaron
□ 333 All-Star 2B: 2.50 1.10 .30
Rod Carew
Joe Morgan
□ 334 All-Star 3B: 2.50 1.10 .30
Brooks Robinson
Ron Santo
□ 335 All-Star SS 1.00 .45 .12
Bert Campaneris
Chris Speier
□ 336 All-Star LF: 3.00 1.35 .35
Bobby Murcer
Pete Rose
□ 337 All-Star CF 1.00 .45 .12
Amos Otis
Cesar Cedeno
□ 338 All-Star RF: 5.00 2.20 .60
Reggie Jackson
Billy Williams
□ 339 All-Star Pitchers: 1.25 .55 .16
Jim Hunter
Rick Wise
□ 340 Thurman Munson 6.00 2.70 .75
□ 341 Dan Driessen 1.00 .45 .12
□ 342 Jim Lonborg .75 .35 .09
□ 343 Royals Team 1.00 .45 .12
□ 344 Mike Caldwell .50 .23 .06
□ 345 Bill North .50 .23 .06
□ 346 Ron Reed .50 .23 .06
□ 347 Sandy Alomar .50 .23 .06
□ 348 Pete Richert .50 .23 .06
□ 349 John Vukovich .50 .23 .06
□ 350 Bob Gibson 5.00 2.20 .60
□ 351 Dwight Evans 3.00 1.35 .35
□ 352 Bill Stoneman .50 .23 .06
□ 353 Rich Coggins .50 .23 .06
□ 354 Chicago Cubs Leaders .75 .35 .09
Whitey Lockman MG
J.C. Martin CO
Hank Aguirre CO
Al Spangler CO
Jim Marshall CO
□ 355 Dave Nelson .50 .23 .06
□ 356 Jerry Koosman 1.00 .45 .12
□ 357 Buddy Bradford .50 .23 .06
□ 358 Dal Maxvill .50 .23 .06
□ 359 Brent Strom .50 .23 .06
□ 360 Greg Luzinski 1.00 .45 .12
□ 361 Don Carrithers .50 .23 .06
□ 362 Hal King .50 .23 .06
□ 363 Yankees Team 1.00 .45 .12
□ 364 Cito Gaston .50 .23 .06
□ 365 Steve Busby .75 .35 .09
□ 366 Larry Hisle .75 .35 .09
□ 367 Norm Cash 1.00 .45 .12
□ 368 Manny Mota .75 .35 .09
□ 369 Paul Lindblad .50 .23 .06
□ 370 Bob Watson .75 .35 .09
□ 371 Jim Slaton .50 .23 .06
□ 372 Ken Reitz .50 .23 .06
□ 373 John Curtis .50 .23 .06
□ 374 Marty Perez .50 .23 .06
□ 375 Earl Williams .50 .23 .06
□ 376 Jorge Orta .50 .23 .06
□ 377 Ron Woods .50 .23 .06
□ 378 Burt Hooton .75 .35 .09
□ 379 Rangers Leaders 1.00 .45 .12
Billy Martin MG
Frank Lucchesi CO
Art Fowler CO
Charlie Silvera CO
Jackie Moore CO
□ 380 Bud Harrelson .75 .35 .09
□ 381 Charlie Sands .50 .23 .06
□ 382 Bob Moose .50 .23 .06
□ 383 Phillies Team 1.00 .45 .12
□ 384 Chris Chambliss .75 .35 .09
□ 385 Don Gullett .75 .35 .09
□ 386 Gary Matthews .75 .35 .09
□ 387 Rich Morales .50 .23 .06
□ 388 Phil Roof .50 .23 .06
□ 389 Gates Brown .50 .23 .06
□ 390 Lou Piniella 1.25 .55 .16
□ 391 Billy Champion .50 .23 .06
□ 392 Dick Green .50 .23 .06
□ 393 Orlando Pena .50 .23 .06
□ 394 Ken Henderson .50 .23 .06
□ 395 Doug Rader .50 .23 .06
□ 396 Tommy Davis .75 .35 .09
□ 397 George Stone .50 .23 .06
□ 398 Duke Sims .50 .23 .06
□ 399 Mike Paul .50 .23 .06
□ 400 Harmon Killebrew 5.00 2.20 .60
□ 401 Elliott Maddox .50 .23 .06
□ 402 Jim Rooker .50 .23 .06
□ 403 Red Sox Leaders .75 .35 .09
Darrell Johnson MG
Eddie Popowski CO
Lee Stange CO
Don Zimmer CO
Don Bryant CO
□ 404 Jim Howarth .50 .23 .06
□ 405 Ellie Rodriguez .50 .23 .06
□ 406 Steve Arlin .50 .23 .06
□ 407 Jim Wohlford .50 .23 .06
□ 408 Charlie Hough 1.00 .45 .12
□ 409 Ike Brown .50 .23 .06
□ 410 Pedro Borbon .50 .23 .06
□ 411 Frank Baker .50 .23 .06
□ 412 Chuck Taylor .50 .23 .06
□ 413 Don Money .50 .23 .06
□ 414 Checklist 397-528 2.50 1.10 .30
□ 415 Gary Gentry .50 .23 .06
□ 416 White Sox Team 1.00 .45 .12
□ 417 Rich Folkers .50 .23 .06
□ 418 Walt Williams .50 .23 .06
□ 419 Wayne Twitchell .50 .23 .06
□ 420 Ray Fosse .50 .23 .06
□ 421 Dan Fife .50 .23 .06
□ 422 Gonzalo Marquez .50 .23 .06
□ 423 Fred Stanley .50 .23 .06
□ 424 Jim Beauchamp .50 .23 .06
□ 425 Pete Broberg .50 .23 .06
□ 426 Rennie Stennett .50 .23 .06
□ 427 Bobby Bolin .50 .23 .06
□ 428 Gary Sutherland .50 .23 .06
□ 429 Dick Lange .50 .23 .06
□ 430 Matty Alou .75 .35 .09
□ 431 Gene Garber 1.00 .45 .12
□ 432 Chris Arnold .50 .23 .06
□ 433 Lerrin LaGrow .50 .23 .06
□ 434 Ken McMullen .50 .23 .06
□ 435 Dave Concepcion 2.50 1.10 .30
□ 436 Don Hood .50 .23 .06
□ 437 Jim Lyttle .50 .23 .06
□ 438 Ed Herrmann .50 .23 .06
□ 439 Norm Miller .50 .23 .06
□ 440 Jim Kaat 1.50 .70 .19
□ 441 Tom Ragland .50 .23 .06
□ 442 Alan Foster .50 .23 .06
□ 443 Tom Hutton .50 .23 .06
□ 444 Vic Davalillo .50 .23 .06
□ 445 George Medich .50 .23 .06
□ 446 Len Randle .50 .23 .06
□ 447 Twins Leaders .75 .35 .09
Frank Quilici MG
Ralph Rowe CO
Bob Rodgers CO
Vern Morgan CO
□ 448 Ron Hodges .50 .23 .06
□ 449 Tom McCraw .50 .23 .06
□ 450 Rich Hebner .75 .35 .09
□ 451 Tommy John 1.50 .70 .19
□ 452 Gene Hiser .50 .23 .06
□ 453 Balor Moore .50 .23 .06
□ 454 Kurt Bevacqua .50 .23 .06
□ 455 Tom Bradley .50 .23 .06
□ 456 Dave Winfield 140.00 65.00 17.50
□ 457 Chuck Goggin .50 .23 .06
□ 458 Jim Ray .50 .23 .06
□ 459 Reds Team 1.00 .45 .12
□ 460 Boog Powell 1.00 .45 .12
□ 461 John Odom .50 .23 .06
□ 462 Luis Alvarado .50 .23 .06
□ 463 Pat Dobson .50 .23 .06
□ 464 Jose Cruz .75 .35 .09
□ 465 Dick Bosman .50 .23 .06
□ 466 Dick Billings .50 .23 .06
□ 467 Winston Llenas .50 .23 .06
□ 468 Pepe Frias .50 .23 .06
□ 469 Joe Decker .50 .23 .06
□ 470 Reggie Jackson ALCS 6.00 2.70 .75
□ 471 Jon Matlack NLCS 1.00 .45 .12
□ 472 Darold Knowles WS .50 .23 .06
□ 473 Willie Mays WS 7.50 3.40 .95
□ 474 Bert Campaneris WS 1.00 .45 .12
□ 475 Rusty Staub WS 1.00 .45 .12
□ 476 Cleon Jones WS 1.00 .45 .12
□ 477 Reggie Jackson WS 6.00 2.70 .75
□ 478 Bert Campaneris WS 1.00 .45 .12
□ 479 World Series Summary 1.00 .45 .12
A's Celebrate; Win
2nd cons. championship
□ 480 Willie Crawford .50 .23 .06
□ 481 Jerry Terrell .50 .23 .06
□ 482 Bob Didier .50 .23 .06
□ 483 Braves Team 1.00 .45 .12
□ 484 Carmen Fanzone .50 .23 .06
□ 485 Felipe Alou 1.00 .45 .12
□ 486 Steve Stone .75 .35 .09
□ 487 Ted Martinez .50 .23 .06
□ 488 Andy Etchebarren .50 .23 .06
□ 489 Pirates Leaders 1.00 .45 .12
Danny Murtaugh MG
Don Osborn CO
Don Leppert CO
Bill Mazeroski CO
Bob Skinner CO
□ 490 Vada Pinson 1.00 .45 .12
□ 491 Roger Nelson .50 .23 .06
□ 492 Mike Rogodzinski .50 .23 .06
□ 493 Joe Hoerner .50 .23 .06
□ 494 Ed Goodson .50 .23 .06
□ 495 Dick McAuliffe .75 .35 .09
□ 496 Tom Murphy .50 .23 .06
□ 497 Bobby Mitchell .50 .23 .06
□ 498 Pat Corrales .50 .23 .06
□ 499 Rusty Torres .50 .23 .06
□ 500 Lee May .75 .35 .09
□ 501 Eddie Leon .50 .23 .06
□ 502 Dave LaRoche .50 .23 .06
□ 503 Eric Soderholm .50 .23 .06
□ 504 Joe Niekro .75 .35 .09
□ 505 Bill Buckner 1.00 .45 .12
□ 506 Ed Farmer .50 .23 .06
□ 507 Larry Stahl .50 .23 .06
□ 508 Expos Team 1.00 .45 .12
□ 509 Jesse Jefferson .50 .23 .06
□ 510 Wayne Garrett .50 .23 .06
□ 511 Toby Harrah .75 .35 .09
□ 512 Joe Lahoud .50 .23 .06
□ 513 Jim Campanis .50 .23 .06
□ 514 Paul Schaal .50 .23 .06
□ 515 Willie Montanez .50 .23 .06
□ 516 Horacio Pina .50 .23 .06
□ 517 Mike Hegan .50 .23 .06

Card	NRMT	VG-E	GOOD
□ 518 Derrel Thomas	.50	.23	.06
□ 519 Bill Sharp	.50	.23	.06
□ 520 Tim McCarver	1.00	.45	.12
□ 521 Indians Leaders	.50	.23	.06
Ken Aspromonte MG			
Clay Bryant CO			
Tony Pacheco CO			
□ 522 J.R. Richard	.75	.35	.09
□ 523 Cecil Cooper	1.00	.45	.12
□ 524 Bill Plummer	.50	.23	.06
□ 525 Clyde Wright	.50	.23	.06
□ 526 Frank Tepedino	.50	.23	.06
□ 527 Bobby Darwin	.50	.23	.06
□ 528 Bill Bonham	.50	.23	.06
□ 529 Horace Clarke	.50	.23	.06
□ 530 Mickey Stanley	.75	.35	.09
□ 531 Expos Leaders	.75	.35	.09
Gene Mauch MG			
Dave Bristol CO			
Cal McLish CO			
Larry Doby CO			
Jerry Zimmerman CO			
□ 532 Skip Lockwood	.50	.23	.06
□ 533 Mike Phillips	.50	.23	.06
□ 534 Eddie Watt	.50	.23	.06
□ 535 Bob Tolan	.50	.23	.06
□ 536 Duffy Dyer	.50	.23	.06
□ 537 Steve Mingori	.50	.23	.06
□ 538 Cesar Tovar	.50	.23	.06
□ 539 Lloyd Allen	.50	.23	.06
□ 540 Bob Robertson	.50	.23	.06
□ 541 Indians Team	1.00	.45	.12
□ 542 Rich Gossage	3.00	1.35	.35
□ 543 Danny Cater	.50	.23	.06
□ 544 Ron Schueler	.50	.23	.06
□ 545 Billy Conigliaro	.75	.35	.09
□ 546 Mike Corkins	.50	.23	.06
□ 547 Glenn Borgmann	.50	.23	.06
□ 548 Sonny Siebert	.50	.23	.06
□ 549 Mike Jorgensen	.50	.23	.06
□ 550 Sam McDowell	.75	.35	.09
□ 551 Von Joshua	.50	.23	.06
□ 552 Denny Doyle	.50	.23	.06
□ 553 Jim Willoughby	.50	.23	.06
□ 554 Tim Johnson	.50	.23	.06
□ 555 Woody Fryman	.50	.23	.06
□ 556 Dave Campbell	.50	.23	.06
□ 557 Jim McGlothlin	.50	.23	.06
□ 558 Bill Fahey	.50	.23	.06
□ 559 Darrell Chaney	.50	.23	.06
□ 560 Mike Cuellar	.75	.35	.09
□ 561 Ed Kranepool	.50	.23	.06
□ 562 Jack Aker	.50	.23	.06
□ 563 Hal McRae	1.00	.45	.12
□ 564 Mike Ryan	.50	.23	.06
□ 565 Milt Wilcox	.50	.23	.06
□ 566 Jackie Hernandez	.50	.23	.06
□ 567 Red Sox Team	1.00	.45	.12
□ 568 Mike Torrez	.75	.35	.09
□ 569 Rick Dempsey	.75	.35	.09
□ 570 Ralph Garr	.75	.35	.09
□ 571 Rich Hand	.50	.23	.06
□ 572 Enzo Hernandez	.50	.23	.06
□ 573 Mike Adams	.50	.23	.06
□ 574 Bill Parsons	.50	.23	.06
□ 575 Steve Garvey	4.00	1.80	.50
□ 576 Scipio Spinks	.50	.23	.06
□ 577 Mike Sadek	.50	.23	.06
□ 578 Ralph Houk MG	.75	.35	.09
□ 579 Cecil Upshaw	.50	.23	.06
□ 580 Jim Spencer	.50	.23	.06
□ 581 Fred Norman	.50	.23	.06
□ 582 Bucky Dent	2.00	.90	.25
□ 583 Marty Pattin	.50	.23	.06
□ 584 Ken Rudolph	.50	.23	.06
□ 585 Merv Rettenmund	.50	.23	.06
□ 586 Jack Brohamer	.50	.23	.06
□ 587 Larry Christenson	.50	.23	.06
□ 588 Hal Lanier	.50	.23	.06
□ 589 Boots Day	.75	.35	.09
□ 590 Rogelio Moret	.50	.23	.06
□ 591 Sonny Jackson	.50	.23	.06
□ 592 Ed Bane	.50	.23	.06
□ 593 Steve Yeager	.50	.23	.06
□ 594 Leroy Stanton	.50	.23	.06
□ 595 Steve Blass	.75	.35	.09
□ 596 Rookie Pitchers	.75	.35	.09
Wayne Garland			
Fred Holdsworth			
Mark Littell			
Dick Pole			
□ 597 Rookie Shortstops	1.50	.70	.19
Dave Chalk			
John Gamble			
Pete MacKanin			
Manny Trillo			
□ 598 Rookie Outfielders:	14.00	6.25	1.75
Dave Augustine			
Ken Griffey			
Steve Ontiveros			
Jim Tyrone			
□ 599 Rookie Pitchers	1.00	.45	.12
Ron Diorio			
Dave Freisleben			
Frank Riccelli			
Greg Shanahan			
□ 600 Rookie Infielders:	5.00	2.20	.60
Ron Cash			
Jim Cox			
Bill Madlock			
Reggie Sanders			
□ 601 Rookie Outfielders:	3.00	1.35	.35
Ed Armbrister			
Rich Bladt			
Brian Downing			
Bake McBride			
□ 602 Rookie Pitchers	.75	.35	.09
Glenn Abbott			
Rick Henninger			
Craig Swan			
Dan Vossler			
□ 603 Rookie Catchers	.75	.35	.09
Barry Foote			
Tom Lundstedt			
Charlie Moore			
Sergio Robles			
□ 604 Rookie Infielders:	5.00	2.20	.60
Terry Hughes			
John Knox			
Andy Thornton			
Frank White			
□ 605 Rookie Pitchers:	4.00	1.80	.50
Vic Albury			
Ken Frailing			
Kevin Kobel			
Frank Tanana			
□ 606 Rookie Outfielders	.75	.35	.09
Jim Fuller			
Wilbur Howard			
Tommy Smith			
Otto Velez			
□ 607 Rookie Shortstops	.75	.35	.09
Leo Foster			
Tom Heintzelman			
Dave Rosello			
Frank Taveras			
□ 608 Rookie Pitchers UER	1.00	.45	.12
Bob Apodaca			
Dick Baney			
John D'Acquisto			
Mike Wallace			
Apodaca is spellled Apodaco			
□ 609 Rico Petrocelli	.75	.35	.09
□ 610 Dave Kingman	1.00	.45	.12
□ 611 Rich Stelmaszek	.50	.23	.06
□ 612 Luke Walker	.50	.23	.06
□ 613 Dan Monzon	.50	.23	.06
□ 614 Adrian Devine	.50	.23	.06
□ 615 John Jeter	.50	.23	.06
□ 616 Larry Gura	.50	.23	.06
□ 617 Ted Ford	.50	.23	.06
□ 618 Jim Mason	.50	.23	.06
□ 619 Mike Anderson	.50	.23	.06
□ 620 Al Downing	.50	.23	.06
□ 621 Bernie Carbo	.50	.23	.06
□ 622 Phil Gagliano	.50	.23	.06
□ 623 Celerino Sanchez	.50	.23	.06
□ 624 Bob Miller	.50	.23	.06
□ 625 Ollie Brown	.50	.23	.06
□ 626 Pirates Team	1.00	.45	.12
□ 627 Carl Taylor	.50	.23	.06
□ 628 Ivan Murrell	.50	.23	.06
□ 629 Rusty Staub	1.00	.45	.12
□ 630 Tommy Agee	.75	.35	.09
□ 631 Steve Barber	.50	.23	.06
□ 632 George Culver	.50	.23	.06
□ 633 Dave Hamilton	.50	.23	.06
□ 634 Braves Leaders	1.00	.45	.12
Eddie Mathews MG			
Herm Starrette CO			
Connie Ryan CO			
Jim Busby CO			
Ken Silvestri CO			
□ 635 John Edwards	.50	.23	.06
□ 636 Dave Goltz	.50	.23	.06
□ 637 Checklist 529-660	2.50	1.10	.30
□ 638 Ken Sanders	.50	.23	.06
□ 639 Joe Lovitto	.50	.23	.06
□ 640 Milt Pappas	.75	.35	.09
□ 641 Chuck Brinkman	.50	.23	.06
□ 642 Terry Harmon	.50	.23	.06
□ 643 Dodgers Team	1.00	.45	.12
□ 644 Wayne Granger	.50	.23	.06
□ 645 Ken Boswell	.50	.23	.06
□ 646 George Foster	1.50	.70	.19
□ 647 Juan Beniquez	.50	.23	.06
□ 648 Terry Crowley	.50	.23	.06
□ 649 Fernando Gonzalez	.50	.23	.06
□ 650 Mike Epstein	.50	.23	.06
□ 651 Leron Lee	.50	.23	.06
□ 652 Gail Hopkins	.50	.23	.06
□ 653 Bob Stinson	.75	.35	.09
□ 654 Jesus Alou	.75	.35	.09
□ 655 Mike Tyson	.50	.23	.06
□ 656 Adrian Garrett	.50	.23	.06
□ 657 Jim Shellenback	.50	.23	.06
□ 658 Lee Lacy	.50	.23	.06
□ 659 Joe Lis	.50	.23	.06
□ 660 Larry Dierker	1.00	.45	.12

1974 O-Pee-Chee Team Checklists

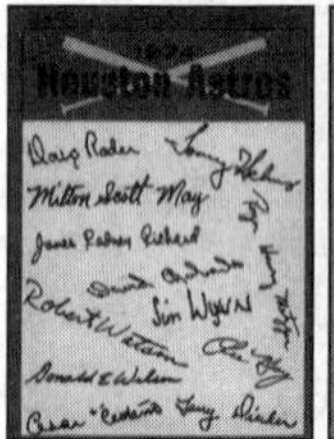
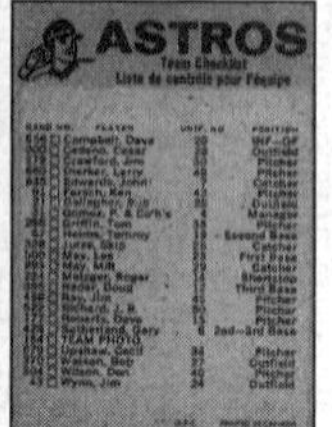

The cards in this 24-card set measure 2 1/2" by 3 1/2". The fronts have red borders and feature the year and team name in a green panel decorated by a crossed bats design, below which is a white area containing facsimile autographs of various players. On a light yellow background, the backs list team members alphabetically, along with their card number, uniform number and position. The words "Team Checklist" appear in French and English. The cards are unnumbered and checklisted below in alphabetical order.

	NRMT	VG-E	GOOD
COMPLETE SET (24)	50.00	22.00	6.25
COMMON TEAM (1-24)	2.50	1.10	.30
□ 1 Atlanta Braves	2.50	1.10	.30
□ 2 Baltimore Orioles	2.50	1.10	.30
□ 3 Boston Red Sox	2.50	1.10	.30
□ 4 California Angels	2.50	1.10	.30
□ 5 Chicago Cubs	2.50	1.10	.30
□ 6 Chicago White Sox	2.50	1.10	.30
□ 7 Cincinnati Reds	2.50	1.10	.30
□ 8 Cleveland Indians	2.50	1.10	.30
□ 9 Detroit Tigers	2.50	1.10	.30
□ 10 Houston Astros	2.50	1.10	.30
□ 11 Kansas City Royals	2.50	1.10	.30
□ 12 Los Angeles Dodgers	2.50	1.10	.30
□ 13 Milwaukee Brewers	2.50	1.10	.30
□ 14 Minnesota Twins	2.50	1.10	.30
□ 15 Montreal Expos	2.50	1.10	.30
□ 16 New York Mets	2.50	1.10	.30
□ 17 New York Yankees	2.50	1.10	.30
□ 18 Oakland A's	2.50	1.10	.30
□ 19 Philadelphia Phillies	2.50	1.10	.30
□ 20 Pittsburgh Pirates	2.50	1.10	.30
□ 21 San Diego Padres	2.50	1.10	.30
□ 22 San Francisco Giants	2.50	1.10	.30
□ 23 St. Louis Cardinals	2.50	1.10	.30
□ 24 Texas Rangers	2.50	1.10	.30

1975 O-Pee-Chee

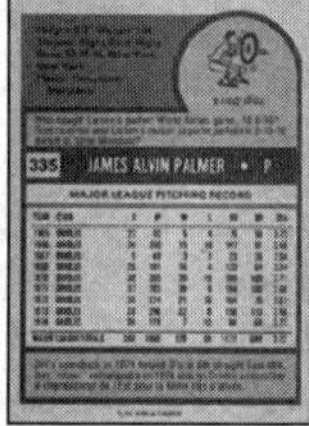

The cards in this 660-card set measure 2 1/2" by 3 1/2". The 1975 O-Pee-Chee cards are very similar to the 1975 Topps cards, yet rather different from previous years' issues. The most prominent change for the fronts is the use of a two-color fram colors surrounding the picture area rather than a single, subdued color. The fronts feature color player photos with rounded corners. The player's name and position, the team name and a facsimile autograph round out the front. The backs are printed in red and green on a yellow-vanilla card stock and carry player biography and statistics in French and English. Cards 189-212 depict the MVPs of both leagues from 1951 through 1974. The first six cards (1-6) feature players breaking records or achieving milestones during the previous season. Cards 306-313 picture league leaders in various statistical categories. Cards 459-466 depict the results of post-season action. Team cards feature a checklist back for players on that team. Remember, the prices below apply only to O-Pee-Chee cards -- they are NOT prices for Topps cards as the Topps cards are generally much more available.

	NRMT	VG-E	GOOD
COMPLETE SET (660)	1000.00	450.00	125.00
COMMON CARD (1-660)	.50	.23	.06
□ 1 Hank Aaron RB	35.00	16.00	4.40
Sets Homer Mark			
□ 2 Lou Brock RB	3.50	1.55	.45
118 Stolen Bases			
□ 3 Bob Gibson RB	3.50	1.55	.45
3000th Strikeout			
□ 4 Al Kaline RB	4.00	1.80	.50
3000 Hit Club			
□ 5 Nolan Ryan RB	35.00	16.00	4.40
Fans 300 for			
3rd Year in a Row			
□ 6 Mike Marshall RB	1.00	.45	.12
Hurls 106 Games			
□ 7 No Hit Pitchers:	15.00	6.75	1.85
Steve Busby			
Dick Bosman			
Nolan Ryan			
□ 8 Rogelio Moret	.50	.23	.06
□ 9 Frank Tepedino	.50	.23	.06
□ 10 Willie Davis	.75	.35	.09
□ 11 Bill Melton	.50	.23	.06
□ 12 David Clyde	.50	.23	.06
□ 13 Gene Locklear	.75	.35	.09
□ 14 Milt Wilcox	.50	.23	.06
□ 15 Jose Cardenal	.50	.23	.06
□ 16 Frank Tanana	2.00	.90	.25
□ 17 Dave Concepcion	2.00	.90	.25
□ 18 Tigers: Team/MG	2.00	.90	.25
Ralph Houk			
□ 19 Jerry Koosman	1.00	.45	.12
□ 20 Thurman Munson	6.00	2.70	.75
□ 21 Rollie Fingers	3.00	1.35	.35
□ 22 Dave Cash	.75	.35	.09
□ 23 Bill Russell	.75	.35	.09
□ 24 Al Fitzmorris	.50	.23	.06
□ 25 Lee May	.75	.35	.09
□ 26 Dave McNally	.75	.35	.09
□ 27 Ken Reitz	.50	.23	.06
□ 28 Tom Murphy	.50	.23	.06
□ 29 Dave Parker	4.00	1.80	.50
□ 30 Bert Blyleven	1.00	.45	.12
□ 31 Dave Rader	.50	.23	.06
□ 32 Reggie Cleveland	.50	.23	.06
□ 33 Dusty Baker	2.00	.90	.25
□ 34 Steve Renko	.50	.23	.06
□ 35 Ron Santo	1.00	.45	.12
□ 36 Joe Lovitto	.50	.23	.06
□ 37 Dave Freisleben	.50	.23	.06
□ 38 Buddy Bell	1.00	.45	.12
□ 39 Andre Thornton	.75	.35	.09
□ 40 Bill Singer	.50	.23	.06
□ 41 Cesar Geronimo	.50	.23	.06
□ 42 Joe Coleman	.50	.23	.06
□ 43 Cleon Jones	.75	.35	.09
□ 44 Pat Dobson	.50	.23	.06
□ 45 Joe Rudi	.75	.35	.09
□ 46 Phillies: Team/MG	2.00	.90	.25
Danny Ozark			
□ 47 Tommy John	1.50	.70	.19
□ 48 Freddie Patek	.50	.23	.06
□ 49 Larry Dierker	.50	.23	.06
□ 50 Brooks Robinson	6.00	2.70	.75
□ 51 Bob Forsch	1.00	.45	.12
□ 52 Darrell Porter	.75	.35	.09
□ 53 Dave Giusti	.50	.23	.06
□ 54 Eric Soderholm	.50	.23	.06
□ 55 Bobby Bonds	2.00	.90	.25
□ 56 Rick Wise	.75	.35	.09
□ 57 Dave Johnson	.75	.35	.09
□ 58 Chuck Taylor	.50	.23	.06
□ 59 Ken Henderson	.50	.23	.06
□ 60 Fergie Jenkins	3.00	1.35	.35
□ 61 Dave Winfield	60.00	27.00	7.50
□ 62 Fritz Peterson	.50	.23	.06
□ 63 Steve Swisher	.50	.23	.06
□ 64 Dave Chalk	.50	.23	.06
□ 65 Don Gullett	1.00	.45	.12
□ 66 Willie Horton	.75	.35	.09
□ 67 Tug McGraw	1.00	.45	.12
□ 68 Ron Blomberg	.50	.23	.06
□ 69 John Odom	.50	.23	.06
□ 70 Mike Schmidt	60.00	27.00	7.50
□ 71 Charlie Hough	1.00	.45	.12
□ 72 Royals: Team/MG	2.00	.90	.25
Jack McKeon			
□ 73 J.R. Richard	.75	.35	.09
□ 74 Mark Belanger	.75	.35	.09
□ 75 Ted Simmons	1.00	.45	.12
□ 76 Ed Sprague	.50	.23	.06
□ 77 Richie Zisk	.75	.35	.09
□ 78 Ray Corbin	.50	.23	.06
□ 79 Gary Matthews	.75	.35	.09
□ 80 Carlton Fisk	15.00	6.75	1.85
□ 81 Ron Reed	.50	.23	.06
□ 82 Pat Kelly	.50	.23	.06
□ 83 Jim Merritt	.50	.23	.06
□ 84 Enzo Hernandez	.50	.23	.06
□ 85 Bill Bonham	.50	.23	.06
□ 86 Joe Lis	.50	.23	.06
□ 87 George Foster	1.50	.70	.19
□ 88 Tom Egan	.50	.23	.06
□ 89 Jim Ray	.50	.23	.06
□ 90 Rusty Staub	1.00	.45	.12
□ 91 Dick Green	.50	.23	.06
□ 92 Cecil Upshaw	.50	.23	.06
□ 93 Dave Lopes	1.00	.45	.12
□ 94 Jim Lonborg	.75	.35	.09
□ 95 John Mayberry	.75	.35	.09
□ 96 Mike Cosgrove	.50	.23	.06
□ 97 Earl Williams	.50	.23	.06
□ 98 Rich Folkers	.50	.23	.06
□ 99 Mike Hegan	.50	.23	.06
□ 100 Willie Stargell	4.00	1.80	.50
□ 101 Expos: Team/MG	2.00	.90	.25
Gene Mauch			
□ 102 Joe Decker	.50	.23	.06
□ 103 Rick Miller	.50	.23	.06
□ 104 Bill Madlock	1.00	.45	.12

☐ 105 Buzz Capra .50 .23 .06
☐ 106 Mike Hargrove 3.00 1.35 .35
☐ 107 Jim Barr .50 .23 .06
☐ 108 Tom Hall .50 .23 .06
☐ 109 George Hendrick .75 .35 .09
☐ 110 Wilbur Wood .50 .23 .06
☐ 111 Wayne Garrett .50 .23 .06
☐ 112 Larry Hardy .50 .23 .06
☐ 113 Elliott Maddox .50 .23 .06
☐ 114 Dick Lange .50 .23 .06
☐ 115 Joe Ferguson .50 .23 .06
☐ 116 Lerrin LaGrow .50 .23 .06
☐ 117 Orioles: Team/MG 2.00 .90 .25
Earl Weaver
☐ 118 Mike Anderson .50 .23 .06
☐ 119 Tommy Helms .50 .23 .06
☐ 120 Steve Busby .75 .35 .09
(photo actually
Fran Healy)
☐ 121 Bill North .50 .23 .06
☐ 122 Al Hrabosky .75 .35 .09
☐ 123 Johnny Briggs .50 .23 .06
☐ 124 Jerry Reuss 1.00 .45 .12
☐ 125 Ken Singleton .75 .35 .09
☐ 126 Checklist 1-132 2.00 .90 .25
☐ 127 Glenn Borgmann .50 .23 .06
☐ 128 Bill Lee .75 .35 .09
☐ 129 Rick Monday .75 .35 .09
☐ 130 Phil Niekro 3.00 1.35 .35
☐ 131 Toby Harrah .75 .35 .09
☐ 132 Randy Moffitt .50 .23 .06
☐ 133 Dan Driessen .75 .35 .09
☐ 134 Ron Hodges .50 .23 .06
☐ 135 Charlie Spikes .50 .23 .06
☐ 136 Jim Mason .50 .23 .06
☐ 137 Terry Forster .50 .23 .06
☐ 138 Del Unser .50 .23 .06
☐ 139 Horacio Pina .50 .23 .06
☐ 140 Steve Garvey 5.00 2.20 .60
☐ 141 Mickey Stanley .75 .35 .09
☐ 142 Bob Reynolds .50 .23 .06
☐ 143 Cliff Johnson .75 .35 .09
☐ 144 Jim Wohlford .50 .23 .06
☐ 145 Ken Holtzman .75 .35 .09
☐ 146 Padres: Team/MG 2.00 .90 .25
John McNamara
☐ 147 Pedro Garcia .50 .23 .06
☐ 148 Jim Rooker .50 .23 .06
☐ 149 Tim Foli .50 .23 .06
☐ 150 Bob Gibson 5.00 2.20 .60
☐ 151 Steve Brye .50 .23 .06
☐ 152 Mario Guerrero .50 .23 .06
☐ 153 Rick Reuschel .75 .35 .09
☐ 154 Mike Lum .50 .23 .06
☐ 155 Jim Bibby .50 .23 .06
☐ 156 Dave Kingman 1.00 .45 .12
☐ 157 Pedro Borbon .50 .23 .06
☐ 158 Jerry Grote .50 .23 .06
☐ 159 Steve Arlin .50 .23 .06
☐ 160 Graig Nettles 2.00 .90 .25
☐ 161 Stan Bahnsen .50 .23 .06
☐ 162 Willie Montanez .50 .23 .06
☐ 163 Jim Brewer .50 .23 .06
☐ 164 Mickey Rivers .75 .35 .09
☐ 165 Doug Rader .75 .35 .09
☐ 166 Woodie Fryman .50 .23 .06
☐ 167 Rich Coggins .50 .23 .06
☐ 168 Bill Greif .50 .23 .06
☐ 169 Cookie Rojas .75 .35 .09
☐ 170 Bert Campaneris .75 .35 .09
☐ 171 Ed Kirkpatrick .50 .23 .06
☐ 172 Red Sox: Team/MG 2.00 .90 .25
Darrell Johnson
☐ 173 Steve Rogers .75 .35 .09
☐ 174 Bake McBride .75 .35 .09
☐ 175 Don Money .75 .35 .09
☐ 176 Burt Hooton .75 .35 .09
☐ 177 Vic Correll .50 .23 .06
☐ 178 Cesar Tovar .50 .23 .06
☐ 179 Tom Bradley .50 .23 .06
☐ 180 Joe Morgan 5.00 2.20 .60
☐ 181 Fred Beene .50 .23 .06
☐ 182 Don Hahn .50 .23 .06
☐ 183 Mel Stottlemyre .75 .35 .09
☐ 184 Jorge Orta .50 .23 .06
☐ 185 Steve Carlton 6.00 2.70 .75
☐ 186 Willie Crawford .50 .23 .06
☐ 187 Denny Doyle .50 .23 .06
☐ 188 Tom Griffin .50 .23 .06
☐ 189 1951 MVP's: 3.50 1.55 .45
Larry (Yogi) Berra
Roy Campanella
(Campy never issued)
☐ 190 1952 MVP's 1.00 .45 .12
Bobby Shantz
Hank Sauer
☐ 191 1953 MVP's: 2.00 .90 .25
Al Rosen
Roy Campanella
☐ 192 1954 MVP's: 4.00 1.80 .50
Yogi Berra
Willie Mays
☐ 193 1955 MVP's: 4.00 1.80 .50
Yogi Berra
Roy Campanella
(Campy never issued)
☐ 194 1956 MVP's: 18.00 8.00 2.20
Mickey Mantle
Don Newcombe
☐ 195 1957 MVP's: 30.00 13.50 3.70
Mickey Mantle
Hank Aaron
☐ 196 1958 MVP's 1.00 .45 .12
Jackie Jensen
Ernie Banks
☐ 197 1959 MVP's: 1.50 .70 .19
Nellie Fox
Ernie Banks
☐ 198 1960 MVP's 1.00 .45 .12
Roger Maris
Dick Groat
☐ 199 1961 MVP's: 3.00 1.35 .35
Roger Maris
Frank Robinson
☐ 200 1962 MVP's: 18.00 8.00 2.20
Mickey Mantle
Maury Wills
(Wills never issued)
☐ 201 1963 MVP's: 1.50 .70 .19
Elston Howard
Sandy Koufax
☐ 202 1964 MVP's: 1.50 .70 .19
Brooks Robinson
Ken Boyer
☐ 203 1965 MVP's: 1.50 .70 .19
Zoilo Versalles
Willie Mays
☐ 204 1966 MVP's: 6.00 2.70 .75
Frank Robinson
Bob Clemente
☐ 205 1967 MVP's: 1.50 .70 .19
Carl Yastrzemski
Orlando Cepeda
☐ 206 1968 MVP's: 1.50 .70 .19
Denny McLain
Bob Gibson
☐ 207 1969 MVP's: 1.50 .70 .19
Harmon Killebrew
Willie McCovey
☐ 208 1970 MVP's: 1.50 .70 .19
Boog Powell
Johnny Bench
☐ 209 1971 MVP's 1.00 .45 .12
Vida Blue
Joe Torre
☐ 210 1972 MVP's: 1.50 .70 .19
Rich Allen
Johnny Bench
☐ 211 1973 MVP's: 6.00 2.70 .75
Reggie Jackson
Pete Rose
☐ 212 1974 MVP's 1.00 .45 .12
Jeff Burroughs
Steve Garvey
☐ 213 Oscar Gamble .75 .35 .09
☐ 214 Harry Parker .50 .23 .06
☐ 215 Bobby Valentine .50 .23 .06
☐ 216 Giants: Team/MG 2.00 .90 .25
Wes Westrum
☐ 217 Lou Piniella 1.25 .55 .16
☐ 218 Jerry Johnson .50 .23 .06
☐ 219 Ed Herrmann .50 .23 .06
☐ 220 Don Sutton 2.50 1.10 .30
☐ 221 Aurelio Rodriguez .50 .23 .06
☐ 222 Dan Spillner .50 .23 .06
☐ 223 Robin Yount 130.00 57.50 16.00
☐ 224 Ramon Hernandez .50 .23 .06
☐ 225 Bob Grich .75 .35 .09
☐ 226 Bill Campbell .50 .23 .06
☐ 227 Bob Watson .75 .35 .09
☐ 228 George Brett 225.00 100.00 28.00
☐ 229 Barry Foote .75 .35 .09
☐ 230 Jim Hunter 3.00 1.35 .35
☐ 231 Mike Tyson .50 .23 .06
☐ 232 Diego Segui .50 .23 .06
☐ 233 Billy Grabarkewitz .50 .23 .06
☐ 234 Tom Grieve .50 .23 .06
☐ 235 Jack Billingham .50 .23 .06
☐ 236 Angels: Team/MG 2.00 .90 .25
Dick Williams
☐ 237 Carl Morton .50 .23 .06
☐ 238 Dave Duncan .50 .23 .06
☐ 239 George Stone .50 .23 .06
☐ 240 Garry Maddox .75 .35 .09
☐ 241 Dick Tidrow .50 .23 .06
☐ 242 Jay Johnstone .75 .35 .09
☐ 243 Jim Kaat 1.00 .45 .12
☐ 244 Bill Buckner 1.00 .45 .12
☐ 245 Mickey Lolich 1.00 .45 .12
☐ 246 Cardinals: Team/MG 2.00 .90 .25
Red Schoendienst
☐ 247 Enos Cabell .50 .23 .06
☐ 248 Randy Jones .75 .35 .09
☐ 249 Danny Thompson .50 .23 .06
☐ 250 Ken Brett .50 .23 .06
☐ 251 Fran Healy .50 .23 .06
☐ 252 Fred Scherman .50 .23 .06
☐ 253 Jesus Alou .50 .23 .06
☐ 254 Mike Torrez .75 .35 .09
☐ 255 Dwight Evans 2.00 .90 .25
☐ 256 Billy Champion .50 .23 .06
☐ 257 Checklist 133-264 2.00 .90 .25
☐ 258 Dave LaRoche .50 .23 .06
☐ 259 Len Randle .50 .23 .06
☐ 260 Johnny Bench 15.00 6.75 1.85
☐ 261 Andy Hassler .50 .23 .06
☐ 262 Rowland Office .50 .23 .06
☐ 263 Jim Perry .75 .35 .09
☐ 264 John Milner .50 .23 .06
☐ 265 Ron Bryant .50 .23 .06
☐ 266 Sandy Alomar .50 .23 .06
☐ 267 Dick Ruthven .50 .23 .06
☐ 268 Hal McRae 1.00 .45 .12
☐ 269 Doug Rau .50 .23 .06
☐ 270 Ron Fairly .75 .35 .09
☐ 271 Jerry Moses .50 .23 .06
☐ 272 Lynn McGlothen .50 .23 .06
☐ 273 Steve Braun .50 .23 .06
☐ 274 Vicente Romo .50 .23 .06
☐ 275 Paul Blair .75 .35 .09
☐ 276 White Sox Team/MG 2.00 .90 .25
Chuck Tanner
☐ 277 Frank Taveras .50 .23 .06
☐ 278 Paul Lindblad .50 .23 .06
☐ 279 Milt May .50 .23 .06
☐ 280 Carl Yastrzemski 6.00 2.70 .75
☐ 281 Jim Slaton .50 .23 .06
☐ 282 Jerry Morales .50 .23 .06
☐ 283 Steve Foucault .50 .23 .06
☐ 284 Ken Griffey 5.00 2.20 .60
☐ 285 Ellie Rodriguez .50 .23 .06
☐ 286 Mike Jorgensen .50 .23 .06
☐ 287 Roric Harrison .50 .23 .06
☐ 288 Bruce Ellingsen .50 .23 .06
☐ 289 Ken Rudolph .50 .23 .06
☐ 290 Jon Matlack .50 .23 .06
☐ 291 Bill Sudakis .50 .23 .06
☐ 292 Ron Schueler .50 .23 .06
☐ 293 Dick Sharon .50 .23 .06
☐ 294 Geoff Zahn .50 .23 .06
☐ 295 Vada Pinson 1.00 .45 .12
☐ 296 Alan Foster .50 .23 .06
☐ 297 Craig Kusick .50 .23 .06
☐ 298 Johnny Grubb .50 .23 .06
☐ 299 Bucky Dent 1.00 .45 .12
☐ 300 Reggie Jackson 25.00 11.00 3.10
☐ 301 Dave Roberts .50 .23 .06
☐ 302 Rick Burleson 1.00 .45 .12
☐ 303 Grant Jackson .50 .23 .06
☐ 304 Pirates: Team/MG 2.00 .90 .25
Danny Murtaugh
☐ 305 Jim Colborn .50 .23 .06
☐ 306 Batting Leaders: 1.50 .70 .19
Rod Carew
Ralph Garr
☐ 307 Home Run Leaders: 3.50 1.55 .45
Dick Allen
Mike Schmidt
☐ 308 RBI Leaders: 1.50 .70 .19
Jeff Burroughs
Johnny Bench
☐ 309 Stolen Base Leaders: 1.50 .70 .19
Bill North
Lou Brock
☐ 310 Victory Leaders: 1.50 .70 .19
Jim Hunter
Fergie Jenkins
Andy Messersmith
Phil Niekro
☐ 311 ERA Leaders: 1.50 .70 .19
Jim Hunter
Buzz Capra
☐ 312 Strikeout Leaders: 25.00 11.00 3.10
Nolan Ryan
Steve Carlton
☐ 313 Leading Firemen 1.00 .45 .12
Terry Forster
Mike Marshall
☐ 314 Buck Martinez .50 .23 .06
☐ 315 Don Kessinger .75 .35 .09
☐ 316 Jackie Brown .50 .23 .06
☐ 317 Joe Lahoud .50 .23 .06
☐ 318 Ernie McAnally .50 .23 .06
☐ 319 Johnny Oates .50 .23 .06
☐ 320 Pete Rose 25.00 11.00 3.10
☐ 321 Rudy May .50 .23 .06
☐ 322 Ed Goodson .50 .23 .06
☐ 323 Fred Holdsworth .50 .23 .06
☐ 324 Ed Kranepool .50 .23 .06
☐ 325 Tony Oliva 1.00 .45 .12
☐ 326 Wayne Twitchell .50 .23 .06
☐ 327 Jerry Hairston .50 .23 .06
☐ 328 Sonny Siebert .50 .23 .06
☐ 329 Ted Kubiak .50 .23 .06
☐ 330 Mike Marshall .75 .35 .09
☐ 331 Indians: Team/MG 2.00 .90 .25
Frank Robinson
☐ 332 Fred Kendall .50 .23 .06
☐ 333 Dick Drago .50 .23 .06
☐ 334 Greg Gross .50 .23 .06
☐ 335 Jim Palmer 5.00 2.20 .60
☐ 336 Rennie Stennett .50 .23 .06
☐ 337 Kevin Kobel .50 .23 .06
☐ 338 Rick Stelmaszek .50 .23 .06
☐ 339 Jim Fregosi .75 .35 .09
☐ 340 Paul Splittorff .50 .23 .06
☐ 341 Hal Breeden .50 .23 .06
☐ 342 Leroy Stanton .50 .23 .06
☐ 343 Danny Frisella .50 .23 .06
☐ 344 Ben Oglivie .75 .35 .09
☐ 345 Clay Carroll .50 .23 .06
☐ 346 Bobby Darwin .50 .23 .06
☐ 347 Mike Caldwell .50 .23 .06
☐ 348 Tony Muser .50 .23 .06
☐ 349 Ray Sadecki .50 .23 .06
☐ 350 Bobby Murcer 1.00 .45 .12
☐ 351 Bob Boone 1.50 .70 .19
☐ 352 Darold Knowles .50 .23 .06
☐ 353 Luis Melendez .50 .23 .06
☐ 354 Dick Bosman .50 .23 .06
☐ 355 Chris Cannizzaro .50 .23 .06
☐ 356 Rico Petrocelli .75 .35 .09
☐ 357 Ken Forsch .50 .23 .06
☐ 358 Al Bumbry .50 .23 .06
☐ 359 Paul Popovich .50 .23 .06
☐ 360 George Scott .75 .35 .09
☐ 361 Dodgers: Team/MG 2.00 .90 .25
Walter Alston
☐ 362 Steve Hargan .50 .23 .06
☐ 363 Carmen Fanzone .50 .23 .06
☐ 364 Doug Bird .50 .23 .06
☐ 365 Bob Bailey .50 .23 .06
☐ 366 Ken Sanders .50 .23 .06
☐ 367 Craig Robinson .50 .23 .06
☐ 368 Vic Albury .50 .23 .06
☐ 369 Merv Rettenmund .50 .23 .06
☐ 370 Tom Seaver 18.00 8.00 2.20
☐ 371 Gates Brown .50 .23 .06
☐ 372 John D'Acquisto .50 .23 .06
☐ 373 Bill Sharp .50 .23 .06
☐ 374 Eddie Watt .50 .23 .06
☐ 375 Roy White .75 .35 .09
☐ 376 Steve Yeager .50 .23 .06
☐ 377 Tom Hilgendorf .50 .23 .06
☐ 378 Derrel Thomas .50 .23 .06
☐ 379 Bernie Carbo .50 .23 .06
☐ 380 Sal Bando .75 .35 .09
☐ 381 John Curtis .50 .23 .06
☐ 382 Don Baylor 3.00 1.35 .35
☐ 383 Jim York .50 .23 .06
☐ 384 Brewers: Team/MG 2.00 .90 .25
Del Crandall
☐ 385 Dock Ellis .50 .23 .06
☐ 386 Checklist 265-396 2.00 .90 .25
☐ 387 Jim Spencer .50 .23 .06
☐ 388 Steve Stone .75 .35 .09
☐ 389 Tony Solaita .50 .23 .06
☐ 390 Ron Cey 1.00 .45 .12
☐ 391 Don DeMola .50 .23 .06
☐ 392 Bruce Bochte 1.00 .45 .12
☐ 393 Gary Gentry .50 .23 .06
☐ 394 Larvell Blanks .50 .23 .06
☐ 395 Bud Harrelson .75 .35 .09
☐ 396 Fred Norman .75 .35 .09
☐ 397 Bill Freehan .75 .35 .09
☐ 398 Elias Sosa .50 .23 .06
☐ 399 Terry Harmon .50 .23 .06
☐ 400 Dick Allen 1.00 .45 .12
☐ 401 Mike Wallace .50 .23 .06
☐ 402 Bob Tolan .50 .23 .06
☐ 403 Tom Buskey .50 .23 .06
☐ 404 Ted Sizemore .50 .23 .06
☐ 405 John Montague .50 .23 .06
☐ 406 Bob Gallagher .50 .23 .06
☐ 407 Herb Washington 1.00 .45 .12
☐ 408 Clyde Wright .50 .23 .06
☐ 409 Bob Robertson .50 .23 .06
☐ 410 Mike Cueller .75 .35 .09
(sic, Cuellar)
☐ 411 George Mitterwald .50 .23 .06
☐ 412 Bill Hands .50 .23 .06
☐ 413 Marty Pattin .50 .23 .06
☐ 414 Manny Mota .75 .35 .09
☐ 415 John Hiller .75 .35 .09
☐ 416 Larry Lintz .50 .23 .06
☐ 417 Skip Lockwood .50 .23 .06
☐ 418 Leo Foster .50 .23 .06
☐ 419 Dave Goltz .50 .23 .06
☐ 420 Larry Bowa 1.00 .45 .12
☐ 421 Mets: Team/MG 2.00 .90 .25
Yogi Berra
☐ 422 Brian Downing 1.00 .45 .12
☐ 423 Clay Kirby .50 .23 .06
☐ 424 John Lowenstein .50 .23 .06
☐ 425 Tito Fuentes .50 .23 .06
☐ 426 George Medich .50 .23 .06
☐ 427 Clarence Gaston 1.00 .45 .12
☐ 428 Dave Hamilton .50 .23 .06
☐ 429 Jim Dwyer .50 .23 .06
☐ 430 Luis Tiant 1.00 .45 .12
☐ 431 Rod Gilbreath .50 .23 .06
☐ 432 Ken Berry .50 .23 .06
☐ 433 Larry Demery .50 .23 .06
☐ 434 Bob Locker .50 .23 .06
☐ 435 Dave Nelson .50 .23 .06
☐ 436 Ken Frailing .50 .23 .06
☐ 437 Al Cowens 1.00 .45 .12
☐ 438 Don Carrithers .50 .23 .06
☐ 439 Ed Brinkman .50 .23 .06
☐ 440 Andy Messersmith .75 .35 .09
☐ 441 Bobby Heise .50 .23 .06

☐ 442 Maximino Leon	.50	.23	.06
☐ 443 Twins: Team/MG	2.00	.90	.25
Frank Quilici			
☐ 444 Gene Garber	.75	.35	.09
☐ 445 Felix Millan	.50	.23	.06
☐ 446 Bart Johnson	.50	.23	.06
☐ 447 Terry Crowley	.50	.23	.06
☐ 448 Frank Duffy	.50	.23	.06
☐ 449 Charlie Williams	.50	.23	.06
☐ 450 Willie McCovey	5.00	2.20	.60
☐ 451 Rick Dempsey	.75	.35	.09
☐ 452 Angel Mangual	.50	.23	.06
☐ 453 Claude Osteen	.75	.35	.09
☐ 454 Doug Griffin	.50	.23	.06
☐ 455 Don Wilson	.50	.23	.06
☐ 456 Bob Coluccio	.50	.23	.06
☐ 457 Mario Mendoza	.50	.23	.06
☐ 458 Ross Grimsley	.50	.23	.06
☐ 459 1974 AL Champs	1.00	.45	.12
A's over Orioles			
(Second base			
action pictured)			
☐ 460 Frank Taveras NCLS	1.50	.70	.19
Steve Garvey			
☐ 461 Reggie Jackson WS	4.00	1.80	.50
☐ 462 World Series Game 2	1.00	.45	.12
(Dodger dugout)			
☐ 463 Rollie Fingers WS	1.50	.70	.19
☐ 464 World Series Game 4	1.00	.45	.12
(A's batter)			
☐ 465 Joe Rudi WS	1.00	.45	.12
☐ 466 World Series Summary:	1.50	.70	.19
A's do it again			
Win 3rd straight			
(A's group)			
☐ 467 Ed Halicki	.50	.23	.06
☐ 468 Bobby Mitchell	.50	.23	.06
☐ 469 Tom Dettore	.50	.23	.06
☐ 470 Jeff Burroughs	.75	.35	.09
☐ 471 Bob Stinson	.50	.23	.06
☐ 472 Bruce Dal Canton	.50	.23	.06
☐ 473 Ken McMullen	.50	.23	.06
☐ 474 Luke Walker	.50	.23	.06
☐ 475 Darrell Evans	1.00	.45	.12
☐ 476 Ed Figueroa	.50	.23	.06
☐ 477 Tom Hutton	.50	.23	.06
☐ 478 Tom Burgmeier	.50	.23	.06
☐ 479 Ken Boswell	.50	.23	.06
☐ 480 Carlos May	.50	.23	.06
☐ 481 Will McEnaney	.75	.35	.09
☐ 482 Tom McCraw	.50	.23	.06
☐ 483 Steve Ontiveros	.50	.23	.06
☐ 484 Glenn Beckert	.50	.23	.06
☐ 485 Sparky Lyle	1.00	.45	.12
☐ 486 Ray Fosse	.50	.23	.06
☐ 487 Astros: Team/MG	2.00	.90	.25
Preston Gomez			
☐ 488 Bill Travers	.50	.23	.06
☐ 489 Cecil Cooper	1.00	.45	.12
☐ 490 Reggie Smith	1.00	.45	.12
☐ 491 Doyle Alexander	.75	.35	.09
☐ 492 Rich Hebner	.75	.35	.09
☐ 493 Don Stanhouse	.50	.23	.06
☐ 494 Pete LaCock	.50	.23	.06
☐ 495 Nelson Briles	.75	.35	.09
☐ 496 Pepe Frias	.50	.23	.06
☐ 497 Jim Nettles	.50	.23	.06
☐ 498 Al Downing	.50	.23	.06
☐ 499 Marty Perez	.50	.23	.06
☐ 500 Nolan Ryan	90.00	40.00	11.00
☐ 501 Bill Robinson	.75	.35	.09
☐ 502 Pat Bourque	.50	.23	.06
☐ 503 Fred Stanley	.50	.23	.06
☐ 504 Buddy Bradford	.50	.23	.06
☐ 505 Chris Speier	.50	.23	.06
☐ 506 Leron Lee	.50	.23	.06
☐ 507 Tom Carroll	.50	.23	.06
☐ 508 Bob Hansen	.50	.23	.06
☐ 509 Dave Hilton	.50	.23	.06
☐ 510 Vida Blue	1.00	.45	.12
☐ 511 Rangers: Team/MG	2.00	.90	.25
Billy Martin			
☐ 512 Larry Milbourne	.50	.23	.06
☐ 513 Dick Pole	.50	.23	.06
☐ 514 Jose Cruz	.75	.35	.09
☐ 515 Manny Sanguillen	.75	.35	.09
☐ 516 Don Hood	.50	.23	.06
☐ 517 Checklist 397-528	2.00	.90	.25
☐ 518 Leo Cardenas	.50	.23	.06
☐ 519 Jim Todd	.50	.23	.06
☐ 520 Amos Otis	.75	.35	.09
☐ 521 Dennis Blair	.50	.23	.06
☐ 522 Gary Sutherland	.50	.23	.06
☐ 523 Tom Paciorek	.50	.23	.06
☐ 524 John Doherty	.50	.23	.06
☐ 525 Tom House	.50	.23	.06
☐ 526 Larry Hisle	.75	.35	.09
☐ 527 Mac Scarce	.50	.23	.06
☐ 528 Eddie Leon	.50	.23	.06
☐ 529 Gary Thomasson	.50	.23	.06
☐ 530 Gaylord Perry	3.00	1.35	.35
☐ 531 Reds: Team/MG	4.00	1.80	.50
Sparky Anderson			
☐ 532 Gorman Thomas	.75	.35	.09
☐ 533 Rudy Meoli	.50	.23	.06
☐ 534 Alex Johnson	.50	.23	.06
☐ 535 Gene Tenace	.75	.35	.09
☐ 536 Bob Moose	.50	.23	.06
☐ 537 Tommy Harper	.75	.35	.09
☐ 538 Duffy Dyer	.50	.23	.06
☐ 539 Jesse Jefferson	.50	.23	.06
☐ 540 Lou Brock	5.00	2.20	.60
☐ 541 Roger Metzger	.50	.23	.06
☐ 542 Pete Broberg	.50	.23	.06
☐ 543 Larry Biittner	.50	.23	.06
☐ 544 Steve Mingori	.50	.23	.06
☐ 545 Billy Williams	3.50	1.55	.45
☐ 546 John Knox	.50	.23	.06
☐ 547 Von Joshua	.50	.23	.06
☐ 548 Charlie Sands	.50	.23	.06
☐ 549 Bill Butler	.50	.23	.06
☐ 550 Ralph Garr	1.00	.45	.12
☐ 551 Larry Christenson	.50	.23	.06
☐ 552 Jack Brohamer	.50	.23	.06
☐ 553 John Boccabella	.50	.23	.06
☐ 554 Rich Gossage	2.00	.90	.25
☐ 555 Al Oliver	1.00	.45	.12
☐ 556 Tim Johnson	.50	.23	.06
☐ 557 Larry Gura	.50	.23	.06
☐ 558 Dave Roberts	.50	.23	.06
☐ 559 Bob Montgomery	.50	.23	.06
☐ 560 Tony Perez	3.00	1.35	.35
☐ 561 A's: Team/MG	2.00	.90	.25
Alvin Dark			
☐ 562 Gary Nolan	.75	.35	.09
☐ 563 Wilbur Howard	.50	.23	.06
☐ 564 Tommy Davis	.75	.35	.09
☐ 565 Joe Torre	1.00	.45	.12
☐ 566 Ray Burris	.50	.23	.06
☐ 567 Jim Sundberg	1.25	.55	.16
☐ 568 Dale Murray	.50	.23	.06
☐ 569 Frank White	1.00	.45	.12
☐ 570 Jim Wynn	.75	.35	.09
☐ 571 Dave Lemanczyk	.50	.23	.06
☐ 572 Roger Nelson	.50	.23	.06
☐ 573 Orlando Pena	.50	.23	.06
☐ 574 Tony Taylor	.75	.35	.09
☐ 575 Gene Clines	.50	.23	.06
☐ 576 Phil Roof	.50	.23	.06
☐ 577 John Morris	.50	.23	.06
☐ 578 Dave Tomlin	.50	.23	.06
☐ 579 Skip Pitlock	.50	.23	.06
☐ 580 Frank Robinson	6.00	2.70	.75
☐ 581 Darrel Chaney	.50	.23	.06
☐ 582 Eduardo Rodriguez	.50	.23	.06
☐ 583 Andy Etchebarren	.50	.23	.06
☐ 584 Mike Garman	.50	.23	.06
☐ 585 Chris Chambliss	.75	.35	.09
☐ 586 Tim McCarver	1.00	.45	.12
☐ 587 Chris Ward	.50	.23	.06
☐ 588 Rick Auerbach	.50	.23	.06
☐ 589 Braves: Team/MG	2.00	.90	.25
Clyde King			
☐ 590 Cesar Cedeno	.75	.35	.09
☐ 591 Glenn Abbott	.50	.23	.06
☐ 592 Balor Moore	.50	.23	.06
☐ 593 Gene Lamont	.50	.23	.06
☐ 594 Jim Fuller	.50	.23	.06
☐ 595 Joe Niekro	1.00	.45	.12
☐ 596 Ollie Brown	.50	.23	.06
☐ 597 Winston Llenas	.50	.23	.06
☐ 598 Bruce Kison	.50	.23	.06
☐ 599 Nate Colbert	.50	.23	.06
☐ 600 Rod Carew	5.00	2.20	.60
☐ 601 Juan Beniquez	.50	.23	.06
☐ 602 John Vukovich	.50	.23	.06
☐ 603 Lew Krausse	.50	.23	.06
☐ 604 Oscar Zamora	.50	.23	.06
☐ 605 John Ellis	.50	.23	.06
☐ 606 Bruce Miller	.50	.23	.06
☐ 607 Jim Holt	.50	.23	.06
☐ 608 Gene Michael	.50	.23	.06
☐ 609 Elrod Hendricks	.50	.23	.06
☐ 610 Ron Hunt	.50	.23	.06
☐ 611 Yankees: Team/MG	2.00	.90	.25
Bill Virdon			
☐ 612 Terry Hughes	.50	.23	.06
☐ 613 Bill Parsons	.50	.23	.06
☐ 614 Rookie Pitchers	1.00	.45	.12
Jack Kucek			
Dyar Miller			
Vern Ruhle			
Paul Siebert			
☐ 615 Rookie Pitchers:	1.50	.70	.19
Pat Darcy			
Dennis Leonard			
Tom Underwood			
Hank Webb			
☐ 616 Rookie Outfielders:	15.00	6.75	1.85
Dave Augustine			
Pepe Mangual			
Jim Rice			
John Scott			
☐ 617 Rookie Infielders:	2.50	1.10	.30
Mike Cubbage			
Doug DeCinces			
Reggie Sanders			
Manny Trillo			
☐ 618 Rookie Pitchers:	1.50	.70	.19
Jamie Easterly			
Tom Johnson			
Scott McGregor			
Rick Rhoden			
☐ 619 Rookie Outfielders	1.00	.45	.12
Benny Ayala			
Nyls Nyman			
Tommy Smith			
Jerry Turner			
☐ 620 Rookie Catcher/OF:	30.00	13.50	3.70
Gary Carter			
Marc Hill			
Danny Meyer			
Leon Roberts			
☐ 621 Rookie Pitchers:	1.50	.70	.19
John Denny			
Rawly Eastwick			
Jim Kern			
Juan Veintidos			
☐ 622 Rookie Outfielders:	6.00	2.70	.75
Ed Armbrister			
Fred Lynn			
Tom Poquette			
Terry Whitfield			
☐ 623 Rookie Infielders:	6.00	2.70	.75
Phil Garner			
Keith Hernandez			
Bob Sheldon			
Tom Veryzer			
☐ 624 Rookie Pitchers	1.00	.45	.12
Doug Konieczny			
Gary Lavelle			
Jim Otten			
Eddie Solomon			
☐ 625 Boog Powell	1.00	.45	.12
☐ 626 Larry Haney	.50	.23	.06
(photo actually			
Dave Duncan)			
☐ 627 Tom Walker	.50	.23	.06
☐ 628 Ron LeFlore	1.00	.45	.12
☐ 629 Joe Hoerner	.50	.23	.06
☐ 630 Greg Luzinski	1.00	.45	.12
☐ 631 Lee Lacy	.50	.23	.06
☐ 632 Morris Nettles	.50	.23	.06
☐ 633 Paul Casanova	.50	.23	.06
☐ 634 Cy Acosta	.50	.23	.06
☐ 635 Chuck Dobson	.50	.23	.06
☐ 636 Charlie Moore	.50	.23	.06
☐ 637 Ted Martinez	.50	.23	.06
☐ 638 Cubs: Team/MG	2.00	.90	.25
Jim Marshall			
☐ 639 Steve Kline	.50	.23	.06
☐ 640 Harmon Killebrew	5.00	2.20	.60
☐ 641 Jim Northrup	.50	.23	.06
☐ 642 Mike Phillips	.50	.23	.06
☐ 643 Brent Strom	.50	.23	.06
☐ 644 Bill Fahey	.50	.23	.06
☐ 645 Danny Cater	.50	.23	.06
☐ 646 Checklist 529-660	2.00	.90	.25
☐ 647 Claudell Washington	1.00	.45	.12
☐ 648 Dave Pagan	.50	.23	.06
☐ 649 Jack Heidemann	.50	.23	.06
☐ 650 Dave May	.50	.23	.06
☐ 651 John Morlan	.50	.23	.06
☐ 652 Lindy McDaniel	.50	.23	.06
☐ 653 Lee Richard	.50	.23	.06
☐ 654 Jerry Terrell	.50	.23	.06
☐ 655 Rico Carty	1.00	.45	.12
☐ 656 Bill Plummer	.50	.23	.06
☐ 657 Bob Oliver	.50	.23	.06
☐ 658 Vic Harris	.50	.23	.06
☐ 659 Bob Apodaca	.50	.23	.06
☐ 660 Hank Aaron	40.00	18.00	5.00

1976 O-Pee-Chee

This is a 660-card standard-size set. The 1976 O-Pee-Chee cards are very similar to the 1976 Topps cards, yet rather different from previous years' issues. The most prominent change is that the backs are much brighter than their American counterparts. The cards parallel the American issue and it is a challenge to find well centered examples of these cards.

	NRMT	VG-E	GOOD
COMPLETE SET (660)	500.00	220.00	60.00
COMMON CARD (1-660)	.30	.14	.04
☐ 1 Hank Aaron RB	16.00	7.25	2.00
Most RBI's, 2262			
☐ 2 Bobby Bonds RB	1.00	.45	.12
Most leadoff			
homers, 32;			
Plus 3 Seasons of			
30 HR's and 30 SB's			
☐ 3 Mickey Lolich RB	.75	.35	.09
Lefthander, Most			
Strikeouts 2679			
☐ 4 Dave Lopes RB	.75	.35	.09
Most consecutive			
SB attempts, 38			
☐ 5 Tom Seaver RB	4.00	1.80	.50
Most cons. seasons			
with 200 SO's, 8			
☐ 6 Rennie Stennett RB	.50	.23	.06
Most hits in a 9			
inning game, 7			
☐ 7 Jim Umbarger	.30	.14	.04
☐ 8 Tito Fuentes	.30	.14	.04
☐ 9 Paul Lindblad	.30	.14	.04
☐ 10 Lou Brock	4.00	1.80	.50
☐ 11 Jim Hughes	.30	.14	.04
☐ 12 Richie Zisk	.50	.23	.06
☐ 13 John Wockenfuss	.30	.14	.04
☐ 14 Gene Garber	.50	.23	.06
☐ 15 George Scott	.50	.23	.06
☐ 16 Bob Apodaca	.30	.14	.04
☐ 17 New York Yankees	1.50	.70	.19
Team Card			
☐ 18 Dale Murray	.30	.14	.04
☐ 19 George Brett	60.00	27.00	7.50
☐ 20 Bob Watson	.50	.23	.06
☐ 21 Dave LaRoche	.30	.14	.04
☐ 22 Bill Russell	.50	.23	.06
☐ 23 Brian Downing	.50	.23	.06
☐ 24 Cesar Geronimo	.50	.23	.06
☐ 25 Mike Torrez	.50	.23	.06
☐ 26 Andre Thornton	.50	.23	.06
☐ 27 Ed Figueroa	.30	.14	.04
☐ 28 Dusty Baker	1.25	.55	.16
☐ 29 Rick Burleson	.30	.14	.04
☐ 30 John Montefusco	.50	.23	.06
☐ 31 Len Randle	.30	.14	.04
☐ 32 Danny Frisella	.30	.14	.04
☐ 33 Bill North	.30	.14	.04
☐ 34 Mike Garman	.30	.14	.04
☐ 35 Tony Oliva	.75	.35	.09
☐ 36 Frank Taveras	.30	.14	.04
☐ 37 John Hiller	.50	.23	.06
☐ 38 Garry Maddox	.50	.23	.06
☐ 39 Pete Broberg	.30	.14	.04
☐ 40 Dave Kingman	.75	.35	.09
☐ 41 Tippy Martinez	.75	.35	.09
☐ 42 Barry Foote	.50	.23	.06
☐ 43 Paul Splittorff	.30	.14	.04
☐ 44 Doug Rader	.30	.14	.04
☐ 45 Boog Powell	.75	.35	.09
☐ 46 Los Angeles Dodgers	1.50	.70	.19
Team Card			
Walt Alston MG			
(Checklist back)			
☐ 47 Jesse Jefferson	.30	.14	.04
☐ 48 Dave Concepcion	1.25	.55	.16
☐ 49 Dave Duncan	.30	.14	.04
☐ 50 Fred Lynn	1.50	.70	.19
☐ 51 Ray Burris	.30	.14	.04
☐ 52 Dave Chalk	.30	.14	.04
☐ 53 Mike Beard	.30	.14	.04
☐ 54 Dave Rader	.30	.14	.04
☐ 55 Gaylord Perry	2.50	1.10	.30
☐ 56 Bob Tolan	.30	.14	.04
☐ 57 Phil Garner	.75	.35	.09
☐ 58 Ron Reed	.30	.14	.04
☐ 59 Larry Hisle	.50	.23	.06
☐ 60 Jerry Reuss	.50	.23	.06
☐ 61 Ron LeFlore	.50	.23	.06
☐ 62 Johnny Oates	.50	.23	.06
☐ 63 Bobby Darwin	.30	.14	.04
☐ 64 Jerry Koosman	.75	.35	.09
☐ 65 Chris Chambliss	.50	.23	.06
☐ 66 Gus Bell FS	.50	.23	.06
Buddy Bell			
☐ 67 Ray Boone FS	.50	.23	.06
Bob Boone			
☐ 68 Joe Coleman FS	.30	.14	.04
Joe Coleman Jr.			
☐ 69 Jim Hegan FS	.30	.14	.04
Mike Hegan			
☐ 70 Roy Smalley FS	.50	.23	.06
Roy Smalley Jr.			
☐ 71 Steve Rogers	.75	.35	.09
☐ 72 Hal McRae	.75	.35	.09
☐ 73 Baltimore Orioles	1.50	.70	.19
Team Card			
Earl Weaver MG			
(Checklist back)			
☐ 74 Oscar Gamble	.50	.23	.06
☐ 75 Larry Dierker	.30	.14	.04
☐ 76 Willie Crawford	.30	.14	.04
☐ 77 Pedro Borbon	.50	.23	.06
☐ 78 Cecil Cooper	.75	.35	.09
☐ 79 Jerry Morales	.30	.14	.04
☐ 80 Jim Kaat	.75	.35	.09
☐ 81 Darrell Evans	.75	.35	.09
☐ 82 Von Joshua	.30	.14	.04
☐ 83 Jim Spencer	.30	.14	.04
☐ 84 Brent Strom	.30	.14	.04
☐ 85 Mickey Rivers	.50	.23	.06
☐ 86 Mike Tyson	.30	.14	.04
☐ 87 Tom Burgmeier	.30	.14	.04

☐ 88 Duffy Dyer .30 .14 .04
☐ 89 Vern Ruhle .30 .14 .04
☐ 90 Sal Bando .50 .23 .06
☐ 91 Tom Hutton .30 .14 .04
☐ 92 Eduardo Rodriguez .30 .14 .04
☐ 93 Mike Phillips .30 .14 .04
☐ 94 Jim Dwyer .30 .14 .04
☐ 95 Brooks Robinson 6.00 2.70 .75
☐ 96 Doug Bird .30 .14 .04
☐ 97 Wilbur Howard .30 .14 .04
☐ 98 Dennis Eckersley 40.00 18.00 5.00
☐ 99 Lee Lacy .30 .14 .04
☐ 100 Jim Hunter 2.50 1.10 .30
☐ 101 Pete LaCock .30 .14 .04
☐ 102 Jim Willoughby .30 .14 .04
☐ 103 Biff Pocoroba .30 .14 .04
☐ 104 Cincinnati Reds 2.00 .90 .25
Team Card
Sparky Anderson MG
(Checklist back)
☐ 105 Gary Lavelle .30 .14 .04
☐ 106 Tom Grieve .30 .14 .04
☐ 107 Dave Roberts .30 .14 .04
☐ 108 Don Kirkwood .30 .14 .04
☐ 109 Larry Lintz .30 .14 .04
☐ 110 Carlos May .30 .14 .04
☐ 111 Danny Thompson .30 .14 .04
☐ 112 Kent Tekulve 1.50 .70 .19
☐ 113 Gary Sutherland .30 .14 .04
☐ 114 Jay Johnstone .50 .23 .06
☐ 115 Ken Holtzman .50 .23 .06
☐ 116 Charlie Moore .30 .14 .04
☐ 117 Mike Jorgensen .50 .23 .06
☐ 118 Boston Red Sox 1.50 .70 .19
Team Card
Darrell Johnson
(Checklist back)
☐ 119 Checklist 1-132 1.50 .70 .19
☐ 120 Rusty Staub .50 .23 .06
☐ 121 Tony Solaita .30 .14 .04
☐ 122 Mike Cosgrove .30 .14 .04
☐ 123 Walt Williams .30 .14 .04
☐ 124 Doug Rau .30 .14 .04
☐ 125 Don Baylor 2.00 .90 .25
☐ 126 Tom Dettore .30 .14 .04
☐ 127 Larvell Blanks .30 .14 .04
☐ 128 Ken Griffey 2.50 1.10 .30
☐ 129 Andy Etchebarren .30 .14 .04
☐ 130 Luis Tiant .75 .35 .09
☐ 131 Bill Stein .30 .14 .04
☐ 132 Don Hood .30 .14 .04
☐ 133 Gary Matthews .50 .23 .06
☐ 134 Mike Ivie .30 .14 .04
☐ 135 Bake McBride .50 .23 .06
☐ 136 Dave Goltz .30 .14 .04
☐ 137 Bill Robinson .50 .23 .06
☐ 138 Lerrin LaGrow .30 .14 .04
☐ 139 Gorman Thomas .50 .23 .06
☐ 140 Vida Blue .75 .35 .09
☐ 141 Larry Parrish .75 .35 .09
☐ 142 Dick Drago .30 .14 .04
☐ 143 Jerry Grote .50 .23 .06
☐ 144 Al Fitzmorris .30 .14 .04
☐ 145 Larry Bowa .75 .35 .09
☐ 146 George Medich .30 .14 .04
☐ 147 Houston Astros 1.50 .70 .19
Team Card
Bill Virdon MG
(Checklist back)
☐ 148 Stan Thomas .30 .14 .04
☐ 149 Tommy Davis .50 .23 .06
☐ 150 Steve Garvey 4.00 1.80 .50
☐ 151 Bill Bonham .30 .14 .04
☐ 152 Leroy Stanton .30 .14 .04
☐ 153 Buzz Capra .30 .14 .04
☐ 154 Bucky Dent .50 .23 .06
☐ 155 Jack Billingham .50 .23 .06
☐ 156 Rico Carty .50 .23 .06
☐ 157 Mike Caldwell .30 .14 .04
☐ 158 Ken Reitz .30 .14 .04
☐ 159 Jerry Terrell .30 .14 .04
☐ 160 Dave Winfield 25.00 11.00 3.10
☐ 161 Bruce Kison .30 .14 .04
☐ 162 Jack Pierce .30 .14 .04
☐ 163 Jim Slaton .30 .14 .04
☐ 164 Pepe Mangual .30 .14 .04
☐ 165 Gene Tenace .50 .23 .06
☐ 166 Skip Lockwood .30 .14 .04
☐ 167 Freddie Patek .50 .23 .06
☐ 168 Tom Hilgendorf .30 .14 .04
☐ 169 Graig Nettles .75 .35 .09
☐ 170 Rick Wise .30 .14 .04
☐ 171 Greg Gross .30 .14 .04
☐ 172 Texas Rangers 1.50 .70 .19
Team Card
Frank Lucchesi MG
(Checklist back)
☐ 173 Steve Swisher .30 .14 .04
☐ 174 Charlie Hough .75 .35 .09
☐ 175 Ken Singleton .50 .23 .06
☐ 176 Dick Lange .30 .14 .04
☐ 177 Marty Perez .30 .14 .04
☐ 178 Tom Buskey .30 .14 .04
☐ 179 George Foster 1.00 .45 .12
☐ 180 Rich Gossage 2.00 .90 .25
☐ 181 Willie Montanez .30 .14 .04
☐ 182 Harry Rasmussen .30 .14 .04
☐ 183 Steve Braun .30 .14 .04
☐ 184 Bill Greif .30 .14 .04
☐ 185 Dave Parker 2.00 .90 .25
☐ 186 Tom Walker .30 .14 .04
☐ 187 Pedro Garcia .30 .14 .04
☐ 188 Fred Scherman .30 .14 .04
☐ 189 Claudell Washington .50 .23 .06
☐ 190 Jon Matlack .50 .23 .06
☐ 191 NL Batting Leaders .75 .35 .09
Bill Madlock
Ted Simmons
Manny Sanguillen
☐ 192 AL Batting Leaders: 2.00 .90 .25
Rod Carew
Fred Lynn
Thurman Munson
☐ 193 NL Home Run Leaders: 3.00 1.35 .35
Mike Schmidt
Dave Kingman
Greg Luzinski
☐ 194 AL Home Run Leaders: 2.50 1.10 .30
Reggie Jackson
George Scott
John Mayberry
☐ 195 NL RBI Leaders: 1.50 .70 .19
Greg Luzinski
Johnny Bench
Tony Perez
☐ 196 AL RBI Leaders .75 .35 .09
George Scott
John Mayberry
Fred Lynn
☐ 197 NL Steals Leaders: 1.50 .70 .19
Dave Lopes
Joe Morgan
Lou Brock
☐ 198 AL Steals Leaders .75 .35 .09
Mickey Rivers
Claudell Washington
Amos Otis
☐ 199 NL Victory Leaders: 1.50 .70 .19
Tom Seaver
Randy Jones
Andy Messersmith
☐ 200 AL Victory Leaders: 1.50 .70 .19
Jim Hunter
Jim Palmer
Vida Blue
☐ 201 NL ERA Leaders 1.50 .70 .19
Randy Jones
Andy Messersmith
Tom Seaver
☐ 202 AL ERA Leaders 5.00 2.20 .60
Jim Palmer
Jim Hunter
Dennis Eckersley
☐ 203 NL Strikeout Leaders 1.50 .70 .19
Tom Seaver
John Montefusco
Andy Messersmith
☐ 204 AL Strikeout Leaders .75 .35 .09
Frank Tanana
Bert Blyleven
Gaylord Perry
☐ 205 Leading Firemen .75 .35 .09
Al Hrabosky
Rich Gossage
☐ 206 Manny Trillo .30 .14 .04
☐ 207 Andy Hassler .30 .14 .04
☐ 208 Mike Lum .30 .14 .04
☐ 209 Alan Ashby .75 .35 .09
☐ 210 Lee May .50 .23 .06
☐ 211 Clay Carroll .30 .14 .04
☐ 212 Pat Kelly .30 .14 .04
☐ 213 Dave Heaverlo .30 .14 .04
☐ 214 Eric Soderholm .30 .14 .04
☐ 215 Reggie Smith .50 .23 .06
☐ 216 Montreal Expos 1.50 .70 .19
Team Card
Karl Kuehl MG
(Checklist back)
☐ 217 Dave Freisleben .30 .14 .04
☐ 218 John Knox .30 .14 .04
☐ 219 Tom Murphy .30 .14 .04
☐ 220 Manny Sanguillen .50 .23 .06
☐ 221 Jim Todd .30 .14 .04
☐ 222 Wayne Garrett .30 .14 .04
☐ 223 Ollie Brown .30 .14 .04
☐ 224 Jim York .30 .14 .04
☐ 225 Roy White .50 .23 .06
☐ 226 Jim Sundberg .50 .23 .06
☐ 227 Oscar Zamora .30 .14 .04
☐ 228 John Hale .30 .14 .04
☐ 229 Jerry Remy .30 .14 .04
☐ 230 Carl Yastrzemski 5.00 2.20 .60
☐ 231 Tom House .30 .14 .04
☐ 232 Frank Duffy .30 .14 .04
☐ 233 Grant Jackson .30 .14 .04
☐ 234 Mike Sadek .30 .14 .04
☐ 235 Bert Blyleven .75 .35 .09
☐ 236 Kansas City Royals 1.50 .70 .19
Team Card
Whitey Herzog MG
(Checklist back)
☐ 237 Dave Hamilton .30 .14 .04
☐ 238 Larry Biittner .30 .14 .04
☐ 239 John Curtis .30 .14 .04
☐ 240 Pete Rose 12.00 5.50 1.50
☐ 241 Hector Torres .30 .14 .04
☐ 242 Dan Meyer .30 .14 .04
☐ 243 Jim Rooker .30 .14 .04
☐ 244 Bill Sharp .30 .14 .04
☐ 245 Felix Millan .30 .14 .04
☐ 246 Cesar Tovar .30 .14 .04
☐ 247 Terry Harmon .30 .14 .04
☐ 248 Dick Tidrow .30 .14 .04
☐ 249 Cliff Johnson .50 .23 .06
☐ 250 Fergie Jenkins 2.50 1.10 .30
☐ 251 Rick Monday .50 .23 .06
☐ 252 Tim Nordbrook .30 .14 .04
☐ 253 Bill Buckner .75 .35 .09
☐ 254 Rudy Meoli .30 .14 .04
☐ 255 Fritz Peterson .30 .14 .04
☐ 256 Rowland Office .30 .14 .04
☐ 257 Ross Grimsley .30 .14 .04
☐ 258 Nyls Nyman .30 .14 .04
☐ 259 Darrel Chaney .30 .14 .04
☐ 260 Steve Busby .30 .14 .04
☐ 261 Gary Thomasson .30 .14 .04
☐ 262 Checklist 133-264 1.50 .70 .19
☐ 263 Lyman Bostock 1.00 .45 .12
☐ 264 Steve Renko .30 .14 .04
☐ 265 Willie Davis .50 .23 .06
☐ 266 Alan Foster .30 .14 .04
☐ 267 Aurelio Rodriguez .30 .14 .04
☐ 268 Del Unser .30 .14 .04
☐ 269 Rick Austin .30 .14 .04
☐ 270 Willie Stargell 3.00 1.35 .35
☐ 271 Jim Lonborg .50 .23 .06
☐ 272 Rick Dempsey .50 .23 .06
☐ 273 Joe Niekro .50 .23 .06
☐ 274 Tommy Harper .50 .23 .06
☐ 275 Rick Manning .30 .14 .04
☐ 276 Mickey Scott .30 .14 .04
☐ 277 Chicago Cubs 1.50 .70 .19
Team Card
Jim Marshall MG
(Checklist back)
☐ 278 Bernie Carbo .30 .14 .04
☐ 279 Roy Howell .30 .14 .04
☐ 280 Burt Hooton .50 .23 .06
☐ 281 Dave May .30 .14 .04
☐ 282 Dan Osborn .30 .14 .04
☐ 283 Merv Rettenmund .30 .14 .04
☐ 284 Steve Ontiveros .30 .14 .04
☐ 285 Mike Cuellar .50 .23 .06
☐ 286 Jim Wohlford .30 .14 .04
☐ 287 Pete Mackanin .30 .14 .04
☐ 288 Bill Campbell .30 .14 .04
☐ 289 Enzo Hernandez .30 .14 .04
☐ 290 Ted Simmons .75 .35 .09
☐ 291 Ken Sanders .30 .14 .04
☐ 292 Leon Roberts .30 .14 .04
☐ 293 Bill Castro .30 .14 .04
☐ 294 Ed Kirkpatrick .30 .14 .04
☐ 295 Dave Cash .30 .14 .04
☐ 296 Pat Dobson .30 .14 .04
☐ 297 Roger Metzger .30 .14 .04
☐ 298 Dick Bosman .30 .14 .04
☐ 299 Champ Summers .30 .14 .04
☐ 300 Johnny Bench 7.50 3.40 .95
☐ 301 Jackie Brown .30 .14 .04
☐ 302 Rick Miller .30 .14 .04
☐ 303 Steve Foucault .30 .14 .04
☐ 304 California Angels 1.50 .70 .19
Team Card
Dick Williams MG
(Checklist back)
☐ 305 Andy Messersmith .50 .23 .06
☐ 306 Rod Gilbreath .30 .14 .04
☐ 307 Al Bumbry .50 .23 .06
☐ 308 Jim Barr .30 .14 .04
☐ 309 Bill Melton .30 .14 .04
☐ 310 Randy Jones .50 .23 .06
☐ 311 Cookie Rojas .30 .14 .04
☐ 312 Don Carrithers .30 .14 .04
☐ 313 Dan Ford .30 .14 .04
☐ 314 Ed Kranepool .30 .14 .04
☐ 315 Al Hrabosky .30 .14 .04
☐ 316 Robin Yount 30.00 13.50 3.70
☐ 317 John Candelaria 2.00 .90 .25
☐ 318 Bob Boone .75 .35 .09
☐ 319 Larry Gura .30 .14 .04
☐ 320 Willie Horton .75 .35 .09
☐ 321 Jose Cruz .50 .23 .06
☐ 322 Glenn Abbott .30 .14 .04
☐ 323 Rob Sperring .30 .14 .04
☐ 324 Jim Bibby .30 .14 .04
☐ 325 Tony Perez 2.00 .90 .25
☐ 326 Dick Pole .30 .14 .04
☐ 327 Dave Moates .30 .14 .04
☐ 328 Carl Morton .30 .14 .04
☐ 329 Joe Ferguson .30 .14 .04
☐ 330 Nolan Ryan 65.00 29.00 8.00
☐ 331 San Diego Padres 1.50 .70 .19
Team Card
John McNamara MG
(Checklist back)
☐ 332 Charlie Williams .30 .14 .04
☐ 333 Bob Coluccio .30 .14 .04
☐ 334 Dennis Leonard .50 .23 .06
☐ 335 Bob Grich .50 .23 .06
☐ 336 Vic Albury .30 .14 .04
☐ 337 Bud Harrelson .50 .23 .06
☐ 338 Bob Bailey .30 .14 .04
☐ 339 John Denny .50 .23 .06
☐ 340 Jim Rice 5.00 2.20 .60
☐ 341 Lou Gehrig ATG 12.00 5.50 1.50
☐ 342 Rogers Hornsby ATG 3.00 1.35 .35
☐ 343 Pie Traynor ATG 1.00 .45 .12
☐ 344 Honus Wagner ATG 5.00 2.20 .60
☐ 345 Babe Ruth ATG 15.00 6.75 1.85
☐ 346 Ty Cobb ATG 8.00 3.60 1.00
☐ 347 Ted Williams ATG 10.00 4.50 1.25
☐ 348 Mickey Cochrane ATG 1.00 .45 .12
☐ 349 Walter Johnson ATG 3.00 1.35 .35
☐ 350 Lefty Grove ATG 1.00 .45 .12
☐ 351 Randy Hundley .30 .14 .04
☐ 352 Dave Giusti .30 .14 .04
☐ 353 Sixto Lezcano .50 .23 .06
☐ 354 Ron Blomberg .30 .14 .04
☐ 355 Steve Carlton 6.00 2.70 .75
☐ 356 Ted Martinez .30 .14 .04
☐ 357 Ken Forsch .30 .14 .04
☐ 358 Buddy Bell .50 .23 .06
☐ 359 Rick Reuschel .50 .23 .06
☐ 360 Jeff Burroughs .50 .23 .06
☐ 361 Detroit Tigers 1.50 .70 .19
Team Card
Ralph Houk MG
(Checklist back)
☐ 362 Will McEnaney .50 .23 .06
☐ 363 Dave Collins .50 .23 .06
☐ 364 Elias Sosa .30 .14 .04
☐ 365 Carlton Fisk 7.50 3.40 .95
☐ 366 Bobby Valentine .30 .14 .04
☐ 367 Bruce Miller .30 .14 .04
☐ 368 Wilbur Wood .30 .14 .04
☐ 369 Frank White .50 .23 .06
☐ 370 Ron Cey .75 .35 .09
☐ 371 Ellie Hendricks .30 .14 .04
☐ 372 Rick Baldwin .30 .14 .04
☐ 373 Johnny Briggs .30 .14 .04
☐ 374 Dan Warthen .30 .14 .04
☐ 375 Ron Fairly .50 .23 .06
☐ 376 Rich Hebner .50 .23 .06
☐ 377 Mike Hegan .30 .14 .04
☐ 378 Steve Stone .50 .23 .06
☐ 379 Ken Boswell .30 .14 .04
☐ 380 Bobby Bonds 1.50 .70 .19
☐ 381 Denny Doyle .30 .14 .04
☐ 382 Matt Alexander .30 .14 .04
☐ 383 John Ellis .30 .14 .04
☐ 384 Philadelphia Phillies 1.50 .70 .19
Team Card
Danny Ozark MG
(Checklist back)
☐ 385 Mickey Lolich .75 .35 .09
☐ 386 Ed Goodson .30 .14 .04
☐ 387 Mike Miley .30 .14 .04
☐ 388 Stan Perzanowski .30 .14 .04
☐ 389 Glenn Adams .30 .14 .04
☐ 390 Don Gullett .75 .35 .09
☐ 391 Jerry Hairston .30 .14 .04
☐ 392 Checklist 265-396 1.50 .70 .19
☐ 393 Paul Mitchell .30 .14 .04
☐ 394 Fran Healy .30 .14 .04
☐ 395 Jim Wynn .50 .23 .06
☐ 396 Bill Lee .50 .23 .06
☐ 397 Tim Foli .30 .14 .04
☐ 398 Dave Tomlin .30 .14 .04
☐ 399 Luis Melendez .30 .14 .04
☐ 400 Rod Carew 4.00 1.80 .50
☐ 401 Ken Brett .30 .14 .04
☐ 402 Don Money .30 .14 .04
☐ 403 Geoff Zahn .30 .14 .04
☐ 404 Enos Cabell .30 .14 .04
☐ 405 Rollie Fingers 2.50 1.10 .30
☐ 406 Ed Herrmann .30 .14 .04
☐ 407 Tom Underwood .30 .14 .04
☐ 408 Charlie Spikes .30 .14 .04
☐ 409 Dave Lemanczyk .30 .14 .04
☐ 410 Ralph Garr .50 .23 .06
☐ 411 Bill Singer .30 .14 .04
☐ 412 Toby Harrah .50 .23 .06
☐ 413 Pete Varney .30 .14 .04
☐ 414 Wayne Garland .30 .14 .04
☐ 415 Vada Pinson .75 .35 .09
☐ 416 Tommy John .75 .35 .09
☐ 417 Gene Clines .30 .14 .04
☐ 418 Jose Morales .30 .14 .04
☐ 419 Reggie Cleveland .30 .14 .04
☐ 420 Joe Morgan 4.00 1.80 .50
☐ 421 Oakland A's 1.50 .70 .19
Team Card
(No MG on front;
checklist back)
☐ 422 Johnny Grubb .30 .14 .04
☐ 423 Ed Halicki .30 .14 .04
☐ 424 Phil Roof .30 .14 .04
☐ 425 Rennie Stennett .30 .14 .04
☐ 426 Bob Forsch .30 .14 .04
☐ 427 Kurt Bevacqua .30 .14 .04
☐ 428 Jim Crawford .30 .14 .04

☐ 429 Fred Stanley	.30	.14	.04
☐ 430 Jose Cardenal	.50	.23	.06
☐ 431 Dick Ruthven	.30	.14	.04
☐ 432 Tom Veryzer	.30	.14	.04
☐ 433 Rick Waits	.30	.14	.04
☐ 434 Morris Nettles	.30	.14	.04
☐ 435 Phil Niekro	2.50	1.10	.30
☐ 436 Bill Fahey	.30	.14	.04
☐ 437 Terry Forster	.30	.14	.04
☐ 438 Doug DeCinces	.50	.23	.06
☐ 439 Rick Rhoden	.50	.23	.06
☐ 440 John Mayberry	.50	.23	.06
☐ 441 Gary Carter	7.50	3.40	.95
☐ 442 Hank Webb	.30	.14	.04
☐ 443 San Francisco Giants	1.50	.70	.19
Team Card			
(No MG on front;			
checklist back)			
☐ 444 Gary Nolan	.50	.23	.06
☐ 445 Rico Petrocelli	.50	.23	.06
☐ 446 Larry Haney	.30	.14	.04
☐ 447 Gene Locklear	.50	.23	.06
☐ 448 Tom Johnson	.30	.14	.04
☐ 449 Bob Robertson	.30	.14	.04
☐ 450 Jim Palmer	4.00	1.80	.50
☐ 451 Buddy Bradford	.30	.14	.04
☐ 452 Tom Hausman	.30	.14	.04
☐ 453 Lou Piniella	1.00	.45	.12
☐ 454 Tom Griffin	.30	.14	.04
☐ 455 Dick Allen	.75	.35	.09
☐ 456 Joe Coleman	.30	.14	.04
☐ 457 Ed Crosby	.30	.14	.04
☐ 458 Earl Williams	.30	.14	.04
☐ 459 Jim Brewer	.30	.14	.04
☐ 460 Cesar Cedeno	.50	.23	.06
☐ 461 NL and AL Champs	.75	.35	.09
Reds sweep Bucs;			
Bosox surprise A's			
☐ 462 World Series	.75	.35	.09
Reds Champs			
☐ 463 Steve Hargan	.30	.14	.04
☐ 464 Ken Henderson	.30	.14	.04
☐ 465 Mike Marshall	.50	.23	.06
☐ 466 Bob Stinson	.30	.14	.04
☐ 467 Woodie Fryman	.30	.14	.04
☐ 468 Jesus Alou	.30	.14	.04
☐ 469 Rawly Eastwick	.30	.14	.04
☐ 470 Bobby Murcer	.50	.23	.06
☐ 471 Jim Burton	.30	.14	.04
☐ 472 Bob Davis	.30	.14	.04
☐ 473 Paul Blair	.50	.23	.06
☐ 474 Ray Corbin	.30	.14	.04
☐ 475 Joe Rudi	.50	.23	.06
☐ 476 Bob Moose	.30	.14	.04
☐ 477 Cleveland Indians	1.50	.70	.19
Team Card			
Frank Robinson MG			
(Checklist back)			
☐ 478 Lynn McGlothen	.30	.14	.04
☐ 479 Bobby Mitchell	.30	.14	.04
☐ 480 Mike Schmidt	25.00	11.00	3.10
☐ 481 Rudy May	.30	.14	.04
☐ 482 Tim Hosley	.30	.14	.04
☐ 483 Mickey Stanley	.30	.14	.04
☐ 484 Eric Raich	.30	.14	.04
☐ 485 Mike Hargrove	.50	.23	.06
☐ 486 Bruce Dal Canton	.30	.14	.04
☐ 487 Leron Lee	.30	.14	.04
☐ 488 Claude Osteen	.50	.23	.06
☐ 489 Skip Jutze	.30	.14	.04
☐ 490 Frank Tanana	.75	.35	.09
☐ 491 Terry Crowley	.30	.14	.04
☐ 492 Martin Pattin	.30	.14	.04
☐ 493 Derrel Thomas	.30	.14	.04
☐ 494 Craig Swan	.30	.14	.04
☐ 495 Nate Colbert	.50	.23	.06
☐ 496 Juan Beniquez	.30	.14	.04
☐ 497 Joe McIntosh	.30	.14	.04
☐ 498 Glenn Borgmann	.30	.14	.04
☐ 499 Mario Guerrero	.30	.14	.04
☐ 500 Reggie Jackson	14.00	6.25	1.75
☐ 501 Billy Champion	.30	.14	.04
☐ 502 Tim McCarver	.75	.35	.09
☐ 503 Elliott Maddox	.30	.14	.04
☐ 504 Pittsburgh Pirates	1.50	.70	.19
Team Card			
Danny Murtaugh MG			
(Checklist back)			
☐ 505 Mark Belanger	.50	.23	.06
☐ 506 George Mitterwald	.30	.14	.04
☐ 507 Ray Bare	.30	.14	.04
☐ 508 Duane Kuiper	.30	.14	.04
☐ 509 Bill Hands	.30	.14	.04
☐ 510 Amos Otis	.50	.23	.06
☐ 511 Jamie Easterley	.30	.14	.04
☐ 512 Ellie Rodriguez	.30	.14	.04
☐ 513 Bart Johnson	.30	.14	.04
☐ 514 Dan Driessen	.50	.23	.06
☐ 515 Steve Yeager	.50	.23	.06
☐ 516 Wayne Granger	.30	.14	.04
☐ 517 John Milner	.30	.14	.04
☐ 518 Doug Flynn	.30	.14	.04
☐ 519 Steve Brye	.30	.14	.04
☐ 520 Willie McCovey	4.00	1.80	.50
☐ 521 Jim Colborn	.30	.14	.04

☐ 522 Ted Sizemore	.30	.14	.04
☐ 523 Bob Montgomery	.30	.14	.04
☐ 524 Pete Falcone	.30	.14	.04
☐ 525 Billy Williams	2.50	1.10	.30
☐ 526 Checklist 397-528	1.50	.70	.19
☐ 527 Mike Anderson	.30	.14	.04
☐ 528 Dock Ellis	.30	.14	.04
☐ 529 Deron Johnson	.30	.14	.04
☐ 530 Don Sutton	1.50	.70	.19
☐ 531 New York Mets	1.50	.70	.19
Team Card			
Joe Frazier MG			
(Checklist back)			
☐ 532 Milt May	.30	.14	.04
☐ 533 Lee Richard	.30	.14	.04
☐ 534 Stan Bahnsen	.30	.14	.04
☐ 535 Dave Nelson	.30	.14	.04
☐ 536 Mike Thompson	.30	.14	.04
☐ 537 Tony Muser	.30	.14	.04
☐ 538 Pat Darcy	.30	.14	.04
☐ 539 John Balaz	.50	.23	.06
☐ 540 Bill Freehan	.50	.23	.06
☐ 541 Steve Mingori	.30	.14	.04
☐ 542 Keith Hernandez	1.50	.70	.19
☐ 543 Wayne Twitchell	.30	.14	.04
☐ 544 Pepe Frias	.30	.14	.04
☐ 545 Sparky Lyle	.50	.23	.06
☐ 546 Dave Rosello	.30	.14	.04
☐ 547 Roric Harrison	.30	.14	.04
☐ 548 Manny Mota	.50	.23	.06
☐ 549 Randy Tate	.30	.14	.04
☐ 550 Hank Aaron	25.00	11.00	3.10
☐ 551 Jerry DaVanon	.30	.14	.04
☐ 552 Terry Humphrey	.30	.14	.04
☐ 553 Randy Moffitt	.30	.14	.04
☐ 554 Ray Fosse	.30	.14	.04
☐ 555 Dyar Miller	.30	.14	.04
☐ 556 Minnesota Twins	1.50	.70	.19
Team Card			
Gene Mauch MG			
(Checklist back)			
☐ 557 Dan Spillner	.30	.14	.04
☐ 558 Clarence Gaston	.75	.35	.09
☐ 559 Clyde Wright	.30	.14	.04
☐ 560 Jorge Orta	.30	.14	.04
☐ 561 Tom Carroll	.30	.14	.04
☐ 562 Adrian Garrett	.30	.14	.04
☐ 563 Larry Demery	.30	.14	.04
☐ 564 Bubble Gum Champ:	.75	.35	.09
Kurt Bevacqua			
☐ 565 Tug McGraw	.50	.23	.06
☐ 566 Ken McMullen	.30	.14	.04
☐ 567 George Stone	.30	.14	.04
☐ 568 Rob Andrews	.30	.14	.04
☐ 569 Nelson Briles	.50	.23	.06
☐ 570 George Hendrick	.50	.23	.06
☐ 571 Don DeMola	.30	.14	.04
☐ 572 Rich Coggins	.30	.14	.04
☐ 573 Bill Travers	.30	.14	.04
☐ 574 Don Kessinger	.50	.23	.06
☐ 575 Dwight Evans	1.50	.70	.19
☐ 576 Maximino Leon	.30	.14	.04
☐ 577 Marc Hill	.30	.14	.04
☐ 578 Ted Kubiak	.30	.14	.04
☐ 579 Clay Kirby	.30	.14	.04
☐ 580 Bert Campaneris	.50	.23	.06
☐ 581 St. Louis Cardinals	1.50	.70	.19
Team Card			
Red Schoendienst MG			
(Checklist back)			
☐ 582 Mike Kekich	.30	.14	.04
☐ 583 Tommy Helms	.30	.14	.04
☐ 584 Stan Wall	.30	.14	.04
☐ 585 Joe Torre	.75	.35	.09
☐ 586 Ron Schueler	.30	.14	.04
☐ 587 Leo Cardenas	.30	.14	.04
☐ 588 Kevin Kobel	.30	.14	.04
☐ 589 Rookie Pitchers:	1.50	.70	.19
Santo Alcala			
Mike Flanagan			
Joe Pactwa			
Pablo Torrealba			
☐ 590 Rookie Outfielders:	1.00	.45	.12
Henry Cruz			
Chet Lemon			
Ellis Valentine			
Terry Whitfield			
☐ 591 Rookie Pitchers	.50	.23	.06
Steve Grilli			
Craig Mitchell			
Jose Sosa			
George Throop			
☐ 592 Rookie Infielders:	6.00	2.70	.75
Willie Randolph			
Dave McKay			
Jerry Royster			
Roy Staiger			
☐ 593 Rookie Pitchers	.50	.23	.06
Larry Anderson			
Ken Crosby			
Mark Littell			
Butch Metzger			
☐ 594 Rookie Catchers/OF	.50	.23	.06
Andy Merchant			
Ed Ott			

Royle Stillman			
Jerry White			
☐ 595 Rookie Pitchers	.50	.23	.06
Art DeFillipis			
Randy Lerch			
Sid Monge			
Steve Barr			
☐ 596 Rookie Infielders	.50	.23	.06
Craig Reynolds			
Lamar Johnson			
Johnnie LeMaster			
Jerry Manuel			
☐ 597 Rookie Pitchers	.50	.23	.06
Don Aase			
Jack Kucek			
Frank LaCorte			
Mike Pazik			
☐ 598 Rookie Outfielders	.50	.23	.06
Hector Cruz			
Jamie Quirk			
Jerry Turner			
Joe Wallis			
☐ 599 Rookie Pitchers	6.00	2.70	.75
Rob Dressler			
Ron Guidry			
Bob McClure			
Pat Zachry			
☐ 600 Tom Seaver	7.50	3.40	.95
☐ 601 Ken Rudolph	.30	.14	.04
☐ 602 Doug Konieczny	.30	.14	.04
☐ 603 Jim Holt	.30	.14	.04
☐ 604 Joe Lovitto	.30	.14	.04
☐ 605 Al Downing	.30	.14	.04
☐ 606 Milwaukee Brewers	1.50	.70	.19
Team Card			
Alex Grammas MG			
(Checklist back)			
☐ 607 Rich Hinton	.30	.14	.04
☐ 608 Vic Correll	.30	.14	.04
☐ 609 Fred Norman	.30	.14	.04
☐ 610 Greg Luzinski	.75	.35	.09
☐ 611 Rich Folkers	.30	.14	.04
☐ 612 Joe Lahoud	.30	.14	.04
☐ 613 Tim Johnson	.30	.14	.04
☐ 614 Fernando Arroyo	.30	.14	.04
☐ 615 Mike Cubbage	.30	.14	.04
☐ 616 Buck Martinez	.30	.14	.04
☐ 617 Darold Knowles	.30	.14	.04
☐ 618 Jack Brohamer	.30	.14	.04
☐ 619 Bill Butler	.30	.14	.04
☐ 620 Al Oliver	.75	.35	.09
☐ 621 Tom Hall	.30	.14	.04
☐ 622 Rick Auerbach	.30	.14	.04
☐ 623 Bob Allietta	.30	.14	.04
☐ 624 Tony Taylor	.50	.23	.06
☐ 625 J.R. Richard	.50	.23	.06
☐ 626 Bob Sheldon	.30	.14	.04
☐ 627 Bill Plummer	.30	.14	.04
☐ 628 John D'Acquisto	.30	.14	.04
☐ 629 Sandy Alomar	.30	.14	.04
☐ 630 Chris Speier	.30	.14	.04
☐ 631 Atlanta Braves	1.50	.70	.19
Team Card			
Dave Bristol MG			
(Checklist back)			
☐ 632 Rogelio Moret	.30	.14	.04
☐ 633 John Stearns	.50	.23	.06
☐ 634 Larry Christenson	.30	.14	.04
☐ 635 Jim Fregosi	.50	.23	.06
☐ 636 Joe Decker	.30	.14	.04
☐ 637 Bruce Bochte	.30	.14	.04
☐ 638 Doyle Alexander	.50	.23	.06
☐ 639 Fred Kendall	.30	.14	.04
☐ 640 Bill Madlock	.75	.35	.09
☐ 641 Tom Paciorek	.50	.23	.06
☐ 642 Dennis Blair	.30	.14	.04
☐ 643 Checklist 529-660	1.50	.70	.19
☐ 644 Tom Bradley	.30	.14	.04
☐ 645 Darrell Porter	.50	.23	.06
☐ 646 John Lowenstein	.30	.14	.04
☐ 647 Ramon Hernandez	.30	.14	.04
☐ 648 Al Cowens	.30	.14	.04
☐ 649 Dave Roberts	.30	.14	.04
☐ 650 Thurman Munson	4.00	1.80	.50
☐ 651 John Odom	.30	.14	.04
☐ 652 Ed Armbrister	.30	.14	.04
☐ 653 Mike Norris	.50	.23	.06
☐ 654 Doug Griffin	.30	.14	.04
☐ 655 Mike Vail	.30	.14	.04
☐ 656 Chicago White Sox	1.50	.70	.19
Team Card			
Chuck Tanner MG			
(Checklist back)			
☐ 657 Roy Smalley	.50	.23	.06
☐ 658 Jerry Johnson	.30	.14	.04
☐ 659 Ben Oglivie	.50	.23	.06
☐ 660 Dave Lopes	1.00	.45	.12

1977 O-Pee-Chee

The 1977 O-Pee-Chee set of 264 standard-size cards is not only much smaller numerically than its American counterpart, but also contains many different poses and is loaded with players from the two Canadian teams, including many players from the inaugural year of the Blue Jays and many single cards of players who were on multiplayer rookie cards. On a white background, the fronts feature

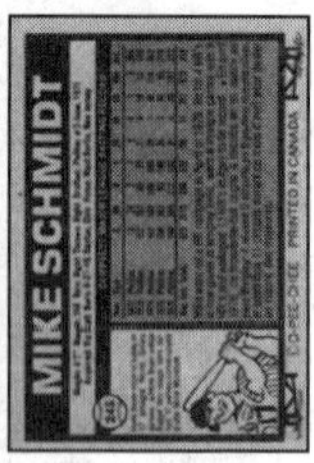

color player photos with thin black borders. The player's name and position, a facsimile autograph, and the team name also appear on the front. The horizontal backs carry player biography and statistics in French and English. The numbering of this set is different than the U.S. issue, the backs have different colors and the words "O-Pee-Chee Printed in Canada" are printed on the back.

	NRMT	VG-E	GOOD
COMPLETE SET (264)	300.00	135.00	38.00
COMMON CARD (1-264)	.25	.11	.03
☐ 1 Batting Leaders	7.50	3.40	.95
George Brett			
Bill Madlock			
☐ 2 Home Run Leaders	2.00	.90	.25
Graig Nettles			
Mike Schmidt			
☐ 3 RBI Leaders	.50	.23	.06
Lee May			
George Foster			
☐ 4 Stolen Base Leaders	.50	.23	.06
Bill North			
Dave Lopes			
☐ 5 Victory Leaders	.75	.35	.09
Jim Palmer			
Randy Jones			
☐ 6 Strikeout Leaders	15.00	6.75	1.85
Nolan Ryan			
Tom Seaver			
☐ 7 ERA Leaders	.50	.23	.06
Mark Fidrych			
John Denny			
☐ 8 Leading Firemen	.50	.23	.06
Bill Campbell			
Rawly Eastwick			
☐ 9 Mike Jorgensen	.35	.16	.04
☐ 10 Jim Hunter	4.00	1.80	.50
☐ 11 Ken Griffey	2.00	.90	.25
☐ 12 Bill Campbell	.25	.11	.03
☐ 13 Otto Velez	.50	.23	.06
☐ 14 Milt May	.25	.11	.03
☐ 15 Dennis Eckersley	6.00	2.70	.75
☐ 16 John Mayberry	.50	.23	.06
☐ 17 Larry Bowa	.50	.23	.06
☐ 18 Don Carrithers	.35	.16	.04
☐ 19 Ken Singleton	.35	.16	.04
☐ 20 Bill Stein	.25	.11	.03
☐ 21 Ken Brett	.25	.11	.03
☐ 22 Gary Woods	.50	.23	.06
☐ 23 Steve Swisher	.25	.11	.03
☐ 24 Don Sutton	2.50	1.10	.30
☐ 25 Willie Stargell	3.50	1.55	.45
☐ 26 Jerry Koosman	.35	.16	.04
☐ 27 Del Unser	.35	.16	.04
☐ 28 Bob Grich	.35	.16	.04
☐ 29 Jim Slaton	.25	.11	.03
☐ 30 Thurman Munson	5.00	2.20	.60
☐ 31 Dan Driessen	.25	.11	.03
☐ 32 Tom Bruno	.50	.23	.06
☐ 33 Larry Hisle	.35	.16	.04
☐ 34 Phil Garner	.35	.16	.04
☐ 35 Mike Hargrove	.35	.16	.04
☐ 36 Jackie Brown	.35	.16	.04
☐ 37 Carl Yastrzemski	5.00	2.20	.60
☐ 38 Dave Roberts	.25	.11	.03
☐ 39 Ray Fosse	.25	.11	.03
☐ 40 Dave McKay	.50	.23	.06
☐ 41 Paul Splittorff	.25	.11	.03
☐ 42 Garry Maddox	.25	.11	.03
☐ 43 Phil Niekro	3.00	1.35	.35
☐ 44 Roger Metzger	.25	.11	.03
☐ 45 Gary Carter	5.00	2.20	.60
☐ 46 Jim Spencer	.25	.11	.03
☐ 47 Ross Grimsley	.25	.11	.03
☐ 48 Bob Bailor	.50	.23	.06
☐ 49 Chris Chambliss	.35	.16	.04
☐ 50 Will McEnaney	.35	.16	.04
☐ 51 Lou Brock	5.00	2.20	.60
☐ 52 Rollie Fingers	3.50	1.55	.45
☐ 53 Chris Speier	.25	.11	.03
☐ 54 Bombo Rivera	.35	.16	.04
☐ 55 Pete Broberg	.25	.11	.03
☐ 56 Bill Madlock	1.00	.45	.12
☐ 57 Rick Rhoden	.25	.11	.03
☐ 58 Blue Jays Coaches	.50	.23	.06
Don Leppert			
Bob Miller			
Jackie Moore			
Harry Warner			
☐ 59 John Candelaria	.35	.16	.04
☐ 60 Ed Kranepool	.25	.11	.03
☐ 61 Dave LaRoche	.25	.11	.03

Card			
☐ 62 Jim Rice	5.00	2.20	.60
☐ 63 Don Stanhouse	.35	.16	.04
☐ 64 Jason Thompson	.35	.16	.04
☐ 65 Nolan Ryan	50.00	22.00	6.25
☐ 66 Tom Poquette	.25	.11	.03
☐ 67 Leon Hooten	.50	.23	.06
☐ 68 Bob Boone	.25	.11	.03
☐ 69 Mickey Rivers	.35	.16	.04
☐ 70 Gary Nolan	.25	.11	.03
☐ 71 Sixto Lezcano	.25	.11	.03
☐ 72 Larry Parrish	.50	.23	.06
☐ 73 Dave Goltz	.25	.11	.03
☐ 74 Bert Campaneris	.35	.16	.04
☐ 75 Vida Blue	.35	.16	.04
☐ 76 Rick Cerone	.50	.23	.06
☐ 77 Ralph Garr	.35	.16	.04
☐ 78 Ken Forsch	.25	.11	.03
☐ 79 Willie Montanez	.25	.11	.03
☐ 80 Jim Palmer	5.00	2.20	.60
☐ 81 Jerry White	.50	.23	.06
☐ 82 Gene Tenace	.35	.16	.04
☐ 83 Bobby Murcer	.35	.16	.04
☐ 84 Garry Templeton	1.25	.55	.16
☐ 85 Bill Singer	.50	.23	.06
☐ 86 Buddy Bell	.35	.16	.04
☐ 87 Luis Tiant	.50	.23	.06
☐ 88 Rusty Staub	.50	.23	.06
☐ 89 Sparky Lyle	.35	.16	.04
☐ 90 Jose Morales	.35	.16	.04
☐ 91 Dennis Leonard	.25	.11	.03
☐ 92 Tommy Smith	.25	.11	.03
☐ 93 Steve Carlton	5.00	2.20	.60
☐ 94 John Scott	.50	.23	.06
☐ 95 Bill Bonham	.25	.11	.03
☐ 96 Dave Lopes	.35	.16	.04
☐ 97 Jerry Reuss	.35	.16	.04
☐ 98 Dave Kingman	.50	.23	.06
☐ 99 Dan Warthen	.35	.16	.04
☐ 100 Johnny Bench	7.50	3.40	.95
☐ 101 Bert Blyleven	2.00	.90	.25
☐ 102 Cecil Cooper	.50	.23	.06
☐ 103 Mike Willis	.50	.23	.06
☐ 104 Dan Ford	.25	.11	.03
☐ 105 Frank Tanana	.50	.23	.06
☐ 106 Bill North	.25	.11	.03
☐ 107 Joe Ferguson	.25	.11	.03
☐ 108 Dick Williams MG	.50	.23	.06
☐ 109 John Denny	.25	.11	.03
☐ 110 Willie Randolph	3.00	1.35	.35
☐ 111 Reggie Cleveland	.35	.16	.04
☐ 112 Doug Howard	.50	.23	.06
☐ 113 Randy Jones	.25	.11	.03
☐ 114 Rico Carty	.50	.23	.06
☐ 115 Mark Fidrych	7.50	3.40	.95
☐ 116 Darrell Porter	.35	.16	.04
☐ 117 Wayne Garrett	.35	.16	.04
☐ 118 Greg Luzinski	.50	.23	.06
☐ 119 Jim Barr	.25	.11	.03
☐ 120 George Foster	1.00	.45	.12
☐ 121 Phil Roof	.50	.23	.06
☐ 122 Bucky Dent	.35	.16	.04
☐ 123 Steve Braun	.25	.11	.03
☐ 124 Checklist 1-132	1.25	.55	.16
☐ 125 Lee May	.35	.16	.04
☐ 126 Woodie Fryman	.35	.16	.04
☐ 127 Jose Cardenal	.25	.11	.03
☐ 128 Doug Rau	.25	.11	.03
☐ 129 Rennie Stennett	.25	.11	.03
☐ 130 Pete Vuckovich	.50	.23	.06
☐ 131 Cesar Cedeno	.35	.16	.04
☐ 132 Jon Matlack	.25	.11	.03
☐ 133 Don Baylor	2.00	.90	.25
☐ 134 Darrel Chaney	.25	.11	.03
☐ 135 Tony Perez	2.50	1.10	.30
☐ 136 Aurelio Rodriguez	.25	.11	.03
☐ 137 Carlton Fisk	7.50	3.40	.95
☐ 138 Wayne Garland	.25	.11	.03
☐ 139 Dave Hilton	.50	.23	.06
☐ 140 Rawly Eastwick	.25	.11	.03
☐ 141 Amos Otis	.35	.16	.04
☐ 142 Tug McGraw	.35	.16	.04
☐ 143 Rod Carew	7.50	3.40	.95
☐ 144 Mike Torrez	.35	.16	.04
☐ 145 Sal Bando	.25	.11	.03
☐ 146 Dock Ellis	.25	.11	.03
☐ 147 Jose Cruz	.35	.16	.04
☐ 148 Alan Ashby	.50	.23	.06
☐ 149 Gaylord Perry	3.00	1.35	.35
☐ 150 Keith Hernandez	1.50	.70	.19
☐ 151 Dave Pagan	.25	.11	.03
☐ 152 Richie Zisk	.25	.11	.03
☐ 153 Steve Rogers	.50	.23	.06
☐ 154 Mark Belanger	.25	.11	.03
☐ 155 Andy Messersmith	.35	.16	.04
☐ 156 Dave Winfield	20.00	9.00	2.50
☐ 157 Chuck Hartenstein	.50	.23	.06
☐ 158 Manny Trillo	.25	.11	.03
☐ 159 Steve Yeager	.25	.11	.03
☐ 160 Cesar Geronimo	.25	.11	.03
☐ 161 Jim Rooker	.25	.11	.03
☐ 162 Tim Foli	.35	.16	.04
☐ 163 Fred Lynn	1.50	.70	.19
☐ 164 Ed Figueroa	.25	.11	.03
☐ 165 Johnny Grubb	.25	.11	.03
☐ 166 Pedro Garcia	.50	.23	.06
☐ 167 Ron LeFlore	.35	.16	.04
☐ 168 Rich Hebner	.25	.11	.03
☐ 169 Larry Herndon	.25	.11	.03
☐ 170 George Brett	40.00	18.00	5.00
☐ 171 Joe Kerrigan	.35	.16	.04
☐ 172 Bud Harrelson	.25	.11	.03
☐ 173 Bobby Bonds	1.50	.70	.19
☐ 174 Bill Travers	.25	.11	.03
☐ 175 John Lowenstein	.50	.23	.06
☐ 176 Butch Wynegar	.25	.11	.03
☐ 177 Pete Falcone	.25	.11	.03
☐ 178 Claudell Washington	.35	.16	.04
☐ 179 Checklist 133-264	1.25	.55	.16
☐ 180 Dave Cash	.35	.16	.04
☐ 181 Fred Norman	.25	.11	.03
☐ 182 Roy White	.25	.11	.03
☐ 183 Marty Perez	.25	.11	.03
☐ 184 Jesse Jefferson	.50	.23	.06
☐ 185 Jim Sundberg	.25	.11	.03
☐ 186 Dan Meyer	.25	.11	.03
☐ 187 Fergie Jenkins	3.00	1.35	.35
☐ 188 Tom Veryzer	.25	.11	.03
☐ 189 Dennis Blair	.35	.16	.04
☐ 190 Rick Manning	.25	.11	.03
☐ 191 Doug Bird	.25	.11	.03
☐ 192 Al Bumbry	.25	.11	.03
☐ 193 Dave Roberts	.25	.11	.03
☐ 194 Larry Christenson	.25	.11	.03
☐ 195 Chet Lemon	.35	.16	.04
☐ 196 Ted Simmons	1.00	.45	.12
☐ 197 Ray Burris	.25	.11	.03
☐ 198 Expos Coaches	.50	.23	.06
Jim Brewer			
Billy Gardner			
Mickey Vernon			
Ozzie Virgil			
☐ 199 Ron Cey	.50	.23	.06
☐ 200 Reggie Jackson	10.00	4.50	1.25
☐ 201 Pat Zachry	.25	.11	.03
☐ 202 Doug Ault	.50	.23	.06
☐ 203 Al Oliver	.50	.23	.06
☐ 204 Robin Yount	20.00	9.00	2.50
☐ 205 Tom Seaver	10.00	4.50	1.25
☐ 206 Joe Rudi	.25	.11	.03
☐ 207 Barry Foote	.35	.16	.04
☐ 208 Toby Harrah	.35	.16	.04
☐ 209 Jeff Burroughs	.25	.11	.03
☐ 210 George Scott	.35	.16	.04
☐ 211 Jim Mason	.50	.23	.06
☐ 212 Vern Ruhle	.25	.11	.03
☐ 213 Fred Kendall	.25	.11	.03
☐ 214 Rick Reuschel	.35	.16	.04
☐ 215 Hal McRae	.50	.23	.06
☐ 216 Chip Lang	.35	.16	.04
☐ 217 Graig Nettles	.25	.11	.03
☐ 218 George Hendrick	.35	.16	.04
☐ 219 Glenn Abbott	.25	.11	.03
☐ 220 Joe Morgan	6.00	2.70	.75
☐ 221 Sam Ewing	.50	.23	.06
☐ 222 George Medich	.25	.11	.03
☐ 223 Reggie Smith	.35	.16	.04
☐ 224 Dave Hamilton	.25	.11	.03
☐ 225 Pepe Frias	.35	.16	.04
☐ 226 Jay Johnstone	.25	.11	.03
☐ 227 J.R. Richard	.35	.16	.04
☐ 228 Doug DeCinces	.35	.16	.04
☐ 229 Dave Lemanczyk	.50	.23	.06
☐ 230 Rick Monday	.25	.11	.03
☐ 231 Manny Sanguillen	.25	.11	.03
☐ 232 John Montefusco	.25	.11	.03
☐ 233 Duane Kuiper	.25	.11	.03
☐ 234 Ellis Valentine	.35	.16	.04
☐ 235 Dick Tidrow	.25	.11	.03
☐ 236 Ben Oglivie	.35	.16	.04
☐ 237 Rick Burleson	.25	.11	.03
☐ 238 Roy Hartsfield MG	.50	.23	.06
☐ 239 Lyman Bostock	.35	.16	.04
☐ 240 Pete Rose	15.00	6.75	1.85
☐ 241 Mike Ivie	.25	.11	.03
☐ 242 Dave Parker	3.00	1.35	.35
☐ 243 Bill Greif	.35	.16	.04
☐ 244 Freddie Patek	.25	.11	.03
☐ 245 Mike Schmidt	20.00	9.00	2.50
☐ 246 Brian Downing	.35	.16	.04
☐ 247 Steve Hargan	.50	.23	.06
☐ 248 Dave Collins	.25	.11	.03
☐ 249 Felix Millan	.25	.11	.03
☐ 250 Don Gullett	.35	.16	.04
☐ 251 Jerry Royster	.25	.11	.03
☐ 252 Earl Williams	.50	.23	.06
☐ 253 Frank Duffy	.25	.11	.03
☐ 254 Tippy Martinez	.25	.11	.03
☐ 255 Steve Garvey	3.00	1.35	.35
☐ 256 Alvis Woods	.50	.23	.06
☐ 257 John Hiller	.35	.16	.04
☐ 258 Dave Concepcion	1.50	.70	.19
☐ 259 Dwight Evans	2.50	1.10	.30
☐ 260 Pete MacKanin	.35	.16	.04
☐ 261 George Brett RB	15.00	6.75	1.85
Most Consec. Games			
Three Or More Hits			
☐ 262 Minnie Minoso RB	.50	.23	.06
Oldest Player To			
Hit Safely			
☐ 263 Jose Morales RB	.50	.23	.06
Most Pinch-hits, Season			
☐ 264 Nolan Ryan RB	20.00	9.00	2.50
Most Seasons 300			
Or More Strikeouts			

1978 O-Pee-Chee

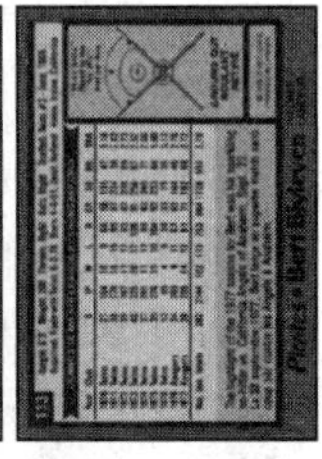

The 242 standard-size cards comprising the 1978 O-Pee-Chee set differ from the cards of the 1978 Topps set by having a higher ratio of cards of players from the two Canadian teams, a practice begun by O-Pee-Chee in 1977 and continued to 1988. The fronts feature white-bordered color player photos, each framed by a colored line. The player's name appears in black lettering at the right of lower white margin. His team name appears in colored cursive lettering, interrupting the framing line at the bottom left of the photo; his position appears within a white baseball icon in an upper corner. The tan and brown horizontal backs carry the player's name, team and position in the brown border at the bottom. Biography, major league statistics, career highlights in both French and English and a bilingual result of an "at bat" in the "Play Ball" game also appear. The asterisked cards have an extra line on the front indicating team change. Double-printed (DP) cards are also noted below. The key card in this set is Eddie Murray.

	NRMT	VG-E	GOOD
COMPLETE SET (242)	225.00	100.00	28.00
COMMON CARD (1-242)	.20	.09	.03
COMMON CARD DP (1-242)	.10	.05	.01
☐ 1 Batting Leaders	1.50	.70	.19
Dave Parker			
Rod Carew			
☐ 2 Home Run Leaders DP	.40	.18	.05
George Foster			
Jim Rice			
☐ 3 RBI Leaders	.40	.18	.05
George Foster			
Larry Hisle			
☐ 4 Stolen Base Leaders DP	.30	.14	.04
Frank Taveras			
Freddie Patek			
☐ 5 Victory Leaders	2.00	.90	.25
Steve Carlton			
Dave Goltz			
Dennis Leonard			
Jim Palmer			
☐ 6 Strikeout Leaders DP	5.00	2.20	.60
Phil Niekro			
Nolan Ryan			
☐ 7 ERA Leaders DP	.30	.14	.04
John Candelaria			
Frank Tanana			
☐ 8 Firemen Leaders	.75	.35	.09
Rollie Fingers			
Bill Campbell			
☐ 9 Steve Rogers DP	.20	.09	.03
☐ 10 Graig Nettles DP	.30	.14	.04
☐ 11 Doug Capilla	.20	.09	.03
☐ 12 George Scott	.30	.14	.04
☐ 13 Gary Woods	.20	.09	.03
☐ 14 Tom Veryzer	.40	.18	.05
Now with Cleveland as of 12-9-77			
☐ 15 Wayne Garland	.20	.09	.03
☐ 16 Amos Otis	.30	.14	.04
☐ 17 Larry Christenson	.20	.09	.03
☐ 18 Dave Cash	.30	.14	.04
☐ 19 Jim Barr	.20	.09	.03
☐ 20 Ruppert Jones	.20	.09	.03
☐ 21 Eric Soderholm	.20	.09	.03
☐ 22 Jesse Jefferson	.20	.09	.03
☐ 23 Jerry Morales	.20	.09	.03
☐ 24 Doug Rau	.20	.09	.03
☐ 25 Rennie Stennett	.20	.09	.03
☐ 26 Lee Mazzilli	.30	.14	.04
☐ 27 Dick Williams MG	.30	.14	.04
☐ 28 Joe Rudi	.30	.14	.04
☐ 29 Robin Yount	15.00	6.75	1.85
☐ 30 Don Gullett DP	.20	.09	.03
☐ 31 Roy Howell DP	.10	.05	.01
☐ 32 Cesar Geronimo	.20	.09	.03
☐ 33 Rick Langford DP	.10	.05	.01
☐ 34 Dan Ford	.20	.09	.03
☐ 35 Gene Tenace	.30	.14	.04
☐ 36 Santo Alcala	.30	.14	.04
☐ 37 Rick Burleson	.20	.09	.03
☐ 38 Dave Rozema	.20	.09	.03
☐ 39 Duane Kuiper	.20	.09	.03
☐ 40 Ron Fairly	.40	.18	.05
Now with California as of 12-8-77			
☐ 41 Dennis Leonard	.30	.14	.04
☐ 42 Greg Luzinski	.40	.18	.05
☐ 43 Willie Montanez	.40	.18	.05
Now with N.Y. Mets as of 12-8-77			
☐ 44 Enos Cabell	.20	.09	.03
☐ 45 Ellis Valentine	.30	.14	.04
☐ 46 Steve Stone	.30	.14	.04
☐ 47 Lee May DP	.30	.14	.04
☐ 48 Roy White	.30	.14	.04
☐ 49 Jerry Garvin	.20	.09	.03
☐ 50 Johnny Bench	5.00	2.20	.60
☐ 51 Garry Templeton	.30	.14	.04
☐ 52 Doyle Alexander	.30	.14	.04
☐ 53 Steve Henderson	.20	.09	.03
☐ 54 Stan Bahnsen	.20	.09	.03
☐ 55 Dan Meyer	.20	.09	.03
☐ 56 Rick Reuschel	.30	.14	.04
☐ 57 Reggie Smith	.30	.14	.04
☐ 58 Blue Jays Team DP	.40	.18	.05
☐ 59 John Montefusco	.20	.09	.03
☐ 60 Dave Parker	1.50	.70	.19
☐ 61 Jim Bibby	.20	.09	.03
☐ 62 Fred Lynn	1.00	.45	.12
☐ 63 Jose Morales	.20	.09	.03
☐ 64 Aurelio Rodriguez	.20	.09	.03
☐ 65 Frank Tanana	.30	.14	.04
☐ 66 Darrell Porter	.30	.14	.04
☐ 67 Otto Velez	.20	.09	.03
☐ 68 Larry Bowa	.40	.18	.05
☐ 69 Jim Hunter	2.50	1.10	.30
☐ 70 George Foster	1.00	.45	.12
☐ 71 Cecil Cooper DP	.30	.14	.04
☐ 72 Gary Alexander DP	.10	.05	.01
☐ 73 Paul Thormodsgard	.20	.09	.03
☐ 74 Toby Harrah	.30	.14	.04
☐ 75 Mitchell Page	.20	.09	.03
☐ 76 Alan Ashby	.20	.09	.03
☐ 77 Jorge Orta	.20	.09	.03
☐ 78 Dave Winfield	12.50	5.50	1.55
☐ 79 Andy Messersmith	.40	.18	.05
Now with N.Y. Yankees as of 12-8-77			
☐ 80 Ken Singleton	.30	.14	.04
☐ 81 Will McEnaney	.30	.14	.04
☐ 82 Lou Piniella	.40	.18	.05
☐ 83 Bob Forsch	.20	.09	.03
☐ 84 Dan Driessen	.20	.09	.03
☐ 85 Dave Lemanczyk	.20	.09	.03
☐ 86 Paul Dade	.20	.09	.03
☐ 87 Bill Campbell	.20	.09	.03
☐ 88 Ron LeFlore	.30	.14	.04
☐ 89 Bill Madlock	.40	.18	.05
☐ 90 Tony Perez DP	1.25	.55	.16
☐ 91 Freddie Patek	.20	.09	.03
☐ 92 Glenn Abbott	.20	.09	.03
☐ 93 Garry Maddox	.20	.09	.03
☐ 94 Steve Staggs	.20	.09	.03
☐ 95 Bobby Murcer	.30	.14	.04
☐ 96 Don Sutton	2.00	.90	.25
☐ 97 Al Oliver	.75	.35	.09
Now with Texas Rangers as of 12-8-77			
☐ 98 Jon Matlack	.30	.14	.04
Now with Texas Rangers as of 12-8-77			
☐ 99 Sam Mejias	.30	.14	.04
☐ 100 Pete Rose DP	5.00	2.20	.60
☐ 101 Randy Jones	.20	.09	.03
☐ 102 Sixto Lezcano	.20	.09	.03
☐ 103 Jim Clancy DP	.10	.05	.01
☐ 104 Butch Wynegar	.20	.09	.03
☐ 105 Nolan Ryan	40.00	18.00	5.00
☐ 106 Wayne Gross	.20	.09	.03
☐ 107 Bob Watson	.30	.14	.04
☐ 108 Joe Kerrigan	.30	.14	.04
Now with Baltimore as of 12-8-77			
☐ 109 Keith Hernandez	1.00	.45	.12
☐ 110 Reggie Jackson	8.00	3.60	1.00
☐ 111 Denny Doyle	.20	.09	.03
☐ 112 Sam Ewing	.30	.14	.04
☐ 113 Bert Blyleven	.50	.23	.06
Now with Pittsburgh as of 12-8-77			
☐ 114 Andre Thornton	.30	.14	.04
☐ 115 Milt May	.20	.09	.03
☐ 116 Jim Colborn	.20	.09	.03
☐ 117 Warren Cromartie	.40	.18	.05
☐ 118 Ted Sizemore	.20	.09	.03
☐ 119 Checklist 1-121	1.25	.55	.16
☐ 120 Tom Seaver	4.00	1.80	.50
☐ 121 Luis Gomez	.20	.09	.03
☐ 122 Jim Spencer	.30	.14	.04
Now with N.Y. Yankees as of 12-12-77			
☐ 123 Leroy Stanton	.20	.09	.03
☐ 124 Luis Tiant	.40	.18	.05
☐ 125 Mark Belanger	.30	.14	.04
☐ 126 Jackie Brown	.20	.09	.03
☐ 127 Bill Buckner	.40	.18	.05
☐ 128 Bill Robinson	.30	.14	.04
☐ 129 Rick Cerone	.30	.14	.04
☐ 130 Ron Cey	.40	.18	.05
☐ 131 Jose Cruz	.30	.14	.04
☐ 132 Len Randle DP	.10	.05	.01
☐ 133 Bob Grich	.30	.14	.04
☐ 134 Jeff Burroughs	.30	.14	.04
☐ 135 Gary Carter	2.50	1.10	.30
☐ 136 Milt Wilcox	.20	.09	.03
☐ 137 Carl Yastrzemski	3.00	1.35	.35
☐ 138 Dennis Eckersley	4.00	1.80	.50
☐ 139 Tim Nordbrook	.20	.09	.03
☐ 140 Ken Griffey	1.00	.45	.12
☐ 141 Bob Boone	.30	.14	.04
☐ 142 Dave Goltz DP	.10	.05	.01

☐ 143 Al Cowens .20 .09 .03
☐ 144 Bill Atkinson .20 .09 .03
☐ 145 Chris Chambliss .30 .14 .04
☐ 146 Jim Slaton .30 .14 .04
Now with Detroit Tigers as of 12-9-77
☐ 147 Bill Stein .20 .09 .03
☐ 148 Bob Bailor .20 .09 .03
☐ 149 J.R. Richard .30 .14 .04
☐ 150 Ted Simmons .30 .14 .04
☐ 151 Rick Manning .20 .09 .03
☐ 152 Lerrin LaGrow .20 .09 .03
☐ 153 Larry Parrish .40 .18 .05
☐ 154 Eddie Murray 125.00 55.00 15.50
☐ 155 Phil Niekro 2.50 1.10 .30
☐ 156 Bake McBride .30 .14 .04
☐ 157 Pete Vuckovich .30 .14 .04
☐ 158 Ivan DeJesus .20 .09 .03
☐ 159 Rick Rhoden .20 .09 .03
☐ 160 Joe Morgan 2.50 1.10 .30
☐ 161 Ed Ott .20 .09 .03
☐ 162 Don Stanhouse .30 .14 .04
☐ 163 Jim Rice 2.00 .90 .25
☐ 164 Bucky Dent .30 .14 .04
☐ 165 Jim Kern .20 .09 .03
☐ 166 Doug Rader .20 .09 .03
☐ 167 Steve Kemp .30 .14 .04
☐ 168 John Mayberry .30 .14 .04
☐ 169 Tim Foli .30 .14 .04
Now with N.Y. Mets as of 12-7-77
☐ 170 Steve Carlton 3.00 1.35 .35
☐ 171 Pepe Frias .30 .14 .04
☐ 172 Pat Zachry .20 .09 .03
☐ 173 Don Baylor .75 .35 .09
☐ 174 Sal Bando DP .30 .14 .04
☐ 175 Alvis Woods .30 .14 .04
☐ 176 Mike Hargrove .40 .18 .05
☐ 177 Vida Blue .30 .14 .04
☐ 178 George Hendrick .30 .14 .04
☐ 179 Jim Palmer 2.50 1.10 .30
☐ 180 Andre Dawson 15.00 6.75 1.85
☐ 181 Paul Moskau .20 .09 .03
☐ 182 Mickey Rivers .40 .18 .05
☐ 183 Checklist 122-242 1.25 .55 .16
☐ 184 Jerry Johnson .30 .14 .04
☐ 185 Willie McCovey 2.50 1.10 .30
☐ 186 Enrique Romo .20 .09 .03
☐ 187 Butch Hobson .20 .09 .03
☐ 188 Rusty Staub .40 .18 .05
☐ 189 Wayne Twitchell .30 .14 .04
☐ 190 Steve Garvey 1.50 .70 .19
☐ 191 Rick Waits .20 .09 .03
☐ 192 Doug DeCinces .30 .14 .04
☐ 193 Tom Murphy .20 .09 .03
☐ 194 Rich Hebner .30 .14 .04
☐ 195 Ralph Garr .30 .14 .04
☐ 196 Bruce Sutter .40 .18 .05
☐ 197 Tom Poquette .20 .09 .03
☐ 198 Wayne Garrett .20 .09 .03
☐ 199 Pedro Borbon .30 .14 .04
☐ 200 Thurman Munson 3.00 1.35 .35
☐ 201 Rollie Fingers 2.50 1.10 .30
☐ 202 Doug Ault .20 .09 .03
☐ 203 Phil Garner DP .30 .14 .04
☐ 204 Lou Brock 2.50 1.10 .30
☐ 205 Ed Kranepool .20 .09 .03
☐ 206 Bobby Bonds .50 .23 .06
Now with White Sox as of 12-15-77
☐ 207 Expos Team DP .40 .18 .05
☐ 208 Bump Wills .20 .09 .03
☐ 209 Gary Matthews .30 .14 .04
☐ 210 Carlton Fisk 4.00 1.80 .50
☐ 211 Jeff Byrd .30 .14 .04
☐ 212 Jason Thompson .20 .09 .03
☐ 213 Larvell Blanks .20 .09 .03
☐ 214 Sparky Lyle .30 .14 .04
☐ 215 George Brett 25.00 11.00 3.10
☐ 216 Del Unser .20 .09 .03
☐ 217 Manny Trillo .20 .09 .03
☐ 218 Roy Hartsfield MG .20 .09 .03
☐ 219 Carlos Lopez .40 .18 .05
Now with Baltimore as of 12-7-77
☐ 220 Dave Concepcion .50 .23 .06
☐ 221 John Candelaria .30 .14 .04
☐ 222 Dave Lopes .30 .14 .04
☐ 223 Tim Blackwell DP .30 .14 .04
Now with Chicago Cubs as of 2-1-78
☐ 224 Chet Lemon .30 .14 .04
☐ 225 Mike Schmidt 12.50 5.50 1.55
☐ 226 Cesar Cedeno .30 .14 .04
☐ 227 Mike Willis .20 .09 .03
☐ 228 Willie Randolph .50 .23 .06
☐ 229 Doug Bair .20 .09 .03
☐ 230 Rod Carew 2.50 1.10 .30
☐ 231 Mike Flanagan .30 .14 .04
☐ 232 Chris Speier .20 .09 .03
☐ 233 Don Aase .30 .14 .04
Now with California as of 12-8-77
☐ 234 Buddy Bell .30 .14 .04
☐ 235 Mark Fidrych 1.50 .70 .19
☐ 236 Lou Brock RB 2.00 .90 .25
Most Steals, Lifetime
☐ 237 Sparky Lyle RB .50 .23 .06
Most Games Pure
Relief, Lifetime
☐ 238 Willie McCovey RB 1.50 .70 .19
Most Times 2 HR's
in Inning, Lifetime
☐ 239 Brooks Robinson RB 2.00 .90 .25
Most Consecutive
Seasons with one club
☐ 240 Pete Rose RB 3.50 1.55 .45
Most Hits, Switch-
hitter, Lifetime
☐ 241 Nolan Ryan RB 15.00 6.75 1.85
Most games 10 or More
Strikeouts, Lifetime
☐ 242 Reggie Jackson RB 4.00 1.80 .50
Most Homers, One
World Series

1979 O-Pee-Chee

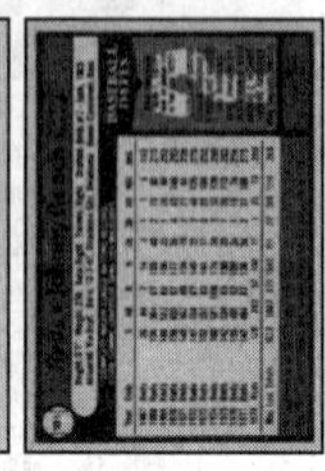

This set is an abridgement of the 1979 Topps set. The 374 standard-size cards comprising the 1979 O-Pee-Chee set differ from the cards of the 1979 Topps set by having a higher ratio of cards of players from the two Canadian teams, a practice begun by O-Pee-Chee in 1977 and continued to 1988. The 1979 O-Pee-Chee set was the largest (374) original baseball card set issued (up to that time) by O-Pee-Chee. The fronts feature white-bordered color player photos. The player's name, position, and team appear in colored lettering within the lower white margin. The green and white horizontal backs carry the player's name, team and position at the top. Biography, major league statistics, career highlights in both French and English and a bilingual trivia question and answer also appear. The asterisked cards have an extra line on the front indicating team change. Double-printed (DP) cards are also noted below. The fronts have an O-Pee-Chee logo in the lower left corner comparable to the Topps logo on the 1979 American Set. The cards are sequenced in the same order as the Topps cards; the O-Pee-Chee cards are in effect a compressed version of the Topps set. The key card in this set is Ozzie Smith.

	NRMT	VG-E	GOOD
COMPLETE SET (374)	200.00	90.00	25.00
COMMON CARD (1-374)	.20	.09	.03
COMMON CARD DP (1-374)	.10	.05	.01

☐ 1 Lee May .50 .23 .06
☐ 2 Dick Drago .20 .09 .03
☐ 3 Paul Dade .20 .09 .03
☐ 4 Ross Grimsley .20 .09 .03
☐ 5 Joe Morgan DP 1.00 .45 .12
☐ 6 Kevin Kobel .20 .09 .03
☐ 7 Terry Forster .20 .09 .03
☐ 8 Paul Molitor 20.00 9.00 2.50
☐ 9 Steve Carlton 2.50 1.10 .30
☐ 10 Dave Goltz .20 .09 .03
☐ 11 Dave Winfield 8.00 3.60 1.00
☐ 12 Dave Rozema .20 .09 .03
☐ 13 Ed Figueroa .20 .09 .03
☐ 14 Alan Ashby .35 .16 .04
Trade with Blue Jays 11-28-78
☐ 15 Dale Murphy 5.00 2.20 .60
☐ 16 Dennis Eckersley 2.00 .90 .25
☐ 17 Ron Blomberg .20 .09 .03
☐ 18 Wayne Twitchell .35 .16 .04
Free Agent as of 3-1-79
☐ 19 Al Hrabosky .20 .09 .03
☐ 20 Fred Norman .20 .09 .03
☐ 21 Steve Garvey DP .75 .35 .09
☐ 22 Willie Stargell 1.50 .70 .19
☐ 23 John Hale .20 .09 .03
☐ 24 Mickey Rivers .35 .16 .04
☐ 25 Jack Brohamer .20 .09 .03
☐ 26 Tom Underwood .20 .09 .03
☐ 27 Mark Belanger .35 .16 .04
☐ 28 Elliott Maddox .20 .09 .03
☐ 29 John Candelaria .35 .16 .04
☐ 30 Shane Rawley .20 .09 .03
☐ 31 Steve Yeager .20 .09 .03
☐ 32 Warren Cromartie .35 .16 .04
☐ 33 Jason Thompson .35 .16 .04
☐ 34 Roger Erickson .20 .09 .03
☐ 35 Gary Matthews .35 .16 .04
☐ 36 Pete Falcone .50 .23 .06
Traded 12-5-78
☐ 37 Dick Tidrow .20 .09 .03
☐ 38 Bob Boone .50 .23 .06
☐ 39 Jim Bibby .20 .09 .03
☐ 40 Len Barker .35 .16 .04
Trade with Rangers 10-3-78
☐ 41 Robin Yount 10.00 4.50 1.25
☐ 42 Sam Mejias .35 .16 .04
Traded 12-14-78
☐ 43 Ray Burris .20 .09 .03
☐ 44 Tom Seaver DP 2.00 .90 .25
☐ 45 Roy Howell .20 .09 .03
☐ 46 Jim Todd .35 .16 .04
Free Agent 3-1-79
☐ 47 Frank Duffy .20 .09 .03
☐ 48 Joel Youngblood .20 .09 .03
☐ 49 Vida Blue .35 .16 .04
☐ 50 Cliff Johnson .20 .09 .03
☐ 51 Nolan Ryan 30.00 13.50 3.70
☐ 52 Ozzie Smith 90.00 40.00 11.00
☐ 53 Jim Sundberg .20 .09 .03
☐ 54 Mike Paxton .20 .09 .03
☐ 55 Lou Whitaker 10.00 4.50 1.25
☐ 56 Dan Schatzeder .20 .09 .03
☐ 57 Rick Burleson .20 .09 .03
☐ 58 Doug Bair .20 .09 .03
☐ 59 Ted Martinez .20 .09 .03
☐ 60 Bob Watson .35 .16 .04
☐ 61 Jim Clancy .20 .09 .03
☐ 62 Rowland Office .20 .09 .03
☐ 63 Bobby Murcer .35 .16 .04
☐ 64 Don Gullett .35 .16 .04
☐ 65 Tom Paciorek .35 .16 .04
☐ 66 Rick Rhoden .20 .09 .03
☐ 67 Duane Kuiper .20 .09 .03
☐ 68 Bruce Boisclair .20 .09 .03
☐ 69 Manny Sarmiento .20 .09 .03
☐ 70 Wayne Cage .20 .09 .03
☐ 71 John Hiller .35 .16 .04
☐ 72 Rick Cerone .20 .09 .03
☐ 73 Dwight Evans .50 .23 .06
☐ 74 Buddy Solomon .20 .09 .03
☐ 75 Roy White .35 .16 .04
☐ 76 Mike Flanagan .50 .23 .06
☐ 77 Tom Johnson .20 .09 .03
☐ 78 Glenn Burke .20 .09 .03
☐ 79 Frank Taveras .20 .09 .03
☐ 80 Don Sutton .75 .35 .09
☐ 81 Leon Roberts .20 .09 .03
☐ 82 George Hendrick .35 .16 .04
☐ 83 Aurelio Rodriguez .20 .09 .03
☐ 84 Ron Reed .20 .09 .03
☐ 85 Alvis Woods .20 .09 .03
☐ 86 Jim Beattie DP .10 .05 .01
☐ 87 Larry Hisle .20 .09 .03
☐ 88 Mike Garman .20 .09 .03
☐ 89 Tim Johnson .20 .09 .03
☐ 90 Paul Splittorff .20 .09 .03
☐ 91 Darrel Chaney .20 .09 .03
☐ 92 Mike Torrez .20 .09 .03
☐ 93 Eric Soderholm .20 .09 .03
☐ 94 Ron Cey .35 .16 .04
☐ 95 Randy Jones .20 .09 .03
☐ 96 Bill Madlock .35 .16 .04
☐ 97 Steve Kemp DP .10 .05 .01
☐ 98 Bob Apodaca .20 .09 .03
☐ 99 Johnny Grubb .20 .09 .03
☐ 100 Larry Milbourne .20 .09 .03
☐ 101 Johnny Bench DP 2.00 .90 .25
☐ 102 Dave Lemanczyk .20 .09 .03
☐ 103 Reggie Cleveland .20 .09 .03
☐ 104 Larry Bowa .35 .16 .04
☐ 105 Denny Martinez 1.50 .70 .19
☐ 106 Bill Travers .20 .09 .03
☐ 107 Willie McCovey 2.00 .90 .25
☐ 108 Wilbur Wood .20 .09 .03
☐ 109 Dennis Leonard .35 .16 .04
☐ 110 Roy Smalley .35 .16 .04
☐ 111 Cesar Geronimo .20 .09 .03
☐ 112 Jesse Jefferson .20 .09 .03
☐ 113 Dave Revering .20 .09 .03
☐ 114 Rich Gossage .50 .23 .06
☐ 115 Steve Stone .50 .23 .06
Free Agent 11-25-78
☐ 116 Doug Flynn .20 .09 .03
☐ 117 Bob Forsch .20 .09 .03
☐ 118 Paul Mitchell .20 .09 .03
☐ 119 Toby Harrah .50 .23 .06
Traded 12-8-78
☐ 120 Steve Rogers .20 .09 .03
☐ 121 Checklist 1-125 DP .60 .25 .07
☐ 122 Balor Moore .20 .09 .03
☐ 123 Rick Reuschel .35 .16 .04
☐ 124 Jeff Burroughs .20 .09 .03
☐ 125 Willie Randolph .35 .16 .04
☐ 126 Bob Stinson .20 .09 .03
☐ 127 Rick Wise .20 .09 .03
☐ 128 Luis Gomez .35 .16 .04
☐ 129 Tommy John 1.00 .45 .12
Signed as Free Agent 11-22-78
☐ 130 Richie Zisk .20 .09 .03
☐ 131 Mario Guerrero .20 .09 .03
☐ 132 Oscar Gamble .35 .16 .04
Trade with Padres 10-25-78
☐ 133 Don Money .20 .09 .03
☐ 134 Joe Rudi .35 .16 .04
☐ 135 Woodie Fryman .20 .09 .03
☐ 136 Butch Hobson .20 .09 .03
☐ 137 Jim Colborn .20 .09 .03
☐ 138 Tom Grieve .35 .16 .04
Traded 12-5-78
☐ 139 Andy Messersmith .35 .16 .04
Free Agent 2-7-79
☐ 140 Andre Thornton .35 .16 .04
☐ 141 Ken Kravec .20 .09 .03
☐ 142 Bobby Bonds .75 .35 .09
Trade with Rangers 10-3-78
☐ 143 Jose Cruz .35 .16 .04
☐ 144 Dave Lopes .35 .16 .04
☐ 145 Jerry Garvin .20 .09 .03
☐ 146 Pepe Frias .20 .09 .03
☐ 147 Mitchell Page .20 .09 .03
☐ 148 Ted Sizemore .35 .16 .04
Traded 2-23-79
☐ 149 Rich Gale .20 .09 .03
☐ 150 Steve Ontiveros .20 .09 .03
☐ 151 Rod Carew 3.00 1.35 .35
Traded 2-5-79
☐ 152 Lary Sorensen DP .10 .05 .01
☐ 153 Willie Montanez .20 .09 .03
☐ 154 Floyd Bannister .35 .16 .04
Traded 12-8-78
☐ 155 Bert Blyleven .50 .23 .06
☐ 156 Ralph Garr .35 .16 .04
☐ 157 Thurman Munson 2.50 1.10 .30
☐ 158 Bob Robertson .35 .16 .04
Free Agent 3-1-79
☐ 159 Jon Matlack .20 .09 .03
☐ 160 Carl Yastrzemski 2.50 1.10 .30
☐ 161 Gaylord Perry 1.00 .45 .12
☐ 162 Mike Tyson .20 .09 .03
☐ 163 Cecil Cooper .35 .16 .04
☐ 164 Pedro Borbon .20 .09 .03
☐ 165 Art Howe DP .20 .09 .03
☐ 166 Joe Coleman .35 .16 .04
Free Agent 3-1-79
☐ 167 George Brett 20.00 9.00 2.50
☐ 168 Gary Alexander .20 .09 .03
☐ 169 Chet Lemon .35 .16 .04
☐ 170 Craig Swan .20 .09 .03
☐ 171 Chris Chambliss .35 .16 .04
☐ 172 John Montague .20 .09 .03
☐ 173 Ron Jackson .35 .16 .04
Traded 12-4-78
☐ 174 Jim Palmer 2.00 .90 .25
☐ 175 Willie Upshaw .50 .23 .06
☐ 176 Tug McGraw .35 .16 .04
☐ 177 Bill Buckner .35 .16 .04
☐ 178 Doug Rau .20 .09 .03
☐ 179 Andre Dawson 8.00 3.60 1.00
☐ 180 Jim Wright .20 .09 .03
☐ 181 Garry Templeton .35 .16 .04
☐ 182 Bill Bonham .20 .09 .03
☐ 183 Lee Mazzilli .20 .09 .03
☐ 184 Alan Trammell 12.00 5.50 1.50
☐ 185 Amos Otis .35 .16 .04
☐ 186 Tom Dixon .20 .09 .03
☐ 187 Mike Cubbage .20 .09 .03
☐ 188 Sparky Lyle .50 .23 .06
Traded 11-10-78
☐ 189 Juan Bernhardt .20 .09 .03
☐ 190 Bump Wills .50 .23 .06
(Texas Rangers)
☐ 191 Dave Kingman .50 .23 .06
☐ 192 Lamar Johnson .20 .09 .03
☐ 193 Lance Rautzhan .20 .09 .03
☐ 194 Ed Herrmann .20 .09 .03
☐ 195 Bill Campbell .20 .09 .03
☐ 196 Gorman Thomas .20 .09 .03
☐ 197 Paul Moskau .20 .09 .03
☐ 198 Dale Murray .20 .09 .03
☐ 199 John Mayberry .35 .16 .04
☐ 200 Phil Garner .35 .16 .04
☐ 201 Dan Ford .35 .16 .04
Traded 12-4-78
☐ 202 Gary Thomasson .35 .16 .04
Traded 2-15-79
☐ 203 Rollie Fingers 1.00 .45 .12
☐ 204 Al Oliver .50 .23 .06
☐ 205 Doug Ault .20 .09 .03
☐ 206 Scott McGregor .35 .16 .04
☐ 207 Dave Cash .20 .09 .03
☐ 208 Bill Plummer .20 .09 .03
☐ 209 Ivan DeJesus .20 .09 .03
☐ 210 Jim Rice 1.50 .70 .19
☐ 211 Ray Knight .35 .16 .04
☐ 212 Paul Hartzell .35 .16 .04
Traded 2-5-79
☐ 213 Tim Foli .20 .09 .03
☐ 214 Butch Wynegar DP .10 .05 .01
☐ 215 Darrell Evans .50 .23 .06
☐ 216 Ken Griffey .75 .35 .09
☐ 217 Doug DeCinces .35 .16 .04
☐ 218 Ruppert Jones .20 .09 .03
☐ 219 Bob Montgomery .20 .09 .03
☐ 220 Rick Manning .20 .09 .03
☐ 221 Chris Speier .20 .09 .03
☐ 222 Bobby Valentine .20 .09 .03
☐ 223 Dave Parker .75 .35 .09
☐ 224 Larry Biittner .20 .09 .03
☐ 225 Ken Clay .20 .09 .03
☐ 226 Gene Tenace .35 .16 .04
☐ 227 Frank White .35 .16 .04
☐ 228 Rusty Staub .50 .23 .06
☐ 229 Lee Lacy .20 .09 .03
☐ 230 Doyle Alexander .20 .09 .03
☐ 231 Bruce Bochte .20 .09 .03
☐ 232 Steve Henderson .20 .09 .03
☐ 233 Jim Lonborg .35 .16 .04
☐ 234 Dave Concepcion .50 .23 .06
☐ 235 Jerry Morales .35 .16 .04
Traded 12-4-78
☐ 236 Len Randle .20 .09 .03
☐ 237 Bill Lee DP .35 .16 .04

Traded 12-7-78			
☐ 238 Bruce Sutter	.35	.16	.04
☐ 239 Jim Essian	.20	.09	.03
☐ 240 Graig Nettles	.50	.23	.06
☐ 241 Otto Velez	.20	.09	.03
☐ 242 Checklist 126-250 DP	.60	.25	.07
☐ 243 Reggie Smith	.35	.16	.04
☐ 244 Stan Bahnsen DP	.10	.05	.01
☐ 245 Garry Maddox DP	.20	.09	.03
☐ 246 Joaquin Andujar	.35	.16	.04
☐ 247 Dan Driessen	.20	.09	.03
☐ 248 Bob Grich	.35	.16	.04
☐ 249 Fred Lynn	.35	.16	.04
☐ 250 Skip Lockwood	.20	.09	.03
☐ 251 Craig Reynolds	.35	.16	.04
Traded 12-5-78			
☐ 252 Willie Horton	.35	.16	.04
☐ 253 Rick Waits	.20	.09	.03
☐ 254 Bucky Dent	.35	.16	.04
☐ 255 Bob Knepper	.20	.09	.03
☐ 256 Miguel Dilone	.20	.09	.03
☐ 257 Bob Owchinko	.20	.09	.03
☐ 258 Al Cowens	.20	.09	.03
☐ 259 Bob Bailor	.20	.09	.03
☐ 260 Larry Christenson	.20	.09	.03
☐ 261 Tony Perez	1.00	.45	.12
☐ 262 Blue Jays Team	1.00	.45	.12
Roy Hartsfield MG			
(Team checklist back)			
☐ 263 Glenn Abbott	.20	.09	.03
☐ 264 Ron Guidry	.35	.16	.04
☐ 265 Ed Kranepool	.20	.09	.03
☐ 266 Charlie Hough	.35	.16	.04
☐ 267 Ted Simmons	.50	.23	.06
☐ 268 Jack Clark	.35	.16	.04
☐ 269 Enos Cabell	.20	.09	.03
☐ 270 Gary Carter	2.00	.90	.25
☐ 271 Sam Ewing	.20	.09	.03
☐ 272 Tom Burgmeier	.20	.09	.03
☐ 273 Freddie Patek	.20	.09	.03
☐ 274 Frank Tanana	.35	.16	.04
☐ 275 Leroy Stanton	.20	.09	.03
☐ 276 Ken Forsch	.20	.09	.03
☐ 277 Ellis Valentine	.20	.09	.03
☐ 278 Greg Luzinski	.35	.16	.04
☐ 279 Rick Bosetti	.20	.09	.03
☐ 280 John Stearns	.20	.09	.03
☐ 281 Enrique Romo	.35	.16	.04
Traded 12-5-78			
☐ 282 Bob Bailey	.20	.09	.03
☐ 283 Sal Bando	.35	.16	.04
☐ 284 Matt Keough	.20	.09	.03
☐ 285 Biff Pocoroba	.20	.09	.03
☐ 286 Mike Lum	.35	.16	.04
Free Agent 3-1-79			
☐ 287 Jay Johnstone	.35	.16	.04
☐ 288 John Montefusco	.20	.09	.03
☐ 289 Ed Ott	.20	.09	.03
☐ 290 Dusty Baker	.50	.23	.06
☐ 291 Rico Carty	.50	.23	.06
Waivers from A's 10-2-78			
☐ 292 Nino Espinosa	.20	.09	.03
☐ 293 Rich Hebner	.20	.09	.03
☐ 294 Cesar Cedeno	.35	.16	.04
☐ 295 Darrell Porter	.20	.09	.03
☐ 296 Rod Gilbreath	.20	.09	.03
☐ 297 Jim Kern	.35	.16	.04
Trade with Indians 10-3-78			
☐ 298 Claudell Washington	.35	.16	.04
☐ 299 Luis Tiant	.50	.23	.06
Signed as Free Agent 11-14-78			
☐ 300 Mike Parrott	.20	.09	.03
☐ 301 Pete Broberg	.35	.16	.04
Free Agent 3-1-79			
☐ 302 Greg Gross	.35	.16	.04
Traded 2-23-79			
☐ 303 Darold Knowles	.35	.16	.04
Free Agent 2-12-79			
☐ 304 Paul Blair	.20	.09	.03
☐ 305 Julio Cruz	.20	.09	.03
☐ 306 Hal McRae	.50	.23	.06
☐ 307 Ken Reitz	.20	.09	.03
☐ 308 Tom Murphy	.20	.09	.03
☐ 309 Terry Whitfield	.20	.09	.03
☐ 310 J.R. Richard	.35	.16	.04
☐ 311 Mike Hargrove	.50	.23	.06
Trade with Rangers 10-25-78			
☐ 312 Rick Dempsey	.35	.16	.04
☐ 313 Phil Niekro	1.50	.70	.19
☐ 314 Bob Stanley	.20	.09	.03
☐ 315 Jim Spencer	.20	.09	.03
☐ 316 George Foster	.35	.16	.04
☐ 317 Dave LaRoche	.20	.09	.03
☐ 318 Rudy May	.20	.09	.03
☐ 319 Jeff Newman	.20	.09	.03
☐ 320 Rick Monday DP	.20	.09	.03
☐ 321 Omar Moreno	.20	.09	.03
☐ 322 Dave McKay	.20	.09	.03
☐ 323 Mike Schmidt	8.00	3.60	1.00
☐ 324 Ken Singleton	.35	.16	.04
☐ 325 Jerry Remy	.20	.09	.03
☐ 326 Bert Campaneris	.35	.16	.04
☐ 327 Pat Zachry	.20	.09	.03
☐ 328 Larry Herndon	.20	.09	.03
☐ 329 Mark Fidrych	1.00	.45	.12
☐ 330 Del Unser	.20	.09	.03
☐ 331 Gene Garber	.35	.16	.04
☐ 332 Bake McBride	.35	.16	.04
☐ 333 Jorge Orta	.20	.09	.03
☐ 334 Don Kirkwood	.20	.09	.03
☐ 335 Don Baylor	.75	.35	.09
☐ 336 Bill Robinson	.35	.16	.04
☐ 337 Manny Trillo	.35	.16	.04
Traded 2-23-79			
☐ 338 Eddie Murray	30.00	13.50	3.70
☐ 339 Tom Hausman	.20	.09	.03
☐ 340 George Scott DP	.20	.09	.03
☐ 341 Rick Sweet	.20	.09	.03
☐ 342 Lou Piniella	.35	.16	.04
☐ 343 Pete Rose	7.50	3.40	.95
Free Agent 12-5-79			
☐ 344 Stan Papi	.35	.16	.04
Traded 12-7-78			
☐ 345 Jerry Koosman	.50	.23	.06
Traded 12-8-78			
☐ 346 Hosken Powell	.20	.09	.03
☐ 347 George Medich	.20	.09	.03
☐ 348 Ron LeFlore DP	.20	.09	.03
☐ 349 Montreal Expos Team	1.00	.45	.12
Dick Williams MG			
(Team checklist back)			
☐ 350 Lou Brock	2.00	.90	.25
☐ 351 Bill North	.20	.09	.03
☐ 352 Jim Hunter DP	.75	.35	.09
☐ 353 Checklist 251-374 DP	.60	.25	.07
☐ 354 Ed Halicki	.20	.09	.03
☐ 355 Tom Hutton	.20	.09	.03
☐ 356 Mike Caldwell	.20	.09	.03
☐ 357 Larry Parrish	.35	.16	.04
☐ 358 Geoff Zahn	.20	.09	.03
☐ 359 Derrel Thomas	.35	.16	.04
Signed as Free Agent 11-14-78			
☐ 360 Carlton Fisk	2.50	1.10	.30
☐ 361 John Henry Johnson	.20	.09	.03
☐ 362 Dave Chalk	.20	.09	.03
☐ 363 Dan Meyer DP	.10	.05	.01
☐ 364 Sixto Lezcano	.20	.09	.03
☐ 365 Rennie Stennett	.20	.09	.03
☐ 366 Mike Willis	.20	.09	.03
☐ 367 Buddy Bell DP	.50	.23	.06
Traded 12-8-78			
☐ 368 Mickey Stanley	.20	.09	.03
☐ 369 Dave Rader	.35	.16	.04
Traded 2-23-79			
☐ 370 Burt Hooton	.20	.09	.03
☐ 371 Keith Hernandez	.75	.35	.09
☐ 372 Bill Stein	.20	.09	.03
☐ 373 Hal Dues	.20	.09	.03
☐ 374 Reggie Jackson DP	2.00	.90	.25

1980 O-Pee-Chee

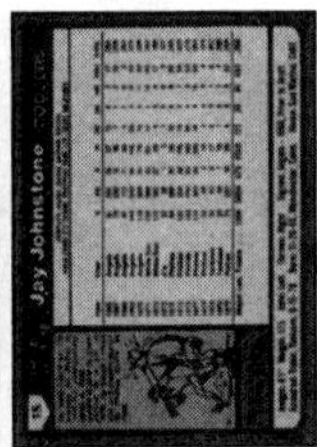

This set is an abridgement of the 1980 Topps set. The cards are printed on white stock rather than the gray stock used by Topps. The 374 standard-size cards also differ from their Topps counterparts by having a higher ratio of cards of players from the two Canadian teams, a practice begun by O-Pee-Chee in 1977 and continued to 1988. The fronts feature white-bordered color player photos framed by a colored line. The player's name appears in the white border at the top and also as a simulated autograph across the photo. The player's position appears within a colored banner at the upper left; his team name appears within a colored banner at the lower right. The blue and white horizontal backs carry the player's name, team and position at the top. Biography, major league statistics and career highlights in both French and English also appear. The cards are numbered on the back. The asterisked cards have an extra line, "Now with (new team name)" on the front indicating team change. Color changes, to correspond to the new team, are apparent on the pennant name and frame on the front. Double-printed (DP) cards are also noted below. The cards in this set were produced in lower quantities than other O-Pee-Chee sets of this era reportedly due to the company being on strike. The cards are sequenced in the same order as the Topps cards.

	NRMT	VG-E	GOOD
COMPLETE SET (374)	90.00	40.00	11.00
COMMON CARD (1-374)	.15	.07	.02
COMMON CARD DP (1-374)	.05	.02	.01

☐ 1 Craig Swan	.15	.07	.02
☐ 2 Dennis Martinez	1.50	.70	.19
☐ 3 Dave Cash	.15	.07	.02
Now With Padres			
☐ 4 Bruce Sutter	.30	.14	.04
☐ 5 Ron Jackson	.15	.07	.02
☐ 6 Balor Moore	.15	.07	.02
☐ 7 Dan Ford	.15	.07	.02
☐ 8 Pat Putnam	.15	.07	.02
☐ 9 Derrel Thomas	.15	.07	.02
☐ 10 Jim Slaton	.15	.07	.02
☐ 11 Lee Mazzilli	.30	.14	.04
☐ 12 Del Unser	.15	.07	.02
☐ 13 Mark Wagner	.15	.07	.02
☐ 14 Vida Blue	.60	.25	.07
☐ 15 Jay Johnstone	.30	.14	.04
☐ 16 Julio Cruz DP	.05	.02	.01
☐ 17 Tony Scott	.15	.07	.02
☐ 18 Jeff Newman DP	.05	.02	.01
☐ 19 Luis Tiant	.30	.14	.04
☐ 20 Carlton Fisk	4.00	1.80	.50
☐ 21 Dave Palmer	.15	.07	.02
☐ 22 Bombo Rivera	.15	.07	.02
☐ 23 Bill Fahey	.15	.07	.02
☐ 24 Frank White	.60	.25	.07
☐ 25 Rico Carty	.30	.14	.04
☐ 26 Bill Bonham DP	.05	.02	.01
☐ 27 Rick Miller	.15	.07	.02
☐ 28 J.R. Richard	.30	.14	.04
☐ 29 Joe Ferguson DP	.05	.02	.01
☐ 30 Bill Madlock	.30	.14	.04
☐ 31 Pete Vuckovich	.15	.07	.02
☐ 32 Doug Flynn	.15	.07	.02
☐ 33 Bucky Dent	.30	.14	.04
☐ 34 Mike Ivie	.15	.07	.02
☐ 35 Bob Stanley	.15	.07	.02
☐ 36 Al Bumbry	.15	.07	.02
☐ 37 Gary Carter	1.25	.55	.16
☐ 38 John Milner DP	.05	.02	.01
☐ 39 Sid Monge	.15	.07	.02
☐ 40 Bill Russell	.30	.14	.04
☐ 41 John Stearns	.15	.07	.02
☐ 42 Dave Stieb	1.00	.45	.12
☐ 43 Ruppert Jones	.15	.07	.02
Now with Yankees			
☐ 44 Bob Owchinko	.15	.07	.02
☐ 45 Ron LeFlore	.30	.14	.04
Now with Expos			
☐ 46 Ted Sizemore	.15	.07	.02
☐ 47 Ted Simmons	.30	.14	.04
☐ 48 Pepe Frias	.15	.07	.02
Now with Rangers			
☐ 49 Ken Landreaux	.15	.07	.02
☐ 50 Manny Trillo	.30	.14	.04
☐ 51 Rick Dempsey	.30	.14	.04
☐ 52 Cecil Cooper	.30	.14	.04
☐ 53 Bill Lee	.30	.14	.04
☐ 54 Victor Cruz	.15	.07	.02
☐ 55 Johnny Bench	5.00	2.20	.60
☐ 56 Rich Dauer	.15	.07	.02
☐ 57 Frank Tanana	.30	.14	.04
☐ 58 Francisco Barrios	.15	.07	.02
☐ 59 Bob Horner	.15	.07	.02
☐ 60 Fred Lynn DP	.30	.14	.04
☐ 61 Bob Knepper	.15	.07	.02
☐ 62 Sparky Lyle	.30	.14	.04
☐ 63 Larry Cox	.15	.07	.02
☐ 64 Dock Ellis	.15	.07	.02
Now with Pirates			
☐ 65 Phil Garner	.30	.14	.04
☐ 66 Greg Luzinski	.30	.14	.04
☐ 67 Checklist 1-125	.30	.14	.04
☐ 68 Dave Lemanczyk	.15	.07	.02
☐ 69 Tony Perez	1.00	.45	.12
Now with Red Sox			
☐ 70 Gary Thomasson	.15	.07	.02
☐ 71 Craig Reynolds	.15	.07	.02
☐ 72 Amos Otis	.30	.14	.04
☐ 73 Biff Pocoroba	.15	.07	.02
☐ 74 Matt Keough	.15	.07	.02
☐ 75 Bill Buckner	.30	.14	.04
☐ 76 John Castino	.15	.07	.02
☐ 77 Rich Gossage	1.00	.45	.12
☐ 78 Gary Alexander	.15	.07	.02
☐ 79 Phil Huffman	.15	.07	.02
☐ 80 Bruce Bochte	.15	.07	.02
☐ 81 Darrell Evans	.30	.14	.04
☐ 82 Terry Puhl	.15	.07	.02
☐ 83 Jason Thompson	.15	.07	.02
☐ 84 Lary Sorensen	.15	.07	.02
☐ 85 Jerry Remy	.15	.07	.02
☐ 86 Tony Brizzolara	.15	.07	.02
☐ 87 Willie Wilson DP	.30	.14	.04
☐ 88 Eddie Murray	20.00	9.00	2.50
☐ 89 Larry Christenson	.15	.07	.02
☐ 90 Bob Randall	.15	.07	.02
☐ 91 Greg Pryor	.15	.07	.02
☐ 92 Glenn Abbott	.15	.07	.02
☐ 93 Jack Clark	.30	.14	.04
☐ 94 Rick Waits	.15	.07	.02
☐ 95 Luis Gomez	.15	.07	.02
Now with Braves			
☐ 96 Burt Hooton	.30	.14	.04
☐ 97 John Henry Johnson	.15	.07	.02
☐ 98 Ray Knight	.30	.14	.04
☐ 99 Rick Reuschel	.30	.14	.04
☐ 100 Champ Summers	.15	.07	.02
☐ 101 Ron Davis	.15	.07	.02
☐ 102 Warren Cromartie	.15	.07	.02
☐ 103 Ken Reitz	.15	.07	.02
☐ 104 Hal McRae	.60	.25	.07
☐ 105 Alan Ashby	.15	.07	.02
☐ 106 Kevin Kobel	.15	.07	.02
☐ 107 Buddy Bell	.30	.14	.04
☐ 108 Dave Goltz	.15	.07	.02
Now with Dodgers			
☐ 109 John Montefusco	.30	.14	.04
☐ 110 Lance Parrish	.30	.14	.04
☐ 111 Mike LaCoss	.15	.07	.02
☐ 112 Jim Rice	.30	.14	.04
☐ 113 Steve Carlton	4.00	1.80	.50
☐ 114 Sixto Lezcano	.15	.07	.02
☐ 115 Ed Halicki	.15	.07	.02
☐ 116 Jose Morales	.15	.07	.02
☐ 117 Dave Concepcion	.60	.25	.07
☐ 118 Joe Cannon	.15	.07	.02
☐ 119 Willie Montanez	.15	.07	.02
Now with Padres			
☐ 120 Lou Piniella	.60	.25	.07
☐ 121 Bill Stein	.15	.07	.02
☐ 122 Dave Winfield	7.50	3.40	.95
☐ 123 Alan Trammell	7.50	3.40	.95
☐ 124 Andre Dawson	7.50	3.40	.95
☐ 125 Marc Hill	.15	.07	.02
☐ 126 Don Aase	.15	.07	.02
☐ 127 Dave Kingman	.30	.14	.04
☐ 128 Checklist 126-250	.30	.14	.04
☐ 129 Dennis Lamp	.15	.07	.02
☐ 130 Phil Niekro	1.50	.70	.19
☐ 131 Tim Foli DP	.05	.02	.01
☐ 132 Jim Clancy	.15	.07	.02
☐ 133 Bill Atkinson	.15	.07	.02
Now with White Sox			
☐ 134 Paul Dade DP	.05	.02	.01
☐ 135 Dusty Baker	.30	.14	.04
☐ 136 Al Oliver	.30	.14	.04
☐ 137 Dave Chalk	.15	.07	.02
☐ 138 Bill Robinson	.15	.07	.02
☐ 139 Robin Yount	10.00	4.50	1.25
☐ 140 Dan Schatzeder	.15	.07	.02
Now with Tigers			
☐ 141 Mike Schmidt DP	5.00	2.20	.60
☐ 142 Ralph Garr	.30	.14	.04
Now with Angels			
☐ 143 Dale Murphy	4.00	1.80	.50
☐ 144 Jerry Koosman	.30	.14	.04
☐ 145 Tom Veryzer	.15	.07	.02
☐ 146 Rick Bosetti	.15	.07	.02
☐ 147 Jim Spencer	.15	.07	.02
☐ 148 Gaylord Perry	1.50	.70	.19
Now with Rangers			
☐ 149 Paul Blair	.30	.14	.04
☐ 150 Don Baylor	.60	.25	.07
☐ 151 Dave Rozema	.15	.07	.02
☐ 152 Steve Garvey	1.00	.45	.12
☐ 153 Elias Sosa	.15	.07	.02
☐ 154 Larry Gura	.15	.07	.02
☐ 155 Tim Johnson	.15	.07	.02
☐ 156 Steve Henderson	.15	.07	.02
☐ 157 Ron Guidry	.30	.14	.04
☐ 158 Mike Edwards	.15	.07	.02
☐ 159 Butch Wynegar	.15	.07	.02
☐ 160 Randy Jones	.15	.07	.02
☐ 161 Denny Walling	.15	.07	.02
☐ 162 Mike Hargrove	.30	.14	.04
☐ 163 Dave Parker	1.00	.45	.12
☐ 164 Roger Metzger	.15	.07	.02
☐ 165 Johnny Grubb	.15	.07	.02
☐ 166 Steve Kemp	.15	.07	.02
☐ 167 Bob Lacey	.15	.07	.02
☐ 168 Chris Speier	.15	.07	.02
☐ 169 Dennis Eckersley	2.00	.90	.25
☐ 170 Keith Hernandez	.30	.14	.04
☐ 171 Claudell Washington	.30	.14	.04
☐ 172 Tom Underwood	.15	.07	.02
Now with Yankees			
☐ 173 Dan Driessen	.15	.07	.02
☐ 174 Al Cowens	.15	.07	.02
Now with Angels			
☐ 175 Rich Hebner	.15	.07	.02
Now with Tigers			
☐ 176 Willie McCovey	2.00	.90	.25
☐ 177 Carney Lansford	.30	.14	.04
☐ 178 Ken Singleton	.30	.14	.04
☐ 179 Jim Essian	.15	.07	.02
☐ 180 Mike Vail	.15	.07	.02
☐ 181 Randy Lerch	.15	.07	.02
☐ 182 Larry Parrish	.30	.14	.04
☐ 183 Checklist 251-374	.30	.14	.04
☐ 184 George Hendrick	.30	.14	.04
☐ 185 Bob Davis	.15	.07	.02
☐ 186 Gary Matthews	.30	.14	.04
☐ 187 Lou Whitaker	6.00	2.70	.75
☐ 188 Darrell Porter DP	.05	.02	.01
☐ 189 Wayne Gross	.15	.07	.02
☐ 190 Bobby Murcer	.30	.14	.04
☐ 191 Willie Aikens	.15	.07	.02
Now with Royals			
☐ 192 Jim Kern	.15	.07	.02
☐ 193 Cesar Cedeno	.30	.14	.04
☐ 194 Joel Youngblood	.15	.07	.02
☐ 195 Ross Grimsley	.15	.07	.02
☐ 196 Jerry Mumphrey	.15	.07	.02
Now with Padres			
☐ 197 Kevin Bell	.15	.07	.02
☐ 198 Garry Maddox	.30	.14	.04
☐ 199 Dave Freisleben	.15	.07	.02
☐ 200 Ed Ott	.15	.07	.02
☐ 201 Enos Cabell	.15	.07	.02
☐ 202 Pete LaCock	.15	.07	.02
☐ 203 Fergie Jenkins	1.50	.70	.19

☐ 204 Milt Wilcox	.15	.07	.02
☐ 205 Ozzie Smith	25.00	11.00	3.10
☐ 206 Ellis Valentine	.15	.07	.02
☐ 207 Dan Meyer	.15	.07	.02
☐ 208 Barry Foote	.15	.07	.02
☐ 209 George Foster	.30	.14	.04
☐ 210 Dwight Evans	.30	.14	.04
☐ 211 Paul Molitor	15.00	6.75	1.85
☐ 212 Tony Solaita	.15	.07	.02
☐ 213 Bill North	.15	.07	.02
☐ 214 Paul Splittorff	.15	.07	.02
☐ 215 Bobby Bonds	.60	.25	.07
Now with Cardinals			
☐ 216 Butch Hobson	.30	.14	.04
☐ 217 Mark Belanger	.30	.14	.04
☐ 218 Grant Jackson	.15	.07	.02
☐ 219 Tom Hutton DP	.05	.02	.01
☐ 220 Pat Zachry	.15	.07	.02
☐ 221 Duane Kuiper	.15	.07	.02
☐ 222 Larry Hisle DP	.05	.02	.01
☐ 223 Mike Krukow	.15	.07	.02
☐ 224 Johnnie LeMaster	.15	.07	.02
☐ 225 Billy Almon	.15	.07	.02
Now with Expos			
☐ 226 Joe Niekro	.30	.14	.04
☐ 227 Dave Revering	.15	.07	.02
☐ 228 Don Sutton	1.00	.45	.12
☐ 229 John Hiller	.15	.07	.02
☐ 230 Alvis Woods	.15	.07	.02
☐ 231 Mark Fidrych	.30	.14	.04
☐ 232 Duffy Dyer	.15	.07	.02
☐ 233 Nino Espinosa	.15	.07	.02
☐ 234 Doug Bair	.15	.07	.02
☐ 235 George Brett	25.00	11.00	3.10
☐ 236 Mike Torrez	.15	.07	.02
☐ 237 Frank Taveras	.15	.07	.02
☐ 238 Bert Blyleven	.60	.25	.07
☐ 239 Willie Randolph	.30	.14	.04
☐ 240 Mike Sadek DP	.05	.02	.01
☐ 241 Jerry Royster	.15	.07	.02
☐ 242 John Denny	.15	.07	.02
Now with Indians			
☐ 243 Rick Monday	.15	.07	.02
☐ 244 Jesse Jefferson	.15	.07	.02
☐ 245 Aurelio Rodriguez	.15	.07	.02
Now with Padres			
☐ 246 Bob Boone	.60	.25	.07
☐ 247 Cesar Geronimo	.15	.07	.02
☐ 248 Bob Shirley	.15	.07	.02
☐ 249 Expos Checklist	.60	.25	.07
☐ 250 Bob Watson	.30	.14	.04
Now with Yankees			
☐ 251 Mickey Rivers	.30	.14	.04
☐ 252 Mike Tyson DP	.05	.02	.01
Now with Cubs			
☐ 253 Wayne Nordhagen	.15	.07	.02
☐ 254 Roy Howell	.15	.07	.02
☐ 255 Lee May	.30	.14	.04
☐ 256 Jerry Martin	.15	.07	.02
☐ 257 Bake McBride	.15	.07	.02
☐ 258 Silvio Martinez	.15	.07	.02
☐ 259 Jim Mason	.15	.07	.02
☐ 260 Tom Seaver	5.00	2.20	.60
☐ 261 Rich Wortham DP	.05	.02	.01
☐ 262 Mike Cubbage	.15	.07	.02
☐ 263 Gene Garber	.15	.07	.02
☐ 264 Bert Campaneris	.30	.14	.04
☐ 265 Tom Buskey	.15	.07	.02
☐ 266 Leon Roberts	.15	.07	.02
☐ 267 Ron Cey	.30	.14	.04
☐ 268 Steve Ontiveros	.15	.07	.02
☐ 269 Mike Caldwell	.15	.07	.02
☐ 270 Nelson Norman	.15	.07	.02
☐ 271 Steve Rogers	.15	.07	.02
☐ 272 Jim Morrison	.15	.07	.02
☐ 273 Clint Hurdle	.15	.07	.02
☐ 274 Dale Murray	.15	.07	.02
☐ 275 Jim Barr	.15	.07	.02
☐ 276 Jim Sundberg DP	.30	.14	.04
☐ 277 Willie Horton	.30	.14	.04
☐ 278 Andre Thornton	.15	.07	.02
☐ 279 Bob Forsch	.15	.07	.02
☐ 280 Joe Strain	.15	.07	.02
☐ 281 Rudy May	.15	.07	.02
Now with Yankees			
☐ 282 Pete Rose	6.00	2.70	.75
☐ 283 Jeff Burroughs	.30	.14	.04
☐ 284 Rick Langford	.15	.07	.02
☐ 285 Ken Griffey	.30	.14	.04
☐ 286 Bill Nahorodny	.15	.07	.02
Now with Braves			
☐ 287 Art Howe	.30	.14	.04
☐ 288 Ed Figueroa	.15	.07	.02
☐ 289 Joe Rudi	.30	.14	.04
☐ 290 Alfredo Griffin	.15	.07	.02
☐ 291 Dave Lopes	.30	.14	.04
☐ 292 Rick Manning	.15	.07	.02
☐ 293 Dennis Leonard	.30	.14	.04
☐ 294 Bud Harrelson	.30	.14	.04
☐ 295 Skip Lockwood	.15	.07	.02
Now with Red Sox			
☐ 296 Roy Smalley	.15	.07	.02
☐ 297 Kent Tekulve	.30	.14	.04
☐ 298 Scot Thompson	.15	.07	.02
☐ 299 Ken Kravec	.15	.07	.02
☐ 300 Blue Jays Checklist	.60	.25	.07
☐ 301 Scott Sanderson	.30	.14	.04
☐ 302 Charlie Moore	.15	.07	.02
☐ 303 Nolan Ryan	30.00	13.50	3.70
Now with Astros			
☐ 304 Bob Bailor	.15	.07	.02
☐ 305 Bob Stinson	.15	.07	.02
☐ 306 Al Hrabosky	.15	.07	.02
Now with Braves			
☐ 307 Mitchell Page	.15	.07	.02
☐ 308 Garry Templeton	.15	.07	.02
☐ 309 Chet Lemon	.30	.14	.04
☐ 310 Jim Palmer	2.00	.90	.25
☐ 311 Rick Cerone	.15	.07	.02
Now with Yankees			
☐ 312 Jon Matlack	.15	.07	.02
☐ 313 Don Money	.15	.07	.02
☐ 314 Reggie Jackson	5.00	2.20	.60
☐ 315 Brian Downing	.15	.07	.02
☐ 316 Woodie Fryman	.15	.07	.02
☐ 317 Alan Bannister	.15	.07	.02
☐ 318 Ron Reed	.15	.07	.02
☐ 319 Willie Stargell	2.00	.90	.25
☐ 320 Jerry Garvin DP	.05	.02	.01
☐ 321 Cliff Johnson	.15	.07	.02
☐ 322 Doug DeCinces	.30	.14	.04
☐ 323 Gene Richards	.15	.07	.02
☐ 324 Joaquin Andujar	.30	.14	.04
☐ 325 Richie Zisk	.15	.07	.02
☐ 326 Bob Grich	.30	.14	.04
☐ 327 Gorman Thomas	.30	.14	.04
☐ 328 Chris Chambliss	.30	.14	.04
Now with Braves			
☐ 329 Blue Jays Prospects	.15	.07	.02
Butch Edge			
Pat Kelly			
Ted Wilborn			
☐ 330 Larry Bowa	.30	.14	.04
☐ 331 Barry Bonnell	.15	.07	.02
Now with Blue Jays			
☐ 332 John Candelaria	.30	.14	.04
☐ 333 Toby Harrah	.30	.14	.04
☐ 334 Larry Biittner	.15	.07	.02
☐ 335 Mike Flanagan	.30	.14	.04
☐ 336 Ed Kranepool	.15	.07	.02
☐ 337 Ken Forsch DP	.05	.02	.01
☐ 338 John Mayberry	.30	.14	.04
☐ 339 Rick Burleson	.15	.07	.02
☐ 340 Milt May	.15	.07	.02
Now with Giants			
☐ 341 Roy White	.15	.07	.02
☐ 342 Joe Morgan	2.00	.90	.25
☐ 343 Rollie Fingers	1.50	.70	.19
☐ 344 Mario Mendoza	.15	.07	.02
☐ 345 Stan Bahnsen	.15	.07	.02
☐ 346 Tug McGraw	.30	.14	.04
☐ 347 Rusty Staub	.30	.14	.04
☐ 348 Tommy John	.60	.25	.07
☐ 349 Ivan DeJesus	.15	.07	.02
☐ 350 Reggie Smith	.30	.14	.04
☐ 351 Expos Prospects	.60	.25	.07
Tony Bernazard			
Randy Miller			
John Tamargo			
☐ 352 Floyd Bannister	.15	.07	.02
☐ 353 Rod Carew DP	1.50	.70	.19
☐ 354 Otto Velez	.15	.07	.02
☐ 355 Gene Tenace	.30	.14	.04
☐ 356 Freddie Patek	.15	.07	.02
Now with Angels			
☐ 357 Elliott Maddox	.15	.07	.02
☐ 358 Pat Underwood	.15	.07	.02
☐ 359 Graig Nettles	.30	.14	.04
☐ 360 Rodney Scott	.15	.07	.02
☐ 361 Terry Whitfield	.15	.07	.02
☐ 362 Fred Norman	.15	.07	.02
Now with Expos			
☐ 363 Sal Bando	.30	.14	.04
☐ 364 Greg Gross	.15	.07	.02
☐ 365 Carl Yastrzemski DP	2.00	.90	.25
☐ 366 Paul Hartzell	.15	.07	.02
☐ 367 Jose Cruz	.30	.14	.04
☐ 368 Shane Rawley	.15	.07	.02
☐ 369 Jerry White	.15	.07	.02
☐ 370 Rick Wise	.15	.07	.02
Now with Padres			
☐ 371 Steve Yeager	.30	.14	.04
☐ 372 Omar Moreno	.15	.07	.02
☐ 373 Bump Wills	.15	.07	.02
☐ 374 Craig Kusick	.15	.07	.02
Now with Padres			

1981 O-Pee-Chee

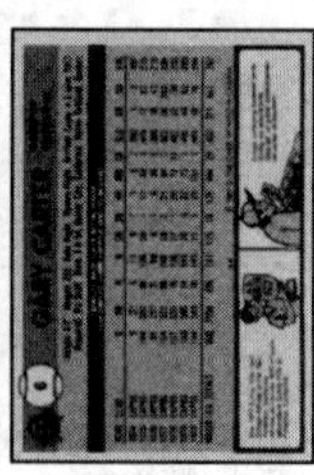

This set is an abridgement of the 1981 Topps set. The 374 standard-size cards comprising the 1981 O-Pee-Chee set differ from the cards of the 1981 Topps set by having a higher ratio of cards of players from the two Canadian teams, a practice begun by O-Pee-Chee in 1977 and continued to 1988. The fronts feature white-bordered color player photos framed by a colored line that is wider at the bottom. The player's name appears in that wider colored area. The player's position and team appear within a colored baseball cap icon at the lower left. The red and white horizontal backs carry the player's name and position at the top. Biography, major league statistics, and career highlights in both French and English also appear. In cases where a player changed teams or was traded before press time, a small line of print on the obverse makes note of the change. Double-printed (DP) cards are also noted below. The card backs are typically found printed on white card stock. There is, however, a "variation" set printed on gray card stock; gray backs are worth 50 percent more than corresponding white backs listed below. Cards of Harold Baines, Kirk Gibson and Tim Raines are featured in their American Rookie Card year.

	NRMT	VG-E	GOOD
COMPLETE SET (374)	50.00	22.00	6.25
COMMON CARD (1-374)	.10	.05	.01
COMMON CARD DP (1-374)	.05	.02	.01
☐ 1 Frank Pastore	.10	.05	.01
☐ 2 Phil Huffman	.10	.05	.01
☐ 3 Len Barker	.10	.05	.01
☐ 4 Robin Yount	2.00	.90	.25
☐ 5 Dave Stieb	.25	.11	.03
☐ 6 Gary Carter	.25	.11	.03
☐ 7 Butch Hobson	.10	.05	.01
Now with Angels			
☐ 8 Lance Parrish	.25	.11	.03
☐ 9 Bruce Sutter	.25	.11	.03
Now with Cardinals			
☐ 10 Mike Flanagan	.25	.11	.03
☐ 11 Paul Mirabella	.10	.05	.01
☐ 12 Craig Reynolds	.10	.05	.01
☐ 13 Joe Charboneau	.50	.23	.06
☐ 14 Dan Driessen	.10	.05	.01
☐ 15 Larry Parrish	.10	.05	.01
☐ 16 Ron Davis	.10	.05	.01
☐ 17 Cliff Johnson	.10	.05	.01
Now with Athletics			
☐ 18 Bruce Bochte	.10	.05	.01
☐ 19 Jim Clancy	.10	.05	.01
☐ 20 Bill Russell	.25	.11	.03
☐ 21 Ron Oester	.10	.05	.01
☐ 22 Danny Darwin	.25	.11	.03
☐ 23 Willie Aikens	.10	.05	.01
☐ 24 Don Stanhouse	.10	.05	.01
☐ 25 Sixto Lezcano	.10	.05	.01
Now with Cardinals			
☐ 26 U.L. Washington	.10	.05	.01
☐ 27 Champ Summers DP	.05	.02	.01
☐ 28 Enrique Romo	.10	.05	.01
☐ 29 Gene Tenace	.25	.11	.03
☐ 30 Jack Clark	.25	.11	.03
☐ 31 Checklist 1-125 DP	.05	.02	.01
☐ 32 Ken Oberkfell	.10	.05	.01
☐ 33 Rick Honeycutt	.10	.05	.01
Now with Rangers			
☐ 34 Al Bumbry	.10	.05	.01
☐ 35 John Tamargo DP	.05	.02	.01
☐ 36 Ed Farmer	.10	.05	.01
☐ 37 Gary Roenicke	.10	.05	.01
☐ 38 Tim Foli DP	.05	.02	.01
☐ 39 Eddie Murray	6.00	2.70	.75
☐ 40 Roy Howell	.10	.05	.01
Now with Brewers			
☐ 41 Bill Gullickson	.50	.23	.06
☐ 42 Jerry White DP	.05	.02	.01
☐ 43 Tim Blackwell	.10	.05	.01
☐ 44 Steve Henderson	.10	.05	.01
☐ 45 Enos Cabell	.10	.05	.01
Now with Giants			
☐ 46 Rick Bosetti	.10	.05	.01
☐ 47 Bill North	.10	.05	.01
☐ 48 Rich Gossage	.50	.23	.06
☐ 49 Bob Shirley	.10	.05	.01
Now with Cardinals			
☐ 50 Dave Lopes	.25	.11	.03
☐ 51 Shane Rawley	.10	.05	.01
☐ 52 Lloyd Moseby	.25	.11	.03
☐ 53 Burt Hooton	.10	.05	.01
☐ 54 Ivan DeJesus	.10	.05	.01
☐ 55 Mike Norris	.10	.05	.01
☐ 56 Del Unser	.10	.05	.01
☐ 57 Dave Revering	.10	.05	.01
☐ 58 Joel Youngblood	.10	.05	.01
☐ 59 Steve McCatty	.10	.05	.01
☐ 60 Willie Randolph	.25	.11	.03
☐ 61 Butch Wynegar	.10	.05	.01
☐ 62 Gary Lavelle	.10	.05	.01
☐ 63 Willie Montanez	.10	.05	.01
☐ 64 Terry Puhl	.10	.05	.01
☐ 65 Scott McGregor	.10	.05	.01
☐ 66 Buddy Bell	.25	.11	.03
☐ 67 Toby Harrah	.25	.11	.03
☐ 68 Jim Rice	.25	.11	.03
☐ 69 Darrell Evans	.25	.11	.03
☐ 70 Al Oliver DP	.25	.11	.03
☐ 71 Hal Dues	.10	.05	.01
☐ 72 Barry Evans DP	.05	.02	.01
☐ 73 Doug Bair	.10	.05	.01
☐ 74 Mike Hargrove	.25	.11	.03
☐ 75 Reggie Smith	.25	.11	.03
☐ 76 Mario Mendoza	.10	.05	.01
Now with Rangers			
☐ 77 Mike Barlow	.10	.05	.01
☐ 78 Garth Iorg	.10	.05	.01
☐ 79 Jeff Reardon	1.50	.70	.19
☐ 80 Roger Erickson	.10	.05	.01
☐ 81 Dave Stapleton	.10	.05	.01
☐ 82 Barry Bonnell	.10	.05	.01
☐ 83 Dave Concepcion	.25	.11	.03
☐ 84 Johnnie LeMaster	.10	.05	.01
☐ 85 Mike Caldwell	.10	.05	.01
☐ 86 Wayne Gross	.10	.05	.01
☐ 87 Rick Camp	.10	.05	.01
☐ 88 Joe Lefebvre	.10	.05	.01
☐ 89 Darrell Jackson	.10	.05	.01
☐ 90 Bake McBride	.10	.05	.01
☐ 91 Tim Stoddard DP	.05	.02	.01
☐ 92 Mike Easler	.10	.05	.01
☐ 93 Jim Bibby	.10	.05	.01
☐ 94 Kent Tekulve	.25	.11	.03
☐ 95 Jim Sundberg	.25	.11	.03
☐ 96 Tommy John	.50	.23	.06
☐ 97 Chris Speier	.10	.05	.01
☐ 98 Clint Hurdle	.10	.05	.01
☐ 99 Phil Garner	.25	.11	.03
☐ 100 Rod Carew	1.50	.70	.19
☐ 101 Steve Stone	.10	.05	.01
☐ 102 Joe Niekro	.10	.05	.01
☐ 103 Jerry Martin	.10	.05	.01
Now with Giants			
☐ 104 Ron LeFlore DP	.05	.02	.01
Now with White Sox			
☐ 105 Jose Cruz	.25	.11	.03
☐ 106 Don Money	.10	.05	.01
☐ 107 Bobby Brown	.10	.05	.01
☐ 108 Larry Herndon	.10	.05	.01
☐ 109 Dennis Eckersley	.75	.35	.09
☐ 110 Carl Yastrzemski	1.50	.70	.19
☐ 111 Greg Minton	.10	.05	.01
☐ 112 Dan Schatzeder	.10	.05	.01
☐ 113 George Brett	8.00	3.60	1.00
☐ 114 Tom Underwood	.10	.05	.01
☐ 115 Roy Smalley	.10	.05	.01
☐ 116 Carlton Fisk	2.00	.90	.25
Now with White Sox			
☐ 117 Pete Falcone	.10	.05	.01
☐ 118 Dale Murphy	1.50	.70	.19
☐ 119 Tippy Martinez	.10	.05	.01
☐ 120 Larry Bowa	.25	.11	.03
☐ 121 Julio Cruz	.10	.05	.01
☐ 122 Jim Gantner	.25	.11	.03
☐ 123 Al Cowens	.10	.05	.01
☐ 124 Jerry Garvin	.10	.05	.01
☐ 125 Andre Dawson	2.00	.90	.25
☐ 126 Charlie Leibrandt	.50	.23	.06
☐ 127 Willie Stargell	1.00	.45	.12
☐ 128 Andre Thornton	.25	.11	.03
☐ 129 Art Howe	.25	.11	.03
☐ 130 Larry Gura	.10	.05	.01
☐ 131 Jerry Remy	.10	.05	.01
☐ 132 Rick Dempsey	.25	.11	.03
☐ 133 Alan Trammell DP	1.00	.45	.12
☐ 134 Mike LaCoss	.10	.05	.01
☐ 135 Gorman Thomas	.10	.05	.01
☐ 136 Expos Future Stars	7.50	3.40	.95
Tim Raines			
Roberto Ramos			
Bobby Pate			
☐ 137 Bill Madlock	.25	.11	.03
☐ 138 Rich Dotson DP	.05	.02	.01
☐ 139 Oscar Gamble	.10	.05	.01
☐ 140 Bob Forsch	.10	.05	.01
☐ 141 Miguel Dilone	.10	.05	.01
☐ 142 Jackson Todd	.10	.05	.01
☐ 143 Dan Meyer	.10	.05	.01
☐ 144 Garry Templeton	.10	.05	.01
☐ 145 Mickey Rivers	.25	.11	.03
☐ 146 Alan Ashby	.10	.05	.01
☐ 147 Dale Berra	.10	.05	.01
☐ 148 Randy Jones	.10	.05	.01
Now with Mets			
☐ 149 Joe Nolan	.10	.05	.01
☐ 150 Mark Fidrych	.50	.23	.06
☐ 151 Tony Armas	.10	.05	.01
☐ 152 Steve Kemp	.10	.05	.01
☐ 153 Jerry Reuss	.25	.11	.03
☐ 154 Rick Langford	.10	.05	.01
☐ 155 Chris Chambliss	.25	.11	.03
☐ 156 Bob McClure	.10	.05	.01
☐ 157 John Wathan	.10	.05	.01
☐ 158 John Curtis	.10	.05	.01
☐ 159 Steve Howe	.25	.11	.03
☐ 160 Garry Maddox	.10	.05	.01
☐ 161 Dan Graham	.10	.05	.01
☐ 162 Doug Corbett	.10	.05	.01
☐ 163 Rob Dressler	.10	.05	.01
☐ 164 Bucky Dent	.25	.11	.03
☐ 165 Alvis Woods	.10	.05	.01
☐ 166 Floyd Bannister	.10	.05	.01
☐ 167 Lee Mazzilli	.10	.05	.01
☐ 168 Don Robinson DP	.05	.02	.01

Card	NRMT	VG-E	GOOD
☐ 169 John Mayberry	.10	.05	.01
☐ 170 Woodie Fryman	.10	.05	.01
☐ 171 Gene Richards	.10	.05	.01
☐ 172 Rick Burleson	.10	.05	.01
Now with Angels			
☐ 173 Bump Wills	.10	.05	.01
☐ 174 Glenn Abbott	.10	.05	.01
☐ 175 Dave Collins	.10	.05	.01
☐ 176 Mike Krukow	.10	.05	.01
☐ 177 Rick Monday	.25	.11	.03
☐ 178 Dave Parker	.25	.11	.03
☐ 179 Rudy May	.10	.05	.01
☐ 180 Pete Rose	3.00	1.35	.35
☐ 181 Elias Sosa	.10	.05	.01
☐ 182 Bob Grich	.25	.11	.03
☐ 183 Fred Norman	.10	.05	.01
☐ 184 Jim Dwyer	.10	.05	.01
Now with Orioles			
☐ 185 Dennis Leonard	.10	.05	.01
☐ 186 Gary Matthews	.10	.05	.01
☐ 187 Ron Hassey DP	.05	.02	.01
☐ 188 Doug DeCinces	.25	.11	.03
☐ 189 Craig Swan	.10	.05	.01
☐ 190 Cesar Cedeno	.25	.11	.03
☐ 191 Rick Sutcliffe	.25	.11	.03
☐ 192 Kiko Garcia	.10	.05	.01
☐ 193 Pete Vuckovich	.10	.05	.01
Now with Brewers			
☐ 194 Tony Bernazard	.10	.05	.01
Now with White Sox			
☐ 195 Keith Hernandez	.25	.11	.03
☐ 196 Jerry Mumphrey	.10	.05	.01
☐ 197 Jim Kern	.10	.05	.01
☐ 198 Jerry Dybzinski	.10	.05	.01
☐ 199 John Lowenstein	.10	.05	.01
☐ 200 George Foster	.25	.11	.03
☐ 201 Phil Niekro	.50	.23	.06
☐ 202 Bill Buckner	.25	.11	.03
☐ 203 Steve Carlton	1.50	.70	.19
☐ 204 John D'Acquisto	.10	.05	.01
Now with Angels			
☐ 205 Rick Reuschel	.25	.11	.03
☐ 206 Dan Quisenberry	.25	.11	.03
☐ 207 Mike Schmidt DP	2.00	.90	.25
☐ 208 Bob Watson	.25	.11	.03
☐ 209 Jim Spencer	.10	.05	.01
☐ 210 Jim Palmer	1.00	.45	.12
☐ 211 Derrel Thomas	.10	.05	.01
☐ 212 Steve Nicosia	.10	.05	.01
☐ 213 Omar Moreno	.10	.05	.01
☐ 214 Richie Zisk	.10	.05	.01
Now with Mariners			
☐ 215 Larry Hisle	.10	.05	.01
☐ 216 Mike Torrez	.10	.05	.01
☐ 217 Rich Hebner	.10	.05	.01
☐ 218 Britt Burns	.10	.05	.01
☐ 219 Ken Landreaux	.10	.05	.01
☐ 220 Tom Seaver	2.00	.90	.25
☐ 221 Bob Davis	.10	.05	.01
Now with Angels			
☐ 222 Jorge Orta	.10	.05	.01
☐ 223 Bobby Bonds	.25	.11	.03
☐ 224 Pat Zachry	.10	.05	.01
☐ 225 Ruppert Jones	.10	.05	.01
☐ 226 Duane Kuiper	.10	.05	.01
☐ 227 Rodney Scott	.10	.05	.01
☐ 228 Tom Paciorek	.10	.05	.01
☐ 229 Rollie Fingers	.75	.35	.09
Now with Brewers			
☐ 230 George Hendrick	.10	.05	.01
☐ 231 Tony Perez	.75	.35	.09
☐ 232 Grant Jackson	.10	.05	.01
☐ 233 Damaso Garcia	.10	.05	.01
☐ 234 Lou Whitaker	1.25	.55	.16
☐ 235 Scott Sanderson	.10	.05	.01
☐ 236 Mike Ivie	.10	.05	.01
☐ 237 Charlie Moore	.10	.05	.01
☐ 238 Blue Jays Rookies	.10	.05	.01
Luis Leal			
Brian Milner			
Ken Schrom			
☐ 239 Rick Miller DP	.05	.02	.01
Now with Red Sox			
☐ 240 Nolan Ryan	10.00	4.50	1.25
☐ 241 Checklist 126-250 DP	.05	.02	.01
☐ 242 Chet Lemon	.10	.05	.01
☐ 243 Dave Palmer	.10	.05	.01
☐ 244 Ellis Valentine	.10	.05	.01
☐ 245 Carney Lansford	.25	.11	.03
Now with Red Sox			
☐ 246 Ed Ott DP	.05	.02	.01
☐ 247 Glenn Hubbard DP	.05	.02	.01
☐ 248 Joey McLaughlin	.10	.05	.01
☐ 249 Jerry Narron	.10	.05	.01
☐ 250 Ron Guidry	.25	.11	.03
☐ 251 Steve Garvey	.50	.23	.06
☐ 252 Victor Cruz	.10	.05	.01
☐ 253 Bobby Murcer	.25	.11	.03
☐ 254 Ozzie Smith	8.00	3.60	1.00
☐ 255 John Stearns	.10	.05	.01
☐ 256 Bill Campbell	.10	.05	.01
☐ 257 Rennie Stennett	.10	.05	.01
☐ 258 Rick Waits	.10	.05	.01
☐ 259 Gary Lucas	.10	.05	.01
☐ 260 Ron Cey	.25	.11	.03
☐ 261 Rickey Henderson	8.00	3.60	1.00
☐ 262 Sammy Stewart	.10	.05	.01
☐ 263 Brian Downing	.10	.05	.01
☐ 264 Mark Bomback	.10	.05	.01
☐ 265 John Candelaria	.25	.11	.03
☐ 266 Renie Martin	.10	.05	.01
☐ 267 Stan Bahnsen	.10	.05	.01
☐ 268 Montreal Expos CL	.50	.23	.06
☐ 269 Ken Forsch	.10	.05	.01
☐ 270 Greg Luzinski	.25	.11	.03
☐ 271 Ron Jackson	.10	.05	.01
☐ 272 Wayne Garland	.10	.05	.01
☐ 273 Milt May	.10	.05	.01
☐ 274 Rick Wise	.10	.05	.01
☐ 275 Dwight Evans	.50	.23	.06
☐ 276 Sal Bando	.25	.11	.03
☐ 277 Alfredo Griffin	.10	.05	.01
☐ 278 Rick Sofield	.10	.05	.01
☐ 279 Bob Knepper	.10	.05	.01
Now with Astros			
☐ 280 Ken Griffey	.25	.11	.03
☐ 281 Ken Singleton	.25	.11	.03
☐ 282 Ernie Whitt	.10	.05	.01
☐ 283 Billy Sample	.10	.05	.01
☐ 284 Jack Morris	.75	.35	.09
☐ 285 Dick Ruthven	.10	.05	.01
☐ 286 Johnny Bench	2.00	.90	.25
☐ 287 Dave Smith	.25	.11	.03
☐ 288 Amos Otis	.25	.11	.03
☐ 289 Dave Goltz	.10	.05	.01
☐ 290 Bob Boone DP	.25	.11	.03
☐ 291 Aurelio Lopez	.10	.05	.01
☐ 292 Tom Hume	.10	.05	.01
☐ 293 Charlie Lea	.10	.05	.01
☐ 294 Bert Blyleven	.50	.23	.06
Now with Indians			
☐ 295 Hal McRae	.25	.11	.03
☐ 296 Bob Stanley	.10	.05	.01
☐ 297 Bob Bailor	.10	.05	.01
Now with Mets			
☐ 298 Jerry Koosman	.25	.11	.03
☐ 299 Elliott Maddox	.10	.05	.01
Now with Yankees			
☐ 300 Paul Molitor	5.00	2.20	.60
☐ 301 Matt Keough	.10	.05	.01
☐ 302 Pat Putnam	.10	.05	.01
☐ 303 Dan Ford	.10	.05	.01
☐ 304 John Castino	.10	.05	.01
☐ 305 Barry Foote	.10	.05	.01
☐ 306 Lou Piniella	.25	.11	.03
☐ 307 Gene Garber	.10	.05	.01
☐ 308 Rick Manning	.10	.05	.01
☐ 309 Don Baylor	.50	.23	.06
☐ 310 Vida Blue DP	.25	.11	.03
☐ 311 Doug Flynn	.10	.05	.01
☐ 312 Rick Rhoden	.10	.05	.01
☐ 313 Fred Lynn	.25	.11	.03
Now with Angels			
☐ 314 Rich Dauer	.10	.05	.01
☐ 315 Kirk Gibson	3.00	1.35	.35
☐ 316 Ken Reitz	.10	.05	.01
Now with Cubs			
☐ 317 Lonnie Smith	.25	.11	.03
☐ 318 Steve Yeager	.10	.05	.01
☐ 319 Rowland Office	.10	.05	.01
☐ 320 Tom Burgmeier	.10	.05	.01
☐ 321 Leon Durham	.25	.11	.03
Now with Cubs			
☐ 322 Neil Allen	.10	.05	.01
☐ 323 Ray Burris	.10	.05	.01
Now with Expos			
☐ 324 Mike Willis	.10	.05	.01
☐ 325 Ray Knight	.25	.11	.03
☐ 326 Rafael Landestoy	.10	.05	.01
☐ 327 Moose Haas	.10	.05	.01
☐ 328 Ross Baumgarten	.10	.05	.01
☐ 329 Joaquin Andujar	.25	.11	.03
☐ 330 Frank White	.25	.11	.03
☐ 331 Toronto Blue Jays CL	.10	.05	.01
☐ 332 Dick Drago	.10	.05	.01
☐ 333 Sid Monge	.10	.05	.01
☐ 334 Joe Sambito	.10	.05	.01
☐ 335 Rick Cerone	.10	.05	.01
☐ 336 Eddie Whitson	.10	.05	.01
☐ 337 Sparky Lyle	.25	.11	.03
☐ 338 Checklist 251-374	.10	.05	.01
☐ 339 Jon Matlack	.10	.05	.01
☐ 340 Ben Oglivie	.10	.05	.01
☐ 341 Dwayne Murphy	.10	.05	.01
☐ 342 Terry Crowley	.10	.05	.01
☐ 343 Frank Taveras	.10	.05	.01
☐ 344 Steve Rogers	.10	.05	.01
☐ 345 Warren Cromartie	.10	.05	.01
☐ 346 Bill Caudill	.10	.05	.01
☐ 347 Harold Baines	2.50	1.10	.30
☐ 348 Frank LaCorte	.10	.05	.01
☐ 349 Glenn Hoffman	.10	.05	.01
☐ 350 J.R. Richard	.10	.05	.01
☐ 351 Otto Velez	.10	.05	.01
☐ 352 Ted Simmons	.25	.11	.03
Now with Brewers			
☐ 353 Terry Kennedy	.10	.05	.01
Now with Padres			
☐ 354 Al Hrabosky	.10	.05	.01
☐ 355 Bob Horner	.25	.11	.03
☐ 356 Cecil Cooper	.25	.11	.03
☐ 357 Bob Welch	.25	.11	.03
☐ 358 Paul Moskau	.10	.05	.01
☐ 359 Dave Rader	.10	.05	.01
Now with Angels			
☐ 360 Willie Wilson	.25	.11	.03
☐ 361 Dave Kingman DP	.25	.11	.03
☐ 362 Joe Rudi	.10	.05	.01
Now with Red Sox			
☐ 363 Rich Gale	.10	.05	.01
☐ 364 Steve Trout	.10	.05	.01
☐ 365 Graig Nettles DP	.25	.11	.03
☐ 366 Lamar Johnson	.05	.02	.01
☐ 367 Denny Martinez	.75	.35	.09
☐ 368 Manny Trillo	.10	.05	.01
☐ 369 Frank Tanana	.25	.11	.03
Now with White Sox			
☐ 370 Reggie Jackson	2.00	.90	.25
☐ 371 Bill Lee	.25	.11	.03
☐ 372 Jay Johnstone	.25	.11	.03
☐ 373 Jason Thompson	.10	.05	.01
☐ 374 Tom Hutton	.10	.05	.01

1981 O-Pee-Chee Posters

The 24 full-color posters comprising the 1981 O-Pee-Chee poster insert set were inserted one per regular wax pack and feature players of the Montreal Expos (numbered 1-12) and the Toronto Blue Jays (numbered 13-24). These posters are typically found with two folds and measure approximately 4 7/8" by 6 7/8". The posters are blank-backed and are numbered at the bottom in French and English. A distinctive red (Expos) or blue (Blue Jays) border surrounds the player photo.

	NRMT	VG-E	GOOD
COMPLETE SET (24)	8.00	3.60	1.00
COMMON CARD (1-24)	.25	.11	.03
☐ 1 Willie Montanez	.25	.11	.03
☐ 2 Rodney Scott	.25	.11	.03
☐ 3 Chris Speier	.25	.11	.03
☐ 4 Larry Parrish	.50	.23	.06
☐ 5 Warren Cromartie	.50	.23	.06
☐ 6 Andre Dawson	2.00	.90	.25
☐ 7 Ellis Valentine	.25	.11	.03
☐ 8 Gary Carter	.50	.23	.06
☐ 9 Steve Rogers	.25	.11	.03
☐ 10 Woodie Fryman	.25	.11	.03
☐ 11 Jerry White	.25	.11	.03
☐ 12 Scott Sanderson	.25	.11	.03
☐ 13 John Mayberry	.25	.11	.03
☐ 14 Damaso Garcia UER	.25	.11	.03
(Misspelled Damasa)			
☐ 15 Alfredo Griffin	.25	.11	.03
☐ 16 Garth Iorg	.25	.11	.03
☐ 17 Alvis Woods	.25	.11	.03
☐ 18 Rick Bosetti	.25	.11	.03
☐ 19 Barry Bonnell	.25	.11	.03
☐ 20 Ernie Whitt	.25	.11	.03
☐ 21 Jim Clancy	.25	.11	.03
☐ 22 Dave Stieb	.50	.23	.06
☐ 23 Otto Velez	.25	.11	.03
☐ 24 Lloyd Moseby	.50	.23	.06

1982 O-Pee-Chee

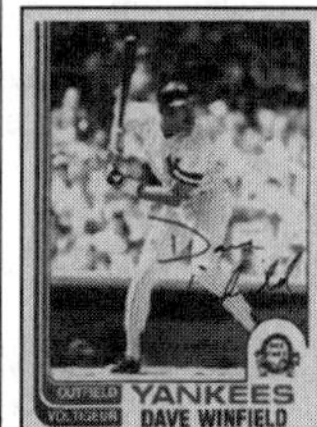

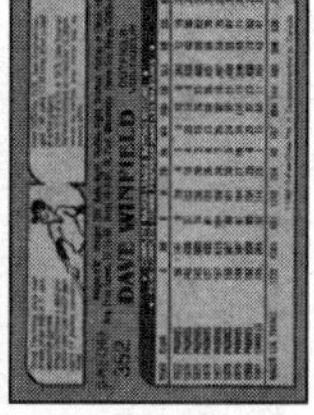

This set is an abridgement of the 1982 Topps set. The 396 standard-size cards comprising the 1982 O-Pee-Chee set differ from the cards of the 1982 Topps set by having a higher ratio of cards of players from the two Canadian teams, a practice begun by O-Pee-Chee in 1977 and continued to 1988. The set contains virtually the same pictures for the players also featured in the 1982 Topps issue, but the O-Pee-Chee photos appear brighter. The fronts feature white-bordered color player photos with colored lines within the wide white margin on the left. The player's name, team and bilingual position appear in colored lettering within the wide bottom margin. The player's name also appears as a simulated autograph across the photo. The blue print on green horizontal backs carry the player's name, bilingual position and biography at the top. The player's major league statistics follow below. The cards are numbered on the back. The asterisked cards have an extra line on the front inside the picture area indicating team change. In Action (IA) and All-Star (AS) cards are indicated in the checklist below; these are included in the set in addition to the player's regular card. The 396 cards in the set were the largest "original" or distinct set total printed up to that time by O-Pee-Chee; the previous high had been 374 in 1979, 1980 and 1981.

	NRMT	VG-E	GOOD
COMPLETE SET (396)	45.00	20.00	5.50
COMMON CARD (1-396)	.10	.05	.01
☐ 1 Dan Spillner	.10	.05	.01
☐ 2 Ken Singleton AS	.10	.05	.01
☐ 3 John Candelaria	.10	.05	.01
☐ 4 Frank Tanana	.25	.11	.03
Traded to Royals Jan. 15/82			
☐ 5 Reggie Smith	.25	.11	.03
☐ 6 Rick Monday	.10	.05	.01
☐ 7 Scott Sanderson	.10	.05	.01
☐ 8 Rich Dauer	.10	.05	.01
☐ 9 Ron Guidry	.25	.11	.03
☐ 10 Ron Guidry IA	.25	.11	.03
☐ 11 Tom Brookens	.10	.05	.01
☐ 12 Moose Haas	.10	.05	.01
☐ 13 Chet Lemon	.10	.05	.01
Traded to Tigers Nov. 27/81			
☐ 14 Steve Howe	.10	.05	.01
☐ 15 Ellis Valentine	.10	.05	.01
☐ 16 Toby Harrah	.25	.11	.03
☐ 17 Darrell Evans	.25	.11	.03
☐ 18 Johnny Bench	2.00	.90	.25
☐ 19 Ernie Whitt	.10	.05	.01
☐ 20 Garry Maddox	.10	.05	.01
☐ 21 Graig Nettles IA	.25	.11	.03
☐ 22 Al Oliver IA	.25	.11	.03
☐ 23 Bob Boone	.25	.11	.03
Traded to Angels Dec. 9/81			
☐ 24 Pete Rose IA	1.50	.70	.19
☐ 25 Jerry Remy	.10	.05	.01
☐ 26 Jorge Orta	.10	.05	.01
Traded to Dodgers Dec 9/81			
☐ 27 Bobby Bonds	.25	.11	.03
☐ 28 Jim Clancy	.10	.05	.01
☐ 29 Dwayne Murphy	.10	.05	.01
☐ 30 Tom Seaver	2.00	.90	.25
☐ 31 Tom Seaver IA	1.00	.45	.12
☐ 32 Claudell Washington	.10	.05	.01
☐ 33 Bob Shirley	.10	.05	.01
☐ 34 Bob Forsch	.10	.05	.01
☐ 35 Willie Aikens	.10	.05	.01
☐ 36 Rod Carew AS	.75	.35	.09
☐ 37 Willie Randolph	.25	.11	.03
☐ 38 Charlie Lea	.10	.05	.01
☐ 39 Lou Whitaker	.75	.35	.09
☐ 40 Dave Parker	.25	.11	.03
☐ 41 Dave Parker IA	.25	.11	.03
☐ 42 Mark Belanger	.25	.11	.03
Traded to Dodgers Dec. 24/81			
☐ 43 Rick Langford	.10	.05	.01
☐ 44 Rollie Fingers IA	.50	.23	.06
☐ 45 Rick Cerone	.10	.05	.01
☐ 46 Johnny Wockenfuss	.10	.05	.01
☐ 47 Jack Morris AS	.25	.11	.03
☐ 48 Cesar Cedeno	.10	.05	.01
Traded to Reds Dec. 18/81			
☐ 49 Alvis Woods	.10	.05	.01
☐ 50 Buddy Bell	.25	.11	.03
☐ 51 Mickey Rivers IA	.10	.05	.01
☐ 52 Steve Rogers	.10	.05	.01
☐ 53 Blue Jays Leaders	.10	.05	.01
John Mayberry			
Dave Stieb			
(Team checklist			
on back)			
☐ 54 Ron Hassey	.10	.05	.01
☐ 55 Rick Burleson	.10	.05	.01
☐ 56 Harold Baines	.50	.23	.06
☐ 57 Craig Reynolds	.10	.05	.01
☐ 58 Carlton Fisk AS	.75	.35	.09
☐ 59 Jim Kern	.10	.05	.01
Traded to Reds Feb. 10/82			
☐ 60 Tony Armas	.10	.05	.01
☐ 61 Warren Cromartie	.10	.05	.01
☐ 62 Graig Nettles	.25	.11	.03
☐ 63 Jerry Koosman	.25	.11	.03
☐ 64 Pat Zachry	.10	.05	.01
☐ 65 Terry Kennedy	.10	.05	.01
☐ 66 Richie Zisk	.10	.05	.01
☐ 67 Rich Gale	.10	.05	.01
Traded to Giants Dec. 10/81			
☐ 68 Steve Carlton	1.50	.70	.19
☐ 69 Greg Luzinski IA	.25	.11	.03
☐ 70 Tim Raines	2.00	.90	.25
☐ 71 Roy Lee Jackson	.10	.05	.01
☐ 72 Carl Yastrzemski	1.50	.70	.19
☐ 73 John Castino	.10	.05	.01
☐ 74 Joe Niekro	.25	.11	.03
☐ 75 Tommy John	.50	.23	.06
☐ 76 Dave Winfield AS	.75	.35	.09
☐ 77 Miguel Dilone	.10	.05	.01
☐ 78 Gary Gray	.10	.05	.01
☐ 79 Tom Hume	.10	.05	.01
☐ 80 Jim Palmer	1.00	.45	.12
☐ 81 Jim Palmer IA	.60	.25	.07
☐ 82 Vida Blue IA	.25	.11	.03

☐ 83 Garth Iorg .10 .05 .01
☐ 84 Rennie Stennett .10 .05 .01
☐ 85 Dave Lopes IA .25 .11 .03
Traded to A's Feb. 8/82
☐ 86 Dave Concepcion .25 .11 .03
☐ 87 Matt Keough .10 .05 .01
☐ 88 Jim Spencer .10 .05 .01
☐ 89 Steve Henderson .10 .05 .01
☐ 90 Nolan Ryan 10.00 4.50 1.25
☐ 91 Carney Lansford .25 .11 .03
☐ 92 Bake McBride .10 .05 .01
☐ 93 Dave Stapleton .10 .05 .01
☐ 94 Expos Team Leaders .10 .05 .01
Warren Cromartie
Bill Gullickson
(Team checklist
on back)
☐ 95 Ozzie Smith 8.00 3.60 1.00
Traded to Cardinals Feb. 11/82
☐ 96 Rich Hebner .10 .05 .01
☐ 97 Tim Foli .10 .05 .01
Traded to Angels Dec. 11/82
☐ 98 Darrell Porter .10 .05 .01
☐ 99 Barry Bonnell .10 .05 .01
☐ 100 Mike Schmidt 3.00 1.35 .35
☐ 101 Mike Schmidt IA 1.50 .70 .19
☐ 102 Dan Briggs .10 .05 .01
☐ 103 Al Cowens .10 .05 .01
☐ 104 Grant Jackson .10 .05 .01
Traded to Royals Jan. 19/82
☐ 105 Kirk Gibson .75 .35 .09
☐ 106 Dan Schatzeder .10 .05 .01
Traded to Giants Dec. 9/81
☐ 107 Juan Berenguer .10 .05 .01
☐ 108 Jack Morris .50 .23 .06
☐ 109 Dave Revering .10 .05 .01
☐ 110 Carlton Fisk 1.50 .70 .19
☐ 111 Carlton Fisk IA .75 .35 .09
☐ 112 Billy Sample .10 .05 .01
☐ 113 Steve McCatty .10 .05 .01
☐ 114 Ken Landreaux .10 .05 .01
☐ 115 Gaylord Perry .75 .35 .09
☐ 116 Elias Sosa .10 .05 .01
☐ 117 Rich Gossage IA .25 .11 .03
☐ 118 Expos Future Stars .50 .23 .06
Terry Francona
Brad Mills
Bryn Smith
☐ 119 Billy Almon .10 .05 .01
☐ 120 Gary Lucas .10 .05 .01
☐ 121 Ken Oberkfell .10 .05 .01
☐ 122 Steve Carlton IA .75 .35 .09
☐ 123 Jeff Reardon .50 .23 .06
☐ 124 Bill Buckner .25 .11 .03
☐ 125 Danny Ainge .75 .35 .09
Voluntarily Retired Nov. 30/81
☐ 126 Paul Splittorff .10 .05 .01
☐ 127 Lonnie Smith .10 .05 .01
Traded to Cardinals Nov. 19/81
☐ 128 Rudy May .10 .05 .01
☐ 129 Checklist 1-132 .10 .05 .01
☐ 130 Julio Cruz .10 .05 .01
☐ 131 Stan Bahnsen .10 .05 .01
☐ 132 Pete Vuckovich .10 .05 .01
☐ 133 Luis Salazar .10 .05 .01
☐ 134 Dan Ford .10 .05 .01
Traded to Orioles Jan. 28/82
☐ 135 Denny Martinez .60 .25 .07
☐ 136 Lary Sorensen .10 .05 .01
☐ 137 Fergie Jenkins .75 .35 .09
Traded to Cubs Dec. 15/81
☐ 138 Rick Camp .10 .05 .01
☐ 139 Wayne Nordhagen .10 .05 .01
☐ 140 Ron LeFlore .25 .11 .03
☐ 141 Rick Sutcliffe .25 .11 .03
☐ 142 Rick Waits .10 .05 .01
☐ 143 Mookie Wilson .75 .35 .09
☐ 144 Greg Minton .10 .05 .01
☐ 145 Bob Horner .25 .11 .03
☐ 146 Joe Morgan IA .60 .25 .07
☐ 147 Larry Gura .10 .05 .01
☐ 148 Alfredo Griffin .10 .05 .01
☐ 149 Pat Putnam .10 .05 .01
☐ 150 Ted Simmons .25 .11 .03
☐ 151 Gary Matthews .25 .11 .03
☐ 152 Greg Luzinski .25 .11 .03
☐ 153 Mike Flanagan .25 .11 .03
☐ 154 Jim Morrison .10 .05 .01
☐ 155 Otto Velez .10 .05 .01
☐ 156 Frank White .25 .11 .03
☐ 157 Doug Corbett .10 .05 .01
☐ 158 Brian Downing .10 .05 .01
☐ 159 Willie Randolph IA .25 .11 .03
☐ 160 Luis Tiant .25 .11 .03
☐ 161 Andre Thornton .10 .05 .01
☐ 162 Amos Otis .25 .11 .03
☐ 163 Paul Mirabella .10 .05 .01
☐ 164 Bert Blyleven .50 .23 .06
☐ 165 Rowland Office .10 .05 .01
☐ 166 Gene Tenace .25 .11 .03
☐ 167 Cecil Cooper .25 .11 .03
☐ 168 Bruce Benedict .10 .05 .01
☐ 169 Mark Clear .10 .05 .01
☐ 170 Jim Bibby .10 .05 .01
☐ 171 Ken Griffey IA .25 .11 .03
Traded to Yankees Nov 4/81
☐ 172 Bill Gullickson .10 .05 .01
☐ 173 Mike Scioscia .10 .05 .01
☐ 174 Doug DeCinces .10 .05 .01
Traded to Angels Jan 28/82
☐ 175 Jerry Mumphrey .10 .05 .01
☐ 176 Rollie Fingers .75 .35 .09
☐ 177 George Foster IA .25 .11 .03
Traded to Mets Feb 10/82
☐ 178 Mitchell Page .10 .05 .01
☐ 179 Steve Garvey .50 .23 .06
☐ 180 Steve Garvey IA .50 .23 .06
☐ 181 Woodie Fryman .10 .05 .01
☐ 182 Larry Herndon .10 .05 .01
Traded to Tigers Dec. 9/81
☐ 183 Frank White IA .25 .11 .03
☐ 184 Alan Ashby .10 .05 .01
☐ 185 Phil Niekro .75 .35 .09
☐ 186 Leon Roberts .10 .05 .01
☐ 187 Rod Carew 1.50 .70 .19
☐ 188 Willie Stargell IA .60 .25 .07
☐ 189 Joel Youngblood .10 .05 .01
☐ 190 J.R. Richard .10 .05 .01
☐ 191 Tim Wallach .50 .23 .06
☐ 192 Broderick Perkins .10 .05 .01
☐ 193 Johnny Grubb .10 .05 .01
☐ 194 Larry Bowa .25 .11 .03
Traded to Cubs Jan. 27/82
☐ 195 Paul Molitor 3.00 1.35 .35
☐ 196 Willie Upshaw .10 .05 .01
☐ 197 Roy Smalley .10 .05 .01
☐ 198 Chris Speier .10 .05 .01
☐ 199 Don Aase .10 .05 .01
☐ 200 George Brett 6.00 2.70 .75
☐ 201 George Brett IA 3.00 1.35 .35
☐ 202 Rick Manning .10 .05 .01
☐ 203 Blue Jays Prospects .50 .23 .06
Jesse Barfield
Brian Milner
Boomer Wells *
☐ 204 Rick Reuschel .25 .11 .03
☐ 205 Neil Allen .10 .05 .01
☐ 206 Leon Durham .10 .05 .01
☐ 207 Jim Gantner .25 .11 .03
☐ 208 Joe Morgan 1.00 .45 .12
☐ 209 Gary Lavelle .10 .05 .01
☐ 210 Keith Hernandez .25 .11 .03
☐ 211 Joe Charboneau .10 .05 .01
☐ 212 Mario Mendoza .10 .05 .01
☐ 213 Willie Randolph AS .25 .11 .03
☐ 214 Lance Parrish .50 .23 .06
☐ 215 Mike Krukow .10 .05 .01
Traded to Phillies Dec. 8/81
☐ 216 Ron Cey .25 .11 .03
☐ 217 Ruppert Jones .10 .05 .01
☐ 218 Dave Lopes .25 .11 .03
Traded to A's Feb. 8/82
☐ 219 Steve Yeager .10 .05 .01
☐ 220 Manny Trillo .10 .05 .01
☐ 221 Dave Concepcion IA .25 .11 .03
☐ 222 Butch Wynegar .10 .05 .01
☐ 223 Lloyd Moseby .10 .05 .01
☐ 224 Bruce Bochte .10 .05 .01
☐ 225 Ed Ott .10 .05 .01
☐ 226 Checklist 133-264 .10 .05 .01
☐ 227 Ray Burris .10 .05 .01
☐ 228 Reggie Smith IA .25 .11 .03
☐ 229 Oscar Gamble .10 .05 .01
☐ 230 Willie Wilson .10 .05 .01
☐ 231 Brian Kingman .10 .05 .01
☐ 232 John Stearns .10 .05 .01
☐ 233 Duane Kuiper .10 .05 .01
Traded to Giants Nov. 16/81
☐ 234 Don Baylor .25 .11 .03
☐ 235 Mike Easler .10 .05 .01
☐ 236 Lou Piniella .25 .11 .03
☐ 237 Robin Yount 1.50 .70 .19
☐ 238 Kevin Saucier .10 .05 .01
☐ 239 Jon Matlack .10 .05 .01
☐ 240 Bucky Dent .25 .11 .03
☐ 241 Bucky Dent IA .25 .11 .03
☐ 242 Milt May .10 .05 .01
☐ 243 Lee Mazzilli .10 .05 .01
☐ 244 Gary Carter .75 .35 .09
☐ 245 Ken Reitz .10 .05 .01
☐ 246 Scott McGregor AS .10 .05 .01
☐ 247 Pedro Guerrero .25 .11 .03
☐ 248 Art Howe .10 .05 .01
☐ 249 Dick Tidrow .10 .05 .01
☐ 250 Tug McGraw .25 .11 .03
☐ 251 Fred Lynn .25 .11 .03
☐ 252 Fred Lynn IA .25 .11 .03
☐ 253 Gene Richards .10 .05 .01
☐ 254 Jorge Bell .10 .05 .01
☐ 255 Tony Perez .50 .23 .06
☐ 256 Tony Perez IA .25 .11 .03
☐ 257 Rich Dotson .10 .05 .01
☐ 258 Bo Diaz .10 .05 .01
Traded to Phillies Nov. 19/81
☐ 259 Rodney Scott .10 .05 .01
☐ 260 Bruce Sutter .25 .11 .03
☐ 261 George Brett AS 3.00 1.35 .35
☐ 262 Rick Dempsey .25 .11 .03
☐ 263 Mike Phillips .10 .05 .01
☐ 264 Jerry Garvin .10 .05 .01
☐ 265 Al Bumbry .10 .05 .01
☐ 266 Hubie Brooks .10 .05 .01
☐ 267 Vida Blue .25 .11 .03
☐ 268 Rickey Henderson 4.00 1.80 .50
☐ 269 Rick Peters .10 .05 .01
☐ 270 Rusty Staub .25 .11 .03
☐ 271 Sixto Lezcano .10 .05 .01
Traded to Padres Dec. 10/81
☐ 272 Bump Wills .10 .05 .01
☐ 273 Gary Allenson .10 .05 .01
☐ 274 Randy Jones .10 .05 .01
☐ 275 Bob Watson .25 .11 .03
☐ 276 Dave Kingman .25 .11 .03
☐ 277 Terry Puhl .10 .05 .01
☐ 278 Jerry Reuss .25 .11 .03
☐ 279 Sammy Stewart .10 .05 .01
☐ 280 Ben Oglivie .10 .05 .01
☐ 281 Kent Tekulve .25 .11 .03
☐ 282 Ken Macha .10 .05 .01
☐ 283 Ron Davis .10 .05 .01
☐ 284 Bob Grich .25 .11 .03
☐ 285 Sparky Lyle .25 .11 .03
☐ 286 Rich Gossage AS .25 .11 .03
☐ 287 Dennis Eckersley .60 .25 .07
☐ 288 Garry Templeton .10 .05 .01
Traded to Padres Dec. 10/81
☐ 289 Bob Stanley .10 .05 .01
☐ 290 Ken Singleton .10 .05 .01
☐ 291 Mickey Hatcher .10 .05 .01
☐ 292 Dave Palmer .10 .05 .01
☐ 293 Damaso Garcia .10 .05 .01
☐ 294 Don Money .10 .05 .01
☐ 295 George Hendrick .10 .05 .01
☐ 296 Steve Kemp .10 .05 .01
Traded to White Sox Nov. 27/81
☐ 297 Dave Smith .10 .05 .01
☐ 298 Bucky Dent AS .10 .05 .01
☐ 299 Steve Trout .10 .05 .01
☐ 300 Reggie Jackson 3.00 1.35 .35
Traded to Angels Jan. 26/82
☐ 301 Reggie Jackson IA 1.50 .70 .19
Traded to Angels Jan. 26/82
☐ 302 Doug Flynn .10 .05 .01
Traded to Rangers Dec. 14/81
☐ 303 Wayne Gross .10 .05 .01
☐ 304 Johnny Bench IA 1.00 .45 .12
☐ 305 Don Sutton .50 .23 .06
☐ 306 Don Sutton IA .25 .11 .03
☐ 307 Mark Bomback .10 .05 .01
☐ 308 Charlie Moore .10 .05 .01
☐ 309 Jeff Burroughs .10 .05 .01
☐ 310 Mike Hargrove .25 .11 .03
☐ 311 Enos Cabell .10 .05 .01
☐ 312 Lenny Randle .10 .05 .01
☐ 313 Ivan DeJesus .10 .05 .01
Traded to Phillies Jan. 27/82
☐ 314 Buck Martinez .10 .05 .01
☐ 315 Burt Hooton .10 .05 .01
☐ 316 Scott McGregor .10 .05 .01
☐ 317 Dick Ruthven .10 .05 .01
☐ 318 Mike Heath .10 .05 .01
☐ 319 Ray Knight .25 .11 .03
Traded to Astros Dec. 18/81
☐ 320 Chris Chambliss .10 .05 .01
☐ 321 Chris Chambliss IA .10 .05 .01
☐ 322 Ross Baumgarten .10 .05 .01
☐ 323 Bill Lee .25 .11 .03
☐ 324 Gorman Thomas .10 .05 .01
☐ 325 Jose Cruz .25 .11 .03
☐ 326 Al Oliver .25 .11 .03
☐ 327 Jackson Todd .10 .05 .01
☐ 328 Ed Farmer .10 .05 .01
Traded to Phillies Jan. 28/82
☐ 329 U.L. Washington .10 .05 .01
☐ 330 Ken Griffey .25 .11 .03
Traded to Yankees Nov. 4/81
☐ 331 John Milner .10 .05 .01
☐ 332 Don Robinson .10 .05 .01
☐ 333 Cliff Johnson .10 .05 .01
☐ 334 Fernando Valenzuela 1.00 .45 .12
☐ 335 Jim Sundberg .25 .11 .03
☐ 336 George Foster .25 .11 .03
Traded to Mets Feb. 10/82
☐ 337 Pete Rose AS 1.50 .70 .19
☐ 338 Dave Lopes AS .25 .11 .03
Traded to A's Feb. 8/82
☐ 339 Mike Schmidt AS 1.50 .70 .19
☐ 340 Dave Concepcion AS .10 .05 .01
☐ 341 Andre Dawson AS .75 .35 .09
☐ 342 George Foster AS .25 .11 .03
Traded to Mets Feb. 10/82
☐ 343 Dave Parker AS .25 .11 .03
☐ 344 Gary Carter AS .25 .11 .03
☐ 345 Fernando Valenzuela AS .50 .23 .06
☐ 346 Tom Seaver AS 1.00 .45 .12
☐ 347 Bruce Sutter AS .25 .11 .03
☐ 348 Darrell Porter IA .10 .05 .01
☐ 349 Dave Collins .10 .05 .01
Traded to Yankees Dec. 23/81
☐ 350 Amos Otis IA .10 .05 .01
☐ 351 Frank Taveras .10 .05 .01
Traded to Expos Dec. 14/81
☐ 352 Dave Winfield 1.50 .70 .19
☐ 353 Larry Parrish .10 .05 .01
☐ 354 Roberto Ramos .10 .05 .01
☐ 355 Dwight Evans .25 .11 .03
☐ 356 Mickey Rivers .10 .05 .01
☐ 357 Butch Hobson .10 .05 .01
☐ 358 Carl Yastrzemski IA .75 .35 .09
☐ 359 Ron Jackson .10 .05 .01
☐ 360 Len Barker .10 .05 .01
☐ 361 Pete Rose 3.00 1.35 .35
☐ 362 Kevin Hickey .10 .05 .01
☐ 363 Rod Carew IA .75 .35 .09
☐ 364 Hector Cruz .10 .05 .01
☐ 365 Bill Madlock .25 .11 .03
☐ 366 Jim Rice .25 .11 .03
☐ 367 Ron Cey IA .25 .11 .03
☐ 368 Luis Leal .10 .05 .01
☐ 369 Dennis Leonard .10 .05 .01
☐ 370 Mike Norris .10 .05 .01
☐ 371 Tom Paciorek .10 .05 .01
Traded to White Sox Dec. 11/81
☐ 372 Willie Stargell 1.00 .45 .12
☐ 373 Dan Driessen .10 .05 .01
☐ 374 Larry Bowa IA .25 .11 .03
Traded to Cubs Jan. 27/82
☐ 375 Dusty Baker .25 .11 .03
☐ 376 Joey McLaughlin .10 .05 .01
☐ 377 Reggie Jackson AS 1.50 .70 .19
Traded to Angels Jan. 26/82
☐ 378 Mike Caldwell .10 .05 .01
☐ 379 Andre Dawson 1.50 .70 .19
☐ 380 Dave Stieb .10 .05 .01
☐ 381 Alan Trammell 1.00 .45 .12
☐ 382 John Mayberry .10 .05 .01
☐ 383 John Wathan .10 .05 .01
☐ 384 Hal McRae .25 .11 .03
☐ 385 Ken Forsch .10 .05 .01
☐ 386 Jerry White .10 .05 .01
☐ 387 Tom Veryzer .10 .05 .01
Traded to Mets Jan. 8/82
☐ 388 Joe Rudi .10 .05 .01
Traded to A's Dec. 4/81
☐ 389 Bob Knepper .10 .05 .01
☐ 390 Eddie Murray 4.00 1.80 .50
☐ 391 Dale Murphy 1.00 .45 .12
☐ 392 Bob Boone IA .25 .11 .03
Traded to Angels Dec. 6/81
☐ 393 Al Hrabosky .10 .05 .01
☐ 394 Checklist 265-396 .10 .05 .01
☐ 395 Omar Moreno .10 .05 .01
☐ 396 Rich Gossage .50 .23 .06

1982 O-Pee-Chee Posters

These 24 full-color posters comprising the 1982 O-Pee-Chee poster insert set were inserted one per regular wax pack and feature players of the Montreal Expos (numbered 13-24) and the Toronto Blue Jays (numbered 1-12). These posters are typically found with two folds and measure approximately 4 7/8" by 6 7/8". The posters are blank-backed and are numbered at the bottom in French and English. A distinctive red (Blue Jays) or blue (Expos) border surrounds the player photo.

	NRMT	VG-E	GOOD
COMPLETE SET (24)	8.00	3.60	1.00
COMMON CARD (1-24)	.25	.11	.03
☐ 1 John Mayberry	.25	.11	.03
☐ 2 Damaso Garcia	.25	.11	.03
☐ 3 Ernie Whitt	.25	.11	.03
☐ 4 Lloyd Moseby	.25	.11	.03
☐ 5 Alvis Woods	.25	.11	.03
☐ 6 Dave Stieb	.50	.23	.06
☐ 7 Roy Lee Jackson	.25	.11	.03
☐ 8 Joey McLaughlin	.25	.11	.03
☐ 9 Luis Leal	.25	.11	.03
☐ 10 Aurelio Rodriguez	.25	.11	.03
☐ 11 Otto Velez	.25	.11	.03
☐ 12 Juan Berenguer UER (Misspelled Berenger)	.25	.11	.03
☐ 13 Warren Cromartie	.25	.11	.03
☐ 14 Rodney Scott	.25	.11	.03
☐ 15 Larry Parrish	.50	.23	.06
☐ 16 Gary Carter	.50	.23	.06
☐ 17 Tim Raines	1.50	.70	.19
☐ 18 Andre Dawson	2.00	.90	.25
☐ 19 Terry Francona	.50	.23	.06
☐ 20 Steve Rogers	.25	.11	.03
☐ 21 Bill Gullickson	.50	.23	.06
☐ 22 Scott Sanderson	.25	.11	.03
☐ 23 Jeff Reardon	1.00	.45	.12
☐ 24 Jerry White	.25	.11	.03

1983 O-Pee-Chee

This set is an abridgement of the 1983 Topps set. The 396 standard-size cards comprising the 1983 O-Pee-Chee set differ from the cards

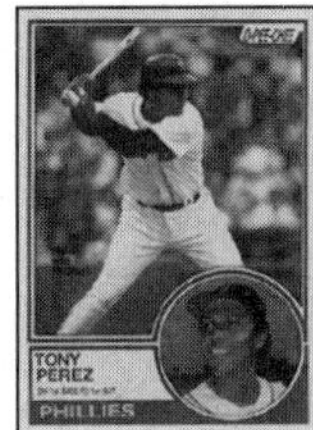

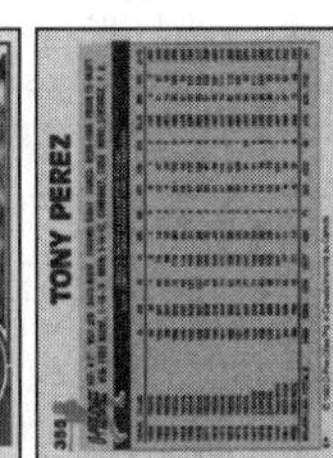

of the 1983 Topps set by having a higher ratio of cards of players from the two Canadian teams, a practice begun by O-Pee-Chee in 1977 and continued to 1988. The set contains virtually the same pictures for the players also featured in the 1983 Topps issue. The fronts feature white-bordered color player action photos framed by a colored line. A circular color player head shot also appears on the front at the lower right. The player's name, team and bilingual position appear at the lower left. The pink and white horizontal backs carry the player's name and biography at the top. The player's major league statistics and bilingual career highlights follow below. The asterisked cards have an extra line on the front inside the picture area indicating team change. The O-Pee-Chee logo appears on the front of every card. Super Veteran (SV) and All-Star (AS) cards are indicated in the checklist below; these are included in the set in addition to the player's regular card. The set features rookie year cards of Tony Gwynn and Ryne Sandberg.

	NRMT	VG-E	GOOD
COMPLETE SET (396)	60.00	27.00	7.50
COMMON CARD (1-396)	.10	.05	.01

	NRMT	VG-E	GOOD
☐ 1 Rusty Staub	.25	.11	.03
☐ 2 Larry Parrish	.10	.05	.01
☐ 3 George Brett	5.00	2.20	.60
☐ 4 Carl Yastrzemski	1.50	.70	.19
☐ 5 Al Oliver SV	.25	.11	.03
☐ 6 Bill Virdon MG	.10	.05	.01
☐ 7 Gene Richards	.10	.05	.01
☐ 8 Steve Balboni	.10	.05	.01
☐ 9 Joey McLaughlin	.10	.05	.01
☐ 10 Gorman Thomas	.10	.05	.01
☐ 11 Chris Chambliss	.25	.11	.03
☐ 12 Ray Burris	.10	.05	.01
☐ 13 Larry Herndon	.10	.05	.01
☐ 14 Ozzie Smith	3.00	1.35	.35
☐ 15 Ron Cey	.25	.11	.03
Now with Cubs			
☐ 16 Willie Wilson	.25	.11	.03
☐ 17 Kent Tekulve	.10	.05	.01
☐ 18 Kent Tekulve SV	.10	.05	.01
☐ 19 Oscar Gamble	.10	.05	.01
☐ 20 Carlton Fisk	1.25	.55	.16
☐ 21 Dale Murphy AS	.50	.23	.06
☐ 22 Randy Lerch	.10	.05	.01
☐ 23 Dale Murphy	.75	.35	.09
☐ 24 Steve Mura	.10	.05	.01
Now with White Sox			
☐ 25 Hal McRae	.25	.11	.03
☐ 26 Dennis Lamp	.10	.05	.01
☐ 27 Ron Washington	.10	.05	.01
☐ 28 Bruce Bochte	.10	.05	.01
☐ 29 Randy Jones	.10	.05	.01
Now with Pirates			
☐ 30 Jim Rice	.25	.11	.03
☐ 31 Bill Gullickson	.25	.11	.03
☐ 32 Dave Concepcion AS	.25	.11	.03
☐ 33 Ted Simmons SV	.25	.11	.03
☐ 34 Bobby Cox MG	.10	.05	.01
☐ 35 Rollie Fingers	.75	.35	.09
☐ 36 Rollie Fingers SV	.50	.23	.06
☐ 37 Mike Hargrove	.25	.11	.03
☐ 38 Roy Smalley	.10	.05	.01
☐ 39 Terry Puhl	.10	.05	.01
☐ 40 Fernando Valenzuela	.50	.23	.06
☐ 41 Garry Maddox	.10	.05	.01
☐ 42 Dale Murray	.50	.23	.06
Now with Yankees			
☐ 43 Bob Dernier	.10	.05	.01
☐ 44 Don Robinson	.10	.05	.01
☐ 45 John Mayberry	.10	.05	.01
☐ 46 Richard Dotson	.10	.05	.01
☐ 47 Wayne Nordhagen	.10	.05	.01
Now with Cubs			
☐ 48 Lary Sorensen	.10	.05	.01
☐ 49 Willie McGee	1.00	.45	.12
☐ 50 Bob Horner	.10	.05	.01
☐ 51 Rusty Staub SV	.25	.11	.03
☐ 52 Tom Seaver	3.00	1.35	.35
Now with Mets			
☐ 53 Chet Lemon	.10	.05	.01
☐ 54 Scott Sanderson	.10	.05	.01
☐ 55 Mookie Wilson	.25	.11	.03
☐ 56 Reggie Jackson	2.00	.90	.25
☐ 57 Tim Blackwell	.10	.05	.01
☐ 58 Keith Moreland	.10	.05	.01
☐ 59 Alvis Woods	.10	.05	.01
Now with Athletics			
☐ 60 Johnny Bench	2.00	.90	.25
☐ 61 Johnny Bench SV	1.00	.45	.12
☐ 62 Jim Gott	.10	.05	.01
☐ 63 Rick Monday	.10	.05	.01
☐ 64 Gary Matthews	.25	.11	.03
☐ 65 Jack Morris	.25	.11	.03
☐ 66 Lou Whitaker	.50	.23	.06
☐ 67 U.L. Washington	.10	.05	.01
☐ 68 Eric Show	.10	.05	.01
☐ 69 Lee Lacy	.10	.05	.01
☐ 70 Steve Carlton	1.25	.55	.16
☐ 71 Steve Carlton SV	.75	.35	.09
☐ 72 Tom Paciorek	.10	.05	.01
☐ 73 Manny Trillo	.10	.05	.01
Now with Indians			
☐ 74 Tony Perez SV	.50	.23	.06
☐ 75 Amos Otis	.25	.11	.03
☐ 76 Rick Mahler	.10	.05	.01
☐ 77 Hosken Powell	.10	.05	.01
☐ 78 Bill Caudill	.10	.05	.01
☐ 79 Dan Petry	.10	.05	.01
☐ 80 George Foster	.25	.11	.03
☐ 81 Joe Morgan	1.00	.45	.12
Now with Phillies			
☐ 82 Burt Hooton	.10	.05	.01
☐ 83 Ryne Sandberg	15.00	6.75	1.85
☐ 84 Alan Ashby	.10	.05	.01
☐ 85 Ken Singleton	.25	.11	.03
☐ 86 Tom Hume	.10	.05	.01
☐ 87 Dennis Leonard	.10	.05	.01
☐ 88 Jim Gantner	.25	.11	.03
☐ 89 Leon Roberts	.10	.05	.01
Now with Royals			
☐ 90 Jerry Reuss	.25	.11	.03
☐ 91 Ben Oglivie	.10	.05	.01
☐ 92 Sparky Lyle SV	.25	.11	.03
☐ 93 John Castino	.10	.05	.01
☐ 94 Phil Niekro	.75	.35	.09
☐ 95 Alan Trammell	.50	.23	.06
☐ 96 Gaylord Perry	.75	.35	.09
☐ 97 Tom Herr	.10	.05	.01
☐ 98 Vance Law	.10	.05	.01
☐ 99 Dickie Noles	.10	.05	.01
☐ 100 Pete Rose	3.00	1.35	.35
☐ 101 Pete Rose SV	1.50	.70	.19
☐ 102 Dave Concepcion	.25	.11	.03
☐ 103 Darrell Porter	.10	.05	.01
☐ 104 Ron Guidry	.25	.11	.03
☐ 105 Don Baylor	.25	.11	.03
Now with Yankees			
☐ 106 Steve Rogers AS	.10	.05	.01
☐ 107 Greg Minton	.10	.05	.01
☐ 108 Glenn Hoffman	.10	.05	.01
☐ 109 Luis Leal	.10	.05	.01
☐ 110 Ken Griffey	.25	.11	.03
☐ 111 Expos Leaders	.25	.11	.03
Al Oliver			
Steve Rogers			
(Team checklist on back)			
☐ 112 Luis Pujols	.10	.05	.01
☐ 113 Julio Cruz	.10	.05	.01
☐ 114 Jim Slaton	.10	.05	.01
☐ 115 Chili Davis	.75	.35	.09
☐ 116 Pedro Guerrero	.25	.11	.03
☐ 117 Mike Ivie	.10	.05	.01
☐ 118 Chris Welsh	.10	.05	.01
☐ 119 Frank Pastore	.10	.05	.01
☐ 120 Len Barker	.10	.05	.01
☐ 121 Chris Speier	.10	.05	.01
☐ 122 Bobby Murcer	.25	.11	.03
☐ 123 Bill Russell	.25	.11	.03
☐ 124 Lloyd Moseby	.10	.05	.01
☐ 125 Leon Durham	.10	.05	.01
☐ 126 Carl Yastrzemski SV	.75	.35	.09
☐ 127 John Candelaria	.10	.05	.01
☐ 128 Phil Garner	.25	.11	.03
☐ 129 Checklist 1-132	.10	.05	.01
☐ 130 Dave Stieb	.10	.05	.01
☐ 131 Geoff Zahn	.10	.05	.01
☐ 132 Todd Cruz	.10	.05	.01
☐ 133 Tony Pena	.25	.11	.03
☐ 134 Hubie Brooks	.10	.05	.01
☐ 135 Dwight Evans	.25	.11	.03
☐ 136 Willie Aikens	.10	.05	.01
☐ 137 Woodie Fryman	.10	.05	.01
☐ 138 Rick Dempsey	.25	.11	.03
☐ 139 Bruce Berenyi	.10	.05	.01
☐ 140 Willie Randolph	.25	.11	.03
☐ 141 Eddie Murray	3.00	1.35	.35
☐ 142 Mike Caldwell	.10	.05	.01
☐ 143 Tony Gwynn	20.00	9.00	2.50
☐ 144 Tommy John SV	.25	.11	.03
☐ 145 Don Sutton	.50	.23	.06
☐ 146 Don Sutton SV	.50	.23	.06
☐ 147 Rick Manning	.10	.05	.01
☐ 148 George Hendrick	.10	.05	.01
☐ 149 Johnny Ray	.10	.05	.01
☐ 150 Bruce Sutter	.25	.11	.03
☐ 151 Bruce Sutter SV	.25	.11	.03
☐ 152 Jay Johnstone	.25	.11	.03
☐ 153 Jerry Koosman	.25	.11	.03
☐ 154 Johnnie LeMaster	.10	.05	.01
☐ 155 Dan Quisenberry	.25	.11	.03
☐ 156 Luis Salazar	.10	.05	.01
☐ 157 Steve Bedrosian	.25	.11	.03
☐ 158 Jim Sundberg	.10	.05	.01
☐ 159 Gaylord Perry SV	.50	.23	.06
☐ 160 Dave Kingman	.25	.11	.03
☐ 161 Dave Kingman SV	.25	.11	.03
☐ 162 Mark Clear	.10	.05	.01
☐ 163 Cal Ripken	15.00	6.75	1.85
☐ 164 Dave Palmer	.10	.05	.01
☐ 165 Dan Driessen	.10	.05	.01
☐ 166 Tug McGraw	.25	.11	.03
☐ 167 Dennis Martinez	.25	.11	.03
☐ 168 Juan Eichelberger	.10	.05	.01
Now with Indians			
☐ 169 Doug Flynn	.10	.05	.01
☐ 170 Steve Howe	.10	.05	.01
☐ 171 Frank White	.25	.11	.03
☐ 172 Mike Flanagan	.25	.11	.03
☐ 173 Andre Dawson AS	.50	.23	.06
☐ 174 Manny Trillo AS	.10	.05	.01
Now with Indians			
☐ 175 Bo Diaz	.10	.05	.01
☐ 176 Dave Righetti	.25	.11	.03
☐ 177 Harold Baines	.50	.23	.06
☐ 178 Vida Blue	.25	.11	.03
☐ 179 Luis Tiant SV	.25	.11	.03
☐ 180 Rickey Henderson	3.00	1.35	.35
☐ 181 Rick Rhoden	.10	.05	.01
☐ 182 Fred Lynn	.25	.11	.03
☐ 183 Ed VandeBerg	.10	.05	.01
☐ 184 Dwayne Murphy	.10	.05	.01
☐ 185 Tim Lollar	.10	.05	.01
☐ 186 Dave Tobik	.10	.05	.01
☐ 187 Tug McGraw SV	.25	.11	.03
☐ 188 Rick Miller	.10	.05	.01
☐ 189 Dan Schatzeder	.10	.05	.01
☐ 190 Cecil Cooper	.25	.11	.03
☐ 191 Jim Beattie	.10	.05	.01
☐ 192 Rich Dauer	.10	.05	.01
☐ 193 Al Cowens	.10	.05	.01
☐ 194 Roy Lee Jackson	.10	.05	.01
☐ 195 Mike Gates	.10	.05	.01
☐ 196 Tommy John	.50	.23	.06
☐ 197 Bob Forsch	.10	.05	.01
☐ 198 Steve Garvey	.50	.23	.06
Now with Padres			
☐ 199 Brad Mills	.10	.05	.01
☐ 200 Rod Carew	1.25	.55	.16
☐ 201 Rod Carew SV	.75	.35	.09
☐ 202 Blue Jays Leaders	.10	.05	.01
Dave Stieb			
Damaso Garcia			
(Team checklist back)			
☐ 203 Floyd Bannister	.10	.05	.01
Now with White Sox			
☐ 204 Bruce Benedict	.10	.05	.01
☐ 205 Dave Parker	.25	.11	.03
☐ 206 Ken Oberkfell	.10	.05	.01
☐ 207 Graig Nettles SV	.25	.11	.03
☐ 208 Sparky Lyle	.25	.11	.03
☐ 209 Jason Thompson	.10	.05	.01
☐ 210 Jack Clark	.25	.11	.03
☐ 211 Jim Kaat	.25	.11	.03
☐ 212 John Stearns	.10	.05	.01
☐ 213 Tom Burgmeier	.10	.05	.01
☐ 214 Jerry White	.10	.05	.01
☐ 215 Mario Soto	.10	.05	.01
☐ 216 Scott McGregor	.10	.05	.01
☐ 217 Tim Stoddard	.10	.05	.01
☐ 218 Bill Laskey	.10	.05	.01
☐ 219 Reggie Jackson SV	1.00	.45	.12
☐ 220 Dusty Baker	.25	.11	.03
☐ 221 Joe Niekro	.25	.11	.03
☐ 222 Damaso Garcia	.10	.05	.01
☐ 223 John Montefusco	.10	.05	.01
☐ 224 Mickey Rivers	.10	.05	.01
☐ 225 Enos Cabell	.10	.05	.01
☐ 226 LaMarr Hoyt	.10	.05	.01
☐ 227 Tim Raines	.50	.23	.06
☐ 228 Joaquin Andujar	.10	.05	.01
☐ 229 Tim Wallach	.25	.11	.03
☐ 230 Fergie Jenkins	.75	.35	.09
☐ 231 Fergie Jenkins SV	.50	.23	.06
☐ 232 Tom Brunansky	.25	.11	.03
☐ 233 Ivan DeJesus	.10	.05	.01
☐ 234 Bryn Smith	.10	.05	.01
☐ 235 Claudell Washington	.10	.05	.01
☐ 236 Steve Renko	.10	.05	.01
☐ 237 Dan Norman	.10	.05	.01
☐ 238 Cesar Cedeno	.25	.11	.03
☐ 239 Dave Stapleton	.10	.05	.01
☐ 240 Rich Gossage	.50	.23	.06
☐ 241 Rich Gossage SV	.25	.11	.03
☐ 242 Bob Stanley	.10	.05	.01
☐ 243 Rich Gale	.10	.05	.01
Now with Reds			
☐ 244 Sixto Lezcano	.10	.05	.01
☐ 245 Steve Sax	.25	.11	.03
☐ 246 Jerry Mumphrey	.10	.05	.01
☐ 247 Dave Smith	.10	.05	.01
☐ 248 Bake McBride	.10	.05	.01
☐ 249 Checklist 133-264	.10	.05	.01
☐ 250 Bill Buckner	.25	.11	.03
☐ 251 Kent Hrbek	.75	.35	.09
☐ 252 Gene Tenace	.10	.05	.01
Now with Pirates			
☐ 253 Charlie Lea	.10	.05	.01
☐ 254 Rick Cerone	.10	.05	.01
☐ 255 Gene Garber	.10	.05	.01
☐ 256 Gene Garber SV	.10	.05	.01
☐ 257 Jesse Barfield	.25	.11	.03
☐ 258 Dave Winfield	1.25	.55	.16
☐ 259 Don Money	.10	.05	.01
☐ 260 Steve Kemp	.10	.05	.01
Now with Yankees			
☐ 261 Steve Yeager	.10	.05	.01
☐ 262 Keith Hernandez	.25	.11	.03
☐ 263 Tippy Martinez	.10	.05	.01
☐ 264 Joe Morgan SV	.50	.23	.06
Now with Phillies			
☐ 265 Joel Youngblood	.10	.05	.01
Now with Giants			
☐ 266 Bruce Sutter AS	.25	.11	.03
☐ 267 Terry Francona	.10	.05	.01
☐ 268 Neil Allen	.10	.05	.01
☐ 269 Ron Oester	.10	.05	.01
☐ 270 Dennis Eckersley	.60	.25	.07
☐ 271 Dale Berra	.10	.05	.01
☐ 272 Al Bumbry	.10	.05	.01
☐ 273 Lonnie Smith	.10	.05	.01
☐ 274 Terry Kennedy	.10	.05	.01
☐ 275 Ray Knight	.25	.11	.03
☐ 276 Mike Norris	.10	.05	.01
☐ 277 Rance Mulliniks	.10	.05	.01
☐ 278 Dan Spillner	.10	.05	.01
☐ 279 Bucky Dent	.25	.11	.03
☐ 280 Bert Blyleven	.50	.23	.06
☐ 281 Barry Bonnell	.10	.05	.01
☐ 282 Reggie Smith	.25	.11	.03
☐ 283 Reggie Smith SV	.25	.11	.03
☐ 284 Ted Simmons	.25	.11	.03
☐ 285 Lance Parrish	.25	.11	.03
☐ 286 Larry Christenson	.10	.05	.01
☐ 287 Ruppert Jones	.10	.05	.01
☐ 288 Bob Welch	.25	.11	.03
☐ 289 John Wathan	.10	.05	.01
☐ 290 Jeff Reardon	.25	.11	.03
☐ 291 Dave Revering	.10	.05	.01
☐ 292 Craig Swan	.10	.05	.01
☐ 293 Graig Nettles	.25	.11	.03
☐ 294 Alfredo Griffin	.10	.05	.01
☐ 295 Jerry Remy	.10	.05	.01
☐ 296 Joe Sambito	.10	.05	.01
☐ 297 Ron LeFlore	.10	.05	.01
☐ 298 Brian Downing	.10	.05	.01
☐ 299 Jim Palmer	1.00	.45	.12
☐ 300 Mike Schmidt	2.50	1.10	.30
☐ 301 Mike Schmidt SV	1.25	.55	.16
☐ 302 Ernie Whitt	.10	.05	.01
☐ 303 Andre Dawson	1.00	.45	.12
☐ 304 Bobby Murcer SV	.25	.11	.03
☐ 305 Larry Bowa	.25	.11	.03
☐ 306 Lee Mazzilli	.10	.05	.01
Now with Pirates			
☐ 307 Lou Piniella	.25	.11	.03
☐ 308 Buck Martinez	.10	.05	.01
☐ 309 Jerry Martin	.10	.05	.01
☐ 310 Greg Luzinski	.25	.11	.03
☐ 311 Al Oliver	.25	.11	.03
☐ 312 Mike Torrez	.10	.05	.01
Now with Mets			
☐ 313 Dick Ruthven	.10	.05	.01
☐ 314 Gary Carter AS	.25	.11	.03
☐ 315 Rick Burleson	.10	.05	.01
☐ 316 Phil Niekro SV	.50	.23	.06
☐ 317 Moose Haas	.10	.05	.01
☐ 318 Carney Lansford	.25	.11	.03
Now with Athletics			
☐ 319 Tim Foli	.10	.05	.01
☐ 320 Steve Rogers	.10	.05	.01
☐ 321 Kirk Gibson	.50	.23	.06
☐ 322 Glenn Hubbard	.10	.05	.01
☐ 323 Luis DeLeon	.10	.05	.01
☐ 324 Mike Marshall	.10	.05	.01
☐ 325 Von Hayes	.10	.05	.01
Now with Phillies			
☐ 326 Garth Iorg	.10	.05	.01
☐ 327 Jose Cruz	.25	.11	.03
☐ 328 Jim Palmer SV	.50	.23	.06
☐ 329 Darrell Evans	.25	.11	.03
☐ 330 Buddy Bell	.25	.11	.03
☐ 331 Mike Krukow	.10	.05	.01
Now with Giants			
☐ 332 Omar Moreno	.10	.05	.01
Now with Astros			
☐ 333 Dave LaRoche	.10	.05	.01
☐ 334 Dave LaRoche SV	.10	.05	.01
☐ 335 Bill Madlock	.25	.11	.03
☐ 336 Garry Templeton	.10	.05	.01
☐ 337 John Lowenstein	.10	.05	.01
☐ 338 Willie Upshaw	.10	.05	.01
☐ 339 Dave Hostetler	.10	.05	.01
☐ 340 Larry Gura	.10	.05	.01
☐ 341 Doug DeCinces	.25	.11	.03
☐ 342 Mike Schmidt AS	1.25	.55	.16
☐ 343 Charlie Hough	.25	.11	.03
☐ 344 Andre Thornton	.10	.05	.01
☐ 345 Jim Clancy	.10	.05	.01
☐ 346 Ken Forsch	.10	.05	.01
☐ 347 Sammy Stewart	.10	.05	.01
☐ 348 Alan Bannister	.10	.05	.01
☐ 349 Checklist 265-396	.10	.05	.01
☐ 350 Robin Yount	1.25	.55	.16
☐ 351 Warren Cromartie	.10	.05	.01
☐ 352 Tim Raines AS	.50	.23	.06
☐ 353 Tony Armas	.10	.05	.01

Now with Red Sox			
□ 354 Tom Seaver SV	1.50	.70	.19
Now with Mets			
□ 355 Tony Perez	.50	.23	.06
Now with Phillies			
□ 356 Toby Harrah	.10	.05	.01
□ 357 Dan Ford	.10	.05	.01
□ 358 Charlie Puleo	.10	.05	.01
Now with Reds			
□ 359 Dave Collins	.10	.05	.01
Now with Blue Jays			
□ 360 Nolan Ryan	10.00	4.50	1.25
□ 361 Nolan Ryan SV	5.00	2.20	.60
□ 362 Bill Almon	.10	.05	.01
Now with Athletics			
□ 363 Eddie Milner	.10	.05	.01
□ 364 Gary Lucas	.10	.05	.01
□ 365 Dave Lopes	.25	.11	.03
□ 366 Bob Boone	.25	.11	.03
□ 367 Biff Pocoroba	.10	.05	.01
□ 368 Richie Zisk	.10	.05	.01
□ 369 Tony Bernazard	.10	.05	.01
□ 370 Gary Carter	.50	.23	.06
□ 371 Paul Molitor	1.50	.70	.19
□ 372 Art Howe	.10	.05	.01
□ 373 Pete Rose AS	1.50	.70	.19
□ 374 Glenn Adams	.10	.05	.01
□ 375 Pete Vuckovich	.10	.05	.01
□ 376 Gary Lavelle	.10	.05	.01
□ 377 Lee May	.25	.11	.03
□ 378 Lee May SV	.25	.11	.03
□ 379 Butch Wynegar	.10	.05	.01
□ 380 Ron Davis	.10	.05	.01
□ 381 Bob Grich	.25	.11	.03
□ 382 Gary Roenicke	.10	.05	.01
□ 383 Jim Kaat SV	.25	.11	.03
□ 384 Steve Carlton AS	.75	.35	.09
□ 385 Mike Easler	.10	.05	.01
□ 386 Rod Carew AS	.75	.35	.09
□ 387 Bob Grich AS	.25	.11	.03
□ 388 George Brett AS	2.50	1.10	.30
□ 389 Robin Yount AS	1.00	.45	.12
□ 390 Reggie Jackson AS	1.00	.45	.12
□ 391 Rickey Henderson AS	1.00	.45	.12
□ 392 Fred Lynn AS	.25	.11	.03
□ 393 Carlton Fisk AS	.60	.25	.07
□ 394 Pete Vuckovich AS	.10	.05	.01
□ 395 Larry Gura AS	.10	.05	.01
□ 396 Dan Quisenberry AS	.10	.05	.01

1984 O-Pee-Chee

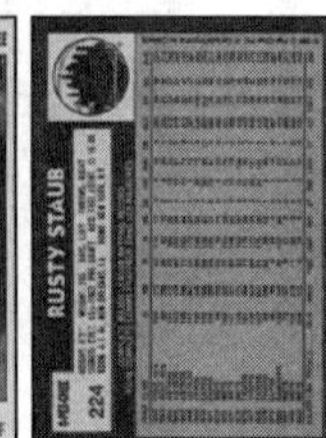

This set is an abridgement of the 1984 Topps set. The 396 standard-size cards comprising the 1984 O-Pee-Chee set differ from the cards of the 1984 Topps set by having a higher ratio of cards of players from the two Canadian teams, a practice begun by O-Pee-Chee in 1977 and continued to 1988. The set contains virtually the same pictures for the players also featured in the 1984 Topps issue. The fronts feature white-bordered color player action photos. A color player head shot also appears on the front at the lower left. The player's name and position appear in colored lettering within the white margin at the lower right. His team name appears in vertical colored lettering within the white margin on the left. The red, white and blue horizontal backs carry the player's name and biography at the top. The player's major league statistics and bilingual career highlights follow below. The asterisked cards have an extra line on the front inside the picture area indicating team change. The O-Pee-Chee logo appears on the front of every card. All-Star (AS) cards are indicated in the checklist below; they are included in the set in addition to the player's regular card. The set features Don Mattingly and Darryl Strawberry in their Rookie Card season.

	NRMT	VG-E	GOOD
COMPLETE SET (396)	35.00	16.00	4.40
COMMON CARD (1-396)	.05	.02	.01
□ 1 Pascual Perez	.05	.02	.01
□ 2 Cal Ripken AS	3.00	1.35	.35
□ 3 Lloyd Moseby AS	.05	.02	.01
□ 4 Mel Hall	.05	.02	.01
□ 5 Willie Wilson	.05	.02	.01
□ 6 Mike Morgan	.05	.02	.01
□ 7 Gary Lucas	.05	.02	.01
Now with Expos			
□ 8 Don Mattingly	10.00	4.50	1.25
□ 9 Jim Gott	.05	.02	.01
□ 10 Robin Yount	.75	.35	.09
□ 11 Joey McLaughlin	.05	.02	.01
□ 12 Billy Sample	.05	.02	.01
□ 13 Oscar Gamble	.05	.02	.01
□ 14 Bill Russell	.05	.02	.01
□ 15 Burt Hooton	.05	.02	.01
□ 16 Omar Moreno	.05	.02	.01
□ 17 Dave Lopes	.15	.07	.02
□ 18 Dale Berra	.05	.02	.01
□ 19 Rance Mulliniks	.05	.02	.01
□ 20 Greg Luzinski	.15	.07	.02
□ 21 Doug Sisk	.05	.02	.01
□ 22 Don Robinson	.05	.02	.01
□ 23 Keith Moreland	.05	.02	.01
□ 24 Richard Dotson	.05	.02	.01
□ 25 Glenn Hubbard	.05	.02	.01
□ 26 Rod Carew	1.00	.45	.12
□ 27 Alan Wiggins	.05	.02	.01
□ 28 Frank Viola	.40	.18	.05
□ 29 Phil Niekro	.50	.23	.06
Now with Yankees			
□ 30 Wade Boggs	2.50	1.10	.30
□ 31 Dave Parker	.15	.07	.02
Now with Reds			
□ 32 Bobby Ramos	.05	.02	.01
□ 33 Tom Burgmeier	.05	.02	.01
□ 34 Eddie Milner	.05	.02	.01
□ 35 Don Sutton	.25	.11	.03
□ 36 Glenn Wilson	.05	.02	.01
□ 37 Mike Krukow	.05	.02	.01
□ 38 Dave Collins	.05	.02	.01
□ 39 Garth Iorg	.05	.02	.01
□ 40 Dusty Baker	.15	.07	.02
□ 41 Tony Bernazard	.05	.02	.01
Now with Indians			
□ 42 Claudell Washington	.05	.02	.01
□ 43 Cecil Cooper	.15	.07	.02
□ 44 Dan Driessen	.05	.02	.01
□ 45 Jerry Mumphrey	.05	.02	.01
□ 46 Rick Rhoden	.05	.02	.01
□ 47 Rudy Law	.05	.02	.01
□ 48 Julio Franco	.40	.18	.05
□ 49 Mike Norris	.05	.02	.01
□ 50 Chris Chambliss	.05	.02	.01
□ 51 Pete Falcone	.05	.02	.01
□ 52 Mike Marshall	.05	.02	.01
□ 53 Amos Otis	.05	.02	.01
Now with Pirates			
□ 54 Jesse Orosco	.05	.02	.01
□ 55 Dave Concepcion	.15	.07	.02
□ 56 Gary Allenson	.05	.02	.01
□ 57 Dan Schatzeder	.05	.02	.01
□ 58 Jerry Remy	.05	.02	.01
□ 59 Carney Lansford	.15	.07	.02
□ 60 Paul Molitor	1.00	.45	.12
□ 61 Chris Codiroli	.05	.02	.01
□ 62 Dave Hostetler	.05	.02	.01
□ 63 Ed VandeBerg	.05	.02	.01
□ 64 Ryne Sandberg	4.00	1.80	.50
□ 65 Kirk Gibson	.25	.11	.03
□ 66 Nolan Ryan	6.00	2.70	.75
□ 67 Gary Ward	.05	.02	.01
Now with Rangers			
□ 68 Luis Salazar	.05	.02	.01
□ 69 Dan Quisenberry AS	.05	.02	.01
□ 70 Gary Matthews	.05	.02	.01
□ 71 Pete O'Brien	.15	.07	.02
□ 72 John Wathan	.05	.02	.01
□ 73 Jody Davis	.05	.02	.01
□ 74 Kent Tekulve	.05	.02	.01
□ 75 Bob Forsch	.05	.02	.01
□ 76 Alfredo Griffin	.05	.02	.01
□ 77 Bryn Smith	.05	.02	.01
□ 78 Mike Torrez	.05	.02	.01
□ 79 Mike Hargrove	.15	.07	.02
□ 80 Steve Rogers	.05	.02	.01
□ 81 Bake McBride	.05	.02	.01
□ 82 Doug DeCinces	.05	.02	.01
□ 83 Richie Zisk	.05	.02	.01
□ 84 Randy Bush	.05	.02	.01
□ 85 Atlee Hammaker	.05	.02	.01
□ 86 Chet Lemon	.05	.02	.01
□ 87 Frank Pastore	.05	.02	.01
□ 88 Alan Trammell	.30	.14	.04
□ 89 Terry Francona	.05	.02	.01
□ 90 Pedro Guerrero	.15	.07	.02
□ 91 Dan Spillner	.05	.02	.01
□ 92 Lloyd Moseby	.05	.02	.01
□ 93 Bob Knepper	.05	.02	.01
□ 94 Ted Simmons AS	.15	.07	.02
□ 95 Aurelio Lopez	.05	.02	.01
□ 96 Bill Buckner	.15	.07	.02
□ 97 LaMarr Hoyt	.05	.02	.01
□ 98 Tom Brunansky	.15	.07	.02
□ 99 Ron Oester	.05	.02	.01
□ 100 Reggie Jackson	1.25	.55	.16
□ 101 Ron Davis	.05	.02	.01
□ 102 Ken Oberkfell	.05	.02	.01
□ 103 Dwayne Murphy	.05	.02	.01
□ 104 Jim Slaton	.05	.02	.01
Now with Angels			
□ 105 Tony Armas	.05	.02	.01
□ 106 Ernie Whitt	.05	.02	.01
□ 107 Johnnie LeMaster	.05	.02	.01
□ 108 Randy Moffitt	.05	.02	.01
□ 109 Terry Forster	.05	.02	.01
□ 110 Ron Guidry	.15	.07	.02
□ 111 Bill Virdon MG	.05	.02	.01
□ 112 Doyle Alexander	.05	.02	.01
□ 113 Lonnie Smith	.05	.02	.01
□ 114 Checklist 1-132	.05	.02	.01
□ 115 Andre Thornton	.05	.02	.01
□ 116 Jeff Reardon	.15	.07	.02
□ 117 Tom Herr	.15	.07	.02
□ 118 Charlie Hough	.15	.07	.02
□ 119 Phil Garner	.15	.07	.02
□ 120 Keith Hernandez	.15	.07	.02
□ 121 Rich Gossage	.25	.11	.03
Now with Padres			
□ 122 Ted Simmons	.15	.07	.02
□ 123 Butch Wynegar	.05	.02	.01
□ 124 Damaso Garcia	.05	.02	.01
□ 125 Britt Burns	.05	.02	.01
□ 126 Bert Blyleven	.15	.07	.02
□ 127 Carlton Fisk	.75	.35	.09
□ 128 Rick Manning	.05	.02	.01
□ 129 Bill Laskey	.05	.02	.01
□ 130 Ozzie Smith	2.00	.90	.25
□ 131 Bo Diaz	.05	.02	.01
□ 132 Tom Paciorek	.05	.02	.01
□ 133 Dave Rozema	.05	.02	.01
□ 134 Dave Stieb	.05	.02	.01
□ 135 Brian Downing	.05	.02	.01
□ 136 Rick Camp	.05	.02	.01
□ 137 Willie Aikens	.05	.02	.01
Now with Blue Jays			
□ 138 Charlie Moore	.05	.02	.01
□ 139 George Frazier	.05	.02	.01
Now with Indians			
□ 140 Storm Davis	.05	.02	.01
□ 141 Glenn Hoffman	.05	.02	.01
□ 142 Charlie Lea	.05	.02	.01
□ 143 Mike Vail	.05	.02	.01
□ 144 Steve Sax	.15	.07	.02
□ 145 Gary Lavelle	.05	.02	.01
□ 146 Gorman Thomas	.05	.02	.01
Now with Mariners			
□ 147 Dan Petry	.05	.02	.01
□ 148 Mark Clear	.05	.02	.01
□ 149 Dave Beard	.05	.02	.01
Now with Mariners			
□ 150 Dale Murphy	.50	.23	.06
□ 151 Steve Trout	.05	.02	.01
□ 152 Tony Pena	.05	.02	.01
□ 153 Geoff Zahn	.05	.02	.01
□ 154 Dave Henderson	.15	.07	.02
□ 155 Frank White	.15	.07	.02
□ 156 Dick Ruthven	.05	.02	.01
□ 157 Gary Gaetti	.25	.11	.03
□ 158 Lance Parrish	.15	.07	.02
□ 159 Joe Price	.05	.02	.01
□ 160 Mario Soto	.05	.02	.01
□ 161 Tug McGraw	.15	.07	.02
□ 162 Bob Ojeda	.05	.02	.01
□ 163 George Hendrick	.05	.02	.01
□ 164 Scott Sanderson	.05	.02	.01
Now with Cubs			
□ 165 Ken Singleton	.05	.02	.01
□ 166 Terry Kennedy	.05	.02	.01
□ 167 Gene Garber	.05	.02	.01
□ 168 Juan Bonilla	.05	.02	.01
□ 169 Larry Parrish	.05	.02	.01
□ 170 Jerry Reuss	.05	.02	.01
□ 171 John Tudor	.05	.02	.01
Now with Pirates			
□ 172 Dave Kingman	.15	.07	.02
□ 173 Garry Templeton	.05	.02	.01
□ 174 Bob Boone	.15	.07	.02
□ 175 Graig Nettles	.15	.07	.02
□ 176 Lee Smith	.50	.23	.06
□ 177 LaMarr Hoyt AS	.05	.02	.01
□ 178 Bill Krueger	.05	.02	.01
□ 179 Buck Martinez	.05	.02	.01
□ 180 Manny Trillo	.05	.02	.01
Now with Giants			
□ 181 Lou Whitaker AS	.15	.07	.02
□ 182 Darryl Strawberry	3.00	1.35	.35
□ 183 Neil Allen	.05	.02	.01
□ 184 Jim Rice AS	.15	.07	.02
□ 185 Sixto Lezcano	.05	.02	.01
□ 186 Tom Hume	.05	.02	.01
□ 187 Garry Maddox	.05	.02	.01
□ 188 Bryan Little	.05	.02	.01
□ 189 Jose Cruz	.15	.07	.02
□ 190 Ben Oglivie	.05	.02	.01
□ 191 Cesar Cedeno	.15	.07	.02
□ 192 Nick Esasky	.05	.02	.01
□ 193 Ken Forsch	.05	.02	.01
□ 194 Jim Palmer	.60	.25	.07
□ 195 Jack Morris	.15	.07	.02
□ 196 Steve Howe	.05	.02	.01
□ 197 Harold Baines	.15	.07	.02
□ 198 Bill Doran	.15	.07	.02
□ 199 Willie Hernandez	.15	.07	.02
□ 200 Andre Dawson	.50	.23	.06
□ 201 Bruce Kison	.05	.02	.01
□ 202 Bobby Cox MG	.15	.07	.02
□ 203 Matt Keough	.05	.02	.01
□ 204 Ron Guidry AS	.15	.07	.02
□ 205 Greg Minton	.05	.02	.01
□ 206 Al Holland	.05	.02	.01
□ 207 Luis Leal	.05	.02	.01
□ 208 Jose Oquendo	.05	.02	.01
□ 209 Leon Durham	.05	.02	.01
□ 210 Joe Morgan	.60	.25	.07
Now with Athletics			
□ 211 Lou Whitaker	.15	.07	.02
□ 212 George Brett	3.00	1.35	.35
□ 213 Bruce Hurst	.05	.02	.01
□ 214 Steve Carlton	1.00	.45	.12
□ 215 Tippy Martinez	.05	.02	.01
□ 216 Ken Landreaux	.05	.02	.01
□ 217 Alan Ashby	.05	.02	.01
□ 218 Dennis Eckersley	.25	.11	.03
□ 219 Craig McMurtry	.05	.02	.01
□ 220 Fernando Valenzuela	.15	.07	.02
□ 221 Cliff Johnson	.05	.02	.01
□ 222 Rick Honeycutt	.05	.02	.01
□ 223 George Brett AS	1.50	.70	.19
□ 224 Rusty Staub	.15	.07	.02
□ 225 Lee Mazzilli	.05	.02	.01
□ 226 Pat Putnam	.05	.02	.01
□ 227 Bob Welch	.05	.02	.01
□ 228 Rick Cerone	.05	.02	.01
□ 229 Lee Lacy	.05	.02	.01
□ 230 Rickey Henderson	1.50	.70	.19
□ 231 Gary Redus	.05	.02	.01
□ 232 Tim Wallach	.15	.07	.02
□ 233 Checklist 133-264	.05	.02	.01
□ 234 Rafael Ramirez	.05	.02	.01
□ 235 Matt Young	.05	.02	.01
□ 236 Ellis Valentine	.05	.02	.01
□ 237 John Castino	.05	.02	.01
□ 238 Eric Show	.05	.02	.01
□ 239 Bob Horner	.05	.02	.01
□ 240 Eddie Murray	1.25	.55	.16
□ 241 Billy Almon	.05	.02	.01
□ 242 Greg Brock	.05	.02	.01
□ 243 Bruce Sutter	.15	.07	.02
□ 244 Dwight Evans	.15	.07	.02
□ 245 Rick Sutcliffe	.15	.07	.02
□ 246 Terry Crowley	.05	.02	.01
□ 247 Fred Lynn	.15	.07	.02
□ 248 Bill Dawley	.05	.02	.01
□ 249 Dave Stapleton	.05	.02	.01
□ 250 Bill Madlock	.05	.02	.01
□ 251 Jim Sundberg	.15	.07	.02
Now with Brewers			
□ 252 Steve Yeager	.05	.02	.01
□ 253 Jim Wohlford	.05	.02	.01
□ 254 Shane Rawley	.05	.02	.01
□ 255 Bruce Benedict	.05	.02	.01
□ 256 Dave Geisel	.05	.02	.01
Now with Mariners			
□ 257 Julio Cruz	.05	.02	.01
□ 258 Luis Sanchez	.05	.02	.01
□ 259 Von Hayes	.05	.02	.01
□ 260 Scott McGregor	.05	.02	.01
□ 261 Tom Seaver	1.50	.70	.19
Now with White Sox			
□ 262 Doug Flynn	.05	.02	.01
□ 263 Wayne Gross	.05	.02	.01
Now with Orioles			
□ 264 Larry Gura	.05	.02	.01
□ 265 John Montefusco	.05	.02	.01
□ 266 Dave Winfield AS	.40	.18	.05
□ 267 Tim Lollar	.05	.02	.01
□ 268 Ron Washington	.05	.02	.01
□ 269 Mickey Rivers	.05	.02	.01
□ 270 Mookie Wilson	.15	.07	.02
□ 271 Moose Haas	.05	.02	.01
□ 272 Rick Dempsey	.15	.07	.02
□ 273 Dan Quisenberry	.05	.02	.01
□ 274 Steve Henderson	.05	.02	.01
□ 275 Len Matuszek	.05	.02	.01
□ 276 Frank Tanana	.15	.07	.02
□ 277 Dave Righetti	.05	.02	.01
□ 278 Jorge Bell	.25	.11	.03
□ 279 Ivan DeJesus	.05	.02	.01
□ 280 Floyd Bannister	.05	.02	.01
□ 281 Dale Murray	.05	.02	.01
□ 282 Andre Robertson	.05	.02	.01
□ 283 Rollie Fingers	.50	.23	.06
□ 284 Tommy John	.25	.11	.03
□ 285 Darrell Porter	.05	.02	.01
□ 286 Lary Sorensen	.05	.02	.01
Now with Athletics			
□ 287 Warren Cromartie	.05	.02	.01
Now playing in Japan			
□ 288 Jim Beattie	.05	.02	.01
□ 289 Blue Jays Leaders	.05	.02	.01
Lloyd Moseby			
Dave Stieb			
(Team checklist back)			
□ 290 Dave Dravecky	.15	.07	.02
□ 291 Eddie Murray AS	.60	.25	.07
□ 292 Greg Bargar	.05	.02	.01
□ 293 Tom Underwood	.05	.02	.01
Now with Orioles			
□ 294 U.L. Washington	.05	.02	.01
□ 295 Mike Flanagan	.05	.02	.01
□ 296 Rich Gedman	.05	.02	.01
□ 297 Bruce Berenyi	.05	.02	.01
□ 298 Jim Gantner	.15	.07	.02
□ 299 Bill Caudill	.05	.02	.01
Now with Athletics			
□ 300 Pete Rose	2.50	1.10	.30
Now with Expos			
□ 301 Steve Kemp	.05	.02	.01
□ 302 Barry Bonnell	.05	.02	.01
Now with Mariners			

Card	NRMT	VG-E	GOOD
☐ 303 Joel Youngblood	.05	.02	.01
☐ 304 Rick Langford	.05	.02	.01
☐ 305 Roy Smalley	.05	.02	.01
☐ 306 Ken Griffey	.15	.07	.02
☐ 307 Al Oliver	.15	.07	.02
☐ 308 Ron Hassey	.05	.02	.01
☐ 309 Len Barker	.05	.02	.01
☐ 310 Willie McGee	.25	.11	.03
☐ 311 Jerry Koosman	.15	.07	.02
Now with Phillies			
☐ 312 Jorge Orta	.05	.02	.01
Now with Royals			
☐ 313 Pete Vuckovich	.05	.02	.01
☐ 314 George Wright	.05	.02	.01
☐ 315 Bob Grich	.15	.07	.02
☐ 316 Jesse Barfield	.15	.07	.02
☐ 317 Willie Upshaw	.05	.02	.01
☐ 318 Bill Gullickson	.05	.02	.01
☐ 319 Ray Burris	.05	.02	.01
Now with Athletics			
☐ 320 Bob Stanley	.05	.02	.01
☐ 321 Ray Knight	.15	.07	.02
☐ 322 Ken Schrom	.05	.02	.01
☐ 323 Johnny Ray	.05	.02	.01
☐ 324 Brian Giles	.05	.02	.01
☐ 325 Darrell Evans	.15	.07	.02
Now with Tigers			
☐ 326 Mike Caldwell	.05	.02	.01
☐ 327 Ruppert Jones	.05	.02	.01
☐ 328 Chris Speier	.05	.02	.01
☐ 329 Bobby Castillo	.05	.02	.01
☐ 330 John Candelaria	.05	.02	.01
☐ 331 Bucky Dent	.15	.07	.02
☐ 332 Expos Leaders	.15	.07	.02
Al Oliver			
Charlie Lea			
(Team checklist back)			
☐ 333 Larry Herndon	.05	.02	.01
☐ 334 Chuck Rainey	.05	.02	.01
☐ 335 Don Baylor	.15	.07	.02
☐ 336 Bob James	.05	.02	.01
☐ 337 Jim Clancy	.05	.02	.01
☐ 338 Duane Kuiper	.05	.02	.01
☐ 339 Roy Lee Jackson	.05	.02	.01
☐ 340 Hal McRae	.15	.07	.02
☐ 341 Larry McWilliams	.05	.02	.01
☐ 342 Tim Foli	.05	.02	.01
Now with Yankees			
☐ 343 Fergie Jenkins	.50	.23	.06
☐ 344 Dickie Thon	.05	.02	.01
☐ 345 Kent Hrbek	.30	.14	.04
☐ 346 Larry Bowa	.15	.07	.02
☐ 347 Buddy Bell	.15	.07	.02
☐ 348 Toby Harrah	.05	.02	.01
Now with Yankees			
☐ 349 Dan Ford	.05	.02	.01
☐ 350 George Foster	.15	.07	.02
☐ 351 Lou Piniella	.15	.07	.02
☐ 352 Dave Stewart	.40	.18	.05
☐ 353 Mike Easler	.05	.02	.01
Now with Red Sox			
☐ 354 Jeff Burroughs	.05	.02	.01
☐ 355 Jason Thompson	.05	.02	.01
☐ 356 Glenn Abbott	.05	.02	.01
☐ 357 Ron Cey	.15	.07	.02
☐ 358 Bob Dernier	.05	.02	.01
☐ 359 Jim Acker	.05	.02	.01
☐ 360 Willie Randolph	.15	.07	.02
☐ 361 Mike Schmidt	1.50	.70	.19
☐ 362 David Green	.05	.02	.01
☐ 363 Cal Ripken	6.00	2.70	.75
☐ 364 Jim Rice	.15	.07	.02
☐ 365 Steve Bedrosian	.05	.02	.01
☐ 366 Gary Carter	.40	.18	.05
☐ 367 Chili Davis	.15	.07	.02
☐ 368 Hubie Brooks	.05	.02	.01
☐ 369 Steve McCatty	.05	.02	.01
☐ 370 Tim Raines	.25	.11	.03
☐ 371 Joaquin Andujar	.05	.02	.01
☐ 372 Gary Roenicke	.05	.02	.01
☐ 373 Ron Kittle	.05	.02	.01
☐ 374 Rich Dauer	.05	.02	.01
☐ 375 Dennis Leonard	.05	.02	.01
☐ 376 Rick Burleson	.05	.02	.01
☐ 377 Eric Rasmussen	.05	.02	.01
☐ 378 Dave Winfield	.75	.35	.09
☐ 379 Checklist 265-396	.05	.02	.01
☐ 380 Steve Garvey	.25	.11	.03
☐ 381 Jack Clark	.15	.07	.02
☐ 382 Odell Jones	.05	.02	.01
☐ 383 Terry Puhl	.05	.02	.01
☐ 384 Joe Niekro	.15	.07	.02
☐ 385 Tony Perez	.25	.11	.03
Now with Reds			
☐ 386 George Hendrick AS	.05	.02	.01
☐ 387 Johnny Ray AS	.05	.02	.01
☐ 388 Mike Schmidt AS	.75	.35	.09
☐ 389 Ozzie Smith AS	1.00	.45	.12
☐ 390 Tim Raines AS	.25	.11	.03
☐ 391 Dale Murphy AS	.25	.11	.03
☐ 392 Andre Dawson AS	.25	.11	.03
☐ 393 Gary Carter AS	.15	.07	.02
☐ 394 Steve Rogers AS	.05	.02	.01
☐ 395 Steve Carlton AS	.50	.23	.06
☐ 396 Jesse Orosco AS	.05	.02	.01

1985 O-Pee-Chee

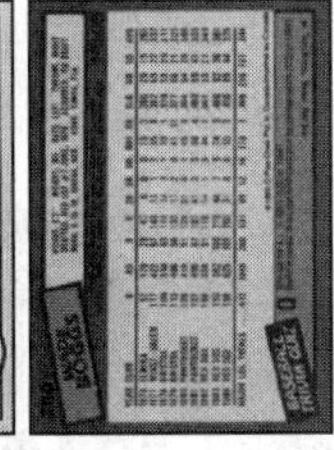

This set is an abridgement of the 1985 Topps set. The 396 standard-size cards comprising the 1985 O-Pee-Chee set differ from the cards of the 1985 Topps set by having a higher ratio of cards of players from the two Canadian teams, a practice begun by O-Pee-Chee in 1977 and continued to 1988. The set contains virtually the same pictures for the players also featured in the 1985 Topps issue. The fronts feature white-bordered color player photos. The player's name, position and team name and logo appear at the bottom of the photo. The green and white horizontal backs carry the player's name and biography at the top. The player's major league statistics and bilingual profile follow below. A bilingual trivia question and answer round out the back. The O-Pee-Chee logo appears on the front of every card. The set features Dwight Gooden and Kirby Puckett in their Rookie Card seasons.

	NRMT	VG-E	GOOD
COMPLETE SET (396)	25.00	11.00	3.10
COMMON CARD (1-396)	.05	.02	.01
☐ 1 Tom Seaver	.40	.18	.05
☐ 2 Gary Lavelle	.05	.02	.01
Traded to Blue Jays 1-26-85			
☐ 3 Tim Wallach	.15	.07	.02
☐ 4 Jim Wohlford	.05	.02	.01
☐ 5 Jeff Robinson	.05	.02	.01
☐ 6 Willie Wilson	.05	.02	.01
☐ 7 Cliff Johnson	.05	.02	.01
Free Agent with Rangers 12-20-84			
☐ 8 Willie Randolph	.15	.07	.02
☐ 9 Larry Herndon	.05	.02	.01
☐ 10 Kirby Puckett	10.00	4.50	1.25
☐ 11 Mookie Wilson	.15	.07	.02
☐ 12 Dave Lopes	.15	.07	.02
Traded to Cubs 8-81-84			
☐ 13 Tim Lollar	.05	.02	.01
Traded to White Sox 12-6-84			
☐ 14 Chris Bando	.05	.02	.01
☐ 15 Jerry Koosman	.05	.02	.01
☐ 16 Bobby Meacham	.05	.02	.01
☐ 17 Mike Scott	.05	.02	.01
☐ 18 Rich Gedman	.05	.02	.01
☐ 19 George Frazier	.05	.02	.01
☐ 20 Chet Lemon	.05	.02	.01
☐ 21 Dave Concepcion	.15	.07	.02
☐ 22 Jason Thompson	.05	.02	.01
☐ 23 Bret Saberhagen	.50	.23	.06
☐ 24 Jesse Barfield	.05	.02	.01
☐ 25 Steve Bedrosian	.05	.02	.01
☐ 26 Roy Smalley	.05	.02	.01
Traded to Twins 2-19-85			
☐ 27 Bruce Berenyi	.05	.02	.01
☐ 28 Butch Wynegar	.05	.02	.01
☐ 29 Alan Ashby	.05	.02	.01
☐ 30 Cal Ripken	4.00	1.80	.50
☐ 31 Luis Leal	.05	.02	.01
☐ 32 Dave Dravecky	.15	.07	.02
☐ 33 Tito Landrum	.05	.02	.01
☐ 34 Pedro Guerrero	.15	.07	.02
☐ 35 Graig Nettles	.15	.07	.02
☐ 36 Fred Breining	.05	.02	.01
☐ 37 Roy Lee Jackson	.05	.02	.01
☐ 38 Steve Henderson	.05	.02	.01
☐ 39 Gary Pettis UER	.05	.02	.01
Photo actually			
Lynn Pettis			
☐ 40 Phil Niekro	.50	.23	.06
☐ 41 Dwight Gooden	2.00	.90	.25
☐ 42 Luis Sanchez	.05	.02	.01
☐ 43 Lee Smith	.30	.14	.04
☐ 44 Dickie Thon	.05	.02	.01
☐ 45 Greg Minton	.05	.02	.01
☐ 46 Mike Flanagan	.05	.02	.01
☐ 47 Bud Black	.05	.02	.01
☐ 48 Tony Fernandez	.15	.07	.02
☐ 49 Carlton Fisk	.40	.18	.05
☐ 50 John Candelaria	.05	.02	.01
☐ 51 Bob Watson	.15	.07	.02
Announced his Retirement			
☐ 52 Rick Leach	.05	.02	.01
☐ 53 Rick Rhoden	.05	.02	.01
☐ 54 Cesar Cedeno	.15	.07	.02
☐ 55 Frank Tanana	.05	.02	.01
☐ 56 Larry Bowa	.15	.07	.02
☐ 57 Willie McGee	.15	.07	.02
☐ 58 Rich Dauer	.05	.02	.01
☐ 59 Jorge Bell	.15	.07	.02
☐ 60 George Hendrick	.05	.02	.01
Traded to Pirates 12-12-84			
☐ 61 Donnie Moore	.05	.02	.01
Drafted by Angels 1-24-85			
☐ 62 Mike Ramsey	.05	.02	.01
☐ 63 Nolan Ryan	3.00	1.35	.35
☐ 64 Mark Bailey	.05	.02	.01
☐ 65 Bill Buckner	.15	.07	.02
☐ 66 Jerry Reuss	.05	.02	.01
☐ 67 Mike Schmidt	1.00	.45	.12
☐ 68 Von Hayes	.05	.02	.01
☐ 69 Phil Bradley	.15	.07	.02
☐ 70 Don Baylor	.15	.07	.02
☐ 71 Julio Cruz	.05	.02	.01
☐ 72 Rick Sutcliffe	.05	.02	.01
☐ 73 Storm Davis	.05	.02	.01
☐ 74 Mike Krukow	.05	.02	.01
☐ 75 Willie Upshaw	.05	.02	.01
☐ 76 Craig Lefferts	.05	.02	.01
☐ 77 Lloyd Moseby	.05	.02	.01
☐ 78 Ron Davis	.05	.02	.01
☐ 79 Rick Mahler	.05	.02	.01
☐ 80 Keith Hernandez	.15	.07	.02
☐ 81 Vance Law	.05	.02	.01
Traded to Expos 12-7-84			
☐ 82 Joe Price	.05	.02	.01
☐ 83 Dennis Lamp	.05	.02	.01
☐ 84 Gary Ward	.05	.02	.01
☐ 85 Mike Marshall	.05	.02	.01
☐ 86 Marvell Wynne	.05	.02	.01
☐ 87 David Green	.05	.02	.01
☐ 88 Bryn Smith	.05	.02	.01
☐ 89 Sixto Lezcano	.05	.02	.01
Free Agent with Pirates 1-26-85			
☐ 90 Rich Gossage	.15	.07	.02
☐ 91 Jeff Burroughs	.05	.02	.01
Purchased by Blue Jays 12-22-84			
☐ 92 Bobby Brown	.05	.02	.01
☐ 93 Oscar Gamble	.05	.02	.01
☐ 94 Rick Dempsey	.15	.07	.02
☐ 95 Jose Cruz	.15	.07	.02
☐ 96 Johnny Ray	.05	.02	.01
☐ 97 Joel Youngblood	.05	.02	.01
☐ 98 Eddie Whitson	.05	.02	.01
Free Agent with 12-28-84			
☐ 99 Milt Wilcox	.05	.02	.01
☐ 100 George Brett	3.00	1.35	.35
☐ 101 Jim Acker	.05	.02	.01
☐ 102 Jim Sundberg	.05	.02	.01
Traded to Royals 1-18-85			
☐ 103 Ozzie Virgil	.05	.02	.01
☐ 104 Mike Fitzgerald	.05	.02	.01
Traded to Expos 12-10-84			
☐ 105 Ron Kittle	.05	.02	.01
☐ 106 Pascual Perez	.05	.02	.01
☐ 107 Barry Bonnell	.05	.02	.01
☐ 108 Lou Whitaker	.25	.11	.03
☐ 109 Gary Roenicke	.05	.02	.01
☐ 110 Alejandro Pena	.05	.02	.01
☐ 111 Doug DeCinces	.05	.02	.01
☐ 112 Doug Flynn	.05	.02	.01
☐ 113 Tom Herr	.15	.07	.02
☐ 114 Bob James	.05	.02	.01
Traded to White Sox 12-7-84			
☐ 115 Rickey Henderson	1.25	.55	.16
Traded to Yankees 12-8-84			
☐ 116 Pete Rose	.75	.35	.09
☐ 117 Greg Gross	.05	.02	.01
☐ 118 Eric Show	.05	.02	.01
☐ 119 Buck Martinez	.05	.02	.01
☐ 120 Steve Kemp	.05	.02	.01
Traded to Pirates 12-20-84			
☐ 121 Checklist 1-132	.05	.02	.01
☐ 122 Tom Brunansky	.15	.07	.02
☐ 123 Dave Kingman	.15	.07	.02
☐ 124 Garry Templeton	.05	.02	.01
☐ 125 Kent Tekulve	.05	.02	.01
☐ 126 Darryl Strawberry	.40	.18	.05
☐ 127 Mark Gubicza	.15	.07	.02
☐ 128 Ernie Whitt	.05	.02	.01
☐ 129 Don Robinson	.05	.02	.01
☐ 130 Al Oliver	.15	.07	.02
Traded to Dodgers 2-4-85			
☐ 131 Mario Soto	.05	.02	.01
☐ 132 Jeff Leonard	.05	.02	.01
☐ 133 Andre Dawson	.25	.11	.03
☐ 134 Bruce Hurst	.05	.02	.01
☐ 135 Bobby Cox MG	.15	.07	.02
(Team checklist back)			
☐ 136 Matt Young	.05	.02	.01
☐ 137 Bob Forsch	.05	.02	.01
☐ 138 Ron Darling	.15	.07	.02
☐ 139 Steve Trout	.05	.02	.01
☐ 140 Geoff Zahn	.05	.02	.01
☐ 141 Ken Forsch	.05	.02	.01
☐ 142 Jerry Willard	.05	.02	.01
☐ 143 Bill Gullickson	.05	.02	.01
☐ 144 Mike Mason	.05	.02	.01
☐ 145 Alvin Davis	.15	.07	.02
☐ 146 Gary Redus	.05	.02	.01
☐ 147 Willie Aikens	.05	.02	.01
☐ 148 Steve Yeager	.05	.02	.01
☐ 149 Dickie Noles	.05	.02	.01
☐ 150 Jim Rice	.15	.07	.02
☐ 151 Moose Haas	.05	.02	.01
☐ 152 Steve Balboni	.05	.02	.01
☐ 153 Frank LaCorte	.05	.02	.01
☐ 154 Argenis Salazar	.05	.02	.01
Drafted by Cardinals 1-24-85			
☐ 155 Bob Grich	.15	.07	.02
☐ 156 Craig Reynolds	.05	.02	.01
☐ 157 Bill Madlock	.05	.02	.01
☐ 158 Pat Tabler	.05	.02	.01
☐ 159 Don Slaught	.05	.02	.01
Traded to Rangers 1-18-85			
☐ 160 Lance Parrish	.15	.07	.02
☐ 161 Ken Schrom	.05	.02	.01
☐ 162 Wally Backman	.05	.02	.01
☐ 163 Dennis Eckersley	.25	.11	.03
☐ 164 Dave Collins	.05	.02	.01
Traded to A's 12-8-84			
☐ 165 Dusty Baker	.15	.07	.02
☐ 166 Claudell Washington	.05	.02	.01
☐ 167 Rick Camp	.05	.02	.01
☐ 168 Garth Iorg	.05	.02	.01
☐ 169 Shane Rawley	.05	.02	.01
☐ 170 George Foster	.15	.07	.02
☐ 171 Tony Bernazard	.05	.02	.01
☐ 172 Don Sutton	.25	.11	.03
Traded to A's 12-8-84			
☐ 173 Jerry Remy	.05	.02	.01
☐ 174 Rick Honeycutt	.05	.02	.01
☐ 175 Dave Parker	.15	.07	.02
☐ 176 Buddy Bell	.15	.07	.02
☐ 177 Steve Garvey	.25	.11	.03
☐ 178 Miguel Dilone	.05	.02	.01
☐ 179 Tommy John	.25	.11	.03
☐ 180 Dave Winfield	.75	.35	.09
☐ 181 Alan Trammell	.25	.11	.03
☐ 182 Rollie Fingers	.50	.23	.06
☐ 183 Larry McWilliams	.05	.02	.01
☐ 184 Carmen Castillo	.05	.02	.01
☐ 185 Al Holland	.05	.02	.01
☐ 186 Jerry Mumphrey	.05	.02	.01
☐ 187 Chris Chambliss	.05	.02	.01
☐ 188 Jim Clancy	.05	.02	.01
☐ 189 Glenn Wilson	.05	.02	.01
☐ 190 Rusty Staub	.15	.07	.02
☐ 191 Ozzie Smith	2.00	.90	.25
☐ 192 Howard Johnson	.15	.07	.02
Traded to Mets 12-7-84			
☐ 193 Jimmy Key	.60	.25	.07
☐ 194 Terry Kennedy	.05	.02	.01
☐ 195 Glenn Hubbard	.05	.02	.01
☐ 196 Pete O'Brien	.05	.02	.01
☐ 197 Keith Moreland	.05	.02	.01
☐ 198 Eddie Milner	.05	.02	.01
☐ 199 Dave Engle	.05	.02	.01
☐ 200 Reggie Jackson	.60	.25	.07
☐ 201 Burt Hooton	.05	.02	.01
Free Agent with Rangers 1-3-85			
☐ 202 Gorman Thomas	.05	.02	.01
☐ 203 Larry Parrish	.05	.02	.01
☐ 204 Bob Stanley	.05	.02	.01
☐ 205 Steve Rogers	.05	.02	.01
☐ 206 Phil Garner	.15	.07	.02
☐ 207 Ed VandeBerg	.05	.02	.01
☐ 208 Jack Clark	.15	.07	.02
Traded to Cardinals 2-1-85			
☐ 209 Bill Campbell	.05	.02	.01
☐ 210 Gary Matthews	.05	.02	.01
☐ 211 Dave Palmer	.05	.02	.01
☐ 212 Tony Perez	.25	.11	.03
☐ 213 Sammy Stewart	.05	.02	.01
☐ 214 John Tudor	.05	.02	.01
Traded to Cardinals 12-12-84			
☐ 215 Bob Brenly	.05	.02	.01
☐ 216 Jim Gantner	.05	.02	.01
☐ 217 Bryan Clark	.05	.02	.01
☐ 218 Doyle Alexander	.05	.02	.01
☐ 219 Bo Diaz	.05	.02	.01
☐ 220 Fred Lynn	.15	.07	.02
Free Agent with Orioles 12-11-84			
☐ 221 Eddie Murray	.75	.35	.09
☐ 222 Hubie Brooks	.05	.02	.01
Traded to Expos 12-10-84			
☐ 223 Tom Hume	.05	.02	.01
☐ 224 Al Cowens	.05	.02	.01
☐ 225 Mike Boddicker	.05	.02	.01
☐ 226 Len Matuszek	.05	.02	.01
☐ 227 Danny Darwin	.05	.02	.01
Traded to Brewers 1-18-85			
☐ 228 Scott McGregor	.05	.02	.01
☐ 229 Dave LaPoint	.05	.02	.01
Traded to Giants 2-1-85			
☐ 230 Gary Carter	.40	.18	.05
Traded to Mets 12-10-84			
☐ 231 Joaquin Andujar	.05	.02	.01
☐ 232 Rafael Ramirez	.05	.02	.01
☐ 233 Wayne Gross	.05	.02	.01
☐ 234 Neil Allen	.05	.02	.01
☐ 235 Garry Maddox	.05	.02	.01
☐ 236 Mark Thurmond	.05	.02	.01
☐ 237 Julio Franco	.25	.11	.03
☐ 238 Ray Burris	.05	.02	.01
Traded to Brewers 12-8-84			
☐ 239 Tim Teufel	.05	.02	.01
☐ 240 Dave Stieb	.05	.02	.01
☐ 241 Brett Butler	.15	.07	.02
☐ 242 Greg Brock	.05	.02	.01
☐ 243 Barbaro Garbey	.05	.02	.01
☐ 244 Greg Walker	.05	.02	.01
☐ 245 Chili Davis	.15	.07	.02
☐ 246 Darrell Porter	.05	.02	.01

- □ 247 Tippy Martinez .05 .02 .01
- □ 248 Terry Forster .05 .02 .01
- □ 249 Harold Baines .15 .07 .02
- □ 250 Jesse Orosco .05 .02 .01
- □ 251 Brad Gulden .05 .02 .01
- □ 252 Mike Hargrove .15 .07 .02
- □ 253 Nick Esasky .05 .02 .01
- □ 254 Frank Williams .05 .02 .01
- □ 255 Lonnie Smith .05 .02 .01
- □ 256 Daryl Sconiers .05 .02 .01
- □ 257 Bryan Little .05 .02 .01
  Traded to White Sox 12-7-84
- □ 258 Terry Francona .05 .02 .01
- □ 259 Mark Langston .50 .23 .06
- □ 260 Dave Righetti .15 .07 .02
- □ 261 Checklist 133-264 .05 .02 .01
- □ 262 Bob Horner .05 .02 .01
- □ 263 Mel Hall .05 .02 .01
- □ 264 John Shelby .05 .02 .01
- □ 265 Juan Samuel .05 .02 .01
- □ 266 Frank Viola .15 .07 .02
- □ 267 Jim Fanning MG .05 .02 .01
  Now Vice President Player, Development and Scouting
- □ 268 Dick Ruthven .05 .02 .01
- □ 269 Bobby Ramos .05 .02 .01
- □ 270 Dan Quisenberry .05 .02 .01
- □ 271 Dwight Evans .15 .07 .02
- □ 272 Andre Thornton .05 .02 .01
- □ 273 Orel Hershiser 1.00 .45 .12
- □ 274 Ray Knight .15 .07 .02
- □ 275 Bill Caudill .05 .02 .01
  Traded to Blue Jays 12-8-84
- □ 276 Charlie Hough .15 .07 .02
- □ 277 Tim Raines .15 .07 .02
- □ 278 Mike Squires .05 .02 .01
- □ 279 Alex Trevino .05 .02 .01
- □ 280 Ron Romanick .05 .02 .01
- □ 281 Tom Niedenfuer .05 .02 .01
- □ 282 Mike Stenhouse .05 .02 .01
  Traded to Twins 1-9-85
- □ 283 Terry Puhl .05 .02 .01
- □ 284 Hal McRae .15 .07 .02
- □ 285 Dan Driessen .05 .02 .01
- □ 286 Rudy Law .05 .02 .01
- □ 287 Walt Terrell .05 .02 .01
  Traded to Tigers 12-7-84
- □ 288 Jeff Kunkel .05 .02 .01
- □ 289 Bob Knepper .05 .02 .01
- □ 290 Cecil Cooper .15 .07 .02
- □ 291 Bob Welch .05 .02 .01
- □ 292 Frank Pastore .05 .02 .01
- □ 293 Dan Schatzeder .05 .02 .01
- □ 294 Tom Nieto .05 .02 .01
- □ 295 Joe Niekro .05 .02 .01
- □ 296 Ryne Sandberg 2.00 .90 .25
- □ 297 Gary Lucas .05 .02 .01
- □ 298 John Castino .05 .02 .01
- □ 299 Bill Doran .05 .02 .01
- □ 300 Rod Carew .50 .23 .06
- □ 301 John Montefusco .05 .02 .01
- □ 302 Johnnie LeMaster .05 .02 .01
- □ 303 Jim Beattie .05 .02 .01
- □ 304 Gary Gaetti .15 .07 .02
- □ 305 Dale Berra .05 .02 .01
  Traded to Yankees 12-20-84
- □ 306 Rick Reuschel .05 .02 .01
- □ 307 Ken Oberkfell .05 .02 .01
- □ 308 Kent Hrbek .25 .11 .03
- □ 309 Mike Witt .05 .02 .01
- □ 310 Manny Trillo .05 .02 .01
- □ 311 Jim Gott .05 .02 .01
  Traded to Giants 1-26-85
- □ 312 LaMarr Hoyt .05 .02 .01
  Traded to Padres 12-6-84
- □ 313 Dave Schmidt .05 .02 .01
- □ 314 Ron Oester .05 .02 .01
- □ 315 Doug Sisk .05 .02 .01
- □ 316 John Lowenstein .05 .02 .01
- □ 317 Derrel Thomas .05 .02 .01
  Traded to Angels 9-6-84
- □ 318 Ted Simmons .15 .07 .02
- □ 319 Darrell Evans .15 .07 .02
- □ 320 Dale Murphy .25 .11 .03
- □ 321 Ricky Horton .05 .02 .01
- □ 322 Ken Phelps .05 .02 .01
- □ 323 Lee Mazzilli .05 .02 .01
- □ 324 Don Mattingly 4.00 1.80 .50
- □ 325 John Denny .05 .02 .01
- □ 326 Ken Singleton .05 .02 .01
- □ 327 Brook Jacoby .05 .02 .01
- □ 328 Greg Luzinski .15 .07 .02
  Announced his Retirement
- □ 329 Bob Ojeda .05 .02 .01
- □ 330 Leon Durham .05 .02 .01
- □ 331 Bill Laskey .05 .02 .01
- □ 332 Ben Oglivie .05 .02 .01
- □ 333 Willie Hernandez .05 .02 .01
- □ 334 Bob Dernier .05 .02 .01
- □ 335 Bruce Benedict .05 .02 .01
- □ 336 Rance Mulliniks .05 .02 .01
- □ 337 Rick Cerone .05 .02 .01
  Traded to Braves 12-6-84
- □ 338 Britt Burns .05 .02 .01
- □ 339 Danny Heep .05 .02 .01
- □ 340 Robin Yount .75 .35 .09
- □ 341 Andy Van Slyke .30 .14 .04
- □ 342 Curt Wilkerson .05 .02 .01
- □ 343 Bill Russell .05 .02 .01
- □ 344 Dave Henderson .05 .02 .01
- □ 345 Charlie Lea .05 .02 .01
- □ 346 Terry Pendleton .60 .25 .07
- □ 347 Carney Lansford .05 .02 .01
- □ 348 Bob Boone .15 .07 .02
- □ 349 Mike Easler .05 .02 .01
- □ 350 Wade Boggs 1.00 .45 .12
- □ 351 Atlee Hammaker .05 .02 .01
- □ 352 Joe Morgan .50 .23 .06
- □ 353 Damaso Garcia .05 .02 .01
- □ 354 Floyd Bannister .05 .02 .01
- □ 355 Bert Blyleven .15 .07 .02
- □ 356 John Butcher .05 .02 .01
- □ 357 Fernando Valenzuela .15 .07 .02
- □ 358 Tony Pena .05 .02 .01
- □ 359 Mike Smithson .05 .02 .01
- □ 360 Steve Carlton .40 .18 .05
- □ 361 Alfredo Griffin .05 .02 .01
  Traded to A's 12-8-84
- □ 362 Craig McMurtry .05 .02 .01
- □ 363 Bill Dawley .05 .02 .01
- □ 364 Richard Dotson .05 .02 .01
- □ 365 Carmelo Martinez .05 .02 .01
- □ 366 Ron Cey .15 .07 .02
- □ 367 Tony Scott .05 .02 .01
- □ 368 Dave Bergman .05 .02 .01
- □ 369 Steve Sax .05 .02 .01
- □ 370 Bruce Sutter .15 .07 .02
- □ 371 Mickey Rivers .05 .02 .01
- □ 372 Kirk Gibson .15 .07 .02
- □ 373 Scott Sanderson .05 .02 .01
- □ 374 Brian Downing .05 .02 .01
- □ 375 Jeff Reardon .15 .07 .02
- □ 376 Frank DiPino .05 .02 .01
- □ 377 Checklist 265-396 .05 .02 .01
- □ 378 Alan Wiggins .05 .02 .01
- □ 379 Charles Hudson .05 .02 .01
- □ 380 Ken Griffey .15 .07 .02
- □ 381 Tom Paciorek .05 .02 .01
- □ 382 Jack Morris .15 .07 .02
- □ 383 Tony Gwynn 3.00 1.35 .35
- □ 384 Jody Davis .05 .02 .01
- □ 385 Jose DeLeon .05 .02 .01
- □ 386 Bob Kearney .05 .02 .01
- □ 387 George Wright .05 .02 .01
- □ 388 Ron Guidry .15 .07 .02
- □ 389 Rick Manning .05 .02 .01
- □ 390 Sid Fernandez .15 .07 .02
- □ 391 Bruce Bochte .05 .02 .01
- □ 392 Dan Petry .05 .02 .01
- □ 393 Tim Stoddard .05 .02 .01
  Free Agent with Padres 1-2-85
- □ 394 Tony Armas .05 .02 .01
- □ 395 Paul Molitor .75 .35 .09
- □ 396 Mike Heath .05 .02 .01

1985 O-Pee-Chee Posters

The 24 full-color posters in the 1985 O-Pee-Chee poster insert set were inserted one per regular wax pack and feature players of the Montreal Expos (numbered 1-12) and the Toronto Blue Jays (numbered 13-24). These posters are typically found with two folds and measure approximately 4 7/8" by 6 7/8". The posters are blank-backed and are numbered at the bottom in French and English. A distinctive blue (Blue Jays) or red (Expos) border surrounds the player photo.

	NRMT	VG-E	GOOD
COMPLETE SET (24)	6.00	2.70	.75
COMMON CARD (1-24)	.25	.11	.03

- □ 1 Mike Fitzgerald .25 .11 .03
- □ 2 Dan Driessen .25 .11 .03
- □ 3 Dave Palmer .25 .11 .03
- □ 4 U.L. Washington .25 .11 .03
- □ 5 Hubie Brooks .25 .11 .03
- □ 6 Tim Wallach .50 .23 .06
- □ 7 Tim Raines .50 .23 .06
- □ 8 Herm Winningham .25 .11 .03
- □ 9 Andre Dawson 1.50 .70 .19
- □ 10 Charlie Lea .25 .11 .03
- □ 11 Steve Rogers .25 .11 .03
- □ 12 Jeff Reardon .50 .23 .06
- □ 13 Buck Martinez .25 .11 .03
- □ 14 Willie Upshaw .25 .11 .03
- □ 15 Damaso Garcia UER .25 .11 .03
  (Misspelled Domaso)
- □ 16 Tony Fernandez .50 .23 .06
- □ 17 Rance Mulliniks .25 .11 .03
- □ 18 George Bell .50 .23 .06
- □ 19 Lloyd Moseby .25 .11 .03
- □ 20 Jesse Barfield .50 .23 .06
- □ 21 Doyle Alexander .25 .11 .03
- □ 22 Dave Stieb .50 .23 .06
- □ 23 Bill Caudill .25 .11 .03
- □ 24 Gary Lavelle .25 .11 .03

1986 O-Pee-Chee

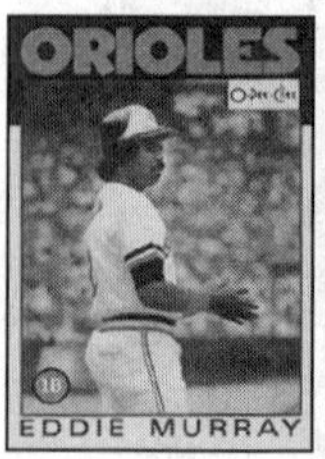

This set is an abridgement of the 1986 Topps set. The 396 standard-size cards comprising the 1986 O-Pee-Chee set differ from the cards of the 1986 Topps set by having a higher ratio of cards of players from the two Canadian teams, a practice begun by O-Pee-Chee in 1977 and continued to 1988. The fronts feature black-and white-bordered color player photos. The player's name appears within the white margin at the bottom. His team name appears within the black margin at the top and his position appears within a colored circle at the photo's lower left. The red horizontal backs carry the player's name and biography at the top. The player's major league statistics follow below. Some backs also have bilingual career highlights, some have bilingual baseball facts and still others have neither. The cards are numbered on the back. The asterisked cards have an extra line on the front inside the picture area indicating team change. The O-Pee-Chee logo appears on the front of every card.

	MINT	NRMT	EXC
COMPLETE SET (396)	12.00	5.50	1.50
COMMON CARD (1-396)	.05	.02	.01

- □ 1 Pete Rose 1.00 .45 .12
- □ 2 Ken Landreaux .05 .02 .01
- □ 3 Rob Picciolo .05 .02 .01
- □ 4 Steve Garvey .15 .07 .02
- □ 5 Andy Hawkins .05 .02 .01
- □ 6 Rudy Law .05 .02 .01
- □ 7 Lonnie Smith .05 .02 .01
- □ 8 Dwayne Murphy .05 .02 .01
- □ 9 Moose Haas .05 .02 .01
- □ 10 Tony Gwynn 1.25 .55 .16
- □ 11 Bob Ojeda .05 .02 .01
  Now with Mets
- □ 12 Jose Uribe .05 .02 .01
- □ 13 Bob Kearney .05 .02 .01
- □ 14 Julio Cruz .05 .02 .01
- □ 15 Eddie Whitson .05 .02 .01
- □ 16 Rick Schu .05 .02 .01
- □ 17 Mike Stenhouse .05 .02 .01
  Now with Red Sox
- □ 18 Lou Thornton .05 .02 .01
- □ 19 Ryne Sandberg .75 .35 .09
- □ 20 Lou Whitaker .10 .05 .01
- □ 21 Mark Brouhard .05 .02 .01
- □ 22 Gary Lavelle .05 .02 .01
- □ 23 Manny Lee .05 .02 .01
- □ 24 Don Slaught .05 .02 .01
- □ 25 Willie Wilson .05 .02 .01
- □ 26 Mike Marshall .05 .02 .01
- □ 27 Ray Knight .10 .05 .01
- □ 28 Mario Soto .05 .02 .01
- □ 29 Dave Anderson .05 .02 .01
- □ 30 Eddie Murray .75 .35 .09
- □ 31 Dusty Baker .10 .05 .01
- □ 32 Steve Yeager .05 .02 .01
  Now with Mariners
- □ 33 Andy Van Slyke .10 .05 .01
- □ 34 Dave Righetti .05 .02 .01
- □ 35 Jeff Reardon .10 .05 .01
- □ 36 Burt Hooton .05 .02 .01
- □ 37 Johnny Ray .05 .02 .01
- □ 38 Glenn Hoffman .05 .02 .01
- □ 39 Rick Mahler .05 .02 .01
- □ 40 Ken Griffey .10 .05 .01
- □ 41 Brad Wellman .05 .02 .01
- □ 42 Joe Hesketh .05 .02 .01
- □ 43 Mark Salas .05 .02 .01
- □ 44 Jorge Orta .05 .02 .01
- □ 45 Damaso Garcia .05 .02 .01
- □ 46 Jim Acker .05 .02 .01
- □ 47 Bill Madlock .05 .02 .01
- □ 48 Bill Almon .05 .02 .01
- □ 49 Rick Manning .05 .02 .01
- □ 50 Dan Quisenberry .05 .02 .01
- □ 51 Jim Gantner .05 .02 .01
- □ 52 Kevin Bass .05 .02 .01
- □ 53 Len Dykstra .75 .35 .09
- □ 54 John Franco .15 .07 .02
- □ 55 Fred Lynn .10 .05 .01
- □ 56 Jim Morrison .05 .02 .01
- □ 57 Bill Doran .05 .02 .01
- □ 58 Leon Durham .05 .02 .01
- □ 59 Andre Thornton .05 .02 .01
- □ 60 Dwight Evans .10 .05 .01
- □ 61 Larry Herndon .05 .02 .01
- □ 62 Bob Boone .10 .05 .01
- □ 63 Kent Hrbek .15 .07 .02
- □ 64 Floyd Bannister .05 .02 .01
- □ 65 Harold Baines .15 .07 .02
- □ 66 Pat Tabler .05 .02 .01
- □ 67 Carmelo Martinez .05 .02 .01
- □ 68 Ed Lynch .05 .02 .01
- □ 69 George Foster .10 .05 .01
- □ 70 Dave Winfield .40 .18 .05
- □ 71 Ken Schrom .05 .02 .01
  Now with Indians
- □ 72 Toby Harrah .05 .02 .01
- □ 73 Jackie Gutierrez .05 .02 .01
  Now with Orioles
- □ 74 Rance Mulliniks .05 .02 .01
- □ 75 Jose DeLeon .05 .02 .01
- □ 76 Ron Romanick .05 .02 .01
- □ 77 Charlie Leibrandt .05 .02 .01
- □ 78 Bruce Benedict .05 .02 .01
- □ 79 Dave Schmidt .05 .02 .01
  Now with White Sox
- □ 80 Darryl Strawberry .15 .07 .02
- □ 81 Wayne Krenchicki .05 .02 .01
- □ 82 Tippy Martinez .05 .02 .01
- □ 83 Phil Garner .10 .05 .01
- □ 84 Darrell Porter .05 .02 .01
  Now with Rangers
- □ 85 Tony Perez .25 .11 .03
  Eric Davis also shown in photo
- □ 86 Tom Waddell .05 .02 .01
- □ 87 Tim Hulett .05 .02 .01
- □ 88 Barbaro Garbey .05 .02 .01
  Now with A's
- □ 89 Randy St. Claire .05 .02 .01
- □ 90 Garry Templeton .05 .02 .01
- □ 91 Tim Teufel .05 .02 .01
  Now with Mets
- □ 92 Al Cowens .05 .02 .01
- □ 93 Scot Thompson .05 .02 .01
- □ 94 Tom Herr .05 .02 .01
- □ 95 Ozzie Virgil .05 .02 .01
  Now with Braves
- □ 96 Jose Cruz .05 .02 .01
- □ 97 Gary Gaetti .10 .05 .01
- □ 98 Roger Clemens 1.00 .45 .12
- □ 99 Vance Law .05 .02 .01
- □ 100 Nolan Ryan 1.50 .70 .19
- □ 101 Mike Smithson .05 .02 .01
- □ 102 Rafael Santana .05 .02 .01
- □ 103 Darrell Evans .10 .05 .01
- □ 104 Rich Gossage .10 .05 .01
- □ 105 Gary Ward .05 .02 .01
- □ 106 Jim Gott .05 .02 .01
- □ 107 Rafael Ramirez .05 .02 .01
- □ 108 Ted Power .05 .02 .01
- □ 109 Ron Guidry .10 .05 .01
- □ 110 Scott McGregor .05 .02 .01
- □ 111 Mike Scioscia .05 .02 .01
- □ 112 Glenn Hubbard .05 .02 .01
- □ 113 U.L. Washington .05 .02 .01
- □ 114 Al Oliver .10 .05 .01
- □ 115 Jay Howell .05 .02 .01
- □ 116 Brook Jacoby .05 .02 .01
- □ 117 Willie McGee .10 .05 .01
- □ 118 Jerry Royster .05 .02 .01
- □ 119 Barry Bonnell .05 .02 .01
- □ 120 Steve Carlton .20 .09 .03
- □ 121 Alfredo Griffin .05 .02 .01
- □ 122 David Green .05 .02 .01
  Now with Brewers
- □ 123 Greg Walker .05 .02 .01
- □ 124 Frank Tanana .05 .02 .01
- □ 125 Dave Lopes .10 .05 .01
- □ 126 Mike Krukow .05 .02 .01
- □ 127 Jack Howell .05 .02 .01
- □ 128 Greg Harris .05 .02 .01
- □ 129 Herm Winningham .05 .02 .01
- □ 130 Alan Trammell .15 .07 .02
- □ 131 Checklist 1-132 .05 .02 .01
- □ 132 Razor Shines .05 .02 .01
- □ 133 Bruce Sutter .10 .05 .01
- □ 134 Carney Lansford .05 .02 .01
- □ 135 Joe Niekro .05 .02 .01
- □ 136 Ernie Whitt .05 .02 .01
- □ 137 Charlie Moore .05 .02 .01
- □ 138 Mel Hall .05 .02 .01
- □ 139 Roger McDowell .05 .02 .01
- □ 140 John Candelaria .05 .02 .01
- □ 141 Bob Rodgers MG .05 .02 .01
  Team checklist back
- □ 142 Manny Trillo .05 .02 .01
  Now with Cubs
- □ 143 Dave Palmer .10 .05 .01
  Now with Braves
- □ 144 Robin Yount .30 .14 .04
- □ 145 Pedro Guerrero .10 .05 .01
- □ 146 Von Hayes .05 .02 .01
- □ 147 Lance Parrish .10 .05 .01
- □ 148 Mike Heath .05 .02 .01
  Now with Cardinals
- □ 149 Brett Butler .10 .05 .01
- □ 150 Joaquin Andujar .05 .02 .01

Now with A's			
☐ 151 Graig Nettles	.10	.05	.01
☐ 152 Pete Vuckovich	.05	.02	.01
☐ 153 Jason Thompson	.05	.02	.01
☐ 154 Bert Roberge	.05	.02	.01
☐ 155 Bob Grich	.10	.05	.01
☐ 156 Roy Smalley	.05	.02	.01
☐ 157 Ron Hassey	.05	.02	.01
☐ 158 Bob Stanley	.05	.02	.01
☐ 159 Orel Hershiser	.40	.18	.05
☐ 160 Chet Lemon	.05	.02	.01
☐ 161 Terry Puhl	.05	.02	.01
☐ 162 Dave LaPoint	.05	.02	.01
Now with Tigers			
☐ 163 Onix Concepcion	.05	.02	.01
☐ 164 Steve Balboni	.05	.02	.01
☐ 165 Mike Davis	.05	.02	.01
☐ 166 Dickie Thon	.05	.02	.01
☐ 167 Zane Smith	.05	.02	.01
☐ 168 Jeff Burroughs	.05	.02	.01
☐ 169 Alex Trevino	.05	.02	.01
Now with Dodgers			
☐ 170 Gary Carter	.10	.05	.01
☐ 171 Tito Landrum	.05	.02	.01
☐ 172 Sammy Stewart	.05	.02	.01
Now with Red Sox			
☐ 173 Wayne Gross	.05	.02	.01
☐ 174 Britt Burns	.05	.02	.01
Now with Yankees			
☐ 175 Steve Sax	.05	.02	.01
☐ 176 Jody Davis	.05	.02	.01
☐ 177 Joel Youngblood	.05	.02	.01
☐ 178 Fernando Valenzuela	.10	.05	.01
☐ 179 Storm Davis	.05	.02	.01
☐ 180 Don Mattingly	1.25	.55	.16
☐ 181 Steve Bedrosian	.05	.02	.01
Now with Phillies			
☐ 182 Jesse Orosco	.05	.02	.01
☐ 183 Gary Roenicke	.05	.02	.01
Now with Yankees			
☐ 184 Don Baylor	.10	.05	.01
☐ 185 Rollie Fingers	.25	.11	.03
☐ 186 Ruppert Jones	.05	.02	.01
☐ 187 Scott Fletcher	.05	.02	.01
Now with Rangers			
☐ 188 Bob Dernier	.05	.02	.01
☐ 189 Mike Mason	.05	.02	.01
☐ 190 George Hendrick	.05	.02	.01
☐ 191 Wally Backman	.05	.02	.01
☐ 192 Oddibe McDowell	.05	.02	.01
☐ 193 Bruce Hurst	.05	.02	.01
☐ 194 Ron Cey	.10	.05	.01
☐ 195 Dave Concepcion	.10	.05	.01
☐ 196 Doyle Alexander	.05	.02	.01
☐ 197 Dale Murray	.05	.02	.01
☐ 198 Mark Langston	.25	.11	.03
☐ 199 Dennis Eckersley	.20	.09	.03
☐ 200 Mike Schmidt	.40	.18	.05
☐ 201 Nick Esasky	.05	.02	.01
☐ 202 Ken Dayley	.05	.02	.01
☐ 203 Rick Cerone	.05	.02	.01
☐ 204 Larry McWilliams	.05	.02	.01
☐ 205 Brian Downing	.05	.02	.01
☐ 206 Danny Darwin	.05	.02	.01
☐ 207 Bill Caudill	.05	.02	.01
☐ 208 Dave Rozema	.05	.02	.01
☐ 209 Eric Show	.05	.02	.01
☐ 210 Brad Komminsk	.05	.02	.01
☐ 211 Chris Bando	.05	.02	.01
☐ 212 Chris Speier	.05	.02	.01
☐ 213 Jim Clancy	.05	.02	.01
☐ 214 Randy Bush	.05	.02	.01
☐ 215 Frank White	.10	.05	.01
☐ 216 Dan Petry	.05	.02	.01
☐ 217 Tim Wallach	.05	.02	.01
☐ 218 Mitch Webster	.05	.02	.01
☐ 219 Dennis Lamp	.05	.02	.01
☐ 220 Bob Horner	.05	.02	.01
☐ 221 Dave Henderson	.05	.02	.01
☐ 222 Dave Smith	.05	.02	.01
☐ 223 Willie Upshaw	.05	.02	.01
☐ 224 Cesar Cedeno	.05	.02	.01
☐ 225 Ron Darling	.05	.02	.01
☐ 226 Lee Lacy	.05	.02	.01
☐ 227 John Tudor	.05	.02	.01
☐ 228 Jim Presley	.05	.02	.01
☐ 229 Bill Gullickson	.05	.02	.01
Now with Reds			
☐ 230 Terry Kennedy	.05	.02	.01
☐ 231 Bob Knepper	.05	.02	.01
☐ 232 Rick Rhoden	.05	.02	.01
☐ 233 Richard Dotson	.05	.02	.01
☐ 234 Jesse Barfield	.05	.02	.01
☐ 235 Butch Wynegar	.05	.02	.01
☐ 236 Jerry Reuss	.05	.02	.01
☐ 237 Juan Samuel	.05	.02	.01
☐ 238 Larry Parrish	.05	.02	.01
☐ 239 Bill Buckner	.10	.05	.01
☐ 240 Pat Sheridan	.05	.02	.01
☐ 241 Tony Fernandez	.05	.02	.01
☐ 242 Rich Thompson	.05	.02	.01
Now with Brewers			
☐ 243 Rickey Henderson	.40	.18	.05
☐ 244 Craig Lefferts	.05	.02	.01
☐ 245 Jim Sundberg	.05	.02	.01
☐ 246 Phil Niekro	.25	.11	.03
☐ 247 Terry Harper	.05	.02	.01
☐ 248 Spike Owen	.05	.02	.01
☐ 249 Bret Saberhagen	.20	.09	.03
☐ 250 Dwight Gooden	.20	.09	.03
☐ 251 Rich Dauer	.05	.02	.01
☐ 252 Keith Hernandez	.10	.05	.01
☐ 253 Bo Diaz	.05	.02	.01
☐ 254 Ozzie Guillen	.15	.07	.02
☐ 255 Tony Armas	.05	.02	.01
☐ 256 Andre Dawson	.15	.07	.02
☐ 257 Doug DeCinces	.05	.02	.01
☐ 258 Tim Burke	.05	.02	.01
☐ 259 Dennis Boyd	.05	.02	.01
☐ 260 Tony Pena	.05	.02	.01
☐ 261 Sal Butera	.05	.02	.01
Now with Reds			
☐ 262 Wade Boggs	.60	.25	.07
☐ 263 Checklist 133-264	.05	.02	.01
☐ 264 Ron Oester	.05	.02	.01
☐ 265 Ron Davis	.05	.02	.01
☐ 266 Keith Moreland	.05	.02	.01
☐ 267 Paul Molitor	.50	.23	.06
☐ 268 John Denny	.05	.02	.01
Now with Reds			
☐ 269 Frank Viola	.10	.05	.01
☐ 270 Jack Morris	.10	.05	.01
☐ 271 Dave Collins	.05	.02	.01
Now with Tigers			
☐ 272 Bert Blyleven	.10	.05	.01
☐ 273 Jerry Willard	.05	.02	.01
☐ 274 Matt Young	.05	.02	.01
☐ 275 Charlie Hough	.10	.05	.01
☐ 276 Dave Dravecky	.10	.05	.01
☐ 277 Garth Iorg	.05	.02	.01
☐ 278 Hal McRae	.10	.05	.01
☐ 279 Curt Wilkerson	.05	.02	.01
☐ 280 Tim Raines	.10	.05	.01
☐ 281 Bill Laskey	.05	.02	.01
Now with Giants			
☐ 282 Jerry Mumphrey	.05	.02	.01
Now with Cubs			
☐ 283 Pat Clements	.05	.02	.01
☐ 284 Bob James	.05	.02	.01
☐ 285 Buddy Bell	.10	.05	.01
☐ 286 Tom Brookens	.05	.02	.01
☐ 287 Dave Parker	.10	.05	.01
☐ 288 Ron Kittle	.05	.02	.01
☐ 289 Johnnie LeMaster	.05	.02	.01
☐ 290 Carlton Fisk	.25	.11	.03
☐ 291 Jimmy Key	.15	.07	.02
☐ 292 Gary Matthews	.05	.02	.01
☐ 293 Marvell Wynne	.05	.02	.01
☐ 294 Danny Cox	.05	.02	.01
☐ 295 Kirk Gibson	.10	.05	.01
☐ 296 Mariano Duncan	.15	.07	.02
☐ 297 Ozzie Smith	1.00	.45	.12
☐ 298 Craig Reynolds	.05	.02	.01
☐ 299 Bryn Smith	.05	.02	.01
☐ 300 George Brett	1.00	.45	.12
☐ 301 Walt Terrell	.05	.02	.01
☐ 302 Greg Gross	.05	.02	.01
☐ 303 Claudell Washington	.05	.02	.01
☐ 304 Howard Johnson	.10	.05	.01
☐ 305 Phil Bradley	.05	.02	.01
☐ 306 R.J. Reynolds	.05	.02	.01
☐ 307 Bob Brenly	.05	.02	.01
☐ 308 Hubie Brooks	.05	.02	.01
☐ 309 Alvin Davis	.05	.02	.01
☐ 310 Donnie Hill	.05	.02	.01
☐ 311 Dick Schofield	.05	.02	.01
☐ 312 Tom Filer	.05	.02	.01
☐ 313 Mike Fitzgerald	.05	.02	.01
☐ 314 Marty Barrett	.05	.02	.01
☐ 315 Mookie Wilson	.10	.05	.01
☐ 316 Alan Knicely	.05	.02	.01
☐ 317 Ed Romero	.05	.02	.01
Now with Red Sox			
☐ 318 Glenn Wilson	.05	.02	.01
☐ 319 Bud Black	.05	.02	.01
☐ 320 Jim Rice	.10	.05	.01
☐ 321 Terry Pendleton	.25	.11	.03
☐ 322 Dave Kingman	.10	.05	.01
☐ 323 Gary Pettis	.05	.02	.01
☐ 324 Dan Schatzeder	.05	.02	.01
☐ 325 Juan Beniquez	.05	.02	.01
Now with Orioles			
☐ 326 Kent Tekulve	.05	.02	.01
☐ 327 Mike Pagliarulo	.05	.02	.01
☐ 328 Pete O'Brien	.05	.02	.01
☐ 329 Kirby Puckett	2.00	.90	.25
☐ 330 Rick Sutcliffe	.05	.02	.01
☐ 331 Alan Ashby	.05	.02	.01
☐ 332 Willie Randolph	.10	.05	.01
☐ 333 Tom Henke	.10	.05	.01
☐ 334 Ken Oberkfell	.05	.02	.01
☐ 335 Don Sutton	.15	.07	.02
☐ 336 Dan Gladden	.05	.02	.01
☐ 337 George Vukovich	.05	.02	.01
☐ 338 Jorge Bell	.10	.05	.01
☐ 339 Jim Dwyer	.05	.02	.01
☐ 340 Cal Ripken	1.50	.70	.19
☐ 341 Willie Hernandez	.05	.02	.01
☐ 342 Gary Redus	.05	.02	.01
Now with Phillies			
☐ 343 Jerry Koosman	.10	.05	.01
☐ 344 Jim Wohlford	.05	.02	.01
☐ 345 Donnie Moore	.05	.02	.01
☐ 346 Floyd Youmans	.05	.02	.01
☐ 347 Gorman Thomas	.05	.02	.01
☐ 348 Cliff Johnson	.05	.02	.01
☐ 349 Ken Howell	.05	.02	.01
☐ 350 Jack Clark	.10	.05	.01
☐ 351 Gary Lucas	.05	.02	.01
Now with Angels			
☐ 352 Bob Clark	.05	.02	.01
☐ 353 Dave Stieb	.05	.02	.01
☐ 354 Tony Bernazard	.05	.02	.01
☐ 355 Lee Smith	.20	.09	.03
☐ 356 Mickey Hatcher	.05	.02	.01
☐ 357 Ed VandeBerg	.05	.02	.01
Now with Dodgers			
☐ 358 Rick Dempsey	.05	.02	.01
☐ 359 Bobby Cox MG	.10	.05	.01
Now General Manager of Atlanta Braves			
Team checklist back			
☐ 360 Lloyd Moseby	.05	.02	.01
☐ 361 Shane Rawley	.05	.02	.01
☐ 362 Garry Maddox	.05	.02	.01
☐ 363 Buck Martinez	.05	.02	.01
☐ 364 Ed Nunez	.05	.02	.01
☐ 365 Luis Leal	.05	.02	.01
☐ 366 Dale Berra	.05	.02	.01
☐ 367 Mike Boddicker	.05	.02	.01
☐ 368 Greg Brock	.05	.02	.01
☐ 369 Al Holland	.05	.02	.01
☐ 370 Vince Coleman	.15	.07	.02
☐ 371 Rod Carew	.20	.09	.03
☐ 372 Ben Oglivie	.05	.02	.01
☐ 373 Lee Mazzilli	.05	.02	.01
☐ 374 Terry Francona	.10	.05	.01
☐ 375 Rich Gedman	.05	.02	.01
☐ 376 Charlie Lea	.05	.02	.01
☐ 377 Joe Carter	1.00	.45	.12
☐ 378 Bruce Bochte	.05	.02	.01
☐ 379 Bobby Meacham	.05	.02	.01
☐ 380 LaMarr Hoyt	.05	.02	.01
☐ 381 Jeff Leonard	.05	.02	.01
☐ 382 Ivan Calderon	.10	.05	.01
☐ 383 Chris Brown	.05	.02	.01
☐ 384 Steve Trout	.05	.02	.01
☐ 385 Cecil Cooper	.10	.05	.01
☐ 386 Cecil Fielder	1.50	.70	.19
☐ 387 Tim Flannery	.05	.02	.01
☐ 388 Chris Codiroli	.05	.02	.01
☐ 389 Glenn Davis	.05	.02	.01
☐ 390 Tom Seaver	.20	.09	.03
☐ 391 Julio Franco	.15	.07	.02
☐ 392 Tom Brunansky	.05	.02	.01
☐ 393 Rob Wilfong	.05	.02	.01
☐ 394 Reggie Jackson	.30	.14	.04
☐ 395 Scott Garrelts	.05	.02	.01
☐ 396 Checklist 265-396	.05	.02	.01

1986 O-Pee-Chee Box Bottoms

O-Pee-Chee printed four different four-card panels on the bottoms of its 1986 wax pack boxes. If cut, each card would measure approximately the standard size. These 16 cards, in alphabetical order and designated A through P, are considered a separate set from the regular issue, but are styled almost exactly the same, differing only in the player photo and colors for the team name, borders and position on the front. The backs are identical, except for the letter designations instead of numbers.

	MINT	NRMT	EXC
COMPLETE SET (16)	8.00	3.60	1.00
COMMON CARD (A-P)	.25	.11	.03
☐ A George Bell	.25	.11	.03
☐ B Wade Boggs	1.00	.45	.12
☐ C George Brett	2.50	1.10	.30
☐ D Vince Coleman	.25	.11	.03
☐ E Carlton Fisk	.75	.35	.09
☐ F Dwight Gooden	.75	.35	.09
☐ G Pedro Guerrero	.25	.11	.03
☐ H Ron Guidry	.50	.23	.06
☐ I Reggie Jackson	1.00	.45	.12
☐ J Don Mattingly	2.50	1.10	.30
☐ K Oddibe McDowell	.25	.11	.03
☐ L Willie McGee	.50	.23	.06
☐ M Dale Murphy	.75	.35	.09
☐ N Pete Rose	1.50	.70	.19
☐ O Bret Saberhagen	.75	.35	.09
☐ P Fernando Valenzuela	.50	.23	.06

1987 O-Pee-Chee

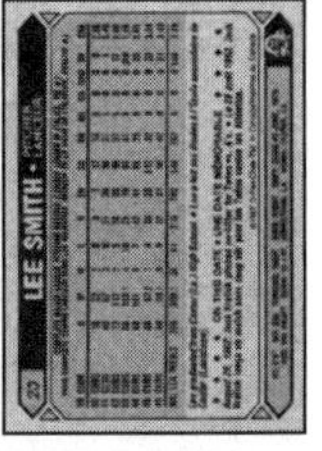

This set is an abridgement of the 1987 Topps set. The 396 standard-size cards comprising the 1987 O-Pee-Chee set differ from the cards of the 1987 Topps set by having a higher ratio of cards of players from the two Canadian teams, a practice begun by O-Pee-Chee in 1977 and continued to 1988. The fronts feature wood grain bordered color player photos. The player's name appears in the colored rectangle at the lower right. His team logo appears at the upper left. The yellow, white and blue horizontal backs carry the player's name and bilingual position at the top. The player's major league statistics follow below. Some backs also have bilingual career highlights, some have bilingual baseball facts and still others have both or neither. The cards are numbered on the back. The asterisked cards have an extra line on the front inside the picture area indicating team change. The O-Pee-Chee logo appears on the front of every card.

	MINT	NRMT	EXC
COMPLETE SET (396)	15.00	6.75	1.85
COMMON CARD (1-396)	.05	.02	.01
☐ 1 Ken Oberkfell	.05	.02	.01
☐ 2 Jack Howell	.05	.02	.01
☐ 3 Hubie Brooks	.05	.02	.01
☐ 4 Bob Grich	.10	.05	.01
☐ 5 Rick Leach	.05	.02	.01
☐ 6 Phil Niekro	.25	.11	.03
☐ 7 Rickey Henderson	.20	.09	.03
☐ 8 Terry Pendleton	.10	.05	.01
☐ 9 Jay Tibbs	.05	.02	.01
☐ 10 Cecil Cooper	.10	.05	.01
☐ 11 Mario Soto	.05	.02	.01
☐ 12 George Bell	.05	.02	.01
☐ 13 Nick Esasky	.05	.02	.01
☐ 14 Larry McWilliams	.05	.02	.01
☐ 15 Dan Quisenberry	.05	.02	.01
☐ 16 Ed Lynch	.05	.02	.01
☐ 17 Pete O'Brien	.05	.02	.01
☐ 18 Luis Aguayo	.05	.02	.01
☐ 19 Matt Young	.05	.02	.01
Now with Dodgers			
☐ 20 Gary Carter	.10	.05	.01
☐ 21 Tom Paciorek	.05	.02	.01
☐ 22 Doug DeCinces	.05	.02	.01
☐ 23 Lee Smith	.15	.07	.02
☐ 24 Jesse Barfield	.05	.02	.01
☐ 25 Bert Blyleven	.10	.05	.01
☐ 26 Greg Brock	.05	.02	.01
Now with Brewers			
☐ 27 Dan Petry	.05	.02	.01
☐ 28 Rick Dempsey	.05	.02	.01
Now with Indians			
☐ 29 Jimmy Key	.10	.05	.01
☐ 30 Tim Raines	.10	.05	.01
☐ 31 Bruce Hurst	.05	.02	.01
☐ 32 Manny Trillo	.05	.02	.01
☐ 33 Andy Van Slyke	.10	.05	.01
☐ 34 Ed VandeBerg	.05	.02	.01
Now with Indians			
☐ 35 Sid Bream	.05	.02	.01
☐ 36 Dave Winfield	.20	.09	.03
☐ 37 Scott Garrelts	.05	.02	.01
☐ 38 Dennis Leonard	.05	.02	.01
☐ 39 Marty Barrett	.05	.02	.01
☐ 40 Dave Righetti	.05	.02	.01
☐ 41 Bo Diaz	.05	.02	.01
☐ 42 Gary Redus	.05	.02	.01
☐ 43 Tom Niedenfuer	.05	.02	.01
☐ 44 Greg Harris	.05	.02	.01
☐ 45 Jim Presley	.05	.02	.01
☐ 46 Danny Gladden	.05	.02	.01
☐ 47 Roy Smalley	.05	.02	.01
☐ 48 Wally Backman	.05	.02	.01
☐ 49 Tom Seaver	.30	.14	.04
☐ 50 Dave Smith	.05	.02	.01
☐ 51 Mel Hall	.05	.02	.01
☐ 52 Tim Flannery	.05	.02	.01
☐ 53 Julio Cruz	.05	.02	.01
☐ 54 Dick Schofield	.05	.02	.01
☐ 55 Tim Wallach	.05	.02	.01
☐ 56 Glenn Davis	.05	.02	.01
☐ 57 Darren Daulton	.20	.09	.03
☐ 58 Chico Walker	.05	.02	.01
☐ 59 Garth Iorg	.05	.02	.01
☐ 60 Tony Pena	.05	.02	.01
☐ 61 Ron Hassey	.05	.02	.01
☐ 62 Dave Dravecky	.10	.05	.01
☐ 63 Jorge Orta	.05	.02	.01
☐ 64 Al Nipper	.05	.02	.01
☐ 65 Tom Browning	.05	.02	.01
☐ 66 Marc Sullivan	.05	.02	.01
☐ 67 Todd Worrell	.10	.05	.01

☐ 68 Glenn Hubbard .05 .02 .01
☐ 69 Carney Lansford .05 .02 .01
☐ 70 Charlie Hough .05 .02 .01
☐ 71 Lance McCullers .05 .02 .01
☐ 72 Walt Terrell .05 .02 .01
☐ 73 Bob Kearney .05 .02 .01
☐ 74 Dan Pasqua .05 .02 .01
☐ 75 Ron Darling .05 .02 .01
☐ 76 Robin Yount .15 .07 .02
☐ 77 Pat Tabler .05 .02 .01
☐ 78 Tom Foley .05 .02 .01
☐ 79 Juan Nieves .05 .02 .01
☐ 80 Wally Joyner .25 .11 .03
☐ 81 Wayne Krenchicki .05 .02 .01
☐ 82 Kirby Puckett .75 .35 .09
☐ 83 Bob Ojeda .05 .02 .01
☐ 84 Mookie Wilson .10 .05 .01
☐ 85 Kevin Bass .05 .02 .01
☐ 86 Kent Tekulve .05 .02 .01
☐ 87 Mark Salas .05 .02 .01
☐ 88 Brian Downing .05 .02 .01
☐ 89 Ozzie Guillen .05 .02 .01
☐ 90 Dave Stieb .05 .02 .01
☐ 91 Rance Mulliniks .05 .02 .01
☐ 92 Mike Witt .05 .02 .01
☐ 93 Charlie Moore .05 .02 .01
☐ 94 Jose Uribe .05 .02 .01
☐ 95 Oddibe McDowell .05 .02 .01
☐ 96 Ray Soff .05 .02 .01
☐ 97 Glenn Wilson .05 .02 .01
☐ 98 Brook Jacoby .05 .02 .01
☐ 99 Darryl Motley .05 .02 .01
Now with Braves
☐ 100 Steve Garvey .15 .07 .02
☐ 101 Frank White .10 .05 .01
☐ 102 Mike Moore .05 .02 .01
☐ 103 Rick Aguilera .10 .05 .01
☐ 104 Buddy Bell .10 .05 .01
☐ 105 Floyd Youmans .05 .02 .01
☐ 106 Lou Whitaker .10 .05 .01
☐ 107 Ozzie Smith .75 .35 .09
☐ 108 Jim Gantner .05 .02 .01
☐ 109 R.J. Reynolds .05 .02 .01
☐ 110 John Tudor .05 .02 .01
☐ 111 Alfredo Griffin .05 .02 .01
☐ 112 Mike Flanagan .05 .02 .01
☐ 113 Neil Allen .05 .02 .01
☐ 114 Ken Griffey .10 .05 .01
☐ 115 Donnie Moore .05 .02 .01
☐ 116 Bob Horner .05 .02 .01
☐ 117 Ron Shepherd .05 .02 .01
☐ 118 Cliff Johnson .05 .02 .01
☐ 119 Vince Coleman .05 .02 .01
☐ 120 Eddie Murray .30 .14 .04
☐ 121 Dwayne Murphy .05 .02 .01
☐ 122 Jim Clancy .05 .02 .01
☐ 123 Ken Landreaux .05 .02 .01
☐ 124 Tom Nieto .05 .02 .01
Now with Twins
☐ 125 Bob Brenly .05 .02 .01
☐ 126 George Brett .75 .35 .09
☐ 127 Vance Law .05 .02 .01
☐ 128 Checklist 1-132 .05 .02 .01
☐ 129 Bob Knepper .05 .02 .01
☐ 130 Dwight Gooden .15 .07 .02
☐ 131 Juan Bonilla .05 .02 .01
☐ 132 Tim Burke .05 .02 .01
☐ 133 Bob McClure .05 .02 .01
☐ 134 Scott Bailes .05 .02 .01
☐ 135 Mike Easler .05 .02 .01
Now with Phillies
☐ 136 Ron Romanick .05 .02 .01
Now with Yankees
☐ 137 Rick Gedman .05 .02 .01
☐ 138 Bob Dernier .05 .02 .01
☐ 139 John Denny .05 .02 .01
☐ 140 Bret Saberhagen .10 .05 .01
☐ 141 Herm Winningham .05 .02 .01
☐ 142 Rick Sutcliffe .05 .02 .01
☐ 143 Ryne Sandberg .40 .18 .05
☐ 144 Mike Scioscia .05 .02 .01
☐ 145 Charlie Kerfeld .05 .02 .01
☐ 146 Jim Rice .10 .05 .01
☐ 147 Steve Trout .05 .02 .01
☐ 148 Jesse Orosco .05 .02 .01
☐ 149 Mike Boddicker .05 .02 .01
☐ 150 Wade Boggs .20 .09 .03
☐ 151 Dane Iorg .05 .02 .01
☐ 152 Rick Burleson .05 .02 .01
Now with Orioles
☐ 153 Duane Ward .10 .05 .01
☐ 154 Rick Reuschel .05 .02 .01
☐ 155 Nolan Ryan .75 .35 .09
☐ 156 Bill Caudill .05 .02 .01
☐ 157 Danny Darwin .05 .02 .01
☐ 158 Ed Romero .05 .02 .01
☐ 159 Bill Almon .05 .02 .01
☐ 160 Julio Franco .10 .05 .01
☐ 161 Kent Hrbek .10 .05 .01
☐ 162 Chili Davis .10 .05 .01
☐ 163 Kevin Gross .05 .02 .01
☐ 164 Carlton Fisk .25 .11 .03
☐ 165 Jeff Reardon .10 .05 .01
Now with Twins
☐ 166 Bob Boone .10 .05 .01
☐ 167 Rick Honeycutt .05 .02 .01
☐ 168 Dan Schatzeder .05 .02 .01
☐ 169 Jim Wohlford .05 .02 .01
☐ 170 Phil Bradley .05 .02 .01
☐ 171 Ken Schrom .05 .02 .01
☐ 172 Ron Oester .05 .02 .01
☐ 173 Juan Beniquez .05 .02 .01
Now with Royals
☐ 174 Tony Armas .05 .02 .01
☐ 175 Bob Stanley .05 .02 .01
☐ 176 Steve Buechele .05 .02 .01
☐ 177 Keith Moreland .05 .02 .01
☐ 178 Cecil Fielder .30 .14 .04
☐ 179 Gary Gaetti .10 .05 .01
☐ 180 Chris Brown .05 .02 .01
☐ 181 Tom Herr .05 .02 .01
☐ 182 Lee Lacy .05 .02 .01
☐ 183 Ozzie Virgil .05 .02 .01
☐ 184 Paul Molitor .25 .11 .03
☐ 185 Roger McDowell .05 .02 .01
☐ 186 Mike Marshall .05 .02 .01
☐ 187 Ken Howell .05 .02 .01
☐ 188 Rob Deer .05 .02 .01
☐ 189 Joe Hesketh .05 .02 .01
☐ 190 Jim Sundberg .05 .02 .01
☐ 191 Kelly Gruber .05 .02 .01
☐ 192 Cory Snyder .05 .02 .01
☐ 193 Dave Concepcion .10 .05 .01
☐ 194 Kirk McCaskill .05 .02 .01
☐ 195 Mike Pagliarulo .05 .02 .01
☐ 196 Rick Manning .05 .02 .01
☐ 197 Brett Butler .10 .05 .01
☐ 198 Tony Gwynn .75 .35 .09
☐ 199 Mariano Duncan .05 .02 .01
☐ 200 Pete Rose .20 .09 .03
☐ 201 John Cangelosi .05 .02 .01
☐ 202 Danny Cox .05 .02 .01
☐ 203 Butch Wynegar .05 .02 .01
Now with Angels
☐ 204 Chris Chambliss .05 .02 .01
☐ 205 Graig Nettles .10 .05 .01
☐ 206 Chet Lemon .05 .02 .01
☐ 207 Don Aase .05 .02 .01
☐ 208 Mike Mason .05 .02 .01
☐ 209 Alan Trammell .15 .07 .02
☐ 210 Lloyd Moseby .05 .02 .01
☐ 211 Richard Dotson .05 .02 .01
☐ 212 Mike Fitzgerald .05 .02 .01
☐ 213 Darrell Porter .05 .02 .01
☐ 214 Checklist 265-396 .05 .02 .01
☐ 215 Mark Langston .15 .07 .02
☐ 216 Steve Farr .05 .02 .01
☐ 217 Dann Bilardello .05 .02 .01
☐ 218 Gary Ward .05 .02 .01
Now with Yankees
☐ 219 Cecilio Guante .05 .02 .01
Now with Yankees
☐ 220 Joe Carter .20 .09 .03
☐ 221 Ernie Whitt .05 .02 .01
☐ 222 Denny Walling .05 .02 .01
☐ 223 Charlie Leibrandt .05 .02 .01
☐ 224 Wayne Tolleson .05 .02 .01
☐ 225 Mike Smithson .05 .02 .01
☐ 226 Zane Smith .05 .02 .01
☐ 227 Terry Puhl .05 .02 .01
☐ 228 Eric Davis .15 .07 .02
☐ 229 Don Mattingly .75 .35 .09
☐ 230 Don Baylor .10 .05 .01
☐ 231 Frank Tanana .05 .02 .01
☐ 232 Tom Brookens .05 .02 .01
☐ 233 Steve Bedrosian .05 .02 .01
☐ 234 Wallace Johnson .05 .02 .01
☐ 235 Alvin Davis .05 .02 .01
☐ 236 Tommy John .10 .05 .01
☐ 237 Jim Morrison .05 .02 .01
☐ 238 Ricky Horton .05 .02 .01
☐ 239 Shane Rawley .05 .02 .01
☐ 240 Steve Balboni .05 .02 .01
☐ 241 Mike Krukow .05 .02 .01
☐ 242 Rick Mahler .05 .02 .01
☐ 243 Bill Doran .05 .02 .01
☐ 244 Mark Clear .05 .02 .01
☐ 245 Willie Upshaw .05 .02 .01
☐ 246 Hal McRae .10 .05 .01
☐ 247 Jose Canseco .60 .25 .07
☐ 248 George Hendrick .05 .02 .01
☐ 249 Doyle Alexander .05 .02 .01
☐ 250 Teddy Higuera .05 .02 .01
☐ 251 Tom Hume .05 .02 .01
☐ 252 Denny Martinez .10 .05 .01
☐ 253 Eddie Milner .05 .02 .01
Now with Giants
☐ 254 Steve Sax .05 .02 .01
☐ 255 Juan Samuel .05 .02 .01
☐ 256 Dave Bergman .05 .02 .01
☐ 257 Bob Forsch .05 .02 .01
☐ 258 Steve Yeager .05 .02 .01
☐ 259 Don Sutton .15 .07 .02
☐ 260 Vida Blue .10 .05 .01
Now with A's
☐ 261 Tom Brunansky .05 .02 .01
☐ 262 Joe Sambito .05 .02 .01
☐ 263 Mitch Webster .05 .02 .01
☐ 264 Checklist 133-264 .05 .02 .01
☐ 265 Darrell Evans .10 .05 .01
☐ 266 Dave Kingman .10 .05 .01
☐ 267 Howard Johnson .05 .02 .01
☐ 268 Greg Pryor .05 .02 .01
☐ 269 Tippy Martinez .05 .02 .01
☐ 270 Jody Davis .05 .02 .01
☐ 271 Steve Carlton .30 .14 .04
☐ 272 Andres Galarraga .60 .25 .07
☐ 273 Fernando Valenzuela .10 .05 .01
☐ 274 Jeff Hearron .05 .02 .01
☐ 275 Ray Knight .10 .05 .01
Now with Orioles
☐ 276 Bill Madlock .05 .02 .01
☐ 277 Tom Henke .05 .02 .01
☐ 278 Gary Pettis .05 .02 .01
☐ 279 Jimy Williams MG .05 .02 .01
team checklist back
☐ 280 Jeffrey Leonard .05 .02 .01
☐ 281 Bryn Smith .05 .02 .01
☐ 282 John Cerutti .05 .02 .01
☐ 283 Gary Roenicke .05 .02 .01
Now with Braves
☐ 284 Joaquin Andujar .05 .02 .01
☐ 285 Dennis Boyd .05 .02 .01
☐ 286 Tim Hulett .05 .02 .01
☐ 287 Craig Lefferts .05 .02 .01
☐ 288 Tito Landrum .05 .02 .01
☐ 289 Manny Lee .05 .02 .01
☐ 290 Leon Durham .05 .02 .01
☐ 291 Johnny Ray .05 .02 .01
☐ 292 Franklin Stubbs .05 .02 .01
☐ 293 Bob Rodgers MG .05 .02 .01
team checklist back
☐ 294 Terry Francona .10 .05 .01
☐ 295 Len Dykstra .15 .07 .02
☐ 296 Tom Candiotti .05 .02 .01
☐ 297 Frank DiPino .05 .02 .01
☐ 298 Craig Reynolds .05 .02 .01
☐ 299 Jerry Hairston .05 .02 .01
☐ 300 Reggie Jackson .30 .14 .04
Now with A's
☐ 301 Luis Aquino .05 .02 .01
☐ 302 Greg Walker .05 .02 .01
☐ 303 Terry Kennedy .05 .02 .01
Now with Orioles
☐ 304 Phil Garner .10 .05 .01
☐ 305 John Franco .10 .05 .01
☐ 306 Bill Buckner .10 .05 .01
☐ 307 Kevin Mitchell .25 .11 .03
Now with Padres
☐ 308 Don Slaught .05 .02 .01
☐ 309 Harold Baines .10 .05 .01
☐ 310 Frank Viola .05 .02 .01
☐ 311 Dave Lopes .10 .05 .01
☐ 312 Cal Ripken .75 .35 .09
☐ 313 John Candelaria .05 .02 .01
☐ 314 Bob Sebra .05 .02 .01
☐ 315 Bud Black .05 .02 .01
☐ 316 Brian Fisher .05 .02 .01
Now with Pirates
☐ 317 Clint Hurdle .05 .02 .01
☐ 318 Earnest Riles .05 .02 .01
☐ 319 Dave LaPoint .05 .02 .01
Now with Cardinals
☐ 320 Barry Bonds 1.25 .55 .16
☐ 321 Tim Stoddard .05 .02 .01
☐ 322 Ron Cey .10 .05 .01
Now with A's
☐ 323 Al Newman .05 .02 .01
☐ 324 Jerry Royster .05 .02 .01
Now with White Sox
☐ 325 Garry Templeton .05 .02 .01
☐ 326 Mark Gubicza .05 .02 .01
☐ 327 Andre Thornton .05 .02 .01
☐ 328 Bob Welch .05 .02 .01
☐ 329 Tony Fernandez .05 .02 .01
☐ 330 Mike Scott .05 .02 .01
☐ 331 Jack Clark .10 .05 .01
☐ 332 Danny Tartabull .05 .02 .01
Now with Royals
☐ 333 Greg Minton .05 .02 .01
☐ 334 Ed Correa .05 .02 .01
☐ 335 Candy Maldonado .05 .02 .01
☐ 336 Dennis Lamp .05 .02 .01
Now with Indians
☐ 337 Sid Fernandez .05 .02 .01
☐ 338 Greg Gross .05 .02 .01
☐ 339 Willie Hernandez .05 .02 .01
☐ 340 Roger Clemens .60 .25 .07
☐ 341 Mickey Hatcher .05 .02 .01
☐ 342 Bob James .05 .02 .01
☐ 343 Jose Cruz .05 .02 .01
☐ 344 Bruce Sutter .05 .02 .01
☐ 345 Andre Dawson .20 .09 .03
☐ 346 Shawon Dunston .10 .05 .01
☐ 347 Scott McGregor .05 .02 .01
☐ 348 Carmelo Martinez .05 .02 .01
☐ 349 Storm Davis .05 .02 .01
Now with Padres
☐ 350 Keith Hernandez .10 .05 .01
☐ 351 Andy McGaffigan .05 .02 .01
☐ 352 Dave Parker .10 .05 .01
☐ 353 Ernie Camacho .05 .02 .01
☐ 354 Eric Show .05 .02 .01
☐ 355 Don Carman .05 .02 .01
☐ 356 Floyd Bannister .05 .02 .01
☐ 357 Willie McGee .10 .05 .01
☐ 358 Atlee Hammaker .05 .02 .01
☐ 359 Dale Murphy .20 .09 .03
☐ 360 Pedro Guerrero .10 .05 .01
☐ 361 Will Clark .60 .25 .07
☐ 362 Bill Campbell .05 .02 .01
☐ 363 Alejandro Pena .05 .02 .01
☐ 364 Dennis Rasmussen .05 .02 .01
☐ 365 Rick Rhoden .05 .02 .01
Now with Yankees
☐ 366 Randy St. Claire .05 .02 .01
☐ 367 Willie Wilson .05 .02 .01
☐ 368 Dwight Evans .10 .05 .01
☐ 369 Moose Haas .05 .02 .01
☐ 370 Fred Lynn .10 .05 .01
☐ 371 Mark Eichhorn .05 .02 .01
☐ 372 Dave Schmidt .05 .02 .01
Now with Orioles
☐ 373 Jerry Reuss .05 .02 .01
☐ 374 Lance Parrish .10 .05 .01
☐ 375 Ron Guidry .10 .05 .01
☐ 376 Jack Morris .10 .05 .01
☐ 377 Willie Randolph .10 .05 .01
☐ 378 Joel Youngblood .05 .02 .01
☐ 379 Darryl Strawberry .15 .07 .02
☐ 380 Rich Gossage .10 .05 .01
☐ 381 Dennis Eckersley .15 .07 .02
☐ 382 Gary Lucas .05 .02 .01
☐ 383 Ron Davis .05 .02 .01
☐ 384 Pete Incaviglia .10 .05 .01
☐ 385 Orel Hershiser .20 .09 .03
☐ 386 Kirk Gibson .10 .05 .01
☐ 387 Don Robinson .05 .02 .01
☐ 388 Darnell Coles .05 .02 .01
☐ 389 Von Hayes .05 .02 .01
☐ 390 Gary Matthews .05 .02 .01
☐ 391 Jay Howell .05 .02 .01
☐ 392 Tim Laudner .05 .02 .01
☐ 393 Rod Scurry .05 .02 .01
☐ 394 Tony Bernazard .05 .02 .01
☐ 395 Damaso Garcia .05 .02 .01
Now with Braves
☐ 396 Mike Schmidt .20 .09 .03

1987 O-Pee-Chee Box Bottoms

O-Pee-Chee printed two different four-card panels on the bottoms of its 1987 wax pack boxes. If cut, each card would measure approximately 2 1/8" by 3". These eight cards, in alphabetical order and designated A through H, are considered a separate set from the regular issue, but are styled almost exactly the same, differing only in the player photo and colors for the team name, borders and position on the front. On the horizontal backs, purple borders frame a yellow panel that presents bilingual text describing an outstanding achievement or milestone in the player's career.

	MINT	NRMT	EXC
COMPLETE SET (8)	4.00	1.80	.50
COMMON CARD (A-H)	.25	.11	.03

	MINT	NRMT	EXC
☐ A Don Baylor	.35	.16	.04
☐ B Steve Carlton	1.00	.45	.12
☐ C Ron Cey	.25	.11	.03
☐ D Cecil Cooper	.25	.11	.03
☐ E Rickey Henderson	1.25	.55	.16
☐ F Jim Rice	.35	.16	.04
☐ G Don Sutton	.50	.23	.06
☐ H Dave Winfield	1.00	.45	.12

1988 O-Pee-Chee

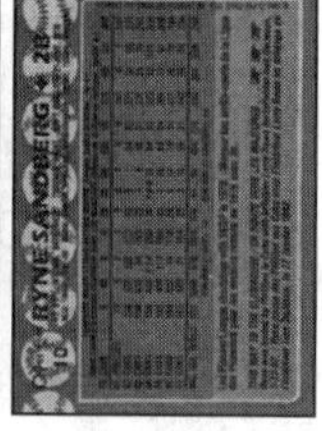

This set is an abridgement of the 1988 Topps set. The 396 standard-size cards comprising the 1988 O-Pee-Chee set differ from the cards of the 1988 Topps set by having a higher ratio of cards of players from the two Canadian teams, a practice begun by O-Pee-Chee in 1977 and continued to 1988. The fronts feature white-bordered color player photos framed by a colored line. The player's name appears in the colored diagonal stripe at the lower right. His team name appears at the top. The orange horizontal backs carry the player's name, position and biography printed across the row of baseball icons at the top. The player's major league statistics follow below. Some backs also have bilingual career highlights, some have bilingual baseball facts and still others have both or neither. The cards are numbered on the back. The asterisked cards have an extra line on the front inside the picture area indicating team change. They are styled like the 1988 Topps regular issue cards. The O-Pee-Chee logo appears on the front of every card. This set includes the first two 1987 draft picks of both the Montreal Expos and the Toronto Blue Jays.

	MINT	NRMT	EXC
COMPLETE SET (396)	12.00	5.50	1.50
COMMON CARD (1-396)	.05	.02	.01

Card	MINT	NRMT	EXC
☐ 1 Chris James	.05	.02	.01
☐ 2 Steve Buechele	.05	.02	.01
☐ 3 Mike Henneman	.05	.02	.01
☐ 4 Eddie Murray	.30	.14	.04
☐ 5 Bret Saberhagen	.10	.05	.01
☐ 6 Nathan Minchey	.05	.02	.01
Expos' second draft choice			
☐ 7 Harold Reynolds	.10	.05	.01
☐ 8 Bo Jackson	.20	.09	.03
☐ 9 Mike Easler	.05	.02	.01
☐ 10 Ryne Sandberg	.30	.14	.04
☐ 11 Mike Young	.05	.02	.01
☐ 12 Tony Phillips	.10	.05	.01
☐ 13 Andres Thomas	.05	.02	.01
☐ 14 Tim Burke	.05	.02	.01
☐ 15 Chili Davis	.10	.05	.01
Now with Angels			
☐ 16 Jim Lindeman	.05	.02	.01
☐ 17 Ron Oester	.05	.02	.01
☐ 18 Craig Reynolds	.05	.02	.01
☐ 19 Juan Samuel	.05	.02	.01
☐ 20 Kevin Gross	.05	.02	.01
☐ 21 Cecil Fielder	.20	.09	.03
☐ 22 Greg Swindell	.05	.02	.01
☐ 23 Jose DeLeon	.05	.02	.01
☐ 24 Jim Deshaies	.05	.02	.01
☐ 25 Andres Galarraga	.20	.09	.03
☐ 26 Mitch Williams	.05	.02	.01
☐ 27 R.J. Reynolds	.05	.02	.01
☐ 28 Jose Nunez	.05	.02	.01
☐ 29 Argenis Salazar	.05	.02	.01
☐ 30 Sid Fernandez	.05	.02	.01
☐ 31 Keith Moreland	.05	.02	.01
☐ 32 John Kruk	.20	.09	.03
☐ 33 Rob Deer	.05	.02	.01
☐ 34 Ricky Horton	.05	.02	.01
☐ 35 Harold Baines	.10	.05	.01
☐ 36 Jamie Moyer	.05	.02	.01
☐ 37 Kevin McReynolds	.05	.02	.01
☐ 38 Ron Darling	.05	.02	.01
☐ 39 Ozzie Smith	.50	.23	.06
☐ 40 Orel Hershiser	.10	.05	.01
☐ 41 Bob Melvin	.05	.02	.01
☐ 42 Alfredo Griffin	.05	.02	.01
Now with Dodgers			
☐ 43 Dick Schofield	.05	.02	.01
☐ 44 Terry Steinbach	.15	.07	.02
☐ 45 Kent Hrbek	.05	.02	.01
☐ 46 Darnell Coles	.05	.02	.01
☐ 47 Jimmy Key	.10	.05	.01
☐ 48 Alan Ashby	.05	.02	.01
☐ 49 Julio Franco	.10	.05	.01
☐ 50 Hubie Brooks	.05	.02	.01
☐ 51 Chris Bando	.05	.02	.01
☐ 52 Fernando Valenzuela	.10	.05	.01
☐ 53 Kal Daniels	.05	.02	.01
☐ 54 Jim Clancy	.05	.02	.01
☐ 55 Phil Bradley	.05	.02	.01
Now with Phillies			
☐ 56 Andy McGaffigan	.05	.02	.01
☐ 57 Mike LaValliere	.05	.02	.01
☐ 58 Dave Magadan	.05	.02	.01
☐ 59 Danny Cox	.05	.02	.01
☐ 60 Rickey Henderson	.15	.07	.02
☐ 61 Jim Rice	.15	.07	.02
☐ 62 Calvin Schiraldi	.05	.02	.01
Now with Cubs			
☐ 63 Jerry Mumphrey	.05	.02	.01
☐ 64 Ken Caminiti	1.00	.45	.12
☐ 65 Leon Durham	.05	.02	.01
☐ 66 Shane Rawley	.05	.02	.01
☐ 67 Ken Oberkfell	.05	.02	.01
☐ 68 Keith Hernandez	.10	.05	.01
☐ 69 Bob Brenly	.05	.02	.01
☐ 70 Roger Clemens	.25	.11	.03
☐ 71 Gary Pettis	.05	.02	.01
Now with Tigers			
☐ 72 Dennis Eckersley	.10	.05	.01
☐ 73 Dave Smith	.05	.02	.01
☐ 74 Cal Ripken	1.50	.70	.19
☐ 75 Joe Carter	.15	.07	.02
☐ 76 Denny Martinez	.10	.05	.01
☐ 77 Juan Beniquez	.05	.02	.01
☐ 78 Tim Laudner	.05	.02	.01
☐ 79 Ernie Whitt	.05	.02	.01
☐ 80 Mark Langston	.10	.05	.01
☐ 81 Dale Sveum	.05	.02	.01
☐ 82 Dion James	.05	.02	.01
☐ 83 Dave Valle	.05	.02	.01
☐ 84 Bill Wegman	.05	.02	.01
☐ 85 Howard Johnson	.05	.02	.01
☐ 86 Benito Santiago	.05	.02	.01
☐ 87 Casey Candaele	.05	.02	.01
☐ 88 Delino DeShields	.75	.35	.09
Expos' first draft choice			
☐ 89 Dave Winfield	.15	.07	.02
☐ 90 Dale Murphy	.15	.07	.02
☐ 91 Jay Howell	.05	.02	.01
Now with Dodgers			
☐ 92 Ken Williams	.05	.02	.01
☐ 93 Bob Sebra	.05	.02	.01
☐ 94 Tim Wallach	.05	.02	.01
☐ 95 Lance Parrish	.05	.02	.01
☐ 96 Todd Benzinger	.05	.02	.01
☐ 97 Scott Garrelts	.05	.02	.01
☐ 98 Jose Guzman	.05	.02	.01
☐ 99 Jeff Reardon	.05	.02	.01
☐ 100 Jack Clark	.10	.05	.01
☐ 101 Tracy Jones	.05	.02	.01
☐ 102 Barry Larkin	.75	.35	.09
☐ 103 Curt Young	.05	.02	.01
☐ 104 Juan Nieves	.05	.02	.01
☐ 105 Terry Pendleton	.10	.05	.01
☐ 106 Rob Ducey	.05	.02	.01
☐ 107 Scott Bailes	.05	.02	.01
☐ 108 Eric King	.05	.02	.01
☐ 109 Mike Pagliarulo	.05	.02	.01
☐ 110 Teddy Higuera	.05	.02	.01
☐ 111 Pedro Guerrero	.05	.02	.01
☐ 112 Chris Brown	.05	.02	.01
☐ 113 Kelly Gruber	.05	.02	.01
☐ 114 Jack Howell	.05	.02	.01
☐ 115 Johnny Ray	.05	.02	.01
☐ 116 Mike Eichhorn	.05	.02	.01
☐ 117 Tony Pena	.05	.02	.01
☐ 118 Bob Welch	.05	.02	.01
Now with Athletics			
☐ 119 Mike Kingery	.05	.02	.01
☐ 120 Kirby Puckett	.75	.35	.09
☐ 121 Charlie Hough	.10	.05	.01
☐ 122 Tony Bernazard	.05	.02	.01
☐ 123 Tom Candiotti	.05	.02	.01
☐ 124 Ray Knight	.10	.05	.01
☐ 125 Bruce Hurst	.05	.02	.01
☐ 126 Steve Jeltz	.05	.02	.01
☐ 127 Ron Guidry	.05	.02	.01
☐ 128 Duane Ward	.05	.02	.01
☐ 129 Greg Minton	.05	.02	.01
☐ 130 Buddy Bell	.10	.05	.01
☐ 131 Denny Walling	.05	.02	.01
☐ 132 Donnie Hill	.05	.02	.01
☐ 133 Wayne Tolleson	.05	.02	.01
☐ 134 Bob Rodgers MG	.05	.02	.01
Team checklist back			
☐ 135 Todd Worrell	.05	.02	.01
☐ 136 Brian Dayett	.05	.02	.01
☐ 137 Chris Bosio	.05	.02	.01
☐ 138 Mitch Webster	.05	.02	.01
☐ 139 Jerry Browne	.05	.02	.01
☐ 140 Jesse Barfield	.05	.02	.01
☐ 141 Doug DeCinces	.05	.02	.01
Now with Cardinals			
☐ 142 Andy Van Slyke	.10	.05	.01
☐ 143 Doug Drabek	.10	.05	.01
☐ 144 Jeff Parrett	.05	.02	.01
☐ 145 Bill Madlock	.05	.02	.01
☐ 146 Larry Herndon	.05	.02	.01
☐ 147 Bill Buckner	.10	.05	.01
☐ 148 Carmelo Martinez	.05	.02	.01
☐ 149 Ken Howell	.05	.02	.01
☐ 150 Eric Davis	.05	.02	.01
☐ 151 Randy Ready	.05	.02	.01
☐ 152 Jeffrey Leonard	.05	.02	.01
☐ 153 Dave Stieb	.05	.02	.01
☐ 154 Jeff Stone	.05	.02	.01
☐ 155 Dave Righetti	.05	.02	.01
☐ 156 Gary Matthews	.05	.02	.01
☐ 157 Gary Carter	.10	.05	.01
☐ 158 Bob Boone	.10	.05	.01
☐ 159 Glenn Davis	.05	.02	.01
☐ 160 Willie McGee	.10	.05	.01
☐ 161 Bryn Smith	.05	.02	.01
☐ 162 Mark McLemore	.05	.02	.01
☐ 163 Dale Mohorcic	.05	.02	.01
☐ 164 Mike Flanagan	.05	.02	.01
☐ 165 Robin Yount	.15	.07	.02
☐ 166 Bill Doran	.05	.02	.01
☐ 167 Rance Mulliniks	.05	.02	.01
☐ 168 Wally Joyner	.15	.07	.02
☐ 169 Cory Snyder	.05	.02	.01
☐ 170 Rich Gossage	.10	.05	.01
☐ 171 Rick Mahler	.05	.02	.01
☐ 172 Henry Cotto	.05	.02	.01
☐ 173 George Bell	.05	.02	.01
☐ 174 B.J. Surhoff	.15	.07	.02
☐ 175 Kevin Bass	.05	.02	.01
☐ 176 Jeff Reed	.05	.02	.01
☐ 177 Frank Tanana	.05	.02	.01
☐ 178 Darryl Strawberry	.10	.05	.01
☐ 179 Lou Whitaker	.10	.05	.01
☐ 180 Terry Kennedy	.05	.02	.01
☐ 181 Mariano Duncan	.05	.02	.01
☐ 182 Ken Phelps	.05	.02	.01
☐ 183 Bob Dernier	.05	.02	.01
Now with Phillies			
☐ 184 Ivan Calderon	.05	.02	.01
☐ 185 Rick Rhoden	.05	.02	.01
☐ 186 Rafael Palmeiro	.60	.25	.07
☐ 187 Kelly Downs	.05	.02	.01
☐ 188 Spike Owen	.05	.02	.01
☐ 189 Bobby Bonilla	.20	.09	.03
☐ 190 Candy Maldonado	.05	.02	.01
☐ 191 John Cerutti	.05	.02	.01
☐ 192 Devon White	.15	.07	.02
☐ 193 Brian Fisher	.05	.02	.01
☐ 194 Alex Sanchez	.05	.02	.01
Blue Jays' first draft choice			
☐ 195 Dan Quisenberry	.05	.02	.01
☐ 196 Dave Engle	.05	.02	.01
☐ 197 Lance McCullers	.05	.02	.01
☐ 198 Franklin Stubbs	.05	.02	.01
☐ 199 Scott Bradley	.05	.02	.01
☐ 200 Wade Boggs	.20	.09	.03
☐ 201 Kirk Gibson	.10	.05	.01
☐ 202 Brett Butler	.10	.05	.01
Now with Giants			
☐ 203 Dave Anderson	.05	.02	.01
☐ 204 Donnie Moore	.05	.02	.01
☐ 205 Nelson Liriano	.05	.02	.01
☐ 206 Danny Gladden	.05	.02	.01
☐ 207 Dan Pasqua	.05	.02	.01
Now with White Sox			
☐ 208 Robby Thompson	.05	.02	.01
☐ 209 Richard Dotson	.05	.02	.01
Now with Yankees			
☐ 210 Willie Randolph	.10	.05	.01
☐ 211 Danny Tartabull	.05	.02	.01
☐ 212 Greg Brock	.05	.02	.01
☐ 213 Albert Hall	.05	.02	.01
☐ 214 Dave Schmidt	.05	.02	.01
☐ 215 Von Hayes	.05	.02	.01
☐ 216 Herm Winningham	.05	.02	.01
☐ 217 Mike Davis	.05	.02	.01
Now with Dodgers			
☐ 218 Charlie Leibrandt	.05	.02	.01
☐ 219 Mike Stanley	.05	.02	.01
☐ 220 Tom Henke	.05	.02	.01
☐ 221 Dwight Evans	.10	.05	.01
☐ 222 Willie Wilson	.05	.02	.01
☐ 223 Stan Jefferson	.05	.02	.01
☐ 224 Mike Dunne	.05	.02	.01
☐ 225 Mike Scioscia	.05	.02	.01
☐ 226 Larry Parrish	.05	.02	.01
☐ 227 Mike Scott	.05	.02	.01
☐ 228 Wallace Johnson	.05	.02	.01
☐ 229 Jeff Musselman	.05	.02	.01
☐ 230 Pat Tabler	.05	.02	.01
☐ 231 Paul Molitor	.25	.11	.03
☐ 232 Bob James	.05	.02	.01
☐ 233 Joe Niekro	.05	.02	.01
☐ 234 Oddibe McDowell	.05	.02	.01
☐ 235 Gary Ward	.05	.02	.01
☐ 236 Ted Power	.05	.02	.01
Now with Royals			
☐ 237 Pascual Perez	.05	.02	.01
☐ 238 Luis Polonia	.10	.05	.01
☐ 239 Mike Diaz	.05	.02	.01
☐ 240 Lee Smith	.10	.05	.01
Now with Red Sox			
☐ 241 Willie Upshaw	.05	.02	.01
☐ 242 Tom Niedenfuer	.05	.02	.01
☐ 243 Tim Raines	.10	.05	.01
☐ 244 Jeff D. Robinson	.05	.02	.01
☐ 245 Rich Gedman	.05	.02	.01
☐ 246 Scott Bankhead	.05	.02	.01
☐ 247 Andre Dawson	.10	.05	.01
☐ 248 Brook Jacoby	.05	.02	.01
☐ 249 Mike Marshall	.05	.02	.01
☐ 250 Nolan Ryan	1.50	.70	.19
☐ 251 Tom Foley	.05	.02	.01
☐ 252 Bob Brower	.05	.02	.01
☐ 253 Checklist	.05	.02	.01
☐ 254 Scott McGregor	.05	.02	.01
☐ 255 Ken Griffey	.05	.02	.01
☐ 256 Ken Schrom	.05	.02	.01
☐ 257 Gary Gaetti	.10	.05	.01
☐ 258 Ed Nunez	.05	.02	.01
☐ 259 Frank Viola	.05	.02	.01
☐ 260 Vince Coleman	.05	.02	.01
☐ 261 Reid Nichols	.05	.02	.01
☐ 262 Tim Flannery	.05	.02	.01
☐ 263 Glenn Braggs	.05	.02	.01
☐ 264 Garry Templeton	.05	.02	.01
☐ 265 Bo Diaz	.05	.02	.01
☐ 266 Matt Nokes	.05	.02	.01
☐ 267 Barry Bonds	1.00	.45	.12
☐ 268 Bruce Ruffin	.05	.02	.01
☐ 269 Ellis Burks	.50	.23	.06
☐ 270 Mike Witt	.05	.02	.01
☐ 271 Ken Gerhart	.05	.02	.01
☐ 272 Lloyd Moseby	.05	.02	.01
☐ 273 Garth Iorg	.05	.02	.01
☐ 274 Mike Greenwell	.10	.05	.01
☐ 275 Kevin Seitzer	.10	.05	.01
☐ 276 Luis Salazar	.05	.02	.01
☐ 277 Shawon Dunston	.05	.02	.01
☐ 278 Rick Reuschel	.05	.02	.01
☐ 279 Randy St.Claire	.05	.02	.01
☐ 280 Pete Incaviglia	.05	.02	.01
☐ 281 Mike Boddicker	.05	.02	.01
☐ 282 Jay Tibbs	.05	.02	.01
☐ 283 Shane Mack	.05	.02	.01
☐ 284 Walt Terrell	.05	.02	.01
☐ 285 Jim Presley	.05	.02	.01
☐ 286 Greg Walker	.05	.02	.01
☐ 287 Dwight Gooden	.10	.05	.01
☐ 288 Jim Morrison	.05	.02	.01
☐ 289 Gene Garber	.05	.02	.01
☐ 290 Tony Fernandez	.05	.02	.01
☐ 291 Ozzie Virgil	.05	.02	.01
☐ 292 Carney Lansford	.05	.02	.01
☐ 293 Jim Acker	.05	.02	.01
☐ 294 Tommy Hinzo	.05	.02	.01
☐ 295 Bert Blyleven	.10	.05	.01
☐ 296 Ozzie Guillen	.10	.05	.01
☐ 297 Zane Smith	.05	.02	.01
☐ 298 Milt Thompson	.05	.02	.01
☐ 299 Len Dykstra	.10	.05	.01
☐ 300 Don Mattingly	.75	.35	.09
☐ 301 Bud Black	.05	.02	.01
☐ 302 Jose Uribe	.05	.02	.01
☐ 303 Manny Lee	.05	.02	.01
☐ 304 Sid Bream	.05	.02	.01
☐ 305 Steve Sax	.05	.02	.01
☐ 306 Billy Hatcher	.05	.02	.01
☐ 307 John Shelby	.05	.02	.01
☐ 308 Lee Mazzilli	.05	.02	.01
☐ 309 Bill Long	.05	.02	.01
☐ 310 Tom Herr	.05	.02	.01
☐ 311 Derek Bell	1.00	.45	.12
Blue Jays' second draft choice			
☐ 312 George Brett	.60	.25	.07
☐ 313 Bob McClure	.05	.02	.01
☐ 314 Jimy Williams MG	.05	.02	.01
Team checklist back			
☐ 315 Dave Parker	.10	.05	.01
Now with Athletics			
☐ 316 Doyle Alexander	.05	.02	.01
☐ 317 Dan Plesac	.05	.02	.01
☐ 318 Mel Hall	.05	.02	.01
☐ 319 Ruben Sierra	.20	.09	.03
☐ 320 Alan Trammell	.10	.05	.01
☐ 321 Mike Schmidt	.20	.09	.03
☐ 322 Wally Ritchie	.05	.02	.01
☐ 323 Rick Leach	.05	.02	.01
☐ 324 Danny Jackson	.05	.02	.01
Now with Reds			
☐ 325 Glenn Hubbard	.05	.02	.01
☐ 326 Frank White	.10	.05	.01
☐ 327 Larry Sheets	.05	.02	.01
☐ 328 John Cangelosi	.05	.02	.01
☐ 329 Bill Gullickson	.05	.02	.01
☐ 330 Eddie Whitson	.05	.02	.01
☐ 331 Brian Downing	.05	.02	.01
☐ 332 Gary Redus	.05	.02	.01
☐ 333 Wally Backman	.05	.02	.01
☐ 334 Dwayne Murphy	.05	.02	.01
☐ 335 Claudell Washington	.05	.02	.01
☐ 336 Dave Concepcion	.10	.05	.01
☐ 337 Jim Gantner	.05	.02	.01
☐ 338 Marty Barrett	.05	.02	.01
☐ 339 Mickey Hatcher	.05	.02	.01
☐ 340 Jack Morris	.10	.05	.01
☐ 341 John Franco	.10	.05	.01
☐ 342 Ron Robinson	.05	.02	.01
☐ 343 Greg Gagne	.05	.02	.01
☐ 344 Steve Bedrosian	.05	.02	.01
☐ 345 Scott Fletcher	.05	.02	.01
☐ 346 Vance Law	.05	.02	.01
Now with Cubs			
☐ 347 Joe Johnson	.05	.02	.01
Now with Angels			
☐ 348 Jim Eisenreich	.15	.07	.02
☐ 349 Alvin Davis	.05	.02	.01
☐ 350 Will Clark	.50	.23	.06
☐ 351 Mike Aldrete	.05	.02	.01
☐ 352 Billy Ripken	.05	.02	.01
☐ 353 Dave Stewart	.10	.05	.01
☐ 354 Neal Heaton	.05	.02	.01
☐ 355 Roger McDowell	.05	.02	.01
☐ 356 John Tudor	.05	.02	.01
☐ 357 Floyd Bannister	.05	.02	.01
Now with Royals			
☐ 358 Rey Quinones	.05	.02	.01
☐ 359 Glenn Wilson	.05	.02	.01
Now with Mariners			
☐ 360 Tony Gwynn	.60	.25	.07
☐ 361 Greg Maddux	3.00	1.35	.35
☐ 362 Juan Castillo	.05	.02	.01
☐ 363 Willie Fraser	.05	.02	.01
☐ 364 Nick Esasky	.05	.02	.01
☐ 365 Floyd Youmans	.05	.02	.01
☐ 366 Chet Lemon	.05	.02	.01
☐ 367 Matt Young	.05	.02	.01
Now with A's			
☐ 368 Gerald Young	.05	.02	.01
☐ 369 Bob Stanley	.05	.02	.01
☐ 370 Jose Canseco	.25	.11	.03
☐ 371 Joe Hesketh	.05	.02	.01
☐ 372 Rick Sutcliffe	.05	.02	.01
☐ 373 Checklist 133-264	.05	.02	.01

Card	MINT	NRMT	EXC
☐ 374 Checklist 265-396	.05	.02	.01
☐ 375 Tom Brunansky	.05	.02	.01
☐ 376 Jody Davis	.05	.02	.01
☐ 377 Sam Horn	.05	.02	.01
☐ 378 Mark Gubicza	.05	.02	.01
☐ 379 Rafael Ramirez Now with Astros	.05	.02	.01
☐ 380 Joe Magrane	.05	.02	.01
☐ 381 Pete O'Brien	.05	.02	.01
☐ 382 Lee Guetterman	.05	.02	.01
☐ 383 Eric Bell	.05	.02	.01
☐ 384 Gene Larkin	.05	.02	.01
☐ 385 Carlton Fisk	.15	.07	.02
☐ 386 Mike Fitzgerald	.05	.02	.01
☐ 387 Kevin Mitchell	.10	.05	.01
☐ 388 Jim Winn	.05	.02	.01
☐ 389 Mike Smithson	.05	.02	.01
☐ 390 Darrell Evans	.10	.05	.01
☐ 391 Terry Leach	.05	.02	.01
☐ 392 Charlie Kerfeld	.05	.02	.01
☐ 393 Mike Krukow	.05	.02	.01
☐ 394 Mark McGwire	1.00	.45	.12
☐ 395 Fred McGriff	.50	.23	.06
☐ 396 DeWayne Buice	.05	.02	.01

1988 O-Pee-Chee Box Bottoms

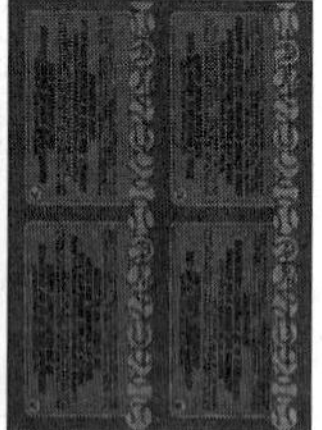

O-Pee-Chee printed four different four-card panels on the bottoms of its 1988 wax pack boxes. If cut, each card would measure approximately the standard size. These 16 cards, in alphabetical order and designated A through P, are considered a separate set from the regular issue but are styled almost exactly the same, differing only in the player photo and colors for the team name, borders and position on the front. The backs are identical, except for the letter designations instead of numbers.

	MINT	NRMT	EXC
COMPLETE SET (16)	8.00	3.60	1.00
COMMON CARD (A-P)	.10	.05	.01
☐ A Don Baylor	.25	.11	.03
☐ B Steve Bedrosian	.10	.05	.01
☐ C Juan Beniquez	.10	.05	.01
☐ D Bob Boone	.25	.11	.03
☐ E Darrell Evans	.25	.11	.03
☐ F Tony Gwynn	1.50	.70	.19
☐ G John Kruk	.50	.23	.06
☐ H Marvell Wynne	.10	.05	.01
☐ I Joe Carter	.50	.23	.06
☐ J Eric Davis	.25	.11	.03
☐ K Howard Johnson	.10	.05	.01
☐ L Darryl Strawberry	.25	.11	.03
☐ M Rickey Henderson	.75	.35	.09
☐ N Nolan Ryan	3.00	1.35	.35
☐ O Mike Schmidt	1.25	.55	.16
☐ P Kent Tekulve	.10	.05	.01

1989 O-Pee-Chee

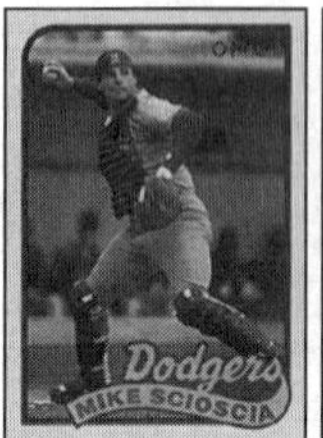

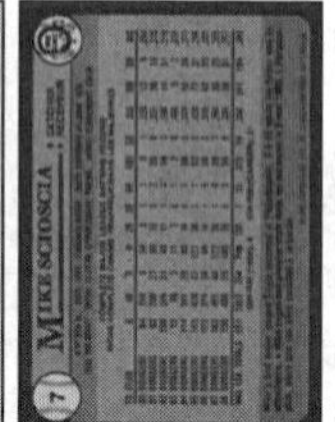

The 1989 O-Pee-Chee baseball set contains 396 standard-size cards that feature white bordered color player photos framed by colored lines. The player's name and team appear at the lower right. The bilingual pinkish horizontal backs are bordered in black and carry the player's biography and statistics.

	MINT	NRMT	EXC
COMPLETE SET (396)	10.00	4.50	1.25
COMPLETE FACT. SET (396)	10.00	4.50	1.25
COMMON CARD (1-396)	.05	.02	.01
☐ 1 Brook Jacoby	.05	.02	.01
☐ 2 Atlee Hammaker	.05	.02	.01
☐ 3 Jack Clark	.05	.02	.01
☐ 4 Dave Stieb	.05	.02	.01
☐ 5 Bud Black	.05	.02	.01
☐ 6 Damon Berryhill	.05	.02	.01
☐ 7 Mike Scioscia	.05	.02	.01
☐ 8 Jose Uribe	.05	.02	.01
☐ 9 Mike Aldrete	.05	.02	.01
☐ 10 Andre Dawson	.10	.05	.01
☐ 11 Bruce Sutter	.05	.02	.01
☐ 12 Dale Sveum	.05	.02	.01
☐ 13 Dan Quisenberry	.05	.02	.01
☐ 14 Tom Niedenfuer	.05	.02	.01
☐ 15 Robby Thompson	.05	.02	.01
☐ 16 Ron Robinson	.05	.02	.01
☐ 17 Brian Downing	.05	.02	.01
☐ 18 Rick Rhoden	.05	.02	.01
☐ 19 Greg Gagne	.05	.02	.01
☐ 20 Allan Anderson	.05	.02	.01
☐ 21 Eddie Whitson	.05	.02	.01
☐ 22 Billy Ripken	.05	.02	.01
☐ 23 Mike Fitzgerald	.05	.02	.01
☐ 24 Shane Rawley	.05	.02	.01
☐ 25 Frank White	.10	.05	.01
☐ 26 Don Mattingly	1.00	.45	.12
☐ 27 Fred Lynn	.05	.02	.01
☐ 28 Mike Moore	.05	.02	.01
☐ 29 Kelly Gruber	.05	.02	.01
☐ 30 Dwight Gooden	.10	.05	.01
☐ 31 Dan Pasqua	.05	.02	.01
☐ 32 Dennis Rasmussen	.05	.02	.01
☐ 33 B.J. Surhoff	.10	.05	.01
☐ 34 Sid Fernandez	.05	.02	.01
☐ 35 John Tudor	.05	.02	.01
☐ 36 Mitch Webster	.05	.02	.01
☐ 37 Doug Drabek	.05	.02	.01
☐ 38 Bobby Witt	.05	.02	.01
☐ 39 Mike Maddux	.05	.02	.01
☐ 40 Steve Sax	.05	.02	.01
☐ 41 Orel Hershiser	.10	.05	.01
☐ 42 Pete Incaviglia	.05	.02	.01
☐ 43 Guillermo Hernandez	.05	.02	.01
☐ 44 Kevin Coffman	.05	.02	.01
☐ 45 Kal Daniels	.05	.02	.01
☐ 46 Carlton Fisk	.25	.11	.03
☐ 47 Carney Lansford	.05	.02	.01
☐ 48 Tim Burke	.05	.02	.01
☐ 49 Alan Trammell	.15	.07	.02
☐ 50 George Bell	.05	.02	.01
☐ 51 Tony Gwynn	.75	.35	.09
☐ 52 Bob Brenly	.05	.02	.01
☐ 53 Ruben Sierra	.10	.05	.01
☐ 54 Otis Nixon	.10	.05	.01
☐ 55 Julio Franco	.10	.05	.01
☐ 56 Pat Tabler	.05	.02	.01
☐ 57 Alvin Davis	.05	.02	.01
☐ 58 Kevin Seitzer	.05	.02	.01
☐ 59 Mark Davis	.05	.02	.01
☐ 60 Tom Brunansky	.05	.02	.01
☐ 61 Jeff Treadway	.05	.02	.01
☐ 62 Alfredo Griffin	.05	.02	.01
☐ 63 Keith Hernandez	.10	.05	.01
☐ 64 Alex Trevino	.05	.02	.01
☐ 65 Rick Reuschel	.05	.02	.01
☐ 66 Bob Walk	.05	.02	.01
☐ 67 Dave Palmer	.05	.02	.01
☐ 68 Pedro Guerrero	.05	.02	.01
☐ 69 Jose Oquendo	.05	.02	.01
☐ 70 Mark McGwire	.75	.35	.09
☐ 71 Mike Boddicker	.05	.02	.01
☐ 72 Wally Backman	.05	.02	.01
☐ 73 Pascual Perez	.05	.02	.01
☐ 74 Joe Hesketh	.05	.02	.01
☐ 75 Tom Henke	.05	.02	.01
☐ 76 Nelson Liriano	.05	.02	.01
☐ 77 Doyle Alexander	.05	.02	.01
☐ 78 Tim Wallach	.05	.02	.01
☐ 79 Scott Bankhead	.05	.02	.01
☐ 80 Cory Snyder	.05	.02	.01
☐ 81 Dave Magadan	.05	.02	.01
☐ 82 Randy Ready	.05	.02	.01
☐ 83 Steve Buechele	.05	.02	.01
☐ 84 Bo Jackson	.15	.07	.02
☐ 85 Kevin McReynolds	.05	.02	.01
☐ 86 Jeff Reardon	.10	.05	.01
☐ 87 Tim Raines (Named Rock on card)	.10	.05	.01
☐ 88 Melido Perez	.05	.02	.01
☐ 89 Dave LaPoint	.05	.02	.01
☐ 90 Vince Coleman	.05	.02	.01
☐ 91 Floyd Youmans	.05	.02	.01
☐ 92 Buddy Bell	.10	.05	.01
☐ 93 Andres Galarraga	.20	.09	.03
☐ 94 Tony Pena	.05	.02	.01
☐ 95 Gerald Young	.05	.02	.01
☐ 96 Rick Cerone	.05	.02	.01
☐ 97 Ken Oberkfell	.05	.02	.01
☐ 98 Larry Sheets	.05	.02	.01
☐ 99 Chuck Crim	.05	.02	.01
☐ 100 Mike Schmidt	.30	.14	.04
☐ 101 Ivan Calderon	.05	.02	.01
☐ 102 Kevin Bass	.05	.02	.01
☐ 103 Chili Davis	.10	.05	.01
☐ 104 Randy Myers	.10	.05	.01
☐ 105 Ron Darling	.05	.02	.01
☐ 106 Willie Upshaw	.05	.02	.01
☐ 107 Jose DeLeon	.05	.02	.01
☐ 108 Fred Manrique	.05	.02	.01
☐ 109 Johnny Ray	.05	.02	.01
☐ 110 Paul Molitor	.30	.14	.04
☐ 111 Rance Mulliniks	.05	.02	.01
☐ 112 Jim Presley	.05	.02	.01
☐ 113 Lloyd Moseby	.05	.02	.01
☐ 114 Lance Parrish	.05	.02	.01
☐ 115 Jody Davis	.05	.02	.01
☐ 116 Matt Nokes	.05	.02	.01
☐ 117 Dave Anderson	.05	.02	.01
☐ 118 Checklist 1-132	.05	.02	.01
☐ 119 Rafael Belliard	.05	.02	.01
☐ 120 Frank Viola	.05	.02	.01
☐ 121 Roger Clemens	.25	.11	.03
☐ 122 Luis Salazar	.05	.02	.01
☐ 123 Mike Stanley	.05	.02	.01
☐ 124 Jim Traber	.05	.02	.01
☐ 125 Mike Krukow	.05	.02	.01
☐ 126 Sid Bream	.05	.02	.01
☐ 127 Joel Skinner	.05	.02	.01
☐ 128 Milt Thompson	.05	.02	.01
☐ 129 Terry Clark	.05	.02	.01
☐ 130 Gerald Perry	.05	.02	.01
☐ 131 Bryn Smith	.05	.02	.01
☐ 132 Kirby Puckett	1.00	.45	.12
☐ 133 Bill Long	.05	.02	.01
☐ 134 Jim Gantner	.05	.02	.01
☐ 135 Jose Rijo	.05	.02	.01
☐ 136 Joey Meyer	.05	.02	.01
☐ 137 Geno Petralli	.05	.02	.01
☐ 138 Wallace Johnson	.05	.02	.01
☐ 139 Mike Flanagan	.05	.02	.01
☐ 140 Shawon Dunston	.05	.02	.01
☐ 141 Eric Plunk	.05	.02	.01
☐ 142 Bobby Bonilla	.15	.07	.02
☐ 143 Jack McDowell	.40	.18	.05
☐ 144 Mookie Wilson	.10	.05	.01
☐ 145 Dave Stewart	.10	.05	.01
☐ 146 Gary Pettis	.05	.02	.01
☐ 147 Eric Show	.05	.02	.01
☐ 148 Eddie Murray	.40	.18	.05
☐ 149 Lee Smith	.10	.05	.01
☐ 150 Fernando Valenzuela	.10	.05	.01
☐ 151 Bob Walk	.05	.02	.01
☐ 152 Harold Baines	.10	.05	.01
☐ 153 Albert Hall	.05	.02	.01
☐ 154 Don Carman	.05	.02	.01
☐ 155 Marty Barrett	.05	.02	.01
☐ 156 Chris Sabo	.05	.02	.01
☐ 157 Bret Saberhagen	.05	.02	.01
☐ 158 Danny Cox	.05	.02	.01
☐ 159 Tom Foley	.05	.02	.01
☐ 160 Jeffrey Leonard	.05	.02	.01
☐ 161 Brady Anderson	1.00	.45	.12
☐ 162 Rich Gossage	.10	.05	.01
☐ 163 Greg Brock	.05	.02	.01
☐ 164 Joe Carter	.15	.07	.02
☐ 165 Mike Dunne	.05	.02	.01
☐ 166 Jeff Russell	.05	.02	.01
☐ 167 Dan Plesac	.05	.02	.01
☐ 168 Willie Wilson	.05	.02	.01
☐ 169 Mike Jackson	.05	.02	.01
☐ 170 Tony Fernandez	.05	.02	.01
☐ 171 Jamie Moyer	.05	.02	.01
☐ 172 Jim Gott	.05	.02	.01
☐ 173 Mel Hall	.05	.02	.01
☐ 174 Mark McGwire	.75	.35	.09
☐ 175 John Shelby	.05	.02	.01
☐ 176 Jeff Parrett	.05	.02	.01
☐ 177 Tim Belcher	.05	.02	.01
☐ 178 Rich Gedman	.05	.02	.01
☐ 179 Ozzie Virgil	.05	.02	.01
☐ 180 Mike Scott	.05	.02	.01
☐ 181 Dickie Thon	.05	.02	.01
☐ 182 Rob Murphy	.05	.02	.01
☐ 183 Oddibe McDowell	.05	.02	.01
☐ 184 Wade Boggs	.20	.09	.03
☐ 185 Claudell Washington	.05	.02	.01
☐ 186 Randy Johnson	1.25	.55	.16
☐ 187 Paul O'Neill	.10	.05	.01
☐ 188 Todd Benzinger	.05	.02	.01
☐ 189 Kevin Mitchell	.10	.05	.01
☐ 190 Mike Witt	.05	.02	.01
☐ 191 Sil Campusano	.05	.02	.01
☐ 192 Ken Gerhart	.05	.02	.01
☐ 193 Bob Rodgers	.05	.02	.01
☐ 194 Floyd Bannister	.05	.02	.01
☐ 195 Ozzie Guillen	.05	.02	.01
☐ 196 Ron Gant	.25	.11	.03
☐ 197 Neal Heaton	.05	.02	.01
☐ 198 Bill Swift	.05	.02	.01
☐ 199 Dave Parker	.15	.07	.02
☐ 200 George Brett	.75	.35	.09
☐ 201 Bo Diaz	.05	.02	.01
☐ 202 Brad Moore	.05	.02	.01
☐ 203 Rob Ducey	.05	.02	.01
☐ 204 Bert Blyleven	.10	.05	.01
☐ 205 Dwight Evans	.10	.05	.01
☐ 206 Roberto Alomar	.75	.35	.09
☐ 207 Henry Cotto	.05	.02	.01
☐ 208 Harold Reynolds	.10	.05	.01
☐ 209 Jose Guzman	.05	.02	.01
☐ 210 Dale Murphy	.15	.07	.02
☐ 211 Mike Pagliarulo	.05	.02	.01
☐ 212 Jay Howell	.05	.02	.01
☐ 213 Rene Gonzales	.05	.02	.01
☐ 214 Scott Garrelts	.05	.02	.01
☐ 215 Kevin Gross	.05	.02	.01
☐ 216 Jack Howell	.05	.02	.01
☐ 217 Kurt Stillwell	.05	.02	.01
☐ 218 Mike LaValliere	.05	.02	.01
☐ 219 Jim Clancy	.05	.02	.01
☐ 220 Gary Gaetti	.05	.02	.01
☐ 221 Hubie Brooks	.05	.02	.01
☐ 222 Bruce Ruffin	.05	.02	.01
☐ 223 Jay Buhner	.25	.11	.03
☐ 224 Cecil Fielder	.10	.05	.01
☐ 225 Willie McGee	.10	.05	.01
☐ 226 Bill Doran	.05	.02	.01
☐ 227 John Farrell	.05	.02	.01
☐ 228 Nelson Santovenia	.05	.02	.01
☐ 229 Jimmy Key	.10	.05	.01
☐ 230 Ozzie Smith	.75	.35	.09
☐ 231 Dave Schmidt	.05	.02	.01
☐ 232 Jody Reed	.05	.02	.01
☐ 233 Gregg Jefferies	.25	.11	.03
☐ 234 Tom Browning	.05	.02	.01
☐ 235 John Kruk	.10	.05	.01
☐ 236 Charles Hudson	.05	.02	.01
☐ 237 Todd Stottlemyre	.15	.07	.02
☐ 238 Don Slaught	.05	.02	.01
☐ 239 Tim Laudner	.05	.02	.01
☐ 240 Greg Maddux	1.25	.55	.16
☐ 241 Brett Butler	.10	.05	.01
☐ 242 Checklist 133-264	.05	.02	.01
☐ 243 Bob Boone	.10	.05	.01
☐ 244 Willie Randolph	.10	.05	.01
☐ 245 Jim Rice	.15	.07	.02
☐ 246 Rey Quinones	.05	.02	.01
☐ 247 Checklist 265-396	.05	.02	.01
☐ 248 Stan Javier	.05	.02	.01
☐ 249 Tim Leary	.05	.02	.01
☐ 250 Cal Ripken	1.50	.70	.19
☐ 251 John Dopson	.05	.02	.01
☐ 252 Billy Hatcher	.05	.02	.01
☐ 253 Robin Yount	.20	.09	.03
☐ 254 Mickey Hatcher	.05	.02	.01
☐ 255 Bob Horner	.05	.02	.01
☐ 256 Benny Santiago	.05	.02	.01
☐ 257 Luis Rivera	.05	.02	.01
☐ 258 Fred McGriff	.20	.09	.03
☐ 259 Dave Wells	.05	.02	.01
☐ 260 Dave Winfield	.25	.11	.03
☐ 261 Rafael Ramirez	.05	.02	.01
☐ 262 Nick Esasky	.05	.02	.01
☐ 263 Barry Bonds	.50	.23	.06
☐ 264 Joe Magrane	.05	.02	.01
☐ 265 Kent Hrbek	.05	.02	.01
☐ 266 Jack Morris	.10	.05	.01
☐ 267 Jeff M. Robinson	.05	.02	.01
☐ 268 Ron Kittle	.05	.02	.01
☐ 269 Candy Maldonado	.05	.02	.01
☐ 270 Wally Joyner	.10	.05	.01
☐ 271 Glenn Braggs	.05	.02	.01
☐ 272 Ron Hassey	.05	.02	.01
☐ 273 Jose Lind	.05	.02	.01
☐ 274 Mark Eichhorn	.05	.02	.01
☐ 275 Danny Tartabull	.05	.02	.01
☐ 276 Paul Kilgus	.05	.02	.01
☐ 277 Mike Davis	.05	.02	.01
☐ 278 Andy McGaffigan	.05	.02	.01
☐ 279 Scott Bradley	.05	.02	.01
☐ 280 Bob Knepper	.05	.02	.01
☐ 281 Gary Redus	.05	.02	.01
☐ 282 Rickey Henderson	.20	.09	.03
☐ 283 Andy Allanson	.05	.02	.01
☐ 284 Rick Leach	.05	.02	.01
☐ 285 John Candelaria	.05	.02	.01
☐ 286 Dick Schofield	.05	.02	.01
☐ 287 Bryan Harvey	.10	.05	.01
☐ 288 Randy Bush	.05	.02	.01
☐ 289 Ernie Whitt	.05	.02	.01
☐ 290 John Franco	.10	.05	.01
☐ 291 Todd Worrell	.05	.02	.01
☐ 292 Teddy Higuera	.05	.02	.01
☐ 293 Keith Moreland	.05	.02	.01
☐ 294 Juan Berenguer	.05	.02	.01
☐ 295 Scott Fletcher	.05	.02	.01
☐ 296 Roger McDowell Now with Indians 12-6-88	.05	.02	.01
☐ 297 Mark Grace	.75	.35	.09
☐ 298 Chris James	.05	.02	.01
☐ 299 Frank Tanana	.05	.02	.01
☐ 300 Darryl Strawberry	.10	.05	.01
☐ 301 Charlie Leibrandt	.05	.02	.01
☐ 302 Gary Ward	.05	.02	.01
☐ 303 Brian Fisher	.05	.02	.01
☐ 304 Terry Steinbach	.10	.05	.01
☐ 305 Dave Smith	.05	.02	.01
☐ 306 Greg Minton	.05	.02	.01
☐ 307 Lance McCullers	.05	.02	.01
☐ 308 Phil Bradley	.05	.02	.01
☐ 309 Terry Kennedy	.05	.02	.01
☐ 310 Rafael Palmeiro	.20	.09	.03
☐ 311 Ellis Burks	.20	.09	.03
☐ 312 Doug Jones	.05	.02	.01
☐ 313 Denny Martinez	.10	.05	.01
☐ 314 Pete O'Brien	.05	.02	.01
☐ 315 Greg Swindell	.05	.02	.01
☐ 316 Walt Weiss	.05	.02	.01
☐ 317 Pete Stanicek	.05	.02	.01
☐ 318 Gene Nelson	.05	.02	.01
☐ 319 Danny Jackson	.05	.02	.01
☐ 320 Lou Whitaker	.10	.05	.01

□ 321 Will Clark .30 .14 .04
□ 322 John Smiley .05 .02 .01
□ 323 Mike Marshall .05 .02 .01
□ 324 Gary Carter .20 .09 .03
□ 325 Jesse Barfield .05 .02 .01
□ 326 Dennis Boyd .05 .02 .01
□ 327 Dave Henderson .05 .02 .01
□ 328 Chet Lemon .05 .02 .01
□ 329 Bob Melvin .05 .02 .01
□ 330 Eric Davis .10 .05 .01
□ 331 Ted Power .05 .02 .01
□ 332 Carmelo Martinez .05 .02 .01
□ 333 Bob Ojeda .05 .02 .01
□ 334 Steve Lyons .05 .02 .01
□ 335 Dave Righetti .05 .02 .01
□ 336 Steve Balboni .05 .02 .01
□ 337 Calvin Schiraldi .05 .02 .01
□ 338 Vance Law .05 .02 .01
□ 339 Zane Smith .05 .02 .01
□ 340 Kirk Gibson .15 .07 .02
□ 341 Jim Deshaies .05 .02 .01
□ 342 Tom Brookens .05 .02 .01
□ 343 Pat Borders .05 .02 .01
□ 344 Devon White .10 .05 .01
□ 345 Charlie Hough .10 .05 .01
□ 346 Rex Hudler .05 .02 .01
□ 347 John Cerutti .05 .02 .01
□ 348 Kirk McCaskill .05 .02 .01
□ 349 Len Dykstra .10 .05 .01
□ 350 Andy Van Slyke .10 .05 .01
□ 351 Jeff D. Robinson .05 .02 .01
□ 352 Rick Schu .05 .02 .01
□ 353 Bruce Benedict .05 .02 .01
□ 354 Bill Wegman .05 .02 .01
□ 355 Mark Langston .05 .02 .01
□ 356 Steve Farr .05 .02 .01
□ 357 Richard Dotson .05 .02 .01
□ 358 Andres Thomas .05 .02 .01
□ 359 Alan Ashby .05 .02 .01
□ 360 Ryne Sandberg .75 .35 .09
□ 361 Kelly Downs .05 .02 .01
□ 362 Jeff Musselman .05 .02 .01
□ 363 Barry Larkin .30 .14 .04
□ 364 Rob Deer .05 .02 .01
□ 365 Mike Henneman .05 .02 .01
□ 366 Nolan Ryan 1.50 .70 .19
□ 367 Johnny Paredes .05 .02 .01
□ 368 Bobby Thigpen .05 .02 .01
□ 369 Mickey Brantley .05 .02 .01
□ 370 Dennis Eckersley .10 .05 .01
□ 371 Manny Lee .05 .02 .01
□ 372 Juan Samuel .05 .02 .01
□ 373 Tracy Jones .05 .02 .01
□ 374 Mike Greenwell .05 .02 .01
□ 375 Terry Pendleton .10 .05 .01
□ 376 Steve Lombardozzi .05 .02 .01
□ 377 Mitch Williams .05 .02 .01
□ 378 Glenn Davis .05 .02 .01
□ 379 Mark Gubicza .05 .02 .01
□ 380 Orel Hershiser WS .10 .05 .01
□ 381 Jimy Williams .05 .02 .01
□ 382 Kirk Gibson WS .15 .07 .02
□ 383 Howard Johnson .05 .02 .01
□ 384 David Cone .20 .09 .03
□ 385 Von Hayes .05 .02 .01
□ 386 Luis Polonia .10 .05 .01
□ 387 Danny Gladden .05 .02 .01
□ 388 Pete Smith .05 .02 .01
□ 389 Jose Canseco .15 .07 .02
□ 390 Mickey Hatcher .05 .02 .01
□ 391 Wil Tejada .05 .02 .01
□ 392 Duane Ward .05 .02 .01
□ 393 Rick Mahler .05 .02 .01
□ 394 Rick Sutcliffe .05 .02 .01
□ 395 Dave Martinez .05 .02 .01
□ 396 Ken Dayley .05 .02 .01

1989 O-Pee-Chee Box Bottoms

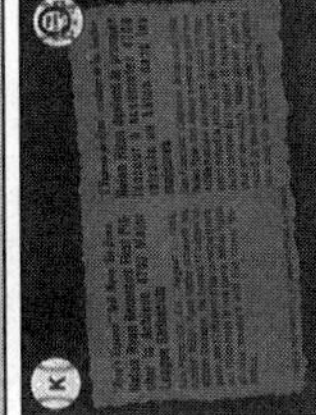

These standard-size box bottom cards feature on their fronts blue-bordered color player photos. The player's name and team appear at the bottom right. The horizontal black back carries bilingual career highlights within a purple panel. The value of the panels uncut is slightly greater, perhaps by 25 percent greater, than the value of the individual cards cut up carefully. The sixteen cards in this set honor players (and one manager) who reached career milestones during the 1988 season.The cards are lettered on the back.

	MINT	NRMT	EXC
COMPLETE SET (16)	6.00	2.70	.75
COMMON CARD (A-K)	.10	.05	.01

□ A George Brett 1.00 .45 .12
(475th Double)
□ B Bill Buckner .15 .07 .02
(2600th Hit)
□ C Darrell Evans .15 .07 .02
(400th Home Run)
□ D Rich Gossage .15 .07 .02
(300th Save)
□ E Greg Gross .10 .05 .01
(125th Pinch Hit)
□ F Rickey Henderson .40 .18 .05
(775th Stolen Base)
□ G Keith Hernandez .15 .07 .02
(125th GW-RBI)
□ H Tom Lasorda MG .25 .11 .03
(1000th Managerial Win)
□ I Jim Rice .15 .07 .02
(1400th Run Batted In)
□ J Cal Ripken 2.00 .90 .25
(1000th Cons. Game)
□ K Nolan Ryan 2.00 .90 .25
(4700th Strikeout)
□ L Mike Schmidt .50 .23 .06
(1000th Long Hit)
□ M Bruce Sutter .10 .05 .01
(300th Save)
□ N Don Sutton .20 .09 .03
(750th Game Started)
□ O Kent Tekulve .10 .05 .01
(1000th Appearance)
□ P Dave Winfield .25 .11 .03
(1400th RBI)

1990 O-Pee-Chee

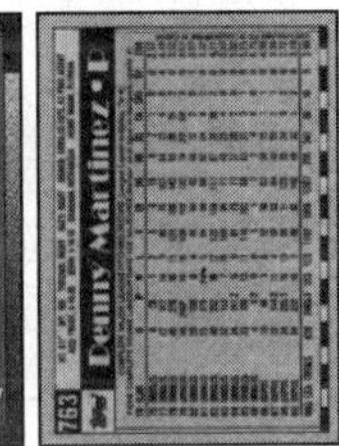

The 1990 O-Pee-Chee baseball set was a 792-card standard-size set. For the first time since 1976, O-Pee-Chee issued the exact same set as Topps. The only distinctions are the bilingual text and the O-Pee-Chee copyright on the backs. The fronts feature color player photos bordered in various colors. The player's name appears at the bottom and his team name is printed at the top. The yellow horizontal backs carry the player's name, biography and position at the top, followed below by major league statistics. Cards 385-407 feature All-Stars, while cards 661-665 are Turn Back the Clock cards. Players appearing in their Rookie Cards year include Delino DeShields (who had been on a 1988 OPC card), Juan Gonzalez, Marquis Grissom, Ben McDonald, Frank Thomas and Larry Walker.

	MINT	NRMT	EXC
COMPLETE SET (792)	25.00	11.00	3.10
COMPLETE FACT.SET (792)	25.00	11.00	3.10
COMMON CARD (1-792)	.05	.02	.01

□ 1 Nolan Ryan 1.50 .70 .19
□ 2 Nolan Ryan Salute .75 .35 .09
New York Mets
□ 3 Nolan Ryan Salute .75 .35 .09
California Angels
□ 4 Nolan Ryan Salute .75 .35 .09
Houston Astros
□ 5 Nolan Ryan Salute .75 .35 .09
Texas Rangers UER
(Says Texas Stadium
rather than
Arlington Stadium)
□ 6 Vince Coleman RB .05 .02 .01
50 consecutive SB's
□ 7 Rickey Henderson RB .20 .09 .03
40 career leadoff HR's
□ 8 Cal Ripken RB .75 .35 .09
20 or more homers for
8 consecutive years
record for shortstops
□ 9 Eric Plunk .05 .02 .01
□ 10 Barry Larkin .15 .07 .02
□ 11 Paul Gibson .05 .02 .01
□ 12 Joe Girardi .10 .05 .01
□ 13 Mark Williamson .05 .02 .01
□ 14 Mike Fetters .05 .02 .01
□ 15 Teddy Higuera .05 .02 .01
□ 16 Kent Anderson .05 .02 .01
□ 17 Kelly Downs .05 .02 .01
□ 18 Carlos Quintana .05 .02 .01
□ 19 Al Newman .05 .02 .01
□ 20 Mark Gubicza .05 .02 .01
□ 21 Jeff Torborg MG .05 .02 .01
□ 22 Bruce Ruffin .05 .02 .01
□ 23 Randy Velarde .05 .02 .01
□ 24 Joe Hesketh .05 .02 .01
□ 25 Willie Randolph .10 .05 .01
□ 26 Don Slaught .05 .02 .01
Now with Pirates
12/4/89
□ 27 Rick Leach .05 .02 .01
□ 28 Duane Ward .05 .02 .01
□ 29 John Cangelosi .05 .02 .01
□ 30 David Cone .20 .09 .03
□ 31 Henry Cotto .05 .02 .01
□ 32 John Farrell .05 .02 .01
□ 33 Greg Walker .05 .02 .01
□ 34 Tony Fossas .05 .02 .01
□ 35 Benito Santiago .05 .02 .01
□ 36 John Costello .05 .02 .01
□ 37 Domingo Ramos .05 .02 .01
□ 38 Wes Gardner .05 .02 .01
□ 39 Curt Ford .05 .02 .01
□ 40 Jay Howell .05 .02 .01
□ 41 Matt Williams .25 .11 .03
□ 42 Jeff M. Robinson .05 .02 .01
□ 43 Dante Bichette .30 .14 .04
□ 44 Roger Salkeld FDP .05 .02 .01
□ 45 Dave Parker UER .10 .05 .01
Born in Jackson
not Calhoun
□ 46 Rob Dibble .05 .02 .01
□ 47 Brian Harper .05 .02 .01
□ 48 Zane Smith .05 .02 .01
□ 49 Tom Lawless .05 .02 .01
□ 50 Glenn Davis .05 .02 .01
□ 51 Doug Rader MG .05 .02 .01
□ 52 Jack Daugherty .05 .02 .01
□ 53 Mike LaCoss .05 .02 .01
□ 54 Joel Skinner .05 .02 .01
□ 55 Darrell Evans UER .10 .05 .01
HR total should be
414, not 424
□ 56 Franklin Stubbs .05 .02 .01
□ 57 Greg Vaughn .20 .09 .03
□ 58 Keith Miller .05 .02 .01
□ 59 Ted Power .05 .02 .01
Now with Pirates
11/21/89
□ 60 George Brett .75 .35 .09
□ 61 Deion Sanders .30 .14 .04
□ 62 Ramon Martinez .15 .07 .02
□ 63 Mike Pagliarulo .05 .02 .01
□ 64 Danny Darwin .05 .02 .01
□ 65 Devon White .10 .05 .01
□ 66 Greg Litton .05 .02 .01
□ 67 Scott Sanderson .05 .02 .01
Now with Athletics
12/13/89
□ 68 Dave Henderson .05 .02 .01
□ 69 Todd Frohwirth .05 .02 .01
□ 70 Mike Greenwell .05 .02 .01
□ 71 Allan Anderson .05 .02 .01
□ 72 Jeff Huson .05 .02 .01
□ 73 Bob Milacki .05 .02 .01
□ 74 Jeff Jackson FDP .05 .02 .01
□ 75 Doug Jones .05 .02 .01
□ 76 Dave Valle .05 .02 .01
□ 77 Dave Bergman .05 .02 .01
□ 78 Mike Flanagan .05 .02 .01
□ 79 Ron Kittle .05 .02 .01
□ 80 Jeff Russell .05 .02 .01
□ 81 Bob Rodgers MG .05 .02 .01
□ 82 Scott Terry .05 .02 .01
□ 83 Hensley Meulens .05 .02 .01
□ 84 Ray Searage .05 .02 .01
□ 85 Juan Samuel .05 .02 .01
Now with Dodgers
12/20/89
□ 86 Paul Kilgus .05 .02 .01
Now with Blue Jays
12/7/89
□ 87 Rick Luecken .05 .02 .01
Now with Braves
12/17/89
□ 88 Glenn Braggs .05 .02 .01
□ 89 Clint Zavaras .05 .02 .01
□ 90 Jack Clark .10 .05 .01
□ 91 Steve Frey .05 .02 .01
□ 92 Mike Stanley .05 .02 .01
□ 93 Shawn Hillegas .05 .02 .01
□ 94 Herm Winningham .05 .02 .01
□ 95 Todd Worrell .05 .02 .01
□ 96 Jody Reed .05 .02 .01
□ 97 Curt Schilling .05 .02 .01
□ 98 Jose Gonzalez .05 .02 .01
□ 99 Rich Monteleone .05 .02 .01
□ 100 Will Clark .15 .07 .02
□ 101 Shane Rawley .05 .02 .01
Now with Red Sox
1/9/90
□ 102 Stan Javier .05 .02 .01
□ 103 Marvin Freeman .05 .02 .01
□ 104 Bob Knepper .05 .02 .01
□ 105 Randy Myers .10 .05 .01
Now with Reds
12/8/89
□ 106 Charlie O'Brien .05 .02 .01
□ 107 Fred Lynn .10 .05 .01
Now with Padres
12/7/89
□ 108 Rod Nichols .05 .02 .01
□ 109 Roberto Kelly .05 .02 .01
□ 110 Tommy Helms MG .05 .02 .01
□ 111 Ed Whited .05 .02 .01
□ 112 Glenn Wilson .05 .02 .01
□ 113 Manny Lee .05 .02 .01
□ 114 Mike Bielecki .05 .02 .01
□ 115 Tony Pena .05 .02 .01
Now with Red Sox
11/28/89
□ 116 Floyd Bannister .05 .02 .01
□ 117 Mike Sharperson .05 .02 .01
□ 118 Erik Hanson .10 .05 .01
□ 119 Billy Hatcher .05 .02 .01
□ 120 John Franco .10 .05 .01
Now with Mets
12/8/89
□ 121 Robin Ventura .20 .09 .03
□ 122 Shawn Abner .05 .02 .01
□ 123 Rich Gedman .05 .02 .01
□ 124 Dave Dravecky .10 .05 .01
□ 125 Kent Hrbek .10 .05 .01
□ 126 Randy Kramer .05 .02 .01
□ 127 Mike Devereaux .05 .02 .01
□ 128 Checklist 1 .05 .02 .01
□ 129 Ron Jones .05 .02 .01
□ 130 Bert Blyleven .10 .05 .01
□ 131 Matt Nokes .05 .02 .01
□ 132 Lance Blankenship .05 .02 .01
□ 133 Ricky Horton .05 .02 .01
□ 134 Earl Cunningham FDP .05 .02 .01
□ 135 Dave Magadan .05 .02 .01
□ 136 Kevin Brown .20 .09 .03
□ 137 Marty Pevey .05 .02 .01
□ 138 Al Leiter .10 .05 .01
□ 139 Greg Brock .05 .02 .01
□ 140 Andre Dawson .10 .05 .01
□ 141 John Hart MG .05 .02 .01
□ 142 Jeff Wetherby .05 .02 .01
□ 143 Rafael Belliard .05 .02 .01
□ 144 Bud Black .05 .02 .01
□ 145 Terry Steinbach .10 .05 .01
□ 146 Rob Richie .05 .02 .01
□ 147 Chuck Finley .10 .05 .01
□ 148 Edgar Martinez .25 .11 .03
□ 149 Steve Farr .05 .02 .01
□ 150 Kirk Gibson .10 .05 .01
□ 151 Rick Mahler .05 .02 .01
□ 152 Lonnie Smith .05 .02 .01
□ 153 Randy Milligan .05 .02 .01
□ 154 Mike Maddux .05 .02 .01
Now with Dodgers
12/21/89
□ 155 Ellis Burks .20 .09 .03
□ 156 Ken Patterson .05 .02 .01
□ 157 Craig Biggio .25 .11 .03
□ 158 Craig Lefferts .05 .02 .01
Now with Padres
12/7/89
□ 159 Mike Felder .05 .02 .01
□ 160 Dave Righetti .05 .02 .01
□ 161 Harold Reynolds .10 .05 .01
□ 162 Todd Zeile .10 .05 .01
□ 163 Phil Bradley .05 .02 .01
□ 164 Jeff Juden FDP .05 .02 .01
□ 165 Walt Weiss .05 .02 .01
□ 166 Bobby Witt .05 .02 .01
□ 167 Kevin Appier .15 .07 .02
□ 168 Jose Lind .05 .02 .01
□ 169 Richard Dotson .05 .02 .01
Now with Royals
12/6/89
□ 170 George Bell .05 .02 .01
□ 171 Russ Nixon MG .05 .02 .01
□ 172 Tom Lampkin .05 .02 .01
□ 173 Tim Belcher .05 .02 .01
□ 174 Jeff Kunkel .05 .02 .01
□ 175 Mike Moore .05 .02 .01
□ 176 Luis Quinones .05 .02 .01
□ 177 Mike Henneman .05 .02 .01
□ 178 Chris James .05 .02 .01
Now with Indians
12/6/89
□ 179 Brian Holton .05 .02 .01
□ 180 Tim Raines .10 .05 .01
□ 181 Juan Agosto .05 .02 .01
□ 182 Mookie Wilson .05 .02 .01
□ 183 Steve Lake .05 .02 .01
□ 184 Danny Cox .05 .02 .01
□ 185 Ruben Sierra .10 .05 .01
□ 186 Dave LaPoint .05 .02 .01
□ 187 Rick Wrona .05 .02 .01
□ 188 Mike Smithson .05 .02 .01
Now with Angels
12/19/89
□ 189 Dick Schofield .05 .02 .01
□ 190 Rick Reuschel .05 .02 .01
□ 191 Pat Borders .05 .02 .01
□ 192 Don August .05 .02 .01
□ 193 Andy Benes .20 .09 .03
□ 194 Glenallen Hill .10 .05 .01
□ 195 Tim Burke .05 .02 .01
□ 196 Gerald Young .05 .02 .01
□ 197 Doug Drabek .05 .02 .01
□ 198 Mike Marshall .05 .02 .01
Now with Mets
12/20/89
□ 199 Sergio Valdez .05 .02 .01
□ 200 Don Mattingly 1.00 .45 .12

□ 201 Cito Gaston MG .05 .02 .01
□ 202 Mike Macfarlane .05 .02 .01
□ 203 Mike Roesler .05 .02 .01
□ 204 Bob Dernier .05 .02 .01
□ 205 Mark Davis .05 .02 .01
Now with Royals
12/11/89
□ 206 Nick Esasky .05 .02 .01
Now with Braves
11/17/89
□ 207 Bob Ojeda .05 .02 .01
□ 208 Brook Jacoby .05 .02 .01
□ 209 Greg Mathews .05 .02 .01
□ 210 Ryne Sandberg .50 .23 .06
□ 211 John Cerutti .05 .02 .01
□ 212 Joe Orsulak .05 .02 .01
□ 213 Scott Bankhead .05 .02 .01
□ 214 Terry Francona .10 .05 .01
□ 215 Kirk McCaskill .05 .02 .01
□ 216 Ricky Jordan .05 .02 .01
□ 217 Don Robinson .05 .02 .01
□ 218 Wally Backman .05 .02 .01
□ 219 Donn Pall .05 .02 .01
□ 220 Barry Bonds .50 .23 .06
□ 221 Gary Mielke .05 .02 .01
□ 222 Kurt Stillwell UER .05 .02 .01
Graduate misspelled
as gradute
□ 223 Tommy Gregg .05 .02 .01
□ 224 Delino DeShields .20 .09 .03
□ 225 Jim Deshaies .05 .02 .01
□ 226 Mickey Hatcher .05 .02 .01
□ 227 Kevin Tapani .10 .05 .01
□ 228 Dave Martinez .05 .02 .01
□ 229 David Wells .05 .02 .01
□ 230 Keith Hernandez .10 .05 .01
Now with Indians
12/7/89
□ 231 Jack McKeon MG .05 .02 .01
□ 232 Darnell Coles .05 .02 .01
□ 233 Ken Hill .20 .09 .03
□ 234 Mariano Duncan .05 .02 .01
□ 235 Jeff Reardon .10 .05 .01
Now with Red Sox
12/6/89
□ 236 Hal Morris .10 .05 .01
Now with Reds
12/12/89
□ 237 Kevin Ritz .05 .02 .01
□ 238 Felix Jose .05 .02 .01
□ 239 Eric Show .05 .02 .01
□ 240 Mark Grace .25 .11 .03
□ 241 Mike Krukow .05 .02 .01
□ 242 Fred Manrique .05 .02 .01
□ 243 Barry Jones .05 .02 .01
□ 244 Bill Schroeder .05 .02 .01
□ 245 Roger Clemens .25 .11 .03
□ 246 Jim Eisenreich .10 .05 .01
□ 247 Jerry Reed .05 .02 .01
□ 248 Dave Anderson .05 .02 .01
Now with Giants,(11/29/89
□ 249 Mike(Texas) Smith .05 .02 .01
□ 250 Jose Canseco .15 .07 .02
□ 251 Jeff Blauser .05 .02 .01
□ 252 Otis Nixon .10 .05 .01
□ 253 Mark Portugal .05 .02 .01
□ 254 Francisco Cabrera .05 .02 .01
□ 255 Bobby Thigpen .05 .02 .01
□ 256 Marvell Wynne .05 .02 .01
□ 257 Jose DeLeon .05 .02 .01
□ 258 Barry Lyons .05 .02 .01
□ 259 Lance McCullers .05 .02 .01
□ 260 Eric Davis .10 .05 .01
□ 261 Whitey Herzog MG .10 .05 .01
□ 262 Checklist 2 .05 .02 .01
□ 263 Mel Stottlemyre Jr. .05 .02 .01
□ 264 Bryan Clutterbuck .05 .02 .01
□ 265 Pete O'Brien .05 .02 .01
Now with Mariners
12/7/89
□ 266 German Gonzalez .05 .02 .01
□ 267 Mark Davidson .05 .02 .01
□ 268 Rob Murphy .05 .02 .01
□ 269 Dickie Thon .05 .02 .01
□ 270 Dave Stewart .10 .05 .01
□ 271 Chet Lemon .05 .02 .01
□ 272 Bryan Harvey .05 .02 .01
□ 273 Bobby Bonilla .10 .05 .01
□ 274 Mauro Gozzo .05 .02 .01
□ 275 Mickey Tettleton .10 .05 .01
□ 276 Gary Thurman .05 .02 .01
□ 277 Lenny Harris .05 .02 .01
□ 278 Pascual Perez .05 .02 .01
Now with Yankees
11/27/89
□ 279 Steve Buechele .05 .02 .01
□ 280 Lou Whitaker .10 .05 .01
□ 281 Kevin Bass .05 .02 .01
Now with Giants
11/20/89
□ 282 Derek Lilliquist .05 .02 .01
□ 283 Joey Belle 1.50 .70 .19
□ 284 Mark Gardner .05 .02 .01
□ 285 Willie McGee .10 .05 .01
□ 286 Lee Guetterman .05 .02 .01
□ 287 Vance Law .05 .02 .01
□ 288 Greg Briley .05 .02 .01
□ 289 Norm Charlton .05 .02 .01
□ 290 Robin Yount .15 .07 .02
□ 291 Dave Johnson MG .10 .05 .01
□ 292 Jim Gott .05 .02 .01
Now with Dodgers
12/7/89
□ 293 Mike Gallego .05 .02 .01
□ 294 Craig McMurtry .05 .02 .01
□ 295 Fred McGriff .15 .07 .02
□ 296 Jeff Ballard .05 .02 .01
□ 297 Tom Herr .05 .02 .01
□ 298 Dan Gladden .05 .02 .01
□ 299 Adam Peterson .05 .02 .01
□ 300 Bo Jackson .10 .05 .01
□ 301 Don Aase .05 .02 .01
□ 302 Marcus Lawton .05 .02 .01
□ 303 Rick Cerone .05 .02 .01
Now with Yankees
12/19/89
□ 304 Marty Clary .05 .02 .01
□ 305 Eddie Murray .50 .23 .06
□ 306 Tom Niedenfuer .05 .02 .01
□ 307 Bip Roberts .05 .02 .01
□ 308 Jose Guzman .05 .02 .01
□ 309 Eric Yelding .05 .02 .01
□ 310 Steve Bedrosian .05 .02 .01
□ 311 Dwight Smith .05 .02 .01
□ 312 Dan Quisenberry .05 .02 .01
□ 313 Gus Polidor .05 .02 .01
□ 314 Donald Harris FDP .05 .02 .01
□ 315 Bruce Hurst .05 .02 .01
□ 316 Carney Lansford .10 .05 .01
□ 317 Mark Guthrie .05 .02 .01
□ 318 Wallace Johnson .05 .02 .01
□ 319 Dion James .05 .02 .01
□ 320 Dave Stieb .05 .02 .01
□ 321 Joe Morgan MG .05 .02 .01
□ 322 Junior Ortiz .05 .02 .01
□ 323 Willie Wilson .05 .02 .01
□ 324 Pete Harnisch .05 .02 .01
□ 325 Robby Thompson .05 .02 .01
□ 326 Tom McCarthy .05 .02 .01
□ 327 Ken Williams .05 .02 .01
□ 328 Curt Young .05 .02 .01
□ 329 Oddibe McDowell .05 .02 .01
□ 330 Ron Darling .05 .02 .01
□ 331 Juan Gonzalez 2.50 1.10 .30
□ 332 Paul O'Neill .10 .05 .01
□ 333 Bill Wegman .05 .02 .01
□ 334 Johnny Ray .05 .02 .01
□ 335 Andy Hawkins .05 .02 .01
□ 336 Ken Griffey Jr. 3.00 1.35 .35
□ 337 Lloyd McClendon .05 .02 .01
□ 338 Dennis Lamp .05 .02 .01
□ 339 Dave Clark .05 .02 .01
Now with Cubs
11/20/89
□ 340 Fernando Valenzuela .10 .05 .01
□ 341 Tom Foley .05 .02 .01
□ 342 Alex Trevino .05 .02 .01
□ 343 Frank Tanana .05 .02 .01
□ 344 George Canale .05 .02 .01
□ 345 Harold Baines .10 .05 .01
□ 346 Jim Presley .05 .02 .01
□ 347 Junior Felix .05 .02 .01
□ 348 Gary Wayne .05 .02 .01
□ 349 Steve Finley .15 .07 .02
□ 350 Bret Saberhagen .05 .02 .01
□ 351 Roger Craig MG .05 .02 .01
□ 352 Bryn Smith .05 .02 .01
Now with Cardinals
11/29/89
□ 353 Sandy Alomar Jr. .20 .09 .03
Now with Indians
12/6/89
□ 354 Stan Belinda .05 .02 .01
□ 355 Marty Barrett .05 .02 .01
□ 356 Randy Ready .05 .02 .01
□ 357 Dave West .05 .02 .01
□ 358 Andres Thomas .05 .02 .01
□ 359 Jimmy Jones .05 .02 .01
□ 360 Paul Molitor .40 .18 .05
□ 361 Randy McCament .05 .02 .01
□ 362 Damon Berryhill .05 .02 .01
□ 363 Dan Petry .05 .02 .01
□ 364 Rolando Roomes .05 .02 .01
□ 365 Ozzie Guillen .05 .02 .01
□ 366 Mike Heath .05 .02 .01
□ 367 Mike Morgan .05 .02 .01
□ 368 Bill Doran .05 .02 .01
□ 369 Todd Burns .05 .02 .01
□ 370 Tim Wallach .05 .02 .01
□ 371 Jimmy Key .10 .05 .01
□ 372 Terry Kennedy .05 .02 .01
□ 373 Alvin Davis .05 .02 .01
□ 374 Steve Cummings .05 .02 .01
□ 375 Dwight Evans .10 .05 .01
□ 376 Checklist 3 UER .05 .02 .01
Higuera misalphabet-
ized in Brewer list
□ 377 Mickey Weston .05 .02 .01
□ 378 Luis Salazar .05 .02 .01
□ 379 Steve Rosenberg .05 .02 .01
□ 380 Dave Winfield .15 .07 .02
□ 381 Frank Robinson MG .20 .09 .03
□ 382 Jeff Musselman .05 .02 .01
□ 383 John Morris .05 .02 .01
□ 384 Pat Combs .05 .02 .01
□ 385 Fred McGriff AS .20 .09 .03
□ 386 Julio Franco AS .05 .02 .01
□ 387 Wade Boggs AS .20 .09 .03
□ 388 Cal Ripken AS .75 .35 .09
□ 389 Robin Yount AS .20 .09 .03
□ 390 Ruben Sierra AS .10 .05 .01
□ 391 Kirby Puckett AS .40 .18 .05
□ 392 Carlton Fisk AS .10 .05 .01
□ 393 Bret Saberhagen AS .05 .02 .01
□ 394 Jeff Ballard AS .05 .02 .01
□ 395 Jeff Russell AS .05 .02 .01
□ 396 A.Bartlett Giamatti .20 .09 .03
COMM MEM
□ 397 Will Clark AS .20 .09 .03
□ 398 Ryne Sandberg AS .25 .11 .03
□ 399 Howard Johnson AS .05 .02 .01
□ 400 Ozzie Smith AS .25 .11 .03
□ 401 Kevin Mitchell AS .05 .02 .01
□ 402 Eric Davis AS .05 .02 .01
□ 403 Tony Gwynn AS .40 .18 .05
□ 404 Craig Biggio AS .20 .09 .03
□ 405 Mike Scott AS .05 .02 .01
□ 406 Joe Magrane AS .05 .02 .01
□ 407 Mark Davis AS .05 .02 .01
Now with Royals
12/11/89
□ 408 Trevor Wilson .05 .02 .01
□ 409 Tom Brunansky .05 .02 .01
□ 410 Joe Boever .05 .02 .01
□ 411 Ken Phelps .05 .02 .01
□ 412 Jamie Moyer .05 .02 .01
□ 413 Brian DuBois .05 .02 .01
□ 414 Frank Thomas FDP 6.00 2.70 .75
□ 415 Shawon Dunston .05 .02 .01
□ 416 Dave Johnson (P) .05 .02 .01
□ 417 Jim Gantner .05 .02 .01
□ 418 Tom Browning .05 .02 .01
□ 419 Beau Allred .05 .02 .01
□ 420 Carlton Fisk .25 .11 .03
□ 421 Greg Minton .05 .02 .01
□ 422 Pat Sheridan .05 .02 .01
□ 423 Fred Toliver .05 .02 .01
Now with Yankees
9/27/89
□ 424 Jerry Reuss .05 .02 .01
□ 425 Bill Landrum .05 .02 .01
□ 426 Jeff Hamilton UER .05 .02 .01
Stats say he fanned
197 times in 1987
but he only had 147 at bats
□ 427 Carmen Castillo .05 .02 .01
□ 428 Steve Davis .05 .02 .01
Now with Dodgers
12/12/89
□ 429 Tom Kelly MG .05 .02 .01
□ 430 Pete Incaviglia .05 .02 .01
□ 431 Randy Johnson .40 .18 .05
□ 432 Damaso Garcia .05 .02 .01
Now with Yankees
12/22/89
□ 433 Steve Olin .10 .05 .01
□ 434 Mark Carreon .05 .02 .01
□ 435 Kevin Seitzer .05 .02 .01
□ 436 Mel Hall .05 .02 .01
□ 437 Les Lancaster .05 .02 .01
□ 438 Greg Myers .05 .02 .01
□ 439 Jeff Parrett .05 .02 .01
□ 440 Alan Trammell .10 .05 .01
□ 441 Bob Kipper .05 .02 .01
□ 442 Jerry Browne .05 .02 .01
□ 443 Cris Carpenter .05 .02 .01
□ 444 Kyle Abbott FDP .05 .02 .01
□ 445 Danny Jackson .05 .02 .01
□ 446 Dan Pasqua .05 .02 .01
□ 447 Atlee Hammaker .05 .02 .01
□ 448 Greg Gagne .05 .02 .01
□ 449 Dennis Rasmussen .05 .02 .01
□ 450 Rickey Henderson .25 .11 .03
□ 451 Mark Lemke .10 .05 .01
□ 452 Luis DeLosSantos .05 .02 .01
□ 453 Jody Davis .05 .02 .01
□ 454 Jeff King .10 .05 .01
□ 455 Jeffrey Leonard .05 .02 .01
□ 456 Chris Gwynn .05 .02 .01
□ 457 Gregg Jefferies .10 .05 .01
□ 458 Bob McClure .05 .02 .01
□ 459 Jim Lefebvre MG .05 .02 .01
□ 460 Mike Scott .05 .02 .01
□ 461 Carlos Martinez .05 .02 .01
□ 462 Denny Walling .05 .02 .01
□ 463 Drew Hall .05 .02 .01
□ 464 Jerome Walton .05 .02 .01
□ 465 Kevin Gross .05 .02 .01
□ 466 Rance Mulliniks .05 .02 .01
□ 467 Juan Nieves .05 .02 .01
□ 468 Bill Ripken .05 .02 .01
□ 469 John Kruk .10 .05 .01
□ 470 Frank Viola .05 .02 .01
□ 471 Mike Brumley .05 .02 .01
Now with Orioles
1/10/90
□ 472 Jose Uribe .05 .02 .01
□ 473 Joe Price .05 .02 .01
□ 474 Rich Thompson .05 .02 .01
□ 475 Bob Welch .05 .02 .01
□ 476 Brad Komminsk .05 .02 .01
□ 477 Willie Fraser .05 .02 .01
□ 478 Mike LaValliere .05 .02 .01
□ 479 Frank White .10 .05 .01
□ 480 Sid Fernandez .05 .02 .01
□ 481 Garry Templeton .05 .02 .01
□ 482 Steve Carter .05 .02 .01
□ 483 Alejandro Pena .05 .02 .01
Now with Mets
12/20/89
□ 484 Mike Fitzgerald .05 .02 .01
□ 485 John Candelaria .05 .02 .01
□ 486 Jeff Treadway .05 .02 .01
□ 487 Steve Searcy .05 .02 .01
□ 488 Ken Oberkfell .05 .02 .01
Now with Astros
12/6/89
□ 489 Nick Leyva MG .05 .02 .01
□ 490 Dan Plesac .05 .02 .01
□ 491 Dave Cochrane .05 .02 .01
□ 492 Ron Oester .05 .02 .01
□ 493 Jason Grimsley .05 .02 .01
□ 494 Terry Puhl .05 .02 .01
□ 495 Lee Smith .10 .05 .01
□ 496 Cecil Espy UER .05 .02 .01
'88 stats have 3 SB's
should be 33
□ 497 Dave Schmidt .05 .02 .01
Now with Expos
12/13/89
□ 498 Rick Schu .05 .02 .01
□ 499 Bill Long .05 .02 .01
□ 500 Kevin Mitchell .05 .02 .01
□ 501 Matt Young .05 .02 .01
Now with Mariners
12/8/89
□ 502 Mitch Webster .05 .02 .01
Now with Indians
11/20/89
□ 503 Randy St.Claire .05 .02 .01
□ 504 Tom O'Malley .05 .02 .01
□ 505 Kelly Gruber .05 .02 .01
□ 506 Tom Glavine .25 .11 .03
□ 507 Gary Redus .05 .02 .01
□ 508 Terry Leach .05 .02 .01
□ 509 Tom Pagnozzi .05 .02 .01
□ 510 Dwight Gooden .10 .05 .01
□ 511 Clay Parker .05 .02 .01
□ 512 Gary Pettis .05 .02 .01
Now with Rangers
11/24/89
□ 513 Mark Eichhorn .05 .02 .01
Now with Angels
12/13/89
□ 514 Andy Allanson .05 .02 .01
□ 515 Len Dykstra .10 .05 .01
□ 516 Tim Leary .05 .02 .01
□ 517 Roberto Alomar .40 .18 .05
□ 518 Bill Krueger .05 .02 .01
□ 519 Bucky Dent MG .05 .02 .01
□ 520 Mitch Williams .05 .02 .01
□ 521 Craig Worthington .05 .02 .01
□ 522 Mike Dunne .05 .02 .01
Now with Padres
12/4/89
□ 523 Jay Bell .10 .05 .01
□ 524 Daryl Boston .05 .02 .01
□ 525 Wally Joyner .10 .05 .01
□ 526 Checklist 4 .05 .02 .01
□ 527 Ron Hassey .05 .02 .01
□ 528 Kevin Wickander UER .05 .02 .01
Monthly scoreboard
strikeout total was 2.2
that was his innings
pitched total
□ 529 Greg A. Harris .05 .02 .01
□ 530 Mark Langston .05 .02 .01
Now with Angels
12/4/89
□ 531 Ken Caminiti .40 .18 .05
□ 532 Cecilio Guante .05 .02 .01
Now with Indians
11/21/89
□ 533 Tim Jones .05 .02 .01
□ 534 Louie Meadows .05 .02 .01
□ 535 John Smoltz .50 .23 .06
□ 536 Bob Geren .05 .02 .01
□ 537 Mark Grant .05 .02 .01
□ 538 Bill Spiers UER .05 .02 .01
Photo actually George Canale
□ 539 Neal Heaton .05 .02 .01
□ 540 Danny Tartabull .05 .02 .01
□ 541 Pat Perry .05 .02 .01
□ 542 Darren Daulton .10 .05 .01
□ 543 Nelson Liriano .05 .02 .01
□ 544 Dennis Boyd .05 .02 .01
Now with Expos
12/7/89
□ 545 Kevin McReynolds .05 .02 .01
□ 546 Kevin Hickey .05 .02 .01
□ 547 Jack Howell .05 .02 .01

Card	MINT	NRMT	EXC
☐ 548 Pat Clements	.05	.02	.01
☐ 549 Don Zimmer MG	.05	.02	.01
☐ 550 Julio Franco	.10	.05	.01
☐ 551 Tim Crews	.05	.02	.01
☐ 552 Mike(Miss.) Smith	.05	.02	.01
☐ 553 Scott Scudder UER	.05	.02	.01
Cedar Rapids			
☐ 554 Jay Buhner	.25	.11	.03
☐ 555 Jack Morris	.10	.05	.01
☐ 556 Gene Larkin	.05	.02	.01
☐ 557 Jeff Innis	.05	.02	.01
☐ 558 Rafael Ramirez	.05	.02	.01
☐ 559 Andy McGaffigan	.05	.02	.01
☐ 560 Steve Sax	.05	.02	.01
☐ 561 Ken Dayley	.05	.02	.01
☐ 562 Chad Kreuter	.05	.02	.01
☐ 563 Alex Sanchez	.05	.02	.01
☐ 564 Tyler Houston FDP	.20	.09	.03
☐ 565 Scott Fletcher	.05	.02	.01
☐ 566 Mark Knudson	.05	.02	.01
☐ 567 Ron Gant	.20	.09	.03
☐ 568 John Smiley	.10	.05	.01
☐ 569 Ivan Calderon	.05	.02	.01
☐ 570 Cal Ripken	1.50	.70	.19
☐ 571 Brett Butler	.10	.05	.01
☐ 572 Greg W. Harris	.05	.02	.01
☐ 573 Danny Heep	.05	.02	.01
☐ 574 Bill Swift	.05	.02	.01
☐ 575 Lance Parrish	.05	.02	.01
☐ 576 Mike Dyer	.05	.02	.01
☐ 577 Charlie Hayes	.05	.02	.01
☐ 578 Joe Magrane	.05	.02	.01
☐ 579 Art Howe MG	.05	.02	.01
☐ 580 Joe Carter	.10	.05	.01
☐ 581 Ken Griffey Sr.	.05	.02	.01
☐ 582 Rick Honeycutt	.05	.02	.01
☐ 583 Bruce Benedict	.05	.02	.01
☐ 584 Phil Stephenson	.05	.02	.01
☐ 585 Kal Daniels	.05	.02	.01
☐ 586 Edwin Nunez	.05	.02	.01
☐ 587 Lance Johnson	.10	.05	.01
☐ 588 Rick Rhoden	.05	.02	.01
☐ 589 Mike Aldrete	.05	.02	.01
☐ 590 Ozzie Smith	.50	.23	.06
☐ 591 Todd Stottlemyre	.05	.02	.01
☐ 592 R.J. Reynolds	.05	.02	.01
☐ 593 Scott Bradley	.05	.02	.01
☐ 594 Luis Sojo	.05	.02	.01
☐ 595 Greg Swindell	.05	.02	.01
☐ 596 Jose DeJesus	.05	.02	.01
☐ 597 Chris Bosio	.05	.02	.01
☐ 598 Brady Anderson	.20	.09	.03
☐ 599 Frank Williams	.05	.02	.01
☐ 600 Darryl Strawberry	.10	.05	.01
☐ 601 Luis Rivera	.05	.02	.01
☐ 602 Scott Garrelts	.05	.02	.01
☐ 603 Tony Armas	.05	.02	.01
☐ 604 Ron Robinson	.05	.02	.01
☐ 605 Mike Scioscia	.05	.02	.01
☐ 606 Storm Davis	.05	.02	.01
Now with Royals			
12/7/89			
☐ 607 Steve Jeltz	.05	.02	.01
☐ 608 Eric Anthony	.05	.02	.01
☐ 609 Sparky Anderson MG	.10	.05	.01
☐ 610 Pedro Guerrero	.05	.02	.01
☐ 611 Walt Terrell	.05	.02	.01
Now with Pirates			
11/29/89			
☐ 612 Dave Gallagher	.05	.02	.01
☐ 613 Jeff Pico	.05	.02	.01
☐ 614 Nelson Santovenia	.05	.02	.01
☐ 615 Rob Deer	.05	.02	.01
☐ 616 Brian Holman	.05	.02	.01
☐ 617 Geronimo Berroa	.10	.05	.01
☐ 618 Ed Whitson	.05	.02	.01
☐ 619 Rob Ducey	.05	.02	.01
☐ 620 Tony Castillo	.05	.02	.01
☐ 621 Melido Perez	.05	.02	.01
☐ 622 Sid Bream	.05	.02	.01
☐ 623 Jim Corsi	.05	.02	.01
☐ 624 Darrin Jackson	.05	.02	.01
☐ 625 Roger McDowell	.05	.02	.01
☐ 626 Bob Melvin	.05	.02	.01
☐ 627 Jose Rijo	.05	.02	.01
☐ 628 Candy Maldonado	.05	.02	.01
Now with Indians			
11/28/89			
☐ 629 Eric Hetzel	.05	.02	.01
☐ 630 Gary Gaetti	.10	.05	.01
☐ 631 John Wetteland	.20	.09	.03
☐ 632 Scott Lusader	.05	.02	.01
☐ 633 Dennis Cook	.05	.02	.01
☐ 634 Luis Polonia	.05	.02	.01
☐ 635 Brian Downing	.05	.02	.01
☐ 636 Jesse Orosco	.05	.02	.01
☐ 637 Craig Reynolds	.05	.02	.01
☐ 638 Jeff Montgomery	.10	.05	.01
☐ 639 Tony LaRussa MG	.10	.05	.01
☐ 640 Rick Sutcliffe	.05	.02	.01
☐ 641 Doug Strange	.05	.02	.01
☐ 642 Jack Armstrong	.05	.02	.01
☐ 643 Alfredo Griffin	.05	.02	.01
☐ 644 Paul Assenmacher	.05	.02	.01
☐ 645 Jose Oquendo	.05	.02	.01
☐ 646 Checklist 5	.05	.02	.01
☐ 647 Rex Hudler	.05	.02	.01
☐ 648 Jim Clancy	.05	.02	.01
☐ 649 Dan Murphy	.05	.02	.01
☐ 650 Mike Witt	.05	.02	.01
☐ 651 Rafael Santana	.05	.02	.01
Now with Indians			
1/10/90			
☐ 652 Mike Boddicker	.05	.02	.01
☐ 653 John Moses	.05	.02	.01
☐ 654 Paul Coleman FDP	.05	.02	.01
☐ 655 Gregg Olson	.05	.02	.01
☐ 656 Mackey Sasser	.05	.02	.01
☐ 657 Terry Mulholland	.05	.02	.01
☐ 658 Donell Nixon	.05	.02	.01
☐ 659 Greg Cadaret	.05	.02	.01
☐ 660 Vince Coleman	.05	.02	.01
☐ 661 Dick Howser TBC'85	.05	.02	.01
UER			
Seaver's 300th on 7/11/85			
should be 8/4/85			
☐ 662 Mike Schmidt TBC'80	.20	.09	.03
☐ 663 Fred Lynn TBC'75	.05	.02	.01
☐ 664 Johnny Bench TBC'70	.20	.09	.03
☐ 665 Sandy Koufax TBC'65	.50	.23	.06
☐ 666 Brian Fisher	.05	.02	.01
☐ 667 Curt Wilkerson	.05	.02	.01
☐ 668 Joe Oliver	.05	.02	.01
☐ 669 Tom Lasorda MG	.25	.11	.03
☐ 670 Dennis Eckersley	.10	.05	.01
☐ 671 Bob Boone	.10	.05	.01
☐ 672 Roy Smith	.05	.02	.01
☐ 673 Joey Meyer	.05	.02	.01
☐ 674 Spike Owen	.05	.02	.01
☐ 675 Jim Abbott	.10	.05	.01
☐ 676 Randy Kutcher	.05	.02	.01
☐ 677 Jay Tibbs	.05	.02	.01
☐ 678 Kirt Manwaring UER	.05	.02	.01
'88 Phoenix stats repeated			
☐ 679 Gary Ward	.05	.02	.01
☐ 680 Howard Johnson	.05	.02	.01
☐ 681 Mike Schooler	.05	.02	.01
☐ 682 Dann Bilardello	.05	.02	.01
☐ 683 Kenny Rogers	.15	.07	.02
☐ 684 Julio Machado	.05	.02	.01
☐ 685 Tony Fernandez	.05	.02	.01
☐ 686 Carmelo Martinez	.05	.02	.01
Now with Phillies			
12/4/89			
☐ 687 Tim Birtsas	.05	.02	.01
☐ 688 Milt Thompson	.05	.02	.01
☐ 689 Rich Yett	.05	.02	.01
Now with Twins			
12/26/89			
☐ 690 Mark McGwire	.60	.25	.07
☐ 691 Chuck Cary	.05	.02	.01
☐ 692 Sammy Sosa	1.00	.45	.12
☐ 693 Calvin Schiraldi	.05	.02	.01
☐ 694 Mike Stanton	.10	.05	.01
☐ 695 Tom Henke	.05	.02	.01
☐ 696 B.J. Surhoff	.10	.05	.01
☐ 697 Mike Davis	.05	.02	.01
☐ 698 Omar Vizquel	.15	.07	.02
☐ 699 Jim Leyland MG	.05	.02	.01
☐ 700 Kirby Puckett	.75	.35	.09
☐ 701 Bernie Williams	1.00	.45	.12
☐ 702 Tony Phillips	.10	.05	.01
Now with Tigers			
12/5/89			
☐ 703 Jeff Brantley	.10	.05	.01
☐ 704 Chip Hale	.05	.02	.01
☐ 705 Claudell Washington	.05	.02	.01
☐ 706 Geno Petralli	.05	.02	.01
☐ 707 Luis Aquino	.05	.02	.01
☐ 708 Larry Sheets	.05	.02	.01
Now with Tigers			
1/10/90			
☐ 709 Juan Berenguer	.05	.02	.01
☐ 710 Von Hayes	.05	.02	.01
☐ 711 Rick Aguilera	.10	.05	.01
☐ 712 Todd Benzinger	.05	.02	.01
☐ 713 Tim Drummond	.05	.02	.01
☐ 714 Marquis Grissom	.50	.23	.06
☐ 715 Greg Maddux	1.25	.55	.16
☐ 716 Steve Balboni	.05	.02	.01
☐ 717 Ron Karkovice	.05	.02	.01
☐ 718 Gary Sheffield	.50	.23	.06
☐ 719 Wally Whitehurst	.05	.02	.01
☐ 720 Andres Galarraga	.20	.09	.03
☐ 721 Lee Mazzilli	.05	.02	.01
☐ 722 Felix Fermin	.05	.02	.01
☐ 723 Jeff D. Robinson	.05	.02	.01
Now with Yankees			
12/4/89			
☐ 724 Juan Bell	.05	.02	.01
☐ 725 Terry Pendleton	.10	.05	.01
☐ 726 Gene Nelson	.05	.02	.01
☐ 727 Pat Tabler	.05	.02	.01
☐ 728 Jim Acker	.05	.02	.01
☐ 729 Bobby Valentine MG	.05	.02	.01
☐ 730 Tony Gwynn	.75	.35	.09
☐ 731 Don Carman	.05	.02	.01
☐ 732 Ernest Riles	.05	.02	.01
☐ 733 John Dopson	.05	.02	.01
☐ 734 Kevin Elster	.05	.02	.01
☐ 735 Charlie Hough	.05	.02	.01
☐ 736 Rick Dempsey	.05	.02	.01
☐ 737 Chris Sabo	.05	.02	.01
☐ 738 Gene Harris	.05	.02	.01
☐ 739 Dale Sveum	.05	.02	.01
☐ 740 Jesse Barfield	.05	.02	.01
☐ 741 Steve Wilson	.05	.02	.01
☐ 742 Ernie Whitt	.05	.02	.01
☐ 743 Tom Candiotti	.05	.02	.01
☐ 744 Kelly Mann	.05	.02	.01
☐ 745 Hubie Brooks	.05	.02	.01
☐ 746 Dave Smith	.05	.02	.01
☐ 747 Randy Bush	.05	.02	.01
☐ 748 Doyle Alexander	.05	.02	.01
☐ 749 Mark Parent UER	.05	.02	.01
'87 BA .80, should be .080			
☐ 750 Dale Murphy	.20	.09	.03
☐ 751 Steve Lyons	.05	.02	.01
☐ 752 Tom Gordon	.05	.02	.01
☐ 753 Chris Speier	.05	.02	.01
☐ 754 Bob Walk	.05	.02	.01
☐ 755 Rafael Palmeiro	.15	.07	.02
☐ 756 Ken Howell	.05	.02	.01
☐ 757 Larry Walker	1.00	.45	.12
☐ 758 Mark Thurmond	.05	.02	.01
☐ 759 Tom Trebelhorn MG	.05	.02	.01
☐ 760 Wade Boggs	.20	.09	.03
☐ 761 Mike Jackson	.05	.02	.01
☐ 762 Doug Dascenzo	.05	.02	.01
☐ 763 Dennis Martinez	.10	.05	.01
☐ 764 Tim Teufel	.05	.02	.01
☐ 765 Chili Davis	.10	.05	.01
☐ 766 Brian Meyer	.05	.02	.01
☐ 767 Tracy Jones	.05	.02	.01
☐ 768 Chuck Crim	.05	.02	.01
☐ 769 Greg Hibbard	.05	.02	.01
☐ 770 Cory Snyder	.05	.02	.01
☐ 771 Pete Smith	.05	.02	.01
☐ 772 Jeff Reed	.05	.02	.01
☐ 773 Dave Leiper	.05	.02	.01
☐ 774 Ben McDonald	.20	.09	.03
☐ 775 Andy Van Slyke	.10	.05	.01
☐ 776 Charlie Leibrandt	.05	.02	.01
Now with Braves			
12/17/89			
☐ 777 Tim Laudner	.05	.02	.01
☐ 778 Mike Jeffcoat	.05	.02	.01
☐ 779 Lloyd Moseby	.05	.02	.01
Now with Tigers			
12/7/89			
☐ 780 Orel Hershiser	.10	.05	.01
☐ 781 Mario Diaz	.05	.02	.01
☐ 782 Jose Alvarez	.05	.02	.01
Now with Giants			
12/4/89			
☐ 783 Checklist 6	.05	.02	.01
☐ 784 Scott Bailes	.05	.02	.01
Now with Angels			
1/9/90			
☐ 785 Jim Rice	.10	.05	.01
☐ 786 Eric King	.05	.02	.01
☐ 787 Rene Gonzales	.05	.02	.01
☐ 788 Frank DiPino	.05	.02	.01
☐ 789 John Wathan MG	.05	.02	.01
☐ 790 Gary Carter	.10	.05	.01
☐ 791 Alvaro Espinoza	.05	.02	.01
☐ 792 Gerald Perry	.05	.02	.01

1990 O-Pee-Chee Box Bottoms

The 1990 O-Pee-Chee box bottom cards comprise four different box bottoms from the bottoms of wax pack boxes, with four cards each, for a total of 16 standard-size cards. The cards are nearly identical to the 1990 Topps Box Bottom cards. The fronts feature green-bordered color player action shots. The player's name appears at the bottom and his team name appears at the upper left. The yellow-green horizontal backs carry player career highlights in both English and French. The cards are lettered (A-P) rather than numbered on the back.

	MINT	NRMT	EXC
COMPLETE SET (16)	5.00	2.20	.60
COMMON CARD (A-P)	.15	.07	.02
☐ A Wade Boggs	.50	.23	.06
☐ B George Brett	1.00	.45	.12
☐ C Andre Dawson	.25	.11	.03
☐ D Darrell Evans	.15	.07	.02
☐ E Dwight Gooden	.25	.11	.03
☐ F Rickey Henderson	.50	.23	.06
☐ G Tom Lasorda MG	.50	.23	.06
☐ H Fred Lynn	.15	.07	.02
☐ I Mark McGwire	.75	.35	.09
☐ J Dave Parker	.25	.11	.03
☐ K Jeff Reardon	.15	.07	.02
☐ L Rick Reuschel	.15	.07	.02
☐ M Jim Rice	.25	.11	.03
☐ N Cal Ripken	2.50	1.10	.30
☐ O Nolan Ryan	2.50	1.10	.30
☐ P Ryne Sandberg	1.00	.45	.12

1991 O-Pee-Chee

The 1991 O-Pee-Chee baseball set contains 792 standard-size cards. For the second time since 1976, O-Pee-Chee issued the exact same set as Topps. The only distinctions are the bilingual text and the O-Pee-Chee copyright on the backs. The fronts feature white-bordered color action player photos framed by two different colored lines. The player's name and position appear at the bottom of the photo, with his team name appearing just above. The Topps 40th anniversary logo appears in the upper left corner. The traded players have their new teams and dates of trade printed on the photo. The pinkish horizontal backs present player biography, statistics and bilingual career highlights. Cards 386-407 are an All-Star subset. Five players are listed as Future Stars: 114 Lance Dickson, 211 Brian Barnes, 561 Tim McIntosh, 587 Jose Offerman, and 594 Rich Garces. Nine players are listed as First Draft Picks: 74 Shane Andrews, 103 Tim Costo, 113 Carl Everett, 278 Alex Fernandez, 471 Mike Lieberthal, 491 Kurt Miller, 529 Marc Newfield, 596 Ronnie Walden and 767 Dan Wilson. The key Rookie Cards are Wes Chamberlain, Brian McRae, Marc Newfield and Phil Plantier.

	MINT	NRMT	EXC
COMPLETE SET (792)	25.00	11.00	3.10
COMPLETE FACT.SET (792)	25.00	11.00	3.10
COMMON CARD (1-792)	.05	.02	.01
☐ 1 Nolan Ryan	1.50	.70	.19
☐ 2 George Brett RB	.40	.18	.05
☐ 3 Carlton Fisk RB	.20	.09	.03
☐ 4 Kevin Maas RB	.05	.02	.01
☐ 5 Cal Ripken RB	.75	.35	.09
☐ 6 Nolan Ryan RB	.75	.35	.09
☐ 7 Ryne Sandberg RB	.15	.07	.02
☐ 8 Bobby Thigpen RB	.05	.02	.01
☐ 9 Darrin Fletcher	.05	.02	.01
☐ 10 Gregg Olson	.05	.02	.01
☐ 11 Roberto Kelly	.05	.02	.01
☐ 12 Paul Assenmacher	.05	.02	.01
☐ 13 Mariano Duncan	.05	.02	.01
☐ 14 Dennis Lamp	.05	.02	.01
☐ 15 Von Hayes	.05	.02	.01
☐ 16 Mike Heath	.05	.02	.01
☐ 17 Jeff Brantley	.05	.02	.01
☐ 18 Nelson Liriano	.05	.02	.01
☐ 19 Jeff D. Robinson	.05	.02	.01
☐ 20 Pedro Guerrero	.05	.02	.01
☐ 21 Joe Morgan MG	.05	.02	.01
☐ 22 Storm Davis	.05	.02	.01
☐ 23 Jim Gantner	.05	.02	.01
☐ 24 Dave Martinez	.05	.02	.01
☐ 25 Tim Belcher	.05	.02	.01
☐ 26 Luis Sojo UER	.05	.02	.01
Born in Barquisimeto			
not Caracas			
Now with Angels			
12/2/90			
☐ 27 Bobby Witt	.05	.02	.01
☐ 28 Alvaro Espinoza	.05	.02	.01
☐ 29 Bob Walk	.05	.02	.01
☐ 30 Gregg Jefferies	.10	.05	.01
☐ 31 Colby Ward	.05	.02	.01
☐ 32 Mike Simms	.05	.02	.01
☐ 33 Barry Jones	.05	.02	.01
☐ 34 Atlee Hammaker	.05	.02	.01
☐ 35 Greg Maddux	1.25	.55	.16
☐ 36 Donnie Hill	.05	.02	.01
☐ 37 Tom Bolton	.05	.02	.01
☐ 38 Scott Bradley	.05	.02	.01
☐ 39 Jim Neidlinger	.05	.02	.01
☐ 40 Kevin Mitchell	.10	.05	.01
☐ 41 Ken Dayley	.05	.02	.01
Now with Blue Jays			
11/26/90			
☐ 42 Chris Hoiles	.10	.05	.01
☐ 43 Roger McDowell	.05	.02	.01
☐ 44 Mike Felder	.05	.02	.01
☐ 45 Chris Sabo	.05	.02	.01
☐ 46 Tim Drummond	.05	.02	.01
☐ 47 Brook Jacoby	.05	.02	.01
☐ 48 Dennis Boyd	.05	.02	.01
☐ 49 Pat Borders	.05	.02	.01
☐ 50 Bob Welch	.05	.02	.01

Card			
☐ 51 Art Howe MG	.05	.02	.01
☐ 52 Francisco Oliveras	.05	.02	.01
☐ 53 Mike Sharperson UER	.05	.02	.01
Born in 1961, not 1960			
☐ 54 Gary Mielke	.05	.02	.01
☐ 55 Jeffrey Leonard	.05	.02	.01
☐ 56 Jeff Parrett	.05	.02	.01
☐ 57 Jack Howell	.05	.02	.01
☐ 58 Mel Stottlemyre Jr.	.05	.02	.01
☐ 59 Eric Yelding	.05	.02	.01
☐ 60 Frank Viola	.05	.02	.01
☐ 61 Stan Javier	.05	.02	.01
☐ 62 Lee Guetterman	.05	.02	.01
☐ 63 Milt Thompson	.05	.02	.01
☐ 64 Tom Herr	.05	.02	.01
☐ 65 Bruce Hurst	.05	.02	.01
☐ 66 Terry Kennedy	.05	.02	.01
☐ 67 Rick Honeycutt	.05	.02	.01
☐ 68 Gary Sheffield	.20	.09	.03
☐ 69 Steve Wilson	.05	.02	.01
☐ 70 Ellis Burks	.10	.05	.01
☐ 71 Jim Acker	.05	.02	.01
☐ 72 Junior Ortiz	.05	.02	.01
☐ 73 Craig Worthington	.05	.02	.01
☐ 74 Shane Andrews	.20	.09	.03
☐ 75 Jack Morris	.10	.05	.01
☐ 76 Jerry Browne	.05	.02	.01
☐ 77 Drew Hall	.05	.02	.01
☐ 78 Geno Petralli	.05	.02	.01
☐ 79 Frank Thomas	3.00	1.35	.35
☐ 80 Fernando Valenzuela	.10	.05	.01
☐ 81 Cito Gaston MG	.05	.02	.01
☐ 82 Tom Glavine	.20	.09	.03
☐ 83 Daryl Boston	.05	.02	.01
☐ 84 Bob McClure	.05	.02	.01
☐ 85 Jesse Barfield	.05	.02	.01
☐ 86 Les Lancaster	.05	.02	.01
☐ 87 Tracy Jones	.05	.02	.01
☐ 88 Bob Tewksbury	.05	.02	.01
☐ 89 Darren Daulton	.10	.05	.01
☐ 90 Danny Tartabull	.05	.02	.01
☐ 91 Greg Colbrunn	.20	.09	.03
☐ 92 Danny Jackson	.05	.02	.01
Now with Cubs			
11/21/90			
☐ 93 Ivan Calderon	.05	.02	.01
☐ 94 John Dopson	.05	.02	.01
☐ 95 Paul Molitor	.40	.18	.05
☐ 96 Trevor Wilson	.05	.02	.01
☐ 97 Brady Anderson	.20	.09	.03
☐ 98 Sergio Valdez	.05	.02	.01
☐ 99 Chris Gwynn	.05	.02	.01
☐ 100 Don Mattingly	1.00	.45	.12
☐ 101 Rob Ducey	.05	.02	.01
☐ 102 Gene Larkin	.05	.02	.01
☐ 103 Tim Costo	.05	.02	.01
☐ 104 Don Robinson	.05	.02	.01
☐ 105 Kevin McReynolds	.05	.02	.01
☐ 106 Ed Nunez	.05	.02	.01
Now with Brewers			
12/4/90			
☐ 107 Luis Polonia	.05	.02	.01
☐ 108 Matt Young	.05	.02	.01
Now with Red Sox			
12/4/90			
☐ 109 Greg Riddoch MG	.05	.02	.01
☐ 110 Tom Henke	.05	.02	.01
☐ 111 Andres Thomas	.05	.02	.01
☐ 112 Frank DiPino	.05	.02	.01
☐ 113 Carl Everett	.20	.09	.03
☐ 114 Lance Dickson	.05	.02	.01
☐ 115 Hubie Brooks	.05	.02	.01
Now with Mets			
12/15/90			
☐ 116 Mark Davis	.05	.02	.01
☐ 117 Dion James	.05	.02	.01
☐ 118 Tom Edens	.05	.02	.01
☐ 119 Carl Nichols	.05	.02	.01
☐ 120 Joe Carter	.10	.05	.01
Now with Blue Jays			
12/5/90			
☐ 121 Eric King	.05	.02	.01
Now with Indians			
12/4/90			
☐ 122 Paul O'Neill	.10	.05	.01
☐ 123 Greg A. Harris	.05	.02	.01
☐ 124 Randy Bush	.05	.02	.01
☐ 125 Steve Bedrosian	.05	.02	.01
Now with Twins			
12/5/90			
☐ 126 Bernard Gilkey	.15	.07	.02
☐ 127 Joe Price	.05	.02	.01
☐ 128 Travis Fryman	.25	.11	.03
Front has SS, back has SS-3B			
☐ 129 Mark Eichhorn	.05	.02	.01
☐ 130 Ozzie Smith	.50	.23	.06
☐ 131 Checklist 1	.05	.02	.01
☐ 132 Jamie Quirk	.05	.02	.01
☐ 133 Greg Briley	.05	.02	.01
☐ 134 Kevin Elster	.05	.02	.01
☐ 135 Jerome Walton	.05	.02	.01
☐ 136 Dave Schmidt	.05	.02	.01
☐ 137 Randy Ready	.05	.02	.01
☐ 138 Jamie Moyer	.05	.02	.01
Now with Cardinals			
1/10/91			
☐ 139 Jeff Treadway	.05	.02	.01
☐ 140 Fred McGriff	.15	.07	.02
Now with Padres			
12/5/90			
☐ 141 Nick Leyva MG	.05	.02	.01
☐ 142 Curt Wilkerson	.05	.02	.01
Now with Pirates			
1/9/91			
☐ 143 John Smiley	.05	.02	.01
☐ 144 Dave Henderson	.05	.02	.01
☐ 145 Lou Whitaker	.10	.05	.01
☐ 146 Dan Plesac	.05	.02	.01
☐ 147 Carlos Baerga	.40	.18	.05
☐ 148 Rey Palacios	.05	.02	.01
☐ 149 Al Osuna UER	.05	.02	.01
Shown with glove on			
right hand			
bio says throws right			
☐ 150 Cal Ripken	1.50	.70	.19
☐ 151 Tom Browning	.05	.02	.01
☐ 152 Mickey Hatcher	.05	.02	.01
☐ 153 Bryan Harvey	.05	.02	.01
☐ 154 Jay Buhner	.20	.09	.03
☐ 155 Dwight Evans	.10	.05	.01
Now with Orioles			
12/6/90			
☐ 156 Carlos Martinez	.05	.02	.01
☐ 157 John Smoltz	.15	.07	.02
☐ 158 Jose Uribe	.05	.02	.01
☐ 159 Joe Boever	.05	.02	.01
☐ 160 Vince Coleman	.05	.02	.01
☐ 161 Tim Leary	.05	.02	.01
☐ 162 Ozzie Canseco	.05	.02	.01
☐ 163 Dave Johnson	.05	.02	.01
☐ 164 Edgar Diaz	.05	.02	.01
☐ 165 Sandy Alomar Jr.	.10	.05	.01
☐ 166 Harold Baines	.10	.05	.01
☐ 167 Randy Tomlin	.05	.02	.01
☐ 168 John Olerud	.10	.05	.01
☐ 169 Luis Aquino	.05	.02	.01
☐ 170 Carlton Fisk	.25	.11	.03
☐ 171 Tony LaRussa MG	.10	.05	.01
☐ 172 Pete Incaviglia	.05	.02	.01
☐ 173 Jason Grimsley	.05	.02	.01
☐ 174 Ken Caminiti	.20	.09	.03
☐ 175 Jack Armstrong	.05	.02	.01
☐ 176 John Orton	.05	.02	.01
☐ 177 Reggie Harris	.05	.02	.01
☐ 178 Dave Valle	.05	.02	.01
☐ 179 Pete Harnisch	.05	.02	.01
Now with Astros			
1/10/91			
☐ 180 Tony Gwynn	.75	.35	.09
☐ 181 Duane Ward	.05	.02	.01
☐ 182 Junior Noboa	.05	.02	.01
☐ 183 Clay Parker	.05	.02	.01
☐ 184 Gary Green	.05	.02	.01
☐ 185 Joe Magrane	.05	.02	.01
☐ 186 Rod Booker	.05	.02	.01
☐ 187 Greg Cadaret	.05	.02	.01
☐ 188 Damon Berryhill	.05	.02	.01
☐ 189 Daryl Irvine	.05	.02	.01
☐ 190 Matt Williams	.15	.07	.02
☐ 191 Willie Blair	.05	.02	.01
Now with Indians			
11/6/90			
☐ 192 Rob Deer	.05	.02	.01
Now with Tigers			
11/21/90			
☐ 193 Felix Fermin	.05	.02	.01
☐ 194 Xavier Hernandez	.05	.02	.01
☐ 195 Wally Joyner	.10	.05	.01
☐ 196 Jim Vatcher	.05	.02	.01
☐ 197 Chris Nabholz	.05	.02	.01
☐ 198 R.J. Reynolds	.05	.02	.01
☐ 199 Mike Hartley	.05	.02	.01
☐ 200 Darryl Strawberry	.10	.05	.01
Now with Dodgers			
11/8/90			
☐ 201 Tom Kelly MG	.05	.02	.01
☐ 202 Jim Leyritz	.10	.05	.01
☐ 203 Gene Harris	.05	.02	.01
☐ 204 Herm Winningham	.05	.02	.01
☐ 205 Mike Perez	.05	.02	.01
☐ 206 Carlos Quintana	.05	.02	.01
☐ 207 Gary Wayne	.05	.02	.01
☐ 208 Willie Wilson	.05	.02	.01
☐ 209 Ken Howell	.05	.02	.01
☐ 210 Lance Parrish	.05	.02	.01
☐ 211 Brian Barnes	.05	.02	.01
☐ 212 Steve Finley	.10	.05	.01
Now with Astros			
1/10/91			
☐ 213 Frank Wills	.05	.02	.01
☐ 214 Joe Girardi	.05	.02	.01
☐ 215 Dave Smith	.05	.02	.01
Now with Cubs			
12/17/90			
☐ 216 Greg Gagne	.05	.02	.01
☐ 217 Chris Bosio	.05	.02	.01
☐ 218 Rick Parker	.05	.02	.01
☐ 219 Jack McDowell	.15	.07	.02
☐ 220 Tim Wallach	.05	.02	.01
☐ 221 Don Slaught	.05	.02	.01
☐ 222 Brian McRae	.50	.23	.06
☐ 223 Allan Anderson	.05	.02	.01
☐ 224 Juan Gonzalez	1.50	.70	.19
☐ 225 Randy Johnson	.25	.11	.03
☐ 226 Alfredo Griffin	.05	.02	.01
☐ 227 Steve Avery UER	.15	.07	.02
Pitched 13 games for			
Durham in 1989, not 2			
☐ 228 Rex Hudler	.05	.02	.01
☐ 229 Rance Mulliniks	.05	.02	.01
☐ 230 Sid Fernandez	.05	.02	.01
☐ 231 Doug Rader MG	.05	.02	.01
☐ 232 Jose DeJesus	.05	.02	.01
☐ 233 Al Leiter	.10	.05	.01
☐ 234 Scott Erickson	.10	.05	.01
☐ 235 Dave Parker	.10	.05	.01
☐ 236 Frank Tanana	.10	.05	.01
☐ 237 Rick Cerone	.05	.02	.01
☐ 238 Mike Dunne	.05	.02	.01
☐ 239 Darren Lewis	.05	.02	.01
Now with Giants			
12/4/90			
☐ 240 Mike Scott	.05	.02	.01
☐ 241 Dave Clark UER	.05	.02	.01
Career totals 19 HR and 5 3B			
should be 22 and 3			
☐ 242 Mike LaCoss	.05	.02	.01
☐ 243 Lance Johnson	.10	.05	.01
☐ 244 Mike Jeffcoat	.05	.02	.01
☐ 245 Kal Daniels	.05	.02	.01
☐ 246 Kevin Wickander	.05	.02	.01
☐ 247 Jody Reed	.05	.02	.01
☐ 248 Tom Gordon	.05	.02	.01
☐ 249 Bob Melvin	.05	.02	.01
☐ 250 Dennis Eckersley	.10	.05	.01
☐ 251 Mark Lemke	.05	.02	.01
☐ 252 Mel Rojas	.10	.05	.01
☐ 253 Garry Templeton	.05	.02	.01
☐ 254 Shawn Boskie	.05	.02	.01
☐ 255 Brian Downing	.05	.02	.01
☐ 256 Greg Hibbard	.05	.02	.01
☐ 257 Tom O'Malley	.05	.02	.01
☐ 258 Chris Hammond	.05	.02	.01
☐ 259 Hensley Meulens	.05	.02	.01
☐ 260 Harold Reynolds	.10	.05	.01
☐ 261 Bud Harrelson MG	.05	.02	.01
☐ 262 Tim Jones	.05	.02	.01
☐ 263 Checklist 2	.05	.02	.01
☐ 264 Dave Hollins	.05	.02	.01
☐ 265 Mark Gubicza	.05	.02	.01
☐ 266 Carmelo Castillo	.05	.02	.01
☐ 267 Mark Knudson	.05	.02	.01
☐ 268 Tom Brookens	.05	.02	.01
☐ 269 Joe Hesketh	.05	.02	.01
☐ 270 Mark McGwire	.60	.25	.07
☐ 271 Omar Olivares	.05	.02	.01
☐ 272 Jeff King	.10	.05	.01
☐ 273 Johnny Ray	.05	.02	.01
☐ 274 Ken Williams	.05	.02	.01
☐ 275 Alan Trammell	.10	.05	.01
☐ 276 Bill Swift	.05	.02	.01
☐ 277 Scott Coolbaugh	.05	.02	.01
Now with Padres			
12/12/90			
☐ 278 Alex Fernandez UER	.15	.07	.02
No '90 White Sox stats			
☐ 279 Jose Gonzalez	.05	.02	.01
☐ 280 Bret Saberhagen	.10	.05	.01
☐ 281 Larry Sheets	.05	.02	.01
☐ 282 Don Carman	.05	.02	.01
☐ 283 Marquis Grissom	.25	.11	.03
☐ 284 Billy Spiers	.05	.02	.01
☐ 285 Jim Abbott	.10	.05	.01
☐ 286 Ken Oberkfell	.05	.02	.01
☐ 287 Mark Grant	.05	.02	.01
☐ 288 Derrick May	.05	.02	.01
☐ 289 Tim Birtsas	.05	.02	.01
☐ 290 Steve Sax	.05	.02	.01
☐ 291 John Wathan MG	.05	.02	.01
☐ 292 Bud Black	.05	.02	.01
☐ 293 Jay Bell	.10	.05	.01
☐ 294 Mike Moore	.05	.02	.01
☐ 295 Rafael Palmeiro	.20	.09	.03
☐ 296 Mark Williamson	.05	.02	.01
☐ 297 Manny Lee	.05	.02	.01
☐ 298 Omar Vizquel	.20	.09	.03
☐ 299 Scott Radinsky	.05	.02	.01
☐ 300 Kirby Puckett	.75	.35	.09
☐ 301 Steve Farr	.05	.02	.01
Now with Yankees			
11/26/90			
☐ 302 Tim Teufel	.05	.02	.01
☐ 303 Mike Boddicker	.05	.02	.01
Now with Royals			
11/21/90			
☐ 304 Kevin Reimer	.05	.02	.01
☐ 305 Mike Scioscia	.05	.02	.01
☐ 306 Lonnie Smith	.05	.02	.01
☐ 307 Andy Benes	.10	.05	.01
☐ 308 Tom Pagnozzi	.05	.02	.01
☐ 309 Norm Charlton	.05	.02	.01
☐ 310 Gary Carter	.10	.05	.01
☐ 311 Jeff Pico	.05	.02	.01
☐ 312 Charlie Hayes	.05	.02	.01
☐ 313 Ron Robinson	.05	.02	.01
☐ 314 Gary Pettis	.05	.02	.01
☐ 315 Roberto Alomar	.40	.18	.05
☐ 316 Gene Nelson	.05	.02	.01
☐ 317 Mike Fitzgerald	.05	.02	.01
☐ 318 Rick Aguilera	.10	.05	.01
☐ 319 Jeff McKnight	.05	.02	.01
☐ 320 Tony Fernandez	.05	.02	.01
Now with Padres			
12/5/90			
☐ 321 Bob Rodgers MG	.05	.02	.01
☐ 322 Terry Shumpert	.05	.02	.01
☐ 323 Cory Snyder	.05	.02	.01
☐ 324 Ron Kittle	.05	.02	.01
☐ 325 Brett Butler	.10	.05	.01
Now with Dodgers			
12/15/90			
☐ 326 Ken Patterson	.05	.02	.01
☐ 327 Ron Hassey	.05	.02	.01
☐ 328 Walt Terrell	.05	.02	.01
☐ 329 Dave Justice UER	.30	.14	.04
Drafted third round on card			
should say fourth pick			
☐ 330 Dwight Gooden	.10	.05	.01
☐ 331 Eric Anthony	.05	.02	.01
☐ 332 Kenny Rogers	.05	.02	.01
Now with White Sox			
12/4/90			
☐ 333 Chipper Jones FDP	5.00	2.20	.60
☐ 334 Todd Benzinger	.05	.02	.01
☐ 335 Mitch Williams	.05	.02	.01
☐ 336 Matt Nokes	.05	.02	.01
☐ 337 Keith Comstock	.05	.02	.01
☐ 338 Luis Rivera	.05	.02	.01
☐ 339 Larry Walker	.25	.11	.03
☐ 340 Ramon Martinez	.20	.09	.03
☐ 341 John Moses	.05	.02	.01
☐ 342 Mickey Morandini	.05	.02	.01
☐ 343 Jose Oquendo	.05	.02	.01
☐ 344 Jeff Russell	.05	.02	.01
☐ 345 Len Dykstra	.10	.05	.01
☐ 346 Jesse Orosco	.05	.02	.01
☐ 347 Greg Vaughn	.10	.05	.01
☐ 348 Todd Stottlemyre	.10	.05	.01
☐ 349 Dave Gallagher	.05	.02	.01
Now with Angels			
12/4/90			
☐ 350 Glenn Davis	.05	.02	.01
☐ 351 Joe Torre MG	.10	.05	.01
☐ 352 Frank White	.10	.05	.01
☐ 353 Tony Castillo	.05	.02	.01
☐ 354 Sid Bream	.05	.02	.01
Now with Braves			
12/5/90			
☐ 355 Chili Davis	.10	.05	.01
☐ 356 Mike Marshall	.05	.02	.01
☐ 357 Jack Savage	.05	.02	.01
☐ 358 Mark Parent	.05	.02	.01
Now with Rangers			
12/12/90			
☐ 359 Chuck Cary	.05	.02	.01
☐ 360 Tim Raines	.10	.05	.01
Now with White Sox			
12/23/90			
☐ 361 Scott Garrelts	.05	.02	.01
☐ 362 Hector Villanueva	.05	.02	.01
☐ 363 Rick Mahler	.05	.02	.01
☐ 364 Dan Pasqua	.05	.02	.01
☐ 365 Mike Schooler	.05	.02	.01
☐ 366 Checklist 3	.05	.02	.01
☐ 367 Dave Walsh	.05	.02	.01
☐ 368 Felix Jose	.05	.02	.01
☐ 369 Steve Searcy	.05	.02	.01
☐ 370 Kelly Gruber	.05	.02	.01
☐ 371 Jeff Montgomery	.05	.02	.01
☐ 372 Spike Owen	.05	.02	.01
☐ 373 Darrin Jackson	.05	.02	.01
☐ 374 Larry Casian	.05	.02	.01
☐ 375 Tony Pena	.05	.02	.01
☐ 376 Mike Harkey	.05	.02	.01
☐ 377 Rene Gonzales	.05	.02	.01
☐ 378 Wilson Alvarez	.20	.09	.03
☐ 379 Randy Velarde	.05	.02	.01
☐ 380 Willie McGee	.10	.05	.01
Now with Giants			
12/3/90			
☐ 381 Jim Leyland MG	.05	.02	.01
☐ 382 Mackey Sasser	.05	.02	.01
☐ 383 Pete Smith	.05	.02	.01
☐ 384 Gerald Perry	.05	.02	.01
Now with Cardinals			
12/13/90			
☐ 385 Mickey Tettleton	.10	.05	.01
Now with Tigers			
1/12/90			
☐ 386 Cecil Fielder AS	.10	.05	.01
☐ 387 Julio Franco AS	.05	.02	.01
☐ 388 Kelly Gruber AS	.05	.02	.01
☐ 389 Alan Trammell AS	.10	.05	.01
☐ 390 Jose Canseco AS	.20	.09	.03
☐ 391 Rickey Henderson AS	.20	.09	.03
☐ 392 Ken Griffey Jr. AS	1.50	.70	.19
☐ 393 Carlton Fisk AS	.20	.09	.03
☐ 394 Bob Welch AS	.05	.02	.01
☐ 395 Chuck Finley AS	.05	.02	.01
☐ 396 Bobby Thigpen AS	.05	.02	.01
☐ 397 Eddie Murray AS	.20	.09	.03

☐ 398 Ryne Sandberg AS .15 .07 .02
☐ 399 Matt Williams AS .20 .09 .03
☐ 400 Barry Larkin AS .20 .09 .03
☐ 401 Barry Bonds AS .25 .11 .03
☐ 402 Darryl Strawberry AS .10 .05 .01
☐ 403 Bobby Bonilla AS .10 .05 .01
☐ 404 Mike Scioscia AS .05 .02 .01
☐ 405 Doug Drabek AS .05 .02 .01
☐ 406 Frank Viola AS .05 .02 .01
☐ 407 John Franco AS .05 .02 .01
☐ 408 Earnie Riles .05 .02 .01
Now with Athletics
12/4/90
☐ 409 Mike Stanley .05 .02 .01
☐ 410 Dave Righetti .05 .02 .01
Now with Giants
12/4/90
☐ 411 Lance Blankenship .05 .02 .01
☐ 412 Dave Bergman .05 .02 .01
☐ 413 Terry Mulholland .05 .02 .01
☐ 414 Sammy Sosa .25 .11 .03
☐ 415 Rick Sutcliffe .05 .02 .01
☐ 416 Randy Milligan .05 .02 .01
☐ 417 Bill Krueger .05 .02 .01
☐ 418 Nick Esasky .05 .02 .01
☐ 419 Jeff Reed .05 .02 .01
☐ 420 Bobby Thigpen .05 .02 .01
☐ 421 Alex Cole .05 .02 .01
☐ 422 Rick Reuschel .05 .02 .01
☐ 423 Rafael Ramirez UER .05 .02 .01
Born 1959, not 1958
☐ 424 Calvin Schiraldi .05 .02 .01
☐ 425 Andy Van Slyke .05 .02 .01
☐ 426 Joe Grahe .05 .02 .01
☐ 427 Rick Dempsey .05 .02 .01
☐ 428 John Barfield .05 .02 .01
☐ 429 Stump Merrill MG .05 .02 .01
☐ 430 Gary Gaetti .10 .05 .01
☐ 431 Paul Gibson .05 .02 .01
☐ 432 Delino DeShields .05 .02 .01
☐ 433 Pat Tabler .05 .02 .01
Now with Blue Jays
12/5/90
☐ 434 Julio Machado .05 .02 .01
☐ 435 Kevin Maas .05 .02 .01
☐ 436 Scott Bankhead .05 .02 .01
☐ 437 Doug Dascenzo .05 .02 .01
☐ 438 Vicente Palacios .05 .02 .01
☐ 439 Dickie Thon .05 .02 .01
☐ 440 George Bell .05 .02 .01
Now with Cubs
12/6/90
☐ 441 Zane Smith .05 .02 .01
☐ 442 Charlie O'Brien .05 .02 .01
☐ 443 Jeff Innis .05 .02 .01
☐ 444 Glenn Braggs .05 .02 .01
☐ 445 Greg Swindell .05 .02 .01
☐ 446 Craig Grebeck .05 .02 .01
☐ 447 John Burkett .05 .02 .01
☐ 448 Craig Lefferts .05 .02 .01
☐ 449 Juan Berenguer .05 .02 .01
☐ 450 Wade Boggs .25 .11 .03
☐ 451 Neal Heaton .05 .02 .01
☐ 452 Bill Schroeder .05 .02 .01
☐ 453 Lenny Harris .05 .02 .01
☐ 454 Kevin Appier .20 .09 .03
☐ 455 Walt Weiss .05 .02 .01
☐ 456 Charlie Leibrandt .05 .02 .01
☐ 457 Todd Hundley .20 .09 .03
☐ 458 Brian Holman .05 .02 .01
☐ 459 Tom Trebelhorn MG .05 .02 .01
☐ 460 Dave Stieb .05 .02 .01
☐ 461 Robin Ventura .20 .09 .03
☐ 462 Steve Frey .05 .02 .01
☐ 463 Dwight Smith .05 .02 .01
☐ 464 Steve Buechele .05 .02 .01
☐ 465 Ken Griffey Sr. .05 .02 .01
☐ 466 Charles Nagy .25 .11 .03
☐ 467 Dennis Cook .05 .02 .01
☐ 468 Tim Hulett .05 .02 .01
☐ 469 Chet Lemon .05 .02 .01
☐ 470 Howard Johnson .05 .02 .01
☐ 471 Mike Lieberthal .20 .09 .03
☐ 472 Kirt Manwaring .05 .02 .01
☐ 473 Curt Young .05 .02 .01
☐ 474 Phil Plantier .10 .05 .01
☐ 475 Teddy Higuera .05 .02 .01
☐ 476 Glenn Wilson .05 .02 .01
☐ 477 Mike Fetters .05 .02 .01
☐ 478 Kurt Stillwell .05 .02 .01
☐ 479 Bob Patterson .05 .02 .01
☐ 480 Dave Magadan .05 .02 .01
☐ 481 Eddie Whitson .05 .02 .01
☐ 482 Tino Martinez .15 .07 .02
☐ 483 Mike Aldrete .05 .02 .01
☐ 484 Dave LaPoint .05 .02 .01
☐ 485 Terry Pendleton .10 .05 .01
Now with Braves
12/3/90
☐ 486 Tommy Greene .05 .02 .01
☐ 487 Rafael Belliard .05 .02 .01
Now with Braves
12/18/90
☐ 488 Jeff Manto .05 .02 .01
☐ 489 Bobby Valentine MG .05 .02 .01
☐ 490 Kirk Gibson .10 .05 .01
Now with Royals
12/1/90
☐ 491 Kurt Miller .05 .02 .01
☐ 492 Ernie Whitt .05 .02 .01
☐ 493 Jose Rijo .05 .02 .01
☐ 494 Chris James .05 .02 .01
☐ 495 Charlie Hough .05 .02 .01
Now with White Sox
12/20/90
☐ 496 Marty Barrett .05 .02 .01
☐ 497 Ben McDonald .10 .05 .01
☐ 498 Mark Salas .05 .02 .01
☐ 499 Melido Perez .05 .02 .01
☐ 500 Will Clark .25 .11 .03
☐ 501 Mike Bielecki .05 .02 .01
☐ 502 Carney Lansford .05 .02 .01
☐ 503 Roy Smith .05 .02 .01
☐ 504 Julio Valera .05 .02 .01
☐ 505 Chuck Finley .10 .05 .01
☐ 506 Darnell Coles .05 .02 .01
☐ 507 Steve Jeltz .05 .02 .01
☐ 508 Mike York .05 .02 .01
☐ 509 Glenallen Hill .05 .02 .01
☐ 510 John Franco .10 .05 .01
☐ 511 Steve Balboni .05 .02 .01
☐ 512 Jose Mesa .10 .05 .01
☐ 513 Jerald Clark .05 .02 .01
☐ 514 Mike Stanton .05 .02 .01
☐ 515 Alvin Davis .05 .02 .01
☐ 516 Karl Rhodes .05 .02 .01
☐ 517 Joe Oliver .05 .02 .01
☐ 518 Cris Carpenter .05 .02 .01
☐ 519 Sparky Anderson MG .10 .05 .01
☐ 520 Mark Grace .25 .11 .03
☐ 521 Joe Orsulak .05 .02 .01
☐ 522 Stan Belinda .05 .02 .01
☐ 523 Rodney McCray .05 .02 .01
☐ 524 Darrel Akerfelds .05 .02 .01
☐ 525 Willie Randolph .10 .05 .01
☐ 526 Moises Alou .15 .07 .02
☐ 527 Checklist 4 .05 .02 .01
☐ 528 Denny Martinez .10 .05 .01
☐ 529 Marc Newfield .25 .11 .03
☐ 530 Roger Clemens .25 .11 .03
☐ 531 Dave Rohde .05 .02 .01
☐ 532 Kirk McCaskill .05 .02 .01
☐ 533 Oddibe McDowell .05 .02 .01
☐ 534 Mike Jackson .05 .02 .01
☐ 535 Ruben Sierra .05 .02 .01
☐ 536 Mike Witt .05 .02 .01
☐ 537 Jose Lind .05 .02 .01
☐ 538 Bip Roberts .05 .02 .01
☐ 539 Scott Terry .05 .02 .01
☐ 540 George Brett .75 .35 .09
☐ 541 Domingo Ramos .05 .02 .01
☐ 542 Rob Murphy .05 .02 .01
☐ 543 Junior Felix .05 .02 .01
☐ 544 Alejandro Pena .05 .02 .01
☐ 545 Dale Murphy .20 .09 .03
☐ 546 Jeff Ballard .05 .02 .01
☐ 547 Mike Pagliarulo .05 .02 .01
☐ 548 Jaime Navarro .05 .02 .01
☐ 549 John McNamara MG .05 .02 .01
☐ 550 Eric Davis .10 .05 .01
☐ 551 Bob Kipper .05 .02 .01
☐ 552 Jeff Hamilton .05 .02 .01
☐ 553 Joe Klink .05 .02 .01
☐ 554 Brian Harper .05 .02 .01
☐ 555 Turner Ward .05 .02 .01
☐ 556 Gary Ward .05 .02 .01
☐ 557 Wally Whitehurst .05 .02 .01
☐ 558 Otis Nixon .10 .05 .01
☐ 559 Adam Peterson .05 .02 .01
☐ 560 Greg Smith .05 .02 .01
Now with Dodgers
12/14/90
☐ 561 Tim McIntosh .05 .02 .01
☐ 562 Jeff Kunkel .05 .02 .01
☐ 563 Brent Knackert .05 .02 .01
☐ 564 Dante Bichette .15 .07 .02
☐ 565 Craig Biggio .15 .07 .02
☐ 566 Craig Wilson .05 .02 .01
☐ 567 Dwayne Henry .05 .02 .01
☐ 568 Ron Karkovice .05 .02 .01
☐ 569 Curt Schilling .05 .02 .01
Now with Astros
1/10/91
☐ 570 Barry Bonds .50 .23 .06
☐ 571 Pat Combs .05 .02 .01
☐ 572 Dave Anderson .05 .02 .01
☐ 573 Rich Rodriguez UER .05 .02 .01
Stats say drafted 4th
but bio says 9th round
☐ 574 John Marzano .05 .02 .01
☐ 575 Robin Yount .25 .11 .03
☐ 576 Jeff Kaiser .05 .02 .01
☐ 577 Bill Doran .05 .02 .01
☐ 578 Dave West .05 .02 .01
☐ 579 Roger Craig MG .05 .02 .01
☐ 580 Dave Stewart .10 .05 .01
☐ 581 Luis Quinones .05 .02 .01
☐ 582 Marty Clary .05 .02 .01
☐ 583 Tony Phillips .10 .05 .01
☐ 584 Kevin Brown .10 .05 .01
☐ 585 Pete O'Brien .05 .02 .01
☐ 586 Fred Lynn .05 .02 .01
☐ 587 Jose Offerman UER .05 .02 .01
Text says signed 7/24/88
but bio says 1986
☐ 588 Mark Whiten .10 .05 .01
☐ 589 Scott Ruskin .05 .02 .01
☐ 590 Eddie Murray .50 .23 .06
☐ 591 Ken Hill .10 .05 .01
☐ 592 B.J. Surhoff .10 .05 .01
☐ 593 Mike Walker .05 .02 .01
☐ 594 Rich Garces .05 .02 .01
☐ 595 Bill Landrum .05 .02 .01
☐ 596 Ronnie Walden .05 .02 .01
☐ 597 Jerry Don Gleaton .05 .02 .01
☐ 598 Sam Horn .05 .02 .01
☐ 599 Greg Myers .05 .02 .01
☐ 600 Bo Jackson .10 .05 .01
☐ 601 Bob Ojeda .05 .02 .01
Now with Dodgers
12/15/90
☐ 602 Casey Candaele .05 .02 .01
☐ 603 Wes Chamberlain .05 .02 .01
☐ 604 Billy Hatcher .05 .02 .01
☐ 605 Jeff Reardon .05 .02 .01
☐ 606 Jim Gott .05 .02 .01
☐ 607 Edgar Martinez .15 .07 .02
☐ 608 Todd Burns .05 .02 .01
☐ 609 Jeff Torborg MG .05 .02 .01
☐ 610 Andres Galarraga .20 .09 .03
☐ 611 Dave Eiland .05 .02 .01
☐ 612 Steve Lyons .05 .02 .01
☐ 613 Eric Show .05 .02 .01
Now with Athletics
12/10/90
☐ 614 Luis Salazar .05 .02 .01
☐ 615 Bert Blyleven .10 .05 .01
☐ 616 Todd Zeile .10 .05 .01
☐ 617 Bill Wegman .05 .02 .01
☐ 618 Sil Campusano .05 .02 .01
☐ 619 David Wells .05 .02 .01
☐ 620 Ozzie Guillen .05 .02 .01
☐ 621 Ted Power .05 .02 .01
Now with Reds
12/14/90
☐ 622 Jack Daugherty .05 .02 .01
☐ 623 Jeff Blauser .05 .02 .01
☐ 624 Tom Candiotti .05 .02 .01
☐ 625 Terry Steinbach .10 .05 .01
☐ 626 Gerald Young .05 .02 .01
☐ 627 Tim Layana .05 .02 .01
☐ 628 Greg Litton .05 .02 .01
☐ 629 Wes Gardner .05 .02 .01
Now with Padres
12/15/90
☐ 630 Dave Winfield .15 .07 .02
☐ 631 Mike Morgan .05 .02 .01
☐ 632 Lloyd Moseby .05 .02 .01
☐ 633 Kevin Tapani .05 .02 .01
☐ 634 Henry Cotto .05 .02 .01
☐ 635 Andy Hawkins .05 .02 .01
☐ 636 Geronimo Pena .05 .02 .01
☐ 637 Bruce Ruffin .05 .02 .01
☐ 638 Mike Macfarlane .05 .02 .01
☐ 639 Frank Robinson MG .20 .09 .03
☐ 640 Andre Dawson .10 .05 .01
☐ 641 Mike Henneman .05 .02 .01
☐ 642 Hal Morris .05 .02 .01
☐ 643 Jim Presley .05 .02 .01
☐ 644 Chuck Crim .05 .02 .01
☐ 645 Juan Samuel .05 .02 .01
☐ 646 Andujar Cedeno .05 .02 .01
☐ 647 Mark Portugal .05 .02 .01
☐ 648 Lee Stevens .05 .02 .01
☐ 649 Bill Sampen .05 .02 .01
☐ 650 Jack Clark .05 .02 .01
Now with Red Sox
12/15/90
☐ 651 Alan Mills .05 .02 .01
☐ 652 Kevin Romine .05 .02 .01
☐ 653 Anthony Telford .05 .02 .01
☐ 654 Paul Sorrento .10 .05 .01
☐ 655 Erik Hanson .05 .02 .01
☐ 656 Checklist 5 .05 .02 .01
☐ 657 Mike Kingery .05 .02 .01
☐ 658 Scott Aldred .05 .02 .01
☐ 659 Oscar Azocar .05 .02 .01
☐ 660 Lee Smith .10 .05 .01
☐ 661 Steve Lake .05 .02 .01
☐ 662 Rob Dibble .05 .02 .01
☐ 663 Greg Brock .05 .02 .01
☐ 664 John Farrell .05 .02 .01
☐ 665 Mike LaValliere .05 .02 .01
☐ 666 Danny Darwin .05 .02 .01
Now with Red Sox
12/19/90
☐ 667 Kent Anderson .05 .02 .01
☐ 668 Bill Long .05 .02 .01
☐ 669 Lou Piniella MG .05 .02 .01
☐ 670 Rickey Henderson .25 .11 .03
☐ 671 Andy McGaffigan .05 .02 .01
☐ 672 Shane Mack .05 .02 .01
☐ 673 Greg Olson UER .05 .02 .01
6 RBI in '88 at Tidewater
and 2 RBI in '87
should be 48 and 15
☐ 674 Kevin Gross .05 .02 .01
Now with Dodgers
12/3/90
☐ 675 Tom Brunansky .05 .02 .01
☐ 676 Scott Champarino .05 .02 .01
☐ 677 Billy Ripken .05 .02 .01
☐ 678 Mark Davidson .05 .02 .01
☐ 679 Bill Bathe .05 .02 .01
☐ 680 David Cone .10 .05 .01
☐ 681 Jeff Schaefer .05 .02 .01
☐ 682 Ray Lankford .25 .11 .03
☐ 683 Derek Lilliquist .05 .02 .01
☐ 684 Milt Cuyler .05 .02 .01
☐ 685 Doug Drabek .05 .02 .01
☐ 686 Mike Gallego .05 .02 .01
☐ 687 John Cerutti .05 .02 .01
☐ 688 Rosario Rodriguez .05 .02 .01
Now with Pirates
12/20/90
☐ 689 John Kruk .10 .05 .01
☐ 690 Orel Hershiser .10 .05 .01
☐ 691 Mike Blowers .05 .02 .01
☐ 692 Efrain Valdez .05 .02 .01
☐ 693 Francisco Cabrera .05 .02 .01
☐ 694 Randy Veres .05 .02 .01
☐ 695 Kevin Seitzer .05 .02 .01
☐ 696 Steve Olin .05 .02 .01
☐ 697 Shawn Abner .05 .02 .01
☐ 698 Mark Guthrie .05 .02 .01
☐ 699 Jim Lefebvre MG .05 .02 .01
☐ 700 Jose Canseco .25 .11 .03
☐ 701 Pascual Perez .05 .02 .01
☐ 702 Tim Naehring .10 .05 .01
☐ 703 Juan Agosto .05 .02 .01
Now with Cardinals
12/14/90
☐ 704 Devon White .05 .02 .01
Now with Blue Jays
12/2/90
☐ 705 Robby Thompson .05 .02 .01
☐ 706 Brad Arnsberg .05 .02 .01
☐ 707 Jim Eisenreich .10 .05 .01
☐ 708 John Mitchell .05 .02 .01
☐ 709 Matt Sinatro .05 .02 .01
☐ 710 Kent Hrbek .05 .02 .01
☐ 711 Jose DeLeon .05 .02 .01
☐ 712 Ricky Jordan .05 .02 .01
☐ 713 Scott Scudder .05 .02 .01
☐ 714 Marvell Wynne .05 .02 .01
☐ 715 Tim Burke .05 .02 .01
☐ 716 Bob Geren .05 .02 .01
☐ 717 Phil Bradley .05 .02 .01
☐ 718 Steve Crawford .05 .02 .01
☐ 719 Keith Miller .05 .02 .01
☐ 720 Cecil Fielder .10 .05 .01
☐ 721 Mark Lee .05 .02 .01
☐ 722 Wally Backman .05 .02 .01
☐ 723 Candy Maldonado .05 .02 .01
☐ 724 David Segui .10 .05 .01
☐ 725 Ron Gant .10 .05 .01
☐ 726 Phil Stephenson .05 .02 .01
☐ 727 Mookie Wilson .05 .02 .01
☐ 728 Scott Sanderson .05 .02 .01
Now with Yankees
12/31/90
☐ 729 Don Zimmer MG .05 .02 .01
☐ 730 Barry Larkin .15 .07 .02
☐ 731 Jeff Gray .05 .02 .01
☐ 732 Franklin Stubbs .05 .02 .01
Now with Brewers
12/5/90
☐ 733 Kelly Downs .05 .02 .01
☐ 734 John Russell .05 .02 .01
☐ 735 Ron Darling .05 .02 .01
☐ 736 Dick Schofield .05 .02 .01
☐ 737 Tim Crews .05 .02 .01
☐ 738 Mel Hall .05 .02 .01
☐ 739 Russ Swan .05 .02 .01
☐ 740 Ryne Sandberg .50 .23 .06
☐ 741 Jimmy Key .10 .05 .01
☐ 742 Tommy Gregg .05 .02 .01
☐ 743 Bryn Smith .05 .02 .01
☐ 744 Nelson Santovenia .05 .02 .01
☐ 745 Doug Jones .05 .02 .01
☐ 746 John Shelby .05 .02 .01
☐ 747 Tony Fossas .05 .02 .01
☐ 748 Al Newman .05 .02 .01
☐ 749 Greg W. Harris .05 .02 .01
☐ 750 Bobby Bonilla .10 .05 .01
☐ 751 Wayne Edwards .05 .02 .01
☐ 752 Kevin Bass .05 .02 .01
☐ 753 Paul Marak UER .05 .02 .01
Stats say drafted in May
but bio says Jan.
☐ 754 Bill Pecota .05 .02 .01
☐ 755 Mark Langston .05 .02 .01
☐ 756 Jeff Huson .05 .02 .01
☐ 757 Mark Gardner .05 .02 .01
☐ 758 Mike Devereaux .05 .02 .01
☐ 759 Bobby Cox MG .05 .02 .01
☐ 760 Benny Santiago .05 .02 .01
☐ 761 Larry Andersen .05 .02 .01
Now with Padres
12/21/90
☐ 762 Mitch Webster .05 .02 .01

☐ 763 Dana Kiecker	.05	.02	.01
☐ 764 Mark Carreon	.05	.02	.01
☐ 765 Shawon Dunston	.05	.02	.01
☐ 766 Jeff M. Robinson	.05	.02	.01
Now with Orioles 1/12/91			
☐ 767 Dan Wilson	.25	.11	.03
☐ 768 Donn Pall	.05	.02	.01
☐ 769 Tim Sherrill	.05	.02	.01
☐ 770 Jay Howell	.05	.02	.01
☐ 771 Gary Redus UER	.05	.02	.01
Born in Tanner, should say Athens			
☐ 772 Kent Mercker UER	.05	.02	.01
Born in Indianapolis should say Dublin, Ohio			
☐ 773 Tom Foley	.05	.02	.01
☐ 774 Dennis Rasmussen	.05	.02	.01
☐ 775 Julio Franco	.10	.05	.01
☐ 776 Brent Mayne	.05	.02	.01
☐ 777 John Candelaria	.05	.02	.01
☐ 778 Dan Gladden	.05	.02	.01
☐ 779 Carmelo Martinez	.05	.02	.01
☐ 780 Randy Myers	.05	.02	.01
☐ 781 Darryl Hamilton	.10	.05	.01
☐ 782 Jim Deshaies	.05	.02	.01
☐ 783 Joel Skinner	.05	.02	.01
☐ 784 Willie Fraser	.05	.02	.01
Now with Blue Jays 12/2/90			
☐ 785 Scott Fletcher	.05	.02	.01
☐ 786 Eric Plunk	.05	.02	.01
☐ 787 Checklist 6	.05	.02	.01
☐ 788 Bob Milacki	.05	.02	.01
☐ 789 Tom Lasorda MG	.20	.09	.03
☐ 790 Ken Griffey Jr.	3.00	1.35	.35
☐ 791 Mike Benjamin	.05	.02	.01
☐ 792 Mike Greenwell	.05	.02	.01

1991 O-Pee-Chee Box Bottoms

The 1991 O-Pee-Chee Box Bottom cards comprise four different box bottoms from the bottoms of wax pack boxes, with four cards each, for a total of 16 standard-size cards. The cards are nearly identical to the 1991 Topps Box Bottom cards. The fronts feature yellow-bordered color player action shots. The player's name and position appear at the bottom and his team name appears just above. The traded players have their new teams and dates of trade printed on the photo. The pink and blue horizontal backs carry player career highlights in both English and French. The cards are lettered (A-P) rather than numbered on the back.

	MINT	NRMT	EXC
COMPLETE SET (16)	4.00	1.80	.50
COMMON CARD (A-P)	.15	.07	.02
☐ A Bert Blyleven	.25	.11	.03
☐ B George Brett	1.00	.45	.12
☐ C Brett Butler	.25	.11	.03
☐ D Andre Dawson	.25	.11	.03
☐ E Dwight Evans	.25	.11	.03
☐ F Carlton Fisk	.25	.11	.03
☐ G Alfredo Griffin	.15	.07	.02
☐ H Rickey Henderson	.50	.23	.06
☐ I Willie McGee	.25	.11	.03
☐ J Dale Murphy	.40	.18	.05
☐ K Eddie Murray	.60	.25	.07
☐ L Dave Parker	.25	.11	.03
☐ M Jeff Reardon	.15	.07	.02
☐ N Nolan Ryan	2.50	1.10	.30
☐ O Juan Samuel	.15	.07	.02
☐ P Robin Yount	.50	.23	.06

1992 O-Pee-Chee

The 1992 O-Pee-Chee set contains 792 standard-size cards. These cards were sold in ten-card wax packs with a stick of bubble gum. The fronts have either posed or action color player photos on a white card face. Different color stripes frame the pictures, and the player's name and team name appear in two short color stripes respectively at the bottom. In English and French, the horizontally oriented backs have biography and complete career batting or pitching record. In addition, some of the cards have a picture of a baseball field and stadium on the back. Special subsets included are Record Breakers (2-5), Prospects (58, 126, 179, 473, 551, 591, 618, 656, 676) and a five-card tribute to Gary Carter (45, 387, 389, 399, 402). Each wax pack wrapper served as an entry blank offering each collector the chance to win one of 1,000 complete factory sets of 1992 O-Pee-Chee Premier baseball cards.

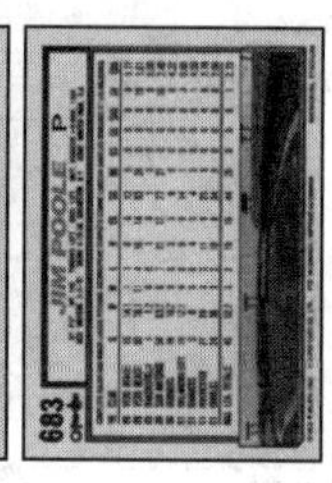

	MINT	NRMT	EXC
COMPLETE SET (792)	25.00	11.00	3.10
COMPLETE FACT.SET (792)	25.00	11.00	3.10
COMMON CARD (1-792)	.05	.02	.01
☐ 1 Nolan Ryan	1.00	.45	.12
☐ 2 Rickey Henderson RB	.15	.07	.02
(Some cards have print marks that show 1.991 on the front)			
☐ 3 Jeff Reardon RB	.05	.02	.01
☐ 4 Nolan Ryan RB	.50	.23	.06
☐ 5 Dave Winfield RB	.15	.07	.02
☐ 6 Brien Taylor	.05	.02	.01
☐ 7 Jim Olander	.05	.02	.01
☐ 8 Bryan Hickerson	.05	.02	.01
☐ 9 Jon Farrell	.05	.02	.01
☐ 10 Wade Boggs	.20	.09	.03
☐ 11 Jack McDowell	.10	.05	.01
☐ 12 Luis Gonzalez	.05	.02	.01
☐ 13 Mike Scioscia	.05	.02	.01
☐ 14 Wes Chamberlain	.05	.02	.01
☐ 15 Dennis Martinez	.10	.05	.01
☐ 16 Jeff Montgomery	.05	.02	.01
☐ 17 Randy Milligan	.05	.02	.01
☐ 18 Greg Cadaret	.05	.02	.01
☐ 19 Jamie Quirk	.05	.02	.01
☐ 20 Bip Roberts	.05	.02	.01
☐ 21 Buck Rodgers MG	.05	.02	.01
☐ 22 Bill Wegman	.05	.02	.01
☐ 23 Chuck Knoblauch	.15	.07	.02
☐ 24 Randy Myers	.05	.02	.01
☐ 25 Ron Gant	.10	.05	.01
☐ 26 Mike Bielecki	.05	.02	.01
☐ 27 Juan Gonzalez	.75	.35	.09
☐ 28 Mike Schooler	.05	.02	.01
☐ 29 Mickey Tettleton	.05	.02	.01
☐ 30 John Kruk	.10	.05	.01
☐ 31 Bryn Smith	.05	.02	.01
☐ 32 Chris Nabholz	.05	.02	.01
☐ 33 Carlos Baerga	.20	.09	.03
☐ 34 Jeff Juden	.05	.02	.01
☐ 35 Dave Righetti	.05	.02	.01
☐ 36 Scott Ruffcorn	.05	.02	.01
☐ 37 Luis Polonia	.05	.02	.01
☐ 38 Tom Candiotti	.05	.02	.01
Now with Dodgers 12-3-91			
☐ 39 Greg Olson	.05	.02	.01
☐ 40 Cal Ripken	2.50	1.10	.30
Lou Gehrig			
☐ 41 Craig Lefferts	.05	.02	.01
☐ 42 Mike Macfarlane	.05	.02	.01
☐ 43 Jose Lind	.05	.02	.01
☐ 44 Rick Aguilera	.05	.02	.01
☐ 45 Gary Carter	.10	.05	.01
☐ 46 Steve Farr	.05	.02	.01
☐ 47 Rex Hudler	.05	.02	.01
☐ 48 Scott Scudder	.05	.02	.01
☐ 49 Damon Berryhill	.05	.02	.01
☐ 50 Ken Griffey Jr.	1.50	.70	.19
☐ 51 Tom Runnells MG	.05	.02	.01
☐ 52 Juan Bell	.05	.02	.01
☐ 53 Tommy Gregg	.05	.02	.01
☐ 54 David Wells	.05	.02	.01
☐ 55 Rafael Palmeiro	.15	.07	.02
☐ 56 Charlie O'Brien	.05	.02	.01
☐ 57 Donn Pall	.05	.02	.01
☐ 58 1992 Prospects C	.15	.07	.02
Brad Ausmus			
Jim Campanis Jr.			
Dave Nilsson			
Doug Robbins			
☐ 59 Mo Vaughn	.50	.23	.06
☐ 60 Tony Fernandez	.05	.02	.01
☐ 61 Paul O'Neill	.10	.05	.01
☐ 62 Gene Nelson	.05	.02	.01
☐ 63 Randy Ready	.05	.02	.01
☐ 64 Bob Kipper	.05	.02	.01
Now with Twins 12-17-91			
☐ 65 Willie McGee	.10	.05	.01
☐ 66 Scott Stahoviak	.10	.05	.01
☐ 67 Luis Salazar	.05	.02	.01
☐ 68 Marvin Freeman	.05	.02	.01
☐ 69 Kenny Lofton	1.50	.70	.19
Now with Indians 12-10-91			
☐ 70 Gary Gaetti	.10	.05	.01
☐ 71 Erik Hanson	.05	.02	.01
☐ 72 Eddie Zosky	.05	.02	.01
☐ 73 Brian Barnes	.05	.02	.01
☐ 74 Scott Leius	.05	.02	.01
☐ 75 Bret Saberhagen	.05	.02	.01
☐ 76 Mike Gallego	.05	.02	.01
☐ 77 Jack Armstrong	.05	.02	.01
Now with Indians 11-15-91			
☐ 78 Ivan Rodriguez	.50	.23	.06
☐ 79 Jesse Orosco	.05	.02	.01
☐ 80 David Justice	.15	.07	.02
☐ 81 Ced Landrum	.05	.02	.01
☐ 82 Doug Simons	.05	.02	.01
☐ 83 Tommy Greene	.05	.02	.01
☐ 84 Leo Gomez	.05	.02	.01
☐ 85 Jose DeLeon	.05	.02	.01
☐ 86 Steve Finley	.10	.05	.01
☐ 87 Bob MacDonald	.05	.02	.01
☐ 88 Darrin Jackson	.05	.02	.01
☐ 89 Neal Heaton	.05	.02	.01
☐ 90 Robin Yount	.15	.07	.02
☐ 91 Jeff Reed	.05	.02	.01
☐ 92 Lenny Harris	.05	.02	.01
☐ 93 Reggie Jefferson	.10	.05	.01
☐ 94 Sammy Sosa	.25	.11	.03
☐ 95 Scott Bailes	.05	.02	.01
☐ 96 Tom McKinnon	.05	.02	.01
☐ 97 Luis Rivera	.05	.02	.01
☐ 98 Mike Harkey	.05	.02	.01
☐ 99 Jeff Treadway	.05	.02	.01
☐ 100 Jose Canseco	.15	.07	.02
☐ 101 Omar Vizquel	.10	.05	.01
☐ 102 Scott Kamieniecki	.05	.02	.01
☐ 103 Ricky Jordan	.05	.02	.01
☐ 104 Jeff Ballard	.05	.02	.01
☐ 105 Felix Jose	.05	.02	.01
☐ 106 Mike Boddicker	.05	.02	.01
☐ 107 Dan Pasqua	.05	.02	.01
☐ 108 Mike Timlin	.05	.02	.01
☐ 109 Roger Craig MG	.05	.02	.01
☐ 110 Ryne Sandberg	.50	.23	.06
☐ 111 Mark Carreon	.05	.02	.01
☐ 112 Oscar Azocar	.05	.02	.01
☐ 113 Mike Greenwell	.05	.02	.01
☐ 114 Mark Portugal	.05	.02	.01
☐ 115 Terry Pendleton	.05	.02	.01
☐ 116 Willie Randolph	.10	.05	.01
Now with Mets 12-20-91			
☐ 117 Scott Terry	.05	.02	.01
☐ 118 Chili Davis	.10	.05	.01
☐ 119 Mark Gardner	.05	.02	.01
☐ 120 Alan Trammell	.10	.05	.01
☐ 121 Derek Bell	.25	.11	.03
☐ 122 Gary Varsho	.05	.02	.01
☐ 123 Bob Ojeda	.05	.02	.01
☐ 124 Shawn Livsey	.05	.02	.01
☐ 125 Chris Hoiles	.05	.02	.01
☐ 126 1992 Prospects 1B	1.00	.45	.12
Ryan Klesko			
John Jaha			
Rico Brogna			
Dave Staton			
☐ 127 Carlos Quintana	.05	.02	.01
☐ 128 Kurt Stillwell	.05	.02	.01
☐ 129 Melido Perez	.05	.02	.01
☐ 130 Alvin Davis	.05	.02	.01
☐ 131 Checklist 1-132	.05	.02	.01
☐ 132 Eric Show	.05	.02	.01
☐ 133 Rance Mulliniks	.05	.02	.01
☐ 134 Darryl Kile	.05	.02	.01
☐ 135 Von Hayes	.05	.02	.01
Now with Angels 12-8-91			
☐ 136 Bill Doran	.05	.02	.01
☐ 137 Jeff D. Robinson	.05	.02	.01
☐ 138 Monty Fariss	.05	.02	.01
☐ 139 Jeff Innis	.05	.02	.01
☐ 140 Mark Grace UER	.20	.09	.03
(Home Calie., should be Calif.)			
☐ 141 Jim Leyland MG UER	.10	.05	.01
(No closed parenthesis after East in 1991)			
☐ 142 Todd Van Poppel	.05	.02	.01
☐ 143 Paul Gibson	.05	.02	.01
☐ 144 Bill Swift	.05	.02	.01
☐ 145 Danny Tartabull	.05	.02	.01
Now with Yankees 1-6-92			
☐ 146 Al Newman	.05	.02	.01
☐ 147 Cris Carpenter	.05	.02	.01
☐ 148 Anthony Young	.05	.02	.01
☐ 149 Brian Bohanon	.05	.02	.01
☐ 150 Roger Clemens UER	.25	.11	.03
(League leading ERA in 1990 not italicized)			
☐ 151 Jeff Hamilton	.05	.02	.01
☐ 152 Charlie Leibrandt	.05	.02	.01
☐ 153 Ron Karkovice	.05	.02	.01
☐ 154 Hensley Meulens	.05	.02	.01
☐ 155 Scott Bankhead	.05	.02	.01
☐ 156 Manny Ramirez	1.50	.70	.19
☐ 157 Keith Miller	.05	.02	.01
Now with Royals 12-11-91			
☐ 158 Todd Frohwirth	.05	.02	.01
☐ 159 Darrin Fletcher	.05	.02	.01
Now with Expos 12-9-91			
☐ 160 Bobby Bonilla	.10	.05	.01
☐ 161 Casey Candaele	.05	.02	.01
☐ 162 Paul Faries	.05	.02	.01
☐ 163 Dana Kiecker	.05	.02	.01
☐ 164 Shane Mack	.05	.02	.01
☐ 165 Mark Langston	.05	.02	.01
☐ 166 Geronimo Pena	.05	.02	.01
☐ 167 Andy Allanson	.05	.02	.01
☐ 168 Dwight Smith	.05	.02	.01
☐ 169 Chuck Crim	.05	.02	.01
Now with Angels 12-10-91			
☐ 170 Alex Cole	.05	.02	.01
☐ 171 Bill Plummer MG	.05	.02	.01
☐ 172 Juan Berenguer	.05	.02	.01
☐ 173 Brian Downing	.05	.02	.01
☐ 174 Steve Frey	.05	.02	.01
☐ 175 Orel Hershiser	.10	.05	.01
☐ 176 Ramon Garcia	.05	.02	.01
☐ 177 Dan Gladden	.05	.02	.01
Now with Tigers 12-19-91			
☐ 178 Jim Acker	.05	.02	.01
☐ 179 1992 Prospects 2B	.05	.02	.01
Bobby DeJardin			
Cesar Bernhardt			
Armando Moreno			
Andy Stankiewicz			
☐ 180 Kevin Mitchell	.05	.02	.01
☐ 181 Hector Villanueva	.05	.02	.01
☐ 182 Jeff Reardon	.05	.02	.01
☐ 183 Brent Mayne	.05	.02	.01
☐ 184 Jimmy Jones	.05	.02	.01
☐ 185 Benito Santiago	.05	.02	.01
☐ 186 Cliff Floyd	.15	.07	.02
☐ 187 Ernie Riles	.05	.02	.01
☐ 188 Jose Guzman	.05	.02	.01
☐ 189 Junior Felix	.05	.02	.01
☐ 190 Glenn Davis	.05	.02	.01
☐ 191 Charlie Hough	.05	.02	.01
☐ 192 Dave Fleming	.05	.02	.01
☐ 193 Omar Olivares	.05	.02	.01
☐ 194 Eric Karros	.25	.11	.03
☐ 195 David Cone	.10	.05	.01
☐ 196 Frank Castillo	.05	.02	.01
☐ 197 Glenn Braggs	.05	.02	.01
☐ 198 Scott Aldred	.05	.02	.01
☐ 199 Jeff Blauser	.05	.02	.01
☐ 200 Len Dykstra	.10	.05	.01
☐ 201 Buck Showalter MG	.15	.07	.02
☐ 202 Rick Honeycutt	.05	.02	.01
☐ 203 Greg Myers	.05	.02	.01
☐ 204 Trevor Wilson	.05	.02	.01
☐ 205 Jay Howell	.05	.02	.01
☐ 206 Luis Sojo	.05	.02	.01
☐ 207 Jack Clark	.05	.02	.01
☐ 208 Julio Machado	.05	.02	.01
☐ 209 Lloyd McClendon	.05	.02	.01
☐ 210 Ozzie Guillen	.05	.02	.01
☐ 211 Jeremy Hernandez	.05	.02	.01
☐ 212 Randy Velarde	.05	.02	.01
☐ 213 Les Lancaster	.05	.02	.01
☐ 214 Andy Mota	.05	.02	.01
☐ 215 Rich Gossage	.10	.05	.01
☐ 216 Brent Gates	.15	.07	.02
☐ 217 Brian Harper	.05	.02	.01
☐ 218 Mike Flanagan	.05	.02	.01
☐ 219 Jerry Browne	.05	.02	.01
☐ 220 Jose Rijo	.05	.02	.01
☐ 221 Skeeter Barnes	.05	.02	.01
☐ 222 Jaime Navarro	.05	.02	.01
☐ 223 Mel Hall	.05	.02	.01
☐ 224 Bret Barberie	.05	.02	.01
☐ 225 Roberto Alomar	.20	.09	.03
☐ 226 Pete Smith	.05	.02	.01
☐ 227 Daryl Boston	.05	.02	.01
☐ 228 Eddie Whitson	.05	.02	.01
☐ 229 Shawn Boskie	.05	.02	.01
☐ 230 Dick Schofield	.05	.02	.01
☐ 231 Brian Drahman	.05	.02	.01
☐ 232 John Smiley	.05	.02	.01
☐ 233 Mitch Webster	.05	.02	.01
☐ 234 Terry Steinbach	.10	.05	.01
☐ 235 Jack Morris	.10	.05	.01
Now with Blue Jays 12-18-91			
☐ 236 Bill Pecota	.05	.02	.01
Now with Mets 12-11-91			
☐ 237 Jose Hernandez	.05	.02	.01
☐ 238 Greg Litton	.05	.02	.01
☐ 239 Brian Holman	.05	.02	.01
☐ 240 Andres Galarraga	.15	.07	.02
☐ 241 Gerald Young	.05	.02	.01
☐ 242 Mike Mussina	.50	.23	.06
☐ 243 Alvaro Espinoza	.05	.02	.01
☐ 244 Darren Daulton	.10	.05	.01
☐ 245 John Smoltz	.15	.07	.02
☐ 246 Jason Pruitt	.05	.02	.01
☐ 247 Chuck Finley	.10	.05	.01
☐ 248 Jim Gantner	.05	.02	.01
☐ 249 Tony Fossas	.05	.02	.01
☐ 250 Ken Griffey Sr.	.05	.02	.01
☐ 251 Kevin Elster	.05	.02	.01
☐ 252 Dennis Rasmussen	.05	.02	.01
☐ 253 Terry Kennedy	.05	.02	.01
☐ 254 Ryan Bowen	.05	.02	.01

☐ 255 Robin Ventura	.10	.05	.01
☐ 256 Mike Aldrete	.05	.02	.01
☐ 257 Jeff Russell	.05	.02	.01
☐ 258 Jim Lindeman	.05	.02	.01
☐ 259 Ron Darling	.05	.02	.01
☐ 260 Devon White	.05	.02	.01
☐ 261 Tom Lasorda MG	.15	.07	.02
☐ 262 Terry Lee	.05	.02	.01
☐ 263 Bob Patterson	.05	.02	.01
☐ 264 Checklist 133-264	.05	.02	.01
☐ 265 Teddy Higuera	.05	.02	.01
☐ 266 Roberto Kelly	.05	.02	.01
☐ 267 Steve Bedrosian	.05	.02	.01
☐ 268 Brady Anderson	.15	.07	.02
☐ 269 Ruben Amaro Jr.	.05	.02	.01
☐ 270 Tony Gwynn	.75	.35	.09
☐ 271 Tracy Jones	.05	.02	.01
☐ 272 Jerry Don Gleaton	.05	.02	.01
☐ 273 Craig Grebeck	.05	.02	.01
☐ 274 Bob Scanlan	.05	.02	.01
☐ 275 Todd Zeile	.05	.02	.01
☐ 276 Shawn Green	.50	.23	.06
☐ 277 Scott Chiamparino	.05	.02	.01
☐ 278 Darryl Hamilton	.05	.02	.01
☐ 279 Jim Clancy	.05	.02	.01
☐ 280 Carlos Martinez	.05	.02	.01
☐ 281 Kevin Appier	.10	.05	.01
☐ 282 John Wehner	.05	.02	.01
☐ 283 Reggie Sanders	.15	.07	.02
☐ 284 Gene Larkin	.05	.02	.01
☐ 285 Bob Welch	.05	.02	.01
☐ 286 Gilberto Reyes	.05	.02	.01
☐ 287 Pete Schourek	.05	.02	.01
☐ 288 Andujar Cedeno	.05	.02	.01
☐ 289 Mike Morgan	.05	.02	.01
Now with Cubs			
12-3-91			
☐ 290 Bo Jackson	.10	.05	.01
☐ 291 Phil Garner MG	.05	.02	.01
☐ 292 Ray Lankford	.15	.07	.02
☐ 293 Mike Henneman	.05	.02	.01
☐ 294 Dave Valle	.05	.02	.01
☐ 295 Alonzo Powell	.05	.02	.01
☐ 296 Tom Brunansky	.05	.02	.01
☐ 297 Kevin Brown	.10	.05	.01
☐ 298 Kelly Gruber	.05	.02	.01
☐ 299 Charles Nagy	.10	.05	.01
☐ 300 Don Mattingly	1.00	.45	.12
☐ 301 Kirk McCaskill	.05	.02	.01
Now with White Sox			
12-28-91			
☐ 302 Joey Cora	.10	.05	.01
☐ 303 Dan Plesac	.05	.02	.01
☐ 304 Joe Oliver	.05	.02	.01
☐ 305 Tom Glavine	.15	.07	.02
☐ 306 Al Shirley	.05	.02	.01
☐ 307 Bruce Ruffin	.05	.02	.01
☐ 308 Craig Shipley	.05	.02	.01
☐ 309 Dave Martinez	.05	.02	.01
Now with Reds			
12-11-91			
☐ 310 Jose Mesa	.10	.05	.01
☐ 311 Henry Cotto	.05	.02	.01
☐ 312 Mike LaValliere	.05	.02	.01
☐ 313 Kevin Tapani	.05	.02	.01
☐ 314 Jeff Huson	.05	.02	.01
☐ 315 Juan Samuel	.05	.02	.01
☐ 316 Curt Schilling	.05	.02	.01
☐ 317 Mike Bordick	.05	.02	.01
☐ 318 Steve Howe	.05	.02	.01
☐ 319 Tony Phillips	.10	.05	.01
☐ 320 George Bell	.05	.02	.01
☐ 321 Lou Piniella MG	.05	.02	.01
☐ 322 Tim Burke	.05	.02	.01
☐ 323 Milt Thompson	.05	.02	.01
☐ 324 Danny Darwin	.05	.02	.01
☐ 325 Joe Orsulak	.05	.02	.01
☐ 326 Eric King	.05	.02	.01
☐ 327 Jay Buhner	.15	.07	.02
☐ 328 Joel Johnston	.05	.02	.01
☐ 329 Franklin Stubbs	.05	.02	.01
☐ 330 Will Clark	.25	.11	.03
☐ 331 Steve Lake	.05	.02	.01
☐ 332 Chris Jones	.05	.02	.01
Now with Astros			
12-19-91			
☐ 333 Pat Tabler	.05	.02	.01
☐ 334 Kevin Gross	.05	.02	.01
☐ 335 Dave Henderson	.05	.02	.01
☐ 336 Greg Anthony	.05	.02	.01
☐ 337 Alejandro Pena	.05	.02	.01
☐ 338 Shawn Abner	.05	.02	.01
☐ 339 Tom Browning	.05	.02	.01
☐ 340 Otis Nixon	.10	.05	.01
☐ 341 Bob Geren	.05	.02	.01
Now with Reds			
12-2-91			
☐ 342 Tim Spehr	.05	.02	.01
☐ 343 John Vander Wal	.05	.02	.01
☐ 344 Jack Daugherty	.05	.02	.01
☐ 345 Zane Smith	.05	.02	.01
☐ 346 Rheal Cormier	.05	.02	.01
☐ 347 Kent Hrbek	.10	.05	.01
☐ 348 Rick Wilkins	.05	.02	.01
☐ 349 Steve Lyons	.05	.02	.01
☐ 350 Gregg Olson	.05	.02	.01
☐ 351 Greg Riddoch MG	.05	.02	.01
☐ 352 Ed Nunez	.05	.02	.01
☐ 353 Braulio Castillo	.05	.02	.01
☐ 354 Dave Bergman	.05	.02	.01
☐ 355 Warren Newson	.05	.02	.01
☐ 356 Luis Quinones	.05	.02	.01
Now with Twins			
1-9-92			
☐ 357 Mike Witt	.05	.02	.01
☐ 358 Ted Wood	.05	.02	.01
☐ 359 Mike Moore	.05	.02	.01
☐ 360 Lance Parrish	.05	.02	.01
☐ 361 Barry Jones	.05	.02	.01
☐ 362 Javier Ortiz	.05	.02	.01
☐ 363 John Candelaria	.05	.02	.01
☐ 364 Glenallen Hill	.05	.02	.01
☐ 365 Duane Ward	.05	.02	.01
☐ 366 Checklist 265-396	.05	.02	.01
☐ 367 Rafael Belliard	.05	.02	.01
☐ 368 Bill Krueger	.05	.02	.01
☐ 369 Steve Whitaker	.05	.02	.01
☐ 370 Shawon Dunston	.05	.02	.01
☐ 371 Dante Bichette	.15	.07	.02
☐ 372 Kip Gross	.05	.02	.01
Now with Dodgers			
11-27-91			
☐ 373 Don Robinson	.05	.02	.01
☐ 374 Bernie Williams	.50	.23	.06
☐ 375 Bert Blyleven	.10	.05	.01
☐ 376 Chris Donnels	.05	.02	.01
☐ 377 Bob Zupcic	.05	.02	.01
☐ 378 Joel Skinner	.05	.02	.01
☐ 379 Steve Chitren	.05	.02	.01
☐ 380 Barry Bonds	.50	.23	.06
☐ 381 Sparky Anderson MG	.10	.05	.01
☐ 382 Sid Fernandez	.05	.02	.01
☐ 383 Dave Hollins	.05	.02	.01
☐ 384 Mark Lee	.05	.02	.01
☐ 385 Tim Wallach	.05	.02	.01
☐ 386 Lance Blankenship	.05	.02	.01
☐ 387 Gary Carter	.15	.07	.02
Tribute			
☐ 388 Ron Tingley	.05	.02	.01
☐ 389 Gary Carter	.15	.07	.02
Tribute			
☐ 390 Gene Harris	.05	.02	.01
☐ 391 Jeff Schaefer	.05	.02	.01
☐ 392 Mark Grant	.05	.02	.01
☐ 393 Carl Willis	.05	.02	.01
☐ 394 Al Leiter	.10	.05	.01
☐ 395 Ron Robinson	.05	.02	.01
☐ 396 Tim Hulett	.05	.02	.01
☐ 397 Craig Worthington	.05	.02	.01
☐ 398 John Orton	.05	.02	.01
☐ 399 Gary Carter	.15	.07	.02
Tribute			
☐ 400 John Dopson	.05	.02	.01
☐ 401 Moises Alou	.15	.07	.02
☐ 402 Gary Carter	.15	.07	.02
Tribute			
☐ 403 Matt Young	.05	.02	.01
☐ 404 Wayne Edwards	.05	.02	.01
☐ 405 Nick Esasky	.05	.02	.01
☐ 406 Dave Eiland	.05	.02	.01
☐ 407 Mike Brumley	.05	.02	.01
☐ 408 Bob Milacki	.05	.02	.01
☐ 409 Geno Petralli	.05	.02	.01
☐ 410 Dave Stewart	.10	.05	.01
☐ 411 Mike Jackson	.05	.02	.01
☐ 412 Luis Aquino	.05	.02	.01
☐ 413 Tim Teufel	.05	.02	.01
☐ 414 Jeff Ware	.05	.02	.01
☐ 415 Jim Deshaies	.05	.02	.01
☐ 416 Ellis Burks	.10	.05	.01
☐ 417 Allan Anderson	.05	.02	.01
☐ 418 Alfredo Griffin	.05	.02	.01
☐ 419 Wally Whitehurst	.05	.02	.01
☐ 420 Sandy Alomar Jr.	.10	.05	.01
☐ 421 Juan Agosto	.05	.02	.01
☐ 422 Sam Horn	.05	.02	.01
☐ 423 Jeff Fassero	.10	.05	.01
☐ 424 Paul McClellan	.05	.02	.01
☐ 425 Cecil Fielder	.10	.05	.01
☐ 426 Tim Raines	.10	.05	.01
☐ 427 Eddie Taubensee	.05	.02	.01
☐ 428 Dennis Boyd	.05	.02	.01
☐ 429 Tony LaRussa MG	.10	.05	.01
☐ 430 Steve Sax	.05	.02	.01
☐ 431 Tom Gordon	.05	.02	.01
☐ 432 Billy Hatcher	.05	.02	.01
☐ 433 Cal Eldred	.05	.02	.01
☐ 434 Wally Backman	.05	.02	.01
☐ 435 Mark Eichhorn	.05	.02	.01
☐ 436 Mookie Wilson	.05	.02	.01
☐ 437 Scott Servais	.05	.02	.01
☐ 438 Mike Maddux	.05	.02	.01
☐ 439 Chico Walker	.05	.02	.01
☐ 440 Doug Drabek	.05	.02	.01
☐ 441 Rob Deer	.05	.02	.01
☐ 442 Dave West	.05	.02	.01
☐ 443 Spike Owen	.05	.02	.01
☐ 444 Tyrone Hill	.05	.02	.01
☐ 445 Matt Williams	.15	.07	.02
☐ 446 Mark Lewis	.05	.02	.01
☐ 447 David Segui	.05	.02	.01
☐ 448 Tom Pagnozzi	.05	.02	.01
☐ 449 Jeff Johnson	.05	.02	.01
☐ 450 Mark McGwire	.50	.23	.06
☐ 451 Tom Henke	.05	.02	.01
☐ 452 Wilson Alvarez	.15	.07	.02
☐ 453 Gary Redus	.05	.02	.01
☐ 454 Darren Holmes	.05	.02	.01
☐ 455 Pete O'Brien	.05	.02	.01
☐ 456 Pat Combs	.05	.02	.01
☐ 457 Hubie Brooks	.05	.02	.01
Now with Angels			
12-10-91			
☐ 458 Frank Tanana	.05	.02	.01
☐ 459 Tom Kelly MG	.05	.02	.01
☐ 460 Andre Dawson	.10	.05	.01
☐ 461 Doug Jones	.05	.02	.01
☐ 462 Rich Rodriguez	.05	.02	.01
☐ 463 Mike Simms	.05	.02	.01
☐ 464 Mike Jeffcoat	.05	.02	.01
☐ 465 Barry Larkin	.15	.07	.02
☐ 466 Stan Belinda	.05	.02	.01
☐ 467 Lonnie Smith	.05	.02	.01
☐ 468 Greg A. Harris	.05	.02	.01
☐ 469 Jim Eisenreich	.05	.02	.01
☐ 470 Pedro Guerrero	.05	.02	.01
☐ 471 Jose DeJesus	.05	.02	.01
☐ 472 Rich Rowland	.05	.02	.01
☐ 473 1992 Prospects 3B UER	.15	.07	.02
Frank Bolick			
Craig Paquette			
Tom Redington			
Paul Russo			
(Line around top border)			
☐ 474 Mike Rossiter	.05	.02	.01
☐ 475 Robby Thompson	.05	.02	.01
☐ 476 Randy Bush	.05	.02	.01
☐ 477 Greg Hibbard	.05	.02	.01
☐ 478 Dale Sveum	.05	.02	.01
Now with Phillies			
12-11-91			
☐ 479 Chito Martinez	.05	.02	.01
☐ 480 Scott Sanderson	.05	.02	.01
☐ 481 Tino Martinez	.10	.05	.01
☐ 482 Jimmy Key	.10	.05	.01
☐ 483 Terry Shumpert	.05	.02	.01
☐ 484 Mike Hartley	.05	.02	.01
☐ 485 Chris Sabo	.05	.02	.01
☐ 486 Bob Walk	.05	.02	.01
☐ 487 John Cerutti	.05	.02	.01
☐ 488 Scott Cooper	.05	.02	.01
☐ 489 Bobby Cox MG	.10	.05	.01
☐ 490 Julio Franco	.10	.05	.01
☐ 491 Jeff Brantley	.10	.05	.01
☐ 492 Mike Devereaux	.05	.02	.01
☐ 493 Jose Offerman	.05	.02	.01
☐ 494 Gary Thurman	.05	.02	.01
☐ 495 Carney Lansford	.05	.02	.01
☐ 496 Joe Grahe	.05	.02	.01
☐ 497 Andy Ashby	.10	.05	.01
☐ 498 Gerald Perry	.05	.02	.01
☐ 499 Dave Otto	.05	.02	.01
☐ 500 Vince Coleman	.05	.02	.01
☐ 501 Rob Mallicoat	.05	.02	.01
☐ 502 Greg Briley	.05	.02	.01
☐ 503 Pascual Perez	.05	.02	.01
☐ 504 Aaron Sele	.25	.11	.03
☐ 505 Bobby Thigpen	.05	.02	.01
☐ 506 Todd Benzinger	.05	.02	.01
☐ 507 Candy Maldonado	.05	.02	.01
☐ 508 Bill Gullickson	.05	.02	.01
☐ 509 Doug Dascenzo	.05	.02	.01
☐ 510 Frank Viola	.05	.02	.01
☐ 511 Kenny Rogers	.10	.05	.01
☐ 512 Mike Heath	.05	.02	.01
☐ 513 Kevin Bass	.05	.02	.01
☐ 514 Kim Batiste	.05	.02	.01
☐ 515 Delino DeShields	.05	.02	.01
☐ 516 Ed Sprague	.10	.05	.01
☐ 517 Jim Gott	.05	.02	.01
☐ 518 Jose Melendez	.05	.02	.01
☐ 519 Hal McRae MG	.05	.02	.01
☐ 520 Jeff Bagwell	1.25	.55	.16
☐ 521 Joe Hesketh	.05	.02	.01
☐ 522 Milt Cuyler	.05	.02	.01
☐ 523 Shawn Hillegas	.05	.02	.01
☐ 524 Don Slaught	.05	.02	.01
☐ 525 Randy Johnson	.25	.11	.03
☐ 526 Doug Piatt	.05	.02	.01
☐ 527 Checklist 397-528	.05	.02	.01
☐ 528 Steve Foster	.05	.02	.01
☐ 529 Joe Girardi	.05	.02	.01
☐ 530 Jim Abbott	.05	.02	.01
☐ 531 Larry Walker	.15	.07	.02
☐ 532 Mike Huff	.05	.02	.01
☐ 533 Mackey Sasser	.05	.02	.01
☐ 534 Benji Gil	.05	.02	.01
☐ 535 Dave Stieb	.05	.02	.01
☐ 536 Willie Wilson	.05	.02	.01
☐ 537 Mark Leiter	.05	.02	.01
☐ 538 Jose Uribe	.05	.02	.01
☐ 539 Thomas Howard	.05	.02	.01
☐ 540 Ben McDonald	.05	.02	.01
☐ 541 Jose Tolentino	.05	.02	.01
☐ 542 Keith Mitchell	.05	.02	.01
☐ 543 Jerome Walton	.05	.02	.01
☐ 544 Cliff Brantley	.05	.02	.01
☐ 545 Andy Van Slyke	.05	.02	.01
☐ 546 Paul Sorrento	.05	.02	.01
☐ 547 Herm Winningham	.05	.02	.01
☐ 548 Mark Guthrie	.05	.02	.01
☐ 549 Joe Torre MG	.10	.05	.01
☐ 550 Darryl Strawberry	.10	.05	.01
☐ 551 1992 Prospects SS UER	2.00	.90	.25
Wilfredo Cordero			
Chipper Jones			
Manny Alexander			
Alex Arias			
(No line around			
top border)			
☐ 552 Dave Gallagher	.05	.02	.01
☐ 553 Edgar Martinez	.10	.05	.01
☐ 554 Donald Harris	.05	.02	.01
☐ 555 Frank Thomas	2.00	.90	.25
☐ 556 Storm Davis	.05	.02	.01
☐ 557 Dickie Thon	.05	.02	.01
☐ 558 Scott Garrelts	.05	.02	.01
☐ 559 Steve Olin	.05	.02	.01
☐ 560 Rickey Henderson	.25	.11	.03
☐ 561 Jose Vizcaino	.05	.02	.01
☐ 562 Wade Taylor	.05	.02	.01
☐ 563 Pat Borders	.05	.02	.01
☐ 564 Jimmy Gonzalez	.05	.02	.01
☐ 565 Lee Smith	.10	.05	.01
☐ 566 Bill Sampen	.05	.02	.01
☐ 567 Dean Palmer	.10	.05	.01
☐ 568 Bryan Harvey	.05	.02	.01
☐ 569 Tony Pena	.05	.02	.01
☐ 570 Lou Whitaker	.10	.05	.01
☐ 571 Randy Tomlin	.05	.02	.01
☐ 572 Greg Vaughn	.10	.05	.01
☐ 573 Kelly Downs	.05	.02	.01
☐ 574 Steve Avery UER	.05	.02	.01
(Should be 13 games			
for Durham in 1989)			
☐ 575 Kirby Puckett	.75	.35	.09
☐ 576 Heathcliff Slocumb	.05	.02	.01
☐ 577 Kevin Seitzer	.05	.02	.01
☐ 578 Lee Guetterman	.05	.02	.01
☐ 579 Johnny Oates MG	.05	.02	.01
☐ 580 Greg Maddux	1.25	.55	.16
☐ 581 Stan Javier	.05	.02	.01
☐ 582 Vicente Palacios	.05	.02	.01
☐ 583 Mel Rojas	.10	.05	.01
☐ 584 Wayne Rosenthal	.05	.02	.01
☐ 585 Lenny Webster	.05	.02	.01
☐ 586 Rod Nichols	.05	.02	.01
☐ 587 Mickey Morandini	.05	.02	.01
☐ 588 Russ Swan	.05	.02	.01
☐ 589 Mariano Duncan	.05	.02	.01
Now with Phillies			
12-10-91			
☐ 590 Howard Johnson	.05	.02	.01
☐ 591 1992 Prospects OF	.15	.07	.02
Jeromy Burnitz			
Jacob Brumfield			
Alan Cockrell			
D.J. Dozier			
☐ 592 Denny Neagle	.15	.07	.02
☐ 593 Steve Decker	.05	.02	.01
☐ 594 Brian Barber	.05	.02	.01
☐ 595 Bruce Hurst	.05	.02	.01
☐ 596 Kent Mercker	.05	.02	.01
☐ 597 Mike Magnante	.05	.02	.01
☐ 598 Jody Reed	.05	.02	.01
☐ 599 Steve Searcy	.05	.02	.01
☐ 600 Paul Molitor	.40	.18	.05
☐ 601 Dave Smith	.05	.02	.01
☐ 602 Mike Fetters	.05	.02	.01
☐ 603 Luis Mercedes	.05	.02	.01
☐ 604 Chris Gwynn	.05	.02	.01
Now with Royals			
12-11-91			
☐ 605 Scott Erickson	.10	.05	.01
☐ 606 Brook Jacoby	.05	.02	.01
☐ 607 Todd Stottlemyre	.10	.05	.01
☐ 608 Scott Bradley	.05	.02	.01
☐ 609 Mike Hargrove MG	.10	.05	.01
☐ 610 Eric Davis	.10	.05	.01
☐ 611 Brian Hunter	.05	.02	.01
☐ 612 Pat Kelly	.05	.02	.01
☐ 613 Pedro Munoz	.05	.02	.01
☐ 614 Al Osuna	.05	.02	.01
☐ 615 Matt Merullo	.05	.02	.01
☐ 616 Larry Andersen	.05	.02	.01
☐ 617 Junior Ortiz	.05	.02	.01
☐ 618 1992 Prospects OF	.05	.02	.01
Cesar Hernandez			
Steve Hosey			
Jeff McNeely			
Dan Peltier			
☐ 619 Danny Jackson	.05	.02	.01
☐ 620 George Brett	.75	.35	.09
☐ 621 Dan Gakeler	.05	.02	.01
☐ 622 Steve Buechele	.05	.02	.01
☐ 623 Bob Tewksbury	.05	.02	.01
☐ 624 Shawn Estes	.25	.11	.03
☐ 625 Kevin McReynolds	.05	.02	.01
☐ 626 Chris Haney	.05	.02	.01
☐ 627 Mike Sharperson	.05	.02	.01

☐ 628 Mark Williamson	.05	.02	.01
☐ 629 Wally Joyner	.10	.05	.01
☐ 630 Carlton Fisk	.15	.07	.02
☐ 631 Armando Reynoso	.05	.02	.01
☐ 632 Felix Fermin	.05	.02	.01
☐ 633 Mitch Williams	.05	.02	.01
☐ 634 Manuel Lee	.05	.02	.01
☐ 635 Harold Baines	.10	.05	.01
☐ 636 Greg W. Harris	.05	.02	.01
☐ 637 Orlando Merced	.05	.02	.01
☐ 638 Chris Bosio	.05	.02	.01
☐ 639 Wayne Housie	.05	.02	.01
☐ 640 Xavier Hernandez	.05	.02	.01
☐ 641 David Howard	.05	.02	.01
☐ 642 Tim Crews	.05	.02	.01
☐ 643 Rick Cerone	.05	.02	.01
☐ 644 Terry Leach	.05	.02	.01
☐ 645 Deion Sanders	.25	.11	.03
☐ 646 Craig Wilson	.05	.02	.01
☐ 647 Marquis Grissom	.10	.05	.01
☐ 648 Scott Fletcher	.05	.02	.01
☐ 649 Norm Charlton	.05	.02	.01
☐ 650 Jesse Barfield	.05	.02	.01
☐ 651 Joe Slusarski	.05	.02	.01
☐ 652 Bobby Rose	.05	.02	.01
☐ 653 Dennis Lamp	.05	.02	.01
☐ 654 Allen Watson	.10	.05	.01
☐ 655 Brett Butler	.10	.05	.01
☐ 656 1992 Prospects OF Rudy Pemberton Henry Rodriguez Lee Tinsley Gerald Williams	.15	.07	.02
☐ 657 Dave Johnson	.05	.02	.01
☐ 658 Checklist 529-660	.05	.02	.01
☐ 659 Brian McRae	.10	.05	.01
☐ 660 Fred McGriff	.15	.07	.02
☐ 661 Bill Landrum	.05	.02	.01
☐ 662 Juan Guzman	.10	.05	.01
☐ 663 Greg Gagne	.05	.02	.01
☐ 664 Ken Hill Now with Expos 11-25-91	.10	.05	.01
☐ 665 Dave Haas	.05	.02	.01
☐ 666 Tom Foley	.05	.02	.01
☐ 667 Roberto Hernandez	.10	.05	.01
☐ 668 Dwayne Henry	.05	.02	.01
☐ 669 Jim Fregosi MG	.05	.02	.01
☐ 670 Harold Reynolds	.10	.05	.01
☐ 671 Mark Whiten	.05	.02	.01
☐ 672 Eric Plunk	.05	.02	.01
☐ 673 Todd Hundley	.10	.05	.01
☐ 674 Mo Sanford	.05	.02	.01
☐ 675 Bobby Witt	.05	.02	.01
☐ 676 1992 Prospects P Sam Militello Pat Mahomes Turk Wendell Roger Salkeld	.05	.02	.01
☐ 677 John Marzano	.05	.02	.01
☐ 678 Joe Klink	.05	.02	.01
☐ 679 Pete Incaviglia	.05	.02	.01
☐ 680 Dale Murphy	.15	.07	.02
☐ 681 Rene Gonzales	.05	.02	.01
☐ 682 Andy Benes	.10	.05	.01
☐ 683 Jim Poole	.05	.02	.01
☐ 684 Trever Miller	.05	.02	.01
☐ 685 Scott Livingstone	.05	.02	.01
☐ 686 Rich DeLucia	.05	.02	.01
☐ 687 Harvey Pulliam	.05	.02	.01
☐ 688 Tim Belcher	.05	.02	.01
☐ 689 Mark Lemke	.05	.02	.01
☐ 690 John Franco	.10	.05	.01
☐ 691 Walt Weiss	.05	.02	.01
☐ 692 Scott Ruskin Now with Reds 12-11-91	.05	.02	.01
☐ 693 Jeff King	.05	.02	.01
☐ 694 Mike Gardiner	.05	.02	.01
☐ 695 Gary Sheffield	.15	.07	.02
☐ 696 Joe Boever	.05	.02	.01
☐ 697 Mike Felder	.05	.02	.01
☐ 698 John Habyan	.05	.02	.01
☐ 699 Cito Gaston MG	.05	.02	.01
☐ 700 Ruben Sierra	.05	.02	.01
☐ 701 Scott Radinsky	.05	.02	.01
☐ 702 Lee Stevens	.05	.02	.01
☐ 703 Mark Wohlers	.15	.07	.02
☐ 704 Curt Young	.05	.02	.01
☐ 705 Dwight Evans	.10	.05	.01
☐ 706 Rob Murphy	.05	.02	.01
☐ 707 Gregg Jefferies Now with Royals 12-11-91	.10	.05	.01
☐ 708 Tom Bolton	.05	.02	.01
☐ 709 Chris James	.05	.02	.01
☐ 710 Kevin Maas	.05	.02	.01
☐ 711 Ricky Bones	.05	.02	.01
☐ 712 Curt Wilkerson	.05	.02	.01
☐ 713 Roger McDowell	.05	.02	.01
☐ 714 Calvin Reese	.10	.05	.01
☐ 715 Craig Biggio	.10	.05	.01
☐ 716 Kirk Dressendorfer	.05	.02	.01
☐ 717 Ken Dayley	.05	.02	.01
☐ 718 B.J. Surhoff	.10	.05	.01
☐ 719 Terry Mulholland	.05	.02	.01
☐ 720 Kirk Gibson	.10	.05	.01
☐ 721 Mike Pagliarulo	.05	.02	.01
☐ 722 Walt Terrell	.05	.02	.01
☐ 723 Jose Oquendo	.05	.02	.01
☐ 724 Kevin Morton	.05	.02	.01
☐ 725 Dwight Gooden	.10	.05	.01
☐ 726 Kirt Manwaring	.05	.02	.01
☐ 727 Chuck McElroy	.05	.02	.01
☐ 728 Dave Burba	.05	.02	.01
☐ 729 Art Howe MG	.05	.02	.01
☐ 730 Ramon Martinez	.10	.05	.01
☐ 731 Donnie Hill	.05	.02	.01
☐ 732 Nelson Santovenia	.05	.02	.01
☐ 733 Bob Melvin	.05	.02	.01
☐ 734 Scott Hatteberg	.05	.02	.01
☐ 735 Greg Swindell Now with Reds 11-15-91	.05	.02	.01
☐ 736 Lance Johnson	.10	.05	.01
☐ 737 Kevin Reimer	.05	.02	.01
☐ 738 Dennis Eckersley	.10	.05	.01
☐ 739 Rob Ducey	.05	.02	.01
☐ 740 Ken Caminiti	.15	.07	.02
☐ 741 Mark Gubicza	.05	.02	.01
☐ 742 Billy Spiers	.05	.02	.01
☐ 743 Darren Lewis	.05	.02	.01
☐ 744 Chris Hammond	.05	.02	.01
☐ 745 Dave Magadan	.05	.02	.01
☐ 746 Bernard Gilkey	.10	.05	.01
☐ 747 Willie Banks	.05	.02	.01
☐ 748 Matt Nokes	.05	.02	.01
☐ 749 Jerald Clark	.05	.02	.01
☐ 750 Travis Fryman	.15	.07	.02
☐ 751 Steve Wilson	.05	.02	.01
☐ 752 Billy Ripken	.05	.02	.01
☐ 753 Paul Assenmacher	.05	.02	.01
☐ 754 Charlie Hayes	.05	.02	.01
☐ 755 Alex Fernandez	.15	.07	.02
☐ 756 Gary Pettis	.05	.02	.01
☐ 757 Rob Dibble	.05	.02	.01
☐ 758 Tim Naehring	.10	.05	.01
☐ 759 Jeff Torborg MG	.05	.02	.01
☐ 760 Ozzie Smith	.50	.23	.06
☐ 761 Mike Fitzgerald	.05	.02	.01
☐ 762 John Burkett	.10	.05	.01
☐ 763 Kyle Abbott	.05	.02	.01
☐ 764 Tyler Green	.05	.02	.01
☐ 765 Pete Harnisch	.05	.02	.01
☐ 766 Mark Davis	.05	.02	.01
☐ 767 Kal Daniels	.05	.02	.01
☐ 768 Jim Thome	1.00	.45	.12
☐ 769 Jack Howell	.05	.02	.01
☐ 770 Sid Bream	.05	.02	.01
☐ 771 Arthur Rhodes	.05	.02	.01
☐ 772 Garry Templeton	.05	.02	.01
☐ 773 Hal Morris	.05	.02	.01
☐ 774 Bud Black	.05	.02	.01
☐ 775 Ivan Calderon	.05	.02	.01
☐ 776 Doug Henry	.05	.02	.01
☐ 777 John Olerud	.10	.05	.01
☐ 778 Tim Leary	.05	.02	.01
☐ 779 Jay Bell	.05	.02	.01
☐ 780 Eddie Murray Now with Mets 11-27-91	.50	.23	.06
☐ 781 Paul Abbott	.05	.02	.01
☐ 782 Phil Plantier	.05	.02	.01
☐ 783 Joe Magrane	.05	.02	.01
☐ 784 Ken Patterson	.05	.02	.01
☐ 785 Albert Belle	.75	.35	.09
☐ 786 Royce Clayton	.10	.05	.01
☐ 787 Checklist 661-792	.05	.02	.01
☐ 788 Mike Stanton	.05	.02	.01
☐ 789 Bobby Valentine MG	.05	.02	.01
☐ 790 Joe Carter	.10	.05	.01
☐ 791 Danny Cox	.05	.02	.01
☐ 792 Dave Winfield Now with Blue Jays 12-19-91	.25	.11	.03

1992 O-Pee-Chee Box Bottoms

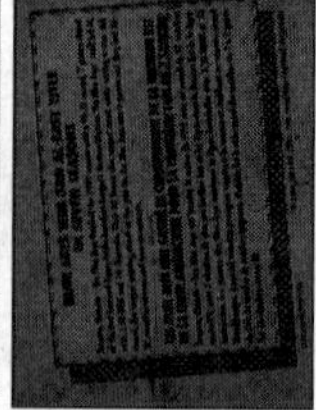

This set consists of four display box bottoms, each featuring one of four team photos of the divisional champions from the 1991 season. The oversized cards measure approximately 5" by 7" and the card's title appears within a ghosted rectangle near the bottom of the white-bordered color photo. The unnumbered horizontal plain-cardboard backs carry the team's season highlights in both English and French in blue lettering.

	MINT	NRMT	EXC
COMPLETE SET (4)	3.00	1.35	.35
COMMON CARD (1-4)	.50	.23	.06
☐ 1 Pirates Prevail	.50	.23	.06
☐ 2 Braves Beat Bucs	.75	.35	.09
☐ 3 Blue Jays Claim Crown	1.00	.45	.12
☐ 4 Kirby Puckett Twins Tally in Tenth	1.50	.70	.19

1993 O-Pee-Chee

The 1993 O-Pee-Chee baseball set consists of 396 standard-size cards. This is the first year that the regular series differs from the series that Topps issued. The set was sold in wax packs with eight cards plus a random insert card from either a four-card World Series Heroes subset or an 18-card World Series Champions subset. The fronts features color action player photos with white borders. The player's name appears in a silver stripe across the bottom that overlaps the O-Pee-Chee logo. The backs display color close-ups next to a panel containing biographical data. The panel and a stripe at the bottom reflect the team colors. A white box in the center of the card contains statistics and bilingual (English and French) career highlights.

	MINT	NRMT	EXC
COMPLETE SET (396)	50.00	22.00	6.25
COMMON CARD (1-396)	.10	.05	.01
☐ 1 Jim Abbott Now with Yankees 12/6/92	.25	.11	.03
☐ 2 Eric Anthony	.10	.05	.01
☐ 3 Harold Baines	.25	.11	.03
☐ 4 Roberto Alomar	.75	.35	.09
☐ 5 Steve Avery	.10	.05	.01
☐ 6 James Austin	.10	.05	.01
☐ 7 Mark Wohlers	.25	.11	.03
☐ 8 Steve Buechele	.10	.05	.01
☐ 9 Pedro Astacio	.10	.05	.01
☐ 10 Moises Alou	.25	.11	.03
☐ 11 Rod Beck	.25	.11	.03
☐ 12 Sandy Alomar	.25	.11	.03
☐ 13 Bret Boone	.25	.11	.03
☐ 14 Bryan Harvey	.10	.05	.01
☐ 15 Bobby Bonilla	.25	.11	.03
☐ 16 Brady Anderson	.50	.23	.06
☐ 17 Andy Benes	.25	.11	.03
☐ 18 Ruben Amaro Jr.	.10	.05	.01
☐ 19 Jay Bell	.10	.05	.01
☐ 20 Kevin Brown	.25	.11	.03
☐ 21 Scott Bankhead Now with Red Sox 12/8/92	.10	.05	.01
☐ 22 Denis Boucher	.10	.05	.01
☐ 23 Kevin Appier	.25	.11	.03
☐ 24 Pat Kelly	.10	.05	.01
☐ 25 Rick Aguilera	.10	.05	.01
☐ 26 George Bell	.10	.05	.01
☐ 27 Steve Farr	.10	.05	.01
☐ 28 Chad Curtis	.10	.05	.01
☐ 29 Jeff Bagwell	2.00	.90	.25
☐ 30 Lance Blankenship	.10	.05	.01
☐ 31 Derek Bell	.25	.11	.03
☐ 32 Damon Berryhill	.10	.05	.01
☐ 33 Ricky Bones	.10	.05	.01
☐ 34 Rheal Cormier	.10	.05	.01
☐ 35 Andre Dawson Now with Red Sox 12/2/92	.25	.11	.03
☐ 36 Brett Butler	.25	.11	.03
☐ 37 Sean Berry	.10	.05	.01
☐ 38 Bud Black	.10	.05	.01
☐ 39 Carlos Baerga	.25	.11	.03
☐ 40 Jay Buhner	.50	.23	.06
☐ 41 Charlie Hough	.25	.11	.03
☐ 42 Sid Fernandez	.10	.05	.01
☐ 43 Luis Mercedes	.10	.05	.01
☐ 44 Jerald Clark Now with Rockies 11/17/92	.10	.05	.01
☐ 45 Wes Chamberlain	.10	.05	.01
☐ 46 Barry Bonds Now with Giants 12/8/92	1.00	.45	.12
☐ 47 Jose Canseco	.60	.25	.07
☐ 48 Tim Belcher	.10	.05	.01
☐ 49 David Nied	.10	.05	.01
☐ 50 George Brett	1.50	.70	.19
☐ 51 Cecil Fielder	.25	.11	.03
☐ 52 Chili Davis Now with Angels 12/11/92	.25	.11	.03
☐ 53 Alex Fernandez	.25	.11	.03
☐ 54 Charlie Hayes Now with Rockies 11/17/92	.10	.05	.01
☐ 55 Rob Ducey	.10	.05	.01
☐ 56 Craig Biggio	.25	.11	.03
☐ 57 Mike Bordick	.10	.05	.01
☐ 58 Pat Borders	.10	.05	.01
☐ 59 Jeff Blauser	.10	.05	.01
☐ 60 Chris Bosio Now with Mariners 12/3/92	.10	.05	.01
☐ 61 Bernard Gilkey	.25	.11	.03
☐ 62 Shawon Dunston	.10	.05	.01
☐ 63 Tom Candiotti	.10	.05	.01
☐ 64 Darrin Fletcher	.10	.05	.01
☐ 65 Jeff Brantley	.10	.05	.01
☐ 66 Albert Belle	1.50	.70	.19
☐ 67 Dave Fleming	.10	.05	.01
☐ 68 John Franco	.25	.11	.03
☐ 69 Glenn Davis	.10	.05	.01
☐ 70 Tony Fernandez Now with Mets 10/26/92	.10	.05	.01
☐ 71 Darren Daulton	.25	.11	.03
☐ 72 Doug Drabek Now with Astros 12/1/92	.10	.05	.01
☐ 73 Julio Franco	.25	.11	.03
☐ 74 Tom Browning	.10	.05	.01
☐ 75 Tom Gordon	.10	.05	.01
☐ 76 Travis Fryman	.25	.11	.03
☐ 77 Scott Erickson	.10	.05	.01
☐ 78 Carlton Fisk	.50	.23	.06
☐ 79 Roberto Kelly Now with Reds 11/3/92	.10	.05	.01
☐ 80 Gary DiSarcina	.10	.05	.01
☐ 81 Ken Caminiti	.50	.23	.06
☐ 82 Ron Darling	.10	.05	.01
☐ 83 Joe Carter	.25	.11	.03
☐ 84 Sid Bream	.10	.05	.01
☐ 85 Cal Eldred	.10	.05	.01
☐ 86 Mark Grace	.75	.35	.09
☐ 87 Eric Davis	.10	.05	.01
☐ 88 Ivan Calderon Now with Red Sox 12/8/92	.10	.05	.01
☐ 89 John Burkett	.10	.05	.01
☐ 90 Felix Fermin	.10	.05	.01
☐ 91 Ken Griffey Jr.	4.00	1.80	.50
☐ 92 Dwight Gooden	.25	.11	.03
☐ 93 Mike Devereaux	.10	.05	.01
☐ 94 Tony Gwynn	2.00	.90	.25
☐ 95 Mariano Duncan	.10	.05	.01
☐ 96 Jeff King	.10	.05	.01
☐ 97 Juan Gonzalez	2.00	.90	.25
☐ 98 Norm Charlton Now with Mariners 11/17/92	.10	.05	.01
☐ 99 Mark Gubicza	.10	.05	.01
☐ 100 Danny Gladden	.10	.05	.01
☐ 101 Greg Gagne Now with Royals 12/8/92	.10	.05	.01
☐ 102 Ozzie Guillen	.10	.05	.01
☐ 103 Don Mattingly	2.00	.90	.25
☐ 104 Damion Easley	.10	.05	.01
☐ 105 Casey Candaele	.10	.05	.01
☐ 106 Dennis Eckersley	.25	.11	.03
☐ 107 David Cone Now with Royals 12/8/92	.25	.11	.03
☐ 108 Ron Gant	.25	.11	.03
☐ 109 Mike Fetters	.10	.05	.01
☐ 110 Mike Harkey	.10	.05	.01
☐ 111 Kevin Gross	.10	.05	.01
☐ 112 Archi Cianfrocco	.10	.05	.01
☐ 113 Will Clark	.60	.25	.07
☐ 114 Glenallen Hill	.10	.05	.01
☐ 115 Erik Hanson	.10	.05	.01
☐ 116 Todd Hundley	.25	.11	.03
☐ 117 Leo Gomez	.10	.05	.01
☐ 118 Bruce Hurst	.10	.05	.01
☐ 119 Len Dykstra	.25	.11	.03
☐ 120 Jose Lind Now with Royals 11/19/92	.10	.05	.01
☐ 121 Jose Guzman Now with Cubs 12/1/92	.10	.05	.01
☐ 122 Rob Dibble	.10	.05	.01
☐ 123 Gregg Jefferies	.25	.11	.03
☐ 124 Bill Gullickson	.10	.05	.01
☐ 125 Brian Harper	.10	.05	.01
☐ 126 Roberto Hernandez	.10	.05	.01
☐ 127 Sam Militello	.10	.05	.01
☐ 128 Junior Felix Now with Marlins 11/17/92	.10	.05	.01
☐ 129 Andujar Cedeno	.10	.05	.01
☐ 130 Rickey Henderson	.60	.25	.07
☐ 131 Bob MacDonald	.10	.05	.01
☐ 132 Tom Glavine	.50	.23	.06
☐ 133 Scott Fletcher	.10	.05	.01

Now with Red Sox
11/30/92
☐ 134 Brian Jordan .25 .11 .03
☐ 135 Greg Maddux 3.00 1.35 .35
Now with Braves
12/9/92
☐ 136 Orel Hershiser .25 .11 .03
☐ 137 Greg Colbrunn .10 .05 .01
☐ 138 Royce Clayton .10 .05 .01
☐ 139 Thomas Howard .10 .05 .01
☐ 140 Randy Johnson .75 .35 .09
☐ 141 Jeff Innis .10 .05 .01
☐ 142 Chris Hoiles .10 .05 .01
☐ 143 Darrin Jackson .10 .05 .01
☐ 144 Tommy Greene .10 .05 .01
☐ 145 Mike LaValliere .10 .05 .01
☐ 146 David Hulse .10 .05 .01
☐ 147 Barry Larkin .60 .25 .07
☐ 148 Wally Joyner .10 .05 .01
☐ 149 Mike Henneman .10 .05 .01
☐ 150 Kent Hrbek .10 .05 .01
☐ 151 Bo Jackson .25 .11 .03
☐ 152 Rich Monteleone .10 .05 .01
☐ 153 Chuck Finley .25 .11 .03
☐ 154 Steve Finley .25 .11 .03
☐ 155 Dave Henderson .10 .05 .01
☐ 156 Kelly Gruber .10 .05 .01
Now with Angels
12/8/92
☐ 157 Brian Hunter .10 .05 .01
☐ 158 Darryl Hamilton .10 .05 .01
☐ 159 Derrick May .10 .05 .01
☐ 160 Jay Howell .10 .05 .01
☐ 161 Wil Cordero .25 .11 .03
☐ 162 Bryan Hickerson .10 .05 .01
☐ 163 Reggie Jefferson .10 .05 .01
☐ 164 Edgar Martinez .25 .11 .03
☐ 165 Nigel Wilson .10 .05 .01
☐ 166 Howard Johnson .10 .05 .01
☐ 167 Tim Hulett .10 .05 .01
☐ 168 Mike Maddux .10 .05 .01
Now with Mets
12/17/92
☐ 169 Dave Hollins .10 .05 .01
☐ 170 Zane Smith .10 .05 .01
☐ 171 Rafael Palmeiro .50 .23 .06
☐ 172 Dave Martinez .10 .05 .01
Now with Giants
12/9/92
☐ 173 Rusty Meacham .10 .05 .01
☐ 174 Mark Leiter .10 .05 .01
☐ 175 Chuck Knoblauch .50 .23 .06
☐ 176 Lance Johnson .25 .11 .03
☐ 177 Matt Nokes .10 .05 .01
☐ 178 Luis Gonzalez .10 .05 .01
☐ 179 Jack Morris .25 .11 .03
☐ 180 David Justice .25 .11 .03
☐ 181 Doug Henry .10 .05 .01
☐ 182 Felix Jose .10 .05 .01
☐ 183 Delino DeShields .10 .05 .01
☐ 184 Rene Gonzales .10 .05 .01
☐ 185 Pete Harnisch .10 .05 .01
☐ 186 Mike Moore .10 .05 .01
Now with Tigers
12/9/92
☐ 187 Juan Guzman .10 .05 .01
☐ 188 John Olerud .25 .11 .03
☐ 189 Ryan Klesko 1.25 .55 .16
☐ 190 John Jaha .50 .23 .06
☐ 191 Ray Lankford .25 .11 .03
☐ 192 Jeff Fassero .10 .05 .01
☐ 193 Darren Lewis .10 .05 .01
☐ 194 Mark Lewis .10 .05 .01
☐ 195 Alan Mills .10 .05 .01
☐ 196 Wade Boggs .60 .25 .07
Now with Yankees
12/15/92
☐ 197 Hal Morris .10 .05 .01
☐ 198 Ron Karkovice .10 .05 .01
☐ 199 Joe Grahe .10 .05 .01
☐ 200 Butch Henry .10 .05 .01
Now with Rockies
11/17/92
☐ 201 Mark McGwire 1.25 .55 .16
☐ 202 Tom Henke .10 .05 .01
Now with Rangers
12/15/92
☐ 203 Ed Sprague .25 .11 .03
☐ 204 Charlie Leibrandt .10 .05 .01
Now with Rangers
12/9/92
☐ 205 Pat Listach .10 .05 .01
☐ 206 Omar Olivares .10 .05 .01
☐ 207 Mike Morgan .10 .05 .01
☐ 208 Eric Karros .50 .23 .06
☐ 209 Marquis Grissom .25 .11 .03
☐ 210 Willie McGee .25 .11 .03
☐ 211 Derek Lilliquist .10 .05 .01
☐ 212 Tino Martinez .25 .11 .03
☐ 213 Jeff Kent .25 .11 .03
☐ 214 Mike Mussina 1.00 .45 .12
☐ 215 Randy Myers .10 .05 .01
Now with Cubs
12/9/92
☐ 216 John Kruk .25 .11 .03
☐ 217 Tom Brunansky .10 .05 .01
☐ 218 Paul O'Neill .25 .11 .03
Now with Yankees
11/3/92
☐ 219 Scott Livingstone .10 .05 .01
☐ 220 John Valentin .25 .11 .03
☐ 221 Eddie Zosky .10 .05 .01
☐ 222 Pete Smith .10 .05 .01
☐ 223 Bill Wegman .10 .05 .01
☐ 224 Todd Zeile .10 .05 .01
☐ 225 Tim Wallach .10 .05 .01
Now with Dodgers
12/24/92
☐ 226 Mitch Williams .10 .05 .01
☐ 227 Tim Wakefield .10 .05 .01
☐ 228 Frank Viola .10 .05 .01
☐ 229 Nolan Ryan 3.00 1.35 .35
☐ 230 Kirk McCaskill .10 .05 .01
☐ 231 Melido Perez .10 .05 .01
☐ 232 Mark Langston .10 .05 .01
☐ 233 Xavier Hernandez .10 .05 .01
☐ 234 Jerry Browne .10 .05 .01
☐ 235 Dave Stieb .10 .05 .01
Now with White Sox
12/8/92
☐ 236 Mark Lemke .10 .05 .01
☐ 237 Paul Molitor .75 .35 .09
Now with Blue Jays
12/7/92
☐ 238 Geronimo Pena .10 .05 .01
☐ 239 Ken Hill .25 .11 .03
☐ 240 Jack Clark .10 .05 .01
☐ 241 Greg Myers .10 .05 .01
☐ 242 Pete Incaviglia .10 .05 .01
Now with Phillies
12/8/92
☐ 243 Ruben Sierra .10 .05 .01
☐ 244 Todd Stottlemyre .10 .05 .01
☐ 245 Pat Hentgen .50 .23 .06
☐ 246 Melvin Nieves .50 .23 .06
☐ 247 Jaime Navarro .10 .05 .01
☐ 248 Donovan Osborne .10 .05 .01
☐ 249 Brian Barnes .10 .05 .01
☐ 250 Cory Snyder .10 .05 .01
Now with Dodgers
12/5/92
☐ 251 Kenny Lofton 1.00 .45 .12
☐ 252 Kevin Mitchell .10 .05 .01
Now with Reds
11/17/92
☐ 253 Dave Magadan .10 .05 .01
Now with Marlins
12/8/92
☐ 254 Ben McDonald .10 .05 .01
☐ 255 Fred McGriff .50 .23 .06
☐ 256 Mickey Morandini .10 .05 .01
☐ 257 Randy Tomlin .10 .05 .01
☐ 258 Dean Palmer .25 .11 .03
☐ 259 Roger Clemens .60 .25 .07
☐ 260 Joe Oliver .10 .05 .01
☐ 261 Jeff Montgomery .10 .05 .01
☐ 262 Tony Phillips .25 .11 .03
☐ 263 Shane Mack .10 .05 .01
☐ 264 Jack McDowell .50 .23 .06
☐ 265 Mike Macfarlane .10 .05 .01
☐ 266 Luis Polonia .10 .05 .01
☐ 267 Doug Jones .10 .05 .01
☐ 268 Terry Steinbach .10 .05 .01
☐ 269 Jimmy Key .25 .11 .03
Now with Yankees
12/10/92
☐ 270 Pat Tabler .10 .05 .01
☐ 271 Otis Nixon .25 .11 .03
☐ 272 Dave Nilsson .10 .05 .01
☐ 273 Tom Pagnozzi .10 .05 .01
☐ 274 Ryne Sandberg 1.50 .70 .19
☐ 275 Ramon Martinez .25 .11 .03
☐ 276 Tim Laker .10 .05 .01
☐ 277 Bill Swift .10 .05 .01
☐ 278 Charles Nagy .25 .11 .03
☐ 279 Harold Reynolds .25 .11 .03
Now with Orioles
12/11/92
☐ 280 Eddie Murray 1.00 .45 .12
☐ 281 Gregg Olson .10 .05 .01
☐ 282 Frank Seminara .10 .05 .01
☐ 283 Terry Mulholland .10 .05 .01
☐ 284 Kevin Reimer .10 .05 .01
Now with Brewers
11/17/92
☐ 285 Mike Greenwell .10 .05 .01
☐ 286 Jose Rijo .10 .05 .01
☐ 287 Brian McRae .10 .05 .01
☐ 288 Frank Tanana .10 .05 .01
Now with Mets
12/10/92
☐ 289 Pedro Munoz .10 .05 .01
☐ 290 Tim Raines .10 .05 .01
☐ 291 Andy Stankiewicz .10 .05 .01
☐ 292 Tim Salmon 1.00 .45 .12
☐ 293 Jimmy Jones .10 .05 .01
☐ 294 Dave Stewart .25 .11 .03
Now with Blue Jays
12/8/92
☐ 295 Mike Timlin .10 .05 .01
☐ 296 Greg Olson .10 .05 .01
☐ 297 Dan Plesac .10 .05 .01
Now with Cubs
12/8/92
☐ 298 Mike Perez .10 .05 .01
☐ 299 Jose Offerman .10 .05 .01
☐ 300 Denny Martinez .25 .11 .03
☐ 301 Robby Thompson .10 .05 .01
☐ 302 Bret Saberhagen .10 .05 .01
☐ 303 Joe Orsulak .10 .05 .01
Now with Mets
12/18/92
☐ 304 Tim Naehring .10 .05 .01
☐ 305 Bip Roberts .10 .05 .01
☐ 306 Kirby Puckett 2.00 .90 .25
☐ 307 Steve Sax .10 .05 .01
☐ 308 Danny Tartabull .10 .05 .01
☐ 309 Jeff Juden .10 .05 .01
☐ 310 Duane Ward .10 .05 .01
☐ 311 Alejandro Pena .10 .05 .01
Now with Pirates
12/10/92
☐ 312 Kevin Seitzer .10 .05 .01
☐ 313 Ozzie Smith 1.00 .45 .12
☐ 314 Mike Piazza 3.00 1.35 .35
☐ 315 Chris Nabholz .10 .05 .01
☐ 316 Tony Pena .10 .05 .01
☐ 317 Gary Sheffield .75 .35 .09
☐ 318 Mark Portugal .10 .05 .01
☐ 319 Walt Weiss .10 .05 .01
Now with Marlins
11/17/92
☐ 320 Manuel Lee .10 .05 .01
Now with Rangers
12/19/92
☐ 321 David Wells .10 .05 .01
☐ 322 Terry Pendleton .10 .05 .01
☐ 323 Billy Spiers .10 .05 .01
☐ 324 Lee Smith .25 .11 .03
☐ 325 Bob Scanlan .10 .05 .01
☐ 326 Mike Scioscia .10 .05 .01
☐ 327 Spike Owen .10 .05 .01
Now with Yankees
12/4/92
☐ 328 Mackey Sasser .10 .05 .01
Now with Mariners
12/23/92
☐ 329 Arthur Rhodes .10 .05 .01
☐ 330 Ben Rivera .10 .05 .01
☐ 331 Ivan Rodriguez 1.00 .45 .12
☐ 332 Phil Plantier .10 .05 .01
Now with Padres
12/10/92
☐ 333 Chris Sabo .10 .05 .01
☐ 334 Mickey Tettleton .10 .05 .01
☐ 335 John Smiley .10 .05 .01
Now with Reds
11/30/92
☐ 336 Bobby Thigpen .10 .05 .01
☐ 337 Randy Velarde .10 .05 .01
☐ 338 Luis Sojo .10 .05 .01
Now with Blue Jays
12/8/92
☐ 339 Scott Servais .10 .05 .01
☐ 340 Bob Welch .10 .05 .01
☐ 341 Devon White .10 .05 .01
☐ 342 Jeff Reardon .10 .05 .01
☐ 343 B.J. Surhoff .25 .11 .03
☐ 344 Bob Tewksbury .10 .05 .01
☐ 345 Jose Vizcaino .10 .05 .01
☐ 346 Mike Sharperson .10 .05 .01
☐ 347 Mel Rojas .10 .05 .01
☐ 348 Matt Williams .50 .23 .06
☐ 349 Steve Olin .10 .05 .01
☐ 350 Mike Schooler .10 .05 .01
☐ 351 Ryan Thompson .10 .05 .01
☐ 352 Cal Ripken 3.00 1.35 .35
☐ 353 Benito Santiago .10 .05 .01
Now with Marlins
12/16/92
☐ 354 Curt Schilling .10 .05 .01
☐ 355 Andy Van Slyke .10 .05 .01
☐ 356 Kenny Rogers .25 .11 .03
☐ 357 Jody Reed .10 .05 .01
Now with Dodgers
11/17/92
☐ 358 Reggie Sanders .50 .23 .06
☐ 359 Kevin McReynolds .10 .05 .01
☐ 360 Alan Trammell .25 .11 .03
☐ 361 Kevin Tapani .10 .05 .01
☐ 362 Frank Thomas 4.00 1.80 .50
☐ 363 Bernie Williams .75 .35 .09
☐ 364 John Smoltz .60 .25 .07
☐ 365 Robin Yount .50 .23 .06
☐ 366 John Wetteland .25 .11 .03
☐ 367 Bob Zupcic .10 .05 .01
☐ 368 Julio Valera .10 .05 .01
☐ 369 Brian Williams .10 .05 .01
☐ 370 Willie Wilson .10 .05 .01
Now with Cubs
12/18/92
☐ 371 Dave Winfield .60 .25 .07
Now with Twins
12/17/92
☐ 372 Deion Sanders .75 .35 .09
☐ 373 Greg Vaughn .25 .11 .03
☐ 374 Todd Worrell .10 .05 .01
Now with Dodgers
12/9/92
☐ 375 Darryl Strawberry .25 .11 .03
☐ 376 John Vander Wal .10 .05 .01
☐ 377 Mike Benjamin .10 .05 .01
☐ 378 Mark Whiten .10 .05 .01
☐ 379 Omar Vizquel .25 .11 .03
☐ 380 Anthony Young .10 .05 .01
☐ 381 Rick Sutcliffe .10 .05 .01
☐ 382 Candy Maldonado .10 .05 .01
Now with Cubs
12/11/92
☐ 383 Francisco Cabrera .10 .05 .01
☐ 384 Larry Walker .50 .23 .06
☐ 385 Scott Cooper .10 .05 .01
☐ 386 Gerald Williams .10 .05 .01
☐ 387 Robin Ventura .25 .11 .03
☐ 388 Carl Willis .10 .05 .01
☐ 389 Lou Whitaker .25 .11 .03
☐ 390 Hipolito Pichardo .10 .05 .01
☐ 391 Rudy Seanez .10 .05 .01
☐ 392 Greg Swindell .10 .05 .01
Now with Astros
12/4/92
☐ 393 Mo Vaughn 1.00 .45 .12
☐ 394 Checklist 1-132 .10 .05 .01
☐ 395 Checklist 133-264 .10 .05 .01
☐ 396 Checklist 265-396 .10 .05 .01

1993 O-Pee-Chee World Champions

This 18-card standard-size set was randomly inserted in 1993 O-Pee-Chee wax packs and features the Toronto Blue Jays, the 1992 World Series Champions. The standard-size cards are similar to the regular issue, with glossy color action player photos with white borders on the fronts. They differ in having a gold (rather than silver) stripe across the bottom, which intersects a 1992 World Champions logo. The backs carry statistics on a burnt orange box against a light blue panel with bilingual (English and French) career highlights.

	MINT	NRMT	EXC
COMPLETE SET (18)	4.00	1.80	.50
COMMON CARD (1-18)	.10	.05	.01
☐ 1 Roberto Alomar	1.00	.45	.12
☐ 2 Pat Borders	.10	.05	.01
☐ 3 Joe Carter	.25	.11	.03
☐ 4 David Cone	.25	.11	.03
☐ 5 Kelly Gruber	.10	.05	.01
☐ 6 Juan Guzman	.25	.11	.03
☐ 7 Tom Henke	.25	.11	.03
☐ 8 Jimmy Key	.25	.11	.03
☐ 9 Manuel Lee	.10	.05	.01
☐ 10 Candy Maldonado	.10	.05	.01
☐ 11 Jack Morris	.25	.11	.03
☐ 12 John Olerud	.25	.11	.03
☐ 13 Ed Sprague	.25	.11	.03
☐ 14 Todd Stottlemyre	.10	.05	.01
☐ 15 Duane Ward	.10	.05	.01
☐ 16 Devon White	.10	.05	.01
☐ 17 Dave Winfield	.75	.35	.09
☐ 18 Cito Gaston MG	.10	.05	.01

1993 O-Pee-Chee World Series Heroes

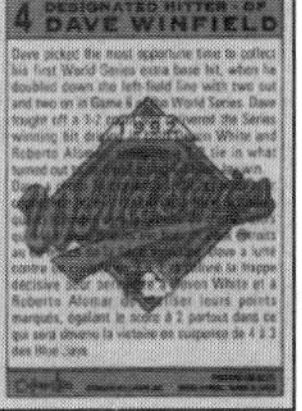

This four-card standard-size set was randomly inserted in 1993 O-Pee-Chee wax packs. These cards were more difficult to find than the 18-card World Series Champions insert set. The fronts feature color action player photos with white borders. The words "World Series Heroes" appear in a dark blue stripe above the picture, while the player's name is printed in the bottom white border. A 1992 World Series logo overlays the picture at the lower right corner. Over a ghosted version of the 1992 World Series logo, the backs summarize, in English and French, the player's outstanding performance in the 1992 World Series. The cards are numbered on the back in alphabetical order by player's name.

	MINT	NRMT	EXC
COMPLETE SET (4)	2.00	.90	.25
COMMON CARD (1-4)	.25	.11	.03
☐ 1 Pat Borders	.25	.11	.03
☐ 2 Jimmy Key	.50	.23	.06
☐ 3 Ed Sprague	.50	.23	.06
☐ 4 Dave Winfield	1.00	.45	.12

1994 O-Pee-Chee

The 1994 O-Pee-Chee baseball set consists of 270 standard-size cards.Production was limited to 2,500 individually numbered cases. Each display box contained 36 packs and one 5" by 7" All-Star Jumbo card. Each foil pack contained 14 regular cards plus eiher one chase card or one redemption card.

	MINT	NRMT	EXC
COMPLETE SET (270)	15.00	6.75	1.85
COMMON CARD (1-270)	.05	.02	.01
☐ 1 Paul Molitor	.40	.18	.05
☐ 2 Kirt Manwaring	.05	.02	.01
☐ 3 Brady Anderson	.20	.09	.03
☐ 4 Scott Cooper	.05	.02	.01
☐ 5 Kevin Stocker	.05	.02	.01
☐ 6 Alex Fernandez	.10	.05	.01
☐ 7 Jeff Montgomery	.05	.02	.01
☐ 8 Danny Tartabull	.05	.02	.01
☐ 9 Damion Easley	.05	.02	.01
☐ 10 Andujar Cedeno	.05	.02	.01
☐ 11 Steve Karsay	.05	.02	.01
☐ 12 Dave Stewart	.10	.05	.01
☐ 13 Fred McGriff	.25	.11	.03
☐ 14 Jaime Navarro	.05	.02	.01
☐ 15 Allen Watson	.05	.02	.01
☐ 16 Ryne Sandberg	.60	.25	.07
☐ 17 Arthur Rhodes	.05	.02	.01
☐ 18 Marquis Grissom	.10	.05	.01
☐ 19 John Burkett	.05	.02	.01
☐ 20 Robby Thompson	.05	.02	.01
☐ 21 Denny Martinez	.10	.05	.01
☐ 22 Ken Griffey Jr.	2.00	.90	.25
☐ 23 Orestes Destrade	.05	.02	.01
☐ 24 Dwight Gooden	.10	.05	.01
☐ 25 Rafael Palmeiro	.20	.09	.03
☐ 26 Pedro A.Martinez	.05	.02	.01
☐ 27 Wes Chamberlain	.05	.02	.01
☐ 28 Juan Gonzalez	1.00	.45	.12
☐ 29 Kevin Mitchell	.05	.02	.01
☐ 30 Dante Bichette	.25	.11	.03
☐ 31 Howard Johnson	.05	.02	.01
☐ 32 Mickey Tettleton	.05	.02	.01
☐ 33 Robin Ventura	.10	.05	.01
☐ 34 Terry Mulholland	.05	.02	.01
☐ 35 Bernie Williams	.40	.18	.05
☐ 36 Eduardo Perez	.05	.02	.01
☐ 37 Rickey Henderson	.30	.14	.04
☐ 38 Terry Pendleton	.05	.02	.01
☐ 39 John Smoltz	.20	.09	.03
☐ 40 Derrick May	.05	.02	.01
☐ 41 Pedro J.Martinez	.10	.05	.01
☐ 42 Mark Portugal	.05	.02	.01
☐ 43 Albert Belle	1.00	.45	.12
☐ 44 Edgar Martinez	.10	.05	.01
☐ 45 Gary Sheffield	.30	.14	.04
☐ 46 Bret Saberhagen	.05	.02	.01
☐ 47 Ricky Gutierrez	.05	.02	.01
☐ 48 Orlando Merced	.05	.02	.01
☐ 49 Mike Greenwell	.05	.02	.01
☐ 50 Jose Rijo	.05	.02	.01
☐ 51 Jeff Granger	.05	.02	.01
☐ 52 Mike Henneman	.05	.02	.01
☐ 53 Dave Winfield	.25	.11	.03
☐ 54 Don Mattingly	1.00	.45	.12
☐ 55 J.T. Snow	.10	.05	.01
☐ 56 Todd Van Poppel	.05	.02	.01
☐ 57 Chipper Jones	1.50	.70	.19
☐ 58 Darryl Hamilton	.05	.02	.01
☐ 59 Delino DeShields	.05	.02	.01
☐ 60 Rondell White	.25	.11	.03
☐ 61 Eric Anthony	.05	.02	.01
☐ 62 Charlie Hough	.10	.05	.01
☐ 63 Sid Fernandez	.05	.02	.01
☐ 64 Derek Bell	.10	.05	.01
☐ 65 Phil Plantier	.05	.02	.01
☐ 66 Curt Schilling	.05	.02	.01
☐ 67 Roger Clemens	.30	.14	.04
☐ 68 Jose Lind	.05	.02	.01
☐ 69 Andres Galarraga	.20	.09	.03
☐ 70 Tim Belcher	.05	.02	.01
☐ 71 Ron Karkovice	.05	.02	.01
☐ 72 Alan Trammell	.10	.05	.01
☐ 73 Pete Harnisch	.05	.02	.01
☐ 74 Mark McGwire	.60	.25	.07
☐ 75 Ryan Klesko	.50	.23	.06
☐ 76 Ramon Martinez	.10	.05	.01
☐ 77 Gregg Jefferies	.10	.05	.01
☐ 78 Steve Buechele	.05	.02	.01
☐ 79 Bill Swift	.05	.02	.01
☐ 80 Matt Williams	.30	.14	.04
☐ 81 Randy Johnson	.25	.11	.03
☐ 82 Mike Mussina	.40	.18	.05
☐ 83 Andy Benes	.10	.05	.01
☐ 84 Dave Staton	.05	.02	.01
☐ 85 Steve Cooke	.05	.02	.01
☐ 86 Andy Van Slyke	.05	.02	.01
☐ 87 Ivan Rodriguez	.40	.18	.05
☐ 88 Frank Viola	.05	.02	.01
☐ 89 Aaron Sele	.05	.02	.01
☐ 90 Ellis Burks	.10	.05	.01
☐ 91 Wally Joyner	.05	.02	.01
☐ 92 Rick Aguilera	.05	.02	.01
☐ 93 Kirby Puckett	1.00	.45	.12
☐ 94 Roberto Hernandez	.05	.02	.01
☐ 95 Mike Stanley	.05	.02	.01
☐ 96 Roberto Alomar	.50	.23	.06
☐ 97 James Mouton	.10	.05	.01
☐ 98 Chad Curtis	.05	.02	.01
☐ 99 Mitch Williams	.05	.02	.01
☐ 100 Carlos Delgado	.60	.25	.07
☐ 101 Greg Maddux	1.25	.55	.16
☐ 102 Brian Harper	.05	.02	.01
☐ 103 Tom Pagnozzi	.05	.02	.01
☐ 104 Jose Offerman	.05	.02	.01
☐ 105 John Wetteland	.10	.05	.01
☐ 106 Carlos Baerga	.30	.14	.04
☐ 107 Dave Magadan	.05	.02	.01
☐ 108 Bobby Jones	.10	.05	.01
☐ 109 Tony Gwynn	1.00	.45	.12
☐ 110 Jeromy Burnitz	.05	.02	.01
☐ 111 Bip Roberts	.05	.02	.01
☐ 112 Carlos Garcia	.05	.02	.01
☐ 113 Jeff Russell	.05	.02	.01
☐ 114 Armando Reynoso	.05	.02	.01
☐ 115 Ozzie Guillen	.05	.02	.01
☐ 116 Bo Jackson	.10	.05	.01
☐ 117 Terry Steinbach	.05	.02	.01
☐ 118 Deion Sanders	.30	.14	.04
☐ 119 Randy Myers	.05	.02	.01
☐ 120 Mark Whiten	.05	.02	.01
☐ 121 Manny Ramirez	.60	.25	.07
☐ 122 Ben McDonald	.05	.02	.01
☐ 123 Darren Daulton	.10	.05	.01
☐ 124 Kevin Young	.05	.02	.01
☐ 125 Barry Larkin	.30	.14	.04
☐ 126 Cecil Fielder	.10	.05	.01
☐ 127 Frank Thomas	2.00	.90	.25
☐ 128 Luis Polonia	.05	.02	.01
☐ 129 Steve Finley	.10	.05	.01
☐ 130 John Olerud	.10	.05	.01
☐ 131 John Jaha	.10	.05	.01
☐ 132 Darren Lewis	.05	.02	.01
☐ 133 Orel Hershiser	.10	.05	.01
☐ 134 Chris Bosio	.05	.02	.01
☐ 135 Ryan Thompson	.05	.02	.01
☐ 136 Chris Sabo	.05	.02	.01
☐ 137 Tommy Greene	.05	.02	.01
☐ 138 Andre Dawson	.10	.05	.01
☐ 139 Roberto Kelly	.05	.02	.01
☐ 140 Ken Hill	.05	.02	.01
☐ 141 Greg Gagne	.05	.02	.01
☐ 142 Julio Franco	.05	.02	.01
☐ 143 Chili Davis	.10	.05	.01
☐ 144 Dennis Eckersley	.10	.05	.01
☐ 145 Joe Carter	.10	.05	.01
☐ 146 Mark Grace	.25	.11	.03
☐ 147 Mike Piazza	1.25	.55	.16
☐ 148 J.R. Phillips	.05	.02	.01
☐ 149 Rich Amaral	.05	.02	.01
☐ 150 Benny Santiago	.05	.02	.01
☐ 151 Jeff King	.05	.02	.01
☐ 152 Dean Palmer	.10	.05	.01
☐ 153 Hal Morris	.05	.02	.01
☐ 154 Mike Macfarlane	.05	.02	.01
☐ 155 Chuck Knoblauch	.25	.11	.03
☐ 156 Pat Kelly	.05	.02	.01
☐ 157 Greg Swindell	.05	.02	.01
☐ 158 Chuck Finley	.10	.05	.01
☐ 159 Devon White	.05	.02	.01
☐ 160 Duane Ward	.05	.02	.01
☐ 161 Sammy Sosa	.25	.11	.03
☐ 162 Javy Lopez	.25	.11	.03
☐ 163 Eric Karros	.10	.05	.01
☐ 164 Royce Clayton	.05	.02	.01
☐ 165 Salomon Torres	.05	.02	.01
☐ 166 Jeff Kent	.05	.02	.01
☐ 167 Chris Hoiles	.05	.02	.01
☐ 168 Len Dykstra	.10	.05	.01
☐ 169 Jose Canseco	.30	.14	.04
☐ 170 Bret Boone	.05	.02	.01
☐ 171 Charlie Hayes	.05	.02	.01
☐ 172 Lou Whitaker	.10	.05	.01
☐ 173 Jack McDowell	.20	.09	.03
☐ 174 Jimmy Key	.10	.05	.01
☐ 175 Mark Langston	.05	.02	.01
☐ 176 Darryl Kile	.05	.02	.01
☐ 177 Juan Guzman	.05	.02	.01
☐ 178 Pat Borders	.05	.02	.01
☐ 179 Cal Eldred	.05	.02	.01
☐ 180 Jose Guzman	.05	.02	.01
☐ 181 Ozzie Smith	.60	.25	.07
☐ 182 Rod Beck	.05	.02	.01
☐ 183 Dave Fleming	.05	.02	.01
☐ 184 Eddie Murray	.50	.23	.06
☐ 185 Cal Ripken	1.50	.70	.19
☐ 186 Dave Hollins	.05	.02	.01
☐ 187 Will Clark	.30	.14	.04
☐ 188 Otis Nixon	.05	.02	.01
☐ 189 Joe Oliver	.05	.02	.01
☐ 190 Roberto Mejia	.05	.02	.01
☐ 191 Felix Jose	.05	.02	.01
☐ 192 Tony Phillips	.10	.05	.01
☐ 193 Wade Boggs	.25	.11	.03
☐ 194 Tim Salmon	.40	.18	.05
☐ 195 Ruben Sierra	.05	.02	.01
☐ 196 Steve Avery	.05	.02	.01
☐ 197 B.J. Surhoff	.05	.02	.01
☐ 198 Todd Zeile	.05	.02	.01
☐ 199 Raul Mondesi	.30	.14	.04
☐ 200 Barry Bonds	.50	.23	.06
☐ 201 Sandy Alomar	.10	.05	.01
☐ 202 Bobby Bonilla	.10	.05	.01
☐ 203 Mike Devereaux	.05	.02	.01
☐ 204 Rickey Bottalico	.25	.11	.03
☐ 205 Kevin Brown	.10	.05	.01
☐ 206 Jason Bere	.05	.02	.01
☐ 207 Reggie Sanders	.10	.05	.01
☐ 208 David Nied	.05	.02	.01
☐ 209 Travis Fryman	.10	.05	.01
☐ 210 James Baldwin	.20	.09	.03
☐ 211 Jim Abbott	.05	.02	.01
☐ 212 Jeff Bagwell	1.00	.45	.12
☐ 213 Bob Welch	.05	.02	.01
☐ 214 Jeff Blauser	.05	.02	.01
☐ 215 Brett Butler	.10	.05	.01
☐ 216 Pat Listach	.05	.02	.01
☐ 217 Bob Tewksbury	.05	.02	.01
☐ 218 Mike Lansing	.05	.02	.01
☐ 219 Wayne Kirby	.05	.02	.01
☐ 220 Chuck Carr	.05	.02	.01
☐ 221 Harold Baines	.10	.05	.01
☐ 222 Jay Bell	.05	.02	.01
☐ 223 Ciff Floyd	.05	.02	.01
☐ 224 Rob Dibble	.05	.02	.01
☐ 225 Kevin Appier	.10	.05	.01
☐ 226 Eric Davis	.05	.02	.01
☐ 227 Matt Walbeck	.05	.02	.01
☐ 228 Tim Raines	.10	.05	.01
☐ 229 Paul O'Neill	.10	.05	.01
☐ 230 Craig Biggio	.10	.05	.01
☐ 231 Brent Gates	.05	.02	.01
☐ 232 Rob Butler	.05	.02	.01
☐ 233 David Justice	.20	.09	.03
☐ 234 Rene Arocha	.05	.02	.01
☐ 235 Mike Morgan	.05	.02	.01
☐ 236 Denis Boucher	.05	.02	.01
☐ 237 Kenny Lofton	.40	.18	.05
☐ 238 Jeff Conine	.10	.05	.01
☐ 239 Bryan Harvey	.05	.02	.01
☐ 240 Danny Jackson	.05	.02	.01
☐ 241 Al Martin	.05	.02	.01
☐ 242 Tom Henke	.05	.02	.01
☐ 243 Erik Hanson	.05	.02	.01
☐ 244 Walt Weiss	.05	.02	.01
☐ 245 Brian McRae	.05	.02	.01
☐ 246 Kevin Tapani	.05	.02	.01
☐ 247 David McCarty	.05	.02	.01
☐ 248 Doug Drabek	.05	.02	.01
☐ 249 Troy Neel	.05	.02	.01
☐ 250 Tom Glavine	.20	.09	.03
☐ 251 Ray Lankford	.10	.05	.01
☐ 252 Wil Cordero	.10	.05	.01
☐ 253 Larry Walker	.20	.09	.03
☐ 254 Charles Nagy	.10	.05	.01
☐ 255 Kirk Rueter	.05	.02	.01
☐ 256 John Franco	.10	.05	.01
☐ 257 John Kruk	.10	.05	.01
☐ 258 Alex Gonzalez	.10	.05	.01
☐ 259 Mo Vaughn	.50	.23	.06
☐ 260 David Cone	.10	.05	.01
☐ 261 Kent Hrbek	.05	.02	.01
☐ 262 Lance Johnson	.10	.05	.01
☐ 263 Luis Gonzalez	.05	.02	.01
☐ 264 Mike Bordick	.05	.02	.01
☐ 265 Ed Sprague	.05	.02	.01
☐ 266 Moises Alou	.10	.05	.01
☐ 267 Omar Vizquel	.10	.05	.01
☐ 268 Jay Buhner	.20	.09	.03
☐ 269 Checklist	.05	.02	.01
☐ 270 Checklist	.05	.02	.01

1994 O-Pee-Chee All-Star Redemptions

Inserted one per pack, this standard-size, 25-card redemption set features some of the game's top stars. White borders surround a color player photo on front. The backs contain redemption information. Any five cards from this set and $20 CDN could be redeemed for a foil version of the jumbo set that was issued one per wax box. The redemption deadline was September 30, 1994.

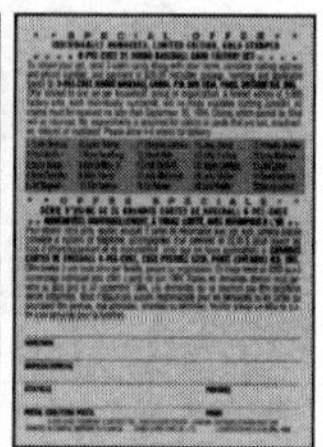

	MINT	NRMT	EXC
COMPLETE SET (25)	12.00	5.50	1.50
COMMON CARD (1-25)	.20	.09	.03
☐ 1 Frank Thomas	4.00	1.80	.50
☐ 2 Paul Molitor	.75	.35	.09
☐ 3 Barry Bonds	.75	.35	.09
☐ 4 Juan Gonzalez	2.00	.90	.25
☐ 5 Jeff Bagwell	2.00	.90	.25
☐ 6 Carlos Baerga	.50	.23	.06
☐ 7 Ryne Sandberg	1.00	.45	.12
☐ 8 Ken Griffey Jr.	4.00	1.80	.50
☐ 9 Mike Piazza	2.50	1.10	.30
☐ 10 Tim Salmon	.50	.23	.06
☐ 11 Marquis Grissom	.40	.18	.05
☐ 12 Albert Belle	2.00	.90	.25
☐ 13 Fred McGriff	.40	.18	.05
☐ 14 Jack McDowell	.20	.09	.03
☐ 15 Cal Ripken	3.00	1.35	.35
☐ 16 John Olerud	.40	.18	.05
☐ 17 Kirby Puckett	2.00	.90	.25
☐ 18 Roger Clemens	.60	.25	.07
☐ 19 Larry Walker	.75	.35	.09
☐ 20 Cecil Fielder	.40	.18	.05
☐ 21 Roberto Alomar	.75	.35	.09
☐ 22 Greg Maddux	2.50	1.10	.30
☐ 23 Joe Carter	.40	.18	.05
☐ 24 David Justice	.40	.18	.05
☐ 25 Kenny Lofton	.75	.35	.09

1994 O-Pee-Chee Jumbo All-Stars

These 5" by 7" parallel cards were included as a bonus at the bottom of every 1994 OPC box. According to published reports, approximately 2,400 of each card was produced.

	MINT	NRMT	EXC
COMPLETE SET (25)	25.00	11.00	3.10
COMMON CARD (1-25)	.40	.18	.05
☐ 1 Frank Thomas	10.00	4.50	1.25
☐ 2 Paul Molitor	2.00	.90	.25
☐ 3 Barry Bonds	2.50	1.10	.30
☐ 4 Juan Gonzalez	5.00	2.20	.60
☐ 5 Jeff Bagwell	5.00	2.20	.60
☐ 6 Carlos Baerga	1.00	.45	.12
☐ 7 Ryne Sandberg	2.50	1.10	.30
☐ 8 Ken Griffey Jr.	10.00	4.50	1.25
☐ 9 Mike Piazza	6.00	2.70	.75
☐ 10 Tim Salmon	2.00	.90	.25
☐ 11 Marquis Grissom	.75	.35	.09
☐ 12 Albert Belle	5.00	2.20	.60
☐ 13 Fred McGriff	1.50	.70	.19
☐ 14 Jack McDowell	.75	.35	.09
☐ 15 Cal Ripken	8.00	3.60	1.00
☐ 16 John Olerud	.75	.35	.09
☐ 17 Kirby Puckett	5.00	2.20	.60
☐ 18 Roger Clemens	2.00	.90	.25
☐ 19 Larry Walker	1.00	.45	.12
☐ 20 Cecil Fielder	.75	.35	.09
☐ 21 Roberto Alomar	2.00	.90	.25
☐ 22 Greg Maddux	6.00	2.70	.75
☐ 23 Joe Carter	.75	.35	.09
☐ 24 David Justice	.75	.35	.09
☐ 25 Kenny Lofton	2.50	1.10	.30

1994 O-Pee-Chee Diamond Dynamos

This 18-card standard-size set was randomly inserted into 1994 OPC packs. According to the company approximately 5,000 sets were produced. The fronts feature player photos as well as red foil lettering while the backs have gold foil stamping. Between one or two cards from this set was included in each box.

	MINT	NRMT	EXC
COMPLETE SET (18)	45.00	20.00	5.50
COMMON CARD (1-18)	2.00	.90	.25

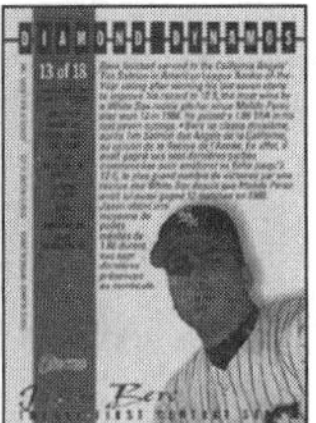

☐ 1 Mike Piazza	20.00	9.00	2.50
☐ 2 Robert Mejia	2.00	.90	.25
☐ 3 Wayne Kirby	2.00	.90	.25
☐ 4 Kevin Stocker	2.00	.90	.25
☐ 5 Chris Gomez	2.00	.90	.25
☐ 6 Bobby Jones	3.00	1.35	.35
☐ 7 David McCarty	2.00	.90	.25
☐ 8 Kirk Rueter	2.00	.90	.25
☐ 9 J.T. Snow	3.00	1.35	.35
☐ 10 Wil Cordero	3.00	1.35	.35
☐ 11 Tim Salmon	7.50	3.40	.95
☐ 12 Jeff Conine	3.00	1.35	.35
☐ 13 Jason Bere	2.00	.90	.25
☐ 14 Greg McMichael	2.00	.90	.25
☐ 15 Brent Gates	3.00	1.35	.35
☐ 16 Allen Watson	2.00	.90	.25
☐ 17 Aaron Sele	3.00	1.35	.35
☐ 18 Carlos Garcia	3.00	1.35	.35

1994 O-Pee-Chee Hot Prospects

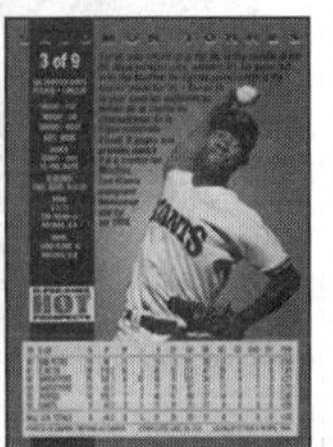

This nine-card standard-size insert set features some of 1994's leading prospects. According to the manufacturer, approximately 6,666 sets were produced. The cards features gold and red foil stamping, player photos on both sides and complete minor league stats. An average of one card was included in each display box.

	MINT	NRMT	EXC
COMPLETE SET (9)	30.00	13.50	3.70
COMMON CARD (1-9)	1.00	.45	.12
☐ 1 Cliff Floyd	1.50	.70	.19
☐ 2 James Mouton	1.00	.45	.12
☐ 3 Salomon Torres	1.00	.45	.12
☐ 4 Raul Mondesi	6.00	2.70	.75
☐ 5 Carlos Delgado	5.00	2.20	.60
☐ 6 Manny Ramirez	10.00	4.50	1.25
☐ 7 Javy Lopez	5.00	2.20	.60
☐ 8 Alex Gonzalez	1.50	.70	.19
☐ 9 Ryan Klesko	8.00	3.60	1.00

1994 O-Pee-Chee World Champions

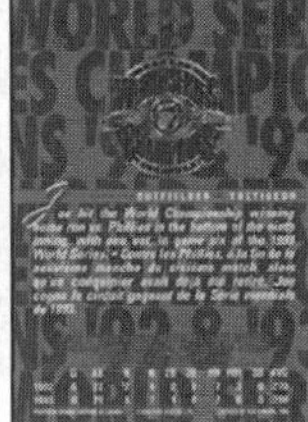

This nine card insert set features members of the 1993 World Series champion Toronto Blue Jays. Randomly inserted in packs at a rate of one in 36, the player is superimposed over a background containing the phrase, "1993 World Series Champions". The backs contain World Series statistics from 1992 and 1993 and highlights.

	MINT	NRMT	EXC
COMPLETE SET (9)	20.00	9.00	2.50
COMMON CARD (1-9)	1.00	.45	.12
☐ 1 Rickey Henderson	4.00	1.80	.50
☐ 2 Devon White	1.00	.45	.12
☐ 3 Paul Molitor	4.00	1.80	.50
☐ 4 Joe Carter	2.00	.90	.25
☐ 5 John Olerud	1.00	.45	.12
☐ 6 Roberto Alomar	4.00	1.80	.50
☐ 7 Ed Sprague	2.00	.90	.25
☐ 8 Pat Borders	1.00	.45	.12
☐ 9 Tony Fernandez	1.00	.45	.12

1991 O-Pee-Chee Premier

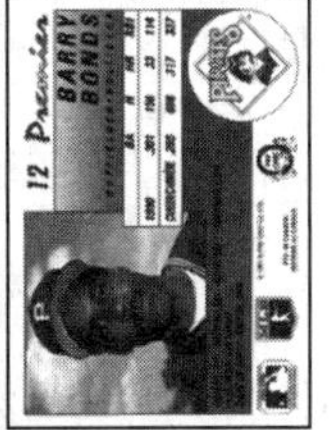

The 1991 OPC Premier set contains 132 standard-size cards. The fronts feature color action player photos on a white card face. All the pictures are bordered in gold above, while the color of the border stripes on the other three sides varies from card to card. The player's name, team name, and position (the last item in English and French) appear below the picture. In a horizontal format, the backs have a color head shot and the team logo in a circular format. Biography and statistics (1990 and career) are presented on an orange and yellow striped background. The cards are arranged in alphabetical order and numbered on the back. Small packs of these cards were given out at the Fan Fest to commemorate the 1991 All-Star Game in Canada.

	MINT	NRMT	EXC
COMPLETE SET (132)	10.00	4.50	1.25
COMPLETE FACT.SET (132)	15.00	6.75	1.85
COMMON CARD (1-132)	.05	.02	.01
☐ 1 Roberto Alomar	.30	.14	.04
☐ 2 Sandy Alomar Jr.	.10	.05	.01
☐ 3 Moises Alou	.15	.07	.02
☐ 4 Brian Barnes	.05	.02	.01
☐ 5 Steve Bedrosian	.05	.02	.01
☐ 6 George Bell	.05	.02	.01
☐ 7 Juan Bell	.05	.02	.01
☐ 8 Albert Belle	1.00	.45	.12
☐ 9 Bud Black	.05	.02	.01
☐ 10 Mike Boddicker	.05	.02	.01
☐ 11 Wade Boggs	.20	.09	.03
☐ 12 Barry Bonds	.40	.18	.05
☐ 13 Denis Boucher	.05	.02	.01
☐ 14 George Brett	.75	.35	.09
☐ 15 Hubie Brooks	.05	.02	.01
☐ 16 Brett Butler	.10	.05	.01
☐ 17 Ivan Calderon	.05	.02	.01
☐ 18 Jose Canseco	.20	.09	.03
☐ 19 Gary Carter	.10	.05	.01
☐ 20 Joe Carter	.10	.05	.01
☐ 21 Jack Clark	.05	.02	.01
☐ 22 Will Clark	.20	.09	.03
☐ 23 Roger Clemens	.25	.11	.03
☐ 24 Alex Cole	.05	.02	.01
☐ 25 Vince Coleman	.05	.02	.01
☐ 26 Jeff Conine	.50	.23	.06
☐ 27 Milt Cuyler	.05	.02	.01
☐ 28 Danny Darwin	.05	.02	.01
☐ 29 Eric Davis	.05	.02	.01
☐ 30 Glenn Davis	.05	.02	.01
☐ 31 Andre Dawson	.10	.05	.01
☐ 32 Ken Dayley	.05	.02	.01
☐ 33 Steve Decker	.05	.02	.01
☐ 34 Delino DeShields	.05	.02	.01
☐ 35 Lance Dickson	.05	.02	.01
☐ 36 Kirk Dressendorfer	.05	.02	.01
☐ 37 Shawon Dunston	.05	.02	.01
☐ 38 Dennis Eckersley	.10	.05	.01
☐ 39 Dwight Evans	.10	.05	.01
☐ 40 Howard Farmer	.05	.02	.01
☐ 41 Junior Felix	.05	.02	.01
☐ 42 Alex Fernandez	.25	.11	.03
☐ 43 Tony Fernandez	.05	.02	.01
☐ 44 Cecil Fielder	.10	.05	.01
☐ 45 Carlton Fisk	.25	.11	.03
☐ 46 Willie Fraser	.05	.02	.01
☐ 47 Gary Gaetti	.05	.02	.01
☐ 48 Andres Galarraga	.15	.07	.02
☐ 49 Ron Gant	.10	.05	.01
☐ 50 Kirk Gibson	.10	.05	.01
☐ 51 Bernard Gilkey	.10	.05	.01
☐ 52 Leo Gomez	.05	.02	.01
☐ 53 Rene Gonzales	.05	.02	.01
☐ 54 Juan Gonzalez	1.00	.45	.12
☐ 55 Dwight Gooden	.10	.05	.01
☐ 56 Ken Griffey Jr.	2.00	.90	.25
☐ 57 Kelly Gruber	.05	.02	.01
☐ 58 Pedro Guerrero	.05	.02	.01
☐ 59 Tony Gwynn	.75	.35	.09
☐ 60 Chris Hammond	.05	.02	.01
☐ 61 Ron Hassey	.05	.02	.01
☐ 62 Rickey Henderson 939 Stolen Bases	.25	.11	.03
☐ 63 Tom Henke	.05	.02	.01
☐ 64 Orel Hershiser	.10	.05	.01
☐ 65 Chris Hoiles	.05	.02	.01
☐ 66 Todd Hundley	.50	.23	.06
☐ 67 Pete Incaviglia	.05	.02	.01
☐ 68 Danny Jackson	.05	.02	.01
☐ 69 Barry Jones	.05	.02	.01
☐ 70 Dave Justice	.40	.18	.05
☐ 71 Jimmy Key	.10	.05	.01
☐ 72 Ray Lankford	.15	.07	.02
☐ 73 Darren Lewis	.05	.02	.01
☐ 74 Kevin Maas	.05	.02	.01
☐ 75 Denny Martinez	.10	.05	.01
☐ 76 Tino Martinez	.15	.07	.02
☐ 77 Don Mattingly	1.00	.45	.12
☐ 78 Willie McGee	.10	.05	.01
☐ 79 Fred McGriff	.20	.09	.03
☐ 80 Hensley Meulens	.05	.02	.01
☐ 81 Kevin Mitchell	.05	.02	.01
☐ 82 Paul Molitor	.40	.18	.05
☐ 83 Mickey Morandini	.05	.02	.01
☐ 84 Jack Morris	.10	.05	.01
☐ 85 Dale Murphy	.15	.07	.02
☐ 86 Eddie Murray	.40	.18	.05
☐ 87 Chris Nabholz	.05	.02	.01
☐ 88 Tim Naehring	.10	.05	.01
☐ 89 Otis Nixon	.10	.05	.01
☐ 90 Jose Offerman	.05	.02	.01
☐ 91 Bob Ojeda	.05	.02	.01
☐ 92 John Olerud	.10	.05	.01
☐ 93 Gregg Olson	.05	.02	.01
☐ 94 Dave Parker	.10	.05	.01
☐ 95 Terry Pendleton	.10	.05	.01
☐ 96 Kirby Puckett	1.00	.45	.12
☐ 97 Tim Raines	.10	.05	.01
☐ 98 Jeff Reardon	.05	.02	.01
☐ 99 Dave Righetti	.05	.02	.01
☐ 100 Cal Ripken	1.50	.70	.19
☐ 101 Mel Rojas	.15	.07	.02
☐ 102 Nolan Ryan 7th No-Hitter	1.50	.70	.19
☐ 103 Ryne Sandberg	.40	.18	.05
☐ 104 Scott Sanderson	.05	.02	.01
☐ 105 Benny Santiago	.05	.02	.01
☐ 106 Pete Schourek	.05	.02	.01
☐ 107 Gary Scott	.05	.02	.01
☐ 108 Terry Shumpert	.05	.02	.01
☐ 109 Ruben Sierra	.05	.02	.01
☐ 110 Doug Simons	.05	.02	.01
☐ 111 Dave Smith	.05	.02	.01
☐ 112 Ozzie Smith	.50	.23	.06
☐ 113 Cory Snyder	.05	.02	.01
☐ 114 Luis Sojo	.05	.02	.01
☐ 115 Dave Stewart	.10	.05	.01
☐ 116 Dave Stieb	.05	.02	.01
☐ 117 Darryl Strawberry	.10	.05	.01
☐ 118 Pat Tabler	.05	.02	.01
☐ 119 Wade Taylor	.05	.02	.01
☐ 120 Bobby Thigpen	.05	.02	.01
☐ 121 Frank Thomas	2.00	.90	.25
☐ 122 Mike Timlin	.05	.02	.01
☐ 123 Alan Trammell	.10	.05	.01
☐ 124 Mo Vaughn	.75	.35	.09
☐ 125 Tim Wallach	.05	.02	.01
☐ 126 Devon White	.05	.02	.01
☐ 127 Mark Whiten	.05	.02	.01
☐ 128 Bernie Williams	.75	.35	.09
☐ 129 Willie Wilson	.05	.02	.01
☐ 130 Dave Winfield	.20	.09	.03
☐ 131 Robin Yount	.20	.09	.03
☐ 132 Checklist 1-132	.05	.02	.01

1992 O-Pee-Chee Premier

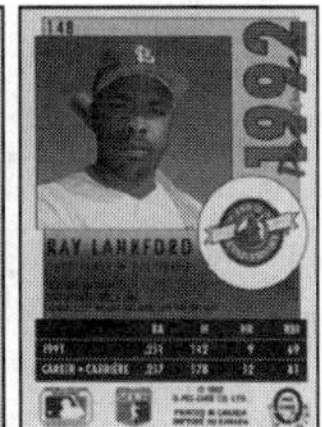

The 1992 OPC Premier baseball set consists of 198 standard-size cards. The fronts feature a mix of color action and posed player photos bordered in white. Gold stripes edge the picture on top and below, while colored stripes edge the pictures on the left and right sides. The player's name, position, and team appear in the bottom white border. In addition to a color head shot, the backs carry biography and the team logo on a panel that shades from green to blue as well as statistics on a black panel.

	MINT	NRMT	EXC
COMPLETE SET (198)	10.00	4.50	1.25
COMPLETE FACT.SET (198)	15.00	6.75	1.85
COMMON CARD (1-198)	.05	.02	.01
☐ 1 Wade Boggs	.20	.09	.03
☐ 2 John Smiley	.05	.02	.01
☐ 3 Checklist 1-99	.05	.02	.01
☐ 4 Ron Gant	.10	.05	.01
☐ 5 Mike Bordick	.05	.02	.01
☐ 6 Charlie Hayes	.05	.02	.01
☐ 7 Kevin Morton	.05	.02	.01
☐ 8 Checklist 100-198	.05	.02	.01
☐ 9 Chris Gwynn	.05	.02	.01
☐ 10 Melido Perez	.05	.02	.01
☐ 11 Dan Gladden	.05	.02	.01
☐ 12 Brian McRae	.15	.07	.02
☐ 13 Dennis Martinez	.10	.05	.01
☐ 14 Bob Scanlan	.05	.02	.01
☐ 15 Julio Franco	.10	.05	.01
☐ 16 Ruben Amaro Jr.	.05	.02	.01
☐ 17 Mo Sanford	.05	.02	.01
☐ 18 Scott Bankhead	.05	.02	.01
☐ 19 Dickie Thon	.05	.02	.01
☐ 20 Chris James	.05	.02	.01
☐ 21 Mike Huff	.05	.02	.01
☐ 22 Orlando Merced	.05	.02	.01
☐ 23 Chris Sabo	.05	.02	.01
☐ 24 Jose Canseco	.20	.09	.03
☐ 25 Reggie Sanders	.25	.11	.03
☐ 26 Chris Nabholz	.05	.02	.01
☐ 27 Kevin Seitzer	.05	.02	.01
☐ 28 Ryan Bowen	.05	.02	.01
☐ 29 Gary Carter	.10	.05	.01
☐ 30 Wayne Rosenthal	.05	.02	.01
☐ 31 Alan Trammell	.10	.05	.01
☐ 32 Doug Drabek	.05	.02	.01
☐ 33 Craig Shipley	.05	.02	.01
☐ 34 Ryne Sandberg	.25	.11	.03
☐ 35 Chuck Knoblauch	.35	.16	.04
☐ 36 Bret Barberie	.05	.02	.01
☐ 37 Tim Naehring	.10	.05	.01
☐ 38 Omar Olivares	.05	.02	.01
☐ 39 Royce Clayton	.10	.05	.01
☐ 40 Brent Mayne	.05	.02	.01
☐ 41 Darrin Fletcher	.05	.02	.01
☐ 42 Howard Johnson	.05	.02	.01
☐ 43 Steve Sax	.05	.02	.01
☐ 44 Greg Swindell	.05	.02	.01
☐ 45 Andre Dawson	.10	.05	.01
☐ 46 Kent Hrbek	.05	.02	.01
☐ 47 Dwight Gooden	.10	.05	.01
☐ 48 Mark Leiter	.05	.02	.01
☐ 49 Tom Glavine	.15	.07	.02
☐ 50 Mo Vaughn	.50	.23	.06
☐ 51 Doug Jones	.05	.02	.01
☐ 52 Brian Barnes	.05	.02	.01
☐ 53 Rob Dibble	.05	.02	.01
☐ 54 Kevin McReynolds	.05	.02	.01
☐ 55 Ivan Rodriguez	.40	.18	.05
☐ 56 Scott Livingstone UER (Photo actually Travis Fryman)	.05	.02	.01
☐ 57 Mike Magnante	.05	.02	.01
☐ 58 Pete Schourek	.05	.02	.01
☐ 59 Frank Thomas	1.50	.70	.19
☐ 60 Kirk McCaskill	.05	.02	.01
☐ 61 Wally Joyner	.05	.02	.01
☐ 62 Rick Aguilera	.10	.05	.01
☐ 63 Eric Karros	.20	.09	.03
☐ 64 Tino Martinez	.10	.05	.01
☐ 65 Bryan Hickerson	.05	.02	.01
☐ 66 Ruben Sierra	.05	.02	.01
☐ 67 Willie Randolph	.10	.05	.01
☐ 68 Bill Landrum	.05	.02	.01
☐ 69 Bip Roberts	.05	.02	.01
☐ 70 Cecil Fielder	.10	.05	.01
☐ 71 Pat Kelly	.05	.02	.01
☐ 72 Kenny Lofton	.75	.35	.09
☐ 73 John Franco	.05	.02	.01
☐ 74 Phil Plantier	.05	.02	.01
☐ 75 Dave Martinez	.05	.02	.01
☐ 76 Warren Newson	.05	.02	.01
☐ 77 Chito Martinez	.05	.02	.01
☐ 78 Brian Hunter	.05	.02	.01
☐ 79 Jack Morris	.10	.05	.01
☐ 80 Eric King	.05	.02	.01
☐ 81 Nolan Ryan	1.00	.45	.12
☐ 82 Bret Saberhagen	.10	.05	.01
☐ 83 Roberto Kelly	.05	.02	.01
☐ 84 Ozzie Smith	.50	.23	.06
☐ 85 Chuck McElroy	.05	.02	.01
☐ 86 Carlton Fisk	.25	.11	.03
☐ 87 Mike Mussina	.50	.23	.06
☐ 88 Mark Carreon	.05	.02	.01
☐ 89 Ken Hill	.10	.05	.01
☐ 90 Rick Cerone	.05	.02	.01
☐ 91 Deion Sanders	.25	.11	.03
☐ 92 Don Mattingly	.75	.35	.09
☐ 93 Danny Tartabull	.05	.02	.01
☐ 94 Keith Miller	.05	.02	.01
☐ 95 Gregg Jefferies	.10	.05	.01
☐ 96 Barry Larkin	.25	.11	.03
☐ 97 Kevin Mitchell	.05	.02	.01
☐ 98 Rick Sutcliffe	.05	.02	.01
☐ 99 Mark McGwire	.50	.23	.06
☐ 100 Albert Belle	.75	.35	.09
☐ 101 Gregg Olson	.05	.02	.01
☐ 102 Kirby Puckett	.75	.35	.09
☐ 103 Luis Gonzalez	.05	.02	.01
☐ 104 Randy Myers	.05	.02	.01
☐ 105 Roger Clemens	.25	.11	.03
☐ 106 Tony Gwynn	.60	.25	.07
☐ 107 Jeff Bagwell	.75	.35	.09
☐ 108 John Wetteland	.10	.05	.01
☐ 109 Bernie Williams	.35	.16	.04
☐ 110 Scott Kamieniecki	.05	.02	.01
☐ 111 Robin Yount	.20	.09	.03
☐ 112 Dean Palmer	.10	.05	.01
☐ 113 Tim Belcher	.05	.02	.01
☐ 114 George Brett	.75	.35	.09
☐ 115 Frank Viola	.05	.02	.01
☐ 116 Kelly Gruber	.05	.02	.01
☐ 117 David Justice	.15	.07	.02

Card	MINT	NRMT	EXC
☐ 118 Scott Leius	.05	.02	.01
☐ 119 Jeff Fassero	.10	.05	.01
☐ 120 Sammy Sosa	.25	.11	.03
☐ 121 Al Osuna	.05	.02	.01
☐ 122 Wilson Alvarez	.15	.07	.02
☐ 123 Jose Offerman	.05	.02	.01
☐ 124 Mel Rojas	.05	.02	.01
☐ 125 Shawon Dunston	.05	.02	.01
☐ 126 Pete Incaviglia	.05	.02	.01
☐ 127 Von Hayes	.05	.02	.01
☐ 128 Dave Gallagher	.05	.02	.01
☐ 129 Eric Davis	.05	.02	.01
☐ 130 Roberto Alomar	.30	.14	.04
☐ 131 Mike Gallego	.05	.02	.01
☐ 132 Robin Ventura	.10	.05	.01
☐ 133 Bill Swift	.05	.02	.01
☐ 134 John Kruk	.10	.05	.01
☐ 135 Craig Biggio	.20	.09	.03
☐ 136 Eddie Taubensee	.05	.02	.01
☐ 137 Cal Ripken	1.00	.45	.12
☐ 138 Charles Nagy	.10	.05	.01
☐ 139 Jose Melendez	.05	.02	.01
☐ 140 Jim Abbott	.10	.05	.01
☐ 141 Paul Molitor	.25	.11	.03
☐ 142 Tom Candiotti	.05	.02	.01
☐ 143 Bobby Bonilla	.10	.05	.01
☐ 144 Matt Williams	.20	.09	.03
☐ 145 Brett Butler	.10	.05	.01
☐ 146 Will Clark	.20	.09	.03
☐ 147 Rickey Henderson	.25	.11	.03
☐ 148 Ray Lankford	.15	.07	.02
☐ 149 Bill Pecota	.05	.02	.01
☐ 150 Dave Winfield	.25	.11	.03
☐ 151 Darren Lewis	.05	.02	.01
☐ 152 Bob MacDonald	.05	.02	.01
☐ 153 David Segui	.05	.02	.01
☐ 154 Benny Santiago	.05	.02	.01
☐ 155 Chuck Finley	.10	.05	.01
☐ 156 Andujar Cedeno	.05	.02	.01
☐ 157 Barry Bonds	.25	.11	.03
☐ 158 Joe Grahe	.05	.02	.01
☐ 159 Frank Castillo	.05	.02	.01
☐ 160 Dave Burba	.05	.02	.01
☐ 161 Leo Gomez	.05	.02	.01
☐ 162 Orel Hershiser	.10	.05	.01
☐ 163 Delino DeShields	.05	.02	.01
☐ 164 Sandy Alomar Jr.	.10	.05	.01
☐ 165 Denny Neagle	.15	.07	.02
☐ 166 Fred McGriff	.25	.11	.03
☐ 167 Ken Griffey Jr.	1.50	.70	.19
☐ 168 Juan Guzman	.10	.05	.01
☐ 169 Bobby Rose	.05	.02	.01
☐ 170 Steve Avery	.10	.05	.01
☐ 171 Rich DeLucia	.05	.02	.01
☐ 172 Mike Timlin	.05	.02	.01
☐ 173 Randy Johnson	.25	.11	.03
☐ 174 Paul Gibson	.05	.02	.01
☐ 175 David Cone	.10	.05	.01
☐ 176 Marquis Grissom	.10	.05	.01
☐ 177 Kurt Stillwell	.05	.02	.01
☐ 178 Mark Whiten	.05	.02	.01
☐ 179 Darryl Strawberry	.10	.05	.01
☐ 180 Mike Morgan	.05	.02	.01
☐ 181 Scott Scudder	.05	.02	.01
☐ 182 George Bell	.05	.02	.01
☐ 183 Alvin Davis	.05	.02	.01
☐ 184 Len Dykstra	.10	.05	.01
☐ 185 Kyle Abbott	.05	.02	.01
☐ 186 Chris Haney	.05	.02	.01
☐ 187 Junior Noboa	.05	.02	.01
☐ 188 Dennis Eckersley	.10	.05	.01
☐ 189 Derek Bell	.25	.11	.03
☐ 190 Lee Smith	.10	.05	.01
☐ 191 Andres Galarraga	.25	.11	.03
☐ 192 Jack Armstrong	.05	.02	.01
☐ 193 Eddie Murray	.35	.16	.04
☐ 194 Joe Carter	.25	.11	.03
☐ 195 Terry Pendleton	.10	.05	.01
☐ 196 Darryl Kile	.10	.05	.01
☐ 197 Rod Beck	.15	.07	.02
☐ 198 Hubie Brooks	.05	.02	.01

1993 O-Pee-Chee Premier

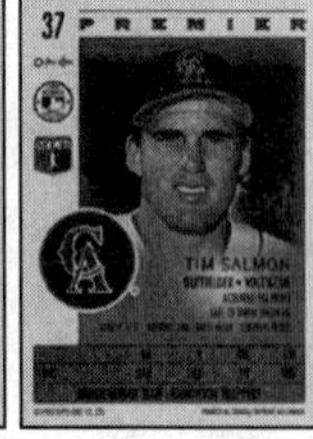

The 1993 OPC Premier set consists of 132 standard-size cards. The foil packs contain eight regular cards and one Star Performer insert card. The white-bordered fronts feature a mix of color action and posed player photos. The player's name and position are printed in the lower left border. The backs carry a color head shot, biography, 1992 statistics, and the team logo. According to O-Pee-Chee, only 4,000 cases were produced.

	MINT	NRMT	EXC
COMPLETE SET (132)	5.00	2.20	.60
COMMON CARD (1-132)	.05	.02	.01
☐ 1 Barry Bonds	.25	.11	.03
☐ 2 Chad Curtis	.05	.02	.01
☐ 3 Chris Bosio	.05	.02	.01
☐ 4 Cal Eldred	.05	.02	.01
☐ 5 Dan Walters	.05	.02	.01
☐ 6 Rene Arocha	.05	.02	.01
☐ 7 Delino DeShields	.05	.02	.01
☐ 8 Spike Owen	.05	.02	.01
☐ 9 Jeff Russell	.05	.02	.01
☐ 10 Phil Plantier	.05	.02	.01
☐ 11 Mike Christopher	.05	.02	.01
☐ 12 Darren Daulton	.10	.05	.01
☐ 13 Scott Cooper	.05	.02	.01
☐ 14 Paul O'Neill	.10	.05	.01
☐ 15 Jimmy Key	.10	.05	.01
☐ 16 Dickie Thon	.05	.02	.01
☐ 17 Greg Gohr	.05	.02	.01
☐ 18 Andre Dawson	.10	.05	.01
☐ 19 Steve Cooke	.05	.02	.01
☐ 20 Tony Fernandez	.05	.02	.01
☐ 21 Mark Gardner	.05	.02	.01
☐ 22 Dave Martinez	.05	.02	.01
☐ 23 Jose Guzman	.05	.02	.01
☐ 24 Chili Davis	.10	.05	.01
☐ 25 Randy Knorr	.05	.02	.01
☐ 26 Mike Piazza	1.00	.45	.12
☐ 27 Benji Gil	.05	.02	.01
☐ 28 Dave Winfield	.20	.09	.03
☐ 29 Wil Cordero	.10	.05	.01
☐ 30 Butch Henry	.05	.02	.01
☐ 31 Eric Young	.15	.07	.02
☐ 32 Orestes Destrade	.05	.02	.01
☐ 33 Randy Myers	.05	.02	.01
☐ 34 Tom Brunansky	.05	.02	.01
☐ 35 Dan Wilson	.05	.02	.01
☐ 36 Juan Guzman	.05	.02	.01
☐ 37 Tim Salmon	.30	.14	.04
☐ 38 Bill Krueger	.05	.02	.01
☐ 39 Larry Walker	.15	.07	.02
☐ 40 David Hulse	.05	.02	.01
☐ 41 Ken Ryan	.05	.02	.01
☐ 42 Jose Lind	.05	.02	.01
☐ 43 Benny Santiago	.05	.02	.01
☐ 44 Ray Lankford	.10	.05	.01
☐ 45 Dave Stewart	.10	.05	.01
☐ 46 Don Mattingly	.75	.35	.09
☐ 47 Fernando Valenzuela	.10	.05	.01
☐ 48 Scott Fletcher	.05	.02	.01
☐ 49 Wade Boggs	.20	.09	.03
☐ 50 Norm Charlton	.05	.02	.01
☐ 51 Carlos Baerga	.15	.07	.02
☐ 52 John Olerud	.10	.05	.01
☐ 53 Willie Wilson	.05	.02	.01
☐ 54 Dennis Moeller	.05	.02	.01
☐ 55 Joe Orsulak	.05	.02	.01
☐ 56 John Smiley	.05	.02	.01
☐ 57 Al Martin	.10	.05	.01
☐ 58 Andres Galarraga	.15	.07	.02
☐ 59 Billy Ripken	.05	.02	.01
☐ 60 Dave Stieb	.05	.02	.01
☐ 61 Dave Magadan	.05	.02	.01
☐ 62 Todd Worrell	.05	.02	.01
☐ 63 Sherman Obando	.05	.02	.01
☐ 64 Kent Bottenfield	.05	.02	.01
☐ 65 Vinny Castilla	.15	.07	.02
☐ 66 Charlie Hayes	.05	.02	.01
☐ 67 Mike Hartley	.05	.02	.01
☐ 68 Harold Baines	.10	.05	.01
☐ 69 John Cummings	.05	.02	.01
☐ 70 J.T. Snow	.25	.11	.03
☐ 71 Graeme Lloyd	.05	.02	.01
☐ 72 Frank Bolick	.05	.02	.01
☐ 73 Doug Drabek	.05	.02	.01
☐ 74 Milt Thompson	.05	.02	.01
☐ 75 Tim Pugh	.05	.02	.01
☐ 76 John Kruk	.10	.05	.01
☐ 77 Tom Henke	.05	.02	.01
☐ 78 Kevin Young	.05	.02	.01
☐ 79 Ryan Thompson	.05	.02	.01
☐ 80 Mike Hampton	.15	.07	.02
☐ 81 Jose Canseco	.15	.07	.02
☐ 82 Mike Lansing	.15	.07	.02
☐ 83 Candy Maldonado	.05	.02	.01
☐ 84 Alex Arias	.05	.02	.01
☐ 85 Troy Neel	.05	.02	.01
☐ 86 Greg Swindell	.05	.02	.01
☐ 87 Tim Wallach	.05	.02	.01
☐ 88 Andy Van Slyke	.05	.02	.01
☐ 89 Harold Reynolds	.10	.05	.01
☐ 90 Bryan Harvey	.05	.02	.01
☐ 91 Jerald Clark	.05	.02	.01
☐ 92 David Cone	.10	.05	.01
☐ 93 Ellis Burks	.10	.05	.01
☐ 94 Scott Bankhead	.05	.02	.01
☐ 95 Pete Incaviglia	.05	.02	.01
☐ 96 Cecil Fielder	.10	.05	.01
☐ 97 Sean Berry	.05	.02	.01
☐ 98 Gregg Jefferies	.10	.05	.01
☐ 99 Billy Brewer	.05	.02	.01
☐ 100 Scott Sanderson	.05	.02	.01
☐ 101 Walt Weiss	.05	.02	.01
☐ 102 Travis Fryman	.10	.05	.01
☐ 103 Barry Larkin	.25	.11	.03
☐ 104 Darren Holmes	.05	.02	.01
☐ 105 Ivan Calderon	.05	.02	.01
☐ 106 Terry Jorgensen	.05	.02	.01
☐ 107 David Nied	.05	.02	.01
☐ 108 Tim Bogar	.05	.02	.01
☐ 109 Roberto Kelly	.05	.02	.01
☐ 110 Mike Moore	.05	.02	.01
☐ 111 Carlos Garcia	.10	.05	.01
☐ 112 Mike Bieleckl	.05	.02	.01
☐ 113 Trevor Hoffman	.15	.07	.02
☐ 114 Rich Amaral	.05	.02	.01
☐ 115 Jody Reed	.05	.02	.01
☐ 116 Charlie Liebrandt	.05	.02	.01
☐ 117 Greg Gagne	.05	.02	.01
☐ 118 Darrell Sherman	.05	.02	.01
☐ 119 Jeff Conine	.10	.05	.01
☐ 120 Tim Laker	.05	.02	.01
☐ 121 Kevin Seitzer	.05	.02	.01
☐ 122 Jeff Mutis	.05	.02	.01
☐ 123 Rico Rossy	.05	.02	.01
☐ 124 Paul Molitor	.25	.11	.03
☐ 125 Cal Ripken	1.00	.45	.12
☐ 126 Greg Maddux	.75	.35	.09
☐ 127 Greg McMichael	.05	.02	.01
☐ 128 Felix Jose	.05	.02	.01
☐ 129 Dick Schofield	.05	.02	.01
☐ 130 Jim Abbott	.10	.05	.01
☐ 131 Kevin Reimer	.05	.02	.01
☐ 132 Checklist 1-132	.05	.02	.01

1993 O-Pee-Chee Premier Star Performers

The 1993 OPC Premier Star Performers 22-card standard-size set was inserted one per 1993 OPC Premier foil packs. The fronts display a gold outer border with a narrow white inner border that frames a color action player photo. The subset title is printed on a green stripe across the top of the photo and the player's name and position are printed below the photo on the lower border. The backs contain a kelly-green border surrounding a white box that carries a player head shot, biography and career summary in both French and English. A ghosted team logo appears beneath the career summary. A parallel set of Foil Star Performers was randomly inserted in foil packs. The gold foil-stamped set logo rests in a lower corner. The Foil Star Performers are valued at a multiple of the regular Star Performers cards.

	MINT	NRMT	EXC
COMPLETE SET (22)	10.00	4.50	1.25
COMMON CARD (1-22)	.10	.05	.01
☐ 1 Frank Thomas	2.00	.90	.25
☐ 2 Fred McGriff	.25	.11	.03
☐ 3 Roberto Alomar	.40	.18	.05
☐ 4 Ryne Sandberg	.60	.25	.07
☐ 5 Edgar Martinez	.15	.07	.02
☐ 6 Gary Sheffield	.30	.14	.04
☐ 7 Juan Gonzalez	1.00	.45	.12
☐ 8 Eric Karros	.20	.09	.03
☐ 9 Ken Griffey Jr.	2.00	.90	.25
☐ 10 Deion Sanders	.25	.11	.03
☐ 11 Kirby Puckett	1.00	.45	.12
☐ 12 Will Clark	.25	.11	.03
☐ 13 Joe Carter	.15	.07	.02
☐ 14 Barry Bonds	.50	.23	.06
☐ 15 Pat Listach	.10	.05	.01
☐ 16 Mark McGwire	.60	.25	.07
☐ 17 Kenny Lofton	.50	.23	.06
☐ 18 Roger Clemens	.30	.14	.04
☐ 19 Greg Maddux	1.25	.55	.16
☐ 20 Nolan Ryan	1.50	.70	.19
☐ 21 Tom Glavine	.20	.09	.03
☐ 22 Dennis Eckersley	.15	.07	.02

1993 O-Pee-Chee Premier Star Performers Foil

This 22 card set is a parallel to the 1993 OPC Premier Star Performers set. These cards were inserted into foil packs but at a lesser rate than the regular Star Performers cards.

	MINT	NRMT	EXC
COMPLETE SET (22)	250.00	110.00	31.00
COMMON CARD (1-22)	2.50	1.10	.30

*STARS: 12.5X to 25X BASIC CARDS

1993 O-Pee-Chee Premier Top Draft Picks

Randomly inserted in foil packs, this four-card standard-size set features the top two draft picks of the Toronto Blue Jays and Montreal

Expos. Each borderless front carries a posed color player photo, with the player's name and team appearing vertically in gold foil within a team color-coded stripe. The set's gold foil-highlighted logo rests in a lower corner. The back carries a posed player color headshot in the upper left of a mottled, light blue panel. The player's team's logo appears alongside and his career highlights follow below.

	MINT	NRMT	EXC
COMPLETE SET (4)	8.00	3.60	1.00
COMMON CARD (1-4)	1.00	.45	.12
☐ 1 B.J. Wallace	1.00	.45	.12
☐ 2 Shannon Stewart	4.00	1.80	.50
☐ 3 Rod Henderson	1.00	.45	.12
☐ 4 Todd Steverson	2.50	1.10	.30

1982 Ohio Hall of Fame set

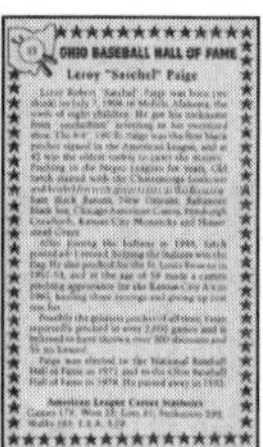

This set of tri-colored cards measures 3" x 6" and contains biographies and statistics on the backs. Cards are numbered and checklisted below.

	NRMT	VG-E	GOOD
COMPLETE SET (65)	60.00	27.00	7.50
COMMON CARD (1-65)	.75	.35	.09
☐ 1 Ohio Hall of Fame	.75	.35	.09
☐ 2 Checklist	.75	.35	.09
☐ 3 Nick Cullop	.75	.35	.09
☐ 4 Dean Chance	.75	.35	.09
☐ 5 Bob Feller	4.00	1.80	.50
☐ 6 Jesse Haines	1.50	.70	.19
☐ 7 Waite Hoyt	1.50	.70	.19
☐ 8 Ernie Lombardi	1.50	.70	.19
☐ 9 Mike Powers	.75	.35	.09
☐ 10 Edd Roush	1.50	.70	.19
☐ 11 Red Ruffing	1.50	.70	.19
☐ 12 Luke Sewell	.75	.35	.09
☐ 13 Tris Speaker	3.00	1.35	.35
☐ 14 Cy Young	3.00	1.35	.35
☐ 15 Walter Alston	1.00	.45	.12
☐ 16 Lou Boudreau	1.50	.70	.19
☐ 17 Warren Giles	1.00	.45	.12
☐ 18 Ted Kluszewski	1.50	.70	.19
☐ 19 William McKinley	1.50	.70	.19
☐ 20 Roger Peckinpaugh	.75	.35	.09
☐ 21 Johnny VanderMeer	1.00	.45	.12
☐ 22 Early Wynn	1.50	.70	.19
☐ 23 Earl Averill	1.50	.70	.19
☐ 24 Stan Coveleskie	1.50	.70	.19
☐ 25 Lefty Grove	2.00	.90	.25
☐ 26 Napolean Lajoie	2.00	.90	.25
☐ 27 Al Lopez	1.00	.45	.12
☐ 28 Eddie Onslow	.75	.35	.09
☐ 29 Branch Rickey	1.00	.45	.12
☐ 30 Frank Robinson	2.50	1.10	.30
☐ 31 George Sisler	1.50	.70	.19
☐ 32 Bob Lemon	1.50	.70	.19
☐ 33 Satchel Paige	5.00	2.20	.60
☐ 34 Bucky Walters	1.00	.45	.12
☐ 35 Gus Bell	.75	.35	.09
☐ 36 Rocky Colavito	1.50	.70	.19
☐ 37 Mel Harder	1.00	.45	.12
☐ 38 Tom Henrich	1.00	.45	.12
☐ 39 Miller Huggins	1.00	.45	.12
☐ 40 Fred Hutchinson	.75	.35	.09
☐ 41 Eppa Rixey	1.50	.70	.19
☐ 42 Joe Sewell	1.50	.70	.19
☐ 43 George Uhle	.75	.35	.09
☐ 44 Bill Veeck	1.00	.45	.12
☐ 45 Estel Crabtree	.75	.35	.09
☐ 46 Harvey Haddix	.75	.35	.09
☐ 47 Noodles Hahn	.75	.35	.09
☐ 48 Joe Jackson	6.00	2.70	.75
☐ 49 Kenesaw Landis	1.00	.45	.12
☐ 50 Thurman Munson	1.50	.70	.19
☐ 51 Gabe Paul	.75	.35	.09
☐ 52 Vada Pinson	1.00	.45	.12
☐ 53 Wally Post	.75	.35	.09

☐ 54 Vic Wertz	.75	.35	.09
☐ 55 Paul Derringer	.75	.35	.09
☐ 56 John Galbreath	.75	.35	.09
☐ 57 Rube Marquard	1.50	.70	.19
☐ 58 Bill McKechnie	1.00	.45	.12
☐ 59 Rocky Nelson	.75	.35	.09
☐ 60 Al Rosen	1.00	.45	.12
☐ 61 Lew Fonseca	.75	.35	.09
☐ 62 Larry MacPhail	.75	.35	.09
☐ 63 Joe Nuxhall	.75	.35	.09
☐ 64 Birdie Tebbetts	.75	.35	.09
☐ 65 Gene Woodling	.75	.35	.09

1959 Oklahoma Today Major Leaguers

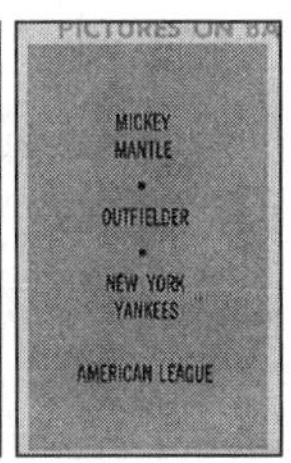

These 20 cards which measure 1 11/16" by 2 3/4" were featured on the back cover of the Summer 1959 Issue of Oklahoma Today. The card fronts feature Black and White photos on color backgrounds (8 green, 8 gold and 4 light blue). The bottom 1/4" of the front has a white panel with the players name in red. The backs are grey with the player's name, position team and league. The checklist below is as the players appear on the uncut covers in 4 rows of 5 cards starting on the top left. In the complete book form -- this set is valued at two to three times the values listed below.

	NRMT	VG-E	GOOD
COMPLETE SET (20)	100.00	45.00	12.50
COMMON CARD (1-20)	2.00	.90	.25
☐ 1 Paul Waner	5.00	2.20	.60
☐ 2 Lloyd Waner	5.00	2.20	.60
☐ 3 Jerry Walker	2.00	.90	.25
☐ 4 Tom Sturdivant	2.00	.90	.25
☐ 5 Warren Spahn	7.50	3.40	.95
☐ 6 Allie Reynolds	3.00	1.35	.35
☐ 7 Dale Mitchell	2.00	.90	.25
☐ 8 Cal McLish	2.00	.90	.25
☐ 9 Von McDaniel	2.00	.90	.25
☐ 10 Lindy McDaniel	2.00	.90	.25
☐ 11 Pepper Martin	4.00	1.80	.50
☐ 12 Mickey Mantle	75.00	34.00	9.50
☐ 13 Carl Hubbell	5.00	2.20	.60
☐ 14 Paul Dean	2.00	.90	.25
☐ 15 Dizzy Dean	5.00	2.20	.60
☐ 16 Don Demeter	2.00	.90	.25
☐ 17 Alvin Dark	2.00	.90	.25
☐ 18 Johnny Callison	3.00	1.35	.35
☐ 19 Harry Brecheen	2.00	.90	.25
☐ 20 Jerry Adair	2.00	.90	.25

1886 Old Judge N167

These cards measure approximately 1 1/2" by 2 1/2". All the players portrayed are members of the New York National team which became the Giants. We have sequenced this set in alphabetical order.

	EX-MT	VG-E	GOOD
COMPLETE SET (14)	30000.00	13500.00	3800.00
COMMON CARD (1-14)	2000.00	900.00	250.00
☐ 1 Roger Connor	3000.00	1350.00	375.00
☐ 2 Larry Corcoran	2000.00	900.00	250.00
☐ 3 Tom Deasley	2000.00	900.00	250.00
☐ 4 Mike Dorgan	2000.00	900.00	250.00
☐ 5 Dude Esterbrook	2000.00	900.00	250.00
☐ 6 Buck Ewing	3000.00	1350.00	375.00
☐ 7 Joe Gerhardt	2000.00	900.00	250.00
☐ 8 Pete Gillespie	2000.00	900.00	250.00
☐ 9 Tim Keefe	3000.00	1350.00	375.00
☐ 10 Jim Mutrie MG	2500.00	1100.00	300.00
☐ 11 James O'Rourke	3000.00	1350.00	375.00
☐ 12 Danny Richardson	2000.00	900.00	250.00
☐ 13 John M. Ward	3000.00	1350.00	375.00
☐ 14 Mickey Welsh (sic)	3000.00	1350.00	375.00

1887-90 Old Judge N172

The Goodwin Company's baseball series depicts hundreds of ballplayers from more than 40 major and minor league teams as well as boxers and wrestlers. The cards (approximately 1 1/2" by 2 1/2") are actually photographs from the Hall studio in New York which were pasted onto thick cardboard. The pictures are sepia in color with either a white or pink cast, and the cards are blank backed. They are found either numbered or unnumbered, with or without a copyright date, and with hand printed or machine printed names. All known cards have the name "Goodwin Co., New York" at the base. The cards were marketed during the period 1887-1890 in packs of "Old Judge" and "Gypsy Queen" cigarettes (cards marked with the latter brand are worth double the values listed below). They have been listed alphabetically and assigned numbers in the checklist below for simplicity's sake; the various poses known for some players also have not been listed for the same reason. Some of the players are pictured in horizontal (HOR) poses. In all, more than 2300 different Goodwin cards are known to collectors, with more being discovered every year. Cards from the "Spotted Tie" sub-series are denoted in the checklist below by SPOT.

	EX-MT	VG-E	GOOD
COMPLETE SET	170000	76500	21200
COMMON CARD	150.00	70.00	19.00
COMMON CARD (DOUBLE)	200.00	90.00	25.00
COMMON BROWNS CHAMP	250.00	110.00	31.00
COMMON CARD (PCL)	2500.00	1100.00	300.00
COMMON SPOTTED TIE	450.00	200.00	55.00
☐ 1 Gus Albert: Cleveland-Milwaukee	150.00	70.00	19.00
☐ 2 Charles Alcott: St. Louis Whites-Mansfield	150.00	70.00	19.00
☐ 3 Alexander: Des Moines	150.00	70.00	19.00
☐ 4 Myron Allen: K.C.	150.00	70.00	19.00
☐ 5 Bob Allen: Pitts.-Phila. N.L.	150.00	70.00	19.00
☐ 6 Uncle Bill Alvord: Toledo-Des Moines	150.00	70.00	19.00
☐ 7 Varney Anderson: St.Paul	1500.00	700.00	190.00
☐ 8 Ed Andrews: Phila.	150.00	70.00	19.00
☐ 9 Ed Andrews and Buster Hoover: Philadelphia	200.00	90.00	25.00
☐ 10 Wally Andrews: Omaha	150.00	70.00	19.00
☐ 11 Bill Annis: Omaha-Worchester	150.00	70.00	19.00
☐ 12A Cap Anson: Chicago (In uniform)	15000.00	6800.00	1900.00
☐ 12B Cap Anson: Chicago (Not in uniform)	2250.00	1000.00	275.00
☐ 13 Old Hoss Ardner: Kansas City-St. Joe	150.00	70.00	19.00
☐ 14 Tug Arundel: Indianapolis-Whites	150.00	70.00	19.00
☐ 15 Jersey Bakley: Cleve.	150.00	70.00	19.00
☐ 16 Clarence Baldwin: Cincinnati	150.00	70.00	19.00
☐ 17 Mark(Fido) Baldwin: Chicago-Columbus	150.00	70.00	19.00
☐ 18 Lady Baldwin: Detroit	150.00	70.00	19.00
☐ 19 James Banning: Wash.	150.00	70.00	19.00
☐ 20 Samuel Barkley: Pittsburgh-K.C.	150.00	70.00	19.00
☐ 22 Bald Billy Barnie: Mgr. Baltimore	175.00	80.00	22.00
☐ 23 Charles Bassett: Indianapolis-N.Y.	150.00	70.00	19.00
☐ 24 Charles Bastian: Phila.-Chicago	150.00	70.00	19.00
☐ 25 Charles Bastian and Schriver: Philadelphia	200.00	90.00	25.00
☐ 26 Ollie Beard: Cinc.	150.00	70.00	19.00
☐ 27 Ebenezer Beatin: Cleve.	150.00	70.00	19.00
☐ 28 Jake Beckley: Eagle Eye Whites-Pittsburgh	600.00	275.00	75.00
☐ 29 Stephen Behel SPOT	1250.00	550.00	160.00
☐ 30 Charles Bennett: Detroit-Boston	150.00	70.00	19.00
☐ 31 Louis Bierbauer: A's	150.00	70.00	19.00
☐ 32 Louis Bierbauer and Robert Gamble: Athletics	200.00	90.00	25.00
☐ 33 Bill Bishop: Pittsburgh-Syracuse	150.00	70.00	19.00
☐ 34 William Blair: A's-Hamiltons	150.00	70.00	19.00
☐ 35 Ned Bligh: Columbus	150.00	70.00	19.00
☐ 36 Bogart: Indianapolis	150.00	70.00	19.00
☐ 37 Boyce: Washington	150.00	70.00	19.00
☐ 38 Jake Boyd: Maroons	175.00	80.00	22.00
☐ 39 Honest John Boyle: St. Louis-Chicago	150.00	70.00	19.00
☐ 40 Handsome Henry Boyle Indianapolis-N.Y.	150.00	70.00	19.00
☐ 41 Nick Bradley: K.C.- Worchester	150.00	70.00	19.00
☐ 42 George(Grin) Bradley Sioux City	150.00	70.00	19.00
☐ 43 Stephen Brady SPOT	500.00	220.00	60.00
☐ 44 Breckinridge: Sacramento PCL	2500.00	1100.00	300.00
☐ 45 Jim Brennan: Kansas City- A's	150.00	70.00	19.00
☐ 46 Timothy Brosnan: Minn.-Sioux City	150.00	70.00	19.00
☐ 47 Cal Broughton: St. Paul	150.00	70.00	19.00
☐ 48 Big Dan Brouthers: Detroit-Boston	500.00	220.00	60.00
☐ 49 Thomas Brown: Pittsburgh-Boston	150.00	70.00	19.00
☐ 50 California Brown: New York	150.00	70.00	19.00
☐ 51 Pete Browning: Gladiator Louisville	300.00	135.00	38.00
☐ 52 Charles Brynan: Chicago-Des Moines	150.00	70.00	19.00
☐ 53 Al Buckenberger MG: Columbus	150.00	70.00	19.00
☐ 54 Dick Buckley: Indianapolis-N.Y.	150.00	70.00	19.00
☐ 55 Charles Buffington: Philadelphia	150.00	70.00	19.00
☐ 56 Ernest Burch: Brooklyn-Whites	150.00	70.00	19.00
☐ 57 Bill Burdick: Omaha-Indianapolis	150.00	70.00	19.00
☐ 58 Black Jack Burdock: Boston-Brooklyn	150.00	70.00	19.00
☐ 59 Robert Burks: Sioux City	150.00	70.00	19.00
☐ 60 George Burnham Watch Mgr. Indianapolis	175.00	80.00	22.00
☐ 61 Burns: Omaha	150.00	70.00	19.00
☐ 62 Jimmy Burns: K.C.	150.00	70.00	19.00
☐ 63 Tommy(Oyster) Burns Baltimore-Brooklyn	150.00	70.00	19.00
☐ 64 Thomas E. Burns: Chicago	150.00	70.00	19.00
☐ 65A Doc Bushong: Brook.	150.00	70.00	19.00
☐ 65B Doc Bushong: Browns Champs	250.00	110.00	31.00
☐ 66 Patsy Cahill: Ind.	150.00	70.00	19.00
☐ 67 Count Campau: Kansas City-Detroit	150.00	70.00	19.00
☐ 68 Jimmy Canavan: Omaha	150.00	70.00	19.00
☐ 69 Bart Cantz: Whites-Baltimore	150.00	70.00	19.00
☐ 70 Handsome Jack Carney Washington	150.00	70.00	19.00
☐ 71 Hick Carpenter Cincinnati	150.00	70.00	19.00
☐ 72 Cliff Carroll: Wash.	150.00	70.00	19.00
☐ 73 Scrappy Carroll: St.Paul-Chicago	150.00	70.00	19.00
☐ 74 Frederick Carroll: Pitts.	150.00	70.00	19.00
☐ 75 Jumbo Cartwright: Kansas City-St. Joe	150.00	70.00	19.00
☐ 76A Bob Caruthers: Parisian Brooklyn	175.00	80.00	22.00
☐ 76B Bob Caruthers: Parisian Browns Champs	300.00	135.00	38.00
☐ 77 Daniel Casey: Phila.	150.00	70.00	19.00
☐ 78 Icebox Chamberlain: St. Louis	150.00	70.00	19.00
☐ 79 Cupid Childs: Phila.-Syracuse	150.00	70.00	19.00
☐ 80 Bob Clark: Washington	150.00	70.00	19.00
☐ 81 Owen Clark: Washington	150.00	70.00	19.00
☐ 82 Clarke and Mickey Hughes: Brooklyn HOR	200.00	90.00	25.00
☐ 83 William(Dad) Clarke: Chicago-Omaha	150.00	70.00	19.00
☐ 84 John Clarkson: Chicago-Boston	500.00	220.00	60.00
☐ 85 Jack Clements: Philadelphia	150.00	70.00	19.00
☐ 86 Elmer Cleveland: Omaha-New York	150.00	70.00	19.00
☐ 87 Monk Cline: K.C.-Sioux City	150.00	70.00	19.00
☐ 88 Cody: Des Moines	150.00	70.00	19.00
☐ 89 John Coleman: Pittsburgh - A's	150.00	70.00	19.00
☐ 90 Bill Collins: New York-Newark	150.00	70.00	19.00
☐ 91 Hub Collins: Louisville-Brooklyn	150.00	70.00	19.00
☐ 92A Charles Comiskey: Browns Champs	900.00	400.00	110.00
☐ 92B Commy Comiskey: St. Louis-Chicago	750.00	350.00	95.00
☐ 93 Pete Connell: Des Moines	150.00	70.00	19.00
☐ 94A Roger Connor: Script	600.00	275.00	75.00
☐ 94B Roger Connor: New York	600.00	275.00	75.00
☐ 95 Richard Conway: Boston-Worchester	150.00	70.00	19.00
☐ 96 Peter Conway: Det.-Pitts.-Ind.	150.00	70.00	19.00
☐ 97 James Conway: K.C.	150.00	70.00	19.00
☐ 98 Paul Cook: Louisville	150.00	70.00	19.00
☐ 99 Jimmy Cooney: Omaha-Chicago	150.00	70.00	19.00
☐ 100 Larry Corcoran: Indianapolis-London	175.00	80.00	22.00
☐ 101 Pop Corkhill: Cincinnati-Brooklyn	150.00	70.00	19.00
☐ 102 Roscoe Coughlin: Maroons-Chicago	175.00	80.00	22.00
☐ 103 Cannon Ball Crane: New York	150.00	70.00	19.00
☐ 104 Samuel Crane: Wash.	150.00	70.00	19.00
☐ 105 Jack Crogan: Maroons	175.00	80.00	22.00
☐ 106 John Crooks: Whites-Omaha	150.00	70.00	19.00
☐ 107 Lave Cross: Louisville-A's-Phila.	150.00	70.00	19.00
☐ 108 Bill Crossley: Milw.	150.00	70.00	19.00
☐ 109A Joe Crotty SPOT	450.00	200.00	55.00
☐ 109B Joe Crotty: Sioux City	150.00	70.00	19.00
☐ 110 Billy Crowell: Cleveland-St. Joe	150.00	70.00	19.00
☐ 111 Jim Cudworth: St. Louis-Worchester	150.00	70.00	19.00
☐ 112 Bert Cunningham: Baltimore-Phila.	150.00	70.00	19.00
☐ 113 Tacks Curtis: St. Joe	150.00	70.00	19.00
☐ 114A Ed Cushman SPOT	500.00	220.00	60.00
☐ 114B Ed Cushman: Toledo	1200.00	550.00	150.00
☐ 115 Tony Cusick: Mil.	1500.00	700.00	190.00
☐ 116 Dailey: Oakland PCL	2500.00	1100.00	300.00
☐ 117 Edward Dailey: Phil.-Wash.-Columbus	150.00	70.00	19.00
☐ 118 Bill Daley: Boston	150.00	70.00	19.00
☐ 119 Con Daley: Boston-Indianapolis	150.00	70.00	19.00
☐ 120 Abner Dalrymple: Pittsburgh-Denver	150.00	70.00	19.00
☐ 121 Tom Daly: Chicago-Wash.-Cleve.	150.00	70.00	19.00
☐ 122 James Daly: Minn.	150.00	70.00	19.00
☐ 123 Law Daniels: K.C.	150.00	70.00	19.00
☐ 124 Dell Darling: Chicago	150.00	70.00	19.00
☐ 125 Wm. Darnbrough: Denver	150.00	70.00	19.00
☐ 126 D. Davin: Milwaukee	150.00	70.00	19.00
☐ 127 Jumbo Davis: K.C.	150.00	70.00	19.00
☐ 128 Pat Dealey: Wash.	150.00	70.00	19.00
☐ 129 Thomas Deasley: New York-Washington	150.00	70.00	19.00
☐ 130 Edward Decker: Phil.	150.00	70.00	19.00
☐ 131 Big Ed Delahanty: Philadelphia	1200.00	550.00	150.00
☐ 132 Jeremiah Denny: Indianapolis-New York	150.00	70.00	19.00
☐ 133 James Devlin: St.L.	150.00	70.00	19.00
☐ 134 Thomas Dolan: Whites-St. Louis-Denver	150.00	70.00	19.00
☐ 135 Jack Donahue: San Francisco PCL	2500.00	1100.00	300.00
☐ 136A James Donahue SPOT	450.00	200.00	55.00
☐ 136B James Donahue: K.C.	150.00	70.00	19.00
☐ 137 James Donnelly: Washington	150.00	70.00	19.00
☐ 138 Dooley: Oakland PCL	2500.00	1100.00	300.00
☐ 139 J. Doran: Omaha	150.00	70.00	19.00
☐ 140 Michael Dorgan: N.Y.	150.00	70.00	19.00
☐ 141 Doyle: San Fran. PCL	2500.00	1100.00	300.00
☐ 142 Homerun Duffe: St.L.	150.00	70.00	19.00
☐ 143 Hugh Duffy: Chicago	600.00	275.00	75.00
☐ 144 Dan Dugdale: Maroons-Minneapolis	175.00	80.00	22.00

☐ 145 Dugrahm: Maroons 175.00 80.00 22.00
☐ 146 Duck Duke: Minn. 150.00 70.00 19.00
☐ 147 Sure Shot Dunlap: Pittsburgh 150.00 70.00 19.00
☐ 148 J. Dunn: Maroons 175.00 80.00 22.00
☐ 149 Jesse(Cyclone)Duryea St. Paul-Cinc. 150.00 70.00 19.00
☐ 150 John Dwyer: Chicago-Maroons 175.00 80.00 22.00
☐ 151 Billy Earle: Cincinnati-St.Paul 150.00 70.00 19.00
☐ 152 Buck Ebright: Wash. 150.00 70.00 19.00
☐ 153 Red Ehret: Louisville 150.00 70.00 19.00
☐ 154 R. Emmerke: Des Moines 150.00 70.00 19.00
☐ 155 Dude Esterbrook: Louisville-Ind.-New York-All Star 150.00 70.00 19.00
☐ 156 Henry Esterday: K.C.-Columbus 150.00 70.00 19.00
☐ 157 Long John Ewing: Louisville-N.Y. 150.00 70.00 19.00
☐ 158 Buck Ewing: New York 500.00 220.00 60.00
☐ 159 Buck Ewing and Mascot: New York 500.00 220.00 60.00
☐ 160 Jay Faatz: Cleveland 150.00 70.00 19.00
☐ 161 Clinkgers Fagan: Kansas City-Denver 150.00 70.00 19.00
☐ 162 William Farmer: Pittsburgh-St. Paul 150.00 70.00 19.00
☐ 163 Sidney Farrar: Philadelphia 175.00 80.00 22.00
☐ 164 John(Moose) Farrell: Wash.-Baltimore 150.00 70.00 19.00
☐ 165 Charles(Duke)Farrell Chicago 150.00 70.00 19.00
☐ 166 Frank Fennelly: Cincinnati-A's 150.00 70.00 19.00
☐ 167 Chas. Ferguson: Phila. 150.00 70.00 19.00
☐ 168 Colonel Ferson: Washington 150.00 70.00 19.00
☐ 169 Wallace Fessenden: Umpire National 175.00 80.00 22.00
☐ 170 Jocko Fields: Pitts. 150.00 70.00 19.00
☐ 171 Fischer: Maroons 175.00 80.00 22.00
☐ 172 Thomas Flanigan: Cleve.-Sioux City 150.00 70.00 19.00
☐ 173 Silver Flint: Chicago 150.00 70.00 19.00
☐ 174 Thomas Flood: St. Joe 150.00 70.00 19.00
☐ 175 Flynn: Omaha 1200.00 550.00 150.00
☐ 176 James Fogarty: Philadelphia 150.00 70.00 19.00
☐ 177 Frank(Monkey)Foreman Baltimore-Cinc. 150.00 70.00 19.00
☐ 178 Thomas Forster: Milwaukee-Hartford 150.00 70.00 19.00
☐ 179A Elmer E. Foster SPOT 450.00 200.00 55.00
☐ 179B Elmer Foster: New York-Chicago 150.00 70.00 19.00
☐ 180 F.W. Foster SPOT T.W. Forster (Sic) 500.00 220.00 60.00
☐ 181A Scissors Foutz: Browns Champ 250.00 110.00 31.00
☐ 181B Scissors Foutz: Brooklyn 150.00 70.00 19.00
☐ 182 Julie Freeman: St.L.-Milwaukee 150.00 70.00 19.00
☐ 183 Will Fry: St. Joe 150.00 70.00 19.00
☐ 184 Fudger: Oakland PCL 2500.00 1100.00 300.00
☐ 185 William Fuller: Milwaukee 150.00 70.00 19.00
☐ 186 Shorty Fuller: St.Louis 150.00 70.00 19.00
☐ 187 Christopher Fullmer: Baltimore 150.00 70.00 19.00
☐ 188 Christopher Fullmer and Tom Tucker: Baltimore HOR 200.00 90.00 25.00
☐ 189 Honest John Gaffney: Mgr. Washington 175.00 80.00 22.00
☐ 190 Pud Galvin: Pitts. 600.00 275.00 75.00
☐ 191 Robert Gamble: A's 150.00 70.00 19.00
☐ 192 Charles Ganzel: Detroit-Boston 150.00 70.00 19.00
☐ 193 Frank(Gid) Gardner: Phila.-Washington 150.00 70.00 19.00
☐ 194 Gid Gardner and Miah Murray: Washington HOR 200.00 90.00 25.00
☐ 195 Ed Gastfield: Omaha 150.00 70.00 19.00
☐ 196 Hank Gastreich: Columbus 150.00 70.00 19.00
☐ 197 Emil Geiss: Chicago 150.00 70.00 19.00
☐ 198 Frenchy Genins: Sioux City 150.00 70.00 19.00
☐ 199 William George: N.Y. 150.00 70.00 19.00
☐ 200 Move Up Joe Gerhardt All Star-Jersey City 150.00 70.00 19.00
☐ 201 Pretzels Getzein: Detroit-Ind. 150.00 70.00 19.00
☐ 202 Lee Gibson: A's 150.00 70.00 19.00
☐ 203 Robert Gilks: Cleve. 150.00 70.00 19.00
☐ 204 Pete Gillespie: N.Y. 150.00 70.00 19.00
☐ 205 Barney Gilligan Washington-Detroit 150.00 70.00 19.00
☐ 206 Frank Gilmore: Wash. 150.00 70.00 19.00
☐ 207 Pebbly Jack Glasscock Indianapolis-N.Y. 175.00 80.00 22.00
☐ 208 Kid Gleason: Phila. 175.00 80.00 22.00
☐ 209A Brother Bill Gleason A's-Louisville 150.00 70.00 19.00
☐ 209B William Bill Gleason Browns Champs 250.00 110.00 31.00
☐ 210 Mouse Glenn: Sioux City 150.00 70.00 19.00
☐ 211 Walt Goldsby: Balt. 150.00 70.00 19.00
☐ 212 Michael Goodfellow: Cleveland-Detroit 150.00 70.00 19.00
☐ 213 George Gore (Pianolegs) New York 150.00 70.00 19.00
☐ 214 Frank Graves: Minn. 150.00 70.00 19.00
☐ 215 William Greenwood: Baltimore-Columbus 150.00 70.00 19.00
☐ 216 Michael Greer: Cleveland-Brooklyn 150.00 70.00 19.00
☐ 217 Mike Griffin: Baltimore-Phila NL 150.00 70.00 19.00
☐ 218 Clark Griffith: Milwaukee 600.00 275.00 75.00
☐ 219 Henry Gruber: Cleve. 150.00 70.00 19.00
☐ 220 Addison Gumbert: Chicago-Boston 150.00 70.00 19.00
☐ 221 Thomas Gunning: Philadelphia-A's 150.00 70.00 19.00
☐ 222 Joseph Gunson: K.C. 150.00 70.00 19.00
☐ 223 George Haddock: Washington 150.00 70.00 19.00
☐ 224 William Hafner: K.C. 150.00 70.00 19.00
☐ 225 Willie Hahm: Chicago Mascot 150.00 70.00 19.00
☐ 226 William Hallman: Philadelphia 150.00 70.00 19.00
☐ 227 Charlie Hallstrom: Minn. 150.00 70.00 19.00
☐ 228 Billy Hamilton: Kansas City-Phila. 750.00 350.00 95.00
☐ 229 Willie Hamm and Ned Williamson: Chicago 200.00 90.00 25.00
☐ 230A Frank Hankinson: SPOT 450.00 200.00 55.00
☐ 230B Frank Hankinson: Kansas City 150.00 70.00 19.00
☐ 231 Ned Hanlon: Det.-Boston-Pitts. 175.00 80.00 22.00
☐ 232 William Hanrahan: Maroons-Minn. 175.00 80.00 22.00
☐ 233 Hapeman: Sacramento PCL 2500.00 1100.00 300.00
☐ 234 Pa Harkins: Brooklyn-Baltimore 150.00 70.00 19.00
☐ 235 William Hart: Cinc.-Des Moines 150.00 70.00 19.00
☐ 236 Wm. Hasamdear: K.C. 150.00 70.00 19.00
☐ 237 Colonel Hatfield: New York 150.00 70.00 19.00
☐ 238 Egyptian Healey: Wash.-Indianapolis 150.00 70.00 19.00
☐ 239 J.C. Healy: Omaha-Denver 150.00 70.00 19.00
☐ 240 Guy Hecker: Louisville 150.00 70.00 19.00
☐ 241 Tony Hellman: Sioux City 150.00 70.00 19.00
☐ 242 Hardie Henderson: Brook.-Pitts.-Balt. 150.00 70.00 19.00
☐ 243 Hardie Henderson and Michael Greer: Brooklyn 200.00 90.00 25.00
☐ 244 Moxie Hengle: Maroons-Minneapolis 175.00 80.00 22.00
☐ 245 John Henry: Phila. 150.00 70.00 19.00
☐ 246 Edward Herr: Whites-Milwaukee 150.00 70.00 19.00
☐ 247 Hunkey Hines: Whites 150.00 70.00 19.00
☐ 248 Paul Hines: Wash.-Indianapolis 150.00 70.00 19.00
☐ 249 Texas Wonder Hoffman: Denver 150.00 70.00 19.00
☐ 250 Eddie Hogan: Cleve. 150.00 70.00 19.00
☐ 251A William Holbert SPOT 450.00 200.00 55.00
☐ 251B William Holbert: Brooklyn-Mets-Jersey City 150.00 70.00 19.00
☐ 252 James(Bugs) Holliday: Des Moines-Cinc. 150.00 70.00 19.00
☐ 253 Charles Hoover: Maroons-Chi.-K.C. 175.00 80.00 22.00
☐ 254 Buster Hoover: Phila.-Toronto 150.00 70.00 19.00
☐ 255 Jack Horner: Milwaukee-New Haven 150.00 70.00 19.00
☐ 256 Jack Horner and E.H. Warner: Milwaukee 200.00 90.00 25.00
☐ 257 Michael Horning: Boston-Balt.-N.Y. 150.00 70.00 19.00
☐ 258 Pete Hotaling: Cleveland 150.00 70.00 19.00
☐ 259 William Howes: Minn.-St. Paul 150.00 70.00 19.00
☐ 260 Dummy Hoy: Washington 500.00 220.00 60.00
☐ 261A Nat Hudson: Browns Champ 250.00 110.00 31.00
☐ 261B Nat Hudson: St. Louis 150.00 70.00 19.00
☐ 262 Mickey Hughes: Brk. 150.00 70.00 19.00
☐ 263 Hungler: Sioux City 150.00 70.00 19.00
☐ 264 Wild Bill Hutchinson: Chicago 150.00 70.00 19.00
☐ 265 John Irwin: Wash.-Wilkes Barre 150.00 70.00 19.00
☐ 266 Cutrate Irwin: Phila.-Boston-Wash. 150.00 70.00 19.00
☐ 267 A.C. Jantzen: Minn. 150.00 70.00 19.00
☐ 268 Frederick Jevne: Minn.-St. Paul 150.00 70.00 19.00
☐ 269 John Johnson: K.C.-Columbus 150.00 70.00 19.00
☐ 270 Richard Johnston: Boston 150.00 70.00 19.00
☐ 271 Jordan: Minneapolis 150.00 70.00 19.00
☐ 272 Heinie Kappell: Columbus-Cincinnati 150.00 70.00 19.00
☐ 273 Keas: Milwaukee 150.00 70.00 19.00
☐ 274 Sir Timothy Keefe: New York 500.00 220.00 60.00
☐ 275 Tim Keefe and Danny Richardson: Stealing 2nd Base New York HOR 450.00 200.00 55.00
☐ 276 George Keefe: Wash. 150.00 70.00 19.00
☐ 277 James Keenan: Cinc. 150.00 70.00 19.00
☐ 278 Mike(King) Kelly 10,000 Chic-Boston 1250.00 550.00 160.00
☐ 279 Honest John Kelly: Mgr. Louisville 175.00 80.00 22.00
☐ 280 Kelly: (Umpire) Western Association 175.00 80.00 22.00
☐ 281 Charles Kelly: Philadelphia 150.00 70.00 19.00
☐ 282 Kelly and Powell: Umpire and Manager Sioux City 200.00 90.00 25.00
☐ 283A Rudolph Kemmler: Browns Champ 250.00 110.00 31.00
☐ 283B Rudolph Kemmler: St. Paul 150.00 70.00 19.00
☐ 284 Theodore Kennedy: Des Moines-Omaha 200.00 90.00 25.00
☐ 285 J.J. Kenyon: Whites-Des Moines 150.00 70.00 19.00
☐ 286 John Kerins: Louisville 150.00 70.00 19.00
☐ 287 Matthew Kilroy: Baltimore-Boston 150.00 70.00 19.00
☐ 288 Charles King: St.L.-Chi. 150.00 70.00 19.00
☐ 289 Aug. Kloff: Minn.-St.Joe 150.00 70.00 19.00
☐ 290 William Klusman: Milwaukee-Denver 150.00 70.00 19.00
☐ 291 Phillip Knell: St. Joe-Phila. 150.00 70.00 19.00
☐ 292 Fred Knouf: St. Louis 150.00 70.00 19.00
☐ 293 Charles Kremmeyer: Sacramento PCL 2500.00 1100.00 300.00
☐ 294 William Krieg: Wash.-St. Joe-Minn. 150.00 70.00 19.00
☐ 295 William Krieg and Aug. Kloff: Minneapolis 200.00 90.00 25.00
☐ 296 Gus Krock: Chicago 150.00 70.00 19.00
☐ 297 Willie Kuehne: Pittsburgh 150.00 70.00 19.00
☐ 298 Frederick Lange: Maroons 175.00 80.00 22.00
☐ 299 Ted Larkin: A's 150.00 70.00 19.00
☐ 300A Arlie Latham: Browns Champ 250.00 110.00 31.00
☐ 300B Arlie Latham: St. Louis-Chicago 175.00 80.00 22.00
☐ 301 John Lauer: Pittsburgh 150.00 70.00 19.00
☐ 302 Lawless: Columbus 150.00 70.00 19.00
☐ 303 John Leighton: Omaha 150.00 70.00 19.00
☐ 304 Levy: San Fran. PCL 2500.00 1100.00 300.00
☐ 305 Tom Loftus MG: Whites-Cleveland 150.00 70.00 19.00
☐ 306 Lohbeck: Cleveland 150.00 70.00 19.00
☐ 307 Herman(Germany)Long Maroons-K.C. 200.00 90.00 25.00
☐ 308 Danny Long: Oak. PCL 2500.00 1100.00 300.00
☐ 309 Tom Lovett: Omaha-Brooklyn 150.00 70.00 19.00
☐ 310 Bobby(Link) Lowe: Milwaukee 200.00 90.00 25.00
☐ 311A Jack Lynch SPOT 500.00 220.00 60.00
☐ 311B John Lynch: All Stars 150.00 70.00 19.00
☐ 312 Dennis Lyons: A's 150.00 70.00 19.00
☐ 313 Harry Lyons: St. L. 150.00 70.00 19.00
☐ 314 Connie Mack: Wash. 1500.00 700.00 190.00
☐ 315 Joe(Reddie) Mack: Louisville 150.00 70.00 19.00
☐ 316 James(Little Mack) Macullar: Des Moines-Milwaukee 150.00 70.00 19.00
☐ 317 Kid Madden: Boston 150.00 70.00 19.00
☐ 318 Daniel Mahoney: St. Joe 150.00 70.00 19.00
☐ 319 Willard(Grasshopper) Maines: St. Paul 150.00 70.00 19.00
☐ 320 Fred Mann: St.Louis-Hartford 150.00 70.00 19.00
☐ 321 Jimmy Manning: K.C. 150.00 70.00 19.00
☐ 322 Charles(Lefty) Marr: Col.-Cinc. 150.00 70.00 19.00
☐ 323 Mascot(Willie Breslin): New York 175.00 80.00 22.00
☐ 324 Samuel Maskery: Milwaukee-Des Moines 150.00 70.00 19.00
☐ 325 Bobby Mathews: A's 150.00 70.00 19.00
☐ 326 Michael Mattimore: New York-A's 150.00 70.00 19.00
☐ 327 Albert Maul: Pitts. 150.00 70.00 19.00
☐ 328A Albert Mays SPOT 450.00 200.00 55.00
☐ 328B Albert Mays: Columbus 150.00 70.00 19.00
☐ 329 James McAleer: Cleveland 150.00 70.00 19.00
☐ 330 Thomas McCarthy: Phila.-St. Louis 500.00 220.00 60.00
☐ 331 John McCarthy: K.C. 150.00 70.00 19.00
☐ 332 James McCauley: Maroons-Phila. 175.00 80.00 22.00
☐ 333 William McClellan: Brooklyn-Denver 150.00 70.00 19.00
☐ 334 John McCormack: Whites 150.00 70.00 19.00
☐ 335 Big Jim McCormick: Chicago-Pittsburgh 150.00 70.00 19.00
☐ 336 McCreachery: Mgr. Indianapolis 175.00 80.00 22.00
☐ 337 Thomas McCullum: Minneapolis 150.00 70.00 19.00
☐ 338 James(Chippy)McGarr: St. Louis-K.C. 150.00 70.00 19.00
☐ 339 Jack McGeachy: Ind. 150.00 70.00 19.00
☐ 340 John McGlone: Cleveland-Detroit 150.00 70.00 19.00
☐ 341 James(Deacon)McGuire Phila.-Toronto 150.00 70.00 19.00
☐ 342 Bill(Gunner) McGunnigle: Mgr. Brooklyn 175.00 80.00 22.00
☐ 343 Ed McKean: Cleveland 150.00 70.00 19.00
☐ 344 Alex McKinnon: Pittsburgh 150.00 70.00 19.00
☐ 345 Thomas McLaughlin SPOT 450.00 200.00 55.00
☐ 346 John(Bid) McPhee: Cincinnati 175.00 80.00 22.00
☐ 347 James McQuaid: Denver 150.00 70.00 19.00
☐ 348 John McQuaid: Umpire Amer. Assoc. 175.00 80.00 22.00
☐ 349 Jame McTamany: Brook.-Col.-K.C. 150.00 70.00 19.00
☐ 350 George McVey: Mil.-Denver-St. Joe 150.00 70.00 19.00
☐ 351 Meegan: San Fran. PCL 2500.00 1100.00 300.00
☐ 352 John Messitt: Omaha 150.00 70.00 19.00
☐ 353 George(Doggie)Miller Pittsburgh 150.00 70.00 19.00
☐ 354 Joseph Miller: Omaha-Minneapolis 150.00 70.00 19.00
☐ 355 Jocko Milligan: St. Louis-Phila. 150.00 70.00 19.00
☐ 356 E.L. Mills: Milwaukee 150.00 70.00 19.00
☐ 357 Minnehan: Minneapolis 150.00 70.00 19.00
☐ 358 Samuel Moffet: Ind. 150.00 70.00 19.00
☐ 359 Honest Morrell: Boston-Washington 150.00 70.00 19.00
☐ 360 Ed Morris (Cannonball): Pittsburgh 150.00 70.00 19.00
☐ 361 Morrisey: St. Paul 150.00 70.00 19.00
☐ 362 Tony(Count) Mullane: Cincinnati 200.00 90.00 25.00
☐ 363 Joseph Mulvey: Philadelphia 150.00 70.00 19.00
☐ 364 P.L. Murphy: St. Paul 150.00 70.00 19.00
☐ 365 Pat J. Murphy: New York 150.00 70.00 19.00
☐ 366 Miah Murray: Wash. 150.00 70.00 19.00
☐ 367 James(Truthful) 175.00 80.00 22.00

Mutrie: Mgr. N.Y.			
☐ 368 George Myers: Indianapolis-Phila.	150.00	70.00	19.00
☐ 369 Al(Cod) Myers: Washington	150.00	70.00	19.00
☐ 370 Thomas Nagle: Omaha-Chi.	150.00	70.00	19.00
☐ 371 Billy Nash: Boston	150.00	70.00	19.00
☐ 372 Jack(Candy) Nelson: SPOT	450.00	200.00	55.00
☐ 373 Kid Nichols: Omaha	900.00	400.00	110.00
☐ 374 Samuel Nichols: Pittsburgh	150.00	70.00	19.00
☐ 375 J.W. Nicholson Maroons-Minn.	175.00	80.00	22.00
☐ 376 Tom Nicholson (Parson) Whites-Cleveland	150.00	70.00	19.00
☐ 377A Nicholls Nicol Browns Champ	250.00	110.00	31.00
☐ 377B Hugh Nicol: Cinc.	150.00	70.00	19.00
☐ 378 Hugh Nicol and Long John Reilly: Cincinnati	200.00	90.00	25.00
☐ 379 Frederick Nyce Whites-Burlington	150.00	70.00	19.00
☐ 380 Doc Oberlander Cleveland-Syracuse	150.00	70.00	19.00
☐ 381 Jack O'Brien Brooklyn-Baltimore	150.00	70.00	19.00
☐ 382 William O'Brien: Washington	150.00	70.00	19.00
☐ 383 William O'Brien and John Irwin: Washington	200.00	90.00	25.00
☐ 384 Darby O'Brien: Brooklyn	150.00	70.00	19.00
☐ 385 John O'Brien: Cleve.	150.00	70.00	19.00
☐ 386 P.J. O'Connell: Omaha-Des Moines	150.00	70.00	19.00
☐ 387 John O'Connor: Cincinnati-Columbus	150.00	70.00	19.00
☐ 388 Hank O'Day: Washington-New York	175.00	80.00	22.00
☐ 389 O'Day Sacramento	150.00	70.00	19.00
☐ 390A James O'Neil: St. Louis-Chicago	150.00	70.00	19.00
☐ 390B James O'Neil: Browns Champs	250.00	110.00	31.00
☐ 391 O'Neill: Oakland PCL	2500.00	1100.00	300.00
☐ 392 Orator O'Rourke: New York	600.00	275.00	75.00
☐ 393 Thomas O'Rourke: Boston-Jersey City	150.00	70.00	19.00
☐ 394A David Orr SPOT	450.00	200.00	55.00
☐ 394B David Orr: All Star-Brooklyn-Columbus	150.00	70.00	19.00
☐ 395 Parsons: Minneapolis	150.00	70.00	19.00
☐ 396 Owen Patton: Minn.-Des Moines	150.00	70.00	19.00
☐ 397 James Peeples: Brooklyn-Columbus	150.00	70.00	19.00
☐ 398 James Peeples and Hardie Henderson: Brooklyn	200.00	90.00	25.00
☐ 399 Hip Perrier: San Francisco PCL	2500.00	1100.00	300.00
☐ 400 Patrick Pettee: Milwaukee-London	150.00	70.00	19.00
☐ 401 Patrick Pettee and Bobby Lowe: Milwaukee	200.00	90.00	25.00
☐ 402 Bob Pettit: Chicago	150.00	70.00	19.00
☐ 403 Dandelion Pfeffer: Chi.	150.00	70.00	19.00
☐ 404 Dick Phelan: Des Moines	150.00	70.00	19.00
☐ 405 William Phillips: Brooklyn-Kansas City	150.00	70.00	19.00
☐ 406 Horace Phillips: Pittsburgh	150.00	70.00	19.00
☐ 407 John Pickett: St. Paul-K.C.-Phila.	150.00	70.00	19.00
☐ 408 George Pinkney: Brooklyn	150.00	70.00	19.00
☐ 409 Thomas Poorman: A's-Milwaukee	150.00	70.00	19.00
☐ 410 Henry Porter: Brooklyn-Kansas City	150.00	70.00	19.00
☐ 411 James Powell: Sioux City	150.00	70.00	19.00
☐ 412 Tom Powers: San Francisco PCL	2500.00	1100.00	300.00
☐ 413 Bill Purcell: (Blondie) Baltimore-A's	150.00	70.00	19.00
☐ 414 Thomas Quinn: Baltimore	150.00	70.00	19.00
☐ 415 Joseph Quinn: Des Moines-Boston	150.00	70.00	19.00
☐ 416A Old Hoss Radbourne: Boston (Portrait)	900.00	400.00	110.00
☐ 416B Old Hoss Radbourne: Boston (Non-portrait)	600.00	275.00	75.00
☐ 417 Shorty Radford: Brooklyn-Cleveland	150.00	70.00	19.00
☐ 418 Tom Ramsey: Louisville	150.00	70.00	19.00
☐ 419 Rehse: Minneapolis	150.00	70.00	19.00
☐ 420 Long John Reilly: Cincinnati	150.00	70.00	19.00
☐ 421 Charles Reilly: (Princeton) St.Paul	150.00	70.00	19.00
☐ 422 Charles Reynolds: Kansas City	150.00	70.00	19.00
☐ 423 Hardie Richardson Detroit-Boston	150.00	70.00	19.00
☐ 424 Danny Richardson: New York	150.00	70.00	19.00
☐ 425 Frank Ringo: St. Paul	150.00	70.00	19.00
☐ 426 Charles Ripslager SPOT	450.00	200.00	55.00
☐ 427 John Roach: New York	150.00	70.00	19.00
☐ 428 Wilbert Robinson Uncle Robbie: A's	750.00	350.00	95.00
☐ 429 M.C. Robinson: Minn.	150.00	70.00	19.00
☐ 430A Yank Robinson: St. Louis	150.00	70.00	19.00
☐ 430B Wm.(Yank) Robinson: Browns Champs	250.00	110.00	31.00
☐ 431 George Rooks: Maroons-Detroit	175.00	80.00	22.00
☐ 432 James(Chief) Roseman SPOT	1000.00	450.00	125.00
☐ 433 Davis Rowe: Mgr. K.C.-Denver	150.00	70.00	19.00
☐ 434 Jack Rowe: Detroit-Pittsburgh	150.00	70.00	19.00
☐ 435 Amos (Hoosier Thunderbolt) Rusie: Ind.-New York	1000.00	450.00	125.00
☐ 436 James Ryan: Chicago	175.00	80.00	22.00
☐ 437 Henry Sage: Des Moines-Toledo	150.00	70.00	19.00
☐ 438 Henry Sage and William Van Dyke: Des Moines-Toledo	200.00	90.00	25.00
☐ 439 Frank Salee Omaha-Boston	150.00	70.00	19.00
☐ 440 Sanders: Omaha	150.00	70.00	19.00
☐ 441 Al(Ben) Sanders: Philadelphia	150.00	70.00	19.00
☐ 442 Frank Scheibeck: Detroit	150.00	70.00	19.00
☐ 443 Albert Schellhase: St. Joseph	150.00	70.00	19.00
☐ 444 William Schenkle: Milwaukee	150.00	70.00	19.00
☐ 445 Bill Schildknecht: Des Moines-Milwaukee	150.00	70.00	19.00
☐ 446 Gus(Pink Whiskers) Schmelz Mgr. Cincinnati	150.00	70.00	19.00
☐ 447 R. F. Schoch: Wash.	150.00	70.00	19.00
☐ 448 Lewis Schoeneck (Jumbo): Maroons-Indianapolis	175.00	80.00	22.00
☐ 449 Pop Schriver: Phila.	150.00	70.00	19.00
☐ 450 John Seery: Ind.	150.00	70.00	19.00
☐ 451 William Serad Cincinnati-Toronto	150.00	70.00	19.00
☐ 452 Edward Seward: A's	150.00	70.00	19.00
☐ 453 George(Orator)Shafer Des Moines	150.00	70.00	19.00
☐ 454 Frank Shafer: St. Paul	150.00	70.00	19.00
☐ 455 Daniel Shannon: Omaha-L'ville-Phila.	150.00	70.00	19.00
☐ 456 William Sharsig: Mgr. Athletics	175.00	80.00	22.00
☐ 457 Samuel Shaw: Baltimore-Newark	150.00	70.00	19.00
☐ 458 John Shaw: Minneapolis	150.00	70.00	19.00
☐ 459 William Shindle: Baltimore-Phila.	150.00	70.00	19.00
☐ 460 George Shock: Wash.	150.00	70.00	19.00
☐ 461 Otto Shomberg: Ind.	150.00	70.00	19.00
☐ 462 Lev Shreve: Ind.	150.00	70.00	19.00
☐ 463 Ed(Baldy) Silch: Brooklyn-Denver	150.00	70.00	19.00
☐ 464 Michael Slattery: New York	150.00	70.00	19.00
☐ 465 Sam(Skyrocket)Smith: Louisville	150.00	70.00	19.00
☐ 466A John(Phenomenal) Smith (Portrait)	1000.00	450.00	125.00
☐ 466B John(Phenomenal) Smith: Balt.-A's (Non-portrait)	175.00	80.00	22.00
☐ 467 Elmer Smith: Cincinnati	150.00	70.00	19.00
☐ 468 Fred(Sam) Smith: Des Moines	150.00	70.00	19.00
☐ 469 George Smith (Germany) Brooklyn	150.00	70.00	19.00
☐ 470 Pop Smith: Pitt.-Bos.-Phila.	150.00	70.00	19.00
☐ 471 Nick Smith: St. Joe	150.00	70.00	19.00
☐ 472 Pop Snyder: Cleve.	150.00	70.00	19.00
☐ 473 P.T. Somers: St. Louis	150.00	70.00	19.00
☐ 474 Joe Sommer: Balt.	150.00	70.00	19.00
☐ 475 Pete Sommers: Chicago-New York	150.00	70.00	19.00
☐ 476 William Sowders: Boston-Pittsburgh	150.00	70.00	19.00
☐ 477 John Sowders: St. Paul-Kansas City	150.00	70.00	19.00
☐ 478 Charles Sprague: Maroons-Chi.-Cleve.	175.00	80.00	22.00
☐ 479 Edward Sproat: Whites	150.00	70.00	19.00
☐ 480 Harry Staley: Whites-Pittsburgh	150.00	70.00	19.00
☐ 481 Daniel Stearns: Des Moines-K.C.	150.00	70.00	19.00
☐ 482 Billy(Cannonball) Stemmyer: Boston-Cleveland	150.00	70.00	19.00
☐ 483 Stengel: Columbus	150.00	70.00	19.00
☐ 484 B.F. Stephens: Milw.	150.00	70.00	19.00
☐ 485 John C. Sterling: Minneapolis	150.00	70.00	19.00
☐ 486 Stockwell: S.F. PCL	2500.00	1100.00	300.00
☐ 487 Harry Stovey: A's-Boston	300.00	135.00	38.00
☐ 488 C. Scott Stratton: Louisville	150.00	70.00	19.00
☐ 489 Joseph Straus: Omaha-Milwaukee	150.00	70.00	19.00
☐ 490 John(Cub) Stricker: Cleveland	150.00	70.00	19.00
☐ 491 J.O. Struck: Milw.	150.00	70.00	19.00
☐ 492 Marty Sullivan: Chicago-Ind.	150.00	70.00	19.00
☐ 493 Michael Sullivan: A's	150.00	70.00	19.00
☐ 494 Billy Sunday: Chicago-Pittsburgh	750.00	350.00	95.00
☐ 495 Sy Sutcliffe: Cleve.	150.00	70.00	19.00
☐ 496 Ezra Sutton: Boston-Milwaukee	150.00	70.00	19.00
☐ 497 Ed Cyrus Swartwood: Brook.-D.Moines-Ham.	150.00	70.00	19.00
☐ 498 Parke Swartzel: K.C.	150.00	70.00	19.00
☐ 499 Peter Sweeney: Wash.	150.00	70.00	19.00
☐ 500 Sylvester: Sacra. PCL	2500.00	1100.00	300.00
☐ 501 Ed(Dimples) Tate: Boston-Baltimore	150.00	70.00	19.00
☐ 502 Patsy Tebeau: Chi.-Cleve.-Minn.	175.00	80.00	22.00
☐ 503 John Tener: Chicago	175.00	80.00	22.00
☐ 504 Bill(Adonis) Terry: Brooklyn	150.00	70.00	19.00
☐ 505 Big Sam Thompson: Detroit-Philadelphia	500.00	220.00	60.00
☐ 506 Silent Mike Tiernan: New York	150.00	70.00	19.00
☐ 507 Ledell Titcomb: N.Y.	150.00	70.00	19.00
☐ 508 Phillip Tomney: Louisville	150.00	70.00	19.00
☐ 509 Stephen Toole: Brooklyn-K.C.-Rochester	150.00	70.00	19.00
☐ 510 George Townsend: A's	150.00	70.00	19.00
☐ 511 William Traffley: Des Moines	150.00	70.00	19.00
☐ 512 George Treadway: St. Paul-Denver	150.00	70.00	19.00
☐ 513 Samuel Trott: Baltimore-Newark	150.00	70.00	19.00
☐ 514 Sam Trott and Tommy(Oyster) Burns: Baltimore HOR	200.00	90.00	25.00
☐ 515 Tom(Foghorn) Tucker: Baltimore	150.00	70.00	19.00
☐ 516 William Tuckerman: St. Paul	150.00	70.00	19.00
☐ 517 Turner: Minneapolis	150.00	70.00	19.00
☐ 518 Lawrence Twitchell: Detroit-Cleveland	150.00	70.00	19.00
☐ 519 James Tyng: Phila.	150.00	70.00	19.00
☐ 520 William Van Dyke: Des Moines-Toledo	150.00	70.00	19.00
☐ 521 George(Rip) VanHaltren Chicago	150.00	70.00	19.00
☐ 522 Harry Vaughn: (Farmer) Louisville-New York	150.00	70.00	19.00
☐ 523 Peek-a-Boo Veach: St. Paul	300.00	135.00	38.00
☐ 524 Veach: Sacra. PCL	2500.00	1100.00	300.00
☐ 525 Leon Viau: Cincinnati	150.00	70.00	19.00
☐ 526 William Vinton: Minneapolis	150.00	70.00	19.00
☐ 527 Joseph Visner: Brooklyn	150.00	70.00	19.00
☐ 528 Christian VonDer Ahe Owner Browns Champs	300.00	135.00	38.00
☐ 529 Joseph Walsh: Omaha	150.00	70.00	19.00
☐ 530 John(Monte) Ward: New York	600.00	275.00	75.00
☐ 531 E.H. Warner: Milwaukee	250.00	110.00	31.00
☐ 532 William Watkins: Mgr. Detroit-Kansas City	175.00	80.00	22.00
☐ 533 Bill Weaver: (Farmer) Louisville	150.00	70.00	19.00
☐ 534 Charles Weber: Sioux City	150.00	70.00	19.00
☐ 535 George Weidman (Stump): Detroit-New York	150.00	70.00	19.00
☐ 536 William Weidner: Columbus	150.00	70.00	19.00
☐ 537A Curtis Welch: Browns Champ	250.00	110.00	31.00
☐ 537B Curtis Welch: A's	150.00	70.00	19.00
☐ 538 Curtis Welch and Bill Gleason: Athletics	200.00	90.00	25.00
☐ 539 Smilin' Mickey Welch: All Star-New York	600.00	275.00	75.00
☐ 540 Jake Wells: K.C.	150.00	70.00	19.00
☐ 541 Frank Wells: Des Moines-Mil.	175.00	80.00	22.00
☐ 542 Joseph Werrick: Louisville-St. Paul	150.00	70.00	19.00
☐ 543 Milton(Buck) West: Minneapolis	150.00	70.00	19.00
☐ 544 Gus(Cannonball) Weyhing: A's	150.00	70.00	19.00
☐ 545 John Weyhing: Athletics-Columbus	150.00	70.00	19.00
☐ 546 Bobby Wheelock: Boston-Detroit	150.00	70.00	19.00
☐ 547 Whitacre: A's	150.00	70.00	19.00
☐ 548 Pat Whitaker: Balt.	150.00	70.00	19.00
☐ 549 Deacon White: Detroit-Pittsburgh	175.00	80.00	22.00
☐ 550 William White: Louisville	150.00	70.00	19.00
☐ 551 Jim(Grasshopper) Whitney: Wash.-Indianapolis	150.00	70.00	19.00
☐ 552 Arthur Whitney: Pittsburgh-New York	150.00	70.00	19.00
☐ 553 G. Whitney: St. Joseph	150.00	70.00	19.00
☐ 554 James Williams: Mgr. Cleveland	175.00	80.00	22.00
☐ 555 Ned Williamson: Chi.	175.00	80.00	22.00
☐ 556 Williamson and Mascot	200.00	90.00	25.00
☐ 557 C.H. Willis: Omaha	150.00	70.00	19.00
☐ 558 Walt Wilmot: Washington-Chicago	150.00	70.00	19.00
☐ 559 George Winkleman: Minneapolis-Hartford	250.00	110.00	31.00
☐ 560 Samuel Wise: Boston-Washington	150.00	70.00	19.00
☐ 561 William Wolf (Chicken) Louisville	150.00	70.00	19.00
☐ 562 George(Dandy) Wood: Philadelphia	150.00	70.00	19.00
☐ 563 Peter Wood: Phila.	150.00	70.00	19.00
☐ 564 Harry Wright: Mgr. Philadelphia	1500.00	700.00	190.00
☐ 565 Charles Zimmer (Chief) Cleveland	150.00	70.00	19.00
☐ 566 Frank Zinn: Athletics	150.00	70.00	19.00

1965 Old London Coins

The Old London set of metal baseball coins was distributed in that company's snack products in 1965. The coins were produced for Old London by Space Magic, Ltd. a Canadian firm which manufactured similar sets in 1964 and 1971. Each metal coin measures 1 1/2" in diameter. The silver-colored backs contain the company logo and a short biographical sketch of the player. Each team is represented by two ballplayers, except for the Mets (1) and the Cardinals (3) -- Tracy Stallard was traded from the former to the latter. The coins are unnumbered and hence they are listed below in alphabetical order within league, e.g., National Leaguers (1-20) and American Leaguers (21-40). Coins found still in their original cellophane wrappers are worth 25 percent more than the values listed below.

	NRMT	VG-E	GOOD
COMPLETE SET (40)	450.00	200.00	55.00
COMMON COIN (1-40)	4.00	1.80	.50
☐ 1 Hank Aaron	50.00	22.00	6.25
☐ 2 Richie Allen	6.00	2.70	.75
☐ 3 Ernie Banks	30.00	13.50	3.70
☐ 4 Ken Boyer	5.00	2.20	.60
☐ 5 Jim Bunning	10.00	4.50	1.25
☐ 6 Orlando Cepeda	8.00	3.60	1.00
☐ 7 Willie Davis	5.00	2.20	.60
☐ 8 Ron Fairly	4.00	1.80	.50
☐ 9 Dick Farrell	4.00	1.80	.50
☐ 10 Bob Friend	4.00	1.80	.50
☐ 11 Dick Groat	5.00	2.20	.60
☐ 12 Ron Hunt	4.00	1.80	.50
☐ 13 Ken Johnson	4.00	1.80	.50
☐ 14 Willie Mays	50.00	22.00	6.25
☐ 15 Bill Mazeroski	6.00	2.70	.75
☐ 16 Vada Pinson	5.00	2.20	.60
☐ 17 Frank Robinson	30.00	13.50	3.70
☐ 18 Tracy Stallard	4.00	1.80	.50
☐ 19 Joe Torre	6.00	2.70	.75
☐ 20 Billy Williams	20.00	9.00	2.50
☐ 21 Bob Allison	4.00	1.80	.50
☐ 22 Dean Chance	4.00	1.80	.50
☐ 23 Rocky Colavito	8.00	3.60	1.00
☐ 24 Vic Davalillo	4.00	1.80	.50
☐ 25 Jim Fregosi	5.00	2.20	.60
☐ 26 Chuck Hinton	4.00	1.80	.50
☐ 27 Al Kaline	30.00	13.50	3.70
☐ 28 Harmon Killebrew	30.00	13.50	3.70
☐ 29 Don Lock	4.00	1.80	.50
☐ 30 Mickey Mantle	125.00	55.00	15.50
☐ 31 Roger Maris	35.00	16.00	4.40
☐ 32 Gary Peters	4.00	1.80	.50
☐ 33 Boog Powell	6.00	2.70	.75
☐ 34 Dick Radatz	4.00	1.80	.50
☐ 35 Brooks Robinson	30.00	13.50	3.70
☐ 36 Leon Wagner	4.00	1.80	.50
☐ 37 Pete Ward	4.00	1.80	.50
☐ 38 Dave Wickersham	4.00	1.80	.50
☐ 39 John Wyatt	4.00	1.80	.50
☐ 40 Carl Yastrzemski	35.00	16.00	4.40

1949 Olmes Studios

This set measures 3 1/2" by 5 1/2" and features Philadelphia players only. Two poses of Ferris Fain exist. The Olmes Studio identification is printed on the back of the postcard

	NRMT	VG-E	GOOD
COMPLETE SET (7)	60.00	27.00	7.50
COMMON CARD (1-7)	10.00	4.50	1.25
☐ 1 Sam Chapman	10.00	4.50	1.25
☐ 2 Ferris Fain	15.00	6.75	1.85
☐ 3 Dick Fowler	10.00	4.50	1.25
☐ 4 Bob Hooper	10.00	4.50	1.25
☐ 5 Robin Roberts	20.00	9.00	2.50
☐ 6 Carl Scheib	10.00	4.50	1.25
☐ 7 Joe Tipton	10.00	4.50	1.25

1932-34 Orbit Pins Numbered PR2

These pins were thought to have been issued some time between 1932 and 1934. The catalog designation for these pins is PR2. These pins are skip-numbered which distinguishes them from the following set designated as PR3 which is unnumbered. Each pin is approximately 13/16" in diameter. On the front of the pin the team nickname is featured in all caps inside quotation marks. Player pictures are set against a green background with the player's name and team in a yellow strip.

	EX-MT	VG-E	GOOD
COMPLETE SET (54)	1200.00	550.00	150.00
COMMON PLAYER (1-72)	15.00	6.75	1.85
COMMON PLAYER (92-120)	20.00	9.00	2.50
☐ 1 Ivy Andrews	15.00	6.75	1.85
☐ 2 Carl Reynolds	15.00	6.75	1.85
☐ 3 Riggs Stephenson	20.00	9.00	2.50
☐ 4 Lon Warneke	15.00	6.75	1.85
☐ 5 Frank Grube	15.00	6.75	1.85
☐ 6 Kiki Cuyler	25.00	11.00	3.10
☐ 7 Marty McManus	15.00	6.75	1.85
☐ 8 Lefty Clark	15.00	6.75	1.85
☐ 9 George Blaeholder	15.00	6.75	1.85
☐ 10 Willie Kamm	15.00	6.75	1.85
☐ 11 Jimmy Dykes	18.00	8.00	2.20
☐ 12 Earl Averill	25.00	11.00	3.10
☐ 13 Pat Malone	15.00	6.75	1.85
☐ 14 Dizzy Dean	75.00	34.00	9.50
☐ 15 Dick Bartell	15.00	6.75	1.85
☐ 16 Guy Bush	15.00	6.75	1.85
☐ 17 Bud Tinning	15.00	6.75	1.85
☐ 18 Jimmy Foxx	50.00	22.00	6.25
☐ 19 Mule Haas	15.00	6.75	1.85
☐ 20 Lew Fonseca	15.00	6.75	1.85
☐ 21 Pepper Martin	20.00	9.00	2.50
☐ 22 Phil Collins	15.00	6.75	1.85
☐ 23 Bill Cissell	15.00	6.75	1.85
☐ 24 Bump Hadley	15.00	6.75	1.85
☐ 25 Smead Jolley	15.00	6.75	1.85
☐ 26 Burleigh Grimes	25.00	11.00	3.10
☐ 27 Dale Alexander	15.00	6.75	1.85
☐ 28 Mickey Cochrane	35.00	16.00	4.40
☐ 29 Mel Harder	18.00	8.00	2.20
☐ 30 Mark Koenig	15.00	6.75	1.85
☐ 31A Lefty O'Doul New York Giants	20.00	9.00	2.50
☐ 31B Lefty O'Doul Brooklyn Dodgers	100.00	45.00	12.50
☐ 32A Woody English	15.00	6.75	1.85
☐ 32B Woody English#(without bat)	75.00	34.00	9.50
☐ 33A Billy Jurges	15.00	6.75	1.85
☐ 33B Billy Jurges (without bat)	75.00	34.00	9.50
☐ 34 Bruce Campbell	15.00	6.75	1.85
☐ 35 Joe Vosmik	15.00	6.75	1.85
☐ 36 Dick Porter	15.00	6.75	1.85
☐ 37 Charlie Grimm	20.00	9.00	2.50
☐ 38 George Earnshaw	15.00	6.75	1.85
☐ 39 Al Simmons	25.00	11.00	3.10
☐ 40 Red Lucas	15.00	6.75	1.85
☐ 51 Wally Berger	15.00	6.75	1.85
☐ 52 Jim Levey	15.00	6.75	1.85
☐ 58 Ernie Lombardi	25.00	11.00	3.10
☐ 64 Jack Burns	15.00	6.75	1.85
☐ 67 Billy Herman	25.00	11.00	3.10
☐ 72 Bill Hallahan	15.00	6.75	1.85
☐ 92 Don Brennan	20.00	9.00	2.50
☐ 96 Sam Byrd	20.00	9.00	2.50
☐ 99 Ben Chapman	20.00	9.00	2.50
☐ 103 Johnny Allen	20.00	9.00	2.50
☐ 107 Tony Lazzeri	35.00	16.00	4.40
☐ 111 Earl Combs	35.00	16.00	4.40
☐ 116 Joe Sewell	35.00	16.00	4.40
☐ 120 Lefty Gomez	45.00	20.00	5.50

1932-34 Orbit Pins Unnumbered PR3

These pins were thought to have been issued some time between 1932 and 1934. The catalog designation for these pins is PR3. These pins are unnumbered which distinguishes them from the set designated as PR2 which is skip-numbered. Each pin is approximately 13/16" in diameter. On the front of the pin the team nickname is featured in all caps inside quotation marks. Player pictures are set against a green background with the player's name and team in a yellow strip.

	EX-MT	VG-E	GOOD
COMPLETE SET (60)	2250.00	1000.00	275.00
COMMON PLAYER (1-60)	30.00	13.50	3.70
☐ 1 Dale Alexander	30.00	13.50	3.70
☐ 2 Ivy Andrews	30.00	13.50	3.70
☐ 3 Earl Averill	50.00	22.00	6.25
☐ 4 (Dick) Bartell	30.00	13.50	3.70
☐ 5 Wally Berger	35.00	16.00	4.40
☐ 6 George Blaeholder	30.00	13.50	3.70
☐ 7 Jack Burns	30.00	13.50	3.70
☐ 8 Guy Bush	35.00	16.00	4.40
☐ 9 Bruce Campbell	30.00	13.50	3.70
☐ 10 Bill Cissell	30.00	13.50	3.70
☐ 11 Lefty Clark	30.00	13.50	3.70
☐ 12 Mickey Cochrane	70.00	32.00	8.75
☐ 13 Phil Collins	30.00	13.50	3.70
☐ 14 Kiki Cuyler	50.00	22.00	6.25
☐ 15 Dizzy Dean	100.00	45.00	12.50
☐ 16 Jimmy Dykes	35.00	16.00	4.40
☐ 17 George Earnshaw	35.00	16.00	4.40
☐ 18 Woody English	30.00	13.50	3.70
☐ 19 Lew Fonseca	30.00	13.50	3.70
☐ 20 Jimmy Foxx	100.00	45.00	12.50
☐ 21 Burleigh Grimes	50.00	22.00	6.25
☐ 22 Charlie Grimm	35.00	16.00	4.40
☐ 23 Lefty Grove	70.00	32.00	8.75
☐ 24 Frank Grube	30.00	13.50	3.70
☐ 25 Mule Haas	30.00	13.50	3.70
☐ 26 Bump Hadley	30.00	13.50	3.70
☐ 27 Chick Hafey	50.00	22.00	6.25
☐ 28 Jesse Haines	50.00	22.00	6.25
☐ 29 Bill Hallahan	30.00	13.50	3.70
☐ 30 Mel Harder	35.00	16.00	4.40
☐ 31 Gabby Hartnett	50.00	22.00	6.25
☐ 32 Babe Herman	40.00	18.00	5.00
☐ 33 Billy Herman	50.00	22.00	6.25
☐ 34 Rogers Hornsby	100.00	45.00	12.50
☐ 35 Roy Johnson	30.00	13.50	3.70
☐ 36 Smead Jolley	30.00	13.50	3.70
☐ 37 Billy Jurges	30.00	13.50	3.70
☐ 38 Willie Kamm	30.00	13.50	3.70
☐ 39 Mark Koenig	35.00	16.00	4.40
☐ 40 Jim Levey	30.00	13.50	3.70
☐ 41 Ernie Lombardi	50.00	22.00	6.25
☐ 42 Red Lucas	30.00	13.50	3.70
☐ 43 Ted Lyons	50.00	22.00	6.25
☐ 44 Connie Mack Mgr. of Athletics	60.00	27.00	7.50
☐ 45 Pat Malone	30.00	13.50	3.70
☐ 46 Pepper Martin	35.00	16.00	4.40
☐ 47 Marty McManus	30.00	13.50	3.70
☐ 48 Lefty O'Doul Brooklyn Dodgers	35.00	16.00	4.40
☐ 49 Dick Porter	30.00	13.50	3.70
☐ 50 Carl Reynolds	30.00	13.50	3.70
☐ 51 Charlie Root	35.00	16.00	4.40
☐ 52 Bob Seeds	30.00	13.50	3.70
☐ 53 Al Simmons	50.00	22.00	6.25
☐ 54 Riggs Stephenson	35.00	16.00	4.40
☐ 55 Bud Tinning	30.00	13.50	3.70
☐ 56 Joe Vosmik	30.00	13.50	3.70
☐ 57 Rube Walberg	30.00	13.50	3.70
☐ 58 Paul Waner	50.00	22.00	6.25
☐ 59 Lon Warneke	30.00	13.50	3.70
☐ 60 Pinky Whitney	30.00	13.50	3.70

1939 Orcajo Photo Art PC786

The postcards in this set measures 3 1/2" by 5 1/2" and comes in three styles. The first contains an Orcajo Photo Art back. Type 2 is marked "Courtesy of Val Decker Packing Co., Piqua Brand Meats" on the front. Type 3 is marked "Metropolitan Clothing Co" on the front. The cards are listed in the checklist below by type. The set is broken down this way: Type 1 are cards 1-26; Type 2 are 27-31 and Type 3 are cards 32-33. The set was issued in 1939 and features a card of Joe DiMaggio, the only apparent non-Cincinnati player. The cards are sepia in color and feature white borders.

	EX-MT	VG-E	GOOD
COMPLETE SET (33)	3500.00	1600.00	450.00
COMMON CARD (1-33)	75.00	34.00	9.50
☐ 1 Wally Berger	100.00	45.00	12.50
☐ 2 Nino Bongiovanni	75.00	34.00	9.50
☐ 3 Frenchy Bordagray	75.00	34.00	9.50
☐ 4 Harry Craft	100.00	45.00	12.50
☐ 5 Ray Davis	75.00	34.00	9.50
☐ 6 Paul Derringer	100.00	45.00	12.50
☐ 7 Joe DiMaggio	750.00	350.00	95.00
☐ 8 Linus Frey	75.00	34.00	9.50
☐ 9 Lee Gamble	75.00	34.00	9.50
☐ 10 Ivan Goodman	75.00	34.00	9.50
☐ 11 Hank Gowdy CO	75.00	34.00	9.50
☐ 12 Lee Grissom	75.00	34.00	9.50
☐ 13 Williard Herschberger Name in White	75.00	34.00	9.50
☐ 14 Eddie Joost	100.00	45.00	12.50
☐ 15 Frank McCormick	75.00	34.00	9.50
☐ 16 Bill McKecknie MG	150.00	70.00	19.00
☐ 17 Billy Meyers	75.00	34.00	9.50
☐ 18 Whitey Moore	75.00	34.00	9.50
☐ 19 Lew Riggs	75.00	34.00	9.50
☐ 20 Les Scarsella	75.00	34.00	9.50
☐ 21 Milburn Shoffner	75.00	34.00	9.50
☐ 22 Junior Thompson	75.00	34.00	9.50
☐ 23 Bucky Walters	100.00	45.00	12.50
☐ 24 Bill Werber	100.00	45.00	12.50
☐ 25 Dick West	75.00	34.00	9.50
☐ 26 Jimmie Wilson	75.00	34.00	9.50
☐ 27 Alan Cooke	75.00	34.00	9.50
☐ 28 Linus Frey small projection	75.00	34.00	9.50
☐ 29 Williard Herschberger Name in black	75.00	34.00	9.50
☐ 30 Ernie Lombardi Name plain	150.00	70.00	19.00
☐ 31 Johnny Vander Meer	125.00	55.00	15.50
☐ 32 Ernie Lombardi name fancy	150.00	70.00	19.00
☐ 33 Johnny Vander Meer	125.00	55.00	15.50

1994 Origins of Baseball

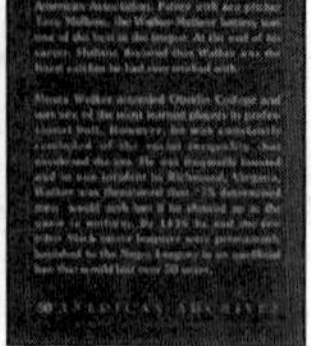

Published by the American Archives Publishing Co. (Beverly Hills, CA), this boxed set of 100 standard-size cards recounts the historic origins of baseball from 1744 to 1899. The fronts features black-bordered sepiatones on its ornately designed fronts. The name of the subject featured in the photo appears in gold-colored lettering near the bottom. The black back is framed by a brownish line and carries historical information in gold-colored lettering set off by a Gothic-style start letter. The cards are numbered on the back. According to the title card, limited edition uncut sheets of the set as well as 8" by 10" reproductions of certain cards were also produced.

	MINT	NRMT	EXC
COMPLETE SET (104)	10.00	4.50	1.25
COMMON CARD (1-100)	.05	.02	.01
☐ 1 Abner Doubleday	.25	.11	.03
☐ 2 Doubleday Field	.05	.02	.01
☐ 3 Rounders 1744	.05	.02	.01
☐ 4 Early Baseball 700 AD	.05	.02	.01
☐ 5 The Knickerbockers	.05	.02	.01
☐ 6 Alexander Cartwright	.25	.11	.03
☐ 7 Baseball in the 1850's	.05	.02	.01
☐ 8 Social Clubs	.05	.02	.01
☐ 9 Brooklyn Eckfords	.05	.02	.01
☐ 10 New England Baseball	.05	.02	.01
☐ 11 Henry Chadwick	.25	.11	.03
☐ 12 Brooklyn Excelsiors	.05	.02	.01
☐ 13 Abraham Lincoln	.75	.35	.09
☐ 14 Andrew Johnson	.15	.07	.02
☐ 15 First Enclosed Park	.05	.02	.01
☐ 16 Brooklyn Atlantics	.05	.02	.01
☐ 17 James Creighton	.15	.07	.02
☐ 18 Baseball in the 1860's	.05	.02	.01
☐ 19 1869 Red Stockings	.05	.02	.01
☐ 20 Cincinnati Celebration	.05	.02	.01
☐ 21 Harry Wright	.25	.11	.03
☐ 22 Boston Ball Club 1872	.05	.02	.01
☐ 23 Arthur Cummings	.25	.11	.03
☐ 24 William Hulbert	.15	.07	.02
☐ 25 George Wright	.25	.11	.03
☐ 26 Albert Spalding	.25	.11	.03
☐ 27 Albert Bushong	.15	.07	.02
☐ 28 Bid McPhee	.15	.07	.02
☐ 29 James O'Rourke	.15	.07	.02
☐ 30 Pud Galvin	.25	.11	.03
☐ 31 Edwin Bligh	.15	.07	.02
☐ 32 William Purcell	.15	.07	.02
☐ 33 Roger Connor	.25	.11	.03
☐ 34 Cincinnati Ball Club	.05	.02	.01
☐ 35 Peter Browning	.15	.07	.02
☐ 36 William Gleason	.15	.07	.02
☐ 37 Paul Hines	.15	.07	.02
☐ 38 Baseball in the 1880's	.05	.02	.01
☐ 39 Robert Carruthers	.15	.07	.02
☐ 40 New York Metropolitans	.05	.02	.01
☐ 41 Saint George's Field	.05	.02	.01
☐ 42 Charles Radbourne	.25	.11	.03
☐ 43 George Andrews	.15	.07	.02
☐ 44 William Hoy	.25	.11	.03
☐ 45 Chicago Ball Club	.05	.02	.01
☐ 46 Cap Anson	.75	.35	.09
☐ 47 John Clarkson	.25	.11	.03
☐ 48 Mike Kelly	.75	.35	.09
☐ 49 Buffalo Bisons 1887	.05	.02	.01
☐ 50 Moses Walker	.75	.35	.09
☐ 51 Detroit Ball Club	.05	.02	.01
☐ 52 Little League	.05	.02	.01
☐ 53 Louisville Ball Club	.05	.02	.01
☐ 54 John Farrell	.15	.07	.02
☐ 55 Walter Latham	.15	.07	.02
☐ 56 Fred Dunlap	.15	.07	.02
☐ 57 Tim Keefe	.25	.11	.03
☐ 58 Cincinnati Ball Club	.05	.02	.01
☐ 59 1889 World Tour	.05	.02	.01
☐ 60 Dan Brouthers	.25	.11	.03
☐ 61 John M. Ward	.25	.11	.03
☐ 62 Albert Spalding	.25	.11	.03
☐ 63 The Baseball Cap	.05	.02	.01
☐ 64 Tom Esterbrook	.15	.07	.02
☐ 65 Mark Baldwin	.15	.07	.02
☐ 66 Tony Mullane	.25	.11	.03
☐ 67 John Glasscock	.15	.07	.02
☐ 68 Amos Rusie	.25	.11	.03
☐ 69 Jake Beckley	.25	.11	.03
☐ 70 Jimmy Collins	.25	.11	.03
☐ 71 Charles Comiskey	.25	.11	.03
☐ 72 Tom Connolly	.25	.11	.03
☐ 73 Mickey Welch	.25	.11	.03
☐ 74 Ed Delahanty	.25	.11	.03
☐ 75 Hugh Duffy	.25	.11	.03
☐ 76 Buck Ewing	.25	.11	.03
☐ 77 Clark Griffith	.25	.11	.03
☐ 78 Kid Nichols	.25	.11	.03
☐ 79 Billy Hamilton	.25	.11	.03
☐ 80 Ban Johnson	.25	.11	.03
☐ 81 Willie Keeler	.25	.11	.03
☐ 82 Bobby Wallace	.25	.11	.03
☐ 83 Napoleon Lajoie	.75	.35	.09
☐ 84 Connie Mack	.75	.35	.09
☐ 85 Fred Clarke	.25	.11	.03
☐ 86 Tommy McCarthy	.25	.11	.03
☐ 87 John McGraw	.75	.35	.09
☐ 88 Jesse Burkett	.25	.11	.03
☐ 89 Frank Chance	.25	.11	.03
☐ 90 Mordecai Brown	.25	.11	.03
☐ 91 New York Nationals	.05	.02	.01
☐ 92 Jack Chesbro	.15	.07	.02
☐ 93 Sam Thompson	.15	.07	.02
☐ 94 Boston vs. New York	.05	.02	.01
☐ 95 Rube Waddell	.25	.11	.03
☐ 96 Joe Kelley	.25	.11	.03

	NRMT	VG-E	GOOD
☐ 97 Addie Joss	.25	.11	.03
☐ 98 Boston Beaneaters	.05	.02	.01
☐ 99 Baltimore Baseball Club	.05	.02	.01
☐ 100 The Game in 1899	.05	.02	.01
☐ z3 Acknowledgments	.05	.02	.01
☐ zNNOO Title card (Proof of ownership)	.05	.02	.01
☐ zNNOO Bibliography card	.05	.02	.01
☐ NNOO Certificate of Authenticity	.05	.02	.01

1954 Orioles Esskay

The cards in this 36-card set measure 2 1/4" by 3 1/2". The 1954 Esskay Meats set contains color, unnumbered cards featuring Baltimore Orioles only. The cards were issued in panels of two on boxes of Esskay hot dogs; consequently, many have grease stains on the cards and are quite difficult to obtain in mint condition. The 1954 Esskay set can be distinguished from the 1955 Esskay set supposedly by the white or off-white (the 1955 set) backs of the cards. The backs of the 1954 cards are also supposedly "waxed" to a greater degree than the 1955 cards. The catalog designation is F181-1. Since the cards are unnumbered, they are ordered below in alphabetical order for convenience.

	NRMT	VG-E	GOOD
COMPLETE SET (36)	3250.00	1450.00	400.00
COMMON CARD (1-36)	100.00	45.00	12.50
☐ 1 Cal Abrams	100.00	45.00	12.50
☐ 2 Neil Berry	100.00	45.00	12.50
☐ 3 Michael Blyzka	100.00	45.00	12.50
☐ 4 Harry Brecheen	125.00	55.00	15.50
☐ 5 Gil Coan	100.00	45.00	12.50
☐ 6 Joe Coleman	100.00	45.00	12.50
☐ 7 Clint Courtney	125.00	55.00	15.50
☐ 8 Charles E. Diering	100.00	45.00	12.50
☐ 9 Jimmie Dykes MG	125.00	55.00	15.50
☐ 10 Frank Fanovich	100.00	45.00	12.50
☐ 11 Howard Fox	100.00	45.00	12.50
☐ 12 Jim Fridley	100.00	45.00	12.50
☐ 13 Chico Garcia	100.00	45.00	12.50
☐ 14 Jehosie Heard	100.00	45.00	12.50
☐ 15 Darrell Johnson	125.00	55.00	15.50
☐ 16 Robert D. Kennedy	125.00	55.00	15.50
☐ 17 Dick Kokos	100.00	45.00	12.50
☐ 18 Dave Koslo	100.00	45.00	12.50
☐ 19 Lou Kretlow	100.00	45.00	12.50
☐ 20 Dick Kryhoski	100.00	45.00	12.50
☐ 21 Bob Kuzava	100.00	45.00	12.50
☐ 22 Don Larsen	175.00	80.00	22.00
☐ 23 Don Lenhardt	100.00	45.00	12.50
☐ 24 Dick Littlefield	100.00	45.00	12.50
☐ 25 Sam Mele	100.00	45.00	12.50
☐ 26 John Lester Moss	100.00	45.00	12.50
☐ 27 Ray L. Murray	100.00	45.00	12.50
☐ 28 Bobo Newsom	125.00	55.00	15.50
☐ 29 Tom Oliver CO	100.00	45.00	12.50
☐ 30 Duane Pillette	100.00	45.00	12.50
☐ 31 Francis M. Skaff CO	100.00	45.00	12.50
☐ 32 Marlin Stuart	100.00	45.00	12.50
☐ 33 Bob Turley	175.00	80.00	22.00
☐ 34 Eddie Waitkus	100.00	45.00	12.50
☐ 35 Vic Wertz	125.00	55.00	15.50
☐ 36 Robert G. Young	100.00	45.00	12.50

1955 Orioles Esskay

The cards in this 27-card set measure 2 1/4" by 3 1/2". The 1955 Esskay Meats set was issued in panels of two on boxes of Esskay hot dogs. This set of full color, blank back, unnumbered cards features Baltimore Orioles only. Many of the players in the 1954 Esskay set were also issued in this set. The catalog designation is F181-2. Since the cards are unnumbered, they are ordered below in alphabetical order for convenience. The 1955 set is supposedly somewhat more difficult to find than the 1954 set.

	NRMT	VG-E	GOOD
COMPLETE SET (27)	2500.00	1100.00	300.00
COMMON CARD (1-27)	100.00	45.00	12.50
☐ 1 Cal Abrams	100.00	45.00	12.50
☐ 2 Robert Alexander	100.00	45.00	12.50
☐ 3 Harry Brecheen	120.00	55.00	15.00
☐ 4 Harry Byrd	100.00	45.00	12.50
☐ 5 Gil Coan	100.00	45.00	12.50
☐ 6 Joe Coleman	100.00	45.00	12.50
☐ 7 William Cox	120.00	55.00	15.00
☐ 8 Charles E. Diering	100.00	45.00	12.50
☐ 9 Walter Evers	120.00	55.00	15.00
☐ 10 Don Johnson	100.00	45.00	12.50
☐ 11 Robert D. Kennedy	120.00	55.00	15.00
☐ 12 Lou Kretlow	100.00	45.00	12.50
☐ 13 Bob Kuzava	100.00	45.00	12.50
☐ 14 Fred Marsh	100.00	45.00	12.50
☐ 15 Charles Maxwell	120.00	55.00	15.00
☐ 16 Jim McDonald	100.00	45.00	12.50
☐ 17 Bill Miller	100.00	45.00	12.50
☐ 18 Willie Miranda	120.00	55.00	15.00
☐ 19 Raymond L. Moore	100.00	45.00	12.50
☐ 20 John Lester Moss	100.00	45.00	12.50
☐ 21 Bobo Newsom	120.00	55.00	15.00
☐ 22 Duane Pillette	100.00	45.00	12.50
☐ 23 Harold W. Smith	100.00	45.00	12.50
☐ 24 Gus Triandos	120.00	55.00	15.00
☐ 25 Eddie Waitkus	100.00	45.00	12.50
☐ 26 Gene Woodling	150.00	70.00	19.00
☐ 27 Robert G. Young	100.00	45.00	12.50

1958 Orioles Jay Publishing

This 12-card set of the Baltimore Orioles measures approximately 5" by 7" and features black-and-white player photos in a white border. These cards were packaged 12 to a packet. The backs are blank. The cards are unnumbered and checklisted below in alphabetical order.

	NRMT	VG-E	GOOD
COMPLETE SET (12)	35.00	16.00	4.40
COMMON CARD (1-12)	3.00	1.35	.35
☐ 1 Bob Boyd	3.00	1.35	.35
☐ 2 Jim Busby	3.00	1.35	.35
☐ 3 Billy Gardner	3.00	1.35	.35
☐ 4 Connie Johnson	3.00	1.35	.35
☐ 5 Billy Loes	3.00	1.35	.35
☐ 6 Willy Miranda	3.50	1.55	.45
☐ 7 Bob Nieman	3.00	1.35	.35
☐ 8 Bill O'Dell	3.00	1.35	.35
☐ 9 Al Pilarcik	3.00	1.35	.35
☐ 10 Paul Richards (MG)	3.50	1.55	.45
☐ 11 Gus Triandos	3.50	1.55	.45
☐ 12 George Zuverink	3.00	1.35	.35

1959 Orioles Jay Publishing

This 12-card set of the Baltimore Orioles measures approximately 5" by 7" and features black-and-white player photos in a white border. These cards were packaged 12 to a packet. The backs are blank. The cards are unnumbered and checklisted below in alphabetical order.

	NRMT	VG-E	GOOD
COMPLETE SET (12)	35.00	16.00	4.40
COMMON CARD (1-12)	2.50	1.10	.30
☐ 1 Bob Boyd	2.50	1.10	.30
☐ 2 Chico Carrasquel	3.00	1.35	.35
☐ 3 Billy Gardner	2.50	1.10	.30
☐ 4 Bob Nieman	2.50	1.10	.30
☐ 5 Billy O'Dell	2.50	1.10	.30
☐ 6 Milt Pappas	3.00	1.35	.35
☐ 7 Brooks Robinson	10.00	4.50	1.25
☐ 8 Willie Tasby	2.50	1.10	.30
☐ 9 Gus Triandos	2.50	1.10	.30
☐ 10 Jerry Walker	2.50	1.10	.30
☐ 11 James(Hoyt) Wilhelm	6.00	2.70	.75
☐ 12 Gene Woodling	2.50	1.10	.30

1960 Orioles Jay Publishing

This 12-card set of the Baltimore Orioles measures approximately 5" by 7" and features black-and-white player photos in a white border. These cards were packaged 12 to a packet and originally sold for 25 cents. The backs are blank. The cards are unnumbered and checklisted below in alphabetical order.

	NRMT	VG-E	GOOD
COMPLETE SET (12)	35.00	16.00	4.40
COMMON CARD (1-12)	2.00	.90	.25
☐ 1 Jackie Brandt	2.00	.90	.25
☐ 2 Marv Breeding	2.00	.90	.25
☐ 3 Jack Fisher	2.00	.90	.25
☐ 4 Ron Hansen	2.00	.90	.25
☐ 5 Milt Pappas	3.00	1.35	.35
☐ 6 Paul Richards MG	3.00	1.35	.35
☐ 7 Brooks Robinson	10.00	4.50	1.25
☐ 8 Willie Tasby	2.00	.90	.25
☐ 9 Gus Triandos	2.00	.90	.25
☐ 10 Jerry Walker	2.00	.90	.25
☐ 11 Hoyt Wilhelm	7.50	3.40	.95
☐ 12 Gene Woodling	3.00	1.35	.35

1964 Orioles Jay Publishing

This 12-card set of the Baltimore Orioles measures approximately 5" by 7". The fronts feature black-and-white posed player photos with the player's and team name printed below in the white border. These cards were packaged 12 to a packet. The backs are blank. The cards are unnumbered and checklisted below in alphabetical order.

	NRMT	VG-E	GOOD
COMPLETE SET (12)	30.00	13.50	3.70
COMMON CARD (1-12)	2.50	1.10	.30
☐ 1 Luis Aparicio	5.00	2.20	.60
☐ 2 Steve Barber	3.00	1.35	.35
☐ 3 Hank Bauer MG	3.50	1.55	.45
☐ 4 Jackie Brandt	2.50	1.10	.30
☐ 5 Chuck Estrada	2.50	1.10	.30
☐ 6 Willie Kirkland	2.50	1.10	.30
☐ 7 John Orsino	2.50	1.10	.30
☐ 8 Milt Pappas	3.00	1.35	.35
☐ 9 Boog Powell	4.00	1.80	.50
☐ 10 Robin Roberts	5.00	2.20	.60
☐ 11 Brooks Robinson	10.00	4.50	1.25
☐ 12 Norm Siebern	2.50	1.10	.30

1970 Orioles

This 15-piece set features blank-backed, white-bordered, 8" X 10" black-and-white photos. The player's name appears in black within the bottom border. A facsimile autograph is printed across the photo. The word "Tadder" is pasted into photos at lower right. Photos are unnumbered and checklisted below in alphabetical order.

	NRMT	VG-E	GOOD
COMPLETE SET (15)	40.00	18.00	5.00
COMMON CARD (1-15)	2.50	1.10	.30
☐ 1 Mark Belanger	3.00	1.35	.35
☐ 2 Don Buford	2.50	1.10	.30
☐ 3 Mike Cuellar	3.50	1.55	.45
☐ 4 Clay Dalrymple	2.50	1.10	.30
☐ 5 Andy Etchebarren	2.50	1.10	.30
☐ 6 Dave Johnson	5.00	2.20	.60
☐ 7 Dave McNally	3.50	1.55	.45
☐ 8 Curt Motton	2.50	1.10	.30
☐ 9 Jim Palmer	7.50	3.40	.95
☐ 10 Boog Powell	5.00	2.20	.60
☐ 11 Merv Rettenmund	2.50	1.10	.30
☐ 12 Frank Robinson	7.50	3.40	.95
☐ 13 Chico Salmon	2.50	1.10	.30
☐ 14 Eddie Watt	2.50	1.10	.30
☐ 15 Earl Weaver MG	3.50	1.55	.45

1971 Orioles

Subtitled "Pictures of Champions," this 16-card set measures 2 1/8" by 2 3/4". Since the card stock is orange, the close-up photos on the fronts are orange-tinted and have orange borders. The orange backs have the jersey number, player's name and the set subtitle. The cards are unnumbered and checklisted below in alphabetical order.

	NRMT	VG-E	GOOD
COMPLETE SET (16)	75.00	34.00	9.50
COMMON CARD (1-16)	4.00	1.80	.50
☐ 1 Mark Belanger	6.00	2.70	.75
☐ 2 Don Buford	4.00	1.80	.50
☐ 3 Mike Cuellar	6.00	2.70	.75
☐ 4 Andy Etchebarren	4.00	1.80	.50
☐ 5 Dick Hall	4.00	1.80	.50
☐ 6 Ellie Hendricks	4.00	1.80	.50
☐ 7 Dave Johnson	7.50	3.40	.95
☐ 8 Dave Leonhard	4.00	1.80	.50
☐ 9 Dave May	4.00	1.80	.50
☐ 10 Dave McNally	6.00	2.70	.75
☐ 11 Jim Palmer	10.00	4.50	1.25
☐ 12 Pete Richert	4.00	1.80	.50
☐ 13 Brooks Robinson	10.00	4.50	1.25
☐ 14 Frank Robinson	10.00	4.50	1.25
☐ 15 Eddie Watt	4.00	1.80	.50
☐ 16 Earl Weaver MG	7.50	3.40	.95

1972 Orioles Police

The 1972 Baltimore Orioles Police/Safety set was issued on a thin unperforated cardboard sheet measuring 12 1/2" by 8". When the players are cut into individual cards, they measure approximately 2 1/2" by 4". The color of the sheet is pale yellow, and consequently the black and white borderless player photos have a similar cast. The player's name, position, and team name appear below the pictures. The backs have different safety messages sponsored by the Office of Traffic Safety, D.C. Department of Motor Vehicles. The cards are unnumbered and checklisted below in alphabetical order.

	NRMT	VG-E	GOOD
COMPLETE SET (10)	30.00	13.50	3.70
COMMON CARD (1-10)	2.00	.90	.25
☐ 1 Mark Belanger	4.00	1.80	.50
☐ 2 Paul Blair	3.00	1.35	.35
☐ 3 Don Buford	3.00	1.35	.35
☐ 4 Mike Cuellar	3.00	1.35	.35
☐ 5 Dave Johnson	4.00	1.80	.50
☐ 6 Dave McNally	4.00	1.80	.50
☐ 7 Boog Powell	5.00	2.20	.60
☐ 8 Brooks Robinson	12.00	5.50	1.50
☐ 9 Merv Rettenmund	2.00	.90	.25
☐ 10 Earl Weaver MG	4.00	1.80	.50

1973 Orioles Johnny Pro

This 25-card set measures approximately 4 1/4" by 7 1/4" and features members of the 1973 Baltimore Orioles. The cards were designed to be pushed-out in a style similar to the 1964 Topps Stand Ups. The sides of the cards have a small advertisement for Johnny Pro Enterprises and even gives a phone number where they could have been reached. Oddly, the Orlando Pena card was not available in a die-cut version. The cards have the player's photo against a distinctive solid green background. The cards are blank backed. There are several variations within the set; the complete set price below includes all of the variation cards. The set is checklisted in order by uniform number. According to informed sources, there were 15,000 sets produced.

	NRMT	VG-E	GOOD
COMPLETE SET (25)	200.00	90.00	25.00
COMMON CARD	4.00	1.80	.50
☐ 1 Al Bumbry	4.00	1.80	.50
☐ 2 Rich Coggins	4.00	1.80	.50
☐ 3A Bobby Grich (Fielding)	8.00	3.60	1.00
☐ 3B Bobby Grich (Batting)	20.00	9.00	2.50
☐ 4 Earl Weaver MG	10.00	4.50	1.25
☐ 5A Brooks Robinson (Fielding)	25.00	11.00	3.10
☐ 5B Brooks Robinson (Batting)	50.00	22.00	6.25
☐ 6 Paul Blair	6.00	2.70	.75
☐ 7 Mark Belanger	6.00	2.70	.75
☐ 8 Andy Etchebarren	4.00	1.80	.50
☐ 10 Elrod Hendricks	4.00	1.80	.50
☐ 11 Terry Crowley	4.00	1.80	.50
☐ 12 Tommy Davis	6.00	2.70	.75
☐ 13 Doyle Alexander	6.00	2.70	.75
☐ 14 Merv Rettenmund	4.00	1.80	.50
☐ 15 Frank Baker	4.00	1.80	.50
☐ 19 Dave McNally	6.00	2.70	.75
☐ 21 Larry Brown	4.00	1.80	.50
☐ 22A Jim Palmer	20.00	9.00	2.50
☐ 22B Jim Palmer (Pitching)	40.00	18.00	5.00
☐ 23 Grant Jackson	4.00	1.80	.50
☐ 25 Don Baylor	8.00	3.60	1.00
☐ 26 John(Boog) Powell	15.00	6.75	1.85
☐ 27 Orlando Pena (NOT die-cut)	15.00	6.75	1.85
☐ 32 Earl Williams	4.00	1.80	.50
☐ 34 Bob Reynolds	4.00	1.80	.50
☐ 35 Mike Cuellar	6.00	2.70	.75
☐ 39 Eddie Watt	4.00	1.80	.50

1976 Orioles English's Chicken Lids

This set features round black-and-white player photos and measures approximately 8 1/4" in diameter. The backs are blank. The cards are unnumbered and checklisted below in alphabetical order; however, the checklist is incomplete. Any known additions to this checklist would be appreciated.

	NRMT	VG-E	GOOD
COMPLETE SET	20.00	9.00	2.50
COMMON CARD	5.00	2.20	.60
☐ 1 Mike Cuellar	5.00	2.20	.60
☐ 2 Ken Holtzman	5.00	2.20	.60
☐ 3 Jim Palmer	10.00	4.50	1.25

1981 Orioles 1966 Franchise

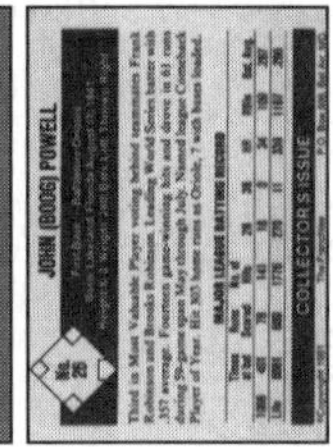

This 32 card standard-size set was issued by the Franchise of Bel Air, Maryland. This set commemorated the 15th anniversary of the first Orioles World Championship.

	NRMT	VG-E	GOOD
COMPLETE SET (32)	60.00	27.00	7.50
COMMON CARD (1-32)	2.00	.90	.25
☐ 1 Title Card	2.00	.90	.25
☐ 2 Team Card	2.00	.90	.25
☐ 3 Luis Aparicio	3.50	1.55	.45
☐ 4 Steve Barber	2.50	1.10	.30
☐ 5 Hank Bauer MG	2.50	1.10	.30
☐ 6 Paul Blair	3.00	1.35	.35
☐ 7 Curt Blefary	2.00	.90	.25
☐ 8 Sam Bowens	2.00	.90	.25
☐ 9 Gene Brabender	2.00	.90	.25
☐ 10 Harry Brecheen CO	2.00	.90	.25
☐ 11 Wally Bunker	2.00	.90	.25
☐ 12 Moe Drabowsky	2.00	.90	.25
☐ 13 Andy Etchebarren	2.00	.90	.25
☐ 14 Eddie Fisher	2.00	.90	.25
☐ 15 Dick Hall	2.00	.90	.25
☐ 16 Larry Haney	2.00	.90	.25
☐ 17 Woodie Held	2.00	.90	.25
☐ 18 Billy Hunter CO	2.00	.90	.25
☐ 19 Bob Johnson	2.00	.90	.25
☐ 20 Dave Johnson	3.50	1.55	.45
☐ 21 Sherm Lollar CO	2.00	.90	.25
☐ 22 Dave McNally	2.50	1.10	.30
☐ 23 John Miller	2.00	.90	.25
☐ 24 Stu Miller	2.00	.90	.25
☐ 25 Jim Palmer	5.00	2.20	.60
☐ 26 John (Boog) Powell	4.00	1.80	.50
☐ 27 Brooks Robinson	5.00	2.20	.60
☐ 28 Frank Robinson	5.00	2.20	.60
☐ 29 Vic Roznovsky	2.00	.90	.25
☐ 30 Russ Snyder	2.00	.90	.25
☐ 31 Eddie Watt	2.00	.90	.25
☐ 32 Gene Woodling CO	2.00	.90	.25

1983 Orioles Postcards

This 30-card set of the Baltimore Orioles measures 3 1/2" by 5 1/8" and features white-bordered, color player portraits with the player's name in the bottom margin. The backs carry a postcard format. The cards are unnumbered and checklisted below in alphabetical order.

	NRMT	VG-E	GOOD
COMPLETE SET (30)	15.00	6.75	1.85
COMMON CARD (1-30)	.50	.23	.06
☐ 1 Joe Altobelli MG	.50	.23	.06
☐ 2 Mike Boddicker	.75	.35	.09
☐ 3 Al Bumbry	.50	.23	.06
☐ 4 Todd Cruz	.50	.23	.06
☐ 5 Rich Dauer	.50	.23	.06
☐ 6 Storm Davis	.75	.35	.09
☐ 7 Rick Dempsey	.75	.35	.09
☐ 8 Jim Dwyer	.50	.23	.06
☐ 9 Mike Flanagan	.50	.23	.06
☐ 10 Dan Ford	.50	.23	.06
☐ 11 Ellie Hendricks CO	.50	.23	.06
☐ 12 John Lowenstein	.50	.23	.06
☐ 13 Dennis Martinez	.75	.35	.09
☐ 14 Tippy Martinez	.50	.23	.06
☐ 15 Scott McGregor	.50	.23	.06
☐ 16 Ray Miller CO	.50	.23	.06
☐ 17 Eddie Murray	3.00	1.35	.35
☐ 18 Joe Nolan	.50	.23	.06
☐ 19 Jim Palmer	2.00	.90	.25
☐ 20 Allan Ramirez	.50	.23	.06
☐ 21 Cal Ripken Jr.	6.00	2.70	.75
☐ 22 Cal Ripken Sr. CO	.50	.23	.06
☐ 23 Gary Roenicke	.50	.23	.06
☐ 24 Ralph Rowe CO	.50	.23	.06
☐ 25 Lenn Sakata	.50	.23	.06
☐ 26 Sammy Stewart	.50	.23	.06
☐ 27 Tim Stoddard	.50	.23	.06
☐ 28 Earl Weaver MG	2.00	.90	.25
☐ 29 Jimmy Williams CO	.50	.23	.06
☐ 30 Memorial Stadium	.50	.23	.06

1984 Orioles English's Discs

This disc set salutes the 1983 Baltimore Orioles Champion team; the discs come into two sizes, measuring either 7 1/4" or 8 3/8" in diameter. The fronts feature a black-and-white head shot on a white background encircled by orange. His name, position, team name biographical information and brief statistics are printed on the white circle. The phrase "English's Salutes" and "1983 Champions" are printed in black print in the orange border. The discs are unnumbered and checklisted below in alphabetical order. The backs are blank so we have sequenced this set in alphabetical order.

	NRMT	VG-E	GOOD
COMPLETE SET (13)	50.00	22.00	6.25
COMMON DISC (1-13)	.50	.23	.06
☐ 1 Mike Boddicker	.50	.23	.06
☐ 2 Rich Dauer	.50	.23	.06
☐ 3 Storm Davis	.50	.23	.06
☐ 4 Rick Dempsey	1.00	.45	.12
☐ 5 Mike Flanagan	1.00	.45	.12
☐ 6 John Lowenstein	.50	.23	.06
☐ 7 Tippy Martinez	.50	.23	.06
☐ 8 Scott McGregor	.50	.23	.06
☐ 9 Eddie Murray	10.00	4.50	1.25
☐ 10 Jim Palmer	6.00	2.70	.75
☐ 11 Cal Ripken	40.00	18.00	5.00
☐ 12 Gary Roenicke	.50	.23	.06
☐ 13 Ken Singleton	1.00	.45	.12

1984 Orioles Team Issue

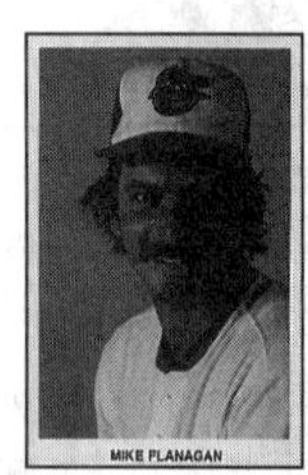

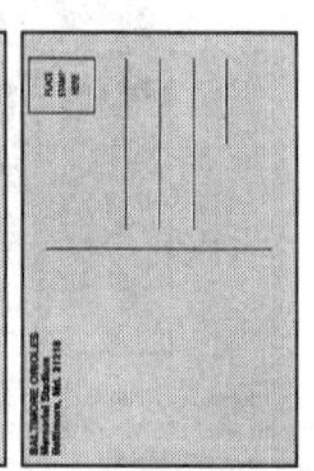

These 29 full-color photos measure approximately 3 1/2 by 5 1/4". They feature members of the 1984 Baltimore Orioles. The person is identified on the bottom of the card. The back is similar to any postcard.

	NRMT	VG-E	GOOD
COMPLETE SET (29)	15.00	6.75	1.85
COMMON CARD (1-29)	.50	.23	.06
☐ 1 Joe Altobelli MG	.50	.23	.06
☐ 2 Benny Ayala	.50	.23	.06
☐ 3 Mike Boddicker	.50	.23	.06
☐ 4 Al Bumbry	.50	.23	.06
☐ 5 Todd Cruz	.50	.23	.06
☐ 6 Rich Dauer	.50	.23	.06
☐ 7 Storm Davis	.50	.23	.06
☐ 8 Rick Dempsey	.75	.35	.09
☐ 9 Jim Dwyer	.50	.23	.06
☐ 10 Mike Flanagan	.75	.35	.09
☐ 11 Dan Ford	.50	.23	.06
☐ 12 Ellie Hendricks CO	.50	.23	.06
☐ 13 John Lowenstein	.50	.23	.06
☐ 14 Dennis Martinez	.75	.35	.09
☐ 15 Tippy Martinez	.50	.23	.06
☐ 16 Scott McGregor	.50	.23	.06
☐ 17 Ray Miller CO	.50	.23	.06
☐ 18 Eddie Murray	2.50	1.10	.30
☐ 19 Joe Nolan	.50	.23	.06
☐ 20 Jim Palmer	2.00	.90	.25
☐ 21 Allan Ramirez	.50	.23	.06
☐ 22 Cal Ripken, Jr.	5.00	2.20	.60
☐ 23 Cal Ripken, Sr. CO	.50	.23	.06
☐ 24 Gary Roenicke	.50	.23	.06
☐ 25 Ralph Rowe CO	.50	.23	.06
☐ 26 Lenn Sakata	.50	.23	.06
☐ 27 Ken Singleton	.75	.35	.09
☐ 28 Sammy Stewart	.50	.23	.06
☐ 29 Jimmy Williams CO	.50	.23	.06

1985 Orioles Health

This 20-card set features color player portraits that measure approximately 3 1/2" by 5 1/4" in a white border. The backs carry a "Health Message" and the player's signature above his name. Some of the players have two cards with the same picture but a different health message on the back. Cal Ripken Jr. has three cards with three different health messages. The cards are unnumbered and checklisted below in alphabetical order. A set in considered complete with any one card of the players for whom more than one card was issued.

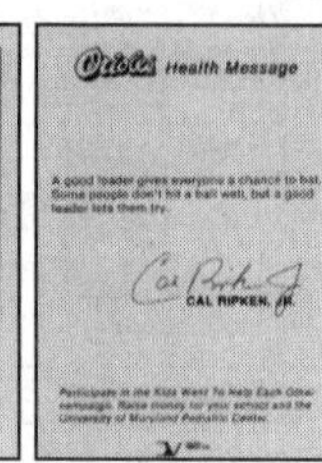

	NRMT	VG-E	GOOD
COMPLETE SET (20)	10.00	4.50	1.25
COMMON CARD (1-20)	.25	.11	.03
☐ 1 Don Aase	.25	.11	.03
☐ 2 Mike Boddicker (2)	.50	.23	.06
☐ 3 Storm Davis	.25	.11	.03
☐ 4 Rick Dempsey (2)	.50	.23	.06
☐ 5 Ken Dixon	.25	.11	.03
☐ 6 Jim Dwyer	.25	.11	.03
☐ 7 Mike Flanagan (2)	.50	.23	.06
☐ 8 Lee Lacy	.25	.11	.03
☐ 9 Fred Lynn (2)	.50	.23	.06
☐ 10 Dennis Martinez	.50	.23	.06
☐ 11 Tippy Martinez	.25	.11	.03
☐ 12 Scott McGregor	.25	.11	.03
☐ 13 Eddie Murray (2)	2.50	1.10	.30
☐ 14 Floyd Rayford (2)	.25	.11	.03
☐ 15 Cal Ripken Jr. (3)	5.00	2.20	.60
☐ 16 Larry Sheets (2)	.25	.11	.03
☐ 17 John Shelby	.25	.11	.03
☐ 18 Earl Weaver MG	1.50	.70	.19
☐ 19 Alan Wiggins	.25	.11	.03
☐ 20 Mike Young	.25	.11	.03

1986 Orioles Greats TCMA

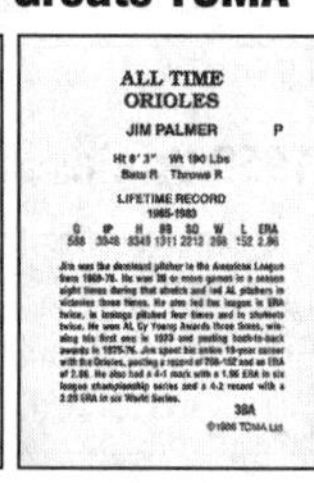

This 12-card standard-size set features some of the best Baltimore Orioles since 1954. The fronts display player photos, his name as well as a position identification. The back has vital statistics, career totals and a biography.

	MINT	NRMT	EXC
COMPLETE SET (12)	6.00	2.70	.75
COMMON CARD (1-12)	.25	.11	.03
☐ 1 Hoyt Wilhelm	.75	.35	.09
☐ 2 Hank Bauer MG	.25	.11	.03
☐ 3 Jim Palmer	1.50	.70	.19
☐ 4 Dave McNally	.50	.23	.06
☐ 5 Paul Blair	.25	.11	.03
☐ 6 Gus Triandos	.25	.11	.03
☐ 7 Frank Robinson	1.50	.70	.19
☐ 8 Ken Singleton	.25	.11	.03
☐ 9 Luis Aparicio	.75	.35	.09
☐ 10 Brooks Robinson	1.50	.70	.19
☐ 11 John "Boog" Powell	.75	.35	.09
☐ 12 Dave Johnson	.50	.23	.06

1987 Orioles French Bray

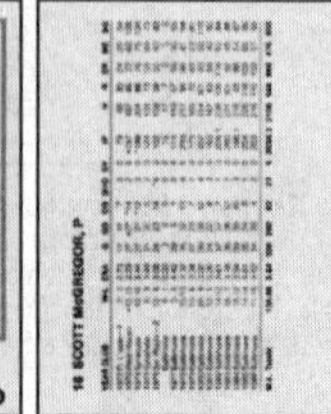

The 1987 French Bray set contains 30 cards (featuring members of the Baltimore Orioles) measuring approximately 2 1/4" by 3". The fronts have facial photos with white and orange borders; the horizontally oriented backs are white and feature career stats. The cards were given away in perforated sheet form on Photo Card Day at the Orioles home game on July 26, 1987. A large team photo was also included as one of the three panels in this perforated card set. The cards are unnumbered except for uniform number.

	MINT	NRMT	EXC
COMPLETE SET (30)	20.00	9.00	2.50
COMMON CARD	.25	.11	.03
☐ 2 Alan Wiggins	.25	.11	.03
☐ 3 Bill Ripken	.50	.23	.06
☐ 6 Floyd Rayford	.25	.11	.03
☐ 7 Cal Ripken Sr. MG	.50	.23	.06
☐ 8 Cal Ripken Jr.	10.00	4.50	1.25
☐ 9 Jim Dwyer	.25	.11	.03
☐ 10 Terry Crowley CO	.25	.11	.03
☐ 15 Terry Kennedy	.25	.11	.03
☐ 16 Scott McGregor	.25	.11	.03
☐ 18 Larry Sheets	.25	.11	.03
☐ 19 Fred Lynn	.50	.23	.06
☐ 20 Frank Robinson CO	2.00	.90	.25
☐ 24 Dave Schmidt	.25	.11	.03
☐ 25 Ray Knight	.75	.35	.09
☐ 27 Lee Lacy	.25	.11	.03
☐ 31 Mark Wiley CO	.25	.11	.03
☐ 32 Mark Williamson	.25	.11	.03
☐ 33 Eddie Murray	3.00	1.35	.35
☐ 38 Ken Gerhart	.25	.11	.03
☐ 39 Ken Dixon	.25	.11	.03
☐ 40 Jimmy Williams CO	.25	.11	.03
☐ 42 Mike Griffin	.25	.11	.03
☐ 43 Mike Young	.25	.11	.03
☐ 44 Elrod Hendricks CO	.25	.11	.03
☐ 45 Eric Bell	.25	.11	.03
☐ 46 Mike Flanagan	.50	.23	.06
☐ 49 Tom Niedenfuer	.25	.11	.03
☐ 52 Mike Boddicker	.50	.23	.06
☐ 54 John Habyan	.25	.11	.03
☐ 57 Tony Arnold	.25	.11	.03

1988 Orioles French Bray

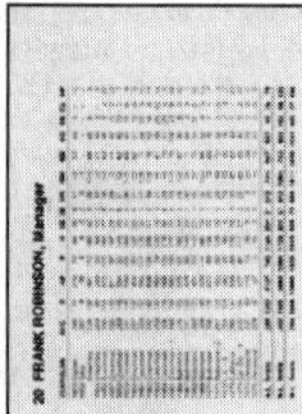

This set was distributed as a perforated set of 30 full-color cards attached to a large team photo on July 31, 1988, the Baltimore Orioles' Photo Card Day. The cards measure approximately 2 1/4" by 3 1/16". Card backs are simply done in black and white with statistics but no narrative or any personal information. Cards are unnumbered except for uniform number. Card front have a thin orange inner border and have the French Bray (Printing and Graphic Communication) logo in the lower right corner.

	MINT	NRMT	EXC
COMPLETE SET (30)	15.00	6.75	1.85
COMMON CARD	.25	.11	.03
☐ 2 Don Buford CO	.25	.11	.03
☐ 6 Joe Orsulak	.25	.11	.03
☐ 7 Bill Ripken	.50	.23	.06
☐ 8 Cal Ripken	7.50	3.40	.95
☐ 9 Jim Dwyer	.25	.11	.03
☐ 10 Terry Crowley CO	.25	.11	.03
☐ 12 Mike Morgan	.25	.11	.03
☐ 14 Mickey Tettleton	1.00	.45	.12
☐ 15 Terry Kennedy	.25	.11	.03
☐ 17 Pete Stanicek	.25	.11	.03
☐ 18 Larry Sheets	.25	.11	.03
☐ 19 Fred Lynn	.75	.35	.09
☐ 20 Frank Robinson MG	1.50	.70	.19
☐ 23 Ozzie Peraza	.25	.11	.03
☐ 24 Dave Schmidt	.25	.11	.03
☐ 25 Rick Schu	.25	.11	.03
☐ 28 Jim Traber	.25	.11	.03
☐ 31 Herm Starrette CO	.25	.11	.03
☐ 33 Eddie Murray	2.50	1.10	.30
☐ 34 Jeff Ballard	.25	.11	.03
☐ 38 Ken Gerhart	.25	.11	.03
☐ 40 Minnie Mendoza CO	.25	.11	.03
☐ 41 Don Aase	.25	.11	.03
☐ 44 Elrod Hendricks CO	.25	.11	.03
☐ 47 John Hart CO	.25	.11	.03
☐ 48 Jose Bautista	.25	.11	.03
☐ 49 Tom Niedenfuer	.25	.11	.03
☐ 52 Mike Boddicker	.50	.23	.06
☐ 53 Jay Tibbs	.25	.11	.03
☐ 88 Rene Gonzales	.25	.11	.03

1989 Orioles French Bray

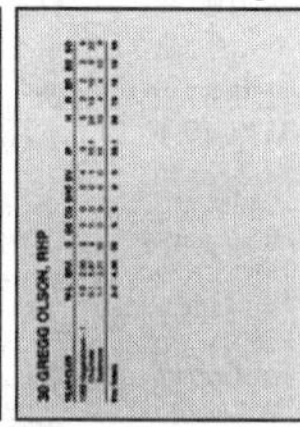

The 1989 French Bray/WWF Orioles set contains 31 cards measuring approximately 2 1/4" by 3". The fronts have facial photos with orange and white borders; the backs are white and feature career stats. The set was given away at a Baltimore home game on May 12, 1989. The cards are numbered by the players' uniform numbers.

	MINT	NRMT	EXC
COMPLETE SET (32)	12.00	5.50	1.50
COMMON CARD	.25	.11	.03
□ 3 Bill Ripken	.25	.11	.03
□ 6 Joe Orsulak	.25	.11	.03
□ 7 Cal Ripken Sr. CO	.50	.23	.06
□ 8 Cal Ripken Jr.	5.00	2.20	.60
□ 9 Brady Anderson	3.00	1.35	.35
□ 10 Steve Finley	1.50	.70	.19
□ 11 Craig Worthington	.25	.11	.03
□ 12 Mike Devereaux	.50	.23	.06
□ 14 Mickey Tettleton	.75	.35	.09
□ 15 Randy Milligan	.25	.11	.03
□ 16 Phil Bradley	.25	.11	.03
□ 18 Bob Milacki	.25	.11	.03
□ 19 Larry Sheets	.25	.11	.03
□ 20 Frank Robinson MG	1.00	.45	.12
□ 21 Mark Thurmond	.25	.11	.03
□ 23 Kevin Hickey	.25	.11	.03
□ 24 Dave Schmidt	.25	.11	.03
□ 28 Jim Traber	.25	.11	.03
□ 29 Jeff Ballard	.25	.11	.03
□ 30 Gregg Olson	.50	.23	.06
□ 31 Al Jackson CO	.25	.11	.03
□ 32 Mark Williamson	.25	.11	.03
□ 36 Bob Melvin	.25	.11	.03
□ 37 Brian Holton	.25	.11	.03
□ 40 Tom McCraw CO	.25	.11	.03
□ 42 Pete Harnisch	.50	.23	.06
□ 43 Francisco Melendez	.25	.11	.03
□ 44 Elrod Hendricks CO	.25	.11	.03
□ 46 Johnny Oates CO	.50	.23	.06
□ 48 Jose Bautista	.25	.11	.03
□ 88 Rene Gonzales	.25	.11	.03
□ NNO Sponsor ad	.25	.11	.03

1991 Orioles Crown

This 501-card set was produced by the Baltimore Orioles in conjunction with Crown Gasoline Stations and Coca-Cola. The cards measure approximately 2 1/2" by 3 1/8" and feature every Oriole player in the team's modern history (1954-1991). The cards were issued in four series, with ten twelve-card sheets per set. The front features a black and white head shot of the player, with a green border and an orange picture frame. The player's name and position appear above the picture, while the Orioles' team logo is superimposed at the lower left corner. In a similar design to the front, the back is printed in black and gray, and presents the player's Orioles statistics and Major League statistics. The sponsors' logos adorn the bottom of the card back, with the card number in the lower right hand corner. The first set was given away at the Orioles May 17th game against the California Angels, and the following day the set went on sale at Baltimore area Crown gasoline stations for 1.99 with an eight gallon fill-up. The second set was given away at the Orioles June 28th game against the Boston Red Sox, and again it went on sale the following day at Crown gasoline stations. The third set was given away at the Orioles August 11th game against the Chicago White Sox and went on sale on the same day. The fourth set went on sale at Crown gasoline stations on September 16. The cards are arranged alphabetically by player and checklisted below accordingly.

	MINT	NRMT	EXC
COMPLETE SET (501)	60.00	27.00	7.50
COMMON CARD (1-501)	.10	.05	.01
□ 1 Don Aase	.10	.05	.01
□ 2 Cal Abrams	.10	.05	.01
□ 3 Jerry Adair	.10	.05	.01
□ 4 Bobby Adams	.10	.05	.01
□ 5 Mike Adamson	.10	.05	.01
□ 6 Jay Aldrich	.10	.05	.01
□ 7 Bob Alexander	.10	.05	.01
□ 8 Doyle Alexander	.25	.11	.03
□ 9 Brady Anderson	1.50	.70	.19
□ 10 John Anderson	.10	.05	.01
□ 11 Mike Anderson	.10	.05	.01
□ 12 Luis Aparicio	1.50	.70	.19
□ 13 Tony Arnold	.10	.05	.01
□ 14 Bobby Avila	.25	.11	.03
□ 15 Benny Ayala	.10	.05	.01
□ 16 Bob Bailor	.10	.05	.01
□ 17 Frank Baker	.10	.05	.01
□ 18 Jeff Ballard	.10	.05	.01
□ 19 George Bamberger	.25	.11	.03
□ 20 Steve Barber	.25	.11	.03
□ 21 Ray(Buddy) Barker	.10	.05	.01
□ 22 Ed Barnowski	.10	.05	.01
□ 23 Jose Bautista	.10	.05	.01
□ 24 Don Baylor	.75	.35	.09
□ 25 Charlie Beamon	.10	.05	.01
□ 26 Fred Beene	.10	.05	.01
□ 27 Mark Belanger	.35	.16	.04
□ 28 Eric Bell	.10	.05	.01
□ 29 Juan Bell	.10	.05	.01
□ 30 Juan Beniquez	.10	.05	.01
□ 31 Neil Berry	.10	.05	.01
□ 32 Frank Bertaina	.10	.05	.01
□ 33 Fred Besana	.10	.05	.01
□ 34 Vern Bickford	.10	.05	.01
□ 35 Babe Birrer	.10	.05	.01
□ 36 Paul Blair	.35	.16	.04
□ 37 Curt Blefary	.25	.11	.03
□ 38 Mike Blyzka	.10	.05	.01
□ 39 Mike Boddicker	.25	.11	.03
□ 40 Juan Bonilla	.10	.05	.01
□ 41 Bob Bonner	.10	.05	.01
□ 42 Dan Boone	.10	.05	.01
□ 43 Rich Bordi	.10	.05	.01
□ 44 Dave Boswell	.10	.05	.01
□ 45 Sam Bowens	.10	.05	.01
□ 46 Bob Boyd	.10	.05	.01
□ 47 Gene Brabender	.10	.05	.01
□ 48 Phil Bradley	.10	.05	.01
□ 49 Jackie Brandt	.10	.05	.01
□ 50 Marv Breeding	.10	.05	.01
□ 51 Jim Brideweser	.10	.05	.01
□ 52 Nelson Briles	.25	.11	.03
□ 53 Dick Brown	.10	.05	.01
□ 54 Hal Brown	.10	.05	.01
□ 55 Larry Brown	.10	.05	.01
□ 56 Mark Brown	.10	.05	.01
□ 57 Marty Brown	.10	.05	.01
□ 58 George Brunet	.10	.05	.01
□ 59 Don Buford	.25	.11	.03
□ 60 Al Bumbry	.25	.11	.03
□ 61 Wally Bunker	.25	.11	.03
□ 62 Leo Burke	.10	.05	.01
□ 63 Rick Burleson	.25	.11	.03
□ 64 Pete Burnside	.10	.05	.01
□ 65 Jim Busby	.10	.05	.01
□ 66 John Buzhardt	.10	.05	.01
□ 67 Harry Byrd	.10	.05	.01
□ 68 Enos Cabell	.10	.05	.01
□ 69 Chico Carrasquel	.25	.11	.03
□ 70 Camilo Carreon	.10	.05	.01
□ 71 Foster Castleman	.10	.05	.01
□ 72 Wayne Causey	.10	.05	.01
□ 73 Art Ceccarelli	.10	.05	.01
□ 74 Bob Chakales	.10	.05	.01
□ 75 Tony Chevez	.10	.05	.01
□ 76 Tom Chism	.10	.05	.01
□ 77 Gino Cimoli	.10	.05	.01
□ 78 Gil Coan	.10	.05	.01
□ 79 Rich Coggins	.10	.05	.01
□ 80 Joe Coleman	.10	.05	.01
□ 81 Rip Coleman	.10	.05	.01
□ 82 Fritz Connally	.10	.05	.01
□ 83 Sandy Consuegra	.10	.05	.01
□ 84 Doug Corbett	.10	.05	.01
□ 85 Mark Corey	.10	.05	.01
□ 86 Clint Courtney	.10	.05	.01
□ 87 Billy Cox	.25	.11	.03
□ 88 Dave Criscione	.10	.05	.01
□ 89 Terry Crowley	.10	.05	.01
□ 90 Todd Cruz	.10	.05	.01
□ 91 Mike Cuellar	.35	.16	.04
□ 92 Angie Dagres	.10	.05	.01
□ 93 Clay Dalrymple	.10	.05	.01
□ 94 Rich Dauer	.10	.05	.01
□ 95 Jerry DaVanon	.10	.05	.01
□ 96 Butch Davis	.10	.05	.01
□ 97 Storm Davis	.25	.11	.03
□ 98 Tommy Davis	.35	.16	.04
□ 99 Doug DeCinces	.35	.16	.04
□ 100 Luis DeLeon	.10	.05	.01
□ 101 Ike Delock	.10	.05	.01
□ 102 Rick Dempsey	.25	.11	.03
□ 103 Mike Devereaux	.35	.16	.04
□ 104 Chuck Diering	.10	.05	.01
□ 105 Gordon Dillard	.10	.05	.01
□ 106 Bill Dillman	.10	.05	.01
□ 107 Mike Dimmel	.10	.05	.01
□ 108 Ken Dixon	.10	.05	.01
□ 109 Pat Dobson	.25	.11	.03
□ 110 Tom Dodd	.10	.05	.01
□ 111 Harry Dorish	.10	.05	.01
□ 112 Moe Drabowsky	.25	.11	.03
□ 113 Dick Drago	.10	.05	.01
□ 114 Walt Dropo	.25	.11	.03
□ 115 Tom Dukes	.10	.05	.01
□ 116 Dave Duncan	.25	.11	.03
□ 117 Ryne Duren	.35	.16	.04
□ 118 Joe Durham	.10	.05	.01
□ 119 Jim Dwyer	.10	.05	.01
□ 120 Jim Dyck	.10	.05	.01
□ 121 Mike Epstein	.25	.11	.03
□ 122 Chuck Essegian	.10	.05	.01
□ 123 Chuck Estrada	.10	.05	.01
□ 124 Andy Etchebarren	.10	.05	.01
□ 125 Hoot Evers	.10	.05	.01
□ 126 Ed Farmer	.10	.05	.01
□ 127 Chico Fernandez	.10	.05	.01
□ 128 Don Ferrarese	.10	.05	.01
□ 129 Jim Finigan	.10	.05	.01
□ 130 Steve Finley	.75	.35	.09
□ 131 Mike Fiore	.10	.05	.01
□ 132 Eddie Fisher	.10	.05	.01
□ 133 Jack Fisher	.10	.05	.01
□ 134 Tom Fisher	.10	.05	.01
□ 135 Mike Flanagan	.35	.16	.04
□ 136 John Flinn	.10	.05	.01
□ 137 Bobby Floyd	.10	.05	.01
□ 138 Hank Foiles	.10	.05	.01
□ 139 Dan Ford	.10	.05	.01
□ 140 Dave Ford	.10	.05	.01
□ 141 Mike Fornieles	.10	.05	.01
□ 142 Howie Fox	.10	.05	.01
□ 143 Tito Francona	.25	.11	.03
□ 144 Joe Frazier	.10	.05	.01
□ 145 Roger Freed	.10	.05	.01
□ 146 Jim Fridley	.10	.05	.01
□ 147 Jim Fuller	.10	.05	.01
□ 148 Joe Gaines	.10	.05	.01
□ 149 Vinicio(Chico) Garcia	.10	.05	.01
□ 150 Kiko Garcia	.10	.05	.01
□ 151 Billy Gardner	.10	.05	.01
□ 152 Wayne Garland	.10	.05	.01
□ 153 Tommy Gastall	.10	.05	.01
□ 154 Jim Gentile	.35	.16	.04
□ 155 Ken Gerhart	.10	.05	.01
□ 156 Paul Gilliford	.10	.05	.01
□ 157 Joe Ginsberg	.10	.05	.01
□ 158 Leo Gomez	.10	.05	.01
□ 159 Rene Gonzales	.10	.05	.01
□ 160 Billy Goodman	.25	.11	.03
□ 161 Dan Graham	.10	.05	.01
□ 162 Ted Gray	.10	.05	.01
□ 163 Gene Green	.10	.05	.01
□ 164 Lenny Green	.10	.05	.01
□ 165 Bobby Grich	.35	.16	.04
□ 166 Nuje Griffin	.10	.05	.01
□ 167 Ross Grimsley	.10	.05	.01
□ 168 Wayne Gross	.10	.05	.01
□ 169 Glenn Gulliver	.10	.05	.01
□ 170 Jackie Gutierrez	.10	.05	.01
□ 171 John Habyan	.10	.05	.01
□ 172 Harvey Haddix	.25	.11	.03
□ 173 Bob Hale	.10	.05	.01
□ 174 Dick Hall	.10	.05	.01
□ 175 Bert Hamric	.10	.05	.01
□ 176 Larry Haney	.10	.05	.01
□ 177 Ron Hansen	.25	.11	.03
□ 178 Jim Hardin	.10	.05	.01
□ 179 Larry Harlow	.10	.05	.01
□ 180 Pete Harnisch	.25	.11	.03
□ 181 Tommy Harper	.25	.11	.03
□ 182 Bob Harrison	.10	.05	.01
□ 183 Roric Harrison	.10	.05	.01
□ 184 Jack Harshman	.10	.05	.01
□ 185 Mike Hart	.10	.05	.01
□ 186 Pete Hartzell	.10	.05	.01
□ 187 Grady Hatton	.10	.05	.01
□ 188 Brad Havens	.10	.05	.01
□ 189 Drungo Hazewood	.10	.05	.01
□ 190 Jehosie Heard	.10	.05	.01
□ 191 Mel Held	.10	.05	.01
□ 192 Woodie Held	.10	.05	.01
□ 193 Ellie Hendricks	.25	.11	.03
□ 194 Leo Hernandez	.10	.05	.01
□ 195 Whitey Herzog	.50	.23	.06
□ 196 Kevin Hickey	.10	.05	.01
□ 197 Billy Hoeft	.10	.05	.01
□ 198 Chris Hoiles	1.00	.45	.12
□ 199 Fred Holdsworth	.10	.05	.01
□ 200 Brian Holton	.10	.05	.01
□ 201 Ken Holtzman	.25	.11	.03
□ 202 Don Hood	.10	.05	.01
□ 203 Sam Horn	.10	.05	.01
□ 204 Art Houtteman	.25	.11	.03
□ 205 Bruce Howard	.10	.05	.01
□ 206 Rex Hudler	.25	.11	.03
□ 207 Phil Huffman	.10	.05	.01
□ 208 Keith Hughes	.10	.05	.01
□ 209 Mark Huismann	.10	.05	.01
□ 210 Tim Hulett	.10	.05	.01
□ 211 Billy Hunter	.10	.05	.01
□ 212 Dave Huppert	.10	.05	.01
□ 213 Jim Hutto	.10	.05	.01
□ 214 Dick Hyde	.10	.05	.01
□ 215 Grant Jackson	.25	.11	.03
□ 216 Lou Jackson	.10	.05	.01
□ 217 Reggie Jackson	5.00	2.20	.60
□ 218 Ron Jackson	.10	.05	.01
□ 219 Jesse Jefferson	.10	.05	.01
□ 220 Stan Jefferson	.10	.05	.01
□ 221 Bob Johnson	.10	.05	.01
□ 222 Connie Johnson	.10	.05	.01
□ 223 Darrell Johnson	.10	.05	.01
□ 224 Dave Johnson	.10	.05	.01
□ 225 Davey Johnson	.50	.23	.06
□ 226 David Johnson	.10	.05	.01
□ 227 Don Johnson	.10	.05	.01
□ 228 Ernie Johnson	.25	.11	.03
□ 229 Gordon Jones	.10	.05	.01
□ 230 Ricky Jones	.10	.05	.01
□ 231 O'Dell Jones	.10	.05	.01
□ 232 Sam Jones	.25	.11	.03
□ 233 George Kell	1.50	.70	.19
□ 234 Frank Kellert	.10	.05	.01
□ 235 Pat Kelly	.25	.11	.03
□ 236 Bob Kennedy	.25	.11	.03
□ 237 Terry Kennedy	.25	.11	.03
□ 238 Joe Kerrigan	.10	.05	.01
□ 239 Mike Kinnunen	.10	.05	.01
□ 240 Willie Kirkland	.10	.05	.01
□ 241 Ron Kittle	.25	.11	.03
□ 242 Billy Klaus	.10	.05	.01
□ 243 Ray Knight	.50	.23	.06
□ 244 Darold Knowles	.10	.05	.01
□ 245 Dick Kokos	.10	.05	.01
□ 246 Brad Komminsk	.10	.05	.01
□ 247 Dave Koslo	.10	.05	.01
□ 248 Wayne Krenchicki	.10	.05	.01
□ 249 Lou Kretlow	.10	.05	.01
□ 250 Dick Kryhoski	.10	.05	.01
□ 251 Bob Kuzava	.10	.05	.01
□ 252 Lee Lacy	.10	.05	.01
□ 253 Hobie Landrith	.10	.05	.01
□ 254 Tito Landrum	.10	.05	.01
□ 255 Don Larsen	.50	.23	.06
□ 256 Charlie Lau	.10	.05	.01
□ 257 Jim Lehew	.10	.05	.01
□ 258 Ken Lehman	.10	.05	.01
□ 259 Don Lenhardt	.10	.05	.01
□ 260 Dave Leonhard	.10	.05	.01
□ 261 Don Leppert	.10	.05	.01
□ 262 Dick Littlefield	.10	.05	.01
□ 263 Charlie Locke	.10	.05	.01
□ 264 Whitey Lockman	.25	.11	.03
□ 265 Billy Loes	.25	.11	.03
□ 266 Ed Lopat	.35	.16	.04
□ 267 Carlos Lopez	.10	.05	.01
□ 268 Marcelino Lopez	.10	.05	.01
□ 269 John Lowenstein	.10	.05	.01
□ 270 Steve Luebber	.10	.05	.01
□ 271 Dick Luebke	.10	.05	.01
□ 272 Fred Lynn	.35	.16	.04
□ 273 Bobby Mabe	.10	.05	.01
□ 274 Elliott Maddox	.10	.05	.01
□ 275 Hank Majeski	.10	.05	.01
□ 276 Roger Marquis	.10	.05	.01
□ 277 Freddie Marsh	.10	.05	.01
□ 278 Jim Marshall	.10	.05	.01
□ 279 Morrie Martin	.10	.05	.01
□ 280 Dennis Martinez	.75	.35	.09
□ 281 Tippy Martinez	.25	.11	.03
□ 282 Tom Matchick	.10	.05	.01
□ 283 Charlie Maxwell	.25	.11	.03
□ 284 Dave May	.10	.05	.01
□ 285 Lee May	.35	.16	.04
□ 286 Rudy May	.25	.11	.03
□ 287 Mike McCormick	.25	.11	.03
□ 288 Ben McDonald	.75	.35	.09
□ 289 Jim McDonald	.10	.05	.01
□ 290 Scott McGregor	.25	.11	.03
□ 291 Mickey McGuire	.10	.05	.01
□ 292 Jeff McKnight	.10	.05	.01
□ 293 Dave McNally	.50	.23	.06
□ 294 Sam Mele	.10	.05	.01
□ 295 Francisco Melendez	.10	.05	.01
□ 296 Bob Melvin	.10	.05	.01
□ 297 Jose Mesa	.75	.35	.09
□ 298 Eddie Miksis	.10	.05	.01
□ 299 Bob Milacki	.10	.05	.01
□ 300 Bill Miller	.10	.05	.01
□ 301 Dyar Miller	.10	.05	.01
□ 302 John Miller	.10	.05	.01
□ 303 Randy Miller	.10	.05	.01
□ 304 Stu Miller	.25	.11	.03
□ 305 Randy Milligan	.10	.05	.01
□ 306 Paul Mirabella	.10	.05	.01
□ 307 Willie Miranda	.10	.05	.01
□ 308 John Mitchell	.10	.05	.01
□ 309 Paul Mitchell	.10	.05	.01
□ 310 Ron Moeller	.10	.05	.01
□ 311 Bob Molinaro	.10	.05	.01
□ 312 Ray Moore	.10	.05	.01
□ 313 Andres Mora	.10	.05	.01
□ 314 Jose Morales	.10	.05	.01
□ 315 Keith Moreland	.10	.05	.01
□ 316 Mike Morgan	.10	.05	.01
□ 317 Dan Morogiello	.10	.05	.01
□ 318 John Morris	.10	.05	.01
□ 319 Les Moss	.10	.05	.01
□ 320 Curt Motton	.10	.05	.01
□ 321 Eddie Murray	5.00	2.20	.60
□ 322 Ray Murray	.10	.05	.01
□ 323 Tony Muser	.10	.05	.01
□ 324 Buster Narum	.10	.05	.01
□ 325 Bob Nelson	.10	.05	.01
□ 326 Roger Nelson	.10	.05	.01
□ 327 Carl Nichols	.10	.05	.01
□ 328 Dave Nicholson	.10	.05	.01
□ 329 Tim Niedenfuer	.10	.05	.01
□ 330 Bob Nieman	.10	.05	.01
□ 331 Donell Nixon	.10	.05	.01
□ 332 Joe Nolan	.10	.05	.01
□ 333 Dickie Noles	.10	.05	.01
□ 334 Tim Nordbrook	.10	.05	.01
□ 335 Jim Northrup	.25	.11	.03
□ 336 Jack O'Connor	.10	.05	.01
□ 337 Billy O'Dell	.25	.11	.03

	MINT	NRMT	EXC
☐ 338 John O'Donoghue	.10	.05	.01
☐ 339 Tom O'Malley	.10	.05	.01
☐ 340 Johnny Oates	.35	.16	.04
☐ 341 Chuck Oertel	.10	.05	.01
☐ 342 Bob Oliver	.10	.05	.01
☐ 343 Gregg Olson	.35	.16	.04
☐ 344 John Orsino	.10	.05	.01
☐ 345 Joe Orsulak	.25	.11	.03
☐ 346 John Pacella	.10	.05	.01
☐ 347 Dave Pagan	.10	.05	.01
☐ 348 Erv Palica	.10	.05	.01
☐ 349 Jim Palmer	5.00	2.20	.60
☐ 350 John Papa	.10	.05	.01
☐ 351 Milt Pappas	.35	.16	.04
☐ 352 Al Pardo	.10	.05	.01
☐ 353 Kelly Paris	.10	.05	.01
☐ 354 Mike Parrott	.10	.05	.01
☐ 355 Tom Patton	.10	.05	.01
☐ 356 Albie Pearson	.25	.11	.03
☐ 357 Orlando Pena	.10	.05	.01
☐ 358 Oswaldo Peraza	.10	.05	.01
☐ 359 Buddy Peterson	.10	.05	.01
☐ 360 Dave Philley	.10	.05	.01
☐ 361 Tom Phoebus	.10	.05	.01
☐ 362 Al Pilarcik	.10	.05	.01
☐ 363 Duane Pillette	.10	.05	.01
☐ 364 Lou Piniella (Pictured wearing a KC Royals cap)	.75	.35	.09
☐ 365 Dave Pope	.10	.05	.01
☐ 366 Arnie Portocarrero	.10	.05	.01
☐ 367 Boog Powell	1.00	.45	.12
☐ 368 Johnny Powers	.10	.05	.01
☐ 369 Carl Powis	.10	.05	.01
☐ 370 Joe Price	.10	.05	.01
☐ 371 Jim Pyburn	.10	.05	.01
☐ 372 Art Quirk	.10	.05	.01
☐ 373 Jamie Quirk	.10	.05	.01
☐ 374 Allan Ramirez	.10	.05	.01
☐ 375 Floyd Rayford	.10	.05	.01
☐ 376 Mike Reinbach	.10	.05	.01
☐ 377 Merv Rettenmund	.10	.05	.01
☐ 378 Bob Reynolds	.10	.05	.01
☐ 379 Del Rice (Wearing St. Louis Cardinals cap)	.10	.05	.01
☐ 380 Pete Richert	.10	.05	.01
☐ 381 Jeff Rineer	.10	.05	.01
☐ 382 Bill Ripken	.25	.11	.03
☐ 383 Cal Ripken	10.00	4.50	1.25
☐ 384 Robin Roberts	1.50	.70	.19
☐ 385 Brooks Robinson	5.00	2.20	.60
☐ 386 Earl Robinson	.10	.05	.01
☐ 387 Eddie Robinson	.10	.05	.01
☐ 388 Frank Robinson	5.00	2.20	.60
☐ 389 Sergio Robles	.10	.05	.01
☐ 390 Aurelio Rodriguez	.10	.05	.01
☐ 391 Vic Rodriguez	.10	.05	.01
☐ 392 Gary Roenicke	.10	.05	.01
☐ 393 Saul Rogovin (Wearing Philadelphia Phillies cap)	.10	.05	.01
☐ 394 Wade Rowdon	.10	.05	.01
☐ 395 Ken Rowe	.10	.05	.01
☐ 396 Willie Royster	.10	.05	.01
☐ 397 Vic Roznovsky	.10	.05	.01
☐ 398 Ken Rudolph	.10	.05	.01
☐ 399 Lenn Sakata	.10	.05	.01
☐ 400 Chico Salmon	.10	.05	.01
☐ 401 Orlando Sanchez (Pictured wearing St. Louis Cardinals cap)	.10	.05	.01
☐ 402 Bob Saverine	.10	.05	.01
☐ 403 Art Schallock	.10	.05	.01
☐ 404 Bill Scherrer (Wearing Detroit Tigers cap)	.10	.05	.01
☐ 405 Curt Schilling	.25	.11	.03
☐ 406 Dave Schmidt	.10	.05	.01
☐ 407 Johnny Schmitz	.10	.05	.01
☐ 408 Jeff Schneider	.10	.05	.01
☐ 409 Rick Schu	.10	.05	.01
☐ 410 Mickey Scott	.10	.05	.01
☐ 411 Kal Segrist	.10	.05	.01
☐ 412 David Segui	.75	.35	.09
☐ 413 Al Severinsen	.10	.05	.01
☐ 414 Larry Sheets	.25	.11	.03
☐ 415 John Shelby	.10	.05	.01
☐ 416 Barry Shetrone	.10	.05	.01
☐ 417 Tom Shopay	.10	.05	.01
☐ 418 Bill Short	.10	.05	.01
☐ 419 Norm Siebern	.25	.11	.03
☐ 420 Nelson Simmons	.10	.05	.01
☐ 421 Ken Singleton	.35	.16	.04
☐ 422 Doug Sisk	.10	.05	.01
☐ 423 Dave Skaggs	.10	.05	.01
☐ 424 Lou Sleater	.10	.05	.01
☐ 425 Al Smith	.25	.11	.03
☐ 426 Billy Smith	.10	.05	.01
☐ 427 Hal Smith	.10	.05	.01
☐ 428 Mike(Texas) Smith	.10	.05	.01
☐ 429 Nate Smith	.10	.05	.01
☐ 430 Nate Snell	.10	.05	.01
☐ 431 Russ Snyder	.10	.05	.01
☐ 432 Don Stanhouse	.10	.05	.01
☐ 433 Pete Stanicek	.10	.05	.01
☐ 434 Herm Starrette	.10	.05	.01
☐ 435 John Stefaro	.10	.05	.01
☐ 436 Gene Stephens	.10	.05	.01
☐ 437 Vern Stephens	.25	.11	.03
☐ 438 Earl Stephenson	.10	.05	.01
☐ 439 Sammy Stewart	.10	.05	.01
☐ 440 Royle Stillman	.10	.05	.01
☐ 441 Wes Stock	.10	.05	.01
☐ 442 Tim Stoddard	.25	.11	.03
☐ 443 Dean Stone	.10	.05	.01
☐ 444 Jeff Stone	.10	.05	.01
☐ 445 Steve Stone	.25	.11	.03
☐ 446 Marlin Stuart	.10	.05	.01
☐ 447 Gordie Sundin	.10	.05	.01
☐ 448 Bill Swaggerty	.10	.05	.01
☐ 449 Willie Tasby	.10	.05	.01
☐ 450 Joe Taylor	.10	.05	.01
☐ 451 Dorn Taylor	.10	.05	.01
☐ 452 Anthony Telford	.10	.05	.01
☐ 453 Johnny Temple	.25	.11	.03
☐ 454 Mickey Tettleton	.50	.23	.06
☐ 455 Valmy Thomas (Wearing Philadelphia Phillies cap)	.10	.05	.01
☐ 456 Bobby Thomson (Wearing Boston Red Sox cap)	.50	.23	.06
☐ 457 Marv Throneberry	.35	.16	.04
☐ 458 Mark Thurmond	.10	.05	.01
☐ 459 Jay Tibbs	.10	.05	.01
☐ 460 Mike Torrez	.25	.11	.03
☐ 461 Jim Traber	.10	.05	.01
☐ 462 Gus Triandos	.35	.16	.04
☐ 463 Paul(Dizzy) Trout (Wearing Detroit Tigers cap)	.25	.11	.03
☐ 464 Bob Turley	.35	.16	.04
☐ 465 Tom Underwood	.10	.05	.01
☐ 466 Fred Valentine	.10	.05	.01
☐ 467 Dave Van Gorder	.10	.05	.01
☐ 468 Dave Vineyard	.10	.05	.01
☐ 469 Ozzie Virgil	.25	.11	.03
☐ 470 Eddie Waitkus	.25	.11	.03
☐ 471 Greg Walker	.10	.05	.01
☐ 472 Jerry Walker	.10	.05	.01
☐ 473 Pete Ward	.10	.05	.01
☐ 474 Carl Warwick	.10	.05	.01
☐ 475 Ron Washington	.10	.05	.01
☐ 476 Eddie Watt	.10	.05	.01
☐ 477 Don Welchel	.10	.05	.01
☐ 478 George Werley	.10	.05	.01
☐ 479 Vic Wertz	.25	.11	.03
☐ 480 Wally Westlake (Wearing a Pittsburgh Pirates cap)	.10	.05	.01
☐ 481 Mickey Weston	.10	.05	.01
☐ 482 Alan Wiggins	.10	.05	.01
☐ 483 Bill Wight	.10	.05	.01
☐ 484 Hoyt Wilhelm	1.50	.70	.19
☐ 485 Dallas Williams	.10	.05	.01
☐ 486 Dick Williams	.35	.16	.04
☐ 487 Earl Williams	.10	.05	.01
☐ 488 Mark Williamson	.10	.05	.01
☐ 489 Jim Wilson	.10	.05	.01
☐ 490 Gene Woodling	.25	.11	.03
☐ 491 Craig Worthington	.10	.05	.01
☐ 492 Bobby Young	.10	.05	.01
☐ 493 Mike Young	.10	.05	.01
☐ 494 Frank Zupo	.10	.05	.01
☐ 495 George Zuverink	.10	.05	.01
☐ 496 Glenn Davis	.25	.11	.03
☐ 497 Dwight Evans	.50	.23	.06
☐ 498 Dave Gallagher	.10	.05	.01
☐ 499 Paul Kilgus	.10	.05	.01
☐ 500 Jeff Robinson	.10	.05	.01
☐ 501 Ernie Whitt	.10	.05	.01

1993 Orioles Crown Action Stand Ups

This set was issued in three distict series through Crown Petroleum service stations. These cards featured mainly retired Orioles players. Even though this set was issued in three distinct series, we have numbered them and priced them as one complete set. However, within each series, we have grouped the cards in alphabetical order.

	MINT	NRMT	EXC
COMPLETE SET (12)	20.00	9.00	2.50
COMMON CARD (1-12)	1.00	.45	.12
☐ 1 Rick Dempsey	1.50	.70	.19
☐ 2 Jim Palmer	4.00	1.80	.50
☐ 3 Brooks Robinson	4.00	1.80	.50
☐ 4 Frank Robinson	4.00	1.80	.50
☐ 5 Bobby Grich	1.50	.70	.19
☐ 6 Tippy Martinez	1.00	.45	.12
☐ 7 Cal Ripken Jr.	7.50	3.40	.95
☐ 8 Earl Weaver MG	3.00	1.35	.35
☐ 9 Paul Blair	1.00	.45	.12
☐ 10 Terry Crowley	1.00	.45	.12
☐ 11 Boog Powell	2.00	.90	.25
☐ 12 Ken Singleton	1.50	.70	.19

1994 Orioles Program

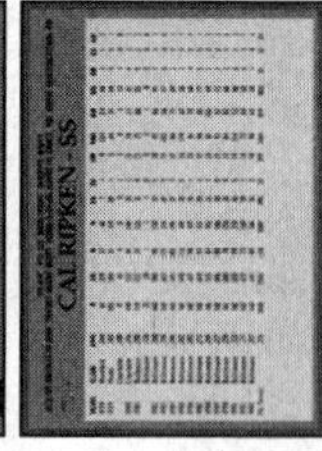

This 108-card set includes all current and minor league players in the Baltimore Orioles' organization. The set was issued in twelve nine-card perforated sheets, with each sheet issued in game day programs which sold for 3.00. Reportedly only 21,000 of each unperforated sheet were produced. Each 7 1/2" by 10 1/2" sheet consists of nine standard-size cards. The fronts feature action and posed color player photos inside a white inner border and an orange outer border. The player's name and position are printed in a black stripe cutting across the bottom of the front. The horizontal backs carry biography and complete career statistics. The cards are unnumbered and checklisted below in alphabetical order.

	MINT	NRMT	EXC
COMPLETE SET (108)	30.00	13.50	3.70
COMMON CARD (1-108)	.20	.09	.03
☐ 1 Manny Alexander	.20	.09	.03
☐ 2 Brady Anderson	1.50	.70	.19
☐ 3 Matt Anderson	.20	.09	.03
☐ 4 Harold Baines	1.00	.45	.12
☐ 5 Miles Barnden	.20	.09	.03
☐ 6 Kimera Bartee	1.00	.45	.12
☐ 7 Juan Bautista	.20	.09	.03
☐ 8 Armando Benitez	.60	.25	.07
☐ 9 Joe Borowski	.20	.09	.03
☐ 10 Brian Brewer	.20	.09	.03
☐ 11 Brandon Bridgers	.20	.09	.03
☐ 12 Cory Brown	.20	.09	.03
☐ 13 Damon Buford	.60	.25	.07
☐ 14 Clayton Byrne	.20	.09	.03
☐ 15 Racco Cafaro	.20	.09	.03
☐ 16 Paul Carey	.20	.09	.03
☐ 17 Carlos Chavez	.20	.09	.03
☐ 18 Eric Chavez	.20	.09	.03
☐ 19 Steve Chitren	.20	.09	.03
☐ 20 Mike Cook	.20	.09	.03
☐ 21 Shawn Curran	.20	.09	.03
☐ 22 Kevin Curtis	.20	.09	.03
☐ 23 Joey Dawley	.20	.09	.03
☐ 24 Jim Dedrick	.20	.09	.03
☐ 25 Cesar Devarez	.20	.09	.03
☐ 26 Mike Devereaux	.60	.25	.07
☐ 27 Brian DuBois	.20	.09	.03
☐ 28 Keith Eaddy	.20	.09	.03
☐ 29 Mark Eichhorn	.20	.09	.03
☐ 30 Scott Emerson	.20	.09	.03
☐ 31 Vaughn Eshelman	.20	.09	.03
☐ 32 Craig Faulkner	.20	.09	.03
☐ 33 Sid Fernandez	.40	.18	.05
☐ 34 Rick Forney	.20	.09	.03
☐ 35 Jim Foster	.20	.09	.03
☐ 36 Jesse Garcia	.20	.09	.03
☐ 37 Mike Garguilo	.20	.09	.03
☐ 38 Rich Gedman	.20	.09	.03
☐ 39 Leo Gomez	.20	.09	.03
☐ 40 Rene Gonzales	.20	.09	.03
☐ 41 Curtis Goodwin	.40	.18	.05
☐ 42 Kris Gresham	.20	.09	.03
☐ 43 Shane Hale	.20	.09	.03
☐ 44 Jeffrey Hammonds	.75	.35	.09
☐ 45 Jimmy Haynes	.60	.25	.07
☐ 46 Chris Hoiles	1.00	.45	.12
☐ 47 Tim Hulett	.20	.09	.03
☐ 48 Matt Jarvis	.20	.09	.03
☐ 49 Scott Klingenbeck	.20	.09	.03
☐ 50 Rick Krivda	.20	.09	.03
☐ 51 David Lamb	.40	.18	.05
☐ 52 Chris Lemp	.20	.09	.03
☐ 53 T.R. Lewis	.20	.09	.03
☐ 54 Bryan Link	.20	.09	.03
☐ 55 John Lombardi	.20	.09	.03
☐ 56 Rob Lukachyk	.20	.09	.03
☐ 57 Calvin Maduro	1.00	.45	.12
☐ 58 Barry Manuel	.20	.09	.03
☐ 59 Lincoln Martin	.20	.09	.03
☐ 60 Scott McClain	.20	.09	.03
☐ 61 Ben McDonald	.75	.35	.09
☐ 62 Kevin McGehee	.20	.09	.03
☐ 63 Mark McLemore	.40	.18	.05
☐ 64 Miguel Mejia	.20	.09	.03
☐ 65 Feliciano Mercedes	.20	.09	.03
☐ 66 Jose Millares	.20	.09	.03
☐ 67 Brent Miller	.20	.09	.03
☐ 68 Alan Mills	.40	.18	.05
☐ 69 Jamie Moyer	.40	.18	.05
☐ 70 Mike Mussina	2.50	1.10	.30
☐ 71 Sherman Obando	.60	.25	.07
☐ 72 Alex Ochoa	1.25	.55	.16
☐ 73 John O'Donoghue	.20	.09	.03
☐ 74 Mike Oquist	.20	.09	.03
☐ 75 Bo Ortiz	.20	.09	.03
☐ 76 Billy Owens	.20	.09	.03
☐ 77 Rafael Palmeiro	2.00	.90	.25
☐ 78 Dave Paveloff	.20	.09	.03
☐ 79 Brad Pennington	.20	.09	.03
☐ 80 Bill Percibal	.40	.18	.05
☐ 81 Jim Poole	.20	.09	.03
☐ 82 Jay Powell	.40	.18	.05
☐ 83 Arthur Rhodes	.60	.25	.07
☐ 84 Matt Riemer	.20	.09	.03
☐ 85 Cal Ripken	5.00	2.20	.60
☐ 86 Kevin Ryan	.20	.09	.03
☐ 87 Chris Sabo	.40	.18	.05
☐ 88 Brian Sackinsky	.20	.09	.03
☐ 89 Francisco Saneaux	.20	.09	.03
☐ 90 Jason Satre	.20	.09	.03
☐ 91 David Segui	.75	.35	.09
☐ 92 Jose Serra	.20	.09	.03
☐ 93 Larry Shenk	.20	.09	.03
☐ 94 Lee Smith	1.00	.45	.12
☐ 95 Lonnie Smith	.60	.25	.07
☐ 96 Mark Smith	.20	.09	.03
☐ 97 Garrett Stephenson	.40	.18	.05
☐ 98 Jeff Tackett	.20	.09	.03
☐ 99 Brad Tyler	.20	.09	.03
☐ 100 Pedro Ulises	.20	.09	.03
☐ 101 Jack Voigt	.20	.09	.03
☐ 102 Jim Walker	.20	.09	.03
☐ 103 B.J. Waszgis	.20	.09	.03
☐ 104 Jim Wawruck	.20	.09	.03
☐ 105 Mel Wearing	.20	.09	.03
☐ 106 Mark Williamson	.20	.09	.03
☐ 107 Brian Wood	.20	.09	.03
☐ 108 Greg Zaun	.20	.09	.03

1994 Orioles U.S. Playing Cards

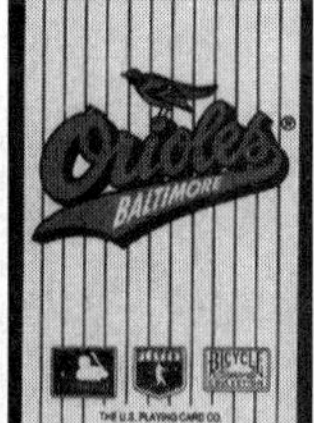

These 56 playing standard-size cards have rounded corners, and feature color posed and action player photos on their white-bordered fronts. The player's name and position appear near the bottom. The white and black backs carry the logos for the Orioles, baseball's 125th Anniversary, MLBPA, and Bicycle Sports Collection. The set is checklisted below in playing card order by suits and assigned numbers to aces (1), jacks (11), queens (12), and kings (13).

	MINT	NRMT	EXC
COMPLETE SET (56)	5.00	2.20	.60
COMMON CARD	.05	.02	.01
☐ 1C Chris Hoiles	.15	.07	.02
☐ 1D Mike Mussina	.30	.14	.04
☐ 1H Cal Ripken Jr.	1.50	.70	.19
☐ 1S Mark McLemore	.05	.02	.01
☐ 2C Mike Cook	.05	.02	.01
☐ 2D Mike Oquist	.05	.02	.01
☐ 2H Harold Baines	.15	.07	.02
☐ 2S Manny Alexander	.05	.02	.01
☐ 3C Paul Carey	.05	.02	.01
☐ 3D Brad Pennington	.05	.02	.01
☐ 3H John O'Donoghue	.05	.02	.01
☐ 3S Kevin McGehee	.05	.02	.01
☐ 4C Jeff Tackett	.05	.02	.01
☐ 4D Jeffrey Hammonds	.15	.07	.02
☐ 4H Sid Fernandez	.05	.02	.01
☐ 4S Jim Poole	.05	.02	.01
☐ 5C Arthur Rhodes	.05	.02	.01
☐ 5D Jack Voigt	.05	.02	.01
☐ 5H Alan Mills	.05	.02	.01
☐ 5S Leo Gomez	.05	.02	.01
☐ 6C Damon Buford	.05	.02	.01
☐ 6D Chris Sabo	.05	.02	.01
☐ 6H Jamie Moyer	.05	.02	.01
☐ 6S Tim Hulett	.05	.02	.01
☐ 7C David Segui	.15	.07	.02
☐ 7D Rafael Palmeiro	.25	.11	.03
☐ 7H Harold Baines	.15	.07	.02
☐ 7S Mike Devereaux	.05	.02	.01
☐ 8C Ben McDonald	.15	.07	.02
☐ 8D Chris Hoiles	.15	.07	.02
☐ 8H Mark McLemore	.05	.02	.01
☐ 8S Brady Anderson	.40	.18	.05
☐ 9C Cal Ripken Jr.	1.50	.70	.19
☐ 9D Jim Poole	.05	.02	.01
☐ 9H Jeff Tackett	.05	.02	.01
☐ 9S Mike Mussina	.30	.14	.04
☐ 10C Brad Pennington	.05	.02	.01
☐ 10D Leo Gomez	.05	.02	.01
☐ 10H Arthur Rhodes	.05	.02	.01
☐ 10S Sherman Obando	.05	.02	.01
☐ 11C Jack Voigt	.05	.02	.01

☐ 11D Tim Hulett	.05	.02	.01
☐ 11H Damon Buford	.05	.02	.01
☐ 11S Alan Mills	.05	.02	.01
☐ 12C Jeffrey Hammonds	.15	.07	.02
☐ 12D Mike Devereaux	.05	.02	.01
☐ 12H David Segui	.15	.07	.02
☐ 12S Jamie Moyer	.05	.02	.01
☐ 13C Rafael Palmeiro	.25	.11	.03
☐ 13D Brady Anderson	.40	.18	.05
☐ 13H Ben McDonald	.15	.07	.02
☐ 13S Harold Baines	.15	.07	.02
☐ NNO Featured Players	.05	.02	.01

1910 Ornate Oval Pins PM1

These pins are very ornate. The issuer of these pins is unknown but it is thought that the pins were produced sometime around 1910 or shortly thereafter. The pins are oval shaped and are approximately 1 1/4" by 1 1/2" including the brass frame border. The photos in the middle are sepia tone. Since these pins are unnumbered, they are listed below in alphabetical order.

	EX-MT	VG-E	GOOD
COMPLETE SET (13)	6000.00	2700.00	750.00
COMMON PLAYER (1-13)	250.00	110.00	31.00
☐ 1 Jimmy Archer	250.00	110.00	31.00
☐ 2 Frank Chance	600.00	275.00	75.00
☐ 3 Ty Cobb	1250.00	550.00	160.00
☐ 4 Al Demaree	250.00	110.00	31.00
☐ 5 Johnny Evers	600.00	275.00	75.00
☐ 6 Dick Hoblitzel	250.00	110.00	31.00
☐ 7 Walter Johnson	750.00	350.00	95.00
☐ 8 Ed Konetchy	250.00	110.00	31.00
☐ 9 Benny Kauff	250.00	110.00	31.00
☐ 10 Napolean Lajoie	600.00	275.00	75.00
☐ 11 Christy Mathewson	750.00	350.00	95.00
☐ 12 Tris Speaker	600.00	275.00	75.00
☐ 13 Joe Tinker	600.00	275.00	75.00

1994 Oscar Mayer Round-Ups

The 1994 Oscar Mayer Superstar Round-Up set consists of 30 circular pop-up cards measuring about 2 1/2" in diameter and features 15 players from the American (1-15) and National (16-30) Leagues. One card was inserted in each specially marked 16-oz. package of Oscar Mayer bologna available in April and May. On-pack and in-store point-of-purchase mail-in offers enabled consumers to order a boxed American and/or National League 15-card set for 1.95 plus proof-of-purchase for each set. The black-bordered fronts feature color action player shots that are perforated and cut out in such a way so that when the tab at the top is pulled, the photo becomes three-dimensional. Also revealed is a trivia question and answer, and the player's statistics. The set's title appears at the top within the black border in blue lettering on American League cards and green lettering on National League cards. The player's name, position, and team appear below the photo. The back displays the player's name, position, team, and career highlights. A color player action cutout appears alongside. The cards are numbered on the front toward the lower right, following alphabetical order by league.

	MINT	NRMT	EXC
COMPLETE SET (30)	12.00	5.50	1.50
COMMON CARD (1-30)	.25	.11	.03
☐ 1 Jim Abbott	.25	.11	.03
☐ 2 Kevin Appier	.50	.23	.06
☐ 3 Roger Clemens	1.00	.45	.12
☐ 4 Cecil Fielder	.75	.35	.09
☐ 5 Juan Gonzalez	2.00	.90	.25
☐ 6 Ken Griffey Jr.	3.00	1.35	.35
☐ 7 Kenny Lofton	1.00	.45	.12
☐ 8 Jack McDowell	.50	.23	.06
☐ 9 Paul Molitor	1.00	.45	.12
☐ 10 Kirby Puckett	2.00	.90	.25
☐ 11 Cal Ripken Jr.	2.50	1.10	.30
☐ 12 Tim Salmon	.75	.35	.09
☐ 13 Ruben Sierra	.25	.11	.03
☐ 14 Frank Thomas	3.00	1.35	.35
☐ 15 Greg Vaughn	.25	.11	.03
☐ 16 Jeff Bagwell	1.50	.70	.19
☐ 17 Barry Bonds	1.00	.45	.12
☐ 18 Bobby Bonilla	.50	.23	.06

☐ 19 Jeff Conine	.50	.23	.06
☐ 20 Lenny Dykstra	.25	.11	.03
☐ 21 Andres Galarraga	.75	.35	.09
☐ 22 Marquis Grissom	.50	.23	.06
☐ 23 Tony Gwynn	2.00	.90	.25
☐ 24 Gregg Jefferies	.25	.11	.03
☐ 25 John Kruk	.25	.11	.03
☐ 26 Greg Maddux	2.00	.90	.25
☐ 27 Mike Piazza	2.00	.90	.25
☐ 28 Jose Rijo	.25	.11	.03
☐ 29 Ryne Sandberg	1.50	.70	.19
☐ 30 Andy Van Slyke	.25	.11	.03

1938 Our National Game Pins PM8

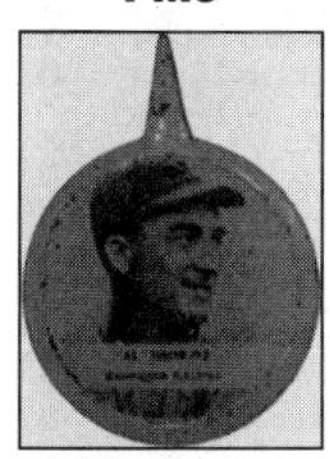

This set of 30 "buttons" (each measuring 7/8" in diameter) do not have a pin back but rather a tab or spike. They are frequently found with paper back "holder". The catalog designation for these "pins" is PM8. The set can be dated at approximately 1938 based on the selection of players in the set. The photo is in black and white but printed in blue tones. Since these buttons are unnumbered, they are listed below in alphabetical order.

	EX-MT	VG-E	GOOD
COMPLETE SET (30)	700.00	325.00	90.00
COMMON PLAYER (1-30)	8.00	3.60	1.00
☐ 1 Wally Berger	8.00	3.60	1.00
☐ 2 Lou Chiozza	8.00	3.60	1.00
☐ 3 Joe Cronin	15.00	6.75	1.85
☐ 4 Frank Crosetti	8.00	3.60	1.00
☐ 5 Dizzy Dean	50.00	22.00	6.25
☐ 6 Frank Demaree	8.00	3.60	1.00
☐ 7 Joe DiMaggio	175.00	80.00	22.00
☐ 8 Bob Feller	40.00	18.00	5.00
☐ 9 Jimmy Foxx	40.00	18.00	5.00
☐ 10 Charlie Gehringer	20.00	9.00	2.50
☐ 11 Lou Gehrig	175.00	80.00	22.00
☐ 12 Lefty Gomez	20.00	9.00	2.50
☐ 13 Hank Greenberg	20.00	9.00	2.50
☐ 14 Bump Hadley	8.00	3.60	1.00
☐ 15 Leo Hartnett	15.00	6.75	1.85
☐ 16 Carl Hubbell	20.00	9.00	2.50
☐ 17 Buddy Lewis	8.00	3.60	1.00
☐ 18 Gus Mancuso	8.00	3.60	1.00
☐ 19 Joe McCarthy MG	12.50	5.50	1.55
☐ 20 Joe Medwick	15.00	6.75	1.85
☐ 21 Joe Moore	8.00	3.60	1.00
☐ 22 Mel Ott	20.00	9.00	2.50
☐ 23 Jake Powell	8.00	3.60	1.00
☐ 24 Jimmy Ripple	8.00	3.60	1.00
☐ 25 Red Ruffing	15.00	6.75	1.85
☐ 26 Hal Schumacher	8.00	3.60	1.00
☐ 27 George Selkirk	10.00	4.50	1.25
☐ 28 Al Simmons	15.00	6.75	1.85
☐ 29 Bill Terry	20.00	9.00	2.50
☐ 30 Harold Trosky	8.00	3.60	1.00

1921 Oxford Confectionery E253

This 20 card set measures 1 5/8" by 2 3/4" and almost the whole front is a player photo. The player's name and team is on the bottom. The backs note that these cards are produced solely for the Oxford Confectionery Company and lists a player checklist.

	EX-MT	VG-E	GOOD
COMPLETE SET (20)	5500.00	2500.00	700.00
COMMON CARD (1-20)	100.00	45.00	12.50
☐ 1 Grover Cleveland Alexander	225.00	100.00	28.00
☐ 2 Dave Bancroft	200.00	90.00	25.00
☐ 3 Max Carey	200.00	90.00	25.00
☐ 4 Ty Cobb	1200.00	550.00	150.00
☐ 5 Eddie Collins	200.00	90.00	25.00
☐ 6 Frankie Frisch	200.00	90.00	25.00
☐ 7 Burleigh Grimes	200.00	90.00	25.00
☐ 8 Bill Holke	100.00	45.00	12.50
☐ 9 Rogers Hornsby	225.00	100.00	28.00
☐ 10 Walter Johnson	500.00	220.00	60.00
☐ 11 Lee Meadows	100.00	45.00	12.50
☐ 12 Cy Perkins	100.00	45.00	12.50
☐ 13 Del Pratt	100.00	45.00	12.50
☐ 14 Edd Roush	200.00	90.00	25.00
☐ 15 Babe Ruth	1800.00	800.00	220.00
☐ 16 Ray Schalk	200.00	90.00	25.00
☐ 17 George Sisler	200.00	90.00	25.00
☐ 18 Tris Speaker	300.00	135.00	38.00
☐ 19 Cy Williams	100.00	45.00	12.50
☐ 20 Whitey Witt	100.00	45.00	12.50

1980-83 Pacific Legends

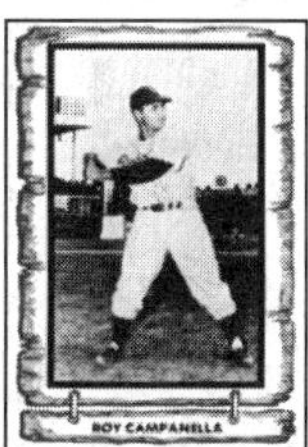

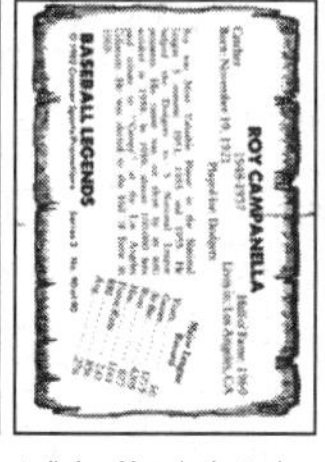

This 120-card standard-size set is actually four 30-card subsets plus a four-card wax box bottom panel. The golden-toned set was distributed by series over several years beginning in 1980 with the first 30 cards. The set was produced by Pacific Trading Cards and is frequently referred to as Cramer Legends, for the founder of Pacific Trading cards, Mike Cramer. Even though the wax box cards are numbered from 121-124 and called "Series 5," the set is considered complete without them.

	NRMT	VG-E	GOOD
COMPLETE SET (120)	30.00	13.50	3.70
COMMON CARD (1-120)	.10	.05	.01
COMMON CARD (121-124)	.50	.23	.06
☐ 1 Babe Ruth	3.00	1.35	.35
☐ 2 Heinie Manush	.20	.09	.03
☐ 3 Rabbit Maranville	.20	.09	.03
☐ 4 Earl Averill	.20	.09	.03
☐ 5 Joe DiMaggio	2.50	1.10	.30
☐ 6 Mickey Mantle	3.00	1.35	.35
☐ 7 Hank Aaron	1.50	.70	.19
☐ 8 Stan Musial	.75	.35	.09
☐ 9 Bill Terry	.20	.09	.03
☐ 10 Sandy Koufax	.50	.23	.06
☐ 11 Ernie Lombardi	.20	.09	.03
☐ 12 Dizzy Dean	.50	.23	.06
☐ 13 Lou Gehrig	2.50	1.10	.30
☐ 14 Walter Alston	.20	.09	.03
☐ 15 Jackie Robinson	1.50	.70	.19
☐ 16 Jimmie Foxx	.35	.16	.04
☐ 17 Billy Southworth	.10	.05	.01
☐ 18 Honus Wagner	.75	.35	.09
☐ 19 Duke Snider	.50	.23	.06
☐ 20 Rogers Hornsby UER (At bat total of 1873 is incorrect)	.50	.23	.06
☐ 21 Paul Waner	.20	.09	.03
☐ 22 Luke Appling	.20	.09	.03
☐ 23 Billy Herman	.20	.09	.03
☐ 24 Lloyd Waner	.20	.09	.03
☐ 25 Fred Hutchinson	.10	.05	.01
☐ 26 Eddie Collins	.20	.09	.03
☐ 27 Lefty Grove	.35	.16	.04
☐ 28 Chuck Connors	.35	.16	.04
☐ 29 Lefty O'Doul	.10	.05	.01
☐ 30 Hank Greenberg	.50	.23	.06
☐ 31 Ty Cobb	2.00	.90	.25
☐ 32 Enos Slaughter	.20	.09	.03
☐ 33 Ernie Banks	.50	.23	.06
☐ 34 Christy Mathewson	.50	.23	.06
☐ 35 Mel Ott	.35	.16	.04
☐ 36 Pie Traynor	.20	.09	.03
☐ 37 Clark Griffith	.20	.09	.03
☐ 38 Mickey Cochrane	.20	.09	.03
☐ 39 Joe Cronin	.20	.09	.03
☐ 40 Leo Durocher	.20	.09	.03
☐ 41 Home Run Baker	.20	.09	.03
☐ 42 Joe Tinker	.20	.09	.03
☐ 43 John McGraw	.20	.09	.03
☐ 44 Bill Dickey	.20	.09	.03
☐ 45 Walter Johnson	.50	.23	.06
☐ 46 Frankie Frisch	.20	.09	.03
☐ 47 Casey Stengel	.35	.16	.04
☐ 48 Willie Mays	1.50	.70	.19
☐ 49 Johnny Mize	.20	.09	.03
☐ 50 Roberto Clemente	2.00	.90	.25
☐ 51 Burleigh Grimes	.20	.09	.03
☐ 52 Pee Wee Reese	.50	.23	.06
☐ 53 Bob Feller	.50	.23	.06
☐ 54 Brooks Robinson	.50	.23	.06
☐ 55 Sam Crawford	.20	.09	.03
☐ 56 Robin Roberts	.35	.16	.04
☐ 57 Warren Spahn	.35	.16	.04
☐ 58 Joe McCarthy	.20	.09	.03
☐ 59 Jocko Conlan	.20	.09	.03
☐ 60 Satchel Paige	1.00	.45	.12
☐ 61 Ted Williams	2.00	.90	.25
☐ 62 George Kelly	.20	.09	.03
☐ 63 Gil Hodges	.35	.16	.04
☐ 64 Jim Bottomley	.20	.09	.03
☐ 65 Al Kaline	.50	.23	.06
☐ 66 Harvey Kuenn	.10	.05	.01
☐ 67 Yogi Berra	.50	.23	.06
☐ 68 Nellie Fox	.10	.05	.01
☐ 69 Harmon Killebrew	.35	.16	.04
☐ 70 Edd Roush	.20	.09	.03
☐ 71 Mordecai Brown	.20	.09	.03
☐ 72 Gabby Hartnett	.20	.09	.03
☐ 73 Early Wynn	.20	.09	.03
☐ 74 Nap Lajoie	.20	.09	.03
☐ 75 Charlie Grimm	.10	.05	.01
☐ 76 Joe Garagiola	.20	.09	.03
☐ 77 Ted Lyons	.10	.05	.01
☐ 78 Mickey Vernon	.10	.05	.01
☐ 79 Lou Boudreau	.20	.09	.03
☐ 80 Al Dark	.10	.05	.01
☐ 81 Ralph Kiner	.35	.16	.04
☐ 82 Phil Rizzuto	.35	.16	.04
☐ 83 Stan Hack	.10	.05	.01
☐ 84 Frank Chance	.20	.09	.03
☐ 85 Ray Schalk	.20	.09	.03
☐ 86 Bill McKechnie	.20	.09	.03
☐ 87 Travis Jackson	.20	.09	.03
☐ 88 Pete Reiser	.10	.05	.01
☐ 89 Carl Hubbell	.35	.16	.04
☐ 90 Roy Campanella	.50	.23	.06
☐ 91 Cy Young	.35	.16	.04
☐ 92 Kiki Cuyler	.20	.09	.03
☐ 93 Chief Bender	.20	.09	.03
☐ 94 Richie Ashburn	.35	.16	.04
☐ 95 Riggs Stephenson	.10	.05	.01
☐ 96 Minnie Minoso	.10	.05	.01
☐ 97 Hack Wilson	.20	.09	.03
☐ 98 Al Lopez	.20	.09	.03
☐ 99 Willie Keeler	.20	.09	.03
☐ 100 Fred Lindstrom	.20	.09	.03
☐ 101 Roger Maris	.35	.16	.04
☐ 102 Roger Bresnahan	.20	.09	.03
☐ 103 Monty Stratton	.20	.09	.03
☐ 104 Goose Goslin	.20	.09	.03
☐ 105 Earle Combs	.20	.09	.03
☐ 106 Pepper Martin	.10	.05	.01
☐ 107 Joe Jackson	1.50	.70	.19
☐ 108 George Sisler	.20	.09	.03
☐ 109 Red Ruffing	.20	.09	.03
☐ 110 Johnny Vander Meer	.10	.05	.01
☐ 111 Herb Pennock	.20	.09	.03
☐ 112 Chuck Klein	.20	.09	.03
☐ 113 Paul Derringer	.10	.05	.01
☐ 114 Addie Joss	.20	.09	.03
☐ 115 Bobby Thomson	.10	.05	.01
☐ 116 Chick Hafey	.20	.09	.03
☐ 117 Lefty Gomez	.20	.09	.03
☐ 118 George Kell	.20	.09	.03
☐ 119 Al Simmons	.20	.09	.03
☐ 120 Bob Lemon	.20	.09	.03
☐ 121 Hoyt Wilhelm (Wax box card)	.50	.23	.06
☐ 122 Arky Vaughan (Wax box card)	.50	.23	.06
☐ 123 Frank Robinson (Wax box card)	1.25	.55	.16
☐ 124 Grover Alexander (Wax box card)	1.00	.45	.12

1988 Pacific Eight Men Out

Eight Men Out
Buck Weaver, Third Baseman
Chicago White Sox

This 110-card standard-size set, produced by Mike Cramer's Pacific Trading Cards of Edmonds, Washington, was released in conjunction with the popular movie of the same name, which told the story of the "fix" of the 1919 World Series between the Cincinnati Reds and the Chicago "Black" Sox. The cards have a raspberry-colored border on the card fronts as well as raspberry-colored print on the white card stock backs. The cards were available either as wax packs or as collated sets. Generally the cards relating to the movie (showing actors) are in full-color whereas the vintage photography showing the actual players involved is in a sepia tone.

	MINT	NRMT	EXC
COMPLETE SET (110)	7.50	3.40	.95
COMMON CARD (1-110)	.05	.02	.01
☐ 1 We're Going To See The Sox	.15	.07	.02
☐ 2 White Sox Win The Pennant	.05	.02	.01
☐ 3 The Series	.05	.02	.01
☐ 4 1919 Chicago White Sox	.05	.02	.01
☐ 5 The Black Sox Scandal	.05	.02	.01
☐ 6 Eddie Cicotte 29-7 in 1919	.15	.07	.02
☐ 7 Buck's Their Favorite	.15	.07	.02
☐ 8 Eddie Collins	.25	.11	.03
☐ 9 Michael Rooker as Chick Gandil	.05	.02	.01
☐ 10 Charlie Sheen as Hap Felsch	.50	.23	.06
☐ 11 James Read as Lefty Williams	.05	.02	.01
☐ 12 John Cusack as	.25	.11	.03

Buck Weaver			
☐ 13 D.B. Sweeney as	.25	.11	.03
Joe Jackson			
☐ 14 David Strathairn as	.05	.02	.01
Eddie Cicotte			
☐ 15 Perry Lang as	.15	.07	.02
Fred McMullin			
☐ 16 Don Harvey as	.05	.02	.01
Swede Risberg			
☐ 17 The Gambler Burns	.05	.02	.01
And Maharg			
☐ 18 Sleepy Bill Burns	.05	.02	.01
☐ 19 The Key is Cicotte	.05	.02	.01
☐ 20 C'mon Betsy	.05	.02	.01
☐ 21 The Fix	.05	.02	.01
☐ 22 Chick Approaches	.05	.02	.01
Cicotte			
☐ 23 Kid Gleason MG	.05	.02	.01
☐ 24 Charles Comiskey OWN	.05	.02	.01
☐ 25 Chick Gandil	.15	.07	.02
1st Baseman			
☐ 26 Swede Risberg	.05	.02	.01
☐ 27 Sport Sullivan	.05	.02	.01
☐ 28 Abe Attell And	.05	.02	.01
Arnold Rothstein			
☐ 29 Hugh Fullerton	.05	.02	.01
Sportswriter			
☐ 30 Ring Lardner	.05	.02	.01
Sportswriter			
☐ 31 Shoeless Joe	.25	.11	.03
His Batting Eye			
☐ 32 Shoeless Joe	.35	.16	.04
☐ 33 Buck Can't Sleep	.05	.02	.01
☐ 34 George 'Buck' Weaver	.15	.07	.02
☐ 35 Hugh and Ring	.05	.02	.01
Confront Kid			
☐ 36 Joe Doesn't Want	.15	.07	.02
To Play			
☐ 37 Shoeless Joe	.35	.16	.04
Jackson			
☐ 38 Sore Arm, Cicotte	.05	.02	.01
Old Man Cicotte			
☐ 39 The Fix Is On	.05	.02	.01
☐ 40 Buck Plays To Win	.05	.02	.01
☐ 41 Hap Makes A	.05	.02	.01
Great Catch			
☐ 42 Hugh and Ring Suspect	.05	.02	.01
☐ 43 Ray Gets Things Going	.05	.02	.01
☐ 44 Lefty Loses Game Two	.05	.02	.01
☐ 45 Lefty Crosses Up	.05	.02	.01
Catcher Ray Schalk			
☐ 46 Chick's RBI Wins	.05	.02	.01
Game Three			
☐ 47 Dickie Kerr Wins	.05	.02	.01
Game Three			
☐ 48 Chick Leaves Buck	.05	.02	.01
At Third			
☐ 49 Williams Loses	.05	.02	.01
Game Five			
☐ 50 Ray Schalk	.05	.02	.01
☐ 51 Schalk Blocks	.05	.02	.01
The Plate			
☐ 52 Schalk Is Thrown Out	.05	.02	.01
☐ 53 Chicago Stickball	.05	.02	.01
Game			
☐ 54 I'm Forever Blowing	.05	.02	.01
Ball Games			
☐ 55 Felsch Scores Jackson	.25	.11	.03
☐ 56 Kerr Wins Game Six	.05	.02	.01
☐ 57 Where's The Money	.05	.02	.01
☐ 58 Cicotte Wins Game	.05	.02	.01
Seven			
☐ 59 Kid Watches Eddie	.05	.02	.01
☐ 60 Lefty Is Threatened	.05	.02	.01
☐ 61 James	.05	.02	.01
Get Your Arm Ready			
Fast			
☐ 62 Shoeless Joe's	.35	.16	.04
Home Run			
☐ 63 Buck Played His Best	.15	.07	.02
☐ 64 Hugh Exposes The Fix	.05	.02	.01
☐ 65 Sign The Petition	.05	.02	.01
☐ 66 Baseball Owners Hire	.05	.02	.01
A Commissioner			
☐ 67 Judge Kenesaw	.15	.07	.02
Mountain Landis			
☐ 68 Grand Jury Summoned	.05	.02	.01
☐ 69 Say It Ain't So,	.25	.11	.03
Joe			
☐ 70 The Swede's A Hard	.05	.02	.01
Guy			
☐ 71 Buck Loves The Game	.05	.02	.01
☐ 72 The Trial	.05	.02	.01
☐ 73 Kid Gleason Takes	.05	.02	.01
The Stand			
☐ 74 The Verdict	.05	.02	.01
☐ 75 Eight Men Out	.05	.02	.01
☐ 76 Oscar(Happy) Felsch	.15	.07	.02
☐ 77 Who's Joe Jackson	.25	.11	.03
☐ 78 Ban Johnson PRES	.15	.07	.02
☐ 79 Judge Landis COMM	.15	.07	.02
☐ 80 Charles Comiskey OWN	.15	.07	.02
☐ 81 Heinie Groh	.05	.02	.01
☐ 82 Slim Sallee	.05	.02	.01
☐ 83 Dutch Ruether	.05	.02	.01
☐ 84 Edd Roush	.25	.11	.03
☐ 85 Morrie Rath	.05	.02	.01
☐ 86 Bill Rariden	.05	.02	.01
☐ 87 Jimmy Ring	.05	.02	.01
☐ 88 Greasy Neale	.15	.07	.02
☐ 89 Pat Moran MG	.05	.02	.01
☐ 90 Adolfo Luque	.05	.02	.01
☐ 91 Larry Kopf	.05	.02	.01
☐ 92 Ray Fisher	.05	.02	.01
☐ 93 Hod Eller	.05	.02	.01
☐ 94 Pat Duncan	.05	.02	.01
☐ 95 Jake Daubert	.05	.02	.01
☐ 96 Red Faber	.25	.11	.03
☐ 97 Dickie Kerr	.05	.02	.01
☐ 98 Shano Collins	.05	.02	.01
☐ 99 Eddie Collins	.25	.11	.03
☐ 100 Ray Schalk	.25	.11	.03
☐ 101 Nemo Leibold	.05	.02	.01
☐ 102 Kid Gleason MG	.15	.07	.02
☐ 103 Swede Risberg	.15	.07	.02
☐ 104 Eddie Cicotte	.15	.07	.02
☐ 105 Fred McMullin	.05	.02	.01
☐ 106 Chick Gandil	.25	.11	.03
☐ 107 Buck Weaver	.25	.11	.03
☐ 108 Lefty Williams	.15	.07	.02
☐ 109 Happy Felsch	.15	.07	.02
☐ 110 Joe Jackson	1.00	.45	.12

1988 Pacific Legends I

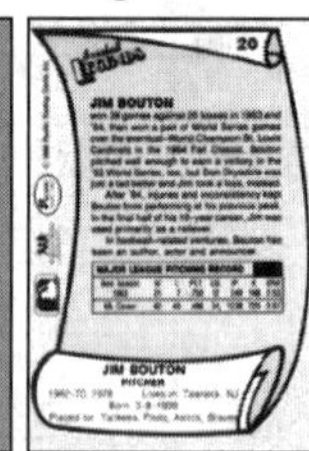

This attractive set of 110 full-color standard-size silver-bordered cards was produced by Mike Cramer's Pacific Trading Cards of Edmonds, Washington. Card backs are printed in yellow, black, and gray on white card stock. The cards were available either as wax packs or as collated sets. The players pictured in the set had retired many years before, but most are still well remembered. The statistics on the card backs give the player's career and "best season" statistics. The set was licensed by Major League Baseball Players Alumni.

	MINT	NRMT	EXC
COMPLETE SET (110)	10.00	4.50	1.25
COMMON CARD (1-110)	.05	.02	.01
☐ 1 Hank Aaron	1.50	.70	.19
☐ 2 Red Schoendienst	.20	.09	.03
☐ 3 Brooks Robinson	.30	.14	.04
☐ 4 Luke Appling	.20	.09	.03
☐ 5 Gene Woodling	.05	.02	.01
☐ 6 Stan Musial	.75	.35	.09
☐ 7 Mickey Mantle	3.00	1.35	.35
☐ 8 Richie Ashburn	.25	.11	.03
☐ 9 Ralph Kiner	.25	.11	.03
☐ 10 Phil Rizzuto	.25	.11	.03
☐ 11 Harvey Haddix	.05	.02	.01
☐ 12 Ken Boyer	.10	.05	.01
☐ 13 Clete Boyer	.05	.02	.01
☐ 14 Ken Harrelson	.10	.05	.01
☐ 15 Robin Roberts	.20	.09	.03
☐ 16 Catfish Hunter	.20	.09	.03
☐ 17 Frank Howard	.10	.05	.01
☐ 18 Jim Perry	.05	.02	.01
☐ 19A Elston Howard ERR	.20	.09	.03
(Reversed negative)			
☐ 19B Elston Howard COR	.20	.09	.03
☐ 20 Jim Bouton	.10	.05	.01
☐ 21 Pee Wee Reese	.25	.11	.03
☐ 22A Mel Stottlemyre ERR	.20	.09	.03
(Spelled Stottlemyer			
on card front)			
☐ 22B Mel Stottlemyre COR	.20	.09	.03
☐ 23 Hank Sauer	.05	.02	.01
☐ 24 Willie Mays	1.50	.70	.19
☐ 25 Tom Tresh	.05	.02	.01
☐ 26 Roy Sievers	.05	.02	.01
☐ 27 Leo Durocher	.20	.09	.03
☐ 28 Al Dark	.05	.02	.01
☐ 29 Tony Kubek	.10	.05	.01
☐ 30 Johnny VanderMeer	.10	.05	.01
☐ 31 Joe Adcock	.05	.02	.01
☐ 32 Bob Lemon	.20	.09	.03
☐ 33 Don Newcombe	.10	.05	.01
☐ 34 Thurman Munson	.25	.11	.03
☐ 35 Earl Battey	.05	.02	.01
☐ 36 Ernie Banks	.50	.23	.06
☐ 37 Matty Alou	.05	.02	.01
☐ 38 Dave McNally	.05	.02	.01
☐ 39 Mickey Lolich	.10	.05	.01
☐ 40 Jackie Robinson	2.00	.90	.25
☐ 41 Allie Reynolds	.10	.05	.01
☐ 42A Don Larsen ERR	.20	.09	.03
(Misspelled Larson			
on card front)			
☐ 42B Don Larsen COR	.20	.09	.03
☐ 43 Fergie Jenkins	.20	.09	.03
☐ 44 Jim Gilliam	.10	.05	.01
☐ 45 Bobby Thomson	.10	.05	.01
☐ 46 Sparky Anderson	.10	.05	.01
☐ 47 Roy Campanella	.50	.23	.06
☐ 48 Marv Throneberry	.05	.02	.01
☐ 49 Bill Virdon	.05	.02	.01
☐ 50 Ted Williams	1.50	.70	.19
☐ 51 Minnie Minoso	.10	.05	.01
☐ 52 Bob Turley	.05	.02	.01
☐ 53 Yogi Berra	.50	.23	.06
☐ 54 Juan Marichal	.20	.09	.03
☐ 55 Duke Snider	.50	.23	.06
☐ 56 Harvey Kuenn	.05	.02	.01
☐ 57 Nellie Fox	.10	.05	.01
☐ 58 Felipe Alou	.10	.05	.01
☐ 59 Tony Oliva	.10	.05	.01
☐ 60 Bill Mazeroski	.20	.09	.03
☐ 61 Bobby Shantz	.05	.02	.01
☐ 62 Mark Fidrych	.20	.09	.03
☐ 63 Johnny Mize	.20	.09	.03
☐ 64 Ralph Terry	.05	.02	.01
☐ 65 Gus Bell	.05	.02	.01
☐ 66 Jerry Koosman	.05	.02	.01
☐ 67 Mike McCormick	.05	.02	.01
☐ 68 Lou Burdette	.05	.02	.01
☐ 69 George Kell	.20	.09	.03
☐ 70 Vic Raschi	.05	.02	.01
☐ 71 Chuck Connors	.25	.11	.03
☐ 72 Ted Kluszewski	.20	.09	.03
☐ 73 Bobby Doerr	.20	.09	.03
☐ 74 Bobby Richardson	.10	.05	.01
☐ 75 Carl Erskine	.10	.05	.01
☐ 76 Hoyt Wilhelm	.20	.09	.03
☐ 77 Bob Purkey	.05	.02	.01
☐ 78 Bob Friend	.05	.02	.01
☐ 79 Monte Irvin	.20	.09	.03
☐ 80A Jim Lonborg ERR	.20	.09	.03
(Misspelled Longborg			
on card front)			
☐ 80B Jim Lonborg COR	.20	.09	.03
☐ 81 Wally Moon	.05	.02	.01
☐ 82 Moose Skowron	.05	.02	.01
☐ 83 Tommy Davis	.05	.02	.01
☐ 84 Enos Slaughter	.20	.09	.03
☐ 85 Sal Maglie UER	.05	.02	.01
(1945-1917 on back)			
☐ 86 Harmon Killebrew	.20	.09	.03
☐ 87 Gil Hodges	.20	.09	.03
☐ 88 Jim Kaat	.10	.05	.01
☐ 89 Roger Maris	.50	.23	.06
☐ 90 Billy Williams	.20	.09	.03
☐ 91 Luis Aparicio	.20	.09	.03
☐ 92 Jim Bunning	.20	.09	.03
☐ 93 Bill Freehan	.10	.05	.01
☐ 94 Orlando Cepeda	.10	.05	.01
☐ 95 Early Wynn	.20	.09	.03
☐ 96 Tug McGraw	.10	.05	.01
☐ 97 Ron Santo	.20	.09	.03
☐ 98 Del Crandall	.05	.02	.01
☐ 99 Sal Bando	.05	.02	.01
☐ 100 Joe DiMaggio	2.50	1.10	.30
☐ 101 Bob Feller	.50	.23	.06
☐ 102 Larry Doby	.05	.02	.01
☐ 103 Rollie Fingers	.20	.09	.03
☐ 104 Al Kaline	.35	.16	.04
☐ 105 Johnny Podres	.05	.02	.01
☐ 106 Lou Boudreau	.20	.09	.03
☐ 107 Zoilo Versalles	.05	.02	.01
☐ 108 Dick Groat	.05	.02	.01
☐ 109 Warren Spahn	.25	.11	.03
☐ 110 Johnny Bench	.50	.23	.06

1989 Pacific Legends II

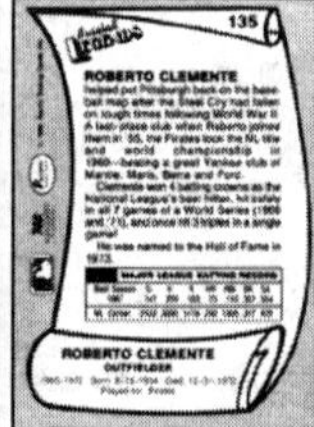

The 1989 Pacific Legends Series II set contains 110 standard-size cards. The fronts have vintage color photos with silver borders. The backs are gray and feature career highlights and lifetime statistics. The cards were distributed as factory sets as well as in ten-card wax packs.

	MINT	NRMT	EXC
COMPLETE SET (110)	10.00	4.50	1.25
COMMON CARD (111-220)	.05	.02	.01
☐ 111 Reggie Jackson	.50	.23	.06
☐ 112 Rich Reese	.05	.02	.01
☐ 113 Frankie Frisch	.20	.09	.03
☐ 114 Ed Kranepool	.05	.02	.01
☐ 115 Al Hrabosky	.05	.02	.01
☐ 116 Eddie Mathews	.20	.09	.03
☐ 117 Ty Cobb	1.50	.70	.19
☐ 118 Jim Davenport	.05	.02	.01
☐ 119 Buddy Lewis	.05	.02	.01
☐ 120 Virgil Trucks	.05	.02	.01
☐ 121 Del Ennis	.05	.02	.01
☐ 122 Dick Radatz	.05	.02	.01
☐ 123 Andy Pafko	.05	.02	.01
☐ 124 Wilbur Wood	.05	.02	.01
☐ 125 Joe Sewell	.20	.09	.03
☐ 126 Herb Score	.05	.02	.01
☐ 127 Paul Waner	.20	.09	.03
☐ 128 Lloyd Waner	.20	.09	.03
☐ 129 Brooks Robinson	.50	.23	.06
☐ 130 Bo Belinsky	.10	.05	.01
☐ 131 Phil Cavarretta	.05	.02	.01
☐ 132 Claude Osteen	.05	.02	.01
☐ 133 Tito Francona	.05	.02	.01
☐ 134 Billy Pierce	.10	.05	.01
☐ 135 Roberto Clemente	1.50	.70	.19
☐ 136 Spud Chandler	.05	.02	.01
☐ 137 Enos Slaughter	.20	.09	.03
☐ 138 Ken Holtzman	.05	.02	.01
☐ 139 John Hopp	.05	.02	.01
☐ 140 Tony LaRussa	.10	.05	.01
☐ 141 Ryne Duren	.05	.02	.01
☐ 142 Glenn Beckert UER	.05	.02	.01
(Misspelled Glen on			
card front)			
☐ 143 Ken Keltner	.05	.02	.01
☐ 144 Hank Bauer	.05	.02	.01
☐ 145 Roger Craig	.10	.05	.01
☐ 146 Frank Baker	.20	.09	.03
☐ 147 Jim O'Toole	.05	.02	.01
☐ 148 Rogers Hornsby	.35	.16	.04
☐ 149 Jose Cardenal	.05	.02	.01
☐ 150 Bobby Doerr	.20	.09	.03
☐ 151 Mickey Cochrane	.20	.09	.03
☐ 152 Gaylord Perry	.20	.09	.03
☐ 153 Frank Thomas	.05	.02	.01
☐ 154 Ted Williams	1.50	.70	.19
☐ 155 Sam McDowell	.05	.02	.01
☐ 156 Bob Feller	.50	.23	.06
☐ 157 Bert Campaneris	.05	.02	.01
☐ 158 Thornton Lee UER	.05	.02	.01
(Misspelled Thorton			
on card front)			
☐ 159 Gary Peters	.05	.02	.01
☐ 160 Joe Medwick	.20	.09	.03
☐ 161 Joe Nuxhall	.05	.02	.01
☐ 162 Joe Schultz	.05	.02	.01
☐ 163 Harmon Killebrew	.25	.11	.03
☐ 164 Bucky Walters	.05	.02	.01
☐ 165 Bob Allison	.05	.02	.01
☐ 166 Lou Boudreau	.20	.09	.03
☐ 167 Joe Cronin	.20	.09	.03
☐ 168 Mike Torrez	.05	.02	.01
☐ 169 Rich Rollins	.05	.02	.01
☐ 170 Tony Cuccinello	.05	.02	.01
☐ 171 Hoyt Wilhelm	.20	.09	.03
☐ 172 Ernie Harwell ANN	.20	.09	.03
☐ 173 George Foster	.05	.02	.01
☐ 174 Lou Gehrig	1.50	.70	.19
☐ 175 Dave Kingman	.20	.09	.03
☐ 176 Babe Ruth	2.00	.90	.25
☐ 177 Joe Black	.05	.02	.01
☐ 178 Roy Face	.05	.02	.01
☐ 179 Earl Weaver MG	.20	.09	.03
☐ 180 Johnny Mize	.20	.09	.03
☐ 181 Roger Cramer	.05	.02	.01
☐ 182 Jim Piersall	.10	.05	.01
☐ 183 Ned Garver	.05	.02	.01
☐ 184 Billy Williams	.20	.09	.03
☐ 185 Lefty Grove	.20	.09	.03
☐ 186 Jim Grant	.05	.02	.01
☐ 187 Elmer Valo	.05	.02	.01
☐ 188 Ewell Blackwell	.05	.02	.01
☐ 189 Mel Ott	.20	.09	.03
☐ 190 Harry Walker	.05	.02	.01
☐ 191 Bill Campbell	.05	.02	.01
☐ 192 Walter Johnson	.25	.11	.03
☐ 193 Catfish Hunter	.20	.09	.03
☐ 194 Charlie Keller	.05	.02	.01
☐ 195 Hank Greenberg	.20	.09	.03
☐ 196 Bobby Murcer	.10	.05	.01
☐ 197 Al Lopez	.20	.09	.03
☐ 198 Vida Blue	.10	.05	.01
☐ 199 Shag Crawford UMP	.05	.02	.01
☐ 200 Arky Vaughan	.20	.09	.03
☐ 201 Smoky Burgess	.05	.02	.01
☐ 202 Rip Sewell	.05	.02	.01
☐ 203 Earl Averill	.20	.09	.03
☐ 204 Milt Pappas	.05	.02	.01
☐ 205 Mel Harder	.05	.02	.01
☐ 206 Sam Jethroe	.05	.02	.01
☐ 207 Randy Hundley	.05	.02	.01
☐ 208 Jesse Haines	.05	.02	.01
☐ 209 Jack Brickhouse ANN	.05	.02	.01
☐ 210 Whitey Ford	.25	.11	.03
☐ 211 Honus Wagner	.50	.23	.06
☐ 212 Phil Niekro	.20	.09	.03
☐ 213 Gary Bell	.05	.02	.01
☐ 214 Jon Matlack	.05	.02	.01
☐ 215 Moe Drabowsky	.05	.02	.01
☐ 216 Edd Roush	.20	.09	.03
☐ 217 Joel Horlen	.05	.02	.01
☐ 218 Casey Stengel	.25	.11	.03

Card	MINT	NRMT	EXC
☐ 219 Burt Hooton	.05	.02	.01
☐ 220 Joe Jackson	1.50	.70	.19

1989-90 Pacific Senior League

The 1989-90 Pacific Trading Cards Senior League set contains 220 standard-size cards. The fronts feature color photos with silver borders and player names and positions at the bottom. The horizontally oriented backs are red, white, and blue, and show vital statistics and career highlights. The cards were distributed as a boxed set with 15 card-sized logo stickers/puzzle pieces as well as in wax packs. There are several In Action cards in the set, designated by IA in the checklist below. The Nettles card was corrected very late according to the set's producer.

	MINT	NRMT	EXC
COMPLETE SET (220)	10.00	4.50	1.25
COMMON CARD (1-220)	.05	.02	.01
☐ 1 Bobby Tolan MG	.10	.05	.01
☐ 2 Sergio Ferrer	.05	.02	.01
☐ 3 David Rajsich	.05	.02	.01
☐ 4 Ron LeFlore	.10	.05	.01
☐ 5 Steve Henderson	.05	.02	.01
☐ 6 Jerry Martin	.05	.02	.01
☐ 7 Gary Rajsich	.05	.02	.01
☐ 8 Elias Sosa	.05	.02	.01
☐ 9 Jon Matlack	.10	.05	.01
☐ 10 Steve Kemp	.10	.05	.01
☐ 11 Lenny Randle	.05	.02	.01
☐ 12 Roy Howell	.05	.02	.01
☐ 13 Milt Wilcox	.05	.02	.01
☐ 14 Alan Bannister	.05	.02	.01
☐ 15 Dock Ellis	.10	.05	.01
☐ 16 Mike Williams	.05	.02	.01
☐ 17 Luis Gomez	.05	.02	.01
☐ 18 Joe Sambito	.05	.02	.01
☐ 19 Bake McBride	.05	.02	.01
☐ 20 Pat Zachry UER (Photo actually Dick Bosman)	.05	.02	.01
☐ 21 Dwight Lowry	.05	.02	.01
☐ 22 Ozzie Virgil Sr. CO	.05	.02	.01
☐ 23 Randy Lerch	.05	.02	.01
☐ 24 Butch Benton	.05	.02	.01
☐ 25 Tom Zimmer CO UER (No bio information)	.05	.02	.01
☐ 26 Al Holland UER (Photo actually Nardi Contreras)	.05	.02	.01
☐ 27 Sammy Stewart	.05	.02	.01
☐ 28 Bill Lee	.10	.05	.01
☐ 29 Ferguson Jenkins	.50	.23	.06
☐ 30 Leon Roberts	.05	.02	.01
☐ 31 Rick Wise	.10	.05	.01
☐ 32 Butch Hobson	.05	.02	.01
☐ 33 Pete LaCock	.05	.02	.01
☐ 34 Bill Campbell	.05	.02	.01
☐ 35 Doug Simunic	.05	.02	.01
☐ 36 Mario Guerrero	.05	.02	.01
☐ 37 Jim Willoughby	.05	.02	.01
☐ 38 Joe Pittman	.05	.02	.01
☐ 39 Mark Bomback	.05	.02	.01
☐ 40 Tommy McMillan	.05	.02	.01
☐ 41 Gary Allenson	.05	.02	.01
☐ 42 Cecil Cooper	.15	.07	.02
☐ 43 John LaRosa	.05	.02	.01
☐ 44 Darrell Brandon	.05	.02	.01
☐ 45 Bernie Carbo	.05	.02	.01
☐ 46 Mike Cuellar	.15	.07	.02
☐ 47 Al Bumbry	.05	.02	.01
☐ 48 Gene Richards	.05	.02	.01
☐ 49 Pedro Borbon	.05	.02	.01
☐ 50 Julio Solo	.05	.02	.01
☐ 51 Ed Nottle MG	.05	.02	.01
☐ 52 Jim Bibby	.05	.02	.01
☐ 53 Doug Griffin CO	.05	.02	.01
☐ 54 Ed Clements	.05	.02	.01
☐ 55 Dalton Jones	.05	.02	.01
☐ 56 Earl Weaver MG	.50	.23	.06
☐ 57 Jesus De La Rosa	.05	.02	.01
☐ 58 Paul Casanova	.05	.02	.01
☐ 59 Frank Riccelli	.05	.02	.01
☐ 60 Rafael Landestoy UER (Misspelled Raphael on card back)	.05	.02	.01
☐ 61 George Hendrick	.10	.05	.01
☐ 62 Cesar Cedeno	.15	.07	.02
☐ 63 Bert Campaneris	.15	.07	.02
☐ 64 Derrel Thomas	.05	.02	.01
☐ 65 Bobby Ramos	.05	.02	.01
☐ 66 Grant Jackson	.05	.02	.01
☐ 67 Steve Whitaker	.05	.02	.01
☐ 68 Pedro Ramos	.05	.02	.01
☐ 69 Joe Hicks UER (No height or weight information)	.05	.02	.01
☐ 70 Taylor Duncan	.05	.02	.01
☐ 71 Tom Shopay	.05	.02	.01
☐ 72 Ken Clay	.05	.02	.01
☐ 73 Mike Kekich	.05	.02	.01
☐ 74 Ed Halicki	.05	.02	.01
☐ 75 Ed Figueroa	.05	.02	.01
☐ 76 Paul Blair	.05	.02	.01
☐ 77 Luis Tiant	.15	.07	.02
☐ 78 Stan Bahnsen	.05	.02	.01
☐ 79 Rennie Stennett	.05	.02	.01
☐ 80 Bobby Molinaro	.05	.02	.01
☐ 81 Jim Gideon	.05	.02	.01
☐ 82 Orlando Gonzalez	.05	.02	.01
☐ 83 Amos Otis	.10	.05	.01
☐ 84 Dennis Leonard	.05	.02	.01
☐ 85 Pat Putnam	.05	.02	.01
☐ 86 Rick Manning	.05	.02	.01
☐ 87 Pat Dobson MG	.05	.02	.01
☐ 88 Marty Castillo	.05	.02	.01
☐ 89 Steve McCatty	.05	.02	.01
☐ 90 Doug Bird	.05	.02	.01
☐ 91 Rick Waits	.05	.02	.01
☐ 92 Ron Jackson	.05	.02	.01
☐ 93 Tim Hosley	.05	.02	.01
☐ 94 Steve Luebber	.05	.02	.01
☐ 95 Rich Gale	.05	.02	.01
☐ 96 Champ Summers	.05	.02	.01
☐ 97 Dave LaRoche	.05	.02	.01
☐ 98 Bobby Jones	.05	.02	.01
☐ 99 Kim Allen	.05	.02	.01
☐ 100 Wayne Garland	.05	.02	.01
☐ 101 Tom Spencer	.05	.02	.01
☐ 102 Dan Driessen	.10	.05	.01
☐ 103 Ron Pruitt	.05	.02	.01
☐ 104 Tim Ireland	.05	.02	.01
☐ 105 Dan Driessen IA	.05	.02	.01
☐ 106 Pepe Frias UER (Misspelled Pepi on card front)	.05	.02	.01
☐ 107 Eric Rasmussen	.05	.02	.01
☐ 108 Don Hood	.05	.02	.01
☐ 109 Joe Coleman CO UER (Photo actually Tony Torchia)	.05	.02	.01
☐ 110 Jim Slaton	.05	.02	.01
☐ 111 Clint Hurdle	.05	.02	.01
☐ 112 Larry Milbourne	.05	.02	.01
☐ 113 Al Holland	.05	.02	.01
☐ 114 George Foster	.10	.05	.01
☐ 115 Graig Nettles MG	.15	.07	.02
☐ 116 Oscar Gamble	.10	.05	.01
☐ 117 Ross Grimsley	.05	.02	.01
☐ 118 Bill Travers	.05	.02	.01
☐ 119 Jose Beniquez	.05	.02	.01
☐ 120 Jerry Grote IA	.05	.02	.01
☐ 121 John D'Acquisto	.05	.02	.01
☐ 122 Tom Murphy	.05	.02	.01
☐ 123 Walt Williams UER (Listed as pitcher)	.05	.02	.01
☐ 124 Roy Thomas	.05	.02	.01
☐ 125 Jerry Grote	.10	.05	.01
☐ 126A Jim Nettles ERR (Writing on bat knob)	.25	.11	.03
☐ 126B Jim Nettles COR	2.50	1.10	.30
☐ 127 Randy Niemann	.05	.02	.01
☐ 128 Bobby Bonds	.50	.23	.06
☐ 129 Ed Glynn	.05	.02	.01
☐ 130 Ed Hicks	.05	.02	.01
☐ 131 Ivan Murrell	.05	.02	.01
☐ 132 Graig Nettles MG	.25	.11	.03
☐ 133 Hal McRae	.25	.11	.03
☐ 134 Pat Kelly	.05	.02	.01
☐ 135 Sammy Stewart	.05	.02	.01
☐ 136 Bruce Kison	.05	.02	.01
☐ 137 Jim Morrison	.05	.02	.01
☐ 138 Omar Moreno	.05	.02	.01
☐ 139 Tom Brown	.05	.02	.01
☐ 140 Steve Dillard	.05	.02	.01
☐ 141 Gary Alexander	.05	.02	.01
☐ 142 Al Oliver	.25	.11	.03
☐ 143 Rick Lysander	.05	.02	.01
☐ 144 Tippy Martinez	.05	.02	.01
☐ 145 Al Cowens	.05	.02	.01
☐ 146 Gene Clines	.05	.02	.01
☐ 147 Willie Aikens	.05	.02	.01
☐ 148 Tommy Moore	.05	.02	.01
☐ 149 Clete Boyer MG	.10	.05	.01
☐ 150 Stan Cliburn	.05	.02	.01
☐ 151 Ken Kravec	.05	.02	.01
☐ 152 Garth Iorg	.05	.02	.01
☐ 153 Rick Peterson	.05	.02	.01
☐ 154 Wayne Nordhagen UER (Misspelled Nordgahen on card back)	.05	.02	.01
☐ 155 Danny Meyer	.05	.02	.01
☐ 156 Wayne Garrett	.05	.02	.01
☐ 157 Wayne Krenchicki	.05	.02	.01
☐ 158 Graig Nettles	.25	.11	.03
☐ 159 Earl Stephenson	.05	.02	.01
☐ 160 Carl Taylor	.05	.02	.01
☐ 161 Rollie Fingers	.50	.23	.06
☐ 162 Toby Harrah	.10	.05	.01
☐ 163 Mickey Rivers	.10	.05	.01
☐ 164 Dave Kingman	.15	.07	.02
☐ 165 Paul Mirabella	.05	.02	.01
☐ 166 Dick Williams MG	.05	.02	.01
☐ 167 Luis Pujols	.05	.02	.01
☐ 168 Tito Landrum	.05	.02	.01
☐ 169 Tom Underwood	.05	.02	.01
☐ 170 Mark Wagner	.05	.02	.01
☐ 171 Odell Jones	.05	.02	.01
☐ 172 Doug Capilla	.05	.02	.01
☐ 173 Alfie Rondon	.05	.02	.01
☐ 174 Lowell Palmer	.05	.02	.01
☐ 175 Juan Eichelberger	.05	.02	.01
☐ 176 Wes Clements	.05	.02	.01
☐ 177 Rodney Scott	.05	.02	.01
☐ 178 Ron Washington	.05	.02	.01
☐ 179 Al Hrabosky	.10	.05	.01
☐ 180 Sid Monge	.05	.02	.01
☐ 181 Randy Johnson	.05	.02	.01
☐ 182 Tim Stoddard	.05	.02	.01
☐ 183 Dick Williams MG	.10	.05	.01
☐ 184 Lee Lacy	.05	.02	.01
☐ 185 Jerry White	.05	.02	.01
☐ 186 Dave Kingman	.15	.07	.02
☐ 187 Checklist 1-110	.05	.02	.01
☐ 188 Jose Cruz	.10	.05	.01
☐ 189 Jamie Easterly	.05	.02	.01
☐ 190 Ike Blessit	.05	.02	.01
☐ 191 Johnny Grubb	.05	.02	.01
☐ 192 Dave Cash	.05	.02	.01
☐ 193 Doug Corbett	.05	.02	.01
☐ 194 Bruce Bochy	.05	.02	.01
☐ 195 Mark Corey	.05	.02	.01
☐ 196 Gil Rondon	.05	.02	.01
☐ 197 Jerry Martin	.05	.02	.01
☐ 198 Gerry Pirtle	.05	.02	.01
☐ 199 Gates Brown MG	.05	.02	.01
☐ 200 Bob Galasso	.05	.02	.01
☐ 201 Bake McBride	.05	.02	.01
☐ 202 Wayne Granger	.05	.02	.01
☐ 203 Larry Milbourne	.05	.02	.01
☐ 204 Tom Paciorek	.05	.02	.01
☐ 205 U.L. Washington	.05	.02	.01
☐ 206 Larvell Blanks	.05	.02	.01
☐ 207 Bob Shirley	.05	.02	.01
☐ 208 Pete Falcone	.05	.02	.01
☐ 209 Sal Butera	.05	.02	.01
☐ 210 Roy Branch	.05	.02	.01
☐ 211 Dyar Miller	.05	.02	.01
☐ 212 Paul Siebert	.05	.02	.01
☐ 213 Ken Reitz	.05	.02	.01
☐ 214 Bill Madlock	.15	.07	.02
☐ 215 Vida Blue	.15	.07	.02
☐ 216 Dave Hilton	.05	.02	.01
☐ 217 Pedro Ramos CO and Charlie Bree CO	.05	.02	.01
☐ 218 Checklist 111-220	.05	.02	.01
☐ 219 Pat Dobson MG and Earl Weaver MG	.15	.07	.02
☐ 220 Curt Flood COMM	.15	.07	.02

1990 Pacific Gwynn Candy Bar

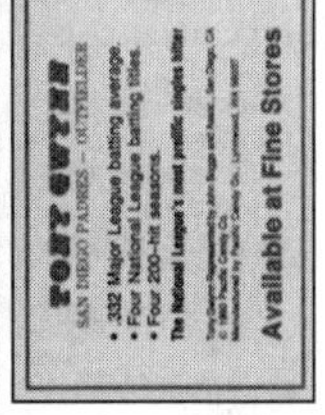

Produced by the Pacific Candy Co., this card features a color action player photo of Tony Gwynn of the San Diego Padres on a tan background in a silver frame and advertises the milk chocolate Tony Gwynn Base Hit Candy Bar. The back displays player information.

	MINT	NRMT	EXC
COMPLETE SET (1)	3.00	1.35	.35
COMMON CARD (1)	3.00	1.35	.35
☐ 1 Tony Gwynn	3.00	1.35	.35

1990 Pacific Legends

The 1990 Pacific Legends issue was a 110-card standard-size set issued by Pacific Trading Cards. The set numbering is basically arranged in two alphabetical sequences. This set was available in both factory set and wax packs form. The set does include some active players, Willie Wilson and Jesse Barfield, the last two players in the set.

	MINT	NRMT	EXC
COMPLETE SET (110)	10.00	4.50	1.25
COMMON CARD (1-110)	.05	.02	.01

Card	MINT	NRMT	EXC
☐ 1 Hank Aaron	.75	.35	.09
☐ 2 Tommie Agee	.05	.02	.01
☐ 3 Luke Appling	.15	.07	.02
☐ 4 Sal Bando	.05	.02	.01
☐ 5 Ernie Banks	.50	.23	.06
☐ 6 Don Baylor	.10	.05	.01
☐ 7 Yogi Berra	.50	.23	.06
☐ 8 Vida Blue	.05	.02	.01
☐ 9 Lou Boudreau	.15	.07	.02
☐ 10 Clete Boyer	.05	.02	.01
☐ 11 George Bamberger	.05	.02	.01
☐ 12 Lou Brock	.25	.11	.03
☐ 13 Ralph Branca	.05	.02	.01
☐ 14 Carl Erskine	.05	.02	.01
☐ 15 Bert Campaneris	.05	.02	.01
☐ 16 Steve Carlton	.25	.11	.03
☐ 17 Rod Carew	.25	.11	.03
☐ 18 Rocky Colavito	.25	.11	.03
☐ 19 Frankie Crosetti	.10	.05	.01
☐ 20 Larry Doby	.10	.05	.01
☐ 21 Bobby Doerr	.15	.07	.02
☐ 22 Walt Dropo	.05	.02	.01
☐ 23 Rick Ferrell	.15	.07	.02
☐ 24 Joe Garagiola	.15	.07	.02
☐ 25 Ralph Garr	.05	.02	.01
☐ 26 Dick Groat	.05	.02	.01
☐ 27 Steve Garvey	.10	.05	.01
☐ 28 Bob Gibson	.25	.11	.03
☐ 29 Don Drysdale	.25	.11	.03
☐ 30 Billy Herman	.15	.07	.02
☐ 31 Bobby Grich	.05	.02	.01
☐ 32 Monte Irvin	.15	.07	.02
☐ 33 Dave Johnson	.05	.02	.01
☐ 34 Don Kessinger	.05	.02	.01
☐ 35 Harmon Killebrew	.15	.07	.02
☐ 36 Ralph Kiner	.15	.07	.02
☐ 37 Vern Law	.05	.02	.01
☐ 38 Ed Lopat	.05	.02	.01
☐ 39 Bill Mazeroski	.15	.07	.02
☐ 40 Rick Monday	.05	.02	.01
☐ 41 Manny Mota	.05	.02	.01
☐ 42 Don Newcombe	.10	.05	.01
☐ 43 Gaylord Perry	.15	.07	.02
☐ 44 Jim Piersall	.10	.05	.01
☐ 45 Johnny Podres	.10	.05	.01
☐ 46 Boog Powell	.15	.07	.02
☐ 47 Robin Roberts	.15	.07	.02
☐ 48 Ron Santo	.15	.07	.02
☐ 49 Herb Score	.10	.05	.01
☐ 50 Enos Slaughter	.15	.07	.02
☐ 51 Warren Spahn	.25	.11	.03
☐ 52 Rusty Staub	.10	.05	.01
☐ 53 Frank Torre	.05	.02	.01
☐ 54 Bob Horner	.05	.02	.01
☐ 55 Lee May	.05	.02	.01
☐ 56 Bill White	.10	.05	.01
☐ 57 Hoyt Wilhelm	.15	.07	.02
☐ 58 Billy Williams	.15	.07	.02
☐ 59 Ted Williams	.75	.35	.09
☐ 60 Tom Seaver	.50	.23	.06
☐ 61 Carl Yastrzemski	.25	.11	.03
☐ 62 Marv Throneberry	.05	.02	.01
☐ 63 Steve Stone	.05	.02	.01
☐ 64 Rico Petrocelli	.05	.02	.01
☐ 65 Orlando Cepeda	.15	.07	.02
☐ 66 Eddie Mathews	.15	.07	.02
☐ 67 Joe Sewell	.15	.07	.02
☐ 68 Catfish Hunter	.15	.07	.02
☐ 69 Alvin Dark	.10	.05	.01
☐ 70 Richie Ashburn	.15	.07	.02
☐ 71 Dusty Baker	.10	.05	.01
☐ 72 George Foster	.05	.02	.01
☐ 73 Eddie Yost	.05	.02	.01
☐ 74 Buddy Bell	.05	.02	.01
☐ 75 Manny Sanguillen	.05	.02	.01
☐ 76 Jim Bunning	.15	.07	.02
☐ 77 Smoky Burgess	.05	.02	.01
☐ 78 Al Rosen	.05	.02	.01
☐ 79 Gene Conley	.05	.02	.01
☐ 80 Dave Dravecky	.05	.02	.01
☐ 81 Charlie Gehringer	.15	.07	.02
☐ 82 Billy Pierce	.05	.02	.01
☐ 83 Willie Horton	.05	.02	.01
☐ 84 Ron Hunt	.05	.02	.01
☐ 85 Bob Feller	.25	.11	.03
☐ 86 George Kell	.15	.07	.02
☐ 87 Dave Kingman	.15	.07	.02
☐ 88 Jerry Koosman	.10	.05	.01
☐ 89 Clem Labine	.05	.02	.01
☐ 90 Tony LaRussa	.10	.05	.01
☐ 91 Dennis Leonard	.05	.02	.01
☐ 92 Dale Long	.05	.02	.01

	MINT	NRMT	EXC
☐ 93 Sparky Lyle	.05	.02	.01
☐ 94 Gil McDougald	.05	.02	.01
☐ 95 Don Mossi	.05	.02	.01
☐ 96 Phil Niekro	.15	.07	.02
☐ 97 Tom Paciorek	.05	.02	.01
☐ 98 Mel Parnell	.05	.02	.01
☐ 99 Lou Piniella	.10	.05	.01
☐ 100 Bobby Richardson	.10	.05	.01
☐ 101 Phil Rizzuto	.25	.11	.03
☐ 102 Brooks Robinson	.25	.11	.03
☐ 103 Pete Runnels	.05	.02	.01
☐ 104 Diego Segui	.05	.02	.01
☐ 105 Bobby Shantz	.05	.02	.01
☐ 106 Bobby Thomson	.10	.05	.01
☐ 107 Joe Torre	.10	.05	.01
☐ 108 Earl Weaver MG	.15	.07	.02
☐ 109 Willie Wilson	.05	.02	.01
☐ 110 Jesse Barfield	.05	.02	.01

1991 Pacific Prototype

This standard-size card was produced by Pacific Trading Cards in order to help them secure a liscense with Major League Baseball. The front has a photo of Ryne Sandberg along with the necessary identification. The back is basically blank. The card has room for vital statistics, a brief biography and some statistics and each section is framed in red. A very limited number of these cards were produced

	MINT	NRMT	EXC
COMPLETE SET (1)	1200.00	550.00	150.00
COMMON CARD (1)	1200.00	550.00	150.00
☐ 1 Ryne Sandberg	1200.00	550.00	150.00

1991 Pacific Ryan Texas Express I

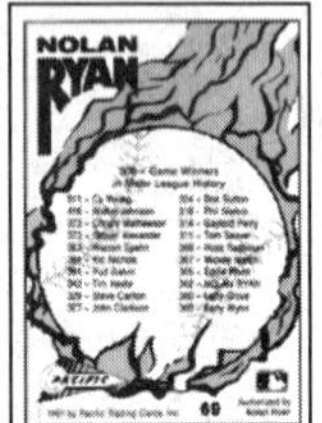

This 110-card standard-size set, Texas Express, traces the career of Nolan Ryan from the start of his career into the 1991 season as well as his personal life with his family on his ranch in Alvin, Texas. This set features glossy full-color photos on the front and either biographical information or an action shot of Ryan on the back which is framed by a fireball. The backs are printed in purple and red on a white background. Inside a flaming baseball design, one finds biography, career highlights, player quote, or an extended caption to the front picture. The cards are numbered on the back. This set was issued by Pacific Trading cards and was the first set featuring an individual baseball player to be sold in wax packs since the 1959 Fleer Ted Williams issue. The cards were available in 12-card foil packs and factory sets. Moreover, eight unnumbered bonus cards (1-6 No Hitters, 1991 25th Season, and Rookie year with the Mets) were produced in quantities of 1,000 of each card in gold foil and 10,000 of each card in silver foil; these bonus cards were randomly inserted in foil packs only. After the first and second series of Pacific Nolan Ryan Texas Express had sold out, Pacific reissued card numbers 1-220 in 1993, and the cards produced in this reissue may be distinguished by the 27th season logo, which was introduced to collectors in the 30-card 27th Season series. Currently there is no value differential between the two types.

	MINT	NRMT	EXC
COMPLETE SET (110)	12.00	5.50	1.50
COMMON CARD (1-110)	.15	.07	.02
☐ 1 Nolan Ryan Future Hall of Famer	.40	.18	.05
☐ 2 Nolan Ryan From Little League to the Major Leagues	.15	.07	.02
☐ 3 Nolan Ryan A Dream Come True	.15	.07	.02
☐ 4 Nolan Ryan Signed by the Mets	.15	.07	.02
☐ 5 Nolan Ryan Fireball Pitcher	.15	.07	.02
☐ 6 Nolan Ryan New York Mets Rookie Pitcher	.15	.07	.02
☐ 7 Nolan Ryan First Major League Win	.15	.07	.02
☐ 8 Nolan Ryan Early in 1969	.15	.07	.02
☐ 9 Nolan Ryan Tensions of a Pennant Race	.15	.07	.02
☐ 10 Nolan Ryan Mets Clinch NL East	.15	.07	.02
☐ 11 Nolan Ryan Gil Hodges Keep the Ball Down	.25	.11	.03
☐ 12 Nolan Ryan Playoff Victory	.15	.07	.02
☐ 13 Nolan Ryan World Series Victory	.15	.07	.02
☐ 14 Nolan Ryan The Amazin' Mets	.15	.07	.02
☐ 15 Nolan Ryan Sets Met Record for Strikeouts	.15	.07	.02
☐ 16 Nolan Ryan One of the Worst Trades in Baseball	.15	.07	.02
☐ 17 Nolan Ryan Slow Start with Mets	.15	.07	.02
☐ 18 Nolan Ryan Pitcher New York Mets	.15	.07	.02
☐ 19 Nolan Ryan Traded to the Angels	.15	.07	.02
☐ 20 Nolan Ryan Meeting New Friends	.15	.07	.02
☐ 21 Nolan Ryan Throwing Fast Balls	.15	.07	.02
☐ 22 Nolan Ryan Move the Ball Around	.15	.07	.02
☐ 23 Nolan Ryan Nolan Heat	.15	.07	.02
☐ 24 Nolan Ryan No-Hitter Number 1	.15	.07	.02
☐ 25 Nolan Ryan Looking Back on Number 1	.15	.07	.02
☐ 26 Nolan Ryan No-Hitter Number 2	.15	.07	.02
☐ 27 Nolan Ryan Single Season Strikeout Record	.15	.07	.02
☐ 28 Nolan Ryan 21 Wins in 1973	.15	.07	.02
☐ 29 Nolan Ryan Fastest Pitch Ever Thrown Clocked at 100.9 MPH	.20	.09	.03
☐ 30 Nolan Ryan No-Hitter Number 3	.20	.09	.03
☐ 31 Nolan Ryan No-Hitter Number 4	.20	.09	.03
☐ 32 Nolan Ryan Frank Tanana	.20	.09	.03
☐ 33 Nolan Ryan Learning Change-Up	.15	.07	.02
☐ 34 Nolan Ryan Pitcher California Angels	.15	.07	.02
☐ 35 Nolan Ryan Joins Astros	.15	.07	.02
☐ 36 Nolan Ryan Starting Pitcher	.20	.09	.03
☐ 37 Nolan Ryan Taking Batting Practice	.15	.07	.02
☐ 38 Nolan Ryan The Game's Greatest Power Pitcher	.15	.07	.02
☐ 39 Nolan Ryan 3,000 Career Strikeout	.15	.07	.02
☐ 40 Nolan Ryan Home Run	.20	.09	.03
☐ 41 Nolan Ryan The Fast Ball Grip	.15	.07	.02
☐ 42 Nolan Ryan Record 5th No-Hitter	.20	.09	.03
☐ 43 Nolan Ryan No-Hitter Number 5	.20	.09	.03
☐ 44 Nolan Ryan A Dream Fulfilled	.15	.07	.02
☐ 45 Nolan Ryan Passes Walter Johnson	.25	.11	.03
☐ 46 Nolan Ryan Strikeout 4000	.20	.09	.03
☐ 47 Nolan Ryan Astros win Western Division Title	.15	.07	.02
☐ 48 Nolan Ryan Pitcher Houston Astros	.15	.07	.02
☐ 49 Nolan Ryan Milestone Strikeouts	.15	.07	.02
☐ 50 Nolan Ryan Post Season Participant	.15	.07	.02
☐ 51 Nolan Ryan Hurling for Houston	.15	.07	.02
☐ 52 Nolan Ryan 135 NL Wins	.15	.07	.02
☐ 53 Nolan Ryan Through with Chew	.15	.07	.02
☐ 54 Nolan Ryan Signed by Rangers 1989	.15	.07	.02
☐ 55 Nolan Ryan Pleasant Change for Nolan	.15	.07	.02
☐ 56 Nolan Ryan Real Special Moment	.15	.07	.02
☐ 57 Nolan Ryan Enters 1989 All-Star Game	.15	.07	.02
☐ 58 Nolan Ryan Pitching in 1989 All-Star Game	.15	.07	.02
☐ 59 Nolan Ryan 5,000 Strikeouts A Standing Ovation	.20	.09	.03
☐ 60 Nolan Ryan Great Moments in 1989	.15	.07	.02
☐ 61 Nolan Ryan Dan Smith	.20	.09	.03
☐ 62 Nolan Ryan Ranger Club Record 16 Strikeouts	.15	.07	.02
☐ 63 Nolan Ryan Last Pitch No-Hitter Number 6	.20	.09	.03
☐ 64 Nolan Ryan Sweet Number 6	.20	.09	.03
☐ 65 Nolan Ryan Oldest To Throw No-Hitter	.15	.07	.02
☐ 66 Nolan Ryan Another Win	.15	.07	.02
☐ 67 Nolan Ryan 20th Pitcher to Win 300 Acknowledging the Fans	.15	.07	.02
☐ 68 Nolan Ryan Brad Arnsberg Geno Petralli 300 Game Win Battery	.20	.09	.03
☐ 69 Nolan Ryan A 300 Game Winner	.15	.07	.02
☐ 70 Nolan Ryan Perfect Mechanics	.15	.07	.02
☐ 71 Nolan Ryan 22 Seasons with 100 or more Strikeouts	.15	.07	.02
☐ 72 Nolan Ryan 11th Strikeout Title	.15	.07	.02
☐ 73 Nolan Ryan 232 Strikeouts in 1990	.15	.07	.02
☐ 74 Nolan Ryan The 1990 Season	.15	.07	.02
☐ 75 Nolan Ryan Pitcher Texas Rangers	.20	.09	.03
☐ 76 Nolan Ryan 1991: Nolan's 25th Season	.15	.07	.02
☐ 77 Nolan Ryan Throwing Spirals	.25	.11	.03
☐ 78 Nolan Ryan Running the Steps	.15	.07	.02
☐ 79 Nolan Ryan Hard Work and Conditioning	.15	.07	.02
☐ 80 Nolan Ryan The Rigid Workout	.15	.07	.02
☐ 81 Nolan Ryan Ryan's Routine	.15	.07	.02
☐ 82 Nolan Ryan Ryan's Routine Between Starts	.15	.07	.02
☐ 83 Nolan Ryan Running in Outfield Before the Big Game	.15	.07	.02
☐ 84 Nolan Ryan B.P. in Texas	.15	.07	.02
☐ 85 Nolan Ryan 18 Career Low-Hitters	.15	.07	.02
☐ 86 Nolan Ryan My Job is to Give My Team a Chance to Win	.15	.07	.02
☐ 87 Nolan Ryan The Spring Workout	.15	.07	.02
☐ 88 Nolan Ryan Power versus Power	.15	.07	.02
☐ 89 Nolan Ryan Awesome Power	.15	.07	.02
☐ 90 Nolan Ryan Blazing Speed	.15	.07	.02
☐ 91 Nolan Ryan The Pick Off	.15	.07	.02
☐ 92 Nolan Ryan A Real Gamer Bloody lip and blood all over jersey)	1.00	.45	.12
☐ 93 Nolan Ryan Jim Sandberg Ranger Battery Mates	.20	.09	.03
☐ 94 Nolan Ryan The Glare	.15	.07	.02
☐ 95 Nolan Ryan The High Leg Kick	.15	.07	.02
☐ 96 Nolan Ryan Day Off from Pitcher	.15	.07	.02
☐ 97 Nolan Ryan A New Ball for Nolan	.15	.07	.02
☐ 98 Nolan Ryan Going to Rosin Bag	.15	.07	.02
☐ 99 Nolan Ryan Time for Relief	.15	.07	.02
☐ 100 Nolan Ryan A Lone Star Legend	.15	.07	.02
☐ 101 Nolan Ryan Fans' Favorite	.15	.07	.02
☐ 102 Nolan Ryan Watching Nolan Pitch	.15	.07	.02
☐ 103 Nolan Ryan Our Family of Five	.15	.07	.02
☐ 104 Nolan Ryan Texas Beefmaster	.15	.07	.02
☐ 105 Nolan Ryan Gentleman Rancher	.15	.07	.02
☐ 106 Nolan Ryan Texas Cowboy Life	.15	.07	.02
☐ 107 Nolan Ryan The Ryan Family	.20	.09	.03
☐ 108 Nolan Ryan Participating in Cutting Horse Contest	.15	.07	.02
☐ 109 Nolan Ryan Nolan Interviews	.15	.07	.02
☐ 110 Nolan Ryan Lynn Nolan Ryan	.35	.16	.04

1991 Pacific Ryan Inserts 8

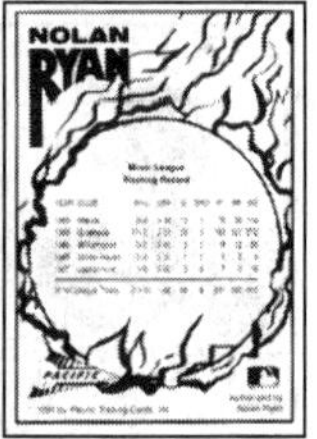

These eight standard-size cards were inserts in 1991 Pacific Nolan Ryan Texas Express foil packs. As with the regular issue, the fronts display glossy color photos that are bordered in silver foil and either purple/red or red/orange border stripes. Inside a flaming baseball design, the back presents either a player photo, statistics, or career highlights. The cards are unnumbered and checklisted below in chronological order. Besides the silver cards, they were also issued on a much more limited basis in gold. The gold versions are valued at quadruple the prices listed below.

	MINT	NRMT	EXC
COMPLETE SET (8)	100.00	45.00	12.50
COMMON CARD (1-8)	15.00	6.75	1.85
☐ 1 Nolan Ryan New York Mets Rookie Pitcher	15.00	6.75	1.85
☐ 2 Nolan Ryan No-Hitter 1	15.00	6.75	1.85
☐ 3 Nolan Ryan No-Hitter 2	15.00	6.75	1.85
☐ 4 Nolan Ryan No-Hitter 3	15.00	6.75	1.85
☐ 5 Nolan Ryan No-Hitter 4	15.00	6.75	1.85
☐ 6 Nolan Ryan No-Hitter 5	15.00	6.75	1.85
☐ 7 Nolan Ryan Sweet 6	15.00	6.75	1.85
☐ 8 Nolan Ryan 1991: Nolan's 25th Season	15.00	6.75	1.85

1991 Pacific Ryan 7th No-Hitter

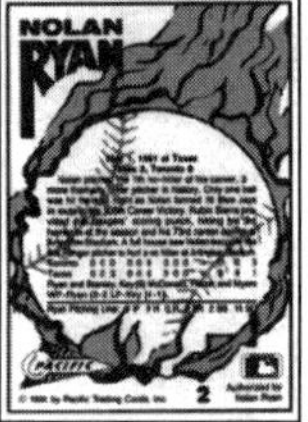

This seven-card set was produced by Pacific Trading Cards Inc. to capture various moments of Nolan Ryan's 7th no-hitter. These cards were produced in the following numbers: 1,000 of each card in gold foil and 10,000 of each card in silver foil. The cards measure the standard size and were randomly inserted in foil packs only. The fronts feature glossy color photos, with silver or gold borders on the sides and faded red borders above and below the picture. In addition, the player's name is written vertically in a multi-colored stripe on the left side of the picture. A flaming baseball in the lower left corner completes the card face. The backs are printed in purple and red on a white background. Inside a flaming baseball design, one finds an extended caption to the front picture. The cards are numbered on the back in the lower left corner. Supposedly as many as half of the cards were destroyed and never released. The prices below refer to the silver versions; the gold versions would be valued at quadruple the prices below.

	MINT	NRMT	EXC
COMPLETE SET (7)	100.00	45.00	12.50
COMMON CARD (1-7)	15.00	6.75	1.85
☐ 1 Nolan Ryan Last Pitch 7th No-Hitter	15.00	6.75	1.85
☐ 2 Nolan Ryan No-Hitter Number 7	15.00	6.75	1.85
☐ 3 Nolan Ryan Number 7 was The Best	15.00	6.75	1.85
☐ 4 Nolan Ryan Time to Celebrate	15.00	6.75	1.85
☐ 5 Nolan Ryan Congratulations from Ranger Fans	15.00	6.75	1.85
☐ 6 Nolan Ryan Mike Stanley Hold the No-Hitter Ball UER Back reads Bryan, should read Ryan	15.00	6.75	1.85
☐ 7 Nolan Ryan All in a Day's Work	15.00	6.75	1.85

1991 Pacific Senior League

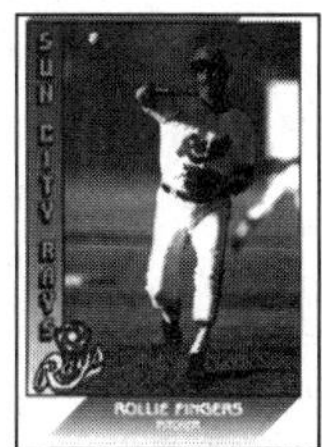

Pacific Trading Cards released this 160-card set just after the Senior League suspended operations. The standard size cards were sold in wax packs and as complete sets. The fronts have glossy color player photos, with white borders and the team name written vertically in a stripe running down the left side of the picture. The backs are mint-colored and feature career highlights. Apparently there are two different versions of cards for the following players: Jim Rice, Rollie Fingers, Vida Blue, Dave Cash, Dan Norman, Ron LeFlore, Cesar Cedeno, Rafael Landestoy, and Dan Driessen.

	MINT	NRMT	EXC
COMPLETE SET (160)	9.00	4.00	1.10
COMMON CARD (1-160)	.05	.02	.01
☐ 1 Dan Driessen	.10	.05	.01
☐ 2 Marty Castillo	.05	.02	.01
☐ 3 Jerry White	.05	.02	.01
☐ 4 Bud Anderson	.05	.02	.01
☐ 5 Ron Jackson	.05	.02	.01
☐ 6 Fred Stanley CO	.05	.02	.01
☐ 7 Steve Luebber	.05	.02	.01
☐ 8 Jerry Terrell CO	.05	.02	.01
☐ 9 Pat Dobson	.10	.05	.01
☐ 10 Ken Kravec	.05	.02	.01
☐ 11 Gil Rondon	.05	.02	.01
☐ 12 Dyar Miller CO	.05	.02	.01
☐ 13 Bobby Molinaro	.05	.02	.01
☐ 14 Jerry Martin	.05	.02	.01
☐ 15 Rick Waits	.05	.02	.01
☐ 16 Steve McCatty	.05	.02	.01
☐ 17 Roger Slagle	.05	.02	.01
☐ 18 Mike Ramsey	.05	.02	.01
☐ 19 Rich Gale	.05	.02	.01
☐ 20 Larry Harlow	.05	.02	.01
☐ 21 Dan Rohn	.05	.02	.01
☐ 22 Don Cooper	.05	.02	.01
☐ 23 Marv Foley	.05	.02	.01
☐ 24 Rafael Landestoy	.05	.02	.01
☐ 25 Eddie Milner	.05	.02	.01
☐ 26 Amos Otis	.10	.05	.01
☐ 27 Odell Jones	.05	.02	.01
☐ 28 Tippy Martinez	.05	.02	.01
☐ 29 Stu Cliburn	.05	.02	.01
☐ 30 Stan Cliburn	.05	.02	.01
☐ 31 Tony Cloninger CO	.05	.02	.01
☐ 32 Jeff Jones	.05	.02	.01
☐ 33 Ken Reitz	.05	.02	.01
☐ 34 Dave Sax	.05	.02	.01
☐ 35 Orlando Gonzalez	.05	.02	.01
☐ 36 Jose Cruz	.10	.05	.01
☐ 37 Mickey Mahler	.05	.02	.01
☐ 38 Derek Botelho	.05	.02	.01
☐ 39 Rick Lysander	.05	.02	.01
☐ 40 Cesar Cedeno	.10	.05	.01
☐ 41 Garth Iorg	.05	.02	.01
☐ 42 Wayne Krenchicki	.05	.02	.01
☐ 43 Clete Boyer CO	.10	.05	.01
☐ 44 Dan Boone	.05	.02	.01
☐ 45 George Vukovich	.05	.02	.01
☐ 46 Omar Moreno	.05	.02	.01
☐ 47 Ron Washington	.05	.02	.01
☐ 48 Ron Washington MVP	.05	.02	.01
☐ 49 Rick Peterson	.05	.02	.01
☐ 50 Tack Wilson	.05	.02	.01
☐ 51 Stan and Stu Cliburn	.05	.02	.01
☐ 52 Rick Lysander POY	.05	.02	.01
☐ 53 Cesar Cedeno and Pete LaCock	.10	.05	.01
☐ 54 Jim Marshall MG and Clete Boyer MG	.05	.02	.01
☐ 55 Doug Simunic	.05	.02	.01
☐ 56 Pat Kelly	.05	.02	.01
☐ 57 Roy Branch	.05	.02	.01
☐ 58 Dave Cash	.10	.05	.01
☐ 59 Bobby Jones	.05	.02	.01
☐ 60 Hector Cruz	.05	.02	.01
☐ 61 Reggie Cleveland	.05	.02	.01
☐ 62 Gary Lance	.05	.02	.01
☐ 63 Ron LeFlore	.10	.05	.01
☐ 64 Dan Norman	.05	.02	.01
☐ 65 Renie Martin	.05	.02	.01
☐ 66 Pete Mackanin MG	.05	.02	.01
☐ 67 Frank Riccelli	.05	.02	.01
☐ 68 Alfie Rondon	.05	.02	.01
☐ 69 Rodney Scott	.05	.02	.01
☐ 70 Jim Tracy	.05	.02	.01
☐ 71 Ed Dennis	.05	.02	.01
☐ 72 Rick Lindell	.05	.02	.01
☐ 73 Stu Pepper	.05	.02	.01
☐ 74 Jeff Youngbauer	.05	.02	.01
☐ 75 Russ Foster	.05	.02	.01
☐ 76 Jeff Capriati	.05	.02	.01
☐ 77 Art DeFreites	.05	.02	.01
☐ 78 Alfie Rondon	.05	.02	.01
☐ 79 Reggie Cleveland IA	.05	.02	.01
☐ 80 Dave Cash	.05	.02	.01
☐ 81 Vida Blue	.15	.07	.02
☐ 82 Ed Glynn	.05	.02	.01
☐ 83 Bob Owchinko	.05	.02	.01
☐ 84 Bill Fleming	.05	.02	.01
☐ 85 Ron and Gary Roenicke	.05	.02	.01
☐ 86 Tom Thompson CO	.05	.02	.01
☐ 87 Derrel Thomas UER (Name misspelled Derrell)	.05	.02	.01
☐ 88 Jim Willoughby	.05	.02	.01
☐ 89 Jim Pankovits	.05	.02	.01
☐ 90 Jack Cooley CO	.05	.02	.01
☐ 91 Lenn Sakata	.05	.02	.01
☐ 92 Mike Brocki	.05	.02	.01
☐ 93 Chuck Fick	.05	.02	.01
☐ 94 Tom Benedict	.05	.02	.01
☐ 95 Anthony Davis	.25	.11	.03
☐ 96 Cardell Camper	.05	.02	.01
☐ 97 Leon Roberts	.05	.02	.01
☐ 98 Roger Erickson	.05	.02	.01
☐ 99 Kim Allen	.05	.02	.01
☐ 100 Dave Skaggs	.05	.02	.01
☐ 101 Joe Decker	.05	.02	.01
☐ 102 U.L. Washington	.05	.02	.01
☐ 103 Don Fletcher	.05	.02	.01
☐ 104 Gary Roenicke	.05	.02	.01
☐ 105 Rich Dauer MG	.05	.02	.01
☐ 106 Ron Roenicke	.05	.02	.01
☐ 107 Mike Norris	.05	.02	.01
☐ 108 Ferguson Jenkins	.50	.23	.06
☐ 109 Ronn Reynolds	.05	.02	.01
☐ 110 Pete Falcone	.05	.02	.01
☐ 111 Gary Allenson	.05	.02	.01
☐ 112 Mark Wagner	.05	.02	.01
☐ 113 Jack Lazorko	.05	.02	.01
☐ 114 Bob Galasso	.05	.02	.01
☐ 115 Ron Davis	.05	.02	.01
☐ 116 Lenny Randle	.05	.02	.01
☐ 117 Ricky Peters	.05	.02	.01
☐ 118 Jim Dwyer	.05	.02	.01
☐ 119 Juan Eichelberger	.05	.02	.01
☐ 120 Pete LaCock	.10	.05	.01
☐ 121 Tony Scott	.05	.02	.01
☐ 122 Rick Lancellotti	.05	.02	.01
☐ 123 Barry Bonnell	.05	.02	.01
☐ 124 Dave Hilton	.05	.02	.01
☐ 125 Bill Campbell	.05	.02	.01
☐ 126 Rollie Fingers	.50	.23	.06
☐ 127 Jim Marshall MG	.05	.02	.01
☐ 128 Razor Shines	.10	.05	.01
☐ 129 Guy Sularz	.05	.02	.01
☐ 130 Roy Thomas	.05	.02	.01
☐ 131 Joel Youngblood	.05	.02	.01
☐ 132 Ernie Camacho	.05	.02	.01
☐ 133 Dave Hilton CO, Jim Marshall MG, and Fred Stanley CO	.05	.02	.01
☐ 134 Ken Landreaux	.05	.02	.01
☐ 135 Dave Rozema	.05	.02	.01
☐ 136 Tom Zimmer CO	.05	.02	.01
☐ 137 Elias Sosa	.05	.02	.01
☐ 138 Ossie Virgil Sr. CO	.05	.02	.01
☐ 139 Al Holland	.05	.02	.01
☐ 140 Milt Wilcox	.05	.02	.01
☐ 141 Jerry Reed	.05	.02	.01
☐ 142 Chris Welsh	.05	.02	.01
☐ 143 Luis Gomez	.05	.02	.01
☐ 144 Steve Henderson	.05	.02	.01
☐ 145 Butch Benton	.05	.02	.01
☐ 146 Bill Lee	.10	.05	.01
☐ 147 Todd Cruz	.05	.02	.01
☐ 148 Jim Rice	.25	.11	.03
☐ 149 Tito Landrum	.05	.02	.01
☐ 150 Ozzie Virgil Jr.	.05	.02	.01
☐ 151 Joe Pittman	.05	.02	.01
☐ 152 Bobby Tolan MG	.05	.02	.01
☐ 153 Len Barker	.05	.02	.01
☐ 154 Dave Rajsich	.05	.02	.01
☐ 155 Glenn Gulliver	.05	.02	.01
☐ 156 Gary Rajsich	.05	.02	.01
☐ 157 Joe Sambito	.05	.02	.01
☐ 158 Frank Vito	.05	.02	.01
☐ 159 Ozzie Virgil Jr./Sr.	.05	.02	.01
☐ 160 Dave and Gary Rajsich	.05	.02	.01

1992 Pacific Ryan Magazine 6

These six standard size cards were inserted (bound) into the July 1992 Volume 2, Issue 2 of Trading Cards magazine as a pair of two-card strips. These are very similar to the hard-to-find inserts that Pacific inserted into the Ryan Texas Express second series foil packs. These "magazine cards" are only differentiable by the fact that they lack the words "Limited Edition" on the copyright line on their backs.

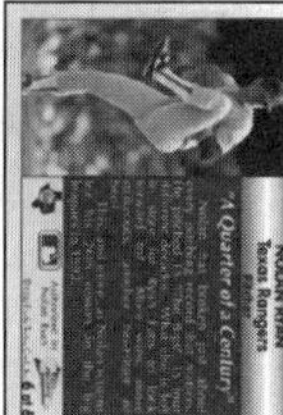

	MINT	NRMT	EXC
COMPLETE SET (6)	8.00	3.60	1.00
COMMON CARD (1-6)	1.50	.70	.19
☐ 1 Nolan Ryan Pitching, side view	1.50	.70	.19
☐ 2 Nolan Ryan Pitching, front view gray uniform	1.50	.70	.19
☐ 3 Nolan Ryan The Texas Express	1.50	.70	.19
☐ 4 Nolan Ryan The Seventh No-Hitter	1.50	.70	.19
☐ 5 Nolan Ryan A Texas Legacy	1.50	.70	.19
☐ 6 Nolan Ryan A Quarter of a Century	1.50	.70	.19

1992 Pacific Ryan Texas Express II

For the second year, Pacific issued a 110-card standard-size set titled Texas Express. A six-card insert set was randomly inserted in foil packs, with 1,000 autographed and numbered of card number 1. The fronts feature glossy posed and action photos (some color, some black-and-white) of Ryan in various stages of his life and career. The pictures are bordered at the top and bottom in varying shades of red, orange and purple. His name is printed in silver vertically down the left edge of the card on either red, orange or purple. A fiery baseball overlaps the border and photo at the bottom. The backs show the fiery baseball with either statistics, career highlights, pictures, or quotes about Nolan printed in blue on the baseball. This set is essentially an extension or second series of the 1991 Pacific Nolan Ryan set and is numbered that way. After the first and second series of Pacific Nolan Ryan Texas Express had sold out, Pacific reissued card numbers 1-220 in 1993, and the cards produced in this reissue may be distinguished by the 27th season logo, which was introduced to collectors in the 30-card 27th Season series. Currently there is no value differential between the two types.

	MINT	NRMT	EXC
COMPLETE SET (110)	10.00	4.50	1.25
COMMON CARD (111-220)	.15	.07	.02
☐ 111 Nolan Ryan The Golden Arm	.25	.11	.03
☐ 112 Nolan Ryan Little League All-Star	.15	.07	.02
☐ 113 Nolan Ryan All-State Pitcher	.15	.07	.02
☐ 114 Nolan Ryan Nolan Ryan Field	.15	.07	.02
☐ 115 Nolan Ryan at Age 20	.15	.07	.02
☐ 116 Nolan Ryan Jacksonville Suns	.15	.07	.02
☐ 117 Nolan Ryan Surrounded By Friends	.15	.07	.02
☐ 118 Nolan Ryan The Cowboy	.20	.09	.03
☐ 119 Nolan Ryan The Simple Life	.15	.07	.02
☐ 120 Nolan Ryan Loves Animals	.15	.07	.02
☐ 121 Nolan Ryan Growing Up in New York	.15	.07	.02
☐ 122 Nolan Ryan New York Strikeout Record	.20	.09	.03
☐ 123 Nolan Ryan Traded	.15	.07	.02
☐ 124 Nolan Ryan Hall of Fame Victims	.25	.11	.03
☐ 125 Nolan Ryan Number 500	.15	.07	.02
☐ 126 Nolan Ryan California Victory	.15	.07	.02
☐ 127 Nolan Ryan 20 Win Season	.15	.07	.02
☐ 128 Nolan Ryan Throwing Heat	.15	.07	.02
☐ 129 Nolan Ryan Strikeout Record	.20	.09	.03
☐ 130 Nolan Ryan Number One	.20	.09	.03
☐ 131 Nolan Ryan 1,000th Strikeout	.15	.07	.02
☐ 132 Nolan Ryan Number Two	.20	.09	.03
☐ 133 Nolan Ryan 2,000th Strikeout	.15	.07	.02
☐ 134 Nolan Ryan Number Three	.20	.09	.03
☐ 135 Nolan Ryan Bob Feller Pure Speed	.25	.11	.03
☐ 136 Nolan Ryan Independence Day Fireworks	.15	.07	.02
☐ 137 Nolan Ryan Fast Ball Pitcher	.15	.07	.02
☐ 138 Nolan Ryan Number Four	.20	.09	.03
☐ 139 Nolan Ryan Free Agent	.15	.07	.02
☐ 140 Nolan Ryan Houston Bound	.15	.07	.02
☐ 141 Nolan Ryan Big Dollars	.15	.07	.02
☐ 142 Nolan Ryan Strong Houston Staff	.20	.09	.03
☐ 143 Nolan Ryan Number Five	.20	.09	.03
☐ 144 Nolan Ryan Astro MVP	.15	.07	.02
☐ 145 Nolan Ryan Western Division Game	.15	.07	.02
☐ 146 Nolan Ryan National League All-Star	.15	.07	.02
☐ 147 Nolan Ryan Major League Record	.15	.07	.02
☐ 148 Nolan Ryan Breaks Walter Johnson's Record	.25	.11	.03
☐ 149 Nolan Ryan Reese Ryan	.25	.11	.03
☐ 150 Nolan Ryan 100th National League Win	.15	.07	.02
☐ 151 Nolan Ryan 4,000th Strikeout	.15	.07	.02
☐ 152 Nolan Ryan League Leader	.15	.07	.02
☐ 153 Nolan Ryan 250th Career Win	.15	.07	.02
☐ 154 Nolan Ryan The Seldom of Swat	.15	.07	.02
☐ 155 Nolan Ryan 4,500th Strikeout	.15	.07	.02
☐ 156 Nolan Ryan Like Father Like Son	.20	.09	.03
☐ 157 Nolan Ryan Spoiled in the Ninth	.15	.07	.02
☐ 158 Nolan Ryan Leaving Houston in Style	.15	.07	.02
☐ 159 Nolan Ryan Houston Star	.15	.07	.02
☐ 160 Nolan Ryan Tests Free Agency	.15	.07	.02
☐ 161 Nolan Ryan Awesome Heat	.15	.07	.02
☐ 162 Nolan Ryan Brotherly Love	.15	.07	.02
☐ 163 Nolan Ryan Astros Return of The Prodigious Son	.15	.07	.02
☐ 164 Nolan Ryan Texas Size Decision	.15	.07	.02
☐ 165 Nolan Ryan Texas Legend	.15	.07	.02
☐ 166 Nolan Ryan Drawing a Crowd	.15	.07	.02
☐ 167 Nolan Ryan Great Start	.15	.07	.02
☐ 168 Nolan Ryan 5,000th Strikeout	.15	.07	.02
☐ 169 Nolan Ryan Texas All-Star	.15	.07	.02
☐ 170 Nolan Ryan Number Six	.20	.09	.03
☐ 171 Nolan Ryan 300th Win	.20	.09	.03
☐ 172 Nolan Ryan 1990 League Leader	.15	.07	.02
☐ 173 Nolan Ryan Man of the Year	.25	.11	.03
☐ 174 Nolan Ryan Spring Training 1991	.15	.07	.02
☐ 175 Nolan Ryan Fast Ball Grip	.15	.07	.02
☐ 176 Nolan Ryan Strong Arm	.15	.07	.02
☐ 177 Nolan Ryan Mike Stanley Stanley's Delight	.20	.09	.03
☐ 178 Nolan Ryan After Nolan's 7th No-Hitter	.20	.09	.03
☐ 179 Nolan Ryan Stretching Before the Game	.15	.07	.02
☐ 180 Nolan Ryan The Rangers Sign Nolan For 1992 and 1993	.15	.07	.02
☐ 181 Nolan Ryan	.15	.07	.02

	MINT	NRMT	EXC
Heading to the Bullpen to Warmup			
□ 182 Nolan Ryan Banker	.15	.07	.02
□ 183 Nolan Ryan Time with Fans	.15	.07	.02
□ 184 Nolan Ryan Solid 1991 Season	.15	.07	.02
□ 185 Nolan Ryan Ranger Team Leader	.15	.07	.02
□ 186 Nolan Ryan Sets More Records	.15	.07	.02
□ 187 Nolan Ryan Number Seven	.20	.09	.03
□ 188 Nolan Ryan Passes Phil Niekro	.20	.09	.03
□ 189 Nolan Ryan Trails Don Sutton	.20	.09	.03
□ 190 Nolan Ryan Ranger Strikeout Mark	.15	.07	.02
□ 191 Nolan Ryan Consecutive K's	.15	.07	.02
□ 192 Nolan Ryan 5,500th Strikeout	.15	.07	.02
□ 193 Nolan Ryan Twenty-Five First Timers	.15	.07	.02
□ 194 Nolan Ryan No-Hitters Ended in the Ninth	.15	.07	.02
□ 195 Nolan Ryan Constant Work-Outs	.15	.07	.02
□ 196 Nolan Ryan In Motion	.15	.07	.02
□ 197 Nolan Ryan Pitching in Fenway Park	.15	.07	.02
□ 198 Nolan Ryan Goose Gossage	.25	.11	.03
□ 199 Nolan Ryan Talking Over Strategy	.15	.07	.02
□ 200 Nolan Ryan Roger Clemens Don't Mess With Texas	.40	.18	.05
□ 201 Nolan Ryan 314-278 Thru 1991	.15	.07	.02
□ 202 Nolan Ryan All-Time Leader	.15	.07	.02
□ 203 Nolan Ryan High Praise	.15	.07	.02
□ 204 Nolan Ryan Bobby Valentine Manager's Delight	.20	.09	.03
□ 205 Nolan Ryan 733 Major League Starts	.15	.07	.02
□ 206 Nolan Ryan The Quarterback	.25	.11	.03
□ 207 Nolan Ryan Hard Work Pays Off	.15	.07	.02
□ 208 Nolan Ryan Tom House Passing Along Wisdom	.20	.09	.03
□ 209 Nolan Ryan Still Dominant	.15	.07	.02
□ 210 Nolan Ryan Fast Ball Is Just a Blur	.15	.07	.02
□ 211 Nolan Ryan Seven No-Hitters	.20	.09	.03
□ 212 Nolan Ryan Training for Perfection	.15	.07	.02
□ 213 Nolan Ryan Edge and Speed	.15	.07	.02
□ 214 Nolan Ryan This One was for Them	.15	.07	.02
□ 215 Nolan Ryan Another Day's Work	.15	.07	.02
□ 216 Nolan Ryan Pick Off at Third	.15	.07	.02
□ 217 Nolan Ryan Ready to Pitch	.15	.07	.02
□ 218 Nolan Ryan Spring Training 1992	.15	.07	.02
□ 219 Nolan Ryan Receives The Victor Award	.20	.09	.03
□ 220 Nolan Ryan 1992: Nolan's 26th Season	.25	.11	.03

1992 Pacific Ryan Gold

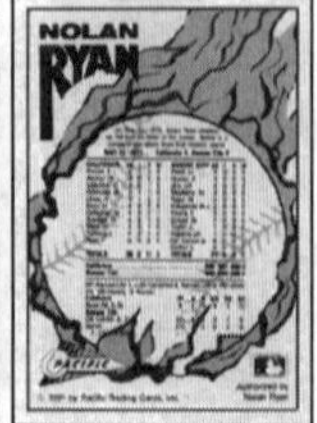

These eight standard size cards were one of two insert subsets randomly packed in 1992 Pacific Nolan Ryan Texas Express II 12-card and 24-card foil packs. Supposedly 10,000 of each card were produced. The cards feature high gloss color action photos of Ryan pitching his seven no-hitters. The pictures are bordered in gold foil and either red/orange (1-4) or purple/red border (5-8) stripes. Inside a flaming baseball design, the backs of cards 1-7 display statistics for that no-hitter while card No. 8 summarizes all seven no-hitters. The cards are unnumbered and checklisted below in chronological order of the events.

	MINT	NRMT	EXC
COMPLETE SET (8)	175.00	80.00	22.00
COMMON CARD (1-8)	25.00	11.00	3.10
□ 1 Nolan Ryan Number One	25.00	11.00	3.10
□ 2 Nolan Ryan Number Two	25.00	11.00	3.10
□ 3 Nolan Ryan Number Three	25.00	11.00	3.10
□ 4 Nolan Ryan Number Four	25.00	11.00	3.10
□ 5 Nolan Ryan Number Five	25.00	11.00	3.10
□ 6 Nolan Ryan Number Six	25.00	11.00	3.10
□ 7 Nolan Ryan Number Seven	25.00	11.00	3.10
□ 8 Nolan Ryan Seven No-Hitters	25.00	11.00	3.10

1992 Pacific Ryan Limited

These six standard size cards were one of two insert subsets randomly packed in 1992 Pacific Nolan Ryan Texas Express II 12-card and 24-card foil packs. Only 3,000 of each card were produced and, as an added bonus, 1,000 of card number 1 were autographed by Ryan. A similar-looking pair of two-card strips was inserted (bound) into all issues of the July 1992 Volume 2, Issue 2 of Trading Cards magazine. However these "magazine cards" lack the words "Limited Edition" on the copyright line on their backs. The six career highlight cards feature high gloss color action photos on their fronts edged by a graded blue stripe on the left side and framed by a white outer border. The Texas Rangers and Pacific logos overlap the picture. The horizontal backs feature a second action color photo. Nolan's name appears in a red, white, and blue bar above a red box containing either career highlights (2, 3, 6), statistics (4) or a poem (5).

	MINT	NRMT	EXC
COMPLETE SET (6)	125.00	55.00	15.50
COMMON CARD (1-6)	25.00	11.00	3.10
□ 1 Nolan Ryan Pitching, side view limited edition on back	25.00	11.00	3.10
□ 2 Nolan Ryan (Pitching, front view gray uniform limited edition on back	25.00	11.00	3.10
□ 3 Nolan Ryan The Texas Express Limited edition on back	25.00	11.00	3.10
□ 4 Nolan Ryan The Seventh No-Hitter Limited edition on back	25.00	11.00	3.10
□ 5 Nolan Ryan A Texas Legacy Limited edition on back	25.00	11.00	3.10
□ 6 Nolan Ryan A Quarter of a Century Limited edition on back	25.00	11.00	3.10

1992 Pacific Seaver

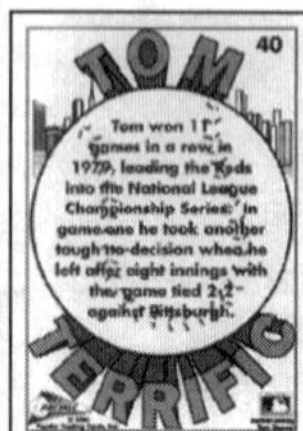

This 110-card standard-size set traces the career of Tom Seaver. The set was sold in 12-card foil packs or as a factory set for $12.95 through a mail-in offer. The fronts feature glossy color player photos with silver, purple, or red borders. Also white border stripes appear on the left and right sides of the pictures. At the lower left corner the nickname "Tom Terrific" in yellow lettering wraps around a white baseball icon. The back design is based on a larger version of this baseball icon, with a second color photo, career summary, or highlights inside the ball. Behind the ball appears a skyline with tall buildings. Autograph cards of Tom Seaver were randomly inserted into packs, they are valued at the bottom of the listings.

	MINT	NRMT	EXC
COMPLETE SET (110)	7.50	3.40	.95
COMMON CARD (1-110)	.10	.05	.01
□ 1 Tom Seaver Stand-out High School Basketball Player	.35	.16	.04
□ 2 Tom Seaver Pro Ball Player	.10	.05	.01
□ 3 Tom Seaver Destined to be a Met	.10	.05	.01
□ 4 Tom Seaver Brave or Met	.10	.05	.01
□ 5 Tom Seaver Mets Luck of the Draw	.10	.05	.01
□ 6 Tom Seaver Sent to Jacksonville	.10	.05	.01
□ 7 Tom Seaver First Major League Win	.10	.05	.01
□ 8 Tom Seaver 1967 Rookie of the Year	.20	.09	.03
□ 9 Tom Seaver Humble Beginnings	.10	.05	.01
□ 10 Tom Seaver Predicting the Future	.10	.05	.01
□ 11 Tom Seaver Rookie All-Star	.10	.05	.01
□ 12 Tom Seaver 16 Wins in 1968	.10	.05	.01
□ 13 Tom Seaver 1968 National League All-Star	.10	.05	.01
□ 14 Tom Seaver The Amazing Mets	.10	.05	.01
□ 15 Tom Seaver 1969 Cy Young Winner	.20	.09	.03
□ 16 Tom Seaver Pitcher of the Year	.20	.09	.03
□ 17 Tom Seaver Strikeout Leader	.10	.05	.01
□ 18 Tom Seaver Ties Major League Record	.10	.05	.01
□ 19 Tom Seaver Mr. Consistency	.10	.05	.01
□ 20 Tom Seaver Finishing in Style	.10	.05	.01
□ 21 Tom Seaver Twenty-Game Winner	.10	.05	.01
□ 22 Tom Seaver Second Cy Young Award	.20	.09	.03
□ 23 Tom Seaver Batting Star	.10	.05	.01
□ 24 Tom Seaver At Bat in the World Series	.10	.05	.01
□ 25 Tom Seaver Championship Series Record	.10	.05	.01
□ 26 Tom Seaver Injury Plagued Season	.10	.05	.01
□ 27 Tom Seaver Comeback	.10	.05	.01
□ 28 Tom Seaver Super September	.10	.05	.01
□ 29 Tom Seaver Sporting News All-Star	.10	.05	.01
□ 30 Tom Seaver Strikeout Record	.10	.05	.01
□ 31 Tom Seaver USC Alumni Star	.10	.05	.01
□ 32 Tom Seaver Winning Smile	.10	.05	.01
□ 33 Tom Seaver One-Hitter	.10	.05	.01
□ 34 Tom Seaver Traded to the Reds	.10	.05	.01
□ 35 Tom Seaver New York Mets Pitcher	.10	.05	.01
□ 36 Tom Seaver Winning with the Reds	.10	.05	.01
□ 37 Tom Seaver No-Hitter	.10	.05	.01
□ 38 Tom Seaver National League Leader	.10	.05	.01
□ 39 Tom Seaver Smooth Swing	.10	.05	.01
□ 40 Tom Seaver No Decision in the Championship Series	.10	.05	.01
□ 41 Tom Seaver Injury Shortened Season	.10	.05	.01
□ 42 Tom Seaver Bouncing Back	.10	.05	.01
□ 43 Tom Seaver Eighth All-Star Appearance	.10	.05	.01
□ 44 Tom Seaver Spring Training 1982	.10	.05	.01
□ 45 Tom Seaver Back to New York	.10	.05	.01
□ 46 Tom Seaver Cincinnati Reds Pitcher	.10	.05	.01
□ 47 Tom Seaver Back in the Big Apple	.10	.05	.01
□ 48 Tom Seaver Opening Day Star	.10	.05	.01
□ 49 Tom Seaver Not Much Run Support	.10	.05	.01
□ 50 Tom Seaver A Pair of Shutouts	.10	.05	.01
□ 51 Tom Seaver 4,000 Inning Mark	.10	.05	.01
□ 52 Tom Seaver One Season in New York	.10	.05	.01
□ 53 Tom Seaver Chicago Bound	.10	.05	.01
□ 54 Tom Seaver Chicago White Sox Pitcher	.20	.09	.03
□ 55 Tom Seaver Win 300	.10	.05	.01
□ 56 Tom Seaver 16 Wins in 1985	.10	.05	.01
□ 57 Tom Seaver Luke Appling Ozzie Guillen Blast From the Past	.10	.05	.01
□ 58 Tom Seaver Moving Up in the Record Book	.10	.05	.01
□ 59 Tom Seaver LaMarr Hoyt Cy Young Winners	.20	.09	.03
□ 60 Tom Seaver Carlton Fisk Two Legends of the Game	.25	.11	.03
□ 61 Tom Seaver Placido Domingo Singing Praise	.20	.09	.03
□ 62 Tom Seaver 300th Win Tribute	.10	.05	.01
□ 63 Tom Seaver Sarah Seaver Anne Seaver Nancy Seaver The Seaver Family	.20	.09	.03
□ 64 Tom Seaver 20th Major League Season	.10	.05	.01
□ 65 Tom Seaver Traded to the Red Sox	.20	.09	.03
□ 66 Tom Seaver Chicago White Sox Career Record	.10	.05	.01
□ 67 Tom Seaver Red Sox Man	.20	.09	.03
□ 68 Tom Seaver Boston Red Sox Pitcher	.20	.09	.03
□ 69 Tom Seaver One Last Try	.10	.05	.01
□ 70 Tom Seaver Major League Records	.10	.05	.01
□ 71 Tom Seaver Lowest National League Career ERA	.10	.05	.01
□ 72 Tom Seaver Pitching in Comiskey Park	.10	.05	.01
□ 73 Tom Seaver 273 National League Wins	.10	.05	.01
□ 74 Tom Seaver 300 Win Honors	.10	.05	.01
□ 75 Tom Seaver 311 Major League Wins	.10	.05	.01
□ 76 Tom Seaver 41 Retired	.10	.05	.01
□ 77 Tom Seaver Championship Series 2.84 ERA	.10	.05	.01
□ 78 Tom Seaver June 1976 Age 32	.10	.05	.01
□ 79 Tom Seaver 8-Time National League All-Star Pitcher	.10	.05	.01
□ 80 Tom Seaver Broadcasting Career	.10	.05	.01
□ 81 Tom Seaver 300th Game Win Celebration	.10	.05	.01
□ 82 Tom Seaver Nolan Ryan	.40	.18	.05
□ 83 Tom Seaver 4th Best ERA All-Time	.10	.05	.01
□ 84 Tom Seaver 15th All-Time in Victories	.10	.05	.01
□ 85 Tom Seaver Nolan Ryan 300 Win Club	.40	.18	.05
□ 86 Tom Seaver#[Hall of Fame	.10	.05	.01
□ 87 Tom Seaver Pitching in Wrigley Field	.10	.05	.01
□ 88 Tom Seaver Power Pitching	.10	.05	.01
□ 89 Tom Seaver Spring Training 1980	.10	.05	.01
□ 90 Tom Seaver Pitching in Riverfront Stadium, 1980	.10	.05	.01
□ 91 Tom Seaver Tom Terrific	.20	.09	.03
□ 92 Tom Seaver Super Seaver	.20	.09	.03
□ 93 Tom Seaver Top 10 All-Time	.10	.05	.01
□ 94 Tom Seaver 16 Opening Day Starting Asignments	.10	.05	.01
□ 95 Tom Seaver	.10	.05	.01

	MINT	NRMT	EXC
3,272 Major League Strikeouts			
☐ 96 Tom Seaver	.10	.05	.01
Six Opening Day Wins			
☐ 97 Tom Seaver	.10	.05	.01
239 Innings Pitched in 1985			
☐ 98 Tom Seaver	.10	.05	.01
A Day Off			
☐ 99 Tom Seaver	.10	.05	.01
Concentration (You Can't Let Up)			
☐ 100 Tom Seaver	.10	.05	.01
Velocity, Movement and Location			
☐ 101 Tom Seaver	.10	.05	.01
Strikeout King			
☐ 102 Tom Seaver	.10	.05	.01
The Most Important Pitch			
☐ 103 Tom Seaver	.10	.05	.01
Cincinnati Reds Number 41			
☐ 104 Tom Seaver	.20	.09	.03
George Thomas Seaver			
☐ 105 Tom Seaver	.10	.05	.01
Dazzling Dean of the Reds' Staff			
☐ 106 Tom Seaver	.20	.09	.03
Receives the Judge Emil Fuchs Award			
☐ 107 Tom Seaver	.10	.05	.01
Boston Mound Ace			
☐ 108 Tom Seaver	.10	.05	.01
Fly Ball to Center			
☐ 109 Tom Seaver	.10	.05	.01
August 4, 1985 Yankee Stadium			
☐ 110 Tom Seaver	.20	.09	.03
Breaking Walter Johnson's Strikeout Record			

1992 Pacific Seaver Inserts 6

These six standard-size cards were one of two insert subsets (depicting career highlights of Tom Seaver) randomly packed in 1992 Pacific Tom Seaver 12-card foil packs. The two insert sets are numbered the same, the primary physical difference being a white border or a gold foil border on the card front. Only 3,000 of each non-gold card were produced and, as an added bonus, 1,000 of card number 1 were autographed by Seaver. According to Pacific, 10,000 of each gold card were produced. However, it seems like the numbers reported by Pacific were actually transposed when the cards were issued. There seem to be more non-gold (White) card issued than Gold cards. The six career highlight cards feature high gloss color action player photos on their fronts edged by a color stripe on the left and framed by a white (or gold) outer border. The 'Tom Terrific' logo overlays the stripe at the lower left corner. The horizontal backs display a second action color photo. Seaver's name and the card subtitle appear in a graded color bar above a color-coded panel containing career highlights. The backs of the gold foil insert cards are identical to those of the regular inserts and are distinguished only by their non-glossy finish. The values for the gold and white versions are the same at this time.

	MINT	NRMT	EXC
COMPLETE SET (6)	125.00	55.00	15.50
COMMON CARD (1-6)	25.00	11.00	3.10
☐ 1 Tom Seaver	25.00	11.00	3.10
Rookie Phenomenon			
☐ 2 Tom Seaver	25.00	11.00	3.10
Miracle Mets			
☐ 3 Tom Seaver	25.00	11.00	3.10
Strikeout Record			
☐ 4 Tom Seaver	25.00	11.00	3.10
No-Hitter			
☐ 5 Tom Seaver	25.00	11.00	3.10
300th Win			
☐ 6 Tom Seaver	25.00	11.00	3.10
Hall of Fame			
☐ AU1 Tom Seaver AU	75.00	34.00	9.50

1993 Pacific Ryan 27th Season

Pacific issued this 30-card set to honor Nolan Ryan being the first player in Major League Baseball history to appear in 27 seasons. The series was available in collector sets inside an attractive complete set box as well as in 25-cent five-card foil packs; the foil packs contained series I, series II, 27th Season series, and randomly inserted bonus cards. The cards measure the standard size and capture Ryan's 1992 highlights. The set features glossy color photos that are bordered in blue and red stripes. The 27th season logo appears in the lower left corner. In a flaming baseball design, the back presents career highlights. The cards are numbered on the back in continuation of the Texas Express first and second series. Beginning in mid-June,

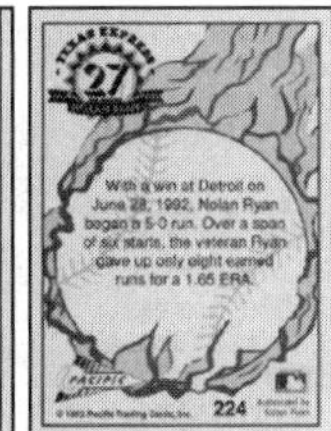

displays of Advil featuring Ryan and two-card packs appeared in stores nationwide. The two-card foil packs were available with the purchase of a bottle of 24 or more Advil Tablets or Caplets. On June 20, 1993, an offer to purchase the entire set was featured in Sunday newspapers. By mailing the Advil proof of purchase and $3.49 plus $1.50 for shipping to Pacific, the complete 30-card set could be obtained; the offer expired Dec. 31, 1993.

	MINT	NRMT	EXC
COMPLETE SET (30)	12.00	5.50	1.50
COMMON CARD (221-250)	.25	.11	.03
☐ 221 Nolan Ryan	.25	.11	.03
Ranger's Opening Night Pitcher			
☐ 222 Nolan Ryan	.25	.11	.03
Slow Start in 1992			
☐ 223 Nolan Ryan	.25	.11	.03
Still Productive			
☐ 224 Nolan Ryan	.25	.11	.03
Getting Hot			
☐ 225 Nolan Ryan	.25	.11	.03
Closing Strong in 1992			
☐ 226 Nolan Ryan	.25	.11	.03
No Decision			
☐ 227 Nolan Ryan	.25	.11	.03
No Run Support			
☐ 228 Nolan Ryan	.25	.11	.03
Two Complete Games			
☐ 229 Nolan Ryan	.25	.11	.03
8 2/3 Inning Shutout			
☐ 230 Nolan Ryan	.25	.11	.03
Multiple Strikeout Games			
☐ 231 Nolan Ryan	.25	.11	.03
Ejected			
☐ 232 Nolan Ryan	.25	.11	.03
319 And Counting			
☐ 233 Nolan Ryan	.25	.11	.03
Strikeout King			
☐ 234 Nolan Ryan	.25	.11	.03
24 of 26 Seasons			
☐ 235 Nolan Ryan	.25	.11	.03
Smile, Nolan			
☐ 236 Nolan Ryan	.25	.11	.03
Texas Ranger Marks			
☐ 237 Nolan Ryan	.25	.11	.03
Ranger Ace			
☐ 238 Nolan Ryan	.25	.11	.03
Another Record			
☐ 239 Nolan Ryan	.25	.11	.03
6th Place All-Time Career Innings Pitched			
☐ 240 Nolan Ryan	.25	.11	.03
27 Games Started in 1992			
☐ 241 Nolan Ryan	.75	.35	.09
Tom Seaver			
☐ 242 Nolan Ryan	.75	.35	.09
Rod Carew Angels' Number 30 Retired			
☐ 243 Nolan Ryan	.25	.11	.03
Angels' Nolan Ryan Night			
☐ 244 Nolan Ryan	.25	.11	.03
Angels' Hall of Fame			
☐ 245 Nolan Ryan	.50	.23	.06
Jimmie Reese Great Friends			
☐ 246 Nolan Ryan	.50	.23	.06
Gene Autry Cowboys			
☐ 247 Nolan Ryan	.25	.11	.03
Spring Training 1993			
☐ 248 Nolan Ryan	.25	.11	.03
Smokin' Fastball			
☐ 249 Nolan Ryan	.25	.11	.03
The Texas Express			
☐ 250 Nolan Ryan	.50	.23	.06
Tom Seaver Pacific Pride			
☐ NNO Pacific Trading Cards	.15	.07	.02
(Advertisement; Cover card)			

1993 Pacific Ryan Farewell McCormick

Given away to fans attending a Texas Rangers game at Arlington Stadium during Nolan Ryan Appreciation Week, this 21-card, standard-size set was produced by Pacific Trading Cards, Inc. for McCormick and Company. The fronts feature posed and action glossy photos of Ryan in various stages of his life and career. The pictures are bordered at the top and bottom in shades of coral red. His name is printed in silver vertically down the left edge of the card on a blue stripe. A logo for "1993 Nolan Ryan Farewell to a Legend" overlaps the corner of the border and the picture. The backs display Ryan's career statistics and milestones superimposed over a ghosted action shot of Ryan. The white-edged card backs have a McCormick logo in the upper left corner, a Brookshire's logo in the upper right corner, and the card number inside a flaming baseball design.

	MINT	NRMT	EXC
COMPLETE SET (21)	10.00	4.50	1.25
COMMON CARD (1-20)	.50	.23	.06
☐ 1 Nolan Ryan	.50	.23	.06
No-Hitter 1			
☐ 2 Nolan Ryan#[No-Hitter 2	.50	.23	.06
☐ 3 Nolan Ryan	.50	.23	.06
No-Hitter 3			
☐ 4 Nolan Ryan	.50	.23	.06
No-Hitter 4			
☐ 5 Nolan Ryan	.50	.23	.06
No-Hitter 5			
☐ 6 Nolan Ryan	.50	.23	.06
Last Pitch No-Hitter 6			
☐ 7 Nolan Ryan	.50	.23	.06
No-Hitter 7			
☐ 8 Nolan Ryan	.50	.23	.06
1st Strikeout			
☐ 9 Nolan Ryan	.50	.23	.06
1,000 Strikeout			
☐ 10 Nolan Ryan	.50	.23	.06
2,000 Strikeout			
☐ 11 Nolan Ryan	.50	.23	.06
3,000th Strikeout			
☐ 12 Nolan Ryan	.50	.23	.06
Breaks Walter Johnson's Record			
☐ 13 Nolan Ryan	.50	.23	.06
4,000 Strikeout			
☐ 14 Nolan Ryan	.50	.23	.06
5,000 Strikeout			
☐ 15 Nolan Ryan	.50	.23	.06
5,500 Strikeout			
☐ 16 Nolan Ryan	.50	.23	.06
First Major League Win			
☐ 17 Nolan Ryan	.50	.23	.06
250th Career Win			
☐ 18 Nolan Ryan	.50	.23	.06
300th Career Win			
☐ 19 Nolan Ryan	.50	.23	.06
Fastest Pitch Ever Thrown Clocked at 100.9 MPH			
☐ 20 Nolan Ryan	.50	.23	.06
A Lone Star Legend			
☐ NNO Title Card	.25	.11	.03
(Manufacturer's Coupon)			

1993 Pacific Ryan Limited

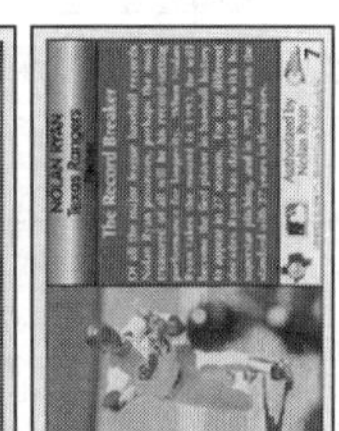

Six more cards (7-12), numbered in continuation of the 1992 set, were issued in 1993 and have a 1993 copyright notice on the card back. The card design was not significantly altered, and the backs contain the words "Limited Edition", as do the first six cards. The cards measure 2 1/2" by 3 1/2". Card numbers 7-12 were issued with gold foil borders, and the production run was 3,000 of each card. Gold foil versions of card Nos. 7-9 were given away only at the Bellevue (WA) Sports Collectors Classic IV each day of the show; card numbers 10-12 were randomly inserted in the 25-cent Changemaker packs. Although the cards are most commonly found with gold borders, white border cards have also been reported. The white border cards are valued at 20 percent of the prices below.

	MINT	NRMT	EXC
COMPLETE SET (6)	125.00	55.00	15.50
COMMON CARD (7-12)	25.00	11.00	3.10
☐ 7 Nolan Ryan	25.00	11.00	3.10
The Record Breaker Limited edition on back			
☐ 8 Nolan Ryan	25.00	11.00	3.10
Strikeout Leader Limited edition on back			
☐ 9 Nolan Ryan	25.00	11.00	3.10
Seven No-Hit Games Limited edition on back			
☐ 10 Nolan Ryan	25.00	11.00	3.10
Baseball Legend Limited edition on back			
☐ 11 Nolan Ryan	25.00	11.00	3.10
Favorite Son Limited edition on back			
☐ 12 Nolan Ryan	25.00	11.00	3.10
Hometown Charm Limited edition on back			

1993 Pacific Ryan Prism Inserts

This 20-card prism set was issued by Pacific to honor the career of Nolan Ryan. The cards were randomly inserted into 1993 Nolan Ryan 25-cent Changemaker five-card packs. The production figures were reportedly 10,000 of each card. The cards measure the standard size and feature a cut-out photo of Nolan Ryan against a prism background. His name appears at the bottom in red letters outlined in white and blue. The horizontal backs show a cut-out photo of Ryan against either a variegated blue or red panel that is bordered by a team color-coded design. Included on the panel are career highlights that correspond to the year the photo was taken. A white outer border rounds out the card back. Gold and silver versions of these sets are known as well. There is not currently enough market information to price these cards.

	MINT	NRMT	EXC
COMPLETE SET (20)	100.00	45.00	12.50
COMMON CARD (1-20)	7.50	3.40	.95
☐ 1 Nolan Ryan	7.50	3.40	.95
Mets - 1965			
☐ 2 Nolan Ryan	7.50	3.40	.95
Mets - 1969			
☐ 3 Nolan Ryan	7.50	3.40	.95
Mets - 1973 1st No-Hitter			
☐ 4 Nolan Ryan	7.50	3.40	.95
Angels - 1973 1st No-Hitter			
☐ 5 Nolan Ryan	7.50	3.40	.95
Angels - 1973			
☐ 6 Nolan Ryan	7.50	3.40	.95
Astros - 1979			
☐ 7 Nolan Ryan	7.50	3.40	.95
Astros - 1981			
☐ 8 Nolan Ryan	7.50	3.40	.95
Astros - 1983			
☐ 9 Nolan Ryan	7.50	3.40	.95
Rangers - 1988			
☐ 10 Nolan Ryan	7.50	3.40	.95
Rangers - 1989 5,000 Strike Outs			
☐ 11 Nolan Ryan	7.50	3.40	.95
Rangers - 1989			
☐ 12 Nolan Ryan	7.50	3.40	.95
Rangers - 1990			
☐ 13 Nolan Ryan	7.50	3.40	.95
Rangers - 1990 6th No-Hitter			
☐ 14 Nolan Ryan	7.50	3.40	.95
Rangers - 1990 300th Win			
☐ 15 Nolan Ryan	7.50	3.40	.95
Rangers - 1991			
☐ 16 Nolan Ryan	7.50	3.40	.95
Rangers - 1991			
☐ 17 Nolan Ryan	7.50	3.40	.95
Rangers - 1991 7th No-Hitter			
☐ 18 Nolan Ryan	7.50	3.40	.95
Rangers - 1992			
☐ 19 Nolan Ryan	7.50	3.40	.95
Rangers - 1992			
☐ 20 Nolan Ryan	7.50	3.40	.95
Rangers - 1993			

1993 Pacific Spanish

Issued in two 330-card series, these 660 standard-size cards represent Pacific's first effort at a nationally distributed, MLB-licensed card set. The fronts display glossy color action photos bordered in white. Two team color-coded stripes, carrying the player's name and position, edge the pictures on the left and bottom respectively, and the team logo appears on a home plate icon at their intersection in the lower left corner. On gradated panels framed by different color edges, the horizontal backs show a color close-up photo, biography, statistics, and brief player profile. All text on both sides is in Spanish. The cards are numbered on the back, grouped alphabetically within teams, and checklisted below alphabetically according to teams in both series. Each series card numbering is alphabetical by players within teams with the teams themselves in order by team nickname. Very early in the printing, Rob Maurer (#313) was printed with, very obviously, someone else's photo on the card. This very tough card is rarely seen in the hobby and since it is so thinly traded there is no established market value. On the Third Annual Latin Night at Yankee Stadium (July 22, 1993; New York Yankees versus California Angels), four-card foil packs, featuring a title card and three player cards, were given away.

	MINT	NRMT	EXC
COMPLETE SET (660)	40.00	18.00	5.00
COMPLETE SERIES 1 (330)	25.00	11.00	3.10
COMPLETE SERIES 2 (330)	17.50	8.00	2.20
COMMON CARD (1-660)	.05	.02	.01
□ 1 Rafael Belliard	.05	.02	.01
□ 2 Sid Bream	.05	.02	.01
□ 3 Francisco Cabrera	.05	.02	.01
□ 4 Marvin Freeman	.05	.02	.01
□ 5 Ron Gant	.10	.05	.01
□ 6 Tom Glavine	.20	.09	.03
□ 7 Brian Hunter	.05	.02	.01
□ 8 David Justice	.30	.14	.04
□ 9 Ryan Klesko	.50	.23	.06
□ 10 Melvin Nieves	.20	.09	.03
□ 11 Deion Sanders	.50	.23	.06
□ 12 John Smoltz	.50	.23	.06
□ 13 Mark Wohlers	.10	.05	.01
□ 14 Brady Anderson	.20	.09	.03
□ 15 Glenn Davis	.05	.02	.01
□ 16 Mike Devereaux	.05	.02	.01
□ 17 Leo Gomez	.05	.02	.01
□ 18 Chris Hoiles	.10	.05	.01
□ 19 Chito Martinez	.05	.02	.01
□ 20 Ben McDonald	.10	.05	.01
□ 21 Mike Mussina	.50	.23	.06
□ 22 Gregg Olson	.05	.02	.01
□ 23 Joe Orsulak	.05	.02	.01
□ 24 Cal Ripken	2.50	1.10	.30
□ 25 David Segui	.05	.02	.01
□ 26 Rick Sutcliffe	.05	.02	.01
□ 27 Wade Boggs	.40	.18	.05
□ 28 Tom Brunansky	.05	.02	.01
□ 29 Ellis Burks	.10	.05	.01
□ 30 Roger Clemens	.50	.23	.06
□ 31 John Dopson	.05	.02	.01
□ 32 John Flaherty	.05	.02	.01
□ 33 Mike Greenwell	.05	.02	.01
□ 34 Tony Pena	.05	.02	.01
□ 35 Carlos Quintana	.05	.02	.01
□ 36 Luis Rivera	.05	.02	.01
□ 37 Mo Vaughn	.75	.35	.09
□ 38 Frank Viola	.10	.05	.01
□ 39 Matt Young	.05	.02	.01
□ 40 Scott Bailes	.05	.02	.01
□ 41 Bert Blyleven	.10	.05	.01
□ 42 Chad Curtis	.05	.02	.01
□ 43 Gary DiSarcina	.05	.02	.01
□ 44 Chuck Finley	.05	.02	.01
□ 45 Mike Fitzgerald	.05	.02	.01
□ 46 Gary Gaetti	.05	.02	.01
□ 47 Rene Gonzales	.05	.02	.01
□ 48 Mark Langston	.05	.02	.01
□ 49 Scott Lewis	.05	.02	.01
□ 50 Luis Polonia	.05	.02	.01
□ 51 Tim Salmon	.75	.35	.09
□ 52 Lee Stevens	.05	.02	.01
□ 53 Steve Buechele	.05	.02	.01
□ 54 Frank Castillo	.05	.02	.01
□ 55 Doug Dascenzo	.05	.02	.01
□ 56 Andre Dawson	.10	.05	.01
□ 57 Shawon Dunston	.05	.02	.01
□ 58 Mark Grace	.35	.16	.04
□ 59 Mike Morgan	.05	.02	.01
□ 60 Luis Salazar	.05	.02	.01
□ 61 Rey Sanchez	.05	.02	.01
□ 62 Ryne Sandberg	.75	.35	.09
□ 63 Dwight Smith	.05	.02	.01
□ 64 Jerome Walton	.05	.02	.01
□ 65 Rick Wilkins	.05	.02	.01
□ 66 Wilson Alvarez	.10	.05	.01
□ 67 George Bell	.05	.02	.01
□ 68 Joey Cora	.10	.05	.01
□ 69 Alex Fernandez	.10	.05	.01
□ 70 Carlton Fisk	.20	.09	.03
□ 71 Craig Grebeck	.05	.02	.01
□ 72 Ozzie Guillen	.05	.02	.01
□ 73 Jack McDowell	.20	.09	.03
□ 74 Scott Radinsky	.05	.02	.01
□ 75 Tim Raines	.10	.05	.01
□ 76 Bobby Thigpen	.05	.02	.01
□ 77 Frank Thomas	3.00	1.35	.35
□ 78 Robin Ventura	.10	.05	.01
□ 79 Tom Browning	.05	.02	.01
□ 80 Jacob Brumfield	.05	.02	.01
□ 81 Rob Dibble	.05	.02	.01
□ 82 Bill Doran	.05	.02	.01
□ 83 Billy Hatcher	.05	.02	.01
□ 84 Barry Larkin	.35	.16	.04
□ 85 Hal Morris	.10	.05	.01
□ 86 Joe Oliver	.05	.02	.01
□ 87 Jeff Reed	.05	.02	.01
□ 88 Jose Rijo	.05	.02	.01
□ 89 Bip Roberts	.05	.02	.01
□ 90 Chris Sabo	.05	.02	.01
□ 91 Sandy Alomar Jr.	.10	.05	.01
□ 92 Brad Arnsberg	.05	.02	.01
□ 93 Carlos Baerga	.40	.18	.05
□ 94 Albert Belle	1.50	.70	.19
□ 95 Felix Fermin	.05	.02	.01
□ 96 Mark Lewis	.05	.02	.01
□ 97 Kenny Lofton	1.25	.55	.16
□ 98 Carlos Martinez	.05	.02	.01
□ 99 Rod Nichols	.05	.02	.01
□ 100 Dave Rohde	.05	.02	.01
□ 101 Scott Scudder	.05	.02	.01
□ 102 Paul Sorrento	.05	.02	.01
□ 103 Mark Whiten	.05	.02	.01
□ 104 Mark Carreon	.05	.02	.01
□ 105 Milt Cuyler	.05	.02	.01
□ 106 Rob Deer	.05	.02	.01
□ 107 Cecil Fielder	.10	.05	.01
□ 108 Travis Fryman	.10	.05	.01
□ 109 Dan Gladden	.05	.02	.01
□ 110 Bill Gullickson	.05	.02	.01
□ 111 Les Lancaster	.05	.02	.01
□ 112 Mark Leiter	.05	.02	.01
□ 113 Tony Phillips	.10	.05	.01
□ 114 Mickey Tettleton	.05	.02	.01
□ 115 Alan Trammell	.10	.05	.01
□ 116 Lou Whitaker	.10	.05	.01
□ 117 Jeff Bagwell	1.50	.70	.19
□ 118 Craig Biggio	.10	.05	.01
□ 119 Joe Boever	.05	.02	.01
□ 120 Casey Candaele	.05	.02	.01
□ 121 Andujar Cedeno	.05	.02	.01
□ 122 Steve Finley	.10	.05	.01
□ 123 Luis Gonzalez	.05	.02	.01
□ 124 Pete Harnisch	.05	.02	.01
□ 125 Jimmy Jones	.05	.02	.01
□ 126 Mark Portugal	.05	.02	.01
□ 127 Rafael Ramirez	.05	.02	.01
□ 128 Mike Simms	.05	.02	.01
□ 129 Eric Yelding	.05	.02	.01
□ 130 Luis Aquino	.05	.02	.01
□ 131 Kevin Appier	.10	.05	.01
□ 132 Mike Boddicker	.05	.02	.01
□ 133 George Brett	1.25	.55	.16
□ 134 Tom Gordon	.05	.02	.01
□ 135 Mark Gubicza	.05	.02	.01
□ 136 David Howard	.05	.02	.01
□ 137 Gregg Jefferies	.10	.05	.01
□ 138 Wally Joyner	.10	.05	.01
□ 139 Brian McRae	.10	.05	.01
□ 140 Jeff Montgomery	.05	.02	.01
□ 141 Terry Shumpert	.05	.02	.01
□ 142 Curtis Wilkerson	.05	.02	.01
□ 143 Brett Butler	.10	.05	.01
□ 144 Eric Davis	.10	.05	.01
□ 145 Kevin Gross	.05	.02	.01
□ 146 Dave Hansen	.05	.02	.01
□ 147 Lenny Harris	.05	.02	.01
□ 148 Carlos Hernandez	.05	.02	.01
□ 149 Orel Hershiser	.10	.05	.01
□ 150 Jay Howell	.05	.02	.01
□ 151 Eric Karros	.20	.09	.03
□ 152 Ramon Martinez	.10	.05	.01
□ 153 Jose Offerman	.05	.02	.01
□ 154 Mike Sharperson	.05	.02	.01
□ 155 Darryl Strawberry	.10	.05	.01
□ 156 Jim Gantner	.05	.02	.01
□ 157 Darryl Hamilton	.05	.02	.01
□ 158 Doug Henry	.05	.02	.01
□ 159 John Jaha	.20	.09	.03
□ 160 Pat Listach	.05	.02	.01
□ 161 Jaime Navarro	.05	.02	.01
□ 162 Dave Nilsson	.10	.05	.01
□ 163 Jesse Orosco	.05	.02	.01
□ 164 Kevin Seitzer	.05	.02	.01
□ 165 B.J. Surhoff	.10	.05	.01
□ 166 Greg Vaughn	.10	.05	.01
□ 167 Robin Yount	.40	.18	.05
□ 168 Rick Aguilera	.05	.02	.01
□ 169 Scott Erickson	.05	.02	.01
□ 170 Mark Guthrie	.05	.02	.01
□ 171 Kent Hrbek	.10	.05	.01
□ 172 Chuck Knoblauch	.50	.23	.06
□ 173 Gene Larkin	.05	.02	.01
□ 174 Shane Mack	.05	.02	.01
□ 175 Pedro Munoz	.05	.02	.01
□ 176 Mike Pagliarulo	.05	.02	.01
□ 177 Kirby Puckett	1.50	.70	.19
□ 178 Kevin Tapani	.05	.02	.01
□ 179 Gary Wayne	.05	.02	.01
□ 180 Moises Alou	.10	.05	.01
□ 181 Brian Barnes	.05	.02	.01
□ 182 Archi Cianfrocco	.05	.02	.01
□ 183 Delino DeShields	.05	.02	.01
□ 184 Darrin Fletcher	.05	.02	.01
□ 185 Marquis Grissom	.10	.05	.01
□ 186 Ken Hill	.10	.05	.01
□ 187 Dennis Martinez	.10	.05	.01
□ 188 Bill Sampen	.05	.02	.01
□ 189 John Vander Wal	.05	.02	.01
□ 190 Larry Walker	.30	.14	.04
□ 191 Tim Wallach	.05	.02	.01
□ 192 Bobby Bonilla	.10	.05	.01
□ 193 Daryl Boston	.05	.02	.01
□ 194 Vince Coleman	.05	.02	.01
□ 195 Kevin Elster	.05	.02	.01
□ 196 Sid Fernandez	.05	.02	.01
□ 197 John Franco	.10	.05	.01
□ 198 Dwight Gooden	.10	.05	.01
□ 199 Howard Johnson	.05	.02	.01
□ 200 Willie Randolph	.05	.02	.01
□ 201 Bret Saberhagen	.10	.05	.01
□ 202 Dick Schofield	.05	.02	.01
□ 203 Pete Schourek	.05	.02	.01
□ 204 Greg Cadaret	.05	.02	.01
□ 205 John Habyan	.05	.02	.01
□ 206 Pat Kelly	.05	.02	.01
□ 207 Kevin Maas	.05	.02	.01
□ 208 Don Mattingly	1.50	.70	.19
□ 209 Matt Nokes	.05	.02	.01
□ 210 Melido Perez	.05	.02	.01
□ 211 Scott Sanderson	.05	.02	.01
□ 212 Andy Stankiewicz	.05	.02	.01
□ 213 Danny Tartabull	.05	.02	.01
□ 214 Randy Velarde	.05	.02	.01
□ 215 Bernie Williams	.60	.25	.07
□ 216 Harold Baines	.10	.05	.01
□ 217 Mike Bordick	.05	.02	.01
□ 218 Scott Brosius	.05	.02	.01
□ 219 Jerry Browne	.05	.02	.01
□ 220 Ron Darling	.05	.02	.01
□ 221 Dennis Eckersley	.10	.05	.01
□ 222 Rickey Henderson	.20	.09	.03
□ 223 Rick Honeycutt	.05	.02	.01
□ 224 Mark McGwire	1.00	.45	.12
□ 225 Ruben Sierra	.05	.02	.01
□ 226 Terry Steinbach	.10	.05	.01
□ 227 Bob Welch	.05	.02	.01
□ 228 Willie Wilson	.05	.02	.01
□ 229 Ruben Amaro	.05	.02	.01
□ 230 Kim Batiste	.05	.02	.01
□ 231 Juan Bell	.05	.02	.01
□ 232 Wes Chamberlain	.05	.02	.01
□ 233 Darren Daulton	.10	.05	.01
□ 234 Mariano Duncan	.05	.02	.01
□ 235 Lenny Dykstra	.10	.05	.01
□ 236 Dave Hollins	.05	.02	.01
□ 237 Stan Javier	.05	.02	.01
□ 238 John Kruk	.10	.05	.01
□ 239 Mickey Morandini	.05	.02	.01
□ 240 Terry Mulholland	.05	.02	.01
□ 241 Mitch Williams	.05	.02	.01
□ 242 Stan Belinda	.05	.02	.01
□ 243 Jay Bell	.10	.05	.01
□ 244 Carlos Garcia	.05	.02	.01
□ 245 Jeff King	.05	.02	.01
□ 246 Mike LaValliere	.05	.02	.01
□ 247 Lloyd McClendon	.05	.02	.01
□ 248 Orlando Merced	.05	.02	.01
□ 249 Paul Miller	.05	.02	.01
□ 250 Gary Redus	.05	.02	.01
□ 251 Don Slaught	.05	.02	.01
□ 252 Zane Smith	.05	.02	.01
□ 253 Andy Van Slyke	.05	.02	.01
□ 254 Tim Wakefield	.05	.02	.01
□ 255 Andy Benes	.10	.05	.01
□ 256 Dann Bilardello	.05	.02	.01
□ 257 Tony Gwynn	1.25	.55	.16
□ 258 Greg W. Harris	.05	.02	.01
□ 259 Darrin Jackson	.05	.02	.01
□ 260 Mike Maddux	.05	.02	.01
□ 261 Fred McGriff	.50	.23	.06
□ 262 Rich Rodriguez	.05	.02	.01
□ 263 Benito Santiago	.10	.05	.01
□ 264 Gary Sheffield	.50	.23	.06
□ 265 Kurt Stillwell	.05	.02	.01
□ 266 Tim Teufel	.05	.02	.01
□ 267 Bud Black	.05	.02	.01
□ 268 John Burkett	.10	.05	.01
□ 269 Will Clark	.40	.18	.05
□ 270 Royce Clayton	.10	.05	.01
□ 271 Bryan Hickerson	.05	.02	.01
□ 272 Chris James	.05	.02	.01
□ 273 Darren Lewis	.05	.02	.01
□ 274 Willie McGee	.10	.05	.01
□ 275 Jim McNamara	.05	.02	.01
□ 276 Francisco Oliveras	.05	.02	.01
□ 277 Robby Thompson	.05	.02	.01
□ 278 Matt Williams	.50	.23	.06
□ 279 Trevor Wilson	.05	.02	.01
□ 280 Bret Boone	.10	.05	.01
□ 281 Greg Briley	.05	.02	.01
□ 282 Jay Buhner	.20	.09	.03
□ 283 Henry Cotto	.05	.02	.01
□ 284 Rich DeLucia	.05	.02	.01
□ 285 Dave Fleming	.05	.02	.01
□ 286 Ken Griffey Jr.	3.00	1.35	.35
□ 287 Erik Hanson	.05	.02	.01
□ 288 Randy Johnson	.40	.18	.05
□ 289 Tino Martinez	.10	.05	.01
□ 290 Edgar Martinez	.10	.05	.01
□ 291 Dave Valle	.05	.02	.01
□ 292 Omar Vizquel	.10	.05	.01
□ 293 Luis Alicea	.05	.02	.01
□ 294 Bernard Gilkey	.10	.05	.01
□ 295 Felix Jose	.05	.02	.01
□ 296 Ray Lankford	.10	.05	.01
□ 297 Omar Olivares	.05	.02	.01
□ 298 Jose Oquendo	.05	.02	.01
□ 299 Tom Pagnozzi	.05	.02	.01
□ 300 Geronimo Pena	.05	.02	.01
□ 301 Gerald Perry	.05	.02	.01
□ 302 Ozzie Smith	.75	.35	.09
□ 303 Lee Smith	.10	.05	.01
□ 304 Bob Tewksbury	.05	.02	.01
□ 305 Todd Zeile	.05	.02	.01
□ 306 Kevin Brown	.10	.05	.01
□ 307 Todd Burns	.05	.02	.01
□ 308 Jose Canseco	.30	.14	.04
□ 309 Hector Fajardo	.05	.02	.01
□ 310 Julio Franco	.10	.05	.01
□ 311 Juan Gonzalez	1.50	.70	.19
□ 312 Jeff Huson	.05	.02	.01
□ 313 Rob Maurer	.05	.02	.01
□ 314 Rafael Palmeiro	.20	.09	.03
□ 315 Dean Palmer	.10	.05	.01
□ 316 Ivan Rodriguez	1.25	.55	.16
□ 317 Nolan Ryan	2.50	1.10	.30
□ 318 Dickie Thon	.05	.02	.01
□ 319 Roberto Alomar	.50	.23	.06
□ 320 Derek Bell	.10	.05	.01
□ 321 Pat Borders	.05	.02	.01
□ 322 Joe Carter	.10	.05	.01
□ 323 Kelly Gruber	.05	.02	.01
□ 324 Juan Guzman	.10	.05	.01
□ 325 Manny Lee	.05	.02	.01
□ 326 Jack Morris	.10	.05	.01
□ 327 John Olerud	.10	.05	.01
□ 328 Ed Sprague	.10	.05	.01
□ 329 Todd Stottlemyre	.10	.05	.01
□ 330 Duane Ward	.05	.02	.01
□ 331 Steve Avery	.10	.05	.01
□ 332 Damon Berryhill	.05	.02	.01
□ 333 Jeff Blauser	.05	.02	.01
□ 334 Mark Lemke	.05	.02	.01
□ 335 Greg Maddux	1.75	.80	.22
□ 336 Kent Mercker	.05	.02	.01
□ 337 Otis Nixon	.10	.05	.01
□ 338 Greg Olson	.05	.02	.01
□ 339 Bill Pecota	.05	.02	.01
□ 340 Terry Pendleton	.10	.05	.01
□ 341 Mike Stanton	.05	.02	.01
□ 342 Todd Frohwirth	.05	.02	.01
□ 343 Tim Hulett	.05	.02	.01
□ 344 Mark McLemore	.05	.02	.01
□ 345 Luis Mercedes	.05	.02	.01
□ 346 Alan Mills	.05	.02	.01
□ 347 Sherman Obando	.05	.02	.01
□ 348 Jim Poole	.05	.02	.01
□ 349 Harold Reynolds	.10	.05	.01
□ 350 Arthur Rhodes	.05	.02	.01
□ 351 Jeff Tackett	.05	.02	.01
□ 352 Fernando Valenzuela	.10	.05	.01
□ 353 Scott Bankhead	.05	.02	.01
□ 354 Ivan Calderon	.05	.02	.01
□ 355 Scott Cooper	.05	.02	.01
□ 356 Danny Darwin	.05	.02	.01
□ 357 Scott Fletcher	.05	.02	.01
□ 358 Tony Fossas	.05	.02	.01
□ 359 Greg A. Harris	.05	.02	.01
□ 360 Joe Hesketh	.05	.02	.01
□ 361 Jose Melendez	.05	.02	.01
□ 362 Paul Quantrill	.05	.02	.01
□ 363 John Valentin	.10	.05	.01
□ 364 Mike Butcher	.05	.02	.01
□ 365 Chuck Crim	.05	.02	.01
□ 366 Chili Davis	.10	.05	.01
□ 367 Damion Easley	.05	.02	.01
□ 368 Steve Frey	.05	.02	.01
□ 369 Joe Grahe	.05	.02	.01
□ 370 Greg Myers	.05	.02	.01
□ 371 John Orton	.05	.02	.01
□ 372 J.T. Snow	.25	.11	.03
□ 373 Ron Tingley	.05	.02	.01
□ 374 Julio Valera	.05	.02	.01
□ 375 Paul Assenmacher	.05	.02	.01
□ 376 Jose Bautista	.05	.02	.01
□ 377 Jose Guzman	.05	.02	.01
□ 378 Greg Hibbard	.05	.02	.01
□ 379 Candy Maldonado	.05	.02	.01
□ 380 Derrick May	.05	.02	.01
□ 381 Dan Plesac	.05	.02	.01
□ 382 Tommy Shields	.05	.02	.01
□ 383 Sammy Sosa	.75	.35	.09
□ 384 Jose Vizcaino	.05	.02	.01
□ 385 Matt Walbeck	.05	.02	.01
□ 386 Ellis Burks	.10	.05	.01
□ 387 Roberto Hernandez	.05	.02	.01
□ 388 Mike Huff	.05	.02	.01
□ 389 Bo Jackson	.10	.05	.01
□ 390 Lance Johnson	.10	.05	.01
□ 391 Ron Karkovice	.05	.02	.01
□ 392 Kirk McCaskill	.05	.02	.01
□ 393 Donn Pall	.05	.02	.01
□ 394 Dan Pasqua	.05	.02	.01
□ 395 Steve Sax	.05	.02	.01
□ 396 Dave Stieb	.05	.02	.01
□ 397 Bobby Ayala	.05	.02	.01
□ 398 Tim Belcher	.05	.02	.01
□ 399 Jeff Branson	.05	.02	.01
□ 400 Cesar Hernandez	.05	.02	.01
□ 401 Roberto Kelly	.05	.02	.01
□ 402 Randy Milligan	.05	.02	.01

☐ 403 Kevin Mitchell	.10	.05	.01
☐ 404 Juan Samuel	.05	.02	.01
☐ 405 Reggie Sanders	.20	.09	.03
☐ 406 John Smiley	.05	.02	.01
☐ 407 Dan Wilson	.20	.09	.03
☐ 408 Mike Christopher	.05	.02	.01
☐ 409 Dennis Cook	.05	.02	.01
☐ 410 Alvaro Espinoza	.05	.02	.01
☐ 411 Glenallen Hill	.05	.02	.01
☐ 412 Reggie Jefferson	.10	.05	.01
☐ 413 Derek Lilliquist	.05	.02	.01
☐ 414 Jose Mesa	.05	.02	.01
☐ 415 Charles Nagy	.10	.05	.01
☐ 416 Junior Ortiz	.05	.02	.01
☐ 417 Eric Plunk	.05	.02	.01
☐ 418 Ted Power	.05	.02	.01
☐ 419 Scott Aldred	.05	.02	.01
☐ 420 Andy Ashby	.05	.02	.01
☐ 421 Freddie Benavides	.05	.02	.01
☐ 422 Dante Bichette	.50	.23	.06
☐ 423 Willie Blair	.05	.02	.01
☐ 424 Vinny Castilla	.20	.09	.03
☐ 425 Jerald Clark	.05	.02	.01
☐ 426 Alex Cole	.05	.02	.01
☐ 427 Andres Galarraga	.20	.09	.03
☐ 428 Joe Girardi	.05	.02	.01
☐ 429 Charlie Hayes	.05	.02	.01
☐ 430 Butch Henry	.05	.02	.01
☐ 431 Darren Holmes	.05	.02	.01
☐ 432 Dale Murphy	.20	.09	.03
☐ 433 David Nied	.05	.02	.01
☐ 434 Jeff Parrett	.05	.02	.01
☐ 435 Steve Reed	.05	.02	.01
☐ 436 Armando Reynoso	.05	.02	.01
☐ 437 Bruce Ruffin	.05	.02	.01
☐ 438 Bryn Smith	.05	.02	.01
☐ 439 Jim Tatum	.05	.02	.01
☐ 440 Eric Young	.20	.09	.03
☐ 441 Skeeter Barnes	.05	.02	.01
☐ 442 Tom Bolton	.05	.02	.01
☐ 443 Kirk Gibson	.10	.05	.01
☐ 444 Chad Kreuter	.05	.02	.01
☐ 445 Bill Krueger	.05	.02	.01
☐ 446 Scott Livingstone	.05	.02	.01
☐ 447 Bob MacDonald	.05	.02	.01
☐ 448 Mike Moore	.05	.02	.01
☐ 449 Mike Munoz	.05	.02	.01
☐ 450 Gary Thurman	.05	.02	.01
☐ 451 David Wells	.05	.02	.01
☐ 452 Alex Arias	.05	.02	.01
☐ 453 Jack Armstrong	.05	.02	.01
☐ 454 Bret Barberie	.05	.02	.01
☐ 455 Ryan Bowen	.05	.02	.01
☐ 456 Cris Carpenter	.05	.02	.01
☐ 457 Chuck Carr	.05	.02	.01
☐ 458 Jeff Conine	.10	.05	.01
☐ 459 Steve Decker	.05	.02	.01
☐ 460 Orestes Destrade	.05	.02	.01
☐ 461 Monty Fariss	.05	.02	.01
☐ 462 Junior Felix	.05	.02	.01
☐ 463 Bryan Harvey	.05	.02	.01
☐ 464 Trevor Hoffman	.20	.09	.03
☐ 465 Charlie Hough	.05	.02	.01
☐ 466 Dave Magadan	.05	.02	.01
☐ 467 Bob McClure	.05	.02	.01
☐ 468 Rob Natal	.05	.02	.01
☐ 469 Scott Pose	.05	.02	.01
☐ 470 Rich Renteria	.05	.02	.01
☐ 471 Benito Santiago	.10	.05	.01
☐ 472 Matt Turner	.05	.02	.01
☐ 473 Walt Weiss	.05	.02	.01
☐ 474 Eric Anthony	.05	.02	.01
☐ 475 Chris Donnels	.05	.02	.01
☐ 476 Doug Drabek	.10	.05	.01
☐ 477 Xavier Hernandez	.05	.02	.01
☐ 478 Doug Jones	.05	.02	.01
☐ 479 Darryl Kile	.05	.02	.01
☐ 480 Scott Servais	.05	.02	.01
☐ 481 Greg Swindell	.05	.02	.01
☐ 482 Eddie Taubensee	.05	.02	.01
☐ 483 Jose Uribe	.05	.02	.01
☐ 484 Brian Williams	.05	.02	.01
☐ 485 Billy Brewer	.05	.02	.01
☐ 486 David Cone	.10	.05	.01
☐ 487 Greg Gagne	.05	.02	.01
☐ 488 Phil Hiatt	.05	.02	.01
☐ 489 Jose Lind	.05	.02	.01
☐ 490 Brent Mayne	.05	.02	.01
☐ 491 Kevin McReynolds	.05	.02	.01
☐ 492 Keith Miller	.05	.02	.01
☐ 493 Hipolito Pichardo	.05	.02	.01
☐ 494 Harvey Pulliam	.05	.02	.01
☐ 495 Rico Rossy	.05	.02	.01
☐ 496 Pedro Astacio	.10	.05	.01
☐ 497 Tom Candiotti	.05	.02	.01
☐ 498 Tom Goodwin	.05	.02	.01
☐ 499 Jim Gott	.05	.02	.01
☐ 500 Pedro Martinez	.20	.09	.03
☐ 501 Roger McDowell	.05	.02	.01
☐ 502 Mike Piazza	4.00	1.80	.50
☐ 503 Jody Reed	.05	.02	.01
☐ 504 Rick Trlicek	.05	.02	.01
☐ 505 Mitch Webster	.05	.02	.01
☐ 506 Steve Wilson	.05	.02	.01
☐ 507 James Austin	.05	.02	.01
☐ 508 Ricky Bones	.05	.02	.01
☐ 509 Alex Diaz	.05	.02	.01
☐ 510 Mike Fetters	.05	.02	.01
☐ 511 Teddy Higuera	.05	.02	.01
☐ 512 Graeme Lloyd	.05	.02	.01
☐ 513 Carlos Maldonado	.05	.02	.01
☐ 514 Josias Manzanillo	.05	.02	.01
☐ 515 Kevin Reimer	.05	.02	.01
☐ 516 Bill Spiers	.05	.02	.01
☐ 517 Bill Wegman	.05	.02	.01
☐ 518 Willie Banks	.05	.02	.01
☐ 519 J.T. Bruett	.05	.02	.01
☐ 520 Brian Harper	.05	.02	.01
☐ 521 Terry Jorgensen	.05	.02	.01
☐ 522 Scott Leius	.05	.02	.01
☐ 523 Pat Mahomes	.05	.02	.01
☐ 524 Dave McCarty	.05	.02	.01
☐ 525 Jeff Reboulet	.05	.02	.01
☐ 526 Mike Trombley	.05	.02	.01
☐ 527 Carl Willis	.05	.02	.01
☐ 528 Dave Winfield	.30	.14	.04
☐ 529 Sean Berry	.05	.02	.01
☐ 530 Frank Bolick	.05	.02	.01
☐ 531 Kent Bottenfield	.05	.02	.01
☐ 532 Wilfredo Cordero	.10	.05	.01
☐ 533 Jeff Fassero	.10	.05	.01
☐ 534 Tim Laker	.05	.02	.01
☐ 535 Mike Lansing	.20	.09	.03
☐ 536 Chris Nabholz	.05	.02	.01
☐ 537 Mel Rojas	.05	.02	.01
☐ 538 John Wetteland	.10	.05	.01
☐ 539 Ted Wood	.05	.02	.01
☐ 540 Mike Draper	.05	.02	.01
☐ 541 Tony Fernandez	.05	.02	.01
☐ 542 Todd Hundley	.20	.09	.03
☐ 543 Jeff Innis	.05	.02	.01
☐ 544 Jeff McKnight	.05	.02	.01
☐ 545 Eddie Murray	1.25	.55	.16
☐ 546 Charlie O'Brien	.05	.02	.01
☐ 547 Frank Tanana	.05	.02	.01
☐ 548 Ryan Thompson	.05	.02	.01
☐ 549 Chico Walker	.05	.02	.01
☐ 550 Anthony Young	.05	.02	.01
☐ 551 Jim Abbott	.10	.05	.01
☐ 552 Wade Boggs	.50	.23	.06
☐ 553 Steve Farr	.05	.02	.01
☐ 554 Neal Heaton	.05	.02	.01
☐ 555 Steve Howe	.05	.02	.01
☐ 556 Dion James	.05	.02	.01
☐ 557 Scott Kamieniecki	.05	.02	.01
☐ 558 Jimmy Key	.10	.05	.01
☐ 559 Jim Leyritz	.05	.02	.01
☐ 560 Paul O'Neill	.10	.05	.01
☐ 561 Spike Owen	.05	.02	.01
☐ 562 Lance Blankenship	.05	.02	.01
☐ 563 Joe Boever	.05	.02	.01
☐ 564 Storm Davis	.05	.02	.01
☐ 565 Kelly Downs	.05	.02	.01
☐ 566 Eric Fox	.05	.02	.01
☐ 567 Rich Gossage	.20	.09	.03
☐ 568 Dave Henderson	.05	.02	.01
☐ 569 Shawn Hillegas	.05	.02	.01
☐ 570 Mike Mohler	.05	.02	.01
☐ 571 Troy Neel	.05	.02	.01
☐ 572 Dale Sveum	.05	.02	.01
☐ 573 Larry Andersen	.05	.02	.01
☐ 574 Bob Ayrault	.05	.02	.01
☐ 575 Jose DeLeon	.05	.02	.01
☐ 576 Jim Eisenreich	.10	.05	.01
☐ 577 Pete Incaviglia	.05	.02	.01
☐ 578 Danny Jackson	.05	.02	.01
☐ 579 Ricky Jordan	.05	.02	.01
☐ 580 Ben Rivera	.05	.02	.01
☐ 581 Curt Schilling	.05	.02	.01
☐ 582 Milt Thompson	.05	.02	.01
☐ 583 David West	.05	.02	.01
☐ 584 John Candelaria	.05	.02	.01
☐ 585 Steve Cooke	.05	.02	.01
☐ 586 Tom Foley	.05	.02	.01
☐ 587 Al Martin	.05	.02	.01
☐ 588 Blas Minor	.05	.02	.01
☐ 589 Dennis Moeller	.05	.02	.01
☐ 590 Denny Neagle	.10	.05	.01
☐ 591 Tom Prince	.05	.02	.01
☐ 592 Randy Tomlin	.05	.02	.01
☐ 593 Bob Walk	.05	.02	.01
☐ 594 Kevin Young	.05	.02	.01
☐ 595 Pat Gomez	.05	.02	.01
☐ 596 Ricky Gutierrez	.05	.02	.01
☐ 597 Gene Harris	.05	.02	.01
☐ 598 Jeremy Hernandez	.05	.02	.01
☐ 599 Phil Plantier	.05	.02	.01
☐ 600 Tim Scott	.05	.02	.01
☐ 601 Frank Seminara	.05	.02	.01
☐ 602 Darrell Sherman	.05	.02	.01
☐ 603 Craig Shipley	.05	.02	.01
☐ 604 Guillermo Velasquez	.05	.02	.01
☐ 605 Dan Walters	.05	.02	.01
☐ 606 Mike Benjamin	.05	.02	.01
☐ 607 Barry Bonds	1.00	.45	.12
☐ 608 Jeff Brantley	.05	.02	.01
☐ 609 Dave Burba	.05	.02	.01
☐ 610 Craig Colbert	.05	.02	.01
☐ 611 Mike Jackson	.05	.02	.01
☐ 612 Kirt Manwaring	.05	.02	.01
☐ 613 Dave Martinez	.05	.02	.01
☐ 614 Dave Righetti	.05	.02	.01
☐ 615 Kevin Rogers	.05	.02	.01
☐ 616 Bill Swift	.05	.02	.01
☐ 617 Rich Amaral	.05	.02	.01
☐ 618 Mike Blowers	.05	.02	.01
☐ 619 Chris Bosio	.05	.02	.01
☐ 620 Norm Charlton	.05	.02	.01
☐ 621 John Cummings	.05	.02	.01
☐ 622 Mike Felder	.05	.02	.01
☐ 623 Bill Haselman	.05	.02	.01
☐ 624 Tim Leary	.05	.02	.01
☐ 625 Pete O'Brien	.05	.02	.01
☐ 626 Russ Swan	.05	.02	.01
☐ 627 Fernando Vina	.05	.02	.01
☐ 628 Rene Arocha	.05	.02	.01
☐ 629 Rod Brewer	.05	.02	.01
☐ 630 Ozzie Canseco	.05	.02	.01
☐ 631 Rheal Cormier	.05	.02	.01
☐ 632 Brian Jordan	.20	.09	.03
☐ 633 Joe Magrane	.05	.02	.01
☐ 634 Donovan Osborne	.05	.02	.01
☐ 635 Mike Perez	.05	.02	.01
☐ 636 Stan Royer	.05	.02	.01
☐ 637 Hector Villanueva	.05	.02	.01
☐ 638 Tracy Woodson	.05	.02	.01
☐ 639 Benji Gil	.05	.02	.01
☐ 640 Tom Henke	.05	.02	.01
☐ 641 David Hulse	.05	.02	.01
☐ 642 Charlie Leibrandt	.05	.02	.01
☐ 643 Robb Nen	.05	.02	.01
☐ 644 Dan Peltier	.05	.02	.01
☐ 645 Billy Ripken	.05	.02	.01
☐ 646 Kenny Rogers	.05	.02	.01
☐ 647 John Russell	.05	.02	.01
☐ 648 Dan Smith	.05	.02	.01
☐ 649 Matt Whiteside	.05	.02	.01
☐ 650 William Canate	.05	.02	.01
☐ 651 Darnell Coles	.05	.02	.01
☐ 652 Al Leiter	.10	.05	.01
☐ 653 Domingo Martinez	.05	.02	.01
☐ 654 Paul Molitor	.75	.35	.09
☐ 655 Luis Sojo	.05	.02	.01
☐ 656 Dave Stewart	.10	.05	.01
☐ 657 Mike Timlin	.05	.02	.01
☐ 658 Turner Ward	.05	.02	.01
☐ 659 Devon White	.10	.05	.01
☐ 660 Eddie Zosky	.05	.02	.01

1993 Pacific Beisbol Amigos

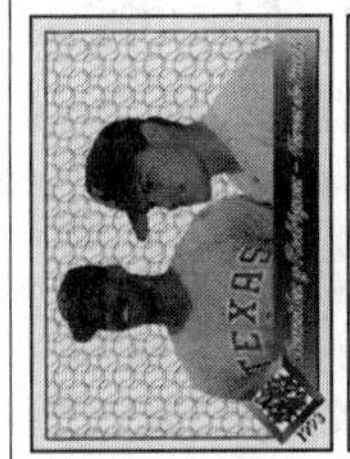

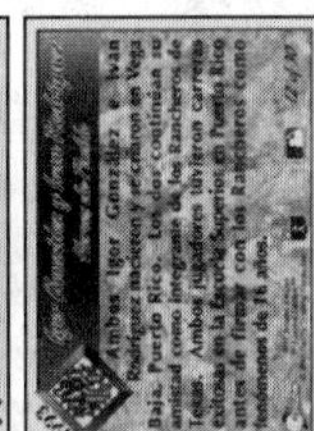

Randomly inserted in 1993 Pacific Spanish second series foil packs, this 30-card standard-size set by Pacific features Hispanic baseball players. The portrait style photos are overlaid on a baseball motif background and edged in white. Across the bottom edge is a diamond-shaped logo for Beisbol Amigos 1993 followed by the players' names pictured on the card. With the exception of the first, all the cards in the set carry photos of two or more players. The horizontal backs are edged in white with a gray marbleized background and list players' career highlights.

	MINT	NRMT	EXC
COMPLETE SET (30)	50.00	22.00	6.25
COMMON CARD (1-30)	1.00	.45	.12
☐ 1 Edgar Martinez	3.00	1.35	.35
☐ 2 Luis Polonia Stan Javier	1.00	.45	.12
☐ 3 George Bell Julio Franco	1.00	.45	.12
☐ 4 Ozzie Guillen Ivan Rodriguez	4.00	1.80	.50
☐ 5 Carlos Baerga Sandy Alomar Jr.	2.00	.90	.25
☐ 6 Intercambio Extranjero Sandy Alomar Jr. Alvaro Espinoza Paul Sorrento Carlos Baerga Felix Fermin Junior Ortiz Jose Mesa Carlos Martinez	2.00	.90	.25
☐ 7 Sandy Alomar Jr. Roberto Alomar	4.00	1.80	.50
☐ 8 Jose Lind Felix Jose	1.00	.45	.12
☐ 9 Ricky Bones Jaime Navarro	1.00	.45	.12
☐ 10 Jamie Navarro Jesse Orosco	1.00	.45	.12
☐ 11 Tino Martinez Edgar Martinez	2.00	.90	.25
☐ 12 Juan Gonzalez Ivan Rodriguez	10.00	4.50	1.25
☐ 13 Juan Gonzalez Julio Franco	6.00	2.70	.75
☐ 14 Julio Franco Jose Canseco Rafael Palmeiro	6.00	2.70	.75
☐ 15 Juan Gonzalez Jose Canseco	12.50	5.50	1.55
☐ 16 Ivan Rodriguez Benji Gil	3.00	1.35	.35
☐ 17 Jose Guzman Frank Castillo	1.00	.45	.12
☐ 18 Rey Sanchez Jose Vizcaino	1.00	.45	.12
☐ 19 Derrick May Sammy Sosa	2.50	1.10	.30
☐ 20 Sammy Sosa UER Candy Maldonado Sammy is from Dominican Republic not Puerto Rico	2.50	1.10	.30
☐ 21 Jose Rijo Juan Samuel	1.00	.45	.12
☐ 22 Freddie Benavides Andres Galarraga	1.50	.70	.19
☐ 23 Guillermo Velasquez Benito Santiago	1.00	.45	.12
☐ 24 Luis Gonzalez Andujar Cedeno	1.00	.45	.12
☐ 25 Wilfredo Cordero Dennis Martinez	1.50	.70	.19
☐ 26 Moises Alou Wilfredo Cordero	1.50	.70	.19
☐ 27 Ozzie Canseco Jose Canseco	3.00	1.35	.35
☐ 28 Jose Oquendo Luis Alicea	1.00	.45	.12
☐ 29 Luis Alicea Rene Arocha	1.00	.45	.12
☐ 30 Geronimo Pena Luis Alicea	1.00	.45	.12

1993 Pacific Spanish Gold Estrellas

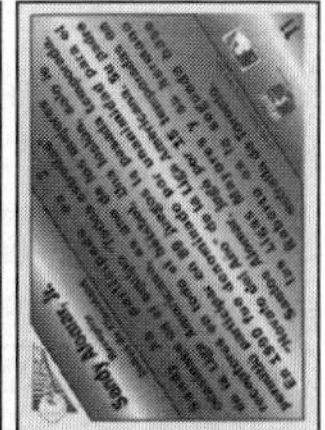

Randomly inserted Spanish first series foil packs, this 20-card standard-size set features the top Latin players at each position. Just 10,000 complete sets were produced for insertion. The fronts display color action player photos within gold foil borders. All the text on this set is in Spanish. The words "Estrellas De Beisbol" (Stars of Baseball) appears vertically to the left of the picture in a variegated blue, purple, and red stripe. The player's name appears at the bottom. The backs are diagonally oriented and carry career hightlights against a red, white, and blue background.

	MINT	NRMT	EXC
COMPLETE SET (20)	40.00	18.00	5.00
COMMON CARD (1-20)	1.00	.45	.12
☐ 1 Moises Alou	2.00	.90	.25
☐ 2 Bobby Bonilla	2.00	.90	.25
☐ 3 Tony Fernandez	1.00	.45	.12
☐ 4 Felix Jose	1.00	.45	.12
☐ 5 Dennis Martinez	2.00	.90	.25
☐ 6 Orlando Merced	1.00	.45	.12
☐ 7 Jose Oquendo	1.50	.70	.19
☐ 8 Geronimo Pena	1.50	.70	.19
☐ 9 Jose Rijo	2.00	.90	.25
☐ 10 Benito Santiago	1.00	.45	.12
☐ 11 Sandy Alomar Jr.	2.00	.90	.25
☐ 12 Carlos Baerga	3.00	1.35	.35
☐ 13 Jose Canseco	7.50	3.40	.95
☐ 14 Juan Gonzalez	10.00	4.50	1.25
☐ 15 Juan Guzman	2.00	.90	.25
☐ 16 Edgar Martinez	5.00	2.20	.60
☐ 17 Rafael Palmeiro	7.50	3.40	.95
☐ 18 Ruben Sierra	3.00	1.35	.35
☐ 19 Danny Tartabull	1.00	.45	.12
☐ 20 Omar Vizquel	3.00	1.35	.35

1993 Pacific Jugadores Calientes

Randomly inserted in 1993 Pacific Spanish second series foil packs,This 36-card standard-size set by Pacific is titled "Jugadores Calientes" and features cut-out action photos of the players over a borderless, prismatic background. The player's name is printed on the lower edge in bold shadowed lettering. The horizontal backs with gray marbleized background carry a close-up, cut-out picture on the left.

The player's name, position, and a career highlight overlay on a ghosted logo of his team with a ghosted action photo. The cards are numbered on the back and are arranged alphabetically according to the American (1-18) and National (19-36) Leagues.

	MINT	NRMT	EXC
COMPLETE SET (36)	175.00	80.00	22.00
COMMON CARD (1-36)	1.50	.70	.19
☐ 1 Rich Amaral	1.50	.70	.19
☐ 2 George Brett	15.00	6.75	1.85
☐ 3 Jay Buhner	4.00	1.80	.50
☐ 4 Roger Clemens	5.00	2.20	.60
☐ 5 Kirk Gibson	2.50	1.10	.30
☐ 6 Juan Gonzalez	15.00	6.75	1.85
☐ 7 Ken Griffey Jr.	30.00	13.50	3.70
☐ 8 Bo Jackson	2.50	1.10	.30
☐ 9 Kenny Lofton	10.00	4.50	1.25
☐ 10 Mark McGwire	10.00	4.50	1.25
☐ 11 Sherman Obando	1.50	.70	.19
☐ 12 John Olerud	2.50	1.10	.30
☐ 13 Carlos Quintana	1.50	.70	.19
☐ 14 Ivan Rodriguez	7.50	3.40	.95
☐ 15 Nolan Ryan	25.00	11.00	3.10
☐ 16 J.T. Snow	3.00	1.35	.35
☐ 17 Fernando Valenzuela	2.50	1.10	.30
☐ 18 Dave Winfield	3.00	1.35	.35
☐ 19 Moises Alou	2.50	1.10	.30
☐ 20 Jeff Bagwell	15.00	6.75	1.85
☐ 21 Barry Bonds	6.00	2.70	.75
☐ 22 Bobby Bonilla	2.50	1.10	.30
☐ 23 Vinny Castilla	3.00	1.35	.35
☐ 24 Andujar Cedeno	1.50	.70	.19
☐ 25 Orestes Destrade	1.50	.70	.19
☐ 26 Andres Galarraga	4.00	1.80	.50
☐ 27 Mark Grace	5.00	2.20	.60
☐ 28 Tony Gwynn	12.00	5.50	1.50
☐ 29 Roberto Kelly	1.50	.70	.19
☐ 30 John Kruk	2.50	1.10	.30
☐ 31 Dave Magadan	1.50	.70	.19
☐ 32 Derrick May	1.50	.70	.19
☐ 33 Orlando Merced	1.50	.70	.19
☐ 34 Mike Piazza	25.00	11.00	3.10
☐ 35 Armando Reynoso	1.50	.70	.19
☐ 36 Jose Vizcaino	1.50	.70	.19

1993 Pacific Spanish Prism Inserts

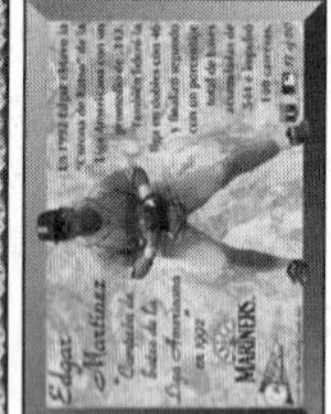

Randomly inserted into Spanish series I foil packs, this 20-card standard-size set highlights top Latin players in Major League Baseball. Ten thousand of these sets were produced for insertion. The fronts display color cut-out player photos against a prism background. The player's name appears below the picture in team color-coded block letters. The backs carry cut-out close-up photos against a marbleized background. The background and borders are team color-coded. Career highlights are featured in Spanish on either side of the picture.

	MINT	NRMT	EXC
COMPLETE SET (20)	100.00	45.00	12.50
COMMON CARD (1-20)	3.00	1.35	.35
☐ 1 Francisco Cabrera	3.00	1.35	.35
☐ 2 Jose Lind	3.00	1.35	.35
☐ 3 Dennis Martinez	5.00	2.20	.60
☐ 4 Ramon Martinez	5.00	2.20	.60
☐ 5 Jose Rijo	3.00	1.35	.35
☐ 6 Benito Santiago	3.00	1.35	.35
☐ 7 Roberto Alomar	10.00	4.50	1.25
☐ 8 Sandy Alomar Jr.	4.00	1.80	.50
☐ 9 Carlos Baerga	6.00	2.70	.75
☐ 10 George Bell	4.00	1.80	.50
☐ 11 Jose Canseco	8.00	3.60	1.00
☐ 12 Alex Fernandez	7.50	3.40	.95
☐ 13 Julio Franco	4.00	1.80	.50
☐ 14 Juan Gonzalez	15.00	6.75	1.85
☐ 15 Ozzie Guillen	5.00	2.20	.60
☐ 16 Teddy Higuera	3.00	1.35	.35
☐ 17 Edgar Martinez	7.50	3.40	.95
☐ 18 Hipolito Pichardo	3.00	1.35	.35
☐ 19 Luis Polonia	3.00	1.35	.35
☐ 20 Ivan Rodriguez	12.50	5.50	1.55

1994 Pacific Promos

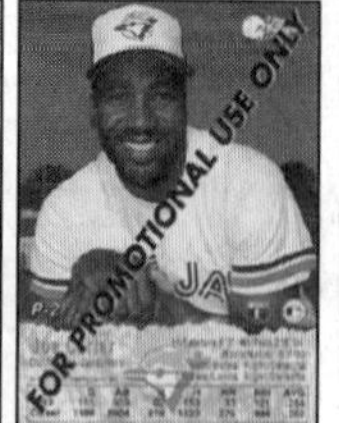

Measuring the standard size, these eight promo cards were issued to show the design of the forthcoming 1994 Pacific Crown Collection set. The cards were given away at the Super Bowl Card Show in Atlanta, to Pacific's master hobby lists of dealers and writers, and used as sales samples. The production run was reportedly approximately 10,000 sets. The fronts feature full-bleed color action player photos, except at the bottom where a gold foil stripe separates the picture from a marbleized team color-coded stripe. The disclaimer "For Promotional Use Only" is stamped diagonally in black lettering across both sides of the card. The cards are arranged alphabetically and numbered on the back with a "P" prefix.

	MINT	NRMT	EXC
COMPLETE SET (8)	10.00	4.50	1.25
COMMON CARD (P1-P8)	.25	.11	.03
☐ P1 Carlos Baerga	.25	.11	.03
☐ P2 Joe Carter	.25	.11	.03
☐ P3 Juan Gonzalez	1.50	.70	.19
☐ P4 Ken Griffey Jr.	3.00	1.35	.35
☐ P5 Greg Maddux	1.75	.80	.22
☐ P6 Mike Piazza	2.50	1.10	.30
☐ P7 Tim Salmon	.75	.35	.09
☐ P8 Frank Thomas	3.00	1.35	.35

1994 Pacific

The 660 standard-size cards comprising this set feature color player action shots on their fronts that are borderless, except at the bottom, where a team color-coded marbleized border set off by a gold-foil line carries the team color-coded player's name. The set's gold-foil-stamped crown logo rests at the lower left. The back carries another color player action photo that is bordered only at the bottom, where the photo appears "torn away," revealing the gray marbleized area that carries the player's name, biography in both English and Spanish, statistics, and a ghosted team logo. The cards are numbered on the back, grouped alphabetically within teams. The set closes with an Award Winners subset (655-660). There are no key Rookie Cards in this set.

	MINT	NRMT	EXC
COMPLETE SET (660)	30.00	13.50	3.70
COMMON CARD (1-660)	.05	.02	.01
COMP.CHECKLIST SET (6)	2.00	.90	.25
COMMON CHECKLIST	.35	.16	.04
☐ 1 Steve Avery	.15	.07	.02
☐ 2 Steve Bedrosian	.05	.02	.01
☐ 3 Damon Berryhill	.05	.02	.01
☐ 4 Jeff Blauser	.05	.02	.01
☐ 5 Sid Bream	.05	.02	.01
☐ 6 Francisco Cabrera	.05	.02	.01
☐ 7 Ramon Caraballo	.05	.02	.01
☐ 8 Ron Gant	.15	.07	.02
☐ 9 Tom Glavine	.30	.14	.04
☐ 10 Chipper Jones	1.50	.70	.19
☐ 11 Dave Justice	.30	.14	.04
☐ 12 Ryan Klesko	.40	.18	.05
☐ 13 Mark Lemke	.05	.02	.01
☐ 14 Javier Lopez	.30	.14	.04
☐ 15 Greg Maddux	1.25	.55	.16
☐ 16 Fred McGriff	.30	.14	.04
☐ 17 Greg McMichael	.05	.02	.01
☐ 18 Kent Mercker	.05	.02	.01
☐ 19 Otis Nixon	.05	.02	.01
☐ 20 Terry Pendleton	.15	.07	.02
☐ 21 Deion Sanders	.30	.14	.04
☐ 22 John Smoltz	.30	.14	.04
☐ 23 Tony Tarasco	.05	.02	.01
☐ 24 Manny Alexander	.05	.02	.01
☐ 25 Brady Anderson	.30	.14	.04
☐ 26 Harold Baines	.15	.07	.02
☐ 27 Damon Buford	.05	.02	.01
☐ 28 Paul Carey	.05	.02	.01
☐ 29 Mike Devereaux	.05	.02	.01
☐ 30 Todd Frohwirth	.05	.02	.01
☐ 31 Leo Gomez	.05	.02	.01
☐ 32 Jeffrey Hammonds	.15	.07	.02
☐ 33 Chris Hoiles	.05	.02	.01
☐ 34 Tim Hulett	.05	.02	.01
☐ 35 Ben McDonald	.05	.02	.01
☐ 36 Mark McLemore	.05	.02	.01
☐ 37 Alan Mills	.05	.02	.01
☐ 38 Mike Mussina	.40	.18	.05
☐ 39 Sherman Obando	.05	.02	.01
☐ 40 Gregg Olson	.05	.02	.01
☐ 41 Mike Pagliarulo	.05	.02	.01
☐ 42 Jim Poole	.05	.02	.01
☐ 43 Harold Reynolds	.05	.02	.01
☐ 44 Cal Ripken	1.50	.70	.19
☐ 45 David Segui	.05	.02	.01
☐ 46 Fernando Valenzuela	.15	.07	.02
☐ 47 Jack Voigt	.05	.02	.01
☐ 48 Scott Bankhead	.05	.02	.01
☐ 49 Roger Clemens	.40	.18	.05
☐ 50 Scott Cooper	.05	.02	.01
☐ 51 Danny Darwin	.05	.02	.01
☐ 52 Andre Dawson	.15	.07	.02
☐ 53 John Dopson	.05	.02	.01
☐ 54 Scott Fletcher	.05	.02	.01
☐ 55 Tony Fossas	.05	.02	.01
☐ 56 Mike Greenwell	.05	.02	.01
☐ 57 Billy Hatcher	.05	.02	.01
☐ 58 Jeff McNeely	.05	.02	.01
☐ 59 Jose Melendez	.05	.02	.01
☐ 60 Tim Naehring	.05	.02	.01
☐ 61 Tony Pena	.05	.02	.01
☐ 62 Carlos Quintana	.05	.02	.01
☐ 63 Paul Quantrill	.05	.02	.01
☐ 64 Luis Rivera	.05	.02	.01
☐ 65 Jeff Russell	.05	.02	.01
☐ 66 Aaron Sele	.15	.07	.02
☐ 67 John Valentin	.15	.07	.02
☐ 68 Mo Vaughn	.50	.23	.06
☐ 69 Frank Viola	.05	.02	.01
☐ 70 Bob Zupcic	.05	.02	.01
☐ 71 Mike Butcher	.05	.02	.01
☐ 72 Rod Correia	.05	.02	.01
☐ 73 Chad Curtis	.05	.02	.01
☐ 74 Chili Davis	.15	.07	.02
☐ 75 Gary DiSarcina	.05	.02	.01
☐ 76 Damion Easley	.05	.02	.01
☐ 77 John Farrell	.05	.02	.01
☐ 78 Chuck Finley	.05	.02	.01
☐ 79 Joe Grahe	.05	.02	.01
☐ 80 Stan Javier	.05	.02	.01
☐ 81 Mark Langston	.15	.07	.02
☐ 82 Phil Leftwich	.05	.02	.01
☐ 83 Torey Lovullo	.05	.02	.01
☐ 84 Joe Magrane	.05	.02	.01
☐ 85 Greg Myers	.05	.02	.01
☐ 86 Eduardo Perez	.05	.02	.01
☐ 87 Luis Polonia	.05	.02	.01
☐ 88 Tim Salmon	.30	.14	.04
☐ 89 J.T. Snow	.15	.07	.02
☐ 90 Kurt Stillwell	.05	.02	.01
☐ 91 Ron Tingley	.05	.02	.01
☐ 92 Chris Turner	.05	.02	.01
☐ 93 Julio Valera	.05	.02	.01
☐ 94 Jose Bautista	.05	.02	.01
☐ 95 Shawn Boskie	.05	.02	.01
☐ 96 Steve Buechele	.05	.02	.01
☐ 97 Frank Castillo	.05	.02	.01
☐ 98 Mark Grace UER (stats have 98 home runs in 1993; should be 14)	.30	.14	.04
☐ 99 Jose Guzman	.05	.02	.01
☐ 100 Mike Harkey	.05	.02	.01
☐ 101 Greg Hibbard	.05	.02	.01
☐ 102 Doug Jennings	.05	.02	.01
☐ 103 Derrick May	.05	.02	.01
☐ 104 Mike Morgan	.05	.02	.01
☐ 105 Randy Myers	.05	.02	.01
☐ 106 Karl Rhodes	.05	.02	.01
☐ 107 Kevin Roberson	.05	.02	.01
☐ 108 Rey Sanchez	.05	.02	.01
☐ 109 Ryne Sandberg	.50	.23	.06
☐ 110 Tommy Shields	.05	.02	.01
☐ 111 Dwight Smith	.05	.02	.01
☐ 112 Sammy Sosa	.30	.14	.04
☐ 113 Jose Vizcaino	.05	.02	.01
☐ 114 Turk Wendell	.05	.02	.01
☐ 115 Rick Wilkins	.05	.02	.01
☐ 116 Willie Wilson	.05	.02	.01
☐ 117 Eduardo Zambrano	.05	.02	.01
☐ 118 Wilson Alvarez	.15	.07	.02
☐ 119 Tim Belcher	.05	.02	.01
☐ 120 Jason Bere	.15	.07	.02
☐ 121 Rodney Bolton	.05	.02	.01
☐ 122 Ellis Burks	.15	.07	.02
☐ 123 Joey Cora	.05	.02	.01
☐ 124 Alex Fernandez	.15	.07	.02
☐ 125 Ozzie Guillen	.05	.02	.01
☐ 126 Craig Grebeck	.05	.02	.01
☐ 127 Roberto Hernandez	.15	.07	.02
☐ 128 Bo Jackson	.15	.07	.02
☐ 129 Lance Johnson	.15	.07	.02
☐ 130 Ron Karkovice	.05	.02	.01
☐ 131 Mike LaValliere	.05	.02	.01
☐ 132 Norberto Martin	.05	.02	.01
☐ 133 Kirk McCaskill	.05	.02	.01
☐ 134 Jack McDowell	.15	.07	.02
☐ 135 Scott Radinsky	.05	.02	.01
☐ 136 Tim Raines	.30	.14	.04
☐ 137 Steve Sax	.05	.02	.01
☐ 138 Frank Thomas	2.00	.90	.25
☐ 139 Dan Pasqua	.05	.02	.01
☐ 140 Robin Ventura	.15	.07	.02
☐ 141 Jeff Branson	.05	.02	.01
☐ 142 Tom Browning	.05	.02	.01
☐ 143 Jacob Brumfield	.05	.02	.01
☐ 144 Tim Costo	.05	.02	.01
☐ 145 Rob Dibble	.05	.02	.01
☐ 146 Brian Dorsett	.05	.02	.01
☐ 147 Steve Foster	.05	.02	.01
☐ 148 Cesar Hernandez	.05	.02	.01
☐ 149 Roberto Kelly	.05	.02	.01
☐ 150 Barry Larkin	.30	.14	.04
☐ 151 Larry Luebbers	.05	.02	.01
☐ 152 Kevin Mitchell	.15	.07	.02
☐ 153 Joe Oliver	.05	.02	.01
☐ 154 Tim Pugh	.05	.02	.01
☐ 155 Jeff Reardon	.15	.07	.02
☐ 156 Jose Rijo	.05	.02	.01
☐ 157 Bip Roberts	.05	.02	.01
☐ 158 Chris Sabo	.05	.02	.01
☐ 159 Juan Samuel	.05	.02	.01
☐ 160 Reggie Sanders	.15	.07	.02
☐ 161 John Smiley	.05	.02	.01
☐ 162 Jerry Spradlin	.05	.02	.01
☐ 163 Gary Varsho	.05	.02	.01
☐ 164 Sandy Alomar Jr.	.15	.07	.02
☐ 165 Albert Belle	.75	.35	.09
☐ 166 Carlos Baerga	.15	.07	.02
☐ 167 Mark Clark	.05	.02	.01
☐ 168 Alvaro Espinoza	.05	.02	.01
☐ 169 Felix Fermin	.05	.02	.01
☐ 170 Reggie Jefferson	.15	.07	.02
☐ 171 Wayne Kirby	.05	.02	.01
☐ 172 Tom Kramer	.05	.02	.01
☐ 173 Kenny Lofton	.60	.25	.07
☐ 174 Jesse Levis	.05	.02	.01
☐ 175 Candy Maldonado	.05	.02	.01
☐ 176 Carlos Martinez	.05	.02	.01
☐ 177 Jose Mesa	.15	.07	.02
☐ 178 Jeff Mutis	.05	.02	.01
☐ 179 Charles Nagy	.15	.07	.02
☐ 180 Bob Ojeda	.05	.02	.01
☐ 181 Junior Ortiz	.05	.02	.01
☐ 182 Eric Plunk	.05	.02	.01
☐ 183 Manny Ramirez	.60	.25	.07
☐ 184 Paul Sorrento	.05	.02	.01
☐ 185 Jeff Treadway	.05	.02	.01
☐ 186 Bill Wertz	.05	.02	.01
☐ 187 Freddie Benavides	.05	.02	.01
☐ 188 Dante Bichette	.30	.14	.04
☐ 189 Willie Blair	.05	.02	.01
☐ 190 Daryl Boston	.05	.02	.01
☐ 191 Pedro Castellano	.05	.02	.01
☐ 192 Vinny Castilla	.30	.14	.04
☐ 193 Jerald Clark	.05	.02	.01
☐ 194 Alex Cole	.05	.02	.01
☐ 195 Andres Galarraga	.30	.14	.04
☐ 196 Joe Girardi	.05	.02	.01
☐ 197 Charlie Hayes	.05	.02	.01
☐ 198 Darren Holmes	.05	.02	.01
☐ 199 Chris Jones	.05	.02	.01
☐ 200 Curt Leskanic	.05	.02	.01
☐ 201 Roberto Mejia	.05	.02	.01
☐ 202 David Nied	.05	.02	.01
☐ 203 J. Owens	.05	.02	.01
☐ 204 Steve Reed	.05	.02	.01
☐ 205 Armando Reynoso	.05	.02	.01
☐ 206 Bruce Ruffin	.05	.02	.01
☐ 207 Keith Shepherd	.05	.02	.01
☐ 208 Jim Tatum	.05	.02	.01
☐ 209 Eric Young	.15	.07	.02
☐ 210 Skeeter Barnes	.05	.02	.01
☐ 211 Danny Bautista	.05	.02	.01
☐ 212 Tom Bolton	.05	.02	.01
☐ 213 Eric Davis	.15	.07	.02
☐ 214 Storm Davis	.05	.02	.01
☐ 215 Cecil Fielder	.15	.07	.02
☐ 216 Travis Fryman	.15	.07	.02
☐ 217 Kirk Gibson	.15	.07	.02
☐ 218 Dan Gladden	.05	.02	.01
☐ 219 John Doherty	.05	.02	.01
☐ 220 Chris Gomez	.05	.02	.01
☐ 221 David Haas	.05	.02	.01
☐ 222 Bill Krueger	.05	.02	.01
☐ 223 Chad Kreuter	.05	.02	.01
☐ 224 Mark Leiter	.05	.02	.01
☐ 225 Bob MacDonald	.05	.02	.01
☐ 226 Mike Moore	.05	.02	.01
☐ 227 Tony Phillips	.15	.07	.02
☐ 228 Rich Rowland	.05	.02	.01
☐ 229 Mickey Tettleton	.05	.02	.01
☐ 230 Alan Trammell	.15	.07	.02
☐ 231 David Wells	.05	.02	.01
☐ 232 Lou Whitaker	.15	.07	.02
☐ 233 Luis Aquino	.05	.02	.01

□ 234 Alex Arias .05 .02 .01
□ 235 Jack Armstrong .05 .02 .01
□ 236 Ryan Bowen .05 .02 .01
□ 237 Chuck Carr .05 .02 .01
□ 238 Matias Carrillo .05 .02 .01
□ 239 Jeff Conine .15 .07 .02
□ 240 Henry Cotto .05 .02 .01
□ 241 Orestes Destrade .05 .02 .01
□ 242 Chris Hammond .05 .02 .01
□ 243 Bryan Harvey .05 .02 .01
□ 244 Charlie Hough .05 .02 .01
□ 245 Richie Lewis .05 .02 .01
□ 246 Mitch Lyden .05 .02 .01
□ 247 Dave Magadan .05 .02 .01
□ 248 Bob Natal .05 .02 .01
□ 249 Benito Santiago .05 .02 .01
□ 250 Gary Sheffield .30 .14 .04
□ 251 Matt Turner .05 .02 .01
□ 252 David Weathers .05 .02 .01
□ 253 Walt Weiss .05 .02 .01
□ 254 Darrell Whitmore .05 .02 .01
□ 255 Nigel Wilson .05 .02 .01
□ 256 Eric Anthony .05 .02 .01
□ 257 Jeff Bagwell .75 .35 .09
□ 258 Kevin Bass .05 .02 .01
□ 259 Craig Biggio .15 .07 .02
□ 260 Ken Caminiti .30 .14 .04
□ 261 Andujar Cedeno .05 .02 .01
□ 262 Chris Donnels .05 .02 .01
□ 263 Doug Drabek .05 .02 .01
□ 264 Tom Edens .05 .02 .01
□ 265 Steve Finley .30 .14 .04
□ 266 Luis Gonzalez .05 .02 .01
□ 267 Pete Harnisch .05 .02 .01
□ 268 Xavier Hernandez .05 .02 .01
□ 269 Todd Jones .05 .02 .01
□ 270 Darryl Kile .05 .02 .01
□ 271 Al Osuna .05 .02 .01
□ 272 Rick Parker .05 .02 .01
□ 273 Mark Portugal .05 .02 .01
□ 274 Scott Servais .05 .02 .01
□ 275 Greg Swindell .05 .02 .01
□ 276 Eddie Taubensee .05 .02 .01
□ 277 Jose Uribe .05 .02 .01
□ 278 Brian Williams .05 .02 .01
□ 279 Kevin Appier .15 .07 .02
□ 280 Billy Brewer .05 .02 .01
□ 281 David Cone .15 .07 .02
□ 282 Greg Gagne .05 .02 .01
□ 283 Tom Gordon .05 .02 .01
□ 284 Chris Gwynn .05 .02 .01
□ 285 John Habyan .05 .02 .01
□ 286 Chris Haney .05 .02 .01
□ 287 Phil Hiatt .05 .02 .01
□ 288 David Howard .05 .02 .01
□ 289 Felix Jose .05 .02 .01
□ 290 Wally Joyner .15 .07 .02
□ 291 Kevin Koslofski .05 .02 .01
□ 292 Jose Lind .05 .02 .01
□ 293 Brent Mayne .05 .02 .01
□ 294 Mike Macfarlane .05 .02 .01
□ 295 Brian McRae .15 .07 .02
□ 296 Kevin McReynolds .05 .02 .01
□ 297 Keith Miller .05 .02 .01
□ 298 Jeff Montgomery .15 .07 .02
□ 299 Hipolito Pichardo .05 .02 .01
□ 300 Rico Rossy .05 .02 .01
□ 301 Curtis Wilkerson .05 .02 .01
□ 302 Pedro Astacio .05 .02 .01
□ 303 Rafael Bournigal .05 .02 .01
□ 304 Brett Butler .15 .07 .02
□ 305 Tom Candiotti .05 .02 .01
□ 306 Omar Daal .05 .02 .01
□ 307 Jim Gott .05 .02 .01
□ 308 Kevin Gross .05 .02 .01
□ 309 Dave Hansen .05 .02 .01
□ 310 Carlos Hernandez .05 .02 .01
□ 311 Orel Hershiser .15 .07 .02
□ 312 Eric Karros .15 .07 .02
□ 313 Pedro Martinez .30 .14 .04
□ 314 Ramon Martinez .15 .07 .02
□ 315 Roger McDowell .05 .02 .01
□ 316 Raul Mondesi .30 .14 .04
□ 317 Jose Offerman .05 .02 .01
□ 318 Mike Piazza 1.25 .55 .16
□ 319 Jody Reed .05 .02 .01
□ 320 Henry Rodriguez .15 .07 .02
□ 321 Cory Snyder .05 .02 .01
□ 322 Darryl Strawberry .15 .07 .02
□ 323 Tim Wallach .05 .02 .01
□ 324 Steve Wilson .05 .02 .01
□ 325 Juan Bell .05 .02 .01
□ 326 Ricky Bones .05 .02 .01
□ 327 Alex Diaz .05 .02 .01
□ 328 Cal Eldred .05 .02 .01
□ 329 Darryl Hamilton .05 .02 .01
□ 330 Doug Henry .05 .02 .01
□ 331 John Jaha .15 .07 .02
□ 332 Pat Listach .05 .02 .01
□ 333 Graeme Lloyd .05 .02 .01
□ 334 Carlos Maldonado .05 .02 .01
□ 335 Angel Miranda .05 .02 .01
□ 336 Jaime Navarro .05 .02 .01
□ 337 Dave Nilsson .15 .07 .02
□ 338 Rafael Novoa .05 .02 .01
□ 339 Troy O'Leary .05 .02 .01
□ 340 Jesse Orosco .05 .02 .01
□ 341 Kevin Seitzer .05 .02 .01
□ 342 Bill Spiers .05 .02 .01
□ 343 William Suero .05 .02 .01
□ 344 B.J. Surhoff .05 .02 .01
□ 345 Dickie Thon .05 .02 .01
□ 346 Jose Valentin .15 .07 .02
□ 347 Greg Vaughn .30 .14 .04
□ 348 Robin Yount .30 .14 .04
□ 349 Willie Banks .05 .02 .01
□ 350 Bernardo Brito .05 .02 .01
□ 351 Scott Erickson .05 .02 .01
□ 352 Mark Guthrie .05 .02 .01
□ 353 Chip Hale .05 .02 .01
□ 354 Brian Harper .05 .02 .01
□ 355 Kent Hrbek .15 .07 .02
□ 356 Terry Jorgensen .05 .02 .01
□ 357 Chuck Knoblauch .30 .14 .04
□ 358 Gene Larkin .05 .02 .01
□ 359 Scott Leius .05 .02 .01
□ 360 Shane Mack .05 .02 .01
□ 361 David McCarty .05 .02 .01
□ 362 Pat Meares .05 .02 .01
□ 363 Pedro Munoz .05 .02 .01
□ 364 Derek Parks .05 .02 .01
□ 365 Kirby Puckett .75 .35 .09
□ 366 Jeff Reboulet .05 .02 .01
□ 367 Kevin Tapani .05 .02 .01
□ 368 Mike Trombley .05 .02 .01
□ 369 George Tsamis .05 .02 .01
□ 370 Carl Willis .05 .02 .01
□ 371 Dave Winfield .30 .14 .04
□ 372 Moises Alou .15 .07 .02
□ 373 Brian Barnes .05 .02 .01
□ 374 Sean Berry .05 .02 .01
□ 375 Frank Bolick .05 .02 .01
□ 376 Wil Cordero .15 .07 .02
□ 377 Delino DeShields .05 .02 .01
□ 378 Jeff Fassero .05 .02 .01
□ 379 Darrin Fletcher .05 .02 .01
□ 380 Cliff Floyd .30 .14 .04
□ 381 Lou Frazier .05 .02 .01
□ 382 Marquis Grissom .15 .07 .02
□ 383 Gil Heredia .05 .02 .01
□ 384 Mike Lansing .15 .07 .02
□ 385 Oreste Marrero .05 .02 .01
□ 386 Dennis Martinez .15 .07 .02
□ 387 Curtis Pride .15 .07 .02
□ 388 Mel Rojas .05 .02 .01
□ 389 Kirk Rueter .05 .02 .01
□ 390 Joe Siddall .05 .02 .01
□ 391 John Vander Wal .05 .02 .01
□ 392 Larry Walker .30 .14 .04
□ 393 John Wetteland .15 .07 .02
□ 394 Rondell White .30 .14 .04
□ 395 Tim Bogar .05 .02 .01
□ 396 Bobby Bonilla .15 .07 .02
□ 397 Jeromy Burnitz .05 .02 .01
□ 398 Mike Draper .05 .02 .01
□ 399 Sid Fernandez .05 .02 .01
□ 400 John Franco .05 .02 .01
□ 401 Dave Gallagher .05 .02 .01
□ 402 Dwight Gooden .15 .07 .02
□ 403 Eric Hillman .05 .02 .01
□ 404 Todd Hundley .15 .07 .02
□ 405 Butch Huskey .15 .07 .02
□ 406 Jeff Innis .05 .02 .01
□ 407 Howard Johnson .05 .02 .01
□ 408 Jeff Kent .05 .02 .01
□ 409 Ced Landrum .05 .02 .01
□ 410 Mike Maddux .05 .02 .01
□ 411 Josias Manzanillo .05 .02 .01
□ 412 Jeff McKnight .05 .02 .01
□ 413 Eddie Murray .50 .23 .06
□ 414 Tito Navarro .05 .02 .01
□ 415 Joe Orsulak .05 .02 .01
□ 416 Bret Saberhagen .15 .07 .02
□ 417 Dave Telgheder .05 .02 .01
□ 418 Ryan Thompson .05 .02 .01
□ 419 Chico Walker .05 .02 .01
□ 420 Jim Abbott .05 .02 .01
□ 421 Wade Boggs .30 .14 .04
□ 422 Mike Gallego .05 .02 .01
□ 423 Mark Hutton .05 .02 .01
□ 424 Dion James .05 .02 .01
□ 425 Domingo Jean .05 .02 .01
□ 426 Pat Kelly .05 .02 .01
□ 427 Jimmy Key .15 .07 .02
□ 428 Jim Leyritz .05 .02 .01
□ 429 Kevin Maas .05 .02 .01
□ 430 Don Mattingly 1.00 .45 .12
□ 431 Bobby Munoz .05 .02 .01
□ 432 Matt Nokes .05 .02 .01
□ 433 Paul O'Neill .15 .07 .02
□ 434 Spike Owen .05 .02 .01
□ 435 Melido Perez .05 .02 .01
□ 436 Lee Smith .15 .07 .02
□ 437 Andy Stankiewicz .05 .02 .01
□ 438 Mike Stanley .05 .02 .01
□ 439 Danny Tartabull .05 .02 .01
□ 440 Randy Velarde .05 .02 .01
□ 441 Bernie Williams .40 .18 .05
□ 442 Gerald Williams .05 .02 .01
□ 443 Mike Witt .05 .02 .01
□ 444 Marcos Armas .05 .02 .01
□ 445 Lance Blankenship .05 .02 .01
□ 446 Mike Bordick .05 .02 .01
□ 447 Ron Darling UER .05 .02 .01
Reversed negative on front
□ 448 Dennis Eckersley .15 .07 .02
□ 449 Brent Gates .05 .02 .01
□ 450 Goose Gossage .15 .07 .02
□ 451 Scott Hemond .05 .02 .01
□ 452 Dave Henderson .05 .02 .01
□ 453 Shawn Hillegas .05 .02 .01
□ 454 Rick Honeycutt .05 .02 .01
□ 455 Scott Lydy .05 .02 .01
□ 456 Mark McGwire .60 .25 .07
□ 457 Henry Mercedes .05 .02 .01
□ 458 Mike Mohler .05 .02 .01
□ 459 Troy Neel .05 .02 .01
□ 460 Edwin Nunez .05 .02 .01
□ 461 Craig Paquette .05 .02 .01
□ 462 Ruben Sierra .15 .07 .02
□ 463 Terry Steinbach .15 .07 .02
□ 464 Todd Van Poppel .05 .02 .01
□ 465 Bob Welch .05 .02 .01
□ 466 Bobby Witt .05 .02 .01
□ 467 Ruben Amaro .05 .02 .01
□ 468 Larry Andersen .05 .02 .01
□ 469 Kim Batiste .05 .02 .01
□ 470 Wes Chamberlain .05 .02 .01
□ 471 Darren Daulton .15 .07 .02
□ 472 Mariano Duncan .05 .02 .01
□ 473 Len Dykstra .15 .07 .02
□ 474 Jim Eisenreich .05 .02 .01
□ 475 Tommy Greene .05 .02 .01
□ 476 Dave Hollins .05 .02 .01
□ 477 Pete Incaviglia .05 .02 .01
□ 478 Danny Jackson .05 .02 .01
□ 479 John Kruk .15 .07 .02
□ 480 Tony Longmire .05 .02 .01
□ 481 Jeff Manto .05 .02 .01
□ 482 Mickey Morandini .05 .02 .01
□ 483 Terry Mulholland .05 .02 .01
□ 484 Todd Pratt .05 .02 .01
□ 485 Ben Rivera .05 .02 .01
□ 486 Curt Schilling .05 .02 .01
□ 487 Kevin Stocker .05 .02 .01
□ 488 Milt Thompson .05 .02 .01
□ 489 David West .05 .02 .01
□ 490 Mitch Williams .05 .02 .01
□ 491 Jeff Ballard .05 .02 .01
□ 492 Jay Bell .15 .07 .02
□ 493 Scott Bullett .05 .02 .01
□ 494 Dave Clark .05 .02 .01
□ 495 Steve Cooke .05 .02 .01
□ 496 Midre Cummings .05 .02 .01
□ 497 Mark Dewey .05 .02 .01
□ 498 Carlos Garcia .05 .02 .01
□ 499 Jeff King .15 .07 .02
□ 500 Al Martin .05 .02 .01
□ 501 Lloyd McClendon .05 .02 .01
□ 502 Orlando Merced .15 .07 .02
□ 503 Blas Minor .05 .02 .01
□ 504 Denny Neagle .15 .07 .02
□ 505 Tom Prince .05 .02 .01
□ 506 Don Slaught .05 .02 .01
□ 507 Zane Smith .05 .02 .01
□ 508 Randy Tomlin .05 .02 .01
□ 509 Andy Van Slyke .15 .07 .02
□ 510 Paul Wagner .05 .02 .01
□ 511 Tim Wakefield .05 .02 .01
□ 512 Bob Walk .05 .02 .01
□ 513 John Wehner .05 .02 .01
□ 514 Kevin Young .05 .02 .01
□ 515 Billy Bean .05 .02 .01
□ 516 Andy Benes .15 .07 .02
□ 517 Derek Bell .15 .07 .02
□ 518 Doug Brocail .05 .02 .01
□ 519 Jarvis Brown .05 .02 .01
□ 520 Phil Clark .05 .02 .01
□ 521 Mark Davis .05 .02 .01
□ 522 Jeff Gardner .05 .02 .01
□ 523 Pat Gomez .05 .02 .01
□ 524 Ricky Gutierrez .05 .02 .01
□ 525 Tony Gwynn .75 .35 .09
□ 526 Gene Harris .05 .02 .01
□ 527 Kevin Higgins .05 .02 .01
□ 528 Trevor Hoffman .15 .07 .02
□ 529 Luis Lopez .05 .02 .01
□ 530 Pedro Martinez .30 .14 .04
□ 531 Melvin Nieves .15 .07 .02
□ 532 Phil Plantier .05 .02 .01
□ 533 Frank Seminara .05 .02 .01
□ 534 Craig Shipley .05 .02 .01
□ 535 Tim Teufel .05 .02 .01
□ 536 Guillermo Velasquez .05 .02 .01
□ 537 Wally Whitehurst .05 .02 .01
□ 538 Rod Beck .15 .07 .02
□ 539 Todd Benzinger .05 .02 .01
□ 540 Barry Bonds .50 .23 .06
□ 541 Jeff Brantley .05 .02 .01
□ 542 Dave Burba .05 .02 .01
□ 543 John Burkett .05 .02 .01
□ 544 Will Clark .30 .14 .04
□ 545 Royce Clayton .15 .07 .02
□ 546 Bryan Hickerson .05 .02 .01
□ 547 Mike Jackson .05 .02 .01
□ 548 Darren Lewis .05 .02 .01
□ 549 Kirt Manwaring .05 .02 .01
□ 550 Dave Martinez .05 .02 .01
□ 551 Willie McGee .05 .02 .01
□ 552 Jeff Reed .05 .02 .01
□ 553 Dave Righetti .05 .02 .01
□ 554 Kevin Rogers .05 .02 .01
□ 555 Steve Scarsone .05 .02 .01
□ 556 Bill Swift .05 .02 .01
□ 557 Robby Thompson .05 .02 .01
□ 558 Salomon Torres .05 .02 .01
□ 559 Matt Williams .30 .14 .04
□ 560 Trevor Wilson .05 .02 .01
□ 561 Rich Amaral .05 .02 .01
□ 562 Mike Blowers .05 .02 .01
□ 563 Chris Bosio .05 .02 .01
□ 564 Jay Buhner .30 .14 .04
□ 565 Norm Charlton .05 .02 .01
□ 566 Jim Converse .05 .02 .01
□ 567 Rich DeLucia .05 .02 .01
□ 568 Mike Felder .05 .02 .01
□ 569 Dave Fleming .05 .02 .01
□ 570 Ken Griffey Jr. 2.00 .90 .25
□ 571 Bill Haselman .05 .02 .01
□ 572 Dwayne Henry .05 .02 .01
□ 573 Brad Holman .05 .02 .01
□ 574 Randy Johnson .30 .14 .04
□ 575 Greg Litton .05 .02 .01
□ 576 Edgar Martinez .15 .07 .02
□ 577 Tino Martinez .15 .07 .02
□ 578 Jeff Nelson .05 .02 .01
□ 579 Marc Newfield .15 .07 .02
□ 580 Roger Salkeld .05 .02 .01
□ 581 Mackey Sasser .05 .02 .01
□ 582 Brian Turang .05 .02 .01
□ 583 Omar Vizquel .15 .07 .02
□ 584 Dave Valle .05 .02 .01
□ 585 Luis Alicea .05 .02 .01
□ 586 Rene Arocha .05 .02 .01
□ 587 Rheal Cormier .05 .02 .01
□ 588 Tripp Cromer .05 .02 .01
□ 589 Bernard Gilkey .15 .07 .02
□ 590 Lee Guetterman .05 .02 .01
□ 591 Gregg Jefferies .30 .14 .04
□ 592 Tim Jones .05 .02 .01
□ 593 Paul Kilgus .05 .02 .01
□ 594 Les Lancaster .05 .02 .01
□ 595 Omar Olivares .05 .02 .01
□ 596 Jose Oquendo .05 .02 .01
□ 597 Donovan Osborne .05 .02 .01
□ 598 Tom Pagnozzi .05 .02 .01
□ 599 Erik Pappas .05 .02 .01
□ 600 Geronimo Pena .05 .02 .01
□ 601 Mike Perez .05 .02 .01
□ 602 Gerald Perry .05 .02 .01
□ 603 Stan Royer .05 .02 .01
□ 604 Ozzie Smith .50 .23 .06
□ 605 Bob Tewksbury .05 .02 .01
□ 606 Allen Watson .05 .02 .01
□ 607 Mark Whiten .05 .02 .01
□ 608 Todd Zeile .05 .02 .01
□ 609 Jeff Bronkey .05 .02 .01
□ 610 Kevin Brown .15 .07 .02
□ 611 Jose Canseco .30 .14 .04
□ 612 Doug Dascenzo .05 .02 .01
□ 613 Butch Davis .05 .02 .01
□ 614 Mario Diaz .05 .02 .01
□ 615 Julio Franco .15 .07 .02
□ 616 Benji Gil .05 .02 .01
□ 617 Juan Gonzalez 1.00 .45 .12
□ 618 Tom Henke .05 .02 .01
□ 619 Jeff Huson .05 .02 .01
□ 620 David Hulse .05 .02 .01
□ 621 Craig Lefferts .05 .02 .01
□ 622 Rafael Palmeiro .30 .14 .04
□ 623 Dean Palmer .15 .07 .02
□ 624 Bob Patterson .05 .02 .01
□ 625 Roger Pavlik .05 .02 .01
□ 626 Gary Redus .05 .02 .01
□ 627 Ivan Rodriguez .50 .23 .06
□ 628 Kenny Rogers .05 .02 .01
□ 629 Jon Shave .05 .02 .01
□ 630 Doug Strange .05 .02 .01
□ 631 Matt Whiteside .05 .02 .01
□ 632 Roberto Alomar .40 .18 .05
□ 633 Pat Borders .05 .02 .01
□ 634 Scott Brow .05 .02 .01
□ 635 Rob Butler .05 .02 .01
□ 636 Joe Carter .15 .07 .02
□ 637 Tony Castillo .05 .02 .01
□ 638 Mark Eichhorn .05 .02 .01
□ 639 Tony Fernandez .05 .02 .01
□ 640 Huck Flener .05 .02 .01
□ 641 Alfredo Griffin .05 .02 .01
□ 642 Juan Guzman .15 .07 .02
□ 643 Rickey Henderson .30 .14 .04
□ 644 Pat Hentgen .15 .07 .02
□ 645 Randy Knorr .05 .02 .01
□ 646 Al Leiter .15 .07 .02
□ 647 Domingo Martinez .05 .02 .01
□ 648 Paul Molitor .40 .18 .05
□ 649 Jack Morris .15 .07 .02
□ 650 John Olerud .05 .02 .01
□ 651 Ed Sprague .15 .07 .02
□ 652 Dave Stewart .15 .07 .02

	MINT	NRMT	EXC
☐ 653 Devon White	.05	.02	.01
☐ 654 Woody Williams	.05	.02	.01
☐ 655 Barry Bonds MVP	.30	.14	.04
☐ 656 Greg Maddux CY	.60	.25	.07
☐ 657 Jack McDowell CY	.05	.02	.01
☐ 658 Mike Piazza ROY	.60	.25	.07
☐ 659 Tim Salmon ROY	.30	.14	.04
☐ 660 Frank Thomas MVP	1.00	.45	.12

1994 Pacific All-Latino

Randomly inserted in Pacific purple foil packs at a rate of one in 25, this 20-card standard-size set spotlights the greatest Latin players chosen by the Pacific staff. Print run was limited to 8,000 sets. The fronts feature a full-bleed color player photo with gold foil stamping. The player's name in gold foil appears on the bottom of the photo. Superimposed on the player's native country's flag, the horizontal backs show a close-up color player photo on the left, while 1993 highlights, printed in English and Spanish, appear on the right. The set subdivides into National League (1-10) and American League (11-20) players.

	MINT	NRMT	EXC
COMPLETE SET (20)	25.00	11.00	3.10
COMMON CARD (1-20)	1.00	.45	.12
☐ 1 Benito Santiago	1.00	.45	.12
☐ 2 Dave Magadan	1.00	.45	.12
☐ 3 Andres Galarraga	3.00	1.35	.35
☐ 4 Luis Gonzalez	1.00	.45	.12
☐ 5 Jose Offerman	1.00	.45	.12
☐ 6 Bobby Bonilla	2.00	.90	.25
☐ 7 Dennis Martinez	1.00	.45	.12
☐ 8 Mariano Duncan	1.00	.45	.12
☐ 9 Orlando Merced	1.00	.45	.12
☐ 10 Jose Rijo	1.00	.45	.12
☐ 11 Danny Tartabull	1.00	.45	.12
☐ 12 Ruben Sierra	1.00	.45	.12
☐ 13 Ivan Rodriguez	6.00	2.70	.75
☐ 14 Juan Gonzalez	12.00	5.50	1.50
☐ 15 Jose Canseco	3.00	1.35	.35
☐ 16 Rafael Palmeiro	3.00	1.35	.35
☐ 17 Roberto Alomar	5.00	2.20	.60
☐ 18 Eduardo Perez	1.00	.45	.12
☐ 19 Alex Fernandez	2.00	.90	.25
☐ 20 Omar Vizquel	2.00	.90	.25

1994 Pacific Gold Prisms

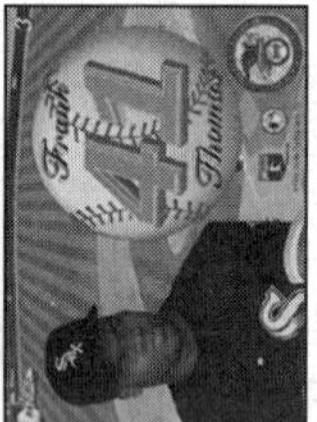

Randomly inserted in Pacific purple foil packs at a rate of one in 25, this 20-card standard-size prismatic 'Home Run Leaders' set honors the top 1993 home run leaders. Print run was reportedly limited to 8,000 sets. The fronts feature a cut-out color player photo against a gold prism background. The player's name appears at the bottom, highlighted in team colors. Superimposed on a baseball field, the horizontal backs show a close-up color player photo on the left, while the number of home runs the player hit in 1993 is highlighted on a large baseball icon on the right. The set subdivides into American League (1-10) and National League (11-20) players.

	MINT	NRMT	EXC
COMPLETE SET (20)	90.00	40.00	11.00
COMMON CARD (1-20)	1.50	.70	.19
☐ 1 Juan Gonzalez	12.00	5.50	1.50
☐ 2 Ken Griffey Jr.	25.00	11.00	3.10
☐ 3 Frank Thomas	25.00	11.00	3.10
☐ 4 Albert Belle	10.00	4.50	1.25
☐ 5 Rafael Palmeiro	3.00	1.35	.35
☐ 6 Joe Carter	2.00	.90	.25
☐ 7 Dean Palmer	2.00	.90	.25
☐ 8 Mickey Tettleton	1.50	.70	.19
☐ 9 Tim Salmon	4.00	1.80	.50
☐ 10 Danny Tartabull	1.50	.70	.19
☐ 11 Barry Bonds	6.00	2.70	.75
☐ 12 Dave Justice	2.00	.90	.25
☐ 13 Matt Williams	3.00	1.35	.35
☐ 14 Fred McGriff	3.00	1.35	.35
☐ 15 Ron Gant	2.00	.90	.25
☐ 16 Mike Piazza	15.00	6.75	1.85
☐ 17 Bobby Bonilla	2.00	.90	.25
☐ 18 Phil Plantier	1.50	.70	.19
☐ 19 Sammy Sosa	4.00	1.80	.50
☐ 20 Rick Wilkins	1.50	.70	.19

1994 Pacific Silver Prisms

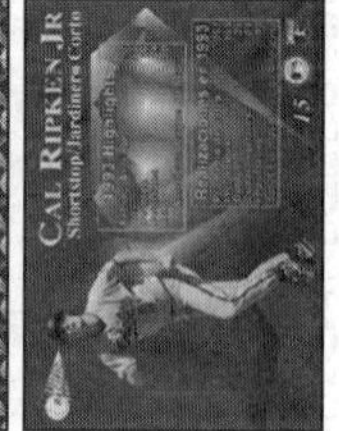

Randomly inserted in Pacific foil packs, this 36-card standard-size set is also known as 'Jewels of the Crown'. The triangular versions were randomly inserted in purple packs and the more common circular one per black retail pack. The print run was reportedly limited to 8,000 sets. The set divides into American League (1-18) and National League (19-36) players. The cards measure the standard size. The fronts feature a cut-out color player photo against a prism background that is either circular or triangular. The player's name appears at the bottom, highlighted in team colors.

	MINT	NRMT	EXC
COMPLETE SET (36)	125.00	55.00	15.50
COMMON CARD (1-36)	1.00	.45	.12
COMP.CIRCULAR SET (36)	60.00	27.00	7.50
COMMON CIRCULAR (1-36)	.50	.23	.06

*CIRCULAR STARS: .25X TO .5X BASIC CARDS

	MINT	NRMT	EXC
☐ 1 Robin Yount	25.00	11.00	3.10
☐ 2 Juan Gonzalez	10.00	4.50	1.25
☐ 3 Rafael Palmeiro	25.00	11.00	3.10
☐ 4 Paul Molitor	4.00	1.80	.50
☐ 5 Roberto Alomar	4.00	1.80	.50
☐ 6 John Olerud	1.50	.70	.19
☐ 7 Randy Johnson	3.00	1.35	.35
☐ 8 Ken Griffey Jr.	20.00	9.00	2.50
☐ 9 Wade Boggs	25.00	11.00	3.10
☐ 10 Don Mattingly	10.00	4.50	1.25
☐ 11 Kirby Puckett	8.00	3.60	1.00
☐ 12 Tim Salmon	3.00	1.35	.35
☐ 13 Frank Thomas	20.00	9.00	2.50
☐ 14 Fernando Valenzuela	1.50	.70	.19
☐ 15 Cal Ripken	15.00	6.75	1.85
☐ 16 Carlos Baerga	1.00	.45	.12
☐ 17 Kenny Lofton	6.00	2.70	.75
☐ 18 Cecil Fielder	1.50	.70	.19
☐ 19 John Burkett	1.00	.45	.12
☐ 20 Andres Galarraga	25.00	11.00	3.10
☐ 21 Charlie Hayes	1.00	.45	.12
☐ 22 Orestes Destrade	1.00	.45	.12
☐ 23 Jeff Conine	1.50	.70	.19
☐ 24 Jeff Bagwell	8.00	3.60	1.00
☐ 25 Mark Grace	25.00	11.00	3.10
☐ 26 Ryne Sandberg	5.00	2.20	.60
☐ 27 Gregg Jefferies	1.00	.45	.12
☐ 28 Barry Bonds	5.00	2.20	.60
☐ 29 Mike Piazza	12.00	5.50	1.50
☐ 30 Greg Maddux	12.00	5.50	1.50
☐ 31 Darren Dalton	1.50	.70	.19
☐ 32 John Kruk	1.50	.70	.19
☐ 33 Lenny Dykstra	1.50	.70	.19
☐ 34 Orlando Merced	1.00	.45	.12
☐ 35 Tony Gwynn	8.00	3.60	1.00
☐ 36 Robby Thompson	1.00	.45	.12

1995 Pacific

This 450-card standard-size set was issued in one series. The full-bleed fronts have action photos; the 'Pacific Collection' logo is on the upper left and the player's name is at the bottom. The horizontal backs have a player photo on the left with 1994 stats and some career highlights on the right. The career highlights are in both English and Spanish. The cards are numbered in the lower right corner. The cards are grouped alphabetically within teams and checklisted below alphabetically according to teams for each league. There are no key Rookie Cards in this set.

	MINT	NRMT	EXC
COMPLETE SET (450)	30.00	13.50	3.70
COMMON CARD (1-450)	.05	.02	.01
☐ 1 Steve Avery	.15	.07	.02
☐ 2 Rafael Belliard	.05	.02	.01
☐ 3 Jeff Blauser	.05	.02	.01
☐ 4 Tom Glavine	.30	.14	.04
☐ 5 David Justice	.30	.14	.04
☐ 6 Mike Kelly	.05	.02	.01
☐ 7 Roberto Kelly	.05	.02	.01
☐ 8 Ryan Klesko	.30	.14	.04
☐ 9 Mark Lemke	.05	.02	.01
☐ 10 Javier Lopez	.30	.14	.04
☐ 11 Greg Maddux	1.25	.55	.16
☐ 12 Fred McGriff	.30	.14	.04
☐ 13 Greg McMichael	.05	.02	.01
☐ 14 Jose Oliva	.05	.02	.01
☐ 15 John Smoltz	.30	.14	.04
☐ 16 Tony Tarasco	.05	.02	.01
☐ 17 Brady Anderson	.30	.14	.04
☐ 18 Harold Baines	.15	.07	.02
☐ 19 Armando Benitez	.05	.02	.01
☐ 20 Mike Devereaux	.05	.02	.01
☐ 21 Leo Gomez	.05	.02	.01
☐ 22 Jeffrey Hammonds	.15	.07	.02
☐ 23 Chris Hoiles	.05	.02	.01
☐ 24 Ben McDonald	.05	.02	.01
☐ 25 Mark McLemore	.05	.02	.01
☐ 26 Jamie Moyer	.05	.02	.01
☐ 27 Mike Mussina	.40	.18	.05
☐ 28 Rafael Palmeiro	.30	.14	.04
☐ 29 Jim Poole	.05	.02	.01
☐ 30 Cal Ripken Jr.	1.50	.70	.19
☐ 31 Lee Smith	.15	.07	.02
☐ 32 Mark Smith	.05	.02	.01
☐ 33 Jose Canseco	.30	.14	.04
☐ 34 Roger Clemens	.40	.18	.05
☐ 35 Scott Cooper	.05	.02	.01
☐ 36 Andre Dawson	.15	.07	.02
☐ 37 Tony Fossas	.05	.02	.01
☐ 38 Mike Greenwell	.05	.02	.01
☐ 39 Chris Howard	.05	.02	.01
☐ 40 Jose Melendez	.05	.02	.01
☐ 41 Nate Minchey	.05	.02	.01
☐ 42 Tim Naehring	.05	.02	.01
☐ 43 Otis Nixon	.05	.02	.01
☐ 44 Carlos Rodriguez	.05	.02	.01
☐ 45 Aaron Sele	.15	.07	.02
☐ 46 Lee Tinsley	.05	.02	.01
☐ 47 Sergio Valdez	.05	.02	.01
☐ 48 John Valentin	.15	.07	.02
☐ 49 Mo Vaughn	.50	.23	.06
☐ 50 Brian Anderson	.05	.02	.01
☐ 51 Garret Anderson	.15	.07	.02
☐ 52 Rod Correia	.05	.02	.01
☐ 53 Chad Curtis	.05	.02	.01
☐ 54 Mark Dalesandro	.05	.02	.01
☐ 55 Chili Davis	.15	.07	.02
☐ 56 Gary DiSarcina	.05	.02	.01
☐ 57 Damion Easley	.05	.02	.01
☐ 58 Jim Edmonds	.30	.14	.04
☐ 59 Jorge Fabregas	.05	.02	.01
☐ 60 Chuck Finley	.15	.07	.02
☐ 61 Bo Jackson	.15	.07	.02
☐ 62 Mark Langston	.05	.02	.01
☐ 63 Eduardo Perez	.05	.02	.01
☐ 64 Tim Salmon	.30	.14	.04
☐ 65 J.T. Snow	.15	.07	.02
☐ 66 Willie Banks	.05	.02	.01
☐ 67 Jose Bautista	.05	.02	.01
☐ 68 Shawon Dunston	.05	.02	.01
☐ 69 Kevin Foster	.05	.02	.01
☐ 70 Mark Grace	.30	.14	.04
☐ 71 Jose Guzman	.05	.02	.01
☐ 72 Jose Hernandez	.05	.02	.01
☐ 73 Blaise Ilsley	.05	.02	.01
☐ 74 Derrick May	.05	.02	.01
☐ 75 Randy Myers	.05	.02	.01
☐ 76 Karl Rhodes	.05	.02	.01
☐ 77 Kevin Roberson	.05	.02	.01
☐ 78 Rey Sanchez	.05	.02	.01
☐ 79 Sammy Sosa	.30	.14	.04
☐ 80 Steve Trachsel	.05	.02	.01
☐ 81 Eddie Zambrano	.05	.02	.01
☐ 82 Wilson Alvarez	.15	.07	.02
☐ 83 Jason Bere	.05	.02	.01
☐ 84 Joey Cora	.05	.02	.01
☐ 85 Jose DeLeon	.05	.02	.01
☐ 86 Alex Fernandez	.15	.07	.02
☐ 87 Julio Franco	.15	.07	.02
☐ 88 Ozzie Guillen	.05	.02	.01
☐ 89 Joe Hall	.05	.02	.01
☐ 90 Roberto Hernandez	.05	.02	.01
☐ 91 Darrin Jackson	.05	.02	.01
☐ 92 Lance Johnson	.15	.07	.02
☐ 93 Norberto Martin	.05	.02	.01
☐ 94 Jack McDowell	.15	.07	.02
☐ 95 Tim Raines	.30	.14	.04
☐ 96 Olmedo Saenz	.05	.02	.01
☐ 97 Frank Thomas	2.00	.90	.25
☐ 98 Robin Ventura	.15	.07	.02
☐ 99 Bret Boone	.15	.07	.02
☐ 100 Jeff Brantley	.05	.02	.01
☐ 101 Jacob Brumfield	.05	.02	.01
☐ 102 Hector Carrasco	.05	.02	.01
☐ 103 Brian Dorsett	.05	.02	.01
☐ 104 Tony Fernandez	.05	.02	.01
☐ 105 Willie Greene	.05	.02	.01
☐ 106 Erik Hanson	.05	.02	.01
☐ 107 Kevin Jarvis	.05	.02	.01
☐ 108 Barry Larkin	.30	.14	.04
☐ 109 Kevin Mitchell	.15	.07	.02
☐ 110 Hal Morris	.05	.02	.01
☐ 111 Jose Rijo	.05	.02	.01
☐ 112 Johnny Ruffin	.05	.02	.01
☐ 113 Deion Sanders	.30	.14	.04
☐ 114 Reggie Sanders	.15	.07	.02
☐ 115 Sandy Alomar Jr.	.05	.02	.01
☐ 116 Ruben Amaro	.05	.02	.01
☐ 117 Carlos Baerga	.15	.07	.02
☐ 118 Albert Belle	.75	.35	.09
☐ 119 Alvaro Espinoza	.05	.02	.01
☐ 120 Rene Gonzales	.05	.02	.01
☐ 121 Wayne Kirby	.05	.02	.01
☐ 122 Kenny Lofton	.50	.23	.06
☐ 123 Candy Maldonado	.05	.02	.01
☐ 124 Dennis Martinez	.15	.07	.02
☐ 125 Eddie Murray	.50	.23	.06
☐ 126 Charles Nagy	.15	.07	.02
☐ 127 Tony Pena	.05	.02	.01
☐ 128 Manny Ramirez	.50	.23	.06
☐ 129 Paul Sorrento	.05	.02	.01
☐ 130 Jim Thome	.40	.18	.05
☐ 131 Omar Vizquel	.15	.07	.02
☐ 132 Dante Bichette	.30	.14	.04
☐ 133 Ellis Burks	.15	.07	.02
☐ 134 Vinny Castilla	.15	.07	.02
☐ 135 Marvin Freeman	.05	.02	.01
☐ 136 Andres Galarraga	.30	.14	.04
☐ 137 Joe Girardi	.05	.02	.01
☐ 138 Charlie Hayes	.05	.02	.01
☐ 139 Mike Kingery	.05	.02	.01
☐ 140 Nelson Liriano	.05	.02	.01
☐ 141 Roberto Mejia	.05	.02	.01
☐ 142 David Nied	.05	.02	.01
☐ 143 Steve Reed	.05	.02	.01
☐ 144 Armando Reynoso	.05	.02	.01
☐ 145 Bruce Ruffin	.05	.02	.01
☐ 146 John VanderWal	.05	.02	.01
☐ 147 Walt Weiss	.05	.02	.01
☐ 148 Skeeter Barnes	.05	.02	.01
☐ 149 Tim Belcher	.15	.07	.02
☐ 150 Junior Felix	.05	.02	.01
☐ 151 Cecil Fielder	.15	.07	.02
☐ 152 Travis Fryman	.15	.07	.02
☐ 153 Kirk Gibson	.15	.07	.02
☐ 154 Chris Gomez	.05	.02	.01
☐ 155 Buddy Groom	.05	.02	.01
☐ 156 Chad Kreuter	.05	.02	.01
☐ 157 Mike Moore	.05	.02	.01
☐ 158 Tony Phillips	.15	.07	.02
☐ 159 Juan Samuel	.05	.02	.01
☐ 160 Mickey Tettleton	.05	.02	.01
☐ 161 Alan Trammell	.15	.07	.02
☐ 162 David Wells	.05	.02	.01
☐ 163 Lou Whitaker	.15	.07	.02
☐ 164 Kurt Abbott	.05	.02	.01
☐ 165 Luis Aquino	.05	.02	.01
☐ 166 Alex Arias	.05	.02	.01
☐ 167 Bret Barberie	.05	.02	.01
☐ 168 Jerry Browne	.05	.02	.01
☐ 169 Chuck Carr	.05	.02	.01
☐ 170 Matias Carrillo	.05	.02	.01
☐ 171 Greg Colbrunn	.05	.02	.01
☐ 172 Jeff Conine	.15	.07	.02
☐ 173 Carl Everett	.05	.02	.01
☐ 174 Robb Nen	.05	.02	.01
☐ 175 Yorkis Perez	.05	.02	.01
☐ 176 Pat Rapp	.05	.02	.01
☐ 177 Benito Santiago	.05	.02	.01
☐ 178 Gary Sheffield	.30	.14	.04
☐ 179 Darrell Whitmore	.05	.02	.01
☐ 180 Jeff Bagwell	.75	.35	.09
☐ 181 Kevin Bass	.05	.02	.01
☐ 182 Craig Biggio	.15	.07	.02
☐ 183 Andujar Cedeno	.05	.02	.01
☐ 184 Doug Drabek	.05	.02	.01
☐ 185 Tony Eusebio	.05	.02	.01
☐ 186 Steve Finley	.15	.07	.02
☐ 187 Luis Gonzalez	.05	.02	.01
☐ 188 Pete Harnisch	.05	.02	.01
☐ 189 John Hudek	.05	.02	.01
☐ 190 Orlando Miller	.05	.02	.01
☐ 191 James Mouton	.05	.02	.01
☐ 192 Roberto Petagine	.05	.02	.01
☐ 193 Shane Reynolds	.05	.02	.01
☐ 194 Greg Swindell	.05	.02	.01
☐ 195 Dave Veres	.05	.02	.01
☐ 196 Kevin Appier	.15	.07	.02
☐ 197 Stan Belinda	.05	.02	.01
☐ 198 Vince Coleman	.05	.02	.01
☐ 199 David Cone	.15	.07	.02
☐ 200 Gary Gaetti	.15	.07	.02
☐ 201 Greg Gagne	.05	.02	.01
☐ 202 Mark Gubicza	.05	.02	.01
☐ 203 Bob Hamelin	.05	.02	.01
☐ 204 Dave Henderson	.05	.02	.01
☐ 205 Felix Jose	.05	.02	.01
☐ 206 Wally Joyner	.15	.07	.02
☐ 207 Jose Lind	.05	.02	.01
☐ 208 Mike Macfarlane	.05	.02	.01
☐ 209 Brian McRae	.15	.07	.02
☐ 210 Jeff Montgomery	.15	.07	.02
☐ 211 Hipolito Pichardo	.05	.02	.01
☐ 212 Pedro Astacio	.05	.02	.01

☐ 213 Brett Butler	.15	.07	.02
☐ 214 Omar Daal	.05	.02	.01
☐ 215 Delino DeShields	.05	.02	.01
☐ 216 Darren Dreifort	.05	.02	.01
☐ 217 Carlos Hernandez	.05	.02	.01
☐ 218 Orel Hershiser	.15	.07	.02
☐ 219 Garey Ingram	.05	.02	.01
☐ 220 Eric Karros	.15	.07	.02
☐ 221 Ramon Martinez	.15	.07	.02
☐ 222 Raul Mondesi	.30	.14	.04
☐ 223 Jose Offerman	.05	.02	.01
☐ 224 Mike Piazza	1.25	.55	.16
☐ 225 Henry Rodriguez	.15	.07	.02
☐ 226 Ismael Valdes	.15	.07	.02
☐ 227 Tim Wallach	.05	.02	.01
☐ 228 Jeff Cirillo	.15	.07	.02
☐ 229 Alex Diaz	.05	.02	.01
☐ 230 Cal Eldred	.05	.02	.01
☐ 231 Mike Fetters	.05	.02	.01
☐ 232 Brian Harper	.05	.02	.01
☐ 233 Ted Higuera	.05	.02	.01
☐ 234 John Jaha	.15	.07	.02
☐ 235 Graeme Lloyd	.05	.02	.01
☐ 236 Jose Mercedes	.05	.02	.01
☐ 237 Jaime Navarro	.05	.02	.01
☐ 238 Dave Nilsson	.15	.07	.02
☐ 239 Jesse Orosco	.05	.02	.01
☐ 240 Jody Reed	.05	.02	.01
☐ 241 Jose Valentin	.15	.07	.02
☐ 242 Greg Vaughn	.15	.07	.02
☐ 243 Turner Ward	.05	.02	.01
☐ 244 Rick Aguilera	.05	.02	.01
☐ 245 Rich Becker	.05	.02	.01
☐ 246 Jim Deshaies	.05	.02	.01
☐ 247 Steve Dunn	.05	.02	.01
☐ 248 Scott Erickson	.05	.02	.01
☐ 249 Kent Hrbek	.15	.07	.02
☐ 250 Chuck Knoblauch	.30	.14	.04
☐ 251 Scott Leius	.05	.02	.01
☐ 252 David McCarty	.05	.02	.01
☐ 253 Pat Meares	.05	.02	.01
☐ 254 Pedro Munoz	.05	.02	.01
☐ 255 Kirby Puckett	.75	.35	.09
☐ 256 Carlos Pulido	.05	.02	.01
☐ 257 Kevin Tapani	.05	.02	.01
☐ 258 Matt Walbeck	.05	.02	.01
☐ 259 Dave Winfield	.30	.14	.04
☐ 260 Moises Alou	.15	.07	.02
☐ 261 Juan Bell	.05	.02	.01
☐ 262 Freddie Benavides	.05	.02	.01
☐ 263 Sean Berry	.05	.02	.01
☐ 264 Wil Cordero	.05	.02	.01
☐ 265 Jeff Fassero	.05	.02	.01
☐ 266 Darrin Fletcher	.05	.02	.01
☐ 267 Cliff Floyd	.15	.07	.02
☐ 268 Marquis Grissom	.15	.07	.02
☐ 269 Gil Heredia	.05	.02	.01
☐ 270 Ken Hill	.05	.02	.01
☐ 271 Pedro J. Martinez	.15	.07	.02
☐ 272 Mel Rojas	.05	.02	.01
☐ 273 Larry Walker	.30	.14	.04
☐ 274 John Wetteland	.15	.07	.02
☐ 275 Rondell White	.15	.07	.02
☐ 276 Tim Bogar	.05	.02	.01
☐ 277 Bobby Bonilla	.15	.07	.02
☐ 278 Rico Brogna	.05	.02	.01
☐ 279 Jeromy Burnitz	.05	.02	.01
☐ 280 John Franco	.05	.02	.01
☐ 281 Eric Hillman	.05	.02	.01
☐ 282 Todd Hundley	.15	.07	.02
☐ 283 Jeff Kent	.05	.02	.01
☐ 284 Mike Maddux	.05	.02	.01
☐ 285 Joe Orsulak	.05	.02	.01
☐ 286 Luis Rivera	.05	.02	.01
☐ 287 Bret Saberhagen	.15	.07	.02
☐ 288 David Segui	.05	.02	.01
☐ 289 Ryan Thompson	.05	.02	.01
☐ 290 Fernando Vina	.05	.02	.01
☐ 291 Jose Vizcaino	.05	.02	.01
☐ 292 Jim Abbott	.05	.02	.01
☐ 293 Wade Boggs	.30	.14	.04
☐ 294 Russ Davis	.05	.02	.01
☐ 295 Mike Gallego	.05	.02	.01
☐ 296 Xavier Hernandez	.05	.02	.01
☐ 297 Steve Howe	.05	.02	.01
☐ 298 Jimmy Key	.15	.07	.02
☐ 299 Don Mattingly	1.00	.45	.12
☐ 300 Terry Mulholland	.05	.02	.01
☐ 301 Paul O'Neill	.15	.07	.02
☐ 302 Luis Polonia	.05	.02	.01
☐ 303 Mike Stanley	.05	.02	.01
☐ 304 Danny Tartabull	.05	.02	.01
☐ 305 Randy Velarde	.05	.02	.01
☐ 306 Bob Wickman	.05	.02	.01
☐ 307 Bernie Williams	.40	.18	.05
☐ 308 Mark Acre	.05	.02	.01
☐ 309 Geronimo Berroa	.05	.02	.01
☐ 310 Mike Bordick	.05	.02	.01
☐ 311 Dennis Eckersley	.15	.07	.02
☐ 312 Rickey Henderson	.30	.14	.04
☐ 313 Stan Javier	.05	.02	.01
☐ 314 Miguel Jimenez	.05	.02	.01
☐ 315 Francisco Matos	.05	.02	.01
☐ 316 Mark McGwire	.60	.25	.07
☐ 317 Troy Neel	.05	.02	.01
☐ 318 Steve Ontiveros	.05	.02	.01
☐ 319 Carlos Reyes	.05	.02	.01
☐ 320 Ruben Sierra	.15	.07	.02
☐ 321 Terry Steinbach	.15	.07	.02
☐ 322 Bob Welch	.05	.02	.01
☐ 323 Bobby Witt	.05	.02	.01
☐ 324 Larry Andersen	.05	.02	.01
☐ 325 Kim Batiste	.05	.02	.01
☐ 326 Darren Daulton	.15	.07	.02
☐ 327 Mariano Duncan	.05	.02	.01
☐ 328 Lenny Dykstra	.15	.07	.02
☐ 329 Jim Eisenreich	.05	.02	.01
☐ 330 Danny Jackson	.05	.02	.01
☐ 331 John Kruk	.15	.07	.02
☐ 332 Tony Longmire	.05	.02	.01
☐ 333 Tom Marsh	.05	.02	.01
☐ 334 Mickey Morandini	.05	.02	.01
☐ 335 Bobby Munoz	.05	.02	.01
☐ 336 Todd Pratt	.05	.02	.01
☐ 337 Tom Quinlan	.05	.02	.01
☐ 338 Kevin Stocker	.05	.02	.01
☐ 339 Fernando Valenzuela	.15	.07	.02
☐ 340 Jay Bell	.15	.07	.02
☐ 341 Dave Clark	.05	.02	.01
☐ 342 Steve Cooke	.05	.02	.01
☐ 343 Carlos Garcia	.05	.02	.01
☐ 344 Jeff King	.15	.07	.02
☐ 345 Jon Lieber	.05	.02	.01
☐ 346 Ravelo Manzanillo	.05	.02	.01
☐ 347 Al Martin	.15	.07	.02
☐ 348 Orlando Merced	.05	.02	.01
☐ 349 Denny Neagle	.15	.07	.02
☐ 350 Alejandro Pena	.05	.02	.01
☐ 351 Don Slaught	.05	.02	.01
☐ 352 Zane Smith	.05	.02	.01
☐ 353 Andy Van Slyke	.15	.07	.02
☐ 354 Rick White	.05	.02	.01
☐ 355 Kevin Young	.05	.02	.01
☐ 356 Andy Ashby	.15	.07	.02
☐ 357 Derek Bell	.15	.07	.02
☐ 358 Andy Benes	.05	.02	.01
☐ 359 Phil Clark	.05	.02	.01
☐ 360 Donnie Elliott	.05	.02	.01
☐ 361 Ricky Gutierrez	.05	.02	.01
☐ 362 Tony Gwynn	.75	.35	.09
☐ 363 Trevor Hoffman	.15	.07	.02
☐ 364 Tim Hyers	.05	.02	.01
☐ 365 Luis Lopez	.05	.02	.01
☐ 366 Jose Martinez	.05	.02	.01
☐ 367 Pedro A. Martinez	.05	.02	.01
☐ 368 Phil Plantier	.05	.02	.01
☐ 369 Bip Roberts	.05	.02	.01
☐ 370 A.J. Sager	.05	.02	.01
☐ 371 Jeff Tabaka	.05	.02	.01
☐ 372 Todd Benzinger	.05	.02	.01
☐ 373 Barry Bonds	.50	.23	.06
☐ 374 John Burkett	.15	.07	.02
☐ 375 Mark Carreon	.05	.02	.01
☐ 376 Royce Clayton	.05	.02	.01
☐ 377 Pat Gomez	.05	.02	.01
☐ 378 Erik Johnson	.05	.02	.01
☐ 379 Darren Lewis	.05	.02	.01
☐ 380 Kirt Manwaring	.05	.02	.01
☐ 381 Dave Martinez	.05	.02	.01
☐ 382 John Patterson	.05	.02	.01
☐ 383 Mark Portugal	.05	.02	.01
☐ 384 Darryl Strawberry	.15	.07	.02
☐ 385 Salomon Torres	.05	.02	.01
☐ 386 Wm. VanLandingham	.05	.02	.01
☐ 387 Matt Williams	.30	.14	.04
☐ 388 Rich Amaral	.05	.02	.01
☐ 389 Bobby Ayala	.05	.02	.01
☐ 390 Mike Blowers	.05	.02	.01
☐ 391 Chris Bosio	.05	.02	.01
☐ 392 Jay Buhner	.30	.14	.04
☐ 393 Jim Converse	.05	.02	.01
☐ 394 Tim Davis	.05	.02	.01
☐ 395 Felix Fermin	.05	.02	.01
☐ 396 Dave Fleming	.05	.02	.01
☐ 397 Goose Gossage	.15	.07	.02
☐ 398 Ken Griffey Jr.	2.00	.90	.25
☐ 399 Randy Johnson	.30	.14	.04
☐ 400 Edgar Martinez	.15	.07	.02
☐ 401 Tino Martinez	.15	.07	.02
☐ 402 Alex Rodriguez	2.50	1.10	.30
☐ 403 Dan Wilson	.15	.07	.02
☐ 404 Luis Alicea	.05	.02	.01
☐ 405 Rene Arocha	.05	.02	.01
☐ 406 Bernard Gilkey	.15	.07	.02
☐ 407 Gregg Jefferies	.15	.07	.02
☐ 408 Ray Lankford	.15	.07	.02
☐ 409 Terry McGriff	.05	.02	.01
☐ 410 Omar Olivares	.05	.02	.01
☐ 411 Jose Oquendo	.05	.02	.01
☐ 412 Vicente Palacios	.05	.02	.01
☐ 413 Geronimo Pena	.05	.02	.01
☐ 414 Mike Perez	.05	.02	.01
☐ 415 Gerald Perry	.05	.02	.01
☐ 416 Ozzie Smith	.50	.23	.06
☐ 417 Bob Tewksbury	.05	.02	.01
☐ 418 Mark Whiten	.05	.02	.01
☐ 419 Todd Zeile	.05	.02	.01
☐ 420 Esteban Beltre	.05	.02	.01
☐ 421 Kevin Brown	.15	.07	.02
☐ 422 Cris Carpenter	.05	.02	.01
☐ 423 Will Clark	.30	.14	.04
☐ 424 Hector Fajardo	.05	.02	.01
☐ 425 Jeff Frye	.05	.02	.01
☐ 426 Juan Gonzalez	1.00	.45	.12
☐ 427 Rusty Greer	.30	.14	.04
☐ 428 Rick Honeycutt	.05	.02	.01
☐ 429 David Hulse	.05	.02	.01
☐ 430 Manny Lee	.05	.02	.01
☐ 431 Junior Ortiz	.05	.02	.01
☐ 432 Dean Palmer	.15	.07	.02
☐ 433 Ivan Rodriguez	.50	.23	.06
☐ 434 Dan Smith	.05	.02	.01
☐ 435 Roberto Alomar	.40	.18	.05
☐ 436 Pat Borders	.05	.02	.01
☐ 437 Scott Brow	.05	.02	.01
☐ 438 Rob Butler	.05	.02	.01
☐ 439 Joe Carter	.15	.07	.02
☐ 440 Tony Castillo	.05	.02	.01
☐ 441 Domingo Cedeno	.05	.02	.01
☐ 442 Brad Cornett	.05	.02	.01
☐ 443 Carlos Delgado	.15	.07	.02
☐ 444 Alex Gonzalez	.15	.07	.02
☐ 445 Juan Guzman	.15	.07	.02
☐ 446 Darren Hall	.05	.02	.01
☐ 447 Paul Molitor	.40	.18	.05
☐ 448 John Olerud	.05	.02	.01
☐ 449 Robert Perez	.05	.02	.01
☐ 450 Devon White	.15	.07	.02

1995 Pacific Gold Crown Die Cuts

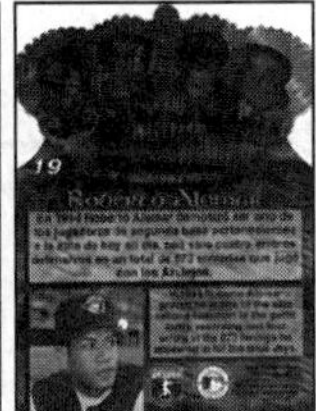

Inserted approximately one in every 18 packs, these cards are in a diecut design. The player photo goes to the full-bleed bottom borders while the top has a gold crown. The player is identified on the bottom. The back of the card features a gold crown, player information in both English and Spanish, and a player photo against a blue background. The cards are sequenced in alphabetical order according to team name.

	MINT	NRMT	EXC
COMPLETE SET (20)	250.00	110.00	31.00
COMMON CARD (1-20)	3.00	1.35	.35
☐ 1 Greg Maddux	25.00	11.00	3.10
☐ 2 Fred McGriff	5.00	2.20	.60
☐ 3 Rafael Palmeiro	5.00	2.20	.60
☐ 4 Cal Ripken Jr.	30.00	13.50	3.70
☐ 5 Jose Canseco	5.00	2.20	.60
☐ 6 Frank Thomas	40.00	18.00	5.00
☐ 7 Albert Belle	15.00	6.75	1.85
☐ 8 Manny Ramirez	10.00	4.50	1.25
☐ 9 Andres Galarraga	5.00	2.20	.60
☐ 10 Jeff Bagwell	15.00	6.75	1.85
☐ 11 Chan Ho Park	3.00	1.35	.35
☐ 12 Raul Mondesi	5.00	2.20	.60
☐ 13 Mike Piazza	25.00	11.00	3.10
☐ 14 Kirby Puckett	15.00	6.75	1.85
☐ 15 Barry Bonds	10.00	4.50	1.25
☐ 16 Ken Griffey Jr.	40.00	18.00	5.00
☐ 17 Alex Rodriguez	40.00	18.00	5.00
☐ 18 Juan Gonzalez	20.00	9.00	2.50
☐ 19 Roberto Alomar	8.00	3.60	1.00
☐ 20 Carlos Delgado	4.00	1.80	.50

1995 Pacific Gold Prisms

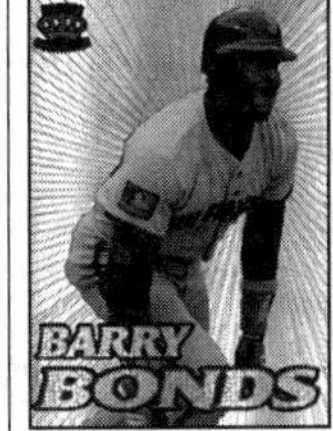

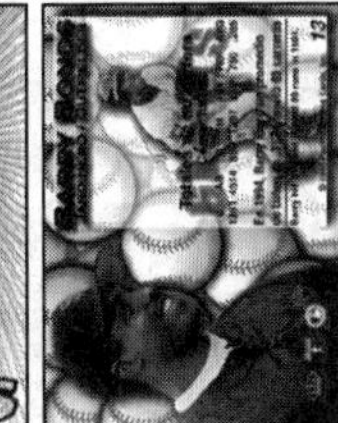

This 36-card standard-size set was inserted approximately one in every 12 packs. The fronts feature a player photo set against a gold metallic background. The player is identified on the bottom of the card. The horizontal backs feature a player photo set against a group of baseballs on the left side. Another photo is on the right along with the player's name, his career totals and some brief information in English and Spanish.

	MINT	NRMT	EXC
COMPLETE SET (36)	150.00	70.00	19.00
COMMON CARD (1-36)	1.50	.70	.19
☐ 1 Jose Canseco	3.00	1.35	.35
☐ 2 Gregg Jefferies	2.00	.90	.25
☐ 3 Fred McGriff	3.00	1.35	.35
☐ 4 Joe Carter	2.00	.90	.25
☐ 5 Tim Salmon	3.00	1.35	.35
☐ 6 Wade Boggs	3.00	1.35	.35
☐ 7 Dave Winfield	3.00	1.35	.35
☐ 8 Bob Hamelin	1.50	.70	.19
☐ 9 Cal Ripken Jr.	20.00	9.00	2.50
☐ 10 Don Mattingly	12.00	5.50	1.50
☐ 11 Juan Gonzalez	12.00	5.50	1.50
☐ 12 Carlos Delgado	2.00	.90	.25
☐ 13 Barry Bonds	6.00	2.70	.75
☐ 14 Albert Belle	10.00	4.50	1.25
☐ 15 Raul Mondesi	3.00	1.35	.35
☐ 16 Jeff Bagwell	10.00	4.50	1.25
☐ 17 Mike Piazza	15.00	6.75	1.85
☐ 18 Rafael Palmeiro	3.00	1.35	.35
☐ 19 Frank Thomas	25.00	11.00	3.10
☐ 20 Matt Williams	3.00	1.35	.35
☐ 21 Ken Griffey Jr.	25.00	11.00	3.10
☐ 22 Will Clark	3.00	1.35	.35
☐ 23 Bobby Bonilla	2.00	.90	.25
☐ 24 Kenny Lofton	6.00	2.70	.75
☐ 25 Paul Molitor	5.00	2.20	.60
☐ 26 Kirby Puckett	10.00	4.50	1.25
☐ 27 David Justice	2.00	.90	.25
☐ 28 Jeff Conine	2.00	.90	.25
☐ 29 Bret Boone	1.50	.70	.19
☐ 30 Larry Walker	3.00	1.35	.35
☐ 31 Cecil Fielder	2.00	.90	.25
☐ 32 Manny Ramirez	6.00	2.70	.75
☐ 33 Javier Lopez	2.00	.90	.25
☐ 34 Jimmy Key	1.50	.70	.19
☐ 35 Andres Galarraga	3.00	1.35	.35
☐ 36 Tony Gwynn	10.00	4.50	1.25

1995 Pacific Latinos Destacados

This 36-card standard size set was inserted approximately one in every nine packs. A literal translation for this set is Hot Hispanics and features only Spanish players. The full-bleed fronts feature color photos with the playeris name at the bottom along with a fire design. The backs have the player's name spelled vertically in the upper left with a sentence in both English and Spanish. The bottom left has the team logo while the right side had a player photo. The cards are numbered and arranged in alphabetical order.

	MINT	NRMT	EXC
COMPLETE SET (36)	50.00	22.00	6.25
COMMON CARD (1-36)	1.00	.45	.12
☐ 1 Roberto Alomar	4.00	1.80	.50
☐ 2 Moises Alou	1.50	.70	.19
☐ 3 Wilson Alvarez	1.50	.70	.19
☐ 4 Carlos Baerga	1.00	.45	.12
☐ 5 Geronimo Berroa	1.00	.45	.12
☐ 6 Jose Canseco	2.50	1.10	.30
☐ 7 Hector Carrasco	1.00	.45	.12
☐ 8 Wil Cordero	1.50	.70	.19
☐ 9 Carlos Delgado	1.50	.70	.19
☐ 10 Damion Easley	1.00	.45	.12
☐ 11 Tony Eusebio	1.00	.45	.12
☐ 12 Hector Fajardo	1.00	.45	.12
☐ 13 Andres Galarraga	2.50	1.10	.30
☐ 14 Carlos Garcia	1.00	.45	.12
☐ 15 Chris Gomez	1.00	.45	.12
☐ 16 Alex Gonzalez	1.50	.70	.19
☐ 17 Juan Gonzalez	10.00	4.50	1.25
☐ 18 Luis Gonzalez	1.00	.45	.12
☐ 19 Felix Jose	1.00	.45	.12
☐ 20 Javier Lopez	2.50	1.10	.30
☐ 21 Luis Lopez	1.00	.45	.12
☐ 22 Dennis Martinez	1.50	.70	.19
☐ 23 Orlando Miller	1.00	.45	.12
☐ 24 Raul Mondesi	2.50	1.10	.30
☐ 25 Jose Oliva	1.00	.45	.12
☐ 26 Rafael Palmeiro	2.50	1.10	.30
☐ 27 Yorkis Perez	1.00	.45	.12
☐ 28 Manny Ramirez	5.00	2.20	.60
☐ 29 Jose Rijo	1.00	.45	.12
☐ 30 Alex Rodriguez	18.00	8.00	2.20
☐ 31 Ivan Rodriguez	5.00	2.20	.60
☐ 32 Carlos Rodriguez	1.00	.45	.12
☐ 33 Sammy Sosa	3.00	1.35	.35
☐ 34 Tony Tarasco	1.00	.45	.12
☐ 35 Ismael Valdes	1.00	.45	.12
☐ 36 Bernie Williams	4.00	1.80	.50

1995 Pacific Harvey Riebe

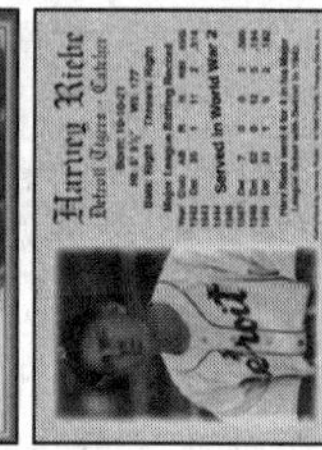

Produced by Pacific, this standard-size card celebrates the baseball career of Harvey Riebe. Inside white and purple borders, the front displays a sepia-tone photo. The horizontal backs have a sepia-tone closeup photo, biography, and major league batting record. The card is unnumbered. Riebe had never before been featured on any card.

	MINT	NRMT	EXC
COMPLETE SET (1)	1.00	.45	.12
COMMON CARD (1)	1.00	.45	.12
☐ 1 Harvey Riebe	1.00	.45	.12

1996 Pacific

This 450-card set was issued in 12-card packs. The fronts feature borderless color action player photos with double-etched gold foil printing. The horizontal backs carry a color player portrait with player information in both English and Spanish and 1995 season player statistics.

	MINT	NRMT	EXC
COMPLETE SET (450)	30.00	13.50	3.70
COMMON CARD (1-450)	.05	.02	.01
☐ 1 Steve Avery	.15	.07	.02
☐ 2 Ryan Klesko	.30	.14	.04
☐ 3 Pedro Borbon	.05	.02	.01
☐ 4 Chipper Jones	1.25	.55	.16
☐ 5 Kent Mercker	.05	.02	.01
☐ 6 Greg Maddux	1.25	.55	.16
☐ 7 Greg McMichael	.05	.02	.01
☐ 8 Mark Wohlers	.15	.07	.02
☐ 9 Fred McGriff	.30	.14	.04
☐ 10 John Smoltz	.30	.14	.04
☐ 11 Rafael Belliard	.05	.02	.01
☐ 12 Mark Lemke	.05	.02	.01
☐ 13 Tom Glavine	.30	.14	.04
☐ 14 Javier Lopez	.30	.14	.04
☐ 15 Jeff Blauser	.05	.02	.01
☐ 16 David Justice	.15	.07	.02
☐ 17 Marquis Grissom	.15	.07	.02
☐ 18 Greg Maddux CY	.60	.25	.07
☐ 19 Randy Myers	.05	.02	.01
☐ 20 Scott Servais	.05	.02	.01
☐ 21 Sammy Sosa	.30	.14	.04
☐ 22 Kevin Foster	.05	.02	.01
☐ 23 Jose Hernandez	.05	.02	.01
☐ 24 Jim Bullinger	.05	.02	.01
☐ 25 Mike Perez	.05	.02	.01
☐ 26 Shawon Dunston	.05	.02	.01
☐ 27 Rey Sanchez	.05	.02	.01
☐ 28 Frank Castillo	.05	.02	.01
☐ 29 Jaime Navarro	.05	.02	.01
☐ 30 Brian McRae	.05	.02	.01
☐ 31 Mark Grace	.30	.14	.04
☐ 32 Roberto Rivera	.05	.02	.01
☐ 33 Luis Gonzalez	.05	.02	.01
☐ 34 Hector Carrasco	.05	.02	.01
☐ 35 Bret Boone	.05	.02	.01
☐ 36 Thomas Howard	.05	.02	.01
☐ 37 Hal Morris	.05	.02	.01
☐ 38 John Smiley	.05	.02	.01
☐ 39 Jeff Brantley	.05	.02	.01
☐ 40 Barry Larkin	.30	.14	.04
☐ 41 Mariano Duncan	.05	.02	.01
☐ 42 Xavier Hernandez	.05	.02	.01
☐ 43 Pete Schourek	.15	.07	.02
☐ 44 Reggie Sanders	.15	.07	.02
☐ 45 Dave Burba	.05	.02	.01
☐ 46 Jeff Branson	.05	.02	.01
☐ 47 Mark Portugal	.05	.02	.01
☐ 48 Ron Gant	.15	.07	.02
☐ 49 Benito Santiago	.05	.02	.01
☐ 50 Barry Larkin MVP	.30	.14	.04
☐ 51 Steve Reed	.05	.02	.01
☐ 52 Kevin Ritz	.05	.02	.01
☐ 53 Dante Bichette	.30	.14	.04
☐ 54 Darren Holmes	.05	.02	.01
☐ 55 Ellis Burks	.15	.07	.02
☐ 56 Walt Weiss	.05	.02	.01
☐ 57 Armando Reynoso	.05	.02	.01
☐ 58 Vinny Castilla	.15	.07	.02
☐ 59 Jason Bates	.05	.02	.01
☐ 60 Mike Kingery	.05	.02	.01
☐ 61 Bryan Rekar	.05	.02	.01
☐ 62 Curtis Leskanic	.05	.02	.01
☐ 63 Bret Saberhagen	.05	.02	.01
☐ 64 Andres Galarraga	.30	.14	.04
☐ 65 Larry Walker	.30	.14	.04
☐ 66 Joe Girardi	.05	.02	.01
☐ 67 Quilvio Veras	.05	.02	.01
☐ 68 Robb Nen	.05	.02	.01
☐ 69 Mario Diaz	.05	.02	.01
☐ 70 Chuck Carr	.05	.02	.01
☐ 71 Alex Arias	.05	.02	.01
☐ 72 Pat Rapp	.05	.02	.01
☐ 73 Rich Garces	.05	.02	.01
☐ 74 Kurt Abbott	.05	.02	.01
☐ 75 Andre Dawson	.15	.07	.02
☐ 76 Greg Colbrunn	.05	.02	.01
☐ 77 John Burkett	.05	.02	.01
☐ 78 Terry Pendleton	.15	.07	.02
☐ 79 Jesus Tavarez	.05	.02	.01
☐ 80 Charles Johnson	.15	.07	.02
☐ 81 Yorkis Perez	.05	.02	.01
☐ 82 Jeff Conine	.15	.07	.02
☐ 83 Gary Sheffield	.30	.14	.04
☐ 84 Brian L. Hunter	.15	.07	.02
☐ 85 Derrick May	.05	.02	.01
☐ 86 Greg Swindell	.05	.02	.01
☐ 87 Derek Bell	.15	.07	.02
☐ 88 Dave Veres	.05	.02	.01
☐ 89 Jeff Bagwell	.75	.35	.09
☐ 90 Todd Jones	.05	.02	.01
☐ 91 Orlando Miller	.05	.02	.01
☐ 92 Pedro A. Martinez	.05	.02	.01
☐ 93 Tony Eusebio	.05	.02	.01
☐ 94 Craig Biggio	.15	.07	.02
☐ 95 Shane Reynolds	.05	.02	.01
☐ 96 James Mouton	.05	.02	.01
☐ 97 Doug Drabek	.05	.02	.01
☐ 98 Dave Magadan	.05	.02	.01
☐ 99 Ricky Gutierrez	.05	.02	.01
☐ 100 Hideo Nomo	.50	.23	.06
☐ 101 Delino DeShields	.05	.02	.01
☐ 102 Tom Candiotti	.05	.02	.01
☐ 103 Mike Piazza	1.25	.55	.16
☐ 104 Ramon Martinez	.15	.07	.02
☐ 105 Pedro Astacio	.05	.02	.01
☐ 106 Chad Fonville	.05	.02	.01
☐ 107 Raul Mondesi	.30	.14	.04
☐ 108 Ismael Valdes	.15	.07	.02
☐ 109 Jose Offerman	.05	.02	.01
☐ 110 Todd Worrell	.15	.07	.02
☐ 111 Eric Karros	.15	.07	.02
☐ 112 Brett Butler	.05	.02	.01
☐ 113 Juan Castro	.05	.02	.01
☐ 114 Roberto Kelly	.05	.02	.01
☐ 115 Omar Daal	.05	.02	.01
☐ 116 Antonio Osuna	.05	.02	.01
☐ 117 Hideo Nomo ROY	.30	.14	.04
☐ 118 Mike Lansing	.05	.02	.01
☐ 119 Mel Rojas	.15	.07	.02
☐ 120 Sean Berry	.05	.02	.01
☐ 121 David Segui	.05	.02	.01
☐ 122 Tavo Alvarez	.05	.02	.01
☐ 123 Pedro Martinez	.15	.07	.02
☐ 124 F.P. Santangelo	.05	.02	.01
☐ 125 Rondell White	.15	.07	.02
☐ 126 Cliff Floyd	.05	.02	.01
☐ 127 Henry Rodriguez	.15	.07	.02
☐ 128 Tony Tarasco	.05	.02	.01
☐ 129 Yamil Benitez	.15	.07	.02
☐ 130 Carlos Perez	.05	.02	.01
☐ 131 Wil Cordero	.05	.02	.01
☐ 132 Jeff Fassero	.05	.02	.01
☐ 133 Moises Alou	.15	.07	.02
☐ 134 John Franco	.05	.02	.01
☐ 135 Rico Brogna	.05	.02	.01
☐ 136 Dave Mlicki	.05	.02	.01
☐ 137 Bill Pulsipher	.15	.07	.02
☐ 138 Jose Vizcaino	.05	.02	.01
☐ 139 Carl Everett	.05	.02	.01
☐ 140 Edgardo Alfonzo	.15	.07	.02
☐ 141 Bobby Jones	.05	.02	.01
☐ 142 Alberto Castillo	.05	.02	.01
☐ 143 Joe Orsulak	.05	.02	.01
☐ 144 Jeff Kent	.05	.02	.01
☐ 145 Ryan Thompson	.05	.02	.01
☐ 146 Jason Isringhausen	.30	.14	.04
☐ 147 Todd Hundley	.15	.07	.02
☐ 148 Alex Ochoa	.15	.07	.02
☐ 149 Charlie Hayes	.05	.02	.01
☐ 150 Michael Mimbs	.05	.02	.01
☐ 151 Darren Daulton	.15	.07	.02
☐ 152 Toby Borland	.05	.02	.01
☐ 153 Andy Van Slyke	.15	.07	.02
☐ 154 Mickey Morandini	.05	.02	.01
☐ 155 Sid Fernandez	.05	.02	.01
☐ 156 Tom Marsh	.05	.02	.01
☐ 157 Kevin Stocker	.05	.02	.01
☐ 158 Paul Quantrill	.05	.02	.01
☐ 159 Gregg Jefferies	.30	.14	.04
☐ 160 Ricky Bottalico	.05	.02	.01
☐ 161 Lenny Dykstra	.15	.07	.02
☐ 162 Mark Whiten	.05	.02	.01
☐ 163 Tyler Green	.05	.02	.01
☐ 164 Jim Eisenreich	.05	.02	.01
☐ 165 Heathcliff Slocumb	.05	.02	.01
☐ 166 Esteban Loaiza	.05	.02	.01
☐ 167 Rich Aude	.05	.02	.01
☐ 168 Jason Christiansen	.05	.02	.01
☐ 169 Ramon Morel	.15	.07	.02
☐ 170 Orlando Merced	.15	.07	.02
☐ 171 Paul Wagner	.05	.02	.01
☐ 172 Jeff King	.15	.07	.02
☐ 173 Jay Bell	.15	.07	.02
☐ 174 Jacob Brumfield	.05	.02	.01
☐ 175 Nelson Liriano	.05	.02	.01
☐ 176 Dan Miceli	.05	.02	.01
☐ 177 Carlos Garcia	.05	.02	.01
☐ 178 Denny Neagle	.15	.07	.02
☐ 179 Angelo Encarnacion	.05	.02	.01
☐ 180 Al Martin	.05	.02	.01
☐ 181 Midre Cummings	.05	.02	.01
☐ 182 Eddie Williams	.05	.02	.01
☐ 183 Roberto Petagine	.05	.02	.01
☐ 184 Tony Gwynn	.75	.35	.09
☐ 185 Andy Ashby	.05	.02	.01
☐ 186 Melvin Nieves	.15	.07	.02
☐ 187 Phil Clark	.05	.02	.01
☐ 188 Brad Ausmus	.05	.02	.01
☐ 189 Bip Roberts	.05	.02	.01
☐ 190 Fernando Valenzuela	.15	.07	.02
☐ 191 Marc Newfield	.15	.07	.02
☐ 192 Steve Finley	.30	.14	.04
☐ 193 Trevor Hoffman	.15	.07	.02
☐ 194 Andujar Cedeno	.05	.02	.01
☐ 195 Jody Reed	.05	.02	.01
☐ 196 Ken Caminiti	.30	.14	.04
☐ 197 Joey Hamilton	.15	.07	.02
☐ 198 Tony Gwynn BAC	.40	.18	.05
☐ 199 Shawn Barton	.05	.02	.01
☐ 200 Deion Sanders	.30	.14	.04
☐ 201 Rikkert Faneyte	.05	.02	.01
☐ 202 Barry Bonds	.50	.23	.06
☐ 203 Matt Williams	.30	.14	.04
☐ 204 Jose Bautista	.05	.02	.01
☐ 205 Mark Leiter	.05	.02	.01
☐ 206 Mark Carreon	.05	.02	.01
☐ 207 Robby Thompson	.05	.02	.01
☐ 208 Terry Mulholland	.05	.02	.01
☐ 209 Rod Beck	.05	.02	.01
☐ 210 Royce Clayton	.05	.02	.01
☐ 211 J.R. Phillips	.05	.02	.01
☐ 212 Kirt Manwaring	.05	.02	.01
☐ 213 Glenallen Hill	.05	.02	.01
☐ 214 William VanLandingham	.05	.02	.01
☐ 215 Scott Cooper	.05	.02	.01
☐ 216 Bernard Gilkey	.15	.07	.02
☐ 217 Allen Watson	.05	.02	.01
☐ 218 Donovan Osborne	.05	.02	.01
☐ 219 Ray Lankford	.15	.07	.02
☐ 220 Tony Fossas	.05	.02	.01
☐ 221 Tom Pagnozzi	.05	.02	.01
☐ 222 John Mabry	.15	.07	.02
☐ 223 Tripp Cromer	.05	.02	.01
☐ 224 Mark Petkovsek	.05	.02	.01
☐ 225 Mike Morgan	.05	.02	.01
☐ 226 Ozzie Smith	.50	.23	.06
☐ 227 Tom Henke	.15	.07	.02
☐ 228 Jose Oquendo	.05	.02	.01
☐ 229 Brian Jordan	.15	.07	.02
☐ 230 Cal Ripken	1.50	.70	.19
☐ 231 Scott Erickson	.05	.02	.01
☐ 232 Harold Baines	.15	.07	.02
☐ 233 Jeff Manto	.05	.02	.01
☐ 234 Jesse Orosco	.05	.02	.01
☐ 235 Jeffrey Hammonds	.05	.02	.01
☐ 236 Brady Anderson	.30	.14	.04
☐ 237 Manny Alexander	.05	.02	.01
☐ 238 Chris Hoiles	.05	.02	.01
☐ 239 Rafael Palmeiro	.30	.14	.04
☐ 240 Ben McDonald	.05	.02	.01
☐ 241 Curtis Goodwin	.05	.02	.01
☐ 242 Bobby Bonilla	.15	.07	.02
☐ 243 Mike Mussina	.40	.18	.05
☐ 244 Kevin Brown	.15	.07	.02
☐ 245 Armando Benitez	.05	.02	.01
☐ 246 Jose Canseco	.30	.14	.04
☐ 247 Erik Hanson	.05	.02	.01
☐ 248 Mo Vaughn	.50	.23	.06
☐ 249 Tim Naehring	.05	.02	.01
☐ 250 Vaughn Eshelman	.05	.02	.01
☐ 251 Mike Greenwell	.05	.02	.01
☐ 252 Troy O'Leary	.05	.02	.01
☐ 253 Tim Wakefield	.05	.02	.01
☐ 254 Dwayne Hosey	.05	.02	.01
☐ 255 John Valentin	.15	.07	.02
☐ 256 Rick Aguilera	.05	.02	.01
☐ 257 Mike Macfarlane	.05	.02	.01
☐ 258 Roger Clemens	.40	.18	.05
☐ 259 Luis Alicea	.05	.02	.01
☐ 260 Mo Vaughn MVP	.30	.14	.04
☐ 261 Mark Langston	.05	.02	.01
☐ 262 Jim Edmonds	.15	.07	.02
☐ 263 Rod Correia	.05	.02	.01
☐ 264 Tim Salmon	.30	.14	.04
☐ 265 J.T. Snow	.15	.07	.02
☐ 266 Orlando Palmeiro	.05	.02	.01
☐ 267 Jorge Fabregas	.05	.02	.01
☐ 268 Jim Abbott	.30	.14	.04
☐ 269 Eduardo Perez	.05	.02	.01
☐ 270 Lee Smith	.15	.07	.02
☐ 271 Gary DiSarcina	.05	.02	.01
☐ 272 Damion Easley	.05	.02	.01
☐ 273 Tony Phillips	.05	.02	.01
☐ 274 Garret Anderson	.30	.14	.04
☐ 275 Chuck Finley	.05	.02	.01
☐ 276 Chili Davis	.05	.02	.01
☐ 277 Lance Johnson	.15	.07	.02
☐ 278 Alex Fernandez	.15	.07	.02
☐ 279 Robin Ventura	.15	.07	.02
☐ 280 Chris Snopek	.05	.02	.01
☐ 281 Brian Keyser	.05	.02	.01
☐ 282 Lyle Mouton	.05	.02	.01
☐ 283 Luis Andujar	.05	.02	.01
☐ 284 Tim Raines	.30	.14	.04
☐ 285 Larry Thomas	.05	.02	.01
☐ 286 Ozzie Guillen	.05	.02	.01
☐ 287 Frank Thomas	2.00	.90	.25
☐ 288 Roberto Hernandez	.15	.07	.02
☐ 289 Dave Martinez	.05	.02	.01
☐ 290 Ray Durham	.30	.14	.04
☐ 291 Ron Karkovice	.05	.02	.01
☐ 292 Wilson Alvarez	.30	.14	.04
☐ 293 Omar Vizquel	.15	.07	.02
☐ 294 Eddie Murray	.50	.23	.06
☐ 295 Sandy Alomar, Jr.	.05	.02	.01
☐ 296 Orel Hershiser	.15	.07	.02
☐ 297 Jose Mesa	.15	.07	.02
☐ 298 Julian Tavarez	.05	.02	.01
☐ 299 Dennis Martinez	.15	.07	.02
☐ 300 Carlos Baerga	.15	.07	.02
☐ 301 Manny Ramirez	.50	.23	.06
☐ 302 Jim Thome	.40	.18	.05
☐ 303 Kenny Lofton	.50	.23	.06
☐ 304 Tony Pena	.05	.02	.01
☐ 305 Alvaro Espinoza	.05	.02	.01
☐ 306 Paul Sorrento	.05	.02	.01
☐ 307 Albert Belle	.75	.35	.09
☐ 308 Danny Bautista	.05	.02	.01
☐ 309 Chris Gomez	.05	.02	.01
☐ 310 Jose Lima	.05	.02	.01
☐ 311 Phil Nevin	.05	.02	.01
☐ 312 Alan Trammell	.15	.07	.02
☐ 313 Chad Curtis	.05	.02	.01
☐ 314 John Flaherty	.05	.02	.01
☐ 315 Travis Fryman	.15	.07	.02
☐ 316 Todd Steverson	.05	.02	.01
☐ 317 Brian Bohanon	.05	.02	.01
☐ 318 Lou Whitaker	.15	.07	.02
☐ 319 Bobby Higginson	.15	.07	.02
☐ 320 Steve Rodriguez	.05	.02	.01
☐ 321 Cecil Fielder	.15	.07	.02
☐ 322 Felipe Lira	.05	.02	.01
☐ 323 Juan Samuel	.05	.02	.01
☐ 324 Bob Hamelin	.05	.02	.01
☐ 325 Tom Goodwin	.15	.07	.02
☐ 326 Johnny Damon	.15	.07	.02
☐ 327 Hipolito Pichardo	.05	.02	.01
☐ 328 Dilson Torres	.05	.02	.01
☐ 329 Kevin Appier	.15	.07	.02
☐ 330 Mark Gubicza	.05	.02	.01
☐ 331 Jon Nunnally	.05	.02	.01
☐ 332 Gary Gaetti	.15	.07	.02
☐ 333 Brent Mayne	.05	.02	.01
☐ 334 Brent Cookson	.05	.02	.01
☐ 335 Tom Gordon	.05	.02	.01
☐ 336 Wally Joyner	.05	.02	.01
☐ 337 Greg Gagne	.05	.02	.01
☐ 338 Fernando Vina	.05	.02	.01
☐ 339 Joe Oliver	.05	.02	.01
☐ 340 John Jaha	.15	.07	.02
☐ 341 Jeff Cirillo	.05	.02	.01
☐ 342 Pat Listach	.05	.02	.01
☐ 343 Dave Nilsson	.15	.07	.02
☐ 344 Steve Sparks	.05	.02	.01
☐ 345 Ricky Bones	.05	.02	.01
☐ 346 David Hulse	.05	.02	.01
☐ 347 Scott Karl	.05	.02	.01
☐ 348 Darryl Hamilton	.05	.02	.01
☐ 349 B.J. Surhoff	.05	.02	.01
☐ 350 Angel Miranda	.05	.02	.01
☐ 351 Sid Roberson	.05	.02	.01
☐ 352 Matt Mieske	.05	.02	.01
☐ 353 Jose Valentin	.05	.02	.01
☐ 354 Matt Lawton	.05	.02	.01
☐ 355 Eddie Guardado	.05	.02	.01
☐ 356 Brad Radke	.05	.02	.01
☐ 357 Pedro Munoz	.05	.02	.01
☐ 358 Scott Stahoviak	.05	.02	.01
☐ 359 Erik Schullstrom	.05	.02	.01
☐ 360 Pat Meares	.05	.02	.01
☐ 361 Marty Cordova	.15	.07	.02
☐ 362 Scott Leius	.05	.02	.01
☐ 363 Matt Walbeck	.05	.02	.01
☐ 364 Rich Becker	.15	.07	.02
☐ 365 Kirby Puckett	.75	.35	.09
☐ 366 Oscar Munoz	.05	.02	.01
☐ 367 Chuck Knoblauch	.30	.14	.04
☐ 368 Marty Cordova ROY	.15	.07	.02

	MINT	NRMT	EXC
☐ 369 Bernie Williams	.40	.18	.05
☐ 370 Mike Stanley	.05	.02	.01
☐ 371 Andy Pettitte	.60	.25	.07
☐ 372 Jack McDowell	.30	.14	.04
☐ 373 Sterling Hitchcock	.05	.02	.01
☐ 374 David Cone	.15	.07	.02
☐ 375 Randy Velarde	.05	.02	.01
☐ 376 Don Mattingly	1.00	.45	.12
☐ 377 Melido Perez	.05	.02	.01
☐ 378 Wade Boggs	.30	.14	.04
☐ 379 Ruben Sierra	.05	.02	.01
☐ 380 Tony Fernandez	.05	.02	.01
☐ 381 John Wetteland	.15	.07	.02
☐ 382 Mariano Rivera	.15	.07	.02
☐ 383 Derek Jeter	1.25	.55	.16
☐ 384 Paul O'Neill	.05	.02	.01
☐ 385 Mark McGwire	.60	.25	.07
☐ 386 Scott Brosius	.15	.07	.02
☐ 387 Don Wengert	.05	.02	.01
☐ 388 Terry Steinbach	.15	.07	.02
☐ 389 Brent Gates	.05	.02	.01
☐ 390 Craig Paquette	.05	.02	.01
☐ 391 Mike Bordick	.15	.07	.02
☐ 392 Ariel Prieto	.05	.02	.01
☐ 393 Dennis Eckersley	.15	.07	.02
☐ 394 Carlos Reyes	.05	.02	.01
☐ 395 Todd Stottlemyre	.05	.02	.01
☐ 396 Rickey Henderson	.30	.14	.04
☐ 397 Geronimo Berroa	.15	.07	.02
☐ 398 Steve Ontiveros	.05	.02	.01
☐ 399 Mike Gallego	.05	.02	.01
☐ 400 Stan Javier	.05	.02	.01
☐ 401 Randy Johnson	.30	.14	.04
☐ 402 Norm Charlton	.05	.02	.01
☐ 403 Mike Blowers	.05	.02	.01
☐ 404 Tino Martinez	.15	.07	.02
☐ 405 Dan Wilson	.05	.02	.01
☐ 406 Andy Benes	.05	.02	.01
☐ 407 Alex Diaz	.05	.02	.01
☐ 408 Edgar Martinez	.15	.07	.02
☐ 409 Chris Bosio	.05	.02	.01
☐ 410 Ken Griffey Jr.	2.00	.90	.25
☐ 411 Luis Sojo	.05	.02	.01
☐ 412 Bob Wolcott	.05	.02	.01
☐ 413 Vince Coleman	.05	.02	.01
☐ 414 Rich Amaral	.05	.02	.01
☐ 415 Jay Buhner	.30	.14	.04
☐ 416 Alex Rodriguez	2.00	.90	.25
☐ 417 Joey Cora	.05	.02	.01
☐ 418 Randy Johnson CY	.30	.14	.04
☐ 419 Edgar Martinez BAC	.15	.07	.02
☐ 420 Ivan Rodriguez	.50	.23	.06
☐ 421 Mark McLemore	.05	.02	.01
☐ 422 Mickey Tettleton	.15	.07	.02
☐ 423 Juan Gonzalez	1.00	.45	.12
☐ 424 Will Clark	.30	.14	.04
☐ 425 Kevin Gross	.05	.02	.01
☐ 426 Dean Palmer	.30	.14	.04
☐ 427 Kenny Rogers	.05	.02	.01
☐ 428 Bob Tewksbury	.05	.02	.01
☐ 429 Benji Gil	.05	.02	.01
☐ 430 Jeff Russell	.05	.02	.01
☐ 431 Rusty Greer	.30	.14	.04
☐ 432 Roger Pavlik	.05	.02	.01
☐ 433 Esteban Beltre	.05	.02	.01
☐ 434 Otis Nixon	.05	.02	.01
☐ 435 Paul Molitor	.40	.18	.05
☐ 436 Carlos Delgado	.15	.07	.02
☐ 437 Ed Sprague	.15	.07	.02
☐ 438 Juan Guzman	.05	.02	.01
☐ 439 Domingo Cedeno	.05	.02	.01
☐ 440 Pat Hentgen	.15	.07	.02
☐ 441 Tomas Perez	.05	.02	.01
☐ 442 John Olerud	.05	.02	.01
☐ 443 Shawn Green	.15	.07	.02
☐ 444 Al Leiter	.05	.02	.01
☐ 445 Joe Carter	.15	.07	.02
☐ 446 Robert Perez	.05	.02	.01
☐ 447 Devon White	.05	.02	.01
☐ 448 Tony Castillo	.05	.02	.01
☐ 449 Alex Gonzalez	.05	.02	.01
☐ 450 Roberto Alomar	.40	.18	.05

1996 Pacific Cramer's Choice

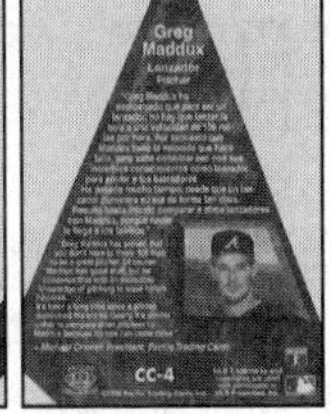

Randomly inserted in packs at a rate of one in 721, this 10-card set features the top Major League Baseball players as chosen by Pacific President and CEO, Michael Cramer. The fronts display a color player cut-out on a pyramid diecut shaped background. The backs carry information about why the player was selected for this set in both English and Spanish.

	MINT	NRMT	EXC
COMPLETE SET (10)	1200.00	550.00	150.00
COMMON CARD (CC1-CC10)	40.00	18.00	5.00
☐ CC1 Roberto Alomar	50.00	22.00	6.25
☐ CC2 Wade Boggs	40.00	18.00	5.00
☐ CC3 Cal Ripken	200.00	90.00	25.00
☐ CC4 Greg Maddux	150.00	70.00	19.00
☐ CC5 Frank Thomas	250.00	110.00	31.00
☐ CC6 Tony Gwynn	100.00	45.00	12.50
☐ CC7 Mike Piazza	175.00	80.00	22.00
☐ CC8 Ken Griffey Jr.	250.00	110.00	31.00
☐ CC9 Manny Ramirez	60.00	27.00	7.50
☐ CC10 Edgar Martinez	40.00	18.00	5.00

1996 Pacific Estrellas Latinas

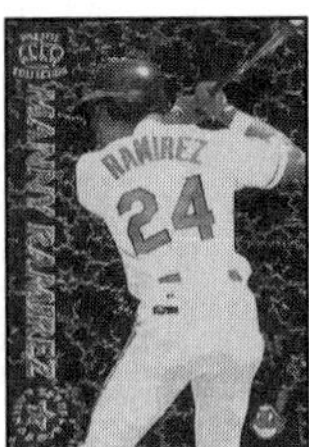

Randomly inserted in packs at a rate of four in 37, this 36-card set salutes the great Latino players in the major leagues today. The fronts feature color player action cut-outs on a black and gold foil background. The horizontal backs carry a player portrait with information about the player in both English and Spanish.

	MINT	NRMT	EXC
COMPLETE SET (36)	50.00	22.00	6.25
COMMON CARD (EL1-EL36)	1.00	.45	.12
☐ EL1 Roberto Alomar	3.00	1.35	.35
☐ EL2 Moises Alou	1.50	.70	.19
☐ EL3 Carlos Baerga	1.00	.45	.12
☐ EL4 Geronimo Berroa	1.00	.45	.12
☐ EL5 Ricky Bones	1.00	.45	.12
☐ EL6 Bobby Bonilla	1.50	.70	.19
☐ EL7 Jose Canseco	2.00	.90	.25
☐ EL8 Vinny Castilla	1.50	.70	.19
☐ EL9 Pedro Martinez	1.50	.70	.19
☐ EL10 John Valentin	1.00	.45	.12
☐ EL11 Andres Galarraga	2.00	.90	.25
☐ EL12 Juan Gonzalez	8.00	3.60	1.00
☐ EL13 Ozzie Guillen	1.00	.45	.12
☐ EL14 Esteban Loaiza	1.00	.45	.12
☐ EL15 Javier Lopez	2.00	.90	.25
☐ EL16 Dennis Martinez	1.00	.45	.12
☐ EL17 Edgar Martinez	1.50	.70	.19
☐ EL18 Tino Martinez	1.50	.70	.19
☐ EL19 Orlando Merced	1.00	.45	.12
☐ EL20 Jose Mesa	1.00	.45	.12
☐ EL21 Raul Mondesi	2.00	.90	.25
☐ EL22 Jaime Navarro	1.00	.45	.12
☐ EL23 Rafael Palmeiro	2.00	.90	.25
☐ EL24 Carlos Perez	1.00	.45	.12
☐ EL25 Manny Ramirez	4.00	1.80	.50
☐ EL26 Alex Rodriguez	15.00	6.75	1.85
☐ EL27 Ivan Rodriguez	4.00	1.80	.50
☐ EL28 David Segui	1.00	.45	.12
☐ EL29 Ruben Sierra	1.00	.45	.12
☐ EL30 Sammy Sosa	2.50	1.10	.30
☐ EL31 Julian Tavarez	1.00	.45	.12
☐ EL32 Ismael Valdes	1.00	.45	.12
☐ EL33 Fernando Valenzuela	1.50	.70	.19
☐ EL34 Quilvio Veras	1.00	.45	.12
☐ EL35 Omar Vizquel	1.50	.70	.19
☐ EL36 Bernie Williams	3.00	1.35	.35

1996 Pacific Gold Crown Die Cuts

Randomly inserted in packs at a rate of one in 37, this 36-card set features 1996 Major League Baseball Super Stars. The fronts display color action player photos with a diecut gold crown at the top and gold foil printing. The backs carry a color player portrait and information about the player in English and Spanish.

	MINT	NRMT	EXC
COMPLETE SET (36)	450.00	200.00	55.00
COMMON CARD (DC1-DC36)	4.00	1.80	.50
☐ DC1 Roberto Alomar	10.00	4.50	1.25
☐ DC2 Will Clark	6.00	2.70	.75
☐ DC3 Johnny Damon	5.00	2.20	.60
☐ DC4 Don Mattingly	25.00	11.00	3.10
☐ DC5 Edgar Martinez	5.00	2.20	.60
☐ DC6 Manny Ramirez	12.00	5.50	1.50
☐ DC7 Mike Piazza	30.00	13.50	3.70
☐ DC8 Quilvio Veras	4.00	1.80	.50
☐ DC9 Rickey Henderson	6.00	2.70	.75
☐ DC10 Jeff Bagwell	20.00	9.00	2.50
☐ DC11 Andres Galarraga	6.00	2.70	.75
☐ DC12 Tim Salmon	6.00	2.70	.75
☐ DC13 Ken Griffey Jr.	50.00	22.00	6.25
☐ DC14 Sammy Sosa	8.00	3.60	1.00
☐ DC15 Cal Ripken	40.00	18.00	5.00
☐ DC16 Raul Mondesi	6.00	2.70	.75
☐ DC17 Jose Canseco	6.00	2.70	.75
☐ DC18 Frank Thomas	50.00	22.00	6.25
☐ DC19 Hideo Nomo	12.00	5.50	1.50
☐ DC20 Wade Boggs	6.00	2.70	.75
☐ DC21 Reggie Sanders	5.00	2.20	.60
☐ DC22 Carlos Baerga	4.00	1.80	.50
☐ DC23 Mo Vaughn	12.00	5.50	1.50
☐ DC24 Ivan Rodriguez	12.00	5.50	1.50
☐ DC25 Kirby Puckett	20.00	9.00	2.50
☐ DC26 Albert Belle	20.00	9.00	2.50
☐ DC27 Vinny Castilla	5.00	2.20	.60
☐ DC28 Greg Maddux	30.00	13.50	3.70
☐ DC29 Dante Bichette	6.00	2.70	.75
☐ DC30 Deion Sanders	6.00	2.70	.75
☐ DC31 Chipper Jones	30.00	13.50	3.70
☐ DC32 Cecil Fielder	5.00	2.20	.60
☐ DC33 Randy Johnson	8.00	3.60	1.00
☐ DC34 Mark McGwire	15.00	6.75	1.85
☐ DC35 Tony Gwynn	20.00	9.00	2.50
☐ DC36 Barry Bonds	12.00	5.50	1.50

1996 Pacific Hometowns

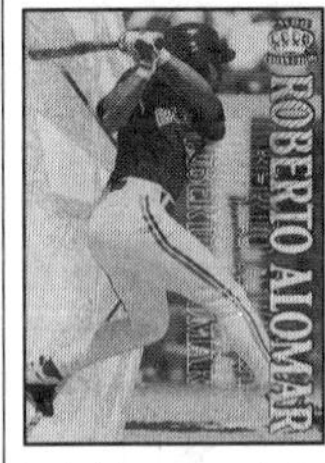

Randomly inserted in packs at a rate of two in 37, this 20-card set features color action player photos with a gold foil border on the left and gold foil printing. The backs carry a player portrait with the player's hometown or city and country and player information printed in both English and Spanish.

	MINT	NRMT	EXC
COMPLETE SET (20)	120.00	55.00	15.00
COMMON CARD (HP1-HP20)	1.50	.70	.19
☐ HP1 Mike Piazza	12.00	5.50	1.50
☐ HP2 Greg Maddux	12.00	5.50	1.50
☐ HP3 Tony Gwynn	8.00	3.60	1.00
☐ HP4 Carlos Baerga	1.50	.70	.19
☐ HP5 Don Mattingly	10.00	4.50	1.25
☐ HP6 Cal Ripken	15.00	6.75	1.85
☐ HP7 Chipper Jones	12.00	5.50	1.50
☐ HP8 Andres Galarraga	2.50	1.10	.30
☐ HP9 Manny Ramirez	5.00	2.20	.60
☐ HP10 Roberto Alomar	4.00	1.80	.50
☐ HP11 Ken Griffey Jr.	20.00	9.00	2.50
☐ HP12 Jose Canseco	2.50	1.10	.30
☐ HP13 Frank Thomas	20.00	9.00	2.50
☐ HP14 Vinny Castilla	2.00	.90	.25
☐ HP15 Roberto Kelly	1.50	.70	.19
☐ HP16 Dennis Martinez	1.50	.70	.19
☐ HP17 Kirby Puckett	8.00	3.60	1.00
☐ HP18 Raul Mondesi	2.50	1.10	.30
☐ HP19 Hideo Nomo	5.00	2.20	.60
☐ HP20 Edgar Martinez	2.00	.90	.25

1996 Pacific Milestones

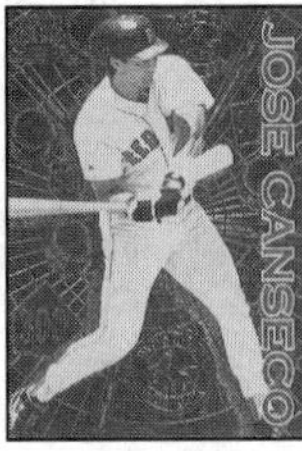

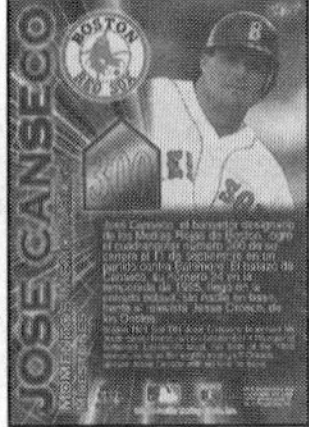

Randomly inserted in packs at a rate of one in 37, this 10-card set denotes the outstanding milestone and record-breaking achievements of baseball's superstars in 1995. The fronts feature a color action player cut-out on a blue foil background with embossed symbols represting the team logo, baseball, and the milestone or achievement. The backs carry a player portrait with the milestone or achievement printed in both English and Spanish.

	MINT	NRMT	EXC
COMPLETE SET (10)	75.00	34.00	9.50
COMMON CARD (M1-M10)	2.50	1.10	.30
☐ M1 Albert Belle	8.00	3.60	1.00
☐ M2 Don Mattingly	10.00	4.50	1.25
☐ M3 Tony Gwynn	8.00	3.60	1.00
☐ M4 Jose Canseco	4.00	1.80	.50
☐ M5 Marty Cordova	2.50	1.10	.30
☐ M6 Wade Boggs	4.00	1.80	.50
☐ M7 Greg Maddux	12.00	5.50	1.50
☐ M8 Eddie Murray	5.00	2.20	.60
☐ M9 Ken Griffey Jr.	20.00	9.00	2.50
☐ M10 Cal Ripken	15.00	6.75	1.85

1996 Pacific October Moments

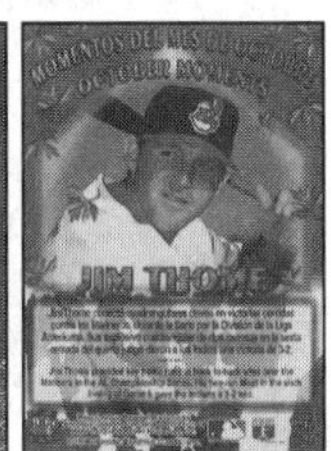

Randomly inserted in packs at a rate of one in 37, this 20-card set highlights 1995 postseason heroics and the players involved. The fronts feature borderless color player action photos with a bronze foil background and printing. The backs carry a player portrait with the heroic action printed in both English and Spanish.

	MINT	NRMT	EXC
COMPLETE SET (20)	150.00	70.00	19.00
COMMON CARD (OM1-OM20)	2.50	1.10	.30
☐ OM1 Carlos Baerga	2.50	1.10	.30
☐ OM2 Albert Belle	12.00	5.50	1.50
☐ OM3 Dante Bichette	4.00	1.80	.50
☐ OM4 Jose Canseco	4.00	1.80	.50
☐ OM5 Tom Glavine	4.00	1.80	.50
☐ OM6 Ken Griffey Jr.	30.00	13.50	3.70
☐ OM7 Randy Johnson	5.00	2.20	.60
☐ OM8 Chipper Jones	20.00	9.00	2.50
☐ OM9 David Justice	3.00	1.35	.35
☐ OM10 Ryan Klesko	5.00	2.20	.60
☐ OM11 Kenny Lofton	8.00	3.60	1.00
☐ OM12 Javier Lopez	3.00	1.35	.35
☐ OM13 Greg Maddux	20.00	9.00	2.50
☐ OM14 Edgar Martinez	3.00	1.35	.35
☐ OM15 Don Mattingly	15.00	6.75	1.85
☐ OM16 Hideo Nomo	8.00	3.60	1.00
☐ OM17 Mike Piazza	20.00	9.00	2.50
☐ OM18 Manny Ramirez	8.00	3.60	1.00
☐ OM19 Reggie Sanders	3.00	1.35	.35
☐ OM20 Jim Thome	6.00	2.70	.75

1996 Pacific/Advil Nolan Ryan

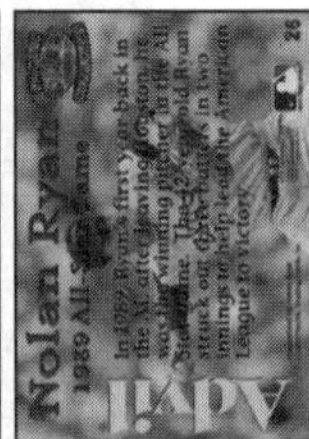

This 27-card standard-size set features all-time strikeout king, Nolan Ryan. The set was available directly with a proof of purchase of Advil products. Each full-bleed card features a different highlight of Ryan's career. There was also an A , B card which were included at retail stores as part of the store display. A collector got a pack with these cards if they a big enough package. They were not available as part of the regular set.

	MINT	NRMT	EXC
COMPLETE SET (27)	15.00	6.75	1.85
COMMON CARD (1-27)	.60	.25	.07
☐ 1 Nolan Ryan New York Mets	.60	.25	.07
☐ 2 Nolan Ryan California Angels	.60	.25	.07
☐ 3 Nolan Ryan Houston Astros	.60	.25	.07
☐ 4 Nolan Ryan Texas Rangers	.60	.25	.07
☐ 5 Nolan Ryan No-Hitter #1	.60	.25	.07
☐ 6 Nolan Ryan No-Hitter #2	.60	.25	.07
☐ 7 Nolan Ryan No-Hitter #3	.60	.25	.07

Card	MINT	NRMT	EXC
☐ 8 Nolan Ryan No-Hitter #4	.60	.25	.07
☐ 9 Nolan Ryan No-Hitter #5	.60	.25	.07
☐ 10 Nolan Ryan No-Hitter #6	.60	.25	.07
☐ 11 Nolan Ryan No-Hitter #7	.60	.25	.07
☐ 12 Nolan Ryan 1st Major League Win	.60	.25	.07
☐ 13 Nolan Ryan 250th Win	.60	.25	.07
☐ 14 Nolan Ryan 300th Win	.60	.25	.07
☐ 15 Nolan Ryan 324th Win	.60	.25	.07
☐ 16 Nolan Ryan 1,000 Strikeout	.60	.25	.07
☐ 17 Nolan Ryan 2,000 Strikeout	.60	.25	.07
☐ 18 Nolan Ryan 3,000 Strikeout	.60	.25	.07
☐ 19 Nolan Ryan Strikeout Record	.60	.25	.07
☐ 20 Nolan Ryan 4,000 Strikeout	.60	.25	.07
☐ 21 Nolan Ryan 5,000 Strikeout	.60	.25	.07
☐ 22 Nolan Ryan World Series Victory	.60	.25	.07
☐ 23 Nolan Ryan Fastest Pitch	.60	.25	.07
☐ 24 Nolan Ryan Ryan Homerun	.60	.25	.07
☐ 25 Nolan Ryan Power Pitcher	.60	.25	.07
☐ 26 Nolan Ryan 1989 All-Star Game	.60	.25	.07
☐ 27 Nolan Ryan Last Appearence	.60	.25	.07
☐ A Nolan Ryan	2.50	1.10	.30
☐ B Nolan Ryan	2.50	1.10	.30

1996 Pacific Baerga Softball

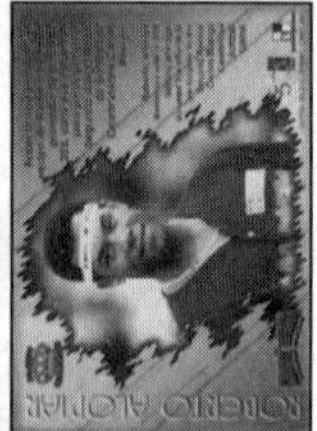

This eight card set features major league baseball players who donated their time to participate in the Second Annual Carlos Baerga Celebrities Softball Game, played Dec. 8 in Bayamon, Puerto Rico. Two cards from the set were distributed to each attendee of the game. The fronts carry colored action player photos from the softball game. The backs display color player portraits with player information in both Spanish and English.

	MINT	NRMT	EXC
COMPLETE SET (8)	6.00	2.70	.75
COMMON CARD (1-8)	.25	.11	.03
☐ 1 Carlos Baerga	.25	.11	.03
☐ 2 Mike Piazza	1.75	.80	.22
☐ 3 Bernie Williams	.35	.16	.04
☐ 4 Frank Thomas	3.00	1.35	.35
☐ 5 Roberto Alomar	.60	.25	.07
☐ 6 Edgar Martinez	.75	.35	.09
☐ 7 Kenny Lofton	1.00	.45	.12
☐ 8 Sammy Sosa	.60	.25	.07

1997 Pacific

This 450-card set was issued in one series and distributed in 12-card packs. The fronts feature color action player photos foiled in gold. The backs carry player information in both English and Spanish with player statistics.

	MINT	NRMT	EXC
COMPLETE SET (450)	40.00	18.00	5.00
COMMON CARD (1-450)	.10	.05	.01
☐ 1 Garret Anderson	.10	.05	.01
☐ 2 George Arias	.10	.05	.01
☐ 3 Chili Davis	.10	.05	.01
☐ 4 Gary DiSarcina	.10	.05	.01
☐ 5 Jim Edmonds	.25	.11	.03
☐ 6 Darin Erstad	1.50	.70	.19
☐ 7 Jorge Fabregas	.10	.05	.01
☐ 8 Chuck Finley	.10	.05	.01
☐ 9 Rex Hudler	.10	.05	.01
☐ 10 Mark Langston	.10	.05	.01
☐ 11 Orlando Palmeiro	.10	.05	.01
☐ 12 Troy Percival	.10	.05	.01
☐ 13 Tim Salmon	.40	.18	.05
☐ 14 J.T. Snow	.10	.05	.01
☐ 15 Randy Velarde	.10	.05	.01
☐ 16 Manny Alexander	.10	.05	.01
☐ 17 Roberto Alomar	.60	.25	.07
☐ 18 Brady Anderson	.25	.11	.03
☐ 19 Armando Benitez	.10	.05	.01
☐ 20 Bobby Bonilla	.25	.11	.03
☐ 21 Rocky Coppinger	.25	.11	.03
☐ 22 Scott Erickson	.10	.05	.01
☐ 23 Jeffrey Hammonds	.10	.05	.01
☐ 24 Chris Hoiles	.10	.05	.01
☐ 25 Eddie Murray	.75	.35	.09
☐ 26 Mike Mussina	.50	.23	.06
☐ 27 Randy Myers	.10	.05	.01
☐ 28 Rafael Palmeiro	.40	.18	.05
☐ 29 Cal Ripken	2.50	1.10	.30
☐ 30 B.J. Surhoff	.10	.05	.01
☐ 31 Tony Tarasco	.10	.05	.01
☐ 32 Esteban Beltre	.10	.05	.01
☐ 33 Darren Bragg	.10	.05	.01
☐ 34 Jose Canseco	.40	.18	.05
☐ 35 Roger Clemens	.60	.25	.07
☐ 36 Wil Cordero	.10	.05	.01
☐ 37 Alex Delgado	.10	.05	.01
☐ 38 Jeff Frye	.10	.05	.01
☐ 39 Nomar Garciaparra	1.25	.55	.16
☐ 40 Tom Gordon	.10	.05	.01
☐ 41 Mike Greenwell	.10	.05	.01
☐ 42 Reggie Jefferson	.10	.05	.01
☐ 43 Tim Naehring	.10	.05	.01
☐ 44 Troy O'Leary	.10	.05	.01
☐ 45 Heathcliff Slocumb	.10	.05	.01
☐ 46 Lee Tinsley	.10	.05	.01
☐ 47 John Valentin	.10	.05	.01
☐ 48 Mo Vaughn	.75	.35	.09
☐ 49 Wilson Alvarez	.10	.05	.01
☐ 50 Harold Baines	.10	.05	.01
☐ 51 Ray Durham	.10	.05	.01
☐ 52 Alex Fernandez	.25	.11	.03
☐ 53 Ozzie Guillen	.10	.05	.01
☐ 54 Roberto Hernandez	.10	.05	.01
☐ 55 Ron Karkovice	.10	.05	.01
☐ 56 Darren Lewis	.10	.05	.01
☐ 57 Norberto Martin	.10	.05	.01
☐ 58 Dave Martinez	.10	.05	.01
☐ 59 Lyle Mouton	.10	.05	.01
☐ 60 Jose Munoz	.10	.05	.01
☐ 61 Tony Phillips	.10	.05	.01
☐ 62 Kevin Tapani	.10	.05	.01
☐ 63 Danny Tartabull	.10	.05	.01
☐ 64 Frank Thomas	3.00	1.35	.35
☐ 65 Robin Ventura	.25	.11	.03
☐ 66 Sandy Alomar Jr.	.10	.05	.01
☐ 67 Albert Belle	1.25	.55	.16
☐ 68 Julio Franco	.10	.05	.01
☐ 69 Brian Giles	.10	.05	.01
☐ 70 Danny Graves	.10	.05	.01
☐ 71 Orel Hershiser	.25	.11	.03
☐ 72 Jeff Kent	.10	.05	.01
☐ 73 Kenny Lofton	.75	.35	.09
☐ 74 Dennis Martinez	.10	.05	.01
☐ 75 Jack McDowell	.10	.05	.01
☐ 76 Jose Mesa	.10	.05	.01
☐ 77 Charles Nagy	.25	.11	.03
☐ 78 Manny Ramirez	.75	.35	.09
☐ 79 Julian Tavarez	.10	.05	.01
☐ 80 Jim Thome	.60	.25	.07
☐ 81 Jose Vizcaino	.10	.05	.01
☐ 82 Omar Vizquel	.25	.11	.03
☐ 83 Brad Ausmus	.10	.05	.01
☐ 84 Kimera Bartee	.10	.05	.01
☐ 85 Raul Casanova	.10	.05	.01
☐ 86 Tony Clark	.50	.23	.06
☐ 87 Travis Fryman	.25	.11	.03
☐ 88 Bobby Higginson	.25	.11	.03
☐ 89 Mark Lewis	.10	.05	.01
☐ 90 Jose Lima	.10	.05	.01
☐ 91 Felipe Lira	.10	.05	.01
☐ 92 Phil Nevin	.10	.05	.01
☐ 93 Melvin Nieves	.10	.05	.01
☐ 94 Curtis Pride	.10	.05	.01
☐ 95 Ruben Sierra	.10	.05	.01
☐ 96 Alan Trammell	.25	.11	.03
☐ 97 Kevin Appier	.25	.11	.03
☐ 98 Tim Belcher	.10	.05	.01
☐ 99 Johnny Damon	.10	.05	.01
☐ 100 Tom Goodwin	.10	.05	.01
☐ 101 Bob Hamelin	.10	.05	.01
☐ 102 David Howard	.10	.05	.01
☐ 103 Jason Jacome	.10	.05	.01
☐ 104 Keith Lockhart	.10	.05	.01
☐ 105 Mike Macfarlane	.10	.05	.01
☐ 106 Jeff Montgomery	.10	.05	.01
☐ 107 Jose Offerman	.10	.05	.01
☐ 108 Hipolito Pichardo	.10	.05	.01
☐ 109 Joe Randa	.10	.05	.01
☐ 110 Bip Roberts	.10	.05	.01
☐ 111 Chris Stynes	.10	.05	.01
☐ 112 Mike Sweeney	.25	.11	.03
☐ 113 Joe Vitiello	.10	.05	.01
☐ 114 Jeromy Burnitz	.10	.05	.01
☐ 115 Chuck Carr	.10	.05	.01
☐ 116 Jeff Cirillo	.10	.05	.01
☐ 117 Mike Fetters	.10	.05	.01
☐ 118 David Hulse	.10	.05	.01
☐ 119 John Jaha	.25	.11	.03
☐ 120 Scott Karl	.10	.05	.01
☐ 121 Jesse Levis	.10	.05	.01
☐ 122 Mark Loretta	.10	.05	.01
☐ 123 Mike Matheny	.10	.05	.01
☐ 124 Ben McDonald	.10	.05	.01
☐ 125 Matt Mieske	.10	.05	.01
☐ 126 Angel Miranda	.10	.05	.01
☐ 127 Dave Nilsson	.10	.05	.01
☐ 128 Jose Valentin	.10	.05	.01
☐ 129 Fernando Vina	.10	.05	.01
☐ 130 Ron Villone	.10	.05	.01
☐ 131 Gerald Williams	.10	.05	.01
☐ 132 Rick Aguilera	.10	.05	.01
☐ 133 Rich Becker	.10	.05	.01
☐ 134 Ron Coomer	.10	.05	.01
☐ 135 Marty Cordova	.25	.11	.03
☐ 136 Eddie Guardado	.10	.05	.01
☐ 137 Denny Hocking	.10	.05	.01
☐ 138 Roberto Kelly	.10	.05	.01
☐ 139 Chuck Knoblauch	.50	.23	.06
☐ 140 Matt Lawton	.10	.05	.01
☐ 141 Pat Meares	.10	.05	.01
☐ 142 Paul Molitor	.60	.25	.07
☐ 143 Greg Myers	.10	.05	.01
☐ 144 Jeff Reboulet	.10	.05	.01
☐ 145 Scott Stahoviak	.10	.05	.01
☐ 146 Todd Walker	1.25	.55	.16
☐ 147 Wade Boggs	.40	.18	.05
☐ 148 David Cone	.25	.11	.03
☐ 149 Mariano Duncan	.10	.05	.01
☐ 150 Cecil Fielder	.25	.11	.03
☐ 151 Dwight Gooden	.25	.11	.03
☐ 152 Derek Jeter	2.00	.90	.25
☐ 153 Jim Leyritz	.10	.05	.01
☐ 154 Tino Martinez	.25	.11	.03
☐ 155 Paul O'Neill	.10	.05	.01
☐ 156 Andy Pettitte	.75	.35	.09
☐ 157 Tim Raines	.10	.05	.01
☐ 158 Mariano Rivera	.25	.11	.03
☐ 159 Ruben Rivera	.40	.18	.05
☐ 160 Kenny Rogers	.10	.05	.01
☐ 161 Darryl Strawberry	.25	.11	.03
☐ 162 John Wetteland	.25	.11	.03
☐ 163 Bernie Williams	.60	.25	.07
☐ 164 Tony Batista	.40	.18	.05
☐ 165 Geronimo Berroa	.10	.05	.01
☐ 166 Mike Bordick	.10	.05	.01
☐ 167 Scott Brosius	.10	.05	.01
☐ 168 Brent Gates	.10	.05	.01
☐ 169 Jason Giambi	.25	.11	.03
☐ 170 Jose Herrera	.10	.05	.01
☐ 171 Brian Lesher	.10	.05	.01
☐ 172 Damon Mashore	.25	.11	.03
☐ 173 Mark McGwire	1.00	.45	.12
☐ 174 Ariel Prieto	.10	.05	.01
☐ 175 Carlos Reyes	.10	.05	.01
☐ 176 Matt Stairs	.10	.05	.01
☐ 177 Terry Steinbach	.10	.05	.01
☐ 178 John Wasdin	.10	.05	.01
☐ 179 Ernie Young	.10	.05	.01
☐ 180 Rich Amaral	.10	.05	.01
☐ 181 Bobby Ayala	.10	.05	.01
☐ 182 Jay Buhner	.40	.18	.05
☐ 183 Rafael Carmona	.10	.05	.01
☐ 184 Norm Charlton	.10	.05	.01
☐ 185 Joey Cora	.10	.05	.01
☐ 186 Ken Griffey Jr.	3.00	1.35	.35
☐ 187 Sterling Hitchcock	.10	.05	.01
☐ 188 Dave Hollins	.10	.05	.01
☐ 189 Randy Johnson	.50	.23	.06
☐ 190 Edgar Martinez	.25	.11	.03
☐ 191 Jamie Moyer	.10	.05	.01
☐ 192 Alex Rodriguez	3.00	1.35	.35
☐ 193 Paul Sorrento	.10	.05	.01
☐ 194 Salomon Torres	.10	.05	.01
☐ 195 Bob Wells	.10	.05	.01
☐ 196 Dan Wilson	.10	.05	.01
☐ 197 Will Clark	.40	.18	.05
☐ 198 Kevin Elster	.10	.05	.01
☐ 199 Rene Gonzales	.10	.05	.01
☐ 200 Juan Gonzalez	1.50	.70	.19
☐ 201 Rusty Greer	.25	.11	.03
☐ 202 Darryl Hamilton	.10	.05	.01
☐ 203 Mike Henneman	.10	.05	.01
☐ 204 Ken Hill	.10	.05	.01
☐ 205 Mark McLemore	.10	.05	.01
☐ 206 Darren Oliver	.10	.05	.01
☐ 207 Dean Palmer	.10	.05	.01
☐ 208 Roger Pavlik	.10	.05	.01
☐ 209 Ivan Rodriguez	.75	.35	.09
☐ 210 Kurt Stillwell	.10	.05	.01
☐ 211 Mickey Tettleton	.10	.05	.01
☐ 212 Bobby Witt	.10	.05	.01
☐ 213 Tilson Brito	.10	.05	.01
☐ 214 Jacob Brumfield	.10	.05	.01
☐ 215 Miguel Cairo	.10	.05	.01
☐ 216 Joe Carter	.25	.11	.03
☐ 217 Felipe Crespo	.10	.05	.01
☐ 218 Carlos Delgado	.25	.11	.03
☐ 219 Alex Gonzalez	.10	.05	.01
☐ 220 Shawn Green	.10	.05	.01
☐ 221 Juan Guzman	.10	.05	.01
☐ 222 Pat Hentgen	.25	.11	.03
☐ 223 Charlie O'Brien	.10	.05	.01
☐ 224 John Olerud	.10	.05	.01
☐ 225 Robert Perez	.10	.05	.01
☐ 226 Tomas Perez	.10	.05	.01
☐ 227 Juan Samuel	.10	.05	.01
☐ 228 Ed Sprague	.10	.05	.01
☐ 229 Mike Timlin	.10	.05	.01
☐ 230 Rafael Belliard	.10	.05	.01
☐ 231 Jermaine Dye	.50	.23	.06
☐ 232 Tom Glavine	.40	.18	.05
☐ 233 Marquis Grissom	.25	.11	.03
☐ 234 Andruw Jones	3.00	1.35	.35
☐ 235 Chipper Jones	2.00	.90	.25
☐ 236 David Justice	.25	.11	.03
☐ 237 Ryan Klesko	.50	.23	.06
☐ 238 Mark Lemke	.10	.05	.01
☐ 239 Javier Lopez	.25	.11	.03
☐ 240 Greg Maddux	2.00	.90	.25
☐ 241 Fred McGriff	.40	.18	.05
☐ 242 Denny Neagle	.10	.05	.01
☐ 243 Eddie Perez	.10	.05	.01
☐ 244 John Smoltz	.50	.23	.06
☐ 245 Mark Wohlers	.10	.05	.01
☐ 246 Brant Brown	.10	.05	.01
☐ 247 Scott Bullett	.10	.05	.01
☐ 248 Leo Gomez	.10	.05	.01
☐ 249 Luis Gonzalez	.10	.05	.01
☐ 250 Mark Grace	.40	.18	.05
☐ 251 Jose Hernandez	.10	.05	.01
☐ 252 Brooks Kieschnick	.25	.11	.03
☐ 253 Brian McRae	.10	.05	.01
☐ 254 Jaime Navarro	.10	.05	.01
☐ 255 Mike Perez	.10	.05	.01
☐ 256 Rey Sanchez	.10	.05	.01
☐ 257 Ryne Sandberg	.75	.35	.09
☐ 258 Scott Servais	.10	.05	.01
☐ 259 Sammy Sosa	.50	.23	.06
☐ 260 Pedro Valdes	.10	.05	.01
☐ 261 Turk Wendell	.10	.05	.01
☐ 262 Bret Boone	.10	.05	.01
☐ 263 Jeff Branson	.10	.05	.01
☐ 264 Jeff Brantley	.10	.05	.01
☐ 265 Dave Burba	.10	.05	.01
☐ 266 Hector Carrasco	.10	.05	.01
☐ 267 Eric Davis	.10	.05	.01
☐ 268 Willie Greene	.10	.05	.01
☐ 269 Lenny Harris	.10	.05	.01
☐ 270 Thomas Howard	.10	.05	.01
☐ 271 Barry Larkin	.40	.18	.05
☐ 272 Hal Morris	.10	.05	.01
☐ 273 Joe Oliver	.10	.05	.01
☐ 274 Eric Owens	.10	.05	.01
☐ 275 Jose Rijo	.10	.05	.01
☐ 276 Reggie Sanders	.25	.11	.03
☐ 277 Eddie Taubensee	.10	.05	.01
☐ 278 Jason Bates	.10	.05	.01
☐ 279 Dante Bichette	.40	.18	.05
☐ 280 Ellis Burks	.25	.11	.03
☐ 281 Vinny Castilla	.25	.11	.03
☐ 282 Andres Galarraga	.40	.18	.05
☐ 283 Quinton McCracken	.10	.05	.01
☐ 284 Jayhawk Owens	.10	.05	.01
☐ 285 Jeff Reed	.10	.05	.01
☐ 286 Bryan Rekar	.10	.05	.01
☐ 287 Armando Reynoso	.10	.05	.01
☐ 288 Kevin Ritz	.10	.05	.01
☐ 289 Bruce Ruffin	.10	.05	.01
☐ 290 John Vander Wal	.10	.05	.01
☐ 291 Larry Walker	.25	.11	.03
☐ 292 Walt Weiss	.10	.05	.01
☐ 293 Eric Young	.25	.11	.03
☐ 294 Kurt Abbott	.10	.05	.01
☐ 295 Alex Arias	.10	.05	.01
☐ 296 Miguel Batista	.10	.05	.01
☐ 297 Kevin Brown	.25	.11	.03
☐ 298 Luis Castillo	.40	.18	.05
☐ 299 Greg Colbrunn	.10	.05	.01
☐ 300 Jeff Conine	.25	.11	.03
☐ 301 Charles Johnson	.10	.05	.01
☐ 302 Al Leiter	.10	.05	.01
☐ 303 Robb Nen	.10	.05	.01
☐ 304 Joe Orsulak	.10	.05	.01
☐ 305 Yorkis Perez	.10	.05	.01
☐ 306 Edgar Renteria	.40	.18	.05
☐ 307 Gary Sheffield	.50	.23	.06
☐ 308 Jesus Tavarez	.10	.05	.01
☐ 309 Quilvio Veras	.10	.05	.01
☐ 310 Devon White	.10	.05	.01
☐ 311 Jeff Bagwell	1.25	.55	.16
☐ 312 Derek Bell	.25	.11	.03
☐ 313 Sean Berry	.10	.05	.01
☐ 314 Craig Biggio	.25	.11	.03
☐ 315 Doug Drabek	.10	.05	.01
☐ 316 Tony Eusebio	.10	.05	.01
☐ 317 Ricky Gutierrez	.10	.05	.01

☐ 318 Xavier Hernandez	.10	.05	.01
☐ 319 Brian L. Hunter	.10	.05	.01
☐ 320 Darryl Kile	.10	.05	.01
☐ 321 Derrick May	.10	.05	.01
☐ 322 Orlando Miller	.10	.05	.01
☐ 323 James Mouton	.10	.05	.01
☐ 324 Bill Spiers	.10	.05	.01
☐ 325 Pedro Astacio	.10	.05	.01
☐ 326 Brett Butler	.10	.05	.01
☐ 327 Juan Castro	.10	.05	.01
☐ 328 Roger Cedeno	.10	.05	.01
☐ 329 Delino DeShields	.10	.05	.01
☐ 330 Karim Garcia	.50	.23	.06
☐ 331 Todd Hollandsworth	.25	.11	.03
☐ 332 Eric Karros	.25	.11	.03
☐ 333 Oreste Marrero	.10	.05	.01
☐ 334 Ramon Martinez	.25	.11	.03
☐ 335 Raul Mondesi	.40	.18	.05
☐ 336 Hideo Nomo	.75	.35	.09
☐ 337 Antonio Osuna	.10	.05	.01
☐ 338 Chan Ho Park	.40	.18	.05
☐ 339 Mike Piazza	2.00	.90	.25
☐ 340 Ismael Valdes	.25	.11	.03
☐ 341 Moises Alou	.25	.11	.03
☐ 342 Omar Daal	.10	.05	.01
☐ 343 Jeff Fassero	.10	.05	.01
☐ 344 Cliff Floyd	.10	.05	.01
☐ 345 Mark Grudzielanek	.10	.05	.01
☐ 346 Mike Lansing	.10	.05	.01
☐ 347 Pedro Martinez	.25	.11	.03
☐ 348 Sherman Obando	.10	.05	.01
☐ 349 Jose Paniagua	.10	.05	.01
☐ 350 Henry Rodriguez	.25	.11	.03
☐ 351 Mel Rojas	.10	.05	.01
☐ 352 F.P. Santangelo	.10	.05	.01
☐ 353 David Segui	.10	.05	.01
☐ 354 Dave Silvestri	.10	.05	.01
☐ 355 Ugueth Urbina	.10	.05	.01
☐ 356 Rondell White	.10	.05	.01
☐ 357 Edgardo Alfonzo	.10	.05	.01
☐ 358 Carlos Baerga	.25	.11	.03
☐ 359 Tim Bogar	.10	.05	.01
☐ 360 Rico Brogna	.10	.05	.01
☐ 361 Alvaro Espinoza	.10	.05	.01
☐ 362 Carl Everett	.10	.05	.01
☐ 363 John Franco	.10	.05	.01
☐ 364 Bernard Gilkey	.10	.05	.01
☐ 365 Todd Hundley	.25	.11	.03
☐ 366 Butch Huskey	.10	.05	.01
☐ 367 Jason Isringhausen	.25	.11	.03
☐ 368 Bobby Jones	.10	.05	.01
☐ 369 Lance Johnson	.10	.05	.01
☐ 370 Brent Mayne	.10	.05	.01
☐ 371 Alex Ochoa	.10	.05	.01
☐ 372 Rey Ordonez	.40	.18	.05
☐ 373 Ron Blazier	.10	.05	.01
☐ 374 Ricky Bottalico	.10	.05	.01
☐ 375 David Doster	.10	.05	.01
☐ 376 Lenny Dykstra	.25	.11	.03
☐ 377 Jim Eisenreich	.10	.05	.01
☐ 378 Bobby Estalella	.40	.18	.05
☐ 379 Gregg Jefferies	.10	.05	.01
☐ 380 Kevin Jordan	.10	.05	.01
☐ 381 Ricardo Jordan	.10	.05	.01
☐ 382 Mickey Morandini	.10	.05	.01
☐ 383 Ricky Otero	.10	.05	.01
☐ 384 Benito Santiago	.10	.05	.01
☐ 385 Gene Schall	.10	.05	.01
☐ 386 Curt Schilling	.10	.05	.01
☐ 387 Kevin Sefcik	.10	.05	.01
☐ 388 Kevin Stocker	.10	.05	.01
☐ 389 Jermaine Allensworth	.25	.11	.03
☐ 390 Jay Bell	.10	.05	.01
☐ 391 Jason Christiansen	.10	.05	.01
☐ 392 Francisco Cordova	.10	.05	.01
☐ 393 Mark Johnson	.10	.05	.01
☐ 394 Jason Kendall	.25	.11	.03
☐ 395 Jeff King	.10	.05	.01
☐ 396 Jon Lieber	.10	.05	.01
☐ 397 Nelson Liriano	.10	.05	.01
☐ 398 Esteban Loaiza	.10	.05	.01
☐ 399 Al Martin	.10	.05	.01
☐ 400 Orlando Merced	.10	.05	.01
☐ 401 Ramon Morel	.10	.05	.01
☐ 402 Luis Alicea	.10	.05	.01
☐ 403 Alan Benes	.25	.11	.03
☐ 404 Andy Benes	.10	.05	.01
☐ 405 Terry Bradshaw	.10	.05	.01
☐ 406 Royce Clayton	.10	.05	.01
☐ 407 Dennis Eckersley	.25	.11	.03
☐ 408 Gary Gaetti	.10	.05	.01
☐ 409 Mike Gallego	.10	.05	.01
☐ 410 Ron Gant	.25	.11	.03
☐ 411 Brian Jordan	.25	.11	.03
☐ 412 Ray Lankford	.25	.11	.03
☐ 413 John Mabry	.10	.05	.01
☐ 414 Willie McGee	.10	.05	.01
☐ 415 Tom Pagnozzi	.10	.05	.01
☐ 416 Ozzie Smith	.75	.35	.09
☐ 417 Todd Stottlemyre	.10	.05	.01
☐ 418 Mark Sweeney	.10	.05	.01
☐ 419 Andy Ashby	.10	.05	.01
☐ 420 Ken Caminiti	.50	.23	.06
☐ 421 Archi Cianfrocco	.10	.05	.01
☐ 422 Steve Finley	.10	.05	.01
☐ 423 Chris Gomez	.10	.05	.01
☐ 424 Tony Gwynn	1.25	.55	.16
☐ 425 Joey Hamilton	.25	.11	.03
☐ 426 Rickey Henderson	.40	.18	.05
☐ 427 Trevor Hoffman	.10	.05	.01
☐ 428 Brian Johnson	.10	.05	.01
☐ 429 Wally Joyner	.10	.05	.01
☐ 430 Scott Livingstone	.10	.05	.01
☐ 431 Jody Reed	.10	.05	.01
☐ 432 Craig Shipley	.10	.05	.01
☐ 433 Fernando Valenzuela	.25	.11	.03
☐ 434 Greg Vaughn	.10	.05	.01
☐ 435 Rich Aurilia	.10	.05	.01
☐ 436 Kim Batiste	.10	.05	.01
☐ 437 Jose Bautista	.10	.05	.01
☐ 438 Rod Beck	.10	.05	.01
☐ 439 Marvin Benard	.10	.05	.01
☐ 440 Barry Bonds	.75	.35	.09
☐ 441 Shawon Dunston	.10	.05	.01
☐ 442 Shawn Estes	.10	.05	.01
☐ 443 Osvaldo Fernandez	.10	.05	.01
☐ 444 Stan Javier	.10	.05	.01
☐ 445 David McCarty	.10	.05	.01
☐ 446 Bill Mueller	.10	.05	.01
☐ 447 Steve Scarsone	.10	.05	.01
☐ 448 Robby Thompson	.10	.05	.01
☐ 449 Rick Wilkins	.10	.05	.01
☐ 450 Matt Williams	.40	.18	.05

1997 Pacific Light Blue

These Light Blue parallel foil cards were found one per pack exclusively in Wal-Mart and Sam's 14-card retail packs. The cards are very similar in design to the scarce Silver parallels randomly seeded in basic packs resulting in a source of confusion for dealers and collectors alike. The Light Blue parallels are not as reflective as the Silvers. Collectors should take extreme caution when purchasing Silver or Light Blue cards.

	MINT	NRMT	EXC
COMPLETE SET (450)	300.00	135.00	38.00
COMMON CARD (1-450)	.25	.11	.03
*STARS: 4X TO 8X BASIC CARDS			
*YOUNG STARS: 3X TO 6X BASIC CARDS			

1997 Pacific Silver

Randomly inserted in packs at a rate of one in 73, this 450-card set is a silver foil parallel version of the regular set and is similar in design. Only 67 of these sets were produced.

	MINT	NRMT	EXC
COMMON CARD (1-450)	15.00	6.75	1.85
*STARS: 75X TO 120X BASIC CARDS			
*YOUNG STARS: 60X TO 100X BASIC CARDS			
☐ 6 Darin Erstad	150.00	70.00	19.00
☐ 25 Eddie Murray	100.00	45.00	12.50
☐ 29 Cal Ripken	300.00	135.00	38.00
☐ 39 Nomar Garciaparra	120.00	55.00	15.00
☐ 48 Mo Vaughn	100.00	45.00	12.50
☐ 64 Frank Thomas	400.00	180.00	50.00
☐ 67 Albert Belle	200.00	90.00	25.00
☐ 73 Kenny Lofton	100.00	45.00	12.50
☐ 78 Manny Ramirez	100.00	45.00	12.50
☐ 146 Todd Walker	120.00	55.00	15.00
☐ 152 Derek Jeter	250.00	110.00	31.00
☐ 156 Andy Pettitte	100.00	45.00	12.50
☐ 173 Mark McGwire	120.00	55.00	15.00
☐ 186 Ken Griffey Jr.	400.00	180.00	50.00
☐ 192 Alex Rodriguez	400.00	180.00	50.00
☐ 200 Juan Gonzalez	200.00	90.00	25.00
☐ 209 Ivan Rodriguez	100.00	45.00	12.50
☐ 234 Andruw Jones	300.00	135.00	38.00
☐ 235 Chipper Jones	250.00	110.00	31.00
☐ 240 Greg Maddux	200.00	90.00	25.00
☐ 257 Ryne Sandberg	100.00	45.00	12.50
☐ 311 Jeff Bagwell	150.00	70.00	19.00
☐ 336 Hideo Nomo	120.00	55.00	15.00
☐ 339 Mike Piazza	250.00	110.00	31.00
☐ 416 Ozzie Smith	100.00	45.00	12.50
☐ 424 Tony Gwynn	150.00	70.00	19.00
☐ 440 Barry Bonds	100.00	45.00	12.50

1997 Pacific Card-Supials

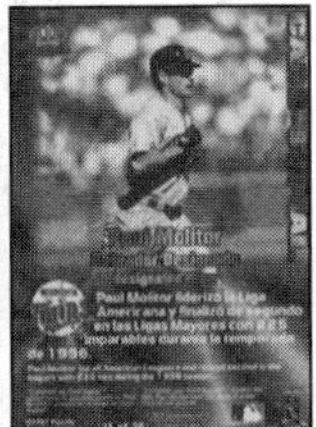

Randomly inserted in packs at a rate of one in 37, this 36-paired-card insert set features color action player photos of some of the greatest players in the Major Leagues. A smaller card was made to pair with the regular size card of the same player. The backs carry a slot for insertion of the small card.

	MINT	NRMT	EXC
COMP.LARGE SET (36)	350.00	160.00	45.00
COMMON LARGE (1-36)	3.00	1.35	.35
☐ 1 Roberto Alomar	6.00	2.70	.75
☐ 2 Brady Anderson	3.00	1.35	.35
☐ 3 Eddie Murray	8.00	3.60	1.00
☐ 4 Cal Ripken	25.00	11.00	3.10
☐ 5 Jose Canseco	4.00	1.80	.50
☐ 6 Mo Vaughn	8.00	3.60	1.00
☐ 7 Frank Thomas	30.00	13.50	3.70
☐ 8 Albert Belle	12.00	5.50	1.50
☐ 9 Omar Vizquel	3.00	1.35	.35
☐ 10 Chuck Knoblauch	5.00	2.20	.60
☐ 11 Paul Molitor	6.00	2.70	.75
☐ 12 Wade Boggs	5.00	2.20	.60
☐ 13 Derek Jeter	20.00	9.00	2.50
☐ 14 Andy Pettitte	8.00	3.60	1.00
☐ 15 Mark McGwire	10.00	4.50	1.25
☐ 16 Jay Buhner	4.00	1.80	.50
☐ 17 Ken Griffey Jr.	30.00	13.50	3.70
☐ 18 Alex Rodriguez	30.00	13.50	3.70
☐ 19 Juan Gonzalez	15.00	6.75	1.85
☐ 20 Ivan Rodriguez	8.00	3.60	1.00
☐ 21 Andruw Jones	30.00	13.50	3.70
☐ 22 Chipper Jones	20.00	9.00	2.50
☐ 23 Ryan Klesko	5.00	2.20	.60
☐ 24 Greg Maddux	20.00	9.00	2.50
☐ 25 Ryne Sandberg	8.00	3.60	1.00
☐ 26 Andres Galarraga	4.00	1.80	.50
☐ 27 Gary Sheffield	5.00	2.20	.60
☐ 28 Jeff Bagwell	12.00	5.50	1.50
☐ 29 Todd Hollandsworth	3.00	1.35	.35
☐ 30 Hideo Nomo	8.00	3.60	1.00
☐ 31 Mike Piazza	20.00	9.00	2.50
☐ 32 Todd Hundley	3.00	1.35	.35
☐ 33 Dennis Eckersley	3.00	1.35	.35
☐ 34 Ken Caminiti	5.00	2.20	.60
☐ 35 Tony Gwynn	12.00	5.50	1.50
☐ 36 Barry Bonds	8.00	3.60	1.00

1997 Pacific Card-Supials Minis

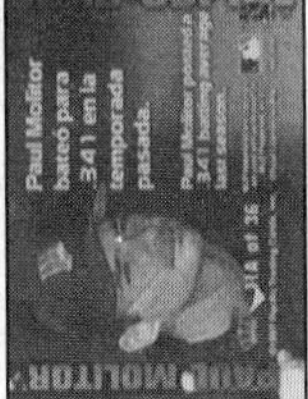

This 36-card mini parallel set measures approximately 1 1/4" by 1 3/4" and was made to be paired with and inserted into the slot in the backs of the cards of the regular size Pacific Card-Supials set to complete the colored action player picture. The backs of this mini set carry a small color head photo and information about the player in Spanish.

	MINT	NRMT	EXC
COMPLETE SET (36)	200.00	90.00	25.00
COMMON CARD (1-36)	2.00	.90	.25
*MINIS: .3X TO .6X BASIC CARD-SUPIALS			

1997 Pacific Cramer's Choice

Randomly inserted in packs at a rate of one in 721, this 10-card set features the top Major League Baseball players as chosen by Pacific President and CEO, Michael Cramer. The fronts display a color player cut-out on a pyramid die-cut shaped background. The backs carry information about why the player was selected for this set in both English and Spanish.

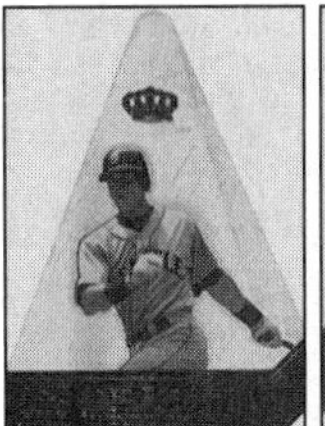

	MINT	NRMT	EXC
COMPLETE SET (10)	1200.00	550.00	150.00
COMMON CARD (1-10)	40.00	18.00	5.00
☐ 1 Roberto Alomar	50.00	22.00	6.25
☐ 2 Frank Thomas	250.00	110.00	31.00
☐ 3 Albert Belle	100.00	45.00	12.50
☐ 4 Andy Pettitte	60.00	27.00	7.50
☐ 5 Ken Griffey Jr.	250.00	110.00	31.00
☐ 6 Alex Rodriguez	250.00	110.00	31.00
☐ 7 Chipper Jones	150.00	70.00	19.00
☐ 8 John Smoltz	40.00	18.00	5.00
☐ 9 Mike Piazza	150.00	70.00	19.00
☐ 10 Tony Gwynn	100.00	45.00	12.50

1997 Pacific Fireworks Die Cuts

Randomly inserted in packs at a rate of one in 73, this 20-card set features color action player photos on a fireworks die-cut background. The backs carry player information in both English and Spanish.

	MINT	NRMT	EXC
COMPLETE SET (20)	450.00	200.00	55.00
COMMON CARD (1-20)	5.00	2.20	.60
☐ 1 Roberto Alomar	10.00	4.50	1.25
☐ 2 Brady Anderson	5.00	2.20	.60
☐ 3 Eddie Murray	12.00	5.50	1.50
☐ 4 Cal Ripken	40.00	18.00	5.00
☐ 5 Frank Thomas	50.00	22.00	6.25
☐ 6 Albert Belle	20.00	9.00	2.50
☐ 7 Derek Jeter	30.00	13.50	3.70
☐ 8 Andy Pettitte	12.00	5.50	1.50
☐ 9 Bernie Williams	10.00	4.50	1.25
☐ 10 Mark McGwire	15.00	6.75	1.85
☐ 11 Ken Griffey Jr.	50.00	22.00	6.25
☐ 12 Alex Rodriguez	50.00	22.00	6.25
☐ 13 Juan Gonzalez	25.00	11.00	3.10
☐ 14 Andruw Jones	50.00	22.00	6.25
☐ 15 Chipper Jones	30.00	13.50	3.70
☐ 16 Hideo Nomo	12.00	5.50	1.50
☐ 17 Mike Piazza	30.00	13.50	3.70
☐ 18 Henry Rodriguez	5.00	2.20	.60
☐ 19 Tony Gwynn	20.00	9.00	2.50
☐ 20 Barry Bonds	12.00	5.50	1.50

1997 Pacific Gold Crown Die Cuts

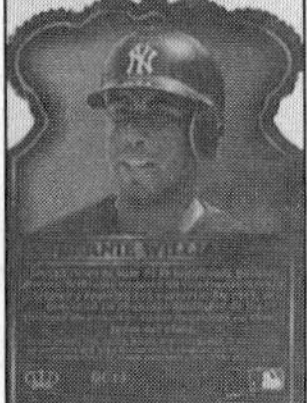

Randomly inserted in packs at a rate of one in 37, this 36-card set honors some of Major League Baseball's Super Stars of today. The fronts feature color action player photos with a die-cut gold crown at the top and gold foil printing. The backs carry player information in both English and Spanish.

	MINT	NRMT	EXC
COMPLETE SET (36)	450.00	200.00	55.00
COMMON CARD (1-36)	4.00	1.80	.50
☐ 1 Roberto Alomar	8.00	3.60	1.00
☐ 2 Brady Anderson	4.00	1.80	.50
☐ 3 Mike Mussina	8.00	3.60	1.00
☐ 4 Eddie Murray	10.00	4.50	1.25
☐ 5 Cal Ripken	30.00	13.50	3.70

	MINT	NRMT	EXC
☐ 6 Jose Canseco	5.00	2.20	.60
☐ 7 Frank Thomas	40.00	18.00	5.00
☐ 8 Albert Belle	15.00	6.75	1.85
☐ 9 Omar Vizquel	4.00	1.80	.50
☐ 10 Wade Boggs	5.00	2.20	.60
☐ 11 Derek Jeter	25.00	11.00	3.10
☐ 12 Andy Pettitte	10.00	4.50	1.25
☐ 13 Mariano Rivera	4.00	1.80	.50
☐ 14 Bernie Williams	8.00	3.60	1.00
☐ 15 Mark McGwire	12.00	5.50	1.50
☐ 16 Ken Griffey Jr.	40.00	18.00	5.00
☐ 17 Edgar Martinez	4.00	1.80	.50
☐ 18 Alex Rodriguez	40.00	18.00	5.00
☐ 19 Juan Gonzalez	20.00	9.00	2.50
☐ 20 Ivan Rodriguez	10.00	4.50	1.25
☐ 21 Andruw Jones	40.00	18.00	5.00
☐ 22 Chipper Jones	25.00	11.00	3.10
☐ 23 Ryan Klesko	6.00	2.70	.75
☐ 24 John Smoltz	6.00	2.70	.75
☐ 25 Ryne Sandberg	10.00	4.50	1.25
☐ 26 Andres Galarraga	5.00	2.20	.60
☐ 27 Edgar Renteria	5.00	2.20	.60
☐ 28 Jeff Bagwell	15.00	6.75	1.85
☐ 29 Todd Hollandsworth	4.00	1.80	.50
☐ 30 Hideo Nomo	10.00	4.50	1.25
☐ 31 Mike Piazza	25.00	11.00	3.10
☐ 32 Todd Hundley	4.00	1.80	.50
☐ 33 Brian Jordan	4.00	1.80	.50
☐ 34 Ken Caminiti	6.00	2.70	.75
☐ 35 Tony Gwynn	15.00	6.75	1.85
☐ 36 Barry Bonds	10.00	4.50	1.25

1997 Pacific Latinos of the Major Leagues

Randomly inserted in packs at a rate of two in 37, this 36-card set salutes the great Latino players in the Major Leagues today. The fronts feature color player action images on a gold foil background of their name. The backs carry player information in both English and Spanish.

	MINT	NRMT	EXC
COMPLETE SET (36)	100.00	45.00	12.50
COMMON CARD (1-36)	1.00	.45	.12
☐ 1 George Arias	1.00	.45	.12
☐ 2 Roberto Alomar	4.00	1.80	.50
☐ 3 Rafael Palmeiro	2.50	1.10	.30
☐ 4 Bobby Bonilla	2.00	.90	.25
☐ 5 Jose Canseco	2.50	1.10	.30
☐ 6 Wilson Alvarez	1.00	.45	.12
☐ 7 Dave Martinez	1.00	.45	.12
☐ 8 Julio Franco	1.00	.45	.12
☐ 9 Manny Ramirez	5.00	2.20	.60
☐ 10 Omar Vizquel	2.00	.90	.25
☐ 11 Marty Cordova	2.00	.90	.25
☐ 12 Roberto Kelly	1.00	.45	.12
☐ 13 Tino Martinez	2.00	.90	.25
☐ 14 Mariano Rivera	2.00	.90	.25
☐ 15 Ruben Rivera	3.00	1.35	.35
☐ 16 Bernie Williams	4.00	1.80	.50
☐ 17 Geronimo Berroa	1.00	.45	.12
☐ 18 Joey Cora	1.00	.45	.12
☐ 19 Edgar Martinez	2.00	.90	.25
☐ 20 Alex Rodriguez	20.00	9.00	2.50
☐ 21 Juan Gonzalez	10.00	4.50	1.25
☐ 22 Ivan Rodriguez	5.00	2.20	.60
☐ 23 Andruw Jones	20.00	9.00	2.50
☐ 24 Javier Lopez	2.00	.90	.25
☐ 25 Sammy Sosa	3.00	1.35	.35
☐ 26 Vinny Castilla	2.00	.90	.25
☐ 27 Andres Galarraga	2.50	1.10	.30
☐ 28 Ramon Martinez	2.00	.90	.25
☐ 29 Raul Mondesi	2.50	1.10	.30
☐ 30 Ismael Valdes	2.00	.90	.25
☐ 31 Pedro Martinez	2.00	.90	.25
☐ 32 Henry Rodriguez	2.00	.90	.25
☐ 33 Carlos Baerga	2.00	.90	.25
☐ 34 Rey Ordonez	2.50	1.10	.30
☐ 35 Fernando Valenzuela	2.00	.90	.25
☐ 36 Osvaldo Fernandez	1.00	.45	.12

1997 Pacific Triple Crown Die Cuts

Randomly inserted in packs at a rate of one in 145, this 20-card set features color player images over a gold foil diamond-shaped background with a die-cut gold crown at the top. The backs carry player information in both English and Spanish.

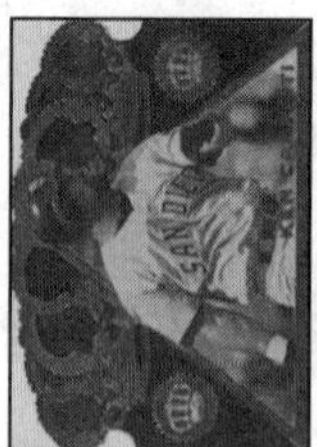

	MINT	NRMT	EXC
COMPLETE SET (20)	750.00	350.00	95.00
COMMON CARD (1-20)	10.00	4.50	1.25
☐ 1 Brady Anderson	10.00	4.50	1.25
☐ 2 Rafael Palmeiro	12.00	5.50	1.50
☐ 3 Mo Vaughn	25.00	11.00	3.10
☐ 4 Frank Thomas	100.00	45.00	12.50
☐ 5 Albert Belle	40.00	18.00	5.00
☐ 6 Jim Thome	20.00	9.00	2.50
☐ 7 Cecil Fielder	10.00	4.50	1.25
☐ 8 Mark McGwire	30.00	13.50	3.70
☐ 9 Ken Griffey Jr.	100.00	45.00	12.50
☐ 10 Alex Rodriguez	100.00	45.00	12.50
☐ 11 Juan Gonzalez	50.00	22.00	6.25
☐ 12 Andruw Jones	100.00	45.00	12.50
☐ 13 Chipper Jones	60.00	27.00	7.50
☐ 14 Dante Bichette	12.00	5.50	1.50
☐ 15 Ellis Burks	10.00	4.50	1.25
☐ 16 Andres Galarraga	12.00	5.50	1.50
☐ 17 Jeff Bagwell	40.00	18.00	5.00
☐ 18 Mike Piazza	60.00	27.00	7.50
☐ 19 Ken Caminiti	15.00	6.75	1.85
☐ 20 Barry Bonds	25.00	11.00	3.10

1995 Pacific Prisms

This 144-card standard-size set was issued for the first time as a stand alone set instead as an insert set. Total production of this product was 2,999 individually numbered cases that contained 20 boxes of 36 packs. The full-bleed fronts feature a player photo against a silver prismatic background with the player's name on the bottom. The backs have a full-color photo with some biographical information. The cards are grouped alphabetically according to teams for each league with AL and NL intermingled. There are no key Rookie Cards in this set. A checklist or team logo card was seeded into every pack.

	MINT	NRMT	EXC
COMPLETE SET (144)	150.00	70.00	19.00
COMMON CARD (1-144)	1.00	.45	.12
COMP.TEAM LOGO SET (28)	5.00	2.20	.60
☐ 1 David Justice	2.00	.90	.25
☐ 2 Ryan Klesko	2.50	1.10	.30
☐ 3 Javier Lopez	2.00	.90	.25
☐ 4 Greg Maddux	10.00	4.50	1.25
☐ 5 Fred McGriff	2.00	.90	.25
☐ 6 Tony Tarasco	1.00	.45	.12
☐ 7 Jeffrey Hammonds	1.50	.70	.19
☐ 8 Mike Mussina	3.00	1.35	.35
☐ 9 Rafael Palmeiro	2.00	.90	.25
☐ 10 Cal Ripken	12.00	5.50	1.50
☐ 11 Lee Smith	1.50	.70	.19
☐ 12 Roger Clemens	3.00	1.35	.35
☐ 13 Scott Cooper	1.00	.45	.12
☐ 14 Mike Greenwell	1.00	.45	.12
☐ 15 Carlos Rodriguez	1.00	.45	.12
☐ 16 Mo Vaughn	4.00	1.80	.50
☐ 17 Chili Davis	1.50	.70	.19
☐ 18 Jim Edmonds	2.00	.90	.25
☐ 19 Jorge Fabregas	1.00	.45	.12
☐ 20 Bo Jackson	1.50	.70	.19
☐ 21 Tim Salmon	2.00	.90	.25
☐ 22 Mark Grace	2.00	.90	.25
☐ 23 Jose Guzman	1.00	.45	.12
☐ 24 Randy Myers	1.00	.45	.12
☐ 25 Rey Sanchez	1.00	.45	.12
☐ 26 Sammy Sosa	2.50	1.10	.30
☐ 27 Wilson Alvarez	1.50	.70	.19
☐ 28 Julio Franco	1.50	.70	.19
☐ 29 Ozzie Guillen	1.00	.45	.12
☐ 30 Jack McDowell	1.50	.70	.19
☐ 31 Frank Thomas	15.00	6.75	1.85
☐ 32 Bret Boone	1.50	.70	.19
☐ 33 Barry Larkin	2.00	.90	.25
☐ 34 Hal Morris	1.00	.45	.12
☐ 35 Jose Rijo	1.00	.45	.12
☐ 36 Deion Sanders	2.00	.90	.25
☐ 37 Carlos Baerga	1.50	.70	.19
☐ 38 Albert Belle	6.00	2.70	.75
☐ 39 Kenny Lofton	4.00	1.80	.50
☐ 40 Dennis Martinez	1.50	.70	.19
☐ 41 Manny Ramirez	4.00	1.80	.50
☐ 42 Omar Vizquel	1.50	.70	.19
☐ 43 Dante Bichette	2.00	.90	.25
☐ 44 Marvin Freeman	1.00	.45	.12
☐ 45 Andres Galarraga	2.00	.90	.25
☐ 46 Mike Kingery	1.00	.45	.12
☐ 47 Danny Bautista	1.00	.45	.12
☐ 48 Cecil Fielder	1.50	.70	.19
☐ 49 Travis Fryman	1.50	.70	.19
☐ 50 Tony Phillips	1.50	.70	.19
☐ 51 Alan Trammell	1.50	.70	.19
☐ 52 Lou Whitaker	1.50	.70	.19
☐ 53 Alex Arias	1.00	.45	.12
☐ 54 Bret Barberie	1.00	.45	.12
☐ 55 Jeff Conine	1.50	.70	.19
☐ 56 Charles Johnson	1.50	.70	.19
☐ 57 Gary Sheffield	2.50	1.10	.30
☐ 58 Jeff Bagwell	6.00	2.70	.75
☐ 59 Craig Biggio	1.50	.70	.19
☐ 60 Doug Drabek	1.00	.45	.12
☐ 61 Tony Eusebio	1.00	.45	.12
☐ 62 Luis Gonzalez	1.00	.45	.12
☐ 63 David Cone	1.50	.70	.19
☐ 64 Bob Hamelin	1.00	.45	.12
☐ 65 Felix Jose	1.00	.45	.12
☐ 66 Wally Joyner	1.50	.70	.19
☐ 67 Brian McRae	1.50	.70	.19
☐ 68 Brett Butler	1.50	.70	.19
☐ 69 Garey Ingram	1.00	.45	.12
☐ 70 Ramon Martinez	1.50	.70	.19
☐ 71 Raul Mondesi	2.00	.90	.25
☐ 72 Mike Piazza	10.00	4.50	1.25
☐ 73 Henry Rodriguez	1.50	.70	.19
☐ 74 Ricky Bones	1.00	.45	.12
☐ 75 Pat Listach	1.00	.45	.12
☐ 76 Dave Nilsson	1.50	.70	.19
☐ 77 Jose Valentin	1.50	.70	.19
☐ 78 Rick Aguilera	1.00	.45	.12
☐ 79 Denny Hocking	1.00	.45	.12
☐ 80 Shane Mack	1.00	.45	.12
☐ 81 Pedro Munoz	1.00	.45	.12
☐ 82 Kirby Puckett	6.00	2.70	.75
☐ 83 Dave Winfield	2.00	.90	.25
☐ 84 Moises Alou	1.50	.70	.19
☐ 85 Wil Cordero	1.00	.45	.12
☐ 86 Cliff Floyd	1.50	.70	.19
☐ 87 Marquis Grissom	1.50	.70	.19
☐ 88 Pedro J. Martinez	1.50	.70	.19
☐ 89 Larry Walker	2.00	.90	.25
☐ 90 Bobby Bonilla	1.50	.70	.19
☐ 91 Jeromy Burnitz	1.00	.45	.12
☐ 92 John Franco	1.00	.45	.12
☐ 93 Jeff Kent	1.00	.45	.12
☐ 94 Jose Vizcaino	1.00	.45	.12
☐ 95 Wade Boggs	2.00	.90	.25
☐ 96 Jimmy Key	1.50	.70	.19
☐ 97 Don Mattingly	8.00	3.60	1.00
☐ 98 Paul O'Neill	1.50	.70	.19
☐ 99 Luis Polonia	1.00	.45	.12
☐ 100 Danny Tartabull	1.00	.45	.12
☐ 101 Geronimo Berroa	1.00	.45	.12
☐ 102 Rickey Henderson	2.00	.90	.25
☐ 103 Ruben Sierra	1.00	.45	.12
☐ 104 Terry Steinbach	1.50	.70	.19
☐ 105 Darren Daulton	1.50	.70	.19
☐ 106 Mariano Duncan	1.00	.45	.12
☐ 107 Lenny Dykstra	1.50	.70	.19
☐ 108 Mike Lieberthal	1.00	.45	.12
☐ 109 Tony Longmire	1.00	.45	.12
☐ 110 Tom Marsh	1.00	.45	.12
☐ 111 Jay Bell	1.50	.70	.19
☐ 112 Carlos Garcia	1.00	.45	.12
☐ 113 Orlando Merced	1.00	.45	.12
☐ 114 Andy Van Slyke	1.50	.70	.19
☐ 115 Derek Bell	1.50	.70	.19
☐ 116 Tony Gwynn	6.00	2.70	.75
☐ 117 Luis Lopez	1.00	.45	.12
☐ 118 Bip Roberts	1.00	.45	.12
☐ 119 Rod Beck	1.00	.45	.12
☐ 120 Barry Bonds	4.00	1.80	.50
☐ 121 Darryl Strawberry	1.50	.70	.19
☐ 122 Wm. Van Landingham	1.00	.45	.12
☐ 123 Matt Williams	2.00	.90	.25
☐ 124 Jay Buhner	2.00	.90	.25
☐ 125 Felix Fermin	1.00	.45	.12
☐ 126 Ken Griffey Jr.	15.00	6.75	1.85
☐ 127 Randy Johnson	2.00	.90	.25
☐ 128 Edgar Martinez	1.50	.70	.19
☐ 129 Alex Rodriguez	20.00	9.00	2.50
☐ 130 Rene Arocha	1.00	.45	.12
☐ 131 Gregg Jefferies	1.50	.70	.19
☐ 132 Mike Perez	1.00	.45	.12
☐ 133 Ozzie Smith	4.00	1.80	.50
☐ 134 Jose Canseco	2.00	.90	.25
☐ 135 Will Clark	2.00	.90	.25
☐ 136 Juan Gonzalez	8.00	3.60	1.00
☐ 137 Ivan Rodriguez	4.00	1.80	.50
☐ 138 Roberto Alomar	3.00	1.35	.35
☐ 139 Joe Carter	1.50	.70	.19
☐ 140 Carlos Delgado	1.50	.70	.19
☐ 141 Alex Gonzalez	1.50	.70	.19
☐ 142 Juan Guzman	1.50	.70	.19
☐ 143 Paul Molitor	3.00	1.35	.35
☐ 144 John Olerud	1.00	.45	.12
☐ CL1 Checklist	.25	.11	.03
☐ CL2 Checklist	.25	.11	.03

1996 Pacific Prisms

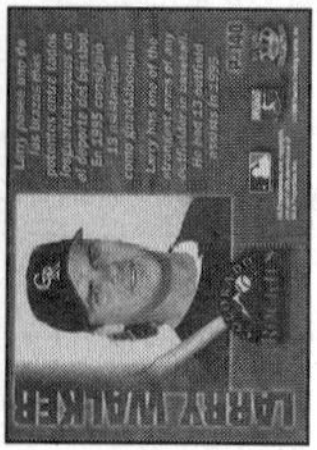

This 144-card set features a color action player cut-out over a double-etched silver foil prismatic background. The backs carry a color player portrait with information about the player in both English and Spanish.

	MINT	NRMT	EXC
COMPLETE SET (144)	150.00	70.00	19.00
COMMON CARD (1-144)	1.00	.45	.12
☐ P1 Tom Glavine	2.00	.90	.25
☐ P2 Chipper Jones	10.00	4.50	1.25
☐ P3 David Justice	1.50	.70	.19
☐ P4 Ryan Klesko	2.50	1.10	.30
☐ P5 Javy Lopez	1.50	.70	.19
☐ P6 Greg Maddux	10.00	4.50	1.25
☐ P7 Fred McGriff	2.00	.90	.25
☐ P8 Frank Castillo	1.00	.45	.12
☐ P9 Luis Gonzalez	1.00	.45	.12
☐ P10 Mark Grace	2.00	.90	.25
☐ P11 Brian McRae	1.00	.45	.12
☐ P12 Jaime Navarro	1.00	.45	.12
☐ P13 Sammy Sosa	2.50	1.10	.30
☐ P14 Bret Boone	1.00	.45	.12
☐ P15 Ron Gant	1.50	.70	.19
☐ P16 Barry Larkin	2.00	.90	.25
☐ P17 Reggie Sanders	1.50	.70	.19
☐ P18 Benito Santiago	1.00	.45	.12
☐ P19 Dante Bichette	2.00	.90	.25
☐ P20 Vinny Castilla	1.50	.70	.19
☐ P21 Andres Galarraga	2.00	.90	.25
☐ P22 Bryan Rekar	1.00	.45	.12
☐ P23 Roberto Alomar	3.00	1.35	.35
☐ P24 Jeff Conine	1.50	.70	.19
☐ P25 Andre Dawson	1.50	.70	.19
☐ P26 Charles Johnson	1.50	.70	.19
☐ P27 Gary Sheffield	2.50	1.10	.30
☐ P28 Quilvio Veras	1.00	.45	.12
☐ P29 Jeff Bagwell	6.00	2.70	.75
☐ P30 Derek Bell	1.50	.70	.19
☐ P31 Craig Biggio	1.50	.70	.19
☐ P32 Tony Eusebio	1.00	.45	.12
☐ P33 Karim Garcia	3.00	1.35	.35
☐ P34 Eric Karros	1.50	.70	.19
☐ P35 Ramon Martinez	1.50	.70	.19
☐ P36 Raul Mondesi	2.00	.90	.25
☐ P37 Hideo Nomo	4.00	1.80	.50
☐ P38 Mike Piazza	10.00	4.50	1.25
☐ P39 Ismael Valdes	1.50	.70	.19
☐ P40 Moises Alou	1.50	.70	.19
☐ P41 Wil Cordero	1.00	.45	.12
☐ P42 Pedro Martinez	1.50	.70	.19
☐ P43 Mel Rojas	1.50	.70	.19
☐ P44 David Segui	1.00	.45	.12
☐ P45 Edfardo Alfonzo	1.50	.70	.19
☐ P46 Rico Brogna	1.00	.45	.12
☐ P47 John Franco	1.00	.45	.12
☐ P48 Jason Isringhausen	1.00	.45	.12
☐ P49 Jose Vizcaino	1.00	.45	.12
☐ P50 Ricky Bottalico	1.00	.45	.12
☐ P51 Darren Daulton	1.50	.70	.19
☐ P52 Lenny Dykstra	1.50	.70	.19
☐ P53 Tyler Green	1.00	.45	.12
☐ P54 Gregg Jefferies	2.00	.90	.25
☐ P55 Jay Bell	1.50	.70	.19
☐ P56 Jason Christiansen	1.00	.45	.12
☐ P57 Carlos Garcia	1.00	.45	.12
☐ P58 Esteban Loaiza	1.00	.45	.12
☐ P59 Orlando Merced	1.50	.70	.19
☐ P60 Andujar Cedeno	1.00	.45	.12
☐ P61 Tony Gwynn	6.00	2.70	.75
☐ P62 Melvin Nieves	1.50	.70	.19
☐ P63 Phil Plantier	1.00	.45	.12
☐ P64 Fernando Valenzuela	1.50	.70	.19
☐ P65 Barry Bonds	4.00	1.80	.50
☐ P66 J.R. Phillips	1.00	.45	.12
☐ P67 Deion Sanders	2.00	.90	.25
☐ P68 Matt Williams	2.00	.90	.25
☐ P69 Bernard Gilkey	1.50	.70	.19
☐ P70 Tom Henke	1.50	.70	.19
☐ P71 Brian Jordan	1.50	.70	.19
☐ P72 Ozzie Smith	4.00	1.80	.50
☐ P73 Manny Alexander	1.00	.45	.12
☐ P74 Bobby Bonilla	1.50	.70	.19
☐ P75 Mike Mussina	3.00	1.35	.35
☐ P76 Rafael Palmeiro	2.00	.90	.25
☐ P77 Cal Ripken	12.00	5.50	1.50
☐ P78 Jose Canseco	2.00	.90	.25
☐ P79 Roger Clemens	3.00	1.35	.35
☐ P80 John Valentin	1.50	.70	.19
☐ P81 Mo Vaughn	4.00	1.80	.50
☐ P82 Tim Wakefield	1.00	.45	.12

☐ P83 Garret Anderson	2.00	.90	.25
☐ P84 Damion Easley	1.00	.45	.12
☐ P85 Jim Edmonds	1.50	.70	.19
☐ P86 Tim Salmon	2.00	.90	.25
☐ P87 Wilson Alvarez	2.00	.90	.25
☐ P88 Alex Fernandez	1.50	.70	.19
☐ P89 Ozzie Guillen	1.00	.45	.12
☐ P90 Roberto Hernandez	1.50	.70	.19
☐ P91 Frank Thomas	15.00	6.75	1.85
☐ P92 Robin Ventura	1.50	.70	.19
☐ P93 Carlos Baerga	1.00	.45	.12
☐ P94 Albert Belle	6.00	2.70	.75
☐ P95 Kenny Lofton	4.00	1.80	.50
☐ P96 Dennis Martinez	1.50	.70	.19
☐ P97 Eddie Murray	4.00	1.80	.50
☐ P98 Manny Ramirez	4.00	1.80	.50
☐ P99 Omar Vizquel	1.50	.70	.19
☐ P100 Chad Curtis	1.00	.45	.12
☐ P101 Cecil Fielder	1.50	.70	.19
☐ P102 Felipe Lira	1.00	.45	.12
☐ P103 Alan Trammell	1.50	.70	.19
☐ P104 Kevin Appier	1.50	.70	.19
☐ P105 Johnny Damon	1.50	.70	.19
☐ P106 Gary Gaetti	1.50	.70	.19
☐ P107 Wally Joyner	1.00	.45	.12
☐ P108 Ricky Bones	1.00	.45	.12
☐ P109 John Jaha	1.50	.70	.19
☐ P110 B.J. Surhoff	1.00	.45	.12
☐ P111 Jose Valentin	1.00	.45	.12
☐ P112 Fernando Vina	1.00	.45	.12
☐ P113 Marty Cordova	1.50	.70	.19
☐ P114 Chuck Knoblauch	2.00	.90	.25
☐ P115 Scott Leius	1.00	.45	.12
☐ P116 Pedro Munoz	1.00	.45	.12
☐ P117 Kirby Puckett	6.00	2.70	.75
☐ P118 Wade Boggs	2.00	.90	.25
☐ P119 Don Mattingly	8.00	3.60	1.00
☐ P120 Jack McDowell	2.00	.90	.25
☐ P121 Paul O'Neill	1.00	.45	.12
☐ P122 Ruben Rivera	3.00	1.35	.35
☐ P123 Bernie Williams	3.00	1.35	.35
☐ P124 Geronimo Berroa	1.50	.70	.19
☐ P125 Rickey Henderson	2.00	.90	.25
☐ P126 Mark McGwire	5.00	2.20	.60
☐ P127 Terry Steinbach	1.50	.70	.19
☐ P128 Danny Tartabull	1.00	.45	.12
☐ P129 Jay Buhner	2.00	.90	.25
☐ P130 Joey Cora	1.00	.45	.12
☐ P131 Ken Griffey, Jr.	15.00	6.75	1.85
☐ P132 Randy Johnson	2.50	1.10	.30
☐ P133 Edgar Martinez	1.50	.70	.19
☐ P134 Tino Martinez	2.00	.90	.25
☐ P135 Will Clark	2.00	.90	.25
☐ P136 Juan Gonzalez	8.00	3.60	1.00
☐ P137 Dean Palmer	2.00	.90	.25
☐ P138 Ivan Rodriguez	4.00	1.80	.50
☐ P139 Mickey Tettleton	1.50	.70	.19
☐ P140 Larry Walker	2.00	.90	.25
☐ P141 Joe Carter	1.50	.70	.19
☐ P142 Carlos Delgado	1.50	.70	.19
☐ P143 Alex Gonzalez	1.00	.45	.12
☐ P144 Paul Molitor	3.00	1.35	.35

1996 Pacific Prisms Gold

This 144-card parallel set features the same design as the Pacific Prisms set except the prismatic background on the front is printed in double-etched gold foil. The horizontal backs contain player information in both English and Spanish.

	MINT	NRMT	EXC
COMPLETE SET (144)	600.00	275.00	75.00
COMMON CARD (1-144)	2.50	1.10	.30
*STARS: 2X to 4X BASIC CARDS			

1996 Pacific Prisms Fence Busters

Randomly inserted in packs at a rate of one in 37, this 20-card set highlights 20 of baseball's hardest hitters. The fronts feature an embossed color player action cut-out with a borderless foil baseball field as background. The backs carry a player photo with information as to why the player was selected for this set in both English and Spanish.

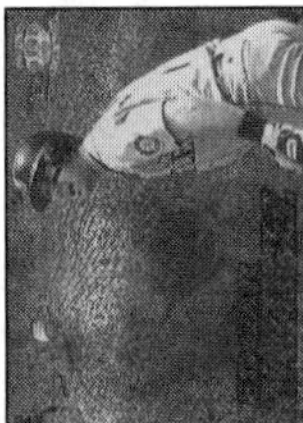

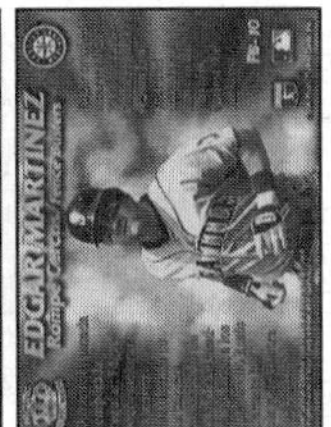

	MINT	NRMT	EXC
COMPLETE SET (20)	180.00	80.00	22.00
COMMON CARD (1-20)	3.00	1.35	.35
☐ FB1 Albert Belle	15.00	6.75	1.85
☐ FB2 Dante Bichette	5.00	2.20	.60
☐ FB3 Barry Bonds	10.00	4.50	1.25
☐ FB4 Jay Buhner	5.00	2.20	.60
☐ FB5 Jose Canseco	5.00	2.20	.60
☐ FB6 Ken Griffey Jr.	40.00	18.00	5.00
☐ FB7 Chipper Jones	25.00	11.00	3.10
☐ FB8 Dave Justice	4.00	1.80	.50
☐ FB9 Eric Karros	4.00	1.80	.50
☐ FB10 Edgar Martinez	4.00	1.80	.50
☐ FB11 Mark McGwire	12.00	5.50	1.50
☐ FB12 Eddie Murray	10.00	4.50	1.25
☐ FB13 Mike Piazza	25.00	11.00	3.10
☐ FB14 Kirby Puckett	15.00	6.75	1.85
☐ FB15 Cal Ripken	30.00	13.50	3.70
☐ FB16 Tim Salmon	5.00	2.20	.60
☐ FB17 Sammy Sosa	6.00	2.70	.75
☐ FB18 Frank Thomas	40.00	18.00	5.00
☐ FB19 Mo Vaughn	10.00	4.50	1.25
☐ FB20 Larry Walker	5.00	2.20	.60

1996 Pacific Prisms Flame Throwers

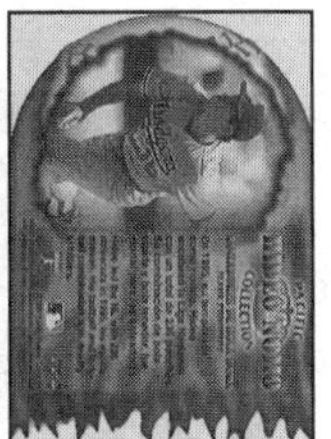

Randomly inserted in packs at a rate of one in 73, this 10-card set features 10 of Major League Baseball's hardest throwing pitchers. The fronts display a color action player photo printed on a diecut baseball-shaped card with gold foil flames indicating the force of the thrown ball. The backs carry another player photo with information of why the player was selected for this set printed in both English and Spanish.

	MINT	NRMT	EXC
COMPLETE SET (10)	150.00	70.00	19.00
COMMON CARD (1-10)	8.00	3.60	1.00
☐ FT1 Randy Johnson	15.00	6.75	1.85
☐ FT2 Mike Mussina	20.00	9.00	2.50
☐ FT3 Roger Clemens	20.00	9.00	2.50
☐ FT4 Tom Glavine	12.00	5.50	1.50
☐ FT5 Hideo Nomo	30.00	13.50	3.70
☐ FT6 Jose Rijo	8.00	3.60	1.00
☐ FT7 Greg Maddux	60.00	27.00	7.50
☐ FT8 David Cone	10.00	4.50	1.25
☐ FT9 Ramon Martinez	10.00	4.50	1.25
☐ FT10 Jose Mesa	8.00	3.60	1.00

1996 Pacific Prisms Red Hot Stars

Randomly inserted in packs at a rate of one in 37, this 20-card set features 20 of Major League Baseball's hottest stars. The fronts display a color action player cut-out on a red foil background. The backs carry a color player photo with information about the player printed in both English and Spanish.

	MINT	NRMT	EXC
COMPLETE SET (20)	250.00	110.00	31.00
COMMON CARD (1-20)	3.00	1.35	.35
☐ RH1 Roberto Alomar	8.00	3.60	1.00
☐ RH2 Jose Canseco	5.00	2.20	.60
☐ RH3 Chipper Jones	25.00	11.00	3.10
☐ RH4 Mike Piazza	25.00	11.00	3.10
☐ RH5 Tim Salmon	5.00	2.20	.60
☐ RH6 Jeff Bagwell	15.00	6.75	1.85
☐ RH7 Ken Griffey Jr.	40.00	18.00	5.00
☐ RH8 Greg Maddux	25.00	11.00	3.10
☐ RH9 Kirby Puckett	15.00	6.75	1.85
☐ RH10 Frank Thomas	40.00	18.00	5.00
☐ RH11 Albert Belle	15.00	6.75	1.85
☐ RH12 Tony Gwynn	15.00	6.75	1.85
☐ RH13 Edgar Martinez	3.00	1.35	.35
☐ RH14 Manny Ramirez	10.00	4.50	1.25
☐ RH15 Barry Bonds	10.00	4.50	1.25
☐ RH16 Wade Boggs	5.00	2.20	.60
☐ RH17 Randy Johnson	6.00	2.70	.75
☐ RH18 Don Mattingly	20.00	9.00	2.50
☐ RH19 Cal Ripken	40.00	18.00	5.00
☐ RH20 Mo Vaughn	10.00	4.50	1.25

1997 Pacific Prisms

The 1997 Pacific Prism set was issued in one series totalling 150 cards and displays color action photos of many of the top players from last season. Foiled in gold, the set features a visually stunning inlaid transparent cel on each card. The backs carry player information in both Spanish and English.

	MINT	NRMT	EXC
COMPLETE SET (150)	175.00	80.00	22.00
COMMON CARD (1-150)	1.00	.45	.12
☐ 1 Chili Davis	1.00	.45	.12
☐ 2 Jim Edmonds	1.50	.70	.19
☐ 3 Darin Erstad	8.00	3.60	1.00
☐ 4 Orlando Palmeiro	1.00	.45	.12
☐ 5 Tim Salmon	2.00	.90	.25
☐ 6 J.T. Snow	1.00	.45	.12
☐ 7 Roberto Alomar	3.00	1.35	.35
☐ 8 Brady Anderson	1.50	.70	.19
☐ 9 Eddie Murray	4.00	1.80	.50
☐ 10 Mike Mussina	3.00	1.35	.35
☐ 11 Rafael Palmeiro	2.00	.90	.25
☐ 12 Cal Ripken	12.00	5.50	1.50
☐ 13 Jose Canseco	2.00	.90	.25
☐ 14 Roger Clemens	3.00	1.35	.35
☐ 15 Nomar Garciaparra	6.00	2.70	.75
☐ 16 Reggie Jefferson	1.00	.45	.12
☐ 17 Mo Vaughn	4.00	1.80	.50
☐ 18 Wilson Alvarez	1.00	.45	.12
☐ 19 Harold Baines	1.00	.45	.12
☐ 20 Alex Fernandez	1.50	.70	.19
☐ 21 Danny Tartabull	1.00	.45	.12
☐ 22 Frank Thomas	15.00	6.75	1.85
☐ 23 Robin Ventura	1.50	.70	.19
☐ 24 Sandy Alomar Jr.	1.00	.45	.12
☐ 25 Albert Belle	6.00	2.70	.75
☐ 26 Kenny Lofton	4.00	1.80	.50
☐ 27 Jim Thome	3.00	1.35	.35
☐ 28 Omar Vizquel	1.50	.70	.19
☐ 29 Raul Casanova	1.00	.45	.12
☐ 30 Tony Clark	2.50	1.10	.30
☐ 31 Travis Fryman	1.50	.70	.19
☐ 32 Bobby Higginson	1.50	.70	.19
☐ 33 Melvin Nieves	1.00	.45	.12
☐ 34 Justin Thompson	1.50	.70	.19
☐ 35 Johnny Damon	1.00	.45	.12
☐ 36 Tom Goodwin	1.00	.45	.12
☐ 37 Jeff Montgomery	1.00	.45	.12
☐ 38 Jose Offerman	1.00	.45	.12
☐ 39 John Jaha	1.50	.70	.19
☐ 40 Jeff Cirillo	1.00	.45	.12
☐ 41 Dave Nilsson	1.00	.45	.12
☐ 42 Jose Valentin	1.00	.45	.12
☐ 43 Fernando Vina	1.00	.45	.12
☐ 44 Marty Cordova	1.50	.70	.19
☐ 45 Roberto Kelly	1.00	.45	.12
☐ 46 Chuck Knoblauch	2.50	1.10	.30
☐ 47 Paul Molitor	3.00	1.35	.35
☐ 48 Todd Walker	6.00	2.70	.75
☐ 49 Wade Boggs	2.00	.90	.25
☐ 50 Cecil Fielder	1.50	.70	.19
☐ 51 Derek Jeter	10.00	4.50	1.25
☐ 52 Tino Martinez	1.50	.70	.19
☐ 53 Andy Pettitte	4.00	1.80	.50
☐ 54 Mariano Rivera	1.50	.70	.19
☐ 55 Bernie Williams	3.00	1.35	.35
☐ 56 Tony Batista	2.00	.90	.25
☐ 57 Geronimo Berroa	1.00	.45	.12
☐ 58 Jason Giambi	1.50	.70	.19
☐ 59 Mark McGwire	5.00	2.20	.60
☐ 60 Terry Steinbach	1.00	.45	.12
☐ 61 Jay Buhner	2.00	.90	.25
☐ 62 Joey Cora	1.00	.45	.12
☐ 63 Ken Griffey Jr.	15.00	6.75	1.85
☐ 64 Edgar Martinez	1.50	.70	.19
☐ 65 Alex Rodriguez	15.00	6.75	1.85
☐ 66 Paul Sorrento	1.00	.45	.12
☐ 67 Will Clark	2.00	.90	.25
☐ 68 Juan Gonzalez	8.00	3.60	1.00
☐ 69 Rusty Greer	1.50	.70	.19
☐ 70 Dean Palmer	1.00	.45	.12
☐ 71 Ivan Rodriguez	4.00	1.80	.50
☐ 72 Joe Carter	1.50	.70	.19
☐ 73 Carlos Delgado	1.50	.70	.19
☐ 74 Juan Guzman	1.00	.45	.12
☐ 75 Pat Hentgen	1.50	.70	.19
☐ 76 Ed Sprague	1.00	.45	.12
☐ 77 Jermaine Dye	2.50	1.10	.30
☐ 78 Andruw Jones	15.00	6.75	1.85
☐ 79 Chipper Jones	10.00	4.50	1.25
☐ 80 Ryan Klesko	2.50	1.10	.30
☐ 81 Javier Lopez	1.50	.70	.19
☐ 82 Greg Maddux	10.00	4.50	1.25
☐ 83 John Smoltz	2.50	1.10	.30
☐ 84 Mark Grace	2.00	.90	.25
☐ 85 Luis Gonzalez	1.00	.45	.12
☐ 86 Brooks Kieschnick	1.50	.70	.19
☐ 87 Jaime Navarro	1.00	.45	.12
☐ 88 Ryne Sandberg	4.00	1.80	.50
☐ 89 Sammy Sosa	2.50	1.10	.30
☐ 90 Bret Boone	1.00	.45	.12
☐ 91 Jeff Brantley	1.00	.45	.12
☐ 92 Eric Davis	1.00	.45	.12
☐ 93 Barry Larkin	2.00	.90	.25
☐ 94 Reggie Sanders	1.50	.70	.19
☐ 95 Ellis Burks	1.50	.70	.19
☐ 96 Dante Bichette	2.00	.90	.25
☐ 97 Vinny Castilla	1.50	.70	.19
☐ 98 Andres Galarraga	2.00	.90	.25
☐ 99 Eric Young	1.50	.70	.19
☐ 100 Kevin Brown	1.50	.70	.19
☐ 101 Jeff Conine	1.50	.70	.19
☐ 102 Charles Johnson	1.00	.45	.12
☐ 103 Edgar Renteria	2.00	.90	.25
☐ 104 Gary Sheffield	2.50	1.10	.30
☐ 105 Jeff Bagwell	6.00	2.70	.75
☐ 106 Derek Bell	1.50	.70	.19
☐ 107 Sean Berry	1.00	.45	.12
☐ 108 Craig Biggio	1.50	.70	.19
☐ 109 Shane Reynolds	1.00	.45	.12
☐ 110 Karim Garcia	2.50	1.10	.30
☐ 111 Todd Hollandsworth	1.50	.70	.19
☐ 112 Ramon Martinez	1.50	.70	.19
☐ 113 Raul Mondesi	2.00	.90	.25
☐ 114 Hideo Nomo	4.00	1.80	.50
☐ 115 Mike Piazza	10.00	4.50	1.25
☐ 116 Ismael Valdes	1.50	.70	.19
☐ 117 Moises Alou	1.50	.70	.19
☐ 118 Mark Grudzielanek	1.00	.45	.12
☐ 119 Pedro Martinez	1.50	.70	.19
☐ 120 Henry Rodriguez	1.50	.70	.19
☐ 121 F.P. Santangelo	1.00	.45	.12
☐ 122 Carlos Baerga	1.50	.70	.19
☐ 123 Bernard Gilkey	1.00	.45	.12
☐ 124 Todd Hundley	1.50	.70	.19
☐ 125 Lance Johnson	1.00	.45	.12
☐ 126 Alex Ochoa	1.00	.45	.12
☐ 127 Rey Ordonez	2.00	.90	.25
☐ 128 Lenny Dykstra	1.50	.70	.19
☐ 129 Gregg Jefferies	1.00	.45	.12
☐ 130 Ricky Otero	1.00	.45	.12
☐ 131 Benito Santiago	1.00	.45	.12
☐ 132 Jermaine Allensworth	1.50	.70	.19
☐ 133 Francisco Cordova	1.00	.45	.12
☐ 134 Carlos Garcia	1.00	.45	.12
☐ 135 Jason Kendall	1.50	.70	.19
☐ 136 Al Martin	1.00	.45	.12
☐ 137 Dennis Eckersley	1.50	.70	.19
☐ 138 Ron Gant	1.50	.70	.19
☐ 139 Brian Jordan	1.50	.70	.19
☐ 140 John Mabry	1.00	.45	.12
☐ 141 Ozzie Smith	4.00	1.80	.50
☐ 142 Ken Caminiti	2.50	1.10	.30
☐ 143 Steve Finley	1.00	.45	.12
☐ 144 Tony Gwynn	6.00	2.70	.75
☐ 145 Wally Joyner	1.00	.45	.12
☐ 146 Fernando Valenzuela	1.50	.70	.19
☐ 147 Barry Bonds	4.00	1.80	.50
☐ 148 Jacob Cruz	1.00	.45	.12
☐ 149 Osvaldo Fernandez	1.00	.45	.12
☐ 150 Matt Williams	2.00	.90	.25

1997 Pacific Prism Light Blue

Distributed exclusively in retail outlets at a rate of 2:37 packs, cards from this 150-card set parallel the standard 1997 Pacific Prisms. The light blue foil fronts easily differentiate them from their bronze basic issue counterparts.

	MINT	NRMT	EXC
COMPLETE SET (150)	900.00	400.00	110.00
COMMON CARD (1-150)	6.00	2.70	.75
*STARS: 3X to 6X BASIC CARDS			

1997 Pacific Prisms Platinum

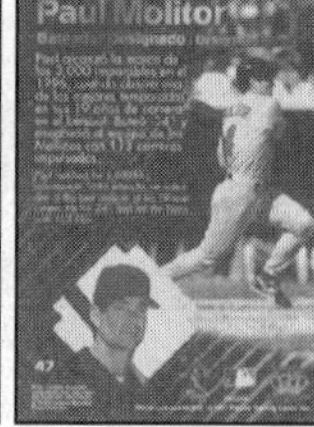

Randomly inserted in packs at a rate of two in 37, this set is a platinum foiled parallel version of the regular set.

	MINT	NRMT	EXC
COMPLETE SET (150)	750.00	350.00	95.00
COMMON CARD (1-150)	5.00	2.20	.60
*STARS: 2.5X TO 5X BASIC CARDS			

1997 Pacific Prisms Gate Attractions

Randomly inserted in packs at a rate of one in 73, this 32-card set features some of the league's current most popular players. The fronts display a player image on a baseball with a borderless photo of the inside of a baseball glove as background. The backs contain player information in both Spanish and English.

	MINT	NRMT	EXC
COMPLETE SET (32)	600.00	275.00	75.00
COMMON CARD (GA1-GA32)	6.00	2.70	.75
☐ GA1 Roberto Alomar	12.00	5.50	1.50
☐ GA2 Brady Anderson	8.00	3.60	1.00
☐ GA3 Cal Ripken	50.00	22.00	6.25
☐ GA4 Frank Thomas	60.00	27.00	7.50
☐ GA5 Kenny Lofton	15.00	6.75	1.85
☐ GA6 Omar Vizquel	6.00	2.70	.75
☐ GA7 Paul Molitor	12.00	5.50	1.50
☐ GA8 Wade Boggs	8.00	3.60	1.00
☐ GA9 Derek Jeter	40.00	18.00	5.00
☐ GA10 Andy Pettitte	15.00	6.75	1.85
☐ GA11 Bernie Williams	12.00	5.50	1.50
☐ GA12 Geronimo Berroa	6.00	2.70	.75
☐ GA13 Mark McGwire	20.00	9.00	2.50
☐ GA14 Ken Griffey Jr.	60.00	27.00	7.50
☐ GA15 Alex Rodriguez	60.00	27.00	7.50
☐ GA16 Juan Gonzalez	30.00	13.50	3.70
☐ GA17 Andruw Jones	60.00	27.00	7.50
☐ GA18 Chipper Jones	40.00	18.00	5.00
☐ GA19 Greg Maddux	40.00	18.00	5.00
☐ GA20 Ryne Sandberg	15.00	6.75	1.85
☐ GA21 Sammy Sosa	12.00	5.50	1.50
☐ GA22 Andres Galarraga	8.00	3.60	1.00
☐ GA23 Jeff Bagwell	25.00	11.00	3.10
☐ GA24 Todd Hollandsworth	8.00	3.60	1.00
☐ GA25 Hideo Nomo	15.00	6.75	1.85
☐ GA26 Mike Piazza	40.00	18.00	5.00
☐ GA27 Todd Hundley	8.00	3.60	1.00
☐ GA28 Lance Johnson	6.00	2.70	.75
☐ GA29 Ozzie Smith	15.00	6.75	1.85
☐ GA30 Ken Caminiti	10.00	4.50	1.25
☐ GA31 Tony Gwynn	25.00	11.00	3.10
☐ GA32 Barry Bonds	15.00	6.75	1.85

1997 Pacific Prisms Gems of the Diamond

Randomly inserted at the rate of approximately two per pack, this 220 card bonus set features color action photos with the player's name printed in the bottom gold border. A diamond replica displays the name of the player's team. The backs carry player information in both Spanish and English.

	MINT	NRMT	EXC
COMPLETE SET (220)	50.00	22.00	6.25
COMMON CARD (GD1-GD220)	.15	.07	.02
☐ GD1 Jim Abbott	.15	.07	.02
☐ GD2 Shawn Boskie	.15	.07	.02
☐ GD3 Gary Disarcina	.15	.07	.02
☐ GD4 Jim Edmonds	.40	.18	.05
☐ GD5 Todd Greene	.15	.07	.02
☐ GD6 Jack Howell	.15	.07	.02
☐ GD7 Jeff Schmidt	.15	.07	.02
☐ GD8 Shad Williams	.15	.07	.02
☐ GD9 Roberto Alomar	1.00	.45	.12
☐ GD10 Cesar Devarez	.15	.07	.02
☐ GD11 Alan Mills	.15	.07	.02
☐ GD12 Eddie Murray	1.25	.55	.16
☐ GD13 Jesse Orosco	.15	.07	.02
☐ GD14 Arthur Rhodes	.15	.07	.02
☐ GD15 Bill Ripken	.15	.07	.02
☐ GD16 Cal Ripken	4.00	1.80	.50
☐ GD17 Mark Smith	.15	.07	.02
☐ GD18 Roger Clemens	1.00	.45	.12
☐ GD19 Vaughn Eshelman	.15	.07	.02
☐ GD20 Rich Garces	.15	.07	.02
☐ GD21 Bill Haselman	.15	.07	.02
☐ GD22 Dwayne Hosey	.15	.07	.02
☐ GD23 Mike Maddux	.15	.07	.02
☐ GD24 Jose Malave	.15	.07	.02
☐ GD25 Aaron Sele	.15	.07	.02
☐ GD26 James Baldwin	.15	.07	.02
☐ GD27 Pat Borders	.15	.07	.02
☐ GD28 Mike Cameron	.75	.35	.09
☐ GD29 Tony Castillo	.15	.07	.02
☐ GD30 Domingo Cedeno	.15	.07	.02
☐ GD31 Greg Norton	.15	.07	.02
☐ GD32 Frank Thomas	5.00	2.20	.60
☐ GD33 Albert Belle	2.00	.90	.25
☐ GD34 Edgar Diaz	.15	.07	.02
☐ GD35 Alan Embree	.15	.07	.02
☐ GD36 Albie Lopez	.15	.07	.02
☐ GD37 Chad Ogea	.15	.07	.02
☐ GD38 Tony Pena	.15	.07	.02
☐ GD39 Joe Roa	.15	.07	.02
☐ GD40 Fausto Cruz	.15	.07	.02
☐ GD41 Joey Eischen	.15	.07	.02
☐ GD42 Travis Fryman	.40	.18	.05
☐ GD43 Mike Myers	.15	.07	.02
☐ GD44 A.J. Sager	.15	.07	.02
☐ GD45 Duane Singleton	.15	.07	.02
☐ GD46 Justin Thompson	.40	.18	.05
☐ GD47 Jeff Granger	.15	.07	.02
☐ GD48 Les Norman	.15	.07	.02
☐ GD49 Jon Nunnally	.15	.07	.02
☐ GD50 Craig Paquette	.15	.07	.02
☐ GD51 Michael Tucker	.15	.07	.02
☐ GD52 Julio Valera	.15	.07	.02
☐ GD53 Kevin Young	.15	.07	.02
☐ GD54 Cal Eldred	.15	.07	.02
☐ GD55 Ramon Garcia	.15	.07	.02
☐ GD56 Marc Newfield	.15	.07	.02
☐ GD57 Al Reyes	.15	.07	.02
☐ GD58 Tim Unroe	.15	.07	.02
☐ GD59 Tim Vanegmond	.15	.07	.02
☐ GD60 Turner Ward	.15	.07	.02
☐ GD61 Bob Wickman	.15	.07	.02
☐ GD62 Chuck Knoblauch	.75	.35	.09
☐ GD63 Paul Molitor	1.00	.45	.12
☐ GD64 Kirby Puckett	2.00	.90	.25
☐ GD65 Tom Quinlan	.15	.07	.02
☐ GD66 Rich Robertson	.15	.07	.02
☐ GD67 Dave Stevens	.15	.07	.02
☐ GD68 Matt Walbeck	.15	.07	.02
☐ GD69 Wade Boggs	.60	.25	.07
☐ GD70 Tony Fernandez	.15	.07	.02
☐ GD71 Andy Fox	.15	.07	.02
☐ GD72 Joe Girardi	.15	.07	.02
☐ GD73 Charlie Hayes	.15	.07	.02
☐ GD74 Pat Kelly	.15	.07	.02
☐ GD75 Jeff Nelson	.15	.07	.02
☐ GD76 Melido Perez	.15	.07	.02
☐ GD77 Mark Acre	.15	.07	.02
☐ GD78 Allen Battle	.15	.07	.02
☐ GD79 Rafael Bournigal	.15	.07	.02
☐ GD80 Mark McGwire	1.50	.70	.19
☐ GD81 Pedro Munoz	.15	.07	.02
☐ GD82 Scott Spiezio	.40	.18	.05
☐ GD83 Don Wengert	.15	.07	.02
☐ GD84 Steve Wojciechowski	.15	.07	.02
☐ GD85 Alex Diaz	.15	.07	.02
☐ GD86 Ken Griffey Jr.	5.00	2.20	.60
☐ GD87 Raul Ibanez	.15	.07	.02
☐ GD88 Mike Jackson	.15	.07	.02
☐ GD89 John Marzano	.15	.07	.02
☐ GD90 Greg McCarthy	.15	.07	.02
☐ GD91 Alex Rodriguez	5.00	2.20	.60
☐ GD92 Andy Sheets	.15	.07	.02
☐ GD93 Mac Suzuki	.15	.07	.02
☐ GD94 Benji Gil	.15	.07	.02
☐ GD95 Juan Gonzalez	2.50	1.10	.30
☐ GD96 Kevin Gross	.15	.07	.02
☐ GD97 Gil Heredia	.15	.07	.02
☐ GD98 Luis Ortiz	.15	.07	.02
☐ GD99 Jeff Russell	.15	.07	.02
☐ GD100 Dave Valle	.15	.07	.02
☐ GD101 Marty Janzen	.15	.07	.02
☐ GD102 Sandy Martinez	.15	.07	.02
☐ GD103 Julio Mosquera	.15	.07	.02
☐ GD104 Otis Nixon	.15	.07	.02
☐ GD105 Paul Spoljaric	.15	.07	.02
☐ GD106 Shannon Stewart	.15	.07	.02
☐ GD107 Woody Williams	.15	.07	.02
☐ GD108 Steve Avery	.15	.07	.02
☐ GD109 Mike Bielecki	.15	.07	.02
☐ GD110 Pedro Borbon	.15	.07	.02
☐ GD111 Ed Giovanola	.15	.07	.02
☐ GD112 Chipper Jones	3.00	1.35	.35
☐ GD113 Greg Maddux	3.00	1.35	.35
☐ GD114 Mike Mordecai	.15	.07	.02
☐ GD115 Terrell Wade	.15	.07	.02
☐ GD116 Terry Adams	.15	.07	.02
☐ GD117 Brian Dorsett	.15	.07	.02
☐ GD118 Doug Glanville	.15	.07	.02
☐ GD119 Tyler Houston	.15	.07	.02
☐ GD120 Robin Jennings	.15	.07	.02
☐ GD121 Ryne Sandberg	1.25	.55	.16
☐ GD122 Terry Shumpert	.15	.07	.02
☐ GD123 Amaury Telemaco	.15	.07	.02
☐ GD124 Steve Trachsel	.15	.07	.02
☐ GD125 Curtis Goodwin	.15	.07	.02
☐ GD126 Mike Kelly	.15	.07	.02
☐ GD127 Chad Mottola	.15	.07	.02
☐ GD128 Mark Portugal	.15	.07	.02
☐ GD129 Roger Salkeld	.15	.07	.02
☐ GD130 John Smiley	.15	.07	.02
☐ GD131 Lee Smith	.40	.18	.05
☐ GD132 Roger Bailey	.15	.07	.02
☐ GD133 Andres Galarraga	.60	.25	.07
☐ GD134 Darren Holmes	.15	.07	.02
☐ GD135 Curtis Leskanic	.15	.07	.02
☐ GD136 Mike Munoz	.15	.07	.02
☐ GD137 Jeff Reed	.15	.07	.02
☐ GD138 Mark Thompson	.15	.07	.02
☐ GD139 Jamey Wright	.40	.18	.05
☐ GD140 Andre Dawson	.40	.18	.05
☐ GD141 Craig Grebeck	.15	.07	.02
☐ GD142 Matt Mantei	.15	.07	.02
☐ GD143 Billy McMillon	.15	.07	.02
☐ GD144 Kurt Miller	.15	.07	.02
☐ GD145 Ralph Milliard	.15	.07	.02
☐ GD146 Bob Natal	.15	.07	.02
☐ GD147 Joe Siddall	.15	.07	.02
☐ GD148 Bob Abreu	.60	.25	.07
☐ GD149 Doug Brocail	.15	.07	.02
☐ GD150 Danny Darwin	.15	.07	.02
☐ GD151 Mike Hampton	.15	.07	.02
☐ GD152 Todd Jones	.15	.07	.02
☐ GD153 Kirt Manwaring	.15	.07	.02
☐ GD154 Alvin Morman	.15	.07	.02
☐ GD155 Billy Ashley	.15	.07	.02
☐ GD156 Tom Candiotti	.15	.07	.02
☐ GD157 Darren Dreifort	.15	.07	.02
☐ GD158 Greg Gagne	.15	.07	.02
☐ GD159 Wilton Guerrero	.75	.35	.09
☐ GD160 Hideo Nomo	1.25	.55	.16
☐ GD161 Mike Piazza	3.00	1.35	.35
☐ GD162 Tom Prince	.15	.07	.02
☐ GD163 Todd Worrell	.15	.07	.02
☐ GD164 Moises Alou	.40	.18	.05
☐ GD165 Shane Andrews	.15	.07	.02
☐ GD166 Derek Aucoin	.15	.07	.02
☐ GD167 Raul Chavez	.15	.07	.02
☐ GD168 Darrin Fletcher	.15	.07	.02
☐ GD169 Mark Leiter	.15	.07	.02
☐ GD170 Henry Rodriguez	.40	.18	.05
☐ GD171 Dave Veres	.15	.07	.02
☐ GD172 Paul Byrd	.15	.07	.02
☐ GD173 Alberto Castillo	.15	.07	.02
☐ GD174 Mark Clark	.15	.07	.02
☐ GD175 Rey Ordonez	.60	.25	.07
☐ GD176 Roberto Petagine	.15	.07	.02
☐ GD177 Andy Tomberlin	.15	.07	.02
☐ GD178 Derek Wallace	.15	.07	.02
☐ GD179 Paul Wilson	.40	.18	.05
☐ GD180 Ruben Amaro Jr.	.15	.07	.02
☐ GD181 Toby Borland	.15	.07	.02
☐ GD182 Rich Hunter	.15	.07	.02
☐ GD183 Tony Longmire	.15	.07	.02
☐ GD184 Wendell Magee	.40	.18	.05
☐ GD185 Bobby Munoz	.15	.07	.02
☐ GD186 Scott Rolen	2.00	.90	.25
☐ GD187 Mike Williams	.15	.07	.02
☐ GD188 Trey Beamon	.15	.07	.02
☐ GD189 Jason Christiansen	.15	.07	.02
☐ GD190 Elmer Dessens	.15	.07	.02
☐ GD191 Angelo Encarnacion	.15	.07	.02
☐ GD192 Carlos Garcia	.15	.07	.02
☐ GD193 Mike Kingery	.15	.07	.02
☐ GD194 Chris Peters	.15	.07	.02
☐ GD195 Tony Womack	.15	.07	.02
☐ GD196 Brian Barber	.15	.07	.02
☐ GD197 David Bell	.15	.07	.02
☐ GD198 Tony Fossas	.15	.07	.02
☐ GD199 Rick Honeycutt	.15	.07	.02
☐ GD200 T.J. Mathews	.15	.07	.02
☐ GD201 Miguel Mejia	.15	.07	.02
☐ GD202 Donovan Osborne	.15	.07	.02
☐ GD203 Ozzie Smith	1.25	.55	.16
☐ GD204 Andres Berumen	.15	.07	.02
☐ GD205 Ken Caminiti	.75	.35	.09
☐ GD206 Chris Gwynn	.15	.07	.02
☐ GD207 Tony Gwynn	2.00	.90	.25
☐ GD208 Rickey Henderson	.60	.25	.07
☐ GD209 Scott Sanders	.15	.07	.02
☐ GD210 Jason Thompson	.15	.07	.02
☐ GD211 Fernando Valenzuela	.40	.18	.05
☐ GD212 Tim Worrell	.15	.07	.02
☐ GD213 Barry Bonds	1.25	.55	.16
☐ GD214 Jay Canizaro	.15	.07	.02
☐ GD215 Doug Creek	.15	.07	.02
☐ GD216 Jacob Cruz	.15	.07	.02
☐ GD217 Glenallen Hill	.15	.07	.02
☐ GD218 Tom Lampkin	.15	.07	.02
☐ GD219 Jim Poole	.15	.07	.02
☐ GD220 Desi Wilson	.15	.07	.02

1997 Pacific Prisms Sizzling Lumber

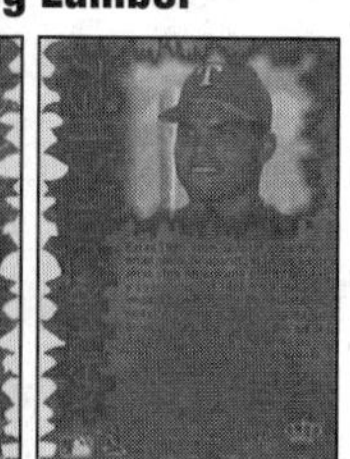

Randomly inserted in packs at a rate of one in 37, this 36-card set features color photos of three top hitters from each of twelve major league teams. The die-cut cards display red-and-gold foil flames coming from a portion of a baseball bat. The three player cards from the same team form a complete bat on fire when laid top to bottom according to the letters found after the card number. Information is printed in both Spanish and English.

	MINT	NRMT	EXC
COMPLETE SET (36)	400.00	180.00	50.00
COMMON CARD (SL1A-SL12B)	4.00	1.80	.50
☐ SL1A Cal Ripken	30.00	13.50	3.70
☐ SL1B Rafael Palmeiro	5.00	2.20	.60
☐ SL1C Roberto Alomar	8.00	3.60	1.00
☐ SL2A Frank Thomas	40.00	18.00	5.00
☐ SL2B Robin Ventura	4.00	1.80	.50
☐ SL2C Harold Baines	4.00	1.80	.50
☐ SL3A Albert Belle	15.00	6.75	1.85
☐ SL3B Manny Ramirez	10.00	4.50	1.25
☐ SL3C Kenny Lofton	10.00	4.50	1.25
☐ SL4A Derek Jeter	25.00	11.00	3.10
☐ SL4B Bernie Williams	8.00	3.60	1.00
☐ SL4C Wade Boggs	5.00	2.20	.60
☐ SL5A Mark McGwire	12.00	5.50	1.50
☐ SL5B Jason Giambi	4.00	1.80	.50
☐ SL5C Geronimo Berroa	4.00	1.80	.50
☐ SL6A Ken Griffey Jr.	40.00	18.00	5.00
☐ SL6B Alex Rodriguez	40.00	18.00	5.00
☐ SL6C Jay Buhner	5.00	2.20	.60
☐ SL7A Juan Gonzalez	20.00	9.00	2.50
☐ SL7B Dean Palmer	4.00	1.80	.50
☐ SL7C Ivan Rodriguez	10.00	4.50	1.25
☐ SL8A Ryan Klesko	6.00	2.70	.75
☐ SL8B Chipper Jones	25.00	11.00	3.10
☐ SL8C Andruw Jones	40.00	18.00	5.00
☐ SL9A Dante Bichette	5.00	2.20	.60
☐ SL9B Andres Galarraga	5.00	2.20	.60
☐ SL9C Vinny Castilla	4.00	1.80	.50
☐ SL10A Jeff Bagwell	15.00	6.75	1.85
☐ SL10B Craig Biggio	4.00	1.80	.50
☐ SL10C Derek Bell	4.00	1.80	.50
☐ SL11A Mike Piazza	25.00	11.00	3.10
☐ SL11B Raul Mondesi	4.00	1.80	.50
☐ SL11C Karim Garcia	6.00	2.70	.75
☐ SL12A Tony Gwynn	15.00	6.75	1.85
☐ SL12B Ken Caminiti	6.00	2.70	.75
☐ SL12C Greg Vaughn	4.00	1.80	.50

1997 Pacific Prisms Sluggers and Hurlers

Randomly inserted in packs at a rate of one in 145, cards from this 24-card set feature top hitters and pitchers for a dozen teams printed in a two-card puzzle style matching the hitter and pitcher from the same team to form a complete background picture displaying the team's name.

	MINT	NRMT	EXC
COMPLETE SET (24)	900.00	400.00	110.00
COMMON CARD (SH1A-SH12B)	6.00	2.70	.75

□ SH1A Cal Ripken	80.00	36.00	10.00
□ SH1B Mike Mussina	20.00	9.00	2.50
□ SH2A Jose Canseco	12.00	5.50	1.50
□ SH2B Roger Clemens	20.00	9.00	2.50
□ SH3A Frank Thomas	100.00	45.00	12.50
□ SH3B Wilson Alvarez	6.00	2.70	.75
□ SH4A Kenny Lofton	25.00	11.00	3.10
□ SH4B Orel Hershiser	8.00	3.60	1.00
□ SH5A Derek Jeter	60.00	27.00	7.50
□ SH5B Andy Pettitte	25.00	11.00	3.10
□ SH6A Ken Griffey Jr.	100.00	45.00	12.50
□ SH6B Randy Johnson	15.00	6.75	1.85
□ SH7A Alex Rodriguez	100.00	45.00	12.50
□ SH7B Jamie Moyer	6.00	2.70	.75
□ SH8A Andruw Jones	100.00	45.00	12.50
□ SH8B Greg Maddux	60.00	27.00	7.50
□ SH9A Chipper Jones	60.00	27.00	7.50
□ SH9B John Smoltz	15.00	6.75	1.85
□ SH10A Jeff Bagwell	40.00	18.00	5.00
□ SH10B Shane Reynolds	6.00	2.70	.75
□ SH11A Mike Piazza	60.00	27.00	7.50
□ SH11B Hideo Nomo	25.00	11.00	3.10
□ SH12A Tony Gwynn	40.00	18.00	5.00
□ SH12B Fernando Valenzuela	8.00	3.60	1.00

1958 Packard Bell

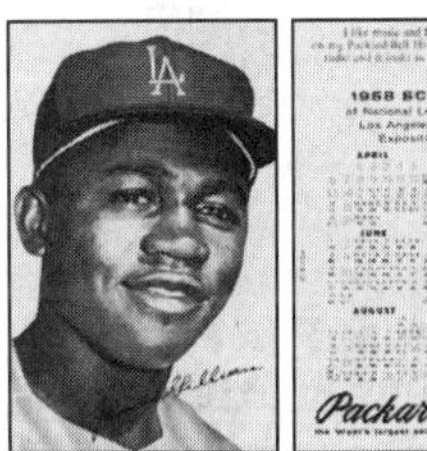

This seven-card set includes members of the Los Angeles Dodgers and San Francisco Giants and was issued in both teams' first year on the West Coast. This black and white, unnumbered set features cards measuring approximately 3 3/8" by 5 3/8". The backs are advertisements for Packard Bell (a television and radio manufacturer) along with a schedule for either the Giants or Dodgers. There were four Giants printed and three Dodgers. The catalog designation for this set is H805-5. Since the cards are unnumbered, they are listed below alphabetically.

	NRMT	VG-E	GOOD
COMPLETE SET (7)	500.00	220.00	60.00
COMMON CARD (1-7)	40.00	18.00	5.00
□ 1 Walt Alston MG	75.00	34.00	9.50
□ 2 Johnny Antonelli	40.00	18.00	5.00
□ 3 Jim Gilliam	50.00	22.00	6.25
□ 4 Gil Hodges	100.00	45.00	12.50
□ 5 Willie Mays	250.00	110.00	31.00
□ 6 Bill Rigney MG	40.00	18.00	5.00
□ 7 Hank Sauer	40.00	18.00	5.00

1969 Padres Volpe

These eight 8 1/2" by 11 cards feature members of the San Diego Padres in their inagural season. These cards feature drawings by noted sport artist Nicholas Volpe on the front. The backs have the Padres logo as well as a biography of Volpe. These cards are unnumbered and we have sequenced them in alphabetical order.

	NRMT	VG-E	GOOD
COMPLETE SET (8)	25.00	11.00	3.10
COMMON CARD (1-8)	2.50	1.10	.30
□ 1 Ollie Brown	4.50	2.00	.55
□ 2 Tommy Dean	2.50	1.10	.30
□ 3 Al Ferrera	2.50	1.10	.30
□ 4 Clarence Gaston	7.50	3.40	.95
□ 5 Preston Gomez MG	4.00	1.80	.50
□ 6 Johnny Podres	4.50	2.00	.55
□ 7 Al Santorini	2.50	1.10	.30
□ 8 Ed Spiezio	2.50	1.10	.30

1972 Padres Team Issue

This 28-card set features borderless black-and-white player photos on the fronts with only the photographers name on the back. The cards are unnumbered and checklisted below in alphabetical order.

	MINT	NRMT	EXC
COMPLETE SET (28)	8.00	3.60	1.00
COMMON CARD (1-28)	.25	.11	.03
□ 1 Ed Acosta	.25	.11	.03
□ 2 Steve Arlin	.25	.11	.03
□ 3 Bob Barton	.25	.11	.03
□ 4 Ollie Brown	.25	.11	.03
□ 5 Mike Caldwell	.25	.11	.03
□ 6 Dave Campbell	.50	.23	.06
□ 7 Nate Colbert	.25	.11	.03
□ 8 Mike Corkins	.25	.11	.03
□ 9 Roger Craig CO	.25	.11	.03
□ 10 Clarence Gaston	1.00	.45	.12
□ 11 Bill Grief	.25	.11	.03
□ 12 Enzo Hernandez	.25	.11	.03
□ 13 Gary Jestadt	.25	.11	.03
□ 14 John Jeter	.25	.11	.03
□ 15 Fred Kendall	.25	.11	.03
□ 16 Clay Kirby	.25	.11	.03
□ 17 Leron Lee	.25	.11	.03
□ 18 Jerry Morales	.25	.11	.03
□ 19 Ivan Murrell	.25	.11	.03
□ 20 Fred Norman	.25	.11	.03
□ 21 Rafeal Robles	.25	.11	.03
□ 22 Gary Ross	.25	.11	.03
□ 23 Mark Schaeffer	.25	.11	.03
□ 24 Ed Spiezio	.25	.11	.03
□ 25 Ron Taylor	.25	.11	.03
□ 26 Darrel Thomas	.25	.11	.03
□ 27 Whitey Wietlemann CO	.25	.11	.03
□ 28 Don Zimmer MG	.50	.23	.06

1974 Padres Dean's

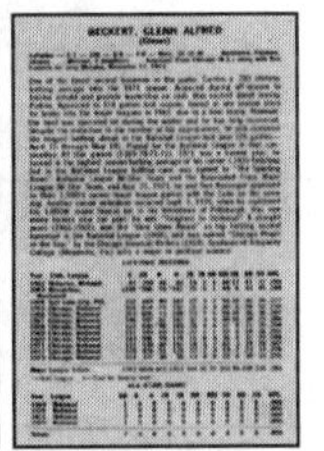

These cards measure 5 1/2" by 8 1/2" and are printed on very thin paper. The fronts feature white-bordered black-and-white player photos with the player's name and position, and sponsor and team logos below the photo. The backs carry the player's career summary, biography and statistics. The cards are unnumbered and checklisted below in alphabetical order. Some of these cards are also known to come with blank backs.

	NRMT	VG-E	GOOD
COMPLETE SET (30)	75.00	34.00	9.50
COMMON CARD (1-30)	2.00	.90	.25
□ 1 Matty Alou	3.00	1.35	.35
□ 2 Bob Barton	2.00	.90	.25
□ 3 Glenn Beckert	2.00	.90	.25
□ 4 Jack Bloomfield CO	2.00	.90	.25
□ 5 Nate Colbert	2.00	.90	.25
□ 6 Mike Corkins	2.00	.90	.25
□ 7 Jim Davenport CO	2.00	.90	.25
□ 8 Dave Freisleben	2.00	.90	.25
□ 9 Cito Gaston	4.00	1.80	.50
□ 10 Bill Greif	2.00	.90	.25
□ 11 John Grubb	2.00	.90	.25
□ 12 Larry Hardy	2.00	.90	.25
□ 13 Enzo Hernandez	2.00	.90	.25
□ 14 Dave Hilton	2.00	.90	.25
□ 15 Randy Jones	5.00	2.20	.60
□ 16 Fred Kendall	2.00	.90	.25
□ 17 Gene Locklear	2.00	.90	.25
□ 18 Willie McCovey	10.00	4.50	1.25
□ 19 John McNamara MG	2.00	.90	.25
□ 20 Rich Morales	2.00	.90	.25
□ 21 Bill Poesdel CO	2.00	.90	.25
□ 22 Dave Roberts	2.00	.90	.25
□ 23 Vicente Romo	2.00	.90	.25
□ 24 Dan Spillner	2.00	.90	.25
□ 25 Derrel Thomas	2.00	.90	.25
□ 26 Bob Tolan	2.00	.90	.25
□ 27 Rich Troedson	2.00	.90	.25
□ 28 Whitey Wietelmann CO	3.00	1.35	.35
□ 29 Bernie Williams	2.00	.90	.25
□ 30 Dave Winfield	20.00	9.00	2.50

1974 Padres McDonald Discs

Measuring approximately 2 3/8" in diameter, members of the 1974 Padres are featured in this set. Among the players featured in this set is Dave Winfield during his Rookie Card season.

	NRMT	VG-E	GOOD
COMPLETE SET (15)	50.00	22.00	6.25
COMMON PLAYER (1-15)	3.00	1.35	.35
□ 1 Matty Alou	5.00	2.20	.60
□ 2 Glen Beckert	3.00	1.35	.35
□ 3 Nate Colbert	4.00	1.80	.50
□ 4 Bill Greif	3.00	1.35	.35
□ 5 John Grubb	3.00	1.35	.35
□ 6 Enzo Hernandez	3.00	1.35	.35
□ 7 Randy Jones	3.00	1.35	.35
□ 8 Fred Kendall	3.00	1.35	.35
□ 9 Willie McCovey	10.00	4.50	1.25
□ 10 John McNamara MG	3.00	1.35	.35
□ 11 Dave Roberts	3.00	1.35	.35
□ 12 Bobby Tolan	4.00	1.80	.50
□ 13 Dave Winfield	20.00	9.00	2.50
□ 14 Ronald McDonald Has giveaway dates	3.00	1.35	.35
□ 15 Padres Sked	3.00	1.35	.35

1977 Padres Schedule Cards

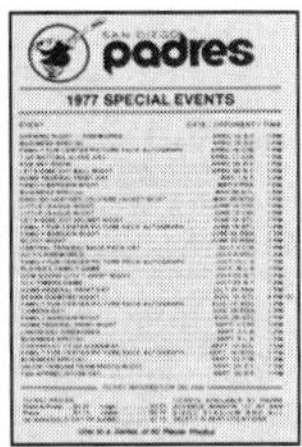

This 89-card set was issued in 1977 and features members of the 1977 San Diego Padres as well as former Padres and others connected with the Padres in some capacity. The cards measure approximately 2 1/4" by 3 3/8" and have brown and white photos on the front of the cards with a schedule of the 1977 Padres special events on the back. A thin line borders the front photo with the team name and player name appearing below in the same sepia tone. The set is checklisted alphabetically in the list below. The complete set price below refers to the set with all variations listed. The blank-backed cards may have been issued in a different year than the other schedule-back cards.

	NRMT	VG-E	GOOD
COMPLETE SET (89)	50.00	22.00	6.25
COMMON CARD (1-65)	.25	.11	.03
□ 1A Bill Almon (Kneeling)	.35	.16	.04
□ 1B Bill Almon (Shown chest up bat on shoulder)	.50	.23	.06
□ 2 Matty Alou	.50	.23	.06
□ 3 Joe Amalfitano CO	.25	.11	.03
□ 4A Steve Arlin (Follow through)	.35	.16	.04
□ 4B Steve Arlin (Glove to chest)	.35	.16	.04
□ 5 Bob Barton	.50	.23	.06
□ 6 Buzzie Bavasi GM	.35	.16	.04
□ 7 Glenn Beckert	.50	.23	.06
□ 8 Vic Bernal	.25	.11	.03
□ 9 Ollie Brown	.50	.23	.06
□ 10A Dave Campbell (Bat on shoulder)	.50	.23	.06
□ 10B Dave Campbell (Kneeling, capless)	.50	.23	.06
□ 11 Mike Champion	.25	.11	.03
□ 12 Mike Champion and Bill Almon	.25	.11	.03
□ 13A Nate Colbert (Shown waist up)	.50	.23	.06
□ 13B Nate Colbert (Shown full figure; blank back)	1.25	.55	.16
□ 14 Nate Colbert and friend (Kneeling next to child with bat)	.50	.23	.06
□ 15 Jerry Coleman ANN	.50	.23	.06
□ 16 Roger Craig CO	.35	.16	.04
□ 17 John D'Acquisto	.25	.11	.03
□ 18 Bob Davis	.25	.11	.03
□ 19 Willie Davis	.75	.35	.09
□ 20 Jim Eakle (Tuba Man)	.50	.23	.06
□ 21A Rollie Fingers (Shown waist up both hands in glove in front of body)	2.00	.90	.25
□ 21B Rollie Fingers (Head shot)	2.00	.90	.25
□ 22A Dave Freisleben (Washington jersey and cap, blank back)	2.50	1.10	.30
□ 22B Dave Freisleben (Kneeling)	.35	.16	.04
□ 23A Clarence Gaston (Bat on shoulder adres on jersey)	1.00	.45	.12
□ 23B Clarence Gaston (Bat on shoulder dre on jersey)	1.00	.45	.12
□ 24 Tom Griffin	.25	.11	.03
□ 25 Johnny Grubb	.35	.16	.04
□ 26A George Hendrick (Shown chest up wearing warm-up jacket)	.50	.23	.06
□ 26B George Hendrick (Shown waist up wearing white jersey)	.50	.23	.06
□ 27 Enzo Hernandez	.25	.11	.03
□ 28 Enzo Hernandez and Nate Colbert	.50	.23	.06
□ 29A Mike Ivie (Batting pose, shown from thighs up)	.50	.23	.06
□ 29B Mike Ivie (Batting pose, shown from shoulders up blank back)	.50	.23	.06
□ 29C Mike Ivie (Bat on shoulder)	.50	.23	.06
□ 30A Randy Jones (Following Through)	.50	.23	.06
□ 30B Randy Jones (Holding Cy Young Award)	1.00	.45	.12
□ 31 Randy Jones and Bowie Kuhn (Randy holding trophy)	1.50	.70	.19
□ 32A Fred Kendall (Batting pose)	.50	.23	.06
□ 32B Fred Kendall (Ball in right hand)	.50	.23	.06
□ 33 Mike Kilkenny (Blank back)	.50	.23	.06
□ 34A Clay Kirby (Follow through)	.50	.23	.06
□ 34B Clay Kirby (Glove near to chest)	.50	.23	.06
□ 35 Ray Kroc OWN (Blank back)	1.25	.55	.16
□ 36 Dave Marshall	.50	.23	.06
□ 37A Willie McCovey With mustache bat on shoulder)	3.00	1.35	.35
□ 37B Willie McCovey Without mustache blank back)	3.00	1.35	.35
□ 38A John McNamara MG (Looking to his left blank back)	.50	.23	.06
□ 38B John McNamara MG (Looking to his right)	.50	.23	.06
□ 38C John McNamara MG (Looking straight ahead, smiling)	.50	.23	.06
□ 39 Luis Melendez	.25	.11	.03
□ 40 Butch Metzger	.25	.11	.03
□ 41 Bob Miller	.25	.11	.03
□ 42A Fred Norman (Short hair, kneeling)	.50	.23	.06
□ 42B Fred Norman (Long hair, arms over head)	.50	.23	.06
□ 43 Bob Owchinko	.25	.11	.03
□ 44 Doug Rader	.50	.23	.06
□ 45 Merv Rettenmund	.25	.11	.03
□ 46A Gene Richards (Shown chest up stands in background)	.50	.23	.06
□ 46B Gene Richards (Shown from thighs up)	.35	.16	.04
□ 47 Dave Roberts	.25	.11	.03
□ 48 Rick Sawyer	.25	.11	.03
□ 49 Bob Shirley	.25	.11	.03
□ 50 Bob Skinner CO	.35	.16	.04
□ 51 Ballard Smith GM	.50	.23	.06
□ 52 Ed Spiezio	.50	.23	.06
□ 53 Dan Spillner	.25	.11	.03
□ 54 Brent Strom	.25	.11	.03
□ 55 Gary Sutherland	.25	.11	.03
□ 56 Gene Tenace	.50	.23	.06
□ 57A Derrell Thomas (Head shot wearing glasses)	.50	.23	.06
□ 57B Derrell Thomas (Kneeling, not wearing glasses)	.50	.23	.06
□ 58A Bobby Tolan (Batting pose)	.50	.23	.06
□ 58B Bobby Tolan (Kneeling, holding cleats in hand)	.50	.23	.06
□ 59 Dave Tomlin	.25	.11	.03
□ 60A Jerry Turner (Batting pose, gloveless wall in background)	.50	.23	.06
□ 60B Jerry Turner (Batting pose both hands gloved)	.50	.23	.06
□ 61 Bobby Valentine	1.00	.45	.12
□ 62 Dave Wehrmeister	.25	.11	.03
□ 63 Whitey Wietelmann CO	.25	.11	.03
□ 64 Don Williams CO	.25	.11	.03
□ 65A Dave Winfield (Batting pose, waist	7.50	3.40	.95

up, field in background)			
☐ 65B Dave Winfield (Batting, stands in background, black bat telescoped)	7.50	3.40	.95
☐ 65C Dave Winfield (Two bats on shoulder)	7.50	3.40	.95
☐ 65D Dave Winfield (Full figure, leaning on bat, blank back)	7.50	3.40	.95

1978 Padres Family Fun

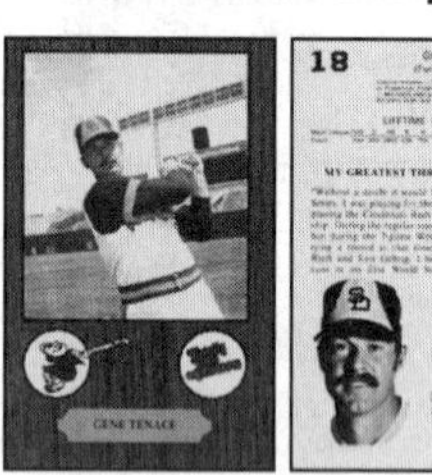

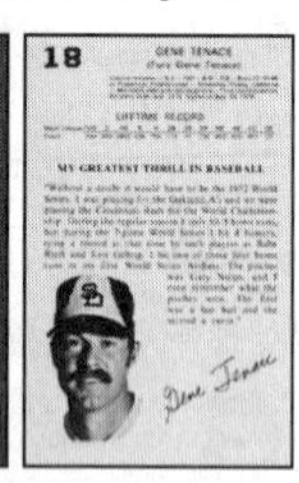

This 39-card set features members of the 1978 San Diego Padres. These large cards measure approximately 3 1/2" by 5 1/2" and are framed in a style similar to the 1962 Topps set with wood-grain borders. The cards have full color photos on the front of the card along with the Padres logo and Family Fun Centers underneath the photo in circles and the name of the player on the bottom of the card. The backs of the card asked each person what their greatest thrill in baseball was. This set is especially noteworthy for having one of the earliest Ozzie Smith cards printed. The set is checklisted alphabetically in the list below.

	NRMT	VG-E	GOOD
COMPLETE SET (39)	50.00	22.00	6.25
COMMON CARD (1-39)	.50	.23	.06
☐ 1 Bill Almon	.50	.23	.06
☐ 2 Tucker Ashford	.50	.23	.06
☐ 3 Chuck Baker	.50	.23	.06
☐ 4 Dave Campbell ANN	.50	.23	.06
☐ 5 Mike Champion	.50	.23	.06
☐ 6 Jerry Coleman ANN	.75	.35	.09
☐ 7 Roger Craig MG	1.00	.45	.12
☐ 8 John D'Acquisto	.50	.23	.06
☐ 9 Bob Davis	.50	.23	.06
☐ 10 Chuck Estrada CO	.75	.35	.09
☐ 11 Rollie Fingers	4.00	1.80	.50
☐ 12 Dave Freisleben	.50	.23	.06
☐ 13 Oscar Gamble	.50	.23	.06
☐ 14 Fernando Gonzalez	.50	.23	.06
☐ 15 Billy Herman CO	1.25	.55	.16
☐ 16 Randy Jones	.75	.35	.09
☐ 17 Ray Kroc OWN	1.25	.55	.16
☐ 18 Mark Lee	.50	.23	.06
☐ 19 Mickey Lolich	1.00	.45	.12
☐ 20 Bob Owchinko	.50	.23	.06
☐ 21 Broderick Perkins	.50	.23	.06
☐ 22 Gaylord Perry	4.00	1.80	.50
☐ 23 Eric Rasmussen	.50	.23	.06
☐ 24 Don Reynolds	.50	.23	.06
☐ 25 Gene Richards	.50	.23	.06
☐ 26 Dave Roberts	.50	.23	.06
☐ 27 Phil Roof CO	.50	.23	.06
☐ 28 Bob Shirley	.50	.23	.06
☐ 29 Ozzie Smith	20.00	9.00	2.50
☐ 30 Dan Spillner	.50	.23	.06
☐ 31 Rick Sweet	.50	.23	.06
☐ 32 Gene Tenace	.75	.35	.09
☐ 33 Derrel Thomas	.50	.23	.06
☐ 34 Jerry Turner	.50	.23	.06
☐ 35 Dave Wehrmeister	.50	.23	.06
☐ 36 Whitey Wietelmann CO	.50	.23	.06
☐ 37 Don Williams CO	.50	.23	.06
☐ 38 Dave Winfield	10.00	4.50	1.25
☐ 39 1978 All-Star Game	.75	.35	.09

1984 Padres Mother's

The cards in this 28-card set measure 2 1/2" by 3 1/2". In 1984, the Los Angeles based Mother's Cookies Co. issued five sets of cards featuring players from major league teams. The San Diego Padres set features current players depicted by photos. Similar to their 1952 and 1953 issues, the cards have rounded corners. The backs of the cards contain the Mother's Cookies logo. The cards were distributed in partial sets to fans at the respective stadiums of the teams involved. Whereas 20 cards were given to each patron, a redemption card, redeemable for eight more cards was included. Unfortunately, the eight cards received by redeeming the coupon were not necessarily the eight needed to complete a set. Hobbyist Barry Colla was involved in the production of these sets.

	NRMT	VG-E	GOOD
COMPLETE SET (28)	20.00	9.00	2.50
COMMON CARD (1-28)	.25	.11	.03
☐ 1 Dick Williams MG	.50	.23	.06
☐ 2 Rich Gossage	1.00	.45	.12
☐ 3 Tim Lollar	.25	.11	.03
☐ 4 Eric Show	.25	.11	.03
☐ 5 Terry Kennedy	.50	.23	.06
☐ 6 Kurt Bevacqua	.50	.23	.06
☐ 7 Steve Garvey	2.00	.90	.25
☐ 8 Garry Templeton	.50	.23	.06
☐ 9 Tony Gwynn	12.50	5.50	1.55
☐ 10 Alan Wiggins	.25	.11	.03
☐ 11 Dave Dravecky	1.50	.70	.19
☐ 12 Tim Flannery	.25	.11	.03
☐ 13 Kevin McReynolds	1.00	.45	.12
☐ 14 Bobby Brown	.25	.11	.03
☐ 15 Ed Whitson	.25	.11	.03
☐ 16 Doug Gwosdz	.25	.11	.03
☐ 17 Luis DeLeon	.25	.11	.03
☐ 18 Andy Hawkins	.50	.23	.06
☐ 19 Craig Lefferts	.50	.23	.06
☐ 20 Carmelo Martinez	.25	.11	.03
☐ 21 Sid Monge	.25	.11	.03
☐ 22 Graig Nettles	1.00	.45	.12
☐ 23 Mario Ramirez	.25	.11	.03
☐ 24 Luis Salazar	.25	.11	.03
☐ 25 Champ Summers	.25	.11	.03
☐ 26 Mark Thurmond	.25	.11	.03
☐ 27 Padres' Coaches Harry Dunlop Jack Krol Ozzie Virgil Norm Sherry Deacon Jones	.25	.11	.03
☐ 28 Padres' Checklist	.25	.11	.03

1984 Padres Smokey

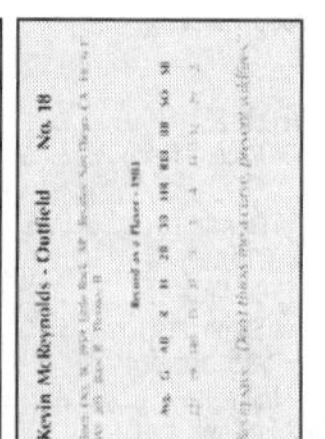

The cards in this 29-card set measure 2 1/2" by 3 3/4". This unnumbered, full color set features the Fire Prevention Bear and a Padres player, coach, manager, or associate on each card. The set was given out at the ballpark at the May 14th game against the Expos. Logos of the California Department of Forestry and the U.S. Forest Service appear in conjunction with a Smokey the Bear logo on the obverse. The set commemorates the 40th birthday of Smokey the Bear. The backs contain short biographical data, statistics and a fire prevention hint from the player pictured on the front.

	NRMT	VG-E	GOOD
COMPLETE SET (29)	12.00	5.50	1.50
COMMON CARD (1-29)	.25	.11	.03
☐ 1 Kurt Bevacqua	.50	.23	.06
☐ 2 Bobby Brown	.25	.11	.03
☐ 3 Dave Campbell ANN	.25	.11	.03
☐ 4 The Chicken Mascot	1.00	.45	.12
☐ 5 Jerry Coleman ANN	.50	.23	.06
☐ 6 Luis DeLeon	.25	.11	.03
☐ 7 Dave Dravecky	1.00	.45	.12
☐ 8 Harry Dunlop CO	.25	.11	.03
☐ 9 Tim Flannery	.25	.11	.03
☐ 10 Steve Garvey	1.50	.70	.19
☐ 11 Doug Gwosdz	.25	.11	.03
☐ 12 Tony Gwynn	5.00	2.20	.60
☐ 13 Doug Harvey UMP	.50	.23	.06
☐ 14 Terry Kennedy	.50	.23	.06
☐ 15 Jack Krol CO	.25	.11	.03
☐ 16 Tim Lollar	.25	.11	.03
☐ 17 Jack McKeon VP Baseball Operations	.25	.11	.03
☐ 18 Kevin McReynolds	.75	.35	.09
☐ 19 Sid Monge	.25	.11	.03
☐ 20 Luis Salazar	.25	.11	.03
☐ 21 Norm Sherry CO	.25	.11	.03
☐ 22 Eric Show	.25	.11	.03
☐ 23 Smokey the Bear	.25	.11	.03
☐ 24 Garry Templeton	.25	.11	.03
☐ 25 Mark Thurmond	.25	.11	.03
☐ 26 Ozzie Virgil CO	.25	.11	.03
☐ 27 Ed Whitson	.25	.11	.03
☐ 28 Alan Wiggins	.25	.11	.03
☐ 29 Dick Williams MG	.50	.23	.06

1985 Padres Mother's

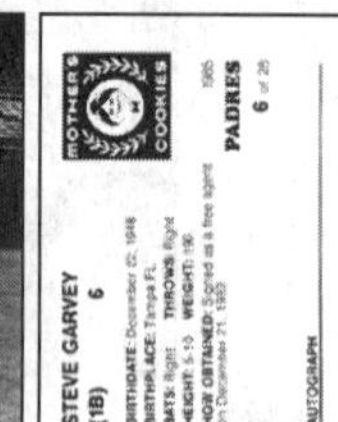

The cards in this 28-card set measure 2 1/2" by 3 1/2". In 1985, the Los Angeles based Mother's Cookies Co. again issued five sets of cards featuring players from major league teams. The San Diego Padres set features current players depicted by photos on cards with rounded corners. The backs of the cards contain the Mother's Cookies logo. Cards were passed out at the stadium on August 11.

	NRMT	VG-E	GOOD
COMPLETE SET (28)	10.00	4.50	1.25
COMMON CARD (1-28)	.25	.11	.03
☐ 1 Dick Williams MG	.50	.23	.06
☐ 2 Tony Gwynn	5.00	2.20	.60
☐ 3 Kevin McReynolds	.50	.23	.06
☐ 4 Graig Nettles	1.00	.45	.12
☐ 5 Rich Gossage	1.00	.45	.12
☐ 6 Steve Garvey	1.50	.70	.19
☐ 7 Garry Templeton	.25	.11	.03
☐ 8 Dave Dravecky	.75	.35	.09
☐ 9 Eric Show	.25	.11	.03
☐ 10 Terry Kennedy	.50	.23	.06
☐ 11 Luis DeLeon	.25	.11	.03
☐ 12 Bruce Bochy	.25	.11	.03
☐ 13 Andy Hawkins	.25	.11	.03
☐ 14 Kurt Bevacqua	.50	.23	.06
☐ 15 Craig Lefferts	.25	.11	.03
☐ 16 Mario Ramirez	.25	.11	.03
☐ 17 LaMarr Hoyt	.25	.11	.03
☐ 18 Jerry Royster	.25	.11	.03
☐ 19 Tim Stoddard	.25	.11	.03
☐ 20 Tim Flannery	.25	.11	.03
☐ 21 Mark Thurmond	.25	.11	.03
☐ 22 Greg Booker	.25	.11	.03
☐ 23 Bobby Brown	.25	.11	.03
☐ 24 Carmelo Martinez	.25	.11	.03
☐ 25 Al Bumbry	.25	.11	.03
☐ 26 Jerry Davis	.25	.11	.03
☐ 27 Padres' Coaches Jack Krol Harry Dunlop Deacon Jones	.25	.11	.03
☐ 28 Padres' Checklist Jack Murphy Stadium	.25	.11	.03

1986 Padres Greats TCMA

This 12-card standard-size set features some of the leading Padres players from their first two decades. The player's photo and name are on the front. The backs are used to give more player information.

	MINT	NRMT	EXC
COMPLETE SET (12)	4.00	1.80	.50
COMMON CARD (1-12)	.25	.11	.03
☐ 1 Nate Colbert	.50	.23	.06
☐ 2 Tito Fuentes	.25	.11	.03
☐ 3 Enzo Hernandez	.25	.11	.03
☐ 4 Dave Roberts	.25	.11	.03
☐ 5 Gene Richards	.25	.11	.03
☐ 6 Ollie Brown	.25	.11	.03
☐ 7 Clarence Gaston	.75	.35	.09
☐ 8 Fred Kendall	.25	.11	.03
☐ 9 Gaylord Perry	1.00	.45	.12
☐ 10 Randy Jones	.50	.23	.06
☐ 11 Rollie Fingers	1.00	.45	.12
☐ 12 Preston Gomez MG	.25	.11	.03

1987 Padres Bohemian Hearth Bread

The Bohemian Hearth Bread Company issued this 22-card set of San Diego Padres. The cards measure 2 1/2" by 3 1/2" and feature a distinctive yellow border on the front of the cards. Card backs provide career year-by-year statistics and are numbered.

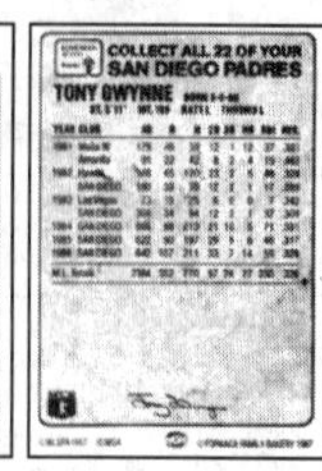

	MINT	NRMT	EXC
COMPLETE SET (22)	50.00	22.00	6.25
COMMON CARD	1.00	.45	.12
☐ 1 Garry Templeton	1.00	.45	.12
☐ 4 Joey Cora	2.50	1.10	.30
☐ 5 Randy Ready	1.00	.45	.12
☐ 6 Steve Garvey	5.00	2.20	.60
☐ 7 Kevin Mitchell	2.50	1.10	.30
☐ 8 John Kruk	4.00	1.80	.50
☐ 9 Benito Santiago	10.00	4.50	1.25
☐ 10 Larry Bowa MG	1.50	.70	.19
☐ 11 Tim Flannery	1.00	.45	.12
☐ 14 Carmelo Martinez	1.00	.45	.12
☐ 16 Marvell Wynne	1.00	.45	.12
☐ 19 Tony Gwynn	25.00	11.00	3.10
☐ 21 James Steels	1.00	.45	.12
☐ 22 Stan Jefferson	1.00	.45	.12
☐ 30 Eric Show	1.00	.45	.12
☐ 31 Ed Whitson	1.00	.45	.12
☐ 34 Storm Davis	1.00	.45	.12
☐ 37 Craig Lefferts	1.00	.45	.12
☐ 40 Andy Hawkins	1.00	.45	.12
☐ 41 Lance McCullers	1.00	.45	.12
☐ 43 Dave Dravecky	4.00	1.80	.50
☐ 54 Rich Gossage	5.00	2.20	.60

1987 Padres Fire Prevention Tips Booklets

These four Fire Prevention Booklets feature members of the 1987 San Diego Padres. The first two booklets issued are somewhat smaller than than the third and fourth book issued. These booklets are unnumbered and we have sequenced them in alphabetical order

	MINT	EXC	G-VG
COMPLETE SET (4)	10.00	4.50	1.25
COMMON CARD (1-4)	2.00	.90	.25
☐ 1 Dave Dravecky Pitching Tips	3.00	1.35	.35
☐ 2 Tim Flannery Fielding Tips	2.00	.90	.25
☐ 3 Lance McCullers Tips on Receiving the Pitch	2.00	.90	.25
☐ 4 Benito Santiago The Pick-Off Move to First	4.00	1.80	.50

1988 Padres Coke

These cards were actually issued as two separate promotions. The first eight cards were issued as a perforated sheet (approximately 7 1/2" by 10 1/2") as a Coca Cola Junior Padres Club promotion. The other 12 cards were issued later on specific game days to members of the Junior Padres Club. All the cards are standard size, 2 1/2" by 3 1/2" and are unnumbered. Cards that were on the perforated panel are indicated by PAN in the checklist below. Since the cards are unnumbered, they are listed below by uniform number, which is featured prominently on the card fronts.

	MINT	NRMT	EXC
COMPLETE SET (21)	35.00	16.00	4.40
COMMON PANEL PLAYER	.50	.23	.06
COMMON NON-PAN PLAYER	1.50	.70	.19
☐ 1 Garry Templeton PAN	.75	.35	.09
☐ 5 Randy Ready PAN	.50	.23	.06
☐ 7 Keith Moreland	1.50	.70	.19
☐ 8 John Kruk	5.00	2.20	.60
☐ 9 Benito Santiago	2.00	.90	.25
☐ 10 Larry Bowa MG PAN	1.00	.45	.12
☐ 11 Tim Flannery PAN	.50	.23	.06
☐ 14 Carmelo Martinez	1.50	.70	.19
☐ 15 Jack McKeon MG	1.50	.70	.19
☐ 19 Tony Gwynn	20.00	9.00	2.50
☐ 22 Stan Jefferson	1.50	.70	.19
☐ 27 Mark Parent	1.50	.70	.19
☐ 30 Eric Show	1.50	.70	.19
☐ 31 Eddie Whitson	1.50	.70	.19
☐ 35 Chris Brown PAN	.50	.23	.06
☐ 41 Lance McCullers	1.50	.70	.19

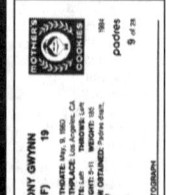

Card	MINT	NRMT	EXC
☐ 45 Jimmy Jones PAN	.50	.23	.06
☐ 48 Mark Davis PAN	.75	.35	.09
☐ 51 Greg Booker	1.50	.70	.19
☐ 55 Mark Grant PAN	.50	.23	.06
☐ NNO Padres Logo PAN (Program explanation on reverse)	.50	.23	.06

1988 Padres Smokey

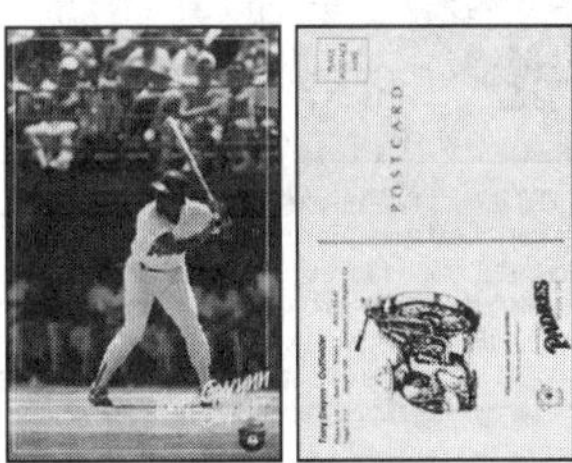

The cards in this 31-card set measure approximately 3 3/4" by 5 3/4". This unnumbered, full color set features the Fire Prevention Bear, Smokey, and a Padres player, coach, manager, or associate on each card. The set was given out at Jack Murphy Stadium to fans under the age of 14 during the Smokey Bear Day game promotion. The logo of the California Department of Forestry appears on the reverse in conjunction with a Smokey the Bear logo on the obverse. The backs contain short biographical data and a fire prevention hint from Smokey. The set is numbered below in alphabetical order. The card backs are actually postcards that can be addressed and mailed. Cards of Larry Bowa and Candy Sierra were printed but were not officially released since they were no longer members of the Padres by the time the cards were to be distributed.

	MINT	NRMT	EXC
COMPLETE SET (31)	30.00	13.50	3.70
COMMON CARD (1-31)	.75	.35	.09
☐ 1 Shawn Abner	.75	.35	.09
☐ 2 Roberto Alomar	10.00	4.50	1.25
☐ 3 Sandy Alomar CO	1.00	.45	.12
☐ 4 Greg Booker	.75	.35	.09
☐ 5 Chris Brown	.75	.35	.09
☐ 6 Mark Davis	1.00	.45	.12
☐ 7 Pat Dobson CO	.75	.35	.09
☐ 8 Tim Flannery	.75	.35	.09
☐ 9 Mark Grant	.75	.35	.09
☐ 10 Tony Gwynn	7.50	3.40	.95
☐ 11 Andy Hawkins	.75	.35	.09
☐ 12 Stan Jefferson	.75	.35	.09
☐ 13 Jimmy Jones	.75	.35	.09
☐ 14 John Kruk	2.00	.90	.25
☐ 15 Dave Leiper	.75	.35	.09
☐ 16 Shane Mack	.75	.35	.09
☐ 17 Carmelo Martinez	.75	.35	.09
☐ 18 Lance McCullers	.75	.35	.09
☐ 19 Keith Moreland	.75	.35	.09
☐ 20 Eric Nolte	.75	.35	.09
☐ 21 Amos Otis CO	.75	.35	.09
☐ 22 Mark Parent	.75	.35	.09
☐ 23 Randy Ready	.75	.35	.09
☐ 24 Greg Riddoch CO	.75	.35	.09
☐ 25 Benito Santiago	1.50	.70	.19
☐ 26 Eric Show	.75	.35	.09
☐ 27 Denny Sommers CO	.75	.35	.09
☐ 28 Garry Templeton	1.00	.45	.12
☐ 29 Dickie Thon	.75	.35	.09
☐ 30 Ed Whitson	.75	.35	.09
☐ 31 Marvell Wynne	.75	.35	.09

1989 Padres Coke

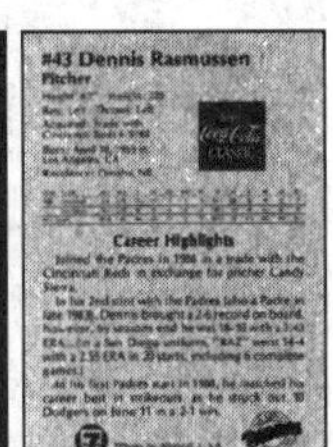

These cards were actually issued as two separate promotions. The first nine cards were issued as a perforated sheet (approximately 7 1/2" by 10 1/2") as a Coca Cola Junior Padres Club promotion. The other 12 cards were issued later on specific game days to members of the Junior Padres Club. All the cards are standard size and are unnumbered. Cards that were on the perforated panel are indicated by PAN in the checklist below. Since the cards are unnumbered, they are listed below in alphabetical order by subject. Marvell Wynne was planned for the set but was not issued since he was traded before the set was released; Walt Terrell also is tougher to find due to his mid-season trade.

	MINT	NRMT	EXC
COMPLETE SET (21)	35.00	16.00	4.40
COMMON PANEL CARD	.50	.23	.06
COMMON NON-PAN CARD	1.50	.70	.19
☐ 1 Roberto Alomar PAN	6.00	2.70	.75
☐ 2 Jack Clark	2.00	.90	.25
☐ 3 Mark Davis	1.50	.70	.19
☐ 4 Tim Flannery	1.50	.70	.19
☐ 5 Mark Grant	1.50	.70	.19
☐ 6 Tony Gwynn	12.50	5.50	1.55
☐ 7 Bruce Hurst	2.00	.90	.25
☐ 8 Chris James	1.50	.70	.19
☐ 9 Carmelo Martinez PAN	.50	.23	.06
☐ 10 Jack McKeon MG PAN	.50	.23	.06
☐ 11 Mark Parent	1.50	.70	.19
☐ 12 Dennis Rasmussen PAN	.50	.23	.06
☐ 13 Randy Ready PAN	.50	.23	.06
☐ 14 Bip Roberts	2.00	.90	.25
☐ 15 Luis Salazar	1.50	.70	.19
☐ 16 Benito Santiago	2.00	.90	.25
☐ 17 Eric Show PAN	.50	.23	.06
☐ 18 Garry Templeton PAN	.50	.23	.06
☐ 19 Walt Terrell SP	7.50	3.40	.95
☐ 20 Ed Whitson PAN	.50	.23	.06
☐ NNO Padres Logo PAN	.50	.23	.06

1989 Padres Magazine

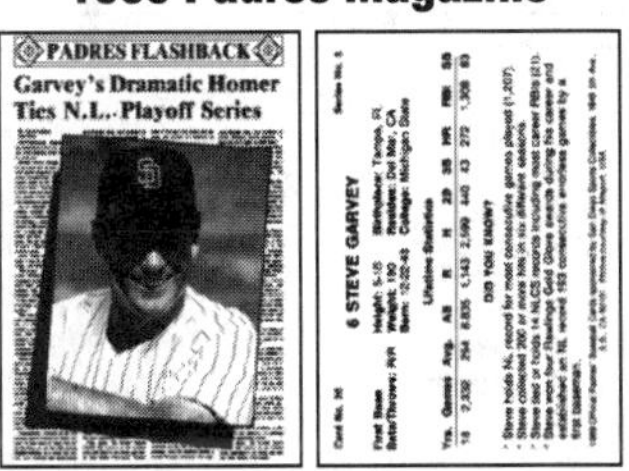

These 2 1/2" by 3 1/2" cards came as an insert in issues of "Padres" magazine sold in San Diego. These cards were sponsored by San Diego Sports Collectibles, a major hobby dealer. The cards feature beautiful full-color photos on the front and interesting did-you-know facts on the back along with one line of career statistics. The cards of retired Padres feature a highlight of their career in San Diego. The suggested retail price of each of the six different Padres magazines was 1.50.

	MINT	NRMT	EXC
COMPLETE SET (24)	15.00	6.75	1.85
COMMON CARD (1-24)	.25	.11	.03
☐ 1 Jack McKeon MG	.25	.11	.03
☐ 2 Sandy Alomar Jr.	1.00	.45	.12
☐ 3 Tony Gwynn	6.00	2.70	.75
☐ 4 Willie McCovey McCovey hits 16th grand slam	1.50	.70	.19
☐ 5 John Kruk	.50	.23	.06
☐ 6 Jack Clark	.50	.23	.06
☐ 7 Eric Show	.25	.11	.03
☐ 8 Rollie Fingers Fingers wins NL Saves title for second time	1.00	.45	.12
☐ 9 The Alomars Sandy Alomar Sr. Sandy Alomar Jr. Roberto Alomar	2.00	.90	.25
☐ 10 Carmelo Martinez	.25	.11	.03
☐ 11 Benito Santiago	.50	.23	.06
☐ 12 Nate Colbert 5 HR's, 13 RBI's in Doubleheader	.25	.11	.03
☐ 13 Mark Davis	.25	.11	.03
☐ 14 Roberto Alomar	6.00	2.70	.75
☐ 15 Tim Flannery	.25	.11	.03
☐ 16 Randy Jones Wins Cy Young Award	.50	.23	.06
☐ 17 Dennis Rasmussen	.25	.11	.03
☐ 18 Greg W. Harris	.25	.11	.03
☐ 19 Garry Templeton	.25	.11	.03
☐ 20 Steve Garvey Home Run ties NLCS	.75	.35	.09
☐ 21 Bruce Hurst	.25	.11	.03
☐ 22 Ed Whitson	.25	.11	.03
☐ 23 Chris James	.25	.11	.03
☐ 24 Gaylord Perry Wins Cy Young in Both Leagues	1.00	.45	.12

1990 Padres Coke

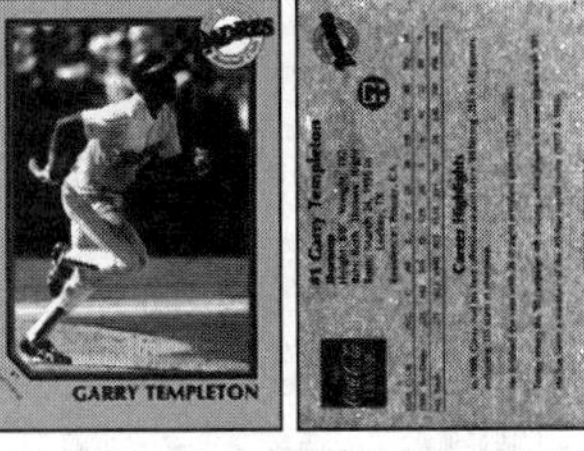

These standard-size cards were issued in two forms: a 7 1/2" by 10 5/8" perforated sheet featuring eight player cards and the Padre logo card (marked by PAN below) as well as 12 individual player cards. The sheet was issued to Coca-Cola Junior Padres Club Members as a starter set, and club members who attended the first six Junior Padres Club games received two additional cards per game. The fronts have color action player photos, with two-toned brown borders on a beige card face. The team logo appears in the upper right corner, and the lower left corner of each picture is cut out to provide space for the player's number and position. In dark brown lettering, the horizontally oriented backs present biography, statistics, and career highlights. The cards are unnumbered and checklisted below in alphabetical order, with the team logo card listed at the end.

	MINT	NRMT	EXC
COMPLETE SET (21)	30.00	13.50	3.70
COMMON PANEL CARD	.50	.23	.06
COMMON NON-PAN CARD	1.25	.55	.16
☐ 1 Roberto Alomar	7.50	3.40	.95
☐ 2 Andy Benes PAN	1.00	.45	.12
☐ 3 Joe Carter	6.00	2.70	.75
☐ 4 Jack Clark	1.50	.70	.19
☐ 5 Mark Grant PAN	.50	.23	.06
☐ 6 Tony Gwynn	10.00	4.50	1.25
☐ 7 Greg W. Harris	1.25	.55	.16
☐ 8 Bruce Hurst	1.25	.55	.16
☐ 9 Craig Lefferts	1.25	.55	.16
☐ 10 Fred Lynn	1.50	.70	.19
☐ 11 Jack McKeon MG PAN	.50	.23	.06
☐ 12 Mike Pagliarulo	1.25	.55	.16
☐ 13 Mark Parent PAN	.50	.23	.06
☐ 14 Dennis Rasmussen PAN	.50	.23	.06
☐ 15 Bip Roberts PAN	.75	.35	.09
☐ 16 Benito Santiago	1.50	.70	.19
☐ 17 Calvin Schiraldi	1.25	.55	.16
☐ 18 Eric Show PAN	.50	.23	.06
☐ 19 Garry Templeton	1.25	.55	.16
☐ 20 Ed Whitson PAN	.50	.23	.06
☐ NNO Padres Logo PAN	.50	.23	.06

1990 Padres Magazine/Unocal

This 24-card set was sponsored by Unocal 76 and was available in the San Diego Padres' game programs for 17.50. The cards were divided into six series, and each series was issued on a 5" by 9" sheet of four cards with a sponsor's coupon. After perforation, the cards measure the standard size. Some players appear in more than one series. The front features a color action player photo with white borders. The player's name is given in a tan stripe below the picture, with the Unocal 76 logo to the right of the name. The backs are printed in black on white and have biography, statistics, and career highlights. Coupons from the magazine were to be turned into Unocal for 25 Jack McKeon, 26 Bip Roberts, and 27 Joe Carter.

	MINT	NRMT	EXC
COMPLETE SET (27)	20.00	9.00	2.50
COMMON CARD (1-24)	.25	.11	.03
COMMON CARD (25-27)	.75	.35	.09
☐ 1 Tony Gwynn	6.00	2.70	.75
☐ 2 Benito Santiago	1.00	.45	.12
☐ 3 Mike Pagliarulo	.25	.11	.03
☐ 4 Dennis Rasmussen	.25	.11	.03
☐ 5 Eric Show	.25	.11	.03
☐ 6 Darrin Jackson	.25	.11	.03
☐ 7 Mark Parent	.25	.11	.03
☐ 8 Padres Announcers Jerry Coleman Rick Monday	.50	.23	.06
☐ 9 Andy Benes	1.25	.55	.16
☐ 10 Roberto Alomar	4.00	1.80	.50
☐ 11 Craig Lefferts	.25	.11	.03
☐ 12 Ed Whitson	.25	.11	.03
☐ 13 Calvin Schiraldi	.25	.11	.03
☐ 14 Garry Templeton	.25	.11	.03
☐ 15 Tony Gwynn	6.00	2.70	.75
☐ 16 Padres Announcers Bob Chandler and Ted Leitner	.25	.11	.03
☐ 17 Fred Lynn	.50	.23	.06
☐ 18 Jack Clark	.50	.23	.06
☐ 19 Mike Dunne	.25	.11	.03
☐ 20 Mark Grant	.25	.11	.03
☐ 21 Benito Santiago	1.00	.45	.12
☐ 22 The Coaches Sandy Alomar Sr. Pat Dobson Amos Otis Greg Riddoch Denny Sommers	.50	.23	.06
☐ 23 Bruce Hurst	.25	.11	.03
☐ 24 Greg W. Harris	.25	.11	.03
☐ 25 Jack McKeon MG	.75	.35	.09
☐ 26 Bip Roberts	1.50	.70	.19
☐ 27 Joe Carter	3.00	1.35	.35

1991 Padres Coke

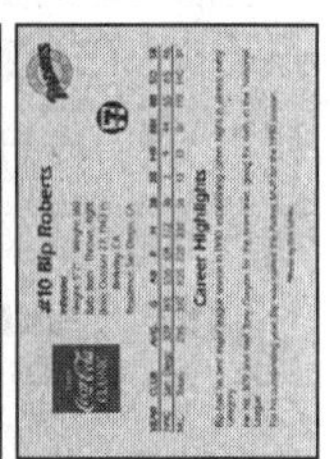

These nine standard-size cards were sponsored by Coca-Cola and issued in perforated sheets that measure approximately 7 3/4" by 10 3/4". They feature on their fronts posed studio shots of players and announcers for the Padres. These photos are set off from their white borders by black and brown lines. Black and brown speckles decorate the white border, but the white margin underneath the photo that carries the player's or announcer's name and position is free of these, as is the upper right corner of the card, which contains the Padres logo. The horizontal backs carry the player's name, position, biography, stats, and career highlights. The logos for the Padres, Coca-Cola, and 7-Eleven round out the back. The cards are unnumbered and checklisted below in alphabetical order.

	MINT	NRMT	EXC
COMPLETE SET (9)	8.00	3.60	1.00
COMMON CARD (1-9)	1.00	.45	.12
☐ 1 Bob Chandler ANN	1.00	.45	.12
☐ 2 Jerry Coleman ANN	1.25	.55	.16
☐ 3 Paul Faries	1.00	.45	.12
☐ 4 Craig Lefferts	1.00	.45	.12
☐ 5 Ted Leitner ANN	1.00	.45	.12
☐ 6 Rick Monday ANN	1.00	.45	.12
☐ 7 Greg Riddoch MG	1.25	.55	.16
☐ 8 Bip Roberts	1.50	.70	.19
☐ 9 Title card	1.00	.45	.12

1991 Padres Magazine/Rally's

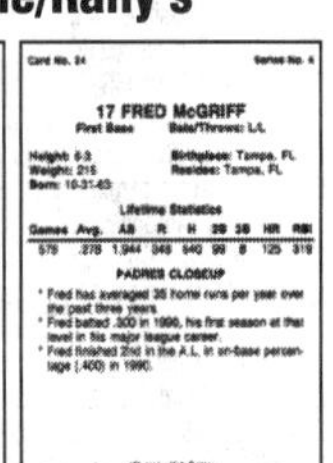

This 30-card set was sponsored by Rally's Hamburgers. The first 27 cards were divided into six series, and each series was issued on a 5" by 9" sheet of four cards with a sponsor's coupon. After perforation, the cards measure the standard size. The front features a color pose shot (from the waist up) of the player, inside a tan baseball diamond framework. Outside the diamond, the card background is dark blue, with white borders. The player's name is given in an orange banner at the bottom of the card. Team and sponsor logos in the upper corners round out the front. The backs are printed in black on white and have biography, statistics, and career highlights.Some players appear on more than one sheet, and there are variations involving Schiraldi, Gardner, and Presley, who were released during the season. For example, on the fourth sheet (13-16), Clark replaced Schiraldi; likewise Hurst replaced Gardner on the fifth sheet (17-20) and Roberts (who also appears on the third sheet) replaced Presley on the sixth sheet (21-24). The last three cards were available as part of a promotion whereby fans could tear out a coupon from the Padres Magazine and bring the coupon to one of eight Rally's Hamburgers locations in San Diego County in order to redeem one card.

	MINT	NRMT	EXC
COMPLETE SET (30)	25.00	11.00	3.10
COMMON CARD (1-24)	.25	.11	.03
COMMON CARD (25-27)	1.00	.45	.12
☐ 1 Greg Riddoch MG	.25	.11	.03
☐ 2 Dennis Rasmussen	.25	.11	.03
☐ 3 Thomas Howard	.25	.11	.03
☐ 4 Tom Lampkin	.25	.11	.03
☐ 5 Bruce Hurst	.25	.11	.03
☐ 6 Darrin Jackson	.25	.11	.03
☐ 7 Jerald Clark	.25	.11	.03
☐ 8 Shawn Abner	.25	.11	.03
☐ 9 Bip Roberts	1.00	.45	.12
☐ 10 Marty Barrett	.25	.11	.03
☐ 11 Jim Vatcher	.25	.11	.03
☐ 12 Greg Gross	.25	.11	.03
☐ 13 Greg W. Harris	.25	.11	.03
☐ 14 Ed Whitson	.25	.11	.03
☐ 15A Calvin Schiraldi SP	3.00	1.35	.35
☐ 15B Jerald Clark	1.00	.45	.12
☐ 16 Rich Rodriguez	.25	.11	.03
☐ 17 Larry Andersen	.25	.11	.03
☐ 18 Andy Benes	1.25	.55	.16
☐ 19A Wes Gardner SP	3.00	1.35	.35
☐ 19B Bruce Hurst	1.00	.45	.12

	MINT	NRMT	EXC
☐ 20 Paul Faries	.25	.11	.03
☐ 21 Craig Lefferts	.25	.11	.03
☐ 22 Tony Gwynn	6.00	2.70	.75
☐ 23A Jim Presley SP	3.00	1.35	.35
☐ 23B Bip Roberts	1.00	.45	.12
☐ 24 Fred McGriff	4.00	1.80	.50
☐ 25 Gaylord Perry	2.00	.90	.25
☐ 26 Benito Santiago	1.00	.45	.12
☐ 27 Tony Fernandez	1.00	.45	.12

1991 Padres Smokey

This 39-card set of the San Diego Padres measures approximately 3 1/2" by 5" and features color player photos on the fronts.

	MINT	NRMT	EXC
COMPLETE SET (39)	15.00	6.75	1.85
COMMON CARD (1-39)	.25	.11	.03
☐ 1 Shawn Abner	.25	.11	.03
☐ 2 Larry Andersen	.25	.11	.03
☐ 3 Andy Benes	1.00	.45	.12
☐ 4 Jerald Clark	.25	.11	.03
☐ 5 Pat Clements	.25	.11	.03
☐ 6 Scott Coolbaugh	.25	.11	.03
☐ 7 John Costello	.25	.11	.03
☐ 8 Bruce Dorsett	.25	.11	.03
☐ 9 Paul Faries	.25	.11	.03
☐ 10 Tony Fernandez	.75	.35	.09
☐ 11 Tony Gwynn	7.50	3.40	.95
☐ 12 Atlee Hammaker	.25	.11	.03
☐ 13 Greg Harris	.25	.11	.03
☐ 14 Thomas Howard	.25	.11	.03
☐ 15 Bruce Hurst	.25	.11	.03
☐ 16 Darrin Jackson	.25	.11	.03
☐ 17 Bruce Kimm CO	.25	.11	.03
☐ 18 Tom Lampkin	.25	.11	.03
☐ 19 Craig Lefferts	.25	.11	.03
☐ 20 Mike Maddux	.25	.11	.03
☐ 21 Fred McGriff	2.00	.90	.25
☐ 22 Joe McIlvaine GM	.25	.11	.03
☐ 23 Jose Melendez	.25	.11	.03
☐ 24 Jose Mota	.25	.11	.03
☐ 25 Adam Peterson	.25	.11	.03
☐ 26 Rob Picciolo CO	.25	.11	.03
☐ 27 Dennis Rasmussen	.25	.11	.03
☐ 28 Merv Rettenmund CO	.25	.11	.03
☐ 29 Greg Riddoch MG	.25	.11	.03
☐ 30 Mike Roarke CO	.25	.11	.03
☐ 31 Bip Roberts	.50	.23	.06
☐ 32 Steve Rosenberg	.25	.11	.03
☐ 33 Benito Santiago	.50	.23	.06
☐ 34 Jim Snyder CO	.25	.11	.03
☐ 35 Phil Stephenson	.25	.11	.03
☐ 36 Tim Teufel	.25	.11	.03
☐ 37 Jim Vatcher	.25	.11	.03
☐ 38 Kevin Ward	.25	.11	.03
☐ 39 Ed Whitson	.25	.11	.03

1992 Padres Carl's Jr.

This 25-card set was sponsored by Carl's Jr. restaurants and issued in perforated nine-card sheets or in a precut set. The cards are printed on thick card stock and measure slightly larger than standard size (2 9/16" by 3 9/16"). The fronts feature color action player photos bordered in white. The team name appears in tan lettering above the picture while the player's position and name are printed in blue lettering beneath the picture. A unique feature about the player's name is that the first and last letter of his name are oversized. On navy blue lettering on a white background, the horizontally oriented backs present statistics, biography, and career highlights. The sponsor logo in pink rounds out the back. The cards are unnumbered and checklisted below in alphabetical order.

	MINT	NRMT	EXC
COMPLETE SET (25)	15.00	6.75	1.85
COMMON CARD (1-25)	.25	.11	.03
☐ 1 Larry Andersen	.25	.11	.03
☐ 2 Oscar Azocar	.25	.11	.03
☐ 3 Andy Benes	1.00	.45	.12
☐ 4 Dann Bilardello	.25	.11	.03
☐ 5 Jerald Clark	.25	.11	.03
☐ 6 Tony Fernandez	.50	.23	.06
☐ 7 Tony Gwynn	6.00	2.70	.75
☐ 8 Greg W. Harris	.25	.11	.03
☐ 9 Bruce Hurst	.50	.23	.06
☐ 10 Darrin Jackson	.25	.11	.03
☐ 11 Craig Lefferts	.25	.11	.03
☐ 12 Mike Maddux	.25	.11	.03
☐ 13 Fred McGriff	3.00	1.35	.35
☐ 14 Jose Melendez	.25	.11	.03
☐ 15 Randy Myers	.75	.35	.09
☐ 16 Greg Riddoch MG	.25	.11	.03
☐ 17 Rich Rodriguez	.25	.11	.03
☐ 18 Benito Santiago	.75	.35	.09
☐ 19 Gary Sheffield	5.00	2.20	.60
☐ 20 Craig Shipley	.25	.11	.03
☐ 21 Kurt Stillwell	.25	.11	.03
☐ 22 Tim Teufel	.25	.11	.03
☐ 23 Kevin Ward	.25	.11	.03
☐ 24 Ed Whitson	.25	.11	.03
☐ 25 All-Star Game Logo	.25	.11	.03

1992 Padres Mother's

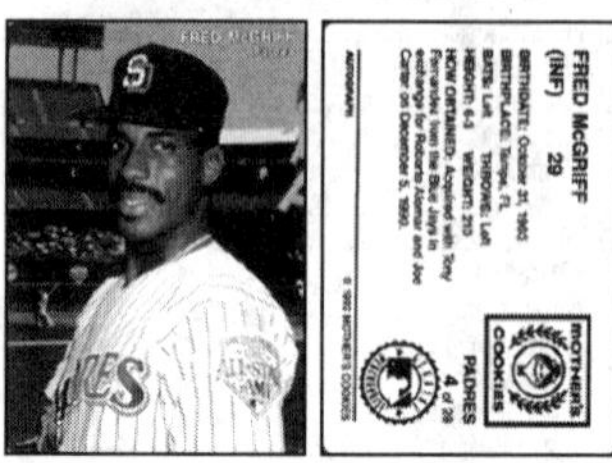

The 1992 Mother's Cookies Padres set contains 28 cards with rounded corners measuring the standard size. The front design has borderless glossy color player photos. The player's name and team name appear in one of the upper corners. The horizontal backs are printed in red and purple, and present biography and a "how obtained" remark where appropriate. A blank slot for the player's autograph rounds out the back.

	MINT	NRMT	EXC
COMPLETE SET (28)	12.00	5.50	1.50
COMMON CARD (1-28)	.25	.11	.03
☐ 1 Greg Riddoch MG	.25	.11	.03
☐ 2 Greg W. Harris	.25	.11	.03
☐ 3 Gary Sheffield	2.00	.90	.25
☐ 4 Fred McGriff	2.50	1.10	.30
☐ 5 Kurt Stillwell	.25	.11	.03
☐ 6 Benito Santiago	.50	.23	.06
☐ 7 Tony Gwynn	4.00	1.80	.50
☐ 8 Tony Fernandez	.50	.23	.06
☐ 9 Jerald Clark	.25	.11	.03
☐ 10 Dave Eiland	.25	.11	.03
☐ 11 Randy Myers	.75	.35	.09
☐ 12 Oscar Azocar	.25	.11	.03
☐ 13 Dann Bilardello	.25	.11	.03
☐ 14 Jose Melendez	.25	.11	.03
☐ 15 Darrin Jackson	.25	.11	.03
☐ 16 Andy Benes	1.00	.45	.12
☐ 17 Tim Teufel	.25	.11	.03
☐ 18 Jeremy Hernandez	.25	.11	.03
☐ 19 Kevin Ward	.25	.11	.03
☐ 20 Bruce Hurst	.25	.11	.03
☐ 21 Larry Andersen	.25	.11	.03
☐ 22 Rich Rodriguez	.25	.11	.03
☐ 23 Pat Clements	.25	.11	.03
☐ 24 Craig Lefferts	.25	.11	.03
☐ 25 Craig Shipley	.25	.11	.03
☐ 26 Mike Maddux	.25	.11	.03
☐ 27 Coaches Jim Snyder Mike Roarke Rob Picciolo Merv Rettenmund Bruce Kimm	.25	.11	.03
☐ 28 Checklist	.25	.11	.03

1992 Padres Police DARE

Sponsored by DARE (Drug Abuse Resistance Education) America, this 30-card standard-size set is printed on thin card stock. The fronts features color action player photos inside white borders. The team logo is printed in the top border while the player's name and position appear in the bottom border. The horizontal backs are divided down the middle, with biography on the left portion and an anti-drug message on the right. DARE logos round out the back. The cards are unnumbered and checklisted below in alphabetical order, with multi-player cards listed at the end.

	MINT	NRMT	EXC
COMPLETE SET (27)	40.00	18.00	5.00
COMMON CARD (1-27)	.75	.35	.09
☐ 1 Oscar Azocar	.75	.35	.09
☐ 2 Bluepper (Mascot)	1.00	.45	.12
☐ 3 Andy Benes	1.50	.70	.19
☐ 4 Jerald Clark	.75	.35	.09
☐ 5 Jim Deshaies	.75	.35	.09
☐ 6 Dave Eiland	.75	.35	.09
☐ 7 Tony Fernandez	1.00	.45	.12
☐ 8 Tony Gwynn	7.50	3.40	.95
☐ 9 Greg W. Harris	.75	.35	.09
☐ 10 Bruce Hurst	.75	.35	.09
☐ 11 Darrin Jackson	.75	.35	.09
☐ 12 Tom Lampkin	.75	.35	.09
☐ 13 Craig Lefferts	2.00	.90	.25
☐ 14 Fred McGriff	5.00	2.20	.60
☐ 15 Rob Picciolo	2.00	.90	.25
☐ 16 Merv Rettenmund CO	.75	.35	.09
☐ 17 Greg Riddoch MG	.75	.35	.09
☐ 18 Benito Santiago	2.00	.90	.25
☐ 19 Frank Seminara	.75	.35	.09
☐ 20 Gary Sheffield	5.00	2.20	.60
☐ 21 Craig Shipley	.75	.35	.09
☐ 22 Phil Stephenson	.75	.35	.09
☐ 23 Kurt Stillwell	.75	.35	.09
☐ 24 Tim Teufel	.75	.35	.09
☐ 25 Dan Walters	.75	.35	.09
☐ 26 Kevin Ward	.75	.35	.09
☐ 27 Jack Murphy Stadium	.75	.35	.09
☐ 28 Coaches Card Bruce Kimm Rob Picciolo Merv Rettenmund Mike Roarke Jim Snyder	.75	.35	.09
☐ 29 Padres Relievers Larry Andersen Mike Maddux Jose Melendez Rich Rodriguez Tim Scott	.75	.35	.09
☐ 30 Fred McGriff Tony Fernandez Gary Sheffield Tony Gwynn	5.00	2.20	.60

1992 Padres Smokey

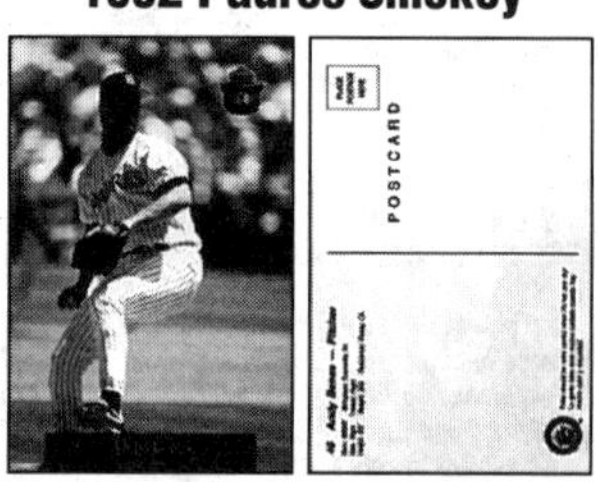

This 36-card set was issued in the postcard format and measures approximately 3 13/16" by 5 11/16". The fronts feature full-bleed color action player photos. The Smokey the Bear logo is superimposed in one of the upper corners while the player's name and position are printed in burnt orange lettering in a navy blue stripe edging the bottom of the card. The left portion of the horizontally oriented backs presents brief biographical information and a fire prevention tip in English and Spanish. The cards are unnumbered and checklisted below in alphabetical order.

	MINT	NRMT	EXC
COMPLETE SET (36)	18.00	8.00	2.20
COMMON CARD (1-36)	.50	.23	.06
☐ 1 Larry Andersen	.50	.23	.06
☐ 2 Oscar Azocar	.50	.23	.06
☐ 3 Andy Benes	1.25	.55	.16
☐ 4 Dann Bilardello	.50	.23	.06
☐ 5 Jerald Clark	.50	.23	.06
☐ 6 Pat Clements	.50	.23	.06
☐ 7 Dave Eiland	.50	.23	.06
☐ 8 Tony Fernandez	.75	.35	.09
☐ 9 Tony Gwynn	8.00	3.60	1.00
☐ 10 Gene Harris	.50	.23	.06
☐ 11 Greg W. Harris	.50	.23	.06
☐ 12 Jeremy Hernandez	.50	.23	.06
☐ 13 Bruce Hurst	.50	.23	.06
☐ 14 Darrin Jackson	.50	.23	.06
☐ 15 Tom Lampkin	.50	.23	.06
☐ 16 Bruce Kimm CO	.50	.23	.06
☐ 17 Craig Lefferts	.50	.23	.06
☐ 18 Mike Maddux	.50	.23	.06
☐ 19 Fred McGriff	1.00	.45	.12
☐ 20 Jose Melendez	.50	.23	.06
☐ 21 Randy Myers	1.25	.55	.16
☐ 22 Gary Pettis	.50	.23	.06
☐ 23 Rob Picciolo CO	.50	.23	.06
☐ 24 Merv Rettenmund CO	.50	.23	.06
☐ 25 Greg Riddoch MG	.50	.23	.06
☐ 26 Mike Roarke CO	.50	.23	.06
☐ 27 Rich Rodriguez	.50	.23	.06
☐ 28 Benito Santiago	1.00	.45	.12
☐ 29 Frank Seminara	.50	.23	.06
☐ 30 Gary Sheffield	4.00	1.80	.50
☐ 31 Craig Shipley	.50	.23	.06
☐ 32 Jim Snyder CO	.50	.23	.06
☐ 33 Dave Staton	.50	.23	.06
☐ 34 Kurt Stillwell	.50	.23	.06
☐ 35 Tim Teufel	.50	.23	.06
☐ 36 Kevin Ward	.50	.23	.06

1993 Padres Mother's

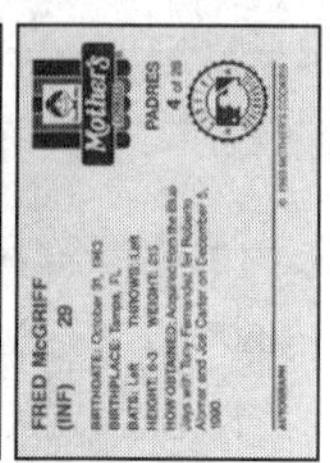

The 1993 Mother's Cookies Padres set consists of 28 standard-size cards with rounded corners. The fronts display full-bleed color player portraits shot from the waist up in stadium settings. The player's name and team name appear in one of the corners. On a white background in red and purple print, the horizontal backs carry biographical information and the sponsor's logo. A blank slot for the player's autograph rounds out the back.

	MINT	NRMT	EXC
COMPLETE SET (28)	12.00	5.50	1.50
COMMON CARD (1-28)	.25	.11	.03
☐ 1 Jim Riggleman MG	.25	.11	.03
☐ 2 Gary Sheffield	2.00	.90	.25
☐ 3 Tony Gwynn	4.00	1.80	.50
☐ 4 Fred McGriff	1.50	.70	.19
☐ 5 Greg W. Harris	.25	.11	.03
☐ 6 Tim Teufel	.25	.11	.03
☐ 7 Dave Eiland	.25	.11	.03
☐ 8 Phil Plantier	.25	.11	.03
☐ 9 Bruce Hurst	.25	.11	.03
☐ 10 Ricky Gutierrez	.25	.11	.03
☐ 11 Rich Rodriguez	.25	.11	.03
☐ 12 Derek Bell	.50	.23	.06
☐ 13 Bob Geren	.25	.11	.03
☐ 14 Andy Benes	1.00	.45	.12
☐ 15 Darrell Sherman	.25	.11	.03
☐ 16 Frank Seminara	.25	.11	.03
☐ 17 Guillermo Velasquez	.25	.11	.03
☐ 18 Gene Harris	.25	.11	.03
☐ 19 Dan Walters	.25	.11	.03
☐ 20 Craig Shipley	.25	.11	.03
☐ 21 Phil Clark	.25	.11	.03
☐ 22 Jeff Gardner	.25	.11	.03
☐ 23 Mike Scioscia	.25	.11	.03
☐ 24 Wally Whitehurst	.25	.11	.03
☐ 25 Roger Mason	.25	.11	.03
☐ 26 Kerry Taylor	.25	.11	.03
☐ 27 Tim Scott	.25	.11	.03
☐ 28 Checklist/Coaches Bruce Bochy Dan Radison Mike Roarke Dave Bialas Rob Picciolo Merv Rettenmund	.25	.11	.03

1994 Padres Mother's

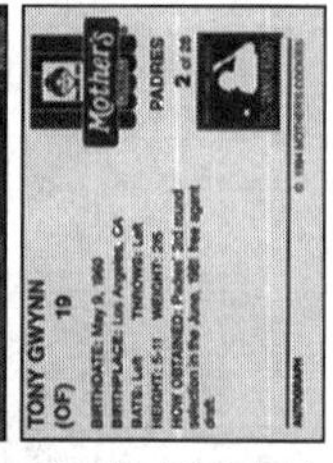

The 1994 Mother's Cookies Padres set consists of 28 standard-size cards with rounded corners. The fronts display full-bleed color player portraits shot from the waist up against a stadium background. The player's name and team name appear in one of the corners. On a white background in red and purple print, the horizontal backs carry biographical information and the sponsor's logo. A blank slot for the player's autograph rounds out the back.

	MINT	NRMT	EXC
COMPLETE SET (28)	8.00	3.60	1.00
COMMON CARD (1-28)	.25	.11	.03
☐ 1 Jim Riggleman MG	.25	.11	.03
☐ 2 Tony Gwynn	2.50	1.10	.30
☐ 3 Andy Benes	1.00	.45	.12
☐ 4 Bip Roberts	.50	.23	.06
☐ 5 Phil Clark	.25	.11	.03
☐ 6 Wally Whitehurst	.25	.11	.03
☐ 7 Archi Cianfrocco	.25	.11	.03
☐ 8 Derek Bell	.50	.23	.06
☐ 9 Ricky Gutierrez	.25	.11	.03
☐ 10 Mark Davis	.25	.11	.03
☐ 11 Phil Plantier	.25	.11	.03
☐ 12 Brian Johnson	.25	.11	.03
☐ 13 Billy Bean	.25	.11	.03
☐ 14 Craig Shipley	.25	.11	.03
☐ 15 Tim Hyers	.25	.11	.03
☐ 16 Gene Harris	.25	.11	.03

□ 17 Scott Sanders	.50	.23	.06
□ 18 A.J. Sager	.25	.11	.03
□ 19 Keith Lockhart	.25	.11	.03
□ 20 Tim Mauser	.25	.11	.03
□ 21 Andy Ashby	.50	.23	.06
□ 22 Brad Ausmus	.25	.11	.03
□ 23 Trevor Hoffman	.50	.23	.06
□ 24 Luis Lopez	.25	.11	.03
□ 25 Doug Brocail	.25	.11	.03
□ 26 Dave Staton	.25	.11	.03
□ 27 Pedro Martinez	.25	.11	.03
□ 28 Checklist/Coaches	.25	.11	.03
Sonny Siebert			
Rob Picciolo			
Dave Bialas			
Dan Radison			
Merv Rettenmund			
Bruce Bochy			

1995 Padres CHP

Sponsored by the California Highway Patrol, this 16-card set features color player photos in a blue frame. The backs carry player information and a safety tip.

	MINT	NRMT	EXC
COMPLETE SET (16)	15.00	6.75	1.85
COMMON CARD (1-16)	.50	.23	.06
□ 1 Tony Gwynn	7.50	3.40	.95
□ 2 Brad Ausmus	.50	.23	.06
□ 3 Andy Ashby	.75	.35	.09
□ 4 Brian Johnson	.50	.23	.06
□ 5 Trevor Hoffman	.75	.35	.09
□ 6 Scott Sanders	.50	.23	.06
□ 7 Bip Roberts	.75	.35	.09
□ 8 Roberto Petagine	.50	.23	.06
□ 9 Fernando Valenzuela	.75	.35	.09
□ 10 Ken Caminiti	2.50	1.10	.30
□ 11 Steve Finley	1.50	.70	.19
□ 12 Andujar Cedeno	.50	.23	.06
□ 13 Jody Reed	.50	.23	.06
□ 14 Eddie Williams	.50	.23	.06
□ 15 Joey Hamilton	1.00	.45	.12
□ 16 Bruce Bochy MG	.50	.23	.06
Chief Don Watkins			

1995 Padres Mother's

The 1995 Mother's Cookies San Diego Padres set consists of 28 standard-size cards with rounded corners. The fronts display posed color player portraits in stadium settings. The player's name and team name appear in one of the top corners. The backs carry biographical information and the sponsor's logo on a white background in red and purple print. A blank slot for the player's autograph rounds out the back.

	MINT	NRMT	EXC
COMPLETE SET (28)	10.00	4.50	1.25
COMMON CARD (1-28)	.25	.11	.03
□ 1 Bruce Bochy MG	.25	.11	.03
□ 2 Tony Gwynn	2.50	1.10	.30
□ 3 Ken Caminiti	2.00	.90	.25
□ 4 Bip Roberts	.50	.23	.06
□ 5 Andujar Cedeno	.25	.11	.03
□ 6 Andy Benes	1.00	.45	.12
□ 7 Phil Clark	.25	.11	.03
□ 8 Fernando Valenzuela	.75	.35	.09
□ 9 Roberto Petagine	.25	.11	.03
□ 10 Brian Johnson	.25	.11	.03
□ 11 Scott Livingstone	.25	.11	.03
□ 12 Brian Williams	.25	.11	.03
□ 13 Jody Reed	.25	.11	.03
□ 14 Steve Finley	1.00	.45	.12
□ 15 Jeff Tabaka	.25	.11	.03
□ 16 Ray Holbert	.25	.11	.03
□ 17 Tim Worrell	.25	.11	.03
□ 18 Eddie Williams	.25	.11	.03
□ 19 Brad Ausmus	.25	.11	.03
□ 20 Willie Blair	.25	.11	.03
□ 21 Trevor Hoffman	.50	.23	.06
□ 22 Scott Sanders	.50	.23	.06
□ 23 Andy Ashby	.50	.23	.06
□ 24 Joey Hamilton	.75	.35	.09
□ 25 Andres Berumen	.25	.11	.03
□ 26 Melvin Nieves	.50	.23	.06
□ 27 Bryce Florie	.25	.11	.03
□ 28 Coaches/Checklist	.50	.23	.06
Merv Rettenmund			
Graig Nettles			
Davey Lopes			
Sonny Siebert			
Rob Picciolo			
Ty Waller			

1996 Padres Mother's

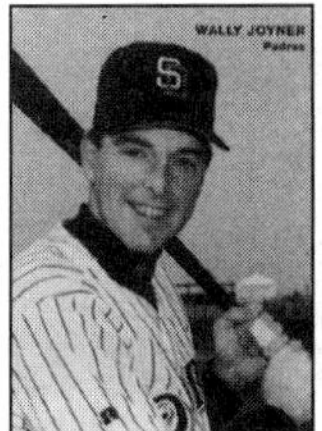

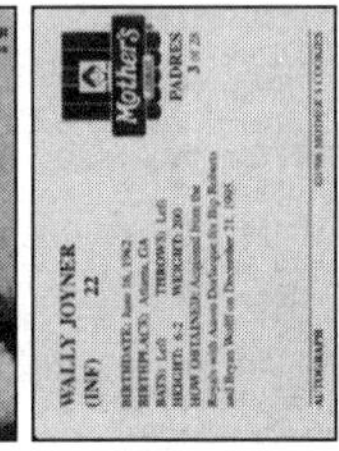

This 28-card set consists of borderless posed color player portraits in stadium settings. The player's and team's names appear in one of the top rounded corners. The backs carry biographical information and the sponsor's logo on a white background in red and purple print. A blank slot for the player's autograph rounds out the back.

	MINT	NRMT	EXC
COMPLETE SET (28)	10.00	4.50	1.25
COMMON CARD (1-28)	.25	.11	.03
□ 1 Bruce Bochy MG	.25	.11	.03
□ 2 Tony Gwynn	2.50	1.10	.30
□ 3 Wally Joyner	.50	.23	.06
□ 4 Rickey Henderson	1.25	.55	.16
□ 5 Ken Caminiti	2.00	.90	.25
□ 6 Scott Sanders	.50	.23	.06
□ 7 Steve Finley	1.00	.45	.12
□ 8 Fernando Valenzuela	.50	.23	.06
□ 9 Brian Johnson	.25	.11	.03
□ 10 Jody Reed	.25	.11	.03
□ 11 Bob Tewksbury	.25	.11	.03
□ 12 Andujar Cedeno	.25	.11	.03
□ 13 Sean Bergman	.25	.11	.03
□ 14 Marc Newfield	.75	.35	.09
□ 15 Craig Shipley	.25	.11	.03
□ 16 Scott Livingstone	.25	.11	.03
□ 17 Trevor Hoffman	.50	.23	.06
□ 18 Doug Bochtler	.25	.11	.03
□ 19 Archi Cianfrocco	.25	.11	.03
□ 20 Joey Hamilton	.50	.23	.06
□ 21 Andy Ashby	.50	.23	.06
□ 22 Chris Gwynn	.25	.11	.03
□ 23 Luis Lopez	.25	.11	.03
□ 24 Tim Worrell	.25	.11	.03
□ 25 Brad Ausmus	.25	.11	.03
□ 26 Willie Blair	.25	.11	.03
□ 27 Bryce Florie	.25	.11	.03
□ 28 Coaches Card CL	.25	.11	.03
Dan Warthen			
Rob Picciolo			
Davey Lopes			
Grady Little			
Tim Flannery			
Merv Rettenmund			

1988 Panini Stickers

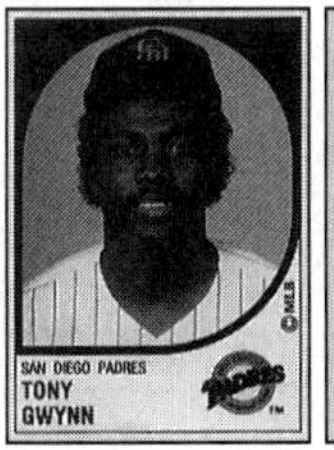

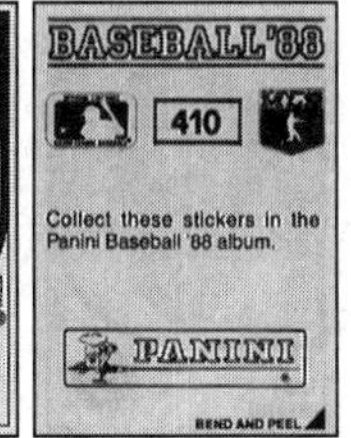

These 480 stickers measure approximately 1 15/16" by 2 11/16" (regular) and 2 1/8" by 2 11/16" (foils). The fronts of the regular stickers have white borders and feature color player head shots on a colored background. The player's name, along with his team name and logo, appear at the bottom. In addition to carrying the stickers' numbers, the white backs carry the logos for MLB, the MLBPA and Panini. There are 80 foil stickers in the set; these foils are essentially the non-player stickers. A 64-page album onto which the stickers could be affixed was available at retail stores (for 59 cents) and was also given away to Little Leaguers as part of a national promotion. The album features Don Mattingly on the front and a photo of a gold glove on the back. The album and the sticker numbering are organized alphabetically by team with AL teams preceding NL teams. The last 26 stickers in the album are actually lettered rather than numbered but are listed below as numbers 455-480. The stickers were also sold at retail outlets packed with the album as a "Complete Collectors Set." The 1988 Panini Sticker set was heavily promoted as Panini entered the baseball sticker market under its own label after producing Topps' stickers for the previous seven years.

	MINT	NRMT	EXC
COMPLETE SET (480)	40.00	18.00	5.00
COMMON STICKER (1-480)	.05	.02	.01
□ 1 1987 WS Trophy	.05	.02	.01
□ 2 Orioles Emblem	.05	.02	.01
□ 3 Orioles Uniform	.05	.02	.01
□ 4 Eric Bell	.05	.02	.01
□ 5 Mike Boddicker	.05	.02	.01
□ 6 Dave Schmidt	.05	.02	.01
□ 7 Terry Kennedy	.05	.02	.01
□ 8 Eddie Murray	1.00	.45	.12
□ 9 Bill Ripken	.05	.02	.01
□ 10 Orioles TL	.05	.02	.01
(Action photo)			
□ 11 Orioles W-L Breakdown	1.50	.70	.19
Cal Ripken IA			
□ 12 Ray Knight	.05	.02	.01
□ 13 Cal Ripken	4.00	1.80	.50
□ 14 Ken Gerhart	.05	.02	.01
□ 15 Fred Lynn	.05	.02	.01
□ 16 Larry Sheets	.05	.02	.01
□ 17 Mike Young	.05	.02	.01
□ 18 Red Sox Emblem	.05	.02	.01
□ 19 Red Sox Uniform	.05	.02	.01
□ 20 Oil Can Boyd	.05	.02	.01
□ 21 Roger Clemens	.75	.35	.09
□ 22 Bruce Hurst	.05	.02	.01
□ 23 Bob Stanley	.05	.02	.01
□ 24 Rich Gedman	.05	.02	.01
□ 25 Dwight Evans	.15	.07	.02
□ 26 Red Sox TL	.05	.02	.01
(Action photo)			
□ 27 Red Sox W-L Breakdown	.05	.02	.01
(Action photo)			
□ 28 Marty Barrett	.05	.02	.01
□ 29 Wade Boggs	.50	.23	.06
□ 30 Spike Owen	.05	.02	.01
□ 31 Ellis Burks	.75	.35	.09
□ 32 Mike Greenwell	.15	.07	.02
□ 33 Jim Rice	.15	.07	.02
□ 34 Angels Emblem	.05	.02	.01
□ 35 Angels Uniform	.05	.02	.01
□ 36 Kirk McCaskill	.05	.02	.01
□ 37 Don Sutton	.30	.14	.04
□ 38 Mike Witt	.05	.02	.01
□ 39 Bob Boone	.15	.07	.02
□ 40 Wally Joyner	.30	.14	.04
□ 41 Mark McLemore	.05	.02	.01
□ 42 Angels TL	.05	.02	.01
(Action photo)			
□ 43 Angels W-L Breakdown	.15	.07	.02
Devon White IA			
□ 44 Jack Howell	.05	.02	.01
□ 45 Dick Schofield	.05	.02	.01
□ 46 Brian Downing	.05	.02	.01
□ 47 Ruppert Jones	.05	.02	.01
□ 48 Gary Pettis	.05	.02	.01
□ 49 Devon White	.30	.14	.04
□ 50 White Sox Emblem	.05	.02	.01
□ 51 White Sox Uniform	.05	.02	.01
□ 52 Floyd Bannister	.05	.02	.01
□ 53 Richard Dotson	.05	.02	.01
□ 54 Bob James	.05	.02	.01
□ 55 Carlton Fisk	.40	.18	.05
□ 56 Greg Walker	.05	.02	.01
□ 57 Fred Manrique	.05	.02	.01
□ 58 White Sox TL	.05	.02	.01
(Action photo)			
□ 59 White Sox W-L	.05	.02	.01
Breakdown			
(Action photo)			
□ 60 Steve Lyons	.05	.02	.01
□ 61 Ozzie Guillen	.15	.07	.02
□ 62 Harold Baines	.15	.07	.02
□ 63 Ivan Calderon	.05	.02	.01
□ 64 Gary Redus	.05	.02	.01
□ 65 Ken Williams	.05	.02	.01
□ 66 Indians Emblem	.05	.02	.01
□ 67 Indians Uniform	.05	.02	.01
□ 68 Scott Bailes	.05	.02	.01
□ 69 Tom Candiotti	.05	.02	.01
□ 70 Greg Swindell	.05	.02	.01
□ 71 Chris Bando	.05	.02	.01
□ 72 Joe Carter	.30	.14	.04
□ 73 Tommy Hinzo	.05	.02	.01
□ 74 Indians TL	.05	.02	.01
(Action photo)			
□ 75 Indians W-L Breakdown	.05	.02	.01
Juan Bonilla IA			
□ 76 Brook Jacoby	.05	.02	.01
□ 77 Julio Franco	.15	.07	.02
□ 78 Brett Butler	.15	.07	.02
□ 79 Mel Hall	.05	.02	.01
□ 80 Cory Snyder	.05	.02	.01
□ 81 Pat Tabler	.05	.02	.01
□ 82 Tigers Emblem	.05	.02	.01
□ 83 Tigers Uniform	.05	.02	.01
□ 84 Willie Hernandez	.05	.02	.01
□ 85 Jack Morris	.15	.07	.02
□ 86 Frank Tanana	.05	.02	.01
□ 87 Walt Terrell	.05	.02	.01
□ 88 Matt Nokes	.05	.02	.01
□ 89 Darrell Evans	.15	.07	.02
□ 90 Tigers TL	.15	.07	.02
Darrell Evans IA			
□ 91 Tigers W-L Breakdown	.30	.14	.04
Carlton Fisk IA			
□ 92 Lou Whitaker	.15	.07	.02
□ 93 Tom Brookens	.05	.02	.01
□ 94 Alan Trammell	.15	.07	.02
□ 95 Kirk Gibson	.15	.07	.02
□ 96 Chet Lemon	.05	.02	.01
□ 97 Pat Sheridan	.05	.02	.01
□ 98 Royals Emblem	.05	.02	.01
□ 99 Royals Uniform	.05	.02	.01
□ 100 Charlie Leibrandt	.05	.02	.01
□ 101 Dan Quisenberry	.05	.02	.01
□ 102 Bret Saberhagen	.15	.07	.02
□ 103 Jamie Quirk	.05	.02	.01
□ 104 George Brett	1.25	.55	.16
□ 105 Frank White	.15	.07	.02
□ 106 Royals TL	.15	.07	.02
Bret Saberhagen IA			
□ 107 Royals W-L Breakdown	.15	.07	.02
Bret Saberhagen IA			
□ 108 Kevin Seitzer	.15	.07	.02
□ 109 Angel Salazar	.05	.02	.01
□ 110 Bo Jackson	.30	.14	.04
□ 111 Lonnie Smith	.05	.02	.01
□ 112 Danny Tartabull	.05	.02	.01
□ 113 Willie Wilson	.05	.02	.01
□ 114 Brewers Emblem	.05	.02	.01
□ 115 Brewers Uniform	.05	.02	.01
□ 116 Ted Higuera	.05	.02	.01
□ 117 Juan Nieves	.05	.02	.01
□ 118 Dan Plesac	.05	.02	.01
□ 119 Bill Wegman	.05	.02	.01
□ 120 B.J. Surhoff	.15	.07	.02
□ 121 Greg Brock	.05	.02	.01
□ 122 Brewers TL	.15	.07	.02
Lou Whitaker IA			
□ 123 Brewers W-L Breakdown	.05	.02	.01
Jim Gantner IA			
□ 124 Jim Gantner	.05	.02	.01
□ 125 Paul Molitor	.75	.35	.09
□ 126 Dale Sveum	.05	.02	.01
□ 127 Glenn Braggs	.05	.02	.01
□ 128 Rob Deer	.05	.02	.01
□ 129 Robin Yount	.40	.18	.05
□ 130 Twins Emblem	.05	.02	.01
□ 131 Twins Uniform	.05	.02	.01
□ 132 Bert Blyleven	.15	.07	.02
□ 133 Jeff Reardon	.15	.07	.02
□ 134 Frank Viola	.05	.02	.01
□ 135 Tim Laudner	.05	.02	.01
□ 136 Kent Hrbek	.15	.07	.02
□ 137 Steve Lombardozzi	.05	.02	.01
□ 138 Twins TL	.05	.02	.01
(Action photo)			
□ 139 Twins W-L Breakdown	.05	.02	.01
(Action photo)			
□ 140 Gary Gaetti	.15	.07	.02
□ 141 Greg Gagne	.05	.02	.01
□ 142 Tom Brunansky	.05	.02	.01
□ 143 Dan Gladden	.05	.02	.01
□ 144 Kirby Puckett	2.00	.90	.25
□ 145 Gene Larkin	.05	.02	.01
□ 146 Team Emblem	.05	.02	.01
New York Yankees			
□ 147 Team Uniform	.05	.02	.01
New York Yankees			
□ 148 Tommy John	.15	.07	.02
□ 149 Rick Rhoden	.05	.02	.01
□ 150 Dave Righetti	.05	.02	.01
□ 151 Rick Cerone	.05	.02	.01
□ 152 Don Mattingly	2.00	.90	.25
□ 153 Willie Randolph	.15	.07	.02
□ 154 1987 Team Leaders	.05	.02	.01
Scott Fletcher IA			
□ 155 1987 W-L Breakdown	.75	.35	.09
Don Mattingly IA			
□ 156 Mike Pagliarulo	.05	.02	.01
□ 157 Wayne Tolleson	.05	.02	.01
□ 158 Rickey Henderson	.40	.18	.05
□ 159 Dan Pasqua	.05	.02	.01
□ 160 Gary Ward	.05	.02	.01
□ 161 Dave Winfield	.50	.23	.06
□ 162 Team Emblem	.05	.02	.01
Oakland A's			
□ 163 Team Uniform	.05	.02	.01
Oakland A's			
□ 164 Dave Stewart	.15	.07	.02
□ 165 Curt Young	.05	.02	.01
□ 166 Terry Steinbach	.30	.14	.04
□ 167 Mark McGwire	3.00	1.35	.35
□ 168 Tony Phillips	.15	.07	.02
□ 169 Carney Lansford	.15	.07	.02
□ 170 1987 Team Leaders	.05	.02	.01
(Action photo)			
□ 171 1987 W-L Breakdown	.05	.02	.01
(Action photo)			
□ 172 Alfredo Griffin	.05	.02	.01
□ 173 Jose Canseco	1.00	.45	.12
□ 174 Mike Davis	.05	.02	.01
□ 175 Reggie Jackson	.50	.23	.06
□ 176 Dwayne Murphy	.05	.02	.01
□ 177 Luis Polonia	.15	.07	.02
□ 178 Team Emblem	.05	.02	.01
Seattle Mariners			
□ 179 Team Uniform	.05	.02	.01
Seattle Mariners			
□ 180 Scott Bankhead	.05	.02	.01
□ 181 Mark Langston	.15	.07	.02
□ 182 Edwin Nunez	.05	.02	.01
□ 183 Scott Bradley	.05	.02	.01

☐ 184 Dave Valle	.05	.02	.01
☐ 185 Alvin Davis	.05	.02	.01
☐ 186 1987 Team Leaders	.05	.02	.01
Rey Quinones IA			
☐ 187 1987 W-L Breakdown	.05	.02	.01
Jack Howell IA			
☐ 188 Harold Reynolds	.15	.07	.02
☐ 189 Jim Presley	.05	.02	.01
☐ 190 Rey Quinones	.05	.02	.01
☐ 191 Phil Bradley	.05	.02	.01
☐ 192 Mickey Brantley	.05	.02	.01
☐ 193 Mike Kingery	.05	.02	.01
☐ 194 Team Emblem	.05	.02	.01
Texas Rangers			
☐ 195 Team Uniform	.05	.02	.01
Texas Rangers			
☐ 196 Edwin Correa	.05	.02	.01
☐ 197 Charlie Hough	.05	.02	.01
☐ 198 Bobby Witt	.05	.02	.01
☐ 199 Mike Stanley	.05	.02	.01
☐ 200 Pete O'Brien	.05	.02	.01
☐ 201 Jerry Browne	.05	.02	.01
☐ 202 1987 Team Leaders	.05	.02	.01
(Action photo)			
☐ 203 1987 W-L Breakdown	.30	.14	.04
Steve Buechele and			
Eddie Murray IA			
☐ 204 Steve Buechele	.05	.02	.01
☐ 205 Larry Parrish	.05	.02	.01
☐ 206 Scott Fletcher	.05	.02	.01
☐ 207 Pete Incaviglia	.05	.02	.01
☐ 208 Oddibe McDowell	.05	.02	.01
☐ 209 Ruben Sierra	.30	.14	.04
☐ 210 Team Emblem	.05	.02	.01
Toronto Blue Jays			
☐ 211 Team Uniform	.05	.02	.01
Toronto Blue Jays			
☐ 212 Mark Eichhorn	.05	.02	.01
☐ 213 Tom Henke	.05	.02	.01
☐ 214 Jimmy Key	.15	.07	.02
☐ 215 Dave Stieb	.05	.02	.01
☐ 216 Ernie Whitt	.05	.02	.01
☐ 217 Willie Upshaw	.05	.02	.01
☐ 218 1987 Team Leaders	.05	.02	.01
Willie Upshaw IA			
☐ 219 1987 W-L Breakdown	.05	.02	.01
Harold Reynolds IA			
☐ 220 Garth Iorg	.05	.02	.01
☐ 221 Kelly Gruber	.05	.02	.01
☐ 222 Tony Fernandez	.05	.02	.01
☐ 223 Jesse Barfield	.05	.02	.01
☐ 224 George Bell	.05	.02	.01
☐ 225 Lloyd Moseby	.05	.02	.01
☐ 226A AL Logo	.05	.02	.01
☐ 226B NL Logo	.05	.02	.01
☐ 227 Terry Kennedy and	.75	.35	.09
Don Mattingly			
☐ 228 Willie Randolph and	.30	.14	.04
Wade Boggs			
☐ 229 Bret Saberhagen	.15	.07	.02
☐ 230 Cal Ripken and	2.00	.90	.25
George Bell			
☐ 231 Rickey Henderson and	.40	.18	.05
Dave Winfield			
☐ 232 Gary Carter and	.15	.07	.02
Jack Clark			
☐ 233 Mike Scott	.05	.02	.01
☐ 234 Ryne Sandberg and	.75	.35	.09
Mike Schmidt			
☐ 235 Ozzie Smith and	.50	.23	.06
Eric Davis			
☐ 236 Andre Dawson and	.15	.07	.02
Darryl Strawberry			
☐ 237 Team Emblem	.05	.02	.01
Atlanta Braves			
☐ 238 Team Uniform	.05	.02	.01
Atlanta Braves			
☐ 239 Rick Mahler	.05	.02	.01
☐ 240 Zane Smith	.05	.02	.01
☐ 241 Ozzie Virgil	.05	.02	.01
☐ 242 Gerald Perry	.05	.02	.01
☐ 243 Glenn Hubbard	.05	.02	.01
☐ 244 Ken Oberkfell	.05	.02	.01
☐ 245 1987 Team Leaders	.05	.02	.01
(Action photo)			
☐ 246 1987 W-L Breakdown	.05	.02	.01
Jeffrey Leonard IA			
☐ 247 Rafael Ramirez	.05	.02	.01
☐ 248 Ken Griffey	.05	.02	.01
☐ 249 Albert Hall	.05	.02	.01
☐ 250 Dion James	.05	.02	.01
☐ 251 Dale Murphy	.30	.14	.04
☐ 252 Gary Roenicke	.05	.02	.01
☐ 253 Team Emblem	.05	.02	.01
Chicago Cubs			
☐ 254 Team Uniform	.05	.02	.01
Chicago Cubs			
☐ 255 Jamie Moyer	.05	.02	.01
☐ 256 Lee Smith	.15	.07	.02
☐ 257 Rick Sutcliffe	.05	.02	.01
☐ 258 Jody Davis	.05	.02	.01
☐ 259 Leon Durham	.05	.02	.01
☐ 260 Ryne Sandberg	1.00	.45	.12
☐ 261 1987 Team Leaders	.05	.02	.01
(Action photo)			
☐ 262 1987 W-L Breakdown	.05	.02	.01
Jody Davis IA			
☐ 263 Keith Moreland	.05	.02	.01
☐ 264 Shawon Dunston	.05	.02	.01
☐ 265 Andre Dawson	.15	.07	.02
☐ 266 Dave Martinez	.05	.02	.01
☐ 267 Jerry Mumphrey	.05	.02	.01
☐ 268 Rafael Palmeiro	.75	.35	.09
☐ 269 Team Emblem	.05	.02	.01
Cincinnati Reds			
☐ 270 Team Uniform	.05	.02	.01
Cincinnati Reds			
☐ 271 John Franco	.15	.07	.02
☐ 272 Ted Power	.05	.02	.01
☐ 273 Bo Diaz	.05	.02	.01
☐ 274 Nick Esasky	.05	.02	.01
☐ 275 Dave Concepcion	.15	.07	.02
☐ 276 Kurt Stillwell	.05	.02	.01
☐ 277 1987 Team Leaders	.15	.07	.02
Dave Parker IA			
☐ 278 1987 W-L Breakdown	.05	.02	.01
(Action photo)			
☐ 279 Buddy Bell	.15	.07	.02
☐ 280 Barry Larkin	1.00	.45	.12
☐ 281 Kal Daniels	.05	.02	.01
☐ 282 Eric Davis	.15	.07	.02
☐ 283 Tracy Jones	.05	.02	.01
☐ 284 Dave Parker	.15	.07	.02
☐ 285 Team Emblem	.05	.02	.01
Houston Astros			
☐ 286 Team Uniform	.05	.02	.01
Houston Astros			
☐ 287 Jim Deshaies	.05	.02	.01
☐ 288 Nolan Ryan	4.00	1.80	.50
☐ 289 Mike Scott	.05	.02	.01
☐ 290 Dave Smith	.05	.02	.01
☐ 291 Alan Ashby	.05	.02	.01
☐ 292 Glenn Davis	.05	.02	.01
☐ 293 1987 Team Leaders	.05	.02	.01
(Action photo)			
☐ 294 1987 W-L Breakdown	.05	.02	.01
(Action photo)			
☐ 295 Bill Doran	.05	.02	.01
☐ 296 Denny Walling	.05	.02	.01
☐ 297 Craig Reynolds	.05	.02	.01
☐ 298 Kevin Bass	.05	.02	.01
☐ 299 Jose Cruz	.05	.02	.01
☐ 300 Billy Hatcher	.05	.02	.01
☐ 301 Team Emblem	.05	.02	.01
Los Angeles Dodgers			
☐ 302 Team Uniform	.05	.02	.01
Los Angeles Dodgers			
☐ 303 Orel Hershiser	.15	.07	.02
☐ 304 Fernando Valenzuela	.15	.07	.02
☐ 305 Bob Welch	.05	.02	.01
☐ 306 Matt Young	.05	.02	.01
☐ 307 Mike Scioscia	.05	.02	.01
☐ 308 Franklin Stubbs	.05	.02	.01
☐ 309 1987 Team Leaders	.05	.02	.01
(Action photo)			
☐ 310 1987 W-L Breakdown	.05	.02	.01
(Action photo)			
☐ 311 Steve Sax	.05	.02	.01
☐ 312 Jeff Hamilton	.05	.02	.01
☐ 313 Dave Anderson	.05	.02	.01
☐ 314 Pedro Guerrero	.05	.02	.01
☐ 315 Mike Marshall	.05	.02	.01
☐ 316 John Shelby	.05	.02	.01
☐ 317 Team Emblem	.05	.02	.01
Montreal Expos			
☐ 318 Team Uniform	.05	.02	.01
Montreal Expos			
☐ 319 Neal Heaton	.05	.02	.01
☐ 320 Bryn Smith	.05	.02	.01
☐ 321 Floyd Youmans	.05	.02	.01
☐ 322 Mike Fitzgerald	.05	.02	.01
☐ 323 Andres Galarraga	.50	.23	.06
☐ 324 Vance Law	.05	.02	.01
☐ 325 1987 Team Leaders	.15	.07	.02
Tim Raines IA			
☐ 326 1987 W-L Breakdown	.15	.07	.02
John Kruk IA			
☐ 327 Tim Wallach	.05	.02	.01
☐ 328 Hubie Brooks	.05	.02	.01
☐ 329 Casey Candaele	.05	.02	.01
☐ 330 Tim Raines	.15	.07	.02
☐ 331 Mitch Webster	.05	.02	.01
☐ 332 Herm Winningham	.05	.02	.01
☐ 333 Team Emblem	.05	.02	.01
New York Mets			
☐ 334 Team Uniform	.05	.02	.01
New York Mets			
☐ 335 Ron Darling	.05	.02	.01
☐ 336 Sid Fernandez	.05	.02	.01
☐ 337 Dwight Gooden	.15	.07	.02
☐ 338 Gary Carter	.15	.07	.02
☐ 339 Keith Hernandez	.15	.07	.02
☐ 340 Wally Backman	.05	.02	.01
☐ 341 1987 Team Leaders	.05	.02	.01
Junior Ortiz IA			
☐ 342 1987 W-L Breakdown	.15	.07	.02
Mookie Wilson,			
Darryl Strawberry,			
and Tim Teufel IA			
☐ 343 Howard Johnson	.05	.02	.01
☐ 344 Rafael Santana	.05	.02	.01
☐ 345 Lenny Dykstra	.15	.07	.02
☐ 346 Kevin McReynolds	.05	.02	.01
☐ 347 Darryl Strawberry	.15	.07	.02
☐ 348 Mookie Wilson	.15	.07	.02
☐ 349 Team Emblem	.05	.02	.01
Philadelphia Phillies			
☐ 350 Team Uniform	.05	.02	.01
Philadelphia Phillies			
☐ 351 Steve Bedrosian	.05	.02	.01
☐ 352 Shane Rawley	.05	.02	.01
☐ 353 Bruce Ruffin	.05	.02	.01
☐ 354 Kent Tekulve	.05	.02	.01
☐ 355 Lance Parrish	.05	.02	.01
☐ 356 Von Hayes	.05	.02	.01
☐ 357 1987 Team Leaders	.05	.02	.01
(Action photo)			
☐ 358 1987 W-L Breakdown	.05	.02	.01
Glenn Wilson IA			
☐ 359 Juan Samuel	.05	.02	.01
☐ 360 Mike Schmidt	1.00	.45	.12
☐ 361 Steve Jeltz	.05	.02	.01
☐ 362 Chris James	.05	.02	.01
☐ 363 Milt Thompson	.05	.02	.01
☐ 364 Glenn Wilson	.05	.02	.01
☐ 365 Team Emblem	.05	.02	.01
Pittsburgh Pirates			
☐ 366 Team Uniform	.05	.02	.01
Pittsburgh Pirates			
☐ 367 Mike Dunne	.05	.02	.01
☐ 368 Brian Fisher	.05	.02	.01
☐ 369 Mike LaValliere	.05	.02	.01
☐ 370 Sid Bream	.05	.02	.01
☐ 371 Jose Lind	.05	.02	.01
☐ 372 Bobby Bonilla	.30	.14	.04
☐ 373 1987 Team Leaders	.30	.14	.04
Bobby Bonilla IA			
☐ 374 1987 W-L Breakdown	.05	.02	.01
(Action photo)			
☐ 375 Al Pedrique	.05	.02	.01
☐ 376 Barry Bonds	1.50	.70	.19
☐ 377 John Cangelosi	.05	.02	.01
☐ 378 Mike Diaz	.05	.02	.01
☐ 379 R.J. Reynolds	.05	.02	.01
☐ 380 Andy Van Slyke	.15	.07	.02
☐ 381 Team Emblem	.05	.02	.01
St. Louis Cardinals			
☐ 382 Team Uniform	.05	.02	.01
St. Louis Cardinals			
☐ 383 Danny Cox	.05	.02	.01
☐ 384 Bob Forsch	.05	.02	.01
☐ 385 Joe Magrane	.05	.02	.01
☐ 386 Todd Worrell	.15	.07	.02
☐ 387 Tony Pena	.05	.02	.01
☐ 388 Jack Clark	.05	.02	.01
☐ 389 1987 Team Leaders	.05	.02	.01
Tommy Herr IA			
☐ 390 1987 W-L Breakdown	.05	.02	.01
(Action photo)			
☐ 391 Tom Herr	.05	.02	.01
☐ 392 Terry Pendleton	.15	.07	.02
☐ 393 Ozzie Smith	1.00	.45	.12
☐ 394 Vince Coleman	.05	.02	.01
☐ 395 Curt Ford	.05	.02	.01
☐ 396 Willie McGee	.15	.07	.02
☐ 397 Team Emblem	.05	.02	.01
San Diego Padres			
☐ 398 Team Uniform	.05	.02	.01
San Diego Padres			
☐ 399 Lance McCullers	.05	.02	.01
☐ 400 Eric Show	.05	.02	.01
☐ 401 Ed Whitson	.05	.02	.01
☐ 402 Benito Santiago	.05	.02	.01
☐ 403 John Kruk	.30	.14	.04
☐ 404 Tim Flannery	.05	.02	.01
☐ 405 1987 Team Leaders	.05	.02	.01
Benito Santiago IA			
☐ 406 1987 W-L Breakdown	.05	.02	.01
(Action photo)			
☐ 407 Randy Ready	.05	.02	.01
☐ 408 Chris Brown	.05	.02	.01
☐ 409 Garry Templeton	.05	.02	.01
☐ 410 Tony Gwynn	1.50	.70	.19
☐ 411 Stan Jefferson	.05	.02	.01
☐ 412 Carmelo Martinez	.05	.02	.01
☐ 413 Team Emblem	.05	.02	.01
San Francisco Giants			
☐ 414 Team Uniform	.05	.02	.01
San Francisco Giants			
☐ 415 Kelly Downs	.05	.02	.01
☐ 416 Scott Garrelts	.05	.02	.01
☐ 417 Mike Krukow	.05	.02	.01
☐ 418 Mike LaCoss	.05	.02	.01
☐ 419 Bob Brenly	.05	.02	.01
☐ 420 Will Clark	1.00	.45	.12
☐ 421 1987 Team Leaders	.30	.14	.04
Will Clark IA			
☐ 422 1987 W-L Breakdown	.05	.02	.01
(Action photo)			
☐ 423 Robby Thompson	.05	.02	.01
☐ 424 Kevin Mitchell	.15	.07	.02
☐ 425 Jose Uribe	.05	.02	.01
☐ 426 Mike Aldrete	.05	.02	.01
☐ 427 Jeffrey Leonard	.05	.02	.01
☐ 428 Candy Maldonado	.05	.02	.01
☐ 429 Mike Schmidt	1.00	.45	.12
☐ 430 Don Mattingly	2.00	.90	.25
☐ 431 Juan Nieves	.05	.02	.01
☐ 432 Paul Molitor	.75	.35	.09
☐ 433 Benito Santiago	.05	.02	.01
☐ 434 Rickey Henderson	.40	.18	.05
☐ 435 Nolan Ryan	4.00	1.80	.50
☐ 436 Kevin Seitzer	.15	.07	.02
☐ 437 Tony Gwynn	1.50	.70	.19
☐ 438 Mark McGwire	3.00	1.35	.35
☐ 439 Howard Johnson	.05	.02	.01
(switch-hitting)			
☐ 440 Steve Bedrosian	.05	.02	.01
☐ 441 Darrell Evans	.15	.07	.02
☐ 442 Eddie Murray	1.00	.45	.12
(switch-hitting)			
☐ 443 Lou Whitaker IA	.15	.07	.02
☐ 444 Kirby Puckett and	1.00	.45	.12
Alan Trammell IA			
☐ 445 Gary Gaetti	.15	.07	.02
☐ 446 Jeffrey Leonard	.05	.02	.01
☐ 447 Tony Pena IA	.05	.02	.01
☐ 448 Kevin Mitchell IA	.15	.07	.02
☐ 449 Tony Pena IA	.05	.02	.01
☐ 450 Randy Bush IA	.05	.02	.01
☐ 451 Minnesota Twins UL	.05	.02	.01
(celebrating)			
☐ 452 Minnesota Twins UR	.05	.02	.01
(celebrating)			
☐ 453 Minnesota Twins LL	.05	.02	.01
(celebrating)			
☐ 454 Minnesota Twins LR	.05	.02	.01
(celebrating)			
☐ 455 Baltimore Orioles A	.05	.02	.01
Pennant and Logo			
☐ 456 Boston Red Sox B	.05	.02	.01
Pennant and Logo			
☐ 457 California Angels C	.05	.02	.01
Pennant and Logo			
☐ 458 Chicago White Sox D	.05	.02	.01
Pennant and Logo			
☐ 459 Cleveland Indians E	.05	.02	.01
Pennant and Logo			
☐ 460 Detroit Tigers F	.05	.02	.01
Pennant and Logo			
☐ 461 Kansas City Royals G	.05	.02	.01
Pennant and Logo			
☐ 462 Milwaukee Brewers H	.05	.02	.01
Pennant and Logo			
☐ 463 Minnesota Twins I	.05	.02	.01
Pennant and Logo			
☐ 464 New York Yankees J	.05	.02	.01
Pennant and Logo			
☐ 465 Oakland A's K	.05	.02	.01
Pennant and Logo			
☐ 466 Seattle Mariners L	.05	.02	.01
Pennant and Logo			
☐ 467 Texas Rangers M	.05	.02	.01
Pennant and Logo			
☐ 468 Toronto Blue Jays N	.05	.02	.01
Pennant and Logo			
☐ 469 Atlanta Braves O	.05	.02	.01
Pennant and Logo			
☐ 470 Chicago Cubs P	.05	.02	.01
Pennant and Logo			
☐ 471 Cincinnati Reds Q	.05	.02	.01
Pennant and Logo			
☐ 472 Houston Astros R	.05	.02	.01
Pennant and Logo			
☐ 473 Los Angeles Dodgers S	.05	.02	.01
Pennant and Logo			
☐ 474 Montreal Expos T	.05	.02	.01
Pennant and Logo			
☐ 475 New York Mets U	.05	.02	.01
Pennant and Logo			
☐ 476 Phila. Phillies W	.05	.02	.01
Pennant and Logo			
☐ 477 Pittsburgh Pirates W	.05	.02	.01
Pennant and Logo			
☐ 478 St. Louis Cardinals X	.05	.02	.01
Pennant and Logo			
☐ 479 San Diego Padres Y	.05	.02	.01
Pennant and Logo			
☐ 480 San Fran. Giants Z	.05	.02	.01
Pennant and Logo			
☐ xx Sticker Album	1.00	.45	.12
Don Mattingly on front			

1989 Panini Stickers

These 480 stickers measure approximately 1 7/8" by 2 11/16" and feature white-bordered color player action shots. Sticker packets contained six stickers (five paper, one foil) and sold for 30 cents. The set includes 80 foil stickers; the first two stickers are foil, then each of the 26 teams has three foils out of its full complement of 16 stickers. An album onto which the stickers could be affixed was available at retail stores. The album featured Jose Canseco on the front cover and an ad for Oscar Mayer on the back. The stickers are organized alphabetically by city with NL teams preceding AL teams. The following subsets are also included: 1988 World Series Trophy (Foil, 1-2), 1988 Highlights (3-9), 1988 League Championship Series (10-15), 1988 World Series (16-29), 1988 NL Stat Leaders (222-226), 1988 All-Stars (227-244), 1988 AL Stat Leaders (245-249) and 1988 Award Winners (474-480).

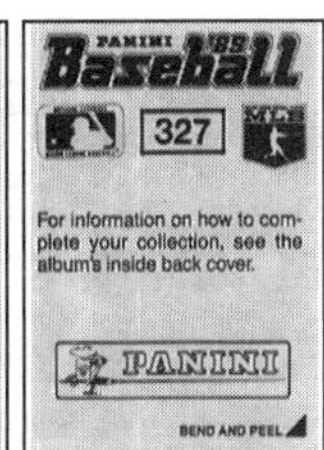

	MINT	NRMT	EXC
COMPLETE SET (480)	20.00	9.00	2.50
COMMON STICKER (1-480)	.05	.02	.01
☐ 1 World Series Trophy	.05	.02	.01
☐ 2 World Series Trophy	.05	.02	.01
☐ 3 Mike Schmidt	.50	.23	.06
☐ 4 Tom Browning	.05	.02	.01
☐ 5 Doug Jones	.05	.02	.01
☐ 6 Wrigley Field	.05	.02	.01
☐ 7 Wade Boggs	.30	.14	.04
☐ 8 Jose Canseco	.50	.23	.06
☐ 9 Orel Hershiser	.10	.05	.01
☐ 10 Oakland wins ALCS	.05	.02	.01
☐ 11 Oakland wins ALCS	.05	.02	.01
☐ 12 Dennis Eckersley ALCS	.10	.05	.01
☐ 13 Orel Hershiser NLCS	.10	.05	.01
☐ 14 Dodgers win NLCS	.05	.02	.01
☐ 15 Dodgers win NLCS	.05	.02	.01
☐ 16 Kirk Gibson	.20	.09	.03
☐ 17 Kirk Gibson	.20	.09	.03
☐ 18 Orel Hershiser	.10	.05	.01
☐ 19 Orel Hershiser	.10	.05	.01
☐ 20 Mark McGwire	1.25	.55	.16
☐ 21 Tim Belcher	.05	.02	.01
☐ 22 Jay Howell	.05	.02	.01
☐ 23 Mickey Hatcher	.05	.02	.01
☐ 24 Mike Davis	.05	.02	.01
☐ 25 Orel Hershiser WS MVP	.10	.05	.01
☐ 26 Dodgers win AS	.05	.02	.01
☐ 27 Dodgers win AS	.05	.02	.01
☐ 28 Dodgers win AS	.05	.02	.01
☐ 29 Dodgers win AS	.05	.02	.01
☐ 30 Atlanta team logo	.05	.02	.01
☐ 31 Jose Alvarez	.05	.02	.01
☐ 32 Tommy Gregg	.05	.02	.01
☐ 33 Paul Assenmacher	.05	.02	.01
☐ 34 Tom Glavine	.75	.35	.09
☐ 35 Rick Mahler	.05	.02	.01
☐ 36 Pete Smith	.05	.02	.01
☐ 37 Atlanta-Fulton County Stadium	.05	.02	.01
☐ 38 Atlanta team lettering	.05	.02	.01
☐ 39 Bruce Sutter	.05	.02	.01
☐ 40 Gerald Perry	.05	.02	.01
☐ 41 Jeff Blauser	.10	.05	.01
☐ 42 Ron Gant	.35	.16	.04
☐ 43 Andres Thomas	.05	.02	.01
☐ 44 Dion James	.05	.02	.01
☐ 45 Dale Murphy	.20	.09	.03
☐ 46 Cubs team logo	.05	.02	.01
☐ 47 Doug Dascenzo	.05	.02	.01
☐ 48 Mike Harkey	.05	.02	.01
☐ 49 Greg Maddux	1.75	.80	.22
☐ 50 Jeff Pico	.05	.02	.01
☐ 51 Rick Sutcliffe	.05	.02	.01
☐ 52 Damon Berryhill	.05	.02	.01
☐ 53 Wrigley Field	.05	.02	.01
☐ 54 Cubs lettering	.05	.02	.01
☐ 55 Mark Grace	.60	.25	.07
☐ 56 Ryne Sandberg	.75	.35	.09
☐ 57 Vance Law	.05	.02	.01
☐ 58 Shawon Dunston	.05	.02	.01
☐ 59 Andre Dawson	.10	.05	.01
☐ 60 Rafael Palmeiro	.30	.14	.04
☐ 61 Mitch Webster	.05	.02	.01
☐ 62 Reds team logo	.05	.02	.01
☐ 63 Jack Armstrong	.05	.02	.01
☐ 64 Chris Sabo	.05	.02	.01
☐ 65 Tom Browning	.05	.02	.01
☐ 66 John Franco	.10	.05	.01
☐ 67 Danny Jackson	.05	.02	.01
☐ 68 Jose Rijo	.05	.02	.01
☐ 69 Riverfront Stadium	.05	.02	.01
☐ 70 Reds team lettering	.05	.02	.01
☐ 71 Bo Diaz	.05	.02	.01
☐ 72 Nick Esasky	.05	.02	.01
☐ 73 Jeff Treadway	.05	.02	.01
☐ 74 Barry Larkin	.60	.25	.07
☐ 75 Kal Daniels	.05	.02	.01
☐ 76 Eric Davis	.10	.05	.01
☐ 77 Paul O'Neill	.10	.05	.01
☐ 78 Astros team logo	.05	.02	.01
☐ 79 Craig Biggio	1.00	.45	.12
☐ 80 John Fishel	.05	.02	.01
☐ 81 Juan Agosto	.05	.02	.01
☐ 82 Bob Knepper	.05	.02	.01
☐ 83 Nolan Ryan	3.00	1.35	.35
☐ 84 Mike Scott	.05	.02	.01
☐ 85 The Astrodome	.05	.02	.01
☐ 86 Astros team lettering	.05	.02	.01
☐ 87 Dave Smith	.05	.02	.01
☐ 88 Glenn Davis	.05	.02	.01
☐ 89 Bill Doran	.05	.02	.01
☐ 90 Rafael Ramirez	.05	.02	.01
☐ 91 Kevin Bass	.05	.02	.01
☐ 92 Billy Hatcher	.05	.02	.01
☐ 93 Gerald Young	.05	.02	.01
☐ 94 Dodgers team logo	.05	.02	.01
☐ 95 Tim Belcher	.05	.02	.01
☐ 96 Tim Crews	.05	.02	.01
☐ 97 Orel Hershiser	.10	.05	.01
☐ 98 Jay Howell	.05	.02	.01
☐ 99 Tim Leary	.05	.02	.01
☐ 100 John Tudor	.05	.02	.01
☐ 101 Dodger Stadium	.05	.02	.01
☐ 102 Dodgers team lettering	.05	.02	.01
☐ 103 Fernando Valenzuela	.10	.05	.01
☐ 104 Mike Scioscia	.05	.02	.01
☐ 105 Mickey Hatcher	.05	.02	.01
☐ 106 Steve Sax	.05	.02	.01
☐ 107 Kirk Gibson	.20	.09	.03
☐ 108 Mike Marshall	.05	.02	.01
☐ 109 John Shelby	.05	.02	.01
☐ 110 Expos team logo	.05	.02	.01
☐ 111 Randy Johnson	1.25	.55	.16
☐ 112 Nelson Santovenia	.05	.02	.01
☐ 113 Tim Burke	.05	.02	.01
☐ 114 Dennis Martinez	.10	.05	.01
☐ 115 Pascual Perez	.05	.02	.01
☐ 116 Bryn Smith	.05	.02	.01
☐ 117 Olympic Stadium	.05	.02	.01
☐ 118 Expos team lettering	.05	.02	.01
☐ 119 Andres Galarraga	.20	.09	.03
☐ 120 Wallace Johnson	.05	.02	.01
☐ 121 Tom Foley	.05	.02	.01
☐ 122 Tim Wallach	.05	.02	.01
☐ 123 Hubie Brooks	.05	.02	.01
☐ 124 Tracy Jones	.05	.02	.01
☐ 125 Tim Raines	.10	.05	.01
☐ 126 Mets team logo	.05	.02	.01
☐ 127 Kevin Elster	.05	.02	.01
☐ 128 Gregg Jefferies	.25	.11	.03
☐ 129 David Cone	.30	.14	.04
☐ 130 Ron Darling	.05	.02	.01
☐ 131 Dwight Gooden	.10	.05	.01
☐ 132 Roger McDowell	.05	.02	.01
☐ 133 Shea Stadium	.05	.02	.01
☐ 134 Mets team lettering	.05	.02	.01
☐ 135 Randy Myers	.10	.05	.01
☐ 136 Gary Carter	.10	.05	.01
☐ 137 Keith Hernandez	.10	.05	.01
☐ 138 Lenny Dykstra	.10	.05	.01
☐ 139 Kevin McReynolds	.05	.02	.01
☐ 140 Darryl Strawberry	.10	.05	.01
☐ 141 Mookie Wilson	.05	.02	.01
☐ 142 Phillies team logo	.05	.02	.01
☐ 143 Ron Jones	.05	.02	.01
☐ 144 Ricky Jordan	.05	.02	.01
☐ 145 Steve Bedrosian	.05	.02	.01
☐ 146 Don Carman	.05	.02	.01
☐ 147 Kevin Gross	.05	.02	.01
☐ 148 Bruce Ruffin	.05	.02	.01
☐ 149 Veterans Stadium	.05	.02	.01
☐ 150 Phillies team lettering	.05	.02	.01
☐ 151 Von Hayes	.05	.02	.01
☐ 152 Juan Samuel	.05	.02	.01
☐ 153 Mike Schmidt	.75	.35	.09
☐ 154 Phil Bradley	.05	.02	.01
☐ 155 Bob Dernier	.05	.02	.01
☐ 156 Chris James	.05	.02	.01
☐ 157 Milt Thompson	.05	.02	.01
☐ 158 Pirates team logo	.05	.02	.01
☐ 159 Randy Kramer	.05	.02	.01
☐ 160 Scott Medvin	.05	.02	.01
☐ 161 Doug Drabek	.05	.02	.01
☐ 162 Mike Dunne	.05	.02	.01
☐ 163 Jim Gott	.05	.02	.01
☐ 164 Jeff D. Robinson	.05	.02	.01
☐ 165 Three Rivers Stadium	.05	.02	.01
☐ 166 Pirates team lettering	.05	.02	.01
☐ 167 John Smiley	.05	.02	.01
☐ 168 Mike LaValliere	.05	.02	.01
☐ 169 Sid Bream	.05	.02	.01
☐ 170 Jose Lind	.05	.02	.01
☐ 171 Bobby Bonilla	.20	.09	.03
☐ 172 Barry Bonds	.75	.35	.09
☐ 173 Andy Van Slyke	.10	.05	.01
☐ 174 Cardinals team logo	.05	.02	.01
☐ 175 Luis Alicea	.05	.02	.01
☐ 176 John Costello	.05	.02	.01
☐ 177 Jose DeLeon	.05	.02	.01
☐ 178 Joe Magrane	.05	.02	.01
☐ 179 Todd Worrell	.05	.02	.01
☐ 180 Tony Pena	.05	.02	.01
☐ 181 Busch Stadium	.05	.02	.01
☐ 182 Cardinals team lettering	.05	.02	.01
☐ 183 Pedro Guerrero	.05	.02	.01
☐ 184 Jose Oquendo	.05	.02	.01
☐ 185 Terry Pendleton	.10	.05	.01
☐ 186 Ozzie Smith	.75	.35	.09
☐ 187 Tom Brunansky	.05	.02	.01
☐ 188 Vince Coleman	.05	.02	.01
☐ 189 Willie McGee	.10	.05	.01
☐ 190 Padres team logo	.05	.02	.01
☐ 191 Roberto Alomar	1.00	.45	.12
☐ 192 Sandy Alomar Jr.	.50	.23	.06
☐ 193 Mark Davis	.05	.02	.01
☐ 194 Andy Hawkins	.05	.02	.01
☐ 195 Dennis Rasmussen	.05	.02	.01
☐ 196 Eric Show	.05	.02	.01
☐ 197 Jack Murphy Stadium	.05	.02	.01
☐ 198 Padres team lettering	.05	.02	.01
☐ 199 Benito Santiago	.05	.02	.01
☐ 200 John Kruk	.10	.05	.01
☐ 201 Randy Ready	.05	.02	.01
☐ 202 Garry Templeton	.05	.02	.01
☐ 203 Tony Gwynn	1.25	.55	.16
☐ 204 Carmelo Martinez	.05	.02	.01
☐ 205 Marvell Wynne	.05	.02	.01
☐ 206 Giants Team Logo	.05	.02	.01
☐ 207 Dennis Cook	.05	.02	.01
☐ 208 Kirt Manwaring	.05	.02	.01
☐ 209 Kelly Downs	.05	.02	.01
☐ 210 Rick Reuschel	.05	.02	.01
☐ 211 Don Robinson	.05	.02	.01
☐ 212 Will Clark	.50	.23	.06
☐ 213 Candlestick Park	.05	.02	.01
☐ 214 Giants team lettering	.05	.02	.01
☐ 215 Robby Thompson	.05	.02	.01
☐ 216 Kevin Mitchell	.05	.02	.01
☐ 217 Jose Uribe	.05	.02	.01
☐ 218 Matt Williams	.75	.35	.09
☐ 219 Mike Aldrete	.05	.02	.01
☐ 220 Brett Butler	.10	.05	.01
☐ 221 Candy Maldonado	.05	.02	.01
☐ 222 Tony Gwynn	1.25	.55	.16
☐ 223 Darryl Strawberry	.10	.05	.01
☐ 224 Andres Galarraga	.20	.09	.03
☐ 225 Orel Hershiser Danny Jackson	.10	.05	.01
☐ 226 Nolan Ryan	3.00	1.35	.35
☐ 227 Dwight Gooden AS	.10	.05	.01
☐ 228 Gary Carter AS	.10	.05	.01
☐ 229 Vince Coleman AS	.05	.02	.01
☐ 230 Andre Dawson AS	.10	.05	.01
☐ 231 Darryl Strawberry AS	.10	.05	.01
☐ 232 Will Clark AS	.20	.09	.03
☐ 233 Ryne Sandberg AS	.35	.16	.04
☐ 234 Bobby Bonilla AS	.20	.09	.03
☐ 235 Ozzie Smith AS	.35	.16	.04
☐ 236 Terry Steinbach AS	.10	.05	.01
☐ 237 Frank Viola AS	.05	.02	.01
☐ 238 Jose Canseco AS	.20	.09	.03
☐ 239 Rickey Henderson AS	.20	.09	.03
☐ 240 Dave Winfield AS	.20	.09	.03
☐ 241 Cal Ripken Jr. AS	1.50	.70	.19
☐ 242 Wade Boggs AS	.20	.09	.03
☐ 243 Paul Molitor AS	.35	.16	.04
☐ 244 Mark McGwire AS	.60	.25	.07
☐ 245 Wade Boggs AS	.20	.09	.03
☐ 246 Jose Canseco	.50	.23	.06
☐ 247 Kirby Puckett	1.50	.70	.19
☐ 248 Frank Viola	.05	.02	.01
☐ 249 Roger Clemens	.60	.25	.07
☐ 250 Orioles team logo	.05	.02	.01
☐ 251 Bob Milacki	.05	.02	.01
☐ 252 Craig Worthington	.05	.02	.01
☐ 253 Jeff Ballard	.05	.02	.01
☐ 254 Tom Niedenfuer	.05	.02	.01
☐ 255 Dave Schmidt	.05	.02	.01
☐ 256 Terry Kennedy	.05	.02	.01
☐ 257 Memorial Stadium	.05	.02	.01
☐ 258 Orioles team lettering	.05	.02	.01
☐ 259 Mickey Tettleton	.10	.05	.01
☐ 260 Eddie Murray	.75	.35	.09
☐ 261 Bill Ripken	.05	.02	.01
☐ 262 Cal Ripken Jr.	3.00	1.35	.35
☐ 263 Joe Orsulak	.05	.02	.01
☐ 264 Larry Sheets	.05	.02	.01
☐ 265 Pete Stanicek	.05	.02	.01
☐ 266 Red Sox team logo	.05	.02	.01
☐ 267 Steve Curry	.05	.02	.01
☐ 268 Jody Reed	.05	.02	.01
☐ 269 Oil Can Boyd	.05	.02	.01
☐ 270 Roger Clemens	.50	.23	.06
☐ 271 Bruce Hurst	.05	.02	.01
☐ 272 Lee Smith	.10	.05	.01
☐ 273 Fenway Park	.05	.02	.01
☐ 274 Red Sox team lettering	.05	.02	.01
☐ 275 Todd Benzinger	.05	.02	.01
☐ 276 Marty Barrett	.05	.02	.01
☐ 277 Wade Boggs	.30	.14	.04
☐ 278 Ellis Burks	.20	.09	.03
☐ 279 Dwight Evans	.10	.05	.01
☐ 280 Mike Greenwell	.05	.02	.01
☐ 281 Jim Rice	.10	.05	.01
☐ 282 Angels team logo	.05	.02	.01
☐ 283 Dante Bichette	1.50	.70	.19
☐ 284 Bryan Harvey	.05	.02	.01
☐ 285 Kirk McCaskill	.05	.02	.01
☐ 286 Mike Witt	.05	.02	.01
☐ 287 Bob Boone	.10	.05	.01
☐ 288 Brian Downing	.05	.02	.01
☐ 289 Anaheim Stadium	.05	.02	.01
☐ 290 Angels team lettering	.05	.02	.01
☐ 291 Wally Joyner	.10	.05	.01
☐ 292 Johnny Ray	.05	.02	.01
☐ 293 Jack Howell	.05	.02	.01
☐ 294 Dick Schofield	.05	.02	.01
☐ 295 Tony Armas	.05	.02	.01
☐ 296 Chili Davis	.10	.05	.01
☐ 297 Devon White	.10	.05	.01
☐ 298 White Sox team logo	.05	.02	.01
☐ 299 Dave Gallagher	.05	.02	.01
☐ 300 Melido Perez	.05	.02	.01
☐ 301 Shawn Hillegas	.05	.02	.01
☐ 302 Jack McDowell	.25	.11	.03
☐ 303 Bobby Thigpen	.05	.02	.01
☐ 304 Carlton Fisk	.25	.11	.03
☐ 305 Comiskey Park	.05	.02	.01
☐ 306 White Sox team lettering	.05	.02	.01
☐ 307 Greg Walker	.05	.02	.01
☐ 308 Steve Lyons	.05	.02	.01
☐ 309 Ozzie Guillen	.05	.02	.01
☐ 310 Harold Baines	.10	.05	.01
☐ 311 Daryl Boston	.05	.02	.01
☐ 312 Lance Johnson	.20	.09	.03
☐ 313 Dan Pasqua	.05	.02	.01
☐ 314 Indians team logo	.05	.02	.01
☐ 315 Luis Medina	.05	.02	.01
☐ 316 Ron Tingley	.05	.02	.01
☐ 317 Tom Candiotti	.05	.02	.01
☐ 318 John Farrell	.05	.02	.01
☐ 319 Doug Jones	.05	.02	.01
☐ 320 Greg Swindell	.05	.02	.01
☐ 321 Cleveland Stadium	.05	.02	.01
☐ 322 Indians team lettering	.05	.02	.01
☐ 323 Andy Allanson	.05	.02	.01
☐ 324 Willie Upshaw	.05	.02	.01
☐ 325 Julio Franco	.10	.05	.01
☐ 326 Brook Jacoby	.05	.02	.01
☐ 327 Joe Carter	.20	.09	.03
☐ 328 Mel Hall	.05	.02	.01
☐ 329 Cory Snyder	.05	.02	.01
☐ 330 Tigers team logo	.05	.02	.01
☐ 331 Paul Gibson	.05	.02	.01
☐ 332 Torey Lovullo	.05	.02	.01
☐ 333 Mike Henneman	.05	.02	.01
☐ 334 Jack Morris	.10	.05	.01
☐ 335 Jeff M. Robinson	.05	.02	.01
☐ 336 Frank Tanana	.05	.02	.01
☐ 337 Tiger Stadium	.05	.02	.01
☐ 338 Tigers team lettering	.05	.02	.01
☐ 339 Matt Nokes	.05	.02	.01
☐ 340 Tom Brookens	.05	.02	.01
☐ 341 Lou Whitaker	.10	.05	.01
☐ 342 Luis Salazar	.05	.02	.01
☐ 343 Alan Trammell	.10	.05	.01
☐ 344 Chet Lemon	.05	.02	.01
☐ 345 Gary Pettis	.05	.02	.01
☐ 346 Royals team logo	.05	.02	.01
☐ 347 Luis de los Santos	.05	.02	.01
☐ 348 Gary Thurman	.05	.02	.01
☐ 349 Steve Farr	.05	.02	.01
☐ 350 Mark Gubicza	.05	.02	.01
☐ 351 Charlie Leibrandt	.05	.02	.01
☐ 352 Bret Saberhagen	.10	.05	.01
☐ 353 Royals Stadium	.05	.02	.01
☐ 354 Royals team lettering	.05	.02	.01
☐ 355 George Brett	1.25	.55	.16
☐ 356 Frank White	.10	.05	.01
☐ 357 Kevin Seitzer	.05	.02	.01
☐ 358 Bo Jackson	.20	.09	.03
☐ 359 Pat Tabler	.05	.02	.01
☐ 360 Danny Tartabull	.05	.02	.01
☐ 361 Willie Wilson	.05	.02	.01
☐ 362 Brewers team logo	.05	.02	.01
☐ 363 Joey Meyer	.05	.02	.01
☐ 364 Gary Sheffield	2.00	.90	.25
☐ 365 Don August	.05	.02	.01
☐ 366 Ted Higuera	.05	.02	.01
☐ 367 Dan Plesac	.05	.02	.01
☐ 368 B.J. Surhoff	.10	.05	.01
☐ 369 Milwaukee County Stadium	.05	.02	.01
☐ 370 Brewers team lettering	.05	.02	.01
☐ 371 Greg Brock	.05	.02	.01
☐ 372 Jim Gantner	.05	.02	.01
☐ 373 Paul Molitor	.75	.35	.09
☐ 374 Dale Sveum	.05	.02	.01
☐ 375 Glenn Braggs	.05	.02	.01
☐ 376 Rob Deer	.05	.02	.01
☐ 377 Robin Yount	.25	.11	.03
☐ 378 Twins team logo	.05	.02	.01
☐ 379 German Gonzalez	.05	.02	.01
☐ 380 Kelvin Torve	.05	.02	.01
☐ 381 Allan Anderson	.05	.02	.01
☐ 382 Jeff Reardon	.10	.05	.01
☐ 383 Frank Viola	.05	.02	.01
☐ 384 Tim Laudner	.05	.02	.01
☐ 385 Hubert H. Humphrey Metrodome	.05	.02	.01
☐ 386 Twins team lettering	.05	.02	.01
☐ 387 Kent Hrbek	.10	.05	.01
☐ 388 Gene Larkin	.05	.02	.01
☐ 389 Gary Gaetti	.05	.02	.01

☐ 390 Greg Gagne	.05	.02	.01
☐ 391 Randy Bush	.05	.02	.01
☐ 392 Dan Gladden	.05	.02	.01
☐ 393 Kirby Puckett	1.50	.70	.19
☐ 394 Yankees team logo	.05	.02	.01
☐ 395 Roberto Kelly	.05	.02	.01
☐ 396 Al Leiter	.10	.05	.01
☐ 397 John Candelaria	.05	.02	.01
☐ 398 Rich Dotson	.05	.02	.01
☐ 399 Rick Rhoden	.05	.02	.01
☐ 400 Dave Righetti	.05	.02	.01
☐ 401 Yankee Stadium	.05	.02	.01
☐ 402 Yankees team lettering	.05	.02	.01
☐ 403 Don Slaught	.05	.02	.01
☐ 404 Don Mattingly	1.50	.70	.19
☐ 405 Willie Randolph	.10	.05	.01
☐ 406 Mike Pagliarulo	.05	.02	.01
☐ 407 Rafael Santana	.05	.02	.01
☐ 408 Rickey Henderson	.25	.11	.03
☐ 409 Dave Winfield	.25	.11	.03
☐ 410 Athletics team logo	.05	.02	.01
☐ 411 Todd Burns	.05	.02	.01
☐ 412 Walt Weiss	.05	.02	.01
☐ 413 Storm Davis	.05	.02	.01
☐ 414 Dennis Eckersley	.10	.05	.01
☐ 415 Dave Stewart	.10	.05	.01
☐ 416 Bob Welch	.05	.02	.01
☐ 417 Oakland Alameda County Coliseum	.05	.02	.01
☐ 418 Athletics team lettering	.05	.02	.01
☐ 419 Terry Steinbach	.10	.05	.01
☐ 420 Mark McGwire	1.25	.55	.16
☐ 421 Carney Lansford	.05	.02	.01
☐ 422 Jose Canseco	.50	.23	.06
☐ 423 Dave Henderson	.05	.02	.01
☐ 424 Dave Parker	.10	.05	.01
☐ 425 Luis Polonia	.10	.05	.01
☐ 426 Mariners team logo	.05	.02	.01
☐ 427 Mario Diaz	.05	.02	.01
☐ 428 Edgar Martinez	.40	.18	.05
☐ 429 Scott Bankhead	.05	.02	.01
☐ 430 Mark Langston	.10	.05	.01
☐ 431 Mike Moore	.05	.02	.01
☐ 432 Scott Bradley	.05	.02	.01
☐ 433 The Kingdome	.05	.02	.01
☐ 434 Mariners team lettering	.05	.02	.01
☐ 435 Alvin Davis	.05	.02	.01
☐ 436 Harold Reynolds	.10	.05	.01
☐ 437 Jim Presley	.05	.02	.01
☐ 438 Rey Quinones	.05	.02	.01
☐ 439 Mickey Brantley	.05	.02	.01
☐ 440 Jay Buhner	.50	.23	.06
☐ 441 Henry Cotto	.05	.02	.01
☐ 442 Rangers team logo	.05	.02	.01
☐ 443 Cecil Espy	.05	.02	.01
☐ 444 Chad Kreuter	.05	.02	.01
☐ 445 Jose Guzman	.05	.02	.01
☐ 446 Charlie Hough	.05	.02	.01
☐ 447 Jeff Russell	.05	.02	.01
☐ 448 Bobby Witt	.05	.02	.01
☐ 449 Arlington Stadium	.05	.02	.01
☐ 450 Rangers team lettering	.05	.02	.01
☐ 451 Geno Petralli	.05	.02	.01
☐ 452 Pete O'Brien	.05	.02	.01
☐ 453 Steve Buechele	.05	.02	.01
☐ 454 Scott Fletcher	.05	.02	.01
☐ 455 Pete Incaviglia	.05	.02	.01
☐ 456 Oddibe McDowell	.05	.02	.01
☐ 457 Ruben Sierra	.10	.05	.01
☐ 458 Blue Jays team logo	.05	.02	.01
☐ 459 Rob Ducey	.05	.02	.01
☐ 460 Todd Stottlemyre	.10	.05	.01
☐ 461 Tom Henke	.05	.02	.01
☐ 462 Jimmy Key	.10	.05	.01
☐ 463 Dave Stieb	.05	.02	.01
☐ 464 Pat Borders	.05	.02	.01
☐ 465 Exhibition Stadium	.05	.02	.01
☐ 466 Blue Jays team lettering	.05	.02	.01
☐ 467 Fred McGriff	.40	.18	.05
☐ 468 Manny Lee	.05	.02	.01
☐ 469 Kelly Gruber	.05	.02	.01
☐ 470 Tony Fernandez	.05	.02	.01
☐ 471 Jesse Barfield	.05	.02	.01
☐ 472 George Bell	.05	.02	.01
☐ 473 Lloyd Moseby	.05	.02	.01
☐ 474 Orel Hershiser	.10	.05	.01
☐ 475 Frank Viola	.05	.02	.01
☐ 476 Chris Sabo	.05	.02	.01
☐ 477 Jose Canseco	.50	.23	.06
☐ 478 Walt Weiss	.05	.02	.01
☐ 479 Kirk Gibson	.20	.09	.03
☐ 480 Jose Canseco	.50	.23	.06
☐ xx Sticker Album (Jose Canseco on front)	.75	.35	.09

1990 Panini Stickers

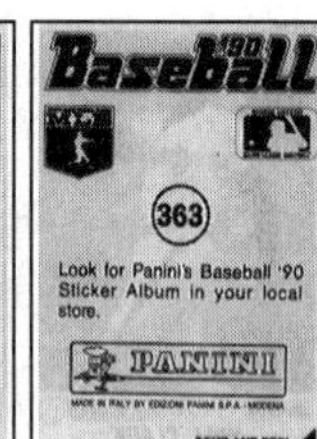

Baseball '90
363
Look for Panini's Baseball '90 Sticker Album in your local store.
PANINI

These 388 stickers measure approximately 2 1/8" by 3" and feature on their fronts white-bordered color player action shots. The player's name and team name, along with a baseball icon, appear within the broad white margin at the bottom. In addition to carrying the stickers' numbers, the white backs carry the logos for MLB, the MLBPA and Panini. Stickers 186-197 are foils. An album onto which the stickers could be affixed was available at retail stores. The album featured Nolan Ryan on the front and an ad for the Panini 1990 Fan Club Pop Star Sticker Collection on the back. The album also featured a four-page insert without stickers on the 1989 post-season. The album and the sticker numbering are organized by team alphabetically by city with AL teams preceding NL teams. Subsets include 1989 AL Stat Leaders (183-185), 1989 League Championship Series (Foil, 186-187), Excellence in the '80s (Foil, 188-197), 1989 All-Stars (198-213), 1989 NL Stat Leaders (214-216), Tomorrow's Headliners (373-382) and 1989 Highlights (383-388).

	MINT	NRMT	EXC
COMPLETE SET (388)	15.00	6.75	1.85
COMMON STICKER (1-388)	.05	.02	.01
☐ 1 Randy Milligan	.05	.02	.01
☐ 2 Gregg Olson	.05	.02	.01
☐ 3 Bill Ripken	.05	.02	.01
☐ 4 Phil Bradley	.05	.02	.01
☐ 5 Joe Orsulak	.05	.02	.01
☐ 6 Bob Milacki	.05	.02	.01
☐ 7 Cal Ripken	2.50	1.10	.30
☐ 8 Mickey Tettleton	.10	.05	.01
☐ 9 Orioles Logo	.05	.02	.01
☐ 10 Orioles Helmet	.05	.02	.01
☐ 11 Craig Worthington	.05	.02	.01
☐ 12 Mike Devereaux	.05	.02	.01
☐ 13 Jeff Ballard	.05	.02	.01
☐ 14 Lee Smith	.10	.05	.01
☐ 15 Marty Barrett	.05	.02	.01
☐ 16 Mike Greenwell	.05	.02	.01
☐ 17 Dwight Evans	.10	.05	.01
☐ 18 John Dopson	.05	.02	.01
☐ 19 Wade Boggs	.35	.16	.04
☐ 20 Mike Boddicker	.05	.02	.01
☐ 21 Ellis Burks	.15	.07	.02
☐ 22 Red Sox Logo	.05	.02	.01
☐ 23 Red Sox Helmet	.05	.02	.01
☐ 24 Roger Clemens	.50	.23	.06
☐ 25 Jody Reed	.05	.02	.01
☐ 26 Nick Esasky	.05	.02	.01
☐ 27 Brian Downing	.05	.02	.01
☐ 28 Bert Blyleven	.10	.05	.01
☐ 29 Devon White	.10	.05	.01
☐ 30 Claudell Washington	.05	.02	.01
☐ 31 Wally Joyner	.10	.05	.01
☐ 32 Chuck Finley	.10	.05	.01
☐ 33 Johnny Ray	.05	.02	.01
☐ 34 Jim Abbott	.10	.05	.01
☐ 35 Angels Logo	.05	.02	.01
☐ 36 Angels Helmet	.05	.02	.01
☐ 37 Kirk McCaskill	.05	.02	.01
☐ 38 Lance Parrish	.05	.02	.01
☐ 39 Chili Davis	.10	.05	.01
☐ 40 Steve Lyons	.05	.02	.01
☐ 41 Ozzie Guillen	.05	.02	.01
☐ 42 Melido Perez	.05	.02	.01
☐ 43 Scott Fletcher	.05	.02	.01
☐ 44 Carlton Fisk	.25	.11	.03
☐ 45 Greg Walker	.05	.02	.01
☐ 46 Dave Gallagher	.05	.02	.01
☐ 47 Ivan Calderon	.05	.02	.01
☐ 48 White Sox Logo	.05	.02	.01
☐ 49 White Sox Helmet	.05	.02	.01
☐ 50 Bobby Thigpen	.05	.02	.01
☐ 51 Ron Kittle	.05	.02	.01
☐ 52 Daryl Boston	.05	.02	.01
☐ 53 John Farrell	.05	.02	.01
☐ 54 Jerry Browne	.05	.02	.01
☐ 55 Pete O'Brien	.05	.02	.01
☐ 56 Cory Snyder	.05	.02	.01
☐ 57 Tom Candiotti	.05	.02	.01
☐ 58 Brook Jacoby	.05	.02	.01
☐ 59 Greg Swindell	.05	.02	.01
☐ 60 Felix Fermin	.05	.02	.01
☐ 61 Indians Logo	.05	.02	.01
☐ 62 Indians Helmet	.05	.02	.01
☐ 63 Doug Jones	.05	.02	.01
☐ 64 Dion James	.05	.02	.01
☐ 65 Joe Carter	.10	.05	.01
☐ 66 Mike Heath	.05	.02	.01
☐ 67 Dave Bergman	.05	.02	.01
☐ 68 Gary Ward	.05	.02	.01
☐ 69 Mike Henneman	.05	.02	.01
☐ 70 Alan Trammell	.10	.05	.01
☐ 71 Lou Whitaker	.10	.05	.01
☐ 72 Frank Tanana	.05	.02	.01
☐ 73 Fred Lynn	.10	.05	.01
☐ 74 Tigers Logo	.05	.02	.01
☐ 75 Tigers Helmet	.05	.02	.01
☐ 76 Jack Morris	.10	.05	.01
☐ 77 Chet Lemon	.05	.02	.01
☐ 78 Gary Pettis	.05	.02	.01
☐ 79 Kurt Stillwell	.05	.02	.01
☐ 80 Jim Eisenreich	.10	.05	.01
☐ 81 Bret Saberhagen	.10	.05	.01
☐ 82 Mark Gubicza	.05	.02	.01
☐ 83 Frank White	.10	.05	.01
☐ 84 Bo Jackson	.10	.05	.01
☐ 85 Jeff Montgomery	.05	.02	.01
☐ 86 Kevin Seitzer	.05	.02	.01
☐ 87 Royals Logo	.05	.02	.01
☐ 88 Royals Helmet	.05	.02	.01
☐ 89 Tom Gordon	.05	.02	.01
☐ 90 Danny Tartabull	.05	.02	.01
☐ 91 George Brett	1.25	.55	.16
☐ 92 Robin Yount	.25	.11	.03
☐ 93 B.J. Surhoff	.10	.05	.01
☐ 94 Jim Gantner	.05	.02	.01
☐ 95 Dan Plesac	.05	.02	.01
☐ 96 Ted Higuera	.05	.02	.01
☐ 97 Glenn Braggs	.05	.02	.01
☐ 98 Paul Molitor	.60	.25	.07
☐ 99 Chris Bosio	.05	.02	.01
☐ 100 Brewers Logo	.05	.02	.01
☐ 101 Brewers Helmet	.05	.02	.01
☐ 102 Rob Deer	.05	.02	.01
☐ 103 Chuck Crim	.05	.02	.01
☐ 104 Greg Brock	.05	.02	.01
☐ 105 Kirby Puckett	1.50	.70	.19
☐ 106 Gary Gaetti	.05	.02	.01
☐ 107 Roy Smith	.05	.02	.01
☐ 108 Jeff Reardon	.10	.05	.01
☐ 109 Randy Bush	.05	.02	.01
☐ 110 Al Newman	.05	.02	.01
☐ 111 Dan Gladden	.05	.02	.01
☐ 112 Kent Hrbek	.10	.05	.01
☐ 113 Twins Logo	.05	.02	.01
☐ 114 Twins Helmet	.05	.02	.01
☐ 115 Greg Gagne	.05	.02	.01
☐ 116 Brian Harper	.05	.02	.01
☐ 117 Allan Anderson	.05	.02	.01
☐ 118 Lee Guetterman	.05	.02	.01
☐ 119 Roberto Kelly	.05	.02	.01
☐ 120 Jesse Barfield	.05	.02	.01
☐ 121 Alvaro Espinoza	.05	.02	.01
☐ 122 Mel Hall	.05	.02	.01
☐ 123 Chuck Cary	.05	.02	.01
☐ 124 Dave Righetti	.05	.02	.01
☐ 125 Don Mattingly	1.50	.70	.19
☐ 126 Yankees Logo	.05	.02	.01
☐ 127 Yankees Helmet	.05	.02	.01
☐ 128 Bob Geren	.05	.02	.01
☐ 129 Steve Sax	.05	.02	.01
☐ 130 Andy Hawkins	.05	.02	.01
☐ 131 Bob Welch	.05	.02	.01
☐ 132 Mark McGwire	1.00	.45	.12
☐ 133 Dave Henderson	.05	.02	.01
☐ 134 Carney Lansford	.05	.02	.01
☐ 135 Walt Weiss	.05	.02	.01
☐ 136 Mike Moore	.05	.02	.01
☐ 137 Dennis Eckersley	.10	.05	.01
☐ 138 Rickey Henderson	.25	.11	.03
☐ 139 Athletics Logo	.05	.02	.01
☐ 140 Athletics Helmet	.05	.02	.01
☐ 141 Dave Stewart	.10	.05	.01
☐ 142 Jose Canseco	.35	.16	.04
☐ 143 Terry Steinbach	.10	.05	.01
☐ 144 Harold Reynolds	.10	.05	.01
☐ 145 Darnell Coles	.05	.02	.01
☐ 146 Brian Holman	.05	.02	.01
☐ 147 Scott Bankhead	.05	.02	.01
☐ 148 Greg Briley	.05	.02	.01
☐ 149 Alvin Davis	.05	.02	.01
☐ 150 Jeffrey Leonard	.05	.02	.01
☐ 151 Mike Schooler	.05	.02	.01
☐ 152 Mariners Logo	.05	.02	.01
☐ 153 Mariners Helmet	.05	.02	.01
☐ 154 Randy Johnson	1.00	.45	.12
☐ 155 Ken Griffey Jr.	3.00	1.35	.35
☐ 156 Dave Valle	.05	.02	.01
☐ 157 Pete Incaviglia	.05	.02	.01
☐ 158 Fred Manrique	.05	.02	.01
☐ 159 Jeff Russell	.05	.02	.01
☐ 160 Nolan Ryan	2.50	1.10	.30
☐ 161 Geno Petralli	.05	.02	.01
☐ 162 Ruben Sierra	.10	.05	.01
☐ 163 Julio Franco	.10	.05	.01
☐ 164 Rafael Palmeiro	.15	.07	.02
☐ 165 Rangers Logo	.05	.02	.01
☐ 166 Rangers Helmet	.05	.02	.01
☐ 167 Harold Baines	.10	.05	.01
☐ 168 Kevin Brown	.15	.07	.02
☐ 169 Steve Buechele	.05	.02	.01
☐ 170 Fred McGriff	.35	.16	.04
☐ 171 Kelly Gruber	.05	.02	.01
☐ 172 Todd Stottlemyre	.10	.05	.01
☐ 173 Dave Stieb	.05	.02	.01
☐ 174 Mookie Wilson	.05	.02	.01
☐ 175 Pat Borders	.05	.02	.01
☐ 176 Tony Fernandez	.05	.02	.01
☐ 177 John Cerutti	.05	.02	.01
☐ 178 Blue Jays Logo	.05	.02	.01
☐ 179 Blue Jays Helmet	.05	.02	.01
☐ 180 George Bell	.05	.02	.01
☐ 181 Jimmy Key	.05	.02	.01
☐ 182 Nelson Liriano	.05	.02	.01
☐ 183 Kirby Puckett	1.50	.70	.19
☐ 184 Carney Lansford	.10	.05	.01
☐ 185 Nolan Ryan	2.50	1.10	.30
☐ 186 AL Logo	.05	.02	.01
☐ 187 NL Logo	.05	.02	.01
☐ 188 World Championship Trophy	.05	.02	.01
☐ 189 '88 World Championship LA Dodgers Ring	.05	.02	.01
☐ 190 '87 World Championship Minnesota Twins Ring	.05	.02	.01
☐ 191 '86 World Championship NY Mets Ring	.05	.02	.01
☐ 192 '85 World Championship KC Royals Ring	.05	.02	.01
☐ 193 '84 World Championship Detroit Tigers Ring	.05	.02	.01
☐ 194 '83 World Championship Baltimore Orioles Ring	.05	.02	.01
☐ 195 '82 World Championship St.Louis Cardinals Ring	.05	.02	.01
☐ 196 '81 World Championship LA Dodgers Ring	.05	.02	.01
☐ 197 '80 World Championship Philadelphia Phillies Ring	.05	.02	.01
☐ 198 Dave Stewart Bo Jackson	.10	.05	.01
☐ 199 Wade Boggs Kirby Puckett	.35	.16	.04
☐ 200 Harold Baines	.10	.05	.01
☐ 201 Julio Franco	.10	.05	.01
☐ 202 Cal Ripken	2.50	1.10	.30
☐ 203 Ruben Sierra	.10	.05	.01
☐ 204 Mark McGwire	1.00	.45	.12
☐ 205 Terry Steinbach	.10	.05	.01
☐ 206 Rick Reuschel Ozzie Smith	.15	.07	.02
☐ 207 Tony Gwynn Will Clark	.60	.25	.07
☐ 208 Kevin Mitchell	.05	.02	.01
☐ 209 Eric Davis	.05	.02	.01
☐ 210 Howard Johnson	.05	.02	.01
☐ 211 Pedro Guerrero	.05	.02	.01
☐ 212 Ryne Sandberg	.75	.35	.09
☐ 213 Benito Santiago	.05	.02	.01
☐ 214 Kevin Mitchell	.05	.02	.01
☐ 215 Mark Davis	.05	.02	.01
☐ 216 Vince Coleman	.05	.02	.01
☐ 217 Jeff Blauser	.05	.02	.01
☐ 218 Jeff Treadway	.05	.02	.01
☐ 219 Tom Glavine	.50	.23	.06
☐ 220 Joe Boever	.05	.02	.01
☐ 221 Oddibe McDowell	.05	.02	.01
☐ 222 Dale Murphy	.15	.07	.02
☐ 223 Derek Lilliquist	.05	.02	.01
☐ 224 Tommy Gregg	.05	.02	.01
☐ 225 Braves Logo	.05	.02	.01
☐ 226 Braves Helmet	.05	.02	.01
☐ 227 Lonnie Smith	.05	.02	.01
☐ 228 John Smoltz	.75	.35	.09
☐ 229 Andres Thomas	.05	.02	.01
☐ 230 Jerome Walton	.05	.02	.01
☐ 231 Ryne Sandberg	.75	.35	.09
☐ 232 Mitch Williams	.05	.02	.01
☐ 233 Rick Sutcliffe	.05	.02	.01
☐ 234 Damon Berryhill	.05	.02	.01
☐ 235 Dwight Smith	.05	.02	.01
☐ 236 Shawon Dunston	.05	.02	.01
☐ 237 Greg Maddux	1.75	.80	.22
☐ 238 Cubs Logo	.05	.02	.01
☐ 239 Cubs Helmet	.05	.02	.01
☐ 240 Andre Dawson	.10	.05	.01
☐ 241 Mark Grace	.15	.07	.02
☐ 242 Mike Bielecki	.05	.02	.01
☐ 243 Jose Rijo	.05	.02	.01
☐ 244 John Franco	.10	.05	.01
☐ 245 Paul O'Neill	.10	.05	.01
☐ 246 Eric Davis	.05	.02	.01
☐ 247 Tom Browning	.05	.02	.01
☐ 248 Chris Sabo	.05	.02	.01
☐ 249 Rob Dibble	.05	.02	.01
☐ 250 Todd Benzinger	.05	.02	.01
☐ 251 Reds Logo	.05	.02	.01
☐ 252 Reds Helmet	.05	.02	.01
☐ 253 Barry Larkin	.35	.16	.04
☐ 254 Rolando Roomes	.05	.02	.01
☐ 255 Danny Jackson	.05	.02	.01
☐ 256 Terry Puhl	.05	.02	.01
☐ 257 Dave Smith	.05	.02	.01
☐ 258 Glenn Davis	.05	.02	.01
☐ 259 Craig Biggio	.30	.14	.04
☐ 260 Ken Caminiti	.50	.23	.06
☐ 261 Kevin Bass	.05	.02	.01
☐ 262 Mike Scott	.05	.02	.01
☐ 263 Gerald Young	.05	.02	.01
☐ 264 Astros Logo	.05	.02	.01
☐ 265 Astros Helmet	.05	.02	.01
☐ 266 Rafael Ramirez	.05	.02	.01
☐ 267 Jim Deshaies	.05	.02	.01
☐ 268 Bill Doran	.05	.02	.01
☐ 269 Fernando Valenzuela	.10	.05	.01
☐ 270 Alfredo Griffin	.05	.02	.01

☐ 271 Kirk Gibson	.10	.05	.01
☐ 272 Mike Marshall	.05	.02	.01
☐ 273 Eddie Murray	.75	.35	.09
☐ 274 Jay Howell	.05	.02	.01
☐ 275 Orel Hershiser	.10	.05	.01
☐ 276 Mike Scioscia	.05	.02	.01
☐ 277 Dodgers Logo	.05	.02	.01
☐ 278 Dodgers Helmet	.05	.02	.01
☐ 279 Willie Randolph	.10	.05	.01
☐ 280 Kal Daniels	.05	.02	.01
☐ 281 Tim Belcher	.05	.02	.01
☐ 282 Pascual Perez	.05	.02	.01
☐ 283 Tim Raines	.10	.05	.01
☐ 284 Andres Galarraga	.35	.16	.04
☐ 285 Spike Owen	.05	.02	.01
☐ 286 Tim Wallach	.05	.02	.01
☐ 287 Mark Langston	.05	.02	.01
☐ 288 Dennis Martinez	.10	.05	.01
☐ 289 Nelson Santovenia	.05	.02	.01
☐ 290 Expos Logo	.05	.02	.01
☐ 291 Expos Helmet	.05	.02	.01
☐ 292 Tom Foley	.05	.02	.01
☐ 293 Dave Martinez	.05	.02	.01
☐ 294 Tim Burke	.05	.02	.01
☐ 295 Ron Darling	.05	.02	.01
☐ 296 Kevin Elster	.05	.02	.01
☐ 297 Dwight Gooden	.10	.05	.01
☐ 298 Gregg Jefferies	.10	.05	.01
☐ 299 Sid Fernandez	.05	.02	.01
☐ 300 Dave Magadan	.05	.02	.01
☐ 301 David Cone	.15	.07	.02
☐ 302 Darryl Strawberry	.10	.05	.01
☐ 303 Mets Logo	.05	.02	.01
☐ 304 Mets Helmet	.05	.02	.01
☐ 305 Kevin McReynolds	.05	.02	.01
☐ 306 Howard Johnson	.05	.02	.01
☐ 307 Randy Myers	.05	.02	.01
☐ 308 Roger McDowell	.05	.02	.01
☐ 309 Tom Herr	.05	.02	.01
☐ 310 John Kruk	.10	.05	.01
☐ 311 Randy Ready	.05	.02	.01
☐ 312 Jeff Parrett	.05	.02	.01
☐ 313 Lenny Dykstra	.10	.05	.01
☐ 314 Ken Howell	.05	.02	.01
☐ 315 Ricky Jordan	.05	.02	.01
☐ 316 Phillies Logo	.05	.02	.01
☐ 317 Phillies Helmet	.05	.02	.01
☐ 318 Dickie Thon	.05	.02	.01
☐ 319 Von Hayes	.05	.02	.01
☐ 320 Dennis Cook	.05	.02	.01
☐ 321 Jay Bell	.10	.05	.01
☐ 322 Barry Bonds	.75	.35	.09
☐ 323 John Smiley	.05	.02	.01
☐ 324 Andy Van Slyke	.10	.05	.01
☐ 325 Bobby Bonilla	.10	.05	.01
☐ 326 Bill Landrum	.05	.02	.01
☐ 327 Randy Kramer	.05	.02	.01
☐ 328 Jose Lind	.05	.02	.01
☐ 329 Pirates Logo	.05	.02	.01
☐ 330 Pirates Helmet	.05	.02	.01
☐ 331 Gary Redus	.05	.02	.01
☐ 332 Doug Drabek	.05	.02	.01
☐ 333 Mike LaValliere	.05	.02	.01
☐ 334 Jose DeLeon	.05	.02	.01
☐ 335 Pedro Guerrero	.05	.02	.01
☐ 336 Vince Coleman	.05	.02	.01
☐ 337 Terry Pendleton	.10	.05	.01
☐ 338 Ozzie Smith	.75	.35	.09
☐ 339 Willie McGee	.10	.05	.01
☐ 340 Todd Worrell	.05	.02	.01
☐ 341 Jose Oquendo	.05	.02	.01
☐ 342 Cardinals Logo	.05	.02	.01
☐ 343 Cardinals Helmet	.05	.02	.01
☐ 344 Tom Brunansky	.05	.02	.01
☐ 345 Milt Thompson	.05	.02	.01
☐ 346 Joe Magrane	.05	.02	.01
☐ 347 Ed Whitson	.05	.02	.01
☐ 348 Jack Clark	.05	.02	.01
☐ 349 Roberto Alomar	.75	.35	.09
☐ 350 Chris James	.05	.02	.01
☐ 351 Tony Gwynn	1.25	.55	.16
☐ 352 Mark Davis	.05	.02	.01
☐ 353 Greg W. Harris	.05	.02	.01
☐ 354 Garry Templeton	.05	.02	.01
☐ 355 Padres Logo	.05	.02	.01
☐ 356 Padres Helmet	.05	.02	.01
☐ 357 Bruce Hurst	.05	.02	.01
☐ 358 Benito Santiago	.05	.02	.01
☐ 359 Bip Roberts	.05	.02	.01
☐ 360 Dave Dravecky	.05	.02	.01
☐ 361 Kevin Mitchell	.05	.02	.01
☐ 362 Craig Lefferts	.05	.02	.01
☐ 363 Will Clark	.35	.16	.04
☐ 364 Steve Bedrosian	.05	.02	.01
☐ 365 Brett Butler	.10	.05	.01
☐ 366 Matt Williams	.35	.16	.04
☐ 367 Scott Garrelts	.05	.02	.01
☐ 368 Giants Logo	.05	.02	.01
☐ 369 Giants Helmet	.05	.02	.01
☐ 370 Rick Reuschel	.05	.02	.01
☐ 371 Robby Thompson	.05	.02	.01
☐ 372 Jose Uribe	.05	.02	.01
☐ 373 Ben McDonald	.25	.11	.03
☐ 374 Carlos Martinez	.05	.02	.01
☐ 375 Steve Olin	.10	.05	.01
☐ 376 Bill Spiers	.05	.02	.01
☐ 377 Junior Felix	.05	.02	.01
☐ 378 Joe Oliver	.05	.02	.01
☐ 379 Eric Anthony	.05	.02	.01
☐ 380 Ramon Martinez	.15	.07	.02
☐ 381 Todd Zeile	.10	.05	.01
☐ 382 Andy Benes	.15	.07	.02
☐ 383 Vince Coleman	.05	.02	.01
☐ 384 Bo Jackson	.10	.05	.01
☐ 385 Howard Johnson	.05	.02	.01
☐ 386 Dave Dravecky	.05	.02	.01
☐ 387 Nolan Ryan	2.50	1.10	.30
☐ 388 Cal Ripken	2.50	1.10	.30
☐ xx Sticker Album (Nolan Ryan on front)	1.50	.70	.19

1991 Panini Stickers

The 1991 Panini baseball set contains 271 stickers measuring 1 1/2" by 2 1/2". The fronts display color action player photos bordered in white. The player's name, positon, brief biography, 1990 statistics and career totals are given beneath the picture. Included in the set are 54 foil stickers of team pennants, logos and league insignias. The stickers may be pasted in a collectible sticker album that measures 8 1/4" by 10 1/2". The stickers are numbered on the back. After a "Year of the No-Hitter 1990" (1-9) subset, the stickers are checklisted alphabetically according to teams within the NL and then the AL.

	MINT	NRMT	EXC
COMPLETE SET (271)	15.00	6.75	1.85
COMMON STICKER (1-271)	.05	.02	.01
☐ 1 Mark Langston	.05	.02	.01
☐ 2 Randy Johnson	.30	.14	.04
☐ 3 Nolan Ryan	2.50	1.10	.30
☐ 4 Dave Stewart	.10	.05	.01
☐ 5 Fernando Valenzuela	.10	.05	.01
☐ 6 Andy Hawkins	.05	.02	.01
☐ 7 Melido Perez	.05	.02	.01
☐ 8 Terry Mulholland	.05	.02	.01
☐ 9 Dave Stieb	.05	.02	.01
☐ 10 Craig Biggio	.30	.14	.04
☐ 11 Jim Deshaies	.05	.02	.01
☐ 12 Dave Smith	.05	.02	.01
☐ 13 Eric Yelding	.05	.02	.01
☐ 14 Astros Pennant	.05	.02	.01
☐ 15 Astros Logo	.05	.02	.01
☐ 16 Mike Scott	.05	.02	.01
☐ 17 Ken Caminiti	.50	.23	.06
☐ 18 Danny Darwin	.05	.02	.01
☐ 19 Glenn Davis	.05	.02	.01
☐ 20 Braves Pennant	.05	.02	.01
☐ 21 Braves Logo	.05	.02	.01
☐ 22 Lonnie Smith	.05	.02	.01
☐ 23 Charlie Leibrandt	.05	.02	.01
☐ 24 Jim Presley	.05	.02	.01
☐ 25 Greg Olson	.05	.02	.01
☐ 26 John Smoltz	.50	.23	.06
☐ 27 Ron Gant	.10	.05	.01
☐ 28 Jeff Treadway	.05	.02	.01
☐ 29 Dave Justice	.30	.14	.04
☐ 30 Jose Oquendo	.05	.02	.01
☐ 31 Joe Magrane	.05	.02	.01
☐ 32 Cardinals Pennant	.05	.02	.01
☐ 33 Cardinals Logo	.05	.02	.01
☐ 34 Todd Zeile	.05	.02	.01
☐ 35 Vince Coleman	.05	.02	.01
☐ 36 Bob Tewksbury	.05	.02	.01
☐ 37 Pedro Guerrero	.05	.02	.01
☐ 38 Lee Smith	.10	.05	.01
☐ 39 Ozzie Smith	.75	.35	.09
☐ 40 Ryne Sandberg	.75	.35	.09
☐ 41 Andre Dawson	.10	.05	.01
☐ 42 Cubs Pennant	.05	.02	.01
☐ 43 Greg Maddux	1.75	.80	.22
☐ 44 Jerome Walton	.05	.02	.01
☐ 45 Cubs Logo	.05	.02	.01
☐ 46 Mike Harkey	.05	.02	.01
☐ 47 Shawon Dunston	.05	.02	.01
☐ 48 Mark Grace	.35	.16	.04
☐ 49 Joe Girardi	.05	.02	.01
☐ 50 Ramon Martinez	.15	.07	.02
☐ 51 Lenny Harris	.05	.02	.01
☐ 52 Mike Morgan	.05	.02	.01
☐ 53 Eddie Murray	.75	.35	.09
☐ 54 Dodgers Pennant	.05	.02	.01
☐ 55 Dodgers Logo	.05	.02	.01
☐ 56 Hubie Brooks	.05	.02	.01
☐ 57 Mike Scioscia	.05	.02	.01
☐ 58 Kal Daniels	.05	.02	.01
☐ 59 Fernando Valenzuela	.10	.05	.01
☐ 60 Expos Pennant	.05	.02	.01
☐ 61 Expos Logo	.05	.02	.01
☐ 62 Spike Owen	.05	.02	.01
☐ 63 Tim Raines	.10	.05	.01
☐ 64 Tim Wallach	.05	.02	.01
☐ 65 Larry Walker	.50	.23	.06
☐ 66 Dave Martinez	.05	.02	.01
☐ 67 Mark Gardner	.05	.02	.01
☐ 68 Dennis Martinez	.10	.05	.01
☐ 69 Delino DeShields	.05	.02	.01
☐ 70 Jeff Brantley	.05	.02	.01
☐ 71 Kevin Mitchell	.05	.02	.01
☐ 72 Giants Pennant	.05	.02	.01
☐ 73 Giants Logo	.05	.02	.01
☐ 74 Don Robinson	.05	.02	.01
☐ 75 Brett Butler	.10	.05	.01
☐ 76 Matt Williams	.35	.16	.04
☐ 77 Robby Thompson	.05	.02	.01
☐ 78 John Burkett	.05	.02	.01
☐ 79 Will Clark	.35	.16	.04
☐ 80 David Cone	.10	.05	.01
☐ 81 Dave Magadan	.05	.02	.01
☐ 82 Mets Pennant	.05	.02	.01
☐ 83 Gregg Jefferies	.10	.05	.01
☐ 84 Frank Viola	.05	.02	.01
☐ 85 Mets Logo	.05	.02	.01
☐ 86 Howard Johnson	.05	.02	.01
☐ 87 John Franco	.10	.05	.01
☐ 88 Darryl Strawberry	.10	.05	.01
☐ 89 Dwight Gooden	.10	.05	.01
☐ 90 Joe Carter	.10	.05	.01
☐ 91 Ed Whitson	.05	.02	.01
☐ 92 Andy Benes	.10	.05	.01
☐ 93 Benito Santiago	.05	.02	.01
☐ 94 Padres Pennant	.05	.02	.01
☐ 95 Padres Logo	.05	.02	.01
☐ 96 Roberto Alomar	.50	.23	.06
☐ 97 Bip Roberts	.05	.02	.01
☐ 98 Jack Clark	.05	.02	.01
☐ 99 Tony Gwynn	1.25	.55	.16
☐ 100 Phillies Pennant	.05	.02	.01
☐ 101 Phillies Logo	.05	.02	.01
☐ 102 Charlie Hayes	.05	.02	.01
☐ 103 Len Dykstra	.10	.05	.01
☐ 104 Dale Murphy	.15	.07	.02
☐ 105 Von Hayes	.05	.02	.01
☐ 106 Dickie Thon	.05	.02	.01
☐ 107 John Kruk	.10	.05	.01
☐ 108 Ken Howell	.05	.02	.01
☐ 109 Darren Daulton	.10	.05	.01
☐ 110 Jay Bell	.05	.02	.01
☐ 111 Bobby Bonilla	.10	.05	.01
☐ 112 Pirates Pennant	.05	.02	.01
☐ 113 Pirates Logo	.05	.02	.01
☐ 114 Barry Bonds	.50	.23	.06
☐ 115 Neal Heaton	.05	.02	.01
☐ 116 Doug Drabek	.05	.02	.01
☐ 117 Jose Lind	.05	.02	.01
☐ 118 Andy Van Slyke	.05	.02	.01
☐ 119 Sid Bream	.05	.02	.01
☐ 120 Paul O'Neill	.10	.05	.01
☐ 121 Randy Myers	.05	.02	.01
☐ 122 Reds Pennant	.05	.02	.01
☐ 123 Mariano Duncan	.05	.02	.01
☐ 124 Eric Davis	.05	.02	.01
☐ 125 Reds Logo	.05	.02	.01
☐ 126 Jack Armstrong	.05	.02	.01
☐ 127 Chris Sabo	.05	.02	.01
☐ 128 Rob Dibble	.05	.02	.01
☐ 129 Barry Larkin	.35	.16	.04
☐ 130 National League Logo	.05	.02	.01
☐ 131 American League Logo	.05	.02	.01
☐ 132 Dave Winfield	.25	.11	.03
☐ 133 Lance Parrish	.05	.02	.01
☐ 134 Chili Davis	.10	.05	.01
☐ 135 Chuck Finley	.10	.05	.01
☐ 136 Angels Pennant	.05	.02	.01
☐ 137 Angels Logo	.05	.02	.01
☐ 138 Johnny Ray	.05	.02	.01
☐ 139 Dante Bichette	.50	.23	.06
☐ 140 Jim Abbott	.10	.05	.01
☐ 141 Wally Joyner	.05	.02	.01
☐ 142 Athletics Pennant	.05	.02	.01
☐ 143 Athletics Logo	.05	.02	.01
☐ 144 Dave Stewart	.10	.05	.01
☐ 145 Mark McGwire	1.00	.45	.12
☐ 146 Rickey Henderson	.35	.16	.04
☐ 147 Walt Weiss	.05	.02	.01
☐ 148 Dennis Eckersley	.10	.05	.01
☐ 149 Jose Canseco	.35	.16	.04
☐ 150 Dave Henderson	.05	.02	.01
☐ 151 Bob Welch	.05	.02	.01
☐ 152 Tony Fernandez	.05	.02	.01
☐ 153 David Wells	.05	.02	.01
☐ 154 Blue Jays Pennant	.05	.02	.01
☐ 155 Blue Jays Logo	.05	.02	.01
☐ 156 Pat Borders	.05	.02	.01
☐ 157 Fred McGriff	.35	.16	.04
☐ 158 George Bell	.05	.02	.01
☐ 159 John Olerud	.15	.07	.02
☐ 160 Dave Stieb	.05	.02	.01
☐ 161 Kelly Gruber	.05	.02	.01
☐ 162 Bill Spiers	.05	.02	.01
☐ 163 Dan Plesac	.05	.02	.01
☐ 164 Brewers Pennant	.05	.02	.01
☐ 165 Mark Knudson	.05	.02	.01
☐ 166 Robin Yount	.25	.11	.03
☐ 167 Brewers Logo	.05	.02	.01
☐ 168 Paul Molitor	.75	.35	.09
☐ 169 B.J. Surhoff	.10	.05	.01
☐ 170 Gary Sheffield	.50	.23	.06
☐ 171 Dave Parker	.10	.05	.01
☐ 172 Sandy Alomar Jr.	.10	.05	.01
☐ 173 Doug Jones	.05	.02	.01
☐ 174 Tom Candiotti	.05	.02	.01
☐ 175 Mitch Webster	.05	.02	.01
☐ 176 Indians Pennant	.05	.02	.01
☐ 177 Indians Logo	.05	.02	.01
☐ 178 Brook Jacoby	.05	.02	.01
☐ 179 Candy Maldonado	.05	.02	.01
☐ 180 Carlos Baerga	.50	.23	.06
☐ 181 Chris James	.05	.02	.01
☐ 182 Mariners Pennant	.05	.02	.01
☐ 183 Mariners Logo	.05	.02	.01
☐ 184 Mike Schooler	.05	.02	.01
☐ 185 Alvin Davis	.05	.02	.01
☐ 186 Erik Hanson	.05	.02	.01
☐ 187 Edgar Martinez	.35	.16	.04
☐ 188 Randy Johnson	.30	.14	.04
☐ 189 Ken Griffey Jr.	3.00	1.35	.35
☐ 190 Jay Buhner	.35	.16	.04
☐ 191 Harold Reynolds	.10	.05	.01
☐ 192 Cal Ripken	2.50	1.10	.30
☐ 193 Gregg Olson	.05	.02	.01
☐ 194 Orioles Pennant	.05	.02	.01
☐ 195 Orioles Logo	.05	.02	.01
☐ 196 Mike Devereaux	.05	.02	.01
☐ 197 Ben McDonald	.10	.05	.01
☐ 198 Craig Worthington	.05	.02	.01
☐ 199 Dave Johnson	.05	.02	.01
☐ 200 Joe Orsulak	.05	.02	.01
☐ 201 Randy Milligan	.05	.02	.01
☐ 202 Ruben Sierra	.05	.02	.01
☐ 203 Bobby Witt	.05	.02	.01
☐ 204 Rangers Pennant	.05	.02	.01
☐ 205 Nolan Ryan	2.50	1.10	.30
☐ 206 Jeff Huson	.05	.02	.01
☐ 207 Rangers Logo	.05	.02	.01
☐ 208 Kevin Brown	.10	.05	.01
☐ 209 Steve Buechele	.05	.02	.01
☐ 210 Julio Franco	.10	.05	.01
☐ 211 Rafael Palmeiro	.35	.16	.04
☐ 212 Ellis Burks	.10	.05	.01
☐ 213 Dwight Evans	.10	.05	.01
☐ 214 Wade Boggs	.30	.14	.04
☐ 215 Roger Clemens	.50	.23	.06
☐ 216 Red Sox Pennant	.05	.02	.01
☐ 217 Red Sox Logo	.05	.02	.01
☐ 218 Jeff Reardon	.05	.02	.01
☐ 219 Tony Pena	.05	.02	.01
☐ 220 Jody Reed	.05	.02	.01
☐ 221 Carlos Quintana	.05	.02	.01
☐ 222 Royals Pennant	.05	.02	.01
☐ 223 Royals Logo	.05	.02	.01
☐ 224 George Brett	1.25	.55	.16
☐ 225 Bret Saberhagen	.10	.05	.01
☐ 226 Bo Jackson	.10	.05	.01
☐ 227 Kevin Seitzer	.05	.02	.01
☐ 228 Mark Gubicza	.05	.02	.01
☐ 229 Jim Eisenreich	.10	.05	.01
☐ 230 Gerald Perry	.05	.02	.01
☐ 231 Tom Gordon	.05	.02	.01
☐ 232 Cecil Fielder	.10	.05	.01
☐ 233 Lou Whitaker	.10	.05	.01
☐ 234 Tigers Pennant	.05	.02	.01
☐ 235 Tigers Logo	.05	.02	.01
☐ 236 Mike Henneman	.05	.02	.01
☐ 237 Mike Heath	.05	.02	.01
☐ 238 Alan Trammell	.10	.05	.01
☐ 239 Lloyd Moseby	.05	.02	.01
☐ 240 Dan Petry	.05	.02	.01
☐ 241 Dave Bergman	.05	.02	.01
☐ 242 Brian Harper	.05	.02	.01
☐ 243 Rick Aguilera	.05	.02	.01
☐ 244 Twins Pennant	.05	.02	.01
☐ 245 Greg Gagne	.05	.02	.01
☐ 246 Gene Larkin	.05	.02	.01
☐ 247 Twins Logo	.05	.02	.01
☐ 248 Kirby Puckett	1.50	.70	.19
☐ 249 Kevin Tapani	.05	.02	.01
☐ 250 Gary Gaetti	.05	.02	.01
☐ 251 Kent Hrbek	.10	.05	.01
☐ 252 Bobby Thigpen	.05	.02	.01
☐ 253 Lance Johnson	.10	.05	.01
☐ 254 Greg Hibbard	.05	.02	.01
☐ 255 Carlton Fisk	.25	.11	.03
☐ 256 White Sox Pennant	.05	.02	.01
☐ 257 White Sox Logo	.05	.02	.01
☐ 258 Ivan Calderon	.05	.02	.01
☐ 259 Barry Jones	.05	.02	.01
☐ 260 Robin Ventura	.15	.07	.02
☐ 261 Ozzie Guillen	.05	.02	.01
☐ 262 Yankees Pennant	.05	.02	.01
☐ 263 Yankees Logo	.05	.02	.01
☐ 264 Kevin Maas	.05	.02	.01
☐ 265 Bob Geren	.05	.02	.01
☐ 266 Dave Righetti	.05	.02	.01
☐ 267 Don Mattingly	1.50	.70	.19
☐ 268 Roberto Kelly	.05	.02	.01
☐ 269 Alvaro Espinoza	.05	.02	.01
☐ 270 Oscar Azocar	.05	.02	.01
☐ 271 Steve Sax	.05	.02	.01

1991 Panini Canadian Top 15

The 1991 Panini Top 15 sticker set consists of 136 stickers and features Major League's best players and teams in various statistical categories. An American and a Canadian version were issued. The stickers resemble cards insofar as they measure the standard size and are printed on a thick cardboard stock. The fronts have glossy color player photos with white borders. The player's name, team and statistical category (the last item in French and English in the Canadian version) appear below the picture. Moreover, the front also has a number (1-4) indicating the player's finish in that category, the statistic and different color emblems for the National League (blue) and the American League (red). The Gold glove winners have a gold emblem, irrespective of league. The set is subdivided according to the following statistical categories, with National League winners listed first (e.g., 1-4) and then American League winners (e.g., 5-8): batting average (1-8); home runs (9-16); runs batted in (17-24); hits (25-32); slugging average (33-40); stolen bases (41-48); runs (49-56); wins (57-64); earned run average (65-72); strikeouts (73-80); saves (81-88); shutouts (89-96); National League logo (97) and gold glove (98-106); American League logo (107) and gold glove (108-16); and team statistical leaders (117-36). The NL logo (97), AL logo (107) and all the team stickers (117-36) are foil.

	MINT	NRMT	EXC
COMPLETE SET (136)	30.00	13.50	3.70
COMMON STICKER (1-136)	.05	.02	.01
□ 1 Willie McGee	.15	.07	.02
□ 2 Eddie Murray	1.25	.55	.16
□ 3 Dave Magadan	.05	.02	.01
□ 4 Lenny Dykstra	.15	.07	.02
□ 5 George Brett	2.00	.90	.25
□ 6 Rickey Henderson	.50	.23	.06
□ 7 Rafael Palmeiro	.50	.23	.06
□ 8 Alan Trammell	.15	.07	.02
□ 9 Ryne Sandberg	1.25	.55	.16
□ 10 Darryl Strawberry	.15	.07	.02
□ 11 Kevin Mitchell	.05	.02	.01
□ 12 Barry Bonds	1.25	.55	.16
□ 13 Cecil Fielder	.15	.07	.02
□ 14 Mark McGwire	1.50	.70	.19
□ 15 Jose Canseco	.60	.25	.07
□ 16 Fred McGriff	.50	.23	.06
□ 17 Matt Williams	.75	.35	.09
□ 18 Bobby Bonilla	.15	.07	.02
□ 19 Joe Carter	.15	.07	.02
□ 20 Barry Bonds	1.25	.55	.16
□ 21 Cecil Fielder	.15	.07	.02
□ 22 Kelly Gruber	.05	.02	.01
□ 23 Mark McGwire	1.50	.70	.19
□ 24 Jose Canseco	.60	.25	.07
□ 25 Brett Butler	.15	.07	.02
□ 26 Lenny Dykstra	.15	.07	.02
□ 27 Ryne Sandberg	1.25	.55	.16
□ 28 Barry Larkin	.40	.18	.05
□ 29 Rafael Palmeiro	.50	.23	.06
□ 30 Wade Boggs	.60	.25	.07
□ 31 Roberto Kelly	.05	.02	.01
□ 32 Mike Greenwell	.05	.02	.01
□ 33 Barry Bonds	1.25	.55	.16
□ 34 Ryne Sandberg	1.25	.55	.16
□ 35 Kevin Mitchell	.05	.02	.01
□ 36 Ron Gant	.15	.07	.02
□ 37 Cecil Fielder	.15	.07	.02
□ 38 Rickey Henderson	.50	.23	.06
□ 39 Jose Canseco	.60	.25	.07
□ 40 Fred McGriff	.50	.23	.06
□ 41 Vince Coleman	.05	.02	.01
□ 42 Eric Yelding	.05	.02	.01
□ 43 Barry Bonds	1.25	.55	.16
□ 44 Brett Butler	.15	.07	.02
□ 45 Rickey Henderson	.50	.23	.06
□ 46 Steve Sax	.05	.02	.01
□ 47 Roberto Kelly	.05	.02	.01
□ 48 Alex Cole	.05	.02	.01
□ 49 Ryne Sandberg	1.25	.55	.16
□ 50 Bobby Bonilla	.15	.07	.02
□ 51 Brett Butler	.15	.07	.02
□ 52 Ron Gant	.15	.07	.02
□ 53 Rickey Henderson	.50	.23	.06
□ 54 Cecil Fielder	.15	.07	.02
□ 55 Harold Reynolds	.15	.07	.02
□ 56 Robin Yount	.40	.18	.05
□ 57 Doug Drabek	.05	.02	.01
□ 58 Ramon Martinez	.30	.14	.04
□ 59 Frank Viola	.05	.02	.01
□ 60 Dwight Gooden	.15	.07	.02
□ 61 Bob Welch	.05	.02	.01
□ 62 Dave Stewart	.15	.07	.02
□ 63 Roger Clemens	.75	.35	.09
□ 64 Dave Stieb	.05	.02	.01
□ 65 Danny Darwin	.05	.02	.01
□ 66 Zane Smith	.05	.02	.01
□ 67 Ed Whitson	.05	.02	.01
□ 68 Frank Viola	.05	.02	.01
□ 69 Roger Clemens	1.00	.45	.12
□ 70 Chuck Finley	.15	.07	.02
□ 71 Dave Stewart	.15	.07	.02
□ 72 Kevin Appier	.30	.14	.04
□ 73 David Cone	.15	.07	.02
□ 74 Dwight Gooden	.15	.07	.02
□ 75 Ramon Martinez	.30	.14	.04
□ 76 Frank Viola	.05	.02	.01
□ 77 Nolan Ryan	3.00	1.35	.35
□ 78 Bobby Witt	.05	.02	.01
□ 79 Erik Hanson	.05	.02	.01
□ 80 Roger Clemens	.75	.35	.09
□ 81 John Franco	.15	.07	.02
□ 82 Randy Myers	.05	.02	.01
□ 83 Lee Smith	.15	.07	.02
□ 84 Craig Lefferts	.05	.02	.01
□ 85 Bobby Thigpen	.05	.02	.01
□ 86 Dennis Eckersley	.15	.07	.02
□ 87 Doug Jones	.05	.02	.01
□ 88 Gregg Olson	.05	.02	.01
□ 89 Mike Morgan	.05	.02	.01
□ 90 Bruce Hurst	.05	.02	.01
□ 91 Mark Gardner	.05	.02	.01
□ 92 Doug Drabek	.05	.02	.01
□ 93 Dave Stewart	.15	.07	.02
□ 94 Roger Clemens	.75	.35	.09
□ 95 Kevin Appier	.30	.14	.04
□ 96 Melido Perez	.05	.02	.01
□ 97 National League	.05	.02	.01
□ 98 Greg Maddux	3.00	1.35	.35
□ 99 Benito Santiago	.05	.02	.01
□ 100 Andres Galarraga	.50	.23	.06
□ 101 Ryne Sandberg	1.25	.55	.16
□ 102 Tim Wallach	.05	.02	.01
□ 103 Ozzie Smith	1.25	.55	.16
□ 104 Tony Gwynn	2.00	.90	.25
□ 105 Barry Bonds	1.25	.55	.16
□ 106 Andy Van Slyke	.15	.07	.02
□ 107 American League	.05	.02	.01
□ 108 Mike Boddicker	.05	.02	.01
□ 109 Sandy Alomar Jr.	.15	.07	.02
□ 110 Mark McGwire	1.50	.70	.19
□ 111 Harold Reynolds	.15	.07	.02
□ 112 Kelly Gruber	.05	.02	.01
□ 113 Ozzie Guillen	.05	.02	.01
□ 114 Ellis Burks	.15	.07	.02
□ 115 Gary Pettis	.05	.02	.01
□ 116 Ken Griffey Jr.	5.00	2.20	.60
□ 117 Cincinnati Reds Highest Batting Average	.05	.02	.01
□ 118 New York Mets Most Home Runs	.05	.02	.01
□ 119 New York Mets Most Runs Scored	.05	.02	.01
□ 120 Chicago Cubs Most Hits	.05	.02	.01
□ 121 Montreal Expos Most Stolen Bases	.05	.02	.01
□ 122 Boston Red Sox Highest Batting Average	.05	.02	.01
□ 123 Detroit Tigers Most Home Runs	.05	.02	.01
□ 124 Toronto Blue Jays Most Runs Scored	.05	.02	.01
□ 125 Boston Red Sox Most Hits	.05	.02	.01
□ 126 Milwaukee Brewers Most Stolen Bases	.05	.02	.01
□ 127 Philadelphia Phillies Most Double Plays	.05	.02	.01
□ 128 Cincinnati Reds Fewest Errors	.05	.02	.01
□ 129 Montreal Expos Best ERA	.05	.02	.01
□ 130 New York Mets Most Shutouts	.05	.02	.01
□ 131 Cincinnati Reds Most Saves	.05	.02	.01
□ 132 California Angels Most Double Plays	.05	.02	.01
□ 133 Toronto Blue Jays Fewest Errors	.05	.02	.01
□ 134 Oakland Athletics Best ERA	.05	.02	.01
□ 135 Oakland Athletics Most Shutouts	.05	.02	.01
□ 136 Chicago White Sox Most Saves	.05	.02	.01

1991 Panini French Stickers

The French version of the 1991 Panini baseball set contains 360 stickers measuring approximately 2 1/8" by 3". The fronts display color action player photos bordered in white. The player's name and team are given beneath the picture. NL players have a blue stripe in the lower left corner, while AL players have a red stripe in the same location. Included in the set are foil stickers of team pennants, logos and league insignias. The stickers may be pasted in a collectible sticker album that measures 8 1/4" by 10 1/2". The stickers are checklisted alphabetically according to teams within the NL and then the AL, with the Canadian teams listed after each league. A special Year of the No-Hitter (352-360) subset is included at the end of the set.

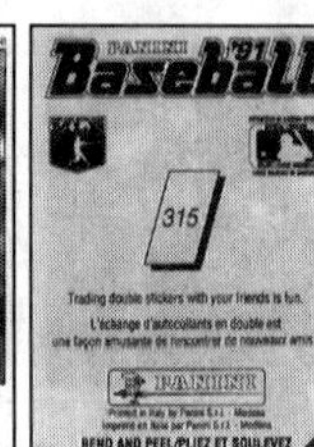

	MINT	NRMT	EXC
COMPLETE SET (360)	25.00	11.00	3.10
COMMON STICKER (1-360)	.05	.02	.01
□ 1 MLB Logo	.05	.02	.01
□ 2 MLBPA Logo	.05	.02	.01
□ 3 Panini Baseball 1991 Logo	.05	.02	.01
□ 4 Astros Pennant	.05	.02	.01
□ 5 Astros Logo	.05	.02	.01
□ 6 Craig Biggio	.30	.14	.04
□ 7 Glenn Davis	.05	.02	.01
□ 8 Casey Candaele	.05	.02	.01
□ 9 Ken Caminiti	.50	.23	.06
□ 10 Rafael Ramirez	.05	.02	.01
□ 11 Glenn Wilson	.05	.02	.01
□ 12 Eric Yelding	.05	.02	.01
□ 13 Franklin Stubbs	.05	.02	.01
□ 14 Mike Scott	.05	.02	.01
□ 15 Danny Darwin	.05	.02	.01
□ 16 Braves Pennant	.05	.02	.01
□ 17 Braves Logo	.05	.02	.01
□ 18 Greg Olson	.05	.02	.01
□ 19 Tommy Gregg	.05	.02	.01
□ 20 Jeff Treadway	.05	.02	.01
□ 21 Jim Presley	.05	.02	.01
□ 22 Jeff Blauser	.05	.02	.01
□ 23 Ron Gant	.15	.07	.02
□ 24 Lonnie Smith	.05	.02	.01
□ 25 Dave Justice	.50	.23	.06
□ 26 John Smoltz	.50	.23	.06
□ 27 Charlie Leibrandt	.05	.02	.01
□ 28 Cardinals Pennant	.05	.02	.01
□ 29 Cardinals Logo	.05	.02	.01
□ 30 Tom Pagnozzi	.05	.02	.01
□ 31 Pedro Guerrero	.05	.02	.01
□ 32 Jose Oquendo	.05	.02	.01
□ 33 Todd Zeile	.05	.02	.01
□ 34 Ozzie Smith	.75	.35	.09
□ 35 Vince Coleman	.05	.02	.01
□ 36 Milt Thompson	.05	.02	.01
□ 37 Rex Hudler	.05	.02	.01
□ 38 Joe Magrane	.05	.02	.01
□ 39 Lee Smith	.15	.07	.02
□ 40 Cubs Pennant	.05	.02	.01
□ 41 Cubs Logo	.05	.02	.01
□ 42 Joe Girardi	.05	.02	.01
□ 43 Mark Grace	.35	.16	.04
□ 44 Ryne Sandberg	.75	.35	.09
□ 45 Luis Salazar	.05	.02	.01
□ 46 Shawon Dunston	.05	.02	.01
□ 47 Dwight Smith	.05	.02	.01
□ 48 Jerome Walton	.05	.02	.01
□ 49 Andre Dawson	.15	.07	.02
□ 50 Greg Maddux	1.75	.80	.22
□ 51 Mike Harkey	.05	.02	.01
□ 52 Dodgers Pennant	.05	.02	.01
□ 53 Dodgers Logo	.05	.02	.01
□ 54 Mike Scioscia	.05	.02	.01
□ 55 Eddie Murray	.75	.35	.09
□ 56 Juan Samuel	.05	.02	.01
□ 57 Lenny Harris	.05	.02	.01
□ 58 Alfredo Griffin	.05	.02	.01
□ 59 Hubie Brooks	.05	.02	.01
□ 60 Kal Daniels	.05	.02	.01
□ 61 Stan Javier	.05	.02	.01
□ 62 Ramon Martinez	.25	.11	.03
□ 63 Mike Morgan	.05	.02	.01
□ 64 Giants Pennant	.05	.02	.01
□ 65 Giants Logo	.05	.02	.01
□ 66 Terry Kennedy	.05	.02	.01
□ 67 Will Clark	.35	.16	.04
□ 68 Robby Thompson	.05	.02	.01
□ 69 Matt Williams	.35	.16	.04
□ 70 Jose Uribe	.05	.02	.01
□ 71 Kevin Mitchell	.05	.02	.01
□ 72 Brett Butler	.15	.07	.02
□ 73 Don Robinson	.05	.02	.01
□ 74 John Burkett	.05	.02	.01
□ 75 Jeff Brantley	.05	.02	.01
□ 76 Mets Pennant	.05	.02	.01
□ 77 Mets Logo	.05	.02	.01
□ 78 Mackey Sasser	.05	.02	.01
□ 79 Dave Magadan	.05	.02	.01
□ 80 Gregg Jefferies	.15	.07	.02
□ 81 Howard Johnson	.05	.02	.01
□ 82 Kevin Elster	.05	.02	.01
□ 83 Kevin McReynolds	.05	.02	.01
□ 84 Daryl Boston	.05	.02	.01
□ 85 Darryl Strawberry	.15	.07	.02
□ 86 Dwight Gooden	.15	.07	.02
□ 87 Frank Viola	.05	.02	.01
□ 88 Padres Pennant	.05	.02	.01
□ 89 Padres Logo	.05	.02	.01
□ 90 Benito Santiago	.05	.02	.01
□ 91 Jack Clark	.05	.02	.01
□ 92 Roberto Alomar	.75	.35	.09
□ 93 Mike Pagliarulo	.05	.02	.01
□ 94 Garry Templeton	.05	.02	.01
□ 95 Joe Carter	.15	.07	.02
□ 96 Bip Roberts	.05	.02	.01
□ 97 Tony Gwynn	1.25	.55	.16
□ 98 Ed Whitson	.05	.02	.01
□ 99 Andy Benes	.15	.07	.02
□ 100 Phillies Pennant	.05	.02	.01
□ 101 Phillies Logo	.05	.02	.01
□ 102 Darren Daulton	.15	.07	.02
□ 103 Ricky Jordan	.05	.02	.01
□ 104 Randy Ready	.05	.02	.01
□ 105 Charlie Hayes	.05	.02	.01
□ 106 Dickie Thon	.05	.02	.01
□ 107 Von Hayes	.05	.02	.01
□ 108 Len Dykstra	.15	.07	.02
□ 109 Dale Murphy	.25	.11	.03
□ 110 Ken Howell	.05	.02	.01
□ 111 Roger McDowell	.05	.02	.01
□ 112 Pirates Pennant	.05	.02	.01
□ 113 Pirates Logo	.05	.02	.01
□ 114 Mike LaValliere	.05	.02	.01
□ 115 Sid Bream	.05	.02	.01
□ 116 Jose Lind	.05	.02	.01
□ 117 Jeff King	.05	.02	.01
□ 118 Jay Bell	.05	.02	.01
□ 119 Barry Bonds	.75	.35	.09
□ 120 Bobby Bonilla	.15	.07	.02
□ 121 Andy Van Slyke	.15	.07	.02
□ 122 Doug Drabek	.05	.02	.01
□ 123 Neal Heaton	.05	.02	.01
□ 124 Reds Pennant	.05	.02	.01
□ 125 Reds Logo	.05	.02	.01
□ 126 Joe Oliver	.05	.02	.01
□ 127 Todd Benzinger	.05	.02	.01
□ 128 Mariano Duncan	.05	.02	.01
□ 129 Chris Sabo	.05	.02	.01
□ 130 Barry Larkin	.40	.18	.05
□ 131 Eric Davis	.05	.02	.01
□ 132 Billy Hatcher	.05	.02	.01
□ 133 Paul O'Neill	.15	.07	.02
□ 134 Jose Rijo	.05	.02	.01
□ 135 Randy Myers	.05	.02	.01
□ 136 Expos Pennant	.05	.02	.01
□ 137 Expos Logo	.05	.02	.01
□ 138 Mike Fitzgerald	.05	.02	.01
□ 139 Andres Galarraga	.35	.16	.04
□ 140 Delino DeShields	.05	.02	.01
□ 141 Tim Wallach	.05	.02	.01
□ 142 Spike Owen	.05	.02	.01
□ 143 Tim Raines	.15	.07	.02
□ 144 Dave Martinez	.05	.02	.01
□ 145 Larry Walker	.50	.23	.06
□ 146 Expos Helmet	.05	.02	.01
□ 147 Dennis Boyd	.05	.02	.01
□ 148 Tim Burke	.05	.02	.01
□ 149 Bill Sampen	.05	.02	.01
□ 150 Dennis Martinez	.15	.07	.02
□ 151 Marquis Grissom	.50	.23	.06
□ 152 Otis Nixon	.15	.07	.02
□ 153 Jerry Goff	.05	.02	.01
□ 154 Steve Frey	.05	.02	.01
□ 155 NL Emblem	.05	.02	.01
□ 156 AL Emblem	.05	.02	.01
□ 157 Benito Santiago	.05	.02	.01
□ 158 Will Clark	.35	.16	.04
□ 159 Ryne Sandberg	.75	.35	.09
□ 160 Chris Sabo	.05	.02	.01
□ 161 Ozzie Smith	.75	.35	.09
□ 162 Kevin Mitchell	.05	.02	.01
□ 163 Len Dykstra	.15	.07	.02
□ 164 Darryl Strawberry	.15	.07	.02
□ 165 Jack Armstrong	.05	.02	.01
□ 166 Sandy Alomar Jr.	.15	.07	.02
□ 167 Mark McGwire	1.00	.45	.12
□ 168 Steve Sax	.05	.02	.01
□ 169 Wade Boggs	.35	.16	.04
□ 170 Cal Ripken	2.50	1.10	.30
□ 171 Rickey Henderson	.40	.18	.05
□ 172 Ken Griffey Jr.	3.00	1.35	.35
□ 173 Jose Canseco	.40	.18	.05
□ 174 Bob Welch	.05	.02	.01
□ 175 Wrigley Field	.05	.02	.01
□ 176 World Series Trophy	.05	.02	.01
□ 177 Angels Pennant	.05	.02	.01
□ 178 Angels Logo	.05	.02	.01
□ 179 Lance Parrish	.05	.02	.01
□ 180 Wally Joyner	.15	.07	.02
□ 181 Johnny Ray	.05	.02	.01
□ 182 Jack Howell	.05	.02	.01
□ 183 Dick Schofield	.05	.02	.01
□ 184 Dave Winfield	.40	.18	.05
□ 185 Devon White	.05	.02	.01
□ 186 Dante Bichette	.40	.18	.05
□ 187 Chuck Finley	.15	.07	.02
□ 188 Jim Abbott	.15	.07	.02
□ 189 Athletics Pennant	.05	.02	.01
□ 190 Athletics Logo	.05	.02	.01
□ 191 Terry Steinbach	.05	.02	.01
□ 192 Mark McGwire	1.00	.45	.12

☐ 193 Willie Randolph	.15	.07	.02
☐ 194 Carney Lansford	.05	.02	.01
☐ 195 Walt Weiss	.05	.02	.01
☐ 196 Rickey Henderson	.35	.16	.04
☐ 197 Dave Henderson	.05	.02	.01
☐ 198 Jose Canseco	.40	.18	.05
☐ 199 Dave Stewart	.15	.07	.02
☐ 200 Dennis Eckersley	.15	.07	.02
☐ 201 Brewers Pennant	.05	.02	.01
☐ 202 Brewers Logo	.05	.02	.01
☐ 203 B.J. Surhoff	.15	.07	.02
☐ 204 Greg Brock	.05	.02	.01
☐ 205 Paul Molitor	.75	.35	.09
☐ 206 Gary Sheffield	.50	.23	.06
☐ 207 Bill Spiers	.05	.02	.01
☐ 208 Robin Yount	.40	.18	.05
☐ 209 Rob Deer	.05	.02	.01
☐ 210 Dave Parker	.15	.07	.02
☐ 211 Mark Knudson	.05	.02	.01
☐ 212 Dan Plesac	.05	.02	.01
☐ 213 Indians Pennant	.05	.02	.01
☐ 214 Indians Logo	.05	.02	.01
☐ 215 Sandy Alomar Jr.	.15	.07	.02
☐ 216 Brook Jacoby	.05	.02	.01
☐ 217 Jerry Browne	.05	.02	.01
☐ 218 Carlos Baerga	.75	.35	.09
☐ 219 Felix Fermin	.05	.02	.01
☐ 220 Candy Maldonado	.05	.02	.01
☐ 221 Cory Snyder	.05	.02	.01
☐ 222 Alex Cole	.05	.02	.01
☐ 223 Tom Candiotti	.05	.02	.01
☐ 224 Doug Jones	.05	.02	.01
☐ 225 Mariners Pennant	.05	.02	.01
☐ 226 Mariners Logo	.05	.02	.01
☐ 227 Dave Valle	.05	.02	.01
☐ 228 Pete O'Brien	.05	.02	.01
☐ 229 Harold Reynolds	.15	.07	.02
☐ 230 Edgar Martinez	.35	.16	.04
☐ 231 Omar Vizquel	.25	.11	.03
☐ 232 Henry Cotto	.05	.02	.01
☐ 233 Ken Griffey Jr.	3.00	1.35	.35
☐ 234 Jay Buhner	.35	.16	.04
☐ 235 Erik Hanson	.05	.02	.01
☐ 236 Mike Schooler	.05	.02	.01
☐ 237 Orioles Pennant	.05	.02	.01
☐ 238 Orioles Logo	.05	.02	.01
☐ 239 Mickey Tettleton	.05	.02	.01
☐ 240 Randy Milligan	.05	.02	.01
☐ 241 Bill Ripken	.05	.02	.01
☐ 242 Craig Worthington	.05	.02	.01
☐ 243 Cal Ripken	2.50	1.10	.30
☐ 244 Steve Finley	.15	.07	.02
☐ 245 Mike Devereaux	.05	.02	.01
☐ 246 Joe Orsulak	.05	.02	.01
☐ 247 Ben McDonald	.15	.07	.02
☐ 248 Gregg Olson	.05	.02	.01
☐ 249 Rangers Pennant	.05	.02	.01
☐ 250 Rangers Logo	.05	.02	.01
☐ 251 Geno Petralli	.05	.02	.01
☐ 252 Rafael Palmeiro	.35	.16	.04
☐ 253 Julio Franco	.15	.07	.02
☐ 254 Steve Buechele	.05	.02	.01
☐ 255 Jeff Huson	.05	.02	.01
☐ 256 Gary Pettis	.05	.02	.01
☐ 257 Ruben Sierra	.05	.02	.01
☐ 258 Pete Incaviglia	.05	.02	.01
☐ 259 Nolan Ryan	2.50	1.10	.30
☐ 260 Bobby Witt	.05	.02	.01
☐ 261 Red Sox Pennant	.05	.02	.01
☐ 262 Red Sox Logo	.05	.02	.01
☐ 263 Tony Pena	.05	.02	.01
☐ 264 Carlos Quintana	.05	.02	.01
☐ 265 Jody Reed	.05	.02	.01
☐ 266 Wade Boggs	.35	.16	.04
☐ 267 Luis Rivera	.05	.02	.01
☐ 268 Mike Greenwell	.05	.02	.01
☐ 269 Ellis Burks	.15	.07	.02
☐ 270 Tom Brunansky	.05	.02	.01
☐ 271 Roger Clemens	.50	.23	.06
☐ 272 Jeff Reardon	.05	.02	.01
☐ 273 Royals Pennant	.05	.02	.01
☐ 274 Royals Logo	.05	.02	.01
☐ 275 Mike Macfarlane	.05	.02	.01
☐ 276 George Brett	1.25	.55	.16
☐ 277 Bill Pecota	.05	.02	.01
☐ 278 Kevin Seitzer	.05	.02	.01
☐ 279 Kurt Stillwell	.05	.02	.01
☐ 280 Jim Eisenreich	.15	.07	.02
☐ 281 Bo Jackson	.15	.07	.02
☐ 282 Danny Tartabull	.05	.02	.01
☐ 283 Bret Saberhagen	.15	.07	.02
☐ 284 Tom Gordon	.05	.02	.01
☐ 285 Tigers Pennant	.05	.02	.01
☐ 286 Tigers Logo	.05	.02	.01
☐ 287 Mike Heath	.05	.02	.01
☐ 288 Cecil Fielder	.15	.07	.02
☐ 289 Lou Whitaker	.15	.07	.02
☐ 290 Tony Phillips	.15	.07	.02
☐ 291 Alan Trammell	.15	.07	.02
☐ 292 Chet Lemon	.05	.02	.01
☐ 293 Lloyd Moseby	.05	.02	.01
☐ 294 Gary Ward	.05	.02	.01
☐ 295 Dan Petry	.05	.02	.01
☐ 296 Jack Morris	.15	.07	.02
☐ 297 Twins Pennant	.05	.02	.01
☐ 298 Twins Logo	.05	.02	.01
☐ 299 Brian Harper	.05	.02	.01
☐ 300 Kent Hrbek	.15	.07	.02
☐ 301 Al Newman	.05	.02	.01
☐ 302 Gary Gaetti	.05	.02	.01
☐ 303 Greg Gagne	.05	.02	.01
☐ 304 Dan Gladden	.05	.02	.01
☐ 305 Kirby Puckett	1.50	.70	.19
☐ 306 Gene Larkin	.05	.02	.01
☐ 307 Kevin Tapani	.05	.02	.01
☐ 308 Rick Aguilera	.05	.02	.01
☐ 309 White Sox Pennant	.05	.02	.01
☐ 310 White Sox Logo	.05	.02	.01
☐ 311 Carlton Fisk	.40	.18	.05
☐ 312 Carlos Martinez	.05	.02	.01
☐ 313 Scott Fletcher	.05	.02	.01
☐ 314 Robin Ventura	.25	.11	.03
☐ 315 Ozzie Guillen	.05	.02	.01
☐ 316 Sammy Sosa	.60	.25	.07
☐ 317 Lance Johnson	.15	.07	.02
☐ 318 Ivan Calderon	.05	.02	.01
☐ 319 Greg Hibbard	.05	.02	.01
☐ 320 Bobby Thigpen	.05	.02	.01
☐ 321 Yankees Pennant	.05	.02	.01
☐ 322 Yankees Logo	.05	.02	.01
☐ 323 Bob Geren	.05	.02	.01
☐ 324 Don Mattingly	1.50	.70	.19
☐ 325 Steve Sax	.05	.02	.01
☐ 326 Jim Leyritz	.05	.02	.01
☐ 327 Alvaro Espinoza	.05	.02	.01
☐ 328 Roberto Kelly	.05	.02	.01
☐ 329 Oscar Azocar	.05	.02	.01
☐ 330 Jesse Barfield	.05	.02	.01
☐ 331 Chuck Cary	.05	.02	.01
☐ 332 Dave Righetti	.05	.02	.01
☐ 333 Blue Jays Pennant	.05	.02	.01
☐ 334 Blue Jays Logo	.05	.02	.01
☐ 335 Pat Borders	.05	.02	.01
☐ 336 Fred McGriff	.35	.16	.04
☐ 337 Manny Lee	.05	.02	.01
☐ 338 Kelly Gruber	.05	.02	.01
☐ 339 Tony Fernandez	.05	.02	.01
☐ 340 George Bell	.05	.02	.01
☐ 341 Mookie Wilson	.05	.02	.01
☐ 342 Junior Felix	.05	.02	.01
☐ 343 Blue Jays Helmet	.05	.02	.01
☐ 344 Dave Stieb	.05	.02	.01
☐ 345 Tom Henke	.05	.02	.01
☐ 346 Greg Myers	.05	.02	.01
☐ 347 Glenallen Hill	.05	.02	.01
☐ 348 John Olerud	.15	.07	.02
☐ 349 Todd Stottlemyre	.15	.07	.02
☐ 350 David Wells	.05	.02	.01
☐ 351 Jimmy Key	.05	.02	.01
☐ 352 Mark Langston	.05	.02	.01
☐ 353 Randy Johnson	.50	.23	.06
☐ 354 Nolan Ryan	2.50	1.10	.30
☐ 355 Dave Stewart	.15	.07	.02
☐ 356 Fernando Valenzuela	.15	.07	.02
☐ 357 Andy Hawkins	.05	.02	.01
☐ 358 Melido Perez	.05	.02	.01
☐ 359 Terry Mulholland	.05	.02	.01
☐ 360 Dave Stieb	.05	.02	.01

1992 Panini Stickers

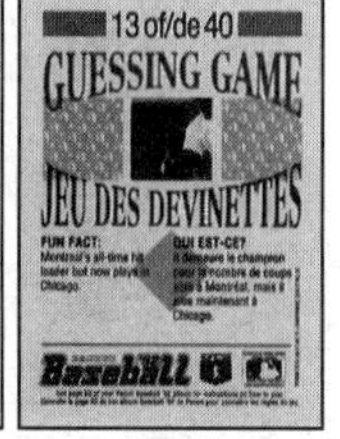

These 288 stickers measure approximately 2 1/8" by 3" and feature on their fronts white-bordered color player action shots that are serrated on their left sides and are framed by a colored line on the remaining three sides. The stickers and album used to store them are organized by team. The Best of the Best AL (144-146), The Best of the Best NL (147-149) and 1991 All-Stars (270-288) are the subsets included within the set.

	MINT	NRMT	EXC
COMPLETE SET (288)	15.00	6.75	1.85
COMMON STICKER (1-288)	.05	.02	.01
☐ 1 Panini Baseball 1992 Logo	.05	.02	.01
☐ 2 MLB Logo	.05	.02	.01
☐ 3 MLBPA Logo	.05	.02	.01
☐ 4 Lance Parrish	.05	.02	.01
☐ 5 Wally Joyner	.10	.05	.01
☐ 6 Luis Sojo	.05	.02	.01
☐ 7 Gary Gaetti	.05	.02	.01
☐ 8 Dick Schofield	.05	.02	.01
☐ 9 Junior Felix	.05	.02	.01
☐ 10 Luis Polonia	.05	.02	.01
☐ 11 Mark Langston	.05	.02	.01
☐ 12 Jim Abbott	.10	.05	.01
☐ 13 Angels Team Logo	.05	.02	.01
☐ 14 Terry Steinbach	.05	.02	.01
☐ 15 Mark McGwire	.75	.35	.09
☐ 16 Mike Gallego	.05	.02	.01
☐ 17 Carney Lansford	.05	.02	.01
☐ 18 Walt Weiss	.05	.02	.01
☐ 19 Jose Canseco	.40	.18	.05
☐ 20 Dave Henderson	.05	.02	.01
☐ 21 Rickey Henderson	.30	.14	.04
☐ 22 Dennis Eckersley	.10	.05	.01
☐ 23 Athletics Team Logo	.05	.02	.01
☐ 24 Pat Borders	.05	.02	.01
☐ 25 John Olerud	.10	.05	.01
☐ 26 Roberto Alomar	.50	.23	.06
☐ 27 Kelly Gruber	.05	.02	.01
☐ 28 Manuel Lee	.05	.02	.01
☐ 29 Joe Carter	.10	.05	.01
☐ 30 Devon White	.05	.02	.01
☐ 31 Candy Maldonado	.05	.02	.01
☐ 32 Dave Stieb	.05	.02	.01
☐ 33 Blue Jays Team Logo	.05	.02	.01
☐ 34 B.J. Surhoff	.10	.05	.01
☐ 35 Franklin Stubbs	.05	.02	.01
☐ 36 Willie Randolph	.10	.05	.01
☐ 37 Jim Gantner	.05	.02	.01
☐ 38 Bill Spiers	.05	.02	.01
☐ 39 Dante Bichette	.25	.11	.03
☐ 40 Robin Yount	.25	.11	.03
☐ 41 Greg Vaughn	.10	.05	.01
☐ 42 Chris Bosio	.05	.02	.01
☐ 43 Brewers Team Logo	.05	.02	.01
☐ 44 Sandy Alomar Jr.	.10	.05	.01
☐ 45 Mike Aldrete	.05	.02	.01
☐ 46 Mark Lewis	.05	.02	.01
☐ 47 Carlos Baerga	.30	.14	.04
☐ 48 Felix Fermin	.05	.02	.01
☐ 49 Mark Whiten	.05	.02	.01
☐ 50 Alex Cole	.05	.02	.01
☐ 51 Albert Belle	1.25	.55	.16
☐ 52 Greg Swindell	.05	.02	.01
☐ 53 Indians Team Logo	.05	.02	.01
☐ 54 Dave Valle	.05	.02	.01
☐ 55 Pete O'Brien	.05	.02	.01
☐ 56 Harold Reynolds	.10	.05	.01
☐ 57 Edgar Martinez	.30	.14	.04
☐ 58 Omar Vizquel	.10	.05	.01
☐ 59 Jay Buhner	.30	.14	.04
☐ 60 Ken Griffey Jr.	2.50	1.10	.30
☐ 61 Greg Briley	.05	.02	.01
☐ 62 Randy Johnson	.30	.14	.04
☐ 63 Mariners Team Logo	.05	.02	.01
☐ 64 Chris Hoiles	.05	.02	.01
☐ 65 Randy Milligan	.05	.02	.01
☐ 66 Bill Ripken	.05	.02	.01
☐ 67 Leo Gomez	.05	.02	.01
☐ 68 Cal Ripken	2.00	.90	.25
☐ 69 Dwight Evans	.10	.05	.01
☐ 70 Mike Devereaux	.05	.02	.01
☐ 71 Joe Orsulak	.05	.02	.01
☐ 72 Gregg Olson	.05	.02	.01
☐ 73 Orioles Team Logo	.05	.02	.01
☐ 74 Ivan Rodriguez	1.00	.45	.12
☐ 75 Rafael Palmeiro	.30	.14	.04
☐ 76 Julio Franco	.10	.05	.01
☐ 77 Dean Palmer	.10	.05	.01
☐ 78 Jeff Huson	.05	.02	.01
☐ 79 Ruben Sierra	.05	.02	.01
☐ 80 Gary Pettis	.05	.02	.01
☐ 81 Juan Gonzalez	1.25	.55	.16
☐ 82 Nolan Ryan	2.00	.90	.25
☐ 83 Rangers Team Logo	.05	.02	.01
☐ 84 Tony Pena	.05	.02	.01
☐ 85 Carlos Quintana	.05	.02	.01
☐ 86 Jody Reed	.05	.02	.01
☐ 87 Wade Boggs	.30	.14	.04
☐ 88 Luis Rivera	.05	.02	.01
☐ 89 Tom Brunansky	.05	.02	.01
☐ 90 Ellis Burks	.10	.05	.01
☐ 91 Mike Greenwell	.05	.02	.01
☐ 92 Roger Clemens	.40	.18	.05
☐ 93 Red Sox Team Logo	.05	.02	.01
☐ 94 Todd Benzinger	.05	.02	.01
☐ 95 Terry Shumpert	.05	.02	.01
☐ 96 Bill Pecota	.05	.02	.01
☐ 97 Kurt Stillwell	.05	.02	.01
☐ 98 Danny Tartabull	.05	.02	.01
☐ 99 Brian McRae	.10	.05	.01
☐ 100 Kirk Gibson	.10	.05	.01
☐ 101 Bret Saberhagen	.10	.05	.01
☐ 102 George Brett	1.00	.45	.12
☐ 103 Royals Team Logo	.05	.02	.01
☐ 104 Mickey Tettleton	.10	.05	.01
☐ 105 Cecil Fielder	.10	.05	.01
☐ 106 Lou Whitaker	.10	.05	.01
☐ 107 Travis Fryman	.15	.07	.02
☐ 108 Alan Trammell	.10	.05	.01
☐ 109 Rob Deer	.05	.02	.01
☐ 110 Milt Cuyler	.05	.02	.01
☐ 111 Lloyd Moseby	.05	.02	.01
☐ 112 Bill Gullickson	.05	.02	.01
☐ 113 Tigers Team Logo	.05	.02	.01
☐ 114 Brian Harper	.05	.02	.01
☐ 115 Kent Hrbek	.10	.05	.01
☐ 116 Chuck Knoblauch	.50	.23	.06
☐ 117 Mike Pagliarulo	.05	.02	.01
☐ 118 Greg Gagne	.05	.02	.01
☐ 119 Shane Mack	.05	.02	.01
☐ 120 Kirby Puckett	1.25	.55	.16
☐ 121 Dan Gladden	.05	.02	.01
☐ 122 Jack Morris	.10	.05	.01
☐ 123 Twins Team Logo	.05	.02	.01
☐ 124 Carlton Fisk	.25	.11	.03
☐ 125 Frank Thomas	2.50	1.10	.30
☐ 126 Joey Cora	.10	.05	.01
☐ 127 Robin Ventura	.10	.05	.01
☐ 128 Ozzie Guillen	.05	.02	.01
☐ 129 Sammy Sosa	.40	.18	.05
☐ 130 Lance Johnson	.10	.05	.01
☐ 131 Tim Raines	.10	.05	.01
☐ 132 Bobby Thigpen	.05	.02	.01
☐ 133 White Sox Team Logo	.05	.02	.01
☐ 134 Matt Nokes	.05	.02	.01
☐ 135 Don Mattingly	1.25	.55	.16
☐ 136 Steve Sax	.05	.02	.01
☐ 137 Pat Kelly	.05	.02	.01
☐ 138 Alvaro Espinoza	.05	.02	.01
☐ 139 Jesse Barfield	.05	.02	.01
☐ 140 Roberto Kelly	.05	.02	.01
☐ 141 Mel Hall	.05	.02	.01
☐ 142 Scott Sanderson	.05	.02	.01
☐ 143 Yankees Team Logo	.05	.02	.01
☐ 144 Cecil Fielder Jose Canseco	.15	.07	.02
☐ 145 Julio Franco	.10	.05	.01
☐ 146 Roger Clemens	.40	.18	.05
☐ 147 Howard Johnson	.05	.02	.01
☐ 148 Terry Pendleton	.05	.02	.01
☐ 149 Dennis Martinez	.10	.05	.01
☐ 150 Astros Team Logo	.05	.02	.01
☐ 151 Craig Biggio	.10	.05	.01
☐ 152 Jeff Bagwell	1.25	.55	.16
☐ 153 Casey Candaele	.05	.02	.01
☐ 154 Ken Caminiti	.40	.18	.05
☐ 155 Andujar Cedeno	.05	.02	.01
☐ 156 Mike Simms	.05	.02	.01
☐ 157 Steve Finley	.10	.05	.01
☐ 158 Luis Gonzalez	.05	.02	.01
☐ 159 Pete Harnisch	.05	.02	.01
☐ 160 Braves Team Logo	.05	.02	.01
☐ 161 Greg Olson	.05	.02	.01
☐ 162 Sid Bream	.05	.02	.01
☐ 163 Mark Lemke	.05	.02	.01
☐ 164 Terry Pendleton	.05	.02	.01
☐ 165 Rafael Belliard	.05	.02	.01
☐ 166 Dave Justice	.25	.11	.03
☐ 167 Ron Gant	.10	.05	.01
☐ 168 Lonnie Smith	.05	.02	.01
☐ 169 Steve Avery	.10	.05	.01
☐ 170 Cardinals Team Logo	.05	.02	.01
☐ 171 Tom Pagnozzi	.05	.02	.01
☐ 172 Pedro Guerrero	.05	.02	.01
☐ 173 Jose Oquendo	.05	.02	.01
☐ 174 Todd Zeile	.05	.02	.01
☐ 175 Ozzie Smith	.60	.25	.07
☐ 176 Felix Jose	.05	.02	.01
☐ 177 Ray Lankford	.15	.07	.02
☐ 178 Jose DeLeon	.05	.02	.01
☐ 179 Lee Smith	.10	.05	.01
☐ 180 Cubs Team Logo	.05	.02	.01
☐ 181 Hector Villanueva	.05	.02	.01
☐ 182 Mark Grace	.25	.11	.03
☐ 183 Ryne Sandberg	.60	.25	.07
☐ 184 Luis Salazar	.05	.02	.01
☐ 185 Shawon Dunston	.05	.02	.01
☐ 186 Andre Dawson	.10	.05	.01
☐ 187 Jerome Walton	.05	.02	.01
☐ 188 George Bell	.05	.02	.01
☐ 189 Greg Maddux	1.50	.70	.19
☐ 190 Dodgers Team Logo	.05	.02	.01
☐ 191 Mike Scioscia	.05	.02	.01
☐ 192 Eddie Murray	.60	.25	.07
☐ 193 Juan Samuel	.05	.02	.01
☐ 194 Lenny Harris	.05	.02	.01
☐ 195 Alfredo Griffin	.05	.02	.01
☐ 196 Darryl Strawberry	.10	.05	.01
☐ 197 Brett Butler	.10	.05	.01
☐ 198 Kal Daniels	.05	.02	.01
☐ 199 Orel Hershiser	.10	.05	.01
☐ 200 Expos Team Logo	.05	.02	.01
☐ 201 Gilberto Reyes	.05	.02	.01
☐ 202 Andres Galarraga	.30	.14	.04
☐ 203 Delino DeShields	.05	.02	.01
☐ 204 Tim Wallach	.05	.02	.01
☐ 205 Spike Owen	.05	.02	.01
☐ 206 Larry Walker	.30	.14	.04
☐ 207 Marquis Grissom	.40	.18	.05
☐ 208 Ivan Calderon	.05	.02	.01
☐ 209 Dennis Martinez	.10	.05	.01
☐ 210 Giants Team Logo	.05	.02	.01
☐ 211 Steve Decker	.05	.02	.01
☐ 212 Will Clark	.30	.14	.04
☐ 213 Robby Thompson	.05	.02	.01
☐ 214 Matt Williams	.40	.18	.05
☐ 215 Jose Uribe	.05	.02	.01
☐ 216 Kevin Bass	.05	.02	.01
☐ 217 Willie McGee	.10	.05	.01
☐ 218 Kevin Mitchell	.05	.02	.01
☐ 219 Dave Righetti	.05	.02	.01
☐ 220 Mets Team Logo	.05	.02	.01
☐ 221 Rick Cerone	.05	.02	.01
☐ 222 Dave Magadan	.05	.02	.01

☐ 223 Gregg Jefferies .10 .05 .01
☐ 224 Howard Johnson .05 .02 .01
☐ 225 Kevin Elster .05 .02 .01
☐ 226 Hubie Brooks .05 .02 .01
☐ 227 Vince Coleman .05 .02 .01
☐ 228 Kevin McReynolds .05 .02 .01
☐ 229 Frank Viola .05 .02 .01
☐ 230 Padres Team Logo .05 .02 .01
☐ 231 Benito Santiago .05 .02 .01
☐ 232 Fred McGriff .30 .14 .04
☐ 233 Bip Roberts .05 .02 .01
☐ 234 Jack Howell .05 .02 .01
☐ 235 Tony Fernandez .05 .02 .01
☐ 236 Tony Gwynn 1.00 .45 .12
☐ 237 Darrin Jackson .05 .02 .01
☐ 238 Bruce Hurst .05 .02 .01
☐ 239 Craig Lefferts .05 .02 .01
☐ 240 Phillies Team Logo .05 .02 .01
☐ 241 Darren Daulton .10 .05 .01
☐ 242 John Kruk .10 .05 .01
☐ 243 Mickey Morandini .05 .02 .01
☐ 244 Charlie Hayes .05 .02 .01
☐ 245 Dickie Thon .05 .02 .01
☐ 246 Dale Murphy .15 .07 .02
☐ 247 Lenny Dykstra .10 .05 .01
☐ 248 Von Hayes .05 .02 .01
☐ 249 Terry Mulholland .05 .02 .01
☐ 250 Pirates Team Logo .05 .02 .01
☐ 251 Mike LaValliere .05 .02 .01
☐ 252 Orlando Merced .05 .02 .01
☐ 253 Jose Lind .05 .02 .01
☐ 254 Steve Buechele .05 .02 .01
☐ 255 Jay Bell .05 .02 .01
☐ 256 Bobby Bonilla .10 .05 .01
☐ 257 Andy Van Slyke .05 .02 .01
☐ 258 Barry Bonds .60 .25 .07
☐ 259 Doug Drabek .05 .02 .01
☐ 260 Reds Team Logo .05 .02 .01
☐ 261 Joe Oliver .05 .02 .01
☐ 262 Hal Morris .05 .02 .01
☐ 263 Bill Doran .05 .02 .01
☐ 264 Chris Sabo .05 .02 .01
☐ 265 Barry Larkin .25 .11 .03
☐ 266 Paul O'Neill .10 .05 .01
☐ 267 Eric Davis .05 .02 .01
☐ 268 Glenn Braggs .05 .02 .01
☐ 269 Jose Rijo .05 .02 .01
☐ 270 Toronto Skydome .05 .02 .01
☐ 271 Sandy Alomar Jr. AS .10 .05 .01
☐ 272 Cecil Fielder AS .10 .05 .01
☐ 273 Roberto Alomar AS .25 .11 .03
☐ 274 Wade Boggs AS .15 .07 .02
☐ 275 Cal Ripken AS 1.00 .45 .12
☐ 276 Dave Henderson AS .05 .02 .01
☐ 277 Ken Griffey Jr. AS 1.25 .55 .16
☐ 278 Rickey Henderson AS .15 .07 .02
☐ 279 Jack Morris AS .10 .05 .01
☐ 280 Benito Santiago AS .05 .02 .01
☐ 281 Will Clark AS .15 .07 .02
☐ 282 Ryne Sandberg AS .30 .14 .04
☐ 283 Chris Sabo AS .05 .02 .01
☐ 284 Ozzie Smith AS .30 .14 .04
☐ 285 Andre Dawson AS .10 .05 .01
☐ 286 Tony Gwynn AS .50 .23 .06
☐ 287 Ivan Calderon AS .05 .02 .01
☐ 288 Tom Glavine AS .10 .05 .01

1993 Panini Stickers

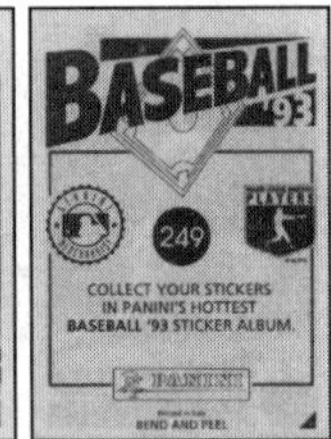

The 300 stickers in this set measure approximately 2 3/8" by 3 3/8" and were to be pasted in a 9" by 11" album. Six stickers were distributed in each 49-cent foil pack. The fronts feature color action player photos with white borders. The player's team name appears on a team color-coded angled bar at the top and the player's name is printed on a second team color-coded bar at the bottom. The team logo is located in the lower left corner. The backs are white and carry the set name, sticker number and manufacturer logo. Ten players from each of the American and National League teams are featured, including one glitter sticker of Panini's Future Stars. One card for each team displays the team's logo on the front. The stickers are numbered on the back and checklisted below according to special subsets and teams.

	MINT	NRMT	EXC
COMPLETE SET (300)	15.00	6.75	1.85
COMMON STICKER (1-300)	.05	.02	.01

☐ 1 Angels Logo .05 .02 .01
☐ 2 Mark Langston .05 .02 .01
☐ 3 Ron Tingley .05 .02 .01
☐ 4 Gary Gaetti .05 .02 .01
☐ 5 Kelly Gruber .05 .02 .01
☐ 6 Gary DiSarcina .05 .02 .01
☐ 7 Damion Easley .05 .02 .01
☐ 8 Luis Polonia .05 .02 .01
☐ 9 Lee Stevens .05 .02 .01
☐ 10 Chad Curtis .05 .02 .01
☐ 11 Rene Gonzales .05 .02 .01
☐ 12 Athletics Logo .05 .02 .01
☐ 13 Dennis Eckersley .10 .05 .01
☐ 14 Terry Steinbach .05 .02 .01
☐ 15 Mark McGwire .75 .35 .09
☐ 16 Mike Bordick .05 .02 .01
☐ 17 Carney Lansford .05 .02 .01
☐ 18 Jerry Browne .05 .02 .01
☐ 19 Rickey Henderson .30 .14 .04
☐ 20 Dave Henderson .05 .02 .01
☐ 21 Ruben Sierra .05 .02 .01
☐ 22 Ron Darling .05 .02 .01
☐ 23 Blue Jays Logo .05 .02 .01
☐ 24 Jack Morris .10 .05 .01
☐ 25 Pat Borders .05 .02 .01
☐ 26 John Olerud .10 .05 .01
☐ 27 Roberto Alomar .50 .23 .06
☐ 28 Luis Sojo .05 .02 .01
☐ 29 Dave Stewart .10 .05 .01
☐ 30 Devon White .05 .02 .01
☐ 31 Joe Carter .10 .05 .01
☐ 32 Derek Bell .10 .05 .01
☐ 33 Juan Guzman .05 .02 .01
☐ 34 Brewers Logo .05 .02 .01
☐ 35 Jaime Navarro .05 .02 .01
☐ 36 B.J. Surhoff .10 .05 .01
☐ 37 Franklin Stubbs .05 .02 .01
☐ 38 Bill Spiers .05 .02 .01
☐ 39 Pat Listach .05 .02 .01
☐ 40 Kevin Seitzer .05 .02 .01
☐ 41 Darryl Hamilton .05 .02 .01
☐ 42 Robin Yount .25 .11 .03
☐ 43 Kevin Reimer .05 .02 .01
☐ 44 Greg Vaughn .10 .05 .01
☐ 45 Indians Logo .05 .02 .01
☐ 46 Charles Nagy .10 .05 .01
☐ 47 Sandy Alomar Jr. .10 .05 .01
☐ 48 Reggie Jefferson .05 .02 .01
☐ 49 Mark Lewis .05 .02 .01
☐ 50 Felix Fermin .05 .02 .01
☐ 51 Carlos Baerga .30 .14 .04
☐ 52 Albert Belle 1.25 .55 .16
☐ 53 Kenny Lofton .75 .35 .09
☐ 54 Mark Whiten .05 .02 .01
☐ 55 Paul Sorrento .05 .02 .01
☐ 56 Mariners Logo .05 .02 .01
☐ 57 Dave Fleming .05 .02 .01
☐ 58 Dave Valle .05 .02 .01
☐ 59 Pete O'Brien .05 .02 .01
☐ 60 Randy Johnson .30 .14 .04
☐ 61 Omar Vizquel .10 .05 .01
☐ 62 Edgar Martinez .30 .14 .04
☐ 63 Ken Griffey Jr. 2.50 1.10 .30
☐ 64 Henry Cotto .05 .02 .01
☐ 65 Jay Buhner .30 .14 .04
☐ 66 Tino Martinez .10 .05 .01
☐ 67 Orioles Logo .05 .02 .01
☐ 68 Ben McDonald .05 .02 .01
☐ 69 Mike Mussina .50 .23 .06
☐ 70 Chris Hoiles .05 .02 .01
☐ 71 Randy Milligan .05 .02 .01
☐ 72 Billy Ripken .05 .02 .01
☐ 73 Cal Ripken 2.00 .90 .25
☐ 74 Leo Gomez .05 .02 .01
☐ 75 Mike Devereaux .05 .02 .01
☐ 76 Brady Anderson .15 .07 .02
☐ 77 Joe Orsulak .05 .02 .01
☐ 78 Rangers Logo .05 .02 .01
☐ 79 Kevin Brown .10 .05 .01
☐ 80 Ivan Rodriguez .60 .25 .07
☐ 81 Rafael Palmeiro .30 .14 .04
☐ 82 Julio Franco .10 .05 .01
☐ 83 Jeff Huson .05 .02 .01
☐ 84 Dean Palmer .10 .05 .01
☐ 85 Jose Canseco .30 .14 .04
☐ 86 Juan Gonzalez 1.25 .55 .16
☐ 87 Nolan Ryan 2.00 .90 .25
☐ 88 Brian Downing .05 .02 .01
☐ 89 Red Sox Logo .05 .02 .01
☐ 90 Roger Clemens .40 .18 .05
☐ 91 Tony Pena .05 .02 .01
☐ 92 Mo Vaughn .60 .25 .07
☐ 93 Scott Cooper .05 .02 .01
☐ 94 Luis Rivera .05 .02 .01
☐ 95 Ellis Burks .10 .05 .01
☐ 96 Mike Greenwell .05 .02 .01
☐ 97 Andre Dawson .10 .05 .01
☐ 98 Ivan Calderon .05 .02 .01
☐ 99 Phil Plantier .05 .02 .01
☐ 100 Royals Logo .05 .02 .01
☐ 101 Kevin Appier .10 .05 .01
☐ 102 Mike Macfarlane .05 .02 .01
☐ 103 Wally Joyner .10 .05 .01
☐ 104 Jim Eisenreich .10 .05 .01
☐ 105 Greg Gagne .05 .02 .01
☐ 106 Gregg Jefferies .10 .05 .01
☐ 107 Kevin McReynolds .05 .02 .01
☐ 108 Brian McRae .10 .05 .01
☐ 109 Keith Miller .05 .02 .01
☐ 110 George Brett 1.00 .45 .12
☐ 111 Tigers Logo .05 .02 .01
☐ 112 Bill Gullickson .05 .02 .01
☐ 113 Mickey Tettleton .05 .02 .01
☐ 114 Cecil Fielder .10 .05 .01
☐ 115 Tony Phillips .10 .05 .01
☐ 116 Scott Livingstone .05 .02 .01
☐ 117 Travis Fryman .10 .05 .01
☐ 118 Dan Gladden .05 .02 .01
☐ 119 Rob Deer .05 .02 .01
☐ 120 Frank Tanana .05 .02 .01
☐ 121 Skeeter Barnes .05 .02 .01
☐ 122 Twins Logo .05 .02 .01
☐ 123 Scott Erickson .05 .02 .01
☐ 124 Brian Harper .05 .02 .01
☐ 125 Kent Hrbek .05 .02 .01
☐ 126 Chuck Knoblauch .40 .18 .05
☐ 127 Willie Banks .05 .02 .01
☐ 128 Scott Leius .05 .02 .01
☐ 129 Shane Mack .05 .02 .01
☐ 130 Kirby Puckett 1.25 .55 .16
☐ 131 Chili Davis .10 .05 .01
☐ 132 Pedro Munoz .05 .02 .01
☐ 133 White Sox Logo .05 .02 .01
☐ 134 Jack McDowell .10 .05 .01
☐ 135 Carlton Fisk .25 .11 .03
☐ 136 Frank Thomas 2.50 1.10 .30
☐ 137 Steve Sax .05 .02 .01
☐ 138 Ozzie Guillen .05 .02 .01
☐ 139 Robin Ventura .10 .05 .01
☐ 140 Tim Raines .10 .05 .01
☐ 141 Lance Johnson .10 .05 .01
☐ 142 Ron Karkovice .05 .02 .01
☐ 143 George Bell .05 .02 .01
☐ 144 Yankees Logo .05 .02 .01
☐ 145 Scott Sanderson .05 .02 .01
☐ 146 Matt Nokes .05 .02 .01
☐ 147 Kevin Maas .05 .02 .01
☐ 148 Randy Velarde .05 .02 .01
☐ 149 Andy Stankiewicz .05 .02 .01
☐ 150 Pat Kelly .05 .02 .01
☐ 151 Paul O'Neill .10 .05 .01
☐ 152 Wade Boggs .30 .14 .04
☐ 153 Danny Tartabull .05 .02 .01
☐ 154 Don Mattingly 1.25 .55 .16
☐ 155 Edgar Martinez LL .10 .05 .01
☐ 156 Kevin Brown LL .10 .05 .01
☐ 157 Dennis Eckersley LL .10 .05 .01
☐ 158 Gary Sheffield LL .15 .07 .02
☐ 159 Tom Glavine LL .60 .25 .07
Greg Maddux
☐ 160 Lee Smith LL .10 .05 .01
☐ 161 Dennis Eckersley CY .10 .05 .01
☐ 162 Dennis Eckersley MVP .10 .05 .01
☐ 163 Pat Listach ROY .05 .02 .01
☐ 164 Greg Maddux CY .75 .35 .09
☐ 165 Barry Bonds MVP .25 .11 .03
☐ 166 Eric Karros ROY .15 .07 .02
☐ 167 Astros Logo .05 .02 .01
☐ 168 Pete Harnisch .05 .02 .01
☐ 169 Eddie Taubensee .05 .02 .01
☐ 170 Jeff Bagwell 1.25 .55 .16
☐ 171 Craig Biggio .10 .05 .01
☐ 172 Andujar Cedeno .05 .02 .01
☐ 173 Ken Caminiti .40 .18 .05
☐ 174 Steve Finley .10 .05 .01
☐ 175 Luis Gonzalez .05 .02 .01
☐ 176 Eric Anthony .05 .02 .01
☐ 177 Casey Candaele .05 .02 .01
☐ 178 Braves Logo .05 .02 .01
☐ 179 Tom Glavine .30 .14 .04
☐ 180 Greg Olson .05 .02 .01
☐ 181 Sid Bream .05 .02 .01
☐ 182 Mark Lemke .05 .02 .01
☐ 183 Jeff Blauser .05 .02 .01
☐ 184 Terry Pendleton .05 .02 .01
☐ 185 Ron Gant .10 .05 .01
☐ 186 Otis Nixon .05 .02 .01
☐ 187 Dave Justice .25 .11 .03
☐ 188 Deion Sanders .40 .18 .05
☐ 189 Cardinals Logo .05 .02 .01
☐ 190 Bob Tewksbury .05 .02 .01
☐ 191 Tom Pagnozzi .05 .02 .01
☐ 192 Lee Smith .10 .05 .01
☐ 193 Geronimo Pena .05 .02 .01
☐ 194 Ozzie Smith .60 .25 .07
☐ 195 Todd Zeile .05 .02 .01
☐ 196 Ray Lankford .10 .05 .01
☐ 197 Bernard Gilkey .10 .05 .01
☐ 198 Felix Jose .05 .02 .01
☐ 199 Donovan Osborne .05 .02 .01
☐ 200 Cubs Logo .05 .02 .01
☐ 201 Mike Morgan .05 .02 .01
☐ 202 Rick Wilkins .05 .02 .01
☐ 203 Mark Grace .40 .18 .05
☐ 204 Ryne Sandberg .60 .25 .07
☐ 205 Shawon Dunston .05 .02 .01
☐ 206 Steve Buechele .05 .02 .01
☐ 207 Kal Daniels .05 .02 .01
☐ 208 Sammy Sosa .40 .18 .05
☐ 209 Derrick May .05 .02 .01
☐ 210 Doug Dascenzo .05 .02 .01
☐ 211 Dodgers Logo .05 .02 .01
☐ 212 Ramon Martinez .10 .05 .01
☐ 213 Mike Sciocia .05 .02 .01
☐ 214 Eric Karros .15 .07 .02
☐ 215 Tim Wallach .05 .02 .01
☐ 216 Jose Offerman .05 .02 .01
☐ 217 Mike Sharperson .05 .02 .01
☐ 218 Brett Butler .10 .05 .01
☐ 219 Darryl Strawberry .10 .05 .01
☐ 220 Lenny Harris .05 .02 .01
☐ 221 Eric Davis .05 .02 .01
☐ 222 Expos Logo .05 .02 .01
☐ 223 Ken Hill .10 .05 .01
☐ 224 Darrin Fletcher .05 .02 .01
☐ 225 Greg Colbrunn .05 .02 .01
☐ 226 Delino DeShields .05 .02 .01
☐ 227 Wil Cordero .05 .02 .01
☐ 228 Dennis Martinez .10 .05 .01
☐ 229 John Vander Wal .05 .02 .01
☐ 230 Marquis Grissom .10 .05 .01
☐ 231 Larry Walker .15 .07 .02
☐ 232 Moises Alou .10 .05 .01
☐ 233 Giants Logo .05 .02 .01
☐ 234 Bill Swift .05 .02 .01
☐ 235 Kirt Manwaring .05 .02 .01
☐ 236 Will Clark .40 .18 .05
☐ 237 Robby Thompson .05 .02 .01
☐ 238 Royce Clayton .05 .02 .01
☐ 239 Matt Williams .40 .18 .05
☐ 240 Willie McGee .05 .02 .01
☐ 241 Mark Leonard .05 .02 .01
☐ 242 Cory Snyder .05 .02 .01
☐ 243 Barry Bonds .50 .23 .06
☐ 244 Mets Logo .05 .02 .01
☐ 245 Dwight Gooden .10 .05 .01
☐ 246 Todd Hundley .10 .05 .01
☐ 247 Eddie Murray .60 .25 .07
☐ 248 Sid Fernandez .05 .02 .01
☐ 249 Tony Fernandez .05 .02 .01
☐ 250 Dave Magadan .05 .02 .01
☐ 251 Howard Johnson .05 .02 .01
☐ 252 Vince Coleman .05 .02 .01
☐ 253 Bobby Bonilla .10 .05 .01
☐ 254 Daryl Boston .05 .02 .01
☐ 255 Padres Logo .05 .02 .01
☐ 256 Bruce Hurst .05 .02 .01
☐ 257 Dan Walters .05 .02 .01
☐ 258 Fred McGriff .40 .18 .05
☐ 259 Kurt Stillwell .05 .02 .01
☐ 260 Craig Shipley .05 .02 .01
☐ 261 Gary Sheffield .40 .18 .05
☐ 262 Tony Gwynn 1.00 .45 .12
☐ 263 Oscar Azocar .05 .02 .01
☐ 264 Darrin Jackson .05 .02 .01
☐ 265 Andy Benes .10 .05 .01
☐ 266 Phillies Logo .05 .02 .01
☐ 267 Terry Mulholland .05 .02 .01
☐ 268 Curt Schilling .05 .02 .01
☐ 269 Darren Daulton .10 .05 .01
☐ 270 John Kruk .10 .05 .01
☐ 271 Mickey Morandini .05 .02 .01
☐ 272 Mariano Duncan .05 .02 .01
☐ 273 Dave Hollins .05 .02 .01
☐ 274 Lenny Dykstra .10 .05 .01
☐ 275 Wes Chamberlain .05 .02 .01
☐ 276 Stan Javier .05 .02 .01
☐ 277 Pirates Logo .05 .02 .01
☐ 278 Zane Smith .05 .02 .01
☐ 279 Tim Wakefield .05 .02 .01
☐ 280 Mike LaValliere .05 .02 .01
☐ 281 Orlando Merced .05 .02 .01
☐ 282 Stan Belinda .05 .02 .01
☐ 283 Jay Bell .05 .02 .01
☐ 284 Jeff King .05 .02 .01
☐ 285 Andy Van Slyke .10 .05 .01
☐ 286 Bob Walk .05 .02 .01
☐ 287 Gary Varsho .05 .02 .01
☐ 288 Reds Logo .05 .02 .01
☐ 289 Jose Rijo .05 .02 .01
☐ 290 Joe Oliver .05 .02 .01
☐ 291 Hal Morris .05 .02 .01
☐ 292 Bip Roberts .05 .02 .01
☐ 293 Barry Larkin .25 .11 .03
☐ 294 Chris Sabo .05 .02 .01
☐ 295 Roberto Kelly .05 .02 .01
☐ 296 Kevin Mitchell .05 .02 .01
☐ 297 Rob Dibble .05 .02 .01
☐ 298 Reggie Sanders .25 .11 .03
☐ 299 Marlins Logo .05 .02 .01
☐ 300 Rockies Logo .10 .05 .01

1994 Panini Stickers

This set of 1994 Panini Baseball consists of 268 stickers measuring approximately 2 3/8" by 3 3/8". The stickers were sold in Panini packets of six, with 50 packets (suggested retail price of 49 cents each) per box. The collectible sticker album measures 9 1/8" by 10 5/8" (suggested retail price of 99 cents) and features eight baseball players on the bright yellow, UV coated cover. The album's inside front cover carries 1993 Team Statistics for the American and National Leagues and also lists the 1993 League Standings. The back inside cover provides information on how to order missing stickers and take advantage of the mail in offer of 30 stickers for $4.00, plus ten '94 Panini wrappers. The sticker fronts feature kelly-green bordered action player shots. A white baseball pennant icon across the bottom carries the player's name and team logo. After presenting the American (5-10) and National League Leaders (11-16), the set is arranged grouped alphabetically within teams and checklisted below alphabetically according to teams for each league.

	MINT	NRMT	EXC
COMPLETE SET (268)	15.00	6.75	1.85
COMMON STICKER (1-268)	.05	.02	.01

	MINT	NRMT	EXC
□ 1 WS Opening Ceremony (Upper left)	.05	.02	.01
□ 2 WS Opening Ceremony (Upper right)	.05	.02	.01
□ 3 WS Opening Ceremony (Lower left)	.05	.02	.01
□ 4 WS Opening Ceremony (Lower right)	.05	.02	.01
□ 5 John Olerud Highest Batting Average	.10	.05	.01
□ 6 Juan Gonzalez Most Home Runs	.50	.23	.06
□ 7 Albert Belle Most Runs Batted In	.50	.23	.06
□ 8 Jack McDowell Most Wins	.10	.05	.01
□ 9 Randy Johnson Most Strikeouts	.25	.11	.03
□ 10 Jeff Montgomery Duane Ward Most Saves (tie)	.05	.02	.01
□ 11 Andres Galarraga Highest Batting Average	.15	.07	.02
□ 12 Barry Bonds Most Home Runs	.30	.14	.04
□ 13 Barry Bonds Most Runs Batted In	.30	.14	.04
□ 14 Tom Glavine John Burkett Most Wins (tie)	.15	.07	.02
□ 15 Jose Rijo Most Strikeouts	.05	.02	.01
□ 16 Randy Myers Most Saves	.05	.02	.01
□ 17 Brady Anderson	.15	.07	.02
□ 18 Harold Baines	.10	.05	.01
□ 19 Mike Devereaux	.05	.02	.01
□ 20 Chris Hoiles	.05	.02	.01
□ 21 Mike Mussina	.40	.18	.05
□ 22 Harold Reynolds	.10	.05	.01
□ 23 Cal Ripken Jr.	1.50	.70	.19
□ 24 David Segui	.05	.02	.01
□ 25 Fernando Valenzuela	.10	.05	.01
□ 26 Roger Clemens	.30	.14	.04
□ 27 Scott Cooper	.05	.02	.01
□ 28 Andre Dawson	.10	.05	.01
□ 29 Scott Fletcher	.05	.02	.01
□ 30 Mike Greenwell	.05	.02	.01
□ 31 Billy Hatcher	.05	.02	.01
□ 32 Tony Pena	.05	.02	.01
□ 33 John Valentin	.10	.05	.01
□ 34 Mo Vaughn	.50	.23	.06
□ 35 Chad Curtis	.05	.02	.01
□ 36 Gary DiSarcina	.05	.02	.01
□ 37 Damion Easley	.05	.02	.01
□ 38 Mark Langston	.05	.02	.01
□ 39 Torey Lovullo	.05	.02	.01
□ 40 Greg Myers	.05	.02	.01
□ 41 Luis Polonia	.05	.02	.01
□ 42 Tim Salmon	.40	.18	.05
□ 43 J.T. Snow	.10	.05	.01
□ 44 George Bell	.05	.02	.01
□ 45 Ellis Burks	.10	.05	.01
□ 46 Joey Cora	.05	.02	.01
□ 47 Ozzie Guillen	.05	.02	.01
□ 48 Roberto Hernandez	.05	.02	.01
□ 49 Bo Jackson	.10	.05	.01
□ 50 Jack McDowell	.10	.05	.01
□ 51 Frank Thomas	2.00	.90	.25
□ 52 Robin Ventura	.10	.05	.01
□ 53 Sandy Alomar Jr.	.05	.02	.01
□ 54 Carlos Baerga	.30	.14	.04
□ 55 Albert Belle	1.00	.45	.12
□ 56 Felix Fermin	.05	.02	.01
□ 57 Wayne Kirby	.05	.02	.01
□ 58 Kenny Lofton	.60	.25	.07
□ 59 Charles Nagy	.10	.05	.01
□ 60 Paul Sorrento	.05	.02	.01
□ 61 Jeff Treadway	.05	.02	.01
□ 62 Eric Davis	.05	.02	.01
□ 63 Cecil Fielder	.10	.05	.01
□ 64 Travis Fryman	.10	.05	.01
□ 65 Bill Gullickson	.05	.02	.01
□ 66 Mike Moore	.05	.02	.01
□ 67 Tony Phillips	.10	.05	.01
□ 68 Mickey Tettleton	.10	.05	.01
□ 69 Alan Trammell	.10	.05	.01
□ 70 Lou Whitaker	.10	.05	.01
□ 71 Kevin Appier	.10	.05	.01
□ 72 Greg Gagne	.05	.02	.01
□ 73 Tom Gordon	.05	.02	.01
□ 74 Felix Jose	.05	.02	.01
□ 75 Wally Joyner	.10	.05	.01
□ 76 Jose Lind	.05	.02	.01
□ 77 Mike Macfarlane	.05	.02	.01
□ 78 Brian McRae	.05	.02	.01
□ 79 Kevin McReynolds	.05	.02	.01
□ 80 Darryl Hamilton	.05	.02	.01
□ 81 Teddy Higuera	.05	.02	.01
□ 82 John Jaha	.10	.05	.01
□ 83 Pat Listach	.05	.02	.01
□ 84 Dave Nilsson	.05	.02	.01
□ 85 Kevin Reimer	.05	.02	.01
□ 86 Kevin Seitzer	.05	.02	.01
□ 87 B.J. Surhoff	.10	.05	.01
□ 88 Greg Vaughn	.05	.02	.01
□ 89 Willie Banks	.05	.02	.01
□ 90 Brian Harper	.05	.02	.01
□ 91 Kent Hrbek	.05	.02	.01
□ 92 Chuck Knoblauch	.40	.18	.05
□ 93 Shane Mack	.05	.02	.01
□ 94 Pat Meares	.05	.02	.01
□ 95 Pedro Munoz	.05	.02	.01
□ 96 Kirby Puckett	1.00	.45	.12
□ 97 Dave Winfield	.25	.11	.03
□ 98 Jim Abbott	.10	.05	.01
□ 99 Wade Boggs	.30	.14	.04
□ 100 Mike Gallego	.05	.02	.01
□ 101 Pat Kelly	.05	.02	.01
□ 102 Don Mattingly	1.00	.45	.12
□ 103 Paul O'Neill	.10	.05	.01
□ 104 Mike Stanley	.05	.02	.01
□ 105 Danny Tartabull	.05	.02	.01
□ 106 Bernie Williams	.50	.23	.06
□ 107 Mike Bordick	.05	.02	.01
□ 108 Dennis Eckersley	.10	.05	.01
□ 109 Dave Henderson	.05	.02	.01
□ 110 Mark McGwire	.60	.25	.07
□ 111 Troy Neel	.05	.02	.01
□ 112 Ruben Sierra	.05	.02	.01
□ 113 Terry Steinbach	.05	.02	.01
□ 114 Todd Van Poppel	.05	.02	.01
□ 115 Bob Welch	.05	.02	.01
□ 116 Bret Boone	.05	.02	.01
□ 117 Jay Buhner	.15	.07	.02
□ 118 Ken Griffey Jr.	2.00	.90	.25
□ 119 Randy Johnson	.30	.14	.04
□ 120 Rich Amaral	.05	.02	.01
□ 121 Edgar Martinez	.25	.11	.03
□ 122 Tino Martinez	.10	.05	.01
□ 123 Dave Valle	.05	.02	.01
□ 124 Omar Vizquel	.10	.05	.01
□ 125 Jose Canseco	.25	.11	.03
□ 126 Julio Franco	.10	.05	.01
□ 127 Juan Gonzalez	1.00	.45	.12
□ 128 Tom Henke	.05	.02	.01
□ 129 Manuel Lee	.05	.02	.01
□ 130 Rafael Palmeiro	.25	.11	.03
□ 131 Dean Palmer	.10	.05	.01
□ 132 Ivan Rodriguez	.50	.23	.06
□ 133 Doug Strange	.05	.02	.01
□ 134 Roberto Alomar	.50	.23	.06
□ 135 Pat Borders	.05	.02	.01
□ 136 Joe Carter	.10	.05	.01
□ 137 Tony Fernandez	.05	.02	.01
□ 138 Juan Guzman	.05	.02	.01
□ 139 Rickey Henderson	.25	.11	.03
□ 140 Paul Molitor	.50	.23	.06
□ 141 John Olerud	.10	.05	.01
□ 142 Devon White	.05	.02	.01
□ 143 Jeff Blauser	.05	.02	.01
□ 144 Ron Gant	.10	.05	.01
□ 145 Tom Glavine	.25	.11	.03
□ 146 Dave Justice	.25	.11	.03
□ 147 Greg Maddux	1.25	.55	.16
□ 148 Fred McGriff	.25	.11	.03
□ 149 Terry Pendleton	.05	.02	.01
□ 150 Deion Sanders	.30	.14	.04
□ 151 John Smoltz	.30	.14	.04
□ 152 Shawon Dunston	.05	.02	.01
□ 153 Mark Grace	.30	.14	.04
□ 154 Derrick May	.05	.02	.01
□ 155 Randy Myers	.05	.02	.01
□ 156 Ryne Sandberg	.50	.23	.06
□ 157 Dwight Smith	.05	.02	.01
□ 158 Sammy Sosa	.30	.14	.04
□ 159 Jose Vizcaino	.05	.02	.01
□ 160 Rick Wilkins	.05	.02	.01
□ 161 Tom Browning	.05	.02	.01
□ 162 Roberto Kelly	.05	.02	.01
□ 163 Barry Larkin	.25	.11	.03
□ 164 Kevin Mitchell	.05	.02	.01
□ 165 Hal Morris	.05	.02	.01
□ 166 Joe Oliver	.05	.02	.01
□ 167 Jose Rijo	.05	.02	.01
□ 168 Chris Sabo	.05	.02	.01
□ 169 Reggie Sanders	.10	.05	.01
□ 170 Freddie Benavides	.05	.02	.01
□ 171 Dante Bichette	.25	.11	.03
□ 172 Vinny Castilla	.15	.07	.02
□ 173 Jerald Clark	.05	.02	.01
□ 174 Andres Galarraga	.25	.11	.03
□ 175 Charlie Hayes	.05	.02	.01
□ 176 Chris Jones	.05	.02	.01
□ 177 Roberto Mejia	.05	.02	.01
□ 178 Eric Young	.10	.05	.01
□ 179 Bret Barberie	.05	.02	.01
□ 180 Chuck Carr	.05	.02	.01
□ 181 Jeff Conine	.25	.11	.03
□ 182 Orestes Destrade	.05	.02	.01
□ 183 Bryan Harvey	.05	.02	.01
□ 184 Rich Renteria	.05	.02	.01
□ 185 Benito Santiago	.05	.02	.01
□ 186 Gary Sheffield	.30	.14	.04
□ 187 Walt Weiss	.05	.02	.01
□ 188 Eric Anthony	.05	.02	.01
□ 189 Jeff Bagwell	1.00	.45	.12
□ 190 Craig Biggio	.10	.05	.01
□ 191 Ken Caminiti	.30	.14	.04
□ 192 Andujar Cedeno	.05	.02	.01
□ 193 Doug Drabek	.05	.02	.01
□ 194 Steve Finley	.15	.07	.02
□ 195 Doug Jones	.05	.02	.01
□ 196 Darryl Kile	.05	.02	.01
□ 197 Brett Butler	.10	.05	.01
□ 198 Tom Candiotti	.05	.02	.01
□ 199 Dave Hansen	.05	.02	.01
□ 200 Orel Hershiser	.10	.05	.01
□ 201 Eric Karros	.10	.05	.01
□ 202 Jose Offerman	.05	.02	.01
□ 203 Mike Piazza	1.25	.55	.16
□ 204 Cory Snyder	.05	.02	.01
□ 205 Darryl Strawberry	.10	.05	.01
□ 206 Moises Alou	.10	.05	.01
□ 207 Sean Berry	.05	.02	.01
□ 208 Wil Cordero	.05	.02	.01
□ 209 Delino DeShields	.05	.02	.01
□ 210 Marquis Grissom	.10	.05	.01
□ 211 Ken Hill	.05	.02	.01
□ 212 Mike Lansing	.05	.02	.01
□ 213 Larry Walker	.15	.07	.02
□ 214 John Wetteland	.10	.05	.01
□ 215 Bobby Bonilla	.10	.05	.01
□ 216 Jeromy Burnitz	.05	.02	.01
□ 217 Dwight Gooden	.10	.05	.01
□ 218 Todd Hundley	.10	.05	.01
□ 219 Howard Johnson	.05	.02	.01
□ 220 Jeff Kent	.05	.02	.01
□ 221 Eddie Murray	.50	.23	.06
□ 222 Bret Saberhagen	.10	.05	.01
□ 223 Ryan Thompson	.05	.02	.01
□ 224 Darren Daulton	.10	.05	.01
□ 225 Mariano Duncan	.05	.02	.01
□ 226 Lenny Dykstra	.10	.05	.01
□ 227 Jim Eisenreich	.10	.05	.01
□ 228 Dave Hollins	.05	.02	.01
□ 229 John Kruk	.10	.05	.01
□ 230 Curt Schilling	.05	.02	.01
□ 231 Kevin Stocker	.05	.02	.01
□ 232 Mitch Williams	.05	.02	.01
□ 233 Jay Bell	.05	.02	.01
□ 234 Steve Cooke	.05	.02	.01
□ 235 Carlos Garcia	.05	.02	.01
□ 236 Jeff King	.05	.02	.01
□ 237 Orlando Merced	.05	.02	.01
□ 238 Don Slaught	.05	.02	.01
□ 239 Zane Smith	.05	.02	.01
□ 240 Andy Van Slyke	.05	.02	.01
□ 241 Kevin Young	.05	.02	.01
□ 242 Bernard Gilkey	.10	.05	.01
□ 243 Gregg Jefferies	.10	.05	.01
□ 244 Brian Jordan	.15	.07	.02
□ 245 Ray Lankford	.10	.05	.01
□ 246 Tom Pagnozzi	.05	.02	.01
□ 247 Geronimo Perez	.05	.02	.01
□ 248 Ozzie Smith	.50	.23	.06
□ 249 Bob Tewksbury	.05	.02	.01
□ 250 Mark Whiten	.05	.02	.01
□ 251 Brad Ausmus	.05	.02	.01
□ 252 Derek Bell	.10	.05	.01
□ 253 Andy Benes	.10	.05	.01
□ 254 Phil Clark	.05	.02	.01
□ 255 Jeff Gardner	.05	.02	.01
□ 256 Tony Gwynn	.75	.35	.09
□ 257 Trevor Hoffman	.10	.05	.01
□ 258 Phil Plantier	.05	.02	.01
□ 259 Craig Shipley	.05	.02	.01
□ 260 Rod Beck	.05	.02	.01
□ 261 Barry Bonds	.60	.25	.07
□ 262 John Burkett	.05	.02	.01
□ 263 Will Clark	.20	.09	.03
□ 264 Royce Clayton	.05	.02	.01
□ 265 Willie McGee	.10	.05	.01
□ 266 Bill Swift	.05	.02	.01
□ 267 Robby Thompson	.05	.02	.01
□ 268 Matt Williams	.30	.14	.04

1995 Panini Stickers

This 156-sticker set measures approximately 1 15/16" by 3" and was distributed by Fleer. The fronts feature color action player photos framed in different colors on a white background. The player's name and team logo appear in a bar at the bottom. The backs carry the sponsor logos. The set closes with team logos (129-156).

	MINT	NRMT	EXC
COMPLETE SET (156)	20.00	9.00	2.50
COMMON STICKER (1-156)	.05	.02	.01

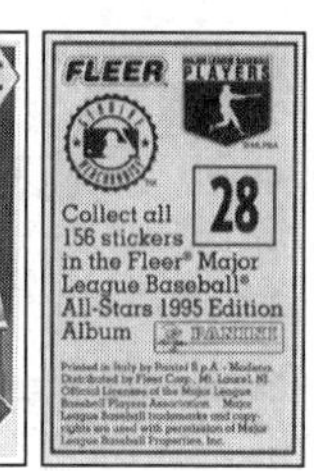

	MINT	NRMT	EXC
□ 1 Tom Glavine	.20	.09	.03
□ 2 Doug Drabek	.05	.02	.01
□ 3 Rod Beck	.05	.02	.01
□ 4 Pedro Martinez	.10	.05	.01
□ 5 Danny Jackson	.05	.02	.01
□ 6 Greg Maddux	1.75	.80	.22
□ 7 Bret Saberhagen	.10	.05	.01
□ 8 Ken Hill	.05	.02	.01
□ 9 Marvin Freeman	.05	.02	.01
□ 10 Andy Benes	.10	.05	.01
□ 11 Wilson Alvarez	.10	.05	.01
□ 12 Jimmy Key	.05	.02	.01
□ 13 Mike Mussina	.60	.25	.07
□ 14 Roger Clemens	.50	.23	.06
□ 15 Pat Hentgen	.25	.11	.03
□ 16 Randy Johnson	.30	.14	.04
□ 17 Lee Smith	.10	.05	.01
□ 18 David Cone	.10	.05	.01
□ 19 Jason Bere	.05	.02	.01
□ 20 Dennis Martinez	.10	.05	.01
□ 21 Darren Daulton	.10	.05	.01
□ 22 Darrin Fletcher	.05	.02	.01
□ 23 Tom Pagnozzi	.05	.02	.01
□ 24 Mike Piazza	1.50	.70	.19
□ 25 Benito Santiago	.05	.02	.01
□ 26 Sandy Alomar Jr.	.05	.02	.01
□ 27 Chris Hoiles	.05	.02	.01
□ 28 Ivan Rodriguez	.75	.35	.09
□ 29 Mike Stanley	.05	.02	.01
□ 30 Dave Nilsson	.05	.02	.01
□ 31 Jeff Bagwell	1.50	.70	.19
□ 32 Mark Grace	.40	.18	.05
□ 33 Gregg Jefferies	.10	.05	.01
□ 34 Andres Galarraga	.40	.18	.05
□ 35 Fred McGriff	.40	.18	.05
□ 36 Will Clark	.40	.18	.05
□ 37 Mo Vaughn	.75	.35	.09
□ 38 Don Mattingly	1.50	.70	.19
□ 39 Frank Thomas	3.00	1.35	.35
□ 40 Cecil Fielder	.10	.05	.01
□ 41 Robby Thompson	.05	.02	.01
□ 42 Delino DeShields	.05	.02	.01
□ 43 Carlos Garcia	.05	.02	.01
□ 44 Bret Boone	.05	.02	.01
□ 45 Craig Biggio	.10	.05	.01
□ 46 Roberto Alomar	.50	.23	.06
□ 47 Chuck Knoblauch	.60	.25	.07
□ 48 Jose Lind	.05	.02	.01
□ 49 Carlos Baerga	.30	.14	.04
□ 50 Lou Whitaker	.10	.05	.01
□ 51 Bobby Bonilla	.10	.05	.01
□ 52 Tim Wallach	.05	.02	.01
□ 53 Todd Zeile	.05	.02	.01
□ 54 Matt Williams	.40	.18	.05
□ 55 Ken Caminiti	.50	.23	.06
□ 56 Robin Ventura	.10	.05	.01
□ 57 Wade Boggs	.30	.14	.04
□ 58 Scott Cooper	.05	.02	.01
□ 59 Travis Fryman	.10	.05	.01
□ 60 Dean Palmer	.10	.05	.01
□ 61 Jay Bell	.05	.02	.01
□ 62 Barry Larkin	.35	.16	.04
□ 63 Ozzie Smith	.75	.35	.09
□ 64 Wil Cordero	.05	.02	.01
□ 65 Royce Clayton	.05	.02	.01
□ 66 Chris Gomez	.05	.02	.01
□ 67 Ozzie Guillen	.05	.02	.01
□ 68 Cal Ripken Jr.	2.50	1.10	.30
□ 69 Omar Vizquel	.10	.05	.01
□ 70 Gary DiSarcina	.05	.02	.01
□ 71 Dante Bichette	.35	.16	.04
□ 72 Lenny Dykstra	.10	.05	.01
□ 73 Barry Bonds	.60	.25	.07
□ 74 Gary Sheffield	.50	.23	.06
□ 75 Larry Walker	.20	.09	.03
□ 76 Raul Mondesi	.60	.25	.07
□ 77 Dave Justice	.25	.11	.03
□ 78 Moises Alou	.10	.05	.01
□ 79 Tony Gwynn	1.25	.55	.16
□ 80 Deion Sanders	.40	.18	.05
□ 81 Kenny Lofton	.75	.35	.09
□ 82 Kirby Puckett	1.50	.70	.19
□ 83 Juan Gonzalez	1.50	.70	.19
□ 84 Jay Buhner	.20	.09	.03
□ 85 Joe Carter	.10	.05	.01
□ 86 Ken Griffey Jr.	3.00	1.35	.35
□ 87 Ruben Sierra	.05	.02	.01
□ 88 Tim Salmon	.50	.23	.06
□ 89 Paul O'Neill	.10	.05	.01
□ 90 Albert Belle	1.50	.70	.19
□ 91 Danny Tartabull	.05	.02	.01
□ 92 Jose Canseco	.35	.16	.04

☐ 93 Harold Baines .10 .05 .01
☐ 94 Kirk Gibson .10 .05 .01
☐ 95 Chili Davis .10 .05 .01
☐ 96 Eddie Murray .75 .35 .09
☐ 97 Bob Hamelin .05 .02 .01
☐ 98 Paul Molitor .75 .35 .09
☐ 99 Raul Mondesi .60 .25 .07
☐ 100 Ryan Klesko .50 .23 .06
☐ 101 Cliff Floyd .05 .02 .01
☐ 102 William VanLandingham .05 .02 .01
☐ 103 Joey Hamilton .20 .09 .03
☐ 104 John Hudek .05 .02 .01
☐ 105 Manny Ramirez .75 .35 .09
☐ 106 Bob Hamelin .05 .02 .01
☐ 107 Rusty Greer .50 .23 .06
☐ 108 Chris Gomez .05 .02 .01
☐ 109 Greg Maddux 1.75 .80 .22
☐ 110 Jeff Bagwell 1.50 .70 .19
☐ 111 Raul Mondesi .60 .25 .07
☐ 112 David Cone .10 .05 .01
☐ 113 Frank Thomas 1.75 .80 .22
☐ 114 Bob Hamelin .05 .02 .01
☐ 115 Tony Gwynn 1.25 .55 .16
☐ 116 Matt Williams .40 .18 .05
☐ 117 Jeff Bagwell 1.50 .70 .19
☐ 118 Craig Biggio .10 .05 .01
☐ 119 Andy Benes .10 .05 .01
☐ 120 Greg Maddux 1.75 .80 .22
☐ 121 John Franco .10 .05 .01
☐ 122 Paul O'Neill .10 .05 .01
☐ 123 Ken Griffey Jr. 3.00 1.35 .35
☐ 124 Kirby Puckett 1.50 .70 .19
☐ 125 Kenny Lofton .75 .35 .09
☐ 126 Randy Johnson .30 .14 .04
☐ 127 Jimmy Key .05 .02 .01
☐ 128 Lee Smith .10 .05 .01
☐ 129 San Francisco Giants .05 .02 .01
☐ 130 Montreal Expos .05 .02 .01
☐ 131 Cincinnati Reds .05 .02 .01
☐ 132 Los Angeles Dodgers .05 .02 .01
☐ 133 New York Mets .05 .02 .01
☐ 134 San Diego Padres .05 .02 .01
☐ 135 Colorado Rockies .05 .02 .01
☐ 136 Pittsburgh Pirates .05 .02 .01
☐ 137 Florida Marlins .05 .02 .01
☐ 138 Philadelphia Phillies .05 .02 .01
☐ 139 Atlanta Braves .05 .02 .01
☐ 140 Houston Astros .05 .02 .01
☐ 141 St. Louis Cardinals .05 .02 .01
☐ 142 Chicago Cubs .05 .02 .01
☐ 143 Cleveland Indians .05 .02 .01
☐ 144 New York Yankees .05 .02 .01
☐ 145 Kansas City Royals .05 .02 .01
☐ 146 Chicago White Sox .05 .02 .01
☐ 147 Baltimore Orioles .05 .02 .01
☐ 148 Seattle Mariners .05 .02 .01
☐ 149 Boston Red Sox .05 .02 .01
☐ 150 California Angels .05 .02 .01
☐ 151 Toronto Blue Jays .05 .02 .01
☐ 152 Detroit Tigers .05 .02 .01
☐ 153 Texas Rangers .05 .02 .01
☐ 154 Oakland Athletics .05 .02 .01
☐ 155 Milwaukee Brewers .05 .02 .01
☐ 156 Minnesota Twins .05 .02 .01

1996 Panini Stickers

This 246-sticker set was distributed as a complete set in a cellophane wrapper with a suggested retail price of $8. A 60-page album to hold the stickers was included with the set. The stickers feature color action player photos with the same lighter image in the background inside a green border. Player information and statistics are found in the album below each sticker. Stickers to finish ones set were available from the Panini Missing Sticker Club at a cost of $4 for 20 different stickers or $4 for 30 stickers as long as 10 wrappers were sent as well.

	MINT	NRMT	EXC
COMPLETE SET (246)	12.00	5.50	1.50
COMMON CARD (1-246)	.05	.02	.01

☐ 1 David Justice .15 .07 .02
☐ 2 Tom Glavine .15 .07 .02
☐ 3 Javier Lopez .05 .02 .01
☐ 4 Greg Maddux .60 .25 .07
☐ 5 Marquis Grissom .10 .05 .01
☐ 6 Atlanta Braves Team Logo .05 .02 .01
☐ 7 Ryan Klesko .20 .09 .03
☐ 8 Chipper Jones .60 .25 .07
☐ 9 Quilvio Veras .05 .02 .01
☐ 10 Chris Hammond .05 .02 .01
☐ 11 Charles Johnson .10 .05 .01
☐ 12 John Burkett .05 .02 .01
☐ 13 Florida Marlins Team Logo .05 .02 .01
☐ 14 Jeff Conine .10 .05 .01
☐ 15 Gary Sheffield .15 .07 .02
☐ 16 Greg Colbrunn .05 .02 .01
☐ 17 Moises Alou .10 .05 .01
☐ 18 Pedro Martinez .10 .05 .01
☐ 19 Rondell White .10 .05 .01
☐ 20 Tony Tarasco .05 .02 .01
☐ 21 Montreal Expos Team Logo .05 .02 .01
☐ 22 Carlos Perez .05 .02 .01
☐ 23 David Segui .05 .02 .01
☐ 24 Wil Cordero .05 .02 .01
☐ 25 Jason Isringhausen .15 .07 .02
☐ 26 Rico Brogna .05 .02 .01
☐ 27 Edgardo Alfonzo .05 .02 .01
☐ 28 Todd Hundley .10 .05 .01
☐ 29 New York Mets Team Logo .05 .02 .01
☐ 30 Bill Pulsipher .05 .02 .01
☐ 31 Carl Everett .05 .02 .01
☐ 32 Jose Vizcaino .05 .02 .01
☐ 33 Lenny Dykstra .10 .05 .01
☐ 34 Charlie Hayes .05 .02 .01
☐ 35 Heathcliff Slocumb .05 .02 .01
☐ 36 Darren Daulton .10 .05 .01
☐ 37 Philadelphia Phillies Team Logo .05 .02 .01
☐ 38 Mickey Morandini .05 .02 .01
☐ 39 Gregg Jefferies .10 .05 .01
☐ 40 Jim Eisenreich .10 .05 .01
☐ 41 Brian McRae .05 .02 .01
☐ 42 Luis Gonzalez .05 .02 .01
☐ 43 Randy Myers .05 .02 .01
☐ 44 Shawon Dunston .05 .02 .01
☐ 45 Chicago Cubs Team Logo .05 .02 .01
☐ 46 Jaime Navarro .05 .02 .01
☐ 47 Mark Grace .20 .09 .03
☐ 48 Sammy Sosa .20 .09 .03
☐ 49 Barry Larkin .20 .09 .03
☐ 50 Pete Schourek .05 .02 .01
☐ 51 John Smiley .05 .02 .01
☐ 52 Reggie Sanders .10 .05 .01
☐ 53 Cincinnati Reds Team Logo .05 .02 .01
☐ 54 Hal Morris .05 .02 .01
☐ 55 Ron Gant .10 .05 .01
☐ 56 Bret Boone .05 .02 .01
☐ 57 Craig Biggio .10 .05 .01
☐ 58 Brian Hunter .05 .02 .01
☐ 59 Jeff Bagwell .50 .23 .06
☐ 60 Shane Reynolds .05 .02 .01
☐ 61 Houston Astros Team Logo .05 .02 .01
☐ 62 Derek Bell .10 .05 .01
☐ 63 Doug Drabek .05 .02 .01
☐ 64 Orlando Miller .05 .02 .01
☐ 65 Jay Bell .05 .02 .01
☐ 66 Dan Miceli .05 .02 .01
☐ 67 Orlando Merced .05 .02 .01
☐ 68 Jeff King .05 .02 .01
☐ 69 Carlos Garcia .05 .02 .01
☐ 70 Pittsburgh Pirates Team Logo .05 .02 .01
☐ 71 Al Martin .05 .02 .01
☐ 72 Denny Neagle .05 .02 .01
☐ 73 Ray Lankford .10 .05 .01
☐ 74 Ozzie Smith .25 .11 .03
☐ 75 Bernard Gilkey .05 .02 .01
☐ 76 John Mabry .10 .05 .01
☐ 77 St. Louis Cardinals Team Logo .05 .02 .01
☐ 78 Brian Jordan .10 .05 .01
☐ 79 Scott Cooper .05 .02 .01
☐ 80 Allen Watson .05 .02 .01
☐ 81 Dante Bichette .15 .07 .02
☐ 82 Bret Saberhagen .05 .02 .01
☐ 83 Walt Weiss .05 .02 .01
☐ 84 Andres Galarraga .15 .07 .02
☐ 85 Colorado Rockies Team Logo .05 .02 .01
☐ 86 Larry Walker .15 .07 .02
☐ 87 Bill Swift .05 .02 .01
☐ 88 Vinny Castilla .10 .05 .01
☐ 89 Raul Mondesi .15 .07 .02
☐ 90 Roger Cedeno .05 .02 .01
☐ 91 Chad Fonville .05 .02 .01
☐ 92 Hideo Nomo .50 .23 .06
☐ 93 Los Angeles Dodgers Team Logo .05 .02 .01
☐ 94 Ramon Martinez .10 .05 .01
☐ 95 Mike Piazza .60 .25 .07
☐ 96 Eric Karros .10 .05 .01
☐ 97 Tony Gwynn .40 .18 .05
☐ 98 Brad Ausmus .05 .02 .01
☐ 99 Trevor Hoffman .05 .02 .01
☐ 100 Ken Caminiti .15 .07 .02
☐ 101 San Diego Padres Team Logo .05 .02 .01
☐ 102 Andy Ashby .05 .02 .01
☐ 103 Steve Finley .15 .07 .02
☐ 104 Joey Hamilton .10 .05 .01
☐ 105 Matt Williams .15 .07 .02
☐ 106 Rod Beck .05 .02 .01
☐ 107 Barry Bonds .25 .11 .03
☐ 108 William VanLandingham .05 .02 .01
☐ 109 San Francisco Giants Team Logo .05 .02 .01
☐ 110 Deion Sanders .20 .09 .03
☐ 111 Royce Clayton .05 .02 .01
☐ 112 Glenallen Hill .05 .02 .01
☐ 113 Tony Gwynn .40 .18 .05
☐ 114 Dante Bichette .15 .07 .02
☐ 115 Dante Bichette .15 .07 .02
☐ 116 Quilvio Veras .05 .02 .01
☐ 117 Hideo Nomo .50 .23 .06
☐ 118 Greg Maddux .60 .25 .07
☐ 119 Randy Myers .05 .02 .01
☐ 120 Edgar Martinez .10 .05 .01
☐ 121 Albert Belle .50 .23 .06
☐ 122 Mo Vaughn .25 .11 .03
☐ 123 Kenny Lofton .25 .11 .03
☐ 124 Randy Johnson .15 .07 .02
☐ 125 Mike Mussina .20 .09 .03
☐ 126 Jose Mesa .05 .02 .01
☐ 127 Mike Mussina .20 .09 .03
☐ 128 Cal Ripken Jr. .75 .35 .09
☐ 129 Rafael Palmeiro .15 .07 .02
☐ 130 Ben McDonald .05 .02 .01
☐ 131 Baltimore Orioles Team Logo .05 .02 .01
☐ 132 Chris Hoiles .05 .02 .01
☐ 133 Bobby Bonilla .10 .05 .01
☐ 134 Brady Anderson .15 .07 .02
☐ 135 Jose Canseco .15 .07 .02
☐ 136 Roger Clemens .15 .07 .02
☐ 137 Mo Vaughn .25 .11 .03
☐ 138 Mike Greenwell .05 .02 .01
☐ 139 Boston Red Sox Team Logo .05 .02 .01
☐ 140 Tim Wakefield .05 .02 .01
☐ 141 John Valentin .05 .02 .01
☐ 142 Tim Naehring .05 .02 .01
☐ 143 Travis Fryman .10 .05 .01
☐ 144 Chad Curtis .05 .02 .01
☐ 145 Felipe Lira .05 .02 .01
☐ 146 Cecil Fielder .10 .05 .01
☐ 147 Detroit Tigers Team Logo .05 .02 .01
☐ 148 John Flaherty .05 .02 .01
☐ 149 Chris Gomez .05 .02 .01
☐ 150 Sean Bergman .05 .02 .01
☐ 151 Don Mattingly .50 .23 .06
☐ 152 Andy Pettitte .40 .18 .05
☐ 153 Wade Boggs .15 .07 .02
☐ 154 Paul O'Neill .05 .02 .01
☐ 155 New York Yankees Team Logo .05 .02 .01
☐ 156 Bernie Williams .20 .09 .03
☐ 157 Jack McDowell .10 .05 .01
☐ 158 David Cone .10 .05 .01
☐ 159 Roberto Alomar .25 .11 .03
☐ 160 Paul Molitor .25 .11 .03
☐ 161 Shawn Green .05 .02 .01
☐ 162 Joe Carter .10 .05 .01
☐ 163 Toronto Blue Jays Team Logo .05 .02 .01
☐ 164 Alex Gonzalez .05 .02 .01
☐ 165 Al Leiter .05 .02 .01
☐ 166 John Olerud .10 .05 .01
☐ 167 Alex Fernandez .10 .05 .01
☐ 168 Ray Durham .10 .05 .01
☐ 169 Lance Johnson .10 .05 .01
☐ 170 Ozzie Guillen .05 .02 .01
☐ 171 Chicago White Sox Team Logo .05 .02 .01
☐ 172 Robin Ventura .10 .05 .01
☐ 173 Frank Thomas 1.00 .45 .12
☐ 174 Tim Raines .10 .05 .01
☐ 175 Albert Belle .50 .23 .06
☐ 176 Manny Ramirez .25 .11 .03
☐ 177 Eddie Murray .25 .11 .03
☐ 178 Orel Hershiser .10 .05 .01
☐ 179 Cleveland Indians Team Logo .05 .02 .01
☐ 180 Kenny Lofton .25 .11 .03
☐ 181 Carlos Baerga .10 .05 .01
☐ 182 Jose Mesa .05 .02 .01
☐ 183 Gary Gaetti .10 .05 .01
☐ 184 Tom Goodwin .05 .02 .01
☐ 185 Kevin Appier .10 .05 .01
☐ 186 Jon Nunnally .05 .02 .01
☐ 187 Kansas City Royals Team Logo .05 .02 .01
☐ 188 Wally Joyner .05 .02 .01
☐ 189 Jeff Montgomery .05 .02 .01
☐ 190 Johnny Damon .10 .05 .01
☐ 191 B.J. Surhoff .10 .05 .01
☐ 192 Ricky Bones .05 .02 .01
☐ 193 John Jaha .10 .05 .01
☐ 194 Dave Nilsson .05 .02 .01
☐ 195 Milwaukee Brewers Team Logo .05 .02 .01
☐ 196 Greg Vaughn .05 .02 .01
☐ 197 Kevin Seitzer .05 .02 .01
☐ 198 Joe Oliver .05 .02 .01
☐ 199 Chuck Knoblauch .15 .07 .02
☐ 200 Kirby Puckett .50 .23 .06
☐ 201 Marty Cordova .10 .05 .01
☐ 202 Pat Meares .05 .02 .01
☐ 203 Minnesota Twins Team Logo .05 .02 .01
☐ 204 Scott Stahoviak .05 .02 .01
☐ 205 Matt Walbeck .05 .02 .01
☐ 206 Pedro Munoz .05 .02 .01
☐ 207 Garret Anderson .10 .05 .01
☐ 208 Chili Davis .05 .02 .01
☐ 209 Tim Salmon .15 .07 .02
☐ 210 J.T. Snow .05 .02 .01
☐ 211 California Angels Team Logo .05 .02 .01
☐ 212 Jim Edmonds .10 .05 .01
☐ 213 Chuck Finley .05 .02 .01
☐ 214 Mark Langston .05 .02 .01
☐ 215 Dennis Eckersley .10 .05 .01
☐ 216 Todd Stottlemyre .05 .02 .01
☐ 217 Geronimo Berroa .05 .02 .01
☐ 218 Mark McGwire .30 .14 .04
☐ 219 Oakland A's Team Logo .05 .02 .01
☐ 220 Brent Gates .05 .02 .01
☐ 221 Terry Steinbach .10 .05 .01
☐ 222 Rickey Henderson .15 .07 .02
☐ 223 Ken Griffey Jr. 1.00 .45 .12
☐ 224 Alex Rodriguez 1.00 .45 .12
☐ 225 Tino Martinez .10 .05 .01
☐ 226 Randy Johnson .15 .07 .02
☐ 227 Seattle Mariners Team Logo .05 .02 .01
☐ 228 Jay Buhner .15 .07 .02
☐ 229 Vince Coleman .05 .02 .01
☐ 230 Edgar Martinez .10 .05 .01
☐ 231 Will Clark .15 .07 .02
☐ 232 Juan Gonzalez .50 .23 .06
☐ 233 Kenny Rogers .05 .02 .01
☐ 234 Ivan Rodriguez .20 .09 .03
☐ 235 Texas Rangers Team Logo .05 .02 .01
☐ 236 Mickey Tettleton .05 .02 .01
☐ 237 Dean Palmer .10 .05 .01
☐ 238 Otis Nixon .05 .02 .01
☐ 239 Hideo Nomo .50 .23 .06
☐ 240 Quilvio Veras .05 .02 .01
☐ 241 Jason Isringhausen .15 .07 .02
☐ 242 Andy Pettitte .40 .18 .05
☐ 243 Chipper Jones .60 .25 .07
☐ 244 Garret Anderson .10 .05 .01
☐ 245 Charles Johnson .10 .05 .01
☐ 246 Marty Cordova .10 .05 .01

1989 PAO Religious Tracts

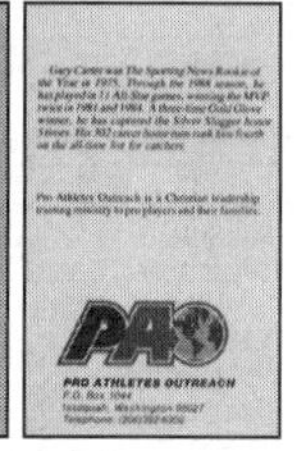

This four-card set features color player photos on a 4 1/8" by 7 5/8" tri-fold card and was distributed by Pro Athletes Outreach, a Christian leadership training ministry to pro players and their families. The front fold displays the player photo with player stories and religious messages printed on the rest of the card. The cards are unnumbered and checklisted below in alphabetical order.

	MINT	NRMT	EXC
COMPLETE SET (4)	6.00	2.70	.75
COMMON CARD (1-4)	1.00	.45	.12

☐ 1 Gary Carter 4.00 1.80 .50
☐ 2 Alvin Davis 2.00 .90 .25
☐ 3 Mike Moore 1.00 .45 .12
☐ 4 Frank Pastore 1.00 .45 .12

1978 Papa Gino's Discs

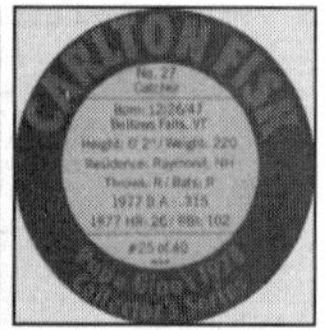

This 40-disc set consists of all American League players with more than half the set being Boston Red Sox players. Papa Gino's was a chain of restaurants located throughout central New England.The discs are 3 3/8" in diameter and have a distinctive thick dark blue border on the front with orange printing. The set was approved by the Major League Baseball Players Association under the auspices of Mike Schechter Associates (MSA) and as such has team logos airbrushed away. The discs are numbered on the back at the bottom; the uniform number is also given at the top of the reverse. The first 25 players in the set are members of the Boston Red Sox. Supposedly eight discs were printed in smaller quantities; these short printed discs are marked SP in the checklist below.

	NRMT	VG-E	GOOD
COMPLETE SET (40)	35.00	16.00	4.40
COMMON DISC (1-40)	.50	.23	.06

☐ 1 Allen Ripley .50 .23 .06
☐ 2 Jerry Remy .50 .23 .06
☐ 3 Jack Brohamer .50 .23 .06
☐ 4 Butch Hobson .50 .23 .06
☐ 5 Dennis Eckersley 3.00 1.35 .35
☐ 6 Sam Bowen SP 1.00 .45 .12
☐ 7 Rick Burleson .50 .23 .06
☐ 8 Carl Yastrzemski 4.00 1.80 .50
☐ 9 Bill Lee 1.00 .45 .12
☐ 10 Bob Montgomery .50 .23 .06
☐ 11 Dick Drago SP 1.00 .45 .12
☐ 12 Bob Stanley SP 1.00 .45 .12
☐ 13 Fred Kendall SP 1.00 .45 .12
☐ 14 Jim Rice SP 3.00 1.35 .35
☐ 15 George Scott 1.00 .45 .12
☐ 16 Tom Burgmeier .50 .23 .06
☐ 17 Frank Duffy SP 1.00 .45 .12
☐ 18 Jim Wright .50 .23 .06
☐ 19 Fred Lynn 1.00 .45 .12

☐ 20 Bob Bailey SP	1.00	.45	.12
☐ 21 Mike Torrez	.50	.23	.06
☐ 22 Bill Campbell SP	1.00	.45	.12
☐ 23 Luis Tiant	2.00	.90	.25
☐ 24 Dwight Evans	2.00	.90	.25
☐ 25 Carlton Fisk	3.00	1.35	.35
☐ 26 Reggie Jackson	4.00	1.80	.50
☐ 27 Thurman Munson	3.00	1.35	.35
☐ 28 Ron Guidry	2.00	.90	.25
☐ 29 Bruce Bochte	.50	.23	.06
☐ 30 Richie Zisk	.50	.23	.06
☐ 31 Jim Palmer	3.00	1.35	.35
☐ 32 Mark Fidrych	2.50	1.10	.30
☐ 33 Frank Tanana	1.00	.45	.12
☐ 34 Buddy Bell	1.00	.45	.12
☐ 35 Rod Carew	3.00	1.35	.35
☐ 36 George Brett	7.50	3.40	.95
☐ 37 Ralph Garr	.50	.23	.06
☐ 38 Larry Hisle	.50	.23	.06
☐ 39 Mitchell Page	.50	.23	.06
☐ 40 John Mayberry	.50	.23	.06

1910-14 People's T216

The cards in this 59-player set measure 1 1/2" by 2 5/8" and contains unnumbered cards. The players have been alphabetized and numbered for reference in the checklist below. The complete set price references only one of each player. Back variations within this set include Kotton, Mino and Virginia Cigarettes.

	EX-MT	VG-E	GOOD
COMPLETE SET (59)	18000.00	8100.00	2200.00
COMMON CARD	80.00	36.00	10.00
☐ 1A Jack Barry Fielding	80.00	36.00	10.00
☐ 1B Jack Barry Fielding	80.00	36.00	10.00
☐ 2 Harry Bemis	80.00	36.00	10.00
☐ 3A Chief Bender Striped Cap Phila Am.	200.00	90.00	25.00
☐ 3B Chief Bender Striped Cap Baltimore Fed	200.00	90.00	25.00
☐ 3C Chief Bender White Cap Phila Am.	200.00	90.00	25.00
☐ 3D Chief Bender White Cap Baltimore Fed	200.00	90.00	25.00
☐ 4 Bill Bergen	80.00	36.00	10.00
☐ 5A Bob Bescher Cincinnati	80.00	36.00	10.00
☐ 5B Bob Bescher St. Louis Fed	80.00	36.00	10.00
☐ 6 Roger Bresnahan	200.00	90.00	25.00
☐ 7A Al Bridwell batting	80.00	36.00	10.00
☐ 7B Al Bridwell Sliding New York Nat'l	80.00	36.00	10.00
☐ 7C Al Bridwell Sliding@(St. Louis Feds	80.00	36.00	10.00
☐ 8 Donie Bush	200.00	90.00	25.00
☐ 9 Doc Casey	80.00	36.00	10.00
☐ 10 Frank Chance	300.00	135.00	38.00
☐ 11A Hal Chase Portrait	160.00	70.00	20.00
☐ 11B Hal Chase Fielding New York Am.	160.00	70.00	20.00
☐ 11C Hal Chase Fielding Buffalo	160.00	70.00	20.00
☐ 12A Ty Cobb Standing Detroit Am.	1800.00	800.00	220.00
☐ 12B Ty Cobb Standing Detroit Americans	1800.00	800.00	220.00
☐ 12C Ty Cobb batting	1800.00	800.00	220.00
☐ 13 Sam Crawford	200.00	90.00	25.00
☐ 13A Eddie Collins Philadelphia Amer.	200.00	90.00	25.00
☐ 13B Eddie Collins Phila Am.	200.00	90.00	25.00
☐ 13C Eddie Collins Chicago Americans	200.00	90.00	25.00
☐ 14 Harry Davis	80.00	36.00	10.00
☐ 15 Ray Demmitt	80.00	36.00	10.00
☐ 17A Bill Donovan Detroit Amer.	80.00	36.00	10.00
☐ 17B Bill Donovan N.Y. Americans	80.00	36.00	10.00
☐ 18A Red Dooin Phila Nat.	80.00	36.00	10.00
☐ 18B Red Dooin Cincinnati	80.00	36.00	10.00
☐ 19A Mickey Doolan Phila Nat.	80.00	36.00	10.00
☐ 19B Mickey Doolan Baltimore Fed.	80.00	36.00	10.00
☐ 20 Patsy Dougherty	80.00	36.00	10.00
☐ 21A Larry Doyle N.Y. Nat'l	80.00	36.00	10.00
☐ 21B Larry Doyle New York Nat'l	80.00	36.00	10.00
☐ 21C Larry Doyle Throwing	80.00	36.00	10.00
☐ 22 Clyde Engle	80.00	36.00	10.00
☐ 23A Johnny Evers Chicago Nat'l	200.00	90.00	25.00
☐ 23B Johnny Evers Boston National	200.00	90.00	25.00
☐ 24 Art Fromme	80.00	36.00	10.00
☐ 25A George Gibson Back Pittsburg Nat'l	80.00	36.00	10.00
☐ 25B George Gibson Back Pittsburgh Nat'l.	80.00	36.00	10.00
☐ 25C George Gibson Front Pittsburg Nat'l	80.00	36.00	10.00
☐ 25D George Gibson Front Pittsburgh Nat'l	80.00	36.00	10.00
☐ 26A Topsy Hartsel Phila Am.	80.00	36.00	10.00
☐ 26B Topsy Hartsel Philadelphia Amer.	80.00	36.00	10.00
☐ 27A Roy Hartzell Catching	80.00	36.00	10.00
☐ 27B Roy Hartzell Batting	80.00	36.00	10.00
☐ 28A Fred Jacklitsch Phila Nat.	80.00	36.00	10.00
☐ 28B Fred Jacklitsch Baltimore Feds	80.00	36.00	10.00
☐ 29A Hugh Jennings Dance: Red	200.00	90.00	25.00
☐ 29B Hugh Jennings Dance; Orange	200.00	90.00	25.00
☐ 30 Red Kleinow	80.00	36.00	10.00
☐ 31A Otto Knabe Phila Nat.	80.00	36.00	10.00
☐ 31B Otto Knabe Baltimore Fed.	80.00	36.00	10.00
☐ 32 John Knight	80.00	36.00	10.00
☐ 33A Nap Lajoie Portrait	400.00	180.00	50.00
☐ 33B Nap Lajoie Fielding Cleveland	400.00	180.00	50.00
☐ 33C Nap Lajoie Fielding Phila Amer.	400.00	180.00	50.00
☐ 34A Hans Lobert Cincinnati	200.00	90.00	25.00
☐ 34B Hans Lobert New York Nat'l	200.00	90.00	25.00
☐ 35 Sherry Magee	80.00	36.00	10.00
☐ 36 Rube Marquard	200.00	90.00	25.00
☐ 37A Christy Mathewson Small Print	500.00	220.00	60.00
☐ 37B Christy Mathewson Large Print	500.00	220.00	60.00
☐ 38A John McGraw MG Small Print	300.00	135.00	38.00
☐ 38B John McGraw MG Large Print	300.00	135.00	38.00
☐ 39 Larry McLean	80.00	36.00	10.00
☐ 40 George McQuillan	80.00	36.00	10.00
☐ 41A Dots Miller Batting	80.00	36.00	10.00
☐ 41B Dots Miller Fielding Pittsburg	80.00	36.00	10.00
☐ 41C Dots Miller Fielding St. Louis Nat'l	80.00	36.00	10.00
☐ 42A Danny Murphy Phila Amer.	80.00	36.00	10.00
☐ 42B Danny Murphy Brooklyn Feds.	80.00	36.00	10.00
☐ 43 Rebel Oakes	80.00	36.00	10.00
☐ 44 Bill O'Hara	80.00	36.00	10.00
☐ 45 Eddie Plank	200.00	90.00	25.00
☐ 46A Germany Schaefer Washington	80.00	36.00	10.00
☐ 46B Germany Schaefer Newark Fed.	80.00	36.00	10.00
☐ 47 Admiral Schlei	80.00	36.00	10.00
☐ 48 Boss Schmidt	80.00	36.00	10.00
☐ 49 Dave Shean	80.00	36.00	10.00
☐ 50 Johnny Siegle	80.00	36.00	10.00
☐ 51 Tris Speaker	400.00	180.00	50.00
☐ 52 Oscar Stanage	80.00	36.00	10.00
☐ 53 George Stovall	80.00	36.00	10.00
☐ 54 Ed Sweeney	80.00	36.00	10.00
☐ 55A Joe Tinker Portrait	200.00	90.00	25.00
☐ 55B Joe Tinker Batting Chicago Nat'l	200.00	90.00	25.00
☐ 55C Joe Tinker Batting Chicago Feds	200.00	90.00	25.00
☐ 56A Honus Wagner Batting Pittsburg Nat'l	700.00	325.00	90.00
☐ 56B Honus Wagner Batting Pittsburgh Nat'l	700.00	325.00	90.00
☐ 56C Honus Wagner Throwing S.S	700.00	325.00	90.00
☐ 56D Honus Wagner Throwing #2b	700.00	325.00	90.00
☐ 57 Hooks Wiltse	80.00	36.00	10.00
☐ 58 Cy Young	400.00	180.00	50.00
☐ 59A Heinie Zimmerman 2B	80.00	36.00	10.00
☐ 59B Heinie Zimmerman 3B	80.00	36.00	10.00

1977 Pepsi Glove Discs

These discs actually form the middle of a glove-shaped tab which was inserted in cartons of Pepsi-Cola during a baseball related promotion. The disc itself measures 3 3/8" in diameter whereas the glove tab is approximately 9" tall. The backs of the discs and the tab tell how you can get a personalized superstar shirt of Pete Rose, Rico Carty, Joe Morgan, or Rick Manning by sending in Pepsi cap liners. The players are shown in "generic" hats, i.e., the team logos have been airbrushed. This set was sanctioned by the Major League Baseball Players Association. The set is quite heavy in Cleveland Indians and Cincinnati Reds.

	NRMT	VG-E	GOOD
COMPLETE SET (72)	60.00	27.00	7.50
COMMON DISC (1-72)	.25	.11	.03
☐ 1 Robin Yount	5.00	2.20	.60
☐ 2 Rod Carew	5.00	2.20	.60
☐ 3 Butch Wynegar	.25	.11	.03
☐ 4 Manny Sanguillen	.25	.11	.03
☐ 5 Mike Hargrove	.50	.23	.06
☐ 6 Larvell Blanks	.25	.11	.03
☐ 7 Jim Kern	.25	.11	.03
☐ 8 Pat Dobson	.25	.11	.03
☐ 9 Rico Carty	.25	.11	.03
☐ 10 John Grubb	.25	.11	.03
☐ 11 Buddy Bell	.50	.23	.06
☐ 12 Rick Manning	.25	.11	.03
☐ 13 Dennis Eckersley	3.00	1.35	.35
☐ 14 Wayne Garland	.25	.11	.03
☐ 15 Dave Laroche	.25	.11	.03
☐ 16 Rick Waits	.25	.11	.03
☐ 17 Ray Fosse	.25	.11	.03
☐ 18 Frank Duffy	.25	.11	.03
☐ 19 Duane Kuiper	.25	.11	.03
☐ 20 Jim Palmer	5.00	2.20	.60
☐ 21 Fred Lynn	.50	.23	.06
☐ 22 Carlton Fisk	5.00	2.20	.60
☐ 23 Carl Yastrzemski	5.00	2.20	.60
☐ 24 Nolan Ryan	10.00	4.50	1.25
☐ 25 Bobby Grich	.50	.23	.06
☐ 26 Ralph Garr	.25	.11	.03
☐ 27 Richie Zisk	.25	.11	.03
☐ 28 Ron LeFlore	.25	.11	.03
☐ 29 Rusty Staub	1.00	.45	.12
☐ 30 Mark Fidrych	2.50	1.10	.30
☐ 31 Willie Horton	.50	.23	.06
☐ 32 George Brett	10.00	4.50	1.25
☐ 33 Amos Otis	.25	.11	.03
☐ 34 Reggie Jackson	5.00	2.20	.60
☐ 35 Don Gullett	.25	.11	.03
☐ 36 Thurman Munson	1.50	.70	.19
☐ 37 Al Hrabosky	.25	.11	.03
☐ 38 Mike Tyson	.25	.11	.03
☐ 39 Gene Tenace	.50	.23	.06
☐ 40 George Hendrick	.25	.11	.03
☐ 41 Chris Speier	.25	.11	.03
☐ 42 John Montefusco	.25	.11	.03
☐ 43 Pete Rose	5.00	2.20	.60
☐ 44 Johnny Bench	5.00	2.20	.60
☐ 45 Dan Driessen	.25	.11	.03
☐ 46 Joe Morgan	3.00	1.35	.35
☐ 47 Dave Concepcion	1.00	.45	.12
☐ 48 George Foster	1.00	.45	.12
☐ 49 Cesar Geronimo	.25	.11	.03
☐ 50 Ken Griffey	1.00	.45	.12
☐ 51 Gary Nolan	.25	.11	.03
☐ 52 Santo Alcala	.25	.11	.03
☐ 53 Jack Billingham	.25	.11	.03
☐ 54 Pedro Borbon	.25	.11	.03
☐ 55 Rawly Eastwick	.25	.11	.03
☐ 56 Fred Norman	.25	.11	.03
☐ 57 Pat Zachry	.25	.11	.03
☐ 58 Jeff Burroughs	.25	.11	.03
☐ 59 Manny Trillo	.25	.11	.03
☐ 60 Bob Watson	1.00	.45	.12
☐ 61 Steve Garvey	1.50	.70	.19
☐ 62 Don Sutton	3.00	1.35	.35
☐ 63 John Candelaria	.25	.11	.03
☐ 64 Willie Stargell	3.00	1.35	.35
☐ 65 Jerry Reuss	.25	.11	.03
☐ 66 Dave Cash	.25	.11	.03
☐ 67 Tom Seaver	5.00	2.20	.60
☐ 68 Jon Matlack	.25	.11	.03
☐ 69 Dave Kingman	1.50	.70	.19
☐ 70 Mike Schmidt	5.00	2.20	.60
☐ 71 Jay Johnstone	1.00	.45	.12
☐ 72 Greg Luzinski	1.00	.45	.12

1978 Pepsi

Sponsored by Pepsi-Cola and produced by MSA, this set of 40 collector cards measures approximately 2 1/8" by 9 1/2" and features members of the Cincinnati Reds and 15 national players. On a red background and inside a star cut-out, the fronts have a sepia toned player portrait in the top part. The player's name appears under the photo, along with short biography. A checklist for the Cincinnati Reds (1-25) and for the 15 National players (26-40) is printed below. The bottom part of the front has information on how to get a deck of Superstar playing cards free for 250 Pepsi capliners. The backs carry an order form and more detailed information. The cards are unnumbered and checklisted below in alphabetical order by grouping.

	NRMT	VG-E	GOOD
COMPLETE SET (40)	75.00	34.00	9.50
COMMON CARD (1-40)	1.00	.45	.12
☐ 1 Sparky Anderson MG	2.50	1.10	.30
☐ 2 Rick Auerbach	1.00	.45	.12
☐ 3 Doug Bair	1.00	.45	.12
☐ 4 Johnny Bench	7.50	3.40	.95
☐ 5 Bill Bonham	1.00	.45	.12
☐ 6 Pedro Borbon	1.00	.45	.12
☐ 7 Dave Collins	1.00	.45	.12
☐ 8 Dave Concepcion	2.50	1.10	.30
☐ 9 Dan Driessen	1.50	.70	.19
☐ 10 George Foster	2.00	.90	.25
☐ 11 Cesar Geronimo	1.00	.45	.12
☐ 12 Ken Griffey	2.50	1.10	.30
☐ 13 Ken Henderson	1.00	.45	.12
☐ 14 Tom Hume	1.00	.45	.12
☐ 15 Junior Kennedy	1.00	.45	.12
☐ 16 Ray Knight	2.00	.90	.25
☐ 17 Mike Lum	1.00	.45	.12
☐ 18 Joe Morgan	5.00	2.20	.60
☐ 19 Paul Moskau	1.00	.45	.12
☐ 20 Fred Norman	1.00	.45	.12
☐ 21 Pete Rose	7.50	3.40	.95
☐ 22 Manny Sarmiento	1.00	.45	.12
☐ 23 Tom Seaver	7.50	3.40	.95
☐ 24 Dave Tomlin	1.00	.45	.12
☐ 25 Don Werner	1.00	.45	.12
☐ 26 Buddy Bell	2.00	.90	.25
☐ 27 Larry Bowa	1.50	.70	.19
☐ 28 George Brett	15.00	6.75	1.85
☐ 29 Jeff Burroughs	1.00	.45	.12
☐ 30 Rod Carew	5.00	2.20	.60
☐ 31 Steve Garvey	3.00	1.35	.35
☐ 32 Reggie Jackson	7.50	3.40	.95
☐ 33 Dave Kingman	2.00	.90	.25
☐ 34 Jerry Koosman	1.50	.70	.19
☐ 35 Bill Madlock	1.50	.70	.19
☐ 36 Jim Palmer	5.00	2.20	.60
☐ 37 Nolan Ryan	15.00	6.75	1.85
☐ 38 Ted Simmons	2.00	.90	.25
☐ 39 Carl Yastrzemski	5.00	2.20	.60
☐ 40 Richie Zisk	1.00	.45	.12

1989 Pepsi McGwire

Each of these 12 standard-size cards depicts Mark McGwire. The cards are printed on rather thin card stock. The cards have a distinctive blue outer border. The Pepsi logo is shown on the front and back of each card. All the pictures used in the set are posed showing McGwire in a generic uniform with a Pepsi patch on his upper arm and his number 25 on his chest; in each case his cap or batting helmet is in the Oakland colors but without their logo. The card backs all contain exactly the same statistical and biographical information, only the card number is different. Reportedly cards were distributed inside specially marked 12-packs of Pepsi in the Northern California area.

	MINT	NRMT	EXC
COMPLETE SET (12)	15.00	6.75	1.85
COMMON CARD (1-12)	1.25	.55	.16
☐ 1 Mark McGwire (Batting stance with left foot lifted)	1.25	.55	.16
☐ 2 Mark McGwire (Fielding position at first base)	1.25	.55	.16
☐ 3 Mark McGwire (Reaching out with glove for ball)	1.25	.55	.16
☐ 4 Mark McGwire (Batting stance in empty stadium)	1.25	.55	.16
☐ 5 Mark McGwire (On one knee with bat)	1.25	.55	.16
☐ 6 Mark McGwire (Stretching for ball at first base)	1.25	.55	.16
☐ 7 Mark McGwire (Smiling with bat on shoulder facing camera)	1.25	.55	.16
☐ 8 Mark McGwire (Holding bat in green windbreaker)	1.25	.55	.16
☐ 9 Mark McGwire (Rawlings bat on left shoulder)	1.25	.55	.16
☐ 10 Mark McGwire (Holding bat parallel to ground in green windbreaker)	1.25	.55	.16
☐ 11 Mark McGwire (Holding bat parallel to ground in uniform, toothy smile)	1.25	.55	.16
☐ 12 Mark McGwire (Serious looking follow through)	1.25	.55	.16

1990 Pepsi Canseco

This ten-card, standard-size set was issued in conjunction with Pepsi-Cola. These blue-bordered cards do not have the team logos. This set is very similar in style to the Pepsi McGwire set issued the year before. All the pictures used in the set are posed showing Canseco in a generic uniform with a Pepsi patch.

	MINT	NRMT	EXC
COMPLETE SET (10)	10.00	4.50	1.25
COMMON CARD (1-10)	1.00	.45	.12
☐ 1 Jose Canseco (Follow Through Waist)	1.00	.45	.12
☐ 2 Jose Canseco (Follow Through Shoulder)	1.00	.45	.12
☐ 3 Jose Canseco (Catching Ball)	1.00	.45	.12
☐ 4 Jose Canseco (Batting Pose)	1.00	.45	.12
☐ 5 Jose Canseco (Glove Over Chest)	1.00	.45	.12
☐ 6 Jose Canseco (Action Follow Through)	1.00	.45	.12
☐ 7 Jose Canseco (Sitting on Dugout Steps)	1.00	.45	.12
☐ 8 Jose Canseco (Waiting for Pitch)	1.00	.45	.12
☐ 9 Jose Canseco (Portrait/Bat at Waist)	1.00	.45	.12
☐ 10 Jose Canseco (Portrait)	1.00	.45	.12

1991 Pepsi Sid Fernandez

A local Hawaii Pepsi bottling company issued a 2-card set of El Sid. He is depicted wearing a "Pepsi" uniform. Back has Pepsi logo and El Sid statistics through 1990.

	MINT	NRMT	EXC
COMPLETE SET (2)	4.00	1.80	.50
COMMON CARD (1-2)	2.00	.90	.25
☐ 1 Sid Fernandez	2.00	.90	.25
☐ 2 Sid Fernandez	2.00	.90	.25

1991 Pepsi Griffeys

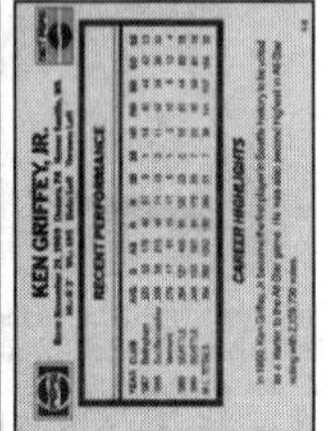

This eight-card standard-size set was sponsored by Pepsi-Cola, and its company logo appears on the front and back of each card. These cards were inserted one per special 12-pack of Pepsi. The color player photos are bordered in red, white, and purple, with Ken Griffey, Jr. in red block lettering below each picture. The backs are either horizontally or vertically oriented and present biographical as well as statistical information in black print on a white background. A ninth card was issued on a very limited basis as only 150 were produced.

	MINT	NRMT	EXC
COMPLETE SET (8)	10.00	4.50	1.25
COMMON CARD (1-6)	1.50	.70	.19
COMMON CARD (7-8)	.50	.23	.06
☐ 1 Ken Griffey Jr. Swinging the bat	1.50	.70	.19
☐ 2 Ken Griffey Jr. Throwing from the outfield	1.50	.70	.19
☐ 3 Ken Griffey Jr. Catching ball at wall	1.50	.70	.19
☐ 4 Ken Griffey Jr. Posing with bat on shoulder	1.50	.70	.19
☐ 5 Ken Griffey Jr. Ken Griffey Sr. Dad seated)	1.50	.70	.19
☐ 6 Ken Griffey Jr. Ken Griffey Sr. Dad standing	1.50	.70	.19
☐ 7 Ken Griffey Sr. At bat	.50	.23	.06
☐ 8 Ken Griffey Sr. Catching fly ball	.50	.23	.06

1991 Pepsi Rickey Henderson

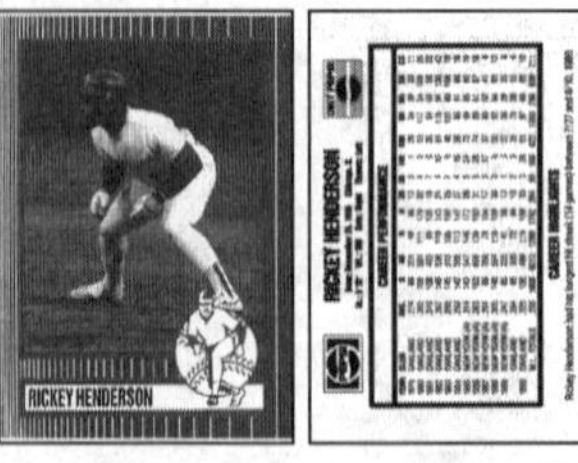

These ten standard-size cards were sponsored by Pepsi and feature Rickey Henderson. The front design has a color player photo, enframed by red borders on blue and white pinstripe background. The white pinstripes become farther and farther apart as one moves toward the right side of the card. An icon of a baseball and baserunner in the lower right corner rounds out the card face. In a horizontal format, the backs have the same career performance statistics but differing career highlights.

	MINT	NRMT	EXC
COMPLETE SET (10)	10.00	4.50	1.25
COMMON CARD (1-10)	1.00	.45	.12
☐ 1 Rickey Henderson (Follow through, left side)	1.00	.45	.12
☐ 2 Rickey Henderson (Running bases)	1.00	.45	.12
☐ 3 Rickey Henderson (Stretching hamstring)	1.00	.45	.12
☐ 4 Rickey Henderson (Ready to run)	1.00	.45	.12
☐ 5 Rickey Henderson (Bat on shoulder)	1.00	.45	.12
☐ 6 Rickey Henderson (Follow through, Right side)	1.00	.45	.12
☐ 7 Rickey Henderson (Squatting with bat)	1.00	.45	.12
☐ 8 Rickey Henderson (After throw)	1.00	.45	.12
☐ 9 Rickey Henderson (Leading off base)	1.00	.45	.12
☐ 10 Rickey Henderson (Warming up with bat)	1.00	.45	.12

1991 Pepsi Rickey Henderson Discs

This four-disc set was issued by Pepsi in honor of Rickey Henderson. The discs measure approximately 2 1/8" in diameter. The fronts feature 3-D color action shots that change to different shots when one holds the discs at a different angle. A purple border with white stars, the player's name, and the sponsor's name encircle the picture. In red and blue print on white, the backs have Henderson's 1990 statistics and his Major League career totals. The discs are unnumbered.

	MINT	NRMT	EXC
COMPLETE SET (4)	6.00	2.70	.75
COMMON DISC (1-4)	1.50	.70	.19
☐ 1 Rickey Henderson Ready to run running bases	1.50	.70	.19
☐ 2 Rickey Henderson Posed with bat Follow through	1.50	.70	.19
☐ 3 Rickey Henderson Leading off base Sliding in	1.50	.70	.19
☐ 4 Rickey Henderson Warming up Follow through	1.50	.70	.19

1991 Pepsi Superstar

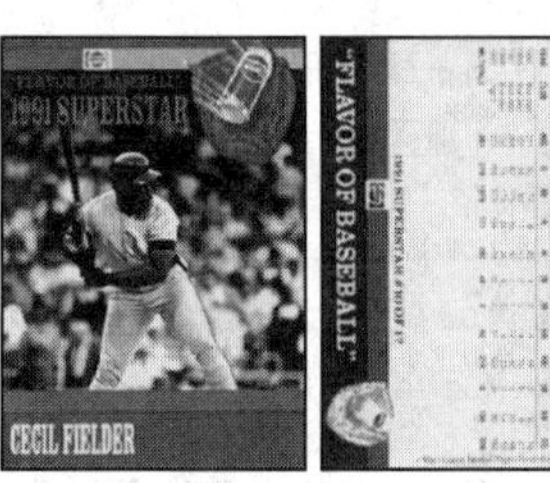

This 17-card set was sponsored by Pepsi-Cola of Florida as part of the "Flavor of Baseball" promotion. The promotion featured a chance to win one of 104 rare, older cards, including one 1952 Mickey Mantle rookie card. The Superstar cards were glued inside specially marked 12 packs of Pepsi-Cola products in Orlando, Tampa, and Miami. It is difficult to remove the cards without creasing them; reportedly area supervisors for Pepsi each received a few sets. The cards measure slightly wider than standard size (2 5/8" by 3 1/2"). The fronts have color action player photos, with a baseball glove "catching" a can of Pepsi superimposed at the upper right corner of the picture. The player photo has two top (purple and red/blue) and two bottom (red and purple) color stripes serving as borders but none on its sides. In a horizontal format, the backs have blue and red stripes, and present Major League statistics as well as biography.

	MINT	NRMT	EXC
COMPLETE SET (17)	50.00	22.00	6.25
COMMON CARD (1-17)	1.25	.55	.16
☐ 1 Dwight Gooden	3.00	1.35	.35
☐ 2 Andre Dawson	3.00	1.35	.35
☐ 3 Ryne Sandberg	10.00	4.50	1.25
☐ 4 Dave Stieb	1.25	.55	.16
☐ 5 Jose Rijo	1.25	.55	.16
☐ 6 Roger Clemens	6.00	2.70	.75
☐ 7 Barry Bonds	5.00	2.20	.60
☐ 8 Cal Ripken	20.00	9.00	2.50
☐ 9 Dave Justice	3.00	1.35	.35
☐ 10 Cecil Fielder	2.00	.90	.25
☐ 11 Don Mattingly	12.50	5.50	1.55
☐ 12 Ozzie Smith	10.00	4.50	1.25
☐ 13 Kirby Puckett	12.50	5.50	1.55
☐ 14 Rafael Palmeiro	2.50	1.10	.30
☐ 15 Bobby Bonilla	2.00	.90	.25
☐ 16 Len Dykstra	2.00	.90	.25
☐ 17 Jose Canseco	5.00	2.20	.60

1992 Pepsi Diet MSA

Issued in two different types of three-card packs, (a clear cello and a white cello with bilingual printing) this 30-card standard-size set was issued by MSA (Michael Schechter Associates) for Diet Pepsi in Canada. The packs were given away free with the purchase of Diet Pepsi or Diet Caffeine Free Pepsi. The glossy color action photos are framed by white borders. The top is edged with a royal blue stripe while a red stripe, with sponsor logos and player's name, edges the bottom. As is typical of MSA sets, the team logos have been airbrushed out. The horizontally oriented backs carry a close-up color photo bordered in red with biography and complete career statistics on a light blue box. A facsimile autograph rounds out the back.

	MINT	NRMT	EXC
COMPLETE SET (30)	20.00	9.00	2.50
COMMON CARD (1-30)	.25	.11	.03
☐ 1 Roger Clemens	1.00	.45	.12
☐ 2 Dwight Gooden	.50	.23	.06
☐ 3 Tom Henke	.25	.11	.03
☐ 4 Dennis Martinez	.50	.23	.06
☐ 5 Tom Glavine	.75	.35	.09
☐ 6 Jack Morris	.50	.23	.06
☐ 7 Dennis Eckersley	.50	.23	.06
☐ 8 Jeff Reardon	.25	.11	.03
☐ 9 Bryan Harvey	.25	.11	.03
☐ 10 Sandy Alomar Jr.	.50	.23	.06
☐ 11 Carlton Fisk	.75	.35	.09
☐ 12 Gary Carter	.50	.23	.06
☐ 13 Cecil Fielder	.50	.23	.06
☐ 14 Will Clark	.75	.35	.09
☐ 15 Roberto Alomar	1.00	.45	.12
☐ 16 Ryne Sandberg	2.00	.90	.25
☐ 17 Cal Ripken	3.00	1.35	.35
☐ 18 Barry Larkin	1.00	.45	.12
☐ 19 Ozzie Smith	1.50	.70	.19
☐ 20 Kelly Gruber	.25	.11	.03
☐ 21 Wade Boggs	1.00	.45	.12
☐ 22 Tim Wallach	.25	.11	.03
☐ 23 Howard Johnson	.25	.11	.03
☐ 24 Jose Canseco	1.00	.45	.12
☐ 25 Joe Carter	.50	.23	.06
☐ 26 Ken Griffey Jr.	4.00	1.80	.50
☐ 27 Kirby Puckett	2.00	.90	.25
☐ 28 Rickey Henderson	1.00	.45	.12
☐ 29 Barry Bonds	1.25	.55	.16
☐ 30 Dave Winfield	.75	.35	.09

1980-96 Perez-Steele Hall of Fame Postcards

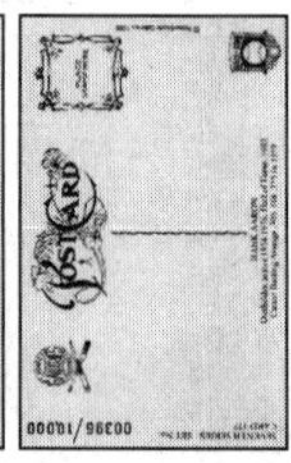

President Ronald Reagan was given the first numbered set issued on May 27th, 1981 at the White House.The sets were also issued with continuation rights. These rights have been transferable over the years. These 3 1/2" by 5 1/2" cards feature noted sports artist Dick Perez drawings. The cards are distributed through Perez Steele galleries. According to the producer, many of these cards are sold to art or postcard collectors. Just 10,000 of these sets were produced.

	NRMT	VG-E	GOOD
COMPLETE SET	1000.00	450.00	125.00
COMMON CARD	1.00	.45	.12
☐ 1 Ty Cobb	35.00	16.00	4.40
☐ 2 Walter Johnson	10.00	4.50	1.25
☐ 3 Christy Mathewson	10.00	4.50	1.25
☐ 4 Babe Ruth	60.00	27.00	7.50
☐ 5 Honus Wagner	10.00	4.50	1.25
☐ 6 Morgan Bulkeley	1.00	.45	.12
☐ 7 Ban Johnson	1.00	.45	.12
☐ 8 Nap Lajoie	5.00	2.20	.60
☐ 9 Connie Mack	5.00	2.20	.60
☐ 10 John McGraw	5.00	2.20	.60
☐ 11 Tris Speaker	5.00	2.20	.60
☐ 12 George Wright	1.00	.45	.12
☐ 13 Cy Young	5.00	2.20	.60
☐ 14 Grover Alexander	5.00	2.20	.60

	MINT	NRMT	EXC
15 Alex. Cartwright	1.00	.45	.12
16 Henry Chadwick	1.00	.45	.12
17 Cap Anson	2.50	1.10	.30
18 Eddie Collins	5.00	2.20	.60
19 Candy Cummings	1.50	.70	.19
20 Charles Comiskey	1.00	.45	.12
21 Buck Ewing	1.50	.70	.19
22 Lou Gehrig	35.00	16.00	4.40
23 Willie Keeler	1.50	.70	.19
24 Hoss Radbourne	1.50	.70	.19
25 George Sisler	15.00	6.75	1.85
26 A.G. Spalding	1.50	.70	.19
27 Rogers Hornsby	5.00	2.20	.60
28 Kenesaw Landis	1.00	.45	.12
29 Roger Bresnahan	1.50	.70	.19
30 Dan Brouthers	1.50	.70	.19
31 Fred Clarke	1.50	.70	.19
32 Jimmy Collins	1.50	.70	.19
33 Ed Delahanty	1.50	.70	.19
34 Hugh Duffy	1.50	.70	.19
35 Hughie Jennings	1.50	.70	.19
36 King Kelly	2.50	1.10	.30
37 Jim O'Rourke	1.50	.70	.19
38 Wilbert Robinson	1.50	.70	.19
39 Jesse Burkett	1.50	.70	.19
40 Frank Chance	5.00	2.20	.60
41 Jack Chesbro	1.50	.70	.19
42 Johnny Evers	5.00	2.20	.60
43 Clark Griffith	1.50	.70	.19
44 Thomas McCarthy	1.50	.70	.19
45 Joe McGinnity	1.50	.70	.19
46 Eddie Plank	1.50	.70	.19
47 Joe Tinker	5.00	2.20	.60
48 Rube Waddell	1.50	.70	.19
49 Ed Walsh	1.50	.70	.19
50 Mickey Cochrane	5.00	2.20	.60
51 Frankie Frisch	5.00	2.20	.60
52 Lefty Grove	5.00	2.20	.60
53 Carl Hubbell	10.00	4.50	1.25
54 Herb Pennock	1.50	.70	.19
55 Pie Traynor	2.50	1.10	.30
56 Mordecai Brown	1.50	.70	.19
57 Charlie Gehringer	2.50	1.10	.30
58 Kid Nichols	1.50	.70	.19
59 Jimmy Foxx	15.00	6.75	1.85
60 Mel Ott	10.00	4.50	1.25
61 Harry Heilmann	1.50	.70	.19
62 Paul Waner	5.00	2.20	.60
63 Edward Barrow	1.00	.45	.12
64 Chief Bender	5.00	2.20	.60
65 Tom Connolly	1.00	.45	.12
66 Dizzy Dean	15.00	6.75	1.85
67 Bill Klem	1.00	.45	.12
68 Al Simmons	5.00	2.20	.60
69 Bobby Wallace	1.50	.70	.19
70 Harry Wright	1.50	.70	.19
71 Bill Dickey	5.00	2.20	.60
72 Rabbit Maranville	1.50	.70	.19
73 Bill Terry	7.50	3.40	.95
74 Frank Baker	1.50	.70	.19
75 Joe DiMaggio	60.00	27.00	7.50
76 Gabby Hartnett	1.50	.70	.19
77 Ted Lyons	1.50	.70	.19
78 Ray Schalk	1.50	.70	.19
79 Dazzy Vance	1.50	.70	.19
80 Joe Cronin	2.50	1.10	.30
81 Hank Greenberg	20.00	9.00	2.50
82 Sam Crawford	5.00	2.20	.60
83 Joe McCarthy	1.00	.45	.12
84 Zack Wheat	1.50	.70	.19
85 Max Carey	1.50	.70	.19
86 Billy Hamilton	1.50	.70	.19
87 Bob Feller	20.00	9.00	2.50
88 Bill McKechnie	1.00	.45	.12
89 Jackie Robinson	25.00	11.00	3.10
90 Edd Roush	2.50	1.10	.30
91 John Clarkson	1.50	.70	.19
92 Elmer Flick	1.50	.70	.19
93 Sam Rice	5.00	2.20	.60
94 Eppa Rixey	1.50	.70	.19
95 Luke Appling	2.50	1.10	.30
96 Red Faber	1.50	.70	.19
97 Burleigh Grimes	1.50	.70	.19
98 Miller Huggins	1.50	.70	.19
99 Tim Keefe	1.50	.70	.19
100 Heinie Manush	1.50	.70	.19
101 John Ward	1.50	.70	.19
102 Pud Galvin	1.50	.70	.19
103 Casey Stengel	10.00	4.50	1.25
104 Ted Williams	60.00	27.00	7.50
105 Branch Rickey	1.50	.70	.19
106 Red Ruffing	1.50	.70	.19
107 Lloyd Waner	1.50	.70	.19
108 Kiki Cuyler	1.50	.70	.19
109 Goose Goslin	5.00	2.20	.60
110 Joe Medwick	1.50	.70	.19
111 Roy Campanella	10.00	4.50	1.25
112 Stan Coveleski	1.50	.70	.19
113 Waite Hoyt	1.50	.70	.19
114 Stan Musial	35.00	16.00	4.40
115 Lou Boudreau	12.00	5.50	1.50
116 Earl Combs	1.50	.70	.19
117 Ford Frick	1.00	.45	.12
118 Jesse Haines	1.50	.70	.19
119 David Bancroft	1.50	.70	.19
120 Jake Beckley	1.50	.70	.19
121 Chick Hafey	1.00	.45	.12
122 Harry Hooper	1.50	.70	.19
123 Joe Kelley	1.50	.70	.19
124 Rube Marquard	5.00	2.20	.60
125 Satchel Paige	25.00	11.00	3.10
126 George Weiss	1.00	.45	.12
127 Yogi Berra	15.00	6.75	1.85
128 Josh Gibson	5.00	2.20	.60
129 Lefty Gomez	2.50	1.10	.30
130 William Harridge	1.00	.45	.12
131 Sandy Koufax	20.00	9.00	2.50
132 Buck Leonard	15.00	6.75	1.85
133 Early Wynn	7.50	3.40	.95
134 Ross Youngs	1.50	.70	.19
135 Roberto Clemente	50.00	22.00	6.25
136 Billy Evans	1.00	.45	.12
137 Monte Irvin	8.00	3.60	1.00
138 George Kelly	1.50	.70	.19
139 Warren Spahn	10.00	4.50	1.25
140 Mickey Welch	1.50	.70	.19
141 Cool Papa Bell	8.00	3.60	1.00
142 Jim Bottomley	1.50	.70	.19
143 Jocko Conlan	1.00	.45	.12
144 Whitey Ford	20.00	9.00	2.50
145 Mickey Mantle	60.00	27.00	7.50
146 Sam Thompson	1.50	.70	.19
147 Earl Averill	2.50	1.10	.30
148 Bucky Harris	1.50	.70	.19
149 Billy Herman	2.50	1.10	.30
150 Judy Johnson	10.00	4.50	1.25
151 Ralph Kiner	10.00	4.50	1.25
152 Oscar Charleston	2.50	1.10	.30
153 Roger Connor	1.50	.70	.19
154 Cal Hubbard	1.00	.45	.12
155 Bob Lemon	8.00	3.60	1.00
156 Fred Lindstrom	1.50	.70	.19
157 Robin Roberts	10.00	4.50	1.25
158 Ernie Banks	15.00	6.75	1.85
159 Martin Dihigo	5.00	2.20	.60
160 John Lloyd	5.00	2.20	.60
161 Al Lopez	12.00	5.50	1.50
162 Amos Rusie	1.50	.70	.19
163 Joe Sewell	1.50	.70	.19
164 Addie Joss	1.50	.70	.19
165 Larry MacPhail	1.00	.45	.12
166 Eddie Mathews	10.00	4.50	1.25
167 Warren Giles	1.00	.45	.12
168 Willie Mays	35.00	16.00	4.40
169 Hack Wilson	1.50	.70	.19
170 Al Kaline	20.00	9.00	2.50
171 Chuck Klein	1.50	.70	.19
172 Duke Snider	20.00	9.00	2.50
173 Tom Yawkey	1.00	.45	.12
174 Rube Foster	1.00	.45	.12
175 Bob Gibson	10.00	4.50	1.25
176 Johnny Mize	2.50	1.10	.30
177 Hank Aaron	20.00	9.00	2.50
178 Happy Chandler	1.00	.45	.12
179 Travis Jackson	1.50	.70	.19
180 Frank Robinson	20.00	9.00	2.50
181 Walter Alston	8.00	3.60	1.00
182 George Kell	8.00	3.60	1.00
183 Juan Marichal	6.00	2.70	.75
184 Brooks Robinson	20.00	9.00	2.50
185 Luis Aparicio	10.00	4.50	1.25
186 Don Drysdale	5.00	2.20	.60
187 Rick Ferrell	1.50	.70	.19
188 Harmon Killebrew	10.00	4.50	1.25
189 Pee Wee Reese	20.00	9.00	2.50
190 Lou Brock	15.00	6.75	1.85
191 Enos Slaughter	8.00	3.60	1.00
192 Arky Vaughan	1.50	.70	.19
193 Hoyt Wilhelm	8.00	3.60	1.00
194 Bobby Doerr	8.00	3.60	1.00
195 Ernie Lombardi	1.50	.70	.19
196 Willie McCovey	6.00	2.70	.75
197 Ray Dandridge	5.00	2.20	.60
198 Catfish Hunter	8.00	3.60	1.00
199 Billy Williams	8.00	3.60	1.00
200 Willie Stargell	6.00	2.70	.75
201 Al Barlick	2.50	1.10	.30
202 Johnny Bench	6.00	2.70	.75
203 Red Schoendienst	8.00	3.60	1.00
204 Carl Yastrzemski	20.00	9.00	2.50
205 Joe Morgan	20.00	9.00	2.50
206 Jim Palmer	6.00	2.70	.75
207 Rod Carew	15.00	6.75	1.85
208 Ferguson Jenkins	10.00	4.50	1.25
209 Tony Lazzeri	1.50	.70	.19
210 Gaylord Perry	8.00	3.60	1.00
211 Bill Veeck	1.00	.45	.12
212 Rollie Fingers	8.00	3.60	1.00
213 Bill McGowan	1.00	.45	.12
214 Hal Newhouser	15.00	6.75	1.85
215 Tom Seaver	20.00	9.00	2.50
216 Reggie Jackson	20.00	9.00	2.50
217 Steve Carlton	15.00	6.75	1.85
218 Leo Durocher	5.00	2.20	.60
219 Phil Rizzuto	20.00	9.00	2.50
220 Richie Ashburn	10.00	4.50	1.25
221 Leon Day	2.50	1.10	.30
222 William Hulbert	1.00	.45	.12
223 Mike Schmidt	20.00	9.00	2.50
224 Vic Willis	5.00	2.20	.60
225 Jim Bunning	10.00	4.50	1.25
226 Bill Foster	5.00	2.20	.60
227 Ned Hanlon	5.00	2.20	.60
228 Earl Weaver	10.00	4.50	1.25
A Abner Doubleday	5.00	2.20	.60
B Stephen C. Clark	1.00	.45	.12
C Paul S. Kerr	1.00	.45	.12
D Edward W. Stack	1.00	.45	.12
E Perez-Steele Galleries	1.00	.45	.12
F George W. Bush Edward W. Stack	2.50	1.10	.30

1989 Perez-Steele Celebration Postcards

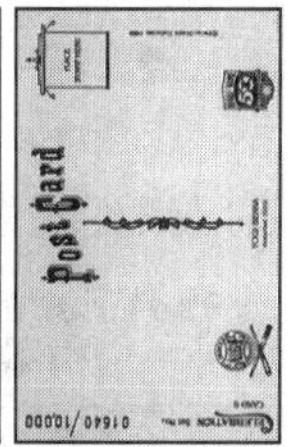

This 44-card set celebrates the 50th Anniversary of the National Baseball Hall of Fame and Museum. The cards measure approximately 3 1/2" by 5 1/2" and feature art work by artist Dick Perez. The backs carry a postcard format.

	MINT	NRMT	EXC
COMPLETE SET (44)	125.00	55.00	15.50
COMMON CARD (1-44)	2.00	.90	.25
1 Hank Aaron	6.00	2.70	.75
2 Luis Aparicio	4.00	1.80	.50
3 Ernie Banks	6.00	2.70	.75
4 Cool Papa Bell	3.50	1.55	.45
5 Johnny Bench	4.00	1.80	.50
6 Yogi Berra	6.00	2.70	.75
7 Lou Boudreau	4.00	1.80	.50
8 Roy Campanella	5.00	2.20	.60
9 Happy Chandler	2.50	1.10	.30
10 Jocko Conlan	2.50	1.10	.30
11 Ray Dandridge	3.00	1.35	.35
12 Bill Dickey	4.00	1.80	.50
13 Bobby Doerr	4.00	1.80	.50
14 Rick Ferrell	3.00	1.35	.35
15 Charlie Gehringer	3.50	1.55	.45
16 Lefty Gomez	4.00	1.80	.50
17 Billy Herman	3.00	1.35	.35
18 Carfish Hunter	4.00	1.80	.50
19 Monte Irvin	4.00	1.80	.50
20 Judy Johnson	4.00	1.80	.50
21 Al Kaline	6.00	2.70	.75
22 George Kell	4.00	1.80	.50
23 Harmon Killebrew	5.00	2.20	.60
24 Ralph Kiner	4.00	1.80	.50
25 Bob Lemon	3.00	1.35	.35
26 Buck Leonard	4.00	1.80	.50
27 Al Lopez	2.50	1.10	.30
28 Mickey Mantle	10.00	4.50	1.25
29 Juan Marichal	4.00	1.80	.50
30 Eddie Mathews	4.00	1.80	.50
31 Willie McCovey	4.00	1.80	.50
32 Johnny Mize	3.50	1.55	.45
33 Stan Musial	6.00	2.70	.75
34 Pee Wee Reese	4.00	1.80	.50
35 Brooks Robinson	5.00	2.20	.60
36 Joe Sewell	3.00	1.35	.35
37 Enos Slaughter	4.00	1.80	.50
38 Duke Snider	4.00	1.80	.50
39 Warren Spahn	5.00	2.20	.60
40 Willie Stargell	4.00	1.80	.50
41 Bill Terry	3.50	1.55	.45
42 Billy Williams	3.00	1.35	.35
43 Ted Williams	10.00	4.50	1.25
44 Carl Yastrzemski	4.00	1.80	.50

1990-92 Perez-Steele Master Works

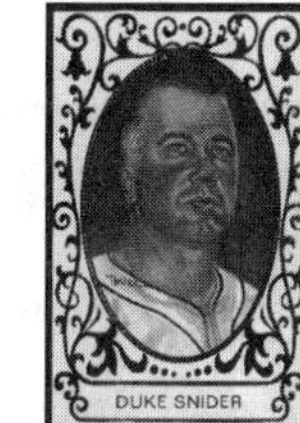

This 50-card set measures 3 1/2" by 5 1/2" and again features the fine artwork of Dick Perez. The set honors living Hall-of Famers at the time of issue and depicts them as if they might have appeared on several vintage card sets. The sets imitated are the Goodwin Champions of 1888, Rose Postcards of 1908, the T205 Gold Borders, 1909 Ramlys and one original design. The sets are numbered and are limited to 10,000 sets. The original issue price for each series was $135.

	MINT	NRMT	EXC
COMPLETE SET (50)	225.00	100.00	28.00
COMMON CARD (1-50)	2.00	.90	.25
1 Charlie Gehringer Ramly	2.00	.90	.25
2 Charlie Gehringer Goodwin	2.00	.90	.25
3 Charlie Gehringer Rose	2.00	.90	.25
4 Charlie Gehringer T205	2.00	.90	.25
5 Charlie Gehringer Original Drawing	2.00	.90	.25
6 Mickey Mantle Ramly	15.00	6.75	1.85
7 Mickey Mantle Goodwin	15.00	6.75	1.85
8 Mickey Mantle Rose	15.00	6.75	1.85
9 Mickey Mantle T205	15.00	6.75	1.85
10 Mickey Mantle Original Drawing	15.00	6.75	1.85
11 Willie Mays Ramly	12.50	5.50	1.55
12 Willie Mays Goodwin	12.50	5.50	1.55
13 Willie Mays Rose	12.50	5.50	1.55
14 Willie Mays T205	12.50	5.50	1.55
15 Willie Mays Original Drawing	12.50	5.50	1.55
16 Duke Snider Ramly	7.50	3.40	.95
17 Duke Snider Goodwin	7.50	3.40	.95
18 Duke Snider Rose	7.50	3.40	.95
19 Duke Snider T205	7.50	3.40	.95
20 Duke Snider Original Drawing	7.50	3.40	.95
21 Warren Spahn Ramly	3.00	1.35	.35
22 Warren Spahn Goodwin	3.00	1.35	.35
23 Warren Sphan Rose	3.00	1.35	.35
24 Warren Spahn T205	3.00	1.35	.35
25 Warren Spahn Original Drawing	3.00	1.35	.35
26 Yogi Berra Ramly	5.00	2.20	.60
27 Yogi Berra Goodwin	5.00	2.20	.60
28 Yogi Berra Rose	5.00	2.20	.60
29 Yogi Berra T205	5.00	2.20	.60
30 Yogi Berra Original Drawing	5.00	2.20	.60
31 Johnny Mize Ramly	2.00	.90	.25
32 Johnny Mize Goodwin	2.00	.90	.25
33 Johnny Mize Rose	2.00	.90	.25
34 Johnny Mize T205	2.00	.90	.25
35 Johnny Mize Original Drawing	2.00	.90	.25
36 Willie Stargell Ramly	3.00	1.35	.35
37 Willie Stargell Goodwin	3.00	1.35	.35
38 Willie Stargell Rose	3.00	1.35	.35
39 Willie Stargell T205	3.00	1.35	.35
40 Willie Stargell Original Drawing	3.00	1.35	.35
41 Ted Williams Ramly	12.50	5.50	1.55
42 Ted Williams Goodwin	12.50	5.50	1.55
43 Ted Williams Rose	12.50	5.50	1.55
44 Ted Williams T205	12.50	5.50	1.55
45 Ted Williams Original Drawing	12.50	5.50	1.55
46 Carl Yastrzemski Ramly	5.00	2.20	.60
47 Carl Yastrzemski Goodwin	5.00	2.20	.60
48 Carl Yastrzemski Rose	5.00	2.20	.60
49 Carl Yastrzemski T205	5.00	2.20	.60
50 Carl Yastrzemski Original Drawing	5.00	2.20	.60

1990-96 Perez-Steele Great Moments

These cards were issued in series of 12 cards each. So far, eight series have been issued. The cards measure 3 1/2" by 5 1/2" and feature leading moments in Hall of Famers careers. These sets are also issued with continuation rights.

	MINT	NRMT	EXC
COMPLETE SET (96)	300.00	135.00	38.00
COMMON CARD	2.00	.90	.25
☐ 1 Babe Ruth	20.00	9.00	2.50
☐ 2 Al Kaline	3.00	1.35	.35
☐ 3 Jackie Robinson	15.00	6.75	1.85
☐ 4 Lou Gehrig	15.00	6.75	1.85
☐ 5 Whitey Ford	5.00	2.20	.60
☐ 6 Christy Mathewson	7.50	3.40	.95
☐ 7 Roy Campanella	5.00	2.20	.60
☐ 8 Walter Johnson	7.50	3.40	.95
☐ 9 Hank Aaron	15.00	6.75	1.85
☐ 10 Cy Young	7.50	3.40	.95
☐ 11 Stan Musial	7.50	3.40	.95
☐ 12 Ty Cobb	15.00	6.75	1.85
☐ 13 Ted Williams	15.00	6.75	1.85
☐ 14 Warren Spahn	3.00	1.35	.35
☐ 15 Paul Waner	3.00	1.35	.35
Lloyd Waner			
☐ 16 Sandy Koufax	7.50	3.40	.95
☐ 17 Robin Roberts	3.00	1.35	.35
☐ 18 Dizzy Dean	5.00	2.20	.60
☐ 19 Mickey Mantle	20.00	9.00	2.50
☐ 20 Satchel Paige	10.00	4.50	1.25
☐ 21 Ernie Banks	7.50	3.40	.95
☐ 22 Willie McCovey	3.00	1.35	.35
☐ 23 Johnny Mize	2.00	.90	.25
☐ 24 Honus Wagner	5.00	2.20	.60
☐ 25 Willie Keeler	2.00	.90	.25
☐ 26 Pee Wee Reese	5.00	2.20	.60
☐ 27 Monte Irvin	2.00	.90	.25
☐ 28 Eddie Mathews	5.00	2.20	.60
☐ 29 Enos Slaughter	3.00	1.35	.35
☐ 30 Rube Marquard	2.00	.90	.25
☐ 31 Charlie Gehringer	3.00	1.35	.35
☐ 32 Roberto Clemente	15.00	6.75	1.85
☐ 33 Duke Snider	7.50	3.40	.95
☐ 34 Ray Dandridge	2.00	.90	.25
☐ 35 Carl Hubbell	3.00	1.35	.35
☐ 36 Bobby Doerr	3.00	1.35	.35
☐ 37 Bill Dickey	3.00	1.35	.35
☐ 38 Willie Stargell	3.00	1.35	.35
☐ 39 Brooks Robinson	5.00	2.20	.60
☐ 40 Joe Tinker	5.00	2.20	.60
Johnny Evers			
Frank Chance			
☐ 41 Billy Herman	2.00	.90	.25
☐ 42 Grover Alexander	5.00	2.20	.60
☐ 43 Luis Aparicio	3.00	1.35	.35
☐ 44 Lefty Gomez	2.00	.90	.25
☐ 45 Eddie Collins	2.00	.90	.25
☐ 46 Judy Johnson	3.00	1.35	.35
☐ 47 Harry Heilmann	2.00	.90	.25
☐ 48 Harmon Killebrew	3.00	1.35	.35
☐ 49 Johnny Bench	7.50	3.40	.95
☐ 50 Max Carey	2.00	.90	.25
☐ 51 Cool Papa Bell	3.00	1.35	.35
☐ 52 Rube Waddell	2.00	.90	.25
☐ 53 Yogi Berra	7.50	3.40	.95
☐ 54 Herb Pennock	2.00	.90	.25
☐ 55 Red Schoendienst	3.00	1.35	.35
☐ 56 Juan Marichal	5.00	2.20	.60
☐ 57 Frankie Frisch	2.00	.90	.25
☐ 58 Buck Leonard	3.00	1.35	.35
☐ 59 George Kell	3.00	1.35	.35
☐ 60 Chuck Klein	2.00	.90	.25
☐ 61 King Kelly	2.00	.90	.25
☐ 62 Catfish Hunter	5.00	2.20	.60
☐ 63 Lou Boudreau	3.00	1.35	.35
☐ 64 Al Lopez	3.00	1.35	.35
☐ 65 Willie Mays	15.00	6.75	1.85
☐ 66 Lou Brock	5.00	2.20	.60
☐ 67 Bob Lemon	3.00	1.35	.35
☐ 68 Joe Sewell	2.00	.90	.25
☐ 69 Billy Williams	3.00	1.35	.35
☐ 70 Rick Ferrell	2.00	.90	.25
☐ 71 Arky Vaughan	2.00	.90	.25
☐ 72 Carl Yastrzemski	7.50	3.40	.95
☐ 73 Tom Seaver	5.00	2.20	.60
☐ 74 Rollie Fingers	4.00	1.80	.50
☐ 75 Ralph Kiner	4.00	1.80	.50
☐ 76 Frank Baker	3.00	1.35	.35
☐ 77 Rod Carew	4.00	1.80	.50
☐ 78 Goose Goslin	3.00	1.35	.35
☐ 79 Gaylord Perry	4.00	1.80	.50
☐ 80 Hack Wilson	4.00	1.80	.50
☐ 81 Hal Newhouser	2.00	.90	.25
☐ 82 Early Wynn	2.00	.90	.25
☐ 83 Bob Feller	5.00	2.20	.60
☐ 84 Branch Rickey	2.00	.90	.25
☐ 85 Jim Palmer	4.00	1.80	.50
☐ 86 Al Barlick	2.00	.90	.25
☐ 87 Mickey Mantle	10.00	4.50	1.25
Willie Mays			
Duke Snider			
☐ 88 Hank Greenberg	4.00	1.80	.50
☐ 89 Joe Morgan	4.00	1.80	.50
☐ 90 Chief Bender	3.00	1.35	.35
☐ 91 Pee Wee Reese	5.00	2.20	.60
Jackie Robinson			
☐ 92 Jim Bottomley	3.00	1.35	.35
☐ 93 Ferguson Jenkins	4.00	1.80	.50
☐ 94 Frank Robinson	5.00	2.20	.60
☐ 95 Hoyt Wilhelm	2.00	.90	.25
☐ 96 Cap Anson	3.00	1.35	.35

1981 Perma-Graphic All-Stars

This set commemorates the starters of the 1981 All-Star game. This 18-card set measure 2 1/8" by 3 3/8" and has rounded corners. Because of the players strike of 1981 plenty of time was available to prepare the player's biography with appropriate notes. The set is framed on the front in red for the National League and blue for the American League.

	NRMT	VG-E	GOOD
COMPLETE SET (18)	50.00	22.00	6.25
COMMON CARD (1-18)	1.00	.45	.12
☐ 1 Gary Carter	6.00	2.70	.75
☐ 2 Dave Concepcion	2.50	1.10	.30
☐ 3 Andre Dawson	6.00	2.70	.75
☐ 4 George Foster	1.00	.45	.12
☐ 5 Davey Lopes	2.50	1.10	.30
☐ 6 Dave Parker	2.50	1.10	.30
☐ 7 Pete Rose	7.50	3.40	.95
☐ 8 Mike Schmidt	8.00	3.60	1.00
☐ 9 Fernando Valenzuela	2.50	1.10	.30
☐ 10 George Brett	12.50	5.50	1.55
☐ 11 Rod Carew	5.00	2.20	.60
☐ 12 Bucky Dent	2.50	1.10	.30
☐ 13 Carlton Fisk	5.00	2.20	.60
☐ 14 Reggie Jackson	6.00	2.70	.75
☐ 15 Jack Morris	4.00	1.80	.50
☐ 16 Willie Randolph	2.50	1.10	.30
☐ 17 Ken Singleton	1.00	.45	.12
☐ 18 Dave Winfield	6.00	2.70	.75

1981 Perma-Graphic Credit Cards

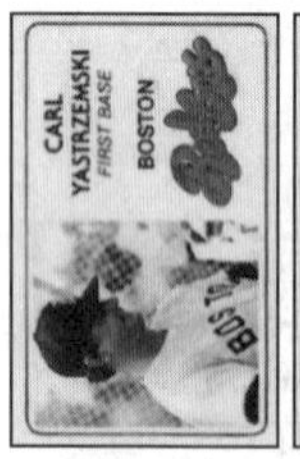

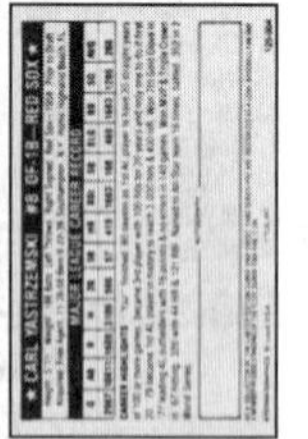

Perma-Graphic began their three-year foray into card manufacturing with this 32-card set of "credit cards" each measuring approximately 2 1/8" by 3 3/8". The set featured 32 of the leading players of 1981. This set's design is split on the front between a full-color photo of the player and an identification of said player while the back has one line of career statistics and lines of career highlights. These sets (made of plastic) were issued with the cooperation of Topps Chewing Gum. This first set of Perma-Graphic cards seems to have been produced in greater quantities than the other five Perma-Graphic sets.

	NRMT	VG-E	GOOD
COMPLETE SET (32)	50.00	22.00	6.25
COMMON CARD (1-32)	1.00	.45	.12
☐ 1 Johnny Bench	4.00	1.80	.50
☐ 2 Mike Schmidt	7.50	3.40	.95
☐ 3 George Brett	10.00	4.50	1.25
☐ 4 Carl Yastrzemski	4.00	1.80	.50
☐ 5 Pete Rose	5.00	2.20	.60
☐ 6 Bob Horner	1.00	.45	.12
☐ 7 Reggie Jackson	6.00	2.70	.75
☐ 8 Keith Hernandez	2.00	.90	.25
☐ 9 George Foster	1.00	.45	.12
☐ 10 Garry Templeton	1.00	.45	.12
☐ 11 Tom Seaver	4.00	1.80	.50
☐ 12 Steve Garvey	2.00	.90	.25
☐ 13 Dave Parker	2.00	.90	.25
☐ 14 Willie Stargell	3.00	1.35	.35
☐ 15 Cecil Cooper	1.00	.45	.12
☐ 16 Steve Carlton	4.00	1.80	.50
☐ 17 Ted Simmons	1.00	.45	.12
☐ 18 Dave Kingman	2.00	.90	.25
☐ 19 Rickey Henderson	10.00	4.50	1.25
☐ 20 Fred Lynn	2.00	.90	.25
☐ 21 Dave Winfield	5.00	2.20	.60
☐ 22 Rod Carew	4.00	1.80	.50
☐ 23 Jim Rice	2.00	.90	.25
☐ 24 Bruce Sutter	2.00	.90	.25
☐ 25 Cesar Cedeno	1.00	.45	.12
☐ 26 Nolan Ryan	12.50	5.50	1.55
☐ 27 Dusty Baker	1.00	.45	.12
☐ 28 Jim Palmer	4.00	1.80	.50
☐ 29 Gorman Thomas	1.00	.45	.12
☐ 30 Ben Oglivie	1.00	.45	.12
☐ 31 Willie Wilson	1.00	.45	.12
☐ 32 Gary Carter	3.00	1.35	.35

1982 Perma-Graphic All-Stars

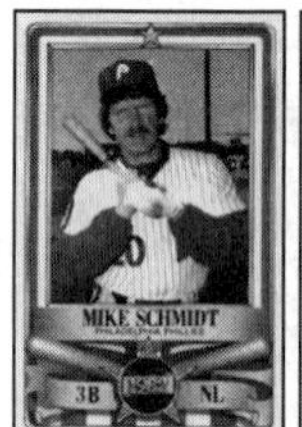

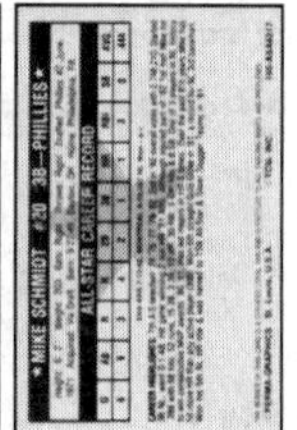

For the second time Perma-Graphic issued a special set commemorating the starters of the 1982 All-Star game. This 18-card set measures 2 1/8" by 3 3/8" and features a colorful design framing the players photo on the front The back again feature one line of complete All-Star game statistics including the 1982 game and career highlites. Perma-Graphic also issued the set in a limited (reportedly 1200 sets produced) "gold" edition, i.e., with a gold tint to the cards. The gold edition cards are valued at a multiplte of the regular set. Please refer to the multiplication table below.

	NRMT	VG-E	GOOD
COMPLETE SET (18)	50.00	22.00	6.25
COMMON CARD (1-18)	1.50	.70	.19
*GOLD CARDS:2X to 3X BASIC CARDS			
☐ 1 Dennis Eckersley			
☐ 2 Cecil Cooper	1.50	.70	.19
☐ 3 Carlton Fisk	5.00	2.20	.60
☐ 4 Robin Yount	5.00	2.20	.60
☐ 5 Bobby Grich	1.50	.70	.19
☐ 6 Rickey Henderson	6.00	2.70	.75
☐ 7 Reggie Jackson	6.00	2.70	.75
☐ 8 Fred Lynn	2.50	1.10	.30
☐ 9 George Brett	10.00	4.50	1.25
☐ 10 Gary Carter	4.00	1.80	.50
☐ 11 Dave Concepcion	1.50	.70	.19
☐ 12 Andre Dawson	4.00	1.80	.50
☐ 13 Tim Raines	2.50	1.10	.30
☐ 14 Dale Murphy	4.00	1.80	.50
☐ 15 Steve Rogers	1.50	.70	.19
☐ 16 Pete Rose	6.00	2.70	.75
☐ 17 Mike Schmidt	6.00	2.70	.75
☐ 18 Manny Trillo	1.50	.70	.19

1982 Perma-Graphic Credit Cards

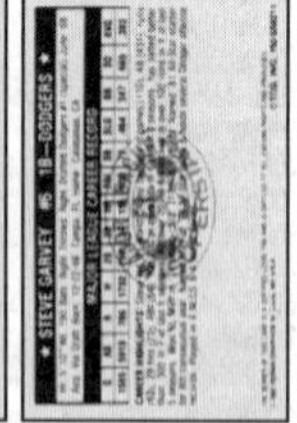

For the second year Perma-Graphic, in association with Topps produced a high-quality set on plastic honoring the leading players in baseball of 1982. The players photo is on the front middle of the card and is framed by a brown border with many innovative designs. This 24-card set features plastic cards each measuring approximately 2 1/8" by 3 3/8". On the card back there is one line of career statistics along with career highlights. Perma-Graphic also issued the set in a limited (reportedly 900 sets produced) "gold" edition, i.e., with a gold tint to the cards. The gold edition cards are valued at a mulitple of the regular cards. Please see information below for the multiplication value. Again in 1982 Perma-Graphic issued these sets in conjuction and with the approval of Topps Chewing Gum.

	NRMT	VG-E	GOOD
COMPLETE SET (24)	50.00	22.00	6.25
COMMON CARD (1-24)	1.00	.45	.12
*GOLD CARDS: 2X to 3X BASIC CARDS			
☐ 1 Johnny Bench	4.00	1.80	.50
☐ 2 Tom Seaver	4.00	1.80	.50
☐ 3 Mike Schmidt	6.00	2.70	.75
☐ 4 Gary Carter	3.00	1.35	.35
☐ 5 Willie Stargell	3.00	1.35	.35
☐ 6 Tim Raines	2.00	.90	.25
☐ 7 Bill Madlock	1.00	.45	.12
☐ 8 Keith Hernandez	2.00	.90	.25
☐ 9 Pete Rose	6.00	2.70	.75
☐ 10 Steve Carlton	4.00	1.80	.50
☐ 11 Steve Garvey	2.00	.90	.25
☐ 12 Fernando Valenzuela	2.00	.90	.25
☐ 13 Carl Yastrzemski	4.00	1.80	.50
☐ 14 Dave Winfield	4.00	1.80	.50
☐ 15 Carney Lansford	1.00	.45	.12
☐ 16 Rollie Fingers	2.50	1.10	.30
☐ 17 Tony Armas	1.00	.45	.12
☐ 18 Cecil Cooper	1.00	.45	.12
☐ 19 George Brett	10.00	4.50	1.25
☐ 20 Reggie Jackson	6.00	2.70	.75
☐ 21 Rod Carew	4.00	1.80	.50
☐ 22 Eddie Murray	7.50	3.40	.95
☐ 23 Rickey Henderson	6.00	2.70	.75
☐ 24 Kirk Gibson	3.00	1.35	.35

1983 Perma-Graphic All-Stars

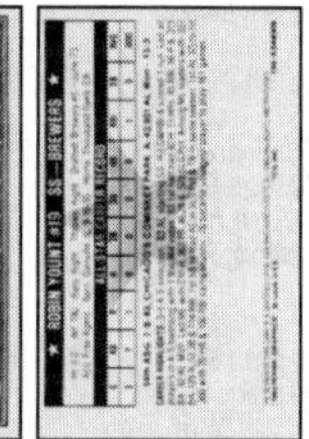

The 1983 All-Star Set was the third set Perma-Graphic issued commemorating the starters of the All-Star game. Again, Perma-Graphic used the Topps photos and issued their sets of plastic cards. This 18-card set features cards each measuring approximately 2 1/8" by 3 3/8". Perma-Graphic also issued the set in a limited "gold" edition, i.e., with a gold tint to the cards. The gold edition cards are valued at a multiple of the regular issue cards. Please see information below for values.

	NRMT	VG-E	GOOD
COMPLETE SET (18)_	50.00	22.00	6.25
COMMON CARD (1-18)	1.25	.55	.16
*GOLD CARDS:2X to3 X BASIC CARDS			
☐ 1 George Brett	10.00	4.50	1.25
☐ 2 Rod Carew	4.00	1.80	.50
☐ 3 Fred Lynn	2.50	1.10	.30
☐ 4 Jim Rice	2.50	1.10	.30
☐ 5 Ted Simmons	1.25	.55	.16
☐ 6 Dave Stieb	1.25	.55	.16
☐ 7 Dave Winfield	4.00	1.80	.50
☐ 8 Manny Trillo	1.25	.55	.16
☐ 9 Robin Yount	4.00	1.80	.50
☐ 10 Gary Carter	3.00	1.35	.35
☐ 11 Andre Dawson	3.00	1.35	.35
☐ 12 Dale Murphy	3.00	1.35	.35
☐ 13 Al Oliver	1.25	.55	.16
☐ 14 Tim Raines	3.00	1.35	.35
☐ 15 Steve Sax	1.25	.55	.16
☐ 16 Mike Schmidt	6.00	2.70	.75
☐ 17 Ozzie Smith	7.50	3.40	.95
☐ 18 Mario Soto	1.25	.55	.16

1983 Perma-Graphic Credit Cards

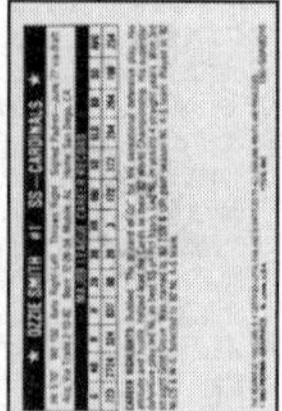

This set was the third straight year Perma-Graphic, with approval from Topps issued their high-quality plastic set. This 36-card set which measures 2 1/8" by 3 3/8" have the players photos framed by colorful backgrounds. The backs again feature one line of career statistics and several informative lines of career highlights. Perma-Graphic also issued the set in a limited (reportedly 1000 sets produced) "gold" edition, i.e., with a gold tint to the cards. The gold edition cards are valued at a multiple of the regular issue cards. Please see information below for values.

	NRMT	VG-E	GOOD
COMPLETE SET (36)	50.00	22.00	6.25
COMMON CARD (1-36)	1.00	.45	.12
*GOLD CARDS:2X to 3X BASIC CARDS			

☐ 1 Bill Buckner	1.00	.45	.12
☐ 2 Steve Carlton	4.00	1.80	.50
☐ 3 Gary Carter	3.00	1.35	.35
☐ 4 Andre Dawson	3.00	1.35	.35
☐ 5 Pedro Guerrero	1.00	.45	.12
☐ 6 George Hendrick	1.00	.45	.12
☐ 7 Keith Hernandez	2.00	.90	.25
☐ 8 Bill Madlock	1.00	.45	.12
☐ 9 Dale Murphy	3.00	1.35	.35
☐ 10 Al Oliver	1.00	.45	.12
☐ 11 Dave Parker	2.00	.90	.25
☐ 12 Darrell Porter	1.00	.45	.12
☐ 13 Pete Rose	6.00	2.70	.75
☐ 14 Mike Schmidt	6.00	2.70	.75
☐ 15 Lonnie Smith	1.00	.45	.12
☐ 16 Ozzie Smith	7.50	3.40	.95
☐ 17 Bruce Sutter	2.00	.90	.25
☐ 18 Fernando Valenzuela	2.00	.90	.25
☐ 19 George Brett	10.00	4.50	1.25
☐ 20 Rod Carew	4.00	1.80	.50
☐ 21 Cecil Cooper	1.00	.45	.12
☐ 22 Doug DeCinces	1.00	.45	.12
☐ 23 Rollie Fingers	2.50	1.10	.30
☐ 24 Damaso Garcia	1.00	.45	.12
☐ 25 Toby Harrah	1.00	.45	.12
☐ 26 Rickey Henderson	6.00	2.70	.75
☐ 27 Reggie Jackson	6.00	2.70	.75
☐ 28 Hal McRae	1.00	.45	.12
☐ 29 Eddie Murray	6.00	2.70	.75
☐ 30 Lance Parrish	2.00	.90	.25
☐ 31 Jim Rice	2.00	.90	.25
☐ 32 Gorman Thomas	1.00	.45	.12
☐ 33 Willie Wilson	1.00	.45	.12
☐ 34 Dave Winfield	4.00	1.80	.50
☐ 35 Carl Yastrzemski	4.00	1.80	.50
☐ 36 Robin Yount	3.00	1.35	.35

1991 Petro-Canada Standups

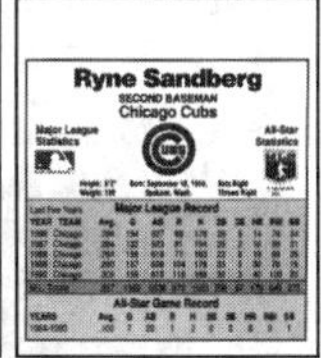

These 3-D action collector cards consist of three cardboard sheets measuring approximately 2 7/8" by 3 13/16" and joined at one end. The front cover has blue and red stripe borders and features either an American or National league logo inside a baseball diamond. The inside cover has a color photo of the crowd at the game. The middle sheet consists of a 3-D standup of the player. The inside of the last sheet has biographical information, career regular season statistics and All-Star game statistics. The back has career highlights in a sky blue box and "Play the All Star Quiz" questions and answers. The set was first released in Toronto at the All-Star Game in conjunction with the All-Star Fanfest. The cards are numbered on the front.

	MINT	NRMT	EXC
COMPLETE SET (26)	10.00	4.50	1.25
COMMON CARD (1-26)	.15	.07	.02

☐ 1 Cal Ripken	2.00	.90	.25
☐ 2 Greg Olson	.15	.07	.02
☐ 3 Roger Clemens	1.00	.45	.12
☐ 4 Ryne Sandberg	1.25	.55	.16
☐ 5 Dave Winfield	.50	.23	.06
☐ 6 Eric Davis	.25	.11	.03
☐ 7 Carlton Fisk	.35	.16	.04
☐ 8 Mike Scott	.15	.07	.02
☐ 9 Sandy Alomar Jr.	.25	.11	.03
☐ 10 Tim Wallach	.15	.07	.02
☐ 11 Cecil Fielder	.50	.23	.06
☐ 12 Dwight Gooden	.25	.11	.03
☐ 13 George Brett	1.50	.70	.19
☐ 14 Dale Murphy	.35	.16	.04
☐ 15 Paul Molitor	.50	.23	.06
☐ 16 Barry Bonds	1.00	.45	.12
☐ 17 Kirby Puckett	1.25	.55	.16
☐ 18 Ozzie Smith	1.25	.55	.16
☐ 19 Don Mattingly	1.25	.55	.16
☐ 20 Will Clark	.75	.35	.09
☐ 21 Rickey Henderson	.50	.23	.06
☐ 22 Orel Hershiser	.25	.11	.03
☐ 23 Ken Griffey Jr.	2.50	1.10	.30
☐ 24 Tony Gwynn	1.25	.55	.16
☐ 25 Nolan Ryan	2.00	.90	.25
☐ 26 Kelly Gruber	.15	.07	.02

1909 Philadelphia Caramel E95

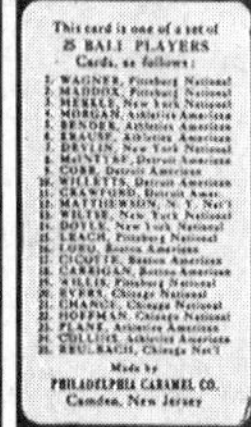
This card is one of a set of
25 BALL PLAYERS
Cards, as follows:
1. WAGNER, Pittsburg National
2. MADDOX, Pittsburg National
3. MERKLE, New York National
4. MORGAN, Athletics American
5. BENDER, Athletics American
6. KRAUSE, Athletics American
7. DEVLIN, New York National
8. McINTYRE, Detroit American
9. COBB, Detroit American
10. WILLETTS, Detroit American
11. CRAWFORD, Detroit Amer.
12. MATTHEWSON, N. Y. Nat'l
13. WILTSE, New York National
14. DOYLE, New York National
15. LEACH, Pittsburg National
16. LORD, Boston American
17. CICOTTE, Boston American
18. CARRIGAN, Boston American
19. WILLIS, Pittsburg National
20. EVERS, Chicago National
21. CHANCE, Chicago National
22. HOFFMAN, Chicago National
23. PLANK, Athletics American
24. COLLINS, Athletics American
25. REULBACH, Chicago Nat'l
Made by
PHILADELPHIA CARAMEL CO.
Camden, New Jersey

The cards in this 25-card set measure 1 1/2" by 2 3/4". This set of color drawings was issued by the Philadelphia Caramel Company about 1909. The back is checklisted with its own numbering system (begins with "1. Wagner"), but has been alphabetized for convenience in this listing. Blank backs found in this set are probably cut from advertising panels and should not be considered as proof cards.

	EX-MT	VG-E	GOOD
COMPLETE SET (25)	4500.00	2000.00	550.00
COMMON CARD (1-25)	75.00	34.00	9.50

☐ 1 Chief Bender	200.00	90.00	25.00
☐ 2 Bill Carrigan	75.00	34.00	9.50
☐ 3 Frank Chance	225.00	100.00	28.00
☐ 4 Eddie Cicotte	150.00	70.00	19.00
☐ 5 Ty Cobb	1250.00	550.00	160.00
☐ 6 Eddie Collins	225.00	100.00	28.00
☐ 7 Sam Crawford	225.00	100.00	28.00
☐ 8 Art Devlin	75.00	34.00	9.50
☐ 9 Larry Doyle	75.00	34.00	9.50
☐ 10 Johnny Evers	200.00	90.00	25.00
☐ 11 Solly Hoffman	75.00	34.00	9.50
☐ 12 Harry Krause	75.00	34.00	9.50
☐ 13 Tommy Leach	75.00	34.00	9.50
☐ 14 Harry Lord	75.00	34.00	9.50
☐ 15 Nick Maddox	75.00	34.00	9.50
☐ 16 Christy Mathewson	500.00	220.00	60.00
☐ 17 Matty McIntyre	75.00	34.00	9.50
☐ 18 Fred Merkle	100.00	45.00	12.50
☐ 19 Harry (Cy) Morgan	75.00	34.00	9.50
☐ 20 Eddie Plank	300.00	135.00	38.00
☐ 21 Ed Reulbach	75.00	34.00	9.50
☐ 22 Honus Wagner	600.00	275.00	75.00
☐ 23 Ed Willett	75.00	34.00	9.50
☐ 24 Vic Willis	100.00	45.00	12.50
☐ 25 Hooks Wiltse	75.00	34.00	9.50

1912 Philadelphia Caramel E96

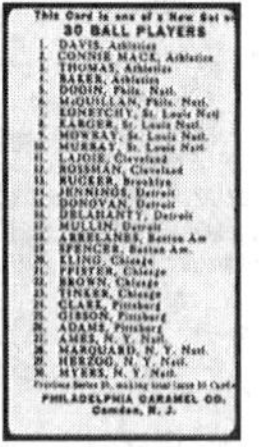
This Card is one of a New Set of
30 BALL PLAYERS
1. DAVIS, Athletics
2. CONNIE MACK, Athletics
3. THOMAS, Athletics
4. BAKER, Athletics
5. DOOIN, Phila. Natl.
6. McQUILLAN, Phila. Natl.
7. KONETCHY, St. Louis Natl.
8. KARGER, St. Louis Natl.
9. MOWRAY, St. Louis Natl.
10. MURRAY, St. Louis Natl.
11. LAJOIE, Cleveland
12. ROSSMAN, Cleveland
13. RUCKER, Brooklyn
14. JENNINGS, Detroit
15. DONOVAN, Detroit
16. DELAHANTY, Detroit
17. MULLIN, Detroit
18. ARRELANES, Boston Am.
19. SPENCER, Boston Am.
20. KLING, Chicago
21. PFISTER, Chicago
22. BROWN, Chicago
23. TINKER, Chicago
24. CLARK, Pittsburg
25. GIBSON, Pittsburg
26. ADAMS, Pittsburg
27. AMES, N. Y. Natl.
28. MARQUARD, N. Y. Natl.
29. HERZOG, N. Y. Natl.
30. MYERS, N. Y. Natl.
PHILADELPHIA CARAMEL CO.
Camden, N. J.

The cards in this 30-card set measure 1 1/2" by 2 3/4". The red printed backs in this set carry the statement "previous Series 25, making total issue 55 cards", and for this reason it is often referred to as the second series of E95. Issued about 1912, the numbering of the original checklist (starts with "1. Davis") has been rearranged alphabetically below. Some blank backs are known.

	EX-MT	VG-E	GOOD
COMPLETE SET (30)	3200.00	1450.00	400.00
COMMON CARD (1-30)	75.00	34.00	9.50

☐ 1 Babe Adams	75.00	34.00	9.50
☐ 2 Red Ames	75.00	34.00	9.50
☐ 3 Frank Arrelanes	75.00	34.00	9.50
☐ 4 J. Frank Baker	175.00	80.00	22.00
☐ 5 Mordecai Brown	150.00	70.00	19.00
☐ 6 Fred Clark (sic)	150.00	70.00	19.00
☐ 7 Harry Davis	75.00	34.00	9.50
☐ 8 Jim Delehanty	75.00	34.00	9.50
☐ 9 Bill Donovan	75.00	34.00	9.50
☐ 10 Red Dooin	75.00	34.00	9.50
☐ 11 George Gibson	75.00	34.00	9.50
☐ 12 Buck Herzog	75.00	34.00	9.50
☐ 13 Hugh Jennings	150.00	70.00	19.00
☐ 14 Ed Karger	75.00	34.00	9.50
☐ 15 Johnny Kling	75.00	34.00	9.50
☐ 16 Ed Konetchy	75.00	34.00	9.50
☐ 17 Napoleon Lajoie	400.00	180.00	50.00
☐ 18 Connie Mack	400.00	180.00	50.00
☐ 19 Rube Marquard	150.00	70.00	19.00
☐ 20 George McQuillan	75.00	34.00	9.50
☐ 21 Chief Meyers	75.00	34.00	9.50
☐ 22 Mike Mowrey	75.00	34.00	9.50
☐ 23 George Mullin	75.00	34.00	9.50
☐ 24 Red Murray	75.00	34.00	9.50
☐ 25 Jack Pfeister	75.00	34.00	9.50
☐ 26 Claude Rossman	75.00	34.00	9.50
☐ 27 Nap Rucker	75.00	34.00	9.50
☐ 28 Tubby Spencer	75.00	34.00	9.50
☐ 29 Ira Thomas	75.00	34.00	9.50
☐ 30 Joe Tinker	150.00	70.00	19.00

1949 Philadelphia Bulletin

This 59-card set features 8" by 10" black-and-white portraits of the Philadelphia A's and Phillies. Six of the portraits were inserted each week in the "Fun Book" section of the "Philadelphia Sunday Bulletin" from May 22 through July 24, 1949. Only five portraits were inserted in the paper the last Sunday. The cards are unnumbered and checklisted below in alphabetical order.

	NRMT	VG-E	GOOD
COMPLETE SET (59)	250.00	110.00	31.00
COMMON CARD (1-59)	3.50	1.55	.45

☐ 1 Richie Ashburn	20.00	9.00	2.50
☐ 2 Joe Astroth	3.50	1.55	.45
☐ 3 Bennie Bengough CO	3.50	1.55	.45
☐ 4 Hank Biasetti	3.50	1.55	.45
☐ 5 Charles Bicknell	3.50	1.55	.45
☐ 6 Buddy Blattner	3.50	1.55	.45
☐ 7 Hank Borowy	3.50	1.55	.45
☐ 8 Lou Brissie	3.50	1.55	.45
☐ 9 Earle Brucker CO	3.50	1.55	.45
☐ 10 Ralph Caballero	3.50	1.55	.45
☐ 11 Sam Chapman	5.00	2.20	.60
☐ 12 Joe Coleman	5.00	2.20	.60
☐ 13 Dusty Cooke CO	3.50	1.55	.45
☐ 14 Thomas Davis	3.50	1.55	.45
☐ 15 Blix Donnelly	3.50	1.55	.45
☐ 16 Jimmy Dykes CO	5.00	2.20	.60
☐ 17 Del Ennis	5.00	2.20	.60
☐ 18 Ferris Fain	5.00	2.20	.60
☐ 19 Dick Fowler	3.50	1.55	.45
☐ 20 Nellie Fox	20.00	9.00	2.50
☐ 21 Mike Guerra	3.50	1.55	.45
☐ 22 Granny Hamner	5.00	2.20	.60
☐ 23 Charley Harris	3.50	1.55	.45
☐ 24 Ken Heintzleman	3.50	1.55	.45
☐ 25 Stan Hollmig	3.50	1.55	.45
☐ 26 Willie Jones	3.50	1.55	.45
☐ 27 Eddie Joost	5.00	2.20	.60
☐ 28 Alex Kellner	3.50	1.55	.45
☐ 29 Jim Konstanty	5.00	2.20	.60
☐ 30 Stan Lopata	5.00	2.20	.60
☐ 31 Connie Mack MG	20.00	9.00	2.50
☐ 32 Earle Mack CO	5.00	2.20	.60
☐ 33 Hank Majeskie	3.50	1.55	.45
☐ 34 Phil Marchildon	3.50	1.55	.45
☐ 35 Jackie Mayo	3.50	1.55	.45
☐ 36 Bill McCahan	3.50	1.55	.45
☐ 37 Barney McCoskey	3.50	1.55	.45
☐ 38 Russ Meyer	5.00	2.20	.60
☐ 39 Eddie Miller	3.50	1.55	.45
☐ 40 Wally Moses	3.50	1.55	.45
☐ 41 Bill Nicholson	3.50	1.55	.45
☐ 42 Cy Perkins CO	3.50	1.55	.45
☐ 43 Robin Roberts	15.00	6.75	1.85
☐ 44 Buddy Rosar	3.50	1.55	.45
☐ 45 Schoolboy Rowe	5.00	2.20	.60
☐ 46 Eddie Sawyer	3.50	1.55	.45
☐ 47 Carl Scheib	3.50	1.55	.45
☐ 48 Andy Seminick	5.00	2.20	.60
☐ 49 Bobby Shantz	5.00	2.20	.60
☐ 50 Ken Silvestri	3.50	1.55	.45
☐ 51 Al Simmons CO	10.00	4.50	1.25
☐ 52 Curt Simmons	10.00	4.50	1.25
☐ 53 Dick Sisler	3.50	1.55	.45
☐ 54 Pete Suder	3.50	1.55	.45
☐ 55 Ken Trinkle	3.50	1.55	.45
☐ 56 Elmer Valo	3.50	1.55	.45
☐ 57 Eddie Waitkus	3.50	1.55	.45
☐ 58 Don White	3.50	1.55	.45
☐ 59 Taft Wright	3.50	1.55	.45

1992 Philadelphia Daily News *

This nine-card set, which is aptly subtitled "Great Moments in Philadelphia Sports," was sponsored by the Philadelphia Daily News. The fronts of the standard-size cards have red borders and feature miniature reproductions of newspaper front pages with famous headlines and memorable photos. Each card captures a great moment in the history of Philadelphia sports. Sports represented are baseball, (cards 1 and 7-8) hockey, (2) basketball, (3-4) football, (5-6) and boxing (9). The backs are printed in gray, black and white and provide text relating to the event commemorated on the card.

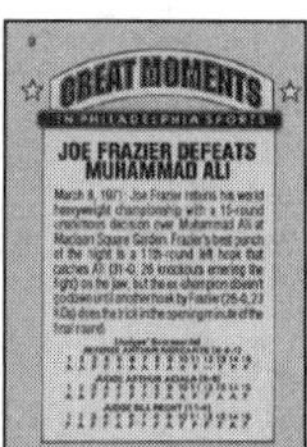

	MINT	NRMT	EXC
COMPLETE SET (9)	3.50	1.55	.45
COMMON CARD (1-9)	.25	.11	.03

☐ 1 We Win Phillies win World Series	.50	.23	.06
☐ 2 God Bless the Flyers Flyers win Stanley Cup	.25	.11	.03
☐ 3 V Villanova wins NCAA Championship	.25	.11	.03
☐ 4 Hoopla Sixers win NBA Championship	.25	.11	.03
☐ 5 Eagles Seek New CO, QB Eagles win NFL Championship	.25	.11	.03
☐ 6 Super Eagles win NFC Championship	.25	.11	.03
☐ 7 Mike Schmidt announces retirement	1.00	.45	.12
☐ 8 City Wild Phillies win NL Championship	.25	.11	.03
☐ 9 Joe Frazier defeats Muhammad Ali	1.00	.45	.12

1943 Phillies Team Issue

This 23-card set of the Philadelphia Phillies measures approximately 6" by 8 1/2" and features black-and-white player photos with white borders. The backs are blank. The cards are unnumbered and checklisted below in alphabetical order.

	NRMT	VG-E	GOOD
COMPLETE SET (23)	75.00	34.00	9.50
COMMON CARD (1-23)	3.00	1.35	.35

☐ 1 Buster Adams	3.00	1.35	.35
☐ 2 Walter Beck	3.00	1.35	.35
☐ 3 Charlie Brewster	3.00	1.35	.35
☐ 4 Paul Busby	3.00	1.35	.35
☐ 5 Bennie Culp	3.00	1.35	.35
☐ 6 Babe Dahlgren	5.00	2.20	.60
☐ 7 Lloyd Dietz	3.00	1.35	.35
☐ 8 George Eyrich	3.00	1.35	.35
☐ 9 Charlie Fuchs	3.00	1.35	.35
☐ 10 Al Gerheauser	3.00	1.35	.35
☐ 11 Si Johnson	3.00	1.35	.35
☐ 12 Newell Kimball	3.00	1.35	.35
☐ 13 Chuck Klein	15.00	6.75	1.85
☐ 14 Jack Kraus	3.00	1.35	.35
☐ 15 Mickey Livingston	3.00	1.35	.35
☐ 16 Merrill May	3.00	1.35	.35
☐ 17 Danny Murtaugh	10.00	4.50	1.25
☐ 18 Ron Northey	3.00	1.35	.35
☐ 19 Tom Padden	3.00	1.35	.35
☐ 20 Schoolboy Rowe	5.00	2.20	.60
☐ 21 Neb Stewart	3.00	1.35	.35
☐ 22 Coaker Triplett	3.00	1.35	.35
☐ 23 Jimmie Wasdell	3.00	1.35	.35

1949 Phillies Lummis Peanut Butter

The cards in this 12-card set measure 3 1/4" by 4 1/4". The 1949 Lummis set of black and white, unnumbered action poses depicts Philadelphia Phillies only. These "cards" are actually stickers and were distributed locally by Lummis Peanut Butter and Sealtest Dairy Products. The prices listed below are for the Sealtest cards. The harder-to-find Lummis variety are worth double the listed values below. The catalog designation is F343.

	NRMT	VG-E	GOOD
COMPLETE SET (12)	800.00	350.00	100.00
COMMON CARD (1-12)	50.00	22.00	6.25
☐ 1 Rich Ashburn	175.00	80.00	22.00
☐ 2 Hank Borowy	50.00	22.00	6.25
☐ 3 Del Ennis	60.00	27.00	7.50
☐ 4 Granny Hamner	50.00	22.00	6.25
☐ 5 Puddinhead Jones	50.00	22.00	6.25
☐ 6 Russ Meyer	50.00	22.00	6.25
☐ 7 Bill Nicholson	50.00	22.00	6.25
☐ 8 Robin Roberts	150.00	70.00	19.00
☐ 9 Schoolboy Rowe	60.00	27.00	7.50
☐ 10 Andy Seminick	60.00	27.00	7.50
☐ 11 Curt Simmons	60.00	27.00	7.50
☐ 12 Ed Waitkus	50.00	22.00	6.25

1958 Phillies Jay Publishing

This 12-card set of the Philadelphia Phillies measures approximately 5" by 7" and features black-and-white player photos in a white border. These cards were packaged 12 to a packet. The backs are blank. The cards are unnumbered and checklisted below in alphabetical order.

	NRMT	VG-E	GOOD
COMPLETE SET (12)	35.00	16.00	4.40
COMMON CARD (1-12)	2.50	1.10	.30
☐ 1 Harry Anderson	2.50	1.10	.30
☐ 2 Richie Ashburn	6.00	2.70	.75
☐ 3 Bob Bowman	2.50	1.10	.30
☐ 4 Dick Farrell	2.50	1.10	.30
☐ 5 Chico Fernandez	2.50	1.10	.30
☐ 6 Granny Hamner	2.50	1.10	.30
☐ 7 Stan Lopata	2.50	1.10	.30
☐ 8 Rip Repulski	2.50	1.10	.30
☐ 9 Robin Roberts	5.00	2.20	.60
☐ 10 Jack Sanford UER Sandford	2.50	1.10	.30
☐ 11 Curt Simmons	3.00	1.35	.35
☐ 12 Mayo Smith MG	2.50	1.10	.30

1960 Phillies Jay Publishing

This 12-card set of the Philadelphia Phillies measures approximately 5" X 7". The fronts feature black-and-white posed player photos with the player's and team name printed below in the white border. These cards were packaged 12 to a packet and originally sold for 25 cents. The backs are blank. The cards are unnumbered and checklisted below in alphabetical order.

	NRMT	VG-E	GOOD
COMPLETE SET (12)	30.00	13.50	3.70
COMMON CARD (1-12)	2.00	.90	.25
☐ 1 Ruben Amaro	2.00	.90	.25
☐ 2 Harry Anderson	2.00	.90	.25
☐ 3 Ed Bouchee	2.00	.90	.25
☐ 4 John Callison	4.00	1.80	.50
☐ 5 Jim Coker	2.00	.90	.25
☐ 6 Al Dark	3.00	1.35	.35
☐ 7 Dick Farrell	2.00	.90	.25
☐ 8 Pancho Herrera	2.00	.90	.25
☐ 9 Jim Owens	2.00	.90	.25
☐ 10 Wally Post	3.00	1.35	.35
☐ 11 Robin Roberts	10.00	4.50	1.25
☐ 12 Eddie Sawyer MG	2.00	.90	.25

1964 Phillies Jay Publishing

This 12-card set of the Philadelphia Phillies measures approximately 5" by 7". The fronts feature black-and-white posed player photos with the player's and team name printed below in the white border. These cards were packaged 12 to a packet. The backs are blank. The cards are unnumbered and checklisted below in alphabetical order.

	NRMT	VG-E	GOOD
COMPLETE SET (12)	30.00	13.50	3.70
COMMON CARD (1-12)	2.00	.90	.25
☐ 1 Ruben Amaro	2.50	1.10	.30
☐ 2 Jack Baldschun	2.00	.90	.25
☐ 3 Jim Bunning	5.00	2.20	.60
☐ 4 John Callison	3.50	1.55	.45
☐ 5 Clay Dalrymple	2.00	.90	.25
☐ 6 Dallas Green	3.50	1.55	.45
☐ 7 Art Mahaffey	2.00	.90	.25
☐ 8 Gene Mauch MG	2.50	1.10	.30
☐ 9 Chris Short	2.00	.90	.25
☐ 10 Tony Taylor	2.50	1.10	.30
☐ 11 Gus Triandos	2.50	1.10	.30
☐ 12 Bob Wine	2.00	.90	.25

1964 Phillies Philadelphia Bulletin

This 27-subject set was produced by the Philadelphia Bulletin, a newspaper. The catalog designation for this set is M130-5. These large, approximately 8" by 10", photo cards are unnumbered and blank backed. The complete set price below includes both Bunning variation cards.

	NRMT	VG-E	GOOD
COMPLETE SET (27)	250.00	110.00	31.00
COMMON CARD (1-27)	6.00	2.70	.75
☐ 1 Richie Allen	25.00	11.00	3.10
☐ 2 Ruben Amaro	7.50	3.40	.95
☐ 3 Jack Baldschun	6.00	2.70	.75
☐ 4 Dennis Bennett	6.00	2.70	.75
☐ 5 John Boozer	6.00	2.70	.75
☐ 6 Johnny Briggs	6.00	2.70	.75
☐ 7 Jim Bunning (2)	25.00	11.00	3.10
☐ 8 Johnny Callison	7.50	3.40	.95
☐ 9 Danny Cater	6.00	2.70	.75
☐ 10 Wes Covington	7.50	3.40	.95
☐ 11 Ray Culp	7.50	3.40	.95
☐ 12 Clay Dalrymple	6.00	2.70	.75
☐ 13 Tony Gonzalez	7.50	3.40	.95
☐ 14 John Herrnstein	6.00	2.70	.75
☐ 15 Alex Johnson	7.50	3.40	.95
☐ 16 Art Mahaffey	6.00	2.70	.75
☐ 17 Gene Mauch MG	7.50	3.40	.95
☐ 18 Vic Power	7.50	3.40	.95
☐ 19 Ed Roebuck	6.00	2.70	.75
☐ 20 Cookie Rojas	7.50	3.40	.95
☐ 21 Bobby Shantz	7.50	3.40	.95
☐ 22 Chris Short	7.50	3.40	.95
☐ 23 Tony Taylor	7.50	3.40	.95
☐ 24 Frank Thomas	7.50	3.40	.95
☐ 25 Gus Triandos	7.50	3.40	.95
☐ 26 Bobby Wine	7.50	3.40	.95
☐ 27 Rick Wise	7.50	3.40	.95

1964 Phillies Team Set

This six-card set of the Philadelphia Phillies measures approximately 3 1/4" by 5 1/2" and feature black-and-white player portraits with a facsimile autograph. The backs are blank. The cards are unnumbered and checklisted below in alphabetical order.

	NRMT	VG-E	GOOD
COMPLETE SET (6)	20.00	9.00	2.50
COMMON CARD (1-6)	3.00	1.35	.35
☐ 1 Jim Bunning	7.50	3.40	.95
☐ 2 Clay Dalrymple	3.00	1.35	.35
☐ 3 Tony Gonzalez	3.00	1.35	.35
☐ 4 Cookie Rojas	4.00	1.80	.50
☐ 5 Chris Short	4.00	1.80	.50
☐ 6 Roy Sievers	4.00	1.80	.50

1965 Phillies Jay Publishing

This 12-card set of the Philadelphia Phillies measures approximately 5" X 7". The fronts feature black-and-white posed player photos with the player's and team's names printed below in the white border.

These cards were packaged 12 to a packet and originally sold for 25 cents. The backs are blank. The cards are unnumbered and checklisted below in alphabetical order.

	NRMT	VG-E	GOOD
COMPLETE SET (12)	25.00	11.00	3.10
COMMON CARD (1-12)	2.00	.90	.25
☐ 1 Ruben Amaro	2.00	.90	.25
☐ 2 Jack Baldschun	2.00	.90	.25
☐ 3 Jim Bunning	7.50	3.40	.95
☐ 4 John Callison	5.00	2.20	.60
☐ 5 Clay Dalrymple	2.00	.90	.25
☐ 6 Dallas Green	3.00	1.35	.35
☐ 7 Art Mahaffey	2.00	.90	.25
☐ 8 Gene Mauch MG	3.00	1.35	.35
☐ 9 Chris Short	2.00	.90	.25
☐ 10 Tony Taylor	3.00	1.35	.35
☐ 11 Gus Triandos	2.00	.90	.25
☐ 12 Bob Wine	2.00	.90	.25

1966 Phillies Team Issue

This 12-card set features black-and-white photos of the 1966 Philadelphia Phillies. The cards are unnumbered and checklisted below in alphabetical order.

	NRMT	VG-E	GOOD
COMPLETE SET (12)	25.00	11.00	3.10
COMMON CARD (1-12)	2.00	.90	.25
☐ 1 Richie Allen	3.50	1.55	.45
☐ 2 Jackie Brandt	2.00	.90	.25
☐ 3 Jim Bunning	4.50	2.00	.55
☐ 4 John Callison	3.50	1.55	.45
☐ 5 Ray Culp	2.00	.90	.25
☐ 6 Clayton Dalrymple	2.00	.90	.25
☐ 7 Tony Gonzalez	2.00	.90	.25
☐ 8 Dick Groat	2.00	.90	.25
☐ 9 Phil Linz	2.00	.90	.25
☐ 10 Cookie Rojas	2.00	.90	.25
☐ 11 Chris Short	2.00	.90	.25
☐ 12 Bill White	2.50	1.10	.30

1967 Phillies Police

The 1967 Philadelphia Phillies Police/Safety set contains 13 cards measuring approximately 2 13/16" by 4 7/16". The black and white posed player photos on the fronts are bordered in white and have the player's signature inscribed across the picture. In blue print on white, the backs have biography, player profile, and a "Safe Driving" emblem at the bottom. Cards can be found where the players' pictured on the fronts do not match the card backs. For example, the Jim Bunning card has a Dick Ellsworth back, the John Briggs card has a Dick Groat back, the Johnny Callison card has a Bill White back, the Clay Dalrymple card has a Chris Short back, and the Gene Mauch card has a Tony Gonzalez back. The cards are unnumbered and checklisted below in alphabetical order.

	NRMT	VG-E	GOOD
COMPLETE SET (13)	65.00	29.00	8.00
COMMON CARD (1-13)	3.00	1.35	.35
☐ 1 Richie Allen	8.00	3.60	1.00
☐ 2 Jim Bunning	15.00	6.75	1.85
☐ 3 John Briggs	3.00	1.35	.35
☐ 4 Johnny Callison	6.00	2.70	.75
☐ 5 Clay Dalrymple	4.00	1.80	.50
☐ 6 Dick Ellsworth	4.00	1.80	.50
☐ 7 Tony Gonzalez	4.00	1.80	.50
☐ 8 Dick Groat	6.00	2.70	.75
☐ 9 Larry Jackson	4.00	1.80	.50
☐ 10 Gene Mauch MG	5.00	2.20	.60
☐ 11 Cookie Rojas	5.00	2.20	.60
☐ 12 Chris Short	4.00	1.80	.50
☐ 13 Bill White	6.00	2.70	.75

1969 Phillies Team Issue

This 12-card set of the Philadelphia Phillies measures approximately 4 1/4" by 7". The fronts freature black-and-white player portraits in a white border. The player's name and team name are printed above. The backs are blank. The cards are unnumbered and checklisted below in alphabetical order.

	NRMT	VG-E	GOOD
COMPLETE SET (12)	25.00	11.00	3.10
COMMON CARD (1-12)	2.00	.90	.25
☐ 1 Richie Allen	3.50	1.55	.45
☐ 2 John Callison	3.50	1.55	.45
☐ 3 Woody Fryman	2.00	.90	.25
☐ 4 Larry Hisle	2.00	.90	.25
☐ 5 Deron Johnson	2.50	1.10	.30
☐ 6 Don Money	2.00	.90	.25
☐ 7 Cookie Rojas	2.50	1.10	.30
☐ 8 Mike Ryan	2.00	.90	.25
☐ 9 Chris Short	2.00	.90	.25
☐ 10 Bob Skinner MG	2.00	.90	.25
☐ 11 Tony Taylor	2.00	.90	.25
☐ 12 Rick Wise	2.00	.90	.25

1970 Phillies Team Issue

This 12-card set of the Philadelphia Phillies measures approximately 4 1/4" by 7" and features black-and-white player photos in a white border. Packaged 12 to a packet with blank backs, the cards are unnumbered and checklisted below in alphabetical order.

	NRMT	VG-E	GOOD
COMPLETE SET (12)	25.00	11.00	3.10
COMMON CARD (1-12)	2.00	.90	.25
☐ 1 Larry Bowa	5.00	2.20	.60
☐ 2 John Briggs	2.00	.90	.25
☐ 3 Denny Doyle	2.00	.90	.25
☐ 4 Larry Hisle	3.00	1.35	.35
☐ 5 Grant Jackson	2.00	.90	.25
☐ 6 Deron Johnson	3.00	1.35	.35
☐ 7 Rick Joseph	2.00	.90	.25
☐ 8 Tim McCarver	4.00	1.80	.50
☐ 9 Don Money	2.00	.90	.25
☐ 10 Chris Short	2.50	1.10	.30
☐ 11 Tony Taylor	2.50	1.10	.30
☐ 12 Rick Wise	2.50	1.10	.30

1971 Phillies Arco Oil

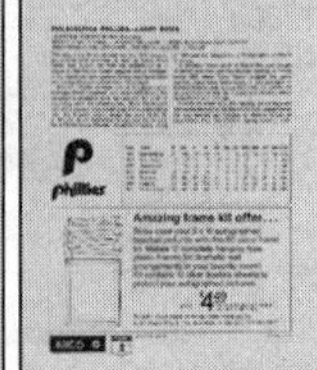

Sponsored by Arco Oil, these 13 pictures of the 1971 Philadelphia Phillies measure approximately 8" by 10" and feature on their fronts white-bordered posed color player photos. The player's name is shown in black lettering within the white margin below the photo. His facsimile autograph appears across the picture. The white back carries the team's and player's names at the top, followed below by position, biography, career highlights, and statistics. An ad at the bottom for picture frames rounds out the back. The cards are unnumbered and checklisted below in alphabetical order.

	NRMT	VG-E	GOOD
COMPLETE SET (13)	35.00	16.00	4.40
COMMON CARD (1-13)	2.50	1.10	.30
☐ 1 Larry Bowa	5.00	2.20	.60
☐ 2 Jim Bunning	7.50	3.40	.95
☐ 3 Roger Freed	2.50	1.10	.30
☐ 4 Terry Harmon	2.50	1.10	.30
☐ 5 Larry Hisle	3.00	1.35	.35
☐ 6 Joe Hoerner	2.50	1.10	.30
☐ 7 Deron Johnson	3.00	1.35	.35
☐ 8 Tim McCarver	5.00	2.20	.60
☐ 9 Don Money	3.00	1.35	.35
☐ 10 Dick Selma	2.50	1.10	.30
☐ 11 Chris Short	3.00	1.35	.35
☐ 12 Tony Taylor	3.00	1.35	.35
☐ 13 Rick Wise	3.00	1.35	.35

1974 Phillies Johnny Pro

This 12-card set measures approximately 3 3/4" by 7 1/8" and features members of the 1974 Philadelphia Phillies. The most significant player in this series is an early card of Mike Schmidt. The cards are designed to be pushed out and have the players photo against a solid white background. The backs are blank and marked the second straight year that Johnny Pro issued cards of a major league team. The set is checklisted by uniform number. According to informed sources, there were less than 15,000 sets produced.

	NRMT	VG-E	GOOD
COMPLETE SET (12)	300.00	135.00	38.00
COMMON CARD	5.00	2.20	.60
☐ 8 Bob Boone	15.00	6.75	1.85
☐ 10 Larry Bowa	7.50	3.40	.95
☐ 16 Dave Cash	5.00	2.20	.60
☐ 19 Greg Luzinski	15.00	6.75	1.85
☐ 20 Mike Schmidt	225.00	100.00	28.00
☐ 22 Mike Anderson	5.00	2.20	.60
☐ 24 Bill Robinson	6.00	2.70	.75
☐ 25 Del Unser	6.00	2.70	.75
☐ 27 Willie Montanez	5.00	2.20	.60
☐ 32 Steve Carlton	50.00	22.00	6.25
☐ 37 Ron Schueler	6.00	2.70	.75
☐ 41 Jim Lonborg	7.50	3.40	.95

1978 Phillies SSPC

This 27 card standard-size set features members of the Philadelphia Phillies giving various skill tips. The cards are numbered 28-54 in continuation of the set begun by the Yankees Diary set.

	NRMT	VG-E	GOOD
COMPLETE SET	10.00	4.50	1.25
COMMON CARD (28-54)	.10	.05	.01
☐ 28 Garry Maddox	.10	.05	.01
☐ 29 Steve Carlton	2.50	1.10	.30
☐ 30 Ron Reed	.10	.05	.01
☐ 31 Greg Luzinski	.50	.23	.06
☐ 32 Bobby Wine CO	.10	.05	.01
☐ 33 Bob Boone	.10	.05	.01
☐ 34 Carroll Beringer CO	.10	.05	.01
☐ 35 Rich Hebner	.10	.05	.01
☐ 36 Ray Ripplemeyer CO	.10	.05	.01
☐ 37 Terry Harmon	.10	.05	.01
☐ 38 Gene Garber	.10	.05	.01
☐ 39 Ted Sizemore	.10	.05	.01
☐ 40 Barry Foote	.10	.05	.01
☐ 41 Tony Taylor CO	.10	.05	.01
☐ 42 Tug McGraw	.25	.11	.03
☐ 43 Jay Johnstone	.25	.11	.03
☐ 44 Randy Lerch	.10	.05	.01
☐ 45 Billy DeMars CO	.10	.05	.01
☐ 46 Mike Schmidt	2.00	.90	.25
☐ 47 Larry Christenson	.10	.05	.01
☐ 48 Tim McCarver	.25	.11	.03
☐ 49 Larry Bowa	.50	.23	.06
☐ 50 Danny Ozark MG	.10	.05	.01
☐ 51 Jerry Martin	.10	.05	.01
☐ 52 Jim Lonborg	.10	.05	.01
☐ 53 Bake McBride	.10	.05	.01
☐ 54 Warren Brusstar	.10	.05	.01

1979 Phillies Burger King

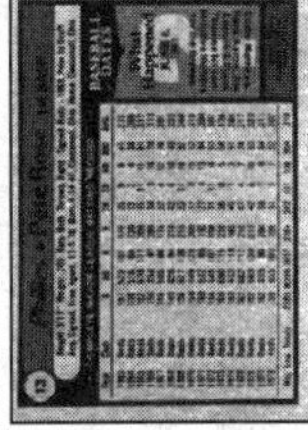

The cards in this 23-card set measure 2 1/2" by 3 1/2". The 1979 Burger King Phillies set follows the regular format of 22 player cards and one unnumbered checklist card. The asterisk indicates where the pose differs from the Topps card of that year. The set features the first card of Pete Rose as a member of the Philadelphia Phillies.

	NRMT	VG-E	GOOD
COMPLETE SET (23)	10.00	4.50	1.25
COMMON CARD (1-22)	.15	.07	.02
☐ 1 Danny Ozark MG *	.25	.11	.03
☐ 2 Bob Boone	.50	.23	.06
☐ 3 Tim McCarver	.50	.23	.06
☐ 4 Steve Carlton	2.50	1.10	.30
☐ 5 Larry Christenson	.15	.07	.02
☐ 6 Dick Ruthven	.15	.07	.02
☐ 7 Ron Reed	.15	.07	.02
☐ 8 Randy Lerch	.15	.07	.02
☐ 9 Warren Brusstar	.15	.07	.02
☐ 10 Tug McGraw	.35	.16	.04
☐ 11 Nino Espinosa *	.15	.07	.02
☐ 12 Doug Bird *	.15	.07	.02
☐ 13 Pete Rose * (Shown as Reds in 1979 Topps)	4.00	1.80	.50
☐ 14 Manny Trillo *	.25	.11	.03
☐ 15 Larry Bowa	.35	.16	.04
☐ 16 Mike Schmidt	4.00	1.80	.50
☐ 17 Pete Mackanin *	.15	.07	.02
☐ 18 Jose Cardenal	.15	.07	.02
☐ 19 Greg Luzinski	.35	.16	.04
☐ 20 Garry Maddox	.25	.11	.03
☐ 21 Bake McBride	.15	.07	.02
☐ 22 Greg Gross *	.15	.07	.02
☐ NNO Checklist Card TP	.05	.02	.01

1979 Phillies Team Issue

This 10-card set of the Philadelphia Phillies was issued in a clear front envelope and was likely sold at the stadium. The set measures approximately 8 3/4" by 11 5/8" and features art work by Todd Alan Gold. Each card displays two action drawings and a portrait of the same player. The backs are blank. The cards are unnumbered and checklisted below in alphabetical order.

	NRMT	VG-E	GOOD
COMPLETE SET (10)	20.00	9.00	2.50
COMMON CARD (1-10)	1.50	.70	.19
☐ 1 Rich Ashburn	3.00	1.35	.35
☐ 2 Bob Boone	2.00	.90	.25
☐ 3 Larry Bowa	2.00	.90	.25
☐ 4 Greg Luzinski	2.00	.90	.25
☐ 5 Garry Maddox	1.50	.70	.19
☐ 6 Bake McBride	1.50	.70	.19
☐ 7 Robin Roberts	2.00	.90	.25
☐ 8 Pete Rose	5.00	2.20	.60
☐ 9 Mike Schmidt	5.00	2.20	.60
☐ 10 Manny Trillo	1.50	.70	.19

1980 Phillies Burger King

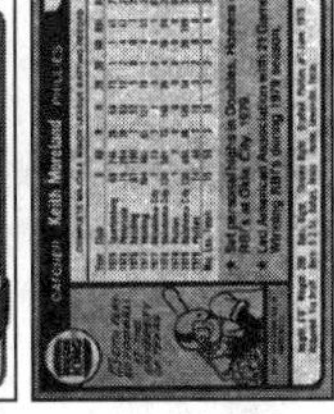

The cards in this 23-card set measure 2 1/2" by 3 1/2". The 1980 edition of Burger King Phillies follows the established pattern of 22 numbered player cards and one unnumbered checklist. Cards marked with asterisks contain poses different from those found in the regular 1980 Topps cards. This was the first Burger King set to carry the Burger King logo and hence does not generate the same confusion that the three previous years do for collectors trying to distinguish Burger King cards from the very similar Topps cards of the same years.

	NRMT	VG-E	GOOD
COMPLETE SET (23)	8.00	3.60	1.00
COMMON CARD (1-22)	.10	.05	.01
☐ 1 Dallas Green MG *	.30	.14	.04
☐ 2 Bob Boone	.30	.14	.04
☐ 3 Keith Moreland *	.20	.09	.03
☐ 4 Pete Rose	4.00	1.80	.50
☐ 5 Manny Trillo	.20	.09	.03
☐ 6 Mike Schmidt	4.00	1.80	.50
☐ 7 Larry Bowa	.20	.09	.03
☐ 8 John Vukovich *	.10	.05	.01
☐ 9 Bake McBride	.10	.05	.01
☐ 10 Garry Maddox	.20	.09	.03
☐ 11 Greg Luzinski	.20	.09	.03
☐ 12 Greg Gross	.10	.05	.01
☐ 13 Del Unser	.10	.05	.01
☐ 14 Lonnie Smith *	.20	.09	.03
☐ 15 Steve Carlton	2.50	1.10	.30
☐ 16 Larry Christenson	.10	.05	.01
☐ 17 Nino Espinosa	.10	.05	.01
☐ 18 Randy Lerch	.10	.05	.01
☐ 19 Dick Ruthven	.10	.05	.01
☐ 20 Tug McGraw	.30	.14	.04
☐ 21 Ron Reed	.10	.05	.01
☐ 22 Kevin Saucier *	.10	.05	.01
☐ NNO Checklist Card TP	.05	.02	.01

1983 Phillies Postcards Great Moments

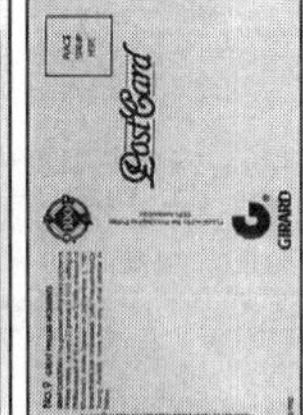

On "Nostalgia Nights" during the Philadelphia Phillies 100th Anniversary season, two collectors' art postcards were presented to fans at every Friday night home game. One card commemorated the great Phillies moments and the players involved in these, and the other card honored great Phillies players and managers that were depicted in the Phillies 1983 calendar. The art work on the card front was reproduced from original watercolors by Dick Perez who is the official artist for the National Baseball Hall of Fame in Cooperstown, New York. The backs carry a postcard format. The 13 cards in the Great Moments set along with the 13 cards in the Great Players and Managers set are combined with a checklist card and a title card to make a 28-card set.

	NRMT	VG-E	GOOD
COMPLETE SET (14)	40.00	18.00	5.00
COMMON CARD (1-14)	2.00	.90	.25
☐ 1 Richie Ashburn	6.00	2.70	.75
☐ 2 Dick Sisler	2.00	.90	.25
Del Ennis			
☐ 3 Art Mahaffey	2.00	.90	.25
☐ 4 Jim Bunning	3.00	1.35	.35
Tony Taylor			
☐ 5 Mike Schmidt	12.00	5.50	1.50
☐ 6 Johnny Callison	3.00	1.35	.35
☐ 7 Grover Alexander	6.00	2.70	.75
☐ 8 Robin Roberts	6.00	2.70	.75
☐ 9 Steve Carlton	6.00	2.70	.75
☐ 10 Tug McGraw	2.00	.90	.25
Del Unser			
☐ 11 Rick Wise	2.00	.90	.25
☐ 12 Greg Luzinski	2.00	.90	.25
Jim Lonborg			
☐ 13 Pete Rose	7.50	3.40	.95

1983 Phillies Postcards Great Players and Managers

On "Nostalgia Nights" during the Philadelphia Phillies 100th Anniversary season, two collectors' art postcards were presented to fans at every Friday night home game. One card honored the great Phillies players and managers that were depicted in the Phillies 1983 calendar, and the other card commemorated great Phillies moments and the players involved in these. The art work on the card front is a reproduction fof original watercolors by Dick Perez, the official artist for the National Baseball Hall of Fame in Cooperstown, New York. The backs carry a postcard format. The 13 cards in the Great Players and Managers set along with the 13 cards in the Great Moments set are combined with a checklist card and a title card to make a 28-card set.

	NRMT	VG-E	GOOD
COMPLETE SET (14)	40.00	18.00	5.00
COMMON CARD	2.00	.90	.25
☐ 1 Chuck Klein	3.00	1.35	.35
Johnny Callison			
Cy Williams			
☐ 2 Robin Roberts	10.00	4.50	1.25
Steve Carlton			
Grover Alexander			
☐ 3 Bob Boone	2.00	.90	.25
Stan Lopata			
Andy Seminick			
Bo Diaz			
☐ 4 Ruben Amaro	2.00	.90	.25
Larry Bowa			
Granny Hamner			
Bobby Wane			
Dave Bancroft			
☐ 5 Ed Delahanty	4.00	1.80	.50
Gavvy Cravath			
Sherry Magee			
☐ 6 Gary Matthews	3.00	1.35	.35
Greg Luzinski			
Del Ennis			
☐ 7 Eddie Waitkus	6.00	2.70	.75
Pete Rose			
Dick Allen			
☐ 8 Tony Taylor	2.00	.90	.25
Manny Trillo			
Cookie Rojas			
☐ 9 Chris Short	3.00	1.35	.35
Curt Simmons			
Jim Bunning			
☐ 10 Willie Jones	10.00	4.50	1.25
Mike Schmidt			
Pinky Whitney			
☐ 11 Eddie Sawyer MG	2.00	.90	.25
Pat Moran MG			
Harry Wright MG			
Dallas Green MG			
☐ 12 Tony Gonzalez	4.00	1.80	.50
Richie Ashburn			
Garry Maddox			
☐ 13 Ron Reed	3.00	1.35	.35
Jim Konstanty			
Tug McGraw			
☐ 14 Checklist	2.00	.90	.25

1983 Phillies Tastykake

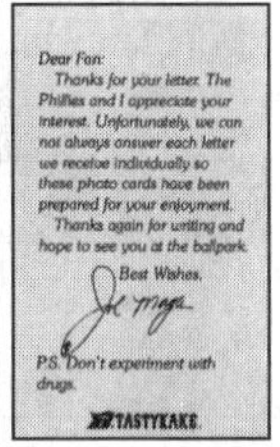

This 31-card set features the Philadelphia Phillies and was sponsored by Tastykake. The cards measure 3 1/2" by 5 1/4" and are printed on thin card stock. Inside white borders, the fronts display posed color headshots with a blue studio background. The backs carry a short letter or slogan from the player and his facsimile autograph. The cards are unnumbered and checklisted below in alphabetical order.

	NRMT	VG-E	GOOD
COMPLETE SET (31)	15.00	6.75	1.85
COMMON CARD (1-31)	.25	.11	.03
☐ 1 Luis Aguayo	.25	.11	.03
☐ 2 Joe Amalfitano CO	.25	.11	.03
☐ 3 Marty Bystrom	.25	.11	.03
☐ 4 Steve Carlton	2.50	1.10	.30
☐ 5 Larry Christenson	.25	.11	.03
☐ 6 Pat Corrales MG	.25	.11	.03
☐ 7 Ivan DeJesus	.25	.11	.03
☐ 8 John Denny	.50	.23	.06
☐ 9 Bob Dernier	.25	.11	.03
☐ 10 Bo Diaz	.25	.11	.03
☐ 11 Ed Farmer	.25	.11	.03
☐ 12 Greg Gross	.25	.11	.03
☐ 13 Von Hayes	.25	.11	.03
☐ 14 Al Holland	.25	.11	.03
☐ 15 Garry Maddox	.50	.23	.06
☐ 16 Gary Matthews	.50	.23	.06
☐ 17 Tug McGraw	.75	.35	.09
☐ 18 Larry Milbourne	.25	.11	.03
☐ 19 Bob Molinaro	.25	.11	.03
☐ 20 Sid Monge	.25	.11	.03
☐ 21 Joe Morgan	2.00	.90	.25

☐ 22 Tony Perez	1.25	.55	.16
☐ 23 Ron Reed	.25	.11	.03
☐ 24 Bill Robinson	.25	.11	.03
☐ 25 Pete Rose	4.00	1.80	.50
☐ 26 Dick Ruthven	.25	.11	.03
☐ 27 Mike Schmidt	4.00	1.80	.50
☐ 28 Ozzie Virgil	.25	.11	.03
☐ 29 Coaches	.25	.11	.03
☐ 30 Philly Phanatic Mascot	.75	.35	.09
☐ 31 Veterans Stadium	.25	.11	.03

1984 Phillies Tastykake

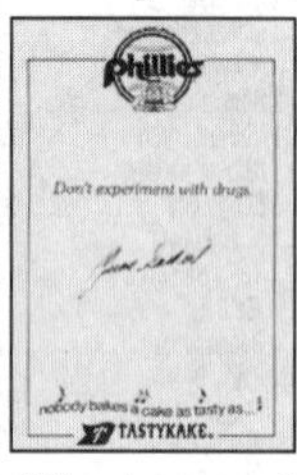

This set features the Philadelphia Phillies and was sponsored by Tastykake. The card fronts feature a colorful picture of the player or subject inside a white border. The cards measure approximately 3 1/2" by 5 1/4". The set was distributed to fans attending a specific game. There were four additional cards which were put out late in the year updating new players (after the first 40 had been out for some time). The update cards are numbered 41-44 after the first group. The card backs contain a brief message (tip) from the player with his facsimile autograph. The cards are unnumbered but the title card gives a numbering system essentially alphabetically within position; that system is used below for the first 40 cards.

	NRMT	VG-E	GOOD
COMPLETE SET (44)	15.00	6.75	1.85
COMMON CARD (1-40)	.25	.11	.03
COMMON CARD (41-44)	.75	.35	.09
☐ 1 Logo Card/Checklist	.25	.11	.03
☐ 2 Team Photo	.50	.23	.06
☐ 3 Phillie Phanatic (Mascot)	.75	.35	.09
☐ 4 Veterans Stadium	.25	.11	.03
☐ 5 Steve Carlton Hall of Fame	2.00	.90	.25
☐ 6 Mike Schmidt Hall of Fame	3.00	1.35	.35
☐ 7 Phillies Broadcasters	.50	.23	.06
☐ 8 Paul Owens MG	.25	.11	.03
☐ 9 Dave Bristol CO	.25	.11	.03
☐ 10 John Felske CO	.25	.11	.03
☐ 11 Deron Johnson CO	.25	.11	.03
☐ 12 Claude Osteen CO	.25	.11	.03
☐ 13 Mike Ryan CO	.25	.11	.03
☐ 14 Larry Andersen	.25	.11	.03
☐ 15 Marty Bystrom	.25	.11	.03
☐ 16 Bill Campbell	.25	.11	.03
☐ 17 Steve Carlton	2.00	.90	.25
☐ 18 John Denny	.50	.23	.06
☐ 19 Tony Ghelfi	.25	.11	.03
☐ 20 Kevin Gross	1.00	.45	.12
☐ 21 Al Holland	.25	.11	.03
☐ 22 Charles Hudson	.25	.11	.03
☐ 23 Jerry Koosman	.75	.35	.09
☐ 24 Tug McGraw	.75	.35	.09
☐ 25 Bo Diaz	.25	.11	.03
☐ 26 Ozzie Virgil	.25	.11	.03
☐ 27 John Wockenfuss	.25	.11	.03
☐ 28 Luis Aguayo	.25	.11	.03
☐ 29 Ivan DeJesus	.25	.11	.03
☐ 30 Kiko Garcia	.25	.11	.03
☐ 31 Len Matuszek	.25	.11	.03
☐ 32 Juan Samuel	.75	.35	.09
☐ 33 Mike Schmidt	3.00	1.35	.35
☐ 34 Tim Corcoran	.25	.11	.03
☐ 35 Greg Gross	.25	.11	.03
☐ 36 Von Hayes	.50	.23	.06
☐ 37 Joe Lefebvre	.25	.11	.03
☐ 38 Sixto Lezcano	.25	.11	.03
☐ 39 Garry Maddox	.50	.23	.06
☐ 40 Glenn Wilson	.25	.11	.03
☐ 41 Don Carman	.75	.35	.09
☐ 42 John Russell	.75	.35	.09
☐ 43 Jeff Stone	.75	.35	.09
☐ 44 Dave Wehrmeister	.75	.35	.09

1985 Phillies CIGNA

This colorful 16-card set (measuring approximately 2 5/8" by 4 1/8") features the Philadelphia Phillies and was also sponsored by CIGNA Corporation. Cards are numbered on the back and contain a safety tip as such the set is frequently categorized and referenced as a safety set. Cards are also numbered by uniform number on the front.

	NRMT	VG-E	GOOD
COMPLETE SET (16)	8.00	3.60	1.00
COMMON CARD (1-16)	.25	.11	.03
☐ 1 Juan Samuel	.50	.23	.06
☐ 2 Von Hayes	.50	.23	.06

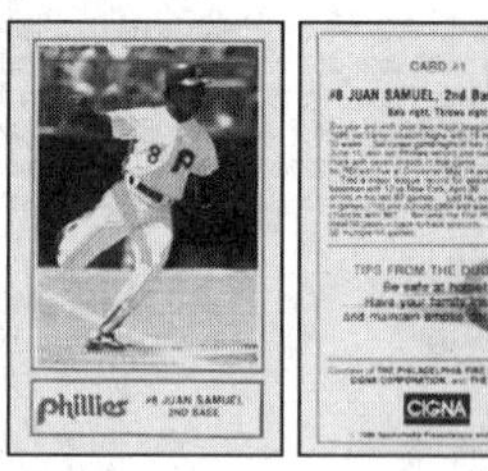

☐ 3 Ozzie Virgil	.25	.11	.03
☐ 4 Mike Schmidt	4.00	1.80	.50
☐ 5 Greg Gross	.25	.11	.03
☐ 6 Tim Corcoran	.25	.11	.03
☐ 7 Jerry Koosman	.50	.23	.06
☐ 8 Jeff Stone	.25	.11	.03
☐ 9 Glenn Wilson	.25	.11	.03
☐ 10 Steve Jeltz	.25	.11	.03
☐ 11 Garry Maddox	.50	.23	.06
☐ 12 Steve Carlton	2.00	.90	.25
☐ 13 John Denny	.50	.23	.06
☐ 14 Kevin Gross	.25	.11	.03
☐ 15 Shane Rawley	.25	.11	.03
☐ 16 Charlie Hudson	.25	.11	.03

1985 Phillies Tastykake

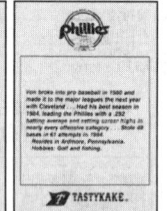

The 1985 Tastykake Philadelphia Phillies set consists of 47 cards, each measuring approximately 3 1/2" by 5 1/4". They feature a color photo of the player framed against white borders. The group shots of the various parts of the teams were posed after the other cards were issued so there are stylistic differences between the group shots and the individual shots. The backs feature brief biographies of the players. The cards are arranged below by position and in alphabetical order within these positions. The set features an early card of Darren Daulton.

	NRMT	VG-E	GOOD
COMPLETE SET (47)	15.00	6.75	1.85
COMMON CARD (1-47)	.25	.11	.03
☐ 1 Checklist Card	.50	.23	.06
☐ 2 John Felske MG	.25	.11	.03
☐ 3 Dave Bristol CO	.25	.11	.03
☐ 4 Lee Elia CO	.25	.11	.03
☐ 5 Claude Osteen CO	.25	.11	.03
☐ 6 Mike Ryan CO	.25	.11	.03
☐ 7 Del Unser CO	.25	.11	.03
☐ 8 John Felske MG and Del Unser CO Dave Bristol CO Lee Elia CO Mike Ryan CO Hank King CO Claude Osteen CO	.25	.11	.03
☐ 9 Pitching Staff Pat Zachry Larry Andersen Charles Hudson Shane Rawley John Denny Steve Carlton Kevin Gross Al Holland Jerry Koosman Don Carman Bill Campbell	.75	.35	.09
☐ 10 Catchers Darren Daulton Bo Diaz Ozzie Virgil	1.50	.70	.19
☐ 11 Infielders Mike Schmidt Steve Jeltz Ivan DeJesus Juan Samuel Luis Aguayo John Russell	1.00	.45	.12
☐ 12 Outfielders Tim Corcoran Greg Gross Von Hayes Joe Lefebvre Jeff Stone Glenn Wilson	.25	.11	.03
☐ 13 Larry Andersen	.25	.11	.03
☐ 14 Steve Carlton	2.00	.90	.25
☐ 15 Don Carman	.25	.11	.03
☐ 16 John Denny	.50	.23	.06
☐ 17 Tony Ghelfi	.25	.11	.03
☐ 18 Kevin Gross	.25	.11	.03
☐ 19 Al Holland	.25	.11	.03
☐ 20 Charles Hudson	.25	.11	.03
☐ 21 Jerry Koosman	.50	.23	.06
☐ 22 Shane Rawley	.25	.11	.03
☐ 23 Pat Zachry	.25	.11	.03
☐ 24 Darren Daulton	2.50	1.10	.30
☐ 25 Bo Diaz	.25	.11	.03
☐ 26 Ozzie Virgil	.25	.11	.03
☐ 27 John Wockenfuss	.25	.11	.03
☐ 28 Luis Aguayo	.25	.11	.03
☐ 29 Kiko Garcia	.25	.11	.03
☐ 30 Steve Jeltz	.25	.11	.03
☐ 31 John Russell	.25	.11	.03
☐ 32 Juan Samuel	.50	.23	.06
☐ 33 Mike Schmidt	3.00	1.35	.35
☐ 34 Tim Corcoran	.25	.11	.03
☐ 35 Greg Gross	.25	.11	.03
☐ 36 Von Hayes	.50	.23	.06
☐ 37 Joe Lefebvre	.25	.11	.03
☐ 38 Garry Maddox	.50	.23	.06
☐ 39 Jeff Stone	.25	.11	.03
☐ 40 Glenn Wilson	.25	.11	.03
☐ 41 Ramon Caraballo and Mike Diaz	.25	.11	.03
☐ 42 Mike Maddux and Rodger Cole	.25	.11	.03
☐ 43 Rick Schu and Chris James	.50	.23	.06
☐ 44 Francisco Melendez and Ken Jackson	.25	.11	.03
☐ 45 Randy Salava and Rocky Childress	.25	.11	.03
☐ 46 Rich Surhoff and Ralph Citarella	.25	.11	.03
☐ 47 Team Photo	.50	.23	.06

1986 Phillies CIGNA

This 16-card set was sponsored by CIGNA Corp. and was given away by the Philadelphia area Fire Departments. Cards measure approximately 2 3/4" by 4 1/8" and feature full color fronts. The card backs are printed in maroon and black on white card stock. Although the uniform numbers are given on the front of the card, the cards are numbered on the back in the order listed below.

	MINT	NRMT	EXC
COMPLETE SET (16)	7.00	3.10	.85
COMMON CARD (1-16)	.25	.11	.03
☐ 1 Juan Samuel	.50	.23	.06
☐ 2 Don Carman	.25	.11	.03
☐ 3 Von Hayes	.50	.23	.06
☐ 4 Kent Tekulve	.50	.23	.06
☐ 5 Greg Gross	.25	.11	.03
☐ 6 Shane Rawley	.25	.11	.03
☐ 7 Darren Daulton	2.00	.90	.25
☐ 8 Kevin Gross	.25	.11	.03
☐ 9 Steve Jeltz	.25	.11	.03
☐ 10 Mike Schmidt	4.00	1.80	.50
☐ 11 Steve Bedrosian	.50	.23	.06
☐ 12 Gary Redus	.25	.11	.03
☐ 13 Charles Hudson	.25	.11	.03
☐ 14 John Russell	.25	.11	.03
☐ 15 Fred Toliver	.25	.11	.03
☐ 16 Glenn Wilson	.25	.11	.03

1986 Phillies Greats TCMA

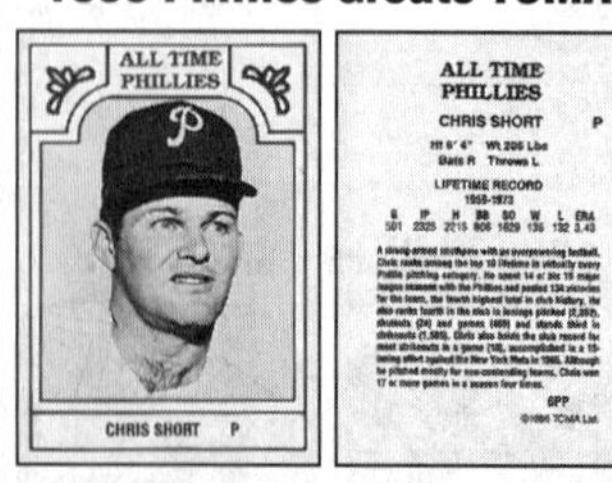

This 12-card standard-size set features some all-time great Phillies. The fronts feature a player photo, his name and position. The backs have vital statistics, a biography and career totals.

	MINT	NRMT	EXC
COMPLETE SET (12)	4.00	1.80	.50
COMMON CARD (1-12)	.25	.11	.03
☐ 1 Chuck Klein	.75	.35	.09
☐ 2 Richie Ashburn	1.00	.45	.12
☐ 3 Del Ennis	.50	.23	.06
☐ 4 Spud Davis	.25	.11	.03
☐ 5 Grover Alexander	1.00	.45	.12
☐ 6 Chris Short	.25	.11	.03
☐ 7 Jim Konstanty	.25	.11	.03
☐ 8 Danny Ozark MG	.25	.11	.03
☐ 9 Larry Bowa	.25	.11	.03
☐ 10 Richie Allen	.50	.23	.06
☐ 11 Don Hurst	.25	.11	.03
☐ 12 Tony Taylor	.25	.11	.03

1986 Phillies Keller's

These cards were printed crudely on the boxes of one-pound packages of butter made by Keller's. The cards are approximately 2 1/2" by 2 3/4" and are very similar to the Meadow Gold cards. The same art was used on the Schmidt card which is in both sets. Both Keller's and Meadow Gold are subsidiaries of Beatrice Foods. The set was licensed by Mike Schechter Associates and the Major League Baseball Players' Association. The set contains only Philadelphia Phillies players. The cards are blank backed and are printed in red, dark blue and yellow on white waxed cardboard. Complete boxes would bring double the values listed below. Since the cards are unnumbered they are listed below in alphabetical order.

	MINT	NRMT	EXC
COMPLETE SET (6)	12.50	5.50	1.55
COMMON CARD (1-6)	.75	.35	.09
☐ 1 Steve Carlton	4.00	1.80	.50
☐ 2 Von Hayes	.75	.35	.09
☐ 3 Gary Redus	.75	.35	.09
☐ 4 Juan Samuel	1.00	.45	.12
☐ 5 Mike Schmidt	6.00	2.70	.75
☐ 6 Glenn Wilson	.75	.35	.09

1986 Phillies Tastykake

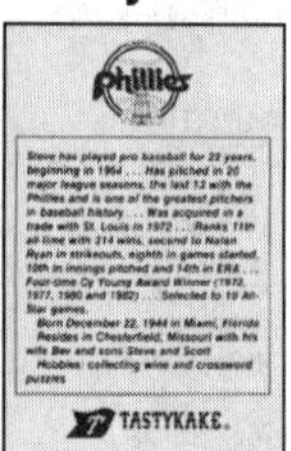

The 1986 Tastykake Philadelphia Phillies set consists of 47 cards, which measure approximately 3 1/2" by 5 1/4". This set features members of the 1986 Philadelphia Phillies. The front of the cards features a full-color photo of the player against white borders while the back has brief biographies. The set has been checklisted for reference below in order by uniform number.

	MINT	NRMT	EXC
COMPLETE SET (47)	12.00	5.50	1.50
COMMON CARD	.25	.11	.03
☐ 2 Jim Davenport CO	.25	.11	.03
☐ 3 Claude Osteen CO	.25	.11	.03
☐ 4 Lee Elia CO	.25	.11	.03
☐ 5 Mike Ryan CO	.25	.11	.03
☐ 6 John Russell	.25	.11	.03
☐ 7 John Felske MG	.25	.11	.03
☐ 8 Juan Samuel	.50	.23	.06
☐ 9 Von Hayes	.25	.11	.03
☐ 10 Darren Daulton	2.00	.90	.25
☐ 11 Tom Foley	.25	.11	.03
☐ 12 Glenn Wilson	.25	.11	.03
☐ 14 Jeff Stone	.25	.11	.03
☐ 15 Rick Schu	.25	.11	.03
☐ 16 Luis Aguayo	.25	.11	.03
☐ 20 Mike Schmidt	3.00	1.35	.35
☐ 21 Greg Gross	.25	.11	.03
☐ 22 Gary Redus	.25	.11	.03
☐ 23 Joe Lefebvre	.25	.11	.03
☐ 24 Milt Thompson	.25	.11	.03
☐ 25 Del Unser CO	.25	.11	.03
☐ 26 Chris James	.25	.11	.03
☐ 27 Kent Tekulve	.50	.23	.06
☐ 28 Shane Rawley	.25	.11	.03
☐ 29 Ronn Reynolds	.25	.11	.03
☐ 30 Steve Jeltz	.25	.11	.03
☐ 31 Garry Maddox	.50	.23	.06
☐ 32 Steve Carlton	2.00	.90	.25
☐ 33 David Shipanoff	.25	.11	.03
☐ 35 Randy Lerch	.25	.11	.03
☐ 36 Robin Roberts	1.50	.70	.19
☐ 39 Dave Rucker	.25	.11	.03
☐ 40 Steve Bedrosian	.50	.23	.06
☐ 41 Tom Hume	.25	.11	.03

	MINT	NRMT	EXC
☐ 42 Don Carman	.25	.11	.03
☐ 43 Fred Toliver	.25	.11	.03
☐ 46 Kevin Gross	.25	.11	.03
☐ 47 Larry Andersen	.25	.11	.03
☐ 48 Dave Stewart	.75	.35	.09
☐ 49 Charles Hudson	.25	.11	.03
☐ 50 Rocky Childress	.25	.11	.03
☐ xx Future Phillies Ramon Caraballo Joe Cipolloni	.25	.11	.03
☐ xx Future Phillies Arturo Gonzalez Mike Maddux	.25	.11	.03
☐ xx Future Phillies Francisco Melendez Ricky Jordan	.50	.23	.06
☐ xx Future Phillies Kevin Ward Randy Day	.25	.11	.03
☐ xx0 Night to Remember 26-7; June 11, 1985	.50	.23	.06
☐ xx Pennant Winning Team 1915 Phillies	.50	.23	.06
☐ xx Pennant Winning Team 1950 Phillies	.50	.23	.06
☐ xx Pennant Winning Team 1980 Phillies	.50	.23	.06
☐ xx Pennant Winning Team 1983 Phillies	.50	.23	.06

1987 Phillies 1950 TCMA

This nine-card standard-size set honors members of the "Whiz Kids" who won the 1950 National League Pennant. The fronts feature player photos, identification and position. The backs carry some biographical information as well as the 1950 stats.

	MINT	NRMT	EXC
COMPLETE SET (9)	4.00	1.80	.50
COMMON CARD (1-9)	.25	.11	.03
☐ 1 Eddie Sawyer MG	.25	.11	.03
☐ 2 Curt Simmons	.50	.23	.06
☐ 3 Jim Konstanty	.50	.23	.06
☐ 4 Eddie Waitkus	.25	.11	.03
☐ 5 Granny Hamner	.25	.11	.03
☐ 6 Del Ennis	.50	.23	.06
☐ 7 Richie Ashburn	1.00	.45	.12
☐ 8 Dick Sisler	.25	.11	.03
☐ 9 Robin Roberts	1.00	.45	.12

1987 Phillies Champion

This four-card set which measures approximately 3" by 4 3/4" (with scratch-off tab) is unusual in that there is no way to determine the player's identity other than knowing and recognizing whose photo it is. The top part of the card has a color photo of the player surrounded in the upper left hand corner with a Champion spark plug logo. The Philadelphia Phillies logo is in the upper right hand part of the card. A Pep Boys ad is in the lower left hand corner of the photo and the WIP Philadelphia Sports Radio promo is in the lower right hand corner of the photo. The set is checklisted alphabetically by subject since the cards are unnumbered.

	MINT	NRMT	EXC
COMPLETE SET (4)	18.00	8.00	2.20
COMMON CARD (1-4)	1.50	.70	.19
☐ 1 Von Hayes	1.50	.70	.19
☐ 2 Steve Jeltz	1.50	.70	.19
☐ 3 Juan Samuel	2.00	.90	.25
☐ 4 Mike Schmidt	15.00	6.75	1.85

1987 Phillies Tastykake

The 1987 Tastykake Philadelphia Phillies set consists of 47 cards which measure approximately 3 1/2" by 5 1/4". The sets again feature full-color photos against a solid white background. There were two number 39s in this set as the Phillies changed personnel during the

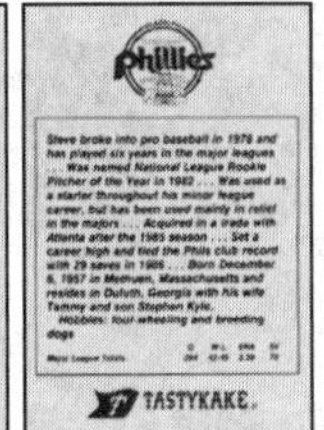

season, Joe Cowley and Bob Scanlan. For convenience uniform numbers are used below as a basis for numbering and checklisting this set.

	MINT	NRMT	EXC
COMPLETE SET (47)	12.00	5.50	1.50
COMMON CARD	.25	.11	.03
☐ 6 John Russell	.25	.11	.03
☐ 7 John Felske MG	.25	.11	.03
☐ 8 Juan Samuel	.50	.23	.06
☐ 9 Von Hayes	.25	.11	.03
☐ 10 Darren Daulton	.75	.35	.09
☐ 11 Greg Legg	.25	.11	.03
☐ 12 Glenn Wilson	.25	.11	.03
☐ 13 Lance Parrish	.75	.35	.09
☐ 14 Jeff Stone	.25	.11	.03
☐ 15 Rick Schu	.25	.11	.03
☐ 16 Luis Aguayo	.25	.11	.03
☐ 17 Ron Roenicke	.25	.11	.03
☐ 18 Chris James	.25	.11	.03
☐ 20 Mike Schmidt	4.00	1.80	.50
☐ 21 Greg Gross	.25	.11	.03
☐ 23 Joe Cipolloni	.25	.11	.03
☐ 24 Milt Thompson	.25	.11	.03
☐ 27 Kent Tekulve	.50	.23	.06
☐ 28 Shane Rawley	.25	.11	.03
☐ 29 Ronn Reynolds	.25	.11	.03
☐ 30 Steve Jeltz	.25	.11	.03
☐ 33 Mike Jackson	.50	.23	.06
☐ 34 Mike Easler	.25	.11	.03
☐ 35 Dan Schatzeder	.25	.11	.03
☐ 37 Ken Howell	.25	.11	.03
☐ 38 Jim Olander	.25	.11	.03
☐ 39A Joe Cowley	.25	.11	.03
☐ 39B Bob Scanlan	.25	.11	.03
☐ 40 Steve Bedrosian	.50	.23	.06
☐ 41 Tom Hume	.25	.11	.03
☐ 42 Don Carman	.25	.11	.03
☐ 43 Freddie Toliver	.25	.11	.03
☐ 44 Mike Maddux	.25	.11	.03
☐ 45 Greg Jelks	.25	.11	.03
☐ 46 Kevin Gross	.25	.11	.03
☐ 47 Bruce Ruffin	.50	.23	.06
☐ 48 Marvin Freeman	.25	.11	.03
☐ 49 Len Watts	.25	.11	.03
☐ 50 Tom Newell	.25	.11	.03
☐ 51 Ken Jackson	.25	.11	.03
☐ 52 Todd Frohwirth	.25	.11	.03
☐ 58 Doug Bair	.25	.11	.03
☐ xx Phillie Phanatic (Mascot)	.75	.35	.09
☐ xx Team Photo	.50	.23	.06
☐ xx Shawn Barton and Rick Lundblade	.25	.11	.03
☐ xx Jeff Kaye and Darren Loy	.25	.11	.03
☐ xx0 Coaches Card Claude Osteen Del Unser Jim Davenport Mike Ryan Lee Elia	.25	.11	.03

1988 Phillies Tastykake

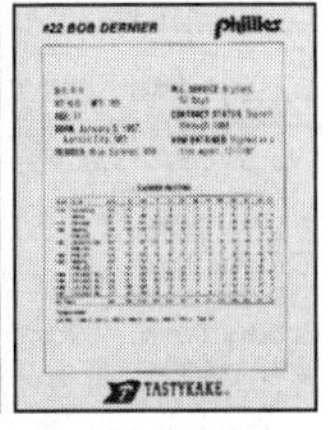

The 1988 Tastykake Philadelphia Phillies set is a 30-card set measuring approximately 4 7/8" by 6 1/4". This set is listed below alphabetically by player. The cards have a full-color photo front and complete player history on the back. There was also a nine-card update set issued later in the year which included a Ricky Jordan card; the update cards are numbered as 31-39 and are blank backed.

	MINT	NRMT	EXC
COMPLETE SET (39)	10.00	4.50	1.25
COMMON CARD (1-30)	.25	.11	.03
COMMON CARD (31-39)	.35	.16	.04
☐ 1 Luis Aguayo	.25	.11	.03
☐ 2 Bill Almon	.25	.11	.03
☐ 3 Steve Bedrosian	.50	.23	.06
☐ 4 Phil Bradley	.25	.11	.03
☐ 5 Jeff Calhoun	.25	.11	.03
☐ 6 Don Carman	.25	.11	.03
☐ 7 Darren Daulton	.50	.23	.06
☐ 8 Bob Dernier	.25	.11	.03
☐ 9A Lee Elia MG (Vertical format)	.50	.23	.06
☐ 9B Lee Elia MG (Horizontal format)	.50	.23	.06
☐ 10 Todd Frohwirth	.25	.11	.03
☐ 11 Greg Gross	.25	.11	.03
☐ 12 Kevin Gross	.25	.11	.03
☐ 13 Von Hayes	.50	.23	.06
☐ 14 Chris James	.25	.11	.03
☐ 15 Steve Jeltz	.25	.11	.03
☐ 16 Mike Maddux	.25	.11	.03
☐ 17 Dave Palmer	.25	.11	.03
☐ 18 Lance Parrish	.50	.23	.06
☐ 19 Shane Rawley	.25	.11	.03
☐ 20 Wally Ritchie	.25	.11	.03
☐ 21 Bruce Ruffin	.25	.11	.03
☐ 22 Juan Samuel	.50	.23	.06
☐ 23 Mike Schmidt	2.00	.90	.25
☐ 24 Kent Tekulve	.50	.23	.06
☐ 25 Milt Thompson	.25	.11	.03
☐ 26 Mike Young	.25	.11	.03
☐ 27 Phillies Prospects Tom Barrett Brad Brink Steve DeAngelis Ron Jones Keith Miller Brad Moore Howard Nichols Shane Turner	.25	.11	.03
☐ 28 Team Card	.50	.23	.06
☐ 29 Phillies Coaches Claude Osteen Del Unser John Vuckovich Dave Bristol Tony Taylor Mike Ryan	.25	.11	.03
☐ 30 Phillie Phanatic (Mascot)	.50	.23	.06
☐ 31 Larry Bowa CO	.75	.35	.09
☐ 32 Lee Elia CO	.35	.16	.04
☐ 33 Jackie Gutierrez	.35	.16	.04
☐ 34 Greg A. Harris	.35	.16	.04
☐ 35 Ricky Jordan	.75	.35	.09
☐ 36 Keith Miller	.35	.16	.04
☐ 37 John Russell	.35	.16	.04
☐ 38 John Vukovich CO	.35	.16	.04
☐ 39 Phillies Announcers Garry Maddox Richie Ashburn Chris Wheeler Harry Kalas Andy Musser	.75	.35	.09

1988 Phillies Topps Ashburn Sheet

This 13-card set was issued on one perforated sheet measuring approximately 10" by 14" commemorating Richie Ashburn's 40 years in baseball. Sponsored by Campbell's, the sheet features 12 smaller versions of different Topps cards printed on a sky-blue and flag background with a bigger 5" by 7" portrait card in the middle. The back of this card displayed his complete Major League batting record and accomplishments. The cards are listed below according to the year they appeared in the Topps sets.

	MINT	NRMT	EXC
COMPLETE SET (13)	8.00	3.60	1.00
COMMON CARD (1-13)	.75	.35	.09
☐ 1 1952 Bowman	.75	.35	.09
☐ 2 1952 Topps	.75	.35	.09
☐ 3 1954 Topps	.75	.35	.09
☐ 4 1956 Topps	.75	.35	.09
☐ 5 1957 Topps	.75	.35	.09
☐ 6 1958 Topps	.75	.35	.09
☐ 7 1959 Topps	.75	.35	.09
☐ 8 1959 Topps with Willie Mays	.75	.35	.09
☐ 9 1960 Topps	.75	.35	.09
☐ 10 1961 Topps	.75	.35	.09
☐ 11 1962 Topps	.75	.35	.09
☐ 12 1963 Topps	.75	.35	.09
☐ 13 1988 Richie Ashburn	1.00	.45	.12

1989 Phillies Tastykake

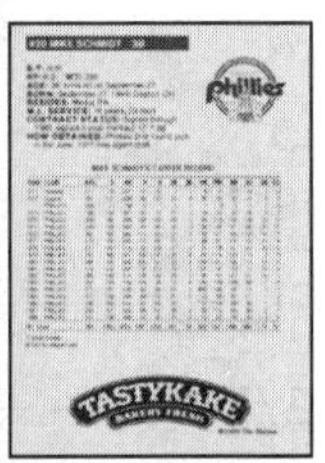

This set was a 36-card set of Philadelphia Phillies measuring approximately 4 1/8" by 6" featuring full-color fronts with complete biographical information and career stats on the back. The set is checklisted alphabetically in the list below. The set was a give away to fans attending the Phillies Tastykake Photocard Night on May 13, 1989 and was later available from a mail-away offer. There was also a nine-player extended set issued later during the 1989 season; the extended players are numbered below in alphabetical order, numbers 37-45. Chris James' card lists him as uniform number 26, but his number is 18, while 26 was Ron Jones' number.

	MINT	NRMT	EXC
COMPLETE SET (45)	10.00	4.50	1.25
COMMON CARD (1-36)	.25	.11	.03
COMMON CARD (37-45)	.35	.16	.04
☐ 1 Steve Bedrosian	.50	.23	.06
☐ 2 Larry Bowa CO	.50	.23	.06
☐ 3 Don Carman	.25	.11	.03
☐ 4 Darren Daulton	1.25	.55	.16
☐ 5 Bob Dernier	.25	.11	.03
☐ 6 Curt Ford	.25	.11	.03
☐ 7 Todd Frohwirth	.25	.11	.03
☐ 8 Greg A. Harris	.25	.11	.03
☐ 9 Von Hayes	.25	.11	.03
☐ 10 Tom Herr	.25	.11	.03
☐ 11 Ken Howell	.25	.11	.03
☐ 12 Chris James UER (Wrong uniform number on card)	.25	.11	.03
☐ 13 Steve Jeltz	.25	.11	.03
☐ 14 Ron Jones	.25	.11	.03
☐ 15 Ricky Jordan	.50	.23	.06
☐ 16 Darold Knowles CO	.25	.11	.03
☐ 17 Steve Lake	.25	.11	.03
☐ 18 Nick Levya MG	.25	.11	.03
☐ 19 Mike Maddux	.25	.11	.03
☐ 20 Alex Madrid	.25	.11	.03
☐ 21 Larry McWilliams	.25	.11	.03
☐ 22 Denis Menke CO	.25	.11	.03
☐ 23 Dwayne Murphy	.25	.11	.03
☐ 24 Tom Nieto	.25	.11	.03
☐ 25 Randy O'Neal	.25	.11	.03
☐ 26 Steve Ontiveros	.25	.11	.03
☐ 27 Jeff Parrett	.25	.11	.03
☐ 28 Bruce Ruffin	.25	.11	.03
☐ 29 Mark Ryal	.25	.11	.03
☐ 30 Mike Ryan CO	.25	.11	.03
☐ 31 Juan Samuel	.50	.23	.06
☐ 32 Mike Schmidt	2.50	1.10	.30
☐ 33 Tony Taylor CO	.25	.11	.03
☐ 34 Dickie Thon	.25	.11	.03
☐ 35 John Vukovich CO	.25	.11	.03
☐ 36 Floyd Youmans	.25	.11	.03
☐ 37 Jim Adduci	.35	.16	.04
☐ 38 Eric Bullock	.35	.16	.04
☐ 39 Dennis Cook	.35	.16	.04
☐ 40 Len Dykstra	1.50	.70	.19
☐ 41 Charlie Hayes	.75	.35	.09
☐ 42 John Kruk	1.00	.45	.12
☐ 43 Roger McDowell	.35	.16	.04
☐ 44 Terry Mulholland	.35	.16	.04
☐ 45 Randy Ready	.35	.16	.04

1990 Phillies Tastykake

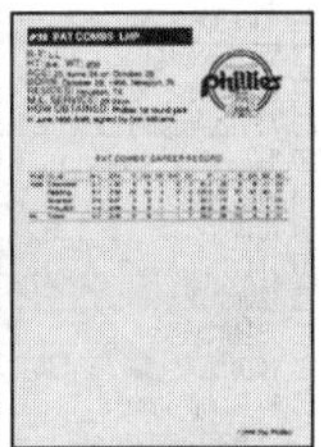

The 1990 Tastykake Philadelphia Phillies set is a 36-card set measuring approximately 4 1/8" by 6" which features players, coaches and manager, four players who have had their uniform numbers retired, broadcasters, and even the Phillies Mascot. The set is checklisted alphabetically, with complete biography and complete stats on the back.

	MINT	NRMT	EXC
COMPLETE SET (36)	10.00	4.50	1.25
COMMON CARD (1-36)	.25	.11	.03

☐ 1 Darrel Akerfelds	.25	.11	.03
☐ 2 Rod Booker	.25	.11	.03
☐ 3 Sil Campusano	.25	.11	.03
☐ 4 Don Carman	.25	.11	.03
☐ 5 Pat Combs	.25	.11	.03
☐ 6 Dennis Cook	.25	.11	.03
☐ 7 Darren Daulton	1.50	.70	.19
☐ 8 Len Dykstra	1.50	.70	.19
☐ 9 Curt Ford	.25	.11	.03
☐ 10 Jason Grimsley	.25	.11	.03
☐ 11 Charlie Hayes	.50	.23	.06
☐ 12 Von Hayes	.25	.11	.03
☐ 13 Tommy Herr	.25	.11	.03
☐ 14 Dave Hollins	.50	.23	.06
☐ 15 Ken Howell	.25	.11	.03
☐ 16 Ron Jones	.25	.11	.03
☐ 17 Ricky Jordan	.25	.11	.03
☐ 18 John Kruk	.50	.23	.06
☐ 19 Steve Lake	.25	.11	.03
☐ 20 Nick Levya MG	.25	.11	.03
☐ 21 Carmelo Martinez	.25	.11	.03
☐ 22 Roger McDowell	.25	.11	.03
☐ 23 Chuck McElroy	.25	.11	.03
☐ 24 Terry Mulholland	.25	.11	.03
☐ 25 Jeff Parrett	.25	.11	.03
☐ 26 Randy Ready	.25	.11	.03
☐ 27 Bruce Ruffin	.25	.11	.03
☐ 28 Dickie Thon	.25	.11	.03
☐ 29 Richie Ashburn	1.25	.55	.16
☐ 30 Steve Carlton	1.50	.70	.19
☐ 31 Robin Roberts	1.25	.55	.16
☐ 32 Mike Schmidt	2.00	.90	.25
☐ 33 Phillie Phanatic	.75	.35	.09
(Mascot)			
☐ 34 Phillie Coaches	.25	.11	.03
Denis Menke			
Mike Ryan			
John Vukovich			
Hal Lanier			
Darold Knowles			
Larry Bowa			
☐ 35 Phillies Broadcasters	.50	.23	.06
Chris Wheeler			
Andy Musser			
Harry Kalas			
Richie Ashburn			
☐ 36 Phillies Broadcasters	.75	.35	.09
Mike Schmidt			
Jim Barniak			
Garry Maddox			

1991 Phillies Medford

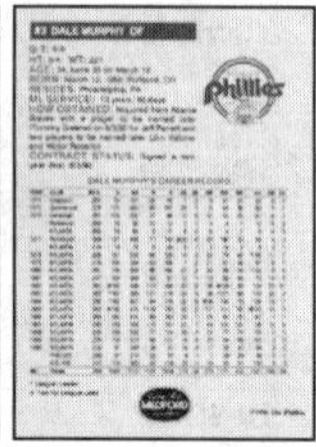

This 35-card set was sponsored by Medford (rather than by Tastykake as in past years), and its company logo is found on the bottom of the reverse. The oversized cards measure approximately 4 1/8" by 6" and feature borderless glossy color action player photos on the obverse. The player's name is given in a red bar at either the top or bottom of the picture. The backs are printed in red and black on white and present biographical as well as statistical information. The cards are unnumbered and checklisted below in alphabetical order.

	MINT	NRMT	EXC
COMPLETE SET (35)	8.00	3.60	1.00
COMMON CARD (1-35)	.15	.07	.02
☐ 1 Darrel Akerfelds	.15	.07	.02
☐ 2 Andy Ashby	.50	.23	.06
☐ 3 Wally Backman	.15	.07	.02
☐ 4 Joe Boever	.15	.07	.02
☐ 5 Rod Booker	.15	.07	.02
☐ 6 Larry Bowa CO	.30	.14	.04
☐ 7 Sil Campusano	.15	.07	.02
☐ 8 Wes Chamberlain	.15	.07	.02
☐ 9 Pat Combs	.15	.07	.02
☐ 10 Danny Cox	.15	.07	.02
☐ 11 Darren Daulton	.75	.35	.09
☐ 12 Jose DeJesus	.15	.07	.02
☐ 13 Len Dykstra	.75	.35	.09
☐ 14 Darrin Fletcher	.15	.07	.02
☐ 15 Tommy Greene	.15	.07	.02
☐ 16 Jason Grimsley	.15	.07	.02
☐ 17 Charlie Hayes	.30	.14	.04
☐ 18 Von Hayes	.15	.07	.02
☐ 19 Dave Hollins	.30	.14	.04
☐ 20 Ken Howell	.15	.07	.02
☐ 21 Ricky Jordan	.15	.07	.02
☐ 22 John Kruk	.50	.23	.06
☐ 23 Steve Lake	.15	.07	.02
☐ 24 Hal Lanier CO	.15	.07	.02
☐ 25 Tim Mauser	.15	.07	.02
☐ 26 Roger McDowell	.15	.07	.02
☐ 27 Denis Menke CO	.15	.07	.02
☐ 28 Mickey Morandini	.30	.14	.04
☐ 29 John Morris	.15	.07	.02
☐ 30 Terry Mulholland	.15	.07	.02
☐ 31 Dale Murphy	.75	.35	.09
☐ 32 Johnny Podres CO	.30	.14	.04
☐ 33 Randy Ready	.15	.07	.02
☐ 34 Dickie Thon	.15	.07	.02
☐ 35 John Vukovich CO	.15	.07	.02

1992 Phillies Medford

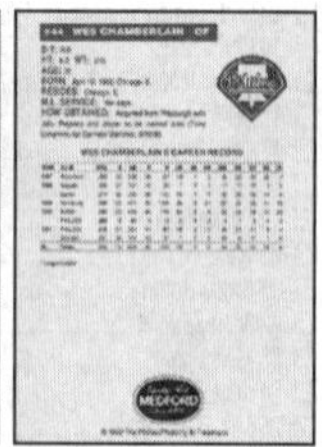

For the second consecutive year, Medford has sponsored a Phillies set, consisting of a first series of 36 cards measuring approximately 4 1/8" by 6" and an extended update series of another ten cards of the same size. The players featured in the update series were mostly mid-season call-ups from the minor leagues. The card fronts feature glossy full-bleed posed color player photos, shot against a studio background. The player's name appears in white lettering in a short red stripe. In black and red print on white, the backs present basic biographical information, career statistics, and the team logo. The sponsor logo at the bottom rounds out the back. The cards are unnumbered and checklisted below alphabetically within series, with the nonplayer cards listed at the end.

	MINT	NRMT	EXC
COMPLETE SET (46)	12.00	5.50	1.50
COMMON CARD (1-36)	.25	.11	.03
COMMON CARD (37-46)	.35	.16	.04
☐ 1 Kyle Abbott	.25	.11	.03
☐ 2 Ruben Amaro	.25	.11	.03
☐ 3 Andy Ashby	.75	.35	.09
☐ 4 Wally Backman	.25	.11	.03
☐ 5 Kim Batiste	.25	.11	.03
☐ 6 Larry Bowa CO	.50	.23	.06
☐ 7 Cliff Brantley	.25	.11	.03
☐ 8 Wes Chamberlain	.25	.11	.03
☐ 9 Danny Cox	.25	.11	.03
☐ 10 Darren Daulton	1.50	.70	.19
☐ 11 Mariano Duncan	.75	.35	.09
☐ 12 Len Dykstra	1.50	.70	.19
☐ 13 Jim Fregosi MG	.50	.23	.06
☐ 14 Tommy Greene	.25	.11	.03
☐ 15 Dave Hollins	.25	.11	.03
☐ 16 Barry Jones	.25	.11	.03
☐ 17 John Kruk	1.25	.55	.16
☐ 18 Steve Lake	.25	.11	.03
☐ 19 Jim Lindeman	.25	.11	.03
☐ 20 Denis Menke CO	.25	.11	.03
☐ 21 Mickey Morandini	.50	.23	.06
☐ 22 Terry Mulholland	.25	.11	.03
☐ 23 Dale Murphy	1.25	.55	.16
☐ 24 Johnny Podres CO	.50	.23	.06
☐ 25 Wally Ritchie	.25	.11	.03
☐ 26 Mel Roberts CO	.25	.11	.03
☐ 27 Mike Ryan CO	.25	.11	.03
☐ 28 Curt Schilling	.25	.11	.03
☐ 29 Steve Searcy	.25	.11	.03
☐ 30 Dale Sveum	.25	.11	.03
☐ 31 John Vukovich	.25	.11	.03
Dugout Assistant			
☐ 32 Mitch Williams	.75	.35	.09
☐ 33 Phillie Phanatic	.75	.35	.09
(Mascot)			
☐ 34 Team Photo	.50	.23	.06
☐ 35 Veterans Stadium	.25	.11	.03
☐ 36 Uniforms Through	.50	.23	.06
The Years			
☐ 37 Bob Ayrault	.35	.16	.04
☐ 38 Brad Brink	.35	.16	.04
☐ 39 Pat Combs	.35	.16	.04
☐ 40 Jeff Grotewold	.35	.16	.04
☐ 41 Mike Hartley	.35	.16	.04
☐ 42 Ricky Jordan	.35	.16	.04
☐ 43 Tom Marsh	.35	.16	.04
☐ 44 Terry Mulholland	.35	.16	.04
☐ 45 Ben Rivera	.35	.16	.04
☐ 46 Don Robinson	.35	.16	.04

1993 Phillies Medford

This 35-card set was sponsored by Medford, and its company logo is found on the bottom of the reverse. The oversized cards measure approximately 4 1/8" by 6" and feature borderless glossy color player action photos on their fronts. The player's name is shown in a red bar, most often in an upper corner. The backs are printed in red and black on white and present biographical as well as statistical information. The Phillies logo in the upper right rounds out the back. The cards are unnumbered and checklisted below in alphabetical order.

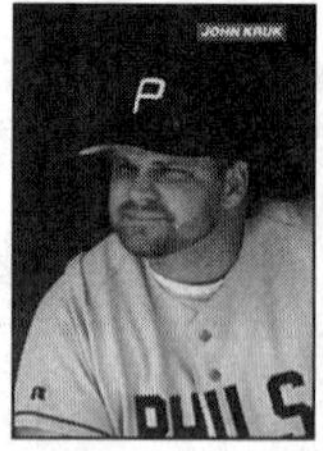

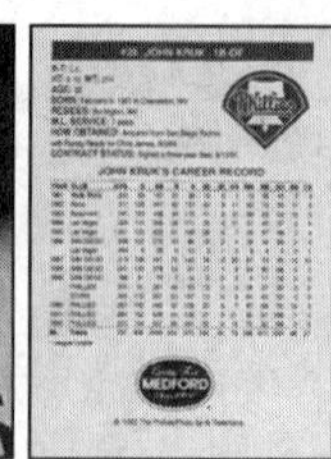

	MINT	NRMT	EXC
COMPLETE SET (35)	8.00	3.60	1.00
COMMON CARD (1-35)	.25	.11	.03
☐ 1 Kyle Abbott	.25	.11	.03
☐ 2 Ruben Amaro	.25	.11	.03
☐ 3 Larry Andersen	.25	.11	.03
☐ 4 Bob Ayrault	.25	.11	.03
☐ 5 Kim Batiste	.25	.11	.03
☐ 6 Juan Bell	.25	.11	.03
☐ 7 Larry Bowa CO	.50	.23	.06
☐ 8 Wes Chamberlain	.25	.11	.03
☐ 9 Darren Daulton	1.00	.45	.12
☐ 10 Jose DeLeon	.25	.11	.03
☐ 11 Mariano Duncan	.75	.35	.09
☐ 12 Len Dykstra	1.00	.45	.12
☐ 13 Jim Eisenreich	.75	.35	.09
☐ 14 Jim Fregosi MG	.50	.23	.06
☐ 15 Tyler Green	.25	.11	.03
☐ 16 Tommy Greene	.25	.11	.03
☐ 17 Dave Hollins	.25	.11	.03
☐ 18 Pete Incaviglia	.75	.35	.09
☐ 19 Danny Jackson	.25	.11	.03
☐ 20 Ricky Jordan	.25	.11	.03
☐ 21 John Kruk	.75	.35	.09
☐ 22 Denis Menke CO	.25	.11	.03
☐ 23 Mickey Morandini	.50	.23	.06
☐ 24 Terry Mulholland	.25	.11	.03
☐ 25 Phillie Phanatic	.50	.23	.06
(Mascot)			
☐ 26 Johnny Podres CO	.50	.23	.06
☐ 27 Todd Pratt	.25	.11	.03
☐ 28 Ben Rivera	.25	.11	.03
☐ 29 Mel Roberts CO	.25	.11	.03
☐ 30 Mike Ryan CO	.25	.11	.03
☐ 31 Curt Schilling	.75	.35	.09
☐ 32 Milt Thompson	.25	.11	.03
☐ 33 John Vukovich CO	.25	.11	.03
☐ 34 David West	.25	.11	.03
☐ 35 Mitch Williams	.50	.23	.06

1994 Phillies Medford

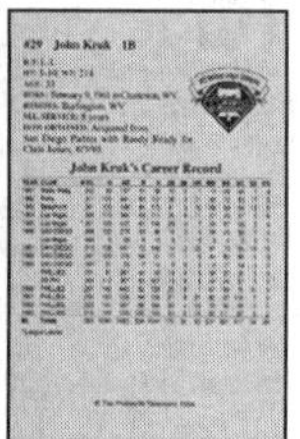

These 36 cards measure approximately 4" by 6" and feature borderless color player photos on their fronts. The player's name appears in white lettering within a red bar on the card face. The white back carries the player's uniform number, name, position, biography, and statistics in red and black lettering. The Phillies logo at the upper right rounds out the card. The cards are unnumbered and checklisted below in alphabetical order.

	MINT	NRMT	EXC
COMPLETE SET (36)	10.00	4.50	1.25
COMMON CARD (1-36)	.25	.11	.03
☐ 1 Larry Andersen	.25	.11	.03
☐ 2 Kim Batiste	.25	.11	.03
☐ 3 Larry Bowa CO	.50	.23	.06
☐ 4 Wes Chamberlain	.25	.11	.03
☐ 5 Norm Charlton	.25	.11	.03
☐ 6 Darren Daulton	1.00	.45	.12
☐ 7 Mariano Duncan	.50	.23	.06
☐ 8 Lenny Dykstra	.75	.35	.09
☐ 9 Jim Eisenreich	.75	.35	.09
☐ 10 Jim Fregosi MG	.25	.11	.03
☐ 11 Tyler Green	.25	.11	.03
☐ 12 Tommy Greene	.25	.11	.03
☐ 13 Dave Hollins	.25	.11	.03
☐ 14 Pete Incaviglia	.50	.23	.06
☐ 15 Danny Jackson	.25	.11	.03
☐ 16 Doug Jones	.50	.23	.06
☐ 17 Ricky Jordan	.25	.11	.03
☐ 18 Jeff Juden	.25	.11	.03
☐ 19 John Kruk	.75	.35	.09
☐ 20 Tony Longmire	.25	.11	.03
☐ 21 Roger Mason	.25	.11	.03
☐ 22 Denis Menke CO	.25	.11	.03
☐ 23 Mickey Morandini	.50	.23	.06
☐ 24 Bobby Munoz	.25	.11	.03
☐ 25 Johnny Podres CO	.50	.23	.06
☐ 26 Todd Pratt	.25	.11	.03
☐ 27 Ben Rivera	.25	.11	.03
☐ 28 Mel Roberts CO	.25	.11	.03
☐ 29 Mike Ryan CO	.25	.11	.03
☐ 30 Curt Schilling	.25	.11	.03
☐ 31 Heathcliff Slocumb	.50	.23	.06
☐ 32 Kevin Stocker	.50	.23	.06
☐ 33 Milt Thompson	.25	.11	.03
☐ 34 John Vukovich CO	.25	.11	.03
☐ 35 David West	.25	.11	.03
☐ 36 Mike Williams	.25	.11	.03

1994 Phillies Mellon

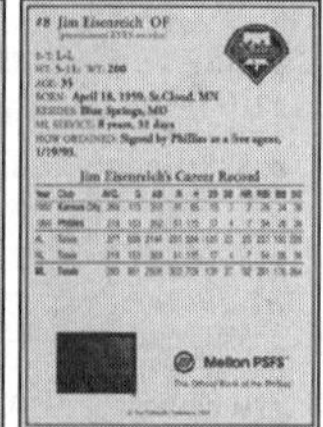

The 1994 Phillies Team Photo/Card Pack was sponsored by Mellon PSFS, "The Official Bank of the Phillies." The set consists of three 12 1/2" by 7" sheets and one 12 1/2" by 3" strip all joined together. The first sheet features a team photo. The second and third sheets consist of two row of five cards each, while the third strip presents one row of five cards. The sheets are perforated and the cards measure the standard-size. The fronts feature color action player photos on a team color-coded background. The logos for baseball's 125th Anniversary and Mellon Bank at the bottom round out the card. The team name appears in a box above the photo, while the player's name is printed inside a banner on the bottom. The backs carry a short player biography and career records. The cards are unnumbered and checklisted below in alphabetical order.

	MINT	NRMT	EXC
COMPLETE SET (26)	8.00	3.60	1.00
COMMON CARD (1-26)	.25	.11	.03
☐ 1 Larry Andersen	.25	.11	.03
☐ 2 Kim Batiste	.25	.11	.03
☐ 3 Shawn Boskie	.25	.11	.03
☐ 4 Darren Daulton	.50	.23	.06
☐ 5 Mariano Duncan	.50	.23	.06
☐ 6 Lenny Dykstra	1.00	.45	.12
☐ 7 Jim Eisenreich	.75	.35	.09
☐ 8 Tommy Greene	.25	.11	.03
☐ 9 Dave Hollins	.25	.11	.03
☐ 10 Pete Incaviglia	.50	.23	.06
☐ 11 Danny Jackson	.25	.11	.03
☐ 12 Doug Jones	.50	.23	.06
☐ 13 Ricky Jordan	.25	.11	.03
☐ 14 John Kruk	1.00	.45	.12
☐ 15 Tony Longmire	.25	.11	.03
☐ 16 Mickey Morandini	.50	.23	.06
☐ 17 Bobby Munoz	.25	.11	.03
☐ 18 Todd Pratt	.25	.11	.03
☐ 19 Paul Quantrill	.25	.11	.03
Billy Hatcher			
☐ 20 Curt Schilling	.75	.35	.09
☐ 21 Heathcliff Slocumb	.50	.23	.06
☐ 22 Kevin Stocker	.50	.23	.06
☐ 23 Milt Thompson	.25	.11	.03
☐ 24 David West	.25	.11	.03
☐ 25 Mike Williams	.25	.11	.03
☐ 26 Large Team Photo	2.00	.90	.25
12 1/2" by 7"			

1994 Phillies U.S. Playing Cards

These 56 playing standard-size cards have rounded corners, and feature color posed and action player photos on their white-bordered fronts. The player's name and position appear near the bottom. The blue and gray backs carry the logos for the Phillies, baseball's 125th Anniversary, MLBPA, and Bicycle Sports Collection. The set is checklisted below in playing card order by suits and assigned numbers to aces (1), jacks (11), queens (12), and kings (13).

	MINT	NRMT	EXC
COMPLETE SET (56)	3.00	1.35	.35
COMMON CARD	.05	.02	.01
☐ 1C Pete Incaviglia	.05	.02	.01
☐ 1D Terry Mulholland	.05	.02	.01

☐ 1H Lenny Dykstra	.25	.11	.03
☐ 1S Dave Hollins	.05	.02	.01
☐ 2C Lenny Dykstra	.25	.11	.03
☐ 2D Brad Brink	.05	.02	.01
☐ 2H Tony Longmire	.05	.02	.01
☐ 2S Danny Jackson	.05	.02	.01
☐ 3C Milt Thompson	.05	.02	.01
☐ 3D Roger Mason	.05	.02	.01
☐ 3H Kim Batiste	.05	.02	.01
☐ 3S Todd Pratt	.05	.02	.01
☐ 4C Mickey Morandini	.15	.07	.02
☐ 4D Mariano Duncan	.05	.02	.01
☐ 4H Pete Incaviglia	.15	.07	.02
☐ 4S David West	.05	.02	.01
☐ 5C Kevin Stocker	.15	.07	.02
☐ 5D Danny Jackson	.05	.02	.01
☐ 5H Ben Rivera	.05	.02	.01
☐ 5S Lenny Dykstra	.25	.11	.03
☐ 6C Terry Mulholland	.05	.02	.01
☐ 6D Jim Eisenreich	.05	.02	.01
☐ 6H Ricky Jordan	.05	.02	.01
☐ 6S Wes Chamberlain	.05	.02	.01
☐ 7C Curt Schilling	.05	.02	.01
☐ 7D John Kruk	.15	.07	.02
☐ 7H Dave Hollins	.05	.02	.01
☐ 7S Tommy Greene	.05	.02	.01
☐ 8C Darren Daulton	.25	.11	.03
☐ 8D David West	.05	.02	.01
☐ 8H Kevin Foster	.05	.02	.01
☐ 8S Tony Longmire	.05	.02	.01
☐ 9C Terry Mulholland	.05	.02	.01
☐ 9D Todd Pratt	.05	.02	.01
☐ 9H Kevin Stocker	.05	.02	.01
☐ 9S Brad Brink	.05	.02	.01
☐ 10C Roger Mason	.05	.02	.01
☐ 10D Wes Chamberlain	.05	.02	.01
☐ 10H Mike Williams	.05	.02	.01
☐ 10S Ricky Jordan	.05	.02	.01
☐ 11C Mariano Duncan	.05	.02	.01
☐ 11D Jim Eisenreich	.15	.07	.02
☐ 11H Milt Thompson	.05	.02	.01
☐ 11S Kim Batiste	.05	.02	.01
☐ 12C Ben Rivera	.05	.02	.01
☐ 12D Mickey Morandini	.05	.02	.01
☐ 12H Curt Schilling	.15	.07	.02
☐ 12S Tyler Green	.05	.02	.01
☐ 13C John Kruk	.15	.07	.02
☐ 13D Tommy Greene	.05	.02	.01
☐ 13H Darren Daulton	.25	.11	.03
☐ 13S Jim Eisenreich	.15	.07	.02
☐ NNO Featured Players	.05	.02	.01

1995 Phillies

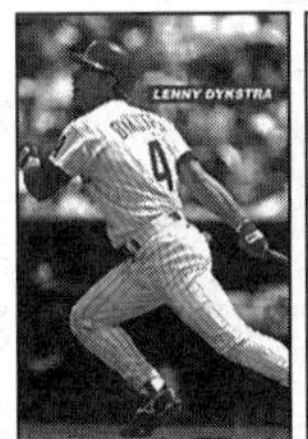
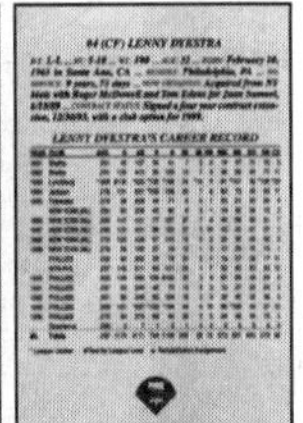

This 36-card set measures approximately 4" by 6". The fronts feature borderless color player photos with the player's name printed in white on a red bar. The white backs carry the player's uniform number, name, position, biography, and statistics in red and black lettering with the team logo below. The cards are unnumbered and checklisted below in alphabetical order.

	MINT	NRMT	EXC
COMPLETE SET (36)	10.00	4.50	1.25
COMMON CARD (1-36)	.25	.11	.03
☐ 1 Kyle Abbott	.25	.11	.03
☐ 2 Richie Ashburn HOF	1.25	.55	.16
☐ 3 Toby Borland	.25	.11	.03
☐ 4 Ricky Bottalico	.50	.23	.06
☐ 5 Larry Bowa CO	.25	.11	.03
☐ 6 Norm Charlton	.50	.23	.06
☐ 7 Darren Daulton	1.25	.55	.16
☐ 8 Mariano Duncan	.50	.23	.06
☐ 9 Lenny Dykstra	.75	.35	.09
☐ 10 Jim Eisenreich	.75	.35	.09
☐ 11 Jim Fregosi MG	.25	.11	.03
☐ 12 Dave Gallagher	.25	.11	.03
☐ 13 Tyler Green	.25	.11	.03
☐ 14 Gene Harris	.25	.11	.03
☐ 15 Charlie Hayes	.50	.23	.06
☐ 16 Dave Hollins	.25	.11	.03
☐ 17 Gregg Jefferies	.75	.35	.09
☐ 18 Tony Longmire	.25	.11	.03
☐ 19 Denis Menke CO	.25	.11	.03
☐ 20 Michael Mimbs	.25	.11	.03
☐ 21 Mickey Morandini	.50	.23	.06
☐ 22 Bobby Munoz	.25	.11	.03
☐ 23 Johnny Podres CO	.50	.23	.06
☐ 24 Paul Quantrill	.25	.11	.03
☐ 25 Randy Ready	.25	.11	.03
☐ 26 Mel Roberts CO	.25	.11	.03
☐ 27 Mike Ryan CO	.25	.11	.03
☐ 28 Curt Schilling	.75	.35	.09
☐ 29 Mike Schmidt HOF	1.50	.70	.19
☐ 30 Heathcliff Slocumb	.75	.35	.09
☐ 31 Kevin Stocker	.50	.23	.06
☐ 32 Gary Varsho	.25	.11	.03
☐ 33 John Vukovich	.25	.11	.03
☐ 34 Lenny Webster	.25	.11	.03
☐ 35 David West	.25	.11	.03
☐ 36 Team Photo	.50	.23	.06

1995 Phillies Mellon

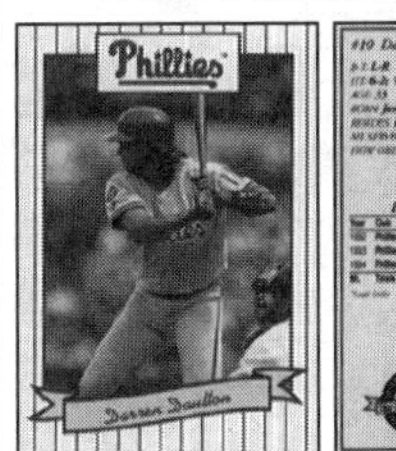
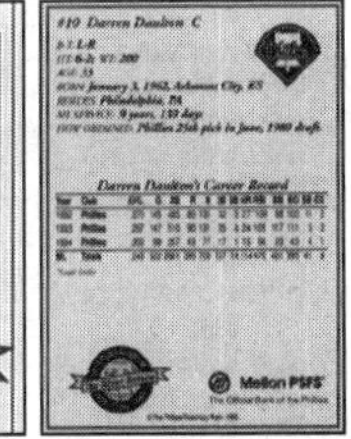

This 25-card set of the Phillies measures the standard size and was issued in perforated sheets. The fronts feature color action player photos on white-and-red pinstripe background. The team name appears in a box above the photo with the player's name printed inside a banner on the bottom. The backs carry a short player biography and career records. The team's Silver Season logo and Mellon Bank's logo at the bottom round out the card. The cards are unnumbered and checklisted below in alphabetical order.

	MINT	NRMT	EXC
COMPLETE SET (25)	6.00	2.70	.75
COMMON CARD (1-25)	.25	.11	.03
☐ 1 Kyle Abbott	.25	.11	.03
☐ 2 Toby Borland	.25	.11	.03
☐ 3 Ricky Bottalico	.50	.23	.06
☐ 4 Norm Charlton	.50	.23	.06
☐ 5 Darren Daulton	1.00	.45	.12
☐ 6 Mariano Duncan	.50	.23	.06
☐ 7 Lenny Dykstra	.50	.23	.06
☐ 8 Jim Eisenreich	.75	.35	.09
☐ 9 Dave Gallagher	.25	.11	.03
☐ 10 Tyler Green	.25	.11	.03
☐ 11 Gene Harris	.25	.11	.03
☐ 12 Charlie Hayes	.50	.23	.06
☐ 13 Dave Hollins	.25	.11	.03
☐ 14 Gregg Jefferies	.75	.35	.09
☐ 15 Tony Longmire	.25	.11	.03
☐ 16 Michael Mimbs	.50	.23	.06
☐ 17 Mickey Morandini	.50	.23	.06
☐ 18 Paul Quantrill	.25	.11	.03
☐ 19 Randy Ready	.25	.11	.03
☐ 20 Curt Schilling	.75	.35	.09
☐ 21 Heathcliff Slocumb	.50	.23	.06
☐ 22 Kevin Stocker	.50	.23	.06
☐ 23 Gary Varsho	.25	.11	.03
☐ 24 Lenny Webster	.25	.11	.03
☐ 25 David West	.25	.11	.03

1996 Phillies Team Issue

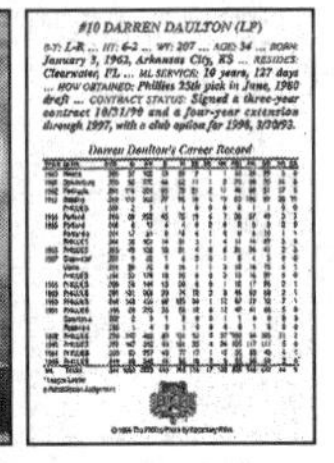

These 4" by 6" cards feature members of the 1996 Philadelphia Phillies. The full-bleed fronts feature color player photos with their names in the upper left corner. The backs have vital statistics and a career record. This set is unumbered and we have checklisted it in alphabetical order.

	MINT	NRMT	EXC
COMPLETE SET (36)	8.00	3.60	1.00
COMMON CARD (1-36)	.25	.11	.03
☐ 1 Howard Battle	.25	.11	.03
☐ 2 Mike Benjamin	.25	.11	.03
☐ 3 Toby Borland	.25	.11	.03
☐ 4 Ricky Bottalico	.50	.23	.06
☐ 5 Larry Bowa CO	.25	.11	.03
☐ 6 Dave Cash CO	.25	.11	.03
☐ 7 Carlos Crawford	.25	.11	.03
☐ 8 Darren Daulton	1.00	.45	.12
☐ 9 Lenny Dykstra	1.00	.45	.12
☐ 10 Jim Eisenreich	.75	.35	.09
☐ 11 Sid Fernandez	.50	.23	.06
☐ 12 Jim Fregosi MG	.25	.11	.03
☐ 13 Steve Frey	.25	.11	.03
☐ 14 Mike Grace	.50	.23	.06
☐ 15 Tyler Green	.25	.11	.03
☐ 16 Pete Incaviglia	.25	.11	.03
☐ 17 Gregg Jefferies	.50	.23	.06
☐ 18 Kevin Jordan	.25	.11	.03
☐ 19 Dave Leiper	.25	.11	.03
☐ 20 Mike Lieberthal	.25	.11	.03
☐ 21 Denis Menke CO	.25	.11	.03
☐ 22 Mike Mimbs	.25	.11	.03
☐ 23 Mickey Morandini	.25	.11	.03
☐ 24 Terry Mulholland	.25	.11	.03
☐ 25 Phillie Phanatic	.50	.23	.06
☐ 26 Johnny Podres CO	.50	.23	.06
☐ 27 Joe Rigoli CO	.25	.11	.03
☐ 28 Ken Ryan	.25	.11	.03
☐ 29 Benito Santiago	.50	.23	.06
☐ 30 Russ Springer	.25	.11	.03
☐ 31 Kevin Stocker	.25	.11	.03
☐ 32 Lee Tinsley	.25	.11	.03
☐ 33 John Vukovich CO	.25	.11	.03
☐ 34 Mark Whiten	.25	.11	.03
☐ 35 Mike Williams	.25	.11	.03
☐ 36 Todd Zeile	.25	.11	.03

1992 Photo File Hall of Fame

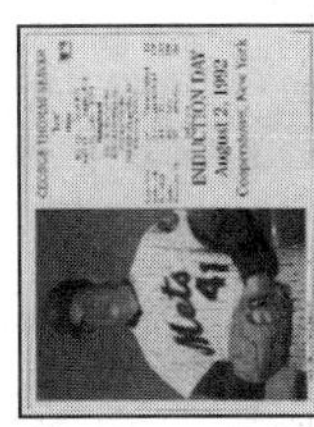

This four-card set produced by Photo File displays color photos of the 1992 Baseball Hall of Fame inductees. The 8" by 10" cards commemorate the induction day ceremonies and include player statistics and biographical information. The cards are checklisted below alphabetically.

	MINT	NRMT	EXC
COMPLETE SET (4)	12.00	5.50	1.50
COMMON CARD (1-4)	2.00	.90	.25
☐ 1 Rollie Fingers	3.00	1.35	.35
☐ 2 Hal Newhouser	2.00	.90	.25
☐ 3 Tom Seaver Pitching	4.00	1.80	.50
☐ 4 Tom Seaver Still photo	4.00	1.80	.50

1993 Photo File Ryan

This eight-card set measures approximately 8" by 10" and commemorates Nolan Ryan's career record seven no-hitters. Each card features a black-and-white or color photo of Ryan as well as the box score from the game. The cards are checklisted below according to the date of the no-hitter.

	MINT	NRMT	EXC
COMPLETE SET j(8)	20.00	9.00	2.50
COMMON CARD (1-8)	2.50	1.10	.30
☐ 1 Nolan Ryan 1st No-Hitter; May 15, 1973	2.50	1.10	.30
☐ 2 Nolan Ryan 2nd No-Hitter; July 15, 1973	2.50	1.10	.30
☐ 3 Nolan Ryan 3rd No-Hitter; September 28, 1974	2.50	1.10	.30
☐ 4 Nolan Ryan 4th No-Hitter; June 1, 1975	2.50	1.10	.30
☐ 5 Nolan Ryan 5th No-Hitter; September 26, 1981	2.50	1.10	.30
☐ 6 Nolan Ryan 6th No-Hitter; June 11, 1990	2.50	1.10	.30
☐ 7 Nolan Ryan 7th No-Hitter; May 1, 1991	2.50	1.10	.30
☐ 8 Title Card	2.50	1.10	.30

1973 Pictureform Clemente

The Roberto Clemente Pictureform set consists of 12 photos and originally sold for $ 2.00. The black-and-white action photos are in a circle format and measure approximately 8 3/16" in diameter. The photos are bordered by an orange or light blue 1 3/8" border and printed on medium weight paper stock. There are five scored lines surrounding the photo that indicate where to fold the picture to form the pictureform. Once assembled, the pictures form a twelve-sided sphere. No lettering is printed on the front and the backs are blank. The photos were packaged with a large folder which displayed a color posed photo of Clemente on the front. On the inside left side were Clemente's career highlights and quotes from his peers. The inside

right contained instructions for assembling the pictureform with line drawn illustrations above and below.

	NRMT	VG-E	GOOD
COMPLETE SET (12)	100.00	45.00	12.50
COMMON CARD (1-12)	10.00	4.50	1.25
☐ 1 Roberto Clemente (Front view batting stance)	10.00	4.50	1.25
☐ 2 Roberto Clemente (Sliding into base)	10.00	4.50	1.25
☐ 3 Roberto Clemente (Fielding, calling player out, umpire in foreground)	10.00	4.50	1.25
☐ 4 Roberto Clemente (Stretching to make the catch at the wall)	10.00	4.50	1.25
☐ 5 Roberto Clemente (Sliding, right arm up)	10.00	4.50	1.25
☐ 6 Roberto Clemente (Batting pose)	10.00	4.50	1.25
☐ 7 Roberto Clemente (Fielding the ball)	10.00	4.50	1.25
☐ 8 Roberto Clemente (Swinging at the ball)	10.00	4.50	1.25
☐ 9 Roberto Clemente (Jumping on fence, looking up)	10.00	4.50	1.25
☐ 10 Roberto Clemente (Sliding into base umpire in foreground)	10.00	4.50	1.25
☐ 11 Roberto Clemente (Reaching back to make the catch)	10.00	4.50	1.25
☐ 12 Roberto Clemente (Hitting a bunt)	10.00	4.50	1.25

1914 Piedmont Stamps T330-2

These attractive stamps are approximately 1 7/16" by 2 5/8" and are unnumbered. Unlike most stamps, these have blue printing on the back. These art stamps were apparently a premium as the stamp back references "Offer expires June 30, 1915." The front designs are similar to T205.

	EX-MT	VG-E	GOOD
COMPLETE SET (64)	7000.00	3200.00	900.00
COMMON PLAYER (1-64)	75.00	34.00	9.50
☐ 1 Cy Barger	75.00	34.00	9.50
☐ 2 Jack Barry	75.00	34.00	9.50
☐ 3 Beals Becker	75.00	34.00	9.50
☐ 4 Joe Birmingham	75.00	34.00	9.50
☐ 5 Walter Blair	75.00	34.00	9.50
☐ 6 Al Bridwell	75.00	34.00	9.50
☐ 7 Mordecai Brown	200.00	90.00	25.00
☐ 8 Howie Camnitz	75.00	34.00	9.50
☐ 9 Bill Carrigan	75.00	34.00	9.50
☐ 10 Frank Chance	250.00	110.00	31.00
☐ 11 Hal Chase	150.00	70.00	19.00
☐ 12 Fred Clarke	200.00	90.00	25.00
☐ 13 Ty Cobb	800.00	350.00	100.00
☐ 14 Eddie Collins	200.00	90.00	25.00
☐ 15 Bill Dahlen	100.00	45.00	12.50
☐ 16 Jake Daubert	100.00	45.00	12.50
☐ 17 Josh Devore	75.00	34.00	9.50
☐ 18 Tom Downey	75.00	34.00	9.50
☐ 19 Larry Doyle	100.00	45.00	12.50
☐ 20 Joe Egan	75.00	34.00	9.50
☐ 21 Clyde Engle	75.00	34.00	9.50
☐ 22 Russ Ford	75.00	34.00	9.50
☐ 23 Arthur Fromme	75.00	34.00	9.50
☐ 24 William Goode	75.00	34.00	9.50
☐ 25 Clark Griffith	200.00	90.00	25.00
☐ 26 Bob Groom	75.00	34.00	9.50
☐ 27 Arnold Houser	75.00	34.00	9.50
☐ 28 Miller Huggins	200.00	90.00	25.00
☐ 29 John Hummel	75.00	34.00	9.50
☐ 30 William Killifer	125.00	55.00	15.50
☐ 31 John Knight	75.00	34.00	9.50

☐ 32 Frank LaPorte	75.00	34.00	9.50
☐ 33 Hans Lobert	75.00	34.00	9.50
☐ 34 Bris Lord	75.00	34.00	9.50
☐ 35 Sherry Magee	75.00	34.00	9.50
☐ 36 George McBride	75.00	34.00	9.50
☐ 37 John McGraw MG	250.00	110.00	31.00
☐ 38 Larry McLean	75.00	34.00	9.50
☐ 39 Chief Meyers	100.00	45.00	12.50
☐ 40 Dots Miller	75.00	34.00	9.50
☐ 41 Michael Mitchell	75.00	34.00	9.50
☐ 42 Pat Moran	75.00	34.00	9.50
☐ 43 Danny Murphy	75.00	34.00	9.50
☐ 44 Jack Murray	75.00	34.00	9.50
☐ 45 Tom Needham	75.00	34.00	9.50
☐ 46 Rebel Oakes	75.00	34.00	9.50
☐ 47 Freddy Parent	75.00	34.00	9.50
☐ 48 Dode Paskert	75.00	34.00	9.50
☐ 49 Lewis Ritchie	75.00	34.00	9.50
☐ 50 John A. Rowan	75.00	34.00	9.50
☐ 51 Germany Schaefer	100.00	45.00	12.50
☐ 52 Tris Speaker	250.00	110.00	31.00
☐ 53 Oscar Stanage	75.00	34.00	9.50
☐ 54 Ira Thomas	75.00	34.00	9.50
☐ 55 Joe Tinker	200.00	90.00	25.00
☐ 56 Terry Turner	100.00	45.00	12.50
☐ 57 Hippo Vaughn	75.00	34.00	9.50
☐ 58 Bobby Wallace	200.00	90.00	25.00
☐ 59 Ed Walsh	200.00	90.00	25.00
☐ 60 Zach Wheat	200.00	90.00	25.00
☐ 61 Kaiser Wilhelm	75.00	34.00	9.50
☐ 62 Ed Willett	75.00	34.00	9.50
☐ 63 J. Owen Wilson	75.00	34.00	9.50
☐ 64 Hooks Wiltse	75.00	34.00	9.50

1969 Pilots Post-Intelligencer

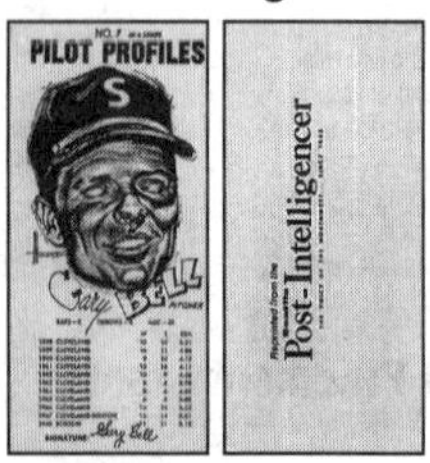

This set was originally inserted into copies of the Seattle Post-Intelligencer in 1969. These cards which measure approximately 2 1/4" b y 5" clearly state that these are reprints from those inserts. Card number five was never issued. The fronts feature drawings; and year by year stats. This set is dated 1969 as that was the only year of the Pilots existence.

	NRMT	VG-E	GOOD
COMPLETE SET (38)	300.00	135.00	38.00
COMMON CARD (1-39)	7.50	3.40	.95
☐ 1 Don Mincher	7.50	3.40	.95
☐ 2 Tommy Harper	10.00	4.50	1.25
☐ 3 Ray Oyler	7.50	3.40	.95
☐ 4 Jerry McNertney	7.50	3.40	.95
☐ 6 Tommy Davis	10.00	4.50	1.25
☐ 7 Gary Bell	7.50	3.40	.95
☐ 8 Chico Salmon	8.00	3.60	1.00
☐ 9 Jack Aker	7.50	3.40	.95
☐ 10 Rich Rollins	7.50	3.40	.95
☐ 11 Diego Segui	8.00	3.60	1.00
☐ 12 Steve Barber	8.00	3.60	1.00
☐ 13 Wayne Comer	7.50	3.40	.95
☐ 14 John Kennedy	7.50	3.40	.95
☐ 15 Buzz Stephen	7.50	3.40	.95
☐ 16 Jim Gosger	7.50	3.40	.95
☐ 17 Mike Ferraro	7.50	3.40	.95
☐ 18 Marty Pattin	7.50	3.40	.95
☐ 19 Gerry Schoen	7.50	3.40	.95
☐ 20 Steve Hovely	7.50	3.40	.95
☐ 21 Frank Crosetti CO	15.00	6.75	1.85
☐ 22 Dick Bates	7.50	3.40	.95
☐ 23 Jose Vidal	7.50	3.40	.95
☐ 24 Bob Richmond	7.50	3.40	.95
☐ 25 Lou Piniella	25.00	11.00	3.10
☐ 26 John Miklos	7.50	3.40	.95
☐ 27 John Morris	7.50	3.40	.95
☐ 28 Larry Haney	7.50	3.40	.95
☐ 29 Mike Marshall	10.00	4.50	1.25
☐ 30 Marv Staehle	7.50	3.40	.95
☐ 31 Gus Gil	7.50	3.40	.95
☐ 32 Sal Maglie CO	10.00	4.50	1.25
☐ 33 Ron Plaza CO	7.50	3.40	.95
☐ 34 Ed O'Brien CO	7.50	3.40	.95
☐ 35 Jim Bouton	15.00	6.75	1.85
☐ 36 Bill Stafford	7.50	3.40	.95
☐ 37 Darrell Brandon	7.50	3.40	.95
☐ 38 Mike Hegan	7.50	3.40	.95
☐ 39 Dick Baney	7.50	3.40	.95

1983 Pilots 69 Galasso

This 43-card standard-size set features members of the Seattle Pilots. The fronts have a player photo with his name and position located under the photo. All of this is surrounded by yellow borders. The backs

have a career history along with their stats for the Pilots. Some sets were issued with specially autographed Jim Bouton cards. The Bouton autographed card adds $5 to the value of the set.

	NRMT	VG-E	GOOD
COMPLETE SET (43)	10.00	4.50	1.25
COMMON CARD (1-43)	.25	.11	.03
☐ 1 Jim Bouton	.75	.35	.09
☐ 2 Joe Schultz MG	.25	.11	.03
☐ 3 Bill Edgerton	.25	.11	.03
☐ 4 Gary Timberlake	.25	.11	.03
☐ 5 Dick Baney	.25	.11	.03
☐ 6 Mike Marshall	.50	.23	.06
☐ 7 Jim Gosger	.25	.11	.03
☐ 8 Mike Hegan	.25	.11	.03
☐ 9 Steve Hovely	.25	.11	.03
☐ 10 Don Mincher	.25	.11	.03
☐ 11 Miguel Fuentes	.25	.11	.03
☐ 12 Dick Bates	.25	.11	.03
☐ 13 John O'Donoghue	.25	.11	.03
☐ 14 Tommy Davis	.50	.23	.06
☐ 15 Jerry McNertney	.25	.11	.03
☐ 16 Rich Rollins	.25	.11	.03
☐ 17 Fred Talbot	.25	.11	.03
☐ 18 John Gelnar	.25	.11	.03
☐ 19 Bob Locker	.25	.11	.03
☐ 20 Frank Crosetti CO	.50	.23	.06
☐ 21 Sal Maglie CO	.50	.23	.06
☐ 22 Sibby Sisti CO	.25	.11	.03
☐ 23 Ron Plaza CO	.25	.11	.03
☐ 24 Federico Velazaquez	.25	.11	.03
☐ 25 Diego Segui	.25	.11	.03
☐ 26 Steve Barber	.25	.11	.03
☐ 27 Jack Aker	.25	.11	.03
☐ 28 Marty Pattin	.25	.11	.03
☐ 29 Ray Oyler	.25	.11	.03
☐ 30 Danny Walton	.25	.11	.03
☐ 31 Merritt Ranew	.25	.11	.03
☐ 32 John Donaldson	.25	.11	.03
☐ 33 Greg Goossen	.50	.23	.06
☐ 34 Gary Bell	.25	.11	.03
☐ 35 Jim Pagliaroni	.25	.11	.03
☐ 36 Mike Ferraro	.25	.11	.03
☐ 37 Tommy Harper	.50	.23	.06
☐ 38 John Morris	.25	.11	.03
☐ 39 Larry Haney	.25	.11	.03
☐ 40 Ron Clark	.25	.11	.03
☐ 41 Steve Whitaker	.25	.11	.03
☐ 42 Wayne Comer	.25	.11	.03
☐ 43 Gene Brabender	.25	.11	.03

1992 Pinnacle

The 1992 Pinnacle set (issued by Score) consists of two series each with 310 standard-size cards. Cards were distributed in first and second series 16-card foil packs and 27-card cello packs. The card fronts feature glossy color player photos, on a black background accented by thin white borders. An anti-counterfeit device appears in the bottom border of each card back. A special ribbed plastic lenticular detector card was made available that allowed the user to view the anti-counterfeit device and unscramble the coding with the word "Pinnacle" appearing. Special subsets featured include '92 Rookie Prospects (52, 55, 168, 247-261, 263-280), Idols (281-286/584-591), Sidelines (287-294/592-596), Draft Picks (295-304), Shades (305-310/601-605), Grips (606-612), and Technicians (614-620). Rookie Cards in the set include Brian Jordan and Manny Ramirez.

	MINT	NRMT	EXC
COMPLETE SET (620)	40.00	18.00	5.00
COMPLETE SERIES 1 (310)	25.00	11.00	3.10
COMPLETE SERIES 2 (310)	15.00	6.75	1.85
COMMON CARD (1-620)	.10	.05	.01
☐ 1 Frank Thomas	3.00	1.35	.35
☐ 2 Benito Santiago	.10	.05	.01
☐ 3 Carlos Baerga	.15	.07	.02
☐ 4 Cecil Fielder	.15	.07	.02
☐ 5 Barry Larkin	.30	.14	.04
☐ 6 Ozzie Smith	.50	.23	.06
☐ 7 Willie McGee	.10	.05	.01
☐ 8 Paul Molitor	.40	.18	.05
☐ 9 Andy Van Slyke	.15	.07	.02
☐ 10 Ryne Sandberg	.50	.23	.06
☐ 11 Kevin Seitzer	.10	.05	.01
☐ 12 Len Dykstra	.15	.07	.02
☐ 13 Edgar Martinez	.15	.07	.02
☐ 14 Rubon Sierra	.15	.07	.02
☐ 15 Howard Johnson	.10	.05	.01
☐ 16 Dave Henderson	.10	.05	.01
☐ 17 Devon White	.15	.07	.02
☐ 18 Terry Pendleton	.15	.07	.02
☐ 19 Steve Finley	.15	.07	.02
☐ 20 Kirby Puckett	.75	.35	.09
☐ 21 Orel Hershiser	.15	.07	.02
☐ 22 Hal Morris	.10	.05	.01
☐ 23 Don Mattingly	1.00	.45	.12
☐ 24 Delino DeShields	.10	.05	.01
☐ 25 Dennis Eckersley	.15	.07	.02
☐ 26 Ellis Burks	.15	.07	.02
☐ 27 Jay Buhner	.30	.14	.04
☐ 28 Matt Williams	.30	.14	.04
☐ 29 Lou Whitaker	.15	.07	.02
☐ 30 Alex Fernandez	.30	.14	.04
☐ 31 Albert Belle	1.00	.45	.12
☐ 32 Todd Zeile	.10	.05	.01
☐ 33 Tony Pena	.10	.05	.01
☐ 34 Jay Bell	.15	.07	.02
☐ 35 Rafael Palmeiro	.30	.14	.04
☐ 36 Wes Chamberlain	.10	.05	.01
☐ 37 George Bell	.10	.05	.01
☐ 38 Robin Yount	.30	.14	.04
☐ 39 Vince Coleman	.10	.05	.01
☐ 40 Bruce Hurst	.10	.05	.01
☐ 41 Harold Baines	.15	.07	.02
☐ 42 Chuck Finley	.10	.05	.01
☐ 43 Ken Caminiti	.30	.14	.04
☐ 44 Ben McDonald	.10	.05	.01
☐ 45 Roberto Alomar	.40	.18	.05
☐ 46 Chili Davis	.15	.07	.02
☐ 47 Bill Doran	.10	.05	.01
☐ 48 Jerald Clark	.10	.05	.01
☐ 49 Jose Lind	.10	.05	.01
☐ 50 Nolan Ryan	1.50	.70	.19
☐ 51 Phil Plantier	.15	.07	.02
☐ 52 Gary DiSarcina	.10	.05	.01
☐ 53 Kevin Bass	.10	.05	.01
☐ 54 Pat Kelly	.10	.05	.01
☐ 55 Mark Wohlers	.30	.14	.04
☐ 56 Walt Weiss	.10	.05	.01
☐ 57 Lenny Harris	.10	.05	.01
☐ 58 Ivan Calderon	.10	.05	.01
☐ 59 Harold Reynolds	.10	.05	.01
☐ 60 George Brett	.75	.35	.09
☐ 61 Gregg Olson	.10	.05	.01
☐ 62 Orlando Merced	.15	.07	.02
☐ 63 Steve Decker	.10	.05	.01
☐ 64 John Franco	.10	.05	.01
☐ 65 Greg Maddux	1.50	.70	.19
☐ 66 Alex Cole	.10	.05	.01
☐ 67 Dave Hollins	.10	.05	.01
☐ 68 Kent Hrbek	.15	.07	.02
☐ 69 Tom Pagnozzi	.10	.05	.01
☐ 70 Jeff Bagwell	1.25	.55	.16
☐ 71 Jim Gantner	.10	.05	.01
☐ 72 Matt Nokes	.10	.05	.01
☐ 73 Brian Harper	.10	.05	.01
☐ 74 Andy Benes	.15	.07	.02
☐ 75 Tom Glavine	.30	.14	.04
☐ 76 Terry Steinbach	.15	.07	.02
☐ 77 Dennis Martinez	.15	.07	.02
☐ 78 John Olerud	.15	.07	.02
☐ 79 Ozzie Guillen	.10	.05	.01
☐ 80 Darryl Strawberry	.15	.07	.02
☐ 81 Gary Gaetti	.15	.07	.02
☐ 82 Dave Righetti	.10	.05	.01
☐ 83 Chris Hoiles	.10	.05	.01
☐ 84 Andujar Cedeno	.10	.05	.01
☐ 85 Jack Clark	.15	.07	.02
☐ 86 David Howard	.10	.05	.01
☐ 87 Bill Gullickson	.10	.05	.01
☐ 88 Bernard Gilkey	.15	.07	.02
☐ 89 Kevin Elster	.10	.05	.01
☐ 90 Kevin Maas	.10	.05	.01
☐ 91 Mark Lewis	.10	.05	.01
☐ 92 Greg Vaughn	.15	.07	.02
☐ 93 Bret Barberie	.10	.05	.01
☐ 94 Dave Smith	.10	.05	.01
☐ 95 Roger Clemens	.40	.18	.05
☐ 96 Doug Drabek	.10	.05	.01
☐ 97 Omar Vizquel	.15	.07	.02
☐ 98 Jose Guzman	.10	.05	.01
☐ 99 Juan Samuel	.10	.05	.01
☐ 100 Dave Justice	.30	.14	.04
☐ 101 Tom Browning	.10	.05	.01
☐ 102 Mark Gubicza	.10	.05	.01
☐ 103 Mickey Morandini	.10	.05	.01
☐ 104 Ed Whitson	.10	.05	.01
☐ 105 Lance Parrish	.10	.05	.01
☐ 106 Scott Erickson	.15	.07	.02
☐ 107 Jack McDowell	.15	.07	.02
☐ 108 Dave Stieb	.10	.05	.01
☐ 109 Mike Moore	.10	.05	.01
☐ 110 Travis Fryman	.30	.14	.04
☐ 111 Dwight Gooden	.15	.07	.02
☐ 112 Fred McGriff	.30	.14	.04
☐ 113 Alan Trammell	.15	.07	.02
☐ 114 Roberto Kelly	.10	.05	.01
☐ 115 Andre Dawson	.15	.07	.02
☐ 116 Bill Landrum	.10	.05	.01
☐ 117 Brian McRae	.15	.07	.02
☐ 118 B.J. Surhoff	.15	.07	.02
☐ 119 Chuck Knoblauch	.30	.14	.04
☐ 120 Steve Olin	.10	.05	.01
☐ 121 Robin Ventura	.15	.07	.02
☐ 122 Will Clark	.30	.14	.04
☐ 123 Tino Martinez	.15	.07	.02
☐ 124 Dale Murphy	.30	.14	.04
☐ 125 Pete O'Brien	.10	.05	.01
☐ 126 Ray Lankford	.30	.14	.04
☐ 127 Juan Gonzalez	1.25	.55	.16
☐ 128 Ron Gant	.15	.07	.02
☐ 129 Marquis Grissom	.15	.07	.02
☐ 130 Jose Canseco	.30	.14	.04
☐ 131 Mike Greenwell	.10	.05	.01
☐ 132 Mark Langston	.15	.07	.02
☐ 133 Brett Butler	.15	.07	.02
☐ 134 Kelly Gruber	.10	.05	.01
☐ 135 Chris Sabo	.10	.05	.01
☐ 136 Mark Grace	.30	.14	.04
☐ 137 Tony Fernandez	.10	.05	.01
☐ 138 Glenn Davis	.10	.05	.01
☐ 139 Pedro Munoz	.10	.05	.01
☐ 140 Craig Biggio	.15	.07	.02
☐ 141 Pete Schourek	.15	.07	.02
☐ 142 Mike Boddicker	.10	.05	.01
☐ 143 Robby Thompson	.10	.05	.01
☐ 144 Mel Hall	.10	.05	.01
☐ 145 Bryan Harvey	.10	.05	.01
☐ 146 Mike LaValliere	.10	.05	.01
☐ 147 John Kruk	.15	.07	.02
☐ 148 Joe Carter	.15	.07	.02
☐ 149 Greg Olson	.10	.05	.01
☐ 150 Julio Franco	.15	.07	.02
☐ 151 Darryl Hamilton	.10	.05	.01
☐ 152 Felix Fermin	.10	.05	.01
☐ 153 Jose Offerman	.10	.05	.01
☐ 154 Paul O'Neill	.15	.07	.02
☐ 155 Tommy Greene	.10	.05	.01
☐ 156 Ivan Rodriguez	.75	.35	.09
☐ 157 Dave Stewart	.15	.07	.02
☐ 158 Jeff Reardon	.15	.07	.02
☐ 159 Felix Jose	.10	.05	.01
☐ 160 Doug Dascenzo	.10	.05	.01
☐ 161 Tim Wallach	.10	.05	.01
☐ 162 Dan Plesac	.10	.05	.01
☐ 163 Luis Gonzalez	.15	.07	.02
☐ 164 Mike Henneman	.10	.05	.01
☐ 165 Mike Devereaux	.10	.05	.01
☐ 166 Luis Polonia	.10	.05	.01
☐ 167 Mike Sharperson	.10	.05	.01
☐ 168 Chris Donnels	.10	.05	.01
☐ 169 Greg W. Harris	.10	.05	.01
☐ 170 Deion Sanders	.30	.14	.04
☐ 171 Mike Schooler	.10	.05	.01
☐ 172 Jose DeJesus	.10	.05	.01
☐ 173 Jeff Montgomery	.15	.07	.02
☐ 174 Milt Cuyler	.10	.05	.01
☐ 175 Wade Boggs	.30	.14	.04
☐ 176 Kevin Tapani	.10	.05	.01
☐ 177 Bill Spiers	.10	.05	.01
☐ 178 Tim Raines	.30	.14	.04
☐ 179 Randy Milligan	.10	.05	.01
☐ 180 Rob Dibble	.10	.05	.01
☐ 181 Kirt Manwaring	.10	.05	.01
☐ 182 Pascual Perez	.10	.05	.01
☐ 183 Juan Guzman	.15	.07	.02
☐ 184 John Smiley	.10	.05	.01
☐ 185 David Segui	.10	.05	.01
☐ 186 Omar Olivares	.10	.05	.01
☐ 187 Joe Slusarski	.10	.05	.01
☐ 188 Erik Hanson	.10	.05	.01
☐ 189 Mark Portugal	.10	.05	.01
☐ 190 Walt Terrell	.10	.05	.01
☐ 191 John Smoltz	.30	.14	.04
☐ 192 Wilson Alvarez	.30	.14	.04
☐ 193 Jimmy Key	.15	.07	.02
☐ 194 Larry Walker	.30	.14	.04
☐ 195 Lee Smith	.15	.07	.02
☐ 196 Pete Harnisch	.10	.05	.01
☐ 197 Mike Harkey	.10	.05	.01
☐ 198 Frank Tanana	.10	.05	.01
☐ 199 Terry Mulholland	.10	.05	.01
☐ 200 Cal Ripken	1.50	.70	.19
☐ 201 Dave Magadan	.10	.05	.01
☐ 202 Bud Black	.10	.05	.01
☐ 203 Terry Shumpert	.10	.05	.01
☐ 204 Mike Mussina	.60	.25	.07
☐ 205 Mo Vaughn	.75	.35	.09
☐ 206 Steve Farr	.10	.05	.01
☐ 207 Darrin Jackson	.10	.05	.01
☐ 208 Jerry Browne	.10	.05	.01
☐ 209 Jeff Russell	.10	.05	.01
☐ 210 Mike Scioscia	.10	.05	.01
☐ 211 Rick Aguilera	.10	.05	.01
☐ 212 Jaime Navarro	.10	.05	.01
☐ 213 Randy Tomlin	.10	.05	.01
☐ 214 Bobby Thigpen	.10	.05	.01

☐ 215 Mark Gardner .10 .05 .01
☐ 216 Norm Charlton .10 .05 .01
☐ 217 Mark McGwire .60 .25 .07
☐ 218 Skeeter Barnes .10 .05 .01
☐ 219 Bob Tewksbury .10 .05 .01
☐ 220 Junior Felix .10 .05 .01
☐ 221 Sam Horn .10 .05 .01
☐ 222 Jody Reed .10 .05 .01
☐ 223 Luis Sojo .10 .05 .01
☐ 224 Jerome Walton .10 .05 .01
☐ 225 Darryl Kile .10 .05 .01
☐ 226 Mickey Tettleton .10 .05 .01
☐ 227 Dan Pasqua .10 .05 .01
☐ 228 Jim Gott .10 .05 .01
☐ 229 Bernie Williams .50 .23 .06
☐ 230 Shane Mack .10 .05 .01
☐ 231 Steve Avery .15 .07 .02
☐ 232 Dave Valle .10 .05 .01
☐ 233 Mark Leonard .10 .05 .01
☐ 234 Spike Owen .10 .05 .01
☐ 235 Gary Sheffield .30 .14 .04
☐ 236 Steve Chitren .10 .05 .01
☐ 237 Zane Smith .10 .05 .01
☐ 238 Tom Gordon .10 .05 .01
☐ 239 Jose Oquendo .10 .05 .01
☐ 240 Todd Stottlemyre .15 .07 .02
☐ 241 Darren Daulton .15 .07 .02
☐ 242 Tim Naehring .15 .07 .02
☐ 243 Tony Phillips .15 .07 .02
☐ 244 Shawon Dunston .10 .05 .01
☐ 245 Manuel Lee .10 .05 .01
☐ 246 Mike Pagliarulo .10 .05 .01
☐ 247 Jim Thome 1.50 .70 .19
☐ 248 Luis Mercedes .10 .05 .01
☐ 249 Cal Eldred .10 .05 .01
☐ 250 Derek Bell .30 .14 .04
☐ 251 Arthur Rhodes .10 .05 .01
☐ 252 Scott Cooper .10 .05 .01
☐ 253 Roberto Hernandez .15 .07 .02
☐ 254 Mo Sanford .10 .05 .01
☐ 255 Scott Servais .10 .05 .01
☐ 256 Eric Karros .30 .14 .04
☐ 257 Andy Mota .10 .05 .01
☐ 258 Keith Mitchell .10 .05 .01
☐ 259 Joel Johnston .10 .05 .01
☐ 260 John Wehner .10 .05 .01
☐ 261 Gino Minutelli .10 .05 .01
☐ 262 Greg Gagne .10 .05 .01
☐ 263 Stan Royer .10 .05 .01
☐ 264 Carlos Garcia .15 .07 .02
☐ 265 Andy Ashby .15 .07 .02
☐ 266 Kim Batiste .10 .05 .01
☐ 267 Julio Valera .10 .05 .01
☐ 268 Royce Clayton .15 .07 .02
☐ 269 Gary Scott .10 .05 .01
☐ 270 Kirk Dressendorfer .10 .05 .01
☐ 271 Sean Berry .15 .07 .02
☐ 272 Lance Dickson .10 .05 .01
☐ 273 Rob Maurer .10 .05 .01
☐ 274 Scott Brosius .10 .05 .01
☐ 275 Dave Fleming .10 .05 .01
☐ 276 Lenny Webster .10 .05 .01
☐ 277 Mike Humphreys .10 .05 .01
☐ 278 Freddie Benavides .10 .05 .01
☐ 279 Harvey Pulliam .10 .05 .01
☐ 280 Jeff Carter .10 .05 .01
☐ 281 Jim Abbott I .30 .14 .04
Nolan Ryan
☐ 282 Wade Boggs I .40 .18 .05
George Brett
☐ 283 Ken Griffey Jr. I .75 .35 .09
Rickey Henderson
☐ 284 Wally Joyner I .15 .07 .02
Dale Murphy
☐ 285 Chuck Knoblauch I .30 .14 .04
Ozzie Smith
☐ 286 Robin Ventura I .50 .23 .06
Lou Gehrig
☐ 287 Robin Yount SIDE .30 .14 .04
☐ 288 Bob Tewksbury SIDE .10 .05 .01
☐ 289 Kirby Puckett SIDE .30 .14 .04
☐ 290 Kenny Lofton SIDE 1.25 .55 .16
☐ 291 Jack McDowell SIDE .10 .05 .01
☐ 292 John Burkett SIDE .10 .05 .01
☐ 293 Dwight Smith SIDE .10 .05 .01
☐ 294 Nolan Ryan SIDE .75 .35 .09
☐ 295 Manny Ramirez DP 4.00 1.80 .50
☐ 296 Cliff Floyd DP UER .75 .35 .09
(Throws right, not left as indicated on back)
☐ 297 Al Shirley DP .15 .07 .02
☐ 298 Brian Barber DP .15 .07 .02
☐ 299 Jon Farrell DP .10 .05 .01
☐ 300 Scott Ruffcorn DP .15 .07 .02
☐ 301 Tyrone Hill DP .10 .05 .01
☐ 302 Benji Gil DP .30 .14 .04
☐ 303 Tyler Green DP .15 .07 .02
☐ 304 Allen Watson DP .15 .07 .02
☐ 305 Jay Buhner SH .30 .14 .04
☐ 306 Roberto Alomar SH .30 .14 .04
☐ 307 Chuck Knoblauch SH .30 .14 .04
☐ 308 Darryl Strawberry SH .15 .07 .02
☐ 309 Danny Tartabull SH .10 .05 .01
☐ 310 Bobby Bonilla SH .15 .07 .02
☐ 311 Mike Felder .10 .05 .01
☐ 312 Storm Davis .10 .05 .01
☐ 313 Tim Teufel .10 .05 .01
☐ 314 Tom Brunansky .10 .05 .01
☐ 315 Rex Hudler .10 .05 .01
☐ 316 Dave Otto .10 .05 .01
☐ 317 Jeff King .15 .07 .02
☐ 318 Dan Gladden .10 .05 .01
☐ 319 Bill Pecota .10 .05 .01
☐ 320 Franklin Stubbs .10 .05 .01
☐ 321 Gary Carter .15 .07 .02
☐ 322 Melido Perez .10 .05 .01
☐ 323 Eric Davis .15 .07 .02
☐ 324 Greg Myers .10 .05 .01
☐ 325 Pete Incaviglia .10 .05 .01
☐ 326 Von Hayes .10 .05 .01
☐ 327 Greg Swindell .10 .05 .01
☐ 328 Steve Sax .10 .05 .01
☐ 329 Chuck McElroy .10 .05 .01
☐ 330 Gregg Jefferies .15 .07 .02
☐ 331 Joe Oliver .10 .05 .01
☐ 332 Paul Faries .10 .05 .01
☐ 333 David West .10 .05 .01
☐ 334 Craig Grebeck .10 .05 .01
☐ 335 Chris Hammond .10 .05 .01
☐ 336 Billy Ripken .10 .05 .01
☐ 337 Scott Sanderson .10 .05 .01
☐ 338 Dick Schofield .10 .05 .01
☐ 339 Bob Milacki .10 .05 .01
☐ 340 Kevin Reimer .10 .05 .01
☐ 341 Jose DeLeon .10 .05 .01
☐ 342 Henry Cotto .10 .05 .01
☐ 343 Daryl Boston .10 .05 .01
☐ 344 Kevin Gross .10 .05 .01
☐ 345 Milt Thompson .10 .05 .01
☐ 346 Luis Rivera .10 .05 .01
☐ 347 Al Osuna .10 .05 .01
☐ 348 Rob Deer .10 .05 .01
☐ 349 Tim Leary .10 .05 .01
☐ 350 Mike Stanton .10 .05 .01
☐ 351 Dean Palmer .15 .07 .02
☐ 352 Trevor Wilson .10 .05 .01
☐ 353 Mark Eichhorn .10 .05 .01
☐ 354 Scott Aldred .10 .05 .01
☐ 355 Mark Whiten .15 .07 .02
☐ 356 Leo Gomez .10 .05 .01
☐ 357 Rafael Belliard .10 .05 .01
☐ 358 Carlos Quintana .10 .05 .01
☐ 359 Mark Davis .10 .05 .01
☐ 360 Chris Nabholz .10 .05 .01
☐ 361 Carlton Fisk .30 .14 .04
☐ 362 Joe Orsulak .10 .05 .01
☐ 363 Eric Anthony .10 .05 .01
☐ 364 Greg Hibbard .10 .05 .01
☐ 365 Scott Leius .10 .05 .01
☐ 366 Hensley Meulens .10 .05 .01
☐ 367 Chris Bosio .10 .05 .01
☐ 368 Brian Downing .10 .05 .01
☐ 369 Sammy Sosa .50 .23 .06
☐ 370 Stan Belinda .10 .05 .01
☐ 371 Joe Grahe .10 .05 .01
☐ 372 Luis Salazar .10 .05 .01
☐ 373 Lance Johnson .15 .07 .02
☐ 374 Kal Daniels .10 .05 .01
☐ 375 Dave Winfield .30 .14 .04
☐ 376 Brook Jacoby .10 .05 .01
☐ 377 Mariano Duncan .10 .05 .01
☐ 378 Ron Darling .10 .05 .01
☐ 379 Randy Johnson .30 .14 .04
☐ 380 Chito Martinez .10 .05 .01
☐ 381 Andres Galarraga .30 .14 .04
☐ 382 Willie Randolph .15 .07 .02
☐ 383 Charles Nagy .15 .07 .02
☐ 384 Tim Belcher .10 .05 .01
☐ 385 Duane Ward .10 .05 .01
☐ 386 Vicente Palacios .10 .05 .01
☐ 387 Mike Gallego .10 .05 .01
☐ 388 Rich DeLucia .10 .05 .01
☐ 389 Scott Radinsky .10 .05 .01
☐ 390 Damon Berryhill .10 .05 .01
☐ 391 Kirk McCaskill .10 .05 .01
☐ 392 Pedro Guerrero .10 .05 .01
☐ 393 Kevin Mitchell .15 .07 .02
☐ 394 Dickie Thon .10 .05 .01
☐ 395 Bobby Bonilla .15 .07 .02
☐ 396 Bill Wegman .10 .05 .01
☐ 397 Dave Martinez .10 .05 .01
☐ 398 Rick Sutcliffe .10 .05 .01
☐ 399 Larry Andersen .10 .05 .01
☐ 400 Tony Gwynn .75 .35 .09
☐ 401 Rickey Henderson .30 .14 .04
☐ 402 Greg Cadaret .10 .05 .01
☐ 403 Keith Miller .10 .05 .01
☐ 404 Bip Roberts .10 .05 .01
☐ 405 Kevin Brown .15 .07 .02
☐ 406 Mitch Williams .10 .05 .01
☐ 407 Frank Viola .10 .05 .01
☐ 408 Darren Lewis .10 .05 .01
☐ 409 Bob Welch .10 .05 .01
☐ 410 Bob Walk .10 .05 .01
☐ 411 Todd Frohwirth .10 .05 .01
☐ 412 Brian Hunter .10 .05 .01
☐ 413 Ron Karkovice .10 .05 .01
☐ 414 Mike Morgan .10 .05 .01
☐ 415 Joe Hesketh .10 .05 .01
☐ 416 Don Slaught .10 .05 .01
☐ 417 Tom Henke .10 .05 .01
☐ 418 Kurt Stillwell .10 .05 .01
☐ 419 Hector Villaneuva .10 .05 .01
☐ 420 Glenallen Hill .10 .05 .01
☐ 421 Pat Borders .10 .05 .01
☐ 422 Charlie Hough .10 .05 .01
☐ 423 Charlie Leibrandt .10 .05 .01
☐ 424 Eddie Murray .50 .23 .06
☐ 425 Jesse Barfield .10 .05 .01
☐ 426 Mark Lemke .10 .05 .01
☐ 427 Kevin McReynolds .10 .05 .01
☐ 428 Gilberto Reyes .10 .05 .01
☐ 429 Ramon Martinez .15 .07 .02
☐ 430 Steve Buechele .10 .05 .01
☐ 431 David Wells .10 .05 .01
☐ 432 Kyle Abbott .10 .05 .01
☐ 433 John Habyan .10 .05 .01
☐ 434 Kevin Appier .15 .07 .02
☐ 435 Gene Larkin .10 .05 .01
☐ 436 Sandy Alomar Jr. .15 .07 .02
☐ 437 Mike Jackson .10 .05 .01
☐ 438 Todd Benzinger .10 .05 .01
☐ 439 Teddy Higuera .10 .05 .01
☐ 440 Reggie Sanders .30 .14 .04
☐ 441 Mark Carreon .10 .05 .01
☐ 442 Bret Saberhagen .15 .07 .02
☐ 443 Gene Nelson .10 .05 .01
☐ 444 Jay Howell .10 .05 .01
☐ 445 Roger McDowell .10 .05 .01
☐ 446 Sid Bream .10 .05 .01
☐ 447 Mackey Sasser .10 .05 .01
☐ 448 Bill Swift .10 .05 .01
☐ 449 Hubie Brooks .10 .05 .01
☐ 450 David Cone .15 .07 .02
☐ 451 Bobby Witt .10 .05 .01
☐ 452 Brady Anderson .30 .14 .04
☐ 453 Lee Stevens .10 .05 .01
☐ 454 Luis Aquino .10 .05 .01
☐ 455 Carney Lansford .15 .07 .02
☐ 456 Carlos Hernandez .10 .05 .01
☐ 457 Danny Jackson .10 .05 .01
☐ 458 Gerald Young .10 .05 .01
☐ 459 Tom Candiotti .10 .05 .01
☐ 460 Billy Hatcher .10 .05 .01
☐ 461 John Wetteland .15 .07 .02
☐ 462 Mike Bordick .15 .07 .02
☐ 463 Don Robinson .10 .05 .01
☐ 464 Jeff Johnson .10 .05 .01
☐ 465 Lonnie Smith .10 .05 .01
☐ 466 Paul Assenmacher .10 .05 .01
☐ 467 Alvin Davis .10 .05 .01
☐ 468 Jim Eisenreich .10 .05 .01
☐ 469 Brent Mayne .10 .05 .01
☐ 470 Jeff Brantley .15 .07 .02
☐ 471 Tim Burke .10 .05 .01
☐ 472 Pat Mahomes .10 .05 .01
☐ 473 Ryan Bowen .10 .05 .01
☐ 474 Bryn Smith .10 .05 .01
☐ 475 Mike Flanagan .10 .05 .01
☐ 476 Reggie Jefferson .15 .07 .02
☐ 477 Jeff Blauser .10 .05 .01
☐ 478 Craig Lefferts .10 .05 .01
☐ 479 Todd Worrell .10 .05 .01
☐ 480 Scott Scudder .10 .05 .01
☐ 481 Kirk Gibson .15 .07 .02
☐ 482 Kenny Rogers .10 .05 .01
☐ 483 Jack Morris .15 .07 .02
☐ 484 Russ Swan .10 .05 .01
☐ 485 Mike Huff .10 .05 .01
☐ 486 Ken Hill .15 .07 .02
☐ 487 Geronimo Pena .10 .05 .01
☐ 488 Charlie O'Brien .10 .05 .01
☐ 489 Mike Maddux .10 .05 .01
☐ 490 Scott Livingstone .10 .05 .01
☐ 491 Carl Willis .10 .05 .01
☐ 492 Kelly Downs .10 .05 .01
☐ 493 Dennis Cook .10 .05 .01
☐ 494 Joe Magrane .10 .05 .01
☐ 495 Bob Kipper .10 .05 .01
☐ 496 Jose Mesa .15 .07 .02
☐ 497 Charlie Hayes .10 .05 .01
☐ 498 Joe Girardi .10 .05 .01
☐ 499 Doug Jones .10 .05 .01
☐ 500 Barry Bonds .50 .23 .06
☐ 501 Bill Krueger .10 .05 .01
☐ 502 Glenn Braggs .10 .05 .01
☐ 503 Eric King .10 .05 .01
☐ 504 Frank Castillo .15 .07 .02
☐ 505 Mike Gardiner .10 .05 .01
☐ 506 Cory Snyder .10 .05 .01
☐ 507 Steve Howe .10 .05 .01
☐ 508 Jose Rijo .10 .05 .01
☐ 509 Sid Fernandez .10 .05 .01
☐ 510 Archi Cianfrocco .10 .05 .01
☐ 511 Mark Guthrie .10 .05 .01
☐ 512 Bob Ojeda .10 .05 .01
☐ 513 John Doherty .10 .05 .01
☐ 514 Dante Bichette .30 .14 .04
☐ 515 Juan Berenguer .10 .05 .01
☐ 516 Jeff M. Robinson .10 .05 .01
☐ 517 Mike Macfarlane .10 .05 .01
☐ 518 Matt Young .10 .05 .01
☐ 519 Otis Nixon .10 .05 .01
☐ 520 Brian Holman .10 .05 .01
☐ 521 Chris Haney .10 .05 .01
☐ 522 Jeff Kent .30 .14 .04
☐ 523 Chad Curtis .30 .14 .04
☐ 524 Vince Horsman .10 .05 .01
☐ 525 Rod Nichols .10 .05 .01
☐ 526 Peter Hoy .10 .05 .01
☐ 527 Shawn Boskie .10 .05 .01
☐ 528 Alejandro Pena .10 .05 .01
☐ 529 Dave Burba .10 .05 .01
☐ 530 Ricky Jordan .10 .05 .01
☐ 531 Dave Silvestri .10 .05 .01
☐ 532 John Patterson UER .10 .05 .01
(Listed as being born in 1960; should be 1967)
☐ 533 Jeff Branson .10 .05 .01
☐ 534 Derrick May .10 .05 .01
☐ 535 Esteban Beltre .10 .05 .01
☐ 536 Jose Melendez .10 .05 .01
☐ 537 Wally Joyner .15 .07 .02
☐ 538 Eddie Taubensee .10 .05 .01
☐ 539 Jim Abbott .10 .05 .01
☐ 540 Brian Williams .10 .05 .01
☐ 541 Donovan Osborne .15 .07 .02
☐ 542 Patrick Lennon .10 .05 .01
☐ 543 Mike Groppuso .10 .05 .01
☐ 544 Jarvis Brown .10 .05 .01
☐ 545 Shawn Livsey .10 .05 .01
☐ 546 Jeff Ware .10 .05 .01
☐ 547 Danny Tartabull .10 .05 .01
☐ 548 Bobby Jones .60 .25 .07
☐ 549 Ken Griffey Jr. 3.00 1.35 .35
☐ 550 Rey Sanchez .10 .05 .01
☐ 551 Pedro Astacio .15 .07 .02
☐ 552 Juan Guerrero .10 .05 .01
☐ 553 Jacob Brumfield .10 .05 .01
☐ 554 Ben Rivera .10 .05 .01
☐ 555 Brian Jordan 1.00 .45 .12
☐ 556 Denny Neagle .30 .14 .04
☐ 557 Cliff Brantley .10 .05 .01
☐ 558 Anthony Young .10 .05 .01
☐ 559 John Vander Wal .10 .05 .01
☐ 560 Monty Fariss .10 .05 .01
☐ 561 Russ Springer .10 .05 .01
☐ 562 Pat Listach .15 .07 .02
☐ 563 Pat Hentgen .30 .14 .04
☐ 564 Andy Stankiewicz .10 .05 .01
☐ 565 Mike Perez .10 .05 .01
☐ 566 Mike Bielecki .10 .05 .01
☐ 567 Butch Henry .10 .05 .01
☐ 568 Dave Nilsson .15 .07 .02
☐ 569 Scott Hatteberg .10 .05 .01
☐ 570 Ruben Amaro Jr. .10 .05 .01
☐ 571 Todd Hundley .15 .07 .02
☐ 572 Moises Alou .30 .14 .04
☐ 573 Hector Fajardo .10 .05 .01
☐ 574 Todd Van Poppel .10 .05 .01
☐ 575 Willie Banks .10 .05 .01
☐ 576 Bob Zupcic .10 .05 .01
☐ 577 J.J. Johnson .15 .07 .02
☐ 578 John Burkett .15 .07 .02
☐ 579 Trever Miller .10 .05 .01
☐ 580 Scott Bankhead .10 .05 .01
☐ 581 Rich Amaral .10 .05 .01
☐ 582 Kenny Lofton 2.50 1.10 .30
☐ 583 Matt Stairs .10 .05 .01
☐ 584 Don Mattingly .40 .18 .05
Rod Carew IDOLS
☐ 585 Steve Avery .15 .07 .02
Jack Morris IDOLS
☐ 586 Roberto Alomar .30 .14 .04
Sandy Alomar SR. IDOLS
☐ 587 Scott Sanderson .15 .07 .02
Catfish Hunter IDOLS
☐ 588 Dave Justice .30 .14 .04
Willie Stargell IDOLS
☐ 589 Rex Hudler .30 .14 .04
Roger Staubach IDOLS
☐ 590 David Cone .15 .07 .02
Jackie Gleason IDOLS
☐ 591 Tony Gwynn .30 .14 .04
Willie Davis IDOLS
☐ 592 Orel Hershiser SIDE .15 .07 .02
☐ 593 John Wetteland SIDE .15 .07 .02
☐ 594 Tom Glavine SIDE .15 .07 .02
☐ 595 Randy Johnson SIDE .30 .14 .04
☐ 596 Jim Gott SIDE .10 .05 .01
☐ 597 Donald Harris .10 .05 .01
☐ 598 Shawn Hare .10 .05 .01
☐ 599 Chris Gardner .10 .05 .01
☐ 600 Rusty Meacham .10 .05 .01
☐ 601 Benito Santiago .10 .05 .01
☐ 602 Eric Davis SHADE .10 .05 .01
☐ 603 Jose Lind SHADE .10 .05 .01
☐ 604 Dave Justice SHADE .15 .07 .02
☐ 605 Tim Raines SHADE .15 .07 .02
☐ 606 Randy Tomlin GRIP .10 .05 .01
☐ 607 Jack McDowell GRIP .10 .05 .01
☐ 608 Greg Maddux GRIP .60 .25 .07
☐ 609 Charles Nagy GRIP .15 .07 .02
☐ 610 Tom Candiotti GRIP .10 .05 .01
☐ 611 David Cone GRIP .15 .07 .02
☐ 612 Steve Avery GRIP .15 .07 .02
☐ 613 Rod Beck GRIP .50 .23 .06
☐ 614 Rickey Henderson TECH .30 .14 .04
☐ 615 Benito Santiago TECH .10 .05 .01
☐ 616 Ruben Sierra TECH .10 .05 .01

☐ 617 Ryne Sandberg TECH	.30	.14	.04
☐ 618 Nolan Ryan TECH	.75	.35	.09
☐ 619 Brett Butler TECH	.10	.05	.01
☐ 620 Dave Justice TECH	.15	.07	.02

1992 Pinnacle Rookie Idols

This 18-card insert set is a spin-off on the Idols subset featured in the regular series. The cards were randomly inserted in Series II wax packs. The set features full-bleed color photos of 18 rookies along with their pick of sports figures or other individuals who had the greatest impact on their careers. Both sides of the cards are horizontally oriented. The fronts carry a close-up photo of the rookie superimposed on an action game shot of his idol.

	MINT	NRMT	EXC
COMPLETE SET (18)	140.00	65.00	17.50
COMMON PAIR (1-18)	3.00	1.35	.35
☐ 1 Reggie Sanders and Eric Davis	8.00	3.60	1.00
☐ 2 Hector Fajardo and Jim Abbott	3.00	1.35	.35
☐ 3 Gary Cooper and George Brett	15.00	6.75	1.85
☐ 4 Mark Wohlers and Roger Clemens	10.00	4.50	1.25
☐ 5 Luis Mercedes and Julio Franco	3.00	1.35	.35
☐ 6 Willie Banks and Doc Gooden	3.00	1.35	.35
☐ 7 Kenny Lofton and Rickey Henderson	30.00	13.50	3.70
☐ 8 Keith Mitchell and Dave Henderson	3.00	1.35	.35
☐ 9 Kim Batiste and Barry Larkin	6.00	2.70	.75
☐ 10 Todd Hundley and Thurman Munson	10.00	4.50	1.25
☐ 11 Eddie Zosky and Cal Ripken	25.00	11.00	3.10
☐ 12 Todd Van Poppel and Nolan Ryan	25.00	11.00	3.10
☐ 13 Jim Thome and Ryne Sandberg	25.00	11.00	3.10
☐ 14 Dave Fleming and Bobby Murcer	3.00	1.35	.35
☐ 15 Royce Clayton and Ozzie Smith	8.00	3.60	1.00
☐ 16 Donald Harris and Darryl Strawberry	3.00	1.35	.35
☐ 17 Chad Curtis and Alan Trammell	4.00	1.80	.50
☐ 18 Derek Bell and Dave Winfield	8.00	3.60	1.00

1992 Pinnacle Slugfest

This 15-card set highlights the games top sluggers.The cards were issued exclusively as an insert with specially marked cello packs. The horizontally oriented fronts feature glossy photos of players at bat. The player's name is printed in gold and the word "Slugfest" is printed in red in a black border across the bottom of the picture.

	MINT	NRMT	EXC
COMPLETE SET (15)	40.00	18.00	5.00
COMMON CARD (1-15)	.75	.35	.09
☐ 1 Cecil Fielder	1.00	.45	.12
☐ 2 Mark McGwire	2.50	1.10	.30
☐ 3 Jose Canseco	1.25	.55	.16
☐ 4 Barry Bonds	2.00	.90	.25
☐ 5 David Justice	1.00	.45	.12
☐ 6 Bobby Bonilla	.75	.35	.09
☐ 7 Ken Griffey Jr.	10.00	4.50	1.25
☐ 8 Ron Gant	1.00	.45	.12
☐ 9 Ryne Sandberg	2.00	.90	.25
☐ 10 Ruben Sierra	.75	.35	.09
☐ 11 Frank Thomas	10.00	4.50	1.25
☐ 12 Will Clark	1.25	.55	.16
☐ 13 Kirby Puckett	3.00	1.35	.35
☐ 14 Cal Ripken	8.00	3.60	1.00
☐ 15 Jeff Bagwell	5.00	2.20	.60

1992 Pinnacle Team 2000

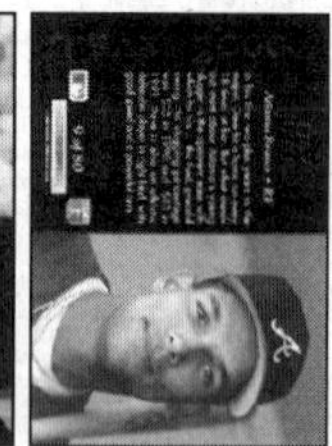

This 80-card standard-size set focuses on young players who were projected to be stars in the year 2000. Cards 1-40 were inserted in Series 1 jumbo packs while cards 41-80 were featured in Series 2 jumbo packs. The fronts features action color player photos. The cards are bordered by a 1/2" black stripe that runs along the left edge and bottom forming a right angle. The two ends of the black stripe are sloped. The words "Team 2000" and the player's name appear in gold foil in the stripe. The team logo is displayed in the lower left corner.

	MINT	NRMT	EXC
COMPLETE SET (80)	30.00	13.50	3.70
COMPLETE SERIES 1 (40)	20.00	9.00	2.50
COMPLETE SERIES 2 (40)	10.00	4.50	1.25
COMMON CARD (1-80)	.15	.07	.02
☐ 1 Mike Mussina	1.00	.45	.12
☐ 2 Phil Plantier	.15	.07	.02
☐ 3 Frank Thomas	5.00	2.20	.60
☐ 4 Travis Fryman	.30	.14	.04
☐ 5 Kevin Appier	.20	.09	.03
☐ 6 Chuck Knoblauch	1.00	.45	.12
☐ 7 Pat Kelly	.15	.07	.02
☐ 8 Ivan Rodriguez	1.25	.55	.16
☐ 9 Dave Justice	.20	.09	.03
☐ 10 Jeff Bagwell	2.00	.90	.25
☐ 11 Marquis Grissom	.20	.09	.03
☐ 12 Andy Benes	.20	.09	.03
☐ 13 Gregg Olson	.15	.07	.02
☐ 14 Kevin Morton	.15	.07	.02
☐ 15 Tim Naehring	.20	.09	.03
☐ 16 Dave Hollins	.15	.07	.02
☐ 17 Sandy Alomar Jr.	.20	.09	.03
☐ 18 Albert Belle	1.50	.70	.19
☐ 19 Charles Nagy	.20	.09	.03
☐ 20 Brian McRae	.20	.09	.03
☐ 21 Larry Walker	.30	.14	.04
☐ 22 Delino DeShields	.15	.07	.02
☐ 23 Jeff Johnson	.15	.07	.02
☐ 24 Bernie Williams	1.25	.55	.16
☐ 25 Jose Offerman	.15	.07	.02
☐ 26 Juan Gonzalez	3.00	1.35	.35
☐ 27A Juan Guzman (Pinnacle logo at top)	.20	.09	.03
☐ 27B Juan Guzman (Pinnacle logo at bottom)	.20	.09	.03
☐ 28 Eric Anthony	.15	.07	.02
☐ 29 Brian Hunter	.15	.07	.02
☐ 30 John Smoltz	.60	.25	.07
☐ 31 Deion Sanders	.30	.14	.04
☐ 32 Greg Maddux	3.00	1.35	.35
☐ 33 Andujar Cedeno	.15	.07	.02
☐ 34 Royce Clayton	.20	.09	.03
☐ 35 Kenny Lofton	2.50	1.10	.30
☐ 36 Cal Eldred	.15	.07	.02
☐ 37 Jim Thome	3.00	1.35	.35
☐ 38 Gary DiSarcina	.15	.07	.02
☐ 39 Brian Jordan	2.00	.90	.25
☐ 40 Chad Curtis	.20	.09	.03
☐ 41 Ben McDonald	.15	.07	.02
☐ 42 Jim Abbott	.15	.07	.02
☐ 43 Robin Ventura	.20	.09	.03
☐ 44 Milt Cuyler	.15	.07	.02
☐ 45 Gregg Jefferies	.20	.09	.03
☐ 46 Scott Radinsky	.15	.07	.02
☐ 47 Ken Griffey Jr.	5.00	2.20	.60
☐ 48 Roberto Alomar	.60	.25	.07
☐ 49 Ramon Martinez	.20	.09	.03
☐ 50 Bret Barberie	.15	.07	.02
☐ 51 Ray Lankford	.30	.14	.04
☐ 52 Leo Gomez	.15	.07	.02
☐ 53 Tommy Greene	.15	.07	.02
☐ 54 Mo Vaughn	1.50	.70	.19
☐ 55 Sammy Sosa	.75	.35	.09
☐ 56 Carlos Baerga	.15	.07	.02
☐ 57 Mark Lewis	.15	.07	.02
☐ 58 Tom Gordon	.15	.07	.02
☐ 59 Gary Sheffield	.60	.25	.07
☐ 60 Scott Erickson	.20	.09	.03
☐ 61 Pedro Munoz	.15	.07	.02
☐ 62 Tino Martinez	.20	.09	.03
☐ 63 Darren Lewis	.15	.07	.02
☐ 64 Dean Palmer	.20	.09	.03
☐ 65 John Olerud	.20	.09	.03
☐ 66 Steve Avery	.20	.09	.03
☐ 67 Pete Harnisch	.15	.07	.02
☐ 68 Luis Gonzalez	.20	.09	.03
☐ 69 Kim Batiste	.15	.07	.02
☐ 70 Reggie Sanders	.30	.14	.04
☐ 71 Luis Mercedes	.15	.07	.02
☐ 72 Todd Van Poppel	.15	.07	.02
☐ 73 Gary Scott	.15	.07	.02
☐ 74 Monty Fariss	.15	.07	.02
☐ 75 Kyle Abbott	.15	.07	.02
☐ 76 Eric Karros	.30	.14	.04
☐ 77 Mo Sanford	.15	.07	.02
☐ 78 Todd Hundley	.75	.35	.09
☐ 79 Reggie Jefferson	.15	.07	.02
☐ 80 Pat Mahomes	.15	.07	.02

1992 Pinnacle Team Pinnacle

This 12-card, double-sided insert set features the National League and American League All-Star team as selected by Pinnacle. The standard-size cards were randomly inserted in Series I wax packs. The cards feature illustrations by sports artist Chris Greco with the National League All-Star on one side and the corresponding American League All-Star by position on the other. The words "Team Pinnacle" are printed vertically down the left side of the card in red for American League on one side and blue for National League on the other.

	MINT	NRMT	EXC
COMPLETE SET (12)	100.00	45.00	12.50
COMMON PAIR (1-12)	5.00	2.20	.60
☐ 1 Roger Clemens and Ramon Martinez	6.00	2.70	.75
☐ 2 Jim Abbott and Steve Avery	5.00	2.20	.60
☐ 3 Ivan Rodriguez and Benito Santiago	8.00	3.60	1.00
☐ 4 Frank Thomas and Will Clark	30.00	13.50	3.70
☐ 5 Roberto Alomar and Ryne Sandberg	15.00	6.75	1.85
☐ 6 Robin Ventura and Matt Williams	6.00	2.70	.75
☐ 7 Cal Ripken and Barry Larkin	30.00	13.50	3.70
☐ 8 Danny Tartabull and Barry Bonds	8.00	3.60	1.00
☐ 9 Ken Griffey Jr. and Brett Butler	20.00	9.00	2.50
☐ 10 Ruben Sierra and Dave Justice	5.00	2.20	.60
☐ 11 Dennis Eckersley and Rob Dibble	5.00	2.20	.60
☐ 12 Scott Radinsky and John Franco	5.00	2.20	.60

1992 Pinnacle Rookies

This 30-card boxed set features top rookies of the 1992 season, with at least one player from each team. A total of 180,000 sets were produced. The fronts feature full-bleed color action player photos except at the bottom where a team-color coded bar carries the player's name (in gold foil lettering) and a black bar has the words "1992 Rookie." The team logo appears in a gold foil circle at the lower right corner.

	MINT	NRMT	EXC
COMPLETE FACT.SET (30)	5.00	2.20	.60
COMMON CARD (1-30)	.10	.05	.01
☐ 1 Luis Mercedes	.10	.05	.01
☐ 2 Scott Cooper	.10	.05	.01
☐ 3 Kenny Lofton	4.00	1.80	.50
☐ 4 John Doherty	.10	.05	.01
☐ 5 Pat Listach	.20	.09	.03
☐ 6 Andy Stankiewicz	.10	.05	.01
☐ 7 Derek Bell	.40	.18	.05
☐ 8 Gary DiSarcina	.10	.05	.01
☐ 9 Roberto Hernandez	.20	.09	.03
☐ 10 Joel Johnston	.10	.05	.01
☐ 11 Pat Mahomes	.10	.05	.01
☐ 12 Todd Van Poppel	.10	.05	.01
☐ 13 Dave Fleming	.20	.09	.03
☐ 14 Monty Fariss	.10	.05	.01
☐ 15 Gary Scott	.10	.05	.01
☐ 16 Moises Alou	.40	.18	.05
☐ 17 Todd Hundley	.20	.09	.03
☐ 18 Kim Batiste	.10	.05	.01
☐ 19 Denny Neagle	.20	.09	.03
☐ 20 Donovan Osborne	.20	.09	.03
☐ 21 Mark Wohlers	.40	.18	.05
☐ 22 Reggie Sanders	.75	.35	.09
☐ 23 Brian Williams	.10	.05	.01
☐ 24 Eric Karros	.75	.35	.09
☐ 25 Frank Seminara	.10	.05	.01
☐ 26 Royce Clayton	.20	.09	.03
☐ 27 Dave Nilsson	.20	.09	.03
☐ 28 Matt Stairs	.10	.05	.01
☐ 29 Chad Curtis	.20	.09	.03
☐ 30 Carlos Hernandez	.10	.05	.01

1992 Pinnacle Mantle

This 30-card standard-size set commemorates the life and career of Mickey Mantle. A total of 180,000 sets were produced. Each set was packaged in a black and blue box that featured a picture of Mantle and a checklist. The fronts feature a mix of black and white, full-color, and colorized photos in a full-bleed design with gold-foil stamping. At the bottom of each photo appears a purple bar bearing his uniform number (7) and name. The horizontal or vertical backs carry a second player photo and summarize chapters from his life and career on a royal blue panel with navy blue borders.

	MINT	NRMT	EXC
COMPLETE SET (30)	20.00	9.00	2.50
COMMON CARD (1-30)	.75	.35	.09
☐ 1 Mickey Mantle Mutt Mantle Father and Son	1.00	.45	.12
☐ 2 Mickey Mantle High School	.75	.35	.09
☐ 3 Mickey Mantle Commerce Comet	.75	.35	.09
☐ 4 Mickey Mantle Spring Training	.75	.35	.09
☐ 5 Mickey Mantle The Beginning	.75	.35	.09
☐ 6 Mickey Mantle Number 6	.75	.35	.09
☐ 7 Mickey Mantle The Rookie	.75	.35	.09
☐ 8 Mickey Mantle Tape-Measure Shots	.75	.35	.09
☐ 9 Mickey Mantle Shortstop	.75	.35	.09
☐ 10 Mickey Mantle Outfield	.75	.35	.09
☐ 11 Mickey Mantle Speed, Speed, Speed	.75	.35	.09
☐ 12 Mickey Mantle Contracts	.75	.35	.09
☐ 13 Mickey Mantle Three-time MVP	.75	.35	.09
☐ 14 Mickey Mantle Triple Crown	.75	.35	.09
☐ 15 Mickey Mantle Series Slam	.75	.35	.09
☐ 16 Mickey Mantle Series Star	.75	.35	.09
☐ 17 Mickey Mantle Switch Hitter	.75	.35	.09
☐ 18 Mickey Mantle Fan Favorite	.75	.35	.09
☐ 19 Mickey Mantle Milestones	.75	.35	.09
☐ 20 Mickey Mantle Enthusiasm	.75	.35	.09
☐ 21 Mickey Mantle Hitting	.75	.35	.09
☐ 22 Mickey Mantle First Base	.75	.35	.09
☐ 23 Mickey Mantle Courage	.75	.35	.09
☐ 24 Mickey Mantle Stan Musial Mick and Stan	1.50	.70	.19
☐ 25 Whitey Ford Yogi Berra Whitey and Yogi	1.00	.45	.12
☐ 26 Mickey Mantle	1.00	.45	.12

Card	MINT	NRMT	EXC
Billy Martin			
Mick and Billy			
☐ 27 Mickey Mantle	1.00	.45	.12
Casey Stengel			
Mick and Casey			
☐ 28 Mickey Mantle	.75	.35	.09
Awards			
☐ 29 Mickey Mantle	.75	.35	.09
Retirement			
☐ 30 Mickey Mantle	1.00	.45	.12
Cooperstown			

1993 Pinnacle

The 1993 Pinnacle set (by Score) contains 620 standard-size cards issued in two series of 310 cards each. Cards were distributed in hobby and retail foil packs and 27-card jumbo superpacks. The fronts feature color action player photos bordered in white and set on a black card face. The player's name appears below the photo, the player's team is above. The set includes the following topical subsets: Rookies (238-288, 575-620), Now and Then (289-296, 470-476), Idols (297-303, 477-483), Hometown Heroes (304-310, 484-490), and Draft Picks (455-469). Rookie Cards in this set include Derek Jeter and Jason Kendall.

	MINT	NRMT	EXC
COMPLETE SET (620)	50.00	22.00	6.25
COMPLETE SERIES 1 (310)	25.00	11.00	3.10
COMPLETE SERIES 2 (310)	25.00	11.00	3.10
COMMON CARD (1-620)	.10	.05	.01

Card	MINT	NRMT	EXC
☐ 1 Gary Sheffield	.50	.23	.06
☐ 2 Cal Eldred	.10	.05	.01
☐ 3 Larry Walker	.50	.23	.06
☐ 4 Deion Sanders	.50	.23	.06
☐ 5 Dave Fleming	.10	.05	.01
☐ 6 Carlos Baerga	.25	.11	.03
☐ 7 Bernie Williams	.60	.25	.07
☐ 8 John Kruk	.25	.11	.03
☐ 9 Jimmy Key	.25	.11	.03
☐ 10 Jeff Bagwell	1.25	.55	.16
☐ 11 Jim Abbott	.10	.05	.01
☐ 12 Terry Steinbach	.25	.11	.03
☐ 13 Bob Tewksbury	.10	.05	.01
☐ 14 Eric Karros	.50	.23	.06
☐ 15 Ryne Sandberg	.75	.35	.09
☐ 16 Will Clark	.50	.23	.06
☐ 17 Edgar Martinez	.25	.11	.03
☐ 18 Eddie Murray	.75	.35	.09
☐ 19 Andy Van Slyke	.25	.11	.03
☐ 20 Cal Ripken Jr.	2.50	1.10	.30
☐ 21 Ivan Rodriguez	.75	.35	.09
☐ 22 Barry Larkin	.50	.23	.06
☐ 23 Don Mattingly	1.50	.70	.19
☐ 24 Gregg Jefferies	.25	.11	.03
☐ 25 Roger Clemens	.60	.25	.07
☐ 26 Cecil Fielder	.25	.11	.03
☐ 27 Kent Hrbek	.25	.11	.03
☐ 28 Robin Ventura	.25	.11	.03
☐ 29 Rickey Henderson	.50	.23	.06
☐ 30 Roberto Alomar	.60	.25	.07
☐ 31 Luis Polonia	.10	.05	.01
☐ 32 Andujar Cedeno	.10	.05	.01
☐ 33 Pat Listach	.10	.05	.01
☐ 34 Mark Grace	.50	.23	.06
☐ 35 Otis Nixon	.10	.05	.01
☐ 36 Felix Jose	.10	.05	.01
☐ 37 Mike Sharperson	.10	.05	.01
☐ 38 Dennis Martinez	.25	.11	.03
☐ 39 Willie McGee	.10	.05	.01
☐ 40 Kenny Lofton	1.25	.55	.16
☐ 41 Randy Johnson	.50	.23	.06
☐ 42 Andy Benes	.25	.11	.03
☐ 43 Bobby Bonilla	.25	.11	.03
☐ 44 Mike Mussina	.60	.25	.07
☐ 45 Len Dykstra	.25	.11	.03
☐ 46 Ellis Burks	.25	.11	.03
☐ 47 Chris Sabo	.10	.05	.01
☐ 48 Jay Bell	.25	.11	.03
☐ 49 Jose Canseco	.50	.23	.06
☐ 50 Craig Biggio	.25	.11	.03
☐ 51 Wally Joyner	.25	.11	.03
☐ 52 Mickey Tettleton	.10	.05	.01
☐ 53 Tim Raines	.50	.23	.06
☐ 54 Brian Harper	.10	.05	.01
☐ 55 Rene Gonzales	.10	.05	.01
☐ 56 Mark Langston	.25	.11	.03
☐ 57 Jack Morris	.25	.11	.03
☐ 58 Mark McGwire	1.00	.45	.12
☐ 59 Ken Caminiti	.50	.23	.06
☐ 60 Terry Pendleton	.25	.11	.03
☐ 61 Dave Nilsson	.25	.11	.03
☐ 62 Tom Pagnozzi	.10	.05	.01
☐ 63 Mike Morgan	.10	.05	.01
☐ 64 Darryl Strawberry	.25	.11	.03
☐ 65 Charles Nagy	.25	.11	.03
☐ 66 Ken Hill	.25	.11	.03
☐ 67 Matt Williams	.50	.23	.06
☐ 68 Jay Buhner	.50	.23	.06
☐ 69 Vince Coleman	.10	.05	.01
☐ 70 Brady Anderson	.50	.23	.06
☐ 71 Fred McGriff	.50	.23	.06
☐ 72 Ben McDonald	.10	.05	.01
☐ 73 Terry Mulholland	.10	.05	.01
☐ 74 Randy Tomlin	.10	.05	.01
☐ 75 Nolan Ryan	2.50	1.10	.30
☐ 76 Frank Viola UER	.10	.05	.01
(Card incorrectly states			
he has a surgically			
repaired elbow)			
☐ 77 Jose Rijo	.10	.05	.01
☐ 78 Shane Mack	.10	.05	.01
☐ 79 Travis Fryman	.25	.11	.03
☐ 80 Jack McDowell	.25	.11	.03
☐ 81 Mark Gubicza	.10	.05	.01
☐ 82 Matt Nokes	.10	.05	.01
☐ 83 Bert Blyleven	.25	.11	.03
☐ 84 Eric Anthony	.10	.05	.01
☐ 85 Mike Bordick	.10	.05	.01
☐ 86 John Olerud	.10	.05	.01
☐ 87 B.J.Surhoff	.25	.11	.03
☐ 88 Bernard Gilkey	.25	.11	.03
☐ 89 Shawon Dunston	.10	.05	.01
☐ 90 Tom Glavine	.50	.23	.06
☐ 91 Brett Butler	.25	.11	.03
☐ 92 Moises Alou	.25	.11	.03
☐ 93 Albert Belle	1.25	.55	.16
☐ 94 Darren Lewis	.10	.05	.01
☐ 95 Omar Vizquel	.25	.11	.03
☐ 96 Dwight Gooden	.25	.11	.03
☐ 97 Gregg Olson	.10	.05	.01
☐ 98 Tony Gwynn	1.25	.55	.16
☐ 99 Darren Daulton	.25	.11	.03
☐ 100 Dennis Eckersley	.25	.11	.03
☐ 101 Rob Dibble	.10	.05	.01
☐ 102 Mike Greenwell	.10	.05	.01
☐ 103 Jose Lind	.10	.05	.01
☐ 104 Julio Franco	.25	.11	.03
☐ 105 Tom Gordon	.10	.05	.01
☐ 106 Scott Livingstone	.10	.05	.01
☐ 107 Chuck Knoblauch	.50	.23	.06
☐ 108 Frank Thomas	3.00	1.35	.35
☐ 109 Melido Perez	.10	.05	.01
☐ 110 Ken Griffey Jr.	3.00	1.35	.35
☐ 111 Harold Baines	.25	.11	.03
☐ 112 Gary Gaetti	.25	.11	.03
☐ 113 Pete Harnisch	.10	.05	.01
☐ 114 David Wells	.10	.05	.01
☐ 115 Charlie Leibrandt	.10	.05	.01
☐ 116 Ray Lankford	.25	.11	.03
☐ 117 Kevin Seitzer	.10	.05	.01
☐ 118 Robin Yount	.50	.23	.06
☐ 119 Lenny Harris	.10	.05	.01
☐ 120 Chris James	.10	.05	.01
☐ 121 Delino DeShields	.10	.05	.01
☐ 122 Kirt Manwaring	.10	.05	.01
☐ 123 Glenallen Hill	.10	.05	.01
☐ 124 Hensley Meulens	.10	.05	.01
☐ 125 Darrin Jackson	.10	.05	.01
☐ 126 Todd Hundley	.25	.11	.03
☐ 127 Dave Hollins	.10	.05	.01
☐ 128 Sam Horn	.10	.05	.01
☐ 129 Roberto Hernandez	.25	.11	.03
☐ 130 Vicente Palacios	.10	.05	.01
☐ 131 George Brett	1.25	.55	.16
☐ 132 Dave Martinez	.10	.05	.01
☐ 133 Kevin Appier	.25	.11	.03
☐ 134 Pat Kelly	.10	.05	.01
☐ 135 Pedro Munoz	.10	.05	.01
☐ 136 Mark Carreon	.10	.05	.01
☐ 137 Lance Johnson	.25	.11	.03
☐ 138 Devon White	.10	.05	.01
☐ 139 Julio Valera	.10	.05	.01
☐ 140 Eddie Taubensee	.10	.05	.01
☐ 141 Willie Wilson	.10	.05	.01
☐ 142 Stan Belinda	.10	.05	.01
☐ 143 John Smoltz	.50	.23	.06
☐ 144 Darryl Hamilton	.10	.05	.01
☐ 145 Sammy Sosa	.50	.23	.06
☐ 146 Carlos Hernandez	.10	.05	.01
☐ 147 Tom Candiotti	.10	.05	.01
☐ 148 Mike Felder	.10	.05	.01
☐ 149 Rusty Meacham	.10	.05	.01
☐ 150 Ivan Calderon	.10	.05	.01
☐ 151 Pete O'Brien	.10	.05	.01
☐ 152 Erik Hanson	.10	.05	.01
☐ 153 Billy Ripken	.10	.05	.01
☐ 154 Kurt Stillwell	.10	.05	.01
☐ 155 Jeff Kent	.25	.11	.03
☐ 156 Mickey Morandini	.10	.05	.01
☐ 157 Randy Milligan	.10	.05	.01
☐ 158 Reggie Sanders	.50	.23	.06
☐ 159 Luis Rivera	.10	.05	.01
☐ 160 Orlando Merced	.25	.11	.03
☐ 161 Dean Palmer	.25	.11	.03
☐ 162 Mike Perez	.10	.05	.01
☐ 163 Scott Erickson	.10	.05	.01
☐ 164 Kevin McReynolds	.10	.05	.01
☐ 165 Kevin Maas	.10	.05	.01
☐ 166 Ozzie Guillen	.10	.05	.01
☐ 167 Rob Deer	.10	.05	.01
☐ 168 Danny Tartabull	.10	.05	.01
☐ 169 Lee Stevens	.10	.05	.01
☐ 170 Dave Henderson	.10	.05	.01
☐ 171 Derek Bell	.25	.11	.03
☐ 172 Steve Finley	.25	.11	.03
☐ 173 Greg Olson	.10	.05	.01
☐ 174 Geronimo Pena	.10	.05	.01
☐ 175 Paul Quantrill	.10	.05	.01
☐ 176 Steve Buechele	.10	.05	.01
☐ 177 Kevin Gross	.10	.05	.01
☐ 178 Tim Wallach	.10	.05	.01
☐ 179 Dave Valle	.10	.05	.01
☐ 180 Dave Silvestri	.10	.05	.01
☐ 181 Bud Black	.10	.05	.01
☐ 182 Henry Rodriguez	.50	.23	.06
☐ 183 Tim Teufel	.10	.05	.01
☐ 184 Mark McLemore	.10	.05	.01
☐ 185 Bret Saberhagen	.25	.11	.03
☐ 186 Chris Hoiles	.10	.05	.01
☐ 187 Ricky Jordan	.10	.05	.01
☐ 188 Don Slaught	.10	.05	.01
☐ 189 Mo Vaughn	.75	.35	.09
☐ 190 Joe Oliver	.10	.05	.01
☐ 191 Juan Gonzalez	1.50	.70	.19
☐ 192 Scott Leius	.10	.05	.01
☐ 193 Milt Cuyler	.10	.05	.01
☐ 194 Chris Haney	.10	.05	.01
☐ 195 Ron Karkovice	.10	.05	.01
☐ 196 Steve Farr	.10	.05	.01
☐ 197 John Orton	.10	.05	.01
☐ 198 Kelly Gruber	.10	.05	.01
☐ 199 Ron Darling	.10	.05	.01
☐ 200 Ruben Sierra	.25	.11	.03
☐ 201 Chuck Finley	.10	.05	.01
☐ 202 Mike Moore	.10	.05	.01
☐ 203 Pat Borders	.10	.05	.01
☐ 204 Sid Bream	.10	.05	.01
☐ 205 Todd Zeile	.10	.05	.01
☐ 206 Rick Wilkins	.10	.05	.01
☐ 207 Jim Gantner	.10	.05	.01
☐ 208 Frank Castillo	.10	.05	.01
☐ 209 Dave Hansen	.10	.05	.01
☐ 210 Trevor Wilson	.10	.05	.01
☐ 211 Sandy Alomar Jr.	.25	.11	.03
☐ 212 Sean Berry	.10	.05	.01
☐ 213 Tino Martinez	.25	.11	.03
☐ 214 Chito Martinez	.10	.05	.01
☐ 215 Dan Walters	.10	.05	.01
☐ 216 John Franco	.10	.05	.01
☐ 217 Glenn Davis	.10	.05	.01
☐ 218 Mariano Duncan	.10	.05	.01
☐ 219 Mike LaValliere	.10	.05	.01
☐ 220 Rafael Palmeiro	.50	.23	.06
☐ 221 Jack Clark	.10	.05	.01
☐ 222 Hal Morris	.10	.05	.01
☐ 223 Ed Sprague	.25	.11	.03
☐ 224 John Valentin	.25	.11	.03
☐ 225 Sam Militello	.10	.05	.01
☐ 226 Bob Wickman	.10	.05	.01
☐ 227 Damion Easley	.10	.05	.01
☐ 228 John Jaha	.50	.23	.06
☐ 229 Bob Ayrault	.10	.05	.01
☐ 230 Mo Sanford	.10	.05	.01
☐ 231 Walt Weiss	.10	.05	.01
☐ 232 Dante Bichette	.50	.23	.06
☐ 233 Steve Decker	.10	.05	.01
☐ 234 Jerald Clark	.10	.05	.01
☐ 235 Bryan Harvey	.10	.05	.01
☐ 236 Joe Girardi	.10	.05	.01
☐ 237 Dave Magadan	.10	.05	.01
☐ 238 David Nied	.10	.05	.01
☐ 239 Eric Wedge	.10	.05	.01
☐ 240 Rico Brogna	.25	.11	.03
☐ 241 J.T.Bruett	.10	.05	.01
☐ 242 Jonathan Hurst	.10	.05	.01
☐ 243 Bret Boone	.25	.11	.03
☐ 244 Manny Alexander	.10	.05	.01
☐ 245 Scooter Tucker	.10	.05	.01
☐ 246 Troy Neel	.10	.05	.01
☐ 247 Eddie Zosky	.10	.05	.01
☐ 248 Melvin Nieves	.50	.23	.06
☐ 249 Ryan Thompson	.10	.05	.01
☐ 250 Shawn Barton	.10	.05	.01
☐ 251 Ryan Klesko	1.00	.45	.12
☐ 252 Mike Piazza	3.00	1.35	.35
☐ 253 Steve Hosey	.10	.05	.01
☐ 254 Shane Reynolds	.50	.23	.06
☐ 255 Dan Wilson	.25	.11	.03
☐ 256 Tom Marsh	.10	.05	.01
☐ 257 Barry Manuel	.10	.05	.01
☐ 258 Paul Miller	.10	.05	.01
☐ 259 Pedro Martinez	.50	.23	.06
☐ 260 Steve Cooke	.10	.05	.01
☐ 261 Johnny Guzman	.10	.05	.01
☐ 262 Mike Butcher	.10	.05	.01
☐ 263 Bien Figueroa	.10	.05	.01
☐ 264 Rich Rowland	.10	.05	.01
☐ 265 Shawn Jeter	.10	.05	.01
☐ 266 Gerald Williams	.10	.05	.01
☐ 267 Derek Parks	.10	.05	.01
☐ 268 Henry Mercedes	.10	.05	.01
☐ 269 David Hulse	.10	.05	.01
☐ 270 Tim Pugh	.10	.05	.01
☐ 271 William Suero	.10	.05	.01
☐ 272 Ozzie Canseco	.10	.05	.01
☐ 273 Fernando Ramsey	.10	.05	.01
☐ 274 Bernardo Brito	.10	.05	.01
☐ 275 Dave Mlicki	.10	.05	.01
☐ 276 Tim Salmon	.75	.35	.09
☐ 277 Mike Raczka	.10	.05	.01
☐ 278 Ken Ryan	.10	.05	.01
☐ 279 Rafael Bournigal	.10	.05	.01
☐ 280 Wil Cordero	.25	.11	.03
☐ 281 Billy Ashley	.10	.05	.01
☐ 282 Paul Wagner	.10	.05	.01
☐ 283 Blas Minor	.10	.05	.01
☐ 284 Rick Trlicek	.10	.05	.01
☐ 285 Willie Greene	.25	.11	.03
☐ 286 Ted Wood	.10	.05	.01
☐ 287 Phil Clark	.10	.05	.01
☐ 288 Jesse Levis	.10	.05	.01
☐ 289 Tony Gwynn NT	.60	.25	.07
☐ 290 Nolan Ryan NT	1.25	.55	.16
☐ 291 Dennis Martinez NT	.10	.05	.01
☐ 292 Eddie Murray NT	.50	.23	.06
☐ 293 Robin Yount NT	.50	.23	.06
☐ 294 George Brett NT	.60	.25	.07
☐ 295 Dave Winfield NT	.50	.23	.06
☐ 296 Bert Blyleven NT	.25	.11	.03
☐ 297 Jeff Bagwell	.50	.23	.06
Carl Yastrzemski			
☐ 298 John Smoltz	.50	.23	.06
Jack Morris			
☐ 299 Larry Walker	.50	.23	.06
Mike Bossy			
☐ 300 Gary Sheffield	.50	.23	.06
Barry Larkin			
☐ 301 Ivan Rodriguez	.50	.23	.06
Carlton Fisk			
☐ 302 Delino DeShields	.50	.23	.06
Malcolm X			
☐ 303 Tim Salmon	.25	.11	.03
Dwight Evans			
☐ 304 Bernard Gilkey HH	.25	.11	.03
☐ 305 Cal Ripken Jr. HH	1.25	.55	.16
☐ 306 Barry Larkin HH	.50	.23	.06
☐ 307 Kent Hrbek HH	.10	.05	.01
☐ 308 Rickey Henderson HH	.50	.23	.06
☐ 309 Darryl Strawberry HH	.25	.11	.03
☐ 310 John Franco HH	.10	.05	.01
☐ 311 Todd Stottlemyre	.25	.11	.03
☐ 312 Luis Gonzalez	.10	.05	.01
☐ 313 Tommy Greene	.10	.05	.01
☐ 314 Randy Velarde	.10	.05	.01
☐ 315 Steve Avery	.25	.11	.03
☐ 316 Jose Oquendo	.10	.05	.01
☐ 317 Rey Sanchez	.10	.05	.01
☐ 318 Greg Vaughn	.25	.11	.03
☐ 319 Orel Hershiser	.25	.11	.03
☐ 320 Paul Sorrento	.10	.05	.01
☐ 321 Royce Clayton	.25	.11	.03
☐ 322 John Vander Wal	.10	.05	.01
☐ 323 Henry Cotto	.10	.05	.01
☐ 324 Pete Schourek	.25	.11	.03
☐ 325 David Segui	.10	.05	.01
☐ 326 Arthur Rhodes	.10	.05	.01
☐ 327 Bruce Hurst	.10	.05	.01
☐ 328 Wes Chamberlain	.10	.05	.01
☐ 329 Ozzie Smith	.75	.35	.09
☐ 330 Scott Cooper	.10	.05	.01
☐ 331 Felix Fermin	.10	.05	.01
☐ 332 Mike Macfarlane	.10	.05	.01
☐ 333 Dan Gladden	.10	.05	.01
☐ 334 Kevin Tapani	.10	.05	.01
☐ 335 Steve Sax	.10	.05	.01
☐ 336 Jeff Montgomery	.25	.11	.03
☐ 337 Gary DiSarcina	.10	.05	.01
☐ 338 Lance Blankenship	.10	.05	.01
☐ 339 Brian Williams	.10	.05	.01
☐ 340 Duane Ward	.10	.05	.01
☐ 341 Chuck McElroy	.10	.05	.01
☐ 342 Joe Magrane	.10	.05	.01
☐ 343 Jaime Navarro	.10	.05	.01
☐ 344 Dave Justice	.50	.23	.06
☐ 345 Jose Offerman	.10	.05	.01
☐ 346 Marquis Grissom	.25	.11	.03
☐ 347 Bill Swift	.10	.05	.01
☐ 348 Jim Thome	1.50	.70	.19
☐ 349 Archi Cianfrocco	.10	.05	.01
☐ 350 Anthony Young	.10	.05	.01
☐ 351 Leo Gomez	.10	.05	.01
☐ 352 Bill Gullickson	.10	.05	.01
☐ 353 Alan Trammell	.50	.23	.06
☐ 354 Dan Pasqua	.10	.05	.01
☐ 355 Jeff King	.25	.11	.03
☐ 356 Kevin Brown	.25	.11	.03
☐ 357 Tim Belcher	.10	.05	.01
☐ 358 Bip Roberts	.10	.05	.01
☐ 359 Brent Mayne	.10	.05	.01
☐ 360 Rheal Cormier	.10	.05	.01
☐ 361 Mark Guthrie	.10	.05	.01
☐ 362 Craig Grebeck	.10	.05	.01
☐ 363 Andy Stankiewicz	.10	.05	.01
☐ 364 Juan Guzman	.25	.11	.03
☐ 365 Bobby Witt	.10	.05	.01
☐ 366 Mark Portugal	.10	.05	.01

Card	MINT	NRMT	EXC
☐ 367 Brian McRae	.25	.11	.03
☐ 368 Mark Lemke	.10	.05	.01
☐ 369 Bill Wegman	.10	.05	.01
☐ 370 Donovan Osborne	.10	.05	.01
☐ 371 Derrick May	.10	.05	.01
☐ 372 Carl Willis	.10	.05	.01
☐ 373 Chris Nabholz	.10	.05	.01
☐ 374 Mark Lewis	.10	.05	.01
☐ 375 John Burkett	.10	.05	.01
☐ 376 Luis Mercedes	.10	.05	.01
☐ 377 Ramon Martinez	.25	.11	.03
☐ 378 Kyle Abbott	.10	.05	.01
☐ 379 Mark Wohlers	.25	.11	.03
☐ 380 Bob Walk	.10	.05	.01
☐ 381 Kenny Rogers	.10	.05	.01
☐ 382 Tim Naehring	.10	.05	.01
☐ 383 Alex Fernandez	.25	.11	.03
☐ 384 Keith Miller	.10	.05	.01
☐ 385 Mike Henneman	.10	.05	.01
☐ 386 Rick Aguilera	.10	.05	.01
☐ 387 George Bell	.10	.05	.01
☐ 388 Mike Gallego	.10	.05	.01
☐ 389 Howard Johnson	.10	.05	.01
☐ 390 Kim Batiste	.10	.05	.01
☐ 391 Jerry Browne	.10	.05	.01
☐ 392 Damon Berryhill	.10	.05	.01
☐ 393 Ricky Bones	.10	.05	.01
☐ 394 Omar Olivares	.10	.05	.01
☐ 395 Mike Harkey	.10	.05	.01
☐ 396 Pedro Astacio	.10	.05	.01
☐ 397 John Wetteland	.25	.11	.03
☐ 398 Rod Beck	.25	.11	.03
☐ 399 Thomas Howard	.10	.05	.01
☐ 400 Mike Devereaux	.10	.05	.01
☐ 401 Tim Wakefield	.25	.11	.03
☐ 402 Curt Schilling	.10	.05	.01
☐ 403 Zane Smith	.10	.05	.01
☐ 404 Bob Zupcic	.10	.05	.01
☐ 405 Tom Browning	.10	.05	.01
☐ 406 Tony Phillips	.25	.11	.03
☐ 407 John Doherty	.10	.05	.01
☐ 408 Pat Mahomes	.10	.05	.01
☐ 409 John Habyan	.10	.05	.01
☐ 410 Steve Olin	.10	.05	.01
☐ 411 Chad Curtis	.25	.11	.03
☐ 412 Joe Grahe	.10	.05	.01
☐ 413 John Patterson	.10	.05	.01
☐ 414 Brian Hunter	.10	.05	.01
☐ 415 Doug Henry	.10	.05	.01
☐ 416 Lee Smith	.25	.11	.03
☐ 417 Bob Scanlan	.10	.05	.01
☐ 418 Kent Mercker	.10	.05	.01
☐ 419 Mel Rojas	.25	.11	.03
☐ 420 Mark Whiten	.10	.05	.01
☐ 421 Carlton Fisk	.50	.23	.06
☐ 422 Candy Maldonado	.10	.05	.01
☐ 423 Doug Drabek	.10	.05	.01
☐ 424 Wade Boggs	.50	.23	.06
☐ 425 Mark Davis	.10	.05	.01
☐ 426 Kirby Puckett	1.25	.55	.16
☐ 427 Joe Carter	.25	.11	.03
☐ 428 Paul Molitor	.60	.25	.07
☐ 429 Eric Davis	.25	.11	.03
☐ 430 Darryl Kile	.10	.05	.01
☐ 431 Jeff Parrett	.10	.05	.01
☐ 432 Jeff Blauser	.10	.05	.01
☐ 433 Dan Plesac	.10	.05	.01
☐ 434 Andres Galarraga	.50	.23	.06
☐ 435 Jim Gott	.10	.05	.01
☐ 436 Jose Mesa	.25	.11	.03
☐ 437 Ben Rivera	.10	.05	.01
☐ 438 Dave Winfield	.50	.23	.06
☐ 439 Norm Charlton	.10	.05	.01
☐ 440 Chris Bosio	.10	.05	.01
☐ 441 Wilson Alvarez	.25	.11	.03
☐ 442 Dave Stewart	.25	.11	.03
☐ 443 Doug Jones	.10	.05	.01
☐ 444 Jeff Russell	.10	.05	.01
☐ 445 Ron Gant	.25	.11	.03
☐ 446 Paul O'Neill	.25	.11	.03
☐ 447 Charlie Hayes	.10	.05	.01
☐ 448 Joe Hesketh	.10	.05	.01
☐ 449 Chris Hammond	.10	.05	.01
☐ 450 Hipolito Pichardo	.10	.05	.01
☐ 451 Scott Radinsky	.10	.05	.01
☐ 452 Bobby Thigpen	.10	.05	.01
☐ 453 Xavier Hernandez	.10	.05	.01
☐ 454 Lonnie Smith	.10	.05	.01
☐ 455 Jamie Arnold DP	.25	.11	.03
☐ 456 B.J. Wallace DP	.10	.05	.01
☐ 457 Derek Jeter DP	6.00	2.70	.75
☐ 458 Jason Kendall DP	2.00	.90	.25
☐ 459 Rick Helling DP	.25	.11	.03
☐ 460 Derek Wallace DP	.10	.05	.01
☐ 461 Sean Lowe DP	.25	.11	.03
☐ 462 Shannon Stewart DP	.50	.23	.06
☐ 463 Benji Grigsby DP	.10	.05	.01
☐ 464 Todd Steverson DP	.25	.11	.03
☐ 465 Dan Serafini DP	.50	.23	.06
☐ 466 Michael Tucker DP	.50	.23	.06
☐ 467 Chris Roberts DP	.25	.11	.03
☐ 468 Pete Janicki DP	.10	.05	.01
☐ 469 Jeff Schmidt DP	.10	.05	.01
☐ 470 Don Mattingly NT	.75	.35	.09
☐ 471 Cal Ripken Jr. NT	1.25	.55	.16
☐ 472 Jack Morris NT	.10	.05	.01
☐ 473 Terry Pendleton NT	.10	.05	.01
☐ 474 Dennis Eckersley NT	.25	.11	.03
☐ 475 Carlton Fisk NT	.25	.11	.03
☐ 476 Wade Boggs NT	.50	.23	.06
☐ 477 Len Dykstra Ken Stabler	.25	.11	.03
☐ 478 Danny Tartabull Jose Tartabull	.10	.05	.01
☐ 479 Jeff Conine Dale Murphy	.25	.11	.03
☐ 480 Gregg Jefferies Ron Cey	.25	.11	.03
☐ 481 Paul Molitor Harmon Killebrew	.30	.14	.04
☐ 482 John Valentin Dave Concepcion	.25	.11	.03
☐ 483 Alex Arias Dave Winfield	.25	.11	.03
☐ 484 Barry Bonds HH	.50	.23	.06
☐ 485 Doug Drabek HH	.10	.05	.01
☐ 486 Dave Winfield HH	.50	.23	.06
☐ 487 Brett Butler HH	.10	.05	.01
☐ 488 Harold Baines HH	.10	.05	.01
☐ 489 David Cone HH	.25	.11	.03
☐ 490 Willie McGee HH	.10	.05	.01
☐ 491 Robby Thompson	.10	.05	.01
☐ 492 Pete Incaviglia	.10	.05	.01
☐ 493 Manuel Lee	.10	.05	.01
☐ 494 Rafael Belliard	.10	.05	.01
☐ 495 Scott Fletcher	.10	.05	.01
☐ 496 Jeff Frye	.10	.05	.01
☐ 497 Andre Dawson	.25	.11	.03
☐ 498 Mike Scioscia	.10	.05	.01
☐ 499 Spike Owen	.10	.05	.01
☐ 500 Sid Fernandez	.10	.05	.01
☐ 501 Joe Orsulak	.10	.05	.01
☐ 502 Benito Santiago	.10	.05	.01
☐ 503 Dale Murphy	.50	.23	.06
☐ 504 Barry Bonds	.75	.35	.09
☐ 505 Jose Guzman	.10	.05	.01
☐ 506 Tony Pena	.10	.05	.01
☐ 507 Greg Swindell	.10	.05	.01
☐ 508 Mike Pagliarulo	.10	.05	.01
☐ 509 Lou Whitaker	.25	.11	.03
☐ 510 Greg Gagne	.10	.05	.01
☐ 511 Butch Henry	.10	.05	.01
☐ 512 Jeff Brantley	.10	.05	.01
☐ 513 Jack Armstrong	.10	.05	.01
☐ 514 Danny Jackson	.10	.05	.01
☐ 515 Junior Felix	.10	.05	.01
☐ 516 Milt Thompson	.10	.05	.01
☐ 517 Greg Maddux	2.00	.90	.25
☐ 518 Eric Young	.50	.23	.06
☐ 519 Jody Reed	.10	.05	.01
☐ 520 Roberto Kelly	.10	.05	.01
☐ 521 Darren Holmes	.10	.05	.01
☐ 522 Craig Lefferts	.10	.05	.01
☐ 523 Charlie Hough	.10	.05	.01
☐ 524 Bo Jackson	.25	.11	.03
☐ 525 Bill Spiers	.10	.05	.01
☐ 526 Orestes Destrade	.10	.05	.01
☐ 527 Greg Hibbard	.10	.05	.01
☐ 528 Roger McDowell	.10	.05	.01
☐ 529 Cory Snyder	.10	.05	.01
☐ 530 Harold Reynolds	.10	.05	.01
☐ 531 Kevin Reimer	.10	.05	.01
☐ 532 Rick Sutcliffe	.10	.05	.01
☐ 533 Tony Fernandez	.10	.05	.01
☐ 534 Tom Brunansky	.10	.05	.01
☐ 535 Jeff Reardon	.25	.11	.03
☐ 536 Chili Davis	.25	.11	.03
☐ 537 Bob Ojeda	.10	.05	.01
☐ 538 Greg Colbrunn	.10	.05	.01
☐ 539 Phil Plantier	.10	.05	.01
☐ 540 Brian Jordan	.50	.23	.06
☐ 541 Pete Smith	.10	.05	.01
☐ 542 Frank Tanana	.10	.05	.01
☐ 543 John Smiley	.10	.05	.01
☐ 544 David Cone	.25	.11	.03
☐ 545 Daryl Boston	.10	.05	.01
☐ 546 Tom Henke	.10	.05	.01
☐ 547 Bill Krueger	.10	.05	.01
☐ 548 Freddie Benavides	.10	.05	.01
☐ 549 Randy Myers	.25	.11	.03
☐ 550 Reggie Jefferson	.25	.11	.03
☐ 551 Kevin Mitchell	.25	.11	.03
☐ 552 Dave Stieb	.10	.05	.01
☐ 553 Bret Barberie	.10	.05	.01
☐ 554 Tim Crews	.10	.05	.01
☐ 555 Doug Dascenzo	.10	.05	.01
☐ 556 Alex Cole	.10	.05	.01
☐ 557 Jeff Innis	.10	.05	.01
☐ 558 Carlos Garcia	.10	.05	.01
☐ 559 Steve Howe	.10	.05	.01
☐ 560 Kirk McCaskill	.10	.05	.01
☐ 561 Frank Seminara	.10	.05	.01
☐ 562 Cris Carpenter	.10	.05	.01
☐ 563 Mike Stanley	.10	.05	.01
☐ 564 Carlos Quintana	.10	.05	.01
☐ 565 Mitch Williams	.10	.05	.01
☐ 566 Juan Bell	.10	.05	.01
☐ 567 Eric Fox	.10	.05	.01
☐ 568 Al Leiter	.25	.11	.03
☐ 569 Mike Stanton	.10	.05	.01
☐ 570 Scott Kamieniecki	.10	.05	.01
☐ 571 Ryan Bowen	.10	.05	.01
☐ 572 Andy Ashby	.25	.11	.03
☐ 573 Bob Welch	.10	.05	.01
☐ 574 Scott Sanderson	.10	.05	.01
☐ 575 Joe Kmak	.10	.05	.01
☐ 576 Scott Pose	.10	.05	.01
☐ 577 Ricky Gutierrez	.10	.05	.01
☐ 578 Mike Trombley	.10	.05	.01
☐ 579 Sterling Hitchcock	.25	.11	.03
☐ 580 Rodney Bolton	.10	.05	.01
☐ 581 Tyler Green	.10	.05	.01
☐ 582 Tim Costo	.10	.05	.01
☐ 583 Tim Laker	.10	.05	.01
☐ 584 Steve Reed	.10	.05	.01
☐ 585 Tom Kramer	.10	.05	.01
☐ 586 Robb Nen	.25	.11	.03
☐ 587 Jim Tatum	.10	.05	.01
☐ 588 Frank Bolick	.10	.05	.01
☐ 589 Kevin Young	.10	.05	.01
☐ 590 Matt Whiteside	.10	.05	.01
☐ 591 Cesar Hernandez	.10	.05	.01
☐ 592 Mike Mohler	.10	.05	.01
☐ 593 Alan Embree	.10	.05	.01
☐ 594 Terry Jorgensen	.10	.05	.01
☐ 595 John Cummings	.10	.05	.01
☐ 596 Domingo Martinez	.10	.05	.01
☐ 597 Benji Gil	.25	.11	.03
☐ 598 Todd Pratt	.10	.05	.01
☐ 599 Rene Arocha	.10	.05	.01
☐ 600 Dennis Moeller	.10	.05	.01
☐ 601 Jeff Conine	.25	.11	.03
☐ 602 Trevor Hoffman	.50	.23	.06
☐ 603 Daniel Smith	.10	.05	.01
☐ 604 Lee Tinsley	.25	.11	.03
☐ 605 Dan Peltier	.10	.05	.01
☐ 606 Billy Brewer	.10	.05	.01
☐ 607 Matt Walbeck	.10	.05	.01
☐ 608 Richie Lewis	.10	.05	.01
☐ 609 J.T. Snow	.50	.23	.06
☐ 610 Pat Gomez	.10	.05	.01
☐ 611 Phil Hiatt	.10	.05	.01
☐ 612 Alex Arias	.10	.05	.01
☐ 613 Kevin Rogers	.10	.05	.01
☐ 614 Al Martin	.25	.11	.03
☐ 615 Greg Gohr	.10	.05	.01
☐ 616 Graeme Lloyd	.10	.05	.01
☐ 617 Kent Bottenfield	.10	.05	.01
☐ 618 Chuck Carr	.10	.05	.01
☐ 619 Darrell Sherman	.10	.05	.01
☐ 620 Mike Lansing	.25	.11	.03

1993 Pinnacle Expansion Opening Day

This nine-card standard-size dual-sided set was issued to commemorate openning day for the two 1993 expansion teams, the Colorado Rockies and the Florida Marlins. The cards were inserted on top of sealed series two hobby boxes. These cards were also available through a mail-in offer. The full-bleed fronts feature glossy color action player photos. Across the bottom is a team color-coded bar containing the player's name, position, and opening day date. A logo for the Expansion Draft is printed in the lower right corner. An anti-counterfeit device is printed in the bottom black border. The backs carry the same design as the fronts with a player from the Rockies appearing on one side and a Marlin's player on the flip side. The cards are numbered on both sides.

	MINT	NRMT	EXC
COMPLETE SET (9)	25.00	11.00	3.10
COMMON PAIR (1-9)	1.50	.70	.19
☐ 1 Charlie Hough David Nied	2.50	1.10	.30
☐ 2 Benito Santiago Joe Girardi	2.50	1.10	.30
☐ 3 Orestes Destrade Andres Galarraga	6.00	2.70	.75
☐ 4 Bret Barberie Eric Young	2.50	1.10	.30
☐ 5 Dave Magadan Charlie Hayes	2.50	1.10	.30
☐ 6 Walt Weiss Freddie Benavides	2.50	1.10	.30
☐ 7 Jeff Conine Jerald Clark	5.00	2.20	.60
☐ 8 Scott Pose Alex Cole	1.50	.70	.19
☐ 9 Junior Felix Dante Bichette	8.00	3.60	1.00

1993 Pinnacle Rookie Team Pinnacle

Cards from this 10-card standard-size set were randomly inserted into one in every 90 series 2 foil packs and each features an American League rookie on one side and a National League rookie on the other. Each double-sided card displays paintings by artist Christopher Greco encased by a bold black border. The cards are numbered on the front and back.

	MINT	NRMT	EXC
COMPLETE SET (10)	100.00	45.00	12.50
COMMON PAIR (1-10)	4.00	1.80	.50
☐ 1 Pedro Martinez Mike Trombley	8.00	3.60	1.00
☐ 2 Kevin Rogers Sterling Hitchcock	4.00	1.80	.50
☐ 3 Mike Piazza Jesse Levis	50.00	22.00	6.25
☐ 4 Ryan Klesko J.T. Snow	20.00	9.00	2.50
☐ 5 John Patterson Bret Boone	8.00	3.60	1.00
☐ 6 Kevin Young Domingo Martinez	4.00	1.80	.50
☐ 7 Wil Cordero Manny Alexander	8.00	3.60	1.00
☐ 8 Steve Hosey Tim Salmon	15.00	6.75	1.85
☐ 9 Ryan Thompson Gerald Williams	4.00	1.80	.50
☐ 10 Melvin Nieves David Hulse	8.00	3.60	1.00

1993 Pinnacle Slugfest

These 30 standard-size cards salute baseball's top hitters and were randomly inserted in series 2 jumbo superpacks. The fronts feature color player action shots that are borderless, except at the bottom, where a black stripe carries the player's name in white lettering. The set's title appears below in black lettering within a gold foil stripe.

	MINT	NRMT	EXC
COMPLETE SET (30)	60.00	27.00	7.50
COMMON CARD (1-30)	1.00	.45	.12
☐ 1 Juan Gonzalez	8.00	3.60	1.00
☐ 2 Mark McGwire	5.00	2.20	.60
☐ 3 Cecil Fielder	1.50	.70	.19
☐ 4 Joe Carter	1.50	.70	.19
☐ 5 Fred McGriff	2.00	.90	.25
☐ 6 Barry Bonds	4.00	1.80	.50
☐ 7 Gary Sheffield	2.50	1.10	.30
☐ 8 Dave Hollins	1.00	.45	.12
☐ 9 Frank Thomas	15.00	6.75	1.85
☐ 10 Danny Tartabull	1.00	.45	.12
☐ 11 Albert Belle	6.00	2.70	.75
☐ 12 Ruben Sierra	1.00	.45	.12
☐ 13 Larry Walker	2.00	.90	.25
☐ 14 Jeff Bagwell	6.00	2.70	.75
☐ 15 David Justice	1.50	.70	.19
☐ 16 Kirby Puckett	6.00	2.70	.75
☐ 17 John Kruk	1.00	.45	.12
☐ 18 Howard Johnson	1.00	.45	.12
☐ 19 Darryl Strawberry	1.50	.70	.19
☐ 20 Will Clark	2.00	.90	.25
☐ 21 Kevin Mitchell	1.00	.45	.12
☐ 22 Mickey Tettleton	1.00	.45	.12
☐ 23 Don Mattingly	6.00	2.70	.75
☐ 24 Jose Canseco	2.00	.90	.25
☐ 25 George Bell	1.00	.45	.12
☐ 26 Andre Dawson	1.50	.70	.19
☐ 27 Ryne Sandberg	4.00	1.80	.50
☐ 28 Ken Griffey Jr.	15.00	6.75	1.85
☐ 29 Carlos Baerga	1.00	.45	.12
☐ 30 Travis Fryman	1.50	.70	.19

1993 Pinnacle Team 2001

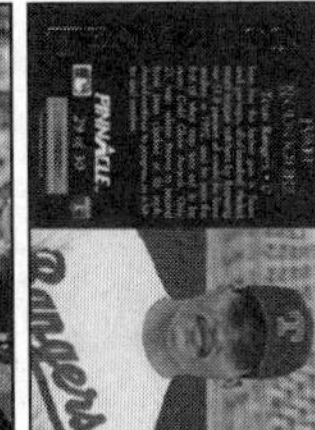

This 30-card standard-size set salutes players expected to be stars in the year 2001. The cards were inserted one per pack in first series jumbo superpacks and feature color player action shots on their fronts. These photos are borderless at the top and right, and black-bordered on the bottom and left. The player's name appears in gold-foil in the bottom margin, and his gold-foil-encircled team logo rests in the bottom left.

	MINT	NRMT	EXC
COMPLETE SET (30)	40.00	18.00	5.00
COMMON CARD (1-30)	.75	.35	.09
☐ 1 Wil Cordero	.75	.35	.09
☐ 2 Cal Eldred	.75	.35	.09
☐ 3 Mike Mussina	3.00	1.35	.35
☐ 4 Chuck Knoblauch	2.50	1.10	.30
☐ 5 Melvin Nieves	1.00	.45	.12
☐ 6 Tim Wakefield	.75	.35	.09
☐ 7 Carlos Baerga	.75	.35	.09
☐ 8 Bret Boone	1.00	.45	.12
☐ 9 Jeff Bagwell	6.00	2.70	.75
☐ 10 Travis Fryman	1.00	.45	.12
☐ 11 Royce Clayton	.75	.35	.09
☐ 12 Delino DeShields	.75	.35	.09
☐ 13 Juan Gonzalez	8.00	3.60	1.00
☐ 14 Pedro Martinez	1.50	.70	.19
☐ 15 Bernie Williams	3.00	1.35	.35
☐ 16 Billy Ashley	.75	.35	.09
☐ 17 Marquis Grissom	1.00	.45	.12
☐ 18 Kenny Lofton	6.00	2.70	.75
☐ 19 Ray Lankford	1.00	.45	.12
☐ 20 Tim Salmon	3.00	1.35	.35
☐ 21 Steve Hosey	.75	.35	.09
☐ 22 Charles Nagy	1.00	.45	.12
☐ 23 Dave Fleming	.75	.35	.09
☐ 24 Reggie Sanders	1.50	.70	.19
☐ 25 Sam Militello	.75	.35	.09
☐ 26 Eric Karros	1.50	.70	.19
☐ 27 Ryan Klesko	5.00	2.20	.60
☐ 28 Dean Palmer	1.00	.45	.12
☐ 29 Ivan Rodriguez	4.00	1.80	.50
☐ 30 Sterling Hitchcock	.75	.35	.09

1993 Pinnacle Team Pinnacle

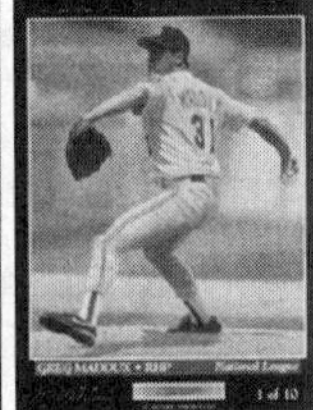

Cards from this ten-card dual-sided set, featuring a selection of top stars paired of by position, were randomly inserted into one in every 24 first series foil packs. Each double-sided card displays paintings by artist Christopher Greco. A special bonus Team Pinnacle card (11) was available to collectors only through a mail-in offer for ten 1993 Pinnacle baseball wrappers plus 1.50 for shipping and handling. Moreover, hobby dealers who ordered Pinnacle received two bonus cards and an advertisement display promoting the offer.

	MINT	NRMT	EXC
COMPLETE SET (10)	90.00	40.00	11.00
COMMON PAIR (1-10/B11)	3.00	1.35	.35
☐ 1 Greg Maddux Mike Mussina	25.00	11.00	3.10
☐ 2 Tom Glavine John Smiley	5.00	2.20	.60
☐ 3 Darren Daulton Ivan Rodriguez	10.00	4.50	1.25
☐ 4 Fred McGriff Frank Thomas	30.00	13.50	3.70
☐ 5 Delino DeShields Carlos Baerga	4.00	1.80	.50
☐ 6 Gary Sheffield Edgar Martinez	8.00	3.60	1.00
☐ 7 Ozzie Smith Pat Listach	10.00	4.50	1.25
☐ 8 Barry Bonds Juan Gonzalez	20.00	9.00	2.50
☐ 9 Andy Van Slyke Kirby Puckett	15.00	6.75	1.85
☐ 10 Larry Walker Joe Carter	8.00	3.60	1.00
☐ B11 Rob Dibble Rick Aguilera	3.00	1.35	.35

1993 Pinnacle Tribute

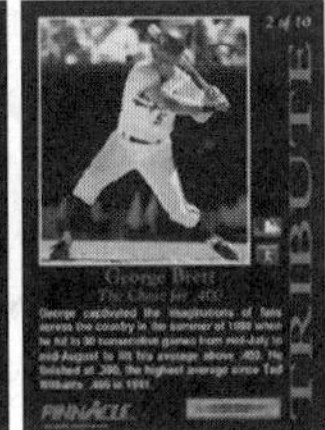

Randomly inserted in second-series packs, these ten standard-size cards pay tribute to two recent retirees from baseball: George Brett (1-5), and Nolan Ryan (6-10). Score estimates that the chances of finding a tribute chase card are not less than one in 24 count good packs. The fronts feature black-bordered color player action shots that are framed by a thin white line. The player's name appears in white lettering within the black bottom margin. Printed vertically, "Tribute" appears in gold foil along the right edge.

	MINT	NRMT	EXC
COMPLETE SET (10)	75.00	34.00	9.50
COMMON BRETT (1-5)	6.00	2.70	.75
COMMON RYAN (6-10)	10.00	4.50	1.25
☐ 1 George Brett Kansas City Royalty	6.00	2.70	.75
☐ 2 George Brett The Chase for .400	6.00	2.70	.75
☐ 3 George Brett Pine Tar Pandemonium	6.00	2.70	.75
☐ 4 George Brett MVP and a World Series, Too	6.00	2.70	.75
☐ 5 George Brett 3,000 or Bust	6.00	2.70	.75
☐ 6 Nolan Ryan The Rookie	10.00	4.50	1.25
☐ 7 Nolan Ryan Angel of No Mercy	10.00	4.50	1.25
☐ 8 Nolan Ryan Astronomical Success	10.00	4.50	1.25
☐ 9 Nolan Ryan 5,000 Ks	10.00	4.50	1.25
☐ 10 Nolan Ryan No-Hitter No. 7	10.00	4.50	1.25

1993 Pinnacle Cooperstown

This 30-card standard-size set features full-bleed color player photos of possible future HOF inductees. A green and gold foil Cooperstown Card logo overlays the bottom of the picture, and the player's name appears in gold foil within the black stripe that edges the bottom. The borderless back has a second color shot above a black background containing a brief career summary. The Cooperstown Card logo overlays the bottom of the picture.

	MINT	NRMT	EXC
COMPLETE SET (30)	8.00	3.60	1.00
COMMON CARD (1-30)	.10	.05	.01
☐ 1 Nolan Ryan	1.50	.70	.19
☐ 2 George Brett	.75	.35	.09
☐ 3 Robin Yount	.25	.11	.03
☐ 4 Carlton Fisk	.25	.11	.03
☐ 5 Dale Murphy	.25	.11	.03
☐ 6 Dennis Eckersley	.25	.11	.03
☐ 7 Rickey Henderson	.30	.14	.04
☐ 8 Ryne Sandberg	.50	.23	.06
☐ 9 Ozzie Smith	.75	.35	.09
☐ 10 Dave Winfield			
☐ 11 Andre Dawson	.25	.11	.03
☐ 12 Kirby Puckett	1.00	.45	.12
☐ 13 Wade Boggs			
☐ 14 Don Mattingly	1.00	.45	.12
☐ 15 Barry Bonds	.50	.23	.06
☐ 16 Will Clark	.30	.14	.04
☐ 17 Cal Ripken	1.50	.70	.19
☐ 18 Roger Clemens	.30	.14	.04
☐ 19 Dwight Gooden	.25	.11	.03
☐ 20 Tony Gwynn	.75	.35	.09
☐ 21 Joe Carter	.25	.11	.03
☐ 22 Ken Griffey Jr.	2.00	.90	.25
☐ 23 Paul Molitor	.40	.18	.05
☐ 24 Frank Thomas	2.00	.90	.25
☐ 25 Juan Gonzalez	1.00	.45	.12
☐ 26 Barry Larkin	.25	.11	.03
☐ 27 Eddie Murray	.50	.23	.06
☐ 28 Cecil Fielder	.25	.11	.03
☐ 29 Roberto Alomar	.40	.18	.05
☐ 30 Mark McGwire	.60	.25	.07

1993 Pinnacle Cooperstown Dufex

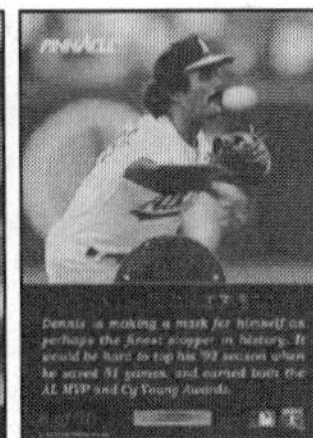

This 30-card standard-size set is a special parallel to the 1993 Pinnacle Cooperstown set. This version, of which no more than 1,000 sets were produced was given out to dealers who attended all the sessions of the 1993 SCAI meeting in Dallas. Since attendance at the convention was less than anticipated, this set was also distributed through other methods.

	MINT	NRMT	EXC
COMPLETE SET (30)	2000.00	900.00	250.00
COMMON CARD (1-30)	25.00	11.00	3.10
☐ 1 Nolan Ryan	300.00	135.00	38.00
☐ 2 George Brett	150.00	70.00	19.00
☐ 3 Robin Yount	50.00	22.00	6.25
☐ 4 Carlton Fisk	50.00	22.00	6.25
☐ 5 Dale Murphy	60.00	27.00	7.50
☐ 6 Dennis Eckersley	50.00	22.00	6.25
☐ 7 Rickey Henderson	60.00	27.00	7.50
☐ 8 Ryne Sandberg	125.00	55.00	15.50
☐ 9 Ozzie Smith	125.00	55.00	15.50
☐ 10 Dave Winfield	75.00	34.00	9.50
☐ 11 Andre Dawson	50.00	22.00	6.25
☐ 12 Kirby Puckett	175.00	80.00	22.00
☐ 13 Wade Boggs	75.00	34.00	9.50
☐ 14 Don Mattingly	175.00	80.00	22.00
☐ 15 Barry Bonds	75.00	34.00	9.50
☐ 16 Will Clark	60.00	27.00	7.50
☐ 17 Cal Ripken	300.00	135.00	38.00
☐ 18 Roger Clemens	75.00	34.00	9.50
☐ 19 Dwight Gooden	50.00	22.00	6.25
☐ 20 Tony Gwynn	150.00	70.00	19.00
☐ 21 Joe Carter	50.00	22.00	6.25
☐ 22 Ken Griffey Jr.	350.00	160.00	45.00
☐ 23 Paul Molitor	75.00	34.00	9.50
☐ 24 Frank Thomas	350.00	160.00	45.00
☐ 25 Juan Gonzalez	175.00	80.00	22.00
☐ 26 Barry Larkin	50.00	22.00	6.25
☐ 27 Eddie Murray	80.00	36.00	10.00
☐ 28 Cecil Fielder	50.00	22.00	6.25
☐ 29 Roberto Alomar	75.00	34.00	9.50
☐ 30 Mark McGwire	100.00	45.00	12.50

1993 Pinnacle DiMaggio

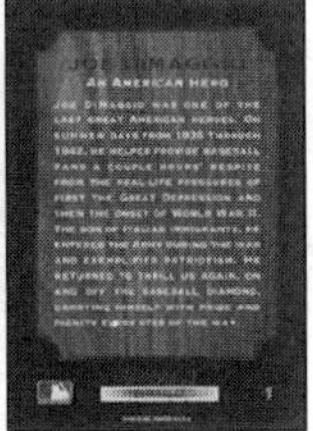

This 30-card set commemorates the life and career of Joe DiMaggio. Production was limited to 209,000 sets, with each set packaged in a black and gold collector's tin that features a color picture of DiMaggio. The black- and gold-bordered cards are standard-size. The fronts feature a mix of black-and-white, full-color, and colorized photos. At the bottom, DiMaggio's name is stamped in gold foil over a wood-grained, gold foil-framed bar. The black backs contain descriptive summaries from chapters in his life printed on a wood-grained background and framed in gold foil. The set includes an authenticator lens that can read the anticounterfeiting pattern at the bottom of the back. A certificate of authenticity card is also included that carries the production number of the set. DiMaggio also signed 9,000 cards for this set. One of 9,000 autographed cards from a special five-card set were randomly inserted into 30-card boxed hobby sets of 1993 Pinnacle Joe DiMaggio.

	MINT	NRMT	EXC
COMPLETE SET (30)	20.00	9.00	2.50
COMMON CARD (1-30)	.75	.35	.09
☐ 1 Joe DiMaggio An American Hero	.75	.35	.09
☐ 2 Joe DiMaggio San Francisco Seals	.75	.35	.09
☐ 3 Joe DiMaggio Seals Farewell	.75	.35	.09
☐ 4 Joe DiMaggio First Game	.75	.35	.09
☐ 5 Joe DiMaggio The Rookie	.75	.35	.09
☐ 6 Joe DiMaggio Rookie All-Star	.75	.35	.09
☐ 7 Joe DiMaggio Fan Favorite	.75	.35	.09
☐ 8 Joe DiMaggio Teammates' Awe	.75	.35	.09
☐ 9 Joe DiMaggio Classic Swing	.75	.35	.09
☐ 10 Joe DiMaggio Joltin' Power	.75	.35	.09
☐ 11 Joe DiMaggio Bob Feller Rapid Robert Feller vs. Joltin' Joe	1.50	.70	.19
☐ 12 Joe DiMaggio The Complete Hitter	.75	.35	.09
☐ 13 Joe DiMaggio Makin' It Look Easy	.75	.35	.09
☐ 14 Joe DiMaggio Extra Swings	.75	.35	.09
☐ 15 Joe DiMaggio The Run Producer	.75	.35	.09
☐ 16 Joe DiMaggio Quiet Confidence	.75	.35	.09
☐ 17 Joe DiMaggio A Link to the Past	.75	.35	.09
☐ 18 Joe DiMaggio Sticks 'n' Bones	.75	.35	.09
☐ 19 Joe DiMaggio Center of Attention	.75	.35	.09
☐ 20 Joe DiMaggio The DiMaggio Mystique	.75	.35	.09
☐ 21 Joe DiMaggio Joe McCarthy MG	1.00	.45	.12
☐ 22 Joe DiMaggio World War II	.75	.35	.09
☐ 23 Joe DiMaggio Fearless Baserunner	.75	.35	.09
☐ 24 Joe DiMaggio The Summer of '41	.75	.35	.09
☐ 25 Joe DiMaggio Career Statistics	.75	.35	.09
☐ 26 Joe DiMaggio No. 45	.75	.35	.09
☐ 27 Joe DiMaggio Chasing (Babe) Ruth	.75	.35	.09
☐ 28 Joe DiMaggio The Final Season	.75	.35	.09
☐ 29 Joe DiMaggio Retirement	.75	.35	.09
☐ 30 Joe DiMaggio Baseball's Greatest Living Player	.75	.35	.09

1993 Pinnacle DiMaggio Autographs

Joe DiMaggio personally signed a total of 9,000 cards, and one autographed card from this five-card set was randomly inserted in selected 30-card boxed 1993 Pinnacle Joe DiMaggio hobby sets. These five autographed cards are slightly smaller (narrower) than standard size and feature white-bordered black-and-white action shots from DiMaggio's career that place special emphasis on the skills that made him great. DiMaggio's signature appears below the photo within the wide white lower margin.

	MINT	NRMT	EXC
COMPLETE SET (5)	1500.00	700.00	190.00
COMMON CARD (1-5)	300.00	135.00	38.00
☐ 1 Joe DiMaggio Spring 1936	300.00	135.00	38.00
☐ 2 Joe DiMaggio Joltin' Joe	300.00	135.00	38.00
☐ 3 Joe DiMaggio The Streak	300.00	135.00	38.00
☐ 4 Joe DiMaggio Opening Day	300.00	135.00	38.00
☐ 5 Joe DiMaggio Ebbets Field	300.00	135.00	38.00

1993 Pinnacle Home Run Club

This 48-card boxed standard-size set features players with outstanding home run statistics. Each set contains a certificate of authenticity card that verifies the set is one of 200,000 sets produced and includes the set number printed on a white bar. The checklist is printed on an outer sleeve that encases the black hinged box. The black fronts display an action photo cut-out that is superimposed over the initials "HR" in multi-colored foil. The words "Home Run" are printed over the "H" of the "HR". The card has an inner gold border with the player's name in a gold bordered box over the picture at the bottom. The silver-bordered backs carry descriptive career highlights on a black background with a ghosted HR logo.

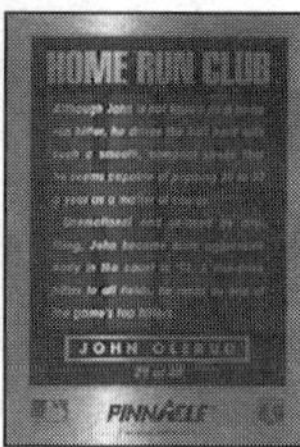

	MINT	NRMT	EXC
COMPLETE SET (48)	25.00	11.00	3.10
COMMON CARD (1-48)	.25	.11	.03

	MINT	NRMT	EXC
□ 1 Juan Gonzalez	2.50	1.10	.30
□ 2 Fred McGriff	.50	.23	.06
□ 3 Cecil Fielder	.50	.23	.06
□ 4 Barry Bonds	1.00	.45	.12
□ 5 Albert Belle	2.50	1.10	.30
□ 6 Gary Sheffield	.75	.35	.09
□ 7 Joe Carter	.50	.23	.06
□ 8 Mark McGwire	1.50	.70	.19
□ 9 Darren Daulton	.35	.16	.04
□ 10 Jose Canseco	.60	.25	.07
□ 11 Dave Hollins	.25	.11	.03
□ 12 Ryne Sandberg	1.50	.70	.19
□ 13 Ken Griffey Jr.	5.00	2.20	.60
□ 14 Larry Walker	.50	.23	.06
□ 15 Rob Deer	.25	.11	.03
□ 16 Andre Dawson	.35	.16	.04
□ 17 Frank Thomas	5.00	2.20	.60
□ 18 Mickey Tettleton	.25	.11	.03
□ 19 Charlie Hayes	.25	.11	.03
□ 20 Ron Gant	.35	.16	.04
□ 21 Rickey Henderson	.60	.25	.07
□ 22 Matt Williams	.50	.23	.06
□ 23 Kevin Mitchell	.25	.11	.03
□ 24 Robin Ventura	.50	.23	.06
□ 25 Dean Palmer	.35	.16	.04
□ 26 Mike Piazza	3.00	1.35	.35
□ 27 J.T. Snow	.50	.23	.06
□ 28 Jeff Bagwell	2.50	1.10	.30
□ 29 John Olerud	.35	.16	.04
□ 30 Greg Vaughn	.35	.16	.04
□ 31 Dave Justice	.50	.23	.06
□ 32 Dave Winfield	.50	.23	.06
□ 33 Danny Tartabull	.25	.11	.03
□ 34 Eric Anthony	.25	.11	.03
□ 35 Eddie Murray	1.25	.55	.16
□ 36 Jay Buhner	.60	.25	.07
□ 37 Derek Bell	.35	.16	.04
□ 38 Will Clark	.75	.35	.09
□ 39 Carlos Baerga	.35	.16	.04
□ 40 Mo Vaughn	1.25	.55	.16
□ 41 Bobby Bonilla	.35	.16	.04
□ 42 Tim Salmon	.75	.35	.09
□ 43 Bo Jackson	.35	.16	.04
□ 44 Howard Johnson	.25	.11	.03
□ 45 Kent Hrbek	.25	.11	.03
□ 46 Ruben Sierra	.25	.11	.03
□ 47 Cal Ripken	4.00	1.80	.50
□ 48 Travis Fryman	.35	.16	.04

1994 Pinnacle Samples

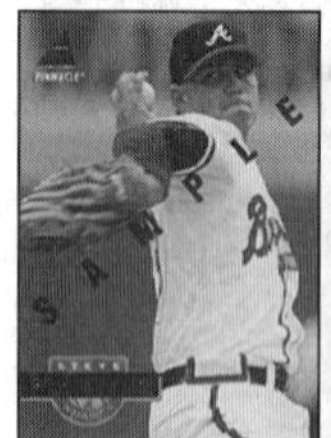

Sealed in a cello pack, these ten-or 11-card standard-size sample groups were issued to preview the new design of the 1994 Pinnacle baseball set. The fronts feature full-bleed color action player photos. In one of the upper corners the new Pinnacle logo appears, consisting of a gold foil triangular "A" with the brand name immediately below in small white lettering. Toward the bottom, the player's last name in gold foil on a black bar overlays a two-color emblem carrying his first name and his team name. On most of the backs, a ghosted version of the front picture forms the background for a player cutout, biography and statistics. Both sides of the cards have "SAMPLE" stenciled across them. The ten-card set was the retail version whereas the 11-card set was for the hobby. The hobby and retail versions are only distinguishable after opening by "Hobby Edition" or "Retail Edition" printed on the title card and the inclusion of an eleventh card, Paul Molitor in the hobby samples set. The cards are numbered in a baseball icon at the upper right. Also a two-card sample strip consisting of Olerud and Alou cards was issued.

	MINT	NRMT	EXC
COMPLETE SET (12)	9.00	4.00	1.10
COMMON CARD	.25	.11	.03

	MINT	NRMT	EXC
□ 2 Carlos Baerga	1.00	.45	.12
□ 3 Sammy Sosa	.75	.35	.09
□ 5 John Olerud	.50	.23	.06
□ 7 Moises Alou	.50	.23	.06
□ 8 Steve Avery	.25	.11	.03
□ 10 Cecil Fielder	.50	.23	.06
□ 11 Greg Maddux	2.00	.90	.25
□ 269 Jeff Granger	.25	.11	.03
□ TR1 Paul Molitor Tribute	2.00	.90	.25
□ NNO Title card Hobby Edition (Pinnacle ad)	.25	.11	.03
□ NNO Title card Retail Edition (Pinnacle ad)	.25	.11	.03
□ NNO Jeff Granger 1994 Museum Collection	1.00	.45	.12

1994 Pinnacle

The 540-card 1994 Pinnacle standard-size set was issued in two series of 270. Cards were issued in hobby and retail foil-wrapped packs. The card fronts feature full-bleed color action player photos with a small foil logo and players name at the base. Subsets include Rookie Prospects (224-261) and Draft Picks (262-270/430-438). Notable Rookie Cards include Derrek Lee, Chan Ho Park and Billy Wagner.

	MINT	NRMT	EXC
COMPLETE SET (540)	30.00	13.50	3.70
COMPLETE SERIES 1 (270)	15.00	6.75	1.85
COMPLETE SERIES 2 (270)	15.00	6.75	1.85
COMMON CARD (1-540)	.10	.05	.01

	MINT	NRMT	EXC
□ 1 Frank Thomas	2.50	1.10	.30
□ 2 Carlos Baerga	.25	.11	.03
□ 3 Sammy Sosa	.50	.23	.06
□ 4 Tony Gwynn	1.00	.45	.12
□ 5 John Olerud	.10	.05	.01
□ 6 Ryne Sandberg	.60	.25	.07
□ 7 Moises Alou	.25	.11	.03
□ 8 Steve Avery	.25	.11	.03
□ 9 Tim Salmon	.50	.23	.06
□ 10 Cecil Fielder	.25	.11	.03
□ 11 Greg Maddux	1.50	.70	.19
□ 12 Barry Larkin	.50	.23	.06
□ 13 Mike Devereaux	.10	.05	.01
□ 14 Charlie Hayes	.10	.05	.01
□ 15 Albert Belle	1.00	.45	.12
□ 16 Andy Van Slyke	.25	.11	.03
□ 17 Mo Vaughn	.60	.25	.07
□ 18 Brian McRae	.25	.11	.03
□ 19 Cal Eldred	.10	.05	.01
□ 20 Craig Biggio	.25	.11	.03
□ 21 Kirby Puckett	1.00	.45	.12
□ 22 Derek Bell	.25	.11	.03
□ 23 Don Mattingly	1.25	.55	.16
□ 24 John Burkett	.10	.05	.01
□ 25 Roger Clemens	.50	.23	.06
□ 26 Barry Bonds	.60	.25	.07
□ 27 Paul Molitor	.50	.23	.06
□ 28 Mike Piazza	1.50	.70	.19
□ 29 Robin Ventura	.25	.11	.03
□ 30 Jeff Conine	.25	.11	.03
□ 31 Wade Boggs	.50	.23	.06
□ 32 Dennis Eckersley	.25	.11	.03
□ 33 Bobby Bonilla	.25	.11	.03
□ 34 Lenny Dykstra	.25	.11	.03
□ 35 Manny Alexander	.10	.05	.01
□ 36 Ray Lankford	.25	.11	.03
□ 37 Greg Vaughn	.50	.23	.06
□ 38 Chuck Finley	.10	.05	.01
□ 39 Todd Benzinger	.10	.05	.01
□ 40 Dave Justice	.50	.23	.06
□ 41 Rob Dibble	.10	.05	.01
□ 42 Tom Henke	.10	.05	.01
□ 43 David Nied	.10	.05	.01
□ 44 Sandy Alomar Jr.	.25	.11	.03
□ 45 Pete Harnisch	.10	.05	.01
□ 46 Jeff Russell	.10	.05	.01
□ 47 Terry Mulholland	.10	.05	.01
□ 48 Kevin Appier	.25	.11	.03
□ 49 Randy Tomlin	.10	.05	.01
□ 50 Cal Ripken Jr.	2.00	.90	.25
□ 51 Andy Benes	.25	.11	.03
□ 52 Jimmy Key	.25	.11	.03
□ 53 Kirt Manwaring	.10	.05	.01
□ 54 Kevin Tapani	.10	.05	.01
□ 55 Jose Guzman	.10	.05	.01
□ 56 Todd Stottlemyre	.10	.05	.01
□ 57 Jack McDowell	.25	.11	.03
□ 58 Orel Hershiser	.25	.11	.03
□ 59 Chris Hammond	.10	.05	.01
□ 60 Chris Nabholz	.10	.05	.01
□ 61 Ruben Sierra	.25	.11	.03
□ 62 Dwight Gooden	.25	.11	.03
□ 63 John Kruk	.25	.11	.03
□ 64 Omar Vizquel	.25	.11	.03
□ 65 Tim Naehring	.10	.05	.01
□ 66 Dwight Smith	.10	.05	.01
□ 67 Mickey Tettleton	.10	.05	.01
□ 68 J.T. Snow	.25	.11	.03
□ 69 Greg McMichael	.10	.05	.01
□ 70 Kevin Mitchell	.25	.11	.03
□ 71 Kevin Brown	.25	.11	.03
□ 72 Scott Cooper	.10	.05	.01
□ 73 Jim Thome	.60	.25	.07
□ 74 Joe Girardi	.10	.05	.01
□ 75 Eric Anthony	.10	.05	.01
□ 76 Orlando Merced	.25	.11	.03
□ 77 Felix Jose	.10	.05	.01
□ 78 Tommy Greene	.10	.05	.01
□ 79 Bernard Gilkey	.25	.11	.03
□ 80 Phil Plantier	.10	.05	.01
□ 81 Danny Tartabull	.10	.05	.01
□ 82 Trevor Wilson	.10	.05	.01
□ 83 Chuck Knoblauch	.50	.23	.06
□ 84 Rick Wilkins	.10	.05	.01
□ 85 Devon White	.10	.05	.01
□ 86 Lance Johnson	.25	.11	.03
□ 87 Eric Karros	.25	.11	.03
□ 88 Gary Sheffield	.50	.23	.06
□ 89 Wil Cordero	.25	.11	.03
□ 90 Ron Darling	.10	.05	.01
□ 91 Darren Daulton	.25	.11	.03
□ 92 Joe Orsulak	.10	.05	.01
□ 93 Steve Cooke	.10	.05	.01
□ 94 Darryl Hamilton	.10	.05	.01
□ 95 Aaron Sele	.25	.11	.03
□ 96 John Doherty	.10	.05	.01
□ 97 Gary DiSarcina	.10	.05	.01
□ 98 Jeff Blauser	.10	.05	.01
□ 99 John Smiley	.10	.05	.01
□ 100 Ken Griffey Jr.	2.50	1.10	.30
□ 101 Dean Palmer	.25	.11	.03
□ 102 Felix Fermin	.10	.05	.01
□ 103 Jerald Clark	.10	.05	.01
□ 104 Doug Drabek	.10	.05	.01
□ 105 Curt Schilling	.10	.05	.01
□ 106 Jeff Montgomery	.25	.11	.03
□ 107 Rene Arocha	.10	.05	.01
□ 108 Carlos Garcia	.10	.05	.01
□ 109 Wally Whitehurst	.10	.05	.01
□ 110 Jim Abbott	.10	.05	.01
□ 111 Royce Clayton	.25	.11	.03
□ 112 Chris Hoiles	.10	.05	.01
□ 113 Mike Morgan	.10	.05	.01
□ 114 Joe Magrane	.10	.05	.01
□ 115 Tom Candiotti	.10	.05	.01
□ 116 Ron Karkovice	.10	.05	.01
□ 117 Ryan Bowen	.10	.05	.01
□ 118 Rod Beck	.25	.11	.03
□ 119 John Wetteland	.25	.11	.03
□ 120 Terry Steinbach	.25	.11	.03
□ 121 Dave Hollins	.10	.05	.01
□ 122 Jeff Kent	.10	.05	.01
□ 123 Ricky Bones	.10	.05	.01
□ 124 Brian Jordan	.50	.23	.06
□ 125 Chad Kreuter	.10	.05	.01
□ 126 John Valentin	.25	.11	.03
□ 127 Hilly Hathaway	.10	.05	.01
□ 128 Wilson Alvarez	.25	.11	.03
□ 129 Tino Martinez	.25	.11	.03
□ 130 Rodney Bolton	.10	.05	.01
□ 131 David Segui	.10	.05	.01
□ 132 Wayne Kirby	.10	.05	.01
□ 133 Eric Young	.25	.11	.03
□ 134 Scott Servais	.10	.05	.01
□ 135 Scott Radinsky	.10	.05	.01
□ 136 Bret Barberie	.10	.05	.01
□ 137 John Roper	.10	.05	.01
□ 138 Ricky Gutierrez	.10	.05	.01
□ 139 Bernie Williams	.50	.23	.06
□ 140 Bud Black	.10	.05	.01
□ 141 Jose Vizcaino	.10	.05	.01
□ 142 Gerald Williams	.10	.05	.01
□ 143 Duane Ward	.10	.05	.01
□ 144 Danny Jackson	.10	.05	.01
□ 145 Allen Watson	.10	.05	.01
□ 146 Scott Fletcher	.10	.05	.01
□ 147 Delino DeShields	.10	.05	.01
□ 148 Shane Mack	.10	.05	.01
□ 149 Jim Eisenreich	.10	.05	.01
□ 150 Troy Neel	.10	.05	.01
□ 151 Jay Bell	.25	.11	.03
□ 152 B.J. Surhoff	.10	.05	.01
□ 153 Mark Whiten	.10	.05	.01
□ 154 Mike Henneman	.10	.05	.01
□ 155 Todd Hundley	.25	.11	.03
□ 156 Greg Myers	.10	.05	.01
□ 157 Ryan Klesko	.50	.23	.06
□ 158 Dave Fleming	.10	.05	.01
□ 159 Mickey Morandini	.10	.05	.01
□ 160 Blas Minor	.10	.05	.01
□ 161 Reggie Jefferson	.25	.11	.03
□ 162 David Hulse	.10	.05	.01
□ 163 Greg Swindell	.10	.05	.01
□ 164 Roberto Hernandez	.25	.11	.03
□ 165 Brady Anderson	.50	.23	.06
□ 166 Jack Armstrong	.10	.05	.01
□ 167 Phil Clark	.10	.05	.01
□ 168 Melido Perez	.10	.05	.01
□ 169 Darren Lewis	.10	.05	.01
□ 170 Sam Horn	.10	.05	.01
□ 171 Mike Harkey	.10	.05	.01
□ 172 Juan Guzman	.25	.11	.03
□ 173 Bob Natal	.10	.05	.01
□ 174 Deion Sanders	.50	.23	.06
□ 175 Carlos Quintana	.10	.05	.01
□ 176 Mel Rojas	.10	.05	.01
□ 177 Willie Banks	.10	.05	.01
□ 178 Ben Rivera	.10	.05	.01
□ 179 Kenny Lofton	.75	.35	.09
□ 180 Leo Gomez	.10	.05	.01
□ 181 Roberto Mejia	.10	.05	.01
□ 182 Mike Perez	.10	.05	.01
□ 183 Travis Fryman	.25	.11	.03
□ 184 Ben McDonald	.10	.05	.01
□ 185 Steve Frey	.10	.05	.01
□ 186 Kevin Young	.10	.05	.01
□ 187 Dave Magadan	.10	.05	.01
□ 188 Bobby Munoz	.10	.05	.01
□ 189 Pat Rapp	.10	.05	.01
□ 190 Jose Offerman	.10	.05	.01
□ 191 Vinny Castilla	.50	.23	.06
□ 192 Ivan Calderon	.10	.05	.01
□ 193 Ken Caminiti	.50	.23	.06
□ 194 Benji Gil	.10	.05	.01
□ 195 Chuck Carr	.10	.05	.01
□ 196 Derrick May	.10	.05	.01
□ 197 Pat Kelly	.10	.05	.01
□ 198 Jeff Brantley	.10	.05	.01
□ 199 Jose Lind	.10	.05	.01
□ 200 Steve Buechele	.10	.05	.01
□ 201 Wes Chamberlain	.10	.05	.01
□ 202 Eduardo Perez	.10	.05	.01
□ 203 Bret Saberhagen	.25	.11	.03
□ 204 Gregg Jefferies	.50	.23	.06
□ 205 Darrin Fletcher	.10	.05	.01
□ 206 Kent Hrbek	.25	.11	.03
□ 207 Kim Batiste	.10	.05	.01
□ 208 Jeff King	.25	.11	.03
□ 209 Donovan Osborne	.10	.05	.01
□ 210 Dave Nilsson	.25	.11	.03
□ 211 Al Martin	.10	.05	.01
□ 212 Mike Moore	.10	.05	.01
□ 213 Sterling Hitchcock	.25	.11	.03
□ 214 Geronimo Pena	.10	.05	.01
□ 215 Kevin Higgins	.10	.05	.01
□ 216 Norm Charlton	.10	.05	.01
□ 217 Don Slaught	.10	.05	.01
□ 218 Mitch Williams	.10	.05	.01
□ 219 Derek Lilliquist	.10	.05	.01
□ 220 Armando Reynoso	.10	.05	.01
□ 221 Kenny Rogers	.10	.05	.01
□ 222 Doug Jones	.10	.05	.01
□ 223 Luis Aquino	.10	.05	.01
□ 224 Mike Oquist	.10	.05	.01
□ 225 Darryl Scott	.10	.05	.01
□ 226 Kurt Abbott	.25	.11	.03
□ 227 Andy Tomberlin	.10	.05	.01
□ 228 Norberto Martin	.10	.05	.01
□ 229 Pedro Castellano	.10	.05	.01
□ 230 Curtis Pride	.25	.11	.03
□ 231 Jeff McNeely	.10	.05	.01
□ 232 Scott Lydy	.10	.05	.01
□ 233 Darren Oliver	.10	.05	.01
□ 234 Danny Bautista	.10	.05	.01
□ 235 Butch Huskey	.25	.11	.03
□ 236 Chipper Jones	2.00	.90	.25
□ 237 Eddie Zambrano	.10	.05	.01
□ 238 Domingo Jean	.10	.05	.01
□ 239 Javier Lopez	.50	.23	.06
□ 240 Nigel Wilson	.10	.05	.01
□ 241 Drew Denson	.10	.05	.01
□ 242 Raul Mondesi	.50	.23	.06
□ 243 Luis Ortiz	.10	.05	.01
□ 244 Manny Ramirez	.75	.35	.09
□ 245 Greg Blosser	.10	.05	.01
□ 246 Rondell White	.50	.23	.06
□ 247 Steve Karsay	.10	.05	.01
□ 248 Scott Stahoviak	.10	.05	.01
□ 249 Jose Valentin	.25	.11	.03
□ 250 Marc Newfield	.25	.11	.03
□ 251 Keith Kessinger	.10	.05	.01
□ 252 Carl Everett	.10	.05	.01
□ 253 John O'Donoghue	.10	.05	.01
□ 254 Turk Wendell	.10	.05	.01
□ 255 Scott Ruffcorn	.10	.05	.01
□ 256 Tony Tarasco	.10	.05	.01
□ 257 Andy Cook	.10	.05	.01
□ 258 Matt Mieske	.10	.05	.01
□ 259 Luis Lopez	.10	.05	.01
□ 260 Ramon Caraballo	.10	.05	.01
□ 261 Salomon Torres	.10	.05	.01
□ 262 Brooks Kieschnick	.50	.23	.06
□ 263 Daron Kirkreit	.25	.11	.03
□ 264 Bill Wagner	.75	.35	.09
□ 265 Matt Drews	1.00	.45	.12
□ 266 Scott Christman	.25	.11	.03
□ 267 Torii Hunter	.25	.11	.03
□ 268 Jamey Wright	.60	.25	.07
□ 269 Jeff Granger	.25	.11	.03

☐ 270 Trot Nixon	.50	.23	.06
☐ 271 Randy Myers	.10	.05	.01
☐ 272 Trevor Hoffman	.25	.11	.03
☐ 273 Bob Wickman	.10	.05	.01
☐ 274 Willie McGee	.10	.05	.01
☐ 275 Hipolito Pichardo	.10	.05	.01
☐ 276 Bobby Witt	.10	.05	.01
☐ 277 Gregg Olson	.10	.05	.01
☐ 278 Randy Johnson	.50	.23	.06
☐ 279 Robb Nen	.25	.11	.03
☐ 280 Paul O'Neill	.25	.11	.03
☐ 281 Lou Whitaker	.25	.11	.03
☐ 282 Chad Curtis	.10	.05	.01
☐ 283 Doug Henry	.10	.05	.01
☐ 284 Tom Glavine	.50	.23	.06
☐ 285 Mike Greenwell	.10	.05	.01
☐ 286 Roberto Kelly	.10	.05	.01
☐ 287 Roberto Alomar	.50	.23	.06
☐ 288 Charlie Hough	.10	.05	.01
☐ 289 Alex Fernandez	.25	.11	.03
☐ 290 Jeff Bagwell	1.00	.45	.12
☐ 291 Wally Joyner	.25	.11	.03
☐ 292 Andujar Cedeno	.10	.05	.01
☐ 293 Rick Aguilera	.10	.05	.01
☐ 294 Darryl Strawberry	.25	.11	.03
☐ 295 Mike Mussina	.50	.23	.06
☐ 296 Jeff Gardner	.10	.05	.01
☐ 297 Chris Gwynn	.10	.05	.01
☐ 298 Matt Williams	.50	.23	.06
☐ 299 Brent Gates	.10	.05	.01
☐ 300 Mark McGwire	.75	.35	.09
☐ 301 Jim Deshaies	.10	.05	.01
☐ 302 Edgar Martinez	.25	.11	.03
☐ 303 Danny Darwin	.10	.05	.01
☐ 304 Pat Meares	.10	.05	.01
☐ 305 Benito Santiago	.10	.05	.01
☐ 306 Jose Canseco	.50	.23	.06
☐ 307 Jim Gott	.10	.05	.01
☐ 308 Paul Sorrento	.10	.05	.01
☐ 309 Scott Kamieniecki	.10	.05	.01
☐ 310 Larry Walker	.50	.23	.06
☐ 311 Mark Langston	.25	.11	.03
☐ 312 John Jaha	.25	.11	.03
☐ 313 Stan Javier	.10	.05	.01
☐ 314 Hal Morris	.10	.05	.01
☐ 315 Robby Thompson	.10	.05	.01
☐ 316 Pat Hentgen	.25	.11	.03
☐ 317 Tom Gordon	.10	.05	.01
☐ 318 Joey Cora	.10	.05	.01
☐ 319 Luis Alicea	.10	.05	.01
☐ 320 Andre Dawson	.25	.11	.03
☐ 321 Darryl Kile	.10	.05	.01
☐ 322 Jose Rijo	.10	.05	.01
☐ 323 Luis Gonzalez	.10	.05	.01
☐ 324 Billy Ashley	.10	.05	.01
☐ 325 David Cone	.25	.11	.03
☐ 326 Bill Swift	.10	.05	.01
☐ 327 Phil Hiatt	.10	.05	.01
☐ 328 Craig Paquette	.10	.05	.01
☐ 329 Bob Welch	.10	.05	.01
☐ 330 Tony Phillips	.25	.11	.03
☐ 331 Archi Cianfrocco	.10	.05	.01
☐ 332 Dave Winfield	.50	.23	.06
☐ 333 David McCarty	.10	.05	.01
☐ 334 Al Leiter	.25	.11	.03
☐ 335 Tom Browning	.10	.05	.01
☐ 336 Mark Grace	.50	.23	.06
☐ 337 Jose Mesa	.25	.11	.03
☐ 338 Mike Stanley	.10	.05	.01
☐ 339 Roger McDowell	.10	.05	.01
☐ 340 Damion Easley	.10	.05	.01
☐ 341 Angel Miranda	.10	.05	.01
☐ 342 John Smoltz	.50	.23	.06
☐ 343 Jay Buhner	.50	.23	.06
☐ 344 Bryan Harvey	.10	.05	.01
☐ 345 Joe Carter	.25	.11	.03
☐ 346 Dante Bichette	.50	.23	.06
☐ 347 Jason Bere	.25	.11	.03
☐ 348 Frank Viola	.10	.05	.01
☐ 349 Ivan Rodriguez	.60	.25	.07
☐ 350 Juan Gonzalez	1.25	.55	.16
☐ 351 Steve Finley	.50	.23	.06
☐ 352 Mike Felder	.10	.05	.01
☐ 353 Ramon Martinez	.25	.11	.03
☐ 354 Greg Gagne	.10	.05	.01
☐ 355 Ken Hill	.10	.05	.01
☐ 356 Pedro Munoz	.10	.05	.01
☐ 357 Todd Van Poppel	.10	.05	.01
☐ 358 Marquis Grissom	.25	.11	.03
☐ 359 Milt Cuyler	.10	.05	.01
☐ 360 Reggie Sanders	.25	.11	.03
☐ 361 Scott Erickson	.10	.05	.01
☐ 362 Billy Hatcher	.10	.05	.01
☐ 363 Gene Harris	.10	.05	.01
☐ 364 Rene Gonzales	.10	.05	.01
☐ 365 Kevin Rogers	.10	.05	.01
☐ 366 Eric Plunk	.10	.05	.01
☐ 367 Todd Zeile	.10	.05	.01
☐ 368 John Franco	.10	.05	.01
☐ 369 Brett Butler	.25	.11	.03
☐ 370 Bill Spiers	.10	.05	.01
☐ 371 Terry Pendleton	.25	.11	.03
☐ 372 Chris Bosio	.10	.05	.01
☐ 373 Orestes Destrade	.10	.05	.01
☐ 374 Dave Stewart	.25	.11	.03
☐ 375 Darren Holmes	.10	.05	.01
☐ 376 Doug Strange	.10	.05	.01
☐ 377 Brian Turang	.10	.05	.01
☐ 378 Carl Willis	.10	.05	.01
☐ 379 Mark McLemore	.10	.05	.01
☐ 380 Bobby Jones	.25	.11	.03
☐ 381 Scott Sanders	.10	.05	.01
☐ 382 Kirk Rueter	.10	.05	.01
☐ 383 Randy Velarde	.10	.05	.01
☐ 384 Fred McGriff	.50	.23	.06
☐ 385 Charles Nagy	.25	.11	.03
☐ 386 Rich Amaral	.10	.05	.01
☐ 387 Geronimo Berroa	.25	.11	.03
☐ 388 Eric Davis	.25	.11	.03
☐ 389 Ozzie Smith	.60	.25	.07
☐ 390 Alex Arias	.10	.05	.01
☐ 391 Brad Ausmus	.10	.05	.01
☐ 392 Cliff Floyd	.50	.23	.06
☐ 393 Roger Salkeld	.10	.05	.01
☐ 394 Jim Edmonds	.50	.23	.06
☐ 395 Jeromy Burnitz	.10	.05	.01
☐ 396 Dave Staton	.10	.05	.01
☐ 397 Rob Butler	.10	.05	.01
☐ 398 Marcos Armas	.10	.05	.01
☐ 399 Darrell Whitmore	.10	.05	.01
☐ 400 Ryan Thompson	.10	.05	.01
☐ 401 Ross Powell	.10	.05	.01
☐ 402 Joe Oliver	.10	.05	.01
☐ 403 Paul Carey	.10	.05	.01
☐ 404 Bob Hamelin	.10	.05	.01
☐ 405 Chris Turner	.10	.05	.01
☐ 406 Nate Minchey	.10	.05	.01
☐ 407 Lonnie Maclin	.10	.05	.01
☐ 408 Harold Baines	.25	.11	.03
☐ 409 Brian Williams	.10	.05	.01
☐ 410 Johnny Ruffin	.10	.05	.01
☐ 411 Julian Tavarez	.25	.11	.03
☐ 412 Mark Hutton	.10	.05	.01
☐ 413 Carlos Delgado	.50	.23	.06
☐ 414 Chris Gomez	.10	.05	.01
☐ 415 Mike Hampton	.25	.11	.03
☐ 416 Alex Diaz	.10	.05	.01
☐ 417 Jeffrey Hammonds	.25	.11	.03
☐ 418 Jayhawk Owens	.10	.05	.01
☐ 419 J.R. Phillips	.10	.05	.01
☐ 420 Cory Bailey	.10	.05	.01
☐ 421 Denny Hocking	.10	.05	.01
☐ 422 Jon Shave	.10	.05	.01
☐ 423 Damon Buford	.10	.05	.01
☐ 424 Troy O'Leary	.10	.05	.01
☐ 425 Tripp Cromer	.10	.05	.01
☐ 426 Albie Lopez	.25	.11	.03
☐ 427 Tony Fernandez	.10	.05	.01
☐ 428 Ozzie Guillen	.10	.05	.01
☐ 429 Alan Trammell	.25	.11	.03
☐ 430 John Wasdin	.60	.25	.07
☐ 431 Marc Valdes	.25	.11	.03
☐ 432 Brian Anderson	.25	.11	.03
☐ 433 Matt Brunson	.25	.11	.03
☐ 434 Wayne Gomes	.25	.11	.03
☐ 435 Jay Powell	.25	.11	.03
☐ 436 Kirk Presley	.50	.23	.06
☐ 437 Jon Ratliff	.25	.11	.03
☐ 438 Derrek Lee	1.50	.70	.19
☐ 439 Tom Pagnozzi	.10	.05	.01
☐ 440 Kent Mercker	.10	.05	.01
☐ 441 Phil Leftwich	.10	.05	.01
☐ 442 Jamie Moyer	.10	.05	.01
☐ 443 John Flaherty	.10	.05	.01
☐ 444 Mark Wohlers	.25	.11	.03
☐ 445 Jose Bautista	.10	.05	.01
☐ 446 Andres Galarraga	.50	.23	.06
☐ 447 Mark Lemke	.10	.05	.01
☐ 448 Tim Wakefield	.10	.05	.01
☐ 449 Pat Listach	.10	.05	.01
☐ 450 Rickey Henderson	.50	.23	.06
☐ 451 Mike Gallego	.10	.05	.01
☐ 452 Bob Tewksbury	.10	.05	.01
☐ 453 Kirk Gibson	.25	.11	.03
☐ 454 Pedro Astacio	.10	.05	.01
☐ 455 Mike Lansing	.25	.11	.03
☐ 456 Sean Berry	.10	.05	.01
☐ 457 Bob Walk	.10	.05	.01
☐ 458 Chili Davis	.25	.11	.03
☐ 459 Ed Sprague	.25	.11	.03
☐ 460 Kevin Stocker	.10	.05	.01
☐ 461 Mike Stanton	.10	.05	.01
☐ 462 Tim Raines	.50	.23	.06
☐ 463 Mike Bordick	.10	.05	.01
☐ 464 David Wells	.10	.05	.01
☐ 465 Tim Laker	.10	.05	.01
☐ 466 Cory Snyder	.10	.05	.01
☐ 467 Alex Cole	.10	.05	.01
☐ 468 Pete Incaviglia	.10	.05	.01
☐ 469 Roger Pavlik	.10	.05	.01
☐ 470 Greg W. Harris	.10	.05	.01
☐ 471 Xavier Hernandez	.10	.05	.01
☐ 472 Erik Hanson	.10	.05	.01
☐ 473 Jesse Orosco	.10	.05	.01
☐ 474 Greg Colbrunn	.10	.05	.01
☐ 475 Harold Reynolds	.10	.05	.01
☐ 476 Greg A. Harris	.10	.05	.01
☐ 477 Pat Borders	.10	.05	.01
☐ 478 Melvin Nieves	.25	.11	.03
☐ 479 Mariano Duncan	.10	.05	.01
☐ 480 Greg Hibbard	.10	.05	.01
☐ 481 Tim Pugh	.10	.05	.01
☐ 482 Bobby Ayala	.10	.05	.01
☐ 483 Sid Fernandez	.10	.05	.01
☐ 484 Tim Wallach	.10	.05	.01
☐ 485 Randy Milligan	.10	.05	.01
☐ 486 Walt Weiss	.10	.05	.01
☐ 487 Matt Walbeck	.10	.05	.01
☐ 488 Mike Macfarlane	.10	.05	.01
☐ 489 Jerry Browne	.10	.05	.01
☐ 490 Chris Sabo	.10	.05	.01
☐ 491 Tim Belcher	.10	.05	.01
☐ 492 Spike Owen	.10	.05	.01
☐ 493 Rafael Palmeiro	.50	.23	.06
☐ 494 Brian Harper	.10	.05	.01
☐ 495 Eddie Murray	.60	.25	.07
☐ 496 Ellis Burks	.25	.11	.03
☐ 497 Karl Rhodes	.10	.05	.01
☐ 498 Otis Nixon	.10	.05	.01
☐ 499 Lee Smith	.25	.11	.03
☐ 500 Bip Roberts	.10	.05	.01
☐ 501 Pedro Martinez	.50	.23	.06
☐ 502 Brian Hunter	.10	.05	.01
☐ 503 Tyler Green	.10	.05	.01
☐ 504 Bruce Hurst	.10	.05	.01
☐ 505 Alex Gonzalez	.25	.11	.03
☐ 506 Mark Portugal	.10	.05	.01
☐ 507 Bob Ojeda	.10	.05	.01
☐ 508 Dave Henderson	.10	.05	.01
☐ 509 Bo Jackson	.25	.11	.03
☐ 510 Bret Boone	.25	.11	.03
☐ 511 Mark Eichhorn	.10	.05	.01
☐ 512 Luis Polonia	.10	.05	.01
☐ 513 Will Clark	.50	.23	.06
☐ 514 Dave Valle	.10	.05	.01
☐ 515 Dan Wilson	.25	.11	.03
☐ 516 Dennis Martinez	.25	.11	.03
☐ 517 Jim Leyritz	.10	.05	.01
☐ 518 Howard Johnson	.10	.05	.01
☐ 519 Jody Reed	.10	.05	.01
☐ 520 Julio Franco	.25	.11	.03
☐ 521 Jeff Reardon	.25	.11	.03
☐ 522 Willie Greene	.25	.11	.03
☐ 523 Shawon Dunston	.10	.05	.01
☐ 524 Keith Mitchell	.10	.05	.01
☐ 525 Rick Helling	.10	.05	.01
☐ 526 Mark Kiefer	.10	.05	.01
☐ 527 Chan Ho Park	.75	.35	.09
☐ 528 Tony Longmire	.10	.05	.01
☐ 529 Rich Becker	.25	.11	.03
☐ 530 Tim Hyers	.10	.05	.01
☐ 531 Darrin Jackson	.10	.05	.01
☐ 532 Jack Morris	.25	.11	.03
☐ 533 Rick White	.10	.05	.01
☐ 534 Mike Kelly	.10	.05	.01
☐ 535 James Mouton	.25	.11	.03
☐ 536 Steve Trachsel	.25	.11	.03
☐ 537 Tony Eusebio	.10	.05	.01
☐ 538 Kelly Stinnett	.10	.05	.01
☐ 539 Paul Spoljaric	.10	.05	.01
☐ 540 Darren Dreifort	.25	.11	.03
☐ SR1 C.Delgado Super Rook.	10.00	4.50	1.25

1994 Pinnacle Artist's Proofs

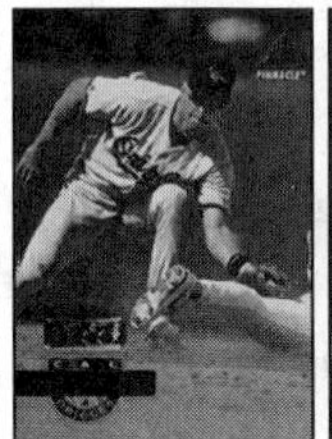

Randomly inserted at a rate of one in 26 hobby and retail packs, cards from this 540-card set parallel that of the basic Pinnacle issue. Each card is embossed with a gold-foil-stamped "Artist's Proof" logo just above the player name. The Pinnacle logo is also done in gold foil. Just 1,000 of each card were printed.

	MINT	NRMT	EXC
COMPLETE SET (540)	3000.00	1350.00	375.00
COMPLETE SERIES 1 (270)	2000.00	900.00	250.00
COMPLETE SERIES 2 (270)	1000.00	450.00	125.00
COMMON CARD (1-540)	2.50	1.10	.30

*STARS: 15X to 30X BASIC CARDS....
*YOUNG STARS: 10X to 20X BASIC CARDS

1994 Pinnacle Museum Collection

This 540-card set is a parallel dufex to that of the basic Pinnacle issue. They were randomly inserted at a rate of one in four hobby and retail packs. A Museum Collection logo replaces the anti-counterfeit device. Only 6,500 of each card were printed. Five cards (#'s 279, 313, 328, 382 and 387) were available only by mailing in a redemption card randomly seeded into packs.

	MINT	NRMT	EXC
COMPLETE SET (540)	800.00	350.00	100.00
COMPLETE SERIES 1 (270)	500.00	220.00	60.00
COMPLETE SERIES 2 (270)	300.00	135.00	38.00
COMMON CARD (1-540)	1.00	.45	.12
TRADE (279/313/328/382/387)	3.00	1.35	.35

*STARS: 6X TO 15X BASIC CARDS....
*YOUNG STARS: 5X TO 12X BASIC CARDS

1994 Pinnacle Rookie Team Pinnacle

These nine double-front standard-size cards of the "Rookie Team Pinnacle" set feature a top AL and a top NL rookie prospect by position. The insertion rate for these is one per 48 packs. These special portrait cards were painted by artists Christopher Greco and Ron DeFelice. The front features the National League player and card number. Both sides contain a gold Rookie Team Pinnacle logo.

	MINT	NRMT	EXC
COMPLETE SET (9)	90.00	40.00	11.00
COMMON PAIR (1-9)	5.00	2.20	.60
☐ 1 Carlos Delgado Javier Lopez	12.00	5.50	1.50
☐ 2 Bob Hamelin J.R. Phillips	5.00	2.20	.60
☐ 3 Jon Shave Keith Kessinger	5.00	2.20	.60
☐ 4 Luis Ortiz Butch Huskey	10.00	4.50	1.25
☐ 5 Kurt Abbott Chipper Jones	40.00	18.00	5.00
☐ 6 Manny Ramirez Rondell White	20.00	9.00	2.50
☐ 7 Jeffrey Hammonds Cliff Floyd	10.00	4.50	1.25
☐ 8 Marc Newfield Nigel Wilson	10.00	4.50	1.25
☐ 9 Mark Hutton Salomon Torres	5.00	2.20	.60

1994 Pinnacle Run Creators

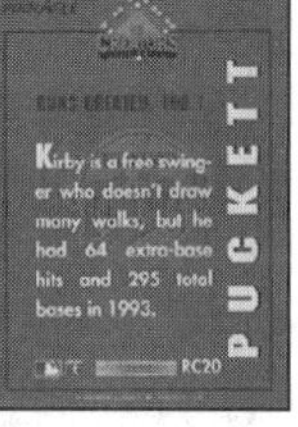

Randomly inserted at an approximate rate of one in four jumbo packs, this 22-card standard-size set spotlights top run producers. The player stands out from a solid background on front. His last name and the Pinnacle logo run up the right border in gold foil. The Run Creators logo is at bottom center. A solid colored back contains the team logo as background to statistical highlights including runs created.

	MINT	NRMT	EXC
COMPLETE SET (44)	150.00	70.00	19.00
COMPLETE SERIES 1 (22)	90.00	40.00	11.00
COMPLETE SERIES 2 (22)	60.00	27.00	7.50
COMMON CARD (RC1-RC44)	1.00	.45	.12
☐ RC1 John Olerud	1.50	.70	.19
☐ RC2 Frank Thomas	20.00	9.00	2.50
☐ RC3 Ken Griffey Jr.	20.00	9.00	2.50
☐ RC4 Paul Molitor	4.00	1.80	.50
☐ RC5 Rafael Palmeiro	2.00	.90	.25
☐ RC6 Roberto Alomar	4.00	1.80	.50
☐ RC7 Juan Gonzalez	10.00	4.50	1.25
☐ RC8 Albert Belle	8.00	3.60	1.00
☐ RC9 Travis Fryman	1.50	.70	.19
☐ RC10 Rickey Henderson	2.00	.90	.25

☐ RC11 Tony Phillips	1.00	.45	.12
☐ RC12 Mo Vaughn	5.00	2.20	.60
☐ RC13 Tim Salmon	3.00	1.35	.35
☐ RC14 Kenny Lofton	6.00	2.70	.75
☐ RC15 Carlos Baerga	1.50	.70	.19
☐ RC16 Greg Vaughn	2.00	.90	.25
☐ RC17 Jay Buhner	2.00	.90	.25
☐ RC18 Chris Hoiles	1.00	.45	.12
☐ RC19 Mickey Tettleton	1.50	.70	.19
☐ RC20 Kirby Puckett	8.00	3.60	1.00
☐ RC21 Danny Tartabull	1.50	.70	.19
☐ RC22 Devon White	1.50	.70	.19
☐ RC23 Barry Bonds	5.00	2.20	.60
☐ RC24 Lenny Dykstra	1.50	.70	.19
☐ RC25 John Kruk	1.50	.70	.19
☐ RC26 Fred McGriff	2.00	.90	.25
☐ RC27 Gregg Jefferies	2.00	.90	.25
☐ RC28 Mike Piazza	12.00	5.50	1.50
☐ RC29 Jeff Blauser	1.00	.45	.12
☐ RC30 Andres Galarraga	2.00	.90	.25
☐ RC31 Darren Daulton	1.50	.70	.19
☐ RC32 Dave Justice	1.50	.70	.19
☐ RC33 Craig Biggio	1.50	.70	.19
☐ RC34 Mark Grace	2.00	.90	.25
☐ RC35 Tony Gwynn	8.00	3.60	1.00
☐ RC36 Jeff Bagwell	8.00	3.60	1.00
☐ RC37 Jay Bell	1.00	.45	.12
☐ RC38 Marquis Grissom	1.50	.70	.19
☐ RC39 Matt Williams	2.00	.90	.25
☐ RC40 Charlie Hayes	1.00	.45	.12
☐ RC41 Dante Bichette	2.00	.90	.25
☐ RC42 Bernard Gilkey	2.00	.90	.25
☐ RC43 Brett Butler	1.50	.70	.19
☐ RC44 Rick Wilkins	1.00	.45	.12

1994 Pinnacle Team Pinnacle

Identical in design to the Rookie Team Pinnacle set, these double-front cards feature top players from each of the nine positions. Randomly inserted in second series hobby and retail packs at a rate of one in 48, these special portrait cards were painted by artists Christopher Greco and Ron DeFelice. The front features the National League player and card number. Both sides contain a gold Team Pinnacle logo.

	MINT	NRMT	EXC
COMPLETE SET (9)	200.00	90.00	25.00
COMMON PAIR (1-9)	8.00	3.60	1.00
☐ 1 Jeff Bagwell Frank Thomas	60.00	27.00	7.50
☐ 2 Carlos Baerga Robby Thompson	12.00	5.50	1.50
☐ 3 Matt Williams Dean Palmer	8.00	3.60	1.00
☐ 4 Cal Ripken Jr. Jay Bell	35.00	16.00	4.40
☐ 5 Ivan Rodriguez Mike Piazza	30.00	13.50	3.70
☐ 6 Lenny Dykstra Ken Griffey Jr.	40.00	18.00	5.00
☐ 7 Juan Gonzalez Barry Bonds	30.00	13.50	3.70
☐ 8 Tim Salmon Dave Justice	8.00	3.60	1.00
☐ 9 Greg Maddux Jack McDowell	30.00	13.50	3.70

1994 Pinnacle Tribute

Randomly inserted in hobby packs at a rate of one in 18, this 18-card set was issued in two series of nine. Showcasing some of the top superstar veterans, the fronts have a color player photo with "Tribute" up the left border in a black stripe. The player's name appears at the bottom with a notation given to describe the player. The backs are primarily black with a close-up photo of the player. The cards are numbered with a TR prefix.

	MINT	NRMT	EXC
COMPLETE SET (18)	100.00	45.00	12.50
COMPLETE SERIES 1 (9)	30.00	13.50	3.70
COMPLETE SERIES 2 (9)	70.00	32.00	8.75
COMMON CARD (TR1-TR18)	1.00	.45	.12
☐ TR1 Paul Molitor	4.00	1.80	.50
☐ TR2 Jim Abbott	1.50	.70	.19
☐ TR3 Dave Winfield	2.50	1.10	.30
☐ TR4 Bo Jackson	1.50	.70	.19
☐ TR5 David Justice	1.50	.70	.19
☐ TR6 Len Dykstra	1.50	.70	.19
☐ TR7 Mike Piazza	12.00	5.50	1.50
☐ TR8 Barry Bonds	5.00	2.20	.60
☐ TR9 Randy Johnson	3.00	1.35	.35
☐ TR10 Ozzie Smith	5.00	2.20	.60
☐ TR11 Mark Whiten	1.00	.45	.12
☐ TR12 Greg Maddux	12.00	5.50	1.50
☐ TR13 Cal Ripken Jr.	15.00	6.75	1.85
☐ TR14 Frank Thomas	20.00	9.00	2.50
☐ TR15 Juan Gonzalez	10.00	4.50	1.25
☐ TR16 Roberto Alomar	4.00	1.80	.50
☐ TR17 Ken Griffey Jr.	20.00	9.00	2.50
☐ TR18 Lee Smith	1.50	.70	.19

1994 Pinnacle The Naturals

These 25 standard-size cards were issued as a boxed set and were printed with Pinnacle's Dufex process, which imparts a metallic appearance to the cards. A certificate of authenticity that carries the set's production number out of 100,000 produced was included with every boxed set. The borderless fronts feature embossed player photos against a textured-foil background. The hand-etched background is enhanced with transparent inks. The backs picture the player on a background of nature photography, including lightning, blue skies and clouds.

	MINT	NRMT	EXC
COMPLETE SET (25)	20.00	9.00	2.50
COMMON CARD (1-25)	.15	.07	.02
☐ 1 Frank Thomas	4.00	1.80	.50
☐ 2 Barry Bonds	1.00	.45	.12
☐ 3 Ken Griffey Jr.	4.00	1.80	.50
☐ 4 Juan Gonzalez	2.00	.90	.25
☐ 5 David Justice	.40	.18	.05
☐ 6 Albert Belle	2.00	.90	.25
☐ 7 Kenny Lofton	1.00	.45	.12
☐ 8 Roberto Alomar	.60	.25	.07
☐ 9 Tim Salmon	.60	.25	.07
☐ 10 Randy Johnson	.75	.35	.09
☐ 11 Kirby Puckett	2.00	.90	.25
☐ 12 Tony Gwynn	1.50	.70	.19
☐ 13 Fred McGriff	.50	.23	.06
☐ 14 Ryne Sandberg	1.00	.45	.12
☐ 15 Greg Maddux	2.50	1.10	.30
☐ 16 Matt Williams	.60	.25	.07
☐ 17 Lenny Dykstra	.15	.07	.02
☐ 18 Gary Sheffield	.60	.25	.07
☐ 19 Mike Piazza	2.50	1.10	.30
☐ 20 Dean Palmer	.15	.07	.02
☐ 21 Travis Fryman	.30	.14	.04
☐ 22 Carlos Baerga	.60	.25	.07
☐ 23 Cal Ripken	2.50	1.10	.30
☐ 24 John Olerud	.30	.14	.04
☐ 25 Roger Clemens	.75	.35	.09
☐ P18 Gary Sheffield Promo	1.00	.45	.12

1994 Pinnacle New Generation

This 25-card standard-size set spotlights 25 of the most prominent prospects to hit the major leagues. Just 100,000 sets were produced, and a certificate of authenticity carrying the set serial number was printed on the back of the display box. The fronts feature borderless color action shots, with the player's name appearing at the bottom along with icons of a baseball and bats. The back displays another borderless color player action shot, with the player's name appearing across the picture. The picture is ghosted on the left side. This ghosted band carries the player's position, biography, and career highlights.

	MINT	NRMT	EXC
COMPLETE SET (25)	5.00	2.20	.60
COMMON CARD (NG1-NG25)	.10	.05	.01
☐ NG1 Tim Salmon	.50	.23	.06
☐ NG2 Mike Piazza	2.50	1.10	.30
☐ NG3 Jason Bere	.25	.11	.03
☐ NG4 Jeffrey Hammonds	.25	.11	.03
☐ NG5 Aaron Sele	.25	.11	.03
☐ NG6 Salomon Torres	.10	.05	.01
☐ NG7 Wilfredo Cordero	.20	.09	.03
☐ NG8 Allen Watson	.10	.05	.01
☐ NG9 J.T. Snow	.10	.05	.01
☐ NG10 Cliff Floyd	.30	.14	.04
☐ NG11 Jeff McNeely	.10	.05	.01
☐ NG12 Butch Huskey	.20	.09	.03
☐ NG13 J.R. Phillips	.10	.05	.01
☐ NG14 Bobby Jones	.25	.11	.03
☐ NG15 Javier Lopez	.50	.23	.06
☐ NG16 Scott Ruffcorn	.10	.05	.01
☐ NG17 Manny Ramirez	1.00	.45	.12
☐ NG18 Carlos Delgado	.40	.18	.05
☐ NG19 Rondell White	.40	.18	.05
☐ NG20 Chipper Jones	2.00	.90	.25
☐ NG21 Billy Ashley	.25	.11	.03
☐ NG22 Nigel Wilson	.10	.05	.01
☐ NG23 Jeromy Burnitz	.10	.05	.01
☐ NG24 Danny Bautista	.10	.05	.01
☐ NG25 Darrell Whitmore	.10	.05	.01
☐ PNG10 Cliff Floyd Promo	1.00	.45	.12

1994 Pinnacle Power Surge

These 25 standard-size cards came in a boxed set from Pinnacle and feature on their fronts borderless color action shots. The player's last name appears in gold foil at the top. His team name in white lettering also appears at the top within a marbleized stripe. On the right side, the marbleized back carries a circular player head shot at the top, followed by his name, team name, statistics, and career highlights. On the left are biography and a small action shot.

	MINT	NRMT	EXC
COMPLETE SET (25)	5.00	2.20	.60
COMMON CARD (1-25)	.10	.05	.01
☐ PS1 David Justice	.25	.11	.03
☐ PS2 Chris Hoiles	.10	.05	.01
☐ PS3 Mo Vaughn	.40	.18	.05
☐ PS4 Tim Salmon	.25	.11	.03
☐ PS5 J.T. Snow	.10	.05	.01
☐ PS6 Frank Thomas	1.50	.70	.19
☐ PS7 Sammy Sosa	.30	.14	.04
☐ PS8 Rick Wilkins	.10	.05	.01
☐ PS9 Robin Ventura	.25	.11	.03
☐ PS10 Reggie Sanders	.25	.11	.03
☐ PS11 Albert Belle	.75	.35	.09
☐ PS12 Carlos Baerga	.30	.14	.04
☐ PS13 Manny Ramirez	.50	.23	.06
☐ PS14 Travis Fryman	.25	.11	.03
☐ PS15 Gary Sheffield	.30	.14	.04
☐ PS16 Jeff Bagwell	.75	.35	.09
☐ PS17 Mike Piazza	1.00	.45	.12
☐ PS18 Eric Karros	.25	.11	.03
☐ PS19 Cliff Floyd	.10	.05	.01
☐ PS20 Mark Whiten	.10	.05	.01
☐ PS21 Phil Plantier	.10	.05	.01
☐ PS22 Derek Bell	.25	.11	.03
☐ PS23 Ken Griffey Jr.	1.50	.70	.19
☐ PS24 Juan Gonzalez	.75	.35	.09
☐ PS25 Dean Palmer	.10	.05	.01
☐ PS12P Carlos Baerga Promo	1.00	.45	.12

1995 Pinnacle Samples

The 1995 Pinnacle Sample set contains nine standard-size cards. The full-bleed color player photos on the front have gold highlighting that looks like the stitching of a baseball. The horizontal backs feature two color photos, biography, player profile, and statistics. The samples are easily distinguished from their regular issue counterparts by zeros in the stat lines. Also the disclaimer "SAMPLE" is diagonally printed across the front and the back.

	MINT	NRMT	EXC
COMPLETE SET (9)	10.00	4.50	1.25
COMMON CARD	.50	.23	.06
☐ 16 Mickey Morandini	.50	.23	.06
☐ 119 Gary Sheffield	1.50	.70	.19

☐ 122 Ivan Rodriguez	2.00	.90	.25
☐ 132 Alex Rodriguez	2.50	1.10	.30
☐ 208 Bo Jackson	.75	.35	.09
☐ 223 Jose Rijo	.50	.23	.06
☐ 224 Ryan Klesko	1.00	.45	.12
☐ US22 Wil Cordero	1.50	.70	.19
☐ NNO Title Card	.50	.23	.06

1995 Pinnacle

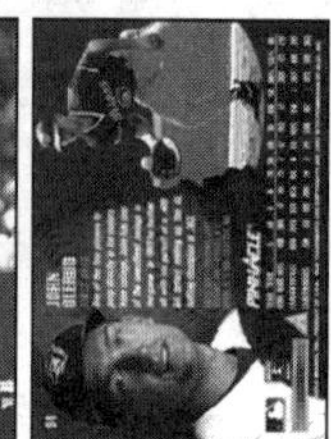

This 450-card standard-size set was issued in two series of 225 cards. They were released in 12-card packs, 24 packs to a box and 18 boxes in a case. The full-bleed fronts feature action photos. The player's last name is printed in black ink against a dramatic gold foil background at the base of the card. There are no notable Rookie Cards in this set.

	MINT	NRMT	EXC
COMPLETE SET (450)	40.00	18.00	5.00
COMPLETE SERIES 1 (225)	20.00	9.00	2.50
COMPLETE SERIES 2 (225)	20.00	9.00	2.50
COMMON CARD (1-450)	.10	.05	.01
☐ 1 Jeff Bagwell	1.25	.55	.16
☐ 2 Roger Clemens	.60	.25	.07
☐ 3 Mark Whiten	.10	.05	.01
☐ 4 Shawon Dunston	.10	.05	.01
☐ 5 Bobby Bonilla	.25	.11	.03
☐ 6 Kevin Tapani	.10	.05	.01
☐ 7 Eric Karros	.25	.11	.03
☐ 8 Cliff Floyd	.25	.11	.03
☐ 9 Pat Kelly	.10	.05	.01
☐ 10 Jeffrey Hammonds	.25	.11	.03
☐ 11 Jeff Conine	.25	.11	.03
☐ 12 Fred McGriff	.50	.23	.06
☐ 13 Chris Bosio	.10	.05	.01
☐ 14 Mike Mussina	.60	.25	.07
☐ 15 Danny Bautista	.10	.05	.01
☐ 16 Mickey Morandini	.10	.05	.01
☐ 17 Chuck Finley	.25	.11	.03
☐ 18 Jim Thome	.60	.25	.07
☐ 19 Luis Ortiz	.10	.05	.01
☐ 20 Walt Weiss	.10	.05	.01
☐ 21 Don Mattingly	1.50	.70	.19
☐ 22 Bob Hamelin	.10	.05	.01
☐ 23 Melido Perez	.10	.05	.01
☐ 24 Keith Mitchell	.10	.05	.01
☐ 25 John Smoltz	.50	.23	.06
☐ 26 Hector Carrasco	.10	.05	.01
☐ 27 Pat Hentgen	.25	.11	.03
☐ 28 Derrick May	.10	.05	.01
☐ 29 Mike Kingery	.10	.05	.01
☐ 30 Chuck Carr	.10	.05	.01
☐ 31 Billy Ashley	.10	.05	.01
☐ 32 Todd Hundley	.25	.11	.03
☐ 33 Luis Gonzalez	.10	.05	.01
☐ 34 Marquis Grissom	.25	.11	.03
☐ 35 Jeff King	.25	.11	.03
☐ 36 Eddie Williams	.10	.05	.01
☐ 37 Tom Pagnozzi	.10	.05	.01
☐ 38 Chris Hoiles	.10	.05	.01
☐ 39 Sandy Alomar Jr.	.10	.05	.01
☐ 40 Mike Greenwell	.10	.05	.01
☐ 41 Lance Johnson	.25	.11	.03
☐ 42 Junior Felix	.10	.05	.01
☐ 43 Felix Jose	.10	.05	.01
☐ 44 Scott Leius	.10	.05	.01
☐ 45 Ruben Sierra	.25	.11	.03
☐ 46 Kevin Seitzer	.10	.05	.01
☐ 47 Wade Boggs	.50	.23	.06
☐ 48 Reggie Jefferson	.25	.11	.03
☐ 49 Jose Canseco	.50	.23	.06
☐ 50 David Justice	.50	.23	.06
☐ 51 John Smiley	.10	.05	.01
☐ 52 Joe Carter	.25	.11	.03
☐ 53 Rick Wilkins	.10	.05	.01
☐ 54 Ellis Burks	.25	.11	.03
☐ 55 Dave Weathers	.10	.05	.01
☐ 56 Pedro Astacio	.10	.05	.01

☐ 57 Ryan Thompson .10 .05 .01
☐ 58 James Mouton .10 .05 .01
☐ 59 Mel Rojas .10 .05 .01
☐ 60 Orlando Merced .10 .05 .01
☐ 61 Matt Williams .50 .23 .06
☐ 62 Bernard Gilkey .25 .11 .03
☐ 63 J.R. Phillips .10 .05 .01
☐ 64 Lee Smith .25 .11 .03
☐ 65 Jim Edmonds .50 .23 .06
☐ 66 Darrin Jackson .10 .05 .01
☐ 67 Scott Cooper .10 .05 .01
☐ 68 Ron Karkovice .10 .05 .01
☐ 69 Chris Gomez .10 .05 .01
☐ 70 Kevin Appier .25 .11 .03
☐ 71 Bobby Jones .25 .11 .03
☐ 72 Doug Drabek .10 .05 .01
☐ 73 Matt Mieske .25 .11 .03
☐ 74 Sterling Hitchcock .25 .11 .03
☐ 75 John Valentin .25 .11 .03
☐ 76 Reggie Sanders .25 .11 .03
☐ 77 Wally Joyner .25 .11 .03
☐ 78 Turk Wendell .10 .05 .01
☐ 79 Charlie Hayes .10 .05 .01
☐ 80 Bret Barberie .10 .05 .01
☐ 81 Troy Neel .10 .05 .01
☐ 82 Ken Caminiti .50 .23 .06
☐ 83 Milt Thompson .10 .05 .01
☐ 84 Paul Sorrento .10 .05 .01
☐ 85 Trevor Hoffman .25 .11 .03
☐ 86 Jay Bell .25 .11 .03
☐ 87 Mark Portugal .10 .05 .01
☐ 88 Sid Fernandez .10 .05 .01
☐ 89 Charles Nagy .25 .11 .03
☐ 90 Jeff Montgomery .25 .11 .03
☐ 91 Chuck Knoblauch .50 .23 .06
☐ 92 Jeff Frye .10 .05 .01
☐ 93 Tony Gwynn 1.25 .55 .16
☐ 94 John Olerud .10 .05 .01
☐ 95 David Nied .10 .05 .01
☐ 96 Chris Hammond .10 .05 .01
☐ 97 Edgar Martinez .25 .11 .03
☐ 98 Kevin Stocker .10 .05 .01
☐ 99 Jeff Fassero .10 .05 .01
☐ 100 Curt Schilling .10 .05 .01
☐ 101 Dave Clark .10 .05 .01
☐ 102 Delino DeShields .10 .05 .01
☐ 103 Leo Gomez .10 .05 .01
☐ 104 Dave Hollins .10 .05 .01
☐ 105 Tim Naehring .10 .05 .01
☐ 106 Otis Nixon .10 .05 .01
☐ 107 Ozzie Guillen .10 .05 .01
☐ 108 Jose Lind .10 .05 .01
☐ 109 Stan Javier .10 .05 .01
☐ 110 Greg Vaughn .25 .11 .03
☐ 111 Chipper Jones 2.00 .90 .25
☐ 112 Ed Sprague .25 .11 .03
☐ 113 Mike Macfarlane .10 .05 .01
☐ 114 Steve Finley .25 .11 .03
☐ 115 Ken Hill .10 .05 .01
☐ 116 Carlos Garcia .10 .05 .01
☐ 117 Lou Whitaker .25 .11 .03
☐ 118 Todd Zeile .10 .05 .01
☐ 119 Gary Sheffield .50 .23 .06
☐ 120 Ben McDonald .10 .05 .01
☐ 121 Pete Harnisch .10 .05 .01
☐ 122 Ivan Rodriguez .75 .35 .09
☐ 123 Wilson Alvarez .25 .11 .03
☐ 124 Travis Fryman .25 .11 .03
☐ 125 Pedro Munoz .10 .05 .01
☐ 126 Mark Lemke .10 .05 .01
☐ 127 Jose Valentin .25 .11 .03
☐ 128 Ken Griffey Jr. 3.00 1.35 .35
☐ 129 Omar Vizquel .25 .11 .03
☐ 130 Milt Cuyler .10 .05 .01
☐ 131 Steve Trachsel .10 .05 .01
☐ 132 Alex Rodriguez 4.00 1.80 .50
☐ 133 Garret Anderson .25 .11 .03
☐ 134 Armando Benitez .10 .05 .01
☐ 135 Shawn Green .25 .11 .03
☐ 136 Jorge Fabregas .10 .05 .01
☐ 137 Orlando Miller .10 .05 .01
☐ 138 Rikkert Faneyte .10 .05 .01
☐ 139 Ismael Valdes .25 .11 .03
☐ 140 Jose Oliva .10 .05 .01
☐ 141 Aaron Small .10 .05 .01
☐ 142 Tim Davis .10 .05 .01
☐ 143 Ricky Bottalico .25 .11 .03
☐ 144 Mike Matheny .10 .05 .01
☐ 145 Roberto Petagine .10 .05 .01
☐ 146 Fausto Cruz .10 .05 .01
☐ 147 Bryce Florie .10 .05 .01
☐ 148 Jose Lima .10 .05 .01
☐ 149 John Hudek .10 .05 .01
☐ 150 Duane Singleton .10 .05 .01
☐ 151 John Mabry .50 .23 .06
☐ 152 Robert Eenhoorn .10 .05 .01
☐ 153 Jon Lieber .10 .05 .01
☐ 154 Garey Ingram .10 .05 .01
☐ 155 Paul Shuey .10 .05 .01
☐ 156 Mike Lieberthal .10 .05 .01
☐ 157 Steve Dunn .10 .05 .01
☐ 158 Charles Johnson .25 .11 .03
☐ 159 Ernie Young .25 .11 .03
☐ 160 Jose Martinez .10 .05 .01
☐ 161 Kurt Miller .10 .05 .01
☐ 162 Joey Eischen .10 .05 .01
☐ 163 Dave Stevens .10 .05 .01
☐ 164 Brian L.Hunter .25 .11 .03
☐ 165 Jeff Cirillo .25 .11 .03
☐ 166 Mark Smith .10 .05 .01
☐ 167 McKay Christensen .25 .11 .03
☐ 168 C.J. Nitkowski .25 .11 .03
☐ 169 Antone Williamson .50 .23 .06
☐ 170 Paul Konerko 2.00 .90 .25
☐ 171 Scott Elarton .50 .23 .06
☐ 172 Jacob Shumate .25 .11 .03
☐ 173 Terrence Long .50 .23 .06
☐ 174 Mark Johnson .25 .11 .03
☐ 175 Ben Grieve 1.50 .70 .19
☐ 176 Jayson Peterson .25 .11 .03
☐ 177 Checklist .10 .05 .01
☐ 178 Checklist .10 .05 .01
☐ 179 Checklist .10 .05 .01
☐ 180 Checklist .10 .05 .01
☐ 181 Brian Anderson .10 .05 .01
☐ 182 Steve Buechele .10 .05 .01
☐ 183 Mark Clark .10 .05 .01
☐ 184 Cecil Fielder .25 .11 .03
☐ 185 Steve Avery .25 .11 .03
☐ 186 Devon White .25 .11 .03
☐ 187 Craig Shipley .10 .05 .01
☐ 188 Brady Anderson .50 .23 .06
☐ 189 Kenny Lofton .75 .35 .09
☐ 190 Alex Cole .10 .05 .01
☐ 191 Brent Gates .10 .05 .01
☐ 192 Dean Palmer .25 .11 .03
☐ 193 Alex Gonzalez .25 .11 .03
☐ 194 Steve Cooke .10 .05 .01
☐ 195 Ray Lankford .25 .11 .03
☐ 196 Mark McGwire 1.00 .45 .12
☐ 197 Marc Newfield .25 .11 .03
☐ 198 Pat Rapp .10 .05 .01
☐ 199 Darren Lewis .10 .05 .01
☐ 200 Carlos Baerga .25 .11 .03
☐ 201 Rickey Henderson .50 .23 .06
☐ 202 Kurt Abbott .10 .05 .01
☐ 203 Kirt Manwaring .10 .05 .01
☐ 204 Cal Ripken 2.50 1.10 .30
☐ 205 Darren Daulton .25 .11 .03
☐ 206 Greg Colbrunn .10 .05 .01
☐ 207 Darryl Hamilton .10 .05 .01
☐ 208 Bo Jackson .25 .11 .03
☐ 209 Tony Phillips .25 .11 .03
☐ 210 Geronimo Berroa .10 .05 .01
☐ 211 Rich Becker .10 .05 .01
☐ 212 Tony Tarasco .10 .05 .01
☐ 213 Karl Rhodes .10 .05 .01
☐ 214 Phil Plantier .10 .05 .01
☐ 215 J.T. Snow .25 .11 .03
☐ 216 Mo Vaughn .75 .35 .09
☐ 217 Greg Gagne .10 .05 .01
☐ 218 Ricky Bones .10 .05 .01
☐ 219 Mike Bordick .10 .05 .01
☐ 220 Chad Curtis .10 .05 .01
☐ 221 Royce Clayton .10 .05 .01
☐ 222 Roberto Alomar .60 .25 .07
☐ 223 Jose Rijo .10 .05 .01
☐ 224 Ryan Klesko .50 .23 .06
☐ 225 Mark Langston .10 .05 .01
☐ 226 Frank Thomas 3.00 1.35 .35
☐ 227 Juan Gonzalez 1.50 .70 .19
☐ 228 Ron Gant .25 .11 .03
☐ 229 Javier Lopez .50 .23 .06
☐ 230 Sammy Sosa .50 .23 .06
☐ 231 Kevin Brown .25 .11 .03
☐ 232 Gary DiSarcina .10 .05 .01
☐ 233 Albert Belle 1.25 .55 .16
☐ 234 Jay Buhner .50 .23 .06
☐ 235 Pedro J.Martinez .25 .11 .03
☐ 236 Bob Tewksbury .10 .05 .01
☐ 237 Mike Piazza 2.00 .90 .25
☐ 238 Darryl Kile .10 .05 .01
☐ 239 Bryan Harvey .10 .05 .01
☐ 240 Andres Galarraga .50 .23 .06
☐ 241 Jeff Blauser .10 .05 .01
☐ 242 Jeff Kent .10 .05 .01
☐ 243 Bobby Munoz .10 .05 .01
☐ 244 Greg Maddux 2.00 .90 .25
☐ 245 Paul O'Neill .25 .11 .03
☐ 246 Lenny Dykstra .25 .11 .03
☐ 247 Todd Van Poppel .10 .05 .01
☐ 248 Bernie Williams .60 .25 .07
☐ 249 Glenallen Hill .10 .05 .01
☐ 250 Duane Ward .10 .05 .01
☐ 251 Dennis Eckersley .25 .11 .03
☐ 252 Pat Mahomes .10 .05 .01
☐ 253 Rusty Greer .50 .23 .06
☐ 254 Roberto Kelly .10 .05 .01
☐ 255 Randy Myers .10 .05 .01
☐ 256 Scott Ruffcorn .10 .05 .01
☐ 257 Robin Ventura .25 .11 .03
☐ 258 Eduardo Perez .10 .05 .01
☐ 259 Aaron Sele .25 .11 .03
☐ 260 Paul Molitor .60 .25 .07
☐ 261 Juan Guzman .25 .11 .03
☐ 262 Darren Oliver .50 .23 .06
☐ 263 Mike Stanley .10 .05 .01
☐ 264 Tom Glavine .50 .23 .06
☐ 265 Rico Brogna .10 .05 .01
☐ 266 Craig Biggio .25 .11 .03
☐ 267 Darrell Whitmore .10 .05 .01
☐ 268 Jimmy Key .25 .11 .03
☐ 269 Will Clark .50 .23 .06
☐ 270 David Cone .25 .11 .03
☐ 271 Brian Jordan .50 .23 .06
☐ 272 Barry Bonds .75 .35 .09
☐ 273 Danny Tartabull .10 .05 .01
☐ 274 Ramon J.Martinez .25 .11 .03
☐ 275 Al Martin .25 .11 .03
☐ 276 Fred McGriff SM .50 .23 .06
☐ 277 Carlos Delgado SM .25 .11 .03
☐ 278 Juan Gonzalez SM .75 .35 .09
☐ 279 Shawn Green SM .25 .11 .03
☐ 280 Carlos Baerga SM .25 .11 .03
☐ 281 Cliff Floyd SM .10 .05 .01
☐ 282 Ozzie Smith SM .50 .23 .06
☐ 283 Alex Rodriguez SM 2.00 .90 .25
☐ 284 Kenny Lofton SM .50 .23 .06
☐ 285 Dave Justice SM .25 .11 .03
☐ 286 Tim Salmon SM .50 .23 .06
☐ 287 Manny Ramirez SM .50 .23 .06
☐ 288 Will Clark SM .50 .23 .06
☐ 289 Garret Anderson SM .25 .11 .03
☐ 290 Billy Ashley SM .10 .05 .01
☐ 291 Tony Gwynn SM .60 .25 .07
☐ 292 Raul Mondesi SM .50 .23 .06
☐ 293 Rafael Palmeiro SM .50 .23 .06
☐ 294 Matt Williams SM .50 .23 .06
☐ 295 Don Mattingly SM .75 .35 .09
☐ 296 Kirby Puckett SM .50 .23 .06
☐ 297 Paul Molitor SM .50 .23 .06
☐ 298 Albert Belle SM .60 .25 .07
☐ 299 Barry Bonds SM .50 .23 .06
☐ 300 Mike Piazza SM 1.00 .45 .12
☐ 301 Jeff Bagwell SM .60 .25 .07
☐ 302 Frank Thomas SM 1.50 .70 .19
☐ 303 Chipper Jones SM 1.00 .45 .12
☐ 304 Ken Griffey Jr. SM 1.50 .70 .19
☐ 305 Cal Ripken Jr. SM 1.25 .55 .16
☐ 306 Eric Anthony .10 .05 .01
☐ 307 Todd Benzinger .10 .05 .01
☐ 308 Jacob Brumfield .10 .05 .01
☐ 309 Wes Chamberlain .10 .05 .01
☐ 310 Tino Martinez .25 .11 .03
☐ 311 Roberto Mejia .10 .05 .01
☐ 312 Jose Offerman .10 .05 .01
☐ 313 David Segui .10 .05 .01
☐ 314 Eric Young .25 .11 .03
☐ 315 Rey Sanchez .10 .05 .01
☐ 316 Raul Mondesi .50 .23 .06
☐ 317 Bret Boone .25 .11 .03
☐ 318 Andre Dawson .25 .11 .03
☐ 319 Brian McRae .25 .11 .03
☐ 320 Dave Nilsson .25 .11 .03
☐ 321 Moises Alou .25 .11 .03
☐ 322 Don Slaught .10 .05 .01
☐ 323 Dave McCarty .10 .05 .01
☐ 324 Mike Huff .10 .05 .01
☐ 325 Rick Aguilera .10 .05 .01
☐ 326 Rod Beck .10 .05 .01
☐ 327 Kenny Rogers .10 .05 .01
☐ 328 Andy Benes .10 .05 .01
☐ 329 Allen Watson .10 .05 .01
☐ 330 Randy Johnson .50 .23 .06
☐ 331 Willie Greene .10 .05 .01
☐ 332 Hal Morris .10 .05 .01
☐ 333 Ozzie Smith .75 .35 .09
☐ 334 Jason Bere .10 .05 .01
☐ 335 Scott Erickson .10 .05 .01
☐ 336 Dante Bichette .50 .23 .06
☐ 337 Willie Banks .10 .05 .01
☐ 338 Eric Davis .25 .11 .03
☐ 339 Rondell White .25 .11 .03
☐ 340 Kirby Puckett 1.25 .55 .16
☐ 341 Deion Sanders .50 .23 .06
☐ 342 Eddie Murray .75 .35 .09
☐ 343 Mike Harkey .10 .05 .01
☐ 344 Joey Hamilton .50 .23 .06
☐ 345 Roger Salkeld .10 .05 .01
☐ 346 Wil Cordero .10 .05 .01
☐ 347 John Wetteland .25 .11 .03
☐ 348 Geronimo Pena .10 .05 .01
☐ 349 Kirk Gibson .25 .11 .03
☐ 350 Manny Ramirez .75 .35 .09
☐ 351 Wm.VanLandingham .10 .05 .01
☐ 352 B.J. Surhoff .25 .11 .03
☐ 353 Ken Ryan .10 .05 .01
☐ 354 Terry Steinbach .25 .11 .03
☐ 355 Bret Saberhagen .25 .11 .03
☐ 356 John Jaha .25 .11 .03
☐ 357 Joe Girardi .10 .05 .01
☐ 358 Steve Karsay .10 .05 .01
☐ 359 Alex Fernandez .25 .11 .03
☐ 360 Salomon Torres .10 .05 .01
☐ 361 John Burkett .25 .11 .03
☐ 362 Derek Bell .25 .11 .03
☐ 363 Tom Henke .10 .05 .01
☐ 364 Gregg Jefferies .25 .11 .03
☐ 365 Jack McDowell .25 .11 .03
☐ 366 Andujar Cedeno .10 .05 .01
☐ 367 Dave Winfield .50 .23 .06
☐ 368 Carl Everett .10 .05 .01
☐ 369 Danny Jackson .10 .05 .01
☐ 370 Jeromy Burnitz .10 .05 .01
☐ 371 Mark Grace .50 .23 .06
☐ 372 Larry Walker .50 .23 .06
☐ 373 Bill Swift .10 .05 .01
☐ 374 Dennis Martinez .25 .11 .03
☐ 375 Mickey Tettleton .10 .05 .01
☐ 376 Mel Nieves .25 .11 .03
☐ 377 Cal Eldred .10 .05 .01
☐ 378 Orel Hershiser .25 .11 .03
☐ 379 David Wells .10 .05 .01
☐ 380 Gary Gaetti .25 .11 .03
☐ 381 Jeromy Burnitz .10 .05 .01
☐ 382 Barry Larkin .50 .23 .06
☐ 383 Jason Jacome .10 .05 .01
☐ 384 Tim Wallach .10 .05 .01
☐ 385 Robby Thompson .10 .05 .01
☐ 386 Frank Viola .10 .05 .01
☐ 387 Dave Stewart .25 .11 .03
☐ 388 Bip Roberts .10 .05 .01
☐ 389 Ron Darling .10 .05 .01
☐ 390 Carlos Delgado .25 .11 .03
☐ 391 Tim Salmon .50 .23 .06
☐ 392 Alan Trammell .25 .11 .03
☐ 393 Kevin Foster .10 .05 .01
☐ 394 Jim Abbott .10 .05 .01
☐ 395 John Kruk .25 .11 .03
☐ 396 Andy Van Slyke .25 .11 .03
☐ 397 Dave Magadan .10 .05 .01
☐ 398 Rafael Palmeiro .50 .23 .06
☐ 399 Mike Devereaux .10 .05 .01
☐ 400 Benito Santiago .10 .05 .01
☐ 401 Brett Butler .25 .11 .03
☐ 402 John Franco .10 .05 .01
☐ 403 Matt Walbeck .10 .05 .01
☐ 404 Terry Pendleton .25 .11 .03
☐ 405 Chris Sabo .10 .05 .01
☐ 406 Andrew Lorraine .25 .11 .03
☐ 407 Dan Wilson .25 .11 .03
☐ 408 Mike Lansing .10 .05 .01
☐ 409 Ray McDavid .25 .11 .03
☐ 410 Shane Andrews .10 .05 .01
☐ 411 Tom Gordon .10 .05 .01
☐ 412 Chad Ogea .10 .05 .01
☐ 413 James Baldwin .25 .11 .03
☐ 414 Russ Davis .10 .05 .01
☐ 415 Ray Holbert .10 .05 .01
☐ 416 Ray Durham .25 .11 .03
☐ 417 Matt Nokes .10 .05 .01
☐ 418 Rod Henderson .10 .05 .01
☐ 419 Gabe White .10 .05 .01
☐ 420 Todd Hollandsworth .50 .23 .06
☐ 421 Midre Cummings .10 .05 .01
☐ 422 Harold Baines .25 .11 .03
☐ 423 Troy Percival .10 .05 .01
☐ 424 Joe Vitiello .10 .05 .01
☐ 425 Andy Ashby .25 .11 .03
☐ 426 Michael Tucker .25 .11 .03
☐ 427 Mark Gubicza .10 .05 .01
☐ 428 Jim Bullinger .10 .05 .01
☐ 429 Jose Malave .10 .05 .01
☐ 430 Pete Schourek .25 .11 .03
☐ 431 Bobby Ayala .10 .05 .01
☐ 432 Marvin Freeman .10 .05 .01
☐ 433 Pat Listach .10 .05 .01
☐ 434 Eddie Taubensee .10 .05 .01
☐ 435 Steve Howe .10 .05 .01
☐ 436 Kent Mercker .10 .05 .01
☐ 437 Hector Fajardo .10 .05 .01
☐ 438 Scott Kamieniecki .10 .05 .01
☐ 439 Robb Nen .10 .05 .01
☐ 440 Mike Kelly .10 .05 .01
☐ 441 Tom Candiotti .10 .05 .01
☐ 442 Albie Lopez .10 .05 .01
☐ 443 Jeff Granger .10 .05 .01
☐ 444 Rich Aude .10 .05 .01
☐ 445 Luis Polonia .10 .05 .01
☐ 446 Frank Thomas CL 1.50 .70 .19
☐ 447 Ken Griffey Jr. CL 1.50 .70 .19
☐ 448 Mike Piazza CL 1.00 .45 .12
☐ 449 Jeff Bagwell CL .60 .25 .07
☐ 450 Checklist 2.00 .90 .25
Jeff Bagwell
Frank Thomas
Ken Griffey Jr.
Mike Piazza

1995 Pinnacle Artist's Proofs

Inserted one per 36 packs, this is a parallel set to the regular Pinnacle issue. The words "Artist Proof" are clearly labeled in silver on the card front. The name on the bottom is also set against a silver background.

	MINT	NRMT	EXC
COMPLETE SET (450)	2000.00	900.00	250.00
COMPLETE SERIES 1 (225)	1000.00	450.00	125.00

	MINT	NRMT	EXC
COMPLETE SERIES 2 (225)	1000.00	450.00	125.00
COMMON CARD (1-450)	3.00	1.35	.35
*STARS: 15X TO 30X BASIC CARDS			
*YOUNG STARS: 15X TO 25X BASIC CARDS			

1995 Pinnacle Museum Collection

Inserted one in four packs, this is a parallel to the regular Pinnacle issue. These cards use the Dufex technology on front and are clearly labeled on the back as Museum Collection cards. Seven series 2 cards (#'S 410, 413, 416, 420, 423, 426 and 444) were available only with randomly inserted trade cards. These trade cards expired Dec. 31, 1995.

	MINT	NRMT	EXC
COMPLETE SET (450)	600.00	275.00	75.00
COMPLETE SERIES 1 (225)	300.00	135.00	38.00
COMPLETE SERIES 2 (225)	300.00	135.00	38.00
COMMON CARD (1-450)	1.00	.45	.12
TRADE (410/413/416/420)	3.00	1.35	.35
TRADE(423/426/444)	3.00	1.35	.35
*STARS: 5X TO 10X BASIC CARDS			
*YOUNG STARS: 4X TO 8X BASIC CARDS			

1995 Pinnacle ETA

This six-card standard-sized set was randomly inserted approximately one in every 24 first series hobby packs. This set features players who were among the leading prospects for major league stardom. The fronts feature a player photo as well as a quick information bit. The player's name is located on the top. The busy full-bleed backs feature a player photo and some quick comments. On the bottom is the player's name and the card is numbered with an "ETA" prefix in the upper left corner.

	MINT	NRMT	EXC
COMPLETE SET (6)	25.00	11.00	3.10
COMMON CARD (1-6)	2.50	1.10	.30
☐ 1 Ben Grieve	15.00	6.75	1.85
☐ 2 Alex Ochoa	4.00	1.80	.50
☐ 3 Joe Vitiello	2.50	1.10	.30
☐ 4 Johnny Damon	6.00	2.70	.75
☐ 5 Trey Beamon	4.00	1.80	.50
☐ 6 Brooks Kieschnick			

1995 Pinnacle Gate Attractions

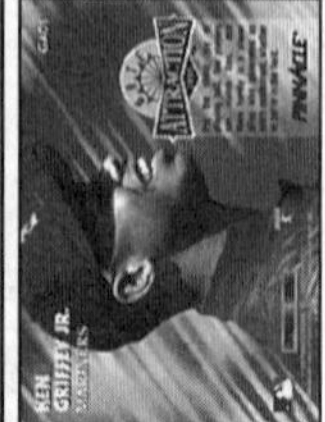

This 18-card standard-size set was inserted approximately one every 12 second series jumbo packs. The fronts feature two photos, with the words "Gate Attraction" at the bottom left. The player is identified on the top. The horizontal full-bleed backs have the player's name on the left, a player photo in the middle and some career information in the lower right. The cards are numbered with a "GA" prefix in the upper right corner.

	MINT	NRMT	EXC
COMPLETE SET (18)	125.00	55.00	15.50
COMMON CARD (GA1-GA18)	2.00	.90	.25
☐ GA1 Ken Griffey Jr.	25.00	11.00	3.10
☐ GA2 Frank Thomas	25.00	11.00	3.10
☐ GA3 Cal Ripken	20.00	9.00	2.50
☐ GA4 Jeff Bagwell	10.00	4.50	1.25
☐ GA5 Mike Piazza	15.00	6.75	1.85
☐ GA6 Barry Bonds	6.00	2.70	.75
☐ GA7 Kirby Puckett	10.00	4.50	1.25
☐ GA8 Albert Belle	10.00	4.50	1.25
☐ GA9 Tony Gwynn	10.00	4.50	1.25
☐ GA10 Raul Mondesi	3.00	1.35	.35
☐ GA11 Will Clark	3.00	1.35	.35
☐ GA12 Don Mattingly	12.00	5.50	1.50
☐ GA13 Roger Clemens	5.00	2.20	.60
☐ GA14 Paul Molitor	5.00	2.20	.60
☐ GA15 Matt Williams	3.00	1.35	.35
☐ GA16 Greg Maddux	15.00	6.75	1.85
☐ GA17 Kenny Lofton	6.00	2.70	.75
☐ GA18 Cliff Floyd	2.00	.90	.25

1995 Pinnacle New Blood

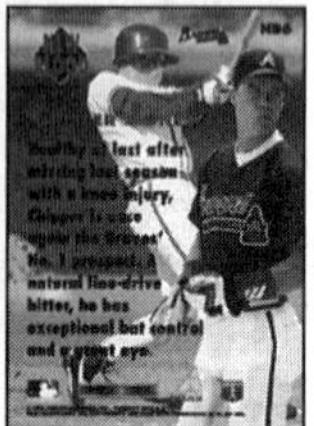

This nine-card standard-size set was inserted approximately one in every 90 second series hobby and retail packs. This set features nine players who were leading prospects entering the 1995 season. The Dufex enhanced fronts feature two player photos. One photo is a color shot while the other one is a black and white background photo. The words "New Blood" and player's name are on the bottom. The full-bleed backs feature two more photos. Player information is set against these photos. The card is numbered with an "NB" prefix in the upper left corner.

	MINT	NRMT	EXC
COMPLETE SET (9)	120.00	55.00	15.00
COMMON CARD (NB1-NB9)	4.00	1.80	.50
☐ NB1 Alex Rodriguez	75.00	34.00	9.50
☐ NB2 Shawn Green	4.00	1.80	.50
☐ NB3 Brian Hunter	10.00	4.50	1.25
☐ NB4 Garret Anderson	5.00	2.20	.60
☐ NB5 Charles Johnson	6.00	2.70	.75
☐ NB6 Chipper Jones	50.00	22.00	6.25
☐ NB7 Carlos Delgado	10.00	4.50	1.25
☐ NB8 Billy Ashley	4.00	1.80	.50
☐ NB9 J.R. Phillips UER Dodgers logo on back Phillips plays for the Giants	4.00	1.80	.50

1995 Pinnacle Performers

These 18 standard-size cards were randomly inserted approximately one in every 12 first series jumbo packs. The full-bleed fronts feature a player photo against a shiny background. The player's name is in white lettering in the upper right corner. The backs have two photos: one a color portrait with the other one being a shaded black and white. There is also some text pertaining to that player. The cards are numbered in the upper right corner with a "PP" prefix.

	MINT	NRMT	EXC
COMPLETE SERIES 1 (18)	100.00	45.00	12.50
COMMON CARD (1-18)	2.00	.90	.25
☐ PP1 Frank Thomas	30.00	13.50	3.70
☐ PP2 Albert Belle	12.00	5.50	1.50
☐ PP3 Barry Bonds	8.00	3.60	1.00
☐ PP4 Juan Gonzalez	15.00	6.75	1.85
☐ PP5 Andres Galarraga	4.00	1.80	.50
☐ PP6 Raul Mondesi	4.00	1.80	.50
☐ PP7 Paul Molitor	6.00	2.70	.75
☐ PP8 Tim Salmon	4.00	1.80	.50
☐ PP9 Mike Piazza	20.00	9.00	2.50
☐ PP10 Gregg Jefferies	3.00	1.35	.35
☐ PP11 Will Clark	4.00	1.80	.50
☐ PP12 Greg Maddux	20.00	9.00	2.50
☐ PP13 Manny Ramirez	8.00	3.60	1.00
☐ PP14 Kirby Puckett	12.00	5.50	1.50
☐ PP15 Shawn Green	3.00	1.35	.35
☐ PP16 Rafael Palmeiro	4.00	1.80	.50
☐ PP17 Paul O'Neill	3.00	1.35	.35
☐ PP18 Jason Bere	2.00	.90	.25

1995 Pinnacle Pin Redemption

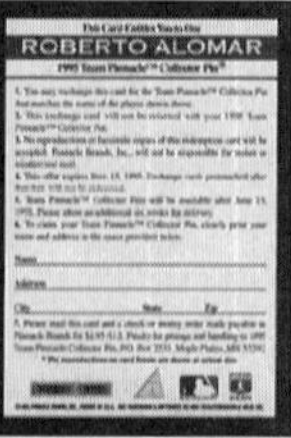

This 18-card standard-size set was randomly inserted in all second series packs. Printed odds indicate that these cards were inserted approximately one every in 48 hobby and retail packs and one in every 36 jumbo packs. The horizontal full-bleed fronts feature an action photo, a team logo and another small player photo. The backs explain the rules for ordering the "Team Pinnacle" Collector Pin. The offer expired on November 15, 1995.

	MINT	NRMT	EXC
COMPLETE SET (18)	80.00	36.00	10.00
COMMON CARD (1-18)	1.00	.45	.12
☐ 1 Greg Maddux	10.00	4.50	1.25
☐ 2 Mike Mussina	3.00	1.35	.35
☐ 3 Mike Piazza	10.00	4.50	1.25
☐ 4 Carlos Delgado	1.50	.70	.19
☐ 5 Jeff Bagwell	6.00	2.70	.75
☐ 6 Frank Thomas	15.00	6.75	1.85
☐ 7 Craig Biggio	1.50	.70	.19
☐ 8 Roberto Alomar	3.00	1.35	.35
☐ 9 Ozzie Smith	4.00	1.80	.50
☐ 10 Cal Ripken Jr.	12.00	5.50	1.50
☐ 11 Matt Williams	2.00	.90	.25
☐ 12 Travis Fryman	1.50	.70	.19
☐ 13 Barry Bonds	4.00	1.80	.50
☐ 14 Ken Griffey Jr.	15.00	6.75	1.85
☐ 15 Dave Justice	1.00	.45	.12
☐ 16 Albert Belle	6.00	2.70	.75
☐ 17 Tony Gwynn	6.00	2.70	.75
☐ 18 Kirby Puckett	6.00	2.70	.75

1995 Pinnacle Pins

These pins were sent to collectors when they redeemed a pin redemption card inserted in series 2 Pinnacle packs. The redemption deadline was November 15, 1995. We have checklisted these pins in the same order as the cards used to redeem for these pins.

	MINT	NRMT	EXC
COMPLETE SET (18)	60.00	27.00	7.50
COMMON PIN (1-18)	1.00	.45	.12
☐ 1 Greg Maddux	10.00	4.50	1.25
☐ 2 Mike Mussina	3.00	1.35	.35
☐ 3 Mike Piazza	10.00	4.50	1.25
☐ 4 Carlos Delgado	1.50	.70	.19
☐ 5 Jeff Bagwell	6.00	2.70	.75
☐ 6 Frank Thomas	15.00	6.75	1.85
☐ 7 Craig Biggio	1.50	.70	.19
☐ 8 Roberto Alomar	3.00	1.35	.35
☐ 9 Ozzie Smith	4.00	1.80	.50
☐ 10 Cal Ripken Jr.	12.00	5.50	1.50
☐ 11 Matt Williams	2.00	.90	.25
☐ 12 Travis Fryman	1.50	.70	.19
☐ 13 Barry Bonds	4.00	1.80	.50
☐ 14 Ken Griffey Jr.	15.00	6.75	1.85
☐ 15 Dave Justice	1.50	.70	.19
☐ 16 Albert Belle	6.00	2.70	.75
☐ 17 Tony Gwynn	6.00	2.70	.75
☐ 18 Kirby Puckett	6.00	2.70	.75

1995 Pinnacle Red Hot

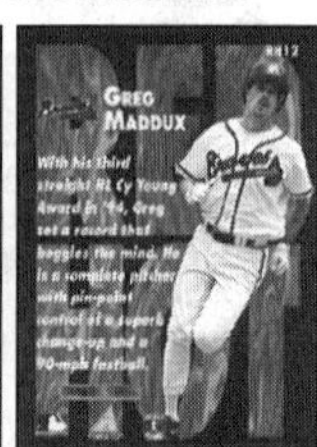

Cards from this 25-card standard-size set were randomly inserted into second series hobby and retail packs. The fronts feature a player photo on the right, with his name, an inset portrait and the words "Red Hot" on the left.

	MINT	NRMT	EXC
COMPLETE SET (25)	80.00	36.00	10.00
COMMON CARD (RH1-RH25)	1.00	.45	.12
☐ RH1 Cal Ripken Jr.	12.00	5.50	1.50
☐ RH2 Ken Griffey Jr.	15.00	6.75	1.85
☐ RH3 Frank Thomas	15.00	6.75	1.85
☐ RH4 Jeff Bagwell	6.00	2.70	.75
☐ RH5 Mike Piazza	10.00	4.50	1.25
☐ RH6 Barry Bonds	4.00	1.80	.50
☐ RH7 Albert Belle	6.00	2.70	.75
☐ RH8 Tony Gwynn	6.00	2.70	.75
☐ RH9 Kirby Puckett	6.00	2.70	.75
☐ RH10 Don Mattingly	8.00	3.60	1.00
☐ RH11 Matt Williams	2.00	.90	.25
☐ RH12 Greg Maddux	10.00	4.50	1.25
☐ RH13 Raul Mondesi	2.00	.90	.25
☐ RH14 Paul Molitor	3.00	1.35	.35
☐ RH15 Manny Ramirez	4.00	1.80	.50
☐ RH16 Joe Carter	1.50	.70	.19
☐ RH17 Will Clark	2.00	.90	.25
☐ RH18 Roger Clemens	3.00	1.35	.35
☐ RH19 Tim Salmon	2.00	.90	.25
☐ RH20 Dave Justice	1.00	.45	.12
☐ RH21 Kenny Lofton	4.00	1.80	.50
☐ RH22 Deion Sanders	2.00	.90	.25
☐ RH23 Roberto Alomar	3.00	1.35	.35
☐ RH24 Cliff Floyd	1.00	.45	.12
☐ RH25 Carlos Baerga	1.00	.45	.12

1995 Pinnacle White Hot

Parallel to the more common Red Hot cards, these cards were randomly seeded exclusively into second series hobby packs. A crystal blue foil background and white lettering on front differentiate these cards from their more common red counterparts.

	MINT	NRMT	EXC
COMPLETE SET (25)	300.00	135.00	38.00
COMMON CARD (WH1-WH25)	4.00	1.80	.50
*WHITE: 2X to 4X RED CARDS			

1995 Pinnacle Team Pinnacle

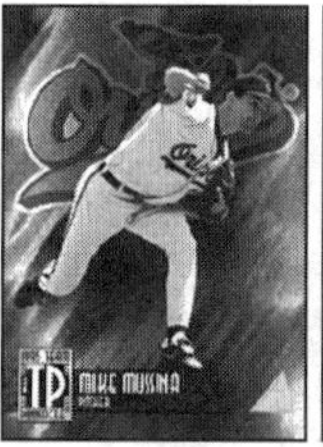

Randomly inserted in series one hobby and retail packs at a rate of one in 90, this nine-card standard-size set showcases the game's top players in an etched-foil design. A player photo is superimposed over the player's team logo. The Team Pinnacle logo, player's name and position are printed in silver foil on a black strip at the bottom left of the card. Cards are numbered with the prefix "TP". All cards were intentionally issued with two variations, whereby one side of the card or the other had the Dufex effect. Regional premiums of up to 25% may exist for the player with the enhanced side.

	MINT	NRMT	EXC
COMPLETE SET (9)	250.00	110.00	31.00
COMMON CARD (1-9)	8.00	3.60	1.00
☐ TP1 Mike Mussina Greg Maddux	40.00	18.00	5.00
☐ TP2 Carlos Delgado Mike Piazza	30.00	13.50	3.70
☐ TP3 Frank Thomas Jeff Bagwell	60.00	27.00	7.50
☐ TP4 Roberto Alomar Craig Biggio	15.00	6.75	1.85
☐ TP5 Cal Ripken Ozzie Smith	50.00	22.00	6.25
☐ TP6 Travis Fryman Matt Williams	8.00	3.60	1.00
☐ TP7 Ken Griffey Jr. Barry Bonds	50.00	22.00	6.25
☐ TP8 Albert Belle David Justice	20.00	9.00	2.50
☐ TP9 Kirby Puckett Tony Gwynn	40.00	18.00	5.00

1995 Pinnacle Upstarts

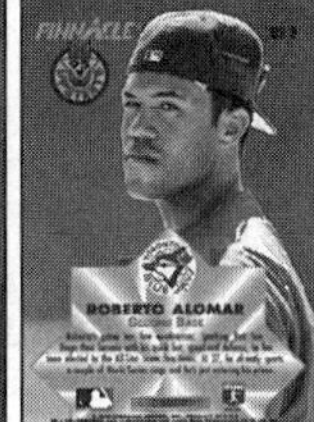

Top young players are featured in this 30-card standard-size set. The cards were randomly inserted in series one hobby and retail packs at a rate of one in eight. Multi-colored foil fronts feature the player in a action cutout set against a star background. The player's name is wrapped around the "Upstarts" logo which is printed on the lower left of the front. The player's team logo is printed at the top right of the front. Backs are full-bleed color action photos of the player and are numbered at the top right with the prefix "US". A gold polygonal box encloses the player's name and '94 stats along with the team logo. The Pinnacle and '95 Upstarts logo are printed on the top left of the back.

	MINT	NRMT	EXC
COMPLETE SET (30)	60.00	27.00	7.50
COMMON CARD (US1-US30)	1.00	.45	.12
☐ US1 Frank Thomas	20.00	9.00	2.50
☐ US2 Roberto Alomar	4.00	1.80	.50
☐ US3 Mike Piazza	12.00	5.50	1.50
☐ US4 Javier Lopez	2.50	1.10	.30
☐ US5 Albert Belle	8.00	3.60	1.00
☐ US6 Carlos Delgado	1.50	.70	.19
☐ US7 Brent Gates	1.00	.45	.12
☐ US8 Tim Salmon	2.50	1.10	.30
☐ US9 Raul Mondesi	2.50	1.10	.30
☐ US10 Juan Gonzalez	10.00	4.50	1.25
☐ US11 Manny Ramirez	5.00	2.20	.60
☐ US12 Sammy Sosa	3.00	1.35	.35
☐ US13 Jeff Kent	1.00	.45	.12
☐ US14 Melvin Nieves	1.00	.45	.12
☐ US15 Rondell White	1.50	.70	.19
☐ US16 Shawn Green	1.50	.70	.19
☐ US17 Bernie Williams	4.00	1.80	.50
☐ US18 Aaron Sele	1.50	.70	.19
☐ US19 Jason Bere	1.00	.45	.12
☐ US20 Joey Hamilton	1.50	.70	.19
☐ US21 Mike Kelly	1.00	.45	.12
☐ US22 Wil Cordero	1.00	.45	.12
☐ US23 Moises Alou	1.50	.70	.19
☐ US24 Roberto Kelly	1.00	.45	.12
☐ US25 Deion Sanders	2.50	1.10	.30
☐ US26 Steve Karsay	1.00	.45	.12
☐ US27 Bret Boone	1.00	.45	.12
☐ US28 Willie Greene	2.50	1.10	.30
☐ US29 Billy Ashley	1.00	.45	.12
☐ US30 Brian Anderson	1.00	.45	.12

1995 Pinnacle FanFest

Available in two-card cello packs, this 30-card standard-size set was issued to commemorate the Pinnacle All-Star FanFest July 7-11 in Arlington, Texas. The fronts feature full-bleed color action photos; at the lower right corner, a gold foil diamond design carries the player's last name and team logo. Between black stripes, the horizontal backs have a player cutout superposed over a photo of The Ballpark in Arlington.

	MINT	NRMT	EXC
COMPLETE SET (30)	40.00	18.00	5.00
COMMON CARD (1-30)	.40	.18	.05
☐ 1 Cal Ripken	5.00	2.20	.60
☐ 2 Roger Clemens	1.00	.45	.12
☐ 3 Don Mattingly	2.50	1.10	.30
☐ 4 Albert Belle	3.00	1.35	.35
☐ 5 Kirby Puckett	3.00	1.35	.35
☐ 6 Cecil Fielder	.60	.25	.07
☐ 7 Kevin Appier	.60	.25	.07
☐ 8 Will Clark	1.00	.45	.12
☐ 9 Juan Gonzalez	3.00	1.35	.35
☐ 10 Ivan Rodriguez	1.50	.70	.19
☐ 11 Ken Griffey Jr.	6.00	2.70	.75
☐ 12 Tim Salmon	.75	.35	.09
☐ 13 Frank Thomas	6.00	2.70	.75
☐ 14 Roberto Alomar	1.25	.55	.16
☐ 15 Rickey Henderson			
☐ 16 Raul Mondesi	.75	.35	.09
☐ 17 Matt Williams	.75	.35	.09
☐ 18 Ozzie Smith	2.00	.90	.25
☐ 19 Deion Sanders	.75	.35	.09
☐ 20 Tony Gwynn	2.50	1.10	.30
☐ 21 Greg Maddux	4.50	2.00	.55
☐ 22 Sammy Sosa	1.00	.45	.12
☐ 23 Mike Piazza	3.50	1.55	.45
☐ 24 Barry Bonds	1.25	.55	.16
☐ 25 Jeff Bagwell	2.50	1.10	.30
☐ 26 Lenny Dykstra	.60	.25	.07
☐ 27 Rico Brogna	.40	.18	.05
☐ 28 Larry Walker	1.00	.45	.12
☐ 29 Gary Sheffield	1.00	.45	.12
☐ 30 Wil Cordero	.40	.18	.05

1996 Pinnacle Samples

This 9-card set was released to preview the first series of the 1996 Pinnacle set. The fronts feature full-bleed color action photos, with a gold foil triangle across the bottom. The backs have a color closeup photo along with statistics and biography. The disclaimer "SAMPLE" is stamped diagonally across both sides of the card.

	MINT	NRMT	EXC
COMPLETE SET (9)	8.00	3.60	1.00
COMMON CARD	.25	.11	.03
☐ 1 Greg Maddux	2.50	1.10	.30
☐ 2 Bill Pulsipher	.50	.23	.06
☐ 3 Dante Bichette	1.25	.55	.16
☐ 4 Mike Piazza	2.50	1.10	.30
☐ 5 Garret Anderson	.50	.23	.06
☐ 165 Ruben Rivera	.75	.35	.09
☐ 166 Tony Clark	1.25	.55	.16
☐ PP2 Mo Vaughn	2.50	1.10	.30
Pinnacle Power			
☐ NNO Title Card	.25	.11	.03

1996 Pinnacle

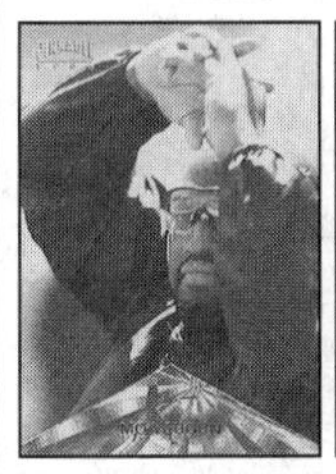

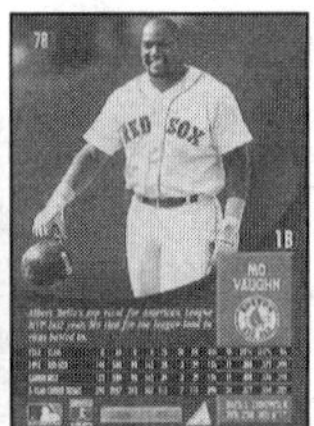

The 1996 Pinnacle set was issued in two separate series of 200 cards each. The 10-card packs retailed for $2.49. On 20-point card stock, the fronts feature full-bleed color action photos, bordered at the bottom by a gold foil triangle. The backs carry a color closeup photo, biography, and statistics. The Series I set features the following topical subsets: The Naturals (134-163), '95 Rookies (164-193) and Checklists (194-200). Series II set features these subsets: Hardball Heroes (30 cards), 300 Series (17 cards), Rookies (25 cards), and Checklists (7 cards). Numbering for the 300 Series subset was based on player's career batting average. At that time, both Paul Molitor and Jeff Bagwell had identical career batting averages of .305, thus Pinnacle numbered both of their 300 Series subset cards as 305. Due to this quirky numbering, the set only runs through card 399, but actually contains 400 cards. A special Cal Ripken Jr. Tribute card was inserted in first series packs at the rate of one in 150.

	MINT	NRMT	EXC
COMPLETE SET (400)	30.00	13.50	3.70
COMPLETE SERIES 1 (200)	15.00	6.75	1.85
COMPLETE SERIES 2 (200)	15.00	6.75	1.85
COMMON CARD (1-399)	.10	.05	.01
☐ 1 Greg Maddux	2.00	.90	.25
☐ 2 Bill Pulsipher	.25	.11	.03
☐ 3 Dante Bichette	.50	.23	.06
☐ 4 Mike Piazza	2.00	.90	.25
☐ 5 Garret Anderson	.50	.23	.06
☐ 6 Steve Finley	.50	.23	.06
☐ 7 Andy Benes	.10	.05	.01
☐ 8 Chuck Knoblauch	.50	.23	.06
☐ 9 Tom Gordon	.10	.05	.01
☐ 10 Jeff Bagwell	1.25	.55	.16
☐ 11 Wil Cordero	.10	.05	.01
☐ 12 John Mabry	.25	.11	.03
☐ 13 Jeff Frye	.10	.05	.01
☐ 14 Travis Fryman	.25	.11	.03
☐ 15 John Wetteland	.25	.11	.03
☐ 16 Jason Bates	.10	.05	.01
☐ 17 Danny Tartabull	.10	.05	.01
☐ 18 Charles Nagy	.25	.11	.03
☐ 19 Robin Ventura	.25	.11	.03
☐ 20 Reggie Sanders	.25	.11	.03
☐ 21 Dave Clark	.10	.05	.01
☐ 22 Jaime Navarro	.10	.05	.01
☐ 23 Joey Hamilton	.25	.11	.03
☐ 24 Al Leiter	.10	.05	.01
☐ 25 Deion Sanders	.50	.23	.06
☐ 26 Tim Salmon	.50	.23	.06
☐ 27 Tino Martinez	.25	.11	.03
☐ 28 Mike Greenwell	.10	.05	.01
☐ 29 Phil Plantier	.10	.05	.01
☐ 30 Bobby Bonilla	.25	.11	.03
☐ 31 Kenny Rogers	.10	.05	.01
☐ 32 Chili Davis	.10	.05	.01
☐ 33 Joe Carter	.25	.11	.03
☐ 34 Mike Mussina	.60	.25	.07
☐ 35 Matt Mieske	.10	.05	.01
☐ 36 Jose Canseco	.50	.23	.06
☐ 37 Brad Radke	.10	.05	.01
☐ 38 Juan Gonzalez	1.50	.70	.19
☐ 39 David Segui	.10	.05	.01
☐ 40 Alex Fernandez	.25	.11	.03
☐ 41 Jeff Kent	.10	.05	.01
☐ 42 Todd Zeile	.25	.11	.03
☐ 43 Darryl Strawberry	.25	.11	.03
☐ 44 Jose Rijo	.10	.05	.01
☐ 45 Ramon Martinez	.25	.11	.03
☐ 46 Manny Ramirez	.75	.35	.09
☐ 47 Gregg Jefferies	.50	.23	.06
☐ 48 Bryan Rekar	.10	.05	.01
☐ 49 Jeff King	.25	.11	.03
☐ 50 John Olerud	.10	.05	.01
☐ 51 Marc Newfield	.25	.11	.03
☐ 52 Charles Johnson	.25	.11	.03
☐ 53 Robby Thompson	.10	.05	.01
☐ 54 Brian L. Hunter	.25	.11	.03
☐ 55 Mike Blowers	.10	.05	.01
☐ 56 Keith Lockhart	.10	.05	.01
☐ 57 Ray Lankford	.25	.11	.03
☐ 58 Tim Wallach	.10	.05	.01
☐ 59 Ivan Rodriguez	.75	.35	.09
☐ 60 Ed Sprague	.25	.11	.03
☐ 61 Paul Molitor	.60	.25	.07
☐ 62 Eric Karros	.25	.11	.03
☐ 63 Glenallen Hill	.25	.11	.03
☐ 64 Jay Bell	.25	.11	.03
☐ 65 Tom Pagnozzi	.10	.05	.01
☐ 66 Greg Colbrunn	.10	.05	.01
☐ 67 Edgar Martinez	.25	.11	.03
☐ 68 Paul Sorrento	.10	.05	.01
☐ 69 Kirt Manwaring	.10	.05	.01
☐ 70 Pete Schourek	.25	.11	.03
☐ 71 Orlando Merced	.25	.11	.03
☐ 72 Shawon Dunston	.10	.05	.01
☐ 73 Ricky Bottalico	.10	.05	.01
☐ 74 Brady Anderson	.50	.23	.06
☐ 75 Steve Ontiveros	.10	.05	.01
☐ 76 Jim Abbott	.50	.23	.06
☐ 77 Carl Everett	.10	.05	.01
☐ 78 Mo Vaughn	.75	.35	.09
☐ 79 Pedro Martinez	.25	.11	.03
☐ 80 Harold Baines	.25	.11	.03
☐ 81 Alan Trammell	.25	.11	.03
☐ 82 Steve Avery	.10	.05	.01
☐ 83 Jeff Cirillo	.10	.05	.01
☐ 84 John Valentin	.25	.11	.03
☐ 85 Bernie Williams	.60	.25	.07
☐ 86 Andre Dawson	.25	.11	.03
☐ 87 Dave Winfield	.50	.23	.06
☐ 88 B.J. Surhoff	.10	.05	.01
☐ 89 Jeff Blauser	.10	.05	.01
☐ 90 Barry Larkin	.50	.23	.06
☐ 91 Cliff Floyd	.10	.05	.01
☐ 92 Sammy Sosa	.50	.23	.06
☐ 93 Andres Galarraga	.50	.23	.06
☐ 94 Dave Nilsson	.25	.11	.03
☐ 95 James Mouton	.10	.05	.01
☐ 96 Marquis Grissom	.25	.11	.03
☐ 97 Matt Williams	.50	.23	.06
☐ 98 John Jaha	.25	.11	.03
☐ 99 Don Mattingly	1.50	.70	.19
☐ 100 Tim Naehring	.10	.05	.01
☐ 101 Kevin Appier	.25	.11	.03
☐ 102 Bobby Higginson	.25	.11	.03
☐ 103 Andy Pettitte	1.00	.45	.12
☐ 104 Ozzie Smith	.75	.35	.09
☐ 105 Kenny Lofton	.75	.35	.09
☐ 106 Ken Caminiti	.50	.23	.06
☐ 107 Walt Weiss	.10	.05	.01
☐ 108 Jack McDowell	.50	.23	.06
☐ 109 Brian McRae	.10	.05	.01
☐ 110 Gary Gaetti	.25	.11	.03
☐ 111 Curtis Goodwin	.10	.05	.01
☐ 112 Dennis Martinez	.25	.11	.03
☐ 113 Omar Vizquel	.25	.11	.03
☐ 114 Chipper Jones	2.00	.90	.25
☐ 115 Mark Gubicza	.10	.05	.01
☐ 116 Ruben Sierra	.10	.05	.01
☐ 117 Eddie Murray	.75	.35	.09
☐ 118 Chad Curtis	.10	.05	.01
☐ 119 Hal Morris	.10	.05	.01
☐ 120 Ben McDonald	.10	.05	.01
☐ 121 Marty Cordova	.25	.11	.03
☐ 122 Ken Griffey Jr. UER	3.00	1.35	.35
Card says Ken homered from both sides			
He is only a left hitter			
☐ 123 Gary Sheffield	.50	.23	.06
☐ 124 Charlie Hayes	.10	.05	.01
☐ 125 Shawn Green	.25	.11	.03
☐ 126 Jason Giambi	.50	.23	.06
☐ 127 Mark Langston	.10	.05	.01
☐ 128 Mark Whiten	.10	.05	.01
☐ 129 Greg Vaughn	.50	.23	.06
☐ 130 Mark McGwire	1.00	.45	.12
☐ 131 Hideo Nomo	.75	.35	.09
☐ 132 Eric Karros	.75	.35	.09
Mike Piazza			
Raul Mondesi			
Hideo Nomo			
☐ 133 Jason Bere	.10	.05	.01
☐ 134 Ken Griffey Jr. NAT	1.50	.70	.19
☐ 135 Frank Thomas NAT	1.50	.70	.19
☐ 136 Cal Ripken NAT	1.25	.55	.16
☐ 137 Albert Belle NAT	.60	.25	.07
☐ 138 Mike Piazza NAT	1.00	.45	.12
☐ 139 Dante Bichette NAT	.50	.23	.06
☐ 140 Sammy Sosa NAT	.50	.23	.06
☐ 141 Mo Vaughn NAT	.50	.23	.06
☐ 142 Tim Salmon NAT	.50	.23	.06
☐ 143 Reggie Sanders NAT	.25	.11	.03
☐ 144 Cecil Fielder NAT	.25	.11	.03
☐ 145 Jim Edmonds NAT	.25	.11	.03
☐ 146 Rafael Palmeiro NAT	.50	.23	.06
☐ 147 Edgar Martinez NAT	.25	.11	.03
☐ 148 Barry Bonds NAT	.50	.23	.06
☐ 149 Manny Ramirez NAT	.25	.11	.03
☐ 150 Larry Walker NAT	.50	.23	.06
☐ 151 Jeff Bagwell NAT	.60	.25	.07
☐ 152 Ron Gant NAT	.25	.11	.03
☐ 153 Andres Galarraga NAT	.50	.23	.06
☐ 154 Eddie Murray NAT	.50	.23	.06
☐ 155 Kirby Puckett NAT	.50	.23	.06
☐ 156 Will Clark NAT	.50	.23	.06
☐ 157 Don Mattingly NAT	.75	.35	.09
☐ 158 Mark McGwire NAT	.50	.23	.06
☐ 159 Dean Palmer NAT	.25	.11	.03
☐ 160 Matt Williams NAT	.50	.23	.06
☐ 161 Fred McGriff NAT	.50	.23	.06
☐ 162 Joe Carter NAT	.25	.11	.03
☐ 163 Juan Gonzalez NAT	.75	.35	.09
☐ 164 Alex Ochoa	.25	.11	.03
☐ 165 Ruben Rivera	.60	.25	.07
☐ 166 Tony Clark	.60	.25	.07
☐ 167 Brian Barber	.10	.05	.01
☐ 168 Matt Lawton	.10	.05	.01
☐ 169 Terrell Wade	.25	.11	.03
☐ 170 Johnny Damon	.25	.11	.03
☐ 171 Derek Jeter	2.00	.90	.25
☐ 172 Phil Nevin	.10	.05	.01
☐ 173 Robert Perez	.10	.05	.01
☐ 174 C.J. Nitkowski	.10	.05	.01
☐ 175 Joe Vitiello	.10	.05	.01
☐ 176 Roger Cedeno	.25	.11	.03
☐ 177 Ron Coomer	.10	.05	.01
☐ 178 Chris Widger	.10	.05	.01
☐ 179 Jimmy Haynes	.10	.05	.01
☐ 180 Mike Sweeney	.60	.25	.07
☐ 181 Howard Battle	.10	.05	.01
☐ 182 John Wasdin	.10	.05	.01
☐ 183 Jim Pittsley	.25	.11	.03
☐ 184 Bob Wolcott	.10	.05	.01
☐ 185 LaTroy Hawkins	.10	.05	.01
☐ 186 Nigel Wilson	.10	.05	.01
☐ 187 Dustin Hermanson	.10	.05	.01
☐ 188 Chris Snopek	.10	.05	.01
☐ 189 Mariano Rivera	.25	.11	.03
☐ 190 Jose Herrera	.10	.05	.01
☐ 191 Chris Stynes	.10	.05	.01
☐ 192 Larry Thomas	.10	.05	.01
☐ 193 David Bell	.10	.05	.01
☐ 194 Frank Thomas CL	1.50	.70	.19
☐ 195 Ken Griffey Jr. CL	1.50	.70	.19
☐ 196 Cal Ripken CL	1.25	.55	.16
☐ 197 Jeff Bagwell CL	.60	.25	.07
☐ 198 Mike Piazza CL	1.00	.45	.12
☐ 199 Barry Bonds CL	.50	.23	.06
☐ 200 Garret Anderson CL	.75	.35	.09
Chipper Jones			
☐ 201 Frank Thomas	3.00	1.35	.35
☐ 202 Michael Tucker	.25	.11	.03
☐ 203 Kirby Puckett	1.25	.55	.16
☐ 204 Alex Gonzalez	.10	.05	.01
☐ 205 Tony Gwynn	1.25	.55	.16
☐ 206 Moises Alou	.25	.11	.03
☐ 207 Albert Belle	1.25	.55	.16
☐ 208 Barry Bonds	.75	.35	.09
☐ 209 Fred McGriff	.50	.23	.06
☐ 210 Dennis Eckersley	.25	.11	.03
☐ 211 Craig Biggio	.25	.11	.03
☐ 212 David Cone	.25	.11	.03
☐ 213 Will Clark	.50	.23	.06
☐ 214 Cal Ripken	2.50	1.10	.30
☐ 215 Wade Boggs	.50	.23	.06
☐ 216 Pete Schourek	.25	.11	.03
☐ 217 Darren Daulton	.25	.11	.03
☐ 218 Carlos Baerga	.25	.11	.03
☐ 219 Larry Walker	.50	.23	.06
☐ 220 Denny Neagle	.25	.11	.03
☐ 221 Jim Edmonds	.25	.11	.03
☐ 222 Lee Smith	.25	.11	.03

☐ 223 Jason Isringhausen	.50	.23	.06
☐ 224 Jay Buhner	.50	.23	.06
☐ 225 John Olerud	.10	.05	.01
☐ 226 Jeff Conine	.25	.11	.03
☐ 227 Dean Palmer	.50	.23	.06
☐ 228 Jim Abbott	.50	.23	.06
☐ 229 Raul Mondesi	.50	.23	.06
☐ 230 Tom Glavine	.50	.23	.06
☐ 231 Kevin Seitzer	.10	.05	.01
☐ 232 Lenny Dykstra	.25	.11	.03
☐ 233 Brian Jordan	.25	.11	.03
☐ 234 Rondell White	.25	.11	.03
☐ 235 Bret Boone	.10	.05	.01
☐ 236 Randy Johnson	.50	.23	.06
☐ 237 Paul O'Neill	.10	.05	.01
☐ 238 Jim Thome	.60	.25	.07
☐ 239 Edgardo Alfonzo	.25	.11	.03
☐ 240 Terry Pendleton	.25	.11	.03
☐ 241 Harold Baines	.25	.11	.03
☐ 242 Roberto Alomar	.60	.25	.07
☐ 243 Mark Grace	.50	.23	.06
☐ 244 Derek Bell	.25	.11	.03
☐ 245 Vinny Castilla	.25	.11	.03
☐ 246 Cecil Fielder	.25	.11	.03
☐ 247 Roger Clemens	.60	.25	.07
☐ 248 Orel Hershiser	.25	.11	.03
☐ 249 J.T. Snow	.25	.11	.03
☐ 250 Rafael Palmeiro	.50	.23	.06
☐ 251 Bret Saberhagen	.10	.05	.01
☐ 252 Todd Hollandsworth	.25	.11	.03
☐ 253 Ryan Klesko	.50	.23	.06
☐ 254 Greg Maddux HH	1.00	.45	.12
☐ 255 Ken Griffey Jr. HH	1.50	.70	.19
☐ 256 Hideo Nomo HH	.50	.23	.06
☐ 257 Frank Thomas HH	1.50	.70	.19
☐ 258 Cal Ripken HH	1.25	.55	.16
☐ 259 Jeff Bagwell HH	.60	.25	.07
☐ 260 Barry Bonds HH	.50	.23	.06
☐ 261 Mo Vaughn HH	.50	.23	.06
☐ 262 Albert Belle HH	.60	.25	.07
☐ 263 Sammy Sosa HH	.50	.23	.06
☐ 264 Reggie Sanders HH	.25	.11	.03
☐ 265 Mike Piazza HH	1.00	.45	.12
☐ 266 Chipper Jones HH	1.00	.45	.12
☐ 267 Tony Gwynn HH	.60	.25	.07
☐ 268 Kirby Puckett HH	.50	.23	.06
☐ 269 Wade Boggs HH	.50	.23	.06
☐ 270 Will Clark HH	.50	.23	.06
☐ 271 Gary Sheffield HH	.50	.23	.06
☐ 272 Dante Bichette HH	.50	.23	.06
☐ 273 Randy Johnson HH	.50	.23	.06
☐ 274 Matt Williams HH	.50	.23	.06
☐ 275 Alex Rodriguez HH	1.50	.70	.19
☐ 276 Tim Salmon HH	.50	.23	.06
☐ 277 Johnny Damon HH	.25	.11	.03
☐ 278 Manny Ramirez HH	.25	.11	.03
☐ 279 Derek Jeter HH	1.00	.45	.12
☐ 280 Eddie Murray HH	.50	.23	.06
☐ 281 Ozzie Smith HH	.50	.23	.06
☐ 282 Garret Anderson HH	.25	.11	.03
☐ 283 Raul Mondesi HH	.50	.23	.06
☐ 284 Terry Steinbach	.25	.11	.03
☐ 285 Carlos Garcia	.10	.05	.01
☐ 286 Dave Justice	.25	.11	.03
☐ 287 Eric Anthony	.10	.05	.01
☐ 288 Benji Gil	.10	.05	.01
☐ 289 Bob Hamelin	.10	.05	.01
☐ 290 Dwayne Hosey	.10	.05	.01
☐ 291 Andy Pettitte	1.00	.45	.12
☐ 292 Rod Beck	.25	.11	.03
☐ 293 Shane Andrews	.10	.05	.01
☐ 294 Julian Tavarez	.10	.05	.01
☐ 295 Willie Greene	.10	.05	.01
☐ 296 Ismael Valdes	.25	.11	.03
☐ 297 Glenallen Hill	.10	.05	.01
☐ 298 Troy Percival	.25	.11	.03
☐ 299 Ray Durham	.50	.23	.06
☐ 300 Jeff Conine 300	.25	.11	.03
☐ 301 Ken Griffey Jr. 300	1.50	.70	.19
☐ 302 Will Clark 300	.50	.23	.06
☐ 303 Mike Greenwell 300	.10	.05	.01
☐ 304 Carlos Baerga 300	.25	.11	.03
☐ 305A Paul Molitor 300	.50	.23	.06
☐ 305B Jeff Bagwell 300	.60	.25	.07
☐ 306 Mark Grace 300	.50	.23	.06
☐ 307 Don Mattingly 300	.75	.35	.09
☐ 308 Hal Morris 300	.10	.05	.01
☐ 309 Butch Huskey	.25	.11	.03
☐ 310 Ozzie Guillen	.10	.05	.01
☐ 311 Erik Hanson	.10	.05	.01
☐ 312 Kenny Lofton 300	.50	.23	.06
☐ 313 Edgar Martinez 300	.25	.11	.03
☐ 314 Kurt Abbott	.10	.05	.01
☐ 315 John Smoltz	.50	.23	.06
☐ 316 Ariel Prieto	.10	.05	.01
☐ 317 Mark Carreon	.10	.05	.01
☐ 318 Kirby Puckett 300	.50	.23	.06
☐ 319 Carlos Perez	.10	.05	.01
☐ 320 Gary DiSarcina	.10	.05	.01
☐ 321 Trevor Hoffman	.25	.11	.03
☐ 322 Mike Piazza 300	1.00	.45	.12
☐ 323 Frank Thomas 300	1.50	.70	.19
☐ 324 Juan Acevedo	.10	.05	.01
☐ 325 Bip Roberts	.10	.05	.01
☐ 326 Javier Lopez	.50	.23	.06
☐ 327 Benito Santiago	.10	.05	.01
☐ 328 Mark Lewis	.10	.05	.01
☐ 329 Royce Clayton	.10	.05	.01
☐ 330 Tom Gordon	.10	.05	.01
☐ 331 Ben McDonald	.10	.05	.01
☐ 332 Dan Wilson	.10	.05	.01
☐ 333 Ron Gant	.25	.11	.03
☐ 334 Wade Boggs 300	.50	.23	.06
☐ 335 Paul Molitor	.60	.25	.07
☐ 336 Tony Gwynn 300	.60	.25	.07
☐ 337 Sean Berry	.10	.05	.01
☐ 338 Rickey Henderson	.50	.23	.06
☐ 339 Wil Cordero	.10	.05	.01
☐ 340 Kent Mercker	.10	.05	.01
☐ 341 Kenny Rogers	.10	.05	.01
☐ 342 Ryne Sandberg	.75	.35	.09
☐ 343 Charlie Hayes	.10	.05	.01
☐ 344 Andy Benes	.10	.05	.01
☐ 345 Sterling Hitchcock	.10	.05	.01
☐ 346 Bernard Gilkey	.25	.11	.03
☐ 347 Julio Franco	.25	.11	.03
☐ 348 Ken Hill	.25	.11	.03
☐ 349 Russ Davis	.10	.05	.01
☐ 350 Mike Blowers	.10	.05	.01
☐ 351 B.J. Surhoff	.10	.05	.01
☐ 352 Lance Johnson	.25	.11	.03
☐ 353 Darryl Hamilton	.10	.05	.01
☐ 354 Shawon Dunston	.10	.05	.01
☐ 355 Rick Aguilera	.10	.05	.01
☐ 356 Danny Tartabull	.10	.05	.01
☐ 357 Todd Stottlemyre	.10	.05	.01
☐ 358 Mike Bordick	.25	.11	.03
☐ 359 Jack McDowell	.50	.23	.06
☐ 360 Todd Zeile	.25	.11	.03
☐ 361 Tino Martinez	.25	.11	.03
☐ 362 Greg Gagne	.10	.05	.01
☐ 363 Mike Kelly	.10	.05	.01
☐ 364 Tim Raines	.50	.23	.06
☐ 365 Ernie Young	.10	.05	.01
☐ 366 Mike Stanley	.10	.05	.01
☐ 367 Wally Joyner	.10	.05	.01
☐ 368 Karim Garcia	.60	.25	.07
☐ 369 Paul Wilson	.25	.11	.03
☐ 370 Sal Fasano	.10	.05	.01
☐ 371 Jason Schmidt	.50	.23	.06
☐ 372 Livan Hernandez	.50	.23	.06
☐ 373 George Arias	.10	.05	.01
☐ 374 Steve Gibralter	.10	.05	.01
☐ 375 Jermaine Dye	.60	.25	.07
☐ 376 Jason Kendall	.50	.23	.06
☐ 377 Brooks Kieschnick	.50	.23	.06
☐ 378 Jeff Ware	.10	.05	.01
☐ 379 Alan Benes	.50	.23	.06
☐ 380 Rey Ordonez	.50	.23	.06
☐ 381 Jay Powell	.10	.05	.01
☐ 382 Osvaldo Fernandez	.25	.11	.03
☐ 383 Wilton Guerrero	1.50	.70	.19
☐ 384 Eric Owens	.10	.05	.01
☐ 385 George Williams	.10	.05	.01
☐ 386 Chan Ho Park	.50	.23	.06
☐ 387 Jeff Suppan	.50	.23	.06
☐ 388 F.P. Santangelo	.10	.05	.01
☐ 389 Terry Adams	.10	.05	.01
☐ 390 Bob Abreu	.50	.23	.06
☐ 391 Quinton McCracken	.10	.05	.01
☐ 392 Mike Busby	.10	.05	.01
☐ 393 Cal Ripken CL	1.25	.55	.16
☐ 394 Ken Griffey Jr. CL	1.50	.70	.19
☐ 395 Frank Thomas CL	1.50	.70	.19
☐ 396 Chipper Jones CL	1.00	.45	.12
☐ 397 Greg Maddux CL	1.00	.45	.12
☐ 398 Mike Piazza CL	1.00	.45	.12
☐ 399 Superstar CL	1.50	.70	.19
☐ CR1 Cal Ripken Tribute	20.00	9.00	2.50

1996 Pinnacle Foil

This 200-card set is a parallel set to the 1996 Pinnacle second series set and was issued in five-card packs which retailed for $2.99. Produced with micro-etched foil fronts, this limited version is similar in design to the regular second series set.

	MINT	NRMT	EXC
COMPLETE SET (200)	25.00	11.00	3.10
COMMON CARD (201-399)	.15	.07	.02
*STARS: 1.5X BASIC CARDS			

1996 Pinnacle Christie Brinkley Collection

Randomly inserted at the rate of one in 23 packs, this 16-card set features the 1995 World Series participants captured by the lens of

supermodel and photographer Christie Brinkley. The fronts feature color player photos in various poses with different backgrounds. The backs carry a color portrait of the player and Ms. Brinkley with an explanation as to why she posed them as she did.

	MINT	NRMT	EXC
COMPLETE SET (16)	75.00	34.00	9.50
COMMON CARD (1-16)	2.00	.90	.25
☐ 1 Greg Maddux	15.00	6.75	1.85
☐ 2 Ryan Klesko	3.00	1.35	.35
☐ 3 Dave Justice	2.50	1.10	.30
☐ 4 Tom Glavine	3.00	1.35	.35
☐ 5 Chipper Jones	15.00	6.75	1.85
☐ 6 Fred McGriff	3.00	1.35	.35
☐ 7 Javier Lopez	2.50	1.10	.30
☐ 8 Marquis Grissom	2.50	1.10	.30
☐ 9 Jason Schmidt	2.50	1.10	.30
☐ 10 Albert Belle	10.00	4.50	1.25
☐ 11 Manny Ramirez	6.00	2.70	.75
☐ 12 Carlos Baerga	2.00	.90	.25
☐ 13 Sandy Alomar	2.50	1.10	.30
☐ 14 Jim Thome	5.00	2.20	.60
☐ 15 Julio Franco	2.00	.90	.25
☐ 16 Kenny Lofton	6.00	2.70	.75
☐ PCB Christie Brinkley Promo On the Beach	3.00	1.35	.35

1996 Pinnacle Essence of the Game

Randomly inserted in hobby packs only at a rate of one in 23, this 18-card standard-size set takes a unique perspective, photographically capturing the persona of 18 of the game's most popular icons. Using a micro-etched print technology, the fronts display a color player cutout on an acetate card studded with stars, with "Essence of the Game" appearing on a holographic design across the top. On the back, this holographic design carries a highlight.

	MINT	NRMT	EXC
COMPLETE SET (18)	150.00	70.00	19.00
COMMON CARD (1-18)	2.00	.90	.25
☐ 1 Cal Ripken	20.00	9.00	2.50
☐ 2 Greg Maddux	15.00	6.75	1.85
☐ 3 Frank Thomas	25.00	11.00	3.10
☐ 4 Matt Williams	3.00	1.35	.35
☐ 5 Chipper Jones	15.00	6.75	1.85
☐ 6 Reggie Sanders	2.00	.90	.25
☐ 7 Ken Griffey Jr.	25.00	11.00	3.10
☐ 8 Kirby Puckett	10.00	4.50	1.25
☐ 9 Hideo Nomo	6.00	2.70	.75
☐ 10 Mike Piazza	15.00	6.75	1.85
☐ 11 Jeff Bagwell	10.00	4.50	1.25
☐ 12 Mo Vaughn	6.00	2.70	.75
☐ 13 Albert Belle	10.00	4.50	1.25
☐ 14 Tim Salmon	3.00	1.35	.35
☐ 15 Don Mattingly	12.00	5.50	1.50
☐ 16 Will Clark	3.00	1.35	.35
☐ 17 Eddie Murray	6.00	2.70	.75
☐ 18 Barry Bonds	6.00	2.70	.75

1996 Pinnacle First Rate

Randomly inserted in retail packs only at a rate of one in 23, this 18-card set features former first-round draft picks who have become major league superstars done in Dufex print.

	MINT	NRMT	EXC
COMPLETE SET (18)	125.00	55.00	15.50
COMMON CARD (1-18)	2.50	1.10	.30
☐ 1 Ken Griffey Jr.	30.00	13.50	3.70
☐ 2 Frank Thomas	30.00	13.50	3.70
☐ 3 Mo Vaughn	8.00	3.60	1.00
☐ 4 Chipper Jones	20.00	9.00	2.50
☐ 5 Alex Rodriguez	30.00	13.50	3.70
☐ 6 Kirby Puckett	12.00	5.50	1.50

☐ 7 Gary Sheffield	5.00	2.20	.60
☐ 8 Matt Williams	4.00	1.80	.50
☐ 9 Barry Bonds	8.00	3.60	1.00
☐ 10 Craig Biggio	3.00	1.35	.35
☐ 11 Robin Ventura	3.00	1.35	.35
☐ 12 Michael Tucker	4.00	1.80	.50
☐ 13 Derek Jeter	20.00	9.00	2.50
☐ 14 Manny Ramirez	8.00	3.60	1.00
☐ 15 Barry Larkin	3.00	1.35	.35
☐ 16 Shawn Green	2.50	1.10	.30
☐ 17 Will Clark	4.00	1.80	.50
☐ 18 Mark McGwire	10.00	4.50	1.25

1996 Pinnacle Power

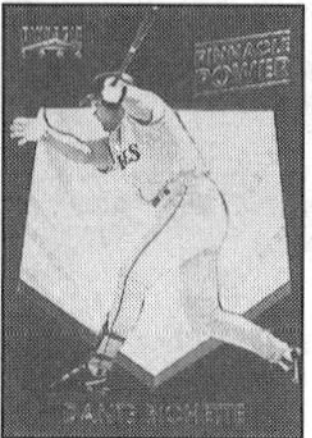

Randomly inserted in packs at a rate of one in 35 retail and hobby packs, or one in 29 jumbo packs, this 20-card set highlights the league's top long-ball hitters in die-cut holographic foil technology. On a black card face, the fronts have a color player cutout superposed over a holographic homeplate. All printing on the front, including the player's name, is stamped in gold foil. The horizontal backs present a color closeup on the left and a player profile on the right.

	MINT	NRMT	EXC
COMPLETE SET (20)	125.00	55.00	15.50
COMMON CARD (1-20)	2.50	1.10	.30
☐ 1 Frank Thomas	30.00	13.50	3.70
☐ 2 Mo Vaughn	8.00	3.60	1.00
☐ 3 Ken Griffey Jr.	30.00	13.50	3.70
☐ 4 Matt Williams	4.00	1.80	.50
☐ 5 Barry Bonds	8.00	3.60	1.00
☐ 6 Reggie Sanders	2.50	1.10	.30
☐ 7 Mike Piazza	20.00	9.00	2.50
☐ 8 Jim Edmonds	3.00	1.35	.35
☐ 9 Dante Bichette	4.00	1.80	.50
☐ 10 Sammy Sosa	5.00	2.20	.60
☐ 11 Jeff Bagwell	12.00	5.50	1.50
☐ 12 Fred McGriff	4.00	1.80	.50
☐ 13 Albert Belle	12.00	5.50	1.50
☐ 14 Tim Salmon	4.00	1.80	.50
☐ 15 Joe Carter	3.00	1.35	.35
☐ 16 Manny Ramirez	8.00	3.60	1.00
☐ 17 Eddie Murray	8.00	3.60	1.00
☐ 18 Cecil Fielder	3.00	1.35	.35
☐ 19 Larry Walker	4.00	1.80	.50
☐ 20 Juan Gonzalez	15.00	6.75	1.85

1996 Pinnacle Project Stardom

This 18-card set was randomly inserted in hobby packs at the rate of one in 35. The fronts feature a color action player photo on a blue foil background with a player portrait framed by silver foil rays depicting a star shining. The backs carry another player portrait with rays coming from behind his head to give the impression of a shining star, and information about the player is printed on the side.

	MINT	NRMT	EXC
COMPLETE SET (18)	150.00	70.00	19.00
COMMON CARD (1-18)	3.00	1.35	.35
☐ 1 Paul Wilson	3.00	1.35	.35
☐ 2 Derek Jeter	30.00	13.50	3.70
☐ 3 Karim Garcia	10.00	4.50	1.25

☐ 4 Johnny Damon	3.00	1.35	.35
☐ 5 Alex Rodriguez	50.00	22.00	6.25
☐ 6 Chipper Jones	30.00	13.50	3.70
☐ 7 Charles Johnson	3.00	1.35	.35
☐ 8 Bob Abreu	5.00	2.20	.60
☐ 9 Alan Benes	5.00	2.20	.60
☐ 10 Richard Hidalgo	5.00	2.20	.60
☐ 11 Brooks Kieschnick	5.00	2.20	.60
☐ 12 Garret Anderson	3.00	1.35	.35
☐ 13 Livan Hernandez	3.00	1.35	.35
☐ 14 Manny Ramirez	12.00	5.50	1.50
☐ 15 Jermaine Dye	8.00	3.60	1.00
☐ 16 Todd Hollandsworth	6.00	2.70	.75
☐ 17 Raul Mondesi	6.00	2.70	.75
☐ 18 Ryan Klesko	8.00	3.60	1.00

1996 Pinnacle Skylines

Randomly inserted in magazine packs at the rate of one in 29, this 18-card set features baseball's best players pictured against their city's skyline and printed on clear plastic stock. The backs carry the same player portrait with information about the player and the city printed below.

	MINT	NRMT	EXC
COMPLETE SET (18)	250.00	110.00	31.00
COMMON CARD (1-18)	6.00	2.70	.75
☐ 1 Ken Griffey Jr.	50.00	22.00	6.25
☐ 2 Frank Thomas	40.00	18.00	5.00
☐ 3 Greg Maddux	30.00	13.50	3.70
☐ 4 Cal Ripken	35.00	16.00	4.40
☐ 5 Albert Belle	20.00	9.00	2.50
☐ 6 Mo Vaughn	12.00	5.50	1.50
☐ 7 Mike Piazza	30.00	13.50	3.70
☐ 8 Wade Boggs	6.00	2.70	.75
☐ 9 Will Clark	6.00	2.70	.75
☐ 10 Barry Bonds	12.00	5.50	1.50
☐ 11 Gary Sheffield	8.00	3.60	1.00
☐ 12 Hideo Nomo	12.00	5.50	1.50
☐ 13 Tony Gwynn	20.00	9.00	2.50
☐ 14 Kirby Puckett	20.00	9.00	2.50
☐ 15 Chipper Jones	30.00	13.50	3.70
☐ 16 Jeff Bagwell	20.00	9.00	2.50
☐ 17 Manny Ramirez	12.00	5.50	1.50
☐ 18 Raul Mondesi	6.00	2.70	.75

1996 Pinnacle Slugfest

Randomly inserted exclusively into one in every 35 series 2 retail packs, cards from this 18 cards set feature a selection of baseball's top slugging stars. The fronts carry a color action player photo on a silver foil starburst background. The backs display a color player photo in a wooden bat with player information on the side.

	MINT	NRMT	EXC
COMPLETE SET (18)	200.00	90.00	25.00
COMMON CARD (1-18)	3.00	1.35	.35
☐ 1 Frank Thomas	40.00	18.00	5.00
☐ 2 Ken Griffey Jr.	40.00	18.00	5.00
☐ 3 Jeff Bagwell	15.00	6.75	1.85
☐ 4 Barry Bonds	10.00	4.50	1.25
☐ 5 Mo Vaughn	10.00	4.50	1.25
☐ 6 Albert Belle	15.00	6.75	1.85
☐ 7 Mike Piazza	25.00	11.00	3.10
☐ 8 Matt Williams	5.00	2.20	.60
☐ 9 Dante Bichette	5.00	2.20	.60
☐ 10 Sammy Sosa	6.00	2.70	.75
☐ 11 Gary Sheffield	6.00	2.70	.75
☐ 12 Reggie Sanders	3.00	1.35	.35
☐ 13 Manny Ramirez	10.00	4.50	1.25
☐ 14 Eddie Murray	10.00	4.50	1.25
☐ 15 Juan Gonzalez	20.00	9.00	2.50
☐ 16 Dean Palmer	3.00	1.35	.35
☐ 17 Rafael Palmeiro	5.00	2.20	.60
☐ 18 Cecil Fielder	4.00	1.80	.50

1996 Pinnacle Starburst

Randomly inserted in first and second series packs at a rate of one in seven, this 200-card quasi-parallel insert set features a select group of major league baseball's hottest superstars derived from the 399-card regular set. Unlike the basic cards, Starburst's are printed on all-foil Dufex card stock. The numbering also differs from the regular issue.

	MINT	NRMT	EXC
COMPLETE SET (200)	600.00	275.00	75.00
COMPLETE SERIES 1 (100)	300.00	135.00	38.00
COMPLETE SERIES 2 (100)	300.00	135.00	38.00
COMMON CARD (1-200)	1.00	.45	.12
☐ 1 Greg Maddux	20.00	9.00	2.50
☐ 2 Bill Pulsipher	1.00	.45	.12
☐ 3 Dante Bichette	4.00	1.80	.50
☐ 4 Mike Piazza	20.00	9.00	2.50
☐ 5 Garret Anderson	1.00	.45	.12
☐ 6 Chuck Knoblauch	4.00	1.80	.50
☐ 7 Jeff Bagwell	12.00	5.50	1.50
☐ 8 Wil Cordero	1.00	.45	.12
☐ 9 Travis Fryman	2.00	.90	.25
☐ 10 Reggie Sanders	2.00	.90	.25
☐ 11 Deion Sanders	4.00	1.80	.50
☐ 12 Tim Salmon	4.00	1.80	.50
☐ 13 Tino Martinez	2.00	.90	.25
☐ 14 Bobby Bonilla	2.00	.90	.25
☐ 15 Joe Carter	2.00	.90	.25
☐ 16 Mike Mussina	6.00	2.70	.75
☐ 17 Jose Canseco	4.00	1.80	.50
☐ 18 Manny Ramirez	8.00	3.60	1.00
☐ 19 Gregg Jefferies	2.00	.90	.25
☐ 20 Charles Johnson	2.00	.90	.25
☐ 21 Brian L. Hunter	2.00	.90	.25
☐ 22 Ray Lankford	2.00	.90	.25
☐ 23 Ivan Rodriguez	8.00	3.60	1.00
☐ 24 Paul Molitor	6.00	2.70	.75
☐ 25 Eric Karros	2.00	.90	.25
☐ 26 Edgar Martinez	2.00	.90	.25
☐ 27 Shawon Dunston	1.00	.45	.12
☐ 28 Mo Vaughn	8.00	3.60	1.00
☐ 29 Pedro J. Martinez	2.00	.90	.25
☐ 30 Marty Cordova	2.00	.90	.25
☐ 31 Ken Caminiti	4.00	1.80	.50
☐ 32 Gary Sheffield	4.00	1.80	.50
☐ 33 Shawn Green	1.00	.45	.12
☐ 34 Cliff Floyd	1.00	.45	.12
☐ 35 Andres Galarraga	4.00	1.80	.50
☐ 36 Matt Williams	4.00	1.80	.50
☐ 37 Don Mattingly	15.00	6.75	1.85
☐ 38 Kevin Appier	2.00	.90	.25
☐ 39 Ozzie Smith	8.00	3.60	1.00
☐ 40 Kenny Lofton	8.00	3.60	1.00
☐ 41 Ken Griffey Jr. UER card mentions him as a swtich-hitter Griffey only bats left	30.00	13.50	3.70
☐ 42 Jack McDowell	2.00	.90	.25
☐ 43 Gary Gaetti	1.00	.45	.12
☐ 44 Dennis Martinez	2.00	.90	.25
☐ 45 Chipper Jones	20.00	9.00	2.50
☐ 46 Eddie Murray	8.00	3.60	1.00
☐ 47 Bernie Williams	6.00	2.70	.75
☐ 48 Andre Dawson	2.00	.90	.25
☐ 49 Dave Winfield	4.00	1.80	.50
☐ 50 B.J. Surhoff	1.00	.45	.12
☐ 51 Barry Larkin	4.00	1.80	.50
☐ 52 Alan Trammell	2.00	.90	.25
☐ 53 Sammy Sosa	4.00	1.80	.50
☐ 54 Hideo Nomo	8.00	3.60	1.00
☐ 55 Mark McGwire	10.00	4.50	1.25
☐ 56 Jay Bell	1.00	.45	.12
☐ 57 Juan Gonzalez	15.00	6.75	1.85
☐ 58 Chili Davis	1.00	.45	.12
☐ 59 Robin Ventura	2.00	.90	.25
☐ 60 John Mabry	2.00	.90	.25
☐ 61 Ken Griffey Jr. NAT	15.00	6.75	1.85
☐ 62 Frank Thomas NAT	15.00	6.75	1.85
☐ 63 Cal Ripken NAT	12.00	5.50	1.50
☐ 64 Albert Belle NAT	6.00	2.70	.75
☐ 65 Mike Piazza NAT	10.00	4.50	1.25
☐ 66 Dante Bichette NAT	4.00	1.80	.50
☐ 67 Sammy Sosa NAT	4.00	1.80	.50
☐ 68 Mo Vaughn NAT	4.00	1.80	.50
☐ 69 Tim Salmon NAT	4.00	1.80	.50
☐ 70 Reggie Sanders NAT	2.00	.90	.25
☐ 71 Cecil Fielder NAT	2.00	.90	.25
☐ 72 Jim Edmonds NAT	2.00	.90	.25
☐ 73 Rafael Palmeiro NAT	4.00	1.80	.50
☐ 74 Edgar Martinez NAT	2.00	.90	.25
☐ 75 Barry Bonds NAT	4.00	1.80	.50
☐ 76 Manny Ramirez NAT	4.00	1.80	.50
☐ 77 Larry Walker NAT	4.00	1.80	.50
☐ 78 Jeff Bagwell NAT	6.00	2.70	.75
☐ 79 Ron Gant NAT	2.00	.90	.25
☐ 80 Andres Galarraga NAT	4.00	1.80	.50
☐ 81 Eddie Murray NAT	4.00	1.80	.50
☐ 82 Kirby Puckett NAT	5.00	2.20	.60
☐ 83 Will Clark NAT	4.00	1.80	.50
☐ 84 Don Mattingly NAT	8.00	3.60	1.00
☐ 85 Mark McGwire NAT	5.00	2.20	.60
☐ 86 Dean Palmer NAT	2.00	.90	.25
☐ 87 Matt Williams NAT	4.00	1.80	.50
☐ 88 Fred McGriff NAT	4.00	1.80	.50
☐ 89 Joe Carter NAT	2.00	.90	.25
☐ 90 Juan Gonzalez NAT	8.00	3.60	1.00
☐ 91 Alex Ochoa	2.00	.90	.25
☐ 92 Ruben Rivera	6.00	2.70	.75
☐ 93 Tony Clark	6.00	2.70	.75
☐ 94 Pete Schourek	1.00	.45	.12
☐ 95 Terrell Wade	2.00	.90	.25
☐ 96 Johnny Damon	2.00	.90	.25
☐ 97 Derek Jeter	20.00	9.00	2.50
☐ 98 Phil Nevin	1.00	.45	.12
☐ 99 Robert Perez	1.00	.45	.12
☐ 100 Dustin Hermanson	1.00	.45	.12
☐ 101 Frank Thomas	30.00	13.50	3.70
☐ 102 Michael Tucker	2.00	.90	.25
☐ 103 Kirby Puckett	12.00	5.50	1.50
☐ 104 Alex Gonzalez	1.00	.45	.12
☐ 105 Tony Gwynn	12.00	5.50	1.50
☐ 106 Moises Alou	2.00	.90	.25
☐ 107 Albert Belle	12.00	5.50	1.50
☐ 108 Barry Bonds	8.00	3.60	1.00
☐ 109 Fred McGriff	4.00	1.80	.50
☐ 110 Dennis Eckersley	2.00	.90	.25
☐ 111 Craig Biggio	2.00	.90	.25
☐ 112 David Cone	2.00	.90	.25
☐ 113 Will Clark	4.00	1.80	.50
☐ 114 Cal Ripken	25.00	11.00	3.10
☐ 115 Wade Boggs	4.00	1.80	.50
☐ 116 Pete Schourek	1.00	.45	.12
☐ 117 Darren Daulton	2.00	.90	.25
☐ 118 Carlos Baerga	2.00	.90	.25
☐ 119 Larry Walker	4.00	1.80	.50
☐ 120 Denny Neagle	2.00	.90	.25
☐ 121 Jim Edmonds	2.00	.90	.25
☐ 122 Lee Smith	2.00	.90	.25
☐ 123 Jason Isringhausen	4.00	1.80	.50
☐ 124 Jay Buhner	4.00	1.80	.50
☐ 125 John Olerud	1.00	.45	.12
☐ 126 Jeff Conine	2.00	.90	.25
☐ 127 Dean Palmer	2.00	.90	.25
☐ 128 Jim Abbott	1.00	.45	.12
☐ 129 Raul Mondesi	4.00	1.80	.50
☐ 130 Tom Glavine	4.00	1.80	.50
☐ 131 Kevin Seitzer	1.00	.45	.12
☐ 132 Lenny Dykstra	2.00	.90	.25
☐ 133 Brian Jordan	2.00	.90	.25
☐ 134 Rondell White	2.00	.90	.25
☐ 135 Bret Boone	1.00	.45	.12
☐ 136 Randy Johnson	4.00	1.80	.50
☐ 137 Paul O'Neill	1.00	.45	.12
☐ 138 Jim Thome	6.00	2.70	.75
☐ 139 Edgardo Alfonzo	1.00	.45	.12
☐ 140 Terry Pendleton	2.00	.90	.25
☐ 141 Harold Baines	2.00	.90	.25
☐ 142 Roberto Alomar	6.00	2.70	.75
☐ 143 Mark Grace	4.00	1.80	.50
☐ 144 Derek Bell	2.00	.90	.25
☐ 145 Vinny Castilla	2.00	.90	.25
☐ 146 Cecil Fielder	2.00	.90	.25
☐ 147 Roger Clemens	6.00	2.70	.75
☐ 148 Orel Hershiser	2.00	.90	.25
☐ 149 J.T. Snow	1.00	.45	.12
☐ 150 Rafael Palmeiro	4.00	1.80	.50
☐ 151 Bret Saberhagen	1.00	.45	.12
☐ 152 Todd Hollandsworth	2.00	.90	.25
☐ 153 Ryan Klesko	4.00	1.80	.50
☐ 154 Greg Maddux HH	10.00	4.50	1.25
☐ 155 Ken Griffey Jr. HH	15.00	6.75	1.85
☐ 156 Hideo Nomo HH	4.00	1.80	.50
☐ 157 Frank Thomas HH	15.00	6.75	1.85
☐ 158 Cal Ripken HH	12.00	5.50	1.50
☐ 159 Jeff Bagwell HH	6.00	2.70	.75
☐ 160 Barry Bonds HH	4.00	1.80	.50
☐ 161 Mo Vaughn HH	4.00	1.80	.50
☐ 162 Albert Belle HH	6.00	2.70	.75
☐ 163 Sammy Sosa HH	4.00	1.80	.50
☐ 164 Reggie Sanders HH	2.00	.90	.25
☐ 165 Mike Piazza HH	10.00	4.50	1.25
☐ 166 Chipper Jones HH	10.00	4.50	1.25
☐ 167 Tony Gwynn HH	6.00	2.70	.75
☐ 168 Kirby Puckett HH	5.00	2.20	.60
☐ 169 Wade Boggs HH	4.00	1.80	.50
☐ 170 Will Clark HH	4.00	1.80	.50
☐ 171 Gary Sheffield HH	4.00	1.80	.50
☐ 172 Dante Bichette HH	4.00	1.80	.50
☐ 173 Randy Johnson HH	4.00	1.80	.50
☐ 174 Matt Williams HH	4.00	1.80	.50
☐ 175 Alex Rodriguez HH	15.00	6.75	1.85
☐ 176 Tim Salmon HH	4.00	1.80	.50
☐ 177 Johnny Damon HH	2.00	.90	.25
☐ 178 Manny Ramirez HH	4.00	1.80	.50
☐ 179 Derek Jeter HH	10.00	4.50	1.25
☐ 180 Eddie Murray HH	4.00	1.80	.50
☐ 181 Ozzie Smith HH	4.00	1.80	.50
☐ 182 Garret Anderson HH	1.00	.45	.12
☐ 183 Raul Mondesi HH	4.00	1.80	.50
☐ 184 Jeff Conine 300	2.00	.90	.25
☐ 185 Ken Griffey Jr. 300	15.00	6.75	1.85
☐ 186 Will Clark 300	4.00	1.80	.50
☐ 187 Mike Greenwell 300	1.00	.45	.12
☐ 188 Carlos Baerga 300	2.00	.90	.25
☐ 189 Paul Molitor 300	4.00	1.80	.50
☐ 190 Jeff Bagwell 300	6.00	2.70	.75
☐ 191 Mark Grace 300	4.00	1.80	.50
☐ 192 Don Mattingly 300	8.00	3.60	1.00
☐ 193 Hal Morris 300	1.00	.45	.12
☐ 194 Kenny Lofton 300	4.00	1.80	.50
☐ 195 Edgar Martinez 300	2.00	.90	.25
☐ 196 Kirby Puckett 300	5.00	2.20	.60
☐ 197 Mike Piazza 300	10.00	4.50	1.25
☐ 198 Frank Thomas 300	15.00	6.75	1.85
☐ 199 Wade Boggs 300	4.00	1.80	.50
☐ 200 Tony Gwynn 300	6.00	2.70	.75

1996 Pinnacle Starburst Artist's Proofs

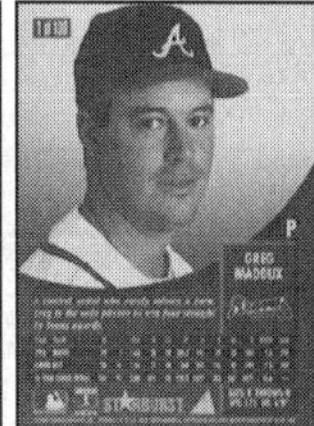

Randomly inserted in packs at a rate of one in 35, this 200-card is a parallel issue to the more common Starburst inserts. The cards are identical to their Starburst counterparts except for the foil "Artist's Proofs" wording on their fronts.

	MINT	NRMT	EXC
COMPLETE SET (200)	2000.00	900.00	250.00
COMPLETE SERIES 1 (100)	1000.00	450.00	125.00
COMPLETE SERIES 2 (100)	1000.00	450.00	125.00
COMMON CARD (1-200)	3.00	1.35	.35

*STARS: 1.5X to 3X BASIC CARDS ...
*YOUNG STARS: 1.25X to 2.5X BASIC CARDS

1996 Pinnacle Team Pinnacle

Randomly inserted in packs at a rate of one in 72, this 9-card set spotlights double-front all-foil Dufex card designs featuring nine top AL and NL players, by position, back-to-back. On a gold foil background displaying a baseball, the fronts present a color player cutout extending beyond the picture frame. "Team Pinnacle," the player's name, and an abbreviation for his position are printed in the bottom border. Only one side of each card is Dufexed.

	MINT	NRMT	EXC
COMPLETE SET (9)	200.00	90.00	25.00
COMMON CARD (1-9)	8.00	3.60	1.00
☐ 1 Frank Thomas Jeff Bagwell	50.00	22.00	6.25
☐ 2 Chuck Knoblauch Craig Biggio	8.00	3.60	1.00
☐ 3 Jim Thome Matt Williams	12.00	5.50	1.50
☐ 4 Barrry Larkin Cal Ripken	40.00	18.00	5.00
☐ 5 Barry Bonds Tim Salmon	15.00	6.75	1.85
☐ 6 Ken Griffey Jr. Reggie Sanders	40.00	18.00	5.00
☐ 7 Albert Belle Sammy Sosa	20.00	9.00	2.50
☐ 8 Ivan Rodriguez Mike Piazza	30.00	13.50	3.70
☐ 9 Greg Maddux Randy Johnson	30.00	13.50	3.70

1996 Pinnacle Team Spirit

Randomly inserted at the rate of one in 72 packs, this 12-card set features color action player images in holographic foil stamping over a silver foil ball outlined in baseball stitching. The backs carry two player photos and player information.

	MINT	NRMT	EXC
COMPLETE SET (12)	300.00	135.00	38.00
COMMON CARD (1-12)	6.00	2.70	.75
□ 1 Greg Maddux	30.00	13.50	3.70
□ 2 Ken Griffey Jr.	50.00	22.00	6.25
□ 3 Derek Jeter	30.00	13.50	3.70
□ 4 Mike Piazza	30.00	13.50	3.70
□ 5 Cal Ripken	40.00	18.00	5.00
□ 6 Frank Thomas	50.00	22.00	6.25
□ 7 Jeff Bagwell	20.00	9.00	2.50
□ 8 Mo Vaughn	12.00	5.50	1.50
□ 9 Albert Belle	20.00	9.00	2.50
□ 10 Chipper Jones	30.00	13.50	3.70
□ 11 Johnny Damon	6.00	2.70	.75
□ 12 Barry Bonds	12.00	5.50	1.50

1996 Pinnacle Team Tomorrow

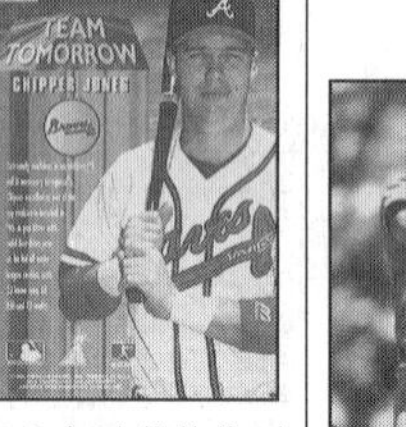

Randomly inserted in jumbo packs at a rate of one in 19, this 10-card set is a jumbo exclusive and features the next crop of superstars. The fronts are printed in an all-foil Dufex design with two of the same color player action cutouts--one close up and the other full-length. The backs carry a color player portrait and information about the player.

	MINT	NRMT	EXC
COMPLETE SET (10)	120.00	55.00	15.00
COMMON CARD (1-10)	3.00	1.35	.35
□ 1 Ruben Rivera	8.00	3.60	1.00
□ 2 Johnny Damon	5.00	2.20	.60
□ 3 Raul Mondesi	6.00	2.70	.75
□ 4 Manny Ramirez	12.00	5.50	1.50
□ 5 Hideo Nomo	12.00	5.50	1.50
□ 6 Chipper Jones	30.00	13.50	3.70
□ 7 Garret Anderson	3.00	1.35	.35
□ 8 Alex Rodriguez	50.00	22.00	6.25
□ 9 Derek Jeter	30.00	13.50	3.70
□ 10 Karim Garcia	10.00	4.50	1.25

1996 Pinnacle FanFest

This standard-size set was issued by Pinnacle in conjunction with the 1996 Pinnacle All-Star FanFest held in Philadelphia and was distributed in two-card poly packs. The Daulton card (#30) features Sportflics technology and was inserted at a rate of about 1:60 packs. The Carlton card (#31) was used for the official FanFest badges; apparently, some loose cards also were given to FanFest volunteers. The Carlton card is not considered part of the complete set. Five other cards (with the same design but no foil stamping or UV coating) were also issued by Pinnacle as part of the celebration. These five cards feature different personalities (most of whom are non-baseball related) involved in the show. The set is considered complete at 30 cards with the Daulton SP.

	MINT	NRMT	EXC
COMPLETE SET (30)	25.00	11.00	3.10
COMMON CARD (1-30)	.25	.11	.03
□ 1 Cal Ripken	2.50	1.10	.30
□ 2 Greg Maddux	1.75	.80	.22
□ 3 Ken Griffey Jr.	3.00	1.35	.35
□ 4 Frank Thomas	3.00	1.35	.35
□ 5 Jeff Bagwell	1.25	.55	.16
□ 6 Hideo Nomo	1.25	.55	.16
□ 7 Tony Gwynn	1.50	.70	.19
□ 8 Albert Belle	2.00	.90	.25
□ 9 Mo Vaughn	1.00	.45	.12
□ 10 Mike Piazza	2.50	1.10	.30
□ 11 Dante Bichette	1.00	.45	.12
□ 12 Ryne Sandberg	1.25	.55	.16
□ 13 Wade Boggs	.60	.25	.07
□ 14 Kirby Puckett	1.50	.70	.19
□ 15 Ozzie Smith	1.25	.55	.16
□ 16 Barry Bonds	1.00	.45	.12
□ 17 Gary Sheffield	.60	.25	.07
□ 18 Barry Larkin	1.00	.45	.12
□ 19 Kevin Seitzer	.25	.11	.03
□ 20 Jay Bell	.25	.11	.03
□ 21 Chipper Jones	2.50	1.10	.30
□ 22 Ivan Rodriguez	.75	.35	.09
□ 23 Cecil Fielder	.50	.23	.06
□ 24 Manny Ramirez	.75	.35	.09
□ 25 Randy Johnson	1.00	.45	.12
□ 26 Moises Alou	.50	.23	.06
□ 27 Mark McGwire	1.50	.70	.19
□ 28 Jason Isringhausen	1.50	.70	.19
□ 29 Joe Carter	.50	.23	.06
□ 30 Darren Daulton SP	10.00	4.50	1.25
□ 31 Steve Carlton	10.00	4.50	1.25
□ BF1 Ben Franklin	5.00	2.20	.60
□ BS1 Bud Selig COMM	10.00	4.50	1.25
□ ER1 Ed Rendell Mayor of Philadelphia	5.00	2.20	.60
□ JS1 John Street City Councilman	5.00	2.20	.60
□ PP1 Phillie Phanatic	10.00	4.50	1.25

1997 Pinnacle

The 1997 Pinnacle set was issued in two series of 200 and ??? cards respectively. Cards were distributed in 10-card hobby and retail packs (SRP $2.49) and 7-card magazine packs. The first series was released in February, 1997. The first series contains the following subsets: Rookies (156-185), Clout (186-197) and Checklists (198-200). Basic card fronts feature full color action shots with dramatic gold foil treatment across the bottom. A conglomeration of legendary players, locales and other regional names of interest related to the specified team of the featured player run in small type within the gold foil borders. Backs feature a small, color mug-shot along with various statistics and information. There are no key Rookie Cards in this set.

	MINT	NRMT	EXC
COMPLETE SERIES 1 (200)	25.00	11.00	3.10
COMMON CARD (1-200)	.10	.05	.01
□ 1 Cecil Fielder	.25	.11	.03
□ 2 Garret Anderson	.10	.05	.01
□ 3 Charles Nagy	.25	.11	.03
□ 4 Darryl Hamilton	.10	.05	.01
□ 5 Greg Myers	.10	.05	.01
□ 6 Eric Davis	.10	.05	.01
□ 7 Jeff Frye	.10	.05	.01
□ 8 Marquis Grissom	.25	.11	.03
□ 9 Curt Schilling	.10	.05	.01
□ 10 Jeff Fassero	.10	.05	.01
□ 11 Alan Benes	.25	.11	.03
□ 12 Orlando Miller	.10	.05	.01
□ 13 Alex Fernandez	.25	.11	.03
□ 14 Andy Pettitte	.75	.35	.09
□ 15 Andre Dawson	.25	.11	.03
□ 16 Mark Grudzielanek	.10	.05	.01
□ 17 Joe Vitiello	.10	.05	.01
□ 18 Juan Gonzalez	1.50	.70	.19
□ 19 Mark Whiten	.10	.05	.01
□ 20 Lance Johnson	.10	.05	.01
□ 21 Trevor Hoffman	.10	.05	.01
□ 22 Marc Newfield	.10	.05	.01
□ 23 Jim Eisenreich	.10	.05	.01
□ 24 Joe Carter	.25	.11	.03
□ 25 Jose Canseco	.40	.18	.05
□ 26 Bill Swift	.10	.05	.01
□ 27 Ellis Burks	.25	.11	.03
□ 28 Ben McDonald	.10	.05	.01
□ 29 Edgar Martinez	.25	.11	.03
□ 30 Jamie Moyer	.10	.05	.01
□ 31 Chan Ho Park	.40	.18	.05
□ 32 Carlos Delgado	.25	.11	.03
□ 33 Kevin Mitchell	.10	.05	.01
□ 34 Carlos Garcia	.10	.05	.01
□ 35 Darryl Strawberry	.25	.11	.03
□ 36 Jim Thome	.60	.25	.07
□ 37 Jose Offerman	.10	.05	.01
□ 38 Ryan Klesko	.50	.23	.06
□ 39 Ruben Sierra	.10	.05	.01
□ 40 Devon White	.10	.05	.01
□ 41 Brian Jordan	.25	.11	.03
□ 42 Tony Gwynn	1.25	.55	.16
□ 43 Rafael Palmeiro	.40	.18	.05
□ 44 Dante Bichette	.40	.18	.05
□ 45 Scott Stahoviak	.10	.05	.01
□ 46 Roger Cedeno	.10	.05	.01
□ 47 Ivan Rodriguez	.75	.35	.09
□ 48 Bob Abreu	.40	.18	.05
□ 49 Darryl Kile	.10	.05	.01
□ 50 Darren Dreifort	.10	.05	.01
□ 51 Shawon Dunston	.10	.05	.01
□ 52 Mark McGwire	1.00	.45	.12
□ 53 Tim Salmon	.40	.18	.05
□ 54 Gene Schall	.10	.05	.01
□ 55 Roger Clemens	.60	.25	.07
□ 56 Rondell White	.10	.05	.01
□ 57 Ed Sprague	.10	.05	.01
□ 58 Craig Paquette	.10	.05	.01
□ 59 David Segui	.10	.05	.01
□ 60 Jaime Navarro	.10	.05	.01
□ 61 Tom Glavine	.40	.18	.05
□ 62 Jeff Brantley	.10	.05	.01
□ 63 Kimera Bartee	.10	.05	.01
□ 64 Fernando Vina	.10	.05	.01
□ 65 Eddie Murray	.75	.35	.09
□ 66 Lenny Dykstra	.25	.11	.03
□ 67 Kevin Elster	.10	.05	.01
□ 68 Vinny Castilla	.25	.11	.03
□ 69 Mike Fetters	.10	.05	.01
□ 70 Brett Butler	.10	.05	.01
□ 71 Robby Thompson	.10	.05	.01
□ 72 Reggie Jefferson	.10	.05	.01
□ 73 Todd Hundley	.25	.11	.03
□ 74 Jeff King	.10	.05	.01
□ 75 Ernie Young	.10	.05	.01
□ 76 Jeff Bagwell	1.25	.55	.16
□ 77 Dan Wilson	.10	.05	.01
□ 78 Paul Molitor	.60	.25	.07
□ 79 Kevin Seitzer	.10	.05	.01
□ 80 Kevin Brown	.25	.11	.03
□ 81 Ron Gant	.25	.11	.03
□ 82 Dwight Gooden	.25	.11	.03
□ 83 Todd Stottlemyre	.10	.05	.01
□ 84 Ken Caminiti	.50	.23	.06
□ 85 James Baldwin	.10	.05	.01
□ 86 Jermaine Dye	.50	.23	.06
□ 87 Harold Baines	.10	.05	.01
□ 88 Pat Hentgen	.25	.11	.03
□ 89 Frank Rodriguez	.10	.05	.01
□ 90 Mark Johnson	.10	.05	.01
□ 91 Jason Kendall	.25	.11	.03
□ 92 Alex Rodriguez	3.00	1.35	.35
□ 93 Alan Trammell	.25	.11	.03
□ 94 Scott Brosius	.10	.05	.01
□ 95 Delino DeShields	.10	.05	.01
□ 96 Chipper Jones	2.00	.90	.25
□ 97 Barry Bonds	.75	.35	.09
□ 98 Brady Anderson	.25	.11	.03
□ 99 Ryne Sandberg	.75	.35	.09
□ 100 Albert Belle	1.25	.55	.16
□ 101 Jeff Cirillo	.10	.05	.01
□ 102 Frank Thomas	3.00	1.35	.35
□ 103 Mike Piazza	2.00	.90	.25
□ 104 Rickey Henderson	.40	.18	.05
□ 105 Rey Ordonez	.40	.18	.05
□ 106 Mark Grace	.40	.18	.05
□ 107 Terry Steinbach	.10	.05	.01
□ 108 Ray Durham	.10	.05	.01
□ 109 Barry Larkin	.40	.18	.05
□ 110 Tony Clark	.50	.23	.06
□ 111 Bernie Williams	.60	.25	.07
□ 112 John Smoltz	.50	.23	.06
□ 113 Moises Alou	.25	.11	.03
□ 114 Alex Gonzalez	.10	.05	.01
□ 115 Rico Brogna	.10	.05	.01
□ 116 Eric Karros	.25	.11	.03
□ 117 Jeff Conine	.25	.11	.03
□ 118 Todd Hollandsworth	.25	.11	.03
□ 119 Troy Percival	.10	.05	.01
□ 120 Paul Wilson	.25	.11	.03
□ 121 Orel Hershiser	.25	.11	.03
□ 122 Ozzie Smith	.75	.35	.09
□ 123 Dave Hollins	.10	.05	.01
□ 124 Ken Hill	.10	.05	.01
□ 125 Rick Wilkins	.10	.05	.01
□ 126 Scott Servais	.10	.05	.01
□ 127 Fernando Valenzuela	.25	.11	.03
□ 128 Mariano Rivera	.25	.11	.03
□ 129 Mark Loretta	.10	.05	.01
□ 130 Shane Reynolds	.10	.05	.01
□ 131 Darren Oliver	.10	.05	.01
□ 132 Steve Trachsel	.10	.05	.01
□ 133 Darren Bragg	.10	.05	.01
□ 134 Jason Dickson	.25	.11	.03
□ 135 Darrin Fletcher	.10	.05	.01
□ 136 Gary Gaetti	.10	.05	.01
□ 137 Joey Cora	.10	.05	.01
□ 138 Terry Pendleton	.10	.05	.01
□ 139 Derek Jeter	2.00	.90	.25
□ 140 Danny Tartabull	.10	.05	.01
□ 141 John Flaherty	.10	.05	.01
□ 142 B.J. Surhoff	.10	.05	.01
□ 143 Mike Sweeney	.25	.11	.03
□ 144 Chad Mottola	.10	.05	.01
□ 145 Andujar Cedeno	.10	.05	.01
□ 146 Tim Belcher	.10	.05	.01
□ 147 Mark Thompson	.10	.05	.01
□ 148 Rafael Bournigal	.10	.05	.01
□ 149 Marty Cordova	.25	.11	.03
□ 150 Osvaldo Fernandez	.10	.05	.01
□ 151 Mike Stanley	.10	.05	.01
□ 152 Ricky Bottalico	.10	.05	.01
□ 153 Donne Wall	.10	.05	.01
□ 154 Omar Vizquel	.25	.11	.03
□ 155 Mike Mussina	.50	.23	.06
□ 156 Brant Brown	.10	.05	.01
□ 157 F.P. Santangelo	.10	.05	.01
□ 158 Ryan Hancock	.10	.05	.01
□ 159 Jeff D'Amico	.25	.11	.03
□ 160 Luis Castillo	.40	.18	.05
□ 161 Darin Erstad	1.50	.70	.19
□ 162 Ugueth Urbina	.10	.05	.01
□ 163 Andruw Jones	3.00	1.35	.35
□ 164 Steve Gibralter	.10	.05	.01
□ 165 Robin Jennings	.10	.05	.01
□ 166 Mike Cameron	.50	.23	.06
□ 167 George Arias	.10	.05	.01
□ 168 Chris Stynes	.10	.05	.01
□ 169 Justin Thompson	.25	.11	.03
□ 170 Jamey Wright	.25	.11	.03
□ 171 Todd Walker	1.25	.55	.16
□ 172 Nomar Garciaparra	1.25	.55	.16
□ 173 Jose Paniagua	.10	.05	.01
□ 174 Marvin Benard	.10	.05	.01
□ 175 Rocky Coppinger	.25	.11	.03
□ 176 Quinton McCracken	.10	.05	.01
□ 177 Amaury Telemaco	.10	.05	.01
□ 178 Neifi Perez	.25	.11	.03
□ 179 Todd Greene	.10	.05	.01
□ 180 Jason Thompson	.10	.05	.01
□ 181 Wilton Guerrero	.50	.23	.06
□ 182 Edgar Renteria	.40	.18	.05
□ 183 Billy Wagner	.25	.11	.03
□ 184 Alex Ochoa	.10	.05	.01
□ 185 Dmitri Young	.25	.11	.03
□ 186 Kenny Lofton CT	.10	.05	.01
□ 187 Andres Galarraga CT	.40	.18	.05
□ 188 Chuck Knoblauch CT	.40	.18	.05
□ 189 Greg Maddux CT	1.00	.45	.12
□ 190 Mo Vaughn CT	.40	.18	.05
□ 191 Cal Ripken CT	1.25	.55	.16
□ 192 Hideo Nomo CT	.10	.05	.01
□ 193 Ken Griffey Jr. CT	1.50	.70	.19
□ 194 Sammy Sosa CT	.40	.18	.05
□ 195 Jay Buhner CT	.25	.11	.03
□ 196 Manny Ramirez CT	.10	.05	.01
□ 197 Matt Williams CT	.25	.11	.03
□ 198 Andruw Jones CL	1.50	.70	.19
□ 199 Darin Erstad CL	.75	.35	.09
□ 200 Trey Beamon CL	.10	.05	.01

1997 Pinnacle Artist's Proofs

After three years of producing Artist's Proofs cards, Pinnacle decided to add some changes to their line of scarce parallel cards. Instead of the typical one per box parallel with a little foil logo on front the set was completely redesigned in 1997. Following a similar promotion run in the 1996 Finest brand, the 200-card first series set was broken down into three different groups of cards; 125 bronze, 50 silver and 25 gold. One in every 47 first series packs contained either a bronze, silver or gold Artist's Proofs card. The gold cards are scarcest (only 300 of each were produced), and silver cards are scarcer than bronze cards. Print runs for the bronze and silver cards were never announced. Each group of cards is easy to identify by their bold color-specific backgrounds (i.e. gold cards have gold backgrounds). All three groups share the same Artist's Proof logo on front.

	MINT	NRMT	EXC
COMMON BRONZE	10.00	4.50	1.25
COMMON SILVER	15.00	6.75	1.85
COMMON GOLD	20.00	9.00	2.50
□ 14 Andy Pettitte G	60.00	27.00	7.50
□ 18 Juan Gonzalez G	125.00	55.00	15.50
□ 25 Jose Canseco S	25.00	11.00	3.10
□ 36 Jim Thome G	50.00	22.00	6.25
□ 38 Ryan Klesko S	30.00	13.50	3.70
□ 42 Tony Gwynn S	80.00	36.00	10.00
□ 43 Rafael Palmeiro S	25.00	11.00	3.10
□ 44 Dante Bichette B	20.00	9.00	2.50
□ 47 Ivan Rodriguez G	60.00	27.00	7.50
□ 52 Mark McGwire S	60.00	27.00	7.50
□ 53 Tim Salmon S	25.00	11.00	3.10
□ 55 Roger Clemens B	30.00	13.50	3.70
□ 61 Tom Glavine S	30.00	13.50	3.70
□ 65 Eddie Murray S	50.00	22.00	6.25

☐ 76 Jeff Bagwell G	100.00	45.00	12.50
☐ 78 Paul Molitor G	50.00	22.00	6.25
☐ 84 Ken Caminiti G	40.00	18.00	5.00
☐ 86 Jermaine Dye S	25.00	11.00	3.10
☐ 91 Jason Kendall S	25.00	11.00	3.10
☐ 92 Alex Rodriguez G	250.00	110.00	31.00
☐ 96 Chipper Jones S	125.00	55.00	15.50
☐ 97 Barry Bonds S	50.00	22.00	6.25
☐ 98 Brady Anderson S	25.00	11.00	3.10
☐ 99 Ryne Sandberg S	50.00	22.00	6.25
☐ 100 Albert Belle G	100.00	45.00	12.50
☐ 102 Frank Thomas G	250.00	110.00	31.00
☐ 103 Mike Piazza S	125.00	55.00	15.50
☐ 109 Barry Larkin S	25.00	11.00	3.10
☐ 110 Tony Clark S	30.00	13.50	3.70
☐ 111 Bernie Williams G	50.00	22.00	6.25
☐ 112 John Smoltz G	40.00	18.00	5.00
☐ 118 Todd Hollandsworth G	30.00	13.50	3.70
☐ 122 Ozzie Smith S	50.00	22.00	6.25
☐ 139 Derek Jeter G	150.00	70.00	19.00
☐ 155 Mike Mussina S	30.00	13.50	3.70
☐ 161 Darin Erstad G	100.00	45.00	12.50
☐ 163 Andruw Jones G	200.00	90.00	25.00
☐ 171 Todd Walker G	80.00	36.00	10.00
☐ 172 Nomar Garciaparra B	40.00	18.00	5.00
☐ 186 Kenny Lofton CT B	30.00	13.50	3.70
☐ 189 Greg Maddux CT S	100.00	45.00	12.50
☐ 190 Mo Vaughn CT S	40.00	18.00	5.00
☐ 191 Cal Ripken CT G	150.00	70.00	19.00
☐ 192 Hideo Nomo CT S	40.00	18.00	5.00
☐ 193 Ken Griffey Jr. CT G	200.00	90.00	25.00
☐ 196 Manny Ramirez CT G	50.00	22.00	6.25
☐ 198 Andruw Jones CL B	80.00	36.00	10.00
☐ 199 Darin Erstad CL B	40.00	18.00	5.00

1997 Pinnacle Museum Collection

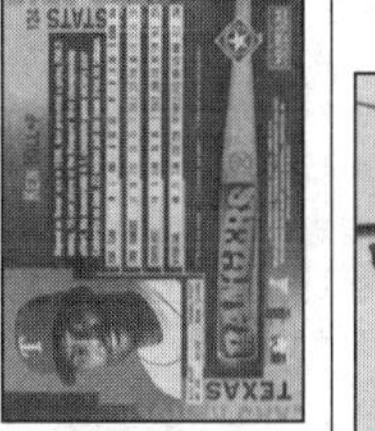

Randomly inserted in all packs at a rate of one in nine, these cards parallel the regular issue. Etched foil fronts differentiate them.

	MINT	NRMT	EXC
COMPLETE SERIES 1 (200)	600.00	275.00	75.00
COMMON CARD (1-200)	1.50	.70	.19

*STARS: 7.5X TO 15X BASIC CARDS
*YOUNG STARS: 6X TO 12X BASIC CARDS

☐ 42 Tony Gwynn	20.00	9.00	2.50
☐ 76 Jeff Bagwell	20.00	9.00	2.50
☐ 92 Alex Rodriguez	50.00	22.00	6.25
☐ 96 Chipper Jones	30.00	13.50	3.70
☐ 100 Albert Belle	20.00	9.00	2.50
☐ 102 Frank Thomas	50.00	22.00	6.25
☐ 103 Mike Piazza	30.00	13.50	3.70
☐ 139 Derek Jeter	30.00	13.50	3.70
☐ 161 Darin Erstad	25.00	11.00	3.10
☐ 163 Andruw Jones	50.00	22.00	6.25
☐ 171 Todd Walker	20.00	9.00	2.50
☐ 172 Nomar Garciaparra	20.00	9.00	2.50
☐ 191 Cal Ripken CT	20.00	9.00	2.50
☐ 193 Ken Griffey Jr. CT	25.00	11.00	3.10
☐ 198 Andruw Jones CL	25.00	11.00	3.10

1997 Pinnacle Cardfrontations

Randomly inserted in hobby packs only at a rate of one in 23, this 20-card set displays color player photos on rainbow holographic foil. The card design features a top pitcher on one side with a top home run hitter on the flip side. Both sides are covered with an opaque peel and reveal protective cover.

	MINT	NRMT	EXC
COMPLETE SET (20)	300.00	135.00	38.00
COMMON CARD (1-20)	5.00	2.20	.60

☐ 1 Greg Maddux Mike Piazza	25.00	11.00	3.10
☐ 2 Tom Glavine Ken Caminiti	6.00	2.70	.75
☐ 3 Randy Johnson Cal Ripken	30.00	13.50	3.70
☐ 4 Kevin Appier Mark McGwire	12.00	5.50	1.50
☐ 5 Andy Pettitte Juan Gonzalez	20.00	9.00	2.50
☐ 6 Pat Hentgen Albert Belle	15.00	6.75	1.85
☐ 7 Hideo Nomo Chipper Jones	25.00	11.00	3.10
☐ 8 Ismael Valdes Sammy Sosa	6.00	2.70	.75
☐ 9 Mike Mussina Manny Ramirez	10.00	4.50	1.25
☐ 10 David Cone Jay Buhner	5.00	2.20	.60
☐ 11 Mark Wohlers Gary Sheffield	6.00	2.70	.75
☐ 12 Alan Benes Barry Bonds	10.00	4.50	1.25
☐ 13 Roger Clemens Ivan Rodriguez	10.00	4.50	1.25
☐ 14 Mariano Rivera Ken Griffey Jr.	40.00	18.00	5.00
☐ 15 Dwight Gooden Frank Thomas	40.00	18.00	5.00
☐ 16 John Wetteland Darin Erstad	20.00	9.00	2.50
☐ 17 John Smoltz Brian Jordan	6.00	2.70	.75
☐ 18 Kevin Brown Jeff Bagwell	15.00	6.75	1.85
☐ 19 Jack McDowell Alex Rodriguez	40.00	18.00	5.00
☐ 20 Charles Nagy Bernie Williams	8.00	3.60	1.00

1997 Pinnacle Home/Away

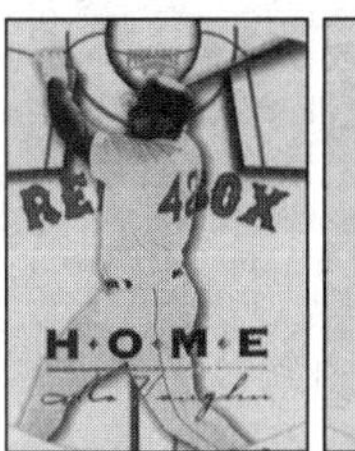
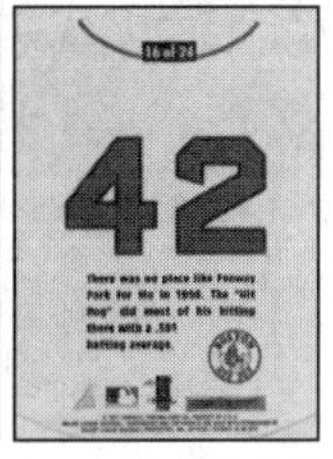

Randomly inserted in retail packs only at a rate of one in 33, this 24-card set features color player photos on die-cut cards.

	MINT	NRMT	EXC
COMPLETE SET (24)	400.00	180.00	50.00
COMMON CARD (1-24)	8.00	3.60	1.00

☐ 1 Chipper Jones	20.00	9.00	2.50
☐ 2 Chipper Jones	20.00	9.00	2.50
☐ 3 Ken Griffey Jr.	30.00	13.50	3.70
☐ 4 Ken Griffey Jr.	30.00	13.50	3.70
☐ 5 Mike Piazza	20.00	9.00	2.50
☐ 6 Mike Piazza	20.00	9.00	2.50
☐ 7 Frank Thomas	30.00	13.50	3.70
☐ 8 Frank Thomas	30.00	13.50	3.70
☐ 9 Jeff Bagwell	12.00	5.50	1.50
☐ 10 Jeff Bagwell	12.00	5.50	1.50
☐ 11 Alex Rodriguez	30.00	13.50	3.70
☐ 12 Alex Rodriguez	30.00	13.50	3.70
☐ 13 Barry Bonds	8.00	3.60	1.00
☐ 14 Barry Bonds	8.00	3.60	1.00
☐ 15 Mo Vaughn	8.00	3.60	1.00
☐ 16 Mo Vaughn	8.00	3.60	1.00
☐ 17 Derek Jeter	20.00	9.00	2.50
☐ 18 Derek Jeter	20.00	9.00	2.50
☐ 19 Mark McGwire	10.00	4.50	1.25
☐ 20 Mark McGwire	10.00	4.50	1.25
☐ 21 Cal Ripken	25.00	11.00	3.10
☐ 22 Cal Ripken	25.00	11.00	3.10
☐ 23 Albert Belle	12.00	5.50	1.50
☐ 24 Albert Belle	12.00	5.50	1.50

1997 Pinnacle Passport to the Majors

Randomly inserted in all first series packs at a rate of one in 36, this 25-card set features color player photos on a bookfold miniature passport card design and honors the rise to fame of some of the League's most high profile superstars.

	MINT	NRMT	EXC
COMPLETE SET (25)	300.00	135.00	38.00
COMMON CARD (1-25)	4.00	1.80	.50

☐ 1 Greg Maddux	25.00	11.00	3.10
☐ 2 Ken Griffey Jr.	40.00	18.00	5.00
☐ 3 Frank Thomas	40.00	18.00	5.00
☐ 4 Cal Ripken	30.00	13.50	3.70
☐ 5 Mike Piazza	25.00	11.00	3.10
☐ 6 Alex Rodriguez	40.00	18.00	5.00
☐ 7 Mo Vaughn	10.00	4.50	1.25

☐ 8 Chipper Jones	25.00	11.00	3.10
☐ 9 Roberto Alomar	8.00	3.60	1.00
☐ 10 Edgar Martinez	4.00	1.80	.50
☐ 11 Javier Lopez	4.00	1.80	.50
☐ 12 Ivan Rodriguez	10.00	4.50	1.25
☐ 13 Juan Gonzalez	20.00	9.00	2.50
☐ 14 Carlos Baerga	4.00	1.80	.50
☐ 15 Sammy Sosa	6.00	2.70	.75
☐ 16 Manny Ramirez	10.00	4.50	1.25
☐ 17 Raul Mondesi	5.00	2.20	.60
☐ 18 Henry Rodriguez	4.00	1.80	.50
☐ 19 Rafael Palmeiro	5.00	2.20	.60
☐ 20 Rey Ordonez	5.00	2.20	.60
☐ 21 Hideo Nomo	10.00	4.50	1.25
☐ 22 Mac Suzuki	4.00	1.80	.50
☐ 23 Chan Ho Park	5.00	2.20	.60
☐ 24 Larry Walker	4.00	1.80	.50
☐ 25 Ruben Rivera	6.00	2.70	.75

1997 Pinnacle Shades

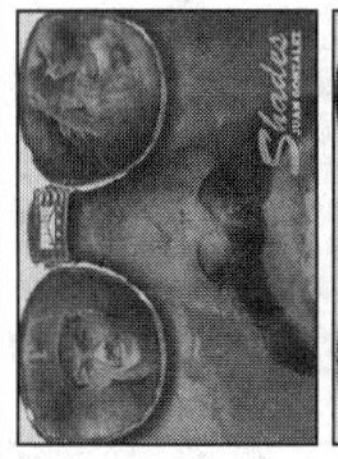
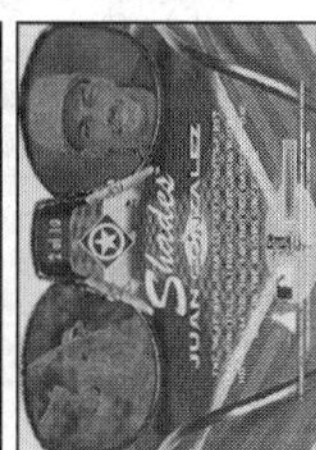

Randomly inserted in packs at a rate of one in 23, this 10-card set features color upclose photos of some of the league's best players wearing their favorite pair of sunglasses. The cards have a die-cut design and mirror mylar finish.

	MINT	NRMT	EXC
COMPLETE SET (10)	120.00	55.00	15.00
COMMON CARD (1-10)	2.50	1.10	.30

☐ 1 Ken Griffey Jr.	25.00	11.00	3.10
☐ 2 Juan Gonzalez	12.00	5.50	1.50
☐ 3 John Smoltz	4.00	1.80	.50
☐ 4 Gary Sheffield	4.00	1.80	.50
☐ 5 Cal Ripken	20.00	9.00	2.50
☐ 6 Mo Vaughn	6.00	2.70	.75
☐ 7 Brian Jordan	2.50	1.10	.30
☐ 8 Mike Piazza	15.00	6.75	1.85
☐ 9 Frank Thomas	25.00	11.00	3.10
☐ 10 Alex Rodriguez	25.00	11.00	3.10

1997 Pinnacle Team Pinnacle

Randomly inserted in packs at a rate of one in 90, this 10-card set matches color player photos of the top American and National League players by position on double-fronted, all-foil Dufex cards. The tenth card is a computer design that makes a full Team Pinnacle picture.

	MINT	NRMT	EXC
COMPLETE SET (10)	325.00	145.00	40.00
COMMON CARD (1-10)	10.00	4.50	1.25

☐ 1 Frank Thomas Jeff Bagwell	60.00	27.00	7.50
☐ 2 Chuck Knoblauch Eric Young	10.00	4.50	1.25
☐ 3 Ken Caminiti Jim Thome	12.00	5.50	1.50
☐ 4 Alex Rodriguez Chipper Jones	60.00	27.00	7.50
☐ 5 Mike Piazza Ivan Rodriguez	40.00	18.00	5.00
☐ 6 Albert Belle Barry Bonds	25.00	11.00	3.10
☐ 7 Ken Griffey Jr. Ellis Burks	50.00	22.00	6.25
☐ 8 Juan Gonzalez Gary Sheffield	30.00	13.50	3.70
☐ 9 John Smoltz Andy Pettitte	15.00	6.75	1.85
☐ 10 Frank Thomas Jeff Bagwell Chuck Knoblauch Eric Young Ken Caminiti Jim Thome Alex Rodriguez Chipper Jones Mike Piazza Ivan Rodriguez Albert Belle Barry Bonds Ken Griffey Jr. Ellis Burks Juan Gonzalez Gary Sheffield John Smoltz Andy Pettitte	60.00	27.00	7.50

1996 Pinnacle Aficionado Promos

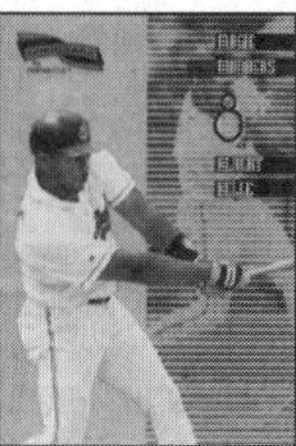
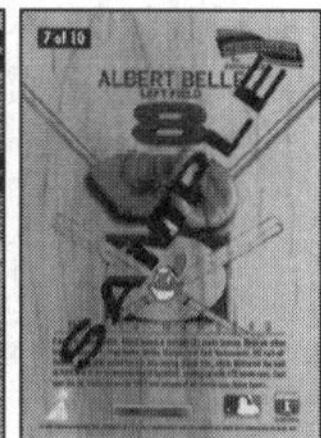

This three-card standard-size set was issued to introduce the new Pinnacle Afficionado brand. The set was distributed to hobby dealers along with promotional information concerning the release.

	MINT	NRMT	EXC
COMPLETE SET (3)	5.00	2.20	.60
COMMON CARD	1.00	.45	.12

☐ 9 Roger Clemens	2.00	.90	.25
☐ 107 Ryan Klesko	1.00	.45	.12
☐ MN7 Albert Belle Magic Number	2.00	.90	.25

1996 Pinnacle Aficionado

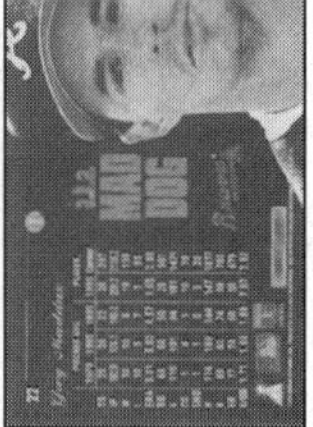

The 1996 Aficionado set was issued in one series totalling 200 cards. The five-card packs retailed for $3.99 and had a special bubble gum scent which was released when the packs were opened. The fronts feature action player photos in sepia tone for players who have played in the Major League for over five years and in color for those who have played less than five years. A heliographic player head print and the player's name printed in gold foil on a wood-look bar round out the front. The backs carry positional comparison statistics between the player and the league average at that position in different eras. Cards numbered 151-160 are a subset titled "Global Reach" and feature color action player cut-outs of international players on a background of a map, a global baseball, and their country's flag.

	MINT	NRMT	EXC
COMPLETE SET (200)	50.00	22.00	6.25
COMMON CARD (1-200)	.25	.11	.03

☐ 1 Jack McDowell	1.00	.45	.12
☐ 2 Jay Bell	.25	.11	.03
☐ 3 Rafael Palmeiro	1.00	.45	.12
☐ 4 Wally Joyner	.25	.11	.03
☐ 5 Ozzie Smith	1.25	.55	.16
☐ 6 Mark McGwire	1.50	.70	.19
☐ 7 Kevin Seitzer	.25	.11	.03
☐ 8 Fred McGriff	1.00	.45	.12
☐ 9 Roger Clemens	1.00	.45	.12
☐ 10 Randy Johnson	1.00	.45	.12
☐ 11 Cecil Fielder	.50	.23	.06
☐ 12 David Cone	.50	.23	.06
☐ 13 Chili Davis	.25	.11	.03
☐ 14 Andres Galarraga	1.00	.45	.12
☐ 15 Joe Carter	.50	.23	.06
☐ 16 Ryne Sandberg	1.25	.55	.16
☐ 17 Paul O'Neill	.25	.11	.03
☐ 18 Cal Ripken	4.00	1.80	.50

☐ 19 Wade Boggs	1.00	.45	.12
☐ 20 Greg Gagne	.25	.11	.03
☐ 21 Edgar Martinez	.50	.23	.06
☐ 22 Greg Maddux	3.00	1.35	.35
☐ 23 Ken Caminiti	1.00	.45	.12
☐ 24 Kirby Puckett	2.00	.90	.25
☐ 25 Craig Biggio	.50	.23	.06
☐ 26 Will Clark	1.00	.45	.12
☐ 27 Ron Gant	.50	.23	.06
☐ 28 Eddie Murray	1.25	.55	.16
☐ 29 Lance Johnson	.50	.23	.06
☐ 30 Tony Gwynn	2.00	.90	.25
☐ 31 Dante Bichette	1.00	.45	.12
☐ 32 Darren Daulton	.50	.23	.06
☐ 33 Danny Tartabull	.25	.11	.03
☐ 34 Jeff King	.25	.11	.03
☐ 35 Tom Glavine	1.00	.45	.12
☐ 36 Rickey Henderson	1.00	.45	.12
☐ 37 Jose Canseco	1.00	.45	.12
☐ 38 Barry Larkin	1.00	.45	.12
☐ 39 Dennis Martinez	.50	.23	.06
☐ 40 Ruben Sierra	.25	.11	.03
☐ 41 Bobby Bonilla	.50	.23	.06
☐ 42 Jeff Conine	.50	.23	.06
☐ 43 Lee Smith	.50	.23	.06
☐ 44 Charlie Hayes	.25	.11	.03
☐ 45 Walt Weiss	.25	.11	.03
☐ 46 Jay Buhner	1.00	.45	.12
☐ 47 Kenny Rogers	.25	.11	.03
☐ 48 Paul Molitor	1.00	.45	.12
☐ 49 Hal Morris	.25	.11	.03
☐ 50 Todd Stottlemyre	.25	.11	.03
☐ 51 Mike Stanley	.25	.11	.03
☐ 52 Mark Grace	1.00	.45	.12
☐ 53 Lenny Dykstra	.50	.23	.06
☐ 54 Andre Dawson	.50	.23	.06
☐ 55 Dennis Eckersley	.50	.23	.06
☐ 56 Ben McDonald	.25	.11	.03
☐ 57 Ray Lankford	.50	.23	.06
☐ 58 Mo Vaughn	1.25	.55	.16
☐ 59 Frank Thomas	5.00	2.20	.60
☐ 60 Julio Franco	.25	.11	.03
☐ 61 Jim Abbott	1.00	.45	.12
☐ 62 Greg Vaughn	1.00	.45	.12
☐ 63 Marquis Grissom	.50	.23	.06
☐ 64 Tino Martinez	.50	.23	.06
☐ 65 Kevin Appier	.50	.23	.06
☐ 66 Matt Williams	1.00	.45	.12
☐ 67 Sammy Sosa	1.00	.45	.12
☐ 68 Larry Walker	1.00	.45	.12
☐ 69 Ivan Rodriguez	1.25	.55	.16
☐ 70 Eric Karros	.50	.23	.06
☐ 71 Bernie Williams	1.00	.45	.12
☐ 72 Carlos Baerga	.50	.23	.06
☐ 73 Jeff Bagwell	2.00	.90	.25
☐ 74 Pete Schourek	.25	.11	.03
☐ 75 Ken Griffey Jr.	5.00	2.20	.60
☐ 76 Bernard Gilkey	.50	.23	.06
☐ 77 Albert Belle	2.00	.90	.25
☐ 78 Chuck Knoblauch	1.00	.45	.12
☐ 79 John Smoltz	1.00	.45	.12
☐ 80 Barry Bonds	1.25	.55	.16
☐ 81 Vinny Castilla	.50	.23	.06
☐ 82 John Olerud	.25	.11	.03
☐ 83 Mike Mussina	1.00	.45	.12
☐ 84 Alex Fernandez	.50	.23	.06
☐ 85 Shawon Dunston	.25	.11	.03
☐ 86 Travis Fryman	.50	.23	.06
☐ 87 Moises Alou	.50	.23	.06
☐ 88 Dean Palmer	.50	.23	.06
☐ 89 Gregg Jefferies	1.00	.45	.12
☐ 90 Jim Thome	1.00	.45	.12
☐ 91 Dave Justice	.50	.23	.06
☐ 92 B.J. Surhoff	.25	.11	.03
☐ 93 Ramon Martinez	.50	.23	.06
☐ 94 Gary Sheffield	1.00	.45	.12
☐ 95 Andy Benes	.25	.11	.03
☐ 96 Reggie Sanders	.50	.23	.06
☐ 97 Roberto Alomar	1.00	.45	.12
☐ 98 Omar Vizquel	.50	.23	.06
☐ 99 Juan Gonzalez	2.50	1.10	.30
☐ 100 Robin Ventura	.50	.23	.06
☐ 101 Jason Isringhausen	1.00	.45	.12
☐ 102 Greg Colbrunn	.25	.11	.03
☐ 103 Brian Jordan	.50	.23	.06
☐ 104 Shawn Green	.25	.11	.03
☐ 105 Brian Hunter	.25	.11	.03
☐ 106 Rondell White	.50	.23	.06
☐ 107 Ryan Klesko	1.00	.45	.12
☐ 108 Sterling Hitchcock	.25	.11	.03
☐ 109 Manny Ramirez	1.25	.55	.16
☐ 110 Bret Boone	.25	.11	.03
☐ 111 Michael Tucker	.50	.23	.06
☐ 112 Julian Tavarez	.25	.11	.03
☐ 113 Benji Gil	.25	.11	.03
☐ 114 Kenny Lofton	1.25	.55	.16
☐ 115 Mike Kelly	.25	.11	.03
☐ 116 Ray Durham	1.00	.45	.12
☐ 117 Trevor Hoffman	.50	.23	.06
☐ 118 Butch Huskey	.50	.23	.06
☐ 119 Phil Nevin	.25	.11	.03
☐ 120 Pedro Martinez	.50	.23	.06
☐ 121 Wil Cordero	.25	.11	.03
☐ 122 Tim Salmon	1.00	.45	.12
☐ 123 Jim Edmonds	.50	.23	.06
☐ 124 Mike Piazza	3.00	1.35	.35
☐ 125 Rico Brogna	.25	.11	.03
☐ 126 John Mabry	.50	.23	.06
☐ 127 Chipper Jones	3.00	1.35	.35
☐ 128 Johnny Damon	.50	.23	.06
☐ 129 Raul Mondesi	1.00	.45	.12
☐ 130 Denny Neagle	.50	.23	.06
☐ 131 Marc Newfield	.50	.23	.06
☐ 132 Hideo Nomo	1.25	.55	.16
☐ 133 Joe Vitiello	.25	.11	.03
☐ 134 Garret Anderson	1.00	.45	.12
☐ 135 Dave Nilsson	.50	.23	.06
☐ 136 Alex Rodriguez	5.00	2.20	.60
☐ 137 Russ Davis	.25	.11	.03
☐ 138 Frank Rodriguez	.25	.11	.03
☐ 139 Royce Clayton	.25	.11	.03
☐ 140 John Valentin	.50	.23	.06
☐ 141 Marty Cordova	.50	.23	.06
☐ 142 Alex Gonzalez	.25	.11	.03
☐ 143 Carlos Delgado	.50	.23	.06
☐ 144 Willie Greene	.25	.11	.03
☐ 145 Cliff Floyd	.25	.11	.03
☐ 146 Bobby Higginson	.50	.23	.06
☐ 147 J.T. Snow	.50	.23	.06
☐ 148 Derek Bell	.50	.23	.06
☐ 149 Edgardo Alfonzo	.50	.23	.06
☐ 150 Charles Johnson	.50	.23	.06
☐ 151 Hideo Nomo GR	1.00	.45	.12
☐ 152 Larry Walker GR	1.00	.45	.12
☐ 153 Bob Abreu GR	1.00	.45	.12
☐ 154 Karim Garcia GR	.50	.23	.06
☐ 155 Dave Nilsson GR	.25	.11	.03
☐ 156 Chan Ho Park GR	1.00	.45	.12
☐ 157 Dennis Martinez GR	.25	.11	.03
☐ 158 Sammy Sosa GR	1.00	.45	.12
☐ 159 Rey Ordonez GR	1.00	.45	.12
☐ 160 Roberto Alomar GR	1.00	.45	.12
☐ 161 George Arias	.25	.11	.03
☐ 162 Jason Schmidt	1.00	.45	.12
☐ 163 Derek Jeter	3.00	1.35	.35
☐ 164 Chris Snopek	.25	.11	.03
☐ 165 Todd Hollandsworth	.50	.23	.06
☐ 166 Sal Fasano	.25	.11	.03
☐ 167 Jay Powell	.25	.11	.03
☐ 168 Paul Wilson	.50	.23	.06
☐ 169 Jim Pittsley	.50	.23	.06
☐ 170 LaTroy Hawkins	.25	.11	.03
☐ 171 Bob Abreu	1.00	.45	.12
☐ 172 Mike Grace	.25	.11	.03
☐ 173 Karim Garcia	1.00	.45	.12
☐ 174 Richard Hidalgo	1.00	.45	.12
☐ 175 Felipe Crespo	.25	.11	.03
☐ 176 Terrell Wade	.50	.23	.06
☐ 177 Steve Gibralter	.25	.11	.03
☐ 178 Jermaine Dye	1.00	.45	.12
☐ 179 Alan Benes	1.00	.45	.12
☐ 180 Wilton Guerrero	2.50	1.10	.30
☐ 181 Brooks Kieschnick	1.00	.45	.12
☐ 182 Roger Cedeno	.50	.23	.06
☐ 183 Osvaldo Fernandez	.50	.23	.06
☐ 184 Matt Lawton	.25	.11	.03
☐ 185 George Williams	.25	.11	.03
☐ 186 Jimmy Haynes	.25	.11	.03
☐ 187 Mike Busby	.50	.23	.06
☐ 188 Chan Ho Park	1.00	.45	.12
☐ 189 Marc Barcelo	.25	.11	.03
☐ 190 Jason Kendall	1.00	.45	.12
☐ 191 Rey Ordonez	1.00	.45	.12
☐ 192 Tyler Houston	.25	.11	.03
☐ 193 John Wasdin	.25	.11	.03
☐ 194 Jeff Suppan	1.00	.45	.12
☐ 195 Jeff Ware	.25	.11	.03
☐ 196 Ken Griffey Jr. CL	2.50	1.10	.30
☐ 197 Albert Belle CL	1.00	.45	.12
☐ 198 Mike Piazza CL	1.50	.70	.19
☐ 199 Greg Maddux CL	1.50	.70	.19
☐ 200 Frank Thomas CL	2.50	1.10	.30

1996 Pinnacle Aficionado Artist's Proofs

Randomly inserted in packs at a rate of one in 35, this 200-card set is a parallel set to the regular Pinnacle Aficionado set. A gold foil stamp in the shape of an artist's pen with the words, "Artist's Proof," printed above the wood-grain look bar containing the player's name distinguishes it from the regular set.

	MINT	NRMT	EXC
COMPLETE SET (200)	2000.00	900.00	250.00
COMMON CARD (1-200)	4.00	1.80	.50

*STARS:15X TO 30X BASIC CARDS ..
*YOUNG STARS: 12.5X TO 25X BASIC CARDS

1996 Pinnacle Aficionado First Pitch Preview

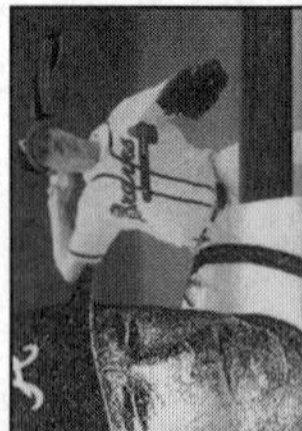

This 100-card set was available through Pinnacle's Web site. Collectors had to answer a series of trivia questions to receive the cards via mail. The set parallels the first 100 cards of the regular issue Aficionado release and thus features only the veteran players that have five or more years of Major League service. The cards are similar in design except for the bronze foil highlights and logo on front designating them as "First Pitch Preview" cards.

	MINT	NRMT	EXC
COMPLETE SET (100)	750.00	350.00	95.00
COMMON CARD (1-100)	1.00	.45	.12

*STARS: 5X TO 10X BASIC CARDS ....

1996 Pinnacle Aficionado Magic Numbers

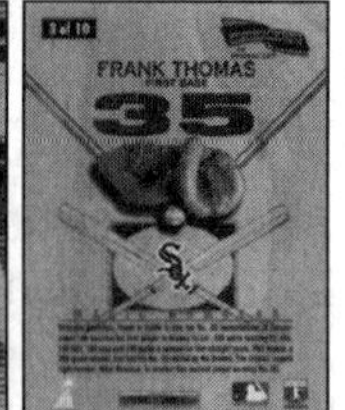

Randomly inserted in packs at a rate of one in 72, this 10-card set is printed on actual maple wood and features ten of of today's top superstars. The fronts feature an embossed color action player cut-out on a wood background. The backs carry trivia regarding the player's jersey number and those players from the past and present who share this same jersey number.

	MINT	NRMT	EXC
COMPLETE SET (10)	250.00	110.00	31.00
COMMON CARD (1-10)	6.00	2.70	.75
☐ 1 Ken Griffey Jr.	50.00	22.00	6.25
☐ 2 Greg Maddux	30.00	13.50	3.70
☐ 3 Frank Thomas	50.00	22.00	6.25
☐ 4 Mo Vaughn	12.00	5.50	1.50
☐ 5 Jeff Bagwell	20.00	9.00	2.50
☐ 6 Chipper Jones	30.00	13.50	3.70
☐ 7 Albert Belle	20.00	9.00	2.50
☐ 8 Cal Ripken	40.00	18.00	5.00
☐ 9 Matt Williams	6.00	2.70	.75
☐ 10 Sammy Sosa	8.00	3.60	1.00

1996 Pinnacle Aficionado Rivals

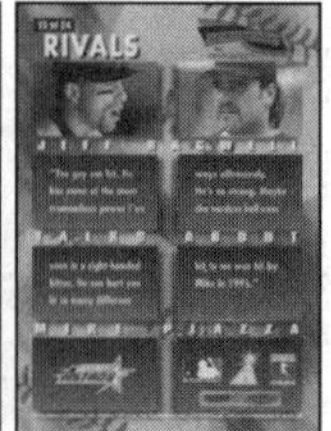

Randomly inserted in packs at a rate of one in 24, this 24-card set features two spot embossed color player photos of rival players. The backs carry a head photo of each and candid player comments on each other.

	MINT	NRMT	EXC
COMPLETE SET (24)	300.00	135.00	38.00
COMMON CARD (1-24)	10.00	4.50	1.25
☐ 1 Ken Griffey Frank Thomas	25.00	11.00	3.10
☐ 2 Frank Thomas Cal Ripken	25.00	11.00	3.10
☐ 3 Cal Ripken Mo Vaughn	15.00	6.75	1.85
☐ 4 Mo Vaughn Ken Griffey Jr.	18.00	8.00	2.20
☐ 5 Ken Griffey Jr. Cal Ripken	25.00	11.00	3.10
☐ 6 Frank Thomas Mo Vaughn	15.00	6.75	1.85
☐ 7 Cal Ripken Ken Griffey Jr.	25.00	11.00	3.10
☐ 8 Mo Vaughn Frank Thomas	15.00	6.75	1.85
☐ 9 Ken Griffey Jr. Mo Vaughn	18.00	8.00	2.20
☐ 10 Frank Thomas Ken Griffey Jr.	25.00	11.00	3.10
☐ 11 Cal Ripken Frank Thomas	25.00	11.00	3.10
☐ 12 Mo Vaughn Cal Ripken	15.00	6.75	1.85
☐ 13 Mike Piazza Jeff Bagwell	10.00	4.50	1.25
☐ 14 Jeff Bagwell Barry Bonds	10.00	4.50	1.25
☐ 15 Jeff Bagwell Mike Piazza	10.00	4.50	1.25
☐ 16 Tony Gwynn Mike Piazza	10.00	4.50	1.25
☐ 17 Mike Piazza Barry Bonds	10.00	4.50	1.25
☐ 18 Jeff Bagwell Tony Gwynn	10.00	4.50	1.25
☐ 19 Barry Bonds Mike Piazza	10.00	4.50	1.25
☐ 20 Tony Gwynn Jeff Bagwell	10.00	4.50	1.25
☐ 21 Mike Piazza Tony Gwynn	10.00	4.50	1.25
☐ 22 Barry Bonds Jeff Bagwell	10.00	4.50	1.25
☐ 23 Tony Gwynn Barry Bonds	10.00	4.50	1.25
☐ 24 Barry Bonds Tony Gwynn	10.00	4.50	1.25

1996 Pinnacle Aficionado Slick Picks

Randomly inserted in packs at a rate of one in 10, this 32-card set honors 32 draft picks for their future all-star abilities. Printed using a spectroetch print technology, the fronts feature a color action player photo on a black background on one side with a black-and-white player portrait on the other. A small simulated autograph and team name are printed below the portrait. The backs carry another color player portrait on a white background with a three-sided black border and information about when the player was drafted printed over a gray number indicating the round the player was selected in.

	MINT	NRMT	EXC
COMPLETE SET (32)	200.00	90.00	25.00
COMMON CARD (1-32)	2.00	.90	.25
☐ 1 Mike Piazza	15.00	6.75	1.85
☐ 2 Cal Ripken	20.00	9.00	2.50
☐ 3 Ken Griffey Jr.	25.00	11.00	3.10
☐ 4 Paul Wilson	2.50	1.10	.30
☐ 5 Frank Thomas	25.00	11.00	3.10
☐ 6 Mo Vaughn	6.00	2.70	.75
☐ 7 Barry Bonds	6.00	2.70	.75
☐ 8 Albert Belle	10.00	4.50	1.25
☐ 9 Jeff Bagwell	10.00	4.50	1.25
☐ 10 Dante Bichette	3.00	1.35	.35
☐ 11 Hideo Nomo	6.00	2.70	.75
☐ 12 Raul Mondesi	3.00	1.35	.35
☐ 13 Manny Ramirez	6.00	2.70	.75
☐ 14 Greg Maddux	15.00	6.75	1.85
☐ 15 Tony Gwynn	10.00	4.50	1.25
☐ 16 Ryne Sandberg	6.00	2.70	.75
☐ 17 Reggie Sanders	2.50	1.10	.30
☐ 18 Derek Jeter	15.00	6.75	1.85
☐ 19 Johnny Damon	2.50	1.10	.30
☐ 20 Alex Rodriguez	25.00	11.00	3.10
☐ 21 Ryan Klesko	4.00	1.80	.50
☐ 22 Jim Thome	5.00	2.20	.60
☐ 23 Kenny Lofton	6.00	2.70	.75
☐ 24 Tino Martinez	2.50	1.10	.30
☐ 25 Randy Johnson	4.00	1.80	.50
☐ 26 Wade Boggs	3.00	1.35	.35
☐ 27 Juan Gonzalez	12.00	5.50	1.50
☐ 28 Kirby Puckett	10.00	4.50	1.25
☐ 29 Tim Salmon	3.00	1.35	.35
☐ 30 Chipper Jones	15.00	6.75	1.85
☐ 31 Garret Anderson	2.00	.90	.25
☐ 32 Eddie Murray	6.00	2.70	.75

1997 Pinnacle Mint

The 1997 Pinnacle Mint set was issued in one series totalling 30 cards and was distributed in packs of three cards and two coins for a

suggested retail price of $3.99. The challenge was to fit the coins with the die-cut cards that pictured the same player on the minted coin. Two die-cut cards were inserted in each pack. Either one bronze, silver or gold card was also included in each pack. The fronts featured color action player images on a sepia player portrait background and a cut-out area for the matching coin. Ryan Klesko's die cut card was distributed to dealers as a promo. Die cut cards are listed below.

	MINT	NRMT	EXC
COMP.DIE CUT SET (30)	20.00	9.00	2.50
☐ 1 Ken Griffey Jr.	2.50	1.10	.30
☐ 2 Frank Thomas	2.50	1.10	.30
☐ 3 Alex Rodriguez	2.50	1.10	.30
☐ 4 Cal Ripken	2.00	.90	.25
☐ 5 Mo Vaughn	.60	.25	.07
☐ 6 Juan Gonzalez	1.25	.55	.16
☐ 7 Mike Piazza	1.50	.70	.19
☐ 8 Albert Belle	1.25	.55	.16
☐ 9 Chipper Jones	1.50	.70	.19
☐ 10 Andruw Jones	2.50	1.10	.30
☐ 11 Greg Maddux	1.50	.70	.19
☐ 12 Hideo Nomo	.60	.25	.07
☐ 13 Jeff Bagwell	1.00	.45	.12
☐ 14 Manny Ramirez	.60	.25	.07
☐ 15 Mark McGwire	.75	.35	.09
☐ 16 Derek Jeter	1.50	.70	.19
☐ 17 Sammy Sosa	.40	.18	.05
☐ 18 Barry Bonds	.60	.25	.07
☐ 19 Chuck Knoblauch	.40	.18	.05
☐ 20 Dante Bichette	.30	.14	.04
☐ 21 Tony Gwynn	1.00	.45	.12
☐ 22 Ken Caminiti	.40	.18	.05
☐ 23 Gary Sheffield	.40	.18	.05
☐ 24 Tim Salmon	.30	.14	.04
☐ 25 Ivan Rodriguez	.60	.25	.07
☐ 26 Henry Rodriguez	.25	.11	.03
☐ 27 Barry Larkin	.30	.14	.04
☐ 28 Ryan Klesko	.60	.25	.07
☐ 29 Brian Jordan	.25	.11	.03
☐ 30 Jay Buhner	.30	.14	.04
☐ P28 Ryan Klesko Promo	3.00	1.35	.35

1997 Pinnacle Mint Bronze

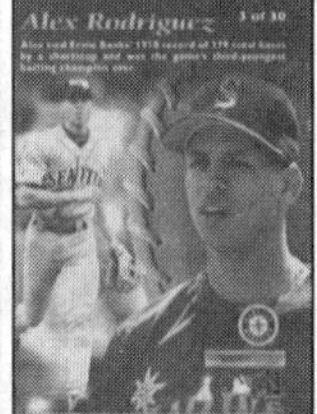

Each pack contained either one bronze, silver or gold card. The bronze versions are the most common. Each bronze card features color action player images on a sepia player portrait background. The player's team name was embossed in a bronze coin replica placed where the coin was to be inserted in the die-cut version. Ryan Klesko's bronze card was distributed to dealers as a promo.

	MINT	NRMT	EXC
COMPLETE SET (30)	40.00	18.00	5.00
COMMON CARD (1-30)	.25	.11	.03
*BRONZE: 1X TO 2X DIE CUT CARDS			
☐ P28 Ryan Klesko Promo	3.00	1.35	.35

1997 Pinnacle Mint Gold

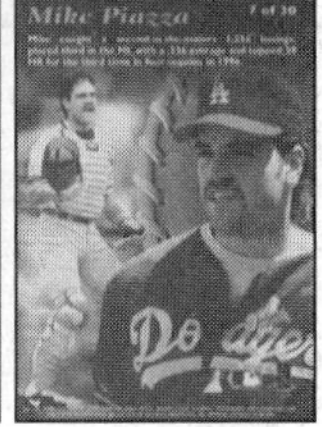

Randomly inserted in packs at a rate of one in 48, this 30-card set is parallel to the regular set and is distinguised from the regular set by the use of full Gold-foil dufex print technologies.

	MINT	NRMT	EXC
COMPLETE SET (30)	500.00	220.00	60.00
COMMON CARD (1-30)	6.00	2.70	.75
*GOLD: 12.5X TO 25X DIE CUT CARDS			

1997 Pinnacle Mint Silver

Randomly inserted in packs at a rate of one in 15, this 30-card set is parallel to the regular set and is similar in design. It is distinguished from the regular set by its silver-foil stamping.

	MINT	NRMT	EXC
COMPLETE SET (30)	250.00	110.00	31.00
COMMON CARD (1-30)	3.00	1.35	.35
*SILVER: 6X TO 12X DIE CUT CARDS			

1997 Pinnacle Mint Coins Brass

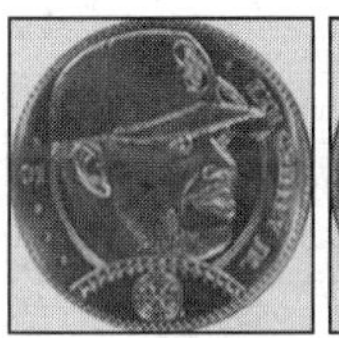

Each pack of Pinnacle Mint contained two coins (a mixture of Brass, Nickel and Gold Plated). The Brass coins were the most common. This set features coins minted in brass with embossed player heads and were made to be matched with the die-cut card version of the same player. Two versions of the Manny Ramirez Brass coin were distributed - an erroneous version with the words "fine silver" printed on back, and a corrected version. Judging from market observations, the "fine silver" version appears to be about four times tougher to find than the corrected. In addition to being inserted in packs, Ryan Klesko's Brass coin was distributed to dealers as a promo.

	MINT	NRMT	EXC
COMP.BRASS SET (30)	60.00	27.00	7.50
COMMON BRASS (1-30)	.75	.35	.09
☐ 1 Ken Griffey Jr.	8.00	3.60	1.00
☐ 2 Frank Thomas	8.00	3.60	1.00
☐ 3 Alex Rodriguez	8.00	3.60	1.00
☐ 4 Cal Ripken	6.00	2.70	.75
☐ 5 Mo Vaughn	2.00	.90	.25
☐ 6 Juan Gonzalez	4.00	1.80	.50
☐ 7 Mike Piazza	5.00	2.20	.60
☐ 8 Albert Belle	4.00	1.80	.50
☐ 9 Chipper Jones	5.00	2.20	.60
☐ 10 Andruw Jones	8.00	3.60	1.00
☐ 11 Greg Maddux	5.00	2.20	.60
☐ 12 Hideo Nomo	2.00	.90	.25
☐ 13 Jeff Bagwell	3.00	1.35	.35
☐ 14A Manny Ramirez COR	2.00	.90	.25
☐ 14B Manny Ramirez ERR. says "Fine Silver" on back	10.00	4.50	1.25
☐ 15 Mark McGwire	2.50	1.10	.30
☐ 16 Derek Jeter	5.00	2.20	.60
☐ 17 Sammy Sosa	1.25	.55	.16
☐ 18 Barry Bonds	2.00	.90	.25
☐ 19 Chuck Knoblauch	1.25	.55	.16
☐ 20 Dante Bichette	1.00	.45	.12
☐ 21 Tony Gwynn	3.00	1.35	.35
☐ 22 Ken Caminiti	1.25	.55	.16
☐ 23 Gary Sheffield	1.25	.55	.16
☐ 24 Tim Salmon	1.00	.45	.12
☐ 25 Ivan Rodriguez	2.00	.90	.25
☐ 26 Henry Rodriguez	.75	.35	.09
☐ 27 Barry Larkin	1.00	.45	.12
☐ 28 Ryan Klesko	1.50	.70	.19
☐ 29 Brian Jordan	.75	.35	.09
☐ 30 Jay Buhner	1.00	.45	.12

1997 Pinnacle Mint Coins Gold-Plated

Randomly inserted in packs at a rate of one in 48, this set is parallel to the regular brass coin set and features 24kt. Gold Plated coins with embossed player heads.

	MINT	NRMT	EXC
COMPLETE SET (30)	750.00	350.00	95.00
COMMON CARD (1-30)	10.00	4.50	1.25
*GOLD PLATED: 6X TO 12X BRASS COINS			

1997 Pinnacle Mint Coins Nickel

Randomly inserted in packs at a rate of one in 20, this set is parallel to the regular brass coin set and features minted Nickel-Silver coins with embossed player heads.

	MINT	NRMT	EXC
COMPLETE SET (30)	300.00	135.00	38.00
COMMON CARD (1-30)	4.00	1.80	.50
*NICKEL: 2.5X TO 5X BRASS COINS..			

1910 Pirates American Caramels E90-2

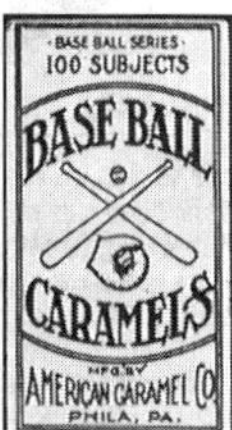

The cards in this 11-card set measure 1 1/2" by 2 3/4". The 1910 E90-2 American Caramels Baseball Star set contains unnumbered cards featuring players from the 1909 Pittsburgh Pirates. The backs of these cards are exactly like the E90-1 cards; however, blue print is used for the names of the players and the teams on the fronts of the cards.

	EX-MT	VG-E	GOOD
COMPLETE SET (11)	1800.00	800.00	220.00
COMMON CARD (1-11)	75.00	34.00	9.50
☐ 1 Babe Adams	75.00	34.00	9.50
☐ 2 Fred Clarke	250.00	110.00	31.00
☐ 3 George Gibson	75.00	34.00	9.50
☐ 4 Ham Hyatt	75.00	34.00	9.50
☐ 5 Tommy Leach	125.00	55.00	15.50
☐ 6 Sam Leever	75.00	34.00	9.50
☐ 7 Nick Maddox	75.00	34.00	9.50
☐ 8 Dots Miller	75.00	34.00	9.50
☐ 9 Deacon Phillippe	125.00	55.00	15.50
☐ 10 Honus Wagner	700.00	325.00	90.00
☐ 11 Chief Wilson	75.00	34.00	9.50

1910 Pirates Hermes Pins

These 12 pins feature members of the defending World Champions Pittsburgh Pirates. The pins measure 1 1/4" and feature black and white photos sets against blue and yellow borders. The players are not identified explicitly but all can be identified. The top of the pin identifies Hermes as the producer of these items. We have sequenced the pins in alphabetical order.

	EX-MT	VG-E	GOOD
COMPLETE SET	2500.00	1100.00	300.00
COMMON PIN	200.00	90.00	25.00
☐ 1 Bill Abstein	200.00	90.00	25.00
☐ 2 Babe Adams	250.00	110.00	31.00
☐ 3 Bobby Byrne	200.00	90.00	25.00
☐ 4 Howie Camnitz	200.00	90.00	25.00
☐ 5 Fred Clarke	400.00	180.00	50.00
☐ 6 George Gibson	200.00	90.00	25.00
☐ 7 Tommy Leach	200.00	90.00	25.00
☐ 8 Sam Leever	200.00	90.00	25.00
☐ 9 Dots Miller	200.00	90.00	25.00
☐ 10 Mike Simon	200.00	90.00	25.00
☐ 11 Honus Wagner	600.00	275.00	75.00
☐ 12 J. Owen Wilson	200.00	90.00	25.00

1910 Pirates Tip-Top D322

This 25-card set of the Pittsburgh Pirates was distributed by Tip-Top Bread and measures approximately 1 13/15" by 2 3/8". The fronts feature pastel paintings of the World Champion Team. The backs carry a checklist, ad for the bakery, and offer to send the complete set for 50 bread labels.

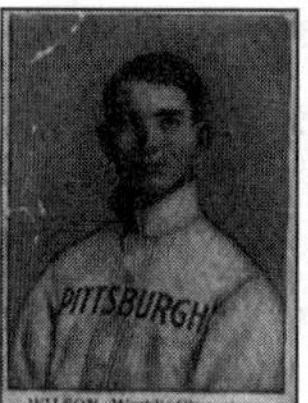

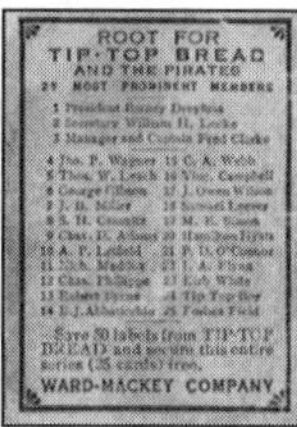

	EX-MT	VG-E	GOOD
COMPLETE SET (25)	7500.00	3400.00	950.00
COMMON CARD (1-25)	250.00	110.00	31.00
☐ 1 Barney Dreyfus PRES	350.00	160.00	45.00
☐ 2 William Locke	250.00	110.00	31.00
☐ 3 Fred Clarke MG	500.00	220.00	60.00
☐ 4 Honrus Wagner	1500.00	700.00	190.00
☐ 5 Tom Leach	250.00	110.00	31.00
☐ 6 George Gibson	250.00	110.00	31.00
☐ 7 Dots Miller	250.00	110.00	31.00
☐ 8 Howie Camnitz	250.00	110.00	31.00
☐ 9 Babe Adams	350.00	160.00	45.00
☐ 10 Lefty Leifield	250.00	110.00	31.00
☐ 11 Nick Maddox	250.00	110.00	31.00
☐ 12 Deacon Philippe	350.00	160.00	45.00
☐ 13 Bobby Byrne	250.00	110.00	31.00
☐ 14 Ed Abbaticchio	250.00	110.00	31.00
☐ 15 Lefty Webb	250.00	110.00	31.00
☐ 16 Vin Campbell	250.00	110.00	31.00
☐ 17 Owen Wilson	350.00	160.00	45.00
☐ 18 Sam Leever	250.00	110.00	31.00
☐ 19 Mike Simon	250.00	110.00	31.00
☐ 20 Ham Hyatt	250.00	110.00	31.00
☐ 21 Paddy O'Connor	250.00	110.00	31.00
☐ 22 John Flynn	250.00	110.00	31.00
☐ 23 Kirby White	250.00	110.00	31.00
☐ 24 Tip Top Boy(Mascot)	250.00	110.00	31.00
☐ 25 Forbes Field	250.00	110.00	31.00

1950 Pirates Team Issue

This set of the Pittsburgh Pirates measures approximately 6 1/2" by 9" and features black-and-white player photos. The backs are blank. The cards are unnumbered and checklisted below in alphabetical order.

	NRMT	VG-E	GOOD
COMPLETE SET (25)	75.00	34.00	9.50
COMMON CARD (1-25)	3.00	1.35	.35
☐ 1 Ted Beard	3.00	1.35	.35
☐ 2 Gus Bell	5.00	2.20	.60
☐ 3 Pete Castiglione	3.00	1.35	.35
☐ 4 Cliff Chambers	3.00	1.35	.35
☐ 5 Dale Coogan	3.00	1.35	.35
☐ 6 Murry Dickson	5.00	2.20	.60
☐ 7 Froilan Fernandez	3.00	1.35	.35
☐ 8 Johnny Hopp	5.00	2.20	.60
☐ 9 Ralph Kiner	10.00	4.50	1.25
☐ 10 Vernon Law	5.00	2.20	.60
☐ 11 Vic Lombardi	3.00	1.35	.35
☐ 12 William MacDonald	3.00	1.35	.35
☐ 13 Clyde McCullough	3.00	1.35	.35
☐ 14 Bill Meyer MG	3.00	1.35	.35
☐ 15 Ray Mueller	3.00	1.35	.35
☐ 16 Danny Murtaugh	5.00	2.20	.60
☐ 17 Jack Phillips	3.00	1.35	.35
☐ 18 Mel Queen	3.00	1.35	.35
☐ 19 Stan Rojek	3.00	1.35	.35
☐ 20 Henry Schenz	3.00	1.35	.35
☐ 21 George Strickland	3.00	1.35	.35
☐ 22 Earl Turner	3.00	1.35	.35
☐ 23 Jim Walsh	3.00	1.35	.35
☐ 24 Bill Werle	3.00	1.35	.35
☐ 25 Wally Westlake	3.00	1.35	.35

1960 Pirates Jay Publishing

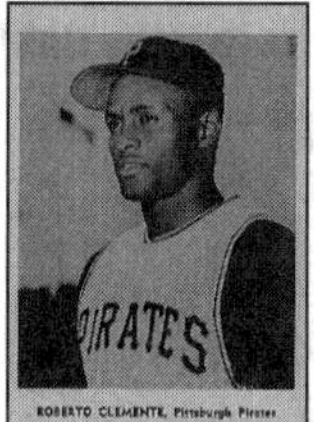

This 12-card set of the Pittsburgh Pirates measures approximately 5" by 7". The fronts feature black-and-white posed player photos with the player's and team name printed below in the white border. These cards were packaged 12 to a packet and originally sold for 50 cents.

The backs are blank. The cards are unnumbered and checklisted below in alphabetical order.

	NRMT	VG-E	GOOD
COMPLETE SET (12)	60.00	27.00	7.50
COMMON CARD (1-12)	2.50	1.10	.30
☐ 1 Smoky Burgess	4.00	1.80	.50
☐ 2 Gino Cimoli	2.50	1.10	.30
☐ 3 Roberto Clemente	30.00	13.50	3.70
☐ 4 Roy Face	4.00	1.80	.50
☐ 5 Bob Friend	3.50	1.55	.45
☐ 6 Dick Groat	4.00	1.80	.50
☐ 7 Harvey Haddix	3.50	1.55	.45
☐ 8 Don Hoak	3.00	1.35	.35
☐ 9 Bill Mazeroski	5.00	2.20	.60
☐ 10 Danny Murtaugh MG	4.00	1.80	.50
☐ 11 Bob Skinner	2.50	1.10	.30
☐ 12 Dick Stuart	3.00	1.35	.35

1960 Pirates Tag-Ons

This 10-card set originally sold for $1.98 and features individually die-cut self-sticking figures in full color on one large sheet measuring approximately 10" by 15 1/2". These flexible color-fast Tag-ons are weatherproof and can be applied to any surface. The figures are checklisted below according to the small black numbers printed on their shoulders.

	NRMT	VG-E	GOOD
COMPLETE SET (10)	60.00	27.00	7.50
COMMON CARD (4-26)	5.00	2.20	.60
☐ 4 Robert Skinner	5.00	2.20	.60
☐ 6 Forrest Burgess	5.00	2.20	.60
☐ 7 Dick Stuart	6.00	2.70	.75
☐ 9 Bill Mazeroski	7.50	3.40	.95
☐ 12 Don Hoak	5.00	2.20	.60
☐ 18 Bill Virdon	6.00	2.70	.75
☐ 19 Bob Friend	5.00	2.20	.60
☐ 21 Roberto Clemente	25.00	11.00	3.10
☐ 24 Dick Groat	6.00	2.70	.75
☐ 26 Elroy Face	6.00	2.70	.75

1961 Pirates Riger Ford

This six-card set was distributed by Ford Motor Company and measures approximately 11" by 14". The fronts feature pencil drawings by Robert Riger of six of the 1960 World Champion Pittsburgh Pirates. The cards are unnumbered and checklisted below in alphabetical order.

	MINT	NRMT	EXC
COMPLETE SET (6)	100.00	45.00	12.50
COMMON CARD (1-6)	10.00	4.50	1.25
☐ 1 Roberto Clemente	50.00	22.00	6.25
☐ 2 Bob Friend	10.00	4.50	1.25
☐ 3 Dick Groat	15.00	6.75	1.85
☐ 4 Don Hoak	10.00	4.50	1.25
☐ 5 Vernon Law	15.00	6.75	1.85
☐ 6 Bill Mazeroski	25.00	11.00	3.10

1961 Pirates Jay Publishing

This 12-card set of the Pittsburgh Pirates measures approximately 5" by 7". The fronts feature black-and-white posed player photos with the player's and team name printed below in the white border. These cards were packaged 12 to a packet. The backs are blank. The cards are unnumbered and checklisted below in alphabetical order.

	NRMT	VG-E	GOOD
COMPLETE SET (12)	45.00	20.00	5.50
COMMON CARD (1-12)	2.50	1.10	.30
☐ 1 Smoky Burgess	3.50	1.25	.45
☐ 2 Roberto Clemente	20.00	9.00	2.50
☐ 3 Roy Face	3.00	1.35	.35
☐ 4 Bob Friend	3.00	1.35	.35
☐ 5 Dick Groat	3.50	1.55	.45
☐ 6 Don Hoak	3.00	1.35	.35
☐ 7 Vern Law	2.50	1.10	.30
☐ 8 Bill Mazeroski	4.00	1.80	.50
☐ 9 Danny Murtaugh MG	3.00	1.35	.35
☐ 10 Bob Skinner	2.50	1.10	.30
☐ 11 Dick Stuart	3.00	1.35	.35
☐ 12 Bill Virdon	3.00	1.35	.35

1963 Pirates IDL

This 26-card set measures approximately 4" by 5" and is blank-backed. The fronts have black and white photos on the top of the card along with the IDL Drug Store logo in the lower left corner of the card and the players name printed in block letters underneath the picture. The only card which has any designation as to position is the manager card of Danny Murtaugh. These cards are unnumbered and feature members of the Pittsburgh Pirates. The catalog designation for the set is H801-13 although it is infrequently referenced. The Stargell card is one of his few cards from 1963, his rookie year for cards.

	NRMT	VG-E	GOOD
COMPLETE SET (26)	150.00	70.00	19.00
COMMON CARD (1-26)	5.00	2.20	.60
☐ 1 Bob Bailey	5.00	2.20	.60
☐ 2 Smoky Burgess	7.50	3.40	.95
☐ 3 Don Cardwell	5.00	2.20	.60
☐ 4 Roberto Clemente	50.00	22.00	6.25
☐ 5 Donn Clendenon	7.50	3.40	.95
☐ 6 Roy Face	7.50	3.40	.95
☐ 7 Earl Francis	5.00	2.20	.60
☐ 8 Bob Friend	7.50	3.40	.95
☐ 9 Joe Gibbon	5.00	2.20	.60
☐ 10 Julio Gotay	5.00	2.20	.60
☐ 11 Harvey Haddix	7.50	3.40	.95
☐ 12 Johnny Logan	7.50	3.40	.95
☐ 13 Bill Mazeroski	10.00	4.50	1.25
☐ 14 Al McBean	5.00	2.20	.60
☐ 15 Danny Murtaugh MG	7.50	3.40	.95
☐ 16 Sam Narron CO	5.00	2.20	.60
☐ 17 Ron Northey CO	5.00	2.20	.60
☐ 18 Frank Oceak CO	5.00	2.20	.60
☐ 19 Jim Pagliaroni	5.00	2.20	.60
☐ 20 Ted Savage	5.00	2.20	.60
☐ 21 Dick Schofield	5.00	2.20	.60
☐ 22 Willie Stargell	25.00	11.00	3.10
☐ 23 Tom Sturdivant	5.00	2.20	.60
☐ 24 Virgil Trucks CO	5.00	2.20	.60
☐ 25 Bob Veale	7.50	3.40	.95
☐ 26 Bill Virdon	7.50	3.40	.95

1963 Pirates Jay Publishing

This 12-card set of the Pittsburgh Pirates measures approximately 5" by 7". The fronts feature black-and-white posed player photos with the player's and team name printed below in the white border. These cards were packaged 12 to a packet. The backs are blank. The cards are unnumbered and checklisted below in alphabetical order.

	NRMT	VG-E	GOOD
COMPLETE SET (12)	40.00	18.00	5.00
COMMON CARD (1-12)	2.50	1.10	.30
☐ 1 Bob Bailey	2.50	1.10	.30
☐ 2 Smoky Burgess	3.50	1.55	.45
☐ 3 Roberto Clemente	25.00	11.00	3.10
☐ 4 Donn Clendenon	2.50	1.10	.30
☐ 5 Roy Face	3.00	1.35	.35
☐ 6 Bob Friend	3.50	1.55	.45
☐ 7 Harvey Haddox	3.00	1.35	.35
☐ 8 Vern Law	2.50	1.10	.30
☐ 9 Bill Mazeroski	4.00	1.80	.50
☐ 10 Danny Murtaugh MG	3.00	1.35	.35
☐ 11 Bob Skinner	2.50	1.10	.30
☐ 12 Bill Virdon	3.00	1.35	.35

1964 Pirates KDKA

This set featured members of the 1964 Pittsburgh Pirates. It was issued by radio station KDKA. The set can be dated to 1964 by the card of Rex Johnston, who only played for the Pirates in that season.

	NRMT	VG-E	GOOD
COMPLETE SET (28)	750.00	350.00	95.00
COMMON CARD (1-28)	20.00	9.00	2.50
☐ 1 Gene Alley	20.00	9.00	2.50
☐ 2 Bob Bailey	20.00	9.00	2.50
☐ 3 Frank Bork	20.00	9.00	2.50
☐ 4 Smoky Burgess	25.00	11.00	3.10
☐ 5 Tom Butters	20.00	9.00	2.50
☐ 6 Don Cardwell	20.00	9.00	2.50
☐ 7 Roberto Clemente	250.00	110.00	31.00
☐ 8 Donn Clendenon	25.00	11.00	3.10
☐ 9 Elroy Face	20.00	9.00	2.50
☐ 10 Gene Freese	20.00	9.00	2.50
☐ 11 Bob Friend	20.00	9.00	2.50
☐ 12 Joe Gibbon	20.00	9.00	2.50
☐ 13 Julio Gotay	20.00	9.00	2.50
☐ 14 Rex Johnston	20.00	9.00	2.50
☐ 15 Vernon Law	20.00	9.00	2.50
☐ 16 Jerry Lynch	20.00	9.00	2.50
☐ 17 Bill Mazeroski	50.00	22.00	6.25
☐ 18 Al McBean	20.00	9.00	2.50
☐ 19 Orlando McFarlane	20.00	9.00	2.50
☐ 20 Manny Mota	25.00	11.00	3.10
☐ 21 Danny Murtaugh MG	25.00	11.00	3.10
☐ 22 Jim Pagliaroni	20.00	9.00	2.50
☐ 23 Dick Schofield	20.00	9.00	2.50
☐ 24 Don Schwall	20.00	9.00	2.50
☐ 25 Tommie Sisk	20.00	9.00	2.50
☐ 26 Willie Stargell	40.00	18.00	5.00
☐ 27 Bob Veale	20.00	9.00	2.50
☐ 28 Bill Virdon	40.00	18.00	5.00

1966 Pirates East Hills

The 1966 East Hills Pirates set consists of 25 large (approximately 3 1/4" by 4 1/4"), full color photos of Pittsburgh Pirate ballplayers. These blank-backed cards are numbered in the lower right corner according to the uniform number of the individual depicted. The set was distributed by various stores located in the East Hills Shopping Center. The catalog number for this set is F405.

	NRMT	VG-E	GOOD
COMPLETE SET (25)	75.00	34.00	9.50
COMMON CARD	.50	.23	.06
☐ 3 Harry Walker MG	.75	.35	.09
☐ 7 Bob Bailey	.50	.23	.06
☐ 8 Willie Stargell	15.00	6.75	1.85
☐ 9 Bill Mazeroski	5.00	2.20	.60
☐ 10 Jim Pagliaroni	.50	.23	.06
☐ 11 Jose Pagan	.50	.23	.06
☐ 12 Jerry May	.50	.23	.06
☐ 14 Gene Alley	1.00	.45	.12
☐ 15 Manny Mota	1.00	.45	.12
☐ 16 Andre Rodgers UER (Andy on card)	.50	.23	.06
☐ 17 Donn Clendenon	1.00	.45	.12
☐ 18 Matty Alou	3.00	1.35	.35
☐ 19 Pete Mikkelsen	.50	.23	.06
☐ 20 Jesse Gonder	.50	.23	.06
☐ 21 Roberto Clemente	50.00	22.00	6.25
☐ 22 Woody Fryman	.75	.35	.09
☐ 24 Jerry Lynch	.50	.23	.06
☐ 25 Tommie Sisk	.50	.23	.06
☐ 26 Roy Face	3.00	1.35	.35
☐ 28 Steve Blass	1.00	.45	.12
☐ 32 Vernon Law	3.00	1.35	.35
☐ 34 Al McBean	.50	.23	.06
☐ 39 Bob Veale	1.00	.45	.12
☐ 43 Don Cardwell	.50	.23	.06
☐ 45 Gene Michael	1.00	.45	.12

1967 Pirates Team Issue

This 24-card set of the Pittsburgh Pirates features color player photos with white borders and measures approximately 3 1/4" by 4 1/4". A facsimile autograph is printed in the wide bottom border. The backs are blank. The cards are unnumbered and checklisted below in alphabetical order.

	NRMT	VG-E	GOOD
COMPLETE SET (24)	75.00	34.00	9.50
COMMON CARD (1-24)	3.00	1.35	.35
☐ 1 Gene Alley	3.00	1.35	.35
☐ 2 Matty Alou	4.00	1.80	.50
☐ 3 Steve Blass	3.00	1.35	.35
☐ 4 Roberto Clemente	20.00	9.00	2.50
☐ 5 Donn Clendenon	4.00	1.80	.50
☐ 6 Roy Face	3.00	1.35	.35
☐ 7 Woody Fryman	3.00	1.35	.35
☐ 8 Jesse Gonder	3.00	1.35	.35
☐ 9 Vernon Law	3.00	1.35	.35
☐ 10 Jerry May	3.00	1.35	.35
☐ 11 Bill Mazeroski	6.00	2.70	.75
☐ 12 Al McBean	3.00	1.35	.35
☐ 13 Pete Mikkelsen	3.00	1.35	.35
☐ 14 Manny Mota	4.00	1.80	.50
☐ 15 Jose Pagan	3.00	1.35	.35
☐ 16 Jim Pagliaroni	3.00	1.35	.35
☐ 17 Juan Pizarro	3.00	1.35	.35
☐ 18 Dennis Ribant	3.00	1.35	.35
☐ 19 Andy Rodgers	3.00	1.35	.35
☐ 20 Tommie Sisk	3.00	1.35	.35
☐ 21 Willie Stargell	7.50	3.40	.95
☐ 22 Bob Veale	3.00	1.35	.35
☐ 23 Harry Walker	3.00	1.35	.35
☐ 24 Maury Wills	5.00	2.20	.60

1968 Pirates KDKA

This 23-card set measures approximately 2 3/8" by 4" and was issued by radio and television station KDKA to promote the Pittsburgh Pirates, whom they were covering at the time. The fronts have the players' photo on the top 2/3 of the card and a facsimile autograph, the players name and position and uniform number on the lower left hand corner and an ad for KDKA on the lower right corner of the card. The back has an advertisment for both KDKA radio and television. The set is checklisted below by uniform number.

	NRMT	VG-E	GOOD
COMPLETE SET (23)	90.00	40.00	11.00
COMMON CARD	2.00	.90	.25
☐ 7 Larry Shepard MG	2.00	.90	.25
☐ 8 Willie Stargell	20.00	9.00	2.50
☐ 9 Bill Mazeroski	8.00	3.60	1.00
☐ 10 Gary Kolb	2.00	.90	.25
☐ 11 Jose Pagan	2.00	.90	.25
☐ 12 Jerry May	2.00	.90	.25
☐ 14 Jim Bunning	6.00	2.70	.75
☐ 15 Manny Mota	3.00	1.35	.35
☐ 17 Donn Clendenon	3.00	1.35	.35
☐ 18 Matty Alou	3.00	1.35	.35
☐ 21 Roberto Clemente	40.00	18.00	5.00
☐ 22 Gene Alley	3.00	1.35	.35
☐ 25 Tommy Sisk	2.00	.90	.25
☐ 26 Roy Face	3.00	1.35	.35
☐ 27 Ron Kline	2.00	.90	.25
☐ 28 Steve Blass	3.00	1.35	.35
☐ 29 Juan Pizzaro	2.00	.90	.25
☐ 30 Maury Wills	6.00	2.70	.75
☐ 34 Al McBean	2.00	.90	.25
☐ 35 Manny Sanguillen	4.00	1.80	.50

	NRMT	VG-E	GOOD
☐ 38 Bob Moose	3.00	1.35	.35
☐ 39 Bob Veale	3.00	1.35	.35
☐ 40 Dave Wickersham	2.00	.90	.25

1968 Pirates Team Issue

This 24-card set of the Pittsburgh Pirates features color player photos with white borders and measures approximately 3 1/4" by 4 1/4". A facsimile autograph is printed in the wide bottom border. The backs are blank. The cards are unnumbered and checklisted below in alphabetical order.

	NRMT	VG-E	GOOD
COMPLETE SET (24)	75.00	34.00	9.50
COMMON CARD (1-24)	3.00	1.35	.35
☐ 1 Gene Alley	3.00	1.35	.35
☐ 2 Matty Alou	5.00	2.20	.60
☐ 3 Steve Blass	3.00	1.35	.35
☐ 4 Jim Bunning	7.50	3.40	.95
☐ 5 Roberto Clemente	20.00	9.00	2.50
☐ 6 Donn Clendenon	4.00	1.80	.50
☐ 7 Roy Face	3.00	1.35	.35
☐ 8 Ronnie Kline	3.00	1.35	.35
☐ 9 Gary Kolb	3.00	1.35	.35
☐ 10 Jerry May	3.00	1.35	.35
☐ 11 Bill Mazeroski	6.00	2.70	.75
☐ 12 Al McBean	3.00	1.35	.35
☐ 13 Bob Moose	3.00	1.35	.35
☐ 14 Manny Mota	4.00	1.80	.50
☐ 15 Jose Pagan	3.00	1.35	.35
☐ 16 Juan Pizarro	3.00	1.35	.35
☐ 17 Manny Sanguillen	4.00	1.80	.50
☐ 18 Jim Shellenback	3.00	1.35	.35
☐ 19 Larry Shepard	3.00	1.35	.35
☐ 20 Tommie Sisk	3.00	1.35	.35
☐ 21 Willie Stargell	7.50	3.40	.95
☐ 22 Bob Veale	3.00	1.35	.35
☐ 23 Dave Wickersham	3.00	1.35	.35
☐ 24 Maury Wills	5.00	2.20	.60

1969 Pirates Jack in the Box

This 12-card set measures approximately 2 1/16" by 3 5/8" and features black-and-white player photos on a white card face. The player's name, team name, position, and batting or pitching record appear below the photo. The backs are blank. The cards are unnumbered and checklisted below in alphabetical order. Pittsburgh is misspelled Pittsburg on the front of the cards.

	NRMT	VG-E	GOOD
COMPLETE SET (12)	60.00	27.00	7.50
COMMON CARD (1-12)	2.00	.90	.25
☐ 1 Gene Alley	3.50	1.55	.45
☐ 2 Dave Cash	5.00	2.20	.60
☐ 3 Dock Ellis	3.50	1.55	.45
☐ 4 Dave Giusti	3.50	1.55	.45
☐ 5 Jerry May	2.00	.90	.25
☐ 6 Bill Mazeroski	7.50	3.40	.95
☐ 7 Al Oliver	7.50	3.40	.95
☐ 8 Jose Pagan	2.00	.90	.25
☐ 9 Fred Patek	3.50	1.55	.45
☐ 10 Bob Robertson	5.00	2.20	.60
☐ 11 Manny Sanguillen	6.00	2.70	.75
☐ 12 Willie Stargell	20.00	9.00	2.50

1969 Pirates Greiner

This eight-card set of the Pittsburgh Pirates, sponsored by Greiner Tire Service, measures approximately 5 1/2" by 8 1/2" and features black-and-white player portraits inside a white border. The player's name and team is printed with a "good luck" message in the wide bottom margin along with the sponsor name, address and phone number. The backs are blank. The cards are unnumbered and checklisted below in alphabetical order.

	NRMT	VG-E	GOOD
COMPLETE SET (8)	125.00	55.00	15.50
COMMON CARD (1-8)	8.50	3.80	1.05
☐ 1 Gene Alley	10.00	4.50	1.25
☐ 2 Matty Alou	15.00	6.75	1.85
☐ 3 Steve Blass	8.50	3.80	1.05
☐ 4 Roberto Clemente	65.00	29.00	8.00
☐ 5 Jerry May	8.50	3.80	1.05
☐ 6 Bill Mazeroski	20.00	9.00	2.50
☐ 7 Larry Shepard MG	8.50	3.80	1.05
☐ 8 Willie Stargell	25.00	11.00	3.10

1970 Pirates Team Issue

This eight-card set of the Pittsburgh Pirates measures approximately 3 1/4" by 4 1/4" and features color player portraits with a facsimile autograph in the wide bottom margin. The cards are unnumbered and checklisted below in alphabetical order.

	NRMT	VG-E	GOOD
COMPLETE SET (8)	50.00	22.00	6.25
COMMON CARD (1-8)	3.00	1.35	.35
☐ 1 Steve Blass	3.00	1.35	.35
☐ 2 Roberto Clemente	15.00	6.75	1.85
☐ 3 Dock Ellis	3.50	1.55	.45
☐ 4 Richie Hebner	3.00	1.35	.35
☐ 5 Al Oliver	5.00	2.20	.60
☐ 6 Bob Robertson	3.00	1.35	.35
☐ 7 Manny Sanguillen	3.50	1.55	.45
☐ 8 Willie Stargell	7.50	3.40	.95

1971 Pirates

The six blank-backed photos comprising this Set "A" of the '71 Pirates measure approximately 7" by 8 3/4" and feature white-bordered posed color player shots. The player's name appears in black lettering within the bottom white margin. The pictures are unnumbered and checklisted below in alphabetical order.

	NRMT	VG-E	GOOD
COMPLETE SET (6)	30.00	13.50	3.70
COMMON CARD (1-6)	4.00	1.80	.50
☐ 1 Nelson Briles	5.00	2.20	.60
☐ 2 Dave Cash	4.00	1.80	.50
☐ 3 Roberto Clemente	20.00	9.00	2.50
☐ 4 Richie Hebner	4.00	1.80	.50
☐ 5 Bob Robertson	4.00	1.80	.50
☐ 6 Luke Walker	4.00	1.80	.50

1971 Pirates Action Photos

These unnumbered cards feature members of the World Champion Pittsburgh Pirates. These cards were issued in two series (1-12, 13-24) and each group is sequenced into alphabetical order.

	NRMT	VG-E	GOOD
COMPLETE SET (24)	60.00	27.00	7.50
COMMON CARD (1-24)	1.00	.45	.12
☐ 1 Gene Alley	1.25	.55	.16
☐ 2 Nelson Briles	1.00	.45	.12
☐ 3 Dave Cash	1.00	.45	.12
☐ 4 Roberto Clemente	30.00	13.50	3.70
☐ 5 Dock Ellis	1.50	.70	.19
☐ 6 Mudcat Grant	1.00	.45	.12
☐ 7 Bob Johnson	1.00	.45	.12
☐ 8 Milt May	1.00	.45	.12
☐ 9 Jose Pagan	1.25	.55	.16
☐ 10 Manny Sanguillen	1.50	.70	.19
☐ 11 Bob Veale	1.00	.45	.12
☐ 12 Luke Walker	1.00	.45	.12
☐ 13 Steve Blass	1.00	.45	.12
☐ 14 Gene Clines	1.00	.45	.12
☐ 15 Vic Davalillo	1.00	.45	.12
☐ 16 Dave Giusti	1.00	.45	.12
☐ 17 Richie Hebner	1.25	.55	.16
☐ 18 Jackie Hernandez	1.00	.45	.12
☐ 19 Bill Mazeroski	2.50	1.10	.30
☐ 20 Bob Moose	1.00	.45	.12
☐ 21 Al Oliver	2.50	1.10	.30
☐ 22 Bob Robertson	1.00	.45	.12
☐ 23 Charlie Sands	1.00	.45	.12
☐ 24 Willie Stargell	3.50	1.55	.45

1971 Pirates Arco Oil

Sponsored by Arco Oil, this 12-card set features photos of the 1971 Pittsburgh Pirates. The cards are unnumbered and checklisted below in alphabetical order.

	NRMT	VG-E	GOOD
COMPLETE SET (12)	75.00	34.00	9.50
COMMON CARD (1-12)	5.00	2.20	.60
☐ 1 Gene Alley	5.00	2.20	.60
☐ 2 Steve Blass	5.00	2.20	.60
☐ 3 Roberto Clemente	25.00	11.00	3.10
☐ 4 Dave Giusti	5.00	2.20	.60
☐ 5 Richie Hebner	5.00	2.20	.60
☐ 6 Bill Mazeroski	7.50	3.40	.95
☐ 7 Bob Moose	5.00	2.20	.60
☐ 8 Al Oliver	7.50	3.40	.95
☐ 9 Bob Robertson	5.00	2.20	.60
☐ 10 Manny Sanguillen	7.50	3.40	.95
☐ 11 Willie Stargell	10.00	4.50	1.25
☐ 12 Luke Walker	5.00	2.20	.60

1975 Pirates

Some of the six cards in this set differ slightly in size, ranging from 3 3/4-4" by 5-5 1/4". The fronts feature white-bordered black-and-white portraits. The player's name is printed in the wider bottom margin. Also a facsimile autograph in blue ink is inscribed across each picture. The backs are blank. The cards are unnumbered and checklisted below in alphabetical order.

	NRMT	VG-E	GOOD
COMPLETE SET (6)	15.00	6.75	1.85
COMMON CARD (1-6)	2.50	1.10	.30
☐ 1 John Candelaria	3.00	1.35	.35
☐ 2 Duffy Dyer	2.50	1.10	.30
☐ 3 Richie Hebner	2.50	1.10	.30
☐ 4 Dave Parker	3.00	1.35	.35
☐ 5 Jerry Reuss	2.50	1.10	.30
☐ 6 Willie Stargell	4.00	1.80	.50

1977 Pirates Post-Gazette Portraits

This 30-card set was distributed in an 8 1/2" by 11" book from the Pittsburgh Post-Gazette. The black-and-white player portraits were detachable and measured approximately 8" by 11". The backs are blank. The cards are unnumbered and checklisted below in alphabetical order.

	NRMT	VG-E	GOOD
COMPLETE SET (30)	20.00	9.00	2.50
COMMON CARD (1-30)	.50	.23	.06
☐ 1 John Candelaria	.75	.35	.09
☐ 2 Larry Demery	.50	.23	.06
☐ 3 Miguel Dilone	.50	.23	.06
☐ 4 Duffy Dyer	.50	.23	.06
☐ 5 Terry Forster	.50	.23	.06
☐ 6 Jim Fregosi	.50	.23	.06
☐ 7 Phil Garner	.75	.35	.09
☐ 8 Fernando Gonzalez	.50	.23	.06
☐ 9 Rich Gossage	1.50	.70	.19
☐ 10 Grant Jackson	.50	.23	.06
☐ 11 Odell Jones	.50	.23	.06
☐ 12 Bruce Kison	.50	.23	.06
☐ 13 Joe Lonnett CO	.50	.23	.06
☐ 14 Mario Mendoza	.50	.23	.06
☐ 15 Al Monchak CO	.50	.23	.06
☐ 16 Omar Moreno	.75	.35	.09
☐ 17 Al Oliver	1.00	.45	.12
☐ 18 Ed Ott	.50	.23	.06
☐ 19 Jose Pagan CO	.50	.23	.06
☐ 20 Dave Parker	1.50	.70	.19
☐ 21 Jerry Reuss	.75	.35	.09
☐ 22 Bill Robinson	.50	.23	.06
☐ 23 Jim Rooker	.50	.23	.06
☐ 24 Larry Sherry CO	.50	.23	.06
☐ 25 Willie Stargell	3.00	1.35	.35
☐ 26 Rennie Stennett	.50	.23	.06
☐ 27 Chuck Tanner MG	.50	.23	.06
☐ 28 Frank Taveras	.50	.23	.06
☐ 29 Kent Tekulve	.75	.35	.09
☐ 30 Bobby Tolan	.50	.23	.06

1985 Pirates

This 23-card set of the Pittsburgh Pirates measures approximately 3 3/8" by 5 1/4" and features white-bordered color player portraits with the player's name, jersey number, and position printed in the wide bottom margin. A facsimile autograph rounds out the front. The backs carry the dates of different games and name of the game sponsor. The cards are unnumbered and checklisted below in alphabetical order.

	NRMT	VG-E	GOOD
COMPLETE SET (23)	6.00	2.70	.75
COMMON CARD (1-23)	.25	.11	.03
☐ 1 Bill Almon	.25	.11	.03
☐ 2 Rafael Belliard	.25	.11	.03
☐ 3 Mike Bielecki	.25	.11	.03
☐ 4 John Candelaria	.50	.23	.06
☐ 5 Jose DeLeon	.25	.11	.03
☐ 6 Tim Foli	.25	.11	.03
☐ 7 George Hendrick	.25	.11	.03
☐ 8 Steve Kemp	.25	.11	.03
☐ 9 Sixto Lezcano	.25	.11	.03
☐ 10 Bill Madlock	.50	.23	.06
☐ 11 Lee Mazzilli	.25	.11	.03
☐ 12 Larry McWilliams	.25	.11	.03
☐ 13 Jim Morrison	.25	.11	.03
☐ 14 Junior Ortiz	.25	.11	.03
☐ 15 Tony Pena	.50	.23	.06
☐ 16 Johnny Ray	.25	.11	.03
☐ 17 Rick Rhoden	.25	.11	.03
☐ 18 Don Robinson	.25	.11	.03
☐ 19 Rod Scurry	.25	.11	.03
☐ 20 Chuck Tanner MG	.50	.23	.06
☐ 21 Jason Thompson	.25	.11	.03
☐ 22 Lee Tunnell	.25	.11	.03
☐ 23 Marvell Wynne	.25	.11	.03

1986 Pirates Greats TCMA

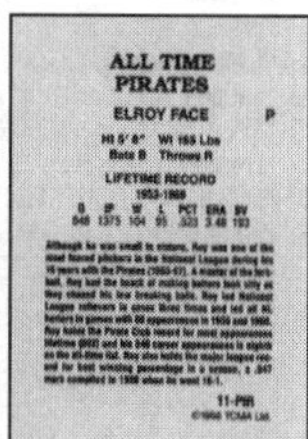

This 12-card standard-size set features all-time leading Pittsburgh Pirates. The player's photo and his name are featured on the front. The back gives more information about that player.

	MINT	NRMT	EXC
COMPLETE SET (12)	7.50	3.40	.95
COMMON CARD (1-12)	.25	.11	.03
☐ 1 Willie Stargell	1.00	.45	.12
☐ 2 Bill Mazeroski	.75	.35	.09
☐ 3 Honus Wagner	1.50	.70	.19
☐ 4 Pie Traynor	1.00	.45	.12
☐ 5 Ralph Kiner	.75	.35	.09
☐ 6 Paul Waner	.75	.35	.09
☐ 7 Roberto Clemente	2.50	1.10	.30
☐ 8 Manny Sanguillen	.25	.11	.03

☐ 9 Vic Willis	.50	.23	.06
☐ 10 Wilbur Cooper	.25	.11	.03
☐ 11 Elroy Face	.25	.11	.03
☐ 12 Danny Murtaugh MG	.25	.11	.03

1987 Pirates 1960 TCMA

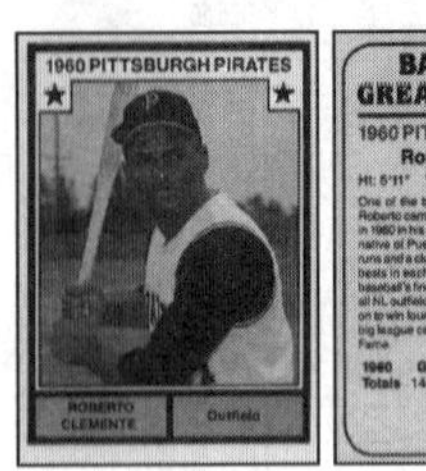

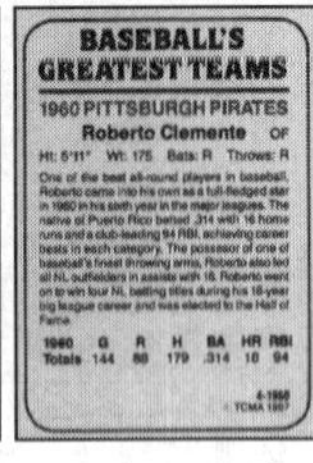

This nine-card standard-size set features members of the 1960 Pittsburgh Pirates. The player photo takes up most of the front with his name noted underneath. The backs give more information about the player as well as their 1960 stats.

	MINT	NRMT	EXC
COMPLETE SET (9)	4.00	1.80	.50
COMMON CARD (1-9)	.25	.11	.03
☐ 1 Dick Stuart	.25	.11	.03
☐ 2 Bill Mazeroski	.75	.35	.09
☐ 3 Dick Groat	.50	.23	.06
☐ 4 Roberto Clemente	2.50	1.10	.30
☐ 5 Bob Skinner	.25	.11	.03
☐ 6 Smoky Burgess	.25	.11	.03
☐ 7 Elroy Face	.50	.23	.06
☐ 8 Bob Friend	.25	.11	.03
☐ 9 Vernon Law	.50	.23	.06

1989 Pirates Very Fine Juice

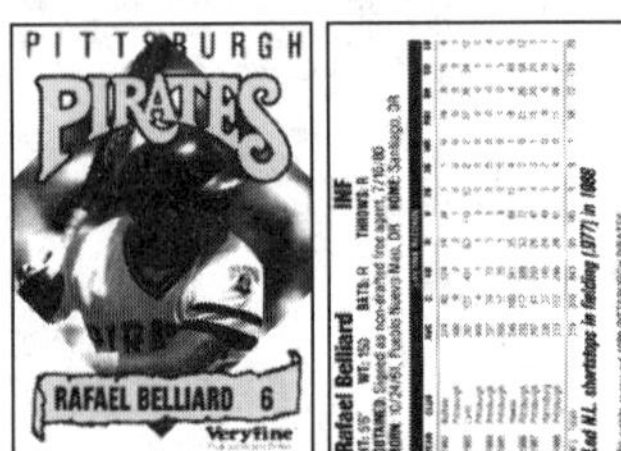

The 1989 Very Fine Juice Pittsburgh Pirates set is a 30-card set with cards measuring approximately 2 1/2" by 3 1/2" featuring the members of the 1989 Pittsburgh Pirates. This set was issued on three separate perforated sheets: two panels contain 15 player cards each, while the third panel serves as a cover for the set and displays color action photos of the Pirates. These panels were given away to fans attending the Pirates home game on April 23, 1989. There was a coupon (expiring on 10/31/89) on the back that could be redeemed for a free can of juice. The cards are numbered by uniform number in the list below. The cards are very colorful.

	MINT	NRMT	EXC
COMPLETE SET (30)	20.00	9.00	2.50
COMMON CARD	.50	.23	.06
☐ 0 Jumior Ortiz	.50	.23	.06
☐ 2 Gary Redus	.50	.23	.06
☐ 3 Jay Bell	1.00	.45	.12
☐ 5 Sid Bream	.75	.35	.09
☐ 6 Rafael Belliard	.50	.23	.06
☐ 10 Jim Leyland MG	.75	.35	.09
☐ 11 Glenn Wilson	.50	.23	.06
☐ 12 Mike LaValliere	.50	.23	.06
☐ 13 Jose Lind	.50	.23	.06
☐ 14 Ken Oberkfell	.50	.23	.06
☐ 15 Doug Drabek	.75	.35	.09
☐ 16 Bob Kipper	.50	.23	.06
☐ 17 Bob Walk	.50	.23	.06
☐ 18 Andy Van Slyke	1.00	.45	.12
☐ 23 R.J. Reynolds	.50	.23	.06
☐ 24 Barry Bonds	6.00	2.70	.75
☐ 25 Bobby Bonilla	1.50	.70	.19
☐ 26 Neal Heaton	.50	.23	.06
☐ 30 Benny Distefano	.50	.23	.06
☐ 31 Ray Miller CO and 37 Tommy Sandt CO	.50	.23	.06
☐ 35 Jim Gott	.50	.23	.06
☐ 36 Bruce Kimm CO and 32 Gene Lamont CO	.50	.23	.06
☐ 39 Milt May CO and 45 Rich Donnelly CO	.50	.23	.06
☐ 41 Mike Dunne	.50	.23	.06
☐ 43 Bill Landrum	.50	.23	.06
☐ 44 John Cangelosi	.50	.23	.06
☐ 49 Jeff D. Robinson	.50	.23	.06
☐ 52 Dorn Taylor	.50	.23	.06
☐ 54 Brian Fisher	.50	.23	.06
☐ 57 John Smiley	1.50	.70	.19

1990 Pirates Homers Cookies

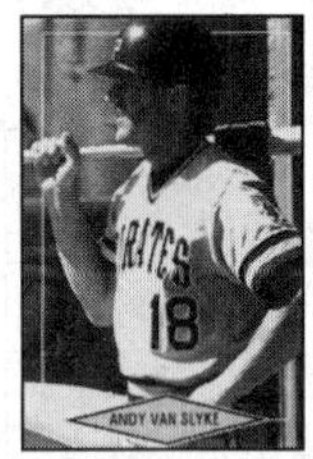

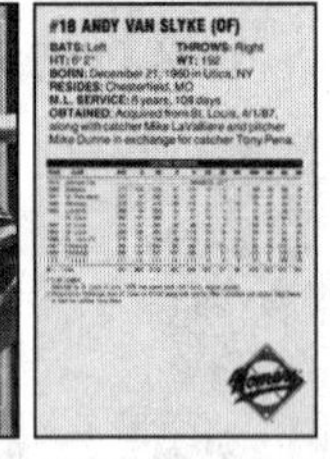

The 1990 Homers Cookies Pittsburgh Pirates set is an attractive 31-card set measuring approximately 4" by 6", used as a giveaway at a Pirates home game. It has been reported that 25,000 of these sets were produced. Four Homers Baseball trivia question cards were also included with the complete set. The fronts are full-color action photos with the backs containing complete statistical information. The set has been checklisted alphabetically below.

	MINT	NRMT	EXC
COMPLETE SET (31)	18.00	8.00	2.20
COMMON CARD (1-31)	.25	.11	.03
☐ 1 Wally Backman	.25	.11	.03
☐ 2 Doug Bair	.25	.11	.03
☐ 3 Rafael Belliard	.25	.11	.03
☐ 4 Jay Bell	1.00	.45	.12
☐ 5 Barry Bonds	6.00	2.70	.75
☐ 6 Bobby Bonilla	2.00	.90	.25
☐ 7 Sid Bream	.50	.23	.06
☐ 8 John Cangelosi	.25	.11	.03
☐ 9 Rich Donnelly CO	.25	.11	.03
☐ 10 Doug Drabek	1.00	.45	.12
☐ 11 Billy Hatcher	.25	.11	.03
☐ 12 Neal Heaton	.25	.11	.03
☐ 13 Jeff King	1.00	.45	.12
☐ 14 Bob Kipper	.25	.11	.03
☐ 15 Randy Kramer	.25	.11	.03
☐ 16 Gene Lamont CO	.50	.23	.06
☐ 17 Bill Landrum	.25	.11	.03
☐ 18 Mike LaValliere	.25	.11	.03
☐ 19 Jim Leyland MG	.50	.23	.06
☐ 20 Jose Lind	.25	.11	.03
☐ 21 Milt May	.25	.11	.03
☐ 22 Ray Miller CO	.25	.11	.03
☐ 23 Ted Power	.25	.11	.03
☐ 24 Gary Redus	.25	.11	.03
☐ 25 R.J. Reynolds	.25	.11	.03
☐ 26 Tommy Sandt CO	.25	.11	.03
☐ 27 Don Slaught	.25	.11	.03
☐ 28 Walt Terrell	.25	.11	.03
☐ 29 Andy Van Slyke	1.00	.45	.12
☐ 30 John Smiley	.50	.23	.06
☐ 31 Bob Walk	.25	.11	.03

1992 Pirates Nationwide Insurance

This 25-card set was sponsored by Nationwide Insurance, the Pittsburgh Bureau of Fire, and West Penn Hospital. The cards are oversized and measure 3 1/2" by 5 3/4". The color action player photos on the front are edged by a thin red and a wider white border. Superimposed at the bottom of the picture are the team logo, the player's name in a yellow banner, and his jersey number in a baseball icon. The backs feature statistical information about the player and fire safety tips. The cards are unnumbered and checklisted below in alphabetical order.

	MINT	NRMT	EXC
COMPLETE SET (25)	12.50	5.50	1.55
COMMON CARD (1-25)	.50	.23	.06
☐ 1 Stan Belinda	.50	.23	.06
☐ 2 Jay Bell	1.00	.45	.12
☐ 3 Barry Bonds	5.00	2.20	.60
☐ 4 Steve Buechele	.50	.23	.06
☐ 5 Terry Collins CO	.50	.23	.06
☐ 6 Rich Donnelly CO	.50	.23	.06
☐ 7 Doug Drabek	1.00	.45	.12
☐ 8 Cecil Espy	.50	.23	.06
☐ 9 Jeff King	1.00	.45	.12
☐ 10 Mike LaValliere	.50	.23	.06
☐ 11 Jim Leyland MG	1.00	.45	.12
☐ 12 Jose Lind	.50	.23	.06
☐ 13 Roger Mason	.50	.23	.06
☐ 14 Milt May CO	.50	.23	.06
☐ 15 Lloyd McClendon	.50	.23	.06
☐ 16 Orlando Merced	1.00	.45	.12
☐ 17 Denny Neagle	1.50	.70	.19
☐ 18 Bob Patterson	.50	.23	.06
☐ 19 Gary Redus	.50	.23	.06
☐ 20 Don Slaught	.50	.23	.06
☐ 21 Zane Smith	.50	.23	.06
☐ 22 Randy Tomlin	.50	.23	.06
☐ 23 Andy Van Slyke	1.00	.45	.12
☐ 24 Gary Varsho	.50	.23	.06
☐ 25 Bob Walk	.50	.23	.06

1993 Pirates Hills

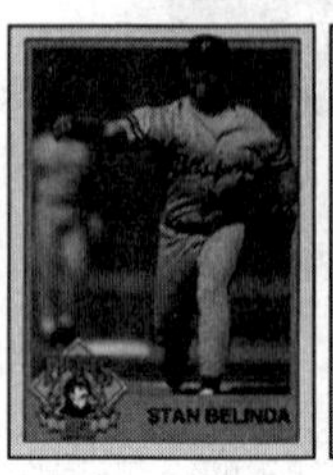

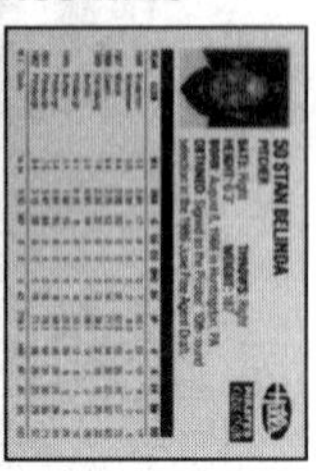

Originally issued in a perforated sheet, these 12 standard-size cards feature on their fronts color player action shots with white outer borders and yellow inner borders. The player's name appears in black lettering within the yellow margin below the photo. The Pirates logo rests at the lower left. The white horizontal back carries a black-and-white player head shot at the upper left, with the player's uniform number, name, position, and biography appearing alongside to the right. Statistics follow below. The cards are unnumbered and checklisted below in alphabetical order.

	MINT	NRMT	EXC
COMPLETE SET (12)	8.00	3.60	1.00
COMMON CARD (1-12)	.75	.35	.09
☐ 1 Stan Belinda	.75	.35	.09
☐ 2 John Candelaria	1.00	.45	.12
☐ 3 Steve Cooke	.75	.35	.09
☐ 4 Jeff King	1.50	.70	.19
☐ 5 Jim Leyland MG	1.00	.45	.12
☐ 6 Al Martin	1.50	.70	.19
☐ 7 Lloyd McClendon	.75	.35	.09
☐ 8 Orlando Merced	1.00	.45	.12
☐ 9 Blas Minor	.75	.35	.09
☐ 10 Denny Neagle	1.50	.70	.19
☐ 11 Tom Prince	.75	.35	.09
☐ 12 Kevin Young	.75	.35	.09

1993 Pirates Nationwide Insurance

These 40 oversized cards measure approximately 3 3/8" by 5 5/8". The color action player photos on the front are edged by a thin black line and a wide white border. The top of the card has a thin red border, and a red block carries the player's name printed in white and the Bucs' Three-Peat logo. The backs include biography and how the player was obtained. The Nationwide Insurance logo at the bottom rounds out the back. On Sunday June 27, children 14 and under were given a set at the Pirates-Phillies game at Three Rivers Stadium. Quintex Mobile Communications/Bell Atlantic is listed as the sponsor on the backs of the giveaway sets. The Parrot card and the Three Rivers card are not included in the Quintex sets.

	MINT	NRMT	EXC
COMPLETE SET (40)	10.00	4.50	1.25
COMMON CARD (1-40)	.25	.11	.03
☐ 1 Stan Belinda	.25	.11	.03
☐ 2 Jay Bell	.75	.35	.09
☐ 3 Steve Blass ANN	.25	.11	.03
☐ 4 John Candelaria	.50	.23	.06
☐ 5 Dave Clark	.25	.11	.03
☐ 6 Terry Collins CO	.25	.11	.03
☐ 7 Steve Cooke	.25	.11	.03
☐ 8 Kent Derdivannis ANN	.25	.11	.03
☐ 9 Rich Donnelly CO	.25	.11	.03
☐ 10 Tom Foley	.25	.11	.03
☐ 11 Lanny Frattare ANN	.25	.11	.03
☐ 12 Carlos Garcia	.50	.23	.06
☐ 13 Jeff King	.75	.35	.09
☐ 14 Jim Leyland MG	.50	.23	.06
☐ 15 Al Martin	.75	.35	.09
☐ 16 Milt May CO	.25	.11	.03
☐ 17 Lloyd McClendon	.25	.11	.03
☐ 18 Orlando Merced	.75	.35	.09
☐ 19 Ray Miller CO	.25	.11	.03
☐ 20 Blas Minor	.25	.11	.03
☐ 21 Dennis Moeller	.25	.11	.03
☐ 22 Denny Neagle	.50	.23	.06
☐ 23 Dave Otto	.25	.11	.03
☐ 24 Pirate Parrot (Mascot)	.50	.23	.06
☐ 25 Tom Prince	.25	.11	.03
☐ 26 Jim Rooker ANN	.25	.11	.03
☐ 27 Tommy Sandt CO	.25	.11	.03
☐ 28 Ted Simmons XGM	.50	.23	.06
☐ 29 Don Slaught	.25	.11	.03
☐ 30 Lonnie Smith	.25	.11	.03
☐ 31 Zane Smith	.25	.11	.03
☐ 32 Randy Tomlin	.25	.11	.03
☐ 33 Andy Van Slyke	.75	.35	.09
☐ 34 Bill Virdon CO	.50	.23	.06
☐ 35 Paul Wagner	.50	.23	.06
☐ 36 Tim Wakefield	.75	.35	.09
☐ 37 Bob Walk	.25	.11	.03
☐ 38 John Wehner	.25	.11	.03
☐ 39 Kevin Young	.25	.11	.03
☐ 40 Three Rivers Stadium	.25	.11	.03

1994 Pirates Quintex

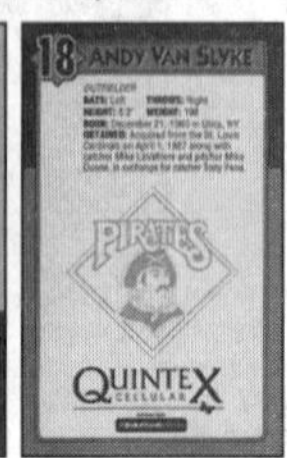

These 29 oversized cards measure approximately 3 1/2" by 5 3/4". The fronts feature color action player photos with team color-coded black and yellow borders. The team name appears in the top part of the photo, while the player's name is printed in a yellow bar under the photo. The backs carry player biography, how the player was obtained, and team and sponsor logos. This set was passed out on July 31, 1994 at the Pirates' home game. A coupon for a cellular transportable bag phone at no charge came with it. The cards are unnumbered and checklisted below in alphabetical order. Cards are also known which say Nationwide Insurance. These cards have the same value as the Qunitex cards.

	MINT	NRMT	EXC
COMPLETE SET (29)	10.00	4.50	1.25
COMMON CARD (1-29)	.25	.11	.03
☐ 1 Jay Bell	.75	.35	.09
☐ 2 Dave Clark	.25	.11	.03
☐ 3 Steve Cooke	.25	.11	.03
☐ 4 Mark Dewey	.25	.11	.03
☐ 5 Rich Donnelly CO	.25	.11	.03
☐ 6 Tom Foley	.25	.11	.03
☐ 7 Carlos Garcia	.75	.35	.09
☐ 8 Brian Hunter	.25	.11	.03
☐ 9 Jeff King	.75	.35	.09
☐ 10 Jim Leyland MG	.50	.23	.06
☐ 11 Ravelo Manzanillo	.25	.11	.03
☐ 12 Al Martin	.75	.35	.09
☐ 13 Milt May CO	.25	.11	.03
☐ 14 Lloyd McClendon	.25	.11	.03
☐ 15 Orlando Merced	.75	.35	.09
☐ 16 Dan Miceli	.25	.11	.03
☐ 17 Ray Miller CO	.25	.11	.03
☐ 18 Denny Neagle	1.00	.45	.12
☐ 19 Pirate Parrot (Mascot)	.50	.23	.06
☐ 20 Tommy Sandt CO	.25	.11	.03
☐ 21 Don Slaught	.25	.11	.03
☐ 22 Zane Smith	.25	.11	.03
☐ 23 Andy Van Slyke	.75	.35	.09
☐ 24 Bill Virdon CO	.50	.23	.06
☐ 25 Paul Wagner	.25	.11	.03
☐ 26 Rick White	.25	.11	.03
☐ 27 Spin Williams CO	.25	.11	.03
☐ 28 Kevin Young	.25	.11	.03
☐ 29 Three Rivers Stadium	.25	.11	.03

1995 Pirates Filmet

This 30-card set of the Pittsburgh Pirates was distributed on Picture Card Night as a perforated sheet measuring approximately 20 1/4" by 13 1/2". The cards themselves measure 2 1/4" by 3 1/4" and feature a color action player photo in a white border. The player's name is printed in yellow in a red banner at the top with the team name in gold running down the side margins. The white backs carry the player's name, position, biography and career information. The cards were created using Kodak Photo CD technology, output, and printed by Filmet Commercial Services. A coupon at the bottom could be used at Filmet locations for film processing. The cards are unnumbered and checklisted below in alphabetical order.

	MINT	NRMT	EXC
COMPLETE SET (30)	8.00	3.60	1.00
COMMON CARD (1-30)	.25	.11	.03
☐ 1 Rich Aude	.25	.11	.03
☐ 2 Jay Bell	.75	.35	.09
☐ 3 Jacob Brumfield	.25	.11	.03
☐ 4 Jason Christiansen	.50	.23	.06

☐ 5 Dave Clark	.25	.11	.03
☐ 6 Steve Cooke	.25	.11	.03
☐ 7 Midre Cummings	.50	.23	.06
☐ 8 Mike Dyer	.25	.11	.03
☐ 9 Angelo Encarnacion	.25	.11	.03
☐ 10 Carlos Garcia	.75	.35	.09
☐ 11 Freddy Garcia	.25	.11	.03
☐ 12 Jim Gott	.25	.11	.03
☐ 13 Mark Johnson	.50	.23	.06
☐ 14 Jeff King	.75	.35	.09
☐ 15 Jim Leyland MG	.50	.23	.06
☐ 16 Jon Lieber	.25	.11	.03
☐ 17 Nelson Liriano	.25	.11	.03
☐ 18 Esteban Loaiza	.25	.11	.03
☐ 19 Al Martin	.75	.35	.09
☐ 20 Jeff McCurry	.25	.11	.03
☐ 21 Orlando Merced	.75	.35	.09
☐ 22 Dan Miceli	.25	.11	.03
☐ 23 Denny Neagle	1.00	.45	.12
☐ 24 Mark Parent	.25	.11	.03
☐ 25 Steve Pegues	.25	.11	.03
☐ 26 Dan Plesac	.25	.11	.03
☐ 27 Don Slaught	.25	.11	.03
☐ 28 Paul Wagner	.25	.11	.03
☐ 29 Rick White	.25	.11	.03
☐ 30 Gary Wilson	.25	.11	.03

1997 Pirates Post-Gazette

This one-card set measures approximately 3 1/2" by 5 3/4" and features a color photo of Pittsburgh Pirates catcher Jason Kendall in a paint-splashed border with a simulated autograph on the front. The back contains player information in a ticket format.

	MINT	NRMT	EXC
COMPLETE SET (1)	5.00	2.20	.60
COMMON CARD (1)	5.00	2.20	.60
☐ 1 Jason Kendall	5.00	2.20	.60

1996 Pitch Postcards HOF

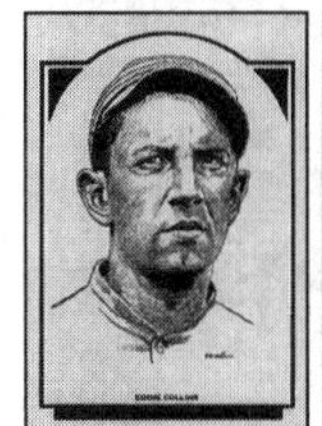
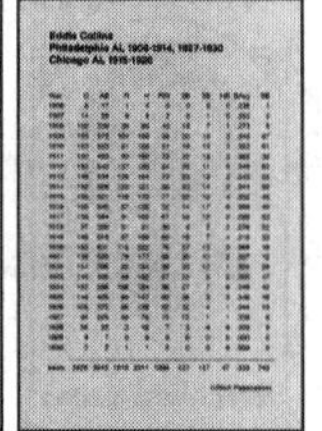

This 12-card set measures approximately 6" by 4" and features black-and-white player drawings. The backs carry player career stats. The cards are unnumbered and checklisted below in alphabetical order.

	MINT	NRMT	EXC
COMPLETE SET (12)	6.00	2.70	.75
COMMON CARD (1-12)	.50	.23	.06
☐ 1 Frank Baker	.50	.23	.06
☐ 2 Frank Chance	.75	.35	.09
☐ 3 Fred Clarke	.50	.23	.06
☐ 4 Eddie Collins	1.00	.45	.12
☐ 5 Sam Crawford	.50	.23	.06
☐ 6 Johnny Evers	.50	.23	.06
☐ 7 Willie Keeler	.50	.23	.06
☐ 8 Nap Lajoie	1.00	.45	.12
☐ 9 Rube Marquard	.50	.23	.06
☐ 10 Eddie Plank	.75	.35	.09
☐ 11 Joe Tinker	.75	.35	.09
☐ 12 Rube Waddell	.50	.23	.06

1939 Play Ball

The cards in this 161-card set measure approximately 2 1/2" by 3 1/8". Gum Incorporated introduced a brief (war-shortened) but innovative era of baseball card production with its set of 1939. The combination of actual player photos (black and white), large card size, and extensive biography proved extremely popular. Player names are found either entirely capitalized or with initial caps only, and a "sample card" overprint is not uncommon. The "sample card" overprint variations are valued at double the prices below. Card number 126 was never issued, and cards 116-162 were produced in lesser quantities than cards 1-115. The catalog designation for this set is R334. A card of Ted Williams in his rookie season as well as an early card of Joe DiMaggio are the key cards in the set.

	EX-MT	VG-E	GOOD
COMPLETE SET (162)	12000.00	5400.00	1500.00
COMMON CARD (1-115)	18.00	8.00	2.20
COMMON CARD (116-162)	90.00	40.00	11.00
WRAPPER (1-CENT)	200.00	90.00	25.00
☐ 1 Jake Powell	75.00	34.00	9.50
☐ 2 Lee Grissom	18.00	8.00	2.20
☐ 3 Red Ruffing	75.00	34.00	9.50
☐ 4 Eldon Auker	18.00	8.00	2.20
☐ 5 Luke Sewell	25.00	11.00	3.10
☐ 6 Leo Durocher	90.00	40.00	11.00
☐ 7 Bobby Doerr	75.00	34.00	9.50
☐ 8 Henry Pippen	18.00	8.00	2.20
☐ 9 James Tobin	18.00	8.00	2.20
☐ 10 James DeShong	18.00	8.00	2.20
☐ 11 Johnny Rizzo	18.00	8.00	2.20
☐ 12 Hershel Martin	18.00	8.00	2.20
☐ 13 Luke Hamlin	18.00	8.00	2.20
☐ 14 Jim Tabor	18.00	8.00	2.20
☐ 15 Paul Derringer	30.00	13.50	3.70
☐ 16 John Peacock	18.00	8.00	2.20
☐ 17 Emerson Dickman	18.00	8.00	2.20
☐ 18 Harry Danning	18.00	8.00	2.20
☐ 19 Paul Dean	30.00	13.50	3.70
☐ 20 Joe Heving	18.00	8.00	2.20
☐ 21 Dutch Leonard	25.00	11.00	3.10
☐ 22 Bucky Walters	25.00	11.00	3.10
☐ 23 Burgess Whitehead	18.00	8.00	2.20
☐ 24 Richard Coffman	18.00	8.00	2.20
☐ 25 George Selkirk	30.00	13.50	3.70
☐ 26 Joe DiMaggio	2400.00	1100.00	300.00
☐ 27 Fred Ostermueller	18.00	8.00	2.20
☐ 28 Sylvester Johnson	18.00	8.00	2.20
☐ 29 John(Jack) Wilson	18.00	8.00	2.20
☐ 30 Bill Dickey	150.00	70.00	19.00
☐ 31 Sam West	18.00	8.00	2.20
☐ 32 Bob Seeds	18.00	8.00	2.20
☐ 33 Del Young	18.00	8.00	2.20
☐ 34 Frank Demaree	18.00	8.00	2.20
☐ 35 Bill Jurges	18.00	8.00	2.20
☐ 36 Frank McCormick	20.00	9.00	2.50
☐ 37 Virgil Davis	18.00	8.00	2.20
☐ 38 Billy Myers	18.00	8.00	2.20
☐ 39 Rick Ferrell	75.00	34.00	9.50
☐ 40 James Bagby Jr.	18.00	8.00	2.20
☐ 41 Lon Warneke	20.00	9.00	2.50
☐ 42 Arndt Jorgens	18.00	8.00	2.20
☐ 43 Melo Almada	18.00	8.00	2.20
☐ 44 Don Heffner	18.00	8.00	2.20
☐ 45 Merrill May	18.00	8.00	2.20
☐ 46 Morris Arnovich	18.00	8.00	2.20
☐ 47 Buddy Lewis	18.00	8.00	2.20
☐ 48 Lefty Gomez	125.00	55.00	15.50
☐ 49 Eddie Miller	18.00	8.00	2.20
☐ 50 Charlie Gehringer	150.00	70.00	19.00
☐ 51 Mel Ott	150.00	70.00	19.00
☐ 52 Tommy Henrich	35.00	16.00	4.40
☐ 53 Carl Hubbell	125.00	55.00	15.50
☐ 54 Harry Gumpert	18.00	8.00	2.20
☐ 55 Arky Vaughan	75.00	34.00	9.50
☐ 56 Hank Greenberg	200.00	90.00	25.00
☐ 57 Buddy Hassett	18.00	8.00	2.20
☐ 58 Lou Chiozza	18.00	8.00	2.20
☐ 59 Ken Chase	18.00	8.00	2.20
☐ 60 Schoolboy Rowe	25.00	11.00	3.10
☐ 61 Tony Cuccinello	20.00	9.00	2.50
☐ 62 Tom Carey	18.00	8.00	2.20
☐ 63 Emmett Mueller	18.00	8.00	2.20
☐ 64 Wally Moses	20.00	9.00	2.50
☐ 65 Harry Craft	20.00	9.00	2.50
☐ 66 Jimmy Ripple	18.00	8.00	2.20
☐ 67 Ed Joost	20.00	9.00	2.50
☐ 68 Fred Sington	18.00	8.00	2.20
☐ 69 Elbie Fletcher	18.00	8.00	2.20
☐ 70 Fred Frankhouse	18.00	8.00	2.20
☐ 71 Monte Pearson	25.00	11.00	3.10
☐ 72 Debs Garms	18.00	8.00	2.20
☐ 73 Hal Schumacher	20.00	9.00	2.50
☐ 74 Cookie Lavagetto	20.00	9.00	2.50
☐ 75 Stan Bordagaray	18.00	8.00	2.20
☐ 76 Goody Rosen	18.00	8.00	2.20
☐ 77 Lew Riggs	18.00	8.00	2.20
☐ 78 Julius Solters	18.00	8.00	2.20
☐ 79 Jo Jo Moore	18.00	8.00	2.20
☐ 80 Pete Fox	18.00	8.00	2.20
☐ 81 Babe Dahlgren	25.00	11.00	3.10
☐ 82 Chuck Klein	125.00	55.00	15.50
☐ 83 Gus Suhr	18.00	8.00	2.20
☐ 84 Skeeter Newsom	18.00	8.00	2.20
☐ 85 Johnny Cooney	18.00	8.00	2.20
☐ 86 Dolph Camilli	20.00	9.00	2.50
☐ 87 Milburn Shoffner	18.00	8.00	2.20
☐ 88 Charlie Keller	35.00	16.00	4.40
☐ 89 Lloyd Waner	75.00	34.00	9.50
☐ 90 Robert Klinger	18.00	8.00	2.20
☐ 91 John Knott	18.00	8.00	2.20
☐ 92 Ted Williams	2400.00	1100.00	300.00
☐ 93 Charles Gelbert	18.00	8.00	2.20
☐ 94 Heinie Manush	75.00	34.00	9.50
☐ 95 Whit Wyatt	20.00	9.00	2.50
☐ 96 Babe Phelps	18.00	8.00	2.20
☐ 97 Bob Johnson	25.00	11.00	3.10
☐ 98 Pinky Whitney	18.00	8.00	2.20
☐ 99 Wally Berger	30.00	13.50	3.70
☐ 100 Buddy Myer	20.00	9.00	2.50
☐ 101 Roger Cramer	20.00	9.00	2.50
☐ 102 Lem Young	18.00	8.00	2.20
☐ 103 Moe Berg	150.00	70.00	19.00
☐ 104 Tom Bridges	20.00	9.00	2.50
☐ 105 Rabbit McNair	18.00	8.00	2.20
☐ 106 Dolly Stark UMP	25.00	11.00	3.10
☐ 107 Joe Vosmik	18.00	8.00	2.20
☐ 108 Frank Hayes	18.00	8.00	2.20
☐ 109 Myril Hoag	18.00	8.00	2.20
☐ 110 Fred Fitzsimmons	20.00	9.00	2.50
☐ 111 Van Lingle Mungo	25.00	11.00	3.10
☐ 112 Paul Waner	90.00	40.00	11.00
☐ 113 Al Schacht	25.00	11.00	3.10
☐ 114 Cecil Travis	20.00	9.00	2.50
☐ 115 Ralph Kress	18.00	8.00	2.20
☐ 116 Gene Desautels	90.00	40.00	11.00
☐ 117 Wayne Ambler	90.00	40.00	11.00
☐ 118 Lynn Nelson	90.00	40.00	11.00
☐ 119 Will Hershberger	100.00	45.00	12.50
☐ 120 Rabbit Warstler	90.00	40.00	11.00
☐ 121 Bill Posedel	90.00	40.00	11.00
☐ 122 George McQuinn	90.00	40.00	11.00
☐ 123 Ray T. Davis	90.00	40.00	11.00
☐ 124 Walter Brown	90.00	40.00	11.00
☐ 125 Cliff Melton	90.00	40.00	11.00
☐ 126 Not issued			
☐ 127 Gil Brack	90.00	40.00	11.00
☐ 128 Joe Bowman	90.00	40.00	11.00
☐ 129 Bill Swift	90.00	40.00	11.00
☐ 130 Bill Brubaker	90.00	40.00	11.00
☐ 131 Mort Cooper	100.00	45.00	12.50
☐ 132 Jim Brown	90.00	40.00	11.00
☐ 133 Lynn Myers	90.00	40.00	11.00
☐ 134 Tot Presnell	90.00	40.00	11.00
☐ 135 Mickey Owen	100.00	45.00	12.50
☐ 136 Roy Bell	90.00	40.00	11.00
☐ 137 Pete Appleton	90.00	40.00	11.00
☐ 138 George Case	100.00	45.00	12.50
☐ 139 Vito Tamulis	90.00	40.00	11.00
☐ 140 Ray Hayworth	90.00	40.00	11.00
☐ 141 Pete Coscarart	90.00	40.00	11.00
☐ 142 Ira Hutchinson	90.00	40.00	11.00
☐ 143 Earl Averill	225.00	100.00	28.00
☐ 144 Zeke Bonura	100.00	45.00	12.50
☐ 145 Hugh Mulcahy	90.00	40.00	11.00
☐ 146 Tom Sunkel	90.00	40.00	11.00
☐ 147 George Coffman	90.00	40.00	11.00
☐ 148 Bill Trotter	90.00	40.00	11.00
☐ 149 Max West	90.00	40.00	11.00
☐ 150 James Walkup	90.00	40.00	11.00
☐ 151 Hugh Casey	100.00	45.00	12.50
☐ 152 Roy Weatherly	90.00	40.00	11.00
☐ 153 Paul Trout	100.00	45.00	12.50
☐ 154 Johnny Hudson	90.00	40.00	11.00
☐ 155 Jimmy Outlaw	90.00	40.00	11.00
☐ 156 Ray Berres	90.00	40.00	11.00
☐ 157 Don Padgett	90.00	40.00	11.00
☐ 158 Bud Thomas	90.00	40.00	11.00
☐ 159 Red Evans	90.00	40.00	11.00
☐ 160 Gene Moore	90.00	40.00	11.00
☐ 161 Lonnie Frey	90.00	40.00	11.00
☐ 162 Whitey Moore	100.00	45.00	12.50

1940 Play Ball

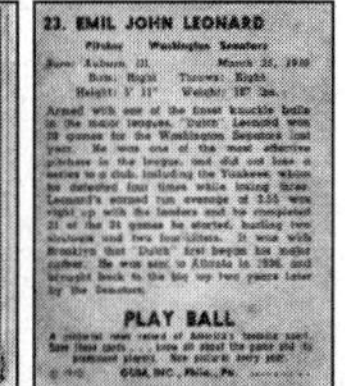

The cards in this 240-card series measure approximately 2 1/2" by 3 1/8". Gum Inc. improved upon its 1939 design by enclosing the 1940 black and white player photo with a frame line and printing the player's name in a panel below the picture (often using a nickname). The set included many Hall of Famers and Old Timers. Cards 1-114 are numbered in team groupings. Cards 181-240 are scarcer than cards 1-180. The backs contain an extensive biography and a dated copyright line. The catalog number for this set is R335. The key cards in the set are the cards of Joe DiMaggio, Shoeless Joe Jackson, and Ted Williams.

	EX-MT	VG-E	GOOD
COMPLETE SET (240)	18000.00	8100.00	2200.00
COMMON CARD (1-120)	20.00	9.00	2.50
COMMON CARD (121-180)	20.00	9.00	2.50
COMMON CARD (181-240)	70.00	32.00	8.75
WRAPPER (1-CENT)	250.00	110.00	31.00
☐ 1 Joe DiMaggio	2700.00	1200.00	350.00
☐ 2 Art Jorgens	22.00	10.00	2.70
☐ 3 Babe Dahlgren	22.00	10.00	2.70
☐ 4 Tommy Henrich	35.00	16.00	4.40
☐ 5 Monte Pearson	22.00	10.00	2.70
☐ 6 Lefty Gomez	150.00	70.00	19.00
☐ 7 Bill Dickey	175.00	80.00	22.00
☐ 8 George Selkirk	22.00	10.00	2.70
☐ 9 Charlie Keller	35.00	16.00	4.40
☐ 10 Red Ruffing	90.00	40.00	11.00
☐ 11 Jake Powell	22.00	10.00	2.70
☐ 12 Johnny Schulte	20.00	9.00	2.50
☐ 13 Jack Knott	20.00	9.00	2.50
☐ 14 Rabbit McNair	20.00	9.00	2.50
☐ 15 George Case	22.00	10.00	2.70
☐ 16 Cecil Travis	22.00	10.00	2.70
☐ 17 Buddy Myer	22.00	10.00	2.70
☐ 18 Charlie Gelbert	20.00	9.00	2.50
☐ 19 Ken Chase	20.00	9.00	2.50
☐ 20 Buddy Lewis	20.00	9.00	2.50
☐ 21 Rick Ferrell	80.00	36.00	10.00
☐ 22 Sammy West	20.00	9.00	2.50
☐ 23 Dutch Leonard	22.00	10.00	2.70
☐ 24 Frank Hayes	20.00	9.00	2.50
☐ 25 Bob Johnson	22.00	10.00	2.70
☐ 26 Wally Moses	22.00	10.00	2.70
☐ 27 Ted Williams	1700.00	750.00	210.00
☐ 28 Gene Desautels	20.00	9.00	2.50
☐ 29 Doc Cramer	22.00	10.00	2.70
☐ 30 Moe Berg	125.00	55.00	15.50
☐ 31 Jack Wilson	20.00	9.00	2.50
☐ 32 Jim Bagby	20.00	9.00	2.50
☐ 33 Fritz Ostermueller	20.00	9.00	2.50
☐ 34 John Peacock	20.00	9.00	2.50
☐ 35 Joe Heving	20.00	9.00	2.50
☐ 36 Jim Tabor	20.00	9.00	2.50
☐ 37 Emerson Dickman	20.00	9.00	2.50
☐ 38 Bobby Doerr	90.00	40.00	11.00
☐ 39 Tom Carey	20.00	9.00	2.50
☐ 40 Hank Greenberg	250.00	110.00	31.00
☐ 41 Charley Gehringer	150.00	70.00	19.00
☐ 42 Bud Thomas	20.00	9.00	2.50
☐ 43 Pete Fox	20.00	9.00	2.50
☐ 44 Dizzy Trout	22.00	10.00	2.70
☐ 45 Red Kress	20.00	9.00	2.50
☐ 46 Earl Averill	90.00	40.00	11.00
☐ 47 Oscar Vitt	20.00	9.00	2.50
☐ 48 Luke Sewell	22.00	10.00	2.70
☐ 49 Stormy Weatherly	20.00	9.00	2.50
☐ 50 Hal Trosky	22.00	10.00	2.70
☐ 51 Don Heffner	20.00	9.00	2.50
☐ 52 Myril Hoag	20.00	9.00	2.50
☐ 53 George McQuinn	22.00	10.00	2.70
☐ 54 Bill Trotter	20.00	9.00	2.50
☐ 55 Slick Coffman	20.00	9.00	2.50
☐ 56 Eddie Miller	22.00	10.00	2.70
☐ 57 Max West	20.00	9.00	2.50
☐ 58 Bill Posedel	20.00	9.00	2.50
☐ 59 Rabbit Warstler	20.00	9.00	2.50
☐ 60 John Cooney	20.00	9.00	2.50
☐ 61 Tony Cuccinello	22.00	10.00	2.70
☐ 62 Buddy Hassett	20.00	9.00	2.50
☐ 63 Pete Coscarart	20.00	9.00	2.50
☐ 64 Van Lingle Mungo	22.00	10.00	2.70
☐ 65 Fred Fitzsimmons	22.00	10.00	2.70
☐ 66 Babe Phelps	20.00	9.00	2.50
☐ 67 Whit Wyatt	22.00	10.00	2.70
☐ 68 Dolph Camilli	22.00	10.00	2.70
☐ 69 Cookie Lavagetto	22.00	10.00	2.70
☐ 70 Luke Hamlin (Hot Potato)	20.00	9.00	2.50
☐ 71 Mel Almada	20.00	9.00	2.50
☐ 72 Chuck Dressen	22.00	10.00	2.70
☐ 73 Bucky Walters	22.00	10.00	2.70
☐ 74 Paul(Duke) Derringer	30.00	13.50	3.70
☐ 75 Frank(Buck) McCormick	22.00	10.00	2.70
☐ 76 Lonny Frey	20.00	9.00	2.50
☐ 77 Willard Hershberger	22.00	10.00	2.70
☐ 78 Lew Riggs	20.00	9.00	2.50
☐ 79 Harry Craft	22.00	10.00	2.70
☐ 80 Billy Myers	20.00	9.00	2.50
☐ 81 Wally Berger	22.00	10.00	2.70
☐ 82 Hank Gowdy CO	22.00	10.00	2.70
☐ 83 Cliff Melton	20.00	9.00	2.50
☐ 84 Jo Jo Moore	20.00	9.00	2.50
☐ 85 Hal Schumacher	22.00	10.00	2.70
☐ 86 Harry Gumbert	20.00	9.00	2.50
☐ 87 Carl Hubbell	125.00	55.00	15.50
☐ 88 Mel Ott	175.00	80.00	22.00
☐ 89 Bill Jurges	20.00	9.00	2.50
☐ 90 Frank Demaree	20.00	9.00	2.50
☐ 91 Bob Seeds	20.00	9.00	2.50
☐ 92 Whitey Whitehead	20.00	9.00	2.50
☐ 93 Harry Danning	20.00	9.00	2.50
☐ 94 Gus Suhr	20.00	9.00	2.50
☐ 95 Hugh Mulcahy	20.00	9.00	2.50
☐ 96 Heinie Mueller	20.00	9.00	2.50
☐ 97 Morry Arnovich	20.00	9.00	2.50
☐ 98 Pinky May	20.00	9.00	2.50
☐ 99 Syl Johnson	20.00	9.00	2.50
☐ 100 Hersh Martin	20.00	9.00	2.50
☐ 101 Del Young	20.00	9.00	2.50
☐ 102 Chuck Klein	100.00	45.00	12.50

☐ 103 Elbie Fletcher	20.00	9.00	2.50
☐ 104 Paul Waner	90.00	40.00	11.00
☐ 105 Lloyd Waner	80.00	36.00	10.00
☐ 106 Pep Young	20.00	9.00	2.50
☐ 107 Arky Vaughan	80.00	36.00	10.00
☐ 108 Johnny Rizzo	20.00	9.00	2.50
☐ 109 Don Padgett	20.00	9.00	2.50
☐ 110 Tom Sunkel	20.00	9.00	2.50
☐ 111 Mickey Owen	30.00	13.50	3.70
☐ 112 Jimmy Brown	20.00	9.00	2.50
☐ 113 Mort Cooper	22.00	10.00	2.70
☐ 114 Lon Warneke	22.00	10.00	2.70
☐ 115 Mike Gonzalez CO	22.00	10.00	2.70
☐ 116 Al Schacht	30.00	13.50	3.70
☐ 117 Dolly Stark UMP	22.00	10.00	2.70
☐ 118 Waite Hoyt	90.00	40.00	11.00
☐ 119 Grover C. Alexander	175.00	80.00	22.00
☐ 120 Walter Johnson	250.00	110.00	31.00
☐ 121 Atley Donald	22.00	10.00	2.70
☐ 122 Sandy Sundra	22.00	10.00	2.70
☐ 123 Hildy Hildebrand	22.00	10.00	2.70
☐ 124 Earle Combs	100.00	45.00	12.50
☐ 125 Art Fletcher	22.00	10.00	2.70
☐ 126 Jake Solters	20.00	9.00	2.50
☐ 127 Muddy Ruel	20.00	9.00	2.50
☐ 128 Pete Appleton	20.00	9.00	2.50
☐ 129 Bucky Harris	80.00	36.00	10.00
☐ 130 Clyde(Deerfoot) Milan	22.00	10.00	2.70
☐ 131 Zeke Bonura	22.00	10.00	2.70
☐ 132 Connie Mack MG	200.00	90.00	25.00
☐ 133 Jimmie Foxx	250.00	110.00	31.00
☐ 134 Joe Cronin	100.00	45.00	12.50
☐ 135 Line Drive Nelson	20.00	9.00	2.50
☐ 136 Cotton Pippen	20.00	9.00	2.50
☐ 137 Bing Miller	20.00	9.00	2.50
☐ 138 Beau Bell	20.00	9.00	2.50
☐ 139 Elden Auker	20.00	9.00	2.50
☐ 140 Dick Coffman	20.00	9.00	2.50
☐ 141 Casey Stengel MG	200.00	90.00	25.00
☐ 142 George Kelly	90.00	40.00	11.00
☐ 143 Gene Moore	20.00	9.00	2.50
☐ 144 Joe Vosmik	20.00	9.00	2.50
☐ 145 Vito Tamulis	20.00	9.00	2.50
☐ 146 Tot Pressnell	20.00	9.00	2.50
☐ 147 Johnny Hudson	20.00	9.00	2.50
☐ 148 Hugh Casey	22.00	10.00	2.70
☐ 149 Pinky Shoffner	20.00	9.00	2.50
☐ 150 Whitey Moore	20.00	9.00	2.50
☐ 151 Edwin Joost	22.00	10.00	2.70
☐ 152 Jimmy Wilson	20.00	9.00	2.50
☐ 153 Bill McKechnie MG	80.00	36.00	10.00
☐ 154 Jumbo Brown	20.00	9.00	2.50
☐ 155 Ray Hayworth	20.00	9.00	2.50
☐ 156 Daffy Dean	35.00	16.00	4.40
☐ 157 Lou Chiozza	20.00	9.00	2.50
☐ 158 Travis Jackson	90.00	40.00	11.00
☐ 159 Pancho Snyder	20.00	9.00	2.50
☐ 160 Hans Lobert CO	20.00	9.00	2.50
☐ 161 Debs Garms	20.00	9.00	2.50
☐ 162 Joe Bowman	20.00	9.00	2.50
☐ 163 Spud Davis	20.00	9.00	2.50
☐ 164 Ray Berres	20.00	9.00	2.50
☐ 165 Bob Klinger	20.00	9.00	2.50
☐ 166 Bill Brubaker	20.00	9.00	2.50
☐ 167 Frankie Frisch MG	90.00	40.00	11.00
☐ 168 Honus Wagner CO	250.00	110.00	31.00
☐ 169 Gabby Street	20.00	9.00	2.50
☐ 170 Tris Speaker	200.00	90.00	25.00
☐ 171 Harry Heilmann	90.00	40.00	11.00
☐ 172 Chief Bender	90.00	40.00	11.00
☐ 173 Larry Lajoie	175.00	80.00	22.00
☐ 174 Johnny Evers	90.00	40.00	11.00
☐ 175 Christy Mathewson	250.00	110.00	31.00
☐ 176 Heinie Manush	90.00	40.00	11.00
☐ 177 Frank Homerun Baker	100.00	45.00	12.50
☐ 178 Max Carey	90.00	40.00	11.00
☐ 179 George Sisler	150.00	70.00	19.00
☐ 180 Mickey Cochrane	150.00	70.00	19.00
☐ 181 Spud Chandler	80.00	36.00	10.00
☐ 182 Knick Knickerbocker	70.00	32.00	8.75
☐ 183 Marvin Breuer	70.00	32.00	8.75
☐ 184 Mule Haas	70.00	32.00	8.75
☐ 185 Joe Kuhel	70.00	32.00	8.75
☐ 186 Taft Wright	70.00	32.00	8.75
☐ 187 Jimmy Dykes MG	80.00	36.00	10.00
☐ 188 Joe Krakauskas	70.00	32.00	8.75
☐ 189 Jim Bloodworth	70.00	32.00	8.75
☐ 190 Charley Berry	70.00	32.00	8.75
☐ 191 John Babich	70.00	32.00	8.75
☐ 192 Dick Siebert	70.00	32.00	8.75
☐ 193 Chubby Dean	70.00	32.00	8.75
☐ 194 Sam Chapman	70.00	32.00	8.75
☐ 195 Dee Miles	70.00	32.00	8.75
☐ 196 Red(Nonny) Nonnenkamp	70.00	32.00	8.75
☐ 197 Lou Finney	70.00	32.00	8.75
☐ 198 Denny Galehouse	70.00	32.00	8.75
☐ 199 Pinky Higgins	70.00	32.00	8.75
☐ 200 Soup Campbell	70.00	32.00	8.75
☐ 201 Barney McCosky	70.00	32.00	8.75
☐ 202 Al Milnar	70.00	32.00	8.75
☐ 203 Bad News Hale	70.00	32.00	8.75
☐ 204 Harry Eisenstat	70.00	32.00	8.75
☐ 205 Rollie Hemsley	70.00	32.00	8.75
☐ 206 Chet Laabs	70.00	32.00	8.75
☐ 207 Gus Mancuso	70.00	32.00	8.75
☐ 208 Lee Gamble	70.00	32.00	8.75
☐ 209 Hy Vandenberg	70.00	32.00	8.75
☐ 210 Bill Lohrman	70.00	32.00	8.75
☐ 211 Pop Joiner	70.00	32.00	8.75
☐ 212 Babe Young	70.00	32.00	8.75
☐ 213 John Rucker	70.00	32.00	8.75
☐ 214 Ken O'Dea	70.00	32.00	8.75
☐ 215 Johnnie McCarthy	70.00	32.00	8.75
☐ 216 Joe Marty	70.00	32.00	8.75
☐ 217 Walter Beck	70.00	32.00	8.75
☐ 218 Wally Millies	70.00	32.00	8.75
☐ 219 Russ Bauers	70.00	32.00	8.75
☐ 220 Mace Brown	70.00	32.00	8.75
☐ 221 Lee Handley	70.00	32.00	8.75
☐ 222 Max Butcher	70.00	32.00	8.75
☐ 223 Hugh Jennings	150.00	70.00	19.00
☐ 224 Pie Traynor	175.00	80.00	22.00
☐ 225 Shoeless Joe Jackson	2500.00	1100.00	300.00
☐ 226 Harry Hooper	150.00	70.00	19.00
☐ 227 Pop Haines	150.00	70.00	19.00
☐ 228 Charley Grimm	80.00	36.00	10.00
☐ 229 Buck Herzog	70.00	32.00	8.75
☐ 230 Red Faber	150.00	70.00	19.00
☐ 231 Dolf Luque	100.00	45.00	12.50
☐ 232 Goose Goslin	150.00	70.00	19.00
☐ 233 Moose Earnshaw	80.00	36.00	10.00
☐ 234 Frank Husk Chance	150.00	70.00	19.00
☐ 235 John J. McGraw	175.00	80.00	22.00
☐ 236 Jim Bottomley	150.00	70.00	19.00
☐ 237 Wee Willie Keeler	250.00	110.00	31.00
☐ 238 Tony Lazzeri	175.00	80.00	22.00
☐ 239 George Uhle	70.00	32.00	8.75
☐ 240 Bill Atwood	100.00	45.00	12.50

1941 Play Ball

The cards in this 72-card set measure approximately 2 1/2" by 3 1/8". Many of the cards in the 1941 Play Ball series are simply color versions of pictures appearing in the 1940 set. This was the only color baseball card set produced by Gum, Inc., and it carries the catalog designation R336. Card numbers 49-72 are slightly more difficult to obtain as they were not issued until 1942. In 1942, numbers 1-48 were also reissued but without the copyright date. The cards were also printed on paper without a cardboard backing; these are generally encountered in sheets or strips. The set features a card of Pee Wee Reese in his rookie year.

	EX-MT	VG-E	GOOD
COMPLETE SET (72)	10000.00	4500.00	1250.00
COMMON CARD (1-48)	40.00	18.00	5.00
COMMON CARD (49-72)	55.00	25.00	7.00
WRAPPER (1-CENT)	750.00	350.00	95.00
☐ 1 Eddie Miller	125.00	55.00	15.50
☐ 2 Max West	40.00	18.00	5.00
☐ 3 Bucky Walters	45.00	20.00	5.50
☐ 4 Paul Derringer	55.00	25.00	7.00
☐ 5 Frank(Buck) McCormick	45.00	20.00	5.50
☐ 6 Carl Hubbell	175.00	80.00	22.00
☐ 7 Harry Danning	40.00	18.00	5.00
☐ 8 Mel Ott	225.00	100.00	28.00
☐ 9 Pinky May	40.00	18.00	5.00
☐ 10 Arky Vaughan	80.00	36.00	10.00
☐ 11 Debs Garms	40.00	18.00	5.00
☐ 12 Jimmy Brown	40.00	18.00	5.00
☐ 13 Jimmy Foxx	300.00	135.00	38.00
☐ 14 Ted Williams	1600.00	700.00	200.00
☐ 15 Joe Cronin	100.00	45.00	12.50
☐ 16 Hal Trosky	45.00	20.00	5.50
☐ 17 Roy Weatherly	40.00	18.00	5.00
☐ 18 Hank Greenberg	300.00	135.00	38.00
☐ 19 Charlie Gehringer	200.00	90.00	25.00
☐ 20 Red Ruffing	100.00	45.00	12.50
☐ 21 Charlie Keller	65.00	29.00	8.00
☐ 22 Bob Johnson	55.00	25.00	7.00
☐ 23 George McQuinn	40.00	18.00	5.00
☐ 24 Dutch Leonard	45.00	20.00	5.50
☐ 25 Gene Moore	40.00	18.00	5.00
☐ 26 Harry Gumpert	40.00	18.00	5.00
☐ 27 Babe Young	40.00	18.00	5.00
☐ 28 Joe Marty	40.00	18.00	5.00
☐ 29 Jack Wilson	40.00	18.00	5.00
☐ 30 Lou Finney	40.00	18.00	5.00
☐ 31 Joe Kuhel	40.00	18.00	5.00
☐ 32 Taft Wright	40.00	18.00	5.00
☐ 33 Al Milnar	40.00	18.00	5.00
☐ 34 Rollie Hemsley	40.00	18.00	5.00
☐ 35 Pinky Higgins	45.00	20.00	5.50
☐ 36 Barney McCosky	40.00	18.00	5.00
☐ 37 Bruce Campbell	40.00	18.00	5.00
☐ 38 Atley Donald	55.00	25.00	7.00
☐ 39 Tom Henrich	65.00	29.00	8.00
☐ 40 John Babich	40.00	18.00	5.00
☐ 41 Frank(Blimp) Hayes	40.00	18.00	5.00
☐ 42 Wally Moses	45.00	20.00	5.50
☐ 43 Al Brancato	40.00	18.00	5.00
☐ 44 Sam Chapman	40.00	18.00	5.00
☐ 45 Eldon Auker	40.00	18.00	5.00
☐ 46 Sid Hudson	40.00	18.00	5.00
☐ 47 Buddy Lewis	40.00	18.00	5.00
☐ 48 Cecil Travis	45.00	20.00	5.50
☐ 49 Babe Dahlgren	65.00	29.00	8.00
☐ 50 Johnny Cooney	55.00	25.00	7.00
☐ 51 Dolph Camilli	65.00	29.00	8.00
☐ 52 Kirby Higbe	55.00	25.00	7.00
☐ 53 Luke Hamlin	55.00	25.00	7.00
☐ 54 Pee Wee Reese	700.00	325.00	90.00
☐ 55 Whit Wyatt	65.00	29.00	8.00
☐ 56 Johnny VanderMeer	100.00	45.00	12.50
☐ 57 Moe Arnovich	55.00	25.00	7.00
☐ 58 Frank Demaree	55.00	25.00	7.00
☐ 59 Bill Jurges	55.00	25.00	7.00
☐ 60 Chuck Klein	225.00	100.00	28.00
☐ 61 Vince DiMaggio	250.00	110.00	31.00
☐ 62 Elbie Fletcher	55.00	25.00	7.00
☐ 63 Dom DiMaggio	250.00	110.00	31.00
☐ 64 Bobby Doerr	175.00	80.00	22.00
☐ 65 Tommy Bridges	65.00	29.00	8.00
☐ 66 Harland Clift	55.00	25.00	7.00
☐ 67 Walt Judnich	55.00	25.00	7.00
☐ 68 John Knott	55.00	25.00	7.00
☐ 69 George Case	65.00	29.00	8.00
☐ 70 Bill Dickey	475.00	210.00	60.00
☐ 71 Joe DiMaggio	2600.00	1150.00	325.00
☐ 72 Lefty Gomez	475.00	210.00	60.00

1991 Playball Will Clark

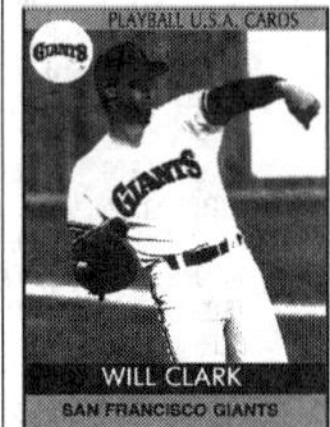

The numbering and card design indicates that this ten-card standard-size set is made up of two five-card sets. The glossy player photos on the first five cards bleed to the sides of the card but are bordered above by a orange stripe and below by black and orange stripes. The glossy color player photos on the second five cards are full bleed without any border stripes. The back design of all cards is horizontally oriented and features the player's name, team name and logo, year and MLB logo in black on a white card stock.

	MINT	NRMT	EXC
COMPLETE SET (10)	6.00	2.70	.75
COMMON CARD (21-25/39-43)	.75	.35	.09
☐ 21 Will Clark Posed, left side from waist up	.75	.35	.09
☐ 22 Will Clark Throwing, follow through	.75	.35	.09
☐ 23 Will Clark Approaching batter's box	.75	.35	.09
☐ 24 Will Clark Head shot in dugout	.75	.35	.09
☐ 25 Will Clark In batter's box Bat in left hand	.75	.35	.09
☐ 39 Will Clark Ready for pitch Bat behind shoulder	.75	.35	.09
☐ 40 Will Clark Left side shot from waist up	.75	.35	.09
☐ 41 Will Clark Follow through with bat	.75	.35	.09
☐ 42 Will Clark Head shot with sunglasses	.75	.35	.09
☐ 43 Will Clark Running to base	.75	.35	.09

1991 Playball Griffey Jr.

The glossy color player photos on the first five cards are full bleed without any border stripes. The glossy player photos on card numbers 1 and 49 bleed to the sides of the card but are bordered above and below by different color stripes. The photo on card number 50 is full bleed, while the unnumbered card has a gold-patterned border. The back design of the cards is horizontally oriented and features the player's name, team name, logo, year and MLB logo in black on a white card stock, except for the unnumbered card, which has a powder blue back.

	MINT	NRMT	EXC
COMPLETE SET	15.00	6.75	1.85
COMMON CARD	1.00	.45	.12
☐ 1 Ken Griffey Jr. Shot from waist up with batter's helmet	1.00	.45	.12
☐ 32 Ken Griffey Jr. Batting practice in batter's cage	1.00	.45	.12
☐ 33 Ken Griffey Jr. Running to catch fly ball	1.00	.45	.12
☐ 34 Ken Griffey Jr. End of swing, close-up	1.00	.45	.12
☐ 35 Ken Griffey Jr. End of swing wearing blue top	1.00	.45	.12
☐ 36 Ken Griffey Jr. Watching ball after swing	1.00	.45	.12
☐ 37 Ken Griffey Jr. Leaning on fence Bat in right hand	1.00	.45	.12
☐ 38 Ken Griffey Jr. Head shot, left side	1.00	.45	.12
☐ 49 Ken Griffey Jr. Head shot, looking up	1.00	.45	.12
☐ 50 Ken Griffey Jr. Middle of swing	1.00	.45	.12
☐ 61 Ken Griffey Jr. Batting stance	1.00	.45	.12
☐ 62 Ken Griffey Jr. In batting cage wearing warm-up suit	1.00	.45	.12
☐ 63 Ken Griffey Jr. Close-up bat on left shoulder	1.00	.45	.12
☐ 64 Ken Griffey Jr. Standing looking over left shoulder	1.00	.45	.12
☐ 65 Ken Griffey Jr. Warming up, on-deck	1.00	.45	.12
☐ 66 Ken Griffey Jr. Portrait, with windbreaker	1.00	.45	.12
☐ xx Ken Griffey Jr. Head shot with sunglasses up	1.00	.45	.12

1991 Playball Mattingly

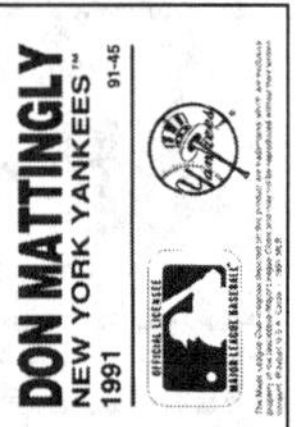

The numbering and card design indicates that this ten-card standard-size set is made up of two five-card sets. The glossy player photos on the first five cards bleed to the sides of the card but are bordered above by a dark blue stripe and below by silver and dark blue stripes. The glossy color player photos on the second five cards are full bleed without any border stripes. The back design of all cards is horizontally oriented and features the player's name, team name, logo, year and MLB logo in black on a white card stock.

	MINT	NRMT	EXC
COMPLETE SET (10)	5.00	2.20	.60
COMMON CARD	.50	.23	.06
☐ 26 Don Mattingly Looking over left shoulder	.50	.23	.06
☐ 27 Don Mattingly Preparing to bat	.50	.23	.06
☐ 28 Don Mattingly Awaiting pitch	.50	.23	.06
☐ 29 Don Mattingly Posed in blue uniform	.50	.23	.06
☐ 30 Don Mattingly Throwing ball	.50	.23	.06
☐ 44 Don Mattingly Beginning of swing	.50	.23	.06
☐ 45 Don Mattingly Posed in batter's helmet	.50	.23	.06
☐ 46 Don Mattingly Wearing practice blue top	.50	.23	.06
☐ 47 Don Mattingly Approaching batter's box	.50	.23	.06
☐ 48 Don Mattingly Watching fly ball	.50	.23	.06

1991 Playball Mattingly Gold

This two-card standard-size set features color action photos framed by gold foil borders. The team logo appears in the upper left corner, while the player's name and team name appear in white lettering at the lower left. The horizontal backs have the player's name, team name, serial number and card number ("91G-X") on the upper portion and MLB and team logos on the lower portion.

	MINT	NRMT	EXC
COMPLETE SET	4.00	1.80	.50
COMMON CARD	2.00	.90	.25
☐ 4 Don Mattingly	2.00	.90	.25
After hit			
bat extended straight ou)			
☐ 5 Don Mattingly	2.00	.90	.25
With glove below chin			

1991 Playball Strawberry

As with the other 1991 Playball sets, this seven-card standard-size set exhibits two different front designs. A blue border stripe above and silver and blue border stripes below frame the glossy color player photos on the first three cards, while the player photos on the last four cards are without any border stripes. The back design of all cards is horizontally oriented and features the player's name, team name, logo, year and MLB logo in black on a white card stock.

	MINT	NRMT	EXC
COMPLETE SET (7)	3.00	1.35	.35
COMMON CARD (53-58/60)	.50	.23	.06
☐ 53 Darryl Strawberry	.50	.23	.06
Left-side close-up			
Bat over shoulder			
☐ 54 Darryl Strawberry	.50	.23	.06
Middle of swing			
☐ 55 Darryl Strawberry	.50	.23	.06
Beginning of swing			
☐ 56 Darryl Strawberry	.50	.23	.06
In batting cage			
☐ 57 Darryl Strawberry	.50	.23	.06
Posed with bat extended			
☐ 58 Darryl Strawberry	.50	.23	.06
Awaiting pitch			
with leg cocked			
☐ 60 Darryl Strawberry	.50	.23	.06
Front pose			
Bat on shoulder			

1992 Playball Griffey Jr.

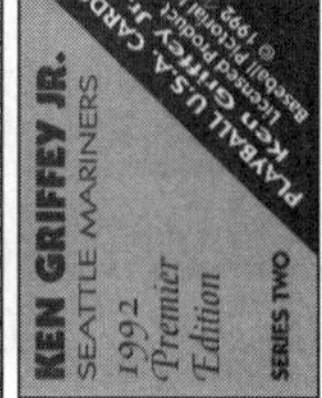

This four-card standard-size set features color action shots of Ken Griffey Jr. These photos are edged in blue and bordered in prismatic gold foil. Ken's name appears in the blue margin at the bottom of the photo. The set year and the manufacturer's name appear at the top and bottom, respectively, within the foil border. The gray-and-black horizontal backs carry the player's name and team, series, and year of issue. The cards are unnumbered.

	MINT	NRMT	EXC
COMPLETE SET (4)	4.00	1.80	.50
COMMON CARD (1-4)	1.00	.45	.12
☐ 1 Ken Griffey Jr.	1.00	.45	.12
With bat in hand			
☐ 2 Ken Griffey Jr.	1.00	.45	.12
Beginning swing			
☐ 3 Ken Griffey Jr.	1.00	.45	.12
Ending swing			
☐ 4 Ken Griffey Jr.	1.00	.45	.12
Running basepaths			

1911 Plow's Candy E300

The cards in this 39-card set measure 3" X 4" with a sepia photograph measuring 2 1/4" X 3 5/16". This set was issued by Plow's Candy Company circa 1911 on thin cardboard with wide borders. The subject's name is printed in block letters outside the bottom frame, and his team is listed directly beneath. The title "Plow's Candy Collection" is printed at the top; the cards are unnumbered and blank-backed. They have been alphabetized and numbered in the checklist below.

	EX-MT	VG-E	GOOD
COMPLETE SET (39)	9000.00	4000.00	1100.00
COMMON CARD (1-39)	225.00	100.00	28.00
☐ 1 Frank Baker	350.00	160.00	45.00
☐ 2 Jack Barry	225.00	100.00	28.00
☐ 3 Joe Benz	225.00	100.00	28.00
☐ 4 Bill Bergen	225.00	100.00	28.00
☐ 5 Mordecai Brown	350.00	160.00	45.00
☐ 6 Bobby Byrne	225.00	100.00	28.00
☐ 7 Nixey Callahan	225.00	100.00	28.00
☐ 8 Hal Chase	250.00	110.00	31.00
☐ 9 Fred Clarke	350.00	160.00	45.00
☐ 10 Ty Cobb	1200.00	550.00	150.00
☐ 11 King Cole	225.00	100.00	28.00
☐ 12 Jim Delahanty	225.00	100.00	28.00
☐ 13 Josh Devore	225.00	100.00	28.00
☐ 14 Bill Donovan	225.00	100.00	28.00
☐ 15 Red Dooin	225.00	100.00	28.00
☐ 16 Robert Harmon	225.00	100.00	28.00
☐ 17 Solly Hoffman	225.00	100.00	28.00
☐ 18 Miller Huggins	350.00	160.00	45.00
☐ 19 John Hummel	225.00	100.00	28.00
☐ 20 Walter Johnson	800.00	350.00	100.00
☐ 21 Johnny Kling	225.00	100.00	28.00
☐ 22 Nap Lajoie	450.00	200.00	55.00
☐ 23 John Lapp	225.00	100.00	28.00
☐ 24 Sherry Magee	225.00	100.00	28.00
☐ 25 Larry McLean	225.00	100.00	28.00
☐ 26 Fred Merkle	250.00	110.00	31.00
☐ 27 Harry Mowrey	225.00	100.00	28.00
☐ 28 Chief Meyers	225.00	100.00	28.00
☐ 29 Rube Oldring	225.00	100.00	28.00
☐ 30 Martin O'Toole	225.00	100.00	28.00
☐ 31 Nap Rucker	225.00	100.00	28.00
☐ 32 Slim Sallee	225.00	100.00	28.00
☐ 33 Jimmy Sheckard	225.00	100.00	28.00
☐ 34 Tris Speaker	450.00	200.00	55.00
☐ 35 Billy Sullivan	250.00	110.00	31.00
☐ 36 Joe Tinker	350.00	160.00	45.00
☐ 37 Ira Thomas	225.00	100.00	28.00
☐ 38 Hippo Vaughn	225.00	100.00	28.00
☐ 39 Ed Walsh	350.00	160.00	45.00

1991 PM Gold Card Prototype

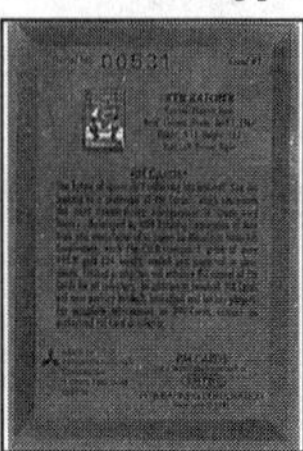

This standard-size card is a prototype for PM cards. Each card contains one gram of pure 999.9 gold (24 karat) and will feature baseball, basketball, football and hockey players (some promos were also printed that do not contain gold). The front design features a color player photo of a fictional player, with a yellow/orange inner border and a gold outer border. The back has the serial number, player biography and an advertisement for PM cards. The cards are numbered on the back.

	MINT	NRMT	EXC
COMPLETE SET (1)	1.00	.45	.12
COMMON CARD	1.00	.45	.12
☐ 1 Ken Katcher	1.00	.45	.12

1992 PM Gold

Distributed by Powell Associates, these PM ("precious metal") cards each contain one gram of pure 24K (999.9 percent) fine gold. These standard-size cards are the product of a technological break through developed by Mitsubishi that makes it possible to put a full color picture on precious metals. Artist Gregory Perillo created the oil paintings of the players reproduced on the card fronts. Production quantities vary for each card. Only 1,000 of card number 1 (a prototype) were produced and distributed to attendees of the Gold Glove charity dinner. The production run of cards number 2 and 3

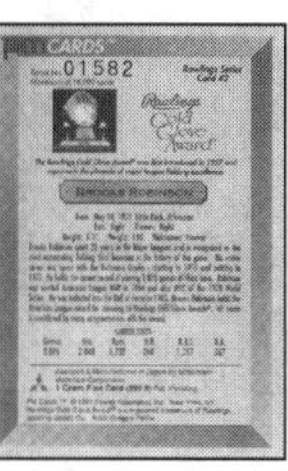

were 10,000 and 1,200 respectively. The card front also has gold borders and the player's name appears in a gold plaque in the bottom gold border. The back has the serial number and career summary. The cards are numbered on the back by "Rawling Series Card number X."

	MINT	NRMT	EXC
COMPLETE SET (3)	40.00	18.00	5.00
COMMON CARD (1-3)	3.00	1.35	.35
☐ 1 Brooks Robinson	20.00	9.00	2.50
Defensive posture, Prototype			
☐ 2 Brooks Robinson	3.00	1.35	.35
Portrait			
☐ 3 Roberto Clemente	25.00	11.00	3.10

1992 PM Gold Ruth Prototype

Distributed by Powell Associates, this Babe Ruth Precious Metal card contains one gram of pure 24K (999.9 percent) fine gold. The card measures the standard size. Artist Gregory Perillo created the oil painting of Ruth that was reproduced on the card front. The card front also has gold borders and the player's name appears in a gold plaque in the bottom gold border. The back has the serial number and career summary. The card is numbered on the back by "Baseball Series Card Number 1."

	MINT	NRMT	EXC
COMPLETE SET	3.00	1.35	.35
COMMON CARD	3.00	1.35	.35
☐ 1 Babe Ruth	3.00	1.35	.35

1993 PM Gold Bench

A one-gram, 24-K gold card featuring former Reds catcher Johnny Bench was given to each attendee at the Third Annual Rawlings Gold Glove Award Charity Dinner held Nov. 18, 1993 at the Sheraton New York. The card was created from an original painting by sports artist Daniel Fruend. The back features a brief biography of the baseball legend.

	MINT	NRMT	EXC
COMPLETE SET	50.00	22.00	6.25
COMMON CARD	50.00	22.00	6.25
☐ 1 Johnny Bench	50.00	22.00	6.25

1947-66 PM10 Stadium Pins 1 3/4'

These pins were sold at the stadiums by the souvenir vendors over a span of many years. The pins were produced in several sizes approximately 1 3/4" in diameter, 2" in diameter, or 2 1/4" in diameter. Most of these pins are in black and white; those showing color are so indicated in the checklist. Reproductions do exist but are fairly easy to spot. The reproductions usually look like they were manufactured yesterday with shiny metal rims and backs, and may have grainy photos. A raised union stamp on the reverse side is a sure sign of a pin's age and authenticity. We realize the foillowing checklist is incomplete. We urge anyone who might have pins that are not checklisted below to pass along the information to us so we can update our files. A simple photo will sufice. No complete set is printed since additions to this checklist are anticapted.

	NRMT	VG-E	GOOD
☐ 1 Hank Aaron	250.00	110.00	31.00
☐ 2 Sandy Amoros	30.00	13.50	3.70
B on cap			
blue background			
☐ 3 Harry Anderson	50.00	22.00	6.25
P on cap			
☐ 4 John Antonelli	30.00	13.50	3.70
NY on cap			
☐ 5 John Antonelli	17.50	8.00	2.20
SF on cap			
☐ 6 Richie Ashburn	75.00	34.00	9.50
Phillies on shirt			
name across shoulders			
gray background			
☐ 7 Dick Bartell	12.00	5.50	1.50
white circle border			
☐ 8 Gus Bell	60.00	27.00	7.50
swinging bat)			
☐ 9 Yogi Berra	80.00	36.00	10.00
NY on cap			
light blue background			
☐ 10 Yogi Berra	60.00	27.00	7.50
NY on cap			
white background			
☐ 11 Yogi Berra	80.00	36.00	10.00
NY on cap			
gray background			
☐ 12 Joe Black	30.00	13.50	3.70
B on cap			
looking forward			
white background			
☐ 13 Joe Black	25.00	11.00	3.10
B on cap			
looking to side			
stands in background			
large print name			
☐ 14 Joe Black	60.00	27.00	7.50
B on cap			
looking to side			
no background			
smaller letters			
☐ 15 Ewel Blackwell	200.00	90.00	25.00
Name on chest			
☐ 16 Don Bollweg	17.50	8.00	2.20
A on cap			
☐ 17 Lou Boudreau	15.00	6.75	1.85
B on cap			
light gray background			
☐ 18 Lou Boudreau	125.00	55.00	15.50
name in red script			
cap in red and blue			
☐ 19 Lou Bourdeau	125.00	55.00	15.50
Circle border, name script			
☐ 20 Bob Bowman	50.00	22.00	6.25
☐ 21 Eddie Bressoud	17.50	8.00	2.20
B on cap			
gray background			
☐ 22 Bill Bruton	17.50	8.00	2.20
☐ 23 Dolph Camilli	17.50	8.00	2.20
Dodgers at top			
white circle border			
☐ 24 Roy Campanella	70.00	32.00	8.75
B on cap			
blue background			
☐ 25 Roy Campanella	50.00	22.00	6.25
B on cap			
white background			
☐ 26 Roy Campanella	50.00	22.00	6.25
B on cap			
teeth showing			
☐ 27 Roy Campanella	200.00	90.00	25.00
Circle border			
☐ 28 Chico Carrasquel	80.00	36.00	10.00
☐ 29 Phil Cavaretta	80.00	36.00	10.00
☐ 30 Orlando Cepeda	30.00	13.50	3.70
SF on cap			
large name			
teeth showing			
gray background			
☐ 31 Orlando Cepeda	30.00	13.50	3.70
SF on cap			
smaller name			
no teeth showing			
natural background			
☐ 32 Roberto Clemente	40.00	18.00	5.00
We Remember			
Clemente			
Recordamos a Clemente			
☐ 33 Gerry Coleman	12.00	5.50	1.50
NY on cap			
light gray background			
☐ 34 Tony Conigliaro	30.00	13.50	3.70
B on cap			
no teeth showing			
gray background			
☐ 35 Tony Conigliaro	30.00	13.50	3.70
B on cap			
teeth showing			
gray background			
☐ 36 Morton Cooper	12.00	5.50	1.50
STL on cap			
white/black background			
☐ 37 Billy Cox	30.00	13.50	3.70
Name on uniform			
☐ 38 Billy Cox	12.00	5.50	1.50
B on cap			
white background			
white name background			
☐ 39 Alvin Dark	12.00	5.50	1.50
☐ 40 Jim Davenport	70.00	32.00	8.75
SF on cap			
☐ 41 Dizzy Dean	30.00	13.50	3.70
black background			
☐ 42 Bill Dickey	125.00	55.00	15.50
☐ 43 Dom DiMaggio	30.00	13.50	3.70
black background			
☐ 44 Dom DiMaggio	15.00	6.75	1.85
white background			
☐ 45 Joe DiMaggio#(green border	200.00	90.00	25.00
☐ 46 Joe DiMaggio	200.00	90.00	25.00
Yankees under name			
facsimile autograph			
☐ 47 Joe DiMaggio	75.00	34.00	9.50

NY on cap
light blue background
☐ 48 Joe DiMaggio 200.00 90.00 25.00
NY on cap
white background
☐ 49 Joe DiMaggio 200.00 90.00 25.00
NY on cap
black background
☐ 50 Joe DiMaggio 275.00 125.00 34.00
Yankees at top
white circle border
☐ 51 Larry Doby 50.00 22.00 6.25
C on cap
looking to side
black background
☐ 52 Larry Doby 80.00 36.00 10.00
Congratulations
☐ 53 Larry Doby 17.50 8.00 2.20
C on cap
looking forward
white background
☐ 54 Luke Easter 50.00 22.00 6.25
☐ 55 Del Ennis 80.00 36.00 10.00
P on cap
Phillies on shirt
gray background
☐ 56 Carl Erskine 30.00 13.50 3.70
B on cap
☐ 57 Ferris Fain 200.00 90.00 25.00
☐ 58 Bob Feller 15.00 6.75 1.85
white background
☐ 59 Bob Feller 150.00 70.00 19.00
gray background
☐ 60 Whitey Ford 85.00 38.00 10.50
NY on cap
white background
☐ 61 Nellie Fox 200.00 90.00 25.00
SOX on cap
foxes in border
☐ 62 Carl Furillo 70.00 32.00 8.75
stands in background
☐ 63 Carl Furillo 80.00 36.00 10.00
blue background
☐ 64 Carl Furillo 80.00 36.00 10.00
white background
☐ 65 Carl Furillo 70.00 32.00 8.75
natural background
☐ 66 Len Gabrielson 70.00 32.00 8.75
SF on cap
☐ 67 Ned Garver 125.00 55.00 15.50
StL on cap
Browns on shirt
white background
☐ 68 Lou Gehrig 350.00 160.00 45.00
Yankees at top
white circle border
☐ 69 Lou Gehrig 300.00 135.00 38.00
Never Forgotten
☐ 70 Jim Gilliam 80.00 36.00 10.00
B on cap
white background
name in smaller print
☐ 71 Jim Gilliam 80.00 36.00 10.00
B on cap
natural background
name in larger print
☐ 72 Lefty Gomez 125.00 55.00 15.50
Yankees at top
☐ 73 Ruben Gomez 12.00 5.50 1.50
SF on cap
white circle border
☐ 74 Billy Goodman 50.00 22.00 6.25
B on cap
white background
☐ 75 Joe Gordon 200.00 90.00 25.00
Yankees
☐ 76 Granny Hamner 80.00 36.00 10.00
Phillies on shirt
name across shoulders
gray background
☐ 77 Ron Hansen 150.00 70.00 19.00
☐ 78 Jim Hart 80.00 36.00 10.00
SF on cap
black circle border
left ear missing
☐ 79 Gabby Hartnett 40.00 18.00 5.00
cap emblem not visible
black background
☐ 80 Grady Hatton 80.00 36.00 10.00
C on cap
Reds on shirt
☐ 81 Jim Hegan 125.00 55.00 15.50
name in red
team name in blue
☐ 82 Tom Henrich 30.00 13.50 3.70
NY on cap
name in border
☐ 83 Tom Henrich 17.50 8.00 2.20
NY on cap
name over shirt
☐ 84 Mike Higgins 12.00 5.50 1.50
B on cap
black background
☐ 85 Gil Hodges 80.00 36.00 10.00
B on cap
orange background
no teeth showing
☐ 86 Gil Hodges 50.00 22.00 6.25
B on cap
white background
no teeth showing
☐ 87 Gil Hodges 50.00 22.00 6.25
no teeth showing
☐ 88 Gil Hodges 80.00 36.00 10.00
B on cap
white background
teeth showing
☐ 89 Rogers Hornsby 200.00 90.00 25.00
☐ 90 Elston Howard 17.50 8.00 2.20
cap turned around
white background
chest protector on
TCMA
☐ 91 Carl Hubbell 80.00 36.00 10.00
sepia tone
☐ 92 Carl Hubbell 25.00 11.00 3.10
black and white
☐ 93 Monte Irvin 60.00 27.00 7.50
NY on cap
New York Giants(at top)
white circle border
☐ 94 Monte Irvin 30.00 13.50 3.70
NY on cap
black background
☐ 95 Monte Irvin 80.00 36.00 10.00
NY on cap
white background
name in white border
teeth plainly showing
☐ 96 Spook Jacobs 17.50 8.00 2.20
A on cap
black/white background
☐ 97 Jackie Jensen 80.00 36.00 10.00
no emblem on cap
name at top
white background
right ear missing
☐ 98 Jackie Jensen 25.00 11.00 3.10
black background
☐ 99 Jackie Jensen 30.00 13.50 3.70
B on cap
natural background
both ears showing
☐ 100 Jackie Jensen Name at Top 125.00 55.00 15.50
☐ 101 Walter Johnson 200.00 90.00 25.00
☐ 102 Willie Jones 80.00 36.00 10.00
P on cap
Phillies on shirt
☐ 103 Harmon Killebrew 150.00 70.00 19.00
W on cap
batting stance
natural background
☐ 104 Ralph Kiner 125.00 55.00 15.50
☐ 105 Ted Kluszewski 50.00 22.00 6.25
C on cap
white background
☐ 106 Ted Kluszewski Name on chest 200.00 90.00
25.00
☐ 107 Jim Konstanty 80.00 36.00 10.00
Phillies on shirt
name across shoulders
gray background
☐ 108 Ed Kranepool 17.50 8.00 2.20
TCMA
☐ 109 Hal Lanier 80.00 36.00 10.00
SF on cap
black circle border
☐ 110 Bill Lee 12.00 5.50 1.50
☐ 111 Bob Lemon 15.00 6.75 1.85
C on cap
☐ 112 Bob Lemon 80.00 36.00 10.00
pitching motion
☐ 113 Jim Lemon 80.00 36.00 10.00
W on cap
batting stance
natural background
☐ 114 Whitey Lockman 15.00 6.75 1.85
NY on cap
gray background
☐ 115 Stan Lopata 80.00 36.00 10.00
Phillies on shirt
name across shoulders
gray background
☐ 116 Sal Maglie 30.00 13.50 3.70
B on cap
natural background
☐ 117 Frank Malzone 50.00 22.00 6.25
B on cap
white background
both ears showing
☐ 118 Frank Malzone 15.00 6.75 1.85
B on cap
natural background
holding bat
right ear missing
☐ 119 Mickey Mantle 175.00 80.00 22.00
NY on cap
blue background
right ear missing
☐ 120 Mickey Mantle 160.00 70.00 20.00
NY on cap
stitched baseball
right ear missing
head and shoulders
☐ 121 Mickey Mantle 160.00 70.00 20.00
NY on cap
blue background
righty batting stance
left hand not visible
name starts at wrist
☐ 122 Mickey Mantle 100.00 45.00 12.50
NY on cap
white background
righty batting stance
left hand not visible
name starts at elbow
☐ 123 Mickey Mantle 50.00 22.00 6.25
NY on cap
white background
righty batting stance
both hands visible
☐ 124 Mickey Mantle 275.00 125.00 34.00
NY on cap
white background
name in white border
eyes almost closed
☐ 125 Mickey Mantle 60.00 27.00 7.50
I Love Mickey
no cap
with Teresa Brewer
each holding a bat
☐ 126 Juan Marichal 80.00 36.00 10.00
SF on cap
black border
☐ 127 Marty Marion 80.00 36.00 10.00
StL on cap
white circle border
☐ 128 Roger Maris 60.00 27.00 7.50
large NY on cap
salmon background
☐ 129 Roger Maris 40.00 18.00 5.00
normal NY on cap
yellow background
☐ 130 Roger Maris 125.00 55.00 15.50
no emblem on cap
white background
☐ 131 Willie Mays 30.00 13.50 3.70
NY on cap
white background
☐ 132 Willie Mays 160.00 70.00 20.00
NY on cap
New York Giants
white circle border
☐ 133 Willie Mays 160.00 70.00 20.00
NY on cap
natural background
☐ 134 Willie Mays 160.00 70.00 20.00
NY on cap
turquoise background
☐ 135 Willie Mays 100.00 45.00 12.50
SF on cap
gray background
white name background
left ear missing
eyes almost closed
☐ 136 Willie Mays 100.00 45.00 12.50
SF on cap
natural background
looking up
tongue showing
☐ 137 Willie Mays 225.00 100.00 28.00
SF on cap
stands in background
white name background
☐ 138 Willie McCovey 40.00 18.00 5.00
no emblem on cap
holding four bats
☐ 139 Gil McDougald 12.00 5.50 1.50
NY on cap
gray background
☐ 140 Cliff Melton 12.00 5.50 1.50
Giants at top
no emblem on cap
white circle border
☐ 141 Bill Meyer 80.00 36.00 10.00
☐ 142 Minnie Minoso 80.00 36.00 10.00
white circle border
name in script
☐ 143 Bill Monbouquette 12.00 5.50 1.50
☐ 144 Don Mueller 12.00 5.50 1.50
NY on cap
white background
no neck showing
☐ 145 Bobby Murcer 17.50 8.00 2.20
NY on cap
white background
head and shoulders
TCMA
☐ 146 Danny Murtaugh 80.00 36.00 10.00
white circle border
☐ 147 Stan Musial 160.00 70.00 20.00
StL on cap
white background
right ear noticeable
☐ 148 Stan Musial 50.00 22.00 6.25
StL on cap
yellow background
right ear missing
☐ 149 Stan Musial 250.00 110.00 31.00
Stan The Man
StL on cap
white background
☐ 150 Don Newcombe 50.00 22.00 6.25
B on cap
blue background
toothy smile
☐ 151 Don Newcombe 17.50 8.00 2.20
B on cap
white background
mouth slightly open
☐ 152 Don Newcombe 50.00 22.00 6.25
B on cap
white background
mouth closed
☐ 153 Don Newcombe 200.00 90.00 25.00
Circle boarder
☐ 154 Dan O'Connell 12.00 5.50 1.50
SF on cap
white circle border
☐ 155 Andy Pafko 100.00 45.00 12.50
☐ 156 Joe Page 30.00 13.50 3.70
NY on cap
white background
☐ 157 Satchel Paige 125.00 55.00 15.50
no emblem on cap
white background
☐ 158 Mel Parnell 12.00 5.50 1.50
B on cap
white background
☐ 159 Joe Pepitone 15.00 6.75 1.85
NY on helmet
white background
looking to side
head and shoulders
TCMA
☐ 160 Gaylord Perry 60.00 27.00 7.50
SF on cap
white background
☐ 161 Johnny Pesky 50.00 22.00 6.25
B on cap
white background
☐ 162 Rico Petrocelli 30.00 13.50 3.70
B on cap
light gray background
☐ 163 Billy Pierce White Sox 200.00 90.00 25.00
☐ 164 Jimmy Piersall 17.50 8.00 2.20
B on cap
white background
☐ 165 Johnny Podres 30.00 13.50 3.70
B on cap
gray/white background
☐ 166 John Pramesa 70.00 32.00 8.75
C on cap
Reds on shirt
gray background
☐ 167 Dick Radatz 25.00 11.00 3.10
B on cap
gray background
☐ 168 Vic Raschi 40.00 18.00 5.00
NY on cap
white background
☐ 169 Pee Wee Reese 70.00 32.00 8.75
B on cap
light gray background
☐ 170 Pee Wee Reese 100.00 45.00 12.50
B on cap
gray background
left ear missing
looking to side
☐ 171 Pee Wee Reese 70.00 32.00 8.75
B on cap
white background
☐ 172 Pee Wee Reese 70.00 32.00 8.75
B on cap
gray background
☐ 173 Pete Reiser 15.00 6.75 1.85
B on cap
Dodgers at top
white circle border
☐ 174 Bill Rigney 12.00 5.50 1.50
☐ 175 Phil Rizzuto 30.00 13.50 3.70
NY on cap
white background
☐ 176 Robin Roberts 17.50 8.00 2.20
P on cap
stands in background
☐ 177 Robin Roberts 80.00 36.00 10.00
P on cap
Phillies on shirt
name across shoulders
☐ 178 Brooks Robinson 250.00 110.00 31.00
☐ 179 Jackie Robinson 60.00 27.00 7.50
B on cap
yellow background
looking serious
☐ 180 Jackie Robinson 250.00 110.00 31.00
Dodgers at bottom
B on cap
red border
I'm Rooting For
Jackie Robinson
☐ 181 Jackie Robinson 150.00 70.00 19.00
B on cap
red border
Rookie of the Year 1947

☐ 182 Jackie Robinson 100.00 45.00 12.50
B on cap
blue background
looking to side
left ear missing
☐ 183 Jackie Robinson 200.00 90.00 25.00
B on cap
gray/white background
looking to side
left ear missing
☐ 184 Jackie Robinson 160.00 70.00 20.00
cap emblem not visible
white background
batting stance
Dodgers at bottom
☐ 185 Jackie Robinson 275.00 125.00 34.00
cap emblem not visible
right ear missing
white background
☐ 186 Jackie Robinson 100.00 45.00 12.50
B on cap
Dodgers on shirt
natural background
☐ 187 Preacher Roe 80.00 36.00 10.00
B on cap
Dodgers on shirt
pitching wind-up
white background
☐ 188 Saul Rogovin 12.00 5.50 1.50
SOX on cap
Chicago White Sox
white circle border
☐ 189 Stan Rojek 80.00 36.00 10.00
P on cap
Pittsburgh Pirates
white circle border
☐ 190 Al Rosen 15.00 6.75 1.85
☐ 191 Red Ruffing 17.50 8.00 2.20
middle name Herbert
☐ 192 Babe Ruth 375.00 170.00 47.50
☐ 193 Jack Sanford 50.00 22.00 6.25
☐ 194 Hank Sauer 200.00 90.00 25.00
☐ 195 Chuck Schilling 50.00 22.00 6.25
B on cap
white background
name at top
☐ 196 Chuck Schilling 50.00 22.00 6.25
name at bottom
☐ 197 George Scott 12.00 5.50 1.50
B on cap
left ear missing
white background
☐ 198 Andy Seminick 80.00 36.00 10.00
☐ 199 Bobby Shantz 80.00 36.00 10.00
gray background
☐ 200 Bobby Shantz 17.50 8.00 2.20
white background
☐ 201 Frank Shea 12.00 5.50 1.50
NY on cap
gray background
☐ 202 Curt Simmons 80.00 36.00 10.00
P on cap
Phillies on shirt
sepia tone
sepia background
☐ 203 Enos Slaughter 80.00 36.00 10.00
StL on cap
black background
☐ 204 Roy Smalley 80.00 36.00 10.00
C on cap
stars in border
white circle border
name in script
☐ 205 Duke Snider 125.00 55.00 15.50
blue background
☐ 206 Duke Snider 160.00 70.00 20.00
stands in background
☐ 207 Duke Snider#(gray background 30.00 13.50
3.70
☐ 208 Dick Stuart 30.00 13.50 3.70
B on cap
light gray background
☐ 209 Hank Thompson 100.00 45.00 12.50
NY on cap
New York Giants
batting pose
white circle border
☐ 210 Bobby Thomson 30.00 13.50 3.70
NY on cap
white background
looking up
☐ 211 Gus Triandos 80.00 36.00 10.00
Oriole on cap
light gray background
☐ 212 Bob Trice 80.00 36.00 10.00
A on cap
natural background
left ear missing
☐ 213 Eddie Waitkus 80.00 36.00 10.00
Phillies on shirt
name across shoulders
gray background
☐ 214 Dixie Walker 30.00 13.50 3.70
cap emblem not visible
Dodgers (at top)
white circle border
☐ 215 Bill Werle 80.00 36.00 10.00
☐ 216 Sam White 12.00 5.50 1.50
partial B on cap
looking up
white background
☐ 217 Ted Williams 100.00 45.00 12.50
cap emblem not visible
name at top
Boston Red Sox
natural background
batting follow-through
☐ 218 Ted Williams 160.00 70.00 20.00
B on cap
white background
white name background
☐ 219 Ted Williams 160.00 70.00 20.00
B on cap
black background
name across shoulders
☐ 220 Ted Williams 160.00 70.00 20.00
B on cap
name at top
natural background
holding bat
white name background
☐ 221 Ted Williams 160.00 70.00 20.00
B on cap
white background
name across shoulders
☐ 222 Ted Williams 60.00 27.00 7.50
B on cap
name at bottom
natural background
holding bat
white name background
☐ 223 Gene Woodling 100.00 45.00 12.50
Oriole on cap
natural background
white name background
☐ 224 Whitlow Wyatt 12.00 5.50 1.50
B on cap
Dodgers (at top)
white circle border
☐ 225 Carl Yastrzemski 100.00 45.00 12.50
gray background
☐ 226 Carl Yastrzemski 100.00 45.00 12.50
white background
☐ 227 Gus Zernial 80.00 36.00 10.00
A on cap
Athletics on shirt
name across chest
gray background
☐ 228 Gus Zernial Name on chest.... 125.00 55.00 15.50

1947-65 PM10 Stadium Pins 2 1/8'

This is more information on stadium pins. Celluoid foxing, cracks, dents, noticeable scratches or rusted metal rims can all reduce the worth of a button or pin. Rusting on the reverse side can sometimes be removed. A missing pin has no effefct on the price. Frequently, the pins were sold with red, white and blue ribbons and or/chains attached to a selection of miniature tin or plastic bats, balls and gloves. The miniature paraphanalia has very little effect on the values as these items are essentially interchangable. If the hanging ties features the same team or player name, this can affect the value of the pin. The pins checklisted below are those in the two larger sizes, close to 2 1/8" in diameter, most are slightly larger or smaller. The Phillies pins are approximately 2 1/4" in diameter, whereas the Yankees and other teams are about 2" in diameter. Again, additions to this checklist is appreciated. And as with the other PM 10 pins, no complete set price is listed.

NRMT VG-E GOOD

☐ 1 Richie Allen 75.00 34.00 9.50
P on cap
light gray background
name across shoulders
☐ 2 Luis Arroyo 40.00 18.00 5.00
NY on cap
white background
name at top
☐ 3 Hank Bauer 60.00 27.00 7.50
NY on cap
white background
name at top
☐ 4 Yogi Berra 150.00 70.00 19.00
NY on cap
white background
name at top
☐ 5 Johnny Blanchard 50.00 22.00 6.25
NY on cap
white background
name at top
☐ 6 Clete Boyer 50.00 22.00 6.25
NY on cap
white background
name at top
☐ 7 Jim Bunning 100.00 45.00 12.50
P on cap
white background
white name background
☐ 8 Johnny Callison 40.00 18.00 5.00
P on cap
white background
white name background
☐ 9 Andy Carey 40.00 18.00 5.00
☐ 10 Gerry Coleman 40.00 18.00 5.00
NY on cap
white background
name at top
name in thin print
☐ 11 Joe Collins 40.00 18.00 5.00
NY on cap
white background
name at top
☐ 12 Del Crandall 40.00 18.00 5.00
M on cap
white background
name at top
☐ 13 Clay Dalrymple 40.00 18.00 5.00
P on cap
white background
white name background
☐ 14 Whitey Ford 125.00 55.00 15.50
NY on cap
light gray background
thin white border
☐ 15 Jim Gilliam 60.00 27.00 7.50
B on cap
white background
name at top
☐ 16 Ruben Gomez 40.00 18.00 5.00
NY on cap
white background
name at top
☐ 17 Elston Howard 75.00 34.00 9.50
NY on cap
white background
name at top
name in thin print
☐ 18 Billy Loes 40.00 18.00 5.00
B on cap
gray background
name at top
☐ 19 Ed Lopat 40.00 18.00 5.00
NY on cap
white background
name at top
☐ 20 Hector Lopez 40.00 18.00 5.00
NY on cap
white background
name at top
☐ 21 Mickey Mantle 250.00 110.00 31.00
NY on cap
light gray background
name at top
☐ 22 Roger Maris 150.00 70.00 19.00
NY on cap
white background
name at top
right ear missing

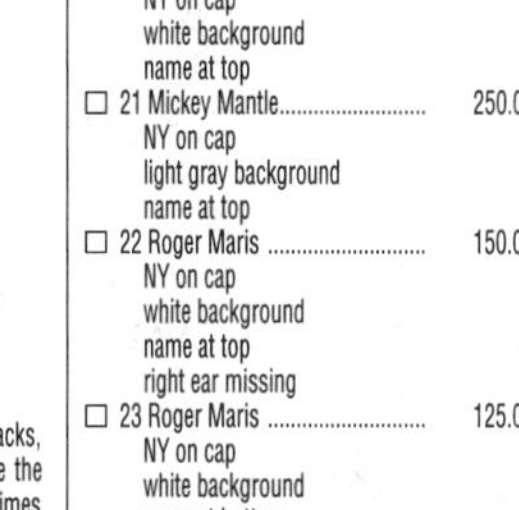

☐ 23 Roger Maris 125.00 55.00 15.50
NY on cap
white background
name at bottom
batting pose
☐ 24 Billy Martin 75.00 34.00 9.50
NY on cap
white background
name at top
right eye sleepy
☐ 25 Willie Mays 200.00 90.00 25.00
NY on cap
white background
name at top
☐ 26 Willie Mays 200.00 90.00 25.00
SF on cap
white background
name at top
☐ 27 Gil McDougald 40.00 18.00 5.00
NY on cap
white background
name at top
☐ 28 Bill Miller 40.00 18.00 5.00
☐ 29 Tom Morgan 40.00 18.00 5.00
NY on cap
light gray background
name at top
☐ 30 Don Newcombe 60.00 27.00 7.50
B on cap
white background
name at top
☐ 31 Irv Noren 40.00 18.00 5.00
NY on cap
white background
name at top
☐ 32 Johnny Podres 60.00 27.00 7.50
B on cap
white background
name at top
☐ 33 Allie Reynolds 60.00 27.00 7.50
☐ 33A Jackie Robinson 400.00 180.00 50.00
☐ 34 Phil Rizzuto 125.00 55.00 15.50
NY on cap
white background
name at top
☐ 35 Chris Short 40.00 18.00 5.00
P on cap
white background
white name background
☐ 36 Roy Sievers 40.00 18.00 5.00
P on cap
white background
white name background
☐ 37 Bill Skowron 40.00 18.00 5.00
☐ 38 Enos Slaughter 75.00 34.00 9.50
NY on cap
white background
name at top
☐ 39 Duke Snider 150.00 70.00 19.00
name at top)
☐ 40 Warren Spahn 100.00 45.00 12.50
M on cap
light gray background
name at top
☐ 41 Ted Williams 200.00 90.00 25.00
B on cap
light gray background
name print splotchy
☐ 42 Bobby Wine 40.00 18.00 5.00
P on cap
white background
white name background
☐ 43 Gene Woodling 60.00 27.00 7.50
NY on cap
black background
thin white border
lefty batting pose
☐ 44 Gene Woodling 40.00 18.00 5.00
NY on cap
white background
name at top

1985 Police Mets/Yankees

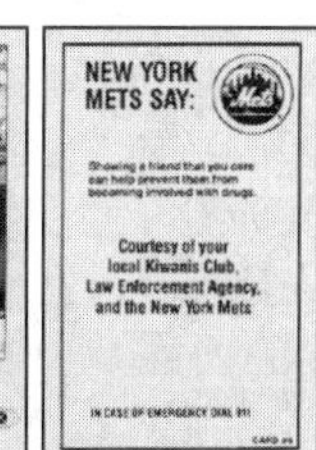

This 12-card set was supposedly issued courtesy of the Kiwanis Club, a local law enforcement agency, and the New York Mets and New York Yankees. The cards measure approximately 2 9/16" by 4 1/16". The fronts feature color player photos with white borders. Beneath the photo, player information appears between the team logo and the Kiwanis International logo. The backs have anti-drug messages introduced by the words "New York Mets Say" or "New York Yankees Say." The cards are numbered on the back and are indicated below by a prefix for Mets or Yankees.

	NRMT	VG-E	GOOD
COMPLETE SET (12)	7.50	3.40	.95
COMMON CARD (M1-M6)	.50	.23	.06
COMMON CARD (Y1-Y6)	.50	.23	.06

☐ M1 George Foster and .... Bill Robinson CO	.50	.23	.06
☐ M2 Davey Johnson MG .... and Gary Carter	1.00	.45	.12
☐ M3 Dwight Gooden	1.50	.70	.19
☐ M4 Mookie Wilson	.50	.23	.06
☐ M5 Keith Hernandez	1.00	.45	.12
☐ M6 Darryl Strawberry	1.00	.45	.12
☐ Y1 Willie Randolph	1.00	.45	.12
☐ Y2 Phil Niekro	1.50	.70	.19
☐ Y3 Ron Guidry	1.00	.45	.12
☐ Y4 Dave Winfield	2.50	1.10	.30
☐ Y5 Dave Righetti	.50	.23	.06
☐ Y6 Billy Martin MG	1.00	.45	.12

1992 Police Avery

Sponsored by the Atlanta Police Athletic League, this card measures the standard-size. One card was given out with each paid admission to a charity auction and autograph session on June 20, 1992. A total of 5,000 cards were produced and each card bears a serial number on the back. The front features a color action photo; the top border is white, while the borders on the other three sides are turquoise. A neon yellow bar at the bottom contains the words "Help Steve Strike Out Drugs." The back has biography, professional pitching record, career highlights and an anti-drug and alcohol quote by Avery. The card is unnumbered.

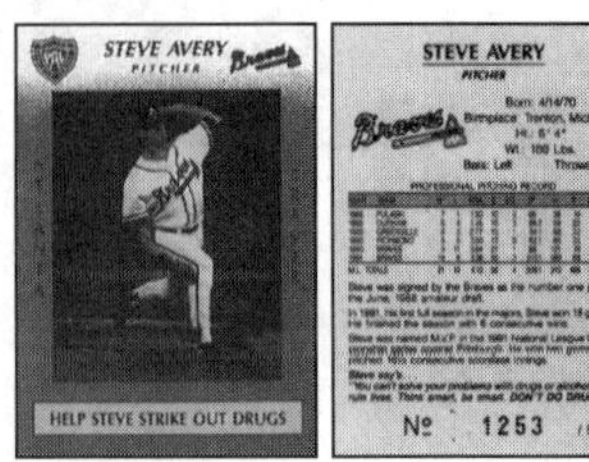

	MINT	NRMT	EXC
COMPLETE SET	3.00	1.35	.35
COMMON CARD	3.00	1.35	.35
☐ 1 Steve Avery	3.00	1.35	.35

1992 Police McGwire

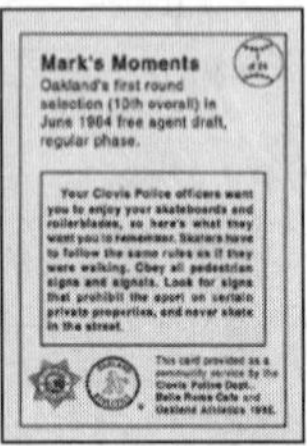

This 24-card standard-size set was sponsored by the Clovis Police Department, The Oakland A's, and 25 Clovis area businesses. The program raised $9,200 in a four-day period. Both businesses and officers gave out 12 1/2" by 18" posters and cards, and graduating DARE students also received cards. The cards were cut from the poster, but some uncut posters (measuring approximately 20" by 25") with the cards still attached were given away to VIPs and sponsors for framing. The fronts feature color action photos of Mark McGwire on a green card face. The pictures have bright yellow borders, and the upper left corner is cut off to display the City of Clovis insignia. The player's name is printed in bright yellow print at the top. The backs features "Mark's Moments" (various facts about McGwire) and public service messages. The cards are numbered on the back.

	MINT	NRMT	EXC
COMPLETE SET (24)	15.00	6.75	1.85
COMMON CARD (1-24)	.75	.35	.09
☐ 1 Mark McGwire	.75	.35	.09
Signing baseball			
☐ 2 Mark McGwire	.75	.35	.09
Reaching to make catch at 1st base			
☐ 3 Mark McGwire	.75	.35	.09
Batting practice, in cage			
☐ 4 Mark McGwire	.75	.35	.09
Squatting, holding bat			
☐ 5 Mark McGwire	.75	.35	.09
In practice jersey			
☐ 6 Mark McGwire	.75	.35	.09
On base			
☐ 7 Mark McGwire	.75	.35	.09
In dugout, posed holding bat			
☐ 8 Mark McGwire	.75	.35	.09
Follow through jersey number visible			
☐ 9 Mark McGwire	.75	.35	.09
Catching pop fly			
☐ 10 Mark McGwire	.75	.35	.09
Follow through bat extended in front			
☐ 11 Mark McGwire	.75	.35	.09
In field, holding glove			
☐ 12 Mark McGwire	.75	.35	.09
Fielding			
☐ 13 Mark McGwire	.75	.35	.09
On deck			
☐ 14 Mark McGwire	.75	.35	.09
Waiting for the pitch, side view			
☐ 15 Mark McGwire	.75	.35	.09
In dugout holding bat across shoulders			
☐ 16 Mark McGwire	.75	.35	.09
Tagging a sliding runner			
☐ 17 Mark McGwire	.75	.35	.09
Being congratulated after scoring			
☐ 18 Mark McGwire	.75	.35	.09
Leading off base			
☐ 19 Mark McGwire	.75	.35	.09
Follow through from the back			
☐ 20 Mark McGwire	.75	.35	.09
On deck bat resting on shoulder			
☐ 21 Mark McGwire	.75	.35	.09
Signing autographs			
☐ 22 Mark McGwire	.75	.35	.09
Preparing bat beside batter's cage			
☐ 23 Mark McGwire	.75	.35	.09
Waiting for a pitch front view			
☐ 24 Mark McGwire	.75	.35	.09
Follow through watching flight of ball			

1913 Polo Grounds WG4

These cards were distributed as part of a baseball game produced around 1913. The cards each measure approximately 2 1/2" by 3 1/2" and have rounded corners. The card fronts show a photo of the player, his name, his team, and the game outcome associated with that particular card. The card backs are printed in green and white and are all the same each showing a panoramic picture of the Polo Grounds inside an ornate frame with a white outer border. Since the cards are unnumbered, they are listed below in alphabetical order.

	EX-MT	VG-E	GOOD
COMPLETE SET (30)	1500.00	700.00	190.00
COMMON CARD (1-30)	35.00	16.00	4.40
☐ 1 Jimmy Archer	35.00	16.00	4.40
☐ 2 Frank Baker	75.00	34.00	9.50
☐ 3 Frank Chance	100.00	45.00	12.50
☐ 4 Larry Cheney	35.00	16.00	4.40
☐ 5 Ty Cobb	300.00	135.00	38.00
☐ 6 Eddie Collins	75.00	34.00	9.50
☐ 7 Larry Doyle	35.00	16.00	4.40
☐ 8 Art Fletcher	35.00	16.00	4.40
☐ 9 Claude Hendrix	35.00	16.00	4.40
☐ 10 Joe Jackson	500.00	220.00	60.00
☐ 11 Hugh Jennings MG	75.00	34.00	9.50
☐ 12 Nap Lajoie	125.00	55.00	15.50
☐ 13 Jimmy Lavender	35.00	16.00	4.40
☐ 14 Fritz Maisel	35.00	16.00	4.40
☐ 15 Rabbit Maranville	75.00	34.00	9.50
☐ 16 Rube Marquard	75.00	34.00	9.50
☐ 17 Christy Mathewson	150.00	70.00	19.00
☐ 18 John McGraw MG	125.00	55.00	15.50
☐ 19 Stuffy McInnis	50.00	22.00	6.25
sic,McInnes			
☐ 20 Chief Meyers	35.00	16.00	4.40
☐ 21 Red Murray	35.00	16.00	4.40
☐ 22 Eddie Plank	100.00	45.00	12.50
☐ 23 Nap Rucker	35.00	16.00	4.40
☐ 24 Reb Russell	35.00	16.00	4.40
☐ 25 Frank Schulte	35.00	16.00	4.40
☐ 26 Jim Scott	35.00	16.00	4.40
☐ 27 Tris Speaker	125.00	55.00	15.50
☐ 28 Honus Wagner	150.00	70.00	19.00
☐ 29 Ed Walsh	75.00	34.00	9.50
☐ 30 Joe Wood	50.00	22.00	6.25

1928 Portraits and Action R315

This 1928 issue contains 88 black and white or yellow and black cards. The cards are blank backed and measure approximately 3 1/4" by 5 1/4". The cards are organized below alphabetically within each type. Type A features the player's name and team inside a white box. Type B features the player's position and team name printed below the frame line on the border. Type C shows the player's name hand lettered at the bottom of the card or near the player's legs. Type D has the position and team printed on the white border. Interestingly, almost all of the C and D type cards (discovered so far) feature members of the Chicago White Sox. Some of these cards are oriented horizontally and are so indicated by HOR in the checklist below.

	EX-MT	VG-E	GOOD
COMPLETE SET (88)	5000.00	2200.00	600.00
COMMON CARD A/B	20.00	9.00	2.50
COMMON CARD C/D	25.00	11.00	3.10
☐ A1 Earl Averill	50.00	22.00	6.25
☐ A2 Benny Bengough	20.00	9.00	2.50
☐ A3 Laurence Benton	20.00	9.00	2.50
☐ A4 Max Bishop	20.00	9.00	2.50
☐ A5 Jim Bottomley	50.00	22.00	6.25
☐ A6 Freddy Fitzsimmons	20.00	9.00	2.50
☐ A7 Jimmy Foxx	200.00	90.00	25.00
☐ A8 Johnny Fredericks	20.00	9.00	2.50
☐ A9 Frank Frisch HOR	75.00	34.00	9.50
☐ A10 Lou Gehrig HOR	400.00	180.00	50.00
☐ A11 Goose Goslin	50.00	22.00	6.25
☐ A12 Burleigh Grimes	50.00	22.00	6.25
☐ A13 Lefty Grove	125.00	55.00	15.50
☐ A14 Mule Haas	20.00	9.00	2.50
☐ A15 Babe Herman	25.00	11.00	3.10
☐ A16 Rogers Hornsby	175.00	80.00	22.00
☐ A17 Carl Hubbell	75.00	34.00	9.50
☐ A18 Travis Jackson	50.00	22.00	6.25
☐ A19 Chuck Klein	75.00	34.00	9.50
☐ A20 Mark Koenig	20.00	9.00	2.50
☐ A21 Tony Lazzeri	25.00	11.00	3.10
☐ A22 Fred Leach	20.00	9.00	2.50
☐ A23 Freddy Lindstrom	50.00	22.00	6.25
☐ A24 Fred Marberry	20.00	9.00	2.50
☐ A25 Bing Miller	20.00	9.00	2.50
☐ A26 Frank O'Doul	25.00	11.00	3.10
☐ A27 Bob O'Farrell	20.00	9.00	2.50
☐ A28 Herbie Pennock	50.00	22.00	6.25
☐ A29 George Pipgras	20.00	9.00	2.50
☐ A30 Andrew Reese	20.00	9.00	2.50
☐ A31 Babe Ruth	500.00	220.00	60.00
☐ A32 Bob Shawkey	20.00	9.00	2.50
☐ A33 Al Simmons	50.00	22.00	6.25
☐ A34 Riggs Stephenson	25.00	11.00	3.10
☐ A35 Bill Terry	75.00	34.00	9.50
☐ A36 Pie Traynor	100.00	45.00	12.50
☐ A37 Dazzy Vance	50.00	22.00	6.25
☐ A38 Paul Waner	50.00	22.00	6.25
☐ A39 Hack Wilson	75.00	34.00	9.50
☐ A40 Tom Zachary	20.00	9.00	2.50
☐ B1 Earl Averill	50.00	22.00	6.25
☐ B2 Benny Bengough	20.00	9.00	2.50
☐ B3 Laurence Benton	20.00	9.00	2.50
☐ B4 Max Bishop	20.00	9.00	2.50
☐ B5 Jim Bottomley	50.00	22.00	6.25
☐ B6 Freddy Fitzsimmons	20.00	9.00	2.50
☐ B7 Jimmy Foxx	150.00	70.00	19.00
☐ B8 Johnny Fredericks	20.00	9.00	2.50
☐ B9 Frank Frisch HOR	125.00	55.00	15.50
☐ B10 Lou Gehrig HOR	400.00	180.00	50.00
☐ B11 Goose Goslin	50.00	22.00	6.25
☐ B12 Burleigh Grimes	50.00	22.00	6.25
☐ B13 Lefty Grove	125.00	55.00	15.50
☐ B14 Mule Haas	20.00	9.00	2.50
☐ B15 Babe Herman	25.00	11.00	3.10
☐ B16 Rogers Hornsby	175.00	80.00	22.00
☐ B17 Carl Hubbell	100.00	45.00	12.50
☐ B18 Travis Jackson	50.00	22.00	6.25
☐ B19 Chuck Klein	75.00	34.00	9.50
☐ B20 Mark Koenig	20.00	9.00	2.50
☐ B21 Tony Lazzeri	25.00	11.00	3.10
☐ B22 Fred Leach	20.00	9.00	2.50
☐ B23 Freddy Lindstrom	50.00	22.00	6.25
☐ B24 Fred Marberry	20.00	9.00	2.50
☐ B25 Bing Miller	20.00	9.00	2.50
☐ B26 Frank O'Doul	25.00	11.00	3.10
☐ B27 Bob O'Farrell	20.00	9.00	2.50
☐ B28 Herb Pennock	50.00	22.00	6.25
☐ B29 George Pipgras	20.00	9.00	2.50
☐ B30 Andrew Reese	20.00	9.00	2.50
☐ B31 Babe Ruth	500.00	220.00	60.00
☐ B32 Bob Shawkey	20.00	9.00	2.50
☐ B33 Al Simmons	50.00	22.00	6.25
☐ B34 Riggs Stephenson	25.00	11.00	3.10
☐ B35 Bill Terry	100.00	45.00	12.50
☐ B36 Pie Traynor	75.00	34.00	9.50
☐ B37 Dazzy Vance	50.00	22.00	6.25
☐ B38 Paul Waner	50.00	22.00	6.25
☐ B39 Hack Wilson	75.00	34.00	9.50
☐ B40 Tom Zachary	20.00	9.00	2.50
☐ C1 Bill Cissell	25.00	11.00	3.10
☐ C2 Harvey Hendricks	25.00	11.00	3.10
☐ C3 Smead Jolley	25.00	11.00	3.10
☐ C4 Carl Reynolds	25.00	11.00	3.10
☐ C5 Art Shires	25.00	11.00	3.10
☐ D1 Bill Cissell	25.00	11.00	3.10
☐ D2 Bud Clancy	25.00	11.00	3.10
☐ D3 Smead Jolley	25.00	11.00	3.10

1929 Portraits and Action R316

The 1929 R316 Portraits and Action Baseball set features 101 unnumbered, blank backed, black and white cards each measuring 3 1/2" by 4 1/2". The name of the player is written in script at the bottom of the card. The Hadley, Haines, Siebold and Todt cards are considered scarce. On the other hand, the Babe Ruth card seems to be one of the more plentiful cards in the set.

	EX-MT	VG-E	GOOD
COMPLETE SET (101)	4500.00	2000.00	550.00
COMMON CARD (1-101)	30.00	13.50	3.70
☐ 1 Ethan N. Allen	30.00	13.50	3.70
☐ 2 Dale Alexander	30.00	13.50	3.70
☐ 3 Larry Benton	30.00	13.50	3.70
☐ 4 Moe Berg	60.00	27.00	7.50
☐ 5 Max Bishop	30.00	13.50	3.70
☐ 6 Del Bissonette	30.00	13.50	3.70
☐ 7 Lucerne A. Blue	30.00	13.50	3.70
☐ 8 James Bottomley	50.00	22.00	6.25
☐ 9 Guy T. Bush	30.00	13.50	3.70
☐ 10 Harold G. Carlson	30.00	13.50	3.70
☐ 11 Owen Carroll	30.00	13.50	3.70
☐ 12 Chalmers W. Cissell	30.00	13.50	3.70
☐ 13 Earl Combs	50.00	22.00	6.25
☐ 14 Hugh M. Critz	30.00	13.50	3.70
☐ 15 H.J. DeBerry	30.00	13.50	3.70
☐ 16 Pete Donohue	30.00	13.50	3.70
☐ 17 Taylor Douthit	30.00	13.50	3.70
☐ 18 Charlie Dressen	40.00	18.00	5.00
☐ 19 Jimmy Dykes	40.00	18.00	5.00
☐ 20 Howard Ehmke	30.00	13.50	3.70
☐ 21 Woody English	30.00	13.50	3.70
☐ 22 Urban Faber	50.00	22.00	6.25
☐ 23 Fred Fitzsimmons	30.00	13.50	3.70
☐ 24 Lewis A. Fonseca	30.00	13.50	3.70
☐ 25 Horace H. Ford	30.00	13.50	3.70
☐ 26 Jimmy Foxx	75.00	34.00	9.50
☐ 27 Frank Frisch	60.00	27.00	7.50
☐ 28 Lou Gehrig	400.00	180.00	50.00
☐ 29 Charles Gehringer	60.00	27.00	7.50
☐ 30 Leon Goslin	50.00	22.00	6.25
☐ 31 George Grantham	30.00	13.50	3.70
☐ 32 Burleigh Grimes	50.00	22.00	6.25
☐ 33 Lefty Grove	60.00	27.00	7.50
☐ 34 Bump Hadley	175.00	80.00	22.00
☐ 35 Chick Hafey	50.00	22.00	6.25
☐ 36 Jesse J. Haines	250.00	110.00	31.00
☐ 37 Harvey Hendrick	30.00	13.50	3.70
☐ 38 Floyd C. Herman	40.00	18.00	5.00
☐ 39 Andy High	30.00	13.50	3.70
☐ 40 Urban J. Hodapp	30.00	13.50	3.70
☐ 41 Frank Hogan	30.00	13.50	3.70
☐ 42 Rogers Hornsby	75.00	34.00	9.50
☐ 43 Waite Hoyt	50.00	22.00	6.25
☐ 44 Willis Hudlin	30.00	13.50	3.70
☐ 45 Frank O. Hurst	30.00	13.50	3.70
☐ 46 Charlie Jamieson	30.00	13.50	3.70
☐ 47 Roy C. Johnson	30.00	13.50	3.70
☐ 48 Percy Jones	30.00	13.50	3.70
☐ 49 Sam Jones	30.00	13.50	3.70
☐ 50 Joseph Judge	30.00	13.50	3.70
☐ 51 Willie Kamm	30.00	13.50	3.70
☐ 52 Chuck Klein	50.00	22.00	6.25
☐ 53 Mark Koenig	30.00	13.50	3.70
☐ 54 Ralph Kress	30.00	13.50	3.70
☐ 55 Fred M. Leach	30.00	13.50	3.70
☐ 56 Fred Lindstrom	50.00	22.00	6.25
☐ 57 Ad Liska	30.00	13.50	3.70
☐ 58 Fred Lucas	30.00	13.50	3.70
☐ 59 Fred Maguire	30.00	13.50	3.70
☐ 60 Perce L. Malone	30.00	13.50	3.70
☐ 61 Harry Manush	50.00	22.00	6.25
☐ 62 Rabbit Maranville	50.00	22.00	6.25
☐ 63 Douglas McWeeney	30.00	13.50	3.70
☐ 64 Oscar Melillo	30.00	13.50	3.70
☐ 65 Bing Miller	30.00	13.50	3.70
☐ 66 Lefty O'Doul	40.00	18.00	5.00
☐ 67 Mel Ott	75.00	34.00	9.50
☐ 68 Herb Pennock	50.00	22.00	6.25
☐ 69 William W. Regan	30.00	13.50	3.70
☐ 70 Harry F. Rice	30.00	13.50	3.70
☐ 71 Sam Rice	50.00	22.00	6.25
☐ 72 Lance Richbourg	30.00	13.50	3.70
☐ 73 Eddie Rommel	30.00	13.50	3.70
☐ 74 Chas. H. Root	30.00	13.50	3.70
☐ 75 Ed Roush	50.00	22.00	6.25
☐ 76 Harold Ruel	30.00	13.50	3.70
☐ 77 Charlie Ruffing	50.00	22.00	6.25
☐ 78 Jack Russell	30.00	13.50	3.70
☐ 79 Babe Ruth DP	350.00	160.00	45.00
☐ 80 Fred Schulte	30.00	13.50	3.70
☐ 81 Joe Sewell	50.00	22.00	6.25
☐ 82 Luke Sewell	40.00	18.00	5.00
☐ 83 Art Shires	30.00	13.50	3.70
☐ 84 Henry Seibold	175.00	80.00	22.00
☐ 85 Al Simmons	50.00	22.00	6.25
☐ 86 Bob Smith	30.00	13.50	3.70
☐ 87 Riggs Stephenson	40.00	18.00	5.00
☐ 88 Bill Terry	60.00	27.00	7.50
☐ 89 Alphonse Thomas	30.00	13.50	3.70
☐ 90 Lafayette Thompson	30.00	13.50	3.70
☐ 91 Phil Todt	175.00	80.00	22.00
☐ 92 Pie Traynor	50.00	22.00	6.25
☐ 93 Dazzy Vance	50.00	22.00	6.25
☐ 94 Lloyd Waner	50.00	22.00	6.25
☐ 95 Paul Waner	50.00	22.00	6.25
☐ 96 Jimmy Welsh	30.00	13.50	3.70
☐ 97 Earl Whitehill	30.00	13.50	3.70
☐ 98 A.C. Whitney	30.00	13.50	3.70
☐ 99 Claude Willoughby	30.00	13.50	3.70
☐ 100 Hack Wilson	60.00	27.00	7.50
☐ 101 Tom Zachary	30.00	13.50	3.70

1960 Post *

These large cards measure approximately 7" by 8 3/4". The 1960 Post Cereal Sports Stars set contains nine cards depicting current baseball, football and basketball players. Each card comprised the entire back of a Grape Nuts Box and is blank backed. The color player photos are set on a colored background surrounded by a wooden frame design and they are unnumbered (assigned numbers below for reference). The catalog designation is F278-26.

	NRMT	VG-E	GOOD
COMPLETE SET (9)	4500.00	2000.00	550.00
COMMON CARD (1-9)	250.00	110.00	31.00

	NRMT	VG-E	GOOD
☐ 1 Bob Cousy Boston Celtics (basketball)	400.00	180.00	50.00
☐ 2 Don Drysdale Los Angeles Dodgers (baseball)	300.00	135.00	38.00
☐ 3 Frank Gifford New York Giants (football)	400.00	180.00	50.00
☐ 4 Al Kaline Detroit Tigers (baseball)	400.00	180.00	50.00
☐ 5 Harmon Killebrew Minnesota Twins (baseball)	250.00	110.00	31.00
☐ 6 Eddie Mathews Milwaukee Braves (baseball)	250.00	110.00	31.00
☐ 7 Mickey Mantle New York Yankees (baseball)	2500.00	1100.00	300.00
☐ 8 Bob Pettit St. Louis Hawks (basketball)	300.00	135.00	38.00
☐ 9 John Unitas Baltimore Colts (football)	500.00	220.00	60.00

1961 Post

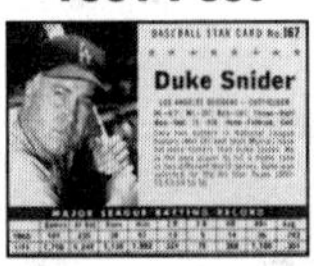

The cards in this 200-card set measure 2 1/2" by 3 1/2". The 1961 Post set was this company's first major set. The cards were available on thick cardbox stock, singly or in various panel sizes from cereal boxes (BOX), or in team sheets, printed on thinner cardboard stock, directly from the Post Cereal Company (COM). It is difficult to differentiate the COM cards from the BOX cards; the thickness of the card stock is the best indicator. Many variations exist and are noted in the checklist below. There are many cards which were produced in lesser quantities; the prices below reflect the relative scarcity of the cards. Cards 10, 23, 70, 73, 94, 113, 135, 163, and 183 are examples of cards printed in limited quantities and hence commanding premium prices. The cards are numbered essentially in team groups, i.e., New York Yankees (1-18), Chicago White Sox (19-34), Detroit (35-46), Boston (47-56), Cleveland (57-67), Baltimore (68-80), Kansas City (81-90), Minnesota (91-100), Milwaukee (101-114), Philadelphia (115-124), Pittsburgh (125-140), San Francisco (141-155), Los Angeles Dodgers (156-170), St. Louis (171-180), Cincinnati (181-190), and Chicago Cubs (191-200). The catalog number is F278-33. The complete set price refers to the maximal set with all variations (357). There was also an album produced by Post to hold the cards.

	NRMT	VG-E	GOOD
COMPLETE SET (357)	3000.00	1350.00	375.00
COMMON CARD (1-200)	3.50	1.55	.45

	NRMT	VG-E	GOOD
☐ 1A Yogi Berra COM	30.00	13.50	3.70
☐ 1B Yogi Berra BOX	30.00	13.50	3.70
☐ 2A Elston Howard COM	5.00	2.20	.60
☐ 2B Elston Howard BOX	5.00	2.20	.60
☐ 3A Bill Skowron COM	5.00	2.20	.60
☐ 3B Bill Skowron BOX	5.00	2.20	.60
☐ 4A Mickey Mantle COM	150.00	70.00	19.00
☐ 4B Mickey Mantle BOX	150.00	70.00	19.00
☐ 5 Bob Turley COM only	20.00	9.00	2.50
☐ 6A Whitey Ford COM	10.00	4.50	1.25
☐ 6B Whitey Ford BOX	10.00	4.50	1.25
☐ 7A Roger Maris COM	30.00	13.50	3.70
☐ 7B Roger Maris BOX	30.00	13.50	3.70
☐ 8A Bobby Richardson COM	5.00	2.20	.60
☐ 8B Bobby Richardson BOX	5.00	2.20	.60
☐ 9A Tony Kubek COM	5.00	2.20	.60
☐ 9B Tony Kubek BOX	5.00	2.20	.60
☐ 10 Gil McDougald BOX only	50.00	22.00	6.25
☐ 11 Cletis Boyer BOX only	3.50	1.55	.45
☐ 12A Hector Lopez COM	3.50	1.55	.45
☐ 12B Hector Lopez BOX	3.50	1.55	.45
☐ 13 Bob Cerv BOX only	3.50	1.55	.45
☐ 14 Ryne Duren BOX only	3.50	1.55	.45
☐ 15 Bobby Shantz BOX only	3.50	1.55	.45
☐ 16 Art Ditmar BOX only	3.50	1.55	.45
☐ 17 Jim Coates BOX only	3.50	1.55	.45
☐ 18 Johnny Blanchard BOX only	3.50	1.55	.45
☐ 19A Luis Aparicio COM	8.00	3.60	1.00
☐ 19B Luis Aparicio BOX	8.00	3.60	1.00
☐ 20A Nellie Fox COM	8.00	3.60	1.00
☐ 20B Nellie Fox BOX	8.00	3.60	1.00
☐ 21A Bill Pierce COM	5.00	2.20	.60
☐ 21B Bill Pierce BOX	5.00	2.20	.60
☐ 22A Early Wynn COM	12.00	5.50	1.50
☐ 22B Early Wynn BOX	12.00	5.50	1.50
☐ 23 Bob Shaw BOX only	100.00	45.00	12.50
☐ 24A Al Smith COM	3.50	1.55	.45
☐ 24B Al Smith BOX	3.50	1.55	.45
☐ 25A Minnie Minoso COM	6.00	2.70	.75
☐ 25B Minnie Minoso BOX	6.00	2.70	.75
☐ 26A Roy Sievers COM	3.50	1.55	.45
☐ 26B Roy Sievers BOX	3.50	1.55	.45
☐ 27A Jim Landis COM	3.50	1.55	.45
☐ 27B Jim Landis BOX	3.50	1.55	.45
☐ 28A Sherm Lollar COM	3.50	1.55	.45
☐ 28B Sherm Lollar BOX	3.50	1.55	.45
☐ 29 Gerry Staley BOX only	3.50	1.55	.45
☐ 30A Gene Freese COM (Reds)	12.00	5.50	1.50
☐ 30B Gene Freese BOX (White Sox)	3.50	1.55	.45
☐ 31 Ted Kluszewski BOX only	5.00	2.20	.60
☐ 32 Turk Lown BOX only	3.50	1.55	.45
☐ 33A Jim Rivera COM	3.50	1.55	.45
☐ 33B Jim Rivera BOX	3.50	1.55	.45
☐ 34 Frank Baumann BOX only	3.50	1.55	.45
☐ 35A Al Kaline COM	20.00	9.00	2.50
☐ 35B Al Kaline BOX	20.00	9.00	2.50
☐ 36A Rocky Colavito COM	7.50	3.40	.95
☐ 36B Rocky Colavito BOX	7.50	3.40	.95
☐ 37A Charlie Maxwell COM	3.50	1.55	.45
☐ 37B Charlie Maxwell BOX	3.50	1.55	.45
☐ 38A Frank Lary COM	3.50	1.55	.45
☐ 38B Frank Lary BOX	3.50	1.55	.45
☐ 39A Jim Bunning COM	8.00	3.60	1.00
☐ 39B Jim Bunning BOX	8.00	3.60	1.00
☐ 40A Norm Cash COM	5.00	2.20	.60
☐ 40B Norm Cash BOX	5.00	2.20	.60
☐ 41A Frank Bolling COM (Braves, Charlie Gehringer in bio)	5.00	2.20	.60
☐ 41B Frank Bolling BOX (Tigers, Charlie Derringer in bio)	7.50	3.40	.95
☐ 42A Don Mossi COM	3.50	1.55	.45
☐ 42B Don Mossi BOX	3.50	1.55	.45
☐ 43A Lou Berberet COM	3.50	1.55	.45
☐ 43B Lou Berberet BOX	3.50	1.55	.45
☐ 44 Dave Sisler BOX only	3.50	1.55	.45
☐ 45 Eddie Yost BOX only	3.50	1.55	.45
☐ 46 Pete Burnside BOX only	3.50	1.55	.45
☐ 47A Pete Runnels COM	5.00	2.20	.60
☐ 47B Pete Runnels BOX	5.00	2.20	.60
☐ 48A Frank Malzone COM	3.50	1.55	.45
☐ 48B Frank Malzone BOX	3.50	1.55	.45
☐ 49A Vic Wertz COM	5.00	2.20	.60
☐ 49B Vic Wertz BOX	5.00	2.20	.60
☐ 50A Tom Brewer COM	3.50	1.55	.45
☐ 50B Tom Brewer BOX	3.50	1.55	.45
☐ 51A Willie Tasby COM (Sold to Wash.)	6.00	2.70	.75
☐ 51B Willie Tasby BOX (No sale mention)	3.50	1.55	.45
☐ 52A Russ Nixon COM	3.50	1.55	.45
☐ 52B Russ Nixon BOX	3.50	1.55	.45
☐ 53A Don Buddin COM	3.50	1.55	.45
☐ 53B Don Buddin BOX	3.50	1.55	.45
☐ 54A Bill Monbouquette COM	3.50	1.55	.45
☐ 54B Bill Monbouquette BOX	3.50	1.55	.45
☐ 55A Frank Sullivan COM (Phillies)	10.00	4.50	1.25
☐ 55B Frank Sullivan BOX (Red Sox)	3.50	1.55	.45
☐ 56A Haywood Sullivan COM	3.50	1.55	.45
☐ 56B Haywood Sullivan BOX	3.50	1.55	.45
☐ 57A Harvey Kuenn COM (Giants)	8.00	3.60	1.00
☐ 57B Harvey Kuenn BOX (Indians)	5.00	2.20	.60
☐ 58A Gary Bell COM	5.00	2.20	.60
☐ 58B Gary Bell BOX	5.00	2.20	.60
☐ 59A Jim Perry COM	3.50	1.55	.45
☐ 59B Jim Perry BOX	3.50	1.55	.45
☐ 60A Jim Grant COM	5.00	2.20	.60
☐ 60B Jim Grant BOX	5.00	2.20	.60
☐ 61A Johnny Temple COM	3.50	1.55	.45
☐ 61B Johnny Temple BOX	3.50	1.55	.45
☐ 62A Paul Foytack COM	3.50	1.55	.45
☐ 62B Paul Foytack BOX	3.50	1.55	.45
☐ 63A Vic Power COM	3.50	1.55	.45
☐ 63B Vic Power BOX	3.50	1.55	.45
☐ 64A Tito Francona COM	3.50	1.55	.45
☐ 64B Tito Francona BOX	3.50	1.55	.45
☐ 65A Ken Aspromonte COM (Sold to L.A.)	7.50	3.40	.95
☐ 65B Ken Aspromonte BOX (No sale mention)	7.50	3.40	.95
☐ 66 Bob Wilson BOX only	3.50	1.55	.45
☐ 67A John Romano COM	3.50	1.55	.45
☐ 67B John Romano BOX	3.50	1.55	.45
☐ 68A Jim Gentile COM	5.00	2.20	.60
☐ 68B Jim Gentile BOX	5.00	2.20	.60
☐ 69A Gus Triandos COM	5.00	2.20	.60
☐ 69B Gus Triandos BOX	5.00	2.20	.60
☐ 70 Gene Woodling BOX only	30.00	13.50	3.70
☐ 71A Milt Pappas COM	5.00	2.20	.60
☐ 71B Milt Pappas BOX	5.00	2.20	.60
☐ 72A Ron Hansen COM	3.50	1.55	.45
☐ 72B Ron Hansen BOX	3.50	1.55	.45
☐ 73 Chuck Estrada COM only	100.00	45.00	12.50
☐ 74A Steve Barber COM	3.50	1.55	.45
☐ 74B Steve Barber BOX	3.50	1.55	.45
☐ 75A Brooks Robinson COM	25.00	11.00	3.10
☐ 75B Brooks Robinson BOX	25.00	11.00	3.10
☐ 76A Jackie Brandt COM	3.50	1.55	.45
☐ 76B Jackie Brandt BOX	3.50	1.55	.45
☐ 77A Marv Breeding COM	3.50	1.55	.45
☐ 77B Marv Breeding BOX	3.50	1.55	.45
☐ 78 Hal Brown BOX only	3.50	1.55	.45
☐ 79 Billy Klaus BOX only	3.50	1.55	.45
☐ 80A Hoyt Wilhelm COM	8.00	3.60	1.00
☐ 80B Hoyt Wilhelm BOX	8.00	3.60	1.00
☐ 81A Jerry Lumpe COM	5.00	2.20	.60
☐ 81B Jerry Lumpe BOX	5.00	2.20	.60
☐ 82A Norm Siebern COM	3.50	1.55	.45
☐ 82B Norm Siebern BOX	3.50	1.55	.45
☐ 83A Bud Daley COM	5.00	2.20	.60
☐ 83B Bud Daley BOX	5.00	2.20	.60
☐ 84A Bill Tuttle COM	3.50	1.55	.45
☐ 84B Bill Tuttle BOX	3.50	1.55	.45
☐ 85A Marv Throneberry COM	5.00	2.20	.60
☐ 85B Marv Throneberry BOX	5.00	2.20	.60
☐ 86A Dick Williams COM	5.00	2.20	.60
☐ 86B Dick Williams BOX	5.00	2.20	.60
☐ 87A Ray Herbert COM	3.50	1.55	.45
☐ 87B Ray Herbert BOX	3.50	1.55	.45
☐ 88A Whitey Herzog COM	5.00	2.20	.60
☐ 88B Whitey Herzog BOX	5.00	2.20	.60
☐ 89A Ken Hamlin COM (Sold to L.A.)	20.00	9.00	2.50
☐ 89B Ken Hamlin BOX (No sale mention)	3.50	1.55	.45
☐ 90A Hank Bauer COM	5.00	2.20	.60
☐ 90B Hank Bauer BOX	5.00	2.20	.60
☐ 91A Bob Allison COM (Minnesota)	6.00	2.70	.75
☐ 91B Bob Allison BOX (Minneapolis)	6.00	2.70	.75
☐ 92A Harmon Killebrew (Minnesota) COM	40.00	18.00	5.00
☐ 92B Harmon Killebrew (Minneapolis) BOX	30.00	13.50	3.70
☐ 93A Jim Lemon COM (Minnesota)	20.00	9.00	2.50
☐ 93B Jim Lemon BOX (Minneapolis)	60.00	27.00	7.50
☐ 94A Chuck Stobbs (Minnesota) COM only	175.00	80.00	22.00
☐ 95A Reno Bertoia COM (Minnesota)	5.00	2.20	.60
☐ 95B Reno Bertoia BOX (Minneapolis)	3.50	1.55	.45
☐ 96A Billy Gardner COM (Minnesota)	5.00	2.20	.60
☐ 96B Billy Gardner BOX (Minneapolis)	3.50	1.55	.45
☐ 97A Earl Battey COM (Minnesota)	5.00	2.20	.60
☐ 97B Earl Battey BOX (Minneapolis)	3.50	1.55	.45
☐ 98A Pedro Ramos COM (Minnesota)	5.00	2.20	.60
☐ 98B Pedro Ramos BOX (Minneapolis)	3.50	1.55	.45
☐ 99A Camilo Pascual COM (Minnesota)	5.00	2.20	.60
☐ 99B Camilo Pascual BOX (Minneapolis)	3.50	1.55	.45
☐ 100A Billy Consolo COM (Minnesota)	5.00	2.20	.60
☐ 100B Billy Consolo BOX (Minneapolis)	3.50	1.55	.45
☐ 101A Warren Spahn COM	25.00	11.00	3.10
☐ 101B Warren Spahn BOX	25.00	11.00	3.10
☐ 102A Lew Burdette COM	5.00	2.20	.60
☐ 102B Lew Burdette BOX	5.00	2.20	.60
☐ 103A Bob Buhl COM	3.50	1.55	.45
☐ 103B Bob Buhl BOX	3.50	1.55	.45
☐ 104A Joe Adcock COM	5.00	2.20	.60
☐ 104B Joe Adcock BOX	5.00	2.20	.60
☐ 105A John Logan COM	5.00	2.20	.60
☐ 105B John Logan BOX	5.00	2.20	.60
☐ 106 Eddie Mathews COM only	30.00	13.50	3.70
☐ 107A Hank Aaron COM	30.00	13.50	3.70
☐ 107B Hank Aaron BOX	30.00	13.50	3.70
☐ 108A Wes Covington COM	3.50	1.55	.45
☐ 108B Wes Covington BOX	3.50	1.55	.45
☐ 109A Bill Bruton COM (Tigers)	6.00	2.70	.75
☐ 109B Bill Bruton BOX (Braves)	6.00	2.70	.75
☐ 110A Del Crandall COM	5.00	2.20	.60
☐ 110B Del Crandall BOX	5.00	2.20	.60
☐ 111 Red Schoendienst BOX only	5.00	2.20	.60
☐ 112 Juan Pizarro BOX only	3.50	1.55	.45
☐ 113 Chuck Cottier BOX only	15.00	6.75	1.85
☐ 114 Al Spangler BOX only	3.50	1.55	.45
☐ 115A Dick Farrell COM	5.00	2.20	.60
☐ 115B Dick Farrell BOX	5.00	2.20	.60
☐ 116A Jim Owens COM	5.00	2.20	.60
☐ 116B Jim Owens BOX	5.00	2.20	.60
☐ 117A Robin Roberts COM	8.00	3.60	1.00
☐ 117B Robin Roberts BOX	8.00	3.60	1.00
☐ 118A Tony Taylor COM	3.50	1.55	.45
☐ 118B Tony Taylor BOX	3.50	1.55	.45
☐ 119A Lee Walls COM	3.50	1.55	.45
☐ 119B Lee Walls BOX	3.50	1.55	.45
☐ 120A Tony Curry COM	3.50	1.55	.45
☐ 120B Tony Curry BOX	3.50	1.55	.45
☐ 121A Pancho Herrera COM	3.50	1.55	.45
☐ 121B Pancho Herrera BOX	3.50	1.55	.45
☐ 122A Ken Walters COM	3.50	1.55	.45
☐ 122B Ken Walters BOX	3.50	1.55	.45
☐ 123A John Callison COM	5.00	2.20	.60
☐ 123B John Callison BOX	5.00	2.20	.60
☐ 124A Gene Conley COM (Red Sox)	12.00	5.50	1.50
☐ 124B Gene Conley BOX (Phillies)	3.50	1.55	.45
☐ 125A Bob Friend COM	5.00	2.20	.60
☐ 125B Bob Friend BOX	5.00	2.20	.60
☐ 126A Vernon Law COM	5.00	2.20	.60
☐ 126B Vernon Law BOX	5.00	2.20	.60
☐ 127A Dick Stuart COM	3.50	1.55	.45
☐ 127B Dick Stuart BOX	3.50	1.55	.45
☐ 128A Bill Mazeroski COM	5.00	2.20	.60
☐ 128B Bill Mazeroski BOX	5.00	2.20	.60
☐ 129A Dick Groat COM	5.00	2.20	.60
☐ 129B Dick Groat BOX	5.00	2.20	.60
☐ 130A Don Hoak COM	3.50	1.55	.45
☐ 130B Don Hoak BOX	3.50	1.55	.45
☐ 131A Bob Skinner COM	3.50	1.55	.45
☐ 131B Bob Skinner BOX	3.50	1.55	.45
☐ 132A Roberto Clemente COM	50.00	22.00	6.25
☐ 132B Roberto Clemente BOX	50.00	22.00	6.25
☐ 133 Roy Face BOX only	5.00	2.20	.60
☐ 134 Harvey Haddix BOX only	3.50	1.55	.45
☐ 135 Bill Virdon BOX only	40.00	18.00	5.00
☐ 136A Gino Cimoli COM	3.50	1.55	.45
☐ 136B Gino Cimoli BOX	3.50	1.55	.45
☐ 137 Rocky Nelson BOX only	3.50	1.55	.45
☐ 138A Smoky Burgess COM	5.00	2.20	.60
☐ 138B Smoky Burgess BOX	5.00	2.20	.60
☐ 139 Hal W. Smith BOX only	3.50	1.55	.45
☐ 140 Wilmer Mizell BOX only	3.50	1.55	.45
☐ 141A Mike McCormick COM	3.50	1.55	.45
☐ 141B Mike McCormick BOX	3.50	1.55	.45
☐ 142A John Antonelli COM (Cleveland)	6.00	2.70	.75
☐ 142B John Antonelli BOX (San Francisco)	5.00	2.20	.60
☐ 143A Sam Jones COM	5.00	2.20	.60
☐ 143B Sam Jones BOX	5.00	2.20	.60
☐ 144A Orlando Cepeda COM	7.00	3.10	.85
☐ 144B Orlando Cepeda BOX	7.00	3.10	.85
☐ 145A Willie Mays COM	35.00	16.00	4.40
☐ 145B Willie Mays BOX	35.00	16.00	4.40
☐ 146A Willie Kirkland (Cleveland) COM	8.00	3.60	1.00
☐ 146B Willie Kirkland (San Francisco) BOX	5.00	2.20	.60
☐ 147A Willie McCovey COM	10.00	4.50	1.25
☐ 147B Willie McCovey BOX	10.00	4.50	1.25
☐ 148A Don Blasingame COM	3.50	1.55	.45
☐ 148B Don Blasingame BOX	3.50	1.55	.45
☐ 149A Jim Davenport COM	5.00	2.20	.60
☐ 149B Jim Davenport BOX	5.00	2.20	.60
☐ 150A Hobie Landrith COM	3.50	1.55	.45
☐ 150B Hobie Landrith BOX	3.50	1.55	.45
☐ 151 Bob Schmidt BOX only	3.50	1.55	.45
☐ 152A Ed Bressoud COM	3.50	1.55	.45
☐ 152B Ed Bressoud BOX	3.50	1.55	.45
☐ 153A Andre Rodgers (no trade mention) BOX only	20.00	9.00	2.50
☐ 153B Andre Rodgers (Traded to Milw.) BOX only	5.00	2.20	.60
☐ 154 Jack Sanford BOX only	3.50	1.55	.45

☐ 155 Billy O'Dell	3.50	1.55	.45
BOX only			
☐ 156A Norm Larker COM	3.50	1.55	.45
☐ 156B Norm Larker BOX	3.50	1.55	.45
☐ 157A Charlie Neal COM	3.50	1.55	.45
☐ 157B Charlie Neal BOX	3.50	1.55	.45
☐ 158A Jim Gilliam COM	6.00	2.70	.75
☐ 158B Jim Gilliam BOX	6.00	2.70	.75
☐ 159A Wally Moon COM	5.00	2.20	.60
☐ 159B Wally Moon BOX	5.00	2.20	.60
☐ 160A Don Drysdale COM	12.00	5.50	1.50
☐ 160B Don Drysdale BOX	12.00	5.50	1.50
☐ 161A Larry Sherry COM	5.00	2.20	.60
☐ 161B Larry Sherry BOX	5.00	2.20	.60
☐ 162 Stan Williams	7.00	3.10	.85
BOX only			
☐ 163 Mel Roach BOX only	90.00	40.00	11.00
☐ 164A Maury Wills COM	10.00	4.50	1.25
☐ 164B Maury Wills BOX	10.00	4.50	1.25
☐ 165 Tommy Davis BOX only	5.00	2.20	.60
☐ 166A John Roseboro COM	3.50	1.55	.45
☐ 166B John Roseboro BOX	3.50	1.55	.45
☐ 167A Duke Snider COM	8.00	3.60	1.00
☐ 167B Duke Snider BOX	8.00	3.60	1.00
☐ 168A Gil Hodges COM	8.00	3.60	1.00
☐ 168B Gil Hodges BOX	8.00	3.60	1.00
☐ 169 John Podres BOX only	3.50	1.55	.45
☐ 170 Ed Roebuck BOX only	3.50	1.55	.45
☐ 171A Ken Boyer COM	8.00	3.60	1.00
☐ 171B Ken Boyer BOX	8.00	3.60	1.00
☐ 172A Joe Cunningham COM	3.50	1.55	.45
☐ 172B Joe Cunningham BOX	3.50	1.55	.45
☐ 173A Daryl Spencer COM	3.50	1.55	.45
☐ 173B Daryl Spencer BOX	3.50	1.55	.45
☐ 174A Larry Jackson COM	3.50	1.55	.45
☐ 174B Larry Jackson BOX	3.50	1.55	.45
☐ 175A Lindy McDaniel COM	3.50	1.55	.45
☐ 175B Lindy McDaniel BOX	3.50	1.55	.45
☐ 176A Bill White COM	5.00	2.20	.60
☐ 176B Bill White BOX	5.00	2.20	.60
☐ 177A Alex Grammas COM	3.50	1.55	.45
☐ 177B Alex Grammas BOX	3.50	1.55	.45
☐ 178A Curt Flood COM	5.00	2.20	.60
☐ 178B Curt Flood BOX	5.00	2.20	.60
☐ 179A Ernie Broglio COM	3.50	1.55	.45
☐ 179B Ernie Broglio BOX	3.50	1.55	.45
☐ 180A Hal Smith COM	3.50	1.55	.45
☐ 180B Hal Smith BOX	3.50	1.55	.45
☐ 181A Vada Pinson COM	5.00	2.20	.60
☐ 181B Vada Pinson BOX	5.00	2.20	.60
☐ 182A Frank Robinson COM	35.00	16.00	4.40
☐ 182B Frank Robinson BOX	35.00	16.00	4.40
☐ 183 Roy McMillan	90.00	40.00	11.00
BOX only			
☐ 184A Bob Purkey COM	3.50	1.55	.45
☐ 184B Bob Purkey BOX	3.50	1.55	.45
☐ 185A Ed Kasko COM	3.50	1.55	.45
☐ 185B Ed Kasko BOX	3.50	1.55	.45
☐ 186A Gus Bell COM	3.50	1.55	.45
☐ 186B Gus Bell BOX	3.50	1.55	.45
☐ 187A Jerry Lynch COM	3.50	1.55	.45
☐ 187B Jerry Lynch BOX	3.50	1.55	.45
☐ 188A Ed Bailey COM	3.50	1.55	.45
☐ 188B Ed Bailey BOX	3.50	1.55	.45
☐ 189A Jim O'Toole COM	3.50	1.55	.45
☐ 189B Jim O'Toole BOX	3.50	1.55	.45
☐ 190A Billy Martin COM	10.00	4.50	1.25
(Sold to Milwaukee)			
☐ 190B Billy Martin BOX	5.00	2.20	.60
(No sale mention)			
☐ 191A Ernie Banks COM	25.00	11.00	3.10
☐ 191B Ernie Banks BOX	25.00	11.00	3.10
☐ 192A Richie Ashburn COM	8.00	3.60	1.00
☐ 192B Richie Ashburn BOX	8.00	3.60	1.00
☐ 193A Frank Thomas COM	40.00	18.00	5.00
☐ 193B Frank Thomas BOX	40.00	18.00	5.00
☐ 194A Don Cardwell COM	3.50	1.55	.45
☐ 194B Don Cardwell BOX	3.50	1.55	.45
☐ 195A George Altman COM	3.50	1.55	.45
☐ 195B George Altman BOX	3.50	1.55	.45
☐ 196A Ron Santo COM	6.00	2.70	.75
☐ 196B Ron Santo BOX	6.00	2.70	.75
☐ 197A Glen Hobbie COM	3.50	1.55	.45
☐ 197B Glen Hobbie BOX	3.50	1.55	.45
☐ 198A Sam Taylor COM	3.50	1.55	.45
☐ 198B Sam Taylor BOX	3.50	1.55	.45
☐ 199A Jerry Kindall COM	3.50	1.55	.45
☐ 199B Jerry Kindall BOX	3.50	1.55	.45
☐ 200A Don Elston COM	5.00	2.20	.60
☐ 200B Don Elston BOX	5.00	2.20	.60

1962 Post

The cards in this 200-player series measure 2 1/2" by 3 1/2" and are oriented horizontally. The 1962 Post set is the easiest of the Post sets to complete. The cards are grouped numerically by team, for example, New York Yankees (1-13), Detroit (14-26), Baltimore (27-36), Cleveland (37-45), Chicago White Sox (46-55), Boston (56-64), Washington (65-73), Los Angeles Angels (74-82), Minnesota (83-91), Kansas City (92-100), Los Angeles Dodgers (101-115), Cincinnati (116-130), San Francisco (131-144), Milwaukee (145-157), St. Louis (158-168), Pittsburgh (169-181), Chicago Cubs (182-191), and Philadelphia (192-200). Cards 5B and 6B were printed on thin stock in a two-card panel and distributed in a Life magazine promotion. The scarce cards are 55, 69, 83, 92, 101, 103, 113, 116, 122, 125, 127, 131, 140, 144, and 158. The checklist for this set is the same as that of 1962 Jello and 1962 Post Canadian, but those sets are considered separate issues. The catalog number for this set is F278-37.

	NRMT	VG-E	GOOD
COMPLETE SET (210)	2000.00	900.00	250.00
COMMON CARD (1-200)	3.00	1.35	.35
☐ 1 Bill Skowron	5.00	2.20	.60
☐ 2 Bobby Richardson	5.00	2.20	.60
☐ 3 Cletis Boyer	4.00	1.80	.50
☐ 4 Tony Kubek	5.00	2.20	.60
☐ 5A Mickey Mantle	150.00	70.00	19.00
☐ 5B Mickey Mantle AD	150.00	70.00	19.00
☐ 6A Roger Maris	25.00	11.00	3.10
☐ 6B Roger Maris AD	25.00	11.00	3.10
☐ 7 Yogi Berra	25.00	11.00	3.10
☐ 8 Elston Howard	5.00	2.20	.60
☐ 9 Whitey Ford	10.00	4.50	1.25
☐ 10 Ralph Terry	3.00	1.35	.35
☐ 11 John Blanchard	3.00	1.35	.35
☐ 12 Luis Arroyo	3.00	1.35	.35
☐ 13 Bill Stafford	3.00	1.35	.35
☐ 14A Norm Cash ERR	20.00	9.00	2.50
(Throws: right)			
☐ 14B Norm Cash COR	4.00	1.80	.50
(Throws: left)			
☐ 15 Jake Wood	3.00	1.35	.35
☐ 16 Steve Boros	3.00	1.35	.35
☐ 17 Chico Fernandez	3.00	1.35	.35
☐ 18 Bill Bruton	3.00	1.35	.35
☐ 19 Rocky Colavito	6.00	2.70	.75
☐ 20 Al Kaline	15.00	6.75	1.85
☐ 21 Dick Brown	3.00	1.35	.35
☐ 22 Frank Lary	3.00	1.35	.35
☐ 23 Don Mossi	3.00	1.35	.35
☐ 24 Phil Regan	3.00	1.35	.35
☐ 25 Charley Maxwell	3.00	1.35	.35
☐ 26 Jim Bunning	7.00	3.10	.85
☐ 27A Jim Gentile	4.00	1.80	.50
(Home: Baltimore)			
☐ 27B Jim Gentile	20.00	9.00	2.50
(Home: San Lorenzo)			
☐ 28 Marv Breeding	3.00	1.35	.35
☐ 29 Brooks Robinson	15.00	6.75	1.85
☐ 30A Ron Hansen	4.00	1.80	.50
(At-Bats)			
☐ 30B Ron Hansen	4.00	1.80	.50
(At Bats)			
☐ 31 Jackie Brandt	3.00	1.35	.35
☐ 32 Dick Williams	4.00	1.80	.50
☐ 33 Gus Triandos	3.00	1.35	.35
☐ 34 Milt Pappas	4.00	1.80	.50
☐ 35 Hoyt Wilhelm	8.00	3.60	1.00
☐ 36 Chuck Estrada	7.50	3.40	.95
☐ 37 Vic Power	3.00	1.35	.35
☐ 38 Johnny Temple	3.00	1.35	.35
☐ 39 Bubba Phillips	3.00	1.35	.35
☐ 40 Tito Francona	3.00	1.35	.35
☐ 41 Willie Kirkland	3.00	1.35	.35
☐ 42 John Romano	3.00	1.35	.35
☐ 43 Jim Perry	3.00	1.35	.35
☐ 44 Woodie Held	3.00	1.35	.35
☐ 45 Chuck Essegian	3.00	1.35	.35
☐ 46 Roy Sievers	3.00	1.35	.35
☐ 47 Nellie Fox	8.00	3.60	1.00
☐ 48 Al Smith	3.00	1.35	.35
☐ 49 Luis Aparicio	7.00	3.10	.85
☐ 50 Jim Landis	3.00	1.35	.35
☐ 51 Minnie Minoso	5.00	2.20	.60
☐ 52 Andy Carey	3.00	1.35	.35
☐ 53 Sherman Lollar	3.00	1.35	.35
☐ 54 Bill Pierce	4.00	1.80	.50
☐ 55 Early Wynn	30.00	13.50	3.70
☐ 56 Chuck Schilling	3.00	1.35	.35
☐ 57 Pete Runnels	3.00	1.35	.35
☐ 58 Frank Malzone	3.00	1.35	.35
☐ 59 Don Buddin	3.00	1.35	.35
☐ 60 Gary Geiger	3.00	1.35	.35
☐ 61 Carl Yastrzemski	40.00	18.00	5.00
☐ 62 Jackie Jensen	4.00	1.80	.50
☐ 63 Jim Pagliaroni	3.00	1.35	.35
☐ 64 Don Schwall	3.00	1.35	.35
☐ 65 Dale Long	3.00	1.35	.35
☐ 66 Chuck Cottier	3.00	1.35	.35
☐ 67 Billy Klaus	3.00	1.35	.35
☐ 68 Coot Veal	3.00	1.35	.35
☐ 69 Marty Keough	40.00	18.00	5.00
☐ 70 Willie Tasby	3.00	1.35	.35
☐ 71 Gene Woodling	3.00	1.35	.35
☐ 72 Gene Green	3.00	1.35	.35
☐ 73 Dick Donovan	3.00	1.35	.35
☐ 74 Steve Bilko	3.00	1.35	.35
☐ 75 Rocky Bridges	3.00	1.35	.35
☐ 76 Eddie Yost	3.00	1.35	.35
☐ 77 Leon Wagner	3.00	1.35	.35
☐ 78 Albie Pearson	3.00	1.35	.35
☐ 79 Ken Hunt	3.00	1.35	.35
☐ 80 Earl Averill	3.00	1.35	.35
☐ 81 Ryne Duren	3.00	1.35	.35
☐ 82 Ted Kluszewski	5.00	2.20	.60
☐ 83 Bob Allison	30.00	13.50	3.70
☐ 84 Billy Martin	5.00	2.20	.60
☐ 85 Harmon Killebrew	10.00	4.50	1.25
☐ 86 Zoilo Versalles	3.00	1.35	.35
☐ 87 Lenny Green	3.00	1.35	.35
☐ 88 Bill Tuttle	3.00	1.35	.35
☐ 89 Jim Lemon	3.00	1.35	.35
☐ 90 Earl Battey	3.00	1.35	.35
☐ 91 Camilo Pascual	3.00	1.35	.35
☐ 92 Norm Siebern	75.00	34.00	9.50
☐ 93 Jerry Lumpe	3.00	1.35	.35
☐ 94 Dick Howser	4.00	1.80	.50
☐ 95A Gene Stephens	4.00	1.80	.50
(Born: Jan. 5)			
☐ 95B Gene Stephens	20.00	9.00	2.50
(Born: Jan. 20)			
☐ 96 Leo Posada	3.00	1.35	.35
☐ 97 Joe Pignatano	3.00	1.35	.35
☐ 98 Jim Archer	3.00	1.35	.35
☐ 99 Haywood Sullivan	3.00	1.35	.35
☐ 100 Art Ditmar	3.00	1.35	.35
☐ 101 Gil Hodges	100.00	45.00	12.50
☐ 102 Charlie Neal	3.00	1.35	.35
☐ 103 Daryl Spencer	30.00	13.50	3.70
☐ 104 Maury Wills	6.00	2.70	.75
☐ 105 Tommy Davis	4.00	1.80	.50
☐ 106 Willie Davis	4.00	1.80	.50
☐ 107 John Roseboro	3.00	1.35	.35
☐ 108 John Podres	4.00	1.80	.50
☐ 109A Sandy Koufax	30.00	13.50	3.70
☐ 109B Sandy Koufax	100.00	45.00	12.50
(With blue lines)			
☐ 110 Don Drysdale	12.00	5.50	1.50
☐ 111 Larry Sherry	4.00	1.80	.50
☐ 112 Jim Gilliam	5.00	2.20	.60
☐ 113 Norm Larker	30.00	13.50	3.70
☐ 114 Duke Snider	8.00	3.60	1.00
☐ 115 Stan Williams	3.00	1.35	.35
☐ 116 Gordy Coleman	100.00	45.00	12.50
☐ 117 Don Blasingame	3.00	1.35	.35
☐ 118 Gene Freese	3.00	1.35	.35
☐ 119 Ed Kasko	3.00	1.35	.35
☐ 120 Gus Bell	3.00	1.35	.35
☐ 121 Vada Pinson	4.00	1.80	.50
☐ 122 Frank Robinson	30.00	13.50	3.70
☐ 123 Bob Purkey	3.00	1.35	.35
☐ 124A Joey Jay	4.00	1.80	.50
☐ 124B Joey Jay	20.00	9.00	2.50
(With blue lines)			
☐ 125 Jim Brosnan	30.00	13.50	3.70
☐ 126 Jim O'Toole	3.00	1.35	.35
☐ 127 Jerry Lynch	75.00	34.00	9.50
☐ 128 Wally Post	3.00	1.35	.35
☐ 129 Ken Hunt	3.00	1.35	.35
☐ 130 Jerry Zimmerman	3.00	1.35	.35
☐ 131 Willie McCovey	100.00	45.00	12.50
☐ 132 Jose Pagan	3.00	1.35	.35
☐ 133 Felipe Alou UER	4.00	1.80	.50
(Misspelled Filipe			
in text)			
☐ 134 Jim Davenport	3.00	1.35	.35
☐ 135 Harvey Kuenn	4.00	1.80	.50
☐ 136 Orlando Cepeda	5.00	2.20	.60
☐ 137 Ed Bailey	3.00	1.35	.35
☐ 138 Sam Jones	3.00	1.35	.35
☐ 139 Mike McCormick	4.00	1.80	.50
☐ 140 Juan Marichal	125.00	55.00	15.50
☐ 141 Jack Sanford	3.00	1.35	.35
☐ 142 Willie Mays	45.00	20.00	5.50
☐ 143 Stu Miller	7.00	3.10	.85
☐ 144 Joe Amalfitano	25.00	11.00	3.10
☐ 145A Joe Adock (sic) ERR	75.00	34.00	9.50
☐ 145B Joe Adcock CORR	4.00	1.80	.50
☐ 146 Frank Bolling	3.00	1.35	.35
☐ 147 Eddie Mathews	12.00	5.50	1.50
☐ 148 Roy McMillan	3.00	1.35	.35
☐ 149 Hank Aaron	40.00	18.00	5.00
☐ 150 Gino Cimoli	3.00	1.35	.35
☐ 151 Frank Thomas	3.00	1.35	.35
☐ 152 Joe Torre	6.00	2.70	.75
☐ 153 Lew Burdette	4.00	1.80	.50
☐ 154 Bob Buhl	3.00	1.35	.35
☐ 155 Carlton Willey	3.00	1.35	.35
☐ 156 Lee Maye	3.00	1.35	.35
☐ 157 Al Spangler	3.00	1.35	.35
☐ 158 Bill White	40.00	18.00	5.00
☐ 159 Ken Boyer	4.00	1.80	.50
☐ 160 Joe Cunningham	3.00	1.35	.35
☐ 161 Carl Warwick	3.00	1.35	.35
☐ 162 Carl Sawatski	3.00	1.35	.35
☐ 163 Lindy McDaniel	3.00	1.35	.35
☐ 164 Ernie Broglio	3.00	1.35	.35
☐ 165 Larry Jackson	3.00	1.35	.35
☐ 166 Curt Flood	4.00	1.80	.50
☐ 167 Curt Simmons	3.00	1.35	.35
☐ 168 Alex Grammas	3.00	1.35	.35
☐ 169 Dick Stuart	3.00	1.35	.35
☐ 170 Bill Mazeroski UER	5.00	2.20	.60
(Bio reads 1959,			
should read 1960)			
☐ 171 Don Hoak	3.00	1.35	.35
☐ 172 Dick Groat	4.00	1.80	.50
☐ 173A Roberto Clemente	60.00	27.00	7.50
☐ 173B Roberto Clemente	175.00	80.00	22.00
(With blue lines)			
☐ 174 Bob Skinner	3.00	1.35	.35
☐ 175 Bill Virdon	4.00	1.80	.50
☐ 176 Smoky Burgess	3.00	1.35	.35
☐ 177 Elroy Face	4.00	1.80	.50
☐ 178 Bob Friend	3.00	1.35	.35
☐ 179 Vernon Law	3.00	1.35	.35
☐ 180 Harvey Haddix	3.00	1.35	.35
☐ 181 Hal Smith	3.00	1.35	.35
☐ 182 Ed Bouchee	3.00	1.35	.35
☐ 183 Don Zimmer	3.00	1.35	.35
☐ 184 Ron Santo	5.00	2.20	.60
☐ 185 Andre Rodgers	3.00	1.35	.35
☐ 186 Richie Ashburn	8.00	3.60	1.00
☐ 187 George Altman	3.00	1.35	.35
☐ 188 Ernie Banks	15.00	6.75	1.85
☐ 189 Sam Taylor	3.00	1.35	.35
☐ 190 Don Elston	3.00	1.35	.35
☐ 191 Jerry Kindall	3.00	1.35	.35
☐ 192 Pancho Herrera	3.00	1.35	.35
☐ 193 Tony Taylor	3.00	1.35	.35
☐ 194 Ruben Amaro	3.00	1.35	.35
☐ 195 Don Demeter	3.00	1.35	.35
☐ 196 Bobby Gene Smith	3.00	1.35	.35
☐ 197 Clay Dalrymple	3.00	1.35	.35
☐ 198 Robin Roberts	8.00	3.60	1.00
☐ 199 Art Mahaffey	3.00	1.35	.35
☐ 200 John Buzhardt	5.00	2.20	.60

1962 Post Canadian

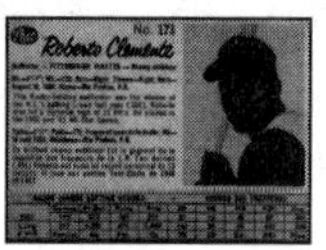

The 200 blank-backed cards comprising the 1962 Post Canadian set measure approximately 2 1/2" by 3 1/2". The set is similar in appearance to the Jell-O set released in the U.S. that same year. The fronts feature a posed color player photo at the upper right. To the left of the photo, the player's name appears in blue cursive lettering, followed below by bilingual biography and career highlights. The cards are numbered on the front. The cards are grouped by team as follows: New York Yankees (1-13), Detroit (14-26), Baltimore (27-36), Cleveland (37-45), Chicago White Sox (46-55), Boston (56-64), Washington (65-73), Los Angeles Angels (74-82), Minnesota (83-91), Kansas City (92-100), Los Angeles Dodgers (101-115), Cincinnati (116-130), San Francisco (131-144), Milwaukee (145-157), St. Louis (158-168), Pittsburgh (169-181), Chicago Cubs (182-191) and Philadelphia (192-200). Maris (6) and Mays (142) are somewhat scarce. Whitey Ford is listed incorrectly with the Dodgers and correctly with the Yankees. The complete set price includes both Whitey Ford variations.

	NRMT	VG-E	GOOD
COMPLETE SET (201)	2500.00	1100.00	300.00
COMMON CARD (1-200)	5.00	2.20	.60
☐ 1 Bill Skowron	7.50	3.40	.95
☐ 2 Bobby Richardson	7.50	3.40	.95
☐ 3 Cletis Boyer	6.00	2.70	.75
☐ 4 Tony Kubek	7.50	3.40	.95
☐ 5 Mickey Mantle	350.00	160.00	45.00
☐ 6 Roger Maris	150.00	70.00	19.00
☐ 7 Yogi Berra	75.00	34.00	9.50
☐ 8 Elston Howard	7.50	3.40	.95
☐ 9A Whitey Ford ERR	75.00	34.00	9.50
(Los Angeles Dodgers)			
☐ 9B Whitey Ford COR	75.00	34.00	9.50
(New York Yankees)			
☐ 10 Ralph Terry	6.00	2.70	.75
☐ 11 John Blanchard	6.00	2.70	.75
☐ 12 Luis Arroyo	5.00	2.20	.60
☐ 13 Bill Stafford	5.00	2.20	.60
☐ 14 Norm Cash	7.50	3.40	.95
☐ 15 Jake Wood	5.00	2.20	.60
☐ 16 Steve Boros	5.00	2.20	.60
☐ 17 Chico Fernandez	5.00	2.20	.60
☐ 18 Bill Bruton	5.00	2.20	.60
☐ 19 Rocky Colavito	10.00	4.50	1.25
☐ 20 Al Kaline	40.00	18.00	5.00
☐ 21 Dick Brown	5.00	2.20	.60
☐ 22 Frank Lary	15.00	6.75	1.85
☐ 23 Don Mossi	6.00	2.70	.75
☐ 24 Phil Regan	5.00	2.20	.60
☐ 25 Charlie Maxwell	5.00	2.20	.60
☐ 26 Jim Bunning	12.50	5.50	1.55
☐ 27 Jim Gentile	6.00	2.70	.75
☐ 28 Marv Breeding	5.00	2.20	.60
☐ 29 Brooks Robinson	40.00	18.00	5.00
☐ 30 Ron Hansen	5.00	2.20	.60
☐ 31 Jackie Brandt	5.00	2.20	.60
☐ 32 Dick Williams	7.50	3.40	.95
☐ 33 Gus Triandos	5.00	2.20	.60
☐ 34 Milt Pappas	6.00	2.70	.75
☐ 35 Hoyt Wilhelm	50.00	22.00	6.25
☐ 36 Chuck Estrada	5.00	2.20	.60
☐ 37 Vic Power	5.00	2.20	.60
☐ 38 Johnny Temple	5.00	2.20	.60
☐ 39 Bubba Phillips	5.00	2.20	.60
☐ 40 Tito Francona	15.00	6.75	1.85
☐ 41 Willie Kirkland	5.00	2.20	.60

Card	NRMT	VG-E	GOOD
☐ 42 John Romano	5.00	2.20	.60
☐ 43 Jim Perry	6.00	2.70	.75
☐ 44 Woodie Held	5.00	2.20	.60
☐ 45 Chuck Essegian	5.00	2.20	.60
☐ 46 Roy Sievers	6.00	2.70	.75
☐ 47 Nellie Fox	12.50	5.50	1.55
☐ 48 Al Smith	5.00	2.20	.60
☐ 49 Luis Aparicio	50.00	22.00	6.25
☐ 50 Jim Landis	5.00	2.20	.60
☐ 51 Minnie Minoso	7.50	3.40	.95
☐ 52 Andy Carey	5.00	2.20	.60
☐ 53 Sherman Lollar	5.00	2.20	.60
☐ 54 Bill Pierce	6.00	2.70	.75
☐ 55 Early Wynn	12.50	5.50	1.55
☐ 56 Chuck Schilling	5.00	2.20	.60
☐ 57 Pete Runnels	6.00	2.70	.75
☐ 58 Frank Malzone	6.00	2.70	.75
☐ 59 Don Buddin	5.00	2.20	.60
☐ 60 Gary Geiger	5.00	2.20	.60
☐ 61 Carl Yastrzemski	100.00	45.00	12.50
☐ 62 Jackie Jensen	6.00	2.70	.75
☐ 63 Jim Pagliaroni	5.00	2.20	.60
☐ 64 Don Schwall	15.00	6.75	1.85
☐ 65 Dale Long	5.00	2.20	.60
☐ 66 Chuck Cottier	5.00	2.20	.60
☐ 67 Billy Klaus	5.00	2.20	.60
☐ 68 Coot Veal	5.00	2.20	.60
☐ 69 Marty Keough	5.00	2.20	.60
☐ 70 Willie Tasby	5.00	2.20	.60
☐ 71 Gene Woodling	6.00	2.70	.75
☐ 72 Gene Green	5.00	2.20	.60
☐ 73 Dick Donovan	5.00	2.20	.60
☐ 74 Steve Bilko	5.00	2.20	.60
☐ 75 Rocky Bridges	5.00	2.20	.60
☐ 76 Eddie Yost	5.00	2.20	.60
☐ 77 Leon Wagner	15.00	6.75	1.85
☐ 78 Albie Pearson	5.00	2.20	.60
☐ 79 Ken L. Hunt	5.00	2.20	.60
☐ 80 Earl Averill	5.00	2.20	.60
☐ 81 Ryne Duren	6.00	2.70	.75
☐ 82 Ted Kluszewski	7.50	3.40	.95
☐ 83 Bob Allison	6.00	2.70	.75
☐ 84 Billy Martin	7.50	3.40	.95
☐ 85 Harmon Killebrew	25.00	11.00	3.10
☐ 86 Zoilo Versalles	6.00	2.70	.75
☐ 87 Lenny Green	15.00	6.75	1.85
☐ 88 Bill Tuttle	5.00	2.20	.60
☐ 89 Jim Lemon	5.00	2.20	.60
☐ 90 Earl Battey	5.00	2.20	.60
☐ 91 Camilo Pascual	6.00	2.70	.75
☐ 92 Norm Siebern	5.00	2.20	.60
☐ 93 Jerry Lumpe	5.00	2.20	.60
☐ 94 Dick Howser	6.00	2.70	.75
☐ 95 Gene Stephens	5.00	2.20	.60
☐ 96 Leo Posada	5.00	2.20	.60
☐ 97 Joe Pignatano	5.00	2.20	.60
☐ 98 Jim Archer	5.00	2.20	.60
☐ 99 Haywood Sullivan	5.00	2.20	.60
☐ 100 Art Ditmar	5.00	2.20	.60
☐ 101 Gil Hodges	25.00	11.00	3.10
☐ 102 Charlie Neal	5.00	2.20	.60
☐ 103 Daryl Spencer	5.00	2.20	.60
☐ 104 Maury Wills	10.00	4.50	1.25
☐ 105 Tommy Davis	20.00	9.00	2.50
☐ 106 Willie Davis	6.00	2.70	.75
☐ 107 John Roseboro	6.00	2.70	.75
☐ 108 John Podres	7.50	3.40	.95
☐ 109 Sandy Koufax	75.00	34.00	9.50
☐ 110 Don Drysdale	25.00	11.00	3.10
☐ 111 Larry Sherry	6.00	2.70	.75
☐ 112 Jim Gilliam	25.00	11.00	3.10
☐ 113 Norm Larker	5.00	2.20	.60
☐ 114 Duke Snider	40.00	18.00	5.00
☐ 115 Stan Williams	5.00	2.20	.60
☐ 116 Gordy Coleman	5.00	2.20	.60
☐ 117 Don Blasingame	15.00	6.75	1.85
☐ 118 Gene Freese	5.00	2.20	.60
☐ 119 Ed Kasko	5.00	2.20	.60
☐ 120 Gus Bell	5.00	2.20	.60
☐ 121 Vada Pinson	7.50	3.40	.95
☐ 122 Frank Robinson	25.00	11.00	3.10
☐ 123 Bob Purkey	15.00	6.75	1.85
☐ 124 Joey Jay	5.00	2.20	.60
☐ 125 Jim Brosnan	5.00	2.20	.60
☐ 126 Jim O'Toole	5.00	2.20	.60
☐ 127 Jerry Lynch	5.00	2.20	.60
☐ 128 Wally Post	6.00	2.70	.75
☐ 129 Ken R. Hunt	5.00	2.20	.60
☐ 130 Jerry Zimmerman	5.00	2.20	.60
☐ 131 Willie McCovey	25.00	11.00	3.10
☐ 132 Jose Pagan	5.00	2.20	.60
☐ 133 Felipe Alou	7.50	3.40	.95
☐ 134 Jim Davenport	5.00	2.20	.60
☐ 135 Harvey Kuenn	5.00	2.20	.60
☐ 136 Orlando Cepeda	10.00	4.50	1.25
☐ 137 Ed Bailey	15.00	6.75	1.85
☐ 138 Sam Jones	5.00	2.20	.60
☐ 139 Mike McCormick	5.00	2.20	.60
☐ 140 Juan Marichal	25.00	11.00	3.10
☐ 141 Jack Sanford	5.00	2.20	.60
☐ 142 Willie Mays	125.00	55.00	15.50
☐ 143 Stu Miller	5.00	2.20	.60
☐ 144 Joe Amalfitano	30.00	13.50	3.70
☐ 145 Joe Adcock	6.00	2.70	.75
☐ 146 Frank Bolling	5.00	2.20	.60
☐ 147 Eddie Mathews	20.00	9.00	2.50
☐ 148 Roy McMillan	5.00	2.20	.60
☐ 149 Hank Aaron	100.00	45.00	12.50
☐ 150 Gino Cimoli	5.00	2.20	.60
☐ 151 Frank Thomas	6.00	2.70	.75
☐ 152 Joe Torre	12.50	5.50	1.55
☐ 153 Lew Burdette	7.50	3.40	.95
☐ 154 Bob Buhl	5.00	2.20	.60
☐ 155 Carlton Willey	5.00	2.20	.60
☐ 156 Lee Maye	5.00	2.20	.60
☐ 157 Al Spangler	5.00	2.20	.60
☐ 158 Bill White	7.50	3.40	.95
☐ 159 Ken Boyer	10.00	4.50	1.25
☐ 160 Joe Cunningham	6.00	2.70	.75
☐ 161 Carl Warwick	15.00	6.75	1.85
☐ 162 Carl Sawatski	5.00	2.20	.60
☐ 163 Lindy McDaniel	5.00	2.20	.60
☐ 164 Ernie Broglio	5.00	2.20	.60
☐ 165 Larry Jackson	5.00	2.20	.60
☐ 166 Curt Flood	7.50	3.40	.95
☐ 167 Curt Simmons	5.00	2.20	.60
☐ 168 Alex Grammas	5.00	2.20	.60
☐ 169 Dick Stuart	5.00	2.20	.60
☐ 170 Bill Mazeroski	10.00	4.50	1.25
☐ 171 Don Hoak	5.00	2.20	.60
☐ 172 Dick Groat	6.00	2.70	.75
☐ 173 Roberto Clemente	175.00	80.00	22.00
☐ 174 Bob Skinner	5.00	2.20	.60
☐ 175 Bill Virdon	6.00	2.70	.75
☐ 176 Smoky Burgess	15.00	6.75	1.85
☐ 177 Elroy Face	7.50	3.40	.95
☐ 178 Bob Friend	5.00	2.20	.60
☐ 179 Vernon Law	6.00	2.70	.75
☐ 180 Harvey Haddix	5.00	2.20	.60
☐ 181 Hal Smith	5.00	2.20	.60
☐ 182 Ed Bouchee	15.00	6.75	1.85
☐ 183 Don Zimmer	5.00	2.20	.60
☐ 184 Ron Santo	7.50	3.40	.95
☐ 185 Andre Rodgers	5.00	2.20	.60
☐ 186 Richie Ashburn	12.50	5.50	1.55
☐ 187 George Altman	5.00	2.20	.60
☐ 188 Ernie Banks	40.00	18.00	5.00
☐ 189 Sam Taylor	5.00	2.20	.60
☐ 190 Don Elston	5.00	2.20	.60
☐ 191 Jerry Kindall	5.00	2.20	.60
☐ 192 Pancho Herrera	5.00	2.20	.60
☐ 193 Tony Taylor	6.00	2.70	.75
☐ 194 Ruben Amaro	5.00	2.20	.60
☐ 195 Don Demeter	5.00	2.20	.60
☐ 196 Bobby Gene Smith	5.00	2.20	.60
☐ 197 Clay Dalrymple	5.00	2.20	.60
☐ 198 Robin Roberts	20.00	9.00	2.50
☐ 199 Art Mahaffey	5.00	2.20	.60
☐ 200 John Buzhardt	6.00	2.70	.75

1963 Post

The cards in this 200-card set measure 2 1/2" by 3 1/2". The players are grouped by team with American Leaguers comprising 1-100 and National Leaguers 101-200. The ordering of teams is as follows: Minnesota (1-11), New York Yankees, Los Angeles Angels (24-34), Chicago White Sox (35-45), Detroit (46-56), Baltimore (57-66), Cleveland (67-76), Boston (77-84), Kansas City (85-92), Washington (93-100), San Francisco (101-112), Los Angeles Dodgers (113-124), Cincinnati (125-136), Pittsburgh (137-147), Milwaukee (148-157), St. Louis (158-168), Chicago Cubs (169-176), Philadelphia (177-184), Houston (185-192), and New York Mets (193-200). In contrast to the 1962 issue, the 1963 Post baseball card series is very difficult to complete. There are many card scarcities reflected in the price list below. Cards of the Post set are easily confused with those of the 1963 Jello set, which are 1/4" narrower (a difference which is often eliminated by bad cutting). The catalog designation is F278-38. There was also an album produced by Post to hold the cards.

	NRMT	VG-E	GOOD
COMPLETE SET (206)	4250.00	1900.00	525.00
COMMON CARD (1-200)	3.50	1.55	.45
☐ 1 Vic Power	6.00	2.70	.75
☐ 2 Bernie Allen	3.50	1.55	.45
☐ 3 Zoilo Versalles	3.50	1.55	.45
☐ 4 Rich Rollins	3.50	1.55	.45
☐ 5 Harmon Killebrew	20.00	9.00	2.50
☐ 6 Lenny Green	45.00	20.00	5.50
☐ 7 Bob Allison	5.00	2.20	.60
☐ 8 Earl Battey	3.50	1.55	.45
☐ 9 Camilo Pascual	3.50	1.55	.45
☐ 10 Jim Kaat	6.00	2.70	.75
☐ 11 Jack Kralick	3.50	1.55	.45
☐ 12 Bill Skowron	5.00	2.20	.60
☐ 13 Bobby Richardson	6.00	2.70	.75
☐ 14 Cletis Boyer	3.50	1.55	.45
☐ 15 Mickey Mantle	350.00	160.00	45.00
☐ 16 Roger Maris	175.00	80.00	22.00
☐ 17 Yogi Berra ERR (Living in Monclair, N.Y.)	25.00	11.00	3.10
☐ 18 Elston Howard	5.00	2.20	.60
☐ 19 Whitey Ford	15.00	6.75	1.85
☐ 20 Ralph Terry	3.50	1.55	.45
☐ 21 John Blanchard	3.50	1.55	.45
☐ 22 Bill Stafford	3.50	1.55	.45
☐ 23 Tom Tresh	3.50	1.55	.45
☐ 24 Steve Bilko	3.50	1.55	.45
☐ 25 Bill Moran	3.50	1.55	.45
☐ 26A Joe Koppe (BA: .277)	3.50	1.55	.45
☐ 26B Joe Koppe (BA: .227)	20.00	9.00	2.50
☐ 27 Felix Torres	3.50	1.55	.45
☐ 28A Leon Wagner (BA: .278)	3.50	1.55	.45
☐ 28B Leon Wagner (BA: .272)	20.00	9.00	2.50
☐ 29 Albie Pearson	3.50	1.55	.45
☐ 30 Lee Thomas UER (Photo actually George Thomas)	100.00	45.00	12.50
☐ 31 Bob Rodgers	3.50	1.55	.45
☐ 32 Dean Chance	3.50	1.55	.45
☐ 33 Ken McBride	3.50	1.55	.45
☐ 34 George Thomas UER (Photo actually Lee Thomas)	3.50	1.55	.45
☐ 35 Joe Cunningham	3.50	1.55	.45
☐ 36 Nellie Fox	8.00	3.60	1.00
☐ 37 Luis Aparicio	8.00	3.60	1.00
☐ 38 Al Smith	45.00	20.00	5.50
☐ 39 Floyd Robinson	125.00	55.00	15.50
☐ 40 Jim Landis	3.50	1.55	.45
☐ 41 Charlie Maxwell	3.50	1.55	.45
☐ 42 Sherman Lollar	3.50	1.55	.45
☐ 43 Early Wynn	8.00	3.60	1.00
☐ 44 Juan Pizarro	3.50	1.55	.45
☐ 45 Ray Herbert	3.50	1.55	.45
☐ 46 Norm Cash	5.00	2.20	.60
☐ 47 Steve Boros	3.50	1.55	.45
☐ 48 Dick McAuliffe	25.00	11.00	3.10
☐ 49 Bill Bruton	5.00	2.20	.60
☐ 50 Rocky Colavito	6.00	2.70	.75
☐ 51 Al Kaline	25.00	11.00	3.10
☐ 52 Dick Brown	3.50	1.55	.45
☐ 53 Jim Bunning	200.00	90.00	25.00
☐ 54 Hank Aguirre	3.50	1.55	.45
☐ 55 Frank Lary	3.50	1.55	.45
☐ 56 Don Mossi	3.50	1.55	.45
☐ 57 Jim Gentile	3.50	1.55	.45
☐ 58 Jackie Brandt	3.50	1.55	.45
☐ 59 Brooks Robinson	25.00	11.00	3.10
☐ 60 Ron Hansen	5.00	2.20	.60
☐ 61 Jerry Adair	200.00	90.00	25.00
☐ 62 Boog Powell	6.00	2.70	.75
☐ 63 Russ Snyder	3.50	1.55	.45
☐ 64 Steve Barber	3.50	1.55	.45
☐ 65 Milt Pappas	5.00	2.20	.60
☐ 66 Robin Roberts	8.00	3.60	1.00
☐ 67 Tito Francona	3.50	1.55	.45
☐ 68 Jerry Kindall	3.50	1.55	.45
☐ 69 Woody Held	3.50	1.55	.45
☐ 70 Bubba Phillips	15.00	6.75	1.85
☐ 71 Chuck Essegian	3.50	1.55	.45
☐ 72 Willie Kirkland	3.50	1.55	.45
☐ 73 Al Luplow	3.50	1.55	.45
☐ 74 Ty Cline	3.50	1.55	.45
☐ 75 Dick Donovan	3.50	1.55	.45
☐ 76 John Romano	3.50	1.55	.45
☐ 77 Pete Runnels	3.50	1.55	.45
☐ 78 Ed Bressoud	3.50	1.55	.45
☐ 79 Frank Malzone	3.50	1.55	.45
☐ 80 Carl Yastrzemski	300.00	135.00	38.00
☐ 81 Gary Geiger	3.50	1.55	.45
☐ 82 Lou Clinton	3.50	1.55	.45
☐ 83 Earl Wilson	3.50	1.55	.45
☐ 84 Bill Monbouquette	3.50	1.55	.45
☐ 85 Norm Siebern	3.50	1.55	.45
☐ 86 Jerry Lumpe	125.00	55.00	15.50
☐ 87 Manny Jimenez	125.00	55.00	15.50
☐ 88 Gino Cimoli	3.50	1.55	.45
☐ 89 Ed Charles	3.50	1.55	.45
☐ 90 Ed Rakow	3.50	1.55	.45
☐ 91 Bob Del Greco	3.50	1.55	.45
☐ 92 Haywood Sullivan	3.50	1.55	.45
☐ 93 Chuck Hinton	3.50	1.55	.45
☐ 94 Ken Retzer	3.50	1.55	.45
☐ 95 Harry Bright	3.50	1.55	.45
☐ 96 Bob Johnson	3.50	1.55	.45
☐ 97 Dave Stenhouse	15.00	6.75	1.85
☐ 98 Chuck Cottier	25.00	11.00	3.10
☐ 99 Tom Cheney	3.50	1.55	.45
☐ 100 Claude Osteen	15.00	6.75	1.85
☐ 101 Orlando Cepeda	6.00	2.70	.75
☐ 102 Chuck Hiller	3.50	1.55	.45
☐ 103 Jose Pagan	3.50	1.55	.45
☐ 104 Jim Davenport	3.50	1.55	.45
☐ 105 Harvey Kuenn	5.00	2.20	.60
☐ 106 Willie Mays	50.00	22.00	6.25
☐ 107 Felipe Alou	5.00	2.20	.60
☐ 108 Tom Haller	125.00	55.00	15.50
☐ 109 Juan Marichal	8.00	3.60	1.00
☐ 110 Jack Sanford	3.50	1.55	.45
☐ 111 Bill O'Dell	3.50	1.55	.45
☐ 112 Willie McCovey	10.00	4.50	1.25
☐ 113 Lee Walls	3.50	1.55	.45
☐ 114 Jim Gilliam	6.00	2.70	.75
☐ 115 Maury Wills	6.00	2.70	.75
☐ 116 Ron Fairly	3.50	1.55	.45
☐ 117 Tommy Davis	5.00	2.20	.60
☐ 118 Duke Snider	10.00	4.50	1.25
☐ 119 Willie Davis	200.00	90.00	25.00
☐ 120 John Roseboro	3.50	1.55	.45
☐ 121 Sandy Koufax	35.00	16.00	4.40
☐ 122 Stan Williams	3.50	1.55	.45
☐ 123 Don Drysdale	9.00	4.00	1.10
☐ 124 Daryl Spencer	3.50	1.55	.45
☐ 125 Gordy Coleman	3.50	1.55	.45
☐ 126 Don Blasingame	3.50	1.55	.45
☐ 127 Leo Cardenas	3.50	1.55	.45
☐ 128 Eddie Kasko	200.00	90.00	25.00
☐ 129 Jerry Lynch	15.00	6.75	1.85
☐ 130 Vada Pinson	6.00	2.70	.75
☐ 131A Frank Robinson (No stripes)	25.00	11.00	3.10
☐ 131B Frank Robinson (Stripes on hat)	50.00	22.00	6.25
☐ 132 John Edwards	3.50	1.55	.45
☐ 133 Joey Jay	3.50	1.55	.45
☐ 134 Bob Purkey	3.50	1.55	.45
☐ 135 Marty Keough	30.00	13.50	3.70
☐ 136 Jim O'Toole	3.50	1.55	.45
☐ 137 Dick Stuart	3.50	1.55	.45
☐ 138 Bill Mazeroski	6.00	2.70	.75
☐ 139 Dick Groat	5.00	2.20	.60
☐ 140 Don Hoak	35.00	16.00	4.40
☐ 141 Bob Skinner	20.00	9.00	2.50
☐ 142 Bill Virdon	5.00	2.20	.60
☐ 143 Roberto Clemente	60.00	27.00	7.50
☐ 144 Smoky Burgess	5.00	2.20	.60
☐ 145 Bob Friend	3.50	1.55	.45
☐ 146 Al McBean	3.50	1.55	.45
☐ 147 Elroy Face	5.00	2.20	.60
☐ 148 Joe Adcock	5.00	2.20	.60
☐ 149 Frank Bolling	3.50	1.55	.45
☐ 150 Roy McMillan	3.50	1.55	.45
☐ 151 Eddie Mathews	20.00	9.00	2.50
☐ 152 Hank Aaron	125.00	55.00	15.50
☐ 153 Del Crandall	35.00	16.00	4.40
☐ 154A Bob Shaw COR	3.50	1.55	.45
☐ 154B Bob Shaw ERR (Two "in 1959" in same sentence)	15.00	6.75	1.85
☐ 155 Lew Burdette	5.00	2.20	.60
☐ 156 Joe Torre	6.00	2.70	.75
☐ 157 Tony Cloninger	3.50	1.55	.45
☐ 158A Bill White (Ht. 6'0")	5.00	2.20	.60
☐ 158B Bill White (Ht. 6';)	5.00	2.20	.60
☐ 159 Julian Javier	3.50	1.55	.45
☐ 160 Ken Boyer	6.00	2.70	.75
☐ 161 Julio Gotay	3.50	1.55	.45
☐ 162 Curt Flood	125.00	55.00	15.50
☐ 163 Charlie James	3.50	1.55	.45
☐ 164 Gene Oliver	3.50	1.55	.45
☐ 165 Ernie Broglio	3.50	1.55	.45
☐ 166 Bob Gibson	9.00	4.00	1.10
☐ 167A Lindy McDaniel (No asterisk)	6.00	2.70	.75
☐ 167B Lindy McDaniel (Asterisk traded line)	6.00	2.70	.75
☐ 168 Ray Washburn	3.50	1.55	.45
☐ 169 Ernie Banks	20.00	9.00	2.50
☐ 170 Ron Santo	6.00	2.70	.75
☐ 171 George Altman	3.50	1.55	.45
☐ 172 Billy Williams	150.00	70.00	19.00
☐ 173 Andre Rodgers	15.00	6.75	1.85
☐ 174 Ken Hubbs	30.00	13.50	3.70
☐ 175 Don Landrum	3.50	1.55	.45
☐ 176 Dick Bertell	20.00	9.00	2.50
☐ 177 Roy Sievers	3.50	1.55	.45
☐ 178 Tony Taylor	3.50	1.55	.45
☐ 179 John Callison	3.50	1.55	.45
☐ 180 Don Demeter	3.50	1.55	.45
☐ 181 Tony Gonzalez	15.00	6.75	1.85
☐ 182 Wes Covington	25.00	11.00	3.10
☐ 183 Art Mahaffey	3.50	1.55	.45
☐ 184 Clay Dalrymple	3.50	1.55	.45
☐ 185 Al Spangler	3.50	1.55	.45
☐ 186 Roman Mejias	3.50	1.55	.45
☐ 187 Bob Aspromonte	375.00	170.00	47.50
☐ 188 Norm Larker	35.00	16.00	4.40
☐ 189 Johnny Temple	3.50	1.55	.45
☐ 190 Carl Warwick	3.50	1.55	.45
☐ 191 Bob Lillis	3.50	1.55	.45
☐ 192 Dick Farrell	3.50	1.55	.45
☐ 193 Gil Hodges	10.00	4.50	1.25
☐ 194 Marv Throneberry	5.00	2.20	.60
☐ 195 Charlie Neal	10.00	4.50	1.25
☐ 196 Frank Thomas	225.00	100.00	28.00
☐ 197 Richie Ashburn	30.00	13.50	3.70
☐ 198 Felix Mantilla	3.50	1.55	.45
☐ 199 Rod Kanehl	20.00	9.00	2.50
☐ 200 Roger Craig	5.00	2.20	.60

1979 Post Garvey Tips

These "Baseball Tips" were printed on boxes of Post Raisin Bran cereal in 1979. Cards 1-6 were on 15 oz. boxes and cards 7-12 were on the larger 20 oz. boxes. The cards are blank backed and feature a lime green background color with a red stitching border around the card. The cards measure approximately 7" by 2 1/16" although as with most

cereal cards they are frequently found badly cut. The set essentially consists of Steve Garvey's advice or tips on various segments and aspects of the game of baseball. Each card shows a crude line drawing demonstrating the skill discussed in the narrative on the card. Each card contains a color drawing of Steve Garvey in the upper left corner of the card along with his facsimile autograph.

	NRMT	VG-E	GOOD
COMPLETE SET (12)	20.00	9.00	2.50
COMMON CARD (1-6)	2.00	.90	.25
COMMON CARD (7-12)	2.50	1.10	.30
☐ 1 The Batting Stance	2.00	.90	.25
☐ 2 Bunting	2.00	.90	.25
☐ 3 Rounding First Base	2.00	.90	.25
☐ 4 The Grip in Throwing	2.00	.90	.25
☐ 5 Fielding a Pop-Up	2.00	.90	.25
☐ 6 Proper Fielding Stances	2.00	.90	.25
☐ 7 On Deck Observation	2.50	1.10	.30
☐ 8 Sliding	2.50	1.10	.30
☐ 9 Hitting to the Opposite Field	2.50	1.10	.30
☐ 10 Throwing from the Outfield	2.50	1.10	.30
☐ 11 Mental Preparation for Each Play	2.50	1.10	.30
☐ 12 Total Conditioning	2.50	1.10	.30

1990 Post

1990 Post Cereal is a 30-card standard-size set issued with the assistance of Mike Schechter Associates. The sets do not have either team logos or other uniform identification on them. There is also a facsimile autograph on the back of the cards. The cards were inserted randomly as a cello pack (with three cards) inside specially marked boxes of Post cereals. The cards feature red, white, and blue fronts with the words, "First Collector Series". Card backs feature a facsimile autograph.

	MINT	NRMT	EXC
COMPLETE SET (30)	8.00	3.60	1.00
COMMON CARD (1-30)	.10	.05	.01
☐ 1 Don Mattingly	1.50	.70	.19
☐ 2 Roger Clemens	.50	.23	.06
☐ 3 Kirby Puckett	1.50	.70	.19
☐ 4 George Brett	1.25	.55	.16
☐ 5 Tony Gwynn	1.25	.55	.16
☐ 6 Ozzie Smith	1.00	.45	.12
☐ 7 Will Clark	.50	.23	.06
☐ 8 Orel Hershiser	.20	.09	.03
☐ 9 Ryne Sandberg	1.00	.45	.12
☐ 10 Darryl Strawberry	.20	.09	.03
☐ 11 Nolan Ryan	2.50	1.10	.30
☐ 12 Mark McGwire	.60	.25	.07
☐ 13 Jim Abbott	.10	.05	.01
☐ 14 Bo Jackson	.20	.09	.03
☐ 15 Kevin Mitchell	.10	.05	.01
☐ 16 Jose Canseco	.50	.23	.06
☐ 17 Wade Boggs	.30	.14	.04
☐ 18 Dale Murphy	.25	.11	.03
☐ 19 Mark Grace	.40	.18	.05
☐ 20 Mike Scott	.10	.05	.01
☐ 21 Cal Ripken	2.50	1.10	.30
☐ 22 Pedro Guerrero	.10	.05	.01
☐ 23 Ken Griffey Jr.	3.00	1.35	.35
☐ 24 Eric Davis	.20	.09	.03
☐ 25 Rickey Henderson	.30	.14	.04
☐ 26 Robin Yount	.25	.11	.03
☐ 27 Von Hayes	.10	.05	.01
☐ 28 Alan Trammell	.20	.09	.03
☐ 29 Dwight Gooden	.20	.09	.03
☐ 30 Joe Carter	.20	.09	.03

1991 Post

This 30-card standard-size set was released early in 1991 by Post Cereal in conjunction with Michael Schechter Associates (MSA). The

players pictured are some of the star players of baseball entering the 1991 season. The design of the set features the Post logo in the upper left hand corner, the MLB logo in the upper right hand corner, and the players name and team underneath the portrait shot of the player pictured on the card. The cards were inserted three-at-a-time in boxes of the following cereals: Post Honeycomb, Super Golden Crisp, Cocoa Pebbles, Fruity Pebbles, Alpha-Bits, and Marshmallow Alpha-Bits. The fronts feature either posed or action color player photos, with blue and yellow borders. The words "1991 Collector Series" appear in a white stripe at the card top. Some cards (numbers 1, 6, 25, and 30) have a banner at the top that reads "Rookie Star". The player's name is given in a white stripe below the picture. The horizontally oriented backs are printed in aqua and dark blue on white and present complete Major League statistical information and a facsimile autograph on the bottom of the card.

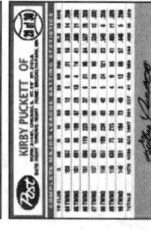

	MINT	NRMT	EXC
COMPLETE SET (30)	8.00	3.60	1.00
COMMON CARD (1-30)	.05	.02	.01
☐ 1 Dave Justice	.20	.09	.03
☐ 2 Mark McGwire	1.00	.45	.12
☐ 3 Will Clark	.25	.11	.03
☐ 4 Jose Canseco	.25	.11	.03
☐ 5 Vince Coleman	.05	.02	.01
☐ 6 Sandy Alomar Jr.	.10	.05	.01
☐ 7 Darryl Strawberry	.10	.05	.01
☐ 8 Len Dykstra	.10	.05	.01
☐ 9 Gregg Jefferies	.10	.05	.01
☐ 10 Tony Gwynn	1.25	.55	.16
☐ 11 Ken Griffey Jr.	3.00	1.35	.35
☐ 12 Roger Clemens	.40	.18	.05
☐ 13 Chris Sabo	.05	.02	.01
☐ 14 Bobby Bonilla	.10	.05	.01
☐ 15 Gary Sheffield	.50	.23	.06
☐ 16 Ryne Sandberg	1.00	.45	.12
☐ 17 Nolan Ryan	2.50	1.10	.30
☐ 18 Barry Larkin	.20	.09	.03
☐ 19 Cal Ripken	2.50	1.10	.30
☐ 20 Jim Abbott	.05	.02	.01
☐ 21 Barry Bonds	.50	.23	.06
☐ 22 Mark Grace	.40	.18	.05
☐ 23 Cecil Fielder	.10	.05	.01
☐ 24 Kevin Mitchell	.05	.02	.01
☐ 25 Todd Zeile	.05	.02	.01
☐ 26 George Brett	1.25	.55	.16
☐ 27 Rickey Henderson	.40	.18	.05
☐ 28 Kirby Puckett	1.50	.70	.19
☐ 29 Don Mattingly	1.50	.70	.19
☐ 30 Kevin Maas	.05	.02	.01

1991 Post Canadian

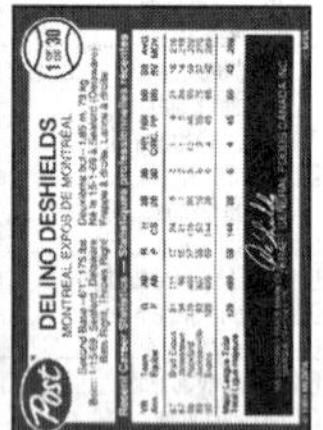

This 30-card Super Stars set was sponsored by Post and features 14 National League and 16 American League players. Two cards were inserted in specially marked boxes of Post Alpha-Bits, Sugar Crisp and Honeycomb sold in Canada. The cards measure the standard size and are bilingual (French and English) on both sides. While all the cards feature color player photos (action or posed) on the fronts, the NL cards (1-14) are accentuated with red stripes while the AL cards (15-30) have royal blue stripes. In a horizontal format, the backs have biography, recent career statistics and a facsimile autograph. The cards are numbered on the back. The side panel also included a checklist, an offer for a baseball player poster-album and an offer to order ten additional cards to complete the set.

	MINT	NRMT	EXC
COMPLETE SET (30)	15.00	6.75	1.85
COMMON CARD (1-30)	.10	.05	.01
☐ 1 Delino DeShields	.10	.05	.01
☐ 2 Tim Wallach	.10	.05	.01
☐ 3 Andres Galarraga	.25	.11	.03
☐ 4 Dave Magadan	.10	.05	.01
☐ 5 Barry Bonds UER (Career BA .256, should be .265)	1.00	.45	.12
☐ 6 Len Dykstra	.20	.09	.03
☐ 7 Andre Dawson	.25	.11	.03
☐ 8 Ozzie Smith	1.25	.55	.16
☐ 9 Will Clark	1.00	.45	.12
☐ 10 Chris Sabo	.10	.05	.01
☐ 11 Eddie Murray	.75	.35	.09
☐ 12 Dave Justice	.40	.18	.05
☐ 13 Benito Santiago	.10	.05	.01
☐ 14 Glenn Davis	.10	.05	.01
☐ 15 Kelly Gruber	.10	.05	.01
☐ 16 Dave Stieb	.10	.05	.01
☐ 17 John Olerud	.20	.09	.03
☐ 18 Roger Clemens	1.00	.45	.12
☐ 19 Cecil Fielder	.20	.09	.03
☐ 20 Kevin Maas	.10	.05	.01
☐ 21 Robin Yount	.50	.23	.06
☐ 22 Cal Ripken	3.00	1.35	.35
☐ 23 Sandy Alomar Jr.	.20	.09	.03
☐ 24 Rickey Henderson	.40	.18	.05
☐ 25 Bobby Thigpen	.10	.05	.01
☐ 26 Ken Griffey Jr.	4.00	1.80	.50
☐ 27 Nolan Ryan	3.00	1.35	.35
☐ 28 Dave Winfield	.50	.23	.06
☐ 29 George Brett	1.50	.70	.19
☐ 30 Kirby Puckett	2.00	.90	.25

1992 Post

This 30-card standard-size set was manufactured by MSA (Michael Schechter Associates) for Post Cereal. Three-card packs were inserted in the following Post cereals: Honeycomb, Super Golden Crisp, Cocoa Pebbles, Fruity Pebbles, Alpha-Bits, Marshmallow Alpha-Bits and, for the first time, Raisin Bran. In the last-mentioned cereal, the cards were protected in cello packs that also had a 50 cent manufacturers coupon good on the next purchase. The other cereals contained tan paper wrapped packs. The complete set could also be obtained via a mail-in offer for 1.00 and five UPC symbols. The fronts feature either posed or action color player photos. A royal blue stripe, which borders the card top, intersects the Post logo at the upper left corner. The player's name and team name appear in a red stripe at the card bottom. The Bagwell and Knoblauch cards display the words "Rookie Star" in a yellow banner at the card top. The horizontally oriented backs show red-bordered posed or action color player photos with biography, statistics and a facsimile autograph on a light-blue box.

	MINT	NRMT	EXC
COMPLETE SET (30)	6.00	2.70	.75
COMMON CARD (1-30)	.05	.02	.01
☐ 1 Jeff Bagwell	.75	.35	.09
☐ 2 Ryne Sandberg	.60	.25	.07
☐ 3 Don Mattingly	1.00	.45	.12
☐ 4 Wally Joyner	.05	.02	.01
☐ 5 Dwight Gooden	.10	.05	.01
☐ 6 Chuck Knoblauch	.50	.23	.06
☐ 7 Kirby Puckett	1.00	.45	.12
☐ 8 Ozzie Smith	.60	.25	.07
☐ 9 Cal Ripken	1.50	.70	.19
☐ 10 Darryl Strawberry	.10	.05	.01
☐ 11 George Brett	.75	.35	.09
☐ 12 Joe Carter	.10	.05	.01
☐ 13 Cecil Fielder	.10	.05	.01
☐ 14 Will Clark	.40	.18	.05
☐ 15 Barry Bonds	.40	.18	.05
☐ 16 Roger Clemens	.40	.18	.05
☐ 17 Paul Molitor	.40	.18	.05
☐ 18 Scott Erickson	.05	.02	.01
☐ 19 Wade Boggs	.30	.14	.04
☐ 20 Ken Griffey Jr.	2.00	.90	.25
☐ 21 Bobby Bonilla	.10	.05	.01
☐ 22 Terry Pendleton	.05	.02	.01
☐ 23 Barry Larkin	.25	.11	.03
☐ 24 Frank Thomas	2.00	.90	.25
☐ 25 Jose Canseco	.40	.18	.05
☐ 26 Tony Gwynn	.75	.35	.09
☐ 27 Nolan Ryan	1.50	.70	.19
☐ 28 Howard Johnson	.05	.02	.01
☐ 29 Dave Justice	.25	.11	.03
☐ 30 Danny Tartabull	.05	.02	.01

1992 Post Canadian

This 18-card Post Super Star II stand-up set was sponsored by Post and measures the standard size. The set features nine American League and nine National League players and is bilingual (French and English) on both sides. The fronts show posed color player photos with team logos airbrushed out. The NL cards (1-9) are accented with a red stripe at the top and bottom of the photo and the AL cards (10-18) are accented with blue stripes. The Post and MLB logos appear in the bottom stripe along with the player's name and team. The backs feature perforated color action player photos that can be displayed standing. As on the front, the NL photos on the back are bordered in red and the AL in blue. The player's name appears in the bottom border.

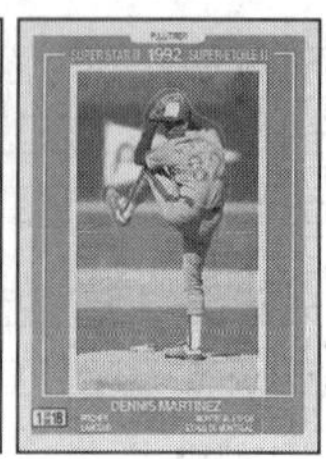

	MINT	NRMT	EXC
COMPLETE SET (18)	15.00	6.75	1.85
COMMON CARD (1-18)	.30	.14	.04
☐ 1 Dennis Martinez	.30	.14	.04
☐ 2 Benito Santiago	.30	.14	.04
☐ 3 Will Clark	.75	.35	.09
☐ 4 Ryne Sandberg	2.50	1.10	.30
☐ 5 Tim Wallach	.30	.14	.04
☐ 6 Ozzie Smith	2.50	1.10	.30
☐ 7 Darryl Strawberry	.50	.23	.06
☐ 8 Brett Butler	.30	.14	.04
☐ 9 Barry Bonds	1.00	.45	.12
☐ 10 Roger Clemens	1.25	.55	.16
☐ 11 Sandy Alomar Jr.	.50	.23	.06
☐ 12 Cecil Fielder	.50	.23	.06
☐ 13 Roberto Alomar	1.00	.45	.12
☐ 14 Kelly Gruber	.30	.14	.04
☐ 15 Cal Ripken	5.00	2.20	.60
☐ 16 Jose Canseco	1.00	.45	.12
☐ 17 Kirby Puckett	2.50	1.10	.30
☐ 18 Rickey Henderson	.75	.35	.09

1993 Post

This 30-card standard-size set features full-bleed action color player photos. The pictures are bordered on two sides by a black stripe containing the phrase "1993 Collector Series" and the player's team and position. A red bar across the bottom of the photo is printed with the player's name. The horizontal backs are black and carry biographical information, career highlights, and statistics. A close-up photo appears at the upper right corner. A red bar containing a facsimile autograph divides the statistics from the other information. Three-packs of cards were found in specially marked boxes of Post Cereal during this promotion. In addition, complete sets were available as a mail-in for five proofs of purchase from any Post Cereal plus 1.00.

	MINT	NRMT	EXC
COMPLETE SET (30)	6.00	2.70	.75
COMMON CARD (1-30)	.05	.02	.01
☐ 1 Dave Fleming	.05	.02	.01
☐ 2 Will Clark	.30	.14	.04
☐ 3 Kirby Puckett	1.00	.45	.12
☐ 4 Roger Clemens	.25	.11	.03
☐ 5 Fred McGriff	.15	.07	.02
☐ 6 Eric Karros	.25	.11	.03
☐ 7 Ken Griffey Jr.	2.00	.90	.25
☐ 8 Tony Gwynn	.75	.35	.09
☐ 9 Cal Ripken	1.50	.70	.19
☐ 10 Cecil Fielder	.10	.05	.01
☐ 11 Gary Sheffield	.30	.14	.04
☐ 12 Don Mattingly	1.00	.45	.12
☐ 13 Ryne Sandberg	.60	.25	.07
☐ 14 Frank Thomas	2.00	.90	.25
☐ 15 Barry Bonds	.40	.18	.05
☐ 16 Paul Molitor	.40	.18	.05
☐ 17 Terry Pendleton	.05	.02	.01
☐ 18 Darren Daulton	.10	.05	.01
☐ 19 Mark McGwire	.60	.25	.07
☐ 20 Nolan Ryan	1.50	.70	.19
☐ 21 Tom Glavine	.25	.11	.03
☐ 22 Roberto Alomar	.50	.23	.06
☐ 23 Juan Gonzalez	1.00	.45	.12
☐ 24 Bobby Bonilla	.10	.05	.01
☐ 25 George Brett	.75	.35	.09
☐ 26 Ozzie Smith	.60	.25	.07
☐ 27 Andy Van Slyke	.05	.02	.01
☐ 28 Barry Larkin	.15	.07	.02
☐ 29 John Kruk	.10	.05	.01
☐ 30 Robin Yount	.20	.09	.03

1993 Post Canadian

This 18-card limited edition stand-up set was sponsored by Post and measures the standard size. The set features American League (1-9) and National League (10-18) players and is printed in French and English. The fronts display color action photos with the team logo

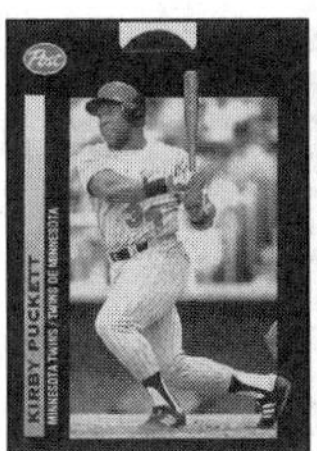

airbrushed out. The black borders have the words "Edition Limite, 1993 Limited Edition" printed in gold lettering at the top and the player's name, position and team printed below the photo. The Post logo appears in the lower left corner. The backs carry a second color action photo with the AL players' names on a blue stripe along the left side and the NL players' names on a bright pink stripe. The cards are numbered on the front.

	MINT	NRMT	EXC
COMPLETE SET (18)	15.00	6.75	1.85
COMMON CARD (1-18)	.15	.07	.02
☐ 1 Pat Borders	.15	.07	.02
☐ 2 Juan Guzman	.15	.07	.02
☐ 3 Roger Clemens	.75	.35	.09
☐ 4 Joe Carter	.50	.23	.06
☐ 5 Roberto Alomar	1.00	.45	.12
☐ 6 Robin Yount	.60	.25	.07
☐ 7 Cal Ripken	3.00	1.35	.35
☐ 8 Kirby Puckett	2.00	.90	.25
☐ 9 Ken Griffey Jr.	4.00	1.80	.50
☐ 10 Darren Daulton	.20	.09	.03
☐ 11 Andy Van Slyke	.15	.07	.02
☐ 12 Bobby Bonilla	.25	.11	.03
☐ 13 Larry Walker	.50	.23	.06
☐ 14 Ryne Sandberg	1.50	.70	.19
☐ 15 Barry Larkin	.50	.23	.06
☐ 16 Gary Sheffield	.60	.25	.07
☐ 17 Ozzie Smith	1.25	.55	.16
☐ 18 Terry Pendleton	.15	.07	.02

1994 Post

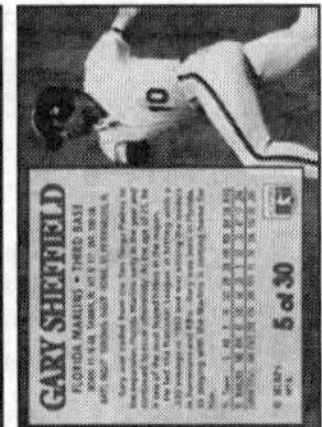

This 30-card standard-size set was sponsored by Post and produced by MSA (Michael Schlechter Associates). The fronts feature color action player photos inside a gold inner border and a forest green marbleized outer border. At the bottom of the picture, a red diagonal stripe with the player's name and team name edges a black triangle that carries the facsimile autograph in gold ink. On the forest green marbleized background, the backs present player information (biography, player profile, and statistics) on a pastel colored panel alongside a color player cutout. As is customary with an MSA set, the set is devoid of team logos or insignias. The cards are numbered on the back "X of 30."

	MINT	NRMT	EXC
COMPLETE SET (30)	5.00	2.20	.60
COMMON CARD (1-30)	.05	.02	.01
☐ 1 Mike Piazza	1.00	.45	.12
☐ 2 Don Mattingly	.75	.35	.09
☐ 3 Juan Gonzalez	.75	.35	.09
☐ 4 Kirby Puckett	.75	.35	.09
☐ 5 Gary Sheffield	.25	.11	.03
☐ 6 Dave Justice	.20	.09	.03
☐ 7 Jack McDowell	.05	.02	.01
☐ 8 Mo Vaughn	.30	.14	.04
☐ 9 Darren Daulton	.10	.05	.01
☐ 10 Bobby Bonilla	.10	.05	.01
☐ 11 Barry Bonds	.30	.14	.04
☐ 12 Barry Larkin	.20	.09	.03
☐ 13 Tony Gwynn	.60	.25	.07
☐ 14 Mark Grace	.25	.11	.03
☐ 15 Ken Griffey Jr.	1.50	.70	.19
☐ 16 Tom Glavine	.20	.09	.03
☐ 17 Cecil Fielder	.10	.05	.01
☐ 18 Roberto Alomar	.50	.23	.06
☐ 19 Mark Whiten	.05	.02	.01
☐ 20 Lenny Dykstra	.10	.05	.01
☐ 21 Frank Thomas	1.50	.70	.19
☐ 22 Will Clark	.25	.11	.03
☐ 23 Andres Galarraga	.20	.09	.03
☐ 24 John Olerud	.10	.05	.01
☐ 25 Cal Ripken	1.25	.55	.16
☐ 26 Tim Salmon	.25	.11	.03
☐ 27 Albert Belle	.75	.35	.09
☐ 28 Gregg Jefferies	.10	.05	.01
☐ 29 Jeff Bagwell	.60	.25	.07
☐ 30 Orlando Merced	.05	.02	.01

1994 Post Canadian

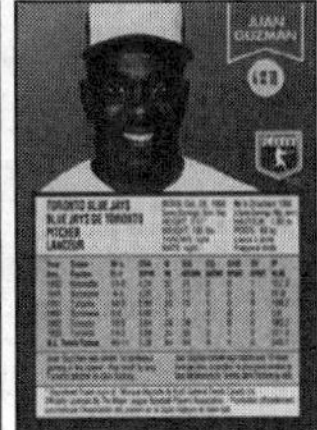

This 18-card set was distributed as single cello-wrapped cards in Canadian Post Alpha-Bits, Honeycomb, Sugar-Crisp, and Marshmallow Alpha-Bits. The cards are slightly smaller than standard-size, measuring 2 1/2" by 3 3/8". Randomly inserted throughout the boxes were Joe Carter HERO cards; 1,000 of these were personally signed. Odds of finding a HERO card were about 1 in 16; odds for finding a signed HERO card were 1 in 3,000. The entire set was available through a mail-in offer for 7 UPC's and $3.49 for postage and handling. An album to display the cards was offered for 2 UPC's and $5.99, plus $4.50 for postage and handling. The fronts feature color player action shots on their borderless fronts. The player's name, team name, and position appear in English and French in a purplish banner near the bottom. The back carries a color player head shot at the top, with his name appearing in yellow lettering at the upper right. Team name, position, biography, statistics, and career highlights in English and French round out the card. The cards are numbered on the back as "X of 18."

	MINT	EXC	G-VG
COMMON PLAYER (1-18)	20.00	9.00	2.50
COMMON CARD (1-18)	.25	.11	.03
*GOLD: 4X BASIC CARDS			
☐ 1 Joe Carter	.50	.23	.06
☐ 2 Paul Molitor	1.00	.45	.12
☐ 3 Roberto Alomar	1.25	.55	.16
☐ 4 John Olerud	.40	.18	.05
☐ 5 Dave Stewart	.40	.18	.05
☐ 6 Juan Guzman	.25	.11	.03
☐ 7 Pat Borders	.25	.11	.03
☐ 8 Larry Walker	.50	.23	.06
☐ 9 Moises Alou	.40	.18	.05
☐ 10 Ken Griffey Jr.	5.00	2.20	.60
☐ 11 Barry Bonds	1.25	.55	.16
☐ 12 Frank Thomas	5.00	2.20	.60
☐ 13 Cal Ripken	4.00	1.80	.50
☐ 14 Mike Piazza	3.00	1.35	.35
☐ 15 Juan Gonzalez	2.50	1.10	.30
☐ 16 Len Dykstra	.40	.18	.05
☐ 17 David Justice	.50	.23	.06
☐ 18 Kirby Puckett	2.50	1.10	.30
☐ NNO Joe Carter AU Hero Card	10.00	4.50	1.25

1995 Post

This 16 card standard-size set was distributed solely in limited in store promotions. Unlike previous years -- the cards were not available in cereal boxes nor directly from the company.

	MINT	NRMT	EXC
COMPLETE SET (16)	12.00	5.50	1.50
COMMON CARD (1-16)	.25	.11	.03
☐ 1 Wade Boggs	.40	.18	.05
☐ 2 Jeff Bagwell	1.25	.55	.16
☐ 3 Greg Maddux	1.75	.80	.22
☐ 4 Ken Griffey Jr.	3.00	1.35	.35
☐ 5 Roberto Alomar	.60	.25	.07
☐ 6 Kirby Puckett	1.50	.70	.19
☐ 7 Tony Gwynn	1.25	.55	.16
☐ 8 Cal Ripken, Jr.	2.50	1.10	.30
☐ 9 Matt Williams	.50	.23	.06
☐ 10 David Justice	.25	.11	.03
☐ 11 Barry Bonds	.75	.35	.09
☐ 12 Mike Piazza	2.00	.90	.25
☐ 13 Albert Belle	1.50	.70	.19
☐ 14 Frank Thomas	3.00	1.35	.35
☐ 15 Len Dykstra	.40	.18	.05
☐ 16 Will Clark	.50	.23	.06

1995 Post Canadian

This 18 card standard-size set was issued one per box. The set was also available via mail-order from the company.

	MINT	NRMT	EXC
COMPLETE SET (18)	50.00	22.00	6.25
COMMON CARD (1-18)	1.00	.45	.12
☐ 1 Ken Griffey, Jr.	10.00	4.50	1.25
☐ 2 Roberto Alomar	3.00	1.35	.35
☐ 3 Paul Molitor	2.50	1.10	.30
☐ 4 Devon White	1.00	.45	.12
☐ 5 Moises Alou	1.50	.70	.19
☐ 6 Ken Hill	1.00	.45	.12
☐ 7 Paul O'Neill	1.00	.45	.12
☐ 8 Joe Carter	2.00	.90	.25
☐ 9 Kirby Puckett	5.00	2.20	.60
☐ 10 Jimmy Key	1.00	.45	.12
☐ 11 Frank Thomas	10.00	4.50	1.25
☐ 12 David Cone	1.50	.70	.19
☐ 13 Tony Gwynn	4.00	1.80	.50
☐ 14 Matt Williams	2.50	1.10	.30
☐ 15 Greg Maddux	6.00	2.70	.75
☐ 16 Jeff Bagwell	4.00	1.80	.50
☐ 17 Barry Bonds	3.00	1.35	.35
☐ 18 Cal Ripken Jr.	8.00	3.60	1.00

1972 Pro Stars Postcards

Printed in Canada by Pro Star Promotions, these 37 blank-backed postcards measure approximately 3 1/2" by 5 1/2" and feature white-bordered color player photos. The player's name appears within the lower white border and also as a facsimile autograph across the bottom of the photo. The postcards are unnumbered and checklisted below in alphabetical order within the Expos team (1-12), National League (13-24) and American League (25-36). In addition to the 36 players listed below, the checklist also carries a listing for 12 posters of major league players.

	NRMT	VG-E	GOOD
COMPLETE SET (37)	100.00	45.00	12.50
COMMON EXPOS (1-12)	1.50	.70	.19
COMMON ALL-STAR (13-36)	2.00	.90	.25
☐ 1 Bob Bailey	2.00	.90	.25
☐ 2 John Boccabella	2.00	.90	.25
☐ 3 Boots Day	1.50	.70	.19
☐ 4 Jim Fairey	1.50	.70	.19
☐ 5 Tim Foli	1.50	.70	.19
☐ 6 Ron Hunt	1.50	.70	.19
☐ 7 Mike Jorgensen	1.50	.70	.19
☐ 8 Ernie McAnally	1.50	.70	.19
☐ 9 Carl Morton	1.50	.70	.19
☐ 10 Steve Renko	1.50	.70	.19
☐ 11 Ken Singleton	3.00	1.35	.35
☐ 12 Bill Stoneman	2.00	.90	.25
☐ 13 Hank Aaron	10.00	4.50	1.25
☐ 14 Johnny Bench	10.00	4.50	1.25
☐ 15 Roberto Clemente	15.00	6.75	1.85
☐ 16 Ferguson Jenkins	4.00	1.80	.50
☐ 17 Juan Marichal	4.00	1.80	.50
☐ 18 Willie Mays	10.00	4.50	1.25
☐ 19 Willie McCovey	6.00	2.70	.75
☐ 20 Frank Robinson	6.00	2.70	.75
☐ 21 Pete Rose	8.00	3.60	1.00
☐ 22 Tom Seaver	8.00	3.60	1.00
☐ 23 Willie Stargell	4.00	1.80	.50
☐ 24 Joe Torre	3.00	1.35	.35
☐ 25 Vida Blue	2.00	.90	.25
☐ 26 Reggie Jackson	8.00	3.60	1.00
☐ 27 Al Kaline	6.00	2.70	.75
☐ 28 Harmon Killebrew	4.00	1.80	.50
☐ 29 Mickey Lolich	3.00	1.35	.35
☐ 30 Dave McNally	2.00	.90	.25
☐ 31 Bill Melton	2.00	.90	.25
☐ 32 Bobby Murcer	3.00	1.35	.35
☐ 33 Fritz Peterson	2.00	.90	.25
☐ 34 Boog Powell	4.00	1.80	.50
☐ 35 Merv Rettenmund	2.00	.90	.25
☐ 36 Brooks Robinson	1.50	.70	.19
☐ 37 Checklist Card	2.00	.90	.25

1994 Pro Mags Promo

These three cards were issued to introduce Pro Mags to the collectible market. They measure 2 1/8 by 3 3/8" and have blank backs. The cards are numbered with a "Promo Mag" logo near the bottom.

	MINT	NRMT	EXC
COMPLETE SET (3)	12.00	5.50	1.50
COMMON CARD (1-3)	3.00	1.35	.35
☐ 1 Ken Griffey	5.00	2.20	.60
☐ 2 Greg Maddux	3.00	1.35	.35
☐ 3 Frank Thomas	5.00	2.20	.60

1994-95 Pro Mags

1994-95 Pro Mags were distributed in rack packs containing five random player magnets, one team magnet, and a checklist. Each player mag has rounded corners and measures 2 1/8" by 3 3/8" (team mags measure 2 1/8" by 3/4"). Fronts feature borderless color player action shots with name at the bottom and a team logo at upper left. The black magnetized backs are blank. The magnets are numbered on the front. Five hundred Joe Carter autograph magnets were randomly inserted into packs as well.

	MINT	NRMT	EXC
COMPLETE SET (140)	80.00	36.00	10.00
COMMON CARD (1-140)	.40	.18	.05
☐ 1 Terry Pendleton	.40	.18	.05
☐ 2 Ryan Klesko	1.25	.55	.16
☐ 3 Fred McGriff	1.50	.70	.19
☐ 4 David Justice	.75	.35	.09
☐ 5 Greg Maddux	3.50	1.55	.45
☐ 6 Brady Anderson	1.00	.45	.12
☐ 7 Ben McDonald	.40	.18	.05
☐ 8 Cal Ripken	5.00	2.20	.60
☐ 9 Mike Mussina	1.50	.70	.19
☐ 10 Jeffrey Hammonds	.40	.18	.05
☐ 11 Roger Clemens	1.50	.70	.19
☐ 12 Andre Dawson	.75	.35	.09
☐ 13 Mike Greenwell	.40	.18	.05
☐ 14 Mo Vaughn	2.00	.90	.25
☐ 15 Otis Nixon	.40	.18	.05
☐ 16 Chad Curtis	.40	.18	.05
☐ 17 Mark Langston	.40	.18	.05
☐ 18 Tim Salmon	1.00	.45	.12
☐ 19 Chuck Finley	.40	.18	.05
☐ 20 Eduardo Perez	.40	.18	.05
☐ 21 Steve Buechele	.40	.18	.05
☐ 22 Mark Grace	1.50	.70	.19
☐ 23 Sammy Sosa	1.25	.55	.16
☐ 24 Derrick May	.40	.18	.05
☐ 25 Shawon Dunston	.40	.18	.05
☐ 26 Jack McDowell	1.00	.45	.12
☐ 27 Tim Raines	.75	.35	.09
☐ 28 Frank Thomas	6.00	2.70	.75
☐ 29 Robin Ventura	.75	.35	.09
☐ 30 Julio Franco	.40	.18	.05
☐ 31 John Smiley	.40	.18	.05
☐ 32 Barry Larkin	1.50	.70	.19
☐ 33 Jose Rijo	.40	.18	.05
☐ 34 Reggie Sanders	.75	.35	.09
☐ 35 Kevin Mitchell	.40	.18	.05
☐ 36 Sandy Alomar	.75	.35	.09
☐ 37 Carlos Baerga	1.50	.70	.19
☐ 38 Albert Belle	3.00	1.35	.35
☐ 39 Manny Ramirez	1.25	.55	.16
☐ 40 Eddie Murray	1.25	.55	.16
☐ 41 Dante Bichette	1.00	.45	.12
☐ 42 Ellis Burks	.75	.35	.09
☐ 43 Andres Galarraga	1.00	.45	.12
☐ 44 Greg Harris	.40	.18	.05
☐ 45 David Nied	.40	.18	.05
☐ 46 Cecil Fielder	.75	.35	.09
☐ 47 Kirk Gibson	.75	.35	.09
☐ 48 Mickey Tettleton	.40	.18	.05
☐ 49 Lou Whitaker	.75	.35	.09
☐ 50 Travis Fryman	.75	.35	.09
☐ 51 Jeff Conine	.75	.35	.09
☐ 52 Charlie Hough	.75	.35	.09
☐ 53 Benito Santiago	.40	.18	.05
☐ 54 Gary Sheffield	1.25	.55	.16
☐ 55 Dave Magadan	.40	.18	.05
☐ 56 Jeff Bagwell	3.00	1.35	.35
☐ 57 Luis Gonzalez	.40	.18	.05
☐ 58 Andujar Cedeno	.40	.18	.05
☐ 59 Craig Biggio	.75	.35	.09
☐ 60 Doug Drabek	.40	.18	.05
☐ 61 Tom Gordon	.40	.18	.05
☐ 62 Brian McRae	.40	.18	.05
☐ 63 David Cone	.75	.35	.09
☐ 64 Wally Joyner	.40	.18	.05
☐ 65 Jeff Montgomery	.40	.18	.05
☐ 66 Eric Karros	.75	.35	.09
☐ 67 Tom Candiotti	.40	.18	.05
☐ 68 Delino DeShields	.40	.18	.05
☐ 69 Orel Hershiser	.75	.35	.09
☐ 70 Mike Piazza	3.50	1.55	.45
☐ 71 Darryl Hamilton	.40	.18	.05
☐ 72 Kevin Seitzer	.40	.18	.05
☐ 73 B.J. Surhoff	.75	.35	.09
☐ 74 John Jaha	.75	.35	.09
☐ 75 Greg Vaughn	.40	.18	.05
☐ 76 Kent Hrbek	.40	.18	.05
☐ 77 Kirby Puckett	3.00	1.35	.35

	MINT	NRMT	EXC
☐ 78 Kevin Tapani	.40	.18	.05
☐ 79 Dave Winfield	1.00	.45	.12
☐ 80 Chuck Knoblauch	1.50	.70	.19
☐ 81 Moises Alou	.75	.35	.09
☐ 82 Wil Cordero	.40	.18	.05
☐ 83 Marquis Grissom	.75	.35	.09
☐ 84 Pedro Martinez	.40	.18	.05
☐ 85 Larry Walker	1.00	.45	.12
☐ 86 Jim Abbott	.40	.18	.05
☐ 87 Wade Boggs	1.25	.55	.16
☐ 88 Don Mattingly	3.00	1.35	.35
☐ 89 Luis Polonia	.40	.18	.05
☐ 90 Danny Tartabull	.40	.18	.05
☐ 91 Bobby Bonilla	.75	.35	.09
☐ 92 Todd Hundley	.75	.35	.09
☐ 93 Dwight Gooden	.75	.35	.09
☐ 94 Jeromy Burnitz	.40	.18	.05
☐ 95 Bret Saberhagen	.40	.18	.05
☐ 96 Dennis Eckersley	.75	.35	.09
☐ 97 Mark McGwire	2.50	1.10	.30
☐ 98 Ruben Sierra	.40	.18	.05
☐ 99 Terry Steinbach	.40	.18	.05
☐ 100 Rickey Henderson	1.50	.70	.19
☐ 101 Darren Daulton	.75	.35	.09
☐ 102 Lenny Dykstra	.75	.35	.09
☐ 103 Dave Hollins	.40	.18	.05
☐ 104 John Kruk	.40	.18	.05
☐ 105 Curt Schilling	.40	.18	.05
☐ 106 Carlos Garcia	.40	.18	.05
☐ 107 Jay Bell	.40	.18	.05
☐ 108 Don Slaught	.40	.18	.05
☐ 109 Andy Van Slyke	.40	.18	.05
☐ 110 Orlando Merced	.40	.18	.05
☐ 111 Ray Lankford	.75	.35	.09
☐ 112 Mark Whiten	.40	.18	.05
☐ 113 Todd Zeile	.40	.18	.05
☐ 114 Ozzie Smith	2.50	1.10	.30
☐ 115 Gregg Jefferies	.40	.18	.05
☐ 116 Derek Bell	.75	.35	.09
☐ 117 Andy Benes	.40	.18	.05
☐ 118 Phil Plantier	.40	.18	.05
☐ 119 Tony Gwynn	3.00	1.35	.35
☐ 120 Bip Roberts	.40	.18	.05
☐ 121 Barry Bonds	2.00	.90	.25
☐ 122 John Burkett	.40	.18	.05
☐ 123 Robby Thompson	.40	.18	.05
☐ 124 Darren Lewis	.40	.18	.05
☐ 125 Willie McGee	.40	.18	.05
☐ 126 Jay Buhner	1.00	.45	.12
☐ 127 Ken Griffey Jr.	6.00	2.70	.75
☐ 128 Randy Johnson	1.25	.55	.16
☐ 129 Eric Anthony	.40	.18	.05
☐ 130 Edgar Martinez	.75	.35	.09
☐ 131 Kevin Brown	.75	.35	.09
☐ 132 Jose Canseco	1.50	.70	.19
☐ 133 Juan Gonzalez	3.00	1.35	.35
☐ 134 Will Clark	1.50	.70	.19
☐ 135 Ivan Rodriguez	1.50	.70	.19
☐ 136 Roberto Alomar	1.25	.55	.16
☐ 137 Joe Carter	.75	.35	.09
☐ 138 Juan Guzman	.40	.18	.05
☐ 139 Paul Molitor	1.50	.70	.19
☐ 140 John Olerud	.75	.35	.09

1996 Pro Mags All-Stars

These 24 magnet cards measure approximately 2" by 3 1/4". The set was distributed in 12-card packs for each league, including 10 players plus an All-Star Game logo and league logo card. The cards have rounded corners and the garish fronts feature the players portrait against either the National or American League background. There is also a league logo and a 1996 All-Star game logo on the front of the card. These cards are numbered in very small print in the lower left hand corner. The American League cards are 1-10, while the National League cards are #11-20.

	MINT	NRMT	EXC
COMPLETE SET (24)	50.00	22.00	6.25
COMMON CARD	.50	.23	.06
☐ 1 Brady Anderson	1.25	.55	.16
☐ 2 Jose Canseco	1.25	.55	.16
☐ 3 Ken Griffey Jr. UER NNO	10.00	4.50	1.25
☐ 4 Kenny Lofton	2.50	1.10	.30
☐ 5 Cal Ripken	8.00	3.60	1.00
☐ 6 Frank Thomas	10.00	4.50	1.25
☐ 7 Ivan Rodriguez	2.50	1.10	.30
☐ 8 Mo Vaughn	2.50	1.10	.30
☐ 9 Albert Belle	6.00	2.70	.75
☐ 10 Alex Rodriguez	10.00	4.50	1.25
☐ 11 Hideo Nomo	6.00	2.70	.75
☐ 12 Greg Maddux	6.00	2.70	.75
☐ 13 Jeff Bagwell	5.00	2.20	.60
☐ 14 Barry Bonds	2.50	1.10	.30
☐ 15 Ryan Klesko	2.00	.90	.25
☐ 16 Mike Piazza	6.00	2.70	.75
☐ 17 David Justice	1.00	.45	.12
☐ 18 Dante Bichette	1.50	.70	.19
☐ 19 Barry Larkin	1.50	.70	.19
☐ 20 Tony Gwynn	6.00	2.70	.75
☐ NNO American League Logo	.50	.23	.06
☐ NNO All-Star Game Logo	.50	.23	.06
☐ NNO National League Logo	.50	.23	.06
☐ NNO All-Star Game Logo	.50	.23	.06

1996 Pro Mags Die Cuts

This 25-card set was issued by Chris Martin Enterprises and features color action figures of some of the stars of Major League Baseball on a die-cut magnet.

	MINT	NRMT	EXC
COMPLETE SET (25)	75.00	34.00	9.50
COMMON CARD (1-25)	1.00	.45	.12
☐ 1 David Justice	1.50	.70	.19
☐ 2 Ryan Klesko	2.00	.90	.25
☐ 3 Fred McGriff	2.00	.90	.25
☐ 4 Cal Ripken Jr.	8.00	3.60	1.00
☐ 5 Bobby Bonilla	1.50	.70	.19
☐ 6 Mo Vaughn	2.50	1.10	.30
☐ 7 Tim Salmon	2.00	.90	.25
☐ 8 Frank Thomas	10.00	4.50	1.25
☐ 9 Barry Larkin	2.50	1.10	.30
☐ 10 Albert Belle	5.00	2.20	.60
☐ 11 Eddie Murray	2.50	1.10	.30
☐ 12 Dante Bichette	2.00	.90	.25
☐ 13 Andres Galarraga	2.00	.90	.25
☐ 14 Cecil Fielder	1.50	.70	.19
☐ 15 Hideo Nomo	4.00	1.80	.50
☐ 16 Mike Piazza	6.00	2.70	.75
☐ 17 Kirby Puckett	5.00	2.20	.60
☐ 18 Don Mattingly	5.00	2.20	.60
☐ 19 Tony Gwynn	4.00	1.80	.50
☐ 20 Barry Bonds	2.50	1.10	.30
☐ 21 Ken Griffey Jr.	10.00	4.50	1.25
☐ 22 Randy Johnson	2.00	.90	.25
☐ 23 Will Clark	2.00	.90	.25
☐ 24 Juan Gonzalez	5.00	2.20	.60
☐ 25 Joe Carter	1.50	.70	.19

1997 Pro Mags

This 79-magnet set is distributed in packs of five with a suggested retail price of $3.99. The fronts feature a color action player image on a white background with a player head photo and team name and logo in a side margin. The magnets are unnumbered and checklisted below in alphabetical order by team.

	MINT	NRMT	EXC
COMPLETE SET (79)	125.00	55.00	15.50
COMMON CARD (1-79)	.50	.23	.06
☐ 1 Andruw Jones	8.00	3.60	1.00
☐ 2 Chipper Jones	5.00	2.20	.60
☐ 3 Greg Maddux	5.00	2.20	.60
☐ 4 John Smoltz	2.00	.90	.25
☐ 5 Brian McRae	.50	.23	.06
☐ 6 Ryne Sandberg	3.00	1.35	.35
☐ 7 Sammy Sosa	2.00	.90	.25
☐ 8 Barry Larkin	1.50	.70	.19
☐ 9 Deion Sanders	1.50	.70	.19
☐ 10 Reggie Sanders	1.00	.45	.12
☐ 11 Dante Bichette	1.50	.70	.19
☐ 12 Ellis Burks	1.00	.45	.12
☐ 13 Andres Galarraga	1.50	.70	.19
☐ 14 Bobby Bonilla	1.00	.45	.12
☐ 15 Jeff Conine	1.00	.45	.12
☐ 16 Gary Sheffield	2.00	.90	.25
☐ 17 Jeff Bagwell	3.00	1.35	.35
☐ 18 Derek Bell	1.00	.45	.12
☐ 19 Shane Reynolds	.50	.23	.06
☐ 20 Eric Karros	1.00	.45	.12
☐ 21 Raul Mondesi	1.50	.70	.19
☐ 22 Hideo Nomo	3.00	1.35	.35
☐ 23 Mike Piazza	5.00	2.20	.60
☐ 24 Wil Cordero	.50	.23	.06
☐ 25 Henry Rodriguez	1.00	.45	.12
☐ 26 Rondell White	.50	.23	.06
☐ 27 Todd Hundley	1.00	.45	.12
☐ 28 Rey Ordonez	1.50	.70	.19
☐ 29 Paul Wilson	1.00	.45	.12
☐ 30 Gregg Jefferies	.50	.23	.06
☐ 31 Mickey Morandini	.50	.23	.06
☐ 32 Jason Kendall	1.00	.45	.12
☐ 33 Al Martin	.50	.23	.06
☐ 34 Brian Jordan	1.00	.45	.12
☐ 35 Ray Lankford	1.00	.45	.12
☐ 36 Tom Pagnozzi	.50	.23	.06
☐ 37 Ken Caminiti	2.00	.90	.25
☐ 38 Tony Gwynn	3.00	1.35	.35
☐ 39 Fernando Valenzuela	1.00	.45	.12
☐ 40 Barry Bonds	2.50	1.10	.30
☐ 41 Garret Anderson	.50	.23	.06
☐ 42 Tim Salmon	1.50	.70	.19
☐ 43 Roberto Alomar	2.50	1.10	.30
☐ 44 Brady Anderson	1.00	.45	.12
☐ 45 Mike Mussina	2.00	.90	.25
☐ 46 Cal Ripken	5.00	2.20	.60
☐ 47 Mike Maddux	.50	.23	.06
☐ 48 Mo Vaughn	3.00	1.35	.35
☐ 49 Tim Wakefield	.50	.23	.06
☐ 50 Albert Belle	4.00	1.80	.50
☐ 51 Frank Thomas	8.00	3.60	1.00
☐ 52 Robin Ventura	1.00	.45	.12
☐ 53 Kenny Lofton	2.50	1.10	.30
☐ 54 Manny Ramirez	2.50	1.10	.30
☐ 55 Travis Fryman	1.00	.45	.12
☐ 56 Kevin Appier	1.00	.45	.12
☐ 57 Johnny Damon	.50	.23	.06
☐ 58 Michael Tucker	.50	.23	.06
☐ 59 John Jaha	1.00	.45	.12
☐ 60 Pat Listach	.50	.23	.06
☐ 61 Marty Cordova	1.00	.45	.12
☐ 62 Chuck Knoblauch	2.00	.90	.25
☐ 63 Paul Molitor	2.50	1.10	.30
☐ 64 Derek Jeter	5.00	2.20	.60
☐ 65 Darryl Strawberry	1.00	.45	.12
☐ 66 Andy Pettitte	2.50	1.10	.30
☐ 67 Bernie Williams	2.50	1.10	.30
☐ 68 Geronimo Berrora	.50	.23	.06
☐ 69 Mark McGwire	3.00	1.35	.35
☐ 70 Jay Buhner	1.50	.70	.19
☐ 71 Ken Griffey, Jr.	8.00	3.60	1.00
☐ 72 Randy Johnson	2.00	.90	.25
☐ 73 Alex Rodriguez	8.00	3.60	1.00
☐ 74 Will Clark	1.50	.70	.19
☐ 75 Juan Gonzalez	4.00	1.80	.50
☐ 76 Ivan Rodriguez	2.50	1.10	.30
☐ 77 Joe Carter	1.00	.45	.12
☐ 78 Carlos Delgado	1.00	.45	.12
☐ 79 Pat Hentgen	1.00	.45	.12

1997 Pro Mags Inspirational Magnets

Randomly inserted in packs at the rate of one in 24, this six-magnet set features color player photos of some of the best and most inspiring players in Major League Baseball today.

	MINT	NRMT	EXC
COMPLETE SET (6)	50.00	22.00	6.25
COMMON CARD (1-6)	7.50	3.40	.95
☐ 1 Ken Griffey Jr.	12.00	5.50	1.50
☐ 2 Frank Thomas	12.00	5.50	1.50
☐ 3 Cal Ripken	10.00	4.50	1.25
☐ 4 Alex Rodriguez	12.00	5.50	1.50
☐ 5 Chipper Jones	7.50	3.40	.95
☐ 6 Derek Jeter	7.50	3.40	.95

1996 Pro Stamps

This 140-stamp set was issued by Chris Martin Enterprises and distributed on 3" by 7 1/2" sheets of six stamps, five players of the same team and team logo. The team logo stamps are unnumbered and not included in the checklist below. Each stamp measures approximately 1 1/2" by 1 15/16". A collector could receive more stamps and become an official Pro Stamps Club member by mailing in the form found on the back of the stamp sheets.

	MINT	NRMT	EXC
COMPLETE SET (140)	75.00	34.00	9.50
COMMON CARD (1-140)	.25	.11	.03
☐ 1 Gary DiSarcina	.25	.11	.03
☐ 2 Tim Salmon	1.00	.45	.12
☐ 3 J.T. Snow	.25	.11	.03
☐ 4 Brian Anderson	.25	.11	.03
☐ 5 Chili Davis	.25	.11	.03
☐ 6 Mark McGwire	1.50	.70	.19
☐ 7 Terry Steinbach	.25	.11	.03
☐ 8 Danny Tartabull	.25	.11	.03
☐ 9 Todd Stottlemyre	.25	.11	.03
☐ 10 Geronimo Berroa	.25	.11	.03
☐ 11 Derek Bell	.50	.23	.06
☐ 12 Craig Biggio	.50	.23	.06
☐ 13 Jeff Bagwell	2.50	1.10	.30
☐ 14 Doug Drabek	.25	.11	.03
☐ 15 Shane Reynolds	.25	.11	.03
☐ 16 Ed Sprague	.25	.11	.03
☐ 17 Pat Hentgen	.50	.23	.06
☐ 18 Joe Carter	.50	.23	.06
☐ 19 John Olerud	.50	.23	.06
☐ 20 Carlos Delgado	.50	.23	.06
☐ 21 Fred McGriff	1.00	.45	.12
☐ 22 Ryan Klesko	1.00	.45	.12
☐ 23 David Justice	.50	.23	.06
☐ 24 Greg Maddux	3.00	1.35	.35
☐ 25 Tom Glavine	1.00	.45	.12
☐ 26 Kevin Seitzer	.25	.11	.03
☐ 27 Greg Vaughn	.25	.11	.03
☐ 28 John Jaha	.50	.23	.06
☐ 29 Pat Listach	.25	.11	.03
☐ 30 Bill Wegman	.25	.11	.03
☐ 31 Brian Jordan	.50	.23	.06
☐ 32 Ray Lankford	.50	.23	.06
☐ 33 Tom Pagnozzi	.25	.11	.03
☐ 34 Bernard Gilkey	.25	.11	.03
☐ 35 Ozzie Smith	2.00	.90	.25
☐ 36 Mark Grace	1.50	.70	.19
☐ 37 Shawon Dunston	.25	.11	.03
☐ 38 Brian McRae	.25	.11	.03
☐ 39 Jaime Navarro	.25	.11	.03
☐ 40 Sammy Sosa	1.00	.45	.12
☐ 41 Mike Piazza	3.00	1.35	.35
☐ 42 Eric Karros	.50	.23	.06
☐ 43 Raul Mondesi	.75	.35	.09
☐ 44 Delino DeShields	.25	.11	.03
☐ 45 Hideo Nomo	2.00	.90	.25
☐ 46 Wilfredo Cordero	.25	.11	.03
☐ 47 Darrin Fletcher	.25	.11	.03
☐ 48 David Segui	.25	.11	.03
☐ 49 Pedro Martinez	.50	.23	.06
☐ 50 Rondell White	.50	.23	.06
☐ 51 Matt Williams	1.00	.45	.12
☐ 52 Barry Bonds	1.25	.55	.16
☐ 53 Deion Sanders	.75	.35	.09
☐ 54 Mark Leiter	.25	.11	.03
☐ 55 Glenallen Hill	.25	.11	.03
☐ 56 Kenny Lofton	1.25	.55	.16
☐ 57 Albert Belle	2.50	1.10	.30
☐ 58 Eddie Murray	1.25	.55	.16
☐ 59 Manny Ramirez	1.25	.55	.16
☐ 60 Charles Nagy	.50	.23	.06
☐ 61 Ken Griffey Jr.	5.00	2.20	.60
☐ 62 Randy Johnson	1.00	.45	.12
☐ 63 Jay Buhner	.75	.35	.09
☐ 64 Edgar Martinez	1.00	.45	.12
☐ 65 Alex Rodriguez	5.00	2.20	.60
☐ 66 Gary Sheffield	1.00	.45	.12
☐ 67 Jeff Conine	.50	.23	.06
☐ 68 Terry Pendleton	.25	.11	.03
☐ 69 Chris Hammond	.25	.11	.03
☐ 70 Greg Colbrunn	.25	.11	.03
☐ 71 Todd Hundley	.50	.23	.06
☐ 72 Jose Vizcaino	.25	.11	.03
☐ 73 Jeff Kent	.25	.11	.03
☐ 74 Rico Brogna	.25	.11	.03
☐ 75 Bobby Jones	.25	.11	.03
☐ 76 Cal Ripken	3.00	1.35	.35
☐ 77 Bobby Bonilla	.50	.23	.06
☐ 78 Brady Anderson	.75	.35	.09
☐ 79 Mike Mussina	1.00	.45	.12
☐ 80 Rafael Palmeiro	.75	.35	.09
☐ 81 Tony Gwynn	2.00	.90	.25
☐ 82 Ken Caminiti	1.00	.45	.12
☐ 83 Andujar Cedeno	.25	.11	.03
☐ 84 Andy Ashby	.25	.11	.03
☐ 85 Jody Reed	.25	.11	.03
☐ 86 Jim Eisenreich	.50	.23	.06
☐ 87 Gregg Jefferies	.25	.11	.03
☐ 88 Mickey Morandini	.25	.11	.03
☐ 89 Paul Quantrill	.25	.11	.03
☐ 90 Darren Daulton	.50	.23	.06
☐ 91 Orlando Merced	.25	.11	.03
☐ 92 Carlos Garcia	.25	.11	.03
☐ 93 Jay Bell	.25	.11	.03
☐ 94 Al Martin	.25	.11	.03
☐ 95 Denny Neagle	.25	.11	.03
☐ 96 Benji Gil	.25	.11	.03
☐ 97 Will Clark	1.00	.45	.12
☐ 98 Juan Gonzalez	2.50	1.10	.30
☐ 99 Ivan Rodriguez	1.25	.55	.16
☐ 100 Dean Palmer	.25	.11	.03
☐ 101 Barry Larkin	.75	.35	.09
☐ 102 Reggie Sanders	.50	.23	.06
☐ 103 Benito Santiago	.25	.11	.03
☐ 104 Jose Rijo	.25	.11	.03
☐ 105 Bret Boone	.25	.11	.03
☐ 106 Mo Vaughn	1.25	.55	.16
☐ 107 Jose Canseco	1.00	.45	.12
☐ 108 Mike Greenwell	.25	.11	.03
☐ 109 John Valentin	.25	.11	.03
☐ 110 Roger Clemens	1.25	.55	.16
☐ 111 Dante Bichette	.75	.35	.09
☐ 112 Vinny Castilla	.50	.23	.06
☐ 113 Andres Galarraga	.75	.35	.09
☐ 114 Larry Walker	.75	.35	.09
☐ 115 Walt Weiss	.25	.11	.03
☐ 116 Tom Goodwin	.25	.11	.03
☐ 117 Keith Lockhart	.25	.11	.03
☐ 118 Mark Gubicza	.25	.11	.03
☐ 119 Jon Nunnally	.25	.11	.03

	MINT	NRMT	EXC
☐ 120 Kevin Appier	.50	.23	.06
☐ 121 Chad Curtis	.25	.11	.03
☐ 122 Phil Nevin	.25	.11	.03
☐ 123 Travis Fryman	.50	.23	.06
☐ 124 Alan Trammell	.50	.23	.06
☐ 125 Cecil Fielder	.50	.23	.06
☐ 126 Chuck Knoblauch	1.00	.45	.12
☐ 127 Kirby Puckett	2.50	1.10	.30
☐ 128 Marty Cordova	.50	.23	.06
☐ 129 Pedro Munoz	.25	.11	.03
☐ 130 Rich Aguilera	.25	.11	.03
☐ 131 Frank Thomas	5.00	2.20	.60
☐ 132 Ozzie Guillen	.25	.11	.03
☐ 133 Robin Ventura	.50	.23	.06
☐ 134 Ron Karkovice	.25	.11	.03
☐ 135 Alex Fernandez	.50	.23	.06
☐ 136 Wade Boggs	.75	.35	.09
☐ 137 Jimmy Key	.25	.11	.03
☐ 138 Paul O'Neill	.25	.11	.03
☐ 139 David Cone	.50	.23	.06
☐ 140 Bernie Williams	1.00	.45	.12

1995 ProMint

This set of 15 diamond cards was produced by ProMint. The embossed gold-foil cards feature 22-karat gold on their fronts and a five-point diamond next to the player's name at the bottom. Each card is individually numbered and packaged in an acrylic holder.

	MINT	NRMT	EXC
COMPLETE SET (15)	375.00	170.00	47.50
COMMON CARD (1-15)	25.00	11.00	3.10
☐ 1 Jeff Bagwell	25.00	11.00	3.10
☐ 2 Albert Belle	25.00	11.00	3.10
☐ 3 Barry Bonds	25.00	11.00	3.10
☐ 4 George Brett	25.00	11.00	3.10
☐ 5 Roger Clemens	25.00	11.00	3.10
☐ 6 Ken Griffey Jr.	35.00	16.00	4.40
☐ 7 Tony Gwynn	25.00	11.00	3.10
☐ 8 Greg Maddux	30.00	13.50	3.70
☐ 9 Don Mattingly	25.00	11.00	3.10
☐ 10 Mike Piazza	25.00	11.00	3.10
☐ 11 Kirby Puckett	25.00	11.00	3.10
☐ 12 Cal Ripken	30.00	13.50	3.70
☐ 13 Nolan Ryan	30.00	13.50	3.70
☐ 14 Ozzie Smith	25.00	11.00	3.10
☐ 15 Frank Thomas	35.00	16.00	4.40

1993 ProMint 22K Gold Bonds

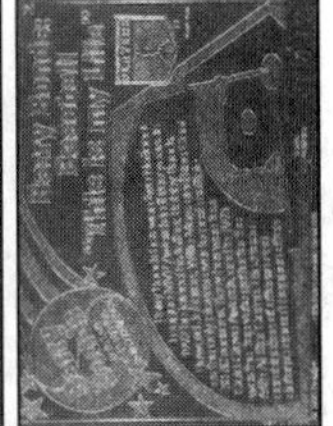

This 22 karat gold card of Barry Bonds measures the standard size and features an embossed image of Bonds bordered by an embossed arrow design. The player's name, along with the ProMint logo, appear near the bottom. The horizontal back carries the player's name within a motion-streaked baseball icon at the upper left. Career highlights appear in the "outfield" of a baseball field design. The card carries its production number at the bottom right, but is otherwise unnumbered.

	MINT	NRMT	EXC
COMPLETE SET	25.00	11.00	3.10
COMMON CARD	25.00	11.00	3.10
☐ 1 Barry Bonds	25.00	11.00	3.10

1990 Pubs.Int'l. Stickers

The 1990 Publications International baseball stickers set contains 648 stickers bound in a book. Subsets of the 648-sticker set include All-Stars from each league, and young stars from each league. The stickers are put into the album over a question which pertains to each player pictured as a clue for where the sticker goes. Good stat information is available on this set in the album/book. The set numbering is ordered by teams. The album spaces are numbered and contain a trivia question answered by the players name. The set/book was licensed by Major League Baseball and MLBPA and was produced by Publications International.

	MINT	NRMT	EXC
COMPLETE SET (648)	40.00	18.00	5.00
COMMON STICKER (1-648)	.05	.02	.01
☐ 1 Dave Anderson	.05	.02	.01
☐ 2 Tim Belcher	.05	.02	.01
☐ 3 Mike Davis	.05	.02	.01
☐ 4 Rick Dempsey	.05	.02	.01
☐ 5 Kirk Gibson	.10	.05	.01
☐ 6 Alfredo Griffin	.05	.02	.01
☐ 7 Jeff Hamilton	.05	.02	.01
☐ 8 Mickey Hatcher	.05	.02	.01
☐ 9 Orel Hershiser	.10	.05	.01
☐ 10 Ricky Horton	.05	.02	.01
☐ 11 Jay Howell	.05	.02	.01
☐ 12 Tim Leary	.05	.02	.01
☐ 13 Mike Marshall	.05	.02	.01
☐ 14 Eddie Murray	.40	.18	.05
☐ 15 Alejandro Pena	.05	.02	.01
☐ 16 Willie Randolph	.10	.05	.01
☐ 17 Mike Scioscia	.05	.02	.01
☐ 18 John Shelby	.05	.02	.01
☐ 19 Franklin Stubbs	.05	.02	.01
☐ 20 John Tudor	.05	.02	.01
☐ 21 Fernando Valenzuela	.10	.05	.01
☐ 22 Todd Benzinger	.05	.02	.01
☐ 23 Tom Browning	.05	.02	.01
☐ 24 Norm Charlton	.05	.02	.01
☐ 25 Kal Daniels	.05	.02	.01
☐ 26 Eric Davis	.05	.02	.01
☐ 27 Bo Diaz	.05	.02	.01
☐ 28 Rob Dibble	.05	.02	.01
☐ 29 John Franco	.05	.02	.01
☐ 30 Ken Griffey	.10	.05	.01
☐ 31 Lenny Harris	.05	.02	.01
☐ 32 Danny Jackson	.05	.02	.01
☐ 33 Barry Larkin	.25	.11	.03
☐ 34 Rick Mahler	.05	.02	.01
☐ 35 Ron Oester	.05	.02	.01
☐ 36 Paul O'Neill	.10	.05	.01
☐ 37 Jeff Reed	.05	.02	.01
☐ 38 Jose Rijo	.05	.02	.01
☐ 39 Chris Sabo	.05	.02	.01
☐ 40 Kent Tekulve	.05	.02	.01
☐ 41 Manny Trillo	.05	.02	.01
☐ 42 Joel Youngblood	.05	.02	.01
☐ 43 Roberto Alomar	.75	.35	.09
☐ 44 Greg Booker	.05	.02	.01
☐ 45 Jack Clark	.10	.05	.01
☐ 46 Jerald Clark	.05	.02	.01
☐ 47 Mark Davis	.05	.02	.01
☐ 48 Tim Flannery	.05	.02	.01
☐ 49 Mark Grant	.05	.02	.01
☐ 50 Tony Gwynn	.75	.35	.09
☐ 51 Bruce Hurst	.05	.02	.01
☐ 52 John Kruk	.10	.05	.01
☐ 53 Dave Leiper	.05	.02	.01
☐ 54 Carmelo Martinez	.05	.02	.01
☐ 55 Mark Parent	.05	.02	.01
☐ 56 Dennis Rasmussen	.05	.02	.01
☐ 57 Randy Ready	.05	.02	.01
☐ 58 Benito Santiago	.10	.05	.01
☐ 59 Eric Show	.05	.02	.01
☐ 60 Garry Templeton	.05	.02	.01
☐ 61 Walt Terrell	.05	.02	.01
☐ 62 Ed Whitson	.05	.02	.01
☐ 63 Marvell Wynne	.05	.02	.01
☐ 64 Brett Butler	.10	.05	.01
☐ 65 Will Clark	.25	.11	.03
☐ 66 Kelly Downs	.05	.02	.01
☐ 67 Scott Garrelts	.05	.02	.01
☐ 68 Rich(Goose) Gossage	.10	.05	.01
☐ 69 Atlee Hammaker	.05	.02	.01
☐ 70 Tracy Jones	.05	.02	.01
☐ 71 Terry Kennedy	.05	.02	.01
☐ 72 Mike Krukow	.05	.02	.01
☐ 73 Mike LaCoss	.05	.02	.01
☐ 74 Craig Lefferts	.05	.02	.01
☐ 75 Candy Maldonado	.05	.02	.01
☐ 76 Kirt Manwaring	.05	.02	.01
☐ 77 Kevin Mitchell	.05	.02	.01
☐ 78 Donell Nixon	.05	.02	.01
☐ 79 Rick Reuschel	.05	.02	.01
☐ 80 Ernest Riles	.05	.02	.01
☐ 81 Don Robinson	.05	.02	.01
☐ 82 Chris Speier	.05	.02	.01
☐ 83 Robby Thompson	.05	.02	.01
☐ 84 Jose Uribe	.05	.02	.01
☐ 85 Juan Agosto	.05	.02	.01
☐ 86 Larry Andersen	.05	.02	.01
☐ 87 Kevin Bass	.05	.02	.01
☐ 88 Craig Biggio	.30	.14	.04
☐ 89 Ken Caminiti	.10	.05	.01
☐ 90 Jim Clancy	.05	.02	.01
☐ 91 Danny Darwin	.05	.02	.01
☐ 92 Glenn Davis	.05	.02	.01
☐ 93 Jim Deshaies	.05	.02	.01
☐ 94 Bill Doran	.05	.02	.01
☐ 95 Bob Forsch	.05	.02	.01
☐ 96 Billy Hatcher	.05	.02	.01
☐ 97 Bob Knepper	.05	.02	.01
☐ 98 Terry Puhl	.05	.02	.01
☐ 99 Rafael Ramirez	.05	.02	.01
☐ 100 Craig Reynolds	.05	.02	.01
☐ 101 Rick Rhoden	.05	.02	.01
☐ 102 Mike Scott	.05	.02	.01
☐ 103 Dave Smith	.05	.02	.01
☐ 104 Alex Trevino	.05	.02	.01
☐ 105 Gerald Young	.05	.02	.01
☐ 106 Jose Alvarez	.05	.02	.01
☐ 107 Paul Assenmacher	.05	.02	.01
☐ 108 Bruce Benedict	.05	.02	.01
☐ 109 Jeff Blauser	.05	.02	.01
☐ 110 Joe Boever	.05	.02	.01
☐ 111 Jody Davis	.05	.02	.01
☐ 112 Darrell Evans	.10	.05	.01
☐ 113 Ron Gant	.15	.07	.02
☐ 114 Tommy Gregg	.05	.02	.01
☐ 115 Dion James	.05	.02	.01
☐ 116 Derek Lilliquist	.05	.02	.01
☐ 117 Dale Murphy	.15	.07	.02
☐ 118 Gerald Perry	.05	.02	.01
☐ 119 Charlie Puleo	.05	.02	.01
☐ 120 John Russell	.05	.02	.01
☐ 121 Lonnie Smith	.05	.02	.01
☐ 122 Pete Smith	.05	.02	.01
☐ 123 Zane Smith	.05	.02	.01
☐ 124 John Smoltz	.30	.14	.04
☐ 125 Bruce Sutter	.10	.05	.01
☐ 126 Andres Thomas	.05	.02	.01
☐ 127 Rick Aguilera	.05	.02	.01
☐ 128 Gary Carter	.10	.05	.01
☐ 129 David Cone	.15	.07	.02
☐ 130 Ron Darling	.05	.02	.01
☐ 131 Len Dykstra	.10	.05	.01
☐ 132 Kevin Elster	.05	.02	.01
☐ 133 Sid Fernandez	.05	.02	.01
☐ 134 Dwight Gooden	.10	.05	.01
☐ 135 Keith Hernandez	.10	.05	.01
☐ 136 Gregg Jefferies	.10	.05	.01
☐ 137 Howard Johnson	.05	.02	.01
☐ 138 Dave Magadan	.05	.02	.01
☐ 139 Lee Mazzilli	.05	.02	.01
☐ 140 Roger McDowell	.05	.02	.01
☐ 141 Kevin McReynolds	.05	.02	.01
☐ 142 Randy Myers	.05	.02	.01
☐ 143 Bob Ojeda	.05	.02	.01
☐ 144 Mackey Sasser	.05	.02	.01
☐ 145 Darryl Strawberry	.10	.05	.01
☐ 146 Tim Teufel	.05	.02	.01
☐ 147 Mookie Wilson	.10	.05	.01
☐ 148 Rafael Belliard	.05	.02	.01
☐ 149 Barry Bonds	.50	.23	.06
☐ 150 Bobby Bonilla	.10	.05	.01
☐ 151 Sid Bream	.05	.02	.01
☐ 152 Benny Distefano	.05	.02	.01
☐ 153 Doug Drabek	.05	.02	.01
☐ 154 Brian Fisher	.05	.02	.01
☐ 155 Jim Gott	.05	.02	.01
☐ 156 Neal Heaton	.05	.02	.01
☐ 157 Bill Landrum	.05	.02	.01
☐ 158 Mike LaValliere	.05	.02	.01
☐ 159 Jose Lind	.05	.02	.01
☐ 160 Junior Ortiz	.05	.02	.01
☐ 161 Tom Prince	.05	.02	.01
☐ 162 Gary Redus	.05	.02	.01
☐ 163 R.J. Reynolds	.05	.02	.01
☐ 164 Jeff Robinson	.05	.02	.01
☐ 165 John Smiley	.05	.02	.01
☐ 166 Andy Van Slyke	.10	.05	.01
☐ 167 Bob Walk	.05	.02	.01
☐ 168 Glenn Wilson	.05	.02	.01
☐ 169 Hubie Brooks	.05	.02	.01
☐ 170 Tim Burke	.05	.02	.01
☐ 171 Mike Fitzgerald	.05	.02	.01
☐ 172 Tom Foley	.05	.02	.01
☐ 173 Andres Galarraga	.25	.11	.03
☐ 174 Kevin Gross	.05	.02	.01
☐ 175 Joe Hesketh	.05	.02	.01
☐ 176 Brian Holman	.05	.02	.01
☐ 177 Rex Hudler	.05	.02	.01
☐ 178 Wallace Johnson	.05	.02	.01
☐ 179 Mark Langston	.10	.05	.01
☐ 180 Dave Martinez	.05	.02	.01
☐ 181 Dennis Martinez	.10	.05	.01
☐ 182 Andy McGaffigan	.05	.02	.01
☐ 183 Otis Nixon	.05	.02	.01
☐ 184 Spike Owen	.05	.02	.01
☐ 185 Pascual Perez	.05	.02	.01
☐ 186 Tim Raines	.10	.05	.01
☐ 187 Nelson Santovenia	.05	.02	.01
☐ 188 Bryn Smith	.05	.02	.01
☐ 189 Tim Wallach	.05	.02	.01
☐ 190 Damon Berryhill	.05	.02	.01
☐ 191 Mike Bielecki	.05	.02	.01
☐ 192 Andre Dawson	.25	.11	.03
☐ 193 Shawon Dunston	.05	.02	.01
☐ 194 Mark Grace	.25	.11	.03
☐ 195 Darrin Jackson	.05	.02	.01
☐ 196 Paul Kilgus	.05	.02	.01
☐ 197 Vance Law	.05	.02	.01
☐ 198 Greg Maddux	1.50	.70	.19
☐ 199 Pat Perry	.05	.02	.01
☐ 200 Jeff Pico	.05	.02	.01
☐ 201 Ryne Sandberg	.50	.23	.06
☐ 202 Scott Sanderson	.05	.02	.01
☐ 203 Calvin Schiraldi	.05	.02	.01
☐ 204 Dwight Smith	.05	.02	.01
☐ 205 Rick Sutcliffe	.05	.02	.01
☐ 206 Gary Varsho	.05	.02	.01
☐ 207 Jerome Walton	.05	.02	.01
☐ 208 Mitch Webster	.05	.02	.01
☐ 209 Curtis Wilkerson	.05	.02	.01
☐ 210 Mitch Williams	.05	.02	.01
☐ 211 Tom Brunansky	.05	.02	.01
☐ 212 Cris Carpenter	.05	.02	.01
☐ 213 Vince Coleman	.05	.02	.01
☐ 214 John Costello	.05	.02	.01
☐ 215 Danny Cox	.05	.02	.01
☐ 216 Ken Dayley	.05	.02	.01
☐ 217 Jose DeLeon	.05	.02	.01
☐ 218 Frank DiPino	.05	.02	.01
☐ 219 Pedro Guerrero	.05	.02	.01
☐ 220 Joe Magrane	.05	.02	.01
☐ 221 Greg Mathews	.05	.02	.01
☐ 222 Willie McGee	.05	.02	.01
☐ 223 Jose Oquendo	.05	.02	.01
☐ 224 Tom Pagnozzi	.05	.02	.01
☐ 225 Tony Pena	.05	.02	.01
☐ 226 Terry Pendleton	.10	.05	.01
☐ 227 Dan Quisenberry	.05	.02	.01
☐ 228 Ozzie Smith	.40	.18	.05
☐ 229 Scott Terry	.05	.02	.01
☐ 230 Milt Thompson	.05	.02	.01
☐ 231 Todd Worrell	.05	.02	.01
☐ 232 Steve Bedrosian	.05	.02	.01
☐ 233 Don Carman	.05	.02	.01
☐ 234 Darren Daulton	.10	.05	.01
☐ 235 Bob Dernier	.05	.02	.01
☐ 236 Marvin Freeman	.05	.02	.01
☐ 237 Greg Harris	.05	.02	.01
☐ 238 Von Hayes	.05	.02	.01
☐ 239 Tom Herr	.05	.02	.01
☐ 240 Ken Howell	.05	.02	.01
☐ 241 Chris James	.05	.02	.01
☐ 242 Steve Jeltz	.05	.02	.01
☐ 243 Ron Jones	.05	.02	.01
☐ 244 Ricky Jordan	.05	.02	.01
☐ 245 Steve Lake	.05	.02	.01
☐ 246 Mike Maddux	.05	.02	.01
☐ 247 Larry McWilliams	.05	.02	.01
☐ 248 Jeff Parrett	.05	.02	.01
☐ 249 Juan Samuel	.05	.02	.01
☐ 250 Mike Schmidt	.60	.25	.07
☐ 251 Dickie Thon	.05	.02	.01
☐ 252 Floyd Youmans	.05	.02	.01
☐ 253 Bobby Bonilla	.10	.05	.01
☐ 254 Will Clark	.25	.11	.03
☐ 255 Eric Davis	.05	.02	.01
☐ 256 Andre Dawson	.25	.11	.03
☐ 257 Bill Doran	.05	.02	.01
☐ 258 John Franco	.05	.02	.01
☐ 259 Kirk Gibson	.10	.05	.01
☐ 260 Dwight Gooden	.10	.05	.01
☐ 261 Tony Gwynn	.75	.35	.09
☐ 262 Keith Hernandez	.10	.05	.01
☐ 263 Orel Hershiser	.10	.05	.01
☐ 264 Danny Jackson	.05	.02	.01
☐ 265 Howard Johnson	.05	.02	.01
☐ 266 Barry Larkin	.25	.11	.03
☐ 267 Joe Magrane	.05	.02	.01
☐ 268 Kevin McReynolds	.05	.02	.01
☐ 269 Tony Pena	.05	.02	.01
☐ 270 Ryne Sandberg	.50	.23	.06
☐ 271 Benito Santiago	.05	.02	.01
☐ 272 Ozzie Smith	.40	.18	.05
☐ 273 Darryl Strawberry	.10	.05	.01
☐ 274 Todd Worrell	.05	.02	.01
☐ 275 Harold Baines	.10	.05	.01
☐ 276 George Bell	.05	.02	.01
☐ 277 Wade Boggs	.25	.11	.03
☐ 278 Bob Boone	.10	.05	.01
☐ 279 Jose Canseco	.25	.11	.03
☐ 280 Joe Carter	.25	.11	.03
☐ 281 Roger Clemens	.25	.11	.03
☐ 282 Dennis Eckersley	.10	.05	.01
☐ 283 Tony Fernandez	.05	.02	.01
☐ 284 Carlton Fisk	.25	.11	.03
☐ 285 Julio Franco	.10	.05	.01
☐ 286 Gary Gaetti	.05	.02	.01
☐ 287 Mike Greenwell	.05	.02	.01
☐ 288 Rickey Henderson	.25	.11	.03
☐ 289 Ted Higuera	.05	.02	.01
☐ 290 Kent Hrbek	.10	.05	.01
☐ 291 Don Mattingly	1.00	.45	.12
☐ 292 Kirby Puckett	.50	.23	.06
☐ 293 Jeff Reardon	.10	.05	.01
☐ 294 Harold Reynolds	.05	.02	.01
☐ 295 Dave Stewart	.10	.05	.01
☐ 296 Alan Trammell	.10	.05	.01
☐ 297 Frank Viola	.05	.02	.01
☐ 298 Dave Winfield	.25	.11	.03
☐ 299 Todd Burns	.05	.02	.01
☐ 300 Greg Cadaret	.05	.02	.01
☐ 301 Jose Canseco	.25	.11	.03
☐ 302 Storm Davis	.05	.02	.01
☐ 303 Dennis Eckersley	.10	.05	.01
☐ 304 Mike Gallego	.05	.02	.01
☐ 305 Ron Hassey	.05	.02	.01
☐ 306 Dave Henderson	.05	.02	.01
☐ 307 Rick Honeycutt	.05	.02	.01
☐ 308 Stan Javier	.05	.02	.01
☐ 309 Carney Lansford	.10	.05	.01
☐ 310 Mark McGwire	.25	.11	.03
☐ 311 Mike Moore	.05	.02	.01
☐ 312 Dave Parker	.10	.05	.01
☐ 313 Eric Plunk	.05	.02	.01
☐ 314 Luis Polonia	.05	.02	.01
☐ 315 Terry Steinbach	.10	.05	.01
☐ 316 Dave Stewart	.10	.05	.01
☐ 317 Walt Weiss	.05	.02	.01
☐ 318 Bob Welch	.05	.02	.01
☐ 319 Curt Young	.05	.02	.01
☐ 320 Allan Anderson	.05	.02	.01
☐ 321 Wally Backman	.05	.02	.01
☐ 322 Doug Baker	.05	.02	.01

☐ 323 Juan Berenguer	.05	.02	.01
☐ 324 Randy Bush	.05	.02	.01
☐ 325 Jim Dwyer	.05	.02	.01
☐ 326 Gary Gaetti	.05	.02	.01
☐ 327 Greg Gagne	.05	.02	.01
☐ 328 Dan Gladden	.05	.02	.01
☐ 329 Brian Harper	.05	.02	.01
☐ 330 Kent Hrbek	.10	.05	.01
☐ 331 Gene Larkin	.05	.02	.01
☐ 332 Tim Laudner	.05	.02	.01
☐ 333 John Moses	.05	.02	.01
☐ 334 Al Newman	.05	.02	.01
☐ 335 Kirby Puckett	.50	.23	.06
☐ 336 Shane Rawley	.05	.02	.01
☐ 337 Jeff Reardon	.10	.05	.01
☐ 338 Steve Shields	.05	.02	.01
☐ 339 Frank Viola	.05	.02	.01
☐ 340 Gary Wayne	.05	.02	.01
☐ 341 Luis Aquino	.05	.02	.01
☐ 342 Floyd Bannister	.05	.02	.01
☐ 343 Bob Boone	.10	.05	.01
☐ 344 George Brett	.75	.35	.09
☐ 345 Bill Buckner	.10	.05	.01
☐ 346 Jim Eisenreich	.05	.02	.01
☐ 347 Steve Farr	.05	.02	.01
☐ 348 Tommy Gordon	.05	.02	.01
☐ 349 Mark Gubicza	.05	.02	.01
☐ 350 Bo Jackson	.10	.05	.01
☐ 351 Charlie Leibrandt	.05	.02	.01
☐ 352 Mike Macfarlane	.05	.02	.01
☐ 353 Jeff Montgomery	.05	.02	.01
☐ 354 Bret Saberhagen	.10	.05	.01
☐ 355 Kevin Seitzer	.05	.02	.01
☐ 356 Kurt Stillwell	.05	.02	.01
☐ 357 Pat Tabler	.05	.02	.01
☐ 358 Danny Tartabull	.05	.02	.01
☐ 359 Gary Thurman	.05	.02	.01
☐ 360 Frank White	.10	.05	.01
☐ 361 Willie Wilson	.05	.02	.01
☐ 362 Jim Abbott	.10	.05	.01
☐ 363 Kent Anderson	.05	.02	.01
☐ 364 Tony Armas	.05	.02	.01
☐ 365 Dante Bichette	.40	.18	.05
☐ 366 Bert Blyleven	.10	.05	.01
☐ 367 Chili Davis	.10	.05	.01
☐ 368 Brian Downing	.05	.02	.01
☐ 369 Chuck Finley	.10	.05	.01
☐ 370 Willie Fraser	.05	.02	.01
☐ 371 Jack Howell	.05	.02	.01
☐ 372 Wally Joyner	.10	.05	.01
☐ 373 Kirk McCaskill	.05	.02	.01
☐ 374 Bob McClure	.05	.02	.01
☐ 375 Greg Minton	.05	.02	.01
☐ 376 Lance Parrish	.10	.05	.01
☐ 377 Dan Petry	.05	.02	.01
☐ 378 Johnny Ray	.05	.02	.01
☐ 379 Dick Schofield	.05	.02	.01
☐ 380 Claudell Washington	.05	.02	.01
☐ 381 Devon White	.10	.05	.01
☐ 382 Mike Witt	.05	.02	.01
☐ 383 Harold Baines	.10	.05	.01
☐ 384 Daryl Boston	.05	.02	.01
☐ 385 Ivan Calderon	.05	.02	.01
☐ 386 Carlton Fisk	.25	.11	.03
☐ 387 Dave Gallagher	.05	.02	.01
☐ 388 Ozzie Guillen	.05	.02	.01
☐ 389 Shawn Hillegas	.05	.02	.01
☐ 390 Barry Jones	.05	.02	.01
☐ 391 Ron Karkovice	.05	.02	.01
☐ 392 Eric King	.05	.02	.01
☐ 393 Ron Kittle	.05	.02	.01
☐ 394 Bill Long	.05	.02	.01
☐ 395 Steve Lyons	.05	.02	.01
☐ 396 Fred Manrique	.05	.02	.01
☐ 397 Donn Pall	.05	.02	.01
☐ 398 Dan Pasqua	.05	.02	.01
☐ 399 Melido Perez	.05	.02	.01
☐ 400 Jerry Reuss	.05	.02	.01
☐ 401 Bobby Thigpen	.05	.02	.01
☐ 402 Greg Walker	.05	.02	.01
☐ 403 Eddie Williams	.05	.02	.01
☐ 404 Buddy Bell	.10	.05	.01
☐ 405 Kevin Brown	.15	.07	.02
☐ 406 Steve Buechele	.05	.02	.01
☐ 407 Cecil Espy	.05	.02	.01
☐ 408 Scott Fletcher	.05	.02	.01
☐ 409 Julio Franco	.10	.05	.01
☐ 410 Cecilio Guante	.05	.02	.01
☐ 411 Jose Guzman	.05	.02	.01
☐ 412 Charlie Hough	.10	.05	.01
☐ 413 Pete Incaviglia	.05	.02	.01
☐ 414 Chad Kreuter	.05	.02	.01
☐ 415 Jeff Kunkel	.05	.02	.01
☐ 416 Rick Leach	.05	.02	.01
☐ 417 Jamie Moyer	.05	.02	.01
☐ 418 Rafael Palmeiro	.25	.11	.03
☐ 419 Geno Petralli	.05	.02	.01
☐ 420 Jeff Russell	.05	.02	.01
☐ 421 Nolan Ryan	2.00	.90	.25
☐ 422 Ruben Sierra	.10	.05	.01
☐ 423 Jim Sundberg	.05	.02	.01
☐ 424 Bobby Witt	.05	.02	.01
☐ 424 Steve Balboni	.05	.02	.01
☐ 426 Scott Bankhead	.05	.02	.01
☐ 427 Scott Bradley	.05	.02	.01
☐ 428 Mickey Brantley	.05	.02	.01
☐ 429 Darnell Coles	.05	.02	.01
☐ 430 Henry Cotto	.05	.02	.01
☐ 431 Alvin Davis	.05	.02	.01
☐ 432 Mario Diaz	.05	.02	.01
☐ 433 Ken Griffey Jr.	3.00	1.35	.35
☐ 434 Erik Hanson	.05	.02	.01
☐ 435 Mike Jackson	.05	.02	.01
☐ 436 Jeffrey Leonard	.05	.02	.01
☐ 437 Edgar Martinez	.25	.11	.03
☐ 438 Tom Niedenfuer	.05	.02	.01
☐ 439 Jim Presley	.05	.02	.01
☐ 440 Jerry Reed	.05	.02	.01
☐ 441 Harold Reynolds	.05	.02	.01
☐ 442 Bill Swift	.05	.02	.01
☐ 443 Steve Trout	.05	.02	.01
☐ 444 David Valle	.05	.02	.01
☐ 445 Omar Vizquel	.15	.07	.02
☐ 446 Marty Barrett	.05	.02	.01
☐ 447 Mike Boddicker	.05	.02	.01
☐ 448 Wade Boggs	.25	.11	.03
☐ 449 Dennis(Oil Can) Boyd	.05	.02	.01
☐ 450 Ellis Burks	.15	.07	.02
☐ 451 Rick Cerone	.05	.02	.01
☐ 452 Roger Clemens	.25	.11	.03
☐ 453 Nick Esasky	.05	.02	.01
☐ 454 Dwight Evans	.10	.05	.01
☐ 455 Wes Gardner	.05	.02	.01
☐ 456 Rich Gedman	.05	.02	.01
☐ 457 Mike Greenwell	.05	.02	.01
☐ 458 Sam Horn	.05	.02	.01
☐ 459 Randy Kutcher	.05	.02	.01
☐ 460 Dennis Lamp	.05	.02	.01
☐ 461 Rob Murphy	.05	.02	.01
☐ 462 Jody Reed	.05	.02	.01
☐ 463 Jim Rice	.10	.05	.01
☐ 464 Lee Smith	.10	.05	.01
☐ 465 Mike Smithson	.05	.02	.01
☐ 466 Bob Stanley	.05	.02	.01
☐ 467 Doyle Alexander	.05	.02	.01
☐ 468 Dave Bergman	.05	.02	.01
☐ 469 Chris Brown	.05	.02	.01
☐ 470 Paul Gibson	.05	.02	.01
☐ 471 Mike Heath	.05	.02	.01
☐ 472 Mike Henneman	.05	.02	.01
☐ 473 Guillermo Hernandez	.05	.02	.01
☐ 474 Charles Hudson	.05	.02	.01
☐ 475 Chet Lemon	.05	.02	.01
☐ 476 Fred Lynn	.10	.05	.01
☐ 477 Keith Moreland	.05	.02	.01
☐ 478 Jack Morris	.10	.05	.01
☐ 479 Matt Nokes	.05	.02	.01
☐ 480 Gary Pettis	.05	.02	.01
☐ 481 Jeff Robinson	.05	.02	.01
☐ 482 Pat Sheridan	.05	.02	.01
☐ 483 Frank Tanana	.05	.02	.01
☐ 484 Alan Trammell	.10	.05	.01
☐ 485 Lou Whitaker	.10	.05	.01
☐ 486 Frank Williams	.05	.02	.01
☐ 487 Kenny Williams	.05	.02	.01
☐ 488 Don August	.05	.02	.01
☐ 489 Mike Birkbeck	.05	.02	.01
☐ 490 Chris Bosio	.05	.02	.01
☐ 491 Glenn Braggs	.05	.02	.01
☐ 492 Greg Brock	.05	.02	.01
☐ 493 Chuck Crim	.05	.02	.01
☐ 494 Rob Deer	.05	.02	.01
☐ 495 Mike Felder	.05	.02	.01
☐ 496 Jim Gantner	.05	.02	.01
☐ 497 Ted Higuera	.05	.02	.01
☐ 498 Joey Meyer	.05	.02	.01
☐ 499 Paul Mirabella	.05	.02	.01
☐ 500 Paul Molitor	.25	.11	.03
☐ 501 Juan Nieves	.05	.02	.01
☐ 502 Charlie O'Brien	.05	.02	.01
☐ 503 Dan Plesac	.05	.02	.01
☐ 504 Gary Sheffield	.30	.14	.04
☐ 505 B.J. Surhoff	.05	.02	.01
☐ 506 Dale Sveum	.05	.02	.01
☐ 507 Bill Wegman	.05	.02	.01
☐ 508 Robin Yount	.25	.11	.03
☐ 509 George Bell	.05	.02	.01
☐ 510 Pat Borders	.05	.02	.01
☐ 511 John Cerutti	.05	.02	.01
☐ 512 Rob Ducey	.05	.02	.01
☐ 513 Tony Fernandez	.05	.02	.01
☐ 514 Mike Flanagan	.05	.02	.01
☐ 515 Kelly Gruber	.05	.02	.01
☐ 516 Tom Henke	.05	.02	.01
☐ 517 Alexis Infante	.05	.02	.01
☐ 518 Jimmy Key	.05	.02	.01
☐ 519 Tom Lawless	.05	.02	.01
☐ 520 Manny Lee	.05	.02	.01
☐ 521 Al Leiter	.05	.02	.01
☐ 522 Nelson Liriano	.05	.02	.01
☐ 523 Fred McGriff	.25	.11	.03
☐ 524 Lloyd Moseby	.05	.02	.01
☐ 525 Rance Mulliniks	.05	.02	.01
☐ 526 Dave Stieb	.05	.02	.01
☐ 527 Todd Stottlemyre	.05	.02	.01
☐ 528 Duane Ward	.05	.02	.01
☐ 529 Ernie Whitt	.05	.02	.01
☐ 530 Jesse Barfield	.05	.02	.01
☐ 531 Bob Brower	.05	.02	.01
☐ 532 John Candelaria	.05	.02	.01
☐ 533 Richard Dotson	.05	.02	.01
☐ 534 Lee Guetterman	.05	.02	.01
☐ 535 Mel Hall	.05	.02	.01
☐ 536 Andy Hawkins	.05	.02	.01
☐ 537 Rickey Henderson	.25	.11	.03
☐ 538 Roberto Kelly	.05	.02	.01
☐ 539 Dave LaPoint	.05	.02	.01
☐ 540 Don Mattingly	1.00	.45	.12
☐ 541 Lance McCullers	.05	.02	.01
☐ 542 Mike Pagliarulo	.05	.02	.01
☐ 543 Clay Parker	.05	.02	.01
☐ 544 Ken Phelps	.05	.02	.01
☐ 545 Dave Righetti	.05	.02	.01
☐ 546 Rafael Santana	.05	.02	.01
☐ 547 Steve Sax	.05	.02	.01
☐ 548 Don Slaught	.05	.02	.01
☐ 549 Wayne Tolleson	.05	.02	.01
☐ 550 Dave Winfield	.25	.11	.03
☐ 551 Andy Allanson	.05	.02	.01
☐ 552 Keith Atherton	.05	.02	.01
☐ 553 Scott Bailes	.05	.02	.01
☐ 554 Bud Black	.05	.02	.01
☐ 555 Jerry Browne	.05	.02	.01
☐ 556 Tom Candiotti	.05	.02	.01
☐ 557 Joe Carter	.25	.11	.03
☐ 558 David Clark	.05	.02	.01
☐ 559 John Farrell	.05	.02	.01
☐ 560 Felix Fermin	.05	.02	.01
☐ 561 Brook Jacoby	.05	.02	.01
☐ 562 Doug Jones	.05	.02	.01
☐ 563 Oddibe McDowell	.05	.02	.01
☐ 564 Luis Medina	.05	.02	.01
☐ 565 Pete O'Brien	.05	.02	.01
☐ 566 Jesse Orosco	.05	.02	.01
☐ 567 Joel Skinner	.05	.02	.01
☐ 568 Cory Snyder	.05	.02	.01
☐ 569 Greg Swindell	.05	.02	.01
☐ 570 Rich Yett	.05	.02	.01
☐ 571 Mike Young	.05	.02	.01
☐ 572 Brady Anderson	.30	.14	.04
☐ 573 Jeff Ballard	.05	.02	.01
☐ 574 Jose Bautista	.05	.02	.01
☐ 575 Phil Bradley	.05	.02	.01
☐ 576 Mike Devereaux	.05	.02	.01
☐ 577 Kevin Hickey	.05	.02	.01
☐ 578 Brian Holton	.05	.02	.01
☐ 579 Bob Melvin	.05	.02	.01
☐ 580 Bob Milacki	.05	.02	.01
☐ 581 Gregg Olson	.05	.02	.01
☐ 582 Joe Orsulak	.05	.02	.01
☐ 583 Bill Ripken	.05	.02	.01
☐ 584 Cal Ripken Jr.	2.00	.90	.25
☐ 585 Dave Schmidt	.05	.02	.01
☐ 586 Larry Sheets	.05	.02	.01
☐ 587 Mickey Tettleton	.10	.05	.01
☐ 588 Mark Thurmond	.05	.02	.01
☐ 589 Jay Tibbs	.05	.02	.01
☐ 590 Jim Traber	.05	.02	.01
☐ 591 Mark Williamson	.05	.02	.01
☐ 592 Craig Worthington	.05	.02	.01
☐ 593 Allan Anderson	.05	.02	.01
☐ 594 Ellis Burks	.15	.07	.02
☐ 595 Ken Griffey Jr.	3.00	1.35	.35
☐ 596 Bo Jackson	.10	.05	.01
☐ 597 Roberto Kelly	.05	.02	.01
☐ 598 Kirk McCaskill	.05	.02	.01
☐ 599 Fred McGriff	.25	.11	.03
☐ 600 Mark McGwire	.25	.11	.03
☐ 601 Bob Milacki	.05	.02	.01
☐ 602 Melido Perez	.05	.02	.01
☐ 603 Jeff Robinson	.05	.02	.01
☐ 604 Gary Sheffield	.30	.14	.04
☐ 605 Ruben Sierra	.10	.05	.01
☐ 606 Greg Swindell	.05	.02	.01
☐ 607 Roberto Alomar	.75	.35	.09
☐ 608 Tim Belcher	.05	.02	.01
☐ 609 Vince Coleman	.05	.02	.01
☐ 610 Kal Daniels	.05	.02	.01
☐ 611 Andres Galarraga	.25	.11	.03
☐ 612 Ron Gant	.15	.07	.02
☐ 613 Mark Grace	.25	.11	.03
☐ 614 Gregg Jefferies	.10	.05	.01
☐ 615 Ricky Jordan	.05	.02	.01
☐ 616 Jose Lind	.05	.02	.01
☐ 617 Kevin Mitchell	.05	.02	.01
☐ 618 Gerald Young	.05	.02	.01
☐ 619 Base	.05	.02	.01
☐ 620 Batting helmets	.05	.02	.01
☐ 621 Bats	.05	.02	.01
☐ 622 Batting gloves	.05	.02	.01
☐ 623 Los Angeles Dodgers	.05	.02	.01
☐ 624 Cincinnati Reds	.05	.02	.01
☐ 625 San Diego Padres	.05	.02	.01
☐ 626 San Francisco Giants	.05	.02	.01
☐ 627 Houston Astros	.05	.02	.01
☐ 628 Atlanta Braves	.05	.02	.01
☐ 629 New York Mets	.05	.02	.01
☐ 630 Pittsburgh Pirates	.05	.02	.01
☐ 631 Montreal Expos	.05	.02	.01
☐ 632 Chicago Cubs	.05	.02	.01
☐ 633 St. Louis Cardinals	.05	.02	.01
☐ 634 Philadelphia Phillies	.05	.02	.01
☐ 635 Oakland Athletics	.05	.02	.01
☐ 636 Minnesota Twins	.05	.02	.01
☐ 637 Kansas City Royals	.05	.02	.01
☐ 638 California Angels	.05	.02	.01
☐ 639 Chicago White Sox	.05	.02	.01
☐ 640 Texas Rangers	.05	.02	.01
☐ 641 Seattle Mariners	.05	.02	.01
☐ 642 Boston Red Sox	.05	.02	.01
☐ 643 Detroit Tigers	.05	.02	.01
☐ 644 Milwaukee Brewers	.05	.02	.01
☐ 645 Toronto Blue Jays	.05	.02	.01
☐ 646 New York Yankees	.05	.02	.01
☐ 647 Cleveland Indians	.05	.02	.01
☐ 648 Baltimore Orioles	.05	.02	.01

1986 Quaker Granola

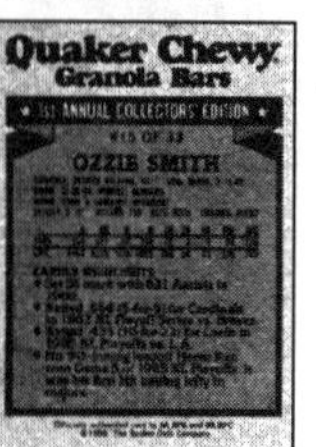

This set of 33 standard-size cards was available in packages of Quaker Oats Chewy Granola, three player cards plus a complete set offer card in each package. The set was also available through a mail-in offer where anyone sending in four UPC seals from Chewy Granola (before 12/31/86) would receive a complete set. The cards were produced by Topps for Quaker Oats. Card backs are printed in red and blue on gray card stock. The cards are numbered on the front and the back. Cards 1-17 feature National League players and cards 18-33 feature American League players. The first three cards in each sequence depict that league's MVP, Cy Young, and Rookie of the Year, respectively. The rest of the cards in each sequence are ordered alphabetically.

	MINT	NRMT	EXC
COMPLETE SET (33)	8.00	3.60	1.00
COMMON CARD (1-33)	.10	.05	.01
☐ 1 Willie McGee	.25	.11	.03
☐ 2 Dwight Gooden	.40	.18	.05
☐ 3 Vince Coleman	.25	.11	.03
☐ 4 Gary Carter	.40	.18	.05
☐ 5 Jack Clark	.10	.05	.01
☐ 6 Steve Garvey	.25	.11	.03
☐ 7 Tony Gwynn	1.00	.45	.12
☐ 8 Dale Murphy	.40	.18	.05
☐ 9 Dave Parker	.25	.11	.03
☐ 10 Tim Raines	.25	.11	.03
☐ 11 Pete Rose	.75	.35	.09
☐ 12 Nolan Ryan	2.00	.90	.25
☐ 13 Ryne Sandberg	.75	.35	.09
☐ 14 Mike Schmidt	.75	.35	.09
☐ 15 Ozzie Smith	.75	.35	.09
☐ 16 Darryl Strawberry	.40	.18	.05
☐ 17 Fernando Valenzuela	.25	.11	.03
☐ 18 Don Mattingly	1.00	.45	.12
☐ 19 Bret Saberhagen	.25	.11	.03
☐ 20 Ozzie Guillen	.25	.11	.03
☐ 21 Bert Blyleven	.25	.11	.03
☐ 22 Wade Boggs	.50	.23	.06
☐ 23 George Brett	1.00	.45	.12
☐ 24 Darrell Evans	.10	.05	.01
☐ 25 Rickey Henderson	.50	.23	.06
☐ 26 Reggie Jackson	.50	.23	.06
☐ 27 Eddie Murray	.75	.35	.09
☐ 28 Phil Niekro	.40	.18	.05
☐ 29 Dan Quisenberry	.10	.05	.01
☐ 30 Jim Rice	.25	.11	.03
☐ 31 Cal Ripken	2.00	.90	.25
☐ 32 Tom Seaver	.40	.18	.05
☐ 33 Dave Winfield	.50	.23	.06
☐ NNO Offer Card for the complete set	.10	.05	.01

1936 R311 Premiums

The 1936 R311 set of Portraits and Team Baseball Photos exist in two different forms, each measuring 6" by 8". Fifteen leather-like or uneven surface cards comprise the first type; these are indicated by the prefix L in the checklist below and are listed first. Twenty eight glossy surface, sepia or black and white cards comprise the second type. These glossy cards are indicated by the prefix G in the checklist below. The Boston Red Sox team exists with or without a sky above the building at the right of the card. Scarcities within the glossy subset include Pepper Martin, Mel Harder, Schoolboy Rowe, and the Dodgers, Pirates, Braves and Columbus team cards; these are asterisked in the checklist below.

	EX-MT	VG-E	GOOD
COMPLETE SET (44)	2400.00	1100.00	300.00
COMMON LEATHER (L1-L15)	30.00	13.50	3.70
COMMON GLOSSY (G1-G28)	20.00	9.00	2.50

	EX-MT	VG-E	GOOD
☐ G1 Earl Averill	40.00	18.00	5.00
☐ G2 James L. "Jim" Bottomley	40.00	18.00	5.00
☐ G3 Gordon S."Mickey" Cochrane	50.00	22.00	6.25
☐ G4 Joe Cronin	40.00	18.00	5.00
☐ G5 Jerome "Dizzy" Dean	75.00	34.00	9.50
☐ G6 Jimmy Dykes	20.00	9.00	2.50
☐ G7 Jimmy Foxx	75.00	34.00	9.50
☐ G8 Frankie Frisch	50.00	22.00	6.25
☐ G9 Henry "Hank" Greenberg	50.00	22.00	6.25
☐ G10 Mel Harder	40.00	18.00	5.00
☐ G11 Ken Keltner	20.00	9.00	2.50
☐ G12 Pepper Martin	150.00	70.00	19.00
☐ G13 Lynwood "Schoolboy" Rowe *	40.00	18.00	5.00
☐ G14 William "Bill" Terry	40.00	18.00	5.00
☐ G15 Harold "Pie" Traynor	40.00	18.00	5.00
☐ G16 American League All Stars 1935	20.00	9.00	2.50
☐ G17 American League Pennant Winners 1934 (Detroit Tigers)	40.00	18.00	5.00
☐ G18 Boston Braves 1935	200.00	90.00	25.00
☐ G19A Boston Red Sox with sky above building at right of the card	20.00	9.00	2.50
☐ G19B Boston Red Sox without sky	75.00	34.00	9.50
☐ G20 Brooklyn Dodgers 1935 *	200.00	90.00	25.00
☐ G21 Chicago White Sox 1935	20.00	9.00	2.50
☐ G22 Columbus Red Birds 1934 Pennant Winners of Amer. Assoc.	20.00	9.00	2.50
☐ G23 National League All Stars 1934	20.00	9.00	2.50
☐ G24 National League Champions 1935 Chicago Cubs	20.00	9.00	2.50
☐ G25 New York Yankees 1935	40.00	18.00	5.00
☐ G26 Pittsburgh Pirates 1935 *	40.00	18.00	5.00
☐ G27 St. Louis Browns 1935	20.00	9.00	2.50
☐ G28 World Champions 1934 St. Louis Cardinals	20.00	9.00	2.50
☐ L1 Paul Derringer	30.00	13.50	3.70
☐ L2 Wes Ferrell	30.00	13.50	3.70
☐ L3 Jimmy Foxx	100.00	45.00	12.50
☐ L4 Charlie Gehringer	75.00	34.00	9.50
☐ L5 Mel Harder	30.00	13.50	3.70
☐ L6 Gabby Hartnett	60.00	27.00	7.50
☐ L7 Rogers Hornsby	100.00	45.00	12.50
☐ L8 Connie Mack	75.00	34.00	9.50
☐ L9 Van Mungo	30.00	13.50	3.70
☐ L10 Steve O'Neill	30.00	13.50	3.70
☐ L11 Charles Ruffing	60.00	27.00	7.50
☐ L12 Joe DiMaggio Frank Crosetti Tony Lazzeri	350.00	160.00	45.00
☐ L13 Arky Vaughan Honus Wagner CO	100.00	45.00	12.50
☐ L14 American League Pennant Winners 1935 Detroit Tigers	30.00	13.50	3.70
☐ L15 National League Pennant Winners 1935 Chicago Cubs	30.00	13.50	3.70

1936 R312 Pastel Photos

The 1936 R312 Baseball Photos set contains 25 color tinted, single player cards, listed with the letter A in the checklist; 14 multiple player cards, listed with the letter B in the checklist; 6 action cards with handwritten signatures, listed with the letter C in the checklist; and 5 action cards with printed titles, listed with the letter D in the checklist. The pictures are reminiscent of a water-color type painting in soft pastels. The Allen card is reportedly more difficult to obtain than other cards in the set.

	EX-MT	VG-E	GOOD
COMPLETE SET (50)	2100.00	950.00	250.00
COMMON CARD (A1-A25)	25.00	11.00	3.10
COMMON CARD (B1-B14)	25.00	11.00	3.10
COMMON CARD (C1-C6)	25.00	11.00	3.10
COMMON CARD (D1-D5)	25.00	11.00	3.10

	EX-MT	VG-E	GOOD
☐ A1 John Thomas Allen	100.00	45.00	12.50
☐ A2 Cy Blanton	25.00	11.00	3.10
☐ A3 Mace Brown	25.00	11.00	3.10
☐ A4 Dolph Camilli	25.00	11.00	3.10
☐ A5 Gordon Cochrane	60.00	27.00	7.50
☐ A6 Rip Collins	25.00	11.00	3.10
☐ A7 Ki Ki Cuyler	40.00	18.00	5.00
☐ A8 Bill Dickey	60.00	27.00	7.50
☐ A9 Joe DiMagio sic, DiMaggio	500.00	220.00	60.00
☐ A10 Chas. Dressen	30.00	13.50	3.70
☐ A11 Benny Frey	25.00	11.00	3.10
☐ A12 Hank Greenberg	60.00	27.00	7.50
☐ A13 Mel Harder	30.00	13.50	3.70
☐ A14 Rogers Hornsby	100.00	45.00	12.50
☐ A15 Ernie Lombardi	40.00	18.00	5.00
☐ A16 Pepper Martin	30.00	13.50	3.70
☐ A17 Johnny Mize	60.00	27.00	7.50
☐ A18 Van L. Mungo	25.00	11.00	3.10
☐ A19 Bud Parmalee	25.00	11.00	3.10
☐ A20 Chas. Ruffing	40.00	18.00	5.00
☐ A21 Eugene Schott	25.00	11.00	3.10
☐ A22 Casey Stengel	100.00	45.00	12.50
☐ A23 Bill Sullivan	25.00	11.00	3.10
☐ A24 Bill Swift	25.00	11.00	3.10
☐ A25 Ralph Winegarner	25.00	11.00	3.10
☐ B1 Ollie Bejma and Rollie Hemsley	25.00	11.00	3.10
☐ B2 Cliff Bolton and Earl Whitehill	25.00	11.00	3.10
☐ B3 Stan Bordagaray and George Earnshaw	25.00	11.00	3.10
☐ B4 Billy Herman Phil Cavarretta, Stan Hack Bill Jurges	25.00	11.00	3.10
☐ B5 Pete Fox Jo Jo White Goose Goslin	25.00	11.00	3.10
☐ B6 Galan, (Billy)Herman, Fred Lindstrom, Gabby Hartnett, Demaree, Cavarretta Hack, Jurges, Klein	25.00	11.00	3.10
☐ B7 Bucky Harris and Joe Cronin	40.00	18.00	5.00
☐ B8 Gabby Hartnett and Lon Warnecke sic, Warneke	30.00	13.50	3.70
☐ B9 Myril Hoag and Lefty Gomez	40.00	18.00	5.00
☐ B10 Allen Sothoron and Rogers Hornsby	40.00	18.00	5.00
☐ B11 Connie Mack MG and Lefty Grove	75.00	34.00	9.50
☐ B12 Taylor Tris Speaker Kiki Cuyler	40.00	18.00	5.00
☐ B13 Dixie Walker Mule Haas Mike Kreevich	25.00	11.00	3.10
☐ B14 Paul Waner Lloyd Waner Big Jim Weaver	40.00	18.00	5.00
☐ C1 Nick Altrock Al Schacht Clowning on the Diamond	30.00	13.50	3.70
☐ C2 Bell (St. Louis) Out At First Zeke Bonura first baseman	25.00	11.00	3.10
☐ C3 Jim Collins (Safe) and Stan Hack	25.00	11.00	3.10
☐ C4 Jimmie Foxx batting with Luke Sewell catching	40.00	18.00	5.00
☐ C5 Al Lopez Traps Two Cubs on Third Base	40.00	18.00	5.00
☐ C6 Pie Traynor and Augie Galan	40.00	18.00	5.00
☐ D1 Alvin Crowder after victory in the World Series	25.00	11.00	3.10
☐ D2 Floyd Vaughan present Pirate Shortstop and Coach Hans Wagner	60.00	27.00	7.50
☐ D3 Gabby Hartnett (crossing home plate after hitting homer...	40.00	18.00	5.00
☐ D4 Kids flock around Schoolboy Rowe as he leaves Cubs park...	25.00	11.00	3.10
☐ D5 Van Atta, St. Louis pitcher out at plate Rick Ferrell Boston, catching	25.00	11.00	3.10

1932 R337 Series Of 24

The cards in this 24-card set measure 2 5/16" by 2 13/16". The "Series of 24" is similar to the MP and Co. issues in terms of style and quality. Produced about 1932, this set is numbered 401-424. The three missing numbers, 403, 413, and 414, probably correspond to the three known unnumbered players.

	EX-MT	VG-E	GOOD
COMPLETE SET (24)	2400.00	1100.00	300.00
COMMON CARD (401-427)	50.00	22.00	6.25

	EX-MT	VG-E	GOOD
☐ 401 Johnny Vergez Giants	50.00	22.00	6.25
☐ 402 Babe Ruth New York Yankees	1000.00	450.00	125.00
☐ 404 George Pipgras Out at First Base	50.00	22.00	6.25
☐ 405 Bill Terry	100.00	45.00	12.50
☐ 406 George Connally Cleveland	50.00	22.00	6.25
☐ 407 Wilson Clark Brooklyn	50.00	22.00	6.25
☐ 408 Lefty Grove Athletics	150.00	70.00	19.00
☐ 409 Henry Johnson Red Sox	50.00	22.00	6.25
☐ 410 Jimmy Dykes White Sox	50.00	22.00	6.25
☐ 411 Henry Hine Schuble Detroit	50.00	22.00	6.25
☐ 412 Washington, Harris Makes Home Run	75.00	34.00	9.50
☐ 415 Al Simmons Safe At Third Base	100.00	45.00	12.50
☐ 416 Heinie Manush A Safe Leap to 2nd Base	75.00	34.00	9.50
☐ 417 Glen Myatt Cleveland	50.00	22.00	6.25
☐ 418 Babe Herman Chicago Cubs	75.00	34.00	9.50
☐ 419 Frank Frisch St. Louis Cardinals	100.00	45.00	12.50
☐ 420 A Safe Slide to the Home Plate	50.00	22.00	6.25
☐ 421 Paul Waner	75.00	34.00	9.50
☐ 422 Jimmy Wilson Cardinals	50.00	22.00	6.25
☐ 423 Charles Grimm Chicago Natl.	75.00	34.00	9.50
☐ 424 Dick Bartell Phila. Natl. at bat	50.00	22.00	6.25
☐ xx Jimmy Fox sic, Jimmie Foxx Athletics unnumbered	150.00	70.00	19.00
☐ xx Roy Johnson Red Sox unnumbered	50.00	22.00	6.25
☐ xx Pie Traynor Pitts,sic, Pittsburgh is out unnumbered	100.00	45.00	12.50

1951 R423 Small Strip

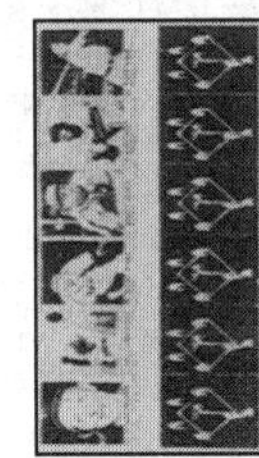

Many numbers of these small and unattractive cards are either unknown or do not exist for this issue of the early 1950s. The cards are printed on thin stock and measure 5/8" by 3/4"; sometimes they are found as a long horizontal strip of 13 cards connected by a perforation. Complete strips intact are worth 50 percent more than the sum of the individual players on the strip. The cards were available with a variety of back colors, red, green, blue, or purple. The cards on the strip are in no apparent order, numerically or alphabetically. The producer's numbering of the cards in the set is very close to alphabetical order. Cards are so small they are sometimes lost. These strips were premiums or prizes in one-cent bubblegum machines; they were folded accordion style and held together by a small metal clip. Obviously, all additions to this list are greatly appreciated.

	NRMT	VG-E	GOOD
COMPLETE SET (88)	175.00	80.00	22.00
COMMON CARD (1-120)	.50	.23	.06

	NRMT	VG-E	GOOD
☐ 1 Richie Ashburn	2.00	.90	.25
☐ 3 Frank Baumholtz	.50	.23	.06
☐ 4 Ralph Branca	.75	.35	.09
☐ 5 Yogi Berra	7.50	3.40	.95
☐ 8 Harry Brecheen	.50	.23	.06
☐ 9 Chico Carrasquel	.50	.23	.06
☐ 10 Jerry Coleman	.50	.23	.06
☐ 11 Walker Cooper	.50	.23	.06
☐ 12 Roy Campanella	7.50	3.40	.95
☐ 13 Phil Cavarretta	.75	.35	.09
☐ 14 Ty Cobb	15.00	6.75	1.85
☐ 17 Frank Crosetti	.75	.35	.09
☐ 18 Larry Doby	.75	.35	.09
☐ 19 Walter Dropo	.50	.23	.06
☐ 20 Alvin Dark	.75	.35	.09
☐ 21 Dizzy Dean	6.00	2.70	.75
☐ 22 Bill Dickey	2.00	.90	.25
☐ 23 Murray Dickson	.50	.23	.06
☐ 24 Dom DiMaggio	1.50	.70	.19
☐ 25 Joe DiMaggio	15.00	6.75	1.85
☐ 28 Bob Elliott	.75	.35	.09
☐ 31 Bob Feller	6.00	2.70	.75
☐ 32 Frank Frisch	1.50	.70	.19
☐ 35 Lou Gehrig	15.00	6.75	1.85
☐ 36 Joe Gordon	.75	.35	.09
☐ 38 Hank Greenberg	2.00	.90	.25
☐ 39 Lefty Grove	2.00	.90	.25
☐ 42 Ken Heintzelman	.50	.23	.06
☐ 44 Jim Hearn	.50	.23	.06
☐ 46 Harry Heilman	1.50	.70	.19
☐ 47 Tommy Henrich	1.00	.45	.12
☐ 48 Roger Hornsby	5.00	2.20	.60
☐ 50 Eddie Joost	.50	.23	.06
☐ 51 Nippy Jones	.50	.23	.06
☐ 54 Walter Johnson	5.00	2.20	.60
☐ 55 Ellis Kinder	.50	.23	.06
☐ 56 Jim Konstanty	.75	.35	.09
☐ 57 George Kell	2.00	.90	.25
☐ 58 Ralph Kiner	2.00	.90	.25
☐ 59 Bob Lemon	2.00	.90	.25
☐ 60 Whitey Lockman	.75	.35	.09
☐ 61 Ed Lopat	.75	.35	.09
☐ 64 Cliff Mapes	.50	.23	.06
☐ 65 Willard Marshall	.50	.23	.06
☐ 67 Connie Mack	2.00	.90	.25
☐ 68 Christy Mathewson	5.00	2.20	.60
☐ 69 Joe Medwick	2.00	.90	.25
☐ 70 Johnny Mize	2.00	.90	.25
☐ 71 Terry Moore	.50	.23	.06
☐ 72 Stan Musial	10.00	4.50	1.25
☐ 73 Hal Newhouser	2.00	.90	.25
☐ 74 Don Newcombe	1.00	.45	.12
☐ 75 Lefty O'Doul	.75	.35	.09
☐ 77 Mel Parnell	.50	.23	.06
☐ 79 Gerald Priddy	.50	.23	.06
☐ 80 Dave Philley	.50	.23	.06
☐ 81 Bob Porterfield	.50	.23	.06
☐ 82 Andy Pafko	.50	.23	.06
☐ 83 Howie Pollet	.50	.23	.06
☐ 84 Herb Pennock	1.50	.70	.19
☐ 85 Al Rosen	.75	.35	.09
☐ 86 Pee Wee Reese	2.00	.90	.25
☐ 87 Del Rice	.50	.23	.06
☐ 89 Allie Reynolds	.75	.35	.09
☐ 92 Babe Ruth	20.00	9.00	2.50
☐ 93 Casey Stengel	2.00	.90	.25
☐ 94 Vern Stephens	.75	.35	.09
☐ 95 Duke Snider	3.00	1.35	.35
☐ 96 Enos Slaughter	2.00	.90	.25
☐ 97 Al Schoendienst	2.00	.90	.25
☐ 98 Gerald Staley	.50	.23	.06
☐ 99 Clyde Shoun	.50	.23	.06
☐ 102 Al Simmons	1.50	.70	.19
☐ 103 George Sisler	1.50	.70	.19
☐ 104 Tris Speaker	2.00	.90	.25
☐ 105 Ed Stanky	.75	.35	.09
☐ 106 Virgil Trucks	.50	.23	.06
☐ 107 Henry Thompson	.50	.23	.06
☐ 109 Dazzy Vance	1.50	.70	.19
☐ 110 Lloyd Waner	1.50	.70	.19
☐ 111 Paul Waner	2.00	.90	.25
☐ 112 Gene Woodling	.50	.23	.06
☐ 113 Ted Williams	15.00	6.75	1.85
☐ 115 Wes Westrum	.50	.23	.06
☐ 117 Eddie Yost	.50	.23	.06
☐ 118 Al Zarilla	.50	.23	.06
☐ 119 Gus Zernial	.50	.23	.06
☐ 120 Sam Zoldak	.50	.23	.06

1993 Rainbow Foods Winfield

This ten-card standard-size set was sponsored by Rainbow Foods, with a portion of the sales proceeds donated to the Minnesota Twins Rookie League youth baseball program. The blue-bordered fronts contain color and sepia photos of Winfield beginning with his college years and following his career in the major leagues. Winfield's name in red script is displayed on a gold stripe under the picture. The Rainbow Foods logo appears in the lower right. The horizontal backs contain a close-up picture on the left and the appropriate statistics and career summary on the right side. Cards 9 and 10 have vertical backs. The cards are numbered on the back. The cards originally sold in five-card packs for 99 cents. Each pack contained four blue-bordered cards and one gold-bordered card. The gold-bordered set is otherwise identical to the blue-bordered set but due to its relative scarcity sells for two to three times the values listed below.

	MINT	NRMT	EXC
COMPLETE SET (10)	7.50	3.40	.95
COMMON CARD (1-10)	.75	.35	.09
☐ 1 Dave Winfield Univ. of Minnesota Outfielder	.75	.35	.09
☐ 2 Dave Winfield Univ. of Minnesota Pitcher	.75	.35	.09
☐ 3 Dave Winfield Univ. of Minnesota Basketball Star	.75	.35	.09
☐ 4 Dave Winfield San Diego Padres 1973-80	.75	.35	.09
☐ 5 Dave Winfield New York Yankees 1981-90	.75	.35	.09
☐ 6 Dave Winfield California Angels 1990-91	.75	.35	.09
☐ 7 Dave Winfield Toronto Blue Jays 1992	.75	.35	.09
☐ 8 Dave Winfield Minnesota Twins 1993-	.75	.35	.09
☐ 9 Dave Winfield 7-Time Golden Glove Winner	.75	.35	.09
☐ 10 Dave Winfield Pride of Minnesota	.75	.35	.09

1984 Ralston Purina

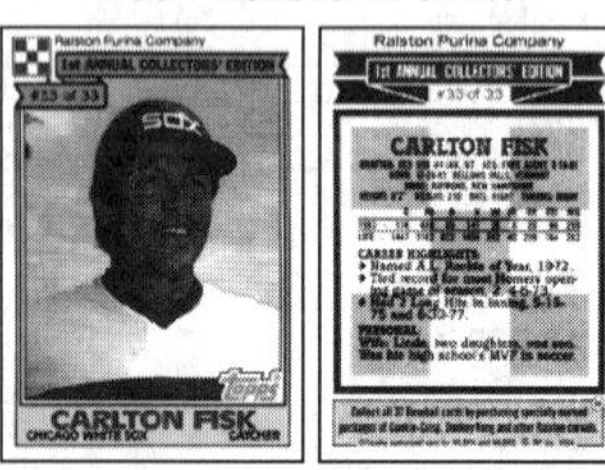

The cards in this 33-card set measure the standard size. In 1984 the Ralston Purina Company issued what it has entitled "The First Annual Collectors Edition of Baseball Cards." The cards feature portrait photos of the players rather than batting action shots. The Topps logo appears along with the Ralston logo on the front of the card. The backs are completely different from the Topps cards of this year; in fact, they contain neither a Topps logo nor a Topps copyright. Large quantities of these cards were obtained by card dealers for direct distribution into the organized hobby, hence the relatively low price of the set.

	MINT	NRMT	EXC
COMPLETE SET (33)	5.00	2.20	.60
COMMON CARD (1-33)	.05	.02	.01
☐ 1 Eddie Murray	.50	.23	.06
☐ 2 Ozzie Smith	.75	.35	.09
☐ 3 Ted Simmons	.05	.02	.01
☐ 4 Pete Rose	.50	.23	.06
☐ 5 Greg Luzinski	.05	.02	.01
☐ 6 Andre Dawson	.25	.11	.03
☐ 7 Dave Winfield	.30	.14	.04
☐ 8 Tom Seaver	.25	.11	.03
☐ 9 Jim Rice	.10	.05	.01
☐ 10 Fernando Valenzuela	.10	.05	.01
☐ 11 Wade Boggs	.50	.23	.06
☐ 12 Dale Murphy	.25	.11	.03
☐ 13 George Brett	.75	.35	.09
☐ 14 Nolan Ryan	1.50	.70	.19
☐ 15 Rickey Henderson	.30	.14	.04
☐ 16 Steve Carlton	.25	.11	.03
☐ 17 Rod Carew	.25	.11	.03
☐ 18 Steve Garvey	.10	.05	.01
☐ 19 Reggie Jackson	.30	.14	.04
☐ 20 Dave Concepcion	.10	.05	.01
☐ 21 Robin Yount	.25	.11	.03
☐ 22 Mike Schmidt	.50	.23	.06
☐ 23 Jim Palmer	.25	.11	.03
☐ 24 Bruce Sutter	.05	.02	.01
☐ 25 Dan Quisenberry	.05	.02	.01
☐ 26 Bill Madlock	.05	.02	.01
☐ 27 Cecil Cooper	.05	.02	.01
☐ 28 Gary Carter	.10	.05	.01
☐ 29 Fred Lynn	.10	.05	.01
☐ 30 Pedro Guerrero	.05	.02	.01
☐ 31 Ron Guidry	.10	.05	.01
☐ 32 Keith Hernandez	.10	.05	.01
☐ 33 Carlton Fisk	.25	.11	.03

1987 Ralston Purina

The Ralston Purina Company issued a set of 15 cards picturing players without their respective team logos. The cards measure approximately 2 1/2" by 3 3/8" and are in full-color on the front. The

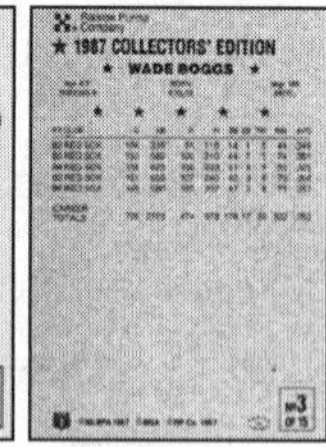

cards are numbered on the back in the lower right hand corner; the player's uniform number is prominently displayed on the front. The cards were distributed as inserts inside packages of certain flavors of Ralston Purina's breakfast cereals. Three cards and a contest card were packaged in cellophane and inserted within the cereal box. The set was also available as an uncut sheet through a mail-in offer. Since the uncut sheets are relatively common, the value of the sheet is essentially the same as the value of the sum of the individual cards. In fact there were two uncut sheets issued, one had "Honey Graham Chex" printed at the top and the other had "Cookie Crisp" printed at the top. Also cards were issued with (cards from cereal boxes) and without (cards cut from the uncut sheets) the words "1987 Collectors Edition" printed in blue on the front. Reportedly 100,000 of the uncut sheets were given away free via instant win certificates inserted in with the cereal or collectors could send in two non-winning contest cards plus 1.00 for each uncut sheet.

	MINT	NRMT	EXC
COMPLETE SET (15)	18.00	8.00	2.20
COMMON CARD (1-15)	.40	.18	.05
☐ 1 Nolan Ryan	5.00	2.20	.60
☐ 2 Steve Garvey	.60	.25	.07
☐ 3 Wade Boggs	1.25	.55	.16
☐ 4 Dave Winfield	1.00	.45	.12
☐ 5 Don Mattingly	2.50	1.10	.30
☐ 6 Don Sutton	.60	.25	.07
☐ 7 Dave Parker	.40	.18	.05
☐ 8 Eddie Murray	1.25	.55	.16
☐ 9 Gary Carter	.60	.25	.07
☐ 10 Roger Clemens	1.25	.55	.16
☐ 11 Fernando Valenzuela	.60	.25	.07
☐ 12 Cal Ripken	5.00	2.20	.60
☐ 13 Ozzie Smith	2.00	.90	.25
☐ 14 Mike Schmidt	1.50	.70	.19
☐ 15 Ryne Sandberg	2.00	.90	.25

1909 Ramly T204

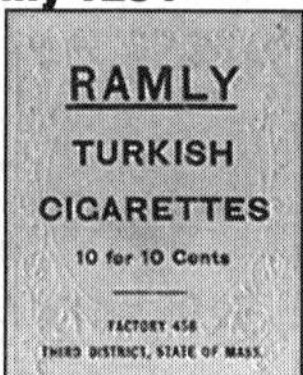

The cards in this 121-card set measure approximately 2" by 2 1/2". The Ramly baseball series, designated T204 in the catalog, contains unnumbered cards. This set is one of the most distinguished ever produced, containing ornate gold borders around a black and white portrait of each player. There are spelling errors, and two distinct backs, "Ramly" and "TTT", are known. There is a premium of up to 25 percent for the "TTT" back. Much of the obverse card detail is actually embossed. The players have been alphabetized and numbered for reference in the checklist below.

	EX-MT	VG-E	GOOD
COMPLETE SET (121)	40000.00	18000.00	5000.00
COMMON CARD (1-121)	250.00	110.00	31.00
☐ 1 Whitey Alperman	250.00	110.00	31.00
☐ 2 John J. Anderson	250.00	110.00	31.00
☐ 3 Jimmy Archer	250.00	110.00	31.00
☐ 4 Frank Arrelanes UER	250.00	110.00	31.00
☐ 5 Jim Ball (Boston NL)	250.00	110.00	31.00
☐ 6 Neal Ball (N.Y. AL)	250.00	110.00	31.00
☐ 7 Frank Bancroft	275.00	125.00	34.00
☐ 8 Johnny Bates	250.00	110.00	31.00
☐ 9 Fred Beebe	250.00	110.00	31.00
☐ 10 George Bell	250.00	110.00	31.00
☐ 11 Chief Bender	600.00	275.00	75.00
☐ 12 Walter Blair	250.00	110.00	31.00
☐ 13 Cliff Blankenship	250.00	110.00	31.00
☐ 14 Frank Bowerman	250.00	110.00	31.00
☐ 15 Kitty Bransfield	250.00	110.00	31.00
☐ 16 Roger Bresnahan	600.00	275.00	75.00
☐ 17 Al Bridwell	250.00	110.00	31.00
☐ 18 Mordecai Brown	600.00	275.00	75.00
☐ 19 Fred Burchell	250.00	110.00	31.00
☐ 20 Jesse Burkett	800.00	350.00	100.00
☐ 21 Bobby Byrnes UER	250.00	110.00	31.00
☐ 22 Bill Carrigan	250.00	110.00	31.00
☐ 23 Frank Chance	800.00	350.00	100.00
☐ 24 Charles Chech	250.00	110.00	31.00
☐ 25 Eddie Cicotte	350.00	160.00	45.00
☐ 26 Otis Clymer	250.00	110.00	31.00
☐ 27 Andrew Coakley	250.00	110.00	31.00
☐ 28 Eddie Collins	800.00	350.00	100.00
☐ 29 Jimmy Collins	800.00	350.00	100.00
☐ 30 Wid Conroy	250.00	110.00	31.00
☐ 31 Jack Coombs	300.00	135.00	38.00
☐ 32 Doc Crandall	250.00	110.00	31.00
☐ 33 Lou Criger	250.00	110.00	31.00
☐ 34 Harry Davis	250.00	110.00	31.00
☐ 35 Art Devlin	250.00	110.00	31.00
☐ 36 Bill Dineen UER	250.00	110.00	31.00
☐ 37 Pat Donahue	250.00	110.00	31.00
☐ 38 Mike Donlin	275.00	125.00	34.00
☐ 39 Wild Bill Donovan	250.00	110.00	31.00
☐ 40 Gus Dorner	250.00	110.00	31.00
☐ 41 Joe Dunn	250.00	110.00	31.00
☐ 42 Kid Elberfield	250.00	110.00	31.00
☐ 43 Johnny Evers	800.00	350.00	100.00
☐ 44 Bob Ewing	250.00	110.00	31.00
☐ 45 George Ferguson	250.00	110.00	31.00
☐ 46 Hobe Ferris	250.00	110.00	31.00
☐ 47 Jerry Freeman	250.00	110.00	31.00
☐ 48 Art Fromme	250.00	110.00	31.00
☐ 49 Bob Ganley	250.00	110.00	31.00
☐ 50 Doc Gessler	250.00	110.00	31.00
☐ 51 Peaches Graham	250.00	110.00	31.00
☐ 52 Clark Griffith	600.00	275.00	75.00
☐ 53 Roy Hartzell	250.00	110.00	31.00
☐ 54 Charlie Hemphill	250.00	110.00	31.00
☐ 55 Dick Hoblitzell UER	250.00	110.00	31.00
☐ 56 George Howard	250.00	110.00	31.00
☐ 57 Harry Howell	250.00	110.00	31.00
☐ 58 Miller Huggins	800.00	350.00	100.00
☐ 59 John Hummel	250.00	110.00	31.00
☐ 60 Walter Johnson	4500.00	2000.00	550.00
☐ 61 Tom Jones	250.00	110.00	31.00
☐ 62 Mike Kahoe	250.00	110.00	31.00
☐ 63 Ed Kargar UER	250.00	110.00	31.00
☐ 64 Willie Keeler	1000.00	450.00	125.00
☐ 65 Ed Konetchey UER	250.00	110.00	31.00
☐ 66 Red Kleinonw	250.00	110.00	31.00
☐ 67 John Knight	250.00	110.00	31.00
☐ 68 Vive Lindaman	250.00	110.00	31.00
☐ 69 Hans Loebert UER	250.00	110.00	31.00
☐ 70 Harry Lord	250.00	110.00	31.00
☐ 71 Harry Lumley	250.00	110.00	31.00
☐ 72 Ernie Lush	250.00	110.00	31.00
☐ 73 Rube Manning	250.00	110.00	31.00
☐ 74 Jimmy McAleer	250.00	110.00	31.00
☐ 75 Amby McConnell	250.00	110.00	31.00
☐ 76 Moose McCormick	250.00	110.00	31.00
☐ 77 Matty McIntyre	250.00	110.00	31.00
☐ 78 Larry McLean	250.00	110.00	31.00
☐ 79 Fred Merkle	300.00	135.00	38.00
☐ 80 Clyde Milan	275.00	125.00	34.00
☐ 81 Mike Mitchell	250.00	110.00	31.00
☐ 82 Pat Moran	250.00	110.00	31.00
☐ 83 Harry Cy Morgan	250.00	110.00	31.00
☐ 84 Tim Murname UER	250.00	110.00	31.00
☐ 85 Danny Murphy	250.00	110.00	31.00
☐ 86 Red Murray	250.00	110.00	31.00
☐ 87 Doc Newton	250.00	110.00	31.00
☐ 88 Simon Nichols UER	250.00	110.00	31.00
☐ 89 Harry Niles	250.00	110.00	31.00
☐ 90 Bill O'Hare UER	250.00	110.00	31.00
☐ 91 Charley O'Leary	250.00	110.00	31.00
☐ 92 Dode Paskert	250.00	110.00	31.00
☐ 93 Barney Pelty	250.00	110.00	31.00
☐ 94 Jack Pfeister UER	250.00	110.00	31.00
☐ 95 Eddie Plank	1250.00	550.00	160.00
☐ 96 Jack Powell	250.00	110.00	31.00
☐ 97 Bugs Raymond	275.00	125.00	34.00
☐ 98 Tom Reilly	250.00	110.00	31.00
☐ 99 Claude Ritchey	250.00	110.00	31.00
☐ 100 Nap Rucker	275.00	125.00	34.00
☐ 101 Ed Ruelbach UER	275.00	125.00	34.00
☐ 102 Slim Sallee	250.00	110.00	31.00
☐ 103 Germany Schaefer	275.00	125.00	34.00
☐ 104 Jimmy Schekard UER	250.00	110.00	31.00
☐ 105 Admiral Schlei	250.00	110.00	31.00
☐ 106 Wildfire Schulte	250.00	110.00	31.00
☐ 107 Jimmy Sebring	250.00	110.00	31.00
☐ 108 Bill Shipke	250.00	110.00	31.00
☐ 109 Charlie Smith	250.00	110.00	31.00
☐ 110 Tubby Spencer	250.00	110.00	31.00
☐ 111 Jake Stahl	300.00	135.00	38.00
☐ 112 Harry Stienfeldt UER	300.00	135.00	38.00
☐ 113 Jim Stephens	250.00	110.00	31.00
☐ 114 Gabby Street	250.00	110.00	31.00
☐ 115 Bill Sweeney	250.00	110.00	31.00
☐ 116 Fred Tenney	250.00	110.00	31.00
☐ 117 Ira Thomas	250.00	110.00	31.00
☐ 118 Joe Tinker	800.00	350.00	100.00
☐ 119 Bob Unglane UER	250.00	110.00	31.00
☐ 120 Heinie Wagner	250.00	110.00	31.00
☐ 121 Bobby Wallace	800.00	350.00	100.00

1978 Rangers Burger King

The cards in this 23-card set measure 2 1/2" by 3 1/2". This set of 22 numbered player cards (featuring the Texas Rangers) and one unnumbered checklist was issued regionally by Burger King in 1978. Asterisks denote poses different from those found in the regular Topps cards of this year.

	NRMT	VG-E	GOOD
COMPLETE SET (23)	15.00	6.75	1.85
COMMON CARD (1-22)	.50	.23	.06
☐ 1 Billy Hunter MG	.50	.23	.06
☐ 2 Jim Sundberg	1.00	.45	.12
☐ 3 John Ellis	.50	.23	.06
☐ 4 Doyle Alexander	.60	.25	.07
☐ 5 Jon Matlack *	.75	.35	.09
☐ 6 Dock Ellis	.50	.23	.06
☐ 7 Doc Medich	.50	.23	.06
☐ 8 Fergie Jenkins *	4.00	1.80	.50
☐ 9 Len Barker	.50	.23	.06
☐ 10 Reggie Cleveland *	.50	.23	.06
☐ 11 Mike Hargrove	1.25	.55	.16
☐ 12 Bump Wills	.50	.23	.06
☐ 13 Toby Harrah	1.00	.45	.12
☐ 14 Bert Campaneris	.75	.35	.09
☐ 15 Sandy Alomar	.60	.25	.07
☐ 16 Kurt Bevacqua	.50	.23	.06
☐ 17 Al Oliver *	1.25	.55	.16
☐ 18 Juan Beniquez	.50	.23	.06
☐ 19 Claudell Washington	1.00	.45	.12
☐ 20 Richie Zisk	.60	.25	.07
☐ 21 John Lowenstein *	.50	.23	.06
☐ 22 Bobby Thompson *	.50	.23	.06
☐ NNO Checklist Card TP	.25	.11	.03

1983 Rangers Affiliated Food

The cards in this 28-card set measure 2 3/8" by 3 1/2". The Affiliated Food Stores chain of Arlington, Texas, produced this set of Texas Rangers late during the 1983 baseball season. Complete sets were given to children 13 and under at the September 3, 1983, Rangers game. The cards are numbered by uniform number and feature the player's name, card number, and the words "1983 Rangers" on the bottom front. The backs contain biographical data, career totals, a small black and white insert picture of the player, and the Affiliated Food Stores' logo. The coaches card is unnumbered.

	NRMT	VG-E	GOOD
COMPLETE SET (28)	5.00	2.20	.60
COMMON CARD	.25	.11	.03
☐ 1 Bill Stein	.25	.11	.03
☐ 2 Mike Richardt	.25	.11	.03
☐ 3 Wayne Tolleson	.25	.11	.03
☐ 5 Billy Sample	.50	.23	.06
☐ 6 Bobby Jones	.25	.11	.03
☐ 7 Bucky Dent	.50	.23	.06
☐ 8 Bobby Johnson	.25	.11	.03
☐ 9 Pete O'Brien	.50	.23	.06
☐ 10 Jim Sundberg	.50	.23	.06
☐ 11 Doug Rader MG	.25	.11	.03
☐ 12 Dave Hostetler	.50	.23	.06
☐ 14 Larry Biittner	.25	.11	.03
☐ 15 Larry Parrish	.50	.23	.06
☐ 17 Mickey Rivers	.50	.23	.06
☐ 21 Odell Jones	.25	.11	.03
☐ 24 Dave Schmidt	.25	.11	.03
☐ 25 Buddy Bell	.75	.35	.09
☐ 26 George Wright	.25	.11	.03
☐ 28 Frank Tanana	.75	.35	.09
☐ 29 John Butcher	.25	.11	.03
☐ 32 Jon Matlack	.25	.11	.03
☐ 40 Rick Honeycutt	.25	.11	.03
☐ 41 Dave Tobik	.25	.11	.03
☐ 44 Danny Darwin	.50	.23	.06
☐ 46 Jim Anderson	.25	.11	.03
☐ 48 Mike Smithson	.25	.11	.03
☐ 49 Charlie Hough	.75	.35	.09
☐ NNO Rangers Coaches Wayne Terwilliger Merv Rettenmund Dick Such Glenn Ezell Rich Donnelly	.25	.11	.03

1984 Rangers Jarvis Press

The cards in this 30-card set measure 2 1/2" by 3 1/2". The Jarvis Press of Dallas issued this full-color regional set of Texas Rangers. Cards are numbered on the front by the players uniform number. The

cards were issued on an uncut sheet. Twenty-seven player cards, a manager card, a trainer card (unnumbered) and a coaches card (unnumbered) comprise this set. The backs are black and white and contain biographical information, statistics, and an additional photo of the player.

	NRMT	VG-E	GOOD
COMPLETE SET (30)	5.00	2.20	.60
COMMON CARD	.25	.11	.03
☐ 1 Bill Stein	.25	.11	.03
☐ 2 Alan Bannister	.25	.11	.03
☐ 3 Wayne Tolleson	.25	.11	.03
☐ 5 Billy Sample	.25	.11	.03
☐ 6 Bobby Jones	.25	.11	.03
☐ 7 Ned Yost	.25	.11	.03
☐ 9 Pete O'Brien	.50	.23	.06
☐ 11 Doug Rader MG	.25	.11	.03
☐ 13 Tommy Dunbar	.25	.11	.03
☐ 14 Jim Anderson	.25	.11	.03
☐ 15 Larry Parrish	.50	.23	.06
☐ 16 Mike Mason	.25	.11	.03
☐ 17 Mickey Rivers	.50	.23	.06
☐ 19 Curtis Wilkerson	.25	.11	.03
☐ 20 Jeff Kunkel	.25	.11	.03
☐ 21 Odell Jones	.25	.11	.03
☐ 24 Dave Schmidt	.25	.11	.03
☐ 25 Buddy Bell	.75	.35	.09
☐ 26 George Wright	.25	.11	.03
☐ 28 Frank Tanana	.75	.35	.09
☐ 30 Marv Foley	.25	.11	.03
☐ 31 Dave Stewart	.50	.23	.06
☐ 32 Gary Ward	.25	.11	.03
☐ 36 Dickie Noles	.25	.11	.03
☐ 43 Donnie Scott	.25	.11	.03
☐ 44 Danny Darwin	.50	.23	.06
☐ 49 Charlie Hough	.75	.35	.09
☐ 53 Joey McLaughlin	.25	.11	.03
☐ NNO Bill Ziegler TR	.25	.11	.03
☐ NNO Rangers Coaches	.25	.11	.03
Merv Rettenmund			
Rich Donnelly			
Glenn Ezell			
Dick Such			
Wayne Terwilliger			

1985 Rangers Performance

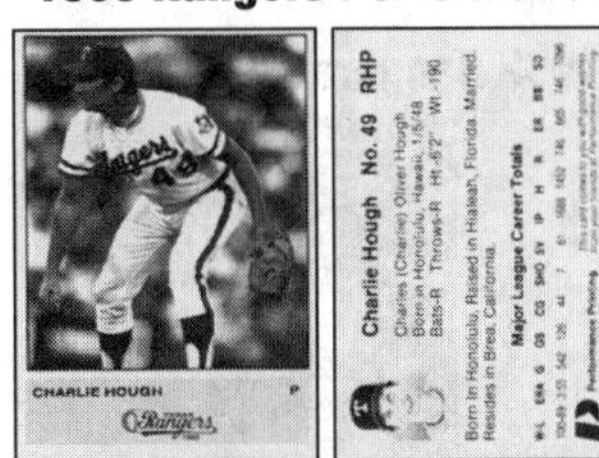

The cards in this 28-card set measure 2 3/8" by 3 1/2". Performance Printing sponsored this full-color regional set of Texas Rangers. Cards are numbered on the back by the players uniform number. The cards were also issued on an uncut sheet. Twenty-five player cards, a manager card, a trainer card (unnumbered) and a coaches card (unnumbered) comprise this set. The backs are black and white and contain biographical information, statistics, and an additional photo of the player.

	NRMT	VG-E	GOOD
☐ 0 Oddibe McDowell	.25	.11	.03
COMPLETE SET (28)	5.00	2.20	.60
COMMON CARD	.25	.11	.03
☐ 1 Bill Stein	.25	.11	.03
☐ 2 Bobby Valentine MG	.50	.23	.06
☐ 3 Wayne Tolleson	.25	.11	.03
☐ 4 Don Slaught	.25	.11	.03
☐ 5 Alan Bannister	.25	.11	.03
☐ 6 Bobby Jones	.25	.11	.03
☐ 7 Glenn Brummer	.25	.11	.03
☐ 8 Luis Pujols	.25	.11	.03
☐ 9 Pete O'Brien	.50	.23	.06
☐ 11 Toby Harrah	.50	.23	.06
☐ 13 Tommy Dunbar	.25	.11	.03
☐ 15 Larry Parrish	.50	.23	.06
☐ 16 Mike Mason	.25	.11	.03
☐ 19 Curtis Wilkerson	.25	.11	.03
☐ 24 Dave Schmidt	.25	.11	.03
☐ 25 Buddy Bell	.75	.35	.09
☐ 27 Greg A. Harris	.25	.11	.03
☐ 30 Dave Rozema	.25	.11	.03
☐ 32 Gary Ward	.25	.11	.03
☐ 36 Dickie Noles	.25	.11	.03
☐ 41 Chris Welsh	.25	.11	.03
☐ 44 Cliff Johnson	.25	.11	.03
☐ 46 Burt Hooton	.25	.11	.03
☐ 48 Dave Stewart	1.00	.45	.12
☐ 49 Charlie Hough	.75	.35	.09
☐ NNO Trainers:Bill Ziegler	.25	.11	.03
and Danny Wheat			
☐ NNO Rangers Coaches	.25	.11	.03
Art Howe			
Rich Donnelly			
Glenn Ezell			
Tom House			
Wayne Terwilliger			

1986 Rangers Greats TCMA

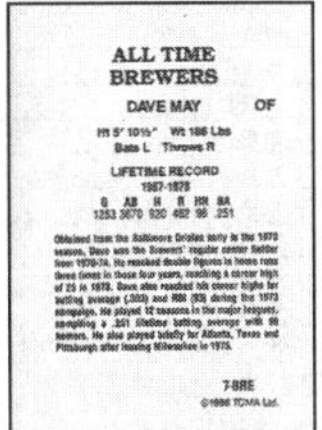

This 12-card standard-size set honors some of the leading Texas Rangers from their first 15 seasons. The player's photo, name and position are noted on the front. The backs have career information, vital statistics as well as a biography.

	MINT	NRMT	EXC
COMPLETE SET (12)	3.00	1.35	.35
COMMON CARD (1-12)	.25	.11	.03
☐ 1 Gaylord Perry	1.00	.45	.12
☐ 2 Jon Matlack	.25	.11	.03
☐ 3 Jim Kern	.25	.11	.03
☐ 4 Billy Hunter MG	.25	.11	.03
☐ 5 Mike Hargrove	.50	.23	.06
☐ 6 Bump Wills	.25	.11	.03
☐ 7 Toby Harrah	.50	.23	.06
☐ 8 Lenny Randle	.25	.11	.03
☐ 9 Al Oliver	.50	.23	.06
☐ 10 Mickey Rivers	.50	.23	.06
☐ 11 Jeff Burroughs	.25	.11	.03
☐ 12 Dick Billings	.25	.11	.03

1986 Rangers Lite

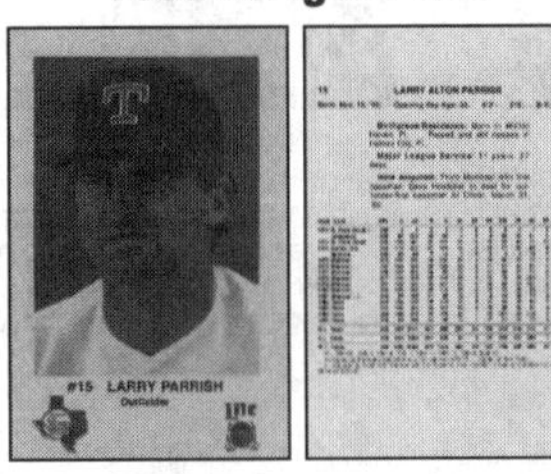

This seven-card set of the Texas Rangers features color player portraits with white borders and measures approximately 4" by 6". The backs carry player biographical information and career statistics. The cards are unnumbered and checklisted below in alphabetical order.

	MINT	NRMT	EXC
COMPLETE SET	4.00	1.80	.50
COMMON CARD	.50	.23	.06
☐ 1 Tim Foli CO	.50	.23	.06
☐ 2 Jose Guzman	.75	.35	.09
☐ 3 Art Howe	.50	.23	.06
☐ 4 Larry Parrish	.75	.35	.09
☐ 5 Darrell Porter	.75	.35	.09
☐ 6 Don Slaught	.50	.23	.06
☐ 7 Curtis Wilkerson	.50	.23	.06

1986 Rangers Performance

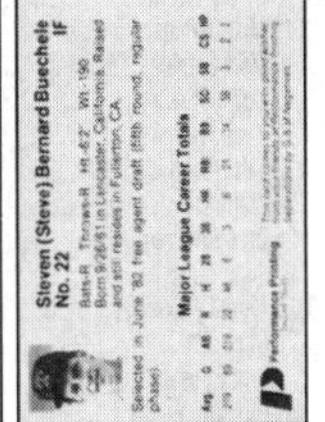

Performance Printing of Dallas produced a 28-card set of Texas Rangers which were given out at the stadium on August 23rd. Cards measure approximately 2 3/8" by 3 1/2" and are in full color. The cards are unnumbered except for uniform number which is given on the card back. Card backs feature black printing on white card stock with a small picture of the player's head in the upper left corner. The set seems to be more desirable than the previous Ranger sets due to the Rangers' 1986 success which was directly related to their outstanding rookie crop including Jose Guzman, Pete Incaviglia, Ruben Sierra, Mitch Williams, and Bobby Witt.

	MINT	NRMT	EXC
COMPLETE SET (28)	10.00	4.50	1.25
COMMON CARD	.25	.11	.03
☐ 0 Oddibe McDowell	.50	.23	.06
☐ 1 Scott Fletcher	.25	.11	.03
☐ 2 Bobby Valentine MG	.50	.23	.06
☐ 3 Ruben Sierra	2.50	1.10	.30
☐ 4 Don Slaught	.25	.11	.03
☐ 9 Pete O'Brien	.50	.23	.06
☐ 11 Toby Harrah	.50	.23	.06
☐ 12 Geno Petralli	.25	.11	.03
☐ 15 Larry Parrish	.50	.23	.06
☐ 16 Mike Mason	.25	.11	.03
☐ 17 Darrell Porter	.50	.23	.06
☐ 18 Edwin Correa	.25	.11	.03
☐ 19 Curtis Wilkerson	.25	.11	.03
☐ 22 Steve Buechele	.50	.23	.06
☐ 23 Jose Guzman	.50	.23	.06
☐ 24 Ricky Wright	.25	.11	.03
☐ 27 Greg A. Harris	.25	.11	.03
☐ 28 Mitch Williams	.75	.35	.09
☐ 29 Pete Incaviglia	1.00	.45	.12
☐ 32 Gary Ward	.25	.11	.03
☐ 34 Dale Mohorcic	.25	.11	.03
☐ 40 Jeff Russell	.50	.23	.06
☐ 44 Tom Paciorek	.25	.11	.03
☐ 46 Mike Loynd	.25	.11	.03
☐ 48 Bobby Witt	1.25	.55	.16
☐ 49 Charlie Hough	.75	.35	.09
☐ NNO Coaching Staff	.25	.11	.03
Art Howe			
Joe Ferguson			
Tim Foli			
Tom Robson			
Tom House			
☐ NNO0 Trainers:Bill Ziegler	.25	.11	.03
and Danny Wheat			

1987 Rangers Mother's

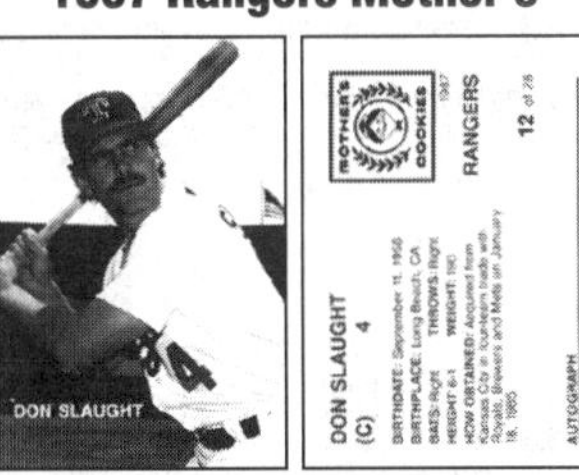

This set consists of 28 full-color, rounded-corner cards each measuring 2 1/2" by 3 1/2". Starter sets (only 20 cards but also including a certificate for eight more cards) were given out at the ballpark and collectors were encouraged to trade to fill in the rest of their set. Cards were originally given out on July 17th during the game against the Yankees. Photos were taken by Barry Colla. The sets were reportedly given out free to the first 25,000 paid admissions at the game.

	MINT	NRMT	EXC
COMPLETE SET (28)	12.00	5.50	1.50
COMMON CARD (1-28)	.25	.11	.03
☐ 1 Bobby Valentine MG	.50	.23	.06
☐ 2 Pete Incaviglia	.75	.35	.09
☐ 3 Charlie Hough	.75	.35	.09
☐ 4 Oddibe McDowell	.50	.23	.06
☐ 5 Larry Parrish	.50	.23	.06
☐ 6 Scott Fletcher	.25	.11	.03
☐ 7 Steve Buechele	.25	.11	.03
☐ 8 Tom Paciorek	.25	.11	.03
☐ 9 Pete O'Brien	.50	.23	.06
☐ 10 Darrell Porter	.50	.23	.06
☐ 11 Greg A. Harris	.25	.11	.03
☐ 12 Don Slaught	.25	.11	.03
☐ 13 Ruben Sierra	2.50	1.10	.30
☐ 14 Curtis Wilkerson	.25	.11	.03
☐ 15 Dale Mohorcic	.25	.11	.03
☐ 16 Ron Meridith	.25	.11	.03
☐ 17 Mitch Williams	.75	.35	.09
☐ 18 Bob Brower	.25	.11	.03
☐ 19 Edwin Correa	.25	.11	.03
☐ 20 Geno Petralli	.25	.11	.03
☐ 21 Mike Loynd	.25	.11	.03
☐ 22 Jerry Browne	.50	.23	.06
☐ 23 Jose Guzman	.25	.11	.03
☐ 24 Jeff Kunkel	.25	.11	.03
☐ 25 Bobby Witt	1.00	.45	.12
☐ 26 Jeff Russell	.50	.23	.06
☐ 27 Rangers' Trainers	.25	.11	.03
Bill Ziegler			
Danny Wheat			
☐ 28 Checklist Card	.25	.11	.03
Tom Robson CO			
Art Howe CO			
Joe Ferguson CO			
Tim Foli CO			
Tom House CO			
Dave Oliver CO			

1987 Rangers Smokey

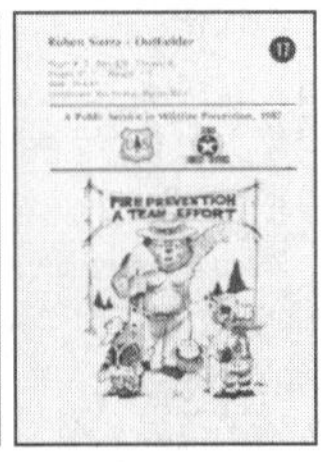

The U.S. Forestry Service (in conjunction with the Texas Rangers) produced this large, attractive 32-card set. The cards feature Smokey the Bear pictured in the upper-right corner of every player's card. The card backs give a cartoon fire safety tip. The cards measure approximately 4 1/4" by 6" and are subtitled "Wildfire Prevention" on the front. Card numbers 4 Mike Mason and 14 Tom Paciorek were withdrawn and were never formally released as part of the set and hence are quite scarce.

	MINT	NRMT	EXC
COMPLETE SET (32)	90.00	40.00	11.00
COMMON CARD (1-32)	.25	.11	.03
☐ 1 Charlie Hough	1.00	.45	.12
☐ 2 Greg A. Harris	.25	.11	.03
☐ 3 Jose Guzman	.25	.11	.03
☐ 4 Mike Mason SP	40.00	18.00	5.00
☐ 5 Dale Mohorcic	.25	.11	.03
☐ 6 Bobby Witt	1.50	.70	.19
☐ 7 Mitch Williams	1.00	.45	.12
☐ 8 Geno Petralli	.25	.11	.03
☐ 9 Don Slaught	.25	.11	.03
☐ 10 Darrell Porter	.25	.11	.03
☐ 11 Steve Buechele	.25	.11	.03
☐ 12 Pete O'Brien	.50	.23	.06
☐ 13 Scott Fletcher	.25	.11	.03
☐ 14 Tom Paciorek SP	40.00	18.00	5.00
☐ 15 Pete Incaviglia	1.00	.45	.12
☐ 16 Oddibe McDowell	.50	.23	.06
☐ 17 Ruben Sierra	2.00	.90	.25
☐ 18 Larry Parrish	.50	.23	.06
☐ 19 Bobby Valentine MG	.50	.23	.06
☐ 20 Tom House CO	.25	.11	.03
☐ 21 Tom Robson CO	.25	.11	.03
☐ 22 Edwin Correa	.25	.11	.03
☐ 23 Mike Stanley	2.00	.90	.25
☐ 24 Joe Ferguson CO	.25	.11	.03
☐ 25 Art Howe CO	.25	.11	.03
☐ 26 Bob Brower	.25	.11	.03
☐ 27 Mike Loynd	.25	.11	.03
☐ 28 Curtis Wilkerson	.25	.11	.03
☐ 29 Tim Foli CO	.25	.11	.03
☐ 30 Dave Oliver CO	.25	.11	.03
☐ 31 Jerry Browne	.50	.23	.06
☐ 32 Jeff Russell	.25	.11	.03

1988 Rangers Mother's

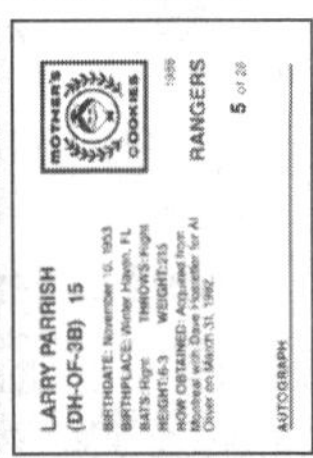

This set consists of 28 full-color, rounded-corner cards each measuring 2 1/2" by 3 1/2". Starter sets (only 20 cards but also including a certificate for eight more cards) were given out at the ballpark and collectors were encouraged to trade to fill in the rest of their set. Cards were originally given out on August 7th. Photos were taken by Barry Colla. The sets were reportedly given out free to the first 25,000 paid admissions at the game.

	MINT	NRMT	EXC
COMPLETE SET (28)	8.00	3.60	1.00
COMMON CARD (1-28)	.25	.11	.03
☐ 1 Bobby Valentine MG	.50	.23	.06
☐ 2 Pete Incaviglia	.50	.23	.06
☐ 3 Charlie Hough	.75	.35	.09
☐ 4 Oddibe McDowell	.50	.23	.06
☐ 5 Larry Parrish	.50	.23	.06
☐ 6 Scott Fletcher	.25	.11	.03
☐ 7 Steve Buechele	.25	.11	.03
☐ 8 Steve Kemp	.25	.11	.03
☐ 9 Pete O'Brien	.50	.23	.06
☐ 10 Ruben Sierra	.75	.35	.09
☐ 11 Mike Stanley	1.00	.45	.12
☐ 12 Jose Cecena	.25	.11	.03

	MINT	NRMT	EXC
□ 13 Cecil Espy	.25	.11	.03
□ 14 Curtis Wilkerson	.25	.11	.03
□ 15 Dale Mohorcic	.25	.11	.03
□ 16 Ray Hayward	.25	.11	.03
□ 17 Mitch Williams	.50	.23	.06
□ 18 Bob Brower	.25	.11	.03
□ 19 Paul Kilgus	.25	.11	.03
□ 20 Geno Petralli	.25	.11	.03
□ 21 James Steels	.25	.11	.03
□ 22 Jerry Browne	.25	.11	.03
□ 23 Jose Guzman	.25	.11	.03
□ 24 DeWayne Vaughn	.25	.11	.03
□ 25 Bobby Witt	1.00	.45	.12
□ 26 Jeff Russell	.50	.23	.06
□ 27 Rangers' Coaches Richard Egan Tom House Art Howe Davey Lopes David Oliver Tom Robson	.25	.11	.03
□ 28 Checklist Card Danny Wheat TR Bill Zeigler TR	.25	.11	.03

1988 Rangers Smokey

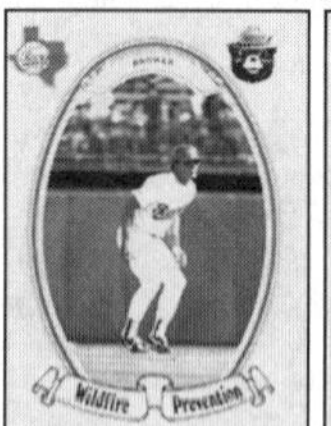

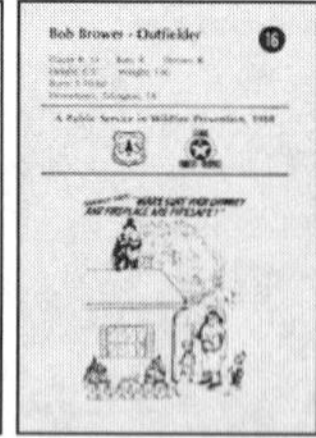

The cards in this 21-card set measure approximately 3 1/2" by 5". This numbered, full color set features the Fire Prevention Bear, Smokey, and a Rangers player (or manager) on each card. The set was given out at Arlington Stadium to fans during the Smokey Bear Day game promotion on August 7th. The logos of the Texas Forest Service and the U.S. Forestry Service appear on the reverse in conjunction with a Smokey the Bear logo on the obverse. The backs contain short biographical data and a fire prevention hint from Smokey.

	MINT	NRMT	EXC
COMPLETE SET (21)	12.00	5.50	1.50
COMMON CARD (1-21)	.50	.23	.06
□ 1 Tom O'Malley	.50	.23	.06
□ 2 Pete O'Brien	.75	.35	.09
□ 3 Geno Petralli	.50	.23	.06
□ 4 Pete Incaviglia	1.00	.45	.12
□ 5 Oddibe McDowell	.75	.35	.09
□ 6 Dale Mohorcic	.50	.23	.06
□ 7 Bobby Witt	1.00	.45	.12
□ 8 Bobby Valentine MG	.75	.35	.09
□ 9 Ruben Sierra	1.00	.45	.12
□ 10 Scott Fletcher	.50	.23	.06
□ 11 Mike Stanley	1.25	.55	.16
□ 12 Steve Buechele	.50	.23	.06
□ 13 Charlie Hough	1.00	.45	.12
□ 14 Larry Parrish	.75	.35	.09
□ 15 Jerry Browne	.50	.23	.06
□ 16 Bob Brower	.50	.23	.06
□ 17 Jeff Russell	.75	.35	.09
□ 18 Edwin Correa	.50	.23	.06
□ 19 Mitch Williams	.75	.35	.09
□ 20 Jose Guzman	.50	.23	.06
□ 21 Curtis Wilkerson	.50	.23	.06

1989 Rangers Mother's

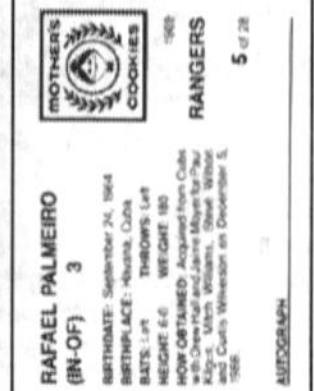

The 1989 Mother's Cookies Texas Rangers set contains 28 standard-size cards with rounded corners. The fronts have borderless color photos, and the horizontally oriented backs have biographical information. Starter sets containing 20 of these cards were given away at a Rangers home game during the 1989 season.

	MINT	NRMT	EXC
COMPLETE SET (28)	15.00	6.75	1.85
COMMON CARD (1-28)	.25	.11	.03
□ 1 Bobby Valentine MG	.50	.23	.06
□ 2 Nolan Ryan	7.50	3.40	.95
□ 3 Julio Franco	1.00	.45	.12
□ 4 Charlie Hough	.75	.35	.09
□ 5 Rafael Palmeiro	2.50	1.10	.30
□ 6 Jeff Russell	.50	.23	.06
□ 7 Ruben Sierra	.50	.23	.06
□ 8 Steve Buechele	.25	.11	.03
□ 9 Buddy Bell	.75	.35	.09
□ 10 Pete Incaviglia	.50	.23	.06
□ 11 Geno Petralli	.25	.11	.03
□ 12 Cecil Espy	.25	.11	.03
□ 13 Scott Fletcher	.25	.11	.03
□ 14 Bobby Witt	.75	.35	.09
□ 15 Brad Arnsberg	.25	.11	.03
□ 16 Rick Leach	.25	.11	.03
□ 17 Jamie Moyer	.25	.11	.03
□ 18 Kevin Brown	2.00	.90	.25
□ 19 Jeff Kunkel	.25	.11	.03
□ 20 Craig McMurtry	.25	.11	.03
□ 21 Kenny Rogers	.75	.35	.09
□ 22 Mike Stanley	.75	.35	.09
□ 23 Cecilio Guante	.25	.11	.03
□ 24 Jim Sundberg	.50	.23	.06
□ 25 Jose Guzman	.25	.11	.03
□ 26 Jeff Stone	.25	.11	.03
□ 27 Rangers' Coaches Dick Egan Tom House Toby Harrah Davey Lopes Dave Oliver Tom Robson	.25	.11	.03
□ 28 Checklist Card Danny Wheat TR Bill Zeigler TR	.25	.11	.03

1989 Rangers Smokey

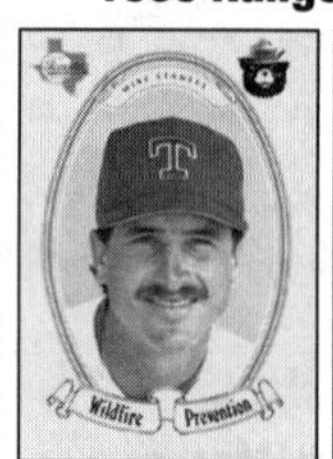

The 1989 Smokey Rangers set features 34 unnumbered cards measuring approximately 4 1/4" by 6". The fronts feature mugshot photos with white borders. The backs feature biographical information and fire prevention tips. The set was given away at a 1989 Rangers' home game.

	MINT	NRMT	EXC
COMPLETE SET (34)	25.00	11.00	3.10
COMMON CARD (1-34)	.50	.23	.06
□ 1 Darrel Akerfelds	.50	.23	.06
□ 2 Brad Arnsberg	.50	.23	.06
□ 3 Buddy Bell	1.00	.45	.12
□ 4 Kevin Brown	2.50	1.10	.30
□ 5 Steve Buechele	.50	.23	.06
□ 6 Dick Egan CO	.50	.23	.06
□ 7 Cecil Espy	.50	.23	.06
□ 8 Scott Fletcher	.50	.23	.06
□ 9 Julio Franco	1.50	.70	.19
□ 10 Cecilio Guante	.50	.23	.06
□ 11 Jose Guzman	.50	.23	.06
□ 12 Drew Hall	.50	.23	.06
□ 13 Toby Harrah CO	.50	.23	.06
□ 14 Charlie Hough	.75	.35	.09
□ 15 Tom House CO	.50	.23	.06
□ 16 Pete Incaviglia	1.00	.45	.12
□ 17 Chad Kreuter	.50	.23	.06
□ 18 Jeff Kunkel	.50	.23	.06
□ 19 Rick Leach	.50	.23	.06
□ 20 Davey Lopes	.75	.35	.09
□ 21 Craig McMurtry	.50	.23	.06
□ 22 Jamie Moyer	.75	.35	.09
□ 23 Dave Oliver CO	.50	.23	.06
□ 24 Rafael Palmeiro	5.00	2.20	.60
□ 25 Geno Petralli	.50	.23	.06
□ 26 Tom Robson CO	.50	.23	.06
□ 27 Kenny Rogers	1.00	.45	.12
□ 28 Jeff Russell	.50	.23	.06
□ 29 Nolan Ryan	10.00	4.50	1.25
□ 30 Ruben Sierra	1.25	.55	.16
□ 31 Mike Stanley	1.00	.45	.12
□ 32 Jim Sundberg	.75	.35	.09
□ 33 Bobby Valentine MG	.75	.35	.09
□ 34 Bobby Witt	1.00	.45	.12

1990 Rangers Mother's

This 28-card, standard-size set features members of the 1990 Texas Rangers. The set has beautiful full-color photos on the front along with biographical information on the back. The set also features the now traditional Mother's Cookies rounded corners. The Rangers cards were distributed on July 22nd to the first 25,000 game attendees in Arlington. They were distributed in 20-card random packets at the game and eight more at the redemption booths. However, both groups of cards were random and there was no guarantee of getting a complete set in the cards. The promotional idea was that the only way one could finish the set was to trade for them. The redemption certificates (for eight more cards) were also able to be redeemed at the 17th Annual Dallas Card Convention on August 18-19, 1990.

	MINT	NRMT	EXC
COMPLETE SET (28)	15.00	6.75	1.85
COMMON CARD (1-28)	.25	.11	.03
□ 1 Bobby Valentine MG	.50	.23	.06
□ 2 Nolan Ryan	7.50	3.40	.95
□ 3 Ruben Sierra	.50	.23	.06
□ 4 Pete Incaviglia	.50	.23	.06
□ 5 Charlie Hough	.75	.35	.09
□ 6 Harold Baines	.75	.35	.09
□ 7 Gino Petralli	.25	.11	.03
□ 8 Jeff Russell	.50	.23	.06
□ 9 Rafael Palmeiro	2.00	.90	.25
□ 10 Julio Franco	1.00	.45	.12
□ 11 Jack Daugherty	.25	.11	.03
□ 12 Gary Pettis	.25	.11	.03
□ 13 Brian Bohanon	.25	.11	.03
□ 14 Steve Buechele	.25	.11	.03
□ 15 Bobby Witt	.75	.35	.09
□ 16 Thad Bosley	.25	.11	.03
□ 17 Gary Mielke	.25	.11	.03
□ 18 Jeff Kunkel	.25	.11	.03
□ 19 Mike Jeffcoat	.25	.11	.03
□ 20 Mike Stanley	.75	.35	.09
□ 21 Kevin Brown	1.50	.70	.19
□ 22 Kenny Rogers	.75	.35	.09
□ 23 Jeff Huson	.25	.11	.03
□ 24 Jamie Moyer	.25	.11	.03
□ 25 Cecil Espy	.25	.11	.03
□ 26 John Russell	.25	.11	.03
□ 27 Coaches Card Dave Oliver Davey Lopes Tom Robson Tom House Toby Harrah	.25	.11	.03
□ 28 Trainers Card Bill Zeigler TR Joe Macko EQ.MG. Marty Stajduhar, Strength and Cond. Danny Wheat ATR	.25	.11	.03

1991 Rangers Mother's

The 1991 Mother's Cookies Texas Rangers set contains 28 cards with rounded corners measuring the standard size. The front design has borderless glossy color player photos, with the locker room as the background. The horizontally oriented backs are printed in red and purple, present biographical information, and have blank slots for player autographs.

	MINT	NRMT	EXC
COMPLETE SET (28)	15.00	6.75	1.85
COMMON CARD (1-28)	.25	.11	.03
□ 1 Bobby Valentine MG	.50	.23	.06
□ 2 Nolan Ryan	6.00	2.70	.75
□ 3 Ruben Sierra	.75	.35	.09
□ 4 Juan Gonzalez	6.00	2.70	.75
□ 5 Steve Buechele	.25	.11	.03
□ 6 Bobby Witt	.75	.35	.09
□ 7 Geno Petralli	.25	.11	.03
□ 8 Jeff Russell	.50	.23	.06
□ 9 Rafael Palmeiro	2.00	.90	.25
□ 10 Julio Franco	.75	.35	.09
□ 11 Jack Daugherty	.25	.11	.03
□ 12 Gary Pettis	.25	.11	.03
□ 13 John Barfield	.25	.11	.03
□ 14 Scott Chiamparino	.25	.11	.03
□ 15 Kevin Reimer	.25	.11	.03
□ 16 Rich Gossage	.75	.35	.09
□ 17 Brian Downing	.50	.23	.06
□ 18 Denny Walling	.25	.11	.03
□ 19 Mike Jeffcoat	.25	.11	.03
□ 20 Mike Stanley	.75	.35	.09
□ 21 Kevin Brown	1.25	.55	.16
□ 22 Kenny Rogers	.75	.35	.09
□ 23 Jeff Huson	.25	.11	.03
□ 24 Mario Diaz	.25	.11	.03
□ 25 Brad Arnsberg	.25	.11	.03
□ 26 John Russell	.25	.11	.03
□ 27 Gerald Alexander	.25	.11	.03
□ 28 Checklist Card Tom Robson CO Toby Harrah CO Orlando Gomez CO Tom House CO Dave Oliver CO Davey Lopes CO	.25	.11	.03

1992 Rangers Mother's

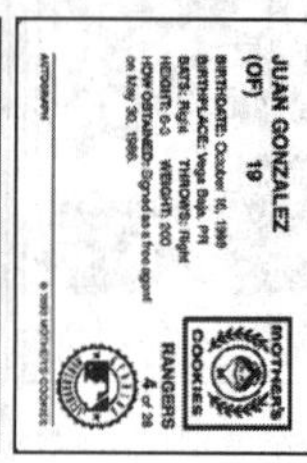

The 1992 Mother's Cookies Rangers set contains 28 cards with rounded corners measuring the standard size. The front design has borderless glossy color player photos in which the players are posed against a blue background. The player's name and team name appear at one of the upper corners. The horizontal backs are printed in red and purple, and present biography and a "how obtained" remark. A blank slot for the player's autograph rounds out the back.

	MINT	NRMT	EXC
COMPLETE SET (28)	15.00	6.75	1.85
COMMON CARD (1-28)	.25	.11	.03
□ 1 Bobby Valentine MG	.50	.23	.06
□ 2 Nolan Ryan	4.00	1.80	.50
□ 3 Ruben Sierra	.75	.35	.09
□ 4 Juan Gonzalez	4.00	1.80	.50
□ 5 Ivan Rodriguez	3.00	1.35	.35
□ 6 Bobby Witt	.75	.35	.09
□ 7 Geno Petralli	.25	.11	.03
□ 8 Jeff Russell	.50	.23	.06
□ 9 Rafael Palmeiro	2.00	.90	.25
□ 10 Julio Franco	.75	.35	.09
□ 11 Jack Daugherty	.25	.11	.03
□ 12 Dickie Thon	.25	.11	.03
□ 13 Floyd Bannister	.25	.11	.03
□ 14 Scott Chiamparino	.25	.11	.03
□ 15 Kevin Reimer	.25	.11	.03
□ 16 Jeff M. Robinson	.25	.11	.03
□ 17 Brian Downing	.50	.23	.06
□ 18 Brian Bohanon	.25	.11	.03
□ 19 Jose Guzman	.25	.11	.03
□ 20 Terry Mathews	.25	.11	.03
□ 21 Kevin Brown	1.25	.55	.16
□ 22 Kenny Rogers	.75	.35	.09
□ 23 Jeff Huson	.25	.11	.03
□ 24 Monty Fariss	.25	.11	.03
□ 25 Al Newman	.25	.11	.03
□ 26 Dean Palmer	2.00	.90	.25
□ 27 John Cangelosi	.25	.11	.03
□ 28 Coaches/Checklist Tom Robson Ray Burris Toby Harrah Dave Oliver Tom House Orlando Gomez	.25	.11	.03

1992 Rangers Team Issue

This 26-card team photo set measures approximately 3" by 5". The fronts feature posed color player photos against a variegated gray studio background. The player's name is printed in black near the top of the card in a white banner. The backs are blank. The cards are unnumbered and checklisted below in alphabetical order.

	MINT	NRMT	EXC
COMPLETE SET (27)	10.00	4.50	1.25
COMMON CARD (1-27)	.25	.11	.03
□ 1 Floyd Bannister	.25	.11	.03
□ 2 Kevin Brown	.75	.35	.09
□ 3 John Cangelosi	.25	.11	.03
□ 4 Scott Chiamparino	.25	.11	.03
□ 5 Jack Daugherty	.25	.11	.03
□ 6 Julio Franco	.50	.23	.06
□ 7 Brian Downing	.50	.23	.06
□ 8 Juan Gonzalez	3.00	1.35	.35
□ 9 Jose Guzman	.25	.11	.03
□ 10 Mike Jeffcoat	.25	.11	.03
□ 11 Jeff Huson	.25	.11	.03
□ 12 Terry Mathews	.25	.11	.03
□ 13 Al Newman	.25	.11	.03
□ 14 Edwin Nunez	.25	.11	.03
□ 15 Rafael Palmeiro	1.25	.55	.16
□ 16 Dean Palmer	1.25	.55	.16
□ 17 Geno Petralli	.25	.11	.03
□ 18 Kevin Reimer	.25	.11	.03

Card	MINT	NRMT	EXC
☐ 19 Ivan Rodriguez	2.00	.90	.25
☐ 20 Kenny Rogers	.50	.23	.06
☐ 21 Jeff Russell	.25	.11	.03
☐ 22 Nolan Ryan	3.00	1.35	.35
☐ 23 Ruben Sierra	.50	.23	.06
☐ 24 Dickie Thon	.25	.11	.03
☐ 25 Bobby Valentine MG	.25	.11	.03
☐ 26 Bobby Witt	.50	.23	.06
☐ 27 Model of New Ballpark	.25	.11	.03

1993 Rangers Dr. Pepper

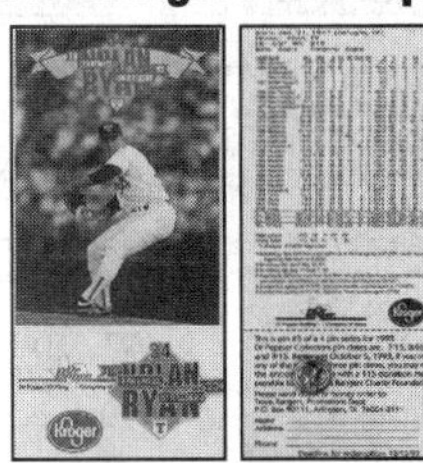

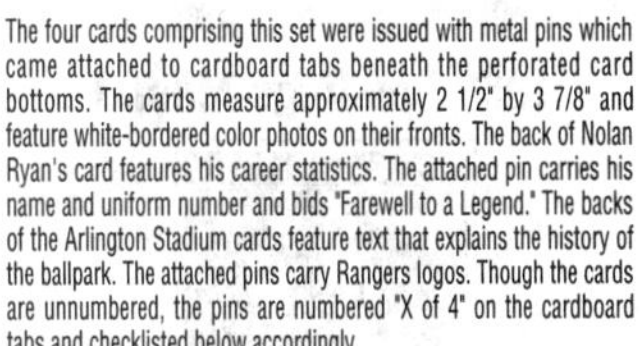

The four cards comprising this set were issued with metal pins which came attached to cardboard tabs beneath the perforated card bottoms. The cards measure approximately 2 1/2" by 3 7/8" and feature white-bordered color photos on their fronts. The back of Nolan Ryan's card features his career statistics. The attached pin carries his name and uniform number and bids "Farewell to a Legend." The backs of the Arlington Stadium cards feature text that explains the history of the ballpark. The attached pins carry Rangers logos. Though the cards are unnumbered, the pins are numbered "X of 4" on the cardboard tabs and checklisted below accordingly.

	MINT	NRMT	EXC
COMPLETE SET (4)	15.00	6.75	1.85
COMMON CARD (1-4)	1.50	.70	.19
☐ 1 Arlington Stadium 1972-1977	1.50	.70	.19
☐ 2 Arlington Stadium 1978-1983	1.50	.70	.19
☐ 3 Nolan Ryan	12.00	5.50	1.50
☐ 4 Arlington Stadium 1984-1993	1.50	.70	.19

1993 Rangers Keebler

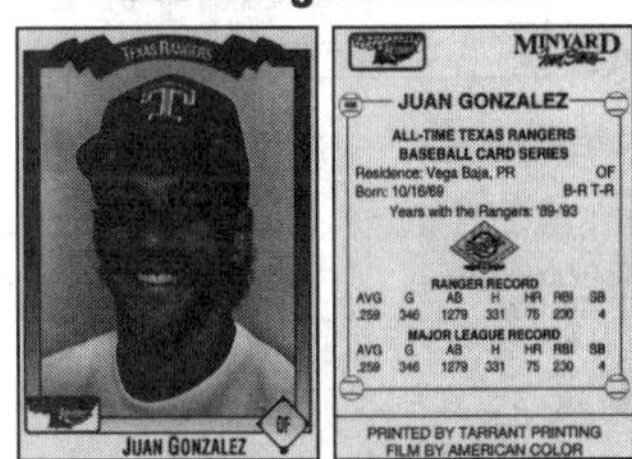

The Keebler All-Time Texas Rangers Card Series was a 468-card set (446 player cards plus 22 stat cards that have SP prefixes) issued in eight series booklets of perforated card sheets that honored everyone who ever wore a Rangers uniform during its 22-year history. The set was sponsored by Keebler and Albertsons food stores. Booklets of perforated sheets were distributed free to 35,000 fans as an in-stadium promotion at specific games. The exception was on April 9, when 42,000 booklets were distributed. Series I highlights 1972 team members, while Series VIII features the 1993 team, with the balance of the Rangers appearing in alphabetical order in Series II-VII. The standard-size cards have white-bordered fronts that display sepia-toned player portraits with "Texas Rangers" printed on a blue banner across the top. A red stripe that fades to pink frames the picture. Keebler's logo is printed in the lower left and the name of the Ranger appears in the white border below the picture. The backs have a biography, years with Rangers, team record, and major league record. The logos for Keebler and Albertsons round out the back.

	MINT	NRMT	EXC
COMPLETE SET (468)	50.00	22.00	6.25
COMMON CARD (1-446)	.10	.05	.01
☐ 1 Ted Williams MG	4.00	1.80	.50
☐ 2 Larry Biittner	.10	.05	.01
☐ 3 Rich Billings	.10	.05	.01
☐ 4 Dick Bosman	.10	.05	.01
☐ 5 Pete Broberg	.10	.05	.01
☐ 6 Jeff Burroughs	.25	.11	.03
☐ 7 Casey Cox	.10	.05	.01
☐ 8 Jim Driscoll	.10	.05	.01
☐ 9 Jan Dukes	.10	.05	.01
☐ 10 Bill Fahey	.10	.05	.01
☐ 11 Ted Ford	.10	.05	.01
☐ 12 Bill Gogolewski	.10	.05	.01
☐ 13 Tom Grieve	.25	.11	.03
☐ 14 Rich Hand	.10	.05	.01
☐ 15 Toby Harrah	.25	.11	.03
☐ 16 Vic Harris	.10	.05	.01
☐ 17 Rich Hinton	.10	.05	.01
☐ 18 Frank Howard	.50	.23	.06
☐ 19 Gerry Janeski	.10	.05	.01
☐ 20 Dalton Jones	.10	.05	.01
☐ 21 Hal King	.10	.05	.01
☐ 22 Ted Kubiak	.10	.05	.01
☐ 23 Steve Lawson	.10	.05	.01
☐ 24 Paul Lindblad	.10	.05	.01
☐ 25 Joe Lovitto	.10	.05	.01
☐ 26 Elliott Maddox	.10	.05	.01
☐ 27 Marty Martinez	.10	.05	.01
☐ 28 Jim Mason	.10	.05	.01
☐ 29 Don Mincher	.10	.05	.01
☐ 30 Dave Nelson	.10	.05	.01
☐ 31 Jim Panther	.10	.05	.01
☐ 32 Mike Paul	.10	.05	.01
☐ 33 Horacio Pina	.10	.05	.01
☐ 34 Tom Ragland	.10	.05	.01
☐ 35 Lenny Randle	.25	.11	.03
☐ 36 Jim Roland	.10	.05	.01
☐ 37 Jim Shellenback	.10	.05	.01
☐ 38 Don Stanhouse	.10	.05	.01
☐ 39 Ken Suarez	.10	.05	.01
☐ 40 Joe Camacho CO	.10	.05	.01
☐ 41 Nellie Fox CO	1.50	.70	.19
☐ 42 Sid Hudson CO	.10	.05	.01
☐ 43 George Susce CO	.10	.05	.01
☐ 44 Wayne Terwilliger CO	.10	.05	.01
☐ 45 Darrel Akerfelds	.10	.05	.01
☐ 46 Doyle Alexander	.25	.11	.03
☐ 47 Gerald Alexander	.10	.05	.01
☐ 48 Brian Allard	.10	.05	.01
☐ 49 Lloyd Allen	.10	.05	.01
☐ 50 Sandy Alomar	.25	.11	.03
☐ 51 Wilson Alvarez	.50	.23	.06
☐ 52 Jim Anderson	.10	.05	.01
☐ 53 Scott Anderson	.10	.05	.01
☐ 54 Brad Arnsberg	.10	.05	.01
☐ 55 Tucker Ashford	.10	.05	.01
☐ 56 Doug Ault	.10	.05	.01
☐ 57 Bob Babcock	.10	.05	.01
☐ 58 Mike Bacsik	.10	.05	.01
☐ 59 Harold Baines	.75	.35	.09
☐ 60 Alan Bannister	.10	.05	.01
☐ 61 Floyd Bannister	.10	.05	.01
☐ 62 John Barfield	.10	.05	.01
☐ 63 Len Barker	.25	.11	.03
☐ 64 Steve Barr	.10	.05	.01
☐ 65 Randy Bass	.10	.05	.01
☐ 66 Lew Beasley	.10	.05	.01
☐ 67 Kevin Belcher	.10	.05	.01
☐ 68 Buddy Bell	.50	.23	.06
☐ 69 Juan Beniquez	.10	.05	.01
☐ 70 Kurt Bevacqua	.25	.11	.03
☐ 71 Jim Bibby	.25	.11	.03
☐ 72 Joe Bitker	.10	.05	.01
☐ 73 Larvell Blanks	.10	.05	.01
☐ 74 Bert Blyleven	.50	.23	.06
☐ 75 Terry Bogener	.10	.05	.01
☐ 76 Tommy Boggs	.10	.05	.01
☐ 77 Dan Boitano	.10	.05	.01
☐ 78 Bobby Bonds	.50	.23	.06
☐ 79 Thad Bosley	.10	.05	.01
☐ 80 Dennis Boyd	.10	.05	.01
☐ 81 Nelson Briles	.25	.11	.03
☐ 82 Ed Brinkman	.10	.05	.01
☐ 83 Bob Brower	.10	.05	.01
☐ 84 Jackie Brown	.10	.05	.01
☐ 85 Larry Brown	.10	.05	.01
☐ 86 Jerry Browne	.10	.05	.01
☐ 87 Glenn Brummer	.10	.05	.01
☐ 88 Kevin Buckley	.10	.05	.01
☐ 89 Steve Buechele	.10	.05	.01
☐ 90 Ray Burris	.10	.05	.01
☐ 91 John Butcher	.10	.05	.01
☐ 92 Bert Campaneris	.25	.11	.03
☐ 93 Mike Campbell	.10	.05	.01
☐ 94 John Cangelosi	.10	.05	.01
☐ 95 Nick Capra	.10	.05	.01
☐ 96 Leo Cardenas	.25	.11	.03
☐ 97 Don Carman	.10	.05	.01
☐ 98 Rico Carty	.25	.11	.03
☐ 99 Don Castle	.10	.05	.01
☐ 100 Jose Cecena	.10	.05	.01
☐ 101 Dave Chalk	.10	.05	.01
☐ 102 Scott Chiamparino	.10	.05	.01
☐ 103 Ken Clay	.10	.05	.01
☐ 104 Reggie Cleveland	.10	.05	.01
☐ 105 Gene Clines	.10	.05	.01
☐ 106 David Clyde	.25	.11	.03
☐ 107 Cris Colon	.10	.05	.01
☐ 108 Merrill Combs CO	.10	.05	.01
☐ 109 Steve Comer	.10	.05	.01
☐ 110 Glen Cook	.10	.05	.01
☐ 111 Scott Coolbaugh	.10	.05	.01
☐ 112 Pat Corrales MG	.10	.05	.01
☐ 113 Edwin Correa	.10	.05	.01
☐ 114 Larry Cox	.10	.05	.01
☐ 115 Keith Creel	.10	.05	.01
☐ 116 Victor Cruz	.10	.05	.01
☐ 117 Mike Cubbage	.10	.05	.01
☐ 118 Bobby Cuellar	.10	.05	.01
☐ 119 Danny Darwin	.50	.23	.06
☐ 120 Jack Daugherty	.10	.05	.01
☐ 121 Doug Davis	.10	.05	.01
☐ 122 Odie Davis	.10	.05	.01
☐ 123 Willie Davis	.25	.11	.03
☐ 124 Bucky Dent	.25	.11	.03
☐ 125 Adrian Devine	.10	.05	.01
☐ 126 Mario Diaz	.10	.05	.01
☐ 127 Rich Donnelly CO	.10	.05	.01
☐ 128 Brian Downing	.25	.11	.03
☐ 129 Tommy Dunbar	.10	.05	.01
☐ 130 Steve Dunning	.10	.05	.01
☐ 131 Dan Duran	.10	.05	.01
☐ 132 Don Durham	.10	.05	.01
☐ 133 Dick Egan CO	.10	.05	.01
☐ 134 Dock Ellis	.25	.11	.03
☐ 135 John Ellis	.10	.05	.01
☐ 136 Mike Epstein	.10	.05	.01
☐ 137 Cecil Espy	.10	.05	.01
☐ 138 Chuck Estrada CO	.10	.05	.01
☐ 139 Glenn Ezell CO	.10	.05	.01
☐ 140 Hector Fajardo	.10	.05	.01
☐ 141 Monty Fariss	.10	.05	.01
☐ 142 Ed Farmer	.10	.05	.01
☐ 143 Jim Farr	.10	.05	.01
☐ 144 Joe Ferguson	.25	.11	.03
☐ 145 Ed Figueroa	.10	.05	.01
☐ 146 Steve Fireovid	.10	.05	.01
☐ 147 Scott Fletcher	.25	.11	.03
☐ 148 Doug Flynn	.10	.05	.01
☐ 149 Marv Foley	.10	.05	.01
☐ 150 Tim Foli	.10	.05	.01
☐ 151 Tony Fossas	.10	.05	.01
☐ 152 Steve Foucault	.10	.05	.01
☐ 153 Art Fowler CO	.10	.05	.01
☐ 154 Jim Fregosi	.25	.11	.03
☐ 155 Pepe Frias	.10	.05	.01
☐ 156 Oscar Gamble	.25	.11	.03
☐ 157 Barbaro Garbey	.10	.05	.01
☐ 158 Dick Gernert CO	.10	.05	.01
☐ 159 Jim Gideon	.10	.05	.01
☐ 160 Jerry Don Gleaton	.10	.05	.01
☐ 161 Orlando Gomez CO	.10	.05	.01
☐ 162 Rich Gossage	.75	.35	.09
☐ 163 Gary Gray	.10	.05	.01
☐ 164 Gary Green	.10	.05	.01
☐ 165 John Grubb	.10	.05	.01
☐ 166 Cecilio Guante	.10	.05	.01
☐ 167 Jose Guzman	.25	.11	.03
☐ 168 Drew Hall	.10	.05	.01
☐ 169 Bill Hands	.10	.05	.01
☐ 170 Steve Hargan	.10	.05	.01
☐ 171 Mike Hargrove	.50	.23	.06
☐ 172 Toby Harrah	.50	.23	.06
☐ 173 Bud Harrelson	.25	.11	.03
☐ 174 Donald Harris	.10	.05	.01
☐ 175 Greg A. Harris	.10	.05	.01
☐ 176 Mike Hart	.10	.05	.01
☐ 177 Bill Haselman	.10	.05	.01
☐ 178 Ray Hayward	.10	.05	.01
☐ 179 Tommy Helms	.10	.05	.01
☐ 180 Ken Henderson	.10	.05	.01
☐ 181 Rick Henninger	.10	.05	.01
☐ 182 Dwayne Henry	.10	.05	.01
☐ 183 Jose Hernandez	.10	.05	.01
☐ 184 Whitey Herzog MG	.50	.23	.06
☐ 185 Chuck Hiller CO	.10	.05	.01
☐ 186 Joe Hoerner	.10	.05	.01
☐ 187 Guy Hoffman	.10	.05	.01
☐ 188 Gary Holle	.10	.05	.01
☐ 189 Rick Honeycutt	.25	.11	.03
☐ 190 Burt Hooton	.25	.11	.03
☐ 191 John Hoover	.10	.05	.01
☐ 192 Willie Horton	.50	.23	.06
☐ 193 Dave Hostetler	.10	.05	.01
☐ 194 Charlie Hough	.50	.23	.06
☐ 195 Tom House	.10	.05	.01
☐ 196 Art Howe CO	.10	.05	.01
☐ 197 Steve Howe	.10	.05	.01
☐ 198 Roy Howell	.10	.05	.01
☐ 199 Charles Hudson	.10	.05	.01
☐ 200 Billy Hunter MG	.10	.05	.01
☐ 201 Pete Incaviglia	.50	.23	.06
☐ 202 Mike Jeffcoat	.10	.05	.01
☐ 203 Ferguson Jenkins	1.50	.70	.19
☐ 204 Alex Johnson	.25	.11	.03
☐ 205 Bobby Johnson	.10	.05	.01
☐ 206 Cliff Johnson	.25	.11	.03
☐ 207 Darrell Johnson MG	.10	.05	.01
☐ 208 John Henry Johnson	.10	.05	.01
☐ 209 Lamar Johnson	.10	.05	.01
☐ 210 Bobby Jones	.10	.05	.01
☐ 211 Odell Jones	.10	.05	.01
☐ 212 Mike Jorgensen	.10	.05	.01
☐ 213 Don Kainer	.10	.05	.01
☐ 214 Mike Kekich	.10	.05	.01
☐ 215 Steve Kemp	.25	.11	.03
☐ 216 Jim Kern	.10	.05	.01
☐ 217 Paul Kilgus	.10	.05	.01
☐ 218 Ed Kirkpatrick	.10	.05	.01
☐ 219 Darold Knowles	.10	.05	.01
☐ 220 Fred Koenig CO	.10	.05	.01
☐ 221 Jim Kremmel	.10	.05	.01
☐ 222 Chad Kreuter	.10	.05	.01
☐ 223 Jeff Kunkel	.10	.05	.01
☐ 224 Bob Lacey	.10	.05	.01
☐ 225 Al Lachowicz	.10	.05	.01
☐ 226 Joe Lahoud	.10	.05	.01
☐ 227 Rick Leach	.10	.05	.01
☐ 228 Danny Leon	.10	.05	.01
☐ 229 Dennis Lewallyn	.10	.05	.01
☐ 230 Rick Lisi	.10	.05	.01
☐ 231 Davey Lopes	.25	.11	.03
☐ 232 John Lowenstein	.10	.05	.01
☐ 233 Mike Loynd	.10	.05	.01
☐ 234 Frank Lucchesi MG	.10	.05	.01
☐ 235 Sparky Lyle	.50	.23	.06
☐ 236 Pete Mackanin	.10	.05	.01
☐ 237 Bill Madlock	.25	.11	.03
☐ 238 Greg Mahlberg	.10	.05	.01
☐ 239 Mickey Mahler	.10	.05	.01
☐ 240 Bob Malloy	.10	.05	.01
☐ 241 Ramon Manon	.10	.05	.01
☐ 242 Fred Manrique	.10	.05	.01
☐ 243 Barry Manuel	.10	.05	.01
☐ 244 Mike Marshall	.25	.11	.03
☐ 245 Billy Martin MG	.75	.35	.09
☐ 246 Mike Mason	.10	.05	.01
☐ 247 Terry Mathews	.10	.05	.01
☐ 248 Jon Matlack	.25	.11	.03
☐ 249 Rob Maurer	.10	.05	.01
☐ 250 Dave May	.10	.05	.01
☐ 251 Scott May	.10	.05	.01
☐ 252 Lee Mazzilli	.10	.05	.01
☐ 253 Larry McCall	.10	.05	.01
☐ 254 Lance McCullers	.10	.05	.01
☐ 255 Oddibe McDowell	.25	.11	.03
☐ 256 Russ McGinnis	.10	.05	.01
☐ 257 Joey McLaughlin	.10	.05	.01
☐ 258 Craig McMurtry	.10	.05	.01
☐ 259 Doc Medich	.10	.05	.01
☐ 260 Dave Meier	.10	.05	.01
☐ 261 Mario Mendoza	.10	.05	.01
☐ 262 Orlando Mercado	.10	.05	.01
☐ 263 Mark Mercer	.10	.05	.01
☐ 264 Ron Meridith	.10	.05	.01
☐ 265 Jim Merritt	.10	.05	.01
☐ 266 Gary Mielke	.10	.05	.01
☐ 267 Eddie Miller	.10	.05	.01
☐ 268 Paul Mirabella	.10	.05	.01
☐ 269 Dave Moates	.10	.05	.01
☐ 270 Dale Mohorcic	.10	.05	.01
☐ 271 Willie Montanez	.10	.05	.01
☐ 272 Tommy Moore	.10	.05	.01
☐ 273 Roger Moret	.10	.05	.01
☐ 274 Jamie Moyer	.10	.05	.01
☐ 275 Dale Murray	.10	.05	.01
☐ 276 Al Newman	.10	.05	.01
☐ 277 Dickie Noles	.10	.05	.01
☐ 278 Eric Nolte	.10	.05	.01
☐ 279 Nelson Norman	.10	.05	.01
☐ 280 Jim Norris	.10	.05	.01
☐ 281 Edwin Nunez	.10	.05	.01
☐ 282 Pete O'Brien	.25	.11	.03
☐ 283 Al Oliver	.50	.23	.06
☐ 284 Tom O'Malley	.10	.05	.01
☐ 285 Tom Paciorek	.50	.23	.06
☐ 286 Ken Pape	.10	.05	.01
☐ 287 Mark Parent	.10	.05	.01
☐ 288 Larry Parrish	.25	.11	.03
☐ 289 Gaylord Perry	1.50	.70	.19
☐ 290 Stan Perzanowski	.10	.05	.01
☐ 291 Fritz Peterson	.10	.05	.01
☐ 292 Mark Petkovsek	.10	.05	.01
☐ 293 Gary Pettis	.10	.05	.01
☐ 294 Jim Piersall CO	.25	.11	.03
☐ 295 John Poloni	.10	.05	.01
☐ 296 Jim Poole	.10	.05	.01
☐ 297 Tom Poquette	.10	.05	.01
☐ 298 Darrell Porter	.25	.11	.03
☐ 299 Ron Pruitt	.10	.05	.01
☐ 300 Greg Pryor	.10	.05	.01
☐ 301 Luis Pujols	.10	.05	.01
☐ 302 Pat Putnam	.10	.05	.01
☐ 303 Doug Rader MG	.10	.05	.01
☐ 304 Dave Rajsich	.10	.05	.01
☐ 305 Kevin Reimer	.10	.05	.01
☐ 306 Merv Rettenmund CO	.10	.05	.01
☐ 307 Mike Richardt	.10	.05	.01
☐ 308 Mickey Rivers	.25	.11	.03
☐ 309 Dave Roberts	.10	.05	.01
☐ 310 Leon Roberts	.10	.05	.01
☐ 311 Jeff M. Robinson	.10	.05	.01
☐ 312 Tom Robson	.10	.05	.01
☐ 313 Wayne Rosenthal	.10	.05	.01
☐ 314 Dave Rozema	.10	.05	.01
☐ 315 Jeff Russell	.25	.11	.03
☐ 316 Connie Ryan MG	.10	.05	.01
☐ 317 Billy Sample	.25	.11	.03
☐ 318 Jim Schaffer CO	.10	.05	.01
☐ 319 Calvin Schiraldi	.10	.05	.01
☐ 320 Dave Schmidt	.10	.05	.01
☐ 321 Donnie Scott	.10	.05	.01
☐ 322 Tony Scruggs	.10	.05	.01
☐ 323 Bob Sebra	.10	.05	.01
☐ 324 Larry See	.10	.05	.01
☐ 325 Sonny Siebert	.10	.05	.01
☐ 326 Ruben Sierra	1.00	.45	.12
☐ 327 Charlie Silvera CO	.10	.05	.01
☐ 328 Duke Sims	.10	.05	.01
☐ 329 Bill Singer	.10	.05	.01
☐ 330 Craig Skok	.10	.05	.01
☐ 331 Don Slaught	.50	.23	.06
☐ 332 Roy Smalley	.10	.05	.01
☐ 333 Dan Smith	.10	.05	.01
☐ 334 Keith Smith	.10	.05	.01
☐ 335 Mike Smithson	.10	.05	.01

Card	MINT	NRMT	EXC
☐ 336 Eric Soderholm	.10	.05	.01
☐ 337 Sammy Sosa	2.00	.90	.25
☐ 338 Jim Spencer	.10	.05	.01
☐ 339 Dick Such CO	.10	.05	.01
☐ 340 Eddie Stanky MG	.25	.11	.03
☐ 341 Mike Stanley	.50	.23	.06
☐ 342 Rusty Staub	.50	.23	.06
☐ 343 James Steels	.10	.05	.01
☐ 344 Bill Stein	.10	.05	.01
☐ 345 Rick Stelmaszek	.10	.05	.01
☐ 346 Ray Stephens	.10	.05	.01
☐ 347 Dave Stewart	.50	.23	.06
☐ 348 Jeff Stone	.10	.05	.01
☐ 349 Bill Sudakis	.10	.05	.01
☐ 350 Jim Sundberg	.25	.11	.03
☐ 351 Rich Surhoff	.10	.05	.01
☐ 352 Greg Tabor	.10	.05	.01
☐ 353 Frank Tanana	.25	.11	.03
☐ 354 Jeff Terpko	.10	.05	.01
☐ 355 Stan Thomas	.10	.05	.01
☐ 356 Bobby Thompson	.10	.05	.01
☐ 357 Danny Thompson	.10	.05	.01
☐ 358 Dickie Thon	.10	.05	.01
☐ 359 Dave Tobik	.10	.05	.01
☐ 360 Wayne Tolleson	.10	.05	.01
☐ 361 Cesar Tovar	.10	.05	.01
☐ 362 Jim Umbarger	.10	.05	.01
☐ 363 Bobby Valentine MG	.25	.11	.03
☐ 364 Ellis Valentine	.25	.11	.03
☐ 365 Ed Vande Berg	.10	.05	.01
☐ 366 DeWayne Vaughn	.10	.05	.01
☐ 367 Mark Wagner	.10	.05	.01
☐ 368 Rick Waits	.10	.05	.01
☐ 369 Duane Walker	.10	.05	.01
☐ 370 Mike Wallace	.10	.05	.01
☐ 371 Denny Walling	.10	.05	.01
☐ 372 Danny Walton	.10	.05	.01
☐ 373 Gary Ward	.10	.05	.01
☐ 374 Claudell Washington	.25	.11	.03
☐ 375 LaRue Washington UER (Misspelled Wasington on card back)	.10	.05	.01
☐ 376 Chris Welsh	.10	.05	.01
☐ 377 Don Werner	.10	.05	.01
☐ 378 Len Whitehouse	.10	.05	.01
☐ 379 Del Wilber MG	.10	.05	.01
☐ 380 Curtis Wilkerson	.10	.05	.01
☐ 381 Matt Williams	.25	.11	.03
☐ 382 Mitch Williams	.50	.23	.06
☐ 383 Bump Wills	.10	.05	.01
☐ 384 Paul Wilmet	.10	.05	.01
☐ 385 Steve Wilson	.10	.05	.01
☐ 386 Bobby Witt	.50	.23	.06
☐ 387 Clyde Wright	.10	.05	.01
☐ 388 George Wright	.10	.05	.01
☐ 389 Ricky Wright	.10	.05	.01
☐ 390 Ned Yost	.10	.05	.01
☐ 391 Don Zimmer MG	.25	.11	.03
☐ 392 Richie Zisk	.25	.11	.03
☐ 393 Kevin Kennedy MG	.25	.11	.03
☐ 394 Steve Balboni	.10	.05	.01
☐ 395 Brian Bohanon	.10	.05	.01
☐ 396 Jeff Bronkey	.10	.05	.01
☐ 397 Kevin Brown	1.00	.45	.12
☐ 398 Todd Burns	.10	.05	.01
☐ 399 Jose Canseco	2.00	.90	.25
☐ 400 Cris Carpenter	.10	.05	.01
☐ 401 Doug Dascenzo	.10	.05	.01
☐ 402 Butch Davis	.10	.05	.01
☐ 403 Steve Dreyer	.10	.05	.01
☐ 404 Rob Ducey	.10	.05	.01
☐ 405 Julio Franco	.50	.23	.06
☐ 406 Jeff Frye	.10	.05	.01
☐ 407 Benji Gil	.25	.11	.03
☐ 408 Juan Gonzalez	6.00	2.70	.75
☐ 409 Tom Henke	.50	.23	.06
☐ 410 David Hulse	.10	.05	.01
☐ 411 Jeff Huson	.10	.05	.01
☐ 412 Chris James	.25	.11	.03
☐ 413 Manuel Lee	.10	.05	.01
☐ 414 Craig Lefferts	.10	.05	.01
☐ 415 Charlie Leibrandt	.25	.11	.03
☐ 416 Gene Nelson	.10	.05	.01
☐ 417 Robb Nen	.60	.25	.07
☐ 418 Darren Oliver	.10	.05	.01
☐ 419 Rafael Palmeiro	2.00	.90	.25
☐ 420 Dean Palmer	1.00	.45	.12
☐ 421 Bob Patterson	.10	.05	.01
☐ 422 Roger Pavlik	.50	.23	.06
☐ 423 Dan Peltier	.10	.05	.01
☐ 424 Geno Petralli	.10	.05	.01
☐ 425 Gary Redus	.10	.05	.01
☐ 426 Rick Reed	.10	.05	.01
☐ 427 Bill Ripken	.10	.05	.01
☐ 428 Ivan Rodriguez	3.00	1.35	.35
☐ 429 Kenny Rogers	.50	.23	.06
☐ 430 John Russell	.10	.05	.01
☐ 431 Nolan Ryan	6.00	2.70	.75
☐ 432 Mike Schooler	.10	.05	.01
☐ 433 Jon Shave	.10	.05	.01
☐ 434 Doug Strange	.10	.05	.01
☐ 435 Matt Whiteside	.10	.05	.01
☐ 436 Mickey Hatcher CO	.10	.05	.01
☐ 437 Perry Hill CO	.10	.05	.01
☐ 438 Jackie Moore CO	.10	.05	.01
☐ 439 Dave Oliver CO	.10	.05	.01
☐ 440 Claude Osteen CO	.10	.05	.01
☐ 441 Willie Upshaw CO	.10	.05	.01
☐ 442 Checklist 1-112	.10	.05	.01
☐ 443 Checklist 113-224	.10	.05	.01
☐ 444 Checklist 225-336	.10	.05	.01
☐ 445 Checklist 337-446	.10	.05	.01
☐ 446 Arlington Stadium	.10	.05	.01
☐ SP1 1972 Team Photo	.25	.11	.03
☐ SP2 Logo	.10	.05	.01
☐ SP3 Logo	.10	.05	.01
☐ SP4 Logo	.10	.05	.01
☐ SP5 Logo	.10	.05	.01
☐ SP6 Home Run Leaders	.25	.11	.03
☐ SP7 RBI Leaders	.25	.11	.03
☐ SP8 Batting Average Leaders	.25	.11	.03
☐ SP9 Win Leaders	.25	.11	.03
☐ SP10 Save Leaders	.25	.11	.03
☐ SP11 Hit Leaders	.25	.11	.03
☐ SP12 Stolen Base Leaders	.25	.11	.03
☐ SP13 Games Played Leaders	.25	.11	.03
☐ SP14 Strikeout Leaders	.25	.11	.03
☐ SP15 ERA Leaders	.25	.11	.03
☐ SP16 Games Pitched Leaders	.25	.11	.03
☐ SP17 Innings Pitched Leaders	.25	.11	.03
☐ SP18 Attendance Records	.25	.11	.03
☐ SP19 Top 20 Crowds	.25	.11	.03
☐ SP20 Hitting Streaks	.25	.11	.03
☐ SP21 All-Stars	.25	.11	.03
☐ SP22 Top Draft Picks	.25	.11	.03

1994 Rangers All-Stars Pins

These pins along with the attached cards honor all Texas Rangers who were selected to the All-Star team during the Rangers stay in Arlington Stadium. The set is sequenced in year order. These pins were given out to all fans at the April 29th, 1994 Rangers game.

	MINT	NRMT	EXC
COMPLETE SET (22)	20.00	9.00	2.50
COMMON PIN (1-22)	1.00	.45	.12
☐ 1 Dave Nelson / Jim Spencer	1.00	.45	.12
☐ 2 Jeff Burroughs / Jim Sundberg	1.00	.45	.12
☐ 3 Mike Hargrove / Toby Harrah	1.50	.70	.19
☐ 4 Toby Harrah	1.00	.45	.12
☐ 5 Bert Campaneris	1.50	.70	.19
☐ 6 Richie Zisk / Jim Sundberg	1.00	.45	.12
☐ 7 Jim Kern	1.00	.45	.12
☐ 8 Al Oliver / Buddy Bell	1.00	.45	.12
☐ 9 Al Oliver / Buddy Bell	1.00	.45	.12
☐ 10 Buddy Bell	1.00	.45	.12
☐ 11 Rick Honeycutt	1.00	.45	.12
☐ 12 Buddy Bell	1.00	.45	.12
☐ 13 Gary Ward	1.00	.45	.12
☐ 14 Charlie Hough	1.50	.70	.19
☐ 15 Larry Parrish	1.00	.45	.12
☐ 16 Jeff Russell	1.00	.45	.12
☐ 17 Julio Franco / Ruben Sierra / Nolan Ryan / Jeff Russell	5.00	2.20	.60
☐ 18 Julio Franco	1.50	.70	.19
☐ 19 Rafael Palmeiro / Ruben Sierra / Julio Franco	2.00	.90	.25
☐ 20 Ivan Rodriguez / Ruben Sierra / Kevin Brown	2.50	1.10	.30
☐ 21 Ivan Rodriguez / Juan Gonzalez	3.00	1.35	.35
☐ 22 Ivan Rodriguez / Will Clark	2.50	1.10	.30

1995 Rangers Crayola

This 36-card set measures approximately 3" by 5". The fronts feature full-bleed color posed player portraits with the team logo, sponsor name, player's name and position in a blue bar across the bottom. The backs are blank. The cards are unnumbered and checklisted below in alphabetical order.

	MINT	NRMT	EXC
COMPLETE SET (36)	10.00	4.50	1.25
COMMON CARD (1-36)	.25	.11	.03
☐ 1 The Ballpark in Arlington	.25	.11	.03
☐ 2 Jose Alberro	.25	.11	.03
☐ 3 Esteban Beltre	.25	.11	.03
☐ 4 Dick Bosman CO	.25	.11	.03
☐ 5 Terry Burrows CO	.25	.11	.03
☐ 6 Will Clark	1.25	.55	.16
☐ 7 Bucky Dent CO	.25	.11	.03
☐ 8 Hector Fajardo	.25	.11	.03
☐ 9 Jeff Frye	.25	.11	.03
☐ 10 Benji Gil	.25	.11	.03
☐ 11 Juan Gonzalez	2.50	1.10	.30
☐ 12 Rusty Greer	1.25	.55	.16
☐ 13 Kevin Gross	.25	.11	.03
☐ 14 Larry Hardy CO	.25	.11	.03
☐ 15 Shawn Hare	.25	.11	.03
☐ 16 Rudy Jaramillo CO	.25	.11	.03
☐ 17 Roger McDowell	.25	.11	.03
☐ 18 Mark McLemore	.25	.11	.03
☐ 19 Ed Napoleon CO	.25	.11	.03
☐ 20 Jerry Narron CO	.25	.11	.03
☐ 21 Chris Nichting	.25	.11	.03
☐ 22 Otis Nixon	.50	.23	.06
☐ 23 Johnny Oates MG	.50	.23	.06
☐ 24 Darren Oliver	.25	.11	.03
☐ 25 Mike Pagliarulo	.25	.11	.03
☐ 26 Dean Palmer	1.00	.45	.12
☐ 27 Roger Pavlik	.50	.23	.06
☐ 28 Ivan Rodriguez	1.50	.70	.19
☐ 29 Kenny Rogers	.50	.23	.06
☐ 30 Jeff Russell	.50	.23	.06
☐ 31 Mickey Tettleton	.50	.23	.06
☐ 32 Bob Tewksbury	.25	.11	.03
☐ 33 David Valle	.25	.11	.03
☐ 34 Jack Voigt	.25	.11	.03
☐ 35 Ed Vosberg	.25	.11	.03
☐ 36 Matt Whiteside	.25	.11	.03

1996 Rangers Mother's

This 28-card set consists of borderless posed color player portraits in stadium settings. The player's and team's names appear in one of the top rounded corners. The backs carry biographical information and the sponsor's logo on a white background in red and purple print. A blank slot for the player's autograph rounds out the back.

	MINT	NRMT	EXC
COMPLETE SET (28)	10.00	4.50	1.25
COMMON CARD (1-28)	.25	.11	.03
☐ 1 Johnny Oates MG	.25	.11	.03
☐ 2 Will Clark	1.25	.55	.16
☐ 3 Juan Gonzalez	2.50	1.10	.30
☐ 4 Ivan Rodriguez	1.50	.70	.19
☐ 5 Darryl Hamilton	.50	.23	.06
☐ 6 Dean Palmer	.75	.35	.09
☐ 7 Mickey Tettleton	.50	.23	.06
☐ 8 Craig Worthington	.25	.11	.03
☐ 9 Rusty Greer	1.25	.55	.16
☐ 10 Kevin Gross	.25	.11	.03
☐ 11 Rick Helling	.25	.11	.03
☐ 12 Kevin Elster	.25	.11	.03
☐ 13 Bobby Witt	.50	.23	.06
☐ 14 Mark McLemore	.25	.11	.03
☐ 15 Warren Newson	.25	.11	.03
☐ 16 Mike Henneman	.25	.11	.03
☐ 17 Ken Hill	.75	.35	.09
☐ 18 Gil Heredia	.25	.11	.03
☐ 19 Roger Pavlik	.25	.11	.03
☐ 20 David Valle	.25	.11	.03
☐ 21 Mark Brandenburg	.25	.11	.03
☐ 22 Kurt Stillwell	.25	.11	.03
☐ 23 Ed Vosberg	.25	.11	.03
☐ 24 Dennis Cook	.25	.11	.03
☐ 25 Damon Buford	.25	.11	.03
☐ 26 Benji Gil	.25	.11	.03
☐ 27 Darren Oliver	.50	.23	.06
☐ 28 Coaches Card CL / Dick Bosman / Bucky Den / Larry Hardy / Rudy Jaramillo / Ed Napoleon / Jerry Narron	.25	.11	.03

1997 Rangers Commemorative Sheet

This 11" by 8 1/2" card was given away at the April 21, 1997, game between the Texas Rangers and the Detroit Tigers and commemorates

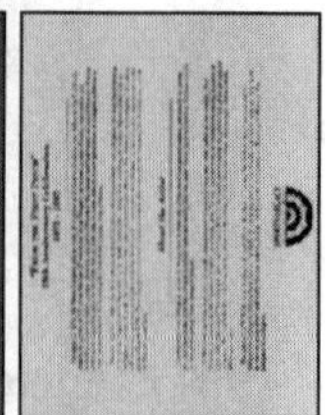

the 25th Anniversary of the Rangers' first game at Arlington Stadium. It also honors former Arlington Mayor, Judge Tom Vandergriff, who was instrumental in biringing Major League Baseball to the North Texas area. The front features art work by sports artist, Vernon Wells, and depicts various present and former Texas Rangers. The back displays information about the 25th anniversary and the artist. Only 50,000 of this card was produced and are sequentially numbered.

	MINT	NRMT	EXC
COMPLETE SET (1)	5.00	2.20	.60
COMMON CARD (1)	5.00	2.20	.60
☐ 1 From the First Pitch	5.00	2.20	.60

1955 Rawlings Musial

This six-card set was actually the side panels of the box containing a Rawlings baseball glove. Rawlings Sporting Goods was headquartered in St. Louis. The cards are numbered and come in two sizes. Cards 1-4 are larger, 2 5/8" by 3 3/4" whereas numbers 1A and 2A are smaller, 2 1/8" by 3 1/8". The cards are blank backed and have a black and white picture on a light blue background.

	NRMT	VG-E	GOOD
COMPLETE SET (6)	1500.00	700.00	190.00
COMMON CARD	200.00	90.00	25.00
☐ 1 Stan Musial (portrait)	300.00	135.00	38.00
☐ 1A Stan Musial (portrait with hand and bat visible)	200.00	90.00	25.00
☐ 2 Stan Musial (kneeling)	300.00	135.00	38.00
☐ 2A Stan Musial (portrait, same picture as number 1	200.00	90.00	25.00
☐ 3 Stan Musial (swinging HOR)	300.00	135.00	38.00
☐ 4 Stan Musial (batting stance)	300.00	135.00	38.00

1961 Rawlings Sporting Goods

This 12-card set measures approximately 8 1/8" by 10 1/8" and features white-bordered, black-and-white player photos. A facsimile autograph and sponsor name is printed in a white box on one side of the picture. The backs are blank. The cards are unnumbered and checklisted below in alphabetical order.

	NRMT	VG-E	GOOD
COMPLETE SET (12)	225.00	100.00	28.00
COMMON CARD (1-12)	10.00	4.50	1.25
☐ 1 Joe Adcock	15.00	6.75	1.85
☐ 2 Ed Bailey	10.00	4.50	1.25
☐ 3 Clete Boyer	15.00	6.75	1.85
☐ 4 Tommy Davis	15.00	6.75	1.85
☐ 5 Mickey Mantle	75.00	34.00	9.50
☐ 6 Wally Moon	15.00	6.75	1.85
☐ 7 Stan Musial	35.00	16.00	4.40
☐ 8 Rocky Nelson	10.00	4.50	1.25
☐ 9 Brooks Robinson	25.00	11.00	3.10
☐ 10 Duke Snider	25.00	11.00	3.10
☐ 11 Warren Spahn	25.00	11.00	3.10
☐ 12 Bob Turley	10.00	4.50	1.25

1964 Rawlings Box

This eight-card set features borderless color player photos that measure 2 3/8" by 4" when properly cut off the glove boxes on which they were printed. The photos are of stars of the day posing with their Rawlings glove prominently displayed, and a facsimile autograph is printed across the bottom of the picture. The cards are unnumbered and checklisted below in alphabetical order. There was also a picture issue of 8" by 9 1/2" Advisory Staff photos given away upon purchase. The same players featured on the boxes were featured on these photos.

	NRMT	VG-E	GOOD
COMPLETE SET (8)	150.00	70.00	20.00
COMMON CARD (1-8)	10.00	4.50	1.25
☐ 1 Ken Boyer	15.00	6.75	1.85
☐ 2 Willie Davis	10.00	4.50	1.25
☐ 3 Dick Groat	10.00	4.50	1.25
☐ 4 Mickey Mantle	50.00	22.00	6.25
☐ 5 Brooks Robinson	25.00	11.00	3.10
☐ 6 Warren Spahn	20.00	9.00	2.50
☐ 7 Tom Tresh	10.00	4.50	1.25
☐ 8 Billy Williams	20.00	9.00	2.50

1976 Rawlings

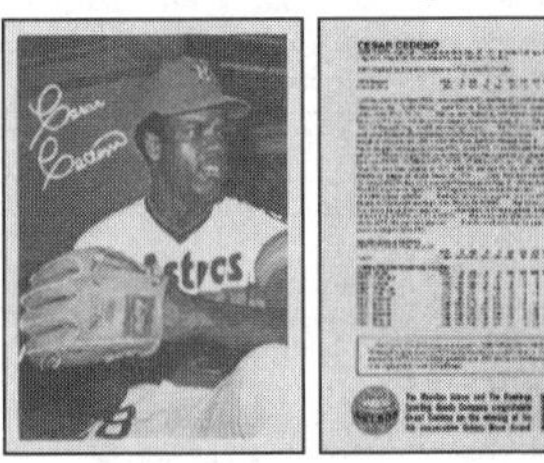

This card was distributed by Rawlings Sporting Goods Company honoring Cesar Cedeno on the winning of his 4th consecutive Golden Glove Award. It measures approximately 5" by 7" and features a color photo in a white border with a white facsimile autograph. The back displays player information and career statistics. This set may be incomplete.

	NRMT	VG-E	GOOD
COMPLETE SET	3.00	1.35	.35
COMMON CARD	3.00	1.35	.35
☐ 1 Cesar Cedeno	3.00	1.35	.35

1977 RC Cola Cans

This 70-can set features black-and white player head photos in white circles measuring 2 1/2" in diameter with no insignia on their caps indicating RC didn't pay the teams for the rights to reproduce their logos. The player's name was printed in red and player information was printed in black in a rectangle below the picture. The cans are unnumbered and checklisted below in alphabetical order. Cans opened from the bottom are worth twice the prices below.

	NRMT	VG-E	GOOD
COMPLETE SET (70)	200.00	90.00	25.00
COMMON CARD (1-70)	2.00	.90	.25
☐ 1 Sal Bando	2.00	.90	.25
☐ 2 Mark Belanger	2.00	.90	.25
☐ 3 Johnny Bench	5.00	2.20	.60
☐ 4 Vida Blue	2.50	1.10	.30
☐ 5 Bobby Bonds	2.50	1.10	.30
☐ 6 Bob Boone	2.50	1.10	.30
☐ 7 Larry Bowa	2.00	.90	.25
☐ 8 Steve Braun	2.00	.90	.25
☐ 9 George Brett	15.00	6.75	1.85
☐ 10 Lou Brock	5.00	2.20	.60
☐ 11 Bert Campaneris	2.50	1.10	.30
☐ 12 Bill Campbell	2.00	.90	.25
☐ 13 Jose Cardenal	2.00	.90	.25
☐ 14 Rod Carew	5.00	2.20	.60
☐ 15 Dave Cash	2.00	.90	.25
☐ 16 Cesar Cedeno	2.00	.90	.25
☐ 17 Ron Cey	2.50	1.10	.30
☐ 18 Chris Chambliss	2.50	1.10	.30
☐ 19 Dave Concepcion	2.00	.90	.25
☐ 20 Mark Fidrych	4.00	1.80	.50
☐ 21 Rollie Fingers	4.00	1.80	.50
☐ 22 George Foster	2.50	1.10	.30
☐ 23 Wayne Garland	2.00	.90	.25
☐ 24 Ralph Garr	2.00	.90	.25
☐ 25 Steve Garvey	4.00	1.80	.50
☐ 26 Bobby Grich	2.50	1.10	.30
☐ 27 Ken Griffey	3.00	1.35	.35
☐ 28 Don Gullett	2.00	.90	.25
☐ 29 Mike Hargrove	2.00	.90	.25
☐ 30 Catfish Hunter	5.00	2.20	.60
☐ 31 Randy Jones	2.00	.90	.25
☐ 32 Dave Kingman	3.00	1.35	.35
☐ 33 Dave LaRoche	2.00	.90	.25
☐ 34 Ron LeFlore	2.00	.90	.25
☐ 35 Greg Luzinski	2.50	1.10	.30
☐ 36 Fred Lynn	2.50	1.10	.30
☐ 37 Bill Madlock	2.50	1.10	.30
☐ 38 Jon Matlack	2.00	.90	.25
☐ 39 Gary Matthews	2.00	.90	.25
☐ 40 Bake McBride	2.00	.90	.25
☐ 41 Hal McRae	2.00	.90	.25
☐ 42 Andy Messersmith	2.00	.90	.25
☐ 43 Rick Monday	2.00	.90	.25
☐ 44 John Montefusco	2.00	.90	.25
☐ 45 Joe Morgan	5.00	2.20	.60
☐ 46 Thurman Munson	4.00	1.80	.50
☐ 47 Al Oliver	2.50	1.10	.30
☐ 48 Amos Otis	2.00	.90	.25
☐ 49 Jim Palmer	5.00	2.20	.60
☐ 50 Dave Parker	3.00	1.35	.35
☐ 51 Fred Patek	2.00	.90	.25
☐ 52 Gaylord Perry	5.00	2.20	.60
☐ 53 Marty Perez	2.00	.90	.25
☐ 54 Tony Perez	2.00	.90	.25
☐ 55 J.R. Richard	2.50	1.10	.30
☐ 56 Pete Rose	7.50	3.40	.95
☐ 57 Joe Rudi	2.00	.90	.25
☐ 58 Mike Schmidt	10.00	4.50	1.25
☐ 59 Tom Seaver	7.50	3.40	.95
☐ 60 Bill Singer	2.00	.90	.25
☐ 61 Rusty Staub	2.00	.90	.25
☐ 62 Don Sutton	4.00	1.80	.50
☐ 63 Gene Tenace	2.00	.90	.25
☐ 64 Luis Tiant	2.50	1.10	.30
☐ 65 Ellis Valentine	2.00	.90	.25
☐ 66 Claudell Washington	2.00	.90	.25
☐ 67 Butch Wynegar	2.00	.90	.25
☐ 68 Carl Yastrzemski	6.00	2.70	.75
☐ 69 Robin Yount	7.50	3.40	.95
☐ 70 Richie Zisk	2.00	.90	.25

1978 RC Cola Cans

This 100-can set is indicated as Collector's Series Two on the cans and features black-and-white player head photos in a white circle with a red border. Player's biographical information is printed beneath in a white circle with red stitching to simulate a baseball. At the top of the ball is a facsimile autograph. The player's career highlights summary is written in paragraph form inside the ball. At the bottom of the ball is the can number, designated as, "No. x of 100." Cans opened from the bottom are worth twice the prices below.

	NRMT	VG-E	GOOD
COMPLETE SET (100)	250.00	110.00	31.00
COMMON CARD (1-100)	2.00	.90	.25
☐ 1 Don Sutton	4.00	1.80	.50
☐ 2 Bill Singer	2.00	.90	.25
☐ 3 Pete Rose	7.50	3.40	.95
☐ 4 Gene Tenace	2.00	.90	.25
☐ 5 Dave Kingman	3.00	1.35	.35
☐ 6 Dave Cash	2.00	.90	.25
☐ 7 Joe Morgan DP	4.00	1.80	.50
☐ 8 Mark Belanger	2.00	.90	.25
☐ 9 Steve Braun	2.00	.90	.25
☐ 10 Butch Wynegar	2.00	.90	.25
☐ 11 Ken Griffey	3.00	1.35	.35
☐ 12 Ron LeFlore	2.00	.90	.25
☐ 13 George Foster	2.00	.90	.25
☐ 14 Tony Perez	4.00	1.80	.50
☐ 15 Thurman Munson	4.00	1.80	.50
☐ 16 Bill Campbell	2.00	.90	.25
☐ 17 Andy Messersmith	2.00	.90	.25
☐ 18 Mike Schmidt	10.00	4.50	1.25
☐ 19 Ron Cey	2.50	1.10	.30
☐ 20 Chris Chambliss	2.50	1.10	.30
☐ 21 Ralph Garr	2.00	.90	.25
☐ 22 Dave LaRoche	2.00	.90	.25
☐ 23 George Brett	15.00	6.75	1.85
☐ 24 Bob Boone	2.50	1.10	.30
☐ 25 Jeff Burroughs	2.00	.90	.25
☐ 26 Bake McBride	2.00	.90	.25
☐ 27 Gary Matthews	2.00	.90	.25
☐ 28 Don Gullett	2.00	.90	.25
☐ 29 Rick Monday	2.00	.90	.25
☐ 30 Al Oliver	2.00	.90	.25
☐ 31 Ellis Valentine	2.00	.90	.25
☐ 32 Mike Hargrove	2.50	1.10	.30
☐ 33 Hal McRae	2.00	.90	.25
☐ 34 Rollie Fingers	5.00	2.20	.60
☐ 35 Dave Parker	4.00	1.80	.50
☐ 36 Tom Seaver DP	5.00	2.20	.60
☐ 37 Wayne Garland	2.00	.90	.25
☐ 38 Jon Matlack	2.00	.90	.25
☐ 39 Richie Zisk	2.00	.90	.25
☐ 40 Joe Rudi	2.00	.90	.25
☐ 41 Sal Bando	2.00	.90	.25
☐ 42 Greg Luzinski	2.00	.90	.25
☐ 43 Vida Blue	2.50	1.10	.30
☐ 44 Bobby Bonds	2.50	1.10	.30
☐ 45 Jim Palmer	5.00	2.20	.60
☐ 46 Claudell Washington	2.00	.90	.25
☐ 47 Dave Concepcion	2.00	.90	.25
☐ 48 Rod Carew DP	4.00	1.80	.50
☐ 49 J.R. Richard	2.00	.90	.25
☐ 50 Rich Gossage	3.00	1.35	.35
☐ 51 Cesar Cedeno	2.00	.90	.25
☐ 52 Bert Campaneris	2.00	.90	.25
☐ 53 Marty Perez	2.00	.90	.25
☐ 54 Bill Madlock	2.00	.90	.25
☐ 55 Amos Otis	2.00	.90	.25
☐ 56 Robin Yount	5.00	2.20	.60
☐ 57 Bobby Grich	2.00	.90	.25
☐ 58 Catfish Hunter	5.00	2.20	.60
☐ 59 Butch Hobson	2.00	.90	.25
☐ 60 Larry Bowa	2.00	.90	.25
☐ 61 Randy Jones	2.00	.90	.25
☐ 62 Richie Hebner	2.00	.90	.25
☐ 63 Fred Patek	2.00	.90	.25
☐ 64 John Denny	2.00	.90	.25
☐ 65 Johnny Bench DP	4.00	1.80	.50
☐ 66 Doyle Alexander	2.00	.90	.25
☐ 67 Dusty Baker	2.50	1.10	.30
☐ 68 Bert Blyleven	3.00	1.35	.35
☐ 69 Lyman Bostock	2.00	.90	.25
☐ 70 Bill Buckner	2.00	.90	.25
☐ 71 Steve Carlton	5.00	2.20	.60
☐ 72 John Candelaria	2.00	.90	.25
☐ 73 Andre Dawson	7.50	3.40	.95
☐ 74 Al Cowens	2.00	.90	.25
☐ 75 Eddie Murray	10.00	4.50	1.25
☐ 76 Dan Driessen	2.00	.90	.25
☐ 77 Jim Rice	3.00	1.35	.35
☐ 78 Garry Maddox	2.00	.90	.25
☐ 79 Larry Hisle	2.00	.90	.25
☐ 80 Al Hrabosky	2.00	.90	.25
☐ 81 Reggie Jackson DP	6.00	2.70	.75
☐ 82 Tommy John	3.00	1.35	.35
☐ 83 Willie McCovey	5.00	2.20	.60
☐ 84 Sparky Lyle	2.50	1.10	.30
☐ 85 Tug McGraw	2.50	1.10	.30
☐ 86 Paul Splittorff	2.00	.90	.25
☐ 87 Bobby Murcer	2.00	.90	.25
☐ 88 Graig Nettles	3.00	1.35	.35
☐ 89 Phil Niekro	5.00	2.20	.60
☐ 90 Lou Piniella	3.00	1.35	.35
☐ 91 Rick Reuschel	2.00	.90	.25
☐ 92 Frank Tanana	2.50	1.10	.30
☐ 93 Nolan Ryan	15.00	6.75	1.85
☐ 94 Garry Templeton	2.00	.90	.25
☐ 95 Reggie Smith	2.00	.90	.25
☐ 96 Bruce Sutter	3.00	1.35	.35
☐ 97 Jason Thompson	2.00	.90	.25
☐ 98 Mike Torrez	2.00	.90	.25
☐ 99 Rick Wise	2.00	.90	.25
☐ 100 Bump Wills	2.00	.90	.25

1978 Reading Remembers

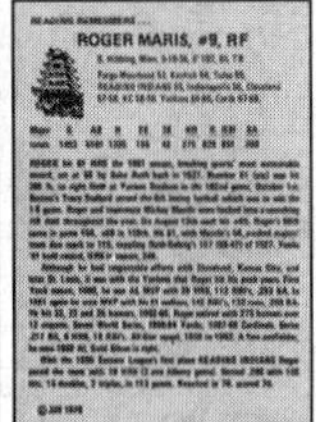

This 23-card set measures 3" by 4". The fronts feature brown and white tinted player action and posted photos. The backs carry the player's name, jersey number, position, biography, statistics, and other player facts. The cards are unnumbered and checklisted below in alphabetical order.

	NRMT	VG-E	GOOD
COMPLETE SET (23)	20.00	9.00	2.00
COMMON CARD (1-33)	.50	.23	.06
☐ 1 Tommy Brown	.50	.23	.06
☐ 2 Doug Clemens	.50	.23	.06
☐ 3 Dom Dallessandro	.50	.23	.06
☐ 4 George Eyrich	.50	.23	.06
☐ 5 Carl Furillo	1.50	.70	.19
☐ 6 Dick Gernert	.50	.23	.06
☐ 7 Randy Gumpert	.50	.23	.06
☐ 8 Bob Katz	.50	.23	.06
☐ 9 Betz Klopp	.50	.23	.06
☐ 20 Whitey Kurowski	.75	.35	.09
☐ 21 Lauer's Park	.50	.23	.06
☐ 22 Jesse Levan	.50	.23	.06
☐ 23 Carl Mathias	.50	.23	.06
☐ 24 Roger Maris	5.00	2.20	.60
☐ 25 Lenny Moore	3.00	1.35	.35
☐ 26 Robin Roberts	5.00	2.20	.60
☐ 27 Harry Schaeffer	.50	.23	.06
☐ 28 Herb Score	1.50	.70	.19
☐ 29 Ty Stofflet	.50	.23	.06
☐ 30 John Updike	.75	.35	.09
☐ 31 Charlie Wagner	.50	.23	.06
☐ 32 Stan Wentzel	.50	.23	.06
☐ 33 Vic Wertz	.50	.23	.06

1910-13 Red Cross T215

The cards in this 167-card set measure 1 1/2" by 2 5/8." There are actually three distinct groupings or types. Type 1 cards have brown captions. Type 2 cards have blue captions. Type 3 cards are distinguished by their "Pirate Cigarettes" backs printed in green ink. The type 3 cards, are so thinly traded that there is no pricing information available on them. According to leading dealers and collectors, these cards were produced for Americans serving their country in the South Seas. The players have been alphabetized within Type and numbered for reference in the checklist below.

	EX-MT	VG-E	GOOD
COMPLETE SET	2000.00	900.00	250.00
COMMON TYPE 1 (1-88)	120.00	55.00	15.00
COMMON TYPE 2 (89-167)	75.00	34.00	9.50
☐ 1 Red Ames	120.00	55.00	15.00
☐ 2 Frank Baker	240.00	110.00	30.00
☐ 3 Neal Ball	120.00	55.00	15.00
☐ 4 Chief Bender (2)	240.00	110.00	30.00
☐ 5 Chief Bender (2)	240.00	110.00	30.00
☐ 6 Al Bridwell	120.00	55.00	15.00
☐ 7 Bobby Byrne	120.00	55.00	15.00
☐ 8 Howie Camnitz	120.00	55.00	15.00
☐ 9 Frank Chance	350.00	160.00	45.00
☐ 10 Hal Chase	300.00	135.00	38.00
☐ 11 Ty Cobb	2000.00	900.00	250.00
☐ 12 Eddie Collins	240.00	110.00	30.00
☐ 13 Wid Conroy	120.00	55.00	15.00
☐ 14 Doc Crandall	120.00	55.00	15.00
☐ 15 Sam Crawford	240.00	110.00	30.00
☐ 16 Birdie Cree	120.00	55.00	15.00
☐ 17 Harry Davis	120.00	55.00	15.00
☐ 18 Josh Devore	120.00	55.00	15.00
☐ 19 Mike Donlin	120.00	55.00	15.00
☐ 20 Mickey Doolan	120.00	55.00	15.00
☐ 21 Patsy Dougherty	120.00	55.00	15.00
☐ 22 Larry Doyle	120.00	55.00	15.00
☐ 23 Larry Doyle	120.00	55.00	15.00
☐ 24 Kid Elberfeld	240.00	110.00	30.00
☐ 25 Russ Ford	120.00	55.00	15.00
☐ 26 Art Fromme	120.00	55.00	15.00
☐ 27 Clark Griffith	240.00	110.00	30.00
☐ 28 Topsy Hartsel	120.00	55.00	15.00
☐ 29 Doc Hoblitzell	120.00	55.00	15.00
☐ 30 Danny Hofman	120.00	55.00	15.00
☐ 31 Del Howard	120.00	55.00	15.00
☐ 32 Miller Huggins	240.00	110.00	30.00
☐ 33 John Hummell	120.00	55.00	15.00
☐ 34 Hugh Jennings (2)	240.00	110.00	30.00
☐ 35 Hugh Jennings (2)	240.00	110.00	30.00
☐ 36 Walter Johnson	600.00	275.00	75.00
☐ 37 Ed Konetchy	240.00	110.00	30.00
☐ 38 Harry Krause	120.00	55.00	15.00
☐ 39 Napolean Lajoie	450.00	200.00	55.00
☐ 40 Arlie Latham	120.00	55.00	15.00
☐ 41 Tommy Leach	120.00	55.00	15.00
☐ 42 Lefty Leifield	120.00	55.00	15.00
☐ 43 Harry Lord	120.00	55.00	15.00
☐ 44 Sherry Magee	120.00	55.00	15.00
☐ 45 Rube Marquard (2)	240.00	110.00	30.00
☐ 46 Rube Marquard (2)	240.00	110.00	30.00
☐ 47 Christy Mathewson	600.00	275.00	75.00
☐ 48 Christy Mathewson	600.00	275.00	75.00
☐ 49 Joe McGinnity	240.00	110.00	30.00
☐ 50 John McGraw (2)	350.00	160.00	45.00
☐ 51 John McGraw (2)	350.00	160.00	45.00
☐ 52 Matty McIntyre	120.00	55.00	15.00
☐ 53 Fred Merkle	240.00	110.00	30.00
☐ 54 Chief Meyers	120.00	55.00	15.00
☐ 55 Dots Miller	120.00	55.00	15.00
☐ 56 George Mullin	120.00	55.00	15.00
☐ 57 Danny Murphy	120.00	55.00	15.00
☐ 58 Red Murray	120.00	55.00	15.00
☐ 59 Rebel Oakes	120.00	55.00	15.00
☐ 60 Charley O'Leary	120.00	55.00	15.00
☐ 61 Dode Paskert	120.00	55.00	15.00
☐ 62 Barney Pelty	120.00	55.00	15.00
☐ 63 Jack Quinn	120.00	55.00	15.00
☐ 64 Ed Reulbach	240.00	110.00	30.00
☐ 65 Nap Rucker	240.00	110.00	30.00
☐ 66 Germany Schaefer	120.00	55.00	15.00
☐ 67 Frank Schulte	120.00	55.00	15.00
☐ 68 Jimmy Sheckard	120.00	55.00	15.00
☐ 69 Frank Smith	120.00	55.00	15.00
☐ 70 Smither	120.00	55.00	15.00
☐ 71 Tris Speaker	450.00	200.00	55.00
☐ 72 Jake Stahl	240.00	110.00	30.00
☐ 73 Harry Steinfeldt	120.00	55.00	15.00
☐ 74 Gabby Street (2)	120.00	55.00	15.00
☐ 75 Gabby Street (2)	120.00	55.00	15.00

☐ 76 William Sweeney	120.00	55.00	15.00
☐ 77 Lee Tannehill	120.00	55.00	15.00
☐ 78 Joe Tinker (2)	240.00	110.00	30.00
☐ 79 Joe Tinker (2)	240.00	110.00	30.00
☐ 80 Honus Wagner	600.00	275.00	75.00
☐ 81 Jack Warhop	120.00	55.00	15.00
☐ 82 Zach Wheat	240.00	110.00	30.00
☐ 83 Doc White	120.00	55.00	15.00
☐ 84 Ed Willett	120.00	55.00	15.00
☐ 85 Owen Wilson	120.00	55.00	15.00
☐ 86 Hooks Wiltse (2)	120.00	55.00	15.00
☐ 87 Hooks Wiltse (2)	120.00	55.00	15.00
☐ 88 Cy Young	450.00	200.00	55.00
☐ 89 Red Ames	75.00	34.00	9.50
☐ 90 Chief Bender (2)	150.00	70.00	19.00
☐ 91 Chief Bender (2)	150.00	70.00	19.00
☐ 92 Roger Bresnahan	150.00	70.00	19.00
☐ 93 Mordecai Brown	150.00	70.00	19.00
☐ 94 Bobby Byrne	75.00	34.00	9.50
☐ 95 Howie Camnitz	75.00	34.00	9.50
☐ 96 Frank Chance	250.00	110.00	31.00
☐ 97 Ty Cobb	1500.00	700.00	190.00
☐ 98 Eddie Collins	150.00	70.00	19.00
☐ 99 Doc Crandall	75.00	34.00	9.50
☐ 100 Birdie Cree	75.00	34.00	9.50
☐ 101 Harry Davis	75.00	34.00	9.50
☐ 102 Josh Devore	75.00	34.00	9.50
☐ 103 Mike Donlin	75.00	34.00	9.50
☐ 104 Mickey Doolan (2)	75.00	34.00	9.50
☐ 105 Mickey Doolan (2)	75.00	34.00	9.50
☐ 106 Patsy Dougherty	75.00	34.00	9.50
☐ 107 Larry Doyle (2)	75.00	34.00	9.50
☐ 108 Larry Doyle (2)	75.00	34.00	9.50
☐ 109 Jean Dubuc	75.00	34.00	9.50
☐ 110 Kid Elberfeld	75.00	34.00	9.50
☐ 111 Johnny Evers	150.00	70.00	19.00
☐ 112 Russ Ford	75.00	34.00	9.50
☐ 113 Art Fromme	75.00	34.00	9.50
☐ 114 Clark Griffith	150.00	70.00	19.00
☐ 115 Bob Groom	75.00	34.00	9.50
☐ 116 Topsy Hartsel	75.00	34.00	9.50
☐ 117 Buck Herzog	75.00	34.00	9.50
☐ 118 Doc Hoblitzell	75.00	34.00	9.50
☐ 119 Solly Hofman	75.00	34.00	9.50
☐ 120 Miller Huggins (2)	300.00	135.00	38.00
☐ 121 Miller Huggins (2)	300.00	135.00	38.00
☐ 122 John Hummel	75.00	34.00	9.50
☐ 123 Hugh Jennings	150.00	70.00	19.00
☐ 124 Walter Johnson	500.00	220.00	60.00
☐ 125 Joe Kelley	150.00	70.00	19.00
☐ 126 Ed Konetchy	75.00	34.00	9.50
☐ 127 Harry Krause	75.00	34.00	9.50
☐ 128 Napolean Lajoie	350.00	160.00	45.00
☐ 129 Joe Lake	75.00	34.00	9.50
☐ 130 Tommy Leach	75.00	34.00	9.50
☐ 131 Lefty Leifield	75.00	34.00	9.50
☐ 132 Harry Lord	75.00	34.00	9.50
☐ 133 Rube Marquard	150.00	70.00	19.00
☐ 134 Christy Mathewson	500.00	220.00	60.00
☐ 135 John McGraw (2)	225.00	100.00	28.00
☐ 136 John McGraw (2)	225.00	100.00	28.00
☐ 137 Larry McLean	75.00	34.00	9.50
☐ 138 Dots Miller	75.00	34.00	9.50
☐ 139 Michael Mitchell	75.00	34.00	9.50
☐ 140 Mike Mowrey	75.00	34.00	9.50
☐ 141 George Mullin	75.00	34.00	9.50
☐ 142 Danny Murphy	75.00	34.00	9.50
☐ 143 Red Murray	75.00	34.00	9.50
☐ 144 Rebel Oakes	75.00	34.00	9.50
☐ 145 Rube Oldring	75.00	34.00	9.50
☐ 146 Charley O'Leary	75.00	34.00	9.50
☐ 147 Dode Paskert	75.00	34.00	9.50
☐ 148 Barney Pelty	75.00	34.00	9.50
☐ 149 William Purtell	75.00	34.00	9.50
☐ 150 Ed Reulbach	75.00	34.00	9.50
☐ 151 Nap Rucker	75.00	34.00	9.50
☐ 152 Germany Schaefer (2)	75.00	34.00	9.50
☐ 153 Germany Schaefer (2)	75.00	34.00	9.50
☐ 154 Frank Schulte	75.00	34.00	9.50
☐ 155 Frank Smith (2)	75.00	34.00	9.50
☐ 156 Frank Smith (2)	75.00	34.00	9.50
☐ 157 Tris Speaker	350.00	160.00	45.00
☐ 158 Jake Stahl	75.00	34.00	9.50
☐ 159 Harry Steinfeldt	75.00	34.00	9.50
☐ 160 Ed Summers	75.00	34.00	9.50
☐ 161 William Sweeney	75.00	34.00	9.50
☐ 162 Joe Tinker	150.00	70.00	19.00
☐ 163 Honus Wagner	500.00	220.00	60.00
☐ 164 Jack Warhop	75.00	34.00	9.50
☐ 165 Doc White	75.00	34.00	9.50
☐ 166 Hooks Wiltse (2)	75.00	34.00	9.50
☐ 167 Hooks Wiltse (2)	75.00	34.00	9.50

1987 Red Foley Sticker Book

The 1987 Red Foley's Best Baseball Book Ever was published by Simon and Schuster and measures 8 1/2" by 11. The book includes 130 stickers, puzzles, quizzes, how-to's, and other trivia features. The stickers appear on 4 insert pages in the middle of the album. Each sticker measures 1 3/8" by 1 7/8" and displays a glossy color player photo bordered in white. The stickers are to be pasted in the appropriate slots next to a trivia question about the player. The stickers are numbered on the front and checklisted below accordingly.

	MINT	NRMT	EXC
COMPLETE SET (130)	12.00	5.50	1.50
COMMON STICKER (1-130)	.05	.02	.01
☐ 1 Julio Franco	.10	.05	.01
☐ 2 Willie Randolph	.10	.05	.01
☐ 3 Jesse Barfield	.05	.02	.01
☐ 4 Mike Witt	.05	.02	.01
☐ 5 Orel Hershiser	.10	.05	.01
☐ 6 Dwight Gooden	.25	.11	.03
☐ 7 Dan Quisenberry	.05	.02	.01
☐ 8 Vince Coleman	.05	.02	.01
☐ 9 Rich Gossage	.10	.05	.01
☐ 10 Kirk Gibson	.10	.05	.01
☐ 11 Joaquin Andujar	.05	.02	.01
☐ 12 David Concepcion	.10	.05	.01
☐ 13 Andre Dawson	.25	.11	.03
☐ 14 Tippy Martinez	.05	.02	.01
☐ 15 Bob James	.05	.02	.01
☐ 16 Ryne Sandberg	.75	.35	.09
☐ 17 Bob Knepper	.05	.02	.01
☐ 18 Bob Stanley	.05	.02	.01
☐ 19 Jim Presley	.05	.02	.01
☐ 20 Greg Gross	.05	.02	.01
☐ 21 Bob Horner	.05	.02	.01
☐ 22 Paul Molitor	.50	.23	.06
☐ 23 Kirby Puckett	1.25	.55	.16
☐ 24 Scott Garrelts	.05	.02	.01
☐ 25 Tony Pena	.05	.02	.01
☐ 26 Charlie Hough	.10	.05	.01
☐ 27 Joe Carter	.40	.18	.05
☐ 28 Dave Winfield	.40	.18	.05
☐ 29 Tony Fernandez	.05	.02	.01
☐ 30 Bobby Grich	.10	.05	.01
☐ 31 Mike Marshall	.05	.02	.01
☐ 32 Keith Hernandez	.10	.05	.01
☐ 33 Dennis Leonard	.05	.02	.01
☐ 34 John Tudor	.05	.02	.01
☐ 35 Kevin McReynolds	.05	.02	.01
☐ 36 Lance Parrish	.10	.05	.01
☐ 37 Carney Lansford	.10	.05	.01
☐ 38 Buddy Bell	.10	.05	.01
☐ 39 Tim Raines	.10	.05	.01
☐ 40 Mike Boddicker	.05	.02	.01
☐ 41 Carlton Fisk	.40	.18	.05
☐ 42 Lee Smith	.25	.11	.03
☐ 43 Glenn Davis	.05	.02	.01
☐ 44 Jim Rice	.10	.05	.01
☐ 45 Mark Langston	.10	.05	.01
☐ 46 Mike Schmidt	1.00	.45	.12
☐ 47 Dale Murphy	.25	.11	.03
☐ 48 Cecil Cooper	.10	.05	.01
☐ 49 Kent Hrbek	.10	.05	.01
☐ 50 Will Clark	.40	.18	.05
☐ 51 Johnny Ray	.05	.02	.01
☐ 52 Darrell Porter	.05	.02	.01
☐ 53 Brook Jacoby	.05	.02	.01
☐ 54 Ron Guidry	.10	.05	.01
☐ 55 Lloyd Moseby	.05	.02	.01
☐ 56 Donnie Moore	.05	.02	.01
☐ 57 Fernando Valenzuela	.10	.05	.01
☐ 58 Darryl Strawberry	.25	.11	.03
☐ 59 Hal McRae	.10	.05	.01
☐ 60 Tommy Herr	.05	.02	.01
☐ 61 Steve Garvey	.25	.11	.03
☐ 62 Alan Trammell	.25	.11	.03
☐ 63 Jose Canseco	.40	.18	.05
☐ 64 Pete Rose	1.25	.55	.16
☐ 65 Jeff Reardon	.10	.05	.01
☐ 66 Eddie Murray	.60	.25	.07
☐ 67 Ozzie Guillen	.05	.02	.01
☐ 68 Jody Davis	.05	.02	.01
☐ 69 Bill Doran	.05	.02	.01
☐ 70 Roger Clemens	.60	.25	.07
☐ 71 Alvin Davis	.05	.02	.01
☐ 72 Von Hayes	.05	.02	.01
☐ 73 Zane Smith	.05	.02	.01
☐ 74 Ted Higuera	.05	.02	.01
☐ 75 Tom Brunansky	.05	.02	.01
☐ 76 Chili Davis	.10	.05	.01
☐ 77 R.J. Reynolds	.05	.02	.01
☐ 78 Oddibe McDowell	.05	.02	.01
☐ 79 Brett Butler	.10	.05	.01
☐ 80 Rickey Henderson	.40	.18	.05
☐ 81 Dave Stieb	.05	.02	.01
☐ 82 Wally Joyner	.75	.35	.09
☐ 83 Pedro Guerrero	.05	.02	.01
☐ 84 Jesse Orosco	.05	.02	.01
☐ 85 Steve Balboni	.05	.02	.01
☐ 86 Willie McGee	.05	.02	.01
☐ 87 Graig Nettles	.10	.05	.01
☐ 88 Lou Whitaker	.10	.05	.01
☐ 89 Jay Howell	.05	.02	.01
☐ 90 Dave Parker	.10	.05	.01
☐ 91 Hubie Brooks	.05	.02	.01
☐ 92 Rick Dempsey	.05	.02	.01
☐ 93 Neil Allen	.05	.02	.01
☐ 94 Shawon Dunston	.05	.02	.01
☐ 95 Jose Cruz	.10	.05	.01
☐ 96 Wade Boggs	.40	.18	.05
☐ 97 Danny Tartabull	.10	.05	.01
☐ 98 Steve Bedrosian	.05	.02	.01
☐ 99 Ken Oberkfell	.05	.02	.01
☐ 100 Ben Oglivie	.05	.02	.01
☐ 101 Bert Blyleven	.10	.05	.01
☐ 102 Jeff Leonard	.05	.02	.01
☐ 103 Rick Rhoden	.05	.02	.01
☐ 104 Larry Parrish	.05	.02	.01
☐ 105 Tony Bernazard	.05	.02	.01
☐ 106 Don Mattingly	1.50	.70	.19
☐ 107 Willie Upshaw	.05	.02	.01
☐ 108 Reggie Jackson	.75	.35	.09
☐ 109 Bill Madlock	.10	.05	.01
☐ 110 Gary Carter	.10	.05	.01
☐ 111 George Brett	1.25	.55	.16
☐ 112 Ozzie Smith	.60	.25	.07
☐ 113 Tony Gwynn	1.25	.55	.16
☐ 114 Jack Morris	.10	.05	.01
☐ 115 Dave Kingman	.10	.05	.01
☐ 116 John Franco	.10	.05	.01
☐ 117 Tim Wallach	.05	.02	.01
☐ 118 Cal Ripken	3.00	1.35	.35
☐ 119 Harold Baines	.10	.05	.01
☐ 120 Leon Durham	.05	.02	.01
☐ 121 Nolan Ryan	3.00	1.35	.35
☐ 122 Dennis(Oil Can) Boyd	.05	.02	.01
☐ 123 Matt Young	.05	.02	.01
☐ 124 Shane Rawley	.05	.02	.01
☐ 125 Bruce Sutter	.10	.05	.01
☐ 126 Robin Yount	.40	.18	.05
☐ 127 Frank Viola	.05	.02	.01
☐ 128 Vida Blue	.10	.05	.01
☐ 129 Rick Reuschel	.05	.02	.01
☐ 130 Pete Incaviglia	.05	.02	.01

1988 Red Foley Sticker Book

The 1988 Red Foley's Best Baseball Book Ever was published by Simon and Schuster and measures 8 1/2" by 11. The book includes 130 stickers (representing 104 players and 26 teams), puzzles, quizzes, how-to's, and other trivia features. The stickers appear on 4 insert pages in the middle of the album. Each sticker measures 1 3/8" by 1 7/8" and displays a glossy color player photo bordered in white. The stickers are to be pasted in the appropriate slots next to a trivia question about the player. The stickers are numbered on the front and present the players in alphabetical order.

	MINT	NRMT	EXC
COMPLETE SET (130)	8.00	3.60	1.00
COMMON STICKER (1-104)	.05	.02	.01
COMMON TEAM (105-130)	.05	.02	.01
☐ 1 Mike Aldrete	.05	.02	.01
☐ 2 Alan Ashby	.05	.02	.01
☐ 3 Harold Baines	.10	.05	.01
☐ 4 Floyd Bannister	.05	.02	.01
☐ 5 Buddy Bell	.10	.05	.01
☐ 6 George Bell	.05	.02	.01
☐ 7 Barry Bonds	1.00	.45	.12
☐ 8 Scott Bradley	.05	.02	.01
☐ 9 Bob Brower	.05	.02	.01
☐ 10 Ellis Burks	.25	.11	.03
☐ 11 Casey Candaele	.05	.02	.01
☐ 12 Jack Clark	.10	.05	.01
☐ 13 Roger Clemens	.40	.18	.05
☐ 14 Kal Daniels	.05	.02	.01
☐ 15 Eric Davis	.05	.02	.01
☐ 16 Mike Davis	.05	.02	.01
☐ 17 Andre Dawson	.10	.05	.01
☐ 18 Rob Deer	.05	.02	.01
☐ 19 Brian Downing	.05	.02	.01
☐ 20 Doug Drabek	.05	.02	.01
☐ 21 Dwight Evans	.10	.05	.01
☐ 22 Sid Fernandez	.05	.02	.01
☐ 23 Carlton Fisk	.40	.18	.05
☐ 24 Scott Fletcher	.05	.02	.01
☐ 25 Julio Franco	.10	.05	.01
☐ 26 Gary Gaetti	.05	.02	.01
☐ 27 Ken Gerhart	.05	.02	.01
☐ 28 Ken Griffey	.10	.05	.01
☐ 29 Pedro Guerrero	.05	.02	.01
☐ 30 Billy Hatcher	.05	.02	.01
☐ 31 Mike Heath	.05	.02	.01
☐ 32 Neal Heaton	.05	.02	.01
☐ 33 Tom Henke	.05	.02	.01
☐ 34 Larry Herndon	.05	.02	.01
☐ 35 Brian Holton	.05	.02	.01
☐ 36 Glenn Hubbard	.05	.02	.01
☐ 37 Bruce Hurst	.05	.02	.01
☐ 38 Bo Jackson	.25	.11	.03
☐ 39 Michael Jackson	.05	.02	.01
☐ 40 Howard Johnson	.05	.02	.01
☐ 41 Wally Joyner	.25	.11	.03
☐ 42 Jimmy Key	.10	.05	.01
☐ 43 Ray Knight	.10	.05	.01
☐ 44 John Kruk	.25	.11	.03
☐ 45 Mike Krukow	.05	.02	.01
☐ 46 Mark Langston	.10	.05	.01
☐ 47 Gene Larkin	.05	.02	.01
☐ 48 Jeff Leonard	.05	.02	.01
☐ 49 Bill Long	.05	.02	.01
☐ 50 Fred Lynn	.10	.05	.01
☐ 51 Dave Magadan	.05	.02	.01
☐ 52 Joe Magrane	.05	.02	.01
☐ 53 Don Mattingly	1.50	.70	.19
☐ 54 Fred McGriff	.75	.35	.09
☐ 55 Mark McGwire	1.00	.45	.12
☐ 56 Kevin McReynolds	.05	.02	.01
☐ 57 Dave Meads	.05	.02	.01
☐ 58 Keith Moreland	.05	.02	.01
☐ 59 Dale Murphy	.25	.11	.03
☐ 60 Juan Nieves	.05	.02	.01
☐ 61 Paul Noce	.05	.02	.01
☐ 62 Matt Nokes	.10	.05	.01
☐ 63 Pete O'Brien	.05	.02	.01
☐ 64 Paul O'Neill	.10	.05	.01
☐ 65 Lance Parrish	.10	.05	.01
☐ 66 Larry Parrish	.05	.02	.01
☐ 67 Tony Pena	.05	.02	.01
☐ 68 Terry Pendleton	.10	.05	.01
☐ 69 Ken Phelps	.05	.02	.01
☐ 70 Dan Plesac	.05	.02	.01
☐ 71 Luis Polonia	.05	.02	.01
☐ 72 Kirby Puckett	1.00	.45	.12
☐ 73 Jeff Reardon	.10	.05	.01
☐ 74 Rick Rhoden	.05	.02	.01
☐ 75 Dave Righetti	.05	.02	.01
☐ 76 Cal Ripken	3.00	1.35	.35
☐ 77 Bret Saberhagen	.10	.05	.01
☐ 78 Benito Santiago	.05	.02	.01
☐ 79 Mike Schmidt	1.00	.45	.12
☐ 80 Dick Schofield	.05	.02	.01
☐ 81 Mike Scott	.05	.02	.01
☐ 82 John Smiley	.05	.02	.01
☐ 83 Cory Snyder	.05	.02	.01
☐ 84 Franklin Stubbs	.05	.02	.01
☐ 85 B.J. Surhoff	.10	.05	.01
☐ 86 Rick Sutcliffe	.05	.02	.01
☐ 87 Pat Tabler	.05	.02	.01
☐ 88 Danny Tartabull	.05	.02	.01
☐ 89 Garry Templeton	.05	.02	.01
☐ 90 Walt Terrell	.05	.02	.01
☐ 91 Andre Thornton	.05	.02	.01
☐ 92 Andy Van Slyke	.10	.05	.01
☐ 93 Ozzie Virgil	.05	.02	.01
☐ 94 Tim Wallach	.05	.02	.01
☐ 95 Gary Ward	.05	.02	.01
☐ 96 Mark Wasinger	.05	.02	.01
☐ 97 Mitch Webster	.05	.02	.01
☐ 98 Bob Welch	.05	.02	.01
☐ 99 Devon White	.25	.11	.03
☐ 100 Frank White	.10	.05	.01
☐ 101 Ed Whitson	.05	.02	.01
☐ 102 Bill Wilkinson	.05	.02	.01
☐ 103 Glenn Wilson	.05	.02	.01
☐ 104 Curt Young	.05	.02	.01
☐ 105 Atlanta Braves	.05	.02	.01
☐ 106 Philadelphia Phillies	.05	.02	.01
☐ 107 San Diego Padres	.05	.02	.01
☐ 108 San Francisco Giants	.05	.02	.01
☐ 109 Baltimore Orioles	.05	.02	.01
☐ 110 Detroit Tigers	.05	.02	.01
☐ 111 Pittsburgh Pirates	.05	.02	.01
☐ 112 Kansas City Royals	.05	.02	.01
☐ 113 Houston Astros	.05	.02	.01
☐ 114 Cleveland Indians	.05	.02	.01
☐ 115 Milwaukee Brewers	.05	.02	.01
☐ 116 St. Louis Cardinals	.05	.02	.01
☐ 117 Chicago White Sox	.05	.02	.01
☐ 118 Toronto Blue Jays	.05	.02	.01
☐ 119 Boston Red Sox	.05	.02	.01
☐ 120 Oakland A's	.05	.02	.01
☐ 121 Chicago Cubs	.05	.02	.01
☐ 122 Seattle Mariners	.05	.02	.01
☐ 123 Texas Rangers	.05	.02	.01
☐ 124 Los Angeles Dodgers	.05	.02	.01
☐ 125 New York Yankees	.05	.02	.01
☐ 126 New York Mets	.05	.02	.01
☐ 127 Minnesota Twins	.05	.02	.01
☐ 128 Montreal Expos	.05	.02	.01
☐ 129 California Angels	.05	.02	.01
☐ 130 Cincinnati Reds	.05	.02	.01

1989 Red Foley Sticker Book

The 1989 Red Foley's Best Baseball Book Ever was published by Simon and Schuster and measures 8 1/2" by 11. The book includes 130 stickers, puzzles, quizzes, how-to's, and other trivia features. The stickers appear on 4 insert pages in the middle of the album. Each sticker measures 1 3/8" by 1 7/8" and displays a glossy color player photo bordered in white. The stickers are to be pasted in the

appropriate slots next to a trivia question about the player. The stickers are numbered on the front and present the players in alphabetical order.

	MINT	NRMT	EXC
COMPLETE SET (130)	15.00	6.75	1.85
COMMON STICKER (1-130)	.05	.02	.01
☐ 1 Doyle Alexander	.05	.02	.01
☐ 2 Luis Alicea	.05	.02	.01
☐ 3 Roberto Alomar	1.25	.55	.16
☐ 4 Alan Ashby	.05	.02	.01
☐ 5 Floyd Bannister	.05	.02	.01
☐ 6 Jesse Barfield	.05	.02	.01
☐ 7 George Bell	.05	.02	.01
☐ 8 Wade Boggs	.40	.18	.05
☐ 9 Barry Bonds	1.00	.45	.12
☐ 10 Bobby Bonilla	.25	.11	.03
☐ 11 Chris Bosio	.05	.02	.01
☐ 12 George Brett	1.25	.55	.16
☐ 13 Hubie Brooks	.05	.02	.01
☐ 14 Tom Brunansky	.05	.02	.01
☐ 15 Tim Burke	.05	.02	.01
☐ 16 Ivan Calderon	.05	.02	.01
☐ 17 Tom Candiotti	.05	.02	.01
☐ 18 Jose Canseco	.40	.18	.05
☐ 19 Gary Carter	.10	.05	.01
☐ 20 Joe Carter	.25	.11	.03
☐ 21 Jack Clark	.10	.05	.01
☐ 22 Will Clark	.40	.18	.05
☐ 23 Roger Clemens	.40	.18	.05
☐ 24 David Cone	.40	.18	.05
☐ 25 Ed Correa	.05	.02	.01
☐ 26 Kal Daniels	.05	.02	.01
☐ 27 Alvin Davis	.05	.02	.01
☐ 28 Chili Davis	.10	.05	.01
☐ 29 Eric Davis	.10	.05	.01
☐ 30 Glenn Davis	.05	.02	.01
☐ 31 Jody Davis	.05	.02	.01
☐ 32 Mark Davis	.05	.02	.01
☐ 33 Andre Dawson	.10	.05	.01
☐ 34 Rob Deer	.05	.02	.01
☐ 35 Jose DeLeon	.05	.02	.01
☐ 36 Bo Diaz	.05	.02	.01
☐ 37 Bill Doran	.05	.02	.01
☐ 38 Shawon Dunston	.05	.02	.01
☐ 39 Dennis Eckersley	.10	.05	.01
☐ 40 Dwight Evans	.10	.05	.01
☐ 41 Tony Fernandez	.05	.02	.01
☐ 42 Brian Fisher	.05	.02	.01
☐ 43 Carlton Fisk	.40	.18	.05
☐ 44 Mike Flanagan	.05	.02	.01
☐ 45 John Franco	.10	.05	.01
☐ 46 Gary Gaetti	.10	.05	.01
☐ 47 Andres Galarraga	.25	.11	.03
☐ 48 Scott Garrelts	.05	.02	.01
☐ 49 Kirk Gibson	.25	.11	.03
☐ 50 Dan Gladden	.05	.02	.01
☐ 51 Dwight Gooden	.10	.05	.01
☐ 52 Pedro Guerrero	.05	.02	.01
☐ 53 Ozzie Guillen	.05	.02	.01
☐ 54 Tony Gwynn	1.25	.55	.16
☐ 55 Mel Hall	.05	.02	.01
☐ 56 Von Hayes	.05	.02	.01
☐ 57 Keith Hernandez	.10	.05	.01
☐ 58 Orel Hershiser	.10	.05	.01
☐ 59 Ted Higuera	.05	.02	.01
☐ 60 Charlie Hough	.10	.05	.01
☐ 61 Jack Howell	.05	.02	.01
☐ 62 Kent Hrbek	.10	.05	.01
☐ 63 Pete Incaviglia	.05	.02	.01
☐ 64 Bo Jackson	.25	.11	.03
☐ 65 Brook Jacoby	.05	.02	.01
☐ 66 Chris James	.05	.02	.01
☐ 67 Lance Johnson	.25	.11	.03
☐ 68 Wally Joyner	.10	.05	.01
☐ 69 Jack Kruk	.10	.05	.01
☐ 70 Mike LaCoss	.05	.02	.01
☐ 71 Mark Langston	.10	.05	.01
☐ 72 Carney Lansford	.10	.05	.01
☐ 73 Barry Larkin	.50	.23	.06
☐ 74 Mike LaValliere	.05	.02	.01
☐ 75 Jose Lind	.05	.02	.01
☐ 76 Fred Lynn	.10	.05	.01
☐ 77 Greg Maddux	4.00	1.80	.50
☐ 78 Candy Maldonado	.05	.02	.01
☐ 79 Don Mattingly	1.50	.70	.19
☐ 80 Mark McGwire	.75	.35	.09
☐ 81 Paul Molitor	.60	.25	.07
☐ 82 Jack Morris	.10	.05	.01
☐ 83 Lloyd Moseby	.05	.02	.01
☐ 84 Dale Murphy	.25	.11	.03
☐ 85 Eddie Murray	.60	.25	.07
☐ 86 Matt Nokes	.05	.02	.01
☐ 87 Pete O'Brien	.05	.02	.01
☐ 88 Rafael Palmeiro	.40	.18	.05
☐ 89 Melido Perez	.05	.02	.01
☐ 90 Gerald Perry	.05	.02	.01
☐ 91 Tim Raines	.10	.05	.01
☐ 92 Willie Randolph	.10	.05	.01
☐ 93 Johnny Ray	.05	.02	.01
☐ 94 Jeff Reardon	.05	.02	.01
☐ 95 Jody Reed	.05	.02	.01
☐ 96 Harold Reynolds	.05	.02	.01
☐ 97 Dave Righetti	.05	.02	.01
☐ 98 Billy Ripken	.05	.02	.01
☐ 99 Cal Ripken Jr.	3.00	1.35	.35
☐ 100 Nolan Ryan	3.00	1.35	.35
☐ 101 Juan Samuel	.05	.02	.01
☐ 102 Benito Santiago	.05	.02	.01
☐ 103 Steve Sax	.05	.02	.01
☐ 104 Mike Schmidt	1.00	.45	.12
☐ 105 Rick Schu	.05	.02	.01
☐ 106 Mike Scott	.05	.02	.01
☐ 107 Kevin Seitzer	.05	.02	.01
☐ 108 Ruben Sierra	.10	.05	.01
☐ 109 Lee Smith	.10	.05	.01
☐ 110 Ozzie Smith	.60	.25	.07
☐ 111 Zane Smith	.05	.02	.01
☐ 112 Dave Stewart	.10	.05	.01
☐ 113 Darryl Strawberry	.10	.05	.01
☐ 114 Bruce Sutter	.10	.05	.01
☐ 115 Bill Swift	.05	.02	.01
☐ 116 Greg Swindell	.05	.02	.01
☐ 117 Frank Tanana	.05	.02	.01
☐ 118 Danny Tartabull	.05	.02	.01
☐ 119 Milt Thompson	.05	.02	.01
☐ 120 Robby Thompson	.05	.02	.01
☐ 121 Alan Trammell	.10	.05	.01
☐ 122 John Tudor	.05	.02	.01
☐ 123 Fernando Valenzuela	.10	.05	.01
☐ 124 Dave Valle	.05	.02	.01
☐ 125 Frank Viola	.05	.02	.01
☐ 126 Ozzie Virgil	.05	.02	.01
☐ 127 Tim Wallach	.05	.02	.01
☐ 128 Dave Winfield	.40	.18	.05
☐ 129 Mike Witt	.05	.02	.01
☐ 130 Robin Yount	.40	.18	.05

1990 Red Foley Sticker Book

The 1990 Red Foley's Best Baseball Book Ever was published by Simon and Schuster and measures 8 1/2" by 11. The book includes 130 stickers (104 players and 26 teams), puzzles, quizzes, how-to's, player-team matchups, and other trivia features. The stickers appear on four insert pages in the middle of the album. Each sticker measures 1 3/8" X 1 7/8" and displays a glossy color player photo bordered in white. The stickers are to be pasted in the appropriate slots next to a trivia question about the player. The stickers are numbered on the front and present the players in alphabetical order.

	MINT	NRMT	EXC
COMPLETE SET (130)	15.00	6.75	1.85
COMMON STICKER (1-104)	.05	.02	.01
COMMON TEAM (105-130)	.05	.02	.01
☐ 1 Allan Anderson	.05	.02	.01
☐ 2 Scott Bailes	.05	.02	.01
☐ 3 Jeff Ballard	.05	.02	.01
☐ 4 Jesse Barfield	.05	.02	.01
☐ 5 Bert Blyleven	.15	.07	.02
☐ 6 Wade Boggs	.40	.18	.05
☐ 7 Barry Bonds	.75	.35	.09
☐ 8 Chris Bosio	.05	.02	.01
☐ 9 George Brett	1.25	.55	.16
☐ 10 Tim Burke	.05	.02	.01
☐ 11 Ellis Burks	.30	.14	.04
☐ 12 Brett Butler	.15	.07	.02
☐ 13 Ivan Calderon	.05	.02	.01
☐ 14 Jose Canseco	.40	.18	.05
☐ 15 Joe Carter	.15	.07	.02
☐ 16 Jack Clark	.15	.07	.02
☐ 17 Will Clark	.40	.18	.05
☐ 18 Roger Clemens	.40	.18	.05
☐ 19 Vince Coleman	.05	.02	.01
☐ 20 Eric Davis	.05	.02	.01
☐ 21 Glenn Davis	.05	.02	.01
☐ 22 Mark Davis	.05	.02	.01
☐ 23 Andre Dawson	.15	.07	.02
☐ 24 Rob Deer	.05	.02	.01
☐ 25 Jose DeLeon	.05	.02	.01
☐ 26 Jim Deshaies	.05	.02	.01
☐ 27 Doug Drabek	.05	.02	.01
☐ 28 Lenny Dykstra	.15	.07	.02
☐ 29 Dennis Eckersley	.15	.07	.02
☐ 30 Steve Farr	.05	.02	.01
☐ 31 Tony Fernandez	.05	.02	.01
☐ 32 Carlton Fisk	.40	.18	.05
☐ 33 John Franco	.05	.02	.01
☐ 34 Julio Franco	.15	.07	.02
☐ 35 Andres Galarraga	.30	.14	.04
☐ 36 Tom Glavine	.40	.18	.05
☐ 37 Dwight Gooden	.15	.07	.02
☐ 38 Mark Grace	.40	.18	.05
☐ 39 Mike Greenwell	.05	.02	.01
☐ 40 Ken Griffey Jr.	5.00	2.20	.60
☐ 41 Kelly Gruber	.05	.02	.01
☐ 42 Pedro Guerrero	.05	.02	.01
☐ 43 Tony Gwynn	1.25	.55	.16
☐ 44 Bryan Harvey	.05	.02	.01
☐ 45 Von Hayes	.05	.02	.01
☐ 46 Willie Hernandez	.05	.02	.01
☐ 47 Tommy Herr	.05	.02	.01
☐ 48 Orel Hershiser	.15	.07	.02
☐ 49 Jay Howell	.05	.02	.01
☐ 50 Kent Hrbek	.15	.07	.02
☐ 51 Bo Jackson	.15	.07	.02
☐ 52 Steve Jeltz	.05	.02	.01
☐ 53 Jimmy Key	.05	.02	.01
☐ 54 Ron Kittle	.05	.02	.01
☐ 55 Mark Langston	.15	.07	.02
☐ 56 Carney Lansford	.15	.07	.02
☐ 57 Barry Larkin	.40	.18	.05
☐ 58 Jeffrey Leonard	.05	.02	.01
☐ 59 Don Mattingly	1.50	.70	.19
☐ 60 Fred McGriff	.40	.18	.05
☐ 61 Mark McGwire	.75	.35	.09
☐ 62 Kevin McReynolds	.05	.02	.01
☐ 63 Randy Myers	.05	.02	.01
☐ 64 Kevin Mitchell	.05	.02	.01
☐ 65 Paul Molitor	.50	.23	.06
☐ 66 Mike Morgan	.05	.02	.01
☐ 67 Dale Murphy	.30	.14	.04
☐ 68 Eddie Murray	.60	.25	.07
☐ 69 Matt Nokes	.05	.02	.01
☐ 70 Greg Olson	.05	.02	.01
☐ 71 Paul O'Neill	.15	.07	.02
☐ 72 Rafael Palmeiro	.30	.14	.04
☐ 73 Lance Parrish	.15	.07	.02
☐ 74 Dan Plesac	.05	.02	.01
☐ 75 Kirby Puckett	.75	.35	.09
☐ 76 Jeff Reardon	.15	.07	.02
☐ 77 Rick Reuschel	.05	.02	.01
☐ 78 Cal Ripken	3.00	1.35	.35
☐ 79 Dave Righetti	.05	.02	.01
☐ 80 Jeff Russell	.05	.02	.01
☐ 81 Nolan Ryan	3.00	1.35	.35
☐ 82 Benito Santiago	.05	.02	.01
☐ 83 Steve Sax	.05	.02	.01
☐ 84 Mike Schooler	.05	.02	.01
☐ 85 Mike Scott	.05	.02	.01
☐ 86 Kevin Seitzer	.05	.02	.01
☐ 87 Dave Smith	.05	.02	.01
☐ 88 Lonnie Smith	.05	.02	.01
☐ 89 Ozzie Smith	.60	.25	.07
☐ 90 John Smoltz	.50	.23	.06
☐ 91 Cory Snyder	.05	.02	.01
☐ 92 Darryl Strawberry	.15	.07	.02
☐ 93 Greg Swindell	.05	.02	.01
☐ 94 Mickey Tettleton	.15	.07	.02
☐ 95 Bobby Thigpen	.05	.02	.01
☐ 96 Alan Trammell	.15	.07	.02
☐ 97 Dave Valle	.05	.02	.01
☐ 98 Andy Van Slyke	.15	.07	.02
☐ 99 Tim Wallach	.05	.02	.01
☐ 100 Jerome Walton	.05	.02	.01
☐ 101 Lou Whitaker	.15	.07	.02
☐ 102 Devon White	.15	.07	.02
☐ 103 Mitch Williams	.05	.02	.01
☐ 104 Glenn Wilson	.05	.02	.01
☐ 105 Cleveland Indians	.05	.02	.01
☐ 106 Texas Rangers	.05	.02	.01
☐ 107 Cincinnati Reds	.05	.02	.01
☐ 108 Baltimore Orioles	.05	.02	.01
☐ 109 Boston Red Sox	.05	.02	.01
☐ 110 Chicago White Sox	.05	.02	.01
☐ 111 Los Angeles Dodgers	.05	.02	.01
☐ 112 Detroit Tigers	.05	.02	.01
☐ 113 Seattle Mariners	.05	.02	.01
☐ 114 Toronto Blue Jays	.05	.02	.01
☐ 115 Montreal Expos	.05	.02	.01
☐ 116 Pittsburgh Pirates	.05	.02	.01
☐ 117 Houston Astros	.05	.02	.01
☐ 118 St. Louis Cardinals	.05	.02	.01
☐ 119 San Diego Padres	.05	.02	.01
☐ 120 California Angels	.05	.02	.01
☐ 121 New York Yankees	.05	.02	.01
☐ 122 Chicago Cubs	.05	.02	.01
☐ 123 Milwaukee Brewers	.05	.02	.01
☐ 124 Minnesota Twins	.05	.02	.01
☐ 125 San Francisco Giants	.05	.02	.01
☐ 126 Kansas City Royals	.05	.02	.01
☐ 127 Oakland A's	.05	.02	.01
☐ 128 New York Mets	.05	.02	.01
☐ 129 Philadelphia Phillies	.05	.02	.01
☐ 130 Atlanta Braves	.05	.02	.01

1991 Red Foley Stickers

The 1991 Red Foley's Best Baseball Book Ever was published by Simon and Schuster and measures 8 1/2" by 11. The 95-page book includes 130 stickers, puzzles, quizzes, how-to's, player-team matchups, and other trivia features. The stickers appear on 4 insert pages in the middle of the album. Each sticker measures 1 3/8" by 1 7/8" and displays a glossy color player photo bordered in white. The stickers are to be pasted in the appropriate slots throughout the sticker album. Stickers 113-130 feature All-Stars. The stickers are numbered on the front and checklisted below accordingly.

	MINT	NRMT	EXC
COMPLETE SET (130)	20.00	9.00	2.50
COMMON STICKER (1-130)	.05	.02	.01
☐ 1 Jim Abbott	.10	.05	.01
☐ 2 Rick Aguilera	.05	.02	.01
☐ 3 Roberto Alomar	1.00	.45	.12
☐ 4 Rob Dibble	.05	.02	.01
☐ 5 Wally Backman	.05	.02	.01
☐ 6 Harold Baines	.10	.05	.01
☐ 7 Steve Bedrosian	.05	.02	.01
☐ 8 Craig Biggio	.25	.11	.03
☐ 9 Wade Boggs	.40	.18	.05
☐ 10 Bobby Bonilla	.10	.05	.01
☐ 11 George Brett	1.25	.55	.16
☐ 12 Greg Brock	.05	.02	.01
☐ 13 Hubie Brooks	.05	.02	.01
☐ 14 Tom Brunansky	.05	.02	.01
☐ 15 Tim Burke	.05	.02	.01
☐ 16 Tom Candiotti	.05	.02	.01
☐ 17 Jose Canseco	.40	.18	.05
☐ 18 Jack Clark	.10	.05	.01
☐ 19 Will Clark	.40	.18	.05
☐ 20 Roger Clemens	.40	.18	.05
☐ 21 Vince Coleman	.05	.02	.01
☐ 22 Kal Daniels	.05	.02	.01
☐ 23 Glenn Davis	.05	.02	.01
☐ 24 Mark Davis	.05	.02	.01
☐ 25 Andre Dawson	.10	.05	.01
☐ 26 Rob Deer	.05	.02	.01
☐ 27 Delino DeShields	.05	.02	.01
☐ 28 Doug Drabek	.05	.02	.01
☐ 29 Shawon Dunston	.05	.02	.01
☐ 30 Len Dykstra	.10	.05	.01
☐ 31 Dennis Eckersley	.10	.05	.01
☐ 32 Kevin Elster	.05	.02	.01
☐ 33 Tony Fernandez	.05	.02	.01
☐ 34 Cecil Fielder	.10	.05	.01
☐ 35 Chuck Finley	.10	.05	.01
☐ 36 Carlton Fisk	.40	.18	.05
☐ 37 Greg Gagne	.05	.02	.01
☐ 38 Ron Gant	.10	.05	.01
☐ 39 Tom Glavine	.25	.11	.03
☐ 40 Dwight Gooden	.10	.05	.01
☐ 41 Ken Griffey Jr.	3.00	1.35	.35
☐ 42 Kelly Gruber	.05	.02	.01
☐ 43 Pedro Guerrero	.05	.02	.01
☐ 44 Ozzie Guillen	.05	.02	.01
☐ 45 Pete Harnisch	.05	.02	.01
☐ 46 Billy Hatcher	.05	.02	.01
☐ 47 Von Hayes	.05	.02	.01
☐ 48 Rickey Henderson	.40	.18	.05
☐ 49 Mike Henneman	.05	.02	.01
☐ 50 Kent Hrbek	.10	.05	.01
☐ 51 Pete Incaviglia	.05	.02	.01
☐ 52 Howard Johnson	.05	.02	.01
☐ 53 Randy Johnson	.75	.35	.09
☐ 54 Doug Jones	.05	.02	.01
☐ 55 Ricky Jordan	.05	.02	.01
☐ 56 Wally Joyner	.10	.05	.01
☐ 57 Roberto Kelly	.05	.02	.01
☐ 58 Barry Larkin	.40	.18	.05
☐ 59 Craig Lefferts	.05	.02	.01
☐ 60 Candy Maldonado	.05	.02	.01
☐ 61 Don Mattingly	1.50	.70	.19
☐ 62 Oddibe McDowell	.05	.02	.01
☐ 63 Roger McDowell	.05	.02	.01
☐ 64 Willie McGee	.05	.02	.01
☐ 65 Fred McGriff	.40	.18	.05
☐ 66 Kevin Mitchell	.05	.02	.01
☐ 67 Mike Morgan	.05	.02	.01
☐ 68 Eddie Murray	.60	.25	.07
☐ 69 Gregg Olson	.05	.02	.01
☐ 70 Joe Orsulak	.05	.02	.01
☐ 71 Dan Petry	.05	.02	.01
☐ 72 Dan Plesac	.05	.02	.01
☐ 73 Jim Presley	.05	.02	.01
☐ 74 Kirby Puckett	1.00	.45	.12
☐ 75 Tim Raines	.10	.05	.01
☐ 76 Jeff Reardon	.10	.05	.01

Card			
☐ 77 Dave Righetti	.05	.02	.01
☐ 78 Cal Ripken	3.00	1.35	.35
☐ 79 Nolan Ryan	3.00	1.35	.35
☐ 80 Bret Saberhagen	.10	.05	.01
☐ 81 Chris Sabo	.05	.02	.01
☐ 82 Ryne Sandberg	.75	.35	.09
☐ 83 Benito Santiago	.05	.02	.01
☐ 84 Steve Sax	.05	.02	.01
☐ 85 Mike Schooler	.05	.02	.01
☐ 86 Mike Scott	.05	.02	.01
☐ 87 Ruben Sierra	.10	.05	.01
☐ 88 Cory Snyder	.05	.02	.01
☐ 89 Dave Stieb	.05	.02	.01
☐ 90 Dave Stewart	.10	.05	.01
☐ 91 Kurt Stillwell	.05	.02	.01
☐ 92 Bobby Thigpen	.05	.02	.01
☐ 93 Alan Trammell	.10	.05	.01
☐ 94 John Tudor	.05	.02	.01
☐ 95 Dave Valle	.05	.02	.01
☐ 96 Andy Van Slyke	.10	.05	.01
☐ 97 Robin Ventura	.25	.11	.03
☐ 98 Frank Viola	.05	.02	.01
☐ 99 Tim Wallach	.05	.02	.01
☐ 100 Matt Williams	.50	.23	.06
☐ 101 Mitch Williams	.05	.02	.01
☐ 102 Dave Winfield	.40	.18	.05
☐ 103 Eric Yelding	.05	.02	.01
☐ 104 Robin Yount	.40	.18	.05
☐ 105 Steve Avery	.25	.11	.03
☐ 106 Travis Fryman	.25	.11	.03
☐ 107 Juan Gonzalez	1.50	.70	.19
☐ 108 Todd Hundley	.25	.11	.03
☐ 109 Ben McDonald	.10	.05	.01
☐ 110 Jose Offerman	.05	.02	.01
☐ 111 Frank Thomas	5.00	2.20	.60
☐ 112 Bernie Williams	.25	.11	.03
☐ 113 Sandy Alomar Jr. AS	.10	.05	.01
☐ 114 Jack Armstrong AS	.05	.02	.01
☐ 115 Wade Boggs AS	.25	.11	.03
☐ 116 Jose Canseco AS	.25	.11	.03
☐ 117 Will Clark AS	.25	.11	.03
☐ 118 Andre Dawson AS	.10	.05	.01
☐ 119 Len Dykstra AS	.10	.05	.01
☐ 120 Ken Griffey Jr. AS	1.50	.70	.19
☐ 121 Rickey Henderson AS	.25	.11	.03
☐ 122 Mark McGwire AS	.40	.18	.05
☐ 123 Kevin Mitchell AS	.05	.02	.01
☐ 124 Cal Ripken AS	1.50	.70	.19
☐ 125 Chris Sabo AS	.05	.02	.01
☐ 126 Ryne Sandberg AS	.40	.18	.05
☐ 127 Steve Sax AS	.05	.02	.01
☐ 128 Mike Scioscia AS	.05	.02	.01
☐ 129 Ozzie Smith AS	.60	.25	.07
☐ 130 Bob Welch AS	.05	.02	.01

1994 Red Foley's Magazine Inserts

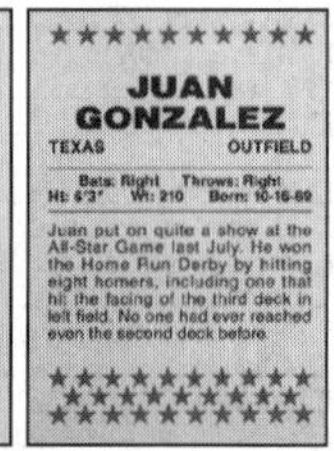

Bound into Red Foley's 1994 Best Baseball Book Ever, these four nine-card perforated sheets feature two-player Team Leaders cards (1-28) and single-player Superstar cards (29-36). If separated from their perforated sheets, the cards would measure the standard size. All the cards feature white-bordered color player action shots on their fronts. Each Team Leaders card has the two players' photos stacked vertically, with their names appearing to the right, and the team name and subset title appearing to the left. A colored stripe also appears on each side of the player photos. The back carries, with one stacked upon the other, each player's name, team, position, biography, and career highlights. The Superstars cards have each player's name appearing above the photo and the subset title appearing below, both accompanied by colored stripes. The back is highlighted by red stars at the top and bottom, and carries the player's name, team, position, biography, and career highlights. The cards are unnumbered and checklisted below in alphabetical order, within each subset. The two-player Team Leaders cards are listed in the order of the players on the top halves of the cards.

	MINT	NRMT	EXC
COMPLETE SET (36)	20.00	9.00	2.50
COMMON CARD (1-36)	.25	.11	.03
☐ 1 Roberto Alomar John Olerud	.25	.11	.03
☐ 2 Jeff Bagwell Doug Drabek	.50	.23	.06
☐ 3 Jay Bell Andy Van Slyke	.25	.11	.03
☐ 4 Albert Belle Carlos Baerga	.75	.35	.09
☐ 5 Andy Benes Tony Gwynn	.75	.35	.09
☐ 6 Bobby Bonilla Dwight Gooden	.25	.11	.03
☐ 7 Jay Buhner Randy Johnson	.50	.23	.06
☐ 8 Jose Canseco Kevin Brown	.25	.11	.03
☐ 9 Will Clark Matt Williams	.75	.35	.09
☐ 10 Cecil Fielder Mike Henneman	.25	.11	.03
☐ 11 Mark Grace Randy Myers	.25	.11	.03
☐ 12 Charlie Hayes Andres Galarraga	.25	.11	.03
☐ 13 John Kruk Tommy Greene	.25	.11	.03
☐ 14 Ray Lankford Ozzie Smith	.25	.11	.03
☐ 15 Barry Larkin Reggie Sanders	.25	.11	.03
☐ 16 Greg Maddux Tom Glavine	1.50	.70	.19
☐ 17 Don Mattingly Jim Abbott	.75	.35	.09
☐ 18 Mark McGwire Dennis Eckersley	.50	.23	.06
☐ 19 Brian McRae David Cone	.25	.11	.03
☐ 20 Mike Piazza Orel Hershiser	1.50	.70	.19
☐ 21 Kirby Puckett Rick Aguilera	1.00	.45	.12
☐ 22 Cal Ripken Mike Mussina	2.00	.90	.25
☐ 23 Tim Salmon Mark Langston	.25	.11	.03
☐ 24 Gary Sheffield Bryan Harvey	.25	.11	.03
☐ 25 Frank Thomas Jack McDowell	2.00	.90	.25
☐ 26 Mo Vaughn Frank Viola	.25	.11	.03
☐ 27 Larry Walker Marquis Grissom	.25	.11	.03
☐ 28 Robin Yount Cal Eldred	.25	.11	.03
☐ 29 Barry Bonds	1.25	.55	.16
☐ 30 Joe Carter	1.00	.45	.12
☐ 31 Roger Clemens	1.00	.45	.12
☐ 32 Juan Gonzalez	2.00	.90	.25
☐ 33 Ken Griffey Jr.	5.00	2.20	.60
☐ 34 Fred McGriff	1.00	.45	.12
☐ 35 Jose Rijo	.25	.11	.03
☐ 36 Ryne Sandberg	1.50	.70	.19

1995 Red Foley

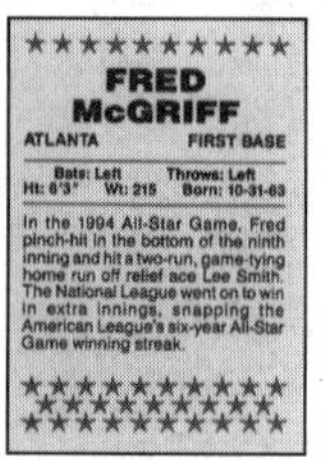

The cards measure standard size. The cards have no numbers so we grouped both single player in alphabetical order and multi-player cards in alphabetical team order.

	MINT	NRMT	EXC
COMPLETE SET (36)	20.00	9.00	2.50
COMMON CARD (1-36)	.25	.11	.03
☐ 1 Barry Bonds	1.50	.70	.19
☐ 2 Joe Carter	1.00	.45	.12
☐ 3 Roger Clemens	1.25	.55	.16
☐ 4 Juan Gonzalez	2.00	.90	.25
☐ 5 Ken Griffey, Jr.	4.00	1.80	.50
☐ 6 Fred McGriff	1.25	.55	.16
☐ 7 Cal Ripken Jr.	4.00	1.80	.50
☐ 8 Frank Thomas	4.00	1.80	.50
☐ 9 David Justice Greg Maddux	1.50	.70	.19
☐ 10 Rafael Palmeiro Mike Mussina	.50	.23	.06
☐ 11 Mo Vaughn Aaron Sele	.75	.35	.09
☐ 12 Tim Salmon Chuck Finley	.25	.11	.03
☐ 13 Mark Grace Randy Myers	.50	.23	.06
☐ 14 Robin Ventura Wilson Alvarez	.25	.11	.03
☐ 15 Barry Larkin Jose Rijo	.25	.11	.03
☐ 16 Albert Belle Carlos Baerga	1.00	.45	.12
☐ 17 Andres Galarraga Dante Bichette	.50	.23	.06
☐ 18 Cecil Fielder Travis Fryman	.50	.23	.06
☐ 19 Gary Sheffield Benito Santiago	.25	.11	.03
☐ 20 Jeff Bagwell Craig Biggio	.50	.23	.06
☐ 21 Brian McRae David Cone	.25	.11	.03
☐ 22 Mike Piazza Orel Hershiser	1.50	.70	.19
☐ 23 Cal Eldred Dave Nilsson	.25	.11	.03
☐ 24 Kirby Puckett Rick Aguilera	.50	.23	.06
☐ 25 Larry Walker Ken Hill	.25	.11	.03
☐ 26 Barry Bonilla Bret Saberhagen	.25	.11	.03
☐ 27 Don Mattingly Jimmy Key	.75	.35	.09
☐ 28 Mark McGwire Dennis Eckersley	.50	.23	.06
☐ 29 John Kruk Lenny Dykstra	.25	.11	.03
☐ 30 Andy Van Slyke Al Martin	.25	.11	.03
☐ 31 Gregg Jefferies Ozzie Smith	.50	.23	.06
☐ 32 Tony Gwynn Andy Benes	1.00	.45	.12
☐ 33 Matt Williams Rod Beck	.25	.11	.03
☐ 34 Jay Buhner Randy Johnson	.25	.11	.03
☐ 35 Jose Canseco Will Clark	.75	.35	.09
☐ 36 Roberto Alomar John Olerud	.25	.11	.03

1954 Red Heart

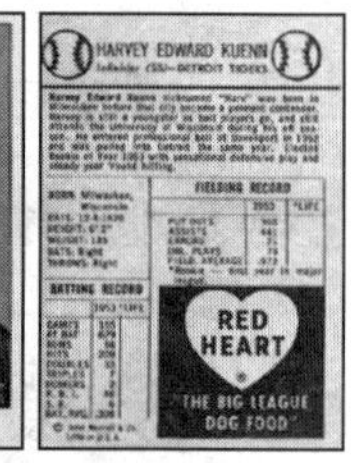

The cards in this 33-card set measure approximately 2 5/8" by 3 3/4". The 1954 Red Heart baseball series was marketed by Red Heart dog food, which, incidentally, was a subsidiary of Morrell Meats. The set consists of three series of eleven unnumbered cards each of which could be ordered from the company via an offer (two can labels plus ten cents for each series) on the can label. Each series has a specific color background (red, green or blue) behind the color player photo. Cards with red backgrounds are considered scarcer and are marked with SP in the checklist (which has been alphabetized and numbered for reference). The catalog designation is F156.

	NRMT	VG-E	GOOD
COMPLETE SET (33)	2000.00	900.00	250.00
COMMON CARD (1-33)	25.00	11.00	3.10
COMMON CARD SP	35.00	16.00	4.40
☐ 1 Richie Ashburn SP	75.00	34.00	9.50
☐ 2 Frank Baumholtz SP	35.00	16.00	4.40
☐ 3 Gus Bell	25.00	11.00	3.10
☐ 4 Billy Cox	30.00	13.50	3.70
☐ 5 Alvin Dark	30.00	13.50	3.70
☐ 6 Carl Erskine SP	40.00	18.00	5.00
☐ 7 Ferris Fain	25.00	11.00	3.10
☐ 8 Dee Fondy	25.00	11.00	3.10
☐ 9 Nellie Fox	60.00	27.00	7.50
☐ 10 Jim Gilliam	35.00	16.00	4.40
☐ 11 Jim Hegan SP	35.00	16.00	4.40
☐ 12 George Kell	50.00	22.00	6.25
☐ 13 Ralph Kiner SP	75.00	34.00	9.50
☐ 14 Ted Kluszewski SP	75.00	34.00	9.50
☐ 15 Harvey Kuenn	30.00	13.50	3.70
☐ 16 Bob Lemon SP	75.00	34.00	9.50
☐ 17 Sherman Lollar	30.00	13.50	3.70
☐ 18 Mickey Mantle	500.00	220.00	60.00
☐ 19 Billy Martin	60.00	27.00	7.50
☐ 20 Gil McDougald SP	40.00	18.00	5.00
☐ 21 Roy McMillan	25.00	11.00	3.10
☐ 22 Minnie Minoso	35.00	16.00	4.40
☐ 23 Stan Musial SP	400.00	180.00	50.00
☐ 24 Billy Pierce	30.00	13.50	3.70
☐ 25 Al Rosen SP	40.00	18.00	5.00
☐ 26 Hank Sauer	25.00	11.00	3.10
☐ 27 Red Schoendienst SP	75.00	34.00	9.50
☐ 28 Enos Slaughter	50.00	22.00	6.25
☐ 29 Duke Snider	150.00	70.00	19.00
☐ 30 Warren Spahn	60.00	27.00	7.50
☐ 31 Sammy White	25.00	11.00	3.10
☐ 32 Eddie Yost	25.00	11.00	3.10
☐ 33 Gus Zernial	30.00	13.50	3.70

1952 Red Man

The cards in this 52-card set measure approximately 3 1/2" by 4" (or 3 1/2" by 3 5/8" without the tab). This Red Man issue was the first nationally available tobacco issue since the T cards of the teens early in this century. This 52-card set contains 26 top players from each league. Cards that have the tab (coupon) attached are generally worth a multiplier of cards without tabs. Please refer to multiplier line below. The 1952 Red Man cards are considered to be the most difficult (of the Red Man sets) to find with tabs. Card numbers are located on the tabs. The prices listed below refer to cards without tabs. The numbering of the set is alphabetical by player within league with the exception of the managers who are listed first.

	NRMT	VG-E	GOOD
COMPLETE SET (52)	750.00	350.00	95.00
COMMON CARD	7.50	3.40	.95
*CARDS WITH TABS:3X BASIC CARDS			
☐ AL1 Casey Stengel MG	25.00	11.00	3.10
☐ AL2 Bobby Avila	7.50	3.40	.95
☐ AL3 Yogi Berra	40.00	18.00	5.00
☐ AL4 Gil Coan	7.50	3.40	.95
☐ AL5 Dom DiMaggio	15.00	6.75	1.85
☐ AL6 Larry Doby	10.00	4.50	1.25
☐ AL7 Ferris Fain	7.50	3.40	.95
☐ AL8 Bob Feller	25.00	11.00	3.10
☐ AL9 Nellie Fox	20.00	9.00	2.50
☐ AL10 Johnny Groth	7.50	3.40	.95
☐ AL11 Jim Hegan	7.50	3.40	.95
☐ AL12 Eddie Joost	7.50	3.40	.95
☐ AL13 George Kell	15.00	6.75	1.85
☐ AL14 Gil McDougald	12.00	5.50	1.50
☐ AL15 Minnie Minoso	12.00	5.50	1.50
☐ AL16 Billy Pierce	10.00	4.50	1.25
☐ AL17 Bob Porterfield	7.50	3.40	.95
☐ AL18 Eddie Robinson	7.50	3.40	.95
☐ AL19 Saul Rogovin	7.50	3.40	.95
☐ AL20 Bobby Shantz	10.00	4.50	1.25
☐ AL21 Vern Stephens	7.50	3.40	.95
☐ AL22 Vic Wertz	7.50	3.40	.95
☐ AL23 Ted Williams	100.00	45.00	12.50
☐ AL24 Early Wynn	15.00	6.75	1.85
☐ AL25 Eddie Yost	7.50	3.40	.95
☐ AL26 Gus Zernial	10.00	4.50	1.25
☐ NL1 Leo Durocher MG	20.00	9.00	2.50
☐ NL2 Richie Ashburn	20.00	9.00	2.50
☐ NL3 Ewell Blackwell	7.50	3.40	.95
☐ NL4 Cliff Chambers	7.50	3.40	.95
☐ NL5 Murry Dickson	7.50	3.40	.95
☐ NL6 Sid Gordon	7.50	3.40	.95
☐ NL7 Granny Hamner	10.00	4.50	1.25
☐ NL8 Jim Hearn	7.50	3.40	.95
☐ NL9 Monte Irvin	15.00	6.75	1.85
☐ NL10 Larry Jansen	7.50	3.40	.95
☐ NL11 Willie Jones	7.50	3.40	.95
☐ NL12 Ralph Kiner	20.00	9.00	2.50
☐ NL13 Whitey Lockman	7.50	3.40	.95
☐ NL14 Sal Maglie	10.00	4.50	1.25
☐ NL15 Willie Mays	75.00	34.00	9.50
☐ NL16 Stan Musial	75.00	34.00	9.50
☐ NL17 Pee Wee Reese	25.00	11.00	3.10
☐ NL18 Robin Roberts	20.00	9.00	2.50
☐ NL19 Red Schoendienst	15.00	6.75	1.85
☐ NL20 Enos Slaughter	20.00	9.00	2.50
☐ NL21 Duke Snider	45.00	20.00	5.50
☐ NL22 Warren Spahn	25.00	11.00	3.10
☐ NL23 Ed Stanky	10.00	4.50	1.25
☐ NL24 Bobby Thomson	12.00	5.50	1.50
☐ NL25 Earl Torgeson	7.50	3.40	.95
☐ NL26 Wes Westrum	7.50	3.40	.95

1953 Red Man

The cards in this 52-card set measure approximately 3 1/2" by 4" (or 3 1/2" by 3 5/8" without the tab). The 1953 Red Man set contains 26 National League stars and 26 American League stars. Card numbers are located both on the write-up of the player and on the tab. Cards that have the tab (coupon) attached are worth a multiplier of cards without tabs. Please refer to the multiplier line below. The prices listed below refer to cards without tabs.

	NRMT	VG-E	GOOD
COMPLETE SET (52)	600.00	275.00	75.00
COMMON CARD	6.00	2.70	.75
*CARDS WITH TABS: 2.5X VALUE			
☐ AL1 Casey Stengel MG	25.00	11.00	3.10
☐ AL2 Hank Bauer	8.00	3.60	1.00
☐ AL3 Yogi Berra	40.00	18.00	5.00
☐ AL4 Walt Dropo	6.00	2.70	.75
☐ AL5 Nellie Fox	20.00	9.00	2.50
☐ AL6 Jackie Jensen	8.00	3.60	1.00
☐ AL7 Eddie Joost	6.00	2.70	.75

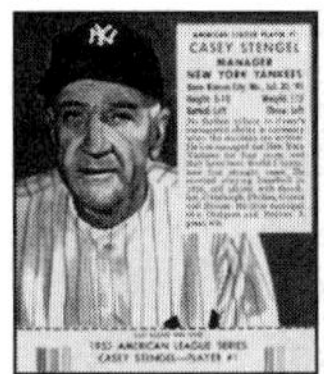
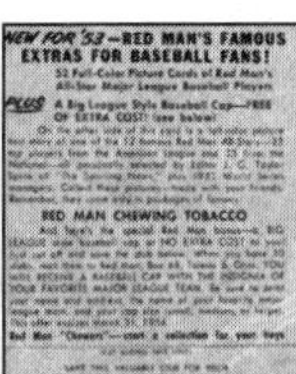

☐ AL8 George Kell	12.00	5.50	1.50
☐ AL9 Dale Mitchell	6.00	2.70	.75
☐ AL10 Phil Rizzuto	25.00	11.00	3.10
☐ AL11 Eddie Robinson	6.00	2.70	.75
☐ AL12 Gene Woodling	10.00	4.50	1.25
☐ AL13 Gus Zernial	8.00	3.60	1.00
☐ AL14 Early Wynn	12.00	5.50	1.50
☐ AL15 Joe Dobson	6.00	2.70	.75
☐ AL16 Billy Pierce	10.00	4.50	1.25
☐ AL17 Bob Lemon	12.00	5.50	1.50
☐ AL18 Johnny Mize	15.00	6.75	1.85
☐ AL19 Bob Porterfield	6.00	2.70	.75
☐ AL20 Bobby Shantz	10.00	4.50	1.25
☐ AL21 Mickey Vernon	10.00	4.50	1.25
☐ AL22 Dom DiMaggio	12.00	5.50	1.50
☐ AL23 Gil McDougald	8.00	3.60	1.00
☐ AL24 Al Rosen	8.00	3.60	1.00
☐ AL25 Mel Parnell	6.00	2.70	.75
☐ AL26 Bobby Avila	6.00	2.70	.75
☐ NL1 Charlie Dressen MG	6.00	2.70	.75
☐ NL2 Bobby Adams	6.00	2.70	.75
☐ NL3 Richie Ashburn	20.00	9.00	2.50
☐ NL4 Joe Black	8.00	3.60	1.00
☐ NL5 Roy Campanella	45.00	20.00	5.50
☐ NL6 Ted Kluszewski	12.00	5.50	1.50
☐ NL7 Whitey Lockman	6.00	2.70	.75
☐ NL8 Sal Maglie	8.00	3.60	1.00
☐ NL9 Andy Pafko	6.00	2.70	.75
☐ NL10 Pee Wee Reese	25.00	11.00	3.10
☐ NL11 Robin Roberts	15.00	6.75	1.85
☐ NL12 Red Schoendienst	12.00	5.50	1.50
☐ NL13 Enos Slaughter	15.00	6.75	1.85
☐ NL14 Duke Snider	45.00	20.00	5.50
☐ NL15 Ralph Kiner	15.00	6.75	1.85
☐ NL16 Hank Sauer	8.00	3.60	1.00
☐ NL17 Del Ennis	8.00	3.60	1.00
☐ NL18 Granny Hamner	8.00	3.60	1.00
☐ NL19 Warren Spahn	25.00	11.00	3.10
☐ NL20 Wes Westrum	6.00	2.70	.75
☐ NL21 Hoyt Wilhelm	12.00	5.50	1.50
☐ NL22 Murry Dickson	6.00	2.70	.75
☐ NL23 Warren Hacker	6.00	2.70	.75
☐ NL24 Gerry Staley	6.00	2.70	.75
☐ NL25 Bobby Thomson	12.00	5.50	1.50
☐ NL26 Stan Musial	75.00	34.00	9.50

1954 Red Man

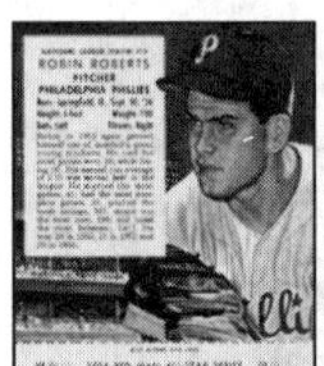

The cards in this 50-card set measure approximately 3 1/2" by 4" (or 3 1/2" by 3 5/8" without the tab). The 1954 Red Man set witnessed a reduction to 25 players from each league. George Kell, Sam Mele, and Dave Philley are known to exist with two different teams. Card number 19 of the National League exists as Enos Slaughter and as Gus Bell. Card numbers are on the write-ups of the players. Cards that have the tab (coupon) attached are worth a multiple of cards without tabs. Please refer to the values below for cards with tabs. The prices listed below refer to cards without tabs. The complete set price below refers to all 54 cards including the four variations.

	NRMT	VG-E	GOOD
COMPLETE SET (54)	750.00	350.00	95.00
COMMON CARD	6.00	2.70	.75
*CARDS WITH TABS:2.5X BASIC CARDS			
☐ AL1 Bobby Avila	6.00	2.70	.75
☐ AL2 Jim Busby	6.00	2.70	.75
☐ AL3 Nellie Fox	20.00	9.00	2.50
☐ AL4A George Kell (Boston)	25.00	11.00	3.10
☐ AL4B George Kell (Chicago)	60.00	27.00	7.50
☐ AL5 Sherman Lollar	6.00	2.70	.75
☐ AL6A Sam Mele (Baltimore)	12.00	5.50	1.50
☐ AL6B Sam Mele (Chicago)	40.00	18.00	5.00
☐ AL7 Minnie Minoso	10.00	4.50	1.25
☐ AL8 Mel Parnell	6.00	2.70	.75
☐ AL9A Dave Philley (Cleveland)	12.00	5.50	1.50
☐ AL9B Dave Philley (Philadelphia)	35.00	16.00	4.40
☐ AL10 Billy Pierce	10.00	4.50	1.25
☐ AL11 Jim Piersall	10.00	4.50	1.25
☐ AL12 Al Rosen	10.00	4.50	1.25
☐ AL13 Mickey Vernon	10.00	4.50	1.25
☐ AL14 Sammy White	6.00	2.70	.75
☐ AL15 Gene Woodling	10.00	4.50	1.25
☐ AL16 Whitey Ford	25.00	11.00	3.10
☐ AL17 Phil Rizzuto	20.00	9.00	2.50
☐ AL18 Bob Porterfield	6.00	2.70	.75
☐ AL19 Chico Carrasquel	10.00	4.50	1.25
☐ AL20 Yogi Berra	40.00	18.00	5.00
☐ AL21 Bob Lemon	12.00	5.50	1.50
☐ AL22 Ferris Fain	6.00	2.70	.75
☐ AL23 Hank Bauer	10.00	4.50	1.25
☐ AL24 Jim Delsing	6.00	2.70	.75
☐ AL25 Gil McDougald	10.00	4.50	1.25
☐ NL1 Richie Ashburn	20.00	9.00	2.50
☐ NL2 Billy Cox	10.00	4.50	1.25
☐ NL3 Del Crandall	10.00	4.50	1.25
☐ NL4 Carl Erskine	10.00	4.50	1.25
☐ NL5 Monte Irvin	12.00	5.50	1.50
☐ NL6 Ted Kluszewski	12.00	5.50	1.50
☐ NL7 Don Mueller	6.00	2.70	.75
☐ NL8 Andy Pafko	6.00	2.70	.75
☐ NL9 Del Rice	6.00	2.70	.75
☐ NL10 Red Schoendienst	12.00	5.50	1.50
☐ NL11 Warren Spahn	20.00	9.00	2.50
☐ NL12 Curt Simmons	10.00	4.50	1.25
☐ NL13 Roy Campanella	45.00	20.00	5.50
☐ NL14 Jim Gilliam	10.00	4.50	1.25
☐ NL15 Pee Wee Reese	25.00	11.00	3.10
☐ NL16 Duke Snider	45.00	20.00	5.50
☐ NL17 Rip Repulski	6.00	2.70	.75
☐ NL18 Robin Roberts	15.00	6.75	1.85
☐ NL19A Enos Slaughter	60.00	27.00	7.50
☐ NL19B Gus Bell	25.00	11.00	3.10
☐ NL20 Johnny Logan	6.00	2.70	.75
☐ NL21 John Antonelli	6.00	2.70	.75
☐ NL22 Gil Hodges	20.00	9.00	2.50
☐ NL23 Eddie Mathews	20.00	9.00	2.50
☐ NL24 Lew Burdette	10.00	4.50	1.25
☐ NL25 Willie Mays	80.00	36.00	10.00

1955 Red Man

The cards in this 50-card set measure approximately 3 1/2" by 4" (or 3 1/2" by 3 5/8" without the tab). The 1955 Red Man set contains 25 players from each league. Card numbers are on the write-ups of the players. Cards that have the tab (coupon) attached are generally worth a multiple of cards which have had their tabs removed. Please see mulitplier values below. The prices listed below refer to cards without tabs.

	NRMT	VG-E	GOOD
COMPLETE SET (50)	500.00	220.00	60.00
COMMON CARD	6.00	2.70	.75
*CARDS WITH TABS:2.5X BASIC CARDS			
☐ AL1 Ray Boone	6.00	2.70	.75
☐ AL2 Jim Busby	6.00	2.70	.75
☐ AL3 Whitey Ford	25.00	11.00	3.10
☐ AL4 Nellie Fox	20.00	9.00	2.50
☐ AL5 Bob Grim	6.00	2.70	.75
☐ AL6 Jack Harshman	6.00	2.70	.75
☐ AL7 Jim Hegan	6.00	2.70	.75
☐ AL8 Bob Lemon	12.00	5.50	1.50
☐ AL9 Irv Noren	6.00	2.70	.75
☐ AL10 Bob Porterfield	6.00	2.70	.75
☐ AL11 Al Rosen	8.00	3.60	1.00
☐ AL12 Mickey Vernon	10.00	4.50	1.25
☐ AL13 Vic Wertz	6.00	2.70	.75
☐ AL14 Early Wynn	12.00	5.50	1.50
☐ AL15 Bobby Avila	6.00	2.70	.75
☐ AL16 Yogi Berra	40.00	18.00	5.00
☐ AL17 Joe Coleman	6.00	2.70	.75
☐ AL18 Larry Doby	10.00	4.50	1.25
☐ AL19 Jackie Jensen	10.00	4.50	1.25
☐ AL20 Pete Runnels	6.00	2.70	.75
☐ AL21 Jim Piersall	8.00	3.60	1.00
☐ AL22 Hank Bauer	8.00	3.60	1.00
☐ AL23 Chico Carrasquel	8.00	3.60	1.00
☐ AL24 Minnie Minoso	8.00	3.60	1.00
☐ AL25 Sandy Consuegra	6.00	2.70	.75
☐ NL1 Richie Ashburn	20.00	9.00	2.50
☐ NL2 Del Crandall	6.00	2.70	.75
☐ NL3 Gil Hodges	20.00	9.00	2.50
☐ NL4 Brooks Lawrence	6.00	2.70	.75
☐ NL5 Johnny Logan	6.00	2.70	.75
☐ NL6 Sal Maglie	8.00	3.60	1.00
☐ NL7 Willie Mays	80.00	36.00	10.00
☐ NL8 Don Mueller	6.00	2.70	.75
☐ NL9 Bill Sarni	6.00	2.70	.75
☐ NL10 Warren Spahn	20.00	9.00	2.50
☐ NL11 Hank Thompson	6.00	2.70	.75
☐ NL12 Hoyt Wilhelm	12.00	5.50	1.50
☐ NL13 John Antonelli	8.00	3.60	1.00
☐ NL14 Carl Erskine	10.00	4.50	1.25
☐ NL15 Granny Hamner	6.00	2.70	.75
☐ NL16 Ted Kluszewski	12.00	5.50	1.50
☐ NL17 Pee Wee Reese	25.00	11.00	3.10
☐ NL18 Red Schoendienst	12.00	5.50	1.50
☐ NL19 Duke Snider	45.00	20.00	5.50
☐ NL20 Frank Thomas	6.00	2.70	.75
☐ NL21 Ray Jablonski	6.00	2.70	.75
☐ NL22 Dusty Rhodes	8.00	3.60	1.00
☐ NL23 Gus Bell	8.00	3.60	1.00
☐ NL24 Curt Simmons	8.00	3.60	1.00
☐ NL25 Marv Grissom	6.00	2.70	.75

1912 Red Sox Boston American Series PC742-1

These cream-colored cards with sepia photo and printing were issued in 1912 by the Boston American newspaper. The set features players from the 1912 Red Sox, who won the World Series. It is reasonable to assume that additional cards will be found. All additions to this checklist are appreciated. Unlike the PC 742-2 Boston Daily American Souvenir set, this set features excellent quality photos.

	EX-MT	VG-E	GOOD
COMPLETE SET (6)	1000.00	450.00	125.00
COMMON CARD (1-6)	150.00	70.00	19.00
☐ 1 Forest Cady	150.00	70.00	19.00
☐ 2 Hub Perdue	150.00	70.00	19.00
☐ 3 Tris Speaker	350.00	160.00	45.00
☐ 4 Jake Stahl	150.00	70.00	19.00
☐ 5 Heinie Wagner	150.00	70.00	19.00
☐ 6 Joe Wood	200.00	90.00	25.00

1912 Red Sox Boston Daily American Souvenir PC742-2

This black and white postcard set was issued in 1912 and features players from the World Champion Boston Red Sox of that year. The printing quality of the cards are rather poor.

	EX-MT	VG-E	GOOD
COMPLETE SET (3)	450.00	200.00	55.00
COMMON CARD (1-3)	150.00	70.00	19.00
☐ 1 Forest Cady	150.00	70.00	19.00
☐ 2 Ray Collins	150.00	70.00	19.00
☐ 3 Heinie Wagner	150.00	70.00	19.00

1942 Red Sox Team Issue

This set of the Boston Red Sox measures approximately 6 1/2" by 9". The black and white photos display fascimile autographs. The backs are blank. The cards are unnumbered and are checklisted below in alphabetical order.

	EX-MT	VG-E	GOOD
COMPLETE SET (25)	100.00	45.00	12.50
COMMON CARD (1-25)	3.00	1.35	.35
☐ 1 Mace Brown	3.00	1.35	.35
☐ 2 Bill Butland	3.00	1.35	.35
☐ 3 Paul Campbell	3.00	1.35	.35
☐ 4 Tom Carey	3.00	1.35	.35
☐ 5 Ken Chase	3.00	1.35	.35
☐ 6 Bill Conroy	3.00	1.35	.35
☐ 7 Joe Cronin	10.00	4.50	1.25
☐ 8 Dominic DiMaggio	5.00	2.20	.60
☐ 9 Joe Dobson	3.00	1.35	.35
☐ 10 Bob Doerr	7.50	3.40	.95
☐ 11 Lou Finney	3.00	1.35	.35
☐ 12 Pete Fox	3.00	1.35	.35
☐ 13 Jimmie Foxx	15.00	6.75	1.85
☐ 14 Tex Hughson	3.00	1.35	.35
☐ 15 Oscar Judd	3.00	1.35	.35
☐ 16 Tony Lupien	3.00	1.35	.35
☐ 17 Dick Newsome	3.00	1.35	.35
☐ 18 Skeeter Newsome	3.00	1.35	.35
☐ 19 John Peacock	3.00	1.35	.35
☐ 20 Johnny Pesky	5.00	2.20	.60
☐ 21 Mike Ryba	3.00	1.35	.35
☐ 22 Jim Tabor	3.00	1.35	.35
☐ 23 Yank Terry	3.00	1.35	.35
☐ 24 Charles Wagner	3.00	1.35	.35
☐ 25 Ted Williams	30.00	13.50	3.70

1943 Red Sox Team Issue

This 24-card set of the Boston Red Sox measures approximately 6 1/2" by 9" and features black-and-white player portraits with a facsimile autograph. The cards are unnumbered and checklisted below in alphabetical order.

	EX-MT	VG-E	GOOD
COMPLETE SET (24)	75.00	34.00	9.50
COMMON CARD (1-24)	3.00	1.35	.35
☐ 1 Mace Brown	3.00	1.35	.35
☐ 2 Ken Chase	3.00	1.35	.35
☐ 3 Bill Conroy	3.00	1.35	.35
☐ 4 Joe Cronin	10.00	4.50	1.25
☐ 5 Joe Dobson	3.00	1.35	.35
☐ 6 Bob Doerr	10.00	4.50	1.25
☐ 7 Pete Fox	3.00	1.35	.35
☐ 8 Ford Garrison	3.00	1.35	.35
☐ 9 Tex Hughson	3.00	1.35	.35
☐ 10 Oscar Judd	3.00	1.35	.35
☐ 11 Andy Karl	3.00	1.35	.35
☐ 12 Eddie Lake	3.00	1.35	.35
☐ 13 John Lazor	3.00	1.35	.35
☐ 14 Lou Luceer	3.00	1.35	.35
☐ 15 Tony Lupien	3.00	1.35	.35
☐ 16 Dee Miles	3.00	1.35	.35
☐ 17 Dick Newsome	3.00	1.35	.35
☐ 18 Skeeter Newsome	3.00	1.35	.35
☐ 19 Roy Partee	3.00	1.35	.35
☐ 20 John Peacock	3.00	1.35	.35
☐ 21 Mike Ryba	3.00	1.35	.35
☐ 22 Al Simmons	15.00	6.75	1.85
☐ 23 Jim Tabor	3.00	1.35	.35
☐ 24 Yank Terry	3.00	1.35	.35

1946 Red Sox Team Issue

These 25 cards measure approximately 6 1/2" by 9". They feature members of the 1946 American League pennant winners Red Sox. The set can be dated by Ernie Andres whose only year in the majors was 1946.

	EX-MT	VG-E	GOOD
COMPLETE SET (25)	125.00	55.00	15.50
COMMON CARD (1-25)	3.00	1.35	.35
☐ 1 Ernie Andres	3.00	1.35	.35
☐ 2 Jim Bagby, Jr	3.00	1.35	.35
☐ 3 Mace Brown	3.00	1.35	.35
☐ 4 Joe Cronin	10.00	4.50	1.25
☐ 5 Leon Culberson	3.00	1.35	.35
☐ 6 Mel Deutsch	3.00	1.35	.35
☐ 7 Dom DiMaggio	10.00	4.50	1.25
☐ 8 Joe Dobson	3.00	1.35	.35
☐ 9 Bob Doerr	10.00	4.50	1.25
☐ 10 Dave Ferriss	3.00	1.35	.35
☐ 11 Mickey Harris	3.00	1.35	.35
☐ 12 Randy Heflin	3.00	1.35	.35
☐ 13 Tex Hughson	3.00	1.35	.35
☐ 14 Earl Johnson	3.00	1.35	.35
☐ 15 Ed McGah	3.00	1.35	.35
☐ 16 George Metkovich	3.00	1.35	.35
☐ 17 Roy Partee	3.00	1.35	.35
☐ 18 Eddie Pellagrini	3.00	1.35	.35
☐ 19 Johnny Pesky	5.00	2.20	.60
☐ 20 Rip Russell	3.00	1.35	.35
☐ 21 Mike Ryba	3.00	1.35	.35
☐ 22 Charlie Wagner	3.00	1.35	.35
☐ 23 Hal Wagner	3.00	1.35	.35
☐ 24 Ted Williams	40.00	18.00	5.00
☐ 25 Rudy York	5.00	2.20	.60

1948 Red Sox Team Issue

These 25 photos measure approximately 6 1/2" by 9". They feature members of the 1948 Boston Red Sox. The photos take up almost the entire surface and are surrounded by white borders. A facsimile autograph is also on each photo. The backs are blank and we have sequenced this set in alphabetical order.

	NRMT	VG-E	GOOD
COMPLETE SET (25)	175.00	80.00	22.00
COMMON CARD (1-25)	3.50	1.55	.45
☐ 1 Matt Batts	3.50	1.55	.45
☐ 2 Dom DiMaggio	15.00	6.75	1.85

☐ 3 Joe Dobson	3.50	1.55	.45
☐ 4 Bobby Doerr	15.00	6.75	1.85
☐ 5 Harry Dorish	3.50	1.55	.45
☐ 6 Dave 'Boo' Ferriss	3.50	1.55	.45
☐ 7 Denny Galehouse	3.50	1.55	.45
☐ 8 Bill Goodman	5.00	2.20	.60
☐ 9 Mickey Harris	3.50	1.55	.45
☐ 10 Billy Hitchcock	3.50	1.55	.45
☐ 11 Earl Johnson	3.50	1.55	.45
☐ 12 Jake Jones	3.50	1.55	.45
☐ 13 Ellis Kinder	3.50	1.55	.45
☐ 14 Jack Kramer	3.50	1.55	.45
☐ 15 Joe McCarthy MG	15.00	6.75	1.85
☐ 16 Maurice McDermott	3.50	1.55	.45
☐ 17 Sam Mele	5.00	2.20	.60
☐ 18 Wally Moses	3.50	1.55	.45
☐ 19 Mel Parnell	5.00	2.20	.60
☐ 20 Johnny Pesky	5.00	2.20	.60
☐ 21 Stan Spence	3.50	1.55	.45
☐ 22 Vern Stephens	5.00	2.20	.60
☐ 23 Chuck Stobbs	3.50	1.55	.45
☐ 24 Birdie Tebbetts	10.00	4.50	1.25
☐ 25 Ted Williams	50.00	22.00	6.25

1953 Red Sox First National Super Market Stores

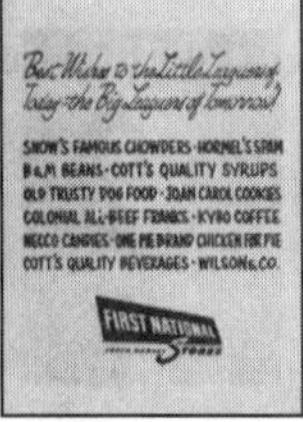

This four-card set features black-and-white player photos and measures approximately 3 3/4" by 5". The backs carry advertising for the stores. The cards are unnumbered and checklisted below in alphabetical order.

	NRMT	VG-E	GOOD
COMPLETE SET (4)	50.00	22.00	6.25
COMMON CARD (1-4)	15.00	6.75	1.85
☐ 1 Bill Goodman	15.00	6.75	1.85
☐ 2 Ellis Kinder	15.00	6.75	1.85
☐ 3 Mel Parnell	17.50	8.00	2.20
☐ 4 Sammy White	15.00	6.75	1.85

1953 Red Sox Team Issue

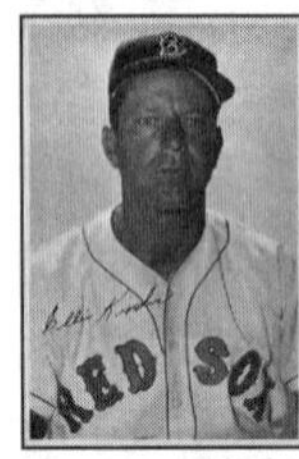

This set of the Boston Red Sox measures approximately 6" by 9". The black-and-white player photos display fascimile autographs. The backs are blank. The cards are unnumbered and checklisted below in alphabetical order.

	NRMT	VG-E	GOOD
COMPLETE SET (30)	100.00	45.00	12.50
COMMON CARD (1-30)	3.00	1.35	.35
☐ 1 Milt Bolling	3.00	1.35	.35
☐ 2 Lou Boudreau MG	7.50	3.40	.95
☐ 3 Harold Brown	3.00	1.35	.35
☐ 4 Bill Consolo	3.00	1.35	.35
☐ 5 Dom DiMaggio	5.00	2.20	.60
☐ 6 Hoot Evers	3.00	1.35	.35
☐ 7 Ben Flowers	3.00	1.35	.35
☐ 8 Hershell Freeman	3.00	1.35	.35
☐ 9 Dick Gernert	3.00	1.35	.35
☐ 10 Bill Goodman	5.00	2.20	.60
☐ 11 Marv Grissom	3.00	1.35	.35
☐ 12 Ken Holcombe	3.00	1.35	.35
☐ 13 Sid Hudson	3.00	1.35	.35
☐ 14 George Kell	7.50	3.40	.95
☐ 15 Bill Kennedy	3.00	1.35	.35
☐ 16 Ellis Kinder	5.00	2.20	.60
☐ 17 Ted Lepcio	3.00	1.35	.35
☐ 18 Johnny Lipon	3.00	1.35	.35
☐ 19 Maurice McDermott	3.00	1.35	.35
☐ 20 John Merson	3.00	1.35	.35
☐ 21 Gus Niarhos	3.00	1.35	.35
☐ 22 Willard Nixon	3.00	1.35	.35
☐ 23 Mel Parnell	5.00	2.20	.60
☐ 24 Jimmy Piersall	7.50	3.40	.95
☐ 25 Gene Stephens	3.00	1.35	.35
☐ 26 Tommy Umphlett	3.00	1.35	.35
☐ 27 Bill Werle	3.00	1.35	.35
☐ 28 Sam White	3.00	1.35	.35
☐ 29 Del Wilber	3.00	1.35	.35
☐ 30 Al Zarilla	3.00	1.35	.35

1958 Red Sox Jay Publishing

This 12-card set of the Boston Red Sox measures approximately 5" by 7" and features black-and-white player photos in a white border. These cards were packaged 12 to a packet. The backs are blank. The cards are unnumbered and checklisted below in alphabetical order.

	NRMT	VG-E	GOOD
COMPLETE SET (12)	35.00	16.00	4.40
COMMON CARD (1-12)	2.50	1.10	.30
☐ 1 Tom Brewer	2.50	1.10	.30
☐ 2 Don Buddin	2.50	1.10	.30
☐ 3 Dick Gernert	2.50	1.10	.30
☐ 4 Mike Higgins MG	2.50	1.10	.30
☐ 5 Jack Jensen	3.00	1.35	.35
☐ 6 Frank Malzone	3.00	1.35	.35
☐ 7 Jim Piersall	3.00	1.35	.35
☐ 8 Pete Runnels	2.50	1.10	.30
☐ 9 Gene Stephens	2.50	1.10	.30
☐ 10 Frank Sullivan	2.50	1.10	.30
☐ 11 Sam White	2.50	1.10	.30
☐ 12 Ted Williams	20.00	9.00	2.50

1959 Red Sox Jay Publishing

This 12-card set of the Boston Red Sox measures approximately 5" by 7" and features black-and-white player photos in a white border. These cards were packaged 12 to a packet and originally sold for 25 cents. The backs are blank. The cards are unnumbered and checklisted below in alphabetical order.

	NRMT	VG-E	GOOD
COMPLETE SET (12)	40.00	18.00	5.00
COMMON CARD (1-12)	2.00	.90	.25
☐ 1 Tom Brewer	2.00	.90	.25
☐ 2 Dick Gernert	2.00	.90	.25
☐ 3 Mike Higgins MG	2.00	.90	.25
☐ 4 Jackie Jensen	5.00	2.20	.60
☐ 5 Frank Malzone	3.00	1.35	.35
☐ 6 Gene Mauch	2.00	.90	.25
☐ 7 Jimmy Piersall	5.00	2.20	.60
☐ 8 Dave Sisler	2.00	.90	.25
☐ 9 Frank Sullivan	2.00	.90	.25
☐ 10 Mickey Vernon	3.00	1.35	.35
☐ 11 Sammy White	2.00	.90	.25
☐ 12 Ted Williams	20.00	9.00	2.50

1960 Red Sox Jay Publishing

This 12-card set of the Boston Red Sox measures approximately 5" by 7" and features black-and-white player photos in a white border. These cards were packaged 12 to a packet. The backs are blank. The cards are unnumbered and checklisted below in alphabetical order.

	NRMT	VG-E	GOOD
COMPLETE SET (12)	35.00	16.00	4.40
COMMON CARD (1-12)	2.00	.90	.25
☐ 1 Tom Brewer	2.00	.90	.25
☐ 2 Don Buddin	2.00	.90	.25
☐ 3 Jerry Casale	2.00	.90	.25
☐ 4 Ike Delock	2.00	.90	.25
☐ 5 Jerry(Pumpsie) Green	2.00	.90	.25
☐ 6 Bill Jurges MG	2.00	.90	.25
☐ 7 Frank Malzone	3.00	1.35	.35
☐ 8 Pete Runnels	2.00	.90	.25
☐ 9 Gene Stephens	2.00	.90	.25
☐ 10 Bobby Thomson	4.00	1.80	.50
☐ 11 Vic Wertz	2.00	.90	.25
☐ 12 Ted Williams	20.00	9.00	2.50

1962 Red Sox Jay Publishing

Like other Jay Publishing issues these black-and-white, blank-backed, white-bordered, 5" X 7" photos. The player's name and team are printed in black within the lower margin. The photos are unnumbered and checklisted below in alphabetical order.

	NRMT	VG-E	GOOD
COMPLETE SET (11)	30.00	13.50	3.70
COMMON CARD (1-11)	2.50	1.10	.30
☐ 1 Ed Bressoud	2.50	1.10	.30
☐ 2 Gene Conley	3.00	1.35	.35
☐ 3 Gary Geiger	2.50	1.10	.30
☐ 4 Mike Higgins MG	2.50	1.10	.30
☐ 5 Frank Malzone	3.50	1.55	.45
☐ 6 Bill Monbouquette	2.50	1.10	.30
☐ 7 Russ Nixon	2.50	1.10	.30
☐ 8 Pete Runnels	2.50	1.10	.30
☐ 9 Charles Schilling	2.50	1.10	.30
☐ 10 Don Schwall	2.50	1.10	.30
☐ 11 Carl Yastrzemski UER (Misspelled Yastremski)	20.00	9.00	2.50

1969 Red Sox Arco Oil

Sponsored by Arco Oil, this 12-card set features photos of the 1969 Boston Red Sox. The cards are unnumbered and checklisted below in alphabetical order.

	NRMT	VG-E	GOOD
COMPLETE SET (12)	60.00	27.00	7.50
COMMON CARD (1-12)	5.00	2.20	.60
☐ 1 Mike Andrews	5.00	2.20	.60
☐ 2 Tony Conigliaro	7.50	3.40	.95
☐ 3 Ray Culp	5.00	2.20	.60
☐ 4 Russ Gibson	5.00	2.20	.60
☐ 5 Dalton Jones	5.00	2.20	.60
☐ 6 Jim Lonborg	7.50	3.40	.95
☐ 7 Sparky Lyle	6.00	2.70	.75
☐ 8 Syd O'Brien	5.00	2.20	.60
☐ 9 Rico Petrocelli	7.50	3.40	.95
☐ 10 Geo. Scott	6.00	2.70	.75
☐ 11 Reggie Smith	7.50	3.40	.95
☐ 12 Carl Yastrzemski	15.00	6.75	1.85

1969 Red Sox Team Issue

This 12-card set of the Boston Red Sox measures approximately 4 1/4" by 7". The fronts display black-and-white player portraits bordered in white. The player's name and team are printed in the top margin. The backs are blank. The cards are unnumbered and checklisted below in alphabetical order.

	NRMT	VG-E	GOOD
COMPLETE SET (12)	30.00	13.50	3.70
COMMON CARD (1-12)	2.00	.90	.25
☐ 1 Mike Andrews	2.00	.90	.25
☐ 2 Tony Conigliaro	5.00	2.20	.60
☐ 3 Russ Gibson	2.00	.90	.25
☐ 4 Dalton Jones	2.00	.90	.25
☐ 5 Bill Landis	2.00	.90	.25
☐ 6 Jim Lonborg	3.00	1.35	.35
☐ 7 Sparky Lyle	5.00	2.20	.60
☐ 8 Rico Petrocelli	3.00	1.35	.35
☐ 9 George Scott	3.00	1.35	.35
☐ 10 Reggie Smith	3.00	1.35	.35
☐ 11 Dick Williams MG	3.00	1.35	.35
☐ 12 Carl Yastrzemski	7.50	3.40	.95

1970 Red Sox Color Photo Post Cards

This set features members of the 1970 Boston Red Sox. These color post cards are unnumbered and we have sequenced them in alphabetical order.

	NRMT	VG-E	GOOD
COMPLETE SET (17)	20.00	9.00	2.50
COMMON CARD (1-17)	1.00	.45	.12
☐ 1 Luis Alvarado	1.00	.45	.12
☐ 2 Mike Andrews	1.00	.45	.12
☐ 3 Ken Brett	1.50	.70	.19
☐ 4 Bill Conigliaro	1.50	.70	.19
☐ 5 Tony Conigliaro	1.50	.70	.19
☐ 6 Ray Culp	1.00	.45	.12
☐ 7 Sparky Lyle	1.50	.70	.19
☐ 8 Gerry Moses	1.00	.45	.12
☐ 9 Mike Nagy	1.00	.45	.12
☐ 10 Gary Peters	1.50	.70	.19
☐ 11 Rico Petrocelli	1.50	.70	.19
☐ 12 George Scott	2.50	1.10	.30
☐ 13 Sonny Siebert	1.00	.45	.12
☐ 14 Reggie Smith	2.50	1.10	.30
☐ 15 Lee Stange	1.00	.45	.12
☐ 16 Carl Yastrzemski	5.00	2.20	.60
☐ 17 Jim Lonborg (oversize)	1.50	.70	.19

1971 Red Sox Arco Oil

Sponsored by Arco Oil, these 12 pictures of the 1971 Boston Red Sox measure approximately 8" by 10" and feature on their fronts white-bordered posed color player photos. The player's name is shown in black lettering within the white margin below the photo. His facsimile autograph appears across the picture. The white back carries the team's and player's names at the top, followed below by position, biography, career highlights, and statistics. An ad at the bottom for picture frames rounds out the back. The cards are unnumbered and checklisted below in alphabetical order.

	NRMT	VG-E	GOOD
COMPLETE SET (12)	40.00	18.00	5.00
COMMON CARD (1-12)	2.50	1.10	.30
☐ 1 Luis Aparicio	7.50	3.40	.95
☐ 2 Ken Brett	3.50	1.55	.45
☐ 3 Billy Conigliaro	4.00	1.80	.50
☐ 4 Ray Culp	2.50	1.10	.30
☐ 5 Doug Griffin	2.50	1.10	.30
☐ 6 Bob Montgomery	2.50	1.10	.30
☐ 7 Gary Peters	3.50	1.55	.45
☐ 8 George Scott	4.00	1.80	.50
☐ 9 Sonny Siebert	2.50	1.10	.30
☐ 10 Reggie Smith	4.00	1.80	.50
☐ 11 Ken Tatum	2.50	1.10	.30
☐ 12 Carl Yastrzemski	10.00	4.50	1.25

1971 Red Sox Team Issue

These 12 photos measure approximately 4 1/4" by 7". The player's name and team are noted on the top with the rest of the front dedicated to a photo. The backs are blank. We have sequenced this set in alphabetical order. The set is dated 1971 as that was Luis Aparicio's first year with the Red Sox and Sparky Lyle's last season with the club.

	NRMT	VG-E	GOOD
COMPLETE SET (12)	25.00	11.00	3.10
COMMON CARD (1-12)	1.50	.70	.19
☐ 1 Luis Aparicio	3.50	1.55	.45
☐ 2 Billy Conigliaro	2.00	.90	.25
☐ 3 Ray Culp	1.50	.70	.19
☐ 4 Duane Josephson	1.50	.70	.19
☐ 5 Jim Lonborg	2.50	1.10	.30
☐ 6 Sparky Lyle	2.50	1.10	.30
☐ 7 Gary Peters	2.00	.90	.25
☐ 8 Rico Petrocelli	2.00	.90	.25
☐ 9 George Scott	2.50	1.10	.30
☐ 10 Sonny Siebert	1.50	.70	.19
☐ 11 Reggie Smith	2.50	1.10	.30
☐ 12 Carl Yastrzemski	4.00	1.80	.50

1976 Red Sox Star Market

This 16-card set of the Boston Red Sox measures approximately 5 7/8" by 9". The white-bordered fronts feature color player head photos

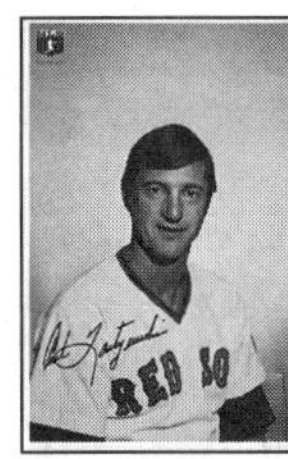

with a facsimile autograph. The backs are blank. The cards are unnumbered and checklisted below in alphabetical order.

	NRMT	VG-E	GOOD
COMPLETE SET (16)	35.00	16.00	4.40
COMMON CARD (1-16)	1.00	.45	.12
□ 1 Rick Burleson	1.50	.70	.19
□ 2 Reggie Cleveland	1.00	.45	.12
□ 3 Cecil Cooper	2.00	.90	.25
□ 4 Denny Doyle	1.00	.45	.12
□ 5 Dwight Evans	4.00	1.80	.50
□ 6 Carlton Fisk	7.50	3.40	.95
□ 7 Tom House	1.00	.45	.12
□ 8 Fergie Jenkins	4.00	1.80	.50
□ 9 Bill Lee	2.00	.90	.25
□ 10 Fred Lynn	3.00	1.35	.35
□ 11 Rick Miller	1.00	.45	.12
□ 12 Rico Petrocelli	2.00	.90	.25
□ 13 Jim Rice	4.00	1.80	.50
□ 14 Luis Tiant	3.00	1.35	.35
□ 15 Rick Wise	1.00	.45	.12
□ 16 Carl Yastrzemski	7.50	3.40	.95

1976-77 Red Sox

This nine-card set of the Boston Red Sox measures approximately 7" by 8 1/2". The fronts feature white-bordered color player action photos with the player's name printed in black in the bottom margin. The backs are blank. The cards are unnumbered and checklisted below in alphabetical order.

	NRMT	VG-E	GOOD
COMPLETE SET (9)	18.00	8.00	2.20
COMMON CARD (1-9)	1.50	.70	.19
□ 1 Rick Burleson	2.00	.90	.25
□ 2 Denny Doyle	1.50	.70	.19
□ 3 Dwight Evans	2.00	.90	.25
□ 4 Carlton Fisk	3.50	1.55	.45
□ 5 Fred Lynn	3.50	1.55	.45
□ 6 Rico Petrocelli	2.50	1.10	.30
□ 7 Jim Rice	3.50	1.55	.45
□ 8 George Scott	2.50	1.10	.30
□ 10 Carl Yastrzemski	4.50	2.00	.55

1979 Red Sox Early Favorites

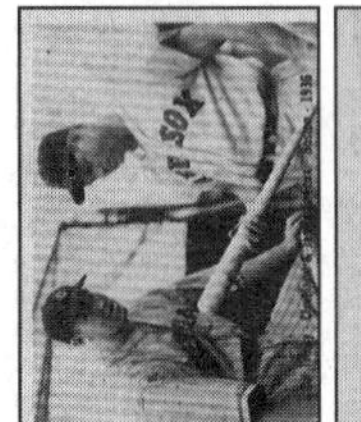

This 25 card set measures 2 1/2" by 3 3/4". The set covers the early years of Tom Yawkey's ownership. The photos are all black and white.

	NRMT	VG-E	GOOD
COMPLETE SET (24)	15.00	6.75	1.85
COMMON CARD (1-24)	.75	.35	.09
□ 1 New Fenway Park	1.00	.45	.12
□ 2 Mrs. Tom Yawkey	.75	.35	.09
Mrs. Eddie Collins			
□ 3 1932 Outfielders	.75	.35	.09
Tom Oliver			
Earl Webb			
Jack Rothrock			
□ 4 Ace Pitchers	.75	.35	.09
John Marcum			
Wes Ferrell			
Lefty Grove			
Fritz Ostermueller			
□ 5 John Gooch	.75	.35	.09
□ 6 Joe Cronin	1.00	.45	.12
Lee Rogers			
Bud Buetter			
Walter Ripley			
Jim Henry			
Alex Mustaikis			
Stewart Bowers			
□ 7 Danny MacFayden	.75	.35	.09
□ 8 Dale Alexander	.75	.35	.09
□ 9 Robert Fothergill	.75	.35	.09
(Fatsy)			
□ 10 Sunday Morning Workout	.75	.35	.09
□ 11 Jimmy Foxx signs ball	1.00	.45	.12
for Mrs. Tom Yawkey			
□ 12 Lefty Grove	1.00	.45	.12
receiving key for new car			
□ 13 Lefty Grove	1.00	.45	.12
Fireball			
□ 14 Jack Rothrock	.75	.35	.09
Urbane Pickering			
□ 15 Tom Daly CO	.75	.35	.09
Al Schact CO			
Herb Pennock CO			
□ 16 Heinie Manush	1.00	.45	.12
Eddie Collins			
□ 17 Tris Speaker	1.25	.55	.16
□ 18 Jimmy Foxx	1.50	.70	.19
□ 19 Smead Jolley	.75	.35	.09
□ 20 Hal Trosky	.75	.35	.09
James Foxx			
□ 21 Harold (Muddy) Ruel	.75	.35	.09
Wilcy (Fireman) Moore			
□ 22 Bob Quinn PR	.75	.35	.09
Shano Collins MG			
□ 23 Tom Oliver	.75	.35	.09
□ 24 Joe Cronin CO	1.00	.45	.12
Herb Pennock CO			
Bud Buetter			

1979 Red Sox Team Issue

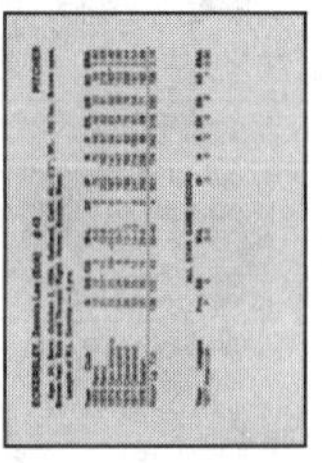

This set of the Boston Red Sox features black-and-white player portraits with biographical and statistical information on the backs except for one card which displays a picture of Garry Hancock on one side and Stan Papi on the other. This set may be incomplete. The cards are unnumbered and checklisted below in alphabetical order.

	NRMT	VG-E	GOOD
COMPLETE SET	6.00	2.70	.75
COMMON CARD	.50	.23	.06
□ 1 Bill Campbell	.50	.23	.06
□ 2 Dennis Eckersley	5.00	2.20	.60
□ 3 Garry Hancock	.50	.23	.06
Stan Papi			
□ 4 Mike Torrez	.50	.23	.06

1981 Red Sox Boston Globe 2nd Series

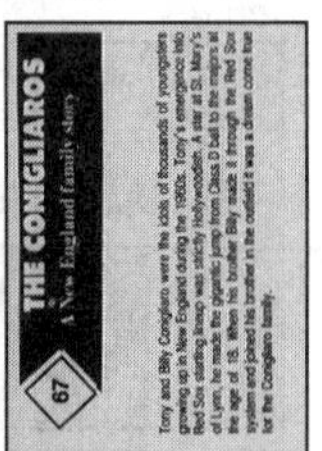

These standard-size cards consist of the second half of the Boston Globe series about famous Red Sox. The black and white photos are surrounded by white borders. The horizontal backs have player information as well as career statistics. This set concentrates on players from the 60's.

	NRMT	VG-E	GOOD
COMPLETE SET (64)	15.00	6.75	1.85
COMMON CARD (65-128)	.25	.11	.03
□ 65 Ted Williams	2.50	1.10	.30
Carl Yastrzemski			
□ 66 Dream Makers	1.00	.45	.12
Dick Williams MG			
Carl Yastrzemski			
Jim Lonborg			
George Scott			
□ 67 Tony Conigliaro	.25	.11	.03
Billy Conigliaro			
□ 68 Jerry Adair	.25	.11	.03
□ 69 Mike Andrews	.25	.11	.03
□ 70 Gary Bell	.25	.11	.03
□ 71 Dennis Bennett	.25	.11	.03
□ 72 Ed Bressoud	.25	.11	.03
□ 73 Ken Brett	.25	.11	.03
□ 74 Lu Clinton	.25	.11	.03
□ 75 Tony Conigliaro	1.25	.55	.16
□ 76 Billy Conigliaro	.25	.11	.03
□ 77 Gene Conley	.25	.11	.03
□ 78 Ray Culp	.25	.11	.03
□ 79 Dick Ellsworth	.25	.11	.03
□ 80 Joe Foy	.25	.11	.03
□ 81 Russ Gibson	.25	.11	.03
□ 82 Jim Gosger	.25	.11	.03
□ 83 Lennie Green	.25	.11	.03
□ 84 Ken Harrelson	.50	.23	.06
□ 85 Tony Horton	.25	.11	.03
□ 86 Elston Howard	1.00	.45	.12
□ 87 Dalton Jones	.25	.11	.03
□ 88 Eddie Kasko	.25	.11	.03
□ 89 Joe Lahoud	.25	.11	.03
□ 90 Jack Lamabe	.25	.11	.03
□ 91 Jim Lonborg	.75	.35	.09
□ 92 Sparky Lyle	.75	.35	.09
□ 93 Felix Mantilla	.25	.11	.03
□ 94 Roman Mejias	.25	.11	.03
□ 95 Don McMahon	.25	.11	.03
□ 96 Dave Morehead	.25	.11	.03
□ 97 Gerry Moses	.25	.11	.03
□ 98 Mike Nagy	.25	.11	.03
□ 99 Russ Nixon	.25	.11	.03
□ 100 Gene Oliver	.25	.11	.03
□ 101 Dan Osinski	.25	.11	.03
□ 102 Rico Petrocelli	.50	.23	.06
□ 103 Juan Pizarro	.25	.11	.03
□ 104 Dick Radatz	.25	.11	.03
□ 105 Vicente Romo	.25	.11	.03
□ 106 Mike Ryan	.25	.11	.03
□ 107 Jose Santiago	.25	.11	.03
□ 108 Chuck Schilling	.25	.11	.03
□ 109 Dick Schofield	.25	.11	.03
□ 110 Don Schwall	.25	.11	.03
□ 111 George Scott	.50	.23	.06
□ 112 Norm Siebern	.25	.11	.03
□ 113 Sonny Seibert	.25	.11	.03
□ 114 Reggie Smith	.50	.23	.06
□ 115 Bill Spanswick	.25	.11	.03
□ 116 Tracy Stallard	.25	.11	.03
□ 117 Lee Stange	.25	.11	.03
□ 118 Jerry Stephenson	.25	.11	.03
□ 119 Dick Stuart	.50	.23	.06
□ 120 Tom Sturdivant	.25	.11	.03
□ 121 Jose Tartabull	.25	.11	.03
□ 122 George Thomas	.25	.11	.03
□ 123 Lee Thomas	.25	.11	.03
□ 124 Bob Tillman	.25	.11	.03
□ 125 Gary Waslewski	.25	.11	.03
□ 126 Dick Williams	.25	.11	.03
□ 127 John Wyatt	.25	.11	.03
□ 128 Carl Yastrzemski	2.50	1.10	.30

1982 Red Sox Coke

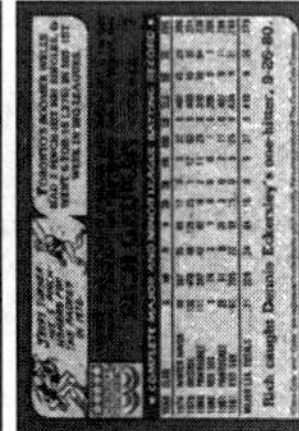

The cards in this 23-card set measure the standard size. This set of Boston Red Sox ballplayers was issued locally in the Boston area as a joint promotion by Brigham's Ice Cream Stores and Coca-Cola. The pictures are identical to those in the Topps regular 1982 issue, except that the colors are brighter and the Brigham and Coke logos appear inside the frame line. The reverses are done in red, black and gray, in contrast to the Topps set, and the number appears to the right of the position listing. The cards were initally distributed in three-card cello packs with an ice cream or Coca-Cola purchase but later became available as sets within the hobby. The unnumbered title or advertising card carries a premium offer on the reverse. The set numbering is in alphabetical order by player's name.

	NRMT	VG-E	GOOD
COMPLETE SET (23)	8.00	3.60	1.00
COMMON CARD (1-22)	.25	.11	.03
□ 1 Gary Allenson	.25	.11	.03
□ 2 Tom Burgmeier	.25	.11	.03
□ 3 Mark Clear	.25	.11	.03
□ 4 Steve Crawford	.25	.11	.03
□ 5 Dennis Eckersley	2.00	.90	.25
□ 6 Dwight Evans	1.25	.55	.16
□ 7 Rich Gedman	.25	.11	.03
□ 8 Garry Hancock	.25	.11	.03
□ 9 Glenn Hoffman	.25	.11	.03
□ 10 Carney Lansford	.50	.23	.06
□ 11 Rick Miller	.25	.11	.03
□ 12 Reid Nichols	.25	.11	.03
□ 13 Bob Ojeda	.50	.23	.06
□ 14 Tony Perez	1.25	.55	.16
□ 15 Chuck Rainey	.25	.11	.03
□ 16 Jerry Remy	.25	.11	.03
□ 17 Jim Rice	1.00	.45	.12
□ 18 Bob Stanley	.50	.23	.06
□ 19 Dave Stapleton	.25	.11	.03
□ 20 Mike Torrez	.50	.23	.06
□ 21 John Tudor	.50	.23	.06
□ 22 Carl Yastrzemski	3.00	1.35	.35
□ NNO Title Card	.15	.07	.02

1986 Red Sox Greats TCMA

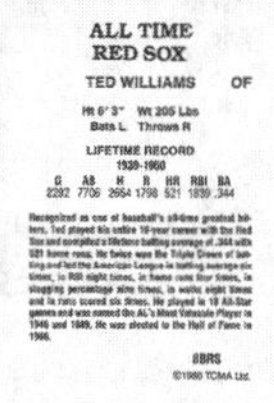

This 12-card standard-size set features all-time leading Red Sox. The player's photo and his name are featured on the front. The back gives more information about that player.

	MINT	NRMT	EXC
COMPLETE SET (12)	7.50	3.40	.95
COMMON CARD (1-12)	.25	.11	.03
□ 1 Sammy White	.25	.11	.03
□ 2 Lefty Grove	1.00	.45	.12
□ 3 Cy Young	1.00	.45	.12
□ 4 Jimmie Foxx	1.00	.45	.12
□ 5 Bobby Doerr	.50	.23	.06
□ 6 Joe Cronin	.25	.11	.03
□ 7 Frank Malzone	.25	.11	.03
□ 8 Ted Williams	2.50	1.10	.30
□ 9 Carl Yastrzemski	1.00	.45	.12
□ 10 Tris Speaker	.75	.35	.09
□ 11 Dick Radatz	.25	.11	.03
□ 12 Dick Williams MG	.25	.11	.03

1987 Red Sox 1946 TCMA

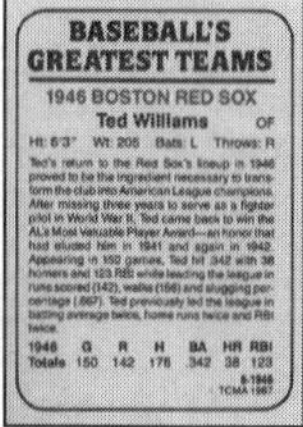

This nine-card standard-size set honors players on the 1946 Red Sox. This team would prove to be the only time Ted Williams would participate in post season play.

	MINT	NRMT	EXC
COMPLETE SET (9)	5.00	2.20	.60
COMMON CARD (1-9)	.25	.11	.03
□ 1 Joe Cronin MG	.50	.23	.06
□ 2 Rudy York	.25	.11	.03
□ 3 Bobby Doerr	.75	.35	.09
□ 4 Johnny Pesky	.50	.23	.06
□ 5 Dom DiMaggio	.75	.35	.09
□ 6 Ted Williams	2.50	1.10	.30
□ 7 Dave "Boo" Ferriss	.25	.11	.03
□ 8 Tex Hughson	.25	.11	.03
□ 9 Mickey Harris	.25	.11	.03

1987 Red Sox Sports Action Postcards

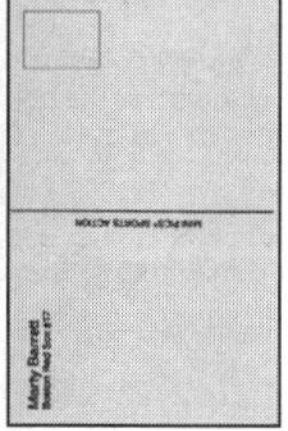

These color postcards featured members of the 1987 Boston Red Sox. They were issued in sets of all ten players.

	MINT	NRMT	EXC
COMPLETE SET (10)	8.00	3.60	1.00
COMMON CARD (1-10)	.50	.23	.06

☐ 1 Marty Barrett	.50	.23	.06
☐ 2 Don Baylor	1.00	.45	.12
☐ 3 Wade Boggs	2.50	1.10	.30
☐ 4 Dennis Boyd	.50	.23	.06
☐ 5 Bill Buckner	.75	.35	.09
☐ 6 Roger Clemens	4.00	1.80	.50
☐ 7 Dwight Evans	1.50	.70	.19
☐ 8 Bruce Hurst	.50	.23	.06
☐ 9 Spike Owen	.50	.23	.06
☐ 10 Jim Rice	1.00	.45	.12

1990 Red Sox Pepsi

The 1990 Pepsi Boston Red Sox set is a 20-card standard-size set, which is checklisted alphabetically below. This set was apparently prepared very early in the 1990 season as Bill Buckner and Lee Smith were still members of the Red Sox in this set. The top of the front of the card have Boston Red Sox printed while the bottom of the card has the players name surrounded by the Pepsi and the Diet Pepsi logo. The backs of the cards have the Score feel to them except the Pepsi and Diet Pepsi logos are again featured prominently on the back of the cards. The cards were supposedly available as a store promotion with one card per specially marked 12-pack of Pepsi. The cards were difficult to remove from the boxes, thus making perfect mint cards worth an extra premium.

	MINT	NRMT	EXC
COMPLETE SET (20)	35.00	16.00	4.40
COMMON CARD (1-20)	1.00	.45	.12
☐ 1 Marty Barrett	1.00	.45	.12
☐ 2 Mike Boddicker	1.00	.45	.12
☐ 3 Wade Boggs	10.00	4.50	1.25
☐ 4 Bill Buckner	2.00	.90	.25
☐ 5 Ellis Burks	4.00	1.80	.50
☐ 6 Roger Clemens	17.50	8.00	2.20
☐ 7 John Dopson	1.00	.45	.12
☐ 8 Dwight Evans	2.50	1.10	.30
☐ 9 Wes Gardner	1.00	.45	.12
☐ 10 Rich Gedman	1.00	.45	.12
☐ 11 Mike Greenwell	2.00	.90	.25
☐ 12 Dennis Lamp	1.00	.45	.12
☐ 13 Rob Murphy	1.00	.45	.12
☐ 14 Tony Pena	1.50	.70	.19
☐ 15 Carlos Quintana	1.00	.45	.12
☐ 16 Jeff Reardon	2.00	.90	.25
☐ 17 Jody Reed	1.50	.70	.19
☐ 18 Luis Rivera	1.00	.45	.12
☐ 19 Kevin Romine	1.00	.45	.12
☐ 20 Lee Smith	3.00	1.35	.35

1991 Red Sox Pepsi

This 20-card set was sponsored by Pepsi and officially licensed by Mike Schechter Associates on behalf of the MLBPA. The 1991 edition consists of 100,000 sets that were available from July 1 through August 10, 1991 in the New England area, with one card per specially marked pack of Pepsi and Diet Pepsi. The promotion also includes a sweepstakes offering a grand prize trip for four to Red Sox Spring training camp. The standard-size cards have color action player photos with a red, white, and blue front design. Two Pepsi logos adorn the card face below the picture. The backs are bordered in red and have a color head shot, biography, professional batting record, and career summary. The cards are unnumbered and checklisted below in alphabetical order.

	MINT	NRMT	EXC
COMPLETE SET (20)	20.00	9.00	2.50
COMMON CARD (1-20)	.75	.35	.09
☐ 1 Tom Bolton	.75	.35	.09
☐ 2 Tom Brunansky	.75	.35	.09
☐ 3 Ellis Burks	2.50	1.10	.30
☐ 4 Jack Clark	1.00	.45	.12
☐ 5 Roger Clemens	10.00	4.50	1.25
☐ 6 Danny Darwin	1.25	.55	.16
☐ 7 Jeff Gray	.75	.35	.09
☐ 8 Mike Greenwell	1.25	.55	.16
☐ 9 Greg A. Harris	.75	.35	.09
☐ 10 Dana Kiecker	.75	.35	.09
☐ 11 Dennis Lamp	.75	.35	.09
☐ 12 John Marzano	.75	.35	.09
☐ 13 Tim Naehring	3.00	1.35	.35
☐ 14 Tony Pena	1.00	.45	.12
☐ 15 Phil Plantier	.75	.35	.09
☐ 16 Carlos Quintana	.75	.35	.09
☐ 17 Jeff Reardon	1.25	.55	.16
☐ 18 Jody Reed	1.00	.45	.12
☐ 19 Luis Rivera	.75	.35	.09
☐ 20 Matt Young	.75	.35	.09

1992 Red Sox Dunkin' Donuts

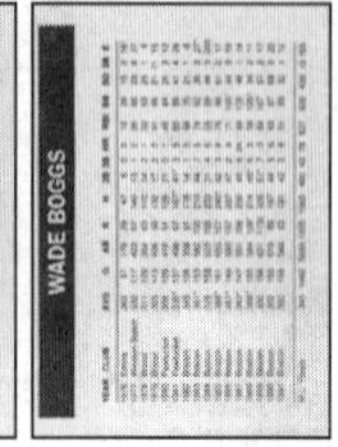

The 1992 Boston Red Sox Player Photo Collection was sponsored by Dunkin' Donuts and WVIT Channel 30 (Connecticut's NBC Station). It consists of three large sheets (each measuring approximately 9 3/8" by 10 3/4") joined together to form one continuous sheet. The first panel displays a color picture of Fenway Park and a WVIT Red Sox Schedule. The second and third panels, which are perforated, feature 15 player cards each. After perforation, the cards measure approximately 2 1/8" by 3 1/8". On a white card face, the fronts have color game shots framed by black border stripes. The player's name, his position, and sponsor logos appear in a bottom white border. On the backs, the player's name appears in a red stripe, and the statistical information is printed in blue on a white background. The cards are unnumbered and checklisted below in alphabetical order. The set was also available sponsored by WJAR-10 TV in Providence, Rhode Island and by Rookie Red Sox Coke via a mail-in offer on 12-packs of Coke in the Boston area for 7.00.

	MINT	NRMT	EXC
COMPLETE SET (30)	12.00	5.50	1.50
COMMON CARD (1-30)	.25	.11	.03
☐ 1 Gary Allenson CO	.25	.11	.03
☐ 2 Wade Boggs	2.00	.90	.25
☐ 3 Tom Bolton	.25	.11	.03
☐ 4 Tom Brunansky	.25	.11	.03
☐ 5 Al Bumbry CO	.25	.11	.03
☐ 6 Ellis Burks	1.25	.55	.16
☐ 7 Rick Burleson CO	.25	.11	.03
☐ 8 Jack Clark	.50	.23	.06
☐ 9 Roger Clemens	5.00	2.20	.60
☐ 10 Danny Darwin	.50	.23	.06
☐ 11 Tony Fossas	.25	.11	.03
☐ 12 Rich Gale CO	.25	.11	.03
☐ 13 Mike Gardiner	.25	.11	.03
☐ 14 Mike Greenwell	.75	.35	.09
☐ 15 Greg A. Harris	.25	.11	.03
☐ 16 Joe Hesketh	.25	.11	.03
☐ 17 Butch Hobson MG	.25	.11	.03
☐ 18 John Marzano	.25	.11	.03
☐ 19 Kevin Morton	.25	.11	.03
☐ 20 Tim Naehring	1.00	.45	.12
☐ 21 Tony Pena	.50	.23	.06
☐ 22 Phil Plantier	.25	.11	.03
☐ 23 Carlos Quintana	.25	.11	.03
☐ 24 Jeff Reardon	.75	.35	.09
☐ 25 Jody Reed	.50	.23	.06
☐ 26 Luis Rivera	.25	.11	.03
☐ 27 Mo Vaughn	5.00	2.20	.60
☐ 28 Frank Viola	.50	.23	.06
☐ 29 Matt Young	.25	.11	.03
☐ 30 Don Zimmer CO	.25	.11	.03

1993 Red Sox Winter Haven Police

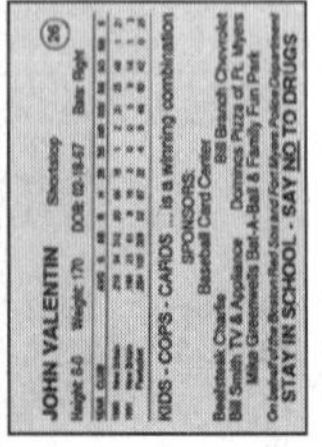

This 28-card standard-size set features players who were invited to the 1993 Red Sox spring training camp. The fronts feature posed studio shots while the backs feature recent stats as well as listing the various sponsors. Many of the stats only go through the 1991 season.

	MINT	NRMT	EXC
COMPLETE SET (28)	10.00	4.50	1.25
COMMON CARD (1-28)	.25	.11	.03
☐ 1 Checklist	.25	.11	.03
☐ 2 Scott Bankhead	.25	.11	.03
☐ 3 Danny Darwin	.50	.23	.06
☐ 4 Andre Dawson	1.00	.45	.12
☐ 5 Scott Fletcher	.25	.11	.03
☐ 6 Billy Hatcher	.25	.11	.03
☐ 7 Jack Clark	.50	.23	.06
☐ 8 Roger Clemens	3.00	1.35	.35
☐ 9 Scott Cooper	.25	.11	.03
☐ 10 John Dopson	.25	.11	.03
☐ 11 Paul Quantrill	.25	.11	.03
☐ 12 Mike Greenwell	.75	.35	.09
☐ 13 Greg A. Harris	.25	.11	.03
☐ 14 Joe Hesketh	.25	.11	.03
☐ 15 Peter Hoy	.25	.11	.03
☐ 16 Daryl Irvine	.25	.11	.03
☐ 17 John Marzano	.25	.11	.03
☐ 18 Jeff McNeely	.25	.11	.03
☐ 19 Tim Naehring	1.00	.45	.12
☐ 20 Matt Young	.25	.11	.03
☐ 21 Jeff Plympton	.25	.11	.03
☐ 22 Bob Melvin	.25	.11	.03
☐ 23 Tony Pena	.25	.11	.03
☐ 24 Luis Rivera	.25	.11	.03
☐ 25 Scott Taylor	.25	.11	.03
☐ 26 John Valentin	1.00	.45	.12
☐ 27 Mo Vaughn	3.00	1.35	.35
☐ 28 Frank Viola	.50	.23	.06

1920 Reds World's Champions PCs

This black and white set of Cincinnati players was issued in 1920 and appears with either of two captions in the border on the front of the card -- World Champions 1919 or National League Champions 1919.

	EX-MT	VG-E	GOOD
COMPLETE SET	1800.00	800.00	220.00
COMMON CARD	75.00	34.00	9.50
☐ 1 Nick Allen	75.00	34.00	9.50
☐ 2 Rube Bressler	75.00	34.00	9.50
☐ 3 Jake Daubert	75.00	34.00	9.50
☐ 4 Pat Duncan	75.00	34.00	9.50
☐ 5 Hod Eller	75.00	34.00	9.50
☐ 6 Ray Fisher	75.00	34.00	9.50
☐ 7 Eddie Gerner	75.00	34.00	9.50
☐ 8 Heine Groh	125.00	55.00	15.50
☐ 9 Larry Kopf	75.00	34.00	9.50
☐ 10 Adolfo Luque	125.00	55.00	15.50
☐ 11 Sherwood Magee	75.00	34.00	9.50
☐ 12 Roy Mitchell	75.00	34.00	9.50
☐ 13 Pat Moran MG	75.00	34.00	9.50
☐ 14 Greasy Neale	125.00	55.00	15.50
☐ 15 Bill Rariden	75.00	34.00	9.50
☐ 16 Morris Rath	75.00	34.00	9.50
☐ 17 Jimmy Ring	75.00	34.00	9.50
☐ 18 Edd Roush	150.00	70.00	19.00
☐ 19 Walter Reuther	75.00	34.00	9.50
☐ 20 Harry Sallee	75.00	34.00	9.50
☐ 21 Hank Schreiber	75.00	34.00	9.50
☐ 22 Charles See	75.00	34.00	9.50
☐ 23 Jimmy Smith	75.00	34.00	9.50
☐ 24 Ivy Wingo	75.00	34.00	9.50
☐ 25 Team Card	400.00	180.00	50.00

1957 Reds Sohio

The 1957 Sohio Cincinnati Reds set consists of 18 perforated photos, approximately 5" by 7", in black and white with facsimile autographs on the front which were designed to be pasted into a special photo album issued by SOHIO (Standard Oil of Ohio). The set features an early Frank Robinson card. These unnumbered cards are listed below in alphabetical order for convenience.

	NRMT	VG-E	GOOD
COMPLETE SET (18)	200.00	90.00	25.00
COMMON CARD (1-18)	7.50	3.40	.95
☐ 1 Ed Bailey	7.50	3.40	.95
☐ 2 Gus Bell	10.00	4.50	1.25
☐ 3 Rocky Bridges	7.50	3.40	.95
☐ 4 Smoky Burgess	10.00	4.50	1.25
☐ 5 Hersh Freeman	7.50	3.40	.95
☐ 6 Alex Grammas	7.50	3.40	.95
☐ 7 Don Gross	7.50	3.40	.95
☐ 8 Warren Hacker	7.50	3.40	.95
☐ 9 Don Hoak	10.00	4.50	1.25
☐ 10 Hal Jeffcoat	7.50	3.40	.95
☐ 11 Johnny Klippstein	7.50	3.40	.95
☐ 12 Ted Kluszewski	50.00	22.00	6.25
☐ 13 Brooks Lawrence	7.50	3.40	.95
☐ 14 Roy McMillan	7.50	3.40	.95
☐ 15 Joe Nuxhall	10.00	4.50	1.25
☐ 16 Wally Post	10.00	4.50	1.25
☐ 17 Frank Robinson	100.00	45.00	12.50
☐ 18 John Temple	10.00	4.50	1.25

1958 Reds Enquirer

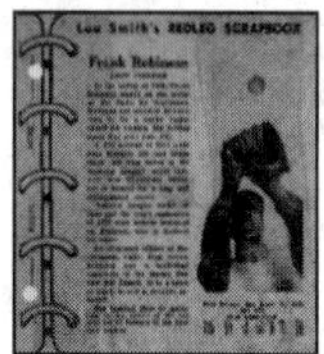

This set consists of Lou Smith's Redleg Scrapbook newspaper clippings from the Cincinnati Enquirer and features black-and-white photos of the members of the 1958 Cincinnati Reds team with information about the players. The clippings were designed to be placed in an album. They are unnumbered and checklisted below in alphabetical order.

	NRMT	VG-E	GOOD
COMPLETE SET (44)	75.00	34.00	9.50
COMMON CARD (1-44)	1.50	.70	.19
☐ 1 Tom Acker	1.50	.70	.19
☐ 2 Chico Alvarez	1.50	.70	.19
☐ 3 Ed Bailey	1.50	.70	.19
☐ 4 Gus Bell	1.50	.70	.19
☐ 5 Steve Bilko	1.50	.70	.19
☐ 6 Smoky Burgess	2.00	.90	.25
☐ 7 Jerry Cade	1.50	.70	.19
☐ 8 George Crowe	2.00	.90	.25
☐ 9 Dutch Dotterer	1.50	.70	.19
☐ 10 Jimmy Dykes CO	2.50	1.10	.30
☐ 11 Tom Ferrick CO	1.50	.70	.19
☐ 12 Dee Fondy	1.50	.70	.19
☐ 13 Hersh Freeman	1.50	.70	.19
☐ 14 Buddy Gilbert	1.50	.70	.19
☐ 15 Harvey Haddix	2.50	1.10	.30
☐ 16 Bob Henrich	1.50	.70	.19
☐ 17 Don Hoak	2.00	.90	.25
☐ 18 Ken Hommel	1.50	.70	.19
☐ 19 Jay Hook	1.50	.70	.19
☐ 20 Hal Jeffcoat	1.50	.70	.19
☐ 21 Bob Kelly	1.50	.70	.19
☐ 22 John Klippstein	1.50	.70	.19
☐ 23 Marty Kutyna	1.50	.70	.19
☐ 24 Brooks Lawrence	2.00	.90	.25
☐ 25 Jerry Lynch	1.50	.70	.19
☐ 26 Roy McMillan	1.50	.70	.19
☐ 27 Joe Nuxhall	2.00	.90	.25
☐ 28 Jim O'Toole	1.50	.70	.19
☐ 29 Stan Palys	1.50	.70	.19
☐ 30 Bob Purkey	1.50	.70	.19
☐ 31 Charley Rabe	1.50	.70	.19
☐ 32 Johnny Riddle CO	1.50	.70	.19
☐ 33 Frank Robinson	10.00	4.50	1.25
☐ 34 Haven Schmidt	1.50	.70	.19
☐ 35 Willard Schmidt	1.50	.70	.19
☐ 36 Dave Skaugstad	1.50	.70	.19
☐ 37 John Smith	1.50	.70	.19
☐ 38 Birdie Tebbetts MG	1.50	.70	.19
☐ 39 John Temple	1.50	.70	.19
☐ 40 Bob Thurman	1.50	.70	.19
☐ 41 Pete Whisenant	1.50	.70	.19
☐ 42 Ted Wieand	1.50	.70	.19
☐ 43 Bill Wight	1.50	.70	.19
☐ 44 Album	15.00	6.75	1.85

1958 Reds Jay Publishing

This 12-card set of the Cincinnati Reds measures approximately 5" by 7" and features black-and-white player photos in a white border. These cards were packaged 12 to a packet. The backs are blank. The cards are unnumbered and checklisted below in alphabetical order.

	NRMT	VG-E	GOOD
COMPLETE SET (12)	30.00	13.50	3.70
COMMON CARD (1-12)	2.00	.90	.25
☐ 1 Ed Bailey	2.00	.90	.25
☐ 2 Gus Bell	2.00	.90	.25
☐ 3 Steve Bilko	2.00	.90	.25
☐ 4 Smoky Burgess	2.50	1.10	.30
☐ 5 George Crowe	2.50	1.10	.30
☐ 6 Harvey Haddix	2.50	1.10	.30

	NRMT	VG-E	GOOD
☐ 7 Don Hoak	2.00	.90	.25
☐ 8 Hal Jeffcoat	2.00	.90	.25
☐ 9 Roy McMillan	2.50	1.10	.30
☐ 10 Bob Purkey	2.00	.90	.25
☐ 11 Frank Robinson	6.00	2.70	.75
☐ 12 Birdie Tebbetts MG	2.50	1.10	.30

1959 Reds Enquirer

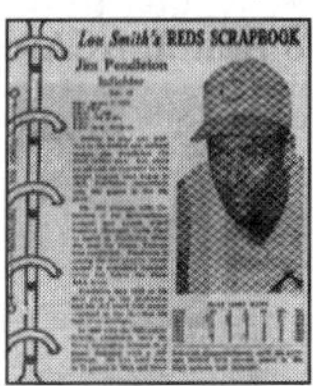

This set consists of Lou Smith's Reds Scrapbook newspaper clippings from the Cincinnati Enquirer and features black-and-white photos of the members of the 1959 Cincinnati Reds team with information about the players. The clippings are unnumbered and checklisted below in alphabetical order.

	NRMT	VG-E	GOOD
COMPLETE SET (28)	35.00	16.00	4.40
COMMON CARD (1-28)	1.50	.70	.19
☐ 1 Tom Acker	1.50	.70	.19
☐ 2 Ed Bailey	1.50	.70	.19
☐ 3 Chuck Coles	2.00	.90	.25
☐ 4 Dutch Dotterer	1.50	.70	.19
☐ 5 Walt Dropo	1.50	.70	.19
☐ 6 Del Ennis	1.50	.70	.19
☐ 7 Jim Fridley	1.50	.70	.19
☐ 8 Buddy Gilbert	1.50	.70	.19
☐ 9 Jesse Gonder	1.50	.70	.19
☐ 10 Bob Henrich	1.50	.70	.19
☐ 11 Hal Jeffcoat	1.50	.70	.19
☐ 12 Brooks Lawrence	2.00	.90	.25
☐ 13 Bobbie Mabe	1.50	.70	.19
☐ 14 Roy McMillan	1.50	.70	.19
☐ 15 Don Newcombe	3.50	1.55	.45
☐ 16 Joe Nuxhall	1.50	.70	.19
☐ 17 Claude Osteen	2.00	.90	.25
☐ 18 Don Pavletich	1.50	.70	.19
☐ 19 Orlando Pena	1.50	.70	.19
☐ 20 Jim Pendleton	1.50	.70	.19
☐ 21 John Powers	1.50	.70	.19
☐ 22 Charley Rabe	1.50	.70	.19
☐ 23 Willard Schmidt	1.50	.70	.19
☐ 24 Mayo Smith MG	2.00	.90	.25
☐ 25 Johnny Temple	1.50	.70	.19
☐ 26 Frank Thomas	1.50	.70	.19
☐ 27 Bob Thurman	1.50	.70	.19
☐ 28 Ted Wieand	1.50	.70	.19

1960 Reds Jay Publishing

This 12-card set of the Cincinnati Reds measures approximately 5" by 7". The fronts feature black-and-white posed player photos with the player's and team name printed below in the white border. These cards were packaged 12 in a packet and originally sold for 25 cents. The backs are blank. The cards are unnumbered and checklisted below in alphabetical order.

	NRMT	VG-E	GOOD
COMPLETE SET (12)	30.00	13.50	3.70
COMMON CARD (1-12)	2.00	.90	.25
☐ 1 Gus Bell	2.00	.90	.25
☐ 2 Dutch Dotterer	2.00	.90	.25
☐ 3 Jay Hook	2.00	.90	.25
☐ 4 Fred Hutchinson MG	3.00	1.35	.35
☐ 5 Roy McMillan	3.00	1.35	.35
☐ 6 Don Newcombe	4.00	1.80	.50
☐ 7 Joe Nuxhall	2.00	.90	.25
☐ 8 Jim O'Toole	2.00	.90	.25
☐ 9 Orlanda Pena	2.00	.90	.25
☐ 10 Vada Pinson	5.00	2.20	.60
☐ 11 Bob Purkey	2.00	.90	.25
☐ 12 Frank Robinson	10.00	4.50	1.25

1961 Reds Jay Publishing

This 12-card set of the Cincinnati Reds measures approximately 5" by 7". The fronts feature black-and-white posed player photos with the player's and team name printed below in the white border. These cards were packaged 12 in a packet. The backs are blank. The cards are unnumbered and checklisted below in alphabetical order.

	NRMT	VG-E	GOOD
COMPLETE SET (12)	35.00	16.00	4.40
COMMON CARD (1-12)	2.50	1.10	.30
☐ 1 Ed Bailey	2.50	1.10	.30
☐ 2 Jim Baumer	2.50	1.10	.30
☐ 3 Gus Bell	3.00	1.35	.35
☐ 4 Gordon Coleman	2.50	1.10	.30
☐ 5 Fred Hutchinson MG	3.00	1.35	.35
☐ 6 Joey Jay	3.00	1.35	.35
☐ 7 Willie Jones	2.50	1.10	.30
☐ 8 Eddie Kasko	2.50	1.10	.30
☐ 9 Jerry Lynch	2.50	1.10	.30
☐ 10 Claude Osteen	3.00	1.35	.35
☐ 11 Vada Pinson	5.00	2.20	.60
☐ 12 Frank Robinson	12.50	5.50	1.55

1962 Reds Enquirer

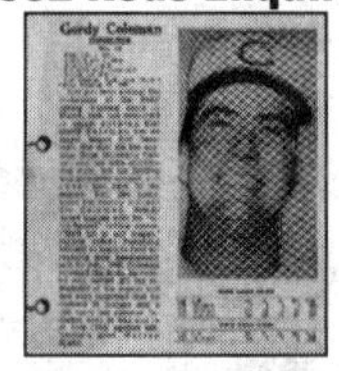

This set consists of newspaper clippings from the Cincinnati Enquirer and features black-and-white photos of the members of the 1962 Cincinnati Reds team with information about the players. They are unnumbered and checklisted below in alphabetical order.

	NRMT	VG-E	GOOD
COMPLETE SET (32)	50.00	22.00	6.25
COMMON CARD (1-32)	1.50	.70	.19
☐ 1 Don Blasingame	1.50	.70	.19
☐ 2 Jim Brosnan	1.50	.70	.19
☐ 3 Leo Cardenas	2.00	.90	.25
☐ 4 Gordy Coleman	1.50	.70	.19
☐ 5 Cliff Cook	1.50	.70	.19
☐ 6 Myron Drabowsky	1.50	.70	.19
☐ 7 John Edwards	1.50	.70	.19
☐ 8 Gene Freese	1.50	.70	.19
☐ 9 Joe Gaines	1.50	.70	.19
☐ 10 Jesse Gonder	1.50	.70	.19
☐ 11 Tom Harper	2.00	.90	.25
☐ 12 Bill Henry	1.50	.70	.19
☐ 13 Dave Hillman	1.50	.70	.19
☐ 14 Ken Hunt	1.50	.70	.19
☐ 15 Fred Hutchinson MG	2.00	.90	.25
☐ 16 Joey Jay	1.50	.70	.19
☐ 17 Darrell Johnson	1.50	.70	.19
☐ 18 Eddie Kasko	1.50	.70	.19
☐ 19 Marty Keough	1.50	.70	.19
☐ 20 John Klippstein	1.50	.70	.19
☐ 21 Jerry Lynch	1.50	.70	.19
☐ 22 Jim Maloney	1.50	.70	.19
☐ 23 Bob Miller	1.50	.70	.19
☐ 24 Jim O'Toole	1.50	.70	.19
☐ 25 Don Pavletich	1.50	.70	.19
☐ 26 Vada Pinson	3.00	1.35	.35
☐ 27 Wally Post	2.00	.90	.25
☐ 28 Bob Purkey	1.50	.70	.19
☐ 29 Frank Robinson	10.00	4.50	1.25
☐ 30 Octavio Rojas	1.50	.70	.19
☐ 31 Hiraldo Ruiz	1.50	.70	.19
☐ 32 Dave Sisler	1.50	.70	.19

1962 Reds Jay Publishing

This 12-card set features members of the Cincinnati Reds. Originally, this set came in a brown envelope that included a "picture pak order form". Printed on thin stock paper, the cards measure approximately 5" by 7". On a white background the fronts have a black-and-white posed player photo. The player's name and team appear in black letters under the photo. The backs are blank. The cards are unnumbered and checklisted below in alphabetical order.

	NRMT	VG-E	GOOD
COMPLETE SET (12)	30.00	13.50	3.70
COMMON CARD (1-12)	2.50	1.10	.30
☐ 1 Jim Brosnan	2.50	1.10	.30
☐ 2 Leo Cardenas	2.50	1.10	.30
☐ 3 Gordon Coleman	2.50	1.10	.30
☐ 4 Jess Gonder	2.50	1.10	.30
☐ 5 Fred Hutchinson MG	3.00	1.35	.35
☐ 6 Joey Jay	3.00	1.35	.35
☐ 7 Eddie Kasko	2.50	1.10	.30
☐ 8 Jerry Lynch	2.50	1.10	.30
☐ 9 Jim O'Toole	3.00	1.35	.35
☐ 10 Vada Pinson	4.50	2.00	.55
☐ 11 Wally Post	3.50	1.55	.45
☐ 12 Frank Robinson	10.00	4.50	1.25

1963 Reds Enquirer

This set consists of newspaper clippings from the Reds' Scrapbook found in the Cincinnati Enquirer and features black-and-white photos of the members of the 1963 Cincinnati Reds team with information about the players. They are unnumbered and checklisted below in alphabetical order.

	NRMT	VG-E	GOOD
COMPLETE SET (33)	75.00	34.00	9.50
COMMON CARD (1-33)	1.50	.70	.19
☐ 1 Don Blasingame	1.50	.70	.19
☐ 2 Harry Bright	1.50	.70	.19
☐ 3 Jim Brosnan	1.50	.70	.19
☐ 4 Leo Cardenas	1.50	.70	.19
☐ 5 Gordy Coleman	1.50	.70	.19
☐ 6 John Edwards	1.50	.70	.19
☐ 7 Sam Ellis	1.50	.70	.19
☐ 8 Hank Foiles	1.50	.70	.19
☐ 9 Gene Freese	1.50	.70	.19
☐ 10 Jesse Gonder	1.50	.70	.19
☐ 11 Tom Harper	2.00	.90	.25
☐ 12 Bill Henry	1.50	.70	.19
☐ 13 Ken Hunt	1.50	.70	.19
☐ 14 Fred Hutchinson MG	2.00	.90	.25
☐ 15 Joey Jay	1.50	.70	.19
☐ 16 Eddie Kasko	1.50	.70	.19
☐ 17 Marty Keough	1.50	.70	.19
☐ 18 John Klippstein	1.50	.70	.19
☐ 19 Jerry Lynch	1.50	.70	.19
☐ 20 Jim Maloney	1.50	.70	.19
☐ 21 Joe Nuxall	1.50	.70	.19
☐ 22 Jim O'Toole	1.50	.70	.19
☐ 23 Jim Owens	1.50	.70	.19
☐ 24 Don Pavletich	1.50	.70	.19
☐ 25 Vada Pinson	3.00	1.35	.35
☐ 26 Wally Post	2.00	.90	.25
☐ 27 Bob Purkey	1.50	.70	.19
☐ 28 Frank Robinson	10.00	4.50	1.25
☐ 29 Dave Sisler	1.50	.70	.19
☐ 30 John Tsitouris	1.50	.70	.19
☐ 31 Ken Walters	1.50	.70	.19
☐ 32 Pete Rose	35.00	16.00	4.40
☐ 33 Al Worthington	1.50	.70	.19

1963 Reds French Bauer Caps

These are a 32 "card" set of (cardboard) milk bottle caps featuring personnel of the Cincinnati Reds. These unattractive cardboard caps are blank-backed and unnumbered; they are numbered below for convenience in alphabetical order. The caps are approximately 1 1/4" in diameter. Blasingame was traded to the Senators early in the '63 season and Spencer was picked up from the Dodgers early in the '63 season; hence their caps are tougher to find than the others. Ken Walters and Don Pavletich also seem to be harder to find.

	NRMT	VG-E	GOOD
COMPLETE SET (32)	400.00	180.00	50.00
COMMON CAP	5.00	2.20	.60
☐ 1 Don Blasingame	12.50	5.50	1.55
☐ 2 Leo Cardenas	7.50	3.40	.95
☐ 3 Gordon Coleman	5.00	2.20	.60
☐ 4 Wm. O. DeWitt OWN	5.00	2.20	.60
☐ 5 John Edwards	5.00	2.20	.60
☐ 6 Jesse Gonder	5.00	2.20	.60
☐ 7 Tommy Harper	7.50	3.40	.95
☐ 8 Bill Henry	5.00	2.20	.60
☐ 9 Fred Hutchinson MG	7.50	3.40	.95
☐ 10 Joey Jay	7.50	3.40	.95
☐ 11 Eddie Kasko	5.00	2.20	.60
☐ 12 Marty Keough	5.00	2.20	.60
☐ 13 Jim Maloney	7.50	3.40	.95
☐ 14 Joe Nuxhall	7.50	3.40	.95
☐ 15 Reggie Otero CO	5.00	2.20	.60
☐ 16 Jim O'Toole	7.50	3.40	.95
☐ 17 Jim Owens	5.00	2.20	.60
☐ 18 Don Pavletich	12.50	5.50	1.55
☐ 19 Vada Pinson	10.00	4.50	1.25
☐ 20 Bob Purkey	5.00	2.20	.60
☐ 21 Dr. Richard Rohde	5.00	2.20	.60
☐ 22 Frank Robinson	50.00	22.00	6.25
☐ 23 Pete Rose	200.00	90.00	25.00
☐ 24 Ray Shore CO	5.00	2.20	.60
☐ 25 Dick Sisler CO	5.00	2.20	.60
☐ 26 Bob Skinner	7.50	3.40	.95
☐ 27 Daryl Spencer	25.00	11.00	3.10
☐ 28 John Tsitouris	5.00	2.20	.60
☐ 29 Jim Turner CO	5.00	2.20	.60
☐ 30 Ken Walters	12.50	5.50	1.55
☐ 31 Al Worthington	5.00	2.20	.60
☐ 32 Dom Zanni	5.00	2.20	.60

1963 Reds Jay Publishing

This 12-card set features members of the Cincinnati Reds. Printed on thin stock paper, the cards measure approximately 5" by 7". On a white background the fronts have a black-and-white posed player photo. The player's name and team appear in black letters under the photo. The backs are blank. The cards are unnumbered and checklisted below in alphabetical order.

	NRMT	VG-E	GOOD
COMPLETE SET (12)	30.00	13.50	3.70
COMMON CARD (1-12)	2.00	.90	.25
☐ 1 Jim Brosnan	2.00	.90	.25
☐ 2 Gordy Coleman	2.00	.90	.25
☐ 3 Fred Hutchinson MG	4.00	1.80	.50
☐ 4 Joey Jay	3.00	1.35	.35
☐ 5 Eddie Kasko	2.00	.90	.25
☐ 6 Marty Keough	2.00	.90	.25
☐ 7 Jerry Lynch	2.00	.90	.25
☐ 8 Jim O'Toole	4.00	1.80	.50
☐ 9 Don Pavletich	2.00	.90	.25
☐ 10 Vada Pinson	5.00	2.20	.60
☐ 11 Bob Purkey	2.00	.90	.25
☐ 12 Frank Robinson	10.00	4.50	1.25

1964 Reds Jay Publishing

This 12-card set of the Cincinnati Reds measures approximately 5" by 7". The fronts feature black-and-white posed player photos with the player's and team name printed below in the white border. These cards were packaged 12 in a packet. The backs are blank. The cards are unnumbered and checklisted below in alphabetical order.

	NRMT	VG-E	GOOD
COMPLETE SET (12)	35.00	16.00	4.40
COMMON CARD (1-12)	2.00	.90	.25
☐ 1 Leo Cardenas	2.00	.90	.25
☐ 2 Gordy Coleman	2.00	.90	.25
☐ 3 Tommy Harper	3.00	1.35	.35
☐ 4 Fred Hutchinson MG	2.00	.90	.25
☐ 5 Joey Jay	3.00	1.35	.35
☐ 6 Jim Maloney	3.00	1.35	.35
☐ 7 Joe Nuxhall	2.00	.90	.25
☐ 8 Jim O'Toole	3.00	1.35	.35
☐ 9 Vada Pinson	4.00	1.80	.50
☐ 10 Bob Purkey	2.00	.90	.25
☐ 11 Frank Robinson	6.00	2.70	.75
☐ 12 Pete Rose	15.00	6.75	1.85

1965 Reds Enquirer

This set consists of newspaper clippings from the Cincinnati Enquirer and features black-and-white photos of the members of the 1965 Cincinnati Reds team with information about the players. They are unnumbered and checklisted below in alphabetical order.

	NRMT	VG-E	GOOD
COMPLETE SET (29)	60.00	27.00	7.50
COMMON CARD (1-29)	1.50	.70	.19

□ 1 Gerry Arrigo	1.50	.70	.19
□ 2 Steve Boros	1.50	.70	.19
□ 3 Leo Cardenas	1.50	.70	.19
□ 4 Jim Coker	1.50	.70	.19
□ 5 Gordy Coleman	1.50	.70	.19
□ 6 Roger Craig	3.00	1.35	.35
□ 7 Ryne Duren	2.00	.90	.25
□ 8 John Edwards	1.50	.70	.19
□ 9 Sammy Ellis	1.50	.70	.19
□ 10 Tommy Harper	2.00	.90	.25
□ 11 Tommy Helms	2.00	.90	.25
□ 12 Bill Henry	1.50	.70	.19
□ 13 Charley James	1.50	.70	.19
□ 14 Joey Jay	1.50	.70	.19
□ 15 Deron Johnson	1.50	.70	.19
□ 16 Marty Keough	1.50	.70	.19
□ 17 Jim Maloney	2.00	.90	.25
□ 18 Bill McCool	1.50	.70	.19
□ 19 Joe Nuxhall	2.00	.90	.25
□ 20 Jim O'Toole	1.50	.70	.19
□ 21 Don Pavletich	1.50	.70	.19
□ 22 Tony Perez	7.50	3.40	.95
□ 23 Vada Pinson	3.00	1.35	.35
□ 24 Frank Robinson	10.00	4.50	1.25
□ 25 Pete Rose	25.00	11.00	3.10
□ 26 Hiraldo S.(Chico) Ruiz	1.50	.70	.19
□ 27 Art Shamsky	1.50	.70	.19
□ 28 Dick Sisler MG	2.00	.90	.25
□ 29 John Tsitouris	1.50	.70	.19

1976 Reds Icee Lids

This unnumbered and blank-backed set of "lids" is complete at 12. Cards are listed below in alphabetical order. They are circular cards with the bottom squared off. The circle is approximately 2" in diameter. The fronts contain the MLB logo as well as the player's name, position and team. The player photo is in black and white with the cap logo removed.

	NRMT	VG-E	GOOD
COMPLETE SET	50.00	22.00	6.25
COMMON LID (1-12)	.50	.23	.06
□ 1 Johnny Bench	15.00	6.75	1.85
□ 2 Dave Concepcion	2.50	1.10	.30
□ 3 Rawley Eastwick	.50	.23	.06
□ 4 George Foster	2.50	1.10	.30
□ 5 Cesar Geronimo	.50	.23	.06
□ 6 Ken Griffey	2.50	1.10	.30
□ 7 Don Gullett	.50	.23	.06
□ 8 Will McEnaney	.50	.23	.06
□ 9 Joe Morgan	7.50	3.40	.95
□ 10 Gary Nolan	.50	.23	.06
□ 11 Tony Perez	5.00	2.20	.60
□ 12 Pete Rose	25.00	11.00	3.10

1976 Reds Kroger

This 16-card set of the Cincinnati Reds measures approximately 5 7/8" by 9". The white-bordered fronts feature color player head photos with a facsimile autograph below. The backs are blank. The cards are unnumbered and checklisted below in alphabetical order.

	NRMT	VG-E	GOOD
COMPLETE SET (16)	25.00	11.00	3.10
COMMON CARD (1-16)	1.00	.45	.12
□ 1 Ed Armbrister	1.00	.45	.12
□ 2 Bob Bailey	1.00	.45	.12
□ 3 Johnny Bench	5.00	2.20	.60
□ 4 Jack Billingham	1.00	.45	.12
□ 5 Dave Concepcion	2.00	.90	.25
□ 6 Dan Driessen	1.00	.45	.12
□ 7 Rawly Eastwick	1.00	.45	.12
□ 8 George Foster	2.00	.90	.25
□ 9 Cesar Geronimo	1.00	.45	.12
□ 10 Ken Griffey	3.00	1.35	.35
□ 11 Don Gullett	1.00	.45	.12
□ 12 Joe Morgan	4.00	1.80	.50
□ 13 Gary Nolan	1.00	.45	.12
□ 14 Fred Norman	1.00	.45	.12
□ 15 Tony Perez	3.00	1.35	.35
□ 16 Pete Rose	7.50	3.40	.95

1976 Reds Posters

This 15-poster set features the 1976 Cincinnati Reds. The color head and shoulders shots measure approximately 5 7/8" by 9" and are printed in thin glossy paper. The pictures are bordered in white and have the players' autographs inscribed across them. The backs are blank and the pictures are checklisted below in alphabetical order.

	NRMT	VG-E	GOOD
COMPLETE SET (15)	40.00	18.00	5.00
COMMON CARD (1-15)	2.00	.90	.25
□ 1 Ed Armbrister	2.00	.90	.25
□ 2 Bob Bailey	2.00	.90	.25
□ 3 Johnny Bench	5.00	2.20	.60
□ 4 Jack Billingham	2.00	.90	.25
□ 5 Dave Concepcion	3.50	1.55	.45
□ 6 Dan Driessen	2.50	1.10	.30
□ 7 Rawly Eastwick	2.00	.90	.25
□ 8 George Foster	3.50	1.55	.45
□ 9 Ken Griffey	3.50	1.55	.45
□ 10 Don Gullett	2.00	.90	.25
□ 11 Joe Morgan	4.00	1.80	.50
□ 12 Gary Nolan	2.00	.90	.25
□ 13 Fred Norman	2.00	.90	.25
□ 14 Tony Perez	4.00	1.80	.50
□ 15 Pete Rose	10.00	4.50	1.25

1980 Reds Enquirer

This set features members of the 1980 Cincinnati Reds. The cards are sequenced by uniform numbers.

	NRMT	VG-E	GOOD
COMPLETE SET	12.50	5.50	1.55
COMMON CARD	.25	.11	.03
□ 2 Russ Nixon CO	.25	.11	.03
□ 3 John McNamara MG	.25	.11	.03
□ 4 Harry Dunlop CO	.25	.11	.03
□ 5 Johnny Bench	4.00	1.80	.50
□ 6 Bill Fischer CO	.25	.11	.03
□ 7 Hector Cruz	.25	.11	.03
□ 9 Vic Correll	.25	.11	.03
□ 11 Ron Plaza CO	.25	.11	.03
□ 12 Harry Spilman	.25	.11	.03
□ 13 Dave Concepcion	1.50	.70	.19
□ 15 George Foster	1.00	.45	.12
□ 16 Ron Oester	.25	.11	.03
□ 19 Don Werner	.25	.11	.03
□ 20 Cesar Geronimo	.25	.11	.03
□ 22 Dan Driessen	.25	.11	.03
□ 23 Rick Auerbach	.25	.11	.03
□ 25 Ray Knight	.75	.35	.09
□ 26 Junior Kennedy	.25	.11	.03
□ 28 Sam Mejias	.25	.11	.03
□ 29 Dave Collins	.25	.11	.03
□ 30 Ken Griffey	1.00	.45	.12
□ 31 Paul Moskau	.25	.11	.03
□ 34 Sheldon Burnside	.25	.11	.03
□ 35 Frank Pastore	.25	.11	.03
□ 36 Mario Soto	.25	.11	.03
□ 37 Dave Tomlin	.25	.11	.03
□ 40 Doug Bair	.25	.11	.03
□ 41 Tom Seaver	2.50	1.10	.30
□ 42 Bill Bonham	.25	.11	.03
□ 44 Charlie Leibrandt	.25	.11	.03
□ 47 Tom Hume	.25	.11	.03
□ 51 Mike LaCoss	.25	.11	.03

1982 Reds Coke

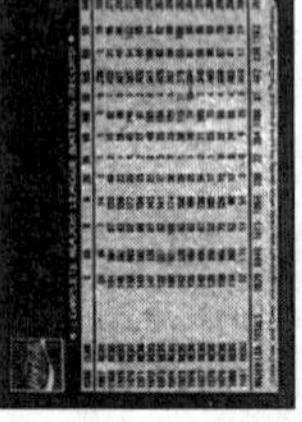

The cards in this 23-card set measure the standard size. The 1982 Coca-Cola Cincinnati Reds set, issued in conjunction with Topps, contains 22 cards of current Reds players. Although the cards of 15 players feature the exact photo used in the Topps' regular issue, the Coke photos have better coloration and appear sharper than their Topps counterparts. Six players, Cedeno, Harris, Hurdle, Kern, Krenchicki, and Trevino are new to the Reds uniform via trades, while Paul Householder had formerly appeared on the Reds' 1982 Topps "Future Stars" card. The cards are numbered 1 to 22 on the red and gray reverse, and the Coke logo appears on both sides of the card. There is an unnumbered title card which contains a premium offer on the reverse. The set numbering is in alphabetical order by player's name.

	NRMT	VG-E	GOOD
COMPLETE SET (23)	8.00	3.60	1.00
COMMON CARD (1-22)	.25	.11	.03
□ 1 Johnny Bench	3.00	1.35	.35
□ 2 Bruce Berenyi	.25	.11	.03
□ 3 Larry Biittner	.25	.11	.03
□ 4 Cesar Cedeno	.50	.23	.06
□ 5 Dave Concepcion	.75	.35	.09
□ 6 Dan Driessen	.25	.11	.03
□ 7 Greg A. Harris	.50	.23	.06
□ 8 Paul Householder	.25	.11	.03
□ 9 Tom Hume	.25	.11	.03
□ 10 Clint Hurdle	.25	.11	.03
□ 11 Jim Kern	.25	.11	.03
□ 12 Wayne Krenchicki	.25	.11	.03
□ 13 Rafael Landestoy	.25	.11	.03
□ 14 Charlie Leibrandt	.25	.11	.03
□ 15 Mike O'Berry	.25	.11	.03
□ 16 Ron Oester	.25	.11	.03
□ 17 Frank Pastore	.25	.11	.03
□ 18 Joe Price	.25	.11	.03
□ 19 Tom Seaver	3.00	1.35	.35
□ 20 Mario Soto	.50	.23	.06
□ 21 Alex Trevino	.25	.11	.03
□ 22 Mike Vail	.25	.11	.03
□ NNO Title Card	.15	.07	.02

1983 Reds Yearbook

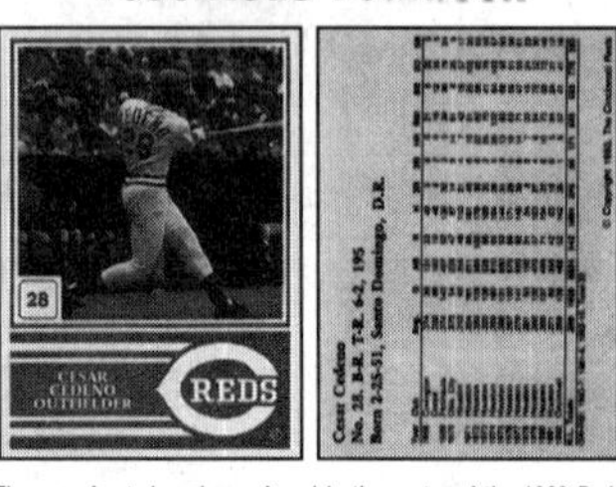

These perforated cards are found in the center of the 1983 Reds Yearbook; they are numbered by uniform number; cards are in full color; backs contain year by year statistical information. The yearbook itself originally sold (cover price) for $3.00. The cards are sequenced in uniform number order.

	NRMT	VG-E	GOOD
COMPLETE SET	5.00	2.20	.60
COMMON CARD	.25	.11	.03
□ 2 Gary Redus	.25	.11	.03
□ 5 Johnny Bench	2.50	1.10	.30
□ 7 Russ Nixon MG	.25	.11	.03
□ 13 Dave Concepcion	.75	.35	.09
□ 16 Ron Oester	.25	.11	.03
□ 20 Eddie Milner	.25	.11	.03
□ 21 Paul Householder	.25	.11	.03
□ 22 Dan Driessen	.25	.11	.03
□ 25 Charlie Puleo	.25	.11	.03
□ 28 Cesar Cedeno	.50	.23	.06
□ 29 Alex Trevino	.25	.11	.03
□ 32 Rich Gale	.25	.11	.03
□ 35 Frank Pastore	.25	.11	.03
□ 36 Mario Soto	.50	.23	.06
□ 38 Bruce Berenyi	.25	.11	.03
□ 47 Tom Hume	.25	.11	.03
□ 49 Joe Price	.25	.11	.03
□ xx Riverfront Stadium	.25	.11	.03

1984 Reds Borden's

This set of eight stickers featuring Eric Davis' first Cincinnati card, was produced as two sheets of four by Borden's Dairy. The sheets are perforated so that the individual stickers may be separated. The sheet of four stickers measures approximately 5 1/2" by 8" whereas the individual stickers measure 2 1/2" by 3 7/8". The backs of the stickers feature discount "cents off" coupons applicable to Borden's products. The fronts feature a full color photo of the player in a bold red border. The stickers are not numbered except that each player's uniform number is given prominently on the front. The sheets are arbitrarily numbered one and two and designated in the checklist below.

	NRMT	VG-E	GOOD
COMPLETE SET (8)	8.00	3.60	1.00
COMMON CARD	.25	.11	.03
□ 2 Gary Redus (sheet 2)	.25	.11	.03
□ 16 Ron Oester (sheet 1)	.25	.11	.03
□ 20 Eddie Milner (sheet 2)	.25	.11	.03
□ 24 Tony Perez (sheet 2)	2.50	1.10	.30
□ 36 Mario Soto (sheet 1)	.25	.11	.03
□ 39 Dave Parker (sheet 1)	1.50	.70	.19
□ 44 Eric Davis (sheet 1)	4.00	1.80	.50
□ 46 Jeff Russell (sheet 2)	.50	.23	.06

1984 Reds Enquirer

This set consists of newspaper clippings from the Cincinnati Enquirer and features black-and-white head photos of the members of the 1984 Cincinnati Reds team with information about the players.

	NRMT	VG-E	GOOD
COMPLETE SET (32)	15.00	6.75	1.85
COMMON CARD (1-32)	.25	.11	.03
□ 1 Tony Perez	1.50	.70	.19
□ 2 Dan Driessen	.25	.11	.03
□ 3 Ron Oester	.25	.11	.03
□ 4 Tom Lawless	.25	.11	.03
□ 5 Dave Concepcion	.75	.35	.09
□ 6 Tom Foley	.25	.11	.03
□ 7 Nick Esasky	.25	.11	.03
□ 8 Wayne Krenchicki	.25	.11	.03
□ 9 Gary Redus	.25	.11	.03
□ 10 Duane Walker	.25	.11	.03
□ 11 Eddie Milner	.25	.11	.03
□ 12 Dave Parker	1.00	.45	.12
□ 13 Cesar Cedeno	.50	.23	.06
□ 14 Dann Bilardello	.25	.11	.03
□ 15 Brad Gulden	.25	.11	.03
□ 16 Jeff Russell	.25	.11	.03
□ 17 Joe Price	.25	.11	.03
□ 18 Bill Scherrer	.25	.11	.03
□ 19 Tom Hume	.25	.11	.03
□ 20 Bruce Berenyi	.25	.11	.03
□ 21 Bob Owchinko	.25	.11	.03
□ 22 Ted Power	.25	.11	.03
□ 23 Frank Pastore	.25	.11	.03
□ 24 John Franco	2.00	.90	.25
□ 25 Mario Soto	.50	.23	.06
□ 26 Eric Davis	5.00	2.20	.60
□ 27 Tommy Helms CO	.25	.11	.03
□ 28 Bruce Kimm CO	.25	.11	.03
□ 29 George Scherger CO	.25	.11	.03
□ 30 Joe Sparks CO	.25	.11	.03
□ 31 Stan Williams CO	.25	.11	.03
□ 32 Vern Rapp MG	.25	.11	.03

1985 Reds Yearbook

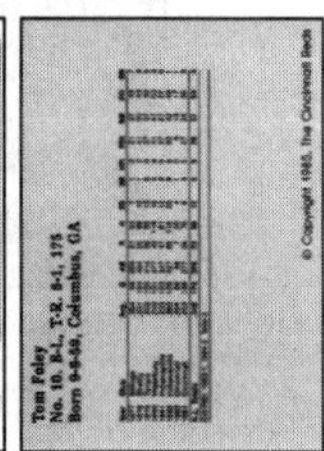

When perforated, these 18 cards measure the standard size. These cards were included as an insert in the 1985 Cincinnati Reds Yearbook. The fronts feature photos, the player's name and his position. The horizontal backs feature vital statistics and career information. We have sequenced this set in alphabetical order.

	NRMT	VG-E	GOOD
COMPLETE SET (18)	7.50	3.40	.95
COMMON CARD (1-18)	.25	.11	.03
□ 1 Cesar Cedeno	.50	.23	.06
□ 2 Dave Concepcion	1.00	.45	.12
□ 3 Eric Davis	2.00	.90	.25
□ 4 Nick Esasky	.25	.11	.03
□ 5 Tom Foley	.25	.11	.03
□ 6 John Franco	1.50	.70	.19
□ 7 Brad Gulden	.25	.11	.03
□ 8 Wayne Krenchicki	.25	.11	.03
□ 9 Eddie Milner	.25	.11	.03
□ 10 Ron Oester	.25	.11	.03
□ 11 Dave Parker	1.00	.45	.12
□ 12 Ted Power	.25	.11	.03
□ 13 Joe Price	.25	.11	.03
□ 14 Pete Rose P/MG	2.00	.90	.25
□ 15 Jeff Russell	.25	.11	.03
□ 16 Mario Soto	.25	.11	.03

☐ 17 Jay Tibbs	.25	.11	.03
☐ 18 Duane Walker	.25	.11	.03

1986 Reds Greats TCMA

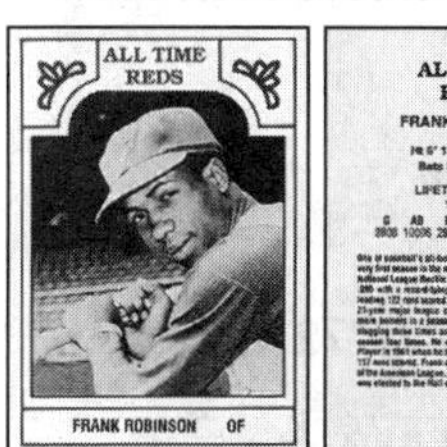

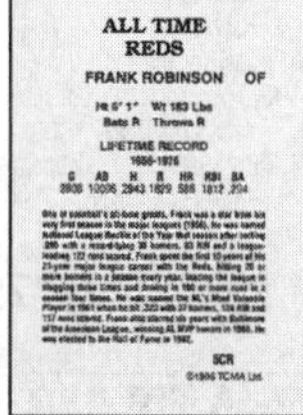

This 12-card standard-size set features some all-time leading Red players. The player's photo, name and position are on the front. The back contains more information about that player.

	MINT	NRMT	EXC
COMPLETE SET (12)	7.50	3.40	.95
COMMON CARD (1-12)	.25	.11	.03
☐ 1 Clay Carroll	.25	.11	.03
☐ 2 Bill McKechnie MG	.50	.23	.06
☐ 3 Paul Derringer	.50	.23	.06
☐ 4 Eppa Rixey	.75	.35	.09
☐ 5 Frank Robinson	1.50	.70	.19
☐ 6 Vada Pinson	.50	.23	.06
☐ 7 Leo Cardenas	.25	.11	.03
☐ 8 Heinie Groh	.25	.11	.03
☐ 9 Ted Kluszewski	.75	.35	.09
☐ 10 Joe Morgan	1.50	.70	.19
☐ 11 Edd Roush	.75	.35	.09
☐ 12 Johnny Bench	2.00	.90	.25

1986 Reds Texas Gold

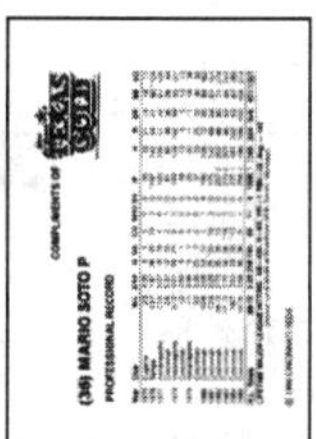

Texas Gold Ice Cream is the sponsor of this 28-card set of Cincinnati Reds. The standard-size cards feature player photos in full color with a red and white border on the front of the card. The set was distributed to fans attending the Reds game at Riverfront Stadium on September 19th. The card backs contain the player's career statistics, uniform number, name, position, and the Texas Gold logo.

	MINT	NRMT	EXC
COMPLETE SET (28)	50.00	22.00	6.25
COMMON CARD	1.00	.45	.12
☐ 6 Bo Diaz	1.00	.45	.12
☐ 9 Max Venable	1.00	.45	.12
☐ 11 Kurt Stillwell	1.25	.55	.16
☐ 12 Nick Esasky	1.00	.45	.12
☐ 13 Dave Concepcion	3.00	1.35	.35
☐ 14A Pete Rose INF	10.00	4.50	1.25
☐ 14B Pete Rose MG	10.00	4.50	1.25
☐ 14C Pete Rose (Commemorative)	10.00	4.50	1.25
☐ 16 Ron Oester	1.00	.45	.12
☐ 20 Eddie Milner	1.00	.45	.12
☐ 22 Sal Butera	1.00	.45	.12
☐ 24 Tony Perez	5.00	2.20	.60
☐ 25 Buddy Bell	1.50	.70	.19
☐ 28 Kal Daniels	1.25	.55	.16
☐ 29 Tracy Jones	1.00	.45	.12
☐ 31 John Franco	2.50	1.10	.30
☐ 32 Tom Browning	1.25	.55	.16
☐ 33 Ron Robinson	1.00	.45	.12
☐ 34 Bill Gullickson	1.00	.45	.12
☐ 36 Mario Soto	1.25	.55	.16
☐ 39 Dave Parker	3.00	1.35	.35
☐ 40 John Denny	1.25	.55	.16
☐ 44 Eric Davis	5.00	2.20	.60
☐ 45 Chris Welsh	1.00	.45	.12
☐ 48 Ted Power	1.00	.45	.12
☐ 49 Joe Price	1.00	.45	.12
☐ NNO Reds Coaches George Scherger Bruce Kimm Billy DeMars Tommy Helms Scott Breeden Jim Lett	1.00	.45	.12
☐ NNO Preferred Customer Card (Discount Coupon)	1.00	.45	.12

1987 Reds Kahn's

This 28-card set was issued to the first 20,000 fans at the August 2nd game between the Reds and the San Francisco Giants at Riverfront

Stadium by Kahn's Wieners. The cards are standard size, 2 1/2" by 3 1/2", and are unnumbered except for uniform number and feature full-color photos bordered in red and white on the front. The Kahn's logo is printed in red in the corner of the reverse. The set features a card of Barry Larkin in his Rookie Card year.

	MINT	NRMT	EXC
COMPLETE SET (28)	25.00	11.00	3.10
COMMON CARD	.50	.23	.06
☐ 6 Bo Diaz	.50	.23	.06
☐ 10 Terry Francona	.50	.23	.06
☐ 11 Kurt Stillwell	.50	.23	.06
☐ 12 Nick Esasky	.50	.23	.06
☐ 13 Dave Concepcion	1.50	.70	.19
☐ 15 Barry Larkin	10.00	4.50	1.25
☐ 16 Ron Oester	.50	.23	.06
☐ 21 Paul O'Neill	4.00	1.80	.50
☐ 23 Lloyd McClendon	.50	.23	.06
☐ 25 Buddy Bell	1.00	.45	.12
☐ 28 Kal Daniels	.75	.35	.09
☐ 29 Tracy Jones	.50	.23	.06
☐ 30 Guy Hoffman	.50	.23	.06
☐ 31 John Franco	1.50	.70	.19
☐ 32 Tom Browning	.75	.35	.09
☐ 33 Ron Robinson	.50	.23	.06
☐ 34 Bill Gullickson	.50	.23	.06
☐ 35 Pat Pacillo	.50	.23	.06
☐ 39 Dave Parker	1.50	.70	.19
☐ 43 Bill Landrum	.50	.23	.06
☐ 44 Eric Davis	3.00	1.35	.35
☐ 46 Rob Murphy	.50	.23	.06
☐ 47 Frank Williams	.50	.23	.06
☐ 48 Ted Power	.50	.23	.06
☐ NNO Pete Rose MG	4.00	1.80	.50
☐ NNO Coaches Card Scott Breeden Billy DeMars Tommy Helms Bruce Kimm Jim Lett Tony Perez	.75	.35	.09
☐ NNO Ad Card Save 25 cents on Corn Dogs	.50	.23	.06
☐ NNO Ad Card Save 30 cents on Smokeys	.50	.23	.06

1988 Reds Kahn's

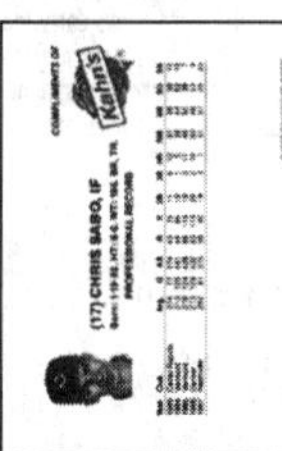

These 26-card standard-size sets were issued to fans at the August 14th game between the Cincinnati Reds and the Atlanta Braves at Riverfront Stadium. The cards are unnumbered except for uniform number and feature full-color photos bordered in red and white on the front. The Kahn's logo is printed in red in the corner of the reverse. The cards are numbered below by uniform number which is listed parenthetically on the front of the cards.

	MINT	NRMT	EXC
COMPLETE SET (26)	15.00	6.75	1.85
COMMON CARD	.25	.11	.03
☐ 6 Bo Diaz	.25	.11	.03
☐ 8 Terry McGriff	.25	.11	.03
☐ 9 Eddie Milner	.25	.11	.03
☐ 10 Leon Durham	.25	.11	.03
☐ 11 Barry Larkin	5.00	2.20	.60
☐ 12 Nick Esasky	.25	.11	.03
☐ 13 Dave Concepcion	1.25	.55	.16
☐ 14 Pete Rose MG	2.50	1.10	.30
☐ 15 Jeff Treadway	.25	.11	.03
☐ 17 Chris Sabo	1.25	.55	.16
☐ 20 Danny Jackson	.25	.11	.03
☐ 21 Paul O'Neill	1.50	.70	.19
☐ 22 Dave Collins	.25	.11	.03
☐ 27 Jose Rijo	.25	.11	.03
☐ 28 Kal Daniels	.25	.11	.03
☐ 29 Tracy Jones	.25	.11	.03
☐ 30 Lloyd McClendon	.25	.11	.03
☐ 31 John Franco	.75	.35	.09
☐ 32 Tom Browning	.50	.23	.06
☐ 33 Ron Robinson	.25	.11	.03
☐ 40 Jack Armstrong	.25	.11	.03
☐ 44 Eric Davis	1.00	.45	.12
☐ 46 Rob Murphy	.25	.11	.03
☐ 47 Frank Williams	.25	.11	.03
☐ 48 Tim Birtsas	.25	.11	.03
☐ NNO Reds Coaches Lee May Tony Perez Bruce Kimm Tommy Helms Jim Lett Scott Breeden	.75	.35	.09

1989 Reds Kahn's

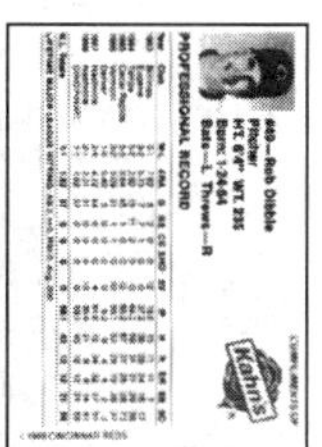

The 1989 Kahn's Reds set contains 28 standard-size cards; each card features a member of the Cincinnati Reds. The fronts have color photos with red borders. The horizontally oriented backs have career stats. The card numbering below is according to uniform number.

	MINT	NRMT	EXC
COMPLETE SET (28)	12.00	5.50	1.50
COMMON CARD	.25	.11	.03
☐ 6 Bo Diaz	.25	.11	.03
☐ 7 Lenny Harris	.50	.23	.06
☐ 11 Barry Larkin	3.00	1.35	.35
☐ 12 Joel Youngblood	.25	.11	.03
☐ 14 Pete Rose MG	2.00	.90	.25
☐ 16 Ron Oester	.25	.11	.03
☐ 17 Chris Sabo	.75	.35	.09
☐ 20 Danny Jackson	.25	.11	.03
☐ 21 Paul O'Neill	1.00	.45	.12
☐ 25 Todd Benzinger	.25	.11	.03
☐ 27 Jose Rijo	.25	.11	.03
☐ 28 Kal Daniels	.25	.11	.03
☐ 29 Herm Winningham	.25	.11	.03
☐ 30 Ken Griffey	.75	.35	.09
☐ 31 John Franco	.75	.35	.09
☐ 32 Tom Browning	.50	.23	.06
☐ 33 Ron Robinson	.25	.11	.03
☐ 34 Jeff Reed	.25	.11	.03
☐ 36 Rolando Roomes	.25	.11	.03
☐ 37 Norm Charlton	1.00	.45	.12
☐ 42 Rick Mahler	.25	.11	.03
☐ 43 Kent Tekulve	.50	.23	.06
☐ 44 Eric Davis	1.00	.45	.12
☐ 48 Tim Birtsas	.25	.11	.03
☐ 49 Rob Dibble	.50	.23	.06
☐ xx Coaches Card Scott Breeden Dave Bristol Tommy Helms Jim Lett Lee May Tony Perez	.50	.23	.06
☐ xx Sponsor Coupon Kahn's Corndogs	.25	.11	.03
☐ xx Sponsor Coupon Kahn's Wieners	.25	.11	.03

1990 Reds Kahn's

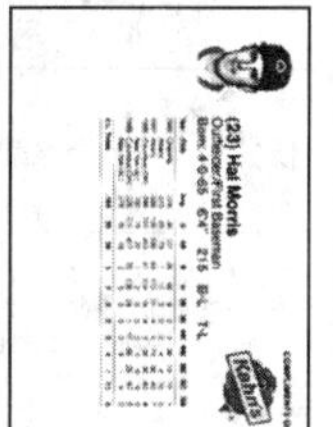

This 27-card, standard size set of Cincinnati Reds was issued by Kahn's Meats. This set which continued a more than 30-year tradition of Kahn's issuing Cincinnati Reds cards had the player's photos framed by red and white borders. The front have full-color photos while the back have a small black and white photo in the upper left hand corner and complete career statistics on the back of the card. The set is checklisted alphabetically since the cards are unnumbered.

	MINT	NRMT	EXC
COMPLETE SET (27)	10.00	4.50	1.25
COMMON CARD (1-27)	.25	.11	.03
☐ 1 Jack Armstrong	.25	.11	.03
☐ 2 Todd Benzinger	.25	.11	.03
☐ 3 Tim Birtsas	.25	.11	.03
☐ 4 Glenn Braggs	.25	.11	.03
☐ 5 Tom Browning	.50	.23	.06
☐ 6 Norm Charlton	.75	.35	.09
☐ 7 Eric Davis	.75	.35	.09
☐ 8 Rob Dibble	.50	.23	.06
☐ 9 Mariano Duncan	.50	.23	.06
☐ 10 Ken Griffey	.75	.35	.09
☐ 11 Billy Hatcher	.25	.11	.03
☐ 12 Barry Larkin	2.50	1.10	.30
☐ 13 Danny Jackson	.25	.11	.03
☐ 14 Tim Layana	.25	.11	.03
☐ 15 Rick Mahler	.25	.11	.03
☐ 16 Hal Morris	.75	.35	.09
☐ 17 Randy Myers	1.00	.45	.12
☐ 18 Ron Oester	.25	.11	.03
☐ 19 Joe Oliver	.25	.11	.03
☐ 20 Paul O'Neill	1.25	.55	.16
☐ 21 Lou Piniella MG	.75	.35	.09
☐ 22 Luis Quinones	.25	.11	.03
☐ 23 Jeff Reed	.25	.11	.03
☐ 24 Jose Rijo	.25	.11	.03
☐ 25 Chris Sabo	.50	.23	.06
☐ 26 Herm Winningham	.25	.11	.03
☐ 27 Red Coaches Jackie Moore Tony Perez Sam Perlozzo Larry Rothschild Stan Williams	.75	.35	.09

1991 Reds Kahn's

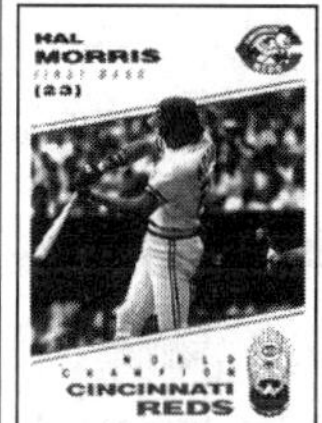

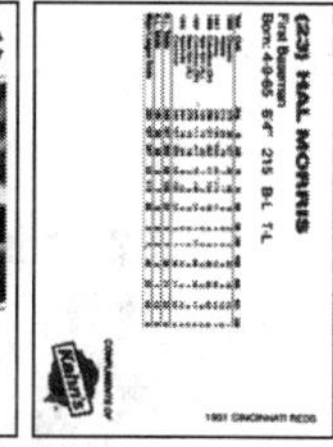

The 1991 Kahn's Cincinnati Reds set contains 28 standard-size cards. The set is skip-numbered by uniform number and includes two Kahn's coupon cards. The front features color action player photos which are mounted diagonally on the card face. Red pinstripe borders frame the picture above and below. The front lettering is printed in red and black on a white background. In a horizontal format the back is printed in red and black, and presents complete statistical information. The Kahn's logo in the lower right corner rounds out the back.

	MINT	NRMT	EXC
COMPLETE SET (28)	8.00	3.60	1.00
COMMON CARD	.25	.11	.03
☐ 0 Schottzie Mascot	.25	.11	.03
☐ 7 Mariano Duncan	.50	.23	.06
☐ 9 Joe Oliver	.25	.11	.03
☐ 10 Luis Quinones	.25	.11	.03
☐ 11 Barry Larkin	2.50	1.10	.30
☐ 15 Glenn Braggs	.25	.11	.03
☐ 17 Chris Sabo	.50	.23	.06
☐ 19 Bill Doran	.25	.11	.03
☐ 21 Paul O'Neill	1.00	.45	.12
☐ 22 Billy Hatcher	.25	.11	.03
☐ 23 Hal Morris	.75	.35	.09
☐ 25 Todd Benzinger	.25	.11	.03
☐ 27 Jose Rijo	.25	.11	.03
☐ 28 Randy Myers	.75	.35	.09
☐ 29 Herm Winningham	.25	.11	.03
☐ 32 Tom Browning	.50	.23	.06
☐ 34 Jeff Reed	.25	.11	.03
☐ 36 Don Carman	.25	.11	.03
☐ 37 Norm Charlton	.75	.35	.09
☐ 40 Jack Armstrong	.25	.11	.03
☐ 41 Lou Piniella MG	.75	.35	.09
☐ 44 Eric Davis	.75	.35	.09
☐ 45 Chris Hammond	.25	.11	.03
☐ 47 Scott Scudder	.25	.11	.03
☐ 48 Ted Power	.25	.11	.03
☐ 49 Rob Dibble	.25	.11	.03
☐ 57 Freddie Benavides	.25	.11	.03
☐ NNO Coaches Card Jackie Moore Tony Perez Sam Perlozzo Larry Rothschild Stan Williams	.50	.23	.06

1991 Reds Pepsi

This 20-card standard-size set was produced by MSA (Michael Schechter Associates) for Pepsi-Cola of Ohio, and Pepsi logos adorn the upper corners of the card face. The cards were placed inside of 24-soda packs of Pepsi, Diet Pepsi, Caffeine-Free Pepsi, Caffeine Free Diet-Pepsi, Mountain Dew, and Diet Mountain Dew. The fronts display color player photos bordered in white and red and with the team logos airbrushed away. The horizontally oriented backs are trimmed in navy

blue and present biography, statistics, and the player's autograph. The cards are unnumbered and checklisted below in alphabetical order.

	MINT	NRMT	EXC
COMPLETE SET (20)	12.00	5.50	1.50
COMMON CARD (1-20)	.50	.23	.06
☐ 1 Jack Armstrong	.50	.23	.06
☐ 2 Todd Benzinger	.50	.23	.06
☐ 3 Glenn Braggs	.50	.23	.06
☐ 4 Tom Browning	.75	.35	.09
☐ 5 Norm Charlton	.75	.35	.09
☐ 6 Eric Davis	1.25	.55	.16
☐ 7 Rob Dibble	.75	.35	.09
☐ 8 Bill Doran	.50	.23	.06
☐ 9 Mariano Duncan	.75	.35	.09
☐ 10 Billy Hatcher	.50	.23	.06
☐ 11 Barry Larkin	3.00	1.35	.35
☐ 12 Hal Morris	1.00	.45	.12
☐ 13 Randy Myers	1.00	.45	.12
☐ 14 Joe Oliver	.50	.23	.06
☐ 15 Paul O'Neill	1.50	.70	.19
☐ 16 Lou Piniella MG	1.00	.45	.12
☐ 17 Jeff Reed	.50	.23	.06
☐ 18 Jose Rijo	.50	.23	.06
☐ 19 Chris Sabo	.75	.35	.09
☐ 20 Herm Winningham	.50	.23	.06

1992 Reds Kahn's

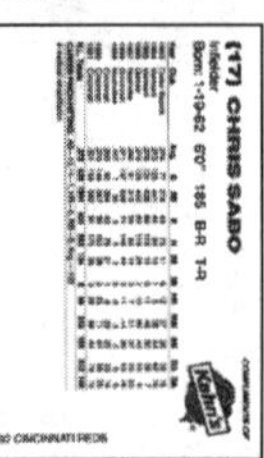

The 1992 Kahn's Cincinnati Reds set consists of 29 standard-size cards. The set included two manufacturer's coupons (one for 50 cents off Kahn's Wieners and another for the same amount off Kahn's Corn Dogs). The fronts feature color action player photos bordered in red. The team name and the player's name appear in white lettering above and below the picture respectively. The team logo overlays the picture at its lower left corner. The horizontally oriented backs have the player's name and sponsor logo in red, while biographical and complete statistical information are printed in black. The cards are skip-numbered by uniform number on both sides and checklisted below accordingly.

	MINT	NRMT	EXC
COMPLETE SET (29)	8.00	3.60	1.00
COMMON CARD	.25	.11	.03
☐ 2 Schottzie	.25	.11	.03
(Mascot)			
☐ 9 Joe Oliver	.25	.11	.03
☐ 10 Bip Roberts	.50	.23	.06
☐ 11 Barry Larkin	2.00	.90	.25
☐ 12 Freddie Benavides	.25	.11	.03
☐ 15 Glenn Braggs	.25	.11	.03
☐ 16 Reggie Sanders	.75	.35	.09
☐ 17 Chris Sabo	.50	.23	.06
☐ 19 Bill Doran	.25	.11	.03
☐ 21 Paul O'Neill	1.00	.45	.12
☐ 23 Hal Morris	.50	.23	.06
☐ 25 Scott Bankhead	.25	.11	.03
☐ 26 Darnell Coles	.25	.11	.03
☐ 27 Jose Rijo	.25	.11	.03
☐ 28 Scott Ruskin	.25	.11	.03
☐ 29 Greg Swindell	.25	.11	.03
☐ 30 Dave Martinez	.25	.11	.03
☐ 31 Tim Belcher	.25	.11	.03
☐ 32 Tom Browning	.50	.23	.06
☐ 34 Jeff Reed	.25	.11	.03
☐ 37 Norm Charlton	.75	.35	.09
☐ 38 Troy Afenir	.25	.11	.03
☐ 41 Lou Piniella MG	.75	.35	.09
☐ 45 Chris Hammond	.25	.11	.03
☐ 48 Dwayne Henry	.25	.11	.03
☐ 49 Rob Dibble	.25	.11	.03
☐ NNO Coaches Card	.50	.23	.06
Jackie Moore			
John McLaren			
Sam Perlozzo			
Tony Perez			
Larry Rothschild			
☐ NNO Manufacturer's Coupon	.25	.11	.03
Kahn's Corn Dogs			
☐ NNO Manufacturer's Coupon	.25	.11	.03
Kahn's Beef Franks			

1993 Reds Kahn's

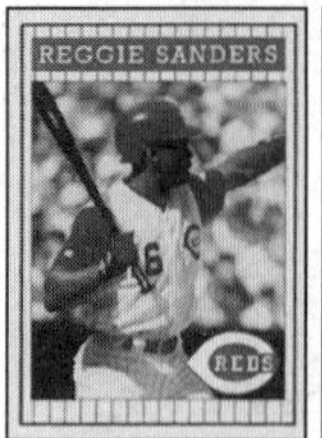

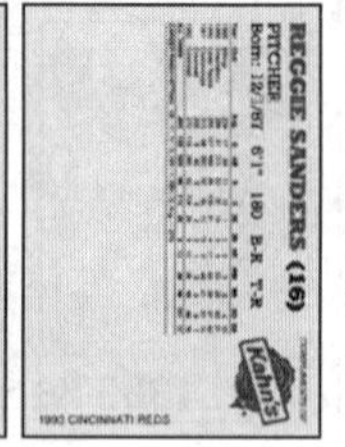

This 27-card standard-size set was issued by Kahn's Meats. The fronts contain an action photo bordered in white with a narrow black inner border. The photo is overlayed on a red pinstriped background with the player's name printed on a red stripe at the top. The set includes two Kahn's coupon cards. In a horizontal format, the backs are printed in red and black and present the player's name, position, number, biography, and statistics. The Kahn's logo in the top right corner rounds out the backs. The cards are unnumbered and checklisted below in alphabetical order.

	MINT	NRMT	EXC
COMPLETE SET (30)	8.00	3.60	1.00
COMMON CARD (1-28)	.25	.11	.03
☐ 1 Bobby Ayala	.25	.11	.03
☐ 2 Tim Belcher	.50	.23	.06
☐ 3 Jeff Branson	.25	.11	.03
☐ 4 Marty Brennaman ANN	.50	.23	.06
Joe Nuxhall ANN			
☐ 5 Tom Browning	.50	.23	.06
☐ 6 Jacob Brumfield	.25	.11	.03
☐ 7 Greg Cadaret	.25	.11	.03
☐ 8 Jose Cardenal CO	.25	.11	.03
Don Gullett CO			
Ray Knight CO			
Dave Miley CO			
Bobby Valentine CO			
☐ 9 Rob Dibble	.50	.23	.06
☐ 10 Davey Johnson MG	.50	.23	.06
☐ 11 Roberto Kelly	.25	.11	.03
☐ 12 Bill Landrum	.25	.11	.03
☐ 13 Barry Larkin	2.00	.90	.25
☐ 14 Randy Milligan	.25	.11	.03
☐ 15 Kevin Mitchell	.50	.23	.06
☐ 16 Hal Morris	.50	.23	.06
☐ 17 Joe Oliver	.25	.11	.03
☐ 18 Tim Pugh	.25	.11	.03
☐ 19 Jeff Reardon	.50	.23	.06
☐ 20 Jose Rijo	.25	.11	.03
☐ 21 Bip Roberts	.50	.23	.06
☐ 22 Chris Sabo	.50	.23	.06
☐ 23 Juan Samuel	.50	.23	.06
☐ 24 Reggie Sanders			
☐ 25 Schottzie (mascot)	.25	.11	.03
Marge Schott			
☐ 26 John Smiley	.50	.23	.06
☐ 27 Gary Varsho	.25	.11	.03
☐ 28 Kevin Wickander	.25	.11	.03
☐ NNO Manufacturer's Coupon	.25	.11	.03
(Kahn's hot dogs)			
☐ NNO Manufacturer's Coupon	.25	.11	.03
(Kahn's corn dogs)			

1994 Reds Kahn's

These 33 standard-size cards were handed out at Riverfront Stadium to fans attending a Reds' home game on August 7. The white-bordered fronts feature color player action shots. The player's name and position appear at the upper left within a vertical red bar stripped into the background on the photo's left side. The horizontal white back carries the player's name and uniform number at the top, followed below by position, biography, and statistics. The red Kahn's logo at the upper right rounds out the card. The cards are unnumbered and checklisted below in alphabetical order.

	MINT	NRMT	EXC
COMPLETE SET (35)	7.50	3.40	.95
COMMON CARD (1-33)	.25	.11	.03
☐ 1 Bret Boone UER	.75	.35	.09
(Misspelled Brett			
on front and back)			
☐ 2 Jeff Branson	.25	.11	.03
☐ 3 Jeff Brantley	.75	.35	.09
☐ 4 Tom Browning	.50	.23	.06
☐ 5 Jacob Brumfield	.25	.11	.03
☐ 6 Hector Carrasco	.25	.11	.03
☐ 7 Rob Dibble	.50	.23	.06
☐ 8 Brian Dorsett	.25	.11	.03
☐ 9 Tony Fernandez	.50	.23	.06
☐ 10 Tim Fortugno UER	.25	.11	.03
(Misspelled Fortungo			
on back)			
☐ 11 Steve Foster	.25	.11	.03
☐ 12 Ron Gant	1.00	.45	.12
☐ 13 Erik Hanson	.25	.11	.03
☐ 14 Lenny Harris	.25	.11	.03
☐ 15 Thomas Howard	.25	.11	.03
☐ 16 Davey Johnson MG	.50	.23	.06
☐ 17 Barry Larkin	2.00	.90	.25
☐ 18 Chuck McElroy	.25	.11	.03
☐ 19 Kevin Mitchell	.50	.23	.06
☐ 20 Hal Morris	.50	.23	.06
☐ 21 Joe Oliver	.25	.11	.03
☐ 22 Tim Pugh	.25	.11	.03
☐ 23 Jose Rijo	.25	.11	.03
☐ 24 John Roper	.25	.11	.03
☐ 25 Johnny Ruffin	.25	.11	.03
☐ 26 Deion Sanders	1.00	.45	.12
☐ 27 Reggie Sanders	.50	.23	.06
☐ 28 Schottzie (Mascot)	.25	.11	.03
☐ 29 Pete Schourek	.50	.23	.06
☐ 30 John Smiley UER	.50	.23	.06
(Front photo is			
Erik Hanson)			
☐ 31 Eddie Taubensee	.25	.11	.03
☐ 32 Jerome Walton	.25	.11	.03
☐ 33 Coaches	.25	.11	.03
Bob Boone			
Don Gullett			
Grant Jackson			
Ray Knight			
Joel Youngblood			
☐ NNO Manufacturer's Coupon	.25	.11	.03
Kahn's Wieners			
☐ NNO Manufacturer's Coupon	.25	.11	.03
Kahn's Corn Dogs			

1995 Reds Kahn's

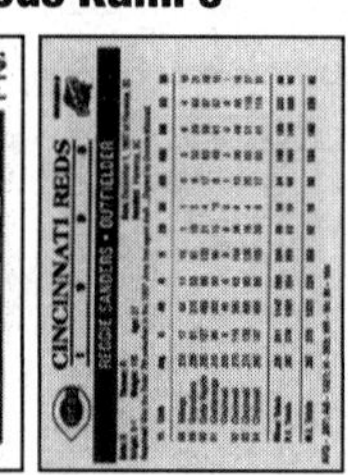

This 34-card standard-size set has white-bordered fronts feature color player action photos. The team name and year appear at the top with the player's name and position printed in a red bar at the bottom. The horizontal white backs carry the team's logo, name and sponsor's logo at the top with the player's name and position in a black bar below. A short player biography and career statistics round out the card. The cards are unnumbered and checklisted below in alphabetical order.

	MINT	NRMT	EXC
COMPLETE SET (36)	7.00	3.10	.85
COMMON CARD (1-36)	.10	.05	.01
☐ 1 Eric Anthony	.10	.05	.01
☐ 2 Damon Berryhill	.10	.05	.01
☐ 3 Bret Boone	.50	.23	.06
☐ 4 Jeff Branson	.10	.05	.01
☐ 5 Jeff Brantley	.50	.23	.06
☐ 6 Hector Carrasco	.10	.05	.01
☐ 7 Ron Gant	.75	.35	.09
☐ 8 Willie Greene	.75	.35	.09
☐ 9 Lenny Harris	.10	.05	.01
☐ 10 Xavier Hernandez	.10	.05	.01
☐ 11 Thomas Howard	.10	.05	.01
☐ 12 Brian Hunter	.10	.05	.01
☐ 13 Mike Jackson	.10	.05	.01
☐ 14 Kevin Jarvis	.10	.05	.01
☐ 15 Davey Johnson MG	.25	.11	.03
☐ 16 Barry Larkin	1.50	.70	.19
☐ 17 Mark Lewis	.50	.23	.06
☐ 18 Chuck McElroy	.10	.05	.01
☐ 19 Hal Morris	.25	.11	.03
☐ 20 C.J. Nitkowski	.10	.05	.01
☐ 21 Brad Pennington	.10	.05	.01
☐ 22 Tim Pugh	.10	.05	.01
☐ 23 Jose Rijo	.10	.05	.01
☐ 24 John Roper	.10	.05	.01
☐ 25 Johnny Ruffin	.10	.05	.01
☐ 26 Deion Sanders	1.00	.45	.12
☐ 27 Reggie Sanders	.25	.11	.03
☐ 28 Benito Santiago	.25	.11	.03
☐ 29 Schottzie (Mascot)	.10	.05	.01
☐ 30 Pete Schourek	.25	.11	.03
☐ 31 John Smiley	.25	.11	.03
☐ 32 Eddie Taubensee	.10	.05	.01
☐ 33 Jerome Walton	.10	.05	.01
☐ 34 Coaches	.10	.05	.01
Ray Knight			
Don Gullett			
Grant Jackson			
Hal McRae			
Joel Youngblood			
☐ NNO Manufacturer's Coupon	.10	.05	.01
Kahn's Hot Dogs			
☐ NNO Manufacturer's Coupon	.10	.05	.01
Kahn's Corn Dogs			

1996 Reds '76 Klosterman

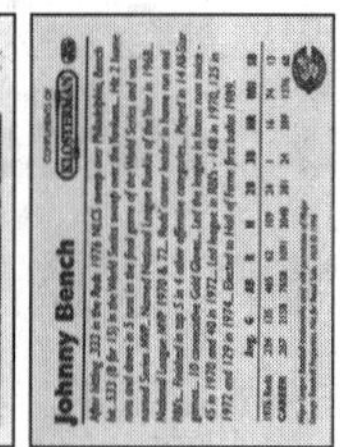

This 10-card set celebrates the 20th anniversary of the Cincinnati Reds 1976 World Championship team. Distributed by Klosterman Baking Co., one card was inserted in bags of Big White Bread product and released to participating Cincinnati-area grocery stores. The fronts feature color action player photos in a white border. The backs carry player career highlights and stats. The cards are unnumbered and checklisted below in alphabetical order.

	MINT	NRMT	EXC
COMPLETE SET (10)	5.00	2.20	.60
COMMON CARD (1-10)	.25	.11	.03
☐ 1 Sparky Anderson MG	.50	.23	.06
☐ 2 Johnny Bench	1.50	.70	.19
☐ 3 Big Four	2.00	.90	.25
Johnny Bench			
Joe Morgan			
Tony Perez			
Pete Rose			
☐ 4 Dave Concepcion	.75	.35	.09
☐ 5 George Foster	.50	.23	.06
☐ 6 Cesar Geronimo	.25	.11	.03
☐ 7 Ken Griffey	.75	.35	.09
☐ 8 Don Gullett	.25	.11	.03
☐ 9 Joe Morgan	1.25	.55	.16
☐ 10 Tony Perez	1.00	.45	.12

1992 Rembrandt Ultra-Pro Promos

The 1992 Rembrandt Ultra-Pro set of 19 standard-size cards was issued one-per-package inside specially marked packages of Rembrandt Ultra-Pro sheets. The cards are numbered with a "P" prefix. The cards contain a high-gloss UV coating and feature an exclusive anti-counterfeiting hologram on the back. The set of the first 18 cards was also available direct from Rembrandt for $35.95 ($37.95 or $39.95) plus $4 shipping and handling along with three (two or one) UPC's or other proofs of purchase.

	MINT	NRMT	EXC
COMPLETE SET (19)	30.00	13.50	3.70
COMMON CARD (P1-P19)	1.00	.45	.12
☐ P1 Bobby Bonilla	2.00	.90	.25
Holding both ends			
of bat across neck			
☐ P2 Bobby Bonilla	2.00	.90	.25
Front pose			
shot from waist up			
☐ P3 Bobby Bonilla	2.00	.90	.25
Follow-through after			
golf swing			
☐ P4 Jose Canseco	3.00	1.35	.35
Posed in car			
☐ P5 Jose Canseco	2.00	.90	.25
Batting stance			
☐ P6 Jose Canseco	2.00	.90	.25
Front pose			
bat resting on shoulder			
☐ P7 Hal Morris	1.00	.45	.12
Front pose			

	MINT	NRMT	EXC
bat resting on shoulder			
☐ P8 Hal Morris	1.00	.45	.12
Posed, tennis racket in hand			
☐ P9 Hal Morris	1.00	.45	.12
Pose, shot from waist up			
☐ P10 Scott Erickson	1.00	.45	.12
Posed, skis on shoulder			
☐ P11 Scott Erickson	1.00	.45	.12
Front pose, shot from waist up			
☐ P12 Scott Erickson	1.00	.45	.12
Batting stance			
☐ P13 Danny Tartabull	1.00	.45	.12
Batting stance			
☐ P14 Danny Tartabull	2.00	.90	.25
Front pose			
bat resting on shoulder			
☐ P15 Danny Tartabull	1.00	.45	.12
Posed, chrome dumbbell in left hand			
☐ P16 Danny Tartabull	2.00	.90	.25
Bobby Bonilla			
Posed in tuxedos			
bat on shoulder			
☐ P17 Bobby Bonilla	2.00	.90	.25
Posed in tuxedo			
☐ P18 Danny Tartabull	5.00	2.20	.60
Bobby Bonilla			
Hologram			
☐ P19 Jose Canseco	3.00	1.35	.35
Holding Ultra-Pro			
sheet filled with cards			

1993 Rembrandt Ultra-Pro Karros

Eric Karros is the exclusive subject of this five-card, standard-size set that celebrates his National League Rookie of the Year award. The full-bleed action photos have a blue bar across the bottom with Karros' name and "Rookie of the Year" in white lettering. The borderless backs carry a head shot in the left with career highlights on the right. Below the picture, Karros' 1992 statistics are listed. The Rembrandt logo appears on a blue bar in the lower left.

	MINT	NRMT	EXC
COMPLETE SET (5)	4.00	1.80	.50
COMMON CARD (1-5)	1.00	.45	.12
☐ 1 Eric Karros	1.00	.45	.12
At bat			
☐ 2 Eric Karros	1.00	.45	.12
In the field			
☐ 3 Eric Karros	1.00	.45	.12
Lifting hand weights			
☐ 4 Eric Karros	1.00	.45	.12
Wearing tux			
☐ 5 Eric Karros	1.00	.45	.12
Dave Hansen			

1994 Rembrandt Ultra-Pro Piazza Promos

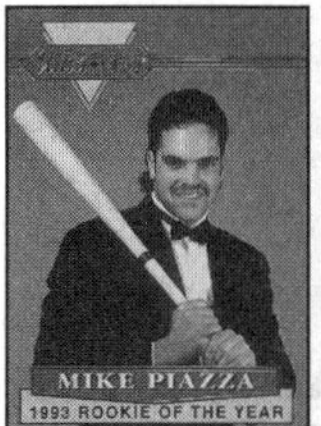

Issued to promote Ultra-Pro's card storage products, these two standard-size cards feature on their borderless fronts color photos of Mike Piazza posed in front of a purple background and holding Ultra-Pro products. His name and the words "1993 Rookie of the Year" appear at the bottom. The pink back carries product information and a facsimile Mike Piazza autograph. The cards are unnumbered.

	MINT	NRMT	EXC
COMPLETE SET (2)	2.00	.90	.25
COMMON CARD (1-2)	1.00	.45	.12
☐ 1 Mike Piazza	1.00	.45	.12
(Holding Ultra-Pro Page)			
☐ 2 Mike Piazza	1.00	.45	.12
(Holding Ultra-Pro			
Mini Top Loader)			

1994 Rembrandt Ultra-Pro Piazza

These six standard-size cards feature on their borderless fronts color photos of Mike Piazza in various game and non-game situations. His name and "1993 Rookie of the Year" appear at the bottom. The pink back has a color head shot of Piazza, with career highlights and statistics below. One of these cards was inserted in each 200-count box of Ultra-Pro Mini Top Loaders. A black vinyl binder for displaying all six cards was also available. The cards are numbered on the back as "X of 6."

	MINT	NRMT	EXC
COMPLETE SET (6)	12.00	5.50	1.50
COMMON CARD (1-6)	2.00	.90	.25
☐ 1 Mike Piazza	2.00	.90	.25
(In tux, holding bat)			
☐ 2 Mike Piazza	2.00	.90	.25
(In uniform, trying to			
make play)			
☐ 3 Mike Piazza	2.00	.90	.25
(In golf shirt,			
golf club on shoulder)			
☐ 4 Mike Piazza	2.00	.90	.25
(In uniform, preparing			
to throw)			
☐ 5 Mike Piazza	2.00	.90	.25
(In golf shirt,			
dumbbell in hand)			
☐ 6 Mike Piazza	2.00	.90	.25
(In uniform, batting			
cut out on foil card)			

1996 Rembrandt Ultra Pro Piazza

This nine-card set is actually a puzzle with each of the cards featuring a different portion of an action photo of Mike Piazza. The complete set could be mailed in for an uncut version of the photo. Gold and silver versions of the puzzle were also produced which, when completed, could be mailed in for monetary prizes. The gold version is distinguished by a gold foil emblem on each piece and could be exchanged for a prize of $250. The silver version displays a silver foil emblem and could be exchanged for $100. The mail-in prize offer expired April 1, 1997.

	MINT	NRMT	EXC
COMPLETE SET (9)	5.00	2.20	.60
COMMON CARD (1-9)	.75	.35	.09
☐ 1 Mike Piazza	.75	.35	.09
(Top of glove)			
☐ 2 Mike Piazza	.75	.35	.09
(Glove and hand ready to catch ball)			
☐ 3 Mike Piazza	.75	.35	.09
(Middle portion of right arm)			
☐ 4 Mike Piazza	.75	.35	.09
(Top of head and face)			
☐ 5 Mike Piazza	.75	.35	.09
(Bottom of face and left elbow)			
☐ 6 Mike Piazza	.75	.35	.09
(Right elbow)			
☐ 7 Mike Piazza	.75	.35	.09
(Word "Pro")			
☐ 8 Mike Piazza	.75	.35	.09
(Right side view and word "Ultra")			
☐ 9 Mike Piazza	.75	.35	.09
(Body's mid-section)			

1992-93 Revolutionary Legends 1

Revolutionary Comics released this Series 1 card set and inserted three cards within each issue of Baseball Legends magazine. The individual cards measure approximately 2 1/2" by 3 5/8" but are combined on one strip and stapled to the center of the magazine. The strip measures 10 1/2" by 2 1/2". These are unauthorized cards according to Revolutionary Comics. The fronts display graphic illustrations by Scott Penzer on a red and black background within an irregular yellow and black border. The black and white backs carry biography, career highlights and career summary. The cards are numbered on the back.

	MINT	NRMT	EXC
COMPLETE SET (15)	10.00	4.50	1.25
COMMON CARD (1-15)	.50	.23	.06
☐ 1 Willie Mays	1.00	.45	.12
Rookie Year 1951			
☐ 2 Willie Mays	1.00	.45	.12
Greaatest Moment			
☐ 3 Willie Mays	1.00	.45	.12
☐ 4 Honus Wagner	.75	.35	.09
Rookie Year 1897			
☐ 5 Honus Wagner	.75	.35	.09
☐ 6 Honus Wagner	.75	.35	.09
Greatest Moment			
☐ 7 Roberto Clemente	1.25	.55	.16
Rookie Year			
☐ 8 Roberto Clemente	1.25	.55	.16
☐ 9 Roberto Clemente	1.25	.55	.16
Greatest Moment			
☐ 10 Yogi Berra	.75	.35	.09
Rookie Year 1947			
☐ 11 Yogi Berra	.75	.35	.09
☐ 12 Yogi Berra	.75	.35	.09
Greatest Moment			
☐ 13 Billy Martin	.50	.23	.06
Rookie Year 1950			
☐ 14 Billy Martin	.50	.23	.06
☐ 15 Billy Martin	.50	.23	.06
Greatest Moment			

1992-93 Revolutionary Superstars 1

1992-93 Baseball Superstars Series 1 was issued by Revolutionary Comics. The cards were inserted in the magazine Baseball Superstars. The cards measure approximately 2 1/2" by 3 5/8" individually and the strip of three measures 10 1/2" by 2 1/2". The graphic illustrations of these superstar players was by Scott Penzer. The fronts display a black background with black and white mottled corner design. The white backs have black print and include biography, career highlights and career summary.

	MINT	NRMT	EXC
COMPLETE SET (15)	12.00	5.50	1.50
COMMON CARD (1-15)	.50	.23	.06
☐ 1 Darryl Strawberry	.50	.23	.06
Rookie Year 1983			
☐ 2 Darryl Strawberry	.50	.23	.06
☐ 3 Darryl Strawberry	.50	.23	.06
Greatest Moment			
☐ 4 Frank Thomas	2.00	.90	.25
Rookie Year 1990			
☐ 5 Frank Thomas	2.00	.90	.25
☐ 6 Frank Thomas	2.00	.90	.25
Greatest Moment			
☐ 7 Ryne Sandberg	1.00	.45	.12
Rookie Year 1981			
☐ 8 Ryne Sandberg	1.00	.45	.12
☐ 9 Ryne Sandberg	1.00	.45	.12
Greatest Moment			
☐ 10 Kirby Puckett	1.00	.45	.12
Rookie Year 1984			
☐ 11 Kirby Puckett	1.00	.45	.12
☐ 12 Kirby Puckett	1.00	.45	.12
Greatest Moment			
☐ 13 Roberto Alomar	.75	.35	.09
Rookie Year 1988			
Sandy Alomar			
Rookie Year 1990			
☐ 14 Roberto Alomar	.75	.35	.09
Sandy Alomar			
☐ 15 Roberto Alomar	.75	.35	.09
Sandy Alomar			
Greatest Moments			

1988 Rini Postcards Dodgers 1

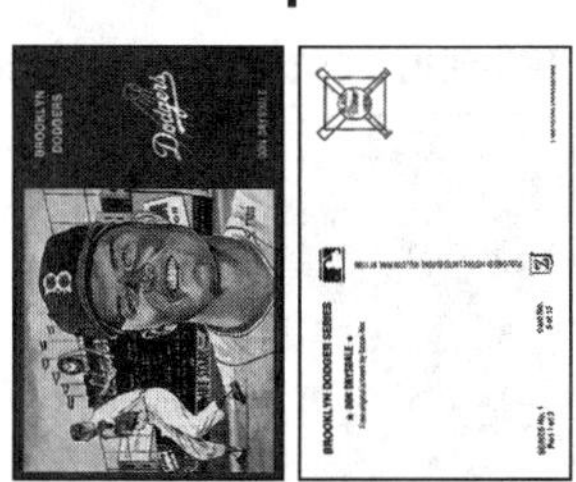

This set of 36 postcards measures 3 1/2" by 5 1/2" and showcases the Brooklyn Dodgers. On a blue background, the horizontal fronts feature color drawings by Susan Rini. There were three subsets in the first series, with 12 cards each. The cards are numbered on the back as "X of 12." Suffixes (A, B, and C) have been arbitrarily assigned to the card numbers below to distinguish between the three subsets.

	MINT	NRMT	EXC
COMPLETE SET (36)	15.00	6.75	1.85
COMMON CARD	.50	.23	.06
☐ 1A Dodgers Sym-Phony Band	.50	.23	.06
☐ 1B Tom Lasorda	2.00	.90	.25
☐ 1C Carl Erskine	1.50	.70	.19
☐ 2A Sandy Amoros	.50	.23	.06
☐ 2B Carl Furillo	1.50	.70	.19
☐ 2C Ebbets Field	.50	.23	.06
☐ 3A Don Newcombe	1.50	.70	.19
☐ 3B Roger Craig	.75	.35	.09
☐ 3C Jackie Robinson	4.00	1.80	.50
☐ 4A Duke Snider	3.00	1.35	.35
☐ 4B Andy Pafko	.75	.35	.09
☐ 4C Red Barber	1.00	.45	.12
Leo Durocher			
☐ 5A Harold(Pee Wee) Reese	3.00	1.35	.35
☐ 5B George Shuba	.50	.23	.06
☐ 5C Red Barber	1.00	.45	.12
☐ 6A Johnny Podres	1.50	.70	.19
☐ 6B Jackie Robinson	2.00	.90	.25
Branch Rickey			
☐ 6C Leo Durocher	2.00	.90	.25
☐ 7A Ralph Branca	.75	.35	.09
☐ 7B Clem Labine	1.50	.70	.19
☐ 7C Gil Hodges	2.00	.90	.25
☐ 8A Don Drysdale	2.00	.90	.25
☐ 8B Larry Mac Phail	.75	.35	.09
☐ 8C Mickey Owen	.50	.23	.06
☐ 9A Roy Campanella	3.00	1.35	.35
☐ 9B Chuck Connors	1.50	.70	.19
☐ 9C Preacher Roe	1.50	.70	.19
☐ 10A Harry Lavagetto	.50	.23	.06
(Cookie)			
☐ 10B Walter O'Malley	1.00	.45	.12
☐ 10C Cal Abrams	.50	.23	.06
☐ 11A Sal Maglie	1.00	.45	.12
☐ 11B Carl Erskine	1.50	.70	.19
☐ 11C Cookie Lavagetto	1.00	.45	.12
☐ 12A Clyde King	.50	.23	.06
☐ 12B Eddie Miksis	.50	.23	.06
☐ 12C Gene Hermanski	.50	.23	.06

1989 Rini Postcards Gehrig

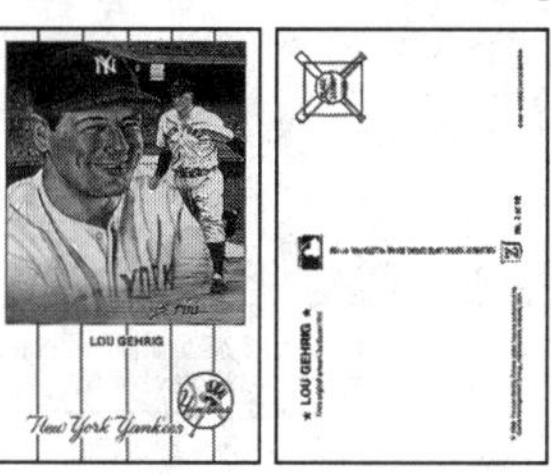

This set of 12 postcards measures 3 1/2" by 5 1/2" and honors Lou Gehrig. The fronts feature color drawings by Susan Rini. The cards are numbered on the back.

	MINT	NRMT	EXC
COMPLETE SET (10)	5.00	2.20	.60
COMMON CARD (1-10)	.50	.23	.06
☐ 1 Lou Gehrig	.50	.23	.06
(With two teammates)			
☐ 2 Lou Gehrig	.50	.23	.06
(Running)			
☐ 3 Lou Gehrig	.50	.23	.06
(Standing with trophy)			
☐ 4 Lou Gehrig	1.00	.45	.12
Babe Ruth			
Sitting Together			
☐ 5 Lou Gehrig	.50	.23	.06
(Batting)			
☐ 6 Lou Gehrig	.50	.23	.06
(Catching the ball)			
☐ 7 Lou Gehrig	.50	.23	.06
(Standing)			
☐ 8 Lou Gehrig	.50	.23	.06
(Standing with glove)			
☐ 9 Lou Gehrig	.50	.23	.06
(Signing a contract)			
☐ 10 Lou Gehrig	.50	.23	.06
(Sliding)			

1989 Rini Postcards Mattingly 1

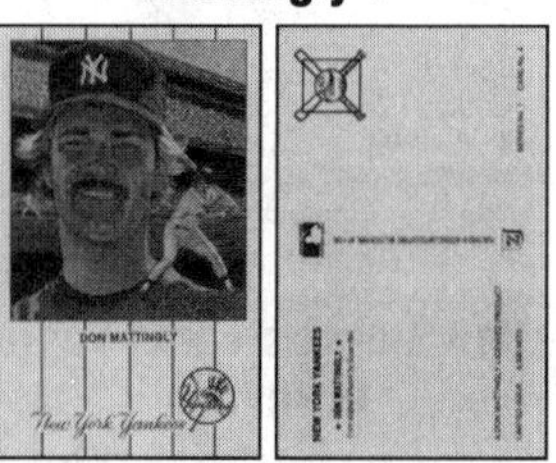

This set of 12 postcards measures 3 1/2" by 5 1/2" and honors Don Mattingly. The fronts feature color drawings by Susan Rini.

	MINT	NRMT	EXC
COMPLETE SET (12)	5.00	2.20	.60
COMMON CARD (1-12)	.50	.23	.06
☐ 1 Don Mattingly	.50	.23	.06
(Batting, seen			
from the back)			
☐ 2 Don Mattingly	.50	.23	.06

	MINT	NRMT	EXC
(Batting)			
☐ 3 Don Mattingly (With bat in both hands)	.50	.23	.06
☐ 4 Don Mattingly (With glove)	.50	.23	.06
☐ 5 Don Mattingly (Batting, seen from the side)	.50	.23	.06
☐ 6 Don Mattingly (Letting go of the bat)	.50	.23	.06
☐ 7 Don Mattingly (Starting to run, bat in right hand)	.50	.23	.06
☐ 8 Don Mattingly (Starting to run, bat in both hands)	.50	.23	.06
☐ 9 Don Mattingly (Batting)	.50	.23	.06
☐ 10 Don Mattingly (Batting)	.50	.23	.06
☐ 11 Don Mattingly (Batting)	.50	.23	.06
☐ 12 Don Mattingly (Batting)	.50	.23	.06

1989 Rini Postcards Mets 1969

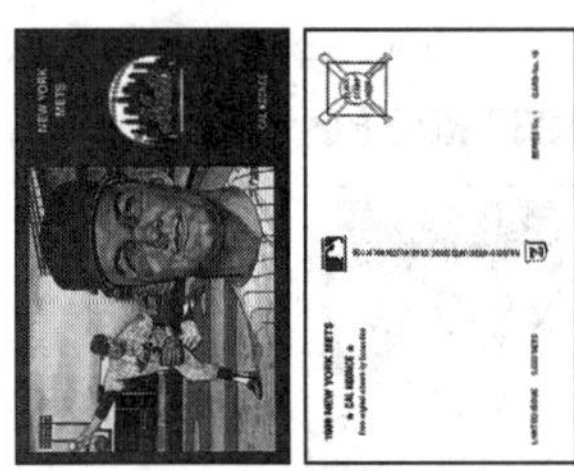

This set of 36 postcards measures 3 1/2" by 5 1/2", were limited to 5,000 produced, and showcases the 1969 New York Mets. On a blue background, the horizontal fronts feature color drawings by Susan Rini. The player cards are sequenced in alphabetical order.

	MINT	NRMT	EXC
COMPLETE SET (36)	15.00	6.75	1.85
COMMON CARD (1-36)	.25	.11	.03
☐ 1 Championship Trophy	.25	.11	.03
☐ 2 Shea Stadium	.25	.11	.03
☐ 3 Tommie Agee	.75	.35	.09
☐ 4 Ken Boswell	.25	.11	.03
☐ 5 Ed Charles	.25	.11	.03
☐ 6 Don Cardwell	.25	.11	.03
☐ 7 Donn Clendenon	.25	.11	.03
☐ 8 Jack DiLauro	.25	.11	.03
☐ 9 Duffy Dyer	.25	.11	.03
☐ 10 Wayne Garrett	.25	.11	.03
☐ 11 Jerry Grote	1.00	.45	.12
☐ 12 Rod Gaspar	.25	.11	.03
☐ 13 Gary Gentry	.25	.11	.03
☐ 14 Bud Harrelson	1.00	.45	.12
☐ 15 Gil Hodges MG	2.00	.90	.25
☐ 16 Cleon Jones	.75	.35	.09
☐ 17 Ed Kranepool	1.00	.45	.12
☐ 18 Cal Koonce	.25	.11	.03
☐ 19 Jerry Koosman	1.50	.70	.19
☐ 20 Jim McAndrew	.25	.11	.03
☐ 21 Tug McGraw	1.00	.45	.12
☐ 22 J.C. Martin	.25	.11	.03
☐ 23 Bob Pfeil	.25	.11	.03
☐ 24 Nolan Ryan	5.00	2.20	.60
☐ 25 Ron Swoboda	.75	.35	.09
☐ 26 Tom Seaver	3.00	1.35	.35
☐ 27 Art Shamsky	.25	.11	.03
☐ 28 Ron Taylor	.25	.11	.03
☐ 29 Al Weis	.25	.11	.03
☐ 30 Joe Pignatano CO	.25	.11	.03
☐ 31 Eddie Yost CO	.25	.11	.03
☐ 32 Ralph Kiner ANN	1.50	.70	.19
☐ 33 Bob Murphy ANN	.25	.11	.03
☐ 34 Lindsey Nelson ANN	.25	.11	.03
☐ 35 Yogi Berra CO	1.50	.70	.19
☐ 36 Rube Walker CO	.25	.11	.03

1989 Rini Postcards Negro League 1

This set of 12 postcards measures 3 1/2" by 5 1/2". The fronts feature color drawings by Susan Rini.

	MINT	NRMT	EXC
COMPLETE SET (12)	5.00	2.20	.60
COMMON CARD (1-12)	.40	.18	.05
☐ 1 Monte Irvin	1.00	.45	.12
☐ 2 Martin Dihigo	.75	.35	.09
☐ 3 Clint Thomas	.40	.18	.05
☐ 4 Buster Haywood	.40	.18	.05
☐ 5 George Giles	.40	.18	.05

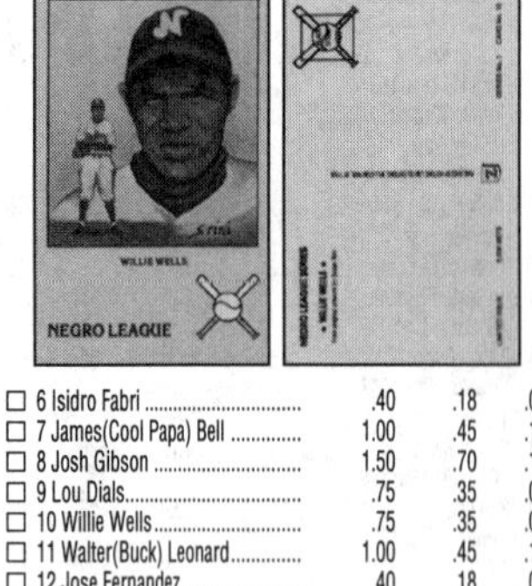

	MINT	NRMT	EXC
☐ 6 Isidro Fabri	.40	.18	.05
☐ 7 James(Cool Papa) Bell	1.00	.45	.12
☐ 8 Josh Gibson	1.50	.70	.19
☐ 9 Lou Dials	.75	.35	.09
☐ 10 Willie Wells	.75	.35	.09
☐ 11 Walter(Buck) Leonard	1.00	.45	.12
☐ 12 Jose Fernandez	.40	.18	.05

1990 Rini Postcards Clemente

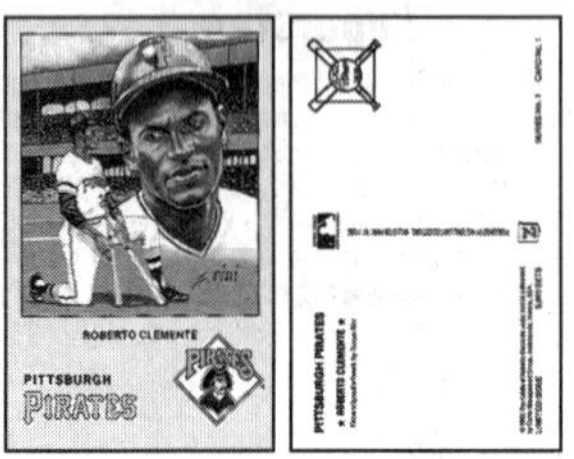

This 12-card set measures approximately 3 1/2" by 5 1/2" and honors Roberto Clemente. The fronts of the postcards feature the artwork of Susan Rini while the back notes that the set is limited to 5,000 copies of each postcard made.

	MINT	NRMT	EXC
COMPLETE SET (12)	5.00	2.20	.60
COMMON CARD (1-12)	.50	.23	.06
☐ 1 Roberto Clemente (Kneeling)	.50	.23	.06
☐ 2 Roberto Clemente (Leaving Batters Box)	.50	.23	.06
☐ 3 Roberto Clemente (Preparing to Swing)	.50	.23	.06
☐ 4 Roberto Clemente (Preparing to Field)	.50	.23	.06
☐ 5 Roberto Clemente (Leaving Batters Box)	.50	.23	.06
☐ 6 Roberto Clemente (Bat at Waist)	.50	.23	.06
☐ 7 Roberto Clemente (Tipping Cap)	.50	.23	.06
☐ 8 Roberto Clemente (Releasing Bat)	.50	.23	.06
☐ 9 Roberto Clemente (Mid-Swing)	.50	.23	.06
☐ 10 Roberto Clemente (Leaping Over Fence)	.50	.23	.06
☐ 11 Roberto Clemente (In Batting Cage)	.50	.23	.06
☐ 12 Roberto Clemente (First step out of batters box)	.50	.23	.06

1990 Rini Postcards Munson

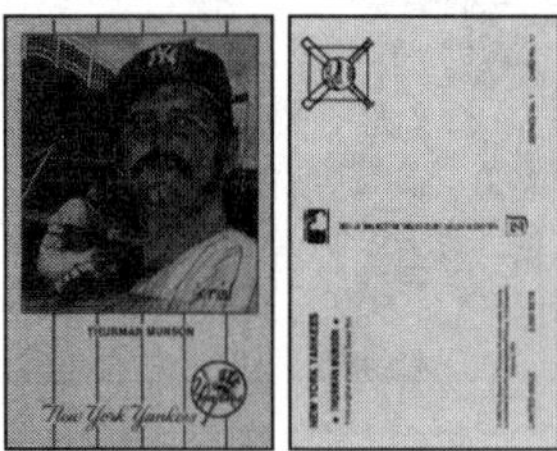

This set of 12 postcards measures 3 1/2" by 5 1/2" and honors Thurman Munson. The fronts feature color drawings by Susan Rini.

	MINT	NRMT	EXC
COMPLETE SET (12)	5.00	2.20	.60
COMMON CARD (1-12)	.50	.23	.06
☐ 1 Thurman Munson (Before a game)	.50	.23	.06
☐ 2 Thurman Munson (Sliding)	.50	.23	.06
☐ 3 Thurman Munson (Throwing a ball)	.50	.23	.06
☐ 4 Thurman Munson (Catching, seen from the back)	.50	.23	.06
☐ 5 Thurman Munson (Standing with bat in right hand)	.50	.23	.06
☐ 6 Thurman Munson (Kneeling)	.50	.23	.06
☐ 7 Thurman Munson (Standing, with catcher's uniform)	.50	.23	.06
☐ 8 Thurman Munson (Catching a ball)	.50	.23	.06
☐ 9 Thurman Munson (Standing with bat in left hand)	.50	.23	.06
☐ 10 Thurman Munson (Walking)	.50	.23	.06
☐ 11 Thurman Munson (Waiting for the ball)	.50	.23	.06
☐ 12 Thurman Munson (Standing)	.50	.23	.06

1990 Rini Postcards Ryan 1

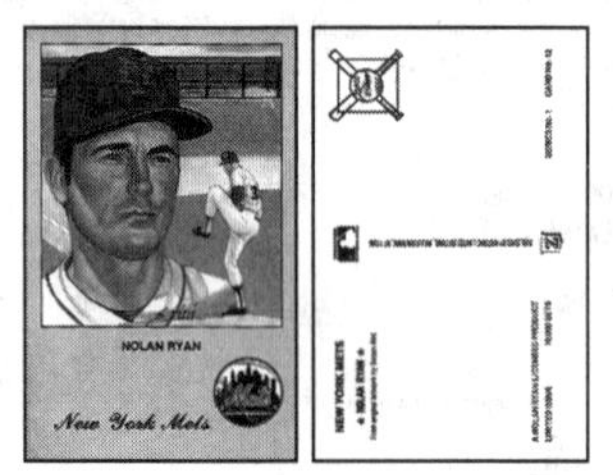

This set of 12 postcards measures 3 1/2" by 5 1/2" and honors Nolan Ryan. On a light blue background, the fronts feature color drawings by Susan Rini.

	MINT	NRMT	EXC
COMPLETE SET (12)	5.00	2.20	.60
COMMON CARD (1-12)	.50	.23	.06
☐ 1 Nolan Ryan (Portrait on the right, pitching for the Rangers on the left)	.50	.23	.06
☐ 2 Nolan Ryan (Portrait on the right, pitching for the Rangers, left leg up, on the left)	.50	.23	.06
☐ 3 Nolan Ryan (Portrait on the right, pitching for the Rangers, ball in right hand, on the left)	.50	.23	.06
☐ 4 Nolan Ryan (Portrait on the right, pitching for the Rangers, right arm stretched out, on the left)	.50	.23	.06
☐ 5 Nolan Ryan (Portrait on the right, pitching for the Rangers, glove in front of left shoulder, on the left)	.50	.23	.06
☐ 6 Nolan Ryan (Portrait on the right, pitching for the Rangers, getting ready to pitch, on the left)	.50	.23	.06
☐ 7 Nolan Ryan (Portrait on the left, pitching for the Rangers, right arm behind head, on the right)	.50	.23	.06
☐ 8 Nolan Ryan (Portrait on the right, pitching for the Rangers, right leg back, on the left)	.50	.23	.06
☐ 9 Nolan Ryan (Portrait on the left, pitching for the Mets, left leg up, on the right)	.50	.23	.06
☐ 10 Nolan Ryan (Portrait on the right, pitching for the Mets, right arm stretched out, on the left)	.50	.23	.06
☐ 11 Nolan Ryan (Portrait on the right, pitching for the Mets, left leg above the ground, on the left)	.50	.23	.06
☐ 12 Nolan Ryan (Portrait on the left, pitching for the Mets, left leg up, on the right)	.50	.23	.06

1990 Rini Postcards Ryan 2

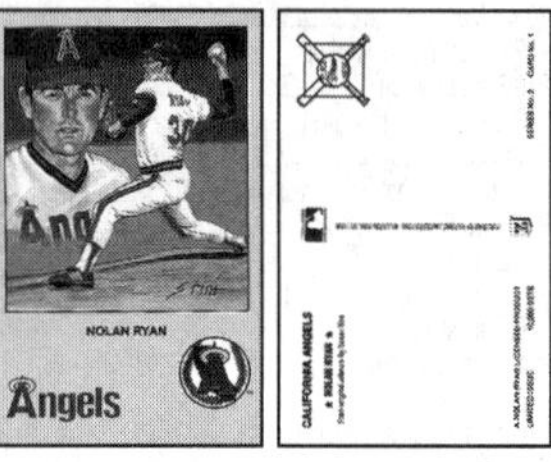

This set of 12 postcards measures 3 1/2" by 5 1/2" and honors Nolan Ryan. On a peach colored background, the fronts feature color drawings by Susan Rini.

	MINT	NRMT	EXC
COMPLETE SET (12)	5.00	2.20	.60
COMMON CARD (1-12)	.50	.23	.06
☐ 1 Nolan Ryan (Portrait on the left, pitching for the Angels, ball behind head, on the right)	.50	.23	.06
☐ 2 Nolan Ryan (Portrait on the left, pitching for the Angels, left leg above ground, on the right)	.50	.23	.06
☐ 3 Nolan Ryan (Portrait on the right, pitching for the Angels, left leg up, on the left)	.50	.23	.06
☐ 4 Nolan Ryan (Portrait on the left, pitching for the Angels, left arm holds the ball, on the right)	.50	.23	.06
☐ 5 Nolan Ryan (Portrait on the right, pitching for the Angels, left leg above ground, on the left)	.50	.23	.06
☐ 6 Nolan Ryan (Portrait on the right, pitching for the Angels, getting ready to pitch, on the left)	.50	.23	.06
☐ 7 Nolan Ryan (Portrait on the right, pitching for the Astros, right arm stretched out, on the left)	.50	.23	.06
☐ 8 Nolan Ryan (Portrait on the right, kneeling, with glove, on the left)	.50	.23	.06
☐ 9 Nolan Ryan (Portrait on the right, pitching for the Astros, left leg slightly above ground, on the left)	.50	.23	.06
☐ 10 Nolan Ryan (Portrait on the right, pitching for the Astros, ball in right hand, on the left)	.50	.23	.06
☐ 11 Nolan Ryan (Portrait on the left, pitching for the Astros, right arm behind head, on the right)	.50	.23	.06
☐ 12 Nolan Ryan (Portrait on the right, pitching for the Astros, right arm stretched out, on the left)	.50	.23	.06

1990 Rini Postcards Yankees Monument Park 1

This set of 12 postcards measures 3 1/2" by 5 1/2". The fronts feature color drawings by Susan Rini.

	MINT	NRMT	EXC
COMPLETE SET (12)	5.00	2.20	.60
COMMON CARD (1-12)	.40	.18	.05
☐ 1 Lou Gehrig	2.00	.90	.25
☐ 2 Babe Ruth	2.50	1.10	.30
☐ 3 Thurman Munson	.75	.35	.09
☐ 4 Elston Howard	.40	.18	.05
☐ 5 Phil Rizzuto	.75	.35	.09
☐ 6 Mickey Mantle	2.50	1.10	.30
☐ 7 Bill Dickey	.75	.35	.09
☐ 8 Lefty Gomez	.60	.25	.07

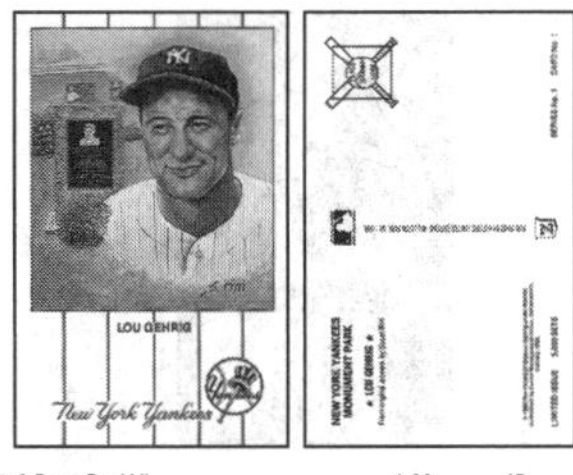

☐ 9 Pope Paul VI	1.00	.45	.12
☐ 10 Jacob Ruppert	.40	.18	.05
☐ 11 Roger Maris	1.00	.45	.12
☐ 12 Joe DiMaggio	1.50	.70	.19

1991 Rini Postcards 1961 Yankees 1

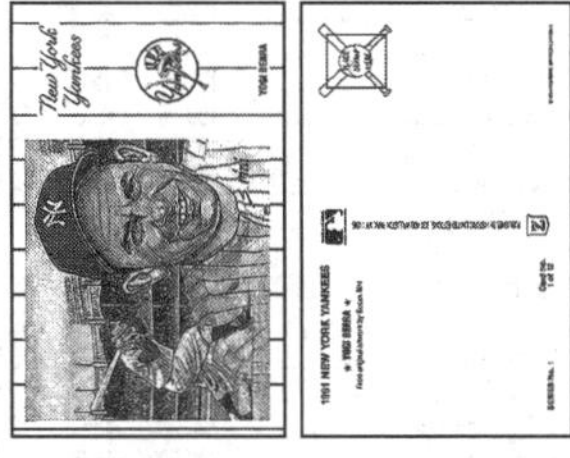

This set of 12 postcards measures 3 1/2" by 5 1/2" and showcases the 1961 New York Yankees. On a white background with blue stripes, the horizontal fronts feature color drawings by Susan Rini. The cards are numbered on the back as "X of 12."

	MINT	NRMT	EXC
COMPLETE SET (12)	5.00	2.20	.60
COMMON CARD (1-12)	.40	.18	.05
☐ 1 Yogi Berra	1.00	.45	.12
☐ 2 Tom Tresh	.60	.25	.07
☐ 3 Bill Skowron	.60	.25	.07
☐ 4 Al Downing	.40	.18	.05
☐ 5 Jim Coates	.40	.18	.05
☐ 6 Luis Arroyo	.40	.18	.05
☐ 7 Johnny Blanchard	.40	.18	.05
☐ 8 Hector Lopez	.40	.18	.05
☐ 9 Tony Kubek	.75	.35	.09
☐ 10 Ralph Houk MG	.60	.25	.07
☐ 11 Bobby Richardson	.75	.35	.09
☐ 12 Clete Boyer	.60	.25	.07

1991 Rini Postcards 1961 Yankees 2

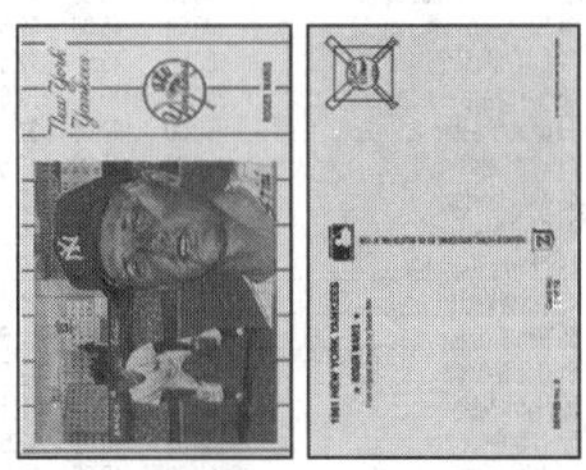

This set of 12 postcards measures 3 1/2" by 5 1/2" and showcases the 1961 New York Yankees. On a white background with blue stripes, the horizontal fronts feature color drawings by Susan Rini. The cards are numbered on the back as "X of 12."

	MINT	NRMT	EXC
COMPLETE SET (12)	5.00	2.20	.60
COMMON CARD (1-12)	.40	.18	.05
☐ 1 Roger Maris	1.00	.45	.12
☐ 2 Jesse Gonder	.40	.18	.05
☐ 3 Danny McDevitt	.40	.18	.05
☐ 4 Leroy Thomas	.40	.18	.05
☐ 5 Billy Gardner	.40	.18	.05
☐ 6 Ralph Terry	.60	.25	.07
☐ 7 Hal Reniff	.40	.18	.05
☐ 8 Earl Torgeson	.40	.18	.05
☐ 9 Art Ditmar	.40	.18	.05
☐ 10 Jack Reed	.40	.18	.05
☐ 11 Johnny James	.40	.18	.05
☐ 12 Elston Howard	.75	.35	.09

1991 Rini Postcards 1961 Yankees 3

This set of 12 postcards measures 3 1/2" by 5 1/2" and showcases the 1961 New York Yankees. On a white background with blue stripes, the horizontal fronts feature color drawings by Susan Rini. The cards are numbered on the back as "X of 12."

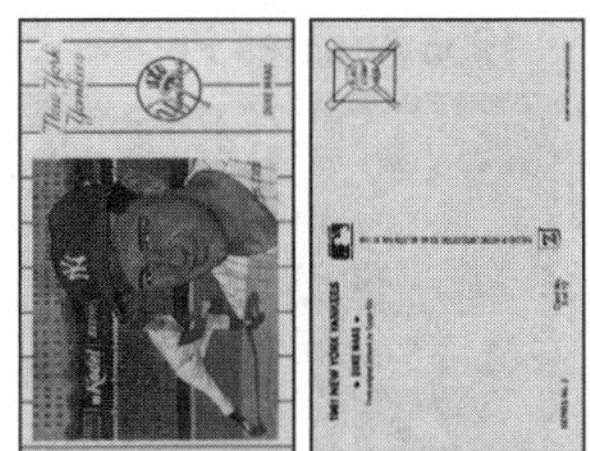

	MINT	NRMT	EXC
COMPLETE SET (12)	5.00	2.20	.60
COMMON CARD (1-12)	.40	.18	.05
☐ 1 Mickey Mantle	2.00	.90	.25
☐ 2 Deron Johnson	.40	.18	.05
☐ 3 Bob Hale	.40	.18	.05
☐ 4 Bill Stafford	.40	.18	.05
☐ 5 Duke Maas	.40	.18	.05
☐ 6 Bob Cerv	.40	.18	.05
☐ 7 Roland Sheldon	.40	.18	.05
☐ 8 Ryne Duren	.60	.25	.07
☐ 9 Bob Turley	.60	.25	.07
☐ 10 Whitey Ford	1.00	.45	.12
☐ 11 Bud Daley	.40	.18	.05
☐ 12 Joe DeMaestri	.40	.18	.05

1991 Rini Postcards Brooklyn Dodgers 2

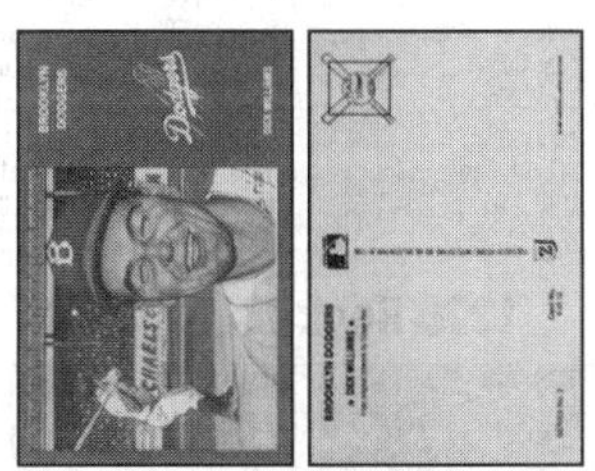

This set of 12 postcards measures 3 1/2" by 5 1/2" and showcases the Brooklyn Dodgers. On a blue background, the horizontal fronts feature color drawings by Susan Rini. The cards are numbered on the back as "X of 12."

	MINT	NRMT	EXC
COMPLETE SET (12)	5.00	2.20	.60
COMMON CARD (1-12)	.40	.18	.05
☐ 1 Charley Dressen	.60	.25	.07
☐ 2 Johnny Roseboro	.60	.25	.07
☐ 3 Eddie Stanky	.60	.25	.07
☐ 4 Goodwin(Goody) Rosen	.40	.18	.05
☐ 5 Ed Head	.40	.18	.05
☐ 6 Dick Williams	.60	.25	.07
☐ 7 Clarence(Bud) Podbielan	.40	.18	.05
☐ 8 Erv Palica	.40	.18	.05
☐ 9 Augie Galan	.40	.18	.05
☐ 10 Billy Loes	.60	.25	.07
☐ 11 Billy Cox	.60	.25	.07
☐ 12 Phil Phifer	.40	.18	.05

1991 Rini Postcards Brooklyn Dodgers 3

This set of 12 postcards measures 3 1/2" by 5 1/2" and showcases the Brooklyn Dodgers. On a blue background, the horizontal fronts feature color drawings by Susan Rini. The cards are numbered on the back as "X of 12."

	MINT	NRMT	EXC
COMPLETE SET (12)	5.00	2.20	.60
COMMON CARD (1-12)	.40	.18	.05
☐ 1 Joe Black	.60	.25	.07
☐ 2 Jack Banta	.40	.18	.05
☐ 3 Whitlow Wyatt	.40	.18	.05
☐ 4 Gino Cimoli	.40	.18	.05
☐ 5 Dolph Camilli	.60	.25	.07
☐ 6 Dan Bankhead	.40	.18	.05
☐ 7 Henry Behrman	.40	.18	.05
☐ 8 Pete Reiser	.75	.35	.09
☐ 9 Chris Van Cuyk	.40	.18	.05
☐ 10 James(Junior) Gilliam	.75	.35	.09
☐ 11 Don Zimmer	.60	.25	.07
☐ 12 Ed Roebuck	.40	.18	.05

1991 Rini Postcards Brooklyn Dodgers 4

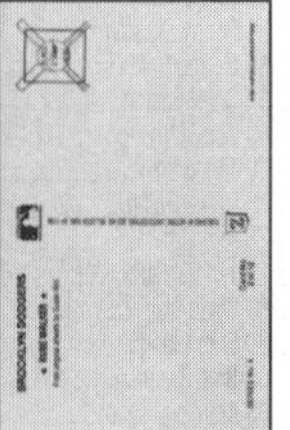

This set of 12 postcards measures 3 1/2" by 5 1/2" and showcases the Brooklyn Dodgers. On a blue background, the horizontal fronts feature color drawings by Susan Rini. The cards are numbered on the back as "X of 12."

	MINT	NRMT	EXC
COMPLETE SET (12)	5.00	2.20	.60
COMMON CARD (1- 12	.40	.18	.05
☐ 1 Billy Herman	1.00	.45	.12
☐ 2 Rube Walker	.40	.18	.05
☐ 3 Tommy Brown	.40	.18	.05
☐ 4 Charles Neal	.40	.18	.05
☐ 5 Kirby Higbe	.60	.25	.07
☐ 6 Bruce Edwards	.40	.18	.05
☐ 7 Joe Hatten	.40	.18	.05
☐ 8 Rex Barney	.40	.18	.05
☐ 9 Al Gionfriddo	.40	.18	.05
☐ 10 Luis Olmo	.40	.18	.05
☐ 11 Dixie Walker	.75	.35	.09
☐ 12 Walter Alston	1.00	.45	.12

1991 Rini Postcards Mattingly II

This set of 12 postcards measures approximately 3 1/2" by 5 1/2" and honors Don Mattingly. On a white background with blue stripes, the fronts feature color drawings by Susan Rini. The backs carry a postcard format.

	MINT	NRMT	EXC
COMPLETE SET (12)	5.00	2.20	.60
COMMON CARD (1-12)	.50	.23	.06
☐ 1 Don Mattingly (Looking to the right and batting seen from back)	.50	.23	.06
☐ 2 Don Mattingly (Looking to the left and batting facing front)	.50	.23	.06
☐ 3 Don Mattingly (Looking to the left and batting in bunting pose)	.50	.23	.06
☐ 4 Don Mattingly (Looking straight ahead and in field position stance)	.50	.23	.06
☐ 5 Don Mattingly (Smiling and at end of batting swing)	.50	.23	.06
☐ 6 Don Mattingly (Looking straight ahead and dropping bat after hitting the ball)	.50	.23	.06
☐ 7 Don Mattingly (Grinning broadly and ready to run to base)	.50	.23	.06
☐ 8 Don Mattingly (Looking to the left and having just swung the bat)	.50	.23	.06
☐ 9 Don Mattingly (Portrait on the left and in middle of swing)	.50	.23	.06
☐ 10 Don Mattingly (Looking straight ahead and at end of swing)	.50	.23	.06
☐ 11 Don Mattingly (With arm raised and in batting stance)	.50	.23	.06
☐ 12 Don Mattingly (With eyes to the right and lifting foot at beginning of swing)	.50	.23	.06

1933 Rittenhouse Candy E285

These cards measure 2 1/4" by 1 7/16" and are found in three colors: red, green or blue. The fronts feature a player photo in the middle surrounded by the suits symbol. The backs either feature one alphabetical character from the words "Rittnebouse Candy Co" or a description of the premium offers. We have sequenced the set in playing order by suit and numbers are assigned to Aces (1), Jacks (11A), Queens (12) and Kings (13).

	EX-MT	VG-E	GOOD
COMPLETE SET (52)	3750.00	1700.00	475.00
COMMON CARD	35.00	16.00	4.40
☐ 1C Doc Cramer	35.00	16.00	4.40
☐ 1D Babe Herman	100.00	45.00	12.50
☐ 1H Mule Haas	35.00	16.00	4.40
☐ 1S Babe Ruth	400.00	180.00	50.00
☐ 2C Bing Miller	35.00	16.00	4.40
☐ 2D Chick Hafey	100.00	45.00	12.50
☐ 2H Gus Mancuso	35.00	16.00	4.40
☐ 2S Billy Herman	100.00	45.00	12.50
☐ 3C Lefty O'Doul	100.00	45.00	12.50
☐ 3D Chuck Klein	100.00	45.00	12.50
☐ 3H George Earnshaw	50.00	22.00	6.25
☐ 3S Frankie Frisch	125.00	55.00	15.50
☐ 4C Mel Ott	125.00	55.00	15.50
☐ 4D Fred Brickell	35.00	16.00	4.40
☐ 4H Leroy Mahaffey	35.00	16.00	4.40
☐ 4S Dick Bartell	35.00	16.00	4.40
☐ 5C Kiki Cuyler	100.00	45.00	12.50
☐ 5D George Davis	35.00	16.00	4.40
☐ 5H Jimmy Dykes	50.00	22.00	6.25
☐ 5S Paul Waner	100.00	45.00	12.50
☐ 6C Hugh Critz	35.00	16.00	4.40
☐ 6D Paul Waner	100.00	45.00	12.50
☐ 6H Rogers Hornsby	150.00	70.00	19.00
☐ 6S Don Hurst	35.00	16.00	4.40
☐ 7C Walter Berger	50.00	22.00	6.25
☐ 7D Sugar Cain	35.00	16.00	4.40
☐ 7H Joe Cronin	100.00	45.00	12.50
☐ 7S Frankie Frisch	100.00	45.00	12.50
☐ 8C Dib Williams	35.00	16.00	4.40
☐ 8D Lefty Grove	125.00	55.00	15.50
☐ 8H Lou Finney	35.00	16.00	4.40
☐ 8S Ed. Cihocki	35.00	16.00	4.40
☐ 9C Hack Wilson	100.00	45.00	12.50
☐ 9D Al Simmons	100.00	45.00	12.50
☐ 9H Spud Davis	35.00	16.00	4.40
☐ 9S Hack Wilson	100.00	45.00	12.50
☐ 10C Pie Traynor	100.00	45.00	12.50
☐ 10D Bill Terry	100.00	45.00	12.50
☐ 10H Lloyd Waner	100.00	45.00	12.50
☐ 10S Jimmy Foxx	125.00	55.00	15.50
☐ 11C Jumbo Elliott	35.00	16.00	4.40
☐ 11D Don Hurst	35.00	16.00	4.40
☐ 11H Pinky Higgins	35.00	16.00	4.40
☐ 11S Jim Bottomley	100.00	45.00	12.50
☐ 12C Pinky Whitney	35.00	16.00	4.40
☐ 12D Lloyd Waner	100.00	45.00	12.50
☐ 12H Eric McNair	35.00	16.00	4.40
☐ 12S Rube Walberg	35.00	16.00	4.40
☐ 13C Babe Ruth	400.00	180.00	50.00
☐ 13D Phil Collins	35.00	16.00	4.40
☐ 13H Gabby Hartnett	100.00	45.00	12.50
☐ 13S Max Bishop	35.00	16.00	4.40

1955 Robert Gould W605

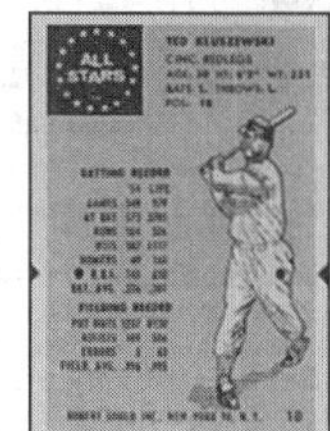

The cards in this 28-card set measure 2 1/2" by 3 1/2". The 1955 Robert F. Gould set of black and white on green cards were toy store cardboard holders for small plastic statues. The statues were attached to the card by a rubber band through two holes on the side of the card. The catalog designation is W605. The cards are numbered in the bottom right corner of the obverse and are blank-backed.

	NRMT	VG-E	GOOD
COMPLETE SET (28)	1350.00	600.00	170.00
COMMON CARD (1-28)	30.00	13.50	3.70
☐ 1 Willie Mays	375.00	170.00	47.50
☐ 2 Gus Zernial	30.00	13.50	3.70
☐ 3 Red Schoendienst	60.00	27.00	7.50
☐ 4 Chico Carrasquel	30.00	13.50	3.70
☐ 5 Jim Hegan	30.00	13.50	3.70
☐ 6 Curt Simmons	35.00	16.00	4.40
☐ 7 Bob Porterfield	30.00	13.50	3.70
☐ 8 Jim Busby	30.00	13.50	3.70
☐ 9 Don Mueller	30.00	13.50	3.70
☐ 10 Ted Kluszewski	60.00	27.00	7.50
☐ 11 Ray Boone	30.00	13.50	3.70

☐ 12 Smoky Burgess	35.00	16.00	4.40
☐ 13 Bob Rush	30.00	13.50	3.70
☐ 14 Early Wynn	60.00	27.00	7.50
☐ 15 Bill Bruton	30.00	13.50	3.70
☐ 16 Gus Bell	30.00	13.50	3.70
☐ 17 Jim Finigan	30.00	13.50	3.70
☐ 18 Granny Hamner	30.00	13.50	3.70
☐ 19 Hank Thompson	30.00	13.50	3.70
☐ 20 Joe Coleman	30.00	13.50	3.70
☐ 21 Don Newcombe	40.00	18.00	5.00
☐ 22 Richie Ashburn	75.00	34.00	9.50
☐ 23 Bobby Thomson	35.00	16.00	4.40
☐ 24 Sid Gordon	30.00	13.50	3.70
☐ 25 Gerry Coleman	35.00	16.00	4.40
☐ 26 Ernie Banks	175.00	80.00	22.00
☐ 27 Billy Pierce	35.00	16.00	4.40
☐ 28 Mel Parnell	35.00	16.00	4.40

1955 Robert Gould Statues

This 28-statue Robert Gould set came attached to a rather bland 2 1/2" X 3 1/2 "player card using a rubber band. The plastic statues are white in color. The below values are for statues only. The cards are priced in the card section under Robert Gould.

	NRMT	VG-E	GOOD
COMPLETE SET (28)	450.00	200.00	55.00
COMMON STATUE (1-28)	15.00	6.75	1.85
☐ 1 Willie Mays	50.00	22.00	6.25
☐ 2 Gus Zernial	15.00	6.75	1.85
☐ 3 Red Schoendienst	25.00	11.00	3.10
☐ 4 Chico Carrasquel	20.00	9.00	2.50
☐ 5 Jim Hegan	15.00	6.75	1.85
☐ 6 Curt Simmons	20.00	9.00	2.50
☐ 7 Bob Porterfield	15.00	6.75	1.85
☐ 8 Jim Busby	15.00	6.75	1.85
☐ 9 Don Mueller	15.00	6.75	1.85
☐ 10 Ted Kluszewski	25.00	11.00	3.10
☐ 11 Ray Boone	15.00	6.75	1.85
☐ 12 Smoky Burgess	20.00	9.00	2.50
☐ 13 Bob Rush	15.00	6.75	1.85
☐ 14 Early Wynn	25.00	11.00	3.10
☐ 15 Bill Bruton	15.00	6.75	1.85
☐ 16 Gus Bell	15.00	6.75	1.85
☐ 17 Jim Finigan	15.00	6.75	1.85
☐ 18 Granny Hamner	15.00	6.75	1.85
☐ 19 Hank Thompson	20.00	9.00	2.50
☐ 20 Joe Coleman	15.00	6.75	1.85
☐ 21 Don Newcombe	25.00	11.00	3.10
☐ 22 Richie Ashburn	35.00	16.00	4.40
☐ 23 Bobby Thomson	20.00	9.00	2.50
☐ 24 Sid Gordon	15.00	6.75	1.85
☐ 25 Gerry Coleman	20.00	9.00	2.50
☐ 26 Ernie Banks	40.00	18.00	5.00
☐ 27 Billy Pierce	20.00	9.00	2.50
☐ 28 Mel Parnell	20.00	9.00	2.50

1993 Rockies U.S. Playing Cards

This 56-card standard-size set celebrates the 1993 Inaugural Year of the Colorado Rockies. The fronts of these rounded-corner cards feature full-color posed and action shots of the players while the backs have the team's purple logo on a silver background with silver pinstripes. The player's name and position appear in a teal bar at the bottom of the photo. Since this set is similar to a playing card set, the set is checklisted below as if it were a playing card deck. In the checklist C means Clubs, D means Diamonds, H means Hearts, S means Spades and JK means Joker. The cards are checklisted in playing order by suits and numbers are assigned to Aces, (1) Jacks, (11) Queens, (12) and Kings (13). Included in the set are a Rockies' opening day player roster card and a 1993 home schedule card. The jokers, home schedule card and the opening day player roster card are unnumbered and listed at the end.

	MINT	NRMT	EXC
COMPLETE SET (56)	4.00	1.80	.50
COMMON CARD	.05	.02	.01
☐ 1C Jim Tatum	.05	.02	.01
☐ 1D Andres Galarraga	.50	.23	.06
☐ 1H Charlie Hayes	.05	.02	.01
☐ 1S David Nied	.05	.02	.01
☐ 2C Charlie Hayes	.15	.07	.02
☐ 2D David Nied	.05	.02	.01
☐ 2H Jim Tatum	.05	.02	.01
☐ 2S Andres Galarraga	.50	.23	.06
☐ 3C Dale Murphy	.25	.11	.03
☐ 3D Dante Bichette	.50	.23	.06
☐ 3H Andy Ashby	.15	.07	.02
☐ 3S Gary Wayne	.05	.02	.01
☐ 4C Scott Aldred	.05	.02	.01
☐ 4D Joe Girardi	.15	.07	.02
☐ 4H Vinny Castilla	.40	.18	.05
☐ 4S Freddie Benavides	.05	.02	.01
☐ 5C Braulio Castillo	.05	.02	.01
☐ 5D Bryn Smith	.05	.02	.01
☐ 5H Steve Reed	.05	.02	.01
☐ 5S Butch Henry	.05	.02	.01
☐ 6C Danny Sheaffer	.05	.02	.01
☐ 6D Darren Holmes	.05	.02	.01
☐ 6H Daryl Boston	.05	.02	.01
☐ 6S Gerald Young	.05	.02	.01
☐ 7C Jerald Clark	.05	.02	.01
☐ 7D Bruce Ruffin	.05	.02	.01
☐ 7H Alex Cole	.05	.02	.01
☐ 7S Jeff Parrett	.05	.02	.01
☐ 8C Willie Blair	.05	.02	.01
☐ 8D Eric Young	.25	.11	.03
☐ 8H Bryn Smith	.05	.02	.01
☐ 8S Braulio Castillo	.05	.02	.01
☐ 9C Daryl Boston	.05	.02	.01
☐ 9D Gerald Young	.05	.02	.01
☐ 9H Danny Sheaffer	.05	.02	.01
☐ 9S Darren Holmes	.05	.02	.01
☐ 10C Andy Ashby	.15	.07	.02
☐ 10D Gary Wayne	.05	.02	.01
☐ 10H Willie Blair	.05	.02	.01
☐ 10S Dale Murphy	.25	.11	.03
☐ 11C Butch Henry	.05	.02	.01
☐ 11D Steve Reed	.05	.02	.01
☐ 11H Dante Bichette	.50	.23	.06
☐ 11S Eric Young	.15	.07	.02
☐ 12C Alex Cole	.05	.02	.01
☐ 12D Jeff Parrett	.05	.02	.01
☐ 12H Jerald Clark	.05	.02	.01
☐ 12S Bruce Ruffin	.05	.02	.01
☐ 13C Vinny Castilla	.40	.18	.05
☐ 13D Freddie Benavides	.05	.02	.01
☐ 13H Scott Aldred	.05	.02	.01
☐ 13S Joe Girardi	.15	.07	.02
☐ JKO National League Logo	.05	.02	.01
☐ NNO 1993 Home Schedule	.05	.02	.01

1994 Rockies Police

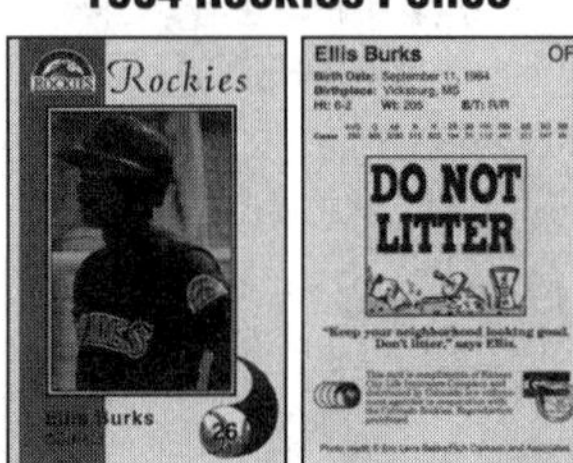

These 27 cards measure approximately 2 5/8" by 4" and feature color action and posed player photos on their yellow-bordered fronts. The player's name and position appear at the lower left. His uniform number appears in a baseball icon at the lower right. A wide purplish stripe that runs down the card near the left edge carries the Rockies logo. The white back carries the player's name and position at the top, followed below by biography, statistics, and safety message, all in purple lettering. The cards are unnumbered and checklisted below in alphabetical order.

	MINT	NRMT	EXC
COMPLETE SET (27)	10.00	4.50	1.25
COMMON CARD (1-27)	.25	.11	.03
☐ 1 Don Baylor MG	.75	.35	.09
☐ 2 Dante Bichette	2.00	.90	.25
☐ 3 Willie Blair	.25	.11	.03
☐ 4 Kent Bottenfield	.25	.11	.03
☐ 5 Ellis Burks	1.50	.70	.19
☐ 6 Vinny Castilla	1.50	.70	.19
☐ 7 Marvin Freeman	.25	.11	.03
☐ 8 Andres Galarraga	2.00	.90	.25
☐ 9 Andres Galarraga 1993 Batting Champ	2.00	.90	.25
☐ 10 Joe Girardi	.25	.11	.03
☐ 11 Mike Harkey	.25	.11	.03
☐ 12 Greg W. Harris	.25	.11	.03
☐ 13 Charlie Hayes	.50	.23	.06
☐ 14 Darren Holmes	.25	.11	.03
☐ 15 Howard Johnson	.25	.11	.03
☐ 16 Nelson Liriano	.25	.11	.03
☐ 17 Roberto Mejia	.25	.11	.03
☐ 18 Mike Munoz	.25	.11	.03
☐ 19 David Nied	.25	.11	.03
☐ 20 Steve Reed	.25	.11	.03
☐ 21 Armando Reynoso	.25	.11	.03
☐ 22 Bruce Ruffin	.25	.11	.03
☐ 23 Danny Sheaffer	.25	.11	.03
☐ 24 Darrell Sherman	.25	.11	.03
☐ 25 Walt Weiss	.50	.23	.06
☐ 26 Eric Young	.50	.23	.06
☐ 27 Coaches Card Larry Bearnarth Dwight Evans Gene Glynn Ron Hassey Bill Plummer Don Zimmer	.25	.11	.03

1995 Rockies Police

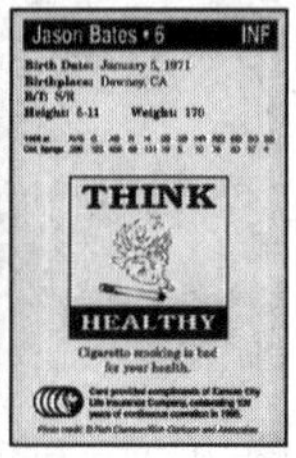

This 12-card set of the Colorado Rockies measures 2 5/8" by 4" and was sponsored by the Kansas City Life Insurance Company. The fronts feature color action player photos in a thin white and tan frame on a black background, with the player's last name and year printed in the right border. The team's logo is at the bottom. The backs carry the player's name, jersey number and position in a black bar across the top followed by biographical information, statistics, and a safety message. The cards are unnumbered and checklisted below in alphabetical order.

	MINT	NRMT	EXC
COMPLETE SET (12)	7.50	3.40	.95
COMMON CARD (1-12)	.25	.11	.03
☐ 1 Jason Bates	.25	.11	.03
☐ 2 Don Baylor MG	.50	.23	.06
☐ 3 Dante Bichette	1.50	.70	.19
☐ 4 Ellis Burks	1.00	.45	.12
☐ 5 Vinny Castilla	1.00	.45	.12
☐ 6 Andres Galarraga	1.50	.70	.19
☐ 7 Joe Girardi	.50	.23	.06
☐ 8 Mike Kingery	.25	.11	.03
☐ 9 Bill Swift	.25	.11	.03
☐ 10 Larry Walker	1.50	.70	.19
☐ 11 Walt Weiss	.50	.23	.06
☐ 12 Eric Young	.75	.35	.09

1996 Rockies Police

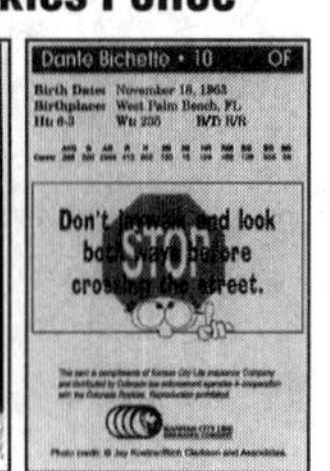

This 27-card set measures approximately 2 5/8" by 4". This set features members of the 1996 Colorado Rockies. The cards are unnumbered and we have sequenced them in alphabetical order. The set was sponsored by Kansas City Life Insurance Company and the back features various safety tips.

	MINT	NRMT	EXC
COMPLETE SET (27)	8.00	3.60	1.00
COMMON CARD (1-27)	.25	.11	.03
☐ 1 Roger Bailey	.25	.11	.03
☐ 2 Jason Bates	.25	.11	.03
☐ 3 Don Baylor MG	.75	.35	.09
☐ 4 Dante Bichette	1.25	.55	.16
☐ 5 Ellis Burks	1.00	.45	.12
☐ 6 Vinny Castilla	.75	.35	.09
☐ 7 Marvin Freeman	.25	.11	.03
☐ 8 Andres Galarraga	1.25	.55	.16
☐ 9 Darren Holmes	.25	.11	.03
☐ 10 Trenidad Hubbard	.25	.11	.03
☐ 11 Curt Leskanic	.25	.11	.03
☐ 12 Quinton McCracken	.25	.11	.03
☐ 13 Mike Munoz	.25	.11	.03
☐ 14 Jayhawk Owens	.25	.11	.03
☐ 15 Lance Painter	.25	.11	.03
☐ 16 Steve Reed	.25	.11	.03
☐ 17 Bryan Rekar	.25	.11	.03
☐ 18 Armando Reynoso	.25	.11	.03
☐ 19 Kevin Ritz	.25	.11	.03
☐ 20 Bruce Ruffin	.25	.11	.03
☐ 21 Bret Saberhagen	.50	.23	.06
☐ 22 Bill Swift	.25	.11	.03
☐ 23 Mark Thompson	.25	.11	.03
☐ 24 John Vander Wal	.25	.11	.03
☐ 25 Larry Walker	1.00	.45	.12
☐ 26 Walt Weiss	.50	.23	.06
☐ 27 Eric Young	.75	.35	.09

1908-09 Rose Company PC760

One of the most attractive postcards ever issued, The Rose Company postcards were issued during the end of the 20th century's first decade. The set features a black and white photo in a circle surrounded by a yellow and green baseball field, crossed bats and small figures. Imprints on the reverse contain the letters TRC, with the loop around the bottom of the C possibly accounting for a lower case "o," giving Co. The Rose Co. baseball series is listed in alphabetical

order by teams in the checklist below-research indicates that each of the 16 major league teams is represented by 12 Rose postcards (to date not all have been found)

	EX-MT	VG-E	GOOD
COMPLETE SET (182)	18500.00	8300.00	2300.00
COMMON CARD (1-182)	100.00	45.00	12.50
☐ 1 Ralph Glaze	100.00	45.00	12.50
☐ 2 Dad Hale	100.00	45.00	12.50
☐ 3 Frank LaPorte	100.00	45.00	12.50
☐ 4 Bris Lord	100.00	45.00	12.50
☐ 5 Tex Pruiett	100.00	45.00	12.50
☐ 6 Jack Thoney	100.00	45.00	12.50
☐ 7 Bob Unglaub	100.00	45.00	12.50
☐ 8 Heinie Wagner	100.00	45.00	12.50
☐ 9 George Winter	100.00	45.00	12.50
☐ 10 Cy Young	500.00	220.00	60.00
☐ 11 Nick Altrock	125.00	55.00	15.50
☐ 12 John Anderson	100.00	45.00	12.50
☐ 13 Jiggs Donohue	100.00	45.00	12.50
☐ 14 Frank Isbell	100.00	45.00	12.50
☐ 15 Fielder Jones	100.00	45.00	12.50
☐ 16 Freddy Parent	100.00	45.00	12.50
☐ 17 Frank Smith	100.00	45.00	12.50
☐ 18 Billy Sullivan	100.00	45.00	12.50
☐ 19 Lee Tannehill	100.00	45.00	12.50
☐ 20 Doc White	100.00	45.00	12.50
☐ 21 Harry Bemis	100.00	45.00	12.50
☐ 22 Joe Birmingham	100.00	45.00	12.50
☐ 23 Bill Bradley	100.00	45.00	12.50
☐ 24 Josh Clarke	100.00	45.00	12.50
☐ 25 Bill Hinchman	100.00	45.00	12.50
☐ 26 Addie Joss	400.00	180.00	50.00
☐ 27 Nap Lajoie	250.00	110.00	31.00
☐ 28 Glen Liebhardt	100.00	45.00	12.50
☐ 29 Bob Rhoads	100.00	45.00	12.50
☐ 30 Terry Turner	100.00	45.00	12.50
☐ 31 Ty Cobb	1000.00	450.00	125.00
☐ 32 Bill Coughlin	100.00	45.00	12.50
☐ 33 Sam Crawford	250.00	110.00	31.00
☐ 34 Bill Donovan	125.00	55.00	15.50
☐ 35 Ed Killian	100.00	45.00	12.50
☐ 36 Matty McIntyre	100.00	45.00	12.50
☐ 37 George Mullin	100.00	45.00	12.50
☐ 38 Charley O'Leary	100.00	45.00	12.50
☐ 39 Claude Rossman	100.00	45.00	12.50
☐ 40 Germany Schaefer	100.00	45.00	12.50
☐ 41 Boss Schmidt	100.00	45.00	12.50
☐ 42 Ed Summers	100.00	45.00	12.50
☐ 43 Hal Chase	250.00	110.00	31.00
☐ 44 Jack Chesbro	250.00	110.00	31.00
☐ 45 Wid Conroy	100.00	45.00	12.50
☐ 46 Kid Elberfeld	100.00	45.00	12.50
☐ 47 Fred Glade	100.00	45.00	12.50
☐ 48 Charlie Hemphill	100.00	45.00	12.50
☐ 49 Willie Keeler	250.00	110.00	31.00
☐ 50 Red Kleinow	100.00	45.00	12.50
☐ 51 Doc Newton	100.00	45.00	12.50
☐ 52 Harry Niles	100.00	45.00	12.50
☐ 53 Al Orth	100.00	45.00	12.50
☐ 54 Jake Stahl	100.00	45.00	12.50
☐ 55 Chief Bender	250.00	110.00	31.00
☐ 56 Jimmy Collins	250.00	110.00	31.00
☐ 57 Jack Coombs	100.00	45.00	12.50
☐ 58 Harry Davis	100.00	45.00	12.50
☐ 59 Jimmy Dygert	100.00	45.00	12.50
☐ 60 Topsy Hartsel	100.00	45.00	12.50
☐ 61 Danny Murphy	100.00	45.00	12.50
☐ 62 Simon Nicholls	100.00	45.00	12.50
☐ 63 Rube Oldring	100.00	45.00	12.50
☐ 64 Eddie Plank	250.00	110.00	31.00
☐ 65 Ossee Schreck	100.00	45.00	12.50
☐ 66 Socks Seybold	100.00	45.00	12.50
☐ 67 Hobe Ferris	100.00	45.00	12.50
☐ 68 Danny Hoffman	100.00	45.00	12.50
☐ 69 Harry Howell	100.00	45.00	12.50
☐ 70 Tom Jones	100.00	45.00	12.50
☐ 71 Jack Powell	100.00	45.00	12.50
☐ 72 Tubby Spencer	100.00	45.00	12.50
☐ 73 George Stone	100.00	45.00	12.50
☐ 74 Rube Waddell	250.00	110.00	31.00
☐ 75 Jimmy Williams	100.00	45.00	12.50
☐ 76 Otis Clymer	100.00	45.00	12.50
☐ 77 Jim Delahanty	100.00	45.00	12.50
☐ 78 Bob Ganley	100.00	45.00	12.50
☐ 79 Jerry Freeman	100.00	45.00	12.50
☐ 80 Walter Johnson	750.00	350.00	95.00
☐ 81 George McBride	100.00	45.00	12.50
☐ 82 Casey Patten	100.00	45.00	12.50
☐ 83 Clyde Milan	100.00	45.00	12.50
☐ 84 Bill Shipke	100.00	45.00	12.50

☐ 85 Charlie Smith	100.00	45.00	12.50
☐ 86 Jack Warner	100.00	45.00	12.50
☐ 87 Ginger Beaumont	100.00	45.00	12.50
☐ 88 Buster Brown	100.00	45.00	12.50
☐ 89 Bill Dahlen	100.00	45.00	12.50
☐ 90 George Ferguson	100.00	45.00	12.50
☐ 91 Vive Lindaman	100.00	45.00	12.50
☐ 92 Claude Ritchey	100.00	45.00	12.50
☐ 93 Whitey Alperman	100.00	45.00	12.50
☐ 94 John Hummel	100.00	45.00	12.50
☐ 95 Harry Lumley	100.00	45.00	12.50
☐ 96 Billy Maloney	100.00	45.00	12.50
☐ 97 Harry MacIntyre	100.00	45.00	12.50
☐ 98 Nap Rucker	100.00	45.00	12.50
☐ 99 Tommy Sheehan	100.00	45.00	12.50
☐ 100 Mordecai Brown	250.00	110.00	31.00
☐ 101 Frank Chance	300.00	135.00	38.00
☐ 102 Johnny Evers	250.00	110.00	31.00
☐ 103 Solly Hofman	100.00	45.00	12.50
☐ 104 John Kling	100.00	45.00	12.50
☐ 105 Orvall Overall	100.00	45.00	12.50
☐ 106 Ed Reulbach	100.00	45.00	12.50
☐ 107 Frank Schulte	100.00	45.00	12.50
☐ 108 Jimmy Sheckard	100.00	45.00	12.50
☐ 109 Jimmy Slagle	100.00	45.00	12.50
☐ 110 Harry Steinfeldt	100.00	45.00	12.50
☐ 111 Joe Tinker	250.00	110.00	31.00
☐ 112 Billy Campbell	100.00	45.00	12.50
☐ 113 Andy Coakley	100.00	45.00	12.50
☐ 114 Bob Ewing	100.00	45.00	12.50
☐ 115 John Ganzel	100.00	45.00	12.50
☐ 116 Miller Huggins	250.00	110.00	31.00
☐ 117 Rudy Hulswitt	100.00	45.00	12.50
☐ 118 Hans Lobert	100.00	45.00	12.50
☐ 119 Larry McLean	100.00	45.00	12.50
☐ 120 Mike Mitchell	100.00	45.00	12.50
☐ 121 Mike Mowery	100.00	45.00	12.50
☐ 122 Dode Paskert	100.00	45.00	12.50
☐ 123 Jake Weimer	100.00	45.00	12.50
☐ 124 Roger Bresnahan	250.00	110.00	31.00
☐ 125 Art Devlin	100.00	45.00	12.50
☐ 126 Mike Donlin	100.00	45.00	12.50
☐ 127 Larry Doyle	100.00	45.00	12.50
☐ 128 Christy Mathewson	750.00	350.00	95.00
☐ 129 Joe McGinnity	250.00	110.00	31.00
☐ 130 Cy Seymour	100.00	45.00	12.50
☐ 131 Spike Shannon	100.00	45.00	12.50
☐ 132 Dummy Taylor	150.00	70.00	19.00
☐ 133 Fred Tenney	100.00	45.00	12.50
☐ 134 Hooks Wiltse	100.00	45.00	12.50
☐ 135 Kitty Bransfield	100.00	45.00	12.50
☐ 136 Buster Brown	100.00	45.00	12.50
☐ 137 Frank Corridon	100.00	45.00	12.50
☐ 138 Red Dooin	100.00	45.00	12.50
☐ 139 Mickey Doolan	100.00	45.00	12.50
☐ 140 Eddie Grant	100.00	45.00	12.50
☐ 141 Otto Knabe	100.00	45.00	12.50
☐ 142 Sherry Magee	100.00	45.00	12.50
☐ 143 George McQuillan	100.00	45.00	12.50
☐ 144 Fred Osborn	100.00	45.00	12.50
☐ 145 Tully Sparks	100.00	45.00	12.50
☐ 146 John Titus	100.00	45.00	12.50
☐ 147 Ed Abbaticchio	100.00	45.00	12.50
☐ 148 Howie Camnitz	100.00	45.00	12.50
☐ 149 Fred Clarke	250.00	110.00	31.00
☐ 150 George Gibson	100.00	45.00	12.50
☐ 151 Jim Kane	100.00	45.00	12.50
☐ 152 Tommy Leach	125.00	55.00	15.50
☐ 153 Nick Maddox	100.00	45.00	12.50
☐ 154 Deacon Philippe	100.00	45.00	12.50
☐ 155 Roy Thomas	100.00	45.00	12.50
☐ 156 Honus Wagner	750.00	350.00	95.00
☐ 157 Owen Wilson	100.00	45.00	12.50
☐ 158 Irv Young	100.00	45.00	12.50
☐ 159 Shad Barry	100.00	45.00	12.50
☐ 160 Fred Beebe	100.00	45.00	12.50
☐ 161 Bobby Byrne	100.00	45.00	12.50
☐ 162 Joe Delahanty	100.00	45.00	12.50
☐ 163 Billy Gilbert	100.00	45.00	12.50
☐ 164 Art Hoelskoetter	100.00	45.00	12.50
☐ 165 Ed Karger	100.00	45.00	12.50
☐ 166 Ed Konetchy	100.00	45.00	12.50
☐ 167 Johnny Lush	100.00	45.00	12.50
☐ 168 Stoney McGlynn	100.00	45.00	12.50
☐ 169 Red Murray	100.00	45.00	12.50
☐ 170 Patsy O'Rourke	100.00	45.00	12.50
☐ 171 Bills	100.00	45.00	12.50
☐ 172 Graham	100.00	45.00	12.50
☐ 173 Halligan	100.00	45.00	12.50
☐ 174 Houser	100.00	45.00	12.50
☐ 175 Moran	100.00	45.00	12.50
☐ 176 Schultz	100.00	45.00	12.50
☐ 177 Steele	100.00	45.00	12.50
☐ 178 Andy Coakley	100.00	45.00	12.50
☐ 179 Knight	100.00	45.00	12.50
☐ 180 Schlei	100.00	45.00	12.50
☐ 181 Spade	100.00	45.00	12.50
☐ 182 Tris Speaker	300.00	135.00	38.00

1905 Rotograph Co. PC782

This rather distinguished looking set mesaures 3 1/4" by 5 3/8" and was printed by the Rotograph Company of New York in 1905. Some of the cards are numbered while others are not. The Clark Griffith card was initially issued with the name misspelled and was later corrected. The Rotograph identificatin is printed on the back of the card. Only New York teams are portrayed.

	EX-MT	VG-E	GOOD
COMPLETE SET (9)	1500.00	700.00	190.00
COMMON CARD (1-9)	100.00	45.00	12.50
☐ 1 Ambrose Puttman	100.00	45.00	12.50
☐ 2 Jack Chesbro (2)	200.00	90.00	25.00
☐ 3 George Brown	100.00	45.00	12.50
☐ 4 Bill Dahlen	100.00	45.00	12.50
☐ 5 John McGraw	300.00	135.00	38.00
☐ 6 Clark Griffill Sic, Griffith	250.00	110.00	31.00
☐ 7 Clark Griffith	250.00	110.00	31.00
☐ 8 Joe McGinnity	250.00	110.00	31.00
☐ 9 Luther Taylor	100.00	45.00	12.50

1905 Rotograph McGinnity

There are two versions of the McGinnity card. One has his first name misspelled Josep and has Rotograph Series marked on the left side of the bottom white border. The other spells his name correctly and has no Rotograph Series marked on the white border at the bottom.

	EX-MT	VG-E	GOOD
COMPLETE SET (2)	500.00	220.00	60.00
COMMON MCGINNITY	250.00	110.00	31.00
☐ 1 Joe McGinnity Spelled Josep	250.00	110.00	31.00
☐ 2 Joe McGinnity Name spelled correctly	250.00	110.00	31.00

1976 Rowe Exhibits

These collector issued exhibits feature the best major leaguers of the pre- World War 2 era. The cards are unnumbered and we have sequenced in alphabetical order by who appears in the upper left corner.

	NRMT	VG-E	GOOD
COMPLETE SET (16)	9.00	4.00	1.10
COMMON CARD (1-16)	.40	.18	.05
☐ 1 Luke Appling Ted Lyons Red Ruffing Red Faber	.40	.18	.05
☐ 2 Jim Bottomley Earle Combs George Sisler Roger Hornsby	.50	.23	.06
☐ 3 Dizzy Dean Stan Musial Jesse Haines Frank Frisch	.75	.35	.09
☐ 4 Joe DiMaggio Lou Gehrig Lefty Gomez Bill Dickey	1.50	.70	.19
☐ 5 Bob Feller Lou Boudreau Earl Averill Bob Lemon	.50	.23	.06
☐ 6 Jimmie Foxx Grover C. Alexander Robin Roberts Eppa Rixey	.40	.18	.05
☐ 7 Hank Greenberg Charlie Gehringer Ty Cobb Goose Goslin	1.00	.45	.12
☐ 8 Chick Hafey Edd Roush Bill McKechnie George Kelly	.40	.18	.05
☐ 9 Fred Lindstrom Billy Herman Kiki Cuyler Gabby Hartnett	.40	.18	.05
☐ 10 Heinie Manush Walter Johnson Bucky Harris Sam Rice	.50	.23	.06
☐ 11 Joe Medwick Max Carey Dazzy Vance Burleigh Grimes	.40	.18	.05
☐ 12 Mel Ott Carl Hubbell Dave Bancroft Bill Terry	.50	.23	.06
☐ 13 Al Simmons Lefty Grove Mickey Cochrane Eddie Collins	.50	.23	.06
☐ 14 Warren Spahn Al Lopez Casey Stengel Rabbit Maranville	.50	.23	.06
☐ 15 Pie Traynor Lloyd Waner Honus Wagner Paul Waner	.50	.23	.06
☐ 16 Ted Williams Herb Pennock Babe Ruth Joe Cronin	1.00	.45	.12

1950-53 Royal Desserts

These cards were issued by Royal desserts over a period of years. These cards measure 2 1/2" by 3 1/2" and even though the same players are featured, variations exist when biographies were changed to keep the cards current. The backs are blank but the cards are numbered on the front. A set is considered complete with only one of each variation.

	NRMT	VG-E	GOOD
COMPLETE SET	1100.00	500.00	140.00
COMMON CARD (1-24)	25.00	11.00	3.10
☐ 1 Stan Musial DP	250.00	110.00	31.00
☐ 2 Pee Wee Reese DP	100.00	45.00	12.50
☐ 3 George Kell	75.00	34.00	9.50
☐ 4 Dom DiMaggio	50.00	22.00	6.25
☐ 5 Warren Spahn	100.00	45.00	12.50
☐ 6A Andy Pafko Chicago Cubs	25.00	11.00	3.10
☐ 6B Andy Pafko Brooklyn Dodgers	100.00	45.00	12.50
☐ 7A Andy Seminick Philadelphia Phillies	25.00	11.00	3.10
☐ 7B Andy Seminick Cincinnati Reds	25.00	11.00	3.10
☐ 8A Lou Brissie Philadelphia A's	25.00	11.00	3.10
☐ 8B Lou Brissie Cleveland Indians	100.00	45.00	12.50
☐ 9 Ewell Blackwell	25.00	11.00	3.10
☐ 10 Bobby Thomson	50.00	22.00	6.25
☐ 11 Phil Rizzuto DP	100.00	45.00	12.50
☐ 12 Tommy Henrich	50.00	22.00	6.25
☐ 13 Joe Gordon	50.00	22.00	6.25
☐ 14A Ray Scarborough Washington Senators	25.00	11.00	3.10
☐ 14B Ray Scarborough Chicago White Sox	100.00	45.00	12.50
☐ 14C Ray Scarborough Boston Red Sox	25.00	11.00	3.10
☐ 15A Stan Rojek Pittsburgh Pirates	25.00	11.00	3.10
☐ 15B Stan Rojek St. Louis Browns	100.00	45.00	12.50
☐ 16 Luke Appling	75.00	34.00	9.50
☐ 17 Willard Marshall	25.00	11.00	3.10
☐ 18 Alvin Dark	50.00	22.00	6.25
☐ 19A Dick Sisler Philadelphia Phillies	25.00	11.00	3.10
☐ 19B Dick Sisler Cincinnati Reds	25.00	11.00	3.10
☐ 20 Johnny Ostrowski	25.00	11.00	3.10
☐ 21A Virgil Trucks Detroit Tigers	25.00	11.00	3.10
☐ 21B Virgil Trucks St. Louis Browns	100.00	45.00	12.50
☐ 22 Eddie Robinson	25.00	11.00	3.10
☐ 23 Nanny Fernandez	100.00	45.00	12.50
☐ 24 Ferris Fain	25.00	11.00	3.10

1952 Royal Premiums

These 16 photos measure approximately 5" by 7". These black and white photos are all facsimile signed with the expression "To a Royal Fan". The backs are blank and sequenced in alphabetical order.

	NRMT	VG-E	GOOD
COMPLETE SET (16)	400.00	180.00	50.00
COMMON CARD (1-16)	15.00	6.75	1.85
☐ 1 Ewell Blackwell	15.00	6.75	1.85
☐ 2 Leland Brissie Jr.	15.00	6.75	1.85
☐ 3 Alvin Dark	20.00	9.00	2.50
☐ 4 Dom DiMaggio	20.00	9.00	2.50
☐ 5 Ferris Fain	15.00	6.75	1.85
☐ 6 George Kell	35.00	16.00	4.40
☐ 7 Stan Musial	100.00	45.00	12.50
☐ 8 Andy Pafko	15.00	6.75	1.85
☐ 9 Pee Wee Reese	50.00	22.00	6.25
☐ 10 Phil Rizzuto	50.00	22.00	6.25
☐ 11 Eddie Robinson	15.00	6.75	1.85
☐ 12 Ray Scarborough	15.00	6.75	1.85
☐ 13 Andy Seminick	15.00	6.75	1.85
☐ 14 Dick Sisler	15.00	6.75	1.85
☐ 15 Warren Spahn	50.00	22.00	6.25
☐ 16 Bobby Thomson	20.00	9.00	2.50

1969 Royals Solon

These 15 blank-backed cards measure approximately 2 1/8" by 3 3/8" and feature blue-screened posed player photos on their white-bordered fronts. The player's name and position, along with the Royals logo, appear in blue lettering in the lower white margin. The cards are unnumbered and checklisted below in alphabetical order.

	NRMT	VG-E	GOOD
COMPLETE SET (15)	15.00	6.75	1.85
COMMON CARD (1-15)	1.00	.45	.12
☐ 1 Jerry Adair	1.50	.70	.19
☐ 2 Wally Bunker	1.00	.45	.12
☐ 3 Moe Drabowsky	1.00	.45	.12
☐ 4 Dick Drago	1.00	.45	.12
☐ 5 Joe Foy	1.00	.45	.12
☐ 6 Joe Gordon MG	1.50	.70	.19
☐ 7 Chuck Harrison	1.00	.45	.12
☐ 8 Mike Hedlund	1.00	.45	.12
☐ 9 Jack Hernandez	1.00	.45	.12
☐ 10 Pat Kelly	1.50	.70	.19
☐ 11 Roger Nelson	1.00	.45	.12
☐ 12 Bob Oliver	1.00	.45	.12
☐ 13 Lou Piniella	3.50	1.55	.45
☐ 14 Ellie Rodriguez	1.50	.70	.19
☐ 15 Dave Wickersham	1.00	.45	.12

1969 Royals Team Issue

This 12-card set of the Kansas City Royals measures approximately 4 1/4" by 7". The fronts display black-and-white player portraits bordered in white. The player's name and team are printed in the top margin. The backs are blank. The cards are unnumbered and checklisted below in alphabetical order.

	NRMT	VG-E	GOOD
COMPLETE SET (1-12)	20.00	9.00	2.50
COMMON CARD (1-12)	1.50	.70	.19
☐ 1 Jerry Adair	2.00	.90	.25
☐ 2 Jimmy Campanis	1.50	.70	.19
☐ 3 Moe Drabowsky	1.50	.70	.19
☐ 4 Mike Fiore	1.50	.70	.19
☐ 5 Joe Foy	1.50	.70	.19
☐ 6 Joe Gordon	2.50	1.10	.30
☐ 7 Pat Kelly	2.00	.90	.25
☐ 8 Joe Keough	1.50	.70	.19
☐ 9 Roger Nelson	1.50	.70	.19
☐ 10 Bob Oliver	1.50	.70	.19
☐ 11 Juan Rios	1.50	.70	.19
☐ 12 Dave Wickersham	1.50	.70	.19

1970 Royals Team Issue

This 38-card set measures approximately 3 3/8" by 5" and features black-and-white player portraits in a white border. A facsimile autograph across the bottom of the picture. The backs are blank. The cards are unnumbered and checklisted below in alphabetical order.

	MINT	NRMT	EXC
COMPLETE SET (38)	20.00	9.00	2.50
COMMON CARD (1-38)	.50	.23	.06
☐ 1 Ted Abernathy	.50	.23	.06
☐ 2 Jerry Adair	.50	.23	.06
☐ 3 Luis Alcaraz	.50	.23	.06

☐ 4 Wally Bunker	.50	.23	.06
☐ 5 Tom Burgmeier	.50	.23	.06
☐ 6 Bill Butler	.50	.23	.06
☐ 7 Jim Campanis	.50	.23	.06
☐ 8 Dan Carnevale CO	.50	.23	.06
☐ 9 Moe Drabowsky	.50	.23	.06
☐ 10 Dick Drago	.50	.23	.06
☐ 11 Harry Dunlop CO	.50	.23	.06
☐ 12 Mike Fiore	.50	.23	.06
☐ 13 Al Fitzmorris	.50	.23	.06
☐ 14 Jack Hernandez	.50	.23	.06
☐ 15 Bob Johnson	.50	.23	.06
☐ 16 Pat Kelly	.50	.23	.06
☐ 17 Joe Keough	.50	.23	.06
☐ 18 Ed Kirkpatrick	.50	.23	.06
☐ 19 Bob Lemon MG	1.50	.70	.19
☐ 20 Pat Locanto	.50	.23	.06
☐ 21 Tommy Matchick	.50	.23	.06
☐ 22 Charlie Metro CO	.50	.23	.06
☐ 23 Aurelio Monteagudo	.50	.23	.06
☐ 24 Dave Morehead	.50	.23	.06
☐ 25 Bob Oliver	.50	.23	.06
☐ 26 Amos Otis	.75	.35	.09
☐ 27 Lou Piniella	2.00	.90	.25
☐ 28 Ellie Rodriguez	.50	.23	.06
☐ 29 Cookie Rojas	.50	.23	.06
☐ 30 Jim Rooker	.50	.23	.06
☐ 31 Paul Schaal	.50	.23	.06
☐ 32 Joe Schultz CO	.75	.35	.09
☐ 33 Bill Sorrell	.50	.23	.06
☐ 34 Rich Stevenson	.50	.23	.06
☐ 35 George Strickland Co	.50	.23	.06
☐ 36 Cedric Tallis GM	.50	.23	.06
☐ 37 Bob"Hawk" Taylor	.50	.23	.06
☐ 38 Ken Wright	.50	.23	.06

1978 Royals

This 27-card set features the Kansas City Royals. The cards measure approximately 3 1/4" by 5". The fronts have black-and-white player portraits with a thin white border. The player's name, position, and team name are printed in a wider border beneath the picture. The backs are blank. The cards are unnumbered and checklisted below in alphabetical order.

	NRMT	VG-E	GOOD
COMPLETE SET (27)	25.00	11.00	3.10
COMMON CARD (1-27)	.75	.35	.09
☐ 1 Doug Bird	.75	.35	.09
☐ 2 Steve Braun	.75	.35	.09
☐ 3 George Brett	5.00	2.20	.60
☐ 4 Al Cowens	.75	.35	.09
☐ 5 Rich Gale	.75	.35	.09
☐ 6 Larry Gura	.75	.35	.09
☐ 7 Whitey Herzog MG	1.50	.70	.19
☐ 8 Al Hrabosky	1.25	.55	.16
☐ 9 Clint Hurdle	.75	.35	.09
☐ 10 Pete LaCock	.75	.35	.09
☐ 11 Dennis Leonard	.75	.35	.09
☐ 12 John Mayberry	1.25	.55	.16
☐ 13 Hal McRae	2.00	.90	.25
☐ 14 Steve Mingori	.75	.35	.09
☐ 15 Dave Nelson	.75	.35	.09
☐ 16 Amos Otis	1.50	.70	.19
☐ 17 Fred Patek	1.25	.55	.16
☐ 18 Marty Pattin	.75	.35	.09
☐ 19 Tom Poquette	.75	.35	.09
☐ 20 Darrell Porter	1.50	.70	.19
☐ 21 Paul Splittorff	.75	.35	.09
☐ 22 Jerry Terrell	.75	.35	.09
☐ 23 U.L. Washington	.75	.35	.09
☐ 24 John Wathan	.75	.35	.09
☐ 25 Frank White	1.25	.55	.16
☐ 26 Willie Wilson	1.50	.70	.19
☐ 27 Joe Zdeb	.75	.35	.09

1979-80 Royals Team Issue

These color photos feature members of the Kansas City Royals. The photos measure approximately 4" by 5 1/4" and have blank backs. A fascimile signature is on each photo and we have sequenced these photos in alphabetical order.

	NRMT	VG-E	GOOD
COMPLETE SET (13)	15.00	6.75	1.85
COMMON CARD (1-13)	1.00	.45	.12
☐ 1 Willie Mays Aikens	1.25	.55	.16
☐ 2 George Brett	5.00	2.20	.60
☐ 3 Larry Gura	1.00	.45	.12
☐ 4 Dennis Leonard	1.00	.45	.12
☐ 5 Renie Martin	1.00	.45	.12
☐ 6 Hal McRae	2.00	.90	.25
☐ 7 Amos Otis	1.50	.70	.19
☐ 8 Dan Quisenberry	1.25	.55	.16
☐ 9 Paul Splitorff	1.00	.45	.12
☐ 10 Jerry Terrell	1.00	.45	.12
☐ 11 U.L Washington	1.00	.45	.12
☐ 12 John Wathan	1.00	.45	.12
☐ 13 Willie Wilson	2.00	.90	.25

1981 Royals Police

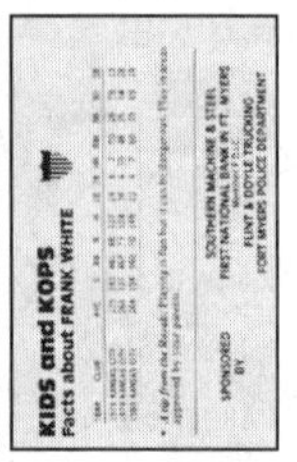

The cards in this ten-card set measure approximately 2 1/2" by 4 1/8". The 1981 Police Kansas City Royals set features full color cards of Royals players. The fronts feature the player's name, position, height and weight, and the Royals' logo in addition to the photo and facsimile autograph of the player. The backs feature player statistics, Tips from the Royals, and identification of the sponsoring organizations. This set can be distinguished from the 1983 Police Royals set by the statistics on the backs of these 1981 cards, whereas the 1983 cards only show a biographical paragraph in the same space.

	NRMT	VG-E	GOOD
COMPLETE SET (10)	30.00	13.50	3.70
COMMON CARD (1-10)	1.50	.70	.19
☐ 1 Willie Aikens	1.50	.70	.19
☐ 2 George Brett	15.00	6.75	1.85
☐ 3 Rich Gale	1.50	.70	.19
☐ 4 Clint Hurdle	2.00	.90	.25
☐ 5 Dennis Leonard	2.00	.90	.25
☐ 6 Hal McRae	3.00	1.35	.35
☐ 7 Amos Otis	2.50	1.10	.30
☐ 8 U.L. Washington	1.50	.70	.19
☐ 9 Frank White	3.00	1.35	.35
☐ 10 Willie Wilson	3.00	1.35	.35

1982 Royals

This set features members of the 1982 Kansas City Royals. Since the cards are unnumbered we have checklisted them below in alphabetical order.

	NRMT	VG-E	GOOD
COMPLETE SET (25)	8.00	3.60	1.00
COMMON CARD (1-25)	.25	.11	.03
☐ 1 Willie Aikens	.25	.11	.03
☐ 2 Mike Armstrong	.25	.11	.03
☐ 3 Vida Blue	.50	.23	.06
☐ 4 George Brett	4.00	1.80	.50
☐ 5 Scott Brown	.25	.11	.03
☐ 6 Onix Concepcion	.25	.11	.03
☐ 7 Dave Frost	.25	.11	.03
☐ 8 Cesar Geronimo	.25	.11	.03
☐ 9 Larry Gura	.25	.11	.03
☐ 10 Dick Howser MG	.25	.11	.03
☐ 11 Dennis Leonard	.25	.11	.03
☐ 12 Jerry Martin	.25	.11	.03
☐ 13 Hal McRae	.75	.35	.09
☐ 14 Amos Otis	.75	.35	.09
☐ 15 Tom Poquette	.25	.11	.03
☐ 16 Greg Pryor	.25	.11	.03
☐ 17 Jamie Quirk	.25	.11	.03
☐ 18 Dan Quisenberry	.75	.35	.09
☐ 19 John Schuerholz GM	.25	.11	.03
☐ 20 Paul Splittorff	.25	.11	.03
☐ 21 U.L. Washington	.25	.11	.03
☐ 22 John Wathan	.25	.11	.03
☐ 23 Dennis Werth	.25	.11	.03
☐ 24 Frank White	.75	.35	.09
☐ 25 Willie Wilson	.75	.35	.09

1983 Royals

Featured in this set are members of the 1983 Kansas City Royals. Since the cards are unnumbered we have checklisted below in alphabetical order.

	NRMT	VG-E	GOOD
COMPLETE SET (32)	10.00	4.50	1.25
COMMON CARD (1-32)	.25	.11	.03
☐ 1 Willie Aikens	.25	.11	.03
☐ 2 Bud Black	.25	.11	.03
☐ 3 Vida Blue	.50	.23	.06
☐ 4 Cloyd Boyer CO	.25	.11	.03
☐ 5 George Brett	3.00	1.35	.35
☐ 6 Rocky Colavito CO	1.25	.55	.16
☐ 7 Onix Concepcion	.25	.11	.03
☐ 8 Keith Creel	.25	.11	.03
☐ 9 Cesar Gernoimo	.25	.11	.03
☐ 10 Larry Gura	.25	.11	.03
☐ 11 Don Hood	.25	.11	.03
☐ 12 Dick Howser MG	.50	.23	.06
☐ 13 Ron Johnson	.25	.11	.03
☐ 14 Dennis Leonard	.25	.11	.03
☐ 15 Jerry Martin	.25	.11	.03
☐ 16 Jose Martinez CO	.25	.11	.03
☐ 17 Hal McRae	.75	.35	.09
☐ 18 Joe Nossek CO	.25	.11	.03
☐ 19 Amos Otis	.75	.35	.09
☐ 20 Greg Pryor	.25	.11	.03
☐ 21 Dan Quisenberry	.75	.35	.09
☐ 22 Steve Renko	.25	.11	.03
☐ 23 Leon Roberts	.25	.11	.03
☐ 24 Jim Schaffer CO	.25	.11	.03
☐ 25 John Schuerholz GM	.25	.11	.03
☐ 26 Joe Simpson	.25	.11	.03
☐ 27 Don Slaught	1.25	.55	.16
☐ 28 Paul Splittorff	.25	.11	.03
☐ 29 U.L. Washington	.25	.11	.03
☐ 30 John Wathan	.25	.11	.03
☐ 31 Frank White	.75	.35	.09
☐ 32 Willie Wilson	.75	.35	.09

1983 Royals Police

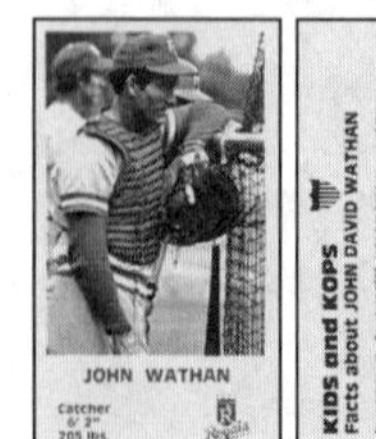

The cards in this ten-card set measure approximately 2 1/2" by 4 1/8". The 1983 Police Kansas City Royals set features full color cards of Royals players. The fronts feature the player's name, height and weight, and the Royals' logo in addition to the player's photo and a facsimile autograph. The backs feature Kids and Cops Facts about the players, Tips from the Royals, and identification of the sponsors of the set. The cards are unnumbered. This set can be distinguished from the 1981 Police Royals set by the absence of statistics on the backs of these 1983 cards, since these 1983 cards only show a brief biographical paragraph.

	NRMT	VG-E	GOOD
COMPLETE SET (10)	25.00	11.00	3.10
COMMON CARD (1-10)	1.50	.70	.19
☐ 1 Willie Aikens	1.50	.70	.19
☐ 2 George Brett	12.50	5.50	1.55
☐ 3 Dennis Leonard	2.00	.90	.25
☐ 4 Hal McRae	3.00	1.35	.35
☐ 5 Amos Otis	3.00	1.35	.35
☐ 6 Dan Quisenberry	3.00	1.35	.35
☐ 7 U.L. Washington	1.50	.70	.19
☐ 8 John Wathan	2.00	.90	.25
☐ 9 Frank White	3.00	1.35	.35
☐ 10 Willie Wilson	3.00	1.35	.35

1986 Royals Greats TCMA

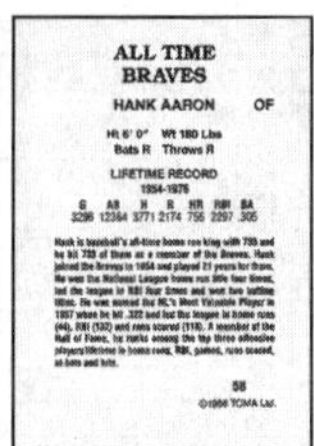

This 12-card strandard-size set features some of the best Kansas City Royals from their first two decades. The player's photo, name and position are noted on the front. There is more personal information about the player on the back.

	MINT	NRMT	EXC
COMPLETE SET (12)	3.00	1.35	.35
COMMON CARD (1-12)	.25	.11	.03
☐ 1 John Mayberry	.50	.23	.06
☐ 2 Cookie Rojas	.25	.11	.03
☐ 3 Fred Patek	.25	.11	.03
☐ 4 Paul Schall	.25	.11	.03
☐ 5 Lou Piniella	.75	.35	.09
☐ 6 Amos Otis	.50	.23	.06
☐ 7 Tom Poquette	.25	.11	.03
☐ 8 Ed Kirkpatrick	.25	.11	.03
☐ 9 Steve Busby	.25	.11	.03
☐ 10 Paul Splittorff	.25	.11	.03
☐ 11 Mark Littell	.25	.11	.03
☐ 12 Jim Frey MG	.25	.11	.03

1986 Royals Kitty Clover Discs

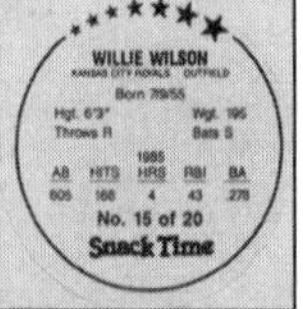

This set of discs was distributed by Kitty Clover in 1986 to commemorate the Kansas City Royals' World Championship in 1985. Each disc measures 2 3/4" in diameter. Each disc has a white border on the front. Inside this white border is a full color photo of the player with his hat on. However the hat's team emblem has been deleted from the picture. The statistics on back of the disc give the player's 1985 pitching or hitting record as well as his vital statistics.

	MINT	NRMT	EXC
COMPLETE SET (20)	18.00	8.00	2.20
COMMON DISC (1-20)	.50	.23	.06
☐ 1 Lonnie Smith	.75	.35	.09
☐ 2 Buddy Biancalana	.50	.23	.06
☐ 3 Bret Saberhagen	2.00	.90	.25
☐ 4 Hal McRae	1.00	.45	.12
☐ 5 Onix Concepcion	.50	.23	.06
☐ 6 Jorge Orta	.50	.23	.06
☐ 7 Bud Black	.50	.23	.06
☐ 8 Dan Quisenberry	1.00	.45	.12
☐ 9 Dane Iorg	.50	.23	.06
☐ 10 Charlie Leibrandt	.75	.35	.09
☐ 11 Pat Sheridan	.50	.23	.06
☐ 12 John Wathan	.50	.23	.06
☐ 13 Frank White	1.00	.45	.12
☐ 14 Darryl Motley	.50	.23	.06
☐ 15 Willie Wilson	1.00	.45	.12
☐ 16 Danny Jackson	.75	.35	.09
☐ 17 Steve Balboni	.50	.23	.06
☐ 18 Jim Sundberg	.75	.35	.09
☐ 19 Mark Gubicza	.75	.35	.09
☐ 20 George Brett	10.00	4.50	1.25

1986 Royals National Photo

The set contains 24 cards which are numbered only by uniform number except for the checklist card and discount card, which entitles the bearer to a 40 percent discount at National Photo. Cards measure approximately 2 7/8" by 4 1/4". Cards were distributed at the stadium on August 14th. The set was supposedly later available for 3.00 directly from the Royals.

	MINT	NRMT	EXC
COMPLETE SET (24)	12.00	5.50	1.50
COMMON CARD	.25	.11	.03
☐ 1 Buddy Biancalana	.25	.11	.03
☐ 3 Jorge Orta	.25	.11	.03
☐ 4 Greg Pryor	.25	.11	.03
☐ 5 George Brett	6.00	2.70	.75
☐ 6 Willie Wilson	1.00	.45	.12
☐ 8 Jim Sundberg	.25	.11	.03
☐ 10 Dick Howser MG	.75	.35	.09
☐ 11 Hal McRae	1.00	.45	.12
☐ 20 Frank White	1.00	.45	.12
☐ 21 Lonnie Smith	.25	.11	.03
☐ 22 Dennis Leonard	.75	.35	.09
☐ 23 Mark Gubicza	.75	.35	.09
☐ 24 Darryl Motley	.25	.11	.03
☐ 25 Danny Jackson	.50	.23	.06
☐ 26 Steve Farr	.50	.23	.06
☐ 29 Dan Quisenberry	1.00	.45	.12
☐ 31 Bret Saberhagen	.75	.35	.09
☐ 35 Lynn Jones	.25	.11	.03
☐ 37 Charlie Leibrandt	.50	.23	.06
☐ 38 Mark Huismann	.25	.11	.03
☐ 40 Bud Black	.25	.11	.03
☐ 45 Steve Balboni	.25	.11	.03
☐ NNO Discount card	.25	.11	.03
☐ NNO Checklist card	.25	.11	.03

1988 Royals Smokey

This set of 28 cards features caricatures of the Kansas City Royals players. The cards are nunmbered on the back except for the unnumbered title/checklist card. The card set was distributed as a giveaway item at the stadium on August 14th to kids age 14 and under. The cards are approximately 3" by 5" and are in full color on the card fronts. The Smokey logo is in the upper right corner of every obverse.

	MINT	NRMT	EXC
COMPLETE SET (28)	12.00	5.50	1.50
COMMON CARD (1-27)	.25	.11	.03
☐ 1 John Wathan MG	.25	.11	.03
☐ 2 Royals Coaches	.50	.23	.06
☐ 3 Willie Wilson	.75	.35	.09
☐ 4 Danny Tartabull	1.00	.45	.12
☐ 5 Bo Jackson	1.50	.70	.19
☐ 6 Gary Thurman	.25	.11	.03
☐ 7 Jerry Don Gleaton	.25	.11	.03
☐ 8 Floyd Bannister	.25	.11	.03
☐ 9 Bud Black	.25	.11	.03
☐ 10 Steve Farr	.50	.23	.06
☐ 11 Gene Garber	.50	.23	.06
☐ 12 Mark Gubicza	.50	.23	.06
☐ 13 Charlie Leibrandt	.50	.23	.06
☐ 14 Ted Power	.25	.11	.03
☐ 15 Dan Quisenberry	.75	.35	.09
☐ 16 Bret Saberhagen	1.00	.45	.12
☐ 17 Mike Macfarlane	1.00	.45	.12
☐ 18 Scotti Madison	.25	.11	.03
☐ 19 Jamie Quirk	.25	.11	.03
☐ 20 George Brett	4.00	1.80	.50
☐ 21 Kevin Seitzer	.75	.35	.09
☐ 22 Bill Pecota	.25	.11	.03
☐ 23 Kurt Stillwell	.25	.11	.03
☐ 24 Brad Wellman	.25	.11	.03
☐ 25 Frank White	.75	.35	.09
☐ 26 Jim Eisenreich	.75	.35	.09
☐ 27 Smokey Bear	.25	.11	.03
☐ NNO Checklist Card	.25	.11	.03

1989 Royals Tastee Discs

This set features members of the 1989 Kansas City Royals. These discs were issued by Tastee-Freez.

	MINT	NRMT	EXC
COMPLETE SET (12)	12.00	5.50	1.50
COMMON DISC (1-12)	.50	.23	.06

	MINT	NRMT	EXC
☐ 1 George Brett	7.50	3.40	.95
☐ 2 Kevin Seitzer	1.00	.45	.12
☐ 3 Pat Tabler	.50	.23	.06
☐ 4 Danny Tartabull	1.00	.45	.12
☐ 5 Willie Wilson	1.00	.45	.12
☐ 6 Bo Jackson	1.50	.70	.19
☐ 7 Frank White	1.50	.70	.19
☐ 8 Kurt Stillwell	.50	.23	.06
☐ 9 Mark Gubicza	1.00	.45	.12
☐ 10 Charlie Leibrandt	1.00	.45	.12
☐ 11 Bret Saberhagen	1.00	.45	.12
☐ 12 Steve Farr	.50	.23	.06

1991 Royals Police

This 27-card set was distributed by the Metropolitan Chiefs and Sheriffs Association. The cards measure approximately 2 5/8" by 4 1/8". The front design has glossy color action photos with white borders. The player's number and name appear below the picture. In blue print, the backs present biography, statistics, and a cartoon with a public service announcement by the player. The cards are unnumbered and checklisted below in alphabetical order, with the coaches' cards listed at the end. Supposedly many of the Bo Jackson cards were burned after Bo was cut from the team.

	MINT	NRMT	EXC
COMPLETE SET (27)	15.00	6.75	1.85
COMMON CARD (1-27)	.25	.11	.03
☐ 1 Kevin Appier	2.00	.90	.25
☐ 2 Luis Aquino	.25	.11	.03
☐ 3 Mike Boddicker	.50	.23	.06
☐ 4 George Brett	5.00	2.20	.60
☐ 5 Steve Crawford	.25	.11	.03
☐ 6 Mark Davis	.50	.23	.06
☐ 7 Storm Davis	.25	.11	.03
☐ 8 Jim Eisenreich	.75	.35	.09
☐ 9 Kirk Gibson	.75	.35	.09
☐ 10 Tom Gordon	.75	.35	.09
☐ 11 Mark Gubicza	.50	.23	.06
☐ 12 Bo Jackson SP	.50	.23	.06
☐ 13 Mike Macfarlane	.75	.35	.09
☐ 14 Andy McGaffigan	.25	.11	.03
☐ 15 Brian McRae	1.50	.70	.19
☐ 16 Jeff Montgomery	.75	.35	.09
☐ 17 Bill Pecota	.25	.11	.03
☐ 18 Bret Saberhagen	.75	.35	.09
☐ 19 Kevin Seitzer	.50	.23	.06
☐ 20 Terry Shumpert	.25	.11	.03
☐ 21 Kurt Stillwell	.25	.11	.03
☐ 22 Danny Tartabull	.75	.35	.09
☐ 23 Gary Thurman	.25	.11	.03
☐ 24 John Wathan MG	.25	.11	.03
☐ 25 Coaches Pat Dodson Adrian Garrett	.25	.11	.03
☐ 26 Coaches Glenn Ezell Lynn Jones Bob Schaefer	.25	.11	.03
☐ 27 Checklist Card	.25	.11	.03

1992 Royals Police

This 27-card set, given out as a promotion at the stadium, was sponsored by the Kansas City Life Insurance Company and distributed by the Metropolitan Chiefs and Sheriffs Association. It is rumored that two cards were pulled prior to release (the cards of Kevin Seitzer, who went to Milwaukee, and Kirk Gibson, who went to Pittsburgh). The cards measure 2 5/8" by 4 1/8" and feature action color player photos with white borders. The team name appears in royal blue on the bottom border, while the player's name and jersey number are in black. The backs are printed in blue on a white background and feature biographical and statistical information as well as a cartoon and a corresponding public service player quote. The sponsors are listed at the bottom. The cards are unnumbered and checklisted below in alphabetical order.

	MINT	NRMT	EXC
COMPLETE SET (27)	10.00	4.50	1.25
COMMON CARD (1-27)	.25	.11	.03
☐ 1 Kevin Appier	1.00	.45	.12
☐ 2 Luis Aquino	.25	.11	.03
☐ 3 Mike Boddicker	.25	.11	.03
☐ 4 George Brett	3.00	1.35	.35
☐ 5 Mark Davis	.25	.11	.03
☐ 6 Jim Eisenreich	.75	.35	.09
☐ 7 Kirk Gibson	.75	.35	.09
☐ 8 Tom Gordon	.50	.23	.06
☐ 9 Mark Gubicza	.50	.23	.06
☐ 10 Chris Gwynn	.25	.11	.03
☐ 11 David Howard	.25	.11	.03
☐ 12 Gregg Jefferies	.75	.35	.09
☐ 13 Joel Johnston	.25	.11	.03
☐ 14 Wally Joyner	.50	.23	.06
☐ 15 Mike Macfarlane	.50	.23	.06
☐ 16 Mike Magnante	.25	.11	.03
☐ 17 Brent Mayne	.25	.11	.03
☐ 18 Brian McRae	.50	.23	.06
☐ 19 Hal McRae MG	.50	.23	.06
☐ 20 Kevin McReynolds	.25	.11	.03
☐ 21 Bob Melvin CO	.25	.11	.03
☐ 22 Keith Miller	.25	.11	.03
☐ 23 Jeff Montgomery	.75	.35	.09
☐ 24 Kevin Seitzer	.50	.23	.06
☐ 25 Terry Shumpert	.25	.11	.03
☐ 26 Gary Thurman	.25	.11	.03
☐ 27 Coaches Glenn Ezell Adrian Garrett Guy Hansen Lynn Jones Bruce Kison Lee May	.25	.11	.03

1993 Royals Police

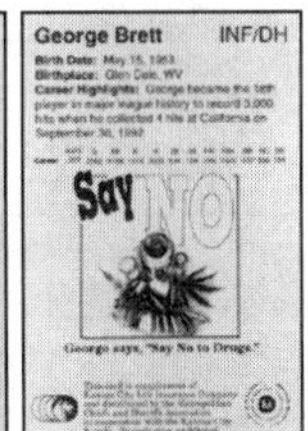

This 27-card set was given away to fans attending the Royals-Twins game of April 10. The set was sponsored by Kansas City Life Insurance and distributed by the Metropolitan Chiefs and Sheriffs Association. The blue-bordered cards measure approximately 2 5/8" by 4" with Royals printed in large royal blue letters with a thin black outline across the top of the card. The player's name, position, uniform number, and the Royals' logo commemorating the team's 25th anniversary rest in the lower margin. The backs contain biography, career highlights, and stats. A safety message and graphic, accompanied by the Kansas City Life and Chiefs-Sheriffs Association logos, round out the back. The cards are unnumbered and checklisted below in alphabetical order.

	MINT	NRMT	EXC
COMPLETE SET (27)	10.00	4.50	1.25
COMMON CARD (1-27)	.25	.11	.03
☐ 1 Hal McRae MG	.50	.23	.06
☐ 2 Kevin Appier	.75	.35	.09
☐ 3 Luis Aquino	.25	.11	.03
☐ 4 Mike Boddicker	.25	.11	.03
☐ 5 George Brett	3.00	1.35	.35
☐ 6 David Cone	1.00	.45	.12
☐ 7 Greg Gagne	.25	.11	.03
☐ 8 Mark Gardner	.25	.11	.03
☐ 9 Tom Gordon	.50	.23	.06
☐ 10 Mark Gubicza	.50	.23	.06
☐ 11 Chris Gwynn	.25	.11	.03
☐ 12 Chris Haney	.25	.11	.03
☐ 13 Felix Jose	.25	.11	.03
☐ 14 Wally Joyner	.50	.23	.06
☐ 15 Kevin Koslofski	.25	.11	.03
☐ 16 Jose Lind	.25	.11	.03
☐ 17 Mike Macfarlane	.50	.23	.06
☐ 18 Brent Mayne	.25	.11	.03
☐ 19 Brian McRae	.50	.23	.06
☐ 20 Kevin McReynolds	.25	.11	.03
☐ 21 Rusty Meacham	.25	.11	.03
☐ 22 Keith Miller	.25	.11	.03
☐ 23 Jeff Montgomery	.50	.23	.06
☐ 24 Hipolito Pichardo	.25	.11	.03
☐ 25 Curtis Wilkerson	.25	.11	.03
☐ 26 Craig Wilson	.25	.11	.03
☐ 27 Royals Coaches Steve Boros Glenn Ezell Guy Hansen Bruce Kison Lee May	.25	.11	.03

1993 Royals Star 25th

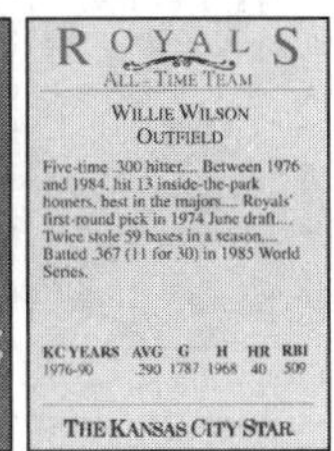

Subtitled "Royals All-Time Team" this 16-card set celebrates the Royals' 25th Anniversary (1969-1993), features great Royals of the past, and was originally issued in a perforated sheet. The sheet measures approximately 10 3/8" by 14 3/8"; after perforation, each card would measure the standard size. The individual cards measure the standard size. They feature color player photos, mostly action shots, on their royal blue- and gold-bordered fronts. The player's name and position appear in the gold-colored bottom margin. The Royals' 25th Anniversary logo rests at the lower right. The white back carries the player's name and position, followed by career highlights and statistics. The cards are unnumbered and checklisted below in alphabetical order.

	MINT	NRMT	EXC
COMPLETE SET (16)	20.00	9.00	2.50
COMMON CARD (1-16)	1.00	.45	.12
☐ 1 George Brett	10.00	4.50	1.25
☐ 2 Steve Busby	1.00	.45	.12
☐ 3 Al Cowens	1.00	.45	.12
☐ 4 Dick Howser MG	1.50	.70	.19
☐ 5 Dennis Leonard	1.50	.70	.19
☐ 6 John Mayberry	1.50	.70	.19
☐ 7 Hal McRae	2.00	.90	.25
☐ 8 Amos Otis	2.00	.90	.25
☐ 9 Fred Patek	1.50	.70	.19
☐ 10 Darrell Porter	1.50	.70	.19
☐ 11 Dan Quisenberry	2.00	.90	.25
☐ 12 Bret Saberhagen	2.00	.90	.25
☐ 13 Paul Splittorff	1.00	.45	.12
☐ 14 Frank White	2.00	.90	.25
☐ 15 Willie Wilson	1.50	.70	.19
☐ 16 Title card	1.00	.45	.12

1996 Royals Police

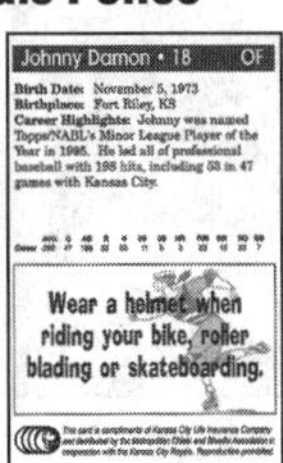

Johnny Damon • 18 OF
Wear a helmet when riding your bike, roller blading or skateboarding.

This 26-card set of the Kansas City Royals measures 2 5/8" by 4" and was sponsored by the Kansas City Life Insurance Company. The fronts feature color action player photos in a thin white border. The backs carry player information, statistics, and a safety message. The cards are unnumbered and checklisted below in alphabetical order.

	MINT	NRMT	EXC
COMPLETE SET (26)	7.50	3.40	.95
COMMON CARD (1-26)	.10	.05	.01
☐ 1 Kevin Appier	.75	.35	.09
☐ 2 Tim Belcher	.10	.05	.01
☐ 3 Bob Boone MG	.10	.05	.01
☐ 4 Melvin Bunch	.25	.11	.03
☐ 5 Terry Clark	.10	.05	.01
☐ 6 Jim Converse	.10	.05	.01
☐ 7 Johnny Damon	3.00	1.35	.35
☐ 8 Tom Goodwin	.25	.11	.03
☐ 9 Mark Gubicza	.25	.11	.03
☐ 10 Bob Hamelin	.10	.05	.01
☐ 11 Chris Haney	.10	.05	.01
☐ 12 David Howard	.10	.05	.01
☐ 13 Rick Huisman	.10	.05	.01
☐ 14 Jason Jacome	.10	.05	.01
☐ 15 Keith Lockhart	.10	.05	.01
☐ 16 Mike Macfarlane	.10	.05	.01
☐ 17 Rusty Meacham	.10	.05	.01
☐ 18 Jeff Montgomery	.25	.11	.03
☐ 19 Les Norman	.10	.05	.01
☐ 20 Jon Nunnally	.25	.11	.03
☐ 21 Jose Offerman	.10	.05	.01
☐ 22 Hipolito Pichardo	.10	.05	.01
☐ 23 Joe Randa	.10	.05	.01
☐ 24 Bip Roberts	.10	.05	.01

☐ 25 Michael Tucker	1.00	.45	.12
☐ 26 Joe Vitiello	.50	.23	.06

1997 Royals Police

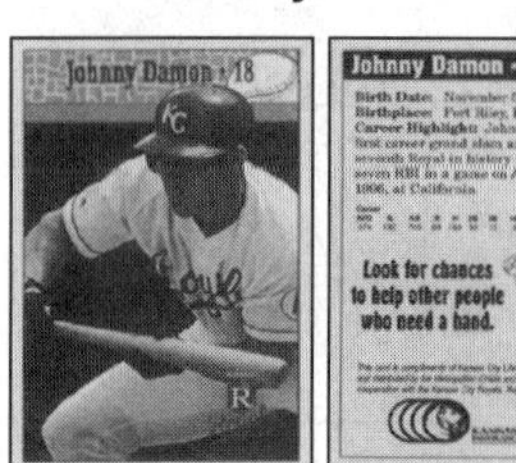

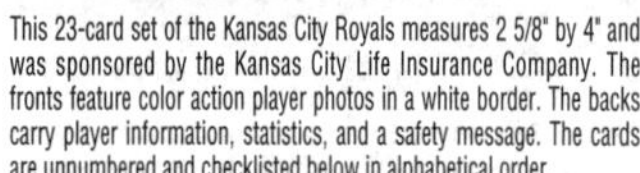

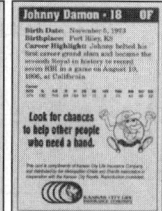

This 23-card set of the Kansas City Royals measures 2 5/8" by 4" and was sponsored by the Kansas City Life Insurance Company. The fronts feature color action player photos in a white border. The backs carry player information, statistics, and a safety message. The cards are unnumbered and checklisted below in alphabetical order.

	MINT	NRMT	EXC
COMPLETE SET (23)	7.50	3.40	.95
COMMON CARD (1-23)	.25	.11	.03
☐ 1 Kevin Appier	.75	.35	.09
☐ 2 Tim Belcher	.25	.11	.03
☐ 3 Jay Bell	.25	.11	.03
☐ 4 Jaime Bluma	.50	.23	.06
☐ 5 Bob Boone MG	.25	.11	.03
☐ 6 Johnny Damon	.75	.35	.09
☐ 7 Chili Davis	.50	.23	.06
☐ 8 Tom Goodwin	.25	.11	.03
☐ 9 Chris Haney	.25	.11	.03
☐ 10 David Howard	.25	.11	.03
☐ 11 Rick Huisman	.25	.11	.03
☐ 12 Jason Jacome	.25	.11	.03
☐ 13 Jeff King	.50	.23	.06
☐ 14 Mike Macfarlane	.25	.11	.03
☐ 15 Jeff Montgomery	.50	.23	.06
☐ 16 Jose Offerman	.25	.11	.03
☐ 17 Craig Paquette	.25	.11	.03
☐ 18 Hipolito Pichardo	.25	.11	.03
☐ 19 Bip Roberts	.25	.11	.03
☐ 20 Jose Rosado	1.00	.45	.12
☐ 21 Mike Sweeney	.75	.35	.09
☐ 22 Joe Vitiello	.25	.11	.03
☐ 23 Sluggerrr(Mascot)	.25	.11	.03

1994 Ryan SSCA

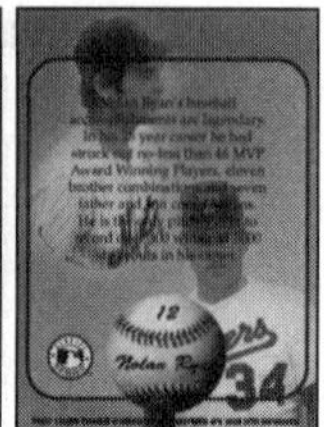

This 12-card set was distributed in sealed factory boxes and are actually official postage stamp cards issued by the Government of Guyana. The fronts feature color photos of Nolan Ryan with a gold foil simulated autograph. The backs carry information about Ryan's career. 1000 redemption cards were randomly seeded into sets which could be redeemed for a special card autographed by Nolan Ryan himself.

	MINT	NRMT	EXC
COMPLETE SET (12)	20.00	9.00	2.50
COMMON CARD (1-12)	2.00	.90	.25
☐ 1 Nolan Ryan Alvin High School pitcher	2.00	.90	.25
☐ 2 Nolan Ryan Mets 8th draft pick, 1965	2.00	.90	.25
☐ 3 Nolan Ryan Pitching for the Mets	2.00	.90	.25
☐ 4 Nolan Ryan Pitching for the Angels	2.00	.90	.25
☐ 5 Nolan Ryan Pitching for the Angels	2.00	.90	.25
☐ 6 Nolan Ryan Laughing portrait	2.00	.90	.25
☐ 7 Nolan Ryan Portrait, Houston Astros red cap	2.00	.90	.25
☐ 8 Nolan Ryan Pitching for the Astros	2.00	.90	.25
☐ 9 Nolan Ryan Smiling portrait, Astros uniform	2.00	.90	.25
☐ 10 Nolan Ryan Pitching for the Rangers	2.00	.90	.25
☐ 11 Nolan Ryan Preparing to pitch	2.00	.90	.25
☐ 12 Nolan Ryan Portrait, Texas Ranger cap	2.00	.90	.25

1936 S and S WG8

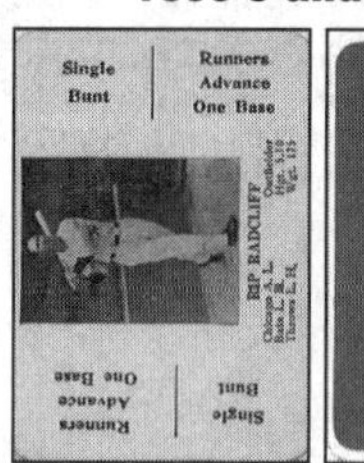

These cards were distributed as part of a baseball game produced in 1936. The cards each measure approximately 2 1/4" by 3 1/2" and have rounded corners. The card fronts are all oriented horizontally and show a small black and white photo of the player, his name, position, his team, vital statistics and the game outcome associated with that particular card. The card backs are evenly split between a plain green back with a thin white border or a plain back on a tannish paper stock. Since the cards are unnumbered, they are listed below in alphabetical order.

	EX-MT	VG-E	GOOD
COMPLETE SET (52)	800.00	350.00	100.00
COMMON CARD (1-52)	10.00	4.50	1.25
☐ 1 Luke Appling	30.00	13.50	3.70
☐ 2 Earl Averill	30.00	13.50	3.70
☐ 3 Zeke Bonura	10.00	4.50	1.25
☐ 4 Dolph Camilli	15.00	6.75	1.85
☐ 5 Ben Cantwell	10.00	4.50	1.25
☐ 6 Phil Cavarretta	25.00	11.00	3.10
☐ 7 Rip Collins	15.00	6.75	1.85
☐ 8 Joe Cronin	50.00	22.00	6.25
☐ 9 Frank Crosetti	25.00	11.00	3.10
☐ 10 Kiki Cuyler	30.00	13.50	3.70
☐ 11 Virgil Davis	10.00	4.50	1.25
☐ 12 Frank Demaree	15.00	6.75	1.85
☐ 13 Paul Derringer	25.00	11.00	3.10
☐ 14 Bill Dickey	60.00	27.00	7.50
☐ 15 Woody English	10.00	4.50	1.25
☐ 16 Fred Fitzsimmons	15.00	6.75	1.85
☐ 17 Rick Ferrell	30.00	13.50	3.70
☐ 18 Pete Fox	10.00	4.50	1.25
☐ 19 Jimmy Foxx	60.00	27.00	7.50
☐ 20 Larry French	10.00	4.50	1.25
☐ 21 Frank Frisch	50.00	22.00	6.25
☐ 22 August Galan	15.00	6.75	1.85
☐ 23 Charlie Gehringer	50.00	22.00	6.25
☐ 24 John Gill	10.00	4.50	1.25
☐ 25 Charles Grimm	25.00	11.00	3.10
☐ 26 Mule Haas	15.00	6.75	1.85
☐ 27 Stan Hack	25.00	11.00	3.10
☐ 28 Bill Hallahan	15.00	6.75	1.85
☐ 29 Mel Harder	25.00	11.00	3.10
☐ 30 Gabby Hartnett	30.00	13.50	3.70
☐ 31 Ray Hayworth	10.00	4.50	1.25
☐ 32 Ralston Hemsley	10.00	4.50	1.25
☐ 33 Bill Herman	30.00	13.50	3.70
☐ 34 Frank Higgins	10.00	4.50	1.25
☐ 35 Carl Hubbell	50.00	22.00	6.25
☐ 36 Bill Jurges	10.00	4.50	1.25
☐ 37 Vernon Kennedy	10.00	4.50	1.25
☐ 38 Chuck Klein	30.00	13.50	3.70
☐ 39 Mike Kreevich	10.00	4.50	1.25
☐ 40 Bill Lee	10.00	4.50	1.25
☐ 41 Joe Medwick	30.00	13.50	3.70
☐ 42 Van Mungo	15.00	6.75	1.85
☐ 43 James O'Dea	10.00	4.50	1.25
☐ 44 Mel Ott	50.00	22.00	6.25
☐ 45 Rip Radcliff	10.00	4.50	1.25
☐ 46 Pie Traynor	30.00	13.50	3.70
☐ 47 Arky Vaughan	30.00	13.50	3.70
☐ 48 Joe Vosmik	10.00	4.50	1.25
☐ 49 Lloyd Waner	30.00	13.50	3.70
☐ 50 Paul Waner	30.00	13.50	3.70
☐ 51 Lon Warneke	15.00	6.75	1.85
☐ 52 Floyd Young	10.00	4.50	1.25

1911 S74 Silks

Issued around 1911, these silk fabric collectibles have designs similar to the designs in the T205 Cigarette card set. The silk itself is 2" by 3" and the image is 1 1/4" by 2 3/8". The line work on the silks is in one color only, with colors of blue, red, brown and several variations between red and brown known to exist. The field or stock color is known in white and several pastel tints. The cards are unnumbered but have been numbered and listed by team alphabetical order and then player alphabetical order within the teams in the checklist below. Turkey Red and Old Mill Cigarettes are among the issuers of these silks. These silks were produced in more than one year and in fact may possibly be broken into two distinct sets. Silks with Helmar and Red Sun backs can also be found; although the Red Sun variations seem to be very scarce. White backgroung silks ave valued 25% higher. Silks which still have the paper ad backing attached are worth double the prices listed below.

	EX-MT	VG-E	GOOD
COMPLETE SET (122)	4000.00	1800.00	500.00
COMMON PLAYER (1-122)	45.00	20.00	5.50
☐ 1 Bill Carrigan	45.00	20.00	5.50
☐ 2 Ed Cicotte	175.00	80.00	22.00
☐ 3 Tris Speaker	250.00	110.00	31.00
☐ 4 Jake Stahl	45.00	20.00	5.50
☐ 5 Hugh Duffy	150.00	70.00	19.00
☐ 6 Amby McConnell	45.00	20.00	5.50
☐ 7 Freddie Parent	45.00	20.00	5.50
☐ 8 Fred Payne	45.00	20.00	5.50
☐ 9 Lee Tannehill	45.00	20.00	5.50
☐ 10 Doc White	45.00	20.00	5.50
☐ 11 Terry Turner	45.00	20.00	5.50
☐ 12 Cy Young	250.00	110.00	31.00
☐ 13 Ty Cobb	1000.00	450.00	125.00
☐ 14 Jim Delahanty	45.00	20.00	5.50
☐ 15 Davy Jones	45.00	20.00	5.50
☐ 16 George Moriarty	45.00	20.00	5.50
☐ 17 George Mullin	45.00	20.00	5.50
☐ 18 Ed Summers	45.00	20.00	5.50
☐ 19 Ed Willett	45.00	20.00	5.50
☐ 20 Hal Chase	100.00	45.00	12.50
☐ 21 Russ Ford	45.00	20.00	5.50
☐ 22 Charlie Hemphill	45.00	20.00	5.50
☐ 23 John Knight	45.00	20.00	5.50
☐ 24 John Quinn	45.00	20.00	5.50
☐ 25 Harry Wolter	45.00	20.00	5.50
☐ 26 Frank Baker	150.00	70.00	19.00
☐ 27 Jack Barry	45.00	20.00	5.50
☐ 28 Chief Bender	150.00	70.00	19.00
☐ 29 Eddie Collins	150.00	70.00	19.00
☐ 30 Jimmy Dygert	45.00	20.00	5.50
☐ 31 Topsy Hartsel	45.00	20.00	5.50
☐ 32 Harry Krause	45.00	20.00	5.50
☐ 33 Danny Murphy	45.00	20.00	5.50
☐ 34 Rube Oldring	45.00	20.00	5.50
☐ 35 Barney Pelty	45.00	20.00	5.50
☐ 36 George Stone	45.00	20.00	5.50
☐ 37 Bobby Wallace	150.00	70.00	19.00
☐ 38 Kid Elberfeld	45.00	20.00	5.50
☐ 39 Walter Johnson	500.00	220.00	60.00
☐ 40 Germany Schaefer	60.00	27.00	7.50
☐ 41 Gabby Street	45.00	20.00	5.50
☐ 42 Fred Beck	45.00	20.00	5.50
☐ 43 Peaches Graham	45.00	20.00	5.50
☐ 44 Buck Herzog	45.00	20.00	5.50
☐ 45 Al Mattern	45.00	20.00	5.50
☐ 46 Dave Shean	45.00	20.00	5.50
☐ 47 Harry Steinfeldt	60.00	27.00	7.50
☐ 48 Cy Barger (2)	45.00	20.00	5.50
☐ 49 George Bell	45.00	20.00	5.50
☐ 50 Bill Bergen	45.00	20.00	5.50
☐ 51 Bill Dahlen	60.00	27.00	7.50
☐ 52 Jake Daubert	60.00	27.00	7.50
☐ 53 John Hummel	45.00	20.00	5.50
☐ 54 Nap Rucker	60.00	27.00	7.50
☐ 55 Doc Scanlan	45.00	20.00	5.50
☐ 56 Red Smith	45.00	20.00	5.50
☐ 57 Zach Wheat	150.00	70.00	19.00
☐ 58 Mordecai Brown	150.00	70.00	19.00
☐ 59 Frank Chance	200.00	90.00	25.00
☐ 60 Johnny Evers	175.00	80.00	22.00
☐ 61 Bill Foxen	45.00	20.00	5.50
☐ 62 Peaches Graham	45.00	20.00	5.50
☐ 63 Johnny Kling	60.00	27.00	7.50
☐ 64 Harry McIntire	45.00	20.00	5.50
☐ 65 Tom Needham	45.00	20.00	5.50
☐ 66 Orval Overall	60.00	27.00	7.50
☐ 67 Ed Reulbach	60.00	27.00	7.50
☐ 68 Frank Schulte	60.00	27.00	7.50
☐ 69 Jimmy Sheckard	45.00	20.00	5.50
☐ 70 Harry Steinfeldt	60.00	27.00	7.50
☐ 71 Joe Tinker	175.00	80.00	22.00
☐ 72 Bob Bescher	45.00	20.00	5.50
☐ 73 Tom Downey	45.00	20.00	5.50
☐ 74 Art Fromme	45.00	20.00	5.50
☐ 75 Eddie Grant	45.00	20.00	5.50
☐ 76 Clark Griffith	45.00	20.00	5.50
☐ 77 Dick Hoblitzell	45.00	20.00	5.50
☐ 78 Mike Mitchell	45.00	20.00	5.50
☐ 79 Red Ames	45.00	20.00	5.50
☐ 80 Beals Becker	45.00	20.00	5.50
☐ 81 Al Bridwell	45.00	20.00	5.50
☐ 82 Doc Crandall	45.00	20.00	5.50
☐ 83 Art Devlin	45.00	20.00	5.50
☐ 84 Josh Devore	45.00	20.00	5.50
☐ 85 Larry Doyle	60.00	27.00	7.50
☐ 86 Art Fletcher	45.00	20.00	5.50
☐ 87 Rube Marquard	150.00	70.00	19.00
☐ 88 Christy Mathewson	500.00	220.00	60.00
☐ 89 John McGraw MG	200.00	90.00	25.00
☐ 90 Fred Merkle	60.00	27.00	7.50
☐ 91 Chief Meyers	60.00	27.00	7.50
☐ 92 Red Murray	45.00	20.00	5.50
☐ 93 Bugs Raymond	45.00	20.00	5.50
☐ 94 Admiral Schlei	45.00	20.00	5.50
☐ 95 Fred Snodgrass	45.00	20.00	5.50
☐ 96 Hooks Wiltse (2)	45.00	20.00	5.50
☐ 97 Johnny Bates	45.00	20.00	5.50
☐ 98 Red Dooin	45.00	20.00	5.50
☐ 99 Mickey Doolan	45.00	20.00	5.50
☐ 100 Bob Ewing	45.00	20.00	5.50
☐ 101 Hans Lobert	45.00	20.00	5.50
☐ 102 Pat Moran	45.00	20.00	5.50
☐ 103 Dode Paskert	45.00	20.00	5.50
☐ 104 Jack Rowan	45.00	20.00	5.50
☐ 105 John Titus	45.00	20.00	5.50
☐ 106 Bobby Byrne	45.00	20.00	5.50
☐ 107 Howie Camnitz	45.00	20.00	5.50
☐ 108 Fred Clarke	150.00	70.00	19.00
☐ 109 John Flynn	45.00	20.00	5.50
☐ 110 George Gibson	45.00	20.00	5.50
☐ 111 Tommy Leach	45.00	20.00	5.50
☐ 112 Lefty Leifield	45.00	20.00	5.50
☐ 113 Dots Miller	45.00	20.00	5.50
☐ 114 Deacon Phillippe	60.00	27.00	7.50
☐ 115 Kirby White	45.00	20.00	5.50
☐ 116 Owen Wilson	45.00	20.00	5.50
☐ 117 Roger Bresnahan (2)	150.00	70.00	19.00
☐ 118 Steve Evans	45.00	20.00	5.50
☐ 119 Arnold Hauser	45.00	20.00	5.50
☐ 120 Miller Huggins	150.00	70.00	19.00
☐ 121 Ed Konetchy	45.00	20.00	5.50
☐ 122 Rebel Oakes	45.00	20.00	5.50

1911 S81 Large Silks

These large and attractive silks are found in two sizes, approximately 5" by 7" or 7" by 9". Unlike the smaller S74 Baseball Silks, these silks are numbered, beginning with number 86 and ending at number 110. The pose of the picture is the same as that of the T3 Turkey Red baseball cards. The silks were issued in 1911 and are frequently found grouped on pillow covers. For some reason the silk of Mathewson appears to be the most plentiful member of this admittedly scarce issue. Therefore no premium typically associated with a Hall of Famer exists for this card.

	EX-MT	VG-E	GOOD
COMPLETE SET (25)	35000.00	15800.00	4400.00
COMMON PLAYER (86-110)	700.00	325.00	90.00
☐ 86 Rube Marquard	1500.00	700.00	190.00
☐ 87 Marty O'Toole	700.00	325.00	90.00
☐ 88 Rube Benton	700.00	325.00	90.00
☐ 89 Grover C. Alexander	2000.00	900.00	250.00
☐ 90 Russ Ford	700.00	325.00	90.00
☐ 91 John McGraw MG	2000.00	900.00	250.00
☐ 92 Nap Rucker	700.00	325.00	90.00
☐ 93 Mike Mitchell	700.00	325.00	90.00
☐ 94 Chief Bender	1500.00	700.00	190.00
☐ 95 Frank Baker	1500.00	700.00	190.00
☐ 96 Napoleon Lajoie	2000.00	900.00	250.00
☐ 97 Joe Tinker	1500.00	700.00	190.00
☐ 98 Sherry Magee	700.00	325.00	90.00
☐ 99 Howie Camnitz	700.00	325.00	90.00
☐ 100 Eddie Collins	1500.00	700.00	190.00
☐ 101 Red Dooin	700.00	325.00	90.00
☐ 102 Ty Cobb	8000.00	3600.00	1000.00
☐ 103 Hugh Jennings MG	1500.00	700.00	190.00
☐ 104 Roger Bresnahan	1500.00	700.00	190.00
☐ 105 Jake Stahl	700.00	325.00	90.00
☐ 106 Tris Speaker	2000.00	900.00	250.00
☐ 107 Ed Walsh	1500.00	700.00	190.00
☐ 108 Christy Mathewson	1200.00	550.00	150.00
☐ 109 Johnny Evers	2000.00	900.00	250.00
☐ 110 Walter Johnson	4000.00	1800.00	500.00

1889 S.F.Hess & Co. N338-1

In contrast to the color drawings in Hess' California League set N321, the players in this series of big league ballplayers are shown in sepia photographs. The cards are blank-backed and unnumbered; they have no printed detail except for the player's name and the advertisement for S.F. Hess and Co.'s Cigarettes found below the picture. Cards denoted by SPOT are "Spotted Ties".

	EX-MT	VG-E	GOOD
COMPLETE SET	13000.00	5800.00	1600.00
COMMON CARD	600.00	275.00	75.00
☐ 1 Bill Brown: New York	600.00	275.00	75.00
☐ 2 Roger Conner (sic) New York	1000.00	450.00	125.00
☐ 3 Ed Crane: New York	600.00	275.00	75.00
☐ 4 Buck Ewing: New York SPOT	1000.00	450.00	125.00
☐ 5 Elmer Foster: New York	600.00	275.00	75.00
☐ 6 William George: New York	600.00	275.00	75.00
☐ 7 Joe Gerhardt: New York SPOT	600.00	275.00	75.00
☐ 8 Charles Getzein: Detroit	600.00	275.00	75.00
☐ 9 George Gore: New York	600.00	275.00	75.00
☐ 10 Gil Hatfield: New York	600.00	275.00	75.00
☐ 11 Arlie Latham: St.Louis	750.00	350.00	95.00
☐ 12 Pat Murphy: New York	600.00	275.00	75.00
☐ 13 Jim Mutrie: New York	750.00	350.00	95.00
☐ 14 Dave Orr: New York SPOT	600.00	275.00	75.00
☐ 15 Danny Richardson: New York	600.00	275.00	75.00
☐ 16 Mike Slattery: New York	600.00	275.00	75.00
☐ 17 Lidell Titcomb: New York	600.00	275.00	75.00
☐ 18 John M. Ward: New York	1000.00	450.00	125.00
☐ 19 Curt Welch: St. Louis	750.00	350.00	95.00
☐ 20 Mickey Welch: New York SPOT	1000.00	450.00	125.00
☐ 21 Arthur Whitney: New York	600.00	275.00	75.00

1976 Safelon Superstar Lunch Bags

There are six variations to the luch bags which were packed 40 per carton. These lunch bags were white plastic with black-and-white drawings on both sides. The player's name and team are printed in black beneath drawing. A facsimile autograph also appears on the bags. All players appear at least once with all the other players in the set.

	NRMT	VG-E	GOOD
COMPLETE SET (15)	75.00	34.00	9.50
COMMON CARD (1-15)	1.00	.45	.12
☐ 1 Hank Aaron Johnny Bench	7.50	3.40	.95
☐ 2 Hank Aaron Fred Lynn	3.00	1.35	.35
☐ 3 Hank Aaron Catfish Hunter	5.00	2.20	.60
☐ 4 Hank Aaron Pete Rose	12.50	5.50	1.55
☐ 5 Hank Aaron Tom Seaver	7.50	3.40	.95
☐ 6 Johnny Bench Pete Rose	10.00	4.50	1.25
☐ 7 Johnny Bench Jim(Catfish) Hunter	4.00	1.80	.50
☐ 8 Johnny Bench Fred Lynn	2.00	.90	.25
☐ 9 Johnny Bench Tom Seaver	10.00	4.50	1.25
☐ 10 Jim Hunter Pete Rose	10.00	4.50	1.25
☐ 11 Jim Hunter Fred Lynn	2.00	.90	.25
☐ 12 Jim Hunter Tom Seaver	7.50	3.40	.95
☐ 13 Fred Lynn Pete Rose	5.00	2.20	.60
☐ 14 Fred Lynn Tom Seaver	3.00	1.35	.35
☐ 15 Pete Rose Tom Seaver	10.00	4.50	1.25

1962 Salada Plastic Coins

There are 221 different players in the 1962 plastic baseball coins marketed in Salada Tea and Junket Pudding mixes. Each plastic coin measures 1 3/8" in diameter. The initial production run consisted of 10 representatives from each of the 18 major league teams. A subsequent run added 20 players from the Mets and the Colt 45's and also dropped 21 of the original subjects, who were replaced by 21 new players assigned higher numbers. The "coin" itself is made of one-color plastic (light or dark) blue, black, orange, red or white) which has a color portrait printed on paper inserted into the obverse surface. A 10-coin, shield-like holder was available for each team. The complete set price below includes all variations. Many of the variations in the set are based on whether or not there are red buttons (RB) or white buttons (WB); these variation coin pairs are designated in the checklist below. Some of the tougher variations include Jackie Brandt listed as on the Orioles; Ed Bressoud with his name misspelled; Dick Williams with his name on the right; Gary Geiger with an "O" on the hat.

	NRMT	VG-E	GOOD
COMPLETE SET (263)	5000.00	2200.00	600.00
COMMON COIN (1-180)	1.50	.70	.19
COMMON COIN (181-221)	5.00	2.20	.60
☐ 1 Jim Gentile	2.50	1.10	.30
☐ 2 Billy Pierce	125.00	55.00	15.50
☐ 3 Chico Fernandez	1.50	.70	.19
☐ 4 Tom Brewer	25.00	11.00	3.10
☐ 5 Woody Held	1.50	.70	.19
☐ 6 Ray Herbert	25.00	11.00	3.10
☐ 7A Ken Aspromonte (Angels)	7.50	3.40	.95
☐ 7B Ken Aspromonte (Cleveland)	2.50	1.10	.30
☐ 8 Whitey Ford	25.00	11.00	3.10
☐ 9A Jim Lemon RB (does not exist)			
☐ 9B Jim Lemon WB	2.50	1.10	.30
☐ 10 Billy Klaus	1.50	.70	.19
☐ 11 Steve Barber	25.00	11.00	3.10
☐ 12 Nellie Fox	7.50	3.40	.95
☐ 13 Jim Bunning	12.00	5.50	1.50
☐ 14 Frank Malzone	1.50	.70	.19
☐ 15 Tito Francona	1.50	.70	.19
☐ 16 Bobby Del Greco	1.50	.70	.19
☐ 17A Steve Bilko RB	7.50	3.40	.95
☐ 17B Steve Bilko WB	2.50	1.10	.30
☐ 18 Tony Kubek	60.00	27.00	7.50
☐ 19 Earl Battey	1.50	.70	.19
☐ 20 Chuck Cottier	1.50	.70	.19
☐ 21 Willie Tasby	1.50	.70	.19
☐ 22 Bob Allison	2.50	1.10	.30
☐ 23 Roger Maris	35.00	16.00	4.40
☐ 24A Earl Averill RB	7.50	3.40	.95
☐ 24B Earl Averill WB	2.50	1.10	.30
☐ 25 Jerry Lumpe	1.50	.70	.19
☐ 26 Jim Grant	25.00	11.00	3.10
☐ 27 Carl Yastrzemski	60.00	27.00	7.50
☐ 28 Rocky Colavito	5.00	2.20	.60
☐ 29 Al Smith	1.50	.70	.19
☐ 30 Jim Busby	25.00	11.00	3.10
☐ 31 Dick Howser	2.50	1.10	.30
☐ 32 Jim Perry	2.50	1.10	.30
☐ 33 Yogi Berra	30.00	13.50	3.70
☐ 34A Ken Hamlin RB	7.50	3.40	.95
☐ 34B Ken Hamlin WB	2.50	1.10	.30
☐ 35 Dale Long	1.50	.70	.19
☐ 36 Harmon Killebrew	25.00	11.00	3.10
☐ 37 Dick Brown	1.50	.70	.19
☐ 38A Gary Geiger (O on hat)	450.00	200.00	55.00
☐ 38B Gary Geiger (no O on hat)	2.50	1.10	.30
☐ 39A Minnie Minoso (White Sox)	50.00	22.00	6.25
☐ 39B Minnie Minoso (Cardinals)	25.00	11.00	3.10
☐ 40 Brooks Robinson	35.00	16.00	4.40
☐ 41 Mickey Mantle	135.00	60.00	17.00
☐ 42 Bennie Daniels	1.50	.70	.19
☐ 43 Billy Martin	6.00	2.70	.75
☐ 44 Vic Power	1.50	.70	.19
☐ 45 Joe Pignatano	1.50	.70	.19
☐ 46A Ryne Duren RB	7.50	3.40	.95
☐ 46B Ryne Duren WB	2.50	1.10	.30
☐ 47A Pete Runnels (2nd base)	7.50	3.40	.95
☐ 47B Pete Runnels (1st base)	3.50	1.55	.45
☐ 48A Dick Williams (name right)	900.00	400.00	110.00
☐ 48B Dick Williams (name left)	5.00	2.20	.60
☐ 49 Jim Landis	1.50	.70	.19
☐ 50 Steve Boros	1.50	.70	.19
☐ 51A Zoilo Versalles RB	7.50	3.40	.95
☐ 51B Zoilo Versalles WB	2.50	1.10	.30
☐ 52A Johnny Temple (Indians)	10.00	4.50	1.25
☐ 52B Johnny Temple (Orioles)	5.00	2.20	.60
☐ 53A Jackie Brandt (Oriole)	5.00	2.20	.60
☐ 53B Jackie Brandt (Orioles)	900.00	400.00	110.00
☐ 54 Joe McClain	1.50	.70	.19
☐ 55 Sherman Lollar	1.50	.70	.19
☐ 56 Gene Stephens	1.50	.70	.19
☐ 57A Leon Wagner RB	7.50	3.40	.95
☐ 57B Leon Wagner WB	2.50	1.10	.30
☐ 58 Frank Lary	1.50	.70	.19
☐ 59 Bill Skowron	3.50	1.55	.45
☐ 60 Vic Wertz	25.00	11.00	3.10
☐ 61 Willie Kirkland	1.50	.70	.19
☐ 62 Leo Posada	1.50	.70	.19
☐ 63A Albie Pearson RB	7.50	3.40	.95
☐ 63B Albie Pearson WB	2.50	1.10	.30
☐ 64 Bobby Richardson	6.00	2.70	.75
☐ 65A Marv Breeding (Shortstop)	7.50	3.40	.95
☐ 65B Marv Breeding (2nd Base)	3.50	1.55	.45
☐ 66 Roy Sievers	100.00	45.00	12.50
☐ 67 Al Kaline	35.00	16.00	4.40
☐ 68A Don Buddin (Red Sox)	7.50	3.40	.95
☐ 68B Don Buddin (Colt .45's)	3.50	1.55	.45
☐ 69A Lenny Green RB	7.50	3.40	.95
☐ 69B Lenny Green WB	2.50	1.10	.30
☐ 70 Gene Green	25.00	11.00	3.10
☐ 71 Luis Aparicio	15.00	6.75	1.85
☐ 72 Norm Cash	3.50	1.55	.45
☐ 73 Jackie Jensen	35.00	16.00	4.40
☐ 74 Bubba Phillips	1.50	.70	.19
☐ 75 James Archer	1.50	.70	.19
☐ 76A Ken Hunt RB	7.50	3.40	.95
☐ 76B Ken Hunt WB	2.50	1.10	.30
☐ 77 Ralph Terry	2.50	1.10	.30
☐ 78 Camilo Pascual	1.50	.70	.19
☐ 79 Marty Keough	25.00	11.00	3.10
☐ 80 Clete Boyer	2.50	1.10	.30
☐ 81 Jim Pagliaroni	1.50	.70	.19
☐ 82A Gene Leek RB	7.50	3.40	.95
☐ 82B Gene Leek WB	2.50	1.10	.30
☐ 83 Jake Wood	1.50	.70	.19
☐ 84 Coot Veal	25.00	11.00	3.10
☐ 85 Norm Siebern	1.50	.70	.19
☐ 86A Andy Carey (White Sox)	35.00	16.00	4.40
☐ 86B Andy Carey (Phillies)	3.50	1.55	.45
☐ 87A Bill Tuttle RB	7.50	3.40	.95
☐ 87B Bill Tuttle WB	2.50	1.10	.30
☐ 88A Jimmy Piersall (Indians)	10.00	4.50	1.25
☐ 88B Jimmy Piersall (Senators)	5.00	2.20	.60
☐ 89 Ron Hansen	30.00	13.50	3.70
☐ 90A Chuck Stobbs RB	7.50	3.40	.95
☐ 90B Chuck Stobbs WB	2.50	1.10	.30
☐ 91A Ken McBride RB	7.50	3.40	.95
☐ 91B Ken McBride WB	2.50	1.10	.30
☐ 92 Bill Bruton	1.50	.70	.19
☐ 93 Gus Triandos	1.50	.70	.19
☐ 94 John Romano	1.50	.70	.19
☐ 95 Elston Howard	6.00	2.70	.75
☐ 96 Gene Woodling	1.50	.70	.19
☐ 97A Early Wynn (pitching)	50.00	22.00	6.25
☐ 97B Early Wynn (portrait)	25.00	11.00	3.10
☐ 98 Milt Pappas	1.50	.70	.19
☐ 99 Bill Monbouquette	1.50	.70	.19
☐ 100 Wayne Causey	1.50	.70	.19
☐ 101 Don Elston	1.50	.70	.19
☐ 102A Charlie Neal (Dodgers)	7.50	3.40	.95
☐ 102B Charlie Neal (Mets)	3.50	1.55	.45
☐ 103 Don Blasingame	1.50	.70	.19
☐ 104 Frank Thomas	30.00	13.50	3.70
☐ 105 Wes Covington	1.50	.70	.19
☐ 106 Chuck Hiller	1.50	.70	.19
☐ 107 Don Hoak	1.50	.70	.19
☐ 108A Bob Lillis (Cardinals)	15.00	6.75	1.85
☐ 108B Bob Lillis (Colt .45's)	5.00	2.20	.60
☐ 109 Sandy Koufax	40.00	18.00	5.00
☐ 110 Gordy Coleman	1.50	.70	.19
☐ 111 Eddie Matthews (sic, Mathews)	25.00	11.00	3.10
☐ 112 Art Mahaffey	1.50	.70	.19
☐ 113A Ed Bailey (red)	10.00	4.50	1.25
☐ 113B Ed Bailey (white)	2.50	1.10	.30
☐ 114 Smoky Burgess	1.50	.70	.19
☐ 115 Bill White	2.50	1.10	.30
☐ 116 Ed Bouchee	25.00	11.00	3.10
☐ 117 Bob Buhl	1.50	.70	.19
☐ 118 Vada Pinson	2.50	1.10	.30
☐ 119 Carl Sawatski	1.50	.70	.19
☐ 120 Dick Stuart	2.50	1.10	.30
☐ 121 Harvey Kuenn	35.00	16.00	4.40
☐ 122 Pancho Herrera	1.50	.70	.19
☐ 123A Don Zimmer (Cubs)	7.50	3.40	.95
☐ 123B Don Zimmer (Mets)	3.50	1.55	.45
☐ 124 Wally Moon	1.50	.70	.19
☐ 125 Joe Adcock	1.50	.70	.19
☐ 126 Joey Jay	1.50	.70	.19
☐ 127A Maury Wills (blue number 3)	15.00	6.75	1.85
☐ 127B Maury Wills (red number 3)	10.00	4.50	1.25
☐ 128 George Altman	1.50	.70	.19
☐ 129A John Buzhardt (Phillies)	10.00	4.50	1.25
☐ 129B John Buzhardt (White Sox)	5.00	2.20	.60
☐ 130 Felipe Alou	2.50	1.10	.30
☐ 131 Bill Mazeroski	2.50	1.10	.30
☐ 132 Ernie Broglio	1.50	.70	.19
☐ 133 John Roseboro	1.50	.70	.19
☐ 134 Mike McCormick	1.50	.70	.19
☐ 135A Charlie Smith (Philadelphia)	7.50	3.40	.95
☐ 135B Charlie Smith (White Sox)	3.50	1.55	.45
☐ 136 Ron Santo	2.50	1.10	.30
☐ 137 Gene Freese	1.50	.70	.19
☐ 138 Dick Groat	2.50	1.10	.30
☐ 139 Curt Flood	2.50	1.10	.30
☐ 140 Frank Bolling	1.50	.70	.19
☐ 141 Clay Dalrymple	1.50	.70	.19
☐ 142 Willie McCovey	30.00	13.50	3.70
☐ 143 Bob Skinner	1.50	.70	.19
☐ 144 Lindy McDaniel	1.50	.70	.19
☐ 145 Glen Hobbie	1.50	.70	.19
☐ 146A Gil Hodges (Dodgers)	50.00	22.00	6.25
☐ 146B Gil Hodges (Mets)	25.00	11.00	3.10
☐ 147 Eddie Kasko	1.50	.70	.19
☐ 148 Gino Cimoli	35.00	16.00	4.40
☐ 149 Willie Mays	85.00	38.00	10.50
☐ 150 Roberto Clemente	90.00	40.00	11.00
☐ 151 Red Schoendienst	2.50	1.10	.30
☐ 152 Joe Torre	2.50	1.10	.30
☐ 153 Bob Purkey	1.50	.70	.19
☐ 154A Tommy Davis (Outfield)	7.50	3.40	.95
☐ 154B Tommy Davis (3rd Base)	2.50	1.10	.30
☐ 155A Andre Rogers ERR (sic, Rodgers)	7.50	3.40	.95
☐ 155B Andre Rodgers COR	2.50	1.10	.30
☐ 156 Tony Taylor	1.50	.70	.19
☐ 157 Bob Friend	1.50	.70	.19
☐ 158A Gus Bell (Reds)	7.50	3.40	.95
☐ 158B Gus Bell (Mets)	3.50	1.55	.45
☐ 159 Roy McMillan	1.50	.70	.19
☐ 160 Carl Warwick	1.50	.70	.19
☐ 161 Willie Davis	2.50	1.10	.30
☐ 162 Sam Jones	40.00	18.00	5.00
☐ 163 Ruben Amaro	1.50	.70	.19
☐ 164 Sammy Taylor	1.50	.70	.19
☐ 165 Frank Robinson	30.00	13.50	3.70
☐ 166 Lew Burdette	2.50	1.10	.30
☐ 167 Ken Boyer	3.50	1.55	.45
☐ 168 Bill Virdon	2.50	1.10	.30
☐ 169 Jim Davenport	1.50	.70	.19
☐ 170 Don Demeter	1.50	.70	.19
☐ 171 Richie Ashburn	40.00	18.00	5.00
☐ 172 Johnny Podres	2.50	1.10	.30
☐ 173A Joe Cunningham (Cardinals)	50.00	22.00	6.25
☐ 173B Joe Cunningham (White Sox)	20.00	9.00	2.50
☐ 174 Elroy Face	2.50	1.10	.30
☐ 175 Orlando Cepeda	6.00	2.70	.75
☐ 176A Bobby Gene Smith (Philadelphia)	7.50	3.40	.95
☐ 176B Bobby Gene Smith (Mets)	3.50	1.55	.45
☐ 177A Ernie Banks (Outfield)	50.00	22.00	6.25
☐ 177B Ernie Banks (Shortstop)	25.00	11.00	3.10
☐ 178A Daryl Spencer (3rd Base)	7.50	3.40	.95
☐ 178B Daryl Spencer (1st Base)	3.50	1.55	.45
☐ 179 Bob Schmidt	25.00	11.00	3.10
☐ 180 Hank Aaron	75.00	34.00	9.50
☐ 181 Hobie Landrith	5.00	2.20	.60
☐ 182A Ed Broussard (sic, Bressoud)	400.00	180.00	50.00
☐ 182B Ed Bressoud (correct)	25.00	11.00	3.10
☐ 183 Felix Mantilla	5.00	2.20	.60
☐ 184 Dick Farrell	5.00	2.20	.60
☐ 185 Bob Miller	5.00	2.20	.60
☐ 186 Don Taussig	5.00	2.20	.60
☐ 187 Pumpsie Green	5.00	2.20	.60
☐ 188 Bobby Shantz	6.00	2.70	.75
☐ 189 Roger Craig	6.00	2.70	.75
☐ 190 Hal Smith	5.00	2.20	.60
☐ 191 Johnny Edwards	5.00	2.20	.60
☐ 192 John DeMerit	5.00	2.20	.60
☐ 193 Joe Amalfitano	5.00	2.20	.60
☐ 194 Norm Larker	5.00	2.20	.60
☐ 195 Al Heist	5.00	2.20	.60
☐ 196 Al Spangler	5.00	2.20	.60
☐ 197 Alex Grammas	5.00	2.20	.60
☐ 198 Jerry Lynch	5.00	2.20	.60
☐ 199 Jim McKnight	5.00	2.20	.60
☐ 200 Jose Pagen (sic, Pagan)	5.00	2.20	.60
☐ 201 Jim Gilliam	15.00	6.75	1.85
☐ 202 Art Ditmar	5.00	2.20	.60
☐ 203 Bud Daley	5.00	2.20	.60
☐ 204 Johnny Callison	6.00	2.70	.75
☐ 205 Stu Miller	5.00	2.20	.60
☐ 206 Russ Snyder	5.00	2.20	.60

☐ 207 Billy Williams	30.00	13.50	3.70
☐ 208 Walt Bond	5.00	2.20	.60
☐ 209 Joe Koppe	5.00	2.20	.60
☐ 210 Don Schwall	10.00	4.50	1.25
☐ 211 Billy Gardner	6.00	2.70	.75
☐ 212 Chuck Estrada	5.00	2.20	.60
☐ 213 Gary Bell	5.00	2.20	.60
☐ 214 Floyd Robinson	5.00	2.20	.60
☐ 215 Duke Snider	55.00	25.00	7.00
☐ 216 Lee Maye	5.00	2.20	.60
☐ 217 Howie Bedell	5.00	2.20	.60
☐ 218 Bob Will	5.00	2.20	.60
☐ 219 Dallas Green	7.50	3.40	.95
☐ 220 Carroll Hardy	5.00	2.20	.60
☐ 221 Danny O'Connell	5.00	2.20	.60

1963 Salada Metal Coins

The 1963 baseball coin set distributed by Salada Tea and Junket Pudding marked a drastic change from the set of the previous year. The coins were made of metal, rather than plastic, with conspicuous red rims for National League players and blue rims for their American League counterparts. Each coin measures 1 1/2" in diameter. The subject's portrait was printed in color on the front, with his name, position, team and 1962 statistics listed on the back. Also on the reverse is located the coin number and the line "Save and Trade 63 All Star Baseball Coins."

	NRMT	VG-E	GOOD
COMPLETE SET (63)	750.00	350.00	95.00
COMMON COIN (1-63)	3.50	1.55	.45
☐ 1 Don Drysdale	20.00	9.00	2.50
☐ 2 Dick Farrell	3.50	1.55	.45
☐ 3 Bob Gibson	20.00	9.00	2.50
☐ 4 Sandy Koufax	40.00	18.00	5.00
☐ 5 Juan Marichal	15.00	6.75	1.85
☐ 6 Bob Purkey	3.50	1.55	.45
☐ 7 Bob Shaw	3.50	1.55	.45
☐ 8 Warren Spahn	20.00	9.00	2.50
☐ 9 Johnny Podres	5.00	2.20	.60
☐ 10 Art Mahaffey	3.50	1.55	.45
☐ 11 Del Crandall	3.50	1.55	.45
☐ 12 John Roseboro	5.00	2.20	.60
☐ 13 Orlando Cepeda	7.50	3.40	.95
☐ 14 Bill Mazeroski	7.50	3.40	.95
☐ 15 Ken Boyer	6.00	2.70	.75
☐ 16 Dick Groat	5.00	2.20	.60
☐ 17 Ernie Banks	30.00	13.50	3.70
☐ 18 Frank Bolling	3.50	1.55	.45
☐ 19 Jim Davenport	3.50	1.55	.45
☐ 20 Maury Wills	6.00	2.70	.75
☐ 21 Willie Davis	5.00	2.20	.60
☐ 22 Willie Mays	75.00	34.00	9.50
☐ 23 Roberto Clemente	75.00	34.00	9.50
☐ 24 Hank Aaron	75.00	34.00	9.50
☐ 25 Matty Alou	5.00	2.20	.60
☐ 26 Johnny Callison	5.00	2.20	.60
☐ 27 Richie Ashburn	15.00	6.75	1.85
☐ 28 Eddie Mathews	20.00	9.00	2.50
☐ 29 Frank Robinson	25.00	11.00	3.10
☐ 30 Billy Williams	15.00	6.75	1.85
☐ 31 George Altman	3.50	1.55	.45
☐ 32 Hank Aguirre	3.50	1.55	.45
☐ 33 Jim Bunning	15.00	6.75	1.85
☐ 34 Dick Donovan	3.50	1.55	.45
☐ 35 Bill Monbouquette	3.50	1.55	.45
☐ 36 Camilo Pascual	5.00	2.20	.60
☐ 37 Dave Stenhouse	3.50	1.55	.45
☐ 38 Ralph Terry	5.00	2.20	.60
☐ 39 Hoyt Wilhelm	15.00	6.75	1.85
☐ 40 Jim Kaat	7.50	3.40	.95
☐ 41 Ken McBride	3.50	1.55	.45
☐ 42 Ray Herbert	3.50	1.55	.45
☐ 43 Milt Pappas	5.00	2.20	.60
☐ 44 Earl Battey	3.50	1.55	.45
☐ 45 Elston Howard	6.00	2.70	.75
☐ 46 John Romano	3.50	1.55	.45
☐ 47 Jim Gentile	5.00	2.20	.60
☐ 48 Billy Moran	3.50	1.55	.45
☐ 49 Rich Rollins	3.50	1.55	.45
☐ 50 Luis Aparicio	15.00	6.75	1.85
☐ 51 Norm Siebern	3.50	1.55	.45
☐ 52 Bobby Richardson	7.50	3.40	.95
☐ 53 Brooks Robinson	25.00	11.00	3.10
☐ 54 Tom Tresh	5.00	2.20	.60
☐ 55 Leon Wagner	3.50	1.55	.45
☐ 56 Mickey Mantle	125.00	55.00	15.50
☐ 57 Roger Maris	40.00	18.00	5.00
☐ 58 Rocky Colavito	7.50	3.40	.95
☐ 59 Frank Thomas	5.00	2.20	.60
☐ 60 Jim Landis	3.50	1.55	.45
☐ 61 Pete Runnels	5.00	2.20	.60
☐ 62 Yogi Berra	30.00	13.50	3.70
☐ 63 Al Kaline	25.00	11.00	3.10

1981 San Diego Sports Collectors

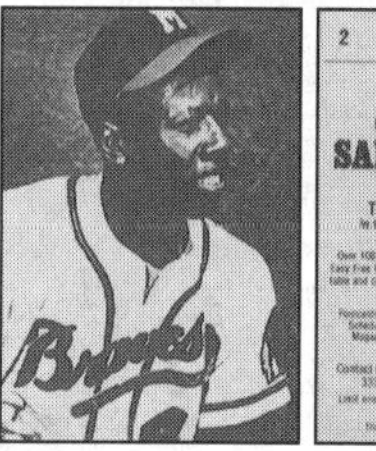

2 Hank Aaron
THIS CARD WORTH
50¢ OFF
ON ADMISSION TO THE
SAN DIEGO SHOW
AUGUST 22 & 23
TOWN & COUNTRY HOTEL

This 20-card standard-size rounded-corner set was presented by the San Diego Sports Collectors Association at the San Diego Show held August 22 and 23, 1981. The fronts feature borderless, glossy, black-and-white player photos. The backs are white and carry the player's name, advertisement information and an offer for 50 cents off admission to the show with the card.

	NRMT	VG-E	GOOD
COMPLETE SET (20)	17.50	8.00	2.20
COMMON CARD (1-20)	.25	.11	.03
☐ 1 Gary Butcher	.25	.11	.03
☐ 2 Hank Aaron	1.50	.70	.19
☐ 3 Duke Snider	1.00	.45	.12
☐ 4 Al Kaline	1.00	.45	.12
☐ 5 Vic Power	.50	.23	.06
☐ 6 Jackie Robinson	1.50	.70	.19
☐ 7 Carl Erskine	.50	.23	.06
☐ 8 Ted Williams (Batting)	2.00	.90	.25
☐ 9 Ted Williams (Portrait)	2.00	.90	.25
☐ 10 Mickey Mantle (Portrait)	2.50	1.10	.30
☐ 11 Mickey Mantle (Holding bat)	2.50	1.10	.30
☐ 12 Mickey Mantle Willie Mays	1.50	.70	.19
☐ 13 Mickey Mantle Stan Musial	1.00	.45	.12
☐ 14 Joe DiMaggio	2.00	.90	.25
☐ 15 Roger Maris (Portrait)	1.50	.70	.19
☐ 16 Roger Maris (Holding bat)	1.50	.70	.19
☐ 17 Lou Gehrig	2.00	.90	.25
☐ 18 Bill Dickey Lou Gehrig	1.00	.45	.12
☐ 19 Lou Gehrig Joe Cronin Bill Dickey Joe DiMaggio	.75	.35	.09
☐ 20 Gary Butcher	.25	.11	.03

1969 SCFS Old Timers

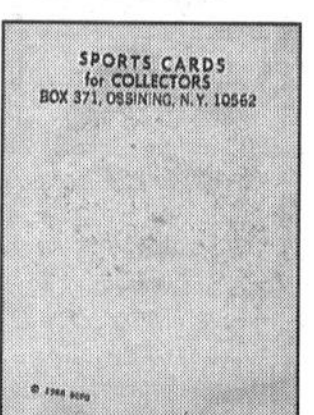

This set measures 3 1/2" X 4 1/4" and features black-and-white artistic renderings of old time baseball players. The player's name, position and years played are printed at the bottom. The backs are blank except for a small stamp at the bottom whi. The cards are numbered on the front. The cards were produced by long time hobbyist Mike Aronstein.

	NRMT	VG-E	GOOD
COMPLETE SET	25.00	11.00	3.10
COMMON CARD	.25	.11	.03
☐ 1 Babe Ruth	5.00	2.20	.60
☐ 2 Rube Marquard	.75	.35	.09
☐ 3 Zack Wheat	.75	.35	.09
☐ 4 John Clarkson	.75	.35	.09
☐ 5 Honus Wagner	1.00	.45	.12
☐ 6 Crab Evers	.75	.35	.09
☐ 7 Bill Dickey	.75	.35	.09
☐ 8 Elmer Smith	.25	.11	.03
☐ 9 Ty Cobb	2.50	1.10	.30
☐ 10 Happy Jack Chesbro	.25	.11	.03
☐ 11 Moon Gibson	.25	.11	.03
☐ 12 Bullet Joe Bush	.25	.11	.03
☐ 13 George Mullin	.25	.11	.03
☐ 14 Buddy Myer	.25	.11	.03
☐ 15 James Collins	.75	.35	.09
☐ 16 William Wambsganss	.25	.11	.03
☐ 17 John Bunny	.25	.11	.03
☐ 18 Dickie Kerr	.25	.11	.03
☐ 19 Connie Mack	.75	.35	.09
☐ 20 Rabbit Maranville	.75	.35	.09
☐ 21 Roger Peckinpaugh	.25	.11	.03
☐ 22 Mickey Cochrane	.75	.35	.09
☐ 23 George Kelly	.75	.35	.09
☐ 24 John Baker	.25	.11	.03
☐ 25 Wally Schang	.25	.11	.03
☐ 26 Eddie Plank	.75	.35	.09
☐ 27 Bill Donovan	.25	.11	.03
☐ 28 Red Faber	.25	.11	.03
☐ 29 Hack Wilson	.75	.35	.09
☐ 30 Three Fingered Brown	.75	.35	.09
☐ 31 Frederick Merkle	.25	.11	.03
☐ 32 Heinie Groh	.25	.11	.03
☐ 33 Stuffy McInnis	.25	.11	.03
☐ 34 Prince Hal Chase	.75	.35	.09
☐ 35 Kenesaw Mountain Landis COMM	.50	.23	.06
☐ 36 Chief Bender	.75	.35	.09
☐ 50 Jimmy Wilson	.25	.11	.03
☐ 55 Jim Thorpe	2.50	1.10	.30

1930 Schutter-Johnson R332

This set of 50 cards was issued by the Schutter-Johnson Candy Corporation around 1930. Each card measures 2 1/4" by 2 7/8". While each card in the series is numbered, the ones in the checklist below are the only ones known at the present time. These black line-drawing cards on a red field are entitled "Major League Secrets" and feature tips from major league players on the reverse.

	EX-MT	VG-E	GOOD
COMPLETE SET (50)	4000.00	1800.00	500.00
COMMON CARD (1-50)	40.00	18.00	5.00
☐ 1 Al Simmons Swings 2 or 3 bats	60.00	27.00	7.50
☐ 2 Lloyd Waner's Batting Stance	60.00	27.00	7.50
☐ 3 Kiki Cuyler's Baserunning Tips	60.00	27.00	7.50
☐ 4 Frank Frisch Chop Bunt	75.00	34.00	9.50
☐ 5 Chick Hafey Get Jump On Fly Balls	60.00	27.00	7.50
☐ 6 Bill Klem UMP Balk	75.00	34.00	9.50
☐ 7 Rogers Hornsby How to Practice Control Pitching Tips)	125.00	55.00	15.50
☐ 8 Carl Mays Underhand Ball	40.00	18.00	5.00
☐ 9 Charles Wrigley UMP Pitcher's feet with no baserunners)	40.00	18.00	5.00
☐ 10 Christy Mathewson Fade-Away Pitch	150.00	70.00	19.00
☐ 11 Bill Dickey Waste Ball	100.00	45.00	12.50
☐ 12 Walter Berger don't step in the bucket	40.00	18.00	5.00
☐ 13 George Earnshaw Curve	40.00	18.00	5.00
☐ 14 Hack Wilson grip bat at extreme end	75.00	34.00	9.50
☐ 15 Charley Grimm testing pitcher at first	40.00	18.00	5.00
☐ 16 Waner Brothers word signs in outfield	60.00	27.00	7.50
☐ 17 Chuck Klein keep eye on ball	60.00	27.00	7.50
☐ 18 Woody English bunt flat-footed	40.00	18.00	5.00
☐ 19 Grover Alexander side arm fastball	75.00	34.00	9.50
☐ 20 Lou Gehrig hit ball where pitched)	350.00	160.00	45.00
☐ 21 Wes Ferrell Wind-up	40.00	18.00	5.00
☐ 22 Carl Hubbell Wind-up Pitching Tips	75.00	34.00	9.50
☐ 23 Pie Traynor Bunting Tips	60.00	27.00	7.50
☐ 24 Gus Mancuso getting under foul ball	40.00	18.00	5.00
☐ 25 Ben Cantwell curve ball grip	40.00	18.00	5.00
☐ 26 Babe Ruth Advice	700.00	325.00	90.00
☐ 27 Goose Goslin throw from outfield	60.00	27.00	7.50
☐ 28 Earle Combs Hands Apart Grip	60.00	27.00	7.50
☐ 29 Kiki Cuyler halfslide	60.00	27.00	7.50
☐ 30 Jimmy Wilson delayed steal	40.00	18.00	5.00
☐ 31 Dizzy Dean curveball	125.00	55.00	15.50
☐ 32 Mickey Cochrane signs	75.00	34.00	9.50
☐ 33 Ted Lyons Knuckle Ball	75.00	34.00	9.50
☐ 34 Si Johnson Slow Ball	40.00	18.00	5.00
☐ 35 Dizzy Dean Fork Ball	125.00	55.00	15.50
☐ 36 Pepper Martin bunting	40.00	18.00	5.00
☐ 37 Joe Cronin Battery Tips	60.00	27.00	7.50
☐ 38 Gabby Hartnett Simple Batting Signs	60.00	27.00	7.50
☐ 39 Oscar Melillo play ball don't let ball play you	40.00	18.00	5.00
☐ 40 Ben Chapman hook slide)	40.00	18.00	5.00
☐ 41 John McGraw MG Coaching Signs	75.00	34.00	9.50
☐ 42 Babe Ruth choke grip	700.00	325.00	90.00
☐ 43 Red Lucas illegal action	40.00	18.00	5.00
☐ 44 Charley Root Holding Runners on First	40.00	18.00	5.00
☐ 45 Dazzy Vance drop pitch	60.00	27.00	7.50
☐ 46 Hugh Critz second baseman's throw	40.00	18.00	5.00
☐ 47 Firpo Marberry Raise Ball	40.00	18.00	5.00
☐ 48 Grover Alexander Full Windup	75.00	34.00	9.50
☐ 49 Lefty Grove fast ball grip	100.00	45.00	12.50
☐ 50 Heine Meine three types of curves	40.00	18.00	5.00

1996 Schwebels Discs

This 20-disc set measures approximately 2 3/4" in diameter. The fronts feature color player portraits in a blue-and-red border with fading stars. The player's name is printed in the top blue border with the year "1996" in the bottom red border. The backs carry the player's name, team, position, biographical information, season and career statistics.

	MINT	NRMT	EXC
COMPLETE SET (20)	15.00	6.75	1.85
COMMON DISC (1-20)	.50	.23	.06
☐ 1 Jim Thome	1.00	.45	.12
☐ 2 Orel Hershiser	.75	.35	.09
☐ 3 Greg Maddux	3.00	1.35	.35
☐ 4 Charles Nagy	.75	.35	.09
☐ 5 Omar Vizquel	.75	.35	.09
☐ 6 Manny Ramirez	1.50	.70	.19
☐ 7 Dennis Martinez	.50	.23	.06
☐ 8 Eddie Murray	1.50	.70	.19
☐ 9 Albert Belle	2.50	1.10	.30
☐ 10 Fred McGriff	2.00	.90	.25
☐ 11 Jack McDowell	.75	.35	.09
☐ 12 Kenny Lofton	2.00	.90	.25
☐ 13 Cal Ripken	4.00	1.80	.50
☐ 14 Jose Mesa	.50	.23	.06
☐ 15 Randy Johnson	1.00	.45	.12
☐ 16 Ken Griffey Jr.	5.00	2.20	.60
☐ 17 Carlos Baerga	.75	.35	.09
☐ 18 Frank Thomas	5.00	2.20	.60
☐ 19 Sandy Alomar	.50	.23	.06
☐ 20 Barry Bonds	1.25	.55	.16

1988 Score Samples

Early in 1988, Score prepared some samples to show prospective dealers and buyers of the new Score cards what they would look like. These sample cards are distinguished by the fact that there is a row of zeroes for the 1987 season statistics since the season was not over when these sample cards were being printed. The cards are standard size and are virtually indistinguishable from the regular 1988 Score cards of the same players except for border color variations in a few instances.

	MINT	NRMT	EXC
COMPLETE SET (6)	40.00	18.00	5.00
COMMON CARD	5.00	2.20	.60

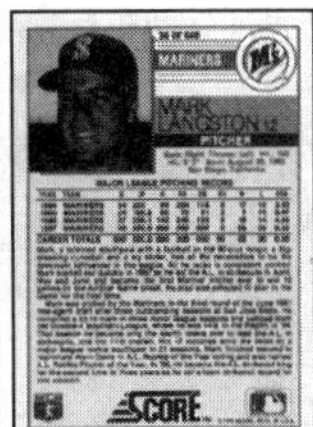

☐ 30 Mark Langston	8.00	3.60	1.00
☐ 48 Tony Pena	5.00	2.20	.60
☐ 71 Keith Moreland	5.00	2.20	.60
☐ 72 Barry Larkin	25.00	11.00	3.10
☐ 121 Dennis Boyd	5.00	2.20	.60
☐ 145 Denny Walling	5.00	2.20	.60

1988 Score

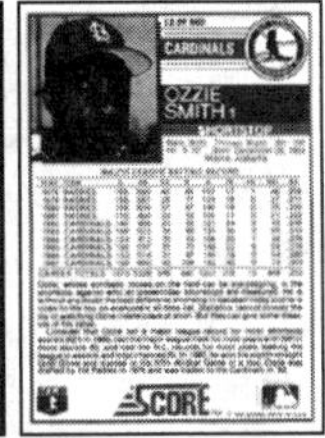

This set consists of 660 standard-size cards. The set was distributed by Major League Marketing and features six distinctive border colors on the front. Subsets include Reggie Jackson Tribute (500-504), Highlights (652-660) and Rookie Prospects (623-647). Card number 501, showing Reggie as a member of the Baltimore Orioles, is one of the few opportunities collectors have to visually remember Reggie's one-year stay with the Orioles. The set is distinguished by the fact that each card back shows a full-color picture of the player. Rookie Cards in this set include Ellis Burks, Ken Caminiti, Ron Gant, Tom Glavine, Gregg Jefferies, Jeff Montgomery, and Matt Williams.

	MINT	NRMT	EXC
COMPLETE SET (660)	10.00	4.50	1.25
COMPLETE FACT.SET (660)	12.00	5.50	1.50
COMMON CARD (1-660)	.05	.02	.01
☐ 1 Don Mattingly	.50	.23	.06
☐ 2 Wade Boggs	.15	.07	.02
☐ 3 Tim Raines	.10	.05	.01
☐ 4 Andre Dawson	.10	.05	.01
☐ 5 Mark McGwire	.60	.25	.07
☐ 6 Kevin Seitzer	.10	.05	.01
☐ 7 Wally Joyner	.15	.07	.02
☐ 8 Jesse Barfield	.05	.02	.01
☐ 9 Pedro Guerrero	.10	.05	.01
☐ 10 Eric Davis	.10	.05	.01
☐ 11 George Brett	.40	.18	.05
☐ 12 Ozzie Smith	.25	.11	.03
☐ 13 Rickey Henderson	.15	.07	.02
☐ 14 Jim Rice	.15	.07	.02
☐ 15 Matt Nokes	.05	.02	.01
☐ 16 Mike Schmidt	.20	.09	.03
☐ 17 Dave Parker	.15	.07	.02
☐ 18 Eddie Murray	.25	.11	.03
☐ 19 Andres Galarraga	.15	.07	.02
☐ 20 Tony Fernandez	.05	.02	.01
☐ 21 Kevin McReynolds	.05	.02	.01
☐ 22 B.J. Surhoff	.10	.05	.01
☐ 23 Pat Tabler	.05	.02	.01
☐ 24 Kirby Puckett	.40	.18	.05
☐ 25 Benny Santiago	.10	.05	.01
☐ 26 Ryne Sandberg	.25	.11	.03
☐ 27 Kelly Downs	.05	.02	.01
(Will Clark in back-ground, out of focus)			
☐ 28 Jose Cruz	.05	.02	.01
☐ 29 Pete O'Brien	.05	.02	.01
☐ 30 Mark Langston	.15	.07	.02
☐ 31 Lee Smith	.10	.05	.01
☐ 32 Juan Samuel	.05	.02	.01
☐ 33 Kevin Bass	.05	.02	.01
☐ 34 R.J. Reynolds	.05	.02	.01
☐ 35 Steve Sax	.05	.02	.01
☐ 36 John Kruk	.15	.07	.02
☐ 37 Alan Trammell	.10	.05	.01
☐ 38 Chris Bosio	.05	.02	.01
☐ 39 Brook Jacoby	.05	.02	.01
☐ 40 Willie McGee UER	.05	.02	.01
(Excited misspelled as excitd)			
☐ 41 Dave Magadan	.05	.02	.01
☐ 42 Fred Lynn	.05	.02	.01
☐ 43 Kent Hrbek	.10	.05	.01
☐ 44 Brian Downing	.05	.02	.01
☐ 45 Jose Canseco	.25	.11	.03
☐ 46 Jim Presley	.05	.02	.01
☐ 47 Mike Stanley	.10	.05	.01
☐ 48 Tony Pena	.05	.02	.01
☐ 49 David Cone	.15	.07	.02
☐ 50 Rick Sutcliffe	.05	.02	.01
☐ 51 Doug Drabek	.10	.05	.01
☐ 52 Bill Doran	.05	.02	.01
☐ 53 Mike Scioscia	.05	.02	.01
☐ 54 Candy Maldonado	.05	.02	.01
☐ 55 Dave Winfield	.15	.07	.02
☐ 56 Lou Whitaker	.10	.05	.01
☐ 57 Tom Henke	.05	.02	.01
☐ 58 Ken Gerhart	.05	.02	.01
☐ 59 Glenn Braggs	.05	.02	.01
☐ 60 Julio Franco	.10	.05	.01
☐ 61 Charlie Leibrandt	.05	.02	.01
☐ 62 Gary Gaetti	.05	.02	.01
☐ 63 Bob Boone	.10	.05	.01
☐ 64 Luis Polonia	.15	.07	.02
☐ 65 Dwight Evans	.10	.05	.01
☐ 66 Phil Bradley	.05	.02	.01
☐ 67 Mike Boddicker	.05	.02	.01
☐ 68 Vince Coleman	.05	.02	.01
☐ 69 Howard Johnson	.05	.02	.01
☐ 70 Tim Wallach	.05	.02	.01
☐ 71 Keith Moreland	.05	.02	.01
☐ 72 Barry Larkin	.30	.14	.04
☐ 73 Alan Ashby	.05	.02	.01
☐ 74 Rick Rhoden	.05	.02	.01
☐ 75 Darrell Evans	.10	.05	.01
☐ 76 Dave Stieb	.10	.05	.01
☐ 77 Dan Plesac	.05	.02	.01
☐ 78 Will Clark UER	.25	.11	.03
(Born 3/17/64, should be 3/13/64)			
☐ 79 Frank White	.10	.05	.01
☐ 80 Joe Carter	.15	.07	.02
☐ 81 Mike Witt	.05	.02	.01
☐ 82 Terry Steinbach	.15	.07	.02
☐ 83 Alvin Davis	.05	.02	.01
☐ 84 Tommy Herr	.10	.05	.01
(Will Clark shown sliding into second)			
☐ 85 Vance Law	.05	.02	.01
☐ 86 Kal Daniels	.05	.02	.01
☐ 87 Rick Honeycutt UER	.05	.02	.01
(Wrong years for stats on back)			
☐ 88 Alfredo Griffin	.05	.02	.01
☐ 89 Bret Saberhagen	.10	.05	.01
☐ 90 Bert Blyleven	.10	.05	.01
☐ 91 Jeff Reardon	.10	.05	.01
☐ 92 Cory Snyder	.05	.02	.01
☐ 93A Greg Walker ERR	2.00	.90	.25
(93 of 66)			
☐ 93B Greg Walker COR	.05	.02	.01
(93 of 660)			
☐ 94 Joe Magrane	.05	.02	.01
☐ 95 Rob Deer	.05	.02	.01
☐ 96 Ray Knight	.10	.05	.01
☐ 97 Casey Candaele	.05	.02	.01
☐ 98 John Cerutti	.05	.02	.01
☐ 99 Buddy Bell	.10	.05	.01
☐ 100 Jack Clark	.10	.05	.01
☐ 101 Eric Bell	.05	.02	.01
☐ 102 Willie Wilson	.05	.02	.01
☐ 103 Dave Schmidt	.05	.02	.01
☐ 104 Dennis Eckersley UER	.10	.05	.01
(Complete games stats are wrong)			
☐ 105 Don Sutton	.15	.07	.02
☐ 106 Danny Tartabull	.05	.02	.01
☐ 107 Fred McGriff	.30	.14	.04
☐ 108 Les Straker	.05	.02	.01
☐ 109 Lloyd Moseby	.05	.02	.01
☐ 110 Roger Clemens	.20	.09	.03
☐ 111 Glenn Hubbard	.05	.02	.01
☐ 112 Ken Williams	.05	.02	.01
☐ 113 Ruben Sierra	.15	.07	.02
☐ 114 Stan Jefferson	.05	.02	.01
☐ 115 Milt Thompson	.05	.02	.01
☐ 116 Bobby Bonilla	.15	.07	.02
☐ 117 Wayne Tolleson	.05	.02	.01
☐ 118 Matt Williams	.75	.35	.09
☐ 119 Chet Lemon	.05	.02	.01
☐ 120 Dale Sveum	.05	.02	.01
☐ 121 Dennis Boyd	.05	.02	.01
☐ 122 Brett Butler	.10	.05	.01
☐ 123 Terry Kennedy	.05	.02	.01
☐ 124 Jack Howell	.05	.02	.01
☐ 125 Curt Young	.05	.02	.01
☐ 126A Dave Valle ERR	.10	.05	.01
(Misspelled Dale on card front)			
☐ 126B Dave Valle COR	.05	.02	.01
☐ 127 Curt Wilkerson	.05	.02	.01
☐ 128 Tim Teufel	.05	.02	.01
☐ 129 Ozzie Virgil	.05	.02	.01
☐ 130 Brian Fisher	.05	.02	.01
☐ 131 Lance Parrish	.05	.02	.01
☐ 132 Tom Browning	.05	.02	.01
☐ 133A Larry Andersen ERR	.10	.05	.01
(Misspelled Anderson on card front)			
☐ 133B Larry Andersen COR	.05	.02	.01
☐ 134A Bob Brenly ERR	.10	.05	.01
(Misspelled Brenley on card front)			
☐ 134B Bob Brenly COR	.05	.02	.01
☐ 135 Mike Marshall	.05	.02	.01
☐ 136 Gerald Perry	.05	.02	.01
☐ 137 Bobby Meacham	.05	.02	.01
☐ 138 Larry Herndon	.05	.02	.01
☐ 139 Fred Manrique	.05	.02	.01
☐ 140 Charlie Hough	.10	.05	.01
☐ 141 Ron Darling	.05	.02	.01
☐ 142 Herm Winningham	.05	.02	.01
☐ 143 Mike Diaz	.05	.02	.01
☐ 144 Mike Jackson	.10	.05	.01
☐ 145 Denny Walling	.05	.02	.01
☐ 146 Robby Thompson	.05	.02	.01
☐ 147 Franklin Stubbs	.05	.02	.01
☐ 148 Albert Hall	.05	.02	.01
☐ 149 Bobby Witt	.05	.02	.01
☐ 150 Lance McCullers	.05	.02	.01
☐ 151 Scott Bradley	.05	.02	.01
☐ 152 Mark McLemore	.05	.02	.01
☐ 153 Tim Laudner	.05	.02	.01
☐ 154 Greg Swindell	.05	.02	.01
☐ 155 Marty Barrett	.05	.02	.01
☐ 156 Mike Heath	.05	.02	.01
☐ 157 Gary Ward	.05	.02	.01
☐ 158A Lee Mazzilli ERR	.10	.05	.01
(Misspelled Mazilli on card front)			
☐ 158B Lee Mazzilli COR	.05	.02	.01
☐ 159 Tom Foley	.05	.02	.01
☐ 160 Robin Yount	.15	.07	.02
☐ 161 Steve Bedrosian	.05	.02	.01
☐ 162 Bob Walk	.05	.02	.01
☐ 163 Nick Esasky	.05	.02	.01
☐ 164 Ken Caminiti	.75	.35	.09
☐ 165 Jose Uribe	.05	.02	.01
☐ 166 Dave Anderson	.05	.02	.01
☐ 167 Ed Whitson	.05	.02	.01
☐ 168 Ernie Whitt	.05	.02	.01
☐ 169 Cecil Cooper	.10	.05	.01
☐ 170 Mike Pagliarulo	.05	.02	.01
☐ 171 Pat Sheridan	.05	.02	.01
☐ 172 Chris Bando	.05	.02	.01
☐ 173 Lee Lacy	.05	.02	.01
☐ 174 Steve Lombardozzi	.05	.02	.01
☐ 175 Mike Greenwell	.15	.07	.02
☐ 176 Greg Minton	.05	.02	.01
☐ 177 Moose Haas	.05	.02	.01
☐ 178 Mike Kingery	.05	.02	.01
☐ 179 Greg A. Harris	.05	.02	.01
☐ 180 Bo Jackson	.15	.07	.02
☐ 181 Carmelo Martinez	.05	.02	.01
☐ 182 Alex Trevino	.05	.02	.01
☐ 183 Ron Oester	.05	.02	.01
☐ 184 Danny Darwin	.05	.02	.01
☐ 185 Mike Krukow	.05	.02	.01
☐ 186 Rafael Palmeiro	.25	.11	.03
☐ 187 Tim Burke	.05	.02	.01
☐ 188 Roger McDowell	.05	.02	.01
☐ 189 Garry Templeton	.05	.02	.01
☐ 190 Terry Pendleton	.10	.05	.01
☐ 191 Larry Parrish	.05	.02	.01
☐ 192 Rey Quinones	.05	.02	.01
☐ 193 Joaquin Andujar	.05	.02	.01
☐ 194 Tom Brunansky	.05	.02	.01
☐ 195 Donnie Moore	.05	.02	.01
☐ 196 Dan Pasqua	.05	.02	.01
☐ 197 Jim Gantner	.05	.02	.01
☐ 198 Mark Eichhorn	.05	.02	.01
☐ 199 John Grubb	.05	.02	.01
☐ 200 Bill Ripken	.10	.05	.01
☐ 201 Sam Horn	.05	.02	.01
☐ 202 Todd Worrell	.05	.02	.01
☐ 203 Terry Leach	.05	.02	.01
☐ 204 Garth Iorg	.05	.02	.01
☐ 205 Brian Dayett	.05	.02	.01
☐ 206 Bo Diaz	.05	.02	.01
☐ 207 Craig Reynolds	.05	.02	.01
☐ 208 Brian Holton	.05	.02	.01
☐ 209 Marvell Wynne UER	.05	.02	.01
(Misspelled Marvelle on card front)			
☐ 210 Dave Concepcion	.10	.05	.01
☐ 211 Mike Davis	.05	.02	.01
☐ 212 Devon White	.15	.07	.02
☐ 213 Mickey Brantley	.05	.02	.01
☐ 214 Greg Gagne	.05	.02	.01
☐ 215 Oddibe McDowell	.05	.02	.01
☐ 216 Jimmy Key	.10	.05	.01
☐ 217 Dave Bergman	.05	.02	.01
☐ 218 Calvin Schiraldi	.05	.02	.01
☐ 219 Larry Sheets	.05	.02	.01
☐ 220 Mike Easler	.05	.02	.01
☐ 221 Kurt Stillwell	.05	.02	.01
☐ 222 Chuck Jackson	.05	.02	.01
☐ 223 Dave Martinez	.05	.02	.01
☐ 224 Tim Leary	.05	.02	.01
☐ 225 Steve Garvey	.15	.07	.02
☐ 226 Greg Mathews	.05	.02	.01
☐ 227 Doug Sisk	.05	.02	.01
☐ 228 Dave Henderson	.05	.02	.01
(Wearing Red Sox uniform; Red Sox logo on back)			
☐ 229 Jimmy Dwyer	.05	.02	.01
☐ 230 Larry Owen	.05	.02	.01
☐ 231 Andre Thornton	.10	.05	.01
☐ 232 Mark Salas	.05	.02	.01
☐ 233 Tom Brookens	.05	.02	.01
☐ 234 Greg Brock	.05	.02	.01
☐ 235 Rance Mulliniks	.05	.02	.01
☐ 236 Bob Brower	.05	.02	.01
☐ 237 Joe Niekro	.05	.02	.01
☐ 238 Scott Bankhead	.05	.02	.01
☐ 239 Doug DeCinces	.05	.02	.01
☐ 240 Tommy John	.10	.05	.01
☐ 241 Rich Gedman	.05	.02	.01
☐ 242 Ted Power	.05	.02	.01
☐ 243 Dave Meads	.05	.02	.01
☐ 244 Jim Sundberg	.05	.02	.01
☐ 245 Ken Oberkfell	.05	.02	.01
☐ 246 Jimmy Jones	.05	.02	.01
☐ 247 Ken Landreaux	.05	.02	.01
☐ 248 Jose Oquendo	.05	.02	.01
☐ 249 John Mitchell	.05	.02	.01
☐ 250 Don Baylor	.15	.07	.02
☐ 251 Scott Fletcher	.05	.02	.01
☐ 252 Al Newman	.05	.02	.01
☐ 253 Carney Lansford	.10	.05	.01
☐ 254 Johnny Ray	.05	.02	.01
☐ 255 Gary Pettis	.05	.02	.01
☐ 256 Ken Phelps	.05	.02	.01
☐ 257 Rick Leach	.05	.02	.01
☐ 258 Tim Stoddard	.05	.02	.01
☐ 259 Ed Romero	.05	.02	.01
☐ 260 Sid Bream	.05	.02	.01
☐ 261A Tom Niedenfuer ERR	.10	.05	.01
(Misspelled Neidenfuer on card front)			
☐ 261B Tom Niedenfuer COR	.05	.02	.01
☐ 262 Rick Dempsey	.05	.02	.01
☐ 263 Lonnie Smith	.05	.02	.01
☐ 264 Bob Forsch	.05	.02	.01
☐ 265 Barry Bonds	.60	.25	.07
☐ 266 Willie Randolph	.10	.05	.01
☐ 267 Mike Ramsey	.05	.02	.01
☐ 268 Don Slaught	.05	.02	.01
☐ 269 Mickey Tettleton	.10	.05	.01
☐ 270 Jerry Reuss	.05	.02	.01
☐ 271 Marc Sullivan	.05	.02	.01
☐ 272 Jim Morrison	.05	.02	.01
☐ 273 Steve Balboni	.05	.02	.01
☐ 274 Dick Schofield	.05	.02	.01
☐ 275 John Tudor	.05	.02	.01
☐ 276 Gene Larkin	.05	.02	.01
☐ 277 Harold Reynolds	.05	.02	.01
☐ 278 Jerry Browne	.05	.02	.01
☐ 279 Willie Upshaw	.05	.02	.01
☐ 280 Ted Higuera	.05	.02	.01
☐ 281 Terry McGriff	.05	.02	.01
☐ 282 Terry Puhl	.05	.02	.01
☐ 283 Mark Wasinger	.05	.02	.01
☐ 284 Luis Salazar	.05	.02	.01
☐ 285 Ted Simmons	.10	.05	.01
☐ 286 John Shelby	.05	.02	.01
☐ 287 John Smiley	.15	.07	.02
☐ 288 Curt Ford	.05	.02	.01
☐ 289 Steve Crawford	.05	.02	.01
☐ 290 Dan Quisenberry	.05	.02	.01
☐ 291 Alan Wiggins	.05	.02	.01
☐ 292 Randy Bush	.05	.02	.01
☐ 293 John Candelaria	.05	.02	.01
☐ 294 Tony Phillips	.15	.07	.02
☐ 295 Mike Morgan	.05	.02	.01
☐ 296 Bill Wegman	.05	.02	.01
☐ 297A Terry Francona ERR	.10	.05	.01
(Misspelled Franconia on card front)			
☐ 297B Terry Francona COR	.05	.02	.01
☐ 298 Mickey Hatcher	.05	.02	.01
☐ 299 Andres Thomas	.05	.02	.01
☐ 300 Bob Stanley	.05	.02	.01
☐ 301 Al Pedrique	.05	.02	.01
☐ 302 Jim Lindeman	.05	.02	.01
☐ 303 Wally Backman	.05	.02	.01
☐ 304 Paul O'Neill	.10	.05	.01
☐ 305 Hubie Brooks	.05	.02	.01
☐ 306 Steve Buechele	.05	.02	.01
☐ 307 Bobby Thigpen	.05	.02	.01
☐ 308 George Hendrick	.05	.02	.01
☐ 309 John Moses	.05	.02	.01
☐ 310 Ron Guidry	.05	.02	.01
☐ 311 Bill Schroeder	.05	.02	.01
☐ 312 Jose Nunez	.05	.02	.01
☐ 313 Bud Black	.05	.02	.01
☐ 314 Joe Sambito	.05	.02	.01
☐ 315 Scott McGregor	.05	.02	.01
☐ 316 Rafael Santana	.05	.02	.01
☐ 317 Frank Williams	.05	.02	.01
☐ 318 Mike Fitzgerald	.05	.02	.01
☐ 319 Rick Mahler	.05	.02	.01
☐ 320 Jim Gott	.05	.02	.01
☐ 321 Mariano Duncan	.05	.02	.01
☐ 322 Jose Guzman	.05	.02	.01
☐ 323 Lee Guetterman	.05	.02	.01
☐ 324 Dan Gladden	.05	.02	.01
☐ 325 Gary Carter	.10	.05	.01
☐ 326 Tracy Jones	.05	.02	.01
☐ 327 Floyd Youmans	.05	.02	.01
☐ 328 Bill Dawley	.05	.02	.01
☐ 329 Paul Noce	.05	.02	.01
☐ 330 Angel Salazar	.05	.02	.01
☐ 331 Goose Gossage	.15	.07	.02
☐ 332 George Frazier	.05	.02	.01

Card			
☐ 333 Ruppert Jones	.05	.02	.01
☐ 334 Billy Joe Robidoux	.05	.02	.01
☐ 335 Mike Scott	.05	.02	.01
☐ 336 Randy Myers	.10	.05	.01
☐ 337 Bob Sebra	.05	.02	.01
☐ 338 Eric Show	.05	.02	.01
☐ 339 Mitch Williams	.10	.05	.01
☐ 340 Paul Molitor	.20	.09	.03
☐ 341 Gus Polidor	.05	.02	.01
☐ 342 Steve Trout	.05	.02	.01
☐ 343 Jerry Don Gleaton	.05	.02	.01
☐ 344 Bob Knepper	.05	.02	.01
☐ 345 Mitch Webster	.05	.02	.01
☐ 346 John Morris	.05	.02	.01
☐ 347 Andy Hawkins	.05	.02	.01
☐ 348 Dave Leiper	.05	.02	.01
☐ 349 Ernest Riles	.05	.02	.01
☐ 350 Dwight Gooden	.10	.05	.01
☐ 351 Dave Righetti	.10	.05	.01
☐ 352 Pat Dodson	.05	.02	.01
☐ 353 John Habyan	.05	.02	.01
☐ 354 Jim Deshaies	.05	.02	.01
☐ 355 Butch Wynegar	.05	.02	.01
☐ 356 Bryn Smith	.05	.02	.01
☐ 357 Matt Young	.05	.02	.01
☐ 358 Tom Pagnozzi	.10	.05	.01
☐ 359 Floyd Rayford	.05	.02	.01
☐ 360 Darryl Strawberry	.10	.05	.01
☐ 361 Sal Butera	.05	.02	.01
☐ 362 Domingo Ramos	.05	.02	.01
☐ 363 Chris Brown	.05	.02	.01
☐ 364 Jose Gonzalez	.05	.02	.01
☐ 365 Dave Smith	.05	.02	.01
☐ 366 Andy McGaffigan	.05	.02	.01
☐ 367 Stan Javier	.05	.02	.01
☐ 368 Henry Cotto	.05	.02	.01
☐ 369 Mike Birkbeck	.05	.02	.01
☐ 370 Len Dykstra	.10	.05	.01
☐ 371 Dave Collins	.05	.02	.01
☐ 372 Spike Owen	.05	.02	.01
☐ 373 Geno Petralli	.05	.02	.01
☐ 374 Ron Karkovice	.05	.02	.01
☐ 375 Shane Rawley	.05	.02	.01
☐ 376 DeWayne Buice	.05	.02	.01
☐ 377 Bill Pecota	.05	.02	.01
☐ 378 Leon Durham	.05	.02	.01
☐ 379 Ed Olwine	.05	.02	.01
☐ 380 Bruce Hurst	.05	.02	.01
☐ 381 Bob McClure	.05	.02	.01
☐ 382 Mark Thurmond	.05	.02	.01
☐ 383 Buddy Biancalana	.05	.02	.01
☐ 384 Tim Conroy	.05	.02	.01
☐ 385 Tony Gwynn	.40	.18	.05
☐ 386 Greg Gross	.05	.02	.01
☐ 387 Barry Lyons	.05	.02	.01
☐ 388 Mike Felder	.05	.02	.01
☐ 389 Pat Clements	.05	.02	.01
☐ 390 Ken Griffey	.05	.02	.01
☐ 391 Mark Davis	.05	.02	.01
☐ 392 Jose Rijo	.05	.02	.01
☐ 393 Mike Young	.05	.02	.01
☐ 394 Willie Fraser	.05	.02	.01
☐ 395 Dion James	.05	.02	.01
☐ 396 Steve Shields	.05	.02	.01
☐ 397 Randy St.Claire	.05	.02	.01
☐ 398 Danny Jackson	.05	.02	.01
☐ 399 Cecil Fielder	.15	.07	.02
☐ 400 Keith Hernandez	.10	.05	.01
☐ 401 Don Carman	.05	.02	.01
☐ 402 Chuck Crim	.05	.02	.01
☐ 403 Rob Woodward	.05	.02	.01
☐ 404 Junior Ortiz	.05	.02	.01
☐ 405 Glenn Wilson	.05	.02	.01
☐ 406 Ken Howell	.05	.02	.01
☐ 407 Jeff Kunkel	.05	.02	.01
☐ 408 Jeff Reed	.05	.02	.01
☐ 409 Chris James	.05	.02	.01
☐ 410 Zane Smith	.05	.02	.01
☐ 411 Ken Dixon	.05	.02	.01
☐ 412 Ricky Horton	.05	.02	.01
☐ 413 Frank DiPino	.05	.02	.01
☐ 414 Shane Mack	.05	.02	.01
☐ 415 Danny Cox	.05	.02	.01
☐ 416 Andy Van Slyke	.10	.05	.01
☐ 417 Danny Heep	.05	.02	.01
☐ 418 John Cangelosi	.05	.02	.01
☐ 419A John Christensen ERR (Christiansen on card front)	.10	.05	.01
☐ 419B John Christensen COR	.05	.02	.01
☐ 420 Joey Cora	.20	.09	.03
☐ 421 Mike LaValliere	.05	.02	.01
☐ 422 Kelly Gruber	.05	.02	.01
☐ 423 Bruce Benedict	.05	.02	.01
☐ 424 Len Matuszek	.05	.02	.01
☐ 425 Kent Tekulve	.05	.02	.01
☐ 426 Rafael Ramirez	.05	.02	.01
☐ 427 Mike Flanagan	.05	.02	.01
☐ 428 Mike Gallego	.05	.02	.01
☐ 429 Juan Castillo	.05	.02	.01
☐ 430 Neal Heaton	.05	.02	.01
☐ 431 Phil Garner	.05	.02	.01
☐ 432 Mike Dunne	.05	.02	.01
☐ 433 Wallace Johnson	.05	.02	.01
☐ 434 Jack O'Connor	.05	.02	.01
☐ 435 Steve Jeltz	.05	.02	.01
☐ 436 Donell Nixon	.05	.02	.01
☐ 437 Jack Lazorko	.05	.02	.01
☐ 438 Keith Comstock	.05	.02	.01
☐ 439 Jeff D. Robinson	.05	.02	.01
☐ 440 Graig Nettles	.10	.05	.01
☐ 441 Mel Hall	.05	.02	.01
☐ 442 Gerald Young	.05	.02	.01
☐ 443 Gary Redus	.05	.02	.01
☐ 444 Charlie Moore	.05	.02	.01
☐ 445 Bill Madlock	.05	.02	.01
☐ 446 Mark Clear	.05	.02	.01
☐ 447 Greg Booker	.05	.02	.01
☐ 448 Rick Schu	.05	.02	.01
☐ 449 Ron Kittle	.05	.02	.01
☐ 450 Dale Murphy	.15	.07	.02
☐ 451 Bob Dernier	.05	.02	.01
☐ 452 Dale Mohorcic	.05	.02	.01
☐ 453 Rafael Belliard	.05	.02	.01
☐ 454 Charlie Puleo	.05	.02	.01
☐ 455 Dwayne Murphy	.05	.02	.01
☐ 456 Jim Eisenreich	.10	.05	.01
☐ 457 David Palmer	.05	.02	.01
☐ 458 Dave Stewart	.15	.07	.02
☐ 459 Pascual Perez	.05	.02	.01
☐ 460 Glenn Davis	.05	.02	.01
☐ 461 Dan Petry	.05	.02	.01
☐ 462 Jim Winn	.05	.02	.01
☐ 463 Darrell Miller	.05	.02	.01
☐ 464 Mike Moore	.05	.02	.01
☐ 465 Mike LaCoss	.05	.02	.01
☐ 466 Steve Farr	.05	.02	.01
☐ 467 Jerry Mumphrey	.05	.02	.01
☐ 468 Kevin Gross	.05	.02	.01
☐ 469 Bruce Bochy	.05	.02	.01
☐ 470 Orel Hershiser	.10	.05	.01
☐ 471 Eric King	.05	.02	.01
☐ 472 Ellis Burks	.40	.18	.05
☐ 473 Darren Daulton	.10	.05	.01
☐ 474 Mookie Wilson	.10	.05	.01
☐ 475 Frank Viola	.05	.02	.01
☐ 476 Ron Robinson	.05	.02	.01
☐ 477 Bob Melvin	.05	.02	.01
☐ 478 Jeff Musselman	.05	.02	.01
☐ 479 Charlie Kerfeld	.05	.02	.01
☐ 480 Richard Dotson	.05	.02	.01
☐ 481 Kevin Mitchell	.10	.05	.01
☐ 482 Gary Roenicke	.05	.02	.01
☐ 483 Tim Flannery	.05	.02	.01
☐ 484 Rich Yett	.05	.02	.01
☐ 485 Pete Incaviglia	.05	.02	.01
☐ 486 Rick Cerone	.05	.02	.01
☐ 487 Tony Armas	.05	.02	.01
☐ 488 Jerry Reed	.05	.02	.01
☐ 489 Dave Lopes	.10	.05	.01
☐ 490 Frank Tanana	.05	.02	.01
☐ 491 Mike Loynd	.05	.02	.01
☐ 492 Bruce Ruffin	.05	.02	.01
☐ 493 Chris Speier	.05	.02	.01
☐ 494 Tom Hume	.05	.02	.01
☐ 495 Jesse Orosco	.05	.02	.01
☐ 496 Robbie Wine UER (Misspelled Robby on card front)	.05	.02	.01
☐ 497 Jeff Montgomery	.20	.09	.03
☐ 498 Jeff Dedmon	.05	.02	.01
☐ 499 Luis Aguayo	.05	.02	.01
☐ 500 Reggie Jackson (Oakland A's)	.15	.07	.02
☐ 501 Reggie Jackson (Baltimore Orioles)	.15	.07	.02
☐ 502 Reggie Jackson (New York Yankees)	.15	.07	.02
☐ 503 Reggie Jackson (California Angels)	.15	.07	.02
☐ 504 Reggie Jackson (Oakland A's)	.15	.07	.02
☐ 505 Billy Hatcher	.05	.02	.01
☐ 506 Ed Lynch	.05	.02	.01
☐ 507 Willie Hernandez	.05	.02	.01
☐ 508 Jose DeLeon	.05	.02	.01
☐ 509 Joel Youngblood	.05	.02	.01
☐ 510 Bob Welch	.05	.02	.01
☐ 511 Steve Ontiveros	.05	.02	.01
☐ 512 Randy Ready	.05	.02	.01
☐ 513 Juan Nieves	.05	.02	.01
☐ 514 Jeff Russell	.05	.02	.01
☐ 515 Von Hayes	.05	.02	.01
☐ 516 Mark Gubicza	.05	.02	.01
☐ 517 Ken Dayley	.05	.02	.01
☐ 518 Don Aase	.05	.02	.01
☐ 519 Rick Reuschel	.05	.02	.01
☐ 520 Mike Henneman	.10	.05	.01
☐ 521 Rick Aguilera	.10	.05	.01
☐ 522 Jay Howell	.05	.02	.01
☐ 523 Ed Correa	.05	.02	.01
☐ 524 Manny Trillo	.05	.02	.01
☐ 525 Kirk Gibson	.10	.05	.01
☐ 526 Wally Ritchie	.05	.02	.01
☐ 527 Al Nipper	.05	.02	.01
☐ 528 Atlee Hammaker	.05	.02	.01
☐ 529 Shawon Dunston	.05	.02	.01
☐ 530 Jim Clancy	.05	.02	.01
☐ 531 Tom Paciorek	.05	.02	.01
☐ 532 Joel Skinner	.05	.02	.01
☐ 533 Scott Garrelts	.05	.02	.01
☐ 534 Tom O'Malley	.05	.02	.01
☐ 535 John Franco	.10	.05	.01
☐ 536 Paul Kilgus	.05	.02	.01
☐ 537 Darrell Porter	.05	.02	.01
☐ 538 Walt Terrell	.05	.02	.01
☐ 539 Bill Long	.05	.02	.01
☐ 540 George Bell	.05	.02	.01
☐ 541 Jeff Sellers	.05	.02	.01
☐ 542 Joe Boever	.05	.02	.01
☐ 543 Steve Howe	.05	.02	.01
☐ 544 Scott Sanderson	.05	.02	.01
☐ 545 Jack Morris	.15	.07	.02
☐ 546 Todd Benzinger	.10	.05	.01
☐ 547 Steve Henderson	.05	.02	.01
☐ 548 Eddie Milner	.05	.02	.01
☐ 549 Jeff M. Robinson	.05	.02	.01
☐ 550 Cal Ripken	.75	.35	.09
☐ 551 Jody Davis	.05	.02	.01
☐ 552 Kirk McCaskill	.05	.02	.01
☐ 553 Craig Lefferts	.05	.02	.01
☐ 554 Darnell Coles	.05	.02	.01
☐ 555 Phil Niekro	.15	.07	.02
☐ 556 Mike Aldrete	.05	.02	.01
☐ 557 Pat Perry	.05	.02	.01
☐ 558 Juan Agosto	.05	.02	.01
☐ 559 Rob Murphy	.05	.02	.01
☐ 560 Dennis Rasmussen	.05	.02	.01
☐ 561 Manny Lee	.05	.02	.01
☐ 562 Jeff Blauser	.15	.07	.02
☐ 563 Bob Ojeda	.05	.02	.01
☐ 564 Dave Dravecky	.10	.05	.01
☐ 565 Gene Garber	.05	.02	.01
☐ 566 Ron Roenicke	.05	.02	.01
☐ 567 Tommy Hinzo	.05	.02	.01
☐ 568 Eric Nolte	.05	.02	.01
☐ 569 Ed Hearn	.05	.02	.01
☐ 570 Mark Davidson	.05	.02	.01
☐ 571 Jim Walewander	.05	.02	.01
☐ 572 Donnie Hill UER (84 Stolen Base total listed as 7)	.05	.02	.01
☐ 573 Jamie Moyer	.05	.02	.01
☐ 574 Ken Schrom	.05	.02	.01
☐ 575 Nolan Ryan	.75	.35	.09
☐ 576 Jim Acker	.05	.02	.01
☐ 577 Jamie Quirk	.05	.02	.01
☐ 578 Jay Aldrich	.05	.02	.01
☐ 579 Claudell Washington	.05	.02	.01
☐ 580 Jeff Leonard	.05	.02	.01
☐ 581 Carmen Castillo	.05	.02	.01
☐ 582 Daryl Boston	.05	.02	.01
☐ 583 Jeff DeWillis	.05	.02	.01
☐ 584 John Marzano	.05	.02	.01
☐ 585 Bill Gullickson	.05	.02	.01
☐ 586 Andy Allanson	.05	.02	.01
☐ 587 Lee Tunnell UER (1987 stat line reads .4.84 ERA)	.05	.02	.01
☐ 588 Gene Nelson	.05	.02	.01
☐ 589 Dave LaPoint	.05	.02	.01
☐ 590 Harold Baines	.10	.05	.01
☐ 591 Bill Buckner	.10	.05	.01
☐ 592 Carlton Fisk	.15	.07	.02
☐ 593 Rick Manning	.05	.02	.01
☐ 594 Doug Jones	.10	.05	.01
☐ 595 Tom Candiotti	.05	.02	.01
☐ 596 Steve Lake	.05	.02	.01
☐ 597 Jose Lind	.10	.05	.01
☐ 598 Ross Jones	.05	.02	.01
☐ 599 Gary Matthews	.05	.02	.01
☐ 600 Fernando Valenzuela	.10	.05	.01
☐ 601 Dennis Martinez	.10	.05	.01
☐ 602 Les Lancaster	.05	.02	.01
☐ 603 Ozzie Guillen	.10	.05	.01
☐ 604 Tony Bernazard	.05	.02	.01
☐ 605 Chili Davis	.15	.07	.02
☐ 606 Roy Smalley	.05	.02	.01
☐ 607 Ivan Calderon	.05	.02	.01
☐ 608 Jay Tibbs	.05	.02	.01
☐ 609 Guy Hoffman	.05	.02	.01
☐ 610 Doyle Alexander	.05	.02	.01
☐ 611 Mike Bielecki	.05	.02	.01
☐ 612 Shawn Hillegas	.05	.02	.01
☐ 613 Keith Atherton	.05	.02	.01
☐ 614 Eric Plunk	.05	.02	.01
☐ 615 Sid Fernandez	.05	.02	.01
☐ 616 Dennis Lamp	.05	.02	.01
☐ 617 Dave Engle	.05	.02	.01
☐ 618 Harry Spilman	.05	.02	.01
☐ 619 Don Robinson	.05	.02	.01
☐ 620 John Farrell	.05	.02	.01
☐ 621 Nelson Liriano	.05	.02	.01
☐ 622 Floyd Bannister	.05	.02	.01
☐ 623 Randy Milligan	.05	.02	.01
☐ 624 Kevin Elster	.15	.07	.02
☐ 625 Jody Reed	.10	.05	.01
☐ 626 Shawn Abner	.05	.02	.01
☐ 627 Kirt Manwaring	.10	.05	.01
☐ 628 Pete Stanicek	.05	.02	.01
☐ 629 Rob Ducey	.05	.02	.01
☐ 630 Steve Kiefer	.05	.02	.01
☐ 631 Gary Thurman	.05	.02	.01
☐ 632 Darrel Akerfelds	.05	.02	.01
☐ 633 Dave Clark	.05	.02	.01
☐ 634 Roberto Kelly	.15	.07	.02
☐ 635 Keith Hughes	.05	.02	.01
☐ 636 John Davis	.05	.02	.01
☐ 637 Mike Devereaux	.15	.07	.02
☐ 638 Tom Glavine	.75	.35	.09
☐ 639 Keith A. Miller	.05	.02	.01
☐ 640 Chris Gwynn UER (Wrong batting and throwing on back)	.10	.05	.01
☐ 641 Tim Crews	.10	.05	.01
☐ 642 Mackey Sasser	.05	.02	.01
☐ 643 Vicente Palacios	.05	.02	.01
☐ 644 Kevin Romine	.05	.02	.01
☐ 645 Gregg Jefferies	.30	.14	.04
☐ 646 Jeff Treadway	.05	.02	.01
☐ 647 Ron Gant	.40	.18	.05
☐ 648 Mark McGwire and Matt Nokes (Rookie Sluggers)	.15	.07	.02
☐ 649 Eric Davis and Tim Raines (Speed and Power)	.10	.05	.01
☐ 650 Don Mattingly and Jack Clark	.20	.09	.03
☐ 651 Tony Fernandez, Alan Trammell, and Cal Ripken	.30	.14	.04
☐ 652 Vince Coleman HL 100 Stolen Bases	.05	.02	.01
☐ 653 Kirby Puckett HL 10 Hits in a Row	.15	.07	.02
☐ 654 Benito Santiago HL Hitting Streak	.05	.02	.01
☐ 655 Juan Nieves HL No Hitter	.05	.02	.01
☐ 656 Steve Bedrosian HL Saves Record	.05	.02	.01
☐ 657 Mike Schmidt HL 500 Homers	.15	.07	.02
☐ 658 Don Mattingly HL Home Run Streak	.25	.11	.03
☐ 659 Mark McGwire HL Rookie HR Record	.30	.14	.04
☐ 660 Paul Molitor HL Hitting Streak	.15	.07	.02

1988 Score Glossy

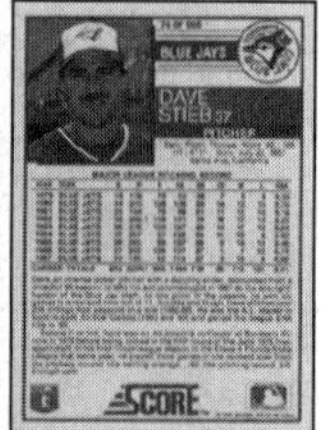

This 660 card set is a parallel to the regular 1988 Score set. According to the manufacturer, 5,000 of these sets were produced. These sets are considered glossy as "UV Coating" was added to the fronts of the card. These sets were issued in factory set versions only and released solely through Major League Marketing's hobby accounts.

	MINT	NRMT	EXC
COMPLETE FACT.SET (660)	200.00	90.00	25.00
COMMON CARD (1-660)	.25	.11	.03
*STARS: 5X to 10X BASIC CARDS			
*ROOKIES: 4X to 8X BASIC CARDS			

1988 Score Box Cards

There are six different wax box bottom panels each featuring three players and a trivia (related to a particular stadium for a given year) question. The players and trivia question cards are individually numbered. The trivia are numbered below with the prefix T in order to avoid confusion. The trivia cards are very unpopular with collectors since they do not picture any players. When panels of four are cut into individuals, the cards are standard size. The card backs of the players feature the respective League logos most prominently.

	MINT	NRMT	EXC
COMPLETE SET (24)	10.00	4.50	1.25
COMMON CARD (1-18)	.25	.11	.03
COMMON TRIVIA (T1-T6)	.10	.05	.01
☐ 1 Terry Kennedy	.25	.11	.03
☐ 2 Don Mattingly	1.50	.70	.19

Card	MINT	NRMT	EXC
□ 3 Willie Randolph	.25	.11	.03
□ 4 Wade Boggs	.60	.25	.07
□ 5 Cal Ripken	3.00	1.35	.35
□ 6 George Bell	.25	.11	.03
□ 7 Rickey Henderson	.60	.25	.07
□ 8 Dave Winfield	.60	.25	.07
□ 9 Bret Saberhagen	.40	.18	.05
□ 10 Gary Carter	.40	.18	.05
□ 11 Jack Clark	.25	.11	.03
□ 12 Ryne Sandberg	1.25	.55	.16
□ 13 Mike Schmidt	.75	.35	.09
□ 14 Ozzie Smith	1.25	.55	.16
□ 15 Eric Davis	.40	.18	.05
□ 16 Andre Dawson	.40	.18	.05
□ 17 Darryl Strawberry	.40	.18	.05
□ 18 Mike Scott	.25	.11	.03
□ T1 Fenway Park '60 Ted Williams Hits To The End	.25	.11	.03
□ T2 Comiskey Park '83 Grand Slam Fred Lynn Breaks Jinx	.10	.05	.01
□ T3 Anaheim Stadium '87 Old Rookie Record Falls Mark McGwire	.25	.11	.03
□ T4 Wrigley Field '38 Gabby Hartnett Gets Pennant Homer	.10	.05	.01
□ T5 Comiskey Park '50 Red Schoendienst Rips Winning HR	.10	.05	.01
□ T6 County Stadium '87 John Farrell Stops Hit Streak Paul Molitor	.10	.05	.01

1988 Score Rookie/Traded

This 110-card standard-size set features traded players (1-65) and rookies (66-110) for the 1988 season. The cards are distinguishable from the regular Score set by the orange borders and by the fact that the numbering on the back has a T suffix. The cards were distributed exclusively in factory set form along with some trivia cards. Apparently Score's first attempt at a Rookie/Traded set was produced very conservatively, resulting in a set which is now recognized as being much tougher to find than the other Rookie/Traded sets from the other major companies of that year. Extended Rookie Cards in this set include Roberto Alomar, Brady Anderson, Craig Biggio, Jay Buhner, Mark Grace, Darryl Hamilton, Jack McDowell, Todd Stottlemyre and Walt Weiss.

	MINT	NRMT	EXC
COMPLETE FACT.SET (110)	50.00	22.00	6.25
COMMON CARD (1T-110T)	.15	.07	.02

Card	MINT	NRMT	EXC
□ 1T Jack Clark	.40	.18	.05
□ 2T Danny Jackson	.15	.07	.02
□ 3T Brett Butler	.40	.18	.05
□ 4T Kurt Stillwell	.15	.07	.02
□ 5T Tom Brunansky	.15	.07	.02
□ 6T Dennis Lamp	.15	.07	.02
□ 7T Jose DeLeon	.15	.07	.02
□ 8T Tom Herr	.15	.07	.02
□ 9T Keith Moreland	.15	.07	.02
□ 10T Kirk Gibson	.40	.18	.05
□ 11T Bud Black	.15	.07	.02
□ 12T Rafael Ramirez	.15	.07	.02
□ 13T Luis Salazar	.15	.07	.02
□ 14T Goose Gossage	.75	.35	.09
□ 15T Bob Welch	.15	.07	.02
□ 16T Vance Law	.15	.07	.02
□ 17T Ray Knight	.40	.18	.05
□ 18T Dan Quisenberry	.15	.07	.02
□ 19T Don Slaught	.15	.07	.02
□ 20T Lee Smith	.40	.18	.05
□ 21T Rick Cerone	.15	.07	.02
□ 22T Pat Tabler	.15	.07	.02
□ 23T Larry McWilliams	.15	.07	.02
□ 24T Ricky Horton	.15	.07	.02
□ 25T Graig Nettles	.40	.18	.05
□ 26T Dan Petry	.15	.07	.02
□ 27T Jose Rijo	.15	.07	.02
□ 28T Chili Davis	.75	.35	.09
□ 29T Dickie Thon	.15	.07	.02
□ 30T Mackey Sasser	.15	.07	.02
□ 31T Mickey Tettleton	.40	.18	.05
□ 32T Rick Dempsey	.15	.07	.02
□ 33T Ron Hassey	.15	.07	.02
□ 34T Phil Bradley	.15	.07	.02
□ 35T Jay Howell	.15	.07	.02
□ 36T Bill Buckner	.40	.18	.05
□ 37T Alfredo Griffin	.15	.07	.02
□ 38T Gary Pettis	.15	.07	.02
□ 39T Calvin Schiraldi	.15	.07	.02
□ 40T John Candelaria	.15	.07	.02
□ 41T Joe Orsulak	.15	.07	.02
□ 42T Willie Upshaw	.15	.07	.02
□ 43T Herm Winningham	.15	.07	.02
□ 44T Ron Kittle	.15	.07	.02
□ 45T Bob Dernier	.15	.07	.02
□ 46T Steve Balboni	.15	.07	.02
□ 47T Steve Shields	.15	.07	.02
□ 48T Henry Cotto	.15	.07	.02
□ 49T Dave Henderson	.15	.07	.02
□ 50T Dave Parker	.75	.35	.09
□ 51T Mike Young	.15	.07	.02
□ 52T Mark Salas	.15	.07	.02
□ 53T Mike Davis	.15	.07	.02
□ 54T Rafael Santana	.15	.07	.02
□ 55T Don Baylor	.75	.35	.09
□ 56T Dan Pasqua	.15	.07	.02
□ 57T Ernest Riles	.15	.07	.02
□ 58T Glenn Hubbard	.15	.07	.02
□ 59T Mike Smithson	.15	.07	.02
□ 60T Richard Dotson	.15	.07	.02
□ 61T Jerry Reuss	.15	.07	.02
□ 62T Mike Jackson	.40	.18	.05
□ 63T Floyd Bannister	.15	.07	.02
□ 64T Jesse Orosco	.15	.07	.02
□ 65T Larry Parrish	.15	.07	.02
□ 66T Jeff Bittiger	.15	.07	.02
□ 67T Ray Hayward	.15	.07	.02
□ 68T Ricky Jordan	.40	.18	.05
□ 69T Tommy Gregg	.15	.07	.02
□ 70T Brady Anderson	12.00	5.50	1.50
□ 71T Jeff Montgomery	.75	.35	.09
□ 72T Darryl Hamilton	.40	.18	.05
□ 73T Cecil Espy	.15	.07	.02
□ 74T Greg Briley	.15	.07	.02
□ 75T Joey Meyer	.15	.07	.02
□ 76T Mike Macfarlane	.75	.35	.09
□ 77T Oswald Peraza	.15	.07	.02
□ 78T Jack Armstrong	.15	.07	.02
□ 79T Don Heinkel	.15	.07	.02
□ 80T Mark Grace	8.00	3.60	1.00
□ 81T Steve Curry	.15	.07	.02
□ 82T Damon Berryhill	.15	.07	.02
□ 83T Steve Ellsworth	.15	.07	.02
□ 84T Pete Smith	.15	.07	.02
□ 85T Jack McDowell	5.00	2.20	.60
□ 86T Rob Dibble	.40	.18	.05
□ 87T Bryan Harvey UER (Games Pitched 47, Innings 5)	.40	.18	.05
□ 88T John Dopson	.15	.07	.02
□ 89T Dave Gallagher	.15	.07	.02
□ 90T Todd Stottlemyre	1.50	.70	.19
□ 91T Mike Schooler	.15	.07	.02
□ 92T Don Gordon	.15	.07	.02
□ 93T Sil Campusano	.15	.07	.02
□ 94T Jeff Pico	.15	.07	.02
□ 95T Jay Buhner	12.00	5.50	1.50
□ 96T Nelson Santovenia	.15	.07	.02
□ 97T Al Leiter	.75	.35	.09
□ 98T Luis Alicea	.40	.18	.05
□ 99T Pat Borders	.40	.18	.05
□ 100T Chris Sabo	.40	.18	.05
□ 101T Tim Belcher	.15	.07	.02
□ 102T Walt Weiss	.40	.18	.05
□ 103T Craig Biggio	8.00	3.60	1.00
□ 104T Don August	.15	.07	.02
□ 105T Roberto Alomar	25.00	11.00	3.10
□ 106T Todd Burns	.15	.07	.02
□ 107T John Costello	.15	.07	.02
□ 108T Melido Perez	.40	.18	.05
□ 109T Darrin Jackson	.40	.18	.05
□ 110T Orestes Destrade	.75	.35	.09

1988 Score Rookie/Traded Glossy

This 110-card standard-size set was issued as a parallel vesion to the regular Score Rookie/Traded set. According to published reports, only 3,000 of these sets were created. The sets were sold solely through Score's dealer's accounts of the time.

	MINT	NRMT	EXC
COMPLETE FACT.SET (110)	150.00	70.00	19.00
COMMON CARD (1T-110T)	.50	.23	.06
*STARS: 2X to 4X BASIC CARDS			
*ROOKIES: 2X to 4X BASIC CARDS			

1988 Score Young Superstars I

This attractive high-gloss 40-card standard-size set of "Young Superstars" was distributed in a small blue box which had the checklist of the set on a side panel of the box. The cards were also distributed as an insert, one per rack pack. These attractive cards are in full color on the front and also have a full-color small portrait on the card back. The cards in this series are distinguishable from the cards in Series II by the fact that this series has a blue and green border on the card front instead of the (Series II) blue and pink border.

	MINT	NRMT	EXC
COMPLETE SET (40)	5.00	2.20	.60
COMMON CARD (1-40)	.10	.05	.01

Card	MINT	NRMT	EXC
□ 1 Mark McGwire	1.25	.55	.16
□ 2 Benito Santiago	.20	.09	.03
□ 3 Sam Horn	.10	.05	.01
□ 4 Chris Bosio	.10	.05	.01
□ 5 Matt Nokes	.10	.05	.01
□ 6 Ken Williams	.10	.05	.01
□ 7 Dion James	.10	.05	.01
□ 8 B.J. Surhoff	.20	.09	.03
□ 9 Joe Magrane	.10	.05	.01
□ 10 Kevin Seitzer	.20	.09	.03
□ 11 Stanley Jefferson	.10	.05	.01
□ 12 Devon White	.40	.18	.05
□ 13 Nelson Liriano	.10	.05	.01
□ 14 Chris James	.10	.05	.01
□ 15 Mike Henneman	.20	.09	.03
□ 16 Terry Steinbach	.40	.18	.05
□ 17 John Kruk	.40	.18	.05
□ 18 Matt Williams	1.50	.70	.19
□ 19 Kelly Downs	.10	.05	.01
□ 20 Bill Ripken	.10	.05	.01
□ 21 Ozzie Guillen	.10	.05	.01
□ 22 Luis Polonia	.20	.09	.03
□ 23 Dave Magadan	.10	.05	.01
□ 24 Mike Greenwell	.10	.05	.01
□ 25 Will Clark	.60	.25	.07
□ 26 Mike Dunne	.10	.05	.01
□ 27 Wally Joyner	.40	.18	.05
□ 28 Robby Thompson	.10	.05	.01
□ 29 Ken Caminiti	1.25	.55	.16
□ 30 Jose Canseco	.60	.25	.07
□ 31 Todd Benzinger	.10	.05	.01
□ 32 Pete Incaviglia	.10	.05	.01
□ 33 John Farrell	.10	.05	.01
□ 34 Casey Candaele	.10	.05	.01
□ 35 Mike Aldrete	.10	.05	.01
□ 36 Ruben Sierra	.20	.09	.03
□ 37 Ellis Burks	.60	.25	.07
□ 38 Tracy Jones	.10	.05	.01
□ 39 Kal Daniels	.10	.05	.01
□ 40 Cory Snyder	.10	.05	.01

1988 Score Young Superstars II

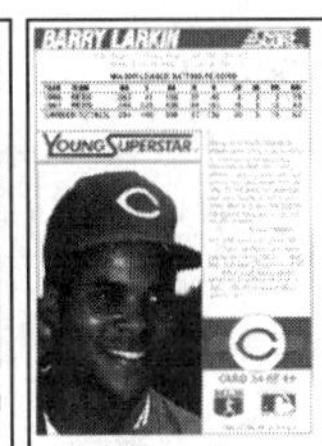

This attractive high-gloss 40-card standard-size set of "Young Superstars" was distributed in a small purple box which had the checklist of the set on a side panel of the box. The cards were not distributed as an insert with rak paks as the first series was, but were only available as a complete set from hobby dealers or through a mail-in offer direct from the company. These attractive cards are in full color on the front and also have a full-color small portrait on the card back. The cards in this series are distinguishable from the cards in Series I by the fact that this series has a blue and pink border on the card front instead of the (Series I) blue and green border.

	MINT	NRMT	EXC
COMPLETE SET (40)	5.00	2.20	.60
COMMON CARD (1-40)	.10	.05	.01

Card	MINT	NRMT	EXC
□ 1 Don Mattingly	1.50	.70	.19
□ 2 Glenn Braggs	.10	.05	.01
□ 3 Dwight Gooden	.20	.09	.03
□ 4 Jose Lind	.10	.05	.01
□ 5 Danny Tartabull	.10	.05	.01
□ 6 Tony Fernandez	.10	.05	.01
□ 7 Julio Franco	.20	.09	.03
□ 8 Andres Galarraga	.75	.35	.09
□ 9 Bobby Bonilla	.30	.14	.04
□ 10 Eric Davis	.20	.09	.03
□ 11 Gerald Young	.10	.05	.01
□ 12 Barry Bonds	1.25	.55	.16
□ 13 Jerry Browne	.10	.05	.01
□ 14 Jeff Blauser	.20	.09	.03
□ 15 Mickey Brantley	.10	.05	.01
□ 16 Floyd Youmans	.10	.05	.01
□ 17 Bret Saberhagen	.20	.09	.03
□ 18 Shawon Dunston	.10	.05	.01
□ 19 Len Dykstra	.20	.09	.03
□ 20 Darryl Strawberry	.20	.09	.03
□ 21 Rick Aguilera	.20	.09	.03
□ 22 Ivan Calderon	.10	.05	.01
□ 23 Roger Clemens	1.25	.55	.16
□ 24 Vince Coleman	.10	.05	.01
□ 25 Gary Thurman	.10	.05	.01
□ 26 Jeff Treadway	.10	.05	.01
□ 27 Oddibe McDowell	.10	.05	.01
□ 28 Fred McGriff	1.00	.45	.12
□ 29 Mark McLemore	.10	.05	.01
□ 30 Jeff Musselman	.10	.05	.01
□ 31 Mitch Williams	.10	.05	.01
□ 32 Dan Plesac	.10	.05	.01
□ 33 Juan Nieves	.10	.05	.01
□ 34 Barry Larkin	1.00	.45	.12
□ 35 Greg Mathews	.10	.05	.01
□ 36 Shane Mack	.10	.05	.01
□ 37 Scott Bankhead	.10	.05	.01
□ 38 Eric Bell	.10	.05	.01
□ 39 Greg Swindell	.10	.05	.01
□ 40 Kevin Elster	.20	.09	.03

1989 Score

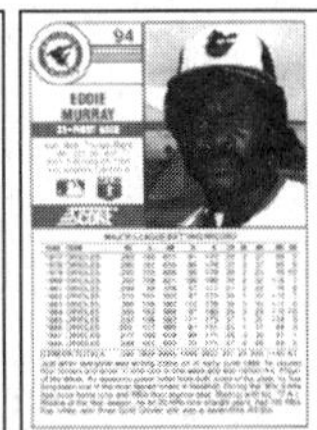

This 660-card standard-size set was distributed by Major League Marketing. Cards were issued primarily in fin-wrapped plastic packs and factory sets. Cards feature six distinctive inner border (inside a white outer border) colors on the front. Subsets include Highlights (652-660) and Rookie Prospects (621-651). Rookie Cards in this set include Sandy Alomar Jr., Brady Anderson, Craig Biggio, Charlie Hayes, Randy Johnson, Ramon Martinez, Gary Sheffield, and John Smoltz.

	MINT	NRMT	EXC
COMPLETE SET (660)	8.00	3.60	1.00
COMPLETE FACT.SET (660)	8.00	3.60	1.00
COMMON CARD (1-660)	.05	.02	.01

Card	MINT	NRMT	EXC
□ 1 Jose Canseco	.15	.07	.02
□ 2 Andre Dawson	.10	.05	.01
□ 3 Mark McGwire UER	.30	.14	.04
□ 4 Benito Santiago	.10	.05	.01
□ 5 Rick Reuschel	.05	.02	.01
□ 6 Fred McGriff	.20	.09	.03
□ 7 Kal Daniels	.05	.02	.01
□ 8 Gary Gaetti	.05	.02	.01
□ 9 Ellis Burks	.15	.07	.02
□ 10 Darryl Strawberry	.10	.05	.01
□ 11 Julio Franco	.10	.05	.01
□ 12 Lloyd Moseby	.05	.02	.01
□ 13 Jeff Pico	.05	.02	.01
□ 14 Johnny Ray	.05	.02	.01
□ 15 Cal Ripken	.75	.35	.09
□ 16 Dick Schofield	.05	.02	.01
□ 17 Mel Hall	.05	.02	.01
□ 18 Bill Ripken	.05	.02	.01
□ 19 Brook Jacoby	.05	.02	.01
□ 20 Kirby Puckett	.40	.18	.05
□ 21 Bill Doran	.05	.02	.01
□ 22 Pete O'Brien	.05	.02	.01
□ 23 Matt Nokes	.05	.02	.01
□ 24 Brian Fisher	.05	.02	.01
□ 25 Jack Clark	.10	.05	.01
□ 26 Gary Pettis	.05	.02	.01
□ 27 Dave Valle	.05	.02	.01
□ 28 Willie Wilson	.05	.02	.01
□ 29 Curt Young	.05	.02	.01
□ 30 Dale Murphy	.15	.07	.02
□ 31 Barry Larkin	.20	.09	.03
□ 32 Dave Stewart	.10	.05	.01
□ 33 Mike LaValliere	.05	.02	.01
□ 34 Glenn Hubbard	.05	.02	.01
□ 35 Ryne Sandberg	.25	.11	.03
□ 36 Tony Pena	.05	.02	.01
□ 37 Greg Walker	.05	.02	.01
□ 38 Von Hayes	.05	.02	.01
□ 39 Kevin Mitchell	.10	.05	.01
□ 40 Tim Raines	.15	.07	.02
□ 41 Keith Hernandez	.10	.05	.01
□ 42 Keith Moreland	.05	.02	.01
□ 43 Ruben Sierra	.10	.05	.01
□ 44 Chet Lemon	.05	.02	.01
□ 45 Willie Randolph	.10	.05	.01
□ 46 Andy Allanson	.05	.02	.01
□ 47 Candy Maldonado	.05	.02	.01
□ 48 Sid Bream	.05	.02	.01
□ 49 Denny Walling	.05	.02	.01
□ 50 Dave Winfield	.15	.07	.02
□ 51 Alvin Davis	.05	.02	.01
□ 52 Cory Snyder	.05	.02	.01
□ 53 Hubie Brooks	.05	.02	.01
□ 54 Chili Davis	.10	.05	.01
□ 55 Kevin Seitzer	.05	.02	.01

☐ 56 Jose Uribe .05 .02 .01
☐ 57 Tony Fernandez .05 .02 .01
☐ 58 Tim Teufel .05 .02 .01
☐ 59 Oddibe McDowell .05 .02 .01
☐ 60 Les Lancaster .05 .02 .01
☐ 61 Billy Hatcher .05 .02 .01
☐ 62 Dan Gladden .05 .02 .01
☐ 63 Marty Barrett .05 .02 .01
☐ 64 Nick Esasky .05 .02 .01
☐ 65 Wally Joyner .10 .05 .01
☐ 66 Mike Greenwell .05 .02 .01
☐ 67 Ken Williams .05 .02 .01
☐ 68 Bob Horner .05 .02 .01
☐ 69 Steve Sax .05 .02 .01
☐ 70 Rickey Henderson .15 .07 .02
☐ 71 Mitch Webster .05 .02 .01
☐ 72 Rob Deer .05 .02 .01
☐ 73 Jim Presley .05 .02 .01
☐ 74 Albert Hall .05 .02 .01
☐ 75 George Brett COR .40 .18 .05
(At age 35)
☐ 75A George Brett ERR .75 .35 .09
(At age 33)
☐ 76 Brian Downing .05 .02 .01
☐ 77 Dave Martinez .05 .02 .01
☐ 78 Scott Fletcher .05 .02 .01
☐ 79 Phil Bradley .05 .02 .01
☐ 80 Ozzie Smith .25 .11 .03
☐ 81 Larry Sheets .05 .02 .01
☐ 82 Mike Aldrete .05 .02 .01
☐ 83 Darnell Coles .05 .02 .01
☐ 84 Len Dykstra .10 .05 .01
☐ 85 Jim Rice .15 .07 .02
☐ 86 Jeff Treadway .05 .02 .01
☐ 87 Jose Lind .05 .02 .01
☐ 88 Willie McGee .05 .02 .01
☐ 89 Mickey Brantley .05 .02 .01
☐ 90 Tony Gwynn .40 .18 .05
☐ 91 R.J. Reynolds .05 .02 .01
☐ 92 Milt Thompson .05 .02 .01
☐ 93 Kevin McReynolds .05 .02 .01
☐ 94 Eddie Murray UER .25 .11 .03
('86 batting .205,
should be .305)
☐ 95 Lance Parrish .05 .02 .01
☐ 96 Ron Kittle .05 .02 .01
☐ 97 Gerald Young .05 .02 .01
☐ 98 Ernie Whitt .05 .02 .01
☐ 99 Jeff Reed .05 .02 .01
☐ 100 Don Mattingly .50 .23 .06
☐ 101 Gerald Perry .05 .02 .01
☐ 102 Vance Law .05 .02 .01
☐ 103 John Shelby .05 .02 .01
☐ 104 Chris Sabo .05 .02 .01
☐ 105 Danny Tartabull .05 .02 .01
☐ 106 Glenn Wilson .05 .02 .01
☐ 107 Mark Davidson .05 .02 .01
☐ 108 Dave Parker .10 .05 .01
☐ 109 Eric Davis .10 .05 .01
☐ 110 Alan Trammell .10 .05 .01
☐ 111 Ozzie Virgil .05 .02 .01
☐ 112 Frank Tanana .05 .02 .01
☐ 113 Rafael Ramirez .05 .02 .01
☐ 114 Dennis Martinez .10 .05 .01
☐ 115 Jose DeLeon .05 .02 .01
☐ 116 Bob Ojeda .05 .02 .01
☐ 117 Doug Drabek .10 .05 .01
☐ 118 Andy Hawkins .05 .02 .01
☐ 119 Greg Maddux .75 .35 .09
☐ 120 Cecil Fielder UER .10 .05 .01
(Photo on back
reversed)
☐ 121 Mike Scioscia .05 .02 .01
☐ 122 Dan Petry .05 .02 .01
☐ 123 Terry Kennedy .05 .02 .01
☐ 124 Kelly Downs .05 .02 .01
☐ 125 Greg Gross UER .05 .02 .01
(Gregg on back)
☐ 126 Fred Lynn .05 .02 .01
☐ 127 Barry Bonds .40 .18 .05
☐ 128 Harold Baines .10 .05 .01
☐ 129 Doyle Alexander .05 .02 .01
☐ 130 Kevin Elster .10 .05 .01
☐ 131 Mike Heath .05 .02 .01
☐ 132 Teddy Higuera .05 .02 .01
☐ 133 Charlie Leibrandt .05 .02 .01
☐ 134 Tim Laudner .05 .02 .01
☐ 135A Ray Knight ERR .15 .07 .02
(Reverse negative)
☐ 135B Ray Knight COR .05 .02 .01
☐ 136 Howard Johnson .05 .02 .01
☐ 137 Terry Pendleton .10 .05 .01
☐ 138 Andy McGaffigan .05 .02 .01
☐ 139 Ken Oberkfell .05 .02 .01
☐ 140 Butch Wynegar .05 .02 .01
☐ 141 Rob Murphy .05 .02 .01
☐ 142 Rich Renteria .05 .02 .01
☐ 143 Jose Guzman .05 .02 .01
☐ 144 Andres Galarraga .15 .07 .02
☐ 145 Ricky Horton .05 .02 .01
☐ 146 Frank DiPino .05 .02 .01
☐ 147 Glenn Braggs .05 .02 .01
☐ 148 John Kruk .10 .05 .01
☐ 149 Mike Schmidt .20 .09 .03
☐ 150 Lee Smith .10 .05 .01
☐ 151 Robin Yount .15 .07 .02
☐ 152 Mark Eichhorn .05 .02 .01
☐ 153 DeWayne Buice .05 .02 .01
☐ 154 B.J. Surhoff .15 .07 .02
☐ 155 Vince Coleman .05 .02 .01
☐ 156 Tony Phillips .15 .07 .02
☐ 157 Willie Fraser .05 .02 .01
☐ 158 Lance McCullers .05 .02 .01
☐ 159 Greg Gagne .05 .02 .01
☐ 160 Jesse Barfield .05 .02 .01
☐ 161 Mark Langston .10 .05 .01
☐ 162 Kurt Stillwell .05 .02 .01
☐ 163 Dion James .05 .02 .01
☐ 164 Glenn Davis .05 .02 .01
☐ 165 Walt Weiss .05 .02 .01
☐ 166 Dave Concepcion .10 .05 .01
☐ 167 Alfredo Griffin .05 .02 .01
☐ 168 Don Heinkel .05 .02 .01
☐ 169 Luis Rivera .05 .02 .01
☐ 170 Shane Rawley .05 .02 .01
☐ 171 Darrell Evans .10 .05 .01
☐ 172 Robby Thompson .05 .02 .01
☐ 173 Jody Davis .05 .02 .01
☐ 174 Andy Van Slyke .10 .05 .01
☐ 175 Wade Boggs UER .15 .07 .02
(Bio says .364,
should be .356)
☐ 176 Garry Templeton .05 .02 .01
('85 stats
off-centered)
☐ 177 Gary Redus .05 .02 .01
☐ 178 Craig Lefferts .05 .02 .01
☐ 179 Carney Lansford .10 .05 .01
☐ 180 Ron Darling .05 .02 .01
☐ 181 Kirk McCaskill .05 .02 .01
☐ 182 Tony Armas .05 .02 .01
☐ 183 Steve Farr .05 .02 .01
☐ 184 Tom Brunansky .05 .02 .01
☐ 185 Bryan Harvey UER .10 .05 .01
('87 games 47,
should be 3)
☐ 186 Mike Marshall .05 .02 .01
☐ 187 Bo Diaz .05 .02 .01
☐ 188 Willie Upshaw .05 .02 .01
☐ 189 Mike Pagliarulo .05 .02 .01
☐ 190 Mike Krukow .05 .02 .01
☐ 191 Tommy Herr .05 .02 .01
☐ 192 Jim Pankovits .05 .02 .01
☐ 193 Dwight Evans .10 .05 .01
☐ 194 Kelly Gruber .05 .02 .01
☐ 195 Bobby Bonilla .15 .07 .02
☐ 196 Wallace Johnson .05 .02 .01
☐ 197 Dave Stieb .05 .02 .01
☐ 198 Pat Borders .10 .05 .01
☐ 199 Rafael Palmeiro .15 .07 .02
☐ 200 Dwight Gooden .10 .05 .01
☐ 201 Pete Incaviglia .10 .05 .01
☐ 202 Chris James .05 .02 .01
☐ 203 Marvell Wynne .05 .02 .01
☐ 204 Pat Sheridan .05 .02 .01
☐ 205 Don Baylor .15 .07 .02
☐ 206 Paul O'Neill .10 .05 .01
☐ 207 Pete Smith .05 .02 .01
☐ 208 Mark McLemore .05 .02 .01
☐ 209 Henry Cotto .05 .02 .01
☐ 210 Kirk Gibson .15 .07 .02
☐ 211 Claudell Washington .05 .02 .01
☐ 212 Randy Bush .05 .02 .01
☐ 213 Joe Carter .15 .07 .02
☐ 214 Bill Buckner .10 .05 .01
☐ 215 Bert Blyleven UER .10 .05 .01
(Wrong birth year)
☐ 216 Brett Butler .10 .05 .01
☐ 217 Lee Mazzilli .05 .02 .01
☐ 218 Spike Owen .05 .02 .01
☐ 219 Bill Swift .05 .02 .01
☐ 220 Tim Wallach .05 .02 .01
☐ 221 David Cone .15 .07 .02
☐ 222 Don Carman .05 .02 .01
☐ 223 Rich Gossage .15 .07 .02
☐ 224 Bob Walk .05 .02 .01
☐ 225 Dave Righetti .05 .02 .01
☐ 226 Kevin Bass .05 .02 .01
☐ 227 Kevin Gross .05 .02 .01
☐ 228 Tim Burke .05 .02 .01
☐ 229 Rick Mahler .05 .02 .01
☐ 230 Lou Whitaker UER .10 .05 .01
(252 games in '85,
should be 152)
☐ 231 Luis Alicea .05 .02 .01
☐ 232 Roberto Alomar .40 .18 .05
☐ 233 Bob Boone .10 .05 .01
☐ 234 Dickie Thon .05 .02 .01
☐ 235 Shawon Dunston .05 .02 .01
☐ 236 Pete Stanicek .05 .02 .01
☐ 237 Craig Biggio .40 .18 .05
(Inconsistent design,
portrait on front)
☐ 238 Dennis Boyd .05 .02 .01
☐ 239 Tom Candiotti .05 .02 .01
☐ 240 Gary Carter .10 .05 .01
☐ 241 Mike Stanley .05 .02 .01
☐ 242 Ken Phelps .05 .02 .01
☐ 243 Chris Bosio .05 .02 .01
☐ 244 Les Straker .05 .02 .01
☐ 245 Dave Smith .05 .02 .01
☐ 246 John Candelaria .05 .02 .01
☐ 247 Joe Orsulak .05 .02 .01
☐ 248 Storm Davis .05 .02 .01
☐ 249 Floyd Bannister UER .05 .02 .01
(ML Batting Record)
☐ 250 Jack Morris .10 .05 .01
☐ 251 Bret Saberhagen .10 .05 .01
☐ 252 Tom Niedenfuer .05 .02 .01
☐ 253 Neal Heaton .05 .02 .01
☐ 254 Eric Show .05 .02 .01
☐ 255 Juan Samuel .05 .02 .01
☐ 256 Dale Sveum .05 .02 .01
☐ 257 Jim Gott .05 .02 .01
☐ 258 Scott Garrelts .05 .02 .01
☐ 259 Larry McWilliams .05 .02 .01
☐ 260 Steve Bedrosian .05 .02 .01
☐ 261 Jack Howell .05 .02 .01
☐ 262 Jay Tibbs .05 .02 .01
☐ 263 Jamie Moyer .05 .02 .01
☐ 264 Doug Sisk .05 .02 .01
☐ 265 Todd Worrell .05 .02 .01
☐ 266 John Farrell .05 .02 .01
☐ 267 Dave Collins .05 .02 .01
☐ 268 Sid Fernandez .05 .02 .01
☐ 269 Tom Brookens .05 .02 .01
☐ 270 Shane Mack .05 .02 .01
☐ 271 Paul Kilgus .05 .02 .01
☐ 272 Chuck Crim .05 .02 .01
☐ 273 Bob Knepper .05 .02 .01
☐ 274 Mike Moore .05 .02 .01
☐ 275 Guillermo Hernandez .05 .02 .01
☐ 276 Dennis Eckersley .10 .05 .01
☐ 277 Graig Nettles .10 .05 .01
☐ 278 Rich Dotson .05 .02 .01
☐ 279 Larry Herndon .05 .02 .01
☐ 280 Gene Larkin .05 .02 .01
☐ 281 Roger McDowell .05 .02 .01
☐ 282 Greg Swindell .05 .02 .01
☐ 283 Juan Agosto .05 .02 .01
☐ 284 Jeff M. Robinson .05 .02 .01
☐ 285 Mike Dunne .05 .02 .01
☐ 286 Greg Mathews .05 .02 .01
☐ 287 Kent Tekulve .05 .02 .01
☐ 288 Jerry Mumphrey .05 .02 .01
☐ 289 Jack McDowell .10 .05 .01
☐ 290 Frank Viola .05 .02 .01
☐ 291 Mark Gubicza .05 .02 .01
☐ 292 Dave Schmidt .05 .02 .01
☐ 293 Mike Henneman .05 .02 .01
☐ 294 Jimmy Jones .05 .02 .01
☐ 295 Charlie Hough .10 .05 .01
☐ 296 Rafael Santana .05 .02 .01
☐ 297 Chris Speier .05 .02 .01
☐ 298 Mike Witt .05 .02 .01
☐ 299 Pascual Perez .05 .02 .01
☐ 300 Nolan Ryan .75 .35 .09
☐ 301 Mitch Williams .05 .02 .01
☐ 302 Mookie Wilson .10 .05 .01
☐ 303 Mackey Sasser .05 .02 .01
☐ 304 John Cerutti .05 .02 .01
☐ 305 Jeff Reardon .10 .05 .01
☐ 306 Randy Myers UER .10 .05 .01
(6 hits in '87,
should be 61)
☐ 307 Greg Brock .05 .02 .01
☐ 308 Bob Welch .05 .02 .01
☐ 309 Jeff D. Robinson .05 .02 .01
☐ 310 Harold Reynolds .05 .02 .01
☐ 311 Jim Walewander .05 .02 .01
☐ 312 Dave Magadan .05 .02 .01
☐ 313 Jim Gantner .05 .02 .01
☐ 314 Walt Terrell .05 .02 .01
☐ 315 Wally Backman .05 .02 .01
☐ 316 Luis Salazar .05 .02 .01
☐ 317 Rick Rhoden .05 .02 .01
☐ 318 Tom Henke .05 .02 .01
☐ 319 Mike Macfarlane .10 .05 .01
☐ 320 Dan Plesac .05 .02 .01
☐ 321 Calvin Schiraldi .05 .02 .01
☐ 322 Stan Javier .05 .02 .01
☐ 323 Devon White .10 .05 .01
☐ 324 Scott Bradley .05 .02 .01
☐ 325 Bruce Hurst .05 .02 .01
☐ 326 Manny Lee .05 .02 .01
☐ 327 Rick Aguilera .15 .07 .02
☐ 328 Bruce Ruffin .05 .02 .01
☐ 329 Ed Whitson .05 .02 .01
☐ 330 Bo Jackson .15 .07 .02
☐ 331 Ivan Calderon .05 .02 .01
☐ 332 Mickey Hatcher .05 .02 .01
☐ 333 Barry Jones .05 .02 .01
☐ 334 Ron Hassey .05 .02 .01
☐ 335 Bill Wegman .05 .02 .01
☐ 336 Damon Berryhill .05 .02 .01
☐ 337 Steve Ontiveros .05 .02 .01
☐ 338 Dan Pasqua .05 .02 .01
☐ 339 Bill Pecota .05 .02 .01
☐ 340 Greg Cadaret .05 .02 .01
☐ 341 Scott Bankhead .05 .02 .01
☐ 342 Ron Guidry .05 .02 .01
☐ 343 Danny Heep .05 .02 .01
☐ 344 Bob Brower .05 .02 .01
☐ 345 Rich Gedman .05 .02 .01
☐ 346 Nelson Santovenia .05 .02 .01
☐ 347 George Bell .05 .02 .01
☐ 348 Ted Power .05 .02 .01
☐ 349 Mark Grant .05 .02 .01
☐ 350A Roger Clemens ERR 2.00 .90 .25
(778 career wins)
☐ 350B Roger Clemens COR .20 .09 .03
(78 career wins)
☐ 351 Bill Long .05 .02 .01
☐ 352 Jay Bell .15 .07 .02
☐ 353 Steve Balboni .05 .02 .01
☐ 354 Bob Kipper .05 .02 .01
☐ 355 Steve Jeltz .05 .02 .01
☐ 356 Jesse Orosco .05 .02 .01
☐ 357 Bob Dernier .05 .02 .01
☐ 358 Mickey Tettleton .10 .05 .01
☐ 359 Duane Ward .05 .02 .01
☐ 360 Darrin Jackson .05 .02 .01
☐ 361 Rey Quinones .05 .02 .01
☐ 362 Mark Grace .20 .09 .03
☐ 363 Steve Lake .05 .02 .01
☐ 364 Pat Perry .05 .02 .01
☐ 365 Terry Steinbach .10 .05 .01
☐ 366 Alan Ashby .05 .02 .01
☐ 367 Jeff Montgomery .10 .05 .01
☐ 368 Steve Buechele .05 .02 .01
☐ 369 Chris Brown .05 .02 .01
☐ 370 Orel Hershiser .10 .05 .01
☐ 371 Todd Benzinger .05 .02 .01
☐ 372 Ron Gant .15 .07 .02
☐ 373 Paul Assenmacher .05 .02 .01
☐ 374 Joey Meyer .05 .02 .01
☐ 375 Neil Allen .05 .02 .01
☐ 376 Mike Davis .05 .02 .01
☐ 377 Jeff Parrett .05 .02 .01
☐ 378 Jay Howell .05 .02 .01
☐ 379 Rafael Belliard .05 .02 .01
☐ 380 Luis Polonia UER .10 .05 .01
(2 triples in '87,
should be 10)
☐ 381 Keith Atherton .05 .02 .01
☐ 382 Kent Hrbek .10 .05 .01
☐ 383 Bob Stanley .05 .02 .01
☐ 384 Dave LaPoint .05 .02 .01
☐ 385 Rance Mulliniks .05 .02 .01
☐ 386 Melido Perez .05 .02 .01
☐ 387 Doug Jones .05 .02 .01
☐ 388 Steve Lyons .05 .02 .01
☐ 389 Alejandro Pena .05 .02 .01
☐ 390 Frank White .10 .05 .01
☐ 391 Pat Tabler .05 .02 .01
☐ 392 Eric Plunk .05 .02 .01
☐ 393 Mike Maddux .05 .02 .01
☐ 394 Allan Anderson .05 .02 .01
☐ 395 Bob Brenly .05 .02 .01
☐ 396 Rick Cerone .05 .02 .01
☐ 397 Scott Terry .05 .02 .01
☐ 398 Mike Jackson .05 .02 .01
☐ 399 Bobby Thigpen UER .05 .02 .01
(Bio says 37 saves in
'88, should be 34)
☐ 400 Don Sutton .15 .07 .02
☐ 401 Cecil Espy .05 .02 .01
☐ 402 Junior Ortiz .05 .02 .01
☐ 403 Mike Smithson .05 .02 .01
☐ 404 Bud Black .05 .02 .01
☐ 405 Tom Foley .05 .02 .01
☐ 406 Andres Thomas .05 .02 .01
☐ 407 Rick Sutcliffe .05 .02 .01
☐ 408 Brian Harper .05 .02 .01
☐ 409 John Smiley .05 .02 .01
☐ 410 Juan Nieves .05 .02 .01
☐ 411 Shawn Abner .05 .02 .01
☐ 412 Wes Gardner .05 .02 .01
☐ 413 Darren Daulton .10 .05 .01
☐ 414 Juan Berenguer .05 .02 .01
☐ 415 Charles Hudson .05 .02 .01
☐ 416 Rick Honeycutt .05 .02 .01
☐ 417 Greg Booker .05 .02 .01
☐ 418 Tim Belcher .05 .02 .01
☐ 419 Don August .05 .02 .01
☐ 420 Dale Mohorcic .05 .02 .01
☐ 421 Steve Lombardozzi .05 .02 .01
☐ 422 Atlee Hammaker .05 .02 .01
☐ 423 Jerry Don Gleaton .05 .02 .01
☐ 424 Scott Bailes .05 .02 .01
☐ 425 Bruce Sutter .05 .02 .01
☐ 426 Randy Ready .05 .02 .01
☐ 427 Jerry Reed .05 .02 .01
☐ 428 Bryn Smith .05 .02 .01
☐ 429 Tim Leary .05 .02 .01
☐ 430 Mark Clear .05 .02 .01
☐ 431 Terry Leach .05 .02 .01
☐ 432 John Moses .05 .02 .01
☐ 433 Ozzie Guillen .05 .02 .01
☐ 434 Gene Nelson .05 .02 .01
☐ 435 Gary Ward .05 .02 .01
☐ 436 Luis Aguayo .05 .02 .01
☐ 437 Fernando Valenzuela .10 .05 .01
☐ 438 Jeff Russell UER .05 .02 .01
(Saves total does
not add up correctly)
☐ 439 Cecilio Guante .05 .02 .01
☐ 440 Don Robinson .05 .02 .01
☐ 441 Rick Anderson .05 .02 .01
☐ 442 Tom Glavine .25 .11 .03

□ 443 Daryl Boston .05 .02 .01
□ 444 Joe Price .05 .02 .01
□ 445 Stewart Cliburn .05 .02 .01
□ 446 Manny Trillo .05 .02 .01
□ 447 Joel Skinner .05 .02 .01
□ 448 Charlie Puleo .05 .02 .01
□ 449 Carlton Fisk .15 .07 .02
□ 450 Will Clark .20 .09 .03
□ 451 Otis Nixon .05 .02 .01
□ 452 Rick Schu .05 .02 .01
□ 453 Todd Stottlemyre UER .10 .05 .01
(ML Batting Record)
□ 454 Tim Birtsas .05 .02 .01
□ 455 Dave Gallagher .05 .02 .01
□ 456 Barry Lyons .05 .02 .01
□ 457 Fred Manrique .05 .02 .01
□ 458 Ernest Riles .05 .02 .01
□ 459 Doug Jennings .05 .02 .01
□ 460 Joe Magrane .05 .02 .01
□ 461 Jamie Quirk .05 .02 .01
□ 462 Jack Armstrong .05 .02 .01
□ 463 Bobby Witt .05 .02 .01
□ 464 Keith A. Miller .05 .02 .01
□ 465 Todd Burns .05 .02 .01
□ 466 John Dopson .05 .02 .01
□ 467 Rich Yett .05 .02 .01
□ 468 Craig Reynolds .05 .02 .01
□ 469 Dave Bergman .05 .02 .01
□ 470 Rex Hudler .05 .02 .01
□ 471 Eric King .05 .02 .01
□ 472 Joaquin Andujar .05 .02 .01
□ 473 Sil Campusano .05 .02 .01
□ 474 Terry Mulholland .05 .02 .01
□ 475 Mike Flanagan .05 .02 .01
□ 476 Greg A. Harris .05 .02 .01
□ 477 Tommy John .10 .05 .01
□ 478 Dave Anderson .05 .02 .01
□ 479 Fred Toliver .05 .02 .01
□ 480 Jimmy Key .10 .05 .01
□ 481 Donell Nixon .05 .02 .01
□ 482 Mark Portugal .05 .02 .01
□ 483 Tom Pagnozzi .05 .02 .01
□ 484 Jeff Kunkel .05 .02 .01
□ 485 Frank Williams .05 .02 .01
□ 486 Jody Reed .05 .02 .01
□ 487 Roberto Kelly .10 .05 .01
□ 488 Shawn Hillegas UER .05 .02 .01
(165 innings in '87,
should be 165.2)
□ 489 Jerry Reuss .05 .02 .01
□ 490 Mark Davis .05 .02 .01
□ 491 Jeff Sellers .05 .02 .01
□ 492 Zane Smith .05 .02 .01
□ 493 Al Newman .05 .02 .01
□ 494 Mike Young .05 .02 .01
□ 495 Larry Parrish .05 .02 .01
□ 496 Herm Winningham .05 .02 .01
□ 497 Carmen Castillo .05 .02 .01
□ 498 Joe Hesketh .05 .02 .01
□ 499 Darrell Miller .05 .02 .01
□ 500 Mike LaCoss .05 .02 .01
□ 501 Charlie Lea .05 .02 .01
□ 502 Bruce Benedict .05 .02 .01
□ 503 Chuck Finley .10 .05 .01
□ 504 Brad Wellman .05 .02 .01
□ 505 Tim Crews .05 .02 .01
□ 506 Ken Gerhart .05 .02 .01
□ 507A Brian Holton ERR .05 .02 .01
(Born 1/25/65 Denver,
should be 11/29/59
in McKeesport)
□ 507B Brian Holton COR 2.00 .90 .25
□ 508 Dennis Lamp .05 .02 .01
□ 509 Bobby Meacham UER .05 .02 .01
('84 games 099)
□ 510 Tracy Jones .05 .02 .01
□ 511 Mike R. Fitzgerald .05 .02 .01
□ 512 Jeff Bittiger .05 .02 .01
□ 513 Tim Flannery .05 .02 .01
□ 514 Ray Hayward .05 .02 .01
□ 515 Dave Leiper .05 .02 .01
□ 516 Rod Scurry .05 .02 .01
□ 517 Carmelo Martinez .05 .02 .01
□ 518 Curtis Wilkerson .05 .02 .01
□ 519 Stan Jefferson .05 .02 .01
□ 520 Dan Quisenberry .05 .02 .01
□ 521 Lloyd McClendon .05 .02 .01
□ 522 Steve Trout .05 .02 .01
□ 523 Larry Andersen .05 .02 .01
□ 524 Don Aase .05 .02 .01
□ 525 Bob Forsch .05 .02 .01
□ 526 Geno Petralli .05 .02 .01
□ 527 Angel Salazar .05 .02 .01
□ 528 Mike Schooler .05 .02 .01
□ 529 Jose Oquendo .05 .02 .01
□ 530 Jay Buhner UER .25 .11 .03
(Wearing 43 on front,
listed as 34 on back)
□ 531 Tom Bolton .05 .02 .01
□ 532 Al Nipper .05 .02 .01
□ 533 Dave Henderson .05 .02 .01
□ 534 John Costello .05 .02 .01
□ 535 Donnie Moore .05 .02 .01
□ 536 Mike Laga .05 .02 .01
□ 537 Mike Gallego .05 .02 .01
□ 538 Jim Clancy .05 .02 .01
□ 539 Joel Youngblood .05 .02 .01
□ 540 Rick Leach .05 .02 .01
□ 541 Kevin Romine .05 .02 .01
□ 542 Mark Salas .05 .02 .01
□ 543 Greg Minton .05 .02 .01
□ 544 Dave Palmer .05 .02 .01
□ 545 Dwayne Murphy UER .05 .02 .01
(Game-sinning)
□ 546 Jim Deshaies .05 .02 .01
□ 547 Don Gordon .05 .02 .01
□ 548 Ricky Jordan .10 .05 .01
□ 549 Mike Boddicker .05 .02 .01
□ 550 Mike Scott .05 .02 .01
□ 551 Jeff Ballard .05 .02 .01
□ 552A Jose Rijo ERR .15 .07 .02
(Uniform listed as
27 on back)
□ 552B Jose Rijo COR .15 .07 .02
(Uniform listed as
24 on back)
□ 553 Danny Darwin .05 .02 .01
□ 554 Tom Browning .05 .02 .01
□ 555 Danny Jackson .05 .02 .01
□ 556 Rick Dempsey .05 .02 .01
□ 557 Jeffrey Leonard .05 .02 .01
□ 558 Jeff Musselman .05 .02 .01
□ 559 Ron Robinson .05 .02 .01
□ 560 John Tudor .05 .02 .01
□ 561 Don Slaught UER .05 .02 .01
(237 games in 1987)
□ 562 Dennis Rasmussen .05 .02 .01
□ 563 Brady Anderson .60 .25 .07
□ 564 Pedro Guerrero .10 .05 .01
□ 565 Paul Molitor .20 .09 .03
□ 566 Terry Clark .05 .02 .01
□ 567 Terry Puhl .05 .02 .01
□ 568 Mike Campbell .05 .02 .01
□ 569 Paul Mirabella .05 .02 .01
□ 570 Jeff Hamilton .05 .02 .01
□ 571 Oswald Peraza .05 .02 .01
□ 572 Bob McClure .05 .02 .01
□ 573 Jose Bautista .05 .02 .01
□ 574 Alex Trevino .05 .02 .01
□ 575 John Franco .10 .05 .01
□ 576 Mark Parent .05 .02 .01
□ 577 Nelson Liriano .05 .02 .01
□ 578 Steve Shields .05 .02 .01
□ 579 Odell Jones .05 .02 .01
□ 580 Al Leiter .10 .05 .01
□ 581 Dave Stapleton .05 .02 .01
□ 582 World Series '88 .10 .05 .01
Orel Hershiser
Jose Canseco
Kirk Gibson
Dave Stewart
□ 583 Donnie Hill .05 .02 .01
□ 584 Chuck Jackson .05 .02 .01
□ 585 Rene Gonzales .05 .02 .01
□ 586 Tracy Woodson .05 .02 .01
□ 587 Jim Adduci .05 .02 .01
□ 588 Mario Soto .05 .02 .01
□ 589 Jeff Blauser .10 .05 .01
□ 590 Jim Traber .05 .02 .01
□ 591 Jon Perlman .05 .02 .01
□ 592 Mark Williamson .05 .02 .01
□ 593 Dave Meads .05 .02 .01
□ 594 Jim Eisenreich .10 .05 .01
□ 595A Paul Gibson P1 1.00 .45 .12
□ 595B Paul Gibson P2 .05 .02 .01
(Airbrushed leg on
player in background)
□ 596 Mike Birkbeck .05 .02 .01
□ 597 Terry Francona .05 .02 .01
□ 598 Paul Zuvella .05 .02 .01
□ 599 Franklin Stubbs .05 .02 .01
□ 600 Gregg Jefferies .15 .07 .02
□ 601 John Cangelosi .05 .02 .01
□ 602 Mike Sharperson .05 .02 .01
□ 603 Mike Diaz .05 .02 .01
□ 604 Gary Varsho .05 .02 .01
□ 605 Terry Blocker .05 .02 .01
□ 606 Charlie O'Brien .05 .02 .01
□ 607 Jim Eppard .05 .02 .01
□ 608 John Davis .05 .02 .01
□ 609 Ken Griffey Sr. .05 .02 .01
□ 610 Buddy Bell .10 .05 .01
□ 611 Ted Simmons UER .10 .05 .01
('78 stats Cardinal)
□ 612 Matt Williams .25 .11 .03
□ 613 Danny Cox .05 .02 .01
□ 614 Al Pedrique .05 .02 .01
□ 615 Ron Oester .05 .02 .01
□ 616 John Smoltz .75 .35 .09
□ 617 Bob Melvin .05 .02 .01
□ 618 Rob Dibble .10 .05 .01
□ 619 Kirt Manwaring .05 .02 .01
□ 620 Felix Fermin .05 .02 .01
□ 621 Doug Dascenzo .05 .02 .01
□ 622 Bill Brennan .05 .02 .01
□ 623 Carlos Quintana .05 .02 .01
□ 624 Mike Harkey UER .05 .02 .01
(13 and 31 walks
in '88, should
be 35 and 33)
□ 625 Gary Sheffield .75 .35 .09
□ 626 Tom Prince .05 .02 .01
□ 627 Steve Searcy .05 .02 .01
□ 628 Charlie Hayes .15 .07 .02
(Listed as outfielder)
□ 629 Felix Jose UER .05 .02 .01
(Modesto misspelled
as Modesta)
□ 630 Sandy Alomar Jr. .20 .09 .03
(Inconsistent design,
portrait on front)
□ 631 Derek Lilliquist .05 .02 .01
□ 632 Geronimo Berroa .10 .05 .01
□ 633 Luis Medina .05 .02 .01
□ 634 Tom Gordon UER .10 .05 .01
(Height 6'0")
□ 635 Ramon Martinez .25 .11 .03
□ 636 Craig Worthington .05 .02 .01
□ 637 Edgar Martinez .15 .07 .02
□ 638 Chad Kreuter .05 .02 .01
□ 639 Ron Jones .05 .02 .01
□ 640 Van Snider .05 .02 .01
□ 641 Lance Blankenship .05 .02 .01
□ 642 Dwight Smith UER .10 .05 .01
(10 HR's in '87,
should be 18)
□ 643 Cameron Drew .05 .02 .01
□ 644 Jerald Clark .05 .02 .01
□ 645 Randy Johnson .75 .35 .09
□ 646 Norm Charlton .10 .05 .01
□ 647 Todd Frohwirth UER .05 .02 .01
(Southpaw on back)
□ 648 Luis De Los Santos .05 .02 .01
□ 649 Tim Jones .05 .02 .01
□ 650 Dave West UER .05 .02 .01
(ML hits 3,
should be 6)
□ 651 Bob Milacki .05 .02 .01
□ 652 Wrigley Field HL .10 .05 .01
(Let There Be Lights)
□ 653 Orel Hershiser HL .10 .05 .01
(The Streak)
□ 654A Wade Boggs HL ERR 1.50 .70 .19
(Wade Whacks 'Em)
("seaason" on back)
□ 654B Wade Boggs HL COR .15 .07 .02
(Wade Whacks 'Em)
□ 655 Jose Canseco HL .15 .07 .02
(One of a Kind)
□ 656 Doug Jones HL .05 .02 .01
(Doug Sets Saves)
□ 657 Rickey Henderson HL .15 .07 .02
(Rickey Rocks 'Em)
□ 658 Tom Browning HL .05 .02 .01
(Tom Perfect Pitches)
□ 659 Mike Greenwell HL .05 .02 .01
(Greenwell Gamers)
□ 660 Boston Red Sox HL .05 .02 .01
(Joe Morgan MG,
Sox Sock 'Em)

1989 Score Rookie/Traded

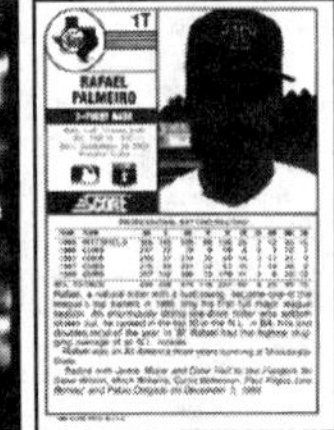

The 1989 Score Rookie and Traded set contains 110 standard-size cards. The set was issued exclusively in factory set form through hobby dealers. The set was distributed in a blue box with 10 Magic Motion trivia cards. The fronts have coral green borders with pink diamonds at the bottom. Cards 1-80 feature traded players; cards 81-110 feature 1989 rookies. Rookie Cards in this set include Jim Abbott, Joey (Albert) Belle, Ken Griffey Jr., Ken Hill and John Wetteland.

	MINT	NRMT	EXC
COMPLETE FACT.SET (110)	8.00	3.60	1.00
COMMON CARD (1T-110T)	.05	.02	.01

□ 1T Rafael Palmeiro .15 .07 .02
□ 2T Nolan Ryan 1.50 .70 .19
□ 3T Jack Clark .10 .05 .01
□ 4T Dave LaPoint .05 .02 .01
□ 5T Mike Moore .05 .02 .01
□ 6T Pete O'Brien .05 .02 .01
□ 7T Jeffrey Leonard .05 .02 .01
□ 8T Rob Murphy .05 .02 .01
□ 9T Tom Herr .05 .02 .01
□ 10T Claudell Washington .05 .02 .01
□ 11T Mike Pagliarulo .05 .02 .01
□ 12T Steve Lake .05 .02 .01
□ 13T Spike Owen .05 .02 .01
□ 14T Andy Hawkins .05 .02 .01
□ 15T Todd Benzinger .05 .02 .01
□ 16T Mookie Wilson .10 .05 .01
□ 17T Bert Blyleven .10 .05 .01
□ 18T Jeff Treadway .05 .02 .01
□ 19T Bruce Hurst .05 .02 .01
□ 20T Steve Sax .05 .02 .01
□ 21T Juan Samuel .05 .02 .01
□ 22T Jesse Barfield .05 .02 .01
□ 23T Carmen Castillo .05 .02 .01
□ 24T Terry Leach .05 .02 .01
□ 25T Mark Langston .10 .05 .01
□ 26T Eric King .05 .02 .01
□ 27T Steve Balboni .05 .02 .01
□ 28T Len Dykstra .10 .05 .01
□ 29T Keith Moreland .05 .02 .01
□ 30T Terry Kennedy .05 .02 .01
□ 31T Eddie Murray .25 .11 .03
□ 32T Mitch Williams .05 .02 .01
□ 33T Jeff Parrett .05 .02 .01
□ 34T Wally Backman .05 .02 .01
□ 35T Julio Franco .10 .05 .01
□ 36T Lance Parrish .05 .02 .01
□ 37T Nick Esasky .05 .02 .01
□ 38T Luis Polonia .10 .05 .01
□ 39T Kevin Gross .05 .02 .01
□ 40T John Dopson .05 .02 .01
□ 41T Willie Randolph .10 .05 .01
□ 42T Jim Clancy .05 .02 .01
□ 43T Tracy Jones .05 .02 .01
□ 44T Phil Bradley .05 .02 .01
□ 45T Milt Thompson .05 .02 .01
□ 46T Chris James .05 .02 .01
□ 47T Scott Fletcher .05 .02 .01
□ 48T Kal Daniels .05 .02 .01
□ 49T Steve Bedrosian .05 .02 .01
□ 50T Rickey Henderson .15 .07 .02
□ 51T Dion James .05 .02 .01
□ 52T Tim Leary .05 .02 .01
□ 53T Roger McDowell .05 .02 .01
□ 54T Mel Hall .05 .02 .01
□ 55T Dickie Thon .05 .02 .01
□ 56T Zane Smith .05 .02 .01
□ 57T Danny Heep .05 .02 .01
□ 58T Bob McClure .05 .02 .01
□ 59T Brian Holton .05 .02 .01
□ 60T Randy Ready .05 .02 .01
□ 61T Bob Melvin .05 .02 .01
□ 62T Harold Baines .10 .05 .01
□ 63T Lance McCullers .05 .02 .01
□ 64T Jody Davis .05 .02 .01
□ 65T Darrell Evans .10 .05 .01
□ 66T Joel Youngblood .05 .02 .01
□ 67T Frank Viola .05 .02 .01
□ 68T Mike Aldrete .05 .02 .01
□ 69T Greg Cadaret .05 .02 .01
□ 70T John Kruk .10 .05 .01
□ 71T Pat Sheridan .05 .02 .01
□ 72T Oddibe McDowell .05 .02 .01
□ 73T Tom Brookens .05 .02 .01
□ 74T Bob Boone .10 .05 .01
□ 75T Walt Terrell .05 .02 .01
□ 76T Joel Skinner .05 .02 .01
□ 77T Randy Johnson .75 .35 .09
□ 78T Felix Fermin .05 .02 .01
□ 79T Rick Mahler .05 .02 .01
□ 80T Richard Dotson .05 .02 .01
□ 81T Cris Carpenter .05 .02 .01
□ 82T Bill Spiers .05 .02 .01
□ 83T Junior Felix .05 .02 .01
□ 84T Joe Girardi .15 .07 .02
□ 85T Jerome Walton .10 .05 .01
□ 86T Greg Litton .05 .02 .01
□ 87T Greg W.Harris .05 .02 .01
□ 88T Jim Abbott .15 .07 .02
□ 89T Kevin Brown .15 .07 .02
□ 90T John Wetteland .40 .18 .05
□ 91T Gary Wayne .05 .02 .01
□ 92T Rich Monteleone .05 .02 .01
□ 93T Bob Geren .05 .02 .01
□ 94T Clay Parker .05 .02 .01
□ 95T Steve Finley .25 .11 .03
□ 96T Gregg Olson .10 .05 .01
□ 97T Ken Patterson .05 .02 .01
□ 98T Ken Hill .40 .18 .05
□ 99T Scott Scudder .05 .02 .01
□ 100T Ken Griffey Jr. 5.00 2.20 .60
□ 101T Jeff Brantley .05 .02 .01
□ 102T Donn Pall .05 .02 .01
□ 103T Carlos Martinez .05 .02 .01
□ 104T Joe Oliver .15 .07 .02
□ 105T Omar Vizquel .40 .18 .05
□ 106T Joey Belle 2.50 1.10 .30
□ 107T Kenny Rogers .10 .05 .01
□ 108T Mark Carreon .05 .02 .01
□ 109T Rolando Roomes .05 .02 .01
□ 110T Pete Harnisch .10 .05 .01

1989 Score Hottest 100 Rookies

This set was distributed by Publications International in January 1989 through many retail stores and chains; the card set was packaged along with a colorful 48-page book for a suggested retail price of 12.95. Supposedly 225,000 sets were produced. The cards measure the standard size and show full color on both sides of the card. The cards were produced by Score as indicated on the card backs. The set is subtitled "Rising Star" on the reverse. The first six cards (1-6) of a 12-card set of Score's trivia cards, subtitled "Rookies to Remember" is

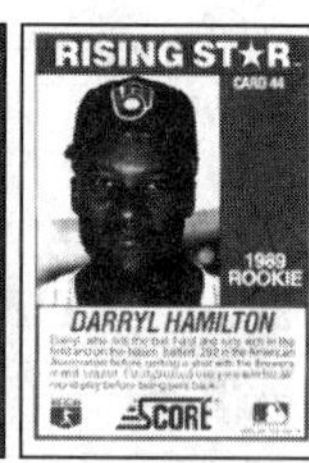

included along with each set. This set is distinguished by the sharp blue borders and the player's first initial inside a yellow triangle in the lower left corner of the obverse. The set features Dave Justice appearing one year before his Rookie Card year.

	MINT	NRMT	EXC
COMPLETE SET (100)	10.00	4.50	1.25
COMMON CARD (1-100)	.05	.02	.01
☐ 1 Gregg Jefferies	.50	.23	.06
☐ 2 Vicente Palacios	.05	.02	.01
☐ 3 Cameron Drew	.05	.02	.01
☐ 4 Doug Dascenzo	.05	.02	.01
☐ 5 Luis Medina	.05	.02	.01
☐ 6 Craig Worthington	.05	.02	.01
☐ 7 Rob Ducey	.05	.02	.01
☐ 8 Hal Morris	.10	.05	.01
☐ 9 Bill Brennan	.05	.02	.01
☐ 10 Gary Sheffield	1.50	.70	.19
☐ 11 Mike Devereaux	.10	.05	.01
☐ 12 Hensley Meulens	.05	.02	.01
☐ 13 Carlos Quintana	.05	.02	.01
☐ 14 Todd Frohwirth	.05	.02	.01
☐ 15 Scott Lusader	.05	.02	.01
☐ 16 Mark Carreon	.05	.02	.01
☐ 17 Torey Lovullo	.05	.02	.01
☐ 18 Randy Velarde	.05	.02	.01
☐ 19 Billy Bean	.05	.02	.01
☐ 20 Lance Blankenship	.05	.02	.01
☐ 21 Chris Gwynn	.05	.02	.01
☐ 22 Felix Jose	.05	.02	.01
☐ 23 Derek Lilliquist	.05	.02	.01
☐ 24 Gary Thurman	.05	.02	.01
☐ 25 Ron Jones	.05	.02	.01
☐ 26 Dave Justice	1.50	.70	.19
☐ 27 Johnny Paredes	.05	.02	.01
☐ 28 Tim Jones	.05	.02	.01
☐ 29 Jose Gonzalez	.05	.02	.01
☐ 30 Geronimo Berroa	.20	.09	.03
☐ 31 Trevor Wilson	.05	.02	.01
☐ 32 Morris Madden	.05	.02	.01
☐ 33 Lance Johnson	.40	.18	.05
☐ 34 Marvin Freeman	.05	.02	.01
☐ 35 Jose Cecena	.05	.02	.01
☐ 36 Jim Corsi	.05	.02	.01
☐ 37 Rolando Roomes	.05	.02	.01
☐ 38 Scott Medvin	.05	.02	.01
☐ 39 Charlie Hayes	.20	.09	.03
☐ 40 Edgar Martinez	.50	.23	.06
☐ 41 Van Snider	.05	.02	.01
☐ 42 John Fishel	.05	.02	.01
☐ 43 Bruce Fields	.05	.02	.01
☐ 44 Darryl Hamilton	.20	.09	.03
☐ 45 Tom Prince	.05	.02	.01
☐ 46 Kirt Manwaring	.05	.02	.01
☐ 47 Steve Searcy	.05	.02	.01
☐ 48 Mike Harkey	.05	.02	.01
☐ 49 German Gonzalez	.05	.02	.01
☐ 50 Tony Perezchica	.05	.02	.01
☐ 51 Chad Kreuter	.05	.02	.01
☐ 52 Luis DeLosSantos	.05	.02	.01
☐ 53 Steve Curry	.05	.02	.01
☐ 54 Greg Briley	.05	.02	.01
☐ 55 Ramon Martinez	.30	.14	.04
☐ 56 Ron Tingley	.05	.02	.01
☐ 57 Randy Kramer	.05	.02	.01
☐ 58 Alex Madrid	.05	.02	.01
☐ 59 Kevin Reimer	.05	.02	.01
☐ 60 Dave Otto	.05	.02	.01
☐ 61 Ken Patterson	.05	.02	.01
☐ 62 Keith Miller	.05	.02	.01
☐ 63 Randy Johnson	1.50	.70	.19
☐ 64 Dwight Smith	.10	.05	.01
☐ 65 Eric Yelding	.05	.02	.01
☐ 66 Bob Geren	.05	.02	.01
☐ 67 Shane Turner	.05	.02	.01
☐ 68 Tom Gordon	.25	.11	.03
☐ 69 Jeff Huson	.05	.02	.01
☐ 70 Marty Brown	.05	.02	.01
☐ 71 Nelson Santovenia	.05	.02	.01
☐ 72 Roberto Alomar	1.50	.70	.19
☐ 73 Mike Schooler	.05	.02	.01
☐ 74 Pete Smith	.05	.02	.01
☐ 75 John Costello	.05	.02	.01
☐ 76 Chris Sabo	.10	.05	.01
☐ 77 Damon Berryhill	.05	.02	.01
☐ 78 Mark Grace	1.25	.55	.16
☐ 79 Melido Perez	.05	.02	.01
☐ 80 Al Leiter	.20	.09	.03
☐ 81 Todd Stottlemyre	.15	.07	.02
☐ 82 Mackey Sasser	.05	.02	.01
☐ 83 Don August	.05	.02	.01
☐ 84 Jeff Treadway	.05	.02	.01
☐ 85 Jody Reed	.05	.02	.01
☐ 86 Mike Campbell	.05	.02	.01
☐ 87 Ron Gant	.50	.23	.06
☐ 88 Ricky Jordan	.05	.02	.01
☐ 89 Terry Clark	.05	.02	.01
☐ 90 Roberto Kelly	.10	.05	.01
☐ 91 Pat Borders	.20	.09	.03
☐ 92 Bryan Harvey	.10	.05	.01
☐ 93 Joey Meyer	.05	.02	.01
☐ 94 Tim Belcher	.05	.02	.01
☐ 95 Walt Weiss	.10	.05	.01
☐ 96 Dave Gallagher	.05	.02	.01
☐ 97 Mike Macfarlane	.10	.05	.01
☐ 98 Craig Biggio	.75	.35	.09
☐ 99 Jack Armstrong	.05	.02	.01
☐ 100 Todd Burns	.05	.02	.01

1989 Score Hottest 100 Stars

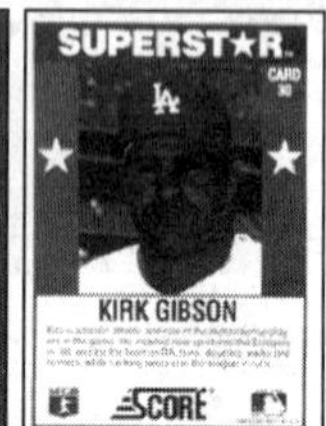

This set was distributed by Publications International in January 1989 through many retail stores and chains; the card set was packaged along with a colorful 48-page book for a suggested retail price of 12.95. Supposedly 225,000 sets were produced. The cards measure the standard size and show full color on both sides of the card. The cards were produced by Score as indicated on the card backs. The set is subtitled "Superstar" on the reverse. The last six cards (7-12) of a 12-card set of Score's trivia cards, subtitled "Rookies to Remember" is included along with each set. This set is distinguished by the sharp red borders and the player's first initial inside a yellow triangle in the upper left corner of the obverse.

	MINT	NRMT	EXC
COMPLETE SET (100)	10.00	4.50	1.25
COMMON CARD (1-100)	.05	.02	.01
☐ 1 Jose Canseco	.30	.14	.04
☐ 2 David Cone	.40	.18	.05
☐ 3 Dave Winfield	.40	.18	.05
☐ 4 George Brett	1.25	.55	.16
☐ 5 Frank Viola	.05	.02	.01
☐ 6 Cory Snyder	.05	.02	.01
☐ 7 Alan Trammell	.10	.05	.01
☐ 8 Dwight Evans	.10	.05	.01
☐ 9 Tim Leary	.05	.02	.01
☐ 10 Don Mattingly	1.50	.70	.19
☐ 11 Kirby Puckett	1.25	.55	.16
☐ 12 Carney Lansford	.05	.02	.01
☐ 13 Dennis Martinez	.10	.05	.01
☐ 14 Kent Hrbek	.10	.05	.01
☐ 15 Dwight Gooden	.10	.05	.01
☐ 16 Dennis Eckersley	.10	.05	.01
☐ 17 Kevin Seitzer	.05	.02	.01
☐ 18 Lee Smith	.10	.05	.01
☐ 19 Danny Tartabull	.05	.02	.01
☐ 20 Gerald Perry	.05	.02	.01
☐ 21 Gary Gaetti	.10	.05	.01
☐ 22 Rick Reuschel	.05	.02	.01
☐ 23 Keith Hernandez	.10	.05	.01
☐ 24 Jeff Reardon	.10	.05	.01
☐ 25 Mark McGwire	1.00	.45	.12
☐ 26 Juan Samuel	.05	.02	.01
☐ 27 Jack Clark	.05	.02	.01
☐ 28 Robin Yount	.40	.18	.05
☐ 29 Steve Bedrosian	.05	.02	.01
☐ 30 Kirk Gibson	.15	.07	.02
☐ 31 Barry Bonds	.50	.23	.06
☐ 32 Dan Plesac	.05	.02	.01
☐ 33 Steve Sax	.05	.02	.01
☐ 34 Jeff M. Robinson	.05	.02	.01
☐ 35 Orel Hershiser	.10	.05	.01
☐ 36 Julio Franco	.10	.05	.01
☐ 37 Dave Righetti	.05	.02	.01
☐ 38 Bob Knepper	.05	.02	.01
☐ 39 Carlton Fisk	.15	.07	.02
☐ 40 Tony Gwynn	1.25	.55	.16
☐ 41 Doug Jones	.05	.02	.01
☐ 42 Bobby Bonilla	.15	.07	.02
☐ 43 Ellis Burks	.15	.07	.02
☐ 44 Pedro Guerrero	.05	.02	.01
☐ 45 Rickey Henderson	.50	.23	.06
☐ 46 Glenn Davis	.05	.02	.01
☐ 47 Benito Santiago	.10	.05	.01
☐ 48 Greg Maddux	1.75	.80	.22
☐ 49 Teddy Higuera	.05	.02	.01
☐ 50 Darryl Strawberry	.10	.05	.01
☐ 51 Ozzie Guillen	.05	.02	.01
☐ 52 Barry Larkin	.60	.25	.07
☐ 53 Tony Fernandez	.05	.02	.01
☐ 54 Ryne Sandberg	.75	.35	.09
☐ 55 Joe Carter	.25	.11	.03
☐ 56 Rafael Palmeiro	.50	.23	.06
☐ 57 Paul Molitor	.60	.25	.07
☐ 58 Eric Davis	.10	.05	.01
☐ 59 Mike Henneman	.05	.02	.01
☐ 60 Mike Scott	.05	.02	.01
☐ 61 Tom Browning	.05	.02	.01
☐ 62 Mark Davis	.05	.02	.01
☐ 63 Tom Henke	.05	.02	.01
☐ 64 Nolan Ryan	2.50	1.10	.30
☐ 65 Fred McGriff	.50	.23	.06
☐ 66 Dale Murphy	.15	.07	.02
☐ 67 Mark Langston	.05	.02	.01
☐ 68 Bobby Thigpen	.05	.02	.01
☐ 69 Mark Gubicza	.05	.02	.01
☐ 70 Mike Greenwell	.10	.05	.01
☐ 71 Ron Darling	.05	.02	.01
☐ 72 Gerald Young	.05	.02	.01
☐ 73 Wally Joyner	.10	.05	.01
☐ 74 Andres Galarraga	.50	.23	.06
☐ 75 Danny Jackson	.05	.02	.01
☐ 76 Mike Schmidt	.60	.25	.07
☐ 77 Cal Ripken	2.00	.90	.25
☐ 78 Alvin Davis	.05	.02	.01
☐ 79 Bruce Hurst	.05	.02	.01
☐ 80 Andre Dawson	.25	.11	.03
☐ 81 Bob Boone	.10	.05	.01
☐ 82 Harold Reynolds	.10	.05	.01
☐ 83 Eddie Murray	.75	.35	.09
☐ 84 Robby Thompson	.05	.02	.01
☐ 85 Will Clark	.60	.25	.07
☐ 86 Vince Coleman	.05	.02	.01
☐ 87 Doug Drabek	.10	.05	.01
☐ 88 Ozzie Smith	.75	.35	.09
☐ 89 Bob Welch	.05	.02	.01
☐ 90 Roger Clemens	.40	.18	.05
☐ 91 George Bell	.05	.02	.01
☐ 92 Andy Van Slyke	.10	.05	.01
☐ 93 Willie McGee	.10	.05	.01
☐ 94 Todd Worrell	.15	.07	.02
☐ 95 Tim Raines	.10	.05	.01
☐ 96 Kevin McReynolds	.05	.02	.01
☐ 97 John Franco	.10	.05	.01
☐ 98 Jim Gott	.05	.02	.01
☐ 99 Johnny Ray	.05	.02	.01
☐ 100 Wade Boggs	.30	.14	.04

1989 Score Scoremasters

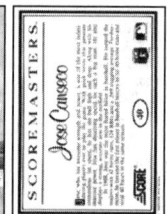

The 1989 Score Scoremasters set contains 42 standard-size cards. The fronts are "pure" with attractively drawn action portraits. The backs feature write-ups of the players' careers. The set was issued in factory set form only.

	MINT	NRMT	EXC
COMPLETE FACT. SET (42)	6.00	2.70	.75
COMMON CARD (1-42)	.05	.02	.01
☐ 1 Bo Jackson	.15	.07	.02
☐ 2 Jerome Walton	.05	.02	.01
☐ 3 Cal Ripken	1.50	.70	.19
☐ 4 Mike Scott	.05	.02	.01
☐ 5 Nolan Ryan	1.50	.70	.19
☐ 6 Don Mattingly	.75	.35	.09
☐ 7 Tom Gordon	.05	.02	.01
☐ 8 Jack Morris	.10	.05	.01
☐ 9 Carlton Fisk	.15	.07	.02
☐ 10 Will Clark	.25	.11	.03
☐ 11 George Brett	.60	.25	.07
☐ 12 Kevin Mitchell	.05	.02	.01
☐ 13 Mark Langston	.05	.02	.01
☐ 14 Dave Stewart	.05	.02	.01
☐ 15 Dale Murphy	.15	.07	.02
☐ 16 Gary Gaetti	.05	.02	.01
☐ 17 Wade Boggs	.25	.11	.03
☐ 18 Eric Davis	.10	.05	.01
☐ 19 Kirby Puckett	1.00	.45	.12
☐ 20 Roger Clemens	.30	.14	.04
☐ 21 Orel Hershiser	.10	.05	.01
☐ 22 Mark Grace	.25	.11	.03
☐ 23 Ryne Sandberg	.60	.25	.07
☐ 24 Barry Larkin	.25	.11	.03
☐ 25 Ellis Burks	.25	.11	.03
☐ 26 Dwight Gooden	.10	.05	.01
☐ 27 Ozzie Smith	.60	.25	.07
☐ 28 Andre Dawson	.10	.05	.01
☐ 29 Julio Franco	.10	.05	.01
☐ 30 Ken Griffey Jr.	2.00	.90	.25
☐ 31 Ruben Sierra	.10	.05	.01
☐ 32 Mark McGwire	.60	.25	.07
☐ 33 Andres Galarraga	.20	.09	.03
☐ 34 Joe Carter	.20	.09	.03
☐ 35 Vince Coleman	.05	.02	.01
☐ 36 Mike Greenwell	.05	.02	.01
☐ 37 Tony Gwynn	.75	.35	.09
☐ 38 Andy Van Slyke	.05	.02	.01
☐ 39 Gregg Jefferies	.20	.09	.03
☐ 40 Jose Canseco	.25	.11	.03
☐ 41 Dave Winfield	.20	.09	.03
☐ 42 Darryl Strawberry	.10	.05	.01

1989 Score Young Superstars I

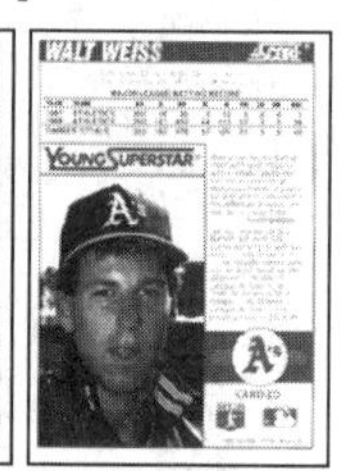

The 1989 Score Young Superstars set I contains 42 standard-size cards. The fronts are pink, white and blue. The vertically oriented backs have color facial shots, 1988 and career stats, and biographical information. One card was included in each 1989 Score rack pack, and the cards were also distributed as a boxed set with five Magic Motion trivia cards.

	MINT	NRMT	EXC
COMPLETE SET (42)	5.00	2.20	.60
COMMON CARD (1-42)	.05	.02	.01
☐ 1 Gregg Jefferies	.30	.14	.04
☐ 2 Jody Reed	.05	.02	.01
☐ 3 Mark Grace	.75	.35	.09
☐ 4 Dave Gallagher	.05	.02	.01
☐ 5 Bo Jackson	.20	.09	.03
☐ 6 Jay Buhner	.60	.25	.07
☐ 7 Melido Perez	.05	.02	.01
☐ 8 Bobby Witt	.05	.02	.01
☐ 9 David Cone	.30	.14	.04
☐ 10 Chris Sabo	.05	.02	.01
☐ 11 Pat Borders	.05	.02	.01
☐ 12 Mark Grant	.05	.02	.01
☐ 13 Mike Macfarlane	.05	.02	.01
☐ 14 Mike Jackson	.05	.02	.01
☐ 15 Ricky Jordan	.05	.02	.01
☐ 16 Ron Gant	.30	.14	.04
☐ 17 Al Leiter	.20	.09	.03
☐ 18 Jeff Parrett	.05	.02	.01
☐ 19 Pete Smith	.05	.02	.01
☐ 20 Walt Weiss	.05	.02	.01
☐ 21 Doug Drabek	.10	.05	.01
☐ 22 Kirt Manwaring	.05	.02	.01
☐ 23 Keith Miller	.05	.02	.01
☐ 24 Damon Berryhill	.05	.02	.01
☐ 25 Gary Sheffield	1.00	.45	.12
☐ 26 Brady Anderson	1.00	.45	.12
☐ 27 Mitch Williams	.05	.02	.01
☐ 28 Roberto Alomar	1.00	.45	.12
☐ 29 Bobby Thigpen	.05	.02	.01
☐ 30 Bryan Harvey UER (47 games in '87)	.10	.05	.01
☐ 31 Jose Rijo	.05	.02	.01
☐ 32 Dave West	.05	.02	.01
☐ 33 Joey Meyer	.05	.02	.01
☐ 34 Allan Anderson	.05	.02	.01
☐ 35 Rafael Palmeiro	.50	.23	.06
☐ 36 Tim Belcher	.05	.02	.01
☐ 37 John Smiley	.05	.02	.01
☐ 38 Mackey Sasser	.05	.02	.01
☐ 39 Greg Maddux	2.00	.90	.25
☐ 40 Ramon Martinez	.50	.23	.06
☐ 41 Randy Myers	.10	.05	.01
☐ 42 Scott Bankhead	.05	.02	.01

1989 Score Young Superstars II

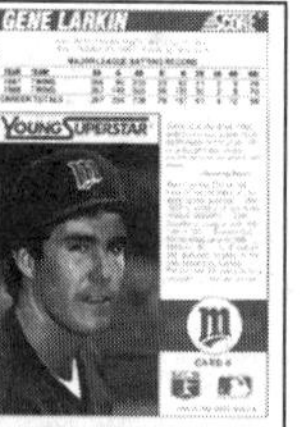

The 1989 Score Young Superstars II set contains 42 standard-size cards. The fronts are orange, white and purple. The vertically oriented backs have color facial shots, 1988 and career stats, and biographical information. The cards were distributed as a boxed set with five Magic Motion trivia cards.

	MINT	NRMT	EXC
COMPLETE SET (42)	4.00	1.80	.50
COMMON CARD (1-42)	.05	.02	.01

☐ 1 Sandy Alomar Jr. .25 .11 .03
☐ 2 Tom Gordon .15 .07 .02
☐ 3 Ron Jones .05 .02 .01
☐ 4 Todd Burns .05 .02 .01
☐ 5 Paul O'Neill .25 .11 .03
☐ 6 Gene Larkin .05 .02 .01
☐ 7 Eric King .05 .02 .01
☐ 8 Jeff M. Robinson .05 .02 .01
☐ 9 Bill Wegman .05 .02 .01
☐ 10 Cecil Espy .05 .02 .01
☐ 11 Jose Guzman .05 .02 .01
☐ 12 Kelly Gruber .05 .02 .01
☐ 13 Duane Ward .05 .02 .01
☐ 14 Mark Gubicza .05 .02 .01
☐ 15 Norm Charlton .15 .07 .02
☐ 16 Jose Oquendo .05 .02 .01
☐ 17 Geronimo Berroa .15 .07 .02
☐ 18 Ken Griffey Jr. 2.50 1.10 .30
☐ 19 Lance McCullers .05 .02 .01
☐ 20 Todd Stottlemyre .15 .07 .02
☐ 21 Craig Worthington .05 .02 .01
☐ 22 Mike Devereaux .05 .02 .01
☐ 23 Tom Glavine .50 .23 .06
☐ 24 Dale Sveum .05 .02 .01
☐ 25 Roberto Kelly .15 .07 .02
☐ 26 Luis Medina .05 .02 .01
☐ 27 Steve Searcy .05 .02 .01
☐ 28 Don August .05 .02 .01
☐ 29 Shawn Hillegas .05 .02 .01
☐ 30 Mike Campbell .05 .02 .01
☐ 31 Mike Harkey .05 .02 .01
☐ 32 Randy Johnson .75 .35 .09
☐ 33 Craig Biggio .50 .23 .06
☐ 34 Mike Schooler .05 .02 .01
☐ 35 Andres Thomas .05 .02 .01
☐ 36 Jerome Walton .05 .02 .01
☐ 37 Cris Carpenter .05 .02 .01
☐ 38 Kevin Mitchell .15 .07 .02
☐ 39 Eddie Williams .05 .02 .01
☐ 40 Chad Kreuter .05 .02 .01
☐ 41 Danny Jackson .05 .02 .01
☐ 42 Kurt Stillwell .05 .02 .01

1990 Score

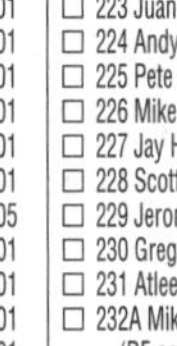

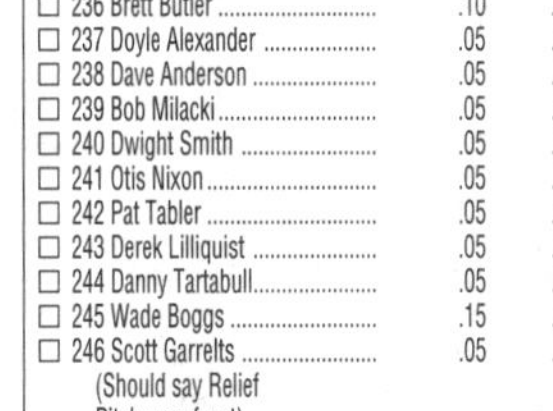
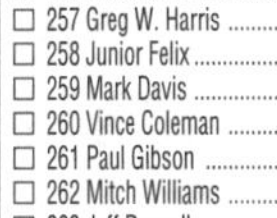
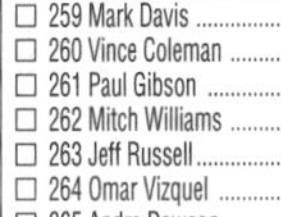

The 1990 Score set contains 704 standard-size cards. The front borders are red, blue, green or white. The vertically oriented backs are white with borders that match the fronts, and feature color mugshots. Subsets include Draft Picks (661-682) and Dream Team (683-695). Rookie Cards of note include Juan Gonzalez, Marquis Grissom, Dave Justice, Chuck Knoblauch, Ben McDonald, Dean Palmer, Sammy Sosa, Frank Thomas, Mo Vaughn, Larry Walker and Bernie Williams. A ten-card set of Dream Team Rookies was inserted into each hobby factory set, but was not included in retail factory sets.

	MINT	NRMT	EXC
COMPLETE SET (704)	10.00	4.50	1.25
COMPLETE RETAIL SET (704)	10.00	4.50	1.25
COMPLETE HOBBY SET (714)	15.00	6.75	1.85
COMMON CARD (1-704)	.05	.02	.01

☐ 1 Don Mattingly .50 .23 .06
☐ 2 Cal Ripken .75 .35 .09
☐ 3 Dwight Evans .10 .05 .01
☐ 4 Barry Bonds .25 .11 .03
☐ 5 Kevin McReynolds .05 .02 .01
☐ 6 Ozzie Guillen .05 .02 .01
☐ 7 Terry Kennedy .05 .02 .01
☐ 8 Bryan Harvey .05 .02 .01
☐ 9 Alan Trammell .10 .05 .01
☐ 10 Cory Snyder .05 .02 .01
☐ 11 Jody Reed .05 .02 .01
☐ 12 Roberto Alomar .25 .11 .03
☐ 13 Pedro Guerrero .05 .02 .01
☐ 14 Gary Redus .05 .02 .01
☐ 15 Marty Barrett .05 .02 .01
☐ 16 Ricky Jordan .05 .02 .01
☐ 17 Joe Magrane .05 .02 .01
☐ 18 Sid Fernandez .05 .02 .01
☐ 19 Richard Dotson .05 .02 .01
☐ 20 Jack Clark .10 .05 .01
☐ 21 Bob Walk .05 .02 .01
☐ 22 Ron Karkovice .05 .02 .01
☐ 23 Lenny Harris .05 .02 .01
☐ 24 Phil Bradley .05 .02 .01
☐ 25 Andres Galarraga .15 .07 .02
☐ 26 Brian Downing .05 .02 .01
☐ 27 Dave Martinez .05 .02 .01
☐ 28 Eric King .05 .02 .01
☐ 29 Barry Lyons .05 .02 .01
☐ 30 Dave Schmidt .05 .02 .01
☐ 31 Mike Boddicker .05 .02 .01
☐ 32 Tom Foley .05 .02 .01
☐ 33 Brady Anderson .15 .07 .02
☐ 34 Jim Presley .05 .02 .01
☐ 35 Lance Parrish .05 .02 .01
☐ 36 Von Hayes .05 .02 .01
☐ 37 Lee Smith .10 .05 .01
☐ 38 Herm Winningham .05 .02 .01
☐ 39 Alejandro Pena .05 .02 .01
☐ 40 Mike Scott .05 .02 .01
☐ 41 Joe Orsulak .05 .02 .01
☐ 42 Rafael Ramirez .05 .02 .01
☐ 43 Gerald Young .05 .02 .01
☐ 44 Dick Schofield .05 .02 .01
☐ 45 Dave Smith .05 .02 .01
☐ 46 Dave Magadan .05 .02 .01
☐ 47 Dennis Martinez .10 .05 .01
☐ 48 Greg Minton .05 .02 .01
☐ 49 Milt Thompson .05 .02 .01
☐ 50 Orel Hershiser .10 .05 .01
☐ 51 Bip Roberts .05 .02 .01
☐ 52 Jerry Browne .05 .02 .01
☐ 53 Bob Ojeda .05 .02 .01
☐ 54 Fernando Valenzuela .10 .05 .01
☐ 55 Matt Nokes .05 .02 .01
☐ 56 Brook Jacoby .05 .02 .01
☐ 57 Frank Tanana .05 .02 .01
☐ 58 Scott Fletcher .05 .02 .01
☐ 59 Ron Oester .05 .02 .01
☐ 60 Bob Boone .10 .05 .01
☐ 61 Dan Gladden .05 .02 .01
☐ 62 Darnell Coles .05 .02 .01
☐ 63 Gregg Olson .05 .02 .01
☐ 64 Todd Burns .05 .02 .01
☐ 65 Todd Benzinger .05 .02 .01
☐ 66 Dale Murphy .15 .07 .02
☐ 67 Mike Flanagan .05 .02 .01
☐ 68 Jose Oquendo .05 .02 .01
☐ 69 Cecil Espy .05 .02 .01
☐ 70 Chris Sabo .05 .02 .01
☐ 71 Shane Rawley .05 .02 .01
☐ 72 Tom Brunansky .05 .02 .01
☐ 73 Vance Law .05 .02 .01
☐ 74 B.J. Surhoff .10 .05 .01
☐ 75 Lou Whitaker .10 .05 .01
☐ 76 Ken Caminiti UER .20 .09 .03
(Euclid, Ohio should be Hanford, California)
☐ 77 Nelson Liriano .05 .02 .01
☐ 78 Tommy Gregg .05 .02 .01
☐ 79 Don Slaught .05 .02 .01
☐ 80 Eddie Murray .25 .11 .03
☐ 81 Joe Boever .05 .02 .01
☐ 82 Charlie Leibrandt .05 .02 .01
☐ 83 Jose Lind .05 .02 .01
☐ 84 Tony Phillips .15 .07 .02
☐ 85 Mitch Webster .05 .02 .01
☐ 86 Dan Plesac .05 .02 .01
☐ 87 Rick Mahler .05 .02 .01
☐ 88 Steve Lyons .05 .02 .01
☐ 89 Tony Fernandez .05 .02 .01
☐ 90 Ryne Sandberg .25 .11 .03
☐ 91 Nick Esasky .05 .02 .01
☐ 92 Luis Salazar .05 .02 .01
☐ 93 Pete Incaviglia .05 .02 .01
☐ 94 Ivan Calderon .05 .02 .01
☐ 95 Jeff Treadway .05 .02 .01
☐ 96 Kurt Stillwell .05 .02 .01
☐ 97 Gary Sheffield .25 .11 .03
☐ 98 Jeffrey Leonard .05 .02 .01
☐ 99 Andres Thomas .05 .02 .01
☐ 100 Roberto Kelly .10 .05 .01
☐ 101 Alvaro Espinoza .05 .02 .01
☐ 102 Greg Gagne .05 .02 .01
☐ 103 John Farrell .05 .02 .01
☐ 104 Willie Wilson .05 .02 .01
☐ 105 Glenn Braggs .05 .02 .01
☐ 106 Chet Lemon .05 .02 .01
☐ 107A Jamie Moyer ERR .05 .02 .01
(Scintilating)
☐ 107B Jamie Moyer COR .10 .05 .01
(Scintillating)
☐ 108 Chuck Crim .05 .02 .01
☐ 109 Dave Valle .05 .02 .01
☐ 110 Walt Weiss .05 .02 .01
☐ 111 Larry Sheets .05 .02 .01
☐ 112 Don Robinson .05 .02 .01
☐ 113 Danny Heep .05 .02 .01
☐ 114 Carmelo Martinez .05 .02 .01
☐ 115 Dave Gallagher .05 .02 .01
☐ 116 Mike LaValliere .05 .02 .01
☐ 117 Bob McClure .05 .02 .01
☐ 118 Rene Gonzales .05 .02 .01
☐ 119 Mark Parent .05 .02 .01
☐ 120 Wally Joyner .10 .05 .01
☐ 121 Mark Gubicza .05 .02 .01
☐ 122 Tony Pena .05 .02 .01
☐ 123 Carmen Castillo .05 .02 .01
☐ 124 Howard Johnson .05 .02 .01
☐ 125 Steve Sax .05 .02 .01
☐ 126 Tim Belcher .05 .02 .01
☐ 127 Tim Burke .05 .02 .01
☐ 128 Al Newman .05 .02 .01
☐ 129 Dennis Rasmussen .05 .02 .01
☐ 130 Doug Jones .05 .02 .01
☐ 131 Fred Lynn .05 .02 .01
☐ 132 Jeff Hamilton .05 .02 .01
☐ 133 German Gonzalez .05 .02 .01
☐ 134 John Morris .05 .02 .01
☐ 135 Dave Parker .10 .05 .01
☐ 136 Gary Pettis .05 .02 .01
☐ 137 Dennis Boyd .05 .02 .01
☐ 138 Candy Maldonado .05 .02 .01
☐ 139 Rick Cerone .05 .02 .01
☐ 140 George Brett .40 .18 .05
☐ 141 Dave Clark .05 .02 .01
☐ 142 Dickie Thon .05 .02 .01
☐ 143 Junior Ortiz .05 .02 .01
☐ 144 Don August .05 .02 .01
☐ 145 Gary Gaetti .10 .05 .01
☐ 146 Kirt Manwaring .05 .02 .01
☐ 147 Jeff Reed .05 .02 .01
☐ 148 Jose Alvarez .05 .02 .01
☐ 149 Mike Schooler .05 .02 .01
☐ 150 Mark Grace .15 .07 .02
☐ 151 Geronimo Berroa .10 .05 .01
☐ 152 Barry Jones .05 .02 .01
☐ 153 Geno Petralli .05 .02 .01
☐ 154 Jim Deshaies .05 .02 .01
☐ 155 Barry Larkin .15 .07 .02
☐ 156 Alfredo Griffin .05 .02 .01
☐ 157 Tom Henke .05 .02 .01
☐ 158 Mike Jeffcoat .05 .02 .01
☐ 159 Bob Welch .05 .02 .01
☐ 160 Julio Franco .10 .05 .01
☐ 161 Henry Cotto .05 .02 .01
☐ 162 Terry Steinbach .10 .05 .01
☐ 163 Damon Berryhill .05 .02 .01
☐ 164 Tim Crews .05 .02 .01
☐ 165 Tom Browning .05 .02 .01
☐ 166 Fred Manrique .05 .02 .01
☐ 167 Harold Reynolds .05 .02 .01
☐ 168A Ron Hassey ERR .05 .02 .01
(27 on back)
☐ 168B Ron Hassey COR .50 .23 .06
(24 on back)
☐ 169 Shawon Dunston .05 .02 .01
☐ 170 Bobby Bonilla .10 .05 .01
☐ 171 Tommy Herr .05 .02 .01
☐ 172 Mike Heath .05 .02 .01
☐ 173 Rich Gedman .05 .02 .01
☐ 174 Bill Ripken .05 .02 .01
☐ 175 Pete O'Brien .05 .02 .01
☐ 176A Lloyd McClendon ERR .50 .23 .06
(Uniform number on back listed as 1)
☐ 176B Lloyd McClendon COR .05 .02 .01
(Uniform number on back listed as 10)
☐ 177 Brian Holton .05 .02 .01
☐ 178 Jeff Blauser .10 .05 .01
☐ 179 Jim Eisenreich .05 .02 .01
☐ 180 Bert Blyleven .10 .05 .01
☐ 181 Rob Murphy .05 .02 .01
☐ 182 Bill Doran .05 .02 .01
☐ 183 Curt Ford .05 .02 .01
☐ 184 Mike Henneman .05 .02 .01
☐ 185 Eric Davis .10 .05 .01
☐ 186 Lance McCullers .05 .02 .01
☐ 187 Steve Davis .05 .02 .01
☐ 188 Bill Wegman .05 .02 .01
☐ 189 Brian Harper .05 .02 .01
☐ 190 Mike Moore .05 .02 .01
☐ 191 Dale Mohorcic .05 .02 .01
☐ 192 Tim Wallach .05 .02 .01
☐ 193 Keith Hernandez .10 .05 .01
☐ 194 Dave Righetti .05 .02 .01
☐ 195A Bret Saberhagen ERR .10 .05 .01
(Joke)
☐ 195B Bret Saberhagen COR .10 .05 .01
(Joker)
☐ 196 Paul Kilgus .05 .02 .01
☐ 197 Bud Black .05 .02 .01
☐ 198 Juan Samuel .05 .02 .01
☐ 199 Kevin Seitzer .05 .02 .01
☐ 200 Darryl Strawberry .10 .05 .01
☐ 201 Dave Stieb .05 .02 .01
☐ 202 Charlie Hough .05 .02 .01
☐ 203 Jack Morris .10 .05 .01
☐ 204 Rance Mulliniks .05 .02 .01
☐ 205 Alvin Davis .05 .02 .01
☐ 206 Jack Howell .05 .02 .01
☐ 207 Ken Patterson .05 .02 .01
☐ 208 Terry Pendleton .10 .05 .01
☐ 209 Craig Lefferts .05 .02 .01
☐ 210 Kevin Brown UER .15 .07 .02
(First mention of '89 Rangers should be '88)
☐ 211 Dan Petry .05 .02 .01
☐ 212 Dave Leiper .05 .02 .01
☐ 213 Daryl Boston .05 .02 .01
☐ 214 Kevin Hickey .05 .02 .01
☐ 215 Mike Krukow .05 .02 .01
☐ 216 Terry Francona .05 .02 .01
☐ 217 Kirk McCaskill .05 .02 .01
☐ 218 Scott Bailes .05 .02 .01
☐ 219 Bob Forsch .05 .02 .01
☐ 220A Mike Aldrete ERR .05 .02 .01
(25 on back)
☐ 220B Mike Aldrete COR .10 .05 .01
(24 on back)
☐ 221 Steve Buechele .05 .02 .01
☐ 222 Jesse Barfield .05 .02 .01
☐ 223 Juan Berenguer .05 .02 .01
☐ 224 Andy McGaffigan .05 .02 .01
☐ 225 Pete Smith .05 .02 .01
☐ 226 Mike Witt .05 .02 .01
☐ 227 Jay Howell .05 .02 .01
☐ 228 Scott Bradley .05 .02 .01
☐ 229 Jerome Walton .05 .02 .01
☐ 230 Greg Swindell .05 .02 .01
☐ 231 Atlee Hammaker .05 .02 .01
☐ 232A Mike Devereaux ERR .05 .02 .01
(RF on front)
☐ 232B Mike Devereaux COR .50 .23 .06
(CF on front)
☐ 233 Ken Hill .15 .07 .02
☐ 234 Craig Worthington .05 .02 .01
☐ 235 Scott Terry .05 .02 .01
☐ 236 Brett Butler .10 .05 .01
☐ 237 Doyle Alexander .05 .02 .01
☐ 238 Dave Anderson .05 .02 .01
☐ 239 Bob Milacki .05 .02 .01
☐ 240 Dwight Smith .05 .02 .01
☐ 241 Otis Nixon .05 .02 .01
☐ 242 Pat Tabler .05 .02 .01
☐ 243 Derek Lilliquist .05 .02 .01
☐ 244 Danny Tartabull .05 .02 .01
☐ 245 Wade Boggs .15 .07 .02
☐ 246 Scott Garrelts .05 .02 .01
(Should say Relief Pitcher on front)
☐ 247 Spike Owen .05 .02 .01
☐ 248 Norm Charlton .05 .02 .01
☐ 249 Gerald Perry .05 .02 .01
☐ 250 Nolan Ryan .75 .35 .09
☐ 251 Kevin Gross .05 .02 .01
☐ 252 Randy Milligan .05 .02 .01
☐ 253 Mike LaCoss .05 .02 .01
☐ 254 Dave Bergman .05 .02 .01
☐ 255 Tony Gwynn .40 .18 .05
☐ 256 Felix Fermin .05 .02 .01
☐ 257 Greg W. Harris .05 .02 .01
☐ 258 Junior Felix .05 .02 .01
☐ 259 Mark Davis .05 .02 .01
☐ 260 Vince Coleman .05 .02 .01
☐ 261 Paul Gibson .05 .02 .01
☐ 262 Mitch Williams .05 .02 .01
☐ 263 Jeff Russell .05 .02 .01
☐ 264 Omar Vizquel .15 .07 .02
☐ 265 Andre Dawson .10 .05 .01
☐ 266 Storm Davis .05 .02 .01
☐ 267 Guillermo Hernandez .05 .02 .01
☐ 268 Mike Felder .05 .02 .01
☐ 269 Tom Candiotti .05 .02 .01
☐ 270 Bruce Hurst .05 .02 .01
☐ 271 Fred McGriff .15 .07 .02
☐ 272 Glenn Davis .05 .02 .01
☐ 273 John Franco .05 .02 .01
☐ 274 Rich Yett .05 .02 .01
☐ 275 Craig Biggio .15 .07 .02
☐ 276 Gene Larkin .05 .02 .01
☐ 277 Rob Dibble .05 .02 .01
☐ 278 Randy Bush .05 .02 .01
☐ 279 Kevin Bass .05 .02 .01
☐ 280A Bo Jackson ERR .10 .05 .01
(Watham)
☐ 280B Bo Jackson COR .10 .05 .01
(Wathan)
☐ 281 Wally Backman .05 .02 .01
☐ 282 Larry Andersen .05 .02 .01
☐ 283 Chris Bosio .05 .02 .01
☐ 284 Juan Agosto .05 .02 .01
☐ 285 Ozzie Smith .25 .11 .03
☐ 286 George Bell .05 .02 .01
☐ 287 Rex Hudler .05 .02 .01
☐ 288 Pat Borders .05 .02 .01
☐ 289 Danny Jackson .05 .02 .01
☐ 290 Carlton Fisk .15 .07 .02
☐ 291 Tracy Jones .05 .02 .01
☐ 292 Allan Anderson .05 .02 .01
☐ 293 Johnny Ray .05 .02 .01
☐ 294 Lee Guetterman .05 .02 .01
☐ 295 Paul O'Neill .10 .05 .01
☐ 296 Carney Lansford .10 .05 .01
☐ 297 Tom Brookens .05 .02 .01
☐ 298 Claudell Washington .05 .02 .01
☐ 299 Hubie Brooks .05 .02 .01
☐ 300 Will Clark .15 .07 .02
☐ 301 Kenny Rogers .10 .05 .01
☐ 302 Darrell Evans .10 .05 .01
☐ 303 Greg Briley .05 .02 .01
☐ 304 Donn Pall .05 .02 .01
☐ 305 Teddy Higuera .05 .02 .01
☐ 306 Dan Pasqua .05 .02 .01
☐ 307 Dave Winfield .15 .07 .02
☐ 308 Dennis Powell .05 .02 .01
☐ 309 Jose DeLeon .05 .02 .01
☐ 310 Roger Clemens UER .20 .09 .03
(Dominate, should say dominant)
☐ 311 Melido Perez .05 .02 .01
☐ 312 Devon White .10 .05 .01
☐ 313 Dwight Gooden .10 .05 .01
☐ 314 Carlos Martinez .05 .02 .01
☐ 315 Dennis Eckersley .10 .05 .01

☐ 316 Clay Parker UER .05 .02 .01
(Height 6'11")
☐ 317 Rick Honeycutt .05 .02 .01
☐ 318 Tim Laudner .05 .02 .01
☐ 319 Joe Carter .10 .05 .01
☐ 320 Robin Yount .15 .07 .02
☐ 321 Felix Jose .05 .02 .01
☐ 322 Mickey Tettleton .10 .05 .01
☐ 323 Mike Gallego .05 .02 .01
☐ 324 Edgar Martinez .15 .07 .02
☐ 325 Dave Henderson .05 .02 .01
☐ 326 Chili Davis .10 .05 .01
☐ 327 Steve Balboni .05 .02 .01
☐ 328 Jody Davis .05 .02 .01
☐ 329 Shawn Hillegas .05 .02 .01
☐ 330 Jim Abbott .10 .05 .01
☐ 331 John Dopson .05 .02 .01
☐ 332 Mark Williamson .05 .02 .01
☐ 333 Jeff D. Robinson .05 .02 .01
☐ 334 John Smiley .10 .05 .01
☐ 335 Bobby Thigpen .05 .02 .01
☐ 336 Garry Templeton .05 .02 .01
☐ 337 Marvell Wynne .05 .02 .01
☐ 338A Ken Griffey Sr. ERR .05 .02 .01
(Uniform number on back listed as 25)
☐ 338B Ken Griffey Sr. COR .50 .23 .06
(Uniform number on back listed as 30)
☐ 339 Steve Finley .15 .07 .02
☐ 340 Ellis Burks .15 .07 .02
☐ 341 Frank Williams .05 .02 .01
☐ 342 Mike Morgan .05 .02 .01
☐ 343 Kevin Mitchell .10 .05 .01
☐ 344 Joel Youngblood .05 .02 .01
☐ 345 Mike Greenwell .05 .02 .01
☐ 346 Glenn Wilson .05 .02 .01
☐ 347 John Costello .05 .02 .01
☐ 348 Wes Gardner .05 .02 .01
☐ 349 Jeff Ballard .05 .02 .01
☐ 350 Mark Thurmond UER .05 .02 .01
(ERA is 192, should be 1.92)
☐ 351 Randy Myers .10 .05 .01
☐ 352 Shawn Abner .05 .02 .01
☐ 353 Jesse Orosco .05 .02 .01
☐ 354 Greg Walker .05 .02 .01
☐ 355 Pete Harnisch .05 .02 .01
☐ 356 Steve Farr .05 .02 .01
☐ 357 Dave LaPoint .05 .02 .01
☐ 358 Willie Fraser .05 .02 .01
☐ 359 Mickey Hatcher .05 .02 .01
☐ 360 Rickey Henderson .15 .07 .02
☐ 361 Mike Fitzgerald .05 .02 .01
☐ 362 Bill Schroeder .05 .02 .01
☐ 363 Mark Carreon .05 .02 .01
☐ 364 Ron Jones .05 .02 .01
☐ 365 Jeff Montgomery .10 .05 .01
☐ 366 Bill Krueger .05 .02 .01
☐ 367 John Cangelosi .05 .02 .01
☐ 368 Jose Gonzalez .05 .02 .01
☐ 369 Greg Hibbard .05 .02 .01
☐ 370 John Smoltz .25 .11 .03
☐ 371 Jeff Brantley .10 .05 .01
☐ 372 Frank White .10 .05 .01
☐ 373 Ed Whitson .05 .02 .01
☐ 374 Willie McGee .05 .02 .01
☐ 375 Jose Canseco .15 .07 .02
☐ 376 Randy Ready .05 .02 .01
☐ 377 Don Aase .05 .02 .01
☐ 378 Tony Armas .05 .02 .01
☐ 379 Steve Bedrosian .05 .02 .01
☐ 380 Chuck Finley .10 .05 .01
☐ 381 Kent Hrbek .10 .05 .01
☐ 382 Jim Gantner .05 .02 .01
☐ 383 Mel Hall .05 .02 .01
☐ 384 Mike Marshall .05 .02 .01
☐ 385 Mark McGwire .30 .14 .04
☐ 386 Wayne Tolleson .05 .02 .01
☐ 387 Brian Holman .05 .02 .01
☐ 388 John Wetteland .15 .07 .02
☐ 389 Darren Daulton .10 .05 .01
☐ 390 Rob Deer .05 .02 .01
☐ 391 John Moses .05 .02 .01
☐ 392 Todd Worrell .05 .02 .01
☐ 393 Chuck Cary .05 .02 .01
☐ 394 Stan Javier .05 .02 .01
☐ 395 Willie Randolph .10 .05 .01
☐ 396 Bill Buckner .05 .02 .01
☐ 397 Robby Thompson .05 .02 .01
☐ 398 Mike Scioscia .05 .02 .01
☐ 399 Lonnie Smith .05 .02 .01
☐ 400 Kirby Puckett .40 .18 .05
☐ 401 Mark Langston .10 .05 .01
☐ 402 Danny Darwin .05 .02 .01
☐ 403 Greg Maddux .60 .25 .07
☐ 404 Lloyd Moseby .05 .02 .01
☐ 405 Rafael Palmeiro .15 .07 .02
☐ 406 Chad Kreuter .05 .02 .01
☐ 407 Jimmy Key .10 .05 .01
☐ 408 Tim Birtsas .05 .02 .01
☐ 409 Tim Raines .15 .07 .02
☐ 410 Dave Stewart .10 .05 .01
☐ 411 Eric Yelding .05 .02 .01
☐ 412 Kent Anderson .05 .02 .01
☐ 413 Les Lancaster .05 .02 .01
☐ 414 Rick Dempsey .05 .02 .01
☐ 415 Randy Johnson .25 .11 .03
☐ 416 Gary Carter .10 .05 .01
☐ 417 Rolando Roomes .05 .02 .01
☐ 418 Dan Schatzeder .05 .02 .01
☐ 419 Bryn Smith .05 .02 .01
☐ 420 Ruben Sierra .10 .05 .01
☐ 421 Steve Jeltz .05 .02 .01
☐ 422 Ken Oberkfell .05 .02 .01
☐ 423 Sid Bream .05 .02 .01
☐ 424 Jim Clancy .05 .02 .01
☐ 425 Kelly Gruber .05 .02 .01
☐ 426 Rick Leach .05 .02 .01
☐ 427 Len Dykstra .10 .05 .01
☐ 428 Jeff Pico .05 .02 .01
☐ 429 John Cerutti .05 .02 .01
☐ 430 David Cone .15 .07 .02
☐ 431 Jeff Kunkel .05 .02 .01
☐ 432 Luis Aquino .05 .02 .01
☐ 433 Ernie Whitt .05 .02 .01
☐ 434 Bo Diaz .05 .02 .01
☐ 435 Steve Lake .05 .02 .01
☐ 436 Pat Perry .05 .02 .01
☐ 437 Mike Davis .05 .02 .01
☐ 438 Cecilio Guante .05 .02 .01
☐ 439 Duane Ward .05 .02 .01
☐ 440 Andy Van Slyke .10 .05 .01
☐ 441 Gene Nelson .05 .02 .01
☐ 442 Luis Polonia .05 .02 .01
☐ 443 Kevin Elster .05 .02 .01
☐ 444 Keith Moreland .05 .02 .01
☐ 445 Roger McDowell .05 .02 .01
☐ 446 Ron Darling .05 .02 .01
☐ 447 Ernest Riles .05 .02 .01
☐ 448 Mookie Wilson .05 .02 .01
☐ 449A Billy Spiers ERR .15 .07 .02
(No birth year)
☐ 449B Billy Spiers COR .05 .02 .01
(Born in 1966)
☐ 450 Rick Sutcliffe .05 .02 .01
☐ 451 Nelson Santovenia .05 .02 .01
☐ 452 Andy Allanson .05 .02 .01
☐ 453 Bob Melvin .05 .02 .01
☐ 454 Benito Santiago .05 .02 .01
☐ 455 Jose Uribe .05 .02 .01
☐ 456 Bill Landrum .05 .02 .01
☐ 457 Bobby Witt .05 .02 .01
☐ 458 Kevin Romine .05 .02 .01
☐ 459 Lee Mazzilli .05 .02 .01
☐ 460 Paul Molitor .20 .09 .03
☐ 461 Ramon Martinez .15 .07 .02
☐ 462 Frank DiPino .05 .02 .01
☐ 463 Walt Terrell .05 .02 .01
☐ 464 Bob Geren .05 .02 .01
☐ 465 Rick Reuschel .05 .02 .01
☐ 466 Mark Grant .05 .02 .01
☐ 467 John Kruk .10 .05 .01
☐ 468 Gregg Jefferies .10 .05 .01
☐ 469 R.J. Reynolds .05 .02 .01
☐ 470 Harold Baines .10 .05 .01
☐ 471 Dennis Lamp .05 .02 .01
☐ 472 Tom Gordon .05 .02 .01
☐ 473 Terry Puhl .05 .02 .01
☐ 474 Curt Wilkerson .05 .02 .01
☐ 475 Dan Quisenberry .05 .02 .01
☐ 476 Oddibe McDowell .05 .02 .01
☐ 477A Zane Smith ERR .05 .02 .01
(Career ERA .393)
☐ 477B Zane Smith COR .05 .02 .01
(career ERA 3.93)
☐ 478 Franklin Stubbs .05 .02 .01
☐ 479 Wallace Johnson .05 .02 .01
☐ 480 Jay Tibbs .05 .02 .01
☐ 481 Tom Glavine .15 .07 .02
☐ 482 Manny Lee .05 .02 .01
☐ 483 Joe Hesketh UER .05 .02 .01
(Says Rookiess on back, should say Rookies)
☐ 484 Mike Bielecki .05 .02 .01
☐ 485 Greg Brock .05 .02 .01
☐ 486 Pascual Perez .05 .02 .01
☐ 487 Kirk Gibson .10 .05 .01
☐ 488 Scott Sanderson .05 .02 .01
☐ 489 Domingo Ramos .05 .02 .01
☐ 490 Kal Daniels .05 .02 .01
☐ 491A David Wells ERR .50 .23 .06
(Reverse negative photo on card back)
☐ 491B David Wells COR .05 .02 .01
☐ 492 Jerry Reed .05 .02 .01
☐ 493 Eric Show .05 .02 .01
☐ 494 Mike Pagliarulo .05 .02 .01
☐ 495 Ron Robinson .05 .02 .01
☐ 496 Brad Komminsk .05 .02 .01
☐ 497 Greg Litton .05 .02 .01
☐ 498 Chris James .05 .02 .01
☐ 499 Luis Quinones .05 .02 .01
☐ 500 Frank Viola .05 .02 .01
☐ 501 Tim Teufel UER .05 .02 .01
(Twins '85, the s is lower case, should be upper case)
☐ 502 Terry Leach .05 .02 .01
☐ 503 Matt Williams UER .15 .07 .02
(Wearing 10 on front, listed as 9 on back)
☐ 504 Tim Leary .05 .02 .01
☐ 505 Doug Drabek .05 .02 .01
☐ 506 Mariano Duncan .05 .02 .01
☐ 507 Charlie Hayes .10 .05 .01
☐ 508 Joey Belle .75 .35 .09
☐ 509 Pat Sheridan .05 .02 .01
☐ 510 Mackey Sasser .05 .02 .01
☐ 511 Jose Rijo .05 .02 .01
☐ 512 Mike Smithson .05 .02 .01
☐ 513 Gary Ward .05 .02 .01
☐ 514 Dion James .05 .02 .01
☐ 515 Jim Gott .05 .02 .01
☐ 516 Drew Hall .05 .02 .01
☐ 517 Doug Bair .05 .02 .01
☐ 518 Scott Scudder .05 .02 .01
☐ 519 Rick Aguilera .10 .05 .01
☐ 520 Rafael Belliard .05 .02 .01
☐ 521 Jay Buhner .15 .07 .02
☐ 522 Jeff Reardon .10 .05 .01
☐ 523 Steve Rosenberg .05 .02 .01
☐ 524 Randy Velarde .05 .02 .01
☐ 525 Jeff Musselman .05 .02 .01
☐ 526 Bill Long .05 .02 .01
☐ 527 Gary Wayne .05 .02 .01
☐ 528 Dave Johnson (P) .05 .02 .01
☐ 529 Ron Kittle .05 .02 .01
☐ 530 Erik Hanson UER .10 .05 .01
(5th line on back says seson, should say season)
☐ 531 Steve Wilson .05 .02 .01
☐ 532 Joey Meyer .05 .02 .01
☐ 533 Curt Young .05 .02 .01
☐ 534 Kelly Downs .05 .02 .01
☐ 535 Joe Girardi .10 .05 .01
☐ 536 Lance Blankenship .05 .02 .01
☐ 537 Greg Mathews .05 .02 .01
☐ 538 Donell Nixon .05 .02 .01
☐ 539 Mark Knudson .05 .02 .01
☐ 540 Jeff Wetherby .05 .02 .01
☐ 541 Darrin Jackson .05 .02 .01
☐ 542 Terry Mulholland .05 .02 .01
☐ 543 Eric Hetzel .05 .02 .01
☐ 544 Rick Reed .05 .02 .01
☐ 545 Dennis Cook .05 .02 .01
☐ 546 Mike Jackson .05 .02 .01
☐ 547 Brian Fisher .05 .02 .01
☐ 548 Gene Harris .05 .02 .01
☐ 549 Jeff King .10 .05 .01
☐ 550 Dave Dravecky .15 .07 .02
☐ 551 Randy Kutcher .05 .02 .01
☐ 552 Mark Portugal .05 .02 .01
☐ 553 Jim Corsi .05 .02 .01
☐ 554 Todd Stottlemyre .10 .05 .01
☐ 555 Scott Bankhead .05 .02 .01
☐ 556 Ken Dayley .05 .02 .01
☐ 557 Rick Wrona .05 .02 .01
☐ 558 Sammy Sosa .75 .35 .09
☐ 559 Keith Miller .05 .02 .01
☐ 560 Ken Griffey Jr. 1.50 .70 .19
☐ 561A Ryne Sandberg HL ERR 8.00 3.60 1.00
(Position on front listed as 3B)
☐ 561B Ryne Sandberg HL COR .15 .07 .02
☐ 562 Billy Hatcher .05 .02 .01
☐ 563 Jay Bell .10 .05 .01
☐ 564 Jack Daugherty .05 .02 .01
☐ 565 Rich Monteleone .05 .02 .01
☐ 566 Bo Jackson AS-MVP .10 .05 .01
☐ 567 Tony Fossas .05 .02 .01
☐ 568 Roy Smith .05 .02 .01
☐ 569 Jaime Navarro .05 .02 .01
☐ 570 Lance Johnson .10 .05 .01
☐ 571 Mike Dyer .05 .02 .01
☐ 572 Kevin Ritz .05 .02 .01
☐ 573 Dave West .05 .02 .01
☐ 574 Gary Mielke .05 .02 .01
☐ 575 Scott Lusader .05 .02 .01
☐ 576 Joe Oliver .05 .02 .01
☐ 577 Sandy Alomar Jr. .15 .07 .02
☐ 578 Andy Benes UER .15 .07 .02
(Extra comma between day and year)
☐ 579 Tim Jones .05 .02 .01
☐ 580 Randy McCament .05 .02 .01
☐ 581 Curt Schilling .05 .02 .01
☐ 582 John Orton .05 .02 .01
☐ 583A Milt Cuyler ERR .50 .23 .06
(998 games)
☐ 583B Milt Cuyler COR .05 .02 .01
(98 games; the extra 9 was ghosted out and may still be visible)
☐ 584 Eric Anthony .10 .05 .01
☐ 585 Greg Vaughn .15 .07 .02
☐ 586 Deion Sanders .20 .09 .03
☐ 587 Jose DeJesus .05 .02 .01
☐ 588 Chip Hale .05 .02 .01
☐ 589 John Olerud .15 .07 .02
☐ 590 Steve Olin .10 .05 .01
☐ 591 Marquis Grissom .50 .23 .06
☐ 592 Moises Alou .40 .18 .05
☐ 593 Mark Lemke .10 .05 .01
☐ 594 Dean Palmer .40 .18 .05
☐ 595 Robin Ventura .15 .07 .02
☐ 596 Tino Martinez .15 .07 .02
☐ 597 Mike Huff .05 .02 .01
☐ 598 Scott Hemond .05 .02 .01
☐ 599 Wally Whitehurst .05 .02 .01
☐ 600 Todd Zeile .10 .05 .01
☐ 601 Glenallen Hill .10 .05 .01
☐ 602 Hal Morris .10 .05 .01
☐ 603 Juan Bell .05 .02 .01
☐ 604 Bobby Rose .05 .02 .01
☐ 605 Matt Merullo .05 .02 .01
☐ 606 Kevin Maas .10 .05 .01
☐ 607 Randy Nosek .05 .02 .01
☐ 608A Billy Bates .10 .05 .01
(Text mentions 12 triples in tenth line)
☐ 608B Billy Bates .10 .05 .01
(Text has no mention of triples)
☐ 609 Mike Stanton .10 .05 .01
☐ 610 Mauro Gozzo .05 .02 .01
☐ 611 Charles Nagy .20 .09 .03
☐ 612 Scott Coolbaugh .05 .02 .01
☐ 613 Jose Vizcaino .15 .07 .02
☐ 614 Greg Smith .05 .02 .01
☐ 615 Jeff Huson .05 .02 .01
☐ 616 Mickey Weston .05 .02 .01
☐ 617 John Pawlowski .05 .02 .01
☐ 618A Joe Skalski ERR .05 .02 .01
(27 on back)
☐ 618B Joe Skalski COR .50 .23 .06
(67 on back)
☐ 619 Bernie Williams 1.00 .45 .12
☐ 620 Shawn Holman .05 .02 .01
☐ 621 Gary Eave .05 .02 .01
☐ 622 Darrin Fletcher UER .10 .05 .01
(Elmherst, should be Elmhurst)
☐ 623 Pat Combs .05 .02 .01
☐ 624 Mike Blowers .15 .07 .02
☐ 625 Kevin Appier .15 .07 .02
☐ 626 Pat Austin .05 .02 .01
☐ 627 Kelly Mann .05 .02 .01
☐ 628 Matt Kinzer .05 .02 .01
☐ 629 Chris Hammond .05 .02 .01
☐ 630 Dean Wilkins .05 .02 .01
☐ 631 Larry Walker UER .60 .25 .07
(Uniform number 55 on front and 33 on back; Home is Maple Ridge, not Maple River)
☐ 632 Blaine Beatty .05 .02 .01
☐ 633A Tommy Barrett ERR .05 .02 .01
(29 on back)
☐ 633B Tommy Barrett COR .50 .23 .06
(14 on back)
☐ 634 Stan Belinda .05 .02 .01
☐ 635 Mike (Tex) Smith .05 .02 .01
☐ 636 Hensley Meulens .05 .02 .01
☐ 637 Juan Gonzalez UER 2.00 .90 .25
(Sarasots on back, should be Sarasota)
☐ 638 Lenny Webster .05 .02 .01
☐ 639 Mark Gardner .05 .02 .01
☐ 640 Tommy Greene .05 .02 .01
☐ 641 Mike Hartley .05 .02 .01
☐ 642 Phil Stephenson .05 .02 .01
☐ 643 Kevin Mmahat .05 .02 .01
☐ 644 Ed Whited .05 .02 .01
☐ 645 Delino DeShields .10 .05 .01
☐ 646 Kevin Blankenship .05 .02 .01
☐ 647 Paul Sorrento .15 .07 .02
☐ 648 Mike Roesler .05 .02 .01
☐ 649 Jason Grimsley .05 .02 .01
☐ 650 Dave Justice .50 .23 .06
☐ 651 Scott Cooper .05 .02 .01
☐ 652 Dave Eiland .05 .02 .01
☐ 653 Mike Munoz .05 .02 .01
☐ 654 Jeff Fischer .05 .02 .01
☐ 655 Terry Jorgensen .05 .02 .01
☐ 656 George Canale .05 .02 .01
☐ 657 Brian DuBois UER .05 .02 .01
(Misspelled Dubois on card)
☐ 658 Carlos Quintana .05 .02 .01
☐ 659 Luis de los Santos .05 .02 .01
☐ 660 Jerald Clark .05 .02 .01
☐ 661 Donald Harris DC .05 .02 .01
☐ 662 Paul Coleman DC .05 .02 .01
☐ 663 Frank Thomas DC 4.00 1.80 .50
☐ 664 Brent Mayne DC .05 .02 .01
☐ 665 Eddie Zosky DC .05 .02 .01
☐ 666 Steve Hosey DC .05 .02 .01
☐ 667 Scott Bryant DC .05 .02 .01
☐ 668 Tom Goodwin DC .15 .07 .02
☐ 669 Cal Eldred DC .15 .07 .02
☐ 670 Earl Cunningham DC .05 .02 .01
☐ 671 Alan Zinter DC .05 .02 .01
☐ 672 Chuck Knoblauch DC .75 .35 .09
☐ 673 Kyle Abbott DC .05 .02 .01
☐ 674 Roger Salkeld DC .05 .02 .01
☐ 675 Maurice Vaughn DC 1.50 .70 .19
☐ 676 Keith(Kiki) Jones DC .05 .02 .01
☐ 677 Tyler Houston DC .15 .07 .02
☐ 678 Jeff Jackson DC .05 .02 .01

	MINT	NRMT	EXC
☐ 679 Greg Gohr DC	.05	.02	.01
☐ 680 Ben McDonald DC	.15	.07	.02
☐ 681 Greg Blosser DC	.05	.02	.01
☐ 682 Willie Green DC UER (Name misspelled on card, should be Greene)	.15	.07	.02
☐ 683A Wade Boggs DT ERR (Text says 215 hits in '89, should be 205)	.15	.07	.02
☐ 683B Wade Boggs DT COR (Text says 205 hits in '89)	.15	.07	.02
☐ 684 Will Clark DT	.15	.07	.02
☐ 685 Tony Gwynn DT UER (Text reads battling instead of batting)	.20	.09	.03
☐ 686 Rickey Henderson DT	.15	.07	.02
☐ 687 Bo Jackson DT	.10	.05	.01
☐ 688 Mark Langston DT	.10	.05	.01
☐ 689 Barry Larkin DT	.15	.07	.02
☐ 690 Kirby Puckett DT	.15	.07	.02
☐ 691 Ryne Sandberg DT	.15	.07	.02
☐ 692 Mike Scott DT	.05	.02	.01
☐ 693A Terry Steinbach DT ERR (cathers)	.10	.05	.01
☐ 693B Terry Steinbach DT COR (catchers)	.10	.05	.01
☐ 694 Bobby Thigpen DT	.05	.02	.01
☐ 695 Mitch Williams DT	.05	.02	.01
☐ 696 Nolan Ryan HL	.40	.18	.05
☐ 697 Bo Jackson FB/BB	.50	.23	.06
☐ 698 Rickey Henderson ALCS-MVP	.15	.07	.02
☐ 699 Will Clark NLCS-MVP	.15	.07	.02
☐ 700 WS Games 1/2 (Dave Stewart Mike Moore)	.10	.05	.01
☐ 701 Lights Out: Candlestick 5:04pm (10/17/89)	.15	.07	.02
☐ 702 WS Game 3 Bashers Blast Giants (Carney Lansford, Rickey Henderson, Jose Canseco, Dave Henderson)	.15	.07	.02
☐ 703 WS Game 4/Wrap-up A's Sweep Battle of the Bay (A's Celebrate)	.05	.02	.01
☐ 704 Wade Boggs HL Wade Raps 200	.15	.07	.02

1990 Score Rookie Dream Team

A ten-card set of Dream Team Rookies was inserted only into hobby factory sets.These standard size cards carry a B prefix on the card number and include a player at each position plus a commemorative card honoring the late Baseball Commissioner A. Bartlett Giamatti.

	MINT	NRMT	EXC
COMPLETE SET (10)	5.00	2.20	.60
COMMON CARD (B1-B10)	.25	.11	.03
☐ B1 A.Bartlett Giamatti COMM MEM	.40	.18	.05
☐ B2 Pat Combs	.25	.11	.03
☐ B3 Todd Zeile	.40	.18	.05
☐ B4 Luis de los Santos	.25	.11	.03
☐ B5 Mark Lemke	.40	.18	.05
☐ B6 Robin Ventura	.75	.35	.09
☐ B7 Jeff Huson	.25	.11	.03
☐ B8 Greg Vaughn	.60	.25	.07
☐ B9 Marquis Grissom	2.00	.90	.25
☐ B10 Eric Anthony	.40	.18	.05

1990 Score Rookie/Traded

The standard-size 110-card1990 Score Rookie and Traded set marked the third consecutive year Score had issued an end of the year set to note trades and give rookies early cards. The set was issued through hobby accounts and only in factory set form. The first 66 cards are traded players while the last 44 cards are rookie cards. Hockey star Eric Lindros is included in this set. Rookie Cards in the set include Carlos Baerga, Derek Bell, Todd Hundley and Ray Lankford.

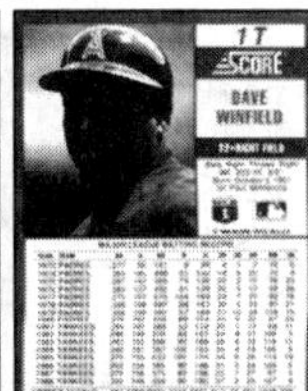

	MINT	NRMT	EXC
COMPLETE FACT.SET (110)	6.00	2.70	.75
COMMON CARD (1T-110T)	.05	.02	.01
☐ 1T Dave Winfield	.15	.07	.02
☐ 2T Kevin Bass	.05	.02	.01
☐ 3T Nick Esasky	.05	.02	.01
☐ 4T Mitch Webster	.05	.02	.01
☐ 5T Pascual Perez	.05	.02	.01
☐ 6T Gary Pettis	.05	.02	.01
☐ 7T Tony Pena	.05	.02	.01
☐ 8T Candy Maldonado	.05	.02	.01
☐ 9T Cecil Fielder	.10	.05	.01
☐ 10T Carmelo Martinez	.05	.02	.01
☐ 11T Mark Langston	.10	.05	.01
☐ 12T Dave Parker	.10	.05	.01
☐ 13T Don Slaught	.05	.02	.01
☐ 14T Tony Phillips	.15	.07	.02
☐ 15T John Franco	.05	.02	.01
☐ 16T Randy Myers	.10	.05	.01
☐ 17T Jeff Reardon	.10	.05	.01
☐ 18T Sandy Alomar Jr.	.15	.07	.02
☐ 19T Joe Carter	.10	.05	.01
☐ 20T Fred Lynn	.05	.02	.01
☐ 21T Storm Davis	.05	.02	.01
☐ 22T Craig Lefferts	.05	.02	.01
☐ 23T Pete O'Brien	.05	.02	.01
☐ 24T Dennis Boyd	.05	.02	.01
☐ 25T Lloyd Moseby	.05	.02	.01
☐ 26T Mark Davis	.05	.02	.01
☐ 27T Tim Leary	.05	.02	.01
☐ 28T Gerald Perry	.05	.02	.01
☐ 29T Don Aase	.05	.02	.01
☐ 30T Ernie Whitt	.05	.02	.01
☐ 31T Dale Murphy	.15	.07	.02
☐ 32T Alejandro Pena	.05	.02	.01
☐ 33T Juan Samuel	.05	.02	.01
☐ 34T Hubie Brooks	.05	.02	.01
☐ 35T Gary Carter	.10	.05	.01
☐ 36T Jim Presley	.05	.02	.01
☐ 37T Wally Backman	.05	.02	.01
☐ 38T Matt Nokes	.05	.02	.01
☐ 39T Dan Petry	.05	.02	.01
☐ 40T Franklin Stubbs	.05	.02	.01
☐ 41T Jeff Huson	.05	.02	.01
☐ 42T Billy Hatcher	.05	.02	.01
☐ 43T Terry Leach	.05	.02	.01
☐ 44T Phil Bradley	.05	.02	.01
☐ 45T Claudell Washington	.05	.02	.01
☐ 46T Luis Polonia	.05	.02	.01
☐ 47T Daryl Boston	.05	.02	.01
☐ 48T Lee Smith	.10	.05	.01
☐ 49T Tom Brunansky	.05	.02	.01
☐ 50T Mike Witt	.05	.02	.01
☐ 51T Willie Randolph	.10	.05	.01
☐ 52T Stan Javier	.05	.02	.01
☐ 53T Brad Komminsk	.05	.02	.01
☐ 54T John Candelaria	.05	.02	.01
☐ 55T Bryn Smith	.05	.02	.01
☐ 56T Glenn Braggs	.05	.02	.01
☐ 57T Keith Hernandez	.10	.05	.01
☐ 58T Ken Oberkfell	.05	.02	.01
☐ 59T Steve Jeltz	.05	.02	.01
☐ 60T Chris James	.05	.02	.01
☐ 61T Scott Sanderson	.05	.02	.01
☐ 62T Bill Long	.05	.02	.01
☐ 63T Rick Cerone	.05	.02	.01
☐ 64T Scott Bailes	.05	.02	.01
☐ 65T Larry Sheets	.05	.02	.01
☐ 66T Junior Ortiz	.05	.02	.01
☐ 67T Francisco Cabrera	.05	.02	.01
☐ 68T Gary DiSarcina	.15	.07	.02
☐ 69T Greg Olson	.05	.02	.01
☐ 70T Beau Allred	.05	.02	.01
☐ 71T Oscar Azocar	.05	.02	.01
☐ 72T Kent Mercker	.10	.05	.01
☐ 73T John Burkett	.10	.05	.01
☐ 74T Carlos Baerga	.30	.14	.04
☐ 75T Dave Hollins	.15	.07	.02
☐ 76T Todd Hundley	.60	.25	.07
☐ 77T Rick Parker	.05	.02	.01
☐ 78T Steve Cummings	.05	.02	.01
☐ 79T Bill Sampen	.05	.02	.01
☐ 80T Jerry Kutzler	.05	.02	.01
☐ 81T Derek Bell	.50	.23	.06
☐ 82T Kevin Tapani	.10	.05	.01
☐ 83T Jim Leyritz	.15	.07	.02
☐ 84T Ray Lankford	.50	.23	.06
☐ 85T Wayne Edwards	.05	.02	.01
☐ 86T Frank Thomas	4.00	1.80	.50
☐ 87T Tim Naehring	.15	.07	.02
☐ 88T Willie Blair	.05	.02	.01
☐ 89T Alan Mills	.05	.02	.01
☐ 90T Scott Radinsky	.05	.02	.01
☐ 91T Howard Farmer	.05	.02	.01
☐ 92T Julio Machado	.05	.02	.01
☐ 93T Rafael Valdez	.05	.02	.01
☐ 94T Shawn Boskie	.05	.02	.01
☐ 95T David Segui	.15	.07	.02
☐ 96T Chris Hoiles	.15	.07	.02
☐ 97T D.J. Dozier	.10	.05	.01
☐ 98T Hector Villanueva	.05	.02	.01
☐ 99T Eric Gunderson	.05	.02	.01
☐ 100T Eric Lindros	2.00	.90	.25
☐ 101T Dave Otto	.05	.02	.01
☐ 102T Dana Kiecker	.05	.02	.01
☐ 103T Tim Drummond	.05	.02	.01
☐ 104T Mickey Pina	.05	.02	.01
☐ 105T Craig Grebeck	.05	.02	.01
☐ 106T Bernard Gilkey	.40	.18	.05
☐ 107T Tim Layana	.05	.02	.01
☐ 108T Scott Chiamparino	.05	.02	.01
☐ 109T Steve Avery	.15	.07	.02
☐ 110T Terry Shumpert	.05	.02	.01

1990 Score 100 Rising Stars

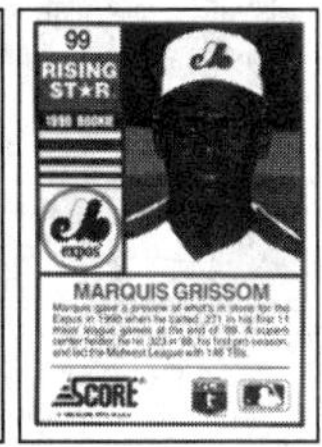

The 1990 Score Rising Stars set contains 100 standard size cards. The fronts are green, blue and white. The vertically oriented backs feature a large color facial shot and career highlights. The cards were distributed as a set in a blister pack, which also included a full color booklet with more information about each player.

	MINT	NRMT	EXC
COMPLETE SET (100)	8.00	3.60	1.00
COMMON CARD (1-100)	.05	.02	.01
☐ 1 Tom Gordon	.10	.05	.01
☐ 2 Jerome Walton	.05	.02	.01
☐ 3 Ken Griffey Jr.	3.00	1.35	.35
☐ 4 Dwight Smith	.05	.02	.01
☐ 5 Jim Abbott	.20	.09	.03
☐ 6 Todd Zeile	.20	.09	.03
☐ 7 Donn Pall	.05	.02	.01
☐ 8 Rick Reed	.05	.02	.01
☐ 9 Joey Belle	2.00	.90	.25
☐ 10 Gregg Jefferies	.30	.14	.04
☐ 11 Kevin Ritz	.05	.02	.01
☐ 12 Charlie Hayes	.10	.05	.01
☐ 13 Kevin Appier	.20	.09	.03
☐ 14 Jeff Huson	.05	.02	.01
☐ 15 Gary Wayne	.05	.02	.01
☐ 16 Eric Yelding	.05	.02	.01
☐ 17 Clay Parker	.05	.02	.01
☐ 18 Junior Felix	.05	.02	.01
☐ 19 Derek Lilliquist	.05	.02	.01
☐ 20 Gary Sheffield	.75	.35	.09
☐ 21 Craig Worthington	.05	.02	.01
☐ 22 Jeff Brantley	.10	.05	.01
☐ 23 Eric Hetzel	.05	.02	.01
☐ 24 Greg W.Harris	.05	.02	.01
☐ 25 John Wetteland	.20	.09	.03
☐ 26 Joe Oliver	.05	.02	.01
☐ 27 Kevin Maas	.05	.02	.01
☐ 28 Kevin Brown	.20	.09	.03
☐ 29 Mike Stanton	.05	.02	.01
☐ 30 Greg Vaughn	.25	.11	.03
☐ 31 Ron Jones	.05	.02	.01
☐ 32 Gregg Olson	.05	.02	.01
☐ 33 Joe Girardi	.10	.05	.01
☐ 34 Ken Hill	.25	.11	.03
☐ 35 Sammy Sosa	1.00	.45	.12
☐ 36 Geronimo Berroa	.10	.05	.01
☐ 37 Omar Vizquel	.30	.14	.04
☐ 38 Dean Palmer	.50	.23	.06
☐ 39 John Olerud	.50	.23	.06
☐ 40 Deion Sanders	.60	.25	.07
☐ 41 Randy Kramer	.05	.02	.01
☐ 42 Scott Lusader	.05	.02	.01
☐ 43 Dave Johnson (P)	.05	.02	.01
☐ 44 Jeff Wetherby	.05	.02	.01
☐ 45 Eric Anthony	.05	.02	.01
☐ 46 Kenny Rogers	.15	.07	.02
☐ 47 Matt Winters	.05	.02	.01
☐ 48 Mauro Gozzo	.05	.02	.01
☐ 49 Carlos Quintana	.05	.02	.01
☐ 50 Bob Geren	.05	.02	.01
☐ 51 Chad Kreuter	.05	.02	.01
☐ 52 Randy Johnson	1.00	.45	.12
☐ 53 Hensley Meulens	.05	.02	.01
☐ 54 Gene Harris	.05	.02	.01
☐ 55 Bill Spiers	.05	.02	.01
☐ 56 Kelly Mann	.05	.02	.01
☐ 57 Tom McCarthy	.05	.02	.01
☐ 58 Steve Finley	.25	.11	.03
☐ 59 Ramon Martinez	.20	.09	.03
☐ 60 Greg Briley	.05	.02	.01
☐ 61 Jack Daugherty	.05	.02	.01
☐ 62 Tim Jones	.05	.02	.01
☐ 63 Doug Strange	.05	.02	.01
☐ 64 John Orton	.05	.02	.01
☐ 65 Scott Scudder	.05	.02	.01
☐ 66 Mark Gardner	.05	.02	.01
☐ 67 Mark Carreon	.05	.02	.01
☐ 68 Bob Milacki	.05	.02	.01
☐ 69 Andy Benes	.20	.09	.03
☐ 70 Carlos Martinez	.05	.02	.01
☐ 71 Jeff King	.10	.05	.01
☐ 72 Brad Arnsberg	.05	.02	.01
☐ 73 Rick Wrona	.05	.02	.01
☐ 74 Cris Carpenter	.05	.02	.01
☐ 75 Dennis Cook	.05	.02	.01
☐ 76 Pete Harnisch	.05	.02	.01
☐ 77 Greg Hibbard	.05	.02	.01
☐ 78 Ed Whited	.05	.02	.01
☐ 79 Scott Coolbaugh	.05	.02	.01
☐ 80 Billy Bates	.05	.02	.01
☐ 81 German Gonzalez	.05	.02	.01
☐ 82 Lance Blankenship	.05	.02	.01
☐ 83 Lenny Harris	.05	.02	.01
☐ 84 Milt Cuyler	.05	.02	.01
☐ 85 Erik Hanson	.10	.05	.01
☐ 86 Kent Anderson	.05	.02	.01
☐ 87 Hal Morris	.10	.05	.01
☐ 88 Mike Brumley	.05	.02	.01
☐ 89 Ken Patterson	.05	.02	.01
☐ 90 Mike Devereaux	.10	.05	.01
☐ 91 Greg Litton	.05	.02	.01
☐ 92 Rolando Roomes	.05	.02	.01
☐ 93 Ben McDonald	.25	.11	.03
☐ 94 Curt Schilling	.05	.02	.01
☐ 95 Jose DeJesus	.05	.02	.01
☐ 96 Robin Ventura	.40	.18	.05
☐ 97 Steve Searcy	.05	.02	.01
☐ 98 Chip Hale	.05	.02	.01
☐ 99 Marquis Grissom	.75	.35	.09
☐ 100 Luis de los Santos	.05	.02	.01

1990 Score 100 Superstars

The 1990 Score Superstars set contains 100 standard size cards. The fronts are red, white, blue and purple. The vertically oriented backs feature a large color facial shot and career highlights. The cards were distributed as a set in a blister pack, which also included a full color booklet with more information about each player.

	MINT	NRMT	EXC
COMPLETE SET (100)	10.00	4.50	1.25
COMMON CARD (1-100)	.05	.02	.01
☐ 1 Kirby Puckett	1.50	.70	.19
☐ 2 Steve Sax	.05	.02	.01
☐ 3 Tony Gwynn	1.25	.55	.16
☐ 4 Willie Randolph	.05	.02	.01
☐ 5 Jose Canseco	.30	.14	.04
☐ 6 Ozzie Smith	1.00	.45	.12
☐ 7 Rick Reuschel	.05	.02	.01
☐ 8 Bill Doran	.05	.02	.01
☐ 9 Mickey Tettleton	.05	.02	.01
☐ 10 Don Mattingly	1.50	.70	.19
☐ 11 Greg Swindell	.05	.02	.01
☐ 12 Bert Blyleven	.10	.05	.01
☐ 13 Dave Stewart	.10	.05	.01
☐ 14 Andres Galarraga	.40	.18	.05
☐ 15 Darryl Strawberry	.10	.05	.01
☐ 16 Ellis Burks	.15	.07	.02
☐ 17 Paul O'Neill	.10	.05	.01
☐ 18 Bruce Hurst	.05	.02	.01
☐ 19 Dave Smith	.05	.02	.01
☐ 20 Carney Lansford	.05	.02	.01
☐ 21 Robby Thompson	.05	.02	.01
☐ 22 Gary Gaetti	.10	.05	.01
☐ 23 Jeff Russell	.05	.02	.01
☐ 24 Chuck Finley	.10	.05	.01
☐ 25 Mark McGwire	.60	.25	.07
☐ 26 Alvin Davis	.05	.02	.01
☐ 27 George Bell	.10	.05	.01
☐ 28 Cory Snyder	.05	.02	.01
☐ 29 Keith Hernandez	.10	.05	.01
☐ 30 Will Clark	.30	.14	.04
☐ 31 Steve Bedrosian	.05	.02	.01
☐ 32 Ryne Sandberg	.75	.35	.09
☐ 33 Tom Browning	.05	.02	.01
☐ 34 Tim Burke	.05	.02	.01
☐ 35 John Smoltz	.50	.23	.06
☐ 36 Phil Bradley	.05	.02	.01
☐ 37 Bobby Bonilla	.10	.05	.01
☐ 38 Kirk McCaskill	.05	.02	.01
☐ 39 Dave Righetti	.05	.02	.01
☐ 40 Bo Jackson	.20	.09	.03

Card	MINT	NRMT	EXC
☐ 41 Alan Trammell	.20	.09	.03
☐ 42 Mike Moore UER (Uniform number is 21, not 23 as on front)	.05	.02	.01
☐ 43 Harold Reynolds	.10	.05	.01
☐ 44 Nolan Ryan	2.50	1.10	.30
☐ 45 Fred McGriff	.30	.14	.04
☐ 46 Brian Downing	.05	.02	.01
☐ 47 Brett Butler	.10	.05	.01
☐ 48 Mike Scioscia	.05	.02	.01
☐ 49 John Franco	.10	.05	.01
☐ 50 Kevin Mitchell	.10	.05	.01
☐ 51 Mark Davis	.05	.02	.01
☐ 52 Glenn Davis	.05	.02	.01
☐ 53 Barry Bonds	.50	.23	.06
☐ 54 Dwight Evans	.05	.02	.01
☐ 55 Terry Steinbach	.10	.05	.01
☐ 56 Dave Gallagher	.05	.02	.01
☐ 57 Roberto Kelly	.20	.09	.03
☐ 58 Rafael Palmeiro	.35	.16	.04
☐ 59 Joe Carter	.25	.11	.03
☐ 60 Mark Grace	.30	.14	.04
☐ 61 Pedro Guerrero	.05	.02	.01
☐ 62 Von Hayes	.05	.02	.01
☐ 63 Benito Santiago	.05	.02	.01
☐ 64 Dale Murphy	.25	.11	.03
☐ 65 John Smiley	.10	.05	.01
☐ 66 Cal Ripken	2.00	.90	.25
☐ 67 Mike Greenwell	.10	.05	.01
☐ 68 Devon White	.10	.05	.01
☐ 69 Ed Whitson	.05	.02	.01
☐ 70 Carlton Fisk	.25	.11	.03
☐ 71 Lou Whitaker	.15	.07	.02
☐ 72 Danny Tartabull	.05	.02	.01
☐ 73 Vince Coleman	.05	.02	.01
☐ 74 Andre Dawson	.10	.05	.01
☐ 75 Tim Raines	.10	.05	.01
☐ 76 George Brett	1.50	.70	.19
☐ 77 Tom Herr	.05	.02	.01
☐ 78 Andy Van Slyke	.05	.02	.01
☐ 79 Roger Clemens	.40	.18	.05
☐ 80 Wade Boggs	.30	.14	.04
☐ 81 Wally Joyner	.10	.05	.01
☐ 82 Lonnie Smith	.05	.02	.01
☐ 83 Howard Johnson	.05	.02	.01
☐ 84 Julio Franco	.10	.05	.01
☐ 85 Ruben Sierra	.10	.05	.01
☐ 86 Dan Plesac	.05	.02	.01
☐ 87 Bobby Thigpen	.05	.02	.01
☐ 88 Kevin Seitzer	.05	.02	.01
☐ 89 Dave Stieb	.05	.02	.01
☐ 90 Rickey Henderson	.40	.18	.05
☐ 91 Jeffrey Leonard	.05	.02	.01
☐ 92 Robin Yount	.25	.11	.03
☐ 93 Mitch Williams	.05	.02	.01
☐ 94 Orel Hershiser	.10	.05	.01
☐ 95 Eric Davis	.10	.05	.01
☐ 96 Mark Langston	.05	.02	.01
☐ 97 Mike Scott	.05	.02	.01
☐ 98 Paul Molitor	.60	.25	.07
☐ 99 Dwight Gooden	.10	.05	.01
☐ 100 Kevin Bass	.05	.02	.01

1990 Score McDonald's

This 25-card standard-size set was produced by Score for McDonald's restaurants; included with the set were 15 World Series Trivia cards. The player cards were given away four to a pack and free with the purchase of fries and a drink, at only 11 McDonald's in the United States (in Idaho and Eastern Oregon) during a special promotion which lasted approximately three weeks. The front has color action player photos, with white and yellow borders on a purple card face that fades as one moves toward the middle of the card. The upper left corner of the picture is cut off to allow space for the McDonald's logo; the player's name and team logo at the bottom round out the card face. The backs have color mugshots, biography, statistics, and career summary.

	MINT	NRMT	EXC
COMPLETE SET (25)	500.00	220.00	60.00
COMMON CARD (1-25)	5.00	2.20	.60
☐ 1 Will Clark	30.00	13.50	3.70
☐ 2 Sandy Alomar Jr.	10.00	4.50	1.25
☐ 3 Julio Franco	5.00	2.20	.60
☐ 4 Carlton Fisk	25.00	11.00	3.10
☐ 5 Rickey Henderson	25.00	11.00	3.10
☐ 6 Matt Williams	40.00	18.00	5.00
☐ 7 John Franco	5.00	2.20	.60
☐ 8 Ryne Sandberg	60.00	27.00	7.50
☐ 9 Kelly Gruber	5.00	2.20	.60
☐ 10 Andre Dawson	25.00	11.00	3.10
☐ 11 Barry Bonds	30.00	13.50	3.70
☐ 12 Gary Sheffield	25.00	11.00	3.10
☐ 13 Ramon Martinez	10.00	4.50	1.25
☐ 14 Len Dykstra	10.00	4.50	1.25
☐ 15 Benito Santiago	5.00	2.20	.60
☐ 16 Cecil Fielder	15.00	6.75	1.85
☐ 17 John Olerud	15.00	6.75	1.85
☐ 18 Roger Clemens	40.00	18.00	5.00
☐ 19 George Brett	60.00	27.00	7.50
☐ 20 George Bell	5.00	2.20	.60
☐ 21 Ozzie Guillen	5.00	2.20	.60
☐ 22 Steve Sax	5.00	2.20	.60
☐ 23 Dave Stewart	5.00	2.20	.60
☐ 24 Ozzie Smith	60.00	27.00	7.50
☐ 25 Robin Yount	25.00	11.00	3.10

1990 Score Sportflics Ryan

This standard-size card was issued by Optigraphics (producer of Score and Sportflics) to commemorate the 11th National Sports Card Collectors Convention held in Arlington, Texas in July of 1990. This card featured a Score front similar to the Ryan 1990 Score highlight card except for the 11th National Convention Logo on the bottom right of the card. On the other side a Ryan Sportflics card was printed that stated (reflected) either Sportflics or 1990 National Sports Collectors Convention on the bottom of the card. This issue was limited to a printing of 600 cards with Ryan himself destroying the printing plates.

	MINT	NRMT	EXC
COMPLETE SET (1)	450.00	200.00	55.00
COMMON CARD (NNO)	450.00	200.00	55.00
☐ NNO Nolan Ryan (No number on back; card back is actually another front in Sportflics style)	450.00	200.00	55.00

1990 Score Young Superstars I

1990 Score Young Superstars I are glossy full color cards featuring 42 standard-size cards of popular young players. The first series was issued with 1990 Score baseball rack packs while the second series was available only via a mailaway from the company.

	MINT	NRMT	EXC
COMPLETE SET (42)	4.00	1.80	.50
COMMON CARD (1-42)	.05	.02	.01
☐ 1 Bo Jackson	.25	.11	.03
☐ 2 Dwight Smith	.05	.02	.01
☐ 3 Joey Belle	2.00	.90	.25
☐ 4 Gregg Olson	.05	.02	.01
☐ 5 Jim Abbott	.20	.09	.03
☐ 6 Felix Fermin	.05	.02	.01
☐ 7 Brian Holman	.05	.02	.01
☐ 8 Clay Parker	.05	.02	.01
☐ 9 Junior Felix	.05	.02	.01
☐ 10 Joe Oliver	.05	.02	.01
☐ 11 Steve Finley	.25	.11	.03
☐ 12 Greg Briley	.05	.02	.01
☐ 13 Greg Vaughn	.30	.14	.04
☐ 14 Bill Spiers	.05	.02	.01
☐ 15 Eric Yelding	.05	.02	.01
☐ 16 Jose Gonzalez	.05	.02	.01
☐ 17 Mark Carreon	.05	.02	.01
☐ 18 Greg W. Harris	.05	.02	.01
☐ 19 Felix Jose	.05	.02	.01
☐ 20 Bob Milacki	.05	.02	.01
☐ 21 Kenny Rogers	.10	.05	.01
☐ 22 Rolando Roomes	.05	.02	.01
☐ 23 Bip Roberts	.10	.05	.01
☐ 24 Jeff Brantley	.10	.05	.01
☐ 25 Jeff Ballard	.05	.02	.01
☐ 26 John Dopson	.05	.02	.01
☐ 27 Ken Patterson	.05	.02	.01
☐ 28 Omar Vizquel	.30	.14	.04
☐ 29 Kevin Brown	.20	.09	.03
☐ 30 Derek Lilliquist	.05	.02	.01
☐ 31 David Wells	.10	.05	.01
☐ 32 Ken Hill	.25	.11	.03
☐ 33 Greg Litton	.05	.02	.01
☐ 34 Rob Ducey	.05	.02	.01
☐ 35 Carlos Martinez	.05	.02	.01
☐ 36 John Smoltz	.50	.23	.06
☐ 37 Lenny Harris	.05	.02	.01
☐ 38 Charlie Hayes	.25	.11	.03
☐ 39 Tommy Gregg	.05	.02	.01
☐ 40 John Wetteland	.30	.14	.04
☐ 41 Jeff Huson	.05	.02	.01
☐ 42 Eric Anthony	.05	.02	.01

1990 Score Young Superstars II

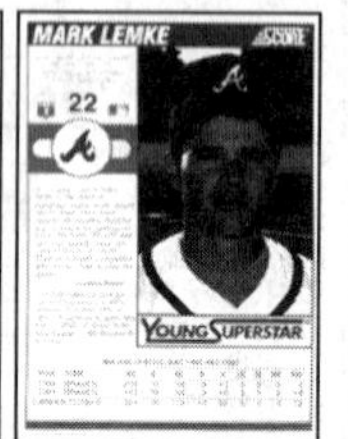

1990 Score Young Superstars II are glossy full color cards featuring 42 standard-size cards of popular young players. Whereas the first series was issued with 1990 Score baseball rack packs, this second series was available only via a mailaway from the company.

	MINT	NRMT	EXC
COMPLETE SET (42)	5.00	2.20	.60
COMMON CARD (1-42)	.05	.02	.01
☐ 1 Todd Zeile	.20	.09	.03
☐ 2 Ben McDonald	.25	.11	.03
☐ 3 Delino DeShields	.25	.11	.03
☐ 4 Pat Combs	.05	.02	.01
☐ 5 John Olerud	.30	.14	.04
☐ 6 Marquis Grissom	.50	.23	.06
☐ 7 Mike Stanton	.05	.02	.01
☐ 8 Robin Ventura	.25	.11	.03
☐ 9 Larry Walker	.75	.35	.09
☐ 10 Dante Bichette	.50	.23	.06
☐ 11 Jack Armstrong	.05	.02	.01
☐ 12 Jay Bell	.15	.07	.02
☐ 13 Andy Benes	.15	.07	.02
☐ 14 Joey Cora	.15	.07	.02
☐ 15 Rob Dibble	.05	.02	.01
☐ 16 Jeff King	.20	.09	.03
☐ 17 Jeff Hamilton	.05	.02	.01
☐ 18 Erik Hanson	.10	.05	.01
☐ 19 Pete Harnisch	.05	.02	.01
☐ 20 Greg Hibbard	.05	.02	.01
☐ 21 Stan Javier	.05	.02	.01
☐ 22 Mark Lemke	.10	.05	.01
☐ 23 Steve Olin	.05	.02	.01
☐ 24 Tommy Greene	.05	.02	.01
☐ 25 Sammy Sosa	1.00	.45	.12
☐ 26 Gary Wayne	.05	.02	.01
☐ 27 Deion Sanders	.75	.35	.09
☐ 28 Steve Wilson	.05	.02	.01
☐ 29 Joe Girardi	.10	.05	.01
☐ 30 John Orton	.05	.02	.01
☐ 31 Kevin Tapani	.20	.09	.03
☐ 32 Carlos Baerga	.25	.11	.03
☐ 33 Glenallen Hill	.10	.05	.01
☐ 34 Mike Blowers	.30	.14	.04
☐ 35 Dave Hollins	.05	.02	.01
☐ 36 Lance Blankenship	.05	.02	.01
☐ 37 Hal Morris	.10	.05	.01
☐ 38 Lance Johnson	.25	.11	.03
☐ 39 Chris Gwynn	.05	.02	.01
☐ 40 Doug Dascenzo	.05	.02	.01
☐ 41 Jerald Clark	.05	.02	.01
☐ 42 Carlos Quintana	.05	.02	.01

1991 Score

The 1991 Score set contains 893 standard-size cards issued in two separate series of 441 and 452 cards each. This set marks the fourth consecutive year that Score has issued a major set but the first time Score issued the set in two series. Cards were distributed in plastic-wrap packs, blister packs and factory sets. The card fronts feature one of four different solid color borders (black, blue, teal and white) framing the full-color photo of the cards. Subsets include Rookie Prospects (331-379), First Draft Picks (380-391, 671-682), AL All-Stars (392-401), Master Blasters (402-406, 689-693), K-Men (407-411, 684-688), Rifleman (412-416, 694-698), NL All-Stars (661-670), No-Hitters (699-707), Franchise (849-874), Award Winners (875-881) and Dream Team (882-893). An American Flag card (737) was issued to honor the American soldiers involved in Desert Storm. Rookie Cards in the set include Jeff Conine, Chipper Jones, Brian McRae, Mike Mussina and Rondell White. There are a number of pitchers whose card backs show Innings Pitched totals which do not equal the added year-by-year total; the following card numbers were affected, 4, 24, 29, 30, 51, 81, 109, 111, 118, 141, 150, 156, 177, 204, 218, 232, 235, 255, 287, 289, 311, and 328.

	MINT	NRMT	EXC
COMPLETE SET (893)	12.00	5.50	1.50
COMPLETE FACT.SET (900)	20.00	9.00	2.50
COMMON CARD (1-893)	.05	.02	.01
☐ 1 Jose Canseco	.15	.07	.02
☐ 2 Ken Griffey Jr.	1.50	.70	.19
☐ 3 Ryne Sandberg	.25	.11	.03
☐ 4 Nolan Ryan	.75	.35	.09
☐ 5 Bo Jackson	.10	.05	.01
☐ 6 Bret Saberhagen UER (In bio, missed misspelled as mised)	.10	.05	.01
☐ 7 Will Clark	.15	.07	.02
☐ 8 Ellis Burks	.10	.05	.01
☐ 9 Joe Carter	.10	.05	.01
☐ 10 Rickey Henderson	.15	.07	.02
☐ 11 Ozzie Guillen	.05	.02	.01
☐ 12 Wade Boggs	.15	.07	.02
☐ 13 Jerome Walton	.05	.02	.01
☐ 14 John Franco	.05	.02	.01
☐ 15 Ricky Jordan UER (League misspelled as legue)	.05	.02	.01
☐ 16 Wally Backman	.05	.02	.01
☐ 17 Rob Dibble	.05	.02	.01
☐ 18 Glenn Braggs	.05	.02	.01
☐ 19 Cory Snyder	.05	.02	.01
☐ 20 Kal Daniels	.05	.02	.01
☐ 21 Mark Langston	.10	.05	.01
☐ 22 Kevin Gross	.05	.02	.01
☐ 23 Don Mattingly UER (First line, ' is missing from Yankee)	.50	.23	.06
☐ 24 Dave Righetti	.05	.02	.01
☐ 25 Roberto Alomar	.20	.09	.03
☐ 26 Robby Thompson	.05	.02	.01
☐ 27 Jack McDowell	.10	.05	.01
☐ 28 Bip Roberts UER (Bio reads playd)	.05	.02	.01
☐ 29 Jay Howell	.05	.02	.01
☐ 30 Dave Stieb UER (17 wins in bio, 18 in stats)	.05	.02	.01
☐ 31 Johnny Ray	.05	.02	.01
☐ 32 Steve Sax	.05	.02	.01
☐ 33 Terry Mulholland	.05	.02	.01
☐ 34 Lee Guetterman	.05	.02	.01
☐ 35 Tim Raines	.15	.07	.02
☐ 36 Scott Fletcher	.05	.02	.01
☐ 37 Lance Parrish	.05	.02	.01
☐ 38 Tony Phillips UER (Born 4/15, should be 4/25)	.10	.05	.01
☐ 39 Todd Stottlemyre	.05	.02	.01
☐ 40 Alan Trammell	.10	.05	.01
☐ 41 Todd Burns	.05	.02	.01
☐ 42 Mookie Wilson	.05	.02	.01
☐ 43 Chris Bosio	.05	.02	.01
☐ 44 Jeffrey Leonard	.05	.02	.01
☐ 45 Doug Jones	.05	.02	.01
☐ 46 Mike Scott UER (In first line, dominate should read dominating)	.05	.02	.01
☐ 47 Andy Hawkins	.05	.02	.01
☐ 48 Harold Reynolds	.05	.02	.01
☐ 49 Paul Molitor	.20	.09	.03
☐ 50 John Farrell	.05	.02	.01
☐ 51 Danny Darwin	.05	.02	.01
☐ 52 Jeff Blauser	.05	.02	.01
☐ 53 John Tudor UER (41 wins in '81)	.05	.02	.01
☐ 54 Milt Thompson	.05	.02	.01
☐ 55 Dave Justice	.15	.07	.02
☐ 56 Greg Olson	.05	.02	.01
☐ 57 Willie Blair	.05	.02	.01
☐ 58 Rick Parker	.05	.02	.01
☐ 59 Shawn Boskie	.05	.02	.01
☐ 60 Kevin Tapani	.05	.02	.01
☐ 61 Dave Hollins	.05	.02	.01
☐ 62 Scott Radinsky	.05	.02	.01
☐ 63 Francisco Cabrera	.05	.02	.01
☐ 64 Tim Layana	.05	.02	.01
☐ 65 Jim Leyritz	.10	.05	.01
☐ 66 Wayne Edwards	.05	.02	.01
☐ 67 Lee Stevens	.05	.02	.01
☐ 68 Bill Sampen UER (Fourth line, long is spelled along)	.05	.02	.01
☐ 69 Craig Grebeck UER (Born in Cerritos,	.05	.02	.01

not Johnstown)
☐ 70 John Burkett .10 .05 .01
☐ 71 Hector Villanueva .05 .02 .01
☐ 72 Oscar Azocar .05 .02 .01
☐ 73 Alan Mills .05 .02 .01
☐ 74 Carlos Baerga .15 .07 .02
☐ 75 Charles Nagy .15 .07 .02
☐ 76 Tim Drummond .05 .02 .01
☐ 77 Dana Kiecker .05 .02 .01
☐ 78 Tom Edens .05 .02 .01
☐ 79 Kent Mercker .05 .02 .01
☐ 80 Steve Avery .15 .07 .02
☐ 81 Lee Smith .10 .05 .01
☐ 82 Dave Martinez .05 .02 .01
☐ 83 Dave Winfield .15 .07 .02
☐ 84 Bill Spiers .05 .02 .01
☐ 85 Dan Pasqua .05 .02 .01
☐ 86 Randy Milligan .05 .02 .01
☐ 87 Tracy Jones .05 .02 .01
☐ 88 Greg Myers .05 .02 .01
☐ 89 Keith Hernandez .10 .05 .01
☐ 90 Todd Benzinger .05 .02 .01
☐ 91 Mike Jackson .05 .02 .01
☐ 92 Mike Stanley .05 .02 .01
☐ 93 Candy Maldonado .05 .02 .01
☐ 94 John Kruk UER .10 .05 .01
(No decimal point
before 1990 BA)
☐ 95 Cal Ripken UER .75 .35 .09
(Genius spelled genuis)
☐ 96 Willie Fraser .05 .02 .01
☐ 97 Mike Felder .05 .02 .01
☐ 98 Bill Landrum .05 .02 .01
☐ 99 Chuck Crim .05 .02 .01
☐ 100 Chuck Finley .10 .05 .01
☐ 101 Kirt Manwaring .05 .02 .01
☐ 102 Jaime Navarro .05 .02 .01
☐ 103 Dickie Thon .05 .02 .01
☐ 104 Brian Downing .05 .02 .01
☐ 105 Jim Abbott .10 .05 .01
☐ 106 Tom Brookens .05 .02 .01
☐ 107 Darryl Hamilton UER .10 .05 .01
(Bio info is for
Jeff Hamilton)
☐ 108 Bryan Harvey .05 .02 .01
☐ 109 Greg A. Harris UER .05 .02 .01
(Shown pitching lefty,
bio says righty)
☐ 110 Greg Swindell .05 .02 .01
☐ 111 Juan Berenguer .05 .02 .01
☐ 112 Mike Heath .05 .02 .01
☐ 113 Scott Bradley .05 .02 .01
☐ 114 Jack Morris .10 .05 .01
☐ 115 Barry Jones .05 .02 .01
☐ 116 Kevin Romine .05 .02 .01
☐ 117 Garry Templeton .05 .02 .01
☐ 118 Scott Sanderson .05 .02 .01
☐ 119 Roberto Kelly .05 .02 .01
☐ 120 George Brett .40 .18 .05
☐ 121 Oddibe McDowell .05 .02 .01
☐ 122 Jim Acker .05 .02 .01
☐ 123 Bill Swift UER .05 .02 .01
(Born 12/27/61,
should be 10/27)
☐ 124 Eric King .05 .02 .01
☐ 125 Jay Buhner .15 .07 .02
☐ 126 Matt Young .05 .02 .01
☐ 127 Alvaro Espinoza .05 .02 .01
☐ 128 Greg Hibbard .05 .02 .01
☐ 129 Jeff M. Robinson .05 .02 .01
☐ 130 Mike Greenwell .05 .02 .01
☐ 131 Dion James .05 .02 .01
☐ 132 Donn Pall UER .05 .02 .01
(1988 ERA in stats 0.00)
☐ 133 Lloyd Moseby .05 .02 .01
☐ 134 Randy Velarde .05 .02 .01
☐ 135 Allan Anderson .05 .02 .01
☐ 136 Mark Davis .05 .02 .01
☐ 137 Eric Davis .10 .05 .01
☐ 138 Phil Stephenson .05 .02 .01
☐ 139 Felix Fermin .05 .02 .01
☐ 140 Pedro Guerrero .05 .02 .01
☐ 141 Charlie Hough .05 .02 .01
☐ 142 Mike Henneman .05 .02 .01
☐ 143 Jeff Montgomery .10 .05 .01
☐ 144 Lenny Harris .05 .02 .01
☐ 145 Bruce Hurst .05 .02 .01
☐ 146 Eric Anthony .05 .02 .01
☐ 147 Paul Assenmacher .05 .02 .01
☐ 148 Jesse Barfield .05 .02 .01
☐ 149 Carlos Quintana .05 .02 .01
☐ 150 Dave Stewart .10 .05 .01
☐ 151 Roy Smith .05 .02 .01
☐ 152 Paul Gibson .05 .02 .01
☐ 153 Mickey Hatcher .05 .02 .01
☐ 154 Jim Eisenreich .10 .05 .01
☐ 155 Kenny Rogers .05 .02 .01
☐ 156 Dave Schmidt .05 .02 .01
☐ 157 Lance Johnson .10 .05 .01
☐ 158 Dave West .05 .02 .01
☐ 159 Steve Balboni .05 .02 .01
☐ 160 Jeff Brantley .05 .02 .01
☐ 161 Craig Biggio .15 .07 .02
☐ 162 Brook Jacoby .05 .02 .01
☐ 163 Dan Gladden .05 .02 .01
☐ 164 Jeff Reardon UER .10 .05 .01
(Total IP shown as
943.2, should be 943.1)
☐ 165 Mark Carreon .05 .02 .01
☐ 166 Mel Hall .05 .02 .01
☐ 167 Gary Mielke .05 .02 .01
☐ 168 Cecil Fielder .10 .05 .01
☐ 169 Darrin Jackson .05 .02 .01
☐ 170 Rick Aguilera .10 .05 .01
☐ 171 Walt Weiss .05 .02 .01
☐ 172 Steve Farr .05 .02 .01
☐ 173 Jody Reed .05 .02 .01
☐ 174 Mike Jeffcoat .05 .02 .01
☐ 175 Mark Grace .15 .07 .02
☐ 176 Larry Sheets .05 .02 .01
☐ 177 Bill Gullickson .05 .02 .01
☐ 178 Chris Gwynn .05 .02 .01
☐ 179 Melido Perez .05 .02 .01
☐ 180 Sid Fernandez UER .05 .02 .01
(779 runs in 1990)
☐ 181 Tim Burke .05 .02 .01
☐ 182 Gary Pettis .05 .02 .01
☐ 183 Rob Murphy .05 .02 .01
☐ 184 Craig Lefferts .05 .02 .01
☐ 185 Howard Johnson .05 .02 .01
☐ 186 Ken Caminiti .15 .07 .02
☐ 187 Tim Belcher .05 .02 .01
☐ 188 Greg Cadaret .05 .02 .01
☐ 189 Matt Williams .15 .07 .02
☐ 190 Dave Magadan .05 .02 .01
☐ 191 Geno Petralli .05 .02 .01
☐ 192 Jeff D. Robinson .05 .02 .01
☐ 193 Jim Deshaies .05 .02 .01
☐ 194 Willie Randolph .10 .05 .01
☐ 195 George Bell .05 .02 .01
☐ 196 Hubie Brooks .05 .02 .01
☐ 197 Tom Gordon .05 .02 .01
☐ 198 Mike Fitzgerald .05 .02 .01
☐ 199 Mike Pagliarulo .05 .02 .01
☐ 200 Kirby Puckett .40 .18 .05
☐ 201 Shawon Dunston .05 .02 .01
☐ 202 Dennis Boyd .05 .02 .01
☐ 203 Junior Felix UER .05 .02 .01
(Text has him in NL)
☐ 204 Alejandro Pena .05 .02 .01
☐ 205 Pete Smith .05 .02 .01
☐ 206 Tom Glavine UER .15 .07 .02
(Lefty spelled leftie)
☐ 207 Luis Salazar .05 .02 .01
☐ 208 John Smoltz .15 .07 .02
☐ 209 Doug Dascenzo .05 .02 .01
☐ 210 Tim Wallach .05 .02 .01
☐ 211 Greg Gagne .05 .02 .01
☐ 212 Mark Gubicza .05 .02 .01
☐ 213 Mark Parent .05 .02 .01
☐ 214 Ken Oberkfell .05 .02 .01
☐ 215 Gary Carter .10 .05 .01
☐ 216 Rafael Palmeiro .15 .07 .02
☐ 217 Tom Niedenfuer .05 .02 .01
☐ 218 Dave LaPoint .05 .02 .01
☐ 219 Jeff Treadway .05 .02 .01
☐ 220 Mitch Williams UER .05 .02 .01
('89 ERA shown as 2.76,
should be 2.64)
☐ 221 Jose DeLeon .05 .02 .01
☐ 222 Mike LaValliere .05 .02 .01
☐ 223 Darrel Akerfelds .05 .02 .01
☐ 224A Kent Anderson ERR .10 .05 .01
(First line, flachy
should read flashy)
☐ 224B Kent Anderson COR .10 .05 .01
(Corrected in
factory sets)
☐ 225 Dwight Evans .10 .05 .01
☐ 226 Gary Redus .05 .02 .01
☐ 227 Paul O'Neill .10 .05 .01
☐ 228 Marty Barrett .05 .02 .01
☐ 229 Tom Browning .05 .02 .01
☐ 230 Terry Pendleton .10 .05 .01
☐ 231 Jack Armstrong .05 .02 .01
☐ 232 Mike Boddicker .05 .02 .01
☐ 233 Neal Heaton .05 .02 .01
☐ 234 Marquis Grissom .15 .07 .02
☐ 235 Bert Blyleven .10 .05 .01
☐ 236 Curt Young .05 .02 .01
☐ 237 Don Carman .05 .02 .01
☐ 238 Charlie Hayes .05 .02 .01
☐ 239 Mark Knudson .05 .02 .01
☐ 240 Todd Zeile .10 .05 .01
☐ 241 Larry Walker UER .15 .07 .02
(Maple River, should
be Maple Ridge)
☐ 242 Jerald Clark .05 .02 .01
☐ 243 Jeff Ballard .05 .02 .01
☐ 244 Jeff King .10 .05 .01
☐ 245 Tom Brunansky .05 .02 .01
☐ 246 Darren Daulton .10 .05 .01
☐ 247 Scott Terry .05 .02 .01
☐ 248 Rob Deer .05 .02 .01
☐ 249 Brady Anderson UER .15 .07 .02
(1990 Hagerstown 1 hit,
should say 13 hits)
☐ 250 Len Dykstra .10 .05 .01
☐ 251 Greg W. Harris .05 .02 .01
☐ 252 Mike Hartley .05 .02 .01
☐ 253 Joey Cora .10 .05 .01
☐ 254 Ivan Calderon .05 .02 .01
☐ 255 Ted Power .05 .02 .01
☐ 256 Sammy Sosa .25 .11 .03
☐ 257 Steve Buechele .05 .02 .01
☐ 258 Mike Devereaux UER .05 .02 .01
(No comma between
city and state)
☐ 259 Brad Komminsk UER .05 .02 .01
(Last text line,
Ba should be BA)
☐ 260 Teddy Higuera .05 .02 .01
☐ 261 Shawn Abner .05 .02 .01
☐ 262 Dave Valle .05 .02 .01
☐ 263 Jeff Huson .05 .02 .01
☐ 264 Edgar Martinez .10 .05 .01
☐ 265 Carlton Fisk .15 .07 .02
☐ 266 Steve Finley .10 .05 .01
☐ 267 John Wetteland .15 .07 .02
☐ 268 Kevin Appier .15 .07 .02
☐ 269 Steve Lyons .05 .02 .01
☐ 270 Mickey Tettleton .10 .05 .01
☐ 271 Luis Rivera .05 .02 .01
☐ 272 Steve Jeltz .05 .02 .01
☐ 273 R.J. Reynolds .05 .02 .01
☐ 274 Carlos Martinez .05 .02 .01
☐ 275 Dan Plesac .05 .02 .01
☐ 276 Mike Morgan UER .05 .02 .01
(Total IP shown as
1149.1, should be 1149)
☐ 277 Jeff Russell .05 .02 .01
☐ 278 Pete Incaviglia .05 .02 .01
☐ 279 Kevin Seitzer UER .05 .02 .01
(Bio has 200 hits twice
and .300 four times,
should be once and
three times)
☐ 280 Bobby Thigpen .05 .02 .01
☐ 281 Stan Javier UER .05 .02 .01
(Born 1/9,
should say 9/1)
☐ 282 Henry Cotto .05 .02 .01
☐ 283 Gary Wayne .05 .02 .01
☐ 284 Shane Mack .05 .02 .01
☐ 285 Brian Holman .05 .02 .01
☐ 286 Gerald Perry .05 .02 .01
☐ 287 Steve Crawford .05 .02 .01
☐ 288 Nelson Liriano .05 .02 .01
☐ 289 Don Aase .05 .02 .01
☐ 290 Randy Johnson .15 .07 .02
☐ 291 Harold Baines .10 .05 .01
☐ 292 Kent Hrbek .10 .05 .01
☐ 293A Les Lancaster ERR .05 .02 .01
(No comma between
Dallas and Texas)
☐ 293B Les Lancaster COR .05 .02 .01
(Corrected in
factory sets)
☐ 294 Jeff Musselman .05 .02 .01
☐ 295 Kurt Stillwell .05 .02 .01
☐ 296 Stan Belinda .05 .02 .01
☐ 297 Lou Whitaker .10 .05 .01
☐ 298 Glenn Wilson .05 .02 .01
☐ 299 Omar Vizquel UER .15 .07 .02
(Born 5/15, should be
4/24, there is a decimal
before GP total for '90)
☐ 300 Ramon Martinez .15 .07 .02
☐ 301 Dwight Smith .05 .02 .01
☐ 302 Tim Crews .05 .02 .01
☐ 303 Lance Blankenship .05 .02 .01
☐ 304 Sid Bream .05 .02 .01
☐ 305 Rafael Ramirez .05 .02 .01
☐ 306 Steve Wilson .05 .02 .01
☐ 307 Mackey Sasser .05 .02 .01
☐ 308 Franklin Stubbs .05 .02 .01
☐ 309 Jack Daugherty UER .05 .02 .01
(Born 6/3/60,
should say July)
☐ 310 Eddie Murray .25 .11 .03
☐ 311 Bob Welch .05 .02 .01
☐ 312 Brian Harper .05 .02 .01
☐ 313 Lance McCullers .05 .02 .01
☐ 314 Dave Smith .05 .02 .01
☐ 315 Bobby Bonilla .10 .05 .01
☐ 316 Jerry Don Gleaton .05 .02 .01
☐ 317 Greg Maddux .60 .25 .07
☐ 318 Keith Miller .05 .02 .01
☐ 319 Mark Portugal .05 .02 .01
☐ 320 Robin Ventura .15 .07 .02
☐ 321 Bob Ojeda .05 .02 .01
☐ 322 Mike Harkey .05 .02 .01
☐ 323 Jay Bell .10 .05 .01
☐ 324 Mark McGwire .30 .14 .04
☐ 325 Gary Gaetti .10 .05 .01
☐ 326 Jeff Pico .05 .02 .01
☐ 327 Kevin McReynolds .05 .02 .01
☐ 328 Frank Tanana .05 .02 .01
☐ 329 Eric Yelding UER .05 .02 .01
(Listed as 6'3"
should be 5'11")
☐ 330 Barry Bonds .25 .11 .03
☐ 331 Brian McRae UER .25 .11 .03
(No comma between
city and state)
☐ 332 Pedro Munoz .10 .05 .01
☐ 333 Daryl Irvine .05 .02 .01
☐ 334 Chris Hoiles .05 .02 .01
☐ 335 Thomas Howard .05 .02 .01
☐ 336 Jeff Schulz .05 .02 .01
☐ 337 Jeff Manto .05 .02 .01
☐ 338 Beau Allred .05 .02 .01
☐ 339 Mike Bordick .15 .07 .02
☐ 340 Todd Hundley .15 .07 .02
☐ 341 Jim Vatcher UER .05 .02 .01
(Height 6'9",
should be 5'9")
☐ 342 Luis Sojo .05 .02 .01
☐ 343 Jose Offerman UER .05 .02 .01
(Born 1969, should
say 1968)
☐ 344 Pete Coachman .05 .02 .01
☐ 345 Mike Benjamin .05 .02 .01
☐ 346 Ozzie Canseco .05 .02 .01
☐ 347 Tim McIntosh .05 .02 .01
☐ 348 Phil Plantier .10 .05 .01
☐ 349 Terry Shumpert .05 .02 .01
☐ 350 Darren Lewis .10 .05 .01
☐ 351 David Walsh .05 .02 .01
☐ 352A Scott Chiamparino .10 .05 .01
ERR (Bats left,
should be right)
☐ 352B Scott Chiamparino .10 .05 .01
COR (corrected in
factory sets)
☐ 353 Julio Valera .05 .02 .01
UER (Progressed mis-
spelled as progessed)
☐ 354 Anthony Telford .05 .02 .01
☐ 355 Kevin Wickander .05 .02 .01
☐ 356 Tim Naehring .10 .05 .01
☐ 357 Jim Poole .05 .02 .01
☐ 358 Mark Whiten UER .10 .05 .01
(Shown hitting lefty,
bio says righty)
☐ 359 Terry Wells .05 .02 .01
☐ 360 Rafael Valdez .05 .02 .01
☐ 361 Mel Stottlemyre Jr. .05 .02 .01
☐ 362 David Segui .10 .05 .01
☐ 363 Paul Abbott .05 .02 .01
☐ 364 Steve Howard .05 .02 .01
☐ 365 Karl Rhodes .05 .02 .01
☐ 366 Rafael Novoa .05 .02 .01
☐ 367 Joe Grahe .05 .02 .01
☐ 368 Darren Reed .05 .02 .01
☐ 369 Jeff McKnight .05 .02 .01
☐ 370 Scott Leius .05 .02 .01
☐ 371 Mark Dewey .05 .02 .01
☐ 372 Mark Lee UER .05 .02 .01
(Shown hitting lefty,
bio says righty, born
in Dakota, should
say North Dakota)
☐ 373 Rosario Rodriguez .05 .02 .01
(Shown hitting lefty,
bio says righty) UER
☐ 374 Chuck McElroy .05 .02 .01
☐ 375 Mike Bell .05 .02 .01
☐ 376 Mickey Morandini .05 .02 .01
☐ 377 Bill Haselman .05 .02 .01
☐ 378 Dave Pavlas .05 .02 .01
☐ 379 Derrick May .05 .02 .01
☐ 380 Jeromy Burnitz FDP .10 .05 .01
☐ 381 Donald Peters FDP .05 .02 .01
☐ 382 Alex Fernandez FDP .15 .07 .02
☐ 383 Mike Mussina FDP 1.00 .45 .12
☐ 384 Dan Smith FDP .05 .02 .01
☐ 385 Lance Dickson FDP .05 .02 .01
☐ 386 Carl Everett FDP .15 .07 .02
☐ 387 Thomas Nevers FDP .05 .02 .01
☐ 388 Adam Hyzdu FDP .05 .02 .01
☐ 389 Todd Van Poppel FDP .10 .05 .01
☐ 390 Rondell White FDP .40 .18 .05
☐ 391 Marc Newfield FDP .15 .07 .02
☐ 392 Julio Franco AS .05 .02 .01
☐ 393 Wade Boggs AS .15 .07 .02
☐ 394 Ozzie Guillen AS .05 .02 .01
☐ 395 Cecil Fielder AS .10 .05 .01
☐ 396 Ken Griffey Jr. AS .75 .35 .09
☐ 397 Rickey Henderson AS .15 .07 .02
☐ 398 Jose Canseco AS .15 .07 .02
☐ 399 Roger Clemens AS .15 .07 .02
☐ 400 Sandy Alomar Jr. AS .10 .05 .01
☐ 401 Bobby Thigpen AS .05 .02 .01
☐ 402 Bobby Bonilla MB .10 .05 .01
☐ 403 Eric Davis MB .10 .05 .01
☐ 404 Fred McGriff MB .15 .07 .02
☐ 405 Glenn Davis MB .05 .02 .01
☐ 406 Kevin Mitchell MB .05 .02 .01
☐ 407 Rob Dibble KM .05 .02 .01
☐ 408 Ramon Martinez KM .15 .07 .02
☐ 409 David Cone KM .10 .05 .01
☐ 410 Bobby Witt KM .05 .02 .01
☐ 411 Mark Langston KM .05 .02 .01
☐ 412 Bo Jackson RIF .10 .05 .01
☐ 413 Shawon Dunston RIF .05 .02 .01
UER (In the baseball,
should say in baseball)
☐ 414 Jesse Barfield RIF .05 .02 .01
☐ 415 Ken Caminiti RIF .15 .07 .02
☐ 416 Benito Santiago RIF .05 .02 .01
☐ 417 Nolan Ryan HL .40 .18 .05

☐ 418 Bobby Thigpen HL UER .05 .02 .01
(Back refers to Hal McRae Jr., should say Brian McRae)
☐ 419 Ramon Martinez HL .15 .07 .02
☐ 420 Bo Jackson HL .10 .05 .01
☐ 421 Carlton Fisk HL .15 .07 .02
☐ 422 Jimmy Key .10 .05 .01
☐ 423 Junior Noboa .05 .02 .01
☐ 424 Al Newman .05 .02 .01
☐ 425 Pat Borders .05 .02 .01
☐ 426 Von Hayes .05 .02 .01
☐ 427 Tim Teufel .05 .02 .01
☐ 428 Eric Plunk UER .05 .02 .01
(Text says Eric's had, no apostrophe needed)
☐ 429 John Moses .05 .02 .01
☐ 430 Mike Witt .05 .02 .01
☐ 431 Otis Nixon .05 .02 .01
☐ 432 Tony Fernandez .05 .02 .01
☐ 433 Rance Mulliniks .05 .02 .01
☐ 434 Dan Petry .05 .02 .01
☐ 435 Bob Geren .05 .02 .01
☐ 436 Steve Frey .05 .02 .01
☐ 437 Jamie Moyer .05 .02 .01
☐ 438 Junior Ortiz .05 .02 .01
☐ 439 Tom O'Malley .05 .02 .01
☐ 440 Pat Combs .05 .02 .01
☐ 441 Jose Canseco DT .15 .07 .02
☐ 442 Alfredo Griffin .05 .02 .01
☐ 443 Andres Galarraga .15 .07 .02
☐ 444 Bryn Smith .05 .02 .01
☐ 445 Andre Dawson .10 .05 .01
☐ 446 Juan Samuel .05 .02 .01
☐ 447 Mike Aldrete .05 .02 .01
☐ 448 Ron Gant .10 .05 .01
☐ 449 Fernando Valenzuela .10 .05 .01
☐ 450 Vince Coleman UER .05 .02 .01
(Should say topped majors in steals four times, not three times)
☐ 451 Kevin Mitchell .10 .05 .01
☐ 452 Spike Owen .05 .02 .01
☐ 453 Mike Bielecki .05 .02 .01
☐ 454 Dennis Martinez .10 .05 .01
☐ 455 Brett Butler .10 .05 .01
☐ 456 Ron Darling .05 .02 .01
☐ 457 Dennis Rasmussen .05 .02 .01
☐ 458 Ken Howell .05 .02 .01
☐ 459 Steve Bedrosian .05 .02 .01
☐ 460 Frank Viola .05 .02 .01
☐ 461 Jose Lind .05 .02 .01
☐ 462 Chris Sabo .05 .02 .01
☐ 463 Dante Bichette .15 .07 .02
☐ 464 Rick Mahler .05 .02 .01
☐ 465 John Smiley .05 .02 .01
☐ 466 Devon White .10 .05 .01
☐ 467 John Orton .05 .02 .01
☐ 468 Mike Stanton .05 .02 .01
☐ 469 Billy Hatcher .05 .02 .01
☐ 470 Wally Joyner .10 .05 .01
☐ 471 Gene Larkin .05 .02 .01
☐ 472 Doug Drabek .05 .02 .01
☐ 473 Gary Sheffield .15 .07 .02
☐ 474 David Wells .05 .02 .01
☐ 475 Andy Van Slyke .10 .05 .01
☐ 476 Mike Gallego .05 .02 .01
☐ 477 B.J. Surhoff .10 .05 .01
☐ 478 Gene Nelson .05 .02 .01
☐ 479 Mariano Duncan .05 .02 .01
☐ 480 Fred McGriff .15 .07 .02
☐ 481 Jerry Browne .05 .02 .01
☐ 482 Alvin Davis .05 .02 .01
☐ 483 Bill Wegman .05 .02 .01
☐ 484 Dave Parker .10 .05 .01
☐ 485 Dennis Eckersley .10 .05 .01
☐ 486 Erik Hanson UER .05 .02 .01
(Basketball misspelled as baseketball)
☐ 487 Bill Ripken .05 .02 .01
☐ 488 Tom Candiotti .05 .02 .01
☐ 489 Mike Schooler .05 .02 .01
☐ 490 Gregg Olson .05 .02 .01
☐ 491 Chris James .05 .02 .01
☐ 492 Pete Harnisch .05 .02 .01
☐ 493 Julio Franco .10 .05 .01
☐ 494 Greg Briley .05 .02 .01
☐ 495 Ruben Sierra .10 .05 .01
☐ 496 Steve Olin .05 .02 .01
☐ 497 Mike Fetters .05 .02 .01
☐ 498 Mark Williamson .05 .02 .01
☐ 499 Bob Tewksbury .05 .02 .01
☐ 500 Tony Gwynn .40 .18 .05
☐ 501 Randy Myers .10 .05 .01
☐ 502 Keith Comstock .05 .02 .01
☐ 503 Craig Worthington UER .05 .02 .01
(DeCinces misspelled DiCinces on back)
☐ 504 Mark Eichhorn UER .05 .02 .01
(Stats incomplete, doesn't have '89 Braves stint)
☐ 505 Barry Larkin .15 .07 .02
☐ 506 Dave Johnson .05 .02 .01
☐ 507 Bobby Witt .05 .02 .01
☐ 508 Joe Orsulak .05 .02 .01
☐ 509 Pete O'Brien .05 .02 .01
☐ 510 Brad Arnsberg .05 .02 .01
☐ 511 Storm Davis .05 .02 .01
☐ 512 Bob Milacki .05 .02 .01
☐ 513 Bill Pecota .05 .02 .01
☐ 514 Glenallen Hill .05 .02 .01
☐ 515 Danny Tartabull .05 .02 .01
☐ 516 Mike Moore .05 .02 .01
☐ 517 Ron Robinson UER .05 .02 .01
(577 K's in 1990)
☐ 518 Mark Gardner .05 .02 .01
☐ 519 Rick Wrona .05 .02 .01
☐ 520 Mike Scioscia .05 .02 .01
☐ 521 Frank Wills .05 .02 .01
☐ 522 Greg Brock .05 .02 .01
☐ 523 Jack Clark .10 .05 .01
☐ 524 Bruce Ruffin .05 .02 .01
☐ 525 Robin Yount .15 .07 .02
☐ 526 Tom Foley .05 .02 .01
☐ 527 Pat Perry .05 .02 .01
☐ 528 Greg Vaughn .10 .05 .01
☐ 529 Wally Whitehurst .05 .02 .01
☐ 530 Norm Charlton .05 .02 .01
☐ 531 Marvell Wynne .05 .02 .01
☐ 532 Jim Gantner .05 .02 .01
☐ 533 Greg Litton .05 .02 .01
☐ 534 Manny Lee .05 .02 .01
☐ 535 Scott Bailes .05 .02 .01
☐ 536 Charlie Leibrandt .05 .02 .01
☐ 537 Roger McDowell .05 .02 .01
☐ 538 Andy Benes .10 .05 .01
☐ 539 Rick Honeycutt .05 .02 .01
☐ 540 Dwight Gooden .10 .05 .01
☐ 541 Scott Garrelts .05 .02 .01
☐ 542 Dave Clark .05 .02 .01
☐ 543 Lonnie Smith .05 .02 .01
☐ 544 Rick Reuschel .05 .02 .01
☐ 545 Delino DeShields UER .05 .02 .01
(Rockford misspelled as Rock Ford in '88)
☐ 546 Mike Sharperson .05 .02 .01
☐ 547 Mike Kingery .05 .02 .01
☐ 548 Terry Kennedy .05 .02 .01
☐ 549 David Cone .10 .05 .01
☐ 550 Orel Hershiser .10 .05 .01
☐ 551 Matt Nokes .05 .02 .01
☐ 552 Eddie Williams .05 .02 .01
☐ 553 Frank DiPino .05 .02 .01
☐ 554 Fred Lynn .05 .02 .01
☐ 555 Alex Cole .05 .02 .01
☐ 556 Terry Leach .05 .02 .01
☐ 557 Chet Lemon .05 .02 .01
☐ 558 Paul Mirabella .05 .02 .01
☐ 559 Bill Long .05 .02 .01
☐ 560 Phil Bradley .05 .02 .01
☐ 561 Duane Ward .05 .02 .01
☐ 562 Dave Bergman .05 .02 .01
☐ 563 Eric Show .05 .02 .01
☐ 564 Xavier Hernandez .05 .02 .01
☐ 565 Jeff Parrett .05 .02 .01
☐ 566 Chuck Cary .05 .02 .01
☐ 567 Ken Hill .10 .05 .01
☐ 568 Bob Welch Hand .05 .02 .01
(Complement should be compliment) UER
☐ 569 John Mitchell .05 .02 .01
☐ 570 Travis Fryman .15 .07 .02
☐ 571 Derek Lilliquist .05 .02 .01
☐ 572 Steve Lake .05 .02 .01
☐ 573 John Barfield .05 .02 .01
☐ 574 Randy Bush .05 .02 .01
☐ 575 Joe Magrane .05 .02 .01
☐ 576 Eddie Diaz .05 .02 .01
☐ 577 Casey Candaele .05 .02 .01
☐ 578 Jesse Orosco .05 .02 .01
☐ 579 Tom Henke .05 .02 .01
☐ 580 Rick Cerone UER .05 .02 .01
(Actually his third go-round with Yankees)
☐ 581 Drew Hall .05 .02 .01
☐ 582 Tony Castillo .05 .02 .01
☐ 583 Jimmy Jones .05 .02 .01
☐ 584 Rick Reed .05 .02 .01
☐ 585 Joe Girardi .10 .05 .01
☐ 586 Jeff Gray .05 .02 .01
☐ 587 Luis Polonia .05 .02 .01
☐ 588 Joe Klink .05 .02 .01
☐ 589 Rex Hudler .05 .02 .01
☐ 590 Kirk McCaskill .05 .02 .01
☐ 591 Juan Agosto .05 .02 .01
☐ 592 Wes Gardner .05 .02 .01
☐ 593 Rich Rodriguez .05 .02 .01
☐ 594 Mitch Webster .05 .02 .01
☐ 595 Kelly Gruber .05 .02 .01
☐ 596 Dale Mohorcic .05 .02 .01
☐ 597 Willie McGee .05 .02 .01
☐ 598 Bill Krueger .05 .02 .01
☐ 599 Bob Walk UER .05 .02 .01
(Cards says he's 33, but actually he's 34)
☐ 600 Kevin Maas .05 .02 .01
☐ 601 Danny Jackson .05 .02 .01
☐ 602 Craig McMurtry UER .05 .02 .01
(Anonymously misspelled anonimously)
☐ 603 Curtis Wilkerson .05 .02 .01
☐ 604 Adam Peterson .05 .02 .01
☐ 605 Sam Horn .05 .02 .01
☐ 606 Tommy Gregg .05 .02 .01
☐ 607 Ken Dayley .05 .02 .01
☐ 608 Carmelo Castillo .05 .02 .01
☐ 609 John Shelby .05 .02 .01
☐ 610 Don Slaught .05 .02 .01
☐ 611 Calvin Schiraldi .05 .02 .01
☐ 612 Dennis Lamp .05 .02 .01
☐ 613 Andres Thomas .05 .02 .01
☐ 614 Jose Gonzalez .05 .02 .01
☐ 615 Randy Ready .05 .02 .01
☐ 616 Kevin Bass .05 .02 .01
☐ 617 Mike Marshall .05 .02 .01
☐ 618 Daryl Boston .05 .02 .01
☐ 619 Andy McGaffigan .05 .02 .01
☐ 620 Joe Oliver .05 .02 .01
☐ 621 Jim Gott .05 .02 .01
☐ 622 Jose Oquendo .05 .02 .01
☐ 623 Jose DeJesus .05 .02 .01
☐ 624 Mike Brumley .05 .02 .01
☐ 625 John Olerud .10 .05 .01
☐ 626 Ernest Riles .05 .02 .01
☐ 627 Gene Harris .05 .02 .01
☐ 628 Jose Uribe .05 .02 .01
☐ 629 Darnell Coles .05 .02 .01
☐ 630 Carney Lansford .10 .05 .01
☐ 631 Tim Leary .05 .02 .01
☐ 632 Tim Hulett .05 .02 .01
☐ 633 Kevin Elster .05 .02 .01
☐ 634 Tony Fossas .05 .02 .01
☐ 635 Francisco Oliveras .05 .02 .01
☐ 636 Bob Patterson .05 .02 .01
☐ 637 Gary Ward .05 .02 .01
☐ 638 Rene Gonzales .05 .02 .01
☐ 639 Don Robinson .05 .02 .01
☐ 640 Darryl Strawberry .10 .05 .01
☐ 641 Dave Anderson .05 .02 .01
☐ 642 Scott Scudder .05 .02 .01
☐ 643 Reggie Harris UER .05 .02 .01
(Hepatitis misspelled as hepititis)
☐ 644 Dave Henderson .05 .02 .01
☐ 645 Ben McDonald .10 .05 .01
☐ 646 Bob Kipper .05 .02 .01
☐ 647 Hal Morris UER .05 .02 .01
(It's should be its)
☐ 648 Tim Birtsas .05 .02 .01
☐ 649 Steve Searcy .05 .02 .01
☐ 650 Dale Murphy .15 .07 .02
☐ 651 Ron Oester .05 .02 .01
☐ 652 Mike LaCoss .05 .02 .01
☐ 653 Ron Jones .05 .02 .01
☐ 654 Kelly Downs .05 .02 .01
☐ 655 Roger Clemens .20 .09 .03
☐ 656 Herm Winningham .05 .02 .01
☐ 657 Trevor Wilson .05 .02 .01
☐ 658 Jose Rijo .05 .02 .01
☐ 659 Dann Bilardello UER .05 .02 .01
(Bio has 13 games, 1 hit, and 32 AB, stats show 19, 2, and 37)
☐ 660 Gregg Jefferies .10 .05 .01
☐ 661 Doug Drabek AS UER .05 .02 .01
(Through is mis-spelled though)
☐ 662 Randy Myers AS .05 .02 .01
☐ 663 Benny Santiago AS .05 .02 .01
☐ 664 Will Clark AS .15 .07 .02
☐ 665 Ryne Sandberg AS .15 .07 .02
☐ 666 Barry Larkin AS UER .15 .07 .02
(Line 13, coolly misspelled cooly)
☐ 667 Matt Williams AS .15 .07 .02
☐ 668 Barry Bonds AS .15 .07 .02
☐ 669 Eric Davis AS .10 .05 .01
☐ 670 Bobby Bonilla AS .10 .05 .01
☐ 671 Chipper Jones FDP 3.00 1.35 .35
☐ 672 Eric Christopherson FDP .05 .02 .01
☐ 673 Robbie Beckett FDP .05 .02 .01
☐ 674 Shane Andrews FDP .15 .07 .02
☐ 675 Steve Karsay FDP .15 .07 .02
☐ 676 Aaron Holbert FDP .05 .02 .01
☐ 677 Donovan Osborne FDP .15 .07 .02
☐ 678 Todd Ritchie FDP .05 .02 .01
☐ 679 Ron Walden FDP .05 .02 .01
☐ 680 Tim Costo FDP .05 .02 .01
☐ 681 Dan Wilson FDP .25 .11 .03
☐ 682 Kurt Miller FDP .05 .02 .01
☐ 683 Mike Lieberthal FDP .15 .07 .02
☐ 684 Roger Clemens KM .15 .07 .02
☐ 685 Doc Gooden KM .10 .05 .01
☐ 686 Nolan Ryan KM .40 .18 .05
☐ 687 Frank Viola KM .05 .02 .01
☐ 688 Erik Hanson KM .05 .02 .01
☐ 689 Matt Williams MB .15 .07 .02
☐ 690 Jose Canseco MB UER .15 .07 .02
(Mammoth misspelled as monmouth)
☐ 691 Darryl Strawberry MB .10 .05 .01
☐ 692 Bo Jackson MB .10 .05 .01
☐ 693 Cecil Fielder MB .10 .05 .01
☐ 694 Sandy Alomar Jr. RF .10 .05 .01
☐ 695 Cory Snyder RF .05 .02 .01
☐ 696 Eric Davis RF .10 .05 .01
☐ 697 Ken Griffey Jr. RF .75 .35 .09
☐ 698 Andy Van Slyke RF UER .05 .02 .01
(Line 2, outfielders does not need)
☐ 699 Langston/Witt NH .05 .02 .01
Mark Langston
Mike Witt
☐ 700 Randy Johnson NH .15 .07 .02
☐ 701 Nolan Ryan NH .40 .18 .05
☐ 702 Dave Stewart NH .05 .02 .01
☐ 703 Fernando Valenzuela NH .10 .05 .01
☐ 704 Andy Hawkins NH .05 .02 .01
☐ 705 Melido Perez NH .05 .02 .01
☐ 706 Terry Mulholland NH .05 .02 .01
☐ 707 Dave Stieb NH .05 .02 .01
☐ 708 Brian Barnes .05 .02 .01
☐ 709 Bernard Gilkey .10 .05 .01
☐ 710 Steve Decker .05 .02 .01
☐ 711 Paul Faries .05 .02 .01
☐ 712 Paul Marak .05 .02 .01
☐ 713 Wes Chamberlain .05 .02 .01
☐ 714 Kevin Belcher .05 .02 .01
☐ 715 Dan Boone UER .05 .02 .01
(IP adds up to 101, but card has 101.2)
☐ 716 Steve Adkins .05 .02 .01
☐ 717 Geronimo Pena .05 .02 .01
☐ 718 Howard Farmer .05 .02 .01
☐ 719 Mark Leonard .05 .02 .01
☐ 720 Tom Lampkin .05 .02 .01
☐ 721 Mike Gardiner .05 .02 .01
☐ 722 Jeff Conine .50 .23 .06
☐ 723 Efrain Valdez .05 .02 .01
☐ 724 Chuck Malone .05 .02 .01
☐ 725 Leo Gomez .05 .02 .01
☐ 726 Paul McClellan .05 .02 .01
☐ 727 Mark Leiter .05 .02 .01
☐ 728 Rich DeLucia UER .05 .02 .01
(Line 2, all told is written alltold)
☐ 729 Mel Rojas .10 .05 .01
☐ 730 Hector Wagner .05 .02 .01
☐ 731 Ray Lankford .15 .07 .02
☐ 732 Turner Ward .05 .02 .01
☐ 733 Gerald Alexander .05 .02 .01
☐ 734 Scott Anderson .05 .02 .01
☐ 735 Tony Perezchica .05 .02 .01
☐ 736 Jimmy Kremers .05 .02 .01
☐ 737 American Flag .15 .07 .02
(Pray for Peace)
☐ 738 Mike York .05 .02 .01
☐ 739 Mike Rochford .05 .02 .01
☐ 740 Scott Aldred .05 .02 .01
☐ 741 Rico Brogna .10 .05 .01
☐ 742 Dave Burba .05 .02 .01
☐ 743 Ray Stephens .05 .02 .01
☐ 744 Eric Gunderson .05 .02 .01
☐ 745 Troy Afenir .05 .02 .01
☐ 746 Jeff Shaw .05 .02 .01
☐ 747 Orlando Merced .15 .07 .02
☐ 748 Omar Olivares UER .05 .02 .01
(Line 9, league is misspelled legaue)
☐ 749 Jerry Kutzler .05 .02 .01
☐ 750 Mo Vaughn UER .50 .23 .06
(44 SB's in 1990)
☐ 751 Matt Stark .05 .02 .01
☐ 752 Randy Hennis .05 .02 .01
☐ 753 Andujar Cedeno .05 .02 .01
☐ 754 Kelvin Torve .05 .02 .01
☐ 755 Joe Kraemer .05 .02 .01
☐ 756 Phil Clark .05 .02 .01
☐ 757 Ed Vosberg .05 .02 .01
☐ 758 Mike Perez .05 .02 .01
☐ 759 Scott Lewis .05 .02 .01
☐ 760 Steve Chitren .05 .02 .01
☐ 761 Ray Young .05 .02 .01
☐ 762 Andres Santana .05 .02 .01
☐ 763 Rodney McCray .05 .02 .01
☐ 764 Sean Berry UER .10 .05 .01
(Name misspelled Barry on card front)
☐ 765 Brent Mayne .05 .02 .01
☐ 766 Mike Simms .05 .02 .01
☐ 767 Glenn Sutko .05 .02 .01
☐ 768 Gary DiSarcina .05 .02 .01
☐ 769 George Brett HL .20 .09 .03
☐ 770 Cecil Fielder HL .10 .05 .01
☐ 771 Jim Presley .05 .02 .01
☐ 772 John Dopson .05 .02 .01
☐ 773 Bo Jackson Breaker .10 .05 .01
☐ 774 Brent Knackert UER .05 .02 .01
(Born in 1954, shown throwing righty, but bio says lefty)
☐ 775 Bill Doran UER .05 .02 .01
(Reds in NL East)
☐ 776 Dick Schofield .05 .02 .01
☐ 777 Nelson Santovenia .05 .02 .01
☐ 778 Mark Guthrie .05 .02 .01
☐ 779 Mark Lemke .05 .02 .01
☐ 780 Terry Steinbach .10 .05 .01
☐ 781 Tom Bolton .05 .02 .01

□ 782 Randy Tomlin	.05	.02	.01
□ 783 Jeff Kunkel	.05	.02	.01
□ 784 Felix Jose	.05	.02	.01
□ 785 Rick Sutcliffe	.05	.02	.01
□ 786 John Cerutti	.05	.02	.01
□ 787 Jose Vizcaino UER	.05	.02	.01
(Offerman, not Opperman)			
□ 788 Curt Schilling	.05	.02	.01
□ 789 Ed Whitson	.05	.02	.01
□ 790 Tony Pena	.05	.02	.01
□ 791 John Candelaria	.05	.02	.01
□ 792 Carmelo Martinez	.05	.02	.01
□ 793 Sandy Alomar Jr. UER	.10	.05	.01
(Indian's should say Indians')			
□ 794 Jim Neidlinger	.05	.02	.01
□ 795 Barry Larkin WS and Chris Sabo	.15	.07	.02
□ 796 Paul Sorrento	.10	.05	.01
□ 797 Tom Pagnozzi	.05	.02	.01
□ 798 Tino Martinez	.15	.07	.02
□ 799 Scott Ruskin UER	.05	.02	.01
(Text says first three seasons but lists averages for four)			
□ 800 Kirk Gibson	.10	.05	.01
□ 801 Walt Terrell	.05	.02	.01
□ 802 John Russell	.05	.02	.01
□ 803 Chili Davis	.10	.05	.01
□ 804 Chris Nabholz	.05	.02	.01
□ 805 Juan Gonzalez	.75	.35	.09
□ 806 Ron Hassey	.05	.02	.01
□ 807 Todd Worrell	.05	.02	.01
□ 808 Tommy Greene	.05	.02	.01
□ 809 Joel Skinner UER	.05	.02	.01
(Joel, not Bob, was drafted in 1979)			
□ 810 Benito Santiago	.05	.02	.01
□ 811 Pat Tabler UER	.05	.02	.01
(Line 3, always misspelled alway)			
□ 812 Scott Erickson UER	.10	.05	.01
(Record spelled rcord)			
□ 813 Moises Alou	.15	.07	.02
□ 814 Dale Sveum	.05	.02	.01
□ 815 Ryne Sandberg MANYR	.15	.07	.02
□ 816 Rick Dempsey	.05	.02	.01
□ 817 Scott Bankhead	.05	.02	.01
□ 818 Jason Grimsley	.05	.02	.01
□ 819 Doug Jennings	.05	.02	.01
□ 820 Tom Herr	.05	.02	.01
□ 821 Rob Ducey	.05	.02	.01
□ 822 Luis Quinones	.05	.02	.01
□ 823 Greg Minton	.05	.02	.01
□ 824 Mark Grant	.05	.02	.01
□ 825 Ozzie Smith UER	.25	.11	.03
(Shortstop misspelled shortsop)			
□ 826 Dave Eiland	.05	.02	.01
□ 827 Danny Heep	.05	.02	.01
□ 828 Hensley Meulens	.05	.02	.01
□ 829 Charlie O'Brien	.05	.02	.01
□ 830 Glenn Davis	.05	.02	.01
□ 831 John Marzano UER	.05	.02	.01
(International mis-spelled Internaional)			
□ 832 Steve Ontiveros	.05	.02	.01
□ 833 Ron Karkovice	.05	.02	.01
□ 834 Jerry Goff	.05	.02	.01
□ 835 Ken Griffey Sr.	.05	.02	.01
□ 836 Kevin Reimer	.05	.02	.01
□ 837 Randy Kutcher UER	.05	.02	.01
(Infectious mis-spelled infectous)			
□ 838 Mike Blowers	.05	.02	.01
□ 839 Mike Macfarlane	.05	.02	.01
□ 840 Frank Thomas UER	2.00	.90	.25
(1989 Sarasota stats, 15 games but 188 AB)			
□ 841 The Griffeys	.75	.35	.09
Ken Griffey Jr. Ken Griffey Sr.			
□ 842 Jack Howell	.05	.02	.01
□ 843 Goose Gozzo	.05	.02	.01
□ 844 Gerald Young	.05	.02	.01
□ 845 Zane Smith	.05	.02	.01
□ 846 Kevin Brown	.10	.05	.01
□ 847 Sil Campusano	.05	.02	.01
□ 848 Larry Andersen	.05	.02	.01
□ 849 Cal Ripken FRAN	.40	.18	.05
□ 850 Roger Clemens FRAN	.15	.07	.02
□ 851 Sandy Alomar Jr. FRAN	.10	.05	.01
□ 852 Alan Trammell FRAN	.10	.05	.01
□ 853 George Brett FRAN	.20	.09	.03
□ 854 Robin Yount FRAN	.15	.07	.02
□ 855 Kirby Puckett FRAN	.15	.07	.02
□ 856 Don Mattingly FRAN	.25	.11	.03
□ 857 Rickey Henderson FRAN	.15	.07	.02
□ 858 Ken Griffey Jr. FRAN	.75	.35	.09
□ 859 Ruben Sierra FRAN	.10	.05	.01
□ 860 John Olerud FRAN	.05	.02	.01
□ 861 Dave Justice FRAN	.10	.05	.01
□ 862 Ryne Sandberg FRAN	.15	.07	.02
□ 863 Eric Davis FRAN	.10	.05	.01
□ 864 Darryl Strawberry FRAN	.10	.05	.01
□ 865 Tim Wallach FRAN	.05	.02	.01
□ 866 Doc Gooden FRAN	.10	.05	.01
□ 867 Len Dykstra FRAN	.10	.05	.01
□ 868 Barry Bonds FRAN	.15	.07	.02
□ 869 Todd Zeile FRAN UER	.05	.02	.01
(Powerful misspelled as poweful)			
□ 870 Benito Santiago FRAN	.05	.02	.01
□ 871 Will Clark FRAN	.15	.07	.02
□ 872 Craig Biggio FRAN	.15	.07	.02
□ 873 Wally Joyner FRAN	.05	.02	.01
□ 874 Frank Thomas FRAN	1.00	.45	.12
□ 875 Rickey Henderson MVP	.15	.07	.02
□ 876 Barry Bonds MVP	.15	.07	.02
□ 877 Bob Welch CY	.05	.02	.01
□ 878 Doug Drabek CY	.05	.02	.01
□ 879 Sandy Alomar Jr ROY	.10	.05	.01
□ 880 Dave Justice ROY	.10	.05	.01
□ 881 Damon Berryhill	.05	.02	.01
□ 882 Frank Viola DT	.05	.02	.01
□ 883 Dave Stewart DT	.05	.02	.01
□ 884 Doug Jones DT	.05	.02	.01
□ 885 Randy Myers DT	.05	.02	.01
□ 886 Will Clark DT	.15	.07	.02
□ 887 Roberto Alomar DT	.20	.09	.03
□ 888 Barry Larkin DT	.15	.07	.02
□ 889 Wade Boggs DT	.15	.07	.02
□ 890 Rickey Henderson DT	.15	.07	.02
□ 891 Kirby Puckett DT	.40	.18	.05
□ 892 Ken Griffey Jr DT	1.50	.70	.19
□ 893 Benny Santiago DT	.05	.02	.01

1991 Score Cooperstown

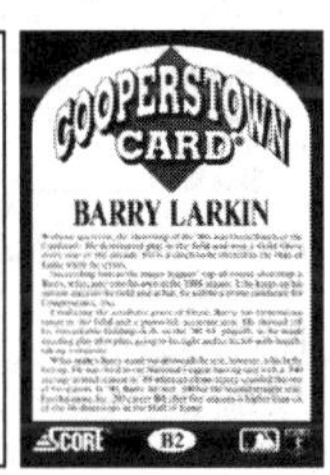

This seven-card standard-size set was available only in complete set form as an insert with 1991 Score factory sets. The card design is not like the regular 1991 Score cards. The card front features a portrait of the player in an oval on a white background. The words "Cooperstown Card" are prominently displayed on the front. The cards are numbered on the back with a B prefix.

	MINT	NRMT	EXC
COMPLETE SET (7)	8.00	3.60	1.00
COMMON CARD (B1-B7)	.50	.23	.06
□ B1 Wade Boggs	.50	.23	.06
□ B2 Barry Larkin	1.00	.45	.12
□ B3 Ken Griffey Jr.	5.00	2.20	.60
□ B4 Rickey Henderson	.50	.23	.06
□ B5 George Brett	1.50	.70	.19
□ B6 Will Clark	.50	.23	.06
□ B7 Nolan Ryan	3.00	1.35	.35

1991 Score Hot Rookies

This ten-card standard-size set was inserted in the one per 1991 Score 100-card blister pack. The front features a color action player photo, with white borders and the words "Hot Rookie" in yellow above the picture. The card background shades from orange to yellow to orange as one moves down the card face. In a horizontal format, the left half of the back has a color head shot, while the right half has career summary.

	MINT	NRMT	EXC
COMPLETE SET (10)	15.00	6.75	1.85
COMMON CARD (1-10)	.50	.23	.06
□ 1 Dave Justice	.75	.35	.09
□ 2 Kevin Maas	.50	.23	.06
□ 3 Hal Morris	.50	.23	.06
□ 4 Frank Thomas	10.00	4.50	1.25
□ 5 Jeff Conine	1.25	.55	.16
□ 6 Sandy Alomar Jr.	.75	.35	.09
□ 7 Ray Lankford	1.25	.55	.16
□ 8 Steve Decker	.50	.23	.06
□ 9 Juan Gonzalez	5.00	2.20	.60
□ 10 Jose Offerman	.50	.23	.06

1991 Score Mantle

This seven-card standard-size set features Mickey Mantle at various points in his career. The fronts are full-color glossy shots of Mantle while the backs are in a horizontal format with a full-color photo and some narrative information. The cards were randomly inserted in second series packs. A limited amount of cards were actually signed by Mantle and stamped with certification press. A similar version of this set was also released to dealers and media members on Score's mailing list and was individually to 5,000 numbered on the back. The cards were sent in seven-card packs. The card number and the set serial number appear on the back.

	MINT	NRMT	EXC
COMPLETE SET (7)	250.00	110.00	31.00
COMMON MANTLE (1-7)	40.00	18.00	5.00
*PROMO CARDS: 1X BASIC CARDS ..			
□ 1 Mickey Mantle	40.00	18.00	5.00
The Rookie (With Billy Martin)			
□ 2 Mickey Mantle	40.00	18.00	5.00
Triple Crown			
□ 3 Mickey Mantle	40.00	18.00	5.00
World Series			
□ 4 Mickey Mantle	40.00	18.00	5.00
Going, Going, Gone			
□ 5 Mickey Mantle	40.00	18.00	5.00
Speed and Grace			
□ 6 Mickey Mantle	40.00	18.00	5.00
A True Yankee			
□ 7 Mickey Mantle	40.00	18.00	5.00
Twilight			
□ AU0 Mickey Mantle AU	500.00	220.00	60.00
(Autographed with certified signature)			

1991 Score Rookie/Traded

The 1991 Score Rookie and Traded contains 110 standard-size player cards and was issued exclusively in factory set form along with 10 "World Series II" magic motion trivia cards through hobby dealers. The front design is identical to the regular issue 1991 Score set except for the distinctive mauve borders and T-suffixed numbering. Cards 1T-80T feature traded players, while cards 81T-110T focus on rookies. Rookie Cards in the set inlcude Jeff Bagwell and Ivan Rodriguez.

	MINT	NRMT	EXC
COMPLETE FACT.SET (110)	4.00	1.80	.50
COMMON CARD (1T-110T)	.05	.02	.01
□ 1T Bo Jackson	.10	.05	.01
□ 2T Mike Flanagan	.05	.02	.01
□ 3T Pete Incaviglia	.05	.02	.01
□ 4T Jack Clark	.10	.05	.01
□ 5T Hubie Brooks	.05	.02	.01
□ 6T Ivan Calderon	.05	.02	.01
□ 7T Glenn Davis	.05	.02	.01
□ 8T Wally Backman	.05	.02	.01
□ 9T Dave Smith	.05	.02	.01
□ 10T Tim Raines	.15	.07	.02
□ 11T Joe Carter	.10	.05	.01
□ 12T Sid Bream	.05	.02	.01
□ 13T George Bell	.05	.02	.01
□ 14T Steve Bedrosian	.05	.02	.01
□ 15T Willie Wilson	.05	.02	.01
□ 16T Darryl Strawberry	.10	.05	.01
□ 17T Danny Jackson	.05	.02	.01
□ 18T Kirk Gibson	.10	.05	.01
□ 19T Willie McGee	.05	.02	.01
□ 20T Junior Felix	.05	.02	.01
□ 21T Steve Farr	.05	.02	.01
□ 22T Pat Tabler	.05	.02	.01
□ 23T Brett Butler	.10	.05	.01
□ 24T Danny Darwin	.05	.02	.01
□ 25T Mickey Tettleton	.10	.05	.01
□ 26T Gary Carter	.10	.05	.01
□ 27T Mitch Williams	.05	.02	.01
□ 28T Candy Maldonado	.05	.02	.01
□ 29T Otis Nixon	.05	.02	.01
□ 30T Brian Downing	.05	.02	.01
□ 31T Tom Candiotti	.05	.02	.01
□ 32T John Candelaria	.05	.02	.01
□ 33T Rob Murphy	.05	.02	.01
□ 34T Deion Sanders	.15	.07	.02
□ 35T Willie Randolph	.10	.05	.01
□ 36T Pete Harnisch	.05	.02	.01
□ 37T Dante Bichette	.15	.07	.02
□ 38T Garry Templeton	.05	.02	.01
□ 39T Gary Gaetti	.10	.05	.01
□ 40T John Cerutti	.05	.02	.01
□ 41T Rick Cerone	.05	.02	.01
□ 42T Mike Pagliarulo	.05	.02	.01
□ 43T Ron Hassey	.05	.02	.01
□ 44T Roberto Alomar	.20	.09	.03
□ 45T Mike Boddicker	.05	.02	.01
□ 46T Bud Black	.05	.02	.01
□ 47T Rob Deer	.05	.02	.01
□ 48T Devon White	.10	.05	.01
□ 49T Luis Sojo	.05	.02	.01
□ 50T Terry Pendleton	.10	.05	.01
□ 51T Kevin Gross	.05	.02	.01
□ 52T Mike Huff	.05	.02	.01
□ 53T Dave Righetti	.05	.02	.01
□ 54T Matt Young	.05	.02	.01
□ 55T Earnest Riles	.05	.02	.01
□ 56T Bill Gullickson	.05	.02	.01
□ 57T Vince Coleman	.05	.02	.01
□ 58T Fred McGriff	.15	.07	.02
□ 59T Franklin Stubbs	.05	.02	.01
□ 60T Eric King	.05	.02	.01
□ 61T Cory Snyder	.05	.02	.01
□ 62T Dwight Evans	.10	.05	.01
□ 63T Gerald Perry	.05	.02	.01
□ 64T Eric Show	.05	.02	.01
□ 65T Shawn Hillegas	.05	.02	.01
□ 66T Tony Fernandez	.05	.02	.01
□ 67T Tim Teufel	.05	.02	.01
□ 68T Mitch Webster	.05	.02	.01
□ 69T Mike Heath	.05	.02	.01
□ 70T Chili Davis	.10	.05	.01
□ 71T Larry Andersen	.05	.02	.01
□ 72T Gary Varsho	.05	.02	.01
□ 73T Juan Berenguer	.05	.02	.01
□ 74T Jack Morris	.10	.05	.01
□ 75T Barry Jones	.05	.02	.01
□ 76T Rafael Belliard	.05	.02	.01
□ 77T Steve Buechele	.05	.02	.01
□ 78T Scott Sanderson	.05	.02	.01
□ 79T Bob Ojeda	.05	.02	.01
□ 80T Curt Schilling	.05	.02	.01
□ 81T Brian Drahman	.05	.02	.01
□ 82T Ivan Rodriguez	1.50	.70	.19
□ 83T David Howard	.05	.02	.01
□ 84T Heathcliff Slocumb	.15	.07	.02
□ 85T Mike Timlin	.05	.02	.01
□ 86T Darryl Kile	.05	.02	.01
□ 87T Pete Schourek	.15	.07	.02
□ 88T Bruce Walton	.05	.02	.01
□ 89T Al Osuna	.05	.02	.01
□ 90T Gary Scott	.05	.02	.01
□ 91T Doug Simons	.05	.02	.01
□ 92T Chris Jones	.05	.02	.01
□ 93T Chuck Knoblauch	.25	.11	.03
□ 94T Dana Allison	.05	.02	.01
□ 95T Erik Pappas	.05	.02	.01
□ 96T Jeff Bagwell	2.50	1.10	.30
□ 97T Kirk Dressendorfer	.05	.02	.01
□ 98T Freddie Benavides	.05	.02	.01
□ 99T Luis Gonzalez	.15	.07	.02
□ 100T Wade Taylor	.05	.02	.01
□ 101T Ed Sprague	.10	.05	.01
□ 102T Bob Scanlan	.05	.02	.01
□ 103T Rick Wilkins	.05	.02	.01
□ 104T Chris Donnels	.05	.02	.01
□ 105T Joe Slusarski	.05	.02	.01
□ 106T Mark Lewis	.05	.02	.01
□ 107T Pat Kelly	.10	.05	.01
□ 108T John Briscoe	.05	.02	.01
□ 109T Luis Lopez	.05	.02	.01
□ 110T Jeff Johnson	.05	.02	.01

1991 Score All-Star Fanfest

This 11-card standard-size set was issued with a 3-D 1946 World Series trivia card. The cards feature on the fronts color action player photos, with red borders above and below the pictures. The card face is lime green with miniature yellow baseballs and blue player icons, and it can be seen at the top and bottom of the card front. The backs have a similar pattern on a white background and present biographical information as well as career highlights. The set features young players, who were apparently projected by Score to be future All-Stars. The cards are numbered on the back as "X of 10."

	MINT	NRMT	EXC
COMPLETE SET (10)	7.50	3.40	.95
COMMON CARD (1-10)	.25	.11	.03
☐ 1 Ray Lankford	2.00	.90	.25
☐ 2 Steve Decker	.25	.11	.03
☐ 3 Gary Scott	.25	.11	.03
☐ 4 Hensley Meulens	.25	.11	.03
☐ 5 Tim Naehring	.75	.35	.09
☐ 6 Mark Whiten	.50	.23	.06
☐ 7 Ed Sprague	.75	.35	.09
☐ 8 Charles Nagy	1.00	.45	.12
☐ 9 Terry Shumpert	.25	.11	.03
☐ 10 Chuck Knoblauch	3.00	1.35	.35
☐ NNO Title Card	.25	.11	.03

1991 Score 100 Rising Stars

The 1991 Score 100 Rising Stars sets were issued by Score with or without special books which goes with the cards. The standard-size cards feature 100 of the most popular rising stars. The fronts of the cards are beautiful full-color photos surrounded by blue and green borders while the backs have a full color photo on the back and give a brief biography of the player. The sets (with the special book with brief biography on the players) are marketed for retail purposes at a suggested price of 12.95.

	MINT	NRMT	EXC
COMPLETE SET (100)	8.00	3.60	1.00
COMMON CARD (1-100)	.05	.02	.01
☐ 1 Sandy Alomar Jr.	.10	.05	.01
☐ 2 Tom Edens	.05	.02	.01
☐ 3 Terry Shumpert	.05	.02	.01
☐ 4 Shawn Boskie	.05	.02	.01
☐ 5 Steve Avery	.25	.11	.03
☐ 6 Deion Sanders	.50	.23	.06
☐ 7 John Burkett	.10	.05	.01
☐ 8 Stan Belinda	.05	.02	.01
☐ 9 Thomas Howard	.05	.02	.01
☐ 10 Wayne Edwards	.05	.02	.01
☐ 11 Rick Parker	.05	.02	.01
☐ 12 Randy Veres	.05	.02	.01
☐ 13 Alex Cole	.05	.02	.01
☐ 14 Scott Chiamparino	.05	.02	.01
☐ 15 Greg Olson	.05	.02	.01
☐ 16 Jose DeJesus	.05	.02	.01
☐ 17 Mike Blowers	.05	.02	.01
☐ 18 Jeff Huson	.05	.02	.01
☐ 19 Willie Blair	.05	.02	.01
☐ 20 Howard Farmer	.05	.02	.01
☐ 21 Larry Walker	.25	.11	.03
☐ 22 Scott Hemond	.05	.02	.01
☐ 23 Mel Stottlemyre Jr.	.05	.02	.01
☐ 24 Mark Whiten	.10	.05	.01
☐ 25 Jeff Schulz	.05	.02	.01
☐ 26 Gary DiSarcina	.05	.02	.01
☐ 27 George Canale	.05	.02	.01
☐ 28 Dean Palmer	.20	.09	.03
☐ 29 Jim Leyritz	.10	.05	.01
☐ 30 Carlos Baerga	1.00	.45	.12
☐ 31 Rafael Valdez	.05	.02	.01
☐ 32 Derek Bell	.25	.11	.03
☐ 33 Francisco Cabrera	.05	.02	.01
☐ 34 Chris Hoiles	.10	.05	.01
☐ 35 Craig Grebeck	.05	.02	.01
☐ 36 Scott Coolbaugh	.05	.02	.01
☐ 37 Kevin Wickander	.05	.02	.01
☐ 38 Marquis Grissom	.30	.14	.04
☐ 39 Chip Hale	.05	.02	.01
☐ 40 Kevin Maas	.05	.02	.01
☐ 41 Juan Gonzalez	2.00	.90	.25
☐ 42 Eric Anthony	.05	.02	.01
☐ 43 Luis Sojo	.05	.02	.01
☐ 44 Paul Sorrento	.10	.05	.01
☐ 45 Dave Justice	.50	.23	.06
☐ 46 Oscar Azocar	.05	.02	.01
☐ 47 Charles Nagy	.20	.09	.03
☐ 48 Robin Ventura	.25	.11	.03
☐ 49 Reggie Harris	.05	.02	.01
☐ 50 Ben McDonald	.25	.11	.03
☐ 51 Hector Villanueva	.05	.02	.01
☐ 52 Kevin Tapani	.10	.05	.01
☐ 53 Brian Bohanon	.05	.02	.01
☐ 54 Tim Layana	.05	.02	.01
☐ 55 Delino DeShields	.10	.05	.01
☐ 56 Beau Allred	.05	.02	.01
☐ 57 Eric Gunderson	.05	.02	.01
☐ 58 Kent Mercker	.05	.02	.01
☐ 59 Juan Bell	.05	.02	.01
☐ 60 Glenallen Hill	.10	.05	.01
☐ 61 David Segui	.10	.05	.01
☐ 62 Alan Mills	.05	.02	.01
☐ 63 Mike Harkey	.05	.02	.01
☐ 64 Bill Sampen	.05	.02	.01
☐ 65 Greg Vaughn	.25	.11	.03
☐ 66 Alex Fernandez	.50	.23	.06
☐ 67 Mike Hartley	.05	.02	.01
☐ 68 Travis Fryman	.30	.14	.04
☐ 69 Dave Rohde	.05	.02	.01
☐ 70 Tom Lampkin	.05	.02	.01
☐ 71 Mark Gardner	.05	.02	.01
☐ 72 Pat Combs	.05	.02	.01
☐ 73 Kevin Appier	.25	.11	.03
☐ 74 Mike Fetters	.10	.05	.01
☐ 75 Greg Myers	.05	.02	.01
☐ 76 Steve Searcy	.05	.02	.01
☐ 77 Tim Naehring	.15	.07	.02
☐ 78 Frank Thomas	3.00	1.35	.35
☐ 79 Todd Hundley	.30	.14	.04
☐ 80 Ed Vosberg	.05	.02	.01
☐ 81 Todd Zeile	.10	.05	.01
☐ 82 Lee Stevens	.05	.02	.01
☐ 83 Scott Radinsky	.05	.02	.01
☐ 84 Hensley Meulens	.05	.02	.01
☐ 85 Brian DuBois	.05	.02	.01
☐ 86 Steve Olin	.05	.02	.01
☐ 87 Julio Machado	.05	.02	.01
☐ 88 Jose Vizcaino	.10	.05	.01
☐ 89 Mark Lemke	.10	.05	.01
☐ 90 Felix Jose	.10	.05	.01
☐ 91 Wally Whitehurst	.05	.02	.01
☐ 92 Dana Kiecker	.05	.02	.01
☐ 93 Mike Munoz	.05	.02	.01
☐ 94 Adam Peterson	.05	.02	.01
☐ 95 Tim Drummond	.05	.02	.01
☐ 96 Dave Hollins	.05	.02	.01
☐ 97 Craig Wilson	.05	.02	.01
☐ 98 Hal Morris	.10	.05	.01
☐ 99 Jose Offerman	.10	.05	.01
☐ 100 John Olerud	.25	.11	.03

1991 Score 100 Superstars

The 1991 Score 100 Superstars sets were issued by Score with or without special books that came with the cards. The standard-size cards feature 100 of the most popular superstars. The fronts of the cards feature beautiful full-color photos surrounded by red, white and blue borders while the backs are surrounded by red and blue borders and feature a full-color photo on the back along with a brief biography. The sets (with the special book with brief biography on the players) are marketed for retail purposes at a suggested price of 12.95.

	MINT	NRMT	EXC
COMPLETE SET (100)	8.00	3.60	1.00
COMMON CARD (1-100)	.05	.02	.01
☐ 1 Jose Canseco	.30	.14	.04
☐ 2 Bo Jackson	.10	.05	.01
☐ 3 Wade Boggs	.30	.14	.04
☐ 4 Will Clark	.40	.18	.05
☐ 5 Ken Griffey Jr.	2.00	.90	.25
☐ 6 Doug Drabek	.10	.05	.01
☐ 7 Kirby Puckett	1.00	.45	.12
☐ 8 Joe Orsulak	.05	.02	.01
☐ 9 Eric Davis	.10	.05	.01
☐ 10 Rickey Henderson	.40	.18	.05
☐ 11 Len Dykstra	.15	.07	.02
☐ 12 Ruben Sierra	.15	.07	.02
☐ 13 Paul Molitor	.40	.18	.05
☐ 14 Ron Gant	.15	.07	.02
☐ 15 Ozzie Guillen	.05	.02	.01
☐ 16 Ramon Martinez	.15	.07	.02
☐ 17 Edgar Martinez	.30	.14	.04
☐ 18 Ozzie Smith	.75	.35	.09
☐ 19 Charlie Hayes	.10	.05	.01
☐ 20 Barry Larkin	.30	.14	.04
☐ 21 Cal Ripken	1.50	.70	.19
☐ 22 Andy Van Slyke	.10	.05	.01
☐ 23 Don Mattingly	1.00	.45	.12
☐ 24 Dave Stewart	.10	.05	.01
☐ 25 Nolan Ryan	1.50	.70	.19
☐ 26 Barry Bonds	.40	.18	.05
☐ 27 Gregg Olson	.05	.02	.01
☐ 28 Chris Sabo	.05	.02	.01
☐ 29 John Franco	.10	.05	.01
☐ 30 Gary Sheffield	.40	.18	.05
☐ 31 Jeff Treadway	.05	.02	.01
☐ 32 Tom Browning	.05	.02	.01
☐ 33 Jose Lind	.05	.02	.01
☐ 34 Dave Magadan	.05	.02	.01
☐ 35 Dale Murphy	.20	.09	.03
☐ 36 Tom Candiotti	.05	.02	.01
☐ 37 Willie McGee	.10	.05	.01
☐ 38 Robin Yount	.30	.14	.04
☐ 39 Mark McGwire	.60	.25	.07
☐ 40 George Bell	.05	.02	.01
☐ 41 Carlton Fisk	.25	.11	.03
☐ 42 Bobby Bonilla	.10	.05	.01
☐ 43 Randy Milligan	.05	.02	.01
☐ 44 Dave Parker	.10	.05	.01
☐ 45 Shawon Dunston	.05	.02	.01
☐ 46 Brian Harper	.05	.02	.01
☐ 47 John Tudor	.05	.02	.01
☐ 48 Ellis Burks	.10	.05	.01
☐ 49 Bob Welch	.05	.02	.01
☐ 50 Roger Clemens	.40	.18	.05
☐ 51 Mike Henneman	.05	.02	.01
☐ 52 Eddie Murray	.50	.23	.06
☐ 53 Kal Daniels	.05	.02	.01
☐ 54 Doug Jones	.05	.02	.01
☐ 55 Craig Biggio	.30	.14	.04
☐ 56 Rafael Palmeiro	.25	.11	.03
☐ 57 Wally Joyner	.05	.02	.01
☐ 58 Tim Wallach	.05	.02	.01
☐ 59 Bret Saberhagen	.10	.05	.01
☐ 60 Ryne Sandberg	.75	.35	.09
☐ 61 Benito Santiago	.05	.02	.01
☐ 62 Darryl Strawberry	.10	.05	.01
☐ 63 Alan Trammell	.15	.07	.02
☐ 64 Kelly Gruber	.05	.02	.01
☐ 65 Dwight Gooden	.10	.05	.01
☐ 66 Dave Winfield	.30	.14	.04
☐ 67 Rick Aguilera	.05	.02	.01
☐ 68 Dave Righetti	.05	.02	.01
☐ 69 Jim Abbott	.10	.05	.01
☐ 70 Frank Viola	.05	.02	.01
☐ 71 Fred McGriff	.25	.11	.03
☐ 72 Steve Sax	.05	.02	.01
☐ 73 Dennis Eckersley	.10	.05	.01
☐ 74 Cory Snyder	.05	.02	.01
☐ 75 Mackey Sasser	.05	.02	.01
☐ 76 Candy Maldonado	.05	.02	.01
☐ 77 Matt Williams	.30	.14	.04
☐ 78 Kent Hrbek	.05	.02	.01
☐ 79 Randy Myers	.10	.05	.01
☐ 80 Gregg Jefferies	.15	.07	.02
☐ 81 Joe Carter	.25	.11	.03
☐ 82 Mike Greenwell	.05	.02	.01
☐ 83 Jack Armstrong	.05	.02	.01
☐ 84 Julio Franco	.05	.02	.01
☐ 85 George Brett	.75	.35	.09
☐ 86 Howard Johnson	.05	.02	.01
☐ 87 Andre Dawson	.10	.05	.01
☐ 88 Cecil Fielder	.25	.11	.03
☐ 89 Tim Raines	.20	.09	.03
☐ 90 Chuck Finley	.10	.05	.01
☐ 91 Mark Grace	.40	.18	.05
☐ 92 Brook Jacoby	.05	.02	.01
☐ 93 Dave Stieb	.05	.02	.01
☐ 94 Tony Gwynn	.75	.35	.09
☐ 95 Bobby Thigpen	.05	.02	.01
☐ 96 Roberto Kelly	.05	.02	.01
☐ 97 Kevin Seitzer	.05	.02	.01
☐ 98 Kevin Mitchell	.05	.02	.01
☐ 99 Dwight Evans	.10	.05	.01
☐ 100 Roberto Alomar	.50	.23	.06

1991 Score Rookies

This 40-card standard-sized set was distributed with five magic motion trivia cards. The fronts feature high glossy color action player photos, on a blue card face with meandering green lines. The picture has a yellow border on its right side, and red and yellow borders below. The words "1991 Rookie" appear to the left of the picture running the length of the card. The team logo in the lower right corner rounds out the card face. On a yellow background, the backs have a color head shot, biography, and career highlights.

	MINT	NRMT	EXC
COMPLETE SET (40)	5.00	2.20	.60
COMMON CARD (1-40)	.05	.02	.01
☐ 1 Mel Rojas	.10	.05	.01
☐ 2 Ray Lankford	.25	.11	.03
☐ 3 Scott Aldred	.05	.02	.01
☐ 4 Turner Ward	.05	.02	.01
☐ 5 Omar Olivares	.05	.02	.01
☐ 6 Mo Vaughn	1.50	.70	.19
☐ 7 Phil Clark	.05	.02	.01
☐ 8 Brent Mayne	.05	.02	.01
☐ 9 Scott Lewis	.05	.02	.01
☐ 10 Brian Barnes	.05	.02	.01
☐ 11 Bernard Gilkey	.60	.25	.07
☐ 12 Steve Decker	.05	.02	.01
☐ 13 Paul Marak	.05	.02	.01
☐ 14 Wes Chamberlain	.05	.02	.01
☐ 15 Kevin Belcher	.05	.02	.01
☐ 16 Steve Adkins	.05	.02	.01
☐ 17 Geronimo Pena	.05	.02	.01
☐ 18 Mark Leonard	.05	.02	.01
☐ 19 Jeff Conine	.50	.23	.06
☐ 20 Leo Gomez	.05	.02	.01
☐ 21 Chuck Malone	.05	.02	.01
☐ 22 Beau Allred	.05	.02	.01
☐ 23 Todd Hundley	.25	.11	.03
☐ 24 Lance Dickson	.05	.02	.01
☐ 25 Mike Benjamin	.05	.02	.01
☐ 26 Jose Offerman	.10	.05	.01
☐ 27 Terry Shumpert	.05	.02	.01
☐ 28 Darren Lewis	.05	.02	.01
☐ 29 Scott Chiamparino	.05	.02	.01
☐ 30 Tim Naehring	.10	.05	.01
☐ 31 David Segui	.10	.05	.01
☐ 32 Karl Rhodes	.05	.02	.01
☐ 33 Mickey Morandini	.10	.05	.01
☐ 34 Chuck McElroy	.05	.02	.01
☐ 35 Tim McIntosh	.05	.02	.01
☐ 36 Derrick May	.05	.02	.01
☐ 37 Rich DeLucia	.05	.02	.01
☐ 38 Tino Martinez	.50	.23	.06
☐ 39 Hensley Meulens	.05	.02	.01
☐ 40 Andujar Cedeno	.05	.02	.01

1991 Score Ryan Life and Times

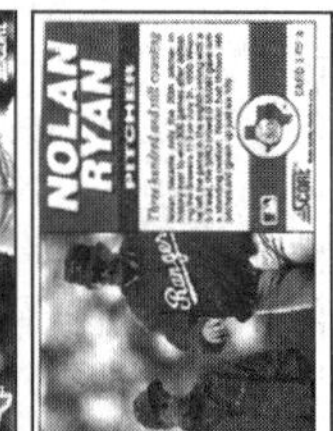

This four-card standard-size set was manufactured by Score to commemorate four significant milestones in Nolan Ryan's illustrious career beginning with his years growing up in Alvin, Texas, his years with the Mets and Angels, with the Astros and Rangers, and his career statistics. Each card commemorates a career milestone (all occur with the Rangers) and features Ryan's color photo on the front. They are part of "The Life and Times of Nolan Ryan," by Tarrant Printing, a special collector set that consists of four volumes (8 1/2" by 11" booklets) along with the cards packaged in a folder. The color action photos on the fronts are full-bleed, except on the left side, where blue and red border stripes run the length of the card. The horizontally oriented backs feature a different color player photo on the left half. The right half is accented with blue and red stripes and has career highlights on a pale yellow background. The cards are numbered on the back.

	MINT	NRMT	EXC
COMPLETE SET (4)	30.00	13.50	3.70
COMMON CARD (1-4)	7.50	3.40	.95
☐ 1 Nolan Ryan 5,000th Career Strikeout	7.50	3.40	.95
☐ 2 Nolan Ryan 6th Career No-Hitter	7.50	3.40	.95
☐ 3 Nolan Ryan HOR 300th Career Victory	7.50	3.40	.95
☐ 4 Nolan Ryan HOR 7th Career No-Hitter	7.50	3.40	.95

1992 Score Samples

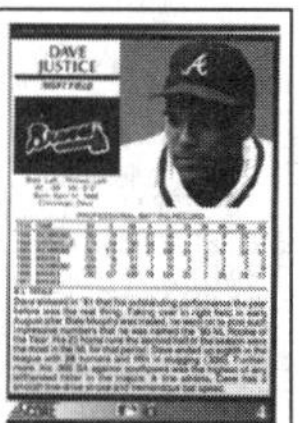

The 1992 Score Preview set contains six standard-size cards done in the same style as the 1992 Score baseball cards. Supposedly the Sandberg and Mack cards are tougher as they were only available at the St. Louis card show that Score attended in November 1991.

	MINT	NRMT	EXC
COMPLETE SET (6)	20.00	9.00	2.50
COMMON CARD (1-6)	1.00	.45	.12
☐ 1 Ken Griffey Jr.	10.00	4.50	1.25
☐ 2 Dave Justice	1.50	.70	.19

☐ 3 Robin Ventura	1.00	.45	.12
☐ 4 Steve Avery	1.00	.45	.12
☐ 5 Ryne Sandberg SP	8.00	3.60	1.00
☐ 6 Shane Mack SP	1.00	.45	.12

1992 Score

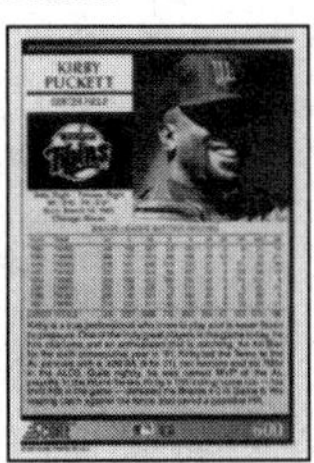

The 1992 Score set marked the second year that Score released their set in two different series. The first series contains 442 cards while the second series contains 451 cards. Cards were distributed in plastic wrapped packs, blister packs, jumbo packs and factory sets. Each pack included a special "World Series II" trivia card. The glossy color action photos on the basic card fronts are bordered above and below by stripes of the same color, and a thicker, different color stripe runs the length of the card to one side of the picture. Topical subsets include Rookie Prospects (395-424/736-772/814-877), No-Hit Club (425-428/784-787), Highlights (429-430), AL All-Stars (431-440; with color montages displaying Chris Greco's player caricatures), Dream Team (441-442/883-893), NL All-Stars (773-782), Highlights (783, 795-797), Draft Picks (799-810), and Memorabilia (878-882). All of the Rookie Prospects (736-772) can be found with or without the Rookie Prospect stripe. Rookie Cards in the set include Vinny Castilla and Manny Ramirez. Chuck Knoblauch, 1991 American League Rookie of the Year, autographed 3,000 of his own 1990 Score Draft Pick cards (card number 672) in gold ink, 2,989 were randomly inserted in Series 2 poly packs, while the other 11 were given away in a sweepstakes. The backs of these Knoblauch autograph cards have special holograms to differentiate them.

	MINT	NRMT	EXC
COMPLETE SET (893)	15.00	6.75	1.85
COMPLETE FACT.SET (910)	20.00	9.00	2.50
COMPLETE SERIES 1 (442)	8.00	3.60	1.00
COMPLETE SERIES 2 (451)	8.00	3.60	1.00
COMMON CARD (1-893)	.05	.02	.01

	MINT	NRMT	EXC
☐ 1 Ken Griffey Jr.	1.50	.70	.19
☐ 2 Nolan Ryan	.75	.35	.09
☐ 3 Will Clark	.15	.07	.02
☐ 4 Dave Justice	.15	.07	.02
☐ 5 Dave Henderson	.05	.02	.01
☐ 6 Bret Saberhagen	.10	.05	.01
☐ 7 Fred McGriff	.15	.07	.02
☐ 8 Erik Hanson	.05	.02	.01
☐ 9 Darryl Strawberry	.10	.05	.01
☐ 10 Dwight Gooden	.10	.05	.01
☐ 11 Juan Gonzalez	.60	.25	.07
☐ 12 Mark Langston	.10	.05	.01
☐ 13 Lonnie Smith	.05	.02	.01
☐ 14 Jeff Montgomery	.10	.05	.01
☐ 15 Roberto Alomar	.20	.09	.03
☐ 16 Delino DeShields	.05	.02	.01
☐ 17 Steve Bedrosian	.05	.02	.01
☐ 18 Terry Pendleton	.10	.05	.01
☐ 19 Mark Carreon	.05	.02	.01
☐ 20 Mark McGwire	.30	.14	.04
☐ 21 Roger Clemens	.20	.09	.03
☐ 22 Chuck Crim	.05	.02	.01
☐ 23 Don Mattingly	.50	.23	.06
☐ 24 Dickie Thon	.05	.02	.01
☐ 25 Ron Gant	.10	.05	.01
☐ 26 Milt Cuyler	.05	.02	.01
☐ 27 Mike Macfarlane	.05	.02	.01
☐ 28 Dan Gladden	.05	.02	.01
☐ 29 Melido Perez	.05	.02	.01
☐ 30 Willie Randolph	.10	.05	.01
☐ 31 Albert Belle	.50	.23	.06
☐ 32 Dave Winfield	.15	.07	.02
☐ 33 Jimmy Jones	.05	.02	.01
☐ 34 Kevin Gross	.05	.02	.01
☐ 35 Andres Galarraga	.15	.07	.02
☐ 36 Mike Devereaux	.05	.02	.01
☐ 37 Chris Bosio	.05	.02	.01
☐ 38 Mike LaValliere	.05	.02	.01
☐ 39 Gary Gaetti	.10	.05	.01
☐ 40 Felix Jose	.05	.02	.01
☐ 41 Alvaro Espinoza	.05	.02	.01
☐ 42 Rick Aguilera	.05	.02	.01
☐ 43 Mike Gallego	.05	.02	.01
☐ 44 Eric Davis	.10	.05	.01
☐ 45 George Bell	.05	.02	.01
☐ 46 Tom Brunansky	.05	.02	.01
☐ 47 Steve Farr	.05	.02	.01
☐ 48 Duane Ward	.05	.02	.01
☐ 49 David Wells	.05	.02	.01
☐ 50 Cecil Fielder	.10	.05	.01
☐ 51 Walt Weiss	.05	.02	.01
☐ 52 Todd Zeile	.05	.02	.01
☐ 53 Doug Jones	.05	.02	.01
☐ 54 Bob Walk	.05	.02	.01
☐ 55 Rafael Palmeiro	.15	.07	.02
☐ 56 Rob Deer	.05	.02	.01
☐ 57 Paul O'Neill	.10	.05	.01
☐ 58 Jeff Reardon	.10	.05	.01
☐ 59 Randy Ready	.05	.02	.01
☐ 60 Scott Erickson	.10	.05	.01
☐ 61 Paul Molitor	.20	.09	.03
☐ 62 Jack McDowell	.10	.05	.01
☐ 63 Jim Acker	.05	.02	.01
☐ 64 Jay Buhner	.15	.07	.02
☐ 65 Travis Fryman	.15	.07	.02
☐ 66 Marquis Grissom	.10	.05	.01
☐ 67 Mike Harkey	.05	.02	.01
☐ 68 Luis Polonia	.05	.02	.01
☐ 69 Ken Caminiti	.15	.07	.02
☐ 70 Chris Sabo	.05	.02	.01
☐ 71 Gregg Olson	.05	.02	.01
☐ 72 Carlton Fisk	.15	.07	.02
☐ 73 Juan Samuel	.05	.02	.01
☐ 74 Todd Stottlemyre	.10	.05	.01
☐ 75 Andre Dawson	.10	.05	.01
☐ 76 Alvin Davis	.05	.02	.01
☐ 77 Bill Doran	.05	.02	.01
☐ 78 B.J. Surhoff	.10	.05	.01
☐ 79 Kirk McCaskill	.05	.02	.01
☐ 80 Dale Murphy	.15	.07	.02
☐ 81 Jose DeLeon	.05	.02	.01
☐ 82 Alex Fernandez	.15	.07	.02
☐ 83 Ivan Calderon	.05	.02	.01
☐ 84 Brent Mayne	.05	.02	.01
☐ 85 Jody Reed	.05	.02	.01
☐ 86 Randy Tomlin	.05	.02	.01
☐ 87 Randy Milligan	.05	.02	.01
☐ 88 Pascual Perez	.05	.02	.01
☐ 89 Hensley Meulens	.05	.02	.01
☐ 90 Joe Carter	.10	.05	.01
☐ 91 Mike Moore	.05	.02	.01
☐ 92 Ozzie Guillen	.05	.02	.01
☐ 93 Shawn Hillegas	.05	.02	.01
☐ 94 Chili Davis	.10	.05	.01
☐ 95 Vince Coleman	.05	.02	.01
☐ 96 Jimmy Key	.10	.05	.01
☐ 97 Billy Ripken	.05	.02	.01
☐ 98 Dave Smith	.05	.02	.01
☐ 99 Tom Bolton	.05	.02	.01
☐ 100 Barry Larkin	.15	.07	.02
☐ 101 Kenny Rogers	.05	.02	.01
☐ 102 Mike Boddicker	.05	.02	.01
☐ 103 Kevin Elster	.05	.02	.01
☐ 104 Ken Hill	.10	.05	.01
☐ 105 Charlie Leibrandt	.05	.02	.01
☐ 106 Pat Combs	.05	.02	.01
☐ 107 Hubie Brooks	.05	.02	.01
☐ 108 Julio Franco	.10	.05	.01
☐ 109 Vicente Palacios	.05	.02	.01
☐ 110 Kal Daniels	.05	.02	.01
☐ 111 Bruce Hurst	.05	.02	.01
☐ 112 Willie McGee	.05	.02	.01
☐ 113 Ted Power	.05	.02	.01
☐ 114 Milt Thompson	.05	.02	.01
☐ 115 Doug Drabek	.05	.02	.01
☐ 116 Rafael Belliard	.05	.02	.01
☐ 117 Scott Garrelts	.05	.02	.01
☐ 118 Terry Mulholland	.05	.02	.01
☐ 119 Jay Howell	.05	.02	.01
☐ 120 Danny Jackson	.05	.02	.01
☐ 121 Scott Ruskin	.05	.02	.01
☐ 122 Robin Ventura	.10	.05	.01
☐ 123 Bip Roberts	.05	.02	.01
☐ 124 Jeff Russell	.05	.02	.01
☐ 125 Hal Morris	.05	.02	.01
☐ 126 Teddy Higuera	.05	.02	.01
☐ 127 Luis Sojo	.05	.02	.01
☐ 128 Carlos Baerga	.10	.05	.01
☐ 129 Jeff Ballard	.05	.02	.01
☐ 130 Tom Gordon	.05	.02	.01
☐ 131 Sid Bream	.05	.02	.01
☐ 132 Rance Mulliniks	.05	.02	.01
☐ 133 Andy Benes	.10	.05	.01
☐ 134 Mickey Tettleton	.05	.02	.01
☐ 135 Rich DeLucia	.05	.02	.01
☐ 136 Tom Pagnozzi	.05	.02	.01
☐ 137 Harold Baines	.10	.05	.01
☐ 138 Danny Darwin	.05	.02	.01
☐ 139 Kevin Bass	.05	.02	.01
☐ 140 Chris Nabholz	.05	.02	.01
☐ 141 Pete O'Brien	.05	.02	.01
☐ 142 Jeff Treadway	.05	.02	.01
☐ 143 Mickey Morandini	.05	.02	.01
☐ 144 Eric King	.05	.02	.01
☐ 145 Danny Tartabull	.05	.02	.01
☐ 146 Lance Johnson	.10	.05	.01
☐ 147 Casey Candaele	.05	.02	.01
☐ 148 Felix Fermin	.05	.02	.01
☐ 149 Rich Rodriguez	.05	.02	.01
☐ 150 Dwight Evans	.10	.05	.01
☐ 151 Joe Klink	.05	.02	.01
☐ 152 Kevin Reimer	.05	.02	.01
☐ 153 Orlando Merced	.05	.02	.01
☐ 154 Mel Hall	.05	.02	.01
☐ 155 Randy Myers	.10	.05	.01
☐ 156 Greg A. Harris	.05	.02	.01
☐ 157 Jeff Brantley	.10	.05	.01
☐ 158 Jim Eisenreich	.05	.02	.01
☐ 159 Luis Rivera	.05	.02	.01
☐ 160 Cris Carpenter	.05	.02	.01
☐ 161 Bruce Ruffin	.05	.02	.01
☐ 162 Omar Vizquel	.10	.05	.01
☐ 163 Gerald Alexander	.05	.02	.01
☐ 164 Mark Guthrie	.05	.02	.01
☐ 165 Scott Lewis	.05	.02	.01
☐ 166 Bill Sampen	.05	.02	.01
☐ 167 Dave Anderson	.05	.02	.01
☐ 168 Kevin McReynolds	.05	.02	.01
☐ 169 Jose Vizcaino	.05	.02	.01
☐ 170 Bob Geren	.05	.02	.01
☐ 171 Mike Morgan	.05	.02	.01
☐ 172 Jim Gott	.05	.02	.01
☐ 173 Mike Pagliarulo	.05	.02	.01
☐ 174 Mike Jeffcoat	.05	.02	.01
☐ 175 Craig Lefferts	.05	.02	.01
☐ 176 Steve Finley	.10	.05	.01
☐ 177 Wally Backman	.05	.02	.01
☐ 178 Kent Mercker	.05	.02	.01
☐ 179 John Cerutti	.05	.02	.01
☐ 180 Jay Bell	.10	.05	.01
☐ 181 Dale Sveum	.05	.02	.01
☐ 182 Greg Gagne	.05	.02	.01
☐ 183 Donnie Hill	.05	.02	.01
☐ 184 Rex Hudler	.05	.02	.01
☐ 185 Pat Kelly	.05	.02	.01
☐ 186 Jeff D. Robinson	.05	.02	.01
☐ 187 Jeff Gray	.05	.02	.01
☐ 188 Jerry Willard	.05	.02	.01
☐ 189 Carlos Quintana	.05	.02	.01
☐ 190 Dennis Eckersley	.10	.05	.01
☐ 191 Kelly Downs	.05	.02	.01
☐ 192 Gregg Jefferies	.10	.05	.01
☐ 193 Darrin Fletcher	.05	.02	.01
☐ 194 Mike Jackson	.05	.02	.01
☐ 195 Eddie Murray	.25	.11	.03
☐ 196 Bill Landrum	.05	.02	.01
☐ 197 Eric Yelding	.05	.02	.01
☐ 198 Devon White	.10	.05	.01
☐ 199 Larry Walker	.15	.07	.02
☐ 200 Ryne Sandberg	.25	.11	.03
☐ 201 Dave Magadan	.05	.02	.01
☐ 202 Steve Chitren	.05	.02	.01
☐ 203 Scott Fletcher	.05	.02	.01
☐ 204 Dwayne Henry	.05	.02	.01
☐ 205 Scott Coolbaugh	.05	.02	.01
☐ 206 Tracy Jones	.05	.02	.01
☐ 207 Von Hayes	.05	.02	.01
☐ 208 Bob Melvin	.05	.02	.01
☐ 209 Scott Scudder	.05	.02	.01
☐ 210 Luis Gonzalez	.10	.05	.01
☐ 211 Scott Sanderson	.05	.02	.01
☐ 212 Chris Donnels	.05	.02	.01
☐ 213 Heathcliff Slocumb	.05	.02	.01
☐ 214 Mike Timlin	.05	.02	.01
☐ 215 Brian Harper	.05	.02	.01
☐ 216 Juan Berenguer UER (Decimal point missing in IP total)	.05	.02	.01
☐ 217 Mike Henneman	.05	.02	.01
☐ 218 Bill Spiers	.05	.02	.01
☐ 219 Scott Terry	.05	.02	.01
☐ 220 Frank Viola	.05	.02	.01
☐ 221 Mark Eichhorn	.05	.02	.01
☐ 222 Ernest Riles	.05	.02	.01
☐ 223 Ray Lankford	.15	.07	.02
☐ 224 Pete Harnisch	.05	.02	.01
☐ 225 Bobby Bonilla	.10	.05	.01
☐ 226 Mike Scioscia	.05	.02	.01
☐ 227 Joel Skinner	.05	.02	.01
☐ 228 Brian Holman	.05	.02	.01
☐ 229 Gilberto Reyes	.05	.02	.01
☐ 230 Matt Williams	.15	.07	.02
☐ 231 Jaime Navarro	.05	.02	.01
☐ 232 Jose Rijo	.05	.02	.01
☐ 233 Atlee Hammaker	.05	.02	.01
☐ 234 Tim Teufel	.05	.02	.01
☐ 235 John Kruk	.10	.05	.01
☐ 236 Kurt Stillwell	.05	.02	.01
☐ 237 Dan Pasqua	.05	.02	.01
☐ 238 Tim Crews	.05	.02	.01
☐ 239 Dave Gallagher	.05	.02	.01
☐ 240 Leo Gomez	.05	.02	.01
☐ 241 Steve Avery	.10	.05	.01
☐ 242 Bill Gullickson	.05	.02	.01
☐ 243 Mark Portugal	.05	.02	.01
☐ 244 Lee Guetterman	.05	.02	.01
☐ 245 Benito Santiago	.05	.02	.01
☐ 246 Jim Gantner	.05	.02	.01
☐ 247 Robby Thompson	.05	.02	.01
☐ 248 Terry Shumpert	.05	.02	.01
☐ 249 Mike Bell	.05	.02	.01
☐ 250 Harold Reynolds	.05	.02	.01
☐ 251 Mike Felder	.05	.02	.01
☐ 252 Bill Pecota	.05	.02	.01
☐ 253 Bill Krueger	.05	.02	.01
☐ 254 Alfredo Griffin	.05	.02	.01
☐ 255 Lou Whitaker	.10	.05	.01
☐ 256 Roy Smith	.05	.02	.01
☐ 257 Jerald Clark	.05	.02	.01
☐ 258 Sammy Sosa	.25	.11	.03
☐ 259 Tim Naehring	.10	.05	.01
☐ 260 Dave Righetti	.05	.02	.01
☐ 261 Paul Gibson	.05	.02	.01
☐ 262 Chris James	.05	.02	.01
☐ 263 Larry Andersen	.05	.02	.01
☐ 264 Storm Davis	.05	.02	.01
☐ 265 Jose Lind	.05	.02	.01
☐ 266 Greg Hibbard	.05	.02	.01
☐ 267 Norm Charlton	.05	.02	.01
☐ 268 Paul Kilgus	.05	.02	.01
☐ 269 Greg Maddux	.75	.35	.09
☐ 270 Ellis Burks	.10	.05	.01
☐ 271 Frank Tanana	.05	.02	.01
☐ 272 Gene Larkin	.05	.02	.01
☐ 273 Ron Hassey	.05	.02	.01
☐ 274 Jeff M. Robinson	.05	.02	.01
☐ 275 Steve Howe	.05	.02	.01
☐ 276 Daryl Boston	.05	.02	.01
☐ 277 Mark Lee	.05	.02	.01
☐ 278 Jose Segura	.05	.02	.01
☐ 279 Lance Blankenship	.05	.02	.01
☐ 280 Don Slaught	.05	.02	.01
☐ 281 Russ Swan	.05	.02	.01
☐ 282 Bob Tewksbury	.05	.02	.01
☐ 283 Geno Petralli	.05	.02	.01
☐ 284 Shane Mack	.05	.02	.01
☐ 285 Bob Scanlan	.05	.02	.01
☐ 286 Tim Leary	.05	.02	.01
☐ 287 John Smoltz	.15	.07	.02
☐ 288 Pat Borders	.05	.02	.01
☐ 289 Mark Davidson	.05	.02	.01
☐ 290 Sam Horn	.05	.02	.01
☐ 291 Lenny Harris	.05	.02	.01
☐ 292 Franklin Stubbs	.05	.02	.01
☐ 293 Thomas Howard	.05	.02	.01
☐ 294 Steve Lyons	.05	.02	.01
☐ 295 Francisco Oliveras	.05	.02	.01
☐ 296 Terry Leach	.05	.02	.01
☐ 297 Barry Jones	.05	.02	.01
☐ 298 Lance Parrish	.05	.02	.01
☐ 299 Wally Whitehurst	.05	.02	.01
☐ 300 Bob Welch	.05	.02	.01
☐ 301 Charlie Hayes	.05	.02	.01
☐ 302 Charlie Hough	.05	.02	.01
☐ 303 Gary Redus	.05	.02	.01
☐ 304 Scott Bradley	.05	.02	.01
☐ 305 Jose Oquendo	.05	.02	.01
☐ 306 Pete Incaviglia	.05	.02	.01
☐ 307 Marvin Freeman	.05	.02	.01
☐ 308 Gary Pettis	.05	.02	.01
☐ 309 Joe Slusarski	.05	.02	.01
☐ 310 Kevin Seitzer	.05	.02	.01
☐ 311 Jeff Reed	.05	.02	.01
☐ 312 Pat Tabler	.05	.02	.01
☐ 313 Mike Maddux	.05	.02	.01
☐ 314 Bob Milacki	.05	.02	.01
☐ 315 Eric Anthony	.05	.02	.01
☐ 316 Dante Bichette	.15	.07	.02
☐ 317 Steve Decker	.05	.02	.01
☐ 318 Jack Clark	.10	.05	.01
☐ 319 Doug Dascenzo	.05	.02	.01
☐ 320 Scott Leius	.05	.02	.01
☐ 321 Jim Lindeman	.05	.02	.01
☐ 322 Bryan Harvey	.05	.02	.01
☐ 323 Spike Owen	.05	.02	.01
☐ 324 Roberto Kelly	.05	.02	.01
☐ 325 Stan Belinda	.05	.02	.01
☐ 326 Joey Cora	.10	.05	.01
☐ 327 Jeff Innis	.05	.02	.01
☐ 328 Willie Wilson	.05	.02	.01
☐ 329 Juan Agosto	.05	.02	.01
☐ 330 Charles Nagy	.10	.05	.01
☐ 331 Scott Bailes	.05	.02	.01
☐ 332 Pete Schourek	.10	.05	.01
☐ 333 Mike Flanagan	.05	.02	.01
☐ 334 Omar Olivares	.05	.02	.01
☐ 335 Dennis Lamp	.05	.02	.01
☐ 336 Tommy Greene	.05	.02	.01
☐ 337 Randy Velarde	.05	.02	.01
☐ 338 Tom Lampkin	.05	.02	.01
☐ 339 John Russell	.05	.02	.01
☐ 340 Bob Kipper	.05	.02	.01
☐ 341 Todd Burns	.05	.02	.01
☐ 342 Ron Jones	.05	.02	.01
☐ 343 Dave Valle	.05	.02	.01
☐ 344 Mike Heath	.05	.02	.01
☐ 345 John Olerud	.10	.05	.01
☐ 346 Gerald Young	.05	.02	.01
☐ 347 Ken Patterson	.05	.02	.01
☐ 348 Les Lancaster	.05	.02	.01
☐ 349 Steve Crawford	.05	.02	.01
☐ 350 John Candelaria	.05	.02	.01
☐ 351 Mike Aldrete	.05	.02	.01
☐ 352 Mariano Duncan	.05	.02	.01
☐ 353 Julio Machado	.05	.02	.01
☐ 354 Ken Williams	.05	.02	.01
☐ 355 Walt Terrell	.05	.02	.01
☐ 356 Mitch Williams	.05	.02	.01
☐ 357 Al Newman	.05	.02	.01
☐ 358 Bud Black	.05	.02	.01
☐ 359 Joe Hesketh	.05	.02	.01
☐ 360 Paul Assenmacher	.05	.02	.01
☐ 361 Bo Jackson	.10	.05	.01
☐ 362 Jeff Blauser	.05	.02	.01
☐ 363 Mike Brumley	.05	.02	.01
☐ 364 Jim Deshaies	.05	.02	.01
☐ 365 Brady Anderson	.15	.07	.02
☐ 366 Chuck McElroy	.05	.02	.01
☐ 367 Matt Merullo	.05	.02	.01
☐ 368 Tim Belcher	.05	.02	.01
☐ 369 Luis Aquino	.05	.02	.01

☐ 370 Joe Oliver .05 .02 .01
☐ 371 Greg Swindell .05 .02 .01
☐ 372 Lee Stevens .05 .02 .01
☐ 373 Mark Knudson .05 .02 .01
☐ 374 Bill Wegman .05 .02 .01
☐ 375 Jerry Don Gleaton .05 .02 .01
☐ 376 Pedro Guerrero .05 .02 .01
☐ 377 Randy Bush .05 .02 .01
☐ 378 Greg W. Harris .05 .02 .01
☐ 379 Eric Plunk .05 .02 .01
☐ 380 Jose DeJesus .05 .02 .01
☐ 381 Bobby Witt .05 .02 .01
☐ 382 Curtis Wilkerson .05 .02 .01
☐ 383 Gene Nelson .05 .02 .01
☐ 384 Wes Chamberlain .05 .02 .01
☐ 385 Tom Henke .05 .02 .01
☐ 386 Mark Lemke .05 .02 .01
☐ 387 Greg Briley .05 .02 .01
☐ 388 Rafael Ramirez .05 .02 .01
☐ 389 Tony Fossas .05 .02 .01
☐ 390 Henry Cotto .05 .02 .01
☐ 391 Tim Hulett .05 .02 .01
☐ 392 Dean Palmer .10 .05 .01
☐ 393 Glenn Braggs .05 .02 .01
☐ 394 Mark Salas .05 .02 .01
☐ 395 Rusty Meacham .05 .02 .01
☐ 396 Andy Ashby .10 .05 .01
☐ 397 Jose Melendez .05 .02 .01
☐ 398 Warren Newson .05 .02 .01
☐ 399 Frank Castillo .10 .05 .01
☐ 400 Chito Martinez .05 .02 .01
☐ 401 Bernie Williams .25 .11 .03
☐ 402 Derek Bell .15 .07 .02
☐ 403 Javier Ortiz .05 .02 .01
☐ 404 Tim Sherrill .05 .02 .01
☐ 405 Rob MacDonald .05 .02 .01
☐ 406 Phil Plantier .10 .05 .01
☐ 407 Troy Afenir .05 .02 .01
☐ 408 Gino Minutelli .05 .02 .01
☐ 409 Reggie Jefferson .10 .05 .01
☐ 410 Mike Remlinger .05 .02 .01
☐ 411 Carlos Rodriguez .05 .02 .01
☐ 412 Joe Redfield .05 .02 .01
☐ 413 Alonzo Powell .05 .02 .01
☐ 414 Scott Livingstone UER .05 .02 .01
(Travis Fryman,
not Woody, should be
referenced on back)
☐ 415 Scott Kamieniecki .05 .02 .01
☐ 416 Tim Spehr .05 .02 .01
☐ 417 Brian Hunter .05 .02 .01
☐ 418 Ced Landrum .05 .02 .01
☐ 419 Bret Barberie .05 .02 .01
☐ 420 Kevin Morton .05 .02 .01
☐ 421 Doug Henry .05 .02 .01
☐ 422 Doug Piatt .05 .02 .01
☐ 423 Pat Rice .05 .02 .01
☐ 424 Juan Guzman .10 .05 .01
☐ 425 Nolan Ryan NH .40 .18 .05
☐ 426 Tommy Greene NH .05 .02 .01
☐ 427 Bob Milacki and .05 .02 .01
Mike Flanagan NH
(Mark Williamson
and Gregg Olson)
☐ 428 Wilson Alvarez NH .10 .05 .01
☐ 429 Otis Nixon HL .05 .02 .01
☐ 430 Rickey Henderson HL .15 .07 .02
☐ 431 Cecil Fielder AS .10 .05 .01
☐ 432 Julio Franco AS .05 .02 .01
☐ 433 Cal Ripken AS .40 .18 .05
☐ 434 Wade Boggs AS .15 .07 .02
☐ 435 Joe Carter AS .15 .07 .02
☐ 436 Ken Griffey Jr. AS .75 .35 .09
☐ 437 Ruben Sierra AS .05 .02 .01
☐ 438 Scott Erickson AS .05 .02 .01
☐ 439 Tom Henke AS .05 .02 .01
☐ 440 Terry Steinbach AS .05 .02 .01
☐ 441 Rickey Henderson DT .15 .07 .02
☐ 442 Ryne Sandberg DT .25 .11 .03
☐ 443 Otis Nixon .05 .02 .01
☐ 444 Scott Radinsky .05 .02 .01
☐ 445 Mark Grace .15 .07 .02
☐ 446 Tony Pena .05 .02 .01
☐ 447 Billy Hatcher .05 .02 .01
☐ 448 Glenallen Hill .05 .02 .01
☐ 449 Chris Gwynn .05 .02 .01
☐ 450 Tom Glavine .15 .07 .02
☐ 451 John Habyan .05 .02 .01
☐ 452 Al Osuna .05 .02 .01
☐ 453 Tony Phillips .10 .05 .01
☐ 454 Greg Cadaret .05 .02 .01
☐ 455 Rob Dibble .05 .02 .01
☐ 456 Rick Honeycutt .05 .02 .01
☐ 457 Jerome Walton .05 .02 .01
☐ 458 Mookie Wilson .05 .02 .01
☐ 459 Mark Gubicza .05 .02 .01
☐ 460 Craig Biggio .10 .05 .01
☐ 461 Dave Cochrane .05 .02 .01
☐ 462 Keith Miller .05 .02 .01
☐ 463 Alex Cole .05 .02 .01
☐ 464 Pete Smith .05 .02 .01
☐ 465 Brett Butler .10 .05 .01
☐ 466 Jeff Huson .05 .02 .01
☐ 467 Steve Lake .05 .02 .01
☐ 468 Lloyd Moseby .05 .02 .01
☐ 469 Tim McIntosh .05 .02 .01
☐ 470 Dennis Martinez .10 .05 .01
☐ 471 Greg Myers .05 .02 .01
☐ 472 Mackey Sasser .05 .02 .01
☐ 473 Junior Ortiz .05 .02 .01
☐ 474 Greg Olson .05 .02 .01
☐ 475 Steve Sax .05 .02 .01
☐ 476 Ricky Jordan .05 .02 .01
☐ 477 Max Venable .05 .02 .01
☐ 478 Brian McRae .10 .05 .01
☐ 479 Doug Simons .05 .02 .01
☐ 480 Rickey Henderson .15 .07 .02
☐ 481 Gary Varsho .05 .02 .01
☐ 482 Carl Willis .05 .02 .01
☐ 483 Rick Wilkins .05 .02 .01
☐ 484 Donn Pall .05 .02 .01
☐ 485 Edgar Martinez .10 .05 .01
☐ 486 Tom Foley .05 .02 .01
☐ 487 Mark Williamson .05 .02 .01
☐ 488 Jack Armstrong .05 .02 .01
☐ 489 Gary Carter .10 .05 .01
☐ 490 Ruben Sierra .10 .05 .01
☐ 491 Gerald Perry .05 .02 .01
☐ 492 Rob Murphy .05 .02 .01
☐ 493 Zane Smith .05 .02 .01
☐ 494 Darryl Kile .05 .02 .01
☐ 495 Kelly Gruber .05 .02 .01
☐ 496 Jerry Browne .05 .02 .01
☐ 497 Darryl Hamilton .05 .02 .01
☐ 498 Mike Stanton .05 .02 .01
☐ 499 Mark Leonard .05 .02 .01
☐ 500 Jose Canseco .15 .07 .02
☐ 501 Dave Martinez .05 .02 .01
☐ 502 Jose Guzman .05 .02 .01
☐ 503 Terry Kennedy .05 .02 .01
☐ 504 Ed Sprague .10 .05 .01
☐ 505 Frank Thomas UER 1.50 .70 .19
(His Gulf Coast League
stats are wrong)
☐ 506 Darren Daulton .10 .05 .01
☐ 507 Kevin Tapani .05 .02 .01
☐ 508 Luis Salazar .05 .02 .01
☐ 509 Paul Faries .05 .02 .01
☐ 510 Sandy Alomar Jr. .10 .05 .01
☐ 511 Jeff King .10 .05 .01
☐ 512 Gary Thurman .05 .02 .01
☐ 513 Chris Hammond .05 .02 .01
☐ 514 Pedro Munoz .05 .02 .01
☐ 515 Alan Trammell .10 .05 .01
☐ 516 Geronimo Pena .05 .02 .01
☐ 517 Rodney McCray UER .05 .02 .01
(Stole 6 bases in
1990, not 5; career
totals are correct at 7)
☐ 518 Manny Lee .05 .02 .01
☐ 519 Junior Felix .05 .02 .01
☐ 520 Kirk Gibson .10 .05 .01
☐ 521 Darrin Jackson .05 .02 .01
☐ 522 John Burkett .10 .05 .01
☐ 523 Jeff Johnson .05 .02 .01
☐ 524 Jim Corsi .05 .02 .01
☐ 525 Robin Yount .15 .07 .02
☐ 526 Jamie Quirk .05 .02 .01
☐ 527 Bob Ojeda .05 .02 .01
☐ 528 Mark Lewis .05 .02 .01
☐ 529 Bryn Smith .05 .02 .01
☐ 530 Kent Hrbek .10 .05 .01
☐ 531 Dennis Boyd .05 .02 .01
☐ 532 Ron Karkovice .05 .02 .01
☐ 533 Don August .05 .02 .01
☐ 534 Todd Frohwirth .05 .02 .01
☐ 535 Wally Joyner .10 .05 .01
☐ 536 Dennis Rasmussen .05 .02 .01
☐ 537 Andy Allanson .05 .02 .01
☐ 538 Goose Gossage .10 .05 .01
☐ 539 John Marzano .05 .02 .01
☐ 540 Cal Ripken .75 .35 .09
☐ 541 Bill Swift UER .05 .02 .01
(Brewers logo on front)
☐ 542 Kevin Appier .10 .05 .01
☐ 543 Dave Bergman .05 .02 .01
☐ 544 Bernard Gilkey .10 .05 .01
☐ 545 Mike Greenwell .05 .02 .01
☐ 546 Jose Uribe .05 .02 .01
☐ 547 Jesse Orosco .05 .02 .01
☐ 548 Bob Patterson .05 .02 .01
☐ 549 Mike Stanley .05 .02 .01
☐ 550 Howard Johnson .05 .02 .01
☐ 551 Joe Orsulak .05 .02 .01
☐ 552 Dick Schofield .05 .02 .01
☐ 553 Dave Hollins .05 .02 .01
☐ 554 David Segui .05 .02 .01
☐ 555 Barry Bonds .25 .11 .03
☐ 556 Mo Vaughn .40 .18 .05
☐ 557 Craig Wilson .05 .02 .01
☐ 558 Bobby Rose .05 .02 .01
☐ 559 Rod Nichols .05 .02 .01
☐ 560 Len Dykstra .10 .05 .01
☐ 561 Craig Grebeck .05 .02 .01
☐ 562 Darren Lewis .05 .02 .01
☐ 563 Todd Benzinger .05 .02 .01
☐ 564 Ed Whitson .05 .02 .01
☐ 565 Jesse Barfield .05 .02 .01
☐ 566 Lloyd McClendon .05 .02 .01
☐ 567 Dan Plesac .05 .02 .01
☐ 568 Danny Cox .05 .02 .01
☐ 569 Skeeter Barnes .05 .02 .01
☐ 570 Bobby Thigpen .05 .02 .01
☐ 571 Deion Sanders .15 .07 .02
☐ 572 Chuck Knoblauch .15 .07 .02
☐ 573 Matt Nokes .05 .02 .01
☐ 574 Herm Winningham .05 .02 .01
☐ 575 Tom Candiotti .05 .02 .01
☐ 576 Jeff Bagwell .60 .25 .07
☐ 577 Brook Jacoby .05 .02 .01
☐ 578 Chico Walker .05 .02 .01
☐ 579 Brian Downing .05 .02 .01
☐ 580 Dave Stewart .10 .05 .01
☐ 581 Francisco Cabrera .05 .02 .01
☐ 582 Rene Gonzales .05 .02 .01
☐ 583 Stan Javier .05 .02 .01
☐ 584 Randy Johnson .15 .07 .02
☐ 585 Chuck Finley .05 .02 .01
☐ 586 Mark Gardner .05 .02 .01
☐ 587 Mark Whiten .10 .05 .01
☐ 588 Garry Templeton .05 .02 .01
☐ 589 Gary Sheffield .15 .07 .02
☐ 590 Ozzie Smith .25 .11 .03
☐ 591 Candy Maldonado .05 .02 .01
☐ 592 Mike Sharperson .05 .02 .01
☐ 593 Carlos Martinez .05 .02 .01
☐ 594 Scott Bankhead .05 .02 .01
☐ 595 Tim Wallach .05 .02 .01
☐ 596 Tino Martinez .10 .05 .01
☐ 597 Roger McDowell .05 .02 .01
☐ 598 Cory Snyder .05 .02 .01
☐ 599 Andujar Cedeno .05 .02 .01
☐ 600 Kirby Puckett .40 .18 .05
☐ 601 Rick Parker .05 .02 .01
☐ 602 Todd Hundley .10 .05 .01
☐ 603 Greg Litton .05 .02 .01
☐ 604 Dave Johnson .05 .02 .01
☐ 605 John Franco .05 .02 .01
☐ 606 Mike Fetters .05 .02 .01
☐ 607 Luis Alicea .05 .02 .01
☐ 608 Trevor Wilson .05 .02 .01
☐ 609 Rob Ducey .05 .02 .01
☐ 610 Ramon Martinez .10 .05 .01
☐ 611 Dave Burba .05 .02 .01
☐ 612 Dwight Smith .05 .02 .01
☐ 613 Kevin Maas .05 .02 .01
☐ 614 John Costello .05 .02 .01
☐ 615 Glenn Davis .05 .02 .01
☐ 616 Shawn Abner .05 .02 .01
☐ 617 Scott Hemond .05 .02 .01
☐ 618 Tom Prince .05 .02 .01
☐ 619 Wally Ritchie .05 .02 .01
☐ 620 Jim Abbott .05 .02 .01
☐ 621 Charlie O'Brien .05 .02 .01
☐ 622 Jack Daugherty .05 .02 .01
☐ 623 Tommy Gregg .05 .02 .01
☐ 624 Jeff Shaw .05 .02 .01
☐ 625 Tony Gwynn .40 .18 .05
☐ 626 Mark Leiter .05 .02 .01
☐ 627 Jim Clancy .05 .02 .01
☐ 628 Tim Layana .05 .02 .01
☐ 629 Jeff Schaefer .05 .02 .01
☐ 630 Lee Smith .10 .05 .01
☐ 631 Wade Taylor .05 .02 .01
☐ 632 Mike Simms .05 .02 .01
☐ 633 Terry Steinbach .10 .05 .01
☐ 634 Shawon Dunston .05 .02 .01
☐ 635 Tim Raines .15 .07 .02
☐ 636 Kirt Manwaring .05 .02 .01
☐ 637 Warren Cromartie .05 .02 .01
☐ 638 Luis Quinones .05 .02 .01
☐ 639 Greg Vaughn .10 .05 .01
☐ 640 Kevin Mitchell .10 .05 .01
☐ 641 Chris Hoiles .05 .02 .01
☐ 642 Tom Browning .05 .02 .01
☐ 643 Mitch Webster .05 .02 .01
☐ 644 Steve Olin .05 .02 .01
☐ 645 Tony Fernandez .05 .02 .01
☐ 646 Juan Bell .05 .02 .01
☐ 647 Joe Boever .05 .02 .01
☐ 648 Carney Lansford .10 .05 .01
☐ 649 Mike Benjamin .05 .02 .01
☐ 650 George Brett .40 .18 .05
☐ 651 Tim Burke .05 .02 .01
☐ 652 Jack Morris .10 .05 .01
☐ 653 Orel Hershiser .10 .05 .01
☐ 654 Mike Schooler .05 .02 .01
☐ 655 Andy Van Slyke .10 .05 .01
☐ 656 Dave Stieb .05 .02 .01
☐ 657 Dave Clark .05 .02 .01
☐ 658 Ben McDonald .05 .02 .01
☐ 659 John Smiley .05 .02 .01
☐ 660 Wade Boggs .15 .07 .02
☐ 661 Eric Bullock .05 .02 .01
☐ 662 Eric Show .05 .02 .01
☐ 663 Lenny Webster .05 .02 .01
☐ 664 Mike Huff .05 .02 .01
☐ 665 Rick Sutcliffe .05 .02 .01
☐ 666 Jeff Manto .05 .02 .01
☐ 667 Mike Fitzgerald .05 .02 .01
☐ 668 Matt Young .05 .02 .01
☐ 669 Dave West .05 .02 .01
☐ 670 Mike Hartley .05 .02 .01
☐ 671 Curt Schilling .05 .02 .01
☐ 672 Brian Bohanon .05 .02 .01
☐ 673 Cecil Espy .05 .02 .01
☐ 674 Joe Grahe .05 .02 .01
☐ 675 Sid Fernandez .05 .02 .01
☐ 676 Edwin Nunez .05 .02 .01
☐ 677 Hector Villanueva .05 .02 .01
☐ 678 Sean Berry .10 .05 .01
☐ 679 Dave Eiland .05 .02 .01
☐ 680 Dave Cone .15 .07 .02
☐ 681 Mike Bordick .10 .05 .01
☐ 682 Tony Castillo .05 .02 .01
☐ 683 John Barfield .05 .02 .01
☐ 684 Jeff Hamilton .05 .02 .01
☐ 685 Ken Dayley .05 .02 .01
☐ 686 Carmelo Martinez .05 .02 .01
☐ 687 Mike Capel .05 .02 .01
☐ 688 Scott Chiamparino .05 .02 .01
☐ 689 Rich Gedman .05 .02 .01
☐ 690 Rich Monteleone .05 .02 .01
☐ 691 Alejandro Pena .05 .02 .01
☐ 692 Oscar Azocar .05 .02 .01
☐ 693 Jim Poole .05 .02 .01
☐ 694 Mike Gardiner .05 .02 .01
☐ 695 Steve Buechele .05 .02 .01
☐ 696 Rudy Seanez .05 .02 .01
☐ 697 Paul Abbott .05 .02 .01
☐ 698 Steve Searcy .05 .02 .01
☐ 699 Jose Offerman .05 .02 .01
☐ 700 Ivan Rodriguez .40 .18 .05
☐ 701 Joe Girardi .05 .02 .01
☐ 702 Tony Perezchica .05 .02 .01
☐ 703 Paul McClellan .05 .02 .01
☐ 704 David Howard .05 .02 .01
☐ 705 Dan Petry .05 .02 .01
☐ 706 Jack Howell .05 .02 .01
☐ 707 Jose Mesa .10 .05 .01
☐ 708 Randy St. Claire .05 .02 .01
☐ 709 Kevin Brown .10 .05 .01
☐ 710 Ron Darling .05 .02 .01
☐ 711 Jason Grimsley .05 .02 .01
☐ 712 John Orton .05 .02 .01
☐ 713 Shawn Boskie .05 .02 .01
☐ 714 Pat Clements .05 .02 .01
☐ 715 Brian Barnes .05 .02 .01
☐ 716 Luis Lopez .05 .02 .01
☐ 717 Bob McClure .05 .02 .01
☐ 718 Mark Davis .05 .02 .01
☐ 719 Dann Bilardello .05 .02 .01
☐ 720 Tom Edens .05 .02 .01
☐ 721 Willie Fraser .05 .02 .01
☐ 722 Curt Young .05 .02 .01
☐ 723 Neal Heaton .05 .02 .01
☐ 724 Craig Worthington .05 .02 .01
☐ 725 Mel Rojas .10 .05 .01
☐ 726 Daryl Irvine .05 .02 .01
☐ 727 Roger Mason .05 .02 .01
☐ 728 Kirk Dressendorfer .05 .02 .01
☐ 729 Scott Aldred .05 .02 .01
☐ 730 Willie Blair .05 .02 .01
☐ 731 Allan Anderson .05 .02 .01
☐ 732 Dana Kiecker .05 .02 .01
☐ 733 Jose Gonzalez .05 .02 .01
☐ 734 Brian Drahman .05 .02 .01
☐ 735 Brad Komminsk .05 .02 .01
☐ 736 Arthur Rhodes .05 .02 .01
☐ 737 Terry Mathews .05 .02 .01
☐ 738 Jeff Fassero .10 .05 .01
☐ 739 Mike Magnante .05 .02 .01
☐ 740 Kip Gross .05 .02 .01
☐ 741 Jim Hunter .05 .02 .01
☐ 742 Jose Mota .05 .02 .01
☐ 743 Joe Bitker .05 .02 .01
☐ 744 Tim Mauser .05 .02 .01
☐ 745 Ramon Garcia .05 .02 .01
☐ 746 Rod Beck .25 .11 .03
☐ 747 Jim Austin .05 .02 .01
☐ 748 Keith Mitchell .05 .02 .01
☐ 749 Wayne Rosenthal .05 .02 .01
☐ 750 Bryan Hickerson .05 .02 .01
☐ 751 Bruce Egloff .05 .02 .01
☐ 752 John Wehner .05 .02 .01
☐ 753 Darren Holmes .05 .02 .01
☐ 754 Dave Hansen .05 .02 .01
☐ 755 Mike Mussina .30 .14 .04
☐ 756 Anthony Young .05 .02 .01
☐ 757 Ron Tingley .05 .02 .01
☐ 758 Ricky Bones .05 .02 .01
☐ 759 Mark Wohlers .15 .07 .02
☐ 760 Wilson Alvarez .15 .07 .02
☐ 761 Harvey Pulliam .05 .02 .01
☐ 762 Ryan Bowen .05 .02 .01
☐ 763 Terry Bross .05 .02 .01
☐ 764 Joel Johnston .05 .02 .01
☐ 765 Terry McDaniel .05 .02 .01
☐ 766 Esteban Beltre .05 .02 .01
☐ 767 Rob Maurer .05 .02 .01
☐ 768 Ted Wood .05 .02 .01
☐ 769 Mo Sanford .05 .02 .01
☐ 770 Jeff Carter .05 .02 .01
☐ 771 Gil Heredia .05 .02 .01
☐ 772 Monty Fariss .05 .02 .01
☐ 773 Will Clark AS .15 .07 .02
☐ 774 Ryne Sandberg AS .15 .07 .02
☐ 775 Barry Larkin AS .15 .07 .02
☐ 776 Howard Johnson AS .05 .02 .01
☐ 777 Barry Bonds AS .15 .07 .02

☐ 778 Brett Butler AS	.05	.02	.01
☐ 779 Tony Gwynn AS	.20	.09	.03
☐ 780 Ramon Martinez AS	.10	.05	.01
☐ 781 Lee Smith AS	.10	.05	.01
☐ 782 Mike Scioscia AS	.05	.02	.01
☐ 783 Dennis Martinez HL UER	.05	.02	.01
(Card has both 13th and 15th perfect game in Major League history)			
☐ 784 Dennis Martinez NH	.05	.02	.01
☐ 785 Mark Gardner NH	.05	.02	.01
☐ 786 Bret Saberhagen NH	.05	.02	.01
☐ 787 Kent Mercker NH	.05	.02	.01
Mark Wohlers			
Alejandro Pena			
☐ 788 Cal Ripken MVP	.40	.18	.05
☐ 789 Terry Pendleton MVP	.05	.02	.01
☐ 790 Roger Clemens CY	.15	.07	.02
☐ 791 Tom Glavine CY	.10	.05	.01
☐ 792 Chuck Knoblauch ROY	.15	.07	.02
☐ 793 Jeff Bagwell ROY	.30	.14	.04
☐ 794 Cal Ripken MANYR	.40	.18	.05
☐ 795 David Cone HL	.10	.05	.01
☐ 796 Kirby Puckett HL	.15	.07	.02
☐ 797 Steve Avery HL	.10	.05	.01
☐ 798 Jack Morris HL	.05	.02	.01
☐ 799 Allen Watson DC	.10	.05	.01
☐ 800 Manny Ramirez DC	2.00	.90	.25
☐ 801 Cliff Floyd DC	.40	.18	.05
☐ 802 Al Shirley DC	.10	.05	.01
☐ 803 Brian Barber DC	.10	.05	.01
☐ 804 Jon Farrell DC	.05	.02	.01
☐ 805 Brent Gates DC	.10	.05	.01
☐ 806 Scott Ruffcorn DC	.10	.05	.01
☐ 807 Tyrone Hill DC	.05	.02	.01
☐ 808 Benji Gil DC	.15	.07	.02
☐ 809 Aaron Sele DC	.15	.07	.02
☐ 810 Tyler Green DC	.10	.05	.01
☐ 811 Chris Jones	.05	.02	.01
☐ 812 Steve Wilson	.05	.02	.01
☐ 813 Freddie Benavides	.05	.02	.01
☐ 814 Don Wakamatsu	.05	.02	.01
☐ 815 Mike Humphreys	.05	.02	.01
☐ 816 Scott Servais	.05	.02	.01
☐ 817 Rico Rossy	.05	.02	.01
☐ 818 John Ramos	.05	.02	.01
☐ 819 Rob Mallicoat	.05	.02	.01
☐ 820 Milt Hill	.05	.02	.01
☐ 821 Carlos Garcia	.10	.05	.01
☐ 822 Stan Royer	.05	.02	.01
☐ 823 Jeff Plympton	.05	.02	.01
☐ 824 Braulio Castillo	.05	.02	.01
☐ 825 David Haas	.05	.02	.01
☐ 826 Luis Mercedes	.05	.02	.01
☐ 827 Eric Karros	.15	.07	.02
☐ 828 Shawn Hare	.05	.02	.01
☐ 829 Reggie Sanders	.15	.07	.02
☐ 830 Tom Goodwin	.10	.05	.01
☐ 831 Dan Gakeler	.05	.02	.01
☐ 832 Stacy Jones	.05	.02	.01
☐ 833 Kim Batiste	.05	.02	.01
☐ 834 Cal Eldred	.05	.02	.01
☐ 835 Chris George	.05	.02	.01
☐ 836 Wayne Housie	.05	.02	.01
☐ 837 Mike Ignasiak	.05	.02	.01
☐ 838 Josias Manzanillo	.05	.02	.01
☐ 839 Jim Olander	.05	.02	.01
☐ 840 Gary Cooper	.05	.02	.01
☐ 841 Royce Clayton	.10	.05	.01
☐ 842 Hector Fajardo	.05	.02	.01
☐ 843 Blaine Beatty	.05	.02	.01
☐ 844 Jorge Pedre	.05	.02	.01
☐ 845 Kenny Lofton	1.00	.45	.12
☐ 846 Scott Brosius	.05	.02	.01
☐ 847 Chris Cron	.05	.02	.01
☐ 848 Denis Boucher	.05	.02	.01
☐ 849 Kyle Abbott	.05	.02	.01
☐ 850 Robert Zupcic	.05	.02	.01
☐ 851 Rheal Cormier	.05	.02	.01
☐ 852 Jim Lewis	.05	.02	.01
☐ 853 Anthony Telford	.05	.02	.01
☐ 854 Cliff Brantley	.05	.02	.01
☐ 855 Kevin Campbell	.05	.02	.01
☐ 856 Craig Shipley	.05	.02	.01
☐ 857 Chuck Carr	.05	.02	.01
☐ 858 Tony Eusebio	.05	.02	.01
☐ 859 Jim Thome	.75	.35	.09
☐ 860 Vinny Castilla	.50	.23	.06
☐ 861 Dann Howitt	.05	.02	.01
☐ 862 Kevin Ward	.05	.02	.01
☐ 863 Steve Wapnick	.05	.02	.01
☐ 864 Rod Brewer	.05	.02	.01
☐ 865 Todd Van Poppel	.05	.02	.01
☐ 866 Jose Hernandez	.05	.02	.01
☐ 867 Amalio Carreno	.05	.02	.01
☐ 868 Calvin Jones	.05	.02	.01
☐ 869 Jeff Gardner	.05	.02	.01
☐ 870 Jarvis Brown	.05	.02	.01
☐ 871 Eddie Taubensee	.05	.02	.01
☐ 872 Andy Mota	.05	.02	.01
☐ 873 Chris Haney	.05	.02	.01
☐ 874 Roberto Hernandez	.10	.05	.01
☐ 875 Laddie Renfroe	.05	.02	.01
☐ 876 Scott Cooper	.05	.02	.01
☐ 877 Armando Reynoso	.05	.02	.01
☐ 878 Ty Cobb MEMO	.25	.11	.03
☐ 879 Babe Ruth MEMO	.30	.14	.04
☐ 880 Honus Wagner MEMO	.20	.09	.03
☐ 881 Lou Gehrig MEMO	.25	.11	.03
☐ 882 Satchel Paige MEMO	.20	.09	.03
☐ 883 Will Clark DT	.15	.07	.02
☐ 884 Cal Ripken DT	2.00	.90	.25
☐ 885 Wade Boggs DT	.15	.07	.02
☐ 886 Kirby Puckett DT	.30	.14	.04
☐ 887 Tony Gwynn DT	.30	.14	.04
☐ 888 Craig Biggio DT	.10	.05	.01
☐ 889 Scott Erickson DT	.05	.02	.01
☐ 890 Tom Glavine DT	.10	.05	.01
☐ 891 Rob Dibble DT	.05	.02	.01
☐ 892 Mitch Williams DT	.05	.02	.01
☐ 893 Frank Thomas DT	1.50	.70	.19
☐ X672 Chuck Knoblauch AU	60.00	27.00	7.50
(1990 Score card, autographed with special hologram on back)			

1992 Score DiMaggio

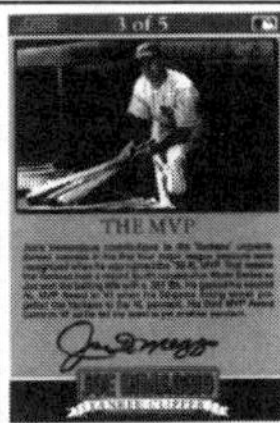

This five-card standard-size insert set was issued in honor of one of baseball's all-time greats, Joe DiMaggio. These cards were randomly inserted in first series packs. According to sources at Score, 30,000 of each card were produced. On a white card face, the fronts have vintage photos that have been colorized and accented by red, white, and blue border stripes. DiMaggio autographed 2,500 cards for this promotion. 2,495 of these cards were inserted in packs while the other five were used as prizes in a mail-in sweepstakes. The autographed cards are individually numbered out of 2,500.

	MINT	NRMT	EXC
COMPLETE SET (5)	150.00	70.00	19.00
COMMON DIMAGGIO (1-5)	30.00	13.50	3.70
☐ 1 Joe DiMaggio	30.00	13.50	3.70
The Minors			
☐ 2 Joe DiMaggio	30.00	13.50	3.70
The Rookie			
☐ 3 Joe DiMaggio	30.00	13.50	3.70
The MVP			
☐ 4 Joe DiMaggio	30.00	13.50	3.70
The Streak			
☐ 5 Joe DiMaggio	30.00	13.50	3.70
The Legend			
☐ AU0 Joe DiMaggio AU	550.00	250.00	70.00
(Autographed with certified signature)			

1992 Score Factory Inserts

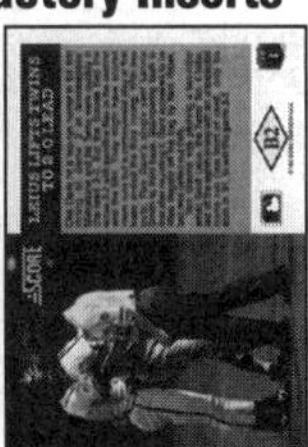

This 17-card insert standard-size set was distributed only in 1992 Score factory sets and consists of four topical subsets. Cards B1-B7 capture a moment from each game of the 1991 World Series. Cards B8-B11 are Cooperstown cards, honoring future Hall of Famers. Cards B12-B14 form a "Joe D" subset paying tribute to Joe DiMaggio. Cards B15-B17, subtitled "Yaz", conclude the set by commemorating Carl Yastrzemski's heroic feats twenty-five years ago in winning the Triple Crown and lifting the Red Sox to their first American League pennant in 21 years. Each subset displayed a different front design. The World Series cards carry full-bleed color action photos except for a blue stripe at the bottom, while the Cooperstown cards have a color portrait on a white card face. Both the DiMaggio and Yastrzemski subsets have action photos with silver borders; they differ in that the DiMaggio photos are black and white, the Yastrzemski photos color. The DiMaggio and Yastrzemski subsets are numbered on the back within each subset (e.g., "1 of 3") and as a part of the 17-card insert set (e.g., "B1"). In the DiMaggio and Yastrzemski subsets, Score varied the insert set slightly in retail versus hobby factory sets. In the hobby set, the DiMaggio cards display different black-and-white photos that are bordered beneath by a dark blue stripe (the stripe is green in the retail factory insert). On the backs, these hobby inserts have a red stripe at the bottom; the same stripe is dark blue on the retail inserts. The Yastrzemski cards in the hobby set have different color photos on their fronts than the retail inserts.

	MINT	NRMT	EXC
COMPLETE SET (17)	6.00	2.70	.75
COMMON WS (B1-B7)	.25	.11	.03
COM.COOPERSTWN (B8-B11)	.75	.35	.09
COMMON DIMAGGIO (B12-B14)	1.50	.70	.19
COMMON YAZ (B15-B17)	.30	.14	.04
☐ B1 Greg Gagne WS	.25	.11	.03
☐ B2 Scott Leius WS	.25	.11	.03
☐ B3 Mark Lemke WS	.25	.11	.03
David Justice			
☐ B4 Lonnie Smith WS	.25	.11	.03
Brian Harper			
☐ B5 David Justice WS	.75	.35	.09
☐ B6 Kirby Puckett WS	3.00	1.35	.35
☐ B7 Gene Larkin WS	.25	.11	.03
☐ B8 Carlton Fisk	.75	.35	.09
☐ B9 Ozzie Smith	2.00	.90	.25
☐ B10 Dave Winfield	.75	.35	.09
☐ B11 Robin Yount	1.00	.45	.12
☐ B12 Joe DiMaggio	1.50	.70	.19
☐ B13 Joe DiMaggio	1.50	.70	.19
☐ B14 Joe DiMaggio	1.50	.70	.19
☐ B15 Carl Yastrzemski	.30	.14	.04
☐ B16 Carl Yastrzemski	.30	.14	.04
☐ B17 Carl Yastrzemski	.30	.14	.04

1992 Score Franchise

This four-card standard-size set features three all-time greats, Stan Musial, Mickey Mantle, and Carl Yastrzemski. Each former player autographed 2,000 of his 1992 Score cards, and 500 of the combo cards were signed by all three. In addition to these signed cards, Score produced 150,000 of each Franchise card, and both signed and unsigned cards were randomly inserted in 1992 Score Series II poly packs, blister packs, and cello packs. The first three cards feature color action photos of each player. The fourth is horizontally oriented and pictures each player in a batting stance. A forest green stripe borders the top and bottom. The words "The Franchise" and the Score logo appear at the top, and the player's name is printed on the green stripe at the bottom. The backs of the first three cards have a close-up photo and a career summary. The fourth card is a combo card, summarizing the career of all three players.

	MINT	NRMT	EXC
COMPLETE SET (4)	30.00	13.50	3.70
COMMON CARD (1-4)	5.00	2.20	.60
☐ 1 Stan Musial	5.00	2.20	.60
☐ 2 Mickey Mantle	12.00	5.50	1.50
☐ 3 Carl Yastrzemski	5.00	2.20	.60
☐ 4 The Franchise Players	10.00	4.50	1.25
Stan Musial			
Mickey Mantle			
Carl Yastrzemski			
☐ AU1 Stan Musial	225.00	100.00	28.00
(Autographed with certified signature)			
☐ AU2 Mickey Mantle	550.00	250.00	70.00
(Autographed with certified signature)			
☐ AU3 Carl Yastrzemski	175.00	80.00	22.00
(Autographed with certified signature)			
☐ AU4 Franchise Players	1600.00	700.00	200.00
Stan Musial			
Mickey Mantle			
Carl Yastrzemski			
(Autographed with certified signatures of all three)			

1992 Score Hot Rookies

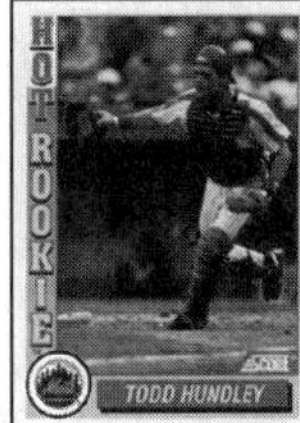

This ten-card standard-size set features color action player photos on a white face. These cards were inserted one per blister pack. The words "Hot Rookie" appear in orange and yellow vertically along the left edge of the photo, and the team logo is in the lower left corner. The player's name is printed in yellow on a red box accented with a shadow detail.

	MINT	NRMT	EXC
COMPLETE SET (10)	15.00	6.75	1.85
COMMON CARD (1-10)	.50	.23	.06
☐ 1 Cal Eldred	.50	.23	.06
☐ 2 Royce Clayton	.75	.35	.09
☐ 3 Kenny Lofton	10.00	4.50	1.25
☐ 4 Todd Van Poppel	.50	.23	.06
☐ 5 Scott Cooper	.50	.23	.06
☐ 6 Todd Hundley	2.00	.90	.25
☐ 7 Tino Martinez	.75	.35	.09
☐ 8 Anthony Telford	.50	.23	.06
☐ 9 Derek Bell	1.50	.70	.19
☐ 10 Reggie Jefferson	.75	.35	.09

1992 Score Impact Players

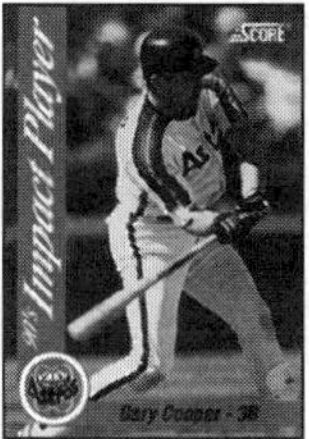

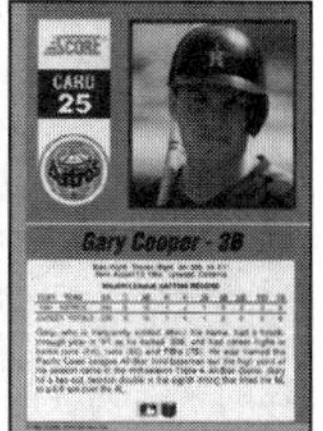

The 1992 Score Impact Players insert set was issued in two series each with 45 standard-size cards with the respective series of the 1992 regular issue Score cards. Five of these cards were inserted in each 1992 Score jumbo pack. The fronts feature full-bleed color action player photos. The pictures are enhanced by a wide vertical stripe running near the left edge containing the words "90's Impact Player" and a narrower stripe at the bottom printed with the player's name.

	MINT	NRMT	EXC
COMPLETE SET (90)	20.00	9.00	2.50
COMPLETE SERIES 1 (45)	14.00	6.25	1.75
COMPLETE SERIES 2 (45)	6.00	2.70	.75
COMMON CARD (1-90)	.15	.07	.02
☐ 1 Chuck Knoblauch	.50	.23	.06
☐ 2 Jeff Bagwell	1.50	.70	.19
☐ 3 Juan Guzman	.25	.11	.03
☐ 4 Milt Cuyler	.15	.07	.02
☐ 5 Ivan Rodriguez	1.00	.45	.12
☐ 6 Rich DeLucia	.15	.07	.02
☐ 7 Orlando Merced	.25	.11	.03
☐ 8 Ray Lankford	.40	.18	.05
☐ 9 Brian Hunter	.15	.07	.02
☐ 10 Roberto Alomar	.50	.23	.06
☐ 11 Wes Chamberlain	.15	.07	.02
☐ 12 Steve Avery	.25	.11	.03
☐ 13 Scott Erickson	.25	.11	.03
☐ 14 Jim Abbott	.15	.07	.02
☐ 15 Mark Whiten	.15	.07	.02
☐ 16 Leo Gomez	.15	.07	.02
☐ 17 Doug Henry	.15	.07	.02
☐ 18 Brent Mayne	.15	.07	.02
☐ 19 Charles Nagy	.25	.11	.03
☐ 20 Phil Plantier	.15	.07	.02
☐ 21 Mo Vaughn	1.00	.45	.12
☐ 22 Craig Biggio	.25	.11	.03
☐ 23 Derek Bell	.40	.18	.05
☐ 24 Royce Clayton	.25	.11	.03
☐ 25 Gary Cooper	.15	.07	.02
☐ 26 Scott Cooper	.15	.07	.02
☐ 27 Juan Gonzalez	1.50	.70	.19
☐ 28 Ken Griffey Jr.	4.00	1.80	.50
☐ 29 Larry Walker	.40	.18	.05
☐ 30 John Smoltz	.50	.23	.06
☐ 31 Todd Hundley	.50	.23	.06
☐ 32 Kenny Lofton	2.00	.90	.25
☐ 33 Andy Mota	.15	.07	.02
☐ 34 Todd Zeile	.15	.07	.02
☐ 35 Arthur Rhodes	.15	.07	.02
☐ 36 Jim Thome	2.50	1.10	.30
☐ 37 Todd Van Poppel	.15	.07	.02
☐ 38 Mark Wohlers	.40	.18	.05
☐ 39 Anthony Young	.15	.07	.02
☐ 40 Sandy Alomar Jr.	.25	.11	.03
☐ 41 John Olerud	.25	.11	.03
☐ 42 Robin Ventura	.25	.11	.03
☐ 43 Frank Thomas	4.00	1.80	.50
☐ 44 Dave Justice	.40	.18	.05
☐ 45 Hal Morris	.15	.07	.02
☐ 46 Ruben Sierra	.15	.07	.02
☐ 47 Travis Fryman	.40	.18	.05
☐ 48 Mike Mussina	.75	.35	.09
☐ 49 Tom Glavine	.40	.18	.05
☐ 50 Barry Larkin	.40	.18	.05
☐ 51 Will Clark UER	.40	.18	.05
Career Totals spelled To als			
☐ 52 Jose Canseco	.40	.18	.05
☐ 53 Bo Jackson	.25	.11	.03
☐ 54 Dwight Gooden	.25	.11	.03
☐ 55 Barry Bonds	.60	.25	.07
☐ 56 Fred McGriff	.40	.18	.05
☐ 57 Roger Clemens	.40	.18	.05
☐ 58 Benito Santiago	.15	.07	.02
☐ 59 Darryl Strawberry	.25	.11	.03

☐ 60 Cecil Fielder	.25	.11	.03
☐ 61 John Franco	.15	.07	.02
☐ 62 Matt Williams	.40	.18	.05
☐ 63 Marquis Grissom	.25	.11	.03
☐ 64 Danny Tartabull	.15	.07	.02
☐ 65 Ron Gant	.25	.11	.03
☐ 66 Paul O'Neill	.25	.11	.03
☐ 67 Devon White	.25	.11	.03
☐ 68 Rafael Palmeiro	.40	.18	.05
☐ 69 Tom Gordon	.15	.07	.02
☐ 70 Shawon Dunston	.15	.07	.02
☐ 71 Rob Dibble	.15	.07	.02
☐ 72 Eddie Zosky	.15	.07	.02
☐ 73 Jack McDowell	.25	.11	.03
☐ 74 Len Dykstra	.25	.11	.03
☐ 75 Ramon Martinez	.25	.11	.03
☐ 76 Reggie Sanders	.25	.11	.03
☐ 77 Greg Maddux	2.50	1.10	.30
☐ 78 Ellis Burks	.40	.18	.05
☐ 79 John Smiley	.15	.07	.02
☐ 80 Roberto Kelly	.15	.07	.02
☐ 81 Ben McDonald	.15	.07	.02
☐ 82 Mark Lewis	.15	.07	.02
☐ 83 Jose Rijo	.15	.07	.02
☐ 84 Ozzie Guillen	.15	.07	.02
☐ 85 Lance Dickson	.15	.07	.02
☐ 86 Kim Batiste	.15	.07	.02
☐ 87 Gregg Olson	.15	.07	.02
☐ 88 Andy Benes	.25	.11	.03
☐ 89 Cal Eldred	.15	.07	.02
☐ 90 David Cone	.25	.11	.03

1992 Score Rookie/Traded

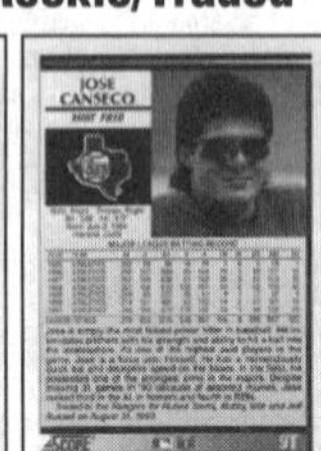

The 1992 Score Rookie and Traded set contains 110 standard-size cards featuring traded veterans and rookies. This set was issued in complete set form and was released through hobby dealers. The fronts display color action player photos edged on one side by an orange stripe that fades to white as one moves down the card face. The player's name appears in a purple bar above the picture, while his position is printed in a purple bar below the picture. The set is arranged numerically such that cards 1T-79T are traded players and cards 80T-110T feature rookies. The only notable Rookie Card in this set features Brian Jordan.

	MINT	NRMT	EXC
COMPLETE FACT.SET (110)	25.00	11.00	3.10
COMMON CARD (1T-110T)	.10	.05	.01

☐ 1T Gary Sheffield	.75	.35	.09
☐ 2T Kevin Seitzer	.10	.05	.01
☐ 3T Danny Tartabull	.10	.05	.01
☐ 4T Steve Sax	.10	.05	.01
☐ 5T Bobby Bonilla	.20	.09	.03
☐ 6T Frank Viola	.10	.05	.01
☐ 7T Dave Winfield	.60	.25	.07
☐ 8T Rick Sutcliffe	.10	.05	.01
☐ 9T Jose Canseco	.75	.35	.09
☐ 10T Greg Swindell	.10	.05	.01
☐ 11T Eddie Murray	.75	.35	.09
☐ 12T Randy Myers	.20	.09	.03
☐ 13T Wally Joyner	.20	.09	.03
☐ 14T Kenny Lofton	8.00	3.60	1.00
☐ 15T Jack Morris	.20	.09	.03
☐ 16T Charlie Hayes	.10	.05	.01
☐ 17T Pete Incaviglia	.10	.05	.01
☐ 18T Kevin Mitchell	.20	.09	.03
☐ 19T Kurt Stillwell	.10	.05	.01
☐ 20T Bret Saberhagen	.20	.09	.03
☐ 21T Steve Buechele	.10	.05	.01
☐ 22T John Smiley	.10	.05	.01
☐ 23T Sammy Sosa	1.25	.55	.16
☐ 24T George Bell	.10	.05	.01
☐ 25T Curt Schilling	.10	.05	.01
☐ 26T Dick Schofield	.10	.05	.01
☐ 27T David Cone	.20	.09	.03
☐ 28T Dan Gladden	.10	.05	.01
☐ 29T Kirk McCaskill	.10	.05	.01
☐ 30T Mike Gallego	.10	.05	.01
☐ 31T Kevin McReynolds	.10	.05	.01
☐ 32T Bill Swift	.10	.05	.01
☐ 33T Dave Martinez	.10	.05	.01
☐ 34T Storm Davis	.10	.05	.01
☐ 35T Willie Randolph	.20	.09	.03
☐ 36T Melido Perez	.10	.05	.01
☐ 37T Mark Carreon	.10	.05	.01
☐ 38T Doug Jones	.10	.05	.01
☐ 39T Gregg Jefferies	.20	.09	.03
☐ 40T Mike Jackson	.10	.05	.01
☐ 41T Dickie Thon	.10	.05	.01
☐ 42T Eric King	.10	.05	.01
☐ 43T Herm Winningham	.10	.05	.01
☐ 44T Derek Lilliquist	.10	.05	.01
☐ 45T Dave Anderson	.10	.05	.01
☐ 46T Jeff Reardon	.20	.09	.03
☐ 47T Scott Bankhead	.10	.05	.01
☐ 48T Cory Snyder	.10	.05	.01
☐ 49T Al Newman	.10	.05	.01
☐ 50T Keith Miller	.10	.05	.01
☐ 51T Dave Burba	.10	.05	.01
☐ 52T Bill Pecota	.10	.05	.01
☐ 53T Chuck Crim	.10	.05	.01
☐ 54T Mariano Duncan	.10	.05	.01
☐ 55T Dave Gallagher	.10	.05	.01
☐ 56T Chris Gwynn	.10	.05	.01
☐ 57T Scott Ruskin	.10	.05	.01
☐ 58T Jack Armstrong	.10	.05	.01
☐ 59T Gary Carter	.20	.09	.03
☐ 60T Andres Galarraga	.35	.16	.04
☐ 61T Ken Hill	.20	.09	.03
☐ 62T Eric Davis	.20	.09	.03
☐ 63T Ruben Sierra	.20	.09	.03
☐ 64T Darrin Fletcher	.10	.05	.01
☐ 65T Tim Belcher	.10	.05	.01
☐ 66T Mike Morgan	.10	.05	.01
☐ 67T Scott Scudder	.10	.05	.01
☐ 68T Tom Candiotti	.10	.05	.01
☐ 69T Hubie Brooks	.10	.05	.01
☐ 70T Kal Daniels	.10	.05	.01
☐ 71T Bruce Ruffin	.10	.05	.01
☐ 72T Billy Hatcher	.10	.05	.01
☐ 73T Bob Melvin	.10	.05	.01
☐ 74T Lee Guetterman	.10	.05	.01
☐ 75T Rene Gonzales	.10	.05	.01
☐ 76T Kevin Bass	.10	.05	.01
☐ 77T Tom Bolton	.10	.05	.01
☐ 78T John Wetteland	.20	.09	.03
☐ 79T Bip Roberts	.10	.05	.01
☐ 80T Pat Listach	.20	.09	.03
☐ 81T John Doherty	.10	.05	.01
☐ 82T Sam Militello	.10	.05	.01
☐ 83T Brian Jordan	2.50	1.10	.30
☐ 84T Jeff Kent	.75	.35	.09
☐ 85T Dave Fleming	.10	.05	.01
☐ 86T Jeff Tackett	.10	.05	.01
☐ 87T Chad Curtis	.35	.16	.04
☐ 88T Eric Fox	.10	.05	.01
☐ 89T Denny Neagle	1.00	.45	.12
☐ 90T Donovan Osborne	.20	.09	.03
☐ 91T Carlos Hernandez	.10	.05	.01
☐ 92T Tim Wakefield	.35	.16	.04
☐ 93T Tim Salmon	5.00	2.20	.60
☐ 94T Dave Nilsson	.20	.09	.03
☐ 95T Mike Perez	.10	.05	.01
☐ 96T Pat Hentgen	.35	.16	.04
☐ 97T Frank Seminara	.10	.05	.01
☐ 98T Ruben Amaro Jr.	.10	.05	.01
☐ 99T Archi Cianfrocco	.10	.05	.01
☐ 100T Andy Stankiewicz	.10	.05	.01
☐ 101T Jim Bullinger	.10	.05	.01
☐ 102T Pat Mahomes	.10	.05	.01
☐ 103T Hipolito Pichardo	.10	.05	.01
☐ 104T Bret Boone	.35	.16	.04
☐ 105T John Vander Wal	.10	.05	.01
☐ 106T Vince Horsman	.10	.05	.01
☐ 107T James Austin	.10	.05	.01
☐ 108T Brian Williams	.10	.05	.01
☐ 109T Dan Walters	.10	.05	.01
☐ 110T Wil Cordero	.20	.09	.03

1992 Score 100 Rising Stars

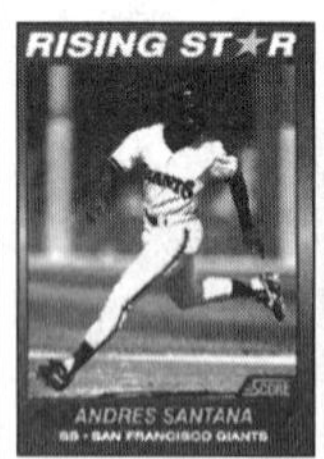

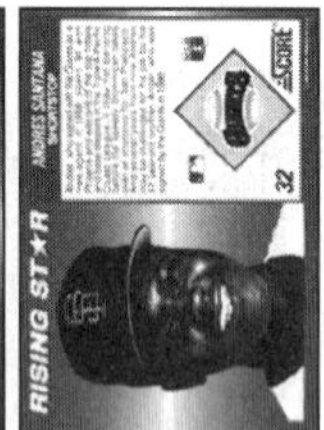

The 1992 Score Rising Stars set contains 100 standard size player cards and six "Magic Motion" trivia cards. The fronts display color action player photos on a card face that shades from green to yellow and back to green. The words "Rising Star" appear above the picture, with the player's name in a blue stripe at the card bottom. The horizontally oriented backs have a color head shot on the left half, with player profile and team logo on the right half.

	MINT	NRMT	EXC
COMPLETE SET (100)	8.00	3.60	1.00
COMMON CARD (1-100)	.05	.02	.01

☐ 1 Milt Cuyler	.05	.02	.01
☐ 2 David Howard	.05	.02	.01
☐ 3 Brian R. Hunter	.05	.02	.01
☐ 4 Darryl Kile	.10	.05	.01
☐ 5 Pat Kelly	.05	.02	.01
☐ 6 Luis Gonzalez	.10	.05	.01
☐ 7 Mike Benjamin	.05	.02	.01
☐ 8 Eric Anthony	.05	.02	.01
☐ 9 Moises Alou	.40	.18	.05
☐ 10 Darren Lewis	.05	.02	.01
☐ 11 Chuck Knoblauch	1.00	.45	.12
☐ 12 Geronimo Pena	.05	.02	.01
☐ 13 Jeff Plympton	.05	.02	.01
☐ 14 Bret Barberie	.05	.02	.01
☐ 15 Chris Haney	.05	.02	.01
☐ 16 Rick Wilkins	.05	.02	.01
☐ 17 Julio Valera	.05	.02	.01
☐ 18 Joe Slusarski	.05	.02	.01
☐ 19 Jose Melendez	.05	.02	.01
☐ 20 Pete Schourek	.20	.09	.03
☐ 21 Jeff Conine	.60	.25	.07
☐ 22 Paul Faries	.05	.02	.01
☐ 23 Scott Kamieniecki	.05	.02	.01
☐ 24 Bernard Gilkey	.40	.18	.05
☐ 25 Wes Chamberlain	.05	.02	.01
☐ 26 Charles Nagy	.40	.18	.05
☐ 27 Juan Guzman	.25	.11	.03
☐ 28 Heath Slocumb	.10	.05	.01
☐ 29 Eddie Taubensee	.10	.05	.01
☐ 30 Cedric Landrum	.05	.02	.01
☐ 31 Jose Offerman	.05	.02	.01
☐ 32 Andres Santana	.05	.02	.01
☐ 33 David Segui	.10	.05	.01
☐ 34 Bernie Williams	1.00	.45	.12
☐ 35 Jeff Bagwell	2.00	.90	.25
☐ 36 Kevin Morton	.05	.02	.01
☐ 37 Kirk Dressendorfer	.05	.02	.01
☐ 38 Mike Fetters	.10	.05	.01
☐ 39 Darren Holmes	.05	.02	.01
☐ 40 Jeff Johnson	.05	.02	.01
☐ 41 Scott Aldred	.05	.02	.01
☐ 42 Kevin Ward	.05	.02	.01
☐ 43 Ray Lankford	.40	.18	.05
☐ 44 Terry Shumpert	.05	.02	.01
☐ 45 Wade Taylor	.05	.02	.01
☐ 46 Rob MacDonald	.05	.02	.01
☐ 47 Jose Mota	.05	.02	.01
☐ 48 Reggie Harris	.05	.02	.01
☐ 49 Mike Remlinger	.05	.02	.01
☐ 50 Mark Lewis	.10	.05	.01
☐ 51 Tino Martinez	.50	.23	.06
☐ 52 Ed Sprague	.10	.05	.01
☐ 53 Freddie Benavides	.05	.02	.01
☐ 54 Rich DeLucia	.05	.02	.01
☐ 55 Brian Drahman	.05	.02	.01
☐ 56 Steve Decker	.05	.02	.01
☐ 57 Scott Livingstone	.05	.02	.01
☐ 58 Mike Timlin	.10	.05	.01
☐ 59 Bob Scanlan	.05	.02	.01
☐ 60 Dean Palmer	.30	.14	.04
☐ 61 Frank Castillo	.05	.02	.01
☐ 62 Mark Leonard	.05	.02	.01
☐ 63 Chuck McElroy	.05	.02	.01
☐ 64 Derek Bell	.30	.14	.04
☐ 65 Andujar Cedeno	.05	.02	.01
☐ 66 Leo Gomez	.05	.02	.01
☐ 67 Rusty Meacham	.05	.02	.01
☐ 68 Dann Howitt	.05	.02	.01
☐ 69 Chris Jones	.05	.02	.01
☐ 70 Dave Cochrane	.05	.02	.01
☐ 71 Carlos Martinez	.05	.02	.01
☐ 72 Hensley Meulens	.05	.02	.01
☐ 73 Rich Reed	.05	.02	.01
☐ 74 Pedro Munoz	.10	.05	.01
☐ 75 Orlando Merced	.10	.05	.01
☐ 76 Chito Martinez	.05	.02	.01
☐ 77 Ivan Rodriguez	1.25	.55	.16
☐ 78 Brian Barnes	.05	.02	.01
☐ 79 Chris Donnels	.05	.02	.01
☐ 80 Todd Hundley	.50	.23	.06
☐ 81 Gary Scott	.05	.02	.01
☐ 82 John Wehner	.05	.02	.01
☐ 83 Al Osuna	.05	.02	.01
☐ 84 Luis Lopez	.05	.02	.01
☐ 85 Brent Mayne	.05	.02	.01
☐ 86 Phil Plantier	.10	.05	.01
☐ 87 Joe Bitker	.05	.02	.01
☐ 88 Scott Cooper	.05	.02	.01
☐ 89 Chris Hammond	.05	.02	.01
☐ 90 Tim Sherrill	.05	.02	.01
☐ 91 Doug Simons	.05	.02	.01
☐ 92 Kip Gross	.05	.02	.01
☐ 93 Tim McIntosh	.05	.02	.01
☐ 94 Larry Casian	.05	.02	.01
☐ 95 Mike Dalton	.05	.02	.01
☐ 96 Lance Dickson	.05	.02	.01
☐ 97 Joe Grahe	.05	.02	.01
☐ 98 Glenn Sutko	.05	.02	.01
☐ 99 Gerald Alexander	.05	.02	.01
☐ 100 Mo Vaughn	1.25	.55	.16

1992 Score 100 Superstars

The 1992 Score Superstars set contains 100 standard-size player cards and six "Magic Motion" trivia cards. The fronts display color action player photos on a card face that shades from reddish-orange to yellow and back to reddish-orange again. The words "Superstar" appear above the pictures, with the player's name in a purple stripe at the card bottom. The horizontally oriented backs have a color head shot on the left half, with player profile and team logo on the right half.

	MINT	NRMT	EXC
COMPLETE SET (100)	8.00	3.60	1.00
COMMON CARD (1-100)	.05	.02	.01

☐ 1 Ken Griffey Jr.	2.00	.90	.25
☐ 2 Scott Erickson	.05	.02	.01
☐ 3 John Smiley	.05	.02	.01
☐ 4 Rick Aguilera	.10	.05	.01
☐ 5 Jeff Reardon	.05	.02	.01
☐ 6 Chuck Finley	.10	.05	.01
☐ 7 Kirby Puckett	1.00	.45	.12
☐ 8 Paul Molitor	.50	.23	.06
☐ 9 Dave Winfield	.25	.11	.03
☐ 10 Mike Greenwell	.05	.02	.01
☐ 11 Bret Saberhagen	.10	.05	.01
☐ 12 Pete Harnisch	.05	.02	.01
☐ 13 Ozzie Guillen	.05	.02	.01
☐ 14 Hal Morris	.05	.02	.01
☐ 15 Tom Glavine	.25	.11	.03
☐ 16 David Cone	.10	.05	.01
☐ 17 Edgar Martinez	.25	.11	.03
☐ 18 Willie McGee	.10	.05	.01
☐ 19 Jim Abbott	.05	.02	.01
☐ 20 Mark Grace	.30	.14	.04
☐ 21 George Brett	.75	.35	.09
☐ 22 Jack McDowell	.10	.05	.01
☐ 23 Don Mattingly	1.00	.45	.12
☐ 24 Will Clark	.30	.14	.04
☐ 25 Dwight Gooden	.10	.05	.01
☐ 26 Barry Bonds	.50	.23	.06
☐ 27 Rafael Palmeiro	.25	.11	.03
☐ 28 Lee Smith	.10	.05	.01
☐ 29 Wally Joyner	.05	.02	.01
☐ 30 Wade Boggs	.30	.14	.04
☐ 31 Tom Henke	.05	.02	.01
☐ 32 Mark Langston	.05	.02	.01
☐ 33 Robin Ventura	.10	.05	.01
☐ 34 Steve Avery	.10	.05	.01
☐ 35 Joe Carter	.25	.11	.03
☐ 36 Benito Santiago	.05	.02	.01
☐ 37 Dave Stieb	.05	.02	.01
☐ 38 Julio Franco	.10	.05	.01
☐ 39 Albert Belle	.75	.35	.09
☐ 40 Dale Murphy	.25	.11	.03
☐ 41 Rob Dibble	.05	.02	.01
☐ 42 Dave Justice	.25	.11	.03
☐ 43 Jose Rijo	.05	.02	.01
☐ 44 Eric Davis	.10	.05	.01
☐ 45 Terry Pendleton	.05	.02	.01
☐ 46 Kevin Maas	.05	.02	.01
☐ 47 Ozzie Smith	.75	.35	.09
☐ 48 Andre Dawson	.25	.11	.03
☐ 49 Sandy Alomar Jr.	.10	.05	.01
☐ 50 Nolan Ryan	1.50	.70	.19
☐ 51 Frank Thomas	2.00	.90	.25
☐ 52 Craig Biggio	.25	.11	.03
☐ 53 Doug Drabek	.05	.02	.01
☐ 54 Bobby Thigpen	.05	.02	.01
☐ 55 Darryl Strawberry	.10	.05	.01
☐ 56 Dennis Eckersley	.10	.05	.01
☐ 57 John Franco	.10	.05	.01
☐ 58 Paul O'Neill	.10	.05	.01
☐ 59 Scott Sanderson	.05	.02	.01
☐ 60 Dave Stewart	.05	.02	.01
☐ 61 Ivan Calderon	.05	.02	.01
☐ 62 Frank Viola	.05	.02	.01
☐ 63 Mark McGwire	.60	.25	.07
☐ 64 Kelly Gruber	.05	.02	.01
☐ 65 Fred McGriff	.25	.11	.03
☐ 66 Cecil Fielder	.25	.11	.03
☐ 67 Jose Canseco	.30	.14	.04
☐ 68 Howard Johnson	.05	.02	.01
☐ 69 Juan Gonzalez	1.00	.45	.12
☐ 70 Tim Wallach	.05	.02	.01
☐ 71 John Olerud	.10	.05	.01
☐ 72 Carlton Fisk	.25	.11	.03
☐ 73 Otis Nixon	.05	.02	.01
☐ 74 Roger Clemens	.40	.18	.05
☐ 75 Ramon Martinez	.10	.05	.01
☐ 76 Ron Gant	.10	.05	.01
☐ 77 Barry Larkin	.30	.14	.04
☐ 78 Eddie Murray	.50	.23	.06
☐ 79 Vince Coleman	.05	.02	.01
☐ 80 Bobby Bonilla	.10	.05	.01
☐ 81 Tony Gwynn	.75	.35	.09
☐ 82 Roberto Alomar	.50	.23	.06
☐ 83 Ellis Burks	.10	.05	.01
☐ 84 Robin Yount	.30	.14	.04
☐ 85 Ryne Sandberg	.75	.35	.09
☐ 86 Len Dykstra	.10	.05	.01
☐ 87 Ruben Sierra	.05	.02	.01
☐ 88 George Bell	.05	.02	.01
☐ 89 Cal Ripken	1.50	.70	.19
☐ 90 Danny Tartabull	.05	.02	.01
☐ 91 Gregg Olson	.05	.02	.01
☐ 92 Dave Henderson	.05	.02	.01

☐ 93 Kevin Mitchell	.05	.02	.01
☐ 94 Ben McDonald	.05	.02	.01
☐ 95 Matt Williams	.30	.14	.04
☐ 96 Roberto Kelly	.05	.02	.01
☐ 97 Dennis Martinez	.10	.05	.01
☐ 98 Kent Hrbek	.05	.02	.01
☐ 99 Felix Jose	.05	.02	.01
☐ 100 Rickey Henderson	.25	.11	.03

1992 Score Coke/Hardees Discs

This 24-disc set measures approximately 3" in diameter. The fronts feature color player action photos in different colored fading borders. The white backs carry player career totals. The cards are unnumbered and checklisted below in alphabetical order.

	MINT	NRMT	EXC
COMPLETE SET (24)	20.00	9.00	2.50
COMMON CARD (1-24)	.25	.11	.03
☐ 1 Roberto Alomar	2.00	.90	.25
☐ 2 Sandy Alomar Jr.	.50	.23	.06
☐ 3 Jeff Bagwell	5.00	2.20	.60
☐ 4 Brett Butler	.50	.23	.06
☐ 5 Roger Clemens	3.00	1.35	.35
☐ 6 Chili Davis	.25	.11	.03
☐ 7 Andre Dawson	1.00	.45	.12
☐ 8 Delino DeShields	.25	.11	.03
☐ 9 Ron Gant	.50	.23	.06
☐ 10 Tom Glavine	1.00	.45	.12
☐ 11 Kelly Gruber	.25	.11	.03
☐ 12 Ozzie Guillen	.25	.11	.03
☐ 13 Dave Henderson	.25	.11	.03
☐ 14 Chuck Knoblauch	2.50	1.10	.30
☐ 15 Paul Molitor	2.00	.90	.25
☐ 16 Hal Morris	.50	.23	.06
☐ 17 Rafael Palmeiro	1.50	.70	.19
☐ 18 Terry Pendleton	.25	.11	.03
☐ 19 Benito Santiago	.25	.11	.03
☐ 20 Ozzie Smith	5.00	2.20	.60
☐ 21 Andy Van Slyke	.50	.23	.06
☐ 22 Devon White	.25	.11	.03
☐ 23 Matt Williams	2.00	.90	.25
☐ 24 Robin Yount	1.50	.70	.19
☐ 25 Title Card CL	.25	.11	.03

1992 Score Pinnacle Promo Panels

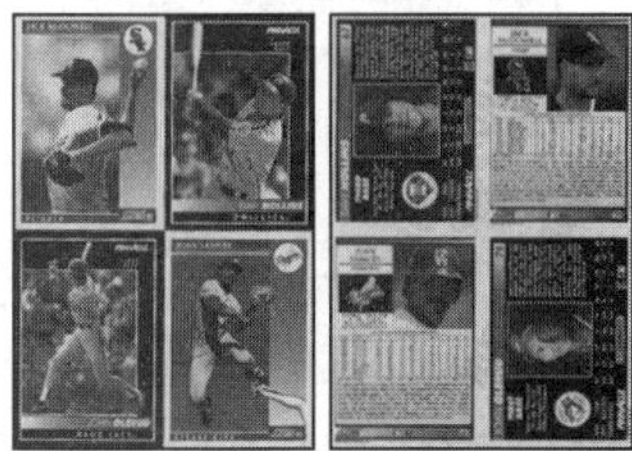

These nine promo panels were issued by Score to illustrate the design of the 1992 Score and 1992 Pinnacle series cards. The Score card is in the upper left of the panel, with a second Score card placed diagonally across in the lower right corner. The Pinnacle cards are diagonally placed in the upper right, and lower left of the promo panel. The promo panel measures approximately 5" by 7". If cut, each of the four cards would measure the standard size. The Score fronts feature a glossy color action photo bordered above and below by a blue bar. Along the left side is a wider green border. The Score backs carry a close-up shot in the upper right corner, with biography, complete career statistics, and player profile printed on a yellow background. The Pinnacle fronts display a glossy color player photos on a black background accented by thin white borders. On a black background the horizontal backs have a close-up player portrait, statistics, and a player profile. An anti-counterfeit device appears in the bottom border of each back. The cards for each set are numbered on the back as in the regular series; the panels themselves, however, are unnumbered. We have sequenced this set according to the player's card number in the upper left corner.

	MINT	NRMT	EXC
COMPLETE SET (25)	75.00	34.00	9.50
COMMON PANEL (1-25)	1.50	.70	.19
☐ 1 Nolan Ryan	10.00	4.50	1.25
Terry Pendleton			
Willie McGee			
Lonnie Smith			
☐ 2 Will Clark			
Mark Langston			
Paul Molitor			
Devon White			
☐ 3 Frank Thomas	10.00	4.50	1.25
David Justice			
Mark Carreon			
Dave Henderson			
☐ 4 Kirby Puckett	10.00	4.50	1.25
Ryne Sandberg			
Roberto Alomar			
Dave Henderson			
☐ 5 Ozzie Smith	3.00	1.35	.35
Darryl Strawberry			
Kevin Seitzer			
Jeff Montgomery			
☐ 6 Robin Yount			
Jay Buhner			
Chuck Crim			
Jimmy Jones			
☐ 7 Don Mattingly	6.00	2.70	.75
Matt Williams			
Dave Winfield			
George Bell			
☐ 8 Orel Hershiser	3.00	1.35	.35
Wes Chamberlain			
Gary Gaetti			
Dickie Thon			
☐ 9 Ron Gant	3.00	1.35	.35
Andres Galarraga			
Bruce Hurst			
Alex Fernandez			
☐ 10 Albert Belle	5.00	2.20	.60
Ellis Burks			
Melido Perez			
Kevin Gross			
☐ 11 Ivan Calderon	1.50	.70	.19
Bill Doran			
Rick Aguilera			
Doug Jones			
☐ 12 Todd Zeile	1.50	.70	.19
Mike Gallego			
Lenny Harris			
Jack Clark			
☐ 13 Harold Baines	1.50	.70	.19
Walt Weiss			
Eric Davis			
Randy Ready			
☐ 14 Nolan Ryan	15.00	6.75	1.85
George Brett			
George Bell			
Rafael Palmeiro			
☐ 15 Chili Davis	1.50	.70	.19
Phil Plantier			
David Wells			
Bob Walk			
☐ 16 John Olerud	1.50	.70	.19
Dave Hollins			
Jack McDowell			
Juan Samuel			
☐ 17 Carlton Fisk	1.50	.70	.19
Kent Hrbek			
Dennis Martinez			
Jim Acker			
☐ 18 Jay Buhner			
Greg Olson			
Terry Steinbach			
Kirk McCaskill			
☐ 19 Jeff Bagwell	5.00	2.20	.60
Darryl Strawberry			
Travis Fryman			
Andre Dawson			
☐ 20 Alex Cole	1.50	.70	.19
Jim Gantner			
Ken Caminiti			
Todd Stottlemyre			
☐ 21 Alex Fernandez			
Bill Gullickson			
Jose Guzman			
Shawn Hillegas			
☐ 22 Beranrd Gilkey	3.00	1.35	.35
Omar Vizquel			
Ivan Calderon			
Ozzie Guillen			
☐ 23 Gary Gaetti	1.50	.70	.19
Doug Drabek			
Brent Mayne			
Tom Bolton			
☐ 24 David Justice	1.50	.70	.19
Kevin Maas			
Jody Reed			
Vince Coleman			
☐ 25 Chili Davis	1.50	.70	.19
Hensley Meulens			
David Howard			
Mark Lewis			

1992 Score Proctor and Gamble

This 18-card standard-size set was produced by Score for Proctor and Gamble as a mail-in premium and contains 18 players from the 1992 All-Star Game line-up. The production run comprised 2,000,000 sets and 25 uncut sheets. A three-card sample set was also produced for sales representatives with a print run of 5,000,000 sets and 25 uncut sheets. The three sample cards, featuring Griffey, Sandberg, and Henderson, are stamped "sample" on the back. Collectors could obtain the set by sending in a required certificate, 99 cents, three UPC

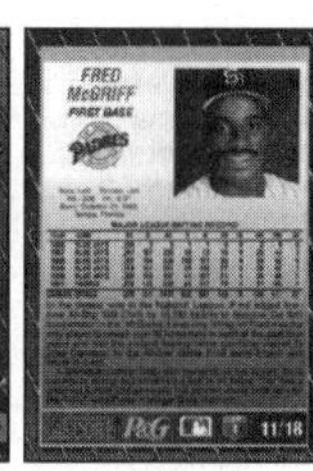

symbols from three different Proctor and Gamble products, and 50 cents for postage and handling. The certificate was published in a flyer inserted in Sunday, August 16 newspapers. The card fronts feature color action player cutouts superimposed on a diagonally striped background showing a large star behind the player. Card numbers 1-9 have a blue star on a graded magenta background, while card numbers 10-18 show a red star on blue-green. The backs display a close-up photo, biographical and statistical information, and career summary on a graded yellow-orange background. The cards are numbered "X/18" at the lower right corner.

	MINT	NRMT	EXC
COMPLETE SET (18)	6.00	2.70	.75
COMMON CARD (1-18)	.10	.05	.01
☐ 1 Sandy Alomar Jr.	.20	.09	.03
☐ 2 Mark McGwire	.60	.25	.07
☐ 3 Roberto Alomar	.50	.23	.06
☐ 4 Wade Boggs	.30	.14	.04
☐ 5 Cal Ripken	2.00	.90	.25
☐ 6 Kirby Puckett	1.00	.45	.12
☐ 7 Ken Griffey Jr.	2.00	.90	.25
☐ 8 Jose Canseco	.30	.14	.04
☐ 9 Kevin Brown	.20	.09	.03
☐ 10 Benito Santiago	.10	.05	.01
☐ 11 Fred McGriff	.25	.11	.03
☐ 12 Ryne Sandberg	.75	.35	.09
☐ 13 Terry Pendleton	.10	.05	.01
☐ 14 Ozzie Smith	.75	.35	.09
☐ 15 Barry Bonds	.50	.23	.06
☐ 16 Tony Gwynn	1.00	.45	.12
☐ 17 Andy Van Slyke	.10	.05	.01
☐ 18 Tom Glavine	.30	.14	.04

1992 Score Rookies

This 40-card boxed set measures the standard size and features glossy color action player photos on a kelly green face with meandering purple stripes. The words "1992 Rookie" are printed in white and red along the left edge of the photo. The player's name appears in white on a red banner at the bottom. The banner and the right edge of the picture are edged in canary yellow. The team logo is superimposed on the photo and the red banner. The back design features close-up player photos with kelly green shadow border on a graded royal blue face. The player's name is printed in red below the picture followed by biography and player profile. The words "1992 Rookie" appear, as on the front, in white and red along the left edge of the card.

	MINT	NRMT	EXC
COMPLETE SET (40)	4.00	1.80	.50
COMMON CARD (1-40)	.05	.02	.01
☐ 1 Todd Van Poppel	.05	.02	.01
☐ 2 Kyle Abbott	.05	.02	.01
☐ 3 Derek Bell	.25	.11	.03
☐ 4 Jim Thome	1.25	.55	.16
☐ 5 Mark Wohlers	.25	.11	.03
☐ 6 Todd Hundley	.50	.23	.06
☐ 7 Arthur Lee Rhodes	.05	.02	.01
☐ 8 John Ramos	.05	.02	.01
☐ 9 Chris George	.05	.02	.01
☐ 10 Kenny Lofton	2.00	.90	.25
☐ 11 Ted Wood	.05	.02	.01
☐ 12 Royce Clayton	.10	.05	.01
☐ 13 Scott Cooper	.05	.02	.01
☐ 14 Anthony Young	.05	.02	.01
☐ 15 Joel Johnston	.05	.02	.01
☐ 16 Andy Mota	.05	.02	.01
☐ 17 Lenny Webster	.05	.02	.01
☐ 18 Andy Ashby	.10	.05	.01
☐ 19 Jose Mota	.05	.02	.01
☐ 20 Tim McIntosh	.05	.02	.01
☐ 21 Terry Bross	.05	.02	.01
☐ 22 Harvey Pulliam	.05	.02	.01
☐ 23 Hector Fajardo	.05	.02	.01
☐ 24 Esteban Beltre	.05	.02	.01
☐ 25 Gary DiSarcina	.05	.02	.01
☐ 26 Mike Humphreys	.05	.02	.01
☐ 27 Jarvis Brown	.05	.02	.01
☐ 28 Gary Cooper	.05	.02	.01
☐ 29 Chris Donnels	.05	.02	.01
☐ 30 Monty Fariss	.05	.02	.01
☐ 31 Eric Karros	.25	.11	.03
☐ 32 Braulio Castillo	.05	.02	.01
☐ 33 Cal Eldred	.10	.05	.01
☐ 34 Tom Goodwin	.05	.02	.01
☐ 35 Reggie Sanders	.25	.11	.03
☐ 36 Scott Servais	.05	.02	.01
☐ 37 Kim Batiste	.05	.02	.01
☐ 38 Eric Wedge	.05	.02	.01
☐ 39 Willie Banks	.05	.02	.01
☐ 40 Mo Sanford	.05	.02	.01

1993 Score

The 1993 Score baseball set consists of 660 standard-size cards issued in one sinle series. The cards were distributed in 16-card poly packs and 35-card jumbo superpacks. The fronts feature color action player photos surrounded by white borders. The player's name appears in the bottom white border, while the team name and position appear in a team color-coded stripe that edges the left side of the picture. Topical subsets featured are Award Winners (481-486), Draft Picks (487-501), All-Star Caricature (502-512 [AL], 522-531 [NL]), Highlights (513-519), World Series Highlights (520-521), Dream Team (532-542) and Rookies (sprinkled throughout the set). Rookie Cards in this set include Derek Jeter and Jason Kendall.

	MINT	NRMT	EXC
COMPLETE SET (660)	40.00	18.00	5.00
COMMON CARD (1-660)	.05	.02	.01
☐ 1 Ken Griffey Jr.	2.00	.90	.25
☐ 2 Gary Sheffield	.15	.07	.02
☐ 3 Frank Thomas	2.00	.90	.25
☐ 4 Ryne Sandberg	.50	.23	.06
☐ 5 Larry Walker	.15	.07	.02
☐ 6 Cal Ripken Jr.	1.50	.70	.19
☐ 7 Roger Clemens	.40	.18	.05
☐ 8 Bobby Bonilla	.10	.05	.01
☐ 9 Carlos Baerga	.10	.05	.01
☐ 10 Darren Daulton	.10	.05	.01
☐ 11 Travis Fryman	.10	.05	.01
☐ 12 Andy Van Slyke	.10	.05	.01
☐ 13 Jose Canseco	.15	.07	.02
☐ 14 Roberto Alomar	.40	.18	.05
☐ 15 Tom Glavine	.15	.07	.02
☐ 16 Barry Larkin	.15	.07	.02
☐ 17 Gregg Jefferies	.10	.05	.01
☐ 18 Craig Biggio	.10	.05	.01
☐ 19 Shane Mack	.05	.02	.01
☐ 20 Brett Butler	.10	.05	.01
☐ 21 Dennis Eckersley	.10	.05	.01
☐ 22 Will Clark	.15	.07	.02
☐ 23 Don Mattingly	1.00	.45	.12
☐ 24 Tony Gwynn	.75	.35	.09
☐ 25 Ivan Rodriguez	.50	.23	.06
☐ 26 Shawon Dunston	.05	.02	.01
☐ 27 Mike Mussina	.40	.18	.05
☐ 28 Marquis Grissom	.10	.05	.01
☐ 29 Charles Nagy	.10	.05	.01
☐ 30 Len Dykstra	.10	.05	.01
☐ 31 Cecil Fielder	.10	.05	.01
☐ 32 Jay Bell	.10	.05	.01
☐ 33 B.J. Surhoff	.10	.05	.01
☐ 34 Bob Tewksbury	.05	.02	.01
☐ 35 Danny Tartabull	.05	.02	.01
☐ 36 Terry Pendleton	.10	.05	.01
☐ 37 Jack Morris	.10	.05	.01
☐ 38 Hal Morris	.05	.02	.01
☐ 39 Luis Polonia	.05	.02	.01
☐ 40 Ken Caminiti	.15	.07	.02
☐ 41 Robin Ventura	.10	.05	.01
☐ 42 Darryl Strawberry	.10	.05	.01
☐ 43 Wally Joyner	.10	.05	.01
☐ 44 Fred McGriff	.15	.07	.02
☐ 45 Kevin Tapani	.05	.02	.01
☐ 46 Matt Williams	.15	.07	.02
☐ 47 Robin Yount	.15	.07	.02
☐ 48 Ken Hill	.10	.05	.01
☐ 49 Edgar Martinez	.10	.05	.01
☐ 50 Mark Grace	.15	.07	.02
☐ 51 Juan Gonzalez	1.00	.45	.12
☐ 52 Curt Schilling	.05	.02	.01
☐ 53 Dwight Gooden	.10	.05	.01
☐ 54 Chris Hoiles	.05	.02	.01
☐ 55 Frank Viola	.05	.02	.01
☐ 56 Ray Lankford	.10	.05	.01
☐ 57 George Brett	.75	.35	.09
☐ 58 Kenny Lofton	.75	.35	.09
☐ 59 Nolan Ryan	1.50	.70	.19

☐ 60 Mickey Tettleton .05 .02 .01
☐ 61 John Smoltz .15 .07 .02
☐ 62 Howard Johnson .05 .02 .01
☐ 63 Eric Karros .15 .07 .02
☐ 64 Rick Aguilera .05 .02 .01
☐ 65 Steve Finley .10 .05 .01
☐ 66 Mark Langston .10 .05 .01
☐ 67 Bill Swift .05 .02 .01
☐ 68 John Olerud .05 .02 .01
☐ 69 Kevin McReynolds .05 .02 .01
☐ 70 Jack McDowell .10 .05 .01
☐ 71 Rickey Henderson .15 .07 .02
☐ 72 Brian Harper .05 .02 .01
☐ 73 Mike Morgan .05 .02 .01
☐ 74 Rafael Palmeiro .15 .07 .02
☐ 75 Dennis Martinez .10 .05 .01
☐ 76 Tino Martinez .10 .05 .01
☐ 77 Eddie Murray .50 .23 .06
☐ 78 Ellis Burks .10 .05 .01
☐ 79 John Kruk .10 .05 .01
☐ 80 Gregg Olson .05 .02 .01
☐ 81 Bernard Gilkey .10 .05 .01
☐ 82 Milt Cuyler .05 .02 .01
☐ 83 Mike LaValliere .05 .02 .01
☐ 84 Albert Belle .75 .35 .09
☐ 85 Bip Roberts .05 .02 .01
☐ 86 Melido Perez .05 .02 .01
☐ 87 Otis Nixon .05 .02 .01
☐ 88 Bill Spiers .05 .02 .01
☐ 89 Jeff Bagwell .75 .35 .09
☐ 90 Orel Hershiser .10 .05 .01
☐ 91 Andy Benes .10 .05 .01
☐ 92 Devon White .05 .02 .01
☐ 93 Willie McGee .05 .02 .01
☐ 94 Ozzie Guillen .05 .02 .01
☐ 95 Ivan Calderon .05 .02 .01
☐ 96 Keith Miller .05 .02 .01
☐ 97 Steve Buechele .05 .02 .01
☐ 98 Kent Hrbek .10 .05 .01
☐ 99 Dave Hollins .05 .02 .01
☐ 100 Mike Bordick .05 .02 .01
☐ 101 Randy Tomlin .05 .02 .01
☐ 102 Omar Vizquel .10 .05 .01
☐ 103 Lee Smith .10 .05 .01
☐ 104 Leo Gomez .05 .02 .01
☐ 105 Jose Rijo .05 .02 .01
☐ 106 Mark Whiten .05 .02 .01
☐ 107 Dave Justice .15 .07 .02
☐ 108 Eddie Taubensee .05 .02 .01
☐ 109 Lance Johnson .10 .05 .01
☐ 110 Felix Jose .05 .02 .01
☐ 111 Mike Harkey .05 .02 .01
☐ 112 Randy Milligan .05 .02 .01
☐ 113 Anthony Young .05 .02 .01
☐ 114 Rico Brogna .10 .05 .01
☐ 115 Bret Saberhagen .10 .05 .01
☐ 116 Sandy Alomar .10 .05 .01
☐ 117 Terry Mulholland .05 .02 .01
☐ 118 Darryl Hamilton .05 .02 .01
☐ 119 Todd Zeile .05 .02 .01
☐ 120 Bernie Williams .40 .18 .05
☐ 121 Zane Smith .05 .02 .01
☐ 122 Derek Bell .10 .05 .01
☐ 123 Deion Sanders .15 .07 .02
☐ 124 Luis Sojo .05 .02 .01
☐ 125 Joe Oliver .05 .02 .01
☐ 126 Craig Grebeck .05 .02 .01
☐ 127 Andujar Cedeno .05 .02 .01
☐ 128 Brian McRae .10 .05 .01
☐ 129 Jose Offerman .05 .02 .01
☐ 130 Pedro Munoz .05 .02 .01
☐ 131 Bud Black .05 .02 .01
☐ 132 Mo Vaughn .50 .23 .06
☐ 133 Bruce Hurst .05 .02 .01
☐ 134 Dave Henderson .05 .02 .01
☐ 135 Tom Pagnozzi .05 .02 .01
☐ 136 Erik Hanson .05 .02 .01
☐ 137 Orlando Merced .10 .05 .01
☐ 138 Dean Palmer .10 .05 .01
☐ 139 John Franco .05 .02 .01
☐ 140 Brady Anderson .15 .07 .02
☐ 141 Ricky Jordan .05 .02 .01
☐ 142 Jeff Blauser .05 .02 .01
☐ 143 Sammy Sosa .15 .07 .02
☐ 144 Bob Walk .05 .02 .01
☐ 145 Delino DeShields .05 .02 .01
☐ 146 Kevin Brown .10 .05 .01
☐ 147 Mark Lemke .05 .02 .01
☐ 148 Chuck Knoblauch .15 .07 .02
☐ 149 Chris Sabo .05 .02 .01
☐ 150 Bobby Witt .05 .02 .01
☐ 151 Luis Gonzalez .05 .02 .01
☐ 152 Ron Karkovice .05 .02 .01
☐ 153 Jeff Brantley .05 .02 .01
☐ 154 Kevin Appier .10 .05 .01
☐ 155 Darrin Jackson .05 .02 .01
☐ 156 Kelly Gruber .05 .02 .01
☐ 157 Royce Clayton .10 .05 .01
☐ 158 Chuck Finley .05 .02 .01
☐ 159 Jeff King .10 .05 .01
☐ 160 Greg Vaughn .10 .05 .01
☐ 161 Geronimo Pena .05 .02 .01
☐ 162 Steve Farr .05 .02 .01
☐ 163 Jose Oquendo .05 .02 .01
☐ 164 Mark Lewis .05 .02 .01
☐ 165 John Wetteland .10 .05 .01
☐ 166 Mike Henneman .05 .02 .01
☐ 167 Todd Hundley .10 .05 .01
☐ 168 Wes Chamberlain .05 .02 .01
☐ 169 Steve Avery .10 .05 .01
☐ 170 Mike Devereaux .05 .02 .01
☐ 171 Reggie Sanders .15 .07 .02
☐ 172 Jay Buhner .15 .07 .02
☐ 173 Eric Anthony .05 .02 .01
☐ 174 John Burkett .05 .02 .01
☐ 175 Tom Candiotti .05 .02 .01
☐ 176 Phil Plantier .05 .02 .01
☐ 177 Doug Henry .05 .02 .01
☐ 178 Scott Leius .05 .02 .01
☐ 179 Kirt Manwaring .05 .02 .01
☐ 180 Jeff Parrett .05 .02 .01
☐ 181 Don Slaught .05 .02 .01
☐ 182 Scott Radinsky .05 .02 .01
☐ 183 Luis Alicea .05 .02 .01
☐ 184 Tom Gordon .05 .02 .01
☐ 185 Rick Wilkins .05 .02 .01
☐ 186 Todd Stottlemyre .10 .05 .01
☐ 187 Moises Alou .10 .05 .01
☐ 188 Joe Grahe .05 .02 .01
☐ 189 Jeff Kent .10 .05 .01
☐ 190 Bill Wegman .05 .02 .01
☐ 191 Kim Batiste .05 .02 .01
☐ 192 Matt Nokes .05 .02 .01
☐ 193 Mark Wohlers .10 .05 .01
☐ 194 Paul Sorrento .05 .02 .01
☐ 195 Chris Hammond .05 .02 .01
☐ 196 Scott Livingstone .05 .02 .01
☐ 197 Doug Jones .05 .02 .01
☐ 198 Scott Cooper .05 .02 .01
☐ 199 Ramon Martinez .10 .05 .01
☐ 200 Dave Valle .05 .02 .01
☐ 201 Mariano Duncan .05 .02 .01
☐ 202 Ben McDonald .05 .02 .01
☐ 203 Darren Lewis .05 .02 .01
☐ 204 Kenny Rogers .05 .02 .01
☐ 205 Manuel Lee .05 .02 .01
☐ 206 Scott Erickson .05 .02 .01
☐ 207 Dan Gladden .05 .02 .01
☐ 208 Bob Welch .05 .02 .01
☐ 209 Greg Olson .05 .02 .01
☐ 210 Dan Pasqua .05 .02 .01
☐ 211 Tim Wallach .05 .02 .01
☐ 212 Jeff Montgomery .10 .05 .01
☐ 213 Derrick May .05 .02 .01
☐ 214 Ed Sprague .10 .05 .01
☐ 215 David Haas .05 .02 .01
☐ 216 Darrin Fletcher .05 .02 .01
☐ 217 Brian Jordan .15 .07 .02
☐ 218 Jaime Navarro .05 .02 .01
☐ 219 Randy Velarde .05 .02 .01
☐ 220 Ron Gant .10 .05 .01
☐ 221 Paul Quantrill .05 .02 .01
☐ 222 Damion Easley .05 .02 .01
☐ 223 Charlie Hough .05 .02 .01
☐ 224 Brad Brink .05 .02 .01
☐ 225 Barry Manuel .05 .02 .01
☐ 226 Kevin Koslofski .05 .02 .01
☐ 227 Ryan Thompson .05 .02 .01
☐ 228 Mike Munoz .05 .02 .01
☐ 229 Dan Wilson .10 .05 .01
☐ 230 Peter Hoy .05 .02 .01
☐ 231 Pedro Astacio .05 .02 .01
☐ 232 Matt Stairs .05 .02 .01
☐ 233 Jeff Reboulet .05 .02 .01
☐ 234 Manny Alexander .05 .02 .01
☐ 235 Willie Banks .05 .02 .01
☐ 236 John Jaha .15 .07 .02
☐ 237 Scooter Tucker .05 .02 .01
☐ 238 Russ Springer .05 .02 .01
☐ 239 Paul Miller .05 .02 .01
☐ 240 Dan Peltier .05 .02 .01
☐ 241 Ozzie Canseco .05 .02 .01
☐ 242 Ben Rivera .05 .02 .01
☐ 243 John Valentin .10 .05 .01
☐ 244 Henry Rodriguez .15 .07 .02
☐ 245 Derek Parks .05 .02 .01
☐ 246 Carlos Garcia .05 .02 .01
☐ 247 Tim Pugh .05 .02 .01
☐ 248 Melvin Nieves .15 .07 .02
☐ 249 Rich Amaral .05 .02 .01
☐ 250 Willie Greene .10 .05 .01
☐ 251 Tim Scott .05 .02 .01
☐ 252 Dave Silvestri .05 .02 .01
☐ 253 Rob Mallicoat .05 .02 .01
☐ 254 Donald Harris .05 .02 .01
☐ 255 Craig Colbert .05 .02 .01
☐ 256 Jose Guzman .05 .02 .01
☐ 257 Domingo Martinez .05 .02 .01
☐ 258 William Suero .05 .02 .01
☐ 259 Juan Guerrero .05 .02 .01
☐ 260 J.T. Snow .15 .07 .02
☐ 261 Tony Pena .05 .02 .01
☐ 262 Tim Fortugno .05 .02 .01
☐ 263 Tom Marsh .05 .02 .01
☐ 264 Kurt Knudsen .05 .02 .01
☐ 265 Tim Costo .05 .02 .01
☐ 266 Steve Shifflett .05 .02 .01
☐ 267 Billy Ashley .05 .02 .01
☐ 268 Jerry Nielsen .05 .02 .01
☐ 269 Pete Young .05 .02 .01
☐ 270 Johnny Guzman .05 .02 .01
☐ 271 Greg Colbrunn .05 .02 .01
☐ 272 Jeff Nelson .05 .02 .01
☐ 273 Kevin Young .05 .02 .01
☐ 274 Jeff Frye .05 .02 .01
☐ 275 J.T. Bruett .05 .02 .01
☐ 276 Todd Pratt .05 .02 .01
☐ 277 Mike Butcher .05 .02 .01
☐ 278 John Flaherty .05 .02 .01
☐ 279 John Patterson .05 .02 .01
☐ 280 Eric Hillman .05 .02 .01
☐ 281 Bien Figueroa .05 .02 .01
☐ 282 Shane Reynolds .15 .07 .02
☐ 283 Rich Rowland .05 .02 .01
☐ 284 Steve Foster .05 .02 .01
☐ 285 Dave Mlicki .05 .02 .01
☐ 286 Mike Piazza 2.00 .90 .25
☐ 287 Mike Trombley .05 .02 .01
☐ 288 Jim Pena .05 .02 .01
☐ 289 Bob Ayrault .05 .02 .01
☐ 290 Henry Mercedes .05 .02 .01
☐ 291 Bob Wickman .05 .02 .01
☐ 292 Jacob Brumfield .05 .02 .01
☐ 293 David Hulse .05 .02 .01
☐ 294 Ryan Klesko .60 .25 .07
☐ 295 Doug Linton .05 .02 .01
☐ 296 Steve Cooke .05 .02 .01
☐ 297 Eddie Zosky .05 .02 .01
☐ 298 Gerald Williams .05 .02 .01
☐ 299 Jonathan Hurst .05 .02 .01
☐ 300 Larry Carter .05 .02 .01
☐ 301 William Pennyfeather .05 .02 .01
☐ 302 Cesar Hernandez .05 .02 .01
☐ 303 Steve Hosey .05 .02 .01
☐ 304 Blas Minor .05 .02 .01
☐ 305 Jeff Grotewald .05 .02 .01
☐ 306 Bernardo Brito .05 .02 .01
☐ 307 Rafael Bournigal .05 .02 .01
☐ 308 Jeff Branson .05 .02 .01
☐ 309 Tom Quinlan .05 .02 .01
☐ 310 Pat Gomez .05 .02 .01
☐ 311 Sterling Hitchcock .10 .05 .01
☐ 312 Kent Bottenfield .05 .02 .01
☐ 313 Alan Trammell .15 .07 .02
☐ 314 Cris Colon .05 .02 .01
☐ 315 Paul Wagner .05 .02 .01
☐ 316 Matt Maysey .05 .02 .01
☐ 317 Mike Stanton .05 .02 .01
☐ 318 Rick Trlicek .05 .02 .01
☐ 319 Kevin Rogers .05 .02 .01
☐ 320 Mark Clark .05 .02 .01
☐ 321 Pedro Martinez .15 .07 .02
☐ 322 Al Martin .10 .05 .01
☐ 323 Mike Macfarlane .05 .02 .01
☐ 324 Rey Sanchez .05 .02 .01
☐ 325 Roger Pavlik .10 .05 .01
☐ 326 Troy Neel .05 .02 .01
☐ 327 Kerry Woodson .05 .02 .01
☐ 328 Wayne Kirby .05 .02 .01
☐ 329 Ken Ryan .05 .02 .01
☐ 330 Jesse Levis .05 .02 .01
☐ 331 James Austin .05 .02 .01
☐ 332 Dan Walters .05 .02 .01
☐ 333 Brian Williams .05 .02 .01
☐ 334 Wil Cordero .10 .05 .01
☐ 335 Bret Boone .10 .05 .01
☐ 336 Hipolito Pichardo .05 .02 .01
☐ 337 Pat Mahomes .05 .02 .01
☐ 338 Andy Stankiewicz .05 .02 .01
☐ 339 Jim Bullinger .05 .02 .01
☐ 340 Archi Cianfrocco .05 .02 .01
☐ 341 Ruben Amaro Jr. .05 .02 .01
☐ 342 Frank Seminara .05 .02 .01
☐ 343 Pat Hentgen .15 .07 .02
☐ 344 Dave Nilsson .10 .05 .01
☐ 345 Mike Perez .05 .02 .01
☐ 346 Tim Salmon .50 .23 .06
☐ 347 Tim Wakefield .10 .05 .01
☐ 348 Carlos Hernandez .05 .02 .01
☐ 349 Donovan Osborne .05 .02 .01
☐ 350 Denny Neagle .10 .05 .01
☐ 351 Sam Militello .05 .02 .01
☐ 352 Eric Fox .05 .02 .01
☐ 353 John Doherty .05 .02 .01
☐ 354 Chad Curtis .10 .05 .01
☐ 355 Jeff Tackett .05 .02 .01
☐ 356 Dave Fleming .05 .02 .01
☐ 357 Pat Listach .05 .02 .01
☐ 358 Kevin Wickander .05 .02 .01
☐ 359 John Vander Wal .05 .02 .01
☐ 360 Arthur Rhodes .05 .02 .01
☐ 361 Bob Scanlan .05 .02 .01
☐ 362 Bob Zupcic .05 .02 .01
☐ 363 Mel Rojas .10 .05 .01
☐ 364 Jim Thome 1.00 .45 .12
☐ 365 Bill Pecota .05 .02 .01
☐ 366 Mark Carreon .05 .02 .01
☐ 367 Mitch Williams .05 .02 .01
☐ 368 Cal Eldred .05 .02 .01
☐ 369 Stan Belinda .05 .02 .01
☐ 370 Pat Kelly .05 .02 .01
☐ 371 Rheal Cormier .05 .02 .01
☐ 372 Juan Guzman .10 .05 .01
☐ 373 Damon Berryhill .05 .02 .01
☐ 374 Gary DiSarcina .05 .02 .01
☐ 375 Norm Charlton .05 .02 .01
☐ 376 Roberto Hernandez .10 .05 .01
☐ 377 Scott Kamieniecki .05 .02 .01
☐ 378 Rusty Meacham .05 .02 .01
☐ 379 Kurt Stillwell .05 .02 .01
☐ 380 Lloyd McClendon .05 .02 .01
☐ 381 Mark Leonard .05 .02 .01
☐ 382 Jerry Browne .05 .02 .01
☐ 383 Glenn Davis .05 .02 .01
☐ 384 Randy Johnson .15 .07 .02
☐ 385 Mike Greenwell .05 .02 .01
☐ 386 Scott Chiamparino .05 .02 .01
☐ 387 George Bell .05 .02 .01
☐ 388 Steve Olin .05 .02 .01
☐ 389 Chuck McElroy .05 .02 .01
☐ 390 Mark Gardner .05 .02 .01
☐ 391 Rod Beck .10 .05 .01
☐ 392 Dennis Rasmussen .05 .02 .01
☐ 393 Charlie Leibrandt .05 .02 .01
☐ 394 Julio Franco .10 .05 .01
☐ 395 Pete Harnisch .05 .02 .01
☐ 396 Sid Bream .05 .02 .01
☐ 397 Milt Thompson .05 .02 .01
☐ 398 Glenallen Hill .05 .02 .01
☐ 399 Chico Walker .05 .02 .01
☐ 400 Alex Cole .05 .02 .01
☐ 401 Trevor Wilson .05 .02 .01
☐ 402 Jeff Conine .10 .05 .01
☐ 403 Kyle Abbott .05 .02 .01
☐ 404 Tom Browning .05 .02 .01
☐ 405 Jerald Clark .05 .02 .01
☐ 406 Vince Horsman .05 .02 .01
☐ 407 Kevin Mitchell .10 .05 .01
☐ 408 Pete Smith .05 .02 .01
☐ 409 Jeff Innis .05 .02 .01
☐ 410 Mike Timlin .05 .02 .01
☐ 411 Charlie Hayes .05 .02 .01
☐ 412 Alex Fernandez .10 .05 .01
☐ 413 Jeff Russell .05 .02 .01
☐ 414 Jody Reed .05 .02 .01
☐ 415 Mickey Morandini .05 .02 .01
☐ 416 Darnell Coles .05 .02 .01
☐ 417 Xavier Hernandez .05 .02 .01
☐ 418 Steve Sax .05 .02 .01
☐ 419 Joe Girardi .05 .02 .01
☐ 420 Mike Fetters .05 .02 .01
☐ 421 Danny Jackson .05 .02 .01
☐ 422 Jim Gott .05 .02 .01
☐ 423 Tim Belcher .05 .02 .01
☐ 424 Jose Mesa .10 .05 .01
☐ 425 Junior Felix .05 .02 .01
☐ 426 Thomas Howard .05 .02 .01
☐ 427 Julio Valera .05 .02 .01
☐ 428 Dante Bichette .15 .07 .02
☐ 429 Mike Sharperson .05 .02 .01
☐ 430 Darryl Kile .05 .02 .01
☐ 431 Lonnie Smith .05 .02 .01
☐ 432 Monty Fariss .05 .02 .01
☐ 433 Reggie Jefferson .10 .05 .01
☐ 434 Bob McClure .05 .02 .01
☐ 435 Craig Lefferts .05 .02 .01
☐ 436 Duane Ward .05 .02 .01
☐ 437 Shawn Abner .05 .02 .01
☐ 438 Roberto Kelly .05 .02 .01
☐ 439 Paul O'Neill .10 .05 .01
☐ 440 Alan Mills .05 .02 .01
☐ 441 Roger Mason .05 .02 .01
☐ 442 Gary Pettis .05 .02 .01
☐ 443 Steve Lake .05 .02 .01
☐ 444 Gene Larkin .05 .02 .01
☐ 445 Larry Andersen .05 .02 .01
☐ 446 Doug Dascenzo .05 .02 .01
☐ 447 Daryl Boston .05 .02 .01
☐ 448 John Candelaria .05 .02 .01
☐ 449 Storm Davis .05 .02 .01
☐ 450 Tom Edens .05 .02 .01
☐ 451 Mike Maddux .05 .02 .01
☐ 452 Tim Naehring .05 .02 .01
☐ 453 John Orton .05 .02 .01
☐ 454 Joey Cora .10 .05 .01
☐ 455 Chuck Crim .05 .02 .01
☐ 456 Dan Plesac .05 .02 .01
☐ 457 Mike Bielecki .05 .02 .01
☐ 458 Terry Jorgensen .05 .02 .01
☐ 459 John Habyan .05 .02 .01
☐ 460 Pete O'Brien .05 .02 .01
☐ 461 Jeff Treadway .05 .02 .01
☐ 462 Frank Castillo .05 .02 .01
☐ 463 Jimmy Jones .05 .02 .01
☐ 464 Tommy Greene .05 .02 .01
☐ 465 Tracy Woodson .05 .02 .01
☐ 466 Rich Rodriguez .05 .02 .01
☐ 467 Joe Hesketh .05 .02 .01
☐ 468 Greg Myers .05 .02 .01
☐ 469 Kirk McCaskill .05 .02 .01
☐ 470 Ricky Bones .05 .02 .01
☐ 471 Lenny Webster .05 .02 .01
☐ 472 Francisco Cabrera .05 .02 .01
☐ 473 Turner Ward .05 .02 .01
☐ 474 Dwayne Henry .05 .02 .01
☐ 475 Al Osuna .05 .02 .01
☐ 476 Craig Wilson .05 .02 .01
☐ 477 Chris Nabholz .05 .02 .01
☐ 478 Rafael Belliard .05 .02 .01
☐ 479 Terry Leach .05 .02 .01

☐ 480 Tim Teufel	.05	.02	.01
☐ 481 Dennis Eckersley AW	.10	.05	.01
☐ 482 Barry Bonds AW	.15	.07	.02
☐ 483 Dennis Eckersley AW	.10	.05	.01
☐ 484 Greg Maddux AW	.60	.25	.07
☐ 485 Pat Listach AW	.05	.02	.01
☐ 486 Eric Karros AW	.15	.07	.02
☐ 487 Jamie Arnold DP	.10	.05	.01
☐ 488 B.J. Wallace DP	.05	.02	.01
☐ 489 Derek Jeter DP	4.00	1.80	.50
☐ 490 Jason Kendall DP	1.25	.55	.16
☐ 491 Rick Helling DP	.10	.05	.01
☐ 492 Derek Wallace DP	.05	.02	.01
☐ 493 Sean Lowe DP	.10	.05	.01
☐ 494 Shannon Stewart DP	.30	.14	.04
☐ 495 Benji Grigsby DP	.05	.02	.01
☐ 496 Todd Steverson DP	.10	.05	.01
☐ 497 Dan Serafini DP	.30	.14	.04
☐ 498 Michael Tucker DP	.15	.07	.02
☐ 499 Chris Roberts DP	.10	.05	.01
☐ 500 Pete Janicki DP	.05	.02	.01
☐ 501 Jeff Schmidt DP	.05	.02	.01
☐ 502 Edgar Martinez AS	.10	.05	.01
☐ 503 Omar Vizquel AS	.10	.05	.01
☐ 504 Ken Griffey Jr. AS	1.00	.45	.12
☐ 505 Kirby Puckett AS	.15	.07	.02
☐ 506 Joe Carter AS	.10	.05	.01
☐ 507 Ivan Rodriguez AS	.15	.07	.02
☐ 508 Jack Morris AS	.05	.02	.01
☐ 509 Dennis Eckersley AS	.10	.05	.01
☐ 510 Frank Thomas AS	1.00	.45	.12
☐ 511 Roberto Alomar AS	.15	.07	.02
☐ 512 Mickey Morandini AS	.05	.02	.01
☐ 513 Dennis Eckersley HL	.10	.05	.01
☐ 514 Jeff Reardon HL	.05	.02	.01
☐ 515 Danny Tartabull HL	.05	.02	.01
☐ 516 Bip Roberts HL	.05	.02	.01
☐ 517 George Brett HL	.40	.18	.05
☐ 518 Robin Yount HL	.15	.07	.02
☐ 519 Kevin Gross HL	.05	.02	.01
☐ 520 Ed Sprague WS	.05	.02	.01
☐ 521 Dave Winfield WS	.15	.07	.02
☐ 522 Ozzie Smith AS	.15	.07	.02
☐ 523 Barry Bonds AS	.15	.07	.02
☐ 524 Andy Van Slyke AS	.05	.02	.01
☐ 525 Tony Gwynn AS	.40	.18	.05
☐ 526 Darren Daulton AS	.10	.05	.01
☐ 527 Greg Maddux AS	.60	.25	.07
☐ 528 Fred McGriff AS	.15	.07	.02
☐ 529 Lee Smith AS	.10	.05	.01
☐ 530 Ryne Sandberg AS	.15	.07	.02
☐ 531 Gary Sheffield AS	.15	.07	.02
☐ 532 Ozzie Smith DT	.15	.07	.02
☐ 533 Kirby Puckett DT	.15	.07	.02
☐ 534 Gary Sheffield DT	.15	.07	.02
☐ 535 Andy Van Slyke DT	.05	.02	.01
☐ 536 Ken Griffey Jr. DT	1.00	.45	.12
☐ 537 Ivan Rodriguez DT	.15	.07	.02
☐ 538 Charles Nagy DT	.10	.05	.01
☐ 539 Tom Glavine DT	.15	.07	.02
☐ 540 Dennis Eckersley DT	.10	.05	.01
☐ 541 Frank Thomas DT	1.00	.45	.12
☐ 542 Roberto Alomar DT	.15	.07	.02
☐ 543 Sean Berry	.05	.02	.01
☐ 544 Mike Schooler	.05	.02	.01
☐ 545 Chuck Carr	.05	.02	.01
☐ 546 Lenny Harris	.05	.02	.01
☐ 547 Gary Scott	.05	.02	.01
☐ 548 Derek Lilliquist	.05	.02	.01
☐ 549 Brian Hunter	.05	.02	.01
☐ 550 Kirby Puckett MOY	.15	.07	.02
☐ 551 Jim Eisenreich	.10	.05	.01
☐ 552 Andre Dawson	.10	.05	.01
☐ 553 David Nied	.05	.02	.01
☐ 554 Spike Owen	.05	.02	.01
☐ 555 Greg Gagne	.05	.02	.01
☐ 556 Sid Fernandez	.05	.02	.01
☐ 557 Mark McGwire	.60	.25	.07
☐ 558 Bryan Harvey	.05	.02	.01
☐ 559 Harold Reynolds	.05	.02	.01
☐ 560 Barry Bonds	.50	.23	.06
☐ 561 Eric Wedge	.05	.02	.01
☐ 562 Ozzie Smith	.50	.23	.06
☐ 563 Rick Sutcliffe	.05	.02	.01
☐ 564 Jeff Reardon	.10	.05	.01
☐ 565 Alex Arias	.05	.02	.01
☐ 566 Greg Swindell	.05	.02	.01
☐ 567 Brook Jacoby	.05	.02	.01
☐ 568 Pete Incaviglia	.05	.02	.01
☐ 569 Butch Henry	.05	.02	.01
☐ 570 Eric Davis	.10	.05	.01
☐ 571 Kevin Seitzer	.05	.02	.01
☐ 572 Tony Fernandez	.05	.02	.01
☐ 573 Steve Reed	.05	.02	.01
☐ 574 Cory Snyder	.05	.02	.01
☐ 575 Joe Carter	.10	.05	.01
☐ 576 Greg Maddux	1.25	.55	.16
☐ 577 Bert Blyleven UER (Should say 3701 career strikeouts)	.10	.05	.01
☐ 578 Kevin Bass	.05	.02	.01
☐ 579 Carlton Fisk	.15	.07	.02
☐ 580 Doug Drabek	.05	.02	.01
☐ 581 Mark Gubicza	.05	.02	.01
☐ 582 Bobby Thigpen	.05	.02	.01
☐ 583 Chili Davis	.10	.05	.01
☐ 584 Scott Bankhead	.05	.02	.01
☐ 585 Harold Baines	.10	.05	.01
☐ 586 Eric Young	.15	.07	.02
☐ 587 Lance Parrish	.05	.02	.01
☐ 588 Juan Bell	.05	.02	.01
☐ 589 Bob Ojeda	.05	.02	.01
☐ 590 Joe Orsulak	.05	.02	.01
☐ 591 Benito Santiago	.05	.02	.01
☐ 592 Wade Boggs	.15	.07	.02
☐ 593 Robby Thompson	.05	.02	.01
☐ 594 Eric Plunk	.05	.02	.01
☐ 595 Hensley Meulens	.05	.02	.01
☐ 596 Lou Whitaker	.10	.05	.01
☐ 597 Dale Murphy	.15	.07	.02
☐ 598 Paul Molitor	.40	.18	.05
☐ 599 Greg W. Harris	.05	.02	.01
☐ 600 Darren Holmes	.05	.02	.01
☐ 601 Dave Martinez	.05	.02	.01
☐ 602 Tom Henke	.05	.02	.01
☐ 603 Mike Benjamin	.05	.02	.01
☐ 604 Rene Gonzales	.05	.02	.01
☐ 605 Roger McDowell	.05	.02	.01
☐ 606 Kirby Puckett	.75	.35	.09
☐ 607 Randy Myers	.10	.05	.01
☐ 608 Ruben Sierra	.10	.05	.01
☐ 609 Wilson Alvarez	.10	.05	.01
☐ 610 David Segui	.05	.02	.01
☐ 611 Juan Samuel	.05	.02	.01
☐ 612 Tom Brunansky	.05	.02	.01
☐ 613 Willie Randolph	.10	.05	.01
☐ 614 Tony Phillips	.10	.05	.01
☐ 615 Candy Maldonado	.05	.02	.01
☐ 616 Chris Bosio	.05	.02	.01
☐ 617 Bret Barberie	.05	.02	.01
☐ 618 Scott Sanderson	.05	.02	.01
☐ 619 Ron Darling	.05	.02	.01
☐ 620 Dave Winfield	.15	.07	.02
☐ 621 Mike Felder	.05	.02	.01
☐ 622 Greg Hibbard	.05	.02	.01
☐ 623 Mike Scioscia	.05	.02	.01
☐ 624 John Smiley	.05	.02	.01
☐ 625 Alejandro Pena	.05	.02	.01
☐ 626 Terry Steinbach	.10	.05	.01
☐ 627 Freddie Benavides	.05	.02	.01
☐ 628 Kevin Reimer	.05	.02	.01
☐ 629 Braulio Castillo	.05	.02	.01
☐ 630 Dave Stieb	.05	.02	.01
☐ 631 Dave Magadan	.05	.02	.01
☐ 632 Scott Fletcher	.05	.02	.01
☐ 633 Cris Carpenter	.05	.02	.01
☐ 634 Kevin Maas	.05	.02	.01
☐ 635 Todd Worrell	.05	.02	.01
☐ 636 Rob Deer	.05	.02	.01
☐ 637 Dwight Smith	.05	.02	.01
☐ 638 Chito Martinez	.05	.02	.01
☐ 639 Jimmy Key	.10	.05	.01
☐ 640 Greg A. Harris	.05	.02	.01
☐ 641 Mike Moore	.05	.02	.01
☐ 642 Pat Borders	.05	.02	.01
☐ 643 Bill Gullickson	.05	.02	.01
☐ 644 Gary Gaetti	.10	.05	.01
☐ 645 David Howard	.05	.02	.01
☐ 646 Jim Abbott	.05	.02	.01
☐ 647 Willie Wilson	.05	.02	.01
☐ 648 David Wells	.05	.02	.01
☐ 649 Andres Galarraga	.15	.07	.02
☐ 650 Vince Coleman	.05	.02	.01
☐ 651 Rob Dibble	.05	.02	.01
☐ 652 Frank Tanana	.05	.02	.01
☐ 653 Steve Decker	.05	.02	.01
☐ 654 David Cone	.10	.05	.01
☐ 655 Jack Armstrong	.05	.02	.01
☐ 656 Dave Stewart	.10	.05	.01
☐ 657 Billy Hatcher	.05	.02	.01
☐ 658 Tim Raines	.15	.07	.02
☐ 659 Walt Weiss	.05	.02	.01
☐ 660 Jose Lind	.05	.02	.01

1993 Score Boys of Summer

Randomly inserted exclusively into one in every four 1993 Score 35-card super packs, cards from this standard-size set feature 30 rookies expected to be the best in their class. The fronts are borderless with a color action player photo superimposed over an illustration of the sun. The player's name appears in cursive lettering within a greenish stripe across the bottom. An early Mike Piazza card highlights this set.

	MINT	NRMT	EXC
COMPLETE SET (30)	60.00	27.00	7.50
COMMON CARD (1-30)	1.00	.45	.12
☐ 1 Billy Ashley	1.00	.45	.12
☐ 2 Tim Salmon	10.00	4.50	1.25
☐ 3 Pedro Martinez	3.00	1.35	.35
☐ 4 Luis Mercedes	1.00	.45	.12
☐ 5 Mike Piazza	30.00	13.50	3.70
☐ 6 Troy Neel	1.00	.45	.12
☐ 7 Melvin Nieves	2.00	.90	.25
☐ 8 Ryan Klesko	10.00	4.50	1.25
☐ 9 Ryan Thompson	1.00	.45	.12
☐ 10 Kevin Young	1.00	.45	.12
☐ 11 Gerald Williams	1.00	.45	.12
☐ 12 Willie Greene	1.50	.70	.19
☐ 13 John Patterson	1.00	.45	.12
☐ 14 Carlos Garcia	1.50	.70	.19
☐ 15 Ed Zosky	1.00	.45	.12
☐ 16 Sean Berry	1.00	.45	.12
☐ 17 Rico Brogna	1.50	.70	.19
☐ 18 Larry Carter	1.00	.45	.12
☐ 19 Bobby Ayala	1.00	.45	.12
☐ 20 Alan Embree	1.00	.45	.12
☐ 21 Donald Harris	1.00	.45	.12
☐ 22 Sterling Hitchcock	1.00	.45	.12
☐ 23 David Nied	1.00	.45	.12
☐ 24 Henry Mercedes	1.00	.45	.12
☐ 25 Ozzie Canseco	1.00	.45	.12
☐ 26 David Hulse	1.00	.45	.12
☐ 27 Al Martin	1.50	.70	.19
☐ 28 Dan Wilson	1.50	.70	.19
☐ 29 Paul Miller	1.00	.45	.12
☐ 30 Rich Rowland	1.00	.45	.12

1993 Score Franchise

This 28-card set honors the top player on each of the major league teams. These cards were randomly inserted into one in every 24 16-card packs. The full-bleed, color action photos on the fronts have the background darkened so that the player stands out. His name appears in white lettering within a team color-coded bar near the bottom, which conjoins with the set logo in the lower left.

	MINT	NRMT	EXC
COMPLETE SET (28)	125.00	55.00	15.50
COMMON CARD (1-28)	1.50	.70	.19
☐ 1 Cal Ripken	25.00	11.00	3.10
☐ 2 Roger Clemens	6.00	2.70	.75
☐ 3 Mark Langston	1.50	.70	.19
☐ 4 Frank Thomas	30.00	13.50	3.70
☐ 5 Carlos Baerga	1.50	.70	.19
☐ 6 Cecil Fielder	2.50	1.10	.30
☐ 7 Gregg Jefferies	2.50	1.10	.30
☐ 8 Robin Yount	4.00	1.80	.50
☐ 9 Kirby Puckett	12.00	5.50	1.50
☐ 10 Don Mattingly	15.00	6.75	1.85
☐ 11 Dennis Eckersley	2.50	1.10	.30
☐ 12 Ken Griffey Jr.	30.00	13.50	3.70
☐ 13 Juan Gonzalez	15.00	6.75	1.85
☐ 14 Roberto Alomar	6.00	2.70	.75
☐ 15 Terry Pendleton	1.50	.70	.19
☐ 16 Ryne Sandberg	8.00	3.60	1.00
☐ 17 Barry Larkin	5.00	2.20	.60
☐ 18 Jeff Bagwell	12.00	5.50	1.50
☐ 19 Brett Butler	1.50	.70	.19
☐ 20 Larry Walker	4.00	1.80	.50
☐ 21 Bobby Bonilla	2.50	1.10	.30
☐ 22 Darren Daulton	2.50	1.10	.30
☐ 23 Andy Van Slyke	1.50	.70	.19
☐ 24 Ray Lankford	2.50	1.10	.30
☐ 25 Gary Sheffield	5.00	2.20	.60
☐ 26 Will Clark	4.00	1.80	.50
☐ 27 Bryan Harvey	1.50	.70	.19
☐ 28 David Nied	1.50	.70	.19

1993 Score Gold Dream Team

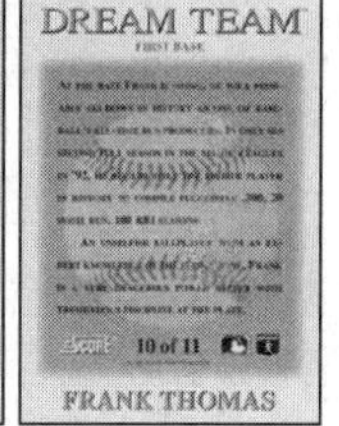

Cards from this 12-card standard-size set feature Score's selection of the best players in baseball at each position. The cards were available only through a mail-in offer. Each card front features sepia tone photos of the players out of uniform, with the exception of Griffey's card (of whom is pictured in his Mariners togs). The photo edges are rounded with an airbrush effect. The words "Dream Team" are printed in gold lettering at the top. The player's name is printed in sepia tones on the bottom edge.

	MINT	NRMT	EXC
COMPLETE SET (12)	6.00	2.70	.75
COMMON CARD (1-11)	.20	.09	.03
☐ 1 Ozzie Smith	.50	.23	.06
☐ 2 Kirby Puckett	.75	.35	.09
☐ 3 Gary Sheffield	.50	.23	.06
☐ 4 Andy Van Slyke	.20	.09	.03
☐ 5 Ken Griffey Jr.	2.00	.90	.25
☐ 6 Ivan Rodriguez	.35	.16	.04
☐ 7 Charles Nagy	.35	.16	.04
☐ 8 Tom Glavine	.50	.23	.06
☐ 9 Dennis Eckersley	.35	.16	.04
☐ 10 Frank Thomas	2.00	.90	.25
☐ 11 Roberto Alomar	.40	.18	.05
☐ NNO Header Card	.50	.23	.06

1993 Score Proctor and Gamble

This ten-card standard-size set was produced by Score as a promotion for Proctor and Gamble. The set was advertised through store displays; the set could be acquired by sending in three UPC symbols and money to cover postage and handling. The fronts display a color action player photo protruding from a diamond-shaped frame. A wide stripe running from the bottom of the card and intersecting the bottom point of the diamond carries the player's name, position, and a picture of the home stadium. The surrounding card face of the front is olive green and accented with gold foil lettering. The name of the city appears in gold print on the reverse side of the card in the center.

	MINT	NRMT	EXC
COMPLETE SET (10)	7.50	3.40	.95
COMMON CARD (1-10)	.25	.11	.03
☐ 1 Wil Cordero	.35	.16	.04
☐ 2 Pedro Martinez	1.00	.45	.12
☐ 3 Bret Boone	.35	.16	.04
☐ 4 Melvin Nieves	.50	.23	.06
☐ 5 Ryan Klesko	4.00	1.80	.50
☐ 6 Ryan Thompson	.25	.11	.03
☐ 7 Kevin Young	.25	.11	.03
☐ 8 Willie Greene	.75	.35	.09
☐ 9 Eric Wedge	.25	.11	.03
☐ 10 David Nied	.25	.11	.03

1994 Score Samples

This 19-card standard-size promo set features dark blue-bordered color player action shots on its fronts. The player's name appears within a team-colored stripe at the bottom of the photo and his team name appears beneath within a grayish stripe. The horizontal back features a narrow-cropped color player action shot on the left side. The player's name appears at the top within a team color-coded stripe and his position appears beneath in a grayish stripe. His team logo, biography, stats and career highlights follow below. The cards are numbered on the back. Each dealer received one basic promo and one "Gold Rush" promo with their order form. The word "SAMPLE" is printed diagonally across the front and back of each card.

	MINT	NRMT	EXC
COMPLETE SET (19)	35.00	16.00	4.40
COMMON CARD	.40	.18	.05
☐ 1 Barry Bonds	1.00	.45	.12
☐ 1GR Barry Bonds	3.00	1.35	.35
☐ 2 John Olerud	.40	.18	.05
☐ 2GR John Olerud	1.25	.55	.16
☐ 3 Ken Griffey Jr.	4.00	1.80	.50
☐ 3GR Ken Griffey Jr.	12.00	5.50	1.50
☐ 4 Jeff Bagwell	1.50	.70	.19
☐ 4GR Jeff Bagwell	5.00	2.20	.60
☐ 5 John Burkett	.40	.18	.05
☐ 5GR John Burkett	1.25	.55	.16

Card	MINT	NRMT	EXC
☐ 6 Jack McDowell	.40	.18	.05
☐ 6GR Jack McDowell	1.25	.55	.16
☐ 7 Albert Belle	2.00	.90	.25
☐ 7GR Albert Belle	6.00	2.70	.75
☐ 8 Andres Galarraga	.75	.35	.09
☐ 8GR Andres Galarraga	2.00	.90	.25
☐ DT5 Barry Larkin	5.00	2.20	.60
☐ NNO Hobby Ad Card	.40	.18	.05
☐ NNO Retail Ad Card	.40	.18	.05

1994 Score

The 1994 Score set of 660 standard-size cards was issued in two series of 330. Cards were distributed in 14-card hobby and retail packs. Each pack contained 13 basic cards plus one Gold Rush parallel card. Cards were also distributed in retail Jumbo packs. 4,875 cases of 1994 Score baseball were printed for the hobby. This figure does not take into account additional product printed for retail outlets. The navy blue bordered card fronts feature color action photos with the player's name and team name appearing on two team color-coded stripes across the bottom. Among the subsets are American League stadiums (317-330) and National League stadiums (647-660). Notable Rookie Cards include Derrek Lee and Billy Wagner.

	MINT	NRMT	EXC
COMPLETE SET (660)	30.00	13.50	3.70
COMPLETE SERIES 1 (330)	15.00	6.75	1.85
COMPLETE SERIES 2 (330)	15.00	6.75	1.85
COMMON CARD (1-660)	.05	.02	.01

Card	MINT	NRMT	EXC
☐ 1 Barry Bonds	.50	.23	.06
☐ 2 John Olerud	.05	.02	.01
☐ 3 Ken Griffey Jr.	2.00	.90	.25
☐ 4 Jeff Bagwell	.75	.35	.09
☐ 5 John Burkett	.05	.02	.01
☐ 6 Jack McDowell	.10	.05	.01
☐ 7 Albert Belle	.75	.35	.09
☐ 8 Andres Galarraga	.15	.07	.02
☐ 9 Mike Mussina	.40	.18	.05
☐ 10 Will Clark	.15	.07	.02
☐ 11 Travis Fryman	.10	.05	.01
☐ 12 Tony Gwynn	.75	.35	.09
☐ 13 Robin Yount	.15	.07	.02
☐ 14 Dave Magadan	.05	.02	.01
☐ 15 Paul O'Neill	.10	.05	.01
☐ 16 Ray Lankford	.10	.05	.01
☐ 17 Damion Easley	.05	.02	.01
☐ 18 Andy Van Slyke	.10	.05	.01
☐ 19 Brian McRae	.10	.05	.01
☐ 20 Ryne Sandberg	.50	.23	.06
☐ 21 Kirby Puckett	.75	.35	.09
☐ 22 Dwight Gooden	.10	.05	.01
☐ 23 Don Mattingly	1.00	.45	.12
☐ 24 Kevin Mitchell	.10	.05	.01
☐ 25 Roger Clemens	.40	.18	.05
☐ 26 Eric Karros	.10	.05	.01
☐ 27 Juan Gonzalez	1.00	.45	.12
☐ 28 John Kruk	.10	.05	.01
☐ 29 Gregg Jefferies	.15	.07	.02
☐ 30 Tom Glavine	.15	.07	.02
☐ 31 Ivan Rodriguez	.50	.23	.06
☐ 32 Jay Bell	.10	.05	.01
☐ 33 Randy Johnson	.15	.07	.02
☐ 34 Darren Daulton	.10	.05	.01
☐ 35 Rickey Henderson	.15	.07	.02
☐ 36 Eddie Murray	.50	.23	.06
☐ 37 Brian Harper	.05	.02	.01
☐ 38 Delino DeShields	.05	.02	.01
☐ 39 Jose Lind	.05	.02	.01
☐ 40 Benito Santiago	.05	.02	.01
☐ 41 Frank Thomas	2.00	.90	.25
☐ 42 Mark Grace	.15	.07	.02
☐ 43 Roberto Alomar	.40	.18	.05
☐ 44 Andy Benes	.10	.05	.01
☐ 45 Luis Polonia	.05	.02	.01
☐ 46 Brett Butler	.10	.05	.01
☐ 47 Terry Steinbach	.10	.05	.01
☐ 48 Craig Biggio	.10	.05	.01
☐ 49 Greg Vaughn	.15	.07	.02
☐ 50 Charlie Hayes	.05	.02	.01
☐ 51 Mickey Tettleton	.05	.02	.01
☐ 52 Jose Rijo	.05	.02	.01
☐ 53 Carlos Baerga	.10	.05	.01
☐ 54 Jeff Blauser	.05	.02	.01
☐ 55 Leo Gomez	.05	.02	.01
☐ 56 Bob Tewksbury	.05	.02	.01
☐ 57 Mo Vaughn	.50	.23	.06
☐ 58 Orlando Merced	.10	.05	.01
☐ 59 Tino Martinez	.10	.05	.01
☐ 60 Lenny Dykstra	.10	.05	.01
☐ 61 Jose Canseco	.15	.07	.02
☐ 62 Tony Fernandez	.05	.02	.01
☐ 63 Donovan Osborne	.05	.02	.01
☐ 64 Ken Hill	.05	.02	.01
☐ 65 Kent Hrbek	.10	.05	.01
☐ 66 Bryan Harvey	.05	.02	.01
☐ 67 Wally Joyner	.10	.05	.01
☐ 68 Derrick May	.05	.02	.01
☐ 69 Lance Johnson	.10	.05	.01
☐ 70 Willie McGee	.05	.02	.01
☐ 71 Mark Langston	.10	.05	.01
☐ 72 Terry Pendleton	.10	.05	.01
☐ 73 Joe Carter	.10	.05	.01
☐ 74 Barry Larkin	.15	.07	.02
☐ 75 Jimmy Key	.10	.05	.01
☐ 76 Joe Girardi	.05	.02	.01
☐ 77 B.J. Surhoff	.05	.02	.01
☐ 78 Pete Harnisch	.05	.02	.01
☐ 79 Lou Whitaker UER (Milt Cuyler pictured on front)	.10	.05	.01
☐ 80 Cory Snyder	.05	.02	.01
☐ 81 Kenny Lofton	.60	.25	.07
☐ 82 Fred McGriff	.15	.07	.02
☐ 83 Mike Greenwell	.05	.02	.01
☐ 84 Mike Perez	.05	.02	.01
☐ 85 Cal Ripken	1.50	.70	.19
☐ 86 Don Slaught	.05	.02	.01
☐ 87 Omar Vizquel	.10	.05	.01
☐ 88 Curt Schilling	.05	.02	.01
☐ 89 Chuck Knoblauch	.15	.07	.02
☐ 90 Moises Alou	.10	.05	.01
☐ 91 Greg Gagne	.05	.02	.01
☐ 92 Bret Saberhagen	.10	.05	.01
☐ 93 Ozzie Guillen	.05	.02	.01
☐ 94 Matt Williams	.15	.07	.02
☐ 95 Chad Curtis	.05	.02	.01
☐ 96 Mike Harkey	.05	.02	.01
☐ 97 Devon White	.05	.02	.01
☐ 98 Walt Weiss	.05	.02	.01
☐ 99 Kevin Brown	.10	.05	.01
☐ 100 Gary Sheffield	.15	.07	.02
☐ 101 Wade Boggs	.15	.07	.02
☐ 102 Orel Hershiser	.10	.05	.01
☐ 103 Tony Phillips	.10	.05	.01
☐ 104 Andujar Cedeno	.05	.02	.01
☐ 105 Bill Spiers	.05	.02	.01
☐ 106 Otis Nixon	.05	.02	.01
☐ 107 Felix Fermin	.05	.02	.01
☐ 108 Bip Roberts	.05	.02	.01
☐ 109 Dennis Eckersley	.10	.05	.01
☐ 110 Dante Bichette	.15	.07	.02
☐ 111 Ben McDonald	.05	.02	.01
☐ 112 Jim Poole	.05	.02	.01
☐ 113 John Dopson	.05	.02	.01
☐ 114 Rob Dibble	.05	.02	.01
☐ 115 Jeff Treadway	.05	.02	.01
☐ 116 Ricky Jordan	.05	.02	.01
☐ 117 Mike Henneman	.05	.02	.01
☐ 118 Willie Blair	.05	.02	.01
☐ 119 Doug Henry	.05	.02	.01
☐ 120 Gerald Perry	.05	.02	.01
☐ 121 Greg Myers	.05	.02	.01
☐ 122 John Franco	.05	.02	.01
☐ 123 Roger Mason	.05	.02	.01
☐ 124 Chris Hammond	.05	.02	.01
☐ 125 Hubie Brooks	.05	.02	.01
☐ 126 Kent Mercker	.05	.02	.01
☐ 127 Jim Abbott	.05	.02	.01
☐ 128 Kevin Bass	.05	.02	.01
☐ 129 Rick Aguilera	.05	.02	.01
☐ 130 Mitch Webster	.05	.02	.01
☐ 131 Eric Plunk	.05	.02	.01
☐ 132 Mark Carreon	.05	.02	.01
☐ 133 Dave Stewart	.10	.05	.01
☐ 134 Willie Wilson	.05	.02	.01
☐ 135 Dave Fleming	.05	.02	.01
☐ 136 Jeff Tackett	.05	.02	.01
☐ 137 Geno Petralli	.05	.02	.01
☐ 138 Gene Harris	.05	.02	.01
☐ 139 Scott Bankhead	.05	.02	.01
☐ 140 Trevor Wilson	.05	.02	.01
☐ 141 Alvaro Espinoza	.05	.02	.01
☐ 142 Ryan Bowen	.05	.02	.01
☐ 143 Mike Moore	.05	.02	.01
☐ 144 Bill Pecota	.05	.02	.01
☐ 145 Jaime Navarro	.05	.02	.01
☐ 146 Jack Daugherty	.05	.02	.01
☐ 147 Bob Wickman	.05	.02	.01
☐ 148 Chris Jones	.05	.02	.01
☐ 149 Todd Stottlemyre	.05	.02	.01
☐ 150 Brian Williams	.05	.02	.01
☐ 151 Chuck Finley	.05	.02	.01
☐ 152 Lenny Harris	.05	.02	.01
☐ 153 Alex Fernandez	.10	.05	.01
☐ 154 Candy Maldonado	.05	.02	.01
☐ 155 Jeff Montgomery	.10	.05	.01
☐ 156 David West	.05	.02	.01
☐ 157 Mark Williamson	.05	.02	.01
☐ 158 Milt Thompson	.05	.02	.01
☐ 159 Ron Darling	.05	.02	.01
☐ 160 Stan Belinda	.05	.02	.01
☐ 161 Henry Cotto	.05	.02	.01
☐ 162 Mel Rojas	.05	.02	.01
☐ 163 Doug Strange	.05	.02	.01
☐ 164 Rene Arocha	.05	.02	.01
☐ 165 Tim Hulett	.05	.02	.01
☐ 166 Steve Avery	.10	.05	.01
☐ 167 Jim Thome	.50	.23	.06
☐ 168 Tom Browning	.05	.02	.01
☐ 169 Mario Diaz	.05	.02	.01
☐ 170 Steve Reed	.05	.02	.01
☐ 171 Scott Livingstone	.05	.02	.01
☐ 172 Chris Donnels	.05	.02	.01
☐ 173 John Jaha	.10	.05	.01
☐ 174 Carlos Hernandez	.05	.02	.01
☐ 175 Dion James	.05	.02	.01
☐ 176 Bud Black	.05	.02	.01
☐ 177 Tony Castillo	.05	.02	.01
☐ 178 Jose Guzman	.05	.02	.01
☐ 179 Torey Lovullo	.05	.02	.01
☐ 180 John Vander Wal	.05	.02	.01
☐ 181 Mike LaValliere	.05	.02	.01
☐ 182 Sid Fernandez	.05	.02	.01
☐ 183 Brent Mayne	.05	.02	.01
☐ 184 Terry Mulholland	.05	.02	.01
☐ 185 Willie Banks	.05	.02	.01
☐ 186 Steve Cooke	.05	.02	.01
☐ 187 Brent Gates	.05	.02	.01
☐ 188 Erik Pappas	.05	.02	.01
☐ 189 Bill Haselman	.05	.02	.01
☐ 190 Fernando Valenzuela	.10	.05	.01
☐ 191 Gary Redus	.05	.02	.01
☐ 192 Danny Darwin	.05	.02	.01
☐ 193 Mark Portugal	.05	.02	.01
☐ 194 Derek Lilliquist	.05	.02	.01
☐ 195 Charlie O'Brien	.05	.02	.01
☐ 196 Matt Nokes	.05	.02	.01
☐ 197 Danny Sheaffer	.05	.02	.01
☐ 198 Bill Gullickson	.05	.02	.01
☐ 199 Alex Arias	.05	.02	.01
☐ 200 Mike Fetters	.05	.02	.01
☐ 201 Brian Jordan	.15	.07	.02
☐ 202 Joe Grahe	.05	.02	.01
☐ 203 Tom Candiotti	.05	.02	.01
☐ 204 Jeremy Hernandez	.05	.02	.01
☐ 205 Mike Stanton	.05	.02	.01
☐ 206 David Howard	.05	.02	.01
☐ 207 Darren Holmes	.05	.02	.01
☐ 208 Rick Honeycutt	.05	.02	.01
☐ 209 Danny Jackson	.05	.02	.01
☐ 210 Rich Amaral	.05	.02	.01
☐ 211 Blas Minor	.05	.02	.01
☐ 212 Kenny Rogers	.05	.02	.01
☐ 213 Jim Leyritz	.05	.02	.01
☐ 214 Mike Morgan	.05	.02	.01
☐ 215 Dan Gladden	.05	.02	.01
☐ 216 Randy Velarde	.05	.02	.01
☐ 217 Mitch Williams	.05	.02	.01
☐ 218 Hipolito Pichardo	.05	.02	.01
☐ 219 Dave Burba	.05	.02	.01
☐ 220 Wilson Alvarez	.10	.05	.01
☐ 221 Bob Zupcic	.05	.02	.01
☐ 222 Francisco Cabrera	.05	.02	.01
☐ 223 Julio Valera	.05	.02	.01
☐ 224 Paul Assenmacher	.05	.02	.01
☐ 225 Jeff Branson	.05	.02	.01
☐ 226 Todd Frohwirth	.05	.02	.01
☐ 227 Armando Reynoso	.05	.02	.01
☐ 228 Rich Rowland	.05	.02	.01
☐ 229 Freddie Benavides	.05	.02	.01
☐ 230 Wayne Kirby	.05	.02	.01
☐ 231 Darryl Kile	.05	.02	.01
☐ 232 Skeeter Barnes	.05	.02	.01
☐ 233 Ramon Martinez	.10	.05	.01
☐ 234 Tom Gordon	.05	.02	.01
☐ 235 Dave Gallagher	.05	.02	.01
☐ 236 Ricky Bones	.05	.02	.01
☐ 237 Larry Andersen	.05	.02	.01
☐ 238 Pat Meares	.05	.02	.01
☐ 239 Zane Smith	.05	.02	.01
☐ 240 Tim Leary	.05	.02	.01
☐ 241 Phil Clark	.05	.02	.01
☐ 242 Danny Cox	.05	.02	.01
☐ 243 Mike Jackson	.05	.02	.01
☐ 244 Mike Gallego	.05	.02	.01
☐ 245 Lee Smith	.10	.05	.01
☐ 246 Todd Jones	.05	.02	.01
☐ 247 Steve Bedrosian	.05	.02	.01
☐ 248 Troy Neel	.05	.02	.01
☐ 249 Jose Bautista	.05	.02	.01
☐ 250 Steve Frey	.05	.02	.01
☐ 251 Jeff Reardon	.10	.05	.01
☐ 252 Stan Javier	.05	.02	.01
☐ 253 Mo Sanford	.05	.02	.01
☐ 254 Steve Sax	.05	.02	.01
☐ 255 Luis Aquino	.05	.02	.01
☐ 256 Domingo Jean	.05	.02	.01
☐ 257 Scott Servais	.05	.02	.01
☐ 258 Brad Pennington	.05	.02	.01
☐ 259 Dave Hansen	.05	.02	.01
☐ 260 Goose Gossage	.10	.05	.01
☐ 261 Jeff Fassero	.05	.02	.01
☐ 262 Junior Ortiz	.05	.02	.01
☐ 263 Anthony Young	.05	.02	.01
☐ 264 Chris Bosio	.05	.02	.01
☐ 265 Ruben Amaro Jr.	.05	.02	.01
☐ 266 Mark Eichhorn	.05	.02	.01
☐ 267 Dave Clark	.05	.02	.01
☐ 268 Gary Thurman	.05	.02	.01
☐ 269 Les Lancaster	.05	.02	.01
☐ 270 Jamie Moyer	.05	.02	.01
☐ 271 Ricky Gutierrez	.05	.02	.01
☐ 272 Greg A.Harris	.05	.02	.01
☐ 273 Mike Benjamin	.05	.02	.01
☐ 274 Gene Nelson	.05	.02	.01
☐ 275 Damon Berryhill	.05	.02	.01
☐ 276 Scott Radinsky	.05	.02	.01
☐ 277 Mike Aldrete	.05	.02	.01
☐ 278 Jerry DiPoto	.05	.02	.01
☐ 279 Chris Haney	.05	.02	.01
☐ 280 Richie Lewis	.05	.02	.01
☐ 281 Jarvis Brown	.05	.02	.01
☐ 282 Juan Bell	.05	.02	.01
☐ 283 Joe Klink	.05	.02	.01
☐ 284 Graeme Lloyd	.05	.02	.01
☐ 285 Casey Candaele	.05	.02	.01
☐ 286 Bob MacDonald	.05	.02	.01
☐ 287 Mike Sharperson	.05	.02	.01
☐ 288 Gene Larkin	.05	.02	.01
☐ 289 Brian Barnes	.05	.02	.01
☐ 290 David McCarty	.05	.02	.01
☐ 291 Jeff Innis	.05	.02	.01
☐ 292 Bob Patterson	.05	.02	.01
☐ 293 Ben Rivera	.05	.02	.01
☐ 294 John Habyan	.05	.02	.01
☐ 295 Rich Rodriguez	.05	.02	.01
☐ 296 Edwin Nunez	.05	.02	.01
☐ 297 Rod Brewer	.05	.02	.01
☐ 298 Mike Timlin	.05	.02	.01
☐ 299 Jesse Orosco	.05	.02	.01
☐ 300 Gary Gaetti	.10	.05	.01
☐ 301 Todd Benzinger	.05	.02	.01
☐ 302 Jeff Nelson	.05	.02	.01
☐ 303 Rafael Belliard	.05	.02	.01
☐ 304 Matt Whiteside	.05	.02	.01
☐ 305 Vinny Castilla	.15	.07	.02
☐ 306 Matt Turner	.05	.02	.01
☐ 307 Eduardo Perez	.05	.02	.01
☐ 308 Joel Johnston	.05	.02	.01
☐ 309 Chris Gomez	.05	.02	.01
☐ 310 Pat Rapp	.05	.02	.01
☐ 311 Jim Tatum	.05	.02	.01
☐ 312 Kirk Rueter	.05	.02	.01
☐ 313 John Flaherty	.05	.02	.01
☐ 314 Tom Kramer	.05	.02	.01
☐ 315 Mark Whiten	.05	.02	.01
☐ 316 Chris Bosio	.05	.02	.01
☐ 317 Baltimore Orioles CL	.05	.02	.01
☐ 318 Boston Red Sox CL UER (Viola listed as 316; should be 331)	.05	.02	.01
☐ 319 California Angels CL	.05	.02	.01
☐ 320 Chicago White Sox CL	.05	.02	.01
☐ 321 Cleveland Indians CL	.05	.02	.01
☐ 322 Detroit Tigers CL	.05	.02	.01
☐ 323 Kansas City Royals CL	.05	.02	.01
☐ 324 Milwaukee Brewers CL	.05	.02	.01
☐ 325 Minnesota Twins CL	.05	.02	.01
☐ 326 New York Yankees CL	.05	.02	.01
☐ 327 Oakland Athletics CL	.05	.02	.01
☐ 328 Seattle Mariners CL	.05	.02	.01
☐ 329 Texas Rangers CL	.05	.02	.01
☐ 330 Toronto Blue Jays CL	.05	.02	.01
☐ 331 Frank Viola	.05	.02	.01
☐ 332 Ron Gant	.10	.05	.01
☐ 333 Charles Nagy	.10	.05	.01
☐ 334 Roberto Kelly	.05	.02	.01
☐ 335 Brady Anderson	.15	.07	.02
☐ 336 Alex Cole	.05	.02	.01
☐ 337 Alan Trammell	.10	.05	.01
☐ 338 Derek Bell	.10	.05	.01
☐ 339 Bernie Williams	.40	.18	.05
☐ 340 Jose Offerman	.05	.02	.01
☐ 341 Bill Wegman	.05	.02	.01
☐ 342 Ken Caminiti	.15	.07	.02
☐ 343 Pat Borders	.05	.02	.01
☐ 344 Kirt Manwaring	.05	.02	.01
☐ 345 Chili Davis	.10	.05	.01
☐ 346 Steve Buechele	.05	.02	.01
☐ 347 Robin Ventura	.10	.05	.01
☐ 348 Teddy Higuera	.05	.02	.01
☐ 349 Jerry Browne	.05	.02	.01
☐ 350 Scott Kamieniecki	.05	.02	.01
☐ 351 Kevin Tapani	.05	.02	.01
☐ 352 Marquis Grissom	.10	.05	.01
☐ 353 Jay Buhner	.15	.07	.02
☐ 354 Dave Hollins	.05	.02	.01
☐ 355 Dan Wilson	.10	.05	.01
☐ 356 Bob Walk	.05	.02	.01
☐ 357 Chris Hoiles	.05	.02	.01
☐ 358 Todd Zeile	.05	.02	.01
☐ 359 Kevin Appier	.10	.05	.01
☐ 360 Chris Sabo	.05	.02	.01
☐ 361 David Segui	.05	.02	.01
☐ 362 Jerald Clark	.05	.02	.01
☐ 363 Tony Pena	.05	.02	.01
☐ 364 Steve Finley	.15	.07	.02
☐ 365 Roger Pavlik	.05	.02	.01
☐ 366 John Smoltz	.15	.07	.02
☐ 367 Scott Fletcher	.05	.02	.01
☐ 368 Jody Reed	.05	.02	.01
☐ 369 David Wells	.05	.02	.01
☐ 370 Jose Vizcaino	.05	.02	.01
☐ 371 Pat Listach	.05	.02	.01
☐ 372 Orestes Destrade	.05	.02	.01
☐ 373 Danny Tartabull	.05	.02	.01

☐ 374 Greg W. Harris	.05	.02	.01
☐ 375 Juan Guzman	.10	.05	.01
☐ 376 Larry Walker	.15	.07	.02
☐ 377 Gary DiSarcina	.05	.02	.01
☐ 378 Bobby Bonilla	.10	.05	.01
☐ 379 Tim Raines	.15	.07	.02
☐ 380 Tommy Greene	.05	.02	.01
☐ 381 Chris Gwynn	.05	.02	.01
☐ 382 Jeff King	.10	.05	.01
☐ 383 Shane Mack	.05	.02	.01
☐ 384 Ozzie Smith	.50	.23	.06
☐ 385 Eddie Zambrano	.05	.02	.01
☐ 386 Mike Devereaux	.05	.02	.01
☐ 387 Erik Hanson	.05	.02	.01
☐ 388 Scott Cooper	.05	.02	.01
☐ 389 Dean Palmer	.10	.05	.01
☐ 390 John Wetteland	.10	.05	.01
☐ 391 Reggie Jefferson	.10	.05	.01
☐ 392 Mark Lemke	.05	.02	.01
☐ 393 Cecil Fielder	.10	.05	.01
☐ 394 Reggie Sanders	.10	.05	.01
☐ 395 Darryl Hamilton	.05	.02	.01
☐ 396 Daryl Boston	.05	.02	.01
☐ 397 Pat Kelly	.05	.02	.01
☐ 398 Joe Orsulak	.05	.02	.01
☐ 399 Ed Sprague	.10	.05	.01
☐ 400 Eric Anthony	.05	.02	.01
☐ 401 Scott Sanderson	.05	.02	.01
☐ 402 Jim Gott	.05	.02	.01
☐ 403 Ron Karkovice	.05	.02	.01
☐ 404 Phil Plantier	.05	.02	.01
☐ 405 David Cone	.10	.05	.01
☐ 406 Robby Thompson	.05	.02	.01
☐ 407 Dave Winfield	.15	.07	.02
☐ 408 Dwight Smith	.05	.02	.01
☐ 409 Ruben Sierra	.10	.05	.01
☐ 410 Jack Armstrong	.05	.02	.01
☐ 411 Mike Felder	.05	.02	.01
☐ 412 Wil Cordero	.10	.05	.01
☐ 413 Julio Franco	.10	.05	.01
☐ 414 Howard Johnson	.05	.02	.01
☐ 415 Mark McLemore	.05	.02	.01
☐ 416 Pete Incaviglia	.05	.02	.01
☐ 417 John Valentin	.10	.05	.01
☐ 418 Tim Wakefield	.05	.02	.01
☐ 419 Jose Mesa	.10	.05	.01
☐ 420 Bernard Gilkey	.10	.05	.01
☐ 421 Kirk Gibson	.10	.05	.01
☐ 422 Dave Justice	.15	.07	.02
☐ 423 Tom Brunansky	.05	.02	.01
☐ 424 John Smiley	.05	.02	.01
☐ 425 Kevin Maas	.05	.02	.01
☐ 426 Doug Drabek	.05	.02	.01
☐ 427 Paul Molitor	.40	.18	.05
☐ 428 Darryl Strawberry	.10	.05	.01
☐ 429 Tim Naehring	.05	.02	.01
☐ 430 Bill Swift	.05	.02	.01
☐ 431 Ellis Burks	.10	.05	.01
☐ 432 Greg Hibbard	.05	.02	.01
☐ 433 Felix Jose	.05	.02	.01
☐ 434 Bret Barberie	.05	.02	.01
☐ 435 Pedro Munoz	.05	.02	.01
☐ 436 Darrin Fletcher	.05	.02	.01
☐ 437 Bobby Witt	.05	.02	.01
☐ 438 Wes Chamberlain	.05	.02	.01
☐ 439 Mackey Sasser	.05	.02	.01
☐ 440 Mark Whiten	.05	.02	.01
☐ 441 Harold Reynolds	.05	.02	.01
☐ 442 Greg Olson	.05	.02	.01
☐ 443 Billy Hatcher	.05	.02	.01
☐ 444 Joe Oliver	.05	.02	.01
☐ 445 Sandy Alomar Jr.	.10	.05	.01
☐ 446 Tim Wallach	.05	.02	.01
☐ 447 Karl Rhodes	.05	.02	.01
☐ 448 Royce Clayton	.10	.05	.01
☐ 449 Cal Eldred	.05	.02	.01
☐ 450 Rick Wilkins	.05	.02	.01
☐ 451 Mike Stanley	.05	.02	.01
☐ 452 Charlie Hough	.05	.02	.01
☐ 453 Jack Morris	.10	.05	.01
☐ 454 Jon Ratliff	.10	.05	.01
☐ 455 Rene Gonzales	.05	.02	.01
☐ 456 Eddie Taubensee	.05	.02	.01
☐ 457 Roberto Hernandez	.10	.05	.01
☐ 458 Todd Hundley	.10	.05	.01
☐ 459 Mike Macfarlane	.05	.02	.01
☐ 460 Mickey Morandini	.05	.02	.01
☐ 461 Scott Erickson	.05	.02	.01
☐ 462 Lonnie Smith	.05	.02	.01
☐ 463 Dave Henderson	.05	.02	.01
☐ 464 Ryan Klesko	.40	.18	.05
☐ 465 Edgar Martinez	.10	.05	.01
☐ 466 Tom Pagnozzi	.05	.02	.01
☐ 467 Charlie Leibrandt	.05	.02	.01
☐ 468 Brian Anderson	.10	.05	.01
☐ 469 Harold Baines	.10	.05	.01
☐ 470 Tim Belcher	.05	.02	.01
☐ 471 Andre Dawson	.10	.05	.01
☐ 472 Eric Young	.10	.05	.01
☐ 473 Paul Sorrento	.05	.02	.01
☐ 474 Luis Gonzalez	.05	.02	.01
☐ 475 Rob Deer	.05	.02	.01
☐ 476 Mike Piazza	1.25	.55	.16
☐ 477 Kevin Reimer	.05	.02	.01
☐ 478 Jeff Gardner	.05	.02	.01
☐ 479 Melido Perez	.05	.02	.01
☐ 480 Darren Lewis	.05	.02	.01
☐ 481 Duane Ward	.05	.02	.01
☐ 482 Rey Sanchez	.05	.02	.01
☐ 483 Mark Lewis	.05	.02	.01
☐ 484 Jeff Conine	.10	.05	.01
☐ 485 Joey Cora	.05	.02	.01
☐ 486 Trot Nixon	.15	.07	.02
☐ 487 Kevin McReynolds	.05	.02	.01
☐ 488 Mike Lansing	.10	.05	.01
☐ 489 Mike Pagliarulo	.05	.02	.01
☐ 490 Mariano Duncan	.05	.02	.01
☐ 491 Mike Bordick	.05	.02	.01
☐ 492 Kevin Young	.05	.02	.01
☐ 493 Dave Valle	.05	.02	.01
☐ 494 Wayne Gomes	.10	.05	.01
☐ 495 Rafael Palmeiro	.15	.07	.02
☐ 496 Deion Sanders	.15	.07	.02
☐ 497 Rick Sutcliffe	.05	.02	.01
☐ 498 Randy Milligan	.05	.02	.01
☐ 499 Carlos Quintana	.05	.02	.01
☐ 500 Chris Turner	.05	.02	.01
☐ 501 Thomas Howard	.05	.02	.01
☐ 502 Greg Swindell	.05	.02	.01
☐ 503 Chad Kreuter	.05	.02	.01
☐ 504 Eric Davis	.10	.05	.01
☐ 505 Dickie Thon	.05	.02	.01
☐ 506 Matt Drews	.60	.25	.07
☐ 507 Spike Owen	.05	.02	.01
☐ 508 Rod Beck	.10	.05	.01
☐ 509 Pat Hentgen	.10	.05	.01
☐ 510 Sammy Sosa	.15	.07	.02
☐ 511 J.T. Snow	.10	.05	.01
☐ 512 Chuck Carr	.05	.02	.01
☐ 513 Bo Jackson	.10	.05	.01
☐ 514 Dennis Martinez	.10	.05	.01
☐ 515 Phil Hiatt	.05	.02	.01
☐ 516 Jeff Kent	.05	.02	.01
☐ 517 Brooks Kieschnick	.40	.18	.05
☐ 518 Kirk Presley	.15	.07	.02
☐ 519 Kevin Seitzer	.05	.02	.01
☐ 520 Carlos Garcia	.05	.02	.01
☐ 521 Mike Blowers	.05	.02	.01
☐ 522 Luis Alicea	.05	.02	.01
☐ 523 David Hulse	.05	.02	.01
☐ 524 Greg Maddux UER (career strikeout totals listed as 113; should be 1134)	1.25	.55	.16
☐ 525 Gregg Olson	.05	.02	.01
☐ 526 Hal Morris	.05	.02	.01
☐ 527 Daron Kirkreit	.10	.05	.01
☐ 528 David Nied	.05	.02	.01
☐ 529 Jeff Russell	.05	.02	.01
☐ 530 Kevin Gross	.05	.02	.01
☐ 531 John Doherty	.05	.02	.01
☐ 532 Matt Brunson	.10	.05	.01
☐ 533 Dave Nilsson	.10	.05	.01
☐ 534 Randy Myers	.05	.02	.01
☐ 535 Steve Farr	.05	.02	.01
☐ 536 Billy Wagner	.60	.25	.07
☐ 537 Darnell Coles	.05	.02	.01
☐ 538 Frank Tanana	.05	.02	.01
☐ 539 Tim Salmon	.15	.07	.02
☐ 540 Kim Batiste	.05	.02	.01
☐ 541 George Bell	.05	.02	.01
☐ 542 Tom Henke	.05	.02	.01
☐ 543 Sam Horn	.05	.02	.01
☐ 544 Doug Jones	.05	.02	.01
☐ 545 Scott Leius	.05	.02	.01
☐ 546 Al Martin	.05	.02	.01
☐ 547 Bob Welch	.05	.02	.01
☐ 548 Scott Christman	.10	.05	.01
☐ 549 Norm Charlton	.05	.02	.01
☐ 550 Mark McGwire	.60	.25	.07
☐ 551 Greg McMichael	.05	.02	.01
☐ 552 Tim Costo	.05	.02	.01
☐ 553 Rodney Bolton	.05	.02	.01
☐ 554 Pedro Martinez	.15	.07	.02
☐ 555 Marc Valdes	.10	.05	.01
☐ 556 Darrell Whitmore	.05	.02	.01
☐ 557 Tim Bogar	.05	.02	.01
☐ 558 Steve Karsay	.05	.02	.01
☐ 559 Danny Bautista	.05	.02	.01
☐ 560 Jeffrey Hammonds	.10	.05	.01
☐ 561 Aaron Sele	.10	.05	.01
☐ 562 Russ Springer	.05	.02	.01
☐ 563 Jason Bere	.10	.05	.01
☐ 564 Billy Brewer	.05	.02	.01
☐ 565 Sterling Hitchcock	.10	.05	.01
☐ 566 Bobby Munoz	.05	.02	.01
☐ 567 Craig Paquette	.05	.02	.01
☐ 568 Bret Boone	.10	.05	.01
☐ 569 Dan Peltier	.05	.02	.01
☐ 570 Jeromy Burnitz	.05	.02	.01
☐ 571 John Wasdin	.40	.18	.05
☐ 572 Chipper Jones	1.50	.70	.19
☐ 573 Jamey Wright	.60	.25	.07
☐ 574 Jeff Granger	.10	.05	.01
☐ 575 Jay Powell	.10	.05	.01
☐ 576 Ryan Thompson	.05	.02	.01
☐ 577 Lou Frazier	.05	.02	.01
☐ 578 Paul Wagner	.05	.02	.01
☐ 579 Brad Ausmus	.05	.02	.01
☐ 580 Jack Voigt	.05	.02	.01
☐ 581 Kevin Rogers	.05	.02	.01
☐ 582 Damon Buford	.05	.02	.01
☐ 583 Paul Quantrill	.05	.02	.01
☐ 584 Marc Newfield	.10	.05	.01
☐ 585 Derrek Lee	1.25	.55	.16
☐ 586 Shane Reynolds	.10	.05	.01
☐ 587 Cliff Floyd	.15	.07	.02
☐ 588 Jeff Schwarz	.05	.02	.01
☐ 589 Ross Powell	.05	.02	.01
☐ 590 Gerald Williams	.05	.02	.01
☐ 591 Mike Trombley	.05	.02	.01
☐ 592 Ken Ryan	.05	.02	.01
☐ 593 John O'Donoghue	.05	.02	.01
☐ 594 Rod Correia	.05	.02	.01
☐ 595 Darrell Sherman	.05	.02	.01
☐ 596 Steve Scarsone	.05	.02	.01
☐ 597 Sherman Obando	.05	.02	.01
☐ 598 Kurt Abbott	.10	.05	.01
☐ 599 Dave Telgheder	.05	.02	.01
☐ 600 Rick Trlicek	.05	.02	.01
☐ 601 Carl Everett	.05	.02	.01
☐ 602 Luis Ortiz	.05	.02	.01
☐ 603 Larry Luebbers	.05	.02	.01
☐ 604 Kevin Roberson	.05	.02	.01
☐ 605 Butch Huskey	.10	.05	.01
☐ 606 Benji Gil	.05	.02	.01
☐ 607 Todd Van Poppel	.05	.02	.01
☐ 608 Mark Hutton	.05	.02	.01
☐ 609 Chip Hale	.05	.02	.01
☐ 610 Matt Maysey	.05	.02	.01
☐ 611 Scott Ruffcorn	.05	.02	.01
☐ 612 Hilly Hathaway	.05	.02	.01
☐ 613 Allen Watson	.05	.02	.01
☐ 614 Carlos Delgado	.15	.07	.02
☐ 615 Roberto Mejia	.05	.02	.01
☐ 616 Turk Wendell	.05	.02	.01
☐ 617 Tony Tarasco	.05	.02	.01
☐ 618 Raul Mondesi	.15	.07	.02
☐ 619 Kevin Stocker	.05	.02	.01
☐ 620 Javier Lopez	.15	.07	.02
☐ 621 Keith Kessinger	.05	.02	.01
☐ 622 Bob Hamelin	.05	.02	.01
☐ 623 John Roper	.05	.02	.01
☐ 624 Lenny Dykstra WS	.05	.02	.01
☐ 625 Joe Carter WS	.10	.05	.01
☐ 626 Jim Abbott HL	.05	.02	.01
☐ 627 Lee Smith HL	.10	.05	.01
☐ 628 Ken Griffey Jr. HL	1.00	.45	.12
☐ 629 Dave Winfield HL	.15	.07	.02
☐ 630 Darryl Kile HL	.05	.02	.01
☐ 631 Frank Thomas AL MVP	1.00	.45	.12
☐ 632 Barry Bonds NL MVP	.15	.07	.02
☐ 633 Jack McDowell AL CY	.05	.02	.01
☐ 634 Greg Maddux NL CY	.60	.25	.07
☐ 635 Tim Salmon AL ROY	.15	.07	.02
☐ 636 Mike Piazza NL ROY	.60	.25	.07
☐ 637 Brian Turang	.05	.02	.01
☐ 638 Rondell White	.15	.07	.02
☐ 639 Nigel Wilson	.05	.02	.01
☐ 640 Torii Hunter	.10	.05	.01
☐ 641 Salomon Torres	.05	.02	.01
☐ 642 Kevin Higgins	.05	.02	.01
☐ 643 Eric Wedge	.05	.02	.01
☐ 644 Roger Salkeld	.05	.02	.01
☐ 645 Manny Ramirez	.60	.25	.07
☐ 646 Jeff McNeely	.05	.02	.01
☐ 647 Atlanta Braves CL	.05	.02	.01
☐ 648 Chicago Cubs CL	.05	.02	.01
☐ 649 Cincinnati Reds CL	.05	.02	.01
☐ 650 Colorado Rockies CL	.05	.02	.01
☐ 651 Florida Marlins CL	.05	.02	.01
☐ 652 Houston Astros CL	.05	.02	.01
☐ 653 Los Angeles Dodgers CL	.05	.02	.01
☐ 654 Montreal Expos CL	.05	.02	.01
☐ 655 New York Mets CL	.05	.02	.01
☐ 656 Philadelphia Phillies CL	.05	.02	.01
☐ 657 Pittsburgh Pirates CL	.05	.02	.01
☐ 658 St. Louis Cardinals CL	.05	.02	.01
☐ 659 San Diego Padres CL	.05	.02	.01
☐ 660 San Francisco Giants CL	.05	.02	.01

1994 Score Gold Rush

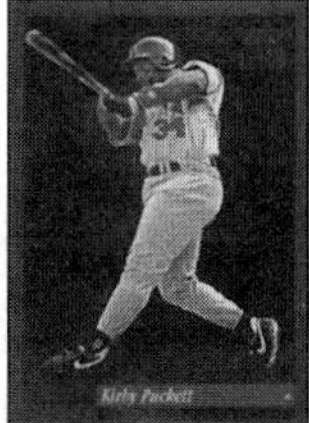

This 660-card standard-size set is parallel to the basic Score issue. This set features metallicized and gold-bordered fronts. Gold Rush cards came one per 14-card pack or super pack. They were also issued two per jumbo. These cards were inserted into both hobby and retail packs.

	MINT	NRMT	EXC
COMPLETE SET (660)	160.00	70.00	20.00
COMPLETE SERIES 1 (330)	80.00	36.00	10.00
COMPLETE SERIES 2 (330)	80.00	36.00	10.00
COMMON CARD (1-660)	.25	.11	.03

*STARS: 2.5X to 5X BASIC CARDS ....
*YOUNG STARS: 2X to 4X BASIC CARDS

1994 Score Boys of Summer

Randomly inserted in super packs at a rate of one in four, this 60-card set features top young stars and hopefuls. The set was issued in two series of 30 cards. The fronts have a color player photo that is outlined by what resembles static electricity. The backgrounds are blurred and the player's name and Boys of Summer logo appear up the right-hand side. An orange back contains a player photo and text.

	MINT	NRMT	EXC
COMPLETE SET (60)	120.00	55.00	15.00
COMPLETE SERIES 1 (30)	50.00	22.00	6.25
COMPLETE SERIES 2 (30)	70.00	32.00	8.75
COMMON CARD (1-60)	1.50	.70	.19
☐ 1 Jeff Conine	3.00	1.35	.35
☐ 2 Aaron Sele	1.50	.70	.19
☐ 3 Kevin Stocker	1.50	.70	.19
☐ 4 Pat Meares	1.50	.70	.19
☐ 5 Jeromy Burnitz	1.50	.70	.19
☐ 6 Mike Piazza	25.00	11.00	3.10
☐ 7 Allen Watson	1.50	.70	.19
☐ 8 Jeffrey Hammonds	1.50	.70	.19
☐ 9 Kevin Roberson	1.50	.70	.19
☐ 10 Hilly Hathaway	1.50	.70	.19
☐ 11 Kirk Rueter	1.50	.70	.19
☐ 12 Eduardo Perez	1.50	.70	.19
☐ 13 Ricky Gutierrez	1.50	.70	.19
☐ 14 Domingo Jean	1.50	.70	.19
☐ 15 David Nied	1.50	.70	.19
☐ 16 Wayne Kirby	1.50	.70	.19
☐ 17 Mike Lansing	1.50	.70	.19
☐ 18 Jason Bere	1.50	.70	.19
☐ 19 Brent Gates	1.50	.70	.19
☐ 20 Javier Lopez	5.00	2.20	.60
☐ 21 Greg McMichael	1.50	.70	.19
☐ 22 David Hulse	1.50	.70	.19
☐ 23 Roberto Mejia	1.50	.70	.19
☐ 24 Tim Salmon	6.00	2.70	.75
☐ 25 Rene Arocha	1.50	.70	.19
☐ 26 Bret Boone	3.00	1.35	.35
☐ 27 David McCarty	1.50	.70	.19
☐ 28 Todd Van Poppel	1.50	.70	.19
☐ 29 Lance Painter	1.50	.70	.19
☐ 30 Erik Pappas	1.50	.70	.19
☐ 31 Chuck Carr	1.50	.70	.19
☐ 32 Mark Hutton	1.50	.70	.19
☐ 33 Jeff McNeely	1.50	.70	.19
☐ 34 Willie Greene	3.00	1.35	.35
☐ 35 Nigel Wilson	1.50	.70	.19
☐ 36 Rondell White	4.00	1.80	.50
☐ 37 Brian Turang	1.50	.70	.19
☐ 38 Manny Ramirez	12.00	5.50	1.50
☐ 39 Salomon Torres	1.50	.70	.19
☐ 40 Melvin Nieves	3.00	1.35	.35
☐ 41 Ryan Klesko	8.00	3.60	1.00
☐ 42 Keith Kessinger	1.50	.70	.19
☐ 43 Brad Ausmus	1.50	.70	.19
☐ 44 Bob Hamelin	1.50	.70	.19
☐ 45 Carlos Delgado	5.00	2.20	.60
☐ 46 Marc Newfield	3.00	1.35	.35
☐ 47 Raul Mondesi	6.00	2.70	.75
☐ 48 Tim Costo	1.50	.70	.19
☐ 49 Pedro Martinez	3.00	1.35	.35
☐ 50 Steve Karsay	1.50	.70	.19
☐ 51 Danny Bautista	1.50	.70	.19
☐ 52 Butch Huskey	3.00	1.35	.35
☐ 53 Kurt Abbott	3.00	1.35	.35
☐ 54 Darrell Sherman	1.50	.70	.19
☐ 55 Damon Buford	1.50	.70	.19
☐ 56 Ross Powell	1.50	.70	.19
☐ 57 Darrell Whitmore	1.50	.70	.19
☐ 58 Chipper Jones	30.00	13.50	3.70
☐ 59 Jeff Granger	1.50	.70	.19
☐ 60 Cliff Floyd	3.00	1.35	.35

1994 Score Cycle

This 20-card set was randomly inserted in second series foil and jumbo packs at a rate of one in 90. The set is arranged according to players with the most singles (1-5), doubles (6-10), triples (11-15) and home runs (16-20). The front contains an oval player photo with "The Cycle" at top and the players name at the bottom. Also at the bottom, is the number of of that particular base hit the player accumulated in 1993. A small baseball diamond appears beneath the oval photo. The back lists the top five of the given base hit category. A dark blue border surrounds both sides. The cards are number with a TC prefix.

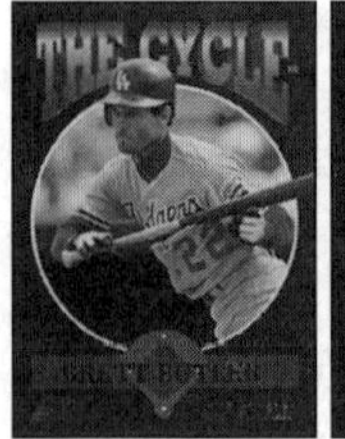

	MINT	NRMT	EXC
COMPLETE SET (20)	150.00	70.00	19.00
COMMON CARD (TC1-TC20)	2.50	1.10	.30
☐ TC1 Brett Butler	5.00	2.20	.60
☐ TC2 Kenny Lofton	15.00	6.75	1.85
☐ TC3 Paul Molitor	10.00	4.50	1.25
☐ TC4 Carlos Baerga	5.00	2.20	.60
☐ TC5 Gregg Jefferies Tony Phillips	5.00	2.20	.60
☐ TC6 John Olerud	2.50	1.10	.30
☐ TC7 Charlie Hayes	2.50	1.10	.30
☐ TC8 Lenny Dykstra	5.00	2.20	.60
☐ TC9 Dante Bichette	6.00	2.70	.75
☐ TC10 Devon White	5.00	2.20	.60
☐ TC11 Lance Johnson	5.00	2.20	.60
☐ TC12 Joey Cora Steve Finley	2.50	1.10	.30
☐ TC13 Tony Fernandez	2.50	1.10	.30
☐ TC14 David Hulse Brett Butler	2.50	1.10	.30
☐ TC15 Jay Bell Brian McRae Mickey Morandini	2.50	1.10	.30
☐ TC16 Juan Gonzalez Barry Bonds	20.00	9.00	2.50
☐ TC17 Ken Griffey Jr.	50.00	22.00	6.25
☐ TC18 Frank Thomas	50.00	22.00	6.25
☐ TC19 Dave Justice	5.00	2.20	.60
☐ TC20 Matt Williams Albert Belle	12.00	5.50	1.50

1994 Score Dream Team

Randomly inserted in first series foil and jumbo packs at a rate of one in 72, this ten-card set feature's baseball's Dream Team as selected by Pinnacle Brands. Banded by forest green stripes above and below, the player photos on the fronts feature ten of baseball's best players sporting historical team uniforms from the 1930's. The set title and player's name appear in gold foil lettering on black bars above and below the picture. The backs carry a color head shot and brief player profile.

	MINT	NRMT	EXC
COMPLETE SET (10)	60.00	27.00	7.50
COMMON CARD (1-10)	2.50	1.10	.30
☐ 1 Mike Mussina	10.00	4.50	1.25
☐ 2 Tom Glavine	6.00	2.70	.75
☐ 3 Don Mattingly	25.00	11.00	3.10
☐ 4 Carlos Baerga	2.50	1.10	.30
☐ 5 Barry Larkin	6.00	2.70	.75
☐ 6 Matt Williams	6.00	2.70	.75
☐ 7 Juan Gonzalez	25.00	11.00	3.10
☐ 8 Andy Van Slyke	2.50	1.10	.30
☐ 9 Larry Walker	6.00	2.70	.75
☐ 10 Mike Stanley	2.50	1.10	.30

1994 Score Gold Stars

Randomly inserted at a rate of one in every 18 hobby packs, this 60-card set features National and American stars. Split into two series of 30 cards, the first series (1-30) comprises of National League players and the second series (31-60) American Leaguers. The fronts feature a color action player photo cut out and superimposed on a foil background. At the bottom, a navy blue triangle carries the set title and the player's name appears in a white bar. The backs have a color close-up shot and a player profile.

	MINT	NRMT	EXC
COMPLETE SET (60)	250.00	110.00	31.00
COMPLETE NL SERIES (30)	100.00	45.00	12.50
COMPLETE AL SERIES (30)	150.00	70.00	19.00
COMMON CARD (1-60)	2.00	.90	.25
☐ 1 Barry Bonds	8.00	3.60	1.00
☐ 2 Orlando Merced	2.00	.90	.25
☐ 3 Mark Grace	4.00	1.80	.50
☐ 4 Darren Daulton	3.00	1.35	.35
☐ 5 Jeff Blauser	2.00	.90	.25
☐ 6 Deion Sanders	4.00	1.80	.50
☐ 7 John Kruk	3.00	1.35	.35
☐ 8 Jeff Bagwell	12.00	5.50	1.50
☐ 9 Gregg Jefferies	4.00	1.80	.50
☐ 10 Matt Williams	4.00	1.80	.50
☐ 11 Andres Galarraga	4.00	1.80	.50
☐ 12 Jay Bell	2.00	.90	.25
☐ 13 Mike Piazza	20.00	9.00	2.50
☐ 14 Ron Gant	3.00	1.35	.35
☐ 15 Barry Larkin	4.00	1.80	.50
☐ 16 Tom Glavine	4.00	1.80	.50
☐ 17 Lenny Dykstra	3.00	1.35	.35
☐ 18 Fred McGriff	4.00	1.80	.50
☐ 19 Andy Van Slyke	3.00	1.35	.35
☐ 20 Gary Sheffield	5.00	2.20	.60
☐ 21 John Burkett	2.00	.90	.25
☐ 22 Dante Bichette	4.00	1.80	.50
☐ 23 Tony Gwynn	12.00	5.50	1.50
☐ 24 Dave Justice	4.00	1.80	.50
☐ 25 Marquis Grissom	3.00	1.35	.35
☐ 26 Bobby Bonilla	3.00	1.35	.35
☐ 27 Larry Walker	4.00	1.80	.50
☐ 28 Brett Butler	3.00	1.35	.35
☐ 29 Robby Thompson	2.00	.90	.25
☐ 30 Jeff Conine	3.00	1.35	.35
☐ 31 Joe Carter	3.00	1.35	.35
☐ 32 Ken Griffey Jr.	30.00	13.50	3.70
☐ 33 Juan Gonzalez	15.00	6.75	1.85
☐ 34 Rickey Henderson	4.00	1.80	.50
☐ 35 Bo Jackson	3.00	1.35	.35
☐ 36 Cal Ripken	25.00	11.00	3.10
☐ 37 John Olerud	3.00	1.35	.35
☐ 38 Carlos Baerga	3.00	1.35	.35
☐ 39 Jack McDowell	4.00	1.80	.50
☐ 40 Cecil Fielder	3.00	1.35	.35
☐ 41 Kenny Lofton	10.00	4.50	1.25
☐ 42 Roberto Alomar	6.00	2.70	.75
☐ 43 Randy Johnson	5.00	2.20	.60
☐ 44 Tim Salmon	5.00	2.20	.60
☐ 45 Frank Thomas	30.00	13.50	3.70
☐ 46 Albert Belle	12.00	5.50	1.50
☐ 47 Greg Vaughn	4.00	1.80	.50
☐ 48 Travis Fryman	3.00	1.35	.35
☐ 49 Don Mattingly	15.00	6.75	1.85
☐ 50 Wade Boggs	4.00	1.80	.50
☐ 51 Mo Vaughn	8.00	3.60	1.00
☐ 52 Kirby Puckett	12.00	5.50	1.50
☐ 53 Devon White	3.00	1.35	.35
☐ 54 Tony Phillips	2.00	.90	.25
☐ 55 Brian Harper	2.00	.90	.25
☐ 56 Chad Curtis	2.00	.90	.25
☐ 57 Paul Molitor	6.00	2.70	.75
☐ 58 Ivan Rodriguez	8.00	3.60	1.00
☐ 59 Rafael Palmeiro	4.00	1.80	.50
☐ 60 Brian McRae	3.00	1.35	.35

1994 Score Rookie/Traded Samples

Issued to preview the designs of Score's 1994 Rookie/Traded set and its inserts, these 11 standard-size cards feature color player action shots on their fronts. The Jackson card is from the one-per-pack Gold Rush insert set. The Palmeiro card represents the randomly inserted Changing Places insert set, and the Ramirez card is an example of the randomly inserted Super Rookies set. Except for the title card, all the cards carry the word "Sample" in diagonal white lettering on their fronts and backs. The cards are numbered on the back with prefixes as shown below.

	MINT	NRMT	EXC
COMPLETE SET (11)	12.00	5.50	1.50
COMMON CARD	.40	.18	.05
☐ CP2 Rafael Palmeiro	3.00	1.35	.35
☐ RT1 Will Clark	1.00	.45	.12
☐ RT2 Lee Smith	.60	.25	.07
☐ RT3 Bo Jackson	.60	.25	.07
☐ RT4 Ellis Burks	.60	.25	.07
☐ RT5 Eddie Murray	2.00	.90	.25
☐ RT6 Delino DeShields	.40	.18	.05
☐ RT102 Carlos Delgado	1.00	.45	.12
☐ SU2 Manny Ramirez	5.00	2.20	.60
☐ NNO Title Card	.40	.18	.05
☐ NNO September Call-Up Redemption Sample	.40	.18	.05

1994 Score Rookie/Traded

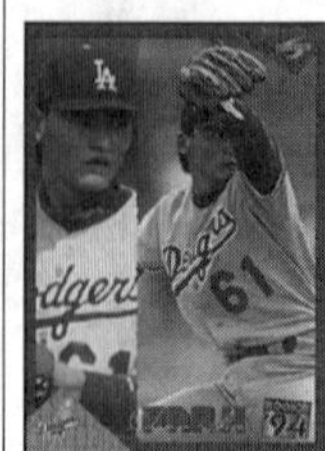
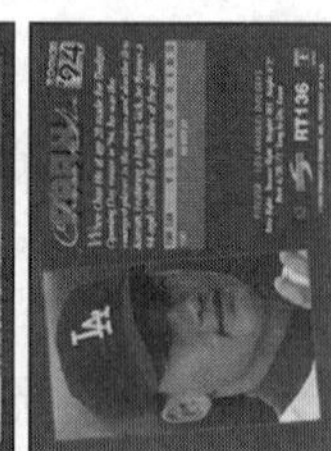

The 1994 Score Rookie and Traded set consists of 165 standard-size cards featuring rookie standouts, traded players, and new young prospects. The set is delineated by traded players (RT1-RT70) and rookies/young prospects (RT71-RT163). The set closes with checklists (RT164-RT165). Each foil pack contained one Gold Rush card. The cards are numbered on the back with an "RT" prefix. Several leading dealers are under the belief that Jose Lima's card (#RT158) was short-printed. A special unnumbered September Call-Up Redemption card could be exchanged for an Alex Rodriguez card. The expiration date was January 31, 1995. Odds of finding a redemption card are approximately one in 240 retail and hobby packs. Rookie Cards include John Mabry and Chan Ho Park.

	MINT	NRMT	EXC
COMPLETE SET (165)	10.00	4.50	1.25
COMMON CARD (RT1-RT165)	.05	.02	.01
☐ RT1 Will Clark	.30	.14	.04
☐ RT2 Lee Smith	.15	.07	.02
☐ RT3 Bo Jackson	.15	.07	.02
☐ RT4 Ellis Burks	.15	.07	.02
☐ RT5 Eddie Murray	.50	.23	.06
☐ RT6 Delino DeShields	.05	.02	.01
☐ RT7 Erik Hanson	.05	.02	.01
☐ RT8 Rafael Palmeiro	.30	.14	.04
☐ RT9 Luis Polonia	.05	.02	.01
☐ RT10 Omar Vizquel	.15	.07	.02
☐ RT11 Kurt Abbott	.15	.07	.02
☐ RT12 Vince Coleman	.05	.02	.01
☐ RT13 Rickey Henderson	.30	.14	.04
☐ RT14 Terry Mulholland	.05	.02	.01
☐ RT15 Greg Hibbard	.05	.02	.01
☐ RT16 Walt Weiss	.05	.02	.01
☐ RT17 Chris Sabo	.05	.02	.01
☐ RT18 Dave Henderson	.05	.02	.01
☐ RT19 Rick Sutcliffe	.05	.02	.01
☐ RT20 Harold Reynolds	.05	.02	.01
☐ RT21 Jack Morris	.15	.07	.02
☐ RT22 Dan Wilson	.15	.07	.02
☐ RT23 Dave Magadan	.05	.02	.01
☐ RT24 Dennis Martinez	.15	.07	.02
☐ RT25 Wes Chamberlain	.05	.02	.01
☐ RT26 Otis Nixon	.05	.02	.01
☐ RT27 Eric Anthony	.05	.02	.01
☐ RT28 Randy Milligan	.05	.02	.01
☐ RT29 Julio Franco	.15	.07	.02
☐ RT30 Kevin McReynolds	.05	.02	.01
☐ RT31 Anthony Young	.05	.02	.01
☐ RT32 Brian Harper	.05	.02	.01
☐ RT33 Gene Harris	.05	.02	.01
☐ RT34 Eddie Taubensee	.05	.02	.01
☐ RT35 David Segui	.05	.02	.01
☐ RT36 Stan Javier	.05	.02	.01
☐ RT37 Felix Fermin	.05	.02	.01
☐ RT38 Darrin Jackson	.05	.02	.01
☐ RT39 Tony Fernandez	.05	.02	.01
☐ RT40 Jose Vizcaino	.05	.02	.01
☐ RT41 Willie Banks	.05	.02	.01
☐ RT42 Brian Hunter	.05	.02	.01
☐ RT43 Reggie Jefferson	.15	.07	.02
☐ RT44 Junior Felix	.05	.02	.01
☐ RT45 Jack Armstrong	.05	.02	.01
☐ RT46 Bip Roberts	.05	.02	.01
☐ RT47 Jerry Browne	.05	.02	.01
☐ RT48 Marvin Freeman	.05	.02	.01
☐ RT49 Jody Reed	.05	.02	.01
☐ RT50 Alex Cole	.05	.02	.01
☐ RT51 Sid Fernandez	.05	.02	.01
☐ RT52 Pete Smith	.05	.02	.01
☐ RT53 Xavier Hernandez	.05	.02	.01
☐ RT54 Scott Sanderson	.05	.02	.01
☐ RT55 Turner Ward	.05	.02	.01
☐ RT56 Rex Hudler	.05	.02	.01
☐ RT57 Deion Sanders	.30	.14	.04
☐ RT58 Sid Bream	.05	.02	.01
☐ RT59 Tony Pena	.05	.02	.01
☐ RT60 Bret Boone	.15	.07	.02
☐ RT61 Bobby Ayala	.05	.02	.01
☐ RT62 Pedro Martinez	.30	.14	.04
☐ RT63 Howard Johnson	.05	.02	.01
☐ RT64 Mark Portugal	.05	.02	.01
☐ RT65 Roberto Kelly	.05	.02	.01
☐ RT66 Spike Owen	.05	.02	.01
☐ RT67 Jeff Treadway	.05	.02	.01
☐ RT68 Mike Harkey	.05	.02	.01
☐ RT69 Doug Jones	.05	.02	.01
☐ RT70 Steve Farr	.05	.02	.01
☐ RT71 Billy Taylor	.05	.02	.01
☐ RT72 Manny Ramirez	.60	.25	.07
☐ RT73 Bob Hamelin	.05	.02	.01
☐ RT74 Steve Karsay	.05	.02	.01
☐ RT75 Ryan Klesko	.40	.18	.05
☐ RT76 Cliff Floyd	.30	.14	.04
☐ RT77 Jeffrey Hammonds	.15	.07	.02
☐ RT78 Javier Lopez	.30	.14	.04
☐ RT79 Roger Salkeld	.05	.02	.01
☐ RT80 Hector Carrasco	.05	.02	.01
☐ RT81 Gerald Williams	.05	.02	.01
☐ RT82 Raul Mondesi	.30	.14	.04
☐ RT83 Sterling Hitchcock	.15	.07	.02
☐ RT84 Danny Bautista	.05	.02	.01
☐ RT85 Chris Turner	.05	.02	.01
☐ RT86 Shane Reynolds	.15	.07	.02
☐ RT87 Rondell White	.30	.14	.04
☐ RT88 Salomon Torres	.05	.02	.01
☐ RT89 Turk Wendell	.05	.02	.01
☐ RT90 Tony Tarasco	.05	.02	.01
☐ RT91 Shawn Green	.15	.07	.02
☐ RT92 Greg Colbrunn	.05	.02	.01
☐ RT93 Eddie Zambrano	.05	.02	.01
☐ RT94 Rich Becker	.15	.07	.02
☐ RT95 Chris Gomez	.05	.02	.01
☐ RT96 John Patterson	.05	.02	.01
☐ RT97 Derek Parks	.05	.02	.01
☐ RT98 Rich Rowland	.05	.02	.01
☐ RT99 James Mouton	.15	.07	.02
☐ RT100 Tim Hyers	.05	.02	.01
☐ RT101 Jose Valentin	.15	.07	.02
☐ RT102 Carlos Delgado	.30	.14	.04
☐ RT103 Robert Eenhoorn	.05	.02	.01
☐ RT104 John Hudek	.05	.02	.01
☐ RT105 Domingo Cedeno	.05	.02	.01
☐ RT106 Denny Hocking	.05	.02	.01
☐ RT107 Greg Pirkl	.05	.02	.01
☐ RT108 Mark Smith	.05	.02	.01
☐ RT109 Paul Shuey	.05	.02	.01
☐ RT110 Jorge Fabregas	.05	.02	.01
☐ RT111 Rikkert Faneyte	.05	.02	.01
☐ RT112 Rob Butler	.05	.02	.01
☐ RT113 Darren Oliver	.05	.02	.01
☐ RT114 Troy O'Leary	.05	.02	.01
☐ RT115 Scott Brow	.05	.02	.01
☐ RT116 Tony Eusebio	.05	.02	.01
☐ RT117 Carlos Reyes	.05	.02	.01
☐ RT118 J.R. Phillips	.05	.02	.01
☐ RT119 Alex Diaz	.05	.02	.01
☐ RT120 Charles Johnson	.30	.14	.04
☐ RT121 Nate Minchey	.05	.02	.01
☐ RT122 Scott Sanders	.05	.02	.01
☐ RT123 Daryl Boston	.05	.02	.01
☐ RT124 Joey Hamilton	.40	.18	.05
☐ RT125 Brian Anderson	.15	.07	.02
☐ RT126 Dan Miceli	.05	.02	.01
☐ RT127 Tom Brunansky	.05	.02	.01
☐ RT128 Dave Staton	.05	.02	.01
☐ RT129 Mike Oquist	.05	.02	.01
☐ RT130 John Mabry	.15	.07	.02
☐ RT131 Norberto Martin	.05	.02	.01
☐ RT132 Hector Fajardo	.05	.02	.01
☐ RT133 Mark Hutton	.05	.02	.01
☐ RT134 Fernando Vina	.05	.02	.01
☐ RT135 Lee Tinsley	.15	.07	.02
☐ RT136 Chan Ho Park	.60	.25	.07
☐ RT137 Paul Spoljaric	.05	.02	.01
☐ RT138 Matias Carrillo	.05	.02	.01
☐ RT139 Mark Kiefer	.05	.02	.01
☐ RT140 Stan Royer	.05	.02	.01
☐ RT141 Bryan Eversgerd	.05	.02	.01
☐ RT142 Brian L.Hunter	.30	.14	.04
☐ RT143 Joe Hall	.05	.02	.01
☐ RT144 Johnny Ruffin	.05	.02	.01
☐ RT145 Alex Gonzalez	.15	.07	.02
☐ RT146 Keith Lockhart	.05	.02	.01
☐ RT147 Tom Marsh	.05	.02	.01
☐ RT148 Tony Longmire	.05	.02	.01
☐ RT149 Keith Mitchell	.05	.02	.01
☐ RT150 Melvin Nieves	.15	.07	.02
☐ RT151 Kelly Stinnett	.05	.02	.01
☐ RT152 Miguel Jimenez	.05	.02	.01
☐ RT153 Jeff Juden	.05	.02	.01
☐ RT154 Matt Walbeck	.05	.02	.01
☐ RT155 Marc Newfield	.15	.07	.02
☐ RT156 Matt Mieske	.05	.02	.01
☐ RT157 Marcus Moore	.05	.02	.01
☐ RT158 Jose Lima SP	1.00	.45	.12
☐ RT159 Mike Kelly	.05	.02	.01
☐ RT160 Jim Edmonds	.40	.18	.05
☐ RT161 Steve Trachsel	.15	.07	.02
☐ RT162 Greg Blosser	.05	.02	.01
☐ RT163 Marc Acre	.05	.02	.01
☐ RT164 AL Checklist	.05	.02	.01
☐ RT165 NL Checklist	.05	.02	.01
☐ HC1 Alex Rodriguez Call-Up Redemption	60.00	27.00	7.50

1994 Score Rookie/Traded Gold Rush

Issued one per pack, these cards are a gold foil version of the 165-card Rookie/Traded set. The differences between the basic card and Gold Rush version are the gold foil borders that surround a metallicized player photo. The only difference on the back is a Gold Rush logo.

	MINT	NRMT	EXC
COMPLETE SET (165)	50.00	22.00	6.25
COMMON CARD (RT1-RT165)	.25	.11	.03

*STARS: 2.5X TO 5X BASIC CARDS ..
*YOUNG STARS: 2X TO 4X BASIC CARDS

1994 Score Rookie/Traded Changing Places

Randomly inserted in both retail and hobby packs at a rate of one in 36 Rookie/Traded packs, this 10-card standard-size set focuses on ten veteran superstar players who were traded prior to or during the 1994 season. Cards fronts feature a color photo with a slanted design. The backs have a short write-up and a distorted photo.

	MINT	NRMT	EXC
COMPLETE SET (10)	30.00	13.50	3.70
COMMON CARD (CP1-CP10)	2.50	1.10	.30
☐ CP1 Will Clark	8.00	3.60	1.00
☐ CP2 Rafael Palmeiro	8.00	3.60	1.00
☐ CP3 Roberto Kelly	2.50	1.10	.30
☐ CP4 Bo Jackson	3.00	1.35	.35
☐ CP5 Otis Nixon	2.50	1.10	.30
☐ CP6 Rickey Henderson	5.00	2.20	.60
☐ CP7 Ellis Burks	3.00	1.35	.35
☐ CP8 Lee Smith	3.00	1.35	.35
☐ CP9 Delino DeShields	2.50	1.10	.30
☐ CP10 Deion Sanders	5.00	2.20	.60

1994 Score Rookie/Traded Super Rookies

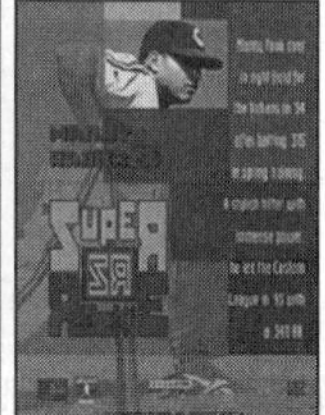

Randomly inserted in hobby packs at a rate of one in 36, this 18-card standard-size set focuses on top rookies of 1994. Odds of finding one of these cards is approximately one in 36 hobby packs. Designed much like the Gold Rush, the cards have an all-foil design. The fronts have a player photo and the backs have a photo that serves as background to the Super Rookies logo and text.

	MINT	NRMT	EXC
COMPLETE SET (18)	80.00	36.00	10.00
COMMON CARD (SU1-SU18)	2.50	1.10	.30
☐ SU1 Carlos Delgado	6.00	2.70	.75
☐ SU2 Manny Ramirez	15.00	6.75	1.85
☐ SU3 Ryan Klesko	10.00	4.50	1.25
☐ SU4 Raul Mondesi	8.00	3.60	1.00
☐ SU5 Bob Hamelin	2.50	1.10	.30
☐ SU6 Steve Karsay	2.50	1.10	.30
☐ SU7 Jeffrey Hammonds	4.00	1.80	.50
☐ SU8 Cliff Floyd	4.00	1.80	.50
☐ SU9 Kurt Abbott	2.50	1.10	.30
☐ SU10 Marc Newfield	4.00	1.80	.50
☐ SU11 Javier Lopez	6.00	2.70	.75
☐ SU12 Rich Becker	2.50	1.10	.30
☐ SU13 Greg Pirkl	2.50	1.10	.30
☐ SU14 Rondell White	5.00	2.20	.60
☐ SU15 James Mouton	2.50	1.10	.30
☐ SU16 Tony Tarasco	2.50	1.10	.30
☐ SU17 Brian Anderson	2.50	1.10	.30
☐ SU18 Jim Edmonds	8.00	3.60	1.00

1995 Score Samples

These ten sample cards were issued to herald the release of the 1995 Score baseball series. The standard-size cards feature on their horizontal and vertical fronts color action player shots with irregular dark green and sand brown borders. The player's name, position and the team logo appear in a blue bar under the picture. The word "Sample" is printed diagonally over the photo. The horizontal backs have the same design as the fronts. They carry another small color headshot on the left, with the player's name, short biography, career highlights and statistics on the right. The word "Sample" is also printed diagonally across the backs.

	MINT	NRMT	EXC
COMPLETE SET (10)	12.00	5.50	1.50
COMMON CARD	.25	.11	.03
☐ 2 Roberto Alomar	1.00	.45	.12
☐ 4 Jose Canseco	.75	.35	.09
☐ 5 Matt Williams	.75	.35	.09
☐ 221 Jeff Bagwell	1.50	.70	.19
☐ 223 Albert Belle	2.00	.90	.25
☐ 224 Chuck Carr	.25	.11	.03
☐ 288 Jorge Fabregas	.25	.11	.03
☐ DP8 McKay Christensen	1.50	.70	.19
☐ HG5 Cal Ripken	6.00	2.70	.75
☐ NNO Title Card	.25	.11	.03

1995 Score

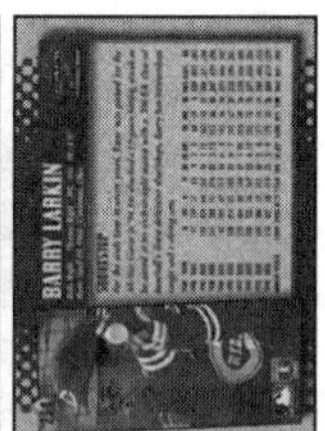

The 1995 Score set consists of 605 standard-size cards issued in hobby, retail and jumbo packs. The horizontal and vertical fronts feature color action player shots with irregular dark green and sand brown borders. The player's name, position and the team logo appear in a blue bar under the photo. The horizontal backs have the same design as the fronts. They carry another small color headshot on the left, with the player's name, short biography, career highlights and statistics on the right. Hobby packs featured a special signed Ryan Klesko (RG1)card. Retail packs also had a Klesko card (SG1) but these were not signed. There are no key Rookie Cards in this set.

	MINT	NRMT	EXC
COMPLETE SET (605)	24.00	11.00	3.00
COMPLETE SERIES 1 (330)	12.00	5.50	1.50
COMPLETE SERIES 2 (275)	12.00	5.50	1.50
COMMON CARD (1-605)	.05	.02	.01
☐ 1 Frank Thomas	2.00	.90	.25
☐ 2 Roberto Alomar	.40	.18	.05
☐ 3 Cal Ripken	1.50	.70	.19
☐ 4 Jose Canseco	.30	.14	.04
☐ 5 Matt Williams	.30	.14	.04
☐ 6 Esteban Beltre	.05	.02	.01
☐ 7 Domingo Cedeno	.05	.02	.01
☐ 8 John Valentin	.15	.07	.02
☐ 9 Glenallen Hill	.05	.02	.01
☐ 10 Rafael Belliard	.05	.02	.01
☐ 11 Randy Myers	.05	.02	.01
☐ 12 Mo Vaughn	.50	.23	.06
☐ 13 Hector Carrasco	.05	.02	.01
☐ 14 Chili Davis	.15	.07	.02
☐ 15 Dante Bichette	.30	.14	.04
☐ 16 Darrin Jackson	.05	.02	.01
☐ 17 Mike Piazza	1.25	.55	.16
☐ 18 Junior Felix	.05	.02	.01
☐ 19 Moises Alou	.15	.07	.02
☐ 20 Mark Gubicza	.05	.02	.01
☐ 21 Bret Saberhagen	.15	.07	.02
☐ 22 Lenny Dykstra	.15	.07	.02
☐ 23 Steve Howe	.05	.02	.01
☐ 24 Mark Dewey	.05	.02	.01
☐ 25 Brian Harper	.05	.02	.01
☐ 26 Ozzie Smith	.50	.23	.06
☐ 27 Scott Erickson	.05	.02	.01
☐ 28 Tony Gwynn	.75	.35	.09
☐ 29 Bob Welch	.05	.02	.01
☐ 30 Barry Bonds	.50	.23	.06
☐ 31 Leo Gomez	.05	.02	.01
☐ 32 Greg Maddux	1.25	.55	.16
☐ 33 Mike Greenwell	.05	.02	.01
☐ 34 Sammy Sosa	.30	.14	.04
☐ 35 Darnell Coles	.05	.02	.01
☐ 36 Tommy Greene	.05	.02	.01
☐ 37 Will Clark	.30	.14	.04
☐ 38 Steve Ontiveros	.05	.02	.01
☐ 39 Stan Javier	.05	.02	.01
☐ 40 Bip Roberts	.05	.02	.01
☐ 41 Paul O'Neill	.15	.07	.02
☐ 42 Bill Haselman	.05	.02	.01
☐ 43 Shane Mack	.05	.02	.01
☐ 44 Orlando Merced	.05	.02	.01
☐ 45 Kevin Seitzer	.05	.02	.01
☐ 46 Trevor Hoffman	.15	.07	.02
☐ 47 Greg Gagne	.05	.02	.01
☐ 48 Jeff Kent	.05	.02	.01
☐ 49 Tony Phillips	.15	.07	.02
☐ 50 Ken Hill	.05	.02	.01
☐ 51 Carlos Baerga	.15	.07	.02
☐ 52 Henry Rodriguez	.15	.07	.02
☐ 53 Scott Sanderson	.05	.02	.01
☐ 54 Jeff Conine	.15	.07	.02
☐ 55 Chris Turner	.05	.02	.01
☐ 56 Ken Caminiti	.30	.14	.04
☐ 57 Harold Baines	.15	.07	.02
☐ 58 Charlie Hayes	.05	.02	.01
☐ 59 Roberto Kelly	.05	.02	.01
☐ 60 John Olerud	.05	.02	.01
☐ 61 Tim Davis	.05	.02	.01
☐ 62 Rich Rowland	.05	.02	.01
☐ 63 Rey Sanchez	.05	.02	.01
☐ 64 Junior Ortiz	.05	.02	.01
☐ 65 Ricky Gutierrez	.05	.02	.01
☐ 66 Rex Hudler	.05	.02	.01
☐ 67 Johnny Ruffin	.05	.02	.01
☐ 68 Jay Buhner	.30	.14	.04
☐ 69 Tom Pagnozzi	.05	.02	.01
☐ 70 Julio Franco	.15	.07	.02
☐ 71 Eric Young	.15	.07	.02
☐ 72 Mike Bordick	.05	.02	.01
☐ 73 Don Slaught	.05	.02	.01
☐ 74 Goose Gossage	.15	.07	.02
☐ 75 Lonnie Smith	.05	.02	.01
☐ 76 Jimmy Key	.15	.07	.02
☐ 77 Dave Hollins	.05	.02	.01
☐ 78 Mickey Tettleton	.05	.02	.01
☐ 79 Luis Gonzalez	.05	.02	.01
☐ 80 Dave Winfield	.30	.14	.04
☐ 81 Ryan Thompson	.05	.02	.01
☐ 82 Felix Jose	.05	.02	.01
☐ 83 Rusty Meacham	.05	.02	.01
☐ 84 Darryl Hamilton	.05	.02	.01
☐ 85 John Wetteland	.15	.07	.02
☐ 86 Tom Brunansky	.05	.02	.01
☐ 87 Mark Lemke	.05	.02	.01
☐ 88 Spike Owen	.05	.02	.01
☐ 89 Shawon Dunston	.05	.02	.01
☐ 90 Wilson Alvarez	.15	.07	.02
☐ 91 Lee Smith	.15	.07	.02
☐ 92 Scott Kamieniecki	.05	.02	.01
☐ 93 Jacob Brumfield	.05	.02	.01
☐ 94 Kirk Gibson	.15	.07	.02
☐ 95 Joe Girardi	.05	.02	.01
☐ 96 Mike Macfarlane	.05	.02	.01
☐ 97 Greg Colbrunn	.05	.02	.01
☐ 98 Ricky Bones	.05	.02	.01
☐ 99 Delino DeShields	.05	.02	.01
☐ 100 Pat Meares	.05	.02	.01
☐ 101 Jeff Fassero	.05	.02	.01
☐ 102 Jim Leyritz	.05	.02	.01
☐ 103 Gary Redus	.05	.02	.01
☐ 104 Terry Steinbach	.15	.07	.02
☐ 105 Kevin McReynolds	.05	.02	.01
☐ 106 Felix Fermin	.05	.02	.01
☐ 107 Danny Jackson	.05	.02	.01
☐ 108 Chris James	.05	.02	.01
☐ 109 Jeff King	.15	.07	.02
☐ 110 Pat Hentgen	.15	.07	.02
☐ 111 Gerald Perry	.05	.02	.01
☐ 112 Tim Raines	.30	.14	.04
☐ 113 Eddie Williams	.05	.02	.01
☐ 114 Jamie Moyer	.05	.02	.01
☐ 115 Bud Black	.05	.02	.01
☐ 116 Chris Gomez	.05	.02	.01
☐ 117 Luis Lopez	.05	.02	.01
☐ 118 Roger Clemens	.40	.18	.05
☐ 119 Javier Lopez	.30	.14	.04
☐ 120 Dave Nilsson	.15	.07	.02
☐ 121 Karl Rhodes	.05	.02	.01
☐ 122 Rick Aguilera	.05	.02	.01
☐ 123 Tony Fernandez	.05	.02	.01
☐ 124 Bernie Williams	.40	.18	.05
☐ 125 James Mouton	.05	.02	.01
☐ 126 Mark Langston	.05	.02	.01
☐ 127 Mike Lansing	.05	.02	.01
☐ 128 Tino Martinez	.15	.07	.02
☐ 129 Joe Orsulak	.05	.02	.01
☐ 130 David Hulse	.05	.02	.01
☐ 131 Pete Incaviglia	.05	.02	.01
☐ 132 Mark Clark	.05	.02	.01
☐ 133 Tony Eusebio	.05	.02	.01
☐ 134 Chuck Finley	.15	.07	.02
☐ 135 Lou Frazier	.05	.02	.01
☐ 136 Craig Grebeck	.05	.02	.01
☐ 137 Kelly Stinnett	.05	.02	.01
☐ 138 Paul Shuey	.05	.02	.01
☐ 139 David Nied	.05	.02	.01
☐ 140 Billy Brewer	.05	.02	.01
☐ 141 Dave Weathers	.05	.02	.01
☐ 142 Scott Leius	.05	.02	.01
☐ 143 Brian Jordan	.30	.14	.04
☐ 144 Melido Perez	.05	.02	.01
☐ 145 Tony Tarasco	.05	.02	.01
☐ 146 Dan Wilson	.15	.07	.02
☐ 147 Rondell White	.15	.07	.02
☐ 148 Mike Henneman	.05	.02	.01
☐ 149 Brian Johnson	.05	.02	.01
☐ 150 Tom Henke	.05	.02	.01
☐ 151 John Patterson	.05	.02	.01
☐ 152 Bobby Witt	.05	.02	.01
☐ 153 Eddie Taubensee	.05	.02	.01
☐ 154 Pat Borders	.05	.02	.01
☐ 155 Ramon Martinez	.15	.07	.02
☐ 156 Mike Kingery	.05	.02	.01
☐ 157 Zane Smith	.05	.02	.01
☐ 158 Benito Santiago	.05	.02	.01
☐ 159 Matias Carrillo	.05	.02	.01
☐ 160 Scott Brosius	.05	.02	.01
☐ 161 Dave Clark	.05	.02	.01
☐ 162 Mark McLemore	.05	.02	.01
☐ 163 Curt Schilling	.05	.02	.01
☐ 164 J.T. Snow	.15	.07	.02
☐ 165 Rod Beck	.05	.02	.01
☐ 166 Scott Fletcher	.05	.02	.01
☐ 167 Bob Tewksbury	.05	.02	.01
☐ 168 Mike LaValliere	.05	.02	.01
☐ 169 Dave Hansen	.05	.02	.01
☐ 170 Pedro Martinez	.15	.07	.02
☐ 171 Kirk Rueter	.05	.02	.01
☐ 172 Jose Lind	.05	.02	.01
☐ 173 Luis Alicea	.05	.02	.01
☐ 174 Mike Moore	.05	.02	.01
☐ 175 Andy Ashby	.15	.07	.02
☐ 176 Jody Reed	.05	.02	.01
☐ 177 Darryl Kile	.05	.02	.01
☐ 178 Carl Willis	.05	.02	.01
☐ 179 Jeromy Burnitz	.05	.02	.01
☐ 180 Mike Gallego	.05	.02	.01
☐ 181 Bill VanLandingham	.05	.02	.01
☐ 182 Sid Fernandez	.05	.02	.01
☐ 183 Kim Batiste	.05	.02	.01
☐ 184 Greg Myers	.05	.02	.01
☐ 185 Steve Avery	.15	.07	.02
☐ 186 Steve Farr	.05	.02	.01
☐ 187 Robb Nen	.05	.02	.01
☐ 188 Dan Pasqua	.05	.02	.01
☐ 189 Bruce Ruffin	.05	.02	.01
☐ 190 Jose Valentin	.15	.07	.02
☐ 191 Willie Banks	.05	.02	.01
☐ 192 Mike Aldrete	.05	.02	.01
☐ 193 Randy Milligan	.05	.02	.01
☐ 194 Steve Karsay	.05	.02	.01
☐ 195 Mike Stanley	.05	.02	.01
☐ 196 Jose Mesa	.05	.02	.01
☐ 197 Tom Browning	.05	.02	.01
☐ 198 John Vander Wal	.05	.02	.01
☐ 199 Kevin Brown	.15	.07	.02
☐ 200 Mike Oquist	.05	.02	.01
☐ 201 Greg Swindell	.05	.02	.01
☐ 202 Eddie Zambrano	.05	.02	.01
☐ 203 Joe Boever	.05	.02	.01
☐ 204 Gary Varsho	.05	.02	.01
☐ 205 Chris Gwynn	.05	.02	.01
☐ 206 David Howard	.05	.02	.01
☐ 207 Jerome Walton	.05	.02	.01
☐ 208 Danny Darwin	.05	.02	.01
☐ 209 Darryl Strawberry	.15	.07	.02
☐ 210 Todd Van Poppel	.05	.02	.01
☐ 211 Scott Livingstone	.05	.02	.01
☐ 212 Dave Fleming	.05	.02	.01
☐ 213 Todd Worrell	.05	.02	.01
☐ 214 Carlos Delgado	.15	.07	.02
☐ 215 Bill Pecota	.05	.02	.01
☐ 216 Jim Lindeman	.05	.02	.01
☐ 217 Rick White	.05	.02	.01
☐ 218 Jose Oquendo	.05	.02	.01
☐ 219 Tony Castillo	.05	.02	.01
☐ 220 Fernando Vina	.05	.02	.01
☐ 221 Jeff Bagwell	.75	.35	.09
☐ 222 Randy Johnson	.30	.14	.04
☐ 223 Albert Belle	.75	.35	.09
☐ 224 Chuck Carr	.05	.02	.01
☐ 225 Mark Leiter	.05	.02	.01
☐ 226 Hal Morris	.05	.02	.01
☐ 227 Robin Ventura	.15	.07	.02
☐ 228 Mike Munoz	.05	.02	.01
☐ 229 Jim Thome	.40	.18	.05
☐ 230 Mario Diaz	.05	.02	.01
☐ 231 John Doherty	.05	.02	.01
☐ 232 Bobby Jones	.15	.07	.02
☐ 233 Raul Mondesi	.30	.14	.04
☐ 234 Ricky Jordan	.05	.02	.01

□ 235 John Jaha .15 .07 .02
□ 236 Carlos Garcia .05 .02 .01
□ 237 Kirby Puckett .75 .35 .09
□ 238 Orel Hershiser .15 .07 .02
□ 239 Don Mattingly 1.00 .45 .12
□ 240 Sid Bream .05 .02 .01
□ 241 Brent Gates .05 .02 .01
□ 242 Tony Longmire .05 .02 .01
□ 243 Robby Thompson .05 .02 .01
□ 244 Rick Sutcliffe .05 .02 .01
□ 245 Dean Palmer .15 .07 .02
□ 246 Marquis Grissom .15 .07 .02
□ 247 Paul Molitor .40 .18 .05
□ 248 Mark Carreon .05 .02 .01
□ 249 Jack Voigt .05 .02 .01
□ 250 Greg McMichael UER .05 .02 .01
(photo on front is Mike Stanton)
□ 251 Damon Berryhill .05 .02 .01
□ 252 Brian Dorsett .05 .02 .01
□ 253 Jim Edmonds .30 .14 .04
□ 254 Barry Larkin .30 .14 .04
□ 255 Jack McDowell .15 .07 .02
□ 256 Wally Joyner .15 .07 .02
□ 257 Eddie Murray .50 .23 .06
□ 258 Lenny Webster .05 .02 .01
□ 259 Milt Cuyler .05 .02 .01
□ 260 Todd Benzinger .05 .02 .01
□ 261 Vince Coleman .05 .02 .01
□ 262 Todd Stottlemyre .05 .02 .01
□ 263 Turner Ward .05 .02 .01
□ 264 Ray Lankford .15 .07 .02
□ 265 Matt Walbeck .05 .02 .01
□ 266 Deion Sanders .30 .14 .04
□ 267 Gerald Williams .05 .02 .01
□ 268 Jim Gott .05 .02 .01
□ 269 Jeff Frye .05 .02 .01
□ 270 Jose Rijo .05 .02 .01
□ 271 Dave Justice .30 .14 .04
□ 272 Ismael Valdes .15 .07 .02
□ 273 Ben McDonald .05 .02 .01
□ 274 Darren Lewis .05 .02 .01
□ 275 Graeme Lloyd .05 .02 .01
□ 276 Luis Ortiz .05 .02 .01
□ 277 Julian Tavarez .05 .02 .01
□ 278 Mark Dalesandro .05 .02 .01
□ 279 Brett Merriman .05 .02 .01
□ 280 Ricky Bottalico .15 .07 .02
□ 281 Robert Eenhoorn .05 .02 .01
□ 282 Rikkert Faneyte .05 .02 .01
□ 283 Mike Kelly .05 .02 .01
□ 284 Mark Smith .05 .02 .01
□ 285 Turk Wendell .05 .02 .01
□ 286 Greg Blosser .05 .02 .01
□ 287 Garey Ingram .05 .02 .01
□ 288 Jorge Fabregas .05 .02 .01
□ 289 Blaise Ilsley .05 .02 .01
□ 290 Joe Hall .05 .02 .01
□ 291 Orlando Miller .05 .02 .01
□ 292 Jose Lima .05 .02 .01
□ 293 Greg O'Halloran .05 .02 .01
□ 294 Mark Kiefer .05 .02 .01
□ 295 Jose Oliva .05 .02 .01
□ 296 Rich Becker .05 .02 .01
□ 297 Brian L. Hunter .15 .07 .02
□ 298 Dave Silvestri .05 .02 .01
□ 299 Armando Benitez .05 .02 .01
□ 300 Darren Dreifort .05 .02 .01
□ 301 John Mabry .30 .14 .04
□ 302 Greg Pirkl .05 .02 .01
□ 303 J.R. Phillips .05 .02 .01
□ 304 Shawn Green .15 .07 .02
□ 305 Roberto Petagine .05 .02 .01
□ 306 Keith Lockhart .05 .02 .01
□ 307 Jonathan Hurst .05 .02 .01
□ 308 Paul Spoljaric .05 .02 .01
□ 309 Mike Lieberthal .05 .02 .01
□ 310 Garret Anderson .15 .07 .02
□ 311 John Johnstone .05 .02 .01
□ 312 Alex Rodriguez 2.50 1.10 .30
□ 313 Kent Mercker HL .05 .02 .01
□ 314 John Valentin HL .05 .02 .01
□ 315 Kenny Rogers HL .05 .02 .01
□ 316 Fred McGriff HL .30 .14 .04
□ 317 Team Checklists .05 .02 .01
□ 318 Team Checklists .05 .02 .01
□ 319 Team Checklists .05 .02 .01
□ 320 Team Checklists .05 .02 .01
□ 321 Team Checklists .05 .02 .01
□ 322 Team Checklists .05 .02 .01
□ 323 Team Checklists .05 .02 .01
□ 324 Team Checklists .05 .02 .01
□ 325 Team Checklists .05 .02 .01
□ 326 Team Checklists .05 .02 .01
□ 327 Team Checklists .05 .02 .01
□ 328 Team Checklists .05 .02 .01
□ 329 Team Checklists .05 .02 .01
□ 330 Team Checklists .05 .02 .01
□ 331 Pedro Munoz .05 .02 .01
□ 332 Ryan Klesko .30 .14 .04
□ 333 Andre Dawson .15 .07 .02
□ 334 Derrick May .05 .02 .01
□ 335 Aaron Sele .15 .07 .02
□ 336 Kevin Mitchell .15 .07 .02
□ 337 Steve Trachsel .05 .02 .01
□ 338 Andres Galarraga .30 .14 .04
□ 339 Terry Pendleton .15 .07 .02
□ 340 Gary Sheffield .30 .14 .04
□ 341 Travis Fryman .15 .07 .02
□ 342 Bo Jackson .15 .07 .02
□ 343 Gary Gaetti .15 .07 .02
□ 344 Brett Butler .15 .07 .02
□ 345 B.J. Surhoff .15 .07 .02
□ 346 Larry Walker .30 .14 .04
□ 347 Kevin Tapani .05 .02 .01
□ 348 Rick Wilkins .05 .02 .01
□ 349 Wade Boggs .30 .14 .04
□ 350 Mariano Duncan .05 .02 .01
□ 351 Ruben Sierra .15 .07 .02
□ 352 Andy Van Slyke .15 .07 .02
□ 353 Reggie Jefferson .15 .07 .02
□ 354 Gregg Jefferies .15 .07 .02
□ 355 Tim Naehring .05 .02 .01
□ 356 John Roper .05 .02 .01
□ 357 Joe Carter .15 .07 .02
□ 358 Kurt Abbott .05 .02 .01
□ 359 Lenny Harris .05 .02 .01
□ 360 Lance Johnson .15 .07 .02
□ 361 Brian Anderson .05 .02 .01
□ 362 Jim Eisenreich .05 .02 .01
□ 363 Jerry Browne .05 .02 .01
□ 364 Mark Grace .30 .14 .04
□ 365 Devon White .15 .07 .02
□ 366 Reggie Sanders .15 .07 .02
□ 367 Ivan Rodriguez .50 .23 .06
□ 368 Kirt Manwaring .05 .02 .01
□ 369 Pat Kelly .05 .02 .01
□ 370 Ellis Burks .15 .07 .02
□ 371 Charles Nagy .15 .07 .02
□ 372 Kevin Bass .05 .02 .01
□ 373 Lou Whitaker .15 .07 .02
□ 374 Rene Arocha .05 .02 .01
□ 375 Derek Parks .05 .02 .01
□ 376 Mark Whiten .05 .02 .01
□ 377 Mark McGwire .60 .25 .07
□ 378 Doug Drabek .05 .02 .01
□ 379 Greg Vaughn .15 .07 .02
□ 380 Al Martin .15 .07 .02
□ 381 Ron Darling .05 .02 .01
□ 382 Tim Wallach .05 .02 .01
□ 383 Alan Trammell .15 .07 .02
□ 384 Randy Velarde .05 .02 .01
□ 385 Chris Sabo .05 .02 .01
□ 386 Wil Cordero .05 .02 .01
□ 387 Darrin Fletcher .05 .02 .01
□ 388 David Segui .05 .02 .01
□ 389 Steve Buechele .05 .02 .01
□ 390 Dave Gallagher .05 .02 .01
□ 391 Thomas Howard .05 .02 .01
□ 392 Chad Curtis .05 .02 .01
□ 393 Cal Eldred .05 .02 .01
□ 394 Jason Bere .05 .02 .01
□ 395 Bret Barberie .05 .02 .01
□ 396 Paul Sorrento .05 .02 .01
□ 397 Steve Finley .15 .07 .02
□ 398 Cecil Fielder .15 .07 .02
□ 399 Eric Karros .15 .07 .02
□ 400 Jeff Montgomery .15 .07 .02
□ 401 Cliff Floyd .15 .07 .02
□ 402 Matt Mieske .15 .07 .02
□ 403 Brian Hunter .05 .02 .01
□ 404 Alex Cole .05 .02 .01
□ 405 Kevin Stocker .05 .02 .01
□ 406 Eric Davis .15 .07 .02
□ 407 Marvin Freeman .05 .02 .01
□ 408 Dennis Eckersley .15 .07 .02
□ 409 Todd Zeile .05 .02 .01
□ 410 Keith Mitchell .05 .02 .01
□ 411 Andy Benes .05 .02 .01
□ 412 Juan Bell .05 .02 .01
□ 413 Royce Clayton .05 .02 .01
□ 414 Ed Sprague .15 .07 .02
□ 415 Mike Mussina .40 .18 .05
□ 416 Todd Hundley .15 .07 .02
□ 417 Pat Listach .05 .02 .01
□ 418 Joe Oliver .05 .02 .01
□ 419 Rafael Palmeiro .30 .14 .04
□ 420 Tim Salmon .30 .14 .04
□ 421 Brady Anderson .30 .14 .04
□ 422 Kenny Lofton .50 .23 .06
□ 423 Craig Biggio .15 .07 .02
□ 424 Bobby Bonilla .15 .07 .02
□ 425 Kenny Rogers .05 .02 .01
□ 426 Derek Bell .15 .07 .02
□ 427 Scott Cooper .05 .02 .01
□ 428 Ozzie Guillen .05 .02 .01
□ 429 Omar Vizquel .15 .07 .02
□ 430 Phil Plantier .05 .02 .01
□ 431 Chuck Knoblauch .30 .14 .04
□ 432 Darren Daulton .15 .07 .02
□ 433 Bob Hamelin .05 .02 .01
□ 434 Tom Glavine .30 .14 .04
□ 435 Walt Weiss .05 .02 .01
□ 436 Jose Vizcaino .05 .02 .01
□ 437 Ken Griffey Jr. 2.00 .90 .25
□ 438 Jay Bell .15 .07 .02
□ 439 Juan Gonzalez 1.00 .45 .12
□ 440 Jeff Blauser .05 .02 .01
□ 441 Rickey Henderson .30 .14 .04
□ 442 Bobby Ayala .05 .02 .01
□ 443 David Cone .15 .07 .02
□ 444 Pedro J. Martinez .15 .07 .02
□ 445 Manny Ramirez .50 .23 .06
□ 446 Mark Portugal .05 .02 .01
□ 447 Damion Easley .05 .02 .01
□ 448 Gary DiSarcina .05 .02 .01
□ 449 Roberto Hernandez .05 .02 .01
□ 450 Jeffrey Hammonds .15 .07 .02
□ 451 Jeff Treadway .05 .02 .01
□ 452 Jim Abbott .05 .02 .01
□ 453 Carlos Rodriguez .05 .02 .01
□ 454 Joey Cora .05 .02 .01
□ 455 Bret Boone .15 .07 .02
□ 456 Danny Tartabull .05 .02 .01
□ 457 John Franco .05 .02 .01
□ 458 Roger Salkeld .05 .02 .01
□ 459 Fred McGriff .30 .14 .04
□ 460 Pedro Astacio .05 .02 .01
□ 461 Jon Lieber .05 .02 .01
□ 462 Luis Polonia .05 .02 .01
□ 463 Geronimo Pena .05 .02 .01
□ 464 Tom Gordon .05 .02 .01
□ 465 Brad Ausmus .05 .02 .01
□ 466 Willie McGee .05 .02 .01
□ 467 Doug Jones .05 .02 .01
□ 468 John Smoltz .30 .14 .04
□ 469 Troy Neel .05 .02 .01
□ 470 Luis Sojo .05 .02 .01
□ 471 John Smiley .05 .02 .01
□ 472 Rafael Bournigal .05 .02 .01
□ 473 Bill Taylor .05 .02 .01
□ 474 Juan Guzman .15 .07 .02
□ 475 Dave Magadan .05 .02 .01
□ 476 Mike Devereaux .05 .02 .01
□ 477 Andujar Cedeno .05 .02 .01
□ 478 Edgar Martinez .15 .07 .02
□ 479 Milt Thompson .05 .02 .01
□ 480 Allen Watson .05 .02 .01
□ 481 Ron Karkovice .05 .02 .01
□ 482 Joey Hamilton .30 .14 .04
□ 483 Vinny Castilla .15 .07 .02
□ 484 Tim Belcher .15 .07 .02
□ 485 Bernard Gilkey .15 .07 .02
□ 486 Scott Servais .05 .02 .01
□ 487 Cory Snyder .05 .02 .01
□ 488 Mel Rojas .05 .02 .01
□ 489 Carlos Reyes .05 .02 .01
□ 490 Chip Hale .05 .02 .01
□ 491 Bill Swift .05 .02 .01
□ 492 Pat Rapp .05 .02 .01
□ 493 Brian McRae .15 .07 .02
□ 494 Mickey Morandini .05 .02 .01
□ 495 Tony Pena .05 .02 .01
□ 496 Danny Bautista .05 .02 .01
□ 497 Armando Reynoso .05 .02 .01
□ 498 Ken Ryan .05 .02 .01
□ 499 Billy Ripken .05 .02 .01
□ 500 Pat Mahomes .05 .02 .01
□ 501 Mark Acre .05 .02 .01
□ 502 Geronimo Berroa .05 .02 .01
□ 503 Norberto Martin .05 .02 .01
□ 504 Chad Kreuter .05 .02 .01
□ 505 Howard Johnson .05 .02 .01
□ 506 Eric Anthony .05 .02 .01
□ 507 Mark Wohlers .15 .07 .02
□ 508 Scott Sanders .05 .02 .01
□ 509 Pete Harnisch .05 .02 .01
□ 510 Wes Chamberlain .05 .02 .01
□ 511 Tom Candiotti .05 .02 .01
□ 512 Albie Lopez .05 .02 .01
□ 513 Denny Neagle .15 .07 .02
□ 514 Sean Berry .05 .02 .01
□ 515 Billy Hatcher .05 .02 .01
□ 516 Todd Jones .05 .02 .01
□ 517 Wayne Kirby .05 .02 .01
□ 518 Butch Henry .05 .02 .01
□ 519 Sandy Alomar Jr. .05 .02 .01
□ 520 Kevin Appier .15 .07 .02
□ 521 Roberto Mejia .05 .02 .01
□ 522 Steve Cooke .05 .02 .01
□ 523 Terry Shumpert .05 .02 .01
□ 524 Mike Jackson .05 .02 .01
□ 525 Kent Mercker .05 .02 .01
□ 526 David Wells .05 .02 .01
□ 527 Juan Samuel .05 .02 .01
□ 528 Salomon Torres .05 .02 .01
□ 529 Duane Ward .05 .02 .01
□ 530 Rob Dibble .05 .02 .01
□ 531 Mike Blowers .05 .02 .01
□ 532 Mark Eichhorn .05 .02 .01
□ 533 Alex Diaz .05 .02 .01
□ 534 Dan Miceli .05 .02 .01
□ 535 Jeff Branson .05 .02 .01
□ 536 Dave Stevens .05 .02 .01
□ 537 Charlie O'Brien .05 .02 .01
□ 538 Shane Reynolds .15 .07 .02
□ 539 Rich Amaral .05 .02 .01
□ 540 Rusty Greer .30 .14 .04
□ 541 Alex Arias .05 .02 .01
□ 542 Eric Plunk .05 .02 .01
□ 543 John Hudek .05 .02 .01
□ 544 Kirk McCaskill .05 .02 .01
□ 545 Jeff Reboulet .05 .02 .01
□ 546 Sterling Hitchcock .15 .07 .02
□ 547 Warren Newson .05 .02 .01
□ 548 Bryan Harvey .05 .02 .01
□ 549 Mike Huff .05 .02 .01
□ 550 Lance Parrish .05 .02 .01
□ 551 Ken Griffey Jr. HIT 1.00 .45 .12
□ 552 Matt Williams HIT .30 .14 .04
□ 553 Roberto Alomar HIT UER .30 .14 .04
(Card says he's a NL All-Star
He plays in the AL)
□ 554 Jeff Bagwell HIT .40 .18 .05
□ 555 Dave Justice HIT .15 .07 .02
□ 556 Cal Ripken Jr. HIT .75 .35 .09
□ 557 Albert Belle HIT .40 .18 .05
□ 558 Mike Piazza HIT .60 .25 .07
□ 559 Kirby Puckett HIT .30 .14 .04
□ 560 Wade Boggs HIT .30 .14 .04
□ 561 Tony Gwynn HIT UER .40 .18 .05
card has him winning AL batting titles
he's played whole career in the NL
□ 562 Barry Bonds HIT .30 .14 .04
□ 563 Mo Vaughn HIT .30 .14 .04
□ 564 Don Mattingly HIT .50 .23 .06
□ 565 Carlos Baerga HIT .15 .07 .02
□ 566 Paul Molitor HIT .30 .14 .04
□ 567 Raul Mondesi HIT .30 .14 .04
□ 568 Manny Ramirez HIT .30 .14 .04
□ 569 Alex Rodriguez HIT 1.25 .55 .16
□ 570 Will Clark HIT .30 .14 .04
□ 571 Frank Thomas HIT 1.00 .45 .12
□ 572 Moises Alou HIT .15 .07 .02
□ 573 Jeff Conine HIT .15 .07 .02
□ 574 Joe Ausanio .05 .02 .01
□ 575 Charles Johnson .15 .07 .02
□ 576 Ernie Young .15 .07 .02
□ 577 Jeff Granger .05 .02 .01
□ 578 Robert Perez .05 .02 .01
□ 579 Melvin Nieves .15 .07 .02
□ 580 Gar Finnvold .05 .02 .01
□ 581 Duane Singleton .05 .02 .01
□ 582 Chan Ho Park .30 .14 .04
□ 583 Fausto Cruz .05 .02 .01
□ 584 Dave Staton .05 .02 .01
□ 585 Denny Hocking .05 .02 .01
□ 586 Nate Minchey .05 .02 .01
□ 587 Marc Newfield .15 .07 .02
□ 588 Jayhawk Owens UER .05 .02 .01
Front Photo is Jim Tatum
□ 589 Darren Bragg .15 .07 .02
□ 590 Kevin King .05 .02 .01
□ 591 Kurt Miller .05 .02 .01
□ 592 Aaron Small .05 .02 .01
□ 593 Troy O'Leary .05 .02 .01
□ 594 Phil Stidham .05 .02 .01
□ 595 Steve Dunn .05 .02 .01
□ 596 Cory Bailey .05 .02 .01
□ 597 Alex Gonzalez .15 .07 .02
□ 598 Jim Bowie .05 .02 .01
□ 599 Jeff Cirillo .15 .07 .02
□ 600 Mark Hutton .05 .02 .01
□ 601 Russ Davis .05 .02 .01
□ 602 Checklist .05 .02 .01
□ 603 Checklist .05 .02 .01
□ 604 Checklist .05 .02 .01
□ 605 Checklist .05 .02 .01
□ RG1 R.Klesko Rook.Greatness 15.00 6.75 1.85
□ SG1 Ryan Klesko AU6100 40.00 18.00 5.00
□ NNO Trade Hall of Gold 1.00 .45 .12

1995 Score Gold Rush

Parallel to the basic Score issue, these cards were inserted one per foil pack and two per jumbo pack. The fronts were printed in gold foil and the backs contain the Gold Rush logo. As part of the Gold Rush program, one Platinum Team Redemption card was randomly inserted in Score packs at a rate of one in 36. This redemption card and up to four Gold Rush team sets (and $2) could be redeemed for platinum versions of the team set(s). The Gold Rush sets that were sent in would be returned with a stamp indicating they were already used for redemption purposes. The Platinum Upgrade offer was good through 7/13/95 for series 1, 10/1/95 for series 2.

	MINT	NRMT	EXC
COMPLETE SET (605)	120.00	55.00	15.00
COMPLETE SERIES 1 (330)	60.00	27.00	7.50
COMPLETE SERIES 2 (275)	60.00	27.00	7.50
COMMON CARD (1-605)	.15	.07	.02
*STARS: 3X to 6X BASIC CARDS			
*YOUNG STARS: 2.5X to 5X BASIC CARDS			

1995 Score Platinum Team Sets

After completing a Score Gold Rush team set in either series, a collector could mail in those cards along with a platinum redemption

card. In return, the collector would receive a complete Platinum Team Set. The cards are similar to the gold cards except they have platinum borders and come in a small card case. The top card is the certificate saying this is a platinum team set. Only 4,950 of each platinum team set was produced.

	MINT	NRMT	EXC
COMPLETE SET (587)	300.00	135.00	38.00
COMPLETE SERIES 1 (316)	200.00	90.00	25.00
COMPLETE SERIES 2 (271)	100.00	45.00	12.50
COMMON CARD	.25	.11	.03
*STARS: 5X to 10X BASIC CARDS			
*YOUNG STARS: 4X to 8X BASIC CARDS			

1995 Score You Trade Em

This skip-numbered 11-card set was available only by redeeming the randomly inserted Score You Trade Em redemption card. The set features a selection of veteran players that were traded to new teams at the beginning of the 1995 season. The numbering and card design parallel the corresponding cards within the regular issue 1995 Score set, but these Trade cards feature the players in their new uniforms.

	MINT	NRMT	EXC
COMPLETE SET (11)	1.50	.70	.19
COMMON CARD	.15	.07	.02
☐ 333T Andre Dawson UER position listed as DH	.40	.18	.05
☐ 339T Terry Pendleton	.15	.07	.02
☐ 344T Brett Butler	.15	.07	.02
☐ 346T Larry Walker	.75	.35	.09
☐ 352T Andy Van Slyke	.15	.07	.02
☐ 392T Chad Curtis	.15	.07	.02
☐ 427T Scott Cooper	.15	.07	.02
☐ 443T David Cone	.40	.18	.05
☐ 452T Jim Abbott	.15	.07	.02
☐ 493T Brian McRae	.15	.07	.02
☐ 530T Rob Dibble	.15	.07	.02
☐ NNO Expired Trade Card	.25	.11	.03

1995 Score Airmail

This 18-card set was randomly inserted in series two jumbo packs at a rate of one in eight. The fronts have a color photo of the player in a home run swing with the sky in the background. Broken red and blue inner borders frame the player. A gold stamp with the words "Air Mail" is prominent in upper left. The backs have a color photo with player information including how many home runs per at-bats he averaged. A sunset serves as background.

	MINT	NRMT	EXC
COMPLETE SET (18)	50.00	22.00	6.25
COMMON CARD (1-18)	2.00	.90	.25
☐ AM1 Bob Hamelin	2.00	.90	.25
☐ AM2 John Mabry	3.00	1.35	.35
☐ AM3 Marc Newfield	2.50	1.10	.30
☐ AM4 Jose Oliva	2.00	.90	.25
☐ AM5 Charles Johnson	2.50	1.10	.30
☐ AM6 Russ Davis	2.00	.90	.25
☐ AM7 Ernie Young	2.00	.90	.25
☐ AM8 Billy Ashley	2.00	.90	.25
☐ AM9 Ryan Klesko	5.00	2.20	.60
☐ AM10 J.R. Phillips	2.00	.90	.25
☐ AM11 Cliff Floyd	2.50	1.10	.30
☐ AM12 Carlos Delgado	4.00	1.80	.50
☐ AM13 Melvin Nieves	2.50	1.10	.30
☐ AM14 Raul Mondesi	4.00	1.80	.50
☐ AM15 Manny Ramirez	8.00	3.60	1.00
☐ AM16 Mike Kelly	2.00	.90	.25
☐ AM17 Alex Rodriguez	30.00	13.50	3.70
☐ AM18 Rusty Greer	4.00	1.80	.50

1995 Score Contest Redemption

These cards were mailed to collectors who correctly identified intentional errors in two Pinnacle print ads depicting baseball scenes.

The Alex Rodriguez card was the prize for the first ad, the Ivan Rodriguez card for the second ad.

	MINT	NRMT	EXC
COMPLETE SET (2)	10.00	4.50	1.25
COMMON CARD (AD1-AD2)	3.00	1.35	.35
☐ AD1 Alex Rodriguez	8.00	3.60	1.00
☐ AD2 Ivan Rodriguez	3.00	1.35	.35

1995 Score Double Gold Champs

This 12-card set was randomly inserted in second series hobby packs at a rate of one in 36. Horizontally-designed fronts have a color action photo with the words "Double Gold Champs" in gold-foil at the bottom above the player's name. The backs have a color photo and a list of the player's accomplishments.

	MINT	NRMT	EXC
COMPLETE SET (12)	100.00	45.00	12.50
COMMON CARD (1-12)	2.50	1.10	.30
☐ GC1 Frank Thomas	20.00	9.00	2.50
☐ GC2 Ken Griffey Jr.	20.00	9.00	2.50
☐ GC3 Barry Bonds	5.00	2.20	.60
☐ GC4 Tony Gwynn	8.00	3.60	1.00
☐ GC5 Don Mattingly	10.00	4.50	1.25
☐ GC6 Greg Maddux	12.00	5.50	1.50
☐ GC7 Roger Clemens	4.00	1.80	.50
☐ GC8 Kenny Lofton	5.00	2.20	.60
☐ GC9 Jeff Bagwell	8.00	3.60	1.00
☐ GC10 Matt Williams	2.50	1.10	.30
☐ GC11 Kirby Puckett	8.00	3.60	1.00
☐ GC12 Cal Ripken	15.00	6.75	1.85

1995 Score Draft Picks

Randomly inserted in first series hobby packs at a rate of one in 36, this 18-card set takes a look at top picks selected in June of 1994. Horizontal fronts have two player photos on a white background. Vertical backs have a player photo and 1994 season's highlights. The cards are numbered with a DP prefix.

	MINT	NRMT	EXC
COMPLETE SET (18)	75.00	34.00	9.50
COMMON CARD (DP1-DP18)	2.50	1.10	.30
☐ DP1 McKay Christensen	2.50	1.10	.30
☐ DP2 Brett Wagner	2.50	1.10	.30
☐ DP3 Paul Wilson	6.00	2.70	.75
☐ DP4 C.J. Nitkowski	2.50	1.10	.30
☐ DP5 Josh Booty	4.00	1.80	.50
☐ DP6 Antone Williamson	6.00	2.70	.75
☐ DP7 Paul Konerko	15.00	6.75	1.85
☐ DP8 Scott Elarton	6.00	2.70	.75
☐ DP9 Jacob Shumate	2.50	1.10	.30
☐ DP10 Terrance Long	5.00	2.20	.60
☐ DP11 Mark Johnson	2.50	1.10	.30
☐ DP12 Ben Grieve	12.00	5.50	1.50
☐ DP13 Doug Million	5.00	2.20	.60
☐ DP14 Jayson Peterson	2.50	1.10	.30
☐ DP15 Dustin Hermanson	2.50	1.10	.30
☐ DP16 Matt Smith	2.50	1.10	.30
☐ DP17 Kevin Witt	3.00	1.35	.35
☐ DP18 Brian Buchanan	2.50	1.10	.30

1995 Score Dream Team

Randomly inserted in first series hobby and retail packs at a rate of one in 72 packs, this 12-card hologram set showcases top performers from the 1994 season. The holographic fronts have two player images. The horizontal backs are not holographic. They are multi-colored with a small player close-up and a brief write-up. The cards are numbered with a DG prefix.

	MINT	NRMT	EXC
COMPLETE SET (12)	150.00	70.00	19.00
COMMON CARD (DG1-DG12)	2.50	1.10	.30
☐ DG1 Frank Thomas	40.00	18.00	5.00
☐ DG2 Roberto Alomar	8.00	3.60	1.00
☐ DG3 Cal Ripken	30.00	13.50	3.70
☐ DG4 Matt Williams	8.00	3.60	1.00
☐ DG5 Mike Piazza	25.00	11.00	3.10
☐ DG6 Albert Belle	15.00	6.75	1.85
☐ DG7 Ken Griffey Jr.	40.00	18.00	5.00
☐ DG8 Tony Gwynn	15.00	6.75	1.85
☐ DG9 Paul Molitor	8.00	3.60	1.00
☐ DG10 Jimmy Key	2.50	1.10	.30
☐ DG11 Greg Maddux	25.00	11.00	3.10
☐ DG12 Lee Smith	5.00	2.20	.60

1995 Score Hall of Gold

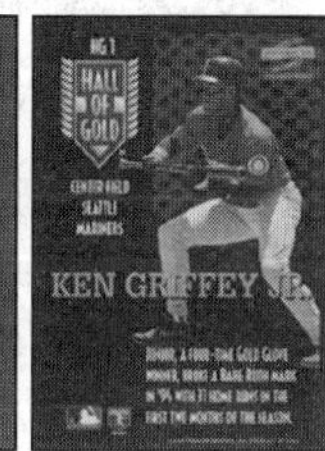

Randomly inserted in packs at a rate one in six, this 110-card multi-series set is a collection of top stars and young hopefuls. Metallic fronts are presented in shades of silver and gold that overlay a player photo. The Hall of Gold logo appears in the upper right-hand corner. Black backs contain a brief write-up and a player photo.

	MINT	NRMT	EXC
COMPLETE SET (110)	80.00	36.00	10.00
COMPLETE SERIES 1 (55)	50.00	22.00	6.25
COMPLETE SERIES 2 (55)	30.00	13.50	3.70
COMMON CARD (HG1-HG110)	.50	.23	.06
☐ HG1 Ken Griffey Jr.	12.00	5.50	1.50
☐ HG2 Matt Williams	1.50	.70	.19
☐ HG3 Roberto Alomar	2.50	1.10	.30
☐ HG4 Jeff Bagwell	5.00	2.20	.60
☐ HG5 Dave Justice	1.00	.45	.12
☐ HG6 Cal Ripken	10.00	4.50	1.25
☐ HG7 Randy Johnson	1.50	.70	.19
☐ HG8 Barry Larkin	1.50	.70	.19
☐ HG9 Albert Belle	5.00	2.20	.60
☐ HG10 Mike Piazza	8.00	3.60	1.00
☐ HG11 Kirby Puckett	5.00	2.20	.60
☐ HG12 Moises Alou	1.00	.45	.12
☐ HG13 Jose Canseco	1.50	.70	.19
☐ HG14 Tony Gwynn	5.00	2.20	.60
☐ HG15 Roger Clemens	2.50	1.10	.30
☐ HG16 Barry Bonds	3.00	1.35	.35
☐ HG17 Mo Vaughn	3.00	1.35	.35
☐ HG18 Greg Maddux	8.00	3.60	1.00
☐ HG19 Dante Bichette	1.50	.70	.19
☐ HG20 Will Clark	1.50	.70	.19
☐ HG21 Lenny Dykstra	1.00	.45	.12
☐ HG22 Don Mattingly	6.00	2.70	.75
☐ HG23 Carlos Baerga	1.00	.45	.12
☐ HG24 Ozzie Smith	3.00	1.35	.35
☐ HG25 Paul Molitor	2.50	1.10	.30
☐ HG26 Paul O'Neill	1.00	.45	.12
☐ HG27 Deion Sanders	1.50	.70	.19
☐ HG28 Jeff Conine	1.00	.45	.12
☐ HG29 John Olerud	.50	.23	.06
☐ HG30 Jose Rijo	.50	.23	.06
☐ HG31 Sammy Sosa	1.50	.70	.19
☐ HG32 Robin Ventura	1.00	.45	.12
☐ HG33 Raul Mondesi	1.50	.70	.19
☐ HG34 Eddie Murray	3.00	1.35	.35
☐ HG35 Marquis Grissom	1.00	.45	.12
☐ HG36 Darryl Strawberry	1.00	.45	.12
☐ HG37 Dave Nilsson	1.00	.45	.12
☐ HG38 Manny Ramirez	3.00	1.35	.35
☐ HG39 Delino DeShields	.50	.23	.06
☐ HG40 Lee Smith	1.00	.45	.12
☐ HG41 Alex Rodriguez	10.00	4.50	1.25
☐ HG42 Julio Franco	.50	.23	.06
☐ HG43 Bret Saberhagen	.50	.23	.06
☐ HG44 Ken Hill	.50	.23	.06
☐ HG45 Roberto Kelly	.50	.23	.06
☐ HG46 Hal Morris	.50	.23	.06
☐ HG47 Jimmy Key	.50	.23	.06
☐ HG48 Terry Steinbach	.50	.23	.06
☐ HG49 Mickey Tettleton	.50	.23	.06
☐ HG50 Tony Phillips	.50	.23	.06
☐ HG51 Carlos Garcia	.50	.23	.06
☐ HG52 Jim Edmonds	1.50	.70	.19
☐ HG53 Rod Beck	.50	.23	.06
☐ HG54 Shane Mack	.50	.23	.06
☐ HG55 Ken Caminiti	1.50	.70	.19
☐ HG56 Frank Thomas	12.00	5.50	1.50
☐ HG57 Kenny Lofton	3.00	1.35	.35
☐ HG58 Juan Gonzalez	6.00	2.70	.75
☐ HG59 Jason Bere	.50	.23	.06
☐ HG60 Joe Carter	1.00	.45	.12
☐ HG61 Gary Sheffield	1.50	.70	.19
☐ HG62 Andres Galarraga	1.50	.70	.19
☐ HG63 Ellis Burks	1.00	.45	.12
☐ HG64 Bobby Bonilla	1.00	.45	.12
☐ HG65 Tom Glavine	1.50	.70	.19
☐ HG66 John Smoltz	1.50	.70	.19
☐ HG67 Fred McGriff	1.50	.70	.19
☐ HG68 Craig Biggio	1.00	.45	.12
☐ HG69 Reggie Sanders	1.00	.45	.12
☐ HG70 Kevin Mitchell	.50	.23	.06
☐ HG71 Larry Walker	1.50	.70	.19
☐ HG72 Carlos Delgado	1.00	.45	.12
☐ HG73 Alex Gonzalez	1.00	.45	.12
☐ HG74 Ivan Rodriguez	3.00	1.35	.35
☐ HG75 Ryan Klesko	1.50	.70	.19
☐ HG76 John Kruk	.50	.23	.06
☐ HG77 Brian McRae	.50	.23	.06
☐ HG78 Tim Salmon	1.50	.70	.19
☐ HG79 Travis Fryman	1.00	.45	.12
☐ HG80 Chuck Knoblauch	1.50	.70	.19
☐ HG81 Jay Bell	.50	.23	.06
☐ HG82 Cecil Fielder	1.00	.45	.12
☐ HG83 Cliff Floyd	1.00	.45	.12
☐ HG84 Ruben Sierra	1.00	.45	.12
☐ HG85 Mike Mussina	2.50	1.10	.30
☐ HG86 Mark Grace	1.50	.70	.19
☐ HG87 Dennis Eckersley	1.00	.45	.12
☐ HG88 Dennis Martinez	1.00	.45	.12
☐ HG89 Rafael Palmeiro	1.50	.70	.19
☐ HG90 Ben McDonald	1.00	.45	.12
☐ HG91 Dave Hollins	.50	.23	.06
☐ HG92 Steve Avery	1.00	.45	.12
☐ HG93 David Cone	1.00	.45	.12
☐ HG94 Darren Daulton	1.00	.45	.12
☐ HG95 Bret Boone	.50	.23	.06
☐ HG96 Wade Boggs	1.50	.70	.19
☐ HG97 Doug Drabek	.50	.23	.06
☐ HG98 Andy Benes	.50	.23	.06
☐ HG99 Jim Thome	2.50	1.10	.30
☐ HG100 Chili Davis	.50	.23	.06
☐ HG101 Jeffrey Hammonds	.50	.23	.06
☐ HG102 Rickey Henderson	1.50	.70	.19
☐ HG103 Brett Butler	1.00	.45	.12
☐ HG104 Tim Wallach	.50	.23	.06
☐ HG105 Wil Cordero	.50	.23	.06
☐ HG106 Mark Whiten	.50	.23	.06
☐ HG107 Bob Hamelin	.50	.23	.06
☐ HG108 Rondell White	1.00	.45	.12
☐ HG109 Devon White	.50	.23	.06
☐ HG110 Tony Tarasco	.50	.23	.06

1995 Score Hall of Gold You Trade Em

This skip-numbered five-card set was available only by redeeming the randomly inserted Hall of Gold Trade card inserted in second series packs of 1995 Score. The set features a selection of veterans that joined new teams prior to the 1995 season. The design and numbering of the cards parallel the regular Hall of Gold inserts.

	MINT	NRMT	EXC
COMPLETE SET (5)	4.00	1.80	.50
COMMON CARD	.50	.23	.06
☐ HG71T Larry Walker	1.50	.70	.19
☐ HG76T John Kruk	.50	.23	.06
☐ HG77T Brian McRae	.50	.23	.06
☐ HG93T David Cone	1.00	.45	.12
☐ HG110T Tony Tarasco	.50	.23	.06
☐ NNO Expired Hall of Gold Trade Card	1.00	.45	.12

1995 Score Rookie Dream Team

This 12-card set was randomly inserted in second series retail and hobby packs at a rate of one in 12. The fronts contain a color photo with a metallic background. The "Rookie Dream Team" title occupy two of the borders. The player's name is at the bottom in gold-foil. The backs are horizontally designed, have a head shot and player information with the sky serving as a background. The cards are numbered with a RDT prefix.

	MINT	NRMT	EXC
COMPLETE SET (12)	60.00	27.00	7.50
COMMON CARD (1-12)	3.00	1.35	.35

Card	MINT	NRMT	EXC
☐ RDT1 J.R. Phillips	3.00	1.35	.35
☐ RDT2 Alex Gonzalez	3.50	1.55	.45
☐ RDT3 Alex Rodriguez	40.00	18.00	5.00
☐ RDT4 Jose Oliva	3.00	1.35	.35
☐ RDT5 Charles Johnson	4.00	1.80	.50
☐ RDT6 Shawn Green	3.50	1.55	.45
☐ RDT7 Brian Hunter	5.00	2.20	.60
☐ RDT8 Garret Anderson	3.50	1.55	.45
☐ RDT9 Julian Tavarez	3.00	1.35	.35
☐ RDT10 Jose Lima	3.00	1.35	.35
☐ RDT11 Armando Benitez	3.00	1.35	.35
☐ RDT12 Ricky Bottalico	3.50	1.55	.45

1995 Score Rules

Randomly inserted in first series jumbo packs, this 30-card standard-size set features top big league players. Card fronts offer a player photo to the left. At right, the player's name is spelled vertically within a green vapor trail left by a baseball that is at the top. A horizontally designed back features three images of the player and a brief write-up. The cards are numbered with an "SR" prefix.

	MINT	NRMT	EXC
COMPLETE SET (30)	125.00	55.00	15.50
COMMON CARD (SR1-SR30)	1.50	.70	.19
☐ SR1 Ken Griffey Jr.	20.00	9.00	2.50
☐ SR2 Frank Thomas	20.00	9.00	2.50
☐ SR3 Mike Piazza	12.00	5.50	1.50
☐ SR4 Jeff Bagwell	8.00	3.60	1.00
☐ SR5 Alex Rodriguez	20.00	9.00	2.50
☐ SR6 Albert Belle	8.00	3.60	1.00
☐ SR7 Matt Williams	2.50	1.10	.30
☐ SR8 Roberto Alomar	4.00	1.80	.50
☐ SR9 Barry Bonds	5.00	2.20	.60
☐ SR10 Raul Mondesi	2.50	1.10	.30
☐ SR11 Jose Canseco	2.50	1.10	.30
☐ SR12 Kirby Puckett	8.00	3.60	1.00
☐ SR13 Fred McGriff	2.50	1.10	.30
☐ SR14 Kenny Lofton	5.00	2.20	.60
☐ SR15 Greg Maddux	12.00	5.50	1.50
☐ SR16 Juan Gonzalez	10.00	4.50	1.25
☐ SR17 Cliff Floyd	1.50	.70	.19
☐ SR18 Cal Ripken Jr.	15.00	6.75	1.85
☐ SR19 Will Clark	2.50	1.10	.30
☐ SR20 Tim Salmon	2.50	1.10	.30
☐ SR21 Paul O'Neill	1.50	.70	.19
☐ SR22 Jason Bere	1.50	.70	.19
☐ SR23 Tony Gwynn	8.00	3.60	1.00
☐ SR24 Manny Ramirez	5.00	2.20	.60
☐ SR25 Don Mattingly	10.00	4.50	1.25
☐ SR26 Dave Justice	2.00	.90	.25
☐ SR27 Javier Lopez	2.00	.90	.25
☐ SR28 Ryan Klesko	2.50	1.10	.30
☐ SR29 Carlos Delgado	2.00	.90	.25
☐ SR30 Mike Mussina	4.00	1.80	.50

1995 Score Rules Jumbos

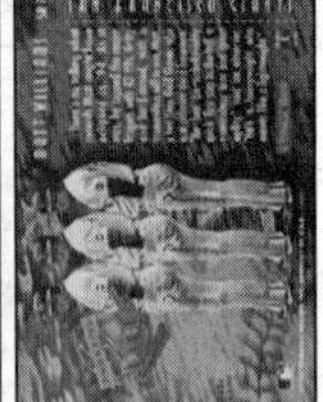

These 30 cards, measuring 7 1/2" by 10 1/2" were issued one per special Score collector kit. The cards are parallels to the regular Score Rules jumbos and were numbered out of 3,000.

	MINT	NRMT	EXC
COMPLETE SET (30)	175.00	80.00	22.00
COMMON CARD (SR1-SR30)	2.00	.90	.25
*JUMBOS: 1.25X BASIC CARDS			

1996 Score Samples

This 8-card set was issued to preview the 1996 Score series. Inside white borders, the fronts feature color action photos with the upper left corner torn off to allow space for the "96 Score" logo. The backs carry a second color closeup photo, biography, statistics, and player profile. The final two cards listed belong to the Rookie subset and have a different front design. All cards have "SAMPLE" stamped diagonally across their front and back.

	MINT	NRMT	EXC
COMPLETE SET (8)	6.00	2.70	.75
COMMON CARD	.50	.23	.06
☐ 3 Ryan Klesko	1.00	.45	.12
☐ 4 Jim Edmonds	.75	.35	.09
☐ 5 Barry Larkin	1.00	.45	.12
☐ 6 Jim Thome	1.00	.45	.12
☐ 7 Raul Mondesi	.75	.35	.09
☐ 110 Derek Bell	.50	.23	.06
☐ 240 Derek Jeter	3.00	1.35	.35
☐ 241 Michael Tucker	.60	.25	.07

1996 Score

This set consists of 517 standard-size cards. These cards were issued in packs of 10 that retailed for 99 cents per pack. The fronts feature an action photo surrounded by white borders. The "Score 96" logo is in the upper left, while the player is identified on the bottom. The backs have season and career stats as well as a player photo and some text. A Cal Ripken tribute card was issued at a rate of 1 every 300 packs.

	MINT	NRMT	EXC
COMPLETE SET (517)	24.00	11.00	3.00
COMPLETE SERIES 1 (275)	12.00	5.50	1.50
COMPLETE SERIES 2 (242)	12.00	5.50	1.50
COMMON CARD (1-517)	.05	.02	.01
☐ 1 Will Clark	.30	.14	.04
☐ 2 Rich Becker	.15	.07	.02
☐ 3 Ryan Klesko	.30	.14	.04
☐ 4 Jim Edmonds	.15	.07	.02
☐ 5 Barry Larkin	.30	.14	.04
☐ 6 Jim Thome	.40	.18	.05
☐ 7 Raul Mondesi	.30	.14	.04
☐ 8 Don Mattingly	1.00	.45	.12
☐ 9 Jeff Conine	.15	.07	.02
☐ 10 Rickey Henderson	.30	.14	.04
☐ 11 Chad Curtis	.05	.02	.01
☐ 12 Darren Daulton	.15	.07	.02
☐ 13 Larry Walker	.30	.14	.04
☐ 14 Carlos Garcia	.05	.02	.01
☐ 15 Carlos Baerga	.15	.07	.02
☐ 16 Tony Gwynn	.75	.35	.09
☐ 17 Jon Nunnally	.05	.02	.01
☐ 18 Deion Sanders	.30	.14	.04
☐ 19 Mark Grace	.30	.14	.04
☐ 20 Alex Rodriguez	2.00	.90	.25
☐ 21 Frank Thomas	2.00	.90	.25
☐ 22 Brian Jordan	.15	.07	.02
☐ 23 J.T. Snow	.15	.07	.02
☐ 24 Shawn Green	.15	.07	.02
☐ 25 Tim Wakefield	.05	.02	.01
☐ 26 Curtis Goodwin	.05	.02	.01
☐ 27 John Smoltz	.30	.14	.04
☐ 28 Devon White	.05	.02	.01
☐ 29 Johnny Damon	.15	.07	.02
☐ 30 Tim Salmon	.30	.14	.04
☐ 31 Rafael Palmeiro	.30	.14	.04
☐ 32 Bernard Gilkey	.15	.07	.02
☐ 33 John Valentin	.15	.07	.02
☐ 34 Randy Johnson	.30	.14	.04
☐ 35 Garret Anderson	.30	.14	.04
☐ 36 Rikkert Faneyte	.05	.02	.01
☐ 37 Ray Durham	.30	.14	.04
☐ 38 Bip Roberts	.05	.02	.01
☐ 39 Jaime Navarro	.05	.02	.01
☐ 40 Mark Johnson	.05	.02	.01
☐ 41 Darren Lewis	.05	.02	.01
☐ 42 Tyler Green	.05	.02	.01
☐ 43 Bill Pulsipher	.15	.07	.02
☐ 44 Jason Giambi	.30	.14	.04
☐ 45 Kevin Ritz	.05	.02	.01
☐ 46 Jack McDowell	.30	.14	.04
☐ 47 Felipe Lira	.05	.02	.01
☐ 48 Rico Brogna	.05	.02	.01
☐ 49 Terry Pendleton	.15	.07	.02
☐ 50 Rondell White	.15	.07	.02
☐ 51 Andre Dawson	.15	.07	.02
☐ 52 Kirby Puckett	.75	.35	.09
☐ 53 Wally Joyner	.05	.02	.01
☐ 54 B.J. Surhoff	.05	.02	.01
☐ 55 Randy Velarde	.05	.02	.01
☐ 56 Greg Vaughn	.30	.14	.04
☐ 57 Roberto Alomar	.40	.18	.05
☐ 58 David Justice	.15	.07	.02
☐ 59 Kevin Seitzer	.05	.02	.01
☐ 60 Cal Ripken	1.50	.70	.19
☐ 61 Ozzie Smith	.50	.23	.06
☐ 62 Mo Vaughn	.50	.23	.06
☐ 63 Ricky Bones	.05	.02	.01
☐ 64 Gary DiSarcina	.05	.02	.01
☐ 65 Matt Williams	.30	.14	.04
☐ 66 Wilson Alvarez	.30	.14	.04
☐ 67 Lenny Dykstra	.15	.07	.02
☐ 68 Brian McRae	.05	.02	.01
☐ 69 Todd Stottlemyre	.05	.02	.01
☐ 70 Bret Boone	.05	.02	.01
☐ 71 Sterling Hitchcock	.05	.02	.01
☐ 72 Albert Belle	.75	.35	.09
☐ 73 Todd Hundley	.15	.07	.02
☐ 74 Vinny Castilla	.15	.07	.02
☐ 75 Moises Alou	.15	.07	.02
☐ 76 Cecil Fielder	.15	.07	.02
☐ 77 Brad Radke	.05	.02	.01
☐ 78 Quilvio Veras	.05	.02	.01
☐ 79 Eddie Murray	.50	.23	.06
☐ 80 James Mouton	.05	.02	.01
☐ 81 Pat Listach	.05	.02	.01
☐ 82 Mark Gubicza	.05	.02	.01
☐ 83 Dave Winfield	.30	.14	.04
☐ 84 Fred McGriff	.30	.14	.04
☐ 85 Darryl Hamilton	.05	.02	.01
☐ 86 Jeffrey Hammonds	.05	.02	.01
☐ 87 Pedro Munoz	.05	.02	.01
☐ 88 Craig Biggio	.15	.07	.02
☐ 89 Cliff Floyd	.05	.02	.01
☐ 90 Tim Naehring	.15	.07	.02
☐ 91 Brett Butler	.05	.02	.01
☐ 92 Kevin Foster	.05	.02	.01
☐ 93 Pat Kelly	.05	.02	.01
☐ 94 John Smiley	.05	.02	.01
☐ 95 Terry Steinbach	.15	.07	.02
☐ 96 Orel Hershiser	.15	.07	.02
☐ 97 Darrin Fletcher	.05	.02	.01
☐ 98 Walt Weiss	.05	.02	.01
☐ 99 John Wetteland	.15	.07	.02
☐ 100 Alan Trammell	.15	.07	.02
☐ 101 Steve Avery	.15	.07	.02
☐ 102 Tony Eusebio	.05	.02	.01
☐ 103 Sandy Alomar Jr.	.05	.02	.01
☐ 104 Joe Girardi	.05	.02	.01
☐ 105 Rick Aguilera	.05	.02	.01
☐ 106 Tony Tarasco	.05	.02	.01
☐ 107 Chris Hammond	.05	.02	.01
☐ 108 Mike Macfarlane	.05	.02	.01
☐ 109 Doug Drabek	.05	.02	.01
☐ 110 Derek Bell	.15	.07	.02
☐ 111 Ed Sprague	.15	.07	.02
☐ 112 Todd Hollandsworth	.15	.07	.02
☐ 113 Otis Nixon	.05	.02	.01
☐ 114 Keith Lockhart	.05	.02	.01
☐ 115 Donovan Osborne	.05	.02	.01
☐ 116 Dave Magadan	.05	.02	.01
☐ 117 Edgar Martinez	.15	.07	.02
☐ 118 Chuck Carr	.05	.02	.01
☐ 119 J.R. Phillips	.05	.02	.01
☐ 120 Sean Bergman	.05	.02	.01
☐ 121 Andujar Cedeno	.05	.02	.01
☐ 122 Eric Young	.15	.07	.02
☐ 123 Al Martin	.05	.02	.01
☐ 124 Mark Lemke	.05	.02	.01
☐ 125 Jim Eisenreich	.05	.02	.01
☐ 126 Benito Santiago	.05	.02	.01
☐ 127 Ariel Prieto	.05	.02	.01
☐ 128 Jim Bullinger	.05	.02	.01
☐ 129 Russ Davis	.05	.02	.01
☐ 130 Jim Abbott	.30	.14	.04
☐ 131 Jason Isringhausen	.30	.14	.04
☐ 132 Carlos Perez	.05	.02	.01
☐ 133 David Segui	.05	.02	.01
☐ 134 Troy O'Leary	.15	.07	.02
☐ 135 Pat Meares	.05	.02	.01
☐ 136 Chris Hoiles	.05	.02	.01
☐ 137 Ismael Valdes	.15	.07	.02
☐ 138 Jose Oliva	.05	.02	.01
☐ 139 Carlos Delgado	.15	.07	.02
☐ 140 Tom Goodwin	.15	.07	.02
☐ 141 Bob Tewksbury	.05	.02	.01
☐ 142 Chris Gomez	.05	.02	.01
☐ 143 Jose Oquendo	.05	.02	.01
☐ 144 Mark Lewis	.05	.02	.01
☐ 145 Salomon Torres	.05	.02	.01
☐ 146 Luis Gonzalez	.05	.02	.01
☐ 147 Mark Carreon	.05	.02	.01
☐ 148 Lance Johnson	.15	.07	.02
☐ 149 Melvin Nieves	.15	.07	.02
☐ 150 Lee Smith	.15	.07	.02
☐ 151 Jacob Brumfield	.05	.02	.01
☐ 152 Armando Benitez	.05	.02	.01
☐ 153 Curt Schilling	.05	.02	.01
☐ 154 Javier Lopez	.30	.14	.04
☐ 155 Frank Rodriguez	.15	.07	.02
☐ 156 Alex Gonzalez	.05	.02	.01
☐ 157 Todd Worrell	.15	.07	.02
☐ 158 Benji Gil	.05	.02	.01
☐ 159 Greg Gagne	.05	.02	.01
☐ 160 Tom Henke	.15	.07	.02
☐ 161 Randy Myers	.05	.02	.01
☐ 162 Joey Cora	.05	.02	.01
☐ 163 Scott Ruffcorn	.05	.02	.01
☐ 164 W. VanLandingham	.05	.02	.01
☐ 165 Tony Phillips	.15	.07	.02
☐ 166 Eddie Williams	.05	.02	.01
☐ 167 Bobby Bonilla	.15	.07	.02
☐ 168 Denny Neagle	.15	.07	.02
☐ 169 Troy Percival	.15	.07	.02
☐ 170 Billy Ashley	.05	.02	.01
☐ 171 Andy Van Slyke	.15	.07	.02
☐ 172 Jose Offerman	.05	.02	.01
☐ 173 Mark Parent	.05	.02	.01
☐ 174 Edgardo Alfonzo	.15	.07	.02
☐ 175 Trevor Hoffman	.15	.07	.02
☐ 176 David Cone	.15	.07	.02
☐ 177 Dan Wilson	.05	.02	.01
☐ 178 Steve Ontiveros	.05	.02	.01
☐ 179 Dean Palmer	.30	.14	.04
☐ 180 Mike Kelly	.05	.02	.01
☐ 181 Jim Leyritz	.05	.02	.01
☐ 182 Ron Karkovice	.05	.02	.01
☐ 183 Kevin Brown	.15	.07	.02
☐ 184 Jose Valentin	.05	.02	.01
☐ 185 Jorge Fabregas	.05	.02	.01
☐ 186 Jose Mesa	.15	.07	.02
☐ 187 Brent Mayne	.05	.02	.01
☐ 188 Carl Everett	.05	.02	.01
☐ 189 Paul Sorrento	.05	.02	.01
☐ 190 Pete Schourek	.30	.14	.04
☐ 191 Scott Kamieniecki	.05	.02	.01
☐ 192 Roberto Hernandez	.15	.07	.02
☐ 193 Randy Johnson RR	.30	.14	.04
☐ 194 Greg Maddux RR	.60	.25	.07
☐ 195 Hideo Nomo RR	.30	.14	.04
☐ 196 David Cone RR	.15	.07	.02
☐ 197 Mike Mussina RR	.30	.14	.04
☐ 198 Andy Benes RR	.05	.02	.01
☐ 199 Kevin Appier RR	.15	.07	.02
☐ 200 John Smoltz RR	.30	.14	.04
☐ 201 John Wetteland RR	.15	.07	.02
☐ 202 Mark Wohlers RR	.15	.07	.02
☐ 203 Stan Belinda	.05	.02	.01
☐ 204 Brian Anderson	.05	.02	.01
☐ 205 Mike Devereaux	.05	.02	.01
☐ 206 Mark Wohlers	.15	.07	.02
☐ 207 Omar Vizquel	.15	.07	.02
☐ 208 Jose Rijo	.05	.02	.01
☐ 209 Willie Blair	.05	.02	.01
☐ 210 Jamie Moyer	.05	.02	.01
☐ 211 Craig Shipley	.05	.02	.01
☐ 212 Shane Reynolds	.15	.07	.02
☐ 213 Chad Fonville	.05	.02	.01
☐ 214 Jose Vizcaino	.05	.02	.01
☐ 215 Sid Fernandez	.05	.02	.01
☐ 216 Andy Ashby	.05	.02	.01
☐ 217 Frank Castillo	.05	.02	.01
☐ 218 Kevin Tapani	.05	.02	.01
☐ 219 Kent Mercker	.05	.02	.01
☐ 220 Karim Garcia	.40	.18	.05
☐ 221 Antonio Osuna	.05	.02	.01
☐ 222 Tim Unroe	.05	.02	.01
☐ 223 Johnny Damon	.15	.07	.02
☐ 224 LaTroy Hawkins	.05	.02	.01
☐ 225 Mariano Rivera	.15	.07	.02
☐ 226 Jose Alberro	.05	.02	.01
☐ 227 Angel Martinez	.05	.02	.01
☐ 228 Jason Schmidt	.30	.14	.04
☐ 229 Tony Clark	.40	.18	.05
☐ 230 Kevin Jordan UER Ricky Jordan pictured on both sides	.05	.02	.01
☐ 231 Mark Thompson	.05	.02	.01
☐ 232 Jim Dougherty	.05	.02	.01
☐ 233 Roger Cedeno	.15	.07	.02
☐ 234 Ugueth Urbina	.05	.02	.01
☐ 235 Ricky Otero	.05	.02	.01
☐ 236 Mark Smith	.05	.02	.01
☐ 237 Brian Barber	.05	.02	.01
☐ 238 Kevin Flora	.05	.02	.01
☐ 239 Joe Rosselli	.05	.02	.01
☐ 240 Derek Jeter	1.25	.55	.16
☐ 241 Michael Tucker	.15	.07	.02
☐ 242 Ben Blomdahl	.05	.02	.01
☐ 243 Joe Vitiello	.05	.02	.01
☐ 244 Todd Steverson	.05	.02	.01
☐ 245 James Baldwin	.15	.07	.02
☐ 246 Alan Embree	.05	.02	.01
☐ 247 Shannon Penn	.05	.02	.01
☐ 248 Chris Stynes	.05	.02	.01
☐ 249 Oscar Munoz	.05	.02	.01
☐ 250 Jose Herrera	.05	.02	.01

251 Scott Sullivan	.05	.02	.01
252 Reggie Williams	.05	.02	.01
253 Mark Grudzielanek	.05	.02	.01
254 Steve Rodriguez	.05	.02	.01
255 Terry Bradshaw	.05	.02	.01
256 F.P. Santangelo	.05	.02	.01
257 Lyle Mouton	.05	.02	.01
258 George Williams	.05	.02	.01
259 Larry Thomas	.05	.02	.01
260 Rudy Pemberton	.05	.02	.01
261 Jim Pittsley	.15	.07	.02
262 Les Norman	.05	.02	.01
263 Ruben Rivera	.40	.18	.05
264 Cesar Devarez	.05	.02	.01
265 Greg Zaun	.05	.02	.01
266 Dustin Hermanson	.15	.07	.02
267 John Frascatore	.05	.02	.01
268 Joe Randa	.05	.02	.01
269 Jeff Bagwell CL	.40	.18	.05
270 Mike Piazza CL	.60	.25	.07
271 Dante Bichette CL	.30	.14	.04
272 Frank Thomas CL	1.00	.45	.12
273 Ken Griffey Jr. CL	1.00	.45	.12
274 Cal Ripken CL	.75	.35	.09
275 Greg Maddux CL Albert Belle	.50	.23	.06
276 Greg Maddux	1.25	.55	.16
277 Pedro Martinez	.15	.07	.02
278 Bobby Higginson	.15	.07	.02
279 Ray Lankford	.15	.07	.02
280 Shawon Dunston	.05	.02	.01
281 Gary Sheffield	.30	.14	.04
282 Ken Griffey, Jr.	2.00	.90	.25
283 Paul Molitor	.40	.18	.05
284 Kevin Appier	.15	.07	.02
285 Chuck Knoblauch	.30	.14	.04
286 Alex Fernandez	.15	.07	.02
287 Steve Finley	.30	.14	.04
288 Jeff Blauser	.05	.02	.01
289 Charles Johnson	.15	.07	.02
290 John Franco	.05	.02	.01
291 Mark Langston	.05	.02	.01
292 Bret Saberhagen	.05	.02	.01
293 John Mabry	.15	.07	.02
294 Ramon Martinez	.15	.07	.02
295 Mike Blowers	.05	.02	.01
296 Paul O'Neill	.05	.02	.01
297 Dave Nilsson	.15	.07	.02
298 Dante Bichette	.30	.14	.04
299 Marty Cordova	.15	.07	.02
300 Jay Bell	.15	.07	.02
301 Mike Mussina	.40	.18	.05
302 Ivan Rodriguez	.50	.23	.06
303 Jose Canseco	.30	.14	.04
304 Jeff Bagwell	.75	.35	.09
305 Manny Ramirez	.50	.23	.06
306 Dennis Martinez	.15	.07	.02
307 Charlie Hayes	.05	.02	.01
308 Joe Carter	.15	.07	.02
309 Travis Fryman	.15	.07	.02
310 Mark McGwire	.60	.25	.07
311 Reggie Sanders UER Photo on front is John Roper	.15	.07	.02
312 Julian Tavarez	.05	.02	.01
313 Jeff Montgomery	.05	.02	.01
314 Andy Benes	.05	.02	.01
315 John Jaha	.15	.07	.02
316 Jeff Kent	.05	.02	.01
317 Mike Piazza	1.25	.55	.16
318 Erik Hanson	.05	.02	.01
319 Kenny Rogers	.05	.02	.01
320 Hideo Nomo	.50	.23	.06
321 Gregg Jefferies	.30	.14	.04
322 Chipper Jones	1.25	.55	.16
323 Jay Buhner	.30	.14	.04
324 Dennis Eckersley	.15	.07	.02
325 Kenny Lofton	.50	.23	.06
326 Robin Ventura	.15	.07	.02
327 Tom Glavine	.30	.14	.04
328 Tim Salmon	.30	.14	.04
329 Andres Galarraga	.30	.14	.04
330 Hal Morris	.05	.02	.01
331 Brady Anderson	.30	.14	.04
332 Chili Davis	.05	.02	.01
333 Roger Clemens	.40	.18	.05
334 Marquis Grissom	.15	.07	.02
335 Mike Greenwell UER Name spelled Jeff on Front	.05	.02	.01
336 Sammy Sosa	.30	.14	.04
337 Ron Gant	.15	.07	.02
338 Ken Caminiti	.30	.14	.04
339 Danny Tartabull	.05	.02	.01
340 Barry Bonds	.50	.23	.06
341 Ben McDonald	.05	.02	.01
342 Ruben Sierra	.05	.02	.01
343 Bernie Williams	.40	.18	.05
344 Wil Cordero	.05	.02	.01
345 Wade Boggs	.30	.14	.04
346 Gary Gaetti	.15	.07	.02
347 Greg Colbrunn	.05	.02	.01
348 Juan Gonzalez	1.00	.45	.12
349 Marc Newfield	.05	.02	.01
350 Charles Nagy	.15	.07	.02
351 Robby Thompson	.05	.02	.01
352 Roberto Petagine	.05	.02	.01
353 Darryl Strawberry	.15	.07	.02
354 Tino Martinez	.15	.07	.02
355 Eric Karros	.15	.07	.02
356 Cal Ripken SS	.75	.35	.09
357 Cecil Fielder SS	.15	.07	.02
358 Kirby Puckett SS	.30	.14	.04
359 Jim Edmonds SS	.15	.07	.02
360 Matt Williams SS	.30	.14	.04
361 Alex Rodriguez SS	1.00	.45	.12
362 Barry Larkin SS	.30	.14	.04
363 Rafael Palmeiro SS	.30	.14	.04
364 David Cone SS	.15	.07	.02
365 Roberto Alomar SS	.30	.14	.04
366 Eddie Murray SS	.30	.14	.04
367 Randy Johnson SS	.30	.14	.04
368 Ryan Klesko SS	.30	.14	.04
369 Raul Mondesi SS	.30	.14	.04
370 Mo Vaughn SS	.30	.14	.04
371 Will Clark SS	.30	.14	.04
372 Carlos Baerga SS	.15	.07	.02
373 Frank Thomas SS	1.00	.45	.12
374 Larry Walker SS	.30	.14	.04
375 Garret Anderson SS	.05	.02	.01
376 Edgar Martinez SS	.15	.07	.02
377 Don Mattingly SS	.50	.23	.06
378 Tony Gwynn SS	.40	.18	.05
379 Albert Belle SS	.40	.18	.05
380 Jason Isringhausen SS	.30	.14	.04
381 Ruben Rivera SS	.30	.14	.04
382 Johnny Damon SS	.15	.07	.02
383 Karim Garcia SS	.05	.02	.01
384 Derek Jeter SS	.50	.23	.06
385 David Justice SS	.05	.02	.01
386 Royce Clayton	.05	.02	.01
387 Mark Whiten	.05	.02	.01
388 Mickey Tettleton	.15	.07	.02
389 Steve Trachsel	.05	.02	.01
390 Danny Bautista	.05	.02	.01
391 Midre Cummings	.05	.02	.01
392 Scott Leius	.05	.02	.01
393 Manny Alexander	.05	.02	.01
394 Brent Gates	.05	.02	.01
395 Rey Sanchez	.05	.02	.01
396 Andy Pettitte	.60	.25	.07
397 Jeff Cirillo	.05	.02	.01
398 Kurt Abbott	.05	.02	.01
399 Lee Tinsley	.05	.02	.01
400 Paul Assenmacher	.05	.02	.01
401 Scott Erickson	.05	.02	.01
402 Todd Zeile	.05	.02	.01
403 Tom Pagnozzi	.05	.02	.01
404 Ozzie Guillen	.05	.02	.01
405 Jeff Frye	.05	.02	.01
406 Kirt Manwaring	.05	.02	.01
407 Chad Ogea	.05	.02	.01
408 Harold Baines	.15	.07	.02
409 Jason Bere	.05	.02	.01
410 Chuck Finley	.05	.02	.01
411 Jeff Fassero	.05	.02	.01
412 Joey Hamilton	.15	.07	.02
413 John Olerud	.05	.02	.01
414 Kevin Stocker	.05	.02	.01
415 Eric Anthony	.05	.02	.01
416 Aaron Sele	.05	.02	.01
417 Chris Bosio	.05	.02	.01
418 Michael Mimbs	.05	.02	.01
419 Orlando Miller	.05	.02	.01
420 Stan Javier	.05	.02	.01
421 Matt Mieske	.05	.02	.01
422 Jason Bates	.05	.02	.01
423 Orlando Merced	.15	.07	.02
424 John Flaherty	.05	.02	.01
425 Reggie Jefferson	.05	.02	.01
426 Scott Stahoviak	.05	.02	.01
427 John Burkett	.05	.02	.01
428 Rod Beck	.05	.02	.01
429 Bill Swift	.05	.02	.01
430 Scott Cooper	.05	.02	.01
431 Mel Rojas	.05	.02	.01
432 Todd Van Poppel	.05	.02	.01
433 Bobby Jones	.05	.02	.01
434 Mike Harkey	.05	.02	.01
435 Sean Berry	.05	.02	.01
436 Glenallen Hill	.05	.02	.01
437 Ryan Thompson	.05	.02	.01
438 Luis Alicea	.05	.02	.01
439 Esteban Loaiza	.05	.02	.01
440 Jeff Reboulet	.05	.02	.01
441 Vince Coleman	.05	.02	.01
442 Ellis Burks	.15	.07	.02
443 Allen Battle	.05	.02	.01
444 Jimmy Key	.15	.07	.02
445 Ricky Bottalico	.05	.02	.01
446 Delino DeShields	.05	.02	.01
447 Albie Lopez	.05	.02	.01
448 Mark Petkovsek	.05	.02	.01
449 Tim Raines	.30	.14	.04
450 Bryan Harvey	.05	.02	.01
451 Pat Hentgen	.15	.07	.02
452 Tim Laker	.05	.02	.01
453 Tom Gordon	.05	.02	.01
454 Phil Plantier	.05	.02	.01
455 Ernie Young	.05	.02	.01
456 Pete Harnisch	.05	.02	.01
457 Roberto Kelly	.05	.02	.01
458 Mark Portugal	.05	.02	.01
459 Mark Leiter	.05	.02	.01
460 Tony Pena	.05	.02	.01
461 Roger Pavlik	.05	.02	.01
462 Jeff King	.15	.07	.02
463 Bryan Rekar	.05	.02	.01
464 Al Leiter	.05	.02	.01
465 Phil Nevin	.05	.02	.01
466 Jose Lima	.05	.02	.01
467 Mike Stanley	.05	.02	.01
468 David McCarty	.05	.02	.01
469 Herb Perry	.05	.02	.01
470 Geronimo Berroa	.15	.07	.02
471 David Wells	.05	.02	.01
472 Vaughn Eshelman	.05	.02	.01
473 Greg Swindell	.05	.02	.01
474 Steve Sparks	.05	.02	.01
475 Luis Sojo	.05	.02	.01
476 Derrick May	.05	.02	.01
477 Joe Oliver	.05	.02	.01
478 Alex Arias	.05	.02	.01
479 Brad Ausmus	.05	.02	.01
480 Gabe White	.05	.02	.01
481 Pat Rapp	.05	.02	.01
482 Damon Buford	.05	.02	.01
483 Turk Wendell	.05	.02	.01
484 Jeff Brantley	.05	.02	.01
485 Curtis Leskanic	.05	.02	.01
486 Robb Nen	.05	.02	.01
487 Lou Whitaker	.15	.07	.02
488 Melido Perez	.05	.02	.01
489 Luis Polonia	.05	.02	.01
490 Scott Brosius	.15	.07	.02
491 Robert Perez	.05	.02	.01
492 Mike Sweeney	.40	.18	.05
493 Mark Loretta	.05	.02	.01
494 Alex Ochoa	.15	.07	.02
495 Matt Lawton	.05	.02	.01
496 Shawn Estes	.15	.07	.02
497 John Wasdin	.05	.02	.01
498 Marc Kroon	.05	.02	.01
499 Chris Snopek	.05	.02	.01
500 Jeff Suppan	.30	.14	.04
501 Terrell Wade	.15	.07	.02
502 Marvin Benard	.05	.02	.01
503 Chris Widger	.05	.02	.01
504 Quinton McCracken	.05	.02	.01
505 Bob Wolcott	.05	.02	.01
506 C.J. Nitkowski	.05	.02	.01
507 Aaron Ledesma	.05	.02	.01
508 Scott Hatteberg	.05	.02	.01
509 Jimmy Haynes	.05	.02	.01
510 Howard Battle	.05	.02	.01
511 Marty Cordova CL	.15	.07	.02
512 Randy Johnson CL	.30	.14	.04
513 Mo Vaughn CL	.30	.14	.04
514 Chan Ho Park CL	.30	.14	.04
515 Greg Maddux CL	.60	.25	.07
516 Barry Larkin CL	.30	.14	.04
517 Tom Glavine CL	.30	.14	.04
NNO Cal Ripken 2131	20.00	9.00	2.50

1996 Score All-Stars

Randomly inserted in jumbo packs at a rate of one in nine, this 20-card set was printed in rainbow holographic prismatic foil.

	MINT	NRMT	EXC
COMPLETE SET (20)	80.00	36.00	10.00
COMMON CARD (1-20)	1.50	.70	.19
1 Frank Thomas	15.00	6.75	1.85
2 Albert Belle	6.00	2.70	.75
3 Ken Griffey Jr.	15.00	6.75	1.85
4 Cal Ripken	12.00	5.50	1.50
5 Mo Vaughn	4.00	1.80	.50
6 Matt Williams	2.50	1.10	.30
7 Barry Bonds	4.00	1.80	.50
8 Dante Bichette	2.50	1.10	.30
9 Tony Gwynn	6.00	2.70	.75
10 Greg Maddux	10.00	4.50	1.25
11 Randy Johnson	2.50	1.10	.30
12 Hideo Nomo	4.00	1.80	.50
13 Tim Salmon	2.50	1.10	.30
14 Jeff Bagwell	6.00	2.70	.75
15 Edgar Martinez	2.00	.90	.25
16 Reggie Sanders	1.50	.70	.19
17 Larry Walker	2.50	1.10	.30
18 Chipper Jones	10.00	4.50	1.25
19 Manny Ramirez	4.00	1.80	.50
20 Eddie Murray	4.00	1.80	.50

1996 Score Big Bats

This 20-card set was randomly inserted in retail packs at a rate of approximately one in 31. The fronts feature a player photo set against a gold-foil background. The words "Big Bats" as well as the player's name is printed in white at the bottom. The backs feature a photo against a multi-colored background. The cards are numbered "X" of 20 in the upper left corner.

	MINT	NRMT	EXC
COMPLETE SET (20)	125.00	55.00	15.50
COMMON CARD (1-20)	2.00	.90	.25
1 Cal Ripken	20.00	9.00	2.50
2 Ken Griffey Jr.	25.00	11.00	3.10
3 Frank Thomas	25.00	11.00	3.10
4 Jeff Bagwell	10.00	4.50	1.25
5 Mike Piazza	15.00	6.75	1.85
6 Barry Bonds	6.00	2.70	.75
7 Matt Williams	3.00	1.35	.35
8 Raul Mondesi	3.00	1.35	.35
9 Tony Gwynn	10.00	4.50	1.25
10 Albert Belle	10.00	4.50	1.25
11 Manny Ramirez	6.00	2.70	.75
12 Carlos Baerga	2.00	.90	.25
13 Mo Vaughn	6.00	2.70	.75
14 Derek Bell	2.00	.90	.25
15 Larry Walker	3.00	1.35	.35
16 Kenny Lofton	6.00	2.70	.75
17 Edgar Martinez	2.50	1.10	.30
18 Reggie Sanders	2.00	.90	.25
19 Eddie Murray	6.00	2.70	.75
20 Chipper Jones	15.00	6.75	1.85

1996 Score Diamond Aces

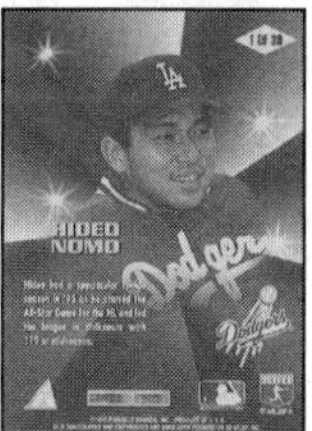

This 30-card set features some of baseball's best players. These cards were inserted approximately one every eight jumbo packs. The fronts display a color player cutout on a computer-generated background with gold foil accenting. On a similar background, the backs carry a color closeup.

	MINT	NRMT	EXC
COMPLETE SET (30)	150.00	70.00	19.00
COMMON CARD (1-30)	2.50	1.10	.30
1 Hideo Nomo	6.00	2.70	.75
2 Brian L.Hunter	2.50	1.10	.30
3 Ray Durham	3.00	1.35	.35
4 Frank Thomas	25.00	11.00	3.10
5 Cal Ripken	20.00	9.00	2.50
6 Barry Bonds	6.00	2.70	.75
7 Greg Maddux	15.00	6.75	1.85
8 Chipper Jones	15.00	6.75	1.85
9 Raul Mondesi	2.50	1.10	.30
10 Mike Piazza	15.00	6.75	1.85
11 Derek Jeter	15.00	6.75	1.85
12 Bill Pulsipher	2.50	1.10	.30
13 Larry Walker	4.00	1.80	.50
14 Ken Griffey Jr.	25.00	11.00	3.10
15 Alex Rodriguez	25.00	11.00	3.10
16 Manny Ramirez	6.00	2.70	.75
17 Mo Vaughn	6.00	2.70	.75
18 Reggie Sanders	2.50	1.10	.30
19 Derek Bell	2.50	1.10	.30
20 Jim Edmonds	3.00	1.35	.35
21 Albert Belle	10.00	4.50	1.25
22 Eddie Murray	6.00	2.70	.75
23 Tony Gwynn	10.00	4.50	1.25
24 Jeff Bagwell	10.00	4.50	1.25
25 Carlos Baerga	2.50	1.10	.30
26 Matt Williams	4.00	1.80	.50
27 Garret Anderson	2.50	1.10	.30
28 Todd Hollandsworth	3.00	1.35	.35
29 Johnny Damon	2.50	1.10	.30
30 Tim Salmon	4.00	1.80	.50

1996 Score Dream Team

This nine-card set was randomly inserted in approximately one in 72 packs. This set features a leading player at each position. The fronts feature a player photo set against a holographic foil background. The words "1995 Dream Team" as well as his name and team are printed on the bottom of the card. The horizontal backs feature a player photo and some text. The cards are numbered in the upper right as "X" of nine.

	MINT	NRMT	EXC
COMPLETE SET (9)	100.00	45.00	12.50
COMMON CARD (1-9)	2.00	.90	.25
☐ 1 Cal Ripken	20.00	9.00	2.50
☐ 2 Frank Thomas	25.00	11.00	3.10
☐ 3 Carlos Baerga	2.00	.90	.25
☐ 4 Matt Williams	3.00	1.35	.35
☐ 5 Mike Piazza	15.00	6.75	1.85
☐ 6 Barry Bonds	6.00	2.70	.75
☐ 7 Ken Griffey Jr.	25.00	11.00	3.10
☐ 8 Manny Ramirez	6.00	2.70	.75
☐ 9 Greg Maddux	15.00	6.75	1.85

1996 Score Dugout Collection

This set is a mini-parallel to the regular issue. Only 110 cards of each Series 1 and Series 2 were selected. Randomly inserted approximately one in every three packs, these cards have all gold foil printing that gives them a shiny copper cast. The words "Dugout Collection" are printed on the back.

	MINT	NRMT	EXC
COMPLETE SERIES 1 (110)	50.00	22.00	6.25
COMMON CARD (A1-A110)	.30	.14	.04
COMPLETE SERIES 2 (110)	50.00	22.00	6.25
COMMON CARD (B1-B110)	.30	.14	.04
☐ A1 Will Clark	1.00	.45	.12
☐ A2 Rich Becker	.30	.14	.04
☐ A3 Ryan Klesko	1.00	.45	.12
☐ A4 Jim Edmonds	.60	.25	.07
☐ A5 Barry Larkin	1.00	.45	.12
☐ A6 Jim Thome	1.50	.70	.19
☐ A7 Raul Mondesi	1.00	.45	.12
☐ A8 Don Mattingly	4.00	1.80	.50
☐ A9 Jeff Conine	.60	.25	.07
☐ A10 Rickey Henderson	1.00	.45	.12
☐ A11 Chad Curtis	.30	.14	.04
☐ A12 Darren Daulton	.60	.25	.07
☐ A13 Larry Walker	1.00	.45	.12
☐ A14 Carlos Baerga	.60	.25	.07
☐ A15 Tony Gwynn	3.00	1.35	.35
☐ A16 Jon Nunnally	.30	.14	.04
☐ A17 Deion Sanders	1.00	.45	.12
☐ A18 Mark Grace	1.00	.45	.12
☐ A19 Alex Rodriguez	8.00	3.60	1.00
☐ A20 Frank Thomas	8.00	3.60	1.00
☐ A21 Brian Jordan	.60	.25	.07
☐ A22 J.T. Snow	.30	.14	.04
☐ A23 Shawn Green	.60	.25	.07
☐ A24 Tim Wakefield	.30	.14	.04
☐ A25 Curtis Goodwin	.30	.14	.04
☐ A26 John Smoltz	1.00	.45	.12
☐ A27 Devon White	.30	.14	.04
☐ A28 Brian L.Hunter	.60	.25	.07
☐ A29 Rusty Greer	1.00	.45	.12
☐ A30 Rafael Palmeiro	1.00	.45	.12
☐ A31 Bernard Gilkey	.60	.25	.07
☐ A32 John Valentin	.60	.25	.07
☐ A33 Randy Johnson	1.00	.45	.12
☐ A34 Garret Anderson	.60	.25	.07
☐ A35 Ray Durham	.30	.14	.04
☐ A36 Bip Roberts	.30	.14	.04
☐ A37 Tyler Green	.30	.14	.04
☐ A38 Bill Pulsipher	.60	.25	.07
☐ A39 Jason Giambi	1.00	.45	.12
☐ A40 Jack McDowell	.60	.25	.07
☐ A41 Rico Brogna	.60	.25	.07
☐ A42 Terry Pendleton	.30	.14	.04
☐ A43 Rondell White	.60	.25	.07
☐ A44 Andre Dawson	.60	.25	.07
☐ A45 Kirby Puckett	3.00	1.35	.35
☐ A46 Wally Joyner	.60	.25	.07
☐ A47 B.J. Surhoff	.30	.14	.04
☐ A48 Randy Velarde	.30	.14	.04
☐ A49 Greg Vaughn	.60	.25	.07
☐ A50 Roberto Alomar	1.50	.70	.19
☐ A51 David Justice	1.00	.45	.12
☐ A52 Cal Ripken	6.00	2.70	.75
☐ A53 Ozzie Smith	2.00	.90	.25
☐ A54 Mo Vaughn	2.00	.90	.25
☐ A55 Gary DiSarcina	.30	.14	.04
☐ A56 Matt Williams	1.00	.45	.12
☐ A57 Lenny Dykstra	.30	.14	.04
☐ A58 Bret Boone	.30	.14	.04
☐ A59 Albert Belle	3.00	1.35	.35
☐ A60 Vinny Castilla	.60	.25	.07
☐ A61 Moises Alou	.60	.25	.07
☐ A62 Cecil Fielder	.60	.25	.07
☐ A63 Brad Radke	.30	.14	.04
☐ A64 Quilvio Veras	.30	.14	.04
☐ A65 Eddie Murray	2.00	.90	.25
☐ A66 Dave Winfield	1.00	.45	.12
☐ A67 Fred McGriff	1.00	.45	.12
☐ A68 Craig Biggio	.60	.25	.07
☐ A69 Cliff Floyd	.60	.25	.07
☐ A70 Tim Naehring	.30	.14	.04
☐ A71 John Wetteland	.60	.25	.07
☐ A72 Alan Trammell	.60	.25	.07
☐ A73 Steve Avery	.60	.25	.07
☐ A74 Rick Aguilera	.60	.25	.07
☐ A75 Derek Bell	.60	.25	.07
☐ A76 Todd Hollandsworth	.60	.25	.07
☐ A77 Edgar Martinez	.60	.25	.07
☐ A78 Mark Lemke	.30	.14	.04
☐ A79 Ariel Prieto	.30	.14	.04
☐ A80 Russ Davis	.30	.14	.04
☐ A81 Jim Abbott	.30	.14	.04
☐ A82 Jason Isringhausen	1.00	.45	.12
☐ A83 Carlos Perez	.30	.14	.04
☐ A84 David Segui	.30	.14	.04
☐ A85 Troy O'Leary	.30	.14	.04
☐ A86 Ismael Valdes	.30	.14	.04
☐ A87 Carlos Delgado	.60	.25	.07
☐ A88 Lee Smith	.60	.25	.07
☐ A89 Javier Lopez	.60	.25	.07
☐ A90 Frank Rodriguez	.30	.14	.04
☐ A91 Alex Gonzalez	.30	.14	.04
☐ A92 Benji Gil	.30	.14	.04
☐ A93 Greg Gagne	.30	.14	.04
☐ A94 Randy Myers	.30	.14	.04
☐ A95 Bobby Bonilla	.60	.25	.07
☐ A96 Billy Ashley	.30	.14	.04
☐ A97 Andy Van Slyke	.60	.25	.07
☐ A98 Edgardo Alfonzo	.30	.14	.04
☐ A99 David Cone	.60	.25	.07
☐ A100 Dean Palmer	.60	.25	.07
☐ A101 Jose Mesa	.30	.14	.04
☐ A102 Karim Garcia	1.50	.70	.19
☐ A103 Johnny Damon	.60	.25	.07
☐ A104 LaTroy Hawkins	.30	.14	.04
☐ A105 Mark Smith	.30	.14	.04
☐ A106 Derek Jeter	5.00	2.20	.60
☐ A107 Michael Tucker	.60	.25	.07
☐ A108 Joe Vitiello	.30	.14	.04
☐ A109 Ruben Rivera	1.50	.70	.19
☐ A110 Greg Zaun	.30	.14	.04
☐ B1 Greg Maddux	5.00	2.20	.60
☐ B2 Pedro Martinez	.60	.25	.07
☐ B3 Bobby Higginson	.60	.25	.07
☐ B4 Ray Lankford	.60	.25	.07
☐ B5 Shawon Dunston	.30	.14	.04
☐ B6 Gary Sheffield	1.00	.45	.12
☐ B7 Ken Griffey Jr.	8.00	3.60	1.00
☐ B8 Paul Molitor	1.00	.45	.12
☐ B9 Kevin Appier	.60	.25	.07
☐ B10 Chuck Knoblauch	1.00	.45	.12
☐ B11 Alex Fernandez	.60	.25	.07
☐ B12 Steve Finley	.60	.25	.07
☐ B13 Jeff Blauser	.30	.14	.04
☐ B14 Charles Johnson	.60	.25	.07
☐ B15 John Franco	.30	.14	.04
☐ B16 Mark Langston	.30	.14	.04
☐ B17 Bret Saberhagen	.30	.14	.04
☐ B18 John Mabry	.60	.25	.07
☐ B19 Ramon Martinez	.60	.25	.07
☐ B20 Mike Blowers	.30	.14	.04
☐ B21 Paul O'Neill	.30	.14	.04
☐ B22 Dave Nilsson	.30	.14	.04
☐ B23 Dante Bichette	1.00	.45	.12
☐ B24 Marty Cordova	.60	.25	.07
☐ B25 Jay Bell	.30	.14	.04
☐ B26 Mike Mussina	1.50	.70	.19
☐ B27 Ivan Rodriguez	1.00	.45	.12
☐ B28 Jose Canseco	1.00	.45	.12
☐ B29 Jeff Bagwell	3.00	1.35	.35
☐ B30 Manny Ramirez	2.00	.90	.25
☐ B31 Dennis Martinez	.60	.25	.07
☐ B32 Charlie Hayes	.30	.14	.04
☐ B33 Joe Carter	.60	.25	.07
☐ B34 Travis Fryman	.60	.25	.07
☐ B35 Mark McGwire	2.50	1.10	.30
☐ B36 Reggie Sanders	.60	.25	.07
☐ B37 Julian Tavarez	.30	.14	.04
☐ B38 Jeff Montgomery	.30	.14	.04
☐ B39 Andy Benes	.30	.14	.04
☐ B40 John Jaha	.60	.25	.07
☐ B41 Jeff Kent	.30	.14	.04
☐ B42 Mike Piazza	5.00	2.20	.60
☐ B43 Erik Hanson	.30	.14	.04
☐ B44 Kenny Rogers	.30	.14	.04
☐ B45 Hideo Nomo	2.00	.90	.25
☐ B46 Gregg Jefferies	.60	.25	.07
☐ B47 Chipper Jones	5.00	2.20	.60
☐ B48 Jay Buhner	1.00	.45	.12
☐ B49 Dennis Eckersley	.60	.25	.07
☐ B50 Kenny Lofton	2.00	.90	.25
☐ B51 Robin Ventura	.60	.25	.07
☐ B52 Tom Glavine	1.00	.45	.12
☐ B53 Tim Salmon	1.00	.45	.12
☐ B54 Andres Galarraga	1.00	.45	.12
☐ B55 Hal Morris	.30	.14	.04
☐ B56 Brady Anderson	1.00	.45	.12
☐ B57 Chili Davis	.30	.14	.04
☐ B58 Roger Clemens	1.50	.70	.19
☐ B59 Marquis Grissom	.60	.25	.07
☐ B60 Mike Greenwell UER	.30	.14	.04
(Front says Jeff Greenwell			
☐ B61 Sammy Sosa	1.00	.45	.12
☐ B62 Ron Gant	.60	.25	.07
☐ B63 Ken Caminiti	1.00	.45	.12
☐ B64 Danny Tartabull	.30	.14	.04
☐ B65 Barry Bonds	2.00	.90	.25
☐ B66 Ben McDonald	.30	.14	.04
☐ B67 Ruben Sierra	.30	.14	.04
☐ B68 Bernie Williams	1.50	.70	.19
☐ B69 Wil Cordero	.30	.14	.04
☐ B70 Wade Boggs	1.00	.45	.12
☐ B71 Gary Gaetti	.30	.14	.04
☐ B72 Greg Colbrunn	.30	.14	.04
☐ B73 Juan Gonzalez	4.00	1.80	.50
☐ B74 Marc Newfield	.30	.14	.04
☐ B75 Charles Nagy	.60	.25	.07
☐ B76 Robby Thompson	.30	.14	.04
☐ B77 Roberto Petagine	.30	.14	.04
☐ B78 Darryl Strawberry	.60	.25	.07
☐ B79 Tino Martinez	.60	.25	.07
☐ B80 Eric Karros	.60	.25	.07
☐ B81 Cal Ripken SS	3.00	1.35	.35
☐ B82 Cecil Fielder SS	.60	.25	.07
☐ B83 Kirby Puckett SS	1.00	.45	.12
☐ B84 Jim Edmonds SS	.60	.25	.07
☐ B85 Matt Williams SS	1.00	.45	.12
☐ B86 Alex Rodriguez SS	4.00	1.80	.50
☐ B87 Barry Larkin SS	.60	.25	.07
☐ B88 Rafael Palmeiro SS	1.00	.45	.12
☐ B89 David Cone SS	.60	.25	.07
☐ B90 Roberto Alomar SS	1.00	.45	.12
☐ B91 Eddie Murray SS	1.00	.45	.12
☐ B92 Randy Johnson SS	1.00	.45	.12
☐ B93 Ryan Klesko SS	1.00	.45	.12
☐ B94 Raul Mondesi SS	1.00	.45	.12
☐ B95 Mo Vaughn SS	.60	.25	.07
☐ B96 Will Clark SS	1.00	.45	.12
☐ B97 Carlos Baerga SS	.60	.25	.07
☐ B98 Frank Thomas SS	4.00	1.80	.50
☐ B99 Larry Walker SS	1.00	.45	.12
☐ B100 Garret Anderson SS	.30	.14	.04
☐ B101 Edgar Martinez SS	.60	.25	.07
☐ B102 Don Mattingly SS	2.00	.90	.25
☐ B103 Tony Gwynn SS	1.50	.70	.19
☐ B104 Albert Belle SS	1.50	.70	.19
☐ B105 Jason Isringhausen SS	1.00	.45	.12
☐ B106 Ruben Rivera SS	1.00	.45	.12
☐ B107 Johnny Damon SS	.60	.25	.07
☐ B108 Karim Garcia SS	1.00	.45	.12
☐ B109 Derek Jeter SS	5.00	2.20	.60
☐ B110 David Justice SS	.60	.25	.07

1996 Score Dugout Collection Artist's Proofs

This set is a parallel to the Dugout Collection set. These cards are different from the regular Dugout Collection as they have the words Artist Proof printed on the front. Randomly inserted one in every 36 packs, this set was printed using Gold Rush all gold-foil card technology .

	MINT	NRMT	EXC
COMPLETE SER.1 SET (110)	350.00	160.00	45.00
COMPLETE SER.2 SET (110)	350.00	160.00	45.00
COMMON CARD (1A-110A)	1.50	.70	.19
COMMON CARD (1B-110B)	1.50	.70	.19

*STARS: 3X TO 6X BASIC CARDS
*YOUNG STARS: 2.5X TO 5X BASIC CARDS

1996 Score Future Franchise

Randomly inserted in retail packs at a rate of one in 72, this 16-card set honors young stars of the game. The fronts feature a color action player cutout on a special holographic foil printed background. The backs carry another player color photo with player information.

	MINT	NRMT	EXC
COMPLETE SET (16)	130.00	57.50	16.00
COMMON CARD (1-16)	4.00	1.80	.50
☐ 1 Jason Isringhausen	4.00	1.80	.50
☐ 2 Chipper Jones	25.00	11.00	3.10
☐ 3 Derek Jeter	25.00	11.00	3.10
☐ 4 Alex Rodriguez	50.00	22.00	6.25
☐ 5 Alex Ochoa	4.00	1.80	.50
☐ 6 Manny Ramirez	12.00	5.50	1.50
☐ 7 Johnny Damon	5.00	2.20	.60
☐ 8 Ruben Rivera	10.00	4.50	1.25
☐ 9 Karim Garcia	10.00	4.50	1.25
☐ 10 Garret Anderson	4.00	1.80	.50
☐ 11 Marty Cordova	6.00	2.70	.75
☐ 12 Bill Pulsipher	4.00	1.80	.50
☐ 13 Hideo Nomo	12.00	5.50	1.50
☐ 14 Marc Newfield	4.00	1.80	.50
☐ 15 Charles Johnson	4.00	1.80	.50
☐ 16 Raul Mondesi	6.00	2.70	.75

1996 Score Gold Stars

Randomly inserted in packs at a rate of one in 15, this 30-card set features borderless color action player photos with a special sepia player cutout inserted behind a gold foil stamp designating the star player. The backs display another player photo with player information.

	MINT	NRMT	EXC
COMPLETE SET (30)	60.00	27.00	7.50
COMMON CARD (1-30)	.75	.35	.09
☐ 1 Ken Griffey Jr.	10.00	4.50	1.25
☐ 2 Frank Thomas	10.00	4.50	1.25
☐ 3 Reggie Sanders	.75	.35	.09
☐ 4 Tim Salmon	1.25	.55	.16
☐ 5 Mike Piazza	6.00	2.70	.75
☐ 6 Tony Gwynn	4.00	1.80	.50
☐ 7 Gary Sheffield	1.50	.70	.19
☐ 8 Matt Williams	1.25	.55	.16
☐ 9 Bernie Williams	2.00	.90	.25
☐ 10 Jason Isringhausen	.75	.35	.09
☐ 11 Albert Belle	4.00	1.80	.50
☐ 12 Chipper Jones	6.00	2.70	.75
☐ 13 Edgar Martinez	1.00	.45	.12
☐ 14 Barry Larkin	1.00	.45	.12
☐ 15 Barry Bonds	2.50	1.10	.30
☐ 16 Jeff Bagwell	4.00	1.80	.50
☐ 17 Greg Maddux	6.00	2.70	.75
☐ 18 Mo Vaughn	2.50	1.10	.30
☐ 19 Ryan Klesko	1.25	.55	.16
☐ 20 Sammy Sosa	1.50	.70	.19
☐ 21 Darren Daulton	1.00	.45	.12
☐ 22 Ivan Rodriguez	2.50	1.10	.30
☐ 23 Dante Bichette	1.25	.55	.16
☐ 24 Hideo Nomo	2.50	1.10	.30
☐ 25 Cal Ripken	8.00	3.60	1.00
☐ 26 Rafael Palmeiro	1.25	.55	.16
☐ 27 Larry Walker	1.25	.55	.16
☐ 28 Carlos Baerga	.75	.35	.09
☐ 29 Randy Johnson	1.50	.70	.19
☐ 30 Manny Ramirez	2.50	1.10	.30

1996 Score Numbers Game

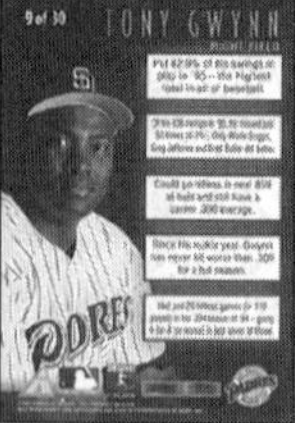

This 30-card set was inserted approximately one in every 15 packs. The fronts feature two player photos. The player's name is spelled vertically on the right while the words "Numbers Game" are printed against a gold-foil background. The backs contain five quick information bytes that feature that player's accomplishments. The cards are numbered as "X" of 30 in the upper left corner.

	MINT	NRMT	EXC
COMPLETE SET (30)	60.00	27.00	7.50
COMMON CARD (1-30)	.75	.35	.09
☐ 1 Cal Ripken	8.00	3.60	1.00
☐ 2 Frank Thomas	10.00	4.50	1.25
☐ 3 Ken Griffey Jr.	10.00	4.50	1.25
☐ 4 Mike Piazza	6.00	2.70	.75
☐ 5 Barry Bonds	2.50	1.10	.30
☐ 6 Greg Maddux	6.00	2.70	.75
☐ 7 Jeff Bagwell	4.00	1.80	.50
☐ 8 Derek Bell	.75	.35	.09
☐ 9 Tony Gwynn	4.00	1.80	.50
☐ 10 Hideo Nomo	2.50	1.10	.30
☐ 11 Raul Mondesi	1.25	.55	.16
☐ 12 Manny Ramirez	2.50	1.10	.30
☐ 13 Albert Belle	4.00	1.80	.50
☐ 14 Matt Williams	1.25	.55	.16
☐ 15 Jim Edmonds	1.00	.45	.12
☐ 16 Edgar Martinez	1.00	.45	.12
☐ 17 Mo Vaughn	2.50	1.10	.30
☐ 18 Reggie Sanders	.75	.35	.09
☐ 19 Chipper Jones	6.00	2.70	.75
☐ 20 Larry Walker	1.25	.55	.16
☐ 21 Juan Gonzalez	5.00	2.20	.60
☐ 22 Kenny Lofton	2.50	1.10	.30
☐ 23 Don Mattingly	5.00	2.20	.60
☐ 24 Ivan Rodriguez	2.50	1.10	.30
☐ 25 Randy Johnson	1.50	.70	.19
☐ 26 Derek Jeter	6.00	2.70	.75
☐ 27 J.T. Snow	.75	.35	.09
☐ 28 Will Clark	1.25	.55	.16
☐ 29 Rafael Palmeiro	1.25	.55	.16
☐ 30 Alex Rodriguez	10.00	4.50	1.25

1996 Score Power Pace

Randomly inserted in retail packs at a rate of one in 31, this 18-card set features homerun hitters. The fronts display color action player cutouts on a gold foil background. The backs carry another player photo with player information including how frequently he can be expected to hit a homerun based on his career at-bats.

	MINT	NRMT	EXC
COMPLETE SET (18)	90.00	40.00	11.00
COMMON CARD (1-18)	2.00	.90	.25
☐ 1 Mark McGwire	8.00	3.60	1.00
☐ 2 Albert Belle	10.00	4.50	1.25
☐ 3 Jay Buhner	3.00	1.35	.35
☐ 4 Frank Thomas	25.00	11.00	3.10
☐ 5 Matt Williams	3.00	1.35	.35
☐ 6 Gary Sheffield	4.00	1.80	.50
☐ 7 Mike Piazza	15.00	6.75	1.85
☐ 8 Larry Walker	3.00	1.35	.35
☐ 9 Mo Vaughn	6.00	2.70	.75
☐ 10 Rafael Palmeiro	3.00	1.35	.35
☐ 11 Dante Bichette	3.00	1.35	.35
☐ 12 Ken Griffey, Jr.	25.00	11.00	3.10
☐ 13 Barry Bonds	6.00	2.70	.75
☐ 14 Manny Ramirez	6.00	2.70	.75
☐ 15 Sammy Sosa	4.00	1.80	.50
☐ 16 Tim Salmon	3.00	1.35	.35
☐ 17 Dave Justice	2.00	.90	.25
☐ 18 Eric Karros	2.00	.90	.25

1996 Score Reflextions

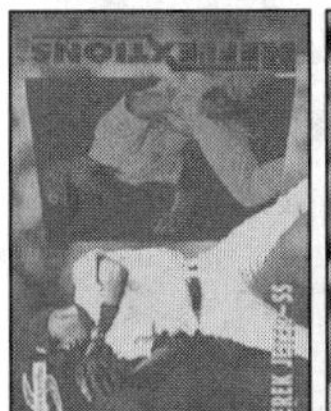

This 20-card set was randomly inserted approximately one in every 31 hobby packs. Two players per card are featured, a veteran player and a younger star playing the same position. These cards feature a mirror effect on the front.

	MINT	NRMT	EXC
COMPLETE SET (20)	125.00	55.00	15.50
COMMON CARD (1-20)	2.00	.90	.25
☐ 1 Cal Ripken Chipper Jones	30.00	13.50	3.70
☐ 2 Ken Griffey Jr. Alex Rodriguez	40.00	18.00	5.00
☐ 3 Frank Thomas Mo Vaughn	25.00	11.00	3.10
☐ 4 Kenny Lofton Brian L.Hunter	6.00	2.70	.75
☐ 5 Don Mattingly J.T.Snow	10.00	4.50	1.25
☐ 6 Manny Ramirez Raul Mondesi	6.00	2.70	.75
☐ 7 Tony Gwynn Garret Anderson	8.00	3.60	1.00
☐ 8 Roberto Alomar Carlos Baerga	6.00	2.70	.75
☐ 9 Andre Dawson Larry Walker	2.00	.90	.25
☐ 10 Barry Larkin Derek Jeter	15.00	6.75	1.85
☐ 11 Barry Bonds Reggie Sanders	6.00	2.70	.75
☐ 12 Mike Piazza Albert Belle	15.00	6.75	1.85
☐ 13 Wade Boggs Edgar Martinez	2.00	.90	.25
☐ 14 David Cone John Smoltz	2.00	.90	.25
☐ 15 Will Clark Jeff Bagwell	10.00	4.50	1.25
☐ 16 Mark McGwire Cecil Fielder	8.00	3.60	1.00
☐ 17 Greg Maddux Mike Mussina	15.00	6.75	1.85
☐ 18 Randy Johnson Hideo Nomo	8.00	3.60	1.00
☐ 19 Jim Thome Dean Palmer	5.00	2.20	.60
☐ 20 Chuck Knoblauch Craig Biggio	2.00	.90	.25

1996 Score Titanic Taters

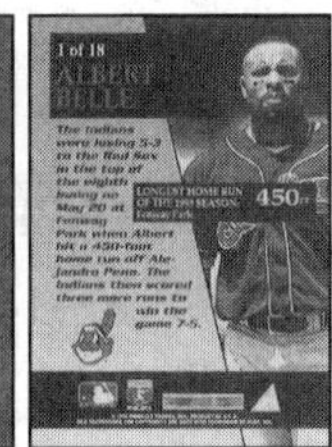

Randomly inserted in hobby packs at a rate of one in 31, this 18-card set features long home run hitters. The fronts display a color action player cutout on a gold foil background of a baseball park. The backs carry another player photo with information about the player's longest home run and the park where it was hit.

	MINT	NRMT	EXC
COMPLETE SET (18)	100.00	45.00	12.50
COMMON CARD (1-18)	2.00	.90	.25
☐ 1 Albert Belle	10.00	4.50	1.25
☐ 2 Frank Thomas	25.00	11.00	3.10
☐ 3 Mo Vaughn	6.00	2.70	.75
☐ 4 Ken Griffey Jr.	25.00	11.00	3.10
☐ 5 Matt Williams	3.00	1.35	.35
☐ 6 Mark McGwire	8.00	3.60	1.00
☐ 7 Dante Bichette	3.00	1.35	.35
☐ 8 Tim Salmon	3.00	1.35	.35
☐ 9 Jeff Bagwell	10.00	4.50	1.25
☐ 10 Rafael Palmeiro	3.00	1.35	.35
☐ 11 Mike Piazza	15.00	6.75	1.85
☐ 12 Cecil Fielder	2.00	.90	.25
☐ 13 Larry Walker	3.00	1.35	.35
☐ 14 Sammy Sosa	4.00	1.80	.50
☐ 15 Manny Ramirez	6.00	2.70	.75
☐ 16 Gary Sheffield	4.00	1.80	.50
☐ 17 Barry Bonds	6.00	2.70	.75
☐ 18 Jay Buhner	3.00	1.35	.35

1997 Score

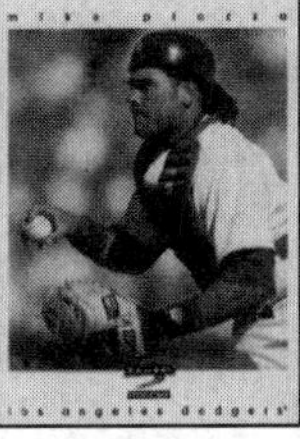
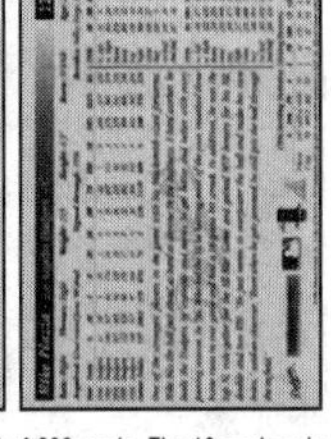

The 1997 Score set has a total of 330 cards. The 10-card packs carried a suggested retail price of $.99 each and were distributed exclusive to retail outlets. The fronts feature color player action photos in a white border. The backs carry player information and career statistics.

	MINT	NRMT	EXC
COMPLETE SET (330)	20.00	9.00	2.50
COMMON CARD (1-330)	.05	.02	.01
☐ 1 Jeff Bagwell	.75	.35	.09
☐ 2 Mickey Tettleton	.05	.02	.01
☐ 3 Johnny Damon	.05	.02	.01
☐ 4 Jeff Conine	.15	.07	.02
☐ 5 Bernie Williams	.40	.18	.05
☐ 6 Will Clark	.25	.11	.03
☐ 7 Ryan Klesko	.30	.14	.04
☐ 8 Cecil Fielder	.15	.07	.02
☐ 9 Paul Wilson	.15	.07	.02
☐ 10 Gregg Jefferies	.05	.02	.01
☐ 11 Chili Davis	.05	.02	.01
☐ 12 Albert Belle	.75	.35	.09
☐ 13 Ken Hill	.05	.02	.01
☐ 14 Cliff Floyd	.05	.02	.01
☐ 15 Jaime Navarro	.05	.02	.01
☐ 16 Ismael Valdes	.15	.07	.02
☐ 17 Jeff King	.05	.02	.01
☐ 18 Chris Bosio	.05	.02	.01
☐ 19 Reggie Sanders	.15	.07	.02
☐ 20 Darren Daulton	.15	.07	.02
☐ 21 Ken Caminiti	.30	.14	.04
☐ 22 Mike Piazza	1.25	.55	.16
☐ 23 Chad Mottola	.05	.02	.01
☐ 24 Darin Erstad	1.00	.45	.12
☐ 25 Dante Bichette	.25	.11	.03
☐ 26 Frank Thomas	2.00	.90	.25
☐ 27 Ben McDonald	.05	.02	.01
☐ 28 Raul Casanova	.05	.02	.01
☐ 29 Kevin Ritz	.05	.02	.01
☐ 30 Garret Anderson	.05	.02	.01
☐ 31 Jason Kendall	.15	.07	.02
☐ 32 Billy Wagner	.15	.07	.02
☐ 33 Dave Justice	.15	.07	.02
☐ 34 Marty Cordova	.15	.07	.02
☐ 35 Derek Jeter	1.25	.55	.16
☐ 36 Trevor Hoffman	.05	.02	.01
☐ 37 Geronimo Berroa	.05	.02	.01
☐ 38 Walt Weiss	.05	.02	.01
☐ 39 Kirt Manwaring	.05	.02	.01
☐ 40 Alex Gonzalez	.05	.02	.01
☐ 41 Sean Berry	.05	.02	.01
☐ 42 Kevin Appier	.15	.07	.02
☐ 43 Rusty Greer	.15	.07	.02
☐ 44 Pete Incaviglia	.05	.02	.01
☐ 45 Rafael Palmeiro	.25	.11	.03
☐ 46 Eddie Murray	.50	.23	.06
☐ 47 Moises Alou	.15	.07	.02
☐ 48 Mark Lewis	.05	.02	.01
☐ 49 Hal Morris	.05	.02	.01
☐ 50 Edgar Renteria	.25	.11	.03
☐ 51 Rickey Henderson	.25	.11	.03
☐ 52 Pat Listach	.05	.02	.01
☐ 53 John Wasdin	.05	.02	.01
☐ 54 James Baldwin	.05	.02	.01
☐ 55 Brian Jordan	.15	.07	.02
☐ 56 Edgar Martinez	.15	.07	.02
☐ 57 Wil Cordero	.05	.02	.01
☐ 58 Danny Tartabull	.05	.02	.01
☐ 59 Keith Lockhart	.05	.02	.01
☐ 60 Rico Brogna	.05	.02	.01
☐ 61 Ricky Bottalico	.05	.02	.01
☐ 62 Terry Pendleton	.05	.02	.01
☐ 63 Bret Boone	.05	.02	.01
☐ 64 Charlie Hayes	.05	.02	.01
☐ 65 Marc Newfield	.05	.02	.01
☐ 66 Sterling Hitchcock	.05	.02	.01
☐ 67 Roberto Alomar	.40	.18	.05
☐ 68 John Jaha	.15	.07	.02
☐ 69 Greg Colbrunn	.05	.02	.01
☐ 70 Sal Fasano	.05	.02	.01
☐ 71 Brooks Kieschnick	.15	.07	.02
☐ 72 Pedro Martinez	.15	.07	.02
☐ 73 Kevin Elster	.05	.02	.01
☐ 74 Ellis Burks	.15	.07	.02
☐ 75 Chuck Finley	.05	.02	.01
☐ 76 John Olerud	.15	.07	.02
☐ 77 Jay Bell	.05	.02	.01
☐ 78 Allen Watson	.05	.02	.01
☐ 79 Darryl Strawberry	.15	.07	.02
☐ 80 Orlando Miller	.05	.02	.01
☐ 81 Jose Herrera	.05	.02	.01
☐ 82 Andy Pettitte	.50	.23	.06
☐ 83 Juan Guzman	.05	.02	.01
☐ 84 Alan Benes	.15	.07	.02
☐ 85 Jack McDowell	.05	.02	.01
☐ 86 Ugueth Urbina	.05	.02	.01
☐ 87 Rocky Coppinger	.15	.07	.02
☐ 88 Jeff Cirillo	.05	.02	.01
☐ 89 Tom Glavine	.25	.11	.03
☐ 90 Robby Thompson	.05	.02	.01
☐ 91 Barry Bonds	.50	.23	.06
☐ 92 Carlos Delgado	.15	.07	.02
☐ 93 Mo Vaughn	.50	.23	.06
☐ 94 Ryne Sandberg	.50	.23	.06
☐ 95 Alex Rodriguez	2.00	.90	.25
☐ 96 Brady Anderson	.15	.07	.02
☐ 97 Scott Brosius	.05	.02	.01
☐ 98 Dennis Eckersley	.15	.07	.02
☐ 99 Brian McRae	.05	.02	.01
☐ 100 Rey Ordonez	.25	.11	.03
☐ 101 John Valentin	.05	.02	.01
☐ 102 Brett Butler	.15	.07	.02
☐ 103 Eric Karros	.15	.07	.02
☐ 104 Harold Baines	.05	.02	.01
☐ 105 Javier Lopez	.15	.07	.02
☐ 106 Alan Trammell	.15	.07	.02
☐ 107 Jim Thome	.30	.14	.04
☐ 108 Frank Rodriguez	.05	.02	.01
☐ 109 Bernard Gilkey	.05	.02	.01
☐ 110 Reggie Jefferson	.05	.02	.01
☐ 111 Scott Stahoviak	.05	.02	.01
☐ 112 Steve Gibralter	.05	.02	.01
☐ 113 Todd Hollandsworth	.15	.07	.02
☐ 114 Ruben Rivera	.25	.11	.03
☐ 115 Dennis Martinez	.05	.02	.01
☐ 116 Mariano Rivera	.15	.07	.02
☐ 117 John Smoltz	.30	.14	.04
☐ 118 John Mabry	.05	.02	.01
☐ 119 Tom Gordon	.05	.02	.01
☐ 120 Alex Ochoa	.05	.02	.01
☐ 121 Jamey Wright	.15	.07	.02
☐ 122 Dave Nilsson	.05	.02	.01
☐ 123 Bobby Bonilla	.15	.07	.02
☐ 124 Al Leiter	.05	.02	.01
☐ 125 Rick Aguilera	.05	.02	.01
☐ 126 Jeff Brantley	.05	.02	.01
☐ 127 Kevin Brown	.15	.07	.02
☐ 128 George Arias	.05	.02	.01
☐ 129 Darren Oliver	.05	.02	.01
☐ 130 Bill Pulsipher	.05	.02	.01
☐ 131 Roberto Hernandez	.05	.02	.01
☐ 132 Delino DeShields	.05	.02	.01
☐ 133 Mark Grudzielanek	.05	.02	.01
☐ 134 John Wetteland	.15	.07	.02
☐ 135 Carlos Baerga	.05	.02	.01
☐ 136 Paul Sorrento	.05	.02	.01
☐ 137 Leo Gomez	.05	.02	.01
☐ 138 Andy Ashby	.05	.02	.01
☐ 139 Julio Franco	.05	.02	.01
☐ 140 Brian Hunter	.05	.02	.01
☐ 141 Jermaine Dye	.25	.11	.03
☐ 142 Tony Clark	.30	.14	.04
☐ 143 Ruben Sierra	.05	.02	.01
☐ 144 Donovan Osborne	.05	.02	.01
☐ 145 Mark McLemore	.05	.02	.01
☐ 146 Terry Steinbach	.05	.02	.01
☐ 147 Bob Wells	.05	.02	.01
☐ 148 Chan Ho Park	.25	.11	.03
☐ 149 Tim Salmon	.25	.11	.03
☐ 150 Paul O'Neill	.05	.02	.01
☐ 151 Cal Ripken	1.50	.70	.19
☐ 152 Wally Joyner	.05	.02	.01
☐ 153 Omar Vizquel	.15	.07	.02
☐ 154 Mike Mussina	.40	.18	.05
☐ 155 Andres Galarraga	.25	.11	.03
☐ 156 Ken Griffey Jr.	2.00	.90	.25
☐ 157 Kenny Lofton	.50	.23	.06
☐ 158 Ray Durham	.05	.02	.01
☐ 159 Hideo Nomo	.50	.23	.06
☐ 160 Ozzie Guillen	.05	.02	.01
☐ 161 Roger Pavlik	.05	.02	.01
☐ 162 Manny Ramirez	.50	.23	.06
☐ 163 Mark Lemke	.05	.02	.01
☐ 164 Mike Stanley	.05	.02	.01
☐ 165 Chuck Knoblauch	.30	.14	.04
☐ 166 Kimera Bartee	.05	.02	.01
☐ 167 Wade Boggs	.25	.11	.03
☐ 168 Jay Buhner	.25	.11	.03
☐ 169 Eric Young	.15	.07	.02
☐ 170 Jose Canseco	.25	.11	.03
☐ 171 Dwight Gooden	.15	.07	.02
☐ 172 Fred McGriff	.25	.11	.03
☐ 173 Sandy Alomar Jr.	.05	.02	.01
☐ 174 Andy Benes	.05	.02	.01
☐ 175 Dean Palmer	.05	.02	.01
☐ 176 Larry Walker	.15	.07	.02
☐ 177 Charles Nagy	.15	.07	.02
☐ 178 David Cone	.15	.07	.02
☐ 179 Mark Grace	.25	.11	.03
☐ 180 Robin Ventura	.15	.07	.02
☐ 181 Roger Clemens	.40	.18	.05
☐ 182 Bobby Witt	.05	.02	.01
☐ 183 Vinny Castilla	.15	.07	.02
☐ 184 Gary Sheffield	.30	.14	.04
☐ 185 Dan Wilson	.05	.02	.01
☐ 186 Roger Cedeno	.05	.02	.01
☐ 187 Mark McGwire	.60	.25	.07
☐ 188 Darren Bragg	.05	.02	.01
☐ 189 Quinton McCracken	.05	.02	.01
☐ 190 Randy Myers	.05	.02	.01
☐ 191 Jeromy Burnitz	.05	.02	.01
☐ 192 Randy Johnson	.30	.14	.04
☐ 193 Chipper Jones	1.25	.55	.16
☐ 194 Greg Vaughn	.05	.02	.01
☐ 195 Travis Fryman	.15	.07	.02
☐ 196 Tim Naehring	.05	.02	.01
☐ 197 B.J. Surhoff	.05	.02	.01
☐ 198 Juan Gonzalez	1.00	.45	.12
☐ 199 Terrell Wade	.05	.02	.01
☐ 200 Jeff Frye	.05	.02	.01
☐ 201 Joey Cora	.05	.02	.01
☐ 202 Raul Mondesi	.25	.11	.03
☐ 203 Ivan Rodriguez	.50	.23	.06
☐ 204 Armando Reynoso	.05	.02	.01
☐ 205 Jeffrey Hammonds	.05	.02	.01
☐ 206 Darren Dreifort	.05	.02	.01
☐ 207 Kevin Seitzer	.05	.02	.01

☐ 208 Tino Martinez	.30	.14	.04
☐ 209 Jim Bruske	.05	.02	.01
☐ 210 Jeff Suppan	.15	.07	.02
☐ 211 Mark Carreon	.05	.02	.01
☐ 212 Wilson Alvarez	.05	.02	.01
☐ 213 John Burkett	.05	.02	.01
☐ 214 Tony Phillips	.05	.02	.01
☐ 215 Greg Maddux	1.25	.55	.16
☐ 216 Mark Whiten	.05	.02	.01
☐ 217 Curtis Pride	.05	.02	.01
☐ 218 Lyle Mouton	.05	.02	.01
☐ 219 Todd Hundley	.15	.07	.02
☐ 220 Greg Gagne	.05	.02	.01
☐ 221 Rich Amaral	.05	.02	.01
☐ 222 Tom Goodwin	.05	.02	.01
☐ 223 Chris Hoiles	.05	.02	.01
☐ 224 Jayhawk Owens	.05	.02	.01
☐ 225 Kenny Rogers	.05	.02	.01
☐ 226 Mike Greenwell	.05	.02	.01
☐ 227 Mark Wohlers	.05	.02	.01
☐ 228 Henry Rodriguez	.15	.07	.02
☐ 229 Robert Perez	.05	.02	.01
☐ 230 Jeff Kent	.05	.02	.01
☐ 231 Darryl Hamilton	.05	.02	.01
☐ 232 Alex Fernandez	.15	.07	.02
☐ 233 Ron Karkovice	.05	.02	.01
☐ 234 Jimmy Haynes	.05	.02	.01
☐ 235 Craig Biggio	.15	.07	.02
☐ 236 Ray Lankford	.15	.07	.02
☐ 237 Lance Johnson	.05	.02	.01
☐ 238 Matt Williams	.25	.11	.03
☐ 239 Chad Curtis	.05	.02	.01
☐ 240 Mark Thompson	.05	.02	.01
☐ 241 Jason Giambi	.15	.07	.02
☐ 242 Barry Larkin	.25	.11	.03
☐ 243 Paul Molitor	.50	.23	.06
☐ 244 Sammy Sosa	.30	.14	.04
☐ 245 Kevin Tapani	.05	.02	.01
☐ 246 Marquis Grissom	.15	.07	.02
☐ 247 Joe Carter	.15	.07	.02
☐ 248 Ramon Martinez	.15	.07	.02
☐ 249 Tony Gwynn	.75	.35	.09
☐ 250 Andy Fox	.05	.02	.01
☐ 251 Troy O'Leary	.05	.02	.01
☐ 252 Warren Newson	.05	.02	.01
☐ 253 Troy Percival	.05	.02	.01
☐ 254 Jamie Moyer	.05	.02	.01
☐ 255 Danny Graves	.05	.02	.01
☐ 256 David Wells	.05	.02	.01
☐ 257 Todd Zeile	.05	.02	.01
☐ 258 Raul Ibanez	.05	.02	.01
☐ 259 Tyler Houston	.05	.02	.01
☐ 260 LaTroy Hawkins	.05	.02	.01
☐ 261 Joey Hamilton	.15	.07	.02
☐ 262 Mike Sweeney	.15	.07	.02
☐ 263 Brant Brown	.05	.02	.01
☐ 264 Pat Hentgen	.15	.07	.02
☐ 265 Mark Johnson	.05	.02	.01
☐ 266 Robb Nen	.05	.02	.01
☐ 267 Justin Thompson	.15	.07	.02
☐ 268 Ron Gant	.15	.07	.02
☐ 269 Jeff D'Amico	.15	.07	.02
☐ 270 Shawn Estes	.05	.02	.01
☐ 271 Derek Bell	.15	.07	.02
☐ 272 Fernando Valenzuela	.15	.07	.02
☐ 273 Tom Pagnozzi	.05	.02	.01
☐ 274 John Burke	.05	.02	.01
☐ 275 Ed Sprague	.05	.02	.01
☐ 276 F.P. Santangelo	.05	.02	.01
☐ 277 Todd Greene	.05	.02	.01
☐ 278 Butch Huskey	.05	.02	.01
☐ 279 Steve Finley	.05	.02	.01
☐ 280 Eric Davis	.05	.02	.01
☐ 281 Shawn Green	.05	.02	.01
☐ 282 Al Martin	.05	.02	.01
☐ 283 Michael Tucker	.05	.02	.01
☐ 284 Shane Reynolds	.05	.02	.01
☐ 285 Matt Mieske	.05	.02	.01
☐ 286 Jose Rosado	.25	.11	.03
☐ 287 Mark Langston	.05	.02	.01
☐ 288 Ralph Milliard	.05	.02	.01
☐ 289 Mike Lansing	.05	.02	.01
☐ 290 Scott Servais	.05	.02	.01
☐ 291 Royce Clayton	.05	.02	.01
☐ 292 Mike Grace	.05	.02	.01
☐ 293 James Mouton	.05	.02	.01
☐ 294 Charles Johnson	.05	.02	.01
☐ 295 Gary Gaetti	.05	.02	.01
☐ 296 Kevin Mitchell	.05	.02	.01
☐ 297 Carlos Garcia	.05	.02	.01
☐ 298 Desi Relaford	.05	.02	.01
☐ 299 Jason Thompson	.05	.02	.01
☐ 300 Osvaldo Fernandez	.05	.02	.01
☐ 301 Fernando Vina	.05	.02	.01
☐ 302 Jose Offerman	.05	.02	.01
☐ 303 Yamil Benitez	.05	.02	.01
☐ 304 J.T. Snow	.05	.02	.01
☐ 305 Rafael Bournigal	.05	.02	.01
☐ 306 Jason Isringhausen	.05	.02	.01
☐ 307 Bobby Higginson	.15	.07	.02
☐ 308 Nerio Rodriguez	.25	.11	.03
☐ 309 Brian Giles	.05	.02	.01
☐ 310 Andruw Jones	2.00	.90	.25
☐ 311 Tony Graffanino	.05	.02	.01
☐ 312 Arquimedez Pozo	.05	.02	.01
☐ 313 Jermaine Allensworth	.15	.07	.02
☐ 314 Jeff Darwin	.05	.02	.01
☐ 315 George Williams	.05	.02	.01
☐ 316 Karim Garcia	.40	.18	.05
☐ 317 Trey Beamon	.05	.02	.01
☐ 318 Mac Suzuki	.05	.02	.01
☐ 319 Robin Jennings	.05	.02	.01
☐ 320 Danny Patterson	.05	.02	.01
☐ 321 Damon Mashore	.15	.07	.02
☐ 322 Wendell Magee	.15	.07	.02
☐ 323 Dax Jones	.05	.02	.01
☐ 324 Kevin Brown	.15	.07	.02
☐ 325 Marvin Benard	.05	.02	.01
☐ 326 Mike Cameron	.30	.14	.04
☐ 327 Marcus Jensen	.05	.02	.01
☐ 328 Eddie Murray CL (1-168)	.25	.11	.03
☐ 329 Paul Molitor CL (169-330)	.25	.11	.03
☐ 330 Todd Hundley CL (inserts)	.15	.07	.02

1997 Score Premium Stock

A special Premium Stock version of the base set was produced exclusively for hobby outlets. The cards parallel the regular issue set except for a grey border, thicker card stock and a prominent gold foil "Premium Stock" logo on front. The cards were distributed in Premium Stock hobby packs.

	MINT	NRMT	EXC
COMPLETE SET (330)	40.00	18.00	5.00
COMMON CARD (1-330)	.10	.05	.01
*STARS: 2X BASIC CARDS			
*YOUNG STARS: 2X BASIC CARDS			

1997 Score Showcase Series

Randomly inserted in hobby and retail packs at a rate of one in seven, this 330-card set is parallel to the regular Score set and is similar in design. It is printed on silver poly laminated card stock which distinguishes it from the regular set.

	MINT	NRMT	EXC
COMPLETE SET (330)	250.00	110.00	31.00
COMMON CARD (1-330)	.50	.23	.06
*STARS: 4X to 8X BASIC CARDS			
*YOUNG STARS: 3X to 6X BASIC CARDS			

1997 Score Showcase Series Artist's Proofs

Randomly inserted in hobby and retail packs at a rate of one in 35, this 330-card set is parallel to the more common Showcase Series set. The cards are printed on holographic laminated card stock with a prismatic foil background and stamped with an Artist's Proof logo on front.

	MINT	NRMT	EXC
COMPLETE SET (330)	1000.00	450.00	125.00
COMMON CARD (1-330)	1.50	.70	.19
*STARS: 15X to 30X BASIC CARDS			
*YOUNG STARS: 10X to 20X BASIC CARDS			

1997 Score Franchise

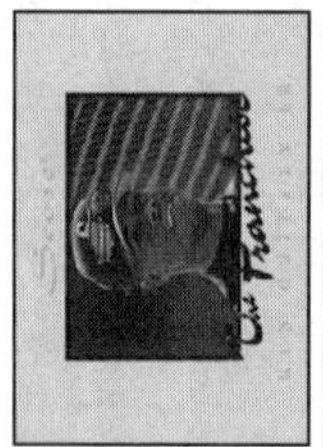
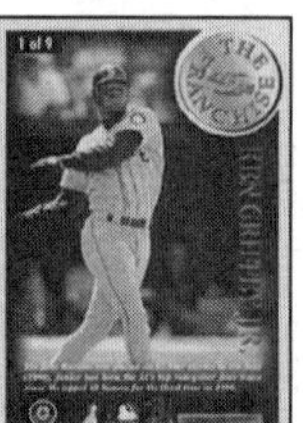

Randomly inserted in hobby packs only at a rate of one in 72, this nine-card set honors superstar players for their irreplaceable contribution to their team. The fronts display sepia player portraits on a white baseball replica background. The backs carry an action player photo with a sentence about the player which explains why he was selected for this set.

	MINT	NRMT	EXC
COMPLETE SET (9)	120.00	55.00	15.00
COMMON CARD (1-9)	5.00	2.20	.60
☐ 1 Ken Griffey Jr.	30.00	13.50	3.70
☐ 2 John Smoltz	5.00	2.20	.60
☐ 3 Cal Ripken	25.00	11.00	3.10
☐ 4 Chipper Jones	20.00	9.00	2.50
☐ 5 Mike Piazza	20.00	9.00	2.50
☐ 6 Albert Belle	12.00	5.50	1.50
☐ 7 Frank Thomas	30.00	13.50	3.70
☐ 8 Sammy Sosa	5.00	2.20	.60
☐ 9 Roberto Alomar	6.00	2.70	.75

1997 Score Franchise Glowing

Randomly inserted in hobby packs only at a rate of one in 240, this nine-card set is parallel to the regular Score Franchise set. Unique glow-in-the-dark ink distinguishes it from the regular set.

	MINT	NRMT	EXC
COMPLETE SET (9)	300.00	135.00	38.00
COMMON CARD (1-9)	12.00	5.50	1.50
GLOWING: 2.5X BASIC FRANCHISE			

1997 Score Highlight Zone

Randomly inserted in hobby packs only at a rate of one in 35, this 18-card set honors those mega-stars who have the incredible ability to consistently make the highlight films. The set is printed on thicker card stock with special foil stamping and a dot matrix holographic background.

	MINT	NRMT	EXC
COMPLETE SET (18)	200.00	90.00	25.00
COMMON CARD (1-18)	5.00	2.20	.60
☐ 1 Frank Thomas	30.00	13.50	3.70
☐ 2 Ken Griffey Jr.	30.00	13.50	3.70
☐ 3 Mo Vaughn	8.00	3.60	1.00
☐ 4 Albert Belle	12.00	5.50	1.50
☐ 5 Mike Piazza	20.00	9.00	2.50
☐ 6 Barry Bonds	8.00	3.60	1.00
☐ 7 Greg Maddux	20.00	9.00	2.50
☐ 8 Sammy Sosa	5.00	2.20	.60
☐ 9 Jeff Bagwell	12.00	5.50	1.50
☐ 10 Alex Rodriguez	30.00	13.50	3.70
☐ 11 Chipper Jones	20.00	9.00	2.50
☐ 12 Brady Anderson	5.00	2.20	.60
☐ 13 Ozzie Smith	6.00	2.70	.75
☐ 14 Edgar Martinez	5.00	2.20	.60
☐ 15 Cal Ripken	25.00	11.00	3.10
☐ 16 Ryan Klesko	5.00	2.20	.60
☐ 17 Randy Johnson	5.00	2.20	.60
☐ 18 Eddie Murray	8.00	3.60	1.00

1997 Score Pitcher Perfect

Randomly inserted in packs at a rate of one in 23, this 15-card set features players photographed by Randy Johnson in unique poses and foil stamping. The backs carry player information.

	MINT	NRMT	EXC
COMPLETE SET (15)	75.00	34.00	9.50
COMMON CARD (1-15)	1.50	.70	.19
☐ 1 Cal Ripken	12.00	5.50	1.50
☐ 2 Alex Rodriguez	15.00	6.75	1.85
☐ 3 Alex Rodriguez Cal Ripken	15.00	6.75	1.85
☐ 4 Edgar Martinez	1.50	.70	.19
☐ 5 Ivan Rodriguez	4.00	1.80	.50
☐ 6 Mark McGwire	5.00	2.20	.60
☐ 7 Tim Salmon	2.00	.90	.25
☐ 8 Chili Davis	1.50	.70	.19
☐ 9 Joe Carter	1.50	.70	.19
☐ 10 Frank Thomas	15.00	6.75	1.85
☐ 11 Will Clark	2.00	.90	.25
☐ 12 Mo Vaughn	4.00	1.80	.50
☐ 13 Wade Boggs	2.00	.90	.25
☐ 14 Ken Griffey Jr.	15.00	6.75	1.85
☐ 15 Randy Johnson	2.50	1.10	.30

1997 Score Stellar Season

Randomly inserted in pre-priced magazine packs only at a rate of one in 17, this 18-card set features players who had a star season. The cards are printed using dot matrix holographic printing.

	MINT	NRMT	EXC
COMPLETE SET (18)	90.00	40.00	11.00
COMMON CARD (1-18)	2.00	.90	.25
☐ 1 Juan Gonzalez	10.00	4.50	1.25
☐ 2 Chuck Knoblauch	3.00	1.35	.35
☐ 3 Jeff Bagwell	8.00	3.60	1.00
☐ 4 John Smoltz	3.00	1.35	.35
☐ 5 Mark McGwire	6.00	2.70	.75
☐ 6 Ken Griffey Jr.	20.00	9.00	2.50
☐ 7 Frank Thomas	20.00	9.00	2.50
☐ 8 Alex Rodriguez	20.00	9.00	2.50
☐ 9 Mike Piazza	12.00	5.50	1.50
☐ 10 Albert Belle	8.00	3.60	1.00
☐ 11 Roberto Alomar	5.00	2.20	.60
☐ 12 Sammy Sosa	3.00	1.35	.35
☐ 13 Mo Vaughn	5.00	2.20	.60
☐ 14 Brady Anderson	2.00	.90	.25
☐ 15 Henry Rodriguez	2.00	.90	.25
☐ 16 Eric Young	2.00	.90	.25
☐ 17 Gary Sheffield	3.00	1.35	.35
☐ 18 Ryan Klesko	3.00	1.35	.35

1997 Score Titanic Taters

Randomly inserted in retail packs only at a rate of one in 35, this 18-card set honors the long-ball ability of some of the league's top sluggers and uses dot matrix holographic printing.

	MINT	NRMT	EXC
COMPLETE SET (18)	125.00	55.00	15.50
COMMON CARD (1-18)	2.50	1.10	.30
☐ 1 Mark McGwire	8.00	3.60	1.00
☐ 2 Mike Piazza	15.00	6.75	1.85
☐ 3 Ken Griffey Jr.	25.00	11.00	3.10
☐ 4 Juan Gonzalez	12.00	5.50	1.50
☐ 5 Frank Thomas	25.00	11.00	3.10
☐ 6 Albert Belle	10.00	4.50	1.25
☐ 7 Sammy Sosa	4.00	1.80	.50
☐ 8 Jeff Bagwell	10.00	4.50	1.25
☐ 9 Todd Hundley	2.50	1.10	.30
☐ 10 Ryan Klesko	4.00	1.80	.50
☐ 11 Brady Anderson	2.50	1.10	.30
☐ 12 Mo Vaughn	6.00	2.70	.75
☐ 13 Jay Buhner	3.00	1.35	.35
☐ 14 Chipper Jones	15.00	6.75	1.85
☐ 15 Barry Bonds	6.00	2.70	.75
☐ 16 Gary Sheffield	4.00	1.80	.50
☐ 17 Alex Rodriguez	25.00	11.00	3.10
☐ 18 Cecil Fielder	2.50	1.10	.30

1997 Score Braves

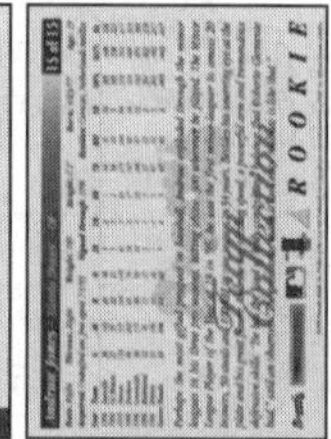

This 15-card set of the Atlanta Braves was issued in five-card packs with a suggested retail of $1.30 each. The fronts feature color player photos with special team specific color foil stamping. The backs carry player information. Only 100 cases were made for each team. Platinum parallel cards were inserted at a rate of 1:6, Premier parallel cards at a rate of 1:31.

	MINT	NRMT	EXC
COMPLETE SET (15)	10.00	4.50	1.25
COMMON CARD (1-15)	.10	.05	.01
☐ 1 Ryan Klesko	.75	.35	.09
☐ 2 Dave Justice	.25	.11	.03
☐ 3 Terry Pendleton	.10	.05	.01
☐ 4 Tom Glavine	.50	.23	.06
☐ 5 Javier Lopez	.25	.11	.03
☐ 6 John Smoltz	.75	.35	.09
☐ 7 Jermaine Dye	.50	.23	.06
☐ 8 Mark Lemke	.10	.05	.01
☐ 9 Fred McGriff	.50	.23	.06
☐ 10 Chipper Jones	3.00	1.35	.35
☐ 11 Terrell Wade	.10	.05	.01
☐ 12 Greg Maddux	3.00	1.35	.35
☐ 13 Mark Wohlers	.25	.11	.03
☐ 14 Marquis Grissom	.25	.11	.03
☐ 15 Andruw Jones	3.00	1.35	.35

1997 Score Braves Platinum

Randomly inserted in packs at the rate of one in six, this 15-card set is parallel to the regular Score Atlanta Braves Team Set. Prismatic foil printing with silver foil stamping distinguishes it from the regular set.

	MINT	NRMT	EXC
COMPLETE SET (15)	40.00	18.00	5.00
COMMON CARD (1-15)	.50	.23	.06
*STARS: 4X BASIC CARDS			

1997 Score Braves Premier

Randomly inserted in packs at the rate of one in 31, this 15-card set is parallel to the regular Score Atlanta Braves Team Set. Prismatic foil printing with special gold foil stamping distinguishes it from the regular set.

	MINT	NRMT	EXC
COMPLETE SET (15)	200.00	90.00	25.00
COMMON CARD (1-15)	2.00	.90	.25
*STARS: 20X BASIC CARDS			

1997 Score Dodgers

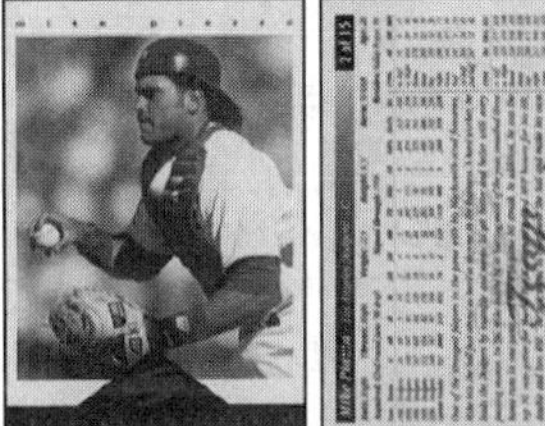
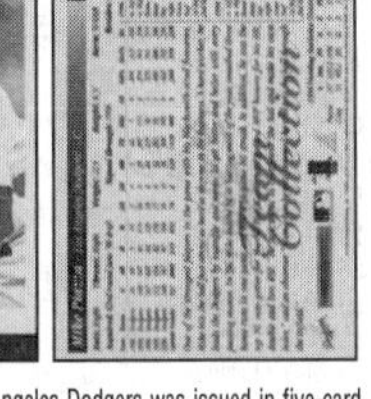

This 15-card set of the Los Angeles Dodgers was issued in five-card packs with a suggested retail price of $1.30 each. The fronts feature color player photos with special team specific color foil stamping. The backs carry player information. Only 100 cases were made for each team. Platinum parallel cards were inserted at a rate of 1:6, Premier parallel cards at a rate of 1:31.

	MINT	NRMT	EXC
COMPLETE SET (15)	5.00	2.20	.60
COMMON CARD (1-15)	.10	.05	.01
☐ 1 Ismael Valdes	.10	.05	.01
☐ 2 Mike Piazza	2.50	1.10	.30
☐ 3 Todd Hollandsworth	.25	.11	.03
☐ 4 Delino DeShields	.10	.05	.01
☐ 5 Chan Ho Park	.50	.23	.06
☐ 6 Roger Cedeno	.10	.05	.01
☐ 7 Raul Mondesi	.75	.35	.09
☐ 8 Darren Dreifort	.10	.05	.01
☐ 9 Jim Bruske	.10	.05	.01
☐ 10 Greg Gagne	.10	.05	.01
☐ 11 Chad Curtis	.10	.05	.01
☐ 12 Ramon Martinez	.25	.11	.03
☐ 13 Brett Butler	.10	.05	.01
☐ 14 Eric Karros	.25	.11	.03
☐ 15 Hideo Nomo	1.50	.70	.19

1997 Score Dodgers Platinum

Randomly inserted in packs at the rate of one in six, this 15-card set is parallel to the regular Score Los Angeles Dodgers Team Set. Prismatic foil printing with silver foil stamping distinguishes it from the regular set.

	MINT	NRMT	EXC
COMPLETE SET (15)	20.00	9.00	2.50
COMMON CARD (1-15)	.40	.18	.05
STARS: 4X BASIC CARDS			

1997 Score Dodgers Premier

Randomly inserted in packs at the rate of one in 31, this 15-card set is parallel to the regular Score Los Angeles Dodgers Team Set. Prismatic foil printing with special gold foil stamping distinguishes it from the regular set.

	MINT	NRMT	EXC
COMPLETE SET (15)	100.00	45.00	12.50
COMMON CARD (1-15)	2.00	.90	.25
*STARS: 20X BASIC CARDS			

1997 Score Indians

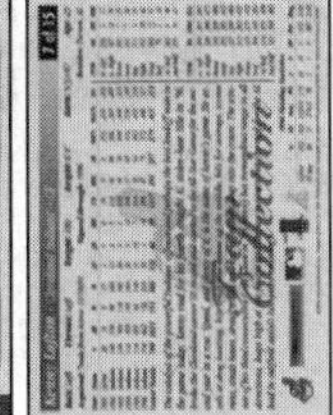

This 15-card set of the Cleveland Indians was issued in five-card packs with a suggested retail price of $1.30 each. The fronts feature color player photos with special team specific color foil stamping. The backs carry player information. Only 100 cases were made for each team. Platinum parallel cards were inserted at a rate of 1:6, Premier parallel cards at a rate of 1:31.

	MINT	NRMT	EXC
COMPLETE SET (15)	6.00	2.70	.75
COMMON CARD (1-15)	.10	.05	.01
☐ 1 Albert Belle	2.00	.90	.25
☐ 2 Jack McDowell	.10	.05	.01
☐ 3 Jim Thome	1.00	.45	.12
☐ 4 Dennis Martinez	.10	.05	.01
☐ 5 Julio Franco	.10	.05	.01
☐ 6 Omar Vizquel	.25	.11	.03
☐ 7 Kenny Lofton	1.50	.70	.19
☐ 8 Manny Ramirez	1.00	.45	.12
☐ 9 Sandy Alomar Jr.	.25	.11	.03
☐ 10 Charles Nagy	.25	.11	.03
☐ 11 Kevin Seitzer	.10	.05	.01
☐ 12 Mark Carreon	.10	.05	.01
☐ 13 Jeff Kent	.10	.05	.01
☐ 14 Danny Graves	.10	.05	.01
☐ 15 Brian Giles	.10	.05	.01

1997 Score Indians Platinum

Randomly inserted in packs at the rate of one in six, this 15-card set is parallel to the regular Score Cleveland Indians Team Set. Prismatic foil printing with silver foil stamping distinguishes it from the regular set.

	MINT	NRMT	EXC
COMPLETE SET (15)	25.00	11.00	3.10
COMMON CARD (1-15)	.40	.18	.05
*STARS: 4X BASIC CARDS			

1997 Score Indians Premier

Randomly inserted in packs at the rate of one in 31, this 15-card set is parallel to the regular Score Cleveland Indians Team Set. Prismatic foil printing with special gold foil stamping distinguishes it from the regular set.

	MINT	NRMT	EXC
COMPLETE SET (15)	125.00	55.00	15.50
COMMON CARD (1-15)	2.00	.90	.25
*STARS: 20X BASIC CARDS			

1997 Score Indians Update

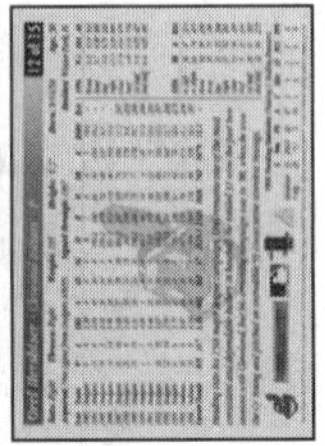

This 15 card set, which is similar in design to the 1997 Score Indians set features some changes from the earlier Indians set. The cards were issued in seven card packs with a suggested retail price of $1.30. An added feature of these packs was that passes to All-Star fanfest were randomly included in the packs. A parallel Tribe collection card was included one every six packs.

	MINT	NRMT	EXC
COMPLETE SET (15)	5.00	2.20	.60
COMMON CARD (1-15)	.10	.05	.01
☐ 1 Matt Williams	1.00	.45	.12
☐ 2 Jack McDowell	.25	.11	.03
☐ 3 Jim Thome	.50	.23	.06
☐ 4 Chad Ogea	.10	.05	.01
☐ 5 Julio Franco	.25	.11	.03
☐ 6 Omar Vizquel	.25	.11	.03
☐ 7 Kenny Lofton	1.25	.55	.16
☐ 8 Manny Ramirez	1.25	.55	.16
☐ 9 Sandy Alomar Jr	.10	.05	.01
☐ 10 Charles Nagy	.25	.11	.03
☐ 11 Kevin Seitzer	.10	.05	.01
☐ 12 Orel Hershiser	.10	.05	.01
☐ 13 Paul Assenmacher	.10	.05	.01
☐ 14 Eric Plunk	.10	.05	.01
☐ 15 Brian Giles	.10	.05	.01

1997 Score Indians Update Tribe Collection

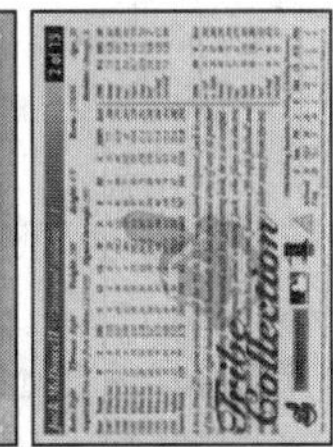

This 15 card set is a parallel to the regular 1997 Score Update Tribe set. These cards were inserted one every six packs. The cards have a metallic sheen on the front and the words "Tribe Collection" on the back.

	MINT	NRMT	EXC
COMPLETE SET (15)	20.00	9.00	2.50
COMMON CARD (1-15)	.40	.18	.05
*TRIBE COLLECTION: 4X BASIC CARDS			

1997 Score Mariners

This 15-card set of the Seattle Mariners was issued in five-card packs with a suggested retail price of $1.30 each. The fronts feature color player photos with special team specific color foil stamping. The backs carry player information. Only 100 cases were made for each team. Platinum parallel cards were inserted at a rate of 1:6, Premier parallel cards at a rate of 1:31.

	MINT	NRMT	EXC
COMPLETE SET (15)	8.00	3.60	1.00
COMMON CARD (1-15)	.10	.05	.01
☐ 1 Chris Bosio	.10	.05	.01
☐ 2 Edgar Martinez	.50	.23	.06
☐ 3 Alex Rodriguez	4.00	1.80	.50
☐ 4 Paul Sorrento	.10	.05	.01
☐ 5 Bob Wells	.10	.05	.01
☐ 6 Ken Griffey Jr.	4.00	1.80	.50
☐ 7 Jay Buhner	.50	.23	.06
☐ 8 Dan Wilson	.25	.11	.03
☐ 9 Randy Johnson	.75	.35	.09
☐ 10 Joey Cora	.10	.05	.01
☐ 11 Mark Whiten	.10	.05	.01
☐ 12 Rich Amaral	.10	.05	.01
☐ 13 Raul Ibanez	.10	.05	.01
☐ 14 Jamie Moyer	.10	.05	.01
☐ 15 Mac Suzuki	.10	.05	.01

1997 Score Mariners Platinum

Randomly inserted in packs at the rate of one in six, this 15-card set is parallel to the regular Score Seattle Mariners Team Set. Prismatic foil printing with silver foil stamping distinguishes it from the regular set.

	MINT	NRMT	EXC
COMPLETE SET (15)	30.00	13.50	3.70
COMMON CARD (1-15)	.40	.18	.05
*STARS: 4X BASIC CARDS			

1997 Score Mariners Premier

Randomly inserted in packs at the rate of one in 31, this 15-card set is parallel to the regular Score Seattle Mariners Team Set. Prismatic foil printing with special gold foil stamping distinguishes it from the regular set.

	MINT	NRMT	EXC
COMPLETE SET (15)	150.00	70.00	19.00
COMMON CARD (1-15)	2.00	.90	.25
*STARS: 20X BASIC CARDS			

1997 Score Orioles

This 15-card set of the Baltimore Orioles was issued in five-card packs with a suggested retail price of $1.30 each. The fronts feature color player photos with special team specific color foil stamping. The backs carry player information. Only 100 cases were made for each team. Platinum parallel cards were inserted at a rate of 1:6, Premier parallel cards at a rate of 1:31.

	MINT	NRMT	EXC
COMPLETE SET (15)	8.00	3.60	1.00
COMMON CARD (1-15)	.10	.05	.01
☐ 1 Rafael Palmeiro	.50	.23	.06
☐ 2 Eddie Murray	1.25	.55	.16
☐ 3 Roberto Alomar	1.25	.55	.16
☐ 4 Rocky Coppinger	.25	.11	.03
☐ 5 Brady Anderson	.75	.35	.09
☐ 6 Bobby Bonilla	.25	.11	.03
☐ 7 Cal Ripken	4.00	1.80	.50
☐ 8 Mike Mussina	1.00	.45	.12
☐ 9 Nerio Rodriguez	.25	.11	.03
☐ 10 Randy Myers	.10	.05	.01
☐ 11 B.J. Surhoff	.25	.11	.03
☐ 12 Jeffrey Hammonds	.10	.05	.01
☐ 13 Chris Hoiles	.10	.05	.01
☐ 14 Jimmy Haynes	.10	.05	.01
☐ 15 David Wells	.10	.05	.01

1997 Score Orioles Platinum

Randomly inserted in packs at the rate of one in six, this 15-card set is parallel to the regular Score Baltimore Orioles Team Set. Prismatic foil printing with silver foil stamping distinguishes it from the regular set.

	MINT	NRMT	EXC
COMPLETE SET (15)	30.00	13.50	3.70
COMMON CARD (1-15)	.40	.18	.05
*STARS: 4X BASIC CARDS			

1997 Score Orioles Premier

Randomly inserted in packs at the rate of one in 31, this 15-card set is parallel to the regular Score Baltimore Orioles Team Set. Prismatic foil printing with special gold foil stamping distinguishes it from the regular set.

	MINT	NRMT	EXC
COMPLETE SET (15)	150.00	70.00	19.00
COMMON CARD (1-15)	2.00	.90	.25
*STARS: 20X BASIC CARDS			

1997 Score Rangers

This 15-card set of the Texas Rangers was issued in five-card packs with a suggested retail price of $1.30 each. The fronts feature color player photos with special team specific color foil stamping. The backs carry player information. Only 100 cases were made for each team. Platinum parallel cards were inserted at a rate of 1:6, Premier parallel cards at a rate of 1:31.

	MINT	NRMT	EXC
COMPLETE SET (15)	5.00	2.20	.60
COMMON CARD (1-15)	.10	.05	.01
☐ 1 Mickey Tettleton	.10	.05	.01
☐ 2 Will Clark	.75	.35	.09
☐ 3 Ken Hill	.10	.05	.01
☐ 4 Rusty Greer	.50	.23	.06
☐ 5 Kevin Elster	.10	.05	.01
☐ 6 Darren Oliver	.10	.05	.01
☐ 7 Mark McLemore	.10	.05	.01
☐ 8 Roger Pavlik	.10	.05	.01
☐ 9 Dean Palmer	.25	.11	.03
☐ 10 Bobby Witt	.10	.05	.01
☐ 11 Juan Gonzalez	3.00	1.35	.35
☐ 12 Ivan Rodriguez	1.50	.70	.19
☐ 13 Darryl Hamilton	.10	.05	.01
☐ 14 John Burkett	.10	.05	.01
☐ 15 Warren Newson	.10	.05	.01

1997 Score Rangers Platinum

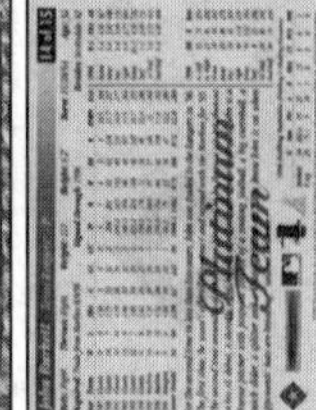

Randomly inserted in packs at the rate of one in six, this 15-card set is parallel to the regular Score Texas Rangers Team Set. Prismatic foil printing with silver foil stamping distinguishes it from the regular set.

	MINT	NRMT	EXC
COMPLETE SET (15)	20.00	9.00	2.50
COMMON CARD (1-15)	.40	.18	.05
*STARS: 4X BASIC CARDS			

1997 Score Rangers Premier

Randomly inserted in packs at the rate of one in 31, this 15-card set is parallel to the regular Score Texas Rangers Team Set. Prismatic foil printing with special gold foil stamping distinguishes it from the regular set.

	MINT	NRMT	EXC
COMPLETE SET (15)	100.00	45.00	12.50
COMMON CARD (1-15)	2.00	.90	.25
*STARS: 20X BASIC CARDS			

1997 Score Red Sox

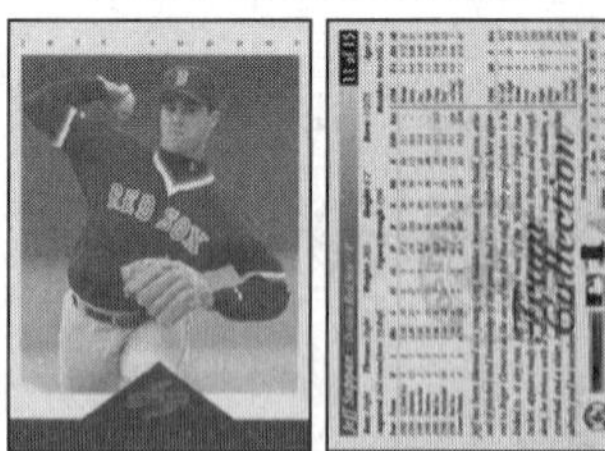
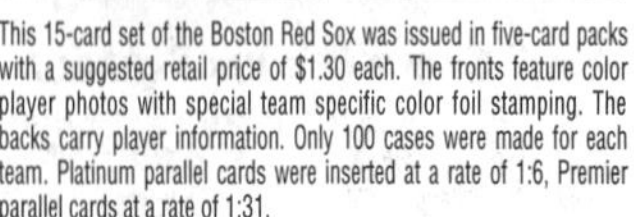

This 15-card set of the Boston Red Sox was issued in five-card packs with a suggested retail price of $1.30 each. The fronts feature color player photos with special team specific color foil stamping. The backs carry player information. Only 100 cases were made for each team. Platinum parallel cards were inserted at a rate of 1:6, Premier parallel cards at a rate of 1:31.

	MINT	NRMT	EXC
COMPLETE SET (15)	5.00	2.20	.60
COMMON CARD (1-15)	.10	.05	.01
☐ 1 Wil Cordero	.10	.05	.01
☐ 2 Mo Vaughn	2.00	.90	.25
☐ 3 John Valentin	.25	.11	.03
☐ 4 Reggie Jefferson	.10	.05	.01
☐ 5 Tom Gordon	.10	.05	.01
☐ 6 Mike Stanley	.10	.05	.01
☐ 7 Jose Canseco	.75	.35	.09
☐ 8 Roger Clemens	1.50	.70	.19
☐ 9 Darren Bragg	.10	.05	.01
☐ 10 Jeff Frye	.10	.05	.01
☐ 11 Jeff Suppan	.25	.11	.03
☐ 12 Mike Greenwell	.10	.05	.01
☐ 13 Arquimedez Pozo	.10	.05	.01
☐ 14 Tim Naehring	.25	.11	.03
☐ 15 Troy O'Leary	.10	.05	.01

1997 Score Red Sox Platinum

Randomly inserted in packs at the rate of one in six, this 15-card set is parallel to the regular Score Boston Red Sox Team Set. Prismatic foil printing with silver foil stamping distinguishes it from the regular set.

	MINT	NRMT	EXC
COMPLETE SET (15)	20.00	9.00	2.50
COMMON CARD (1-15)	.40	.18	.05
*STARS: 4X BASIC CARDS			

1997 Score Red Sox Premier

Randomly inserted in packs at the rate of one in 31, this 15-card set is parallel to the regular Score Boston Red Sox Team Set. Prismatic foil printing with special gold foil stamping distinguishes it from the regular set.

	MINT	NRMT	EXC
COMPLETE SET (15)	100.00	45.00	12.50
COMMON CARD (1-15)	2.00	.90	.25
*STARS: 20X BASIC CARDS			

1997 Score Rockies

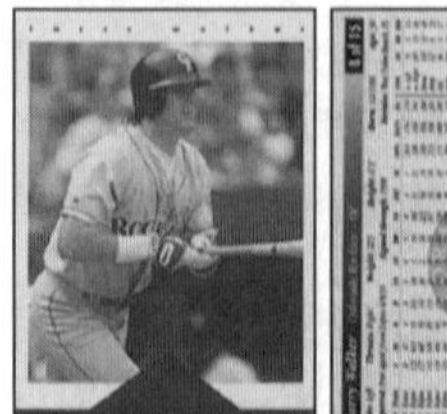

This 15-card set of the Colorado Rockies was issued in five-card packs with a suggested retail price of $1.30 each. The fronts feature color player photos with special team specific color foil stamping. The backs carry player information. Only 100 cases were made for each team. Platinum parallel cards were inserted at a rate of 1:6, Premier parallel cards at a rate of 1:31.

	MINT	NRMT	EXC
COMPLETE SET (15)	5.00	2.20	.60
COMMON CARD (1-15)	.15	.07	.02
☐ 1 Dante Bichette	1.25	.55	.16
☐ 2 Kevin Ritz	.15	.07	.02
☐ 3 Walt Weiss	.15	.07	.02
☐ 4 Ellis Burks	.75	.35	.09
☐ 5 Jamey Wright	.25	.11	.03
☐ 6 Andres Galarraga	1.25	.55	.16
☐ 7 Eric Young	.25	.11	.03
☐ 8 Larry Walker	1.00	.45	.12
☐ 9 Vinny Castilla	.25	.11	.03
☐ 10 Quinton McCracken	.15	.07	.02
☐ 11 Armando Reynoso	.15	.07	.02
☐ 12 Jayhawk Owens	.15	.07	.02
☐ 13 Mark Thompson	.15	.07	.02
☐ 14 Bruce Ruffin	.15	.07	.02
☐ 15 John Burke	.15	.07	.02

1997 Score Rockies Platinum

Randomly inserted in packs at the rate of one in six, this 15-card set is parallel to the regular Score Colorado Rockies Team Set. Prismatic foil printing with silver foil stamping distinguishes it from the regular set.

	MINT	NRMT	EXC
COMPLETE SET (15)	20.00	9.00	2.50
COMMON CARD (1-15)	.40	.18	.05
*STARS: 4X BASIC CARDS			

1997 Score Rockies Premier

Randomly inserted in packs at the rate of one in 31, this 15-card set is parallel to the regular Score Colorado Rockies Team Set. Prismatic foil printing with special gold foil stamping distinguishes it from the regular set.

	MINT	NRMT	EXC
COMPLETE SET (15)	100.00	45.00	12.50
COMMON CARD (1-15)	3.00	1.35	.35
*STARS: 20X BASIC CARDS			

1997 Score White Sox

This 15-card set of the Chicago White Sox was issued in five-card packs with a suggested retail price of $1.30 each. The fronts feature color player photos with special team specific color foil stamping. The backs carry player information. Only 100 cases were made for each team. Platinum parallel cards were inserted at a rate of 1:6, Premier parallel cards at a rate of 1:31.

	MINT	NRMT	EXC
COMPLETE SET (15)	5.00	2.20	.60
COMMON CARD (1-15)	.10	.05	.01
☐ 1 Frank Thomas	3.50	1.55	.45
☐ 2 James Baldwin	.10	.05	.01
☐ 3 Danny Tartabull	.10	.05	.01
☐ 4 Jeff Darwin	.10	.05	.01
☐ 5 Harold Baines	.10	.05	.01
☐ 6 Roberto Hernandez	.10	.05	.01
☐ 7 Ray Durham	.25	.11	.03
☐ 8 Robin Ventura	.50	.23	.06
☐ 9 Wilson Alvarez	.10	.05	.01
☐ 10 Lyle Mouton	.10	.05	.01
☐ 11 Alex Fernandez	.25	.11	.03
☐ 12 Ron Karkovice	.10	.05	.01
☐ 13 Kevin Tapani	.10	.05	.01
☐ 14 Tony Phillips	.10	.05	.01
☐ 15 Mike Cameron	.25	.11	.03

1997 Score White Sox Platinum

Randomly inserted in packs at the rate of one in six, this 15-card set is parallel to the regular Score Chicago White Sox Team Set. Prismatic foil printing with silver foil stamping distinguishes it from the regular set.

	MINT	NRMT	EXC
COMPLETE SET (15)	20.00	9.00	2.50
COMMON CARD (1-15)	.40	.18	.05
*STARS: 4X BASIC CARDS			

1997 Score White Sox Premier

Randomly inserted in packs at the rate of one in 31, this 15-card set is parallel to the regular Score Chicago White Sox Team Set. Prismatic foil printing with special gold foil stamping distinguishes it from the regular set.

	MINT	NRMT	EXC
COMPLETE SET (15)	100.00	45.00	12.50
COMMON CARD (1-15)	2.00	.90	.25
*STARS: 20X BASIC CARDS			

1997 Score Yankees

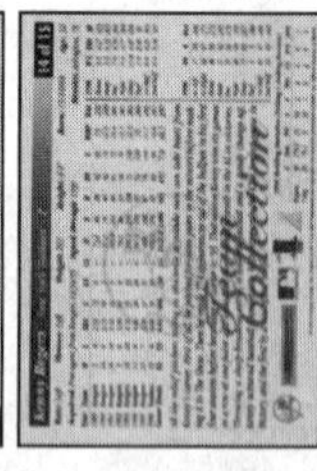

This 15-card set of the New York Yankees was issued in five-card packs with a suggested retail price of $1.30 each. The fronts feature color player photos with special team specific color foil stamping. The backs carry player information. Only 100 cases were made for each team. Platinum parallel cards were inserted at a rate of 1:6, Premier parallel cards at a rate of 1:31.

	MINT	NRMT	EXC
COMPLETE SET (15)	8.00	3.60	1.00
COMMON CARD (1-15)	.10	.05	.01
☐ 1 Bernie Williams	1.50	.70	.19
☐ 2 Cecil Fielder	.25	.11	.03
☐ 3 Derek Jeter	3.00	1.35	.35
☐ 4 Darryl Strawberry	.25	.11	.03
☐ 5 Andy Pettitte	1.50	.70	.19
☐ 6 Ruben Rivera	.50	.23	.06
☐ 7 Mariano Rivera	.25	.11	.03
☐ 8 John Wetteland	.25	.11	.03
☐ 9 Paul O'Neill	.10	.05	.01
☐ 10 Wade Boggs	.75	.35	.09
☐ 11 Dwight Gooden	.25	.11	.03
☐ 12 David Cone	.25	.11	.03
☐ 13 Tino Martinez	.25	.11	.03
☐ 14 Kenny Rogers	.10	.05	.01
☐ 15 Andy Fox	.10	.05	.01

1997 Score Yankees Platinum

Randomly inserted in packs at the rate of one in six, this 15-card set is parallel to the regular Score New York Yankees Team Set. Prismatic foil printing with silver foil stamping distinguishes it from the regular set.

	MINT	NRMT	EXC
COMPLETE SET (15)	30.00	13.50	3.70
COMMON CARD (1-15)	.40	.18	.05
*STARS: 4X BASIC CARDS			

1997 Score Yankees Premier

Randomly inserted in packs at the rate of one in 31, this 15-card set is parallel to the regular Score New York Yankees Team Set. Prismatic foil printing with special gold foil stamping distinguishes it from the regular set.

	MINT	NRMT	EXC
COMPLETE SET (15)	150.00	70.00	19.00
COMMON CARD (1-15)	2.00	.90	.25
*STARS: 20X BASIC CARDS			

1887 Scraps Die Cuts

These cards are unnumbered; they are ordered below alphabetially within team. The first nine players (1-9) are St. Louis and the second nine (10-18) are Detroit players.

	EX-MT	VG-E	GOOD
COMPLETE SET (18)	2500.00	1100.00	300.00
COMMON CARD (1-18)	125.00	55.00	15.50
☐ 1 Doc Bushong	125.00	55.00	15.50
☐ 2 Bob Caruthers	125.00	55.00	15.50
☐ 3 Charles Comiskey	250.00	110.00	31.00
☐ 4 Dave. Foutz	125.00	55.00	15.50
☐ 5 Bill Gleason	175.00	80.00	22.00
☐ 6 Arlie Latham	150.00	70.00	19.00
☐ 7 Tip O'Neill	125.00	55.00	15.50
☐ 8 Yank Robinson	125.00	55.00	15.50
☐ 9 Curt Welch	150.00	70.00	19.00
☐ 10 C.W. Bennett	125.00	55.00	15.50
☐ 11 Dan Brouthers	250.00	110.00	31.00
☐ 12 Fred Dunlap	125.00	55.00	15.50
☐ 13 Charlie Getzen (sic)	125.00	55.00	15.50
☐ 14 Ned Hanlon	125.00	55.00	15.50
☐ 15 Hardie Richardson	125.00	55.00	15.50
☐ 16 Jack Rowe	125.00	55.00	15.50
☐ 17 Sam Thompson	250.00	110.00	31.00
☐ 18 Deacon White	125.00	55.00	15.50

1946 Sears-East St. Louis PC783

This black and white blank-backed set measures 3 1/2" by 5 3/8" and was issued in 1946 and given away by Sears at their East St. Louis location. The set features players from St. Louis teams. Two poses of John Miller exist.

	EX-MT	VG-E	GOOD
COMPLETE SET (60)	4500.00	2000.00	550.00
COMMON CARD (1-60)	75.00	34.00	9.50
☐ 1 Buster Adams	75.00	34.00	9.50
☐ 2 Red Barrett	75.00	34.00	9.50
☐ 3 Johnny Beazley	75.00	34.00	9.50
☐ 4 John Berardino	125.00	55.00	15.50
☐ 5 Frank Biscan	75.00	34.00	9.50
☐ 6 Al Brazle	75.00	34.00	9.50
☐ 7 Ken Burkhart	75.00	34.00	9.50
☐ 8 Jerry Burmeister	75.00	34.00	9.50
☐ 9 Mark Christman	75.00	34.00	9.50
☐ 10 Joffre Cross	75.00	34.00	9.50
☐ 11 Babe Dahlgren	100.00	45.00	12.50
☐ 12 Murray Dickson	75.00	34.00	9.50
☐ 13 Bob Dillinger	75.00	34.00	9.50
☐ 14 Erv Dusak	75.00	34.00	9.50
☐ 15 Eddie Dyer MG	75.00	34.00	9.50
☐ 16 Bill Endicott	75.00	34.00	9.50
☐ 17 Stanley Ferens	75.00	34.00	9.50
☐ 18 Denny Galehouse	75.00	34.00	9.50
☐ 19 Mike Gonzales CO	75.00	34.00	9.50
☐ 20 Joe Grace	75.00	34.00	9.50
☐ 21 Jeff Heath	75.00	34.00	9.50
☐ 22 Henry Helf	75.00	34.00	9.50
☐ 23 Fred Hoffman	75.00	34.00	9.50
☐ 24 Walt Judnich	75.00	34.00	9.50
☐ 25 Ellis Kinder	75.00	34.00	9.50
☐ 26 Lou Klein	75.00	34.00	9.50
☐ 27 Clyde Kluttz	75.00	34.00	9.50
☐ 28 Jack Kramer	75.00	34.00	9.50
☐ 29 Howard Krist	75.00	34.00	9.50
☐ 30 Chet Laabs	75.00	34.00	9.50
☐ 31 John Lucadello	75.00	34.00	9.50
☐ 32 Frank Mancuso	75.00	34.00	9.50
☐ 33 Marty Marion	125.00	55.00	15.50
☐ 34 Fred Martin	75.00	34.00	9.50
☐ 35 George McQuillen	75.00	34.00	9.50
☐ 36 John Miller (2)	75.00	34.00	9.50
☐ 37 Terry Moore	100.00	45.00	12.50
☐ 38 Bob Muncrief	75.00	34.00	9.50
☐ 39 Stan Musial	300.00	135.00	38.00
☐ 40 Howie Pollet	75.00	34.00	9.50
☐ 41 Nelson Potter	75.00	34.00	9.50
☐ 42 Del Rice	75.00	34.00	9.50
☐ 43 Red Schoendienst	125.00	55.00	15.50
☐ 44 Ken Sears	75.00	34.00	9.50
☐ 45 Walt Sessi	75.00	34.00	9.50
☐ 46 Luke Sewell MG	100.00	45.00	12.50
☐ 47 Joe Schultz	75.00	34.00	9.50
☐ 48 Tex Shirley	75.00	34.00	9.50
☐ 49 Dick Sisler	75.00	34.00	9.50
☐ 50 Enos Slaughter	150.00	70.00	19.00
☐ 51 Vern Stephens	100.00	45.00	12.50
☐ 52 Chuck Stevens	75.00	34.00	9.50
☐ 53 Max Surkont	75.00	34.00	9.50
☐ 54 Zack Taylor MG	75.00	34.00	9.50
☐ 55 Harry Walker	100.00	45.00	12.50
☐ 56 Buzzy Wares	75.00	34.00	9.50
☐ 57 Ernie White	75.00	34.00	9.50
☐ 58 Ted Wilks	75.00	34.00	9.50
☐ 59 Al Zarilla	75.00	34.00	9.50
☐ 60 Sam Zoldak	75.00	34.00	9.50

1993 Select Samples

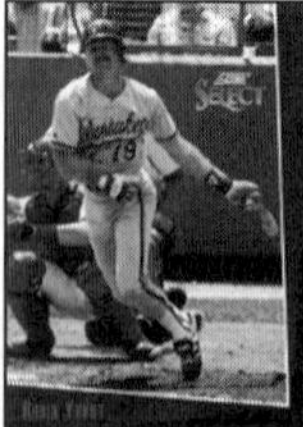

These eight promo cards were issued to provide dealers with a preview of Score's new Select series cards. The cards measure the standard size feature glossy color player photos edged on two sides by a two-toned green border area. The back design is similar to the fronts but with a smaller player photo to create space for player profile and statistics. These promo cards are distinguished from the regular issue by the zeroes in the statistic lines.

	MINT	NRMT	EXC
COMPLETE SET (8)	25.00	11.00	3.10
COMMON CARD	1.00	.45	.12

□ 22 Robin Yount	4.00	1.80	.50
□ 24 Don Mattingly	12.00	5.50	1.50
□ 26 Sandy Alomar Jr.	2.00	.90	.25
□ 41 Gary Sheffield	4.00	1.80	.50
□ 56 Brady Anderson	3.00	1.35	.35
□ 65 Rob Dibble	1.00	.45	.12
□ 75 John Smiley	1.00	.45	.12
□ 79 Mitch Williams	1.00	.45	.12

1993 Select

Seeking a niche in the premium, mid-price market, Score produced a new 405-card standard-size set entitled Select in 1993. The set includes regular players, rookies, and draft picks, and was sold in 15-card hobby and retail packs and 28-card super packs. The front photos, composed either horizontally or vertically, are ultra-violet coated while the two-toned green borders received a matte finish. The player's name appears in mustard-colored lettering in the bottom border. Subset cards include Draft Picks and Rookies, both sprinkled throughout the latter part of the set. Rookie Cards in this set include Derek Jeter and Jason Kendall.

	MINT	NRMT	EXC
COMPLETE SET (405)	30.00	13.50	3.70
COMMON CARD (1-405)	.10	.05	.01

□ 1 Barry Bonds	.75	.35	.09
□ 2 Ken Griffey Jr.	3.00	1.35	.35
□ 3 Will Clark	.40	.18	.05
□ 4 Kirby Puckett	1.25	.55	.16
□ 5 Tony Gwynn	1.25	.55	.16
□ 6 Frank Thomas	3.00	1.35	.35
□ 7 Tom Glavine	.40	.18	.05
□ 8 Roberto Alomar	.60	.25	.07
□ 9 Andre Dawson	.25	.11	.03
□ 10 Ron Darling	.10	.05	.01
□ 11 Bobby Bonilla	.25	.11	.03
□ 12 Danny Tartabull	.10	.05	.01
□ 13 Darren Daulton	.25	.11	.03
□ 14 Roger Clemens	.60	.25	.07
□ 15 Ozzie Smith	.75	.35	.09
□ 16 Mark McGwire	1.00	.45	.12
□ 17 Terry Pendleton	.25	.11	.03
□ 18 Cal Ripken	2.50	1.10	.30
□ 19 Fred McGriff	.40	.18	.05
□ 20 Cecil Fielder	.25	.11	.03
□ 21 Darryl Strawberry	.25	.11	.03
□ 22 Robin Yount	.40	.18	.05
□ 23 Barry Larkin	.40	.18	.05
□ 24 Don Mattingly	1.50	.70	.19
□ 25 Craig Biggio	.25	.11	.03
□ 26 Sandy Alomar Jr.	.25	.11	.03
□ 27 Larry Walker	.40	.18	.05
□ 28 Junior Felix	.10	.05	.01
□ 29 Eddie Murray	.75	.35	.09
□ 30 Robin Ventura	.25	.11	.03
□ 31 Greg Maddux	2.00	.90	.25
□ 32 Dave Winfield	.40	.18	.05
□ 33 John Kruk	.25	.11	.03
□ 34 Wally Joyner	.25	.11	.03
□ 35 Andy Van Slyke	.25	.11	.03
□ 36 Chuck Knoblauch	.40	.18	.05
□ 37 Tom Pagnozzi	.10	.05	.01
□ 38 Dennis Eckersley	.25	.11	.03
□ 39 Dave Justice	.40	.18	.05
□ 40 Juan Gonzalez	1.50	.70	.19
□ 41 Gary Sheffield	.40	.18	.05
□ 42 Paul Molitor	.60	.25	.07
□ 43 Delino DeShields	.10	.05	.01
□ 44 Travis Fryman	.25	.11	.03
□ 45 Hal Morris	.10	.05	.01
□ 46 Greg Olson	.10	.05	.01
□ 47 Ken Caminiti	.40	.18	.05
□ 48 Wade Boggs	.40	.18	.05
□ 49 Orel Hershiser	.25	.11	.03
□ 50 Albert Belle	1.25	.55	.16
□ 51 Bill Swift	.10	.05	.01
□ 52 Mark Langston	.25	.11	.03
□ 53 Joe Girardi	.10	.05	.01
□ 54 Keith Miller	.10	.05	.01
□ 55 Gary Carter	.25	.11	.03
□ 56 Brady Anderson	.40	.18	.05
□ 57 Dwight Gooden	.25	.11	.03
□ 58 Julio Franco	.25	.11	.03
□ 59 Lenny Dykstra	.25	.11	.03
□ 60 Mickey Tettleton	.10	.05	.01
□ 61 Randy Tomlin	.10	.05	.01
□ 62 B.J. Surhoff	.25	.11	.03
□ 63 Todd Zeile	.10	.05	.01
□ 64 Roberto Kelly	.10	.05	.01
□ 65 Rob Dibble	.10	.05	.01
□ 66 Leo Gomez	.10	.05	.01
□ 67 Doug Jones	.10	.05	.01
□ 68 Ellis Burks	.25	.11	.03
□ 69 Mike Scioscia	.10	.05	.01
□ 70 Charles Nagy	.25	.11	.03
□ 71 Cory Snyder	.10	.05	.01
□ 72 Devon White	.10	.05	.01
□ 73 Mark Grace	.40	.18	.05
□ 74 Luis Polonia	.10	.05	.01
□ 75 John Smiley 2X	.10	.05	.01
□ 76 Carlton Fisk	.40	.18	.05
□ 77 Luis Sojo	.10	.05	.01
□ 78 George Brett	1.25	.55	.16
□ 79 Mitch Williams	.10	.05	.01
□ 80 Kent Hrbek	.25	.11	.03
□ 81 Jay Bell	.25	.11	.03
□ 82 Edgar Martinez	.25	.11	.03
□ 83 Lee Smith	.25	.11	.03
□ 84 Deion Sanders	.40	.18	.05
□ 85 Bill Gullickson	.10	.05	.01
□ 86 Paul O'Neill	.25	.11	.03
□ 87 Kevin Seitzer	.10	.05	.01
□ 88 Steve Finley	.25	.11	.03
□ 89 Mel Hall	.10	.05	.01
□ 90 Nolan Ryan	2.50	1.10	.30
□ 91 Eric Davis	.25	.11	.03
□ 92 Mike Mussina	.60	.25	.07
□ 93 Tony Fernandez	.10	.05	.01
□ 94 Frank Viola	.10	.05	.01
□ 95 Matt Williams	.40	.18	.05
□ 96 Joe Carter	.25	.11	.03
□ 97 Ryne Sandberg	.75	.35	.09
□ 98 Jim Abbott	.10	.05	.01
□ 99 Marquis Grissom	.25	.11	.03
□ 100 George Bell	.10	.05	.01
□ 101 Howard Johnson	.10	.05	.01
□ 102 Kevin Appier	.25	.11	.03
□ 103 Dale Murphy	.40	.18	.05
□ 104 Shane Mack	.10	.05	.01
□ 105 Jose Lind	.10	.05	.01
□ 106 Rickey Henderson	.40	.18	.05
□ 107 Bob Tewksbury	.10	.05	.01
□ 108 Kevin Mitchell	.25	.11	.03
□ 109 Steve Avery	.25	.11	.03
□ 110 Candy Maldonado	.10	.05	.01
□ 111 Bip Roberts	.10	.05	.01
□ 112 Lou Whitaker	.25	.11	.03
□ 113 Jeff Bagwell	1.25	.55	.16
□ 114 Dante Bichette	.40	.18	.05
□ 115 Brett Butler	.25	.11	.03
□ 116 Melido Perez	.10	.05	.01
□ 117 Andy Benes	.25	.11	.03
□ 118 Randy Johnson	.40	.18	.05
□ 119 Willie McGee	.10	.05	.01
□ 120 Jody Reed	.10	.05	.01
□ 121 Shawon Dunston	.10	.05	.01
□ 122 Carlos Baerga	.25	.11	.03
□ 123 Bret Saberhagen	.25	.11	.03
□ 124 John Olerud	.10	.05	.01
□ 125 Ivan Calderon	.10	.05	.01
□ 126 Bryan Harvey	.10	.05	.01
□ 127 Terry Mulholland	.10	.05	.01
□ 128 Ozzie Guillen	.10	.05	.01
□ 129 Steve Buechele	.10	.05	.01
□ 130 Kevin Tapani	.10	.05	.01
□ 131 Felix Jose	.10	.05	.01
□ 132 Terry Steinbach	.25	.11	.03
□ 133 Ron Gant	.25	.11	.03
□ 134 Harold Reynolds	.10	.05	.01
□ 135 Chris Sabo	.10	.05	.01
□ 136 Ivan Rodriguez	.75	.35	.09
□ 137 Eric Anthony	.10	.05	.01
□ 138 Mike Henneman	.10	.05	.01
□ 139 Robby Thompson	.10	.05	.01
□ 140 Scott Fletcher	.10	.05	.01
□ 141 Bruce Hurst	.10	.05	.01
□ 142 Kevin Maas	.10	.05	.01
□ 143 Tom Candiotti	.10	.05	.01
□ 144 Chris Hoiles	.10	.05	.01
□ 145 Mike Morgan	.10	.05	.01
□ 146 Mark Whiten	.10	.05	.01
□ 147 Dennis Martinez	.25	.11	.03
□ 148 Tony Pena	.10	.05	.01
□ 149 Dave Magadan	.10	.05	.01
□ 150 Mark Lewis	.10	.05	.01
□ 151 Mariano Duncan	.10	.05	.01
□ 152 Gregg Jefferies	.25	.11	.03
□ 153 Doug Drabek	.10	.05	.01
□ 154 Brian Harper	.10	.05	.01
□ 155 Ray Lankford	.25	.11	.03
□ 156 Carney Lansford	.25	.11	.03
□ 157 Mike Sharperson	.10	.05	.01
□ 158 Jack Morris	.25	.11	.03
□ 159 Otis Nixon	.10	.05	.01
□ 160 Steve Sax	.10	.05	.01
□ 161 Mark Lemke	.10	.05	.01
□ 162 Rafael Palmeiro	.40	.18	.05
□ 163 Jose Rijo	.10	.05	.01
□ 164 Omar Vizquel	.25	.11	.03
□ 165 Sammy Sosa	.40	.18	.05
□ 166 Milt Cuyler	.10	.05	.01
□ 167 John Franco	.10	.05	.01
□ 168 Darryl Hamilton	.10	.05	.01
□ 169 Ken Hill	.25	.11	.03
□ 170 Mike Devereaux	.10	.05	.01
□ 171 Don Slaught	.10	.05	.01
□ 172 Steve Farr	.10	.05	.01
□ 173 Bernard Gilkey	.25	.11	.03
□ 174 Mike Fetters	.10	.05	.01
□ 175 Vince Coleman	.10	.05	.01
□ 176 Kevin McReynolds	.10	.05	.01
□ 177 John Smoltz	.40	.18	.05
□ 178 Greg Gagne	.10	.05	.01
□ 179 Greg Swindell	.10	.05	.01
□ 180 Juan Guzman	.25	.11	.03
□ 181 Kal Daniels	.10	.05	.01
□ 182 Rick Sutcliffe	.10	.05	.01
□ 183 Orlando Merced	.25	.11	.03
□ 184 Bill Wegman	.10	.05	.01
□ 185 Mark Gardner	.10	.05	.01
□ 186 Rob Deer	.10	.05	.01
□ 187 Dave Hollins	.10	.05	.01
□ 188 Jack Clark	.10	.05	.01
□ 189 Brian Hunter	.10	.05	.01
□ 190 Tim Wallach	.10	.05	.01
□ 191 Tim Belcher	.10	.05	.01
□ 192 Walt Weiss	.10	.05	.01
□ 193 Kurt Stillwell	.10	.05	.01
□ 194 Charlie Hayes	.10	.05	.01
□ 195 Willie Randolph	.25	.11	.03
□ 196 Jack McDowell	.25	.11	.03
□ 197 Jose Offerman	.10	.05	.01
□ 198 Chuck Finley	.10	.05	.01
□ 199 Darrin Jackson	.10	.05	.01
□ 200 Kelly Gruber	.10	.05	.01
□ 201 John Wetteland	.25	.11	.03
□ 202 Jay Buhner	.40	.18	.05
□ 203 Mike LaValliere	.10	.05	.01
□ 204 Kevin Brown	.25	.11	.03
□ 205 Luis Gonzalez	.10	.05	.01
□ 206 Rick Aguilera	.10	.05	.01
□ 207 Norm Charlton	.10	.05	.01
□ 208 Mike Bordick	.10	.05	.01
□ 209 Charlie Leibrandt	.10	.05	.01
□ 210 Tom Brunansky	.10	.05	.01
□ 211 Tom Henke	.10	.05	.01
□ 212 Randy Milligan	.10	.05	.01
□ 213 Ramon Martinez	.25	.11	.03
□ 214 Mo Vaughn	.75	.35	.09
□ 215 Randy Myers	.25	.11	.03
□ 216 Greg Hibbard	.10	.05	.01
□ 217 Wes Chamberlain	.10	.05	.01
□ 218 Tony Phillips	.25	.11	.03
□ 219 Pete Harnisch	.10	.05	.01
□ 220 Mike Gallego	.10	.05	.01
□ 221 Bud Black	.10	.05	.01
□ 222 Greg Vaughn	.25	.11	.03
□ 223 Milt Thompson	.10	.05	.01
□ 224 Ben McDonald	.10	.05	.01
□ 225 Billy Hatcher	.10	.05	.01
□ 226 Paul Sorrento	.10	.05	.01
□ 227 Mark Gubicza	.10	.05	.01
□ 228 Mike Greenwell	.10	.05	.01
□ 229 Curt Schilling	.10	.05	.01
□ 230 Alan Trammell	.40	.18	.05
□ 231 Zane Smith	.10	.05	.01
□ 232 Bobby Thigpen	.10	.05	.01
□ 233 Greg Olson	.10	.05	.01
□ 234 Joe Orsulak	.10	.05	.01
□ 235 Joe Oliver	.10	.05	.01
□ 236 Tim Raines	.40	.18	.05
□ 237 Juan Samuel	.10	.05	.01
□ 238 Chili Davis	.25	.11	.03
□ 239 Spike Owen	.10	.05	.01
□ 240 Dave Stewart	.25	.11	.03
□ 241 Jim Eisenreich	.25	.11	.03
□ 242 Phil Plantier	.10	.05	.01
□ 243 Sid Fernandez	.10	.05	.01
□ 244 Dan Gladden	.10	.05	.01
□ 245 Mickey Morandini	.10	.05	.01
□ 246 Tino Martinez	.25	.11	.03
□ 247 Kirt Manwaring	.10	.05	.01
□ 248 Dean Palmer	.25	.11	.03
□ 249 Tom Browning	.10	.05	.01
□ 250 Brian McRae	.25	.11	.03
□ 251 Scott Leius	.10	.05	.01
□ 252 Bert Blyleven	.25	.11	.03
□ 253 Scott Erickson	.10	.05	.01
□ 254 Bob Welch	.10	.05	.01
□ 255 Pat Kelly	.10	.05	.01
□ 256 Felix Fermin	.10	.05	.01
□ 257 Harold Baines	.25	.11	.03
□ 258 Duane Ward	.10	.05	.01
□ 259 Bill Spiers	.10	.05	.01
□ 260 Jaime Navarro	.10	.05	.01
□ 261 Scott Sanderson	.10	.05	.01
□ 262 Gary Gaetti	.25	.11	.03
□ 263 Bob Ojeda	.10	.05	.01
□ 264 Jeff Montgomery	.25	.11	.03
□ 265 Scott Bankhead	.10	.05	.01
□ 266 Lance Johnson	.25	.11	.03
□ 267 Rafael Belliard	.10	.05	.01
□ 268 Kevin Reimer	.10	.05	.01
□ 269 Benito Santiago	.10	.05	.01
□ 270 Mike Moore	.10	.05	.01
□ 271 Dave Fleming	.10	.05	.01
□ 272 Moises Alou	.25	.11	.03
□ 273 Pat Listach	.10	.05	.01
□ 274 Reggie Sanders	.40	.18	.05
□ 275 Kenny Lofton	1.25	.55	.16
□ 276 Donovan Osborne	.10	.05	.01
□ 277 Rusty Meacham	.10	.05	.01
□ 278 Eric Karros	.40	.18	.05
□ 279 Andy Stankiewicz	.10	.05	.01
□ 280 Brian Jordan	.40	.18	.05
□ 281 Gary DiSarcina	.10	.05	.01
□ 282 Mark Wohlers	.25	.11	.03
□ 283 Dave Nilsson	.25	.11	.03
□ 284 Anthony Young	.10	.05	.01
□ 285 Jim Bullinger	.10	.05	.01
□ 286 Derek Bell	.25	.11	.03
□ 287 Brian Williams	.10	.05	.01
□ 288 Julio Valera	.10	.05	.01
□ 289 Dan Walters	.10	.05	.01
□ 290 Chad Curtis	.25	.11	.03
□ 291 Michael Tucker DP	.40	.18	.05
□ 292 Bob Zupcic	.10	.05	.01
□ 293 Todd Hundley	.25	.11	.03
□ 294 Jeff Tackett	.10	.05	.01
□ 295 Greg Colbrunn	.10	.05	.01
□ 296 Cal Eldred	.10	.05	.01
□ 297 Chris Roberts DP	.25	.11	.03
□ 298 John Doherty	.10	.05	.01
□ 299 Denny Neagle	.25	.11	.03
□ 300 Arthur Rhodes	.10	.05	.01
□ 301 Mark Clark	.10	.05	.01
□ 302 Scott Cooper	.10	.05	.01
□ 303 Jamie Arnold DP	.25	.11	.03
□ 304 Jim Thome	1.50	.70	.19
□ 305 Frank Seminara	.10	.05	.01
□ 306 Kurt Knudsen	.10	.05	.01
□ 307 Tim Wakefield	.25	.11	.03
□ 308 John Jaha	.40	.18	.05
□ 309 Pat Hentgen	.40	.18	.05
□ 310 B.J. Wallace DP	.10	.05	.01
□ 311 Roberto Hernandez	.25	.11	.03
□ 312 Hipolito Pichardo	.10	.05	.01
□ 313 Eric Fox	.10	.05	.01
□ 314 Willie Banks	.10	.05	.01
□ 315 Sam Militello	.10	.05	.01
□ 316 Vince Horsman	.10	.05	.01
□ 317 Carlos Hernandez	.10	.05	.01
□ 318 Jeff Kent	.25	.11	.03
□ 319 Mike Perez	.10	.05	.01
□ 320 Scott Livingstone	.10	.05	.01
□ 321 Jeff Conine	.25	.11	.03
□ 322 James Austin	.10	.05	.01
□ 323 John Vander Wal	.10	.05	.01
□ 324 Pat Mahomes	.10	.05	.01
□ 325 Pedro Astacio	.10	.05	.01
□ 326 Bret Boone UER (Misspelled Brett)	.25	.11	.03
□ 327 Matt Stairs	.10	.05	.01
□ 328 Damion Easley	.10	.05	.01
□ 329 Ben Rivera	.10	.05	.01
□ 330 Reggie Jefferson	.25	.11	.03
□ 331 Luis Mercedes	.10	.05	.01
□ 332 Kyle Abbott	.10	.05	.01
□ 333 Eddie Taubensee	.10	.05	.01
□ 334 Tim McIntosh	.10	.05	.01
□ 335 Phil Clark	.10	.05	.01
□ 336 Wil Cordero	.25	.11	.03
□ 337 Russ Springer	.10	.05	.01
□ 338 Craig Colbert	.10	.05	.01
□ 339 Tim Salmon	.75	.35	.09
□ 340 Braulio Castillo	.10	.05	.01
□ 341 Donald Harris	.10	.05	.01
□ 342 Eric Young	.40	.18	.05
□ 343 Bob Wickman	.10	.05	.01
□ 344 John Valentin	.25	.11	.03
□ 345 Dan Wilson	.25	.11	.03
□ 346 Steve Hosey	.10	.05	.01
□ 347 Mike Piazza	3.00	1.35	.35
□ 348 Willie Greene	.25	.11	.03
□ 349 Tom Goodwin	.10	.05	.01
□ 350 Eric Hillman	.10	.05	.01
□ 351 Steve Reed	.10	.05	.01
□ 352 Dan Serafini DP	.50	.23	.06
□ 353 Todd Steverson DP	.25	.11	.03
□ 354 Benji Grigsby DP	.10	.05	.01
□ 355 Shannon Stewart DP	.50	.23	.06
□ 356 Sean Lowe DP	.25	.11	.03
□ 357 Derek Wallace DP	.10	.05	.01
□ 358 Rick Helling DP	.25	.11	.03
□ 359 Jason Kendall DP	2.00	.90	.25
□ 360 Derek Jeter DP	6.00	2.70	.75
□ 361 David Cone	.25	.11	.03
□ 362 Jeff Reardon	.25	.11	.03
□ 363 Bobby Witt	.10	.05	.01
□ 364 Jose Canseco	.40	.18	.05
□ 365 Jeff Russell	.10	.05	.01
□ 366 Ruben Sierra	.25	.11	.03
□ 367 Alan Mills	.10	.05	.01
□ 368 Matt Nokes	.10	.05	.01
□ 369 Pat Borders	.10	.05	.01
□ 370 Pedro Munoz	.10	.05	.01
□ 371 Danny Jackson	.10	.05	.01
□ 372 Geronimo Pena	.10	.05	.01
□ 373 Craig Lefferts	.10	.05	.01
□ 374 Joe Grahe	.10	.05	.01
□ 375 Roger McDowell	.10	.05	.01
□ 376 Jimmy Key	.25	.11	.03
□ 377 Steve Olin	.10	.05	.01
□ 378 Glenn Davis	.10	.05	.01
□ 379 Rene Gonzales	.10	.05	.01
□ 380 Manuel Lee	.10	.05	.01

	MINT	NRMT	EXC
☐ 381 Ron Karkovice	.10	.05	.01
☐ 382 Sid Bream	.10	.05	.01
☐ 383 Gerald Williams	.10	.05	.01
☐ 384 Lenny Harris	.10	.05	.01
☐ 385 J.T. Snow	.40	.18	.05
☐ 386 Dave Stieb	.10	.05	.01
☐ 387 Kirk McCaskill	.10	.05	.01
☐ 388 Lance Parrish	.10	.05	.01
☐ 389 Craig Grebeck	.10	.05	.01
☐ 390 Rick Wilkins	.10	.05	.01
☐ 391 Manny Alexander	.10	.05	.01
☐ 392 Mike Schooler	.10	.05	.01
☐ 393 Bernie Williams	.60	.25	.07
☐ 394 Kevin Koslofski	.10	.05	.01
☐ 395 Willie Wilson	.10	.05	.01
☐ 396 Jeff Parrett	.10	.05	.01
☐ 397 Mike Harkey	.10	.05	.01
☐ 398 Frank Tanana	.10	.05	.01
☐ 399 Doug Henry	.10	.05	.01
☐ 400 Royce Clayton	.25	.11	.03
☐ 401 Eric Wedge	.10	.05	.01
☐ 402 Derrick May	.10	.05	.01
☐ 403 Carlos Garcia	.10	.05	.01
☐ 404 Henry Rodriguez	.40	.18	.05
☐ 405 Ryan Klesko	1.00	.45	.12

1993 Select Aces

This 24-card standard-size set features some of the top starting pitchers in both leagues. The cards were randomly inserted into one in every eight 28-card super packs. The fronts display an action player pose cut out and superimposed on a metallic variegated red and silver diamond design. The diamond itself rests on a background consisting of silver metallic streaks that emanate from the center of the card. In imitation of playing card design, the fronts have a large "A" for Ace in upper left and lower right corners. The player's name in the upper right corner rounds out the card face.

	MINT	NRMT	EXC
COMPLETE SET (24)	80.00	36.00	10.00
COMMON CARD (1-24)	2.50	1.10	.30
☐ 1 Roger Clemens	10.00	4.50	1.25
☐ 2 Tom Glavine	8.00	3.60	1.00
☐ 3 Jack McDowell	5.00	2.20	.60
☐ 4 Greg Maddux	30.00	13.50	3.70
☐ 5 Jack Morris	5.00	2.20	.60
☐ 6 Dennis Martinez	5.00	2.20	.60
☐ 7 Kevin Brown	5.00	2.20	.60
☐ 8 Dwight Gooden	5.00	2.20	.60
☐ 9 Kevin Appier	5.00	2.20	.60
☐ 10 Mike Morgan	2.50	1.10	.30
☐ 11 Juan Guzman	5.00	2.20	.60
☐ 12 Charles Nagy	5.00	2.20	.60
☐ 13 John Smiley	2.50	1.10	.30
☐ 14 Ken Hill	5.00	2.20	.60
☐ 15 Bob Tewksbury	2.50	1.10	.30
☐ 16 Doug Drabek	5.00	2.20	.60
☐ 17 John Smoltz	8.00	3.60	1.00
☐ 18 Greg Swindell	2.50	1.10	.30
☐ 19 Bruce Hurst	2.50	1.10	.30
☐ 20 Mike Mussina	10.00	4.50	1.25
☐ 21 Cal Eldred	2.50	1.10	.30
☐ 22 Melido Perez	2.50	1.10	.30
☐ 23 Dave Fleming	2.50	1.10	.30
☐ 24 Kevin Tapani	2.50	1.10	.30

1993 Select Chase Rookies

This 21-card standard-size set showcases 1992's best rookies. The cards were randomly inserted into one in every eighteen 15-card hobby packs. The fronts exhibit Score's "dufex" printing process, in which a color photo is printed on a metallic base creating an unusual, three-dimensional look. The pictures are tilted slightly to the left and edged on the left and bottom by red metallic borders.

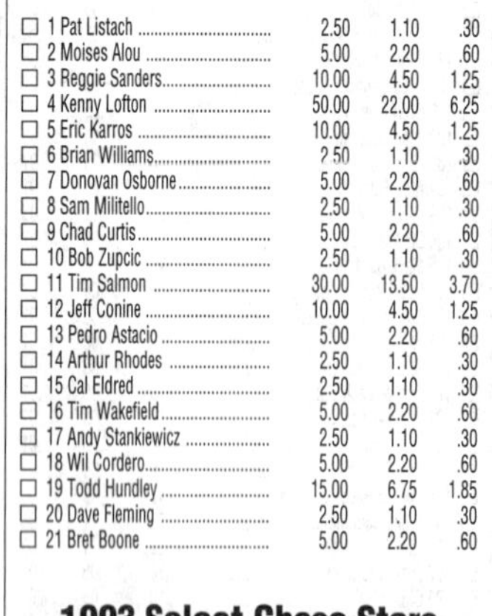

	MINT	NRMT	EXC
COMPLETE SET (21)	150.00	70.00	19.00
COMMON CARD (1-21)	2.50	1.10	.30
☐ 1 Pat Listach	2.50	1.10	.30
☐ 2 Moises Alou	5.00	2.20	.60
☐ 3 Reggie Sanders	10.00	4.50	1.25
☐ 4 Kenny Lofton	50.00	22.00	6.25
☐ 5 Eric Karros	10.00	4.50	1.25
☐ 6 Brian Williams	2.50	1.10	.30
☐ 7 Donovan Osborne	5.00	2.20	.60
☐ 8 Sam Militello	2.50	1.10	.30
☐ 9 Chad Curtis	5.00	2.20	.60
☐ 10 Bob Zupcic	2.50	1.10	.30
☐ 11 Tim Salmon	30.00	13.50	3.70
☐ 12 Jeff Conine	10.00	4.50	1.25
☐ 13 Pedro Astacio	5.00	2.20	.60
☐ 14 Arthur Rhodes	2.50	1.10	.30
☐ 15 Cal Eldred	2.50	1.10	.30
☐ 16 Tim Wakefield	5.00	2.20	.60
☐ 17 Andy Stankiewicz	2.50	1.10	.30
☐ 18 Wil Cordero	5.00	2.20	.60
☐ 19 Todd Hundley	15.00	6.75	1.85
☐ 20 Dave Fleming	2.50	1.10	.30
☐ 21 Bret Boone	5.00	2.20	.60

1993 Select Chase Stars

This 24-card standard-size set showcases the top players in Major League Baseball. The cards were randomly inserted into one in every eighteen retail 15-card packs. The fronts exhibit Score's "dufex" printing process, in which a color photo is printed on a metallic base creating an unusual, three-dimensional look. The pictures are tilted slightly to the left and edged on the left and bottom by green metallic borders.

	MINT	NRMT	EXC
COMPLETE SET (24)	150.00	70.00	19.00
COMMON CARD (1-24)	2.00	.90	.25
☐ 1 Fred McGriff	5.00	2.20	.60
☐ 2 Ryne Sandberg	10.00	4.50	1.25
☐ 3 Ozzie Smith	10.00	4.50	1.25
☐ 4 Gary Sheffield	6.00	2.70	.75
☐ 5 Darren Daulton	4.00	1.80	.50
☐ 6 Andy Van Slyke	2.00	.90	.25
☐ 7 Barry Bonds	10.00	4.50	1.25
☐ 8 Tony Gwynn	15.00	6.75	1.85
☐ 9 Greg Maddux	25.00	11.00	3.10
☐ 10 Tom Glavine	5.00	2.20	.60
☐ 11 John Franco	2.00	.90	.25
☐ 12 Lee Smith	4.00	1.80	.50
☐ 13 Cecil Fielder	4.00	1.80	.50
☐ 14 Roberto Alomar	8.00	3.60	1.00
☐ 15 Cal Ripken	30.00	13.50	3.70
☐ 16 Edgar Martinez	5.00	2.20	.60
☐ 17 Ivan Rodriguez	10.00	4.50	1.25
☐ 18 Kirby Puckett	15.00	6.75	1.85
☐ 19 Ken Griffey Jr.	40.00	18.00	5.00
☐ 20 Joe Carter	4.00	1.80	.50
☐ 21 Roger Clemens	8.00	3.60	1.00
☐ 22 Dave Fleming	2.00	.90	.25
☐ 23 Paul Molitor	8.00	3.60	1.00
☐ 24 Dennis Eckersley	4.00	1.80	.50

1993 Select Stat Leaders

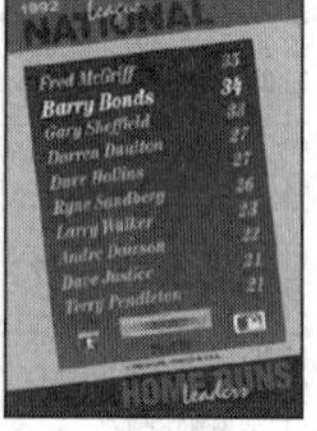

Featuring 45 cards from each league, these 90 Stat Leaders were inserted one per 1993 Score pack in every regular pack and super pack. The fronts feature color player action photos that are borderless on the sides and have oblique green borders at the top and bottom. The player's name appears within an oblique orange stripe across the bottom of the photo. The player's league appears within the top border, and the set's title appears within the bottom border.

	MINT	NRMT	EXC
COMPLETE SET (90)	12.00	5.50	1.50
COMMON CARD (1-90)	.15	.07	.02
☐ 1 Edgar Martinez	.30	.14	.04
☐ 2 Kirby Puckett	.75	.35	.09
☐ 3 Frank Thomas	2.00	.90	.25
☐ 4 Gary Sheffield	.30	.14	.04
☐ 5 Andy Van Slyke	.30	.14	.04
☐ 6 John Kruk	.30	.14	.04
☐ 7 Kirby Puckett	.75	.35	.09
☐ 8 Carlos Baerga	.30	.14	.04
☐ 9 Paul Molitor	.40	.18	.05
☐ 10 Terry Pendleton	.15	.07	.02
Andy Van Slyke			
☐ 11 Ryne Sandberg	.50	.23	.06
☐ 12 Mark Grace	.30	.14	.04
☐ 13 Frank Thomas	1.00	.45	.12
Edgar Martinez			
☐ 14 Don Mattingly	.50	.23	.06
Robin Yount			
☐ 15 Ken Griffey	2.00	.90	.25
☐ 16 Andy Van Slyke	.30	.14	.04
☐ 17 Mariano Duncan	.30	.14	.04
Will Clark			
Ray Lankford			
☐ 18 Marquis Grissom	.30	.14	.04
Terry Pendleton			
☐ 19 Lance Johnson	.30	.14	.04
☐ 20 Mike Devereaux	.15	.07	.02
☐ 21 Brady Anderson	.30	.14	.04
☐ 22 Deion Sanders	.30	.14	.04
☐ 23 Steve Finley	.30	.14	.04
☐ 24 Andy Van Slyke	.30	.14	.04
☐ 25 Juan Gonzalez	1.00	.45	.12
☐ 26 Mark McGwire	.60	.25	.07
☐ 27 Cecil Fielder	.30	.14	.04
☐ 28 Fred McGriff	.30	.14	.04
☐ 29 Barry Bonds	.50	.23	.06
☐ 30 Gary Sheffield	.30	.14	.04
☐ 31 Cecil Fielder	.30	.14	.04
☐ 32 Joe Carter	.30	.14	.04
☐ 33 Frank Thomas	2.00	.90	.25
☐ 34 Darren Daulton	.30	.14	.04
☐ 35 Terry Pendleton	.30	.14	.04
☐ 36 Fred McGriff	.30	.14	.04
☐ 37 Tony Phillips	.30	.14	.04
☐ 38 Frank Thomas	2.00	.90	.25
☐ 39 Roberto Alomar	.40	.18	.05
☐ 40 Barry Bonds	.50	.23	.06
☐ 41 Dave Hollins	.15	.07	.02
☐ 42 Andy Van Slyke	.30	.14	.04
☐ 43 Mark McGwire	.60	.25	.07
☐ 44 Edgar Martinez	.30	.14	.04
☐ 45 Frank Thomas	2.00	.90	.25
☐ 46 Barry Bonds	.50	.23	.06
☐ 47 Gary Sheffield	.30	.14	.04
☐ 48 Fred McGriff	.30	.14	.04
☐ 49 Frank Thomas	2.00	.90	.25
☐ 50 Danny Tartabull	.15	.07	.02
☐ 51 Roberto Alomar	.40	.18	.05
☐ 52 Barry Bonds	.50	.23	.06
☐ 53 John Kruk	.30	.14	.04
☐ 54 Brett Butler	.30	.14	.04
☐ 55 Kenny Lofton	.75	.35	.09
☐ 56 Pat Listach	.15	.07	.02
☐ 57 Brady Anderson	.30	.14	.04
☐ 58 Marquis Grissom	.30	.14	.04
☐ 59 Delino DeShields	.15	.07	.02
☐ 60 Bip Roberts	.30	.14	.04
Steve Finley			
☐ 61 Jack McDowell	.30	.14	.04
☐ 62 Kevin Brown	.30	.14	.04
Roger Clemens			
☐ 63 Charles Nagy	.30	.14	.04
Melido Perez			
☐ 64 Terry Mulholland	.15	.07	.02
☐ 65 Curt Schilling	.15	.07	.02
Doug Drabek			
☐ 66 Greg Maddux	1.00	.45	.12
John Smoltz			
☐ 67 Dennis Eckersley	.30	.14	.04
☐ 68 Rick Aguilera	.15	.07	.02
☐ 69 Jeff Montgomery	.30	.14	.04
☐ 70 Lee Smith	.30	.14	.04
☐ 71 Randy Myers	.30	.14	.04
☐ 72 John Wetteland	.30	.14	.04
☐ 73 Randy Johnson	.30	.14	.04
☐ 74 Melido Perez	.15	.07	.02
☐ 75 Roger Clemens	.40	.18	.05
☐ 76 John Smoltz	.30	.14	.04
☐ 77 David Cone	.30	.14	.04
☐ 78 Greg Maddux	1.25	.55	.16
☐ 79 Roger Clemens	.40	.18	.05
☐ 80 Kevin Appier	.30	.14	.04
☐ 81 Mike Mussina	.40	.18	.05
☐ 82 Bill Swift	.15	.07	.02
☐ 83 Bob Tewksbury	.15	.07	.02
☐ 84 Greg Maddux	1.25	.55	.16
☐ 85 Jack Morris	.30	.14	.04
Kevin Brown			
☐ 86 Jack McDowell	.30	.14	.04
☐ 87 Roger Clemens	.40	.18	.05
Mike Mussina			
☐ 88 Tom Glavine	1.00	.45	.12
Greg Maddux			
☐ 89 Ken Hill	.30	.14	.04
Bob Tewksbury			
☐ 90 Mike Morgan	.15	.07	.02
Dennis Martinez			

1993 Select Triple Crown

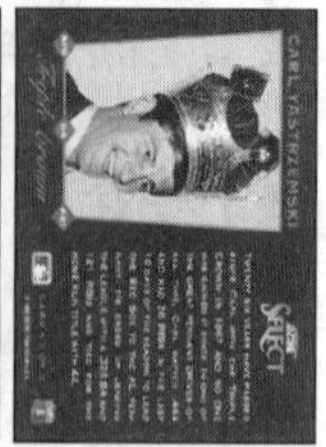

Honoring the three most recent Triple Crown winners since 1993, cards from this 3-card standard-size set were randomly inserted in 15-card hobby packs. The fronts exhibit Score's "dufex" printing process, in which a color photo is printed on a metallic base creating an unusual, three-dimensional look. The color player photos on the fronts have a forest green metallic border. The player's name and the year he won the Triple Crown appear above the picture, while the words "Triple Crown" are written in script beneath it.

	MINT	NRMT	EXC
COMPLETE SET (3)	110.00	50.00	14.00
COMMON CARD (1-3)	20.00	9.00	2.50
☐ 1 Mickey Mantle	80.00	36.00	10.00
☐ 2 Carl Yastrzemski	20.00	9.00	2.50
☐ 3 Frank Robinson	20.00	9.00	2.50

1993 Select Rookie/Traded

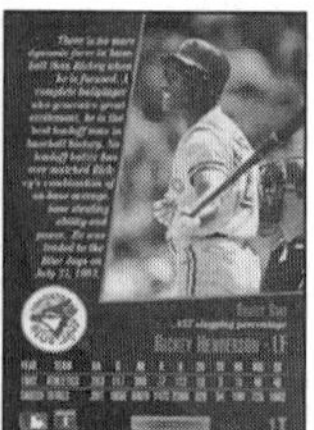

These 150 standard-size cards feature rookies and traded veteran players. The production run comprised 1,950 individually numbered cases. Cards were distributed in foil packs. Card design is similar to the regular 1993 Select cards excpt for the dramatic royal blue borders (instead of emerald green for the regular cards) and T-suffixed numbering. There are no key Rookie Cards in this set. Two Rookie of the Year insert cards and a Nolan Ryan Tribute card were randomly inserted in the foil packs. The chances of finding a Nolan Ryan card was listed at not less than one per 288 packs. The two ROY cards, featuring American League Rookie of the Year, Tim Salmon and National League Rookie of the Year, Mike Piazza were randomly inserted into one in every 576 packs.

	MINT	NRMT	EXC
COMPLETE SET (150)	20.00	9.00	2.50
COMMON CARD (1T-150T)	.10	.05	.01
☐ 1T Rickey Henderson	.50	.23	.06
☐ 2T Rob Deer	.10	.05	.01
☐ 3T Tim Belcher	.10	.05	.01
☐ 4T Gary Sheffield	1.00	.45	.12
☐ 5T Fred McGriff	.75	.35	.09
☐ 6T Mark Whiten	.10	.05	.01
☐ 7T Jeff Russell	.10	.05	.01
☐ 8T Harold Baines	.25	.11	.03
☐ 9T Dave Winfield	.50	.23	.06
☐ 10T Ellis Burks	.25	.11	.03
☐ 11T Andre Dawson	.25	.11	.03
☐ 12T Gregg Jefferies	.25	.11	.03
☐ 13T Jimmy Key	.25	.11	.03
☐ 14T Harold Reynolds	.10	.05	.01
☐ 15T Tom Henke	.10	.05	.01
☐ 16T Paul Molitor	1.25	.55	.16
☐ 17T Wade Boggs	.50	.23	.06
☐ 18T David Cone	.25	.11	.03
☐ 19T Tony Fernandez	.10	.05	.01
☐ 20T Roberto Kelly	.10	.05	.01
☐ 21T Paul O'Neill	.25	.11	.03
☐ 22T Jose Lind	.10	.05	.01
☐ 23T Barry Bonds	1.50	.70	.19
☐ 24T Dave Stewart	.25	.11	.03
☐ 25T Randy Myers	.25	.11	.03
☐ 26T Benito Santiago	.10	.05	.01
☐ 27T Tim Wallach	.10	.05	.01
☐ 28T Greg Gagne	.10	.05	.01
☐ 29T Kevin Mitchell	.25	.11	.03
☐ 30T Jim Abbott	.10	.05	.01
☐ 31T Lee Smith	.25	.11	.03
☐ 32T Bobby Munoz	.10	.05	.01
☐ 33T Mo Sanford	.10	.05	.01
☐ 34T John Roper	.10	.05	.01
☐ 35T David Hulse	.10	.05	.01
☐ 36T Pedro Martinez	.50	.23	.06

Card	MINT	NRMT	EXC
□ 37T Chuck Carr	.10	.05	.01
□ 38T Armando Reynoso	.10	.05	.01
□ 39T Ryan Thompson	.10	.05	.01
□ 40T Carlos Garcia	.10	.05	.01
□ 41T Matt Whiteside	.10	.05	.01
□ 42T Benji Gil	.25	.11	.03
□ 43T Rodney Bolton	.10	.05	.01
□ 44T J.T. Snow	.50	.23	.06
□ 45T David McCarty	.10	.05	.01
□ 46T Paul Quantrill	.10	.05	.01
□ 47T Al Martin	.25	.11	.03
□ 48T Lance Painter	.10	.05	.01
□ 49T Lou Frazier	.10	.05	.01
□ 50T Eduardo Perez	.10	.05	.01
□ 51T Kevin Young	.10	.05	.01
□ 52T Mike Trombley	.10	.05	.01
□ 53T Sterling Hitchcock	1.00	.45	.12
□ 54T Tim Bogar	.10	.05	.01
□ 55T Hilly Hathaway	.10	.05	.01
□ 56T Wayne Kirby	.10	.05	.01
□ 57T Craig Paquette	.10	.05	.01
□ 58T Bret Boone	.25	.11	.03
□ 59T Greg McMichael	.25	.11	.03
□ 60T Mike Lansing	.25	.11	.03
□ 61T Brent Gates	.25	.11	.03
□ 62T Rene Arocha	.10	.05	.01
□ 63T Ricky Gutierrez	.10	.05	.01
□ 64T Kevin Rogers	.10	.05	.01
□ 65T Ken Ryan	.10	.05	.01
□ 66T Phil Hiatt	.10	.05	.01
□ 67T Pat Meares	.25	.11	.03
□ 68T Troy Neel	.10	.05	.01
□ 69T Steve Cooke	.10	.05	.01
□ 70T Sherman Obando	.10	.05	.01
□ 71T Blas Minor	.10	.05	.01
□ 72T Angel Miranda	.10	.05	.01
□ 73T Tom Kramer	.10	.05	.01
□ 74T Chip Hale	.10	.05	.01
□ 75T Brad Pennington	.10	.05	.01
□ 76T Graeme Lloyd	.10	.05	.01
□ 77T Darrell Whitmore	.10	.05	.01
□ 78T David Nied	.10	.05	.01
□ 79T Todd Van Poppel	.10	.05	.01
□ 80T Chris Gomez	.25	.11	.03
□ 81T Jason Bere	.25	.11	.03
□ 82T Jeffrey Hammonds	.25	.11	.03
□ 83T Brad Ausmus	.10	.05	.01
□ 84T Kevin Stocker	.25	.11	.03
□ 85T Jeromy Burnitz	.10	.05	.01
□ 86T Aaron Sele	.25	.11	.03
□ 87T Roberto Mejia	.10	.05	.01
□ 88T Kirk Rueter	.10	.05	.01
□ 89T Kevin Roberson	.10	.05	.01
□ 90T Allen Watson	.10	.05	.01
□ 91T Charlie Leibrandt	.10	.05	.01
□ 92T Eric Davis	.25	.11	.03
□ 93T Jody Reed	.10	.05	.01
□ 94T Danny Jackson	.10	.05	.01
□ 95T Gary Gaetti	.25	.11	.03
□ 96T Norm Charlton	.10	.05	.01
□ 97T Doug Drabek	.10	.05	.01
□ 98T Scott Fletcher	.10	.05	.01
□ 99T Greg Swindell	.10	.05	.01
□ 100T John Smiley	.10	.05	.01
□ 101T Kevin Reimer	.10	.05	.01
□ 102T Andres Galarraga	.50	.23	.06
□ 103T Greg Hibbard	.10	.05	.01
□ 104T Chris Hammond	.10	.05	.01
□ 105T Darnell Coles	.10	.05	.01
□ 106T Mike Felder	.10	.05	.01
□ 107T Jose Guzman	.10	.05	.01
□ 108T Chris Bosio	.10	.05	.01
□ 109T Spike Owen	.10	.05	.01
□ 110T Felix Jose	.10	.05	.01
□ 111T Cory Snyder	.10	.05	.01
□ 112T Craig Lefferts	.10	.05	.01
□ 113T David Wells	.10	.05	.01
□ 114T Pete Incaviglia	.10	.05	.01
□ 115T Mike Pagliarulo	.10	.05	.01
□ 116T Dave Magadan	.10	.05	.01
□ 117T Charlie Hough	.10	.05	.01
□ 118T Ivan Calderon	.10	.05	.01
□ 119T Manuel Lee	.10	.05	.01
□ 120T Bob Patterson	.10	.05	.01
□ 121T Bob Ojeda	.10	.05	.01
□ 122T Scott Bankhead	.10	.05	.01
□ 123T Greg Maddux	4.00	1.80	.50
□ 124T Chili Davis	.25	.11	.03
□ 125T Milt Thompson	.10	.05	.01
□ 126T Dave Martinez	.10	.05	.01
□ 127T Frank Tanana	.10	.05	.01
□ 128T Phil Plantier	.10	.05	.01
□ 129T Juan Samuel	.10	.05	.01
□ 130T Eric Young	.50	.23	.06
□ 131T Joe Orsulak	.10	.05	.01
□ 132T Derek Bell	.25	.11	.03
□ 133T Darrin Jackson	.10	.05	.01
□ 134T Tom Brunansky	.10	.05	.01
□ 135T Jeff Reardon	.25	.11	.03
□ 136T Kevin Higgins	.10	.05	.01
□ 137T Joel Johnston	.10	.05	.01
□ 138T Rick Trlicek	.10	.05	.01
□ 139T Richie Lewis	.10	.05	.01
□ 140T Jeff Gardner	.10	.05	.01
□ 141T Jack Voigt	.10	.05	.01
□ 142T Rod Correia	.10	.05	.01
□ 143T Billy Brewer	.10	.05	.01
□ 144T Terry Jorgensen	.10	.05	.01
□ 145T Rich Amaral	.10	.05	.01
□ 146T Sean Berry	.10	.05	.01
□ 147T Dan Peltier	.10	.05	.01
□ 148T Paul Wagner	.10	.05	.01
□ 149T Damon Buford	.10	.05	.01
□ 150T Wil Cordero	.25	.11	.03
□ NR1 Nolan Ryan Tribute	125.00	55.00	15.50
□ ROY1 Tim Salmon AL ROY	25.00	11.00	3.10
□ ROY2 Mike Piazza NL ROY	80.00	36.00	10.00

1993 Select Rookie/Traded All-Star Rookies

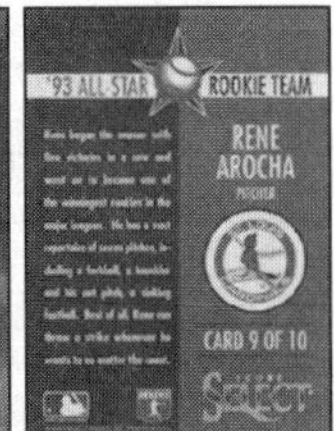

This ten-card standard-size set was randomly inserted in foil packs of 1993 Select Rookie and Traded. The insertion rate was reportedly not less than one in 36 packs. The cards feature on their fronts color player action shots that have a grainy metallic appearance. These photos are borderless, except at the top, where the silver-colored player's name is displayed upon red and blue metallic stripes. The set's title appears within a metallic silver-colored stripe near the bottom, which has a star-and-baseball icon emblazoned over its center. This combination of the set's title, stripe, and star-and-baseball icon reappears at the top of the non-metallic back, but in a red, white, and blue design. The player's name, position, and team logo are shown on the red-colored right half of the card. His career highlights appear in white lettering on the blue-colored left half.

	MINT	NRMT	EXC
COMPLETE SET (10)	150.00	70.00	19.00
COMMON CARD (1-10)	5.00	2.20	.60

Card	MINT	NRMT	EXC
□ 1 Jeff Conine	12.00	5.50	1.50
□ 2 Brent Gates	8.00	3.60	1.00
□ 3 Mike Lansing	8.00	3.60	1.00
□ 4 Kevin Stocker	8.00	3.60	1.00
□ 5 Mike Piazza	80.00	36.00	10.00
□ 6 Jeffrey Hammonds	8.00	3.60	1.00
□ 7 David Hulse	5.00	2.20	.60
□ 8 Tim Salmon	25.00	11.00	3.10
□ 9 Rene Arocha	5.00	2.20	.60
□ 10 Greg McMichael	5.00	2.20	.60

1994 Select Samples

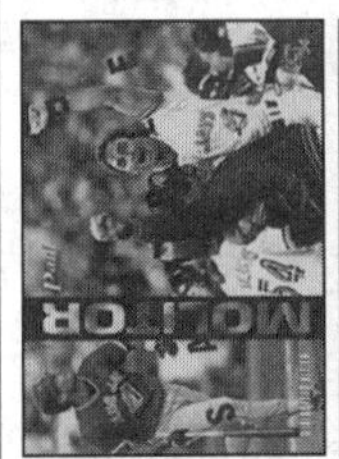

Issued to preview the designs of the 1994 Score Select set and its inserts, these nine standard-size cards feature color player action shots on their fronts -- except for the Kruk card (24), which pictures him dozing, and so could hardly qualify as an "action shot." The cards are from the regular series, except for the Dykstra card, the Floyd card, and the Klesko card. Except for the title card, all the cards carry the word "Sample" in diagonal black lettering on their fronts and backs.

	MINT	NRMT	EXC
COMPLETE SET (9)	8.00	3.60	1.00
COMMON CARD	.25	.11	.03

Card	MINT	NRMT	EXC
□ 3 Paul Molitor	1.50	.70	.19
□ 17 Kirby Puckett	3.00	1.35	.35
□ 19 Randy Johnson	1.00	.45	.12
□ 24 John Kruk	.25	.11	.03
□ 51 Jose Lind	.25	.11	.03
□ 197 Ryan Klesko 94 Rookie Prospect	1.50	.70	.19
□ CC1 Lenny Dykstra Crown Contenders	1.50	.70	.19
□ RS1 Cliff Floyd Rookie Surge '94	1.50	.70	.19
□ NNO Title Card	.25	.11	.03

1994 Select

Measuring the standard size, the 1994 Select set consists of 420 cards that were issued in two series of 210. The horizontal fronts feature a color player action photo and a duo-tone player shot. The backs are vertical and contain a photo, 1993 and career statistics and

highlights. Special Dave Winfield and Cal Ripken cards were inserted in first series packs. A Paul Molitor MVP card and a Carlos Delgado Rookie of the Year card were inserted in second series packs. The insertion rate for ech card was one in 360 packs. Rookie Cards include Kurt Abbott, Brian Anderson and Chan Ho Park.

	MINT	NRMT	EXC
COMPLETE SET (420)	30.00	13.50	3.70
COMPLETE SERIES 1 (210)	18.00	8.00	2.20
COMPLETE SERIES 2 (210)	12.00	5.50	1.50
COMMON CARD (1-420)	.10	.05	.01

Card	MINT	NRMT	EXC
□ 1 Ken Griffey Jr.	3.00	1.35	.35
□ 2 Greg Maddux	2.00	.90	.25
□ 3 Paul Molitor	.60	.25	.07
□ 4 Mike Piazza	2.00	.90	.25
□ 5 Jay Bell	.25	.11	.03
□ 6 Frank Thomas	3.00	1.35	.35
□ 7 Barry Larkin	.50	.23	.06
□ 8 Paul O'Neill	.25	.11	.03
□ 9 Darren Daulton	.25	.11	.03
□ 10 Mike Greenwell	.10	.05	.01
□ 11 Chuck Carr	.10	.05	.01
□ 12 Joe Carter	.25	.11	.03
□ 13 Lance Johnson	.25	.11	.03
□ 14 Jeff Blauser	.10	.05	.01
□ 15 Chris Hoiles	.10	.05	.01
□ 16 Rick Wilkins	.10	.05	.01
□ 17 Kirby Puckett	1.25	.55	.16
□ 18 Larry Walker	.50	.23	.06
□ 19 Randy Johnson	.50	.23	.06
□ 20 Bernard Gilkey	.25	.11	.03
□ 21 Devon White	.10	.05	.01
□ 22 Randy Myers	.10	.05	.01
□ 23 Don Mattingly	1.50	.70	.19
□ 24 John Kruk	.25	.11	.03
□ 25 Ozzie Guillen	.10	.05	.01
□ 26 Jeff Conine	.25	.11	.03
□ 27 Mike Macfarlane	.10	.05	.01
□ 28 Dave Hollins	.10	.05	.01
□ 29 Chuck Knoblauch	.50	.23	.06
□ 30 Ozzie Smith	.75	.35	.09
□ 31 Harold Baines	.25	.11	.03
□ 32 Ryne Sandberg	.75	.35	.09
□ 33 Ron Karkovice	.10	.05	.01
□ 34 Terry Pendleton	.25	.11	.03
□ 35 Wally Joyner	.25	.11	.03
□ 36 Mike Mussina	.60	.25	.07
□ 37 Felix Jose	.10	.05	.01
□ 38 Derrick May	.10	.05	.01
□ 39 Scott Cooper	.10	.05	.01
□ 40 Jose Rijo	.10	.05	.01
□ 41 Robin Ventura	.25	.11	.03
□ 42 Charlie Hayes	.10	.05	.01
□ 43 Jimmy Key	.25	.11	.03
□ 44 Eric Karros	.25	.11	.03
□ 45 Ruben Sierra	.25	.11	.03
□ 46 Ryan Thompson	.10	.05	.01
□ 47 Brian McRae	.25	.11	.03
□ 48 Pat Hentgen	.25	.11	.03
□ 49 John Valentin	.25	.11	.03
□ 50 Al Martin	.10	.05	.01
□ 51 Jose Lind	.10	.05	.01
□ 52 Kevin Stocker	.10	.05	.01
□ 53 Mike Gallego	.10	.05	.01
□ 54 Dwight Gooden	.25	.11	.03
□ 55 Brady Anderson	.50	.23	.06
□ 56 Jeff King	.25	.11	.03
□ 57 Mark McGwire	1.00	.45	.12
□ 58 Sammy Sosa	.50	.23	.06
□ 59 Ryan Bowen	.10	.05	.01
□ 60 Mark Lemke	.10	.05	.01
□ 61 Roger Clemens	.60	.25	.07
□ 62 Brian Jordan	.50	.23	.06
□ 63 Andres Galarraga	.50	.23	.06
□ 64 Kevin Appier	.25	.11	.03
□ 65 Don Slaught	.10	.05	.01
□ 66 Mike Blowers	.10	.05	.01
□ 67 Wes Chamberlain	.10	.05	.01
□ 68 Troy Neel	.10	.05	.01
□ 69 John Wetteland	.25	.11	.03
□ 70 Joe Girardi	.10	.05	.01
□ 71 Reggie Sanders	.25	.11	.03
□ 72 Edgar Martinez	.25	.11	.03
□ 73 Todd Hundley	.25	.11	.03
□ 74 Pat Borders	.10	.05	.01
□ 75 Roberto Mejia	.10	.05	.01
□ 76 David Cone	.25	.11	.03
□ 77 Tony Gwynn	1.25	.55	.16
□ 78 Jim Abbott	.10	.05	.01
□ 79 Jay Buhner	.50	.23	.06
□ 80 Mark McLemore	.10	.05	.01
□ 81 Wil Cordero	.25	.11	.03
□ 82 Pedro Astacio	.10	.05	.01
□ 83 Bob Tewksbury	.10	.05	.01
□ 84 Dave Winfield	.50	.23	.06
□ 85 Jeff Kent	.10	.05	.01
□ 86 Todd Van Poppel	.10	.05	.01
□ 87 Steve Avery	.25	.11	.03
□ 88 Mike Lansing	.25	.11	.03
□ 89 Lenny Dykstra	.25	.11	.03
□ 90 Jose Guzman	.10	.05	.01
□ 91 Brian R. Hunter	.10	.05	.01
□ 92 Tim Raines	.50	.23	.06
□ 93 Andre Dawson	.25	.11	.03
□ 94 Joe Orsulak	.10	.05	.01
□ 95 Ricky Jordan	.10	.05	.01
□ 96 Billy Hatcher	.10	.05	.01
□ 97 Jack McDowell	.25	.11	.03
□ 98 Tom Pagnozzi	.10	.05	.01
□ 99 Darryl Strawberry	.25	.11	.03
□ 100 Mike Stanley	.10	.05	.01
□ 101 Bret Saberhagen	.25	.11	.03
□ 102 Willie Greene	.25	.11	.03
□ 103 Bryan Harvey	.10	.05	.01
□ 104 Tim Bogar	.10	.05	.01
□ 105 Jack Voigt	.10	.05	.01
□ 106 Brad Ausmus	.10	.05	.01
□ 107 Ramon Martinez	.25	.11	.03
□ 108 Mike Perez	.10	.05	.01
□ 109 Jeff Montgomery	.25	.11	.03
□ 110 Danny Darwin	.10	.05	.01
□ 111 Wilson Alvarez	.25	.11	.03
□ 112 Kevin Mitchell	.25	.11	.03
□ 113 David Nied	.10	.05	.01
□ 114 Rich Amaral	.10	.05	.01
□ 115 Stan Javier	.10	.05	.01
□ 116 Mo Vaughn	.75	.35	.09
□ 117 Ben McDonald	.10	.05	.01
□ 118 Tom Gordon	.10	.05	.01
□ 119 Carlos Garcia	.10	.05	.01
□ 120 Phil Plantier	.10	.05	.01
□ 121 Mike Morgan	.10	.05	.01
□ 122 Pat Meares	.10	.05	.01
□ 123 Kevin Young	.10	.05	.01
□ 124 Jeff Fassero	.10	.05	.01
□ 125 Gene Harris	.10	.05	.01
□ 126 Bob Welch	.10	.05	.01
□ 127 Walt Weiss	.10	.05	.01
□ 128 Bobby Witt	.10	.05	.01
□ 129 Andy Van Slyke	.25	.11	.03
□ 130 Steve Cooke	.10	.05	.01
□ 131 Mike Devereaux	.10	.05	.01
□ 132 Joey Cora	.10	.05	.01
□ 133 Bret Barberie	.10	.05	.01
□ 134 Orel Hershiser	.25	.11	.03
□ 135 Ed Sprague	.25	.11	.03
□ 136 Shawon Dunston	.10	.05	.01
□ 137 Alex Arias	.10	.05	.01
□ 138 Archi Cianfrocco	.10	.05	.01
□ 139 Tim Wallach	.10	.05	.01
□ 140 Bernie Williams	.60	.25	.07
□ 141 Karl Rhodes	.10	.05	.01
□ 142 Pat Kelly	.10	.05	.01
□ 143 Dave Magadan	.10	.05	.01
□ 144 Kevin Tapani	.10	.05	.01
□ 145 Eric Young	.25	.11	.03
□ 146 Derek Bell	.25	.11	.03
□ 147 Dante Bichette	.50	.23	.06
□ 148 Geronimo Pena	.10	.05	.01
□ 149 Joe Oliver	.10	.05	.01
□ 150 Orestes Destrade	.10	.05	.01
□ 151 Tim Naehring	.10	.05	.01
□ 152 Ray Lankford	.25	.11	.03
□ 153 Phil Clark	.10	.05	.01
□ 154 David McCarty	.10	.05	.01
□ 155 Tommy Greene	.10	.05	.01
□ 156 Wade Boggs	.50	.23	.06
□ 157 Kevin Gross	.10	.05	.01
□ 158 Hal Morris	.10	.05	.01
□ 159 Moises Alou	.25	.11	.03
□ 160 Rick Aguilera	.10	.05	.01
□ 161 Curt Schilling	.10	.05	.01
□ 162 Chip Hale	.10	.05	.01
□ 163 Tino Martinez	.25	.11	.03
□ 164 Mark Whiten	.10	.05	.01
□ 165 Dave Stewart	.25	.11	.03
□ 166 Steve Buechele	.10	.05	.01
□ 167 Bobby Jones	.25	.11	.03
□ 168 Darrin Fletcher	.10	.05	.01
□ 169 John Smiley	.10	.05	.01
□ 170 Cory Snyder	.10	.05	.01
□ 171 Scott Erickson	.10	.05	.01
□ 172 Kirk Rueter	.10	.05	.01
□ 173 Dave Fleming	.10	.05	.01
□ 174 John Smoltz	.50	.23	.06
□ 175 Ricky Gutierrez	.10	.05	.01
□ 176 Mike Bordick	.10	.05	.01
□ 177 Chan Ho Park	1.00	.45	.12
□ 178 Alex Gonzalez	.25	.11	.03
□ 179 Steve Karsay	.10	.05	.01
□ 180 Jeffrey Hammonds	.25	.11	.03
□ 181 Manny Ramirez	1.00	.45	.12
□ 182 Salomon Torres	.10	.05	.01
□ 183 Raul Mondesi	.50	.23	.06
□ 184 James Mouton	.25	.11	.03
□ 185 Cliff Floyd	.50	.23	.06

☐ 186 Danny Bautista .10 .05 .01
☐ 187 Kurt Abbott .25 .11 .03
☐ 188 Javier Lopez .50 .23 .06
☐ 189 John Patterson .10 .05 .01
☐ 190 Greg Blosser .10 .05 .01
☐ 191 Bob Hamelin .10 .05 .01
☐ 192 Tony Eusebio .10 .05 .01
☐ 193 Carlos Delgado .50 .23 .06
☐ 194 Chris Gomez .10 .05 .01
☐ 195 Kelly Stinnett .10 .05 .01
☐ 196 Shane Reynolds .25 .11 .03
☐ 197 Ryan Klesko .60 .25 .07
☐ 198 Jim Edmonds UER .60 .25 .07
Mark Dalesandro pictured on front
☐ 199 James Hurst .10 .05 .01
☐ 200 Dave Staton .10 .05 .01
☐ 201 Rondell White .50 .23 .06
☐ 202 Keith Mitchell .10 .05 .01
☐ 203 Darren Oliver .10 .05 .01
☐ 204 Mike Matheny .10 .05 .01
☐ 205 Chris Turner .10 .05 .01
☐ 206 Matt Mieske .10 .05 .01
☐ 207 NL Team Checklist .10 .05 .01
☐ 208 NL Team Checklist .10 .05 .01
☐ 209 AL Team Checklist .10 .05 .01
☐ 210 AL Team Checklist .10 .05 .01
☐ 211 Barry Bonds .75 .35 .09
☐ 212 Juan Gonzalez 1.50 .70 .19
☐ 213 Jim Eisenreich .10 .05 .01
☐ 214 Ivan Rodriguez .75 .35 .09
☐ 215 Tony Phillips .25 .11 .03
☐ 216 John Jaha .25 .11 .03
☐ 217 Lee Smith .25 .11 .03
☐ 218 Bip Roberts .10 .05 .01
☐ 219 Dave Hansen .10 .05 .01
☐ 220 Pat Listach .10 .05 .01
☐ 221 Willie McGee .10 .05 .01
☐ 222 Damion Easley .10 .05 .01
☐ 223 Dean Palmer .25 .11 .03
☐ 224 Mike Moore .10 .05 .01
☐ 225 Brian Harper .10 .05 .01
☐ 226 Gary DiSarcina .10 .05 .01
☐ 227 Delino DeShields .10 .05 .01
☐ 228 Otis Nixon .10 .05 .01
☐ 229 Roberto Alomar .60 .25 .07
☐ 230 Mark Grace .50 .23 .06
☐ 231 Kenny Lofton 1.00 .45 .12
☐ 232 Gregg Jefferies .50 .23 .06
☐ 233 Cecil Fielder .25 .11 .03
☐ 234 Jeff Bagwell 1.25 .55 .16
☐ 235 Albert Belle 1.25 .55 .16
☐ 236 Dave Justice .50 .23 .06
☐ 237 Tom Henke .10 .05 .01
☐ 238 Bobby Bonilla .25 .11 .03
☐ 239 John Olerud .10 .05 .01
☐ 240 Robby Thompson .10 .05 .01
☐ 241 Dave Valle .10 .05 .01
☐ 242 Marquis Grissom .25 .11 .03
☐ 243 Greg Swindell .10 .05 .01
☐ 244 Todd Zeile .10 .05 .01
☐ 245 Dennis Eckersley .25 .11 .03
☐ 246 Jose Offerman .10 .05 .01
☐ 247 Greg McMichael .10 .05 .01
☐ 248 Tim Belcher .10 .05 .01
☐ 249 Cal Ripken Jr. 2.50 1.10 .30
☐ 250 Tom Glavine .50 .23 .06
☐ 251 Luis Polonia .10 .05 .01
☐ 252 Bill Swift .10 .05 .01
☐ 253 Juan Guzman .25 .11 .03
☐ 254 Rickey Henderson .50 .23 .06
☐ 255 Terry Mulholland .10 .05 .01
☐ 256 Gary Sheffield .50 .23 .06
☐ 257 Terry Steinbach .25 .11 .03
☐ 258 Brett Butler .25 .11 .03
☐ 259 Jason Bere .25 .11 .03
☐ 260 Doug Strange .10 .05 .01
☐ 261 Kent Hrbek .25 .11 .03
☐ 262 Graeme Lloyd .10 .05 .01
☐ 263 Lou Frazier .10 .05 .01
☐ 264 Charles Nagy .25 .11 .03
☐ 265 Bret Boone .25 .11 .03
☐ 266 Kirk Gibson .25 .11 .03
☐ 267 Kevin Brown .25 .11 .03
☐ 268 Fred McGriff .50 .23 .06
☐ 269 Matt Williams .50 .23 .06
☐ 270 Greg Gagne .10 .05 .01
☐ 271 Mariano Duncan .10 .05 .01
☐ 272 Jeff Russell .10 .05 .01
☐ 273 Eric Davis .25 .11 .03
☐ 274 Shane Mack .10 .05 .01
☐ 275 Jose Vizcaino .10 .05 .01
☐ 276 Jose Canseco .50 .23 .06
☐ 277 Roberto Hernandez .25 .11 .03
☐ 278 Royce Clayton .25 .11 .03
☐ 279 Carlos Baerga .25 .11 .03
☐ 280 Pete Incaviglia .10 .05 .01
☐ 281 Brent Gates .10 .05 .01
☐ 282 Jeromy Burnitz .10 .05 .01
☐ 283 Chili Davis .25 .11 .03
☐ 284 Pete Harnisch .10 .05 .01
☐ 285 Alan Trammell .25 .11 .03
☐ 286 Eric Anthony .10 .05 .01
☐ 287 Ellis Burks .25 .11 .03
☐ 288 Julio Franco .25 .11 .03
☐ 289 Jack Morris .25 .11 .03
☐ 290 Erik Hanson .10 .05 .01
☐ 291 Chuck Finley .10 .05 .01
☐ 292 Reggie Jefferson .25 .11 .03
☐ 293 Kevin McReynolds .10 .05 .01
☐ 294 Greg Hibbard .10 .05 .01
☐ 295 Travis Fryman .25 .11 .03
☐ 296 Craig Biggio .25 .11 .03
☐ 297 Kenny Rogers .10 .05 .01
☐ 298 Dave Henderson .10 .05 .01
☐ 299 Jim Thome .75 .35 .09
☐ 300 Rene Arocha .10 .05 .01
☐ 301 Pedro Munoz .10 .05 .01
☐ 302 David Hulse .10 .05 .01
☐ 303 Greg Vaughn .50 .23 .06
☐ 304 Darren Lewis .10 .05 .01
☐ 305 Deion Sanders .50 .23 .06
☐ 306 Danny Tartabull .10 .05 .01
☐ 307 Darryl Hamilton .10 .05 .01
☐ 308 Andujar Cedeno .10 .05 .01
☐ 309 Tim Salmon .50 .23 .06
☐ 310 Tony Fernandez .10 .05 .01
☐ 311 Alex Fernandez .25 .11 .03
☐ 312 Roberto Kelly .10 .05 .01
☐ 313 Harold Reynolds .10 .05 .01
☐ 314 Chris Sabo .10 .05 .01
☐ 315 Howard Johnson .10 .05 .01
☐ 316 Mark Portugal .10 .05 .01
☐ 317 Rafael Palmeiro .50 .23 .06
☐ 318 Pete Smith .10 .05 .01
☐ 319 Will Clark .50 .23 .06
☐ 320 Henry Rodriguez .25 .11 .03
☐ 321 Omar Vizquel .25 .11 .03
☐ 322 David Segui .10 .05 .01
☐ 323 Lou Whitaker .25 .11 .03
☐ 324 Felix Fermin .10 .05 .01
☐ 325 Spike Owen .10 .05 .01
☐ 326 Darryl Kile .10 .05 .01
☐ 327 Chad Kreuter .10 .05 .01
☐ 328 Rod Beck .25 .11 .03
☐ 329 Eddie Murray .75 .35 .09
☐ 330 B.J. Surhoff .10 .05 .01
☐ 331 Mickey Tettleton .10 .05 .01
☐ 332 Pedro Martinez .50 .23 .06
☐ 333 Roger Pavlik .10 .05 .01
☐ 334 Eddie Taubensee .10 .05 .01
☐ 335 John Doherty .10 .05 .01
☐ 336 Jody Reed .10 .05 .01
☐ 337 Aaron Sele .25 .11 .03
☐ 338 Leo Gomez .10 .05 .01
☐ 339 Dave Nilsson .25 .11 .03
☐ 340 Rob Dibble .10 .05 .01
☐ 341 John Burkett .10 .05 .01
☐ 342 Wayne Kirby .10 .05 .01
☐ 343 Dan Wilson .25 .11 .03
☐ 344 Armando Reynoso .10 .05 .01
☐ 345 Chad Curtis .10 .05 .01
☐ 346 Dennis Martinez .25 .11 .03
☐ 347 Cal Eldred .10 .05 .01
☐ 348 Luis Gonzalez .10 .05 .01
☐ 349 Doug Drabek .10 .05 .01
☐ 350 Jim Leyritz .10 .05 .01
☐ 351 Mark Langston .25 .11 .03
☐ 352 Darrin Jackson .10 .05 .01
☐ 353 Sid Fernandez .10 .05 .01
☐ 354 Benito Santiago .10 .05 .01
☐ 355 Kevin Seitzer .10 .05 .01
☐ 356 Bo Jackson .25 .11 .03
☐ 357 David Wells .10 .05 .01
☐ 358 Paul Sorrento .10 .05 .01
☐ 359 Ken Caminiti .50 .23 .06
☐ 360 Eduardo Perez .10 .05 .01
☐ 361 Orlando Merced .25 .11 .03
☐ 362 Steve Finley .50 .23 .06
☐ 363 Andy Benes .25 .11 .03
☐ 364 Manuel Lee .10 .05 .01
☐ 365 Todd Benzinger .10 .05 .01
☐ 366 Sandy Alomar Jr. .25 .11 .03
☐ 367 Rex Hudler .10 .05 .01
☐ 368 Mike Henneman .10 .05 .01
☐ 369 Vince Coleman .10 .05 .01
☐ 370 Kirt Manwaring .10 .05 .01
☐ 371 Ken Hill .10 .05 .01
☐ 372 Glenallen Hill .10 .05 .01
☐ 373 Sean Berry .10 .05 .01
☐ 374 Geronimo Berroa .25 .11 .03
☐ 375 Duane Ward .10 .05 .01
☐ 376 Allen Watson .10 .05 .01
☐ 377 Marc Newfield .25 .11 .03
☐ 378 Dan Miceli .10 .05 .01
☐ 379 Denny Hocking .10 .05 .01
☐ 380 Mark Kiefer .10 .05 .01
☐ 381 Tony Tarasco .10 .05 .01
☐ 382 Tony Longmire .10 .05 .01
☐ 383 Brian Anderson .25 .11 .03
☐ 384 Fernando Vina .10 .05 .01
☐ 385 Hector Carrasco .10 .05 .01
☐ 386 Mike Kelly .10 .05 .01
☐ 387 Greg Colbrunn .10 .05 .01
☐ 388 Roger Salkeld .10 .05 .01
☐ 389 Steve Trachsel .25 .11 .03
☐ 390 Rich Becker .25 .11 .03
☐ 391 Billy Taylor .10 .05 .01
☐ 392 Rich Rowland .10 .05 .01
☐ 393 Carl Everett .10 .05 .01
☐ 394 Johnny Ruffin .10 .05 .01
☐ 395 Keith Lockhart .10 .05 .01
☐ 396 J.R. Phillips .10 .05 .01
☐ 397 Sterling Hitchcock .25 .11 .03
☐ 398 Jorge Fabregas .10 .05 .01
☐ 399 Jeff Granger .25 .11 .03
☐ 400 Eddie Zambrano .10 .05 .01
☐ 401 Rikkert Faneyte .10 .05 .01
☐ 402 Gerald Williams .10 .05 .01
☐ 403 Joey Hamilton .60 .25 .07
☐ 404 Joe Hall .10 .05 .01
☐ 405 John Hudek .10 .05 .01
☐ 406 Roberto Petagine .25 .11 .03
☐ 407 Charles Johnson .50 .23 .06
☐ 408 Mark Smith .10 .05 .01
☐ 409 Jeff Juden .10 .05 .01
☐ 410 Carlos Pulido .10 .05 .01
☐ 411 Paul Shuey .10 .05 .01
☐ 412 Rob Butler .10 .05 .01
☐ 413 Mark Acre .10 .05 .01
☐ 414 Greg Pirkl .10 .05 .01
☐ 415 Melvin Nieves .25 .11 .03
☐ 416 Tim Hyers .10 .05 .01
☐ 417 NL Checklist .10 .05 .01
☐ 418 NL Checklist .10 .05 .01
☐ 419 AL Checklist .10 .05 .01
☐ 420 AL Checklist .10 .05 .01
☐ RY1 Carlos Delgado 10.00 4.50 1.25
☐ SS1 Cal Ripken Jr. 60.00 27.00 7.50
Salute
☐ SS2 Dave Winfield 10.00 4.50 1.25
Salute
☐ MVP1 Paul Molitor 15.00 6.75 1.85

1994 Select Crown Contenders

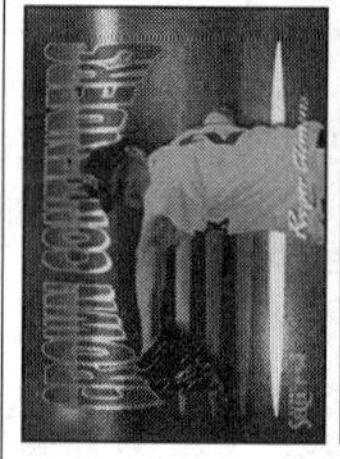
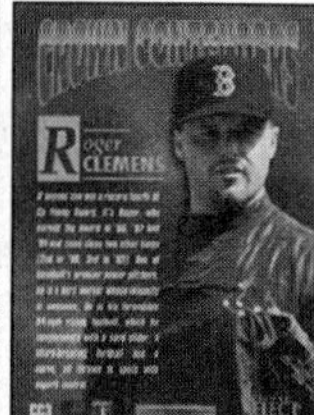

This ten-card set showcases top contenders for various awards such as batting champion, Cy Young Award winner and Most Valuable Player. The cards were inserted in first series packs at a rate of one in 24 and measure the standard size. The horizontal fronts feature color action player shots on a holographic gold foil background. The backs carry a color player close-up photo and highlights. The cards are numbered on the back with a CC prefix.

	MINT	NRMT	EXC
COMPLETE SET (10)	100.00	45.00	12.50
COMMON CARD (CC1-CC10)	3.00	1.35	.35
☐ CC1 Lenny Dykstra	3.00	1.35	.35
☐ CC2 Greg Maddux	15.00	6.75	1.85
☐ CC3 Roger Clemens	5.00	2.20	.60
☐ CC4 Randy Johnson	4.00	1.80	.50
☐ CC5 Frank Thomas	25.00	11.00	3.10
☐ CC6 Barry Bonds	6.00	2.70	.75
☐ CC7 Juan Gonzalez	12.00	5.50	1.50
☐ CC8 John Olerud	3.00	1.35	.35
☐ CC9 Mike Piazza	15.00	6.75	1.85
☐ CC10 Ken Griffey Jr.	25.00	11.00	3.10

1994 Select Rookie Surge

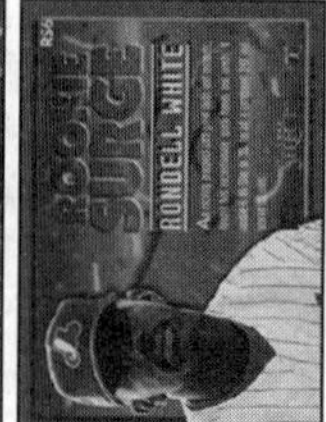

This 18-card standard-size set showcased potential top rookies for 1994. The set was divided into two series of nine cards. The cards were randomly inserted in packs at a rate of one in 48. The fronts exhibit Score's 'dufex' printing process, in which a color photo is printed on a metallic base creating an unusual, three-dimensional look. On a multi-colored background, the horizontal backs present a color player headshot. The cards are numbered on the back with an RS prefix.

	MINT	NRMT	EXC
COMPLETE SET (18)	90.00	40.00	11.00
COMPLETE SERIES 1 (9)	40.00	18.00	5.00
COMPLETE SERIES 2 (9)	50.00	22.00	6.25
COMMON CARD (RS1-RS18)	2.50	1.10	.30
☐ RS1 Cliff Floyd	5.00	2.20	.60
☐ RS2 Bob Hamelin	2.50	1.10	.30
☐ RS3 Ryan Klesko	15.00	6.75	1.85
☐ RS4 Carlos Delgado	10.00	4.50	1.25
☐ RS5 Jeffrey Hammonds	5.00	2.20	.60
☐ RS6 Rondell White	8.00	3.60	1.00
☐ RS7 Salomon Torres	2.50	1.10	.30
☐ RS8 Steve Karsay	2.50	1.10	.30
☐ RS9 Javier Lopez	10.00	4.50	1.25
☐ RS10 Manny Ramirez	25.00	11.00	3.10
☐ RS11 Tony Tarasco	2.50	1.10	.30
☐ RS12 Kurt Abbott	2.50	1.10	.30
☐ RS13 Chan Ho Park	12.00	5.50	1.50
☐ RS14 Rich Becker	5.00	2.20	.60
☐ RS15 James Mouton	5.00	2.20	.60
☐ RS16 Alex Gonzalez	5.00	2.20	.60
☐ RS17 Raul Mondesi	12.00	5.50	1.50
☐ RS18 Steve Trachsel	2.50	1.10	.30

1994 Select Skills

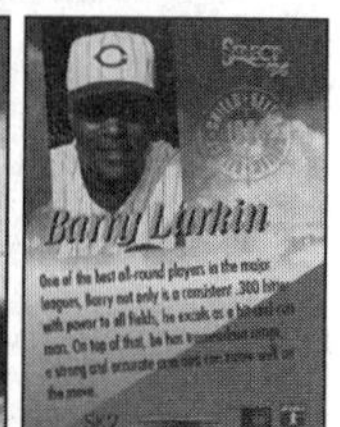

This 10-card standard-size set takes an up close look at the leagues top statistical leaders. The cards were randomly inserted in second series packs at a rate of approximately one in 24. A foil front has a holographic appearance that allows the player to stand out. The bottom of the front notes the player as being the best at something. For example, the front of Barry Bonds' card notes, "Select's Best Run Producer". The back has a small photo with text. The cards are numbered with an "SK" prefix.

	MINT	NRMT	EXC
COMPLETE SET (10)	60.00	27.00	7.50
COMMON CARD (SK1-SK10)	4.00	1.80	.50
☐ SK1 Randy Johnson	8.00	3.60	1.00
☐ SK2 Barry Larkin	6.00	2.70	.75
☐ SK3 Lenny Dykstra	4.00	1.80	.50
☐ SK4 Kenny Lofton	15.00	6.75	1.85
☐ SK5 Juan Gonzalez	25.00	11.00	3.10
☐ SK6 Barry Bonds	12.00	5.50	1.50
☐ SK7 Marquis Grissom	5.00	2.20	.60
☐ SK8 Ivan Rodriguez	12.00	5.50	1.50
☐ SK9 Larry Walker	5.00	2.20	.60
☐ SK10 Travis Fryman	5.00	2.20	.60

1995 Select Samples

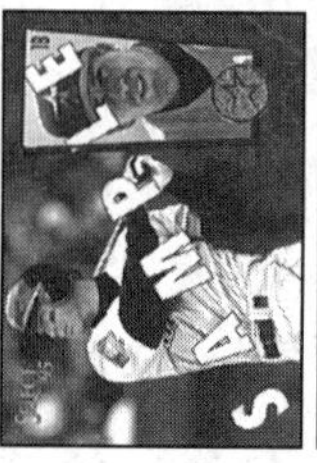

This 4-card set was issued to preview the 1995 Select series. On horizontal fronts, the regular issue cards display a full-bleed color action photo edged on the right by a team color-coded marbleized trapezoid. A color closeup photo is superposed over the trapezoid. The backs carry player profile and statistics printed on a black-and-white closeup photo. Both sides of each card have the disclaimer "SAMPLE" diagonally stamped across the pictures.

	MINT	NRMT	EXC
COMPLETE SET (4)	15.00	6.75	1.85
COMMON CARD	1.00	.45	.12
☐ 34 Roberto Alomar	2.50	1.10	.30
☐ 37 Jeff Bagwell	4.00	1.80	.50
☐ 241 Alex Rodriguez	10.00	4.50	1.25
☐ NNO Title Card	1.00	.45	.12

1995 Select

This 250-card set was issued in 12-card packs with 24 packs per box and 24 boxes per case. There was an announced production run of 4,950 cases. These horizontal cards feature an action photo over most of the card with the playeris profile and name on the right side. The "Select 95" logo is in the upper left corner. The vertical backs have a black and white photo on the top. The middle of the card is dedicated to a brief biography as well as seasonal and career stats. A specific important stat is included at the bottom of the card. A special card of Hideo Nomo (#251) was issued to hobby dealers who had bought cases of the Select product.

	MINT	NRMT	EXC
COMPLETE SET (250)	15.00	6.75	1.85
COMMON CARD (1-250)	.05	.02	.01

☐ 1 Cal Ripken Jr.	1.50	.70	.19
☐ 2 Robin Ventura	.15	.07	.02
☐ 3 Al Martin	.15	.07	.02
☐ 4 Jeff Frye	.05	.02	.01
☐ 5 Darryl Strawberry	.15	.07	.02
☐ 6 Chan Ho Park	.30	.14	.04
☐ 7 Steve Avery	.15	.07	.02
☐ 8 Bret Boone	.15	.07	.02
☐ 9 Danny Tartabull	.05	.02	.01
☐ 10 Dante Bichette	.30	.14	.04
☐ 11 Rondell White	.15	.07	.02
☐ 12 Dave McCarty	.05	.02	.01
☐ 13 Bernard Gilkey	.15	.07	.02
☐ 14 Mark McGwire	.60	.25	.07
☐ 15 Ruben Sierra	.15	.07	.02
☐ 16 Wade Boggs	.30	.14	.04
☐ 17 Mike Piazza	1.25	.55	.16
☐ 18 Jeffrey Hammonds	.15	.07	.02
☐ 19 Mike Mussina	.40	.18	.05
☐ 20 Darryl Kile	.05	.02	.01
☐ 21 Greg Maddux	1.25	.55	.16
☐ 22 Frank Thomas	2.00	.90	.25
☐ 23 Kevin Appier	.15	.07	.02
☐ 24 Jay Bell	.15	.07	.02
☐ 25 Kirk Gibson	.15	.07	.02
☐ 26 Pat Hentgen	.15	.07	.02
☐ 27 Joey Hamilton	.30	.14	.04
☐ 28 Bernie Williams	.40	.18	.05
☐ 29 Aaron Sele	.15	.07	.02
☐ 30 Delino DeShields	.05	.02	.01
☐ 31 Danny Bautista	.05	.02	.01
☐ 32 Jim Thome	.40	.18	.05
☐ 33 Rikkert Faneyte	.05	.02	.01
☐ 34 Roberto Alomar	.40	.18	.05
☐ 35 Paul Molitor	.40	.18	.05
☐ 36 Allen Watson	.05	.02	.01
☐ 37 Jeff Bagwell	.75	.35	.09
☐ 38 Jay Buhner	.30	.14	.04
☐ 39 Marquis Grissom	.15	.07	.02
☐ 40 Jim Edmonds	.30	.14	.04
☐ 41 Ryan Klesko	.30	.14	.04
☐ 42 Fred McGriff	.30	.14	.04
☐ 43 Tony Tarasco	.05	.02	.01
☐ 44 Darren Daulton	.15	.07	.02
☐ 45 Marc Newfield	.15	.07	.02
☐ 46 Barry Bonds	.50	.23	.06
☐ 47 Bobby Bonilla	.15	.07	.02
☐ 48 Greg Pirkl	.05	.02	.01
☐ 49 Steve Karsay	.05	.02	.01
☐ 50 Bob Hamelin	.05	.02	.01
☐ 51 Javier Lopez	.30	.14	.04
☐ 52 Barry Larkin	.30	.14	.04
☐ 53 Kevin Young	.05	.02	.01
☐ 54 Sterling Hitchcock	.15	.07	.02
☐ 55 Tom Glavine	.30	.14	.04
☐ 56 Carlos Delgado	.15	.07	.02
☐ 57 Darren Oliver	.30	.14	.04
☐ 58 Cliff Floyd	.15	.07	.02
☐ 59 Tim Salmon	.30	.14	.04
☐ 60 Albert Belle	.75	.35	.09
☐ 61 Salomon Torres	.05	.02	.01
☐ 62 Gary Sheffield	.30	.14	.04
☐ 63 Ivan Rodriguez	.50	.23	.06
☐ 64 Charles Nagy	.15	.07	.02
☐ 65 Eduardo Perez	.05	.02	.01
☐ 66 Terry Steinbach	.15	.07	.02
☐ 67 Dave Justice	.30	.14	.04
☐ 68 Jason Bere	.05	.02	.01
☐ 69 Dave Nilsson	.15	.07	.02
☐ 70 Brian Anderson	.05	.02	.01
☐ 71 Billy Ashley	.05	.02	.01
☐ 72 Roger Clemens	.40	.18	.05
☐ 73 Jimmy Key	.15	.07	.02
☐ 74 Wally Joyner	.15	.07	.02
☐ 75 Andy Benes	.05	.02	.01
☐ 76 Ray Lankford	.15	.07	.02
☐ 77 Jeff Kent	.05	.02	.01
☐ 78 Moises Alou	.15	.07	.02
☐ 79 Kirby Puckett	.75	.35	.09
☐ 80 Joe Carter	.15	.07	.02
☐ 81 Manny Ramirez	.50	.23	.06
☐ 82 J.R. Phillips	.05	.02	.01
☐ 83 Matt Mieske	.15	.07	.02
☐ 84 John Olerud	.05	.02	.01
☐ 85 Andres Galarraga	.30	.14	.04
☐ 86 Juan Gonzalez	1.00	.45	.12
☐ 87 Pedro Martinez	.15	.07	.02
☐ 88 Dean Palmer	.15	.07	.02
☐ 89 Ken Griffey Jr.	2.00	.90	.25
☐ 90 Brian Jordan	.30	.14	.04
☐ 91 Hal Morris	.05	.02	.01
☐ 92 Lenny Dykstra	.15	.07	.02
☐ 93 Wil Cordero	.05	.02	.01
☐ 94 Tony Gwynn	.75	.35	.09
☐ 95 Alex Gonzalez	.05	.02	.01
☐ 96 Cecil Fielder	.15	.07	.02
☐ 97 Mo Vaughn	.50	.23	.06
☐ 98 John Valentin	.15	.07	.02
☐ 99 Will Clark	.30	.14	.04
☐ 100 Geronimo Pena	.05	.02	.01
☐ 101 Don Mattingly	1.00	.45	.12
☐ 102 Charles Johnson	.15	.07	.02
☐ 103 Raul Mondesi	.30	.14	.04
☐ 104 Reggie Sanders	.15	.07	.02
☐ 105 Royce Clayton	.05	.02	.01
☐ 106 Reggie Jefferson	.15	.07	.02
☐ 107 Craig Biggio	.15	.07	.02
☐ 108 Jack McDowell	.15	.07	.02
☐ 109 James Mouton	.05	.02	.01
☐ 110 Mike Greenwell	.05	.02	.01
☐ 111 David Cone	.15	.07	.02
☐ 112 Matt Williams	.30	.14	.04
☐ 113 Garret Anderson	.15	.07	.02
☐ 114 Carlos Garcia	.05	.02	.01
☐ 115 Alex Fernandez	.15	.07	.02
☐ 116 Deion Sanders	.30	.14	.04
☐ 117 Chili Davis	.15	.07	.02
☐ 118 Mike Kelly	.05	.02	.01
☐ 119 Jeff Conine	.15	.07	.02
☐ 120 Kenny Lofton	.50	.23	.06
☐ 121 Rafael Palmeiro	.30	.14	.04
☐ 122 Chuck Knoblauch	.30	.14	.04
☐ 123 Ozzie Smith	.50	.23	.06
☐ 124 Carlos Baerga	.15	.07	.02
☐ 125 Brett Butler	.15	.07	.02
☐ 126 Sammy Sosa	.30	.14	.04
☐ 127 Ellis Burks	.15	.07	.02
☐ 128 Bret Saberhagen	.15	.07	.02
☐ 129 Doug Drabek	.05	.02	.01
☐ 130 Dennis Martinez	.15	.07	.02
☐ 131 Paul O'Neill	.15	.07	.02
☐ 132 Travis Fryman	.15	.07	.02
☐ 133 Brent Gates	.05	.02	.01
☐ 134 Rickey Henderson	.30	.14	.04
☐ 135 Randy Johnson	.30	.14	.04
☐ 136 Mark Langston	.05	.02	.01
☐ 137 Greg Colbrunn	.05	.02	.01
☐ 138 Jose Rijo	.05	.02	.01
☐ 139 Bryan Harvey	.05	.02	.01
☐ 140 Dennis Eckersley	.15	.07	.02
☐ 141 Ron Gant	.15	.07	.02
☐ 142 Carl Everett	.05	.02	.01
☐ 143 Jeff Granger	.05	.02	.01
☐ 144 Ben McDonald	.05	.02	.01
☐ 145 Kurt Abbott UER	.05	.02	.01
(Mariners logo on front			
☐ 146 Jim Abbott	.05	.02	.01
☐ 147 Jason Jacome	.05	.02	.01
☐ 148 Rico Brogna	.05	.02	.01
☐ 149 Cal Eldred	.05	.02	.01
☐ 150 Rich Becker	.05	.02	.01
☐ 151 Pete Harnisch	.05	.02	.01
☐ 152 Roberto Petagine	.05	.02	.01
☐ 153 Jacob Brumfield	.05	.02	.01
☐ 154 Todd Hundley	.15	.07	.02
☐ 155 Roger Cedeno	.15	.07	.02
☐ 156 Harold Baines	.15	.07	.02
☐ 157 Steve Dunn	.05	.02	.01
☐ 158 Tim Belk	.05	.02	.01
☐ 159 Marty Cordova	.30	.14	.04
☐ 160 Russ Davis	.05	.02	.01
☐ 161 Jose Malave	.05	.02	.01
☐ 162 Brian Hunter	.30	.14	.04
☐ 163 Andy Pettitte	.75	.35	.09
☐ 164 Brooks Kieschnick	.30	.14	.04
☐ 165 Midre Cummings	.05	.02	.01
☐ 166 Frank Rodriguez	.15	.07	.02
☐ 167 Chad Mottola	.15	.07	.02
☐ 168 Brian Barber	.05	.02	.01
☐ 169 Tim Unroe	.15	.07	.02
☐ 170 Shane Andrews	.05	.02	.01
☐ 171 Kevin Flora	.05	.02	.01
☐ 172 Ray Durham	.15	.07	.02
☐ 173 Chipper Jones	1.25	.55	.16
☐ 174 Butch Huskey	.15	.07	.02
☐ 175 Ray McDavid	.15	.07	.02
☐ 176 Jeff Cirillo	.15	.07	.02
☐ 177 Terry Pendleton	.15	.07	.02
☐ 178 Scott Ruffcorn	.05	.02	.01
☐ 179 Ray Holbert	.05	.02	.01
☐ 180 Joe Randa	.05	.02	.01
☐ 181 Jose Oliva	.05	.02	.01
☐ 182 Andy Van Slyke	.15	.07	.02
☐ 183 Albie Lopez	.05	.02	.01
☐ 184 Chad Curtis	.05	.02	.01
☐ 185 Ozzie Guillen	.05	.02	.01
☐ 186 Chad Ogea	.05	.02	.01
☐ 187 Dan Wilson	.15	.07	.02
☐ 188 Tony Fernandez	.05	.02	.01
☐ 189 John Smoltz	.30	.14	.04
☐ 190 Willie Greene	.05	.02	.01
☐ 191 Darren Lewis	.05	.02	.01
☐ 192 Orlando Miller	.05	.02	.01
☐ 193 Kurt Miller	.05	.02	.01
☐ 194 Andrew Lorraine	.15	.07	.02
☐ 195 Ernie Young	.15	.07	.02
☐ 196 Jimmy Haynes	.15	.07	.02
☐ 197 Raul Casanova	.50	.23	.06
☐ 198 Joe Vitiello	.05	.02	.01
☐ 199 Brad Woodall	.05	.02	.01
☐ 200 Juan Acevedo	.05	.02	.01
☐ 201 Michael Tucker	.15	.07	.02
☐ 202 Shawn Green	.15	.07	.02
☐ 203 Alex Rodriguez	2.50	1.10	.30
☐ 204 Julian Tavarez	.05	.02	.01
☐ 205 Jose Lima	.05	.02	.01
☐ 206 Wilson Alvarez	.15	.07	.02
☐ 207 Rich Aude	.05	.02	.01
☐ 208 Armando Benitez	.05	.02	.01
☐ 209 Dwayne Hosey	.05	.02	.01
☐ 210 Gabe White	.05	.02	.01
☐ 211 Joey Eischen	.05	.02	.01
☐ 212 Bill Pulsipher	.15	.07	.02
☐ 213 Robby Thompson	.05	.02	.01
☐ 214 Toby Borland	.05	.02	.01
☐ 215 Rusty Greer	.30	.14	.04
☐ 216 Fausto Cruz	.05	.02	.01
☐ 217 Luis Ortiz	.05	.02	.01
☐ 218 Duane Singleton	.05	.02	.01
☐ 219 Troy Percival	.05	.02	.01
☐ 220 Gregg Jefferies	.15	.07	.02
☐ 221 Mark Grace	.30	.14	.04
☐ 222 Mickey Tettleton	.05	.02	.01
☐ 223 Phil Plantier	.05	.02	.01
☐ 224 Larry Walker	.30	.14	.04
☐ 225 Ken Caminiti	.30	.14	.04
☐ 226 Dave Winfield	.30	.14	.04
☐ 227 Brady Anderson	.30	.14	.04
☐ 228 Kevin Brown	.15	.07	.02
☐ 229 Andujar Cedeno	.05	.02	.01
☐ 230 Roberto Kelly	.05	.02	.01
☐ 231 Jose Canseco	.30	.14	.04
☐ 232 Scott Ruffcorn ST	.05	.02	.01
☐ 233 Billy Ashley ST	.05	.02	.01
☐ 234 J.R. Phillips ST	.05	.02	.01
☐ 235 Chipper Jones ST	.60	.25	.07
☐ 236 Charles Johnson ST	.15	.07	.02
☐ 237 Midre Cummings ST	.05	.02	.01
☐ 238 Brian L.Hunter SH	.15	.07	.02
☐ 239 Garret Anderson ST	.15	.07	.02
☐ 240 Shawn Green SH	.15	.07	.02
☐ 241 Alex Rodriguez ST	1.25	.55	.16
☐ 242 Frank Thomas CL	1.00	.45	.12
☐ 243 Ken Griffey Jr. CL	1.00	.45	.12
☐ 244 Albert Belle CL	.40	.18	.05
☐ 245 Cal Ripken Jr. CL	.75	.35	.09
☐ 246 Barry Bonds CL	.25	.11	.03
☐ 247 Raul Mondesi CL	.30	.14	.04
☐ 248 Mike Piazza CL	.60	.25	.07
☐ 249 Jeff Bagwell CL	.40	.18	.05
☐ 250 Jeff Bagwell Ken Griffey Jr. Frank Thomas Mike Piazza CL	1.50	.70	.19
☐ 251S Hideo Nomo	2.50	1.10	.30

1995 Select Artist's Proofs

This 250-card set is parallel to the regular Select set. These cards were inserted at a rate of one per 24 packs. The only difference between these cards and the regular issue cards are the words "Artist's Proof" printed in the lower left corner. The Hideo Nomo card was randomly distributed directly to hobby dealers and was never inserted in packs.

	MINT	NRMT	EXC
COMPLETE SET (250)	5500.00	2500.00	700.00
COMMON CARD (1-250)	8.00	3.60	1.00
*STARS: 35X TO 60X BASIC CARDS ..			
*YOUNG STARS: 30X TO 50X BASIC CARDS			
☐ 1 Cal Ripken	300.00	135.00	38.00
☐ 17 Mike Piazza	125.00	55.00	15.50
☐ 21 Greg Maddux	300.00	135.00	38.00
☐ 22 Frank Thomas	300.00	135.00	38.00
☐ 37 Jeff Bagwell	100.00	45.00	12.50
☐ 60 Albert Belle	125.00	55.00	15.50
☐ 79 Kirby Puckett	100.00	45.00	12.50
☐ 86 Juan Gonzalez	75.00	34.00	9.50
☐ 89 Ken Griffey Jr.	300.00	135.00	38.00
☐ 94 Tony Gwynn	100.00	45.00	12.50
☐ 101 Don Mattingly	150.00	70.00	19.00
☐ 163 Andy Pettitte	30.00	13.50	3.70
☐ 173 Chipper Jones	150.00	70.00	19.00
☐ 203 Alex Rodriguez	50.00	22.00	6.25
☐ 241 Alex Rodriguez SH	60.00	27.00	7.50
☐ 242 Frank Thomas CL	150.00	70.00	19.00
☐ 243 Ken Griffey Jr. CL	150.00	70.00	19.00
☐ 245 Cal Ripken CL	150.00	70.00	19.00
☐ 250 Jeff Bagwell CL Frank Thomas Ken Griffey Jr. Mike Piazza	275.00	125.00	34.00
☐ 251S Hideo Nomo	100.00	45.00	12.50

1995 Select Big Sticks

Randomly inserted in packs, these 12 cards feature leading hitters. The fronts picture the playeris photo against a metallic background. The words "Big Sticks 95" as well as the player's name is on the bottom. The player's team is noted in the middle of the background. The backs contain a player photo, personal information as well as some notes about his career. The cards are numbered in the upper right corner with a "BS" prefix.

	MINT	NRMT	EXC
COMPLETE SET (12)	150.00	70.00	19.00
COMMON CARD (1-12)	4.00	1.80	.50
☐ BS1 Frank Thomas	30.00	13.50	3.70
☐ BS2 Ken Griffey Jr.	30.00	13.50	3.70
☐ BS3 Cal Ripken Jr.	25.00	11.00	3.10
☐ BS4 Mike Piazza	20.00	9.00	2.50
☐ BS5 Don Mattingly	15.00	6.75	1.85
☐ BS6 Will Clark	4.00	1.80	.50
☐ BS7 Tony Gwynn	12.00	5.50	1.50
☐ BS8 Jeff Bagwell	12.00	5.50	1.50
☐ BS9 Barry Bonds	8.00	3.60	1.00
☐ BS10 Paul Molitor	6.00	2.70	.75
☐ BS11 Matt Williams	4.00	1.80	.50
☐ BS12 Albert Belle	12.00	5.50	1.50

1995 Select Can't Miss

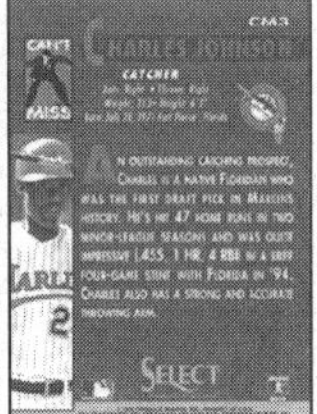

These 12 cards featuring promising young players were inserted one per 24 packs. The player is pictured against a wavy red background. His last name is identified on the bottom left with the "Can't Miss" logo directly above the name. In the middle of the "Can't Miss" logo is a drawing of an umpire signaling safe. The backs have a blue background and include an inset photo, some professional information and biographical data. The cards are numbered with a "CM" prefix in the upper right corner.

	MINT	NRMT	EXC
COMPLETE SET (12)	60.00	27.00	7.50
COMMON CARD (1-12)	2.00	.90	.25
☐ CM1 Cliff Floyd	2.00	.90	.25
☐ CM2 Ryan Klesko	5.00	2.20	.60
☐ CM3 Charles Johnson	2.00	.90	.25
☐ CM4 Raul Mondesi	4.00	1.80	.50
☐ CM5 Manny Ramirez	8.00	3.60	1.00
☐ CM6 Billy Ashley	2.00	.90	.25
☐ CM7 Alex Gonzalez	2.00	.90	.25
☐ CM8 Carlos Delgado	4.00	1.80	.50
☐ CM9 Garret Anderson	2.50	1.10	.30
☐ CM10 Alex Rodriguez	25.00	11.00	3.10
☐ CM11 Chipper Jones	20.00	9.00	2.50
☐ CM12 Shawn Green	2.00	.90	.25

1995 Select Sure Shots

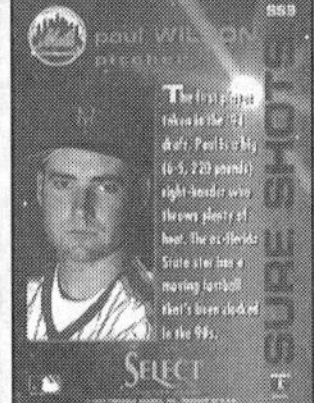

These 10 cards were randomly inserted into packs. This set features some of the top 1994 draft picks. The fronts feature the player's photo against a gold metallic background. The phrase "Sure Shots" is printed on gold ink against a blue background on the left. The player is identified in white ink on the bottom. The backs contain some information about the player as well as an inset photo. All this information is set against a blue background with a white light effect. The cards are numbered with an "SS" prefix in the upper right corner.

	MINT	NRMT	EXC
COMPLETE SET (10)	100.00	45.00	12.50
COMMON CARD (1-10)	5.00	2.20	.60
□ SS1 Ben Grieve	25.00	11.00	3.10
□ SS2 Kevin Witt			
□ SS3 Mark Farris	5.00	2.20	.60
□ SS4 Paul Konerko	30.00	13.50	3.70
□ SS5 Dustin Hermanson	5.00	2.20	.60
□ SS6 Ramon Castro	5.00	2.20	.60
□ SS7 McKay Christensen	5.00	2.20	.60
□ SS8 Brian Buchanan	5.00	2.20	.60
□ SS9 Paul Wilson	12.00	5.50	1.50
□ SS10 Terrence Long	10.00	4.50	1.25

1996 Select

The 1996 Select set was issued in one series totalling 200 cards. The 10-card packs retail for $1.99 each. The fronts feature a color action player photo over most of the card with a small player photo framed and name in gold foil printing. The backs carry another player photo, player information and statistics. The set contains the topical subsets: Lineup Leaders (151-160) and Rookies (161-195).

	MINT	NRMT	EXC
COMPLETE SET (200)	15.00	6.75	1.85
COMMON CARD (1-200)	.05	.02	.01
□ 1 Wade Boggs	.50	.23	.06
□ 2 Shawn Green	.25	.11	.03
□ 3 Andres Galarraga	.50	.23	.06
□ 4 Bill Pulsipher	.25	.11	.03
□ 5 Chuck Knoblauch	.50	.23	.06
□ 6 Ken Griffey Jr.	2.00	.90	.25
□ 7 Greg Maddux	1.25	.55	.16
□ 8 Manny Ramirez	.50	.23	.06
□ 9 Ivan Rodriguez	.50	.23	.06
□ 10 Tim Salmon	.50	.23	.06
□ 11 Frank Thomas	2.00	.90	.25
□ 12 Jeff Bagwell	.75	.35	.09
□ 13 Travis Fryman	.25	.11	.03
□ 14 Kenny Lofton	.50	.23	.06
□ 15 Matt Williams	.50	.23	.06
□ 16 Jay Bell	.25	.11	.03
□ 17 Ken Caminiti	.50	.23	.06
□ 18 Ray Lankford	.25	.11	.03
□ 19 Cal Ripken	1.50	.70	.19
□ 20 Roger Clemens	.40	.18	.05
□ 21 Carlos Baerga	.25	.11	.03
□ 22 Mike Piazza	1.25	.55	.16
□ 23 Gregg Jefferies	.50	.23	.06
□ 24 Reggie Sanders	.25	.11	.03
□ 25 Rondell White	.25	.11	.03
□ 26 Sammy Sosa	.50	.23	.06
□ 27 Kevin Appier	.25	.11	.03
□ 28 Kevin Seitzer	.05	.02	.01
□ 29 Gary Sheffield	.50	.23	.06
□ 30 Mike Mussina	.40	.18	.05
□ 31 Mark McGwire	.60	.25	.07
□ 32 Barry Larkin	.50	.23	.06
□ 33 Marc Newfield	.25	.11	.03
□ 34 Ismael Valdes	.25	.11	.03
□ 35 Marty Cordova	.25	.11	.03
□ 36 Albert Belle	.75	.35	.09
□ 37 Johnny Damon	.25	.11	.03
□ 38 Garret Anderson	.50	.23	.06
□ 39 Cecil Fielder	.25	.11	.03
□ 40 John Mabry	.25	.11	.03
□ 41 Chipper Jones	1.25	.55	.16
□ 42 Omar Vizquel	.25	.11	.03
□ 43 Jose Rijo	.05	.02	.01
□ 44 Charles Johnson	.25	.11	.03
□ 45 Alex Rodriguez	2.00	.90	.25
□ 46 Rico Brogna	.05	.02	.01
□ 47 Joe Carter	.25	.11	.03
□ 48 Mo Vaughn	.50	.23	.06
□ 49 Moises Alou	.25	.11	.03
□ 50 Raul Mondesi	.50	.23	.06
□ 51 Robin Ventura	.25	.11	.03
□ 52 Jim Thome	.40	.18	.05
□ 53 David Justice	.25	.11	.03
□ 54 Jeff King	.25	.11	.03
□ 55 Brian L.Hunter	.25	.11	.03
□ 56 Juan Gonzalez	1.00	.45	.12
□ 57 John Olerud	.05	.02	.01
□ 58 Rafael Palmeiro	.50	.23	.06
□ 59 Tony Gwynn	.75	.35	.09
□ 60 Eddie Murray	.50	.23	.06
□ 61 Jason Isringhausen	.50	.23	.06
□ 62 Dante Bichette	.50	.23	.06
□ 63 Randy Johnson	.50	.23	.06
□ 64 Kirby Puckett	.75	.35	.09
□ 65 Jim Edmonds	.25	.11	.03
□ 66 David Cone	.25	.11	.03
□ 67 Ozzie Smith	.50	.23	.06
□ 68 Fred McGriff	.50	.23	.06
□ 69 Darren Daulton	.25	.11	.03
□ 70 Edgar Martinez	.25	.11	.03
□ 71 J.T. Snow	.25	.11	.03
□ 72 Butch Huskey	.25	.11	.03
□ 73 Hideo Nomo	.50	.23	.06
□ 74 Pedro Martinez	.25	.11	.03
□ 75 Bobby Bonilla	.25	.11	.03
□ 76 Jeff Conine	.25	.11	.03
□ 77 Ryan Klesko	.50	.23	.06
□ 78 Bernie Williams	.40	.18	.05
□ 79 Andre Dawson	.25	.11	.03
□ 80 Trevor Hoffman	.25	.11	.03
□ 81 Mark Grace	.50	.23	.06
□ 82 Benji Gil	.05	.02	.01
□ 83 Eric Karros	.25	.11	.03
□ 84 Pete Schourek	.05	.02	.01
□ 85 Edgardo Alfonzo	.25	.11	.03
□ 86 Jay Buhner	.50	.23	.06
□ 87 Vinny Castilla	.25	.11	.03
□ 88 Bret Boone	.05	.02	.01
□ 89 Ray Durham	.50	.23	.06
□ 90 Brian Jordan	.25	.11	.03
□ 91 Jose Canseco	.50	.23	.06
□ 92 Paul O'Neill	.05	.02	.01
□ 93 Chili Davis	.05	.02	.01
□ 94 Tom Glavine	.50	.23	.06
□ 95 Julian Tavarez	.05	.02	.01
□ 96 Derek Bell	.25	.11	.03
□ 97 Will Clark	.50	.23	.06
□ 98 Larry Walker	.50	.23	.06
□ 99 Denny Neagle	.25	.11	.03
□ 100 Alex Fernandez	.25	.11	.03
□ 101 Barry Bonds	.50	.23	.06
□ 102 Ben McDonald	.05	.02	.01
□ 103 Andy Pettitte	.60	.25	.07
□ 104 Tino Martinez	.25	.11	.03
□ 105 Sterling Hitchcock	.05	.02	.01
□ 106 Royce Clayton	.05	.02	.01
□ 107 Jim Abbott	.50	.23	.06
□ 108 Rickey Henderson	.50	.23	.06
□ 109 Ramon Martinez	.25	.11	.03
□ 110 Paul Molitor	.40	.18	.05
□ 111 Dennis Eckersley	.25	.11	.03
□ 112 Alex Gonzalez	.05	.02	.01
□ 113 Marquis Grissom	.25	.11	.03
□ 114 Greg Vaughn	.50	.23	.06
□ 115 Lance Johnson	.25	.11	.03
□ 116 Todd Stottlemyre	.05	.02	.01
□ 117 Jack McDowell	.25	.11	.03
□ 118 Ruben Sierra	.05	.02	.01
□ 119 Brady Anderson	.50	.23	.06
□ 120 Julio Franco	.25	.11	.03
□ 121 Brooks Kieschnick	.50	.23	.06
□ 122 Roberto Alomar	.40	.18	.05
□ 123 Greg Gagne	.05	.02	.01
□ 124 Wally Joyner	.05	.02	.01
□ 125 John Smoltz	.50	.23	.06
□ 126 John Valentin	.25	.11	.03
□ 127 Russ Davis	.05	.02	.01
□ 128 Joe Vitiello	.05	.02	.01
□ 129 Shawon Dunston	.05	.02	.01
□ 130 Frank Rodriguez	.05	.02	.01
□ 131 Charlie Hayes	.05	.02	.01
□ 132 Andy Benes	.05	.02	.01
□ 133 B.J. Surhoff	.05	.02	.01
□ 134 Dave Nilsson	.25	.11	.03
□ 135 Carlos Delgado	.25	.11	.03
□ 136 Walt Weiss	.05	.02	.01
□ 137 Mike Stanley	.05	.02	.01
□ 138 Greg Colbrunn	.05	.02	.01
□ 139 Mike Kelly	.05	.02	.01
□ 140 Ryne Sandberg	.50	.23	.06
□ 141 Lee Smith	.25	.11	.03
□ 142 Dennis Martinez	.25	.11	.03
□ 143 Bernard Gilkey	.25	.11	.03
□ 144 Lenny Dykstra	.05	.02	.01
□ 145 Danny Tartabull	.05	.02	.01
□ 146 Dean Palmer	.50	.23	.06
□ 147 Craig Biggio	.25	.11	.03
□ 148 Juan Acevedo	.05	.02	.01
□ 149 Michael Tucker	.25	.11	.03
□ 150 Bobby Higginson	.25	.11	.03
□ 151 Ken Griffey Jr. LUL	1.00	.45	.12
□ 152 Frank Thomas LUL	1.00	.45	.12
□ 153 Cal Ripken LUL	.75	.35	.09
□ 154 Albert Belle LUL	.40	.18	.05
□ 155 Mike Piazza LUL	.60	.25	.07
□ 156 Barry Bonds LUL	.50	.23	.06
□ 157 Sammy Sosa LUL	.50	.23	.06
□ 158 Mo Vaughn LUL	.50	.23	.06
□ 159 Greg Maddux LUL	.60	.25	.07
□ 160 Jeff Bagwell LUL	.40	.18	.05
□ 161 Derek Jeter	1.25	.55	.16
□ 162 Paul Wilson	.25	.11	.03
□ 163 Chris Snopek	.05	.02	.01
□ 164 Jason Schmidt	.50	.23	.06
□ 165 Jimmy Haynes	.05	.02	.01
□ 166 George Arias	.05	.02	.01
□ 167 Steve Gibralter	.05	.02	.01
□ 168 Bob Wolcott	.05	.02	.01
□ 169 Jason Kendall	.50	.23	.06
□ 170 Greg Zaun	.05	.02	.01
□ 171 Quinton McCracken	.05	.02	.01
□ 172 Alan Benes	.50	.23	.06
□ 173 Rey Ordonez	.50	.23	.06
□ 174 Livan Hernandez	.50	.23	.06
□ 175 Osvaldo Fernandez	.25	.11	.03
□ 176 Marc Barcelo	.05	.02	.01
□ 177 Sal Fasano	.05	.02	.01
□ 178 Mike Grace	.05	.02	.01
□ 179 Chan Ho Park	.50	.23	.06
□ 180 Robert Perez	.05	.02	.01
□ 181 Todd Hollandsworth	.25	.11	.03
□ 182 Wilton Guerrero	1.00	.45	.12
□ 183 John Wasdin	.05	.02	.01
□ 184 Jim Pittsley	.25	.11	.03
□ 185 LaTroy Hawkins	.05	.02	.01
□ 186 Jay Powell	.05	.02	.01
□ 187 Felipe Crespo	.05	.02	.01
□ 188 Jermaine Dye	.40	.18	.05
□ 189 Bob Abreu	.50	.23	.06
□ 190 Matt Luke	.05	.02	.01
□ 191 Richard Hidalgo	.50	.23	.06
□ 192 Karim Garcia	.40	.18	.05
□ 193 Marvin Benard	.05	.02	.01
□ 194 Andy Fox	.05	.02	.01
□ 195 Terrell Wade	.25	.11	.03
□ 196 Frank Thomas CL	1.00	.45	.12
□ 197 Ken Griffey Jr. CL	1.00	.45	.12
□ 198 Greg Maddux CL	.60	.25	.07
□ 199 Mike Piazza CL	.60	.25	.07
□ 200 Cal Ripken CL	.75	.35	.09

1996 Select Artist's Proofs

Randomly inserted one in 35 packs, this 200-card set is parallel and similar in design to the regular set. The difference is the holographic foil-stamped Artist's Proof logo on the card front.

	MINT	NRMT	EXC
COMPLETE SET (200)	2000.00	900.00	250.00
COMMON CARD (1-200)	3.00	1.35	.35

*STARS: 20X TO 40X BASIC CARDS..
*YOUNG STARS: 15X TO 30X BASIC CARDS

1996 Select Claim To Fame

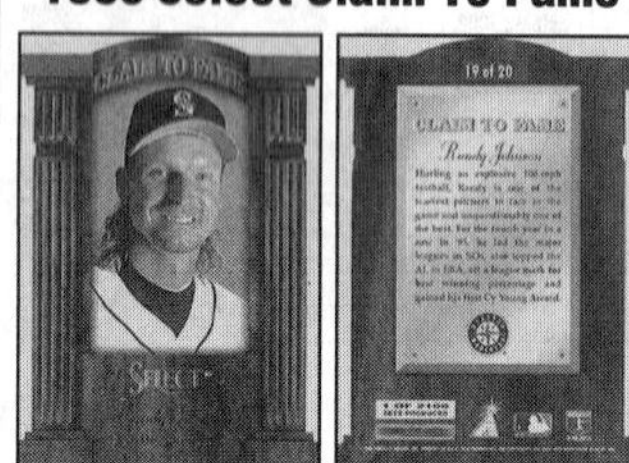

Randomly inserted in packs at a rate of one in 72, this 20-card set features potential Hall of Famers. The fronts display a color player portrait on a diecut plaque similar to the ones that enshrine Hall of Famers. The backs carry information about the player's claim to fame. Only 2100 of these sets were produced.

	MINT	NRMT	EXC
COMPLETE SET (20)	325.00	145.00	40.00
COMMON CARD (1-20)	4.00	1.80	.50
□ 1 Cal Ripken	40.00	18.00	5.00
□ 2 Greg Maddux	30.00	13.50	3.70
□ 3 Ken Griffey Jr.	50.00	22.00	6.25
□ 4 Frank Thomas	50.00	22.00	6.25
□ 5 Mo Vaughn	12.00	5.50	1.50
□ 6 Albert Belle	20.00	9.00	2.50
□ 7 Jeff Bagwell	20.00	9.00	2.50
□ 8 Sammy Sosa	8.00	3.60	1.00
□ 9 Reggie Sanders	4.00	1.80	.50
□ 10 Hideo Nomo	12.00	5.50	1.50
□ 11 Chipper Jones	30.00	13.50	3.70
□ 12 Mike Piazza	30.00	13.50	3.70
□ 13 Matt Williams	6.00	2.70	.75
□ 14 Tony Gwynn	20.00	9.00	2.50
□ 15 Johnny Damon	4.00	1.80	.50
□ 16 Dante Bichette	6.00	2.70	.75
□ 17 Kirby Puckett	20.00	9.00	2.50
□ 18 Barry Bonds	12.00	5.50	1.50
□ 19 Randy Johnson	8.00	3.60	1.00
□ 20 Eddie Murray	12.00	5.50	1.50

1996 Select En Fuego

Randomly inserted in packs at a rate of one in 48, this 25-card set is printed with all-foil Dufex technology, etched highlights and transparent inks that make each card shine. Spanish for "on fire," En Fuego is an expression popularized by ESPN sportscaster Dan Patrick, who provides the commentary for each player on the card back. The fronts feature color action player photos while the backs display more player photos and the commentary.

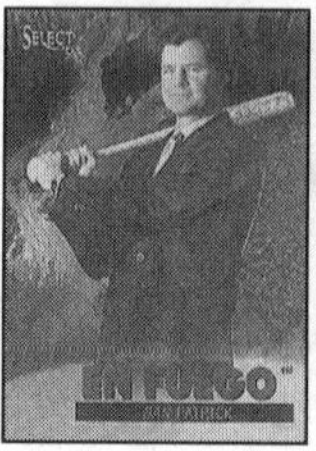

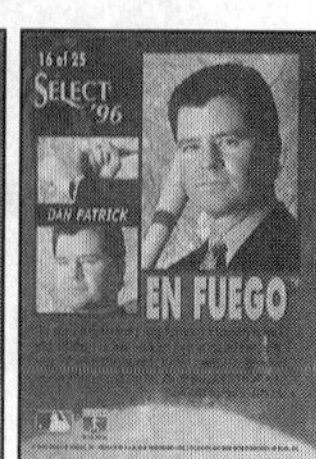

	MINT	NRMT	EXC
COMPLETE SET (25)	300.00	135.00	38.00
COMMON CARD (1-25)	3.00	1.35	.35
□ 1 Ken Griffey Jr.	40.00	18.00	5.00
□ 2 Frank Thomas	40.00	18.00	5.00
□ 3 Cal Ripken	30.00	13.50	3.70
□ 4 Greg Maddux	25.00	11.00	3.10
□ 5 Jeff Bagwell	15.00	6.75	1.85
□ 6 Barry Bonds	10.00	4.50	1.25
□ 7 Mo Vaughn	10.00	4.50	1.25
□ 8 Albert Belle	15.00	6.75	1.85
□ 9 Sammy Sosa	6.00	2.70	.75
□ 10 Reggie Sanders	3.00	1.35	.35
□ 11 Mike Piazza	25.00	11.00	3.10
□ 12 Chipper Jones	25.00	11.00	3.10
□ 13 Tony Gwynn	15.00	6.75	1.85
□ 14 Kirby Puckett	15.00	6.75	1.85
□ 15 Wade Boggs	5.00	2.20	.60
□ 16 Dan Patrick	8.00	3.60	1.00
□ 17 Gary Sheffield	6.00	2.70	.75
□ 18 Dante Bichette	5.00	2.20	.60
□ 19 Randy Johnson	6.00	2.70	.75
□ 20 Matt Williams	5.00	2.20	.60
□ 21 Alex Rodriguez	40.00	18.00	5.00
□ 22 Tim Salmon	5.00	2.20	.60
□ 23 Johnny Damon	3.00	1.35	.35
□ 24 Manny Ramirez	10.00	4.50	1.25
□ 25 Hideo Nomo	10.00	4.50	1.25

1996 Select Team Nucleus

Randomly inserted in packs at a rate of one in 18, this 28-card set is printed on clear plastic with holographic and micro-etched highlights and gold foil stamping. The fronts feature color pictures of three team players with the backs displaying the same photos, the players' names, and a sentence stating why these players are special.

	MINT	NRMT	EXC
COMPLETE SET (28)	100.00	45.00	12.50
COMMON CARD (1-28)	2.00	.90	.25
□ 1 Albert Belle Manny Ramirez Carlos Baerga	10.00	4.50	1.25
□ 2 Ray Lankford Brian Jordan Ozzie Smith	4.00	1.80	.50
□ 3 Jay Bell Jeff King Denny Neagle	2.00	.90	.25
□ 4 Dante Bichette Andres Galarraga Larry Walker	4.00	1.80	.50
□ 5 Mark McGwire Mike Bordick Terry Steinbach	4.00	1.80	.50
□ 6 Bernie Williams Wade Boggs David Cone	5.00	2.20	.60
□ 7 Joe Carter Alex Gonzalez Shawn Green	2.00	.90	.25
□ 8 Roger Clemens Mo Vaughn Jose Canseco	6.00	2.70	.75
□ 9 Ken Griffey Jr. Edgar Martinez Randy Johnson	15.00	6.75	1.85
□ 10 Gregg Jefferies Darren Daulton Len Dykstra	2.00	.90	.25
□ 11 Mike Piazza Raul Mondesi Hideo Nomo	12.00	5.50	1.50
□ 12 Greg Maddux Chipper Jones Ryan Klesko	20.00	9.00	2.50
□ 13 Cecil Fielder	2.00	.90	.25

	MINT	NRMT	EXC
Travis Fryman			
Phil Nevin			
☐ 14 Ivan Rodriguez	10.00	4.50	1.25
Will Clark			
Juan Gonzalez			
☐ 15 Ryne Sandberg	6.00	2.70	.75
Sammy Sosa			
Mark Grace			
☐ 16 Gary Sheffield	2.00	.90	.25
Charles Johnson			
Andre Dawson			
☐ 17 Johnny Damon	2.00	.90	.25
Michael Tucker			
Kevin Appier			
☐ 18 Barry Bonds	4.00	1.80	.50
Matt Williams			
Rod Beck			
☐ 19 Kirby Puckett	6.00	2.70	.75
Chuck Knoblauch			
Marty Cordova			
☐ 20 Cal Ripken	12.00	5.50	1.50
Barry Bonilla			
Mike Mussina			
☐ 21 Jason Isringhausen	2.00	.90	.25
Bill Pulsipher			
Rico Brogna			
☐ 22 Tony Gwynn	6.00	2.70	.75
Ken Caminiti			
Mark Newfield			
☐ 23 Tim Salmon	2.00	.90	.25
Garret Anderson			
Jim Edmonds			
☐ 24 Moises Alou	2.00	.90	.25
Rondell White			
Cliff Floyd			
☐ 25 Barry Larkin	2.00	.90	.25
Reggie Sanders			
Bret Boone			
☐ 26 Jeff Bagwell	6.00	2.70	.75
Craig Biggio			
Derek Bell			
☐ 27 Frank Thomas	12.00	5.50	1.50
Robin Ventura			
Alex Fernandez			
☐ 28 John Jaha	2.00	.90	.25
Greg Vaughn			
Kevin Seitzer			

1995 Select Certified Samples

This 8-card set was issued to preview the premier edition of the Select Certified series. This hobby-only issue is distinguished by 24-point cardstock, a metallic sheen, and double lamination. The cards have the word "SAMPLE" stamped diagonally across both sides.

	MINT	NRMT	EXC
COMPLETE SET (8)	16.00	7.25	2.00
COMMON CARD	.75	.35	.09
☐ 2 Reggie Sanders	.75	.35	.09
☐ 3 Cal Ripken	10.00	4.50	1.25
Gold Team			
☐ 10 Mo Vaughn	1.25	.55	.16
☐ 39 Mike Piazza	4.00	1.80	.50
☐ 50 Mark McGwire	1.50	.70	.19
☐ 75 Roberto Alomar	1.25	.55	.16
☐ 89 Larry Walker	1.00	.45	.12
☐ 110 Ray Durham	.75	.35	.09

1995 Select Certified

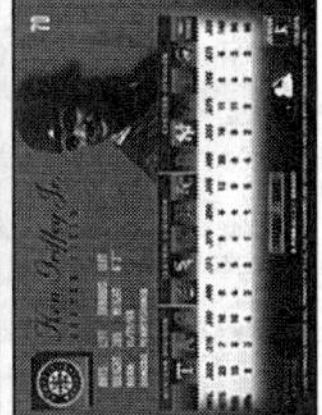

This 135-card standard-size set was issued through hobby outlets only. This product was issued in six-card packs. The cards are made with 24-point stock and are all metallic and double laminated. The fronts feature a player photo, his name in the lower right and the "Select '95 Certified" logo in the upper right. The horizontal backs feature a team by team seasonal summary and a player photo. The cards are numbered in the upper right corner. Rookie Cards in this set include Bobby Higginson and Hideo Nomo. Card #18 was never printed; Cal Ripken is featured on a special card numbered 2131, which is included in the complete set of 135.

	MINT	NRMT	EXC
COMPLETE SET (135)	50.00	22.00	6.25
COMMON CARD (1-135)	.25	.11	.03
☐ 1 Barry Bonds	1.25	.55	.16
☐ 2 Reggie Sanders	.40	.18	.05
☐ 3 Terry Steinbach	.40	.18	.05
☐ 4 Eduardo Perez	.25	.11	.03
☐ 5 Frank Thomas	5.00	2.20	.60
☐ 6 Wil Cordero	.25	.11	.03
☐ 7 John Olerud	.25	.11	.03
☐ 8 Deion Sanders	.75	.35	.09
☐ 9 Mike Mussina	1.00	.45	.12
☐ 10 Mo Vaughn	1.25	.55	.16
☐ 11 Will Clark	.75	.35	.09
☐ 12 Chili Davis	.40	.18	.05
☐ 13 Jimmy Key	.40	.18	.05
☐ 14 Eddie Murray	1.25	.55	.16
☐ 15 Bernard Gilkey	.40	.18	.05
☐ 16 David Cone	.40	.18	.05
☐ 17 Tim Salmon	.75	.35	.09
☐ 19 Steve Ontiveros	.25	.11	.03
☐ 20 Andres Galarraga	.75	.35	.09
☐ 21 Don Mattingly	2.50	1.10	.30
☐ 22 Kevin Appier	.40	.18	.05
☐ 23 Paul Molitor	1.00	.45	.12
☐ 24 Edgar Martinez	.40	.18	.05
☐ 25 Andy Benes	.25	.11	.03
☐ 26 Rafael Palmeiro	.75	.35	.09
☐ 27 Barry Larkin	.75	.35	.09
☐ 28 Gary Sheffield	.75	.35	.09
☐ 29 Wally Joyner	.40	.18	.05
☐ 30 Wade Boggs	.75	.35	.09
☐ 31 Rico Brogna	.25	.11	.03
☐ 32 Eddie Murray 3000th Hit	1.25	.55	.16
☐ 33 Kirby Puckett	2.00	.90	.25
☐ 34 Bobby Bonilla	.40	.18	.05
☐ 35 Hal Morris	.25	.11	.03
☐ 36 Moises Alou	.40	.18	.05
☐ 37 Javier Lopez	.75	.35	.09
☐ 38 Chuck Knoblauch	.75	.35	.09
☐ 39 Mike Piazza	3.00	1.35	.35
☐ 40 Travis Fryman	.40	.18	.05
☐ 41 Rickey Henderson	.75	.35	.09
☐ 42 Jim Thome	1.00	.45	.12
☐ 43 Carlos Baerga	.40	.18	.05
☐ 44 Dean Palmer	.40	.18	.05
☐ 45 Kirk Gibson	.40	.18	.05
☐ 46 Bret Saberhagen	.40	.18	.05
☐ 47 Cecil Fielder	.40	.18	.05
☐ 48 Manny Ramirez	1.25	.55	.16
☐ 49 Derek Bell	.40	.18	.05
☐ 50 Mark McGwire	1.50	.70	.19
☐ 51 Jim Edmonds	.75	.35	.09
☐ 52 Robin Ventura	.40	.18	.05
☐ 53 Ryan Klesko	.75	.35	.09
☐ 54 Jeff Bagwell	2.00	.90	.25
☐ 55 Ozzie Smith	1.25	.55	.16
☐ 56 Albert Belle	2.00	.90	.25
☐ 57 Darren Daulton	.40	.18	.05
☐ 58 Jeff Conine	.40	.18	.05
☐ 59 Greg Maddux	3.00	1.35	.35
☐ 60 Lenny Dykstra	.40	.18	.05
☐ 61 Randy Johnson	.75	.35	.09
☐ 62 Fred McGriff	.75	.35	.09
☐ 63 Ray Lankford	.40	.18	.05
☐ 64 David Justice	.75	.35	.09
☐ 65 Paul O'Neill	.40	.18	.05
☐ 66 Tony Gwynn	2.00	.90	.25
☐ 67 Matt Williams	.75	.35	.09
☐ 68 Dante Bichette	.75	.35	.09
☐ 69 Craig Biggio	.40	.18	.05
☐ 70 Ken Griffey Jr.	5.00	2.20	.60
☐ 71 J.T. Snow	.40	.18	.05
☐ 72 Cal Ripken	4.00	1.80	.50
☐ 73 Jay Bell	.40	.18	.05
☐ 74 Joe Carter	.40	.18	.05
☐ 75 Roberto Alomar	1.00	.45	.12
☐ 76 Benji Gil	.25	.11	.03
☐ 77 Ivan Rodriguez	1.25	.55	.16
☐ 78 Raul Mondesi	.75	.35	.09
☐ 79 Cliff Floyd	.40	.18	.05
☐ 80 Eric Karros	1.00	.45	.12
Mike Piazza			
Raul Mondesi			
☐ 81 Royce Clayton	.25	.11	.03
☐ 82 Billy Ashley	.25	.11	.03
☐ 83 Joey Hamilton	.75	.35	.09
☐ 84 Sammy Sosa	.75	.35	.09
☐ 85 Jason Bere	.25	.11	.03
☐ 86 Dennis Martinez	.40	.18	.05
☐ 87 Greg Vaughn	.40	.18	.05
☐ 88 Roger Clemens	1.00	.45	.12
☐ 89 Larry Walker	.75	.35	.09
☐ 90 Mark Grace	.75	.35	.09
☐ 91 Kenny Lofton	1.25	.55	.16
☐ 92 Carlos Perez	.40	.18	.05
☐ 93 Roger Cedeno	.40	.18	.05
☐ 94 Scott Ruffcorn	.25	.11	.03
☐ 95 Jim Pittsley	.75	.35	.09
☐ 96 Andy Pettitte	2.00	.90	.25
☐ 97 James Baldwin	.40	.18	.05
☐ 98 Hideo Nomo	5.00	2.20	.60
☐ 99 Ismael Valdes	.40	.18	.05
☐ 100 Armando Benitez	.25	.11	.03
☐ 101 Jose Malave	.25	.11	.03
☐ 102 Bob Higginson	1.25	.55	.16
☐ 103 LaTroy Hawkins	.25	.11	.03
☐ 104 Russ Davis	.25	.11	.03
☐ 105 Shawn Green	.40	.18	.05
☐ 106 Joe Vitiello	.25	.11	.03
☐ 107 Chipper Jones	3.00	1.35	.35
☐ 108 Shane Andrews	.25	.11	.03
☐ 109 Jose Oliva	.25	.11	.03
☐ 110 Ray Durham	.40	.18	.05
☐ 111 Jon Nunnally	.40	.18	.05
☐ 112 Alex Gonzalez	.40	.18	.05
☐ 113 Vaughn Eshelman	.25	.11	.03
☐ 114 Marty Cordova	.75	.35	.09
☐ 115 Mark Grudzielanek	1.25	.55	.16
☐ 116 Brian L.Hunter	.40	.18	.05
☐ 117 Charles Johnson	.40	.18	.05
☐ 118 Alex Rodriguez	6.00	2.70	.75
☐ 119 David Bell	.25	.11	.03
☐ 120 Todd Hollandsworth	.75	.35	.09
☐ 121 Joe Randa	.25	.11	.03
☐ 122 Derek Jeter	3.00	1.35	.35
☐ 123 Frank Rodriguez	.40	.18	.05
☐ 124 Curtis Goodwin	.40	.18	.05
☐ 125 Bill Pulsipher	.40	.18	.05
☐ 126 John Mabry	.75	.35	.09
☐ 127 Julian Tavarez	.25	.11	.03
☐ 128 Edgardo Alfonzo	.40	.18	.05
☐ 129 Orlando Miller	.25	.11	.03
☐ 130 Juan Acevedo	.25	.11	.03
☐ 131 Jeff Cirillo	.40	.18	.05
☐ 132 Roberto Petagine	.25	.11	.03
☐ 133 Antonio Osuna	.25	.11	.03
☐ 134 Michael Tucker	.40	.18	.05
☐ 135 Garret Anderson	.40	.18	.05
☐ 2131 Cal Ripken TRIB	5.00	2.20	.60

1995 Select Certified Mirror Gold

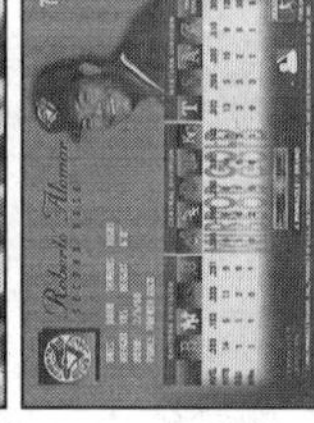

This 135-card set is a parallel to the regular issue. Pinnacle used their all-holographic foil technology on the fronts. The backs are identical to the regular issue but the words "Mirror Gold" are in the middle. These cards were inserted approximately one every five packs.

	MINT	NRMT	EXC
COMPLETE SET (135)	900.00	400.00	110.00
COMMON CARD (1-135)	2.50	1.10	.30

*STARS: 7.5X TO 15X BASIC CARDS
*YOUNG STARS: 6X TO 12X BASIC CARDS

1995 Select Certified Checklists

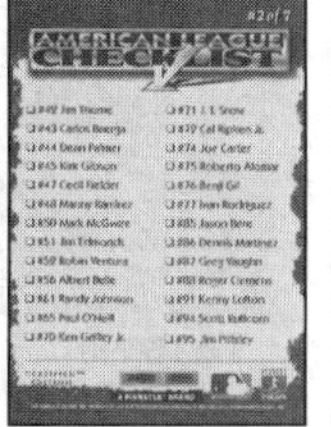

This seven-card standard-size set was inserted one per Select Certified pack. These cards were not made of the same card stock as the regular Certified cards.

	MINT	NRMT	EXC
COMPLETE SET (7)	4.00	1.80	.50
COMMON CARD (1-7)	.25	.11	.03
☐ 1 Ken Griffey Jr.	1.00	.45	.12
☐ 2 Frank Thomas	1.00	.45	.12
☐ 3 Cal Ripken	.75	.35	.09
☐ 4 Jeff Bagwell	.40	.18	.05
☐ 5 Mike Piazza	.60	.25	.07
☐ 6 Barry Bonds	.25	.11	.03
☐ 7 Manny Ramirez	.25	.11	.03
Raul Mondesi			

1995 Select Certified Future

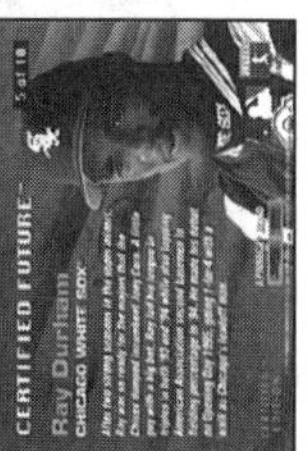

This ten-card set was inserted approximately one in every 19 packs. Ten leading 1995 rookie players are included in this set. These cards were produced using Pinnacle's Dufex technology. The fronts feature a player photo with his name on the bottom. The words "Certified Future" are spelled vertically on the right. The horizontal backs feature some textual information and a player photo.

	MINT	NRMT	EXC
COMPLETE SET (10)	75.00	34.00	9.50
COMMON CARD (1-10)	2.50	1.10	.30
☐ 1 Chipper Jones	20.00	9.00	2.50
☐ 2 Curtis Goodwin	2.50	1.10	.30
☐ 3 Hideo Nomo	12.00	5.50	1.50
☐ 4 Shawn Green	8.00	3.60	1.00
☐ 5 Ray Durham	5.00	2.20	.60
☐ 6 Todd Hollandsworth	4.00	1.80	.50
☐ 7 Brian L.Hunter	4.00	1.80	.50
☐ 8 Carlos Delgado	4.00	1.80	.50
☐ 9 Michael Tucker UER	8.00	3.60	1.00
(front photo is Jon Nunnally)			
☐ 10 Alex Rodriguez	30.00	13.50	3.70

1995 Select Certified Gold Team

This 12-card was inserted approximately one in every 41 packs. This set features some of the leading players in baseball. These cards feature double-sided all-gold-foil Dufex technology.

	MINT	NRMT	EXC
COMPLETE SET (12)	300.00	135.00	38.00
COMMON CARD (1-12)	8.00	3.60	1.00
☐ 1 Ken Griffey Jr.	60.00	27.00	7.50
☐ 2 Frank Thomas	60.00	27.00	7.50
☐ 3 Cal Ripken	50.00	22.00	6.25
☐ 4 Jeff Bagwell	25.00	11.00	3.10
☐ 5 Mike Piazza	40.00	18.00	5.00
☐ 6 Barry Bonds	15.00	6.75	1.85
☐ 7 Matt Williams	8.00	3.60	1.00
☐ 8 Don Mattingly	30.00	13.50	3.70
☐ 9 Will Clark	8.00	3.60	1.00
☐ 10 Tony Gwynn	25.00	11.00	3.10
☐ 11 Kirby Puckett	25.00	11.00	3.10
☐ 12 Jose Canseco	8.00	3.60	1.00

1995 Select Certified Potential Unlimited 1975

Cards from this 20-card set were randomly inserted into one in every 29 packs. The cards feature Pinnacle's all-foil Dufex printing technology. The fronts have a player photo in the middle. The words "Potential Unlimited" appear in the upper left and the player's name appears in the bottom left. The horizontal back has a player photo and some text set against a background of a baseball. Only 1,975 sets were made and each card is numbered 1 of 1,975 at the bottom right.

	MINT	NRMT	EXC
COMPLETE SET (20)	250.00	110.00	31.00
COMMON CARD (1-20)	5.00	2.20	.60

☐ 1 Cliff Floyd	8.00	3.60	1.00
☐ 2 Manny Ramirez	25.00	11.00	3.10
☐ 3 Raul Mondesi	12.00	5.50	1.50
☐ 4 Scott Ruffcorn	5.00	2.20	.60
☐ 5 Billy Ashley	5.00	2.20	.60
☐ 6 Alex Gonzalez	8.00	3.60	1.00
☐ 7 Midre Cummings	5.00	2.20	.60
☐ 8 Charles Johnson	8.00	3.60	1.00
☐ 9 Garret Anderson	8.00	3.60	1.00
☐ 10 Hideo Nomo	40.00	18.00	5.00
☐ 11 Chipper Jones	60.00	27.00	7.50
☐ 12 Curtis Goodwin	5.00	2.20	.60
☐ 13 Frank Rodriguez	5.00	2.20	.60
☐ 14 Shawn Green	8.00	3.60	1.00
☐ 15 Ray Durham	8.00	3.60	1.00
☐ 16 Todd Hollandsworth	12.00	5.50	1.50
☐ 17 Brian L.Hunter	12.00	5.50	1.50
☐ 18 Carlos Delgado	12.00	5.50	1.50
☐ 19 Michael Tucker	8.00	3.60	1.00
☐ 20 Alex Rodriguez	100.00	45.00	12.50

1995 Select Certified Potential Unlimited 903

One of these twenty different cards were randomly placed into sealed boxes of 1995 Select Certified. The cards are parallel to the more plentiful 1975 versions except for the production numbering on back. Only 903 sets were made and each card is numbered 1 of 903 at the bottom right of the card back.

	MINT	NRMT	EXC
COMPLETE SET (20)	450.00	200.00	55.00
COMMON CARD (1-20)	6.00	2.70	.75
*903: 1.25X 1975 CARDS			

1996 Select Certified

The 1996 Select Certified hobby only set was issued in one series totalling 144 cards. Each six-card pack sells for $4.99. Printed on special 24-point silver mirror mylar card stock, the fronts feature a color player photo on a gray and black background. The backs carry another color player photo with information about his playing abilities.

	MINT	NRMT	EXC
COMPLETE SET (144)	40.00	18.00	5.00
COMMON CARD (1-144)	.15	.07	.02

☐ 1 Frank Thomas	5.00	2.20	.60
☐ 2 Tino Martinez	.40	.18	.05
☐ 3 Gary Sheffield	.60	.25	.07
☐ 4 Kenny Lofton	1.25	.55	.16
☐ 5 Joe Carter	.40	.18	.05
☐ 6 Alex Rodriguez	5.00	2.20	.60
☐ 7 Chipper Jones	3.00	1.35	.35
☐ 8 Roger Clemens	1.00	.45	.12
☐ 9 Jay Bell	.15	.07	.02
☐ 10 Eddie Murray	1.25	.55	.16
☐ 11 Will Clark	.60	.25	.07
☐ 12 Mike Mussina	1.00	.45	.12
☐ 13 Hideo Nomo	1.25	.55	.16
☐ 14 Andres Galarraga	.60	.25	.07
☐ 15 Marc Newfield	.40	.18	.05
☐ 16 Jason Isringhausen	.60	.25	.07
☐ 17 Randy Johnson	.60	.25	.07
☐ 18 Chuck Knoblauch	.60	.25	.07
☐ 19 J.T. Snow	.40	.18	.05
☐ 20 Mark McGwire	1.50	.70	.19
☐ 21 Tony Gwynn	2.00	.90	.25
☐ 22 Albert Belle	2.00	.90	.25
☐ 23 Gregg Jefferies	.60	.25	.07
☐ 24 Reggie Sanders	.40	.18	.05
☐ 25 Bernie Williams	1.00	.45	.12
☐ 26 Ray Lankford	.40	.18	.05
☐ 27 Johnny Damon	.40	.18	.05
☐ 28 Ryne Sandberg	1.25	.55	.16
☐ 29 Rondell White	.40	.18	.05
☐ 30 Mike Piazza	3.00	1.35	.35
☐ 31 Barry Bonds	1.25	.55	.16
☐ 32 Greg Maddux	3.00	1.35	.35
☐ 33 Craig Biggio	.40	.18	.05
☐ 34 John Valentin	.40	.18	.05
☐ 35 Ivan Rodriguez	1.25	.55	.16
☐ 36 Rico Brogna	.15	.07	.02
☐ 37 Tim Salmon	.60	.25	.07
☐ 38 Sterling Hitchcock	.15	.07	.02
☐ 39 Charles Johnson	.40	.18	.05
☐ 40 Travis Fryman	.40	.18	.05
☐ 41 Barry Larkin	.60	.25	.07
☐ 42 Tom Glavine	.60	.25	.07
☐ 43 Marty Cordova	.40	.18	.05
☐ 44 Shawn Green	.15	.07	.02
☐ 45 Ben McDonald	.15	.07	.02
☐ 46 Robin Ventura	.40	.18	.05
☐ 47 Ken Griffey Jr.	5.00	2.20	.60
☐ 48 Orlando Merced	.15	.07	.02
☐ 49 Paul O'Neill	.15	.07	.02
☐ 50 Ozzie Smith	1.25	.55	.16
☐ 51 Manny Ramirez	1.25	.55	.16
☐ 52 Ismael Valdes	.40	.18	.05
☐ 53 Cal Ripken	4.00	1.80	.50
☐ 54 Jeff Bagwell	2.00	.90	.25
☐ 55 Greg Vaughn	.60	.25	.07
☐ 56 Juan Gonzalez	2.50	1.10	.30
☐ 57 Raul Mondesi	.60	.25	.07
☐ 58 Carlos Baerga	.40	.18	.05
☐ 59 Sammy Sosa	.60	.25	.07
☐ 60 Mike Kelly	.15	.07	.02
☐ 61 Edgar Martinez	.40	.18	.05
☐ 62 Kirby Puckett	2.00	.90	.25
☐ 63 Cecil Fielder	.40	.18	.05
☐ 64 David Cone	.40	.18	.05
☐ 65 Moises Alou	.40	.18	.05
☐ 66 Fred McGriff	.60	.25	.07
☐ 67 Mo Vaughn	1.25	.55	.16
☐ 68 Edgardo Alfonzo	.40	.18	.05
☐ 69 Jim Thome	1.00	.45	.12
☐ 70 Rickey Henderson	.60	.25	.07
☐ 71 Dante Bichette	.60	.25	.07
☐ 72 Lenny Dykstra	.40	.18	.05
☐ 73 Benji Gil	.15	.07	.02
☐ 74 Wade Boggs	.60	.25	.07
☐ 75 Jim Edmonds	.40	.18	.05
☐ 76 Michael Tucker	.40	.18	.05
☐ 77 Carlos Delgado	.40	.18	.05
☐ 78 Butch Huskey	.40	.18	.05
☐ 79 Billy Ashley	.15	.07	.02
☐ 80 Dean Palmer	.60	.25	.07
☐ 81 Paul Molitor	1.00	.45	.12
☐ 82 Ryan Klesko	.60	.25	.07
☐ 83 Brian L.Hunter	.40	.18	.05
☐ 84 Jay Buhner	.60	.25	.07
☐ 85 Larry Walker	.60	.25	.07
☐ 86 Mike Bordick	.40	.18	.05
☐ 87 Matt Williams	.60	.25	.07
☐ 88 Jack McDowell	.60	.25	.07
☐ 89 Hal Morris	.15	.07	.02
☐ 90 Brian Jordan	.40	.18	.05
☐ 91 Andy Pettitte	1.50	.70	.19
☐ 92 Melvin Nieves	.40	.18	.05
☐ 93 Pedro Martinez	.40	.18	.05
☐ 94 Mark Grace	.60	.25	.07
☐ 95 Garret Anderson	.60	.25	.07
☐ 96 Andre Dawson	.40	.18	.05
☐ 97 Ray Durham	.60	.25	.07
☐ 98 Jose Canseco	.60	.25	.07
☐ 99 Roberto Alomar	1.00	.45	.12
☐ 100 Derek Jeter	3.00	1.35	.35
☐ 101 Alan Benes	.60	.25	.07
☐ 102 Karim Garcia	1.00	.45	.12
☐ 103 Robin Jennings	.15	.07	.02
☐ 104 Bob Abreu	.60	.25	.07
☐ 105 Sal Fasano UER (name on front is Livan Hernandez)	.15	.07	.02
☐ 106 Steve Gibralter	.15	.07	.02
☐ 107 Jermaine Dye	1.00	.45	.12
☐ 108 Jason Kendall	.60	.25	.07
☐ 109 Mike Grace	.15	.07	.02
☐ 110 Jason Schmidt	.60	.25	.07
☐ 111 Paul Wilson	.40	.18	.05
☐ 112 Rey Ordonez	.60	.25	.07
☐ 113 Wilton Guerrero	1.50	.70	.19
☐ 114 Brooks Kieschnick	.60	.25	.07
☐ 115 George Arias	.15	.07	.02
☐ 116 Osvaldo Fernandez	.40	.18	.05
☐ 117 Todd Hollandsworth	.40	.18	.05
☐ 118 John Wasdin	.15	.07	.02
☐ 119 Eric Owens	.15	.07	.02
☐ 120 Chan Ho Park	.60	.25	.07
☐ 121 Mark Loretta	.15	.07	.02
☐ 122 Richard Hidalgo	.60	.25	.07
☐ 123 Jeff Suppan	.60	.25	.07
☐ 124 Jim Pittsley	.40	.18	.05
☐ 125 LaTroy Hawkins	.15	.07	.02
☐ 126 Chris Snopek	.15	.07	.02
☐ 127 Justin Thompson	.40	.18	.05
☐ 128 Jay Powell	.15	.07	.02
☐ 129 Alex Ochoa	.40	.18	.05
☐ 130 Felipe Crespo	.15	.07	.02
☐ 131 Matt Lawton	.15	.07	.02
☐ 132 Jimmy Haynes	.15	.07	.02
☐ 133 Terrell Wade	.40	.18	.05
☐ 134 Ruben Rivera	1.00	.45	.12
☐ 135 Frank Thomas PP	2.50	1.10	.30
☐ 136 Ken Griffey Jr. PP	2.50	1.10	.30
☐ 137 Greg Maddux PP	1.50	.70	.19
☐ 138 Mike Piazza PP	1.50	.70	.19
☐ 139 Cal Ripken PP	2.00	.90	.25
☐ 140 Albert Belle PP	1.00	.45	.12
☐ 141 Mo Vaughn PP	.60	.25	.07
☐ 142 Chipper Jones PP	1.50	.70	.19
☐ 143 Hideo Nomo PP	.60	.25	.07
☐ 144 Ryan Klesko PP	.60	.25	.07

1996 Select Certified Artist's Proofs

Randomly inserted in packs at a rate of one in 12, this 144-card set is parallel to the base set with only 500 sets being produced. The design is similar to the regular set with the exception of a holographic gold foil Artist's proof stamp on the front.

	MINT	NRMT	EXC
COMPLETE SET (144)	2000.00	900.00	250.00
COMMON CARD (1-144)	3.00	1.35	.35
*STARS: 8X TO 20X BASIC CARDS			
*YOUNG STARS: 6X TO 15X BASIC CARDS			

☐ 1 Frank Thomas	1000.00	450.00	125.00
☐ 3 Gary Sheffield	150.00	70.00	19.00
☐ 4 Kenny Lofton	250.00	110.00	31.00
☐ 6 Alex Rodriguez	1000.00	450.00	125.00
☐ 7 Chipper Jones	600.00	275.00	75.00
☐ 8 Roger Clemens	175.00	80.00	22.00
☐ 10 Eddie Murray	250.00	110.00	31.00
☐ 12 Mike Mussina	150.00	70.00	19.00
☐ 13 Hideo Nomo	250.00	110.00	31.00
☐ 18 Chuck Knoblauch	135.00	60.00	17.00
☐ 20 Mark McGwire	300.00	135.00	38.00
☐ 21 Tony Gwynn	450.00	200.00	55.00
☐ 22 Albert Belle	500.00	220.00	60.00
☐ 25 Bernie Williams	150.00	70.00	19.00
☐ 28 Ryne Sandberg	225.00	100.00	28.00
☐ 30 Mike Piazza	600.00	275.00	75.00
☐ 31 Barry Bonds	225.00	100.00	28.00
☐ 32 Greg Maddux	600.00	275.00	75.00
☐ 35 Ivan Rodriguez	250.00	110.00	31.00
☐ 47 Ken Griffey Jr.	1000.00	450.00	125.00
☐ 50 Ozzie Smith	225.00	100.00	28.00
☐ 51 Manny Ramirez	200.00	90.00	25.00
☐ 53 Cal Ripken	750.00	350.00	95.00
☐ 54 Jeff Bagwell	450.00	200.00	55.00
☐ 56 Juan Gonzalez	500.00	220.00	60.00
☐ 59 Sammy Sosa	150.00	70.00	19.00
☐ 62 Kirby Puckett	450.00	200.00	55.00
☐ 67 Mo Vaughn	200.00	90.00	25.00
☐ 69 Jim Thome	150.00	70.00	19.00
☐ 74 Wade Boggs	135.00	60.00	17.00
☐ 81 Paul Molitor	200.00	90.00	25.00
☐ 82 Ryan Klesko	150.00	70.00	19.00
☐ 91 Andy Pettitte	200.00	90.00	25.00
☐ 99 Roberto Alomar	200.00	90.00	25.00
☐ 100 Derek Jeter	600.00	275.00	75.00
☐ 102 Karim Garcia	135.00	60.00	17.00
☐ 113 Wilton Guerrero	150.00	70.00	19.00
☐ 135 Frank Thomas PP	500.00	220.00	60.00
☐ 136 Ken Griffey Jr. PP	500.00	220.00	60.00
☐ 137 Greg Maddux PP	250.00	110.00	31.00
☐ 138 Mike Piazza PP	250.00	110.00	31.00
☐ 139 Cal Ripken PP	400.00	180.00	50.00
☐ 140 Albert Belle PP	200.00	90.00	25.00
☐ 142 Chipper Jones PP	250.00	110.00	31.00

1996 Select Certified Certified Blue

Randomly inserted in packs at a rate of one in 50, this 144-card set is parallel to the base set with only 180 sets being produced. This set is a blue all-foil rendition of the base set.

	MINT	NRMT	EXC
COMPLETE SET (144)	5000.00	2200.00	600.00
COMMON CARD (1-144)	8.00	3.60	1.00
*STARS: 8X to 20X BASIC CARDS			
*YOUNG STARS: 20X to 40X BASIC CARDS			

1996 Select Certified Certified Red

Randomly inserted in packs at a rate of one in five, this 144-card set is parallel to the base set with only 1,800 sets being produced. This set is a red all-foil rendition of the base set.

	MINT	NRMT	EXC
COMPLETE SET (144)	700.00	325.00	90.00
COMMON CARD (1-144)	1.00	.45	.12
*STARS: 4X to 8X BASIC CARDS			
*YOUNG STARS: 3X to 6X BASIC CARDS			

1996 Select Certified Mirror Blue

Randomly inserted in packs at a rate of one in 200, this 144-card set is parallel to the base set with only 45 sets being produced. This set is a blue holographic foil rendition of the base set. No set price has been provided due to scarcity.

	MINT	NRMT	EXC
COMMON CARD (1-144)	40.00	18.00	5.00
*STARS: 125X TO 200X BASIC CARDS			
*YOUNG STARS: 90X TO 150X BASIC CARDS			

1996 Select Certified Mirror Gold

Randomly inserted in packs at a rate of one in 300, this 144-card set is parallel to the base set with only 30 sets being produced. This set is a gold holographic foil rendition of the base set. No set price has been provided due to scarcity.

	MINT	NRMT	EXC
COMMON CARD (1-144)	100.00	45.00	12.50
*STARS: 300X TO 500X BASIC CARDS			
*YOUNG STARS: 250X TO 400X BASIC CARDS			

☐ 1 Frank Thomas	2500.00	1100.00	300.00
☐ 3 Gary Sheffield	400.00	180.00	50.00
☐ 4 Kenny Lofton	750.00	350.00	95.00
☐ 6 Alex Rodriguez	2500.00	1100.00	300.00
☐ 7 Chipper Jones	1500.00	700.00	190.00
☐ 8 Roger Clemens	450.00	200.00	55.00
☐ 10 Eddie Murray	750.00	350.00	95.00
☐ 11 Will Clark	300.00	135.00	38.00
☐ 12 Mike Mussina	500.00	220.00	60.00
☐ 13 Hideo Nomo	650.00	300.00	80.00
☐ 14 Andres Galarraga	250.00	110.00	31.00
☐ 17 Randy Johnson	400.00	180.00	50.00
☐ 18 Chuck Knoblauch	400.00	180.00	50.00
☐ 20 Mark McGwire	800.00	350.00	100.00
☐ 21 Tony Gwynn	1000.00	450.00	125.00
☐ 22 Albert Belle	1200.00	550.00	150.00
☐ 25 Bernie Williams	400.00	180.00	50.00
☐ 28 Ryne Sandberg	600.00	275.00	75.00
☐ 30 Mike Piazza	1500.00	700.00	190.00
☐ 31 Barry Bonds	700.00	325.00	90.00
☐ 32 Greg Maddux	1500.00	700.00	190.00

☐ 35 Ivan Rodriguez	600.00	275.00	75.00
☐ 37 Tim Salmon	250.00	110.00	31.00
☐ 41 Barry Larkin	250.00	110.00	31.00
☐ 42 Tom Glavine	250.00	110.00	31.00
☐ 47 Ken Griffey Jr.	2500.00	1100.00	300.00
☐ 50 Ozzie Smith	600.00	275.00	75.00
☐ 51 Manny Ramirez	600.00	275.00	75.00
☐ 53 Cal Ripken	2000.00	900.00	250.00
☐ 54 Jeff Bagwell	1200.00	550.00	150.00
☐ 56 Juan Gonzalez	1500.00	700.00	190.00
☐ 59 Sammy Sosa	450.00	200.00	55.00
☐ 61 Edgar Martinez	250.00	110.00	31.00
☐ 62 Kirby Puckett	1200.00	550.00	150.00
☐ 66 Fred McGriff	250.00	110.00	31.00
☐ 67 Mo Vaughn	600.00	275.00	75.00
☐ 69 Jim Thome	500.00	220.00	60.00
☐ 70 Rickey Henderson	250.00	110.00	31.00
☐ 71 Dante Bichette	250.00	110.00	31.00
☐ 74 Wade Boggs	400.00	180.00	50.00
☐ 81 Paul Molitor	500.00	220.00	60.00
☐ 82 Ryan Klesko	400.00	180.00	50.00
☐ 84 Jay Buhner	250.00	110.00	31.00
☐ 85 Larry Walker	250.00	110.00	31.00
☐ 87 Matt Williams	350.00	160.00	45.00
☐ 91 Andy Pettitte	600.00	275.00	75.00
☐ 98 Jose Canseco	300.00	135.00	38.00
☐ 99 Roberto Alomar	500.00	220.00	60.00
☐ 100 Derek Jeter	1200.00	550.00	150.00
☐ 102 Karim Garcia	400.00	180.00	50.00
☐ 107 Jermaine Dye	400.00	180.00	50.00
☐ 108 Jason Kendall	250.00	110.00	31.00
☐ 112 Rey Ordonez	300.00	135.00	38.00
☐ 113 Wilton Guerrero	300.00	135.00	38.00
☐ 117 Todd Hollandsworth	250.00	110.00	31.00
☐ 134 Ruben Rivera	400.00	180.00	50.00
☐ 135 Frank Thomas PP	1200.00	550.00	150.00
☐ 136 Ken Griffey Jr. PP	1200.00	550.00	150.00
☐ 137 Greg Maddux PP	700.00	325.00	90.00
☐ 138 Mike Piazza PP	700.00	325.00	90.00
☐ 139 Cal Ripken PP	1000.00	450.00	125.00
☐ 140 Albert Belle PP	600.00	275.00	75.00
☐ 141 Mo Vaughn PP	250.00	110.00	31.00
☐ 142 Chipper Jones PP	700.00	325.00	90.00
☐ 143 Hideo Nomo PP	250.00	110.00	31.00

1996 Select Certified Mirror Red

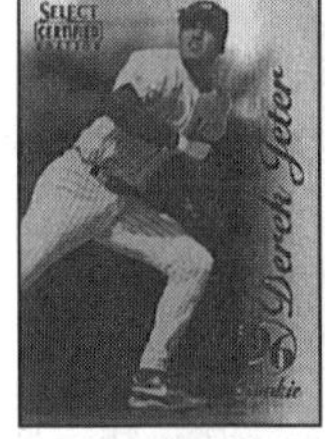

Randomly inserted in packs at a rate of one in 100, this 144-card set is parallel to the base set with only 90 sets being produced. This set is a red holographic foil rendition of the base set. No set price has been provided due to scarcity.

	MINT	NRMT	EXC
COMMON CARD (1-144)	20.00	9.00	2.50
*STARS: 60X TO 100X BASIC CARDS			
*YOUNG STARS: 50X TO 80X BASIC CARDS			
☐ 1 Frank Thomas	500.00	220.00	60.00
☐ 3 Gary Sheffield	80.00	36.00	10.00
☐ 4 Kenny Lofton	125.00	55.00	15.50
☐ 6 Alex Rodriguez	500.00	220.00	60.00
☐ 7 Chipper Jones	300.00	135.00	38.00
☐ 8 Roger Clemens	90.00	40.00	11.00
☐ 10 Eddie Murray	125.00	55.00	15.50
☐ 12 Mike Mussina	80.00	36.00	10.00
☐ 13 Hideo Nomo	125.00	55.00	15.50
☐ 18 Chuck Knoblauch	80.00	36.00	10.00
☐ 20 Mark McGwire	150.00	70.00	19.00
☐ 21 Tony Gwynn	200.00	90.00	25.00
☐ 22 Albert Belle	250.00	110.00	31.00
☐ 25 Bernie Williams	100.00	45.00	12.50
☐ 28 Ryne Sandberg	125.00	55.00	15.50
☐ 30 Mike Piazza	300.00	135.00	38.00
☐ 31 Barry Bonds	125.00	55.00	15.50
☐ 32 Greg Maddux	300.00	135.00	38.00
☐ 35 Ivan Rodriguez	125.00	55.00	15.50
☐ 47 Ken Griffey Jr.	500.00	220.00	60.00
☐ 50 Ozzie Smith	125.00	55.00	15.50
☐ 51 Manny Ramirez	100.00	45.00	12.50
☐ 53 Cal Ripken	400.00	180.00	50.00
☐ 54 Jeff Bagwell	200.00	90.00	25.00
☐ 56 Juan Gonzalez	250.00	110.00	31.00
☐ 59 Sammy Sosa	80.00	36.00	10.00
☐ 62 Kirby Puckett	200.00	90.00	25.00
☐ 67 Mo Vaughn	125.00	55.00	15.50
☐ 69 Jim Thome	80.00	36.00	10.00
☐ 74 Wade Boggs	70.00	32.00	8.75
☐ 81 Paul Molitor	100.00	45.00	12.50
☐ 82 Ryan Klesko	70.00	32.00	8.75
☐ 91 Andy Pettitte	125.00	55.00	15.50
☐ 99 Roberto Alomar	100.00	45.00	12.50
☐ 100 Derek Jeter	300.00	135.00	38.00
☐ 102 Karim Garcia	70.00	32.00	8.75
☐ 113 Wilton Guerrero	80.00	36.00	10.00
☐ 135 Frank Thomas PP	250.00	110.00	31.00
☐ 136 Ken Griffey Jr. PP	250.00	110.00	31.00
☐ 137 Greg Maddux PP	120.00	55.00	15.00
☐ 138 Mike Piazza PP	120.00	55.00	15.00
☐ 139 Cal Ripken PP	200.00	90.00	25.00
☐ 140 Albert Belle PP	100.00	45.00	12.50
☐ 142 Chipper Jones PP	120.00	55.00	15.00

1996 Select Certified Interleague Preview

Randomly inserted in packs at a rate of one in 42, this 25-card set gets ready for the start of interleague play in the 1997 season. Printed on Silver Prime Frost foil stock with gold lettering, the fronts feature color player cutouts of two opposing players. The backs carry another color cutout of the two players with information as to why they are a great matchup.

	MINT	NRMT	EXC
COMPLETE SET (25)	400.00	180.00	50.00
COMMON CARD (1-25)	6.00	2.70	.75
☐ 1 Ken Griffey Jr. / Hideo Nomo	60.00	27.00	7.50
☐ 2 Greg Maddux / Mo Vaughn	40.00	18.00	5.00
☐ 3 Frank Thomas / Sammy Sosa	40.00	18.00	5.00
☐ 4 Mike Piazza / Jim Edmonds	30.00	13.50	3.70
☐ 5 Ryan Klesko / Roger Clemens	12.00	5.50	1.50
☐ 6 Derek Jeter / Rey Ordonez	30.00	13.50	3.70
☐ 7 Johnny Damon / Ray Lankford	6.00	2.70	.75
☐ 8 Manny Ramirez / Reggie Sanders	12.00	5.50	1.50
☐ 9 Barry Bonds / Jay Buhner	15.00	6.75	1.85
☐ 10 Jason Isringhausen / Wade Boggs	6.00	2.70	.75
☐ 11 David Cone / Chipper Jones	30.00	13.50	3.70
☐ 12 Jeff Bagwell / Will Clark	20.00	9.00	2.50
☐ 13 Tony Gwynn / Randy Johnson	25.00	11.00	3.10
☐ 14 Cal Ripken / Tom Glavine	40.00	18.00	5.00
☐ 15 Kirby Puckett / Andy Benes	12.00	5.50	1.50
☐ 16 Gary Sheffield / Mike Mussina	15.00	6.75	1.85
☐ 17 Raul Mondesi / Tim Salmon	10.00	4.50	1.25
☐ 18 Rondell White / Carlos Delgado	6.00	2.70	.75
☐ 19 Cecil Fielder / Ryne Sandberg	12.00	5.50	1.50
☐ 20 Kenny Lofton / Brian L.Hunter	12.00	5.50	1.50
☐ 21 Paul Wilson / Paul O'Neill	6.00	2.70	.75
☐ 22 Ismael Valdes / Edgar Martinez	6.00	2.70	.75
☐ 23 Matt Williams / Mark McGwire	15.00	6.75	1.85
☐ 24 Albert Belle / Barry Larkin	20.00	9.00	2.50
☐ 25 Brady Anderson / Marquis Grissom	8.00	3.60	1.00

1996 Select Certified Select Few

Randomly inserted in packs at a rate of one in 60, this 18-card set honors superstar athletes with unmatched playing field talents. Utilizing the all-new Dot Matrix hologram technology, the fronts feature color action player cutouts. The backs carry player information. Several of the cards were erroneously printed without player's name on the front. These uncorrected errors are worth the same as the corrected cards.

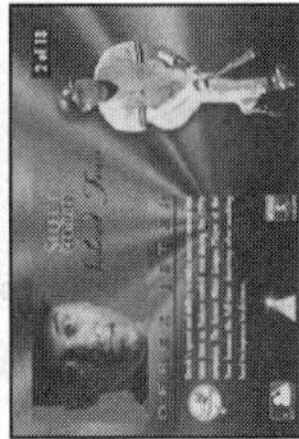

	MINT	NRMT	EXC
COMPLETE SET (18)	300.00	135.00	38.00
COMMON CARD (1-18)	6.00	2.70	.75
☐ 1 Sammy Sosa	8.00	3.60	1.00
☐ 2 Derek Jeter	30.00	13.50	3.70
☐ 3 Ken Griffey Jr.	50.00	22.00	6.25
☐ 4 Albert Belle	20.00	9.00	2.50
☐ 5 Cal Ripken	40.00	18.00	5.00
☐ 6 Greg Maddux	30.00	13.50	3.70
☐ 7 Frank Thomas	50.00	22.00	6.25
☐ 8 Mo Vaughn	12.00	5.50	1.50
☐ 9 Chipper Jones	30.00	13.50	3.70
☐ 10 Mike Piazza	30.00	13.50	3.70
☐ 11 Ryan Klesko	8.00	3.60	1.00
☐ 12 Hideo Nomo	12.00	5.50	1.50
☐ 13 Alan Benes	6.00	2.70	.75
☐ 14 Manny Ramirez	12.00	5.50	1.50
☐ 15 Gary Sheffield	8.00	3.60	1.00
☐ 16 Barry Bonds	12.00	5.50	1.50
☐ 17 Matt Williams	6.00	2.70	.75
☐ 18 Johnny Damon	6.00	2.70	.75

1909 Senators Barr-Farnham Postcards

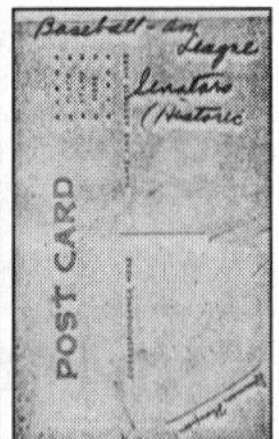

This extremely rare set of real photo postcards was produced by Barr-Farnham Picture Postcards Co. located in Washington, DC in 1909. Ten cards have been positively identified but there are undoubtedly others, probably every member of the team. There is a strong possibility there is a team postcard as well. All additions to this checklist are greatly appreciated. All views show a full body close up of the player taken on the outfield grass with the ball park in the background.

	EX-MT	VG-E	GOOD
COMPLETE SET (10)	1500.00	700.00	190.00
COMMON CARD (1-10)	200.00	90.00	25.00
☐ 1 Otis Clymer	200.00	90.00	25.00
☐ 2 Wid Conroy	200.00	90.00	25.00
☐ 3 Bob Ganley	200.00	90.00	25.00
☐ 4 Dolly Gray	200.00	90.00	25.00
☐ 5 Bob Groom	200.00	90.00	25.00
☐ 6 Walter Johnson	750.00	350.00	95.00
☐ 7 George McBride	200.00	90.00	25.00
☐ 8 Charlie Smith	200.00	90.00	25.00
☐ 9 Jesse Tannehill	200.00	90.00	25.00
☐ 10 Bob Unglaub	200.00	90.00	25.00

1947 Senators Gunther Beer PC

These postcards usually featuring two players on the front were issued around 1947-48 based on the players in the set. The cards feature the players photos on the front along with their names in big bold black letters on the bottom. The backs have room for messages to be sent, usually from the Senators annoucer of the time, Arch MacDonald. This listing may be incomplete so additions are welcome.

	NRMT	VG-E	GOOD
COMPLETE SET	750.00	340.00	95.00
COMMON CARD	75.00	34.00	9.50
☐ 1 Joe Kuhel	75.00	34.00	9.50
☐ 2 Al Evans / Scott Cary	75.00	34.00	9.50
☐ 3 Tom Ferrick / Harold Keller	75.00	34.00	9.50
☐ 4 Mickey Haefner / Forrest Thompson	75.00	34.00	9.50
☐ 5 Sid Hudson / Al Kozar	75.00	34.00	9.50
☐ 6 Walter Masterson / Rick Ferrell	100.00	45.00	12.50
☐ 7 Tom McBride / Milo Candini	75.00	34.00	9.50
☐ 8 Marino Pieretti / Leon Culberson	75.00	34.00	9.50
☐ 9 Sherrard Robertson / Eddie Lyons	75.00	34.00	9.50
☐ 10 Ray Scarborough / Kenneth McCreight	75.00	34.00	9.50
☐ 11 Mickey Vernon / Gil Coan	100.00	45.00	12.50

1958 Senators Jay Publishing

This 12-card set of the Washington Senators measures approximately 5" by 7" and features black-and-white player photos in a white border. These cards were packaged 12 to a packet. The backs are blank. The cards are unnumbered and checklisted below in alphabetical order.

	NRMT	VG-E	GOOD
COMPLETE SET (12)	30.00	13.50	3.70
COMMON CARD (1-12)	2.50	1.10	.30
☐ 1 Rocky Bridges	3.00	1.35	.35
☐ 2 Truman Clevenger	2.50	1.10	.30
☐ 3 Clint Courtney	2.50	1.10	.30
☐ 4 Dick Hyde	2.50	1.10	.30
☐ 5 Cookie Lavagetto MG	3.00	1.35	.35
☐ 6 Jim Lemon	2.50	1.10	.30
☐ 7 Camilo Pascual	2.50	1.10	.30
☐ 8 Albie Pearson	2.50	1.10	.30
☐ 9 Herb Plews	2.50	1.10	.30
☐ 10 Pedro Ramos	2.50	1.10	.30
☐ 11 Roy Sievers	2.50	1.10	.30
☐ 12 Eddie Yost	2.50	1.10	.30

1960 Senators Jay Publishing

This 12-card set of the Washington Senators measures approximately 5" by 7" and features black-and-white player photos in a white border. These cards were packaged 12 to a packet. The backs are blank. The cards are unnumbered and checklisted below in alphabetical order.

	NRMT	VG-E	GOOD
COMPLETE SET (12)	30.00	13.50	3.70
COMMON CARD (1-12)	2.00	.90	.25
☐ 1 Bob Allison	3.00	1.35	.35
☐ 2 Julio Becquer	2.00	.90	.25
☐ 3 Truman Clevenger	2.00	.90	.25
☐ 4 Billy Consolo	2.00	.90	.25
☐ 5 Dan Dobbek	2.00	.90	.25
☐ 6 William(Billy) Gardner	3.00	1.35	.35
☐ 7 Harmon Killebrew	7.50	3.40	.95
☐ 8 Steve Korchek	2.00	.90	.25
☐ 9 Cookie Lavagetto MG	3.00	1.35	.35
☐ 10 Jim Lemon	2.00	.90	.25
☐ 11 Camilo Pascual	2.00	.90	.25
☐ 12 Pedro Ramos	2.00	.90	.25

1961 Senators Jay Publishing

Produced by Jay Publishing, this 12-card set features members of the Washington Senators. Originally, this set came in a plastic sack that included a "picture pak order form" and sold for 25 cents. Printed on thin stock paper, the cards measure approximately 5" by 7". On a white background the fronts have a black-and-white posed player photo. The player's name and team appear in black letters under the photo. The backs are blank. The cards are unnumbered and checklisted below in alphabetical order.

	NRMT	VG-E	GOOD
COMPLETE SET (12)	30.00	13.50	3.70
COMMON CARD (1-12)	2.50	1.10	.30
☐ 1 Pete Burnside	2.50	1.10	.30
☐ 2 Chuck Cottier	2.50	1.10	.30
☐ 3 Bernie Daniels	3.50	1.55	.45
☐ 4 Bob Johnson	2.50	1.10	.30
☐ 5 Marty Kutyna	2.50	1.10	.30
☐ 6 Joe McClain	2.50	1.10	.30
☐ 7 Danny O'Connell	2.50	1.10	.30
☐ 8 Ken Retzer	2.50	1.10	.30
☐ 9 Willie Tasby	3.00	1.35	.35
☐ 10 Mickey Vernon MG	3.50	1.55	.45
☐ 11 Gene Wooding	3.00	1.35	.35
☐ 12 Marion Zipfel	2.50	1.10	.30

1970 Senators Police Yellow

The 1970 Washington Senators Police set was issued on a thin unperforated cardboard sheet measuring approximately 12 1/2" by 8". The sheet is divided into ten cards by thin black lines. When the players are cut into individual cards, they measure approximately 2 1/2" by 4". The color of the sheet is yellow, and consequently the black and white borderless player photos have a similar cast. The player's name, position, and team name appear below the pictures. The backs have different safety messages sponsored by the Office of Traffic Safety, D.C. Department of Motor Vehicles. The cards are unnumbered and checklisted below in alphabetical order.

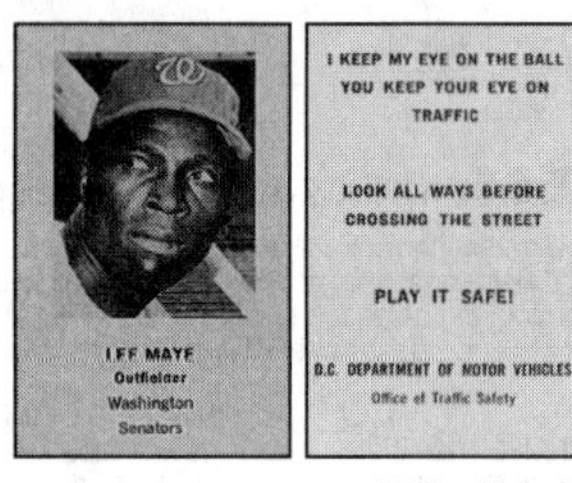

	NRMT	VG-E	GOOD
COMPLETE SET (10)	30.00	13.50	3.70
COMMON CARD (1-10)	2.50	1.10	.30
□ 1 Dick Bosman	3.50	1.55	.45
□ 2 Eddie Brinkman	3.50	1.55	.45
□ 3 Paul Casanova	3.50	1.55	.45
□ 4 Mike Epstein	3.50	1.55	.45
□ 5 Frank Howard	7.50	3.40	.95
□ 6 Darold Knowles	2.50	1.10	.30
□ 7 Lee Maye	2.50	1.10	.30
□ 8 Aurelio Rodriguez	3.50	1.55	.45
□ 9 John Roseboro	3.50	1.55	.45
□ 10 Ed Stroud	2.50	1.10	.30

1971 Senators Police Pink

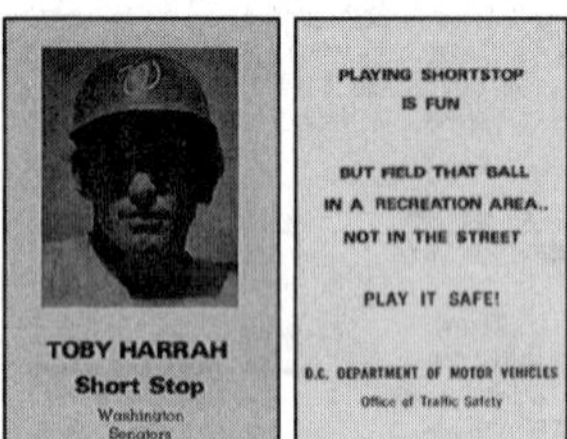

The 1971 Washington Senators Police set was issued on a thin unperforated cardboard sheet measuring approximately 12 1/2" by 8". In contrast to the previous year's issue, the sheet is not divided up into separate cards by thin black lines. If the sheet were cut into individual player cards, each player's card would measure approximately 2 1/2" by 4". The color of the sheet ranges from pink to peach, and consequently the black and white borderless player photos have a similar cast. The player's name, position, and team name appear below the pictures. The backs have different safety messages sponsored by the Office of Traffic Safety, D.C. Department of Motor Vehicles. The cards are unnumbered and checklisted below in alphabetical order. The set is dated by the fact that it is Denny McLain's only year on the Senators.

	NRMT	VG-E	GOOD
COMPLETE SET (10)	30.00	13.50	3.70
COMMON CARD (1-10)	2.50	1.10	.30
□ 1 Dick Bosman	3.50	1.55	.45
□ 2 Paul Casanova	3.50	1.55	.45
□ 3 Tim Cullen	2.50	1.10	.30
□ 4 Joe Foy	2.50	1.10	.30
□ 5 Toby Harrah	6.00	2.70	.75
□ 6 Frank Howard	7.50	3.40	.95
□ 7 Elliott Maddox	3.50	1.55	.45
□ 8 Tom McCraw	3.50	1.55	.45
□ 9 Denny McLain	6.00	2.70	.75
□ 10 Don Wert	2.50	1.10	.30

1910 Sepia Anon PC796

This sepia with white border set measures 3 1/2" by 5 1/2", was issued circa 1910 and features 25 cards of popular players of the era. No markings are found either on the front or on the backs to indicate a manufacturer or issuer. The Cobb and Wagner card spells Honus' name as Honas. The same checklist is also used for the PC Novelty Cultery Co set. The pictures in that set have been reduced and enclosed in an ornate frame border. Postcards by either issuer are valued the same.

	EX-MT	VG-E	GOOD
COMPLETE SET (25)	7500.00	3400.00	950.00
COMMON CARD (1-25)	150.00	70.00	19.00
□ 1 Roger Bresnahan Full catching pose	300.00	135.00	38.00
□ 2 Al Bridwell Stooped fielding	150.00	70.00	19.00
□ 3 Mordecai Brown Pitching - left leg up	250.00	110.00	31.00
□ 4 Ty Cobb Batting to hips	1200.00	550.00	150.00
□ 5 Ty Cobb Honus Wagner Shaking Hands	800.00	350.00	100.00
□ 6 Frank Chance MG Throwing	300.00	135.00	38.00
□ 7 Hal Chase Fielding at first	250.00	110.00	31.00
□ 8 Eddie Collins Batting	250.00	110.00	31.00
□ 9 Sam Crawford Batting	250.00	110.00	31.00
□ 10 Johnny Evers Germany Schaefer Standing	250.00	110.00	31.00
□ 11 Art Devlin Glove outstretched	150.00	70.00	19.00
□ 12 Red Dooin Arms High Ball in one hand; Glove the other	150.00	70.00	19.00
□ 13 Sam Frock Portrait	150.00	70.00	19.00
□ 14 George Gibson Full catching position	150.00	70.00	19.00
□ 15 Artie Hoffman Fielding for high one	150.00	70.00	19.00
□ 16 Walter Johnson Pitching	600.00	275.00	75.00
□ 17 Nap Lajoie Full batting pose	350.00	160.00	45.00
□ 18 Harry Lord Throwing	150.00	70.00	19.00
□ 19 Christy Mathewson Pitching -- right leg up	600.00	275.00	75.00
□ 20 Orvall Overall Pitching -- left leg up	150.00	70.00	19.00
□ 21 Eddie Plank Portrait -- hand over head	250.00	110.00	31.00
□ 22 Tris Speaker Batting pose	300.00	135.00	38.00
□ 23 Charley Street Full catching about to throw	175.00	80.00	22.00
□ 24 Honus Wagner Full batting pose	500.00	220.00	60.00
□ 25 Ed Walsh Full bunting pose	250.00	110.00	31.00

1977 Sertoma Stars

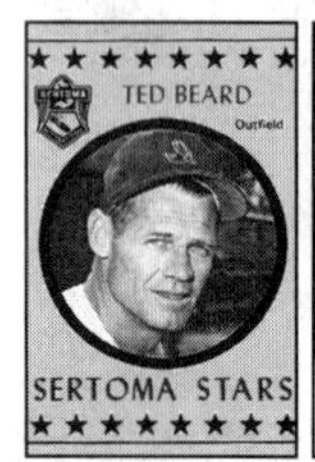

This 25-card set measures approximately 2 3/4" by 4 1/4". The fronts feature a black-and-white player portrait in a black-framed circle on a yellow background. The player's name, position, sponsor logo, and card name are printed in black and red between a top and bottom row of black stars which border the card. The backs carry a puzzle piece which, when placed in the right position, form a picture of the 1913 Pittsburgh Nationals. The cards are unnumbered and checklisted below in alphabetical order.

	NRMT	VG-E	GOOD
COMPLETE SET (25)	25.00	11.00	3.10
COMMON CARD (1-25)	.25	.11	.03
□ 1 Bernie Allen	.25	.11	.03
□ 2 Frank(Home Run) Baker	1.00	.45	.12
□ 3 Ted Beard	.25	.11	.03
□ 4 Don Buford	.25	.11	.03
□ 5 Eddie Cicotte	1.00	.45	.12
□ 6 Roberto Clemente	3.00	1.35	.35
□ 7 Dom Dallessandro	.25	.11	.03
□ 8 Carl Erskine	.50	.23	.06
□ 9 Nellie Fox	1.00	.45	.12
□ 10 Lou Gehrig	3.00	1.35	.35
□ 11 Joe Jackson	3.00	1.35	.35
□ 12 Len Johnston	.25	.11	.03
□ 13 Benny Kauff	.25	.11	.03
□ 14 Dick Kenworthy	.25	.11	.03
□ 15 Harmon Killebrew	1.00	.45	.12
□ 16 Bob(Lefty) Logan	.25	.11	.03
□ 17 Willie Mays	3.00	1.35	.35
□ 18 Satchell Paige	3.00	1.35	.35
□ 19 Edd Roush	1.00	.45	.12
□ 20 Chico Ruiz	.25	.11	.03
□ 21 Babe Ruth	5.00	2.20	.60
□ 22 Herb Score	.50	.23	.06
□ 23 George Sisler	1.00	.45	.12
□ 24 George(Buck) Weaver	1.00	.45	.12
□ 25 Early Wynn	1.00	.45	.12

1961 Seven-Eleven

The 1961 7-Eleven set consists of 30 cards, each measuring approximately 2 7/16" by 3 3/8". The checklist card states that this is the first series, and that a new series was to be released every two weeks (though apparently no other series were issued). The cards are printed on pink cardboard stock and the backs are blank. The fronts have a black and white headshot in the upper left portion and brief biographical information to the right of the picture. The player's name appears across the top of each front. The remainder of the front carries "1960 Hi Lites," which consist of a list of dates and the player's achievements on those dates. The team name across the bottom of the card rounds out the front. The cards are numbered on the front in the lower right corner.

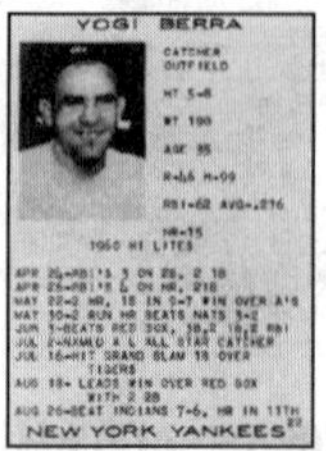

	NRMT	VG-E	GOOD
COMPLETE SET (30)	450.00	200.00	55.00
COMMON CARD (1-29)	6.00	2.70	.75
□ 1 Dave Sisler	6.00	2.70	.75
□ 2 Don Mossi	7.50	3.40	.95
□ 3 Joey Jay	6.00	2.70	.75
□ 4 Bob Purkey	6.00	2.70	.75
□ 5 Jack Fisher	6.00	2.70	.75
□ 6 John Romano	6.00	2.70	.75
□ 7 Russ Snyder	6.00	2.70	.75
□ 8 Johnny Temple	6.00	2.70	.75
□ 9 Roy Sievers	7.50	3.40	.95
□ 10 Ron Hansen	6.00	2.70	.75
□ 11 Pete Runnels	7.50	3.40	.95
□ 12 Gene Woodling	7.50	3.40	.95
□ 13 Clint Courtney	6.00	2.70	.75
□ 14 Whitey Herzog	10.00	4.50	1.25
□ 15 Warren Spahn	30.00	13.50	3.70
□ 16 Stan Musial	60.00	27.00	7.50
□ 17 Willie Mays	75.00	34.00	9.50
□ 18 Ken Boyer	10.00	4.50	1.25
□ 19 Joe Cunningham	7.50	3.40	.95
□ 20 Orlando Cepeda	15.00	6.75	1.85
□ 21 Gil Hodges	15.00	6.75	1.85
□ 22 Yogi Berra	40.00	18.00	5.00
□ 23 Ernie Banks	40.00	18.00	5.00
□ 24 Lou Burdette	10.00	4.50	1.25
□ 25 Roger Maris	50.00	22.00	6.25
□ 26 Charlie Smith	6.00	2.70	.75
□ 27 Jimmie Foxx	15.00	6.75	1.85
□ 28 Mel Ott	15.00	6.75	1.85
□ 29 Don Nottebart	6.00	2.70	.75
□ NNO Checklist Card	20.00	9.00	2.50

1983 Seven-Eleven Coins

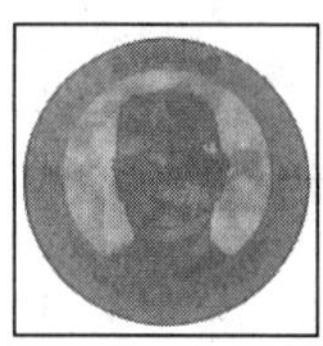

The coins in this 12-coin set measure approximately 1 3/4" diameter. This set of action coins was released by 7-Eleven stores in the Los Angeles area. Given out with large Slurpee drinks, the set features Los Angeles Dodgers (blue background) and California Angels (red background) on plastic discs. The fronts feature two pictures (portrait and action) of each player, each of which can be seen by moving the coin slightly to one side or another. Brief statistics fill the backs of these coins. The coins are numbered by uniform number on the front; in addition, an individual coin number can be found on the back.

	NRMT	VG-E	GOOD
COMPLETE SET (12)	8.00	3.60	1.00
COMMON COIN (1-12)	.25	.11	.03
□ 1 Rod Carew	2.00	.90	.25
□ 2 Steve Sax	.50	.23	.06
□ 3 Fred Lynn	.50	.23	.06
□ 4 Pedro Guerrero	.50	.23	.06
□ 5 Reggie Jackson	2.50	1.10	.30
□ 6 Dusty Baker	.40	.18	.05
□ 7 Doug DeCinces	.40	.18	.05
□ 8 Fernando Valenzuela	.75	.35	.09
□ 9 Tommy John	.50	.23	.06
□ 10 Rick Monday	.25	.11	.03
□ 11 Bobby Grich	.25	.11	.03
□ 12 Greg Brock	.25	.11	.03

1984 Seven-Eleven Coins

The coins in this 72 coin set measure approximately 1 3/4" diameter. For the second year in a row, 7-Eleven issued sets of coins (officially called Slurpee Discs). The fronts feature two pictures (portrait and action) of each player, each of which can be seen by moving the coin slightly to one side or another. There were, in effect, three different sets of 24 coins corresponding to an East, Central and West region. The letter suffix after the number in the checklist below denotes the region of issue, East (E), Central (C), or West (W). Of the total 72 coins, only 60 different players appear. Six players appear in all three sets. The repeat players are Andre Dawson, Robin Yount, Dale Murphy, George Brett, Mike Schmidt and Eddie Murray. Each team is represented by at least one player and as one might expect, players within the three groups favor the teams of the geographical location in

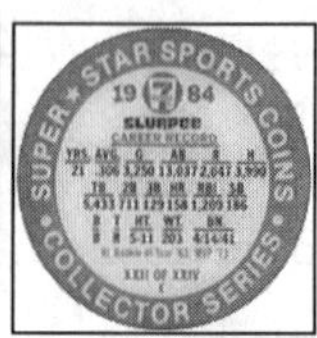

which that particular group was issued. Coins are numbered on the back, which is different from the uniform number which is on the front of the coin.

	NRMT	VG-E	GOOD
COMPLETE SET (72)	40.00	18.00	5.00
COMMON COIN	.20	.09	.03
□ C1 Andre Dawson	.50	.23	.06
□ C2 Robin Yount	.75	.35	.09
□ C3 Dale Murphy	.50	.23	.06
□ C4 Mike Schmidt	1.50	.70	.19
□ C5 George Brett	2.00	.90	.25
□ C6 Eddie Murray	1.25	.55	.16
□ C7 Bruce Sutter	.30	.14	.04
□ C8 Cecil Cooper	.30	.14	.04
□ C9 Willie McGee	.40	.18	.05
□ C10 Mike Hargrove	.30	.14	.04
□ C11 Kent Hrbek	.30	.14	.04
□ C12 Carlton Fisk	1.00	.45	.12
□ C13 Mario Soto	.20	.09	.03
□ C14 Lonnie Smith	.20	.09	.03
□ C15 Gary Carter	.50	.23	.06
□ C16 Lou Whitaker	.30	.14	.04
□ C17 Ron Kittle	.20	.09	.03
□ C18 Paul Molitor	1.00	.45	.12
□ C19 Ozzie Smith	1.50	.70	.19
□ C20 Fergie Jenkins	.50	.23	.06
□ C21 Ted Simmons	.30	.14	.04
□ C22 Pete Rose	2.00	.90	.25
□ C23 LaMarr Hoyt	.20	.09	.03
□ C24 Dan Quisenberry	.20	.09	.03
□ E1 Andre Dawson	.50	.23	.06
□ E2 Robin Yount	.75	.35	.09
□ E3 Dale Murphy	.50	.23	.06
□ E4 Mike Schmidt	1.50	.70	.19
□ E5 George Brett	2.00	.90	.25
□ E6 Eddie Murray	1.25	.55	.16
□ E7 Dave Winfield	1.00	.45	.12
□ E8 Tom Seaver	1.25	.55	.16
□ E9 Mike Boddicker	.20	.09	.03
□ E10 Wade Boggs	1.50	.70	.19
□ E11 Bill Madlock	.20	.09	.03
□ E12 Steve Carlton	1.00	.45	.12
□ E13 Dave Stieb	.20	.09	.03
□ E14 Cal Ripken	5.00	2.20	.60
□ E15 Jim Rice	.30	.14	.04
□ E16 Ron Guidry	.30	.14	.04
□ E17 Darryl Strawberry	.75	.35	.09
□ E18 Tony Pena	.20	.09	.03
□ E19 John Denny	.20	.09	.03
□ E20 Tim Raines	.40	.18	.05
□ E21 Rick Dempsey	.20	.09	.03
□ E22 Rich Gossage	.40	.18	.05
□ E23 Gary Matthews	.20	.09	.03
□ E24 Keith Hernandez	.30	.14	.04
□ W1 Andre Dawson	.50	.23	.06
□ W2 Robin Yount	1.00	.45	.12
□ W3 Dale Murphy	.50	.23	.06
□ W4 Mike Schmidt	1.50	.70	.19
□ W5 George Brett	2.00	.90	.25
□ W6 Eddie Murray	1.25	.55	.16
□ W7 Steve Garvey	.40	.18	.05
□ W8 Rod Carew	1.00	.45	.12
□ W9 Fernando Valenzuela	.30	.14	.04
□ W10 Bob Horner	.20	.09	.03
□ W11 Buddy Bell	.30	.14	.04
□ W12 Reggie Jackson	1.25	.55	.16
□ W13 Nolan Ryan	4.00	1.80	.50
□ W14 Pedro Guerrero	.30	.14	.04
□ W15 Atlee Hammaker	.20	.09	.03
□ W16 Fred Lynn	.30	.14	.04
□ W17 Terry Kennedy	.20	.09	.03
□ W18 Dusty Baker	.30	.14	.04
□ W19 Jose Cruz	.30	.14	.04
□ W20 Steve Rogers	.20	.09	.03
□ W21 Rickey Henderson	1.00	.45	.12
□ W22 Steve Sax	.30	.14	.04
□ W23 Dickie Thon	.20	.09	.03
□ W24 Matt Young	.20	.09	.03

1985 Seven-Eleven Coins

These "3-D" type coins are very similar to those of the preceding years except that in 1985 7-Eleven issued six subsets. The subsets are

Central (C), Detroit (D), Eastern (E), Great Lakes (G), Southeast (S) and Western (W). The letter suffix after the number in the checklist below denotes the region of issue. Each of the six subsets is numbered and contains 16 coins except for the Tigers set which contains only 14 and was distributed in somewhat smaller supply. Each coin measures approximately 1 3/4" in diameter.

	NRMT	VG-E	GOOD
COMPLETE SET (94)	50.00	22.00	6.25
COMMON COIN	.20	.09	.03
☐ C1 Nolan Ryan	4.00	1.80	.50
☐ C2 George Brett	2.00	.90	.25
☐ C3 Dave Winfield	.75	.35	.09
☐ C4 Mike Schmidt	1.50	.70	.19
☐ C5 Bruce Sutter	.30	.14	.04
☐ C6 Joaquin Andujar	.20	.09	.03
☐ C7 Willie Hernandez	.20	.09	.03
☐ C8 Wade Boggs	1.25	.55	.16
☐ C9 Gary Carter	.50	.23	.06
☐ C10 Jose Cruz	.20	.09	.03
☐ C11 Kent Hrbek	.40	.18	.05
☐ C12 Reggie Jackson	1.25	.55	.16
☐ C13 Lance Parrish	.30	.14	.04
☐ C14 Terry Puhl	.20	.09	.03
☐ C15 Dan Quisenberry	.20	.09	.03
☐ C16 Ozzie Smith	1.25	.55	.16
☐ D1 Lou Whitaker	.40	.18	.05
☐ D2 Sparky Anderson MG	.30	.14	.04
☐ D3 Darrell Evans	.30	.14	.04
☐ D4 Larry Herndon	.20	.09	.03
☐ D5 Dave Rozema	.20	.09	.03
☐ D6 Milt Wilcox	.20	.09	.03
☐ D7 Dan Petry	.20	.09	.03
☐ D8 Alan Trammell	.50	.23	.06
☐ D9 Aurelio Lopez	.20	.09	.03
☐ D10 Willie Hernandez	.20	.09	.03
☐ D11 Chet Lemon	.20	.09	.03
☐ D12 Jack Morris	.30	.14	.04
☐ D13 Kirk Gibson	.30	.14	.04
☐ D14 Lance Parrish	.30	.14	.04
☐ E1 Eddie Murray	1.00	.45	.12
☐ E2 George Brett	2.00	.90	.25
☐ E3 Steve Carlton	1.00	.45	.12
☐ E4 Jim Rice	.30	.14	.04
☐ E5 Dave Winfield	.75	.35	.09
☐ E6 Mike Boddicker	.20	.09	.03
☐ E7 Wade Boggs	1.25	.55	.16
☐ E8 Dwight Evans	.40	.18	.05
☐ E9 Dwight Gooden	1.50	.70	.19
☐ E10 Keith Hernandez	.30	.14	.04
☐ E11 Bill Madlock	.20	.09	.03
☐ E12 Don Mattingly	4.00	1.80	.50
☐ E13 Dave Righetti	.30	.14	.04
☐ E14 Cal Ripken	5.00	2.20	.60
☐ E15 Juan Samuel	.20	.09	.03
☐ E16 Mike Schmidt	1.50	.70	.19
☐ G1 Willie Hernandez	.20	.09	.03
☐ G2 George Brett	2.00	.90	.25
☐ G3 Dave Winfield	.75	.35	.09
☐ G4 Eddie Murray	1.00	.45	.12
☐ G5 Bruce Sutter	.30	.14	.04
☐ G6 Harold Baines	.30	.14	.04
☐ G7 Bert Blyleven	.40	.18	.05
☐ G8 Leon Durham	.20	.09	.03
☐ G9 Chet Lemon	.20	.09	.03
☐ G10 Pete Rose	2.00	.90	.25
☐ G11 Ryne Sandberg	2.50	1.10	.30
☐ G12 Tom Seaver	1.25	.55	.16
☐ G13 Mario Soto	.20	.09	.03
☐ G14 Rick Sutcliffe	.20	.09	.03
☐ G15 Alan Trammell	.50	.23	.06
☐ G16 Robin Yount	.75	.35	.09
☐ S1 Dale Murphy	.50	.23	.06
☐ S2 Steve Carlton	1.00	.45	.12
☐ S3 Nolan Ryan	4.00	1.80	.50
☐ S4 Bruce Sutter	.30	.14	.04
☐ S5 Dave Winfield	.75	.35	.09
☐ S6 Steve Bedrosian	.20	.09	.03
☐ S7 Andre Dawson	.50	.23	.06
☐ S8 Kirk Gibson	.30	.14	.04
☐ S9 Fred Lynn	.30	.14	.04
☐ S10 Gary Matthews	.20	.09	.03
☐ S11 Phil Niekro	.50	.23	.06
☐ S12 Tim Raines	.30	.14	.04
☐ S13 Darryl Strawberry	.40	.18	.05
☐ S14 Dave Stieb	.30	.14	.04
☐ S15 Willie Upshaw	.20	.09	.03
☐ S16 Lou Whitaker	.40	.18	.05
☐ W1 Mike Schmidt	1.50	.70	.19
☐ W2 Jim Rice	.30	.14	.04
☐ W3 Dale Murphy	.50	.23	.06
☐ W4 Eddie Murray	1.00	.45	.12
☐ W5 Dave Winfield	.75	.35	.09
☐ W6 Rod Carew	1.00	.45	.12
☐ W7 Alvin Davis	.20	.09	.03
☐ W8 Steve Garvey	.40	.18	.05
☐ W9 Rich Gossage	.40	.18	.05
☐ W10 Pedro Guerrero	.30	.14	.04
☐ W11 Tony Gwynn	4.00	1.80	.50
☐ W12 Rickey Henderson	1.00	.45	.12
☐ W13 Reggie Jackson	1.25	.55	.16
☐ W14 Jeff Leonard	.20	.09	.03
☐ W15 Alejandro Pena	.20	.09	.03
☐ W16 Fernando Valenzuela	.30	.14	.04

1986 Seven-Eleven Coins

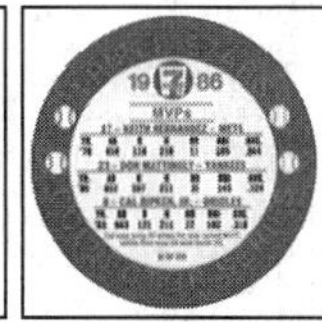

Four subsets of 16 coins each were distributed regionally by the 7-Eleven chain of convenience stores. The letter suffix after the number in the checklist below denotes the region of issue. The regions were Central (C), East (E), South (S) and West (W). The first eight coins in each region are the same; the last eight (9-16) in each region were apparently selected to showcase players from that area. Except for Dwight Gooden all other coins feature three players on each card depending on how you tilt the coin to see one of the three players. The three players are typically related by position. Each coin measures approximately 1 3/4" in diameter.

	MINT	NRMT	EXC
COMPLETE SET (64)	40.00	18.00	5.00
COMMON COIN	.20	.09	.03
☐ C1 Dwight Gooden	1.00	.45	.12
☐ C2 Wade Boggs	2.00	.90	.25
George Brett			
Pete Rose			
☐ C3 Keith Hernandez	3.00	1.35	.35
Don Mattingly			
Cal Ripken			
☐ C4 Harold Baines	.30	.14	.04
Pedro Guerrero			
Dave Parker			
☐ C5 Dale Murphy	.40	.18	.05
Jim Rice			
Mike Schmidt			
☐ C6 Ron Guidry	.30	.14	.04
Bret Saberhagen			
Fernando Valenzuela			
☐ C7 Goose Gossage	.30	.14	.04
Dan Quisenberry			
Bruce Sutter			
☐ C8 Steve Carlton	3.00	1.35	.35
Nolan Ryan			
Tom Seaver			
☐ C9 Willie Hernandez	1.00	.45	.12
Ryne Sandberg			
Robin Yount			
☐ C10 Bert Blyleven	.30	.14	.04
Jack Morris			
Rick Sutcliffe			
☐ C11 Rollie Fingers	.30	.14	.04
Bob James			
Lee Smith			
☐ C12 Carlton Fisk	.30	.14	.04
Lance Parrish			
Tony Pena			
☐ C13 Shawon Dunston	.30	.14	.04
Ozzie Guillen			
Earnie Riles			
☐ C14 Brett Butler	.30	.14	.04
Chet Lemon			
Willie Wilson			
☐ C15 Tom Brunansky	.20	.09	.03
Cecil Cooper			
Darrell Evans			
☐ C16 Kirk Gibson	.30	.14	.04
Paul Molitor			
Greg Walker			
☐ E1 Dwight Gooden	1.00	.45	.12
☐ E2 Wade Boggs	2.00	.90	.25
George Brett			
Pete Rose			
☐ E3 Keith Hernandez	3.00	1.35	.35
Don Mattingly			
Cal Ripken			
☐ E4 Harold Baines	.30	.14	.04
Pedro Guerrero			
Dave Parker			
☐ E5 Dale Murphy	.40	.18	.05
Jim Rice			
Mike Schmidt			
☐ E6 Ron Guidry	.30	.14	.04
Bret Saberhagen			
Fernando Valenzuela			
☐ E7 Goose Gossage	.30	.14	.04
Dan Quisenberry			
Bruce Sutter			
☐ E8 Steve Carlton	3.00	1.35	.35
Nolan Ryan			
Tom Seaver			
☐ E9 Steve Lyons	.20	.09	.03
Rick Schu			
Larry Sheets			
☐ E10 Jeff Reardon	.20	.09	.03
Dave Righetti			
Bob Stanley			
☐ E11 George Bell	.75	.35	.09
Darryl Strawberry			
Dave Winfield			
☐ E12 Rickey Henderson	.40	.18	.05
Tim Raines			
Juan Samuel			
☐ E13 Andre Dawson	1.00	.45	.12
Dwight Evans			
Eddie Murray			
☐ E14 Mike Boddicker	.20	.09	.03
Ron Darling			
Dave Stieb			
☐ E15 Tim Burke	.20	.09	.03
Brian Fisher			
Roger McDowell			
☐ E16 Jesse Barfield	.30	.14	.04
Gary Carter			
Fred Lynn			
☐ S1 Dwight Gooden	1.00	.45	.12
☐ S2 Wade Boggs	2.00	.90	.25
George Brett			
Pete Rose			
☐ S3 Keith Hernandez	3.00	1.35	.35
Don Mattingly			
Cal Ripken			
☐ S4 Harold Baines	.30	.14	.04
Pedro Guerrero			
Dave Parker			
☐ S5 Dale Murphy	1.00	.45	.12
Jim Rice			
Mike Schmidt			
☐ S6 Ron Guidry	.30	.14	.04
Bret Saberhagen			
Fernando Valenzuela			
☐ S7 Goose Gossage	.30	.14	.04
Dan Quisenberry			
Bruce Sutter			
☐ S8 Steve Carlton	3.00	1.35	.35
Nolan Ryan			
Tom Seaver			
☐ S9 Vince Coleman	.30	.14	.04
Eric Davis			
Oddibe McDowell			
☐ S10 Buddy Bell	1.00	.45	.12
Ozzie Smith			
Lou Whitaker			
☐ S11 Mike Scott	.20	.09	.03
Mario Soto			
John Tudor			
☐ S12 Jeff Lahti	.20	.09	.03
Ted Power			
Dave Smith			
☐ S13 Jack Clark	.30	.14	.04
Jose Cruz			
Bob Horner			
☐ S14 Bill Doran	.20	.09	.03
Tommy Herr			
Ron Oester			
☐ S15 Tom Browning	.20	.09	.03
Joe Hesketh			
Todd Worrell			
☐ S16 Willie McGee	1.00	.45	.12
Jerry Mumphrey			
Pete Rose			
☐ W1 Dwight Gooden	1.00	.45	.12
☐ W2 Wade Boggs	2.00	.90	.25
George Brett			
Pete Rose			
☐ W3 Keith Hernandez	3.00	1.35	.35
Don Mattingly			
Cal Ripken			
☐ W4 Harold Baines	.30	.14	.04
Pedro Guerrero			
Dave Parker			
☐ W5 Dale Murphy	1.00	.45	.12
Jim Rice			
Mike Schmidt			
☐ W6 Ron Guidry	.30	.14	.04
Bret Saberhagen			
Fernando Valenzuela			
☐ W7 Goose Gossage	.30	.14	.04
Dan Quisenberry			
Bruce Sutter			
☐ W8 Steve Carlton	3.00	1.35	.35
Nolan Ryan			
Tom Seaver			
☐ W9 Reggie Jackson	.40	.18	.05
Dave Kingman			
Gorman Thomas			
☐ W10 Rod Carew	1.25	.55	.16
Tony Gwynn			
Carney Lansford			
☐ W11 Phil Bradley	.20	.09	.03
Mike Marshall			
Graig Nettles			
☐ W12 Andy Hawkins	.30	.14	.04
Orel Hershiser			
Mike Witt			
☐ W13 Chris Brown	.20	.09	.03
Ivan Calderon			
Mariano Duncan			
☐ W14 Steve Garvey	.30	.14	.04
Bill Madlock			
Jim Presley			
☐ W15 Jay Howell	.20	.09	.03
Donnie Moore			
Edwin Nunez			
☐ W16 Karl Best	.20	.09	.03
Stewart Cliburn			
Steve Ontiveros			

1987 Seven-Eleven Coins

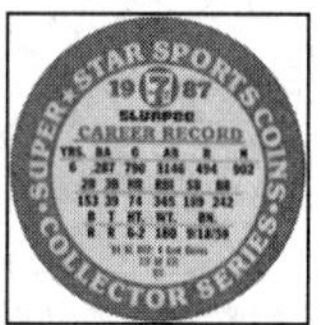

These "3-D" type coins are very similar to those of the preceding years except that in 1987 7-Eleven issued five subsets. The subsets are Detroit (D), East (E), Chicago (C), Mideast (M) and West (W). Each subset has a different color border on the back. The West subset is actually eight Dodgers and eight Angels. The Mideast subset is actually four each from the Mets, Cubs, Red Sox and Orioles. The East subset is actually five each from the Mets, Red Sox and Yankees. The letter prefix before the number in the checklist below denotes the region of issue. Each of the five subsets is numbered and contains between 12 and 16 coins. Each coin measures 1 3/4" in diameter.

	MINT	NRMT	EXC
COMPLETE SET (75)	45.00	20.00	5.50
COMMON COIN	.20	.09	.03
☐ C1 Harold Baines	.30	.14	.04
☐ C2 Jody Davis	.20	.09	.03
☐ C3 John Cangelosi	.20	.09	.03
☐ C4 Shawon Dunston	.30	.14	.04
☐ C5 Dave Cochrane	.20	.09	.03
☐ C6 Leon Durham	.20	.09	.03
☐ C7 Carlton Fisk	.50	.23	.06
☐ C8 Dennis Eckersley	.40	.18	.05
☐ C9 Ozzie Guillen	.20	.09	.03
☐ C10 Gary Matthews	.20	.09	.03
☐ C11 Ron Karkovice	.20	.09	.03
☐ C12 Keith Moreland	.20	.09	.03
☐ C13 Bobby Thigpen	.20	.09	.03
☐ C14 Ryne Sandberg	1.50	.70	.19
☐ C15 Greg Walker	.20	.09	.03
☐ C16 Lee Smith	.40	.18	.05
☐ D1 Darnell Coles	.20	.09	.03
☐ D2 Darrell Evans	.30	.14	.04
☐ D3 Kirk Gibson	.40	.18	.05
☐ D4 Willie Hernandez	.20	.09	.03
☐ D5 Larry Herndon	.20	.09	.03
☐ D6 Chet Lemon	.20	.09	.03
☐ D7 Dwight Lowry	.20	.09	.03
☐ D8 Jack Morris	.30	.14	.04
☐ D9 Dan Petry	.20	.09	.03
☐ D10 Frank Tanana	.20	.09	.03
☐ D11 Alan Trammell	.40	.18	.05
☐ D12 Lou Whitaker	.30	.14	.04
☐ E1 Gary Carter	.50	.23	.06
☐ E2 Don Baylor	.30	.14	.04
☐ E3 Rickey Henderson	.60	.25	.07
☐ E4 Lenny Dykstra	.30	.14	.04
☐ E5 Wade Boggs	.75	.35	.09
☐ E6 Mike Pagliarulo	.20	.09	.03
☐ E7 Dwight Gooden	.50	.23	.06
☐ E8 Roger Clemens	1.50	.70	.19
☐ E9 Dave Righetti	.20	.09	.03
☐ E10 Keith Hernandez	.30	.14	.04
☐ E11 Pat Dodson	.20	.09	.03
☐ E12 Don Mattingly	2.50	1.10	.30
☐ E13 Darryl Strawberry	.40	.18	.05
☐ E14 Jim Rice	.30	.14	.04
☐ E15 Dave Winfield	.60	.25	.07
☐ M1 Gary Carter	.50	.23	.06
☐ M2 Marty Barrett	.20	.09	.03
☐ M3 Jody Davis	.20	.09	.03
☐ M4 Don Aase	.20	.09	.03
☐ M5 Lenny Dykstra	.30	.14	.04
☐ M6 Wade Boggs	.75	.35	.09
☐ M7 Keith Moreland	.20	.09	.03
☐ M8 Mike Boddicker	.20	.09	.03
☐ M9 Dwight Gooden	.50	.23	.06
☐ M10 Roger Clemens	1.50	.70	.19
☐ M11 Ryne Sandberg	1.50	.70	.19
☐ M12 Eddie Murray	1.00	.45	.12
☐ M13 Keith Hernandez	.30	.14	.04
☐ M14 Jim Rice	.30	.14	.04
☐ M15 Lee Smith	.40	.18	.05
☐ M16 Cal Ripken	4.00	1.80	.50
☐ W1 Doug DeCinces	.20	.09	.03
☐ W2 Mariano Duncan	.20	.09	.03
☐ W3 Wally Joyner	.30	.14	.04
☐ W4 Pedro Guerrero	.20	.09	.03
☐ W5 Kirk McCaskill	.20	.09	.03
☐ W6 Orel Hershiser	.50	.23	.06
☐ W7 Gary Pettis	.20	.09	.03
☐ W8 Mike Marshall	.20	.09	.03
☐ W9 Dick Schofield	.20	.09	.03
☐ W10 Steve Sax	.20	.09	.03
☐ W11 Don Sutton	.50	.23	.06
☐ W12 Mike Scioscia	.20	.09	.03
☐ W13 Devon White	.30	.14	.04
☐ W14 Franklin Stubbs	.20	.09	.03
☐ W15 Mike Witt	.20	.09	.03
☐ W16 Fernando Valenzuela	.40	.18	.05

1991 Seven-Eleven 3-D Coins National

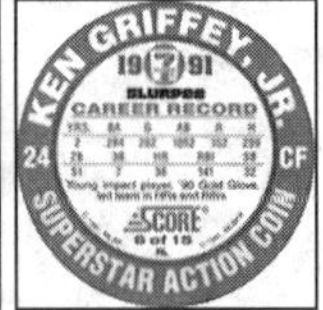

Measuring 1 3/4" in diameter, these 15 discs have 3-D color player photos on their fronts. Depending on how the disc is tilted, either a head shot or an action photo appears. The player's name, his number and position and the team name are printed in the red border around the photo. The backs carry the player's name, number, position, career record and the words "Superstar Action Coin" in yellow letters in the bottom part of the red border. The discs are numbered on the back as "X of 15."

	MINT	NRMT	EXC
COMPLETE SET (15)	8.00	3.60	1.00
COMMON COIN (1-15)	.20	.09	.03
□ 1 Wade Boggs	.60	.25	.07
□ 2 Barry Bonds	1.00	.45	.12
□ 3 Roger Clemens	.75	.35	.09
□ 4 Lenny Dykstra	.30	.14	.04
□ 5 Dwight Gooden	.30	.14	.04
□ 6 Ken Griffey Jr.	4.00	1.80	.50
□ 7 Rickey Henderson	.50	.23	.06
□ 8 Gregg Jefferies	.30	.14	.04
□ 9 Roberto Kelly	.20	.09	.03
□ 10 Kevin Maas	.20	.09	.03
□ 11 Don Mattingly	2.00	.90	.25
□ 12 Mickey Morandini	.20	.09	.03
□ 13 Dale Murphy	.40	.18	.05
□ 14 Darryl Strawberry	.30	.14	.04
□ 15 Frank Viola	.20	.09	.03

1991 Seven-Eleven Coins

This 120-coin set was produced by Score for 7-Eleven. The Superstar sport coins measure approximately 1 3/4" in diameter, and they were attached to the bottom of specially-marked Slurpee cups. The coins were reportedly available through May, or while supplies lasted. These "magic motion" coins have color player pictures on the fronts and different colored borders. The backs have career statistics and brief player profiles. A total of 81 players are featured in the eight regional subsets issued. The subsets are Atlantic (A), Florida (F), Midwest (MW), Northern California (NC), Metro Northeast (NE), Northwest (NW), Southern California (SC) and Texas (T). Ken Griffey Jr. is the only player issued in all eight subsets. The letter suffix before the number in the checklist denotes the region of issue.

	MINT	NRMT	EXC
COMPLETE SET (120)	75.00	34.00	9.50
COMMON COIN	.20	.09	.03
□ A1 Glenn Davis	.20	.09	.03
□ A2 Dwight Evans	.30	.14	.04
□ A3 Leo Gomez	.20	.09	.03
□ A4 Ken Griffey Jr.	4.00	1.80	.50
□ A5 Rickey Henderson	.50	.23	.06
□ A6 Jose Canseco	.50	.23	.06
□ A7 Dave Justice	.40	.18	.05
□ A8 Ben McDonald	.30	.14	.04
□ A9 Randy Milligan	.20	.09	.03
□ A10 Gregg Olson	.20	.09	.03
□ A11 Kirby Puckett	1.50	.70	.19
□ A12 Bill Ripken	.20	.09	.03
□ A13 Cal Ripken	3.00	1.35	.35
□ A14 Nolan Ryan	3.00	1.35	.35
□ A15 David Segui	.20	.09	.03
□ F1 Barry Bonds	1.00	.45	.12
□ F2 George Brett	1.50	.70	.19
□ F3 Roger Clemens	.75	.35	.09
□ F4 Glenn Davis	.20	.09	.03
□ F5 Alex Fernandez	.50	.23	.06
□ F6 Cecil Fielder	.40	.18	.05
□ F7 Ken Griffey Jr.	4.00	1.80	.50
□ F8 Dwight Gooden	.30	.14	.04
□ F9 Dave Justice	.40	.18	.05
□ F10 Barry Larkin	.40	.18	.05
□ F11 Ramon Martinez	.40	.18	.05
□ F12 Jose Offerman	.20	.09	.03
□ F13 Kirby Puckett	1.50	.70	.19
□ F14 Nolan Ryan	3.00	1.35	.35
□ F15 Terry Shumpert	.20	.09	.03
□ M1 George Brett	1.50	.70	.19
□ M2 Andre Dawson	.40	.18	.05
□ M3 Cecil Fielder	.40	.18	.05
□ M4 Carlton Fisk	.50	.23	.06
□ M5 Travis Fryman	.40	.18	.05
□ M6 Mark Grace	.50	.23	.06
□ M7 Ken Griffey Jr.	4.00	1.80	.50
□ M8 Ozzie Guillen	.20	.09	.03
□ M9 Alex Fernandez	.50	.23	.06
□ M10 Ray Lankford	.40	.18	.05
□ M11 Ryne Sandberg	1.50	.70	.19
□ M12 Ozzie Smith	1.00	.45	.12
□ M13 Bobby Thigpen	.20	.09	.03
□ M14 Frank Thomas	4.00	1.80	.50
□ M15 Alan Trammell	.30	.14	.04
□ NE4 Lenny Dykstra	.30	.14	.04
□ NW4 Ken Griffey Jr. Ken Griffey Sr.	1.00	.45	.12
□ T1 Craig Biggio	.40	.18	.05
□ T2 Barry Bonds	1.00	.45	.12
□ T3 Jose Canseco	.50	.23	.06
□ T4 Roger Clemens	.75	.35	.09
□ T5 Glenn Davis	.20	.09	.03
□ T6 Julio Franco	.30	.14	.04
□ T7 Juan Gonzalez	2.00	.90	.25
□ T8 Ken Griffey Jr.	4.00	1.80	.50
□ T9 Mike Scott	.20	.09	.03
□ T10 Rafael Palmeiro	.50	.23	.06
□ T11 Nolan Ryan	3.00	1.35	.35
□ T12 Ryne Sandberg	1.50	.70	.19
□ T13 Ruben Sierra	.20	.09	.03
□ T14 Todd Van Poppel	.20	.09	.03
□ T15 Bobby Witt	.20	.09	.03
□ NC1 John Burkett	.20	.09	.03
□ NC2 Jose Canseco	.50	.23	.06
□ NC3 Will Clark	.50	.23	.06
□ NC4 Steve Decker	.20	.09	.03
□ NC5 Dennis Eckersley	.30	.14	.04
□ NC6 Ken Griffey Jr.	4.00	1.80	.50
□ NC7 Rickey Henderson	.50	.23	.06
□ NC8 Nolan Ryan	3.00	1.35	.35
□ NC9 Mark McGwire	.75	.35	.09
□ NC10 Kevin Mitchell	.20	.09	.03
□ NC11 Terry Steinbach	.30	.14	.04
□ NC12 Dave Stewart	.30	.14	.04
□ NC13 Todd Van Poppel	.20	.09	.03
□ NC14 Bob Welch	.20	.09	.03
□ NC15 Matt Williams	1.00	.45	.12
□ NE1 Wade Boggs	.60	.25	.07
□ NE2 Barry Bonds	1.00	.45	.12
□ NE3 Roger Clemens	.75	.35	.09
□ NE5 Dwight Gooden	.30	.14	.04
□ NE6 Ken Griffey Jr.	4.00	1.80	.50
□ NE7 Rickey Henderson	.50	.23	.06
□ NE8 Gregg Jefferies	.30	.14	.04
□ NE9 Roberto Kelly	.20	.09	.03
□ NE10 Kevin Maas	.20	.09	.03
□ NE11 Don Mattingly	2.00	.90	.25
□ NE12 Mickey Morandini	.20	.09	.03
□ NE13 Dale Murphy	.40	.18	.05
□ NE14 Darryl Strawberry	.30	.14	.04
□ NE15 Frank Viola	.20	.09	.03
□ NW1 George Brett	1.50	.70	.19
□ NW2 Jose Canseco	.50	.23	.06
□ NW3 Alvin Davis	.20	.09	.03
□ NW5 Ken Griffey Jr.	4.00	1.80	.50
□ NW6 Erik Hanson	.20	.09	.03
□ NW7 Rickey Henderson	.50	.23	.06
□ NW8 Ryne Sandberg	1.50	.70	.19
□ NW9 Randy Johnson	.75	.35	.09
□ NW10 Dave Justice	.40	.18	.05
□ NW11 Edgar Martinez	.50	.23	.06
□ NW12 Tino Martinez	.40	.18	.05
□ NW13 Harold Reynolds	.30	.14	.04
□ NW14 Nolan Ryan	3.00	1.35	.35
□ NW15 Mike Schooler	.20	.09	.03
□ SC1 Jim Abbott	.30	.14	.04
□ SC2 Jose Canseco	.50	.23	.06
□ SC3 Ken Griffey Jr.	4.00	1.80	.50
□ SC4 Tony Gwynn	2.00	.90	.25
□ SC5 Orel Hershiser	.30	.14	.04
□ SC6 Eric Davis	.20	.09	.03
□ SC7 Wally Joyner	.30	.14	.04
□ SC8 Ramon Martinez	.40	.18	.05
□ SC9 Fred McGriff	.40	.18	.05
□ SC10 Eddie Murray	1.00	.45	.12
□ SC11 Jose Offerman	.20	.09	.03
□ SC12 Nolan Ryan	3.00	1.35	.35
□ SC13 Benito Santiago	.20	.09	.03
□ SC14 Darryl Strawberry	.30	.14	.04
□ SC15 Fernando Valenzuela	.30	.14	.04

1992 Seven-Eleven Coins

These 26 discs, "Superstar Action Coins," measure approximately 1 3/4" in diameter and feature "Magic Motion" plastic-coated photos that alternate between a posed head shot and an action shot as the disc is moved. The photos are encircled by a yellow line and bordered in red. The player's name, team, position and uniform number appear in white lettering within the red border around the photo. The back carries the player's name in yellow lettering within the black border around the statistics table in the central yellow portion.

	MINT	NRMT	EXC
COMPLETE SET (26)	12.50	5.50	1.55
COMMON COIN (1-26)	.20	.09	.03
□ 1 Dwight Gooden	.30	.14	.04
□ 2 Don Mattingly	1.50	.70	.19
□ 3 Roger Clemens	.75	.35	.09
□ 4 Ivan Calderon	.20	.09	.03
□ 5 Roberto Alomar	.75	.35	.09
□ 6 Sandy Alomar Jr.	.30	.14	.04
□ 7 Andy Van Slyke	.20	.09	.03
□ 8 Lenny Dykstra	.30	.14	.04
□ 9 Cal Ripken	3.00	1.35	.35
□ 10 Dave Justice	.40	.18	.05
□ 11 Nolan Ryan	3.00	1.35	.35
□ 12 Craig Biggio	.30	.14	.04
□ 13 Barry Larkin	.40	.18	.05
□ 14 Ozzie Smith	.75	.35	.09
□ 15 Ryne Sandberg	1.00	.45	.12
□ 16 Frank Thomas	3.00	1.35	.35
□ 17 Robin Yount	.40	.18	.05
□ 18 Kirby Puckett	1.25	.55	.16
□ 19 Cecil Fielder	.40	.18	.05
□ 20 Will Clark	.50	.23	.06
□ 21 Jose Canseco	.50	.23	.06
□ 22 Jim Abbott	.20	.09	.03
□ 23 Tony Gwynn	1.25	.55	.16
□ 24 Darryl Strawberry	.30	.14	.04
□ 25 George Brett	1.25	.55	.16
□ 26 Ken Griffey Jr.	3.00	1.35	.35

1975 Shakey's Pizza

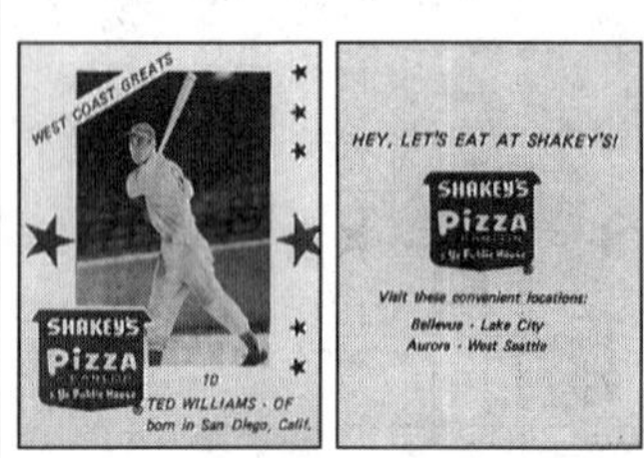

This 18-card set measures 2 3/4" by 3 1/2" and features black-and-white players photos on a white card face. The red Shakey's Pizza logo overlaps the lower left corner of the picture. The phrase "West Coast Greats" cuts diagonally across the upper left corner of the picture. The player's name is printed below the photo in red. Red and brown stars accent the margins. The backs carry a Shakey's Pizza advertisement encouraging consumers to visit Shakey's Pizza parlors in Bellevue, Lake City, Aurora and West Seattle. The DiMaggio back has an offer for $1.00 off on a family-size pizza. The cards are numbered on the front below the picture.

	NRMT	VG-E	GOOD
COMPLETE SET (18)	60.00	27.00	7.50
COMMON CARD (1-18)	3.00	1.35	.35
□ 1 Joe DiMaggio	15.00	6.75	1.85
□ 2 Paul Waner	4.00	1.80	.50
□ 3 Lefty Gomez	4.00	1.80	.50
□ 4 Earl Averill	4.00	1.80	.50
□ 5 Ernie Lombardi	4.00	1.80	.50
□ 6 Joe Cronin	4.00	1.80	.50
□ 7 George Burns	3.00	1.35	.35
□ 8 Casey Stengel	8.00	3.60	1.00
□ 9 Sam Crawford	4.00	1.80	.50
□ 10 Ted Williams	15.00	6.75	1.85
□ 11 Fred Hutchinson	3.00	1.35	.35
□ 12 Duke Snider	8.00	3.60	1.00
□ 13 Hal Chase	3.00	1.35	.35
□ 14 Bobby Doerr	4.00	1.80	.50
□ 15 Arky Vaughan	4.00	1.80	.50
□ 16 Tony Lazzeri	4.00	1.80	.50
□ 17 Lefty O'Doul	3.00	1.35	.35
□ 18 Stan Hack	3.00	1.35	.35

1976 Shakey's Pizza

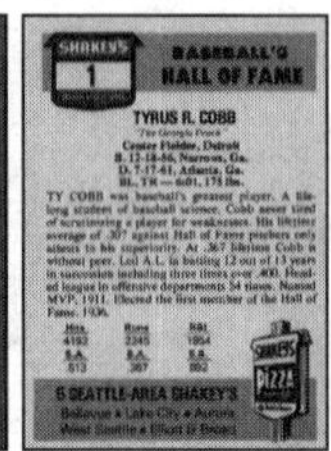

The 1976 Shakey's Pizza set contains 159 standard-size cards. The cards were part of a promotion at five Seattle-area Shakey's restaurants, and the "A" card could be exchanged for $1.00 off on any family-size pizza. The set is arranged according to year of induction into the Baseball Hall of Fame. The fronts feature vintage black and white player photos framed by red and white border stripes against a blue card face. The player's name appears in a baseball icon at the bottom of the picture. The backs have biography, career summary and player statistics.

	NRMT	VG-E	GOOD
COMPLETE SET (159)	50.00	22.00	6.25
COMMON CARD (1-158)	.10	.05	.01
□ 1 Ty Cobb	5.00	2.20	.60
□ 2 Babe Ruth	7.50	3.40	.95
□ 3 Walter Johnson	1.50	.70	.19
□ 4 Christy Mathewson	1.50	.70	.19
□ 5 Honus Wagner	2.00	.90	.25
□ 6 Nap Lajoie	1.50	.70	.19
□ 7 Tris Speaker	.75	.35	.09
□ 8 Cy Young	1.50	.70	.19
□ 9 Morgan G. Bulkeley	.10	.05	.01
□ 10 Ban Johnson PRES	.10	.05	.01
□ 11 John McGraw	1.00	.45	.12
□ 12 Connie Mack	1.00	.45	.12
□ 13 George Wright	.25	.11	.03
□ 14 Grover Cleveland Alexander	.75	.35	.09
□ 15 Alexander Cartwright	.10	.05	.01
□ 16 Henry Chadwick	.10	.05	.01
□ 17 Eddie Collins	.75	.35	.09
□ 18 Lou Gehrig	5.00	2.20	.60
□ 19 Willie Keeler	.25	.11	.03
□ 20 George Sisler	.75	.35	.09
□ 21 Cap Anson	.75	.35	.09
□ 22 Charles Comiskey	.25	.11	.03
□ 23 Candy Cummings	.25	.11	.03
□ 24 Buck Ewing	.25	.11	.03
□ 25 Old Hoss Radbourne	.25	.11	.03
□ 26 Al Spalding	.25	.11	.03
□ 27 Rogers Hornsby	1.00	.45	.12
□ 28 Kenesaw Landis COMM	.10	.05	.01
□ 29 Roger Bresnahan	.25	.11	.03
□ 30 Dan Brouthers	.25	.11	.03
□ 31 Fred Clarke	.25	.11	.03
□ 32 Jimmy Collins	.25	.11	.03
□ 33 Ed Delahanty	.25	.11	.03
□ 34 Hugh Duffy	.25	.11	.03
□ 35 Hugh Jennings	.25	.11	.03
□ 36 Mike(King) Kelly	.25	.11	.03
□ 37 Jim O'Rourke	.25	.11	.03
□ 38 Wilbert Robinson	.25	.11	.03
□ 39 Jesse Burkett	.25	.11	.03
□ 40 Frank Chance	.75	.35	.09
□ 41 Jack Chesbro	.25	.11	.03
□ 42 Johnny Evers	.75	.35	.09
□ 43 Clark Griffith	.25	.11	.03
□ 44 Tommy McCarthy	.25	.11	.03
□ 45 Joe McGinnity	.25	.11	.03
□ 46 Eddie Plank	.25	.11	.03
□ 47 Joe Tinker	.75	.35	.09
□ 48 Rube Waddell	.25	.11	.03
□ 49 Ed Walsh	.25	.11	.03
□ 50 Mickey Cochrane	.75	.35	.09
□ 51 Frankie Frisch	.25	.11	.03
□ 52 Lefty Grove	.75	.35	.09
□ 53 Carl Hubbell	.25	.11	.03
□ 54 Herb Pennock	.25	.11	.03
□ 55 Pie Traynor	.75	.35	.09
□ 56 Charley Gehringer	.25	.11	.03
□ 57 Mordecai Brown	.25	.11	.03
□ 58 Kid Nichols	.25	.11	.03
□ 59 Jimmie Foxx	1.00	.45	.12
□ 60 Mel Ott	.75	.35	.09
□ 61 Harry Heilmann	.25	.11	.03
□ 62 Paul Waner	.25	.11	.03
□ 63 Dizzy Dean	1.00	.45	.12
□ 64 Al Simmons	.25	.11	.03
□ 65 Ed Barrow	.10	.05	.01
□ 66 Chief Bender	.25	.11	.03
□ 67 Tommy Connolly	.10	.05	.01
□ 68 Bill Klem	.10	.05	.01
□ 69 Bobby Wallace	.25	.11	.03
□ 70 Harry Wright	.25	.11	.03
□ 71 Bill Dickey	.75	.35	.09
□ 72 Rabbit Maranville	.25	.11	.03
□ 73 Bill Terry	.25	.11	.03
□ 74 Joe DiMaggio	5.00	2.20	.60
□ 75 Gabby Hartnett	.25	.11	.03
□ 76 Ted Lyons	.25	.11	.03
□ 77 Dazzy Vance	.25	.11	.03
□ 78 Home Run Baker	.25	.11	.03
□ 79 Ray Schalk	.25	.11	.03
□ 80 Joe Cronin	.25	.11	.03
□ 81 Hank Greenberg	.75	.35	.09
□ 82 Sam Crawford	.25	.11	.03
□ 83 Joe McCarthy MG	.10	.05	.01
□ 84 Zack Wheat	.25	.11	.03
□ 85 Max Carey	.25	.11	.03
□ 86 Billy Hamilton	.25	.11	.03
□ 87 Bob Feller	1.00	.45	.12
□ 88 Jackie Robinson	5.00	2.20	.60
□ 89 Bill McKechnie	.10	.05	.01
□ 90 Edd Roush	.25	.11	.03
□ 91 John Clarkson	.25	.11	.03
□ 92 Elmer Flick	.25	.11	.03
□ 93 Sam Rice	.25	.11	.03
□ 94 Eppa Rixey	.25	.11	.03
□ 95 Luke Appling	.25	.11	.03
□ 96 Red Faber	.25	.11	.03
□ 97 Burleigh Grimes	.25	.11	.03
□ 98 Miller Huggins	.25	.11	.03
□ 99 Tim Keefe	.25	.11	.03
□ 100 Heinie Manush	.25	.11	.03
□ 101 Monte Ward	.25	.11	.03
□ 102 Pud Galvin	.25	.11	.03
□ 103 Ted Williams	5.00	2.20	.60
□ 104 Casey Stengel	1.00	.45	.12
□ 105 Red Ruffing	.25	.11	.03
□ 106 Branch Rickey	.10	.05	.01

Card	NRMT	VG-E	GOOD
☐ 107 Lloyd Waner	.25	.11	.03
☐ 108 Joe Medwick	.25	.11	.03
☐ 109 Kiki Cuyler	.25	.11	.03
☐ 110 Goose Goslin	.25	.11	.03
☐ 111 Roy Campanella	1.00	.45	.12
☐ 112 Stan Musial	2.00	.90	.25
☐ 113 Stan Coveleski	.25	.11	.03
☐ 114 Waite Hoyt	.25	.11	.03
☐ 115 Lou Boudreau	.25	.11	.03
☐ 116 Earle Combs	.25	.11	.03
☐ 117 Ford Frick COMM	.10	.05	.01
☐ 118 Jesse Haines	.25	.11	.03
☐ 119 Dave Bancroft	.25	.11	.03
☐ 120 Jake Beckley	.25	.11	.03
☐ 121 Chick Hafey	.25	.11	.03
☐ 122 Harry Hooper	.25	.11	.03
☐ 123 Joe Kelley	.25	.11	.03
☐ 124 Rube Marquard	.25	.11	.03
☐ 125 Satchel Paige	2.00	.90	.25
☐ 126 George Weiss GM	.10	.05	.01
☐ 127 Yogi Berra	1.00	.45	.12
☐ 128 Josh Gibson	2.00	.90	.25
☐ 129 Lefty Gomez	.25	.11	.03
☐ 130 Will Harridge PRES	.10	.05	.01
☐ 131 Sandy Koufax	1.00	.45	.12
☐ 132 Buck Leonard	.25	.11	.03
☐ 133 Early Wynn	.25	.11	.03
☐ 134 Ross Youngs	.25	.11	.03
☐ 135 Roberto Clemente	5.00	2.20	.60
☐ 136 Billy Evans	.10	.05	.01
☐ 137 Monte Irvin	.25	.11	.03
☐ 138 George Kelly	.25	.11	.03
☐ 139 Warren Spahn	.25	.11	.03
☐ 140 Mickey Welch	.10	.05	.01
☐ 141 Cool Papa Bell	.10	.05	.01
☐ 142 Jim Bottomley	.10	.05	.01
☐ 143 Jocko Conlan	.10	.05	.01
☐ 144 Whitey Ford	.10	.05	.01
☐ 145 Mickey Mantle	7.50	3.40	.95
☐ 146 Sam Thompson	.25	.11	.03
☐ 147 Earl Averill	.25	.11	.03
☐ 148 Bucky Harris	.25	.11	.03
☐ 149 Billy Herman	.25	.11	.03
☐ 150 Judy Johnson	.25	.11	.03
☐ 151 Ralph Kiner	.75	.35	.09
☐ 152 Oscar Charleston	.25	.11	.03
☐ 153 Roger Connor	.25	.11	.03
☐ 154 Cal Hubbard	.25	.11	.03
☐ 155 Bob Lemon	.25	.11	.03
☐ 156 Fred Lindstrom	.25	.11	.03
☐ 157 Robin Roberts	.75	.35	.09
☐ 158 Robin Roberts Same picture and text as previous card	.75	.35	.09
☐ A Earl Averill	.10	.05	.01

1977 Shakey's Pizza

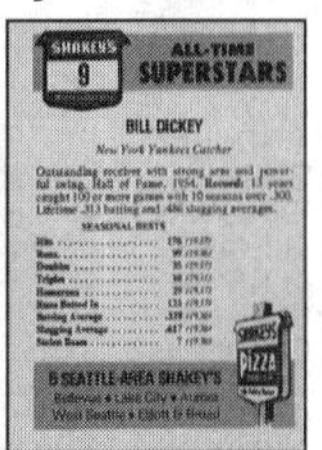

In this 28-card commemorative set, cards A-C were issued in honor of baseball's "1977 WASSCA Convention Superstars." Cards 1-25 honor "All-Time Superstars." They were available at five Seattle area Shakey's: Bellevue, Lake City, Aurora, West Seattle and at Elliott and Broad. The cards measure 2 1/4" by 3" and feature posed and action black-and-white player photos with faded maroon borders. A blue facsimile autograph runs across the bottom of each picture. The backs carry the player's name, career highlights and statistics in the form of "Seasonal Bests."

	NRMT	VG-E	GOOD
COMPLETE SET (28)	50.00	22.00	6.25
COMMON CARD (1-25)	1.00	.45	.12
☐ 1 Connie Mack	1.50	.70	.19
☐ 2 John McGraw	1.00	.45	.12
☐ 3 Cy Young	1.50	.70	.19
☐ 4 Walter Johnson	1.50	.70	.19
☐ 5 Grover C. Alexander	1.50	.70	.19
☐ 6 Christy Mathewson	1.50	.70	.19
☐ 7 Lefty Grove	1.50	.70	.19
☐ 8 Mickey Cochrane	1.00	.45	.12
☐ 9 Bill Dickey	1.00	.45	.12
☐ 10 Lou Gehrig	6.00	2.70	.75
☐ 11 George Sisler	1.00	.45	.12
☐ 12 Cap Anson	1.00	.45	.12
☐ 13 Jimmie Foxx	1.50	.70	.19
☐ 14 Rogers Hornsby	3.00	1.35	.35
☐ 15 Nap Lajoie	1.50	.70	.19
☐ 16 Eddie Collins	1.00	.45	.12
☐ 17 Pie Traynor	1.00	.45	.12
☐ 18 Honus Wagner	1.50	.70	.19
☐ 19 Ty Cobb	6.00	2.70	.75
☐ 20 Babe Ruth	7.50	3.40	.95
☐ 21 Joe Jackson	5.00	2.20	.60
☐ 22 Tris Speaker	1.00	.45	.12
☐ 23 Ted Williams	5.00	2.20	.60
☐ 24 Joe DiMaggio	5.00	2.20	.60
☐ 25 Stan Musial	3.00	1.35	.35
☐ A Earl Averill	.75	.35	.09
☐ B Johnny Mize	.75	.35	.09
☐ C Bob Johnson	.50	.23	.06

1975 Sheraton Great Plains Greats

This 26-card set was sponsored by Sheraton Hotels. The set was also issued as an uncut sheet, which included a card No. 25 (Lloyd Waner) that was never distributed because Waner did not sign a release form. Cards are 2 5/8" by 3 3/4". The front features a black and white player photo with colored border on a white card face. The player's name appears in a diamond at the bottom of the picture. The back has an advertisement for Sheraton.

	NRMT	VG-E	GOOD
COMPLETE SET (26)	20.00	9.00	2.50
COMMON CARD (1-25)	.25	.11	.03
☐ 1 Bob Feller	1.50	.70	.19
☐ 2 Carl Hubbell	1.50	.70	.19
☐ 3 Jocko Conlan	.50	.23	.06
☐ 4 Hal Trosky	.25	.11	.03
☐ 5 Allie Reynolds	.25	.11	.03
☐ 6 Burleigh Grimes	1.00	.45	.12
☐ 7 Jake Beckley	.50	.23	.06
☐ 8 Al Simmons	1.00	.45	.12
☐ 9 Paul Waner	1.00	.45	.12
☐ 10 Chief Bender	1.00	.45	.12
☐ 11 Fred Clarke	.50	.23	.06
☐ 12 Jim Bottomley	.50	.23	.06
☐ 13 Dave Bancroft	.50	.23	.06
☐ 14 Bing Miller	.25	.11	.03
☐ 15 Walter Johnson	2.50	1.10	.30
☐ 16 Grover Alexander	2.50	1.10	.30
☐ 17 Bob Johnson	.25	.11	.03
☐ 18 Roger Maris	2.50	1.10	.30
☐ 19 Ken Keltner	.25	.11	.03
☐ 20 Red Faber	.50	.23	.06
☐ 21 Cool Papa Bell	1.50	.70	.19
☐ 22 Yogi Berra	1.50	.70	.19
☐ 23 Fred Lindstrom	.50	.23	.06
☐ 24 Ray Schalk	.50	.23	.06
☐ 25 Lloyd Waner	.50	.23	.06
☐ xx Checklist	.25	.11	.03

1962 Shirriff Plastic Coins

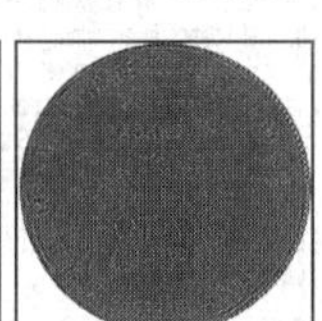

There are 221 different players in this 1962 set of plastic baseball coins marketed in Canada by Shirriff Potato Chips. The set is very similar to the American Salada coin set except for the printing on the reverse of the coin and the relative scarcitites of the coins in the set. Since the Shirriff coins were produced after the Salada coins, there are not the many gradations of scarcities and variations as in the Salada set. Each plastic coin measures approximately 1 3/8" in diameter. The "coin" itself is made of one-color plastic (light or dark) blue, black, orange, red or white) which has a color portrait printed on paper inserted into the obverse surface.

	NRMT	VG-E	GOOD
COMPLETE SET (221)	1600.00	700.00	200.00
COMMON COIN (1-221)	4.00	1.80	.50
☐ 1 Jim Gentile	5.00	2.20	.60
☐ 2 Billy Pierce	5.00	2.20	.60
☐ 3 Chico Fernandez	4.00	1.80	.50
☐ 4 Tom Brewer	4.00	1.80	.50
☐ 5 Woody Held	5.00	2.20	.60
☐ 6 Ray Herbert	4.00	1.80	.50
☐ 7 Ken Aspromonte	5.00	2.20	.60
☐ 8 Whitey Ford	25.00	11.00	3.10
☐ 9 Jim Lemon	5.00	2.20	.60
☐ 10 Billy Klaus	4.00	1.80	.50
☐ 11 Steve Barber	5.00	2.20	.60
☐ 12 Nellie Fox	15.00	6.75	1.85
☐ 13 Jim Bunning	15.00	6.75	1.85
☐ 14 Frank Malzone	5.00	2.20	.60
☐ 15 Tito Francona	4.00	1.80	.50
☐ 16 Bobby Del Greco	4.00	1.80	.50
☐ 17 Steve Bilko	4.00	1.80	.50
☐ 18 Tony Kubek	8.00	3.60	1.00
☐ 19 Earl Battey	4.00	1.80	.50
☐ 20 Chuck Cottier	4.00	1.80	.50
☐ 21 Willie Tasby	4.00	1.80	.50
☐ 22 Bob Allison	5.00	2.20	.60
☐ 23 Roger Maris	35.00	16.00	4.40
☐ 24 Earl Averill	4.00	1.80	.50
☐ 25 Jerry Lumpe	4.00	1.80	.50
☐ 26 Jim Grant	4.00	1.80	.50
☐ 27 Carl Yastrzemski	30.00	13.50	3.70
☐ 28 Rocky Colavito	10.00	4.50	1.25
☐ 29 Al Smith	4.00	1.80	.50
☐ 30 Jim Busby	5.00	2.20	.60
☐ 31 Dick Howser	5.00	2.20	.60
☐ 32 Jim Perry	5.00	2.20	.60
☐ 33 Yogi Berra	30.00	13.50	3.70
☐ 34 Ken Hamlin	4.00	1.80	.50
☐ 35 Dale Long	4.00	1.80	.50
☐ 36 Harmon Killebrew	20.00	9.00	2.50
☐ 37 Dick Brown	4.00	1.80	.50
☐ 38 Gary Geiger	5.00	2.20	.60
☐ 39 Minnie Minoso	8.00	3.60	1.00
☐ 40 Brooks Robinson	25.00	11.00	3.10
☐ 41 Mickey Mantle	150.00	70.00	19.00
☐ 42 Bennie Daniels	4.00	1.80	.50
☐ 43 Billy Martin	8.00	3.60	1.00
☐ 44 Vic Power	4.00	1.80	.50
☐ 45 Joe Pignatano	4.00	1.80	.50
☐ 46 Ryne Duren	5.00	2.20	.60
☐ 47 Pete Runnels	5.00	2.20	.60
☐ 48 Dick Williams	5.00	2.20	.60
☐ 49 Jim Landis	4.00	1.80	.50
☐ 50 Steve Boros	4.00	1.80	.50
☐ 51 Zoilo Versalles	5.00	2.20	.60
☐ 52 Johnny Temple	5.00	2.20	.60
☐ 53 Jackie Brandt	5.00	2.20	.60
☐ 54 Joe McClain	4.00	1.80	.50
☐ 55 Sherman Lollar	4.00	1.80	.50
☐ 56 Gene Stephens	4.00	1.80	.50
☐ 57 Leon Wagner	4.00	1.80	.50
☐ 58 Frank Lary	5.00	2.20	.60
☐ 59 Bill Skowron	6.00	2.70	.75
☐ 60 Vic Wertz	5.00	2.20	.60
☐ 61 Willie Kirkland	4.00	1.80	.50
☐ 62 Leo Posada	4.00	1.80	.50
☐ 63 Albie Pearson	4.00	1.80	.50
☐ 64 Bobby Richardson	8.00	3.60	1.00
☐ 65 Marv Breeding	4.00	1.80	.50
☐ 66 Roy Sievers	5.00	2.20	.60
☐ 67 Al Kaline	30.00	13.50	3.70
☐ 68 Don Buddin	4.00	1.80	.50
☐ 69 Lenny Green	4.00	1.80	.50
☐ 70 Gene Green	5.00	2.20	.60
☐ 71 Luis Aparicio	15.00	6.75	1.85
☐ 72 Norm Cash	8.00	3.60	1.00
☐ 73 Jackie Jensen	6.00	2.70	.75
☐ 74 Bubba Phillips	4.00	1.80	.50
☐ 75 James Archer	4.00	1.80	.50
☐ 76 Ken Hunt	4.00	1.80	.50
☐ 77 Ralph Terry	5.00	2.20	.60
☐ 78 Camilo Pascual	5.00	2.20	.60
☐ 79 Marty Keough	5.00	2.20	.60
☐ 80 Clete Boyer	5.00	2.20	.60
☐ 81 Jim Pagliaroni	4.00	1.80	.50
☐ 82 Gene Leek	4.00	1.80	.50
☐ 83 Jake Wood	4.00	1.80	.50
☐ 84 Coot Veal	4.00	1.80	.50
☐ 85 Norm Siebern	4.00	1.80	.50
☐ 86 Andy Carey	5.00	2.20	.60
☐ 87 Bill Tuttle	5.00	2.20	.60
☐ 88 Jimmy Piersall	6.00	2.70	.75
☐ 89 Ron Hansen	5.00	2.20	.60
☐ 90 Chuck Stobbs	4.00	1.80	.50
☐ 91 Ken McBride	4.00	1.80	.50
☐ 92 Bill Bruton	4.00	1.80	.50
☐ 93 Gus Triandos	5.00	2.20	.60
☐ 94 John Romano	4.00	1.80	.50
☐ 95 Elston Howard	8.00	3.60	1.00
☐ 96 Gene Woodling	5.00	2.20	.60
☐ 97 Early Wynn	15.00	6.75	1.85
☐ 98 Milt Pappas	5.00	2.20	.60
☐ 99 Bill Monbouquette	4.00	1.80	.50
☐ 100 Wayne Causey	4.00	1.80	.50
☐ 101 Don Elston	4.00	1.80	.50
☐ 102 Charlie Neal	4.00	1.80	.50
☐ 103 Don Blasingame	4.00	1.80	.50
☐ 104 Frank Thomas	5.00	2.20	.60
☐ 105 Wes Covington	4.00	1.80	.50
☐ 106 Chuck Hiller	4.00	1.80	.50
☐ 107 Don Hoak	5.00	2.20	.60
☐ 108 Bob Lillis	4.00	1.80	.50
☐ 109 Sandy Koufax	35.00	16.00	4.40
☐ 110 Gordy Coleman	4.00	1.80	.50
☐ 111 Eddie Mathews UER (Misspelled Matthews)	25.00	11.00	3.10
☐ 112 Art Mahaffey	4.00	1.80	.50
☐ 113 Ed Bailey	4.00	1.80	.50
☐ 114 Smokey Burgess	5.00	2.20	.60
☐ 115 Bill White	6.00	2.70	.75
☐ 116 Ed Bouchee	5.00	2.20	.60
☐ 117 Bob Buhl	4.00	1.80	.50
☐ 118 Vada Pinson	6.00	2.70	.75
☐ 119 Carl Sawatski	4.00	1.80	.50
☐ 120 Dick Stuart	5.00	2.20	.60
☐ 121 Harvey Kuenn	6.00	2.70	.75
☐ 122 Pancho Herrera	4.00	1.80	.50
☐ 123 Don Zimmer	5.00	2.20	.60
☐ 124 Wally Moon	5.00	2.20	.60
☐ 125 Joe Adcock	5.00	2.20	.60
☐ 126 Joey Jay	4.00	1.80	.50
☐ 127 Maury Wills	8.00	3.60	1.00
☐ 128 George Altman	4.00	1.80	.50
☐ 129 John Buzhardt	5.00	2.20	.60
☐ 130 Felipe Alou	6.00	2.70	.75
☐ 131 Bill Mazeroski	8.00	3.60	1.00
☐ 132 Ernie Broglio	5.00	2.20	.60
☐ 133 John Roseboro	5.00	2.20	.60
☐ 134 Mike McCormick	4.00	1.80	.50
☐ 135 Charlie Smith	4.00	1.80	.50
☐ 136 Ron Santo	8.00	3.60	1.00
☐ 137 Gene Freese	4.00	1.80	.50
☐ 138 Dick Groat	6.00	2.70	.75
☐ 139 Curt Flood	6.00	2.70	.75
☐ 140 Frank Bolling	4.00	1.80	.50
☐ 141 Clay Dalrymple	4.00	1.80	.50
☐ 142 Willie McCovey	25.00	11.00	3.10
☐ 143 Bob Skinner	4.00	1.80	.50
☐ 144 Lindy McDaniel	4.00	1.80	.50
☐ 145 Glen Hobbie	4.00	1.80	.50
☐ 146 Gil Hodges	15.00	6.75	1.85
☐ 147 Eddie Kasko	4.00	1.80	.50
☐ 148 Gino Cimoli	5.00	2.20	.60
☐ 149 Willie Mays	50.00	22.00	6.25
☐ 150 Roberto Clemente	75.00	34.00	9.50
☐ 151 Red Schoendienst	15.00	6.75	1.85
☐ 152 Joe Torre	10.00	4.50	1.25
☐ 153 Bob Purkey	4.00	1.80	.50
☐ 154 Tommy Davis	6.00	2.70	.75
☐ 155 Andre Rodgers	4.00	1.80	.50
☐ 156 Tony Taylor	5.00	2.20	.60
☐ 157 Bob Friend	5.00	2.20	.60
☐ 158 Gus Bell	5.00	2.20	.60
☐ 159 Roy McMillan	4.00	1.80	.50
☐ 160 Carl Warwick	4.00	1.80	.50
☐ 161 Willie Davis	5.00	2.20	.60
☐ 162 Sam Jones	5.00	2.20	.60
☐ 163 Ruben Amaro	5.00	2.20	.60
☐ 164 Sammy Taylor	4.00	1.80	.50
☐ 165 Frank Robinson	25.00	11.00	3.10
☐ 166 Lew Burdette	5.00	2.20	.60
☐ 167 Ken Boyer	8.00	3.60	1.00
☐ 168 Bill Virdon	5.00	2.20	.60
☐ 169 Jim Davenport	4.00	1.80	.50
☐ 170 Don Demeter	4.00	1.80	.50
☐ 171 Richie Ashburn	15.00	6.75	1.85
☐ 172 Johnny Podres	5.00	2.20	.60
☐ 173 Joe Cunningham	5.00	2.20	.60
☐ 174 Elroy Face	5.00	2.20	.60
☐ 175 Orlando Cepeda	10.00	4.50	1.25
☐ 176 Bobby Gene Smith	4.00	1.80	.50
☐ 177 Ernie Banks	30.00	13.50	3.70
☐ 178 Daryl Spencer	4.00	1.80	.50
☐ 179 Bob Schmidt	5.00	2.20	.60
☐ 180 Hank Aaron	50.00	22.00	6.25
☐ 181 Hobie Landrith	4.00	1.80	.50
☐ 182 Ed Bressoud	5.00	2.20	.60
☐ 183 Felix Mantilla	4.00	1.80	.50
☐ 184 Dick Farrell	4.00	1.80	.50
☐ 185 Bob Miller	4.00	1.80	.50
☐ 186 Don Taussig	4.00	1.80	.50
☐ 187 Pumpsie Green	4.00	1.80	.50
☐ 188 Bobby Shantz	5.00	2.20	.60
☐ 189 Roger Craig	10.00	4.50	1.25
☐ 190 Hal Smith	4.00	1.80	.50
☐ 191 Johnny Edwards	4.00	1.80	.50
☐ 192 John DeMerit	4.00	1.80	.50
☐ 193 Joe Amalfitano	4.00	1.80	.50
☐ 194 Norm Larker	4.00	1.80	.50
☐ 195 Al Heist	4.00	1.80	.50
☐ 196 Al Spangler	4.00	1.80	.50
☐ 197 Alex Grammas	4.00	1.80	.50
☐ 198 Jerry Lynch	4.00	1.80	.50
☐ 199 Jim McKnight	4.00	1.80	.50
☐ 200 Jose Pagan UER (Misspelled Pagen)	4.00	1.80	.50
☐ 201 Jim Gilliam	8.00	3.60	1.00
☐ 202 Art Ditmar	4.00	1.80	.50
☐ 203 Bud Daley	4.00	1.80	.50
☐ 204 Johnny Callison	5.00	2.20	.60
☐ 205 Stu Miller	4.00	1.80	.50
☐ 206 Russ Snyder	4.00	1.80	.50
☐ 207 Billy Williams	20.00	9.00	2.50
☐ 208 Walt Bond	4.00	1.80	.50
☐ 209 Joe Koppe	4.00	1.80	.50
☐ 210 Don Schwall	5.00	2.20	.60
☐ 211 Billy Gardner	5.00	2.20	.60
☐ 212 Chuck Estrada	4.00	1.80	.50
☐ 213 Gary Bell	4.00	1.80	.50
☐ 214 Floyd Robinson	4.00	1.80	.50
☐ 215 Duke Snider	35.00	16.00	4.40
☐ 216 Lee Maye	4.00	1.80	.50
☐ 217 Howie Bedell	4.00	1.80	.50
☐ 218 Bob Will	4.00	1.80	.50
☐ 219 Dallas Green	5.00	2.20	.60
☐ 220 Carroll Hardy	4.00	1.80	.50
☐ 221 Danny O'Connell	4.00	1.80	.50

1991 SilverStar Holograms

These hologram cards measure the standard size and were issued to commemorate outstanding achievements of the players. The backs of the hologram cards are brightly colored and have statistics as well as a player profile. Each card also comes with a 2 1/16" by 5 3/8" blank-backed ticket. The tickets have a color player photo, serial number, and a description of the achievement honored. The Henderson hologram honors him as the all-time stolen base leader; the Ryan hologram celebrates his 7th no-hitter; and the Justice hologram commemorates his two-run homer against the Reds on October 1 that led to a 7-6 Braves' victory during the NL West pennant race. The

cards are unnumbered and checklisted below chronologically by release dates. Cards numbered 5 though 8 were released later and are unnumbered. These cards are sequenced in alphabetical order.

	MINT	NRMT	EXC
COMPLETE SET (8)	12.00	5.50	1.50
COMMON CARD (1-8)	.50	.23	.06
☐ 1 Rickey Henderson On May 1, 1991 Rickey broke Lou Brock's all-time Ô	2.00	.90	.25
☐ 2 Nolan Ryan The Express walked off May 1, 1991 with his 7th no-hitter	3.00	1.35	.35
☐ 3 Dave Justice On October 1, 1991 Justice crushed a two-run homer Ô	1.00	.45	.12
☐ 4 Cal Ripken September, 1991 Cal went on a rampage and was named AL POM Ô	3.00	1.35	.35
☐ 5 Will Clark	2.00	.90	.25
☐ 6 Roger Clemens	2.00	.90	.25
☐ 7 Rawlings Gold Glove	.50	.23	.06
☐ 8 Darryl Strawberry	1.50	.70	.19

1991 Simon and Schuster More Little Big Leaguers

This 96-page album was published by Simon and Schuster and includes boyhood stories of today's pro baseball players. Moreover, five 8 1/2" by 11" sheets of cards (9 cards per sheet) are inserted at the end of the album; after perforation, the cards measure the standard size. The fronts feature black and white photos of these players as kids. The pictures are bordered in green on a white card face. The backs have the same design, only with biography and career summary in place of the picture. The cards are unnumbered and checklisted below in alphabetical order.

	MINT	NRMT	EXC
COMPLETE SET (45)	8.00	3.60	1.00
COMMON CARD (1-45)	.10	.05	.01
☐ 1 Jim Abbott	.10	.05	.01
☐ 2 Jesse Barfield	.10	.05	.01
☐ 3 Kevin Bass	.10	.05	.01
☐ 4 Craig Biggio	.35	.16	.04
☐ 5 Phil Bradley	.10	.05	.01
☐ 6 Jeff Brantley	.10	.05	.01
☐ 7 Tom Brunansky	.10	.05	.01
☐ 8 Ken Caminiti	.35	.16	.04
☐ 9 Will Clark	.50	.23	.06
☐ 10 Vince Coleman	.10	.05	.01
☐ 11 David Cone	.25	.11	.03
☐ 12 Alvin Davis	.10	.05	.01
☐ 13 Andre Dawson	.35	.16	.04
☐ 14 Bill Doran	.10	.05	.01
☐ 15 Nick Esasky	.10	.05	.01
☐ 16 Dwight Gooden	.25	.11	.03
☐ 17 Tom Gordon	.10	.05	.01
☐ 18 Ken Griffey Jr.	2.00	.90	.25
☐ 19 Kevin Gross	.10	.05	.01
☐ 20 Kelly Gruber	.10	.05	.01
☐ 21 Lee Guetterman	.10	.05	.01
☐ 22 Terry Kennedy	.10	.05	.01
☐ 23 John Kruk	.25	.11	.03
☐ 24 Bill Landrum	.10	.05	.01
☐ 25 Mark Langston	.10	.05	.01
☐ 26 Barry Larkin	.50	.23	.06
☐ 27 Dave Magadan	.10	.05	.01
☐ 28 Don Mattingly	1.00	.45	.12
☐ 29 Mark McGwire	.60	.25	.07
☐ 30 Kevin Mitchell	.10	.05	.01
☐ 31 Bob Ojeda	.10	.05	.01
☐ 32 Gregg Olson	.10	.05	.01
☐ 33 Terry Pendleton	.10	.05	.01
☐ 34 Ted Power	.10	.05	.01
☐ 35 Kirby Puckett	1.00	.45	.12
☐ 36 Terry Puhl	.10	.05	.01
☐ 37 Bret Saberhagen	.10	.05	.01
☐ 38 Chris Sabo	.10	.05	.01
☐ 39 Kevin Seitzer	.10	.05	.01
☐ 40 Don Slaught	.10	.05	.01
☐ 41 Lonnie Smith	.10	.05	.01
☐ 42 Darryl Strawberry	.25	.11	.03
☐ 43 Mickey Tettleton	.10	.05	.01
☐ 44 Bobby Thigpen	.10	.05	.01
☐ 45 Frank White	.10	.05	.01

1995 Skin Bracer

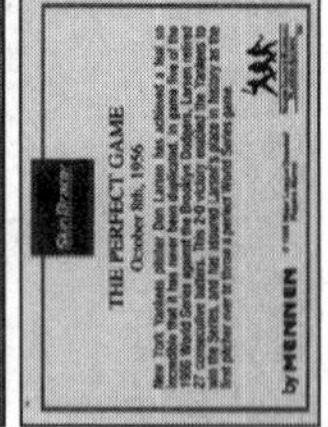

Sponsored by Colgate-Palmolive Co., this 3-card standard-size set was included in specially marked Skin Bracer toiletries bags and 5-ounce Skin Bracer gift cartons. Also autographed 8" by 10" photos commemorating the same players and events were available for $7.99 with a proof-of-purchase from Skin Bracer, Afta skin conditioner or Colgate shave cream. The autographed photo offer was available via in-store tear pads and on-pack. The horizontal fronts feature sepia-tone action photos accented with thin gold border stripes. The player's name appears on a short green bar. The backs carry a description of the significant event portrayed on each card front. The cards are unnumbered and checklisted below in alphabetical order.

	MINT	NRMT	EXC
COMPLETE SET (3)	15.00	6.75	1.85
COMMON CARD (1-3)	5.00	2.20	.60
☐ 1 Don Larsen WS Perfect Game	5.00	2.20	.60
☐ 2 Bill Mazeroski WS-ending Home Run	5.00	2.20	.60
☐ 3 Bobby Thomson Shot Heard 'Round the World	5.00	2.20	.60

1987 Smokey American League

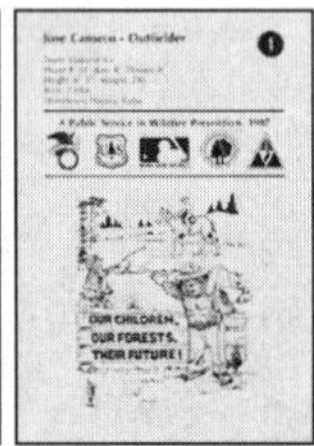

The U.S. Forestry Service (in conjunction with Major League Baseball) produced this large, attractive 14-player card set to commemorate the 43rd birthday of Smokey. The cards feature Smokey the Bear pictured on every card with the player. The card backs give a fire safety tip. The cards measure approximately 4" by 6" and are subtitled "National Smokey Bear Day 1987" on the front. The cards were printed on an uncut (but perforated) sheet that measured 18" by 24".

	MINT	NRMT	EXC
COMPLETE SET (16)	8.00	3.60	1.00
COMMON CARD (1-16)	.25	.11	.03
☐ 1 Jose Canseco	2.00	.90	.25
☐ 2 Dennis Oil Can Boyd	.25	.11	.03
☐ 3 John Candelaria	.25	.11	.03
☐ 4 Harold Baines	.50	.23	.06
☐ 5 Joe Carter	1.00	.45	.12
☐ 6 Jack Morris	.50	.23	.06
☐ 7 Buddy Biancalana	.25	.11	.03
☐ 8 Kirby Puckett	4.00	1.80	.50
☐ 9 Mike Pagliarulo	.25	.11	.03
☐ 10 Larry Sheets	.25	.11	.03
☐ 11 Mike Moore	.25	.11	.03
☐ 12 Charlie Hough	.25	.11	.03
☐ 13 National Smokey Bear Day 1987	.25	.11	.03
☐ 14 Tom Henke	.50	.23	.06
☐ 15 Jim Gantner	.25	.11	.03
☐ 16 American League Smokey Bear Day 1987	.25	.11	.03

1987 Smokey National League

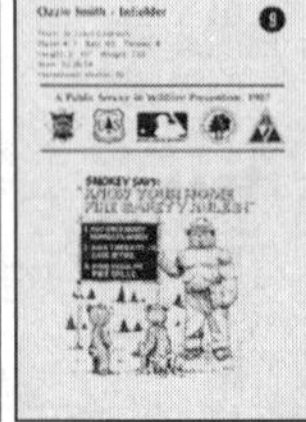

The U.S. Forestry Service (in conjunction with Major League Baseball) produced this large, attractive 14 player card set to commemorate the 43rd birthday of Smokey. The cards feature Smokey the Bear pictured on every card with the player. The card backs give a fire safety tip. The cards measure approximately 4" by 6" and are subtitled "National Smokey Bear Day 1987" on the front. The set price below does not include the more difficult variation cards.

	MINT	NRMT	EXC
COMPLETE SET (15)	7.00	3.10	.85
COMMON CARD (1-15)	.25	.11	.03
☐ 1 Steve Sax	.25	.11	.03
☐ 2A Dale Murphy Holding bat	3.00	1.35	.35
☐ 2B Dale Murphy No bat arm around Smokey	12.50	5.50	1.55
☐ 3A Jody Davis Kneeling with Smokey	.50	.23	.06
☐ 3B Jody Davis Standing, shaking Smokey's hand	7.50	3.40	.95
☐ 4 Bill Gullickson	.25	.11	.03
☐ 5 Mike Scott	.25	.11	.03
☐ 6 Roger McDowell	.25	.11	.03
☐ 7 Steve Bedrosian	.25	.11	.03
☐ 8 Johnny Ray	.25	.11	.03
☐ 9 Ozzie Smith	2.50	1.10	.30
☐ 10 Steve Garvey	.50	.23	.06
☐ 11 National Smokey Bear Day	.25	.11	.03
☐ 12 Mike Krukow	.25	.11	.03
☐ 13 Smokey the Bear	.25	.11	.03
☐ 14 Mike Fitzgerald	.25	.11	.03
☐ 15 National League Logo	.25	.11	.03

1994 Snapple Dean Chance

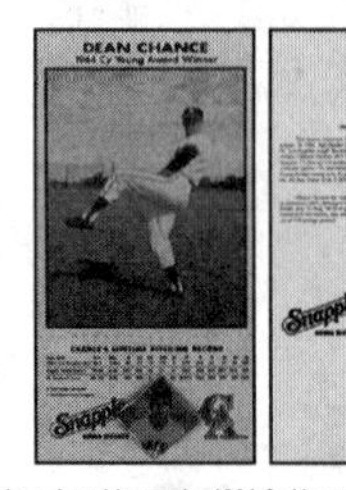

This pin and card honor the 1964 Cy Young Award-Winning pitching ace Dean Chance. The diamond-shaped pin measures about one inch from corner to corner and features a posed color photo of Chance. The card is 2 1/2" by 5 1/8" and features on its white-bordered front a photo of Chance in his windup. His lifetime pitching record appears below the photo in an area set off by a perforated line. The Snapple and California Angels logo rest at the bottom. The plain white back carries career highlights and the Snapple and Angels logos.

	MINT	NRMT	EXC
COMPLETE SET	2.00	.90	.25
COMMON CARD	2.00	.90	.25
☐ 1 Dean Chance	2.00	.90	.25

1989 Socko Hershiser

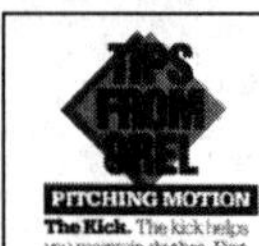

The 1989 Socko Orel Hershiser set contains seven unnumbered standard-size cards. The fronts are blue, green and yellow, and feature full color photos of Hershiser with the Dodger logos airbrushed out. The backs are white and include "Tips from Orel." The cards were distributed as a promotional set through Socko beverages.

	MINT	NRMT	EXC
COMPLETE SET (7)	6.00	2.70	.75
COMMON CARD (1-7)	1.00	.45	.12
☐ 1 Orel Hershiser The Kick	2.00	.90	.25
☐ 2 Orel Hershiser The Follow-Through	2.00	.90	.25
☐ 3 Orel Hershiser The Release	2.00	.90	.25
☐ 4 Orel Hershiser Backing Up The Catcher	2.00	.90	.25
☐ 5 Orel Hershiser Barehanding the Ball	2.00	.90	.25
☐ 6 Orel Hershiser The Grip	2.00	.90	.25
☐ 7 Orel Hershiser Pitching from the Stretch	2.00	.90	.25

1995 Sonic/Pepsi Greats

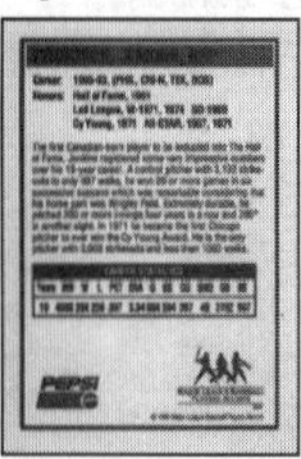

This 12-card standard-size set was released at Sonic restaurants which served Pepsi products. Some players apparently signed cards for this set. The cards were issued in three-card cello packs. The fronts display color player photos inside red borders. Team logos have been airbrushed off hats and jerseys. In blue print on a white background, the backs present career summary, honors received, player profile, and career statistics. The cards are unnumbered and checklisted below in alphabetical order.

	MINT	NRMT	EXC
COMPLETE SET (12)	7.00	3.10	.85
COMMON CARD (1-12)	.50	.23	.06
☐ 1 Bert Campaneris	.50	.23	.06
☐ 2 George Foster	.50	.23	.06
☐ 3 Steve Garvey	.75	.35	.09
☐ 4 Ferguson Jenkins	1.00	.45	.12
☐ 5 Tommy John	.50	.23	.06
☐ 6 Harmon Killebrew	1.00	.45	.12
☐ 7 Sparky Lyle	.50	.23	.06
☐ 8 Fred Lynn	.50	.23	.06
☐ 9 Joe Morgan	1.00	.45	.12
☐ 10 Graig Nettles	.50	.23	.06
☐ 11 Warren Spahn	1.00	.45	.12
☐ 12 Maury Wills	.75	.35	.09

1905 Souvenir Postcard Shop of Cleveland PC785

These distinguished looking black and white cards measures 3 1/4" by 5 1/2" and is similar to PC 782 in appearance and it was also issued in 1905. The Souvenir Postcard Shop of Cleveland identification appears on the front of the card. The backs are devoid of company identification.

	EX-MT	VG-E	GOOD
COMPLETE SET	3000.00	1350.00	375.00
COMMON CARD	150.00	70.00	19.00
☐ 1 Harry Bay	150.00	70.00	19.00
☐ 2 Harry Bemis	150.00	70.00	19.00
☐ 3 Bill Bernhard	150.00	70.00	19.00
☐ 4 Bill Bradley	150.00	70.00	19.00
☐ 5 Fred Buelow	150.00	70.00	19.00
☐ 6 Chuck Carr	150.00	70.00	19.00
☐ 7 Frank Donahue	150.00	70.00	19.00
☐ 8 Elmer Flick	250.00	110.00	31.00
☐ 9 Otto Hess	150.00	70.00	19.00
☐ 10 Jay Jackson	150.00	70.00	19.00
☐ 11 Addie Joss	300.00	135.00	38.00
☐ 12 Nick Kahl	150.00	70.00	19.00
☐ 13 Nap Lajoie	750.00	350.00	95.00
☐ 14 Earl Moore	150.00	70.00	19.00
☐ 15 Robert Rhoads	150.00	70.00	19.00
☐ 16 George Stovall	200.00	90.00	25.00
☐ 17 Terry Turner	200.00	90.00	25.00
☐ 18 Ernest Vinson	150.00	70.00	19.00

1993 SP

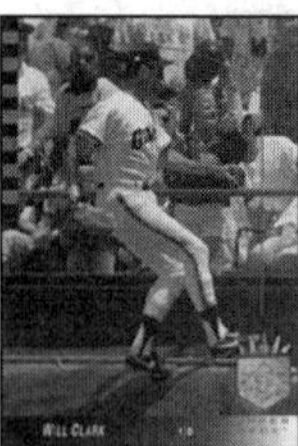

This 290-card standard-size set features fronts with action color player photos. The player's name and position appear within a team-colored stripe at the bottom edge that shades from dark to light, left to right. A team color-checkered stripe is in the upper left and the team name in a gold-lettered arc appears at the top with a gold underline that extends down the right side. The copper foil-stamped SP logo appears at the bottom right. The back displays an action shot of the player in the top half with a team color-checkered stripe in the upper right. The bottom half carries the player's biography, statistics, and career highlights. Special subsets include All Star players (1-18) and Foil Prospects (271-290). Cards 19-270 are in alphabetical order by team nickname. Notable Rookie Cards include Johnny Damon and Derek Jeter.

	MINT	NRMT	EXC
COMPLETE SET (290)	75.00	34.00	9.50
COMMON CARD (1-270)	.15	.07	.02
FOIL PROSPECTS (271-290)	.50	.23	.06

□ 1 Roberto Alomar AS	1.50	.70	.19
□ 2 Wade Boggs AS	1.00	.45	.12
□ 3 Joe Carter AS	.50	.23	.06
□ 4 Ken Griffey Jr. AS	8.00	3.60	1.00
□ 5 Mark Langston AS	.50	.23	.06
□ 6 John Olerud AS	.15	.07	.02
□ 7 Kirby Puckett AS	3.00	1.35	.35
□ 8 Cal Ripken Jr. AS	6.00	2.70	.75
□ 9 Ivan Rodriguez AS	2.00	.90	.25
□ 10 Barry Bonds AS	2.00	.90	.25
□ 11 Darren Daulton AS	.50	.23	.06
□ 12 Marquis Grissom AS	.50	.23	.06
□ 13 David Justice AS	1.00	.45	.12
□ 14 John Kruk AS	.50	.23	.06
□ 15 Barry Larkin AS	1.00	.45	.12
□ 16 Terry Mulholland AS	.15	.07	.02
□ 17 Ryne Sandberg AS	2.00	.90	.25
□ 18 Gary Sheffield AS	1.00	.45	.12
□ 19 Chad Curtis	.50	.23	.06
□ 20 Chili Davis	.50	.23	.06
□ 21 Gary DiSarcina	.15	.07	.02
□ 22 Damion Easley	.15	.07	.02
□ 23 Chuck Finley	.15	.07	.02
□ 24 Luis Polonia	.15	.07	.02
□ 25 Tim Salmon	2.00	.90	.25
□ 26 J.T. Snow	1.00	.45	.12
□ 27 Russ Springer	.15	.07	.02
□ 28 Jeff Bagwell	3.00	1.35	.35
□ 29 Craig Biggio	.50	.23	.06
□ 30 Ken Caminiti	1.00	.45	.12
□ 31 Andujar Cedeno	.15	.07	.02
□ 32 Doug Drabek	.15	.07	.02
□ 33 Steve Finley	.50	.23	.06
□ 34 Luis Gonzalez	.15	.07	.02
□ 35 Pete Harnisch	.15	.07	.02
□ 36 Darryl Kile	.15	.07	.02
□ 37 Mike Bordick	.15	.07	.02
□ 38 Dennis Eckersley	.50	.23	.06
□ 39 Brent Gates	.50	.23	.06
□ 40 Rickey Henderson	1.00	.45	.12
□ 41 Mark McGwire	2.50	1.10	.30
□ 42 Craig Paquette	.15	.07	.02
□ 43 Ruben Sierra	.50	.23	.06
□ 44 Terry Steinbach	.50	.23	.06
□ 45 Todd Van Poppel	.15	.07	.02
□ 46 Pat Borders	.15	.07	.02
□ 47 Tony Fernandez	.15	.07	.02
□ 48 Juan Guzman	.50	.23	.06
□ 49 Pat Hentgen	1.00	.45	.12
□ 50 Paul Molitor	1.50	.70	.19
□ 51 Jack Morris	.50	.23	.06
□ 52 Ed Sprague	.50	.23	.06
□ 53 Duane Ward	.15	.07	.02
□ 54 Devon White	.15	.07	.02
□ 55 Steve Avery	.50	.23	.06
□ 56 Jeff Blauser	.15	.07	.02
□ 57 Ron Gant	.50	.23	.06
□ 58 Tom Glavine	1.00	.45	.12
□ 59 Greg Maddux	5.00	2.20	.60
□ 60 Fred McGriff	1.00	.45	.12
□ 61 Terry Pendleton	.50	.23	.06
□ 62 Deion Sanders	1.00	.45	.12
□ 63 John Smoltz	1.00	.45	.12
□ 64 Cal Eldred	.15	.07	.02
□ 65 Darryl Hamilton	.15	.07	.02
□ 66 John Jaha	1.00	.45	.12
□ 67 Pat Listach	.15	.07	.02
□ 68 Jaime Navarro	.15	.07	.02
□ 69 Kevin Reimer	.15	.07	.02
□ 70 B.J. Surhoff	.50	.23	.06
□ 71 Greg Vaughn	.50	.23	.06
□ 72 Robin Yount	1.00	.45	.12
□ 73 Rene Arocha	.15	.07	.02
□ 74 Bernard Gilkey	.50	.23	.06
□ 75 Gregg Jefferies	.50	.23	.06
□ 76 Ray Lankford	.50	.23	.06
□ 77 Tom Pagnozzi	.15	.07	.02
□ 78 Lee Smith	.50	.23	.06
□ 79 Ozzie Smith	2.00	.90	.25
□ 80 Bob Tewksbury	.15	.07	.02
□ 81 Mark Whiten	.15	.07	.02
□ 82 Steve Buechele	.15	.07	.02
□ 83 Mark Grace	1.00	.45	.12
□ 84 Jose Guzman	.15	.07	.02
□ 85 Derrick May	.15	.07	.02
□ 86 Mike Morgan	.15	.07	.02
□ 87 Randy Myers	.50	.23	.06
□ 88 Kevin Roberson	.15	.07	.02
□ 89 Sammy Sosa	1.00	.45	.12
□ 90 Rick Wilkins	.15	.07	.02
□ 91 Brett Butler	.50	.23	.06
□ 92 Eric Davis	.50	.23	.06
□ 93 Orel Hershiser	.50	.23	.06
□ 94 Eric Karros	1.00	.45	.12
□ 95 Ramon Martinez	.50	.23	.06
□ 96 Raul Mondesi	2.50	1.10	.30
□ 97 Jose Offerman	.15	.07	.02
□ 98 Mike Piazza	8.00	3.60	1.00
□ 99 Darryl Strawberry	.50	.23	.06
□ 100 Moises Alou	.50	.23	.06
□ 101 Wil Cordero	.50	.23	.06
□ 102 Delino DeShields	.15	.07	.02
□ 103 Darrin Fletcher	.15	.07	.02
□ 104 Ken Hill	.50	.23	.06
□ 105 Mike Lansing	.50	.23	.06
□ 106 Dennis Martinez	.50	.23	.06
□ 107 Larry Walker	1.00	.45	.12
□ 108 John Wetteland	.50	.23	.06
□ 109 Rod Beck	.50	.23	.06
□ 110 John Burkett	.15	.07	.02
□ 111 Will Clark	1.00	.45	.12
□ 112 Royce Clayton	.50	.23	.06
□ 113 Darren Lewis	.15	.07	.02
□ 114 Willie McGee	.15	.07	.02
□ 115 Bill Swift	.15	.07	.02
□ 116 Robby Thompson	.15	.07	.02
□ 117 Matt Williams	1.00	.45	.12
□ 118 Sandy Alomar Jr.	.50	.23	.06
□ 119 Carlos Baerga	.50	.23	.06
□ 120 Albert Belle	3.00	1.35	.35
□ 121 Reggie Jefferson	.50	.23	.06
□ 122 Wayne Kirby	.15	.07	.02
□ 123 Kenny Lofton	2.50	1.10	.30
□ 124 Carlos Martinez	.15	.07	.02
□ 125 Charles Nagy	.50	.23	.06
□ 126 Paul Sorrento	.15	.07	.02
□ 127 Rich Amaral	.15	.07	.02
□ 128 Jay Buhner	1.00	.45	.12
□ 129 Norm Charlton	.15	.07	.02
□ 130 Dave Fleming	.15	.07	.02
□ 131 Erik Hanson	.15	.07	.02
□ 132 Randy Johnson	1.00	.45	.12
□ 133 Edgar Martinez	.50	.23	.06
□ 134 Tino Martinez	.50	.23	.06
□ 135 Omar Vizquel	.50	.23	.06
□ 136 Bret Barberie	.15	.07	.02
□ 137 Chuck Carr	.15	.07	.02
□ 138 Jeff Conine	.50	.23	.06
□ 139 Orestes Destrade	.15	.07	.02
□ 140 Chris Hammond	.15	.07	.02
□ 141 Bryan Harvey	.15	.07	.02
□ 142 Benito Santiago	.15	.07	.02
□ 143 Walt Weiss	.15	.07	.02
□ 144 Darrell Whitmore	.15	.07	.02
□ 145 Tim Bogar	.15	.07	.02
□ 146 Bobby Bonilla	.50	.23	.06
□ 147 Jeromy Burnitz	.15	.07	.02
□ 148 Vince Coleman	.15	.07	.02
□ 149 Dwight Gooden	.50	.23	.06
□ 150 Todd Hundley	.50	.23	.06
□ 151 Howard Johnson	.15	.07	.02
□ 152 Eddie Murray	2.00	.90	.25
□ 153 Bret Saberhagen	.50	.23	.06
□ 154 Brady Anderson	1.00	.45	.12
□ 155 Mike Devereaux	.15	.07	.02
□ 156 Jeffrey Hammonds	.50	.23	.06
□ 157 Chris Hoiles	.15	.07	.02
□ 158 Ben McDonald	.15	.07	.02
□ 159 Mark McLemore	.15	.07	.02
□ 160 Mike Mussina	1.50	.70	.19
□ 161 Gregg Olson	.15	.07	.02
□ 162 David Segui	.15	.07	.02
□ 163 Derek Bell	.50	.23	.06
□ 164 Andy Benes	.50	.23	.06
□ 165 Archi Cianfrocco	.15	.07	.02
□ 166 Ricky Gutierrez	.15	.07	.02
□ 167 Tony Gwynn	3.00	1.35	.35
□ 168 Gene Harris	.15	.07	.02
□ 169 Trevor Hoffman	1.00	.45	.12
□ 170 Ray McDavid	.50	.23	.06
□ 171 Phil Plantier	.15	.07	.02
□ 172 Mariano Duncan	.15	.07	.02
□ 173 Len Dykstra	.50	.23	.06
□ 174 Tommy Greene	.15	.07	.02
□ 175 Dave Hollins	.15	.07	.02
□ 176 Pete Incaviglia	.15	.07	.02
□ 177 Mickey Morandini	.15	.07	.02
□ 178 Curt Schilling	.15	.07	.02
□ 179 Kevin Stocker	.50	.23	.06
□ 180 Mitch Williams	.15	.07	.02
□ 181 Stan Belinda	.15	.07	.02
□ 182 Jay Bell	.50	.23	.06
□ 183 Steve Cooke	.15	.07	.02
□ 184 Carlos Garcia	.15	.07	.02
□ 185 Jeff King	.50	.23	.06
□ 186 Orlando Merced	.50	.23	.06
□ 187 Don Slaught	.15	.07	.02
□ 188 Andy Van Slyke	.50	.23	.06
□ 189 Kevin Young	.15	.07	.02
□ 190 Kevin Brown	.50	.23	.06
□ 191 Jose Canseco	1.00	.45	.12
□ 192 Julio Franco	.50	.23	.06
□ 193 Benji Gil	.50	.23	.06
□ 194 Juan Gonzalez	4.00	1.80	.50
□ 195 Tom Henke	.15	.07	.02
□ 196 Rafael Palmeiro	1.00	.45	.12
□ 197 Dean Palmer	.50	.23	.06
□ 198 Nolan Ryan	6.00	2.70	.75
□ 199 Roger Clemens	1.50	.70	.19
□ 200 Scott Cooper	.15	.07	.02
□ 201 Andre Dawson	.50	.23	.06
□ 202 Mike Greenwell	.15	.07	.02
□ 203 Carlos Quintana	.15	.07	.02
□ 204 Jeff Russell	.15	.07	.02
□ 205 Aaron Sele	.50	.23	.06
□ 206 Mo Vaughn	2.00	.90	.25
□ 207 Frank Viola	.15	.07	.02
□ 208 Rob Dibble	.15	.07	.02
□ 209 Roberto Kelly	.15	.07	.02
□ 210 Kevin Mitchell	.50	.23	.06
□ 211 Hal Morris	.15	.07	.02
□ 212 Joe Oliver	.15	.07	.02
□ 213 Jose Rijo	.15	.07	.02
□ 214 Bip Roberts	.15	.07	.02
□ 215 Chris Sabo	.15	.07	.02
□ 216 Reggie Sanders	1.00	.45	.12
□ 217 Dante Bichette	1.00	.45	.12
□ 218 Jerald Clark	.15	.07	.02
□ 219 Alex Cole	.15	.07	.02
□ 220 Andres Galarraga	1.00	.45	.12
□ 221 Joe Girardi	.15	.07	.02
□ 222 Charlie Hayes	.15	.07	.02
□ 223 Roberto Mejia	.15	.07	.02
□ 224 Armando Reynoso	.15	.07	.02
□ 225 Eric Young	1.00	.45	.12
□ 226 Kevin Appier	.50	.23	.06
□ 227 George Brett	3.00	1.35	.35
□ 228 David Cone	.50	.23	.06
□ 229 Phil Hiatt	.15	.07	.02
□ 230 Felix Jose	.15	.07	.02
□ 231 Wally Joyner	.50	.23	.06
□ 232 Mike Macfarlane	.15	.07	.02
□ 233 Brian McRae	.50	.23	.06
□ 234 Jeff Montgomery	.50	.23	.06
□ 235 Rob Deer	.15	.07	.02
□ 236 Cecil Fielder	.50	.23	.06
□ 237 Travis Fryman	.50	.23	.06
□ 238 Mike Henneman	.15	.07	.02
□ 239 Tony Phillips	.50	.23	.06
□ 240 Mickey Tettleton	.15	.07	.02
□ 241 Alan Trammell	1.00	.45	.12
□ 242 David Wells	.15	.07	.02
□ 243 Lou Whitaker	.50	.23	.06
□ 244 Rick Aguilera	.15	.07	.02
□ 245 Scott Erickson	.15	.07	.02
□ 246 Brian Harper	.15	.07	.02
□ 247 Kent Hrbek	.50	.23	.06
□ 248 Chuck Knoblauch	1.00	.45	.12
□ 249 Shane Mack	.15	.07	.02
□ 250 David McCarty	.15	.07	.02
□ 251 Pedro Munoz	.15	.07	.02
□ 252 Dave Winfield	1.00	.45	.12
□ 253 Alex Fernandez	.50	.23	.06
□ 254 Ozzie Guillen	.15	.07	.02
□ 255 Bo Jackson	.50	.23	.06
□ 256 Lance Johnson	.50	.23	.06
□ 257 Ron Karkovice	.15	.07	.02
□ 258 Jack McDowell	.50	.23	.06
□ 259 Tim Raines	1.00	.45	.12
□ 260 Frank Thomas	8.00	3.60	1.00
□ 261 Robin Ventura	.50	.23	.06
□ 262 Jim Abbott	.15	.07	.02
□ 263 Steve Farr	.15	.07	.02
□ 264 Jimmy Key	.50	.23	.06
□ 265 Don Mattingly	4.00	1.80	.50
□ 266 Paul O'Neill	.50	.23	.06
□ 267 Mike Stanley	.15	.07	.02
□ 268 Danny Tartabull	.15	.07	.02
□ 269 Bob Wickman	.15	.07	.02
□ 270 Bernie Williams	1.50	.70	.19
□ 271 Jason Bere FOIL	.50	.23	.06
□ 272 Roger Cedeno FOIL	2.50	1.10	.30
□ 273 Johnny Damon FOIL	6.00	2.70	.75
□ 274 Russ Davis FOIL	1.00	.45	.12
□ 275 Carlos Delgado FOIL	2.50	1.10	.30
□ 276 Carl Everett FOIL	.50	.23	.06
□ 277 Cliff Floyd FOIL	.50	.23	.06
□ 278 Alex Gonzalez FOIL	1.00	.45	.12
□ 279 Derek Jeter FOIL	24.00	11.00	3.00
□ 280 Chipper Jones FOIL	12.00	5.50	1.50
□ 281 Javier Lopez FOIL	2.00	.90	.25
□ 282 Chad Mottola FOIL	1.00	.45	.12
□ 283 Marc Newfield FOIL	.50	.23	.06
□ 284 Eduardo Perez FOIL	.50	.23	.06
□ 285 Manny Ramirez FOIL	6.00	2.70	.75
□ 286 Todd Steverson FOIL	.50	.23	.06
□ 287 Michael Tucker FOIL	1.00	.45	.12
□ 288 Allen Watson FOIL	.50	.23	.06
□ 289 Rondell White FOIL	1.50	.70	.19
□ 290 Dmitri Young FOIL	2.50	1.10	.30

1993 SP Platinum Power

Cards from this 20-card standard-size set were randomly inserted in packs and feature power hitters from the American and National Leagues. The color action cut-out shot is superimposed on a royal blue background that contains lettering for Upper Deck Platinum Power and about the player. The top edge of the front is cut out in an arc with a copper foil stripe containing the player's name. The copper foil-stamped Platinum Power logo appears in the lower right. The back displays a color action player photo over the same royal blue background as depicted on the front. On a white background below the player photo is a career summary. The cards are numbered on the back with a "PP" prefix alphabetically by player's name.

	MINT	NRMT	EXC
COMPLETE SET (20)	140.00	65.00	17.50
COMMON CARD (PP1-PP20)	4.00	1.80	.50
□ PP1 Albert Belle	15.00	6.75	1.85
□ PP2 Barry Bonds	10.00	4.50	1.25
□ PP3 Joe Carter	4.00	1.80	.50
□ PP4 Will Clark	5.00	2.20	.60
□ PP5 Darren Daulton	4.00	1.80	.50
□ PP6 Cecil Fielder	4.00	1.80	.50
□ PP7 Ron Gant	4.00	1.80	.50
□ PP8 Juan Gonzalez	20.00	9.00	2.50
□ PP9 Ken Griffey Jr.	40.00	18.00	5.00
□ PP10 Dave Hollins	4.00	1.80	.50
□ PP11 David Justice	4.00	1.80	.50
□ PP12 Fred McGriff	5.00	2.20	.60
□ PP13 Mark McGwire	12.00	5.50	1.50
□ PP14 Dean Palmer	4.00	1.80	.50
□ PP15 Mike Piazza	25.00	11.00	3.10
□ PP16 Tim Salmon	8.00	3.60	1.00
□ PP17 Ryne Sandberg	10.00	4.50	1.25
□ PP18 Gary Sheffield	6.00	2.70	.75
□ PP19 Frank Thomas	40.00	18.00	5.00
□ PP20 Matt Williams	5.00	2.20	.60

1994 SP Previews

These 15 cards were distributed regionally as inserts in second series Upper Deck hobby packs. They were inserted at a rate of one in 35. The manner of distribution was five cards per Central, East and West region. The cards are nearly identical to the basic SP issue. Card fronts differ in that the region is at bottom right where the team name is located on the SP cards.

	MINT	NRMT	EXC
COMPLETE SET (15)	180.00	80.00	22.00
COMPLETE CENTRAL (5)	85.00	38.00	10.50
COMPLETE EAST (5)	40.00	18.00	5.00
COMPLETE WEST (5)	55.00	25.00	7.00
COMMON CARD	2.50	1.10	.30
□ CR1 Jeff Bagwell	12.00	5.50	1.50
□ CR2 Michael Jordan	30.00	13.50	3.70
□ CR3 Kirby Puckett	12.00	5.50	1.50
□ CR4 Manny Ramirez	10.00	4.50	1.25
□ CR5 Frank Thomas	30.00	13.50	3.70
□ ER1 Roberto Alomar	5.00	2.20	.60
□ ER2 Cliff Floyd	2.50	1.10	.30
□ ER3 Javier Lopez	3.00	1.35	.35
□ ER4 Don Mattingly	12.00	5.50	1.50
□ ER5 Cal Ripken	25.00	11.00	3.10
□ WR1 Barry Bonds	8.00	3.60	1.00
□ WR2 Juan Gonzalez	15.00	6.75	1.85
□ WR3 Ken Griffey Jr.	30.00	13.50	3.70
□ WR4 Mike Piazza	20.00	9.00	2.50
□ WR5 Tim Salmon	5.00	2.20	.60

1994 SP

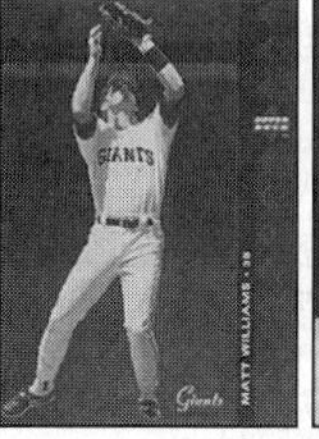

This 200-card standard-size set primarily contains the game's top players and prospects. The first 20 cards in the set are Foil Prospects which are brighter and more metallic than the rest of the set. Cards 21-200 are in alphabetical order by team nickname. In either case, card fronts have a metallic finish with color player photos and a gold right-hand border. The backs contain a color player photo, 1993, career and best season statistics. The left side has a black border. The Upper Deck hologram on back is gold. Rookie Cards include Derrek Lee, Chan Ho Park and Alex Rodriguez.

	MINT	NRMT	EXC
COMPLETE SET (200)	65.00	29.00	8.00
COMMON CARD (21-200)	.15	.07	.02
□ 1 Mike Bell FOIL	1.50	.70	.19
□ 2 D.J. Boston FOIL	.30	.14	.04
□ 3 Johnny Damon FOIL	1.50	.70	.19

	MINT	NRMT	EXC
☐ 4 Brad Fullmer FOIL	2.00	.90	.25
☐ 5 Joey Hamilton FOIL	1.50	.70	.19
☐ 6 Todd Hollandsworth FOIL	2.00	.90	.25
☐ 7 Brian L. Hunter FOIL	1.25	.55	.16
☐ 8 LaTroy Hawkins FOIL	.30	.14	.04
☐ 9 Brooks Kieschnick FOIL	1.50	.70	.19
☐ 10 Derrek Lee FOIL	5.00	2.20	.60
☐ 11 Trot Nixon FOIL	1.00	.45	.12
☐ 12 Alex Ochoa FOIL	.30	.14	.04
☐ 13 Chan Ho Park FOIL	2.50	1.10	.30
☐ 14 Kirk Presley FOIL	.60	.25	.07
☐ 15 Alex Rodriguez FOIL	45.00	20.00	5.50
☐ 16 Jose Silva FOIL	.60	.25	.07
☐ 17 Terrell Wade FOIL	1.50	.70	.19
☐ 18 Billy Wagner FOIL	2.50	1.10	.30
☐ 19 Glenn Williams FOIL	1.00	.45	.12
☐ 20 Preston Wilson FOIL	.30	.14	.04
☐ 21 Brian Anderson	.30	.14	.04
☐ 22 Chad Curtis	.15	.07	.02
☐ 23 Chili Davis	.30	.14	.04
☐ 24 Bo Jackson	.30	.14	.04
☐ 25 Mark Langston	.30	.14	.04
☐ 26 Tim Salmon	.60	.25	.07
☐ 27 Jeff Bagwell	1.50	.70	.19
☐ 28 Craig Biggio	.30	.14	.04
☐ 29 Ken Caminiti	.60	.25	.07
☐ 30 Doug Drabek	.15	.07	.02
☐ 31 John Hudek	.15	.07	.02
☐ 32 Greg Swindell	.15	.07	.02
☐ 33 Brent Gates	.15	.07	.02
☐ 34 Rickey Henderson	.60	.25	.07
☐ 35 Steve Karsay	.15	.07	.02
☐ 36 Mark McGwire	1.25	.55	.16
☐ 37 Ruben Sierra	.30	.14	.04
☐ 38 Terry Steinbach	.30	.14	.04
☐ 39 Roberto Alomar	.75	.35	.09
☐ 40 Joe Carter	.30	.14	.04
☐ 41 Carlos Delgado	.60	.25	.07
☐ 42 Alex Gonzalez	.30	.14	.04
☐ 43 Juan Guzman	.30	.14	.04
☐ 44 Paul Molitor	.75	.35	.09
☐ 45 John Olerud	.15	.07	.02
☐ 46 Devon White	.15	.07	.02
☐ 47 Steve Avery	.30	.14	.04
☐ 48 Jeff Blauser	.15	.07	.02
☐ 49 Tom Glavine	.60	.25	.07
☐ 50 David Justice	.60	.25	.07
☐ 51 Roberto Kelly	.15	.07	.02
☐ 52 Ryan Klesko	.75	.35	.09
☐ 53 Javier Lopez	.60	.25	.07
☐ 54 Greg Maddux	2.50	1.10	.30
☐ 55 Fred McGriff	.60	.25	.07
☐ 56 Ricky Bones	.15	.07	.02
☐ 57 Cal Eldred	.15	.07	.02
☐ 58 Brian Harper	.15	.07	.02
☐ 59 Pat Listach	.15	.07	.02
☐ 60 B.J. Surhoff	.15	.07	.02
☐ 61 Greg Vaughn	.60	.25	.07
☐ 62 Bernard Gilkey	.30	.14	.04
☐ 63 Gregg Jefferies	.60	.25	.07
☐ 64 Ray Lankford	.30	.14	.04
☐ 65 Ozzie Smith	1.00	.45	.12
☐ 66 Bob Tewksbury	.15	.07	.02
☐ 67 Mark Whiten	.15	.07	.02
☐ 68 Todd Zeile	.15	.07	.02
☐ 69 Mark Grace	.60	.25	.07
☐ 70 Randy Myers	.15	.07	.02
☐ 71 Ryne Sandberg	1.00	.45	.12
☐ 72 Sammy Sosa	.60	.25	.07
☐ 73 Steve Trachsel	.30	.14	.04
☐ 74 Rick Wilkins	.15	.07	.02
☐ 75 Brett Butler	.30	.14	.04
☐ 76 Delino DeShields	.15	.07	.02
☐ 77 Orel Hershiser	.30	.14	.04
☐ 78 Eric Karros	.30	.14	.04
☐ 79 Raul Mondesi	.60	.25	.07
☐ 80 Mike Piazza	2.50	1.10	.30
☐ 81 Tim Wallach	.15	.07	.02
☐ 82 Moises Alou	.30	.14	.04
☐ 83 Cliff Floyd	.60	.25	.07
☐ 84 Marquis Grissom	.30	.14	.04
☐ 85 Pedro J. Martinez	.60	.25	.07
☐ 86 Larry Walker	.60	.25	.07
☐ 87 John Wetteland	.30	.14	.04
☐ 88 Rondell White	.60	.25	.07
☐ 89 Rod Beck	.30	.14	.04
☐ 90 Barry Bonds	1.00	.45	.12
☐ 91 John Burkett	.15	.07	.02
☐ 92 Royce Clayton	.30	.14	.04
☐ 93 Billy Swift	.15	.07	.02
☐ 94 Robby Thompson	.15	.07	.02
☐ 95 Matt Williams	.60	.25	.07
☐ 96 Carlos Baerga	.30	.14	.04
☐ 97 Albert Belle	1.50	.70	.19
☐ 98 Kenny Lofton	1.25	.55	.16
☐ 99 Dennis Martinez	.30	.14	.04
☐ 100 Eddie Murray	1.00	.45	.12
☐ 101 Manny Ramirez	1.25	.55	.16
☐ 102 Eric Anthony	.15	.07	.02
☐ 103 Chris Bosio	.15	.07	.02
☐ 104 Jay Buhner	.60	.25	.07
☐ 105 Ken Griffey Jr.	4.00	1.80	.50
☐ 106 Randy Johnson	.60	.25	.07
☐ 107 Edgar Martinez	.30	.14	.04
☐ 108 Chuck Carr	.15	.07	.02
☐ 109 Jeff Conine	.30	.14	.04
☐ 110 Carl Everett	.15	.07	.02
☐ 111 Chris Hammond	.15	.07	.02
☐ 112 Bryan Harvey	.15	.07	.02
☐ 113 Charles Johnson	.60	.25	.07
☐ 114 Gary Sheffield	.60	.25	.07
☐ 115 Bobby Bonilla	.30	.14	.04
☐ 116 Dwight Gooden	.30	.14	.04
☐ 117 Todd Hundley	.30	.14	.04
☐ 118 Bobby Jones	.30	.14	.04
☐ 119 Jeff Kent	.15	.07	.02
☐ 120 Bret Saberhagen	.30	.14	.04
☐ 121 Jeffrey Hammonds	.30	.14	.04
☐ 122 Chris Hoiles	.15	.07	.02
☐ 123 Ben McDonald	.15	.07	.02
☐ 124 Mike Mussina	.75	.35	.09
☐ 125 Rafael Palmeiro	.60	.25	.07
☐ 126 Cal Ripken Jr.	3.00	1.35	.35
☐ 127 Lee Smith	.30	.14	.04
☐ 128 Derek Bell	.30	.14	.04
☐ 129 Andy Benes	.30	.14	.04
☐ 130 Tony Gwynn	1.50	.70	.19
☐ 131 Trevor Hoffman	.30	.14	.04
☐ 132 Phil Plantier	.15	.07	.02
☐ 133 Bip Roberts	.15	.07	.02
☐ 134 Darren Daulton	.30	.14	.04
☐ 135 Lenny Dykstra	.30	.14	.04
☐ 136 Dave Hollins	.15	.07	.02
☐ 137 Danny Jackson	.15	.07	.02
☐ 138 John Kruk	.30	.14	.04
☐ 139 Kevin Stocker	.15	.07	.02
☐ 140 Jay Bell	.30	.14	.04
☐ 141 Carlos Garcia	.15	.07	.02
☐ 142 Jeff King	.30	.14	.04
☐ 143 Orlando Merced	.30	.14	.04
☐ 144 Andy Van Slyke	.30	.14	.04
☐ 145 Rick White	.15	.07	.02
☐ 146 Jose Canseco	.60	.25	.07
☐ 147 Will Clark	.60	.25	.07
☐ 148 Juan Gonzalez	2.00	.90	.25
☐ 149 Rick Helling	.15	.07	.02
☐ 150 Dean Palmer	.30	.14	.04
☐ 151 Ivan Rodriguez	1.00	.45	.12
☐ 152 Roger Clemens	.75	.35	.09
☐ 153 Scott Cooper	.15	.07	.02
☐ 154 Andre Dawson	.30	.14	.04
☐ 155 Mike Greenwell	.15	.07	.02
☐ 156 Aaron Sele	.30	.14	.04
☐ 157 Mo Vaughn	1.00	.45	.12
☐ 158 Bret Boone	.30	.14	.04
☐ 159 Barry Larkin	.60	.25	.07
☐ 160 Kevin Mitchell	.30	.14	.04
☐ 161 Jose Rijo	.15	.07	.02
☐ 162 Deion Sanders	.60	.25	.07
☐ 163 Reggie Sanders	.30	.14	.04
☐ 164 Dante Bichette	.60	.25	.07
☐ 165 Ellis Burks	.30	.14	.04
☐ 166 Andres Galarraga	.60	.25	.07
☐ 167 Charlie Hayes	.15	.07	.02
☐ 168 David Nied	.15	.07	.02
☐ 169 Walt Weiss	.15	.07	.02
☐ 170 Kevin Appier	.30	.14	.04
☐ 171 David Cone	.30	.14	.04
☐ 172 Jeff Granger	.30	.14	.04
☐ 173 Felix Jose	.15	.07	.02
☐ 174 Wally Joyner	.30	.14	.04
☐ 175 Brian McRae	.30	.14	.04
☐ 176 Cecil Fielder	.30	.14	.04
☐ 177 Travis Fryman	.30	.14	.04
☐ 178 Mike Henneman	.15	.07	.02
☐ 179 Tony Phillips	.30	.14	.04
☐ 180 Mickey Tettleton	.15	.07	.02
☐ 181 Alan Trammell	.30	.14	.04
☐ 182 Rick Aguilera	.15	.07	.02
☐ 183 Rich Becker	.30	.14	.04
☐ 184 Scott Erickson	.15	.07	.02
☐ 185 Chuck Knoblauch	.60	.25	.07
☐ 186 Kirby Puckett	1.50	.70	.19
☐ 187 Dave Winfield	.60	.25	.07
☐ 188 Wilson Alvarez	.30	.14	.04
☐ 189 Jason Bere	.30	.14	.04
☐ 190 Alex Fernandez	.30	.14	.04
☐ 191 Julio Franco	.30	.14	.04
☐ 192 Jack McDowell	.30	.14	.04
☐ 193 Frank Thomas	4.00	1.80	.50
☐ 194 Robin Ventura	.30	.14	.04
☐ 195 Jim Abbott	.15	.07	.02
☐ 196 Wade Boggs	.60	.25	.07
☐ 197 Jimmy Key	.30	.14	.04
☐ 198 Don Mattingly	2.00	.90	.25
☐ 199 Paul O'Neill	.30	.14	.04
☐ 200 Danny Tartabull	.15	.07	.02

1994 SP Die Cuts

This 200-card die-cut set is parallel to that of the basic SP issue. The cards were inserted one per SP pack. The difference, of course, is the unique die-cut shape. The backs have a silver Upper Deck hologram as opposed to gold on the basic issue.

	MINT	NRMT	EXC
COMPLETE SET (200)	150.00	70.00	19.00
COMMON CARD (1-200)	.25	.11	.03

*STARS: 1.5X to 3X BASIC CARDS ....
*YOUNG STARS: 1X to 2X BASIC CARDS

1994 SP Holoviews

Randomly inserted in SP foil packs at a rate of one in five, this 38-card set contains top stars and prospects. Card fronts have a color player photo with a black and blue border to the right with which the player's name appears. A player hologram that runs the width of the card is at the bottom. The backs are primarily blue with a player photo and text.

	MINT	NRMT	EXC
COMPLETE SET (38)	150.00	70.00	19.00
COMMON CARD (1-38)	2.00	.90	.25
☐ 1 Roberto Alomar	6.00	2.70	.75
☐ 2 Kevin Appier	3.00	1.35	.35
☐ 3 Jeff Bagwell	12.00	5.50	1.50
☐ 4 Barry Bonds	4.00	1.80	.50
☐ 5 Roger Clemens	6.00	2.70	.75
☐ 6 Carlos Delgado	4.00	1.80	.50
☐ 7 Cecil Fielder	3.00	1.35	.35
☐ 8 Cliff Floyd	2.00	.90	.25
☐ 9 Travis Fryman	3.00	1.35	.35
☐ 10 Andres Galarraga	4.00	1.80	.50
☐ 11 Juan Gonzalez	15.00	6.75	1.85
☐ 12 Ken Griffey Jr.	30.00	13.50	3.70
☐ 13 Tony Gwynn	12.00	5.50	1.50
☐ 14 Jeffrey Hammonds	2.00	.90	.25
☐ 15 Bo Jackson	3.00	1.35	.35
☐ 16 Michael Jordan	35.00	16.00	4.40
☐ 17 David Justice	3.00	1.35	.35
☐ 18 Steve Karsay	2.00	.90	.25
☐ 19 Jeff Kent	2.00	.90	.25
☐ 20 Brooks Kieschnick	3.00	1.35	.35
☐ 21 Ryan Klesko	6.00	2.70	.75
☐ 22 John Kruk	2.00	.90	.25
☐ 23 Barry Larkin	4.00	1.80	.50
☐ 24 Pat Listach	2.00	.90	.25
☐ 25 Don Mattingly	15.00	6.75	1.85
☐ 26 Mark McGwire	10.00	4.50	1.25
☐ 27 Raul Mondesi	5.00	2.20	.60
☐ 28 Trot Nixon	3.00	1.35	.35
☐ 29 Mike Piazza	20.00	9.00	2.50
☐ 30 Kirby Puckett	12.00	5.50	1.50
☐ 31 Manny Ramirez	10.00	4.50	1.25
☐ 32 Cal Ripken	25.00	11.00	3.10
☐ 33 Alex Rodriguez	45.00	20.00	5.50
☐ 34 Tim Salmon	5.00	2.20	.60
☐ 35 Gary Sheffield	5.00	2.20	.60
☐ 36 Ozzie Smith	8.00	3.60	1.00
☐ 37 Sammy Sosa	5.00	2.20	.60
☐ 38 Andy Van Slyke	2.00	.90	.25

1994 SP Holoviews Die Cuts

Parallel to the blue Holoview set, this 38-card red-bordered issue was also randomly inserted in SP packs. They are much more difficult to pull than the blue version with an insertion rate of one in 75. Card fronts have a color player photo with a black and red border to the right with which the player's name appears. A player hologram that runs the width of the card is at the bottom. The backs are primarily red with a player photo and text.

	MINT	NRMT	EXC
COMPLETE SET (38)	2000.00	900.00	250.00
COMMON CARD (1-38)	12.00	5.50	1.50
☐ 1 Roberto Alomar	50.00	22.00	6.25
☐ 3 Jeff Bagwell	100.00	45.00	12.50
☐ 4 Barry Bonds	30.00	13.50	3.70
☐ 5 Roger Clemens	50.00	22.00	6.25
☐ 6 Carlos Delgado	30.00	13.50	3.70
☐ 10 Andres Galarraga	30.00	13.50	3.70
☐ 11 Juan Gonzalez	125.00	55.00	15.50
☐ 12 Ken Griffey Jr.	250.00	110.00	31.00
☐ 13 Tony Gwynn	100.00	45.00	12.50
☐ 16 Michael Jordan	300.00	135.00	38.00
☐ 20 Brooks Kieschnick	30.00	13.50	3.70
☐ 21 Ryan Klesko	50.00	22.00	6.25
☐ 23 Barry Larkin	30.00	13.50	3.70
☐ 25 Don Mattingly	120.00	55.00	15.00
☐ 26 Mark McGwire	75.00	34.00	9.50
☐ 27 Raul Mondesi	40.00	18.00	5.00
☐ 29 Mike Piazza	150.00	70.00	19.00
☐ 30 Kirby Puckett	100.00	45.00	12.50
☐ 31 manny Ramirez	75.00	34.00	9.50
☐ 32 Cal Ripken	200.00	90.00	25.00
☐ 33 Alex Rodriguez	325.00	145.00	40.00
☐ 34 Tim Salmon	50.00	22.00	6.25
☐ 35 Gary Sheffield	40.00	18.00	5.00
☐ 36 Ozzie Smith	60.00	27.00	7.50
☐ 37 Sammy Sosa	40.00	18.00	5.00

1995 SP

This set consists of 207 cards being sold in eight-card, hobby-only packs with a suggested retail price of $3.99. The fronts have full-bleed photos and a large chevron on the left. The chevron consists of red and gold foil for American League players and blue and gold for National Leaguers. The backs have a photo with player information and statistics at the bottom. The backs also have a gold hologram to prevent counterfeiting. Subsets featured are Salute (1-4) and Premier Prospects (5-24). The only notable Rookie Card in this set is Hideo Nomo.

	MINT	NRMT	EXC
COMPLETE SET (207)	40.00	18.00	5.00
COMMON CARD (1-207)	.15	.07	.02
☐ 1 Cal Ripken Salute	3.00	1.35	.35
☐ 2 Nolan Ryan Salute	2.50	1.10	.30
☐ 3 George Brett Salute	1.00	.45	.12
☐ 4 Mike Schmidt Salute	.75	.35	.09
☐ 5 Dustin Hermanson FOIL	.30	.14	.04
☐ 6 Antonio Osuna FOIL	.30	.14	.04
☐ 7 Mark Grudzielanek FOIL	1.00	.45	.12
☐ 8 Ray Durham FOIL	.60	.25	.07
☐ 9 Ugueth Urbina FOIL	.30	.14	.04
☐ 10 Ruben Rivera FOIL	1.50	.70	.19
☐ 11 Curtis Goodwin FOIL	.30	.14	.04
☐ 12 Jimmy Hurst FOIL	.30	.14	.04
☐ 13 Jose Malave FOIL	.30	.14	.04
☐ 14 Hideo Nomo FOIL	4.00	1.80	.50
☐ 15 Juan Acevedo FOIL	.30	.14	.04
☐ 16 Tony Clark FOIL	1.25	.55	.16
☐ 17 Jim Pittsley FOIL	.60	.25	.07
☐ 18 Freddy Garcia FOIL	.30	.14	.04
☐ 19 Carlos Perez FOIL	.30	.14	.04
☐ 20 Raul Casanova FOIL	.50	.23	.06
☐ 21 Quilvio Veras FOIL	.30	.14	.04
☐ 22 Edgardo Alfonzo FOIL	.30	.14	.04
☐ 23 Marty Cordova FOIL	.60	.25	.07
☐ 24 C.J. Nitkowski FOIL	.30	.14	.04
☐ 25 Wade Boggs CL	.60	.25	.07
☐ 26 Dave Winfield CL	.60	.25	.07
☐ 27 Eddie Murray CL	1.00	.45	.12
☐ 28 David Justice	.60	.25	.07
☐ 29 Marquis Grissom	.30	.14	.04
☐ 30 Fred McGriff	.60	.25	.07
☐ 31 Greg Maddux	2.50	1.10	.30
☐ 32 Tom Glavine	.60	.25	.07
☐ 33 Steve Avery	.30	.14	.04
☐ 34 Chipper Jones	2.50	1.10	.30
☐ 35 Sammy Sosa	.60	.25	.07
☐ 36 Jaime Navarro	.15	.07	.02
☐ 37 Randy Myers	.15	.07	.02
☐ 38 Mark Grace	.60	.25	.07
☐ 39 Todd Zeile	.15	.07	.02
☐ 40 Brian McRae	.30	.14	.04
☐ 41 Reggie Sanders	.30	.14	.04
☐ 42 Ron Gant	.30	.14	.04
☐ 43 Deion Sanders	.60	.25	.07
☐ 44 Bret Boone	.30	.14	.04
☐ 45 Barry Larkin	.60	.25	.07
☐ 46 Jose Rijo	.15	.07	.02
☐ 47 Jason Bates	.15	.07	.02
☐ 48 Andres Galarraga	.60	.25	.07
☐ 49 Bill Swift	.15	.07	.02
☐ 50 Larry Walker	.60	.25	.07
☐ 51 Vinny Castilla	.30	.14	.04
☐ 52 Dante Bichette	.60	.25	.07
☐ 53 Jeff Conine	.30	.14	.04
☐ 54 John Burkett	.30	.14	.04
☐ 55 Gary Sheffield	.60	.25	.07
☐ 56 Andre Dawson	.30	.14	.04
☐ 57 Terry Pendleton	.30	.14	.04
☐ 58 Charles Johnson	.30	.14	.04
☐ 59 Brian L. Hunter	.30	.14	.04
☐ 60 Jeff Bagwell	1.50	.70	.19
☐ 61 Craig Biggio	.30	.14	.04
☐ 62 Phil Nevin	.15	.07	.02
☐ 63 Doug Drabek	.15	.07	.02
☐ 64 Derek Bell	.30	.14	.04
☐ 65 Raul Mondesi	.60	.25	.07
☐ 66 Eric Karros	.30	.14	.04
☐ 67 Roger Cedeno	.30	.14	.04
☐ 68 Delino DeShields	.15	.07	.02
☐ 69 Ramon Martinez	.30	.14	.04
☐ 70 Mike Piazza	2.50	1.10	.30
☐ 71 Billy Ashley	.15	.07	.02
☐ 72 Jeff Fassero	.15	.07	.02
☐ 73 Shane Andrews	.15	.07	.02
☐ 74 Wil Cordero	.15	.07	.02
☐ 75 Tony Tarasco	.15	.07	.02
☐ 76 Rondell White	.30	.14	.04

☐ 77 Pedro J. Martinez	.30	.14	.04
☐ 78 Moises Alou	.30	.14	.04
☐ 79 Rico Brogna	.15	.07	.02
☐ 80 Bobby Bonilla	.30	.14	.04
☐ 81 Jeff Kent	.15	.07	.02
☐ 82 Brett Butler	.30	.14	.04
☐ 83 Bobby Jones	.30	.14	.04
☐ 84 Bill Pulsipher	.30	.14	.04
☐ 85 Bret Saberhagen	.30	.14	.04
☐ 86 Gregg Jefferies	.30	.14	.04
☐ 87 Lenny Dykstra	.30	.14	.04
☐ 88 Dave Hollins	.15	.07	.02
☐ 89 Charlie Hayes	.15	.07	.02
☐ 90 Darren Daulton	.30	.14	.04
☐ 91 Curt Schilling	.15	.07	.02
☐ 92 Heathcliff Slocumb	.15	.07	.02
☐ 93 Carlos Garcia	.15	.07	.02
☐ 94 Denny Neagle	.30	.14	.04
☐ 95 Jay Bell	.30	.14	.04
☐ 96 Orlando Merced	.15	.07	.02
☐ 97 Dave Clark	.15	.07	.02
☐ 98 Bernard Gilkey	.30	.14	.04
☐ 99 Scott Cooper	.15	.07	.02
☐ 100 Ozzie Smith	1.00	.45	.12
☐ 101 Tom Henke	.15	.07	.02
☐ 102 Ken Hill	.15	.07	.02
☐ 103 Brian Jordan	.60	.25	.07
☐ 104 Ray Lankford	.30	.14	.04
☐ 105 Tony Gwynn	1.50	.70	.19
☐ 106 Andy Benes	.15	.07	.02
☐ 107 Ken Caminiti	.60	.25	.07
☐ 108 Steve Finley	.30	.14	.04
☐ 109 Joey Hamilton	.60	.25	.07
☐ 110 Bip Roberts	.15	.07	.02
☐ 111 Eddie Williams	.15	.07	.02
☐ 112 Rod Beck	.15	.07	.02
☐ 113 Matt Williams	.60	.25	.07
☐ 114 Glenallen Hill	.15	.07	.02
☐ 115 Barry Bonds	1.00	.45	.12
☐ 116 Robby Thompson	.15	.07	.02
☐ 117 Mark Portugal	.15	.07	.02
☐ 118 Brady Anderson	.60	.25	.07
☐ 119 Mike Mussina	.75	.35	.09
☐ 120 Rafael Palmeiro	.60	.25	.07
☐ 121 Chris Hoiles	.15	.07	.02
☐ 122 Harold Baines	.30	.14	.04
☐ 123 Jeffrey Hammonds	.30	.14	.04
☐ 124 Tim Naehring	.15	.07	.02
☐ 125 Mo Vaughn	1.00	.45	.12
☐ 126 Mike Macfarlane	.15	.07	.02
☐ 127 Roger Clemens	.75	.35	.09
☐ 128 John Valentin	.30	.14	.04
☐ 129 Aaron Sele	.30	.14	.04
☐ 130 Jose Canseco	.60	.25	.07
☐ 131 J.T. Snow	.30	.14	.04
☐ 132 Mark Langston	.15	.07	.02
☐ 133 Chili Davis	.30	.14	.04
☐ 134 Chuck Finley	.30	.14	.04
☐ 135 Tim Salmon	.60	.25	.07
☐ 136 Tony Phillips	.30	.14	.04
☐ 137 Jason Bere	.15	.07	.02
☐ 138 Robin Ventura	.30	.14	.04
☐ 139 Tim Raines	.60	.25	.07
☐ 140 Frank Thomas COR	4.00	1.80	.50
☐ 140A Frank Thomas ERR	8.00	3.60	1.00
☐ 141 Alex Fernandez	.30	.14	.04
☐ 142 Jim Abbott	.15	.07	.02
☐ 143 Wilson Alvarez	.30	.14	.04
☐ 144 Carlos Baerga	.30	.14	.04
☐ 145 Albert Belle	1.50	.70	.19
☐ 146 Jim Thome	.75	.35	.09
☐ 147 Dennis Martinez	.30	.14	.04
☐ 148 Eddie Murray	1.00	.45	.12
☐ 149 Dave Winfield	.60	.25	.07
☐ 150 Kenny Lofton	1.00	.45	.12
☐ 151 Manny Ramirez	1.00	.45	.12
☐ 152 Chad Curtis	.15	.07	.02
☐ 153 Lou Whitaker	.30	.14	.04
☐ 154 Alan Trammell	.30	.14	.04
☐ 155 Cecil Fielder	.30	.14	.04
☐ 156 Kirk Gibson	.30	.14	.04
☐ 157 Michael Tucker	.30	.14	.04
☐ 158 Jon Nunnally	.30	.14	.04
☐ 159 Wally Joyner	.30	.14	.04
☐ 160 Kevin Appier	.30	.14	.04
☐ 161 Jeff Montgomery	.30	.14	.04
☐ 162 Greg Gagne	.15	.07	.02
☐ 163 Ricky Bones	.15	.07	.02
☐ 164 Cal Eldred	.15	.07	.02
☐ 165 Greg Vaughn	.30	.14	.04
☐ 166 Kevin Seitzer	.15	.07	.02
☐ 167 Jose Valentin	.30	.14	.04
☐ 168 Joe Oliver	.15	.07	.02
☐ 169 Rick Aguilera	.15	.07	.02
☐ 170 Kirby Puckett	1.50	.70	.19
☐ 171 Scott Stahoviak	.15	.07	.02
☐ 172 Kevin Tapani	.15	.07	.02
☐ 173 Chuck Knoblauch	.60	.25	.07
☐ 174 Rich Becker	.15	.07	.02
☐ 175 Don Mattingly	2.00	.90	.25
☐ 176 Jack McDowell	.30	.14	.04
☐ 177 Jimmy Key	.30	.14	.04
☐ 178 Paul O'Neill	.30	.14	.04
☐ 179 John Wetteland	.30	.14	.04
☐ 180 Wade Boggs	.60	.25	.07
☐ 181 Derek Jeter	2.50	1.10	.30
☐ 182 Rickey Henderson	.60	.25	.07
☐ 183 Terry Steinbach	.30	.14	.04
☐ 184 Ruben Sierra	.30	.14	.04
☐ 185 Mark McGwire	1.25	.55	.16
☐ 186 Todd Stottlemyre	.15	.07	.02
☐ 187 Dennis Eckersley	.30	.14	.04
☐ 188 Alex Rodriguez	5.00	2.20	.60
☐ 189 Randy Johnson	.60	.25	.07
☐ 190 Ken Griffey Jr.	4.00	1.80	.50
☐ 191 Tino Martinez UER Mike Blowers pictured on back	.30	.14	.04
☐ 192 Jay Buhner	.60	.25	.07
☐ 193 Edgar Martinez	.30	.14	.04
☐ 194 Mickey Tettleton	.15	.07	.02
☐ 195 Juan Gonzalez	2.00	.90	.25
☐ 196 Benji Gil	.15	.07	.02
☐ 197 Dean Palmer	.30	.14	.04
☐ 198 Ivan Rodriguez	1.00	.45	.12
☐ 199 Kenny Rogers	.15	.07	.02
☐ 200 Will Clark	.60	.25	.07
☐ 201 Roberto Alomar	.75	.35	.09
☐ 202 David Cone	.30	.14	.04
☐ 203 Paul Molitor	.75	.35	.09
☐ 204 Shawn Green	.30	.14	.04
☐ 205 Joe Carter	.30	.14	.04
☐ 206 Alex Gonzalez	.30	.14	.04
☐ 207 Pat Hentgen	.30	.14	.04

1995 SP Silver

This 207-card set parallels that of the regular SP set and was inserted one per pack. The only difference between the regular 180 cards in the two sets is that the chevron of the parallel version on the left side of the front uses rainbow-colored foil instead of blue or red. The subset cards have a die-cut design to differentiate them from the regular edition cards. The only other difference is the silver (rather than gold) hologram on the back.

	MINT	NRMT	EXC
COMPLETE SET (207)	100.00	45.00	12.50
COMMON CARD (1-207)	.25	.11	.03

*STARS: 1.5X to 3X BASIC CARDS ....
*YOUNG STARS: 1.25X to 2.5X BASIC CARDS

1995 SP Platinum Power

This 20-card set was randomly inserted in packs at a rate of one in five. This die-cut set is comprised of the top home run hitters in baseball. The fronts have an action photo with a bronze background and rays of light coming out of the "SP" emblem at bottom right. The backs have a player photo in a box at the middle of the card with player statistics at the bottom. The set is sequenced in alphabetical order.

	MINT	NRMT	EXC
COMPLETE SET (20)	20.00	9.00	2.50
COMMON CARD (PP1-PP20)	.50	.23	.06
☐ PP1 Jeff Bagwell	2.00	.90	.25
☐ PP2 Barry Bonds	1.25	.55	.16
☐ PP3 Ron Gant	.50	.23	.06
☐ PP4 Fred McGriff	.75	.35	.09
☐ PP5 Raul Mondesi	.75	.35	.09
☐ PP6 Mike Piazza	3.00	1.35	.35
☐ PP7 Larry Walker	.75	.35	.09
☐ PP8 Matt Williams	.75	.35	.09
☐ PP9 Albert Belle	2.00	.90	.25
☐ PP10 Cecil Fielder	.60	.25	.07
☐ PP11 Juan Gonzalez	2.50	1.10	.30
☐ PP12 Ken Griffey Jr.	5.00	2.20	.60
☐ PP13 Mark McGwire	1.50	.70	.19
☐ PP14 Eddie Murray	1.25	.55	.16
☐ PP15 Manny Ramirez	1.25	.55	.16
☐ PP16 Cal Ripken	4.00	1.80	.50
☐ PP17 Tim Salmon	.75	.35	.09
☐ PP18 Frank Thomas	5.00	2.20	.60
☐ PP19 Jim Thome	1.00	.45	.12
☐ PP20 Mo Vaughn	1.25	.55	.16

1995 SP Special FX

This 48-card set was randomly inserted in packs at a rate of one in 75. The set is comprised of the top names in baseball. The fronts have an action photo on a sky-colored foil background. There is also a hologram of the player's face that allows you to see a 50-degree, 3-D image. The backs have a photo with player information and statistics. The cards are numbered on the back "X/48."

	MINT	NRMT	EXC
COMPLETE SET (48)	1300.00	575.00	160.00
COMMON CARD (1-48)	10.00	4.50	1.25
☐ 1 Jose Canseco	20.00	9.00	2.50
☐ 2 Roger Clemens	25.00	11.00	3.10
☐ 3 Mo Vaughn	40.00	18.00	5.00
☐ 4 Tim Salmon	20.00	9.00	2.50
☐ 5 Chuck Finley	10.00	4.50	1.25
☐ 6 Robin Ventura	12.50	5.50	1.55
☐ 7 Jason Bere	10.00	4.50	1.25
☐ 8 Carlos Baerga	10.00	4.50	1.25
☐ 9 Albert Belle	60.00	27.00	7.50
☐ 10 Kenny Lofton	40.00	18.00	5.00
☐ 11 Manny Ramirez	40.00	18.00	5.00
☐ 12 Jeff Montgomery	10.00	4.50	1.25
☐ 13 Kirby Puckett	60.00	27.00	7.50
☐ 14 Wade Boggs	15.00	6.75	1.85
☐ 15 Don Mattingly	75.00	34.00	9.50
☐ 16 Cal Ripken	125.00	55.00	15.50
☐ 17 Ruben Sierra	10.00	4.50	1.25
☐ 18 Ken Griffey Jr.	150.00	70.00	19.00
☐ 19 Randy Johnson	25.00	11.00	3.10
☐ 20 Alex Rodriguez	150.00	70.00	19.00
☐ 21 Will Clark	20.00	9.00	2.50
☐ 22 Juan Gonzalez	75.00	34.00	9.50
☐ 23 Roberto Alomar	30.00	13.50	3.70
☐ 24 Joe Carter	12.50	5.50	1.55
☐ 25 Alex Gonzalez	10.00	4.50	1.25
☐ 26 Paul Molitor	30.00	13.50	3.70
☐ 27 Ryan Klesko	25.00	11.00	3.10
☐ 28 Fred McGriff	20.00	9.00	2.50
☐ 29 Greg Maddux	100.00	45.00	12.50
☐ 30 Sammy Sosa	25.00	11.00	3.10
☐ 31 Bret Boone	10.00	4.50	1.25
☐ 32 Barry Larkin	20.00	9.00	2.50
☐ 33 Reggie Sanders	12.50	5.50	1.55
☐ 34 Dante Bichette	20.00	9.00	2.50
☐ 35 Andres Galarraga	20.00	9.00	2.50
☐ 36 Charles Johnson	12.50	5.50	1.55
☐ 37 Gary Sheffield	25.00	11.00	3.10
☐ 38 Jeff Bagwell	60.00	27.00	7.50
☐ 39 Craig Biggio	12.50	5.50	1.55
☐ 40 Eric Karros	12.50	5.50	1.55
☐ 41 Billy Ashley	10.00	4.50	1.25
☐ 42 Raul Mondesi	20.00	9.00	2.50
☐ 43 Mike Piazza	100.00	45.00	12.50
☐ 44 Rondell White	12.50	5.50	1.55
☐ 45 Bret Saberhagen	10.00	4.50	1.25
☐ 46 Tony Gwynn	60.00	27.00	7.50
☐ 47 Melvin Nieves	10.00	4.50	1.25
☐ 48 Matt Williams	20.00	9.00	2.50

1996 SP Previews FanFest

These eight standard-size cards were issued to promote the 1996 Upper Deck SP Issue. The fronts feature a color action photo as well as a small inset player shot. The 1996 All-Star game logo as well as the SP logo are on the bottom left corner. The backs have another photo as well as some biographical information.

	MINT	NRMT	EXC
COMPLETE SET (8)	40.00	18.00	5.00
COMMON CARD (1-8)	1.50	.70	.19
☐ 1 Ken Griffey Jr.	12.00	5.50	1.50
☐ 2 Frank Thomas	12.00	5.50	1.50
☐ 3 Albert Belle	6.00	2.70	.75
☐ 4 Mo Vaughn	3.00	1.35	.35
☐ 5 Barry Bonds	3.00	1.35	.35
☐ 6 Mike Piazza	10.00	4.50	1.25
☐ 7 Matt Williams	1.50	.70	.19
☐ 8 Sammy Sosa	2.00	.90	.25

1996 SP

The 1996 SP set was issued in one series totalling 188 cards. The eight-card packs retail for $4.19 each. Cards number 1-20 feature color action player photos with "Premier Prospects" printed in silver foil across the top and the player's name and team at the bottom in the border. The backs carry player information and statistics. Cards number 21-185 display unique player photos with an outer wood-grain border and inner thin platinum foil border as well as a small inset player shot. The backs carry another color player photo with unique player statistics depending on his position. The only notable Rookie Card in this set is Darin Erstad.

	MINT	NRMT	EXC
COMPLETE SET (188)	40.00	18.00	5.00
COMMON CARDS (1-188)	.15	.07	.02
☐ 1 Rey Ordonez FOIL	.60	.25	.07
☐ 2 George Arias FOIL	.15	.07	.02
☐ 3 Osvaldo Fernandez FOIL	.30	.14	.04
☐ 4 Darin Erstad FOIL	6.00	2.70	.75
☐ 5 Paul Wilson FOIL	.30	.14	.04
☐ 6 Richard Hidalgo FOIL	.60	.25	.07
☐ 7 Justin Thompson FOIL	.30	.14	.04
☐ 8 Jimmy Haynes FOIL	.15	.07	.02
☐ 9 Edgar Renteria FOIL	.60	.25	.07
☐ 10 Ruben Rivera FOIL	.60	.25	.07
☐ 11 Chris Snopek FOIL	.15	.07	.02
☐ 12 Billy Wagner FOIL	.60	.25	.07
☐ 13 Mike Grace FOIL	.15	.07	.02
☐ 14 Todd Greene FOIL	.30	.14	.04
☐ 15 Karim Garcia FOIL	.75	.35	.09
☐ 16 John Wasdin FOIL	.15	.07	.02
☐ 17 Jason Kendall FOIL	.60	.25	.07
☐ 18 Bob Abreu FOIL	.60	.25	.07
☐ 19 Jermaine Dye FOIL	.75	.35	.09
☐ 20 Jason Schmidt FOIL	.60	.25	.07
☐ 21 Javy Lopez	.30	.14	.04
☐ 22 Ryan Klesko	.60	.25	.07
☐ 23 Tom Glavine	.60	.25	.07
☐ 24 John Smoltz	.60	.25	.07
☐ 25 Greg Maddux	2.50	1.10	.30
☐ 26 Chipper Jones	2.50	1.10	.30
☐ 27 Fred McGriff	.60	.25	.07
☐ 28 David Justice	.30	.14	.04
☐ 29 Roberto Alomar	.75	.35	.09
☐ 30 Cal Ripken	3.00	1.35	.35
☐ 31 B.J. Surhoff	.15	.07	.02
☐ 32 Bobby Bonilla	.30	.14	.04
☐ 33 Mike Mussina	.75	.35	.09
☐ 34 Randy Myers	.15	.07	.02
☐ 35 Rafael Palmeiro	.60	.25	.07
☐ 36 Brady Anderson	.60	.25	.07
☐ 37 Tim Naehring	.15	.07	.02
☐ 38 Jose Canseco	.60	.25	.07
☐ 39 Roger Clemens	.75	.35	.09
☐ 40 Mo Vaughn	1.00	.45	.12
☐ 41 Jose Valentin	.15	.07	.02
☐ 42 Kevin Mitchell	.15	.07	.02
☐ 43 Chili Davis	.15	.07	.02
☐ 44 Garret Anderson	.60	.25	.07
☐ 45 Tim Salmon	.60	.25	.07
☐ 46 Chuck Finley	.15	.07	.02
☐ 47 Troy Percival	.15	.07	.02
☐ 48 Jim Abbott	.60	.25	.07
☐ 49 J.T. Snow	.15	.07	.02
☐ 50 Jim Edmonds	.30	.14	.04
☐ 51 Sammy Sosa	.60	.25	.07
☐ 52 Brian McRae	.15	.07	.02
☐ 53 Ryne Sandberg	1.00	.45	.12
☐ 54 Jaime Navarro	.15	.07	.02
☐ 55 Mark Grace	.60	.25	.07
☐ 56 Harold Baines	.30	.14	.04
☐ 57 Robin Ventura	.30	.14	.04
☐ 58 Tony Phillips	.30	.14	.04
☐ 59 Alex Fernandez	.30	.14	.04
☐ 60 Frank Thomas	4.00	1.80	.50
☐ 61 Ray Durham	.60	.25	.07
☐ 62 Bret Boone	.15	.07	.02
☐ 63 Reggie Sanders	.30	.14	.04
☐ 64 Pete Schourek	.15	.07	.02
☐ 65 Barry Larkin	.60	.25	.07
☐ 66 John Smiley	.15	.07	.02
☐ 67 Carlos Baerga	.15	.07	.02
☐ 68 Jim Thome	.75	.35	.09
☐ 69 Eddie Murray	1.00	.45	.12
☐ 70 Albert Belle	1.50	.70	.19
☐ 71 Dennis Martinez	.30	.14	.04

	MINT	NRMT	EXC
☐ 72 Jack McDowell	.60	.25	.07
☐ 73 Kenny Lofton	1.00	.45	.12
☐ 74 Manny Ramirez	1.00	.45	.12
☐ 75 Dante Bichette	.60	.25	.07
☐ 76 Vinny Castilla	.30	.14	.04
☐ 77 Andres Galarraga	.60	.25	.07
☐ 78 Walt Weiss	.15	.07	.02
☐ 79 Ellis Burks	.30	.14	.04
☐ 80 Larry Walker	.60	.25	.07
☐ 81 Cecil Fielder	.30	.14	.04
☐ 82 Melvin Nieves	.30	.14	.04
☐ 83 Travis Fryman	.30	.14	.04
☐ 84 Chad Curtis	.15	.07	.02
☐ 85 Alan Trammell	.30	.14	.04
☐ 86 Gary Sheffield	.60	.25	.07
☐ 87 Charles Johnson	.30	.14	.04
☐ 88 Andre Dawson	.30	.14	.04
☐ 89 Jeff Conine	.30	.14	.04
☐ 90 Greg Colbrunn	.15	.07	.02
☐ 91 Derek Bell	.30	.14	.04
☐ 92 Brian L.Hunter	.30	.14	.04
☐ 93 Doug Drabek	.15	.07	.02
☐ 94 Craig Biggio	.30	.14	.04
☐ 95 Jeff Bagwell	1.50	.70	.19
☐ 96 Kevin Appier	.30	.14	.04
☐ 97 Jeff Montgomery	.15	.07	.02
☐ 98 Michael Tucker	.30	.14	.04
☐ 99 Bip Roberts	.15	.07	.02
☐ 100 Johnny Damon	.30	.14	.04
☐ 101 Eric Karros	.30	.14	.04
☐ 102 Raul Mondesi	.60	.25	.07
☐ 103 Ramon Martinez	.30	.14	.04
☐ 104 Ismael Valdes	.30	.14	.04
☐ 105 Mike Piazza	2.50	1.10	.30
☐ 106 Hideo Nomo	1.00	.45	.12
☐ 107 Chan Ho Park	.60	.25	.07
☐ 108 Ben McDonald	.15	.07	.02
☐ 109 Kevin Seitzer	.15	.07	.02
☐ 110 Greg Vaughn	.60	.25	.07
☐ 111 Jose Valentin	.15	.07	.02
☐ 112 Rick Aguilera	.15	.07	.02
☐ 113 Marty Cordova	.30	.14	.04
☐ 114 Brad Radke	.15	.07	.02
☐ 115 Kirby Puckett	1.50	.70	.19
☐ 116 Chuck Knoblauch	.60	.25	.07
☐ 117 Paul Molitor	.75	.35	.09
☐ 118 Pedro Martinez	.30	.14	.04
☐ 119 Mike Lansing	.15	.07	.02
☐ 120 Rondell White	.30	.14	.04
☐ 121 Moises Alou	.30	.14	.04
☐ 122 Mark Grudzielanek	.30	.14	.04
☐ 123 Jeff Fassero	.15	.07	.02
☐ 124 Rico Brogna	.15	.07	.02
☐ 125 Jason Isringhausen	.15	.07	.02
☐ 126 Jeff Kent	.15	.07	.02
☐ 127 Bernard Gilkey	.30	.14	.04
☐ 128 Todd Hundley	.30	.14	.04
☐ 129 David Cone	.30	.14	.04
☐ 130 Andy Pettitte	1.25	.55	.16
☐ 131 Wade Boggs	.60	.25	.07
☐ 132 Paul O'Neill	.15	.07	.02
☐ 133 Ruben Sierra	.15	.07	.02
☐ 134 John Wetteland	.30	.14	.04
☐ 135 Derek Jeter	2.50	1.10	.30
☐ 136 Geronimo Berroa	.30	.14	.04
☐ 137 Terry Steinbach	.30	.14	.04
☐ 138 Ariel Prieto	.15	.07	.02
☐ 139 Scott Brosius	.15	.07	.02
☐ 140 Mark McGwire	1.25	.55	.16
☐ 141 Lenny Dykstra	.30	.14	.04
☐ 142 Todd Zeile	.30	.14	.04
☐ 143 Benito Santiago	.15	.07	.02
☐ 144 Mickey Morandini	.15	.07	.02
☐ 145 Gregg Jefferies	.60	.25	.07
☐ 146 Denny Neagle	.30	.14	.04
☐ 147 Orlando Merced	.30	.14	.04
☐ 148 Charlie Hayes	.15	.07	.02
☐ 149 Carlos Garcia	.15	.07	.02
☐ 150 Jay Bell	.30	.14	.04
☐ 151 Ray Lankford	.30	.14	.04
☐ 152 Alan Benes Andy Benes	.60	.25	.07
☐ 153 Dennis Eckersley	.30	.14	.04
☐ 154 Gary Gaetti	.30	.14	.04
☐ 155 Ozzie Smith	1.00	.45	.12
☐ 156 Ron Gant	.30	.14	.04
☐ 157 Brian Jordan	.30	.14	.04
☐ 158 Ken Caminiti	.60	.25	.07
☐ 159 Rickey Henderson	.60	.25	.07
☐ 160 Tony Gwynn	1.50	.70	.19
☐ 161 Wally Joyner	.15	.07	.02
☐ 162 Andy Ashby	.15	.07	.02
☐ 163 Steve Finley	.60	.25	.07
☐ 164 Glenallen Hill	.15	.07	.02
☐ 165 Matt Williams	.60	.25	.07
☐ 166 Barry Bonds	1.00	.45	.12
☐ 167 William VanLandingham	.15	.07	.02
☐ 168 Rod Beck	.30	.14	.04
☐ 169 Randy Johnson	.60	.25	.07
☐ 170 Ken Griffey Jr.	4.00	1.80	.50
☐ 171 Alex Rodriguez	4.00	1.80	.50
☐ 172 Edgar Martinez	.30	.14	.04
☐ 173 Jay Buhner	.60	.25	.07
☐ 174 Russ Davis	.15	.07	.02
☐ 175 Juan Gonzalez	2.00	.90	.25
☐ 176 Mickey Tettleton	.30	.14	.04
☐ 177 Will Clark	.60	.25	.07
☐ 178 Ken Hill	.30	.14	.04
☐ 179 Dean Palmer	.60	.25	.07
☐ 180 Ivan Rodriguez	1.00	.45	.12
☐ 181 Carlos Delgado	.30	.14	.04
☐ 182 Alex Gonzalez	.15	.07	.02
☐ 183 Shawn Green	.15	.07	.02
☐ 184 Juan Guzman	.15	.07	.02
☐ 185 Joe Carter	.30	.14	.04
☐ 186 Hideo Nomo CL	.60	.25	.07
☐ 187 Cal Ripken CL	1.50	.70	.19
☐ 188 Ken Griffey Jr. CL	2.00	.90	.25

1996 SP Baseball Heroes

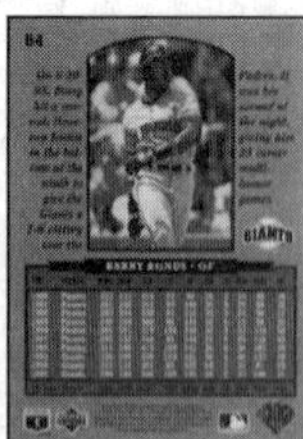

This 10-card set was randomly inserted at the rate of one in 96 packs. It continues the insert set that was started in 1990 featuring ten of the top players in baseball. The fronts feature color action player photos with the team logo on an embossed foil background. The backs carry another color player photo, player information and statistics.

	MINT	NRMT	EXC
COMPLETE SET (10)	300.00	135.00	38.00
COMMON CARD (82-90/HDR)	15.00	6.75	1.85
☐ 82 Frank Thomas	60.00	27.00	7.50
☐ 83 Albert Belle	25.00	11.00	3.10
☐ 84 Barry Bonds	15.00	6.75	1.85
☐ 85 Chipper Jones	40.00	18.00	5.00
☐ 86 Hideo Nomo	15.00	6.75	1.85
☐ 87 Mike Piazza	40.00	18.00	5.00
☐ 88 Manny Ramirez	15.00	6.75	1.85
☐ 89 Greg Maddux	40.00	18.00	5.00
☐ 90 Ken Griffey Jr.	60.00	27.00	7.50
☐ NNO Ken Griffey Jr. HDR	60.00	27.00	7.50

1996 SP Marquee Matchups

Randomly inserted at the rate of one in five packs, this 20-card set highlights two superstars' cards with a common matching stadium background photograph in a blue border. Each card features double foil stamping and embossed player images. The backs carry player information.

	MINT	NRMT	EXC
COMPLETE SET (20)	40.00	18.00	5.00
COMMON CARD (MM1-MM20)	1.00	.45	.12
☐ MM1 Ken Griffey Jr.	8.00	3.60	1.00
☐ MM2 Hideo Nomo	2.00	.90	.25
☐ MM3 Derek Jeter	5.00	2.20	.60
☐ MM4 Rey Ordonez	1.00	.45	.12
☐ MM5 Tim Salmon	1.00	.45	.12
☐ MM6 Mike Piazza	5.00	2.20	.60
☐ MM7 Mark McGwire	2.50	1.10	.30
☐ MM8 Barry Bonds	2.00	.90	.25
☐ MM9 Cal Ripken	6.00	2.70	.75
☐ MM10 Greg Maddux	5.00	2.20	.60
☐ MM11 Albert Belle	4.00	1.80	.50
☐ MM12 Barry Larkin	1.00	.45	.12
☐ MM13 Jeff Bagwell	3.00	1.35	.35
☐ MM14 Juan Gonzalez	3.00	1.35	.35
☐ MM15 Frank Thomas	8.00	3.60	1.00
☐ MM16 Sammy Sosa	1.25	.55	.16
☐ MM17 Mike Mussina	1.50	.70	.19
☐ MM18 Chipper Jones	5.00	2.20	.60
☐ MM19 Roger Clemens	1.00	.45	.12
☐ MM20 Fred McGriff	1.00	.45	.12

1996 SP Marquee Matchup Die Cuts

Randomly inserted at the rate of one in 61 packs, this 20-card set is a diecut version of the regular Marquee Matchup set with the border being red instead of blue.

	MINT	NRMT	EXC
COMPLETE SET (20)	200.00	90.00	25.00
COMMON CARD (MM1-MM20)	5.00	2.20	.60
*STARS: 2.5X TO 5X BASIC CARDS ..			

1996 SP Special FX

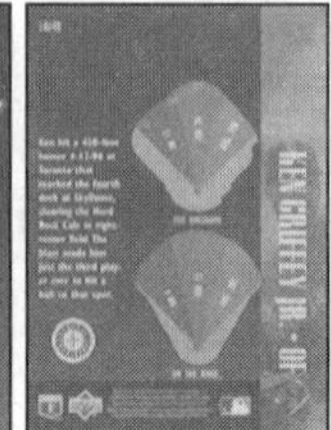

Randomly inserted at the rate of one in 5 packs, this 48-card set features a color action player cutout on a gold foil background with a holoview diamond shaped insert containing a black-and-white player portrait. A wide blue border runs vertically down one side of the card. The backs carry player information and statistics at home and away in baseball field designs on a blue background.

	MINT	NRMT	EXC
COMPLETE SET (48)	175.00	80.00	22.00
COMMON CARD (1-48)	2.00	.90	.25
☐ 1 Greg Maddux	12.00	5.50	1.50
☐ 2 Eric Karros	2.50	1.10	.30
☐ 3 Mike Piazza	12.00	5.50	1.50
☐ 4 Raul Mondesi	2.50	1.10	.30
☐ 5 Hideo Nomo	5.00	2.20	.60
☐ 6 Jim Edmonds	2.50	1.10	.30
☐ 7 Jason Isringhausen	2.00	.90	.25
☐ 8 Jay Buhner	2.50	1.10	.30
☐ 9 Barry Larkin	2.50	1.10	.30
☐ 10 Ken Griffey Jr.	20.00	9.00	2.50
☐ 11 Gary Sheffield	3.00	1.35	.35
☐ 12 Craig Biggio	2.50	1.10	.30
☐ 13 Paul Wilson	2.50	1.10	.30
☐ 14 Rondell White	2.50	1.10	.30
☐ 15 Chipper Jones	12.00	5.50	1.50
☐ 16 Kirby Puckett	8.00	3.60	1.00
☐ 17 Ron Gant	2.50	1.10	.30
☐ 18 Wade Boggs	2.50	1.10	.30
☐ 19 Fred McGriff	2.50	1.10	.30
☐ 20 Cal Ripken	15.00	6.75	1.85
☐ 21 Jason Kendall	2.50	1.10	.30
☐ 22 Johnny Damon	2.50	1.10	.30
☐ 23 Kenny Lofton	5.00	2.20	.60
☐ 24 Roberto Alomar	4.00	1.80	.50
☐ 25 Barry Bonds	5.00	2.20	.60
☐ 26 Dante Bichette	2.50	1.10	.30
☐ 27 Mark McGwire	6.00	2.70	.75
☐ 28 Rafael Palmeiro	2.50	1.10	.30
☐ 29 Juan Gonzalez	10.00	4.50	1.25
☐ 30 Albert Belle	8.00	3.60	1.00
☐ 31 Randy Johnson	3.00	1.35	.35
☐ 32 Jose Canseco	2.50	1.10	.30
☐ 33 Sammy Sosa	3.00	1.35	.35
☐ 34 Eddie Murray	5.00	2.20	.60
☐ 35 Frank Thomas	20.00	9.00	2.50
☐ 36 Tom Glavine	2.50	1.10	.30
☐ 37 Matt Williams	2.50	1.10	.30
☐ 38 Roger Clemens	4.00	1.80	.50
☐ 39 Paul Molitor	4.00	1.80	.50
☐ 40 Tony Gwynn	8.00	3.60	1.00
☐ 41 Mo Vaughn	5.00	2.20	.60
☐ 42 Tim Salmon	2.50	1.10	.30
☐ 43 Manny Ramirez	5.00	2.20	.60
☐ 44 Jeff Bagwell	8.00	3.60	1.00
☐ 45 Edgar Martinez	2.50	1.10	.30
☐ 46 Rey Ordonez	2.50	1.10	.30
☐ 47 Osvaldo Fernandez	2.00	.90	.25
☐ 48 Derek Jeter	12.00	5.50	1.50

1996 SP Special FX Die Cuts

Randomly inserted at the rate of one in 75 packs, this 48-card set is a diecut version of the Holoview insert set. The design is the same except for the diecut top of the card, and the wide one-sided border and back background is red instead of blue.

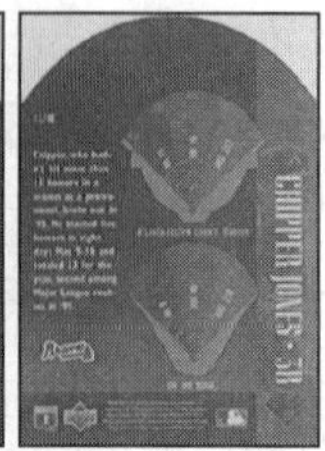

	MINT	NRMT	EXC
COMPLETE SET (48)	800.00	350.00	100.00
COMMON CARD (1-48)	10.00	4.50	1.25
*STARS: 2.5X TO 5X BASIC CARDS ..			

1995 SP Championship

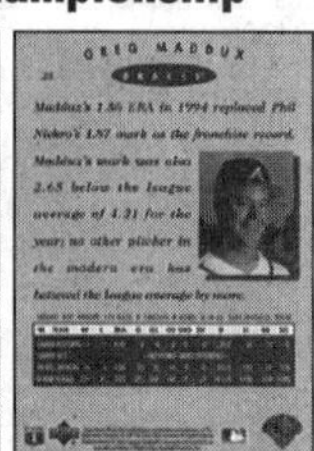

This set contains 200 cards that were sold in six-card retail packs for a suggested price of $2.99. The fronts have a full-bleed action photo with the words "SP Championship Series" in gold-foil in the bottom left-hand corner. In the bottom right-hand corner is the team's name in blue (National League) and red (American League) foil. The backs have a small head shot and player information. Statistics and team name are also on the back in blue or red just like on the front. Subsets featured are Diamonds in the Rough (1-20), October Legends (100-114) and Major League Profiles. Rookie Cards in this set include Bobby Higginson and Hideo Nomo.

	MINT	NRMT	EXC
COMPLETE SET (200)	40.00	18.00	5.00
COMMON CARD (1-200)	.15	.07	.02
☐ 1 Hideo Nomo	4.00	1.80	.50
☐ 2 Roger Cedeno	.30	.14	.04
☐ 3 Curtis Goodwin	.30	.14	.04
☐ 4 Jon Nunnally	.30	.14	.04
☐ 5 Bill Pulsipher	.30	.14	.04
☐ 6 Garret Anderson	.30	.14	.04
☐ 7 Dustin Hermanson	.30	.14	.04
☐ 8 Marty Cordova	.60	.25	.07
☐ 9 Ruben Rivera	1.25	.55	.16
☐ 10 Ariel Prieto	.30	.14	.04
☐ 11 Edgardo Alfonzo	.30	.14	.04
☐ 12 Ray Durham	.30	.14	.04
☐ 13 Quilvio Veras	.15	.07	.02
☐ 14 Ugueth Urbina	.15	.07	.02
☐ 15 Carlos Perez	.30	.14	.04
☐ 16 Glenn Dishman	.30	.14	.04
☐ 17 Jeff Suppan	.60	.25	.07
☐ 18 Jason Bates	.15	.07	.02
☐ 19 Jason Isringhausen	.60	.25	.07
☐ 20 Derek Jeter	2.50	1.10	.30
☐ 21 Fred McGriff MLP	.60	.25	.07
☐ 22 Marquis Grissom	.30	.14	.04
☐ 23 Fred McGriff	.60	.25	.07
☐ 24 Tom Glavine	.60	.25	.07
☐ 25 Greg Maddux	2.50	1.10	.30
☐ 26 Chipper Jones	2.50	1.10	.30
☐ 27 Sammy Sosa MLP	.60	.25	.07
☐ 28 Randy Myers	.15	.07	.02
☐ 29 Mark Grace	.60	.25	.07
☐ 30 Sammy Sosa	.60	.25	.07
☐ 31 Todd Zeile	.15	.07	.02
☐ 32 Brian McRae	.30	.14	.04
☐ 33 Ron Gant MLP	.30	.14	.04
☐ 34 Reggie Sanders	.30	.14	.04
☐ 35 Ron Gant	.30	.14	.04
☐ 36 Barry Larkin	.60	.25	.07
☐ 37 Bret Boone	.30	.14	.04
☐ 38 John Smiley	.15	.07	.02
☐ 39 Larry Walker MLP	.60	.25	.07
☐ 40 Andres Galarraga	.60	.25	.07
☐ 41 Bill Swift	.15	.07	.02
☐ 42 Larry Walker	.60	.25	.07
☐ 43 Vinny Castilla	.30	.14	.04
☐ 44 Dante Bichette	.60	.25	.07
☐ 45 Jeff Conine MLP	.30	.14	.04
☐ 46 Charles Johnson	.30	.14	.04
☐ 47 Gary Sheffield	.60	.25	.07
☐ 48 Andre Dawson	.30	.14	.04
☐ 49 Jeff Conine	.30	.14	.04
☐ 50 Jeff Bagwell MLP	.75	.35	.09
☐ 51 Phil Nevin	.15	.07	.02
☐ 52 Craig Biggio	.30	.14	.04
☐ 53 Brian L. Hunter	.30	.14	.04
☐ 54 Doug Drabek	.15	.07	.02
☐ 55 Jeff Bagwell	1.50	.70	.19
☐ 56 Derek Bell	.30	.14	.04
☐ 57 Mike Piazza MLP	1.25	.55	.16

☐ 58 Raul Mondesi	.60	.25	.07
☐ 59 Eric Karros	.30	.14	.04
☐ 60 Mike Piazza	2.50	1.10	.30
☐ 61 Ramon Martinez	.30	.14	.04
☐ 62 Billy Ashley	.15	.07	.02
☐ 63 Rondell White MLP	.30	.14	.04
☐ 64 Jeff Fassero	.15	.07	.02
☐ 65 Moises Alou	.30	.14	.04
☐ 66 Tony Tarasco	.15	.07	.02
☐ 67 Rondell White	.30	.14	.04
☐ 68 Pedro J. Martinez	.30	.14	.04
☐ 69 Bobby Jones MLP	.30	.14	.04
☐ 70 Bobby Bonilla	.30	.14	.04
☐ 71 Bobby Jones	.30	.14	.04
☐ 72 Bret Saberhagen	.30	.14	.04
☐ 73 Darren Daulton MLP	.15	.07	.02
☐ 74 Darren Daulton	.30	.14	.04
☐ 75 Gregg Jefferies	.30	.14	.04
☐ 76 Tyler Green	.15	.07	.02
☐ 77 Heathcliff Slocumb	.15	.07	.02
☐ 78 Lenny Dykstra	.30	.14	.04
☐ 79 Jay Bell MLP	.30	.14	.04
☐ 80 Denny Neagle	.30	.14	.04
☐ 81 Orlando Merced	.15	.07	.02
☐ 82 Jay Bell	.30	.14	.04
☐ 83 Ozzie Smith MLP	.60	.25	.07
☐ 84 Ken Hill	.15	.07	.02
☐ 85 Ozzie Smith	1.00	.45	.12
☐ 86 Bernard Gilkey	.30	.14	.04
☐ 87 Ray Lankford	.30	.14	.04
☐ 88 Tony Gwynn MLP	.75	.35	.09
☐ 89 Ken Caminiti	.60	.25	.07
☐ 90 Tony Gwynn	1.50	.70	.19
☐ 91 Joey Hamilton	.60	.25	.07
☐ 92 Bip Roberts	.15	.07	.02
☐ 93 Deion Sanders MLP	.60	.25	.07
☐ 94 Glenallen Hill	.15	.07	.02
☐ 95 Matt Williams	.60	.25	.07
☐ 96 Barry Bonds	1.00	.45	.12
☐ 97 Rod Beck	.15	.07	.02
☐ 98 Eddie Murray CL	.60	.25	.07
☐ 99 Cal Ripken Jr. CL	1.50	.70	.19
☐ 100 Roberto Alomar OL	.60	.25	.07
☐ 101 George Brett OL	1.00	.45	.12
☐ 102 Joe Carter OL	.30	.14	.04
☐ 103 Will Clark OL	.60	.25	.07
☐ 104 Dennis Eckersley OL	.30	.14	.04
☐ 105 Whitey Ford OL	.60	.25	.07
☐ 106 Steve Garvey OL	.30	.14	.04
☐ 107 Kirk Gibson OL	.30	.14	.04
☐ 108 Orel Hershiser OL	.30	.14	.04
☐ 109 Reggie Jackson OL	.60	.25	.07
☐ 110 Paul Molitor OL	.60	.25	.07
☐ 111 Kirby Puckett OL	.60	.25	.07
☐ 112 Mike Schmidt OL	.75	.35	.09
☐ 113 Dave Stewart OL	.15	.07	.02
☐ 114 Alan Trammell OL	.30	.14	.04
☐ 115 Cal Ripken Jr. MLP	1.50	.70	.19
☐ 116 Brady Anderson	.60	.25	.07
☐ 117 Mike Mussina	.75	.35	.09
☐ 118 Rafael Palmeiro	.60	.25	.07
☐ 119 Chris Hoiles	.15	.07	.02
☐ 120 Cal Ripken	3.00	1.35	.35
☐ 121 Mo Vaughn MLP	.60	.25	.07
☐ 122 Roger Clemens	.75	.35	.09
☐ 123 Tim Naehring	.15	.07	.02
☐ 124 John Valentin	.30	.14	.04
☐ 125 Mo Vaughn	1.00	.45	.12
☐ 126 Tim Wakefield	.15	.07	.02
☐ 127 Jose Canseco	.60	.25	.07
☐ 128 Rick Aguilera	.15	.07	.02
☐ 129 Chili Davis MLP	.30	.14	.04
☐ 130 Lee Smith	.30	.14	.04
☐ 131 Jim Edmonds	.60	.25	.07
☐ 132 Chuck Finley	.30	.14	.04
☐ 133 Chili Davis	.30	.14	.04
☐ 134 J.T. Snow	.30	.14	.04
☐ 135 Tim Salmon	.60	.25	.07
☐ 136 Frank Thomas MLP	2.00	.90	.25
☐ 137 Jason Bere	.15	.07	.02
☐ 138 Robin Ventura	.30	.14	.04
☐ 139 Tim Raines	.60	.25	.07
☐ 140 Frank Thomas	4.00	1.80	.50
☐ 141 Alex Fernandez	.30	.14	.04
☐ 142 Eddie Murray MLP	.60	.25	.07
☐ 143 Carlos Baerga	.30	.14	.04
☐ 144 Eddie Murray	1.00	.45	.12
☐ 145 Albert Belle	1.50	.70	.19
☐ 146 Jim Thome	.75	.35	.09
☐ 147 Dennis Martinez	.30	.14	.04
☐ 148 Dave Winfield	.60	.25	.07
☐ 149 Kenny Lofton	1.00	.45	.12
☐ 150 Manny Ramirez	1.00	.45	.12
☐ 151 Cecil Fielder MLP	.30	.14	.04
☐ 152 Lou Whitaker	.30	.14	.04
☐ 153 Alan Trammell	.30	.14	.04
☐ 154 Kirk Gibson	.30	.14	.04
☐ 155 Cecil Fielder	.30	.14	.04
☐ 156 Bobby Higginson	1.00	.45	.12
☐ 157 Kevin Appier MLP	.30	.14	.04
☐ 158 Wally Joyner	.30	.14	.04
☐ 159 Jeff Montgomery	.30	.14	.04
☐ 160 Kevin Appier	.30	.14	.04
☐ 161 Gary Gaetti	.30	.14	.04
☐ 162 Greg Gagne	.15	.07	.02
☐ 163 Ricky Bones MLP	.15	.07	.02
☐ 164 Greg Vaughn	.30	.14	.04
☐ 165 Kevin Seitzer	.15	.07	.02
☐ 166 Ricky Bones	.15	.07	.02
☐ 167 Kirby Puckett MLP	.60	.25	.07
☐ 168 Pedro Munoz	.15	.07	.02
☐ 169 Chuck Knoblauch	.60	.25	.07
☐ 170 Kirby Puckett	1.50	.70	.19
☐ 171 Don Mattingly MLP	1.00	.45	.12
☐ 172 Wade Boggs	.60	.25	.07
☐ 173 Paul O'Neill	.30	.14	.04
☐ 174 John Wetteland	.30	.14	.04
☐ 175 Don Mattingly	2.00	.90	.25
☐ 176 Jack McDowell	.30	.14	.04
☐ 177 Mark McGwire MLP	.60	.25	.07
☐ 178 Rickey Henderson	.60	.25	.07
☐ 179 Terry Steinbach	.30	.14	.04
☐ 180 Ruben Sierra	.30	.14	.04
☐ 181 Mark McGwire	1.25	.55	.16
☐ 182 Dennis Eckersley	.30	.14	.04
☐ 183 Ken Griffey Jr. MLP	2.00	.90	.25
☐ 184 Alex Rodriguez	5.00	2.20	.60
☐ 185 Ken Griffey Jr.	4.00	1.80	.50
☐ 186 Randy Johnson	.60	.25	.07
☐ 187 Jay Buhner	.60	.25	.07
☐ 188 Edgar Martinez	.30	.14	.04
☐ 189 Will Clark MLP	.60	.25	.07
☐ 190 Juan Gonzalez	2.00	.90	.25
☐ 191 Benji Gil	.15	.07	.02
☐ 192 Ivan Rodriguez	1.00	.45	.12
☐ 193 Kenny Rogers	.15	.07	.02
☐ 194 Will Clark	.60	.25	.07
☐ 195 Paul Molitor MLP	.60	.25	.07
☐ 196 Roberto Alomar	.75	.35	.09
☐ 197 David Cone	.30	.14	.04
☐ 198 Paul Molitor	.75	.35	.09
☐ 199 Shawn Green	.30	.14	.04
☐ 200 Joe Carter	.30	.14	.04
☐ CR1 Cal Ripken 2131 DC	175.00	80.00	22.00
☐ CR1 Cal Ripken, Jr. Tribute	60.00	27.00	7.50

1995 SP Championship Die Cuts

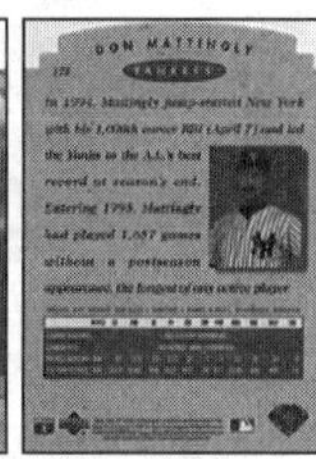

This 200-card set parallels the regular SP Championship set and was inserted one per pack. The only difference between the sets is the die-cut bordered design.

	MINT	NRMT	EXC
COMPLETE SET (200)	150.00	70.00	19.00
COMMON CARD (1-200)	.25	.11	.03
*STARS: 1.5X to 3X BASIC CARDS			
*YOUNG STARS: 1.25X to 2.5X BASIC CARDS			

1995 SP Championship Classic Performances

Cards from this 10-card set were randomly inserted in packs at a rate of one in 15. The set consists of 10 of the most memorable highlights since the 1969 Miracle Mets. The fronts have a series action photo highlighted with the words "Classic Performances" at the top in gold-foil enclosed by red. The backs have a color head shot with information and statistics from the series.

	MINT	NRMT	EXC
COMPLETE SET (10)	40.00	18.00	5.00
COMMON CARD (CP1-CP10)	2.00	.90	.25
☐ CP1 Reggie Jackson	4.00	1.80	.50
☐ CP2 Nolan Ryan	15.00	6.75	1.85
☐ CP3 Kirk Gibson	3.00	1.35	.35
☐ CP4 Joe Carter	3.00	1.35	.35
☐ CP5 George Brett	8.00	3.60	1.00
☐ CP6 Roberto Alomar	4.00	1.80	.50
☐ CP7 Ozzie Smith	5.00	2.20	.60
☐ CP8 Kirby Puckett	8.00	3.60	1.00
☐ CP9 Bret Saberhagen	2.00	.90	.25
☐ CP10 Steve Garvey	3.00	1.35	.35

1995 SP Championship Classic Performances Die Cuts

Cards from this 10-card set parallel the more common Classic Performances cards. These die cut inserts were seeded into one in every 72 packs. The die cut borders differentiate these cards from the basic Classic Performances inserts.

	MINT	NRMT	EXC
COMPLETE SET (10)	200.00	90.00	25.00
COMMON CARD (CP1-CP10)	10.00	4.50	1.25
*DIE CUTS: 2.5X to 5X BASIC CARDS			

1995 SP Championship Fall Classic

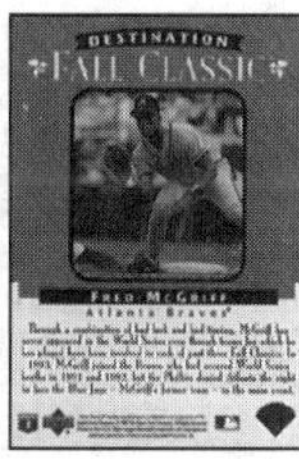

This nine-card set was randomly inserted in packs at a rate of one in 40. The set is comprised of players who had never been to the World Series prior to the 1995 Fall Classic. The fronts have a color-action photo with the game background in foil. There is a grain-colored border with the word "Destination" at the top in bronze-foil and "Fall Classic" underneath in black. The backs have a small, color picture inside a black box with player information underneath. Diecut versions were inserted at a rate of one in 72 packs and are valued at 1.5X to 3X the prices below.

	MINT	NRMT	EXC
COMPLETE SET (9)	125.00	55.00	15.50
COMMON CARD (1-9)	4.00	1.80	.50
☐ 1 Ken Griffey Jr.	30.00	13.50	3.70
☐ 2 Frank Thomas	30.00	13.50	3.70
☐ 3 Albert Belle	12.00	5.50	1.50
☐ 4 Mike Piazza	20.00	9.00	2.50
☐ 5 Don Mattingly	15.00	6.75	1.85
☐ 6 Hideo Nomo	15.00	6.75	1.85
☐ 7 Greg Maddux	20.00	9.00	2.50
☐ 8 Fred McGriff	4.00	1.80	.50
☐ 9 Barry Bonds	6.00	2.70	.75

1995 SP Championship Fall Classic Die Cuts

Cards from this 9-card set parallel the more common Fall Classic cards. These die cut inserts were seeded into one in every 72 packs. The die cut borders differentiate these cards from the basic Fall Classic inserts.

	MINT	NRMT	EXC
COMPLETE SET (9)	250.00	110.00	31.00
COMMON CARD (1-9)	8.00	3.60	1.00
*DIE CUTS: 1X to 2X BASIC CARDS			

1993 Spectrum Gold Signature Griffey Jr.

This standard-size card features Ken Griffey Jr. Each of the 4,000 gold signature cards comes with a certificate of authenticity.

	MINT	NRMT	EXC
COMPLETE SET (1)	8.00	3.60	1.00
COMMON CARD	8.00	3.60	1.00
☐ 1 Ken Griffey Jr.	8.00	3.60	1.00

1993 Spectrum Gold Signature Herman

This card honors Hall of Fame second baseman Billy Herman. Each of the 4,000 gold signature cards comes with a certificate of authenticity.

	MINT	NRMT	EXC
COMPLETE SET (1)	2.00	.90	.25
COMMON CARD	2.00	.90	.25
☐ 1 Billy Herman	2.00	.90	.25

1993 Spectrum Gold Signature Seaver

This card honors Tom Seaver, whose career 311 wins and 3,640 strikeouts earned him a first year induction into the Hall of Fame. Each of the 5,000 gold signature cards comes with a certificate of authenticity.

	MINT	NRMT	EXC
COMPLETE SET (1)	4.00	1.80	.50
COMMON CARD	4.00	1.80	.50
☐ 1 Tom Seaver	4.00	1.80	.50

1993 Spectrum HOF I

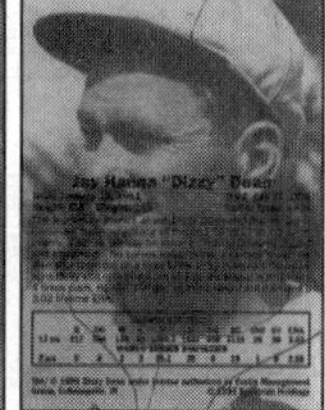

This five-card standard-size set features on its fronts borderless black-and-white vintage player photos that are trimmed in gold foil. The word "Spectrum" is printed diagonally in gold foil across the upper left corner. The card back carries a borderless ghosted black-and-white vintage player photo that provides the background for the player's career highlights. The set includes an official certificate of authenticity giving the set serial number and the production run figures (5,000). The cards are numbered on the back. There was also a Gold Signature version (5,000 sets produced) of the cards which are similar to the regular 1993 Spectrum HOF set, except for the addition of embossed facsimile 24-karat gold signatures across their fronts. The regular cards may also be distinguished from the "Gold Signature" series by different vintage player photos. Each of the Signature cards comes with its own 1/2" Lucite card holder and carries a serial number out of a 5,000-card production run. The Gold Signature cards are valued at two to three times the prices listed below.

	MINT	NRMT	EXC
COMPLETE SET (5)	6.00	2.70	.75
COMMON CARD (1-5)	1.00	.45	.12
☐ 1 Babe Ruth	2.00	.90	.25
☐ 2 Ty Cobb	1.50	.70	.19
☐ 3 Satchel Paige	1.25	.55	.16
☐ 4 Rogers Hornsby	1.00	.45	.12
☐ 5 Dizzy Dean	1.00	.45	.12

1993 Spectrum HOF II

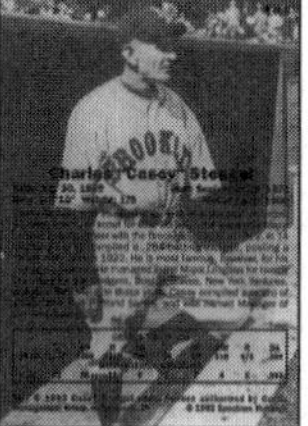

This five-card standard-size set features on its fronts borderless black-and-white vintage player photos that are trimmed in gold foil. "Spectrum" is printed diagonally in gold foil across the upper left corner. Cards are distinguishable from the "Gold Signature" series not only by the absence of embossed signatures but also by different vintage player photos. The back carries a borderless ghosted black-and-white vintage player photo that provides the background for the player's career highlights. The set includes an official certificate of authenticity giving the set serial number and the production run figures (5,000). The cards are numbered on the back. There was also a Gold Signature version (5,000 sets produced) of the cards which are similar to the regular 1993 Spectrum HOF set, except for the addition of embossed facsimile 24-karat gold signatures across their fronts. The regular cards may also be distinguished from the "Gold Signature" series by different vintage player photos. Each of the Signature cards comes with its own 1/2" Lucite card holder and carries a serial number out of a 5,000-card production run. The Gold Signature cards are valued at two to three times the prices listed below. The Grover Alexander card was also issued as a promo, with the disclaimer "For Promotional Use Only" in an oval on the back.

	MINT	NRMT	EXC
COMPLETE SET (5)	6.00	2.70	.75
COMMON CARD (1-5)	1.00	.45	.12
☐ 1 Lou Gehrig	2.00	.90	.25
☐ 2 Grover Alexander	1.00	.45	.12
☐ 3 Honus Wagner	1.50	.70	.19
☐ 4 Cy Young	1.50	.70	.19
☐ 5 Casey Stengel	1.50	.70	.19

1993 Spectrum Ryan 10

This ten-card set was produced by Spectrum Holdings Group, Inc. to commemorate Nolan Ryan's career. A card certifying authenticity is included in the set which indicates that 5,000 sets were produced. The full-bleed color fronts carry action shots of Ryan. A gold line forms an inner border with Ryan's name and position printed in gold lettering on a black and silver bar. The backs present career highlights superimposed over a ghosted full-bleed color photo. The cards are numbered on the back. There is a Gold Signature version (5,000 sets produced) of the cards which are identical to the regular 1993 Spectrum Nolan Ryan set, except for the addition of embossed facsimile gold signatures across their fronts. The Gold Signature cards are valued at double the prices listed below.

	MINT	NRMT	EXC
COMPLETE SET (10)	15.00	6.75	1.85
COMMON CARD (1-10)	1.50	.70	.19
☐ 1 Nolan Ryan Breaking In	1.50	.70	.19
☐ 2 Nolan Ryan The '69 Miracle Mets	1.50	.70	.19
☐ 3 Nolan Ryan Traded to The California Angels	1.50	.70	.19
☐ 4 Nolan Ryan Strikeout Record Breaker	1.50	.70	.19
☐ 5 Nolan Ryan Signs With The Houston Astros	1.50	.70	.19
☐ 6 Nolan Ryan Signs With The Texas Rangers	1.50	.70	.19
☐ 7 Nolan Ryan The King Of The K	1.50	.70	.19
☐ 8 Nolan Ryan 7 Career No-Hitters	1.50	.70	.19
☐ 9 Nolan Ryan Career Win Number 300	1.50	.70	.19
☐ 10 Nolan Ryan A Brilliant Career	1.50	.70	.19

1993 Spectrum Ryan 23K

Produced by Spectrum Holdings Group, Inc., this three-card set was accompanied by a certificate of authenticity carrying the set serial number and the production figures (10,000). Fronts feature a color player cutout on a 23k gold background. The player's name and position appear in a blue bar toward the bottom. The top of the back is edged by a black stripe; beneath on a blue panel are career summary, career highlights and statistics.

	MINT	NRMT	EXC
COMPLETE SET (3)	18.00	8.00	2.20
COMMON CARD (1-3)	6.00	2.70	.75
☐ 1 Nolan Ryan	6.00	2.70	.75
☐ 2 Nolan Ryan Season Records	6.00	2.70	.75
☐ 3 Nolan Ryan Career Records	6.00	2.70	.75

1993 Spectrum Ryan 5

This five-card standard-size set was produced by Spectrum Holdings Group, Inc. to celebrate Nolan Ryan's career. The set included a certificate of authenticity carrying the set serial number and the production run figures (5,000). The full-bleed fronts display color action shots that are framed by a thin gold inner border. The player's name appears on a black and silver bar outlined in gold. A gold seal carrying one of Ryan's records adorns each front and easily distinguishes this set from the 1993 Spectrum Ryan 10 set. Only the first card carries an embossed facsimile gold signature across it. On the same ghosted full-bleed action shot, backs summarize several of Ryan's outstanding pitching achievements. The cards are numbered on the back in the upper right corner.

	MINT	NRMT	EXC
COMPLETE SET (5)	8.00	3.60	1.00
COMMON CARD (1-5)	2.00	.90	.25
☐ 1 Nolan Ryan No-Hitters	2.00	.90	.25
☐ 2 Nolan Ryan Strikeouts	2.00	.90	.25
☐ 3 Nolan Ryan Strikeouts/9 Innings	2.00	.90	.25
☐ 4 Nolan Ryan Hits/9 Innings	2.00	.90	.25
☐ 5 Nolan Ryan Record Breaker	2.00	.90	.25

1993 Spectrum Ryan Tribute Sheet

This blank-backed borderless color sheet measures 8 1/2" by 11" and pays tribute to Nolan Ryan for his record-breaking 27 major league seasons. It features two color action shots of Ryan that are obliquely superimposed upon a background consisting of artificial turf, home plate, a ball and glove and Ryan's jersey. His gold signature appears in the lower left, below the Spectrum gold seal containing the production number out of a total of 5,000.

	MINT	NRMT	EXC
COMPLETE SET (1)	5.00	2.20	.60
COMMON CARD	5.00	2.20	.60
☐ 1 Nolan Ryan Sheet	5.00	2.20	.60

1926 Sport Company of America

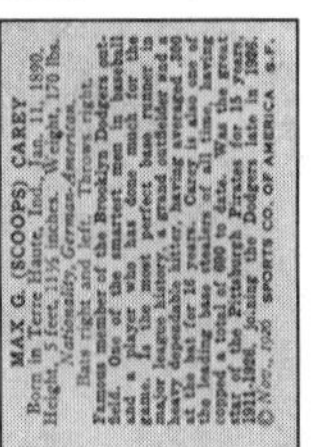

This 49-card set is actually part of a larger set of 151 cards featuring players from different sports. These 49 cards represent the baseball set and display black-and-white player photos within a fancy frame. The player's name and sport are printed at the bottom. The backs carry a short player biography and statistics. The cards came in a small glassine envelope along with a coupon that could be redeemed for sporting equipment. The cards are unnumbered and checklisted below in alphabetical order.

	EX-MT	VG-E	GOOD
COMPLETE BASEBALL SET (49)	1500.00	700.00	190.00
COMMON CARD (1-49)	10.00	4.50	1.25
☐ 1 Babe Adams	15.00	6.75	1.85
☐ 2 Grover Alexander	50.00	22.00	6.25
☐ 3 Nick Altrock	10.00	4.50	1.25
☐ 4 Dave Bancroft	30.00	13.50	3.70
☐ 5 Jesse Barnes	10.00	4.50	1.25
☐ 6 Ossie Bluege	10.00	4.50	1.25
☐ 7 Jim Bottomley	25.00	11.00	3.10
☐ 8 Max Carey	25.00	11.00	3.10
☐ 9 Ty Cobb	300.00	135.00	38.00
☐ 10 Mickey Cochrane	30.00	13.50	3.70
☐ 11 Eddie Collins	30.00	13.50	3.70
☐ 12 Stan Coveleski	25.00	11.00	3.10
☐ 13 Kiki Cuyler	25.00	11.00	3.10
☐ 14 Hank DeBerry	10.00	4.50	1.25
☐ 15 Jack Fournier	10.00	4.50	1.25
☐ 16 Goose Goslin	25.00	11.00	3.10
☐ 17 Charley Grimm	15.00	6.75	1.85
☐ 18 Bucky Harris	25.00	11.00	3.10
☐ 19 Gabby Hartnett	25.00	11.00	3.10
☐ 20 Fred Hofmann	10.00	4.50	1.25
☐ 21 Rogers Hornsby	40.00	18.00	5.00
☐ 22 Waite Hoyt	25.00	11.00	3.10
☐ 23 Walter Johnson	75.00	34.00	9.50
☐ 24 Joe Judge	10.00	4.50	1.25
☐ 25 Willie Kamm	10.00	4.50	1.25
☐ 26 Tony Lazzeri	25.00	11.00	3.10
☐ 27 Rabbit Maranville	25.00	11.00	3.10
☐ 28 Firpo Marberry	10.00	4.50	1.25
☐ 29 Rube Marquard	25.00	11.00	3.10
☐ 30 Stuffy McInnis	10.00	4.50	1.25
☐ 31 Babe Pinelli	10.00	4.50	1.25
☐ 32 Wally Pipp	10.00	4.50	1.25
☐ 33 Dutch Ruether	10.00	4.50	1.25
☐ 34 Sam Rice	25.00	11.00	3.10
☐ 35 Emory Rigney	10.00	4.50	1.25
☐ 36 Babe Ruth	500.00	220.00	60.00
☐ 37 Ray Schalk	25.00	11.00	3.10
☐ 38 Joe Sewell	25.00	11.00	3.10
☐ 39 Urban Shocker	15.00	6.75	1.85
☐ 40 Al Simmons	25.00	11.00	3.10
☐ 41 George Sisler	30.00	13.50	3.70
☐ 42 Tris Speaker	40.00	18.00	5.00
☐ 43 Pie Traynor	30.00	13.50	3.70
☐ 44 George Uhle	10.00	4.50	1.25
☐ 45 Paul Waner	30.00	13.50	3.70
☐ 46 Aaron Ward	10.00	4.50	1.25
☐ 47 Ken Williams	15.00	6.75	1.85
☐ 48 Glenn Wright	10.00	4.50	1.25
☐ 49 Emil Yde	10.00	4.50	1.25

1933 Sport Kings R338

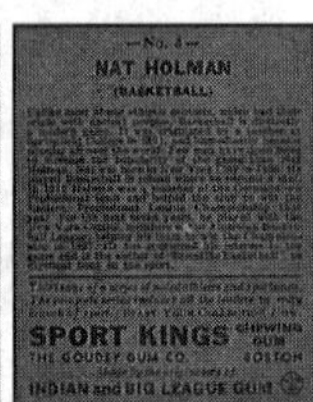

The cards in this 48-card set measure 2 3/8" by 2 7/8". The 1933 Sport Kings set, issued by the Goudey Gum Company, contains cards for the most famous athletic heroes of the times. No less than 18 different sports are represented in the set. The baseball cards of Cobb, Hubbell, and Ruth, and the football cards of Rockne and Thorpe command premium prices. All these cards are priced in the Basketball Annual guide; we have priced only the baseball cards in this volume.

	EX-MT	VG-E	GOOD
COMPLETE SET (48)	12500.00	5600.00	1600.00
COMMON CARD (1-24)	60.00	27.00	7.50
COMMON CARD (25-36)	75.00	34.00	9.50
COMMON CARD (37-48)	100.00	45.00	12.50
WRAPPER	30.00	13.50	3.70
☐ 1 Ty Cobb: baseball	1800.00	800.00	220.00
☐ 2 Babe Ruth: baseball	3500.00	1600.00	450.00
☐ 3 Nat Holman: basketball	350.00	160.00	45.00
☐ 4 Red Grange: football	450.00	200.00	55.00
☐ 5 Ed Wachter: basketball	125.00	55.00	15.50
☐ 6 Jim Thorpe: football	500.00	220.00	60.00
☐ 7 Bobby Walthour, Sr.: cycling	60.00	27.00	7.50
☐ 8 Walter Hagen: golf	200.00	90.00	25.00
☐ 9 Ed Blood: skiing	60.00	27.00	7.50
☐ 10 Anton Lekang: skiing	60.00	27.00	7.50
☐ 11 Claude Jewtraw: ice skating	60.00	27.00	7.50
☐ 12 Bobby McLean: ice skating	60.00	27.00	7.50
☐ 13 Laverne Fator: jockey	60.00	27.00	7.50
☐ 14 Jim Londos: wrestling	75.00	34.00	9.50
☐ 15 Reggie McNamara: bicycling	60.00	27.00	7.50
☐ 16 Bill Tilden: tennis	100.00	45.00	12.50
☐ 17 Jack Dempsey: boxing	350.00	160.00	45.00
☐ 18 Gene Tunney: boxing	250.00	110.00	31.00
☐ 19 Eddie Shore: hockey	400.00	180.00	50.00
☐ 20 Duke Kahanamoku: swim	225.00	100.00	28.00
☐ 21 John Weissmuller: swimming	350.00	160.00	45.00
☐ 22 Gene Sarazen: golf	175.00	80.00	22.00
☐ 23 Vincent Richards: tennis	60.00	27.00	7.50
☐ 24 Howie Morenz: hockey	400.00	180.00	50.00
☐ 25 Ralph Snoddy: speedboat	75.00	34.00	9.50
☐ 26 James R. Wedell: aviator	75.00	34.00	9.50
☐ 27 Col. R. Turner: aviator	75.00	34.00	9.50
☐ 28 James Doolittle: aviator	125.00	55.00	15.50
☐ 29 Ace Bailey: hockey	300.00	135.00	38.00
☐ 30 Ching Johnson: hockey	300.00	135.00	38.00
☐ 31 Bobby Walthour, Jr.: cycling	75.00	34.00	9.50
☐ 32 Joe Lapchick: basketball	400.00	180.00	50.00
☐ 33 Eddie Burke: basketball	250.00	110.00	31.00
☐ 34 Irving Jaffee: ice skating	75.00	34.00	9.50
☐ 35 Knute Rockne: football	600.00	275.00	75.00
☐ 36 Willie Hoppe: billiards	100.00	45.00	12.50
☐ 37 Helene Madison: swimming	100.00	45.00	12.50
☐ 38 Bobby Jones: golf	400.00	180.00	50.00
☐ 39 Jack Westrope: jockey	100.00	45.00	12.50
☐ 40 Don George: wrestling	100.00	45.00	12.50
☐ 41 Jim Browning: wrestling	100.00	45.00	12.50
☐ 42 Carl Hubbell: baseball	450.00	200.00	55.00
☐ 43 Primo Carnera: boxing	150.00	70.00	19.00
☐ 44 Max Baer: boxing	250.00	110.00	31.00
☐ 45 Babe Didrickson: track	600.00	275.00	75.00
☐ 46 Ellsworth Vines: tennis	125.00	55.00	15.50
☐ 47 J.H. Stevens: bob-sled	100.00	45.00	12.50
☐ 48 L. Seppala: dog-sled	125.00	55.00	15.50

1953 Sport Magazine Premiums

This 10-card set features 5 1/2" by 7" color portraits taken by photographer Ozzie Sweet. The cards are unnumbered and checklisted below in alphabetical order.

	NRMT	VG-E	GOOD
COMPLETE SET (10)	60.00	27.00	7.50
COMMON CARD (1-10)	5.00	2.20	.60
☐ 1 Joe Black	6.00	2.70	.75
☐ 2 Bob Cousy	10.00	4.50	1.25
☐ 3 Elroy Hirsch	8.00	3.60	1.00
☐ 4 Rocky Marciano	10.00	4.50	1.25
☐ 5 Bob Mathias	8.00	3.60	1.00
☐ 6 Stan Musial	10.00	4.50	1.25
☐ 7 John Olszewski	5.00	2.20	.60
☐ 8 Allie Reynolds	6.00	2.70	.75
☐ 9 Robin Roberts	8.00	3.60	1.00
☐ 10 Bobby Shantz	5.00	2.20	.60

1985-86 Sportflics Prototypes

The 1985-86 Sportflics Proof set contains four standard-size unnumbered cards, one mini (1 5/16" by 1 5/16") Joe DiMaggio card, and one trivia card (1 3/4" by 2"). The standard-size cards resemble regular 1986 Sportflics cards, but have different photos and stats only through 1984. One of the Winfield cards has a bio only; unfortunately the biographical statements on the back are incorrect in several instances. The DiMaggio card has black and white photos on the front, and career totals on the back. The trivia card is the same as those distributed with 1986 Sportflics, except it shows the major league baseball logo on the front. These test cards were apparently produced in limited quantity to show Major League Baseball and the Major League Baseball Players Association what Sportflics was proposing in order to be a new licensee for producing cards. These cards are very difficult to find and are considerably rarer than the Sportflics Test cards which were given out after the Sportflics license had been granted.

	NRMT	VG-E	GOOD
COMPLETE SET (5)	150.00	70.00	19.00
COMMON CARD (1-5)	5.00	2.20	.60
☐ 1 Joe DiMaggio (Small size)	75.00	34.00	9.50
☐ 2 Mike Schmidt (Stats on back)	50.00	22.00	6.25
☐ 3 Bruce Sutter (Stats on back)	5.00	2.20	.60
☐ 4 Dave Winfield (Biographical back)	15.00	6.75	1.85
☐ 5 Dave Winfield (Stats on back)	25.00	11.00	3.10

1985-86 Sportflics Samples

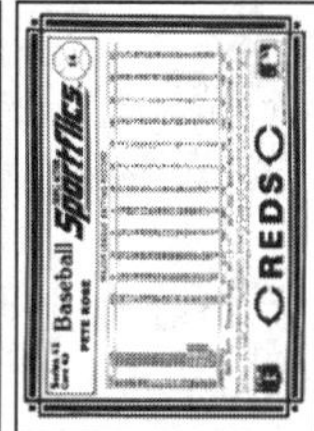

This three-card pack was a test, distributed freely by salesmen to potential buyers to show them what the new Sportflics product would look like. The set is sometimes referred to as the Vendor Sample Kit. Some of these packs even found their way to the retail counters. They are not rare although they are obviously much less common than the regular issue of Sportflics. The cards show statistics only up through 1984. The copyright date on the card backs shows 1986. The cards are standard size.

	NRMT	VG-E	GOOD
COMPLETE SET (3)	40.00	18.00	5.00
COMMON CARD	15.00	6.75	1.85
☐ 1 RBI Sluggers	15.00	6.75	1.85
Mike Schmidt			
Dale Murphy			
Jim Rice			
☐ 43 Pete Rose	15.00	6.75	1.85
(Pictured with bat-			
ting helmet; Pete			
is number 50 in			
regular 1986 set)			
☐ 45 Tom Seaver	15.00	6.75	1.85
(Tom is number 25 in			
regular 1986 set)			

1986 Sportflics

This 200-card standard-size set was marketed with 133 small trivia cards. This inaugural set for Sportflics was initially fairly well received by collectors. Sportflics was distributed by Major League Marketing; the company also maintained distribution agreements with Wrigley and Amurol. The set features 139 single player "magic motion" cards (which can be tilted to show three different pictures of the same player), 50 "Tri-Stars" (which show three different players), 10 "Big Six" cards (which show six players who share similar achievements), and one World Champs card featuring 12 members of the victorious Kansas City Royals. Some of the cards also have (limited production and rarely seen) proof versions with some player selection differences; a proof version of number 178 includes Jim Wilson instead of Mark Funderburk. Also a proof of number 179 with Karl Best, Mark Funderburk, Andres Galarraga, Dwayne Henry, Pete Incaviglia, and Todd Worrell was produced. The following sequences can be found to be in alphabetical order, 26-49, 76-99, 101-124, 151-174, and 187-199. Cards 1-24 seem to be Sportflics' selection of top players and cards 25, 50, 100, 125, and 175 all set milestones or records during the 1985 season. The Robin Yount Yankee error (#42A) is not considered part of the complete set.

	MINT	NRMT	EXC
COMPLETE SET (200)	20.00	9.00	2.50
COMPLETE FACT.SET (200)	20.00	9.00	2.50
COMMON CARD (1-200)	.05	.02	.01
☐ 1 George Brett	1.00	.45	.12
☐ 2 Don Mattingly	1.25	.55	.16
☐ 3 Wade Boggs	.40	.18	.05
☐ 4 Eddie Murray	.60	.25	.07
☐ 5 Dale Murphy	.15	.07	.02
☐ 6 Rickey Henderson	.15	.07	.02
☐ 7 Harold Baines	.10	.05	.01
☐ 8 Cal Ripken	2.50	1.10	.30
☐ 9 Orel Hershiser	.15	.07	.02
☐ 10 Bret Saberhagen	.15	.07	.02
☐ 11 Tim Raines	.10	.05	.01
☐ 12 Fernando Valenzuela	.10	.05	.01
☐ 13 Tony Gwynn	1.25	.55	.16
☐ 14 Pedro Guerrero	.05	.02	.01
☐ 15 Keith Hernandez	.10	.05	.01
☐ 16 Earnie Riles	.05	.02	.01
☐ 17 Jim Rice	.10	.05	.01
☐ 18 Ron Guidry	.10	.05	.01
☐ 19 Willie McGee	.10	.05	.01
☐ 20 Ryne Sandberg	1.00	.45	.12
☐ 21 Kirk Gibson	.10	.05	.01
☐ 22 Ozzie Guillen	.15	.07	.02
☐ 23 Dave Parker	.10	.05	.01
☐ 24 Vince Coleman	.15	.07	.02
☐ 25 Tom Seaver	.60	.25	.07
☐ 26 Brett Butler	.10	.05	.01
☐ 27 Steve Carlton	.50	.23	.06
☐ 28 Gary Carter	.10	.05	.01
☐ 29 Cecil Cooper	.10	.05	.01
☐ 30 Jose Cruz	.05	.02	.01
☐ 31 Alvin Davis	.05	.02	.01
☐ 32 Dwight Evans	.10	.05	.01
☐ 33 Julio Franco	.10	.05	.01
☐ 34 Damaso Garcia	.05	.02	.01
☐ 35 Steve Garvey	.15	.07	.02
☐ 36 Kent Hrbek	.10	.05	.01
☐ 37 Reggie Jackson	.60	.25	.07
☐ 38 Fred Lynn	.10	.05	.01
☐ 39 Paul Molitor	.75	.35	.09
☐ 40 Jim Presley	.05	.02	.01
☐ 41 Dave Righetti	.05	.02	.01
☐ 42A Robin Yount ERR	20.00	9.00	2.50
New York Yankees			
☐ 42B Robin Yount COR	.40	.18	.05
Milwaukee Brewers			
☐ 43 Nolan Ryan	2.50	1.10	.30
☐ 44 Mike Schmidt	.75	.35	.09
☐ 45 Lee Smith	.15	.07	.02
☐ 46 Rick Sutcliffe	.05	.02	.01
☐ 47 Bruce Sutter	.10	.05	.01
☐ 48 Lou Whitaker	.10	.05	.01
☐ 49 Dave Winfield	.15	.07	.02
☐ 50 Pete Rose	.75	.35	.09
☐ 51 NL MVP's	.50	.23	.06
Ryne Sandberg			
Steve Garvey			
Pete Rose			
☐ 52 Slugging Stars	.50	.23	.06
George Brett			
Harold Baines			
Jim Rice			
☐ 53 No-Hitters	.10	.05	.01
Phil Niekro			
Jerry Reuss			
Mike Witt			
☐ 54 Big Hitters	1.50	.70	.19
Don Mattingly			
Cal Ripken			
Robin Yount			
☐ 55 Bullpen Aces	.10	.05	.01
Dan Quisenberry			
Goose Gossage			
Lee Smith			
☐ 56 Rookies of The Year	.50	.23	.06
Darryl Strawberry			
Steve Sax			
Pete Rose			
☐ 57 AL MVP's	1.00	.45	.12
Cal Ripken			
Don Baylor			
Reggie Jackson			
☐ 58 Repeat Batting Champs	.50	.23	.06
Dave Parker			
Bill Madlock			
Pete Rose			
☐ 59 Cy Young Winners	.10	.05	.01
LaMarr Hoyt			
Mike Flanagan			
Ron Guidry			
☐ 60 Double Award Winners	.15	.07	.02
Fernando Valenzuela			
Rick Sutcliffe			
Tom Seaver			
☐ 61 Home Run Champs	.25	.11	.03
Reggie Jackson			
Jim Rice			
Tony Armas			
☐ 62 NL MVP's	.25	.11	.03
Keith Hernandez			
Dale Murphy			
Mike Schmidt			
☐ 63 AL MVP's	.50	.23	.06
Robin Yount			
George Brett			
Fred Lynn			
☐ 64 Comeback Players	.05	.02	.01
Bert Blyleven			
Jerry Koosman			
John Denny			
☐ 65 Cy Young Relievers	.10	.05	.01
Willie Hernandez			
Rollie Fingers			
Bruce Sutter			
☐ 66 Rookies of The Year	.10	.05	.01
Bob Horner			
Andre Dawson			
Gary Matthews			
☐ 67 Rookies of The Year	.25	.11	.03
Ron Kittle			
Carlton Fisk			
Tom Seaver			
☐ 68 Home Run Champs	.15	.07	.02
Mike Schmidt			
George Foster			
Dave Kingman			
☐ 69 Double Award Winners	1.00	.45	.12
Cal Ripken			
Rod Carew			
Pete Rose			
☐ 70 Cy Young Winners	.25	.11	.03
Rick Sutcliffe			
Steve Carlton			
Tom Seaver			
☐ 71 Top Sluggers	.25	.11	.03
Reggie Jackson			
Fred Lynn			
Robin Yount			
☐ 72 Rookies of The Year	.10	.05	.01
Dave Righetti			
Fernando Valenzuela			
Rick Sutcliffe			
☐ 73 Rookies of The Year	1.00	.45	.12
Fred Lynn			
Eddie Murray			
Cal Ripken			
☐ 74 Rookies of The Year	.10	.05	.01
Alvin Davis			
Lou Whitaker			
Rod Carew			
☐ 75 Batting Champs	.75	.35	.09
Don Mattingly			
Wade Boggs			
Carney Lansford			
☐ 76 Jesse Barfield	.05	.02	.01
☐ 77 Phil Bradley	.05	.02	.01
☐ 78 Chris Brown	.05	.02	.01
☐ 79 Tom Browning	.05	.02	.01
☐ 80 Tom Brunansky	.05	.02	.01
☐ 81 Bill Buckner	.10	.05	.01
☐ 82 Chili Davis	.10	.05	.01
☐ 83 Mike Davis	.05	.02	.01
☐ 84 Rich Gedman	.05	.02	.01
☐ 85 Willie Hernandez	.05	.02	.01
☐ 86 Ron Kittle	.05	.02	.01
☐ 87 Lee Lacy	.05	.02	.01
☐ 88 Bill Madlock	.05	.02	.01
☐ 89 Mike Marshall	.05	.02	.01
☐ 90 Keith Moreland	.05	.02	.01
☐ 91 Graig Nettles	.10	.05	.01
☐ 92 Lance Parrish	.05	.02	.01
☐ 93 Kirby Puckett	1.25	.55	.16
☐ 94 Juan Samuel	.05	.02	.01
☐ 95 Steve Sax	.05	.02	.01
☐ 96 Dave Stieb	.05	.02	.01
☐ 97 Darryl Strawberry	.15	.07	.02
☐ 98 Willie Upshaw	.05	.02	.01
☐ 99 Frank Viola	.10	.05	.01
☐ 100 Dwight Gooden	.50	.23	.06
☐ 101 Joaquin Andujar	.05	.02	.01
☐ 102 George Bell	.05	.02	.01
☐ 103 Bert Blyleven	.10	.05	.01
☐ 104 Mike Boddicker	.05	.02	.01
☐ 105 Britt Burns	.05	.02	.01
☐ 106 Rod Carew	.50	.23	.06
☐ 107 Jack Clark	.10	.05	.01
☐ 108 Danny Cox	.05	.02	.01
☐ 109 Ron Darling	.05	.02	.01
☐ 110 Andre Dawson	.15	.07	.02
☐ 111 Leon Durham	.05	.02	.01
☐ 112 Tony Fernandez	.05	.02	.01
☐ 113 Tommy Herr	.05	.02	.01
☐ 114 Teddy Higuera	.10	.05	.01
☐ 115 Bob Horner	.05	.02	.01
☐ 116 Dave Kingman	.10	.05	.01
☐ 117 Jack Morris	.10	.05	.01
☐ 118 Dan Quisenberry	.05	.02	.01
☐ 119 Jeff Reardon	.10	.05	.01
☐ 120 Bryn Smith	.05	.02	.01
☐ 121 Ozzie Smith	1.00	.45	.12
☐ 122 John Tudor	.05	.02	.01
☐ 123 Tim Wallach	.05	.02	.01
☐ 124 Willie Wilson	.05	.02	.01
☐ 125 Carlton Fisk	.40	.18	.05
☐ 126 RBI Sluggers	.10	.05	.01
Gary Carter			
Al Oliver			
George Foster			
☐ 127 Run Scorers	.50	.23	.06
Tim Raines			
Ryne Sandberg			
Keith Hernandez			
☐ 128 Run Scorers	1.00	.45	.12
Paul Molitor			
Cal Ripken			
Willie Wilson			
☐ 129 No-Hitters	.10	.05	.01
John Candelaria			
Dennis Eckersley			
Bob Forsch			
☐ 130 World Series MVP's	.50	.23	.06
Pete Rose			
Ron Cey			
Rollie Fingers			
☐ 131 All-Star Game MVP's	.10	.05	.01
Dave Concepcion			
George Foster			
Bill Madlock			
☐ 132 Cy Young Winners	.05	.02	.01
John Denny			
Fernando Valenzuela			
Vida Blue			
☐ 133 Comeback Players	.05	.02	.01
Rich Dotson			
Joaquin Andujar			
Doyle Alexander			
☐ 134 Big Winners	.10	.05	.01
Rick Sutcliffe			
Tom Seaver			
John Denny			
☐ 135 Veteran Pitchers	.25	.11	.03
Tom Seaver			
Phil Niekro			
Don Sutton			
☐ 136 Rookies of The Year	.10	.05	.01
Dwight Gooden			
Vince Coleman			
Alfredo Griffin			
☐ 137 All-Star Game MVP's	.10	.05	.01
Gary Carter			
Fred Lynn			
Steve Garvey			
☐ 138 Veteran Hitters	.50	.23	.06
Tony Perez			
Rusty Staub			
Pete Rose			
☐ 139 Power Hitters	.40	.18	.05
Mike Schmidt			
Jim Rice			
George Foster			
☐ 140 Batting Champs	.50	.23	.06
Tony Gwynn			
Al Oliver			
Bill Buckner			
☐ 141 No-Hitters	1.00	.45	.12
Nolan Ryan			
Jack Morris			
Dave Righetti			
☐ 142 No-Hitters	.15	.07	.02
Tom Seaver			
Bert Blyleven			
Vida Blue			
☐ 143 Strikeout Kings	1.00	.45	.12
Nolan Ryan			
Fernando Valenzuela			
Dwight Gooden			
☐ 144 Base Stealers	.10	.05	.01
Tim Raines			
Willie Wilson			
Davey Lopes			
☐ 145 RBI Sluggers	.10	.05	.01
Tony Armas			
Cecil Cooper			
Eddie Murray			
☐ 146 AL MVP's	.25	.11	.03
Rod Carew			
Jim Rice			
Rollie Fingers			
☐ 147 World Series MVP's	.15	.07	.02
Alan Trammell			
Rick Dempsey			
Reggie Jackson			
☐ 148 World Series MVP's	.15	.07	.02
Darrell Porter			
Pedro Guerrero			
Mike Schmidt			
☐ 149 ERA Leaders	.05	.02	.01
Mike Boddicker			
Rick Sutcliffe			
Ron Guidry			
☐ 150 Comeback Players	.15	.07	.02
Reggie Jackson			
Dave Kingman			
Fred Lynn			
☐ 151 Buddy Bell	.10	.05	.01
☐ 152 Dennis Boyd	.05	.02	.01
☐ 153 Dave Concepcion	.10	.05	.01
☐ 154 Brian Downing	.05	.02	.01
☐ 155 Shawon Dunston	.10	.05	.01
☐ 156 John Franco	.15	.07	.02
☐ 157 Scott Garrelts	.05	.02	.01
☐ 158 Bob James	.05	.02	.01
☐ 159 Charlie Leibrandt	.05	.02	.01
☐ 160 Oddibe McDowell	.05	.02	.01
☐ 161 Roger McDowell	.05	.02	.01
☐ 162 Mike Moore	.05	.02	.01
☐ 163 Phil Niekro	.15	.07	.02
☐ 164 Al Oliver	.10	.05	.01
☐ 165 Tony Pena	.05	.02	.01
☐ 166 Ted Power	.05	.02	.01
☐ 167 Mike Scioscia	.05	.02	.01
☐ 168 Mario Soto	.05	.02	.01
☐ 169 Bob Stanley	.05	.02	.01
☐ 170 Garry Templeton	.05	.02	.01
☐ 171 Andre Thornton	.05	.02	.01
☐ 172 Alan Trammell	.15	.07	.02
☐ 173 Doug DeCinces	.05	.02	.01
☐ 174 Greg Walker	.05	.02	.01
☐ 175 Don Sutton	.10	.05	.01
☐ 176 1985 Award Winners	.75	.35	.09
Ozzie Guillen			
Bret Saberhagen			
Don Mattingly			
Vince Coleman			
Dwight Gooden			
Willie McGee			
☐ 177 1985 Hot Rookies	.05	.02	.01
Stew Cliburn			
Brian Fisher UER			
(Photo actually			
Mike Pagliarulo)			

Joe Hesketh			
Joe Orsulak			
Mark Salas			
Larry Sheets			
178 1986 Rookies To Watch	2.50	1.10	.30
Jose Canseco			
Mark Funderburk			
Mike Greenwell			
Steve Lombardozzi UER			
(Photo actually			
Mark Salas)			
Billy Joe Robidoux			
Danny Tartabull			
179 1985 Gold Glovers	.75	.35	.09
George Brett			
Ron Guidry			
Keith Hernandez			
Don Mattingly			
Willie McGee			
Dale Murphy			
180 Active Lifetime .300	.75	.35	.09
Wade Boggs			
George Brett			
Rod Carew			
Cecil Cooper			
Don Mattingly			
Willie Wilson			
181 Active Lifetime .300	.50	.23	.06
Tony Gwynn			
Bill Madlock			
Pedro Guerrero			
Dave Parker			
Pete Rose			
Keith Hernandez			
182 1985 Milestones	.75	.35	.09
Rod Carew			
Phil Niekro			
Pete Rose			
Nolan Ryan			
Tom Seaver			
Matt Tallman (fan)			
183 1985 Triple Crown	.75	.35	.09
Wade Boggs			
Darrell Evans			
Don Mattingly			
Willie McGee			
Dale Murphy			
Dave Parker			
184 1985 Highlights	.75	.35	.09
Wade Boggs			
Dwight Gooden			
Rickey Henderson			
Don Mattingly			
Willie McGee			
John Tudor			
185 1985 20 Game Winners	.10	.05	.01
Dwight Gooden			
Ron Guidry			
John Tudor			
Joaquin Andujar			
Bret Saberhagen			
Tom Browning			
186 World Series Champs	.15	.07	.02
Lonnie Smith			
Dane Iorg			
Willie Wilson			
Charlie Leibrandt			
George Brett			
Bret Saberhagen			
Darryl Motley			
Dan Quisenberry			
Danny Jackson			
Jim Sundberg			
Steve Balboni			
Frank White			
187 Hubie Brooks	.05	.02	.01
188 Glenn Davis	.05	.02	.01
189 Darrell Evans	.10	.05	.01
190 Rich Gossage	.10	.05	.01
191 Andy Hawkins	.05	.02	.01
192 Jay Howell	.05	.02	.01
193 LaMarr Hoyt	.05	.02	.01
194 Davey Lopes	.05	.02	.01
195 Mike Scott	.05	.02	.01
196 Ted Simmons	.10	.05	.01
197 Gary Ward	.05	.02	.01
198 Bob Welch	.05	.02	.01
199 Mike Young	.05	.02	.01
200 Buddy Biancalana	.05	.02	.01

1986 Sportflics Rookies

This set of 50 three-phase "animated" standard-size cards features top rookies of 1986 as well as a few outstanding rookies from the past. These "Magic Motion" cards feature a distinctive light blue border on the front of the card. Cards were distributed in a light blue box, which also contained 34 trivia cards, each measuring 1 3/4" by 2". There are 47 single player cards along with two Tri-Stars and one Big Six. The statistics on the card backs are inclusive up through the just-completed 1986 season.

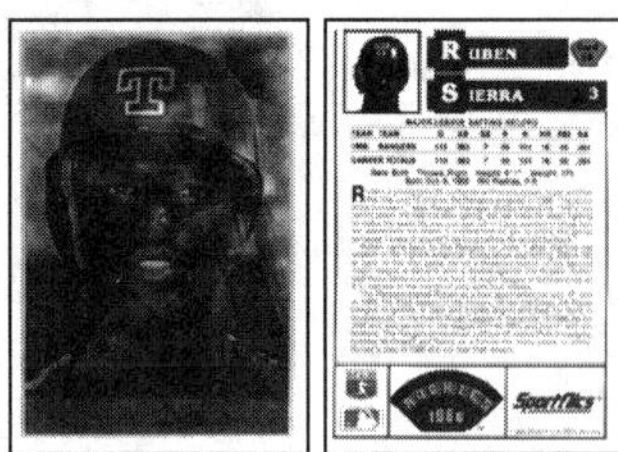

	MINT	NRMT	EXC
COMPLETE SET (50)	10.00	4.50	1.25
COMPLETE FACT.SET (50)	10.00	4.50	1.25
COMMON CARD (1-50)	.10	.05	.01
1 John Kruk	.60	.25	.07
2 Edwin Correa	.10	.05	.01
3 Pete Incaviglia	.20	.09	.03
4 Dale Sveum	.10	.05	.01
5 Juan Nieves	.10	.05	.01
6 Will Clark	1.50	.70	.19
7 Wally Joyner	.60	.25	.07
8 Lance McCullers	.10	.05	.01
9 Scott Bailes	.10	.05	.01
10 Dan Plesac	.10	.05	.01
11 Jose Canseco	2.00	.90	.25
12 Bobby Witt	.20	.09	.03
13 Barry Bonds	3.00	1.35	.35
14 Andres Thomas	.10	.05	.01
15 Jim Deshaies	.10	.05	.01
16 Ruben Sierra	.60	.25	.07
17 Steve Lombardozzi	.10	.05	.01
18 Cory Snyder	.10	.05	.01
19 Reggie Williams	.10	.05	.01
20 Mitch Williams	.10	.05	.01
21 Glenn Braggs	.10	.05	.01
22 Danny Tartabull	.20	.09	.03
23 Charlie Kerfeld	.10	.05	.01
24 Paul Assenmacher	.10	.05	.01
25 Robby Thompson	.20	.09	.03
26 Bobby Bonilla	.50	.23	.06
27 Andres Galarraga	1.50	.70	.19
28 Billy Joe Robidoux	.10	.05	.01
29 Bruce Ruffin	.10	.05	.01
30 Greg Swindell	.20	.09	.03
31 John Cangelosi	.10	.05	.01
32 Jim Traber	.10	.05	.01
33 Russ Morman	.10	.05	.01
34 Barry Larkin	2.00	.90	.25
35 Todd Worrell	.20	.09	.03
36 John Cerutti	.10	.05	.01
37 Mike Kingery	.10	.05	.01
38 Mark Eichhorn	.10	.05	.01
39 Scott Bankhead	.10	.05	.01
40 Bo Jackson	.75	.35	.09
41 Greg Mathews	.10	.05	.01
42 Eric King	.10	.05	.01
43 Kal Daniels	.10	.05	.01
44 Calvin Schiraldi	.10	.05	.01
45 Mickey Brantley	.10	.05	.01
46 Tri-Stars	.75	.35	.09
Willie Mays			
Pete Rose			
Fred Lynn			
47 Tri-Stars	.50	.23	.06
Tom Seaver			
Fernando Valenzuela			
Dwight Gooden			
48 Big Six	1.00	.45	.12
Eddie Murray			
Lou Whitaker			
Dave Righetti			
Steve Sax			
Cal Ripken			
Darryl Strawberry			
49 Kevin Mitchell	.20	.09	.03
50 Mike Diaz	.10	.05	.01

1986 Sportflics Decade Greats Samples

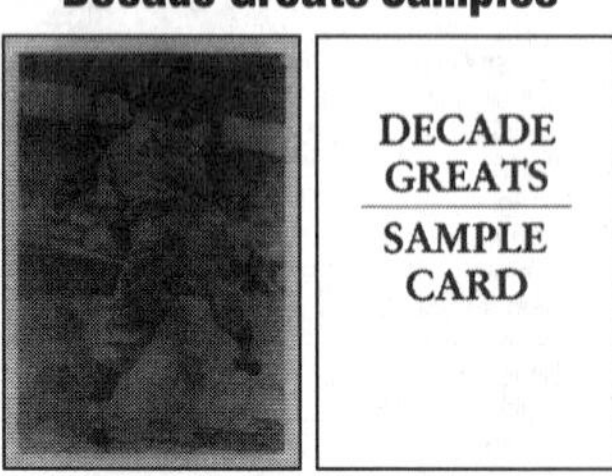

These standard-size cards features 3-D images of Dwight Gooden and Mel Ott. Depending on how the card is tilted, either an action shot or a portrait appears. The front has a white border. The white back carries the words "Decade Greats Sample Card" in large blue letters. The cards are unnumbered.

	MINT	NRMT	EXC
COMPLETE SET (2)	7.50	3.40	.95
COMMON CARD	3.50	1.55	.45
1 Dwight Gooden	3.50	1.55	.45
2 Mel Ott	5.00	2.20	.60

1986 Sportflics Decade Greats

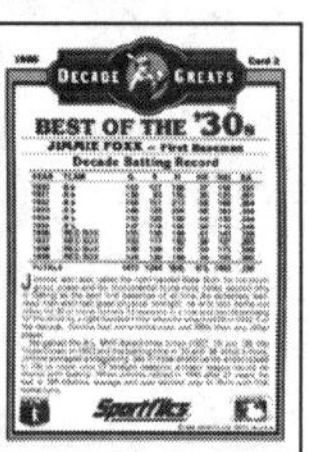

This set of 75 three-phase "animated" standard-size cards was produced by Sportflics and manufactured by Opti-Graphics of Arlington, Texas. The cards feature both sepia (players of the '30s and '40s) and full color cards. The concept of the set was that the best players at each position for each decade (from the '30s to the '80s) were chosen. The bios were written by Les Woodcock. Also included with the set in the specially designed collector box are 51 trivia cards with historical questions about the six decades of All-Star games. Sample cards of Dwight Gooden and Mel Ott, which are blank backed except for being stamped "Sample" on the back, also exist.

	MINT	NRMT	EXC
COMPLETE SET (75)	20.00	9.00	2.50
COMPLETE FACT.SET (75)	20.00	9.00	2.50
COMMON CARD (1-75)	.15	.07	.02
1 Babe Ruth	3.00	1.35	.35
2 Jimmie Foxx	.50	.23	.06
3 Lefty Grove	.50	.23	.06
4 Hank Greenberg	.50	.23	.06
5 Al Simmons	.25	.11	.03
6 Carl Hubbell	.35	.16	.04
7 Joe Cronin	.25	.11	.03
8 Mel Ott	.50	.23	.06
9 Lefty Gomez	.50	.23	.06
10 Lou Gehrig	3.00	1.35	.35
(Best '30s Player)			
11 Pie Traynor	.35	.16	.04
12 Charlie Gehringer	.35	.16	.04
13 Best '30s Catchers	.25	.11	.03
Bill Dickey			
Mickey Cochrane			
Gabby Hartnett			
14 Best '30s Pitchers	.35	.16	.04
Dizzy Dean			
Red Ruffing			
Paul Derringer			
15 Best '30s Outfielders	.25	.11	.03
Paul Waner			
Joe Medwick			
Earl Averill			
16 Bob Feller	.75	.35	.09
17 Lou Boudreau	.35	.16	.04
18 Enos Slaughter	.35	.16	.04
19 Hal Newhouser	.35	.16	.04
20 Joe DiMaggio	3.00	1.35	.35
21 Pee Wee Reese	.50	.23	.06
22 Phil Rizzuto	.50	.23	.06
23 Ernie Lombardi	.25	.11	.03
24 Best '40s Infielders	.35	.16	.04
Johnny Mize			
Joe Gordon			
George Kell			
25 Ted Williams	3.00	1.35	.35
(Best '40s Player)			
26 Mickey Mantle	4.00	1.80	.50
27 Warren Spahn	.50	.23	.06
28 Jackie Robinson	1.50	.70	.19
29 Ernie Banks	.50	.23	.06
30 Stan Musial	1.00	.45	.12
(Best '50s Player)			
31 Yogi Berra	.75	.35	.09
32 Duke Snider	.75	.35	.09
33 Roy Campanella	1.00	.45	.12
34 Eddie Mathews	.50	.23	.06
35 Ralph Kiner	.35	.16	.04
36 Early Wynn	.35	.16	.04
37 Double Play Duo	.50	.23	.06
Nellie Fox			
Luis Aparicio			
38 Best '50s First Base	.15	.07	.02
Gil Hodges			
Ted Kluszewski			
Mickey Vernon			
39 Best '50s Pitchers	.25	.11	.03
Bob Lemon			
Don Newcombe			
Robin Roberts			
40 Henry Aaron	1.50	.70	.19
41 Frank Robinson	.35	.16	.04
42 Bob Gibson	.35	.16	.04
43 Roberto Clemente	2.00	.90	.25
44 Whitey Ford	.60	.25	.07
45 Brooks Robinson	.75	.35	.09
46 Juan Marichal	.35	.16	.04
47 Carl Yastrzemski	.75	.35	.09
48 Best '60s First Base	.35	.16	.04
Willie McCovey			
Harmon Killebrew			
Orlando Cepeda			
49 Best '60s Catchers	.15	.07	.02
Joe Torre			
Elston Howard			
Bill Freehan			
50 Willie Mays	1.50	.70	.19
(Best '50s Player)			
51 Best '60s Outfielders	.35	.16	.04
Al Kaline			
Tony Oliva			
Billy Williams			
52 Tom Seaver	.75	.35	.09
53 Reggie Jackson	.75	.35	.09
54 Steve Carlton	.60	.25	.07
55 Mike Schmidt	1.50	.70	.19
56 Joe Morgan	.50	.23	.06
57 Jim Rice	.25	.11	.03
58 Jim Palmer	.50	.23	.06
59 Lou Brock	.35	.16	.04
60 Pete Rose	1.50	.70	.19
(Best '70s Player)			
61 Steve Garvey	.35	.16	.04
62 Best '70s Catchers	.50	.23	.06
Thurman Munson			
Carlton Fisk			
Ted Simmons			
63 Best '70s Pitchers	1.50	.70	.19
Vida Blue			
Catfish Hunter			
Nolan Ryan			
64 George Brett	2.00	.90	.25
65 Don Mattingly	2.50	1.10	.30
66 Fernando Valenzuela	.15	.07	.02
67 Dale Murphy			
68 Wade Boggs	.60	.25	.07
69 Rickey Henderson			
70 Eddie Murray	.75	.35	.09
(Best '80s Player)			
71 Ron Guidry	.15	.07	.02
72 Best '80s Catchers	.25	.11	.03
Gary Carter			
Lance Parrish			
Tony Pena			
73 Best '80s Infielders	2.00	.90	.25
Cal Ripken			
Lou Whitaker			
Robin Yount			
74 Best '80s Outfielders	.35	.16	.04
Pedro Guerrero			
Tim Raines			
Dave Winfield			
75 Dwight Gooden			

1987 Sportflics

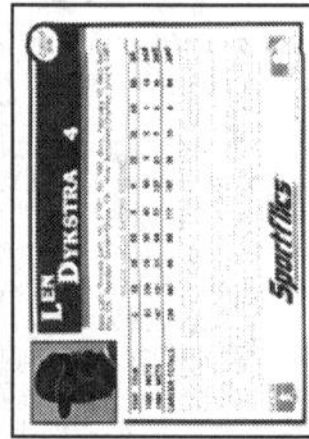

This 200-card standard-size color set was produced by Sportflics and again features three sequence action pictures on each card. Also included with the cards were 136 small team logo and trivia cards. There are 165 individual players, 20 Tri-Stars (the top three players in each league at each position), and 15 other miscellaneous multi-player cards. The cards feature a red border on the front. A full-color face shot of the player is printed on the back of the card. Cards are numbered on the back in the upper right corner. The cards in the factory-collated sets are copyrighted 1986, while the cards in the wax packs are copyrighted 1987 or show no copyright year on the back. Cards from wax packs with 1987 copyright are 1-35, 41-75, 81-115, 121-155, and 161-195; the rest of the numbers (when taken from wax packs) are found without a copyright year.

	MINT	NRMT	EXC
COMPLETE SET (200)	25.00	11.00	3.10
COMPLETE FACT.SET (200)	30.00	13.50	3.70
COMMON CARD (1-200)	.10	.05	.01
1 Don Mattingly	1.50	.70	.19
2 Wade Boggs	.40	.18	.05
3 Dale Murphy	.40	.18	.05
4 Rickey Henderson	.40	.18	.05
5 George Brett	1.25	.55	.16
6 Eddie Murray	.75	.35	.09
7 Kirby Puckett	1.50	.70	.19
8 Ryne Sandberg	1.25	.55	.16
9 Cal Ripken	3.00	1.35	.35
10 Roger Clemens	.75	.35	.09
11 Ted Higuera	.10	.05	.01
12 Steve Sax	.10	.05	.01
13 Chris Brown	.10	.05	.01
14 Jesse Barfield	.10	.05	.01
15 Kent Hrbek	.20	.09	.03
16 Robin Yount	.40	.18	.05
17 Glenn Davis	.10	.05	.01
18 Hubie Brooks	.10	.05	.01

☐ 19 Mike Scott .10 .05 .01
☐ 20 Darryl Strawberry .30 .14 .04
☐ 21 Alvin Davis .10 .05 .01
☐ 22 Eric Davis .20 .09 .03
☐ 23 Danny Tartabull .10 .05 .01
☐ 24A Cory Snyder ERR '86 1.00 .45 .12
(Photo on front
is Pat Tabler)
☐ 24B Cory Snyder ERR '87 .50 .23 .06
(Photos on front and
back are Pat Tabler)
☐ 24C Cory Snyder COR '86 .50 .23 .06
☐ 25 Pete Rose 1.00 .45 .12
☐ 26 Wally Joyner .40 .18 .05
☐ 27 Pedro Guerrero .10 .05 .01
☐ 28 Tom Seaver .75 .35 .09
☐ 29 Bob Knepper .10 .05 .01
☐ 30 Mike Schmidt .75 .35 .09
☐ 31 Tony Gwynn 1.50 .70 .19
☐ 32 Don Slaught .10 .05 .01
☐ 33 Todd Worrell .20 .09 .03
☐ 34 Tim Raines .20 .09 .03
☐ 35 Dave Parker .20 .09 .03
☐ 36 Bob Ojeda .10 .05 .01
☐ 37 Pete Incaviglia .20 .09 .03
☐ 38 Bruce Hurst .10 .05 .01
☐ 39 Bobby Witt .20 .09 .03
☐ 40 Steve Garvey .20 .09 .03
☐ 41 Dave Winfield .40 .18 .05
☐ 42 Jose Cruz .10 .05 .01
☐ 43 Orel Hershiser .20 .09 .03
☐ 44 Reggie Jackson .75 .35 .09
☐ 45 Chili Davis .20 .09 .03
☐ 46 Robby Thompson .20 .09 .03
☐ 47 Dennis Boyd .10 .05 .01
☐ 48 Kirk Gibson .20 .09 .03
☐ 49 Fred Lynn .20 .09 .03
☐ 50 Gary Carter .20 .09 .03
☐ 51 George Bell .10 .05 .01
☐ 52 Pete O'Brien .10 .05 .01
☐ 53 Ron Darling .10 .05 .01
☐ 54 Paul Molitor 1.00 .45 .12
☐ 55 Mike Pagliarulo .10 .05 .01
☐ 56 Mike Boddicker .10 .05 .01
☐ 57 Dave Righetti .10 .05 .01
☐ 58 Len Dykstra .30 .14 .04
☐ 59 Mike Witt .10 .05 .01
☐ 60 Tony Bernazard .10 .05 .01
☐ 61 John Kruk .30 .14 .04
☐ 62 Mike Krukow .10 .05 .01
☐ 63 Sid Fernandez .10 .05 .01
☐ 64 Gary Gaetti .10 .05 .01
☐ 65 Vince Coleman .10 .05 .01
☐ 66 Pat Tabler .10 .05 .01
☐ 67 Mike Scioscia .10 .05 .01
☐ 68 Scott Garrelts .10 .05 .01
☐ 69 Brett Butler .20 .09 .03
☐ 70 Bill Buckner .20 .09 .03
☐ 71A Dennis Rasmussen .50 .23 .06
ERR '86 copyright
(Photo on back
is John Montefusco)
☐ 71B Dennis Rasmussen .20 .09 .03
COR '87 copyright
(Photo with mustache)
☐ 72 Tim Wallach .10 .05 .01
☐ 73 Bob Horner .10 .05 .01
☐ 74 Willie McGee .10 .05 .01
☐ 75 Tri-Stars .60 .25 .07
Don Mattingly
Wally Joyner
Eddie Murray
☐ 76A Jesse Orosco COR .20 .09 .03
'86 copyright
☐ 76B Jesse Orosco ERR .10 .05 .01
'87 copyright
(Number on back is 96)
☐ 77 Tri-Stars .20 .09 .03
Todd Worrell
Jeff Reardon
Dave Smith
☐ 78 Candy Maldonado .10 .05 .01
☐ 79 Tri-Stars .30 .14 .04
Ozzie Smith
Hubie Brooks
Shawon Dunston
☐ 80 Tri-Stars .40 .18 .05
George Bell
Jose Canseco
Jim Rice
☐ 81 Bert Blyleven .20 .09 .03
☐ 82 Mike Marshall .10 .05 .01
☐ 83 Ron Guidry .20 .09 .03
☐ 84 Julio Franco .20 .09 .03
☐ 85 Willie Wilson .10 .05 .01
☐ 86 Lee Lacy .10 .05 .01
☐ 87 Jack Morris .20 .09 .03
☐ 88 Ray Knight .10 .05 .01
☐ 89 Phil Bradley .10 .05 .01
☐ 90 Jose Canseco 1.00 .45 .12
☐ 91 Gary Ward .10 .05 .01
☐ 92 Mike Easler .10 .05 .01
☐ 93 Tony Pena .10 .05 .01
☐ 94 Dave Smith .10 .05 .01
☐ 95 Will Clark 1.00 .45 .12
☐ 96 Lloyd Moseby .10 .05 .01
(See also 76B)
☐ 97 Jim Rice .20 .09 .03
☐ 98 Shawon Dunston .10 .05 .01
☐ 99 Don Sutton .20 .09 .03
☐ 100 Dwight Gooden .30 .14 .04
☐ 101 Lance Parrish .10 .05 .01
☐ 102 Mark Langston .20 .09 .03
☐ 103 Floyd Youmans .10 .05 .01
☐ 104 Lee Smith .30 .14 .04
☐ 105 Willie Hernandez .10 .05 .01
☐ 106 Doug DeCinces .10 .05 .01
☐ 107 Ken Schrom .10 .05 .01
☐ 108 Don Carman .10 .05 .01
☐ 109 Brook Jacoby .10 .05 .01
☐ 110 Steve Bedrosian .10 .05 .01
☐ 111 Tri-Stars .30 .14 .04
Roger Clemens
Jack Morris
Ted Higuera
☐ 112 Tri-Stars .20 .09 .03
Marty Barrett
Tony Bernazard
Lou Whitaker
☐ 113 Tri-Stars 1.25 .55 .16
Cal Ripken
Scott Fletcher
Tony Fernandez
☐ 114 Tri-Stars .50 .23 .06
Wade Boggs
George Brett
Gary Gaetti
☐ 115 Tri-Stars .30 .14 .04
Mike Schmidt
Chris Brown
Tim Wallach
☐ 116 Tri-Stars .30 .14 .04
Ryne Sandberg
Johnny Ray
Bill Doran
☐ 117 Tri-Stars .50 .23 .06
Dave Parker
Tony Gwynn
Kevin Bass
☐ 118 Big Six Rookies .20 .09 .03
Ty Gainey
Terry Steinbach
Dave Clark
Pat Dodson
Phil Lombardi
Benito Santiago
☐ 119 Hi-Lite Tri-Stars .10 .05 .01
Dave Righetti
Fernando Valenzuela
Mike Scott
☐ 120 Tri-Stars .20 .09 .03
Fernando Valenzuela
Mike Scott
Dwight Gooden
☐ 121 Johnny Ray .10 .05 .01
☐ 122 Keith Moreland .10 .05 .01
☐ 123 Juan Samuel .10 .05 .01
☐ 124 Wally Backman .10 .05 .01
☐ 125 Nolan Ryan 3.00 1.35 .35
☐ 126 Greg A. Harris .10 .05 .01
☐ 127 Kirk McCaskill .10 .05 .01
☐ 128 Dwight Evans .20 .09 .03
☐ 129 Rick Rhoden .10 .05 .01
☐ 130 Bill Madlock .10 .05 .01
☐ 131 Oddibe McDowell .10 .05 .01
☐ 132 Darrell Evans .20 .09 .03
☐ 133 Keith Hernandez .20 .09 .03
☐ 134 Tom Brunansky .10 .05 .01
☐ 135 Kevin McReynolds .10 .05 .01
☐ 136 Scott Fletcher .10 .05 .01
☐ 137 Lou Whitaker .20 .09 .03
☐ 138 Carney Lansford .20 .09 .03
☐ 139 Andre Dawson .30 .14 .04
☐ 140 Carlton Fisk .40 .18 .05
☐ 141 Buddy Bell .20 .09 .03
☐ 142 Ozzie Smith 1.25 .55 .16
☐ 143 Dan Pasqua .10 .05 .01
☐ 144 Kevin Mitchell .30 .14 .04
☐ 145 Bret Saberhagen .20 .09 .03
☐ 146 Charlie Kerfeld .10 .05 .01
☐ 147 Phil Niekro .30 .14 .04
☐ 148 John Candelaria .10 .05 .01
☐ 149 Rich Gedman .10 .05 .01
☐ 150 Fernando Valenzuela .20 .09 .03
☐ 151 Tri-Stars .20 .09 .03
Gary Carter
Mike Scioscia
Tony Pena
☐ 152 Tri-Stars .20 .09 .03
Tim Raines
Jose Cruz
Vince Coleman
☐ 153 Tri-Stars .20 .09 .03
Jesse Barfield
Harold Baines
Dave Winfield
☐ 154 Tri-Stars .10 .05 .01
Lance Parrish
Don Slaught
Rich Gedman
☐ 155 Tri-Stars .20 .09 .03
Dale Murphy
Kevin McReynolds
Eric Davis
☐ 156 Hi-Lite Tri-Stars .30 .14 .04
Don Sutton
Mike Schmidt
Jim Deshaies
☐ 157 Speedburners .20 .09 .03
Rickey Henderson
John Cangelosi
Gary Pettis
☐ 158 Big Six Rookies 1.50 .70 .19
Randy Asadoor
Casey Candaele
Kevin Seitzer
Rafael Palmeiro
Tim Pyznarski
Dave Cochrane
☐ 159 Big Six .75 .35 .09
Don Mattingly
Rickey Henderson
Roger Clemens
Dale Murphy
Eddie Murray
Dwight Gooden
☐ 160 Roger McDowell .10 .05 .01
☐ 161 Brian Downing .10 .05 .01
☐ 162 Bill Doran .10 .05 .01
☐ 163 Don Baylor .20 .09 .03
☐ 164A Alfredo Griffin ERR .20 .09 .03
(No uniform number
on card back) '87
☐ 164B Alfredo Griffin .20 .09 .03
COR '86
☐ 165 Don Aase .10 .05 .01
☐ 166 Glenn Wilson .10 .05 .01
☐ 167 Dan Quisenberry .10 .05 .01
☐ 168 Frank White .20 .09 .03
☐ 169 Cecil Cooper .20 .09 .03
☐ 170 Jody Davis .10 .05 .01
☐ 171 Harold Baines .20 .09 .03
☐ 172 Rob Deer .10 .05 .01
☐ 173 John Tudor .10 .05 .01
☐ 174 Larry Parrish .10 .05 .01
☐ 175 Kevin Bass .10 .05 .01
☐ 176 Joe Carter .30 .14 .04
☐ 177 Mitch Webster .10 .05 .01
☐ 178 Dave Kingman .20 .09 .03
☐ 179 Jim Presley .10 .05 .01
☐ 180 Mel Hall .10 .05 .01
☐ 181 Shane Rawley .10 .05 .01
☐ 182 Marty Barrett .10 .05 .01
☐ 183 Damaso Garcia .10 .05 .01
☐ 184 Bobby Grich .10 .05 .01
☐ 185 Leon Durham .10 .05 .01
☐ 186 Ozzie Guillen .20 .09 .03
☐ 187 Tony Fernandez .10 .05 .01
☐ 188 Alan Trammell .30 .14 .04
☐ 189 Jim Clancy .10 .05 .01
☐ 190 Bo Jackson .50 .23 .06
☐ 191 Bob Forsch .10 .05 .01
☐ 192 John Franco .20 .09 .03
☐ 193 Von Hayes .10 .05 .01
☐ 194 Tri-Stars .10 .05 .01
Don Aase
Dave Righetti
Mark Eichhorn
☐ 195 Tri-Stars .50 .23 .06
Keith Hernandez
Will Clark
Glenn Davis
☐ 196 Hi-Lite Tri-Stars .30 .14 .04
Roger Clemens
Joe Cowley
Bob Horner
☐ 197 Big Six .75 .35 .09
George Brett
Hubie Brooks
Tony Gwynn
Ryne Sandberg
Tim Raines
Wade Boggs
☐ 198 Tri-Stars .60 .25 .07
Kirby Puckett
Rickey Henderson
Fred Lynn
☐ 199 Speedburners .20 .09 .03
Tim Raines
Vince Coleman
Eric Davis
☐ 200 Steve Carlton .60 .25 .07

1987 Sportflics Dealer Panels

These "Magic Motion" card panels of four were issued only to dealers who were ordering other Sportflics product in quantity. If cut into individual cards, the interior white borders will be slightly narrower than the regular issue Sportflics since the panels of four measure a shade under 4 7/8" by 6 7/8". The cards have a 1986 copyright on the back same as the factory collated sets. Other than the slight difference in size, these cards are essentially styled the same as the regular issue of 1987 Sportflics. This set of sixteen top players was accompanied by the inclusion of four smaller panels of four team logo/team fact cards. The 16 small team cards correspond directly to the 16 players in the sets. The checklist below prices the panels and gives the card number for each player, which is the same as the player's card number in the Sportflics regular set.

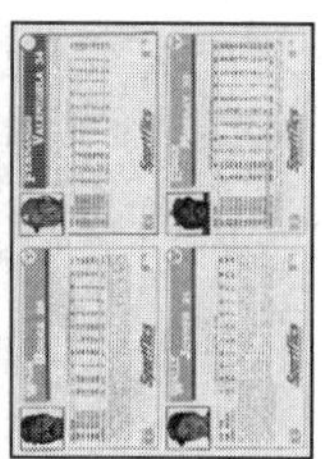

	MINT	NRMT	EXC
COMPLETE SET (4)	18.00	8.00	2.20
COMMON PANEL (1-4)	3.00	1.35	.35
☐ 1 Don Mattingly 1	6.00	2.70	.75
Roger Clemens 10			
Mike Schmidt 30			
Tim Raines 34			
☐ 2 Wade Boggs 2	3.00	1.35	.35
Eddie Murray 6			
Wally Joyner 26			
Fernando Valenzuela 150			
☐ 3 Dale Murphy 3			
Tony Gwynn 31			
Jim Rice 97			
Keith Hernandez 133			
☐ 4 Rickey Henderson 4	8.00	3.60	1.00
George Brett 5			
Cal Ripken 9			
Dwight Gooden 100			

1987 Sportflics Rookies I

These "Magic Motion" cards were issued as a series of 25 cards packaged in its own complete set box, along with 17 trivia cards. Cards are standard sized. The three front photos show the player in two action poses and one portrait pose. The card backs also provide a full-color photo (1 3/8" by 2 1/4") of the player as well as the usual statistics and biographical notes. The front photos are framed by a wide, round-cornered, red border and have the player's name and uniform number at the bottom. The cards in the set are numbered essentially in alphabetical order by player's name.

	MINT	NRMT	EXC
COMPLETE SET (25)	6.00	2.70	.75
COMPLETE FACT.SET (25)	6.00	2.70	.75
COMMON CARD (1-25)	.10	.05	.01
☐ 1 Eric Bell	.10	.05	.01
☐ 2 Chris Bosio	.20	.09	.03
☐ 3 Bob Brower	.10	.05	.01
☐ 4 Jerry Browne	.10	.05	.01
☐ 5 Ellis Burks	1.00	.45	.12
☐ 6 Casey Candaele	.10	.05	.01
☐ 7 Ken Gerhart	.10	.05	.01
☐ 8 Mike Greenwell	.20	.09	.03
☐ 9 Stan Jefferson	.10	.05	.01
☐ 10 Dave Magadan	.10	.05	.01
☐ 11 Joe Magrane	.10	.05	.01
☐ 12 Fred McGriff	1.50	.70	.19
☐ 13 Mark McGwire	1.50	.70	.19
☐ 14 Mark McLemore	.20	.09	.03
☐ 15 Jeff Musselman	.10	.05	.01
☐ 16 Matt Nokes	.10	.05	.01
☐ 17 Paul O'Neill	.40	.18	.05
☐ 18 Luis Polonia	.20	.09	.03
☐ 19 Benito Santiago	.20	.09	.03
☐ 20 Kevin Seitzer	.40	.18	.05
☐ 21 John Smiley	.20	.09	.03
☐ 22 Terry Steinbach	.40	.18	.05
☐ 23 B.J. Surhoff	.40	.18	.05
☐ 24 Devon White	.40	.18	.05
☐ 25 Matt Williams	2.00	.90	.25

1987 Sportflics Rookies II

These "Magic Motion" cards were issued as a series of 25 cards packaged in its own complete set box along with 17 trivia cards. Cards are standard sized. In this second set the card numbering begins with number 26. The three front photos show the player in two action poses and one portrait pose. The card backs also provide a full-color photo (approximately 1 3/8" by 2 1/4") of the player as well as

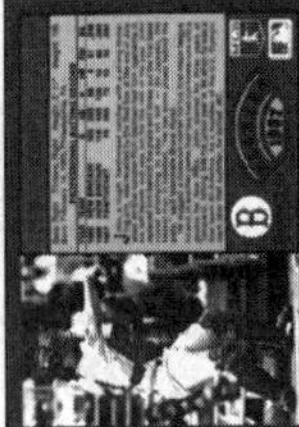

the usual statistics and biographical notes. The front photos are framed by a wide, round-cornered, red border and have the player's name and uniform number at the bottom.

	MINT	NRMT	EXC
COMPLETE SET (25)	5.00	2.20	.60
COMPLETE FACT.SET (25)	5.00	2.20	.60
COMMON CARD (26-50)	.10	.05	.01
☐ 26 DeWayne Buice	.10	.05	.01
☐ 27 Willie Fraser	.10	.05	.01
☐ 28 Billy Ripken	.10	.05	.01
☐ 29 Mike Henneman	.20	.09	.03
☐ 30 Shawn Hillegas	.10	.05	.01
☐ 31 Shane Mack	.10	.05	.01
☐ 32 Rafael Palmeiro	2.50	1.10	.30
☐ 33 Mike Jackson	.10	.05	.01
☐ 34 Gene Larkin	.10	.05	.01
☐ 35 Jimmy Jones	.10	.05	.01
☐ 36 Gerald Young	.10	.05	.01
☐ 37 Ken Caminiti	2.50	1.10	.30
☐ 38 Sam Horn	.10	.05	.01
☐ 39 David Cone	1.25	.55	.16
☐ 40 Mike Dunne	.10	.05	.01
☐ 41 Ken Williams	.10	.05	.01
☐ 42 John Morris	.10	.05	.01
☐ 43 Jim Lindeman	.10	.05	.01
☐ 44 Mike Stanley	.20	.09	.03
☐ 45 Les Straker	.10	.05	.01
☐ 46 Jeff M. Robinson	.10	.05	.01
☐ 47 Todd Benzinger	.10	.05	.01
☐ 48 Jeff Blauser	.30	.14	.04
☐ 49 John Marzano	.10	.05	.01
☐ 50 Keith Miller	.10	.05	.01

1987 Sportflics Rookie Packs

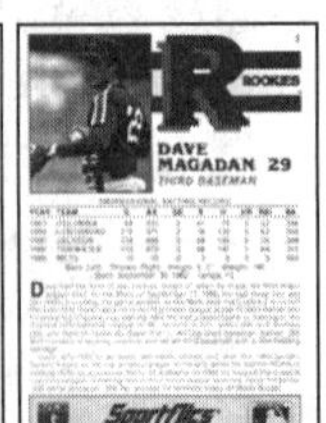

This two pack-set consists of ten "rookie" players and two trivia cards. Each of the two different packs had half the set and the outside of the wrapper told which cards were inside. Each card below has the pack number indicated by P1 or P2. The cards measure the standard size. Dealers received one rookie pack with every Team Preview set they ordered. The card backs also feature a full-color small photo of the player.

	MINT	NRMT	EXC
COMPLETE SET (10)	8.00	3.60	1.00
COMMON CARD (1-10)	.40	.18	.05
☐ 1 Terry Steinbach P2	.75	.35	.09
☐ 2 Rafael Palmeiro P1	4.00	1.80	.50
☐ 3 Dave Magadan P2	.60	.25	.07
☐ 4 Marvin Freeman P2	.40	.18	.05
☐ 5 Brick Smith P2	.40	.18	.05
☐ 6 B.J. Surhoff P1	1.00	.45	.12
☐ 7 John Smiley P1	.75	.35	.09
☐ 8 Alonzo Powell P2	.40	.18	.05
☐ 9 Benito Santiago P1	.75	.35	.09
☐ 10 Devon White P1	1.00	.45	.12

1987 Sportflics Superstar Discs

These 18 discs, measuring approximately 4 5/8" in diameter, featured leading players. The player's photo was surrounded by a red border. Player information is located on the back

	MINT	EXC	G-VG
COMPLETE SET (18)	40.00	18.00	5.00
COMMON DISC (1-18)	1.00	.45	.12
☐ 1 Joe Carter	2.00	.90	.25
☐ 2 Mike Scott	1.00	.45	.12
☐ 3 Ryne Sandberg	5.00	2.20	.60
☐ 4 Mike Schmidt	3.00	1.35	.35
☐ 5 Dale Murphy	2.00	.90	.25
☐ 6 Fernando Valenzuela	1.50	.70	.19
☐ 7 Tony Gwynn	5.00	2.20	.60
☐ 8 Cal Ripken Jr.	10.00	4.50	1.25
☐ 9 Gary Carter	3.00	1.35	.35
☐ 10 Cory Snyder	1.00	.45	.12
☐ 11 Kirby Puckett	5.00	2.20	.60
☐ 12 George Brett	5.00	2.20	.60
☐ 13 Keith Hernandez	1.50	.70	.19
☐ 14 Rickey Henderson	2.50	1.10	.30
☐ 15 Tim Raines	1.50	.70	.19
☐ 16 Bo Jackson	1.50	.70	.19
☐ 17 Pete Rose	5.00	2.20	.60
☐ 18 Eric Davis	1.00	.45	.12

1987 Sportflics Team Logo

These cards, issued one per major league team, featured all-time leaders from all the major league teams.

	MINT	NRMT	EXC
COMPLETE SET (26)	20.00	9.00	2.50
COMMON CARD (1-26)	1.00	.45	.12
☐ 1 Texas Rangers All-Time Team Leaders	1.00	.45	.12
☐ 2 New York Mets All-Time Team Leaders	1.00	.45	.12
☐ 3 Cleveland Indians All-Time Team Leaders	1.00	.45	.12
☐ 4 Cincinnati Reds All-Time Team Leaders	1.00	.45	.12
☐ 5 Toronto Blue Jays All-Time Team Leaders	1.00	.45	.12
☐ 6 Philadelphia Phillies All-Time Team Leaders	1.00	.45	.12
☐ 7 New York Yankees All-Time Team Leaders	1.00	.45	.12
☐ 8 Houston Astros All-Time Team Leaders	1.00	.45	.12
☐ 9 Boston Red Sox All-Time Team Leaders	1.00	.45	.12
☐ 10 San Francisco Giants All-Time Team Leaders	1.00	.45	.12
☐ 11 California Angels All-Time Team Leaders	1.00	.45	.12
☐ 12 St. Louis Cardinals All-Time Team Leaders	1.00	.45	.12
☐ 13 Kansas City Royals All-Time Team Leaders	1.00	.45	.12
☐ 14 Los Angeles Dodgers All-Time Team Leaders	1.00	.45	.12
☐ 15 Detroit Tigers All-Time Team Leaders	1.00	.45	.12
☐ 16 San Diego Padres All-Time Team Leaders	1.00	.45	.12
☐ 17 Minnesota Twins All-Time Team Leaders	1.00	.45	.12
☐ 18 Pittsburgh Pirates All-Time Team Leaders	1.00	.45	.12
☐ 19 Milwaukee Brewers All-Time Team Leaders	1.00	.45	.12
☐ 20 Montreal Expos All-Time Team Leaders	1.00	.45	.12
☐ 21 Baltimore Orioles All-Time Team Leaders	1.00	.45	.12
☐ 22 Chicago Cubs All-Time Team Leaders	1.00	.45	.12
☐ 23 Oakland Athletics All-Time Team Leaders	1.00	.45	.12
☐ 24 Atlanta Braves All-Time Team Leaders	1.00	.45	.12
☐ 25 Seattle Mariners All-Time Team Leaders	1.00	.45	.12
☐ 26 Chicago White Sox All-Time Team Leaders	1.00	.45	.12

1987 Sportflics Team Preview

This 26-card standard-size set features a card for each Major League team. Each card shows 12 different players on that team via four "Magic Motion" trios. The narrative on the back gives Outlook, Newcomers to Watch, and Summary for each team. The list of players appearing on the front is given at the bottom of the reverse of each card. The was distributed as a complete set in its own box along with 26 team logo trivia cards measuring approximately 1 3/4" by 2".

	MINT	NRMT	EXC
COMPLETE SET (26)	10.00	4.50	1.25
COMMON CARD (1-26)	.30	.14	.04
☐ 1 Texas Rangers Pete Incaviglia Mitch Williams Bobby Witt Greg Harris Don Slaught Oddibe McDowell Pete O'Brien Ruben Sierra Larry Parrish Scott Fletcher Charlie Hough Mike Loynd	.30	.14	.04
☐ 2 New York Mets Bob Ojeda Lenny Dykstra Darryl Strawberry Dwight Gooden Ron Darling Sid Fernandez Keith Hernandez Gary Carter Dave Magadan Randy Myers Kevin McReynolds Wally Backman	.30	.14	.04
☐ 3 Cleveland Indians Joe Carter Mel Hall Cory Snyder Pat Tabler Julio Franco Phil Niekro Brook Jacoby Greg Swindell Tom Candiotti Ken Schrom Brett Butler Tony Bernazard	.30	.14	.04
☐ 4 Cincinnati Reds Eric Davis Dave Parker Bill Gullickson John Franco Pete Rose Barry Larkin Tom Browning Kal Daniels Tracy Jones Buddy Bell Paul O'Neill Rob Murphy	.50	.23	.06
☐ 5 Toronto Blue Jays Willie Upshaw Tony Fernandez Glenallen Hill Jimmy Key George Bell Dave Stieb John Cerutti Tom Henke Mark Eichhorn Lloyd Moseby Jesse Barfield Fred McGriff	.30	.14	.04
☐ 6 Philadelphia Phillies Von Hayes Steve Bedrosian Kevin Gross Shane Rawley Glenn Wilson Bruce Ruffin Don Carman Marvin Freeman Milt Thompson Mike Schmidt Juan Samuel Kent Tekulve	.50	.23	.06
☐ 7 New York Yankees Bob Tewksbury Dave Righetti Dave Winfield Don Mattingly Dennis Rasmussen Mike Pagliarulo Rickey Henderson Don Pasqua Joel Skinner Willie Randolph Phil Lombardi Rick Rhoden	1.25	.55	.16
☐ 8 Houston Astros Glenn Davis Bob Knepper Kevin Bass Nolan Ryan Jose Cruz Ty Gainey Mike Scott Charlie Kerfeld Dave Smith Bill Doran Robby Wine Jim Deshaies	1.50	.70	.19
☐ 9 Boston Red Sox Wade Boggs Roger Clemens Dennis Boyd Dwight Evans Pat Dodson Dave Henderson Bruce Hurst Don Baylor Marty Barrett Calvin Schiraldi Mike Greenwell Jim Rice	.50	.23	.06
☐ 10 San Francisco Giants Chris Brown Mike Krukow Will Clark Chili Davis Robby Thompson Kelly Downs Jeff Leonard Terry Mulholland Bob Brenly Scott Garrelts Candy Maldonado Mark Grant	.50	.23	.06
☐ 11 California Angels Don Sutton Mike Witt Donnie Moore Wally Joyner John Candelaria Doug DeCinces Brian Downing Kirk McCaskill Devon White Gary Pettis Ruppert Jones Darrell Miller	.30	.14	.04
☐ 12 St. Louis Cardinals Terry Pendleton Tom Herr Todd Worrell Jack Clark John Tudor Bob Forsch Danny Cox Vince Coleman Willie McGee Ozzie Smith Joe Magrane Andy Van Slyke	.50	.23	.06
☐ 13 Kansas City Royals Bo Jackson Danny Tartabull George Brett Mark Gubicza Bret Saberhagen Willie Wilson Kevin Seitzer Frank White Charlie Leibrandt Dan Quisenberry Hal McRae Lonnie Smith	1.00	.45	.12
☐ 14 Los Angeles Dodgers Mike Scioscia Steve Fax Fernando Valenzuela Reggie Williams Mike Marshall Mariano Duncan Orel Hershiser Franklin Stubbs Matt Young Pedro Guerrero Jose Gonzalez Ralph Bryant	.30	.14	.04
☐ 15 Detroit Tigers Lou Whitaker Dan Petry Alan Trammell Chet Lemon Jack Morris Frank Tanana Darnell Coles Darrell Evans Dwight Lowry Kirk Gibson Willie Hernandez Eric King	.50	.23	.06
☐ 16 San Diego Padres Tony Gwynn John Kruk Kevin Mitchell Lance McCullers Shane Mack Craig Lefferts Steve Garvey	.50	.23	.06

Benny Santiago			
Randy Asadoor			
Andy Hawkins			
Jim Jones			
Ed Wojna			
☐ 17 Minnesota Twins	1.00	.45	.12
Gary Gaetti			
Roy Smalley			
Kirby Puckett			
Frank Viola			
Mark Salas			
Bert Blyleven			
Tom Brunansky			
Kent Hrbek			
Joe Klink			
Steve Lombardozzi			
Greg Gagne			
Jeff Reardon			
☐ 18 Pittsburgh Pirates	.50	.23	.06
John Smiley			
Sid Bream			
Mike Diaz			
Tony Pena			
Johnny Ray			
Jim Morrison			
R.J. Reynolds			
Barry Bonds			
Joe Orsulak			
Bobby Bonilla			
Bob Patterson			
Brian Fisher			
☐ 19 Milwaukee Brewers	.50	.23	.06
Ernest Riles			
Rob Deer			
Billy Jo Robidoux			
Dan Plesac			
Dale Sveum			
Teddy Higuera			
Robin Yount			
Glen Braggs			
B.J. Surhoff			
Paul Molitor			
Juan Nieves			
Tim Pyznarski			
☐ 20 Montreal Expos	.30	.14	.04
Floyd Youmans			
Tim Burke			
Casey Candaele			
Randy St. Claire			
Tim Wallach			
Alonzo Powell			
Mitch Webster			
Mike Fitzgerald			
Dave Collins			
Andres Galarraga			
Hubie Brooks			
Billy More			
☐ 21 Baltimore Orioles	2.00	.90	.25
Don Aase			
Mike Boddicker			
Eric Bell			
Larry Sheets			
Jim Traber			
Terry Kennedy			
Fred Lynn			
Cal Ripken Jr.			
Eddie Murray			
Lee Lacy			
Ray Knight			
Ken Gerhart			
☐ 22 Chicago Cubs	1.50	.70	.19
Ryne Sandberg			
Leon Durham			
Rafael Palmeiro			
Jody Davis			
Keith Moreland			
Scott Sanderson			
Shawon Dunston			
Lee Smith			
Jerry Mumphrey			
Dave Martinez			
Greg Maddux			
Dennis Eckersley			
☐ 23 Oakland Athletics	.50	.23	.06
Terry Steinbach			
Mike Davis			
Carney Lansford			
Jose Canseco			
Mark McGwire			
Rob Nelson			
Jose Rijo			
Dwayne Murphy			
Curt Young			
Tony Phillips			
Alfredo Griffin			
Reggie Jackson			
☐ 24 Atlanta Braves	.30	.14	.04
Rick Mahler			
Ken Oberkfell			
Gene Garber			
Andres Thomas			
Dale Murphy			
Ken Griffey			
David Palmer			
Paul Assenmacher			
Dion James			
Zane Smith			
Tom Glavine			
Glenn Hubbard			
☐ 25 Seattle Mariners	.30	.14	.04
Dave Valle			
Donell Nixon			
Scott Bradley			
Ken Phelps			
Mike Moore			
Mark Langston			
Alvin Davis			
Mickey Brantley			
Scott Bankhead			
Jim Presley			
Phil Bradley			
Steve Fireovid			
☐ 26 Chicago White Sox	.30	.14	.04
Carlton Fisk			
Harold Baines			
Joe Cowley			
John Cangelosi			
Ozzie Guillen			
Bobby Thigpen			
Greg Walker			
Ron Hassey			
Bob James			
Ron Karkovice			
Dave Cochrane			
Russ Mormon			

1988 Sportflics

This 225-card standard-size full-color set was produced by Sportflics and again features three sequence action pictures on each card. There are 219 individual players, three Highlights trios, and three Rookie Prospect trio cards. The cards feature a red border on the front. A full-color action picture of the player is printed on the back of the card.

	MINT	NRMT	EXC
COMPLETE SET (225)	30.00	13.50	3.70
COMPLETE FACT.SET (225)	30.00	13.50	3.70
COMMON CARD (1-225)	.10	.05	.01
☐ 1 Don Mattingly	1.50	.70	.19
☐ 2 Tim Raines	.20	.09	.03
☐ 3 Andre Dawson	.20	.09	.03
☐ 4 George Bell	.10	.05	.01
☐ 5 Joe Carter	.30	.14	.04
☐ 6 Matt Nokes	.10	.05	.01
☐ 7 Dave Winfield	.40	.18	.05
☐ 8 Kirby Puckett	1.50	.70	.19
☐ 9 Will Clark	.50	.23	.06
☐ 10 Eric Davis	.20	.09	.03
☐ 11 Rickey Henderson	.40	.18	.05
☐ 12 Ryne Sandberg	1.25	.55	.16
☐ 13 Jesse Barfield UER	.10	.05	.01
(Misspelled Jessie			
on card back)			
☐ 14 Ozzie Guillen	.10	.05	.01
☐ 15 Bret Saberhagen	.20	.09	.03
☐ 16 Tony Gwynn	1.50	.70	.19
☐ 17 Kevin Seitzer	.20	.09	.03
☐ 18 Jack Clark	.20	.09	.03
☐ 19 Danny Tartabull	.10	.05	.01
☐ 20 Ted Higuera	.10	.05	.01
☐ 21 Charlie Leibrandt UER	.10	.05	.01
(Misspelled Liebrandt			
on card front)			
☐ 22 Benito Santiago	.20	.09	.03
☐ 23 Fred Lynn	.10	.05	.01
☐ 24 Robby Thompson	.10	.05	.01
☐ 25 Alan Trammell	.20	.09	.03
☐ 26 Tony Fernandez	.10	.05	.01
☐ 27 Rick Sutcliffe	.10	.05	.01
☐ 28 Gary Carter	.20	.09	.03
☐ 29 Cory Snyder	.10	.05	.01
☐ 30 Lou Whitaker	.20	.09	.03
☐ 31 Keith Hernandez	.20	.09	.03
☐ 32 Mike Witt	.10	.05	.01
☐ 33 Harold Baines	.20	.09	.03
☐ 34 Robin Yount	.40	.18	.05
☐ 35 Mike Schmidt	.75	.35	.09
☐ 36 Dion James	.10	.05	.01
☐ 37 Tom Candiotti	.10	.05	.01
☐ 38 Tracy Jones	.10	.05	.01
☐ 39 Nolan Ryan	3.00	1.35	.35
☐ 40 Fernando Valenzuela	.20	.09	.03
☐ 41 Vance Law	.10	.05	.01
☐ 42 Roger McDowell	.10	.05	.01
☐ 43 Carlton Fisk	.40	.18	.05
☐ 44 Scott Garrelts	.10	.05	.01
☐ 45 Lee Guetterman	.10	.05	.01
☐ 46 Mark Langston	.20	.09	.03
☐ 47 Willie Randolph	.20	.09	.03
☐ 48 Bill Doran	.10	.05	.01
☐ 49 Larry Parrish	.10	.05	.01
☐ 50 Wade Boggs	.40	.18	.05
☐ 51 Shane Rawley	.10	.05	.01
☐ 52 Alvin Davis	.10	.05	.01
☐ 53 Jeff Reardon	.20	.09	.03
☐ 54 Jim Presley	.10	.05	.01
☐ 55 Kevin Bass	.10	.05	.01
☐ 56 Kevin McReynolds	.10	.05	.01
☐ 57 B.J. Surhoff	.20	.09	.03
☐ 58 Julio Franco	.20	.09	.03
☐ 59 Eddie Murray	.75	.35	.09
☐ 60 Jody Davis	.10	.05	.01
☐ 61 Todd Worrell	.10	.05	.01
☐ 62 Von Hayes	.10	.05	.01
☐ 63 Billy Hatcher	.10	.05	.01
☐ 64 John Kruk	.30	.14	.04
☐ 65 Tom Henke	.10	.05	.01
☐ 66 Mike Scott	.10	.05	.01
☐ 67 Vince Coleman	.10	.05	.01
☐ 68 Ozzie Smith	1.25	.55	.16
☐ 69 Ken Williams	.10	.05	.01
☐ 70 Steve Bedrosian	.10	.05	.01
☐ 71 Luis Polonia	.20	.09	.03
☐ 72 Brook Jacoby	.10	.05	.01
☐ 73 Ron Darling	.10	.05	.01
☐ 74 Lloyd Moseby	.10	.05	.01
☐ 75 Wally Joyner	.30	.14	.04
☐ 76 Dan Quisenberry	.10	.05	.01
☐ 77 Scott Fletcher	.10	.05	.01
☐ 78 Kirk McCaskill	.10	.05	.01
☐ 79 Paul Molitor	1.00	.45	.12
☐ 80 Mike Aldrete	.10	.05	.01
☐ 81 Neal Heaton	.10	.05	.01
☐ 82 Jeffrey Leonard	.10	.05	.01
☐ 83 Dave Magadan	.10	.05	.01
☐ 84 Danny Cox	.10	.05	.01
☐ 85 Lance McCullers	.10	.05	.01
☐ 86 Jay Howell	.10	.05	.01
☐ 87 Charlie Hough	.10	.05	.01
☐ 88 Gene Garber	.10	.05	.01
☐ 89 Jesse Orosco	.10	.05	.01
☐ 90 Don Robinson	.10	.05	.01
☐ 91 Willie McGee	.10	.05	.01
☐ 92 Bert Blyleven	.20	.09	.03
☐ 93 Phil Bradley	.10	.05	.01
☐ 94 Terry Kennedy	.10	.05	.01
☐ 95 Kent Hrbek	.20	.09	.03
☐ 96 Juan Samuel	.10	.05	.01
☐ 97 Pedro Guerrero	.10	.05	.01
☐ 98 Sid Bream	.10	.05	.01
☐ 99 Devon White	.30	.14	.04
☐ 100 Mark McGwire	1.00	.45	.12
☐ 101 Dave Parker	.20	.09	.03
☐ 102 Glenn Davis	.10	.05	.01
☐ 103 Greg Walker	.10	.05	.01
☐ 104 Rick Rhoden	.10	.05	.01
☐ 105 Mitch Webster	.10	.05	.01
☐ 106 Len Dykstra	.20	.09	.03
☐ 107 Gene Larkin	.10	.05	.01
☐ 108 Floyd Youmans	.10	.05	.01
☐ 109 Andy Van Slyke	.20	.09	.03
☐ 110 Mike Scioscia	.10	.05	.01
☐ 111 Kirk Gibson	.20	.09	.03
☐ 112 Kal Daniels	.10	.05	.01
☐ 113 Ruben Sierra	.30	.14	.04
☐ 114 Sam Horn	.10	.05	.01
☐ 115 Ray Knight	.10	.05	.01
☐ 116 Jimmy Key	.20	.09	.03
☐ 117 Bo Diaz	.10	.05	.01
☐ 118 Mike Greenwell	.20	.09	.03
☐ 119 Barry Bonds	1.25	.55	.16
☐ 120 Reggie Jackson UER	.75	.35	.09
(463 lifetime homers)			
☐ 121 Mike Pagliarulo	.10	.05	.01
☐ 122 Tommy John	.20	.09	.03
☐ 123 Bill Madlock	.10	.05	.01
☐ 124 Ken Caminiti	1.00	.45	.12
☐ 125 Gary Ward	.10	.05	.01
☐ 126 Candy Maldonado	.10	.05	.01
☐ 127 Harold Reynolds	.10	.05	.01
☐ 128 Joe Magrane	.10	.05	.01
☐ 129 Mike Henneman	.10	.05	.01
☐ 130 Jim Gantner	.10	.05	.01
☐ 131 Bobby Bonilla	.30	.14	.04
☐ 132 John Farrell	.10	.05	.01
☐ 133 Frank Tanana	.10	.05	.01
☐ 134 Zane Smith	.10	.05	.01
☐ 135 Dave Righetti	.10	.05	.01
☐ 136 Rick Reuschel	.10	.05	.01
☐ 137 Dwight Evans	.20	.09	.03
☐ 138 Howard Johnson	.10	.05	.01
☐ 139 Terry Leach	.10	.05	.01
☐ 140 Casey Candaele	.10	.05	.01
☐ 141 Tom Herr	.10	.05	.01
☐ 142 Tony Pena	.10	.05	.01
☐ 143 Lance Parrish	.10	.05	.01
☐ 144 Ellis Burks	.60	.25	.07
☐ 145 Pete O'Brien	.10	.05	.01
☐ 146 Mike Boddicker	.10	.05	.01
☐ 147 Buddy Bell	.20	.09	.03
☐ 148 Bo Jackson	.30	.14	.04
☐ 149 Frank White	.20	.09	.03
☐ 150 George Brett	1.25	.55	.16
☐ 151 Tim Wallach	.10	.05	.01
☐ 152 Cal Ripken	3.00	1.35	.35
☐ 153 Brett Butler	.20	.09	.03
☐ 154 Gary Gaetti	.10	.05	.01
☐ 155 Darryl Strawberry	.20	.09	.03
☐ 156 Alfredo Griffin	.10	.05	.01
☐ 157 Marty Barrett	.10	.05	.01
☐ 158 Jim Rice	.30	.14	.04
☐ 159 Terry Pendleton	.20	.09	.03
☐ 160 Orel Hershiser	.20	.09	.03
☐ 161 Larry Sheets	.10	.05	.01
☐ 162 Dave Stewart UER	.20	.09	.03
(Braves logo)			
☐ 163 Shawon Dunston	.10	.05	.01
☐ 164 Keith Moreland	.10	.05	.01
☐ 165 Ken Oberkfell	.10	.05	.01
☐ 166 Ivan Calderon	.10	.05	.01
☐ 167 Bob Welch	.10	.05	.01
☐ 168 Fred McGriff	.50	.23	.06
☐ 169 Pete Incaviglia	.10	.05	.01
☐ 170 Dale Murphy	.40	.18	.05
☐ 171 Mike Dunne	.10	.05	.01
☐ 172 Chili Davis	.20	.09	.03
☐ 173 Milt Thompson	.10	.05	.01
☐ 174 Terry Steinbach	.30	.14	.04
☐ 175 Oddibe McDowell	.10	.05	.01
☐ 176 Jack Morris	.20	.09	.03
☐ 177 Sid Fernandez	.10	.05	.01
☐ 178 Ken Griffey	.10	.05	.01
☐ 179 Lee Smith	.20	.09	.03
☐ 180 Highlights 1987	.40	.18	.05
Kirby Puckett			
Juan Nieves			
Mike Schmidt			
☐ 181 Brian Downing	.10	.05	.01
☐ 182 Andres Galarraga	.40	.18	.05
☐ 183 Rob Deer	.10	.05	.01
☐ 184 Greg Brock	.10	.05	.01
☐ 185 Doug DeCinces	.10	.05	.01
☐ 186 Johnny Ray	.10	.05	.01
☐ 187 Hubie Brooks	.10	.05	.01
☐ 188 Darrell Evans	.20	.09	.03
☐ 189 Mel Hall	.10	.05	.01
☐ 190 Jim Deshaies	.10	.05	.01
☐ 191 Dan Plesac	.10	.05	.01
☐ 192 Willie Wilson	.10	.05	.01
☐ 193 Mike LaValliere	.10	.05	.01
☐ 194 Tom Brunansky	.10	.05	.01
☐ 195 John Franco	.20	.09	.03
☐ 196 Frank Viola	.10	.05	.01
☐ 197 Bruce Hurst	.10	.05	.01
☐ 198 John Tudor	.10	.05	.01
☐ 199 Bob Forsch	.10	.05	.01
☐ 200 Dwight Gooden	.20	.09	.03
☐ 201 Jose Canseco	.50	.23	.06
☐ 202 Carney Lansford	.20	.09	.03
☐ 203 Kelly Downs	.10	.05	.01
☐ 204 Glenn Wilson	.10	.05	.01
☐ 205 Pat Tabler	.10	.05	.01
☐ 206 Mike Davis	.10	.05	.01
☐ 207 Roger Clemens	.60	.25	.07
☐ 208 Dave Smith	.10	.05	.01
☐ 209 Curt Young	.10	.05	.01
☐ 210 Mark Eichhorn	.10	.05	.01
☐ 211 Juan Nieves	.10	.05	.01
☐ 212 Bob Boone	.20	.09	.03
☐ 213 Don Sutton	.20	.09	.03
☐ 214 Willie Upshaw	.10	.05	.01
☐ 215 Jim Clancy	.10	.05	.01
☐ 216 Bill Ripken	.10	.05	.01
☐ 217 Ozzie Virgil	.10	.05	.01
☐ 218 Dave Concepcion	.20	.09	.03
☐ 219 Alan Ashby	.10	.05	.01
☐ 220 Mike Marshall	.10	.05	.01
☐ 221 Highlights 1987	.20	.09	.03
Mark McGwire			
Paul Molitor			
Vince Coleman			
☐ 222 Highlights 1987	.60	.25	.07
Benito Santiago			
Steve Bedrosian			
Don Mattingly			
☐ 223 Rookie Prospects	1.50	.70	.19
Shawn Abner			
Jay Buhner			
Gary Thurman			
☐ 224 Rookie Prospects	.10	.05	.01
Tim Crews			
Vicente Palacios			
John Davis			
☐ 225 Rookie Prospects	.20	.09	.03
Jody Reed			
Jeff Treadway			
Keith Miller			

1988 Sportflics Gamewinners

This 25-card set of "Gamewinners" was distributed in a green and yellow box along with 17 trivia cards by Weiser Card Company of New Jersey. The 25 players selected for the set show a strong New York preference. The set was ostensibly produced for use as a youth organizational fund raiser. The cards are the standard size and are done in the typical Sportflics' Magic Motion (three picture) style.

	MINT	NRMT	EXC
COMPLETE FACT.SET (25)	4.00	1.80	.50
COMMON CARD (1-25)	.10	.05	.01
☐ 1 Don Mattingly	2.00	.90	.25
☐ 2 Mark McGwire	1.25	.55	.16
☐ 3 Wade Boggs	.50	.23	.06
☐ 4 Will Clark	1.00	.45	.12
☐ 5 Eric Davis	.20	.09	.03
☐ 6 Willie Randolph	.10	.05	.01
☐ 7 Dave Winfield	.40	.18	.05
☐ 8 Rickey Henderson	.40	.18	.05
☐ 9 Dwight Gooden	.20	.09	.03
☐ 10 Benito Santiago	.20	.09	.03
☐ 11 Keith Hernandez	.20	.09	.03
☐ 12 Juan Samuel	.10	.05	.01
☐ 13 Kevin Seitzer	.20	.09	.03
☐ 14 Gary Carter	.20	.09	.03
☐ 15 Darryl Strawberry	.20	.09	.03
☐ 16 Rick Rhoden	.10	.05	.01
☐ 17 Howard Johnson	.10	.05	.01
☐ 18 Matt Nokes	.10	.05	.01
☐ 19 Dave Righetti	.10	.05	.01
☐ 20 Roger Clemens	1.00	.45	.12
☐ 21 Mike Schmidt	1.00	.45	.12
☐ 22 Kevin McReynolds	.10	.05	.01
☐ 23 Mike Pagliarulo	.10	.05	.01
☐ 24 Kevin Elster	.20	.09	.03
☐ 25 Jack Clark	.10	.05	.01

1989 Sportflics

This 225-card standard-size full-color set was produced by Sportflics (distributed by Major League Marketing) and again features three sequence action pictures on each card. There are 220 individual players, two Highlights trios, and three Rookie Prospect trio cards. The cards feature a white border on the front with red and blue inner trim colors. A full-color action picture of the player is printed on the back of the card.

	MINT	NRMT	EXC
COMPLETE SET (225)	30.00	13.50	3.70
COMPLETE FACT.SET (225)	30.00	13.50	3.70
COMMON CARD (1-225)	.10	.05	.01
☐ 1 Jose Canseco	.40	.18	.05
☐ 2 Wally Joyner	.20	.09	.03
☐ 3 Roger Clemens	.60	.25	.07
☐ 4 Greg Swindell	.10	.05	.01
☐ 5 Jack Morris	.20	.09	.03
☐ 6 Mickey Brantley	.10	.05	.01
☐ 7 Jim Presley	.10	.05	.01
☐ 8 Pete O'Brien	.10	.05	.01
☐ 9 Jesse Barfield	.10	.05	.01
☐ 10 Frank Viola	.10	.05	.01
☐ 11 Kevin Bass	.10	.05	.01
☐ 12 Glenn Wilson	.10	.05	.01
☐ 13 Chris Sabo	.10	.05	.01
☐ 14 Fred McGriff	.40	.18	.05
☐ 15 Mark Grace	.75	.35	.09
☐ 16 Devon White	.20	.09	.03
☐ 17 Juan Samuel	.10	.05	.01
☐ 18 Lou Whitaker UER (Card back says Bats: Right and Throws: Left)	.20	.09	.03
☐ 19 Greg Walker	.10	.05	.01
☐ 20 Roberto Alomar	1.50	.70	.19
☐ 21 Mike Schmidt	.75	.35	.09
☐ 22 Benito Santiago	.10	.05	.01
☐ 23 Dave Stewart	.20	.09	.03
☐ 24 Dave Winfield	.40	.18	.05
☐ 25 George Bell	.10	.05	.01
☐ 26 Jack Clark	.20	.09	.03
☐ 27 Doug Drabek	.10	.05	.01
☐ 28 Ron Gant	.40	.18	.05
☐ 29 Glenn Braggs	.10	.05	.01
☐ 30 Rafael Palmeiro	.50	.23	.06
☐ 31 Brett Butler	.20	.09	.03
☐ 32 Ron Darling	.10	.05	.01
☐ 33 Alvin Davis	.10	.05	.01
☐ 34 Bob Walk	.10	.05	.01
☐ 35 Dave Stieb	.10	.05	.01
☐ 36 Orel Hershiser	.20	.09	.03
☐ 37 John Farrell	.10	.05	.01
☐ 38 Doug Jones	.10	.05	.01
☐ 39 Kelly Downs	.10	.05	.01
☐ 40 Bob Boone	.20	.09	.03
☐ 41 Gary Sheffield UER (7 career triples, should be 0)	2.00	.90	.25
☐ 42 Doug Dascenzo	.10	.05	.01
☐ 43 Chad Kreuter	.10	.05	.01
☐ 44 Ricky Jordan	.10	.05	.01
☐ 45 Dave West	.10	.05	.01
☐ 46 Danny Tartabull	.10	.05	.01
☐ 47 Teddy Higuera	.10	.05	.01
☐ 48 Gary Gaetti	.10	.05	.01
☐ 49 Dave Parker	.20	.09	.03
☐ 50 Don Mattingly	1.50	.70	.19
☐ 51 David Cone	.30	.14	.04
☐ 52 Kal Daniels	.10	.05	.01
☐ 53 Carney Lansford	.20	.09	.03
☐ 54 Mike Marshall	.10	.05	.01
☐ 55 Kevin Seitzer	.10	.05	.01
☐ 56 Mike Henneman	.10	.05	.01
☐ 57 Bill Doran	.10	.05	.01
☐ 58 Steve Sax	.10	.05	.01
☐ 59 Lance Parrish	.10	.05	.01
☐ 60 Keith Hernandez	.20	.09	.03
☐ 61 Jose Uribe	.10	.05	.01
☐ 62 Jose Lind	.10	.05	.01
☐ 63 Steve Bedrosian	.10	.05	.01
☐ 64 George Brett UER (Text says .380 in 1980, should be .390)	1.25	.55	.16
☐ 65 Kirk Gibson	.30	.14	.04
☐ 66 Cal Ripken	3.00	1.35	.35
☐ 67 Mitch Webster	.10	.05	.01
☐ 68 Fred Lynn	.10	.05	.01
☐ 69 Eric Davis	.20	.09	.03
☐ 70 Bo Jackson	.30	.14	.04
☐ 71 Kevin Elster	.10	.05	.01
☐ 72 Rick Reuschel	.10	.05	.01
☐ 73 Tim Burke	.10	.05	.01
☐ 74 Mark Davis	.10	.05	.01
☐ 75 Claudell Washington	.10	.05	.01
☐ 76 Lance McCullers	.10	.05	.01
☐ 77 Mike Moore	.10	.05	.01
☐ 78 Robby Thompson	.10	.05	.01
☐ 79 Roger McDowell	.10	.05	.01
☐ 80 Danny Jackson	.10	.05	.01
☐ 81 Tim Leary	.10	.05	.01
☐ 82 Bobby Witt	.10	.05	.01
☐ 83 Jim Gott	.10	.05	.01
☐ 84 Andy Hawkins	.10	.05	.01
☐ 85 Ozzie Guillen	.10	.05	.01
☐ 86 John Tudor	.10	.05	.01
☐ 87 Todd Burns	.10	.05	.01
☐ 88 Dave Gallagher	.10	.05	.01
☐ 89 Jay Buhner	.75	.35	.09
☐ 90 Gregg Jefferies	.30	.14	.04
☐ 91 Bob Welch	.10	.05	.01
☐ 92 Charlie Hough	.10	.05	.01
☐ 93 Tony Fernandez	.10	.05	.01
☐ 94 Ozzie Virgil	.10	.05	.01
☐ 95 Andre Dawson	.20	.09	.03
☐ 96 Hubie Brooks	.10	.05	.01
☐ 97 Kevin McReynolds	.10	.05	.01
☐ 98 Mike LaValliere	.10	.05	.01
☐ 99 Terry Pendleton	.20	.09	.03
☐ 100 Wade Boggs	.40	.18	.05
☐ 101 Dennis Eckersley	.20	.09	.03
☐ 102 Mark Gubicza	.10	.05	.01
☐ 103 Frank Tanana	.10	.05	.01
☐ 104 Joe Carter	.30	.14	.04
☐ 105 Ozzie Smith	1.25	.55	.16
☐ 106 Dennis Martinez	.20	.09	.03
☐ 107 Jeff Treadway	.10	.05	.01
☐ 108 Greg Maddux	3.00	1.35	.35
☐ 109 Bret Saberhagen	.20	.09	.03
☐ 110 Dale Murphy	.40	.18	.05
☐ 111 Rob Deer	.10	.05	.01
☐ 112 Pete Incaviglia	.10	.05	.01
☐ 113 Vince Coleman	.10	.05	.01
☐ 114 Tim Wallach	.10	.05	.01
☐ 115 Nolan Ryan	3.00	1.35	.35
☐ 116 Walt Weiss	.10	.05	.01
☐ 117 Brian Downing	.10	.05	.01
☐ 118 Melido Perez	.10	.05	.01
☐ 119 Terry Steinbach	.20	.09	.03
☐ 120 Mike Scott	.10	.05	.01
☐ 121 Tim Belcher	.10	.05	.01
☐ 122 Mike Boddicker	.10	.05	.01
☐ 123 Len Dykstra	.20	.09	.03
☐ 124 Fernando Valenzuela	.20	.09	.03
☐ 125 Gerald Young	.10	.05	.01
☐ 126 Tom Henke	.10	.05	.01
☐ 127 Dave Henderson	.10	.05	.01
☐ 128 Dan Plesac	.10	.05	.01
☐ 129 Chili Davis	.20	.09	.03
☐ 130 Bryan Harvey	.10	.05	.01
☐ 131 Don August	.10	.05	.01
☐ 132 Mike Harkey	.10	.05	.01
☐ 133 Luis Polonia	.20	.09	.03
☐ 134 Craig Worthington	.10	.05	.01
☐ 135 Joey Meyer	.10	.05	.01
☐ 136 Barry Larkin	.40	.18	.05
☐ 137 Glenn Davis	.10	.05	.01
☐ 138 Mike Scioscia	.10	.05	.01
☐ 139 Andres Galarraga	.40	.18	.05
☐ 140 Dwight Gooden	.20	.09	.03
☐ 141 Keith Moreland	.10	.05	.01
☐ 142 Kevin Mitchell	.10	.05	.01
☐ 143 Mike Greenwell	.10	.05	.01
☐ 144 Mel Hall	.10	.05	.01
☐ 145 Rickey Henderson	.40	.18	.05
☐ 146 Barry Bonds	.75	.35	.09
☐ 147 Eddie Murray	.75	.35	.09
☐ 148 Lee Smith	.20	.09	.03
☐ 149 Julio Franco	.20	.09	.03
☐ 150 Tim Raines	.20	.09	.03
☐ 151 Mitch Williams	.10	.05	.01
☐ 152 Tim Laudner	.10	.05	.01
☐ 153 Mike Pagliarulo	.10	.05	.01
☐ 154 Floyd Bannister	.10	.05	.01
☐ 155 Gary Carter	.20	.09	.03
☐ 156 Kirby Puckett	1.50	.70	.19
☐ 157 Harold Baines	.20	.09	.03
☐ 158 Dave Righetti	.10	.05	.01
☐ 159 Mark Langston	.20	.09	.03
☐ 160 Tony Gwynn	1.50	.70	.19
☐ 161 Tom Brunansky	.10	.05	.01
☐ 162 Vance Law	.10	.05	.01
☐ 163 Kelly Gruber	.10	.05	.01
☐ 164 Gerald Perry	.10	.05	.01
☐ 165 Harold Reynolds	.10	.05	.01
☐ 166 Andy Van Slyke	.20	.09	.03
☐ 167 Jimmy Key	.20	.09	.03
☐ 168 Jeff Reardon	.20	.09	.03
☐ 169 Milt Thompson	.10	.05	.01
☐ 170 Will Clark	.40	.18	.05
☐ 171 Chet Lemon	.10	.05	.01
☐ 172 Pat Tabler	.10	.05	.01
☐ 173 Jim Rice	.30	.14	.04
☐ 174 Billy Hatcher	.10	.05	.01
☐ 175 Bruce Hurst	.10	.05	.01
☐ 176 John Franco	.20	.09	.03
☐ 177 Van Snider	.10	.05	.01
☐ 178 Ron Jones	.10	.05	.01
☐ 179 Jerald Clark	.10	.05	.01
☐ 180 Tom Browning	.10	.05	.01
☐ 181 Von Hayes	.10	.05	.01
☐ 182 Bobby Bonilla	.30	.14	.04
☐ 183 Todd Worrell	.10	.05	.01
☐ 184 John Kruk	.20	.09	.03
☐ 185 Scott Fletcher	.10	.05	.01
☐ 186 Willie Wilson	.10	.05	.01
☐ 187 Jody Davis	.10	.05	.01
☐ 188 Kent Hrbek	.20	.09	.03
☐ 189 Ruben Sierra	.20	.09	.03
☐ 190 Shawon Dunston	.10	.05	.01
☐ 191 Ellis Burks	.30	.14	.04
☐ 192 Brook Jacoby	.10	.05	.01
☐ 193 Jeff M. Robinson	.10	.05	.01
☐ 194 Rich Dotson	.10	.05	.01
☐ 195 Johnny Ray	.10	.05	.01
☐ 196 Cory Snyder	.10	.05	.01
☐ 197 Mike Witt	.10	.05	.01
☐ 198 Marty Barrett	.10	.05	.01
☐ 199 Robin Yount	.40	.18	.05
☐ 200 Mark McGwire	1.00	.45	.12
☐ 201 Ryne Sandberg	1.25	.55	.16
☐ 202 John Candelaria	.10	.05	.01
☐ 203 Matt Nokes	.10	.05	.01
☐ 204 Dwight Evans	.20	.09	.03
☐ 205 Darryl Strawberry	.20	.09	.03
☐ 206 Willie McGee	.10	.05	.01
☐ 207 Bobby Thigpen	.10	.05	.01
☐ 208 B.J. Surhoff	.20	.09	.03
☐ 209 Paul Molitor	1.00	.45	.12
☐ 210 Jody Reed	.10	.05	.01
☐ 211 Doyle Alexander	.10	.05	.01
☐ 212 Dennis Rasmussen	.10	.05	.01
☐ 213 Kevin Gross	.10	.05	.01
☐ 214 Kirk McCaskill	.10	.05	.01
☐ 215 Alan Trammell	.20	.09	.03
☐ 216 Damon Berryhill	.10	.05	.01
☐ 217 Rick Sutcliffe	.10	.05	.01
☐ 218 Don Slaught	.10	.05	.01
☐ 219 Carlton Fisk	.40	.18	.05
☐ 220 Allan Anderson	.10	.05	.01
☐ 221 Jose Canseco / Wade Boggs / Mike Greenwell	.30	.14	.04
☐ 222 Orel Hershiser / Dennis Eckersley / Tom Browning	.20	.09	.03
☐ 223 Gary Sheffield / Gregg Jefferies / Sandy Alomar Jr.	2.00	.90	.25
☐ 224 Bob Milacki / Randy Johnson / Ramon Martinez	3.00	1.35	.35
☐ 225 Cameron Drew / Geronimo Berroa / Ron Jones	.30	.14	.04

1990 Sportflics

The 1990 Sportflics set contains 225 standard-size cards. On the fronts, the black, white, orange, and yellow borders surround two photos, which can each be seen depending on the angle. The set is considered an improvement over the previous years' versions by many collectors due to the increased clarity of the fronts, caused by having two images rather than three. The backs are dominated by large color photos.

	MINT	NRMT	EXC
COMPLETE SET (225)	30.00	13.50	3.70
COMPLETE FACT.SET (225)	30.00	13.50	3.70
COMMON CARD (1-225)	.10	.05	.01
☐ 1 Kevin Mitchell	.10	.05	.01
☐ 2 Wade Boggs	.40	.18	.05
☐ 3 Cory Snyder	.10	.05	.01
☐ 4 Paul O'Neill	.20	.09	.03
☐ 5 Will Clark	.40	.18	.05
☐ 6 Tony Fernandez	.10	.05	.01
☐ 7 Ken Griffey Jr.	5.00	2.20	.60
☐ 8 Nolan Ryan	3.00	1.35	.35
☐ 9 Rafael Palmeiro	.50	.23	.06
☐ 10 Jesse Barfield	.10	.05	.01
☐ 11 Kirby Puckett	1.50	.70	.19
☐ 12 Steve Sax	.10	.05	.01
☐ 13 Fred McGriff	.40	.18	.05
☐ 14 Gregg Jefferies	.20	.09	.03
☐ 15 Mark Grace	.60	.25	.07
☐ 16 Ozzie Smith	1.25	.55	.16
☐ 17 George Bell	.10	.05	.01
☐ 18 Robin Yount	.40	.18	.05
☐ 19 Glenn Davis	.10	.05	.01
☐ 20 Jeffrey Leonard	.10	.05	.01
☐ 21 Chili Davis	.20	.09	.03
☐ 22 Craig Biggio	.40	.18	.05
☐ 23 Jose Canseco	.40	.18	.05
☐ 24 Derek Lilliquist	.10	.05	.01
☐ 25 Chris Bosio	.10	.05	.01
☐ 26 Dave Stieb	.10	.05	.01
☐ 27 Bobby Thigpen	.10	.05	.01
☐ 28 Jack Clark	.20	.09	.03
☐ 29 Kevin Ritz	.20	.09	.03
☐ 30 Tom Gordon	.10	.05	.01
☐ 31 Bryan Harvey	.10	.05	.01
☐ 32 Jim Deshaies	.10	.05	.01
☐ 33 Terry Steinbach	.20	.09	.03
☐ 34 Tom Glavine	.40	.18	.05
☐ 35 Bob Welch	.10	.05	.01
☐ 36 Charlie Hayes	.10	.05	.01
☐ 37 Jeff Reardon	.20	.09	.03
☐ 38 Joe Orsulak	.10	.05	.01
☐ 39 Scott Garrelts	.10	.05	.01
☐ 40 Bob Boone	.20	.09	.03
☐ 41 Scott Bankhead	.10	.05	.01
☐ 42 Tom Henke	.10	.05	.01
☐ 43 Greg Briley	.10	.05	.01
☐ 44 Teddy Higuera	.10	.05	.01
☐ 45 Pat Borders	.10	.05	.01
☐ 46 Kevin Seitzer	.10	.05	.01
☐ 47 Bruce Hurst	.10	.05	.01
☐ 48 Ozzie Guillen	.10	.05	.01
☐ 49 Wally Joyner	.20	.09	.03
☐ 50 Mike Greenwell	.10	.05	.01
☐ 51 Gary Gaetti	.10	.05	.01
☐ 52 Gary Sheffield UER (Uniform listed as 21, should be 1)	.60	.25	.07
☐ 53 Dennis Martinez	.20	.09	.03
☐ 54 Ryne Sandberg	1.25	.55	.16
☐ 55 Mike Scott	.10	.05	.01
☐ 56 Todd Benzinger	.10	.05	.01
☐ 57 Kelly Gruber	.10	.05	.01
☐ 58 Jose Lind	.10	.05	.01
☐ 59 Allan Anderson	.10	.05	.01
☐ 60 Robby Thompson	.10	.05	.01
☐ 61 John Smoltz	.60	.25	.07
☐ 62 Mark Davis	.10	.05	.01
☐ 63 Tom Herr	.10	.05	.01
☐ 64 Randy Johnson	.75	.35	.09
☐ 65 Lonnie Smith	.10	.05	.01
☐ 66 Pedro Guerrero	.10	.05	.01
☐ 67 Jerome Walton	.10	.05	.01
☐ 68 Ramon Martinez	.30	.14	.04
☐ 69 Tim Raines	.20	.09	.03
☐ 70 Matt Williams	.50	.23	.06
☐ 71 Joe Oliver	.10	.05	.01
☐ 72 Nick Esasky	.10	.05	.01
☐ 73 Kevin Brown	.30	.14	.04
☐ 74 Walt Weiss	.10	.05	.01
☐ 75 Roger McDowell	.10	.05	.01

76 Jose DeLeon	.10	.05	.01
77 Brian Downing	.10	.05	.01
78 Jay Howell	.10	.05	.01
79 Jose Uribe	.10	.05	.01
80 Ellis Burks	.30	.14	.04
81 Sammy Sosa	2.00	.90	.25
82 Johnny Ray	.10	.05	.01
83 Danny Darwin	.10	.05	.01
84 Carney Lansford	.20	.09	.03
85 Jose Oquendo	.10	.05	.01
86 John Cerutti	.10	.05	.01
87 Dave Winfield	.40	.18	.05
88 Dave Righetti	.10	.05	.01
89 Danny Jackson	.10	.05	.01
90 Andy Benes	.30	.14	.04
91 Tom Browning	.10	.05	.01
92 Pete O'Brien	.10	.05	.01
93 Roberto Alomar	1.00	.45	.12
94 Bret Saberhagen	.20	.09	.03
95 Phil Bradley	.10	.05	.01
96 Doug Jones	.10	.05	.01
97 Eric Davis	.20	.09	.03
98 Tony Gwynn	1.50	.70	.19
99 Jim Abbott	.20	.09	.03
100 Cal Ripken	3.00	1.35	.35
101 Andy Van Slyke	.20	.09	.03
102 Dan Plesac	.10	.05	.01
103 Lou Whitaker	.20	.09	.03
104 Steve Bedrosian	.10	.05	.01
105 Dave Gallagher	.10	.05	.01
106 Keith Hernandez	.20	.09	.03
107 Duane Ward	.10	.05	.01
108 Andre Dawson	.20	.09	.03
109 Howard Johnson	.10	.05	.01
110 Mark Langston	.20	.09	.03
111 Jerry Browne	.10	.05	.01
112 Alvin Davis	.10	.05	.01
113 Sid Fernandez	.10	.05	.01
114 Mike Devereaux	.10	.05	.01
115 Benito Santiago	.10	.05	.01
116 Bip Roberts	.10	.05	.01
117 Craig Worthington	.10	.05	.01
118 Kevin Elster	.10	.05	.01
119 Harold Reynolds	.10	.05	.01
120 Joe Carter	.20	.09	.03
121 Brian Harper	.10	.05	.01
122 Frank Viola	.10	.05	.01
123 Jeff Ballard	.10	.05	.01
124 John Kruk	.20	.09	.03
125 Harold Baines	.20	.09	.03
126 Tom Candiotti	.10	.05	.01
127 Kevin McReynolds	.10	.05	.01
128 Mookie Wilson	.10	.05	.01
129 Danny Tartabull	.10	.05	.01
130 Craig Lefferts	.10	.05	.01
131 Jose DeJesus	.10	.05	.01
132 John Orton	.10	.05	.01
133 Curt Schilling	.10	.05	.01
134 Marquis Grissom	1.25	.55	.16
135 Greg Vaughn	.30	.14	.04
136 Brett Butler	.20	.09	.03
137 Rob Deer	.10	.05	.01
138 John Franco	.10	.05	.01
139 Keith Moreland	.10	.05	.01
140 Dave Smith	.10	.05	.01
141 Mark McGwire	1.00	.45	.12
142 Vince Coleman	.10	.05	.01
143 Barry Bonds	.75	.35	.09
144 Mike Henneman	.10	.05	.01
145 Dwight Gooden	.20	.09	.03
146 Darryl Strawberry	.20	.09	.03
147 Von Hayes	.10	.05	.01
148 Andres Galarraga	.40	.18	.05
149 Roger Clemens	.60	.25	.07
150 Don Mattingly	1.50	.70	.19
151 Joe Magrane	.10	.05	.01
152 Dwight Smith	.10	.05	.01
153 Ricky Jordan	.10	.05	.01
154 Alan Trammell	.20	.09	.03
155 Brook Jacoby	.10	.05	.01
156 Len Dykstra	.20	.09	.03
157 Mike LaValliere	.10	.05	.01
158 Julio Franco	.20	.09	.03
159 Joey Belle	3.00	1.35	.35
160 Barry Larkin	.40	.18	.05
161 Rick Reuschel	.10	.05	.01
162 Nelson Santovenia	.10	.05	.01
163 Mike Scioscia	.10	.05	.01
164 Damon Berryhill	.10	.05	.01
165 Todd Worrell	.10	.05	.01
166 Jim Eisenreich	.10	.05	.01
167 Ivan Calderon	.10	.05	.01
168 Mauro Gozzo	.10	.05	.01
169 Kirk McCaskill	.10	.05	.01
170 Dennis Eckersley	.20	.09	.03
171 Mickey Tettleton	.20	.09	.03
172 Chuck Finley	.20	.09	.03
173 Dave Magadan	.10	.05	.01
174 Terry Pendleton	.20	.09	.03
175 Willie Randolph	.20	.09	.03
176 Jeff Huson	.10	.05	.01
177 Todd Zeile	.20	.09	.03
178 Steve Olin	.30	.14	.04
179 Eric Anthony	.10	.05	.01
180 Scott Coolbaugh	.10	.05	.01
181 Rick Sutcliffe	.10	.05	.01
182 Tim Wallach	.10	.05	.01
183 Paul Molitor	1.00	.45	.12
184 Roberto Kelly	.10	.05	.01
185 Mike Moore	.10	.05	.01
186 Junior Felix	.10	.05	.01
187 Mike Schooler	.10	.05	.01
188 Ruben Sierra	.20	.09	.03
189 Dale Murphy	.40	.18	.05
190 Dan Gladden	.10	.05	.01
191 John Smiley	.10	.05	.01
192 Jeff Russell	.10	.05	.01
193 Bert Blyleven	.20	.09	.03
194 Dave Stewart	.20	.09	.03
195 Bobby Bonilla	.20	.09	.03
196 Mitch Williams	.10	.05	.01
197 Orel Hershiser	.20	.09	.03
198 Kevin Bass	.10	.05	.01
199 Tim Burke	.10	.05	.01
200 Bo Jackson	.20	.09	.03
201 David Cone	.30	.14	.04
202 Gary Pettis	.10	.05	.01
203 Kent Hrbek	.20	.09	.03
204 Carlton Fisk	.40	.18	.05
205 Bob Geren	.10	.05	.01
206 Bill Spiers	.10	.05	.01
207 Oddibe McDowell	.10	.05	.01
208 Rickey Henderson	.40	.18	.05
209 Ken Caminiti	.75	.35	.09
210 Devon White	.20	.09	.03
211 Greg Maddux	3.00	1.35	.35
212 Ed Whitson	.10	.05	.01
213 Carlos Martinez	.10	.05	.01
214 George Brett	1.25	.55	.16
215 Gregg Olson	.10	.05	.01
216 Kenny Rogers	.20	.09	.03
217 Dwight Evans	.20	.09	.03
218 Pat Tabler	.10	.05	.01
219 Jeff Treadway	.10	.05	.01
220 Scott Fletcher	.10	.05	.01
221 Deion Sanders	.50	.23	.06
222 Robin Ventura	.50	.23	.06
223 Chip Hale	.10	.05	.01
224 Tommy Greene	.10	.05	.01
225 Dean Palmer	.75	.35	.09

1994 Sportflics Samples

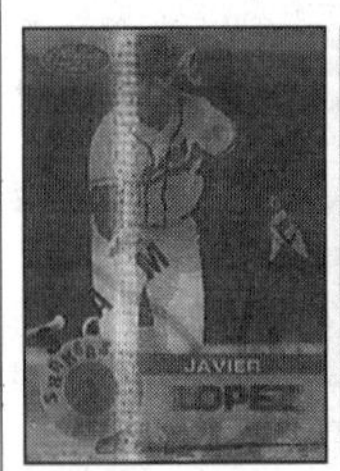

Enclosed in a cello pack, this four-card standard-size set was issued to give dealers a preview of the design of the forthcoming 1994 Sportflics 2000 series. The fronts feature two images that alternate when the card is tilted slightly. The design of the backs varies slightly, but all have a second color player photo and player information. The disclaimer "SAMPLE" is stenciled diagonally across the front and back of each card. In addition to the whole set being sent to dealers, all Wal-Mart greeters were given Len Dysktra cards to give out to promote this product.

	MINT	NRMT	EXC
COMPLETE SET (4)	6.00	2.70	.75
COMMON CARD (1-4)	.50	.23	.06
1 Len Dykstra	.75	.35	.09
7 Javier Lopez	1.50	.70	.19
193 Greg Maddux	5.00	2.20	.60
NNO Sportflics 2000 '94 Hobby Baseball (Ad card)	.50	.23	.06

1994 Sportflics

After a three-year hiatus, Pinnacle resumed producing these lenticular "three-dimensional" cards, issued in hobby and retail packs. Each of the 193 "Magic Motion" cards features two images, which alternate when the card is viewed from different angles and creates the illusion of movement. Cards 176-193 are Starflics featuring top stars. The two commemorative cards, featuring Cliff Floyd and Paul Molitor, were inserted at a rate of one in every 360 packs.

	MINT	NRMT	EXC
COMPLETE SET (193)	25.00	11.00	3.10
COMMON CARD (1-193)	.10	.05	.01
1 Lenny Dykstra	.25	.11	.03
2 Mike Stanley	.10	.05	.01
3 Alex Fernandez	.25	.11	.03
4 Mark McGwire UER (name spelled McGuire on front)	1.00	.45	.12
5 Eric Karros	.25	.11	.03
6 Dave Justice	.50	.23	.06

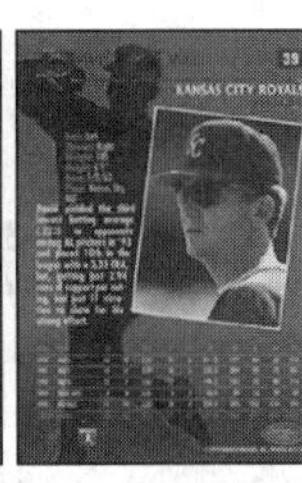

7 Jeff Bagwell	1.25	.55	.16
8 Darren Lewis	.10	.05	.01
9 David McCarty	.10	.05	.01
10 Albert Belle	1.25	.55	.16
11 Ben McDonald	.10	.05	.01
12 Joe Carter	.25	.11	.03
13 Benito Santiago	.10	.05	.01
14 Rob Dibble	.10	.05	.01
15 Roger Clemens	.60	.25	.07
16 Travis Fryman	.25	.11	.03
17 Doug Drabek	.10	.05	.01
18 Jay Buhner	.50	.23	.06
19 Orlando Merced	.25	.11	.03
20 Ryan Klesko	.60	.25	.07
21 Chuck Finley	.10	.05	.01
22 Dante Bichette	.50	.23	.06
23 Wally Joyner	.25	.11	.03
24 Robin Yount	.50	.23	.06
25 Tony Gwynn	1.25	.55	.16
26 Allen Watson	.10	.05	.01
27 Rick Wilkins	.10	.05	.01
28 Gary Sheffield	.50	.23	.06
29 John Burkett	.10	.05	.01
30 Randy Johnson	.50	.23	.06
31 Roberto Alomar	.60	.25	.07
32 Fred McGriff	.50	.23	.06
33 Ozzie Guillen	.10	.05	.01
34 Jimmy Key	.25	.11	.03
35 Juan Gonzalez	1.50	.70	.19
36 Wil Cordero	.25	.11	.03
37 Aaron Sele	.25	.11	.03
38 Mark Langston	.25	.11	.03
39 David Cone	.25	.11	.03
40 John Jaha	.25	.11	.03
41 Ozzie Smith	.75	.35	.09
42 Kirby Puckett	1.25	.55	.16
43 Kenny Lofton	1.00	.45	.12
44 Mike Mussina	.60	.25	.07
45 Ryne Sandberg	.75	.35	.09
46 Robby Thompson	.10	.05	.01
47 Bryan Harvey	.10	.05	.01
48 Marquis Grissom	.25	.11	.03
49 Bobby Bonilla	.25	.11	.03
50 Dennis Eckersley	.25	.11	.03
51 Curt Schilling	.10	.05	.01
52 Andy Benes	.25	.11	.03
53 Greg Maddux	2.00	.90	.25
54 Bill Swift	.10	.05	.01
55 Andres Galarraga	.50	.23	.06
56 Tony Phillips	.25	.11	.03
57 Darryl Hamilton	.10	.05	.01
58 Duane Ward	.10	.05	.01
59 Bernie Williams	.60	.25	.07
60 Steve Avery	.25	.11	.03
61 Eduardo Perez	.10	.05	.01
62 Jeff Conine	.25	.11	.03
63 Dave Winfield	.50	.23	.06
64 Phil Plantier	.10	.05	.01
65 Ray Lankford	.25	.11	.03
66 Robin Ventura	.25	.11	.03
67 Mike Piazza	2.00	.90	.25
68 Jason Bere	.25	.11	.03
69 Cal Ripken	2.50	1.10	.30
70 Frank Thomas	3.00	1.35	.35
71 Carlos Baerga	.25	.11	.03
72 Darryl Kile	.10	.05	.01
73 Ruben Sierra	.25	.11	.03
74 Gregg Jefferies UER Name spelled Jeffries on front	.50	.23	.06
75 John Olerud	.10	.05	.01
76 Andy Van Slyke	.25	.11	.03
77 Larry Walker	.50	.23	.06
78 Cecil Fielder	.25	.11	.03
79 Andre Dawson	.25	.11	.03
80 Tom Glavine	.50	.23	.06
81 Sammy Sosa	.50	.23	.06
82 Charlie Hayes	.10	.05	.01
83 Chuck Knoblauch	.50	.23	.06
84 Kevin Appier	.25	.11	.03
85 Dean Palmer	.25	.11	.03
86 Royce Clayton	.25	.11	.03
87 Moises Alou	.25	.11	.03
88 Ivan Rodriguez	.75	.35	.09
89 Tim Salmon	.50	.23	.06
90 Ron Gant	.25	.11	.03
91 Barry Bonds	.75	.35	.09
92 Jack McDowell	.25	.11	.03
93 Alan Trammell	.25	.11	.03
94 Doc Gooden	.25	.11	.03
95 Jay Bell	.25	.11	.03
96 Devon White	.10	.05	.01
97 Wilson Alvarez	.25	.11	.03
98 Jim Thome	.75	.35	.09
99 Ramon Martinez	.25	.11	.03
100 Kent Hrbek	.25	.11	.03
101 John Kruk	.25	.11	.03
102 Wade Boggs	.50	.23	.06
103 Greg Vaughn	.50	.23	.06
104 Tom Henke	.10	.05	.01
105 Brian Jordan	.50	.23	.06
106 Paul Molitor	.60	.25	.07
107 Cal Eldred	.10	.05	.01
108 Deion Sanders	.50	.23	.06
109 Barry Larkin	.50	.23	.06
110 Mike Greenwell	.10	.05	.01
111 Jeff Blauser	.10	.05	.01
112 Jose Rijo	.10	.05	.01
113 Pete Harnisch	.10	.05	.01
114 Chris Hoiles	.10	.05	.01
115 Edgar Martinez	.25	.11	.03
116 Juan Guzman	.25	.11	.03
117 Todd Zeile	.10	.05	.01
118 Danny Tartabull	.10	.05	.01
119 Chad Curtis	.10	.05	.01
120 Mark Grace	.50	.23	.06
121 J.T. Snow	.25	.11	.03
122 Mo Vaughn	.75	.35	.09
123 Lance Johnson	.25	.11	.03
124 Eric Davis	.25	.11	.03
125 Orel Hershiser	.25	.11	.03
126 Kevin Mitchell	.25	.11	.03
127 Don Mattingly	1.50	.70	.19
128 Darren Daulton	.25	.11	.03
129 Rod Beck	.25	.11	.03
130 Charles Nagy	.25	.11	.03
131 Mickey Tettleton	.10	.05	.01
132 Kevin Brown	.25	.11	.03
133 Pat Hentgen	.25	.11	.03
134 Terry Mulholland	.10	.05	.01
135 Steve Finley	.50	.23	.06
136 John Smoltz	.50	.23	.06
137 Frank Viola	.10	.05	.01
138 Jim Abbott	.10	.05	.01
139 Matt Williams	.50	.23	.06
140 Bernard Gilkey	.25	.11	.03
141 Jose Canseco	.50	.23	.06
142 Mark Whiten	.10	.05	.01
143 Ken Griffey Jr.	3.00	1.35	.35
144 Rafael Palmeiro	.50	.23	.06
145 Dave Hollins	.10	.05	.01
146 Will Clark	.50	.23	.06
147 Paul O'Neill	.25	.11	.03
148 Bobby Jones	.25	.11	.03
149 Butch Huskey	.25	.11	.03
150 Jeffrey Hammonds	.25	.11	.03
151 Manny Ramirez	1.00	.45	.12
152 Bob Hamelin	.10	.05	.01
153 Kurt Abbott	.25	.11	.03
154 Scott Stahoviak	.10	.05	.01
155 Steve Hosey	.10	.05	.01
156 Salomon Torres	.10	.05	.01
157 Sterling Hitchcock	.25	.11	.03
158 Nigel Wilson	.10	.05	.01
159 Luis Lopez	.10	.05	.01
160 Chipper Jones	2.50	1.10	.30
161 Norberto Martin	.10	.05	.01
162 Raul Mondesi	.50	.23	.06
163 Steve Karsay	.10	.05	.01
164 J.R. Phillips	.10	.05	.01
165 Marc Newfield	.25	.11	.03
166 Mark Hutton	.10	.05	.01
167 Curtis Pride	.25	.11	.03
168 Carl Everett	.10	.05	.01
169 Scott Ruffcorn	.10	.05	.01
170 Turk Wendell	.10	.05	.01
171 Jeff McNeely	.10	.05	.01
172 Javier Lopez	.50	.23	.06
173 Cliff Floyd	.50	.23	.06
174 Rondell White	.50	.23	.06
175 Scott Lydy	.10	.05	.01
176 Frank Thomas AS	1.50	.70	.19
177 Roberto Alomar AS	.50	.23	.06
178 Travis Fryman AS	.25	.11	.03
179 Cal Ripken AS	1.25	.55	.16
180 Chris Hoiles AS	.10	.05	.01
181 Ken Griffey Jr. AS	1.50	.70	.19
182 Juan Gonzalez AS	.50	.23	.06
183 Joe Carter AS	.25	.11	.03
184 Jack McDowell AS	.10	.05	.01
185 Fred McGriff AS	.50	.23	.06
186 Robby Thompson AS	.10	.05	.01
187 Matt Williams AS	.50	.23	.06
188 Jay Bell AS	.10	.05	.01
189 Mike Piazza AS	1.00	.45	.12
190 Barry Bonds AS	.50	.23	.06
191 Lenny Dykstra AS	.10	.05	.01
192 Dave Justice AS	.25	.11	.03
193 Greg Maddux AS	1.00	.45	.12
NNO Cliff Floyd Special	4.00	1.80	.50
NNO Paul Molitor Special	15.00	6.75	1.85

1994 Sportflics Movers

These 12 standard-size chase cards were randomly inserted in retail foil packs and picture the game's top veterans. The insertion rate was one in every 24 packs. Fronts feature the dual image effect with the player's name appearing in dual image. The name "Movers" appears in a circular design off to the left of the player's name.

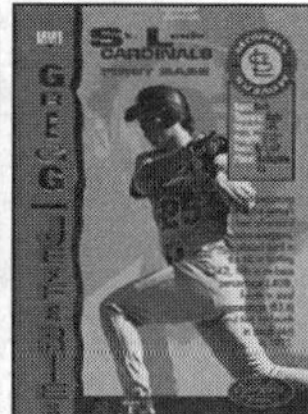

	MINT	NRMT	EXC
COMPLETE SET (12)	50.00	22.00	6.25
COMMON CARD (MM1-MM12)	1.50	.70	.19
☐ MM1 Gregg Jefferies	1.50	.70	.19
☐ MM2 Ryne Sandberg	8.00	3.60	1.00
☐ MM3 Cecil Fielder	2.00	.90	.25
☐ MM4 Kirby Puckett	10.00	4.50	1.25
☐ MM5 Tony Gwynn	10.00	4.50	1.25
☐ MM6 Andres Galarraga	3.00	1.35	.35
☐ MM7 Sammy Sosa	4.00	1.80	.50
☐ MM8 Rickey Henderson	3.00	1.35	.35
☐ MM9 Don Mattingly	12.00	5.50	1.50
☐ MM10 Joe Carter	2.00	.90	.25
☐ MM11 Carlos Baerga	1.50	.70	.19
☐ MM12 Lenny Dykstra	1.50	.70	.19

1994 Sportflics Shakers

These 12 standard-size chase cards were randomly inserted in hobby foil packs and picture baseball's elite young players. The insertion rate was one in every 24 packs. Fronts feature the dual image effect with the player's name also appearing as dual image. The name "Shakers" appears in a circular design off to the left of the player's name.

	MINT	NRMT	EXC
COMPLETE SET (12)	70.00	32.00	8.75
COMMON CARD (SH1-SH12)	2.00	.90	.25
☐ SH1 Kenny Lofton	12.00	5.50	1.50
☐ SH2 Tim Salmon	5.00	2.20	.60
☐ SH3 Jeff Bagwell	15.00	6.75	1.85
☐ SH4 Jason Bere	2.00	.90	.25
☐ SH5 Salomon Torres	2.00	.90	.25
☐ SH6 Rondell White	4.00	1.80	.50
☐ SH7 Javier Lopez	5.00	2.20	.60
☐ SH8 Dean Palmer	3.00	1.35	.35
☐ SH9 Jim Thome	8.00	3.60	1.00
☐ SH10 J.T. Snow	2.00	.90	.25
☐ SH11 Mike Piazza	20.00	9.00	2.50
☐ SH12 Manny Ramirez	10.00	4.50	1.25

1994 Sportflics Rookie/Traded Samples

This set of nine standard-size sample cards previews the 1994 Sportflics Rookie/Traded series. On the fronts, two color game-action photos are overlayed to create a multi-dimensional card that changes images when the card is rotated. On a red and black geometric design, the backs carry a color head shot, biography, and statistics. Both sides have the word "SAMPLE" running diagonally from the lower left to the upper right corner. The cards are numbered on the back. Reportedly due to the baseball strike of 1994, the actual set these samples previewed was never produced or released.

	MINT	NRMT	EXC
COMPLETE SET (9)	8.00	3.60	1.00
COMMON CARD	.50	.23	.06
☐ 1 Will Clark	2.00	.90	.25
☐ 14 Bret Boone	.50	.23	.06
☐ 20 Ellis Burks	1.00	.45	.12
☐ 25 Deion Sanders	2.50	1.10	.30
☐ 65 Chris Turner	.50	.23	.06
☐ 82 Tony Tarasco	.50	.23	.06
☐ 102 Rich Becker	.50	.23	.06
☐ GG1 Gary Sheffield Going, Going, Gone	2.00	.90	.25
☐ NNO Title Card	.50	.23	.06

1994 Sportflics Rookie/Traded

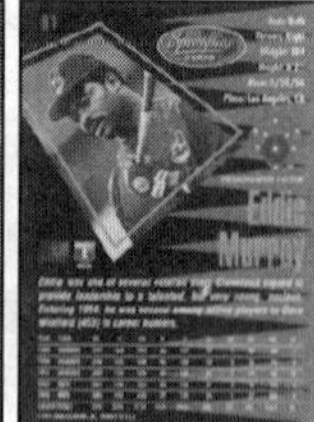

This set of 150 standard-size cards was distributed in five-card retail packs at a suggested price of $1.89. The set features top rookies and traded players. This set was released only through retail (non-hobby) outlets. The fronts feature the "Magic Motion" printing with two action views of the player which change with the tilting of the card. The playeris name is printed in red and expands and contracts with the tilting of the card. Numbered backs include a player biography and career stats and the 1994 performance of the rookie or how the player was acquired in a trade. A full-color photo of the player is framed at an angle with a red and black background. Rookie Cards in this set include Chan Ho Park and Alex Rodriguez.

	MINT	NRMT	EXC
COMPLETE SET (150)	25.00	11.00	3.10
COMMON CARD (1-150)	.15	.07	.02
☐ 1 Will Clark	.60	.25	.07
☐ 2 Sid Fernandez	.15	.07	.02
☐ 3 Joe Magrane	.15	.07	.02
☐ 4 Pete Smith	.15	.07	.02
☐ 5 Roberto Kelly	.15	.07	.02
☐ 6 Delino DeShields	.15	.07	.02
☐ 7 Brian Harper	.15	.07	.02
☐ 8 Darrin Jackson	.15	.07	.02
☐ 9 Omar Vizquel	.30	.14	.04
☐ 10 Luis Polonia	.15	.07	.02
☐ 11 Reggie Jefferson	.30	.14	.04
☐ 12 Geronimo Berroa	.30	.14	.04
☐ 13 Mike Harkey	.15	.07	.02
☐ 14 Bret Boone	.30	.14	.04
☐ 15 Dave Henderson	.15	.07	.02
☐ 16 Pedro J.Martinez	.60	.25	.07
☐ 17 Jose Vizcaino	.15	.07	.02
☐ 18 Xavier Hernandez	.15	.07	.02
☐ 19 Eddie Taubensee	.15	.07	.02
☐ 20 Ellis Burks	.30	.14	.04
☐ 21 Turner Ward	.15	.07	.02
☐ 22 Terry Mulholland	.15	.07	.02
☐ 23 Howard Johnson	.15	.07	.02
☐ 24 Vince Coleman	.15	.07	.02
☐ 25 Deion Sanders	.60	.25	.07
☐ 26 Rafael Palmeiro	.60	.25	.07
☐ 27 Dave Weathers	.15	.07	.02
☐ 28 Kent Mercker	.15	.07	.02
☐ 29 Gregg Olson	.15	.07	.02
☐ 30 Cory Bailey	.15	.07	.02
☐ 31 Brian L.Hunter	.60	.25	.07
☐ 32 Garey Ingram	.15	.07	.02
☐ 33 Daniel Smith	.15	.07	.02
☐ 34 Denny Hocking	.15	.07	.02
☐ 35 Charles Johnson	.60	.25	.07
☐ 36 Otis Nixon	.15	.07	.02
☐ 37 Hector Fajardo	.15	.07	.02
☐ 38 Lee Smith	.30	.14	.04
☐ 39 Phil Stidham	.15	.07	.02
☐ 40 Melvin Nieves	.30	.14	.04
☐ 41 Julio Franco	.30	.14	.04
☐ 42 Greg Gohr	.15	.07	.02
☐ 43 Steve Dunn	.15	.07	.02
☐ 44 Tony Fernandez	.15	.07	.02
☐ 45 Toby Borland	.15	.07	.02
☐ 46 Paul Shuey	.15	.07	.02
☐ 47 Shawn Hare	.15	.07	.02
☐ 48 Shawn Green	.30	.14	.04
☐ 49 Julian Tavarez	.30	.14	.04
☐ 50 Ernie Young	.15	.07	.02
☐ 51 Chris Sabo	.15	.07	.02
☐ 52 Greg O'Halloran	.15	.07	.02
☐ 53 Donnie Elliott	.15	.07	.02
☐ 54 Jim Converse	.15	.07	.02
☐ 55 Ray Holbert	.15	.07	.02
☐ 56 Keith Lockhart	.15	.07	.02
☐ 57 Tony Longmire	.15	.07	.02
☐ 58 Jorge Fabregas	.15	.07	.02
☐ 59 Ravelo Manzanillo	.15	.07	.02
☐ 60 Marcus Moore	.15	.07	.02
☐ 61 Carlos Rodriguez	.15	.07	.02
☐ 62 Mark Portugal	.15	.07	.02
☐ 63 Yorkis Perez	.15	.07	.02
☐ 64 Dan Miceli	.15	.07	.02
☐ 65 Chris Turner	.15	.07	.02
☐ 66 Mike Oquist	.15	.07	.02
☐ 67 Tom Quinlan	.15	.07	.02
☐ 68 Matt Walbeck	.15	.07	.02
☐ 69 Dave Staton	.15	.07	.02
☐ 70 Wm.VanLandingham	.30	.14	.04
☐ 71 Dave Stevens	.15	.07	.02
☐ 72 Domingo Cedeno	.15	.07	.02
☐ 73 Alex Diaz	.15	.07	.02
☐ 74 Darren Bragg	.30	.14	.04
☐ 75 James Hurst	.15	.07	.02
☐ 76 Alex Gonzalez	.30	.14	.04
☐ 77 Steve Dreyer	.15	.07	.02
☐ 78 Robert Fenhoorn	.15	.07	.02
☐ 79 Derek Parks	.15	.07	.02
☐ 80 Jose Valentin	.30	.14	.04
☐ 81 Wes Chamberlain	.15	.07	.02
☐ 82 Tony Tarasco	.15	.07	.02
☐ 83 Steve Traschel	.30	.14	.04
☐ 84 Willie Banks	.15	.07	.02
☐ 85 Rob Butler	.15	.07	.02
☐ 86 Miguel Jimenez	.15	.07	.02
☐ 87 Gerald Williams	.15	.07	.02
☐ 88 Aaron Small	.15	.07	.02
☐ 89 Matt Mieske	.15	.07	.02
☐ 90 Tim Hyers	.15	.07	.02
☐ 91 Eddie Murray	1.25	.55	.16
☐ 92 Dennis Martinez	.30	.14	.04
☐ 93 Tony Eusebio	.15	.07	.02
☐ 94 Brian Anderson	.30	.14	.04
☐ 95 Blaise Ilsley	.15	.07	.02
☐ 96 Johnny Ruffin	.15	.07	.02
☐ 97 Carlos Reyes	.15	.07	.02
☐ 98 Greg Pirkl	.15	.07	.02
☐ 99 Jack Morris	.30	.14	.04
☐ 100 John Mabry	.40	.18	.05
☐ 101 Mike Kelly	.15	.07	.02
☐ 102 Rich Becker	.30	.14	.04
☐ 103 Chris Gomez	.15	.07	.02
☐ 104 Jim Edmonds	1.00	.45	.12
☐ 105 Rich Rowland	.15	.07	.02
☐ 106 Damon Buford	.15	.07	.02
☐ 107 Mark Kiefer	.15	.07	.02
☐ 108 Matias Carrillo	.15	.07	.02
☐ 109 James Mouton	.30	.14	.04
☐ 110 Kelly Stinnett	.15	.07	.02
☐ 111 Billy Ashley	.15	.07	.02
☐ 112 Fausto Cruz	.15	.07	.02
☐ 113 Roberto Petagine	.30	.14	.04
☐ 114 Joe Hall	.15	.07	.02
☐ 115 Brian Johnson	.15	.07	.02
☐ 116 Kevin Jarvis	.15	.07	.02
☐ 117 Tim Davis	.15	.07	.02
☐ 118 John Patterson	.15	.07	.02
☐ 119 Stan Royer	.15	.07	.02
☐ 120 Jeff Juden	.15	.07	.02
☐ 121 Bryan Eversgerd	.15	.07	.02
☐ 122 Chan Ho Park	1.50	.70	.19
☐ 123 Shane Reynolds	.30	.14	.04
☐ 124 Danny Bautista	.15	.07	.02
☐ 125 Rikkert Faneyte	.15	.07	.02
☐ 126 Carlos Pulido	.15	.07	.02
☐ 127 Mike Matheny	.15	.07	.02
☐ 128 Hector Carrasco	.15	.07	.02
☐ 129 Eddie Zambrano	.15	.07	.02
☐ 130 Lee Tinsley	.30	.14	.04
☐ 131 Roger Salkeld	.15	.07	.02
☐ 132 Carlos Delgado	.60	.25	.07
☐ 133 Troy O'Leary	.15	.07	.02
☐ 134 Keith Mitchell	.15	.07	.02
☐ 135 Lance Painter	.15	.07	.02
☐ 136 Nate Minchey	.15	.07	.02
☐ 137 Eric Anthony	.15	.07	.02
☐ 138 Rafael Bournigal	.15	.07	.02
☐ 139 Joey Hamilton	1.00	.45	.12
☐ 140 Bobby Munoz	.15	.07	.02
☐ 141 Rex Hudler	.15	.07	.02
☐ 142 Alex Cole	.15	.07	.02
☐ 143 Stan Javier	.15	.07	.02
☐ 144 Jose Oliva	.30	.14	.04
☐ 145 Tom Brunansky	.15	.07	.02
☐ 146 Greg Colbrunn	.15	.07	.02
☐ 147 Luis S.Lopez	.15	.07	.02
☐ 148 Alex Rodriguez	15.00	6.75	1.85
☐ 149 Darryl Strawberry	.30	.14	.04
☐ 150 Bo Jackson	.30	.14	.04
☐ R01 R.Klesko ROY M.Ramirez	20.00	9.00	2.50

1994 Sportflics Rookie/Traded Artist's Proofs

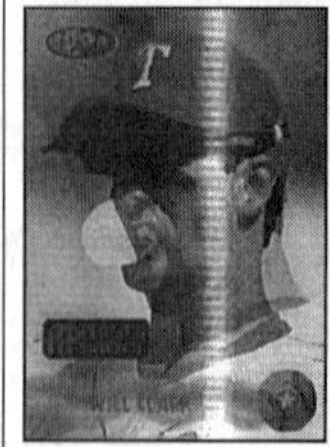
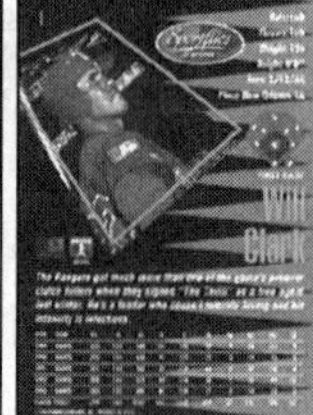

This set of cards parallels the 150 regular issue Rookie/Traded cards and are embellished with the gold foil "Artist's Proof" stamp. They were randomly inserted in at a rate of one in 24 packs.

	MINT	NRMT	EXC
COMPLETE SET (150)	2400.00	1100.00	300.00
COMMON CARD (1-150)	10.00	4.50	1.25
*STARS: 40X TO 80X BASIC CARDS ..			
*YOUNG STARS: 25X TO 50X BASIC CARDS			
☐ 1 Will Clark	50.00	22.00	6.25
☐ 26 Rafael Palmeiro	50.00	22.00	6.25
☐ 31 Brian L.Hunter	40.00	18.00	5.00
☐ 91 Eddie Murray	100.00	45.00	12.50
☐ 100 John Mabry	30.00	13.50	3.70
☐ 104 Jim Edmonds	60.00	27.00	7.50
☐ 122 Chan Ho Park	50.00	22.00	6.25
☐ 132 Carlos Delgado	40.00	18.00	5.00
☐ 139 Joey Hamilton	50.00	22.00	6.25
☐ 148 Alex Rodriguez	600.00	275.00	75.00

1994 Sportflics Rookie/Traded Going Going Gone

Randomly inserted in packs at a rate of one in 18, this 12-card set features big hitters. Sportflics used its "Magic Mirror" technology to produce two images when the card is tilted. The Going, Going, Gone logo is placed at the top left of the front and a gold strip runs vertically on the left side. The player's name is printed in black on top of the gold strip. It expands and contracts when the card is moved. Borderless backs are numbered with the prefix "GG" and have a dark background containing a blurred stadium. The player's close-up picture is bordered with a biography box and name on the left. The playeris slugging percentage, number of home runs and RBI totals are printed on the right side of the back with a shadow effect.

	MINT	NRMT	EXC
COMPLETE SET (12)	90.00	40.00	11.00
COMMON CARD (GG1-GG12)	3.00	1.35	.35
☐ GG1 Gary Sheffield	4.00	1.80	.50
☐ GG2 Matt Williams	3.00	1.35	.35
☐ GG3 Juan Gonzalez	12.00	5.50	1.50
☐ GG4 Ken Griffey Jr.	25.00	11.00	3.10
☐ GG5 Mike Piazza	15.00	6.75	1.85
☐ GG6 Frank Thomas	25.00	11.00	3.10
☐ GG7 Tim Salmon	3.00	1.35	.35
☐ GG8 Barry Bonds	6.00	2.70	.75
☐ GG9 Fred McGriff	3.00	1.35	.35
☐ GG10 Cecil Fielder	3.00	1.35	.35
☐ GG11 Albert Belle	10.00	4.50	1.25
☐ GG12 Joe Carter	3.00	1.35	.35

1994 Sportflics Rookie/Traded Rookie Starflics

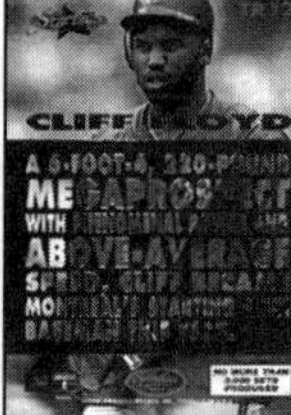

Randomly inserted in packs at a rate of one in 36, these 3-D cards highlight the rookie sensations of 1994. Horizontal fronts feature the player in a full-color action shot with a smaller, mirror image of the player set off in the blue background. The Starflics logo, player's name and team logo are printed on the left side of the front. Backs are borderless and carry full-color action shots of the player. The player's name is printed in gold foil and a player background is printed with reverse type on gold foil.

	MINT	NRMT	EXC
COMPLETE SET (18)	225.00	100.00	28.00
COMMON CARD (TR1-TR18)	5.00	2.20	.60
☐ TR1 John Hudek	5.00	2.20	.60
☐ TR2 Manny Ramirez	30.00	13.50	3.70
☐ TR3 Jeffrey Hammonds	8.00	3.60	1.00
☐ TR4 Carlos Delgado	12.00	5.50	1.50
☐ TR5 Javier Lopez	12.00	5.50	1.50
☐ TR6 Alex Gonzalez	8.00	3.60	1.00
☐ TR7 Raul Mondesi	15.00	6.75	1.85
☐ TR8 Bob Hamelin	5.00	2.20	.60
☐ TR9 Ryan Klesko	20.00	9.00	2.50
☐ TR10 Brian Anderson	5.00	2.20	.60

	MINT	NRMT	EXC
☐ TR11 Alex Rodriguez	100.00	45.00	12.50
☐ TR12 Cliff Floyd	8.00	3.60	1.00
☐ TR13 Chan Ho Park	8.00	3.60	1.00
☐ TR14 Steve Karsay	5.00	2.20	.60
☐ TR15 Rondell White	10.00	4.50	1.25
☐ TR16 Shawn Green	8.00	3.60	1.00
☐ TR17 Rich Becker	5.00	2.20	.60
☐ TR18 Charles Johnson			

1994 Sportflics FanFest All-Stars

At Fanfest, collectors received redemption coupons at various locations. These redemption coupons could be turned in at certain distribution centers for the Sportflics cards. It is noted on the backs that 10,000 sets were produced. The cards measure the standard size. The borderless fronts carry two-dimensional color action photos featuring an American League player and a National League player. The player's names appear in the upper left and bottom right corners. The backs carry headshots and statistics for each player. According to reports, between 10-20 percent of the mintage of this set was destroyed at the end of fanfest.

	MINT	NRMT	EXC
COMPLETE SET (9)	50.00	22.00	6.25
COMMON CARD (AS1-AS9)	2.50	1.10	.30
☐ AS1 Fred McGriff	10.00	4.50	1.25
Frank Thomas			
☐ AS2 Ryne Sandberg	8.00	3.60	1.00
Roberto Alomar			
☐ AS3 Matt Williams	2.50	1.10	.30
Travis Fryman			
☐ AS4 Ozzie Smith	12.00	5.50	1.50
Cal Ripken Jr.			
☐ AS5 Mike Piazza	6.00	2.70	.75
Ivan Rodriguez			
☐ AS6 Barry Bonds	5.00	2.20	.60
Juan Gonzalez			
☐ AS7 Lenny Dykstra	8.00	3.60	1.00
Ken Griffey Jr.			
☐ AS8 Gary Sheffield	4.00	1.80	.50
Kirby Puckett			
☐ AS9 Greg Maddux	10.00	4.50	1.25
Mike Mussina			

1995 Sportflix Samples

This nine-card set features samples of the 1995 Sportlix series. The cards are numbered below according to their numbers in the regular series. This apparently is one of the scarcest promo sets in recent years -- it is rumored that only 200 to 300 of each card were produced.

	MINT	NRMT	EXC
COMPLETE SET (9)	300.00	135.00	38.00
COMMON CARD	10.00	4.50	1.25
☐ 3 Fred McGriff	20.00	9.00	2.50
☐ 20 Frank Thomas	100.00	45.00	12.50
☐ 105 Manny Ramirez	30.00	13.50	3.70
☐ 122 Cal Ripken	100.00	45.00	12.50
☐ 128 Roberto Alomar	30.00	13.50	3.70
☐ 152 Russ Davis	10.00	4.50	1.25
☐ 162 Chipper Jones	75.00	34.00	9.50
☐ DE2 Matt Williams (Detonator)	20.00	9.00	2.50
☐ NNO Title card	10.00	4.50	1.25

1995 Sportflix

This 170 card standard-size set was released by Pinnacle brands. The set was issued in 5 card packs that had a suggested retail price of $1.89 per pack. Thirty-six of these packs are contained in a full box. Jumbo packs were also issued: these packs contained 8 cards per pack and had 36 packs in a box. Card fronts feature Pinnacle's "Magic Motion" printing which shows the player in two different action shots when the card is tilted. The player's position is printed diagonally on the top right with the team logo underneath. Horizontal backs feature

a full-color player photo on the right. Subsets include a rookies section (141-165) and a checklist grouping (166-170). There are no key Rookie Cards in this set.

	MINT	NRMT	EXC
COMPLETE SET (170)	20.00	9.00	2.50
COMMON CARD (1-170)	.10	.05	.01
☐ 1 Ken Griffey Jr.	3.00	1.35	.35
☐ 2 Jeffrey Hammonds	.25	.11	.03
☐ 3 Fred McGriff	.50	.23	.06
☐ 4 Rickey Henderson	.50	.23	.06
☐ 5 Derrick May	.10	.05	.01
☐ 6 Robin Ventura	.25	.11	.03
☐ 7 Royce Clayton	.10	.05	.01
☐ 8 Paul Molitor	.60	.25	.07
☐ 9 Charlie Hayes	.10	.05	.01
☐ 10 David Nied	.10	.05	.01
☐ 11 Ellis Burks	.25	.11	.03
☐ 12 Bernard Gilkey	.25	.11	.03
☐ 13 Don Mattingly	1.50	.70	.19
☐ 14 Albert Belle	1.25	.55	.16
☐ 15 Doug Drabek	.10	.05	.01
☐ 16 Tony Gwynn	1.25	.55	.16
☐ 17 Delino DeShields	.10	.05	.01
☐ 18 Bobby Bonilla	.25	.11	.03
☐ 19 Cliff Floyd	.25	.11	.03
☐ 20 Frank Thomas	3.00	1.35	.35
☐ 21 Raul Mondesi	.50	.23	.06
☐ 22 Dave Nilsson	.25	.11	.03
☐ 23 Todd Zeile	.10	.05	.01
☐ 24 Bernie Williams	.60	.25	.07
☐ 25 Kirby Puckett	1.25	.55	.16
☐ 26 David Cone	.25	.11	.03
☐ 27 Darren Daulton	.25	.11	.03
☐ 28 Marquis Grissom	.25	.11	.03
☐ 29 Randy Johnson	.50	.23	.06
☐ 30 Jeff Kent	.10	.05	.01
☐ 31 Orlando Merced	.10	.05	.01
☐ 32 Dave Justice	.50	.23	.06
☐ 33 Ivan Rodriguez	.75	.35	.09
☐ 34 Kirk Gibson	.25	.11	.03
☐ 35 Alex Fernandez	.25	.11	.03
☐ 36 Rick Wilkins	.10	.05	.01
☐ 37 Andy Benes	.10	.05	.01
☐ 38 Bret Saberhagen	.25	.11	.03
☐ 39 Billy Ashley	.10	.05	.01
☐ 40 Jose Rijo	.10	.05	.01
☐ 41 Matt Williams	.50	.23	.06
☐ 42 Lenny Dykstra	.25	.11	.03
☐ 43 Jay Bell	.25	.11	.03
☐ 44 Reggie Jefferson	.25	.11	.03
☐ 45 Greg Maddux	2.00	.90	.25
☐ 46 Gary Sheffield	.50	.23	.06
☐ 47 Bret Boone	.25	.11	.03
☐ 48 Jeff Bagwell	1.25	.55	.16
☐ 49 Ben McDonald	.10	.05	.01
☐ 50 Eric Karros	.25	.11	.03
☐ 51 Roger Clemens	.60	.25	.07
☐ 52 Sammy Sosa	.50	.23	.06
☐ 53 Barry Bonds	.75	.35	.09
☐ 54 Joey Hamilton	.50	.23	.06
☐ 55 Brian Jordan	.50	.23	.06
☐ 56 Wil Cordero	.10	.05	.01
☐ 57 Aaron Sele	.25	.11	.03
☐ 58 Paul O'Neill	.25	.11	.03
☐ 59 Carlos Garcia	.10	.05	.01
☐ 60 Mike Mussina	.60	.25	.07
☐ 61 John Olerud	.10	.05	.01
☐ 62 Kevin Appier	.25	.11	.03
☐ 63 Matt Mieske	.25	.11	.03
☐ 64 Carlos Baerga	.25	.11	.03
☐ 65 Ryan Klesko	.50	.23	.06
☐ 66 Jimmy Key	.25	.11	.03
☐ 67 James Mouton	.10	.05	.01
☐ 68 Tim Salmon	.50	.23	.06
☐ 69 Hal Morris	.10	.05	.01
☐ 70 Albie Lopez	.10	.05	.01
☐ 71 Dave Hollins	.10	.05	.01
☐ 72 Greg Colbrunn	.10	.05	.01
☐ 73 Juan Gonzalez	1.50	.70	.19
☐ 74 Wally Joyner	.25	.11	.03
☐ 75 Bob Hamelin	.10	.05	.01
☐ 76 Brady Anderson	.50	.23	.06
☐ 77 Deion Sanders	.50	.23	.06
☐ 78 Javier Lopez	.50	.23	.06
☐ 79 Brian McRae	.25	.11	.03
☐ 80 Craig Biggio	.25	.11	.03
☐ 81 Kenny Lofton	.75	.35	.09
☐ 82 Cecil Fielder	.25	.11	.03
☐ 83 Mike Piazza	2.00	.90	.25
☐ 84 Rafael Palmeiro	.50	.23	.06
☐ 85 Jim Thome	.60	.25	.07
☐ 86 Ruben Sierra	.25	.11	.03
☐ 87 Mark Langston	.10	.05	.01
☐ 88 John Valentin	.25	.11	.03
☐ 89 Shawon Dunston	.10	.05	.01
☐ 90 Travis Fryman	.25	.11	.03
☐ 91 Chuck Knoblauch	.50	.23	.06
☐ 92 Dean Palmer	.25	.11	.03
☐ 93 Robby Thompson	.10	.05	.01
☐ 94 Barry Larkin	.50	.23	.06
☐ 95 Darren Lewis	.10	.05	.01
☐ 96 Andres Galarraga	.50	.23	.06
☐ 97 Tony Phillips	.25	.11	.03
☐ 98 Mo Vaughn	.75	.35	.09
☐ 99 Pedro Martinez	.25	.11	.03
☐ 100 Chad Curtis	.10	.05	.01
☐ 101 Brent Gates	.10	.05	.01
☐ 102 Pat Hentgen	.25	.11	.03
☐ 103 Rico Brogna	.10	.05	.01
☐ 104 Carlos Delgado	.25	.11	.03
☐ 105 Manny Ramirez	.75	.35	.09
☐ 106 Mike Greenwell	.10	.05	.01
☐ 107 Wade Boggs	.50	.23	.06
☐ 108 Ozzie Smith	.75	.35	.09
☐ 109 Rusty Greer	.50	.23	.06
☐ 110 Willie Greene	.10	.05	.01
☐ 111 Chili Davis	.25	.11	.03
☐ 112 Reggie Sanders	.25	.11	.03
☐ 113 Roberto Kelly	.10	.05	.01
☐ 114 Tom Glavine	.50	.23	.06
☐ 115 Moises Alou	.25	.11	.03
☐ 116 Dennis Eckersley	.25	.11	.03
☐ 117 Danny Tartabull	.10	.05	.01
☐ 118 Jeff Conine	.25	.11	.03
☐ 119 Will Clark	.50	.23	.06
☐ 120 Joe Carter	.25	.11	.03
☐ 121 Mark McGwire	1.00	.45	.12
☐ 122 Cal Ripken Jr.	2.50	1.10	.30
☐ 123 Danny Jackson	.10	.05	.01
☐ 124 Phil Plantier	.10	.05	.01
☐ 125 Dante Bichette	.50	.23	.06
☐ 126 Jack McDowell	.25	.11	.03
☐ 127 Jose Canseco	.50	.23	.06
☐ 128 Roberto Alomar	6.00	2.70	.75
☐ 129 Rondell White	.25	.11	.03
☐ 130 Ray Lankford	.25	.11	.03
☐ 131 Ryan Thompson	.10	.05	.01
☐ 132 Ken Caminiti	.50	.23	.06
☐ 133 Gregg Jefferies	.25	.11	.03
☐ 134 Omar Vizquel	.25	.11	.03
☐ 135 Mark Grace	.50	.23	.06
☐ 136 Derek Bell	.25	.11	.03
☐ 137 Mickey Tettleton	.10	.05	.01
☐ 138 Wilson Alvarez	.25	.11	.03
☐ 139 Larry Walker	.50	.23	.06
☐ 140 Bo Jackson	.25	.11	.03
☐ 141 Alex Rodriguez	4.00	1.80	.50
☐ 142 Orlando Miller	.10	.05	.01
☐ 143 Shawn Green	.25	.11	.03
☐ 144 Steve Dunn	.10	.05	.01
☐ 145 Midre Cummings	.10	.05	.01
☐ 146 Chan Ho Park	.50	.23	.06
☐ 147 Jose Oliva	.10	.05	.01
☐ 148 Armando Benitez	.10	.05	.01
☐ 149 J.R. Phillips	.10	.05	.01
☐ 150 Charles Johnson	.25	.11	.03
☐ 151 Garret Anderson	.25	.11	.03
☐ 152 Russ Davis	.10	.05	.01
☐ 153 Brian L.Hunter	.25	.11	.03
☐ 154 Ernie Young	.25	.11	.03
☐ 155 Marc Newfield	.25	.11	.03
☐ 156 Greg Pirkl	.10	.05	.01
☐ 157 Scott Ruffcorn	.10	.05	.01
☐ 158 Rikkert Faneyte	.10	.05	.01
☐ 159 Duane Singleton	.10	.05	.01
☐ 160 Gabe White	.10	.05	.01
☐ 161 Alex Gonzalez	.25	.11	.03
☐ 162 Chipper Jones	2.00	.90	.25
☐ 163 Mike Kelly	.10	.05	.01
☐ 164 Kurt Miller	.10	.05	.01
☐ 165 Roberto Petagine	.10	.05	.01
☐ 166 Jeff Bagwell CL	.60	.25	.07
☐ 167 Mike Piazza CL	1.00	.45	.12
☐ 168 Ken Griffey Jr. CL	1.50	.70	.19
☐ 169 Frank Thomas CL	1.50	.70	.19
☐ 170 Barry Bonds CL	1.25	.55	.16
Cal Ripken			

1995 Sportflix Artist's Proofs

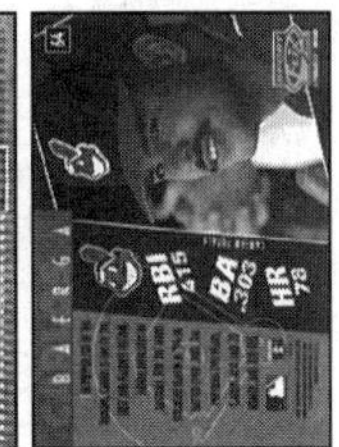

Cards from this 170-card parallel set were randomly inserted in packs at a rate of one in 36. Only 700 sets were printed. The "Artist's Proof" logo is printed in gold foil at the bottom right and the player's last name expands and contracts with the tilting of the card.

	MINT	NRMT	EXC
COMPLETE SET (170)	1000.00	450.00	125.00
COMMON CARD (1-170)	2.50	1.10	.30

*STARS: 12.5X TO 25X BASIC CARDS
*YOUNG STARS: 10X TO 20X BASIC CARDS

1995 Sportflix Detonators

Randomly inserted in packs at a rate of one in 16, this nine-card set highlights power hitters. The player is featured in a full-color cutout action shot atop a gold column with his name inscribed. The background is set back and is lit up with fireworks. The player's team logo and a rocket with the word "Detonators" is printed along the bottom of the card. A blue-sky with a Greek column serves as a backdrop for the borderless backs. A full-color shot of the player is pictured in the column and a short synopsis of the playeris '94 performance is printed in black type on the right side of the back. Backs are numbered with the prefix "DE".

	MINT	NRMT	EXC
COMPLETE SET (9)	30.00	13.50	3.70
COMMON CARD (1-9)	1.00	.45	.12
☐ DE1 Jeff Bagwell	4.00	1.80	.50
☐ DE2 Matt Williams	2.00	.90	.25
☐ DE3 Ken Griffey Jr.	10.00	4.50	1.25
☐ DE4 Frank Thomas	10.00	4.50	1.25
☐ DE5 Mike Piazza	6.00	2.70	.75
☐ DE6 Barry Bonds	2.50	1.10	.30
☐ DE7 Albert Belle	4.00	1.80	.50
☐ DE8 Cliff Floyd	1.00	.45	.12
☐ DE9 Juan Gonzalez	5.00	2.20	.60

1995 Sportflix Double Take

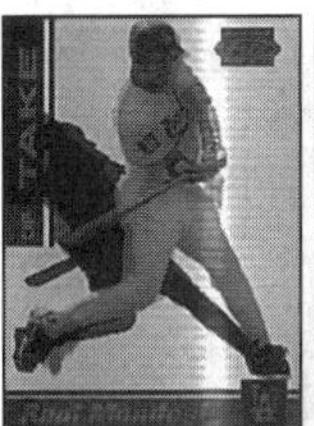

Randomly inserted in packs at a rate of one in 48, this 12-card set features two stars in one see-through 3-D card. Fronts feature the Sportflix "Magic Motion" process that allows the viewer to see two different images when the card is tilted. The players' names are reverse-printed across a red bar with the corresponding team logo on the bottom right. When the card is titled, the player's picture, name and team logo appear. "Double Take" is printed vertically on the left side of the card. Backs are see through and contain only the card number.

	MINT	NRMT	EXC
COMPLETE SET (12)	150.00	70.00	19.00
COMMON CARD (1-12)	5.00	2.20	.60
☐ 1 Jeff Bagwell	30.00	13.50	3.70
Frank Thomas			
☐ 2 Will Clark	5.00	2.20	.60
Fred McGriff			
☐ 3 Roberto Alomar	5.00	2.20	.60
Jeff Kent			
☐ 4 Matt Williams	5.00	2.20	.60
Wade Boggs			
☐ 5 Cal Ripken Jr.	20.00	9.00	2.50
Ozzie Smith			
☐ 6 Alex Rodriguez	20.00	9.00	2.50
Wil Cordero			
☐ 7 Mike Piazza	15.00	6.75	1.85
Carlos Delgado			
☐ 8 Kenny Lofton	6.00	2.70	.75
Dave Justice			
☐ 9 Barry Bonds	25.00	11.00	3.10
Ken Griffey Jr.			
☐ 10 Albert Belle	10.00	4.50	1.25
Raul Mondesi			
☐ 11 Tony Gwynn	15.00	6.75	1.85
Kirby Puckett			
☐ 12 Jimmy Key	12.00	5.50	1.50
Greg Maddux			

1995 Sportflix Hammer Team

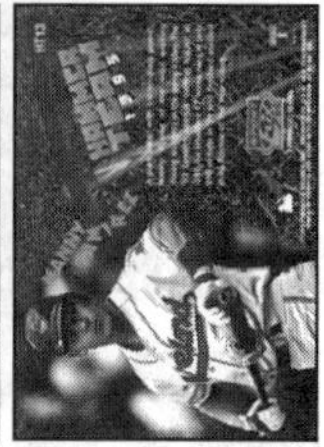

This 18-card set was inserted randomly in packs at a rate of one in 48 and looks at the league's top hitters. The 3-D fronts feature a full-color cutout of the player in action set against a backdrop of blue sky and basepaths. Sledgehammers are placed in the foreground and background of the fronts, while the player's name is printed at the bottom of the card against a green grass background. Full-bleed, horizontal backs are numbered with the prefix "HT" and picture the player in full color. A swinging sledgehammer is in motion against a backdrop of green grass while a 1994 player synopsis is printed in white type underneath the hammer.

	MINT	NRMT	EXC
COMPLETE SET (18)	25.00	11.00	3.10
COMMON CARD (1-18)	.50	.23	.06
☐ HT1 Ken Griffey Jr.	5.00	2.20	.60
☐ HT2 Frank Thomas	5.00	2.20	.60
☐ HT3 Jeff Bagwell	2.00	.90	.25
☐ HT4 Mike Piazza	3.00	1.35	.35
☐ HT5 Cal Ripken Jr.	4.00	1.80	.50
☐ HT6 Albert Belle	2.00	.90	.25
☐ HT7 Barry Bonds	1.25	.55	.16
☐ HT8 Don Mattingly	2.50	1.10	.30
☐ HT9 Will Clark	.50	.23	.06
☐ HT10 Tony Gwynn	2.00	.90	.25
☐ HT11 Matt Williams	.50	.23	.06
☐ HT12 Kirby Puckett	2.00	.90	.25
☐ HT13 Manny Ramirez	1.25	.55	.16
☐ HT14 Fred McGriff	.50	.23	.06
☐ HT15 Juan Gonzalez	2.50	1.10	.30
☐ HT16 Kenny Lofton	1.25	.55	.16
☐ HT17 Raul Mondesi	.50	.23	.06
☐ HT18 Tim Salmon	.50	.23	.06

1995 Sportflix ProMotion

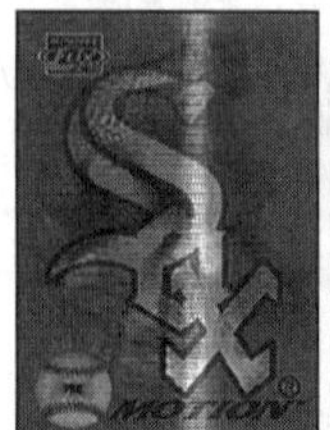

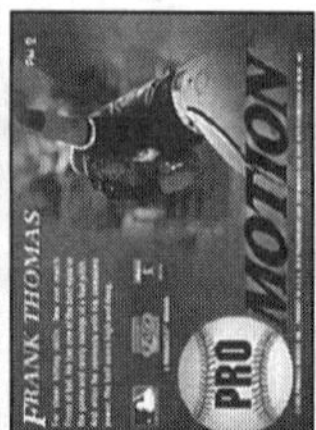

Randomly inserted in jumbo packs at a rate of one in 18, this 12-card set features top stars in the "Magic Motion" technology. Card fronts are coordinated in team colors and depict the player in a full-color action photo. The player's team logo is displayed when tilted. The horizontal backs feature the player in an action shot and are numbered with the prefix "PM". The player's name appears in white type across the top while the "Pro-Motion" logo is printed in black across the bottom of the back.

	MINT	NRMT	EXC
COMPLETE SET (12)	150.00	70.00	19.00
COMMPN CARD (PM1-PM12)	5.00	2.20	.60
☐ PM1 Ken Griffey Jr.	40.00	18.00	5.00
☐ PM2 Frank Thomas	40.00	18.00	5.00
☐ PM3 Cal Ripken Jr.	30.00	13.50	3.70
☐ PM4 Jeff Bagwell	15.00	6.75	1.85
☐ PM5 Mike Piazza	25.00	11.00	3.10
☐ PM6 Matt Williams	5.00	2.20	.60
☐ PM7 Albert Belle	15.00	6.75	1.85
☐ PM8 Jose Canseco	5.00	2.20	.60
☐ PM9 Don Mattingly	20.00	9.00	2.50
☐ PM10 Barry Bonds	10.00	4.50	1.25
☐ PM11 Will Clark	5.00	2.20	.60
☐ PM12 Kirby Puckett	15.00	6.75	1.85

1996 Sportflix

With retail only distribution, this 144 card set comes in five card packs that retail for $1.99. Regular cards picture two different pieces of photography. By flicking the wrist, one image disappears and another appears. Some cards use two different photos, and others use sequence action photography to create the illusion of animation. The wording in the bottom border also changes with movement. The set contains the UC3 Subset (97-120), Rookies Subset (121-141), and Checklists (142-144). The UC3 Subset features veteran superstars in 3-D animation. The 21-card Rookie subset carries color player photos on a background of part of a baseball that changes into a wooden baseball bat section when moved. Eight of the Rookies subset cards

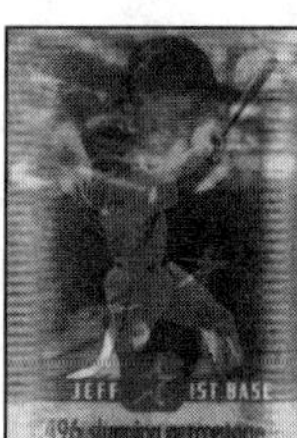

were made in jumbo (5 X 7") format, renumbered out of eight, and inserted as "chiptoppers" in retail boxes. These cards are valued at 15 times the corresponding basic card.

	MINT	NRMT	EXC
COMPLETE SET (144)	30.00	13.50	3.70
COMMON CARD (1-144)	.10	.05	.01
☐ 1 Wade Boggs	.50	.23	.06
☐ 2 Tim Salmon	.50	.23	.06
☐ 3 Will Clark	.50	.23	.06
☐ 4 Dante Bichette	.50	.23	.06
☐ 5 Barry Bonds	.75	.35	.09
☐ 6 Kirby Puckett	1.25	.55	.16
☐ 7 Albert Belle	1.25	.55	.16
☐ 8 Greg Maddux	2.00	.90	.25
☐ 9 Tony Gwynn	1.25	.55	.16
☐ 10 Mike Piazza	2.00	.90	.25
☐ 11 Ivan Rodriguez	.75	.35	.09
☐ 12 Marty Cordova	.25	.11	.03
☐ 13 Frank Thomas	3.00	1.35	.35
☐ 14 Raul Mondesi	.50	.23	.06
☐ 15 Johnny Damon	.25	.11	.03
☐ 16 Mark McGwire	1.00	.45	.12
☐ 17 Len Dykstra	.25	.11	.03
☐ 18 Ken Griffey Jr.	3.00	1.35	.35
☐ 19 Chipper Jones	2.00	.90	.25
☐ 20 Alex Rodriguez	3.00	1.35	.35
☐ 21 Jeff Bagwell	1.25	.55	.16
☐ 22 Jim Edmonds	.25	.11	.03
☐ 23 Edgar Martinez	.25	.11	.03
☐ 24 David Cone	.25	.11	.03
☐ 25 Tom Glavine	.50	.23	.06
☐ 26 Eddie Murray	.75	.35	.09
☐ 27 Paul Molitor	.60	.25	.07
☐ 28 Ryan Klesko	.50	.23	.06
☐ 29 Rafael Palmeiro	.50	.23	.06
☐ 30 Manny Ramirez	.75	.35	.09
☐ 31 Mo Vaughn	.75	.35	.09
☐ 32 Rico Brogna	.10	.05	.01
☐ 33 Marc Newfield	.25	.11	.03
☐ 34 J.T. Snow	.25	.11	.03
☐ 35 Reggie Sanders	.25	.11	.03
☐ 36 Fred McGriff	.50	.23	.06
☐ 37 Craig Biggio	.25	.11	.03
☐ 38 Jeff King	.25	.11	.03
☐ 39 Kenny Lofton	.75	.35	.09
☐ 40 Gary Gaetti	.25	.11	.03
☐ 41 Eric Karros	.25	.11	.03
☐ 42 Jason Isringhausen	.50	.23	.06
☐ 43 B.J. Surhoff	.10	.05	.01
☐ 44 Michael Tucker	.25	.11	.03
☐ 45 Gary Sheffield	.50	.23	.06
☐ 46 Chili Davis	.10	.05	.01
☐ 47 Bobby Bonilla	.25	.11	.03
☐ 48 Hideo Nomo	.75	.35	.09
☐ 49 Ray Durham	.50	.23	.06
☐ 50 Phil Nevin	.10	.05	.01
☐ 51 Randy Johnson	.50	.23	.06
☐ 52 Bill Pulsipher	.10	.05	.01
☐ 53 Ozzie Smith	.75	.35	.09
☐ 54 Cal Ripken	2.50	1.10	.30
☐ 55 Cecil Fielder	.25	.11	.03
☐ 56 Matt Williams	.50	.23	.06
☐ 57 Sammy Sosa	.50	.23	.06
☐ 58 Roger Clemens	.60	.25	.07
☐ 59 Brian L.Hunter	.25	.11	.03
☐ 60 Barry Larkin	.50	.23	.06
☐ 61 Charles Johnson	.25	.11	.03
☐ 62 David Justice	.25	.11	.03
☐ 63 Garret Anderson	.50	.23	.06
☐ 64 Rondell White	.25	.11	.03
☐ 65 Derek Bell	.25	.11	.03
☐ 66 Andres Galarraga	.50	.23	.06
☐ 67 Moises Alou	.25	.11	.03
☐ 68 Travis Fryman	.25	.11	.03
☐ 69 Pedro J. Martinez	.25	.11	.03
☐ 70 Carlos Baerga	.25	.11	.03
☐ 71 John Valentin	.25	.11	.03
☐ 72 Larry Walker	.50	.23	.06
☐ 73 Roberto Alomar	.60	.25	.07
☐ 74 Mike Mussina	.60	.25	.07
☐ 75 Kevin Appier	.25	.11	.03
☐ 76 Bernie Williams	.60	.25	.07
☐ 77 Ray Lankford	.25	.11	.03
☐ 78 Gregg Jefferies	.50	.23	.06
☐ 79 Robin Ventura	.25	.11	.03
☐ 80 Kenny Rogers	.10	.05	.01
☐ 81 Paul O'Neill	.10	.05	.01
☐ 82 Mark Grace	.50	.23	.06
☐ 83 Deion Sanders	.50	.23	.06
☐ 84 Tino Martinez	.25	.11	.03
☐ 85 Joe Carter	.25	.11	.03
☐ 86 Pete Schourek	.10	.05	.01
☐ 87 Jack McDowell	.50	.23	.06
☐ 88 John Mabry	.25	.11	.03
☐ 89 Darren Daulton	.25	.11	.03
☐ 90 Jim Thome	.60	.25	.07
☐ 91 Jay Buhner	.50	.23	.06
☐ 92 Jay Bell	.10	.05	.01
☐ 93 Kevin Seitzer	.10	.05	.01
☐ 94 Jose Canseco	.50	.23	.06
☐ 95 Juan Gonzalez	1.50	.70	.19
☐ 96 Jeff Conine	.25	.11	.03
☐ 97 Chipper Jones UC3	1.00	.45	.12
☐ 98 Ken Griffey Jr. UC3	1.50	.70	.19
☐ 99 Frank Thomas UC3	1.50	.70	.19
☐ 100 Cal Ripken UC3	1.25	.55	.16
☐ 101 Albert Belle UC3	.60	.25	.07
☐ 102 Mike Piazza UC3	1.00	.45	.12
☐ 103 Dante Bichette UC3	.50	.23	.06
☐ 104 Sammy Sosa UC3	.50	.23	.06
☐ 105 Mo Vaughn UC3	.50	.23	.06
☐ 106 Tim Salmon UC3	.50	.23	.06
☐ 107 Reggie Sanders UC3	.25	.11	.03
☐ 108 Gary Sheffield UC3	.50	.23	.06
☐ 109 Ruben Rivera UC3	.50	.23	.06
☐ 110 Rafael Palmeiro UC3	.50	.23	.06
☐ 111 Edgar Martinez UC3	.25	.11	.03
☐ 112 Barry Bonds UC3	.50	.23	.06
☐ 113 Manny Ramirez UC3	.25	.11	.03
☐ 114 Larry Walker UC3	.50	.23	.06
☐ 115 Jeff Bagwell UC3	.60	.25	.07
☐ 116 Matt Williams UC3	.50	.23	.06
☐ 117 Mark McGwire UC3	.50	.23	.06
☐ 118 Johnny Damon UC3	.25	.11	.03
☐ 119 Eddie Murray UC3	.50	.23	.06
☐ 120 Jay Buhner UC3	.50	.23	.06
☐ 121 Tim Unroe	.10	.05	.01
☐ 122 Todd Hollandsworth	.25	.11	.03
☐ 123 Tony Clark	.60	.25	.07
☐ 124 Roger Cedeno	.25	.11	.03
☐ 125 Jim Pittsley	.25	.11	.03
☐ 126 Ruben Rivera	.60	.25	.07
☐ 127 Bob Wolcott	.10	.05	.01
☐ 128 Chan Ho Park	.50	.23	.06
☐ 129 Chris Snopek	.10	.05	.01
☐ 130 Alex Ochoa	.25	.11	.03
☐ 131 Yamil Benitez	.25	.11	.03
☐ 132 Jimmy Haynes	.10	.05	.01
☐ 133 Dustin Hermanson	.25	.11	.03
☐ 134 Shawn Estes	.25	.11	.03
☐ 135 Howard Battle	.10	.05	.01
☐ 136 Matt Lawton	.10	.05	.01
☐ 137 Terrell Wade	.25	.11	.03
☐ 138 Jason Schmidt	.50	.23	.06
☐ 139 Derek Jeter	2.00	.90	.25
☐ 140 Shannon Stewart	.10	.05	.01
☐ 141 Chris Stynes	.10	.05	.01
☐ 142 Ken Griffey Jr. CL	1.50	.70	.19
☐ 143 Greg Maddux CL	1.00	.45	.12
☐ 144 Cal Ripken CL	1.25	.55	.16

1996 Sportflix Artist's Proofs

Inserted at the rate of one in 30, cards from this 144-card set are parallel to the regular set. A gold-foil stamped Artist's Proof logo distinguish them from their regular issue counterparts.

	MINT	NRMT	EXC
COMPLETE SET (144)	1000.00	450.00	125.00
COMMON CARD (1-144)	3.00	1.35	.35

*STARS: 15X TO 30X BASIC CARDS ..
*YOUNG STARS: 12.5X TO 25X BASIC CARDS

1996 Sportflix Double Take

Randomly inserted in jumbo packs, this 12-card set features color player photos of 2 players per card that play the same position.

	MINT	NRMT	EXC
COMPLETE SET (12)	120.00	55.00	15.00
COMMON CARD (1-12)	5.00	2.20	.60
☐ 1 Barry Larkin Cal Ripken	15.00	6.75	1.85
☐ 2 Roberto Alomar Craig Biggio	5.00	2.20	.60
☐ 3 Chipper Jones Matt Williams	12.00	5.50	1.50
☐ 4 Ken Griffey Ruben Rivera	20.00	9.00	2.50
☐ 5 Greg Maddux Hideo Nomo	12.00	5.50	1.50
☐ 6 Frank Thomas Mo Vaughn	20.00	9.00	2.50
☐ 7 Ivan Rodriguez Mike Piazza	12.00	5.50	1.50
☐ 8 Albert Belle Barry Bonds	10.00	4.50	1.25
☐ 9 Alex Rodriguez Derek Jeter	25.00	11.00	3.10
☐ 10 Kirby Puckett Tony Gwynn	15.00	6.75	1.85
☐ 11 Manny Ramirez Sammy Sosa	6.00	2.70	.75
☐ 12 Jeff Bagwell Rico Brogna	6.00	2.70	.75

1996 Sportflix Hit Parade

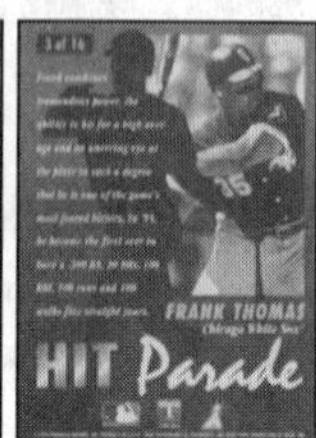

With an insertion rate of one in 35, this 16-card set features color player photos of hitters in 3D with a background scene in full-motion animation.

	MINT	NRMT	EXC
COMPLCTE SET (16)	120.00	55.00	15.00
COMMON CARD (1-16)	2.50	1.10	.30
☐ 1 Ken Griffey Jr.	20.00	9.00	2.50
☐ 2 Cal Ripken	15.00	6.75	1.85
☐ 3 Frank Thomas	20.00	9.00	2.50
☐ 4 Mike Piazza	12.00	5.50	1.50
☐ 5 Mo Vaughn	5.00	2.20	.60
☐ 6 Albert Belle	8.00	3.60	1.00
☐ 7 Jeff Bagwell	8.00	3.60	1.00
☐ 8 Matt Williams	2.50	1.10	.30
☐ 9 Sammy Sosa	3.00	1.35	.35
☐ 10 Kirby Puckett	8.00	3.60	1.00
☐ 11 Dante Bichette	2.50	1.10	.30
☐ 12 Gary Sheffield	3.00	1.35	.35
☐ 13 Tony Gwynn	8.00	3.60	1.00
☐ 14 Wade Boggs	2.50	1.10	.30
☐ 15 Chipper Jones	12.00	5.50	1.50
☐ 16 Barry Bonds	5.00	2.20	.60

1996 Sportflix Power Surge

With an insertion rate of one in 35, this retail only 24-card set is pinted on clear plastic and is a 3-D parallel rendition of the UC3 subset found in the regular Sportflix set.

	MINT	NRMT	EXC
COMPLETE SET (24)	225.00	100.00	28.00
COMMON CARD (1-24)	3.00	1.35	.35
☐ 1 Chipper Jones	25.00	11.00	3.10
☐ 2 Ken Griffey Jr.	40.00	18.00	5.00
☐ 3 Frank Thomas	40.00	18.00	5.00
☐ 4 Cal Ripken	30.00	13.50	3.70
☐ 5 Albert Belle	15.00	6.75	1.85
☐ 6 Mike Piazza	25.00	11.00	3.10
☐ 7 Dante Bichette	5.00	2.20	.60
☐ 8 Sammy Sosa	6.00	2.70	.75
☐ 9 Mo Vaughn	10.00	4.50	1.25
☐ 10 Tim Salmon	5.00	2.20	.60
☐ 11 Reggie Sanders	3.00	1.35	.35
☐ 12 Gary Sheffield	6.00	2.70	.75
☐ 13 Ruben Rivera	6.00	2.70	.75
☐ 14 Rafael Palmeiro	5.00	2.20	.60
☐ 15 Edgar Martinez	3.00	1.35	.35
☐ 16 Barry Bonds	10.00	4.50	1.25
☐ 17 Manny Ramirez	10.00	4.50	1.25
☐ 18 Larry Walker	5.00	2.20	.60
☐ 19 Jeff Bagwell	15.00	6.75	1.85
☐ 20 Matt Williams	5.00	2.20	.60
☐ 21 Mark McGwire	12.00	5.50	1.50
☐ 22 Johnny Damon	3.00	1.35	.35
☐ 23 Eddie Murray	10.00	4.50	1.25
☐ 24 Jay Buhner	5.00	2.20	.60

1996 Sportflix ProMotion

Inserted at the rate of one in 17, this 20-card set uses morphing technology and multi-phase animation to turn a player's photo into a bat, a ball, a glove, or a catcher's mask.

	MINT	NRMT	EXC
COMPLETE SET (20)	100.00	45.00	12.50
COMMON CARD (1-20)	1.00	.45	.12
☐ 1 Cal Ripken	12.00	5.50	1.50
☐ 2 Greg Maddux	10.00	4.50	1.25
☐ 3 Mo Vaughn	4.00	1.80	.50
☐ 4 Albert Belle	6.00	2.70	.75
☐ 5 Mike Piazza	10.00	4.50	1.25
☐ 6 Ken Griffey Jr.	15.00	6.75	1.85
☐ 7 Frank Thomas	15.00	6.75	1.85
☐ 8 Jeff Bagwell	6.00	2.70	.75
☐ 9 Hideo Nomo	4.00	1.80	.50
☐ 10 Chipper Jones	10.00	4.50	1.25
☐ 11 Tony Gwynn	6.00	2.70	.75
☐ 12 Don Mattingly	8.00	3.60	1.00
☐ 13 Dante Bichette	2.00	.90	.25
☐ 14 Matt Williams	2.00	.90	.25
☐ 15 Manny Ramirez	4.00	1.80	.50
☐ 16 Barry Bonds	4.00	1.80	.50
☐ 17 Reggie Sanders	1.50	.70	.19
☐ 18 Tim Salmon	2.00	.90	.25
☐ 19 Ruben Rivera	2.50	1.10	.30
☐ 20 Garret Anderson	1.00	.45	.12

1911 Sporting Life M116

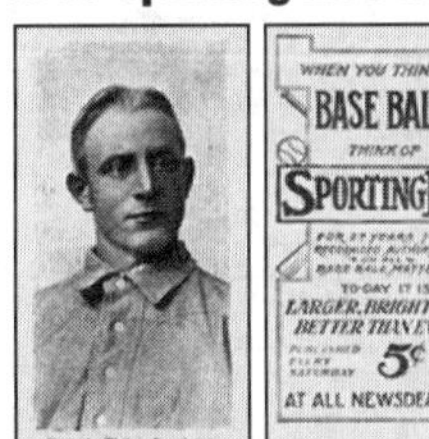

The cards in this 288-card set measure approximately 1 1/2" by 2 5/8". The Sporting Life set was offered as a premium to the publication's subscribers in 1911. Each of the 24 series of 12 cards came in an envelope printed with a list of the players within. Cards marked with an asterisk are also found with a special blue background and are worth double the listed price. McConnell appears with both Boston AL (common) and Chicago White Sox (scarce); McQuillan appears with Phillies (common) and Cincinnati (scarce). Cards are numbered in the checklist below alphabetically within team. Teams are ordered alphabetically within league: Boston AL (1-19), Chicago AL (20-36), Cleveland (37-52), Detroit (53-73), New York AL (74-84), Philadelphia AL (85-105), St. Louis AL (106-120), Washington (121-134), Boston NL (135-147), Brooklyn (148-164), Chicago NL (165-185), Cincinnati (186-203), New York NL (204-223), Philadelphia NL (224-242), Pittsburgh (243-261), and St. Louis (262-279). Cards 280-288 feature minor leaguers and are somewhat more difficult to find since most are from the tougher higher series.

	EX-MT	VG-E	GOOD
COMPLETE SET (290)	30000.00	13500.00	3800.00
COMMON MAJOR (1-279)	50.00	22.00	6.25
COMMON MINOR (280-288)	50.00	22.00	6.25
COMMON S19-S24	100.00	45.00	12.50
☐ 1 Frank Arellanes	50.00	22.00	6.25
☐ 2 Bill Carrigan	50.00	22.00	6.25
☐ 3 Ed Cicotte	125.00	55.00	15.50
☐ 4 Ray Collins S24	100.00	45.00	12.50
☐ 5 Pat Donahue	50.00	22.00	6.25
☐ 6 Patsy Donovan MG S21	100.00	45.00	12.50
☐ 7 Arthur Engle	50.00	22.00	6.25
☐ 8 Larry Gardner S24	100.00	45.00	12.50
☐ 9 Charles Hall	50.00	22.00	6.25
☐ 10 Harry Hooper S23	300.00	135.00	38.00
☐ 11 Edwin Karger	50.00	22.00	6.25
☐ 12 Harry Lord *	50.00	22.00	6.25
☐ 13 Thomas Madden S24	100.00	45.00	12.50
☐ 14A Amby McConnell (Boston AL)	50.00	22.00	6.25
☐ 14B Amby McConnell (Chicago AL)	2000.00	900.00	250.00
☐ 15 Tris Speaker S23	600.00	275.00	75.00
☐ 16 Jake Stahl	60.00	27.00	7.50
☐ 17 John Thoney	50.00	22.00	6.25
☐ 18 Heinie Wagner	60.00	27.00	7.50
☐ 19 Joe Wood S23	200.00	90.00	25.00
☐ 20 Lena Blackburn UER (Sic, Blackburne)	50.00	22.00	6.25
☐ 21 James J. Block S21	100.00	45.00	12.50
☐ 22 Patsy Dougherty	50.00	22.00	6.25
☐ 23 Hugh Duffy MG	125.00	55.00	15.50
☐ 24 Ed Hahn	50.00	22.00	6.25
☐ 25 Paul Meloan S24	100.00	45.00	12.50
☐ 26 Fred Parent	50.00	22.00	6.25
☐ 27 Frederick Payne S21	100.00	45.00	12.50
☐ 28 William Purtell	50.00	22.00	6.25
☐ 29 James Scott S23	100.00	45.00	12.50
☐ 30 Frank Smith	50.00	22.00	6.25
☐ 31 Billy Sullivan	60.00	27.00	7.50
☐ 32 Lee Tannehill	50.00	22.00	6.25
☐ 33 Ed Walsh	125.00	55.00	15.50
☐ 34 Guy(Doc) White	50.00	22.00	6.25
☐ 35 Irv Young	50.00	22.00	6.25
☐ 36 Dutch Zwilling S24	100.00	45.00	12.50
☐ 37 Harry Bemis	50.00	22.00	6.25
☐ 38 Charles Berger	50.00	22.00	6.25
☐ 39 Joseph Birmingham	50.00	22.00	6.25
☐ 40 Hugh Bradley	50.00	22.00	6.25
☐ 41 Nig Clarke	50.00	22.00	6.25
☐ 42 Cy Falkenberg	50.00	22.00	6.25
☐ 43 Elmer Flick	150.00	70.00	19.00
☐ 44 Addie Joss	200.00	90.00	25.00
☐ 45 Napoleon Lajoie *	300.00	135.00	38.00
☐ 46 Frederick Linke S20	100.00	45.00	12.50
☐ 47 B.(Bris) Lord	50.00	22.00	6.25
☐ 48 Deacon McGuire MG	50.00	22.00	6.25
☐ 49 Harry Niles	50.00	22.00	6.25
☐ 50 George Stovall	50.00	22.00	6.25
☐ 51 Terry Turner	50.00	22.00	6.25
☐ 52 Cy Young	400.00	180.00	50.00
☐ 53 Heine Beckendorf	50.00	22.00	6.25
☐ 54 Donie Bush	50.00	22.00	6.25
☐ 55 Ty Cobb *	2000.00	900.00	250.00
☐ 56 Sam Crawford *	150.00	70.00	19.00
☐ 57 Jim Delehanty	60.00	27.00	7.50
☐ 58 Bill Donovan	50.00	22.00	6.25
☐ 59 Hugh Jennings MG *	125.00	55.00	15.50
☐ 60 Davy Jones	50.00	22.00	6.25
☐ 61 Tom Jones	50.00	22.00	6.25
☐ 62 Chick Lathers S21	100.00	45.00	12.50
☐ 63 Matty McIntyre	50.00	22.00	6.25
☐ 64 George Moriarty	60.00	27.00	7.50
☐ 65 George Mullin	50.00	22.00	6.25
☐ 66 Charley O'Leary	50.00	22.00	6.25
☐ 67 Hub Pernoll S23	100.00	45.00	12.50
☐ 68 Boss Schmidt	50.00	22.00	6.25
☐ 69 Oscar Stanage	50.00	22.00	6.25
☐ 70 Sailor Stroud S21	100.00	45.00	12.50
☐ 71 Ed Summers	50.00	22.00	6.25
☐ 72 Ed Willett	50.00	22.00	6.25
☐ 73 Ralph Works	50.00	22.00	6.25
☐ 74 Jimmy Austin S19	100.00	45.00	12.50
☐ 75 Hal Chase *	100.00	45.00	12.50
☐ 76 Birdie Cree	50.00	22.00	6.25
☐ 77 Lou Criger	50.00	22.00	6.25
☐ 78 Russ Ford S23	100.00	45.00	12.50
☐ 79 Earle Gardner S23	100.00	45.00	12.50
☐ 80 John Knight S19	100.00	45.00	12.50
☐ 81 Frank LaPorte	50.00	22.00	6.25
☐ 82 George Stallings MG	50.00	22.00	6.25
☐ 83 Jeff Sweeney S19	100.00	45.00	12.50
☐ 84 Harry Wolter	50.00	22.00	6.25
☐ 85 Tommy Atkins S24	100.00	45.00	12.50
☐ 86 Frank Baker	150.00	70.00	19.00
☐ 87 Jack Barry	60.00	27.00	7.50
☐ 88 Chief Bender *	100.00	45.00	12.50
☐ 89 Eddie Collins *	150.00	70.00	19.00
☐ 90 Jack Coombs	100.00	45.00	12.50
☐ 91 Harry Davis *	50.00	22.00	6.25
☐ 92 Jimmy Dygert	50.00	22.00	6.25
☐ 93 Topsy Hartsel	50.00	22.00	6.25
☐ 94 Heinie Heitmuller	50.00	22.00	6.25
☐ 95 Harry Krause	50.00	22.00	6.25
☐ 96 Jack Lapp S24	100.00	45.00	12.50
☐ 97 Paddy Livingstone	50.00	22.00	6.25
☐ 98 Connie Mack MG	250.00	110.00	31.00
☐ 99 Stuffy McInnis S24 UER (Misspelled McInnes on card)	100.00	45.00	12.50
☐ 100 Cy Morgan	50.00	22.00	6.25
☐ 101 Danny Murphy	50.00	22.00	6.25
☐ 102 Rube Oldring	50.00	22.00	6.25
☐ 103 Eddie Plank	300.00	135.00	38.00
☐ 104 Amos Strunk S24	100.00	45.00	12.50
☐ 105 Ira Thomas *	50.00	22.00	6.25
☐ 106 Bill Bailey	50.00	22.00	6.25
☐ 107 Dode Criss S19	100.00	45.00	12.50
☐ 108 Bert Graham	50.00	22.00	6.25
☐ 109 Roy Hartzell	50.00	22.00	6.25
☐ 110 Danny Hoffman	50.00	22.00	6.25
☐ 111 Harry Howell	50.00	22.00	6.25
☐ 112 Joe Lake S19	100.00	45.00	12.50
☐ 113 Jack O'Conner	50.00	22.00	6.25
☐ 114 Barney Pelty	50.00	22.00	6.25
☐ 115 Jack Powell	50.00	22.00	6.25
☐ 116 Al Schweitzer	50.00	22.00	6.25
☐ 117 Jim Stephens	50.00	22.00	6.25
☐ 118 George Stone	50.00	22.00	6.25
☐ 119 Rube Waddell	150.00	70.00	19.00
☐ 120 Bobby Wallace	100.00	45.00	12.50
☐ 121 Wid Conroy	50.00	22.00	6.25
☐ 122 Kid Elberfeld	50.00	22.00	6.25
☐ 123 Eddie Foster	50.00	22.00	6.25
☐ 124 Doc Gessler	50.00	22.00	6.25
☐ 125 Walter Johnson	700.00	325.00	90.00
☐ 126 Red Killifer S22	100.00	45.00	12.50
☐ 127 Jimmy McAleer MG	50.00	22.00	6.25
☐ 128 George McBride S21	100.00	45.00	12.50
☐ 129 Clyde Milan	60.00	27.00	7.50
☐ 130 Warren Miller S23	100.00	45.00	12.50
☐ 131 Doc Reisling	50.00	22.00	6.25
☐ 132 Germany Schaefer	60.00	27.00	7.50
☐ 133 Gabby Street	50.00	22.00	6.25
☐ 134 Bob Unglaub	50.00	22.00	6.25
☐ 135 Fred Beck	50.00	22.00	6.25
☐ 136 Buster Brown	50.00	22.00	6.25
☐ 137 Cliff Curtis S23	100.00	45.00	12.50
☐ 138 George Ferguson	50.00	22.00	6.25
☐ 139 Samuel Frock S20	100.00	45.00	12.50
☐ 140 Peaches Graham	50.00	22.00	6.25
☐ 141 Buck Herzog	50.00	22.00	6.25
☐ 142 Fred Lake MG	50.00	22.00	6.25
☐ 143 Bayard Sharpe S23	100.00	45.00	12.50
☐ 144 David Shean S20	100.00	45.00	12.50
☐ 145 Charlie Smith S22	100.00	45.00	12.50
☐ 146 Harry Smith	50.00	22.00	6.25
☐ 147 Bill Sweeney	50.00	22.00	6.25
☐ 148 Cy Barger	50.00	22.00	6.25
☐ 149 George Bell	50.00	22.00	6.25
☐ 150 Bill Bergen	50.00	22.00	6.25
☐ 151 Al Burch	50.00	22.00	6.25
☐ 152 Bill Dahlen MG	60.00	27.00	7.50
☐ 153 William Davidson S21	100.00	45.00	12.50
☐ 154 Frank Dessau S21	100.00	45.00	12.50
☐ 155 Tex Erwin S20	100.00	45.00	12.50
☐ 156 John Hummel	50.00	22.00	6.25
☐ 157 George Hunter	50.00	22.00	6.25
☐ 158 Tim Jordan *	50.00	22.00	6.25
☐ 159 Ed Lennox	50.00	22.00	6.25
☐ 160 Pryor McElveen	50.00	22.00	6.25
☐ 161 Tommy McMillan	50.00	22.00	6.25
☐ 162 Nap Rucker	60.00	27.00	7.50
☐ 163 Doc Scanlon UER (Sic, Scanlan)	50.00	22.00	6.25
☐ 164 Kaiser Wilhelm	50.00	22.00	6.25
☐ 165 Jimmy Archer S22	100.00	45.00	12.50
☐ 166 Ginger Beaumont	50.00	22.00	6.25
☐ 167 Mordecai Brown *	150.00	70.00	19.00
☐ 168 Frank Chance *	200.00	90.00	25.00
☐ 169 Johnny Evers	150.00	70.00	19.00
☐ 170 Solly Hofman	50.00	22.00	6.25
☐ 171 John Kane	50.00	22.00	6.25
☐ 172 Johnny Kling	50.00	22.00	6.25
☐ 173 Rube Kroh	50.00	22.00	6.25
☐ 174 Harry McIntire	50.00	22.00	6.25
☐ 175 Tom Needham	50.00	22.00	6.25
☐ 176 Orvie Overall	50.00	22.00	6.25
☐ 177 Big Jeff Pfeffer S23	100.00	45.00	12.50
☐ 178 Jack Pfiester	50.00	22.00	6.25
☐ 179 Ed Reulbach	60.00	27.00	7.50
☐ 180 Lew Richie	50.00	22.00	6.25
☐ 181 Frank Schulte	50.00	22.00	6.25
☐ 182 Jimmy Sheckard	50.00	22.00	6.25
☐ 183 Harry Steinfeldt	60.00	27.00	7.50
☐ 184 Joe Tinker	150.00	70.00	19.00
☐ 185 Heinie Zimmerman S19	100.00	45.00	12.50
☐ 186 Fred Beebe	50.00	22.00	6.25
☐ 187 Bob Bescher	50.00	22.00	6.25
☐ 188 Chappy Charles	50.00	22.00	6.25
☐ 189 Tommy Clarke S20	100.00	45.00	12.50
☐ 190 Tom Downey	50.00	22.00	6.25
☐ 191 Jim Doyle	50.00	22.00	6.25
☐ 192 Dick Egan UER (Sic, Egan)	50.00	22.00	6.25
☐ 193 Art Fromme	50.00	22.00	6.25
☐ 194 Harry Gaspar S19	100.00	45.00	12.50
☐ 195 Clark Griffith MG	125.00	55.00	15.50
☐ 196 Doc Hoblitzel	50.00	22.00	6.25
☐ 197 Hans Lobert	50.00	22.00	6.25
☐ 198 Larry McLean	50.00	22.00	6.25
☐ 199 Mike Mitchell	50.00	22.00	6.25
☐ 200 Art Phelan S23	100.00	45.00	12.50
☐ 201 Jack Rowan	50.00	22.00	6.25
☐ 202 Bob Space UER (Sic, Spade)	50.00	22.00	6.25
☐ 203 George Suggs	50.00	22.00	6.25
☐ 204 Red Ames S22	100.00	45.00	12.50
☐ 205 Al Bridwell	50.00	22.00	6.25
☐ 206 Doc Crandall	50.00	22.00	6.25
☐ 207 Art Devlin	50.00	22.00	6.25
☐ 208 Josh Devore S19	100.00	45.00	12.50
☐ 209 Larry Doyle *	60.00	27.00	7.50
☐ 210 Art Fletcher S22	100.00	45.00	12.50
☐ 211 Christy Mathewson *	700.00	325.00	90.00
☐ 212 John McGraw MG	200.00	90.00	25.00
☐ 213 Fred Merkle	60.00	27.00	7.50
☐ 214 Red Murray	50.00	22.00	6.25
☐ 215 Chief Meyers S23 UER (Misspelled Myers on card)	100.00	45.00	12.50
☐ 216 Bugs Raymond	60.00	27.00	7.50
☐ 217 Admiral Schlei	50.00	22.00	6.25
☐ 218 Cy Seymour	50.00	22.00	6.25
☐ 219 Tillie Shafer S19	100.00	45.00	12.50
☐ 220 Fred Snodgrass	60.00	27.00	7.50
☐ 221 Fred Tenney *	50.00	22.00	6.25
☐ 222 Art Wilson S23	100.00	45.00	12.50
☐ 223 Hooks Wiltse	50.00	22.00	6.25
☐ 224 Johnny Bates	50.00	22.00	6.25
☐ 225 Kitty Bransfeld	50.00	22.00	6.25
☐ 226 Red Dooin *	50.00	22.00	6.25
☐ 227 Mickey Doolan	50.00	22.00	6.25
☐ 228 Bob Ewing	50.00	22.00	6.25
☐ 229 Bill Foxen	50.00	22.00	6.25
☐ 230 Eddie Grant	50.00	22.00	6.25
☐ 231 Fred Jacklitsch	50.00	22.00	6.25
☐ 232 Otto Knabe	50.00	22.00	6.25
☐ 233 Sherry Magee	50.00	22.00	6.25
☐ 234A Geo.McQuillan * (Philadelphia NL)	50.00	22.00	6.25
☐ 234B Geo.McQuillan (Cincinnati NL)	2000.00	900.00	250.00
☐ 235 Earl Moore	50.00	22.00	6.25
☐ 236 Pat Moran	50.00	22.00	6.25
☐ 237 Lew Moren	50.00	22.00	6.25
☐ 238 Dode Paskert S19	100.00	45.00	12.50
☐ 239 Lou Schettler S20	100.00	45.00	12.50
☐ 240 Tully Sparks	50.00	22.00	6.25
☐ 241 John Titus S23	100.00	45.00	12.50
☐ 242A Jimmy Walsh S20 (Dark background)	150.00	70.00	19.00
☐ 242B Jimmy Walsh S22 (White background)	150.00	70.00	19.00
☐ 243 Ed Abbaticchio	50.00	22.00	6.25
☐ 244 Babe Adams	60.00	27.00	7.50
☐ 245 Bobby Byrne	50.00	22.00	6.25
☐ 246 Howie Camnitz	50.00	22.00	6.25
☐ 247 Vin Campbell S21	100.00	45.00	12.50
☐ 248 Fred Clarke	125.00	55.00	15.50
☐ 249 John Flynn S20	100.00	45.00	12.50
☐ 250 George Gibson *	50.00	22.00	6.25
☐ 251 Ham Hyatt	50.00	22.00	6.25
☐ 252 Fred Leach *	50.00	22.00	6.25
☐ 253 Sam Leever	50.00	22.00	6.25
☐ 254 Lefty Leifield	50.00	22.00	6.25
☐ 255 Nick Maddox	50.00	22.00	6.25
☐ 256 Dots Miller	50.00	22.00	6.25
☐ 257 Paddy O'Conner	50.00	22.00	6.25
☐ 258 Deacon Phillipe	60.00	27.00	7.50
☐ 259 Mike Simon S21	100.00	45.00	12.50
☐ 260 Hans Wagner *	700.00	325.00	90.00
☐ 261 Chief Wilson	50.00	22.00	6.25
☐ 262 Les Bachman UER (Sic, Backman)	50.00	22.00	6.25
☐ 263 Jack Bliss S21	100.00	45.00	12.50
☐ 264 Roger Bresnahan *	125.00	55.00	15.50
☐ 265 Frank Corridon	50.00	22.00	6.25
☐ 266 Ray Demmitt S22	100.00	45.00	12.50
☐ 267 Rube Ellis	50.00	22.00	6.25
☐ 268 Steve Evans S23	100.00	45.00	12.50
☐ 269 Bob Harmon S20	100.00	45.00	12.50
☐ 270 Miller Huggins	125.00	55.00	15.50
☐ 271 Rudy Hulswitt	50.00	22.00	6.25
☐ 272 Ed Konetchy	50.00	22.00	6.25
☐ 273 Johnny Lush	50.00	22.00	6.25
☐ 274 Al Mattern	50.00	22.00	6.25
☐ 275 Mike Mowery S21	100.00	45.00	12.50
☐ 276 Rebel Oakes S24	100.00	45.00	12.50
☐ 277 Ed Phelps	50.00	22.00	6.25
☐ 278 Slim Sallee	50.00	22.00	6.25
☐ 279 Vic Willis	125.00	55.00	15.50
☐ 280 Coveleski: Louisville S22 UER (Misspelled Coveleskie on card)	150.00	70.00	19.00
☐ 281 Foster: Rochester S19	100.00	45.00	12.50
☐ 282 Frill: Jersey City S20	100.00	45.00	12.50
☐ 283 Hughes: Rochester S23	100.00	45.00	12.50
☐ 284 Krueger: Sacramento S20	100.00	45.00	12.50
☐ 285 Mitchell: Rochester S19	100.00	45.00	12.50
☐ 286 O'Hara: Toronto	50.00	22.00	6.25
☐ 287 Perring: Columbus S20	100.00	45.00	12.50
☐ 288 Ray: Western League S24	100.00	45.00	12.50

1911 Sporting Life Cabinets W600

These large and attractive cabinet-type cards were issued by the Sporting Life Publishing Company around 1911. The exact number of cards in the set is not known but is estimated to be about 450. The cards are not numbered and might appear to have a slight reddish or sepia tinit. Many are found still in the glassine envelope in which they were issued. The backs are blank.

	EX-MT	VG-E	GOOD
COMPLETE SET	50000.00	22500.00	6200.00
COMMON CARD	100.00	45.00	12.50

Card	EX-MT	VG-E	GOOD
☐ 1 Bill Abstein	100.00	45.00	12.50
☐ 2 Babe Adams	100.00	45.00	12.50
☐ 3 Whitey Alperman	100.00	45.00	12.50
☐ 4 Nick Altrock	150.00	70.00	19.00
☐ 5 Red Ames	100.00	45.00	12.50
☐ 6 Frank Arelanes	100.00	45.00	12.50
☐ 7 Charlie Armbruster	100.00	45.00	12.50
☐ 8 Bill Armour MG	100.00	45.00	12.50
☐ 9 Harry Arndt	100.00	45.00	12.50
☐ 10 Harry Aubrey	100.00	45.00	12.50
☐ 11 Jimmy Austin	150.00	70.00	19.00
☐ 12 Charlie Babb	100.00	45.00	12.50
☐ 13 Frank Baker	600.00	275.00	75.00
☐ 14 Jap Barbeau	100.00	45.00	12.50
☐ 15 Cy Barger	100.00	45.00	12.50
☐ 16 Jimmy Barrett	100.00	45.00	12.50
☐ 17 Shad Barry	100.00	45.00	12.50
☐ 18 Jack Barry	100.00	45.00	12.50
☐ 19 Harry Barton	100.00	45.00	12.50
☐ 20 Emil Batch	100.00	45.00	12.50
☐ 21 Johnny Bates	100.00	45.00	12.50
☐ 22 Harry Bay	100.00	45.00	12.50
☐ 23 Ginger Beaumont	100.00	45.00	12.50
☐ 24 Fred Beck	100.00	45.00	12.50
☐ 25 Henie Beckendorf	100.00	45.00	12.50
☐ 26 Fred Beebe	100.00	45.00	12.50
☐ 27 George Bell	100.00	45.00	12.50
☐ 28 Harry Bemis	100.00	45.00	12.50
☐ 29 Chief Bender	400.00	180.00	50.00
☐ 30 Pug Bennett	100.00	45.00	12.50
☐ 31 Bill Bergen	100.00	45.00	12.50
☐ 32 C. Berger	100.00	45.00	12.50
☐ 33 Bill Bernhard	100.00	45.00	12.50
☐ 34 Bob Bescher	100.00	45.00	12.50
☐ 35 W. Beville	100.00	45.00	12.50
☐ 36 Lena Blackburne	100.00	45.00	12.50
☐ 37 Elmer Bliss	100.00	45.00	12.50
☐ 38 Frank Bowerman	100.00	45.00	12.50
☐ 39 Bill Bradley	100.00	45.00	12.50
☐ 40 W. Bradley	100.00	45.00	12.50
☐ 41 Dave Brain	100.00	45.00	12.50
☐ 42 Kitty Bransfield	100.00	45.00	12.50
☐ 43 Roger Bresnahan	400.00	180.00	50.00
☐ 44 Al Bridwell	100.00	45.00	12.50
☐ 45 Buster Brown	100.00	45.00	12.50
☐ 46 Mordecai Brown	400.00	180.00	50.00
☐ 47 Sam Brown	100.00	45.00	12.50
☐ 48 George Browne	100.00	45.00	12.50
☐ 49 Jimmy Burke	100.00	45.00	12.50
☐ 50 Nixey Callahan	100.00	45.00	12.50
☐ 51 Howie Camnitz	100.00	45.00	12.50
☐ 52 Rip Cannell	100.00	45.00	12.50
☐ 53 Joe Cantillon MG	100.00	45.00	12.50
☐ 54 Pat Carney	100.00	45.00	12.50
☐ 55 Charlie Carr	100.00	45.00	12.50
☐ 56 Bill Carrigan	100.00	45.00	12.50
☐ 57 Doc Casey	100.00	45.00	12.50
☐ 58 Frank Chance	1000.00	450.00	125.00
☐ 59 Hal Chase	200.00	90.00	25.00
☐ 60 Jack Chesbro	400.00	180.00	50.00
☐ 61 Eddie Cicotte	300.00	135.00	38.00
☐ 62 Fred Clarke	600.00	275.00	75.00
☐ 63 Nig Clarke	100.00	45.00	12.50
☐ 64 T. Clarke	100.00	45.00	12.50
☐ 65 Walter Clarkson	100.00	45.00	12.50
☐ 66 Otis Clymer	100.00	45.00	12.50
☐ 67 Andy Coakley	100.00	45.00	12.50
☐ 68 Ty Cobb	3000.00	1350.00	375.00
☐ 69 Eddie Collins	400.00	180.00	50.00
☐ 70 Jimmy Collins	600.00	275.00	75.00
☐ 71 Bunk Congalton	100.00	45.00	12.50
☐ 72 Wid Conroy	100.00	45.00	12.50
☐ 73 Duff Cooley	100.00	45.00	12.50
☐ 74 Jack Coombs	250.00	110.00	31.00
☐ 75 Frank Corridon	100.00	45.00	12.50
☐ 76 Bill Coughlin	100.00	45.00	12.50
☐ 77 Ernie Courtney	100.00	45.00	12.50
☐ 78 Doc Crandall	100.00	45.00	12.50
☐ 79 Sam Crawford	400.00	180.00	50.00
☐ 80 Lou Criger	100.00	45.00	12.50
☐ 81 Dode Criss	100.00	45.00	12.50
☐ 82 John Cronin	150.00	70.00	19.00
☐ 83 Lave Cross	100.00	45.00	12.50
☐ 84 Monte Cross	100.00	45.00	12.50
☐ 85 Clarence Currie	100.00	45.00	12.50
☐ 86 Bill Dahlen	150.00	70.00	19.00
☐ 87 George Davis	100.00	45.00	12.50
☐ 88 Harry Davis	100.00	45.00	12.50
☐ 89 Jim Delehanty	150.00	70.00	19.00
☐ 90 Art Devlin	150.00	70.00	19.00
☐ 91 Pop Dillon	100.00	45.00	12.50
☐ 92 Bill Dineen	100.00	45.00	12.50
☐ 93 John Dobbs	100.00	45.00	12.50
☐ 94 Ed Doheny	100.00	45.00	12.50
☐ 95 Cozy Dolan	100.00	45.00	12.50
☐ 96 Jiggs Donahue	100.00	45.00	12.50
☐ 97 Mike Donlin	150.00	70.00	19.00
☐ 98 Patsy Donovan	100.00	45.00	12.50
☐ 99 Bill Donovan	100.00	45.00	12.50
☐ 100 Red Dooin	100.00	45.00	12.50
☐ 101 Mickey Doolan	100.00	45.00	12.50
☐ 102 Tom Doran	100.00	45.00	12.50
☐ 103 Gus Dorner	100.00	45.00	12.50
☐ 104 Patsy Dougherty	100.00	45.00	12.50
☐ 105 Tom Downey	100.00	45.00	12.50
☐ 106 Red Downs	100.00	45.00	12.50
☐ 107 Jim Doyle	100.00	45.00	12.50
☐ 108 Joe Doyle	100.00	45.00	12.50
☐ 109 Larry Doyle	100.00	45.00	12.50
☐ 110 Hugh Duffy	400.00	180.00	50.00
☐ 111 Bill Duggleby	100.00	45.00	12.50
☐ 112 Gus Dundon	100.00	45.00	12.50
☐ 113 Jack Dunleavy	100.00	45.00	12.50
☐ 114 Jack Dunn	100.00	45.00	12.50
☐ 115 Jimmy Dygert	100.00	45.00	12.50
☐ 116 Dick Egan	100.00	45.00	12.50
☐ 117 Kid Elberfeld	150.00	70.00	19.00
☐ 118 Claude Elliott	100.00	45.00	12.50
☐ 119 Rube Ellis	100.00	45.00	12.50
☐ 120 Johnny Evers	600.00	275.00	75.00
☐ 121 Bob Ewing	100.00	45.00	12.50
☐ 122 Cy Falkenberg	100.00	45.00	12.50
☐ 123 John Farrell	100.00	45.00	12.50
☐ 124 George Ferguson	100.00	45.00	12.50
☐ 125 Hobe Ferris	100.00	45.00	12.50
☐ 126 Tom Fisher	100.00	45.00	12.50
☐ 127 Patsy Flaherty	100.00	45.00	12.50
☐ 128 John Flynn	100.00	45.00	12.50
☐ 129 Bill Foxen	100.00	45.00	12.50
☐ 130 Chick Fraser	100.00	45.00	12.50
☐ 131 Bill Friel	100.00	45.00	12.50
☐ 132 Art Fromme	100.00	45.00	12.50
☐ 133 Dave Fultz	100.00	45.00	12.50
☐ 134 Bob Ganley	100.00	45.00	12.50
☐ 135 John Ganzel	100.00	45.00	12.50
☐ 136 Ned Garvin	100.00	45.00	12.50
☐ 137 Harry Gasper	100.00	45.00	12.50
☐ 138 Phil Geier	100.00	45.00	12.50
☐ 139 Doc Gessler	100.00	45.00	12.50
☐ 140 George Gibson	100.00	45.00	12.50
☐ 141 Norwood Gibson	100.00	45.00	12.50
☐ 142 Billy Gilbert	100.00	45.00	12.50
☐ 143 Fred Glade	100.00	45.00	12.50
☐ 144 Harry Gleason	150.00	70.00	19.00
☐ 145 Eddie Grant	100.00	45.00	12.50
☐ 146 Danny Green	100.00	45.00	12.50
☐ 147 Ed Gremminger	100.00	45.00	12.50
☐ 148 Clark Griffith	400.00	180.00	50.00
☐ 149 Moose Grimshaw	100.00	45.00	12.50
☐ 150 H. Hackett	100.00	45.00	12.50
☐ 151 Ed Hahn	100.00	45.00	12.50
☐ 152 Noodles Hahn	100.00	45.00	12.50
☐ 153 Charley Hall	100.00	45.00	12.50
☐ 154 Bill Hallman	100.00	45.00	12.50
☐ 155 Ned Hanlon MG	150.00	70.00	19.00
☐ 156 Bob Harmon	100.00	45.00	12.50
☐ 157 Jack Harper	100.00	45.00	12.50
☐ 158 Hub Hart	100.00	45.00	12.50
☐ 159 Topsy Hartsel	100.00	45.00	12.50
☐ 160 Roy Hartzell	100.00	45.00	12.50
☐ 161 Charlie Hemphill	100.00	45.00	12.50
☐ 162 Weldon Henley	100.00	45.00	12.50
☐ 163 Otto Hess	100.00	45.00	12.50
☐ 164 Piano Legs Hickman	100.00	45.00	12.50
☐ 165 Hunter Hill	100.00	45.00	12.50
☐ 166 Homer Hillebrand	100.00	45.00	12.50
☐ 167 Harry Hinchman	100.00	45.00	12.50
☐ 168 Bill Hinchman	100.00	45.00	12.50
☐ 169 Dick Hoblitzel	100.00	45.00	12.50
☐ 170 Danny Hoffman	100.00	45.00	12.50
☐ 171 Solly Hofman	100.00	45.00	12.50
☐ 172 Bill Hogg	100.00	45.00	12.50
☐ 173 A. Holesketter	100.00	45.00	12.50
☐ 174 Ducky Holmes	100.00	45.00	12.50
☐ 175 Del Howard	100.00	45.00	12.50
☐ 176 Harry Howell	100.00	45.00	12.50
☐ 177 J. Huelsman	100.00	45.00	12.50
☐ 178 Miller Huggins	400.00	180.00	50.00
☐ 179 Jim Hughes	100.00	45.00	12.50
☐ 180 Tom Hughes	100.00	45.00	12.50
☐ 181 Rudy Hulswitt	100.00	45.00	12.50
☐ 182 John Hummell	100.00	45.00	12.50
☐ 183 Ham Hyatt	100.00	45.00	12.50
☐ 184 Frank Isbell	100.00	45.00	12.50
☐ 185 Fred Jacklitsch	100.00	45.00	12.50
☐ 186 Joe Jackson	2000.00	900.00	250.00
☐ 187 H. Jacobson	100.00	45.00	12.50
☐ 188 Hugh Jennings MG	400.00	180.00	50.00
☐ 189 Charlie Jones	100.00	45.00	12.50
☐ 190 Davy Jones	100.00	45.00	12.50
☐ 191 Oscar Jones	100.00	45.00	12.50
☐ 192 Tom Jones	100.00	45.00	12.50
☐ 193 Dutch Jordan	100.00	45.00	12.50
☐ 194 Mike Kahoe	100.00	45.00	12.50
☐ 195 Ed Karger	100.00	45.00	12.50
☐ 196 Bob Keefe	100.00	45.00	12.50
☐ 197 Willie Keeler	750.00	350.00	95.00
☐ 198 Bill Keister	100.00	45.00	12.50
☐ 199 Joe Kelley	400.00	180.00	50.00
☐ 200 Brickyard Kennedy	100.00	45.00	12.50
☐ 201 Ed Killian	100.00	45.00	12.50
☐ 202 J. Kissinger	100.00	45.00	12.50
☐ 203 Mal Kittridge	100.00	45.00	12.50
☐ 204 Red Kleinrow	100.00	45.00	12.50
☐ 205 Johnny Kling	200.00	90.00	25.00
☐ 206 Ben Koehler	100.00	45.00	12.50
☐ 207 Ed Konetchy	100.00	45.00	12.50
☐ 208 Harry Krause	100.00	45.00	12.50
☐ 209 Otto Krueger	100.00	45.00	12.50
☐ 210 Candy LaChance	100.00	45.00	12.50
☐ 211 Nap Lajoie	1000.00	450.00	125.00
☐ 212 Joe Lake	100.00	45.00	12.50
☐ 213 Frank Laporte	100.00	45.00	12.50
☐ 214 L. Laroy	100.00	45.00	12.50
☐ 215 Tommy Leach	150.00	70.00	19.00
☐ 216 Watty Lee	100.00	45.00	12.50
☐ 217 Sam Leever	100.00	45.00	12.50
☐ 218 Phil Lewis	100.00	45.00	12.50
☐ 219 Vive Lindaman	100.00	45.00	12.50
☐ 220 Paddy Livingstone	100.00	45.00	12.50
☐ 221 Hans Lobert	150.00	70.00	19.00
☐ 222 Herman Long	100.00	45.00	12.50
☐ 223 Bris Lord	100.00	45.00	12.50
☐ 224 Harry Lord	150.00	70.00	19.00
☐ 225 Harry Lumley	100.00	45.00	12.50
☐ 226 Carl Lundgren	100.00	45.00	12.50
☐ 227 Johnny Lush	100.00	45.00	12.50
☐ 228 Connie Mack MG	750.00	350.00	95.00
☐ 229 Nick Maddox	100.00	45.00	12.50
☐ 230 Sherry Magee	150.00	70.00	19.00
☐ 231 George Magoon	100.00	45.00	12.50
☐ 232 John Malarkey	100.00	45.00	12.50
☐ 233 Billy Maloney	100.00	45.00	12.50
☐ 234 Doc Marshall	100.00	45.00	12.50
☐ 235 Christy Mathewson	1500.00	700.00	190.00
☐ 236 Jimmy McAleer	100.00	45.00	12.50
☐ 237 Sport McAlister	100.00	45.00	12.50
☐ 238 Jack McCarthy	100.00	45.00	12.50
☐ 239 John McCloskey	100.00	45.00	12.50
☐ 240 Amby McConnell	100.00	45.00	12.50
☐ 241 Moose McCormick	100.00	45.00	12.50
☐ 242 Chappie McFarland	100.00	45.00	12.50
☐ 243 Herm McFarland	100.00	45.00	12.50
☐ 244 Dan McGann	100.00	45.00	12.50
☐ 245 Joe McGinnity	400.00	180.00	50.00
☐ 246 John McGraw MG	750.00	350.00	95.00
☐ 247 Harry McIntyre	100.00	45.00	12.50
☐ 248 Matty McIntyre	100.00	45.00	12.50
☐ 249 Larry McLean	100.00	45.00	12.50
☐ 250 Fred Merkle	250.00	110.00	31.00
☐ 251 Sam Mertes	100.00	45.00	12.50
☐ 252 Clyde Milan	100.00	45.00	12.50
☐ 253 Dots Miller	100.00	45.00	12.50
☐ 254 Billy Milligan	100.00	45.00	12.50
☐ 255 Fred Mitchell	100.00	45.00	12.50
☐ 256 Mike Mitchell	100.00	45.00	12.50
☐ 257 Earl Moore	100.00	45.00	12.50
☐ 258 Pat Moran	150.00	70.00	19.00
☐ 259 Lew Moren	100.00	45.00	12.50
☐ 260 Cy Morgan	100.00	45.00	12.50
☐ 261 E. Moriarty	100.00	45.00	12.50
☐ 262 Mike Mowery	100.00	45.00	12.50
☐ 263 George Mullin	100.00	45.00	12.50
☐ 264 Danny Murphy	100.00	45.00	12.50
☐ 265 Red Murray	100.00	45.00	12.50
☐ 266 W. Murray	100.00	45.00	12.50
☐ 267 D. Needham	100.00	45.00	12.50
☐ 268 Doc Newton	100.00	45.00	12.50
☐ 269 Harry Niles	100.00	45.00	12.50
☐ 270 Rabbit Nill	100.00	45.00	12.50
☐ 271 Pete Noonan	100.00	45.00	12.50
☐ 272 Jack O'Brien	100.00	45.00	12.50
☐ 273 Pete O'Brien	100.00	45.00	12.50
☐ 274 Rube Oldring	100.00	45.00	12.50
☐ 275 Charley O'Leary	100.00	45.00	12.50
☐ 276 Jack O'Neil	100.00	45.00	12.50
☐ 277 Mike O'Neil	100.00	45.00	12.50
☐ 278 Al Orth	100.00	45.00	12.50
☐ 279 Orvie Overall	100.00	45.00	12.50
☐ 280 Frank Owens	100.00	45.00	12.50
☐ 281 Freddie Parent	100.00	45.00	12.50
☐ 282 Dode Paskert	100.00	45.00	12.50
☐ 283 Jim Pastorious	100.00	45.00	12.50
☐ 284 Roy Paterson	100.00	45.00	12.50
☐ 285 Fred Payne	100.00	45.00	12.50
☐ 286 Barney Pelty	100.00	45.00	12.50
☐ 287 Big Jeff Pfeiffer	100.00	45.00	12.50
☐ 288 Jack Pfiester	100.00	45.00	12.50
☐ 289 Ed Phelps	100.00	45.00	12.50
☐ 290 Deacon Phillippe	200.00	90.00	25.00
☐ 291 Bill Phillips	100.00	45.00	12.50
☐ 292 Eddie Plank	750.00	350.00	95.00
☐ 293 Ed Poole	100.00	45.00	12.50
☐ 294 Jack Powell	100.00	45.00	12.50
☐ 295 Billy Purtell	100.00	45.00	12.50
☐ 296 Ambrose Puttman	100.00	45.00	12.50
☐ 297 Tommy Raub	100.00	45.00	12.50
☐ 298 Fred Raymer	100.00	45.00	12.50
☐ 299 Bill Reidy	100.00	45.00	12.50
☐ 300 Ed Reulbach	200.00	90.00	25.00
☐ 301 Bob Rhoads	100.00	45.00	12.50
☐ 302 D. Richie	100.00	45.00	12.50
☐ 303 Claude Ritchey	100.00	45.00	12.50
☐ 304 Lew Ritter	100.00	45.00	12.50
☐ 305 C. Robinson	100.00	45.00	12.50
☐ 306 George Rohe	100.00	45.00	12.50
☐ 307 Claude Rossman	100.00	45.00	12.50
☐ 308 Frank Roth	100.00	45.00	12.50
☐ 309 Jack Rowan	100.00	45.00	12.50
☐ 310 Slim Sallee	100.00	45.00	12.50
☐ 311 Germany Schaefer	100.00	45.00	12.50
☐ 312 Admiral Schiel	100.00	45.00	12.50
☐ 313 Boss Schmidt	100.00	45.00	12.50
☐ 314 Frank Schulte	100.00	45.00	12.50
☐ 315 Al Schweitzer	100.00	45.00	12.50
☐ 316 T. Sebring	100.00	45.00	12.50
☐ 317 Kip Selbach	100.00	45.00	12.50
☐ 318 Cy Seymour	100.00	45.00	12.50
☐ 319 Spike Shannon	100.00	45.00	12.50
☐ 320 Danny Shay	100.00	45.00	12.50
☐ 321 Dave Shean	100.00	45.00	12.50
☐ 322 Jimmy Sheckard	100.00	45.00	12.50
☐ 323 Ed Siever	100.00	45.00	12.50
☐ 324 Jimmy Slagle	100.00	45.00	12.50
☐ 325 Jack Slattery	100.00	45.00	12.50
☐ 326 Charlie Smith	100.00	45.00	12.50
☐ 327 E. Smith	100.00	45.00	12.50
☐ 328 Frank Smith	100.00	45.00	12.50
☐ 329 Harry Smith	100.00	45.00	12.50
☐ 330 Homer Smoot	100.00	45.00	12.50
☐ 331 Tully Sparks	100.00	45.00	12.50
☐ 332 Chick Stahl	100.00	45.00	12.50
☐ 333 Jake Stahl	250.00	110.00	31.00
☐ 334 Joe Stanley	100.00	45.00	12.50
☐ 335 Harry Steinfeldt	200.00	90.00	25.00
☐ 336 George Stone	100.00	45.00	12.50
☐ 337 George Stovall	100.00	45.00	12.50
☐ 338 Jesss Stovall	100.00	45.00	12.50
☐ 339 Sammy Strang	100.00	45.00	12.50
☐ 340 Elmer Stricklett	100.00	45.00	12.50
☐ 341 Willie Sudhoff	100.00	45.00	12.50
☐ 342 Joe Sugden	100.00	45.00	12.50
☐ 343 Billy Sullivan	100.00	45.00	12.50
☐ 344 Ed Summers	100.00	45.00	12.50
☐ 345 Bill Sweeney	100.00	45.00	12.50
☐ 346 Lee Tannehill	100.00	45.00	12.50
☐ 347 Jack Taylor	100.00	45.00	12.50
☐ 348 Dummy Taylor	100.00	45.00	12.50
☐ 349 Fred Tenney	100.00	45.00	12.50
☐ 350 Ira Thomas	100.00	45.00	12.50
☐ 351 Jack Thoney	100.00	45.00	12.50
☐ 352 Joe Tinker	400.00	180.00	50.00
☐ 353 Terry Turner	100.00	45.00	12.50
☐ 354 Bob Unglaub	100.00	45.00	12.50
☐ 355 George Van Haltren	100.00	45.00	12.50
☐ 356 Bucky Veil	100.00	45.00	12.50
☐ 357 Rube Waddell	600.00	275.00	75.00
☐ 358 Heinie Wagner	100.00	45.00	12.50
☐ 359 Honus Wagner	1250.00	550.00	160.00
☐ 360 Bobby Wallace	400.00	180.00	50.00
☐ 361 Ed Walsh	600.00	275.00	75.00
☐ 362 Jack Warner	100.00	45.00	12.50
☐ 363 Art Weaver	100.00	45.00	12.50
☐ 364 Jake Weimer	100.00	45.00	12.50
☐ 365 Kirby White	100.00	45.00	12.50
☐ 366 Bob Wicker	100.00	45.00	12.50
☐ 367 F. Wilhelm	100.00	45.00	12.50
☐ 368 Ed Willett	100.00	45.00	12.50
☐ 369 Jimmy Williams	100.00	45.00	12.50
☐ 370 Otto Williams	100.00	45.00	12.50
☐ 371 Hooks Wiltse	100.00	45.00	12.50
☐ 372 George Winter	100.00	45.00	12.50
☐ 373 Bill Wolfe	100.00	45.00	12.50
☐ 374 Harry Wolverton	100.00	45.00	12.50
☐ 375 Joe Yeager	100.00	45.00	12.50
☐ 376 Cy Young	1250.00	550.00	160.00
☐ 377 Irv Young	100.00	45.00	12.50
☐ 378 Chief Zimmer	100.00	45.00	12.50
☐ 379 Henie Zimmerman	100.00	45.00	12.50

1909-13 Sporting News Supplements M101-2

These 100 8" x 10" sepia supplements were inserted in various issues of the Sporting News. We have identified the player and then given the date of the issue in which this supplement appears. The set is sequenced in order of appearence. No photos were issued between 4/14 and 8/25 in 1910. No photos were issued between 3/30 and 10/19 in 1911. No photos were issued between 1/18 and 10/03 in 1912.

	EX-MT	VG-E	GOOD
COMPLETE SET (101)	7500.00	3400.00	950.00
COMMON CARD (1-101)	40.00	18.00	5.00
☐ 1 Roger Bresnahan St. Louis NL 7/22/09	150.00	70.00	19.00
☐ 2 Denton T. Young, Cleveland AL and Louis Criger, St. Louis AL	200.00	90.00	25.00

Card	EX-MT	VG-E	GOOD
7/29/09			
☐ 3 Christopher Mathewson New York-N 8/5/09	400.00	180.00	50.00
☐ 4 Nap Lajoie Cleve 8/10/09	250.00	110.00	31.00
☐ 5 Tyrus R. Cobb Detroit 8/12/09	500.00	220.00	60.00
☐ 6 Napoleon Lajoie Cleveland 8/19/09	250.00	110.00	31.00
☐ 7 Sherwood N. Magee Philadelphia-N 8/26/09	40.00	18.00	5.00
☐ 8 Frank L. Chance Chicago-N 9/02/09	250.00	110.00	31.00
☐ 9 Edward Walsh Chicago-A 9/9/09	125.00	55.00	15.50
☐ 10 Nap Rucker Brooklyn 9/16/09	40.00	18.00	5.00
☐ 11 Honus Wagner Pittsburgh 9/23/09	400.00	180.00	50.00
☐ 12 Hugh Jennings MG Detroit 9/30/09	125.00	55.00	15.50
☐ 13 Fred C. Clarke Pittsburgh 10/07/09	200.00	90.00	25.00
☐ 14 Ban Johnson AL PRES 10/14/09	200.00	90.00	25.00
☐ 15 Charles A. Comiskey OWN Chicago White Sox 10/21/09	150.00	70.00	19.00
☐ 16 Edward Collins Philadelphia-A 10/28/09	150.00	70.00	19.00
☐ 17 James A. McAleer Washington 11/04/09	40.00	18.00	5.00
☐ 18 Pittsburgh Pirates 11/11/09	100.00	45.00	12.50
☐ 19 Detroit Team 11/18/09	100.00	45.00	12.50
☐ 20 George Bell Brooklyn 11/25/09	40.00	18.00	5.00
☐ 21 Tris Speaker Boston-A 12/02/09	300.00	135.00	38.00
☐ 22 Mordecai Brown Chicago-N 12/09/09	200.00	90.00	25.00
☐ 23 Hal Chase New York-A 12/16/09	100.00	45.00	12.50
☐ 24 Thomas W. Leach Pittsburgh 12/23/09	60.00	27.00	7.50
☐ 25 Owen Bush Detroit 12/30/09	40.00	18.00	5.00
☐ 26 John J. Evers Chicago-N 1/6/10	150.00	70.00	19.00
☐ 27 Harry Krause Philadelphia-A 1/13/10	40.00	18.00	5.00
☐ 28 Babe Adams Pittsburgh 1/20/10	40.00	18.00	5.00
☐ 29 Addie Joss Cleveland 1/27/10	250.00	110.00	31.00
☐ 30 Orval Overall Chicago-N 2/3/10	40.00	18.00	5.00
☐ 31 Samuel E. Crawford Detroit 2/10/10	200.00	90.00	25.00
☐ 32 Fred Merkle New York-N 2/17/10	60.00	27.00	7.50
☐ 33 George Mullin Detroit 2/24/10	40.00	18.00	5.00
☐ 34 Edward Konetchy St. Louis-N 3/3/10	40.00	18.00	5.00
☐ 35 George Gibson Pitt. Bugs Raymond NY NL 3/10/10	40.00	18.00	5.00
☐ 36 Ty Cobb Detroit Hans Wagner Pittsburgh 3/17/10	400.00	180.00	50.00
☐ 37 Connie Mack MG Phila.-AL 3/24/10	300.00	135.00	38.00
☐ 38 Bill Evans UMP Silk O'Loughlin UMP Bill Klem UMP Bill Johnston UMP 3/31/10	40.00	18.00	5.00
☐ 39 Edward Plank Philadelphia-AL 4/7/10	150.00	70.00	19.00
☐ 40 Walter Johnson Gabby Street Wash. 9/1/10	300.00	135.00	38.00
☐ 41 John C. Kling Chicago-N 9/8/10	40.00	18.00	5.00
☐ 42 Frank Baker Philadelphia-A 9/15/10	150.00	70.00	19.00
☐ 43 Charles S. Dooin Philadelphia-A 9/22/10	40.00	18.00	5.00
☐ 44 Wm. F. Carrigan Boston-A 9/29/10	40.00	18.00	5.00
☐ 45 John B. McLean Cincinnati 10/06/10	40.00	18.00	5.00
☐ 46 John W. Coombs Philadelphia-A 10/13/10	60.00	27.00	7.50
☐ 47 Jos. B. Tinker Chicago-N 10/20/10	200.00	90.00	25.00
☐ 48 John I. Taylor OWN Boston-A 10/27/10	40.00	18.00	5.00
☐ 49 Russell Ford New York-A 11/03/10	40.00	18.00	5.00
☐ 50 Leonard L. Cole Chicago-N 11/10/10	40.00	18.00	5.00
☐ 51 Harry Lord Chicago-A 11/17/10	40.00	18.00	5.00
☐ 52 Philadelphia-A Team 11/24/10	100.00	45.00	12.50
☐ 53 Chicago-N Team 12/1/10	100.00	45.00	12.50
☐ 54 Charles A. Bender Philadelphia-A 12/08/10	125.00	55.00	15.50
☐ 55 Arthur Hofman Chicago-N 12/15/10	40.00	18.00	5.00
☐ 56 Bobby Wallace St. Louis-A 12/21/10	125.00	55.00	15.50
☐ 57 John J. McGraw MG New York-N 12/28/10	300.00	135.00	38.00
☐ 58 Harry H. Davis 1/5/11 Philadelphia-A	40.00	18.00	5.00
☐ 59 James P. Archer Chicago-N 1/12/11	40.00	18.00	5.00
☐ 60 Ira Thomas Philadelphia-A 1/19/11	40.00	18.00	5.00
☐ 61 Robert Byrnes Pittsbutrgh 1/26/11	40.00	18.00	5.00
☐ 62 Clyde Milan Washington 2/2/11	40.00	18.00	5.00
☐ 63 John T. Meyer New York-N 2/9/11	40.00	18.00	5.00
☐ 64 Robert Bescher Cincinnati 2/16/11	40.00	18.00	5.00
☐ 65 John J. Barry Philadelphia-A 2/23/11	40.00	18.00	5.00
☐ 66 Frank Schulte Chicago-N 3/2/11	40.00	18.00	5.00
☐ 67 C. Harris White Chicago-A 3/9/11	40.00	18.00	5.00
☐ 68 Lawrence Doyle New York-N 3/16/11	40.00	18.00	5.00
☐ 69 Joe Jackson Cleveland 3/23/11	750.00	350.00	95.00
☐ 70 Martin J. O'Toole William Kelly Pittsburgh 10/26/11	40.00	18.00	5.00
☐ 71 Vean Gregg Cleveland 11/2/11	40.00	18.00	5.00
☐ 72 Richard W. Marquard New York-N 11/9/11	150.00	70.00	19.00
☐ 73 John E. McInnis Philadelphia-N 11/16/11	60.00	27.00	7.50
☐ 74 Grover C. Alexander Philadelphia-N 11/23/11	250.00	110.00	31.00
☐ 75 Del Gainor Detroit 11/30/11	40.00	18.00	5.00
☐ 76 Fred Snodgrass New York-N 12/7/11	60.00	27.00	7.50
☐ 77 James J. Callahan Chicago-A 12/14/11	60.00	27.00	7.50
☐ 78 Robert Harmon St. Louis-N 12/21/11	40.00	18.00	5.00
☐ 79 George Stovall Cleveland 12/28/11	40.00	18.00	5.00
☐ 80 Zack D. Wheat Brooklyn 1/4/12	150.00	70.00	19.00
☐ 81 Frank 'Ping' Bodie Chicago-A 1/11/12	40.00	18.00	5.00
☐ 82 Boston-A Team 10/10/1912	100.00	45.00	12.50
☐ 83 New York-NTeam 10/17/1912	100.00	45.00	12.50
☐ 84 Jake Stahl MG Boston-A 10/24/12	60.00	27.00	7.50
☐ 85 Joe Wood Boston-A 10/31/12	60.00	27.00	7.50
☐ 86 Charles Wagner Boston-A 11/07/12	40.00	18.00	5.00
☐ 87 Lew Ritchie Chicago-N 11/14/12	40.00	18.00	5.00
☐ 88 Clark Griffith MG Washington 11/21/12	125.00	55.00	15.50
☐ 89 Arnold Houser St. Louis-N 11/28/12	40.00	18.00	5.00
☐ 90 Charles Herzog New York-N 12/05/12	40.00	18.00	5.00
☐ 91 James Lavender Chicago-N 12/12/12	40.00	18.00	5.00
☐ 92 Jeff Tesreau New York-N 12/19/12	40.00	18.00	5.00
☐ 93 August Herrmann OWN Cinc chairman, National Commission	60.00	27.00	7.50
☐ 94 Jake Daubert Brooklyn 10/23/13	60.00	27.00	7.50
☐ 95 Heinie Zimmerman Chicago-N 10/30/13	40.00	18.00	5.00
☐ 96 Ray Schalk Chicago-A 11/07/13	150.00	70.00	19.00
☐ 97 Hans Lobert Philadelphia-N 11/13/13	40.00	18.00	5.00
☐ 98 Albert W. Demaree New York-N 11/20/13	40.00	18.00	5.00
☐ 99 Arthur Fletcher New York-N 11/27/13	40.00	18.00	5.00
☐ 100 Charles A. Somers OWN Cleveland 12/04/13	40.00	18.00	5.00
☐ 101 Joe Birmingham MG Cleveland 12/11/13	40.00	18.00	5.00

1915 Sporting News M101-5

The cards in this 200-card set measure approximately 1 5/8 by 3". The 1915 M101-5 series of black and white, numbered baseball cards is very similar in style to M101-4. The set was offered as a marketing promotion by C.C. Spink and Son, publishers of The Sporting News ("The Baseball Paper of the World"). Most of the players in this also appear in the M101-4 set. Those cards which are asterisked in the checklist below are those cards which do not appear in the companion M101-4 set issued the next year.

	EX-MT	VG-E	GOOD
COMPLETE SET (200)	25000.00	11200.00	3100.00
COMMON CARD (1-200)	45.00	20.00	5.50

Card	EX-MT	VG-E	GOOD
☐ 1 Babe Adams	50.00	22.00	6.25
☐ 2 Sam Agnew	45.00	20.00	5.50
☐ 3 Ed Ainsmith	45.00	20.00	5.50
☐ 4 Grover Cleveland Alexander	250.00	110.00	31.00
☐ 5 Leon Ames	45.00	20.00	5.50
☐ 6 Jimmy Archer	45.00	20.00	5.50
☐ 7 Jimmy Austin	45.00	20.00	5.50
☐ 8 Frank Baker	100.00	45.00	12.50
☐ 9 Dave Bancroft	90.00	40.00	11.00
☐ 10 Jack Barry	50.00	22.00	6.25
☐ 11 Zinn Beck	45.00	20.00	5.50
☐ 12 Luke Boone *	50.00	22.00	6.25
☐ 13 Joe Benz	45.00	20.00	5.50
☐ 14 Bob Bescher	45.00	20.00	5.50
☐ 15 Al Betzel	45.00	20.00	5.50
☐ 16 Roger Bresnahan *	100.00	45.00	12.50
☐ 17 Eddie Burns	45.00	20.00	5.50
☐ 18 George J. Burns	45.00	20.00	5.50
☐ 19 Joe Bush	50.00	22.00	6.25
☐ 20 Owen Bush *	50.00	22.00	6.25
☐ 21 Art Butler	45.00	20.00	5.50
☐ 22 Bobby Byrne	45.00	20.00	5.50
☐ 23 Mordecai Brown	90.00	40.00	11.00
☐ 24 Jimmy Callahan	45.00	20.00	5.50
☐ 25 Ray Caldwell	45.00	20.00	5.50
☐ 26 Max Carey	90.00	40.00	11.00
☐ 27 George Chalmers	45.00	20.00	5.50
☐ 28 Frank Chance MG *	150.00	70.00	19.00
☐ 29 Ray Chapman	60.00	27.00	7.50
☐ 30 Larry Cheney	45.00	20.00	5.50
☐ 31 Ed Cicotte	125.00	55.00	15.50
☐ 32 Tommy Clarke	45.00	20.00	5.50
☐ 33 Eddie Collins	100.00	45.00	12.50
☐ 34 Shano Collins	45.00	20.00	5.50
☐ 35 Charles Comiskey OWN	100.00	45.00	12.50
☐ 36 Joe Connolly	45.00	20.00	5.50
☐ 37 L.(Doc) Cook *	50.00	22.00	6.25
☐ 38 Jack Coombs *	100.00	45.00	12.50
☐ 39 Dan Costello *	50.00	22.00	6.25
☐ 40 Harry Coveleskie	50.00	22.00	6.25
☐ 41 Gavvy Cravath	50.00	22.00	6.25
☐ 42 Sam Crawford	90.00	40.00	11.00
☐ 43 Jean Dale	45.00	20.00	5.50
☐ 44 Jake Daubert	50.00	22.00	6.25
☐ 45 G.A. Davis Jr. *	50.00	22.00	6.25
☐ 46 Charles Deal	45.00	20.00	5.50
☐ 47 Frank Demaree	45.00	20.00	5.50
☐ 48 Bill Doak	45.00	20.00	5.50
☐ 49 Bill Donovan	45.00	20.00	5.50
☐ 50 Red Dooin	45.00	20.00	5.50
☐ 51 Mike Doolan	45.00	20.00	5.50
☐ 52 Larry Doyle	50.00	22.00	6.25
☐ 53 Jean Dubuc	45.00	20.00	5.50
☐ 54 Oscar Dugey	45.00	20.00	5.50
☐ 55 John Evers	100.00	45.00	12.50
☐ 56 Red Faber	90.00	40.00	11.00
☐ 57 Happy Felsch	125.00	55.00	15.50
☐ 58 Bill Fischer	45.00	20.00	5.50
☐ 59 Ray Fisher	45.00	20.00	5.50
☐ 60 Max Flack	45.00	20.00	5.50
☐ 61 Art Fletcher	45.00	20.00	5.50
☐ 62 Eddie Foster	45.00	20.00	5.50
☐ 63 Jacques Fournier	45.00	20.00	5.50
☐ 64 Del Gainer	45.00	20.00	5.50
☐ 65 Larry Gardner	45.00	20.00	5.50
☐ 66 Joe Gedeon	45.00	20.00	5.50
☐ 67 Gus Getz	45.00	20.00	5.50
☐ 68 George Gibson	45.00	20.00	5.50
☐ 69 Wilbur Good	45.00	20.00	5.50
☐ 70 Hank Gowdy	50.00	22.00	6.25
☐ 71 Jack Graney	45.00	20.00	5.50
☐ 72 Tommy Griffith	45.00	20.00	5.50
☐ 73 Heinie Groh	50.00	22.00	6.25
☐ 74 Earl Hamilton	45.00	20.00	5.50
☐ 75 Bob Harmon	45.00	20.00	5.50
☐ 76 Roy Hartzell	45.00	20.00	5.50
☐ 77 Claude Hendrix	45.00	20.00	5.50
☐ 78 Olaf Henriksen	45.00	20.00	5.50
☐ 79 John Henry	45.00	20.00	5.50
☐ 80 Buck Herzog	45.00	20.00	5.50
☐ 81 Hugh High	45.00	20.00	5.50
☐ 82 Dick Hoblitzell	45.00	20.00	5.50
☐ 83 Harry Hooper	90.00	40.00	11.00
☐ 84 Ivan Howard	45.00	20.00	5.50
☐ 85 Miller Huggins	90.00	40.00	11.00
☐ 86 Joe Jackson	4500.00	2000.00	550.00
☐ 87 William James	45.00	20.00	5.50
☐ 88 Harold Janvrin	45.00	20.00	5.50
☐ 89 Hughie Jennings MG	90.00	40.00	11.00
☐ 90 Walter Johnson	650.00	300.00	80.00
☐ 91 Fielder Jones	45.00	20.00	5.50
☐ 92 Benny Kauff	45.00	20.00	5.50
☐ 93 Bill Killefer	45.00	20.00	5.50
☐ 94 Ed Konetchy	45.00	20.00	5.50
☐ 95 Napoleon Lajoie	300.00	135.00	38.00

	EX-MT	VG-E	GOOD
☐ 96 Jack Lapp	45.00	20.00	5.50
☐ 97 John Lavan	45.00	20.00	5.50
☐ 98 Jimmy Lavender	45.00	20.00	5.50
☐ 99 Nemo Leibold	45.00	20.00	5.50
☐ 100 Hub Leonard	50.00	22.00	6.25
☐ 101 Duffy Lewis	50.00	22.00	6.25
☐ 102 Hans Lobert	45.00	20.00	5.50
☐ 103 Tom Long	45.00	20.00	5.50
☐ 104 Fred Luderus	45.00	20.00	5.50
☐ 105 Connie Mack MG	200.00	90.00	25.00
☐ 106 Lee Magee	45.00	20.00	5.50
☐ 107 Al Mamaux	45.00	20.00	5.50
☐ 108 Leslie Mann	45.00	20.00	5.50
☐ 109 Rabbit Maranville	90.00	40.00	11.00
☐ 110 Rube Marquard	90.00	40.00	11.00
☐ 111 Armando Marsans *	50.00	22.00	6.25
☐ 112 J.E.(Erskine) Mayer	45.00	20.00	5.50
☐ 113 George McBride	45.00	20.00	5.50
☐ 114 John McGraw	150.00	70.00	19.00
☐ 115 Jack McInnis	50.00	22.00	6.25
☐ 116 Fred Merkle	50.00	22.00	6.25
☐ 117 Chief Meyers	45.00	20.00	5.50
☐ 118 Clyde Milan	50.00	22.00	6.25
☐ 119 Otto Miller	45.00	20.00	5.50
☐ 120 Willie Mitchell	45.00	20.00	5.50
☐ 121 Fred Mollwitz	45.00	20.00	5.50
☐ 122 J.H.(Herbie) Moran *	50.00	22.00	6.25
☐ 123 Pat Moran MG	45.00	20.00	5.50
☐ 124 Ray Morgan	45.00	20.00	5.50
☐ 125 George Moriarty	45.00	20.00	5.50
☐ 126 Guy Morton	45.00	20.00	5.50
☐ 127 Eddie Murphy	45.00	20.00	5.50
☐ 128 Jack Murray *	50.00	22.00	6.25
☐ 129 Hy Myers	45.00	20.00	5.50
☐ 130 Bert Niehoff	45.00	20.00	5.50
☐ 131 Les Nunamaker *	50.00	22.00	6.25
☐ 132 Rube Oldring	45.00	20.00	5.50
☐ 133 Oliver O'Mara	45.00	20.00	5.50
☐ 134 Steve O'Neill	50.00	22.00	6.25
☐ 135 Dode Paskert	45.00	20.00	5.50
☐ 136 Roger Peckinpaugh	50.00	22.00	6.25
☐ 137 E.J.(Jeff) Pfeffer *	50.00	22.00	6.25
☐ 138 George Pierce *	50.00	22.00	6.25
☐ 139 Wally Pipp	60.00	27.00	7.50
☐ 140 Del Pratt	45.00	20.00	5.50
☐ 141 Bill Rariden	45.00	20.00	5.50
☐ 142 Eppa Rixey	90.00	40.00	11.00
☐ 143 Davey Robertson	45.00	20.00	5.50
☐ 144 Wilbert Robinson MG	150.00	70.00	19.00
☐ 145 Bob Roth	45.00	20.00	5.50
☐ 146 Eddie Rousch	100.00	45.00	12.50
☐ 147 Clarence Rowland MG	45.00	20.00	5.50
☐ 148 Nap Rucker	50.00	22.00	6.25
☐ 149 Dick Rudolph	45.00	20.00	5.50
☐ 150 Reb Russell	45.00	20.00	5.50
☐ 151 Babe Ruth	6000.00	2700.00	750.00
☐ 152 Vic Saier	45.00	20.00	5.50
☐ 153 Slim Sallee	45.00	20.00	5.50
☐ 154 Germany Schaefer *	50.00	22.00	6.25
☐ 155 Ray Schalk	90.00	40.00	11.00
☐ 156 Wally Schang	50.00	22.00	6.25
☐ 157 Charles Schmidt *	50.00	22.00	6.25
☐ 158 Frank Schulte	45.00	20.00	5.50
☐ 159 Jim Scott	45.00	20.00	5.50
☐ 160 Everett Scott	50.00	22.00	6.25
☐ 161 Tom Seaton	45.00	20.00	5.50
☐ 162 Howard Shanks	45.00	20.00	5.50
☐ 163 Bob Shawkey	50.00	22.00	6.25
☐ 164 Ernie Shore	50.00	22.00	6.25
☐ 165 Bert Shotton	45.00	20.00	5.50
☐ 166 George Sisler	150.00	70.00	19.00
☐ 167 Red Smith	45.00	20.00	5.50
☐ 168 Fred Snodgrass	50.00	22.00	6.25
☐ 169 George Stallings MG	45.00	20.00	5.50
☐ 170 Oscar Stanage	45.00	20.00	5.50
☐ 171 Charles Stengel	650.00	300.00	80.00
☐ 172 Milton Stock	45.00	20.00	5.50
☐ 173 Amos Strunk	45.00	20.00	5.50
☐ 174 Billy Sullivan	50.00	22.00	6.25
☐ 175 Jeff Tesreau	45.00	20.00	5.50
☐ 176 Jim Thorpe *	4000.00	1800.00	500.00
☐ 177 Joe Tinker	100.00	45.00	12.50
☐ 178 Fred Toney	45.00	20.00	5.50
☐ 179 Terry Turner	45.00	20.00	5.50
☐ 180 Jim Vaughn	45.00	20.00	5.50
☐ 181 Bobby Veach	45.00	20.00	5.50
☐ 182 James Viox	45.00	20.00	5.50
☐ 183 Oscar Vitt	45.00	20.00	5.50
☐ 184 Honus Wagner	650.00	300.00	80.00
☐ 185 Clarence Walker	45.00	20.00	5.50
☐ 186 Zack Wheat	90.00	40.00	11.00
☐ 187 Ed Walsh	90.00	40.00	11.00
☐ 188 Buck Weaver	150.00	70.00	19.00
☐ 189 Carl Weilman	45.00	20.00	5.50
☐ 190 George Whitted	45.00	20.00	5.50
☐ 191 Fred Williams	45.00	20.00	5.50
☐ 192 Arthur Wilson	45.00	20.00	5.50
☐ 193 Chief Wilson	45.00	20.00	5.50
☐ 194 Ivy Wingo	45.00	20.00	5.50
☐ 195 Meldon Wolfgang	45.00	20.00	5.50
☐ 196 Joe Wood	90.00	40.00	11.00
☐ 197 Steve Yerkes	45.00	20.00	5.50
☐ 198 Rollie Zeider	45.00	20.00	5.50
☐ 199 Heinie Zimmerman	45.00	20.00	5.50
☐ 200 Dutch Zwilling	45.00	20.00	5.50

1915 Sporting News PC757

These postcards feature color, a rare commodity in early baseball postcards. The inscription "published by the Sporting News" appears on the front of the card along with the player's name and team. The postcards are believed to have been issued as premiums, and the set is believed to be complete at six cards.

	EX-MT	VG-E	GOOD
COMPLETE SET (6)	1500.00	700.00	190.00
COMMON CARD (1-6)	100.00	45.00	12.50
☐ 1 Roger Bresnahan	250.00	110.00	31.00
☐ 2 Ty Cobb	600.00	275.00	75.00
☐ 3 Eddie Collins	250.00	110.00	31.00
☐ 4 Vean Gregg	100.00	45.00	12.50
☐ 5 Walter Johnson Gabby Street	250.00	110.00	31.00
☐ 6 Rube Marquard	200.00	90.00	25.00

1916 Sporting News M101-4

The cards in this 200-card set measure approximately 1 5/8" by 3". Issued in 1916 as a premium offer, the M101-4 set features black and white photos of current ballplayers. Each card is numbered and the reverse carries Sporting News advertising. The fronts are the same as D329, H801-9 and the unclassified Famous and Barr set. Most of the players in this also appear in the M101-5 set. Those cards which are asterisked in the checklist below are those cards which do not appear in the companion M101-5 set issued the year before.

	EX-MT	VG-E	GOOD
COMPLETE SET (200)	20000.00	9000.00	2500.00
COMMON CARD (1-200)	40.00	18.00	5.00
☐ 1 Babe Adams	45.00	20.00	5.50
☐ 2 Sam Agnew	45.00	20.00	5.50
☐ 3 Eddie Ainsmith	40.00	18.00	5.00
☐ 4 Grover Cleveland Alexander	250.00	110.00	31.00
☐ 5 Leon Ames	45.00	20.00	5.50
☐ 6 Jimmy Archer	45.00	20.00	5.50
☐ 7 Jimmy Austin	45.00	20.00	5.50
☐ 8 H.D.(Doug) Baird *	45.00	20.00	5.50
☐ 9 Frank Baker	100.00	45.00	12.50
☐ 10 Dave Bancroft	80.00	36.00	10.00
☐ 11 Jack Barry	45.00	20.00	5.50
☐ 12 Zinn Beck	40.00	18.00	5.00
☐ 13 Chief Bender *	100.00	45.00	12.50
☐ 14 Joe Benz	40.00	18.00	5.00
☐ 15 Bob Bescher	40.00	18.00	5.00
☐ 16 Al Betzel	40.00	18.00	5.00
☐ 17 Mordecai Brown	80.00	36.00	10.00
☐ 18 Eddie Burns	40.00	18.00	5.00
☐ 19 George H. Burns *	45.00	20.00	5.50
☐ 20 George J. Burns	40.00	18.00	5.00
☐ 21 Joe Bush	45.00	20.00	5.50
☐ 22 Donie Bush *	45.00	20.00	5.50
☐ 23 Art Butler	40.00	18.00	5.00
☐ 24 Bobbie Byrne	40.00	18.00	5.00
☐ 25 Forrest Cady *	45.00	20.00	5.50
☐ 26 Jim Callahan	40.00	18.00	5.00
☐ 27 Ray Caldwell	40.00	18.00	5.00
☐ 28 Max Carey	80.00	36.00	10.00
☐ 29 George Chalmers	40.00	18.00	5.00
☐ 30 Ray Chapman	60.00	27.00	7.50
☐ 31 Larry Cheney	40.00	18.00	5.00
☐ 32 Ed Cicotte	125.00	55.00	15.50
☐ 33 Tommy Clarke	40.00	18.00	5.00
☐ 34 Eddie Collins	100.00	45.00	12.50
☐ 35 Shano Collins	40.00	18.00	5.00
☐ 36 Charles Comiskey OWN	100.00	45.00	12.50
☐ 37 Joe Connolly	40.00	18.00	5.00
☐ 38 Ty Cobb *	2000.00	900.00	250.00
☐ 39 Harry Coveleskie	40.00	18.00	5.00
☐ 40 Gavvy Cravath	45.00	20.00	5.50
☐ 41 Sam Crawford	80.00	36.00	10.00
☐ 42 Jean Dale	40.00	18.00	5.00
☐ 43 Jake Daubert	45.00	20.00	5.50
☐ 44 Charles Deal	40.00	18.00	5.00
☐ 45 Frank Demaree	40.00	18.00	5.00
☐ 46 Josh Devore *	45.00	20.00	5.50
☐ 47 William Doak	40.00	18.00	5.00
☐ 48 Bill Donovan	40.00	18.00	5.00
☐ 49 Red Dooin	40.00	18.00	5.00
☐ 50 Mike Doolan	40.00	18.00	5.00
☐ 51 Larry Doyle	45.00	20.00	5.50
☐ 52 Jean Dubuc	40.00	18.00	5.00
☐ 53 Oscar J. Dugey	40.00	18.00	5.00
☐ 54 John Evers	100.00	45.00	12.50
☐ 55 Red Faber	80.00	36.00	10.00
☐ 56 Happy Felsch	125.00	55.00	15.50
☐ 57 Bill Fischer	40.00	18.00	5.00
☐ 58 Ray Fisher	40.00	18.00	5.00
☐ 59 Max Flack	40.00	18.00	5.00
☐ 60 Art Fletcher	40.00	18.00	5.00
☐ 61 Eddie Foster	40.00	18.00	5.00
☐ 62 Jacques Fournier	40.00	18.00	5.00
☐ 63 Del Gainer	40.00	18.00	5.00
☐ 64 Chick Gandil *	150.00	70.00	19.00
☐ 65 Larry Gardner	45.00	20.00	5.50
☐ 66 Joe Gedeon	45.00	20.00	5.50
☐ 67 Gus Getz	45.00	20.00	5.50
☐ 68 George Gibson	45.00	20.00	5.50
☐ 69 Wilbur Good	40.00	18.00	5.00
☐ 70 Hank Gowdy	50.00	22.00	6.25
☐ 71 Jack Graney	45.00	20.00	5.50
☐ 72 Clark Griffith *	100.00	45.00	12.50
☐ 73 Tommy Griffith	40.00	18.00	5.00
☐ 74 Heinie Groh	45.00	20.00	5.50
☐ 75 Earl Hamilton	40.00	18.00	5.00
☐ 76 Bob Harmon	40.00	18.00	5.00
☐ 77 Topsy Hartzell	40.00	18.00	5.00
☐ 78 Claude Hendrix	40.00	18.00	5.00
☐ 79 Olaf Henriksen	40.00	18.00	5.00
☐ 80 John Henry	40.00	18.00	5.00
☐ 81 Buck Herzog	40.00	18.00	5.00
☐ 82 Hugh High	40.00	18.00	5.00
☐ 83 Dick Hoblitzell	40.00	18.00	5.00
☐ 84 Harry Hooper	80.00	36.00	10.00
☐ 85 Ivan Howard	40.00	18.00	5.00
☐ 86 Miller Huggins	80.00	36.00	10.00
☐ 87 Joe Jackson	4500.00	2000.00	550.00
☐ 88 William James	40.00	18.00	5.00
☐ 89 Harold Janvrin	40.00	18.00	5.00
☐ 90 Hughie Jennings MG	80.00	36.00	10.00
☐ 91 Walter Johnson	600.00	275.00	75.00
☐ 92 Fielder Jones	40.00	18.00	5.00
☐ 93 Joe Judge *	45.00	20.00	5.50
☐ 94 Benny Kauff	40.00	18.00	5.00
☐ 95 Bill Killifer	40.00	18.00	5.00
☐ 96 Ed Konetchy	40.00	18.00	5.00
☐ 97 Nap Lajoie	250.00	110.00	31.00
☐ 98 Jack Lapp	40.00	18.00	5.00
☐ 99 John Lavan	40.00	18.00	5.00
☐ 100 Jimmy Lavender	40.00	18.00	5.00
☐ 101 Nemo Leibold	40.00	18.00	5.00
☐ 102 Hub Leonard	45.00	20.00	5.50
☐ 103 Duffy Lewis	45.00	20.00	5.50
☐ 104 Hans Lobert	40.00	18.00	5.00
☐ 105 Tom Long	40.00	18.00	5.00
☐ 106 Fred Luderus	40.00	18.00	5.00
☐ 107 Connie Mack MG	200.00	90.00	25.00
☐ 108 Lee Magee	40.00	18.00	5.00
☐ 109 Sherry Magee *	45.00	20.00	5.50
☐ 110 Al Mamaux	40.00	18.00	5.00
☐ 111 Leslie Mann	40.00	18.00	5.00
☐ 112 Rabbit Maranville	80.00	36.00	10.00
☐ 113 Rube Marquard	80.00	36.00	10.00
☐ 114 J.E.(Erskine) Mayer	40.00	18.00	5.00
☐ 115 George McBride	40.00	18.00	5.00
☐ 116 John McGraw MG	150.00	70.00	19.00
☐ 117 Jack McInnis	45.00	20.00	5.50
☐ 118 Fred Merkle	45.00	20.00	5.50
☐ 119 Chief Meyers	40.00	18.00	5.00
☐ 120 Clyde Milan	40.00	18.00	5.00
☐ 121 John Miller *	45.00	20.00	5.50
☐ 122 Otto Miller	40.00	18.00	5.00
☐ 123 Willie Mitchell	40.00	18.00	5.00
☐ 124 Fred Mollwitz	40.00	18.00	5.00
☐ 125 Pat Moran MG	40.00	18.00	5.00
☐ 126 Ray Morgan	40.00	18.00	5.00
☐ 127 George Moriarty	40.00	18.00	5.00
☐ 128 Guy Morton	40.00	18.00	5.00
☐ 129 Mike Mowrey *	45.00	20.00	5.50
☐ 130 Eddie Murphy	40.00	18.00	5.00
☐ 131 Hy Myers	40.00	18.00	5.00
☐ 132 Bert Niehoff	40.00	18.00	5.00
☐ 133 Rube Oldring	40.00	18.00	5.00
☐ 134 Oliver O'Mara	40.00	18.00	5.00
☐ 135 Steve O'Neill	45.00	20.00	5.50
☐ 136 Dode Paskert	40.00	18.00	5.00
☐ 137 Roger Peckinpaugh	45.00	20.00	5.50
☐ 138 Wally Pipp	60.00	27.00	7.50
☐ 139 Del Pratt	40.00	18.00	5.00
☐ 140 Pat Ragan *	45.00	20.00	5.50
☐ 141 Bill Rariden	40.00	18.00	5.00
☐ 142 Eppa Rixey	80.00	36.00	10.00
☐ 143 Davey Robertson	40.00	18.00	5.00
☐ 144 Wilbert Robinson MG	150.00	70.00	19.00
☐ 145 Bob Roth	40.00	18.00	5.00
☐ 146 Eddie Roush	100.00	45.00	12.50
☐ 147 Clarence Rowland MG	40.00	18.00	5.00
☐ 148 Nap Rucker	50.00	22.00	6.25
☐ 149 Dick Rudolph	45.00	20.00	5.50
☐ 150 Reb Russell	40.00	18.00	5.00
☐ 151 Babe Ruth	6000.00	2700.00	750.00
☐ 152 Vic Saier	40.00	18.00	5.00
☐ 153 Slim Sallee	45.00	20.00	5.50
☐ 154 Ray Schalk	80.00	36.00	10.00
☐ 155 Wally Schang	45.00	20.00	5.50
☐ 156 Frank Schulte	40.00	18.00	5.00
☐ 157 Everett Scott	45.00	20.00	5.50
☐ 158 Jim Scott	40.00	18.00	5.00
☐ 159 Tom Seaton	40.00	18.00	5.00
☐ 160 Howard Shanks	40.00	18.00	5.00
☐ 161 Bob Shawkey	45.00	20.00	5.50
☐ 162 Ernie Shore	45.00	20.00	5.50
☐ 163 Burt Shotton	40.00	18.00	5.00
☐ 164 George Sisler	150.00	70.00	19.00
☐ 165 Red Smith	40.00	18.00	5.00
☐ 166 Fred Snodgrass	45.00	20.00	5.50
☐ 167 George Stallings MG	40.00	18.00	5.00
☐ 168 Oscar Stanage	40.00	18.00	5.00
☐ 169 Casey Stengel	600.00	275.00	75.00
☐ 170 Milton Stock	40.00	18.00	5.00
☐ 171 Amos Strunk	40.00	18.00	5.00
☐ 172 Billy Sullivan	45.00	20.00	5.50
☐ 173 Jeff Tesreau	40.00	18.00	5.00
☐ 174 Joe Tinker	100.00	45.00	12.50
☐ 175 Fred Toney	40.00	18.00	5.00
☐ 176 Terry Turner	40.00	18.00	5.00
☐ 177 George Tyler *	45.00	20.00	5.50
☐ 178 Jim Vaughn	40.00	18.00	5.00
☐ 179 Bobby Veach	40.00	18.00	5.00
☐ 180 James Viox	40.00	18.00	5.00
☐ 181 Oscar Vitt	40.00	18.00	5.00
☐ 182 Honus Wagner	600.00	275.00	75.00
☐ 183 Clarence Walker	40.00	18.00	5.00
☐ 184 Ed Walsh	80.00	36.00	10.00
☐ 185 Bill Wambsganss *	45.00	20.00	5.50
☐ 186 Buck Weaver	150.00	70.00	19.00
☐ 187 Carl Weilman	40.00	18.00	5.00
☐ 188 Zack Wheat	80.00	36.00	10.00
☐ 189 George Whitted	40.00	18.00	5.00
☐ 190 Fred Williams	40.00	18.00	5.00
☐ 191 Arthur Wilson	40.00	18.00	5.00
☐ 192 Chief Wilson	40.00	18.00	5.00
☐ 193 Ivy Wingo	40.00	18.00	5.00
☐ 194 Meldon Wolfgang	40.00	18.00	5.00
☐ 195 Joe Wood	80.00	36.00	10.00
☐ 196 Steve Yerkes	40.00	18.00	5.00
☐ 197 Pep Young * (Detroit Tigers)	45.00	20.00	5.50
☐ 198 Rollie Zeider	45.00	20.00	5.50
☐ 199 Heinie Zimmerman	45.00	20.00	5.50
☐ 200 Dutch Zwilling	45.00	20.00	5.50

1926 Sporting News Supplements M101-7

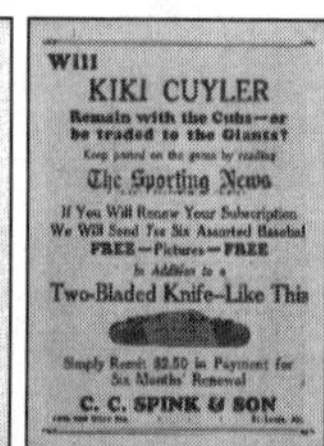

These 11 cards were included as inserts of the "Sporting News" publication. They are known to come in two sizes, 7" by 10" and 10" by 14 1/2". We have basically sequenced this set in alphabetical order.

	EX-MT	VG-E	GOOD
COMPLETE SET (11)	1200.00	550.00	150.00
COMMON CARD (1-11)	75.00	34.00	9.50
☐ 1 Kiki Cuyler	125.00	55.00	15.50
☐ 2 Babe Ruth	400.00	180.00	50.00
☐ 3 Rogers Hornsby	250.00	110.00	31.00
☐ 4 Tony Lazzeri	100.00	45.00	12.50
☐ 5 Heinie Manush	125.00	55.00	15.50
☐ 6 John Mostil	75.00	34.00	9.50
☐ 7 Sam Rice	75.00	34.00	9.50
☐ 8 Al Simmons	150.00	70.00	19.00
☐ 9 Pie Traynor	150.00	70.00	19.00
☐ 10 George Uhle	75.00	34.00	9.50
☐ 11 Glenn Wright	75.00	34.00	9.50

1888-89 Sporting Times M117

These 27 cards which measure 7 1/2" by 4 1/2" were included as premiums in the Sporting Times weekly newspaper. The cards are sequenced in alphabetical order and some of the other photos (most noticably) the Anson were used in other sets.

	EX-MT	VG-E	GOOD
COMPLETE SET (27)	15000.00	6800.00	1900.00
COMMON CARD (1-27)	400.00	180.00	50.00
☐ 1 Cap Anson	1500.00	700.00	190.00
☐ 2 Jersey Bakely	400.00	180.00	50.00
☐ 3 Dan Brouthers	900.00	400.00	110.00
☐ 4 Doc Bushong	400.00	180.00	50.00
☐ 5 Jack Clements	400.00	180.00	50.00
☐ 6 Charles Comiskey	1000.00	450.00	125.00
☐ 7 Hank O'Day	400.00	180.00	50.00
☐ 8 Jerry Denny	400.00	180.00	50.00
☐ 9 Buck Ewing	800.00	350.00	100.00
☐ 10 Dude Esterbrook	400.00	180.00	50.00
☐ 11 Jay Faatz	400.00	180.00	50.00
☐ 12 Pud Galvin	800.00	350.00	100.00
☐ 13 Jack Glasscock	500.00	220.00	60.00
☐ 14 Tim Keefe	800.00	350.00	100.00
☐ 15 King Kelly	800.00	350.00	100.00
☐ 16 Matt Kilroy	400.00	180.00	50.00

☐ 17 Arlie Latham	400.00	180.00	50.00
☐ 18 Doggie Miller	400.00	180.00	50.00
☐ 19 Fred Pfeffer	400.00	180.00	50.00
☐ 20 Henry Porter	400.00	180.00	50.00
☐ 21 Toad Ramsey	400.00	180.00	50.00
☐ 22 John Reilly	400.00	180.00	50.00
☐ 23 Elmer Smith	400.00	180.00	50.00
☐ 24 Harry Stovey	400.00	180.00	50.00
☐ 25 Sam Thompson	800.00	350.00	100.00
☐ 26 John Montgomery Ward	800.00	350.00	100.00
☐ 27 Curt Welch	800.00	350.00	100.00

1981 Sportrait Hall of Fame

This 25-card set measures approximately 3 5/8" by 5" and features a Hall of Fame player's sketch by Stan Sypulski inside a thin color frame on a white background. The player's name and card number are printed at the bottom in the frame color. The backs are blank.

	NRMT	VG-E	GOOD
COMPLETE SET (25)	20.00	9.00	2.50
COMMON CARD (1-25)	.25	.11	.03
☐ 1 Honus Wagner	1.00	.45	.12
☐ 2 Miller Huggins	.50	.23	.06
☐ 3 Babe Ruth	4.00	1.80	.50
☐ 4 Connie Mack	.50	.23	.06
☐ 5 Ty Cobb	3.00	1.35	.35
☐ 6 Lou Gehrig	3.00	1.35	.35
☐ 7 Eddie Collins	.75	.35	.09
☐ 8 Chuck Klein	.50	.23	.06
☐ 9 Ted Williams	3.00	1.35	.35
☐ 10 Jimmy Foxx	1.00	.45	.12
☐ 11 Frank Baker	.50	.23	.06
☐ 12 Nap Lajoie	.75	.35	.09
☐ 13 Casey Stengel	.75	.35	.09
☐ 14 Joe DiMaggio	3.00	1.35	.35
☐ 15 Mickey Mantle	4.00	1.80	.50
☐ 16 Frank Frisch	.50	.23	.06
☐ 17 Bill Terry	.50	.23	.06
☐ 18 Jackie Robinson	2.50	1.10	.30
☐ 19 Sam Rice	.50	.23	.06
☐ 20 Mickey Cochrane	.50	.23	.06
☐ 21 George Sisler	.75	.35	.09
☐ 22 Bob Feller	1.00	.45	.12
☐ 23 Walter Johnson	1.00	.45	.12
☐ 24 Tris Speaker	1.00	.45	.12
☐ NNO Checklist	.25	.11	.03

1984 Sports Design Products West

This 24-card standard-sized set featured the drawings of sports artist Doug West. The set was produced and distributed by Sports Design Products (Charlie Mandel).

	NRMT	VG-E	GOOD
COMPLETE SET (24)	6.00	2.70	.75
COMMON CARD (1-24)	.10	.05	.01
☐ 1 Jackie Robinson	1.00	.45	.12
☐ 2 Luis Aparicio	.25	.11	.03
☐ 3 Roberto Clemente	1.00	.45	.12
☐ 4 Mickey Mantle	1.50	.70	.19
☐ 5 Joe DiMaggio	1.00	.45	.12
☐ 6 Willie Stargell	.25	.11	.03
☐ 7 Brooks Robinson	.35	.16	.04
☐ 8 Ty Cobb	1.00	.45	.12
☐ 9 Don Drysdale	.25	.11	.03
☐ 10 Bob Feller	.35	.16	.04
☐ 11 Stan Musial	.50	.23	.06
☐ 12 Al Kaline	.25	.11	.03
☐ 13 Willie Mays	.75	.35	.09
☐ 14 Willie McCovey	.25	.11	.03
☐ 15 Thurman Munson	.10	.05	.01
☐ 16 Charlie Gehringer	.25	.11	.03
☐ 17 Eddie Mathews	.25	.11	.03
☐ 18 Carl Yastrzemski	.25	.11	.03
☐ 19 Warren Spahn	.25	.11	.03
☐ 20 Ted Williams	1.00	.45	.12
☐ 21 Ernie Banks	.35	.16	.04
☐ 22 Roy Campanella	.35	.16	.04
☐ 23 Harmon Killebrew	.25	.11	.03
☐ 24 Duke Snider	.25	.11	.03

1986 Sports Design J.D. McCarthy

This 24-card standard-size set features the photography of J.D. McCarthy. The fronts have a similar design to the 1969 Topps issue, while the back identifies the player.

	MINT	NRMT	EXC
COMPLETE SET (24)	7.50	3.40	.95
COMMON CARD (1-24)	.10	.05	.01
☐ 1 J.D. McCarthy Ted Williams	.50	.23	.06
☐ 2 Lou Brock	.35	.16	.04
☐ 3 Carl Yastrzemski	.35	.16	.04
☐ 4 Mickey Mantle	2.00	.90	.25
☐ 5 Roger Maris	1.00	.45	.12
☐ 6 Walter Alston	.10	.05	.01
☐ 7 Ernie Banks	.50	.23	.06
☐ 8 Billy Williams	.35	.16	.04
☐ 9 Hank Aaron	1.50	.70	.19
☐ 10 Brooks Robinson	.50	.23	.06
☐ 11 Joe DiMaggio	1.50	.70	.19
☐ 12 Casey Stengel	.35	.16	.04
☐ 13 Juan Marichal	.50	.23	.06
☐ 14 Jim Bunning	.35	.16	.04
☐ 15 Matty Alou	.10	.05	.01
☐ 16 Eddie Mathews	.25	.11	.03
☐ 17 Sandy Koufax	1.00	.45	.12
☐ 18 Roberto Clemente	1.50	.70	.19
☐ 19 Gil Hodges Ernie Banks	.50	.23	.06
☐ 20 Duke Snider	.35	.16	.04
☐ 21 Robin Roberts	.25	.11	.03
☐ 22 Willie Mays	1.50	.70	.19
☐ 23 Willie Stargell	.25	.11	.03
☐ 24 Whitey Ford	.35	.16	.04

1946-49 Sports Exchange W603

These cards measuring approximately 7" by 10" were issued by Sports Exchange between 1946 and 1949. The cards are numbered but we have sequenced them alphabetically within series.

	EX-MT	VG-E	GOOD
COMPLETE SET	2500.00	1100.00	300.00
COMMON CARD	10.00	4.50	1.25
☐ 1-1A Phil Cavaretta	12.50	5.50	1.55
☐ 1-1B Bill Dickey	40.00	18.00	5.00
☐ 1-2 John 'Al' Benton	10.00	4.50	1.25
☐ 1-3 Harry Brecheen	12.50	5.50	1.55
☐ 1-4 Jimmy Foxx	50.00	22.00	6.25
☐ 1-5 Edwin Dyer	10.00	4.50	1.25
☐ 1-6 Ewell Blackwell	12.50	5.50	1.55
☐ 1-7 Floyd Bevens	10.00	4.50	1.25
☐ 1-8 Nick Altrock	10.00	4.50	1.25
☐ 1-9 George Case	10.00	4.50	1.25
☐ 1-10 Lu Blue	10.00	4.50	1.25
☐ 1-11 Ralph Branca- Ken Keltner	12.50	5.50	1.55
☐ 1-12 Gene Bearden	10.00	4.50	1.25
☐ 2-1A Walker Cooper	10.00	4.50	1.25
☐ 2-1B Bob Doerr	15.00	6.75	1.85
☐ 2-2 Lou Boudreau	30.00	13.50	3.70
☐ 2-3 Dom DiMaggio	15.00	6.75	1.85
☐ 2-4 Frank Frisch	30.00	13.50	3.70
☐ 2-5 Charlie Grimm	12.50	5.50	1.55
☐ 2-6 Jimmy Outlaw	10.00	4.50	1.25
☐ 2-7 Hugh Casey	10.00	4.50	1.25
☐ 2-8 Mark Christman	10.00	4.50	1.25
☐ 2-9 Jake Early	10.00	4.50	1.25
☐ 2-10 Bruce Edwards	10.00	4.50	1.25
☐ 2-11 Mickey Cochrane- Bob Dillinger	15.00	6.75	1.85
☐ 2-12 Ben Chapman	10.00	4.50	1.25
☐ 3-1A Dave Ferriss	10.00	4.50	1.25
☐ 3-1B Bob Feller	30.00	13.50	3.70
☐ 3-2 Spud Chandler	12.50	5.50	1.55
☐ 3-3 Del Ennis	12.50	5.50	1.55
☐ 3-4 Lou Gehrig	200.00	90.00	25.00
☐ 3-5 William Herman	20.00	9.00	2.50
☐ 3-6 Andy Pafko	10.00	4.50	1.25
☐ 3-7 Sam Chapman	10.00	4.50	1.25
☐ 3-8 Earle Combs	20.00	9.00	2.50
☐ 3-9 Carl Furillo	15.00	6.75	1.85
☐ 3-10 Elbie Fletcher	10.00	4.50	1.25
☐ 3-11 Dizzy Dean- Edwin Joost	20.00	9.00	2.50
☐ 3-12 Steve Gromek	10.00	4.50	1.25
☐ 4-1A George Kurowski	10.00	4.50	1.25
☐ 4-1B Hank Greenberg	25.00	11.00	3.10
☐ 4-2 Jeff Heath	10.00	4.50	1.25
☐ 4-3 Al Evans	10.00	4.50	1.25
☐ 4-4 Lefty Grove	50.00	22.00	6.25
☐ 4-5 Ted Lyons	20.00	9.00	2.50
☐ 4-6 Harold "Pee Wee" Reese	25.00	11.00	3.10
☐ 4-7 Joe DiMaggio	150.00	70.00	19.00
☐ 4-8 Travis Jackson	10.00	4.50	1.25
☐ 4-9 Augie Galan	10.00	4.50	1.25
☐ 4-10 Joe Gordon	12.50	5.50	1.55
☐ 4-11 Joe Jackson- Wally Westlake	125.00	55.00	15.50
☐ 4-12 Jim Hegan	10.00	4.50	1.25
☐ 5-1A Marty Marion	12.50	5.50	1.55
☐ 5-1B George McQuinn	10.00	4.50	1.25
☐ 5-2 Kirby Higbe	10.00	4.50	1.25
☐ 5-3 John Lindell	10.00	4.50	1.25
☐ 5-4 Bill Hallahan	10.00	4.50	1.25
☐ 5-5 Frank "Lefty" O'Doul	12.50	5.50	1.55
☐ 5-6 Phil Rizzuto	40.00	18.00	5.00
☐ 5-7 Tom Henrich	12.50	5.50	1.55
☐ 5-8 Bob Muncrief	10.00	4.50	1.25
☐ 5-9 Berthold Haas	10.00	4.50	1.25
☐ 5-10 Tommy Holmes	12.50	5.50	1.55
☐ 5-11 Larry Jansen- Yogi Berra	20.00	9.00	2.50
☐ 5-12 Bob Lemon	20.00	9.00	2.50
☐ 6-1A Truett'Rip' Sewell	10.00	4.50	1.25
☐ 6-1B Ray Mueller	10.00	4.50	1.25
☐ 6-2 Tex Hughson	10.00	4.50	1.25
☐ 6-3 John Mize	20.00	9.00	2.50
☐ 6-4 Rogers Hornsby	50.00	22.00	6.25
☐ 6-5 Steve O'Neil	10.00	4.50	1.25
☐ 6-6 Buddy Rosar	10.00	4.50	1.25
☐ 6-7 Ralph Kiner	20.00	9.00	2.50
☐ 6-9 John Hopp	10.00	4.50	1.25
☐ 6-10 Bill Johnson	10.00	4.50	1.25
☐ 6-11 Harry Lowrey- Heinie Manush	12.50	5.50	1.55
☐ 6-12 Billy Meyer	10.00	4.50	1.25
☐ 7-1A Ed Stanky	12.50	5.50	1.55
☐ 7-1B Hal Newhouser	15.00	6.75	1.85
☐ 7-2 Stan Musial	75.00	34.00	9.50
☐ 7-3 Johnny Pesky	12.50	5.50	1.55
☐ 7-4 Carl Hubbell	25.00	11.00	3.10
☐ 7-5 Herb Pennock	20.00	9.00	2.50
☐ 7-6 Johnny Sain	12.50	5.50	1.55
☐ 7-7 Harry Lavagetto	12.50	5.50	1.55
☐ 7-8 Joe Page	12.50	5.50	1.55
☐ 7-9 John 'Buddy' Kelly	10.00	4.50	1.25
☐ 7-10 Phil Masi	10.00	4.50	1.25
☐ 7-12 Dale Mitchell	10.00	4.50	1.25
☐ 8-1A Fred'Dixie' Walker	10.00	4.50	1.25
☐ 8-1B Dick Wakefield	10.00	4.50	1.25
☐ 8-2 Howie Pollet	10.00	4.50	1.25
☐ 8-3 Harold Reiser	12.50	5.50	1.55
☐ 8-4 Babe Ruth	250.00	110.00	31.00
☐ 8-5 Luke Sewell	12.50	5.50	1.55
☐ 8-6 Dizzy Trout	10.00	4.50	1.25
☐ 8-7 Vic Lombardi	10.00	4.50	1.25
☐ 8-8 Honus Wagner	75.00	34.00	9.50
☐ 8-9 Ray Lamanno	10.00	4.50	1.25
☐ 8-10 George Munger	10.00	4.50	1.25
☐ 8-12 Red Rolfe	10.00	4.50	1.25
☐ 9-1B Ted Williams	125.00	55.00	15.50
☐ 9-2 Enos Slaughter	20.00	9.00	2.50
☐ 9-3 Aaron Robinson	10.00	4.50	1.25
☐ 9-4 Lewis 'Hack' Wilson	25.00	11.00	3.10
☐ 9-5 William Southworth MG	10.00	4.50	1.25
☐ 9-6 Harry Walker	10.00	4.50	1.25
☐ 9-7 Cecil Travis	10.00	4.50	1.25
☐ 9-8 Mickey Witek	10.00	4.50	1.25
☐ 9-9 Warren Spahn	30.00	13.50	3.70
☐ 9-10 Vern Stephens	10.00	4.50	1.25
☐ 9-12 Sibbi Sisti	10.00	4.50	1.25
☐ 10-3 Bos. Red Sox-1946	12.50	5.50	1.55
☐ 10-12 Zach Taylor MG	10.00	4.50	1.25
☐ 11-3 St.L.Cardinals-1946	12.50	5.50	1.55
☐ 11-12 Earl Torgeson	10.00	4.50	1.25
☐ 12-12 Mickey Vernon	12.50	5.50	1.55

1977 Sports Illustrated Ad Cards*

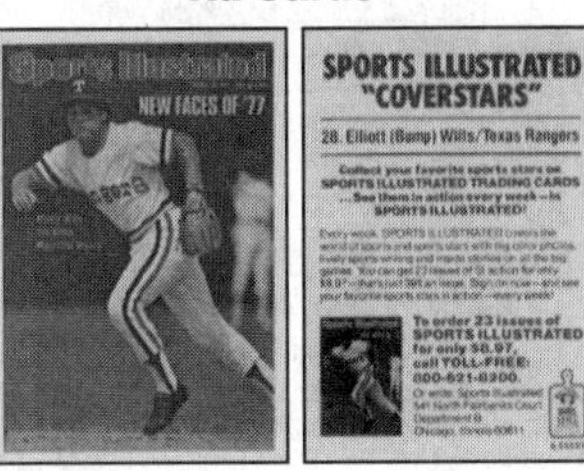

This set is a multi-sport set and features cards with action player photos from various sports as they appeared on different covers of Sports Illustrated Magazine. The cards measure approximately 3 1/2" by 4 3/4" with the backs displaying the player's name and team name and information on how to subscribe to the magazine at a special rate. The checklist is incomplete.

	NRMT	VG-E	GOOD
COMPLETE SET	3.00	1.35	.35
COMMON CARD	3.00	1.35	.35
☐ 1 Elliott(Bump) Wills Texas Rangers	3.00	1.35	.35

1989-91 Sports Illustrated For Kids I

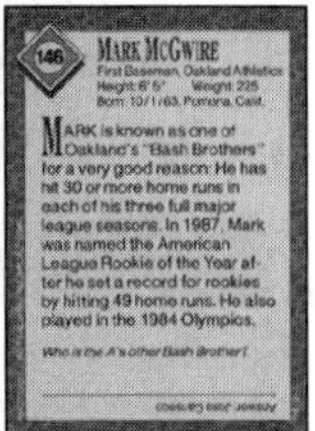

These standard-sized cards were inserted into SI for Kids issues. The first series ran from January 1989 through December 1991. For complete information and a complete checklist please refer to our annual Basketball guide. We have checklisted and priced only the baseball cards here.

	MINT	NRMT	EXC
COMPLETE BB SUBSET (60)	75.00	34.00	9.50
COMMON BB CARD	.25	.11	.03
☐ 5 Orel Hershiser	.50	.23	.06
☐ 11 Jose Canseco	1.25	.55	.16
☐ 20 Darryl Strawberry	.50	.23	.06
☐ 31 Mike Greenwell	.25	.11	.03
☐ 33 Tony Gwynn	4.00	1.80	.50
☐ 35 Frank Viola	.25	.11	.03
☐ 37 Don Mattingly	6.00	2.70	.75
☐ 43 Ozzie Smith	2.50	1.10	.30
☐ 46 Rickey Henderson	.75	.35	.09
☐ 48 Chris Sabo	.25	.11	.03
☐ 52 Andre Dawson	.75	.35	.09
☐ 56 Alan Trammell	.75	.35	.09
☐ 60 Roger Clemens	2.00	.90	.25
☐ 63 Andres Galarraga	.75	.35	.09
☐ 64 John Franco	.25	.11	.03
☐ 69 Cal Ripken	15.00	6.75	1.85
☐ 70 Will Clark	1.25	.55	.16
☐ 75 Bo Jackson	.75	.35	.09
☐ 81 Nolan Ryan	12.00	5.50	1.50
☐ 90 Mike Schmidt	2.50	1.10	.30
☐ 112 Kevin Mitchell	.25	.11	.03
☐ 121 Ryne Sandberg	2.50	1.10	.30
☐ 127 Robin Yount	1.00	.45	.12
☐ 133 Dave Stewart	.25	.11	.03
☐ 140 Eric Davis	.50	.23	.06
☐ 144 Mike Scott	.25	.11	.03
☐ 146 Mark McGwire	2.50	1.10	.30
☐ 151 Dwight Gooden	.50	.23	.06
☐ 158 Ken Griffey Jr.	12.00	5.50	1.50
☐ 162 George Brett	5.00	2.20	.60
☐ 165 Ruben Sierra	.50	.23	.06
☐ 167 Kirby Puckett	4.00	1.80	.50
☐ 171 Carlton Fisk	.75	.35	.09
☐ 172 Fred McGriff	1.25	.55	.16
☐ 176 Wade Boggs	1.25	.55	.16
☐ 178 Tim Raines	.50	.23	.06
☐ 181 Bobby Bonilla	.25	.11	.03
☐ 189 Kelly Gruber	.25	.11	.03
☐ 197 Dennis Eckersley	.75	.35	.09
☐ 205 Cecil Fielder	.75	.35	.09
☐ 212 Jackie Robinson	4.00	1.80	.50
☐ 216 Babe Ruth	4.00	1.80	.50
☐ 229 Barry Bonds	2.50	1.10	.30
☐ 240 Jose Rijo	.25	.11	.03
☐ 248 Sandy Alomar Jr.	.50	.23	.06
☐ 251 Ron Gant	.50	.23	.06
☐ 259 David Justice	1.25	.55	.16
☐ 261 Bob Welch	.25	.11	.03
☐ 266 Doug Drabek	.25	.11	.03
☐ 268 Rafael Palmeiro	.75	.35	.09
☐ 271 Paul Molitor	1.50	.70	.19
☐ 275 Bobby Thigpen	.25	.11	.03
☐ 279 Edgar Martinez	1.25	.55	.16
☐ 282 Dave Winfield	1.25	.55	.16
☐ 283 Mark Grace	.75	.35	.09
☐ 288 Dwight Evans	.25	.11	.03
☐ 289 Dave Henderson	.25	.11	.03
☐ 294 Lee Smith	.50	.23	.06
☐ 303 Ramon Martinez	.50	.23	.06
☐ 321 Ty Cobb	2.00	.90	.25

1992-97 Sports Illustrated For Kids II

These standard-sized cards were inserted into SI for Kids magazines. This is the second series which began in January 1992 and have continued through the present. A complete checklist with

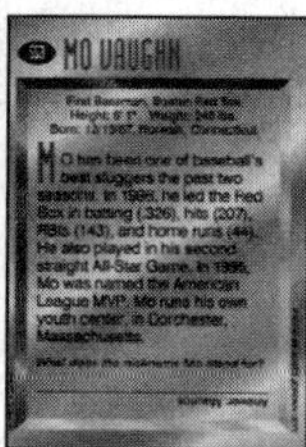

comprehensive pricing is found in our Basketball annual. We have checklisted and priced only baseball cards here.

	MINT	NRMT	EXC
COMPLETE BB SUBSET (84)	100.00	45.00	12.50
COMMON CARD	.25	.11	.03
☐ 24 Terry Pendleton	.25	.11	.03
☐ 29 Kirby Puckett	2.50	1.10	.30
☐ 36 Roger Clemens	1.50	.70	.19
☐ 40 Tom Glavine	1.25	.55	.16
☐ 45 Frank Thomas	8.00	3.60	1.00
☐ 50 Jim Abbott	.25	.11	.03
☐ 54 Roberto Alomar	2.00	.90	.25
☐ 64 Matt Williams	1.00	.45	.12
☐ 68 Bobby Bonilla	.25	.11	.03
☐ 72 Chuck Finley	.25	.11	.03
☐ 75 Danny Tartabull	.25	.11	.03
☐ 81 Jack Morris	.50	.23	.06
☐ 86 Will Clark	.75	.35	.09
☐ 108 Lou Gehrig	3.00	1.35	.35
☐ 121 Juan Gonzalez	3.00	1.35	.35
☐ 132 Cal Ripken	10.00	4.50	1.25
☐ 136 Jack McDowell	.25	.11	.03
☐ 144 Marquis Grissom	.50	.23	.06
☐ 145 Andy Van Slyke	.25	.11	.03
☐ 152 Dennis Eckersley	.50	.23	.06
☐ 157 Barry Bonds	1.50	.70	.19
☐ 162 Greg Maddux	8.00	3.60	1.00
☐ 168 Nolan Ryan	8.00	3.60	1.00
☐ 170 Dave Winfield	.75	.35	.09
☐ 173 Ken Griffey Jr.	8.00	3.60	1.00
☐ 178 Wade Boggs	.75	.35	.09
☐ 185 Kirk Gibson	.50	.23	.06
☐ 187 Albert Belle	3.00	1.35	.35
☐ 190 John Burkett	.25	.11	.03
☐ 196 John Kruk	.25	.11	.03
☐ 199 Randy Johnson	1.50	.70	.19
☐ 204 Lou Whitaker	.50	.23	.06
☐ 212 Yogi Berra	1.00	.45	.12
☐ 236 Lenny Dykstra	.25	.11	.03
☐ 244 Carlos Baerga	.25	.11	.03
☐ 254 Joe Carter	.75	.35	.09
☐ 266 Chuck Carr	.25	.11	.03
☐ 268 Julie Croteau	.25	.11	.03
☐ 270 Michael Jordan	10.00	4.50	1.25
☐ 274 Andres Galarraga	.75	.35	.09
☐ 278 Jeff Bagwell	2.50	1.10	.30
☐ 281 John Olerud	.25	.11	.03
☐ 288 Tony Gwynn	2.50	1.10	.30
☐ 292 Gregg Jefferies	.25	.11	.03
☐ 297 Mo Vaughn	1.50	.70	.19
☐ 298 Moises Alou	.75	.35	.09
☐ 305 Jimmy Key	.50	.23	.06
☐ 311 Mike Mussina	1.25	.55	.16
☐ 313 Mike Piazza	3.00	1.35	.35
☐ 320 Stan Musial	2.00	.90	.25
☐ 327 Matt Williams	.75	.35	.09
☐ 343 Frank Thomas	3.00	1.35	.35
☐ 359 Kenny Lofton	2.50	1.10	.30
☐ 362 Raul Mondesi	1.00	.45	.12
☐ 381 David Cone	.50	.23	.06
☐ 386 Brady Anderson	.75	.35	.09
☐ 390 Eric Karros	.50	.23	.06
☐ 391 Paul O'Neill	.50	.23	.06
☐ 398 Eddie Murray	1.50	.70	.19
☐ 402 Barry Larkin	1.50	.70	.19
☐ 407 Edgar Martinez	.50	.23	.06
☐ 412 Mark McGwire	1.00	.45	.12
☐ 416 Albert Belle	1.25	.55	.16
☐ 430 Mark Grace	.75	.35	.09
☐ 433 Chuck Knoblauch	.75	.35	.09
☐ 447 Chipper Jones	3.00	1.35	.35
☐ 451 Tom Glavine	.50	.23	.06
☐ 455 Cal Ripken	4.00	1.80	.50
☐ 462 Jeff Conine	.75	.35	.09
☐ 470 Hideo Nomo	2.50	1.10	.30
☐ 475 Bernie Williams	1.00	.45	.12
☐ 478 Craig Biggio	.50	.23	.06
☐ 485 Jose Mesa	.25	.11	.03
☐ 497 Roberto Alomar	1.00	.45	.12
☐ 503 John Smoltz	.75	.35	.09
☐ 505 Henry Rodriguez	.25	.11	.03
☐ 513 Rey Ordonez	.25	.11	.03
☐ 516 Ellis Burks	.50	.23	.06
☐ 518 Ivan Rodriguez	1.00	.45	.12
☐ 543 Alex Rodriguez	4.00	1.80	.50
☐ 553 Mo Vaughn	1.00	.45	.12
☐ 561 Andy Pettitte	1.00	.45	.12
☐ 562 Barry Bonds	1.00	.45	.12
☐ 582 Andruw Jones	3.00	1.35	.35

1968 Sports Memorabilia All-Time Greats

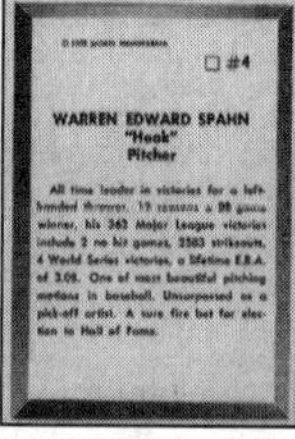

This 15-card standard-size set features some of the leading players of all-time. The fronts have crude drawings of the players, while the backs have a player biography.

	NRMT	VG-E	GOOD
COMPLETE SET (15)	25.00	11.00	3.10
COMMON CARD (1-15)	1.00	.45	.12
☐ 1 Checklist	1.00	.45	.12
☐ 2 Connie Mack	1.50	.70	.19
☐ 3 Walter Johnson	2.00	.90	.25
☐ 4 Warren Spahn	1.50	.70	.19
☐ 5 Christy Mathewson	2.00	.90	.25
☐ 6 Lefty Grove	1.50	.70	.19
☐ 7 Mickey Cochrane	1.00	.45	.12
☐ 8 Bill Dickey	1.00	.45	.12
☐ 9 Tris Speaker	1.50	.70	.19
☐ 10 Ty Cobb	3.00	1.35	.35
☐ 11 Babe Ruth	5.00	2.20	.60
☐ 12 Lou Gehrig	3.00	1.35	.35
☐ 13 Rogers Hornsby	2.00	.90	.25
☐ 14 Honus Wagner	2.00	.90	.25
☐ 15 Pie Traynor	1.00	.45	.12

1987 Sports Reading

These 9" by 14" cards were issued to promote education and sports. They are part of of a reading series for schools. These cards all feature various fun facts about major leaguers. The cards have photos on both sides along with history about a specific event.

	MINT	NRMT	EXC
COMPLETE SET	125.00	55.00	15.50
COMMON CARD (1-40)	.75	.35	.09
☐ 1 Carlos May	.75	.35	.09
☐ 2 Babe Ruth	15.00	6.75	1.85
☐ 3 Eddie Gaedel	2.00	.90	.25
☐ 4 Cesar Gutierrez	.75	.35	.09
☐ 5 Ted Williams	12.50	5.50	1.55
☐ 6 Pete Gray	2.50	1.10	.30
☐ 7 Hank Aaron	10.00	4.50	1.25
☐ 8 Virgil Trucks	.75	.35	.09
☐ 9 Bob Gibson	4.00	1.80	.50
☐ 10 Johnny Vander Meer	.75	.35	.09
☐ 11 Ron Hansen	.75	.35	.09
☐ 12 Roger Clemens	5.00	2.20	.60
☐ 13 Dwight Gooden	1.50	.70	.19
☐ 14 Jimmy Piersall	.75	.35	.09
☐ 15 Dale Long	.75	.35	.09
☐ 16 Herb Score	.75	.35	.09
☐ 17 Dizzy Dean Paul Dean	1.50	.70	.19
☐ 18 Stan Musial	7.50	3.40	.95
☐ 19 Pete Rose	10.00	4.50	1.25
☐ 20 Cy Young	4.00	1.80	.50
☐ 21 Don Mattingly	7.50	3.40	.95
☐ 22 Pete Rose Tom Seaver Nolan Ryan Phil Niekro	10.00	4.50	1.25
☐ 23 Minnie Minoso	1.50	.70	.19
☐ 24 Walter Cooper Mort Cooper	.75	.35	.09
☐ 25 Jim Thorpe	6.00	2.70	.75
☐ 26 Robert Moses Grove	4.00	1.80	.50
☐ 27 Roberto Clemente	12.50	5.50	1.55
☐ 28 Lou Gehrig	12.50	5.50	1.55
☐ 29 Shea Stadium, 1969	.75	.35	.09
☐ 30 Yankee Stadium	.75	.35	.09
☐ 31 Carl Hubbell	3.00	1.35	.35
☐ 32 Wade Boggs	3.00	1.35	.35
☐ 33 Harvey Haddix	.75	.35	.09
☐ 34 Harold Reiser	.75	.35	.09
☐ 35 Jackie Robinson	12.50	5.50	1.55
☐ 36 Walter Johnson	4.00	1.80	.50
☐ 37 The Hall of Fame	.75	.35	.09
☐ 38 Lou Boudreau	1.50	.70	.19
☐ 39 Hank Greenberg	3.00	1.35	.35
☐ 40 Fernando Valenzuela	1.50	.70	.19

1977-79 Sportscaster

This listing just covers the baseball cards covered in this 2,194 card set. The cards have rounded corners and measure 4 11/16" by 6 1/4". The color action photos are full-bleed except at the top, where a color stripe carries the sport, card title and various emblems. In a two-column format, the backs provide copious commentary. All cards are numbered on the back with a distributor's number (e.g. 01 021), followed by the pack number and individual card number (02-08 means the eighth card in the second set). A complete set listing as well as complete pricing can be found in our basketball annual.

	NRMT	VG-E	GOOD
COMPLETE BB SUBSET (142)	600.00	275.00	75.00
COMMON CARD	1.00	.45	.12
☐ 121 Tom Seaver Baseball	4.00	1.80	.50
☐ 208 Joe DiMaggio Baseball	10.00	4.50	1.25
☐ 216 1969 Mets Mets Win Nolan Ryan Baseball	8.00	3.60	1.00
☐ 316 Henry Aaron Baseball	5.00	2.20	.60
☐ 422 Johnny Bench Baseball	4.00	1.80	.50
☐ 511 Babe Ruth Baseball	8.00	3.60	1.00
☐ 514 Bobby Thomson Baseball	1.50	.70	.19
☐ 522 The 1927 Yankees Baseball	2.00	.90	.25
☐ 624 Johnny Vander Meer Baseball	1.50	.70	.19
☐ 716 Roger Maris Mickey Mantle Baseball	12.00	5.50	1.50
☐ 804 Pete Rose Baseball	6.00	2.70	.75
☐ 923 Jackie Robinson Baseball	10.00	4.50	1.25
☐ 1007 Rod Carew Baseball	2.50	1.10	.30
☐ 10122 400-Homer Club Duke Snider Baseball	10.00	4.50	1.25
☐ 10201 Mike Flanagan Baseball	8.00	3.60	1.00
☐ 10210 Boston's Fenway Fenway Park Baseball	8.00	3.60	1.00
☐ 10224 Jim Piersall Baseball	10.00	4.50	1.25
☐ 1106 Willie Mays Baseball	6.00	2.70	.75
☐ 1109 The Rules Hank Aaron Baseball	3.00	1.35	.35
☐ 1207 Ernie Banks Baseball	3.00	1.35	.35
☐ 1303 Ted Williams Baseball	10.00	4.50	1.25
☐ 1409 The Oakland A's 1971-75 Four A's Stars Catfish Hunter Rollie Fingers Reggie Jackson Sal Bando Baseball	3.00	1.35	.35
☐ 1410 Jim Hunter Baseball	3.00	1.35	.35
☐ 1411 Maury Wills Baseball	2.00	.90	.25
☐ 1509 A Century and a Half of BB Johnny Bench Baseball	2.50	1.10	.30
☐ 1607 Brooks Robinson Baseball	2.50	1.10	.30
☐ 1704 Randy Jones Baseball	1.00	.45	.12
☐ 1805 Joe Morgan Baseball	2.50	1.10	.30
☐ 1811 Mark Fidrych Baseball	2.50	1.10	.30
☐ 1816 Lingo II Earl Weaver Baseball	1.50	.70	.19
☐ 1920 Gaylord Perry Baseball	1.50	.70	.19
☐ 2005 Thurman Munson Baseball	4.00	1.80	.50
☐ 2104 Lingo I Dodger Pitcher Baseball	1.00	.45	.12
☐ 2105 Joe Rudi Baseball	1.00	.45	.12
☐ 2109 Vada Pinson Baseball	1.50	.70	.19
☐ 2116 Stan Musial Baseball	5.00	2.20	.60
☐ 2304 Nolan Ryan Baseball	25.00	11.00	3.10
☐ 2323 Warren Spahn Baseball	3.00	1.35	.35
☐ 2416 Lou Brock Baseball	2.50	1.10	.30
☐ 2518 Frank Tanana Baseball	1.50	.70	.19
☐ 2615 Jim Palmer Baseball	4.00	1.80	.50
☐ 2702 Steve Carlton Baseball	3.00	1.35	.35
☐ 2721 Dave Kingman Baseball	1.50	.70	.19
☐ 2902 The Perfect Game Sandy Koufax Baseball	4.00	1.80	.50
☐ 2922 At-A-Glance Reference Tom Seaver Ball Sports	2.50	1.10	.30
☐ 3003 Triple Crown Carl Yastrzemski Baseball	3.00	1.35	.35
☐ 3016 Ron Cey Baseball	1.50	.70	.19
☐ 3101 Instruction Rod Carew Baseball	3.00	1.35	.35
☐ 3201 The 3000 Hit Club Roberto Clemente Baseball	20.00	9.00	2.50
☐ 3204 Tommy John Baseball	2.00	.90	.25
☐ 3217 Cy Young Awards Tom Seaver Baseball	3.00	1.35	.35
☐ 3305 Keeping Score Fan Scorekeeping Baseball	1.00	.45	.12
☐ 3402 Four Home Runs in A Game Mike Schmidt Baseball	8.00	3.60	1.00
☐ 3419 All-Star Game Joe Morgan Steve Garvey Baseball	2.50	1.10	.30
☐ 3424 Greg Luzinski Baseball	1.50	.70	.19
☐ 3502 Infield Fly Rule Bobby Grich Baseball	1.50	.70	.19
☐ 3504 John Candelaria Baseball	1.50	.70	.19
☐ 3515 Interference Johnny Bench Baseball	3.00	1.35	.35
☐ 3601 Ron LeFlore Baseball	1.50	.70	.19
☐ 3709 Pickoff Luis Tiant Baseball	1.50	.70	.19
☐ 3722 NCAA Tournament Texas A,M/Texas Baseball	1.00	.45	.12
☐ 3809 George Brett Baseball	20.00	9.00	2.50
☐ 3810 Jim Rice Baseball			
☐ 3902 Rundown Mets vs. Astros Baseball	1.50	.70	.19
☐ 3904 Measurements Memorial Stadium Baseball	1.00	.45	.12
☐ 4001 Garry Templeton Baseball	1.50	.70	.19
☐ 4002 Jeff Burroughs Baseball	1.50	.70	.19
☐ 4103 Relief Pitching Mike Marshall Baseball	1.50	.70	.19
☐ 4107 Triple Play Bill Wambsganss Baseball	1.50	.70	.19
☐ 4208 Dave Parker Dave Kingman Baseball			
☐ 4209 Bert Blyleven Baseball	1.50	.70	.19
☐ 4307 Rick Reuschel Baseball	1.50	.70	.19
☐ 4417 Hidden Ball Trick A's/Red Sox Baseball	1.50	.70	.19
☐ 4517 Hit and Run George Foster Baseball	2.00	.90	.25
☐ 4522 Hitting the Cutoff Man: Red Sox Player	1.50	.70	.19

Baseball			
☐ 4622 Amateur Draft	1.50	.70	.19
Rick Monday			
Baseball			
☐ 4702 Great Moments	2.50	1.10	.30
Ferguson Jenkins			
Baseball			
☐ 4705 Great Moments	3.00	1.35	.35
Bob Gibson			
Baseball			
☐ 5007 Dennis Eckersley	4.00	1.80	.50
Baseball			
☐ 5102 The Double Steal	1.50	.70	.19
Davey Lopes			
Baseball			
☐ 5103 Cy Young	3.00	1.35	.35
Baseball			
☐ 5202 Gene Tenace	1.50	.70	.19
Baseball			
☐ 5209 Great Moments	2.00	.90	.25
Mickey Lolich			
Baseball			
☐ 5307 Andre Thornton	1.50	.70	.19
Baseball			
☐ 5408 Great Moments	2.50	1.10	.30
Carl Yastrzemski			
Baseball			
☐ 5409 Freddie Patek	1.50	.70	.19
Baseball			
☐ 5503 Lyman Bostock	1.50	.70	.19
Baseball			
☐ 5613 Carlton Fisk	12.00	5.50	1.50
Baseball			
☐ 5702 Dave Winfield	15.00	6.75	1.85
Baseball			
☐ 5801 Shea Stadium	2.50	1.10	.30
Baseball			
☐ 5802 Busch Memorial	2.50	1.10	.30
Stadium			
Baseball			
☐ 5805 Fenway Park	5.00	2.20	.60
Baseball			
☐ 5812 Baltimore Memorial	2.50	1.10	.30
Stadium			
Baseball			
☐ 5814 Yankee Stadium	5.00	2.20	.60
Baseball			
☐ 5818 Candlestick Park	4.00	1.80	.50
Baseball			
☐ 5821 Veterans Stadium	2.50	1.10	.30
Baseball			
☐ 5823 Dodger Stadium	2.50	1.10	.30
Baseball			
☐ 5920 Frank Robinson	8.00	3.60	1.00
Baseball			
☐ 6023 Sandy Koufax	10.00	4.50	1.25
Baseball			
☐ 6102 Ron Guidry			
Baseball			
☐ 6116 Roberto Clemente	30.00	13.50	3.70
Baseball			
☐ 6204 Don Larsen's	5.00	2.20	.60
Perfect Game			
Baseball			
☐ 6318 Gil Hodges	8.00	3.60	1.00
Baseball			
☐ 6518 Vida Blue	4.00	1.80	.50
Baseball			
☐ 6615 Designated Hitter	5.00	2.20	.60
Rusty Staub			
Baseball			
☐ 6701 Steve Garvey	5.00	2.20	.60
Baseball			
☐ 6715 The Presidential Ball	5.00	2.20	.60
Pres.William Taft			
Baseball			
☐ 6810 7th Game of the	4.00	1.80	.50
World Series			
Bert Campaneris			
Baseball			
☐ 6818 Babe Ruth Baseball	4.00	1.80	.50
Ed Figueroa			
Baseball			
☐ 6906 Roy Campanella	10.00	4.50	1.25
Baseball			
☐ 6917 Little League To	4.00	1.80	.50
Big Leagues			
Hector Torres			
Baseball			
☐ 7013 Daffy Dean	5.00	2.20	.60
Dizzy Dean			
Baseball			
☐ 7103 J.R. Richard	4.00	1.80	.50
Baseball			
☐ 7213 Hitting Pitchers	8.00	3.60	1.00
Don Drysdale			
Baseball			
☐ 7315 Emmett Ashford	4.00	1.80	.50
Baseball			
☐ 7401 Forever Blowing	5.00	2.20	.60
Bubbles			
Davey Lopes			
Baseball			
☐ 7410 Phil Niekro	8.00	3.60	1.00
Baseball			
☐ 7423 Ken Forsch	4.00	1.80	.50
Bob Forsch			
Baseball			
☐ 7509 Tommy Lasorda	8.00	3.60	1.00
Baseball			
☐ 7515 Hack Wilson	5.00	2.20	.60
Baseball			
☐ 7524 The Firemen	8.00	3.60	1.00
Goose Gossage			
Baseball			
☐ 7611 Iron Mike	2.50	1.10	.30
Pitching Machine			
Baseball			
☐ 7619 Training Camps	2.50	1.10	.30
Spring Training			
Baseball			
☐ 7708 Monty Stratton	5.00	2.20	.60
Baseball			
☐ 7713 Ron Taylor	4.00	1.80	.50
Baseball			
☐ 7816 Willie McCovey	8.00	3.60	1.00
Baseball			
☐ 7911 Craig Swan	4.00	1.80	.50
Baseball			
☐ 8021 Umpires Strike	6.00	2.70	.75
Ump Picket Line			
Ron Luciano and others			
Baseball			
☐ 8124 Wrigley Marathon	20.00	9.00	2.50
Mike Schmidt			
Baseball			
☐ 8219 Bobby Bonds	8.00	3.60	1.00
Baseball			
☐ 8309 Billy Martin	10.00	4.50	1.25
Baseball			
☐ 8321 Brother vs. Brother	8.00	3.60	1.00
Joe Niekro			
Baseball			
☐ 8408 Triple Play	8.00	3.60	1.00
Rick Burleson			
Baseball			
☐ 8415 The Money Game	10.00	4.50	1.25
Dennis Eckersley			
Baseball			
☐ 8418 Clemente Award	8.00	3.60	1.00
Andre Thornton			
Beyond Sports			
☐ 8504 Like Father	8.00	3.60	1.00
Like Son			
Roy Smalley			
Baseball			
☐ 8608 Danny Ainge	60.00	27.00	7.50
Baseball/Basketball			
☐ 8712 Lee Mazzilli	8.00	3.60	1.00
Baseball			
☐ 8718 Steve Dembrowski	5.00	2.20	.60
Baseball			
☐ 8720 Hutch Award	20.00	9.00	2.50
Al Kaline			
Beyond Sports			
☐ 8803 Dave Winfield	20.00	9.00	2.50
Baseball			
☐ 8824 Cape Cod League	6.00	2.70	.75
Jim Beattie			
Baseball			

1976 Sportstix

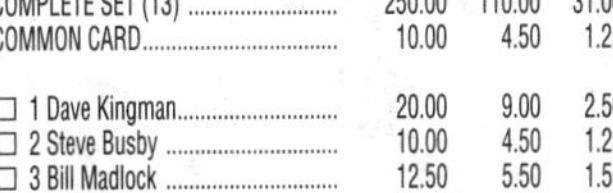

This set features color action photos of some of the favorite sport stars printed on various geometric shaped stickers with peel off backing. These are all that are known to date -- however, other groups may surface -- if so -- any additions to this checklist are appreciated.

	NRMT	VG-E	GOOD
COMPLETE SET (13)	250.00	110.00	31.00
COMMON CARD	10.00	4.50	1.25
☐ 1 Dave Kingman	20.00	9.00	2.50
☐ 2 Steve Busby	10.00	4.50	1.25
☐ 3 Bill Madlock	12.50	5.50	1.55
☐ 4 Jeff Burroughs	10.00	4.50	1.25
☐ 5 Ted Simmons	15.00	6.75	1.85
☐ 6 Randy Jones	10.00	4.50	1.25
☐ 7 Buddy Bell	12.50	5.50	1.55
☐ 8 Dave Cash	10.00	4.50	1.25
☐ 9 Jerry Grote	10.00	4.50	1.25
☐ 10 Dave Lopes	10.00	4.50	1.25
☐ A Willie Mays	30.00	13.50	3.70
☐ C Roberto Clemente	50.00	22.00	6.25
☐ D Mickey Mantle	75.00	34.00	9.50

1982 Spotbilt Brett

This one card standard-size set features Kansas City Royals star George Brett. This card features Brett's picture on the card. The letters GB5 (his uniform number) are on the top with the Spot-Bilt words and logo on the bottom. The horizontal back has vital statistics, career stats as well as some career highlights.

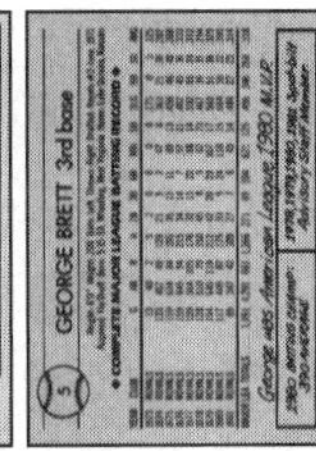

	NRMT	VG-E	GOOD
COMPLETE SET (1)	1.00	.45	.12
COMMON CARD (1)	1.00	.45	.12
☐ 5 George Brett	1.00	.45	.12

1996 SPx

This 1996 SPx set was issued in one series totalling 60 cards. The one-card packs had a suggested retail price of $3.49. Printed on 32 pt. card stock with Holoview technology and a perimeter diecut design, the set features color player photos with a Holography background on the fronts and decorative foil stamping on the back. Two special cards are included in the set: a Ken Griffey Jr. Commemorative card was inserted one in every 75 packs and a Mike Piazza Tribute card inserted one in every 95 packs. An autographed version of each of these cards was inserted at the rate of one in 2,000.

	MINT	NRMT	EXC
COMPLETE SET (60)	100.00	45.00	12.50
COMMON CARD (1-60)	1.00	.45	.12
☐ 1 Greg Maddux	6.00	2.70	.75
☐ 2 Chipper Jones	6.00	2.70	.75
☐ 3 Fred McGriff	1.50	.70	.19
☐ 4 Tom Glavine	1.50	.70	.19
☐ 5 Cal Ripken	8.00	3.60	1.00
☐ 6 Roberto Alomar	2.00	.90	.25
☐ 7 Rafael Palmeiro	1.50	.70	.19
☐ 8 Jose Canseco	1.50	.70	.19
☐ 9 Roger Clemens	2.00	.90	.25
☐ 10 Mo Vaughn	2.50	1.10	.30
☐ 11 Jim Edmonds	1.25	.55	.16
☐ 12 Tim Salmon	1.50	.70	.19
☐ 13 Sammy Sosa	1.50	.70	.19
☐ 14 Ryne Sandberg	2.50	1.10	.30
☐ 15 Mark Grace	1.50	.70	.19
☐ 16 Frank Thomas	10.00	4.50	1.25
☐ 17 Barry Larkin	1.25	.55	.16
☐ 18 Kenny Lofton	2.50	1.10	.30
☐ 19 Albert Belle	4.00	1.80	.50
☐ 20 Eddie Murray	2.50	1.10	.30
☐ 21 Manny Ramirez	2.50	1.10	.30
☐ 22 Dante Bichette	1.50	.70	.19
☐ 23 Larry Walker	1.50	.70	.19
☐ 24 Vinny Castilla	1.25	.55	.16
☐ 25 Andres Galarraga	1.50	.70	.19
☐ 26 Cecil Fielder	1.25	.55	.16
☐ 27 Gary Sheffield	1.50	.70	.19
☐ 28 Craig Biggio	1.25	.55	.16
☐ 29 Jeff Bagwell	4.00	1.80	.50
☐ 30 Derek Bell	1.25	.55	.16
☐ 31 Johnny Damon	1.25	.55	.16
☐ 32 Eric Karros	1.25	.55	.16
☐ 33 Mike Piazza	6.00	2.70	.75
☐ 34 Raul Mondesi	1.50	.70	.19
☐ 35 Hideo Nomo	2.50	1.10	.30
☐ 36 Kirby Puckett	4.00	1.80	.50
☐ 37 Paul Molitor	1.25	.55	.16
☐ 38 Marty Cordova	1.25	.55	.16
☐ 39 Rondell White	1.25	.55	.16
☐ 40 Jason Isringhausen	1.00	.45	.12
☐ 41 Paul Wilson	1.25	.55	.16
☐ 42 Rey Ordonez	1.50	.70	.19
☐ 43 Derek Jeter	6.00	2.70	.75
☐ 44 Wade Boggs	1.50	.70	.19
☐ 45 Mark McGwire	3.00	1.35	.35
☐ 46 Jason Kendall	1.50	.70	.19
☐ 47 Ron Gant	1.25	.55	.16
☐ 48 Ozzie Smith	2.50	1.10	.30
☐ 49 Tony Gwynn	4.00	1.80	.50
☐ 50 Ken Caminiti	1.50	.70	.19
☐ 51 Barry Bonds	2.50	1.10	.30
☐ 52 Matt Williams	1.50	.70	.19
☐ 53 Osvaldo Fernandez	1.25	.55	.16
☐ 54 Jay Buhner	1.50	.70	.19
☐ 55 Ken Griffey Jr.	10.00	4.50	1.25
☐ 56 Randy Johnson	1.50	.70	.19
☐ 57 Alex Rodriguez	10.00	4.50	1.25
☐ 58 Juan Gonzalez	5.00	2.20	.60
☐ 59 Joe Carter	1.25	.55	.16
☐ 60 Carlos Delgado	1.25	.55	.16
☐ KG1 Ken Griffey Jr. Comm.	16.00	7.25	2.00
☐ MP1 Mike Piazza Trib.	12.00	5.50	1.50
☐ KGAU Ken Griffey Jr. Auto.	350.00	160.00	45.00
☐ MPAU Mike Piazza Auto.	225.00	100.00	28.00

1996 SPx Gold

Parallel to the regular version, this 60-card set was randomly inserted in hobby packs only at a rate of one in 7. The design is similar to the regular set with the exception being the gold foil borders on front.

	MINT	NRMT	EXC
COMPLETE SET (60)	300.00	135.00	38.00
COMMON CARD (1-60)	4.00	1.80	.50
*STARS: 1.5X TO 4X BASIC CARDS ..			

1996 SPx Bound for Glory

Randomly inserted in packs at a rate of one in 24, this 10-card set features players with a chance to be long remembered. The fronts display color player photos with a diecut perimeter design and a Holography background. The words, "Bound for Glory" are printed at the top. The backs carry decorative foil stamping.

	MINT	NRMT	EXC
COMPLETE SET (10)	150.00	70.00	19.00
COMMON CARD (1-10)	6.00	2.70	.75
☐ 1 Ken Griffey Jr.	30.00	13.50	3.70
☐ 2 Frank Thomas	30.00	13.50	3.70
☐ 3 Barry Bonds	8.00	3.60	1.00
☐ 4 Cal Ripken	25.00	11.00	3.10
☐ 5 Greg Maddux	20.00	9.00	2.50
☐ 6 Chipper Jones	20.00	9.00	2.50
☐ 7 Roberto Alomar	6.00	2.70	.75
☐ 8 Manny Ramirez	8.00	3.60	1.00
☐ 9 Tony Gwynn	12.00	5.50	1.50
☐ 10 Mike Piazza	20.00	9.00	2.50

1981 Squirt

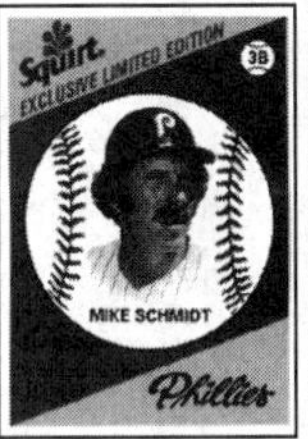

The cards in this 22-panel set consist of 33 different individual cards, each measuring the standard-size. The set was also available as two-card panels measuring approximately 2 1/2" by 10 1/2". Cards numbered 1-11 appear twice, whereas cards 12-33 appear only once in the 22-panel set. The pattern for pairings was 1/12 and 1/23, 2/13 and 2/24, 3/14 and 3/25, and so forth on up to 11/22 and 11/33. Two card panels have a value equal to the sum of the individual cards on the panel. Supposedly panels 4/15, 4/26, 5/27, and 6/28 are more difficult to find than the other panels and are marked as SP in the checklist below.

	NRMT	VG-E	GOOD
COMPLETE PANEL SET	25.00	11.00	3.10
COMPLETE IND. SET	15.00	6.75	1.85
COMMON PANEL	.50	.23	.06
COMMON CARD (1-11) DP	.25	.11	.03
COMMON CARD (12-33)	.25	.11	.03
☐ 1 George Brett DP	3.00	1.35	.35
☐ 2 George Foster DP	.25	.11	.03
☐ 3 Ben Oglivie DP	.25	.11	.03
☐ 4 Steve Garvey DP	.50	.23	.06
☐ 5 Reggie Jackson DP	1.00	.45	.12
☐ 6 Bill Buckner DP	.25	.11	.03
☐ 7 Jim Rice DP	.50	.23	.06
☐ 8 Mike Schmidt DP	2.00	.90	.25
☐ 9 Rod Carew DP	.75	.35	.09
☐ 10 Dave Parker DP	.40	.18	.05
☐ 11 Pete Rose DP	2.00	.90	.25
☐ 12 Garry Templeton	.25	.11	.03
☐ 13 Rick Burleson	.25	.11	.03
☐ 14 Dave Kingman	.25	.11	.03
☐ 15 Eddie Murray SP	8.00	3.60	1.00
☐ 16 Don Sutton	.75	.35	.09
☐ 17 Dusty Baker	.50	.23	.06

☐ 18 Jack Clark	.25	.11	.03
☐ 19 Dave Winfield	1.25	.55	.16
☐ 20 Johnny Bench	1.50	.70	.19
☐ 21 Lee Mazzilli	.25	.11	.03
☐ 22 Al Oliver	.50	.23	.06
☐ 23 Jerry Mumphrey	.25	.11	.03
☐ 24 Tony Armas	.25	.11	.03
☐ 25 Fred Lynn	.50	.23	.06
☐ 26 Ron LeFlore SP	1.00	.45	.12
☐ 27 Steve Kemp SP	1.00	.45	.12
☐ 28 Rickey Henderson SP	8.00	3.60	1.00
☐ 29 John Castino	.25	.11	.03
☐ 30 Cecil Cooper	.25	.11	.03
☐ 31 Bruce Bochte	.25	.11	.03
☐ 32 Joe Charboneau	.25	.11	.03
☐ 33 Chet Lemon	.25	.11	.03

1982 Squirt

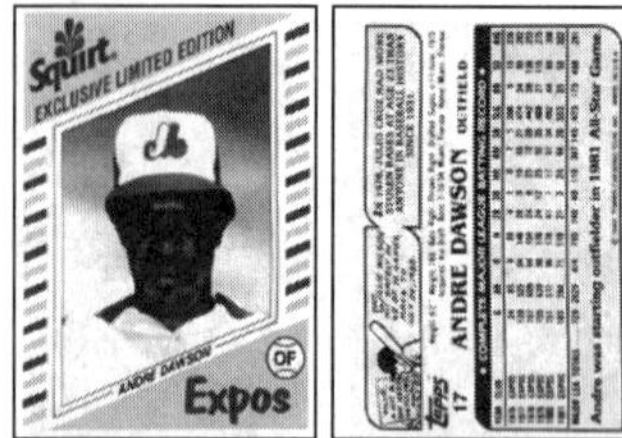

The cards in this 22-card set measure the standard size. Although the 1982 "Exclusive Limited Edition" was prepared for Squirt by Topps, the format and pictures are completely different from the regular Topps cards of this year. Each color picture is obliquely cut and the word Squirt is printed in red in the top left corner. The cards are numbered 1 through 22 and the reverses are yellow and black on white. The cards were issued on four types of panels: (1) yellow attachment card at top with picture card in center and scratch-off game at bottom; (2) yellow attachment card at top with scratch-off game in center and picture card at bottom; (3) white attachment card at top with "Collect all 22" panel in center and picture card at bottom; (4) two card panel with attachment card at top. The two card panels have parallel cards; that is, numbers 1 and 12 together, numbers 2 and 13 together, etc. Two card panels have a value equal to the sum of the individual cards on the panel. The two types (1 and 2) with the scratch-off games are more slightly difficult to obtain than the other two types and hence command prices double those below.

	NRMT	VG-E	GOOD
COMPLETE SET (22)	7.50	3.40	.95
COMMON CARD (1-22)	.25	.11	.03
☐ 1 Cecil Cooper	.50	.23	.06
☐ 2 Jerry Remy	.25	.11	.03
☐ 3 George Brett	3.00	1.35	.35
☐ 4 Alan Trammell	.75	.35	.09
☐ 5 Reggie Jackson	1.25	.55	.16
☐ 6 Kirk Gibson	.75	.35	.09
☐ 7 Dave Winfield	1.00	.45	.12
☐ 8 Carlton Fisk	1.00	.45	.12
☐ 9 Ron Guidry	.50	.23	.06
☐ 10 Dennis Leonard	.25	.11	.03
☐ 11 Rollie Fingers	.50	.23	.06
☐ 12 Pete Rose	2.00	.90	.25
☐ 13 Phil Garner	.25	.11	.03
☐ 14 Mike Schmidt	2.00	.90	.25
☐ 15 Dave Concepcion	.50	.23	.06
☐ 16 George Hendrick	.25	.11	.03
☐ 17 Andre Dawson	.75	.35	.09
☐ 18 George Foster	.50	.23	.06
☐ 19 Gary Carter	.75	.35	.09
☐ 20 Fernando Valenzuela	.50	.23	.06
☐ 21 Tom Seaver	.75	.35	.09
☐ 22 Bruce Sutter	.50	.23	.06

1975 SSPC 18

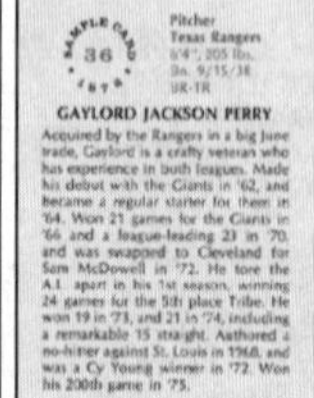

This 18-card promo standard-size set was released the year before the 1976 SSPC 630-card set. Like the 1976 "Pure Card" set, the cards feature white-bordered color player photos on their otherwise plain fronts. The back carries the player's position, team, and biography in red lettering at the upper right. The player's uniform number appears in red within a black-lettered circle formed by the words "Sample Card 1976" at the upper left. Shown below are the player's full name and his career highlights in black lettering. The card number appears on the back at the bottom, as does the copyright date, 1975. These cards were also included as inserts in the Winter 1975 issue of Collectors Quarterly.

	NRMT	VG-E	GOOD
COMPLETE SET (18)	18.00	8.00	2.20
COMMON CARD (1-18)	.75	.35	.09
☐ 1 Harry Parker	.75	.35	.09
☐ 2 Jim Bibby	.75	.35	.09
☐ 3 Mike Wallace	.75	.35	.09
☐ 4 Tony Muser	.75	.35	.09
☐ 5 Yogi Berra MG	6.00	2.70	.75
☐ 6 Preston Gomez MG	.75	.35	.09
☐ 7 Jack McKeon MG	.75	.35	.09
☐ 8 Sam McDowell	1.25	.55	.16
☐ 9 Gaylord Perry	5.00	2.20	.60
☐ 10 Fred Scherman	.75	.35	.09
☐ 11 Willie Davis	.75	.35	.09
☐ 12 Don Hopkins	.75	.35	.09
☐ 13 Whitey Herzog MG	1.25	.55	.16
☐ 14 Ray Sadecki	.75	.35	.09
☐ 15 Stan Bahnsen	.75	.35	.09
☐ 16 Bob Oliver	.75	.35	.09
☐ 17 Denny Doyle	.75	.35	.09
☐ 18 Deron Johnson	.75	.35	.09

1975 SSPC 42

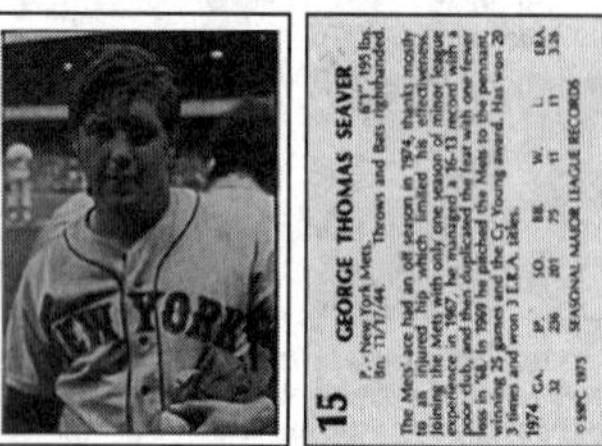

This 42-card standard-size set features posed color player photos with white borders. The horizontal backs are plain white card stock and carry the player's name, biographical information, career highlights, and statistics.

	NRMT	VG-E	GOOD
COMPLETE SET (42)	75.00	34.00	9.50
COMMON CARD (1-42)	.50	.23	.06
☐ 1 Wilbur Wood	.50	.23	.06
☐ 2 Johnny Sain CO	1.00	.45	.12
☐ 3 Bill Melton	.50	.23	.06
☐ 4 Dick Allen	1.50	.70	.19
☐ 5 Jim Palmer	5.00	2.20	.60
☐ 6 Brooks Robinson	6.00	2.70	.75
☐ 7 Tommy Davis	1.00	.45	.12
☐ 8 Frank Robinson MG	5.00	2.20	.60
☐ 9 Vada Pinson	1.00	.45	.12
☐ 10 Nolan Ryan	20.00	9.00	2.50
☐ 11 Reggie Jackson	7.50	3.40	.95
☐ 12 Vida Blue	1.00	.45	.12
☐ 13 Sal Bando	1.00	.45	.12
☐ 14 Bert Campaneris	1.00	.45	.12
☐ 15 Tom Seaver	6.00	2.70	.75
☐ 16 Bud Harrelson	1.00	.45	.12
☐ 17 Jerry Koosman	1.00	.45	.12
☐ 18 David Nelson	.50	.23	.06
☐ 19 Ted Williams	10.00	4.50	1.25
☐ 20 Tony Oliva	1.50	.70	.19
☐ 21 Mickey Lolich	1.00	.45	.12
☐ 22 Amos Otis	.50	.23	.06
☐ 23 Carl Yastrzemski	5.00	2.20	.60
☐ 24 Mike Cuellar	1.00	.45	.12
☐ 25 Doc Medich	.50	.23	.06
☐ 26 Cesar Cedeno	.50	.23	.06
☐ 27 Jeff Burroughs	1.00	.45	.12
☐ 28 Sparky Lyle and Ted Williams	5.00	2.20	.60
☐ 29 Johnny Bench	6.00	2.70	.75
☐ 30 Gaylord Perry	4.00	1.80	.50
☐ 31 John Mayberry	.50	.23	.06
☐ 32 Rod Carew	5.00	2.20	.60
☐ 33 Whitey Ford CO	5.00	2.20	.60
☐ 34 Al Kaline	5.00	2.20	.60
☐ 35 Willie Mays CO	10.00	4.50	1.25
☐ 36 Warren Spahn	5.00	2.20	.60
☐ 37 Mickey Mantle	20.00	9.00	2.50
☐ 38 Norm Cash	1.50	.70	.19
☐ 39 Steve Busby	.50	.23	.06
☐ 40 Yogi Berra MG	5.00	2.20	.60
☐ 41 Harvey Kuenn CO	.50	.23	.06
☐ 42 The Alou Brothers Felipe Alou Matty Alou Jesus Alou	1.00	.45	.12

1975 SSPC Puzzle Back

The 24 cards in this set measure approximately 3 1/2" by 4 1/4" and feature posed color player photos with white borders on the front. The player's name, position, and team are printed at the bottom. The backs are the pieces of a puzzle that shows a 17" by 21" black-and-white photo of Nolan Ryan and Catfish Hunter. When the puzzle is assembled, the player's names appear at the bottom. The name and address of Sports Stars Publishing Company is printed around the left, top, and right edges. The cards are unnumbered and checklisted below in alphabetical order.

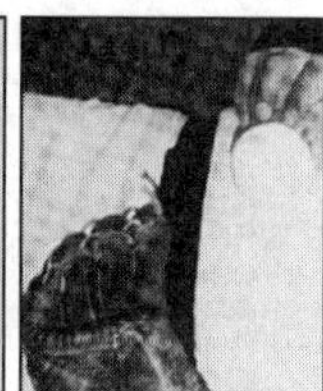

	NRMT	VG-E	GOOD
COMPLETE SET (24)	35.00	16.00	4.40
COMMON CARD (1-24)	.35	.16	.04
☐ 1 Hank Aaron	6.00	2.70	.75
☐ 2 Johnny Bench	3.00	1.35	.35
☐ 3 Bobby Bonds	1.00	.45	.12
☐ 4 Jeff Burroughs	.35	.16	.04
☐ 5 Rod Carew	2.00	.90	.25
☐ 6 Dave Cash	.35	.16	.04
☐ 7 Cesar Cedeno	.35	.16	.04
☐ 8 Bucky Dent	1.00	.45	.12
☐ 9 Rollie Fingers	1.50	.70	.19
☐ 10 Steve Garvey	1.00	.45	.12
☐ 11 John Grubb	.35	.16	.04
☐ 12 Reggie Jackson	5.00	2.20	.60
☐ 13 Jim Kaat	1.00	.45	.12
☐ 14 Greg Luzinski	.50	.23	.06
☐ 15 Fred Lynn	1.00	.45	.12
☐ 16 Bill Madlock	.50	.23	.06
☐ 17 Andy Messersmith	.35	.16	.04
☐ 18 Thurman Munson	2.00	.90	.25
☐ 19 Jim Palmer	2.50	1.10	.30
☐ 20 Dave Parker	1.50	.70	.19
☐ 21 Jim Rice	1.25	.55	.16
☐ 22 Pete Rose	3.00	1.35	.35
☐ 23 Tom Seaver	3.00	1.35	.35
☐ 24 Chris Speier	.35	.16	.04

1975 SSPC Samples

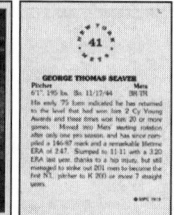

This six-card standard-size set features posed color player photos with white borders. The backs are white card stock and have either a horizontal or vertical format. Each card carries the player's name, biographical information, and career highlights. The horizontal backs also carry statistics. The cards are unnumbered and checklisted below in alphabetical order.

	NRMT	VG-E	GOOD
COMPLETE SET (6)	30.00	13.50	3.70
COMMON CARD (1-6)	1.00	.45	.12
☐ 1 Hank Aaron	7.50	3.40	.95
☐ 2 Catfish Hunter	2.50	1.10	.30
☐ 3 Dave Kingman	1.00	.45	.12
☐ 4 Mickey Mantle	15.00	6.75	1.85
☐ 5 Willie Mays	7.50	3.40	.95
☐ 6 Tom Seaver	5.00	2.20	.60

1976 SSPC

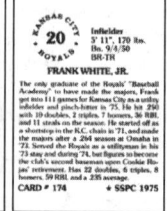

The cards in this 630-card set measure 2 1/2" by 3 1/2". The 1976 "Pure Card" set issued by TCMA derives its name from the lack of borders, logos, signatures, etc., which often clutter up the picture areas of some baseball sets. It differs from other sets produced by this company in that it cannot be re-issued due to an agreement entered into by the manufacturer. Thus, while not technically a legitimate issue, it is significant because it cannot be reprinted, unlike other collector issues. The cards are numbered in team groups, i.e., Atlanta (1-21), Cincinnati (22-46), Houston (47-65), Los Angeles (66-91), San Francisco (92-113), San Diego (114-133), Chicago White Sox (134-158), Kansas City (159-185), California (186-204), Minnesota (205-225), Milwaukee (226-251), Texas (252-273), St. Louis (274-300), Chicago Cubs (301-321), Montreal (322-351), Detroit (352-373), Baltimore (374-401), Boston (402-424), New York Yankees (425-455), Philadelphia (456-477), Oakland (478-503), Cleveland (504-532), New York Mets (533-560), and Pittsburgh (561-586). The rest of the numbers are filled in with checklists (589-595), miscellaneous players, and a heavy dose of coaches. There are a few instances in the set where the team identified on the back is different from the team shown on the front due to trades made after the completion of the 1975 season. The set features rookie year cards of Dennis Eckersley and Willie Randolph as well as early cards of George Brett, Gary Carter, and Robin Yount. The card backs were edited by Keith Olbermann, prior to his ESPN broadcasting days.

	NRMT	VG-E	GOOD
COMPLETE SET (630)	90.00	40.00	11.00
COMMON CARD (1-630)	.10	.05	.01
☐ 1 Buzz Capra	.10	.05	.01
☐ 2 Tom House	.10	.05	.01
☐ 3 Max Leon	.10	.05	.01
☐ 4 Carl Morton	.10	.05	.01
☐ 5 Phil Niekro	4.00	1.80	.50
☐ 6 Mike Thompson	.10	.05	.01
☐ 7 Elias Sosa	.10	.05	.01
☐ 8 Larvell Blanks	.10	.05	.01
☐ 9 Darrell Evans	.30	.14	.04
☐ 10 Rod Gilbreath	.10	.05	.01
☐ 11 Mike Lum	.10	.05	.01
☐ 12 Craig Robinson	.10	.05	.01
☐ 13 Earl Williams	.10	.05	.01
☐ 14 Vic Correll	.10	.05	.01
☐ 15 Biff Pocoroba	.10	.05	.01
☐ 16 Dusty Baker	.50	.23	.06
☐ 17 Ralph Garr	.20	.09	.03
☐ 18 Cito Gaston	.50	.23	.06
☐ 19 Dave May	.10	.05	.01
☐ 20 Rowland Office	.10	.05	.01
☐ 21 Bob Beall	.10	.05	.01
☐ 22 Sparky Anderson MG	1.00	.45	.12
☐ 23 Jack Billingham	.10	.05	.01
☐ 24 Pedro Borbon	.10	.05	.01
☐ 25 Clay Carroll	.10	.05	.01
☐ 26 Pat Darcy	.10	.05	.01
☐ 27 Don Gullett	.20	.09	.03
☐ 28 Clay Kirby	.10	.05	.01
☐ 29 Gary Nolan	.20	.09	.03
☐ 30 Fred Norman	.10	.05	.01
☐ 31 Johnny Bench	6.00	2.70	.75
☐ 32 Bill Plummer	.10	.05	.01
☐ 33 Darrel Chaney	.10	.05	.01
☐ 34 Dave Concepcion	.50	.23	.06
☐ 35 Terry Crowley	.10	.05	.01
☐ 36 Dan Driessen	.20	.09	.03
☐ 37 Doug Flynn	.10	.05	.01
☐ 38 Joe Morgan	4.00	1.80	.50
☐ 39 Tony Perez	2.00	.90	.25
☐ 40 Ken Griffey	1.25	.55	.16
☐ 41 Pete Rose	10.00	4.50	1.25
☐ 42 Ed Armbrister	.10	.05	.01
☐ 43 John Vukovich	.10	.05	.01
☐ 44 George Foster	1.00	.45	.12
☐ 45 Cesar Geronimo	.10	.05	.01
☐ 46 Merv Rettenmund	.10	.05	.01
☐ 47 Jim Crawford	.10	.05	.01
☐ 48 Ken Forsch	.10	.05	.01
☐ 49 Doug Konieczny	.10	.05	.01
☐ 50 Joe Niekro	.30	.14	.04
☐ 51 Cliff Johnson	.10	.05	.01
☐ 52 Skip Jutze	.10	.05	.01
☐ 53 Milt May	.10	.05	.01
☐ 54 Rob Andrews	.10	.05	.01
☐ 55 Ken Boswell	.10	.05	.01
☐ 56 Tommy Helms	.20	.09	.03
☐ 57 Roger Metzger	.10	.05	.01
☐ 58 Larry Milbourne	.10	.05	.01
☐ 59 Doug Rader	.20	.09	.03
☐ 60 Bob Watson	.50	.23	.06
☐ 61 Enos Cabell	.10	.05	.01
☐ 62 Jose Cruz	.30	.14	.04
☐ 63 Cesar Cedeno	.30	.14	.04
☐ 64 Greg Gross	.10	.05	.01
☐ 65 Wilbur Howard	.10	.05	.01
☐ 66 Al Downing	.10	.05	.01
☐ 67 Burt Hooton	.10	.05	.01
☐ 68 Charlie Hough	.50	.23	.06
☐ 69 Tommy John	1.00	.45	.12
☐ 70 Andy Messersmith	.20	.09	.03
☐ 71 Doug Rau	.10	.05	.01
☐ 72 Rick Rhoden	.20	.09	.03
☐ 73 Don Sutton	3.00	1.35	.35
☐ 74 Rick Auerbach	.10	.05	.01
☐ 75 Ron Cey	.50	.23	.06
☐ 76 Ivan DeJesus	.10	.05	.01
☐ 77 Steve Garvey	2.00	.90	.25
☐ 78 Lee Lacy	.10	.05	.01
☐ 79 Dave Lopes	.20	.09	.03
☐ 80 Ken McMullen	.10	.05	.01
☐ 81 Joe Ferguson	.10	.05	.01
☐ 82 Paul Powell	.10	.05	.01
☐ 83 Steve Yeager	.10	.05	.01
☐ 84 Willie Crawford	.10	.05	.01
☐ 85 Henry Cruz	.10	.05	.01
☐ 86 Charlie Manuel	.10	.05	.01
☐ 87 Manny Mota	.20	.09	.03
☐ 88 Tom Paciorek	.30	.14	.04
☐ 89 Jim Wynn	.20	.09	.03
☐ 90 Walt Alston MG	1.00	.45	.12
☐ 91 Bill Buckner	.50	.23	.06
☐ 92 Jim Barr	.10	.05	.01
☐ 93 Mike Caldwell	.10	.05	.01

☐ 94 John D'Acquisto	.10	.05	.01
☐ 95 Dave Heaverlo	.10	.05	.01
☐ 96 Gary Lavelle	.10	.05	.01
☐ 97 John Montefusco	.20	.09	.03
☐ 98 Charlie Williams	.10	.05	.01
☐ 99 Chris Arnold	.10	.05	.01
☐ 100 Marc Hill	.10	.05	.01
☐ 101 Dave Rader	.10	.05	.01
☐ 102 Bruce Miller	.10	.05	.01
☐ 103 Willie Montanez	.10	.05	.01
☐ 104 Steve Ontiveros	.10	.05	.01
☐ 105 Chris Speier	.20	.09	.03
☐ 106 Derrel Thomas	.10	.05	.01
☐ 107 Gary Thomasson	.10	.05	.01
☐ 108 Glenn Adams	.10	.05	.01
☐ 109 Von Joshua	.10	.05	.01
☐ 110 Gary Matthews	.20	.09	.03
☐ 111 Bobby Murcer	.50	.23	.06
☐ 112 Horace Speed	.10	.05	.01
☐ 113 Wes Westrum MG	.10	.05	.01
☐ 114 Rich Folkers	.10	.05	.01
☐ 115 Alan Foster	.10	.05	.01
☐ 116 Dave Freisleben	.10	.05	.01
☐ 117 Dan Frisella	.10	.05	.01
☐ 118 Randy Jones	.20	.09	.03
☐ 119 Dan Spillner	.10	.05	.01
☐ 120 Larry Hardy	.10	.05	.01
☐ 121 Randy Hundley	.20	.09	.03
☐ 122 Fred Kendall	.10	.05	.01
☐ 123 John McNamara MG	.10	.05	.01
☐ 124 Tito Fuentes	.10	.05	.01
☐ 125 Enzo Hernandez	.10	.05	.01
☐ 126 Steve Huntz	.10	.05	.01
☐ 127 Mike Ivie	.10	.05	.01
☐ 128 Hector Torres	.10	.05	.01
☐ 129 Ted Kubiak	.10	.05	.01
☐ 130 John Grubb	.10	.05	.01
☐ 131 John Scott	.10	.05	.01
☐ 132 Bob Tolan	.20	.09	.03
☐ 133 Dave Winfield	18.00	8.00	2.20
☐ 134 Bill Gogolewski	.10	.05	.01
☐ 135 Dan Osborn	.10	.05	.01
☐ 136 Jim Kaat	1.00	.45	.12
☐ 137 Claude Osteen	.20	.09	.03
☐ 138 Cecil Upshaw	.10	.05	.01
☐ 139 Wilbur Wood	.20	.09	.03
☐ 140 Lloyd Allen	.10	.05	.01
☐ 141 Brian Downing	.30	.14	.04
☐ 142 Jim Essian	.10	.05	.01
☐ 143 Bucky Dent	.20	.09	.03
☐ 144 Jorge Orta	.10	.05	.01
☐ 145 Lee Richard	.10	.05	.01
☐ 146 Bill Stein	.10	.05	.01
☐ 147 Ken Henderson	.10	.05	.01
☐ 148 Carlos May	.10	.05	.01
☐ 149 Nyls Nyman	.10	.05	.01
☐ 150 Bob Coluccio	.10	.05	.01
☐ 151 Chuck Tanner MG	.20	.09	.03
☐ 152 Pat Kelly	.10	.05	.01
☐ 153 Jerry Hairston	.10	.05	.01
☐ 154 Pete Varney	.10	.05	.01
☐ 155 Bill Melton	.10	.05	.01
☐ 156 Rich Gossage	1.50	.70	.19
☐ 157 Terry Forster	.20	.09	.03
☐ 158 Rich Hinton	.10	.05	.01
☐ 159 Nelson Briles	.10	.05	.01
☐ 160 Al Fitzmorris	.10	.05	.01
☐ 161 Steve Mingori	.10	.05	.01
☐ 162 Marty Pattin	.10	.05	.01
☐ 163 Paul Splittorff	.10	.05	.01
☐ 164 Dennis Leonard	.20	.09	.03
☐ 165 Buck Martinez	.20	.09	.03
☐ 166 Bob Stinson	.10	.05	.01
☐ 167 George Brett	30.00	13.50	3.70
☐ 168 Harmon Killebrew	4.00	1.80	.50
☐ 169 John Mayberry	.20	.09	.03
☐ 170 Fred Patek	.20	.09	.03
☐ 171 Cookie Rojas	.20	.09	.03
☐ 172 Rodney Scott	.10	.05	.01
☐ 173 Tony Solaita	.10	.05	.01
☐ 174 Frank White	.50	.23	.06
☐ 175 Al Cowens	.10	.05	.01
☐ 176 Hal McRae	.50	.23	.06
☐ 177 Amos Otis	.30	.14	.04
☐ 178 Vada Pinson	.30	.14	.04
☐ 179 Jim Wohlford	.10	.05	.01
☐ 180 Doug Bird	.10	.05	.01
☐ 181 Mark Littell	.10	.05	.01
☐ 182 Bob McClure	.10	.05	.01
☐ 183 Steve Busby	.20	.09	.03
☐ 184 Fran Healy	.10	.05	.01
☐ 185 Whitey Herzog MG	.30	.14	.04
☐ 186 Andy Hassler	.10	.05	.01
☐ 187 Nolan Ryan	30.00	13.50	3.70
☐ 188 Bill Singer	.10	.05	.01
☐ 189 Frank Tanana	.50	.23	.06
☐ 190 Ed Figueroa	.10	.05	.01
☐ 191 Dave Collins	.20	.09	.03
☐ 192 Dick Williams MG	.20	.09	.03
☐ 193 Ellie Rodriguez	.10	.05	.01
☐ 194 Dave Chalk	.10	.05	.01
☐ 195 Winston Llenas	.10	.05	.01
☐ 196 Rudy Meoli	.10	.05	.01
☐ 197 Orlando Ramirez	.10	.05	.01
☐ 198 Jerry Remy	.10	.05	.01

☐ 199 Billy Smith	.10	.05	.01
☐ 200 Bruce Bochte	.10	.05	.01
☐ 201 Joe Lahoud	.10	.05	.01
☐ 202 Morris Nettles	.10	.05	.01
☐ 203 Mickey Rivers	.20	.09	.03
☐ 204 Leroy Stanton	.10	.05	.01
☐ 205 Vic Albury	.10	.05	.01
☐ 206 Tom Burgmeier	.10	.05	.01
☐ 207 Bill Butler	.10	.05	.01
☐ 208 Bill Campbell	.10	.05	.01
☐ 209 Ray Corbin	.10	.05	.01
☐ 210 Joe Decker	.10	.05	.01
☐ 211 Jim Hughes	.10	.05	.01
☐ 212 Ed Bane UER (Photo actually Mike Pazik)	.10	.05	.01
☐ 213 Glenn Borgmann	.10	.05	.01
☐ 214 Rod Carew	6.00	2.70	.75
☐ 215 Steve Brye	.10	.05	.01
☐ 216 Dan Ford	.10	.05	.01
☐ 217 Tony Oliva	1.00	.45	.12
☐ 218 Dave Goltz	.10	.05	.01
☐ 219 Bert Blyleven	.75	.35	.09
☐ 220 Larry Hisle	.20	.09	.03
☐ 221 Steve Braun	.10	.05	.01
☐ 222 Jerry Terrell	.10	.05	.01
☐ 223 Eric Soderholm	.10	.05	.01
☐ 224 Phil Roof	.10	.05	.01
☐ 225 Danny Thompson	.10	.05	.01
☐ 226 Jim Colborn	.10	.05	.01
☐ 227 Tom Murphy	.10	.05	.01
☐ 228 Ed Rodriguez	.10	.05	.01
☐ 229 Jim Slaton	.10	.05	.01
☐ 230 Ed Sprague	.10	.05	.01
☐ 231 Charlie Moore	.10	.05	.01
☐ 232 Darrell Porter	.20	.09	.03
☐ 233 Kurt Bevacqua	.20	.09	.03
☐ 234 Pedro Garcia	.10	.05	.01
☐ 235 Mike Hegan	.10	.05	.01
☐ 236 Don Money	.20	.09	.03
☐ 237 George Scott	.20	.09	.03
☐ 238 Robin Yount	15.00	6.75	1.85
☐ 239 Hank Aaron	15.00	6.75	1.85
☐ 240 Rob Ellis	.10	.05	.01
☐ 241 Sixto Lezcano	.20	.09	.03
☐ 242 Bob Mitchell	.10	.05	.01
☐ 243 Gorman Thomas	.20	.09	.03
☐ 244 Bill Travers	.10	.05	.01
☐ 245 Pete Broberg	.10	.05	.01
☐ 246 Bill Sharp	.10	.05	.01
☐ 247 Bobby Darwin	.10	.05	.01
☐ 248 Rick Austin UER (Photo actually Larry Anderson)	.10	.05	.01
☐ 249 Larry Anderson UER (Photo actually Rick Austin)	.10	.05	.01
☐ 250 Tom Bianco	.10	.05	.01
☐ 251 Lafayette Currence	.10	.05	.01
☐ 252 Steve Foucault	.10	.05	.01
☐ 253 Bill Hands	.10	.05	.01
☐ 254 Steve Hargan	.10	.05	.01
☐ 255 Fergie Jenkins	4.00	1.80	.50
☐ 256 Bob Sheldon	.10	.05	.01
☐ 257 Jim Umbarger	.10	.05	.01
☐ 258 Clyde Wright	.10	.05	.01
☐ 259 Bill Fahey	.10	.05	.01
☐ 260 Jim Sundberg	.30	.14	.04
☐ 261 Leo Cardenas	.10	.05	.01
☐ 262 Jim Fregosi	.30	.14	.04
☐ 263 Mike Hargrove	.20	.09	.03
☐ 264 Toby Harrah	.20	.09	.03
☐ 265 Roy Howell	.10	.05	.01
☐ 266 Lenny Randle	.10	.05	.01
☐ 267 Roy Smalley	.20	.09	.03
☐ 268 Jim Spencer	.10	.05	.01
☐ 269 Jeff Burroughs	.20	.09	.03
☐ 270 Tom Grieve	.20	.09	.03
☐ 271 Joe Lovitto	.10	.05	.01
☐ 272 Frank Lucchesi MG	.10	.05	.01
☐ 273 Dave Nelson	.10	.05	.01
☐ 274 Ted Simmons	1.00	.45	.12
☐ 275 Lou Brock	5.00	2.20	.60
☐ 276 Ron Fairly	.20	.09	.03
☐ 277 Bake McBride	.10	.05	.01
☐ 278 Reggie Smith	.30	.14	.04
☐ 279 Willie Davis	.20	.09	.03
☐ 280 Ken Reitz	.10	.05	.01
☐ 281 Buddy Bradford	.10	.05	.01
☐ 282 Luis Melendez	.10	.05	.01
☐ 283 Mike Tyson	.10	.05	.01
☐ 284 Ted Sizemore	.10	.05	.01
☐ 285 Mario Guerrero	.10	.05	.01
☐ 286 Larry Lintz	.10	.05	.01
☐ 287 Ken Rudolph	.10	.05	.01
☐ 288 Dick Billings	.10	.05	.01
☐ 289 Jerry Mumphrey	.20	.09	.03
☐ 290 Mike Wallace	.10	.05	.01
☐ 291 Al Hrabosky	.20	.09	.03
☐ 292 Ken Reynolds	.10	.05	.01
☐ 293 Mike Garman	.10	.05	.01
☐ 294 Bob Forsch	.20	.09	.03
☐ 295 John Denny	.20	.09	.03
☐ 296 Harry Rasmussen	.10	.05	.01
☐ 297 Lynn McGlothen	.10	.05	.01

☐ 298 Mike Barlow	.10	.05	.01
☐ 299 Greg Terlecky	.10	.05	.01
☐ 300 Red Schoendienst MG	.75	.35	.09
☐ 301 Rick Reuschel	.30	.14	.04
☐ 302 Steve Stone	.20	.09	.03
☐ 303 Bill Bonham	.10	.05	.01
☐ 304 Oscar Zamora	.10	.05	.01
☐ 305 Ken Frailing	.10	.05	.01
☐ 306 Milt Wilcox	.10	.05	.01
☐ 307 Darold Knowles	.10	.05	.01
☐ 308 Jim Marshall MG	.10	.05	.01
☐ 309 Bill Madlock	.75	.35	.09
☐ 310 Jose Cardenal	.20	.09	.03
☐ 311 Rick Monday	.20	.09	.03
☐ 312 Jerry Morales	.10	.05	.01
☐ 313 Tim Hosley	.10	.05	.01
☐ 314 Gene Hiser	.10	.05	.01
☐ 315 Don Kessinger	.20	.09	.03
☐ 316 Manny Trillo	.20	.09	.03
☐ 317 Pete LaCock	.10	.05	.01
☐ 318 George Mitterwald	.10	.05	.01
☐ 319 Steve Swisher	.10	.05	.01
☐ 320 Rob Sperring	.10	.05	.01
☐ 321 Vic Harris	.10	.05	.01
☐ 322 Ron Dunn	.10	.05	.01
☐ 323 Jose Morales	.10	.05	.01
☐ 324 Pete Mackanin	.10	.05	.01
☐ 325 Jim Cox	.10	.05	.01
☐ 326 Larry Parrish	.20	.09	.03
☐ 327 Mike Jorgensen	.10	.05	.01
☐ 328 Tim Foli	.10	.05	.01
☐ 329 Hal Breeden	.10	.05	.01
☐ 330 Nate Colbert	.20	.09	.03
☐ 331 Pepe Frias	.10	.05	.01
☐ 332 Pat Scanlon	.10	.05	.01
☐ 333 Bob Bailey	.10	.05	.01
☐ 334 Gary Carter	6.00	2.70	.75
☐ 335 Pepe Mangual	.10	.05	.01
☐ 336 Larry Biittner	.10	.05	.01
☐ 337 Jim Lyttle	.10	.05	.01
☐ 338 Gary Roenicke	.30	.14	.04
☐ 339 Tony Scott	.10	.05	.01
☐ 340 Jerry White	.10	.05	.01
☐ 341 Jim Dwyer	.10	.05	.01
☐ 342 Ellis Valentine	.20	.09	.03
☐ 343 Fred Scherman	.10	.05	.01
☐ 344 Dennis Blair	.10	.05	.01
☐ 345 Woodie Fryman	.10	.05	.01
☐ 346 Chuck Taylor	.10	.05	.01
☐ 347 Dan Warthen	.10	.05	.01
☐ 348 Dan Carrithers	.10	.05	.01
☐ 349 Steve Rogers	.20	.09	.03
☐ 350 Dale Murray	.10	.05	.01
☐ 351 Duke Snider CO	3.00	1.35	.35
☐ 352 Ralph Houk MG	.20	.09	.03
☐ 353 John Hiller	.10	.05	.01
☐ 354 Mickey Lolich	.50	.23	.06
☐ 355 Dave Lemancyzk	.10	.05	.01
☐ 356 Lerrin LaGrow	.10	.05	.01
☐ 357 Fred Arroyo	.10	.05	.01
☐ 358 Joe Coleman	.10	.05	.01
☐ 359 Ben Oglivie	.20	.09	.03
☐ 360 Willie Horton	.20	.09	.03
☐ 361 John Knox	.10	.05	.01
☐ 362 Leon Roberts	.10	.05	.01
☐ 363 Ron LeFlore	.20	.09	.03
☐ 364 Gary Sutherland	.10	.05	.01
☐ 365 Dan Meyer	.10	.05	.01
☐ 366 Aurelio Rodriguez	.10	.05	.01
☐ 367 Tom Veryzer	.10	.05	.01
☐ 368 Jack Pierce	.10	.05	.01
☐ 369 Gene Michael	.20	.09	.03
☐ 370 Billy Baldwin	.10	.05	.01
☐ 371 Gates Brown	.10	.05	.01
☐ 372 Mickey Stanley	.20	.09	.03
☐ 373 Terry Humphrey	.10	.05	.01
☐ 374 Doyle Alexander	.20	.09	.03
☐ 375 Mike Cuellar	.30	.14	.04
☐ 376 Wayne Garland	.10	.05	.01
☐ 377 Ross Grimsley	.10	.05	.01
☐ 378 Grant Jackson	.10	.05	.01
☐ 379 Dyar Miller	.10	.05	.01
☐ 380 Jim Palmer	5.00	2.20	.60
☐ 381 Mike Torrez	.20	.09	.03
☐ 382 Mike Willis	.10	.05	.01
☐ 383 Dave Duncan	.20	.09	.03
☐ 384 Ellie Hendricks	.10	.05	.01
☐ 385 Jim Hutto	.10	.05	.01
☐ 386 Bob Bailor	.10	.05	.01
☐ 387 Doug DeCinces	.30	.14	.04
☐ 388 Bob Grich	.30	.14	.04
☐ 389 Lee May	.30	.14	.04
☐ 390 Tony Muser	.10	.05	.01
☐ 391 Tim Nordbrook	.10	.05	.01
☐ 392 Brooks Robinson	5.00	2.20	.60
☐ 393 Royle Stillman	.10	.05	.01
☐ 394 Don Baylor	1.00	.45	.12
☐ 395 Paul Blair	.20	.09	.03
☐ 396 Al Bumbry	.10	.05	.01
☐ 397 Larry Harlow	.10	.05	.01
☐ 398 Tommy Davis	.20	.09	.03
☐ 399 Jim Northrup	.20	.09	.03
☐ 400 Ken Singleton	.20	.09	.03
☐ 401 Tom Shopay	.10	.05	.01
☐ 402 Fred Lynn	1.25	.55	.16

☐ 403 Carlton Fisk	6.00	2.70	.75
☐ 404 Cecil Cooper	.50	.23	.06
☐ 405 Jim Rice	3.00	1.35	.35
☐ 406 Juan Beniquez	.10	.05	.01
☐ 407 Denny Doyle	.10	.05	.01
☐ 408 Dwight Evans	1.25	.55	.16
☐ 409 Carl Yastrzemski	6.00	2.70	.75
☐ 410 Rick Burleson	.10	.05	.01
☐ 411 Bernie Carbo	.10	.05	.01
☐ 412 Doug Griffin	.10	.05	.01
☐ 413 Rico Petrocelli	.20	.09	.03
☐ 414 Bob Montgomery	.10	.05	.01
☐ 415 Tim Blackwell	.10	.05	.01
☐ 416 Rick Miller	.10	.05	.01
☐ 417 Darrell Johnson MG	.10	.05	.01
☐ 418 Jim Burton	.10	.05	.01
☐ 419 Jim Willoughby	.10	.05	.01
☐ 420 Rogelio Moret	.10	.05	.01
☐ 421 Bill Lee	.20	.09	.03
☐ 422 Dick Drago	.10	.05	.01
☐ 423 Diego Segui	.10	.05	.01
☐ 424 Luis Tiant	.50	.23	.06
☐ 425 Jim Hunter	4.00	1.80	.50
☐ 426 Rick Sawyer	.10	.05	.01
☐ 427 Rudy May	.10	.05	.01
☐ 428 Dick Tidrow	.10	.05	.01
☐ 429 Sparky Lyle	.50	.23	.06
☐ 430 Doc Medich	.10	.05	.01
☐ 431 Pat Dobson	.10	.05	.01
☐ 432 Dave Pagan	.10	.05	.01
☐ 433 Thurman Munson	3.00	1.35	.35
☐ 434 Chris Chambliss	.50	.23	.06
☐ 435 Roy White	.20	.09	.03
☐ 436 Walt Williams	.10	.05	.01
☐ 437 Graig Nettles	.75	.35	.09
☐ 438 Rick Dempsey	.20	.09	.03
☐ 439 Bobby Bonds	1.00	.45	.12
☐ 440 Ed Herrmann	.10	.05	.01
☐ 441 Sandy Alomar	.20	.09	.03
☐ 442 Fred Stanley	.10	.05	.01
☐ 443 Terry Whitfield	.10	.05	.01
☐ 444 Rich Bladt	.10	.05	.01
☐ 445 Lou Piniella	.75	.35	.09
☐ 446 Rich Coggins	.10	.05	.01
☐ 447 Ed Brinkman	.10	.05	.01
☐ 448 Jim Mason	.10	.05	.01
☐ 449 Larry Murray	.10	.05	.01
☐ 450 Ron Blomberg	.10	.05	.01
☐ 451 Elliott Maddox	.10	.05	.01
☐ 452 Kerry Dineen	.10	.05	.01
☐ 453 Billy Martin MG	1.25	.55	.16
☐ 454 Dave Bergman	.10	.05	.01
☐ 455 Otto Velez	.10	.05	.01
☐ 456 Joe Hoerner	.10	.05	.01
☐ 457 Tug McGraw	.50	.23	.06
☐ 458 Gene Garber	.20	.09	.03
☐ 459 Steve Carlton	6.00	2.70	.75
☐ 460 Larry Christenson	.10	.05	.01
☐ 461 Tom Underwood	.10	.05	.01
☐ 462 Jim Lonborg	.20	.09	.03
☐ 463 Jay Johnstone	.30	.14	.04
☐ 464 Larry Bowa	.30	.14	.04
☐ 465 Dave Cash	.10	.05	.01
☐ 466 Ollie Brown	.10	.05	.01
☐ 467 Greg Luzinski	.50	.23	.06
☐ 468 Johnny Oates	.50	.23	.06
☐ 469 Mike Anderson	.10	.05	.01
☐ 470 Mike Schmidt	20.00	9.00	2.50
☐ 471 Bob Boone	.75	.35	.09
☐ 472 Tom Hutton	.10	.05	.01
☐ 473 Rich Allen	1.00	.45	.12
☐ 474 Tony Taylor	.20	.09	.03
☐ 475 Jerry Martin	.10	.05	.01
☐ 476 Danny Ozark MG	.10	.05	.01
☐ 477 Dick Ruthven	.10	.05	.01
☐ 478 Jim Todd	.10	.05	.01
☐ 479 Paul Lindblad	.10	.05	.01
☐ 480 Rollie Fingers	4.00	1.80	.50
☐ 481 Vida Blue	.30	.14	.04
☐ 482 Ken Holtzman	.20	.09	.03
☐ 483 Dick Bosman	.10	.05	.01
☐ 484 Sonny Siebert	.10	.05	.01
☐ 485 Glenn Abbott	.10	.05	.01
☐ 486 Stan Bahnsen	.10	.05	.01
☐ 487 Mike Norris	.20	.09	.03
☐ 488 Alvin Dark MG	.20	.09	.03
☐ 489 Claudell Washington	.20	.09	.03
☐ 490 Joe Rudi	.20	.09	.03
☐ 491 Bill North	.10	.05	.01
☐ 492 Bert Campaneris	.20	.09	.03
☐ 493 Gene Tenace	.20	.09	.03
☐ 494 Reggie Jackson	10.00	4.50	1.25
☐ 495 Phil Garner	.20	.09	.03
☐ 496 Billy Williams	4.00	1.80	.50
☐ 497 Sal Bando	.20	.09	.03
☐ 498 Jim Holt	.10	.05	.01
☐ 499 Ted Martinez	.10	.05	.01
☐ 500 Ray Fosse	.10	.05	.01
☐ 501 Matt Alexander	.10	.05	.01
☐ 502 Larry Haney	.10	.05	.01
☐ 503 Angel Mangual	.10	.05	.01
☐ 504 Fred Beene	.10	.05	.01
☐ 505 Tom Buskey	.10	.05	.01
☐ 506 Dennis Eckersley	15.00	6.75	1.85
☐ 507 Roric Harrison	.10	.05	.01

☐ 508 Don Hood	.10	.05	.01
☐ 509 Jim Kern	.10	.05	.01
☐ 510 Dave LaRoche	.10	.05	.01
☐ 511 Fritz Peterson	.10	.05	.01
☐ 512 Jim Strickland	.10	.05	.01
☐ 513 Rick Waits	.10	.05	.01
☐ 514 Alan Ashby	.30	.14	.04
☐ 515 John Ellis	.10	.05	.01
☐ 516 Rick Cerone	.30	.14	.04
☐ 517 Buddy Bell	.30	.14	.04
☐ 518 Jack Brohamer	.10	.05	.01
☐ 519 Rico Carty	.20	.09	.03
☐ 520 Ed Crosby	.10	.05	.01
☐ 521 Frank Duffy	.10	.05	.01
☐ 522 Duane Kuiper UER (Photo actually Rick Manning)	.10	.05	.01
☐ 523 Joe Lis	.10	.05	.01
☐ 524 Boog Powell	1.00	.45	.12
☐ 525 Frank Robinson	5.00	2.20	.60
☐ 526 Oscar Gamble	.20	.09	.03
☐ 527 George Hendrick	.20	.09	.03
☐ 528 John Lowenstein	.10	.05	.01
☐ 529 Rick Manning UER (Photo actually Duane Kuiper)	.20	.09	.03
☐ 530 Tommy Smith	.10	.05	.01
☐ 531 Charlie Spikes	.10	.05	.01
☐ 532 Steve Kline	.10	.05	.01
☐ 533 Ed Kranepool	.20	.09	.03
☐ 534 Mike Vail	.10	.05	.01
☐ 535 Del Unser	.10	.05	.01
☐ 536 Felix Millan	.10	.05	.01
☐ 537 Rusty Staub	.50	.23	.06
☐ 538 Jesus Alou	.10	.05	.01
☐ 539 Wayne Garrett	.10	.05	.01
☐ 540 Mike Phillips	.10	.05	.01
☐ 541 Joe Torre	.75	.35	.09
☐ 542 Dave Kingman	.75	.35	.09
☐ 543 Gene Clines	.10	.05	.01
☐ 544 Jack Heidemann	.10	.05	.01
☐ 545 Bud Harrelson	.20	.09	.03
☐ 546 John Stearns	.20	.09	.03
☐ 547 John Milner	.10	.05	.01
☐ 548 Bob Apodaca	.10	.05	.01
☐ 549 Skip Lockwood	.10	.05	.01
☐ 550 Ken Sanders	.10	.05	.01
☐ 551 Tom Seaver	7.50	3.40	.95
☐ 552 Rick Baldwin	.10	.05	.01
☐ 553 Hank Webb	.10	.05	.01
☐ 554 Jon Matlack	.10	.05	.01
☐ 555 Randy Tate	.10	.05	.01
☐ 556 Tom Hall	.10	.05	.01
☐ 557 George Stone	.10	.05	.01
☐ 558 Craig Swan	.10	.05	.01
☐ 559 Jerry Cram	.10	.05	.01
☐ 560 Roy Staiger	.10	.05	.01
☐ 561 Kent Tekulve	.20	.09	.03
☐ 562 Jerry Reuss	.20	.09	.03
☐ 563 John Candelaria	.30	.14	.04
☐ 564 Larry Demery	.10	.05	.01
☐ 565 Dave Giusti	.10	.05	.01
☐ 566 Jim Rooker	.10	.05	.01
☐ 567 Ramon Hernandez	.10	.05	.01
☐ 568 Bruce Kison	.10	.05	.01
☐ 569 Ken Brett	.10	.05	.01
☐ 570 Bob Moose	.10	.05	.01
☐ 571 Manny Sanguillen	.20	.09	.03
☐ 572 Dave Parker	3.00	1.35	.35
☐ 573 Willie Stargell	4.00	1.80	.50
☐ 574 Richie Zisk	.20	.09	.03
☐ 575 Rennie Stennett	.10	.05	.01
☐ 576 Al Oliver	.75	.35	.09
☐ 577 Bill Robinson	.20	.09	.03
☐ 578 Bob Robertson	.10	.05	.01
☐ 579 Rich Hebner	.20	.09	.03
☐ 580 Ed Kirkpatrick	.10	.05	.01
☐ 581 Duffy Dyer	.10	.05	.01
☐ 582 Craig Reynolds	.10	.05	.01
☐ 583 Frank Taveras	.10	.05	.01
☐ 584 Willie Randolph	3.00	1.35	.35
☐ 585 Art Howe	.20	.09	.03
☐ 586 Danny Murtaugh MG	.20	.09	.03
☐ 587 Rick McKinney	.10	.05	.01
☐ 588 Ed Goodson	.10	.05	.01
☐ 589 Checklist 1 George Brett Al Cowens	5.00	2.20	.60
☐ 590 Checklist 2 Keith Hernandez Lou Brock	1.25	.55	.16
☐ 591 Checklist 3 Jerry Koosman Duke Snider	1.50	.70	.19
☐ 592 Checklist 4 Maury Wills John Knox	.20	.09	.03
☐ 593A Checklist 5 ERR Jim Hunter Nolan Ryan (Noland on front)	20.00	9.00	2.50
☐ 593B Checklist 5 COR Jim Hunter Nolan Ryan	10.00	4.50	1.25
☐ 594 Checklist 6 Ralph Branca Carl Erskine Pee Wee Reese	.30	.14	.04
☐ 595 Checklist 7 Willie Mays Herb Score	2.00	.90	.25
☐ 596 Larry Cox	.10	.05	.01
☐ 597 Gene Mauch MG	.20	.09	.03
☐ 598 Whitey Wietelmann CO	.10	.05	.01
☐ 599 Wayne Simpson	.10	.05	.01
☐ 600 Mel Thomason	.10	.05	.01
☐ 601 Ike Hampton	.10	.05	.01
☐ 602 Ken Crosby	.10	.05	.01
☐ 603 Ralph Rowe	.10	.05	.01
☐ 604 Jim Tyrone	.10	.05	.01
☐ 605 Mick Kelleher	.10	.05	.01
☐ 606 Mario Mendoza	.10	.05	.01
☐ 607 Mike Rogodzinski	.10	.05	.01
☐ 608 Bob Gallagher	.10	.05	.01
☐ 609 Jerry Koosman	.30	.14	.04
☐ 610 Joe Frazier MG	.10	.05	.01
☐ 611 Karl Kuehl MG	.10	.05	.01
☐ 612 Frank LaCorte	.10	.05	.01
☐ 613 Ray Bare	.10	.05	.01
☐ 614 Billy Muffett CO	.10	.05	.01
☐ 615 Bill Laxton	.10	.05	.01
☐ 616 Willie Mays CO	10.00	4.50	1.25
☐ 617 Phil Cavarretta CO	.20	.09	.03
☐ 618 Ted Kluszewski CO	.50	.23	.06
☐ 619 Elston Howard CO	.30	.14	.04
☐ 620 Alex Grammas CO	.10	.05	.01
☐ 621 Mickey Vernon CO	.10	.05	.01
☐ 622 Dick Sisler CO	.10	.05	.01
☐ 623 Harvey Haddix CO	.10	.05	.01
☐ 624 Bobby Winkles CO	.10	.05	.01
☐ 625 John Pesky CO	.20	.09	.03
☐ 626 Jim Davenport CO	.10	.05	.01
☐ 627 Dave Tomlin	.10	.05	.01
☐ 628 Roger Craig CO	.20	.09	.03
☐ 629 Joe Amalfitano CO	.10	.05	.01
☐ 630 Jim Reese CO	.50	.23	.06

1976 SSPC 1887 World Series

This 18-card standard-size set was inserted into the Fall 1976 Collectors Quarterly issue. Many of the players featured have few cards issued of them during their career. The fronts feature drawings while the backs talk about the 1887 World Series.

	NRMT	VG-E	GOOD
COMPLETE SET (18)	12.50	5.50	1.55
COMMON CARD (1-18)	.50	.23	.06
☐ 1 Bob Caruthers	.75	.35	.09
☐ 2 Dave Foutz	.50	.23	.06
☐ 3 Arlie Latham	.75	.35	.09
☐ 4 Charlie Getzein	.50	.23	.06
☐ 5 Jack Rowe	.50	.23	.06
☐ 6 Fred Dunlap	.50	.23	.06
☐ 7 Tip O'Neill	.75	.35	.09
☐ 8 Curt Welch	.75	.35	.09
☐ 9 Kid Gleason	1.00	.45	.12
☐ 10 Sam Thompson	1.50	.70	.19
☐ 11 Ned Hanlon	1.50	.70	.19
☐ 12 Dan Brouthers	1.50	.70	.19
☐ 13 Doc Bushong	.50	.23	.06
☐ 14 Charles Comiskey	3.00	1.35	.35
☐ 15 Yank Robinson	.50	.23	.06
☐ 16 Charlie Bennett	.75	.35	.09
☐ 17 Hardy Richardson	.50	.23	.06
☐ 18 Deacon White	.75	.35	.09

1976 SSPC Yankees Old-Timers Day

These nine standard-size cards were inserted in the Collectors Quarterly Spring 1976 edition. The cards feature the player's photo and his name on the bottom. The backs form a puzzle of four Yankee greats: Billy Martin, Joe DiMaggio, Whitey Ford and Mickey Mantle. The cards are unnummbered and thus sequenced in alphabetical order.

	NRMT	VG-E	GOOD
COMPLETE SET (9)	8.00	3.60	1.00
COMMON CARD (1-9)	.25	.11	.03
☐ 1 Earl Averill	.50	.23	.06
☐ 2 Joe DiMaggio	3.00	1.35	.35
☐ 3 Tommy Henrich	.35	.16	.04
☐ 4 Billy Herman	.50	.23	.06
☐ 5 Monte Irvin	.50	.23	.06
☐ 6 Jim Konstanty	.25	.11	.03
☐ 7 Mickey Mantle	3.00	1.35	.35
☐ 8 Pee Wee Reese	1.00	.45	.12
☐ 9 Bobby Thomson	.35	.16	.04

1978 SSPC 270

This 270-card set was issued as magazine (All-Star Gallery) inserts in sets of three panels, with each panel measuring approximately 7 1/4" by 10 3/4". Each of the three panels contains nine cards. If cut, the individual cards would measure the standard size (2 1/2" by 3 1/2"). The fronts display color posed and action player photos with thin black inner borders and white outer borders. The backs carry the player's name, biographical information, and career summary. The cards are checklisted below alphabetically according to teams as

follows: New York Yankees (1-27)), Philadelphia Phillies (28-54), Los Angeles Dodgers (55-81), Texas Rangers (82-108), Cincinnati Reds (109-135), Chicago White Sox (136-162), Boston Red Sox (163-189), California Angels (190-216), Kansas City Royals (217-243), and Chicago Cubs (244-270). The pricing below is for individual cards.

	NRMT	VG-E	GOOD
COMPLETE SET (270)	50.00	22.00	6.25
COMMON CARD (1-270)	.10	.05	.01
☐ 1 Thurman Munson	1.50	.70	.19
☐ 2 Cliff Johnson	.10	.05	.01
☐ 3 Lou Piniella	.50	.23	.06
☐ 4 Dell Alston	.10	.05	.01
☐ 5 Yankee Stadium	.10	.05	.01
☐ 6 Ken Holtzman	.20	.09	.03
☐ 7 Chris Chambliss	.35	.16	.04
☐ 8 Roy White	.20	.09	.03
☐ 9 Ed Figueroa	.10	.05	.01
☐ 10 Dick Tidrow	.10	.05	.01
☐ 11 Sparky Lyle	.35	.16	.04
☐ 12 Fred Stanley	.10	.05	.01
☐ 13 Mickey Rivers	.20	.09	.03
☐ 14 Billy Martin MG	.50	.23	.06
☐ 15 George Zeber	.10	.05	.01
☐ 16 Ken Clay	.10	.05	.01
☐ 17 Ron Guidry	.35	.16	.04
☐ 18 Don Gullett	.20	.09	.03
☐ 19 Fran Healy	.10	.05	.01
☐ 20 Paul Blair	.10	.05	.01
☐ 21 Mickey Klutts	.10	.05	.01
☐ 22 Yankees Team Photo	.20	.09	.03
☐ 23 Catfish Hunter	1.50	.70	.19
☐ 24 Bucky Dent	.20	.09	.03
☐ 25 Graig Nettles	.50	.23	.06
☐ 26 Reggie Jackson	3.00	1.35	.35
☐ 27 Willie Randolph	.35	.16	.04
☐ 28 Garry Maddox	.20	.09	.03
☐ 29 Steve Carlton	2.00	.90	.25
☐ 30 Ron Reed	.10	.05	.01
☐ 31 Greg Luzinski	.35	.16	.04
☐ 32 Bobby Wine CO	.10	.05	.01
☐ 33 Bob Boone	.35	.16	.04
☐ 34 Carroll Beringer CO	.10	.05	.01
☐ 35 Richie Hebner	.20	.09	.03
☐ 36 Ray Rippelmeyer CO	.10	.05	.01
☐ 37 Terry Harmon	.10	.05	.01
☐ 38 Gene Garber	.20	.09	.03
☐ 39 Ted Sizemore	.10	.05	.01
☐ 40 Barry Foote	.10	.05	.01
☐ 41 Tony Taylor CO	.10	.05	.01
☐ 42 Tug McGraw	.50	.23	.06
☐ 43 Jay Johnstone	.35	.16	.04
☐ 44 Randy Lerch	.10	.05	.01
☐ 45 Billy DeMars CO	.10	.05	.01
☐ 46 Mike Schmidt	5.00	2.20	.60
☐ 47 Larry Christenson	.10	.05	.01
☐ 48 Tim McCarver	.50	.23	.06
☐ 49 Larry Bowa	.35	.16	.04
☐ 50 Danny Ozark MG	.10	.05	.01
☐ 51 Jerry Martin	.10	.05	.01
☐ 52 Jim Lonborg	.20	.09	.03
☐ 53 Bake McBride	.10	.05	.01
☐ 54 Warren Brusstar	.10	.05	.01
☐ 55 Burt Hooton	.20	.09	.03
☐ 56 Bill Russell	.20	.09	.03
☐ 57 Dusty Baker	.35	.16	.04
☐ 58 Reggie Smith	.35	.16	.04
☐ 59 Rick Rhoden	.10	.05	.01
☐ 60 Jerry Grote	.10	.05	.01
☐ 61 Bill Butler	.10	.05	.01
☐ 62 Ron Cey	.35	.16	.04
☐ 63 Tom Lasorda MG	.60	.25	.07
☐ 64 Teddy Martinez	.10	.05	.01
☐ 65 Ed Goodson	.10	.05	.01
☐ 66 Vic Davalillo	.10	.05	.01
☐ 67 Davey Lopes	.20	.09	.03
☐ 68 Terry Forster	.10	.05	.01
☐ 69 Lee Lacy	.10	.05	.01
☐ 70 Mike Garman	.10	.05	.01
☐ 71 Steve Garvey	.75	.35	.09
☐ 72 Johnny Oates	.35	.16	.04
☐ 73 Steve Yeager	.10	.05	.01
☐ 74 Rafael Landestoy	.10	.05	.01
☐ 75 Tommy John	.50	.23	.06
☐ 76 Glenn Burke	.10	.05	.01
☐ 77 Rick Monday	.20	.09	.03
☐ 78 Doug Rau	.10	.05	.01
☐ 79 Manny Mota	.20	.09	.03
☐ 80 Don Sutton	1.00	.45	.12
☐ 81 Charlie Hough	.35	.16	.04
☐ 82 Mike Hargrove	.20	.09	.03
☐ 83 Jim Sundberg	.20	.09	.03
☐ 84 Fergie Jenkins	1.50	.70	.19
☐ 85 Paul Lindblad	.10	.05	.01
☐ 86 Sandy Alomar	.10	.05	.01
☐ 87 John Lowenstein	.10	.05	.01
☐ 88 Claudell Washington	.20	.09	.03
☐ 89 Toby Harrah	.20	.09	.03
☐ 90 Jim Umbarger	.10	.05	.01
☐ 91 Len Barker	.10	.05	.01
☐ 92 Dave May	.10	.05	.01
☐ 93 Kurt Bevacqua	.10	.05	.01
☐ 94 Jim Mason	.10	.05	.01
☐ 95 Bump Wills	.10	.05	.01
☐ 96 Dock Ellis	.10	.05	.01
☐ 97 Bill Fahey	.10	.05	.01
☐ 98 Richie Zisk	.10	.05	.01
☐ 99 Jon Matlack	.10	.05	.01
☐ 100 John Ellis	.10	.05	.01
☐ 101 Bert Campaneris	.20	.09	.03
☐ 102 Doc Medich	.10	.05	.01
☐ 103 Juan Beniquez	.10	.05	.01
☐ 104 Billy Hunter MG	.10	.05	.01
☐ 105 Doyle Alexander	.20	.09	.03
☐ 106 Roger Moret	.10	.05	.01
☐ 107 Mike Jorgensen	.10	.05	.01
☐ 108 Al Oliver	.35	.16	.04
☐ 109 Fred Norman	.10	.05	.01
☐ 110 Ray Knight	.60	.25	.07
☐ 111 Pedro Borbon	.10	.05	.01
☐ 112 Bill Bonham	.10	.05	.01
☐ 113 George Foster	.50	.23	.06
☐ 114 Doug Bair	.10	.05	.01
☐ 115 Cesar Geronimo	.10	.05	.01
☐ 116 Tom Seaver	2.00	.90	.25
☐ 117 Mario Soto	.20	.09	.03
☐ 118 Ken Griffey	.35	.16	.04
☐ 119 Mike Lum	.10	.05	.01
☐ 120 Tom Hume	.10	.05	.01
☐ 121 Joe Morgan	1.50	.70	.19
☐ 122 Manny Sarmiento	.10	.05	.01
☐ 123 Dan Driessen	.20	.09	.03
☐ 124 Ed Armbrister	.10	.05	.01
☐ 125 Champ Summers	.10	.05	.01
☐ 126 Rick Auerbach	.10	.05	.01
☐ 127 Doug Capilla	.10	.05	.01
☐ 128 Johnny Bench	2.00	.90	.25
☐ 129 Sparky Anderson MG	.50	.23	.06
☐ 130 Raul Ferreyra	.10	.05	.01
☐ 131 Dale Murray	.10	.05	.01
☐ 132 Pete Rose	3.00	1.35	.35
☐ 133 Dave Concepcion	.35	.16	.04
☐ 134 Junior Kennedy	.10	.05	.01
☐ 135 Dave Collins	.20	.09	.03
☐ 136 Mike Eden	.10	.05	.01
☐ 137 Lamar Johnson	.10	.05	.01
☐ 138 Ron Schueler	.10	.05	.01
☐ 139 Bob Lemon MG	.50	.23	.06
☐ 140 Bobby Bonds	.50	.23	.06
☐ 141 Thad Bosley	.10	.05	.01
☐ 142 Jorge Orta	.10	.05	.01
☐ 143 Wilbur Wood	.10	.05	.01
☐ 144 Francisco Barrios	.10	.05	.01
☐ 145 Greg Prior	.10	.05	.01
☐ 146 Chet Lemon	.20	.09	.03
☐ 147 Mike Squires	.10	.05	.01
☐ 148 Eric Soderholm	.10	.05	.01
☐ 149 Reggie Sanders	.10	.05	.01
☐ 150 Kevin Bell	.10	.05	.01
☐ 151 Alan Bannister	.10	.05	.01
☐ 152 Henry Cruz	.10	.05	.01
☐ 153 Larry Doby CO	.35	.16	.04
☐ 154 Don Kessinger	.20	.09	.03
☐ 155 Ralph Garr	.20	.09	.03
☐ 156 Bill Nahorodny	.10	.05	.01
☐ 157 Ron Blomberg	.10	.05	.01
☐ 158 Bob Molinaro	.10	.05	.01
☐ 159 Junior Moore	.10	.05	.01
☐ 160 Minnie Minoso CO	.35	.16	.04
☐ 161 Lerrin LaGrow	.10	.05	.01
☐ 162 Wayne Nordhagen	.10	.05	.01
☐ 163 Ramon Aviles	.10	.05	.01
☐ 164 Bob Stanley	.35	.16	.04
☐ 165 Reggie Cleveland	.10	.05	.01
☐ 166 Jack Brohamer	.10	.05	.01
☐ 167 Bill Lee	.20	.09	.03
☐ 168 Jim Burton	.10	.05	.01
☐ 169 Bill Campbell	.10	.05	.01
☐ 170 Mike Torrez	.10	.05	.01
☐ 171 Dick Drago	.10	.05	.01
☐ 172 Butch Hobson	.10	.05	.01
☐ 173 Bob Bailey	.10	.05	.01
☐ 174 Fred Lynn	.20	.09	.03
☐ 175 Rick Burleson	.20	.09	.03
☐ 176 Luis Tiant	.35	.16	.04
☐ 177 Ted Williams CO	5.00	2.20	.60
☐ 178 Dennis Eckersley	1.50	.70	.19
☐ 179 Don Zimmer MG	.10	.05	.01
☐ 180 Carlton Fisk	1.50	.70	.19
☐ 181 Dwight Evans	.50	.23	.06
☐ 182 Fred Kendall	.10	.05	.01
☐ 183 George Scott	.20	.09	.03
☐ 184 Frank Duffy	.10	.05	.01
☐ 185 Bernie Carbo	.10	.05	.01
☐ 186 Jerry Remy	.10	.05	.01
☐ 187 Carl Yastrzemski	2.00	.90	.25

☐ 188 Allen Ripley	.10	.05	.01
☐ 189 Jim Rice	.75	.35	.09
☐ 190 Ken Landreaux	.10	.05	.01
☐ 191 Paul Hartzell	.10	.05	.01
☐ 192 Ken Brett	.10	.05	.01
☐ 193 Dave Garcia MG	.10	.05	.01
☐ 194 Bobby Grich	.35	.16	.04
☐ 195 Lyman Bostock Jr.	.35	.16	.04
☐ 196 Ike Hampton	.10	.05	.01
☐ 197 Dave LaRoche	.10	.05	.01
☐ 198 Dave Chalk	.10	.05	.01
☐ 199 Rick Miller	.10	.05	.01
☐ 200 Floyd Rayford	.10	.05	.01
☐ 201 Willie Aikens	.20	.09	.03
☐ 202 Balor Moore	.10	.05	.01
☐ 203 Nolan Ryan	15.00	6.75	1.85
☐ 204 Danny Goodwin	.10	.05	.01
☐ 205 Ron Fairly	.20	.09	.03
☐ 206 Dyar Miller	.10	.05	.01
☐ 207 Carney Lansford	.60	.25	.07
☐ 208 Don Baylor	.50	.23	.06
☐ 209 Gil Flores	.10	.05	.01
☐ 210 Terry Humphrey	.10	.05	.01
☐ 211 Frank Tanana	.50	.23	.06
☐ 212 Chris Knapp	.10	.05	.01
☐ 213 Ron Jackson	.10	.05	.01
☐ 214 Joe Rudi	.20	.09	.03
☐ 215 Tony Solaita	.10	.05	.01
☐ 216 Rance Mulliniks	.10	.05	.01
☐ 217 George Brett	12.50	5.50	1.55
☐ 218 Doug Bird	.10	.05	.01
☐ 219 Hal McRae	.50	.23	.06
☐ 220 Dennis Leonard	.20	.09	.03
☐ 221 Darrell Porter	.20	.09	.03
☐ 222 Randy McGilberry	.10	.05	.01
☐ 223 Pete LaCock	.10	.05	.01
☐ 224 Whitey Herzog MG	.35	.16	.04
☐ 225 Andy Hassler	.10	.05	.01
☐ 226 Joe Lahoud	.10	.05	.01
☐ 227 Amos Otis	.20	.09	.03
☐ 228 Al Hrabosky	.20	.09	.03
☐ 229 Clint Hurdle	.10	.05	.01
☐ 230 Paul Splittorff	.10	.05	.01
☐ 231 Marty Pattin	.10	.05	.01
☐ 232 Frank White	.35	.16	.04
☐ 233 John Wathan	.10	.05	.01
☐ 234 Freddie Patek	.20	.09	.03
☐ 235 Rich Gale	.10	.05	.01
☐ 236 U.L. Washington	.10	.05	.01
☐ 237 Larry Gura	.10	.05	.01
☐ 238 Jim Colborn	.10	.05	.01
☐ 239 Tom Poquette	.10	.05	.01
☐ 240 Al Cowens	.10	.05	.01
☐ 241 Willie Wilson	.50	.23	.06
☐ 242 Steve Mingori	.10	.05	.01
☐ 243 Jerry Terrell	.10	.05	.01
☐ 244 Larry Biittner	.10	.05	.01
☐ 245 Rick Reuschel	.20	.09	.03
☐ 246 Dave Rader	.10	.05	.01
☐ 247 Paul Reuschel	.10	.05	.01
☐ 248 Heity Cruz	.10	.05	.01
☐ 249 Woodie Fryman	.10	.05	.01
☐ 250 Steve Ontiveros	.10	.05	.01
☐ 251 Mike Gordon	.10	.05	.01
☐ 252 Dave Kingman	.50	.23	.06
☐ 253 Gene Clines	.10	.05	.01
☐ 254 Bruce Sutter	.35	.16	.04
☐ 255 Willie Hernandez	.20	.09	.03
☐ 256 Ivan DeJesus	.10	.05	.01
☐ 257 Greg Gross	.10	.05	.01
☐ 258 Larry Cox	.10	.05	.01
☐ 259 Joe Wallis	.10	.05	.01
☐ 260 Dennis Lamp	.10	.05	.01
☐ 261 Ray Burris	.10	.05	.01
☐ 262 Bill Caudill	.10	.05	.01
☐ 263 Donnie Moore	.10	.05	.01
☐ 264 Bill Buckner	.35	.16	.04
☐ 265 Bobby Murcer	.35	.16	.04
☐ 266 Dave Roberts	.10	.05	.01
☐ 267 Mike Krukow	.10	.05	.01
☐ 268 Herman Franks MG	.10	.05	.01
☐ 269 Mick Kelleher	.10	.05	.01
☐ 270 Rudy Meoli	.10	.05	.01

1980-87 SSPC HOF

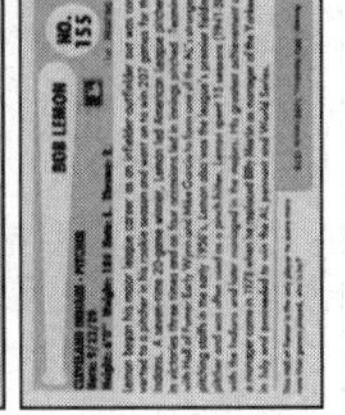

The 1980 SSPC set was commonly known as the Baseball Immortals set. This standard-size set honored all of the members of the Hall of Fame. When the set was first issued the first 10,000 sets made indicated first printing on the back. This set continued to be issued as new additions were inducted into the Hall of Fame.

	NRMT	VG-E	GOOD
COMPLETE SET (199)	30.00	13.50	3.70
COMMON CARD (1-199)	.05	.02	.01
☐ 1 Babe Ruth	2.00	.90	.25
☐ 2 Ty Cobb	1.50	.70	.19
☐ 3 Walter Johnson	.75	.35	.09
☐ 4 Christy Mathewson	.75	.35	.09
☐ 5 Honus Wagner	1.00	.45	.12
☐ 6 Morgan Bulkeley	.05	.02	.01
☐ 7 Ban Johnson	.05	.02	.01
☐ 8 Larry Lajoie	.50	.23	.06
☐ 9 Connie Mack	.25	.11	.03
☐ 10 John McGraw	.25	.11	.03
☐ 11 Tris Speaker	.25	.11	.03
☐ 12 George Wright	.05	.02	.01
☐ 13 Cy Young	.75	.35	.09
☐ 14 Grover Alexander	.75	.35	.09
☐ 15 Alexander Cartwright	.05	.02	.01
☐ 16 Henry Chadwick	.05	.02	.01
☐ 17 Cap Anson	.25	.11	.03
☐ 18 Eddie Collins	.15	.07	.02
☐ 19 Charles Comiskey	.05	.02	.01
☐ 20 Candy Cummings	.05	.02	.01
☐ 21 Buck Ewing	.05	.02	.01
☐ 22 Lou Gehrig	1.50	.70	.19
☐ 23 Willie Keeler	.05	.02	.01
☐ 24 Hoss Radbourne	.05	.02	.01
☐ 25 George Sisler	.15	.07	.02
☐ 26 Albert Spalding	.05	.02	.01
☐ 27 Rogers Hornsby	.75	.35	.09
☐ 28 Judge Landis	.05	.02	.01
☐ 29 Roger Bresnahan	.05	.02	.01
☐ 30 Dan Brouthers	.05	.02	.01
☐ 31 Fred Clarke	.05	.02	.01
☐ 32 James Collins	.05	.02	.01
☐ 33 Ed Delahanty	.05	.02	.01
☐ 34 Hugh Duffy	.05	.02	.01
☐ 35 Hughie Jennings	.05	.02	.01
☐ 36 Mike(King) Kelly	.15	.07	.02
☐ 37 James O'Rourke	.05	.02	.01
☐ 38 Wilbert Robinson	.05	.02	.01
☐ 39 Jesse Burkett	.05	.02	.01
☐ 40 Frank Chance	.15	.07	.02
☐ 41 Jack Chesbro	.05	.02	.01
☐ 42 John Evers	.15	.07	.02
☐ 43 Clark Griffith	.05	.02	.01
☐ 44 Thomas McCarthy	.05	.02	.01
☐ 45 Joe McGinnity	.05	.02	.01
☐ 46 Eddie Plank	.15	.07	.02
☐ 47 Joe Tinker	.15	.07	.02
☐ 48 Rube Waddell	.15	.07	.02
☐ 49 Ed Walsh	.05	.02	.01
☐ 50 Mickey Cochrane	.15	.07	.02
☐ 51 Frankie Frisch	.15	.07	.02
☐ 52 Lefty Grove	.15	.07	.02
☐ 53 Carl Hubbell	.25	.11	.03
☐ 54 Herb Pennock	.05	.02	.01
☐ 55 Pie Traynor	.15	.07	.02
☐ 56 Three Finger Brown	.05	.02	.01
☐ 57 Charlie Gehringer	.15	.07	.02
☐ 58 Kid Nichols	.05	.02	.01
☐ 59 Jimmie Foxx	.75	.35	.09
☐ 60 Mel Ott	.50	.23	.06
☐ 61 Harry Heilmann	.05	.02	.01
☐ 62 Paul Waner	.15	.07	.02
☐ 63 Ed Barrow	.05	.02	.01
☐ 64 Chief Bender	.05	.02	.01
☐ 65 Tom Connolly	.05	.02	.01
☐ 66 Dizzy Dean	.75	.35	.09
☐ 67 Bill Klem	.05	.02	.01
☐ 68 Al Simmons	.15	.07	.02
☐ 69 Bobby Wallace	.05	.02	.01
☐ 70 Harry Wright	.05	.02	.01
☐ 71 Bill Dickey	.25	.11	.03
☐ 72 Rabbit Maranville	.05	.02	.01
☐ 73 Bill Terry	.15	.07	.02
☐ 74 Home Run Baker	.15	.07	.02
☐ 75 Joe DiMaggio	1.50	.70	.19
☐ 76 Gabby Hartnett	.05	.02	.01
☐ 77 Ted Lyons	.05	.02	.01
☐ 78 Ray Schalk	.05	.02	.01
☐ 79 Dazzy Vance	.05	.02	.01
☐ 80 Joe Cronin	.15	.07	.02
☐ 81 Hank Greenberg	.15	.07	.02
☐ 82 Sam Crawford	.05	.02	.01
☐ 83 Joe McCarthy	.05	.02	.01
☐ 84 Zack Wheat	.05	.02	.01
☐ 85 Max Carey	.05	.02	.01
☐ 86 Billy Hamilton	.05	.02	.01
☐ 87 Bob Feller	.75	.35	.09
☐ 88 Bill McKechnie	.05	.02	.01
☐ 89 Jackie Robinson	1.00	.45	.12
☐ 90 Ed Roush	.05	.02	.01
☐ 91 John Clarkson	.05	.02	.01
☐ 92 Elmer Flick	.05	.02	.01
☐ 93 Sam Rice	.05	.02	.01
☐ 94 Eppa Rixey	.05	.02	.01
☐ 95 Luke Appling	.05	.02	.01
☐ 96 Red Faber	.05	.02	.01
☐ 97 Burleigh Grimes	.05	.02	.01
☐ 98 Miller Huggins	.05	.02	.01
☐ 99 Tim Keefe	.05	.02	.01
☐ 100 Heinie Manush	.05	.02	.01
☐ 101 John Ward	.05	.02	.01
☐ 102 Pud Galvin	.05	.02	.01
☐ 103 Casey Stengel	.25	.11	.03
☐ 104 Ted Williams	1.00	.45	.12
☐ 105 Branch Rickey	.15	.07	.02
☐ 106 Red Ruffing	.05	.02	.01
☐ 107 Lloyd Waner	.05	.02	.01
☐ 108 Kiki Cuyler	.05	.02	.01
☐ 109 Goose Goslin	.05	.02	.01
☐ 110 Joe Medwick	.05	.02	.01
☐ 111 Roy Campanella	.50	.23	.06
☐ 112 Stan Coveleski	.05	.02	.01
☐ 113 Waite Hoyt	.05	.02	.01
☐ 114 Stan Musial	.75	.35	.09
☐ 115 Lou Boudreau	.05	.02	.01
☐ 116 Earle Combs	.05	.02	.01
☐ 117 Ford Frick	.05	.02	.01
☐ 118 Jesse Haines	.05	.02	.01
☐ 119 Dave Bancroft	.05	.02	.01
☐ 120 Jake Beckley	.05	.02	.01
☐ 121 Chick Hafey	.05	.02	.01
☐ 122 Harry Hooper	.05	.02	.01
☐ 123 Joe Kelley	.05	.02	.01
☐ 124 Rube Marquard	.05	.02	.01
☐ 125 Satchel Paige	.50	.23	.06
☐ 126 George Weiss	.05	.02	.01
☐ 127 Yogi Berra	.75	.35	.09
☐ 128 Josh Gibson	.50	.23	.06
☐ 129 Lefty Gomez	.15	.07	.02
☐ 130 Will Harridge	.05	.02	.01
☐ 131 Sandy Koufax	.75	.35	.09
☐ 132 Buck Leonard	.15	.07	.02
☐ 133 Early Wynn	.15	.07	.02
☐ 134 Ross Youngs	.05	.02	.01
☐ 135 Roberto Clemente	1.00	.45	.12
☐ 136 Billy Evans	.05	.02	.01
☐ 137 Monte Irvin	.15	.07	.02
☐ 138 George Kelly	.05	.02	.01
☐ 139 Warren Spahn	.15	.07	.02
☐ 140 Mickey Welch	.05	.02	.01
☐ 141 Cool Papa Bell	.15	.07	.02
☐ 142 Jim Bottomley	.05	.02	.01
☐ 143 Jocko Conlan	.05	.02	.01
☐ 144 Whitey Ford	.25	.11	.03
☐ 145 Mickey Mantle	1.50	.70	.19
☐ 146 Sam Thompson	.05	.02	.01
☐ 147 Earl Averill	.05	.02	.01
☐ 148 Bucky Harris	.05	.02	.01
☐ 149 Billy Herman	.05	.02	.01
☐ 150 Judy Johnson	.05	.02	.01
☐ 151 Ralph Kiner	.15	.07	.02
☐ 152 Oscar Charleston	.05	.02	.01
☐ 153 Roger Connor	.05	.02	.01
☐ 154 Cal Hubbard	.05	.02	.01
☐ 155 Bob Lemon	.05	.02	.01
☐ 156 Fred Lindstrom	.05	.02	.01
☐ 157 Robin Roberts	.15	.07	.02
☐ 158 Ernie Banks	.50	.23	.06
☐ 159 Martin Dihigo	.05	.02	.01
☐ 160 John Henry Lloyd	.05	.02	.01
☐ 161 Al Lopez	.05	.02	.01
☐ 162 Amos Rusie	.05	.02	.01
☐ 163 Joe Sewell	.05	.02	.01
☐ 164 Addie Joss	.05	.02	.01
☐ 165 Larry McPhail	.05	.02	.01
☐ 166 Eddie Mathews	.15	.07	.02
☐ 167 Warren Giles	.05	.02	.01
☐ 168 Willie Mays	1.00	.45	.12
☐ 169 Hack Wilson	.05	.02	.01
☐ 170 Duke Snider	.75	.35	.09
☐ 171 Al Kaline	.75	.35	.09
☐ 172 Chuck Klein	.05	.02	.01
☐ 173 Tom Yawkey	.05	.02	.01
☐ 174 Bob Gibson	.50	.23	.06
☐ 175 Rube Foster	.05	.02	.01
☐ 176 Johnny Mize	.05	.02	.01
☐ 177 Hank Aaron	1.00	.45	.12
☐ 178 Frank Robinson	.50	.23	.06
☐ 179 Happy Chandler	.05	.02	.01
☐ 180 Travis Jackson	.05	.02	.01
☐ 181 Brooks Robinson	.25	.11	.03
☐ 182 Juan Marichal	.25	.11	.03
☐ 183 George Kell	.15	.07	.02
☐ 184 Walter Alston	.05	.02	.01
☐ 185 Harmon Killebrew	.25	.11	.03
☐ 186 Luis Aparicio	.15	.07	.02
☐ 187 Don Drysdale	.15	.07	.02
☐ 188 Pee Wee Reese	.25	.11	.03
☐ 189 Rick Ferrell	.05	.02	.01
☐ 190 Willie McCovey	.25	.11	.03
☐ 191 Ernie Lombardi	.05	.02	.01
☐ 192 Bobby Doerr	.05	.02	.01
☐ 193 Arky Vaughan	.05	.02	.01
☐ 194 Enos Slaughter	.50	.23	.06
☐ 195 Lou Brock	.50	.23	.06
☐ 196 Hoyt Wilhelm	.50	.23	.06
☐ 197 Billy Williams	.50	.23	.06
☐ 198 Jim Hunter	.50	.23	.06
☐ 199 Ray Dandridge	.05	.02	.01

1992 St. Vincent HOF Heroes Stamps

This 12-card standard-size set was issued by the St. Vincent Philatelic Services, Ltd. The peel-away stamps are official legal postage in St. Vincent and the Grenadines. The fronts have a head shot of various HOFers in sepia tones on a gold background that fades to red. The

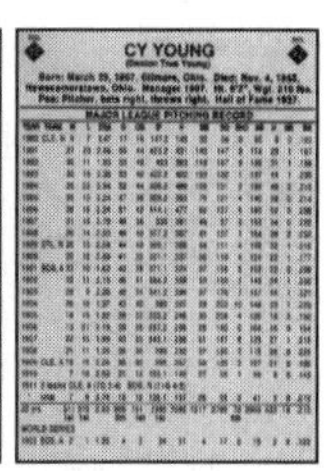

borders have a stamp edge design with an inner border of green. A blue banner across the top carries the words Baseball Hall of Fame Heroes and is placed over a baseball. The card's stamp value of $4.00 is shown in the top right. The lower margin carries the year the player entered the major leagues, his name and final year in the majors. The backs carry the player's name, biography and career statistics.

	MINT	NRMT	EXC
COMPLETE SET (12)	10.00	4.50	1.25
COMMON STAMP (1-12)	.50	.23	.06
☐ 1 Ty Cobb	2.00	.90	.25
☐ 2 Dizzy Dean	.50	.23	.06
☐ 3 Bob Feller	.50	.23	.06
☐ 4 Whitey Ford	.50	.23	.06
☐ 5 Lou Gehrig	3.00	1.35	.35
☐ 6 Rogers Hornsby	.50	.23	.06
☐ 7 Mel Ott	.50	.23	.06
☐ 8 Satchel Paige	.75	.35	.09
☐ 9 Babe Ruth	3.00	1.35	.35
☐ 10 Casey Stengel	.50	.23	.06
☐ 11 Honus Wagner	1.00	.45	.12
☐ 12 Cy Young	.75	.35	.09

1997 St. Vincent HOF Heroes Stamps

This 17-card set commemorates the 50th anniversary of Jackie Robinson breaking Baseball's color barrier. The set features color head portraits of 16 different Black Hall of Famers on 1 3/16" by 1 9/16" $1 stamps. The player's name and year he entered the Hall of Fame are printed down the left. The last stamp listed in the checklist is a $6 stamp and honors Jackie Robinson. It measures approximately 2 3/4" by 4 1/8". The stamps were designed to be placed in a 9" by 8" album with a black-and-white picture of Jackie Robinson in action on the cover. The stamps are unnumbered and checklisted below in alphabetical order.

	MINT	NRMT	EXC
COMPLETE SET (17)	12.00	5.50	1.50
COMMON CARD (1-17)	.50	.23	.06
☐ 1 Hank Aaron	2.00	.90	.25
☐ 2 Ernie Banks	.75	.35	.09
☐ 3 Lou Brock	.50	.23	.06
☐ 4 Roy Campanella	.75	.35	.09
☐ 5 Rod Carew	.50	.23	.06
☐ 6 Roberto Clemente	3.00	1.35	.35
☐ 7 Bob Gibson	.50	.23	.06
☐ 8 Monte Irvin	.50	.23	.06
☐ 9 Reggie Jackson	.75	.35	.09
☐ 10 Ferguson Jenkins	.50	.23	.06
☐ 11 Willie McCovey	.50	.23	.06
☐ 12 Joe Morgan	.50	.23	.06
☐ 13 Satchel Paige	.75	.35	.09
☐ 14 Frank Robinson	.75	.35	.09
☐ 15 Willie Stargell	.50	.23	.06
☐ 16 Billy Williams	.50	.23	.06
☐ 17 Jackie Robinson	5.00	2.20	.60

1991 Stadium Club Pre-Production

The exact origins of this scarce 50-card set is unclear, but speculation is that Topps distributed single cards or uncut strips to its employees and/or major candy wholesale accounts. The card fronts are very similar to the player's corresponding regular Stadium Club cards with the addition of an extra horizontal gold foil stripe at the bottom. The backs of all 50 cards are identical -- unnumbered with a reproduction of Jose Canseco's 1986 Topps Traded card.

	MINT	NRMT	EXC
COMPLETE SET (50)	1000.00	450.00	125.00
COMMON CARD (1-50)	15.00	6.75	1.85
☐ 1 Allan Anderson	15.00	6.75	1.85
☐ 2 Steve Balboni	15.00	6.75	1.85
☐ 3 Jeff Ballard	15.00	6.75	1.85

☐ 4 Jesse Barfield	15.00	6.75	1.85
☐ 5 Andy Benes	25.00	11.00	3.10
☐ 6 Bobby Bonilla	25.00	11.00	3.10
☐ 7 Chris Bosio	15.00	6.75	1.85
☐ 8 Daryl Boston	15.00	6.75	1.85
☐ 9 Chuck Cary	15.00	6.75	1.85
☐ 10 Pat Combs	15.00	6.75	1.85
☐ 11 Delino DeShields	15.00	6.75	1.85
☐ 12 Shawon Dunston	15.00	6.75	1.85
☐ 13 Alvaro Espinoza	15.00	6.75	1.85
☐ 14 Sid Fernandez	15.00	6.75	1.85
☐ 15 Bob Geren	15.00	6.75	1.85
☐ 16 Brian Holman	15.00	6.75	1.85
☐ 17 Jay Howell	15.00	6.75	1.85
☐ 18 Stan Javier	15.00	6.75	1.85
☐ 19 Dave Johnson	15.00	6.75	1.85
☐ 20 Howard Johnson	15.00	6.75	1.85
☐ 21 Kevin Maas	15.00	6.75	1.85
☐ 22 Shane Mack	15.00	6.75	1.85
☐ 23 Joe Magrane	15.00	6.75	1.85
☐ 24 Denny Martinez	15.00	6.75	1.85
☐ 25 Don Mattingly	150.00	70.00	19.00
☐ 26 Ben McDonald	25.00	11.00	3.10
☐ 27 Eddie Murray	75.00	34.00	9.50
☐ 28 Matt Nokes	15.00	6.75	1.85
☐ 29 Greg Olson	15.00	6.75	1.85
☐ 30 Gregg Olson	15.00	6.75	1.85
☐ 31 Jose Oquendo	15.00	6.75	1.85
☐ 32 Tony Phillips	15.00	6.75	1.85
☐ 33 Rafael Ramirez	15.00	6.75	1.85
☐ 34 Dennis Rasmussen	15.00	6.75	1.85
☐ 35 Billy Ripken	15.00	6.75	1.85
☐ 36 Nolan Ryan	250.00	110.00	31.00
☐ 37 Bill Sampen	15.00	6.75	1.85
☐ 38 Steve Sax	15.00	6.75	1.85
☐ 39 Mike Scioscia	15.00	6.75	1.85
☐ 40 David Segui	15.00	6.75	1.85
☐ 41 Zane Smith	15.00	6.75	1.85
☐ 42 B.J. Surhoff	15.00	6.75	1.85
☐ 43 Bobby Thigpen	15.00	6.75	1.85
☐ 44 Alan Trammell	25.00	11.00	3.10
☐ 45 Fernando Valenzuela	25.00	11.00	3.10
☐ 46 Andy Van Slyke	15.00	6.75	1.85
☐ 47 Hector Villanueva	15.00	6.75	1.85
☐ 48 Larry Walker	40.00	18.00	5.00
☐ 49 Walt Weiss	15.00	6.75	1.85
☐ 50 Bob Walk	15.00	6.75	1.85

1991 Stadium Club

This 600-card standard size set marked Topps first premium quality set. The set was issued in two separate series of 300 cards each. Cards were distributed in plastic wrapped packs. Series II cards were also available at McDonald's restaurants in the Northeast at three cards per pack. The set created a stir in the hobby upon release with dazzling full-color borderless photos and slick, glossy card stock. The back of each card has the basic biographical information as well as making use of the Fastball BARS system and an inset photo of the player's Topps rookie card. Rookie Cards include Jeff Bagwell, Jeff Conine and Brian McRae.

	MINT	NRMT	EXC
COMPLETE SET (600)	100.00	45.00	12.50
COMPLETE SERIES 1 (300)	60.00	27.00	7.50
COMPLETE SERIES 2 (300)	40.00	18.00	5.00
COMMON CARD (1-600)	.15	.07	.02

☐ 1 Dave Stewart TUX	.60	.25	.07
☐ 2 Wally Joyner	.30	.14	.04
☐ 3 Shawon Dunston	.15	.07	.02
☐ 4 Darren Daulton	.30	.14	.04
☐ 5 Will Clark	.60	.25	.07
☐ 6 Sammy Sosa	1.25	.55	.16
☐ 7 Dan Plesac	.15	.07	.02
☐ 8 Marquis Grissom	.75	.35	.09
☐ 9 Erik Hanson	.15	.07	.02
☐ 10 Geno Petralli	.15	.07	.02
☐ 11 Jose Rijo	.15	.07	.02
☐ 12 Carlos Quintana	.15	.07	.02
☐ 13 Junior Ortiz	.15	.07	.02
☐ 14 Bob Walk	.15	.07	.02
☐ 15 Mike Macfarlane	.15	.07	.02
☐ 16 Eric Yelding	.15	.07	.02
☐ 17 Bryn Smith	.15	.07	.02
☐ 18 Bip Roberts	.15	.07	.02
☐ 19 Mike Scioscia	.15	.07	.02
☐ 20 Mark Williamson	.15	.07	.02
☐ 21 Don Mattingly	2.50	1.10	.30
☐ 22 John Franco	.15	.07	.02
☐ 23 Chet Lemon	.15	.07	.02
☐ 24 Tom Henke	.15	.07	.02
☐ 25 Jerry Browne	.15	.07	.02
☐ 26 Dave Justice	.75	.35	.09
☐ 27 Mark Langston	.30	.14	.04
☐ 28 Damon Berryhill	.15	.07	.02
☐ 29 Kevin Bass	.15	.07	.02
☐ 30 Scott Fletcher	.15	.07	.02
☐ 31 Moises Alou	1.50	.70	.19
☐ 32 Dave Valle	.15	.07	.02
☐ 33 Jody Reed	.15	.07	.02
☐ 34 Dave West	.15	.07	.02
☐ 35 Kevin McReynolds	.15	.07	.02
☐ 36 Pat Combs	.15	.07	.02
☐ 37 Eric Davis	.30	.14	.04
☐ 38 Bret Saberhagen	.30	.14	.04
☐ 39 Stan Javier	.15	.07	.02
☐ 40 Chuck Cary	.15	.07	.02
☐ 41 Tony Phillips	.30	.14	.04
☐ 42 Lee Smith	.30	.14	.04
☐ 43 Tim Teufel	.15	.07	.02
☐ 44 Lance Dickson	.15	.07	.02
☐ 45 Greg Litton	.15	.07	.02
☐ 46 Teddy Higuera	.15	.07	.02
☐ 47 Edgar Martinez	.30	.14	.04
☐ 48 Steve Avery	.60	.25	.07
☐ 49 Walt Weiss	.15	.07	.02
☐ 50 David Segui	.30	.14	.04
☐ 51 Andy Benes	.30	.14	.04
☐ 52 Karl Rhodes	.15	.07	.02
☐ 53 Neal Heaton	.15	.07	.02
☐ 54 Danny Gladden	.15	.07	.02
☐ 55 Luis Rivera	.15	.07	.02
☐ 56 Kevin Brown	.30	.14	.04
☐ 57 Frank Thomas	10.00	4.50	1.25
☐ 58 Terry Mulholland	.15	.07	.02
☐ 59 Dick Schofield	.15	.07	.02
☐ 60 Ron Darling	.15	.07	.02
☐ 61 Sandy Alomar Jr.	.30	.14	.04
☐ 62 Dave Stieb	.15	.07	.02
☐ 63 Alan Trammell	.30	.14	.04
☐ 64 Matt Nokes	.15	.07	.02
☐ 65 Lenny Harris	.15	.07	.02
☐ 66 Milt Thompson	.15	.07	.02
☐ 67 Storm Davis	.15	.07	.02
☐ 68 Joe Oliver	.15	.07	.02
☐ 69 Andres Galarraga	.60	.25	.07
☐ 70 Ozzie Guillen	.15	.07	.02
☐ 71 Ken Howell	.15	.07	.02
☐ 72 Garry Templeton	.15	.07	.02
☐ 73 Derrick May	.15	.07	.02
☐ 74 Xavier Hernandez	.15	.07	.02
☐ 75 Dave Parker	.30	.14	.04
☐ 76 Rick Aguilera	.30	.14	.04
☐ 77 Robby Thompson	.15	.07	.02
☐ 78 Pete Incaviglia	.15	.07	.02
☐ 79 Bob Welch	.15	.07	.02
☐ 80 Randy Milligan	.15	.07	.02
☐ 81 Chuck Finley	.30	.14	.04
☐ 82 Alvin Davis	.15	.07	.02
☐ 83 Tim Naehring	.30	.14	.04
☐ 84 Jay Bell	.30	.14	.04
☐ 85 Joe Magrane	.15	.07	.02
☐ 86 Howard Johnson	.15	.07	.02
☐ 87 Jack McDowell	.30	.14	.04
☐ 88 Kevin Seitzer	.15	.07	.02
☐ 89 Bruce Ruffin	.15	.07	.02
☐ 90 Fernando Valenzuela	.30	.14	.04
☐ 91 Terry Kennedy	.15	.07	.02
☐ 92 Barry Larkin	.60	.25	.07
☐ 93 Larry Walker	1.00	.45	.12
☐ 94 Luis Salazar	.15	.07	.02
☐ 95 Gary Sheffield	1.00	.45	.12
☐ 96 Bobby Witt	.15	.07	.02
☐ 97 Lonnie Smith	.15	.07	.02
☐ 98 Bryan Harvey	.15	.07	.02
☐ 99 Mookie Wilson	.15	.07	.02
☐ 100 Dwight Gooden	.30	.14	.04
☐ 101 Lou Whitaker	.30	.14	.04
☐ 102 Ron Karkovice	.15	.07	.02
☐ 103 Jesse Barfield	.15	.07	.02
☐ 104 Jose DeJesus	.15	.07	.02
☐ 105 Benito Santiago	.15	.07	.02
☐ 106 Brian Holman	.15	.07	.02
☐ 107 Rafael Ramirez	.15	.07	.02
☐ 108 Ellis Burks	.30	.14	.04
☐ 109 Mike Bielecki	.15	.07	.02
☐ 110 Kirby Puckett	2.00	.90	.25
☐ 111 Terry Shumpert	.15	.07	.02
☐ 112 Chuck Crim	.15	.07	.02
☐ 113 Todd Benzinger	.15	.07	.02
☐ 114 Brian Barnes	.15	.07	.02
☐ 115 Carlos Baerga	.60	.25	.07
☐ 116 Kal Daniels	.15	.07	.02
☐ 117 Dave Johnson	.15	.07	.02
☐ 118 Andy Van Slyke	.30	.14	.04
☐ 119 John Burkett	.30	.14	.04
☐ 120 Rickey Henderson	.60	.25	.07
☐ 121 Tim Jones	.15	.07	.02
☐ 122 Daryl Irvine	.15	.07	.02
☐ 123 Ruben Sierra	.30	.14	.04
☐ 124 Jim Abbott	.30	.14	.04
☐ 125 Daryl Boston	.15	.07	.02
☐ 126 Greg Maddux	3.00	1.35	.35
☐ 127 Von Hayes	.15	.07	.02
☐ 128 Mike Fitzgerald	.15	.07	.02
☐ 129 Wayne Edwards	.15	.07	.02
☐ 130 Greg Briley	.15	.07	.02
☐ 131 Rob Dibble	.15	.07	.02
☐ 132 Gene Larkin	.15	.07	.02
☐ 133 David Wells	.15	.07	.02
☐ 134 Steve Balboni	.15	.07	.02
☐ 135 Greg Vaughn	.30	.14	.04
☐ 136 Mark Davis	.15	.07	.02
☐ 137 Dave Rhode	.15	.07	.02
☐ 138 Eric Show	.15	.07	.02
☐ 139 Bobby Bonilla	.30	.14	.04
☐ 140 Dana Kiecker	.15	.07	.02
☐ 141 Gary Pettis	.15	.07	.02
☐ 142 Dennis Boyd	.15	.07	.02
☐ 143 Mike Benjamin	.15	.07	.02
☐ 144 Luis Polonia	.15	.07	.02
☐ 145 Doug Jones	.15	.07	.02
☐ 146 Al Newman	.15	.07	.02
☐ 147 Alex Fernandez	1.50	.70	.19
☐ 148 Bill Doran	.15	.07	.02
☐ 149 Kevin Elster	.15	.07	.02
☐ 150 Len Dykstra	.30	.14	.04
☐ 151 Mike Gallego	.15	.07	.02
☐ 152 Tim Belcher	.15	.07	.02
☐ 153 Jay Buhner	.60	.25	.07
☐ 154 Ozzie Smith UER (Rookie card is 1979, but card back says '78)	1.25	.55	.16
☐ 155 Jose Canseco	.60	.25	.07
☐ 156 Gregg Olson	.15	.07	.02
☐ 157 Charlie O'Brien	.15	.07	.02
☐ 158 Frank Tanana	.15	.07	.02
☐ 159 George Brett	2.00	.90	.25
☐ 160 Jeff Huson	.15	.07	.02
☐ 161 Kevin Tapani	.15	.07	.02
☐ 162 Jerome Walton	.15	.07	.02
☐ 163 Charlie Hayes	.15	.07	.02
☐ 164 Chris Bosio	.15	.07	.02
☐ 165 Chris Sabo	.15	.07	.02
☐ 166 Lance Parrish	.15	.07	.02
☐ 167 Don Robinson	.15	.07	.02
☐ 168 Manny Lee	.15	.07	.02
☐ 169 Dennis Rasmussen	.15	.07	.02
☐ 170 Wade Boggs	.60	.25	.07
☐ 171 Bob Geren	.15	.07	.02
☐ 172 Mackey Sasser	.15	.07	.02
☐ 173 Julio Franco	.30	.14	.04
☐ 174 Otis Nixon	.15	.07	.02
☐ 175 Bert Blyleven	.30	.14	.04
☐ 176 Craig Biggio	.60	.25	.07
☐ 177 Eddie Murray	1.25	.55	.16
☐ 178 Randy Tomlin	.15	.07	.02
☐ 179 Tino Martinez	.60	.25	.07
☐ 180 Carlton Fisk	.60	.25	.07
☐ 181 Dwight Smith	.15	.07	.02
☐ 182 Scott Garrelts	.15	.07	.02
☐ 183 Jim Gantner	.15	.07	.02
☐ 184 Dickie Thon	.15	.07	.02
☐ 185 John Farrell	.15	.07	.02
☐ 186 Cecil Fielder	.30	.14	.04
☐ 187 Glenn Braggs	.15	.07	.02
☐ 188 Allan Anderson	.15	.07	.02
☐ 189 Kurt Stillwell	.15	.07	.02
☐ 190 Jose Oquendo	.15	.07	.02
☐ 191 Joe Orsulak	.15	.07	.02
☐ 192 Ricky Jordan	.15	.07	.02
☐ 193 Kelly Downs	.15	.07	.02
☐ 194 Delino DeShields	.15	.07	.02
☐ 195 Omar Vizquel	.60	.25	.07
☐ 196 Mark Carreon	.15	.07	.02
☐ 197 Mike Harkey	.15	.07	.02
☐ 198 Jack Howell	.15	.07	.02
☐ 199 Lance Johnson	.30	.14	.04
☐ 200 Nolan Ryan TUX	5.00	2.20	.60
☐ 201 John Marzano	.15	.07	.02
☐ 202 Doug Drabek	.15	.07	.02
☐ 203 Mark Lemke	.15	.07	.02
☐ 204 Steve Sax	.15	.07	.02
☐ 205 Greg Harris	.15	.07	.02
☐ 206 B.J. Surhoff	.30	.14	.04
☐ 207 Todd Burns	.15	.07	.02
☐ 208 Jose Gonzalez	.15	.07	.02
☐ 209 Mike Scott	.15	.07	.02
☐ 210 Dave Magadan	.15	.07	.02
☐ 211 Dante Bichette	.75	.35	.09
☐ 212 Trevor Wilson	.15	.07	.02
☐ 213 Hector Villanueva	.15	.07	.02
☐ 214 Dan Pasqua	.15	.07	.02
☐ 215 Greg Colbrunn	.30	.14	.04
☐ 216 Mike Jeffcoat	.15	.07	.02
☐ 217 Harold Reynolds	.15	.07	.02
☐ 218 Paul O'Neill	.30	.14	.04
☐ 219 Mark Guthrie	.15	.07	.02
☐ 220 Barry Bonds	1.25	.55	.16
☐ 221 Jimmy Key	.30	.14	.04
☐ 222 Billy Ripken	.15	.07	.02
☐ 223 Tom Pagnozzi	.15	.07	.02
☐ 224 Bo Jackson	.30	.14	.04
☐ 225 Sid Fernandez	.15	.07	.02
☐ 226 Mike Marshall	.15	.07	.02
☐ 227 John Kruk	.30	.14	.04
☐ 228 Mike Fetters	.15	.07	.02
☐ 229 Eric Anthony	.15	.07	.02
☐ 230 Ryne Sandberg	1.25	.55	.16
☐ 231 Carney Lansford	.30	.14	.04
☐ 232 Melido Perez	.15	.07	.02
☐ 233 Jose Lind	.15	.07	.02
☐ 234 Darryl Hamilton	.30	.14	.04
☐ 235 Tom Browning	.15	.07	.02
☐ 236 Spike Owen	.15	.07	.02
☐ 237 Juan Gonzalez	8.00	3.60	1.00
☐ 238 Felix Fermin	.15	.07	.02
☐ 239 Keith Miller	.15	.07	.02
☐ 240 Mark Gubicza	.15	.07	.02
☐ 241 Kent Anderson	.15	.07	.02
☐ 242 Alvaro Espinoza	.15	.07	.02
☐ 243 Dale Murphy	.60	.25	.07
☐ 244 Orel Hershiser	.30	.14	.04
☐ 245 Paul Molitor	1.00	.45	.12
☐ 246 Eddie Whitson	.15	.07	.02
☐ 247 Joe Girardi	.30	.14	.04
☐ 248 Kent Hrbek	.30	.14	.04
☐ 249 Bill Sampen	.15	.07	.02
☐ 250 Kevin Mitchell	.30	.14	.04
☐ 251 Mariano Duncan	.15	.07	.02
☐ 252 Scott Bradley	.15	.07	.02
☐ 253 Mike Greenwell	.15	.07	.02
☐ 254 Tom Gordon	.15	.07	.02
☐ 255 Todd Zeile	.30	.14	.04
☐ 256 Bobby Thigpen	.15	.07	.02
☐ 257 Gregg Jefferies	.30	.14	.04
☐ 258 Kenny Rogers	.15	.07	.02
☐ 259 Shane Mack	.15	.07	.02
☐ 260 Zane Smith	.15	.07	.02
☐ 261 Mitch Williams	.15	.07	.02
☐ 262 Jim Deshaies	.15	.07	.02
☐ 263 Dave Winfield	.60	.25	.07
☐ 264 Ben McDonald	.30	.14	.04
☐ 265 Randy Ready	.15	.07	.02
☐ 266 Pat Borders	.15	.07	.02
☐ 267 Jose Uribe	.15	.07	.02
☐ 268 Derek Lilliquist	.15	.07	.02
☐ 269 Greg Brock	.15	.07	.02
☐ 270 Ken Griffey Jr.	10.00	4.50	1.25
☐ 271 Jeff Gray	.15	.07	.02
☐ 272 Danny Tartabull	.15	.07	.02
☐ 273 Denny Martinez	.30	.14	.04
☐ 274 Robin Ventura	.60	.25	.07
☐ 275 Randy Myers	.30	.14	.04
☐ 276 Jack Daugherty	.15	.07	.02
☐ 277 Greg Gagne	.15	.07	.02
☐ 278 Jay Howell	.15	.07	.02
☐ 279 Mike LaValliere	.15	.07	.02
☐ 280 Rex Hudler	.15	.07	.02
☐ 281 Mike Simms	.15	.07	.02
☐ 282 Kevin Maas	.15	.07	.02
☐ 283 Jeff Ballard	.15	.07	.02
☐ 284 Dave Henderson	.15	.07	.02
☐ 285 Pete O'Brien	.15	.07	.02
☐ 286 Brook Jacoby	.15	.07	.02
☐ 287 Mike Henneman	.15	.07	.02
☐ 288 Greg Olson	.15	.07	.02
☐ 289 Greg Myers	.15	.07	.02
☐ 290 Mark Grace	.60	.25	.07
☐ 291 Shawn Abner	.15	.07	.02
☐ 292 Frank Viola	.15	.07	.02
☐ 293 Lee Stevens	.15	.07	.02
☐ 294 Jason Grimsley	.15	.07	.02
☐ 295 Matt Williams	.60	.25	.07
☐ 296 Ron Robinson	.15	.07	.02
☐ 297 Tom Brunansky	.15	.07	.02
☐ 298 Checklist 1-100	.15	.07	.02
☐ 299 Checklist 101-200	.15	.07	.02
☐ 300 Checklist 201-300	.15	.07	.02
☐ 301 Darryl Strawberry	.30	.14	.04
☐ 302 Bud Black	.15	.07	.02
☐ 303 Harold Baines	.30	.14	.04
☐ 304 Roberto Alomar	1.00	.45	.12
☐ 305 Norm Charlton	.15	.07	.02
☐ 306 Gary Thurman	.15	.07	.02
☐ 307 Mike Felder	.15	.07	.02
☐ 308 Tony Gwynn	2.00	.90	.25
☐ 309 Roger Clemens	1.00	.45	.12
☐ 310 Andre Dawson	.30	.14	.04
☐ 311 Scott Radinsky	.15	.07	.02
☐ 312 Bob Melvin	.15	.07	.02
☐ 313 Kirk McCaskill	.15	.07	.02
☐ 314 Pedro Guerrero	.15	.07	.02
☐ 315 Walt Terrell	.15	.07	.02
☐ 316 Sam Horn	.15	.07	.02
☐ 317 Wes Chamberlain UER (Card listed as 1989 Debut card, should be 1990)	.15	.07	.02
☐ 318 Pedro Munoz	.30	.14	.04
☐ 319 Roberto Kelly	.15	.07	.02
☐ 320 Mark Portugal	.15	.07	.02
☐ 321 Tim McIntosh	.15	.07	.02
☐ 322 Jesse Orosco	.15	.07	.02
☐ 323 Gary Green	.15	.07	.02
☐ 324 Greg Harris	.15	.07	.02
☐ 325 Hubie Brooks	.15	.07	.02
☐ 326 Chris Nabholz	.15	.07	.02
☐ 327 Terry Pendleton	.30	.14	.04
☐ 328 Eric King	.15	.07	.02
☐ 329 Chili Davis	.30	.14	.04
☐ 330 Anthony Telford	.15	.07	.02
☐ 331 Kelly Gruber	.15	.07	.02
☐ 332 Dennis Eckersley	.30	.14	.04
☐ 333 Mel Hall	.15	.07	.02
☐ 334 Bob Kipper	.15	.07	.02
☐ 335 Willie McGee	.15	.07	.02
☐ 336 Steve Olin	.15	.07	.02

Card			
337 Steve Buechele	.15	.07	.02
338 Scott Leius	.15	.07	.02
339 Hal Morris	.15	.07	.02
340 Jose Offerman	.15	.07	.02
341 Kent Mercker	.15	.07	.02
342 Ken Griffey Sr.	.15	.07	.02
343 Pete Harnisch	.15	.07	.02
344 Kirk Gibson	.30	.14	.04
345 Dave Smith	.15	.07	.02
346 Dave Martinez	.15	.07	.02
347 Atlee Hammaker	.15	.07	.02
348 Brian Downing	.15	.07	.02
349 Todd Hundley	2.00	.90	.25
350 Candy Maldonado	.15	.07	.02
351 Dwight Evans	.30	.14	.04
352 Steve Searcy	.15	.07	.02
353 Gary Gaetti	.30	.14	.04
354 Jeff Reardon	.30	.14	.04
355 Travis Fryman	1.50	.70	.19
356 Dave Righetti	.15	.07	.02
357 Fred McGriff	.60	.25	.07
358 Don Slaught	.15	.07	.02
359 Gene Nelson	.15	.07	.02
360 Billy Spiers	.15	.07	.02
361 Lee Guetterman	.15	.07	.02
362 Darren Lewis	.30	.14	.04
363 Duane Ward	.15	.07	.02
364 Lloyd Moseby	.15	.07	.02
365 John Smoltz	1.00	.45	.12
366 Felix Jose	.15	.07	.02
367 David Cone	.30	.14	.04
368 Wally Backman	.15	.07	.02
369 Jeff Montgomery	.30	.14	.04
370 Rich Garces	.15	.07	.02
371 Billy Hatcher	.15	.07	.02
372 Bill Swift	.15	.07	.02
373 Jim Eisenreich	.30	.14	.04
374 Rob Ducey	.15	.07	.02
375 Tim Crews	.15	.07	.02
376 Steve Finley	.30	.14	.04
377 Jeff Blauser	.15	.07	.02
378 Willie Wilson	.15	.07	.02
379 Gerald Perry	.15	.07	.02
380 Jose Mesa	.30	.14	.04
381 Pat Kelly	.30	.14	.04
382 Matt Merullo	.15	.07	.02
383 Ivan Calderon	.15	.07	.02
384 Scott Chiamparino	.15	.07	.02
385 Lloyd McClendon	.15	.07	.02
386 Dave Bergman	.15	.07	.02
387 Ed Sprague	.30	.14	.04
388 Jeff Bagwell	6.00	2.70	.75
389 Brett Butler	.30	.14	.04
390 Larry Andersen	.15	.07	.02
391 Glenn Davis	.15	.07	.02
392 Alex Cole UER	.15	.07	.02
(Front photo actually			
Otis Nixon)			
393 Mike Heath	.15	.07	.02
394 Danny Darwin	.15	.07	.02
395 Steve Lake	.15	.07	.02
396 Tim Layana	.15	.07	.02
397 Terry Leach	.15	.07	.02
398 Bill Wegman	.15	.07	.02
399 Mark McGwire	1.50	.70	.19
400 Mike Boddicker	.15	.07	.02
401 Steve Howe	.15	.07	.02
402 Bernard Gilkey	.30	.14	.04
403 Thomas Howard	.15	.07	.02
404 Rafael Belliard	.15	.07	.02
405 Tom Candiotti	.15	.07	.02
406 Rene Gonzales	.15	.07	.02
407 Chuck McElroy	.15	.07	.02
408 Paul Sorrento	.30	.14	.04
409 Randy Johnson	1.00	.45	.12
410 Brady Anderson	.60	.25	.07
411 Dennis Cook	.15	.07	.02
412 Mickey Tettleton	.30	.14	.04
413 Mike Stanton	.15	.07	.02
414 Ken Oberkfell	.15	.07	.02
415 Rick Honeycutt	.15	.07	.02
416 Nelson Santovenia	.15	.07	.02
417 Bob Tewksbury	.15	.07	.02
418 Brent Mayne	.15	.07	.02
419 Steve Farr	.15	.07	.02
420 Phil Stephenson	.15	.07	.02
421 Jeff Russell	.15	.07	.02
422 Chris James	.15	.07	.02
423 Tim Leary	.15	.07	.02
424 Gary Carter	.30	.14	.04
425 Glenallen Hill	.15	.07	.02
426 Matt Young UER	.15	.07	.02
(Card mentions 83T/Tr			
as RC, but 84T shown)			
427 Sid Bream	.15	.07	.02
428 Greg Swindell	.15	.07	.02
429 Scott Aldred	.15	.07	.02
430 Cal Ripken	4.00	1.80	.50
431 Bill Landrum	.15	.07	.02
432 Earnest Riles	.15	.07	.02
433 Danny Jackson	.15	.07	.02
434 Casey Candaele	.15	.07	.02
435 Ken Hill	.30	.14	.04
436 Jaime Navarro	.15	.07	.02
437 Lance Blankenship	.15	.07	.02
438 Randy Velarde	.15	.07	.02
439 Frank DiPino	.15	.07	.02
440 Carl Nichols	.15	.07	.02
441 Jeff M. Robinson	.15	.07	.02
442 Deion Sanders	.75	.35	.09
443 Vicente Palacios	.15	.07	.02
444 Devon White	.30	.14	.04
445 John Cerutti	.15	.07	.02
446 Tracy Jones	.15	.07	.02
447 Jack Morris	.30	.14	.04
448 Mitch Webster	.15	.07	.02
449 Bob Ojeda	.15	.07	.02
450 Oscar Azocar	.15	.07	.02
451 Luis Aquino	.15	.07	.02
452 Mark Whiten	.30	.14	.04
453 Stan Belinda	.15	.07	.02
454 Ron Gant	.30	.14	.04
455 Jose DeLeon	.15	.07	.02
456 Mark Salas UER	.15	.07	.02
(Back has 85T photo,			
but calls it 86T)			
457 Junior Felix	.15	.07	.02
458 Wally Whitehurst	.15	.07	.02
459 Phil Plantier	.30	.14	.04
460 Juan Berenguer	.15	.07	.02
461 Franklin Stubbs	.15	.07	.02
462 Joe Boever	.15	.07	.02
463 Tim Wallach	.15	.07	.02
464 Mike Moore	.15	.07	.02
465 Albert Belle	3.00	1.35	.35
466 Mike Witt	.15	.07	.02
467 Craig Worthington	.15	.07	.02
468 Jerald Clark	.15	.07	.02
469 Scott Terry	.15	.07	.02
470 Milt Cuyler	.15	.07	.02
471 John Smiley	.15	.07	.02
472 Charles Nagy	1.00	.45	.12
473 Alan Mills	.15	.07	.02
474 John Russell	.15	.07	.02
475 Bruce Hurst	.15	.07	.02
476 Andujar Cedeno	.15	.07	.02
477 Dave Eiland	.15	.07	.02
478 Brian McRae	.75	.35	.09
479 Mike LaCoss	.15	.07	.02
480 Chris Gwynn	.15	.07	.02
481 Jamie Moyer	.15	.07	.02
482 John Olerud	.30	.14	.04
483 Efrain Valdez	.15	.07	.02
484 Sil Campusano	.15	.07	.02
485 Pascual Perez	.15	.07	.02
486 Gary Redus	.15	.07	.02
487 Andy Hawkins	.15	.07	.02
488 Cory Snyder	.15	.07	.02
489 Chris Hoiles	.15	.07	.02
490 Ron Hassey	.15	.07	.02
491 Gary Wayne	.15	.07	.02
492 Mark Lewis	.15	.07	.02
493 Scott Coolbaugh	.15	.07	.02
494 Gerald Young	.15	.07	.02
495 Juan Samuel	.15	.07	.02
496 Willie Fraser	.15	.07	.02
497 Jeff Treadway	.15	.07	.02
498 Vince Coleman	.15	.07	.02
499 Cris Carpenter	.15	.07	.02
500 Jack Clark	.30	.14	.04
501 Kevin Appier	.75	.35	.09
502 Rafael Palmeiro	.60	.25	.07
503 Hensley Meulens	.15	.07	.02
504 George Bell	.15	.07	.02
505 Tony Pena	.15	.07	.02
506 Roger McDowell	.15	.07	.02
507 Luis Sojo	.15	.07	.02
508 Mike Schooler	.15	.07	.02
509 Robin Yount	.60	.25	.07
510 Jack Armstrong	.15	.07	.02
511 Rick Cerone	.15	.07	.02
512 Curt Wilkerson	.15	.07	.02
513 Joe Carter	.30	.14	.04
514 Tim Burke	.15	.07	.02
515 Tony Fernandez	.15	.07	.02
516 Ramon Martinez	.60	.25	.07
517 Tim Hulett	.15	.07	.02
518 Terry Steinbach	.30	.14	.04
519 Pete Smith	.15	.07	.02
520 Ken Caminiti	.75	.35	.09
521 Shawn Boskie	.15	.07	.02
522 Mike Pagliarulo	.15	.07	.02
523 Tim Raines	.60	.25	.07
524 Alfredo Griffin	.15	.07	.02
525 Henry Cotto	.15	.07	.02
526 Mike Stanley	.15	.07	.02
527 Charlie Leibrandt	.15	.07	.02
528 Jeff King	.30	.14	.04
529 Eric Plunk	.15	.07	.02
530 Tom Lampkin	.15	.07	.02
531 Steve Bedrosian	.15	.07	.02
532 Tom Herr	.15	.07	.02
533 Craig Lefferts	.15	.07	.02
534 Jeff Reed	.15	.07	.02
535 Mickey Morandini	.15	.07	.02
536 Greg Cadaret	.15	.07	.02
537 Ray Lankford	1.50	.70	.19
538 John Candelaria	.15	.07	.02
539 Rob Deer	.15	.07	.02
540 Brad Arnsberg	.15	.07	.02
541 Mike Sharperson	.15	.07	.02
542 Jeff D. Robinson	.15	.07	.02
543 Mo Vaughn	5.00	2.20	.60
544 Jeff Parrett	.15	.07	.02
545 Willie Randolph	.30	.14	.04
546 Herm Winningham	.15	.07	.02
547 Jeff Innis	.15	.07	.02
548 Chuck Knoblauch	3.00	1.35	.35
549 Tommy Greene UER	.15	.07	.02
(Born in North Carolina,			
not South Carolina)			
550 Jeff Hamilton	.15	.07	.02
551 Barry Jones	.15	.07	.02
552 Ken Dayley	.15	.07	.02
553 Rick Dempsey	.15	.07	.02
554 Greg Smith	.15	.07	.02
555 Mike Devereaux	.15	.07	.02
556 Keith Comstock	.15	.07	.02
557 Paul Faries	.15	.07	.02
558 Tom Glavine	.60	.25	.07
559 Craig Grebeck	.15	.07	.02
560 Scott Erickson	.30	.14	.04
561 Joel Skinner	.15	.07	.02
562 Mike Morgan	.15	.07	.02
563 Dave Gallagher	.15	.07	.02
564 Todd Stottlemyre	.15	.07	.02
565 Rich Rodriguez	.15	.07	.02
566 Craig Wilson	.15	.07	.02
567 Jeff Brantley	.15	.07	.02
568 Scott Kamieniecki	.15	.07	.02
569 Steve Decker	.15	.07	.02
570 Juan Agosto	.15	.07	.02
571 Tommy Gregg	.15	.07	.02
572 Kevin Wickander	.15	.07	.02
573 Jamie Quirk UER	.15	.07	.02
(Rookie card is 1976,			
but card back is 1990)			
574 Jerry Don Gleaton	.15	.07	.02
575 Chris Hammond	.15	.07	.02
576 Luis Gonzalez	.60	.25	.07
577 Russ Swan	.15	.07	.02
578 Jeff Conine	1.50	.70	.19
579 Charlie Hough	.15	.07	.02
580 Jeff Kunkel	.15	.07	.02
581 Darrel Akerfelds	.15	.07	.02
582 Jeff Manto	.15	.07	.02
583 Alejandro Pena	.15	.07	.02
584 Mark Davidson	.15	.07	.02
585 Bob MacDonald	.15	.07	.02
586 Paul Assenmacher	.15	.07	.02
587 Dan Wilson	.75	.35	.09
588 Tom Bolton	.15	.07	.02
589 Brian Harper	.15	.07	.02
590 John Habyan	.15	.07	.02
591 John Orton	.15	.07	.02
592 Mark Gardner	.15	.07	.02
593 Turner Ward	.15	.07	.02
594 Bob Patterson	.15	.07	.02
595 Ed Nunez	.15	.07	.02
596 Gary Scott UER	.15	.07	.02
(Major League Batting			
Record should be			
Minor League)			
597 Scott Bankhead	.15	.07	.02
598 Checklist 301-400	.15	.07	.02
599 Checklist 401-500	.15	.07	.02
600 Checklist 501-600	.15	.07	.02

1991 Stadium Club Charter Member *

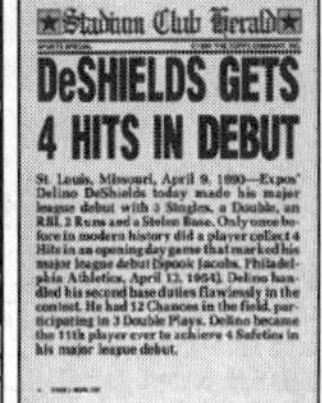

This 50-card multi-sport standard-size set was sent to charter members in the Topps Stadium Club. The sports represented in the set are baseball (1-32), football (33-41), and hockey (42-50). The cards feature on the fronts full-bleed posed and action glossy color player photos. The player's name is shown in the light blue stripe that intersects the Stadium Club logo near the bottom of the picture. The words "Charter Member" are printed in gold foil lettering immediately below the stripe. The back design features a newspaper-like masthead (The Stadium Club Herald) complete with a headline announcing a major event in the player's season with copy below providing more information about the event. The cards are unnumbered and arranged below alphabetically within sports. Topps apparently made two printings of this set, which are most easily identifiable by the small asterisks on the bottom left of the card backs. The first printing cards have one asterisk, the second printing cards have two. The display box that contained the cards also included a Nolan Ryan bronze metallic card and a key chain. Very early members of the Stadium Club received a large size bronze metallic Nolan Ryan 1990 Topps card. This card is valued at between $150-200.

	MINT	NRMT	EXC
COMPLETE SET (50)	20.00	9.00	2.50
COMMON CARD (1-50)	.10	.05	.01
1 Sandy Alomar	.20	.09	.03
2 George Brett	1.25	.55	.16
3 Barry Bonds	1.00	.45	.12
4 Ellis Burks	.20	.09	.03
5 Eric Davis	.10	.05	.01
6 Delino DeShields	.10	.05	.01
7 Doug Drabek	.10	.05	.01
8 Cecil Fielder	.20	.09	.03
9 Carlton Fisk	.40	.18	.05
10 Ken Griffey Jr.	4.00	1.80	.50
and Ken Griffey Sr.			
11 Billy Hatcher	.10	.05	.01
12 Andy Hawkins	.10	.05	.01
13 Rickey Henderson	.40	.18	.05
A.L. Recognizes			
Rickey As MVP			
14 Rickey Henderson	.40	.18	.05
Rickey is A.L.'s			
Leading Thief			
15 Randy Johnson	.75	.35	.09
16 Dave Justice	.50	.23	.06
17 Mark Langston	.10	.05	.01
and Mike Witt			
18 Kevin Maas	.10	.05	.01
19 Ramon Martinez	.30	.14	.04
20 Willie McGee	.10	.05	.01
21 Terry Mulholland	.10	.05	.01
22 Jose Offerman	.10	.05	.01
23 Melido Perez	.10	.05	.01
24 Nolan Ryan	3.00	1.35	.35
A No-Hitter For			
The Ages			
25 Nolan Ryan	3.00	1.35	.35
Nolan Ryan Earns			
300th Career Win			
26 Ryne Sandberg	1.00	.45	.12
27 Dave Stewart	.10	.05	.01
28 Dave Stieb	.10	.05	.01
29 Bobby Thigpen	.10	.05	.01
30 Fernando Valenzuela	.20	.09	.03
31 Frank Viola	.10	.05	.01
32 Bob Welch	.10	.05	.01
33 Ottis Anderson	.10	.05	.01
Anderson, MVP of			
Super Bowl XXV			
34 Ottis Anderson	.10	.05	.01
Ottis The Giant			
Reaches 10,000			
35 Randall Cunningham	.20	.09	.03
36 Warren Moon	.40	.18	.05
37 Barry Sanders	1.50	.70	.19
38 Pete Stoyanovich	.10	.05	.01
39 Lawrence Taylor	.40	.18	.05
40 Derrick Thomas	.20	.09	.03
41 Richmond Webb	.10	.05	.01
42 Ed Belfour	.50	.23	.06
Belfour Cops			
The Vezina			
43 Ed Belfour	.50	.23	.06
Belfour Is Top Goalie			
44 Ray Bourque	.50	.23	.06
45 Paul Coffey	.50	.23	.06
46 Wayne Gretzky	4.00	1.80	.50
Gretzky Takes			
No. 2000			
47 Wayne Gretzky	4.00	1.80	.50
The 700 Club			
48 Brett Hull	.75	.35	.09
Brett's All Hart			
49 Brett Hull	.75	.35	.09
Hull Joins 50-50			
Club			
50 Mario Lemieux	3.00	1.35	.35
NNO Nolan Ryan Bronze Medallion	10.00	4.50	1.25

1991 Stadium Club Members Only *

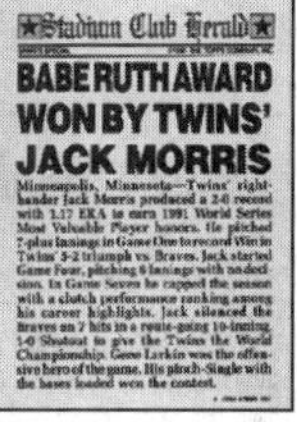

This 50-card multi-sport standard-size set was sent in three installments to members in the Topps Stadium Club. The first and second installments featured baseball players (card numbers 1-10 and 11-30), while the third spotlighted football (31-37) and hockey (38-50) players. The cards feature on the fronts full-bleed posed and action glossy color player photos. The player's name is shown in the light blue stripe that intersects the Stadium Club logo near the bottom of the picture. The words "Members Only" are printed in gold foil lettering immediately below the stripe. The back design features a newspaper-like masthead (The Stadium Club Herald) complete with a headline announcing a major event in the player's season with copy below providing more information about the event. The cards are unnumbered and arranged below alphabetically according to and within installments.

	MINT	NRMT	EXC
COMPLETE SET (50)	20.00	9.00	2.50
COMMON CARD (1-50)	.10	.05	.01
☐ 1 Wilson Alvarez	.30	.14	.04
☐ 2 Andy Ashby	.10	.05	.01
☐ 3 Tommy Greene	.10	.05	.01
☐ 4 Rickey Henderson	.40	.18	.05
Rickey Is Top			
Thief in History			
☐ 5 Denny Martinez	.30	.14	.04
☐ 6 Paul Molitor	.60	.25	.07
☐ 7 Nolan Ryan	3.00	1.35	.35
Ryan Extends Record			
With 7th No-Hitter			
☐ 8 Robby Thompson	.10	.05	.01
☐ 9 Dave Winfield	.50	.23	.06
☐ 10 Orioles No-Hitter	.10	.05	.01
Bob Milacki			
Mike Flanagan			
Mark Williamson			
Gregg Olson			
Chris Hoiles (C)			
☐ 11 Jeff Bagwell	1.50	.70	.19
☐ 12 Roger Clemens	.50	.23	.06
☐ 13 David Cone	.30	.14	.04
☐ 14 Carlton Fisk	.40	.18	.05
☐ 15 Julio Franco	.10	.05	.01
☐ 16 Tom Glavine	.50	.23	.06
☐ 17 Pete Harnisch	.10	.05	.01
☐ 18 Rickey Henderson	.40	.18	.05
Rickey Leads A.L. In			
Thefts For 11th Time			
☐ 19 Howard Johnson	.10	.05	.01
☐ 20 Chuck Knoblauch	.60	.25	.07
☐ 21 Ray Lankford			
☐ 22 Jack Morris	.30	.14	.04
☐ 23 Terry Pendleton	.30	.14	.04
NL's Leading Batsman			
☐ 24 Terry Pendleton	.30	.14	.04
Close MVP Race			
Favors Terry			
☐ 25 Jeff Reardon	.10	.05	.01
☐ 26 Cal Ripken	3.00	1.35	.35
☐ 27 Nolan Ryan	3.00	1.35	.35
Ryan's 22nd Straight			
Year With Over			
100 Strikeouts			
☐ 28 Bret Saberhagen	.10	.05	.01
☐ 29 AL Home Run Leaders	.50	.23	.06
Cecil Fielder			
Jose Canseco			
☐ 30 Braves No Hitter	.40	.18	.05
Kent Mercker			
Mark Wohlers			
Alejandro Pena			
☐ 31 Art Monk	.30	.14	.04
☐ 32 Warren Moon	.40	.18	.05
☐ 33 Leonard Russell	.10	.05	.01
☐ 34 Mark Rypien	.10	.05	.01
☐ 35 Barry Sanders	1.50	.70	.19
☐ 36 Emmitt Smith	3.00	1.35	.35
☐ 37 Tony Zendejas	.10	.05	.01
☐ 38 Pavel Bure	1.25	.55	.16
☐ 39 Guy Carbonneau	.10	.05	.01
☐ 40 Paul Coffey	.50	.23	.06
☐ 41 Mike Gartner	.30	.14	.04
Mike Makes It Two			
☐ 42 Mike Gartner	.30	.14	.04
Mike Makes It 500			
☐ 43 Michel Goulet	.10	.05	.01
☐ 44 Wayne Gretzky	4.00	1.80	.50
☐ 45 Brett Hull	.75	.35	.09
☐ 46 Brian Leetch	.50	.23	.06
☐ 47 Mario Lemieux	3.00	1.35	.35
Mario Repeats As MVP			
☐ 48 Mario Lemieux	3.00	1.35	.35
Lemieux Takes 3rd			
Ross Trophy			
☐ 49 Mark Messier	.75	.35	.09
☐ 50 Patrick Roy	2.50	1.10	.30

1992 Stadium Club Dome

The 1992 Stadium Club Dome set (issued by Topps) features 100 top draft picks, 56 1991 All-Star Game cards, 25 1991 Team U.S.A. cards, and 19 1991 Championship and World Series cards, all packaged in a factory set box inside a molded-plastic SkyDome display. Topps actually references this set as a 1991 set and the copyright lines on the card backs say 1991, but the set was released well into 1992. The standard-size cards display full-bleed glossy player photos on the fronts. The player's name appears in an sky-blue stripe that is accented by parallel gold stripes. Rookie Cards in this set include Shawn Green, Todd Hollandsworth, Alex Ochoa and Manny Ramirez.

	MINT	NRMT	EXC
COMPLETE FACT.SET (200)	12.00	5.50	1.50
COMMON CARD (1-200)	.10	.05	.01

	MINT	NRMT	EXC
☐ 1 Terry Adams	.20	.09	.03
☐ 2 Tommy Adams	.10	.05	.01
☐ 3 Rick Aguilera	.10	.05	.01
☐ 4 Ron Allen	.10	.05	.01
☐ 5 Roberto Alomar	.40	.18	.05
☐ 6 Sandy Alomar	.20	.09	.03
☐ 7 Greg Anthony	.10	.05	.01
☐ 8 James Austin	.10	.05	.01
☐ 9 Steve Avery	.20	.09	.03
☐ 10 Harold Baines	.20	.09	.03
☐ 11 Brian Barber	.20	.09	.03
☐ 12 Jon Barnes	.10	.05	.01
☐ 13 George Bell	.10	.05	.01
☐ 14 Doug Bennett	.10	.05	.01
☐ 15 Sean Bergman	.20	.09	.03
☐ 16 Craig Biggio	.20	.09	.03
☐ 17 Bill Bliss	.10	.05	.01
☐ 18 Wade Boggs	.30	.14	.04
☐ 19 Bobby Bonilla	.20	.09	.03
☐ 20 Russell Brock	.10	.05	.01
☐ 21 Tarrik Brock	.10	.05	.01
☐ 22 Tom Browning	.10	.05	.01
☐ 23 Brett Butler	.20	.09	.03
☐ 24 Ivan Calderon	.10	.05	.01
☐ 25 Joe Carter	.30	.14	.04
☐ 26 Joe Caruso	.10	.05	.01
☐ 27 Dan Cholowsky	.10	.05	.01
☐ 28 Will Clark	.30	.14	.04
☐ 29 Roger Clemens	.40	.18	.05
☐ 30 Shawn Curran	.10	.05	.01
☐ 31 Chris Curtis	.10	.05	.01
☐ 32 Chili Davis	.20	.09	.03
☐ 33 Andre Dawson	.20	.09	.03
☐ 34 Joe DeBerry	.10	.05	.01
☐ 35 John Dettmer	.10	.05	.01
☐ 36 Rob Dibble	.10	.05	.01
☐ 37 John Donati	.10	.05	.01
☐ 38 Dave Doorneweerd	.10	.05	.01
☐ 39 Darren Dreifort	.20	.09	.03
☐ 40 Mike Durant	.10	.05	.01
☐ 41 Chris Durkin	.10	.05	.01
☐ 42 Dennis Eckersley	.20	.09	.03
☐ 43 Brian Edmondson	.10	.05	.01
☐ 44 Vaughn Eshelman	.20	.09	.03
☐ 45 Shawn Estes	.30	.14	.04
☐ 46 Jorge Fabregas	.20	.09	.03
☐ 47 Jon Farrell	.10	.05	.01
☐ 48 Cecil Fielder	.20	.09	.03
☐ 49 Carlton Fisk	.30	.14	.04
☐ 50 Tim Flannelly	.10	.05	.01
☐ 51 Cliff Floyd	.75	.35	.09
☐ 52 Julio Franco	.20	.09	.03
☐ 53 Greg Gagne	.10	.05	.01
☐ 54 Chris Gambs	.10	.05	.01
☐ 55 Ron Gant	.20	.09	.03
☐ 56 Brent Gates	.20	.09	.03
☐ 57 Dwayne Gerald	.10	.05	.01
☐ 58 Jason Giambi	1.50	.70	.19
☐ 59 Benji Gil	.30	.14	.04
☐ 60 Mark Gipner	.10	.05	.01
☐ 61 Danny Gladden	.10	.05	.01
☐ 62 Tom Glavine	.30	.14	.04
☐ 63 Jimmy Gonzalez	.10	.05	.01
☐ 64 Jeff Granger	.20	.09	.03
☐ 65 Dan Grapenthien	.10	.05	.01
☐ 66 Dennis Gray	.10	.05	.01
☐ 67 Shawn Green	.60	.25	.07
☐ 68 Tyler Green	.20	.09	.03
☐ 69 Todd Greene	.30	.14	.04
☐ 70 Ken Griffey Jr.	2.50	1.10	.30
☐ 71 Kelly Gruber	.10	.05	.01
☐ 72 Ozzie Guillen	.10	.05	.01
☐ 73 Tony Gwynn	.75	.35	.09
☐ 74 Shane Halter	.10	.05	.01
☐ 75 Jeffrey Hammonds	.30	.14	.04
☐ 76 Larry Hanlon	.10	.05	.01
☐ 77 Pete Harnisch	.10	.05	.01
☐ 78 Mike Harrison	.10	.05	.01
☐ 79 Bryan Harvey	.10	.05	.01
☐ 80 Scott Hatteberg	.10	.05	.01
☐ 81 Rick Helling	.10	.05	.01
☐ 82 Dave Henderson	.10	.05	.01
☐ 83 Rickey Henderson	.30	.14	.04
☐ 84 Tyrone Hill	.10	.05	.01
☐ 85 Todd Hollandsworth	1.50	.70	.19
☐ 86 Brian Holliday	.10	.05	.01
☐ 87 Terry Horn	.10	.05	.01
☐ 88 Jeff Hostetler	.10	.05	.01
☐ 89 Kent Hrbek	.20	.09	.03
☐ 90 Mark Hubbard	.10	.05	.01
☐ 91 Charles Johnson	.75	.35	.09
☐ 92 Howard Johnson	.10	.05	.01
☐ 93 Todd Johnson	.10	.05	.01
☐ 94 Bobby Jones	.60	.25	.07
☐ 95 Dan Jones	.10	.05	.01
☐ 96 Felix Jose	.10	.05	.01
☐ 97 David Justice	.30	.14	.04
☐ 98 Jimmy Key	.20	.09	.03
☐ 99 Marc Kroon	.20	.09	.03
☐ 100 John Kruk	.20	.09	.03
☐ 101 Mark Langston	.20	.09	.03
☐ 102 Barry Larkin	.30	.14	.04
☐ 103 Mike LaValliere	.10	.05	.01
☐ 104 Scott Leius	.10	.05	.01
☐ 105 Mark Lemke	.10	.05	.01
☐ 106 Donnie Leshnock	.10	.05	.01
☐ 107 Jimmy Lewis	.10	.05	.01
☐ 108 Shane Livesy	.10	.05	.01
☐ 109 Ryan Long	.10	.05	.01
☐ 110 Trevor Mallory	.10	.05	.01
☐ 111 Denny Martinez	.20	.09	.03
☐ 112 Justin Mashore	.10	.05	.01
☐ 113 Jason McDonald	.20	.09	.03
☐ 114 Jack McDowell	.20	.09	.03
☐ 115 Tom McKinnon	.10	.05	.01
☐ 116 Billy McMillon	.20	.09	.03
☐ 117 Buck McNabb	.20	.09	.03
☐ 118 Jim Mecir	.10	.05	.01
☐ 119 Dan Melendez	.10	.05	.01
☐ 120 Shawn Miller	.20	.09	.03
☐ 121 Trever Miller	.10	.05	.01
☐ 122 Paul Molitor	.40	.18	.05
☐ 123 Vincent Moore	.10	.05	.01
☐ 124 Mike Morgan	.10	.05	.01
☐ 125 Jack Morris WS	.20	.09	.03
☐ 126 Jack Morris AS	.10	.05	.01
☐ 127 Sean Mulligan	.10	.05	.01
☐ 128 Eddie Murray AS	.50	.23	.06
☐ 129 Mike Neill	.10	.05	.01
☐ 130 Phil Nevin	.20	.09	.03
☐ 131 Mark O'Brien	.10	.05	.01
☐ 132 Alex Ochoa	1.00	.45	.12
☐ 133 Chad Ogea	.50	.23	.06
☐ 134 Greg Olson	.10	.05	.01
☐ 135 Paul O'Neill	.20	.09	.03
☐ 136 Jared Osentowski	.10	.05	.01
☐ 137 Mike Pagliarulo	.10	.05	.01
☐ 138 Rafael Palmeiro	.30	.14	.04
☐ 139 Rodney Pedraza	.10	.05	.01
☐ 140 Tony Phillips (P)	.10	.05	.01
☐ 141 Scott Pisciotta	.20	.09	.03
☐ 142 Christopher Pritchett	.10	.05	.01
☐ 143 Jason Pruitt	.10	.05	.01
☐ 144 Kirby Puckett WS UER	.75	.35	.09
(Championship series			
AB and BA is wrong)			
☐ 145 Kirby Puckett AS	.75	.35	.09
☐ 146 Manny Ramirez	4.00	1.80	.50
☐ 147 Eddie Ramos	.10	.05	.01
☐ 148 Mark Ratekin	.10	.05	.01
☐ 149 Jeff Reardon	.20	.09	.03
☐ 150 Sean Rees	.10	.05	.01
☐ 151 Calvin Reese	.30	.14	.04
☐ 152 Desmond Relaford	.20	.09	.03
☐ 153 Eric Richardson	.10	.05	.01
☐ 154 Cal Ripken	2.00	.90	.25
☐ 155 Chris Roberts	.20	.09	.03
☐ 156 Mike Robertson	.10	.05	.01
☐ 157 Steve Rodriguez	.10	.05	.01
☐ 158 Mike Rossiter	.10	.05	.01
☐ 159 Scott Ruffcorn	.20	.09	.03
☐ 160 Chris Sabo	.10	.05	.01
☐ 161 Juan Samuel	.10	.05	.01
☐ 162 Ryne Sandberg UER	.50	.23	.06
(On 5th line, prior			
misspelled as prilor)			
☐ 163 Scott Sanderson	.10	.05	.01
☐ 164 Benny Santiago	.10	.05	.01
☐ 165 Gene Schall	.10	.05	.01
☐ 166 Chad Schoenvogel	.10	.05	.01
☐ 167 Chris Seelbach	.20	.09	.03
☐ 168 Aaron Sele	.30	.14	.04
☐ 169 Basil Shabazz	.10	.05	.01
☐ 170 Al Shirley	.20	.09	.03
☐ 171 Paul Shuey	.10	.05	.01
☐ 172 Ruben Sierra	.30	.14	.04
☐ 173 John Smiley	.10	.05	.01
☐ 174 Lee Smith	.20	.09	.03
☐ 175 Ozzie Smith	.50	.23	.06
☐ 176 Tim Smith	.10	.05	.01
☐ 177 Zane Smith	.10	.05	.01
☐ 178 John Smoltz	.30	.14	.04
☐ 179 Scott Stahoviak	.30	.14	.04
☐ 180 Kennie Steenstra	.10	.05	.01
☐ 181 Kevin Stocker	.10	.05	.01
☐ 182 Chris Stynes	.20	.09	.03
☐ 183 Danny Tartabull	.10	.05	.01
☐ 184 Brien Taylor	.20	.09	.03
☐ 185 Todd Taylor	.10	.05	.01
☐ 186 Larry Thomas	.10	.05	.01
☐ 187 Ozzie Timmons	.20	.09	.03
(See also 188)			
☐ 188 David Tuttle UER	.10	.05	.01
(Mistakenly numbered			
as 187 on card)			
☐ 189 Andy Van Slyke	.20	.09	.03
☐ 190 Frank Viola	.10	.05	.01
☐ 191 Michael Walkden	.10	.05	.01
☐ 192 Jeff Ware	.10	.05	.01
☐ 193 Allen Watson	.20	.09	.03
☐ 194 Steve Whitaker	.10	.05	.01
☐ 195 Jerry Willard	.10	.05	.01
☐ 196 Craig Wilson	.10	.05	.01
☐ 197 Chris Wimmer	.10	.05	.01
☐ 198 Steve Wojciechowski	.10	.05	.01
☐ 199 Joel Wolfe	.10	.05	.01
☐ 200 Ivan Zweig	.10	.05	.01

1992 Stadium Club

The 1992 Stadium Club baseball card set consists of 900 standard-size cards issued in three series of 300 cards each. Cards were issued in plastic wrapped packs. A card-like application form for membership in Topps Stadium Club was inserted in each pack. The glossy color player photos on the fronts are full-bleed. The "Topps Stadium Club" logo is superimposed at the bottom of the card face, with the player's name appearing immediately below the logo. Some cards in the set have the Stadium Club logo printed upside down. The backs display a mini reprint of the player's rookie card and "BARS" (Baseball Analysis and Reporting System) statistics. Card numbers 591-610 form a "Members Choice" subset. The only notable Rookie Card in this set features Bill Pulsipher.

	MINT	NRMT	EXC
COMPLETE SET (900)	60.00	27.00	7.50
COMPLETE SERIES 1 (300)	20.00	9.00	2.50
COMPLETE SERIES 2 (300)	20.00	9.00	2.50
COMPLETE SERIES 3 (300)	20.00	9.00	2.50
COMMON CARD (1-900)	.10	.05	.01
☐ 1 Cal Ripken UER	2.00	.90	.25
(Misspelled Ripkin			
on card back)			
☐ 2 Eric Yelding	.10	.05	.01
☐ 3 Geno Petralli	.10	.05	.01
☐ 4 Wally Backman	.10	.05	.01
☐ 5 Milt Cuyler	.10	.05	.01
☐ 6 Kevin Bass	.10	.05	.01
☐ 7 Dante Bichette	.30	.14	.04
☐ 8 Ray Lankford	.30	.14	.04
☐ 9 Mel Hall	.10	.05	.01
☐ 10 Joe Carter	.15	.07	.02
☐ 11 Juan Samuel	.10	.05	.01
☐ 12 Jeff Montgomery	.15	.07	.02
☐ 13 Glenn Braggs	.10	.05	.01
☐ 14 Henry Cotto	.10	.05	.01
☐ 15 Deion Sanders	.30	.14	.04
☐ 16 Dick Schofield	.10	.05	.01
☐ 17 David Cone	.15	.07	.02
☐ 18 Chili Davis	.15	.07	.02
☐ 19 Tom Foley	.10	.05	.01
☐ 20 Ozzie Guillen	.10	.05	.01
☐ 21 Luis Salazar	.10	.05	.01
☐ 22 Terry Steinbach	.15	.07	.02
☐ 23 Chris James	.10	.05	.01
☐ 24 Jeff King	.15	.07	.02
☐ 25 Carlos Quintana	.10	.05	.01
☐ 26 Mike Maddux	.10	.05	.01
☐ 27 Tommy Greene	.10	.05	.01
☐ 28 Jeff Russell	.10	.05	.01
☐ 29 Steve Finley	.15	.07	.02
☐ 30 Mike Flanagan	.10	.05	.01
☐ 31 Darren Lewis	.10	.05	.01
☐ 32 Mark Lee	.10	.05	.01
☐ 33 Willie Fraser	.10	.05	.01
☐ 34 Mike Henneman	.10	.05	.01
☐ 35 Kevin Maas	.10	.05	.01
☐ 36 Dave Hansen	.10	.05	.01
☐ 37 Erik Hanson	.10	.05	.01
☐ 38 Bill Doran	.10	.05	.01
☐ 39 Mike Boddicker	.10	.05	.01
☐ 40 Vince Coleman	.10	.05	.01
☐ 41 Devon White	.15	.07	.02
☐ 42 Mark Gardner	.10	.05	.01
☐ 43 Scott Lewis	.10	.05	.01
☐ 44 Juan Berenguer	.10	.05	.01
☐ 45 Carney Lansford	.15	.07	.02
☐ 46 Curt Wilkerson	.10	.05	.01
☐ 47 Shane Mack	.10	.05	.01
☐ 48 Bip Roberts	.10	.05	.01
☐ 49 Greg A. Harris	.10	.05	.01
☐ 50 Ryne Sandberg	.50	.23	.06
☐ 51 Mark Whiten	.15	.07	.02
☐ 52 Jack McDowell	.15	.07	.02
☐ 53 Jimmy Jones	.10	.05	.01
☐ 54 Steve Lake	.10	.05	.01
☐ 55 Bud Black	.10	.05	.01
☐ 56 Dave Valle	.10	.05	.01

☐ 57 Kevin Reimer .10 .05 .01
☐ 58 Rich Gedman UER .10 .05 .01
(Wrong BARS chart used)
☐ 59 Travis Fryman .30 .14 .04
☐ 60 Steve Avery .15 .07 .02
☐ 61 Francisco de la Rosa .10 .05 .01
☐ 62 Scott Hemond .10 .05 .01
☐ 63 Hal Morris .10 .05 .01
☐ 64 Hensley Meulens .10 .05 .01
☐ 65 Frank Castillo .15 .07 .02
☐ 66 Gene Larkin .10 .05 .01
☐ 67 Jose DeLeon .10 .05 .01
☐ 68 Al Osuna .10 .05 .01
☐ 69 Dave Cochrane .10 .05 .01
☐ 70 Robin Ventura .15 .07 .02
☐ 71 John Cerutti .10 .05 .01
☐ 72 Kevin Gross .10 .05 .01
☐ 73 Ivan Calderon .10 .05 .01
☐ 74 Mike Macfarlane .10 .05 .01
☐ 75 Stan Belinda .10 .05 .01
☐ 76 Shawn Hillegas .10 .05 .01
☐ 77 Pat Borders .10 .05 .01
☐ 78 Jim Vatcher .10 .05 .01
☐ 79 Bobby Rose .10 .05 .01
☐ 80 Roger Clemens .40 .18 .05
☐ 81 Craig Worthington .10 .05 .01
☐ 82 Jeff Treadway .10 .05 .01
☐ 83 Jamie Quirk .10 .05 .01
☐ 84 Randy Bush .10 .05 .01
☐ 85 Anthony Young .10 .05 .01
☐ 86 Trevor Wilson .10 .05 .01
☐ 87 Jaime Navarro .10 .05 .01
☐ 88 Les Lancaster .10 .05 .01
☐ 89 Pat Kelly .10 .05 .01
☐ 90 Alvin Davis .10 .05 .01
☐ 91 Larry Andersen .10 .05 .01
☐ 92 Rob Deer .10 .05 .01
☐ 93 Mike Sharperson .10 .05 .01
☐ 94 Lance Parrish .10 .05 .01
☐ 95 Cecil Espy .10 .05 .01
☐ 96 Tim Spehr .10 .05 .01
☐ 97 Dave Stieb .10 .05 .01
☐ 98 Terry Mulholland .10 .05 .01
☐ 99 Dennis Boyd .10 .05 .01
☐ 100 Barry Larkin .30 .14 .04
☐ 101 Ryan Bowen .10 .05 .01
☐ 102 Felix Fermin .10 .05 .01
☐ 103 Luis Alicea .10 .05 .01
☐ 104 Tim Hulett .10 .05 .01
☐ 105 Rafael Belliard .10 .05 .01
☐ 106 Mike Gallego .10 .05 .01
☐ 107 Dave Righetti .10 .05 .01
☐ 108 Jeff Schaefer .10 .05 .01
☐ 109 Ricky Bones .10 .05 .01
☐ 110 Scott Erickson .15 .07 .02
☐ 111 Matt Nokes .10 .05 .01
☐ 112 Bob Scanlan .10 .05 .01
☐ 113 Tom Candiotti .10 .05 .01
☐ 114 Sean Berry .15 .07 .02
☐ 115 Kevin Morton .10 .05 .01
☐ 116 Scott Fletcher .10 .05 .01
☐ 117 B.J. Surhoff .15 .07 .02
☐ 118 Dave Magadan UER .10 .05 .01
(Born Tampa, not Tamps)
☐ 119 Bill Gullickson .10 .05 .01
☐ 120 Marquis Grissom .15 .07 .02
☐ 121 Lenny Harris .10 .05 .01
☐ 122 Wally Joyner .15 .07 .02
☐ 123 Kevin Brown .15 .07 .02
☐ 124 Braulio Castillo .10 .05 .01
☐ 125 Eric King .10 .05 .01
☐ 126 Mark Portugal .10 .05 .01
☐ 127 Calvin Jones .10 .05 .01
☐ 128 Mike Heath .10 .05 .01
☐ 129 Todd Van Poppel .10 .05 .01
☐ 130 Benny Santiago .10 .05 .01
☐ 131 Gary Thurman .10 .05 .01
☐ 132 Joe Girardi .10 .05 .01
☐ 133 Dave Eiland .10 .05 .01
☐ 134 Orlando Merced .15 .07 .02
☐ 135 Joe Orsulak .10 .05 .01
☐ 136 John Burkett .15 .07 .02
☐ 137 Ken Dayley .10 .05 .01
☐ 138 Ken Hill .15 .07 .02
☐ 139 Walt Terrell .10 .05 .01
☐ 140 Mike Scioscia .10 .05 .01
☐ 141 Junior Felix .10 .05 .01
☐ 142 Ken Caminiti .30 .14 .04
☐ 143 Carlos Baerga .15 .07 .02
☐ 144 Tony Fossas .10 .05 .01
☐ 145 Craig Grebeck .10 .05 .01
☐ 146 Scott Bradley .10 .05 .01
☐ 147 Kent Mercker .10 .05 .01
☐ 148 Derrick May .10 .05 .01
☐ 149 Jerald Clark .10 .05 .01
☐ 150 George Brett .75 .35 .09
☐ 151 Luis Quinones .10 .05 .01
☐ 152 Mike Pagliarulo .10 .05 .01
☐ 153 Jose Guzman .10 .05 .01
☐ 154 Charlie O'Brien .10 .05 .01
☐ 155 Darren Holmes .10 .05 .01
☐ 156 Joe Boever .10 .05 .01
☐ 157 Rich Monteleone .10 .05 .01
☐ 158 Reggie Harris .10 .05 .01
☐ 159 Roberto Alomar .40 .18 .05
☐ 160 Robby Thompson .10 .05 .01
☐ 161 Chris Hoiles .10 .05 .01
☐ 162 Tom Pagnozzi .10 .05 .01
☐ 163 Omar Vizquel .15 .07 .02
☐ 164 John Candelaria .10 .05 .01
☐ 165 Terry Shumpert .10 .05 .01
☐ 166 Andy Mota .10 .05 .01
☐ 167 Scott Bailes .10 .05 .01
☐ 168 Jeff Blauser .10 .05 .01
☐ 169 Steve Olin .10 .05 .01
☐ 170 Doug Drabek .10 .05 .01
☐ 171 Dave Bergman .10 .05 .01
☐ 172 Eddie Whitson .10 .05 .01
☐ 173 Gilberto Reyes .10 .05 .01
☐ 174 Mark Grace .30 .14 .04
☐ 175 Paul O'Neill .15 .07 .02
☐ 176 Greg Cadaret .10 .05 .01
☐ 177 Mark Williamson .10 .05 .01
☐ 178 Casey Candaele .10 .05 .01
☐ 179 Candy Maldonado .10 .05 .01
☐ 180 Lee Smith .15 .07 .02
☐ 181 Harold Reynolds .10 .05 .01
☐ 182 David Justice .30 .14 .04
☐ 183 Lenny Webster .10 .05 .01
☐ 184 Donn Pall .10 .05 .01
☐ 185 Gerald Alexander .10 .05 .01
☐ 186 Jack Clark .15 .07 .02
☐ 187 Stan Javier .10 .05 .01
☐ 188 Ricky Jordan .10 .05 .01
☐ 189 Franklin Stubbs .10 .05 .01
☐ 190 Dennis Eckersley .15 .07 .02
☐ 191 Danny Tartabull .10 .05 .01
☐ 192 Pete O'Brien .10 .05 .01
☐ 193 Mark Lewis .10 .05 .01
☐ 194 Mike Felder .10 .05 .01
☐ 195 Mickey Tettleton .10 .05 .01
☐ 196 Dwight Smith .10 .05 .01
☐ 197 Shawn Abner .10 .05 .01
☐ 198 Jim Leyritz UER .10 .05 .01
(Career totals less
than 1991 totals)
☐ 199 Mike Devereaux .10 .05 .01
☐ 200 Craig Biggio .15 .07 .02
☐ 201 Kevin Elster .10 .05 .01
☐ 202 Rance Mulliniks .10 .05 .01
☐ 203 Tony Fernandez .10 .05 .01
☐ 204 Allan Anderson .10 .05 .01
☐ 205 Herm Winningham .10 .05 .01
☐ 206 Tim Jones .10 .05 .01
☐ 207 Ramon Martinez .15 .07 .02
☐ 208 Teddy Higuera .10 .05 .01
☐ 209 John Kruk .15 .07 .02
☐ 210 Jim Abbott .10 .05 .01
☐ 211 Dean Palmer .15 .07 .02
☐ 212 Mark Davis .10 .05 .01
☐ 213 Jay Buhner .30 .14 .04
☐ 214 Jesse Barfield .10 .05 .01
☐ 215 Kevin Mitchell .15 .07 .02
☐ 216 Mike LaValliere .10 .05 .01
☐ 217 Mark Wohlers .30 .14 .04
☐ 218 Dave Henderson .10 .05 .01
☐ 219 Dave Smith .10 .05 .01
☐ 220 Albert Belle 1.00 .45 .12
☐ 221 Spike Owen .10 .05 .01
☐ 222 Jeff Gray .10 .05 .01
☐ 223 Paul Gibson .10 .05 .01
☐ 224 Bobby Thigpen .10 .05 .01
☐ 225 Mike Mussina .60 .25 .07
☐ 226 Darrin Jackson .10 .05 .01
☐ 227 Luis Gonzalez .15 .07 .02
☐ 228 Greg Briley .10 .05 .01
☐ 229 Brent Mayne .10 .05 .01
☐ 230 Paul Molitor .40 .18 .05
☐ 231 Al Leiter .15 .07 .02
☐ 232 Andy Van Slyke .15 .07 .02
☐ 233 Ron Tingley .10 .05 .01
☐ 234 Bernard Gilkey .15 .07 .02
☐ 235 Kent Hrbek .15 .07 .02
☐ 236 Eric Karros .30 .14 .04
☐ 237 Randy Velarde .10 .05 .01
☐ 238 Andy Allanson .10 .05 .01
☐ 239 Willie McGee .10 .05 .01
☐ 240 Juan Gonzalez 1.25 .55 .16
☐ 241 Karl Rhodes .10 .05 .01
☐ 242 Luis Mercedes .10 .05 .01
☐ 243 Billy Swift .10 .05 .01
☐ 244 Tommy Gregg .10 .05 .01
☐ 245 David Howard .10 .05 .01
☐ 246 Dave Hollins .10 .05 .01
☐ 247 Kip Gross .10 .05 .01
☐ 248 Walt Weiss .10 .05 .01
☐ 249 Mackey Sasser .10 .05 .01
☐ 250 Cecil Fielder .15 .07 .02
☐ 251 Jerry Browne .10 .05 .01
☐ 252 Doug Dascenzo .10 .05 .01
☐ 253 Darryl Hamilton .10 .05 .01
☐ 254 Dann Bilardello .10 .05 .01
☐ 255 Luis Rivera .10 .05 .01
☐ 256 Larry Walker .30 .14 .04
☐ 257 Ron Karkovice .10 .05 .01
☐ 258 Bob Tewksbury .10 .05 .01
☐ 259 Jimmy Key .15 .07 .02
☐ 260 Bernie Williams .50 .23 .06
☐ 261 Gary Wayne .10 .05 .01
☐ 262 Mike Simms UER .10 .05 .01
(Reversed negative)
☐ 263 John Orton .10 .05 .01
☐ 264 Marvin Freeman .10 .05 .01
☐ 265 Mike Jeffcoat .10 .05 .01
☐ 266 Roger Mason .10 .05 .01
☐ 267 Edgar Martinez .15 .07 .02
☐ 268 Henry Rodriguez .30 .14 .04
☐ 269 Sam Horn .10 .05 .01
☐ 270 Brian McRae .15 .07 .02
☐ 271 Kirt Manwaring .10 .05 .01
☐ 272 Mike Bordick .15 .07 .02
☐ 273 Chris Sabo .10 .05 .01
☐ 274 Jim Olander .10 .05 .01
☐ 275 Greg W. Harris .10 .05 .01
☐ 276 Dan Gakeler .10 .05 .01
☐ 277 Bill Sampen .10 .05 .01
☐ 278 Joel Skinner .10 .05 .01
☐ 279 Curt Schilling .10 .05 .01
☐ 280 Dale Murphy .30 .14 .04
☐ 281 Lee Stevens .10 .05 .01
☐ 282 Lonnie Smith .10 .05 .01
☐ 283 Manuel Lee .10 .05 .01
☐ 284 Shawn Boskie .10 .05 .01
☐ 285 Kevin Seitzer .10 .05 .01
☐ 286 Stan Royer .10 .05 .01
☐ 287 John Dopson .10 .05 .01
☐ 288 Scott Bullett .10 .05 .01
☐ 289 Ken Patterson .10 .05 .01
☐ 290 Todd Hundley .15 .07 .02
☐ 291 Tim Leary .10 .05 .01
☐ 292 Brett Butler .15 .07 .02
☐ 293 Gregg Olson .10 .05 .01
☐ 294 Jeff Brantley .15 .07 .02
☐ 295 Brian Holman .10 .05 .01
☐ 296 Brian Harper .10 .05 .01
☐ 297 Brian Bohanon .10 .05 .01
☐ 298 Checklist 1-100 .10 .05 .01
☐ 299 Checklist 101-200 .10 .05 .01
☐ 300 Checklist 201-300 .10 .05 .01
☐ 301 Frank Thomas 3.00 1.35 .35
☐ 302 Lloyd McClendon .10 .05 .01
☐ 303 Brady Anderson .30 .14 .04
☐ 304 Julio Valera .10 .05 .01
☐ 305 Mike Aldrete .10 .05 .01
☐ 306 Joe Oliver .10 .05 .01
☐ 307 Todd Stottlemyre .15 .07 .02
☐ 308 Rey Sanchez .10 .05 .01
☐ 309 Gary Sheffield UER .30 .14 .04
(Listed as 5'1",
should be 5'11")
☐ 310 Andujar Cedeno .10 .05 .01
☐ 311 Kenny Rogers .10 .05 .01
☐ 312 Bruce Hurst .10 .05 .01
☐ 313 Mike Schooler .10 .05 .01
☐ 314 Mike Benjamin .10 .05 .01
☐ 315 Chuck Finley .10 .05 .01
☐ 316 Mark Lemke .10 .05 .01
☐ 317 Scott Livingstone .10 .05 .01
☐ 318 Chris Nabholz .10 .05 .01
☐ 319 Mike Humphreys .10 .05 .01
☐ 320 Pedro Guerrero .10 .05 .01
☐ 321 Willie Banks .10 .05 .01
☐ 322 Tom Goodwin .15 .07 .02
☐ 323 Hector Wagner .10 .05 .01
☐ 324 Wally Ritchie .10 .05 .01
☐ 325 Mo Vaughn .75 .35 .09
☐ 326 Joe Klink .10 .05 .01
☐ 327 Cal Eldred .10 .05 .01
☐ 328 Daryl Boston .10 .05 .01
☐ 329 Mike Huff .10 .05 .01
☐ 330 Jeff Bagwell 1.25 .55 .16
☐ 331 Bob Milacki .10 .05 .01
☐ 332 Tom Prince .10 .05 .01
☐ 333 Pat Tabler .10 .05 .01
☐ 334 Ced Landrum .10 .05 .01
☐ 335 Reggie Jefferson .15 .07 .02
☐ 336 Mo Sanford .10 .05 .01
☐ 337 Kevin Ritz .10 .05 .01
☐ 338 Gerald Perry .10 .05 .01
☐ 339 Jeff Hamilton .10 .05 .01
☐ 340 Tim Wallach .10 .05 .01
☐ 341 Jeff Huson .10 .05 .01
☐ 342 Jose Melendez .10 .05 .01
☐ 343 Willie Wilson .10 .05 .01
☐ 344 Mike Stanton .10 .05 .01
☐ 345 Joel Johnston .10 .05 .01
☐ 346 Lee Guetterman .10 .05 .01
☐ 347 Francisco Oliveras .10 .05 .01
☐ 348 Dave Burba .10 .05 .01
☐ 349 Tim Crews .10 .05 .01
☐ 350 Scott Leius .10 .05 .01
☐ 351 Danny Cox .10 .05 .01
☐ 352 Wayne Housie .10 .05 .01
☐ 353 Chris Donnels .10 .05 .01
☐ 354 Chris George .10 .05 .01
☐ 355 Gerald Young .10 .05 .01
☐ 356 Roberto Hernandez .15 .07 .02
☐ 357 Neal Heaton .10 .05 .01
☐ 358 Todd Frohwirth .10 .05 .01
☐ 359 Jose Vizcaino .10 .05 .01
☐ 360 Jim Thome 1.50 .70 .19
☐ 361 Craig Wilson .10 .05 .01
☐ 362 Dave Haas .10 .05 .01
☐ 363 Billy Hatcher .10 .05 .01
☐ 364 John Barfield .10 .05 .01
☐ 365 Luis Aquino .10 .05 .01
☐ 366 Charlie Leibrandt .10 .05 .01
☐ 367 Howard Farmer .10 .05 .01
☐ 368 Bryn Smith .10 .05 .01
☐ 369 Mickey Morandini .10 .05 .01
☐ 370 Jose Canseco .30 .14 .04
(See also 597)
☐ 371 Jose Uribe .10 .05 .01
☐ 372 Bob MacDonald .10 .05 .01
☐ 373 Luis Sojo .10 .05 .01
☐ 374 Craig Shipley .10 .05 .01
☐ 375 Scott Bankhead .10 .05 .01
☐ 376 Greg Gagne .10 .05 .01
☐ 377 Scott Cooper .10 .05 .01
☐ 378 Jose Offerman .10 .05 .01
☐ 379 Billy Spiers .10 .05 .01
☐ 380 John Smiley .10 .05 .01
☐ 381 Jeff Carter .10 .05 .01
☐ 382 Heathcliff Slocumb .10 .05 .01
☐ 383 Jeff Tackett .10 .05 .01
☐ 384 John Kiely .10 .05 .01
☐ 385 John Vander Wal .10 .05 .01
☐ 386 Omar Olivares .10 .05 .01
☐ 387 Ruben Sierra .15 .07 .02
☐ 388 Tom Gordon .10 .05 .01
☐ 389 Charles Nagy .15 .07 .02
☐ 390 Dave Stewart .15 .07 .02
☐ 391 Pete Harnisch .10 .05 .01
☐ 392 Tim Burke .10 .05 .01
☐ 393 Roberto Kelly .10 .05 .01
☐ 394 Freddie Benavides .10 .05 .01
☐ 395 Tom Glavine .30 .14 .04
☐ 396 Wes Chamberlain .10 .05 .01
☐ 397 Eric Gunderson .10 .05 .01
☐ 398 Dave West .10 .05 .01
☐ 399 Ellis Burks .15 .07 .02
☐ 400 Ken Griffey Jr. 3.00 1.35 .35
☐ 401 Thomas Howard .10 .05 .01
☐ 402 Juan Guzman .15 .07 .02
☐ 403 Mitch Webster .10 .05 .01
☐ 404 Matt Merullo .10 .05 .01
☐ 405 Steve Buechele .10 .05 .01
☐ 406 Danny Jackson .10 .05 .01
☐ 407 Felix Jose .10 .05 .01
☐ 408 Doug Piatt .10 .05 .01
☐ 409 Jim Eisenreich .10 .05 .01
☐ 410 Bryan Harvey .10 .05 .01
☐ 411 Jim Austin .10 .05 .01
☐ 412 Jim Poole .10 .05 .01
☐ 413 Glenallen Hill .10 .05 .01
☐ 414 Gene Nelson .10 .05 .01
☐ 415 Ivan Rodriguez .75 .35 .09
☐ 416 Frank Tanana .10 .05 .01
☐ 417 Steve Decker .10 .05 .01
☐ 418 Jason Grimsley .10 .05 .01
☐ 419 Tim Layana .10 .05 .01
☐ 420 Don Mattingly 1.00 .45 .12
☐ 421 Jerome Walton .10 .05 .01
☐ 422 Rob Ducey .10 .05 .01
☐ 423 Andy Benes .15 .07 .02
☐ 424 John Marzano .10 .05 .01
☐ 425 Gene Harris .10 .05 .01
☐ 426 Tim Raines .30 .14 .04
☐ 427 Bret Barberie .10 .05 .01
☐ 428 Harvey Pulliam .10 .05 .01
☐ 429 Cris Carpenter .10 .05 .01
☐ 430 Howard Johnson .10 .05 .01
☐ 431 Orel Hershiser .15 .07 .02
☐ 432 Brian Hunter .10 .05 .01
☐ 433 Kevin Tapani .10 .05 .01
☐ 434 Rick Reed .10 .05 .01
☐ 435 Ron Witmeyer .15 .07 .02
☐ 436 Gary Gaetti .15 .07 .02
☐ 437 Alex Cole .10 .05 .01
☐ 438 Chito Martinez .10 .05 .01
☐ 439 Greg Litton .10 .05 .01
☐ 440 Julio Franco .15 .07 .02
☐ 441 Mike Munoz .10 .05 .01
☐ 442 Erik Pappas .10 .05 .01
☐ 443 Pat Combs .10 .05 .01
☐ 444 Lance Johnson .15 .07 .02
☐ 445 Ed Sprague .15 .07 .02
☐ 446 Mike Greenwell .10 .05 .01
☐ 447 Milt Thompson .10 .05 .01
☐ 448 Mike Magnante .10 .05 .01
☐ 449 Chris Haney .10 .05 .01
☐ 450 Robin Yount .30 .14 .04
☐ 451 Rafael Ramirez .10 .05 .01
☐ 452 Gino Minutelli .10 .05 .01
☐ 453 Tom Lampkin .10 .05 .01
☐ 454 Tony Perezchica .10 .05 .01
☐ 455 Dwight Gooden .15 .07 .02
☐ 456 Mark Guthrie .10 .05 .01
☐ 457 Jay Howell .10 .05 .01
☐ 458 Gary DiSarcina .10 .05 .01
☐ 459 John Smoltz .30 .14 .04
☐ 460 Will Clark .30 .14 .04
☐ 461 Dave Otto .10 .05 .01
☐ 462 Rob Maurer .10 .05 .01
☐ 463 Dwight Evans .15 .07 .02
☐ 464 Tom Brunansky .10 .05 .01
☐ 465 Shawn Hare .10 .05 .01
☐ 466 Geronimo Pena .10 .05 .01
☐ 467 Alex Fernandez .30 .14 .04
☐ 468 Greg Myers .10 .05 .01
☐ 469 Jeff Fassero .15 .07 .02

☐ 470 Len Dykstra .15 .07 .02
☐ 471 Jeff Johnson .10 .05 .01
☐ 472 Russ Swan .10 .05 .01
☐ 473 Archie Corbin .10 .05 .01
☐ 474 Chuck McElroy .10 .05 .01
☐ 475 Mark McGwire .60 .25 .07
☐ 476 Wally Whitehurst .10 .05 .01
☐ 477 Tim McIntosh .10 .05 .01
☐ 478 Sid Bream .10 .05 .01
☐ 479 Jeff Juden .10 .05 .01
☐ 480 Carlton Fisk .30 .14 .04
☐ 481 Jeff Plympton .10 .05 .01
☐ 482 Carlos Martinez .10 .05 .01
☐ 483 Jim Gott .10 .05 .01
☐ 484 Bob McClure .10 .05 .01
☐ 485 Tim Teufel .10 .05 .01
☐ 486 Vicente Palacios .10 .05 .01
☐ 487 Jeff Reed .10 .05 .01
☐ 488 Tony Phillips .15 .07 .02
☐ 489 Mel Rojas .15 .07 .02
☐ 490 Ben McDonald .10 .05 .01
☐ 491 Andres Santana .10 .05 .01
☐ 492 Chris Beasley .10 .05 .01
☐ 493 Mike Timlin .10 .05 .01
☐ 494 Brian Downing .10 .05 .01
☐ 495 Kirk Gibson .15 .07 .02
☐ 496 Scott Sanderson .10 .05 .01
☐ 497 Nick Esasky .10 .05 .01
☐ 498 Johnny Guzman .10 .05 .01
☐ 499 Mitch Williams .10 .05 .01
☐ 500 Kirby Puckett .75 .35 .09
☐ 501 Mike Harkey .10 .05 .01
☐ 502 Jim Gantner .10 .05 .01
☐ 503 Bruce Egloff .10 .05 .01
☐ 504 Josias Manzanillo .10 .05 .01
☐ 505 Delino DeShields .10 .05 .01
☐ 506 Rheal Cormier .10 .05 .01
☐ 507 Jay Bell .15 .07 .02
☐ 508 Rich Rowland .10 .05 .01
☐ 509 Scott Servais .10 .05 .01
☐ 510 Terry Pendleton .15 .07 .02
☐ 511 Rich DeLucia .10 .05 .01
☐ 512 Warren Newson .10 .05 .01
☐ 513 Paul Faries .10 .05 .01
☐ 514 Kal Daniels .10 .05 .01
☐ 515 Jarvis Brown .10 .05 .01
☐ 516 Rafael Palmeiro .30 .14 .04
☐ 517 Kelly Downs .10 .05 .01
☐ 518 Steve Chitren .10 .05 .01
☐ 519 Moises Alou .30 .14 .04
☐ 520 Wade Boggs .30 .14 .04
☐ 521 Pete Schourek .15 .07 .02
☐ 522 Scott Terry .10 .05 .01
☐ 523 Kevin Appier .15 .07 .02
☐ 524 Gary Redus .10 .05 .01
☐ 525 George Bell .10 .05 .01
☐ 526 Jeff Kaiser .10 .05 .01
☐ 527 Alvaro Espinoza .10 .05 .01
☐ 528 Luis Polonia .10 .05 .01
☐ 529 Darren Daulton .15 .07 .02
☐ 530 Norm Charlton .10 .05 .01
☐ 531 John Olerud .15 .07 .02
☐ 532 Dan Plesac .10 .05 .01
☐ 533 Billy Ripken .10 .05 .01
☐ 534 Rod Nichols .10 .05 .01
☐ 535 Joey Cora .15 .07 .02
☐ 536 Harold Baines .15 .07 .02
☐ 537 Bob Ojeda .10 .05 .01
☐ 538 Mark Leonard .10 .05 .01
☐ 539 Danny Darwin .10 .05 .01
☐ 540 Shawon Dunston .10 .05 .01
☐ 541 Pedro Munoz .10 .05 .01
☐ 542 Mark Gubicza .10 .05 .01
☐ 543 Kevin Baez .10 .05 .01
☐ 544 Todd Zeile .10 .05 .01
☐ 545 Don Slaught .10 .05 .01
☐ 546 Tony Eusebio .10 .05 .01
☐ 547 Alonzo Powell .10 .05 .01
☐ 548 Gary Pettis .10 .05 .01
☐ 549 Brian Barnes .10 .05 .01
☐ 550 Lou Whitaker .15 .07 .02
☐ 551 Keith Mitchell .10 .05 .01
☐ 552 Oscar Azocar .10 .05 .01
☐ 553 Stu Cole .10 .05 .01
☐ 554 Steve Wapnick .10 .05 .01
☐ 555 Derek Bell .30 .14 .04
☐ 556 Luis Lopez .10 .05 .01
☐ 557 Anthony Telford .10 .05 .01
☐ 558 Tim Mauser .10 .05 .01
☐ 559 Glen Sutko .10 .05 .01
☐ 560 Darryl Strawberry .15 .07 .02
☐ 561 Tom Bolton .10 .05 .01
☐ 562 Cliff Young .10 .05 .01
☐ 563 Bruce Walton .10 .05 .01
☐ 564 Chico Walker .10 .05 .01
☐ 565 John Franco .10 .05 .01
☐ 566 Paul McClellan .10 .05 .01
☐ 567 Paul Abbott .10 .05 .01
☐ 568 Gary Varsho .10 .05 .01
☐ 569 Carlos Maldonado .10 .05 .01
☐ 570 Kelly Gruber .10 .05 .01
☐ 571 Jose Oquendo .10 .05 .01
☐ 572 Steve Frey .10 .05 .01
☐ 573 Tino Martinez .15 .07 .02
☐ 574 Bill Haselman .10 .05 .01
☐ 575 Eric Anthony .10 .05 .01
☐ 576 John Habyan .10 .05 .01
☐ 577 Jeff McNeely .10 .05 .01
☐ 578 Chris Bosio .10 .05 .01
☐ 579 Joe Grahe .10 .05 .01
☐ 580 Fred McGriff .30 .14 .04
☐ 581 Rick Honeycutt .10 .05 .01
☐ 582 Matt Williams .30 .14 .04
☐ 583 Cliff Brantley .10 .05 .01
☐ 584 Rob Dibble .10 .05 .01
☐ 585 Skeeter Barnes .10 .05 .01
☐ 586 Greg Hibbard .10 .05 .01
☐ 587 Randy Milligan .10 .05 .01
☐ 588 Checklist 301-400 .10 .05 .01
☐ 589 Checklist 401-500 .10 .05 .01
☐ 590 Checklist 501-600 .10 .05 .01
☐ 591 Frank Thomas MC 1.50 .70 .19
☐ 592 David Justice MC .15 .07 .02
☐ 593 Roger Clemens MC .30 .14 .04
☐ 594 Steve Avery MC .15 .07 .02
☐ 595 Cal Ripken MC 1.00 .45 .12
☐ 596 Barry Larkin MC UER .30 .14 .04
(Ranked in AL,
should be NL)
☐ 597 Jose Canseco MC UER .30 .14 .04
(Mistakenly numbered
370 on card back)
☐ 598 Will Clark MC .30 .14 .04
☐ 599 Cecil Fielder MC .15 .07 .02
☐ 600 Ryne Sandberg MC .30 .14 .04
☐ 601 Chuck Knoblauch MC .30 .14 .04
☐ 602 Dwight Gooden MC .15 .07 .02
☐ 603 Ken Griffey Jr. MC 1.50 .70 .19
☐ 604 Barry Bonds MC .30 .14 .04
☐ 605 Nolan Ryan MC 1.00 .45 .12
☐ 606 Jeff Bagwell MC .60 .25 .07
☐ 607 Robin Yount MC .30 .14 .04
☐ 608 Bobby Bonilla MC .15 .07 .02
☐ 609 George Brett MC .40 .18 .05
☐ 610 Howard Johnson MC .10 .05 .01
☐ 611 Esteban Beltre .10 .05 .01
☐ 612 Mike Christopher .10 .05 .01
☐ 613 Troy Afenir .10 .05 .01
☐ 614 Mariano Duncan .10 .05 .01
☐ 615 Doug Henry .10 .05 .01
☐ 616 Doug Jones .10 .05 .01
☐ 617 Alvin Davis .10 .05 .01
☐ 618 Craig Lefferts .10 .05 .01
☐ 619 Kevin McReynolds .10 .05 .01
☐ 620 Barry Bonds .50 .23 .06
☐ 621 Turner Ward .10 .05 .01
☐ 622 Joe Magrane .10 .05 .01
☐ 623 Mark Parent .10 .05 .01
☐ 624 Tom Browning .10 .05 .01
☐ 625 John Smiley .10 .05 .01
☐ 626 Steve Wilson .10 .05 .01
☐ 627 Mike Gallego .10 .05 .01
☐ 628 Sammy Sosa .50 .23 .06
☐ 629 Rico Rossy .10 .05 .01
☐ 630 Royce Clayton .15 .07 .02
☐ 631 Clay Parker .10 .05 .01
☐ 632 Pete Smith .10 .05 .01
☐ 633 Jeff McKnight .10 .05 .01
☐ 634 Jack Daugherty .10 .05 .01
☐ 635 Steve Sax .10 .05 .01
☐ 636 Joe Hesketh .10 .05 .01
☐ 637 Vince Horsman .10 .05 .01
☐ 638 Eric King .10 .05 .01
☐ 639 Joe Boever .10 .05 .01
☐ 640 Jack Morris .15 .07 .02
☐ 641 Arthur Rhodes .10 .05 .01
☐ 642 Bob Melvin .10 .05 .01
☐ 643 Rick Wilkins .10 .05 .01
☐ 644 Scott Scudder .10 .05 .01
☐ 645 Bip Roberts .10 .05 .01
☐ 646 Julio Valera .10 .05 .01
☐ 647 Kevin Campbell .10 .05 .01
☐ 648 Steve Searcy .10 .05 .01
☐ 649 Scott Kamieniecki .10 .05 .01
☐ 650 Kurt Stillwell .10 .05 .01
☐ 651 Bob Welch .10 .05 .01
☐ 652 Andres Galarraga .30 .14 .04
☐ 653 Mike Jackson .10 .05 .01
☐ 654 Bo Jackson .15 .07 .02
☐ 655 Sid Fernandez .10 .05 .01
☐ 656 Mike Bielecki .10 .05 .01
☐ 657 Jeff Reardon .15 .07 .02
☐ 658 Wayne Rosenthal .10 .05 .01
☐ 659 Eric Bullock .10 .05 .01
☐ 660 Eric Davis .15 .07 .02
☐ 661 Randy Tomlin .10 .05 .01
☐ 662 Tom Edens .10 .05 .01
☐ 663 Rob Murphy .10 .05 .01
☐ 664 Leo Gomez .10 .05 .01
☐ 665 Greg Maddux 1.50 .70 .19
☐ 666 Greg Vaughn .15 .07 .02
☐ 667 Wade Taylor .10 .05 .01
☐ 668 Brad Arnsberg .10 .05 .01
☐ 669 Mike Moore .10 .05 .01
☐ 670 Mark Langston .15 .07 .02
☐ 671 Barry Jones .10 .05 .01
☐ 672 Bill Landrum .10 .05 .01
☐ 673 Greg Swindell .10 .05 .01
☐ 674 Wayne Edwards .10 .05 .01
☐ 675 Greg Olson .10 .05 .01
☐ 676 Bill Pulsipher .50 .23 .06
☐ 677 Bobby Witt .10 .05 .01
☐ 678 Mark Carreon .10 .05 .01
☐ 679 Patrick Lennon .10 .05 .01
☐ 680 Ozzie Smith .50 .23 .06
☐ 681 John Briscoe .10 .05 .01
☐ 682 Matt Young .10 .05 .01
☐ 683 Jeff Conine .30 .14 .04
☐ 684 Phil Stephenson .10 .05 .01
☐ 685 Ron Darling .10 .05 .01
☐ 686 Bryan Hickerson .10 .05 .01
☐ 687 Dale Sveum .10 .05 .01
☐ 688 Kirk McCaskill .10 .05 .01
☐ 689 Rich Amaral .10 .05 .01
☐ 690 Danny Tartabull .10 .05 .01
☐ 691 Donald Harris .10 .05 .01
☐ 692 Doug Davis .10 .05 .01
☐ 693 John Farrell .10 .05 .01
☐ 694 Paul Gibson .10 .05 .01
☐ 695 Kenny Lofton 2.50 1.10 .30
☐ 696 Mike Fetters .10 .05 .01
☐ 697 Rosario Rodriguez .10 .05 .01
☐ 698 Chris Jones .10 .05 .01
☐ 699 Jeff Manto .10 .05 .01
☐ 700 Rick Sutcliffe .10 .05 .01
☐ 701 Scott Bankhead .10 .05 .01
☐ 702 Donnie Hill .10 .05 .01
☐ 703 Todd Worrell .10 .05 .01
☐ 704 Rene Gonzales .10 .05 .01
☐ 705 Rick Cerone .10 .05 .01
☐ 706 Tony Pena .10 .05 .01
☐ 707 Paul Sorrento .10 .05 .01
☐ 708 Gary Scott .10 .05 .01
☐ 709 Junior Noboa .10 .05 .01
☐ 710 Wally Joyner .15 .07 .02
☐ 711 Charlie Hayes .10 .05 .01
☐ 712 Rich Rodriguez .10 .05 .01
☐ 713 Rudy Seanez .10 .05 .01
☐ 714 Jim Bullinger .10 .05 .01
☐ 715 Jeff M. Robinson .10 .05 .01
☐ 716 Jeff Branson .10 .05 .01
☐ 717 Andy Ashby .15 .07 .02
☐ 718 Dave Burba .10 .05 .01
☐ 719 Rich Gossage .15 .07 .02
☐ 720 Randy Johnson .30 .14 .04
☐ 721 David Wells .10 .05 .01
☐ 722 Paul Kilgus .10 .05 .01
☐ 723 Dave Martinez .10 .05 .01
☐ 724 Denny Neagle .30 .14 .04
☐ 725 Andy Stankiewicz .10 .05 .01
☐ 726 Rick Aguilera .10 .05 .01
☐ 727 Junior Ortiz .10 .05 .01
☐ 728 Storm Davis .10 .05 .01
☐ 729 Don Robinson .10 .05 .01
☐ 730 Ron Gant .15 .07 .02
☐ 731 Paul Assenmacher .10 .05 .01
☐ 732 Mike Gardiner .10 .05 .01
☐ 733 Milt Hill .10 .05 .01
☐ 734 Jeremy Hernandez .10 .05 .01
☐ 735 Ken Hill .15 .07 .02
☐ 736 Xavier Hernandez .10 .05 .01
☐ 737 Gregg Jefferies .15 .07 .02
☐ 738 Dick Schofield .10 .05 .01
☐ 739 Ron Robinson .10 .05 .01
☐ 740 Sandy Alomar .15 .07 .02
☐ 741 Mike Stanley .10 .05 .01
☐ 742 Butch Henry .10 .05 .01
☐ 743 Floyd Bannister .10 .05 .01
☐ 744 Brian Drahman .10 .05 .01
☐ 745 Dave Winfield .30 .14 .04
☐ 746 Bob Walk .10 .05 .01
☐ 747 Chris James .10 .05 .01
☐ 748 Don Prybylinski .10 .05 .01
☐ 749 Dennis Rasmussen .10 .05 .01
☐ 750 Rickey Henderson .30 .14 .04
☐ 751 Chris Hammond .10 .05 .01
☐ 752 Bob Kipper .10 .05 .01
☐ 753 Dave Rohde .10 .05 .01
☐ 754 Hubie Brooks .10 .05 .01
☐ 755 Bret Saberhagen .15 .07 .02
☐ 756 Jeff D. Robinson .10 .05 .01
☐ 757 Pat Listach .15 .07 .02
☐ 758 Bill Wegman .10 .05 .01
☐ 759 John Wetteland .15 .07 .02
☐ 760 Phil Plantier .15 .07 .02
☐ 761 Wilson Alvarez .30 .14 .04
☐ 762 Scott Aldred .10 .05 .01
☐ 763 Armando Reynoso .10 .05 .01
☐ 764 Todd Benzinger .10 .05 .01
☐ 765 Kevin Mitchell .15 .07 .02
☐ 766 Gary Sheffield .30 .14 .04
☐ 767 Allan Anderson .10 .05 .01
☐ 768 Rusty Meacham .10 .05 .01
☐ 769 Rick Parker .10 .05 .01
☐ 770 Nolan Ryan 2.00 .90 .25
☐ 771 Jeff Ballard .10 .05 .01
☐ 772 Cory Snyder .10 .05 .01
☐ 773 Denis Boucher .10 .05 .01
☐ 774 Jose Gonzalez .10 .05 .01
☐ 775 Juan Guerrero .10 .05 .01
☐ 776 Ed Nunez .10 .05 .01
☐ 777 Scott Ruskin .10 .05 .01
☐ 778 Terry Leach .10 .05 .01
☐ 779 Carl Willis .10 .05 .01
☐ 780 Bobby Bonilla .15 .07 .02
☐ 781 Duane Ward .10 .05 .01
☐ 782 Joe Slusarski .10 .05 .01
☐ 783 David Segui .10 .05 .01
☐ 784 Kirk Gibson .15 .07 .02
☐ 785 Frank Viola .10 .05 .01
☐ 786 Keith Miller .10 .05 .01
☐ 787 Mike Morgan .10 .05 .01
☐ 788 Kim Batiste .10 .05 .01
☐ 789 Sergio Valdez .10 .05 .01
☐ 790 Eddie Taubensee .10 .05 .01
☐ 791 Jack Armstrong .10 .05 .01
☐ 792 Scott Fletcher .10 .05 .01
☐ 793 Steve Farr .10 .05 .01
☐ 794 Dan Pasqua .10 .05 .01
☐ 795 Eddie Murray .50 .23 .06
☐ 796 John Morris .10 .05 .01
☐ 797 Francisco Cabrera .10 .05 .01
☐ 798 Mike Perez .10 .05 .01
☐ 799 Ted Wood .10 .05 .01
☐ 800 Jose Rijo .10 .05 .01
☐ 801 Danny Gladden .10 .05 .01
☐ 802 Archi Cianfrocco .10 .05 .01
☐ 803 Monty Fariss .10 .05 .01
☐ 804 Roger McDowell .10 .05 .01
☐ 805 Randy Myers .15 .07 .02
☐ 806 Kirk Dressendorfer .10 .05 .01
☐ 807 Zane Smith .10 .05 .01
☐ 808 Glenn Davis .10 .05 .01
☐ 809 Torey Lovullo .10 .05 .01
☐ 810 Andre Dawson .15 .07 .02
☐ 811 Bill Pecota .10 .05 .01
☐ 812 Ted Power .10 .05 .01
☐ 813 Willie Blair .10 .05 .01
☐ 814 Dave Fleming .10 .05 .01
☐ 815 Chris Gwynn .10 .05 .01
☐ 816 Jody Reed .10 .05 .01
☐ 817 Mark Dewey .10 .05 .01
☐ 818 Kyle Abbott .10 .05 .01
☐ 819 Tom Henke .10 .05 .01
☐ 820 Kevin Seitzer .10 .05 .01
☐ 821 Al Newman .10 .05 .01
☐ 822 Tim Sherrill .10 .05 .01
☐ 823 Chuck Crim .10 .05 .01
☐ 824 Darren Reed .10 .05 .01
☐ 825 Tony Gwynn .75 .35 .09
☐ 826 Steve Foster .10 .05 .01
☐ 827 Steve Howe .10 .05 .01
☐ 828 Brook Jacoby .10 .05 .01
☐ 829 Rodney McCray .10 .05 .01
☐ 830 Chuck Knoblauch .30 .14 .04
☐ 831 John Wehner .10 .05 .01
☐ 832 Scott Garrelts .10 .05 .01
☐ 833 Alejandro Pena .10 .05 .01
☐ 834 Jeff Parrett UER .10 .05 .01
(Kentucky)
☐ 835 Juan Bell .10 .05 .01
☐ 836 Lance Dickson .10 .05 .01
☐ 837 Darryl Kile .10 .05 .01
☐ 838 Efrain Valdez .10 .05 .01
☐ 839 Bob Zupcic .10 .05 .01
☐ 840 George Bell .10 .05 .01
☐ 841 Dave Gallagher .10 .05 .01
☐ 842 Tim Belcher .10 .05 .01
☐ 843 Jeff Shaw .10 .05 .01
☐ 844 Mike Fitzgerald .10 .05 .01
☐ 845 Gary Carter .15 .07 .02
☐ 846 John Russell .10 .05 .01
☐ 847 Eric Hillman .10 .05 .01
☐ 848 Mike Witt .10 .05 .01
☐ 849 Curt Wilkerson .10 .05 .01
☐ 850 Alan Trammell .15 .07 .02
☐ 851 Rex Hudler .10 .05 .01
☐ 852 Mike Walkden .10 .05 .01
☐ 853 Kevin Ward .10 .05 .01
☐ 854 Tim Naehring .15 .07 .02
☐ 855 Bill Swift .10 .05 .01
☐ 856 Damon Berryhill .10 .05 .01
☐ 857 Mark Eichhorn .10 .05 .01
☐ 858 Hector Villanueva .10 .05 .01
☐ 859 Jose Lind .10 .05 .01
☐ 860 Denny Martinez .15 .07 .02
☐ 861 Bill Krueger .10 .05 .01
☐ 862 Mike Kingery .10 .05 .01
☐ 863 Jeff Innis .10 .05 .01
☐ 864 Derek Lilliquist .10 .05 .01
☐ 865 Reggie Sanders .30 .14 .04
☐ 866 Ramon Garcia .10 .05 .01
☐ 867 Bruce Ruffin .10 .05 .01
☐ 868 Dickie Thon .10 .05 .01
☐ 869 Melido Perez .10 .05 .01
☐ 870 Ruben Amaro .10 .05 .01
☐ 871 Alan Mills .10 .05 .01
☐ 872 Matt Sinatro .10 .05 .01
☐ 873 Eddie Zosky .10 .05 .01
☐ 874 Pete Incaviglia .10 .05 .01
☐ 875 Tom Candiotti .10 .05 .01
☐ 876 Bob Patterson .10 .05 .01
☐ 877 Neal Heaton .10 .05 .01
☐ 878 Terrel Hansen .10 .05 .01
☐ 879 Dave Eiland .10 .05 .01
☐ 880 Von Hayes .10 .05 .01
☐ 881 Tim Scott .10 .05 .01
☐ 882 Otis Nixon .10 .05 .01
☐ 883 Herm Winningham .10 .05 .01
☐ 884 Dion James .10 .05 .01

☐ 885 Dave Wainhouse	.10	.05	.01
☐ 886 Frank DiPino	.10	.05	.01
☐ 887 Dennis Cook	.10	.05	.01
☐ 888 Jose Mesa	.15	.07	.02
☐ 889 Mark Leiter	.10	.05	.01
☐ 890 Willie Randolph	.15	.07	.02
☐ 891 Craig Colbert	.10	.05	.01
☐ 892 Dwayne Henry	.10	.05	.01
☐ 893 Jim Lindeman	.10	.05	.01
☐ 894 Charlie Hough	.10	.05	.01
☐ 895 Gil Heredia	.10	.05	.01
☐ 896 Scott Champarino	.10	.05	.01
☐ 897 Lance Blankenship	.10	.05	.01
☐ 898 Checklist 601-700	.10	.05	.01
☐ 899 Checklist 701-800	.10	.05	.01
☐ 900 Checklist 801-900	.10	.05	.01

1992 Stadium Club First Draft Picks

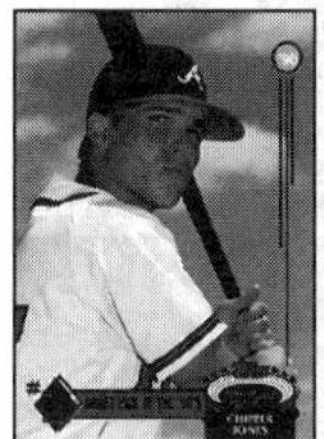

This three-card standard-size set, featuring Major League Baseball's Number 1 draft pick for 1990, 1991, and 1992, was randomly inserted into 1992 Stadium Club Series III packs at an approximate rate of 1:72. One card also was mailed to each member of Topps Stadium Club. The cards feature on the fronts full-bleed posed color player photos. The player's draft year is printed on an orange circle in the upper right corner and is accented by gold foil stripes of varying lengths that run vertically down the right edge of the card. The player's name appears on the Stadium Club logo at the bottom. The number "1" is gold-foil stamped in a black diamond at the lower left and is followed by a red stripe gold-foil stamped with the words "Draft Pick of the '90s". The back design features color photos on a black and red background with the player's signature gold-foil stamped across the bottom of the photo and gold foil bars running down the right edge of the picture. The team name and biographical information is included in a yellow and white box.

	MINT	NRMT	EXC
COMPLETE SET (3)	20.00	9.00	2.50
COMMON CARD (1-3)	1.00	.45	.12
☐ 1 Chipper Jones	18.00	8.00	2.20
☐ 2 Brien Taylor	1.00	.45	.12
☐ 3 Phil Nevin	2.00	.90	.25

1992 Stadium Club Master Photos

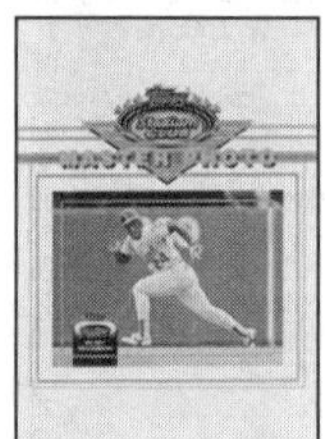

In the first package of materials sent to 1992 Topps Stadium Club members, along with an 11-card boxed set, members received a randomly chosen "Master Photo" printed on (approximately) 5" by 7" white card stock to demonstrate how the photos are cropped to create a borderless design. Each master photo has the Topps Stadium Club logo and the words "Master Photo" above a gold foil picture frame enclosing the color player photo. The backs are blank. The cards are unnumbered and checklisted below alphabetically. Master photos were also available through a special promotion at Walmart as an insert one-per-box in specially marked wax boxes of regular Topps Stadium Club cards.

	MINT	NRMT	EXC
COMPLETE SET (15)	25.00	11.00	3.10
COMMON CARD (1-15)	.50	.23	.06
☐ 1 Wade Boggs	.75	.35	.09
☐ 2 Barry Bonds	1.25	.55	.16
☐ 3 Jose Canseco	1.00	.45	.12
☐ 4 Will Clark	1.00	.45	.12
☐ 5 Cecil Fielder	.60	.25	.07
☐ 6 Dwight Gooden	.60	.25	.07
☐ 7 Ken Griffey Jr.	5.00	2.20	.60
☐ 8 Rickey Henderson	.75	.35	.09
☐ 9 Lance Johnson	.60	.25	.07
☐ 10 Cal Ripken	5.00	2.20	.60
☐ 11 Nolan Ryan	5.00	2.20	.60
☐ 12 Deion Sanders	.75	.35	.09
☐ 13 Darryl Strawberry	.60	.25	.07
☐ 14 Danny Tartabull	.50	.23	.06
☐ 15 Frank Thomas	5.00	2.20	.60

1992 Stadium Club East Coast National

These cards were selected from the regular Stadium Club series and were printed for the Gloria Rothstein's East Coast National Convention. The fronts feature borderless color player photos with the East Coast National Convention logo printed in gold foil in a top corner while the backs display a mini reprint of the player's rookie card and "BARS" (Baseball Analysis and Reporting System) statistics. The cards are checklisted below according to their numbers in the regular series.

	MINT	NRMT	EXC
COMPLETE SET (100)	150.00	70.00	19.00
COMMON CARD	1.00	.45	.12
☐ 601 Chuck Knoblauch MC	7.50	3.40	.95
☐ 602 Doc Gooden MC	4.00	1.80	.50
☐ 603 Ken Griffey Jr. MC	40.00	18.00	5.00
☐ 604 Barry Bonds MC	7.50	3.40	.95
☐ 605 Nolan Ryan MC	40.00	18.00	5.00
☐ 606 Jeff Bagwell MC	20.00	9.00	2.50
☐ 607 Robin Yount MC	6.00	2.70	.75
☐ 608 Bobby Bonilla MC	2.00	.90	.25
☐ 609 George Brett MC	20.00	9.00	2.50
☐ 610 Howard Johnson MC	1.00	.45	.12
☐ 611 Esteban Beltre	1.00	.45	.12
☐ 612 Mike Christopher	1.00	.45	.12
☐ 613 Troy Afenir	1.00	.45	.12
☐ 619 Kevin McReynolds	1.00	.45	.12
☐ 620 Barry Bonds	15.00	6.75	1.85
☐ 622 Joe Magrane	1.00	.45	.12
☐ 623 Mark Parent	1.00	.45	.12
☐ 626 Steve Wilson	1.00	.45	.12
☐ 629 Rico Rossy	1.00	.45	.12
☐ 631 Clay Parker	1.00	.45	.12
☐ 633 Jeff McKnight	1.00	.45	.12
☐ 637 Vince Horsman	1.00	.45	.12
☐ 638 Eric King	1.00	.45	.12
☐ 639 Joe Boever	1.00	.45	.12
☐ 641 Arthur Rhodes	2.00	.90	.25
☐ 647 Kevin Campbell	1.00	.45	.12
☐ 653 Mike Jackson	1.00	.45	.12
☐ 661 Randy Tomlin	1.00	.45	.12
☐ 665 Greg Maddux	25.00	11.00	3.10
☐ 668 Brad Arnsberg	1.00	.45	.12
☐ 671 Barry Jones	1.00	.45	.12
☐ 672 Bill Landrum	1.00	.45	.12
☐ 673 Greg Swindell	1.00	.45	.12
☐ 676 Bill Pulsipher	5.00	2.20	.60
☐ 679 Patrick Lennon	1.00	.45	.12
☐ 681 John Briscoe	1.00	.45	.12
☐ 684 Phil Stephenson	1.00	.45	.12
☐ 685 Ron Darling	1.00	.45	.12
☐ 686 Bryan Hickerson	1.00	.45	.12
☐ 688 Kirk McCaskill	1.00	.45	.12
☐ 689 Rich Amaral	1.00	.45	.12
☐ 692 Doug Davis	1.00	.45	.12
☐ 693 John Farrell	1.00	.45	.12
☐ 700 Rick Sutcliffe	2.00	.90	.25
☐ 704 Rene Gonzalez	1.00	.45	.12
☐ 713 Rudy Seanez	1.00	.45	.12
☐ 714 Jim Bullinger	1.00	.45	.12
☐ 716 Jeff Branson	1.00	.45	.12
☐ 717 Andy Ashby	4.00	1.80	.50
☐ 725 Andy Stankiewicz	1.00	.45	.12
☐ 733 Milt Hill	1.00	.45	.12
☐ 739 Ron Robinson	1.00	.45	.12
☐ 742 Butch Henry	1.00	.45	.12
☐ 747 Chris James	1.00	.45	.12
☐ 749 Dennis Rasmussen	1.00	.45	.12
☐ 753 Dave Rohde	1.00	.45	.12
☐ 757 Pat Listach	2.00	.90	.25
☐ 758 Bill Wegman	1.00	.45	.12
☐ 763 Armando Reynoso	1.00	.45	.12
☐ 765 Kevin Mitchell	2.00	.90	.25
☐ 766 Gary Sheffield	7.50	3.40	.95
☐ 769 Rick Parker	1.00	.45	.12
☐ 771 Jeff Ballard	1.00	.45	.12
☐ 772 Cory Snyder	1.00	.45	.12
☐ 774 Jose Gonzalez	1.00	.45	.12
☐ 775 Juan Guerrero	1.00	.45	.12
☐ 776 Ed Nunez	1.00	.45	.12
☐ 778 Terry Leach	1.00	.45	.12
☐ 782 Joe Slusarski	1.00	.45	.12
☐ 784 Kirk Gibson	2.00	.90	.25
☐ 788 Kim Batiste	1.00	.45	.12
☐ 802 Archi Cianfrocco	1.00	.45	.12
☐ 806 Kirk Dressendorfer	1.00	.45	.12
☐ 807 Zane Smith	1.00	.45	.12
☐ 814 Dave Fleming	1.00	.45	.12
☐ 815 Chris Gwynn	1.00	.45	.12
☐ 817 Mark Dewey	1.00	.45	.12
☐ 819 Tom Henke	2.00	.90	.25
☐ 822 Tim Sherrill	1.00	.45	.12
☐ 826 Steve Foster	1.00	.45	.12
☐ 831 John Wehner	1.00	.45	.12
☐ 832 Scott Garrelts	1.00	.45	.12
☐ 840 George Bell	2.00	.90	.25
☐ 841 Dave Gallagher	1.00	.45	.12
☐ 846 John Russell	1.00	.45	.12
☐ 847 Eric Hillman	1.00	.45	.12
☐ 852 Mike Walkden	1.00	.45	.12
☐ 855 Bill Swift	1.00	.45	.12
☐ 864 Derek Lilliquist	1.00	.45	.12
☐ 876 Bob Patterson	1.00	.45	.12
☐ 878 Terrel Hansen	1.00	.45	.12
☐ 881 Tim Scott	1.00	.45	.12
☐ 886 Frank DiPino	1.00	.45	.12
☐ 891 Craig Colbert	1.00	.45	.12
☐ 892 Dwayne Henry	1.00	.45	.12
☐ 893 Jim Lindeman	1.00	.45	.12
☐ 895 Gil Heredia	1.00	.45	.12
☐ 898 Checklist	1.00	.45	.12
☐ 899 Checklist	1.00	.45	.12
☐ 900 Checklist	1.00	.45	.12

1992 Stadium Club Members Only *

This 50-card standard-size set was sent to 1992 Stadium Club members in four installments. In addition to the Stadium Club cards, the first installment included one "Top Draft Picks of the '90s" card (as a bonus) and a randomly chosen "Master Photo" printed on 5" by 7" white card stock. The third and fourth installments included hockey and football players in addition to baseball players. The cards feature full-bleed glossy color player photos. The fronts of the regular cards have the words "Members Only" printed in gold foil at the bottom along with the player's name and the Stadium Club logo. The backs feature a stadium scene with the scoreboard displaying, in yellow neon, a career highlight. The cards are unnumbered and checklisted below alphabetically, with the two-player cards listed at the end.

	MINT	NRMT	EXC
COMPLETE SET (50)	30.00	13.50	3.70
COMMON CARD (1-50)	.10	.05	.01
☐ 1 Carlos Baerga	.20	.09	.03
☐ 2 Wade Boggs	.40	.18	.05
☐ 3 Barry Bonds	.75	.35	.09
☐ 4 Bret Boone	.10	.05	.01
☐ 5 Pat Borders	.10	.05	.01
☐ 6 George Brett	1.25	.55	.16
☐ 7 George Brett	1.25	.55	.16
☐ 8 Jim Bullinger	.10	.05	.01
☐ 9 Gary Carter	.20	.09	.03
☐ 10 Andujar Cedeno	.10	.05	.01
☐ 11 Roger Clemens and Matt Young	.50	.23	.06
☐ 12 Dennis Eckersley	.20	.09	.03
☐ 13 Dennis Eckersley	.20	.09	.03
☐ 14 Dave Eiland	.10	.05	.01
☐ 15 Ken Griffey Jr.	3.00	1.35	.35
☐ 16 Kevin Gross	.10	.05	.01
☐ 17 Bo Jackson	.20	.09	.03
☐ 18 Eric Karros	.50	.23	.06
☐ 19 Pat Listach	.10	.05	.01
☐ 20 Greg Maddux	2.50	1.10	.30
☐ 21 Mickey Morandini	.10	.05	.01
☐ 22 Jack Morris	.20	.09	.03
☐ 23 Eddie Murray	.75	.35	.09
☐ 24 Eddie Murray	.75	.35	.09
☐ 25 Bip Roberts	.10	.05	.01
☐ 26 Nolan Ryan 27 Seasons	3.00	1.35	.35
☐ 27 Nolan Ryan 1993 Seasons His Finale	3.00	1.35	.35
☐ 28 Gary Sheffield and Dwight Gooden	.40	.18	.05
☐ 29 Gary Sheffield and Fred McGriff	.50	.23	.06
☐ 30 Lee Smith	.20	.09	.03
☐ 31 Ozzie Smith (2,000th Hit)	1.25	.55	.16
☐ 32 Ozzie Smith (7,000th Career Assist)	1.25	.55	.16
☐ 33 Ozzie Smith	1.25	.55	.16
☐ 34 Bobby Thigpen	.10	.05	.01
☐ 35 Dave Winfield	.20	.09	.03
☐ 36 Robin Yount	.40	.18	.05
☐ 37 Troy Aikman	3.00	1.35	.35
☐ 38 Dale Carter	.10	.05	.01
☐ 39 Art Monk	.20	.09	.03
☐ 40 Frank Reich	.10	.05	.01
☐ 41 Emmitt Smith	3.00	1.35	.35
☐ 42 Steve Young	1.50	.70	.19
☐ 43 Neil Brady	.10	.05	.01
☐ 44 Mike Gartner	.20	.09	.03
☐ 45 Chris Kontos	.10	.05	.01
☐ 46 Jari Kurri	.60	.25	.07
☐ 47 Eric Lindros	3.00	1.35	.35
☐ 48 Reggie Savage	.10	.05	.01
☐ 49 Teemu Selanne Selanne Rewrites Record Books	1.00	.45	.12
☐ 50 Teemu Selanne Teemu Bests Bossy	1.00	.45	.12

1992 Stadium Club National Convention

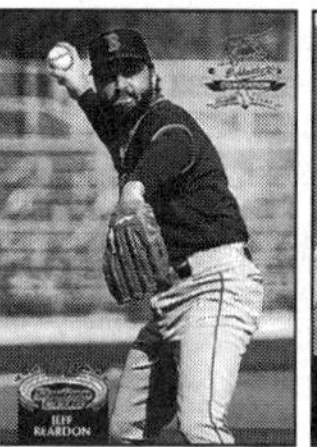

These cards were selected from the regular Stadium Club series and were printed for the National Convention in Atlanta. The fronts feature borderless color player photos with the National Convention logo printed in gold foil in a top corner while the backs display a mini reprint of the player's rookie card and "BARS" (Baseball Analysis and Reporting System) statistics. The cards are checklisted below according to their numbers in the regular series.

	MINT	NRMT	EXC
COMPLETE SET (100)	150.00	70.00	19.00
COMMON CARD	1.00	.45	.12
☐ 616 Doug Jones	1.00	.45	.12
☐ 617 Alvin Davis	1.00	.45	.12
☐ 618 Craig Lefferts	1.00	.45	.12
☐ 621 Turner Ward	1.00	.45	.12
☐ 625 John Smiley	1.00	.45	.12
☐ 627 Mike Gallego	1.00	.45	.12
☐ 630 Royce Clayton	4.00	1.80	.50
☐ 634 Jack Daugherty	1.00	.45	.12
☐ 635 Steve Sax	1.00	.45	.12
☐ 636 Joe Hesketh	1.00	.45	.12
☐ 643 Rick Wilkins	1.00	.45	.12
☐ 644 Scott Scudder	1.00	.45	.12
☐ 645 Bip Roberts	1.00	.45	.12
☐ 650 Kurt Stillwell	1.00	.45	.12
☐ 652 Andres Galarraga	6.00	2.70	.75
☐ 657 Jeff Reardon	2.00	.90	.25
☐ 660 Eric Davis	2.00	.90	.25
☐ 662 Tom Edens	1.00	.45	.12
☐ 675 Greg Olson	1.00	.45	.12
☐ 678 Mark Carreon	1.00	.45	.12
☐ 680 Ozzie Smith	40.00	18.00	5.00
☐ 682 Matt Young	1.00	.45	.12
☐ 690 Danny Tartabull	1.00	.45	.12
☐ 691 Donald Harris	1.00	.45	.12
☐ 695 Kenny Lofton	25.00	11.00	3.10
☐ 697 Rosario Rodriguez	1.00	.45	.12
☐ 701 Scott Bankhead	1.00	.45	.12
☐ 705 Rick Cerone	1.00	.45	.12
☐ 706 Tony Pena	1.00	.45	.12
☐ 709 Junior Noboa	1.00	.45	.12
☐ 710 Wally Joyner	2.00	.90	.25
☐ 711 Charlie Hayes	1.00	.45	.12
☐ 712 Rich Rodriguez	1.00	.45	.12
☐ 721 David Wells	1.00	.45	.12
☐ 723 Dave Martinez	1.00	.45	.12
☐ 726 Rick Aguilera	2.00	.90	.25
☐ 727 Junior Ortiz	1.00	.45	.12
☐ 729 Don Robinson	1.00	.45	.12
☐ 730 Ron Gant	2.00	.90	.25
☐ 731 Paul Assenmacher	1.00	.45	.12
☐ 732 Mark Gardiner	1.00	.45	.12
☐ 735 Ken Hill	2.00	.90	.25
☐ 736 Xavier Hernandez	1.00	.45	.12
☐ 737 Gregg Jefferies	2.00	.90	.25
☐ 740 Sandy Alomar	2.00	.90	.25
☐ 741 Mike Stanley	1.00	.45	.12
☐ 744 Brian Drahman	1.00	.45	.12
☐ 746 Bob Walk	1.00	.45	.12
☐ 751 Chris Hammond	1.00	.45	.12
☐ 759 John Wetteland	4.00	1.80	.50
☐ 760 Phil Plantier	1.00	.45	.12
☐ 761 Wilson Alvarez	2.00	.90	.25
☐ 773 Dennis Boucher	1.00	.45	.12
☐ 777 Scott Ruskin	1.00	.45	.12
☐ 779 Carl Willis	1.00	.45	.12
☐ 783 David Segui	2.00	.90	.25
☐ 786 Keith Miller	1.00	.45	.12
☐ 790 Eddie Taubensee	1.00	.45	.12
☐ 791 Jack Armstrong	1.00	.45	.12
☐ 792 Scott Fletcher	1.00	.45	.12
☐ 793 Steve Farr	1.00	.45	.12
☐ 794 Dan Pasqua	1.00	.45	.12
☐ 797 Francisco Cabrera	1.00	.45	.12

☐ 798 Mike Perez	1.00	.45	.12
☐ 801 Danny Gladden	1.00	.45	.12
☐ 803 Monty Fariss	1.00	.45	.12
☐ 804 Roger McDowell	1.00	.45	.12
☐ 805 Randy Myers	2.00	.90	.25
☐ 808 Glenn Davis	1.00	.45	.12
☐ 809 Torey Lovullo	1.00	.45	.12
☐ 816 Jody Reed	1.00	.45	.12
☐ 825 Tony Gwynn	50.00	22.00	6.25
☐ 827 Steve Howe	1.00	.45	.12
☐ 828 Brook Jacoby	1.00	.45	.12
☐ 829 Rodney McCray	1.00	.45	.12
☐ 830 Chuck Knoblauch	15.00	6.75	1.85
☐ 835 Juan Bell	1.00	.45	.12
☐ 836 Lance Dickson	1.00	.45	.12
☐ 837 Darryl Kile	1.00	.45	.12
☐ 842 Tim Belcher	1.00	.45	.12
☐ 843 Jeff Shaw	1.00	.45	.12
☐ 844 Mike Fitzgerald	1.00	.45	.12
☐ 845 Gary Carter	4.00	1.80	.50
☐ 850 Alan Trammell	4.00	1.80	.50
☐ 851 Rex Hudler	1.00	.45	.12
☐ 856 Damon Berryhill	1.00	.45	.12
☐ 857 Mark Eichhorn	1.00	.45	.12
☐ 858 Hector Villanueva	1.00	.45	.12
☐ 860 Denny Martinez	2.00	.90	.25
☐ 865 Reggie Sanders	4.00	1.80	.50
☐ 869 Melido Perez	1.00	.45	.12
☐ 874 Pete Incaviglia	1.00	.45	.12
☐ 875 Tom Candiotti	1.00	.45	.12
☐ 877 Neal Heaton	1.00	.45	.12
☐ 879 Dave Eiland	1.00	.45	.12
☐ 882 Otis Nixon	2.00	.90	.25
☐ 883 Herm Winningham	1.00	.45	.12
☐ 884 Dion James	1.00	.45	.12
☐ 887 Dennis Cook	1.00	.45	.12
☐ 894 Charlie Hough	1.00	.45	.12

1993 Stadium Club Murphy

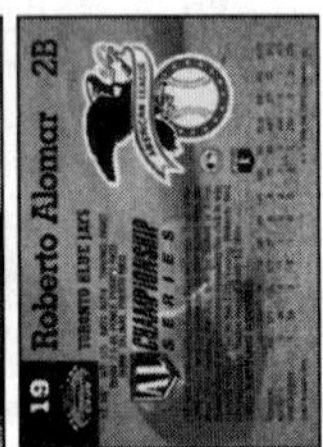

This 200-card boxed set features 1992 All-Star Game cards, 1992 Team USA cards, and 1992 Championship and World Series cards. Topps actually refers to this set as a 1992 issue, but the set was released in 1993. The standard-size cards display full-bleed posed and action color player shots on the fronts. The player's name appears below the Topps Stadium Club logo in the lower right with parallel gold foil stripes intersecting the logo. The horizontal back presents the player's biography, statistics, and highlights on a ghosted photo. This set is housed in a replica of San Diego's Jack Murphy Stadium, site of the 1992 All-Star Game. Production was limited to 8,000 cases, with 16 boxes per case. The set includes 100 Draft Pick cards, 56 All-Star cards, 25 Team USA cards, and 19 cards commemorating the 1992 National and American League Championship Series and the World Series. Notable Rookie Cards in this set include Trey Beamon, Derek Jeter and Jason Kendall.

	MINT	NRMT	EXC
COMPLETE FACT.SET (212)	30.00	13.50	3.70
COMPLETE SET (200)	25.00	11.00	3.10
COMMON CARD (1-200)	.10	.05	.01

☐ 1 Dave Winfield	.50	.23	.06
☐ 2 Juan Guzman	.25	.11	.03
☐ 3 Tony Gwynn	1.25	.55	.16
☐ 4 Chris Roberts	.25	.11	.03
☐ 5 Benny Santiago	.10	.05	.01
☐ 6 Sherard Clinkscales	.10	.05	.01
☐ 7 Jon Nunnally	.25	.11	.03
☐ 8 Chuck Knoblauch	.50	.23	.06
☐ 9 Bob Wolcott	.50	.23	.06
☐ 10 Steve Rodriguez	.10	.05	.01
☐ 11 Mark Williams	.10	.05	.01
☐ 12 Danny Clyburn	1.00	.45	.12
☐ 13 Darren Dreifort	.10	.05	.01
☐ 14 Andy Van Slyke	.25	.11	.03
☐ 15 Wade Boggs	.50	.23	.06
☐ 16 Scott Patton	.10	.05	.01
☐ 17 Gary Sheffield	.50	.23	.06
☐ 18 Ron Villone	.25	.11	.03
☐ 19 Roberto Alomar	.60	.25	.07
☐ 20 Marc Valdes	.10	.05	.01
☐ 21 Daron Kirkreit	.10	.05	.01
☐ 22 Jeff Granger	.10	.05	.01
☐ 23 Levon Largusa	.10	.05	.01
☐ 24 Jimmy Key	.25	.11	.03
☐ 25 Kevin Pearson	.10	.05	.01
☐ 26 Michael Moore	.10	.05	.01
☐ 27 Preston Wilson	.50	.23	.06
☐ 28 Kirby Puckett	1.25	.55	.16
☐ 29 Tim Crabtree	.10	.05	.01
☐ 30 Bip Roberts	.10	.05	.01
☐ 31 Kelly Gruber	.10	.05	.01
☐ 32 Tony Fernandez	.10	.05	.01
☐ 33 Jason Angel	.10	.05	.01
☐ 34 Calvin Murray	.10	.05	.01
☐ 35 Chad McConnell	.10	.05	.01
☐ 36 Jason Moler	.10	.05	.01
☐ 37 Mark Lemke	.10	.05	.01
☐ 38 Tom Knauss	.10	.05	.01
☐ 39 Larry Mitchell	.10	.05	.01
☐ 40 Doug Mirabelli	.10	.05	.01
☐ 41 Everott Stull II	.30	.14	.04
☐ 42 Chris Wimmer	.10	.05	.01
☐ 43 Dan Serafini	.50	.23	.06
☐ 44 Ryne Sandberg	.75	.35	.09
☐ 45 Steve Lyons	25.00	11.00	3.10
☐ 46 Ryan Freeburg	.10	.05	.01
☐ 47 Ruben Sierra	.25	.11	.03
☐ 48 David Mysel	.10	.05	.01
☐ 49 Joe Hamilton	.10	.05	.01
☐ 50 Steve Rodriguez	.10	.05	.01
☐ 51 Tim Wakefield	.25	.11	.03
☐ 52 Scott Gentile	.10	.05	.01
☐ 53 Doug Jones	.10	.05	.01
☐ 54 Willie Brown	.10	.05	.01
☐ 55 Chad Mottola	.25	.11	.03
☐ 56 Ken Griffey Jr.	3.00	1.35	.35
☐ 57 Jon Lieber	.25	.11	.03
☐ 58 Denny Martinez	.25	.11	.03
☐ 59 Joe Petcka	.10	.05	.01
☐ 60 Benji Simonton	.10	.05	.01
☐ 61 Brett Backlund	.10	.05	.01
☐ 62 Damon Berryhill	.10	.05	.01
☐ 63 Juan Guzman	.25	.11	.03
☐ 64 Doug Hecker	.10	.05	.01
☐ 65 Jamie Arnold	.25	.11	.03
☐ 66 Bob Tewksbury	.10	.05	.01
☐ 67 Tim Leger	.10	.05	.01
☐ 68 Todd Etler	.25	.11	.03
☐ 69 Lloyd McClendon	.10	.05	.01
☐ 70 Kurt Ehmann	.10	.05	.01
☐ 71 Rick Magdaleno	.25	.11	.03
☐ 72 Tom Pagnozzi	.10	.05	.01
☐ 73 Jeffrey Hammonds	.25	.11	.03
☐ 74 Joe Carter	.25	.11	.03
☐ 75 Chris Holt	.10	.05	.01
☐ 76 Charles Johnson	.50	.23	.06
☐ 77 Bob Walk	.10	.05	.01
☐ 78 Fred McGriff	.50	.23	.06
☐ 79 Tom Evans	.25	.11	.03
☐ 80 Scott Klingenbeck	.10	.05	.01
☐ 81 Chad McConnell	.10	.05	.01
☐ 82 Chris Eddy	.10	.05	.01
☐ 83 Phil Nevin	.10	.05	.01
☐ 84 John Kruk	.25	.11	.03
☐ 85 Tony Sheffield	.10	.05	.01
☐ 86 John Smoltz	.50	.23	.06
☐ 87 Trevor Humphry	.10	.05	.01
☐ 88 Charles Nagy	.25	.11	.03
☐ 89 Sean Runyan	.10	.05	.01
☐ 90 Mike Gulan	.10	.05	.01
☐ 91 Darren Daulton	.25	.11	.03
☐ 92 Otis Nixon	.10	.05	.01
☐ 93 Nomar Garciaparra	5.00	2.20	.60
☐ 94 Larry Walker	.50	.23	.06
☐ 95 Hut Smith	.10	.05	.01
☐ 96 Rick Helling	.25	.11	.03
☐ 97 Roger Clemens	.60	.25	.07
☐ 98 Ron Gant	.25	.11	.03
☐ 99 Kenny Felder	.10	.05	.01
☐ 100 Steve Murphy	.10	.05	.01
☐ 101 Mike Smith	.25	.11	.03
☐ 102 Terry Pendleton	.25	.11	.03
☐ 103 Tim Davis	.10	.05	.01
☐ 104 Jeff Patzke	.50	.23	.06
☐ 105 Craig Wilson	.10	.05	.01
☐ 106 Tom Glavine	.50	.23	.06
☐ 107 Mark Langston	.25	.11	.03
☐ 108 Mark Thompson	.10	.05	.01
☐ 109 Eric Owens	.25	.11	.03
☐ 110 Keith Johnson	.10	.05	.01
☐ 111 Robin Ventura	.25	.11	.03
☐ 112 Ed Sprague	.25	.11	.03
☐ 113 Jeff Schmidt	.10	.05	.01
☐ 114 Don Wengert	.10	.05	.01
☐ 115 Craig Biggio	.25	.11	.03
☐ 116 Kenny Carlyle	.10	.05	.01
☐ 117 Derek Jeter	8.00	3.60	1.00
☐ 118 Manuel Lee	.10	.05	.01
☐ 119 Jeff Haas	.10	.05	.01
☐ 120 Roger Bailey	.10	.05	.01
☐ 121 Sean Lowe	.25	.11	.03
☐ 122 Rick Aguilera	25.00	11.00	3.10
☐ 123 Sandy Alomar	.25	.11	.03
☐ 124 Derek Wallace	.10	.05	.01
☐ 125 B.J. Wallace	.10	.05	.01
☐ 126 Greg Maddux	2.00	.90	.25
☐ 127 Tim Moore	.10	.05	.01
☐ 128 Lee Smith	.25	.11	.03
☐ 129 Todd Steverson	.10	.05	.01
☐ 130 Chris Widger	.10	.05	.01
☐ 131 Paul Molitor	.60	.25	.07
☐ 132 Chris Smith	.10	.05	.01
☐ 133 Chris Gomez	.25	.11	.03
☐ 134 Jimmy Baron	.10	.05	.01
☐ 135 John Smoltz	.50	.23	.06
☐ 136 Pat Borders	.10	.05	.01
☐ 137 Donnie Leshnock	.10	.05	.01
☐ 138 Gus Gandarillos	.10	.05	.01
☐ 139 Will Clark	.50	.23	.06
☐ 140 Ryan Luzinski	.25	.11	.03
☐ 141 Cal Ripken	2.50	1.10	.30
☐ 142 B.J. Wallace	.10	.05	.01
☐ 143 Trey Beamon	.60	.25	.07
☐ 144 Norm Charlton	.10	.05	.01
☐ 145 Mike Mussina	.60	.25	.07
☐ 146 Billy Owens	.10	.05	.01
☐ 147 Ozzie Smith	.75	.35	.09
☐ 148 Jason Kendall	2.00	.90	.25
☐ 149 Mike Matthews	.25	.11	.03
☐ 150 David Spykstra	.10	.05	.01
☐ 151 Benji Grigsby	.10	.05	.01
☐ 152 Sean Smith	.25	.11	.03
☐ 153 Mark McGwire	1.00	.45	.12
☐ 154 David Cone	.25	.11	.03
☐ 155 Shon Walker	.30	.14	.04
☐ 156 Jason Giambi	1.00	.45	.12
☐ 157 Jack McDowell	.25	.11	.03
☐ 158 Paxton Briley	.10	.05	.01
☐ 159 Edgar Martinez	.25	.11	.03
☐ 160 Brian Sackinsky	.10	.05	.01
☐ 161 Barry Bonds	.75	.35	.09
☐ 162 Roberto Kelly	25.00	11.00	3.10
☐ 163 Jeff Alkire	.10	.05	.01
☐ 164 Mike Sharperson	.10	.05	.01
☐ 165 Jamie Taylor	.10	.05	.01
☐ 166 John Saffer	.10	.05	.01
☐ 167 Jerry Browne	.10	.05	.01
☐ 168 Travis Fryman	.25	.11	.03
☐ 169 Brady Anderson	.50	.23	.06
☐ 170 Chris Roberts	.25	.11	.03
☐ 171 Lloyd Peever	.10	.05	.01
☐ 172 Francisco Cabrera	.10	.05	.01
☐ 173 Ramiro Martinez	.10	.05	.01
☐ 174 Jeff Alkire	.10	.05	.01
☐ 175 Ivan Rodriguez	.75	.35	.09
☐ 176 Kevin Brown	.10	.05	.01
☐ 177 Chad Roper	.25	.11	.03
☐ 178 Rod Henderson	.10	.05	.01
☐ 179 Dennis Eckersley	.25	.11	.03
☐ 180 Shannon Stewart	.50	.23	.06
☐ 181 DeShawn Warren	.25	.11	.03
☐ 182 Lonnie Smith	25.00	11.00	3.10
☐ 183 Willie Adams	.10	.05	.01
☐ 184 Jeff Montgomery	.25	.11	.03
☐ 185 Damon Hollins	.50	.23	.06
☐ 186 Byron Mathews	.10	.05	.01
☐ 187 Harold Baines	.25	.11	.03
☐ 188 Rick Greene	.10	.05	.01
☐ 189 Carlos Baerga	.25	.11	.03
☐ 190 Brandon Cromer	.25	.11	.03
☐ 191 Roberto Alomar	.60	.25	.07
☐ 192 Rich Ireland	.10	.05	.01
☐ 193 Steve Montgomery	.10	.05	.01
☐ 194 Brant Brown	.10	.05	.01
☐ 195 Ritchie Moody	.10	.05	.01
☐ 196 Michael Tucker	.50	.23	.06
☐ 197 Jason Varitek	.75	.35	.09
☐ 198 David Manning	.10	.05	.01
☐ 199 Marquis Riley	.10	.05	.01
☐ 200 Jason Giambi	1.00	.45	.12

1993 Stadium Club Murphy Master Photos

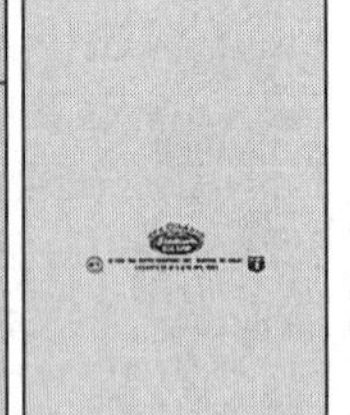

One Murphy Master Photo was included in each 1993 Stadium Club Murphy Special factory set. Each of these twelve uncropped Murphy Master Photos is inlaid in a 5" by 7" white frame and bordered with a prismatic foil trim. The photo within parallels the corresponding player's regular issue Murphy card. The cards are unnumbered and checklisted below in alphabetical order.

	MINT	NRMT	EXC
COMPLETE SET (12)	5.00	2.20	.60
COMMON MASTER PHOTO	.10	.05	.01

☐ 1 Sandy Alomar AS	.10	.05	.01
☐ 2 Tom Glavine AS	.50	.23	.06
☐ 3 Ken Griffey Jr. AS	3.00	1.35	.35
☐ 4 Tony Gwynn AS	1.25	.55	.16
☐ 5 Chuck Knoblauch AS	.50	.23	.06
☐ 6 Chad Mottola '92	.10	.05	.01
☐ 7 Kirby Puckett AS	1.25	.55	.16
☐ 8 Chris Roberts USA	.10	.05	.01
☐ 9 Ryne Sandberg AS	.75	.35	.09
☐ 10 Gary Sheffield AS	.50	.23	.06
☐ 11 Larry Walker AS	.50	.23	.06
☐ 12 Preston Wilson '92	.25	.11	.03

1993 Stadium Club

The 1993 Stadium Club baseball set consists of 750 standard-size cards issued in three series of 300, 300, and 150 cards respectively. The fronts display full-bleed glossy color player photos. A red stripe carrying the player's name and edged on the bottom by a gold stripe cuts across the bottom of the picture. A white baseball icon with gold motion streaks rounds out the front. Award Winner and League Leader cards are studded with gold foil stars. On a background consisting of an artistic drawing of a baseball player's arm extended with ball in glove, the backs carry a second color action photo, biographical information, 1992 Stats Player Profile, the player's ranking (either on his team and/or the AL or NL), statistics, and a miniature reproduction of his Topps rookie card. Each series closes with a Members Choice subset (291-300, 591-600, and 746-750).

	MINT	NRMT	EXC
COMPLETE SET (750)	60.00	27.00	7.50
COMPLETE SERIES 1 (300)	20.00	9.00	2.50
COMPLETE SERIES 2 (300)	25.00	11.00	3.10
COMPLETE SERIES 3 (150)	15.00	6.75	1.85
COMMON CARD (1-750)	.10	.05	.01

☐ 1 Pat Borders	.10	.05	.01
☐ 2 Greg Maddux	2.00	.90	.25
☐ 3 Daryl Boston	.10	.05	.01
☐ 4 Bob Ayrault	.10	.05	.01
☐ 5 Tony Phillips IF	.10	.05	.01
☐ 6 Damion Easley	.10	.05	.01
☐ 7 Kip Gross	.10	.05	.01
☐ 8 Jim Thome	1.50	.70	.19
☐ 9 Tim Belcher	.10	.05	.01
☐ 10 Gary Wayne	.10	.05	.01
☐ 11 Sam Militello	.10	.05	.01
☐ 12 Mike Magnante	.10	.05	.01
☐ 13 Tim Wakefield	.25	.11	.03
☐ 14 Tim Hulett	.10	.05	.01
☐ 15 Rheal Cormier	.10	.05	.01
☐ 16 Juan Guerrero	.10	.05	.01
☐ 17 Rich Gossage	.25	.11	.03
☐ 18 Tim Laker	.10	.05	.01
☐ 19 Darrin Jackson	.10	.05	.01
☐ 20 Jack Clark	.10	.05	.01
☐ 21 Roberto Hernandez	.25	.11	.03
☐ 22 Dean Palmer	.25	.11	.03
☐ 23 Harold Reynolds	.10	.05	.01
☐ 24 Dan Plesac	.10	.05	.01
☐ 25 Brent Mayne	.10	.05	.01
☐ 26 Pat Hentgen	.50	.23	.06
☐ 27 Luis Sojo	.10	.05	.01
☐ 28 Ron Gant	.25	.11	.03
☐ 29 Paul Gibson	.10	.05	.01
☐ 30 Bip Roberts	.10	.05	.01
☐ 31 Mickey Tettleton	.10	.05	.01
☐ 32 Randy Velarde	.10	.05	.01
☐ 33 Brian McRae	.25	.11	.03
☐ 34 Wes Chamberlain	.10	.05	.01
☐ 35 Wayne Kirby	.10	.05	.01
☐ 36 Rey Sanchez	.10	.05	.01
☐ 37 Jesse Orosco	.10	.05	.01
☐ 38 Mike Stanton	.10	.05	.01
☐ 39 Royce Clayton	.25	.11	.03
☐ 40 Cal Ripken UER (Place of birth Havre de Grave; should be Havre de Grace)	2.50	1.10	.30
☐ 41 John Dopson	.10	.05	.01
☐ 42 Gene Larkin	.10	.05	.01
☐ 43 Tim Raines	.50	.23	.06
☐ 44 Randy Myers	.25	.11	.03
☐ 45 Clay Parker	.10	.05	.01
☐ 46 Mike Scioscia	.10	.05	.01
☐ 47 Pete Incaviglia	.10	.05	.01
☐ 48 Todd Van Poppel	.10	.05	.01
☐ 49 Ray Lankford	.25	.11	.03
☐ 50 Eddie Murray	.75	.35	.09
☐ 51 Barry Bonds COR	.75	.35	.09
☐ 51A Barry Bonds ERR (Missing four stars over name to indicate NL MVP)	.75	.35	.09
☐ 52 Gary Thurman	.10	.05	.01
☐ 53 Bob Wickman	.10	.05	.01
☐ 54 Joey Cora	.25	.11	.03
☐ 55 Kenny Rogers	.10	.05	.01
☐ 56 Mike Devereaux	.10	.05	.01
☐ 57 Kevin Seitzer	.10	.05	.01
☐ 58 Rafael Belliard	.10	.05	.01
☐ 59 David Wells	.10	.05	.01
☐ 60 Mark Clark	.10	.05	.01
☐ 61 Carlos Baerga	.25	.11	.03
☐ 62 Scott Brosius	.10	.05	.01
☐ 63 Jeff Grotewold	.10	.05	.01
☐ 64 Rick Wrona	.10	.05	.01

☐ 65 Kurt Knudsen .10 .05 .01
☐ 66 Lloyd McClendon .10 .05 .01
☐ 67 Omar Vizquel .25 .11 .03
☐ 68 Jose Vizcaino .10 .05 .01
☐ 69 Rob Ducey .10 .05 .01
☐ 70 Casey Candaele .10 .05 .01
☐ 71 Ramon Martinez .25 .11 .03
☐ 72 Todd Hundley .25 .11 .03
☐ 73 John Marzano .10 .05 .01
☐ 74 Derek Parks .10 .05 .01
☐ 75 Jack McDowell .25 .11 .03
☐ 76 Tim Scott .10 .05 .01
☐ 77 Mike Mussina .60 .25 .07
☐ 78 Delino DeShields .10 .05 .01
☐ 79 Chris Bosio .10 .05 .01
☐ 80 Mike Bordick .10 .05 .01
☐ 81 Rod Beck .25 .11 .03
☐ 82 Ted Power .10 .05 .01
☐ 83 John Kruk .25 .11 .03
☐ 84 Steve Shifflett .10 .05 .01
☐ 85 Danny Tartabull .10 .05 .01
☐ 86 Mike Greenwell .10 .05 .01
☐ 87 Jose Melendez .10 .05 .01
☐ 88 Craig Wilson .10 .05 .01
☐ 89 Melvin Nieves .50 .23 .06
☐ 90 Ed Sprague .25 .11 .03
☐ 91 Willie McGee .10 .05 .01
☐ 92 Joe Orsulak .10 .05 .01
☐ 93 Jeff King .25 .11 .03
☐ 94 Dan Pasqua .10 .05 .01
☐ 95 Brian Harper .10 .05 .01
☐ 96 Joe Oliver .10 .05 .01
☐ 97 Shane Turner .10 .05 .01
☐ 98 Lenny Harris .10 .05 .01
☐ 99 Jeff Parrett .10 .05 .01
☐ 100 Luis Polonia .10 .05 .01
☐ 101 Kent Bottenfield .10 .05 .01
☐ 102 Albert Belle 1.25 .55 .16
☐ 103 Mike Maddux .10 .05 .01
☐ 104 Randy Tomlin .10 .05 .01
☐ 105 Andy Stankiewicz .10 .05 .01
☐ 106 Rico Rossy .10 .05 .01
☐ 107 Joe Hesketh .10 .05 .01
☐ 108 Dennis Powell .10 .05 .01
☐ 109 Derrick May .10 .05 .01
☐ 110 Pete Harnisch .10 .05 .01
☐ 111 Kent Mercker .10 .05 .01
☐ 112 Scott Fletcher .10 .05 .01
☐ 113 Rex Hudler .10 .05 .01
☐ 114 Chico Walker .10 .05 .01
☐ 115 Rafael Palmeiro .50 .23 .06
☐ 116 Mark Leiter .10 .05 .01
☐ 117 Pedro Munoz .10 .05 .01
☐ 118 Jim Bullinger .10 .05 .01
☐ 119 Ivan Calderon .10 .05 .01
☐ 120 Mike Timlin .10 .05 .01
☐ 121 Rene Gonzales .10 .05 .01
☐ 122 Greg Vaughn .25 .11 .03
☐ 123 Mike Flanagan .10 .05 .01
☐ 124 Mike Hartley .10 .05 .01
☐ 125 Jeff Montgomery .25 .11 .03
☐ 126 Mike Gallego .10 .05 .01
☐ 127 Don Slaught .10 .05 .01
☐ 128 Charlie O'Brien .10 .05 .01
☐ 129 Jose Offerman .10 .05 .01
(Can be found with home town missing on back)
☐ 130 Mark Wohlers .25 .11 .03
☐ 131 Eric Fox .10 .05 .01
☐ 132 Doug Strange .10 .05 .01
☐ 133 Jeff Frye .10 .05 .01
☐ 134 Wade Boggs UER .50 .23 .06
(Redundantly lists lefty breakdown)
☐ 135 Lou Whitaker .25 .11 .03
☐ 136 Craig Grebeck .10 .05 .01
☐ 137 Rich Rodriguez .10 .05 .01
☐ 138 Jay Bell .25 .11 .03
☐ 139 Felix Fermin .10 .05 .01
☐ 140 Denny Martinez .25 .11 .03
☐ 141 Eric Anthony .10 .05 .01
☐ 142 Roberto Alomar .60 .25 .07
☐ 143 Darren Lewis .10 .05 .01
☐ 144 Mike Blowers .10 .05 .01
☐ 145 Scott Bankhead .10 .05 .01
☐ 146 Jeff Reboulet .10 .05 .01
☐ 147 Frank Viola .10 .05 .01
☐ 148 Bill Pecota .10 .05 .01
☐ 149 Carlos Hernandez .10 .05 .01
☐ 150 Bobby Witt .10 .05 .01
☐ 151 Sid Bream .10 .05 .01
☐ 152 Todd Zeile .10 .05 .01
☐ 153 Dennis Cook .10 .05 .01
☐ 154 Brian Bohanon .10 .05 .01
☐ 155 Pat Kelly .10 .05 .01
☐ 156 Milt Cuyler .10 .05 .01
☐ 157 Juan Bell .10 .05 .01
☐ 158 Randy Milligan .10 .05 .01
☐ 159 Mark Gardner .10 .05 .01
☐ 160 Pat Tabler .10 .05 .01
☐ 161 Jeff Reardon .25 .11 .03
☐ 162 Ken Patterson .10 .05 .01
☐ 163 Bobby Bonilla .25 .11 .03
☐ 164 Tony Pena .10 .05 .01
☐ 165 Greg Swindell .10 .05 .01
☐ 166 Kirk McCaskill .10 .05 .01
☐ 167 Doug Drabek .10 .05 .01
☐ 168 Franklin Stubbs .10 .05 .01
☐ 169 Ron Tingley .10 .05 .01
☐ 170 Willie Banks .10 .05 .01
☐ 171 Sergio Valdez .10 .05 .01
☐ 172 Mark Lemke .10 .05 .01
☐ 173 Robin Yount .50 .23 .06
☐ 174 Storm Davis .10 .05 .01
☐ 175 Dan Walters .10 .05 .01
☐ 176 Steve Farr .10 .05 .01
☐ 177 Curt Wilkerson .10 .05 .01
☐ 178 Luis Alicea .10 .05 .01
☐ 179 Russ Swan .10 .05 .01
☐ 180 Mitch Williams .10 .05 .01
☐ 181 Wilson Alvarez .25 .11 .03
☐ 182 Carl Willis .10 .05 .01
☐ 183 Craig Biggio .25 .11 .03
☐ 184 Sean Berry .10 .05 .01
☐ 185 Trevor Wilson .10 .05 .01
☐ 186 Jeff Tackett .10 .05 .01
☐ 187 Ellis Burks .25 .11 .03
☐ 188 Jeff Branson .10 .05 .01
☐ 189 Matt Nokes .10 .05 .01
☐ 190 John Smiley .10 .05 .01
☐ 191 Danny Gladden .10 .05 .01
☐ 192 Mike Boddicker .10 .05 .01
☐ 193 Roger Pavlik .25 .11 .03
☐ 194 Paul Sorrento .10 .05 .01
☐ 195 Vince Coleman .10 .05 .01
☐ 196 Gary DiSarcina .10 .05 .01
☐ 197 Rafael Bournigal .10 .05 .01
☐ 198 Mike Schooler .10 .05 .01
☐ 199 Scott Ruskin .10 .05 .01
☐ 200 Frank Thomas 3.00 1.35 .35
☐ 201 Kyle Abbott .10 .05 .01
☐ 202 Mike Perez .10 .05 .01
☐ 203 Andre Dawson .25 .11 .03
☐ 204 Bill Swift .10 .05 .01
☐ 205 Alejandro Pena .10 .05 .01
☐ 206 Dave Winfield .50 .23 .06
☐ 207 Andujar Cedeno .10 .05 .01
☐ 208 Terry Steinbach .25 .11 .03
☐ 209 Chris Hammond .10 .05 .01
☐ 210 Todd Burns .10 .05 .01
☐ 211 Hipolito Pichardo .10 .05 .01
☐ 212 John Kiely .10 .05 .01
☐ 213 Tim Teufel .10 .05 .01
☐ 214 Lee Guetterman .10 .05 .01
☐ 215 Geronimo Pena .10 .05 .01
☐ 216 Brett Butler .25 .11 .03
☐ 217 Bryan Hickerson .10 .05 .01
☐ 218 Rick Trlicek .10 .05 .01
☐ 219 Lee Stevens .10 .05 .01
☐ 220 Roger Clemens .60 .25 .07
☐ 221 Carlton Fisk .50 .23 .06
☐ 222 Chili Davis .25 .11 .03
☐ 223 Walt Terrell .10 .05 .01
☐ 224 Jim Eisenreich .25 .11 .03
☐ 225 Ricky Bones .10 .05 .01
☐ 226 Henry Rodriguez .50 .23 .06
☐ 227 Ken Hill .25 .11 .03
☐ 228 Rick Wilkins .10 .05 .01
☐ 229 Ricky Jordan .10 .05 .01
☐ 230 Bernard Gilkey .25 .11 .03
☐ 231 Tim Fortugno .10 .05 .01
☐ 232 Geno Petralli .10 .05 .01
☐ 233 Jose Rijo .10 .05 .01
☐ 234 Jim Leyritz .10 .05 .01
☐ 235 Kevin Campbell .10 .05 .01
☐ 236 Al Osuna .10 .05 .01
☐ 237 Pete Smith .10 .05 .01
☐ 238 Pete Schourek .25 .11 .03
☐ 239 Moises Alou .25 .11 .03
☐ 240 Donn Pall .10 .05 .01
☐ 241 Denny Neagle .25 .11 .03
☐ 242 Dan Peltier .10 .05 .01
☐ 243 Scott Scudder .10 .05 .01
☐ 244 Juan Guzman .25 .11 .03
☐ 245 Dave Burba .10 .05 .01
☐ 246 Rick Sutcliffe .10 .05 .01
☐ 247 Tony Fossas .10 .05 .01
☐ 248 Mike Munoz .10 .05 .01
☐ 249 Tim Salmon .75 .35 .09
☐ 250 Rob Murphy .10 .05 .01
☐ 251 Roger McDowell .10 .05 .01
☐ 252 Lance Parrish .10 .05 .01
☐ 253 Cliff Brantley .10 .05 .01
☐ 254 Scott Leius .10 .05 .01
☐ 255 Carlos Martinez .10 .05 .01
☐ 256 Vince Horsman .10 .05 .01
☐ 257 Oscar Azocar .10 .05 .01
☐ 258 Craig Shipley .10 .05 .01
☐ 259 Ben McDonald .10 .05 .01
☐ 260 Jeff Brantley .10 .05 .01
☐ 261 Damon Berryhill .10 .05 .01
☐ 262 Joe Grahe .10 .05 .01
☐ 263 Dave Hansen .10 .05 .01
☐ 264 Rich Amaral .10 .05 .01
☐ 265 Tim Pugh .10 .05 .01
☐ 266 Dion James .10 .05 .01
☐ 267 Frank Tanana .10 .05 .01
☐ 268 Stan Belinda .10 .05 .01
☐ 269 Jeff Kent .25 .11 .03
☐ 270 Bruce Ruffin .10 .05 .01
☐ 271 Xavier Hernandez .10 .05 .01
☐ 272 Darrin Fletcher .10 .05 .01
☐ 273 Tino Martinez .25 .11 .03
☐ 274 Benny Santiago .10 .05 .01
☐ 275 Scott Radinsky .10 .05 .01
☐ 276 Mariano Duncan .10 .05 .01
☐ 277 Kenny Lofton 1.25 .55 .16
☐ 278 Dwight Smith .10 .05 .01
☐ 279 Joe Carter .25 .11 .03
☐ 280 Tim Jones .10 .05 .01
☐ 281 Jeff Huson .10 .05 .01
☐ 282 Phil Plantier .10 .05 .01
☐ 283 Kirby Puckett 1.25 .55 .16
☐ 284 Johnny Guzman .10 .05 .01
☐ 285 Mike Morgan .10 .05 .01
☐ 286 Chris Sabo .10 .05 .01
☐ 287 Matt Williams .50 .23 .06
☐ 288 Checklist 1-100 .10 .05 .01
☐ 289 Checklist 101-200 .10 .05 .01
☐ 290 Checklist 201-300 .10 .05 .01
☐ 291 Dennis Eckersley MC .25 .11 .03
☐ 292 Eric Karros MC .50 .23 .06
☐ 293 Pat Listach MC .10 .05 .01
☐ 294 Andy Van Slyke MC .10 .05 .01
☐ 295 Robin Ventura MC .25 .11 .03
☐ 296 Tom Glavine MC .50 .23 .06
☐ 297 Juan Gonzalez MC UER .75 .35 .09
(Misspelled Gonzales)
☐ 298 Travis Fryman MC .25 .11 .03
☐ 299 Larry Walker MC .50 .23 .06
☐ 300 Gary Sheffield MC .50 .23 .06
☐ 301 Chuck Finley .10 .05 .01
☐ 302 Luis Gonzalez .10 .05 .01
☐ 303 Darryl Hamilton .10 .05 .01
☐ 304 Bien Figueroa .10 .05 .01
☐ 305 Ron Darling .10 .05 .01
☐ 306 Jonathan Hurst .10 .05 .01
☐ 307 Mike Sharperson .10 .05 .01
☐ 308 Mike Christopher .10 .05 .01
☐ 309 Marvin Freeman .10 .05 .01
☐ 310 Jay Buhner .50 .23 .06
☐ 311 Butch Henry .10 .05 .01
☐ 312 Greg W. Harris .10 .05 .01
☐ 313 Darren Daulton .25 .11 .03
☐ 314 Chuck Knoblauch .50 .23 .06
☐ 315 Greg A. Harris .10 .05 .01
☐ 316 John Franco .10 .05 .01
☐ 317 John Wehner .10 .05 .01
☐ 318 Donald Harris .10 .05 .01
☐ 319 Benny Santiago .10 .05 .01
☐ 320 Larry Walker .50 .23 .06
☐ 321 Randy Knorr .10 .05 .01
☐ 322 Ramon Martinez .25 .11 .03
☐ 323 Mike Stanley .10 .05 .01
☐ 324 Bill Wegman .10 .05 .01
☐ 325 Tom Candiotti .10 .05 .01
☐ 326 Glenn Davis .10 .05 .01
☐ 327 Chuck Crim .10 .05 .01
☐ 328 Scott Livingstone .10 .05 .01
☐ 329 Eddie Taubensee .10 .05 .01
☐ 330 George Bell .10 .05 .01
☐ 331 Edgar Martinez .25 .11 .03
☐ 332 Paul Assenmacher .10 .05 .01
☐ 333 Steve Hosey .10 .05 .01
☐ 334 Mo Vaughn .75 .35 .09
☐ 335 Bret Saberhagen .25 .11 .03
☐ 336 Mike Trombley .10 .05 .01
☐ 337 Mark Lewis .10 .05 .01
☐ 338 Terry Pendleton .25 .11 .03
☐ 339 Dave Hollins .10 .05 .01
☐ 340 Jeff Conine .25 .11 .03
☐ 341 Bob Tewksbury .10 .05 .01
☐ 342 Billy Ashley .10 .05 .01
☐ 343 Zane Smith .10 .05 .01
☐ 344 John Wetteland .25 .11 .03
☐ 345 Chris Hoiles .10 .05 .01
☐ 346 Frank Castillo .10 .05 .01
☐ 347 Bruce Hurst .10 .05 .01
☐ 348 Kevin McReynolds .10 .05 .01
☐ 349 Dave Henderson .10 .05 .01
☐ 350 Ryan Bowen .10 .05 .01
☐ 351 Sid Fernandez .10 .05 .01
☐ 352 Mark Whiten .10 .05 .01
☐ 353 Nolan Ryan 2.50 1.10 .30
☐ 354 Rick Aguilera .10 .05 .01
☐ 355 Mark Langston .25 .11 .03
☐ 356 Jack Morris .25 .11 .03
☐ 357 Rob Deer .10 .05 .01
☐ 358 Dave Fleming .10 .05 .01
☐ 359 Lance Johnson .25 .11 .03
☐ 360 Joe Millette .10 .05 .01
☐ 361 Wil Cordero .25 .11 .03
☐ 362 Chito Martinez .10 .05 .01
☐ 363 Scott Servais .10 .05 .01
☐ 364 Bernie Williams .60 .25 .07
☐ 365 Pedro Martinez .50 .23 .06
☐ 366 Ryne Sandberg .75 .35 .09
☐ 367 Brad Ausmus .10 .05 .01
☐ 368 Scott Cooper .10 .05 .01
☐ 369 Rob Dibble .10 .05 .01
☐ 370 Walt Weiss .10 .05 .01
☐ 371 Mark Davis .10 .05 .01
☐ 372 Orlando Merced .25 .11 .03
☐ 373 Mike Jackson .10 .05 .01
☐ 374 Kevin Appier .25 .11 .03
☐ 375 Esteban Beltre .10 .05 .01
☐ 376 Joe Slusarski .10 .05 .01
☐ 377 William Suero .10 .05 .01
☐ 378 Pete O'Brien .10 .05 .01
☐ 379 Alan Embree .10 .05 .01
☐ 380 Lenny Webster .10 .05 .01
☐ 381 Eric Davis .25 .11 .03
☐ 382 Duane Ward .10 .05 .01
☐ 383 John Habyan .10 .05 .01
☐ 384 Jeff Bagwell 1.25 .55 .16
☐ 385 Ruben Amaro .10 .05 .01
☐ 386 Julio Valera .10 .05 .01
☐ 387 Robin Ventura .25 .11 .03
☐ 388 Archi Cianfrocco .10 .05 .01
☐ 389 Skeeter Barnes .10 .05 .01
☐ 390 Tim Costo .10 .05 .01
☐ 391 Luis Mercedes .10 .05 .01
☐ 392 Jeremy Hernandez .10 .05 .01
☐ 393 Shawon Dunston .10 .05 .01
☐ 394 Andy Van Slyke .25 .11 .03
☐ 395 Kevin Maas .10 .05 .01
☐ 396 Kevin Brown .25 .11 .03
☐ 397 J.T. Bruett .10 .05 .01
☐ 398 Darryl Strawberry .25 .11 .03
☐ 399 Tom Pagnozzi .10 .05 .01
☐ 400 Sandy Alomar Jr. .25 .11 .03
☐ 401 Keith Miller .10 .05 .01
☐ 402 Rich DeLucia .10 .05 .01
☐ 403 Shawn Abner .10 .05 .01
☐ 404 Howard Johnson .10 .05 .01
☐ 405 Mike Benjamin .10 .05 .01
☐ 406 Roberto Mejia .10 .05 .01
☐ 407 Mike Butcher .10 .05 .01
☐ 408 Deion Sanders UER .50 .23 .06
(Braves on front and Yankees on back)
☐ 409 Todd Stottlemyre .25 .11 .03
☐ 410 Scott Kamieniecki .10 .05 .01
☐ 411 Doug Jones .10 .05 .01
☐ 412 John Burkett .10 .05 .01
☐ 413 Lance Blankenship .10 .05 .01
☐ 414 Jeff Parrett .10 .05 .01
☐ 415 Barry Larkin .50 .23 .06
☐ 416 Alan Trammell .50 .23 .06
☐ 417 Mark Kiefer .10 .05 .01
☐ 418 Gregg Olson .10 .05 .01
☐ 419 Mark Grace .50 .23 .06
☐ 420 Shane Mack .10 .05 .01
☐ 421 Bob Walk .10 .05 .01
☐ 422 Curt Schilling .10 .05 .01
☐ 423 Erik Hanson .10 .05 .01
☐ 424 George Brett 1.25 .55 .16
☐ 425 Reggie Jefferson .25 .11 .03
☐ 426 Mark Portugal .10 .05 .01
☐ 427 Ron Karkovice .10 .05 .01
☐ 428 Matt Young .10 .05 .01
☐ 429 Troy Neel .10 .05 .01
☐ 430 Hector Fajardo .10 .05 .01
☐ 431 Dave Righetti .10 .05 .01
☐ 432 Pat Listach .10 .05 .01
☐ 433 Jeff Innis .10 .05 .01
☐ 434 Bob MacDonald .10 .05 .01
☐ 435 Brian Jordan .50 .23 .06
☐ 436 Jeff Blauser .10 .05 .01
☐ 437 Mike Myers .10 .05 .01
☐ 438 Frank Seminara .10 .05 .01
☐ 439 Rusty Meacham .10 .05 .01
☐ 440 Greg Briley .10 .05 .01
☐ 441 Derek Lilliquist .10 .05 .01
☐ 442 John Vander Wal .10 .05 .01
☐ 443 Scott Erickson .10 .05 .01
☐ 444 Bob Scanlan .10 .05 .01
☐ 445 Todd Frohwirth .10 .05 .01
☐ 446 Tom Goodwin .10 .05 .01
☐ 447 William Pennyfeather .10 .05 .01
☐ 448 Travis Fryman .25 .11 .03
☐ 449 Mickey Morandini .10 .05 .01
☐ 450 Greg Olson .10 .05 .01
☐ 451 Trevor Hoffman .50 .23 .06
☐ 452 Dave Magadan .10 .05 .01
☐ 453 Shawn Jeter .10 .05 .01
☐ 454 Andres Galarraga .50 .23 .06
☐ 455 Ted Wood .10 .05 .01
☐ 456 Freddie Benavides .10 .05 .01
☐ 457 Junior Felix .10 .05 .01
☐ 458 Alex Cole .10 .05 .01
☐ 459 John Orton .10 .05 .01
☐ 460 Eddie Zosky .10 .05 .01
☐ 461 Dennis Eckersley .25 .11 .03
☐ 462 Lee Smith .25 .11 .03
☐ 463 John Smoltz .50 .23 .06
☐ 464 Ken Caminiti .50 .23 .06
☐ 465 Melido Perez .10 .05 .01
☐ 466 Tom Marsh .10 .05 .01
☐ 467 Jeff Nelson .10 .05 .01
☐ 468 Jesse Levis .10 .05 .01
☐ 469 Chris Nabholz .10 .05 .01
☐ 470 Mike Macfarlane .10 .05 .01
☐ 471 Reggie Sanders .50 .23 .06
☐ 472 Chuck McElroy .10 .05 .01
☐ 473 Kevin Gross .10 .05 .01
☐ 474 Matt Whiteside .10 .05 .01
☐ 475 Cal Eldred .10 .05 .01
☐ 476 Dave Gallagher .10 .05 .01
☐ 477 Len Dykstra .25 .11 .03
☐ 478 Mark McGwire 1.00 .45 .12

Card	MINT	NRMT	EXC
□ 479 David Segui	.10	.05	.01
□ 480 Mike Henneman	.10	.05	.01
□ 481 Bret Barberie	.10	.05	.01
□ 482 Steve Sax	.10	.05	.01
□ 483 Dave Valle	.10	.05	.01
□ 484 Danny Darwin	.10	.05	.01
□ 485 Devon White	.10	.05	.01
□ 486 Eric Plunk	.10	.05	.01
□ 487 Jim Gott	.10	.05	.01
□ 488 Scooter Tucker	.10	.05	.01
□ 489 Omar Olivares	.10	.05	.01
□ 490 Greg Myers	.10	.05	.01
□ 491 Brian Hunter	.10	.05	.01
□ 492 Kevin Tapani	.10	.05	.01
□ 493 Rich Monteleone	.10	.05	.01
□ 494 Steve Buechele	.10	.05	.01
□ 495 Bo Jackson	.25	.11	.03
□ 496 Mike LaValliere	.10	.05	.01
□ 497 Mark Leonard	.10	.05	.01
□ 498 Daryl Boston	.10	.05	.01
□ 499 Jose Canseco	.50	.23	.06
□ 500 Brian Barnes	.10	.05	.01
□ 501 Randy Johnson	.50	.23	.06
□ 502 Tim McIntosh	.10	.05	.01
□ 503 Cecil Fielder	.25	.11	.03
□ 504 Derek Bell	.25	.11	.03
□ 505 Kevin Koslofski	.10	.05	.01
□ 506 Darren Holmes	.10	.05	.01
□ 507 Brady Anderson	.50	.23	.06
□ 508 John Valentin	.25	.11	.03
□ 509 Jerry Browne	.10	.05	.01
□ 510 Fred McGriff	.50	.23	.06
□ 511 Pedro Astacio	.10	.05	.01
□ 512 Gary Gaetti	.25	.11	.03
□ 513 John Burke	.10	.05	.01
□ 514 Dwight Gooden	.25	.11	.03
□ 515 Thomas Howard	.10	.05	.01
□ 516 Darrell Whitmore UER (11 games played in 1992; should be 121)	.10	.05	.01
□ 517 Ozzie Guillen	.10	.05	.01
□ 518 Darryl Kile	.10	.05	.01
□ 519 Rich Rowland	.10	.05	.01
□ 520 Carlos Delgado	.75	.35	.09
□ 521 Doug Henry	.10	.05	.01
□ 522 Greg Colbrunn	.10	.05	.01
□ 523 Tom Gordon	.10	.05	.01
□ 524 Ivan Rodriguez	.75	.35	.09
□ 525 Kent Hrbek	.25	.11	.03
□ 526 Eric Young	.50	.23	.06
□ 527 Rod Brewer	.10	.05	.01
□ 528 Eric Karros	.50	.23	.06
□ 529 Marquis Grissom	.25	.11	.03
□ 530 Rico Brogna	.25	.11	.03
□ 531 Sammy Sosa	.50	.23	.06
□ 532 Bret Boone	.25	.11	.03
□ 533 Luis Rivera	.10	.05	.01
□ 534 Hal Morris	.10	.05	.01
□ 535 Monty Fariss	.10	.05	.01
□ 536 Leo Gomez	.10	.05	.01
□ 537 Wally Joyner	.25	.11	.03
□ 538 Tony Gwynn	1.25	.55	.16
□ 539 Mike Williams	.10	.05	.01
□ 540 Juan Gonzalez	1.50	.70	.19
□ 541 Ryan Klesko	1.00	.45	.12
□ 542 Ryan Thompson	.10	.05	.01
□ 543 Chad Curtis	.25	.11	.03
□ 544 Orel Hershiser	.25	.11	.03
□ 545 Carlos Garcia	.10	.05	.01
□ 546 Bob Welch	.10	.05	.01
□ 547 Vinny Castilla	.50	.23	.06
□ 548 Ozzie Smith	.75	.35	.09
□ 549 Luis Salazar	.10	.05	.01
□ 550 Mark Guthrie	.10	.05	.01
□ 551 Charles Nagy	.25	.11	.03
□ 552 Alex Fernandez	.25	.11	.03
□ 553 Mel Rojas	.25	.11	.03
□ 554 Orestes Destrade	.10	.05	.01
□ 555 Mark Gubicza	.10	.05	.01
□ 556 Steve Finley	.25	.11	.03
□ 557 Don Mattingly	1.50	.70	.19
□ 558 Rickey Henderson	.50	.23	.06
□ 559 Tommy Greene	.10	.05	.01
□ 560 Arthur Rhodes	.10	.05	.01
□ 561 Alfredo Griffin	.10	.05	.01
□ 562 Will Clark	.50	.23	.06
□ 563 Bob Zupcic	.10	.05	.01
□ 564 Chuck Carr	.10	.05	.01
□ 565 Henry Cotto	.10	.05	.01
□ 566 Billy Spiers	.10	.05	.01
□ 567 Jack Armstrong	.10	.05	.01
□ 568 Kurt Stillwell	.10	.05	.01
□ 569 David McCarty	.10	.05	.01
□ 570 Joe Vitiello	.25	.11	.03
□ 571 Gerald Williams	.10	.05	.01
□ 572 Dale Murphy	.50	.23	.06
□ 573 Scott Aldred	.10	.05	.01
□ 574 Bill Gullickson	.10	.05	.01
□ 575 Bobby Thigpen	.10	.05	.01
□ 576 Glenallen Hill	.10	.05	.01
□ 577 Dwayne Henry	.10	.05	.01
□ 578 Calvin Jones	.10	.05	.01
□ 579 Al Martin	.25	.11	.03
□ 580 Ruben Sierra	.25	.11	.03
□ 581 Andy Benes	.25	.11	.03
□ 582 Anthony Young	.10	.05	.01
□ 583 Shawn Boskie	.10	.05	.01
□ 584 Scott Pose	.10	.05	.01
□ 585 Mike Piazza	3.00	1.35	.35
□ 586 Donovan Osborne	.10	.05	.01
□ 587 James Austin	.10	.05	.01
□ 588 Checklist 301-400	.10	.05	.01
□ 589 Checklist 401-500	.10	.05	.01
□ 590 Checklist 501-600	.10	.05	.01
□ 591 Ken Griffey Jr. MC	1.50	.70	.19
□ 592 Ivan Rodriguez MC	.50	.23	.06
□ 593 Carlos Baerga MC	.25	.11	.03
□ 594 Fred McGriff MC	.50	.23	.06
□ 595 Mark McGwire MC	.50	.23	.06
□ 596 Roberto Alomar MC	.50	.23	.06
□ 597 Kirby Puckett MC	.50	.23	.06
□ 598 Marquis Grissom MC	.25	.11	.03
□ 599 John Smoltz MC	.50	.23	.06
□ 600 Ryne Sandberg MC	.50	.23	.06
□ 601 Wade Boggs	.50	.23	.06
□ 602 Jeff Reardon	.25	.11	.03
□ 603 Billy Ripken	.10	.05	.01
□ 604 Bryan Harvey	.10	.05	.01
□ 605 Carlos Quintana	.10	.05	.01
□ 606 Greg Hibbard	.10	.05	.01
□ 607 Ellis Burks	.25	.11	.03
□ 608 Greg Swindell	.10	.05	.01
□ 609 Dave Winfield	.50	.23	.06
□ 610 Charlie Hough	.10	.05	.01
□ 611 Chili Davis	.25	.11	.03
□ 612 Jody Reed	.10	.05	.01
□ 613 Mark Williamson	.10	.05	.01
□ 614 Phil Plantier	.10	.05	.01
□ 615 Jim Abbott	.10	.05	.01
□ 616 Dante Bichette	.50	.23	.06
□ 617 Mark Eichhorn	.10	.05	.01
□ 618 Gary Sheffield	.50	.23	.06
□ 619 Richie Lewis	.10	.05	.01
□ 620 Joe Girardi	.10	.05	.01
□ 621 Jaime Navarro	.10	.05	.01
□ 622 Willie Wilson	.10	.05	.01
□ 623 Scott Fletcher	.10	.05	.01
□ 624 Bud Black	.10	.05	.01
□ 625 Tom Brunansky	.10	.05	.01
□ 626 Steve Avery	.25	.11	.03
□ 627 Paul Molitor	.60	.25	.07
□ 628 Gregg Jefferies	.25	.11	.03
□ 629 Dave Stewart	.25	.11	.03
□ 630 Javier Lopez	.75	.35	.09
□ 631 Greg Gagne	.10	.05	.01
□ 632 Roberto Kelly	.10	.05	.01
□ 633 Mike Fetters	.10	.05	.01
□ 634 Ozzie Canseco	.10	.05	.01
□ 635 Jeff Russell	.10	.05	.01
□ 636 Pete Incaviglia	.10	.05	.01
□ 637 Tom Henke	.10	.05	.01
□ 638 Chipper Jones	4.00	1.80	.50
□ 639 Jimmy Key	.25	.11	.03
□ 640 Dave Martinez	.10	.05	.01
□ 641 Dave Stieb	.10	.05	.01
□ 642 Milt Thompson	.10	.05	.01
□ 643 Alan Mills	.10	.05	.01
□ 644 Tony Fernandez	.10	.05	.01
□ 645 Randy Bush	.10	.05	.01
□ 646 Joe Magrane	.10	.05	.01
□ 647 Ivan Calderon	.10	.05	.01
□ 648 Jose Guzman	.10	.05	.01
□ 649 John Olerud	.10	.05	.01
□ 650 Tom Glavine	.50	.23	.06
□ 651 Julio Franco	.25	.11	.03
□ 652 Armando Reynoso	.10	.05	.01
□ 653 Felix Jose	.10	.05	.01
□ 654 Ben Rivera	.10	.05	.01
□ 655 Andre Dawson	.25	.11	.03
□ 656 Mike Harkey	.10	.05	.01
□ 657 Kevin Seitzer	.10	.05	.01
□ 658 Lonnie Smith	.10	.05	.01
□ 659 Norm Charlton	.10	.05	.01
□ 660 David Justice	.50	.23	.06
□ 661 Fernando Valenzuela	.25	.11	.03
□ 662 Dan Wilson	.25	.11	.03
□ 663 Mark Gardner	.10	.05	.01
□ 664 Doug Dascenzo	.10	.05	.01
□ 665 Greg Maddux	2.00	.90	.25
□ 666 Harold Baines	.25	.11	.03
□ 667 Randy Myers	.25	.11	.03
□ 668 Harold Reynolds	.10	.05	.01
□ 669 Candy Maldonado	.10	.05	.01
□ 670 Al Leiter	.25	.11	.03
□ 671 Jerald Clark	.10	.05	.01
□ 672 Doug Drabek	.10	.05	.01
□ 673 Kirk Gibson	.25	.11	.03
□ 674 Steve Reed	.10	.05	.01
□ 675 Mike Felder	.10	.05	.01
□ 676 Ricky Gutierrez	.10	.05	.01
□ 677 Spike Owen	.10	.05	.01
□ 678 Otis Nixon	.10	.05	.01
□ 679 Scott Sanderson	.10	.05	.01
□ 680 Mark Carreon	.10	.05	.01
□ 681 Troy Percival	.25	.11	.03
□ 682 Kevin Stocker	.25	.11	.03
□ 683 Jim Converse	.10	.05	.01
□ 684 Barry Bonds	.75	.35	.09
□ 685 Greg Gohr	.10	.05	.01
□ 686 Tim Wallach	.10	.05	.01
□ 687 Matt Mieske	.25	.11	.03
□ 688 Robby Thompson	.10	.05	.01
□ 689 Brien Taylor	.10	.05	.01
□ 690 Kirt Manwaring	.10	.05	.01
□ 691 Mike Lansing	.25	.11	.03
□ 692 Steve Decker	.10	.05	.01
□ 693 Mike Moore	.10	.05	.01
□ 694 Kevin Mitchell	.25	.11	.03
□ 695 Phil Hiatt	.10	.05	.01
□ 696 Tony Tarasco	.25	.11	.03
□ 697 Benji Gil	.25	.11	.03
□ 698 Jeff Juden	.10	.05	.01
□ 699 Kevin Reimer	.10	.05	.01
□ 700 Andy Ashby	.25	.11	.03
□ 701 John Jaha	.50	.23	.06
□ 702 Tim Bogar	.10	.05	.01
□ 703 David Cone	.25	.11	.03
□ 704 Willie Greene	.25	.11	.03
□ 705 David Hulse	.10	.05	.01
□ 706 Cris Carpenter	.10	.05	.01
□ 707 Ken Griffey Jr.	3.00	1.35	.35
□ 708 Steve Bedrosian	.10	.05	.01
□ 709 Dave Nilsson	.25	.11	.03
□ 710 Paul Wagner	.10	.05	.01
□ 711 B.J. Surhoff	.25	.11	.03
□ 712 Rene Arocha	.10	.05	.01
□ 713 Manuel Lee	.10	.05	.01
□ 714 Brian Williams	.10	.05	.01
□ 715 Sherman Obando	.10	.05	.01
□ 716 Terry Mulholland	.10	.05	.01
□ 717 Paul O'Neill	.25	.11	.03
□ 718 David Nied	.10	.05	.01
□ 719 J.T. Snow	.50	.23	.06
□ 720 Nigel Wilson	.10	.05	.01
□ 721 Mike Bielecki	.10	.05	.01
□ 722 Kevin Young	.10	.05	.01
□ 723 Charlie Leibrandt	.10	.05	.01
□ 724 Frank Bolick	.10	.05	.01
□ 725 Jon Shave	.10	.05	.01
□ 726 Steve Cooke	.10	.05	.01
□ 727 Domingo Martinez	.10	.05	.01
□ 728 Todd Worrell	.10	.05	.01
□ 729 Jose Lind	.10	.05	.01
□ 730 Jim Tatum	.10	.05	.01
□ 731 Mike Hampton	.50	.23	.06
□ 732 Mike Draper	.10	.05	.01
□ 733 Henry Mercedes	.10	.05	.01
□ 734 John Johnstone	.10	.05	.01
□ 735 Mitch Webster	.10	.05	.01
□ 736 Russ Springer	.10	.05	.01
□ 737 Rob Natal	.10	.05	.01
□ 738 Steve Howe	.10	.05	.01
□ 739 Darrell Sherman	.10	.05	.01
□ 740 Pat Mahomes	.10	.05	.01
□ 741 Alex Arias	.10	.05	.01
□ 742 Damon Buford	.10	.05	.01
□ 743 Charlie Hayes	.10	.05	.01
□ 744 Guillermo Velasquez	.10	.05	.01
□ 745 Checklist 601-750 UER (650 Tom Glavine)	.10	.05	.01
□ 746 Frank Thomas MC	1.50	.70	.19
□ 747 Barry Bonds MC	.50	.23	.06
□ 748 Roger Clemens MC	.50	.23	.06
□ 749 Joe Carter MC	.25	.11	.03
□ 750 Greg Maddux MC	1.00	.45	.12

1993 Stadium Club First Day Issue

Two thousand of each 1993 Stadium Club baseball card were produced on the first day and then randomly inserted in packs at a rate of 1:24. These standard-size cards are identical to the regular-issue 1993 Stadium Club cards, except for the embossed prismatic-foil "1st Day Production" logo stamped in an upper corner. Some of the logos have been transferred from "common" 1st day cards to the fronts of better players.

	MINT	NRMT	EXC
COMPLETE SET (750)	2000.00	900.00	250.00
COMPLETE SERIES 1 (300)	700.00	325.00	90.00
COMPLETE SERIES 2 (300)	800.00	350.00	100.00
COMPLETE SERIES 3 (150)	500.00	220.00	60.00
COMMON CARD (1-750)	1.00	.45	.12
*STARS: 12.5X to 30X BASIC CARDS			
*YOUNG STARS: 8X to 20X BASIC CARDS			

1993 Stadium Club Members Only Parallel

These standard-sized cards were issued in complete set form only through Topps' Stadium Club. These cards are the same as the

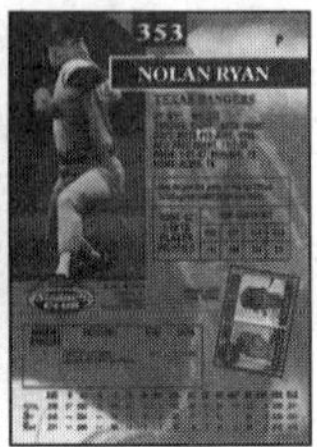

regular Stadium Club cards except they are imprinted with the Stadium Club logo on the front. The set includes parallel versions of both the basic cards and the insert cards. Only the inserts cards have been priced below. Please use the multiplier for values on the basic cards. These sets were issued at an approximate cost of $200 to Stadium Club members.

	MINT	NRMT	EXC
COMPLETE FACT.SET (760)	150.00	70.00	19.00
COMMON CARD (1-750)	.25	.11	.03
*STARS: 2X to 4X BASIC CARDS	1.00	.45	.12
*YOUNG STARS: 1.5X to 3X BASIC CARDS			
*ROOKIES: 1.5X to 3X BASIC CARDS			
□ MA1 Robin Yount	3.00	1.35	.35
□ MA2 George Brett	8.00	3.60	1.00
□ MA3 David Nied	1.00	.45	.12
□ MA4 Nigel Wilson	1.00	.45	.12
□ MB1 Will Clark / Mark McGwire	2.00	.90	.25
□ MB2 Dwight Gooden / Don Mattingly	3.00	1.35	.35
□ MB3 Ryne Sandberg / Frank Thomas	10.00	4.50	1.25
□ MB4 Darryl Strawberry / Ken Griffey	8.00	3.60	1.00
□ MC1 David Nied	1.00	.45	.12
□ MC2 Charlie Hough	1.00	.45	.12

1993 Stadium Club Inserts

This 10-card set was randomly inserted in all series of Stadium Club packs, the first four in series 1, the second four in series 2 and the last two in series 3. The themes of the standard-size cards differ from series to series, but the basic design -- borderless color action shots on the fronts -- remains the same throughout. The series 1 and 3 cards are numbered on the back, the series 2 cards are unnumbered.

	MINT	NRMT	EXC
COMPLETE SET (10)	16.00	7.25	2.00
COMPLETE SERIES 1 (4)	5.00	2.20	.60
COMPLETE SERIES 2 (4)	10.00	4.50	1.25
COMPLETE SERIES 3 (2)	2.00	.90	.25
COMMON SER.1 CARD (A1-A4)	.50	.23	.06
COMMON SER.2 CARD (B1-B4)	1.25	.55	.16
COMMON SER.3 CARD (C1-C2)	.50	.23	.06
□ A1 Robin Yount / 3000 Hit Club	1.00	.45	.12
□ A2 George Brett / 3000 Hit Club	4.00	1.80	.50
□ A3 David Nied / First Draft Pick of the Rockies	.50	.23	.06
□ A4 Nigel Wilson / 1st DP Marlins	.50	.23	.06
□ B1 Will Clark / Mark McGwire / Pacific Terrific	1.25	.55	.16
□ B2 Dwight Gooden / Don Mattingly / Broadway Stars NY	1.50	.70	.19
□ B3 Ryne Sandberg / Frank Thomas / Second City Sluggers	5.00	2.20	.60
□ B4 Darryl Strawberry / Ken Griffey Jr. / Pacific Terrific	4.00	1.80	.50
□ C1 David Nied UER / Colorado Rockies Firsts (Misspelled pitch-hitter on back)	.50	.23	.06
□ C2 Charlie Hough / Florida Marlins Firsts	.50	.23	.06

1993 Stadium Club Master Photos

Each of the three Stadium Club series features Master Photos, uncropped versions of the regular Stadium Club cards. Each Master

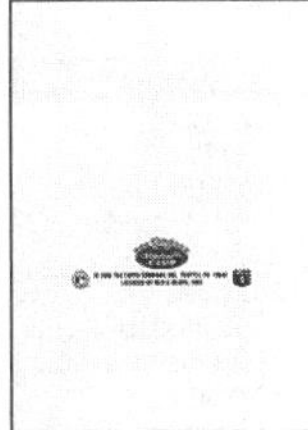

Photo is inlaid in a 5" by 7" white frame and bordered with a prismatic foil trim. The Master Photos were made available to the public in two ways. First, one in every 24 packs included a Master Photo winner card redeemable for a group of three Master Photos until Jan. 31, 1994. Second, each hobby box contained one Master Photo. The cards are unnumbered and checklisted below in alphabetical order within series I (1-12), II (13-24), and III (25-30). Two different versions of these master photos were issued, one with and one without the "Members Only" gold foil seal at the upper right corner. The "Members Only" Master Photos were only available with the direct-mail solicited 750-card Stadium Club Members Only set.

	MINT	NRMT	EXC
COMPLETE SET (30)	24.00	11.00	3.00
COMPLETE SERIES 1 (12)	6.00	2.70	.75
COMPLETE SERIES 2 (12)	8.00	3.60	1.00
COMPLETE SERIES 3 (6)	10.00	4.50	1.25
COMMON CARD	.25	.11	.03
☐ 1 Carlos Baerga	.50	.23	.06
☐ 2 Delino DeShields	.25	.11	.03
☐ 3 Brian McRae	.50	.23	.06
☐ 4 Sam Militello	.25	.11	.03
☐ 5 Joe Oliver	.25	.11	.03
☐ 6 Kirby Puckett	2.00	.90	.25
☐ 7 Cal Ripken	4.00	1.80	.50
☐ 8 Bip Roberts	.25	.11	.03
☐ 9 Mike Scioscia	.25	.11	.03
☐ 10 Rick Sutcliffe	.25	.11	.03
☐ 11 Danny Tartabull	.25	.11	.03
☐ 12 Tim Wakefield	.25	.11	.03
☐ 13 George Brett	2.00	.90	.25
☐ 14 Jose Canseco	.75	.35	.09
☐ 15 Will Clark	.75	.35	.09
☐ 16 Travis Fryman	.50	.23	.06
☐ 17 Dwight Gooden	.50	.23	.06
☐ 18 Mark Grace	.75	.35	.09
☐ 19 Rickey Henderson	.75	.35	.09
☐ 20 Mark McGwire MC	1.50	.70	.19
☐ 21 Nolan Ryan	4.00	1.80	.50
☐ 22 Ruben Sierra	.50	.23	.06
☐ 23 Darryl Strawberry	.50	.23	.06
☐ 24 Larry Walker	.75	.35	.09
☐ 25 Barry Bonds	1.25	.55	.16
☐ 26 Ken Griffey Jr.	5.00	2.20	.60
☐ 27 Greg Maddux	3.00	1.35	.35
☐ 28 David Nied	.25	.11	.03
☐ 29 J.T. Snow	.75	.35	.09
☐ 30 Brien Taylor	.25	.11	.03

1993 Stadium Club Members Only *

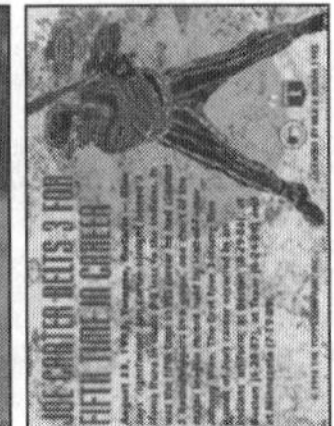

This 59-card standard-size set was mailed out to Stadium Club Members in four separate mailings. Each box contained several sports. The fronts have full-bleed color action player photos with the words "Members Only" printed in gold foil at the bottom along with the player's name and the Stadium Club logo. On a multi-colored background, the horizontal backs carry player information and a computer generated drawing of a baseball player. The cards are unnumbered and checklisted below alphabetically according to sport as follows: baseball (1-28), basketball (29-44), football (45-53), and hockey (54-59).

	MINT	NRMT	EXC
COMPLETE SET (59)	40.00	18.00	5.00
COMMON CARD (1-59)	.15	.07	.02
☐ 1 Jim Abbott	.15	.07	.02
☐ 2 Barry Bonds	.75	.35	.09
☐ 3 Chris Bosio	.15	.07	.02
☐ 4 George Brett	1.25	.55	.16
☐ 5 Jay Buhner	.40	.18	.05
☐ 6 Joe Carter	.25	.11	.03
Belts 3 for Fifth Time in Career			
☐ 7 Joe Carter	.25	.11	.03
Carter's Dramatics Give Jays Series Crown			
☐ 8 Carlton Fisk	.40	.18	.05
☐ 9 Travis Fryman	.25	.11	.03
☐ 10 Mark Grace	.40	.18	.05
☐ 11 Ken Griffey Jr.	3.00	1.35	.35
☐ 12 Darryl Kile	.15	.07	.02
☐ 13 Darren Lewis	.15	.07	.02
☐ 14 Greg Maddux	2.50	1.10	.30
☐ 15 Jack McDowell	.15	.07	.02
☐ 16 Paul Molitor	.75	.35	.09
☐ 17 Eddie Murray	.75	.35	.09
☐ 18 Mike Piazza	3.00	1.35	.35
Home Run Record for Rookie Catchers			
☐ 19 Mike Piazza	3.00	1.35	.35
NL Rookie Honors			
☐ 20 Kirby Puckett	1.50	.70	.19
☐ 21 Jeff Reardon	.15	.07	.02
☐ 22 Tim Salmon	.60	.25	.07
☐ 23 Curt Schilling	.15	.07	.02
☐ 24 Lee Smith	.25	.11	.03
☐ 25 Dave Stewart	.15	.07	.02
☐ 26 Frank Thomas	3.00	1.35	.35
☐ 27 Mark Whiten	.15	.07	.02
☐ 28 Dave Winfield	.35	.16	.04
☐ 29 Danny Ainge	.25	.11	.03
☐ 30 Mark Eaton	.15	.07	.02
☐ 31 Patrick Ewing	.75	.35	.09
☐ 32 Anfernee Hardaway	4.00	1.80	.50
☐ 33 Houston Rockets	.25	.11	.03
Carl Herrera Rockets Tie Mark for Best Start			
☐ 34 Michael Jordan	5.00	2.20	.60
☐ 35 Hakeem Olajuwon	1.50	.70	.19
☐ 36 Shaquille O'Neal	2.50	1.10	.30
☐ 37 Cliff Robinson	.25	.11	.03
☐ 38 David Robinson	1.50	.70	.19
☐ 39 Brian Shaw	.15	.07	.02
☐ 40 John Stockton	.75	.35	.09
☐ 41 Isiah Thomas	.50	.23	.06
☐ 42 Chris Webber	1.50	.70	.19
☐ 43 Dominique Wilkins	.40	.18	.05
☐ 44 Micheal Williams	.15	.07	.02
☐ 45 Morten Andersen	.15	.07	.02
☐ 46 Jerome Bettis	1.00	.45	.12
☐ 47 Steve Christie	.15	.07	.02
☐ 48 Jim Kelly	.40	.18	.05
☐ 49 Dan Marino	3.00	1.35	.35
☐ 50 Sterling Sharpe	.40	.18	.05
☐ 51 Emmitt Smith	3.00	1.35	.35
☐ 52 Dana Stubblefield	.25	.11	.03
☐ 53 Steve Young	1.50	.70	.19
☐ 54 Peter Bondra	.50	.23	.06
☐ 55 Mike Gartner	.25	.11	.03
☐ 56 Mario Lemieux	2.50	1.10	.30
☐ 57 Mike Richter	.50	.23	.06
☐ 58 Patrick Roy	2.00	.90	.25
☐ 59 Teemu Selanne	1.00	.45	.12

1993 Stadium Club Angels

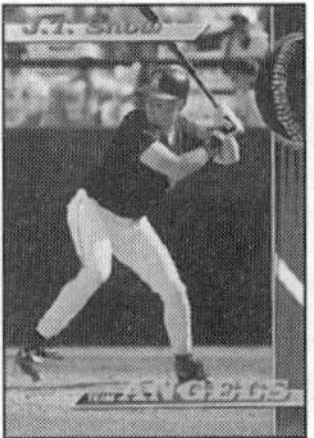

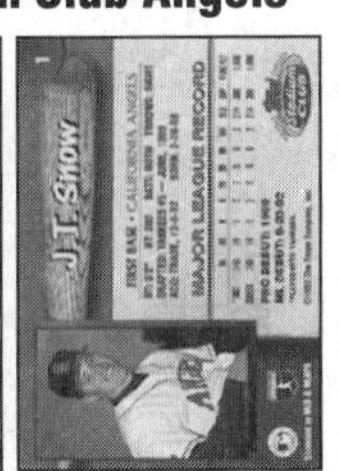

This 30-card standard-size set features the 1993 California Angels. The full-bleed color fronts display primarily color player action photos with a few posed. Along the top left edge the player's name is printed in purple on an orange bar, with the words "Team Angels" appearing on a gray bar across the lower right edge. The right edge has a wide green bar with a gold foil-stamped baseball icon at the top. The horizontal backs are green and present a close-up photo of the player on the left with biography and statistics on the right. The set was issued in hobby (plastic box) and retail (blister) form.

	MINT	NRMT	EXC
COMPLETE SET (30)	5.00	2.20	.60
COMMON CARD (1-30)	.10	.05	.01
☐ 1 J.T. Snow	.40	.18	.05
☐ 2 Chuck Crim	.10	.05	.01
☐ 3 Chili Davis	.20	.09	.03
☐ 4 Mark Langston	.20	.09	.03
☐ 5 Ron Tingley	.10	.05	.01
☐ 6 Eduardo Perez	.10	.05	.01
☐ 7 Scott Sanderson	.10	.05	.01
☐ 8 Jorge Fabregas	.10	.05	.01
☐ 9 Troy Percival	.20	.09	.03
☐ 10 Rod Correia	.10	.05	.01
☐ 11 Greg Myers	.10	.05	.01
☐ 12 Steve Frey	.10	.05	.01
☐ 13 Tim Salmon	2.50	1.10	.30
☐ 14 Scott Lewis	.10	.05	.01
☐ 15 Rene Gonzales	.10	.05	.01
☐ 16 Chuck Finley	.20	.09	.03
☐ 17 John Orton	.10	.05	.01
☐ 18 Joe Grahe	.10	.05	.01
☐ 19 Luis Polonia	.10	.05	.01
☐ 20 John Farrell	.10	.05	.01
☐ 21 Damion Easley	.10	.05	.01
☐ 22 Gene Nelson	.10	.05	.01
☐ 23 Chad Curtis	.20	.09	.03
☐ 24 Russ Springer	.10	.05	.01
☐ 25 DeShawn Warren	.20	.09	.03
☐ 26 Darryl Scott	.10	.05	.01
☐ 27 Gary DiSarcina	.10	.05	.01
☐ 28 Jerry Nielsen	.10	.05	.01
☐ 29 Torey Lovullo	.10	.05	.01
☐ 30 Julio Valera	.10	.05	.01

1993 Stadium Club Astros

This 30-card standard-size set features the 1993 Houston Astros. The full-bleed color fronts display primarily color player action photos with a few posed. Along the top left edge the player's name is printed in blue on an orange bar, with the words "Team Astros" appearing on a gray bar across the lower right edge. The right edge has a wide green bar with a gold foil-stamped baseball icon at the top. The horizontal backs are green and present a close-up photo of the player on the left with biography and statistics on the right. The set was issued in hobby (plastic box) and retail (blister) form.

	MINT	NRMT	EXC
COMPLETE SET (30)	5.00	2.20	.60
COMMON CARD (1-30)	.10	.05	.01
☐ 1 Doug Drabek	.20	.09	.03
☐ 2 Eddie Taubensee	.20	.09	.03
☐ 3 James Mouton	.35	.16	.04
☐ 4 Ken Caminiti	.75	.35	.09
☐ 5 Chris James	.10	.05	.01
☐ 6 Jeff Juden	.10	.05	.01
☐ 7 Eric Anthony	.10	.05	.01
☐ 8 Jeff Bagwell	2.00	.90	.25
☐ 9 Greg Swindell	.10	.05	.01
☐ 10 Steve Finley	.50	.23	.06
☐ 11 Al Osuna	.10	.05	.01
☐ 12 Gary Mota	.10	.05	.01
☐ 13 Scott Servais	.10	.05	.01
☐ 14 Craig Biggio	.50	.23	.06
☐ 15 Doug Jones	.10	.05	.01
☐ 16 Rob Mallicoat	.10	.05	.01
☐ 17 Darryl Kile	.20	.09	.03
☐ 18 Kevin Bass	.10	.05	.01
☐ 19 Pete Harnisch	.10	.05	.01
☐ 20 Andujar Cedeno	.10	.05	.01
☐ 21 Brian L.Hunter	1.00	.45	.12
☐ 22 Brian Williams	.10	.05	.01
☐ 23 Chris Donnels	.10	.05	.01
☐ 24 Xavier Hernandez	.10	.05	.01
☐ 25 Todd Jones	.10	.05	.01
☐ 26 Luis Gonzalez	.20	.09	.03
☐ 27 Rick Parker	.10	.05	.01
☐ 28 Casey Candaele	.10	.05	.01
☐ 29 Tony Eusebio	.10	.05	.01
☐ 30 Mark Portugal	.10	.05	.01

1993 Stadium Club Athletics

This 30-card standard-size set features the 1993 Oakland Athletics. The full-bleed color fronts display primarily color player action photos with a few posed. Along the top left edge the player's name is printed in green on an orange bar, with the words "Team Athletics" appearing on a gray bar across the lower right edge. The right edge has a wide green bar with a gold foil-stamped baseball icon at the top. The horizontal backs are green and present a close-up photo of the player on the left with biography and statistics on the right. The set was issued in hobby (plastic box) and retail (blister) form.

	MINT	NRMT	EXC
COMPLETE SET (30)	4.00	1.80	.50
COMMON CARD (1-30)	.10	.05	.01
☐ 1 Dennis Eckersley	.50	.23	.06
☐ 2 Lance Blankenship	.10	.05	.01
☐ 3 Mike Mohler	.10	.05	.01
☐ 4 Jerry Browne	.10	.05	.01
☐ 5 Kevin Seitzer	.25	.11	.03
☐ 6 Storm Davis	.10	.05	.01
☐ 7 Mark McGwire	1.50	.70	.19
☐ 8 Rickey Henderson	.75	.35	.09
☐ 9 Terry Steinbach	.35	.16	.04
☐ 10 Ruben Sierra	.25	.11	.03
☐ 11 Dave Henderson	.10	.05	.01
☐ 12 Bob Welch	.10	.05	.01
☐ 13 Rick Honeycutt	.10	.05	.01
☐ 14 Ron Darling	.10	.05	.01
☐ 15 Joe Boever	.10	.05	.01
☐ 16 Bobby Witt	.10	.05	.01
☐ 17 Izzy Molina	.10	.05	.01
☐ 18 Mike Bordick	.25	.11	.03
☐ 19 Brent Gates	.25	.11	.03
☐ 20 Shawn Hillegas	.10	.05	.01
☐ 21 Scott Hemond	.10	.05	.01
☐ 22 Todd Van Poppel	.10	.05	.01
☐ 23 Johnny Guzman	.10	.05	.01
☐ 24 Scott Lydy	.10	.05	.01
☐ 25 Scott Baker	.10	.05	.01
☐ 26 Todd Revenig	.10	.05	.01
☐ 27 Scott Brosius	.25	.11	.03
☐ 28 Troy Neel	.10	.05	.01
☐ 29 Dale Sveum	.10	.05	.01
☐ 30 Mike Neill	.10	.05	.01

1993 Stadium Club Braves

This 30-card standard-size set features the 1993 Atlanta Braves. The full-bleed color fronts display primarily color player action photos with a few posed. Along the top left edge the player's name is printed in red on a blue bar, with the words "Team Braves" appearing on a gray bar across the lower right edge. The right edge has a wide green bar with a gold foil-stamped baseball icon at the top. The horizontal backs are green and present a close-up photo of the player on the left with biography and statistics on the right. The set was issued in hobby (plastic box) and retail (blister) form.

	MINT	NRMT	EXC
COMPLETE SET (30)	8.00	3.60	1.00
COMMON CARD (1-30)	.10	.05	.01
☐ 1 Tom Glavine	.75	.35	.09
☐ 2 Bill Pecota	.10	.05	.01
☐ 3 David Justice	.50	.23	.06
☐ 4 Mark Lemke	.10	.05	.01
☐ 5 Jeff Blauser	.25	.11	.03
☐ 6 Ron Gant	.35	.16	.04
☐ 7 Greg Olson	.10	.05	.01
☐ 8 Francisco Cabrera	.10	.05	.01
☐ 9 Chipper Jones	3.00	1.35	.35
☐ 10 Steve Avery	.30	.14	.04
☐ 11 Kent Mercker	.10	.05	.01
☐ 12 John Smoltz	.75	.35	.09
☐ 13 Pete Smith	.10	.05	.01
☐ 14 Damon Berryhill	.10	.05	.01
☐ 15 Sid Bream	.10	.05	.01
☐ 16 Otis Nixon	.25	.11	.03
☐ 17 Mike Stanton	.10	.05	.01
☐ 18 Greg Maddux	2.50	1.10	.30
☐ 19 Jay Howell	.10	.05	.01
☐ 20 Rafael Belliard	.10	.05	.01
☐ 21 Terry Pendleton	.25	.11	.03
☐ 22 Deion Sanders	.75	.35	.09
☐ 23 Brian R. Hunter	.10	.05	.01
☐ 24 Marvin Freeman	.10	.05	.01
☐ 25 Mark Wohlers	.50	.23	.06
☐ 26 Ryan Klesko	1.00	.45	.12
☐ 27 Javier Lopez	.75	.35	.09
☐ 28 Melvin Nieves			
☐ 29 Tony Tarasco	.25	.11	.03
☐ 30 Ramon Caraballo	.10	.05	.01

1993 Stadium Club Cardinals

This 30-card standard-size set features the 1993 St. Louis Cardinals. The full-bleed color fronts display primarily color player action photos with a few posed. Along the top left edge the player's name is printed in red on a gray bar, with the words "Team Cardinals" appearing on a gray bar across the lower right edge. The right edge has a wide green bar with a gold foil-stamped baseball icon at the top. The horizontal backs are green and present a close-up photo of the player on the left with biography and statistics on the right. The set was issued in hobby (plastic box) and retail (blister) form.

	MINT	NRMT	EXC
COMPLETE SET (30)	4.00	1.80	.50
COMMON CARD (1-30)	.10	.05	.01

Card			
☐ 1 Ozzie Smith	2.00	.90	.25
☐ 2 Rene Arocha	.10	.05	.01
☐ 3 Bernard Gilkey	.40	.18	.05
☐ 4 Jose Oquendo	.10	.05	.01
☐ 5 Mike Perez	.10	.05	.01
☐ 6 Tom Pagnozzi	.10	.05	.01
☐ 7 Rod Brewer	.10	.05	.01
☐ 8 Joe Magrane	.10	.05	.01
☐ 9 Todd Zeile	.25	.11	.03
☐ 10 Bob Tewksbury	.10	.05	.01
☐ 11 Darrel Deak	.10	.05	.01
☐ 12 Gregg Jefferies	.35	.16	.04
☐ 13 Lee Smith	.35	.16	.04
☐ 14 Ozzie Canseco	.10	.05	.01
☐ 15 Tom Urbani	.10	.05	.01
☐ 16 Donovan Osborne	.35	.16	.04
☐ 17 Ray Lankford	.50	.23	.06
☐ 18 Rheal Cormier	.10	.05	.01
☐ 19 Allen Watson	.25	.11	.03
☐ 20 Geronimo Pena	.10	.05	.01
☐ 21 Rob Murphy	.10	.05	.01
☐ 22 Tracy Woodson	.10	.05	.01
☐ 23 Basil Shabazz	10	.05	.01
☐ 24 Omar Olivares	.10	.05	.01
☐ 25 Brian Jordan	.75	.35	.09
☐ 26 Les Lancaster	.10	.05	.01
☐ 27 Sean Lowe	.10	.05	.01
☐ 28 Hector Villanueva	.10	.05	.01
☐ 29 Brian Barber	.25	.11	.03
☐ 30 Aaron Holbert	.10	.05	.01

1993 Stadium Club Cubs

This 30-card standard-size set features the 1993 Chicago Cubs. The full-bleed color fronts display primarily color player action photos with a few posed. Along the top left edge the player's name is printed in red on a light blue bar, with the words "Team Cubs" appearing on a gray bar across the lower right edge. The right edge has a wide green bar with a gold foil-stamped baseball icon at the top. The horizontal backs are green and present a close-up photo of the player on the left with biography and statistics on the right. The set was issued in hobby (plastic box) and retail (blister) form.

	MINT	NRMT	EXC
COMPLETE SET (30)	4.00	1.80	.50
COMMON CARD (1-30)	.10	.05	.01
☐ 1 Ryne Sandberg	2.00	.90	.25
☐ 2 Sammy Sosa	.75	.35	.09
☐ 3 Greg Hibbard	.10	.05	.01
☐ 4 Candy Maldonado	.10	.05	.01
☐ 5 Willie Wilson	.10	.05	.01
☐ 6 Dan Plesac	.10	.05	.01
☐ 7 Steve Buechele	.10	.05	.01
☐ 8 Mark Grace	.75	.35	.09
☐ 9 Shawon Dunston	.10	.05	.01
☐ 10 Steve Lake	.10	.05	.01
☐ 11 Dwight Smith	.10	.05	.01
☐ 12 Derrick May	.10	.05	.01
☐ 13 Paul Assenmacher	.10	.05	.01
☐ 14 Mike Harkey	.10	.05	.01
☐ 15 Lance Dickson	.10	.05	.01
☐ 16 Randy Myers	.25	.11	.03
☐ 17 Mike Morgan	.10	.05	.01
☐ 18 Chuck McElroy	.10	.05	.01
☐ 19 Jose Guzman	.10	.05	.01
☐ 20 Jose Vizcaino	.25	.11	.03
☐ 21 Frank Castillo	.10	.05	.01
☐ 22 Bob Scanlan	.10	.05	.01
☐ 23 Rick Wilkins	.10	.05	.01
☐ 24 Rey Sanchez	.10	.05	.01
☐ 25 Phil Dauphin	.10	.05	.01
☐ 26 Jim Bullinger	.10	.05	.01
☐ 27 Jessie Hollins	.10	.05	.01
☐ 28 Matt Walbeck	.10	.05	.01
☐ 29 Fernando Ramsey	.10	.05	.01
☐ 30 Jose Bautista	.10	.05	.01

1993 Stadium Club Dodgers

This 30-card standard-size set features the 1993 Los Angeles Dodgers. The full-bleed color fronts display primarily color player action photos with a few posed. Along the top left edge the player's name is printed in blue on a red bar, with the words "Team Dodgers" appearing on a gray bar across the lower right edge. The right edge has a wide green bar with a gold foil-stamped baseball icon at the top. The horizontal backs are green and present a close-up photo of the player on the left with biography and statistics on the right. The set was issued in hobby (plastic box) and retail (blister) form.

	MINT	NRMT	EXC
COMPLETE SET (30)	8.00	3.60	1.00
COMMON CARD (1-30)	.10	.05	.01
☐ 1 Darryl Strawberry	.25	.11	.03
☐ 2 Pedro Martinez	.35	.16	.04
☐ 3 Jody Reed	.10	.05	.01
☐ 4 Carlos Hernandez	.10	.05	.01
☐ 5 Kevin Gross	.10	.05	.01
☐ 6 Mike Piazza	3.00	1.35	.35
☐ 7 Jim Gott	.10	.05	.01
☐ 8 Eric Karros	.50	.23	.06
☐ 9 Mike Sharperson	.10	.05	.01
☐ 10 Ramon Martinez	.35	.16	.04
☐ 11 Tim Wallach	.10	.05	.01
☐ 12 Pedro Astacio	.25	.11	.03
☐ 13 Lenny Harris	.10	.05	.01
☐ 14 Brett Butler	.35	.16	.04
☐ 15 Raul Mondesi	1.25	.55	.16
☐ 16 Todd Worrell	.25	.11	.03
☐ 17 Jose Offerman	.10	.05	.01
☐ 18 Mitch Webster	.10	.05	.01
☐ 19 Tom Candiotti	.10	.05	.01
☐ 20 Eric Davis	.25	.11	.03
☐ 21 Michael Moore	.10	.05	.01
☐ 22 Billy Ashley	.25	.11	.03
☐ 23 Orel Hershiser	.25	.11	.03
☐ 24 Roger Cedeno	.25	.11	.03
☐ 25 Roger McDowell	.10	.05	.01
☐ 26 Mike James	.10	.05	.01
☐ 27 Steve Wilson	.10	.05	.01
☐ 28 Todd Hollandsworth	1.00	.45	.12
☐ 29 Cory Snyder	.10	.05	.01
☐ 30 Todd Williams	.10	.05	.01

1993 Stadium Club Giants

This 30-card standard-size set features the 1993 San Francisco Giants. The full-bleed color fronts display primarily color player action photos with a few posed. Along the top left edge the player's name is printed in yellow on an orange bar, with the words "Team Giants" appearing on a gray bar across the lower right edge. The right edge has a wide green bar with a gold foil-stamped baseball icon at the top. The horizontal backs are green and present a close-up photo of the player on the left with biography and statistics on the right. The set was issued in hobby (plastic box) and retail (blister) form.

	MINT	NRMT	EXC
COMPLETE SET (30)	4.00	1.80	.50
COMMON CARD (1-30)	.10	.05	.01
☐ 1 Barry Bonds	1.00	.45	.12
☐ 2 Dave Righetti	.10	.05	.01
☐ 3 Matt Williams	.75	.35	.09
☐ 4 Royce Clayton	.25	.11	.03
☐ 5 Salomon Torres	.10	.05	.01
☐ 6 Kirt Manwaring	.10	.05	.01
☐ 7 J.R. Phillips	.10	.05	.01
☐ 8 Kevin Rogers	.10	.05	.01
☐ 9 Will Clark	.75	.35	.09
☐ 10 John Burkett	.25	.11	.03
☐ 11 Willie McGee	.10	.05	.01
☐ 12 Rod Beck	.25	.11	.03
☐ 13 Jeff Reed	.10	.05	.01
☐ 14 Jeff Brantley	.10	.05	.01
☐ 15 Steve Hosey	.10	.05	.01
☐ 16 Chris Hancock	.10	.05	.01
☐ 17 Adell Davenport	.10	.05	.01
☐ 18 Mike Jackson	.10	.05	.01
☐ 19 Dave Martinez	.10	.05	.01
☐ 20 Bill Swift	.10	.05	.01
☐ 21 Steve Scarsone	.10	.05	.01
☐ 22 Trevor Wilson	.10	.05	.01
☐ 23 Mark Carreon	.10	.05	.01
☐ 24 Bud Black	.10	.05	.01
☐ 25 Darren Lewis	.10	.05	.01
☐ 26 Dan Carlson	.10	.05	.01
☐ 27 Craig Colbert	.10	.05	.01
☐ 28 Greg Brummett	.10	.05	.01
☐ 29 Bryan Hickerson	.10	.05	.01
☐ 30 Robby Thompson	.10	.05	.01

1993 Stadium Club Mariners

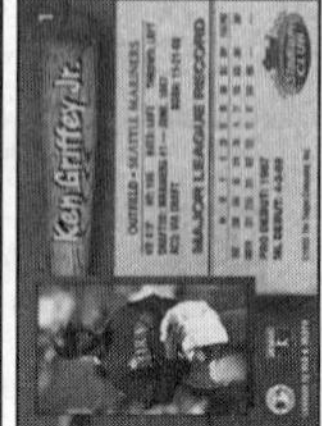

This 30-card standard-size set features the 1993 Seattle Mariners. The full-bleed color fronts display primarily color player action photos with a few posed. Along the top left edge the player's name is printed in yellow on a blue bar, with the words "Team Mariners" appearing on a gray bar across the lower right edge. The right edge has a wide green bar with a gold foil-stamped baseball icon at the top. The horizontal backs are green and present a close-up photo of the player on the left with biography and statistics on the right. The set was issued in hobby (plastic box) and retail (blister) form.

	MINT	NRMT	EXC
COMPLETE SET (30)	8.00	3.60	1.00
COMMON CARD (1-30)	.10	.05	.01
☐ 1 Ken Griffey Jr.	4.00	1.80	.50
☐ 2 Desi Relaford	.35	.16	.04
☐ 3 Dave Wainhouse	.10	.05	.01
☐ 4 Rich Amaral	.10	.05	.01
☐ 5 Brian Deak	.10	.05	.01
☐ 6 Bret Boone	.35	.16	.04
☐ 7 Bill Haselman	.10	.05	.01
☐ 8 Dave Fleming	.10	.05	.01
☐ 9 Fernando Vina	.10	.05	.01
☐ 10 Greg Litton	.10	.05	.01
☐ 11 Mackey Sasser	.10	.05	.01
☐ 12 Lee Tinsley	.10	.05	.01
☐ 13 Norm Charlton	.20	.09	.03
☐ 14 Russ Swan	.10	.05	.01
☐ 15 Brian Holman	.10	.05	.01
☐ 16 Randy Johnson	1.25	.55	.16
☐ 17 Erik Hanson	.20	.09	.03
☐ 18 Tino Martinez	.75	.35	.09
☐ 19 Marc Newfield	.50	.23	.06
☐ 20 Dave Valle	.10	.05	.01
☐ 21 John Cummings	.10	.05	.01
☐ 22 Mike Hampton	.30	.14	.04
☐ 23 Jay Buhner	.75	.35	.09
☐ 24 Edgar Martinez	.75	.35	.09
☐ 25 Omar Vizquel	.35	.16	.04
☐ 26 Pete O'Brien	.10	.05	.01
☐ 27 Brian Turang	.10	.05	.01
☐ 28 Chris Bosio	.10	.05	.01
☐ 29 Mike Felder	.10	.05	.01
☐ 30 Shawn Estes	.75	.35	.09

1993 Stadium Club Marlins

This 30-card standard-size set features the 1993 Florida Marlins. The full-bleed color fronts display primarily color player action photos with a few posed. Along the top left edge the player's name is printed in orange on a sea green bar, with the words "Team Marlins" appearing on a gray bar across the lower right edge. The right edge has a wide green bar with a gold foil-stamped baseball icon at the top. The horizontal backs are green and present a close-up photo of the player on the left with biography and statistics on the right. The set was issued in hobby (plastic box) and retail (blister) form as well as being distributed in shrinkwrapped cardboard boxes with a manager card pictured on it.

	MINT	NRMT	EXC
COMPLETE SET (30)	4.00	1.80	.50
COMMON CARD (1-30)	.10	.05	.01
☐ 1 Nigel Wilson	.10	.05	.01
☐ 2 Bryan Harvey	.10	.05	.01
☐ 3 Bob McClure	.10	.05	.01
☐ 4 Alex Arias	.10	.05	.01
☐ 5 Walt Weiss	.25	.11	.03
☐ 6 Charlie Hough	.10	.05	.01
☐ 7 Scott Chiamparino	.10	.05	.01
☐ 8 Junior Felix	.10	.05	.01
☐ 9 Jack Armstrong	.10	.05	.01
☐ 10 Dave Magadan	.10	.05	.01
☐ 11 Cris Carpenter	.10	.05	.01
☐ 12 Benito Santiago	.25	.11	.03
☐ 13 Jeff Conine	1.00	.45	.12
☐ 14 Jerry Don Gleaton	.10	.05	.01
☐ 15 Steve Decker	.10	.05	.01
☐ 16 Ryan Bowen	.10	.05	.01
☐ 17 Ramon Martinez	.10	.05	.01
☐ 18 Bret Barberie	.10	.05	.01
☐ 19 Monty Fariss	.10	.05	.01
☐ 20 Trevor Hoffman	.50	.23	.06
☐ 21 Scott Pose	.10	.05	.01
☐ 22 Mike Myers	.10	.05	.01
☐ 23 Geronimo Berroa	.25	.11	.03
☐ 24 Darrell Whitmore	.10	.05	.01
☐ 25 Chuck Carr	.10	.05	.01
☐ 26 Dave Weathers	.10	.05	.01
☐ 27 Matt Turner	.10	.05	.01
☐ 28 Jose Martinez	.10	.05	.01
☐ 29 Orestes Destrade	.10	.05	.01
☐ 30 Carl Everett	.25	.11	.03

1993 Stadium Club Phillies

This 30-card standard-size set features the 1993 Philadelphia Phillies. The full-bleed color fronts display primarily color player action photos with a few posed. Along the top left edge the player's name is printed in blue on a coral bar, with the words "Team Phillies" appearing on a gray bar across the lower right edge. The right edge has a wide green bar with a gold foil-stamped baseball icon at the top. The horizontal backs are green and present a close-up photo of the player on the left with biography and statistics on the right. The set was issued in hobby (plastic box) and retail (blister) form.

	MINT	NRMT	EXC
COMPLETE SET (30)	4.00	1.80	.50
COMMON CARD (1-30)	.10	.05	.01
☐ 1 Darren Daulton	.50	.23	.06
☐ 2 Larry Andersen	.10	.05	.01
☐ 3 Kyle Abbott	.10	.05	.01
☐ 4 Chad McConnell	.10	.05	.01
☐ 5 Danny Jackson	.10	.05	.01
☐ 6 Kevin Stocker	.25	.11	.03
☐ 7 Jim Eisenreich	.35	.16	.04
☐ 8 Mickey Morandini	.25	.11	.03
☐ 9 Bob Ayrault	.10	.05	.01
☐ 10 Doug Lindsey	.10	.05	.01
☐ 11 Dave Hollins	.10	.05	.01
☐ 12 Dave West	.10	.05	.01
☐ 13 Wes Chamberlain	.10	.05	.01
☐ 14 Curt Schilling	.35	.16	.04
☐ 15 Len Dykstra	.35	.16	.04
☐ 16 Trevor Humphry	.10	.05	.01
☐ 17 Terry Mulholland	.25	.11	.03
☐ 18 Gene Schall	.25	.11	.03
☐ 19 Mike Lieberthal	.50	.23	.06
☐ 20 Ben Rivera	.10	.05	.01
☐ 21 Mariano Duncan	.10	.05	.01
☐ 22 Pete Incaviglia	.25	.11	.03
☐ 23 Ron Blazier	.10	.05	.01
☐ 24 Jeff Jackson	.10	.05	.01
☐ 25 Jose DeLeon	.10	.05	.01
☐ 26 Ron Lockett	.10	.05	.01
☐ 27 Tommy Greene	.10	.05	.01
☐ 28 Milt Thompson	.10	.05	.01
☐ 29 Mitch Williams	.25	.11	.03
☐ 30 John Kruk	.35	.16	.04

1993 Stadium Club Rangers

This 30-card standard-size set features the 1993 Texas Rangers. The full-bleed color fronts display primarily color player action photos with a few posed. Along the top left edge the player's name is printed in blue on a coral red bar, with the words "Team Rangers" appearing on a gray bar across the lower right edge. The right edge has a wide green bar with a gold foil-stamped baseball icon at the top. The horizontal backs are green and present a close-up photo of the player on the left with biography and statistics on the right. The set was issued in hobby (plastic box) and retail (blister) form.

	MINT	NRMT	EXC
COMPLETE SET (30)	8.00	3.60	1.00
COMMON CARD (1-30)	.10	.05	.01

	MINT	NRMT	EXC
☐ 1 Nolan Ryan	4.00	1.80	.50
☐ 2 Ritchie Moody	.10	.05	.01
☐ 3 Matt Whiteside	.10	.05	.01
☐ 4 David Hulse	.10	.05	.01
☐ 5 Roger Pavlik	.25	.11	.03
☐ 6 Dan Smith	.10	.05	.01
☐ 7 Donald Harris	.10	.05	.01
☐ 8 Butch Davis	.10	.05	.01
☐ 9 Benji Gil	.25	.11	.03
☐ 10 Ivan Rodriguez	1.00	.45	.12
☐ 11 Dean Palmer	.35	.16	.04
☐ 12 Jeff Huson	.10	.05	.01
☐ 13 Rob Maurer	.10	.05	.01
☐ 14 Gary Redus	.10	.05	.01
☐ 15 Doug Dascenzo	.10	.05	.01
☐ 16 Charlie Leibrandt	.10	.05	.01
☐ 17 Tom Henke	.25	.11	.03
☐ 18 Manuel Lee	.10	.05	.01
☐ 19 Kenny Rogers	.25	.11	.03
☐ 20 Kevin Brown	.50	.23	.06
☐ 21 Juan Gonzalez	2.00	.90	.25
☐ 22 Geno Petralli	.10	.05	.01
☐ 23 John Russell	.10	.05	.01
☐ 24 Robb Nen	.25	.11	.03
☐ 25 Julio Franco	.25	.11	.03
☐ 26 Rafael Palmeiro	.75	.35	.09
☐ 27 Todd Burns	.10	.05	.01
☐ 28 Jose Canseco	1.00	.45	.12
☐ 29 Billy Ripken	.10	.05	.01
☐ 30 Dan Peltier	.10	.05	.01

1993 Stadium Club Rockies

This 30-card standard-size set features the 1993 Colorado Rockies. The full-bleed color fronts display primarily color player action photos with a few posed. Along the top left edge the player's name is printed in gray on a purple bar, with the words "Team Rockies" appearing on a gray bar across the lower right edge. The right edge has a wide green bar with a gold foil-stamped baseball icon at the top. The horizontal backs are green and present a close-up photo of the player on the left with biography and statistics on the right. The set was issued in hobby (plastic box) and retail (blister) form as well as being distributed in shrinkwrapped cardboard boxes with a manager card pictured on it.

	MINT	NRMT	EXC
COMPLETE SET (30)	5.00	2.20	.60
COMMON CARD (1-30)	.10	.05	.01
☐ 1 David Nied	.10	.05	.01
☐ 2 Quinton McCracken	.10	.05	.01
☐ 3 Charlie Hayes	.25	.11	.03
☐ 4 Bryn Smith	.10	.05	.01
☐ 5 Dante Bichette	1.00	.45	.12
☐ 6 Alex Cole	.10	.05	.01
☐ 7 Scott Aldred	.10	.05	.01
☐ 8 Roberto Mejia	.10	.05	.01
☐ 9 Jeff Parrett	.10	.05	.01
☐ 10 Joe Girardi	.25	.11	.03
☐ 11 Andres Galarraga	.75	.35	.09
☐ 12 Daryl Boston	.10	.05	.01
☐ 13 Jerald Clark	.10	.05	.01
☐ 14 Gerald Young	.10	.05	.01
☐ 15 Bruce Ruffin	.10	.05	.01
☐ 16 Rudy Seanez	.10	.05	.01
☐ 17 Darren Holmes	.10	.05	.01
☐ 18 Andy Ashby	.25	.11	.03
☐ 19 Chris Jones	.10	.05	.01
☐ 20 Mark Thompson	.35	.16	.04
☐ 21 Freddie Benavides	.10	.05	.01
☐ 22 Eric Wedge	.10	.05	.01
☐ 23 Vinny Castilla	.75	.35	.09
☐ 24 Butch Henry	.10	.05	.01
☐ 25 Jim Tatum	.10	.05	.01
☐ 26 Steve Reed	.10	.05	.01
☐ 27 Eric Young	.35	.16	.04
☐ 28 Danny Sheaffer	.10	.05	.01
☐ 29 Roger Bailey	.10	.05	.01
☐ 30 Brad Ausmus	.10	.05	.01

1993 Stadium Club Royals

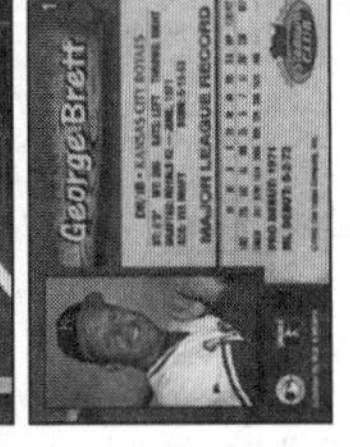

This 30-card standard-size set features the 1993 Kansas City Royals. The full-bleed color fronts display primarily color player action photos with a few posed. Along the top left edge the player's name is printed in yellow on a blue bar, with the words "Team Royals" appearing on a gray bar across the lower right edge. The right edge has a wide green bar with a gold foil-stamped baseball icon at the top. The horizontal backs are green and present a close-up photo of the player on the left with biography and statistics on the right. The set was issued in hobby (plastic box) and retail (blister) form.

	MINT	NRMT	EXC
COMPLETE SET (30)	4.00	1.80	.50
COMMON CARD (1-30)	.10	.05	.01
☐ 1 George Brett	2.00	.90	.25
☐ 2 Mike Macfarlane	.10	.05	.01
☐ 3 Tom Gordon	.25	.11	.03
☐ 4 Wally Joyner	.25	.11	.03
☐ 5 Kevin Appier	.35	.16	.04
☐ 6 Phil Hiatt	.10	.05	.01
☐ 7 Keith Miller	.10	.05	.01
☐ 8 Hipolito Pichardo	.10	.05	.01
☐ 9 Chris Gwynn	.10	.05	.01
☐ 10 Jose Lind	.10	.05	.01
☐ 11 Mark Gubicza	.10	.05	.01
☐ 12 Dennis Rasmussen	.10	.05	.01
☐ 13 Mike Magnante	.10	.05	.01
☐ 14 Joe Vitiello	.10	.05	.01
☐ 15 Kevin McReynolds	.10	.05	.01
☐ 16 Greg Gagne	.10	.05	.01
☐ 17 David Cone	.50	.23	.06
☐ 18 Brent Mayne	.10	.05	.01
☐ 19 Jeff Montgomery	.25	.11	.03
☐ 20 Joe Randa	.10	.05	.01
☐ 21 Felix Jose	.10	.05	.01
☐ 22 Bill Sampen	.10	.05	.01
☐ 23 Curt Wilkerson	.10	.05	.01
☐ 24 Mark Gardner	.10	.05	.01
☐ 25 Brian McRae	.25	.11	.03
☐ 26 Hubie Brooks	.10	.05	.01
☐ 27 Chris Eddy	.10	.05	.01
☐ 28 Harvey Pulliam	.10	.05	.01
☐ 29 Rusty Meacham	.10	.05	.01
☐ 30 Danny Miceli	.25	.11	.03

1993 Stadium Club White Sox

This 30-card standard-size set features the 1993 Chicago White Sox. The full-bleed color fronts display primarily color player action photos with a few posed. Along the top left edge the player's name is printed in light blue on a gray bar, with the words "Team White Sox" appearing on a gray bar across the lower right edge. The right edge has a wide green bar with a gold foil-stamped baseball icon at the top. The horizontal backs are green and present a close-up photo of the player on the left with biography and statistics on the right. The set was issued in hobby (plastic box) and retail (blister) form.

	MINT	NRMT	EXC
COMPLETE SET (30)	8.00	3.60	1.00
COMMON CARD (1-30)	.10	.05	.01
☐ 1 Frank Thomas	3.00	1.35	.35
☐ 2 Bo Jackson	.25	.11	.03
☐ 3 Rod Bolton	.10	.05	.01
☐ 4 Dave Stieb	.10	.05	.01
☐ 5 Tim Raines	.25	.11	.03
☐ 6 Joey Cora	.25	.11	.03
☐ 7 Warren Newson	.10	.05	.01
☐ 8 Roberto Hernandez	.25	.11	.03
☐ 9 Brandon Wilson	.10	.05	.01
☐ 10 Wilson Alvarez	.25	.11	.03
☐ 11 Dan Pasqua	.10	.05	.01
☐ 12 Ozzie Guillen	.25	.11	.03
☐ 13 Robin Ventura	.50	.23	.06
☐ 14 Craig Grebeck	.10	.05	.01
☐ 15 Lance Johnson	.25	.11	.03
☐ 16 Carlton Fisk	.50	.23	.06
☐ 17 Ron Karkovice	.10	.05	.01
☐ 18 Jack McDowell	.25	.11	.03
☐ 19 Scott Radinsky	.10	.05	.01
☐ 20 Bobby Thigpen	.10	.05	.01
☐ 21 Donn Pall	.10	.05	.01
☐ 22 George Bell	.10	.05	.01
☐ 23 Alex Fernandez	.75	.35	.09
☐ 24 Mike Huff	.10	.05	.01
☐ 25 Jason Bere	.25	.11	.03
☐ 26 Johnny Ruffin	.10	.05	.01
☐ 27 Ellis Burks	.50	.23	.06
☐ 28 Kirk McCaskill	.10	.05	.01
☐ 29 Terry Leach	.10	.05	.01
☐ 30 Shawn Gilbert	.10	.05	.01

1993 Stadium Club Yankees

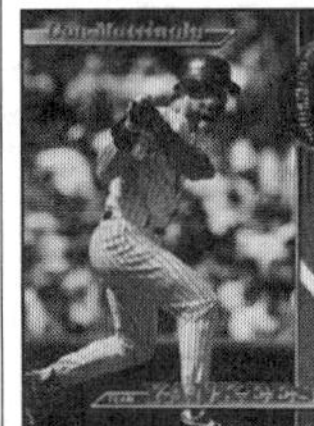

This 30-card standard-size set features the 1993 New York Yankees. The full-bleed color fronts display primarily color player action photos with a few posed. Along the top left edge the player's name is printed in gray on a purple bar, with the words "Team Yankees" appearing on a gray bar across the lower right edge. The right edge has a wide green bar with a gold foil-stamped baseball icon at the top. The horizontal backs are green and present a close-up photo of the player on the left with biography and statistics on the right. The set was issued in hobby (plastic box) and retail (blister) form.

	MINT	NRMT	EXC
COMPLETE SET (30)	6.00	2.70	.75
COMMON CARD (1-30)	.10	.05	.01
☐ 1 Don Mattingly	2.50	1.10	.30
☐ 2 Jim Abbott	.25	.11	.03
☐ 3 Matt Nokes	.10	.05	.01
☐ 4 Danny Tartabull	.25	.11	.03
☐ 5 Wade Boggs	.75	.35	.09
☐ 6 Melido Perez	.10	.05	.01
☐ 7 Steve Farr	.10	.05	.01
☐ 8 Kevin Maas	.10	.05	.01
☐ 9 Randy Velarde	.10	.05	.01
☐ 10 Mike Humphreys	.10	.05	.01
☐ 11 Mike Gallego	.10	.05	.01
☐ 12 Mike Stanley	.25	.11	.03
☐ 13 Jimmy Key	.35	.16	.04
☐ 14 Paul O'Neill	.35	.16	.04
☐ 15 Spike Owen	.10	.05	.01
☐ 16 Pat Kelly	.10	.05	.01
☐ 17 Sterling Hitchcock	.10	.05	.01
☐ 18 Mike Witt	.10	.05	.01
☐ 19 Scott Kamieniecki	.10	.05	.01
☐ 20 John Habyan	.10	.05	.01
☐ 21 Bernie Williams	1.25	.55	.16
☐ 22 Brien Taylor	.10	.05	.01
☐ 23 Rick Monteleone	.10	.05	.01
☐ 24 Mark Hutton	.10	.05	.01
☐ 25 Robert Eenhoorn	.10	.05	.01
☐ 26 Gerald Williams	.10	.05	.01
☐ 27 Sam Militello	.10	.05	.01
☐ 28 Bob Wickman	.10	.05	.01
☐ 29 Andy Stankiewicz	.10	.05	.01
☐ 30 Domingo Jean	.10	.05	.01

1993 Stadium Club Ultra-Pro

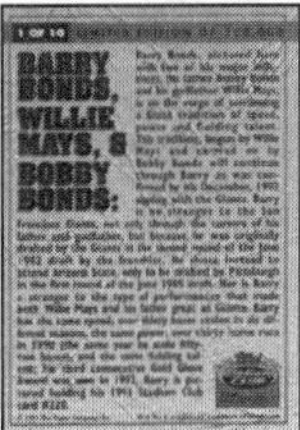

The ten cards in this set measure the standard size and were available singly as limited edition random inserts in the Topps Stadium Club Ultra-Pro Platinum collector pages refill packs (1-6) and individual semi-rigid card protector packs (7-10). The cards feature full-bleed posed color player photos. A red stripe across the bottom is accented with a prismatic gold-foil stripe and contains the player's name in prismatic gold-foil lettering. This stripe design intersects the Stadium Club/Ultra-Pro logo. The backs carry player profile within an aqua outline against a stucco-textured background. The cards are numbered on the back. In light of a marketing partnership with the Rembrandt Company, this ten-card set was produced by Stadium Club to mark the launch of a new accessory line of premium card storage accessory products. Reportedly no more than 150,000 sets were produced. Willie Mays is Barry Bonds' godfather.

	MINT	NRMT	EXC
COMPLETE SET (10)	20.00	9.00	2.50
COMMON CARD (1-10)	1.00	.45	.12
☐ 1 Barry Bonds Willie Mays Bobby Bonds	2.50	1.10	.30
☐ 2 Willie Mays Leaning on bat	3.00	1.35	.35
☐ 3 Bobby Bonds Kneeling, leaning on bat	1.00	.45	.12
☐ 4 Barry Bonds Bat extended	2.00	.90	.25
☐ 5 Barry Bonds Bobby Bonds	2.00	.90	.25
☐ 6 Willie Mays Squatting posture, glove in hand	3.00	1.35	.35
☐ 7 Barry Bonds Dressed in suit	2.00	.90	.25
☐ 8 Bobby Bonds Willie Mays	2.00	.90	.25
☐ 9 Willie Mays Kneeling, bat in right hand	3.00	1.35	.35
☐ 10 Barry Bonds Dressed in tuxedo	2.00	.90	.25

1994 Stadium Club Pre-Production

Issued to herald the release of 1994 Stadium Club Series I, the nine standard-size cards comprising this promo set feature on their fronts borderless color player action shots. The player's last name appears in white lettering within a red foil-stamped rectangle at the bottom; his first name appears alongside in black "typewritten" lettering within a division color-coded "tearaway." The red foil-stamped Stadium Club logo appears in an upper corner. The back carries a color player action cutout superposed upon a blue and black background. The player's name, team, biography, career highlights, and statistics appear in lettering of several different colors and typefaces. The cards have the disclaimer "Pre-Production Sample" printed vertically running down the left edge of the back.

	MINT	NRMT	EXC
COMPLETE SET (9)	6.00	2.70	.75
COMMON CARD	.50	.23	.06
☐ 6 Al Martin	.50	.23	.06
☐ 15 Junior Ortiz	.50	.23	.06
☐ 36 Tim Salmon	1.00	.45	.12
☐ 56 Jerry Spradlin	.50	.23	.06
☐ 122 Tom Pagnozzi	.50	.23	.06
☐ 123 Ron Gant	.75	.35	.09
☐ 125 Dennis Eckersley	.75	.35	.09
☐ 135 Jose Lind	.50	.23	.06
☐ 238 Barry Bonds	2.00	.90	.25

1994 Stadium Club

The 720 standard-size cards comprising this set were issued two series of 270 and a third series of 180. Card fronts feature borderless color player action photos. The player's last name appears in white lettering within a red-foil-stamped rectangle at the bottom. His first name appears alongside in black "typewritten" lettering within a division color-coded "tearaway." The red-foil-stamped Stadium Club logo appears in an upper corner. The back carries a color player action cutout superimposed upon a blue and black background. The player's name, team, biography, career highlights and statistics appear in lettering of several different colors and typefaces. There are a number of subsets including Home Run Club (258-268), Tale of Two Players (525/526), Division Leaders (527-532), Quick Starts (533-538), Career Contributors (541-543), Rookie Rocker (626-630), Rookie Rocket (631-634) and Fantastic Finishes (714-719). The only notable Rookie Card is Chan Ho Park.

	MINT	NRMT	EXC
COMPLETE SET (720)	55.00	25.00	7.00
COMPLETE SERIES 1 (270)	20.00	9.00	2.50
COMPLETE SERIES 2 (270)	20.00	9.00	2.50
COMPLETE SERIES 3 (180)	15.00	6.75	1.85
COMMON CARD (1-720)	.10	.05	.01

☐ 1 Robin Yount .40 .18 .05
☐ 2 Rick Wilkins .10 .05 .01
☐ 3 Steve Scarsone .10 .05 .01
☐ 4 Gary Sheffield .40 .18 .05
☐ 5 George Brett UER 1.25 .55 .16
(birthdate listed as 1963; should be 1953)
☐ 6 Al Martin .10 .05 .01
☐ 7 Joe Oliver .10 .05 .01
☐ 8 Stan Belinda .10 .05 .01
☐ 9 Denny Hocking .10 .05 .01
☐ 10 Roberto Alomar .60 .25 .07
☐ 11 Luis Polonia .10 .05 .01
☐ 12 Scott Hemond .10 .05 .01
☐ 13 Jody Reed .10 .05 .01
☐ 14 Mel Rojas .10 .05 .01
☐ 15 Junior Ortiz .10 .05 .01
☐ 16 Harold Baines .25 .11 .03
☐ 17 Brad Pennington .10 .05 .01
☐ 18 Jay Bell .25 .11 .03
☐ 19 Tom Henke .10 .05 .01
☐ 20 Jeff Branson .10 .05 .01
☐ 21 Roberto Mejia .10 .05 .01
☐ 22 Pedro Munoz .10 .05 .01
☐ 23 Matt Nokes .10 .05 .01
☐ 24 Jack McDowell .25 .11 .03
☐ 25 Cecil Fielder .25 .11 .03
☐ 26 Tony Fossas .10 .05 .01
☐ 27 Jim Eisenreich .10 .05 .01
☐ 28 Anthony Young .10 .05 .01
☐ 29 Chuck Carr .10 .05 .01
☐ 30 Jeff Treadway .10 .05 .01
☐ 31 Chris Nabholz .10 .05 .01
☐ 32 Tom Candiotti .10 .05 .01
☐ 33 Mike Maddux .10 .05 .01
☐ 34 Nolan Ryan 2.50 1.10 .30
☐ 35 Luis Gonzalez .10 .05 .01
☐ 36 Tim Salmon .40 .18 .05
☐ 37 Mark Whiten .10 .05 .01
☐ 38 Roger McDowell .10 .05 .01
☐ 39 Royce Clayton .25 .11 .03
☐ 40 Troy Neel .10 .05 .01
☐ 41 Mike Harkey .10 .05 .01
☐ 42 Darrin Fletcher .10 .05 .01
☐ 43 Wayne Kirby .10 .05 .01
☐ 44 Rich Amaral .10 .05 .01
☐ 45 Robb Nen UER .25 .11 .03
(Nenn on back)
☐ 46 Tim Teufel .10 .05 .01
☐ 47 Steve Cooke .10 .05 .01
☐ 48 Jeff McNeely .10 .05 .01
☐ 49 Jeff Montgomery .25 .11 .03
☐ 50 Skeeter Barnes .10 .05 .01
☐ 51 Scott Stahoviak .10 .05 .01
☐ 52 Pat Kelly .10 .05 .01
☐ 53 Brady Anderson .40 .18 .05
☐ 54 Mariano Duncan .10 .05 .01
☐ 55 Brian Bohanon .10 .05 .01
☐ 56 Jerry Spradlin .10 .05 .01
☐ 57 Ron Karkovice .10 .05 .01
☐ 58 Jeff Gardner .10 .05 .01
☐ 59 Bobby Bonilla .25 .11 .03
☐ 60 Tino Martinez .25 .11 .03
☐ 61 Todd Benzinger .10 .05 .01
☐ 62 Steve Trachsel .25 .11 .03
☐ 63 Brian Jordan .40 .18 .05
☐ 64 Steve Bedrosian .10 .05 .01
☐ 65 Brent Gates .10 .05 .01
☐ 66 Shawn Green .25 .11 .03
☐ 67 Sean Berry .10 .05 .01
☐ 68 Joe Klink .10 .05 .01
☐ 69 Fernando Valenzuela .25 .11 .03
☐ 70 Andy Tomberlin .10 .05 .01
☐ 71 Tony Pena .10 .05 .01
☐ 72 Eric Young .25 .11 .03
☐ 73 Chris Gomez .10 .05 .01
☐ 74 Paul O'Neill .25 .11 .03
☐ 75 Ricky Gutierrez .10 .05 .01
☐ 76 Brad Holman .10 .05 .01
☐ 77 Lance Painter .10 .05 .01
☐ 78 Mike Butcher .10 .05 .01
☐ 79 Sid Bream .10 .05 .01
☐ 80 Sammy Sosa .40 .18 .05
☐ 81 Felix Fermin .10 .05 .01
☐ 82 Todd Hundley .25 .11 .03
☐ 83 Kevin Higgins .10 .05 .01
☐ 84 Todd Pratt .10 .05 .01
☐ 85 Ken Griffey Jr. 3.00 1.35 .35
☐ 86 John O'Donoghue .10 .05 .01
☐ 87 Rick Renteria .10 .05 .01
☐ 88 John Burkett .10 .05 .01
☐ 89 Jose Vizcaino .10 .05 .01
☐ 90 Kevin Seitzer .10 .05 .01
☐ 91 Bobby Witt .10 .05 .01
☐ 92 Chris Turner .10 .05 .01
☐ 93 Omar Vizquel .25 .11 .03
☐ 94 David Justice .40 .18 .05
☐ 95 David Segui .10 .05 .01
☐ 96 Dave Hollins .10 .05 .01
☐ 97 Doug Strange .10 .05 .01
☐ 98 Jerald Clark .10 .05 .01
☐ 99 Mike Moore .10 .05 .01
☐ 100 Joey Cora .10 .05 .01
☐ 101 Scott Kamieniecki .10 .05 .01
☐ 102 Andy Benes .25 .11 .03
☐ 103 Chris Bosio .10 .05 .01
☐ 104 Rey Sanchez .10 .05 .01
☐ 105 John Jaha .25 .11 .03
☐ 106 Otis Nixon .10 .05 .01
☐ 107 Rickey Henderson .40 .18 .05
☐ 108 Jeff Bagwell 1.25 .55 .16
☐ 109 Gregg Jefferies .40 .18 .05
☐ 110 Roberto Alomar .40 .18 .05
Paul Molitor
John Olerud
☐ 111 Ron Gant .40 .18 .05
David Justice
Fred McGriff
☐ 112 Juan Gonzalez .40 .18 .05
Rafael Palmeiro
Dean Palmer
☐ 113 Greg Swindell .10 .05 .01
☐ 114 Bill Haselman .10 .05 .01
☐ 115 Phil Plantier .10 .05 .01
☐ 116 Ivan Rodriguez .75 .35 .09
☐ 117 Kevin Tapani .10 .05 .01
☐ 118 Mike LaValliere .10 .05 .01
☐ 119 Tim Costo .10 .05 .01
☐ 120 Mickey Morandini .10 .05 .01
☐ 121 Brett Butler .25 .11 .03
☐ 122 Tom Pagnozzi .10 .05 .01
☐ 123 Ron Gant .25 .11 .03
☐ 124 Damion Easley .10 .05 .01
☐ 125 Dennis Eckersley .25 .11 .03
☐ 126 Matt Mieske .10 .05 .01
☐ 127 Cliff Floyd .40 .18 .05
☐ 128 Julian Tavarez .25 .11 .03
☐ 129 Arthur Rhodes .10 .05 .01
☐ 130 Dave West .10 .05 .01
☐ 131 Tim Naehring .10 .05 .01
☐ 132 Freddie Benavides .10 .05 .01
☐ 133 Paul Assenmacher .10 .05 .01
☐ 134 David McCarty .10 .05 .01
☐ 135 Jose Lind .10 .05 .01
☐ 136 Reggie Sanders .25 .11 .03
☐ 137 Don Slaught .10 .05 .01
☐ 138 Andujar Cedeno .10 .05 .01
☐ 139 Rob Deer .10 .05 .01
☐ 140 Mike Piazza UER 2.00 .90 .25
(listed as outfielder)
☐ 141 Moises Alou .25 .11 .03
☐ 142 Tom Foley .10 .05 .01
☐ 143 Benito Santiago .10 .05 .01
☐ 144 Sandy Alomar .25 .11 .03
☐ 145 Carlos Hernandez .10 .05 .01
☐ 146 Luis Alicea .10 .05 .01
☐ 147 Tom Lampkin .10 .05 .01
☐ 148 Ryan Klesko .60 .25 .07
☐ 149 Juan Guzman .25 .11 .03
☐ 150 Scott Servais .10 .05 .01
☐ 151 Tony Gwynn 1.25 .55 .16
☐ 152 Tim Wakefield .10 .05 .01
☐ 153 David Nied .10 .05 .01
☐ 154 Chris Haney .10 .05 .01
☐ 155 Danny Bautista .10 .05 .01
☐ 156 Randy Velarde .10 .05 .01
☐ 157 Darrin Jackson .10 .05 .01
☐ 158 J.R. Phillips .10 .05 .01
☐ 159 Greg Gagne .10 .05 .01
☐ 160 Luis Aquino .10 .05 .01
☐ 161 John Vander Wal .10 .05 .01
☐ 162 Randy Myers .10 .05 .01
☐ 163 Ted Power .10 .05 .01
☐ 164 Scott Brosius .10 .05 .01
☐ 165 Len Dykstra .25 .11 .03
☐ 166 Jacob Brumfield .10 .05 .01
☐ 167 Bo Jackson .25 .11 .03
☐ 168 Eddie Taubensee .10 .05 .01
☐ 169 Carlos Baerga .25 .11 .03
☐ 170 Tim Bogar .10 .05 .01
☐ 171 Jose Canseco .40 .18 .05
☐ 172 Greg Blosser UER .10 .05 .01
(Gregg on front)
☐ 173 Chili Davis .25 .11 .03
☐ 174 Randy Knorr .10 .05 .01
☐ 175 Mike Perez .10 .05 .01
☐ 176 Henry Rodriguez .25 .11 .03
☐ 177 Brian Turang .10 .05 .01
☐ 178 Roger Pavlik .10 .05 .01
☐ 179 Aaron Sele .25 .11 .03
☐ 180 Fred McGriff .40 .18 .05
Gary Sheffield
☐ 181 J.T. Snow .25 .11 .03
Tim Salmon
☐ 182 Roberto Hernandez .25 .11 .03
☐ 183 Jeff Reboulet .10 .05 .01
☐ 184 John Doherty .10 .05 .01
☐ 185 Danny Sheaffer .10 .05 .01
☐ 186 Bip Roberts .10 .05 .01
☐ 187 Denny Martinez .25 .11 .03
☐ 188 Darryl Hamilton .10 .05 .01
☐ 189 Eduardo Perez .10 .05 .01
☐ 190 Pete Harnisch .10 .05 .01
☐ 191 Rich Gossage .25 .11 .03
☐ 192 Mickey Tettleton .10 .05 .01
☐ 193 Lenny Webster .10 .05 .01
☐ 194 Lance Johnson .25 .11 .03
☐ 195 Don Mattingly 1.50 .70 .19
☐ 196 Gregg Olson .10 .05 .01
☐ 197 Mark Gubicza .10 .05 .01
☐ 198 Scott Fletcher .10 .05 .01
☐ 199 Jon Shave .10 .05 .01
☐ 200 Tim Mauser .10 .05 .01
☐ 201 Jeromy Burnitz .10 .05 .01
☐ 202 Rob Dibble .10 .05 .01
☐ 203 Will Clark .40 .18 .05
☐ 204 Steve Buechele .10 .05 .01
☐ 205 Brian Williams .10 .05 .01
☐ 206 Carlos Garcia .10 .05 .01
☐ 207 Mark Clark .10 .05 .01
☐ 208 Rafael Palmeiro .40 .18 .05
☐ 209 Eric Davis .25 .11 .03
☐ 210 Pat Meares .10 .05 .01
☐ 211 Chuck Finley .10 .05 .01
☐ 212 Jason Bere .25 .11 .03
☐ 213 Gary DiSarcina .10 .05 .01
☐ 214 Tony Fernandez .10 .05 .01
☐ 215 B.J. Surhoff .10 .05 .01
☐ 216 Lee Guetterman .10 .05 .01
☐ 217 Tim Wallach .10 .05 .01
☐ 218 Kirt Manwaring .10 .05 .01
☐ 219 Albert Belle 1.25 .55 .16
☐ 220 Doc Gooden .25 .11 .03
☐ 221 Archi Cianfrocco .10 .05 .01
☐ 222 Terry Mulholland .10 .05 .01
☐ 223 Hipolito Pichardo .10 .05 .01
☐ 224 Kent Hrbek .25 .11 .03
☐ 225 Craig Grebeck .10 .05 .01
☐ 226 Todd Jones .10 .05 .01
☐ 227 Mike Bordick .10 .05 .01
☐ 228 John Olerud .10 .05 .01
☐ 229 Jeff Blauser .10 .05 .01
☐ 230 Alex Arias .10 .05 .01
☐ 231 Bernard Gilkey .25 .11 .03
☐ 232 Denny Neagle .25 .11 .03
☐ 233 Pedro Borbon .10 .05 .01
☐ 234 Dick Schofield .10 .05 .01
☐ 235 Matias Carrillo .10 .05 .01
☐ 236 Juan Bell .10 .05 .01
☐ 237 Mike Hampton .25 .11 .03
☐ 238 Barry Bonds .75 .35 .09
☐ 239 Cris Carpenter .10 .05 .01
☐ 240 Eric Karros .25 .11 .03
☐ 241 Greg McMichael .10 .05 .01
☐ 242 Pat Hentgen .25 .11 .03
☐ 243 Tim Pugh .10 .05 .01
☐ 244 Vinny Castilla .40 .18 .05
☐ 245 Charlie Hough .10 .05 .01
☐ 246 Bobby Munoz .10 .05 .01
☐ 247 Kevin Baez .10 .05 .01
☐ 248 Todd Frohwirth .10 .05 .01
☐ 249 Charlie Hayes .10 .05 .01
☐ 250 Mike Macfarlane .10 .05 .01
☐ 251 Danny Darwin .10 .05 .01
☐ 252 Ben Rivera .10 .05 .01
☐ 253 Dave Henderson .10 .05 .01
☐ 254 Steve Avery .25 .11 .03
☐ 255 Tim Belcher .10 .05 .01
☐ 256 Dan Plesac .10 .05 .01
☐ 257 Jim Thome .75 .35 .09
☐ 258 Albert Belle HR .60 .25 .07
☐ 259 Barry Bonds HR .40 .18 .05
☐ 260 Ron Gant HR .25 .11 .03
☐ 261 Juan Gonzalez HR .75 .35 .09
☐ 262 Ken Griffey Jr. HR 1.50 .70 .19
☐ 263 David Justice HR .25 .11 .03
☐ 264 Fred McGriff HR .40 .18 .05
☐ 265 Rafael Palmeiro HR .40 .18 .05
☐ 266 Mike Piazza HR 1.00 .45 .12
☐ 267 Frank Thomas HR 1.50 .70 .19
☐ 268 Matt Williams HR .40 .18 .05
☐ 269 Checklist 1-135 .10 .05 .01
☐ 270 Checklist 136-270 .10 .05 .01
☐ 271 Mike Stanley .10 .05 .01
☐ 272 Tony Tarasco .10 .05 .01
☐ 273 Teddy Higuera .10 .05 .01
☐ 274 Ryan Thompson .10 .05 .01
☐ 275 Rick Aguilera .10 .05 .01
☐ 276 Ramon Martinez .25 .11 .03
☐ 277 Orlando Merced .25 .11 .03
☐ 278 Guillermo Velasquez .10 .05 .01
☐ 279 Mark Hutton .10 .05 .01
☐ 280 Larry Walker .40 .18 .05
☐ 281 Kevin Gross .10 .05 .01
☐ 282 Jose Offerman .10 .05 .01
☐ 283 Jim Leyritz .10 .05 .01
☐ 284 Jamie Moyer .10 .05 .01
☐ 285 Frank Thomas 3.00 1.35 .35
☐ 286 Derek Bell .25 .11 .03
☐ 287 Derrick May .10 .05 .01
☐ 288 Dave Winfield .40 .18 .05
☐ 289 Curt Schilling .10 .05 .01
☐ 290 Carlos Quintana .10 .05 .01
☐ 291 Bob Natal .10 .05 .01
☐ 292 David Cone .25 .11 .03
☐ 293 Al Osuna .10 .05 .01
☐ 294 Bob Hamelin .10 .05 .01
☐ 295 Chad Curtis .10 .05 .01
☐ 296 Danny Jackson .10 .05 .01
☐ 297 Bob Welch .10 .05 .01
☐ 298 Felix Jose .10 .05 .01
☐ 299 Jay Buhner .40 .18 .05
☐ 300 Joe Carter .25 .11 .03
☐ 301 Kenny Lofton 1.00 .45 .12
☐ 302 Kirk Rueter .10 .05 .01
☐ 303 Kim Batiste .10 .05 .01
☐ 304 Mike Morgan .10 .05 .01
☐ 305 Pat Borders .10 .05 .01
☐ 306 Rene Arocha .10 .05 .01
☐ 307 Ruben Sierra .25 .11 .03
☐ 308 Steve Finley .40 .18 .05
☐ 309 Travis Fryman .25 .11 .03
☐ 310 Zane Smith .10 .05 .01
☐ 311 Willie Wilson .10 .05 .01
☐ 312 Trevor Hoffman .25 .11 .03
☐ 313 Terry Pendleton .25 .11 .03
☐ 314 Salomon Torres .10 .05 .01
☐ 315 Robin Ventura .25 .11 .03
☐ 316 Randy Tomlin .10 .05 .01
☐ 317 Dave Stewart .25 .11 .03
☐ 318 Mike Benjamin .10 .05 .01
☐ 319 Matt Turner .10 .05 .01
☐ 320 Manny Ramirez 1.00 .45 .12
☐ 321 Kevin Young .10 .05 .01
☐ 322 Ken Caminiti .40 .18 .05
☐ 323 Joe Girardi .10 .05 .01
☐ 324 Jeff McKnight .10 .05 .01
☐ 325 Gene Harris .10 .05 .01
☐ 326 Devon White .10 .05 .01
☐ 327 Darryl Kile .10 .05 .01
☐ 328 Craig Paquette .10 .05 .01
☐ 329 Cal Eldred .10 .05 .01
☐ 330 Bill Swift .10 .05 .01
☐ 331 Alan Trammell .25 .11 .03
☐ 332 Armando Reynoso .10 .05 .01
☐ 333 Brent Mayne .10 .05 .01
☐ 334 Chris Donnels .10 .05 .01
☐ 335 Darryl Strawberry .25 .11 .03
☐ 336 Dean Palmer .25 .11 .03
☐ 337 Frank Castillo .10 .05 .01
☐ 338 Jeff King .25 .11 .03
☐ 339 John Franco .10 .05 .01
☐ 340 Kevin Appier .25 .11 .03
☐ 341 Lance Blankenship .10 .05 .01
☐ 342 Mark McLemore .10 .05 .01
☐ 343 Pedro Astacio .10 .05 .01
☐ 344 Rich Batchelor .10 .05 .01
☐ 345 Ryan Bowen .10 .05 .01
☐ 346 Terry Steinbach .25 .11 .03
☐ 347 Troy O'Leary .10 .05 .01
☐ 348 Willie Blair .10 .05 .01
☐ 349 Wade Boggs .40 .18 .05
☐ 350 Tim Raines .40 .18 .05
☐ 351 Scott Livingstone .10 .05 .01
☐ 352 Rod Correia .10 .05 .01
☐ 353 Ray Lankford .25 .11 .03
☐ 354 Pat Listach .10 .05 .01
☐ 355 Milt Thompson .10 .05 .01
☐ 356 Miguel Jimenez .10 .05 .01
☐ 357 Marc Newfield .25 .11 .03
☐ 358 Mark McGwire 1.00 .45 .12
☐ 359 Kirby Puckett 1.25 .55 .16
☐ 360 Kent Mercker .10 .05 .01
☐ 361 John Kruk .25 .11 .03
☐ 362 Jeff Kent .10 .05 .01
☐ 363 Hal Morris .10 .05 .01
☐ 364 Edgar Martinez .25 .11 .03
☐ 365 Dave Magadan .10 .05 .01
☐ 366 Dante Bichette .40 .18 .05
☐ 367 Chris Hammond .10 .05 .01
☐ 368 Bret Saberhagen .25 .11 .03
☐ 369 Billy Ripken .10 .05 .01
☐ 370 Bill Gullickson .10 .05 .01
☐ 371 Andre Dawson .25 .11 .03
☐ 372 Roberto Kelly .10 .05 .01
☐ 373 Cal Ripken 2.50 1.10 .30
☐ 374 Craig Biggio .25 .11 .03
☐ 375 Dan Pasqua .10 .05 .01
☐ 376 Dave Nilsson .25 .11 .03
☐ 377 Duane Ward .10 .05 .01
☐ 378 Greg Vaughn .40 .18 .05
☐ 379 Jeff Fassero .10 .05 .01
☐ 380 Jerry DiPoto .10 .05 .01
☐ 381 John Patterson .10 .05 .01
☐ 382 Kevin Brown .25 .11 .03
☐ 383 Kevin Roberson .10 .05 .01
☐ 384 Joe Orsulak .10 .05 .01
☐ 385 Hilly Hathaway .10 .05 .01
☐ 386 Mike Greenwell .10 .05 .01
☐ 387 Orestes Destrade .10 .05 .01
☐ 388 Mike Gallego .10 .05 .01
☐ 389 Ozzie Guillen .10 .05 .01
☐ 390 Raul Mondesi .40 .18 .05
☐ 391 Scott Lydy .10 .05 .01
☐ 392 Tom Urbani .10 .05 .01
☐ 393 Wil Cordero .25 .11 .03
☐ 394 Tony Longmire .10 .05 .01
☐ 395 Todd Zeile .10 .05 .01
☐ 396 Scott Cooper .10 .05 .01
☐ 397 Ryne Sandberg .75 .35 .09
☐ 398 Ricky Bones .10 .05 .01
☐ 399 Phil Clark .10 .05 .01
☐ 400 Orel Hershiser .25 .11 .03
☐ 401 Mike Henneman .10 .05 .01
☐ 402 Mark Lemke .10 .05 .01
☐ 403 Mark Grace .40 .18 .05
☐ 404 Ken Ryan .10 .05 .01
☐ 405 John Smoltz .40 .18 .05
☐ 406 Jeff Conine .25 .11 .03
☐ 407 Greg Harris .10 .05 .01

☐ 408 Doug Drabek .10 .05 .01
☐ 409 Dave Fleming .10 .05 .01
☐ 410 Danny Tartabull .10 .05 .01
☐ 411 Chad Kreuter .10 .05 .01
☐ 412 Brad Ausmus .10 .05 .01
☐ 413 Ben McDonald .10 .05 .01
☐ 414 Barry Larkin .40 .18 .05
☐ 415 Bret Barberie .10 .05 .01
☐ 416 Chuck Knoblauch .40 .18 .05
☐ 417 Ozzie Smith .75 .35 .09
☐ 418 Ed Sprague .25 .11 .03
☐ 419 Matt Williams .40 .18 .05
☐ 420 Jeremy Hernandez .10 .05 .01
☐ 421 Jose Bautista .10 .05 .01
☐ 422 Kevin Mitchell .25 .11 .03
☐ 423 Manuel Lee .10 .05 .01
☐ 424 Mike Devereaux .10 .05 .01
☐ 425 Omar Olivares .10 .05 .01
☐ 426 Rafael Belliard .10 .05 .01
☐ 427 Richie Lewis .10 .05 .01
☐ 428 Ron Darling .10 .05 .01
☐ 429 Shane Mack .10 .05 .01
☐ 430 Tim Hulett .10 .05 .01
☐ 431 Wally Joyner .25 .11 .03
☐ 432 Wes Chamberlain .10 .05 .01
☐ 433 Tom Browning .10 .05 .01
☐ 434 Scott Radinsky .10 .05 .01
☐ 435 Rondell White .40 .18 .05
☐ 436 Rod Beck .25 .11 .03
☐ 437 Rheal Cormier .10 .05 .01
☐ 438 Randy Johnson .40 .18 .05
☐ 439 Pete Schourek .25 .11 .03
☐ 440 Mo Vaughn .75 .35 .09
☐ 441 Mike Timlin .10 .05 .01
☐ 442 Mark Langston .25 .11 .03
☐ 443 Lou Whitaker .25 .11 .03
☐ 444 Kevin Stocker .10 .05 .01
☐ 445 Ken Hill .10 .05 .01
☐ 446 John Wetteland .25 .11 .03
☐ 447 J.T. Snow .25 .11 .03
☐ 448 Erik Pappas .10 .05 .01
☐ 449 David Hulse .10 .05 .01
☐ 450 Darren Daulton .25 .11 .03
☐ 451 Chris Hoiles .10 .05 .01
☐ 452 Bryan Harvey .10 .05 .01
☐ 453 Darren Lewis .10 .05 .01
☐ 454 Andres Galarraga .40 .18 .05
☐ 455 Joe Hesketh .10 .05 .01
☐ 456 Jose Valentin .25 .11 .03
☐ 457 Dan Peltier .10 .05 .01
☐ 458 Joe Boever .10 .05 .01
☐ 459 Kevin Rogers .10 .05 .01
☐ 460 Craig Shipley .10 .05 .01
☐ 461 Alvaro Espinoza .10 .05 .01
☐ 462 Wilson Alvarez .25 .11 .03
☐ 463 Cory Snyder .10 .05 .01
☐ 464 Candy Maldonado .10 .05 .01
☐ 465 Blas Minor .10 .05 .01
☐ 466 Rod Bolton .10 .05 .01
☐ 467 Kenny Rogers .10 .05 .01
☐ 468 Greg Myers .10 .05 .01
☐ 469 Jimmy Key .25 .11 .03
☐ 470 Tony Castillo .10 .05 .01
☐ 471 Mike Stanton .10 .05 .01
☐ 472 Deion Sanders .40 .18 .05
☐ 473 Tito Navarro .10 .05 .01
☐ 474 Mike Gardiner .10 .05 .01
☐ 475 Steve Reed .10 .05 .01
☐ 476 John Roper .10 .05 .01
☐ 477 Mike Trombley .10 .05 .01
☐ 478 Charles Nagy .25 .11 .03
☐ 479 Larry Casian .10 .05 .01
☐ 480 Eric Hillman .10 .05 .01
☐ 481 Bill Wertz .10 .05 .01
☐ 482 Jeff Schwarz .10 .05 .01
☐ 483 John Valentin .25 .11 .03
☐ 484 Carl Willis .10 .05 .01
☐ 485 Gary Gaetti .25 .11 .03
☐ 486 Bill Pecota .10 .05 .01
☐ 487 John Smiley .10 .05 .01
☐ 488 Mike Mussina .60 .25 .07
☐ 489 Mike Ignasiak .10 .05 .01
☐ 490 Billy Brewer .10 .05 .01
☐ 491 Jack Voigt .10 .05 .01
☐ 492 Mike Munoz .10 .05 .01
☐ 493 Lee Tinsley .25 .11 .03
☐ 494 Bob Wickman .10 .05 .01
☐ 495 Roger Salkeld .10 .05 .01
☐ 496 Thomas Howard .10 .05 .01
☐ 497 Mark Davis .10 .05 .01
☐ 498 Dave Clark .10 .05 .01
☐ 499 Turk Wendell .10 .05 .01
☐ 500 Rafael Bournigal .10 .05 .01
☐ 501 Chip Hale .10 .05 .01
☐ 502 Matt Whiteside .10 .05 .01
☐ 503 Brian Koelling .10 .05 .01
☐ 504 Jeff Reed .10 .05 .01
☐ 505 Paul Wagner .10 .05 .01
☐ 506 Torey Lovullo .10 .05 .01
☐ 507 Curtis Leskanic .25 .11 .03
☐ 508 Derek Lilliquist .10 .05 .01
☐ 509 Joe Magrane .10 .05 .01
☐ 510 Mackey Sasser .10 .05 .01
☐ 511 Lloyd McClendon .10 .05 .01
☐ 512 Jayhawk Owens .10 .05 .01
☐ 513 Woody Williams .10 .05 .01
☐ 514 Gary Redus .10 .05 .01
☐ 515 Tim Spehr .10 .05 .01
☐ 516 Jim Abbott .10 .05 .01
☐ 517 Lou Frazier .10 .05 .01
☐ 518 Erik Plantenberg .10 .05 .01
☐ 519 Tim Worrell .10 .05 .01
☐ 520 Brian McRae .25 .11 .03
☐ 521 Chan Ho Park 1.00 .45 .12
☐ 522 Mark Wohlers .25 .11 .03
☐ 523 Geronimo Pena .10 .05 .01
☐ 524 Andy Ashby .25 .11 .03
☐ 525 Tim Raines TALE .25 .11 .03
☐ 526 Paul Molitor TALE .40 .18 .05
☐ 527 Joe Carter DL .25 .11 .03
☐ 528 Frank Thomas DL UER 1.50 .70 .19
(listed as third in RBI in 1993; was actually second)
☐ 529 Ken Griffey Jr. DL 1.50 .70 .19
☐ 530 David Justice DL .25 .11 .03
☐ 531 Gregg Jefferies DL .25 .11 .03
☐ 532 Barry Bonds DL .40 .18 .05
☐ 533 John Kruk QS .10 .05 .01
☐ 534 Roger Clemens QS .40 .18 .05
☐ 535 Cecil Fielder QS .25 .11 .03
☐ 536 Ruben Sierra QS .25 .11 .03
☐ 537 Tony Gwynn QS .60 .25 .07
☐ 538 Tom Glavine QS .40 .18 .05
☐ 539 Checklist 271-405 UER .10 .05 .01
(number on back is 269)
☐ 540 Checklist 406-540 UER .10 .05 .01
(numbered 270 on back)
☐ 541 Ozzie Smith ATL .40 .18 .05
☐ 542 Eddie Murray ATL .75 .35 .09
☐ 543 Lee Smith ATL .25 .11 .03
☐ 544 Greg Maddux 2.00 .90 .25
☐ 545 Denis Boucher .10 .05 .01
☐ 546 Mark Gardner .10 .05 .01
☐ 547 Bo Jackson .25 .11 .03
☐ 548 Eric Anthony .10 .05 .01
☐ 549 Delino DeShields .10 .05 .01
☐ 550 Turner Ward .10 .05 .01
☐ 551 Scott Sanderson .10 .05 .01
☐ 552 Hector Carrasco .10 .05 .01
☐ 553 Tony Phillips .25 .11 .03
☐ 554 Melido Perez .10 .05 .01
☐ 555 Mike Felder .10 .05 .01
☐ 556 Jack Morris .25 .11 .03
☐ 557 Rafael Palmeiro .40 .18 .05
☐ 558 Shane Reynolds .25 .11 .03
☐ 559 Pete Incaviglia .10 .05 .01
☐ 560 Greg Harris .10 .05 .01
☐ 561 Matt Walbeck .10 .05 .01
☐ 562 Todd Van Poppel .10 .05 .01
☐ 563 Todd Stottlemyre .10 .05 .01
☐ 564 Ricky Bones .10 .05 .01
☐ 565 Mike Jackson .10 .05 .01
☐ 566 Kevin McReynolds .10 .05 .01
☐ 567 Melvin Nieves .25 .11 .03
☐ 568 Juan Gonzalez 1.50 .70 .19
☐ 569 Frank Viola .10 .05 .01
☐ 570 Vince Coleman .10 .05 .01
☐ 571 Brian Anderson .25 .11 .03
☐ 572 Omar Vizquel .25 .11 .03
☐ 573 Bernie Williams .60 .25 .07
☐ 574 Tom Glavine .40 .18 .05
☐ 575 Mitch Williams .10 .05 .01
☐ 576 Shawon Dunston .10 .05 .01
☐ 577 Mike Lansing .25 .11 .03
☐ 578 Greg Pirkl .10 .05 .01
☐ 579 Sid Fernandez .10 .05 .01
☐ 580 Doug Jones .10 .05 .01
☐ 581 Walt Weiss .10 .05 .01
☐ 582 Tim Belcher .10 .05 .01
☐ 583 Alex Fernandez .25 .11 .03
☐ 584 Alex Cole .10 .05 .01
☐ 585 Greg Cadaret .10 .05 .01
☐ 586 Bob Tewksbury .10 .05 .01
☐ 587 Dave Hansen .10 .05 .01
☐ 588 Kurt Abbott .25 .11 .03
☐ 589 Rick White .10 .05 .01
☐ 590 Kevin Bass .10 .05 .01
☐ 591 Geronimo Berroa .25 .11 .03
☐ 592 Jaime Navarro .10 .05 .01
☐ 593 Steve Farr .10 .05 .01
☐ 594 Jack Armstrong .10 .05 .01
☐ 595 Steve Howe .10 .05 .01
☐ 596 Jose Rijo .10 .05 .01
☐ 597 Otis Nixon .10 .05 .01
☐ 598 Robby Thompson .10 .05 .01
☐ 599 Kelly Stinnett .10 .05 .01
☐ 600 Carlos Delgado .40 .18 .05
☐ 601 Brian Johnson .10 .05 .01
☐ 602 Gregg Olson .10 .05 .01
☐ 603 Jim Edmonds .60 .25 .07
☐ 604 Mike Blowers .10 .05 .01
☐ 605 Lee Smith .25 .11 .03
☐ 606 Pat Rapp .10 .05 .01
☐ 607 Mike Magnante .10 .05 .01
☐ 608 Karl Rhodes .10 .05 .01
☐ 609 Jeff Juden .10 .05 .01
☐ 610 Rusty Meacham .10 .05 .01
☐ 611 Pedro Martinez .40 .18 .05
☐ 612 Todd Worrell .10 .05 .01
☐ 613 Stan Javier .10 .05 .01
☐ 614 Mike Hampton .25 .11 .03
☐ 615 Jose Guzman .10 .05 .01
☐ 616 Xavier Hernandez .10 .05 .01
☐ 617 David Wells .10 .05 .01
☐ 618 John Habyan .10 .05 .01
☐ 619 Chris Nabholz .10 .05 .01
☐ 620 Bobby Jones .25 .11 .03
☐ 621 Chris James .10 .05 .01
☐ 622 Ellis Burks .25 .11 .03
☐ 623 Erik Hanson .10 .05 .01
☐ 624 Pat Meares .10 .05 .01
☐ 625 Harold Reynolds .10 .05 .01
☐ 626 Bob Hamelin RR .10 .05 .01
☐ 627 Manny Ramirez RR .40 .18 .05
☐ 628 Ryan Klesko RR .40 .18 .05
☐ 629 Carlos Delgado RR .40 .18 .05
☐ 630 Javier Lopez RR .40 .18 .05
☐ 631 Steve Karsay RR .10 .05 .01
☐ 632 Rick Helling RR .10 .05 .01
☐ 633 Steve Trachsel RR .25 .11 .03
☐ 634 Hector Carrasco RR .10 .05 .01
☐ 635 Andy Stankiewicz .10 .05 .01
☐ 636 Paul Sorrento .10 .05 .01
☐ 637 Scott Erickson .10 .05 .01
☐ 638 Chipper Jones 2.50 1.10 .30
☐ 639 Luis Polonia .10 .05 .01
☐ 640 Howard Johnson .10 .05 .01
☐ 641 John Dopson .10 .05 .01
☐ 642 Jody Reed .10 .05 .01
☐ 643 Lonnie Smith .10 .05 .01
☐ 644 Mark Portugal .10 .05 .01
☐ 645 Paul Molitor .60 .25 .07
☐ 646 Paul Assenmacher .10 .05 .01
☐ 647 Hubie Brooks .10 .05 .01
☐ 648 Gary Wayne .10 .05 .01
☐ 649 Sean Berry .10 .05 .01
☐ 650 Roger Clemens .60 .25 .07
☐ 651 Brian L.Hunter .40 .18 .05
☐ 652 Wally Whitehurst .10 .05 .01
☐ 653 Allen Watson .10 .05 .01
☐ 654 Rickey Henderson .40 .18 .05
☐ 655 Sid Bream .10 .05 .01
☐ 656 Dan Wilson .25 .11 .03
☐ 657 Ricky Jordan .10 .05 .01
☐ 658 Sterling Hitchcock .25 .11 .03
☐ 659 Darrin Jackson .10 .05 .01
☐ 660 Junior Felix .10 .05 .01
☐ 661 Tom Brunansky .10 .05 .01
☐ 662 Jose Vizcaino .10 .05 .01
☐ 663 Mark Leiter .10 .05 .01
☐ 664 Gil Heredia .10 .05 .01
☐ 665 Fred McGriff .40 .18 .05
☐ 666 Will Clark .40 .18 .05
☐ 667 Al Leiter .25 .11 .03
☐ 668 James Mouton .25 .11 .03
☐ 669 Billy Bean .10 .05 .01
☐ 670 Scott Leius .10 .05 .01
☐ 671 Bret Boone .25 .11 .03
☐ 672 Darren Holmes .10 .05 .01
☐ 673 Dave Weathers .10 .05 .01
☐ 674 Eddie Murray .75 .35 .09
☐ 675 Felix Fermin .10 .05 .01
☐ 676 Chris Sabo .10 .05 .01
☐ 677 Billy Spiers .10 .05 .01
☐ 678 Aaron Sele .25 .11 .03
☐ 679 Juan Samuel .10 .05 .01
☐ 680 Julio Franco .25 .11 .03
☐ 681 Heathcliff Slocumb .25 .11 .03
☐ 682 Denny Martinez .25 .11 .03
☐ 683 Jerry Browne .10 .05 .01
☐ 684 Pedro Martinez .25 .11 .03
☐ 685 Rex Hudler .10 .05 .01
☐ 686 Willie McGee .10 .05 .01
☐ 687 Andy Van Slyke .25 .11 .03
☐ 688 Pat Mahomes .10 .05 .01
☐ 689 Dave Henderson .10 .05 .01
☐ 690 Tony Eusebio .10 .05 .01
☐ 691 Rick Sutcliffe .10 .05 .01
☐ 692 Willie Banks .10 .05 .01
☐ 693 Alan Mills .10 .05 .01
☐ 694 Jeff Treadway .10 .05 .01
☐ 695 Alex Gonzalez .25 .11 .03
☐ 696 David Segui .10 .05 .01
☐ 697 Rick Helling .10 .05 .01
☐ 698 Bip Roberts .10 .05 .01
☐ 699 Jeff Cirillo .50 .23 .06
☐ 700 Terry Mulholland .10 .05 .01
☐ 701 Marvin Freeman .10 .05 .01
☐ 702 Jason Bere .25 .11 .03
☐ 703 Javier Lopez .40 .18 .05
☐ 704 Greg Hibbard .10 .05 .01
☐ 705 Tommy Greene .10 .05 .01
☐ 706 Marquis Grissom .25 .11 .03
☐ 707 Brian Harper .10 .05 .01
☐ 708 Steve Karsay .10 .05 .01
☐ 709 Jeff Brantley .10 .05 .01
☐ 710 Jeff Russell .10 .05 .01
☐ 711 Bryan Hickerson .10 .05 .01
☐ 712 Jim Pittsley .60 .25 .07
☐ 713 Bobby Ayala .10 .05 .01
☐ 714 John Smoltz .40 .18 .05
☐ 715 Jose Rijo .10 .05 .01
☐ 716 Greg Maddux 1.00 .45 .12
☐ 717 Matt Williams .40 .18 .05
☐ 718 Frank Thomas 1.50 .70 .19
☐ 719 Ryne Sandberg .40 .18 .05
☐ 720 Checklist .10 .05 .01

1994 Stadium Club First Day Issue

Randomly inserted in one of every 24 packs, these First Day Production cards are identical to the regular issues except for a special 1st Day foil stamp engraved on the front of each card. No more than 2,000 of each Stadium Club card was issued as First Day Issue. Some FDI logos have been transferred from "common" players to the front of "star" players.

	MINT	NRMT	EXC
COMPLETE SET (720)	2700.00	1200.00	350.00
COMPLETE SERIES 1 (270)	1200.00	550.00	150.00
COMPLETE SERIES 2 (270)	1000.00	450.00	125.00
COMPLETE SERIES 3 (180)	500.00	220.00	60.00
COMMON CARD (1-720)	2.00	.90	.25

*STARS: 15X to 30X BASIC CARDS....
*YOUNG STARS: 12.5X to 25X BASIC CARDS

1994 Stadium Club Golden Rainbow

Parallel to the basic Stadium Club set, Golden Rainbows differ in that the player's last name on front has gold refracting foil over it. The cards were inserted one per Stadium Club foil pack and two per jumbo.

	MINT	NRMT	EXC
COMPLETE SET (720)	170.00	75.00	21.00
COMPLETE SERIES 1 (270)	65.00	29.00	8.00
COMPLETE SERIES 2 (270)	65.00	29.00	8.00
COMPLETE SERIES 3 (180)	40.00	18.00	5.00
COMMON CARD (1-720)	.25	.11	.03

*STARS: 2X to 4X BASIC CARDS.......
*YOUNG STARS: 1.5X to 3X BASIC CARDS

1994 Stadium Club Members Only Parallel

This set, issued only to Topps Stadium Club Members, is a parallel of the regular Stadium Club set. This set was issued in factory set form only and includes parallel versions of both the basic issue and insert cards from the 1994 Stadium Club set. According to Topps, 5,000 sets were produced. Only the insert cards have been listed below. Please use the multiplier for values on the basic issue cards.

	MINT	NRMT	EXC
COMPLETE FACT.SET (770)	200.00	90.00	25.00
COMMON CARD (1-720)	.25	.11	.03

*MEMBERS ONLY: 4X BASIC CARDS

☐ F1 Jeff Bagwell 4.00 1.80 .50
☐ F2 Albert Belle 5.00 2.20 .60
☐ F3 Barry Bonds 2.50 1.10 .30
☐ F4 Juan Gonzalez 5.00 2.20 .60
☐ F5 Ken Griffey Jr. 10.00 4.50 1.25
☐ F6 Marquis Grissom 1.00 .45 .12
☐ F7 David Justice 1.00 .45 .12
☐ F8 Mike Piazza 8.00 3.60 1.00
☐ F9 Tim Salmon
☐ F10 Frank Thomas 10.00 4.50 1.25

Card	MINT	NRMT	EXC
☐ DD1 Mike Piazza	12.00	5.50	1.50
☐ DD2 Dave Winfield	1.50	.70	.19
☐ DD3 John Kruk	1.00	.45	.12
☐ DD4 Cal Ripken	15.00	6.75	1.85
☐ DD5 Kirby Puckett	8.00	3.60	1.00
☐ DD6 Barry Bonds	4.00	1.80	.50
☐ DD7 Ken Griffey Jr.	15.00	6.75	1.85
☐ DD8 Tim Salmon	2.50	1.10	.30
☐ DD9 Frank Thomas	15.00	6.75	1.85
☐ DD10 Jeff Kent	1.00	.45	.12
☐ DD11 Randy Johnson	3.00	1.35	.35
☐ DD12 Darren Daulton	1.00	.45	.12
☐ ST1 Atlanta Braves	8.00	3.60	1.00
(Jeff Blauser			
Terry Pendleton)			
☐ ST2 Chicago Cubs	1.50	.70	.19
(Sammy Sosa			
Derrick May)			
☐ ST3 Cincinnati Reds	2.00	.90	.25
(Reggie Sanders			
Barry Larkin)			
☐ ST4 Colorado Rockies	1.50	.70	.19
(Vinny Castilla			
Eric Young)			
☐ ST5 Florida Marlins	1.50	.70	.19
(Alex Arias)			
☐ ST6 Houston Astros	1.50	.70	.19
(Eric Anthony			
Steve Finley)			
☐ ST7 Los Angeles Dodgers	2.00	.90	.25
(Mike Piazza)			
☐ ST8 Montreal Expos	1.50	.70	.19
(Marquis Grissom)			
☐ ST9 New York Mets	1.50	.70	.19
(Bobby Bonilla)			
☐ ST10 Philadelphia Phillies	1.50	.70	.19
(Mickey Morandini)			
☐ ST11 Pittsburgh Pirates	1.50	.70	.19
(Andy Van Slyke			
Jay Bell)			
☐ ST12 St. Louis Cardinals	1.50	.70	.19
(Todd Zeile			
Gregg Jefferies)			
☐ ST13 San Diego Padres	1.50	.70	.19
(Ricky Gutierrez)			
☐ ST14 San Francisco Giants	2.00	.90	.25
(Matt Williams			
Kirt Manwaring)			
☐ ST15 Baltimore Orioles	4.00	1.80	.50
(Cal Ripken)			
☐ ST16 Boston Red Sox	4.00	1.80	.50
(Luis Rivera			
John Valentin)			
☐ ST17 California Angels	1.50	.70	.19
(Tim Salmon)			
☐ ST18 Chicago White Sox	1.50	.70	.19
(Joey Cora)			
☐ ST19 Cleveland Indians	4.00	1.80	.50
(Kenny Lofton			
Carlos Baerga			
Albert Belle)			
☐ ST20 Detroit Tigers	1.50	.70	.19
(Alan Trammell			
Tony Phillips)			
☐ ST21 Kansas City Royals	1.50	.70	.19
Jose Lind			
Curt Wilkerson)			
☐ ST22 Milwaukee Brewers	1.50	.70	.19
(Julio Navarro			
John Jaha			
Cal Eldred)			
☐ ST23 Minnesota Twins	1.50	.70	.19
(Kirby Puckett			
Kent Hrbek)			
☐ ST24 New York Yankees	2.00	.90	.25
Don Mattingly			
Bernie Williams)			
☐ ST25 Oakland Athletics	1.50	.70	.19
(Mike Bordick			
Brent Gates)			
☐ ST26 Seattle Mariners	4.00	1.80	.50
(Jay Buhner			
Mike Blowers)			
☐ ST27 Texas Rangers	2.00	.90	.25
(Ivan Rodriguez			
Dean Palmer			
Jose Canseco			
Juan Gonzalez)			
☐ ST28 Toronto Blue Jays	1.50	.70	.19
(John Olerud)			

1994 Stadium Club Dugout Dirt

Randomly inserted at a rate of one per six packs, these standard-size cards feature some of baseball's most popular and colorful players by sports cartoonists Daniel Guidera and Steve Benson. The cards resemble basic Stadium Club cards except for a Dugout Dirt logo at the bottom. Backs contain a cartoon. Cards 1-4 were found in first series packs with cards 5-8 and 9-12 were inserted in second series and third series packs respectively.

	MINT	NRMT	EXC
COMPLETE SET (12)	10.00	4.50	1.25
COMPLETE SERIES 1 (4)	5.00	2.20	.60
COMPLETE SERIES 2 (4)	3.00	1.35	.35
COMPLETE SERIES 3 (4)	3.00	1.35	.35
COMMON CARD (DD1-DD12)	.25	.11	.03
☐ DD1 Mike Piazza	2.00	.90	.25
☐ DD2 Dave Winfield	.50	.23	.06
☐ DD3 John Kruk	.25	.11	.03
☐ DD4 Cal Ripken	2.50	1.10	.30
☐ DD5 Jack McDowell	.50	.23	.06
☐ DD6 Barry Bonds	.75	.35	.09
☐ DD7 Ken Griffey Jr.	3.00	1.35	.35
☐ DD8 Tim Salmon	.50	.23	.06
☐ DD9 Frank Thomas	3.00	1.35	.35
☐ DD10 Jeff Kent	.25	.11	.03
☐ DD11 Randy Johnson	.50	.23	.06
☐ DD12 Darren Daulton	.25	.11	.03

1994 Stadium Club Finest

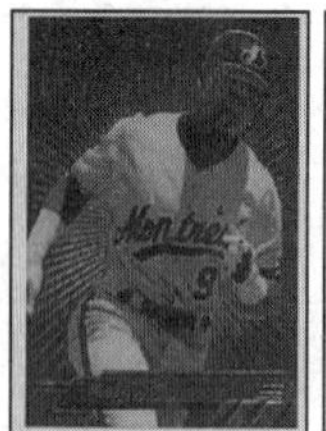

This set contains 10 standard-size metallic cards of top players. They were randomly inserted one in 24 third series packs. The fronts feature a color player photo with a red and yellow background. Backs contain a color player photo with 1993 and career statistics. Jumbo versions measuring approximately five inches by seven inches were issued for retail repacks.

	MINT	NRMT	EXC
COMPLETE SET (10)	35.00	16.00	4.40
COMMON CARD (F1-F10)	1.00	.45	.12
*JUMBOS: 1.5X BASIC CARDS			
☐ F1 Jeff Bagwell	4.00	1.80	.50
☐ F2 Albert Belle	4.00	1.80	.50
☐ F3 Barry Bonds	2.50	1.10	.30
☐ F4 Juan Gonzalez	5.00	2.20	.60
☐ F5 Ken Griffey Jr.	10.00	4.50	1.25
☐ F6 Marquis Grissom	1.00	.45	.12
☐ F7 David Justice	1.00	.45	.12
☐ F8 Mike Piazza	6.00	2.70	.75
☐ F9 Tim Salmon	1.50	.70	.19
☐ F10 Frank Thomas	10.00	4.50	1.25

1994 Stadium Club Super Teams

Randomly inserted at a rate of one per 24 first series packs only, this 28-card standard-size features one card for each of the 28 MLB teams. Collectors holding team cards could redeem them for special prizes if those teams won a division title, a league championship, or the World Series. But, since the strike affected the 1994 season, Topps postponed the promotion until the 1995 season. The expiration was pushed back to January 31, 1996.

	MINT	NRMT	EXC
COMPLETE SET (28)	50.00	22.00	6.25
COMMON TEAM (1-28)	1.50	.70	.19
☐ ST1 Atlanta Braves	10.00	4.50	1.25
(Jeff Blauser			
Terry Pendleton)			
☐ ST2 Chicago Cubs	1.50	.70	.19
(Sammy Sosa			
Derrick May)			
☐ ST3 Cincinnati Reds	3.00	1.35	.35
(Reggie Sanders			
Barry Larkin)			
☐ ST4 Colorado Rockies	1.50	.70	.19
(Vinny Castilla			
Eric Young)			
☐ ST5 Florida Marlins	1.50	.70	.19
(Alex Arias)			
☐ ST6 Houston Astros	1.50	.70	.19
(Eric Anthony			
Steve Finley)			
☐ ST7 Los Angeles Dodgers	6.00	2.70	.75
(Mike Piazza)			
☐ ST8 Montreal Expos	1.50	.70	.19
(Marquis Grissom)			
☐ ST9 New York Mets	1.50	.70	.19
(Bobby Bonilla)			
☐ ST10 Philadelphia Phillies	1.50	.70	.19
(Mickey Morandini)			
☐ ST11 Pittsburgh Pirates	1.50	.70	.19
(Andy Van Slyke			
Jay Bell)			
☐ ST12 St. Louis Cardinals	1.50	.70	.19
(Todd Zeile			
Gregg Jefferies)			
☐ ST13 San Diego Padres	1.50	.70	.19
(Ricky Gutierrez)			
☐ ST14 San Francisco Giants	2.00	.90	.25
(Matt Williams			
Kirt Manwaring)			
☐ ST15 Baltimore Orioles	8.00	3.60	1.00
(Cal Ripken)			
☐ ST16 Boston Red Sox	2.00	.90	.25
(Luis Rivera			
John Valentin)			
☐ ST17 California Angels	1.50	.70	.19
(Tim Salmon)			
☐ ST18 Chicago White Sox	1.50	.70	.19
(Joey Cora)			
☐ ST19 Cleveland Indians	8.00	3.60	1.00
(Kenny Lofton			
Carlos Baerga			
Albert Belle)			
☐ ST20 Detroit Tigers	1.50	.70	.19
(Alan Trammell			
Tony Phillips)			
☐ ST21 Kansas City Royals	1.50	.70	.19
Jose Lind			
Curt Wilkerson)			
☐ ST22 Milwaukee Brewers	1.50	.70	.19
(Julio Navarro			
John Jaha			
Cal Eldred)			
☐ ST23 Minnesota Twins	4.00	1.80	.50
(Kirby Puckett			
Kent Hrbek)			
☐ ST24 New York Yankees	5.00	2.20	.60
Don Mattingly			
Bernie Williams)			
☐ ST25 Oakland Athletics	1.50	.70	.19
(Mike Bordick			
Brent Gates)			
☐ ST26 Seattle Mariners	2.00	.90	.25
(Jay Buhner			
Mike Blowers)			
☐ ST27 Texas Rangers	5.00	2.20	.60
(Ivan Rodriguez			
Dean Palmer			
Jose Canseco			
Juan Gonzalez)			
☐ ST28 Toronto Blue Jays	1.50	.70	.19
(John Olerud)			

1994 Stadium Club Members Only

Issued to Stadium Club members, this 50-card standard-size set features 45 regular Stadium Club cards as well as five Stadium Club Finest cards. The fronts have full-bleed color action player photos. The player's name is printed in the bottom left corner, and the words 'Topps Stadium Club Members Only' appear in one of the top corners. On a black background, the horizontal backs carry a color player close-up shot, and a player profile.

	MINT	NRMT	EXC
COMPLETE SET (50)	20.00	9.00	2.50
COMMON CARD (1-50)	.10	.05	.01
☐ 1 Juan Gonzalez	1.50	.70	.19
☐ 2 Tom Henke	.10	.05	.01
☐ 3 John Kruk	.10	.05	.01
☐ 4 Paul Molitor	.75	.35	.09
☐ 5 David Justice	.40	.18	.05
☐ 6 Rafael Palmeiro	.40	.18	.05
☐ 7 John Smoltz	.50	.23	.06
☐ 8 Matt Williams	.40	.18	.05
☐ 9 John Olerud	.10	.05	.01
☐ 10 Mark Grace	.40	.18	.05
☐ 11 Joe Carter	.30	.14	.04
☐ 12 Wilson Alvarez	.10	.05	.01
☐ 13 Len Dykstra	.20	.09	.03
☐ 14 Kevin Appier	.20	.09	.03
☐ 15 Andres Galarraga	.30	.14	.04
☐ 16 Mark Langston	.10	.05	.01
☐ 17 Ken Griffey Jr.	3.00	1.35	.35
☐ 18 Albert Belle	1.50	.70	.19
☐ 19 Gregg Jefferies	.10	.05	.01
☐ 20 Duane Ward	.10	.05	.01
☐ 21 Jack McDowell	.10	.05	.01
☐ 22 Randy Johnson	.50	.23	.06
☐ 23 Tom Glavine	.30	.14	.04
☐ 24 Barry Bonds	.75	.35	.09
☐ 25 Chuck Carr	.10	.05	.01
☐ 26 Ron Gant	.20	.09	.03
☐ 27 Kenny Lofton	.75	.35	.09
☐ 28 Mike Piazza	2.50	1.10	.30
☐ 29 Frank Thomas	3.00	1.35	.35
☐ 30 Fred McGriff	.40	.18	.05
☐ 31 Bryan Harvey	.10	.05	.01
☐ 32 John Burkett	.10	.05	.01
☐ 33 Roberto Alomar	.75	.35	.09
☐ 34 Cecil Fielder	.20	.09	.03
☐ 35 Marquis Grissom	.20	.09	.03
☐ 36 Randy Myers	.10	.05	.01
☐ 37 Tony Phillips	.10	.05	.01
☐ 38 Rickey Henderson	.30	.14	.04
☐ 39 Luis Polonia	.10	.05	.01
☐ 40 Jose Rijo	.10	.05	.01
☐ 41 Jeff Montgomery	.10	.05	.01
☐ 42 Greg Maddux	2.50	1.10	.30
☐ 43 Tony Gwynn	1.50	.70	.19
☐ 44 Rod Beck	.10	.05	.01
☐ 45 Carlos Baerga	.20	.09	.03
☐ 46 Wil Cordero FIN	.75	.35	.09
☐ 47 Tim Salmon FIN	1.50	.70	.19
☐ 48 Mike Lansing FIN	.75	.35	.09
☐ 49 J.T. Snow FIN	.75	.35	.09
☐ 50 Jeff Conine FIN	1.00	.45	.12

1994 Stadium Club Members Only Finest Bronze

Available only to members who purchase the Members Only baseball set, this 3-card set is the first edition of Topps Finest Bronze cards. Measuring 2 3/4" by 3 3/4", the cards are mounted on bronze and factory sealed in clear resin. On a colorful reflective background, the fronts display a player cutout that is highlighted by a circle design. In black lettering, the horizontal backs present biography as well as major and minor league batting record.

	MINT	NRMT	EXC
COMPLETE SET (3)	60.00	27.00	7.50
COMMON CARD (1-3)	10.00	4.50	1.25
☐ 1 Barry Bonds	10.00	4.50	1.25
☐ 2 Ken Griffey Jr.	30.00	13.50	3.70
☐ 3 Frank Thomas	30.00	13.50	3.70

1994 Stadium Club Team

This 360-card standard-size set features 30 players from 12 teams. The fronts feature full-bleed color action photos that are edged on the bottom and right by a gradated black-and-green pattern. The player's name is printed in gold foil in the bottom stripe, while a line of gold squares accents the right stripe and intersects the team name (also in gold foil). On a gradated green and black background, the backs carry a color head shot, biography, and statistics. The cards are numbered on the back and checklisted below alphabetically according to teams.

	MINT	NRMT	EXC
COMPLETE SET (360)	30.00	13.50	3.70
COMMON CARD (1-360)	.05	.02	.01

Card	MINT	NRMT	EXC
□ 1 Barry Bonds	.75	.35	.09
□ 2 Royce Clayton	.15	.07	.02
□ 3 Kirt Manwaring	.05	.02	.01
□ 4 J.R. Phillips	.05	.02	.01
□ 5 Robby Thompson	.05	.02	.01
□ 6 Willie McGee	.25	.11	.03
□ 7 Steve Hosey	.05	.02	.01
□ 8 Dave Burba	.05	.02	.01
□ 9 Steve Scarsone	.05	.02	.01
□ 10 Salomon Torres	.05	.02	.01
□ 11 Bryan Hickerson	.05	.02	.01
□ 12 Mike Benjamin	.05	.02	.01
□ 13 Mark Carreon	.05	.02	.01
□ 14 Rich Monteleone	.05	.02	.01
□ 15 Dave Martinez	.05	.02	.01
□ 16 Bill Swift	.05	.02	.01
□ 17 Jeff Reed	.05	.02	.01
□ 18 John Patterson	.05	.02	.01
□ 19 Darren Lewis	.05	.02	.01
□ 20 Mark Portugal	.05	.02	.01
□ 21 Trevor Wilson	.05	.02	.01
□ 22 Matt Williams	.50	.23	.06
□ 23 Kevin Rogers	.05	.02	.01
□ 24 Luis Mercedes	.05	.02	.01
□ 25 Mike Jackson	.05	.02	.01
□ 26 Steve Frey	.05	.02	.01
□ 27 Tony Menendez	.05	.02	.01
□ 28 John Burkett	.05	.02	.01
□ 29 Todd Benzinger	.05	.02	.01
□ 30 Rod Beck	.15	.07	.02
□ 31 Greg Maddux	2.00	.90	.25
□ 32 Steve Avery	.15	.07	.02
□ 33 Milt Hill	.05	.02	.01
□ 34 Charlie O'Brien	.05	.02	.01
□ 35 John Smoltz	.60	.25	.07
□ 36 Jarvis Brown	.05	.02	.01
□ 37 Dave Gallagher	.05	.02	.01
□ 38 Ryan Klesko	1.00	.45	.12
□ 39 Kent Mercker	.05	.02	.01
□ 40 Terry Pendleton	.15	.07	.02
□ 41 Ron Gant	.35	.16	.04
□ 42 Pedro Borbon Jr.	.05	.02	.01
□ 43 Steve Bedrosian	.05	.02	.01
□ 44 Ramon Caraballo	.05	.02	.01
□ 45 Tyler Houston	.25	.11	.03
□ 46 Mark Lemke	.05	.02	.01
□ 47 Fred McGriff	.50	.23	.06
□ 48 Jose Oliva	.05	.02	.01
□ 49 David Justice	.35	.16	.04
□ 50 Chipper Jones	2.50	1.10	.30
□ 51 Tony Tarasco	.05	.02	.01
□ 52 Javier Lopez	.50	.23	.06
□ 53 Mark Wohlers	.15	.07	.02
□ 54 Deion Sanders	.50	.23	.06
□ 55 Greg McMichael	.05	.02	.01
□ 56 Tom Glavine	.25	.11	.03
□ 57 Bill Pecota	.05	.02	.01
□ 58 Mike Stanton	.05	.02	.01
□ 59 Rafael Belliard	.05	.02	.01
□ 60 Jeff Blauser	.15	.07	.02
□ 61 Bryan Harvey	.05	.02	.01
□ 62 Bret Barberie	.05	.02	.01
□ 63 Rick Renteria	.05	.02	.01
□ 64 Chris Hammond	.05	.02	.01
□ 65 Pat Rapp	.05	.02	.01
□ 66 Nigel Wilson	.05	.02	.01
□ 67 Gary Sheffield	.60	.25	.07
□ 68 Jerry Browne	.05	.02	.01
□ 69 Charlie Hough	.05	.02	.01
□ 70 Orestes Destrade	.05	.02	.01
□ 71 Mario Diaz	.05	.02	.01
□ 72 Ryan Bowen	.05	.02	.01
□ 73 Carl Everett	.15	.07	.02
□ 74 Richie Lewis	.05	.02	.01
□ 75 Bob Natal	.05	.02	.01
□ 76 Rich Rodriguez	.05	.02	.01
□ 77 Darrell Whitmore	.05	.02	.01
□ 78 Matt Turner	.05	.02	.01
□ 79 Benito Santiago	.15	.07	.02
□ 80 Robb Nen	.15	.07	.02
□ 81 Dave Magadan	.05	.02	.01
□ 82 Brian Drahman	.05	.02	.01
□ 83 Mark Gardner	.05	.02	.01
□ 84 Chuck Carr	.05	.02	.01
□ 85 Alex Arias	.05	.02	.01
□ 86 Kurt Abbott	.25	.11	.03
□ 87 Joe Klink	.05	.02	.01
□ 88 Jeff Mutis	.05	.02	.01
□ 89 Dave Weathers	.05	.02	.01
□ 90 Jeff Conine	.50	.23	.06
□ 91 Andres Galarraga	.25	.11	.03
□ 92 Vinny Castilla	.35	.16	.04
□ 93 Roberto Mejia	.05	.02	.01
□ 94 Darrell Sherman	.05	.02	.01
□ 95 Mike Harkey	.05	.02	.01
□ 96 Danny Sheaffer	.05	.02	.01
□ 97 Pedro Castellano	.05	.02	.01
□ 98 Walt Weiss	.05	.02	.01
□ 99 Greg W. Harris	.05	.02	.01
□ 100 Jayhawk Owens	.05	.02	.01
□ 101 Bruce Ruffin	.05	.02	.01
□ 102 Mike Munoz	.05	.02	.01
□ 103 Armando Reynoso	.05	.02	.01
□ 104 Eric Young	.15	.07	.02
□ 105 Dante Bichette	.50	.23	.06
□ 106 Marvin Freeman	.05	.02	.01
□ 107 Joe Girardi	.05	.02	.01
□ 108 Kent Bottenfield	.05	.02	.01
□ 109 Howard Johnson	.05	.02	.01
□ 110 Nelson Liriano	.05	.02	.01
□ 111 David Nied	.05	.02	.01
□ 112 Steve Reed	.05	.02	.01
□ 113 Eric Wedge	.05	.02	.01
□ 114 Charlie Hayes	.15	.07	.02
□ 115 Ellis Burks	.35	.16	.04
□ 116 Willie Blair	.05	.02	.01
□ 117 Darren Holmes	.05	.02	.01
□ 118 Curtis Leskanic	.05	.02	.01
□ 119 Lance Painter	.05	.02	.01
□ 120 Jim Tatum	.05	.02	.01
□ 121 Frank Thomas	3.00	1.35	.35
□ 122 Jack McDowell	.25	.11	.03
□ 123 Ron Karkovice	.05	.02	.01
□ 124 Mike LaValliere	.05	.02	.01
□ 125 Scott Radinsky	.05	.02	.01
□ 126 Robin Ventura	.35	.16	.04
□ 127 Scott Ruffcorn	.05	.02	.01
□ 128 Steve Sax	.05	.02	.01
□ 129 Roberto Hernandez	.15	.07	.02
□ 130 Jose DeLeon	.05	.02	.01
□ 131 Rod Bolton	.05	.02	.01
□ 132 Wilson Alvarez	.25	.11	.03
□ 133 Craig Grebeck	.05	.02	.01
□ 134 Lance Johnson	.25	.11	.03
□ 135 Kirk McCaskill	.05	.02	.01
□ 136 Tim Raines	.15	.07	.02
□ 137 Jeff Schwarz	.05	.02	.01
□ 138 Warren Newson	.05	.02	.01
□ 139 Norberto Martin	.05	.02	.01
□ 140 Mike Huff	.05	.02	.01
□ 141 Ozzie Guillen	.15	.07	.02
□ 142 Alex Fernandez	.35	.16	.04
□ 143 Joey Cora	.05	.02	.01
□ 144 Jason Bere	.15	.07	.02
□ 145 James Baldwin	.35	.16	.04
□ 146 Esteban Beltre	.05	.02	.01
□ 147 Julio Franco	.15	.07	.02
□ 148 Matt Merullo	.05	.02	.01
□ 149 Dan Pasqua	.05	.02	.01
□ 150 Darrin Jackson	.05	.02	.01
□ 151 Joe Carter	.50	.23	.06
□ 152 Danny Cox	.05	.02	.01
□ 153 Roberto Alomar	.75	.35	.09
□ 154 Woody Williams	.05	.02	.01
□ 155 Duane Ward	.05	.02	.01
□ 156 Ed Sprague	.15	.07	.02
□ 157 Domingo Martinez	.05	.02	.01
□ 158 Pat Hentgen	.50	.23	.06
□ 159 Shawn Green	.50	.23	.06
□ 160 Dick Schofield	.05	.02	.01
□ 161 Paul Molitor	.75	.35	.09
□ 162 Darnell Coles	.05	.02	.01
□ 163 Willie Canate	.05	.02	.01
□ 164 Domingo Cedeno	.05	.02	.01
□ 165 Pat Borders	.05	.02	.01
□ 166 Greg Cadaret	.05	.02	.01
□ 167 Tony Castillo	.05	.02	.01
□ 168 Carlos Delgado	.50	.23	.06
□ 169 Scott Brow	.05	.02	.01
□ 170 Juan Guzman	.15	.07	.02
□ 171 Al Leiter	.15	.07	.02
□ 172 John Olerud	.15	.07	.02
□ 173 Todd Stottlemyre	.15	.07	.02
□ 174 Devon White	.15	.07	.02
□ 175 Paul Spoljaric	.05	.02	.01
□ 176 Randy Knorr	.05	.02	.01
□ 177 Huck Flener	.05	.02	.01
□ 178 Rob Butler	.05	.02	.01
□ 179 Dave Stewart	.15	.07	.02
□ 180 Mike Timlin	.15	.07	.02
□ 181 Don Mattingly	1.50	.70	.19
□ 182 Mark Hutton	.05	.02	.01
□ 183 Mike Gallego	.05	.02	.01
□ 184 Jim Abbott	.15	.07	.02
□ 185 Paul Gibson	.05	.02	.01
□ 186 Scott Kamieniecki	.05	.02	.01
□ 187 Sam Horn	.05	.02	.01
□ 188 Melido Perez	.05	.02	.01
□ 189 Randy Velarde	.05	.02	.01
□ 190 Gerald Williams	.05	.02	.01
□ 191 Dave Silvestri	.05	.02	.01
□ 192 Jim Leyritz	.15	.07	.02
□ 193 Steve Howe	.05	.02	.01
□ 194 Russ Davis	.25	.11	.03
□ 195 Paul Assenmacher	.05	.02	.01
□ 196 Pat Kelly	.05	.02	.01
□ 197 Mike Stanley	.15	.07	.02
□ 198 Bernie Williams	.50	.23	.06
□ 199 Paul O'Neill	.15	.07	.02
□ 200 Donn Pall	.05	.02	.01
□ 201 Xavier Hernandez	.05	.02	.01
□ 202 James Austin	.05	.02	.01
□ 203 Sterling Hitchcock	.15	.07	.02
□ 204 Wade Boggs	.60	.25	.07
□ 205 Jimmy Key	.15	.07	.02
□ 206 Matt Nokes	.05	.02	.01
□ 207 Terry Mulholland	.05	.02	.01
□ 208 Luis Polonia	.05	.02	.01
□ 209 Danny Tartabull	.15	.07	.02
□ 210 Bob Wickman	.05	.02	.01
□ 211 Len Dykstra	.15	.07	.02
□ 212 Kim Batiste	.05	.02	.01
□ 213 Tony Longmire	.05	.02	.01
□ 214 Bobby Munoz	.05	.02	.01
□ 215 Pete Incaviglia	.05	.02	.01
□ 216 Doug Jones	.05	.02	.01
□ 217 Mariano Duncan	.05	.02	.01
□ 218 Jeff Juden	.05	.02	.01
□ 219 Milt Thompson	.05	.02	.01
□ 220 Dave West	.05	.02	.01
□ 221 Roger Mason	.05	.02	.01
□ 222 Tommy Greene	.05	.02	.01
□ 223 Larry Andersen	.05	.02	.01
□ 224 Jim Eisenreich	.15	.07	.02
□ 225 Dave Hollins	.05	.02	.01
□ 226 John Kruk	.15	.07	.02
□ 227 Todd Pratt	.05	.02	.01
□ 228 Ricky Jordan	.05	.02	.01
□ 229 Curt Schilling	.15	.07	.02
□ 230 Mike Williams	.05	.02	.01
□ 231 Heathcliff Slocumb	.15	.07	.02
□ 232 Ben Rivera	.05	.02	.01
□ 233 Mike Lieberthal	.05	.02	.01
□ 234 Mickey Morandini	.05	.02	.01
□ 235 Danny Jackson	.05	.02	.01
□ 236 Kevin Foster	.05	.02	.01
□ 237 Darren Daulton	.15	.07	.02
□ 238 Wes Chamberlain	.05	.02	.01
□ 239 Tyler Green	.15	.07	.02
□ 240 Kevin Stocker	.15	.07	.02
□ 241 Juan Gonzalez	1.50	.70	.19
□ 242 Rick Honeycutt	.05	.02	.01
□ 243 Bruce Hurst	.05	.02	.01
□ 244 Steve Dreyer	.05	.02	.01
□ 245 Brian Bohanon	.05	.02	.01
□ 246 Benji Gil	.05	.02	.01
□ 247 Jon Shave	.05	.02	.01
□ 248 Manuel Lee	.05	.02	.01
□ 249 Donald Harris	.05	.02	.01
□ 250 Jose Canseco	.60	.25	.07
□ 251 David Hulse	.05	.02	.01
□ 252 Kenny Rogers	.15	.07	.02
□ 253 Jeff Huson	.05	.02	.01
□ 254 Dan Peltier	.05	.02	.01
□ 255 Mike Scioscia	.05	.02	.01
□ 256 Jack Armstrong	.05	.02	.01
□ 257 Rob Ducey	.05	.02	.01
□ 258 Will Clark	.60	.25	.07
□ 259 Cris Carpenter	.05	.02	.01
□ 260 Kevin Brown	.15	.07	.02
□ 261 Jeff Frye	.05	.02	.01
□ 262 Jay Howell	.05	.02	.01
□ 263 Roger Pavlik	.05	.02	.01
□ 264 Gary Redus	.05	.02	.01
□ 265 Ivan Rodriguez	.75	.35	.09
□ 266 Matt Whiteside	.05	.02	.01
□ 267 Doug Strange	.05	.02	.01
□ 268 Billy Ripken	.05	.02	.01
□ 269 Dean Palmer	.25	.11	.03
□ 270 Tom Henke	.15	.07	.02
□ 271 Cal Ripken	3.00	1.35	.35
□ 272 Mark McLemore	.05	.02	.01
□ 273 Sid Fernandez	.05	.02	.01
□ 274 Sherman Obando	.05	.02	.01
□ 275 Paul Carey	.05	.02	.01
□ 276 Mike Oquist	.05	.02	.01
□ 277 Alan Mills	.05	.02	.01
□ 278 Harold Baines	.15	.07	.02
□ 279 Mike Mussina	.60	.25	.07
□ 280 Arthur Rhodes	.05	.02	.01
□ 281 Kevin McGehee	.05	.02	.01
□ 282 Mark Eichhorn	.05	.02	.01
□ 283 Damon Buford	.05	.02	.01
□ 284 Ben McDonald	.15	.07	.02
□ 285 David Segui	.15	.07	.02
□ 286 Brad Pennington	.05	.02	.01
□ 287 Jamie Moyer	.05	.02	.01
□ 288 Chris Hoiles	.15	.07	.02
□ 289 Mike Cook	.05	.02	.01
□ 290 Brady Anderson	.50	.23	.06
□ 291 Chris Sabo	.05	.02	.01
□ 292 Jack Voigt	.05	.02	.01
□ 293 Jim Poole	.05	.02	.01
□ 294 Jeff Tackett	.05	.02	.01
□ 295 Rafael Palmeiro	.50	.23	.06
□ 296 Alex Ochoa	.50	.23	.06
□ 297 John O'Donoghue	.05	.02	.01
□ 298 Tim Hulett	.05	.02	.01
□ 299 Mike Devereaux	.05	.02	.01
□ 300 Manny Alexander	.05	.02	.01
□ 301 Ozzie Smith	1.25	.55	.16
□ 302 Omar Olivares	.05	.02	.01
□ 303 Rheal Cormier	.05	.02	.01
□ 304 Donovan Osborne	.15	.07	.02
□ 305 Mark Whiten	.05	.02	.01
□ 306 Todd Zeile	.15	.07	.02
□ 307 Geronimo Pena	.05	.02	.01
□ 308 Brian Jordan	.35	.16	.04
□ 309 Luis Alicea	.05	.02	.01
□ 310 Ray Lankford	.35	.16	.04
□ 311 Stan Royer	.05	.02	.01
□ 312 Bob Tewksbury	.05	.02	.01
□ 313 Jose Oquendo	.05	.02	.01
□ 314 Steve Dixon	.05	.02	.01
□ 315 Rene Arocha	.05	.02	.01
□ 316 Bernard Gilkey	.25	.11	.03
□ 317 Gregg Jefferies	.25	.11	.03
□ 318 Rob Murphy	.05	.02	.01
□ 319 Tom Pagnozzi	.05	.02	.01
□ 320 Mike Perez	.05	.02	.01
□ 321 Tom Urbani	.05	.02	.01
□ 322 Allen Watson	.15	.07	.02
□ 323 Erik Pappas	.05	.02	.01
□ 324 Paul Kilgus	.05	.02	.01
□ 325 John Habyan	.05	.02	.01
□ 326 Rod Brewer	.05	.02	.01
□ 327 Rich Batchelor	.05	.02	.01
□ 328 Tripp Cromer	.05	.02	.01
□ 329 Gerald Perry	.05	.02	.01
□ 330 Les Lancaster	.05	.02	.01
□ 331 Ryne Sandberg	1.25	.55	.16
□ 332 Derrick May	.05	.02	.01
□ 333 Steve Buechele	.05	.02	.01
□ 334 Willie Banks	.05	.02	.01
□ 335 Larry Luebbers	.05	.02	.01
□ 336 Tommy Shields	.05	.02	.01
□ 337 Eric Yelding	.05	.02	.01
□ 338 Rey Sanchez	.05	.02	.01
□ 339 Mark Grace	.60	.25	.07
□ 340 Jose Bautista	.05	.02	.01
□ 341 Frank Castillo	.05	.02	.01
□ 342 Jose Guzman	.05	.02	.01
□ 343 Rafael Novoa	.05	.02	.01
□ 344 Karl Rhodes	.05	.02	.01
□ 345 Steve Trachsel	.05	.02	.01
□ 346 Rick Wilkins	.05	.02	.01
□ 347 Sammy Sosa	.50	.23	.06
□ 348 Kevin Roberson	.05	.02	.01
□ 349 Mark Parent	.05	.02	.01
□ 350 Randy Myers	.15	.07	.02
□ 351 Glenallen Hill	.15	.07	.02
□ 352 Lance Dickson	.05	.02	.01
□ 353 Shawn Boskie	.05	.02	.01
□ 354 Shawon Dunston	.05	.02	.01
□ 355 Dan Plesac	.05	.02	.01
□ 356 Jose Vizcaino	.05	.02	.01
□ 357 Willie Wilson	.05	.02	.01
□ 358 Turk Wendell	.05	.02	.01
□ 359 Mike Morgan	.05	.02	.01
□ 360 Jim Bullinger	.05	.02	.01

1994 Stadium Club Team First Day Issue

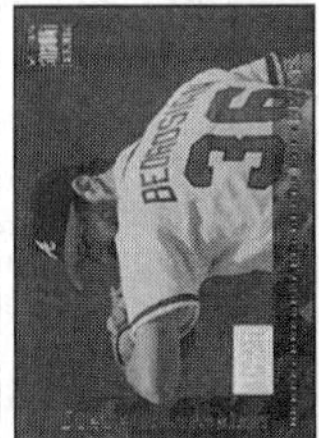

This 360-card standard-size set features 30 players from 12 teams. First Day Issue cards were randomly packed one in every six 12-card packs; the odds of finding these insert cards in 20-card jumbo packs are one in three. Also one 1st Day Issue card was included in the 30-card team sets sold in blister packs. They are identical in design with the regular Stadium Club Team cards except for a holographic "1st Day Issue" emblem on the fronts.

	MINT	NRMT	EXC
COMPLETE SET (360)	600.00	275.00	75.00
COMMON CARD (1-360)	2.00	.90	.25

*STARS: 10X to 20X BASIC CARDS....
*YOUNG STARS: 7.5X to 15X BASIC CARDS

1994 Stadium Club Team Finest

This 12-card standard-size set consists of one player from each of the 12 teams featured in the 1994 Stadium Club team series. The cards were randomly inserted in 12-card foil packs. Also one card was included in the 30-card team sets sold in blister packs. The cards are identical in design with the regular series, except for the metallic sheen characteristic of the Finest series.

	MINT	NRMT	EXC
COMPLETE SET (12)	30.00	13.50	3.70
COMMON CARD (1-12)	1.00	.45	.12
□ 1 Roberto Alomar	2.50	1.10	.30
□ 2 Barry Bonds	2.50	1.10	.30

☐ 3 Len Dykstra	1.00	.45	.12
☐ 4 Andres Galarraga	1.50	.70	.19
☐ 5 Juan Gonzalez	5.00	2.20	.60
☐ 6 David Justice	1.00	.45	.12
☐ 7 Don Mattingly	5.00	2.20	.60
☐ 8 Cal Ripken	8.00	3.60	1.00
☐ 9 Ryne Sandberg	4.00	1.80	.50
☐ 10 Gary Sheffield	2.00	.90	.25
☐ 11 Ozzie Smith	4.00	1.80	.50
☐ 12 Frank Thomas	10.00	4.50	1.25

1995 Stadium Club

The 1995 Stadium Club baseball card collection was issued in three series of 270, 225 and 135 standard-size cards for a total of 630. The cards were distributed in 14-card packs at a suggested retail price of $2.50 and contained 24 packs per box. Cards feature players in full-bleed action photos with team logo and player's name in gold foil at the bottom of the card. Backs feature statistical bar graphs and action photos of players. Notable Rookie Cards include Mark Grudzielanek, Bobby Higginson and Hideo Nomo.

	MINT	NRMT	EXC
COMPLETE SET (630)	60.00	27.00	7.50
COMPLETE SERIES 1 (270)	25.00	11.00	3.10
COMPLETE SERIES 2 (225)	20.00	9.00	2.50
COMPLETE SERIES 3 (135)	15.00	6.75	1.85
COMMON CARD (1-630)	.10	.05	.01

☐ 1 Cal Ripken	2.50	1.10	.30
☐ 2 Bo Jackson	.25	.11	.03
☐ 3 Bryan Harvey	.10	.05	.01
☐ 4 Curt Schilling	.10	.05	.01
☐ 5 Bruce Ruffin	.10	.05	.01
☐ 6 Travis Fryman	.25	.11	.03
☐ 7 Jim Abbott	.10	.05	.01
☐ 8 David McCarty	.10	.05	.01
☐ 9 Gary Gaetti	.25	.11	.03
☐ 10 Roger Clemens	.60	.25	.07
☐ 11 Carlos Garcia	.10	.05	.01
☐ 12 Lee Smith	.25	.11	.03
☐ 13 Bobby Ayala	.10	.05	.01
☐ 14 Charles Nagy	.25	.11	.03
☐ 15 Lou Frazier	.10	.05	.01
☐ 16 Rene Arocha	.10	.05	.01
☐ 17 Carlos Delgado	.25	.11	.03
☐ 18 Steve Finley	.25	.11	.03
☐ 19 Ryan Klesko	.50	.23	.06
☐ 20 Cal Eldred	.10	.05	.01
☐ 21 Rey Sanchez	.10	.05	.01
☐ 22 Ken Hill	.10	.05	.01
☐ 23 Benito Santiago	.10	.05	.01
☐ 24 Julian Tavarez	.10	.05	.01
☐ 25 Jose Vizcaino	.10	.05	.01
☐ 26 Andy Benes	.10	.05	.01
☐ 27 Mariano Duncan	.10	.05	.01
☐ 28 Checklist A	.10	.05	.01
☐ 29 Shawon Dunston	.10	.05	.01
☐ 30 Rafael Palmeiro	.50	.23	.06
☐ 31 Dean Palmer	.25	.11	.03
☐ 32 Andres Galarraga	.50	.23	.06
☐ 33 Joey Cora	.10	.05	.01
☐ 34 Mickey Tettleton	.10	.05	.01
☐ 35 Barry Larkin	.50	.23	.06
☐ 36 Carlos Baerga	.25	.11	.03
☐ 37 Orel Hershiser	.25	.11	.03
☐ 38 Jody Reed	.10	.05	.01
☐ 39 Paul Molitor	.60	.25	.07
☐ 40 Jim Edmonds	.50	.23	.06
☐ 41 Bob Tewksbury	.10	.05	.01
☐ 42 John Patterson	.10	.05	.01
☐ 43 Ray McDavid	.25	.11	.03
☐ 44 Zane Smith	.10	.05	.01
☐ 45 Bret Saberhagen SE	.10	.05	.01
☐ 46 Greg Maddux SE	1.00	.45	.12
☐ 47 Frank Thomas SE	1.50	.70	.19
☐ 48 Carlos Baerga SE	.25	.11	.03
☐ 49 Billy Spiers	.10	.05	.01
☐ 50 Stan Javier	.10	.05	.01
☐ 51 Rex Hudler	.10	.05	.01
☐ 52 Denny Hocking	.10	.05	.01
☐ 53 Todd Worrell	.10	.05	.01
☐ 54 Mark Clark	.10	.05	.01
☐ 55 Hipolito Pichardo	.10	.05	.01
☐ 56 Bob Wickman	.10	.05	.01
☐ 57 Raul Mondesi	.50	.23	.06
☐ 58 Steve Cooke	.10	.05	.01
☐ 59 Rod Beck	.10	.05	.01
☐ 60 Tim Davis	.10	.05	.01
☐ 61 Jeff Kent	.10	.05	.01
☐ 62 John Valentin	.25	.11	.03
☐ 63 Alex Arias	.10	.05	.01
☐ 64 Steve Reed	.10	.05	.01
☐ 65 Ozzie Smith	.75	.35	.09
☐ 66 Terry Pendleton	.25	.11	.03
☐ 67 Kenny Rogers	.10	.05	.01
☐ 68 Vince Coleman	.10	.05	.01
☐ 69 Tom Pagnozzi	.10	.05	.01
☐ 70 Roberto Alomar	.60	.25	.07
☐ 71 Darrin Jackson	.10	.05	.01
☐ 72 Dennis Eckersley	.25	.11	.03
☐ 73 Jay Buhner	.50	.23	.06
☐ 74 Darren Lewis	.10	.05	.01
☐ 75 Dave Weathers	.10	.05	.01
☐ 76 Matt Walbeck	.10	.05	.01
☐ 77 Brad Ausmus	.10	.05	.01
☐ 78 Danny Bautista	.10	.05	.01
☐ 79 Bob Hamelin	.10	.05	.01
☐ 80 Steve Trachsel	.10	.05	.01
☐ 81 Ken Ryan	.10	.05	.01
☐ 82 Chris Turner	.10	.05	.01
☐ 83 David Segui	.10	.05	.01
☐ 84 Ben McDonald	.10	.05	.01
☐ 85 Wade Boggs	.50	.23	.06
☐ 86 John VanderWal	.10	.05	.01
☐ 87 Sandy Alomar Jr.	.10	.05	.01
☐ 88 Ron Karkovice	.10	.05	.01
☐ 89 Doug Jones	.10	.05	.01
☐ 90 Gary Sheffield	.50	.23	.06
☐ 91 Ken Caminiti	.50	.23	.06
☐ 92 Chris Bosio	.10	.05	.01
☐ 93 Kevin Tapani	.10	.05	.01
☐ 94 Walt Weiss	.10	.05	.01
☐ 95 Erik Hanson	.10	.05	.01
☐ 96 Ruben Sierra	.25	.11	.03
☐ 97 Nomar Garciaparra	2.00	.90	.25
☐ 98 Terrence Long	.50	.23	.06
☐ 99 Jacob Shumate	.25	.11	.03
☐ 100 Paul Wilson	.50	.23	.06
☐ 101 Kevin Witt	.25	.11	.03
☐ 102 Paul Konerko	2.00	.90	.25
☐ 103 Ben Grieve	1.50	.70	.19
☐ 104 Mark Johnson	.25	.11	.03
☐ 105 Cade Gaspar	.25	.11	.03
☐ 106 Mark Farris	.25	.11	.03
☐ 107 Dustin Hermanson	.25	.11	.03
☐ 108 Scott Elarton	.50	.23	.06
☐ 109 Doug Million	.50	.23	.06
☐ 110 Matt Smith	.25	.11	.03
☐ 111 Brian Buchanan	.25	.11	.03
☐ 112 Jayson Peterson	.25	.11	.03
☐ 113 Bret Wagner	.25	.11	.03
☐ 114 C.J. Nitkowski	.25	.11	.03
☐ 115 Ramon Castro	.25	.11	.03
☐ 116 Rafael Bournigal	.10	.05	.01
☐ 117 Jeff Fassero	.10	.05	.01
☐ 118 Bobby Bonilla	.25	.11	.03
☐ 119 Ricky Gutierrez	.10	.05	.01
☐ 120 Roger Pavlik	.10	.05	.01
☐ 121 Mike Greenwell	.10	.05	.01
☐ 122 Deion Sanders	.50	.23	.06
☐ 123 Charlie Hayes	.10	.05	.01
☐ 124 Paul O'Neill	.25	.11	.03
☐ 125 Jay Bell	.25	.11	.03
☐ 126 Royce Clayton	.10	.05	.01
☐ 127 Willie Banks	.10	.05	.01
☐ 128 Mark Wohlers	.25	.11	.03
☐ 129 Todd Jones	.10	.05	.01
☐ 130 Todd Stottlemyre	.10	.05	.01
☐ 131 Will Clark	.50	.23	.06
☐ 132 Wilson Alvarez	.25	.11	.03
☐ 133 Chili Davis	.25	.11	.03
☐ 134 Dave Burba	.10	.05	.01
☐ 135 Chris Hoiles	.10	.05	.01
☐ 136 Jeff Blauser	.10	.05	.01
☐ 137 Jeff Reboulet	.10	.05	.01
☐ 138 Bret Saberhagen	.25	.11	.03
☐ 139 Kirk Rueter	.10	.05	.01
☐ 140 Dave Nilsson	.25	.11	.03
☐ 141 Pat Borders	.10	.05	.01
☐ 142 Ron Darling	.10	.05	.01
☐ 143 Derek Bell	.25	.11	.03
☐ 144 Dave Hollins	.10	.05	.01
☐ 145 Juan Gonzalez	1.50	.70	.19
☐ 146 Andre Dawson	.25	.11	.03
☐ 147 Jim Thome	.60	.25	.07
☐ 148 Larry Walker	.50	.23	.06
☐ 149 Mike Piazza	2.00	.90	.25
☐ 150 Mike Perez	.10	.05	.01
☐ 151 Steve Avery	.25	.11	.03
☐ 152 Dan Wilson	.25	.11	.03
☐ 153 Andy Van Slyke	.25	.11	.03
☐ 154 Junior Felix	.10	.05	.01
☐ 155 Jack McDowell	.25	.11	.03
☐ 156 Danny Tartabull	.10	.05	.01
☐ 157 Willie Blair	.10	.05	.01
☐ 158 Wm.VanLandingham	.10	.05	.01
☐ 159 Robb Nen	.10	.05	.01
☐ 160 Lee Tinsley	.10	.05	.01
☐ 161 Ismael Valdes	.25	.11	.03
☐ 162 Juan Guzman	.25	.11	.03
☐ 163 Scott Servais	.10	.05	.01
☐ 164 Cliff Floyd	.25	.11	.03
☐ 165 Allen Watson	.10	.05	.01
☐ 166 Eddie Taubensee	.10	.05	.01
☐ 167 Scott Hemond	.10	.05	.01
☐ 168 Jeff Tackett	.10	.05	.01
☐ 169 Chad Curtis	.10	.05	.01
☐ 170 Rico Brogna	.10	.05	.01
☐ 171 Luis Polonia	.10	.05	.01
☐ 172 Checklist B	.10	.05	.01
☐ 173 Lance Johnson	.25	.11	.03
☐ 174 Sammy Sosa	.50	.23	.06
☐ 175 Mike Macfarlane	.10	.05	.01
☐ 176 Darryl Hamilton	.10	.05	.01
☐ 177 Rick Aguilera	.10	.05	.01
☐ 178 Dave West	.10	.05	.01
☐ 179 Mike Gallego	.10	.05	.01
☐ 180 Marc Newfield	.25	.11	.03
☐ 181 Steve Buechele	.10	.05	.01
☐ 182 David Wells	.10	.05	.01
☐ 183 Tom Glavine	.50	.23	.06
☐ 184 Joe Girardi	.10	.05	.01
☐ 185 Craig Biggio	.25	.11	.03
☐ 186 Eddie Murray	.75	.35	.09
☐ 187 Kevin Gross	.10	.05	.01
☐ 188 Sid Fernandez	.10	.05	.01
☐ 189 John Franco	.10	.05	.01
☐ 190 Bernard Gilkey	.25	.11	.03
☐ 191 Matt Williams	.50	.23	.06
☐ 192 Darrin Fletcher	.10	.05	.01
☐ 193 Jeff Conine	.25	.11	.03
☐ 194 Ed Sprague	.25	.11	.03
☐ 195 Eduardo Perez	.10	.05	.01
☐ 196 Scott Livingstone	.10	.05	.01
☐ 197 Ivan Rodriguez	.75	.35	.09
☐ 198 Orlando Merced	.10	.05	.01
☐ 199 Ricky Bones	.10	.05	.01
☐ 200 Javier Lopez	.50	.23	.06
☐ 201 Miguel Jimenez	.10	.05	.01
☐ 202 Terry McGriff	.10	.05	.01
☐ 203 Mike Lieberthal	.10	.05	.01
☐ 204 David Cone	.25	.11	.03
☐ 205 Todd Hundley	.25	.11	.03
☐ 206 Ozzie Guillen	.10	.05	.01
☐ 207 Alex Cole	.10	.05	.01
☐ 208 Tony Phillips	.25	.11	.03
☐ 209 Jim Eisenreich	.10	.05	.01
☐ 210 Greg Vaughn BES	.10	.05	.01
☐ 211 Barry Larkin BES	.50	.23	.06
☐ 212 Don Mattingly BES	.75	.35	.09
☐ 213 Mark Grace BES	.50	.23	.06
☐ 214 Jose Canseco BES	.50	.23	.06
☐ 215 Joe Carter BES	.25	.11	.03
☐ 216 David Cone BES	.25	.11	.03
☐ 217 Sandy Alomar Jr. BES	.10	.05	.01
☐ 218 Al Martin BES	.10	.05	.01
☐ 219 Roberto Kelly BES	.10	.05	.01
☐ 220 Paul Sorrento	.10	.05	.01
☐ 221 Tony Fernandez	.10	.05	.01
☐ 222 Stan Belinda	.10	.05	.01
☐ 223 Mike Stanley	.10	.05	.01
☐ 224 Doug Drabek	.10	.05	.01
☐ 225 Todd Van Poppel	.10	.05	.01
☐ 226 Matt Mieske	.25	.11	.03
☐ 227 Tino Martinez	.25	.11	.03
☐ 228 Andy Ashby	.25	.11	.03
☐ 229 Midre Cummings	.10	.05	.01
☐ 230 Jeff Frye	.10	.05	.01
☐ 231 Hal Morris	.10	.05	.01
☐ 232 Jose Lind	.10	.05	.01
☐ 233 Shawn Green	.25	.11	.03
☐ 234 Rafael Belliard	.10	.05	.01
☐ 235 Randy Myers	.10	.05	.01
☐ 236 Frank Thomas CE	1.50	.70	.19
☐ 237 Darren Daulton CE	.10	.05	.01
☐ 238 Sammy Sosa CE	.50	.23	.06
☐ 239 Cal Ripken CE	1.25	.55	.16
☐ 240 Jeff Bagwell CE	.60	.25	.07
☐ 241 Ken Griffey Jr.	3.00	1.35	.35
☐ 242 Brett Butler	.25	.11	.03
☐ 243 Derrick May	.10	.05	.01
☐ 244 Pat Listach	.10	.05	.01
☐ 245 Mike Bordick	.10	.05	.01
☐ 246 Mark Langston	.10	.05	.01
☐ 247 Randy Velarde	.10	.05	.01
☐ 248 Julio Franco	.25	.11	.03
☐ 249 Chuck Knoblauch	.50	.23	.06
☐ 250 Bill Gullickson	.10	.05	.01
☐ 251 Dave Henderson	.10	.05	.01
☐ 252 Bret Boone	.25	.11	.03
☐ 253 Al Martin	.25	.11	.03
☐ 254 Armando Benitez	.10	.05	.01
☐ 255 Wil Cordero	.10	.05	.01
☐ 256 Al Leiter	.25	.11	.03
☐ 257 Luis Gonzalez	.10	.05	.01
☐ 258 Charlie O'Brien	.10	.05	.01
☐ 259 Tim Wallach	.10	.05	.01
☐ 260 Scott Sanders	.10	.05	.01
☐ 261 Tom Henke	.10	.05	.01
☐ 262 Otis Nixon	.10	.05	.01
☐ 263 Darren Daulton	.25	.11	.03
☐ 264 Manny Ramirez	.75	.35	.09
☐ 265 Bret Barberie	.10	.05	.01
☐ 266 Mel Rojas	.10	.05	.01
☐ 267 John Burkett	.25	.11	.03
☐ 268 Brady Anderson	.50	.23	.06
☐ 269 John Roper	.10	.05	.01
☐ 270 Shane Reynolds	.10	.05	.01
☐ 271 Barry Bonds	.75	.35	.09
☐ 272 Alex Fernandez	.25	.11	.03
☐ 273 Brian McRae	.25	.11	.03
☐ 274 Todd Zeile	.10	.05	.01
☐ 275 Greg Swindell	.10	.05	.01
☐ 276 Johnny Ruffin	.10	.05	.01
☐ 277 Troy Neel	.10	.05	.01
☐ 278 Eric Karros	.25	.11	.03
☐ 279 John Hudek	.10	.05	.01
☐ 280 Thomas Howard	.10	.05	.01
☐ 281 Joe Carter	.25	.11	.03
☐ 282 Mike Devereaux	.10	.05	.01
☐ 283 Butch Henry	.10	.05	.01
☐ 284 Reggie Jefferson	.25	.11	.03
☐ 285 Mark Lemke	.10	.05	.01
☐ 286 Jeff Montgomery	.25	.11	.03
☐ 287 Ryan Thompson	.10	.05	.01
☐ 288 Paul Shuey	.10	.05	.01
☐ 289 Mark McGwire	1.00	.45	.12
☐ 290 Bernie Williams	.60	.25	.07
☐ 291 Mickey Morandini	.10	.05	.01
☐ 292 Scott Leius	.10	.05	.01
☐ 293 David Hulse	.10	.05	.01
☐ 294 Greg Gagne	.10	.05	.01
☐ 295 Moises Alou	.25	.11	.03
☐ 296 Geronimo Berroa	.10	.05	.01
☐ 297 Eddie Zambrano	.10	.05	.01
☐ 298 Alan Trammell	.25	.11	.03
☐ 299 Don Slaught	.10	.05	.01
☐ 300 Jose Rijo	.10	.05	.01
☐ 301 Joe Ausanio	.10	.05	.01
☐ 302 Tim Raines	.50	.23	.06
☐ 303 Melido Perez	.10	.05	.01
☐ 304 Kent Mercker	.10	.05	.01
☐ 305 James Mouton	.10	.05	.01
☐ 306 Luis Lopez	.10	.05	.01
☐ 307 Mike Kingery	.10	.05	.01
☐ 308 Willie Greene	.10	.05	.01
☐ 309 Cecil Fielder	.25	.11	.03
☐ 310 Scott Kamieniecki	.10	.05	.01
☐ 311 Mike Greenwell BES	.10	.05	.01
☐ 312 Bobby Bonilla BES	.25	.11	.03
☐ 313 Andres Galarraga BES	.50	.23	.06
☐ 314 Cal Ripken BES	1.25	.55	.16
☐ 315 Matt Williams BES	.50	.23	.06
☐ 316 Tom Pagnozzi BES	.10	.05	.01
☐ 317 Len Dykstra BES	.25	.11	.03
☐ 318 Frank Thomas BES	1.50	.70	.19
☐ 319 Kirby Puckett BES	.50	.23	.06
☐ 320 Mike Piazza BES	1.00	.45	.12
☐ 321 Jason Jacome	.10	.05	.01
☐ 322 Brian Hunter	.10	.05	.01
☐ 323 Brent Gates	.10	.05	.01
☐ 324 Jim Converse	.10	.05	.01
☐ 325 Damion Easley	.10	.05	.01
☐ 326 Dante Bichette	.50	.23	.06
☐ 327 Kurt Abbott	.10	.05	.01
☐ 328 Scott Cooper	.10	.05	.01
☐ 329 Mike Henneman	.10	.05	.01
☐ 330 Orlando Miller	.10	.05	.01
☐ 331 John Kruk	.25	.11	.03
☐ 332 Jose Oliva	.10	.05	.01
☐ 333 Reggie Sanders	.25	.11	.03
☐ 334 Omar Vizquel	.25	.11	.03
☐ 335 Devon White	.25	.11	.03
☐ 336 Mike Morgan	.10	.05	.01
☐ 337 J.R. Phillips	.10	.05	.01
☐ 338 Gary DiSarcina	.10	.05	.01
☐ 339 Joey Hamilton	.50	.23	.06
☐ 340 Randy Johnson	.50	.23	.06
☐ 341 Jim Leyritz	.10	.05	.01
☐ 342 Bobby Jones	.25	.11	.03
☐ 343 Jaime Navarro	.10	.05	.01
☐ 344 Bip Roberts	.10	.05	.01
☐ 345 Steve Karsay	.10	.05	.01
☐ 346 Kevin Stocker	.10	.05	.01
☐ 347 Jose Canseco	.50	.23	.06
☐ 348 Bill Wegman	.10	.05	.01
☐ 349 Rondell White	.25	.11	.03
☐ 350 Mo Vaughn	.75	.35	.09
☐ 351 Joe Orsulak	.10	.05	.01
☐ 352 Pat Meares	.10	.05	.01
☐ 353 Albie Lopez	.10	.05	.01
☐ 354 Edgar Martinez	.25	.11	.03
☐ 355 Brian Jordan	.50	.23	.06
☐ 356 Tommy Greene	.10	.05	.01
☐ 357 Chuck Carr	.10	.05	.01
☐ 358 Pedro Astacio	.10	.05	.01
☐ 359 Russ Davis	.10	.05	.01
☐ 360 Chris Hammond	.10	.05	.01
☐ 361 Gregg Jefferies	.25	.11	.03
☐ 362 Shane Mack	.10	.05	.01
☐ 363 Fred McGriff	.50	.23	.06
☐ 364 Pat Rapp	.10	.05	.01
☐ 365 Bill Swift	.10	.05	.01
☐ 366 Checklist	.10	.05	.01
☐ 367 Robin Ventura	.25	.11	.03
☐ 368 Bobby Witt	.10	.05	.01
☐ 369 Karl Rhodes	.10	.05	.01
☐ 370 Eddie Williams	.10	.05	.01
☐ 371 John Jaha	.25	.11	.03
☐ 372 Steve Howe	.10	.05	.01
☐ 373 Leo Gomez	.10	.05	.01
☐ 374 Hector Fajardo	.10	.05	.01
☐ 375 Jeff Bagwell	1.25	.55	.16
☐ 376 Mark Acre	.10	.05	.01
☐ 377 Wayne Kirby	.10	.05	.01
☐ 378 Mark Portugal	.10	.05	.01

☐ 379 Jesus Tavarez	.10	.05	.01
☐ 380 Jim Lindeman	.10	.05	.01
☐ 381 Don Mattingly	1.50	.70	.19
☐ 382 Trevor Hoffman	.25	.11	.03
☐ 383 Chris Gomez	.10	.05	.01
☐ 384 Garret Anderson	.25	.11	.03
☐ 385 Bobby Munoz	.10	.05	.01
☐ 386 Jon Lieber	.10	.05	.01
☐ 387 Rick Helling	.10	.05	.01
☐ 388 Marvin Freeman	.10	.05	.01
☐ 389 Juan Castillo	.10	.05	.01
☐ 390 Jeff Cirillo	.25	.11	.03
☐ 391 Sean Berry	.10	.05	.01
☐ 392 Hector Carrasco	.10	.05	.01
☐ 393 Mark Grace	.50	.23	.06
☐ 394 Pat Kelly	.10	.05	.01
☐ 395 Tim Naehring	.10	.05	.01
☐ 396 Greg Pirkl	.10	.05	.01
☐ 397 John Smoltz	.50	.23	.06
☐ 398 Robby Thompson	.10	.05	.01
☐ 399 Rick White	.10	.05	.01
☐ 400 Frank Thomas	3.00	1.35	.35
☐ 401 Jeff Conine CS	.25	.11	.03
☐ 402 Jose Valentin CS	.10	.05	.01
☐ 403 Carlos Baerga CS	.25	.11	.03
☐ 404 Rick Aguilera CS	.10	.05	.01
☐ 405 Wilson Alvarez CS	.10	.05	.01
☐ 406 Juan Gonzalez CS	.75	.35	.09
☐ 407 Barry Larkin CS	.50	.23	.06
☐ 408 Ken Hill CS	.10	.05	.01
☐ 409 Chuck Carr CS	.10	.05	.01
☐ 410 Tim Raines CS	.25	.11	.03
☐ 411 Bryan Eversgerd	.10	.05	.01
☐ 412 Phil Plantier	.10	.05	.01
☐ 413 Josias Manzanillo	.10	.05	.01
☐ 414 Roberto Kelly	.10	.05	.01
☐ 415 Rickey Henderson	.50	.23	.06
☐ 416 John Smiley	.10	.05	.01
☐ 417 Kevin Brown	.25	.11	.03
☐ 418 Jimmy Key	.25	.11	.03
☐ 419 Wally Joyner	.25	.11	.03
☐ 420 Roberto Hernandez	.10	.05	.01
☐ 421 Felix Fermin	.10	.05	.01
☐ 422 Checklist	.10	.05	.01
☐ 423 Greg Vaughn	.25	.11	.03
☐ 424 Ray Lankford	.25	.11	.03
☐ 425 Greg Maddux	2.00	.90	.25
☐ 426 Mike Mussina	.60	.25	.07
☐ 427 Geronimo Pena	.10	.05	.01
☐ 428 David Nied	.10	.05	.01
☐ 429 Scott Erickson	.10	.05	.01
☐ 430 Kevin Mitchell	.25	.11	.03
☐ 431 Mike Lansing	.10	.05	.01
☐ 432 Brian Anderson	.10	.05	.01
☐ 433 Jeff King	.25	.11	.03
☐ 434 Ramon Martinez	.25	.11	.03
☐ 435 Kevin Seitzer	.10	.05	.01
☐ 436 Salomon Torres	.10	.05	.01
☐ 437 Brian L.Hunter	.25	.11	.03
☐ 438 Melvin Nieves	.25	.11	.03
☐ 439 Mike Kelly	.10	.05	.01
☐ 440 Marquis Grissom	.25	.11	.03
☐ 441 Chuck Finley	.25	.11	.03
☐ 442 Len Dykstra	.25	.11	.03
☐ 443 Ellis Burks	.25	.11	.03
☐ 444 Harold Baines	.25	.11	.03
☐ 445 Kevin Appier	.25	.11	.03
☐ 446 David Justice	.50	.23	.06
☐ 447 Darryl Kile	.10	.05	.01
☐ 448 John Olerud	.10	.05	.01
☐ 449 Greg McMichael	.10	.05	.01
☐ 450 Kirby Puckett	1.25	.55	.16
☐ 451 Jose Valentin	.25	.11	.03
☐ 452 Rick Wilkins	.10	.05	.01
☐ 453 Arthur Rhodes	.10	.05	.01
☐ 454 Pat Hentgen	.25	.11	.03
☐ 455 Tom Gordon	.10	.05	.01
☐ 456 Tom Candiotti	.10	.05	.01
☐ 457 Jason Bere	.10	.05	.01
☐ 458 Wes Chamberlain	.10	.05	.01
☐ 459 Greg Colbrunn	.10	.05	.01
☐ 460 John Doherty	.10	.05	.01
☐ 461 Kevin Foster	.10	.05	.01
☐ 462 Mark Whiten	.10	.05	.01
☐ 463 Terry Steinbach	.25	.11	.03
☐ 464 Aaron Sele	.25	.11	.03
☐ 465 Kirt Manwaring	.10	.05	.01
☐ 466 Darren Hall	.10	.05	.01
☐ 467 Delino DeShields	.10	.05	.01
☐ 468 Andujar Cedeno	.10	.05	.01
☐ 469 Billy Ashley	.10	.05	.01
☐ 470 Kenny Lofton	.75	.35	.09
☐ 471 Pedro Munoz	.10	.05	.01
☐ 472 John Wetteland	.25	.11	.03
☐ 473 Tim Salmon	.50	.23	.06
☐ 474 Denny Neagle	.25	.11	.03
☐ 475 Tony Gwynn	1.25	.55	.16
☐ 476 Vinny Castilla	.25	.11	.03
☐ 477 Steve Dreyer	.10	.05	.01
☐ 478 Jeff Shaw	.10	.05	.01
☐ 479 Chad Ogea	.10	.05	.01
☐ 480 Scott Ruffcorn	.10	.05	.01
☐ 481 Lou Whitaker	.25	.11	.03
☐ 482 J.T. Snow	.25	.11	.03
☐ 483 Rich Rowland	.10	.05	.01
☐ 484 Denny Martinez	.25	.11	.03
☐ 485 Pedro Martinez	.25	.11	.03
☐ 486 Rusty Greer	.50	.23	.06
☐ 487 Dave Fleming	.10	.05	.01
☐ 488 John Dettmer	.10	.05	.01
☐ 489 Albert Belle	1.25	.55	.16
☐ 490 Ravelo Manzanillo	.10	.05	.01
☐ 491 Henry Rodriguez	.25	.11	.03
☐ 492 Andrew Lorraine	.25	.11	.03
☐ 493 Dwayne Hosey	.10	.05	.01
☐ 494 Mike Blowers	.10	.05	.01
☐ 495 Turner Ward	.10	.05	.01
☐ 496 Fred McGriff EC	.50	.23	.06
☐ 497 Sammy Sosa EC	.50	.23	.06
☐ 498 Barry Larkin EC	.50	.23	.06
☐ 499 Andres Galarraga EC	.50	.23	.06
☐ 500 Gary Sheffield EC	.50	.23	.06
☐ 501 Jeff Bagwell EC	.60	.25	.07
☐ 502 Mike Piazza EC	1.00	.45	.12
☐ 503 Moises Alou EC	.25	.11	.03
☐ 504 Bobby Bonilla EC	.25	.11	.03
☐ 505 Darren Daulton EC	.25	.11	.03
☐ 506 Jeff King EC	.25	.11	.03
☐ 507 Ray Lankford EC	.25	.11	.03
☐ 508 Tony Gwynn EC	.60	.25	.07
☐ 509 Barry Bonds EC	.50	.23	.06
☐ 510 Cal Ripken EC	1.25	.55	.16
☐ 511 Mo Vaughn EC	.50	.23	.06
☐ 512 Tim Salmon EC	.50	.23	.06
☐ 513 Frank Thomas EC	1.50	.70	.19
☐ 514 Albert Belle EC	.60	.25	.07
☐ 515 Cecil Fielder EC	.25	.11	.03
☐ 516 Kevin Appier EC	.25	.11	.03
☐ 517 Greg Vaughn EC	.25	.11	.03
☐ 518 Kirby Puckett EC	.50	.23	.06
☐ 519 Paul O'Neill EC	.10	.05	.01
☐ 520 Ruben Sierra EC	.10	.05	.01
☐ 521 Ken Griffey Jr. EC	1.50	.70	.19
☐ 522 Will Clark EC	.50	.23	.06
☐ 523 Joe Carter EC	.25	.11	.03
☐ 524 Antonio Osuna	.10	.05	.01
☐ 525 Glenallen Hill	.10	.05	.01
☐ 526 Alex Gonzalez	.25	.11	.03
☐ 527 Dave Stewart	.25	.11	.03
☐ 528 Ron Gant	.25	.11	.03
☐ 529 Jason Bates	.10	.05	.01
☐ 530 Mike Macfarlane	.10	.05	.01
☐ 531 Esteban Loaiza	.10	.05	.01
☐ 532 Joe Randa	.10	.05	.01
☐ 533 Dave Winfield	.50	.23	.06
☐ 534 Danny Darwin	.10	.05	.01
☐ 535 Pete Harnisch	.10	.05	.01
☐ 536 Joey Cora	.10	.05	.01
☐ 537 Jaime Navarro	.10	.05	.01
☐ 538 Marty Cordova	.50	.23	.06
☐ 539 Andujar Cedeno	.10	.05	.01
☐ 540 Mickey Tettleton	.10	.05	.01
☐ 541 Andy Van Slyke	.25	.11	.03
☐ 542 Carlos Perez	.25	.11	.03
☐ 543 Chipper Jones	2.00	.90	.25
☐ 544 Tony Fernandez	.10	.05	.01
☐ 545 Tom Henke	.10	.05	.01
☐ 546 Pat Borders	.10	.05	.01
☐ 547 Chad Curtis	.10	.05	.01
☐ 548 Ray Durham	.25	.11	.03
☐ 549 Joe Oliver	.10	.05	.01
☐ 550 Jose Mesa	.10	.05	.01
☐ 551 Steve Finley	.25	.11	.03
☐ 552 Otis Nixon	.10	.05	.01
☐ 553 Jacob Brumfield	.10	.05	.01
☐ 554 Bill Swift	.10	.05	.01
☐ 555 Quilvio Veras	.10	.05	.01
☐ 556 Hideo Nomo UER Wins and IP totals reversed	3.00	1.35	.35
☐ 557 Joe Vitiello	.10	.05	.01
☐ 558 Mike Perez	.10	.05	.01
☐ 559 Charlie Hayes	.10	.05	.01
☐ 560 Brad Radke	.25	.11	.03
☐ 561 Darren Bragg	.25	.11	.03
☐ 562 Orel Hershiser	.25	.11	.03
☐ 563 Edgardo Alfonzo	.25	.11	.03
☐ 564 Doug Jones	.10	.05	.01
☐ 565 Andy Pettitte	1.25	.55	.16
☐ 566 Benito Santiago	.10	.05	.01
☐ 567 John Burkett	.25	.11	.03
☐ 568 Brad Clontz	.10	.05	.01
☐ 569 Jim Abbott	.10	.05	.01
☐ 570 Joe Rosselli	.10	.05	.01
☐ 571 Mark Grudzielanek	.75	.35	.09
☐ 572 Dustin Hermanson	.25	.11	.03
☐ 573 Benji Gil	.10	.05	.01
☐ 574 Mark Whiten	.10	.05	.01
☐ 575 Mike Ignasiak	.10	.05	.01
☐ 576 Kevin Ritz	.10	.05	.01
☐ 577 Paul Quantrill	.10	.05	.01
☐ 578 Andre Dawson	.25	.11	.03
☐ 579 Jerald Clark	.10	.05	.01
☐ 580 Frank Rodriguez	.25	.11	.03
☐ 581 Mark Kiefer	.10	.05	.01
☐ 582 Trevor Wilson	.10	.05	.01
☐ 583 Gary Wilson	.10	.05	.01
☐ 584 Andy Stankiewicz	.10	.05	.01
☐ 585 Felipe Lira	.10	.05	.01
☐ 586 Mike Mimbs	.25	.11	.03
☐ 587 Jon Nunnally	.25	.11	.03
☐ 588 Tomas Perez	.25	.11	.03
☐ 589 Checklist	.10	.05	.01
☐ 590 Todd Hollandsworth	.50	.23	.06
☐ 591 Roberto Petagine	.10	.05	.01
☐ 592 Mariano Rivera	.25	.11	.03
☐ 593 Mark McLemore	.10	.05	.01
☐ 594 Bobby Witt	.10	.05	.01
☐ 595 Jose Offerman	.10	.05	.01
☐ 596 Jason Christiansen	.10	.05	.01
☐ 597 Jeff Manto	.10	.05	.01
☐ 598 Jim Dougherty	.10	.05	.01
☐ 599 Juan Acevedo	.10	.05	.01
☐ 600 Troy O'Leary	.10	.05	.01
☐ 601 Ron Villone	.10	.05	.01
☐ 602 Tripp Cromer	.10	.05	.01
☐ 603 Steve Scarsone	.10	.05	.01
☐ 604 Lance Parrish	.10	.05	.01
☐ 605 Ozzie Timmons	.10	.05	.01
☐ 606 Ray Holbert	.10	.05	.01
☐ 607 Tony Phillips	.25	.11	.03
☐ 608 Phil Plantier	.10	.05	.01
☐ 609 Shane Andrews	.10	.05	.01
☐ 610 Heathcliff Slocumb	.10	.05	.01
☐ 611 Bobby Higginson	.75	.35	.09
☐ 612 Bob Tewksbury	.10	.05	.01
☐ 613 Terry Pendleton	.25	.11	.03
☐ 614 Scott Cooper TA	.10	.05	.01
☐ 615 John Wetteland TA	.25	.11	.03
☐ 616 Ken Hill TA	.10	.05	.01
☐ 617 Marquis Grissom TA	.25	.11	.03
☐ 618 Larry Walker TA	.50	.23	.06
☐ 619 Derek Bell TA	.25	.11	.03
☐ 620 David Cone TA	.25	.11	.03
☐ 621 Ken Caminiti TA	.50	.23	.06
☐ 622 Jack McDowell TA	.10	.05	.01
☐ 623 Vaughn Eshelman TA	.10	.05	.01
☐ 624 Brian McRae TA	.10	.05	.01
☐ 625 Gregg Jefferies TA	.10	.05	.01
☐ 626 Kevin Brown TA	.25	.11	.03
☐ 627 Lee Smith TA	.25	.11	.03
☐ 628 Tony Tarasco TA	.10	.05	.01
☐ 629 Brett Butler TA	.10	.05	.01
☐ 630 Jose Canseco TA	.50	.23	.06

1995 Stadium Club First Day Issue

Parallel to the basic first series Stadium Club issue, these cards, were primarily inserted in second series Topps packs. They were also inserted at a rate of ten per Topps factory set. Some logos have been transferred from "common" players to the fronts of "star" players. Nine double printed cards were issued in both first and second series Topps packs. Those cards are as follows: 29, 39, 79, 96, 131, 149, 153, 168 and 197.

	MINT	NRMT	EXC
COMPLETE SET (270)	275.00	125.00	34.00
COMMON CARD (1-270)	1.00	.45	.12
COMMON DP (29/39/79/96)	.50	.23	.06
COMMON DP (153/168/197)	.50	.23	.06

*STARS: 7.5X to 15X BASIC CARDS
*YOUNG STARS: 6X to 12X BASIC CARDS
*DOUBLE PRINT STARS: 2X to 4X BASIC CARDS

1995 Stadium Club Members Only Parallel

This set is a parallel to the regular 1995 Stadium Club set.These cards are identical to their regular issue counterparts except for the distinctive "Members Only" logo. According to Topps, only 4,000 factory sets were issued through the Topps Stadium Club at a price of $200 each. A certificate of authenicity carrying the serial number accompanied each set. In addition to the 630 regular cards, the factory set includes Members Only versions of the following inserts: Crystal Ball, Clear Cut, Power Zone, Ring Leaders, Super Skills, Virtual Extremists and Virtual Reality (listed separately). Only the insert cards are listed below. Please use the multipliers for values on the basic cards.

	MINT	NRMT	EXC
SET W/O VIRTUAL REALITY (755)	250.00	110.00	31.00
COMMON REG.CARD (1-630)	.25	.11	.03

*MEMBERS ONLY: 4X BASIC CARDS

	MINT	NRMT	EXC
☐ CB1 Chipper Jones	15.00	6.75	1.85
☐ CB2 Dustin Hermanson	2.00	.90	.25
☐ CB3 Ray Durham	2.00	.90	.25
☐ CB4 Phil Nevin	1.00	.45	.12
☐ CB5 Billy Ashley	1.00	.45	.12
☐ CB6 Shawn Green	2.00	.90	.25
☐ CB7 Jason Bates	1.00	.45	.12
☐ CB8 Benji Gil	1.00	.45	.12
☐ CB9 Marty Cordova	3.00	1.35	.35
☐ CB10 Quilvio Veras	2.00	.90	.25
☐ CB11 Mark Grudzielanek	3.00	1.35	.35
☐ CB12 Ruben Rivera	6.00	2.70	.75
☐ CB13 Bill Pulsipher	2.00	.90	.25
☐ CB14 Derek Jeter	15.00	6.75	1.85
☐ CB15 LaTroy Hawkins	1.00	.45	.12
☐ CC1 Mike Piazza	12.00	5.50	1.50
☐ CC2 Ruben Sierra	1.00	.45	.12
☐ CC3 Tony Gwynn	8.00	3.60	1.00
☐ CC4 Frank Thomas	15.00	6.75	1.85
☐ CC5 Fred McGriff	2.00	.90	.25
☐ CC6 Rafael Palmeiro	1.00	.45	.12
☐ CC7 Bobby Bonilla	1.00	.45	.12
☐ CC8 Chili Davis	1.00	.45	.12
☐ CC9 Hal Morris	1.00	.45	.12
☐ CC10 Jose Canseco	2.50	1.10	.30
☐ CC11 Jay Bell	1.00	.45	.12
☐ CC12 Kirby Puckett	8.00	3.60	1.00
☐ CC13 Gary Sheffield	3.00	1.35	.35
☐ CC14 Bob Hamelin	1.00	.45	.12
☐ CC15 Jeff Bagwell	6.00	2.70	.75
☐ CC16 Albert Belle	8.00	3.60	1.00
☐ CC17 Sammy Sosa	3.00	1.35	.35
☐ CC18 Ken Griffey Jr.	15.00	6.75	1.85
☐ CC19 Todd Zeile	1.00	.45	.12
☐ CC20 Mo Vaughn	4.00	1.80	.50
☐ CC21 Moises Alou	1.50	.70	.19
☐ CC22 Paul O'Neill	1.50	.70	.19
☐ CC23 Andres Galarraga	1.00	.45	.12
☐ CC24 Greg Vaughn	1.50	.70	.19
☐ CC25 Len Dykstra	1.50	.70	.19
☐ CC26 Joe Carter	.50	.23	.06
☐ CC27 Barry Bonds	4.00	1.80	.50
☐ CC28 Cecil Fielder	1.50	.70	.19
☐ PZ1 Jeff Bagwell	6.00	2.70	.75
☐ PZ2 Albert Belle	8.00	3.60	1.00
☐ PZ3 Barry Bonds	4.00	1.80	.50
☐ PZ4 Joe Carter	2.00	.90	.25
☐ PZ5 Cecil Fielder	1.50	.70	.19
☐ PZ6 Andres Galarraga	2.00	.90	.25
☐ PZ7 Ken Griffey Jr.	15.00	6.75	1.85
☐ PZ8 Paul Molitor	4.00	1.80	.50
☐ PZ9 Fred McGriff	2.00	.90	.25
☐ PZ10 Rafael Palmeiro	2.00	.90	.25
☐ PZ11 Frank Thomas	15.00	6.75	1.85
☐ PZ12 Matt Williams	2.00	.90	.25
☐ RL1 Jeff Bagwell	6.00	2.70	.75
☐ RL2 Mark McGwire	5.00	2.20	.60
☐ RL3 Ozzie Smith	4.00	1.80	.50
☐ RL4 Paul Molitor	4.00	1.80	.50
☐ RL5 Darryl Strawberry	.50	.23	.06
☐ RL6 Eddie Murray	4.00	1.80	.50
☐ RL7 Tony Gwynn	8.00	3.60	1.00
☐ RL8 Jose Canseco	2.50	1.10	.30
☐ RL9 Howard Johnson	1.00	.45	.12
☐ RL10 Andre Dawson	2.00	.90	.25
☐ RL11 Matt Williams	2.00	.90	.25
☐ RL12 Tim Raines	1.50	.70	.19
☐ RL13 Fred McGriff	2.00	.90	.25
☐ RL14 Ken Griffey Jr.	15.00	6.75	1.85
☐ RL15 Gary Sheffield	3.00	1.35	.35
☐ RL16 Dennis Eckersley	1.50	.70	.19
☐ RL17 Kevin Mitchell	1.00	.45	.12
☐ RL18 Will Clark	2.50	1.10	.30
☐ RL19 Darren Daulton	1.00	.45	.12
☐ RL20 Paul O'Neill	1.50	.70	.19
☐ RL21 Julio Franco	1.00	.45	.12
☐ RL22 Albert Belle	8.00	3.60	1.00
☐ RL23 Juan Gonzalez	8.00	3.60	1.00
☐ RL24 Kirby Puckett	8.00	3.60	1.00
☐ RL25 Joe Carter	2.00	.90	.25
☐ RL26 Frank Thomas	15.00	6.75	1.85
☐ RL27 Cal Ripken	15.00	6.75	1.85
☐ RL28 John Olerud	1.00	.45	.12
☐ RL29 Ruben Sierra	1.00	.45	.12
☐ RL30 Barry Bonds	4.00	1.80	.50
☐ RL31 Cecil Fielder	1.50	.70	.19
☐ RL32 Roger Clemens	3.00	1.35	.35
☐ RL33 Don Mattingly	8.00	3.60	1.00
☐ RL34 Terry Pendleton	1.50	.70	.19
☐ RL35 Rickey Henderson	2.00	.90	.25
☐ RL36 Dave Winfield	2.00	.90	.25
☐ RL37 Edgar Martinez	2.00	.90	.25
☐ RL38 Wade Boggs	1.00	.45	.12
☐ RL39 Willie McGee	1.00	.45	.12
☐ RL40 Andres Galarraga	2.00	.90	.25
☐ SS1 Roberto Alomar	4.00	1.80	.50
☐ SS2 Barry Bonds	4.00	1.80	.50
☐ SS3 Jay Buhner	1.00	.45	.12
☐ SS4 Chuck Carr	1.00	.45	.12
☐ SS5 Don Mattingly	8.00	3.60	1.00
☐ SS6 Raul Mondesi	2.00	.90	.25

☐ SS7 Tim Salmon	2.00	.90	.25
☐ SS8 Deion Sanders	2.00	.90	.25
☐ SS9 Devon White	1.00	.45	.12
☐ SS10 Mark Whiten	1.00	.45	.12
☐ SS11 Ken Griffey Jr.	15.00	6.75	1.85
☐ SS12 Marquis Grissom	1.50	.70	.19
☐ SS13 Paul O'Neill	1.50	.70	.19
☐ SS14 Kenny Lofton	4.00	1.80	.50
☐ SS15 Larry Walker	3.00	1.35	.35
☐ SS16 Scott Cooper	1.00	.45	.12
☐ SS17 Barry Larkin	2.00	.90	.25
☐ SS18 Matt Williams	2.00	.90	.25
☐ SS19 John Wetteland	1.50	.70	.19
☐ SS20 Randy Johnson	3.00	1.35	.35
☐ VRE1 Barry Bonds	4.00	1.80	.50
☐ VRE2 Ken Griffey Jr.	15.00	6.75	1.85
☐ VRE3 Jeff Bagwell	6.00	2.70	.75
☐ VRE4 Albert Belle	8.00	3.60	1.00
☐ VRE5 Frank Thomas	15.00	6.75	1.85
☐ VRE6 Tony Gwynn	8.00	3.60	1.00
☐ VRE7 Kenny Lofton	4.00	1.80	.50
☐ VRE8 Deion Sanders	2.00	.90	.25
☐ VRE9 Ken Hill	1.00	.45	.12
☐ VRE10 Jimmy Key	1.50	.70	.19

1995 Stadium Club Super Team Division Winners

Each of these six team sets was available exclusively by mailing in the corresponding winning 1994 Super Team card. Each team set was distributed in a clear plastic sealed wrapper and included ten player cards and a Super Team card (of which was stamped "REDEEMED" on back). The card design and numbering for the player cards parallels regular issue 1995 Stadium Club cards. In fact, the only way to tell these cards apart is by the gold foil "Division Winner" logo on each card front. The cards are listed below alphabetically by team; the prefixes B, D, I, M, R and RS have been added to denote Braves, Dodgers, Indians, Mariners, Reds and Red Sox.

	MINT	NRMT	EXC
COMP.BRAVES SET (11)	8.00	3.60	1.00
COMP.DODGERS SET (11)	8.00	3.60	1.00
COMP.INDIANS SET (11)	6.00	2.70	.75
COMP.MARINERS SET (11)	6.00	2.70	.75
COMP.REDS SET (11)	3.00	1.35	.35
COMP.RED SOX SET (11)	4.00	1.80	.50
COMMON CARD	.25	.11	.03

☐ B1T Braves DW Super Team Jeff Blauser Terry Pendleton	.50	.23	.06
☐ B19 Ryan Klesko	.75	.35	.09
☐ B128 Mark Wohlers	.25	.11	.03
☐ B151 Steve Avery	.25	.11	.03
☐ B183 Tom Glavine	.60	.25	.07
☐ B200 Javy Lopez	.60	.25	.07
☐ B393 Fred McGriff	.60	.25	.07
☐ B397 John Smoltz	.75	.35	.09
☐ B425 Greg Maddux	3.00	1.35	.35
☐ B446 Dave Justice	.60	.25	.07
☐ B543 Chipper Jones	3.00	1.35	.35
☐ D7T Dodgers DW Super Team Mike Piazza	1.00	.45	.12
☐ D57 Raul Mondesi	.60	.25	.07
☐ D149 Mike Piazza	3.00	1.35	.35
☐ D161 Ismael Valdez	.50	.23	.06
☐ D242 Brett Butler	.40	.18	.05
☐ D259 Tim Wallach	.25	.11	.03
☐ D278 Eric Karros	.40	.18	.05
☐ D434 Ramon Martinez	.40	.18	.05
☐ D456 Tom Candiotti	.25	.11	.03
☐ D467 Delino DeShields	.25	.11	.03
☐ D556 Hideo Nomo	5.00	2.20	.60
☐ I19T Indians DW Super Team Carlos Baerga Albert Belle Kenny Lofton	1.00	.45	.12
☐ I36 Carlos Baerga	.40	.18	.05
☐ I147 Jim Thome	1.00	.45	.12
☐ I186 Eddie Murray	1.25	.55	.16
☐ I264 Manny Ramirez	1.25	.55	.16
☐ I334 Omar Vizquel	.40	.18	.05
☐ I470 Kenny Lofton	1.25	.55	.16
☐ I484 Dennis Martinez	.40	.18	.05
☐ I489 Albert Belle	2.00	.90	.25
☐ I550 Jose Mesa	.25	.11	.03
☐ I562 Orel Hershiser	.40	.18	.05
☐ M26T Mariners DW Super Team Mike Blowers Jay Buhner	.50	.23	.06
☐ M73 Jay Buhner	.60	.25	.07
☐ M92 Chris Bosio	.25	.11	.03
☐ M152 Dan Wilson	.40	.18	.05
☐ M227 Tino Martinez	.60	.25	.07
☐ M241 Ken Griffey Jr.	5.00	2.20	.60
☐ M340 Randy Johnson	.75	.35	.09
☐ M354 Edgar Martinez	.50	.23	.06
☐ M421 Felix Fermin	.25	.11	.03
☐ M494 Mike Blowers	.25	.11	.03
☐ M536 Joey Cora	.25	.11	.03
☐ RE3T Reds DW Super Team Barry Larkin Reggie Sanders	.75	.35	.09
☐ RE35 Barry Larkin	.60	.25	.07
☐ RE231 Hal Morris	.25	.11	.03
☐ RE252 Bret Boone	.25	.11	.03
☐ RE280 Thomas Howard	.25	.11	.03
☐ RE300 Jose Rijo	.25	.11	.03
☐ RE333 Reggie Sanders	.40	.18	.05
☐ RE392 Hector Carrasco	.25	.11	.03
☐ RE416 John Smiley	.25	.11	.03
☐ RE528 Ron Gant	.40	.18	.05
☐ RE566 Benito Santiago	.25	.11	.03
☐ RS1T Red Sox DW Super Team Luis Rivera John Valentin	.50	.23	.06
☐ RS10 Roger Clemens	1.25	.55	.16
☐ RS62 John Valentin	.25	.11	.03
☐ RS121 Mike Greenwell	.25	.11	.03
☐ RS160 Lee Tinsley	.25	.11	.03
☐ RS347 Jose Canseco	.60	.25	.07
☐ RS350 Mo Vaughn	1.25	.55	.16
☐ RS395 Tim Naehring	.25	.11	.03
☐ RS464 Aaron Sele	.25	.11	.03
☐ RS530 Mike Macfarlane	.25	.11	.03
☐ RS600 Troy O'Leary	.25	.11	.03

1995 Stadium Club Super Team World Series

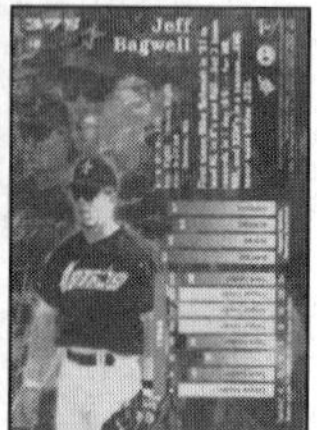

Because of the strike-interrupted season, the 1994 Stadium Club Super Team insert program had to be finished up with the 1995 product. Collectors who redeemed the 1994 Atlanta Braves Super Team card received: 1) a complete 630-card 1995 Stadium Club parallel set stamped with a special gold foil World Series logo (of which was mailed in two separate series of 585 and 45 cards) 2) a Division Winner parallel Braves team set along with the winner card stamped "redeemed" on its back 3) a jumbo-sized (3" by 5") parallel Master Photo Braves team set. Collectors who redeemed the 1994 Cleveland Indians Super Team card got parallel Indians Division Winner and Master Photo team sets. Collectors who redeemed the 1994 Super Team card of a division winner (Dodgers, Mariners, Red Sox and Reds) received a Division Winner parallel team set of the respective team that they sent in. All of these winner cards parallel the 1995 Stadium Club regular series cards.

	MINT	NRMT	EXC
COMP.WORLD SERIES SET (585)	100.00	45.00	12.50
COMP.SER.3 EC AND TA SET (45)	15.00	6.75	1.85
COMMON CARD (1-630)	.15	.07	.02

*STARS: 1X to 2X BASIC CARDS
*YOUNG STARS: .75X to 1.5X BASIC CARDS

1995 Stadium Club Super Team Master Photos

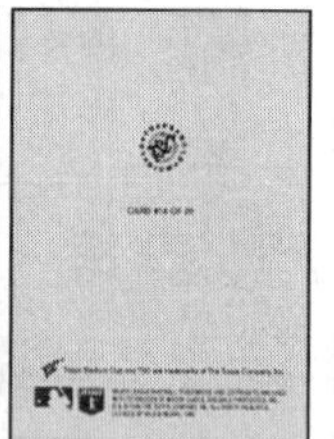

This 20-card set was distributed in two separate 10-card sealed team bags. The cards were available exclusively by mailing in a Braves or Indians 1994 Super Team card. These oversized cards (5" by 7") feature a reproduction of the player's standard 1995 Stadium Club card enframed around a shining blue background. Unlike the standard issue cards they parallel, these are numbered X of 20.

	MINT	NRMT	EXC
COMPLETE SET (20)	22.00	10.00	2.70
COMP.BRAVES SET (10)	12.00	5.50	1.50
COMP.INDIANS SET (10)	10.00	4.50	1.25
COMMON CARD (1-20)	.50	.23	.06

☐ 1 Steve Avery	.50	.23	.06
☐ 2 Tom Glavine	1.00	.45	.12
☐ 3 Chipper Jones	5.00	2.20	.60
☐ 4 Dave Justice	1.00	.45	.12
☐ 5 Ryan Klesko	1.25	.55	.16
☐ 6 Javy Lopez	1.00	.45	.12
☐ 7 Greg Maddux	5.00	2.20	.60
☐ 8 Fred McGriff	1.00	.45	.12
☐ 9 John Smoltz	1.25	.55	.16
☐ 10 Mark Wohlers	.50	.23	.06
☐ 11 Carlos Baerga	.50	.23	.06
☐ 12 Albert Belle	3.00	1.35	.35
☐ 13 Orel Hershiser	.75	.35	.09
☐ 14 Kenny Lofton	2.00	.90	.25
☐ 15 Dennis Martinez	.50	.23	.06
☐ 16 Jose Mesa	.50	.23	.06
☐ 17 Eddie Murray	2.00	.90	.25
☐ 18 Manny Ramirez	2.00	.90	.25
☐ 19 Jim Thome	1.50	.70	.19
☐ 20 Omar Vizquel	.75	.35	.09

1995 Stadium Club Clear Cut

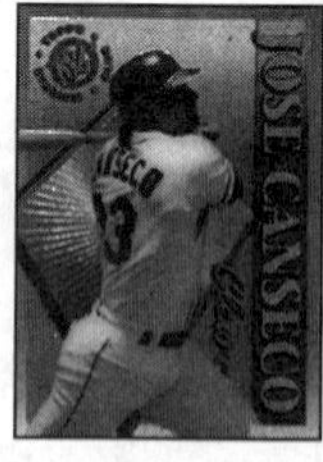

Randomly inserted at a rate of one in 16 packs, this 28-card set features a full color action photo of the player against a clear acetate background with the player's name printed vertically. Backs highlight the season achievement of the player on a thin horizontal strip.

	MINT	NRMT	EXC
COMPLETE SET (28)	100.00	45.00	12.50
COMPLETE SET (14)	50.00	22.00	6.25
COMPLETE SERIES 2 (14)	50.00	22.00	6.25
COMMON CARD (CC1-CC28)	1.50	.70	.19

☐ CC1 Mike Piazza	15.00	6.75	1.85
☐ CC2 Ruben Sierra	3.00	1.35	.35
☐ CC3 Tony Gwynn	10.00	4.50	1.25
☐ CC4 Frank Thomas	25.00	11.00	3.10
☐ CC5 Fred McGriff			
☐ CC6 Rafael Palmeiro			
☐ CC7 Bobby Bonilla	3.00	1.35	.35
☐ CC8 Chili Davis	3.00	1.35	.35
☐ CC9 Hal Morris	1.50	.70	.19
☐ CC10 Jose Canseco			
☐ CC11 Jay Bell	1.50	.70	.19
☐ CC12 Kirby Puckett	10.00	4.50	1.25
☐ CC13 Gary Sheffield	4.00	1.80	.50
☐ CC14 Bob Hamelin	1.50	.70	.19
☐ CC15 Jeff Bagwell	10.00	4.50	1.25
☐ CC16 Albert Belle	10.00	4.50	1.25
☐ CC17 Sammy Sosa	4.00	1.80	.50
☐ CC18 Ken Griffey Jr.	25.00	11.00	3.10
☐ CC19 Todd Zeile	1.50	.70	.19
☐ CC20 Mo Vaughn	6.00	2.70	.75
☐ CC21 Moises Alou	3.00	1.35	.35
☐ CC22 Paul O'Neill	3.00	1.35	.35
☐ CC23 Andres Galarraga			
☐ CC24 Greg Vaughn	3.00	1.35	.35
☐ CC25 Len Dykstra	3.00	1.35	.35
☐ CC26 Joe Carter	3.00	1.35	.35
☐ CC27 Barry Bonds	6.00	2.70	.75
☐ CC28 Cecil Fielder	3.00	1.35	.35

1995 Stadium Club Crunch Time

This 20-card standard-size set features home run hitters and was randomly inserted in first series rack packs. Fronts are action illustrations of players on gold foil paper with the Crunch Time logo and player's name printed in gold foil at the bottom of the card. The horizontal backs include a pie chart and statistics of player offensive output and player action photos. The cards are numbered as "X" of 20 in the upper right corner.

	MINT	NRMT	EXC
COMPLETE SET (20)	40.00	18.00	5.00
COMMON CARD (1-20)	.75	.35	.09

☐ 1 Jeff Bagwell	4.00	1.80	.50
☐ 2 Kirby Puckett	4.00	1.80	.50
☐ 3 Frank Thomas	10.00	4.50	1.25
☐ 4 Albert Belle	4.00	1.80	.50
☐ 5 Julio Franco	.75	.35	.09
☐ 6 Jose Canseco	1.25	.55	.16
☐ 7 Paul Molitor	2.00	.90	.25
☐ 8 Joe Carter	1.00	.45	.12
☐ 9 Ken Griffey Jr.	10.00	4.50	1.25
☐ 10 Larry Walker	1.25	.55	.16
☐ 11 Dante Bichette	1.25	.55	.16
☐ 12 Carlos Baerga	.75	.35	.09
☐ 13 Fred McGriff	1.25	.55	.16
☐ 14 Ruben Sierra	.75	.35	.09
☐ 15 Will Clark	1.25	.55	.16
☐ 16 Moises Alou	1.00	.45	.12
☐ 17 Rafael Palmeiro	1.25	.55	.16
☐ 18 Travis Fryman	1.00	.45	.12
☐ 19 Barry Bonds	2.50	1.10	.30
☐ 20 Cal Ripken	8.00	3.60	1.00

1995 Stadium Club Crystal Ball

This 15-card standard-size set was inserted into series three packs at a rate of one in 24. Fifteen leading 1995 rookies and prospects were featured in this set. The fronts feature a player photo in the middle with the words "Crystal Ball" on the top with the player's name on the bottom. The backs have season-by-season stats with a sentence about the player's accomplishments during that season. A player photo in the upper right is set in a crystal ball. The player is identified on the top and the cards are numbered with a "CB" prefix in the upper left corner.

	MINT	NRMT	EXC
COMPLETE SET (15)	75.00	34.00	9.50
COMMON CARD (CB1-CB15)	2.00	.90	.25

☐ CB1 Chipper Jones	25.00	11.00	3.10
☐ CB2 Dustin Hermanson	2.00	.90	.25
☐ CB3 Ray Durham	4.00	1.80	.50
☐ CB4 Phil Nevin	2.00	.90	.25
☐ CB5 Billy Ashley	2.00	.90	.25
☐ CB6 Shawn Green	4.00	1.80	.50
☐ CB7 Jason Bates	2.00	.90	.25
☐ CB8 Benji Gil	2.00	.90	.25
☐ CB9 Marty Cordova	8.00	3.60	1.00
☐ CB10 Quilvio Veras	2.00	.90	.25
☐ CB11 Mark Grudzielanek	6.00	2.70	.75
☐ CB12 Ruben Rivera	12.00	5.50	1.50
☐ CB13 Bill Pulsipher	2.00	.90	.25
☐ CB14 Derek Jeter	25.00	11.00	3.10
☐ CB15 LaTroy Hawkins	2.00	.90	.25

1995 Stadium Club Phone Cards

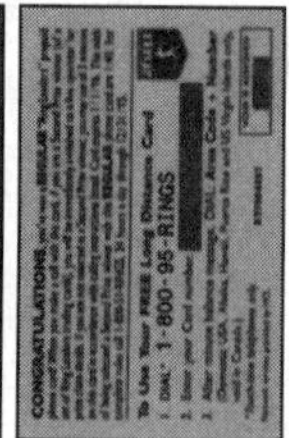

These phone cards were randomly inserted into packs. The prizes for these cards were as follows. The Gold Winner card was redeemable for the ring depicted on the front of the card. The silver winner card was redeemable for a set of all 39 phone cards. The regular winner card was redeemable for a ring leaders set. The fronts feature a photo of a specific ring while the backs have game information. If the card was not a winner for any of the prizes, it was still good for three minutes of time. The phone cards expired on January 1, 1996. If the PIN number is revealed the value is a percentage of an untouched card.

	MINT	NRMT	EXC
COMPLETE REGULAR SET (13)	40.00	18.00	5.00
COMMON REGULAR CARD	4.00	1.80	.50
COMPLETE SILVER SET (13)	75.00	34.00	9.50
COMMON SILVER CARD	8.00	3.60	1.00
COMPLETE GOLD SET (13)	150.00	70.00	19.00
COMMON GOLD CARD	15.00	6.75	1.85

*PIN NUMBER REVEALED: .25X to .50X BASIC CARDS

1995 Stadium Club Power Zone

This 12-card standard-size set was inserted into series three packs at a rate of one in 24. The fronts feature a player photo and his name on the right. The left side of the card has the bat powering through an explosion. The words "Power Zone" are on the bottom. The horizontal backs feature a close-up photo, some vital information as well as some seasonal highlights. The cards are numbered in the upper right corner with a "PZ" prefix. The set is sequenced in alphabetical order.

	MINT	NRMT	EXC
COMPLETE SET (12)	90.00	40.00	11.00
COMMON CARD (PZ1-PZ12)	2.00	.90	.25

□ PZ1 Jeff Bagwell	12.00	5.50	1.50
□ PZ2 Albert Belle	12.00	5.50	1.50
□ PZ3 Barry Bonds	8.00	3.60	1.00
□ PZ4 Joe Carter	2.00	.90	.25
□ PZ5 Cecil Fielder	2.00	.90	.25
□ PZ6 Andres Galarraga	4.00	1.80	.50
□ PZ7 Ken Griffey Jr.	30.00	13.50	3.70
□ PZ8 Paul Molitor	6.00	2.70	.75
□ PZ9 Fred McGriff	4.00	1.80	.50
□ PZ10 Rafael Palmeiro	4.00	1.80	.50
□ PZ11 Frank Thomas	30.00	13.50	3.70
□ PZ12 Matt Williams	4.00	1.80	.50

1995 Stadium Club Ring Leaders

Randomly inserted in packs, this set features players who have won various awards or titles. This set was also redeemable as a prize with winning regular phone cards. This set features Stadium Club's "Power Matrix Technology," which makes the cards shine and glow. The horizontal fronts feature a player photo, rings in both upper corners as well as other designs that make for a very busy front. The backs have information on how the player earned his rings, along with a player photo and some other pertinent information.

	MINT	NRMT	EXC
COMPLETE SET (40)	175.00	80.00	22.00
COMPLETE SERIES 1 (20)	65.00	29.00	8.00
COMPLETE SERIES 2 (20)	110.00	50.00	14.00
COMMON CARD (RL1-RL40)	2.00	.90	.25
□ RL1 Jeff Bagwell	12.00	5.50	1.50
□ RL2 Mark McGwire	10.00	4.50	1.25
□ RL3 Ozzie Smith	8.00	3.60	1.00
□ RL4 Paul Molitor	6.00	2.70	.75
□ RL5 Darryl Strawberry	3.00	1.35	.35
□ RL6 Eddie Murray	8.00	3.60	1.00
□ RL7 Tony Gwynn	12.00	5.50	1.50
□ RL8 Jose Canseco	4.00	1.80	.50
□ RL9 Howard Johnson	2.00	.90	.25
□ RL10 Andre Dawson	3.00	1.35	.35
□ RL11 Matt Williams	4.00	1.80	.50
□ RL12 Tim Raines	3.00	1.35	.35
□ RL13 Fred McGriff	4.00	1.80	.50
□ RL14 Ken Griffey Jr.	30.00	13.50	3.70
□ RL15 Gary Sheffield	5.00	2.20	.60
□ RL16 Dennis Eckersley	3.00	1.35	.35
□ RL17 Kevin Mitchell	2.00	.90	.25
□ RL18 Will Clark	4.00	1.80	.50
□ RL19 Darren Daulton	3.00	1.35	.35
□ RL20 Paul O'Neill	2.00	.90	.25
□ RL21 Julio Franco	2.00	.90	.25
□ RL22 Albert Belle	12.00	5.50	1.50
□ RL23 Juan Gonzalez	15.00	6.75	1.85
□ RL24 Kirby Puckett	12.00	5.50	1.50
□ RL25 Joe Carter	3.00	1.35	.35
□ RL26 Frank Thomas	30.00	13.50	3.70
□ RL27 Cal Ripken	25.00	11.00	3.10
□ RL28 John Olerud	2.00	.90	.25
□ RL29 Ruben Sierra	2.00	.90	.25
□ RL30 Barry Bonds	8.00	3.60	1.00
□ RL31 Cecil Fielder	3.00	1.35	.35
□ RL32 Roger Clemens	6.00	2.70	.75
□ RL33 Don Mattingly	15.00	6.75	1.85
□ RL34 Terry Pendleton	2.00	.90	.25
□ RL35 Rickey Henderson	4.00	1.80	.50
□ RL36 Dave Winfield	4.00	1.80	.50
□ RL37 Edgar Martinez	3.00	1.35	.35
□ RL38 Wade Boggs	4.00	1.80	.50
□ RL39 Willie McGee	2.00	.90	.25
□ RL40 Andres Galarraga	4.00	1.80	.50

1995 Stadium Club Super Skills

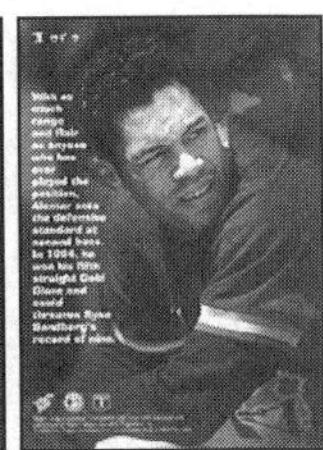

This 20-card set was randomly inserted into hobby packs. The full-bleed front features a player photo against a multi-colored background. The background was enhanced using Stadium Club's "Power Matrix" Technology. The "Super Skills" logo is in the lower left corner. The backs have a full-bleed photo with a description of the player's special skill. The cards are numbered in the upper left as "X" of 9.

	MINT	NRMT	EXC
COMPLETE SET (20)	80.00	36.00	10.00
COMPLETE SERIES 1 (9)	35.00	16.00	4.40
COMPLETE SERIES 2 (11)	45.00	20.00	5.50
COMMON CARD (SS1-SS20)	1.50	.70	.19
□ SS1 Roberto Alomar	5.00	2.20	.60
□ SS2 Barry Bonds	6.00	2.70	.75
□ SS3 Jay Buhner	3.00	1.35	.35
□ SS4 Chuck Carr	1.50	.70	.19
□ SS5 Don Mattingly	12.00	5.50	1.50
□ SS6 Raul Mondesi	3.00	1.35	.35
□ SS7 Tim Salmon	3.00	1.35	.35
□ SS8 Deion Sanders	3.00	1.35	.35
□ SS9 Devon White	1.50	.70	.19
□ SS10 Mark Whiten	1.50	.70	.19
□ SS11 Ken Griffey Jr.	25.00	11.00	3.10
□ SS12 Marquis Grissom	2.00	.90	.25
□ SS13 Paul O'Neill	2.00	.90	.25
□ SS14 Kenny Lofton	6.00	2.70	.75
□ SS15 Larry Walker	3.00	1.35	.35
□ SS16 Scott Cooper	1.50	.70	.19
□ SS17 Barry Larkin	3.00	1.35	.35
□ SS18 Matt Williams	3.00	1.35	.35
□ SS19 John Wetteland	2.00	.90	.25
□ SS20 Randy Johnson	4.00	1.80	.50

1995 Stadium Club Virtual Extremists

This 10-card set was inserted randomly into second series rack packs. The fronts feature a player photo against a baseball backdrop. The words "VR Extremist" are spelled vertically down the right side while the player name is in silver foil on the bottom. All of this is surrounded by blue and purple borders. The horizontal backs feature projected full-season 1994 stats. The cards are numbered with a "VRE" prefix in the upper right corner.

	MINT	NRMT	EXC
COMPLETE SET (10)	120.00	55.00	15.00
COMMON CARD (VRE1-VRE10)	2.50	1.10	.30
□ VRE1 Barry Bonds	10.00	4.50	1.25
□ VRE2 Ken Griffey Jr.	40.00	18.00	5.00
□ VRE3 Jeff Bagwell	15.00	6.75	1.85
□ VRE4 Albert Belle	15.00	6.75	1.85
□ VRE5 Frank Thomas	40.00	18.00	5.00
□ VRE6 Tony Gwynn	15.00	6.75	1.85
□ VRE7 Kenny Lofton	10.00	4.50	1.25
□ VRE8 Deion Sanders			
□ VRE9 Ken Hill	2.50	1.10	.30
□ VRE10 Jimmy Key	2.50	1.10	.30

1995 Stadium Club Virtual Reality

This 270-card standard-size set parallels a selection of cards from the regular 1995 Stadium Club set. Differences include the words "Virtual Reality" printed above the player's name and the numbering on the back. These cards were inserted in the first two Stadium Club series on a one per pack, two per rack pack basis.

	MINT	NRMT	EXC
COMPLETE SET (270)	90.00	40.00	11.00
COMPLETE SERIES 1 (135)	45.00	20.00	5.50
COMPLETE SERIES 2 (135)	45.00	20.00	5.50
COMMON CARD (1-270)	.25	.11	.03
□ 1 Cal Ripken	5.00	2.20	.60
□ 2 Travis Fryman	.50	.23	.06
□ 3 Jim Abbott	.25	.11	.03
□ 4 Gary Gaetti	.25	.11	.03
□ 5 Roger Clemens	1.00	.45	.12
□ 6 Carlos Garcia	.25	.11	.03
□ 7 Lee Smith	.50	.23	.06
□ 8 Bobby Ayala	.25	.11	.03
□ 9 Charles Nagy	.50	.23	.06
□ 10 Rene Arocha	.25	.11	.03
□ 11 Carlos Delgado	.50	.23	.06
□ 12 Steve Finley	.50	.23	.06
□ 13 Ryan Klesko	1.00	.45	.12
□ 14 Cal Eldred	.25	.11	.03
□ 15 Rey Sanchez	.25	.11	.03
□ 16 Ken Hill	.25	.11	.03
□ 17 Jose Vizcaino	.25	.11	.03
□ 18 Andy Benes	.50	.23	.06
□ 19 Shawon Dunston	.25	.11	.03
□ 20 Rafael Palmeiro	1.00	.45	.12
□ 21 Dean Palmer	.50	.23	.06
□ 22 Joey Cora	.25	.11	.03
□ 23 Mickey Tettleton	.25	.11	.03
□ 24 Barry Larkin	1.00	.45	.12
□ 25 Carlos Baerga	.50	.23	.06
□ 26 Orel Hershiser	.50	.23	.06
□ 27 Jody Reed	.25	.11	.03
□ 28 Paul Molitor	1.25	.55	.16
□ 29 Jim Edmonds	1.00	.45	.12
□ 30 Bob Tewksbury	.25	.11	.03
□ 31 Ray McDavid	.25	.11	.03
□ 32 Stan Javier	.25	.11	.03
□ 33 Todd Worrell	.25	.11	.03
□ 34 Bob Wickman	.25	.11	.03
□ 35 Raul Mondesi	1.00	.45	.12
□ 36 Rod Beck	.25	.11	.03
□ 37 Jeff Kent	.25	.11	.03
□ 38 John Valentin	.50	.23	.06
□ 39 Ozzie Smith	1.25	.55	.16
□ 40 Terry Pendleton	.50	.23	.06
□ 41 Kenny Rogers	.25	.11	.03
□ 42 Vince Coleman	.25	.11	.03
□ 43 Roberto Alomar	1.25	.55	.16
□ 44 Darrin Jackson	.25	.11	.03
□ 45 Dennis Eckersley	.50	.23	.06
□ 46 Jay Buhner	1.00	.45	.12
□ 47 Dave Weathers	.25	.11	.03
□ 48 Danny Bautista	.25	.11	.03
□ 49 Bob Hamelin	.25	.11	.03
□ 50 Steve Trachsel	.25	.11	.03
□ 51 Ben McDonald	.25	.11	.03
□ 52 Wade Boggs	1.00	.45	.12
□ 53 Sandy Alomar Jr.	.25	.11	.03
□ 54 Ron Karkovice	.25	.11	.03
□ 55 Doug Jones	.25	.11	.03
□ 56 Gary Sheffield	1.00	.45	.12
□ 57 Ken Caminiti	1.00	.45	.12
□ 58 Kevin Tapani	.25	.11	.03
□ 59 Ruben Sierra	.50	.23	.06
□ 60 Bobby Bonilla	.50	.23	.06
□ 61 Deion Sanders	1.00	.45	.12
□ 62 Charlie Hayes	.25	.11	.03
□ 63 Paul O'Neill	.50	.23	.06
□ 64 Jay Bell	.25	.11	.03
□ 65 Todd Jones	.25	.11	.03
□ 66 Todd Stottlemyre	.25	.11	.03
□ 67 Will Clark	1.00	.45	.12
□ 68 Wilson Alvarez	.25	.11	.03
□ 69 Chili Davis	.50	.23	.06
□ 70 Chris Hoiles	.25	.11	.03
□ 71 Bret Saberhagen	.50	.23	.06
□ 72 Dave Nilsson	.25	.11	.03
□ 73 Derek Bell	.50	.23	.06
□ 74 Juan Gonzalez	3.00	1.35	.35
□ 75 Andre Dawson	.50	.23	.06
□ 76 Jim Thome	1.25	.55	.16
□ 77 Larry Walker	1.00	.45	.12
□ 78 Mike Piazza	4.00	1.80	.50
□ 79 Dan Wilson	.25	.11	.03
□ 80 Junior Felix	.25	.11	.03
□ 81 Jack McDowell	.50	.23	.06
□ 82 Danny Tartabull	.25	.11	.03
□ 83 William Van Landingham	.25	.11	.03
□ 84 Robb Nen	.25	.11	.03
□ 85 Ismael Valdes	.50	.23	.06
□ 86 Juan Guzman	.25	.11	.03
□ 87 Cliff Floyd	.25	.11	.03
□ 88 Rico Brogna	.25	.11	.03
□ 89 Luis Polonia	.25	.11	.03
□ 90 Lance Johnson	.50	.23	.06
□ 91 Sammy Sosa	1.00	.45	.12
□ 92 Dave West	.25	.11	.03
□ 93 Tom Glavine	1.00	.45	.12
□ 94 Joe Girardi	.25	.11	.03
□ 95 Craig Biggio	.50	.23	.06
□ 96 Eddie Murray	1.50	.70	.19
□ 97 Kevin Gross	.25	.11	.03
□ 98 John Franco	.25	.11	.03
□ 99 Matt Williams	1.00	.45	.12
□ 100 Darrin Fletcher	.25	.11	.03
□ 101 Jeff Conine	.50	.23	.06
□ 102 Ed Sprague	.25	.11	.03
□ 103 Ivan Rodriguez	1.25	.55	.16
□ 104 Orlando Merced	.25	.11	.03
□ 105 Ricky Bones	.25	.11	.03
□ 106 David Cone	.50	.23	.06
□ 107 Todd Hundley	.50	.23	.06
□ 108 Alex Cole	.25	.11	.03
□ 109 Tony Phillips	.50	.23	.06
□ 110 Jim Eisenreich	.25	.11	.03
□ 111 Paul Sorrento	.25	.11	.03
□ 112 Mike Stanley	.25	.11	.03
□ 113 Doug Drabek	.25	.11	.03
□ 114 Matt Mieske	.25	.11	.03
□ 115 Tino Martinez	.50	.23	.06
□ 116 Midre Cummings	.25	.11	.03
□ 117 Hal Morris	.25	.11	.03
□ 118 Shawn Green	.50	.23	.06
□ 119 Randy Myers	.25	.11	.03
□ 120 Ken Griffey Jr.	6.00	2.70	.75
□ 121 Brett Butler	.50	.23	.06
□ 122 Julio Franco	.50	.23	.06
□ 123 Chuck Knoblauch	1.00	.45	.12
□ 124 Bret Boone	.25	.11	.03
□ 125 Wil Cordero	.25	.11	.03
□ 126 Luis Gonzalez	.25	.11	.03
□ 127 Tim Wallach	.25	.11	.03
□ 128 Scott Sanders	.25	.11	.03
□ 129 Tom Henke	.25	.11	.03
□ 130 Otis Nixon	.25	.11	.03
□ 131 Darren Daulton	.50	.23	.06
□ 132 Manny Ramirez	1.50	.70	.19
□ 133 Bret Barberie	.25	.11	.03
□ 134 Brady Anderson	1.00	.45	.12
□ 135 Shane Reynolds	.50	.23	.06
□ 136 Barry Bonds	1.50	.70	.19
□ 137 Alex Fernandez	.50	.23	.06
□ 138 Brian McRae	.50	.23	.06
□ 139 Todd Zeile	.25	.11	.03
□ 140 Greg Swindell	.25	.11	.03
□ 141 Troy Neel	.25	.11	.03
□ 142 Eric Karros	.50	.23	.06
□ 143 John Hudek	.25	.11	.03
□ 144 Joe Carter	.50	.23	.06
□ 145 Mike Devereaux	.25	.11	.03
□ 146 Butch Henry	.25	.11	.03
□ 147 Mark Lemke	.25	.11	.03
□ 148 Jeff Montgomery	.25	.11	.03
□ 149 Ryan Thompson	.25	.11	.03
□ 150 Bernie Williams	1.00	.45	.12
□ 151 Scott Leius	.25	.11	.03
□ 152 Greg Gagne	.25	.11	.03
□ 153 Moises Alou	.50	.23	.06
□ 154 Geronimo Berroa	.50	.23	.06
□ 155 Alan Trammell	.50	.23	.06
□ 156 Don Slaught	.25	.11	.03
□ 157 Jose Rijo	.25	.11	.03
□ 158 Tim Raines	.50	.23	.06
□ 159 Melido Perez	.25	.11	.03
□ 160 Kent Mercker	.25	.11	.03
□ 161 James Mouton	.25	.11	.03
□ 162 Luis Lopez	.25	.11	.03
□ 163 Mike Kingery	.25	.11	.03
□ 164 Cecil Fielder	.50	.23	.06
□ 165 Scott Kamieniecki	.25	.11	.03
□ 166 Brent Gates	.25	.11	.03
□ 167 Jason Jacome	.25	.11	.03
□ 168 Dante Bichette	1.00	.45	.12
□ 169 Kurt Abbott	.25	.11	.03
□ 170 Mike Henneman	.25	.11	.03
□ 171 John Kruk	.50	.23	.06
□ 172 Jose Oliva	.25	.11	.03
□ 173 Reggie Sanders	.50	.23	.06
□ 174 Omar Vizquel	.50	.23	.06
□ 175 Devon White	.25	.11	.03
□ 176 Mark McGwire	2.00	.90	.25
□ 177 Gary DiSarcina	.25	.11	.03
□ 178 Joey Hamilton	1.00	.45	.12
□ 179 Randy Johnson	1.00	.45	.12
□ 180 Jim Leyritz	.25	.11	.03
□ 181 Bobby Jones	.25	.11	.03
□ 182 Bip Roberts	.25	.11	.03
□ 183 Jose Canseco	1.00	.45	.12
□ 184 Mo Vaughn	1.50	.70	.19
□ 185 Edgar Martinez	.50	.23	.06
□ 186 Tommy Greene	.25	.11	.03
□ 187 Chuck Carr	.25	.11	.03
□ 188 Pedro Astacio	.25	.11	.03
□ 189 Shane Mack	.25	.11	.03
□ 190 Fred McGriff	1.00	.45	.12
□ 191 Pat Rapp	.25	.11	.03
□ 192 Bill Swift	.25	.11	.03
□ 193 Robin Ventura	.50	.23	.06
□ 194 Bobby Witt	.25	.11	.03
□ 195 Steve Howe	.25	.11	.03
□ 196 Leo Gomez	.25	.11	.03
□ 197 Hector Fajardo	.25	.11	.03
□ 198 Jeff Bagwell	2.50	1.10	.30
□ 199 Rondell White	.50	.23	.06
□ 200 Don Mattingly	3.00	1.35	.35
□ 201 Trevor Hoffman	.50	.23	.06
□ 202 Chris Gomez	.25	.11	.03

☐ 203 Bobby Munoz	.25	.11	.03
☐ 204 Marvin Freeman	.25	.11	.03
☐ 205 Sean Berry	.25	.11	.03
☐ 206 Mark Grace	1.00	.45	.12
☐ 207 Pat Kelly	.25	.11	.03
☐ 208 Eddie Williams	.25	.11	.03
☐ 209 Frank Thomas	6.00	2.70	.75
☐ 210 Bryan Eversgerd	.25	.11	.03
☐ 211 Phil Plantier	.25	.11	.03
☐ 212 Roberto Kelly	.25	.11	.03
☐ 213 Rickey Henderson	1.00	.45	.12
☐ 214 John Smiley	.25	.11	.03
☐ 215 Kevin Brown	.50	.23	.06
☐ 216 Jimmy Key	.25	.11	.03
☐ 217 Wally Joyner	.50	.23	.06
☐ 218 Roberto Hernandez	.25	.11	.03
☐ 219 Felix Fermin	.25	.11	.03
☐ 220 Greg Vaughn	.50	.23	.06
☐ 221 Ray Lankford	.50	.23	.06
☐ 222 Greg Maddux	4.00	1.80	.50
☐ 223 Mike Mussina	1.25	.55	.16
☐ 224 David Nied	.25	.11	.03
☐ 225 Scott Erickson	.25	.11	.03
☐ 226 Kevin Mitchell	.25	.11	.03
☐ 227 Brian Anderson	.25	.11	.03
☐ 228 Jeff King	.25	.11	.03
☐ 229 Ramon Martinez	.50	.23	.06
☐ 230 Kevin Seitzer	.25	.11	.03
☐ 231 Marquis Grissom	.50	.23	.06
☐ 232 Chuck Finley	.25	.11	.03
☐ 233 Len Dykstra	.50	.23	.06
☐ 234 Ellis Burks	.50	.23	.06
☐ 235 Harold Baines	.50	.23	.06
☐ 236 Kevin Appier	.50	.23	.06
☐ 237 David Justice	.50	.23	.06
☐ 238 Darryl Kile	.25	.11	.03
☐ 239 John Olerud	.25	.11	.03
☐ 240 Greg McMichael	.25	.11	.03
☐ 241 Kirby Puckett	2.50	1.10	.30
☐ 242 Jose Valentin	.25	.11	.03
☐ 243 Rick Wilkins	.25	.11	.03
☐ 244 Pat Hentgen	.50	.23	.06
☐ 245 Tom Gordon	.25	.11	.03
☐ 246 Tom Candiotti	.25	.11	.03
☐ 247 Jason Bere	.25	.11	.03
☐ 248 Wes Chamberlain	.25	.11	.03
☐ 249 Jeff Cirillo	.25	.11	.03
☐ 250 Kevin Foster	.25	.11	.03
☐ 251 Mark Whiten	.25	.11	.03
☐ 252 Terry Steinbach	.50	.23	.06
☐ 253 Aaron Sele	.25	.11	.03
☐ 254 Kirt Manwaring	.25	.11	.03
☐ 255 Delino DeShields	.25	.11	.03
☐ 256 Andujar Cedeno	.25	.11	.03
☐ 257 Kenny Lofton	1.50	.70	.19
☐ 258 John Wetteland	.50	.23	.06
☐ 259 Tim Salmon	1.00	.45	.12
☐ 260 Denny Neagle	.50	.23	.06
☐ 261 Tony Gwynn	2.50	1.10	.30
☐ 262 Lou Whitaker	.50	.23	.06
☐ 263 J.T. Snow	.25	.11	.03
☐ 264 Denny Martinez	.50	.23	.06
☐ 265 Pedro Martinez	.50	.23	.06
☐ 266 Rusty Greer	1.00	.45	.12
☐ 267 Dave Fleming	.25	.11	.03
☐ 268 John Dettmer	.25	.11	.03
☐ 269 Albert Belle	3.00	1.35	.35
☐ 270 Henry Rodriguez	.50	.23	.06

1995 Stadium Club Virtual Reality Members Only

These cards parallel the regular 1995 Stadium Club Stadium Club Virtual Reality cards. The only difference is that they all have a Stadium Club Members Only logo imprinted on the front. These cards were distributed as part of the package of material that members of the "Stadium Club Members Only" club received when they ordered the 1995 parallel master set.

	MINT	NRMT	EXC
COMPLETE FACT.SET (270)	100.00	45.00	12.50
COMMON CARD (1-270)	.25	.11	.03
*MEMBERS ONLY: 2X BASIC CARDS			

1995 Stadium Club Members Only

Topps produced a 50-card boxed set for each of the four major sports. With their club membership, members received one set of their choice and had the option of purchasing additional sets for $10.00 each. Player section was based on 1994 leaders from both leagues in various statistical categories. The five Finest cards (46-50) represent Topps' selection of the top rookies of 1994. The color action photos on the fronts have brightly-colored backgrounds and carry the distinctive Topps Stadium Club Members Only gold foil seal. The backs present a second color photo and player profile.

	MINT	NRMT	EXC
COMPLETE SET (50)	20.00	9.00	2.50
COMMON CARD (1-50)	.10	.05	.01
☐ 1 Moises Alou	.20	.09	.03
☐ 2 Jeff Bagwell	1.25	.55	.16
☐ 3 Albert Belle	1.50	.70	.19
☐ 4 Andy Benes	.10	.05	.01
☐ 5 Dante Bichette	.40	.18	.05
☐ 6 Craig Biggio	.20	.09	.03
☐ 7 Wade Boggs	.30	.14	.04
☐ 8 Barry Bonds	.75	.35	.09
☐ 9 Brett Butler	.10	.05	.01
☐ 10 Jose Canseco	.30	.14	.04
☐ 11 Joe Carter	.20	.09	.03
☐ 12 Vince Coleman	.10	.05	.01
☐ 13 Jeff Conine	.20	.09	.03
☐ 14 Cecil Fielder	.20	.09	.03
☐ 15 John Franco	.10	.05	.01
☐ 16 Julio Franco	.10	.05	.01
☐ 17 Travis Fryman	.20	.09	.03
☐ 18 Andres Galarraga	.30	.14	.04
☐ 19 Ken Griffey Jr.	3.00	1.35	.35
☐ 20 Marquis Grissom	.20	.09	.03
☐ 21 Tony Gwynn	1.50	.70	.19
☐ 22 Ken Hill	.10	.05	.01
☐ 23 Randy Johnson	.60	.25	.07
☐ 24 Lance Johnson	.10	.05	.01
☐ 25 Jimmy Key	.20	.09	.03
☐ 26 Chuck Knoblauch	.50	.23	.06
☐ 27 Ray Lankford	.20	.09	.03
☐ 28 Darren Lewis	.10	.05	.01
☐ 29 Kenny Lofton	.75	.35	.09
☐ 30 Greg Maddux	2.50	1.10	.30
☐ 31 Fred McGriff	.30	.14	.04
☐ 32 Kevin Mitchell	.10	.05	.01
☐ 33 Paul Molitor	.75	.35	.09
☐ 34 Hal Morris	.10	.05	.01
☐ 35 Paul O'Neill	.20	.09	.03
☐ 36 Rafael Palmeiro	.30	.14	.04
☐ 37 Tony Phillips	.10	.05	.01
☐ 38 Mike Piazza	2.50	1.10	.30
☐ 39 Kirby Puckett	1.50	.70	.19
☐ 40 Cal Ripken	3.00	1.35	.35
☐ 41 Deion Sanders	.30	.14	.04
☐ 42 Lee Smith	.20	.09	.03
☐ 43 Frank Thomas	3.00	1.35	.35
☐ 44 Larry Walker	.50	.23	.06
☐ 45 Matt Williams	.30	.14	.04
☐ 46 Manny Ramirez	.75	.35	.09
☐ 47 Joey Hamilton	.30	.14	.04
☐ 48 Raul Mondesi	.30	.14	.04
☐ 49 Bob Hamelin	.10	.05	.01
☐ 50 Ryan Klesko	.30	.14	.04

1995 Stadium Club Members Only Finest Bronze

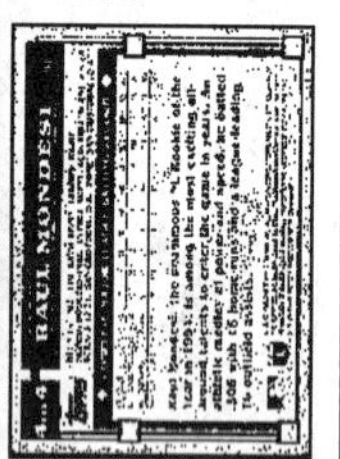

As a special bonus along with the complete 1995 Stadium Club Members Only factory set, members received these four cards featuring the 1994 Rookie of the Year and Cy Young Award Winners. The first shipment included series 1 and 2 cards as well as two of the Finest Bronze cards. The second shipment included series 3 cards and the remaining two Finest Bronze cards. The cards feature chromium metallized graphics, mounted on bronze and factory sealed in clear resin. Also, collectors got one of thsese cards if they only ordered one series. Bob Hamelin (series 1), Greg Maddux (Series 2) and David Cone (series 3). Mondesi was only available if one bought a complete set.

	MINT	NRMT	EXC
COMPLETE SET (4)	50.00	22.00	6.25
COMMON CARD (1-4)	3.00	1.35	.35
☐ 1 Bob Hamelin	3.00	1.35	.35
☐ 2 Greg Maddux	40.00	18.00	5.00
☐ 3 David Cone	5.00	2.20	.60
☐ 4 Raul Mondesi	10.00	4.50	1.25

1996 Stadium Club

The 1996 Stadium Club set consists of 450 cards. The product was primarily distributed in first and second series foil-wrapped packs.There was also a factory set, which included the Mantle insert

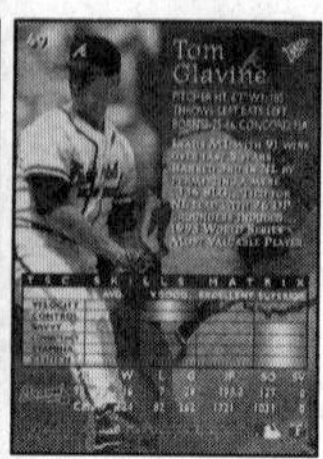

cards, packaged in cereal box type cartons and made available through retail outlets. Card fronts feature glossy, full-bleed color action photos. At the bottom, the player's name is gold foil stamped on a team color-coded nameplate that is highlighted by gold foil stamping. The colorful backs carry biography, highlights, and the TSC Skills Matrix. The set includes a Team TSC subset (181-270). These subset cards were slightly shortprinted in comparison to the other cards in the set.

	MINT	NRMT	EXC
COMPLETE SET (450)	70.00	32.00	8.75
COMP.CEREAL FACT.SET (454)	80.00	36.00	10.00
COMPLETE SERIES 1 (225)	35.00	16.00	4.40
COMPLETE SERIES 2 (225)	35.00	16.00	4.40
COMMON CARD (1-180/271-450)	.10	.05	.01
COMMON TSC SP (181-270)	.25	.11	.03
☐ 1 Hideo Nomo	.75	.35	.09
☐ 2 Paul Molitor	.60	.25	.07
☐ 3 Garret Anderson	.50	.23	.06
☐ 4 Jose Mesa	.25	.11	.03
☐ 5 Vinny Castilla	.25	.11	.03
☐ 6 Mike Mussina	.60	.25	.07
☐ 7 Ray Durham	.50	.23	.06
☐ 8 Jack McDowell	.50	.23	.06
☐ 9 Juan Gonzalez	1.50	.70	.19
☐ 10 Chipper Jones	2.00	.90	.25
☐ 11 Deion Sanders	.50	.23	.06
☐ 12 Rondell White	.25	.11	.03
☐ 13 Tom Henke	.25	.11	.03
☐ 14 Derek Bell	.25	.11	.03
☐ 15 Randy Myers	.10	.05	.01
☐ 16 Randy Johnson	.50	.23	.06
☐ 17 Len Dykstra	.25	.11	.03
☐ 18 Bill Pulsipher	.25	.11	.03
☐ 19 Greg Colbrunn	.10	.05	.01
☐ 20 David Wells	.10	.05	.01
☐ 21 Chad Curtis	.10	.05	.01
☐ 22 Roberto Hernandez	.25	.11	.03
☐ 23 Kirby Puckett	1.25	.55	.16
☐ 24 Joe Vitiello	.10	.05	.01
☐ 25 Roger Clemens	.60	.25	.07
☐ 26 Al Martin	.10	.05	.01
☐ 27 Chad Ogea	.10	.05	.01
☐ 28 David Segui	.10	.05	.01
☐ 29 Joey Hamilton	.25	.11	.03
☐ 30 Dan Wilson	.10	.05	.01
☐ 31 Chad Fonville	.10	.05	.01
☐ 32 Bernard Gilkey	.25	.11	.03
☐ 33 Kevin Seitzer	.10	.05	.01
☐ 34 Shawn Green	.25	.11	.03
☐ 35 Rick Aguilera	.10	.05	.01
☐ 36 Gary DiSarcina	.10	.05	.01
☐ 37 Jaime Navarro	.10	.05	.01
☐ 38 Doug Jones	.10	.05	.01
☐ 39 Brent Gates	.10	.05	.01
☐ 40 Dean Palmer	.50	.23	.06
☐ 41 Pat Rapp	.10	.05	.01
☐ 42 Tony Clark	.60	.25	.07
☐ 43 Bill Swift	.10	.05	.01
☐ 44 Randy Velarde	.10	.05	.01
☐ 45 Matt Williams	.50	.23	.06
☐ 46 John Mabry	.25	.11	.03
☐ 47 Mike Fetters	.10	.05	.01
☐ 48 Orlando Miller	.10	.05	.01
☐ 49 Tom Glavine	.50	.23	.06
☐ 50 Delino DeShields	.10	.05	.01
☐ 51 Scott Erickson	.10	.05	.01
☐ 52 Andy Van Slyke	.25	.11	.03
☐ 53 Jim Bullinger	.10	.05	.01
☐ 54 Lyle Mouton	.10	.05	.01
☐ 55 Bret Saberhagen	.10	.05	.01
☐ 56 Benito Santiago	.10	.05	.01
☐ 57 Dan Miceli	.10	.05	.01
☐ 58 Carl Everett	.10	.05	.01
☐ 59 Rod Beck	.10	.05	.01
☐ 60 Phil Nevin	.10	.05	.01
☐ 61 Jason Giambi	.50	.23	.06
☐ 62 Paul Menhart	.10	.05	.01
☐ 63 Eric Karros	.25	.11	.03
☐ 64 Allen Watson	.10	.05	.01
☐ 65 Jeff Cirillo	.10	.05	.01
☐ 66 Lee Smith	.25	.11	.03
☐ 67 Sean Berry	.10	.05	.01
☐ 68 Luis Sojo	.10	.05	.01
☐ 69 Jeff Montgomery	.10	.05	.01
☐ 70 Todd Hundley	.25	.11	.03
☐ 71 John Burkett	.10	.05	.01
☐ 72 Mark Gubicza	.10	.05	.01
☐ 73 Don Mattingly	1.50	.70	.19
☐ 74 Jeff Brantley	.10	.05	.01
☐ 75 Matt Walbeck	.10	.05	.01
☐ 76 Steve Parris	.10	.05	.01
☐ 77 Ken Caminiti	.50	.23	.06
☐ 78 Kirt Manwaring	.10	.05	.01
☐ 79 Greg Vaughn	.50	.23	.06
☐ 80 Pedro Martinez	.25	.11	.03
☐ 81 Benji Gil	.10	.05	.01
☐ 82 Heathcliff Slocumb	.10	.05	.01
☐ 83 Joe Girardi	.10	.05	.01
☐ 84 Sean Bergman	.10	.05	.01
☐ 85 Matt Karchner	.10	.05	.01
☐ 86 Butch Huskey	.25	.11	.03
☐ 87 Mike Morgan	.10	.05	.01
☐ 88 Todd Worrell	.25	.11	.03
☐ 89 Mike Bordick	.10	.05	.01
☐ 90 Bip Roberts	.10	.05	.01
☐ 91 Mike Hampton	.10	.05	.01
☐ 92 Troy O'Leary	.10	.05	.01
☐ 93 Wally Joyner	.10	.05	.01
☐ 94 Dave Stevens	.10	.05	.01
☐ 95 Cecil Fielder	.25	.11	.03
☐ 96 Wade Boggs	.50	.23	.06
☐ 97 Hal Morris	.10	.05	.01
☐ 98 Mickey Tettleton	.25	.11	.03
☐ 99 Jeff Kent	.10	.05	.01
☐ 100 Denny Martinez	.25	.11	.03
☐ 101 Luis Gonzalez	.10	.05	.01
☐ 102 John Jaha	.25	.11	.03
☐ 103 Javier Lopez	.50	.23	.06
☐ 104 Mark McGwire	1.00	.45	.12
☐ 105 Ken Griffey Jr.	3.00	1.35	.35
☐ 106 Darren Daulton	.25	.11	.03
☐ 107 Bryan Rekar	.10	.05	.01
☐ 108 Mike Macfarlane	.10	.05	.01
☐ 109 Gary Gaetti	.25	.11	.03
☐ 110 Shane Reynolds	.10	.05	.01
☐ 111 Pat Meares	.10	.05	.01
☐ 112 Jason Schmidt	.50	.23	.06
☐ 113 Otis Nixon	.10	.05	.01
☐ 114 John Franco	.10	.05	.01
☐ 115 Marc Newfield	.25	.11	.03
☐ 116 Andy Benes	.10	.05	.01
☐ 117 Ozzie Guillen	.10	.05	.01
☐ 118 Brian Jordan	.25	.11	.03
☐ 119 Terry Pendleton	.10	.05	.01
☐ 120 Chuck Finley	.10	.05	.01
☐ 121 Scott Stahoviak	.10	.05	.01
☐ 122 Sid Fernandez	.10	.05	.01
☐ 123 Derek Jeter	2.00	.90	.25
☐ 124 John Smiley	.10	.05	.01
☐ 125 David Bell	.10	.05	.01
☐ 126 Brett Butler	.10	.05	.01
☐ 127 Doug Drabek	.10	.05	.01
☐ 128 J.T. Snow	.25	.11	.03
☐ 129 Joe Carter	.25	.11	.03
☐ 130 Dennis Eckersley	.25	.11	.03
☐ 131 Marty Cordova	.25	.11	.03
☐ 132 Greg Maddux	2.00	.90	.25
☐ 133 Tom Goodwin	.25	.11	.03
☐ 134 Andy Ashby	.10	.05	.01
☐ 135 Paul Sorrento	.10	.05	.01
☐ 136 Ricky Bones	.10	.05	.01
☐ 137 Shawon Dunston	.10	.05	.01
☐ 138 Moises Alou	.25	.11	.03
☐ 139 Mickey Morandini	.10	.05	.01
☐ 140 Ramon Martinez	.25	.11	.03
☐ 141 Royce Clayton	.10	.05	.01
☐ 142 Brad Ausmus	.10	.05	.01
☐ 143 Kenny Rogers	.10	.05	.01
☐ 144 Tim Naehring	.10	.05	.01
☐ 145 Chris Gomez	.10	.05	.01
☐ 146 Bobby Bonilla	.25	.11	.03
☐ 147 Wilson Alvarez	.50	.23	.06
☐ 148 Johnny Damon	.25	.11	.03
☐ 149 Pat Hentgen	.25	.11	.03
☐ 150 Andres Galarraga	.50	.23	.06
☐ 151 David Cone	.25	.11	.03
☐ 152 Lance Johnson	.25	.11	.03
☐ 153 Carlos Garcia	.10	.05	.01
☐ 154 Doug Johns	.10	.05	.01
☐ 155 Midre Cummings	.10	.05	.01
☐ 156 Steve Sparks	.10	.05	.01
☐ 157 Sandy Martinez	.10	.05	.01
☐ 158 Wm. Van Landingham	.10	.05	.01
☐ 159 David Justice	.50	.23	.06
☐ 160 Mark Grace	.50	.23	.06
☐ 161 Robb Nen	.10	.05	.01
☐ 162 Mike Greenwell	.10	.05	.01
☐ 163 Brad Radke	.10	.05	.01
☐ 164 Edgardo Alfonzo	.25	.11	.03
☐ 165 Mark Leiter	.10	.05	.01
☐ 166 Walt Weiss	.10	.05	.01
☐ 167 Mel Rojas	.25	.11	.03
☐ 168 Bret Boone	.10	.05	.01
☐ 169 Ricky Bottalico	.10	.05	.01
☐ 170 Bobby Higginson	.25	.11	.03
☐ 171 Trevor Hoffman	.25	.11	.03
☐ 172 Jay Bell	.10	.05	.01
☐ 173 Gabe White	.10	.05	.01
☐ 174 Curtis Goodwin	.10	.05	.01
☐ 175 Tyler Green	.10	.05	.01
☐ 176 Roberto Alomar	.60	.25	.07
☐ 177 Sterling Hitchcock	.10	.05	.01
☐ 178 Ryan Klesko	.50	.23	.06
☐ 179 Donne Wall	.10	.05	.01
☐ 180 Brian McRae	.10	.05	.01

□ 181 Will Clark TSC SP	.50	.23	.06
□ 182 Frank Thomas TSC SP	4.00	1.80	.50
□ 183 Jeff Bagwell TSC SP	1.50	.70	.19
□ 184 Mo Vaughn TSC SP	1.00	.45	.12
□ 185 Tino Martinez TSC SP	.25	.11	.03
□ 186 Craig Biggio TSC SP	.25	.11	.03
□ 187 Chuck Knoblauch TSC SP	.50	.23	.06
□ 188 Carlos Baerga TSC SP	.25	.11	.03
□ 189 Quilvio Veras TSC SP	.25	.11	.03
□ 190 Luis Alicea TSC SP	.25	.11	.03
□ 191 Jim Thome TSC SP	.75	.35	.09
□ 192 Mike Blowers TSC SP	.25	.11	.03
□ 193 Robin Ventura TSC SP	.25	.11	.03
□ 194 Jeff King TSC SP	.25	.11	.03
□ 195 Tony Phillips TSC SP	.25	.11	.03
□ 196 John Valentin TSC SP	.50	.23	.06
□ 197 Barry Larkin TSC SP	.50	.23	.06
□ 198 Cal Ripken TSC SP	3.00	1.35	.35
□ 199 Omar Vizquel TSC SP	.25	.11	.03
□ 200 Kurt Abbott TSC SP	.25	.11	.03
□ 201 Albert Belle TSC SP	2.00	.90	.25
□ 202 Barry Bonds TSC SP	1.00	.45	.12
□ 203 Ron Gant TSC SP	.25	.11	.03
□ 204 Dante Bichette TSC SP	.50	.23	.06
□ 205 Jeff Conine TSC SP	.25	.11	.03
□ 206 Jim Edmonds TSC SP UER	.25	.11	.03
Greg Myers pictured on front			
□ 207 Stan Javier TSC SP	.25	.11	.03
□ 208 Kenny Lofton TSC SP	1.00	.45	.12
□ 209 Ray Lankford TSC SP	.25	.11	.03
□ 210 Bernie Williams TSC SP	.60	.25	.07
□ 211 Jay Buhner TSC SP	.50	.23	.06
□ 212 Paul O'Neill TSC SP	.10	.05	.01
□ 213 Tim Salmon TSC SP	.50	.23	.06
□ 214 Reggie Sanders TSC SP	.25	.11	.03
□ 215 Manny Ramirez TSC SP	1.00	.45	.12
□ 216 Mike Piazza TSC SP	2.50	1.10	.30
□ 217 Mike Stanley TSC SP	.25	.11	.03
□ 218 Tony Eusebio TSC SP	.25	.11	.03
□ 219 Chris Hoiles TSC SP	.25	.11	.03
□ 220 Ron Karkovice TSC SP	.25	.11	.03
□ 221 Edgar Martinez TSC SP	.25	.11	.03
□ 222 Chili Davis TSC SP	.50	.23	.06
□ 223 Jose Canseco TSC SP	.50	.23	.06
□ 224 Eddie Murray TSC SP	1.00	.45	.12
□ 225 Geronimo Berroa TSC SP	.25	.11	.03
□ 226 Chipper Jones TSC SP	2.50	1.10	.30
□ 227 Garret Anderson TSC SP	.50	.23	.06
□ 228 Marty Cordova TSC SP	.25	.11	.03
□ 229 Jon Nunnally TSC SP	.25	.11	.03
□ 230 Brian L.Hunter TSC SP	.25	.11	.03
□ 231 Shawn Green TSC SP	.25	.11	.03
□ 232 Ray Durham TSC SP	.50	.23	.06
□ 233 Alex Gonzalez TSC SP	.25	.11	.03
□ 234 Bobby Higginson TSC SP	.25	.11	.03
□ 235 Randy Johnson TSC SP	.50	.23	.06
□ 236 Al Leiter TSC SP	.25	.11	.03
□ 237 Tom Glavine TSC SP	.50	.23	.06
□ 238 Kenny Rogers TSC SP	.25	.11	.03
□ 239 Mike Hampton TSC SP	.25	.11	.03
□ 240 David Wells TSC SP	.25	.11	.03
□ 241 Jim Abbott TSC SP	.50	.23	.06
□ 242 Denny Neagle TSC SP	.25	.11	.03
□ 243 Wilson Alvarez TSC SP	.50	.23	.06
□ 244 John Smiley TSC SP	.25	.11	.03
□ 245 Greg Maddux TSC SP	2.50	1.10	.30
□ 246 Andy Ashby TSC SP	.25	.11	.03
□ 247 Hideo Nomo TSC SP	1.00	.45	.12
□ 248 Pat Rapp TSC SP	.25	.11	.03
□ 249 Tim Wakefield TSC SP	.25	.11	.03
□ 250 John Smoltz TSC SP	.60	.25	.07
□ 251 Joey Hamilton TSC SP	.25	.11	.03
□ 252 Frank Castillo TSC SP	.25	.11	.03
□ 253 Denny Martinez TSC SP	.25	.11	.03
□ 254 Jaime Navarro TSC SP	.25	.11	.03
□ 255 Karim Garcia TSC SP	.75	.35	.09
□ 256 Bob Abreu TSC SP	.50	.23	.06
□ 257 Butch Huskey TSC SP	.50	.23	.06
□ 258 Ruben Rivera TSC SP	.75	.35	.09
□ 259 Johnny Damon TSC SP	.25	.11	.03
□ 260 Derek Jeter TSC SP	2.50	1.10	.30
□ 261 Dennis Eckersley TSC SP	.25	.11	.03
□ 262 Jose Mesa TSC SP	.25	.11	.03
□ 263 Tom Henke TSC SP	.25	.11	.03
□ 264 Rick Aguilera TSC SP	.25	.11	.03
□ 265 Randy Myers TSC SP	.25	.11	.03
□ 266 John Franco TSC SP	.10	.05	.01
□ 267 Jeff Brantley TSC SP	.25	.11	.03
□ 268 John Wetteland TSC SP	.25	.11	.03
□ 269 Mark Wohlers TSC SP	.25	.11	.03
□ 270 Rod Beck TSC SP	.25	.11	.03
□ 271 Barry Larkin	.50	.23	.06
□ 272 Paul O'Neill	.10	.05	.01
□ 273 Bobby Jones	.10	.05	.01
□ 274 Will Clark	.50	.23	.06
□ 275 Steve Avery	.25	.11	.03
□ 276 Jim Edmonds	.25	.11	.03
□ 277 John Olerud	.10	.05	.01
□ 278 Carlos Perez	.10	.05	.01
□ 279 Chris Hoiles	.10	.05	.01
□ 280 Jeff Conine	.25	.11	.03
□ 281 Jim Eisenreich	.10	.05	.01
□ 282 Jason Jacome	.10	.05	.01
□ 283 Ray Lankford	.25	.11	.03
□ 284 John Wasdin	.10	.05	.01

□ 285 Frank Thomas	3.00	1.35	.35
□ 286 Jason Isringhausen	.50	.23	.06
□ 287 Glenallen Hill	.25	.11	.03
□ 288 Esteban Loaiza	.10	.05	.01
□ 289 Bernie Williams	.60	.25	.07
□ 290 Curtis Leskanic	.10	.05	.01
□ 291 Scott Cooper	.10	.05	.01
□ 292 Curt Schilling	.10	.05	.01
□ 293 Eddie Murray	.75	.35	.09
□ 294 Rick Krivda	.10	.05	.01
□ 295 Domingo Cedeno	.10	.05	.01
□ 296 Jeff Fassero	.10	.05	.01
□ 297 Albert Belle	1.25	.55	.16
□ 298 Craig Biggio	.25	.11	.03
□ 299 Fernando Vina	.10	.05	.01
□ 300 Edgar Martinez	.25	.11	.03
□ 301 Tony Gwynn	1.25	.55	.16
□ 302 Felipe Lira	.10	.05	.01
□ 303 Mo Vaughn	.75	.35	.09
□ 304 Alex Fernandez	.25	.11	.03
□ 305 Keith Lockhart	.10	.05	.01
□ 306 Roger Pavlik	.10	.05	.01
□ 307 Lee Tinsley	.10	.05	.01
□ 308 Omar Vizquel	.25	.11	.03
□ 309 Scott Servais	.10	.05	.01
□ 310 Danny Tartabull	.10	.05	.01
□ 311 Chili Davis	.10	.05	.01
□ 312 Cal Eldred	.10	.05	.01
□ 313 Roger Cedeno	.10	.05	.01
□ 314 Chris Hammond	.10	.05	.01
□ 315 Rusty Greer	.50	.23	.06
□ 316 Brady Anderson	.50	.23	.06
□ 317 Ron Villone	.10	.05	.01
□ 318 Mark Carreon	.10	.05	.01
□ 319 Larry Walker	.50	.23	.06
□ 320 Pete Harnisch	.10	.05	.01
□ 321 Robin Ventura	.25	.11	.03
□ 322 Tim Belcher	.10	.05	.01
□ 323 Tony Tarasco	.10	.05	.01
□ 324 Juan Guzman	.10	.05	.01
□ 325 Kenny Lofton	.75	.35	.09
□ 326 Kevin Foster	.10	.05	.01
□ 327 Wil Cordero	.10	.05	.01
□ 328 Troy Percival	.25	.11	.03
□ 329 Turk Wendell	.25	.11	.03
□ 330 Thomas Howard	.10	.05	.01
□ 331 Carlos Baerga	.25	.11	.03
□ 332 B.J. Surhoff	.10	.05	.01
□ 333 Jay Buhner	.50	.23	.06
□ 334 Andujar Cedeno	.10	.05	.01
□ 335 Jeff King	.25	.11	.03
□ 336 Dante Bichette	.50	.23	.06
□ 337 Alan Trammell	.25	.11	.03
□ 338 Scott Leius	.10	.05	.01
□ 339 Chris Snopek	.10	.05	.01
□ 340 Roger Bailey	.10	.05	.01
□ 341 Jacob Brumfield	.10	.05	.01
□ 342 Jose Canseco	.50	.23	.06
□ 343 Rafael Palmeiro	.50	.23	.06
□ 344 Quilvio Veras	.10	.05	.01
□ 345 Darrin Fletcher	.10	.05	.01
□ 346 Carlos Delgado	.25	.11	.03
□ 347 Tony Eusebio	.10	.05	.01
□ 348 Ismael Valdes	.25	.11	.03
□ 349 Terry Steinbach	.25	.11	.03
□ 350 Orel Hershiser	.25	.11	.03
□ 351 Kurt Abbott	.10	.05	.01
□ 352 Jody Reed	.10	.05	.01
□ 353 David Howard	.10	.05	.01
□ 354 Ruben Sierra	.10	.05	.01
□ 355 John Ericks	.10	.05	.01
□ 356 Buck Showalter MG	.10	.05	.01
□ 357 Jim Thome	.60	.25	.07
□ 358 Geronimo Berroa	.25	.11	.03
□ 359 Robby Thompson	.10	.05	.01
□ 360 Jose Vizcaino	.10	.05	.01
□ 361 Jeff Frye	.10	.05	.01
□ 362 Kevin Appier	.25	.11	.03
□ 363 Pat Kelly	.10	.05	.01
□ 364 Ron Gant	.25	.11	.03
□ 365 Luis Alicea	.10	.05	.01
□ 366 Armando Benitez	.10	.05	.01
□ 367 Rico Brogna	.10	.05	.01
□ 368 Manny Ramirez	.75	.35	.09
□ 369 Mike Lansing	.10	.05	.01
□ 370 Sammy Sosa	.50	.23	.06
□ 371 Don Wengert	.10	.05	.01
□ 372 Dave Nilsson	.25	.11	.03
□ 373 Sandy Alomar	.10	.05	.01
□ 374 Joey Cora	.10	.05	.01
□ 375 Larry Thomas	.10	.05	.01
□ 376 John Valentin	.25	.11	.03
□ 377 Kevin Ritz	.10	.05	.01
□ 378 Steve Finley	.50	.23	.06
□ 379 Frank Rodriguez	.25	.11	.03
□ 380 Ivan Rodriguez	.75	.35	.09
□ 381 Alex Ochoa	.25	.11	.03
□ 382 Mark Lemke	.10	.05	.01
□ 383 Scott Brosius	.25	.11	.03
□ 384 James Mouton	.10	.05	.01
□ 385 Mark Langston	.10	.05	.01
□ 386 Ed Sprague	.25	.11	.03
□ 387 Joe Oliver	.10	.05	.01
□ 388 Steve Ontiveros	.10	.05	.01
□ 389 Rey Sanchez	.10	.05	.01

□ 390 Mike Henneman	.10	.05	.01
□ 391 Jose Valentin	.10	.05	.01
□ 392 Tom Candiotti	.10	.05	.01
□ 393 Damon Buford	.10	.05	.01
□ 394 Erik Hanson	.10	.05	.01
□ 395 Mark Smith	.10	.05	.01
□ 396 Pete Schourek	.10	.05	.01
□ 397 John Flaherty	.10	.05	.01
□ 398 Dave Martinez	.10	.05	.01
□ 399 Tommy Greene	.10	.05	.01
□ 400 Gary Sheffield	.50	.23	.06
□ 401 Glenn Dishman	.10	.05	.01
□ 402 Barry Bonds	.75	.35	.09
□ 403 Tom Pagnozzi	.10	.05	.01
□ 404 Todd Stottlemyre	.10	.05	.01
□ 405 Tim Salmon	.50	.23	.06
□ 406 John Hudek	.10	.05	.01
□ 407 Fred McGriff	.50	.23	.06
□ 408 Orlando Merced	.10	.05	.01
□ 409 Brian Barber	.10	.05	.01
□ 410 Ryan Thompson	.10	.05	.01
□ 411 Mariano Rivera	.25	.11	.03
□ 412 Eric Young	.25	.11	.03
□ 413 Chris Bosio	.10	.05	.01
□ 414 Chuck Knoblauch	.50	.23	.06
□ 415 Jamie Moyer	.10	.05	.01
□ 416 Chan Ho Park	.50	.23	.06
□ 417 Mark Portugal	.10	.05	.01
□ 418 Tim Raines	.50	.23	.06
□ 419 Antonio Osuna	.10	.05	.01
□ 420 Todd Zeile	.25	.11	.03
□ 421 Steve Wojciechowski	.10	.05	.01
□ 422 Marquis Grissom	.25	.11	.03
□ 423 Norm Charlton	.10	.05	.01
□ 424 Cal Ripken	2.50	1.10	.30
□ 425 Gregg Jefferies	.50	.23	.06
□ 426 Mike Stanton	.10	.05	.01
□ 427 Tony Fernandez	.25	.11	.03
□ 428 Jose Rijo	.10	.05	.01
□ 429 Jeff Bagwell	1.25	.55	.16
□ 430 Raul Mondesi	.50	.23	.06
□ 431 Travis Fryman	.25	.11	.03
□ 432 Ron Karkovice	.10	.05	.01
□ 433 Alan Benes	.50	.23	.06
□ 434 Tony Phillips	.10	.05	.01
□ 435 Reggie Sanders	.25	.11	.03
□ 436 Andy Pettitte	1.00	.45	.12
□ 437 Matt Lawton	.10	.05	.01
□ 438 Jeff Blauser	.10	.05	.01
□ 439 Michael Tucker	.25	.11	.03
□ 440 Mark Loretta	.10	.05	.01
□ 441 Charlie Hayes	.10	.05	.01
□ 442 Mike Piazza	2.00	.90	.25
□ 443 Shane Andrews	.10	.05	.01
□ 444 Jeff Suppan	.50	.23	.06
□ 445 Steve Rodriguez	.10	.05	.01
□ 446 Mike Matheny	.10	.05	.01
□ 447 Trenidad Hubbard	.10	.05	.01
□ 448 Denny Hocking	.25	.11	.03
□ 449 Mark Grudzielanek	.25	.11	.03
□ 450 Joe Randa	.10	.05	.01

1996 Stadium Club Members Only Parallel

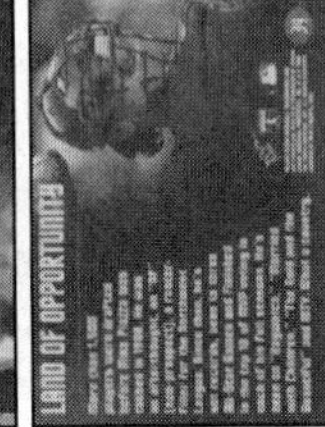

This set, of which only 750 were produced is a parallel to the regular 1996 Stadium Club set. The cards are embossed with a "Members Only" logo and were available only to members of Topps' Stadium Club. The set includes a parallel of the complete 450-card basic set plus the following inserts: Bash and Burn, Mickey Mantle Heroes, Megaheroes, Metalists, Midsummer Matchups, Power Packed, Power Streak, Prime Cuts and TSC Awards. Only the inserts cards are priced below. Please refer to the multiplier for value on parallels to the basic issue cards.

	MINT	NRMT	EXC
COMP.SET W/INSERTS (555)	500.00	220.00	60.00
COMPLETE BASE SET (450)	200.00	90.00	25.00
COMMON CARD (1-450)	.25	.11	.03
COMMON MANTLE (M1-M19)	5.00	2.20	.60
*MEMBERS ONLY: 6X BASIC CARDS			
□ M1 Jeff Bagwell	8.00	3.60	1.00
□ M2 Barry Bonds	5.00	2.20	.60
□ M3 Jose Canseco	2.50	1.10	.30
□ M4 Roger Clemens	4.00	1.80	.50
□ M5 Dennis Eckersley	1.00	.45	.12
□ M6 Greg Maddux	20.00	9.00	2.50
□ M7 Cal Ripken	20.00	9.00	2.50
□ M8 Frank Thomas	20.00	9.00	2.50
□ BB1 Sammy Sosa	3.00	1.35	.35
□ BB2 Barry Bonds	5.00	2.20	.60
□ BB3 Reggie Sanders	1.50	.70	.19
□ BB4 Craig Biggio	1.50	.70	.19
□ BB5 Raul Mondesi	1.50	.70	.19
□ BB6 Ron Gant	1.50	.70	.19
□ BB7 Ray Lankford	1.50	.70	.19
□ BB8 Glenallen Hill	1.00	.45	.12
□ BB9 Chad Curtis	1.00	.45	.12
□ BB10 John Valentin	1.00	.45	.12
□ MH1 Frank Thomas	20.00	9.00	2.50
□ MH2 Ken Griffey Jr.	20.00	9.00	2.50
□ MH3 Hideo Nomo	5.00	2.20	.60
□ MH4 Ozzie Smith	8.00	3.60	1.00
□ MH5 Will Clark	2.50	1.10	.30
□ MH6 Jack McDowell	1.00	.45	.12
□ MH7 Andres Galarraga	2.00	.90	.25
□ MH8 Roger Clemens	4.00	1.80	.50
□ MH9 Deion Sanders	2.00	.90	.25
□ MH10 Mo Vaughn	5.00	2.20	.60
□ MM1 Hideo Nomo Randy Johnson	6.00	2.70	.75
□ MM2 Mike Piazza Ivan Rodriguez	12.00	5.50	1.50
□ MM3 Fred McGriff Frank Thomas	20.00	9.00	2.50
□ MM4 Craig Biggio Carlos Baerga	2.00	.90	.25
□ MM5 Vinny Castilla Wade Boggs	2.50	1.10	.30
□ MM6 Barry Larkin Cal Ripken	20.00	9.00	2.50
□ MM7 Barry Bonds Albert Belle	12.00	5.50	1.50
□ MM8 Len Dykstra Kenny Lofton	5.00	2.20	.60
□ MM9 Tony Gwynn Kirby Puckett	12.00	5.50	1.50
□ MM10 Ron Gant Edgar Martinez	2.00	.90	.25
□ PC1 Albert Belle	10.00	4.50	1.25
□ PC2 Barry Bonds	5.00	2.20	.60
□ PC3 Ken Griffey Jr.	20.00	9.00	2.50
□ PC4 Tony Gwynn	10.00	4.50	1.25
□ PC5 Edgar Martinez	1.50	.70	.19
□ PC6 Rafael Palmeiro	2.00	.90	.25
□ PC7 Mike Piazza	12.00	5.50	1.50
□ PC8 Frank Thomas	20.00	9.00	2.50
□ PP1 Albert Belle	10.00	4.50	1.25
□ PP2 Mark McGwire	6.00	2.70	.75
□ PP3 Jose Canseco	2.50	1.10	.30
□ PP4 Mike Piazza	12.00	5.50	1.50
□ PP5 Ron Gant	1.50	.70	.19
□ PP6 Ken Griffey Jr.	20.00	9.00	2.50
□ PP7 Mo Vaughn	5.00	2.20	.60
□ PP8 Cecil Fielder	1.50	.70	.19
□ PP9 Tim Salmon	2.00	.90	.25
□ PP10 Frank Thomas	20.00	9.00	2.50
□ PP11 Juan Gonzalez	10.00	4.50	1.25
□ PP12 Andres Galarraga	2.00	.90	.25
□ PP13 Fred McGriff	2.00	.90	.25
□ PP14 Jay Buhner	2.00	.90	.25
□ PP15 Dante Bichette	2.00	.90	.25
□ PS1 Randy Johnson	4.00	1.80	.50
□ PS2 Hideo Nomo	5.00	2.20	.60
□ PS3 Albert Belle	10.00	4.50	1.25
□ PS4 Dante Bichette	2.00	.90	.25
□ PS5 Jay Buhner	2.00	.90	.25
□ PS6 Frank Thomas	20.00	9.00	2.50
□ PS7 Mark McGwire	6.00	2.70	.75
□ PS8 Rafael Palmeiro	2.00	.90	.25
□ PS9 Mo Vaughn	5.00	2.20	.60
□ PS10 Sammy Sosa	3.00	1.35	.35
□ PS11 Larry Walker	2.50	1.10	.30
□ PS12 Gary Gaetti	1.00	.45	.12
□ PS13 Tim Salmon	2.00	.90	.25
□ PS14 Barry Bonds	5.00	2.20	.60
□ PS15 Jim Edmonds	1.50	.70	.19
□ TSCA1 Cal Ripken	20.00	9.00	2.50
□ TSCA2 Albert Belle	10.00	4.50	1.25
□ TSCA3 Tom Glavine	2.00	.90	.25
□ TSCA4 Jeff Conine	1.50	.70	.19
□ TSCA5 Ken Griffey Jr.	20.00	9.00	2.50
□ TSCA6 Hideo Nomo	5.00	2.20	.60
□ TSCA7 Greg Maddux	15.00	6.75	1.85
□ TSCA8 Chipper Jones	15.00	6.75	1.85
□ TSCA9 Randy Johnson	4.00	1.80	.50
□ TSCA10 Jose Mesa	1.00	.45	.12

1996 Stadium Club Bash and Burn

Randomly inserted in packs at a rate of one in 29 (retail) and one in 48 (hobby), this ten card set features power/speed players. The fronts carry photos of the players hitting with a baseball background. The backs display photos of the same players running down the baseline on a background of flames.

	MINT	NRMT	EXC
COMPLETE SET (10)	30.00	13.50	3.70
COMMON CARD (BB1-BB10)	2.00	.90	.25
□ BB1 Sammy Sosa	8.00	3.60	1.00
□ BB2 Barry Bonds	12.00	5.50	1.50
□ BB3 Reggie Sanders	4.00	1.80	.50
□ BB4 Craig Biggio	4.00	1.80	.50
□ BB5 Raul Mondesi	6.00	2.70	.75

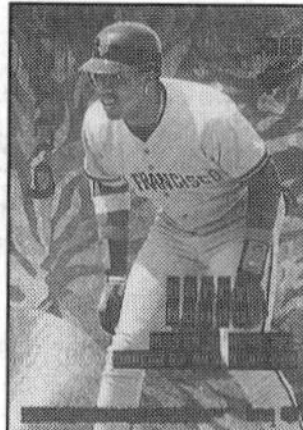

☐ BB6 Ron Gant	4.00	1.80	.50
☐ BB7 Ray Lankford	4.00	1.80	.50
☐ BB8 Glenallen Hill	2.00	.90	.25
☐ BB9 Chad Curtis	2.00	.90	.25
☐ BB10 John Valentin	4.00	1.80	.50

1996 Stadium Club Extreme Players Bronze

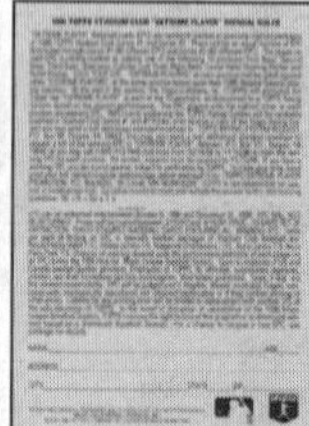

One hundred and seventy nine different players were featured on Extreme Player game cards randomly issued in 1996 Stadium Club first and second series packs. Each player has three versions: Bronze, Silver and Gold. All of these cards parallel their corresponding regular issue card except for the Bronze foil "Extreme Players" logo on each card front and the "EP" suffix on the card number, thus creating a skip-numbered set. The Bronze cards listed below were seeded at a rate of 1:12 packs. At the conclusion of the 1996 regular season, an Extreme Player from each of ten positions was identified as a winner based on scores calculated from their actual playing statistics. The 10 winning players are noted with a "W" below. Prior to the December 31st, 1996 deadline, each of the ten winning Extreme Players Bronze cards was redeemable for a 10-card set of Extreme Winners Bronze.

	MINT	NRMT	EXC
COMP.BRONZE SET (179)	250.00	110.00	31.00
COMP.BRONZE SER.1 (90)	125.00	55.00	15.50
COMP.BRONZE SER.2 (89)	125.00	55.00	15.50
COMMON BRONZE	.75	.35	.09

☐ 1 Hideo Nomo	4.00	1.80	.50
☐ 3 Garret Anderson	.75	.35	.09
☐ 4 Jose Mesa	.75	.35	.09
☐ 5 Vinny Castilla	1.50	.70	.19
☐ 6 Mike Mussina	3.00	1.35	.35
☐ 7 Ray Durham	.75	.35	.09
☐ 8 Jack McDowell	1.50	.70	.19
☐ 9 Juan Gonzalez	8.00	3.60	1.00
☐ 10 Chipper Jones	10.00	4.50	1.25
☐ 11 Deion Sanders	2.00	.90	.25
☐ 12 Rondell White	1.50	.70	.19
☐ 13 Tom Henke	.75	.35	.09
☐ 14 Derek Bell	1.50	.70	.19
☐ 15 Randy Myers	.75	.35	.09
☐ 16 Randy Johnson	2.50	1.10	.30
☐ 17 Len Dykstra	1.50	.70	.19
☐ 18 Bill Pulsipher	.75	.35	.09
☐ 21 Chad Curtis	.75	.35	.09
☐ 22 Roberto Hernandez	.75	.35	.09
☐ 23 Kirby Puckett	6.00	2.70	.75
☐ 25 Roger Clemens	3.00	1.35	.35
☐ 31 Chad Fonville	.75	.35	.09
☐ 32 Bernard Gilkey	1.50	.70	.19
☐ 34 Shawn Green	.75	.35	.09
☐ 35 Rick Aguilera	.75	.35	.09
☐ 40 Dean Palmer	1.50	.70	.19
☐ 45 Matt Williams	2.00	.90	.25
☐ 49 Tom Glavine	2.00	.90	.25
☐ 50 Delino DeShields	.75	.35	.09
☐ 56 Benito Santiago	.75	.35	.09
☐ 59 Rod Beck	.75	.35	.09
☐ 63 Eric Karros	1.50	.70	.19
☐ 66 Lee Smith	1.50	.70	.19
☐ 69 Jeff Montgomery	.75	.35	.09
☐ 70 Todd Hundley	1.50	.70	.19
☐ 73 Don Mattingly	8.00	3.60	1.00
☐ 77 Ken Caminiti W	5.00	2.20	.60
☐ 80 Pedro Martinez	1.50	.70	.19
☐ 82 Heathcliff Slocumb	.75	.35	.09
☐ 83 Joe Girardi	.75	.35	.09
☐ 88 Todd Worrell W	1.50	.70	.19
☐ 90 Bip Roberts	.75	.35	.09
☐ 95 Cecil Fielder	1.50	.70	.19
☐ 96 Wade Boggs	2.00	.90	.25
☐ 98 Mickey Tettleton	.75	.35	.09
☐ 99 Jeff Kent	.75	.35	.09
☐ 100 Denny Martinez	1.50	.70	.19
☐ 101 Luis Gonzalez	.75	.35	.09
☐ 103 Javy Lopez	1.50	.70	.19
☐ 104 Mark McGwire	5.00	2.20	.60
☐ 105 Ken Griffey Jr. W	30.00	13.50	3.70
☐ 106 Darren Daulton	1.50	.70	.19
☐ 108 Mike Macfarlane	.75	.35	.09
☐ 110 Shane Reynolds	.75	.35	.09
☐ 114 John Franco	.75	.35	.09
☐ 116 Andy Benes	.75	.35	.09
☐ 118 Brian Jordan	1.50	.70	.19
☐ 119 Terry Pendleton	1.50	.70	.19
☐ 120 Chuck Finley	.75	.35	.09
☐ 123 Derek Jeter	10.00	4.50	1.25
☐ 124 John Smiley	.75	.35	.09
☐ 126 Brett Butler	.75	.35	.09
☐ 127 Doug Drabek	.75	.35	.09
☐ 128 J.T. Snow	.75	.35	.09
☐ 129 Joe Carter	1.50	.70	.19
☐ 130 Dennis Eckersley	1.50	.70	.19
☐ 131 Marty Cordova	1.50	.70	.19
☐ 132 Greg Maddux W	25.00	11.00	3.10
☐ 135 Paul Sorrento	.75	.35	.09
☐ 137 Shawon Dunston	.75	.35	.09
☐ 138 Moises Alou	1.50	.70	.19
☐ 140 Ramon Martinez	1.50	.70	.19
☐ 141 Royce Clayton	.75	.35	.09
☐ 143 Kenny Rogers	.75	.35	.09
☐ 144 Tim Naehring	.75	.35	.09
☐ 145 Chris Gomez	.75	.35	.09
☐ 146 Bobby Bonilla	1.50	.70	.19
☐ 148 Johnny Damon	1.50	.70	.19
☐ 150 Andres Galarraga W	4.00	1.80	.50
☐ 151 David Cone	1.50	.70	.19
☐ 152 Lance Johnson	1.50	.70	.19
☐ 159 David Justice	1.50	.70	.19
☐ 160 Mark Grace	2.00	.90	.25
☐ 161 Robb Nen	.75	.35	.09
☐ 162 Mike Greenwell	.75	.35	.09
☐ 167 Mel Rojas	.75	.35	.09
☐ 168 Bret Boone	.75	.35	.09
☐ 172 Jay Bell	.75	.35	.09
☐ 176 Roberto Alomar	3.00	1.35	.35
☐ 178 Ryan Klesko	2.00	.90	.25
☐ 271 Barry Larkin W	4.00	1.80	.50
☐ 272 Paul O'Neill	.75	.35	.09
☐ 274 Will Clark	2.00	.90	.25
☐ 275 Steve Avery	.75	.35	.09
☐ 276 Jim Edmonds	1.50	.70	.19
☐ 277 John Olerud	.75	.35	.09
☐ 279 Chris Hoiles	.75	.35	.09
☐ 280 Jeff Conine	1.50	.70	.19
☐ 283 Ray Lankford	1.50	.70	.19
☐ 285 Frank Thomas	15.00	6.75	1.85
☐ 286 Jason Isringhausen	2.00	.90	.25
☐ 287 Glenallen Hill	.75	.35	.09
☐ 289 Bernie Williams	3.00	1.35	.35
☐ 290 Eddie Murray	4.00	1.80	.50
☐ 296 Jeff Fassero	.75	.35	.09
☐ 297 Albert Belle	6.00	2.70	.75
☐ 298 Craig Biggio	1.50	.70	.19
☐ 300 Edgar Martinez	1.50	.70	.19
☐ 301 Tony Gwynn	6.00	2.70	.75
☐ 303 Mo Vaughn	4.00	1.80	.50
☐ 304 Alex Fernandez	1.50	.70	.19
☐ 308 Omar Vizquel	1.50	.70	.19
☐ 310 Danny Tartabull	.75	.35	.09
☐ 316 Brady Anderson	2.00	.90	.25
☐ 319 Larry Walker	2.00	.90	.25
☐ 321 Robin Ventura	1.50	.70	.19
☐ 325 Kenny Lofton	4.00	1.80	.50
☐ 327 Wil Cordero	.75	.35	.09
☐ 328 Troy Percival	.75	.35	.09
☐ 331 Carlos Baerga	1.50	.70	.19
☐ 333 Jay Buhner	2.00	.90	.25
☐ 335 Jeff King	.75	.35	.09
☐ 336 Dante Bichette	2.00	.90	.25
☐ 337 Alan Trammell	1.50	.70	.19
☐ 342 Jose Canseco	2.00	.90	.25
☐ 343 Rafael Palmeiro	2.00	.90	.25
☐ 344 Quilvio Veras	.75	.35	.09
☐ 345 Darrin Fletcher	.75	.35	.09
☐ 347 Tony Eusebio	.75	.35	.09
☐ 348 Ismael Valdes	1.50	.70	.19
☐ 349 Terry Steinbach	1.50	.70	.19
☐ 350 Orel Hershiser	1.50	.70	.19
☐ 351 Kurt Abbott	.75	.35	.09
☐ 354 Ruben Sierra	.75	.35	.09
☐ 357 Jim Thome	3.00	1.35	.35
☐ 358 Geronimo Berroa	.75	.35	.09
☐ 359 Robby Thompson	.75	.35	.09
☐ 360 Jose Vizcaino	.75	.35	.09
☐ 362 Kevin Appier	1.50	.70	.19
☐ 364 Ron Gant	1.50	.70	.19
☐ 367 Rico Brogna	.75	.35	.09
☐ 368 Manny Ramirez	4.00	1.80	.50
☐ 370 Sammy Sosa	2.00	.90	.25
☐ 373 Sandy Alomar	.75	.35	.09
☐ 378 Steve Finley	1.50	.70	.19
☐ 380 Ivan Rodriguez	3.00	1.35	.35
☐ 382 Mark Lemke	.75	.35	.09
☐ 385 Mark Langston	.75	.35	.09
☐ 386 Ed Sprague	.75	.35	.09
☐ 388 Steve Ontiveros	.75	.35	.09
☐ 392 Tom Candiotti	.75	.35	.09
☐ 394 Erik Hanson	.75	.35	.09
☐ 396 Pete Schourek	.75	.35	.09
☐ 400 Gary Sheffield W	5.00	2.20	.60
☐ 402 Barry Bonds W	8.00	3.60	1.00
☐ 403 Tom Pagnozzi	.75	.35	.09
☐ 404 Todd Stottlemyre	.75	.35	.09
☐ 405 Tim Salmon	2.00	.90	.25
☐ 407 Fred McGriff	2.00	.90	.25
☐ 408 Orlando Merced	.75	.35	.09
☐ 412 Eric Young	1.50	.70	.19
☐ 414 Chuck Knoblauch W	5.00	2.20	.60
☐ 417 Mark Portugal	.75	.35	.09
☐ 418 Tim Raines	1.50	.70	.19
☐ 420 Todd Zeile	.75	.35	.09
☐ 422 Marquis Grissom	1.50	.70	.19
☐ 423 Norm Charlton	.75	.35	.09
☐ 424 Cal Ripken	12.00	5.50	1.50
☐ 425 Gregg Jefferies	1.50	.70	.19
☐ 428 Jose Rijo	.75	.35	.09
☐ 429 Jeff Bagwell	6.00	2.70	.75
☐ 430 Raul Mondesi	2.00	.90	.25
☐ 431 Travis Fryman	1.50	.70	.19
☐ 434 Tony Phillips	.75	.35	.09
☐ 435 Reggie Sanders	1.50	.70	.19
☐ 436 Andy Pettitte	5.00	2.20	.60
☐ 438 Jeff Blauser	.75	.35	.09
☐ 441 Charlie Hayes	.75	.35	.09
☐ 442 Mike Piazza W	20.00	9.00	2.50

1996 Stadium Club Extreme Players Gold

These Gold cards, randomly seeded into first and second series packs at a rate of 1:48, parallel the more common Bronze and Silver Extreme Players inserts. The Gold cards can be identified by their holographic gold "Extreme Players" logo on front. Prior to the December 31st, 1996 deadline, each of the the ten winning Extreme Players Gold cards were redeemable on a card for card basis for an attractive metal-based Finest-style gold upgrade card of the corresponding player.

	MINT	NRMT	EXC
COMPLETE SET (179)	800.00	350.00	100.00
COMPLETE SERIES 1 (90)	400.00	180.00	50.00
COMPLETE SERIES 2 (89)	400.00	180.00	50.00
COMMON CARD (1-179)	2.50	1.10	.30

*GOLD: 3X BRONZE EXTREME CARDS

1996 Stadium Club Extreme Players Silver

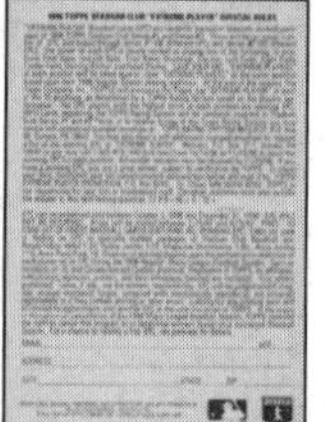

These Silver cards, randomly seeded into first and second series packs at a rate of 1:24, parallel the more common Bronze Extreme Players inserts. The Silver cards can be identified by their holographic silver "Extreme Players" logo on front. Prior to the December 31st, 1996 deadline, each of the the ten winning Extreme Players Silver cards were redeemable for an upgraded 10-card set of Extreme Winners Silver cards.

	MINT	NRMT	EXC
COMPLETE SET (179)	400.00	180.00	50.00
COMPLETE SERIES 1 (90)	200.00	90.00	25.00
COMPLETE SERIES 2 (89)	200.00	90.00	25.00
COMMON CARD (1-179)	1.25	.55	.16

*SILVER: 1.5X BRONZE EXTREME CARDS

1996 Stadium Club Extreme Winners Bronze

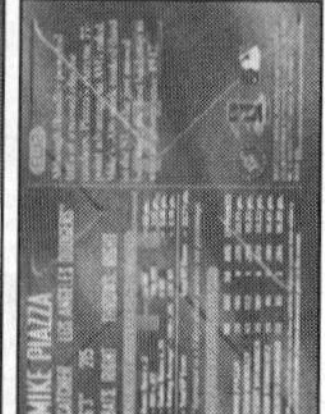

This 10-card skip-numbered set was only available to collectors who redeemed one of the ten winning Bronze Extreme Players cards before the December 31st, 1996 deadline. The cards parallel the Extreme Players cards inserted in Stadium Club packs except for their distinctive diffraction foil fronts.

	MINT	NRMT	EXC
COMPLETE SET (10)	25.00	11.00	3.10
COMMON CARD (EW1-EW10)	.50	.23	.06

☐ EW1 Greg Maddux	6.00	2.70	.75
☐ EW2 Mike Piazza	6.00	2.70	.75
☐ EW3 Andres Galarraga	1.25	.55	.16
☐ EW4 Chuck Knoblauch	1.50	.70	.19
☐ EW5 Ken Caminiti	1.50	.70	.19
☐ EW6 Barry Larkin	1.25	.55	.16
☐ EW7 Barry Bonds	2.50	1.10	.30
☐ EW8 Ken Griffey Jr.	10.00	4.50	1.25
☐ EW9 Gary Sheffield	1.50	.70	.19
☐ EW10 Todd Worrell	.50	.23	.06

1996 Stadium Club Extreme Winners Gold

Lucky collectors who mailed in a winning Extreme Players Gold card (randomly inserted in 1996 Stadium Club packs) received a beautiful glass-coated, metal-backed Finest style card of the same player in return. The Extreme Winners Gold cards are slightly larger than standard-sized cards and much thicker and heavier. Collectors started to receive the cards around early March, 1997.

	MINT	NRMT	EXC
COMPLETE SET (10)	400.00	180.00	50.00
COMMON CARD (EW1-EW10)	8.00	3.60	1.00

*STARS: 7.5X TO 15X BRONZE WINNERS

1996 Stadium Club Extreme Winners Silver

Lucky collectors who mailed in a winning Extreme Players Silver card (randomly inserted in 1996 Stadium Club packs) received a Finest style card of the same player in return. The Extreme Winners Silver cards are standard-sized and feature refractive silver backgrounds. Collectors started to receive the cards around early March, 1997.

	MINT	NRMT	EXC
COMPLETE SET (10)	75.00	34.00	9.50
COMMON CARD (EW1-EW10)	1.50	.70	.19

*STARS: 1.5X TO 3X BRONZE WINNERS

1996 Stadium Club Mantle

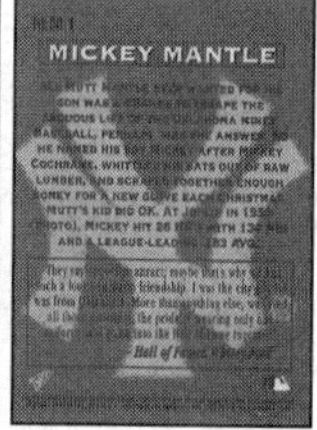

Randomly inserted at a rate of one card in every 24 packs in series 1, one in 12 packs in series 2, this 19-card retrospective set chronicles Mantle's career with classic photography, celebrity quotes and highlights from each year. The cards are double foil-stamped. The series 1 cards feature black-and-white photos, series 2 color photos. Mantle's name is printed across a silver foil facade of Yankee Stadium on each card top.

	MINT	NRMT	EXC
COMPLETE SET (19)	170.00	75.00	21.00
COMPLETE SERIES 1 (9)	110.00	50.00	14.00
COMPLETE SERIES 2 (10)	60.00	27.00	7.50
COMMON MANTLE (MM1-MM9)	14.00	6.25	1.75
COMMON MANTLE (MM10-MM-19)	8.00	3.60	1.00

☐ MM1 Mickey Mantle Batting Follow Through, 1950	14.00	6.25	1.75
☐ MM2 Mickey Mantle	14.00	6.25	1.75
☐ MM3 Mickey Mantle Locker room shot, 1951	14.00	6.25	1.75
☐ MM4 Mickey Mantle	14.00	6.25	1.75
☐ MM5 Mickey Mantle	14.00	6.25	1.75
☐ MM6 Mickey Mantle	14.00	6.25	1.75
☐ MM7 Mickey Mantle	14.00	6.25	1.75
☐ MM8 Mickey Mantle	14.00	6.25	1.75
☐ MM9 Mickey Mantle	14.00	6.25	1.75

Batting both ways, 1959			
☐ MM10 Mickey Mantle	8.00	3.60	1.00
☐ MM11 Mickey Mantle	8.00	3.60	1.00
Beating out hit, 1961			
☐ MM12 Mickey Mantle	8.00	3.60	1.00
Roger Maris 1961			
☐ MM13 Mickey Mantle	8.00	3.60	1.00
☐ MM14 Mickey Mantle	8.00	3.60	1.00
☐ MM15 Mickey Mantle	8.00	3.60	1.00
Smiling Pose, 1964			
☐ MM16 Mickey Mantle	8.00	3.60	1.00
☐ MM17 Mickey Mantle	8.00	3.60	1.00
☐ MM18 Mickey Mantle	8.00	3.60	1.00
☐ MM19 Mickey Mantle	8.00	3.60	1.00

1996 Stadium Club Megaheroes

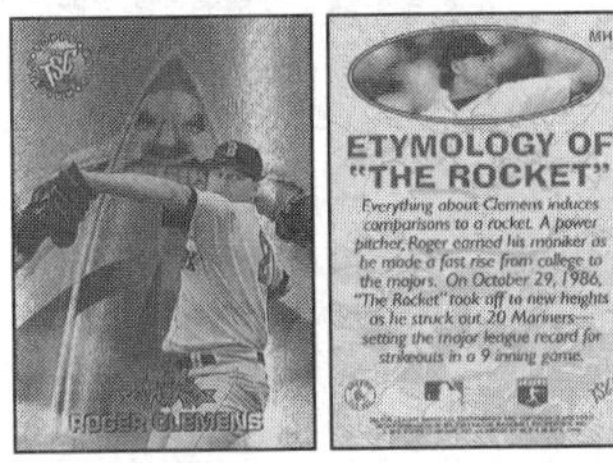

Randomly inserted at a rate of one in every 48 hobby and 24 retail packs, this 10-card set features super-heroic players matched with a comic book-style illustration depicting their nicknames. The fronts display a color player cutout superposed on diffraction foilboard illustrating the player's nickname. On a textured background, the backs present a closeup photo (in an oval format) and a career highlight in the form of an etymology of his nickname.

	MINT	NRMT	EXC
COMPLETE SET (10)	50.00	22.00	6.25
COMMON CARD (MH1-MH10)	1.50	.70	.19
☐ MH1 Frank Thomas	20.00	9.00	2.50
☐ MH2 Ken Griffey Jr.	20.00	9.00	2.50
☐ MH3 Hideo Nomo	5.00	2.20	.60
☐ MH4 Ozzie Smith	5.00	2.20	.60
☐ MH5 Will Clark	2.50	1.10	.30
☐ MH6 Jack McDowell	1.50	.70	.19
☐ MH7 Andres Galarraga	2.50	1.10	.30
☐ MH8 Roger Clemens	4.00	1.80	.50
☐ MH9 Deion Sanders	2.50	1.10	.30
☐ MH10 Mo Vaughn	5.00	2.20	.60

1996 Stadium Club Metalists

Randomly inserted in packs at a rate of one in 96 (retail) and one in 48 (hobby), this eight-card set features players with two or more MLB awards and is printed on laser-cut foil board.

	MINT	NRMT	EXC
COMPLETE SET (8)	50.00	22.00	6.25
COMMON CARD (M1-M8)	2.00	.90	.25
☐ M1 Jeff Bagwell	8.00	3.60	1.00
☐ M2 Barry Bonds	5.00	2.20	.60
☐ M3 Jose Canseco	3.00	1.35	.35
☐ M4 Roger Clemens	4.00	1.80	.50
☐ M5 Dennis Eckersley	2.00	.90	.25
☐ M6 Greg Maddux	12.00	5.50	1.50
☐ M7 Cal Ripken	15.00	6.75	1.85
☐ M8 Frank Thomas	20.00	9.00	2.50

1996 Stadium Club Midsummer Matchups

Randomly inserted at a rate of one in every 48 hobby and 24 retail packs, this 10-card set salutes 1995 National League and American League All-Stars as they are matched back-to-back by position on these two-sided etched foil cards. Each side features a color player cutout on a screened background of 1995 All-Star game emblems. On each side, the lower right corner is peeled back to reveal space for the American or National League logo.

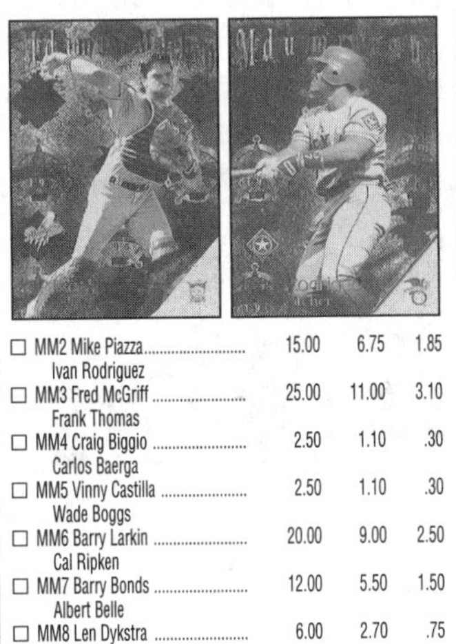

	MINT	NRMT	EXC
COMPLETE SET (10)	100.00	45.00	12.50
COMMON CARD (M1-M10)	2.50	1.10	.30
☐ MM1 Hideo Nomo	8.00	3.60	1.00
Randy Johnson			
☐ MM2 Mike Piazza	15.00	6.75	1.85
Ivan Rodriguez			
☐ MM3 Fred McGriff	25.00	11.00	3.10
Frank Thomas			
☐ MM4 Craig Biggio	2.50	1.10	.30
Carlos Baerga			
☐ MM5 Vinny Castilla	2.50	1.10	.30
Wade Boggs			
☐ MM6 Barry Larkin	20.00	9.00	2.50
Cal Ripken			
☐ MM7 Barry Bonds	12.00	5.50	1.50
Albert Belle			
☐ MM8 Len Dykstra	6.00	2.70	.75
Kenny Lofton			
☐ MM9 Tony Gwynn	20.00	9.00	2.50
Kirby Puckett			
☐ MM10 Ron Gant	2.50	1.10	.30
Edgar Martinez			

1996 Stadium Club Power Packed

Randomly inserted in packs at a rate of one in 48, this 15-card set features the biggest, most powerful hitters in the League. Printed on Power Matrix, the cards carry diagrams showing where the players hit the ball over the fence and how far.

	MINT	NRMT	EXC
COMPLETE SET (15)	80.00	36.00	10.00
COMMON CARD (PP1-PP15)	2.00	.90	.25
☐ PP1 Albert Belle	10.00	4.50	1.25
☐ PP2 Mark McGwire	8.00	3.60	1.00
☐ PP3 Jose Canseco	3.00	1.35	.35
☐ PP4 Mike Piazza	15.00	6.75	1.85
☐ PP5 Ron Gant	2.00	.90	.25
☐ PP6 Ken Griffey Jr.	25.00	11.00	3.10
☐ PP7 Mo Vaughn	6.00	2.70	.75
☐ PP8 Cecil Fielder	2.00	.90	.25
☐ PP9 Tim Salmon	3.00	1.35	.35
☐ PP10 Frank Thomas	25.00	11.00	3.10
☐ PP11 Juan Gonzalez	12.00	5.50	1.50
☐ PP12 Andres Galarraga	3.00	1.35	.35
☐ PP13 Fred McGriff	3.00	1.35	.35
☐ PP14 Jay Buhner	3.00	1.35	.35
☐ PP15 Dante Bichette	3.00	1.35	.35

1996 Stadium Club Power Streak

Randomly inserted at a rate of one in every 24 hobby packs and 48 retail packs, this 15-card set spotlights baseball's most awesome power hitters and strikeout artists. The cards feature Topps' Power Matrix technology. The fronts display a color player cutout on a silver metallic and holographic background featuring a baseball. The backs carry a small color photo and biography; in addition, the player's batting prowess is presented under three topics: 1995 Power Profile, Power Stroke, and Power Zone.

	MINT	NRMT	EXC
COMPLETE SET (15)	70.00	32.00	8.75
COMMON CARD (PS1-PS15)	1.50	.70	.19
☐ PS1 Randy Johnson	4.00	1.80	.50
☐ PS2 Hideo Nomo	6.00	2.70	.75
☐ PS3 Albert Belle	10.00	4.50	1.25
☐ PS4 Dante Bichette	3.00	1.35	.35
☐ PS5 Jay Buhner	3.00	1.35	.35
☐ PS6 Frank Thomas	25.00	11.00	3.10
☐ PS7 Mark McGwire	8.00	3.60	1.00
☐ PS8 Rafael Palmeiro	3.00	1.35	.35
☐ PS9 Mo Vaughn	6.00	2.70	.75
☐ PS10 Sammy Sosa	4.00	1.80	.50
☐ PS11 Larry Walker	3.00	1.35	.35
☐ PS12 Gary Gaetti	1.50	.70	.19
☐ PS13 Tim Salmon	3.00	1.35	.35
☐ PS14 Barry Bonds	6.00	2.70	.75
☐ PS15 Jim Edmonds	2.00	.90	.25

1996 Stadium Club Prime Cuts

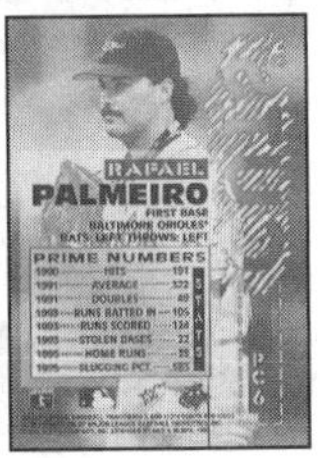

Randomly inserted at a rate of one in every 36 hobby and 72 retail packs, this 8-card set this set highlights eight hitters with the purest swings. These laser-cut cards feature diffraction gold foil. The cards are numbered on the back with a "PC" prefix.

	MINT	NRMT	EXC
COMPLETE SET (8)	60.00	27.00	7.50
COMMON CARD (PC1-PC8)	2.00	.90	.25
☐ PC1 Albert Belle	8.00	3.60	1.00
☐ PC2 Barry Bonds	5.00	2.20	.60
☐ PC3 Ken Griffey Jr.	20.00	9.00	2.50
☐ PC4 Tony Gwynn	8.00	3.60	1.00
☐ PC5 Edgar Martinez	2.00	.90	.25
☐ PC6 Rafael Palmeiro	3.00	1.35	.35
☐ PC7 Mike Piazza	12.00	5.50	1.50
☐ PC8 Frank Thomas	20.00	9.00	2.50

1996 Stadium Club TSC Awards

Randomly inserted in packs at a rate of one in 24 (retail) and one in 48 (hobby), this ten-card set features players whom TSC baseball experts voted to win various awards and is printed on diffraction foil.

	MINT	NRMT	EXC
COMPLETE SET (10)	40.00	18.00	5.00
COMMON CARD (1-10)	1.50	.70	.19
☐ 1 Cal Ripken	12.00	5.50	1.50
☐ 2 Albert Belle	6.00	2.70	.75
☐ 3 Tom Glavine	2.50	1.10	.30
☐ 4 Jeff Conine	2.00	.90	.25
☐ 5 Ken Griffey Jr.	15.00	6.75	1.85
☐ 6 Hideo Nomo	4.00	1.80	.50
☐ 7 Greg Maddux	10.00	4.50	1.25
☐ 8 Chipper Jones	10.00	4.50	1.25
☐ 9 Randy Johnson	2.50	1.10	.30
☐ 10 Jose Mesa	1.50	.70	.19

1996 Stadium Club Members Only

This 50-card set features color player photos of Topps' selection of 45 (#1-45) of the top 1995 American and National League players. The set includes five Finest Cards (#46-50) which represent Topps' selection of the top rookies from 1995. The backs carry information about the player.

	MINT	NRMT	EXC
COMPLETE SET (50)	20.00	9.00	2.50
COMMON CARD (1-50)	.10	.05	.01
☐ 1 Carlos Baerga	.20	.09	.03
☐ 2 Derek Bell	.20	.09	.03
☐ 3 Albert Belle	1.50	.70	.19
☐ 4 Dante Bichette	.30	.14	.04
☐ 5 Craig Biggio	.20	.09	.03
☐ 6 Wade Boggs	.30	.14	.04
☐ 7 Barry Bonds	.75	.35	.09
☐ 8 Jay Buhner	.30	.14	.04
☐ 9 Vinny Castilla	.20	.09	.03
☐ 10 Jeff Conine	.20	.09	.03
☐ 11 Jim Edmonds	.20	.09	.03
☐ 12 Steve Finley	.20	.09	.03
☐ 13 Andres Galarraga	.30	.14	.04
☐ 14 Mark Grace	.30	.14	.04
☐ 15 Tony Gwynn	1.50	.70	.19
☐ 16 Lance Johnson	.20	.09	.03
☐ 17 Randy Johnson	.50	.23	.06
☐ 18 Eric Karros	.20	.09	.03
☐ 19 Chuck Knoblauch	.40	.18	.05
☐ 20 Barry Larkin	.40	.18	.05
☐ 21 Kenny Lofton	.75	.35	.09
☐ 22 Greg Maddux	2.50	1.10	.30
☐ 23 Edgar Martinez	.20	.09	.03
☐ 24 Tino Martinez	.20	.09	.03
☐ 25 Mark McGwire	1.00	.45	.12
☐ 26 Brian McRae	.10	.05	.01
☐ 27 Jose Mesa	.10	.05	.01
☐ 28 Eddie Murray	.75	.35	.09
☐ 29 Mike Mussina	.50	.23	.06
☐ 30 Randy Myers	.10	.05	.01
☐ 31 Hideo Nomo	.75	.35	.09
☐ 32 Rafael Palmeiro	.30	.14	.04
☐ 33 Tony Phillips	.10	.05	.01
☐ 34 Mike Piazza	2.50	1.10	.30
☐ 35 Kirby Puckett	1.50	.70	.19
☐ 36 Manny Ramirez	.75	.35	.09
☐ 37 Tim Salmon	.30	.14	.04
☐ 38 Reggie Sanders	.20	.09	.03
☐ 39 Sammy Sosa	.40	.18	.05
☐ 40 Frank Thomas	3.00	1.35	.35
☐ 41 Jim Thome	.60	.25	.07
☐ 42 John Valentin	.10	.05	.01
☐ 43 Mo Vaughn	.75	.35	.09
☐ 44 Quilvio Veras	.10	.05	.01
☐ 45 Larry Walker	.40	.18	.05
☐ 46 Hideo Nomo FIN	2.00	.90	.25
☐ 47 Marty Cordova FIN	.50	.23	.06
☐ 48 Chipper Jones FIN	3.00	1.35	.35
☐ 49 Garret Anderson FIN	.30	.14	.04
☐ 50 Andy Pettitte FIN	2.00	.90	.25

1997 Stadium Club Pre-Production

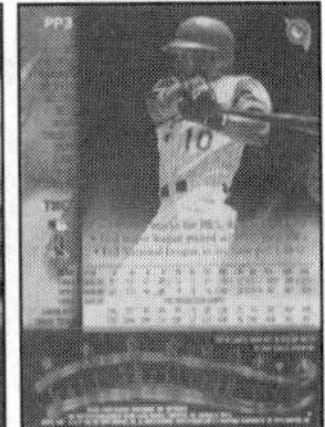

Each Topps wholesale account received one of these three Pre-Production sample cards along with their order forms for 1997 Stadium Club Series 1 baseball. The cards were designed to provide wholesale customers with a sneak preview of the upcoming Stadium Club release. The design parallels the regular issue cards excpt for the PP-prefixed numbering. In addition, the term "Pre-Production Sample" replaces the line of 1996 statistics on back.

	MINT	NRMT	EXC
COMPLETE SET (3)	5.00	2.20	.60
COMMON CARD (PP1-PP3)	1.00	.45	.12
☐ PP1 Chipper Jones	3.00	1.35	.35
☐ PP2 Kenny Lofton	2.00	.90	.25
☐ PP3 Gary Sheffield	1.00	.45	.12

1997 Stadium Club

Cards from the 195-card first series set were distributed in eight-card hobby and retail packs (SRP $3) and 13-card hobby collector packs (SRP $5). Card fronts feature color action player photos printed on 20

pt. card stock with Topps Super Color processing, Hi-gloss laminating, embossing and double foil stamping. The backs carry player information and statistics. In addition to the standard selection of major leaguers, the set contains a 15-card TSC 2000 subset (181-195) featuring a selection of top young prospects. These subset cards were inserted one in every two eight-card first series packs and one per 13-card first series pack. First series cards were released in February, 1997. The 195-card Series 2 set was issued in six-card retail packs with a suggested retail price of $2 and in nine-card hobby packs with a suggested retail price of $3. The second series set features a 15-card Stadium Sluggers subset (376-390) with an insertion rate of one in every two hobby and three retail Series 2 packs. Second series cards were released in April, 1997.

	MINT	NRMT	EXC
COMPLETE SERIES 1 (195)	40.00	18.00	5.00
COMMON CARD (1-195)	.10	.05	.01
COMMON TSC 2000 (181-195)	.25	.11	.03

☐ 1 Chipper Jones	2.00	.90	.25
☐ 2 Gary Sheffield	.50	.23	.06
☐ 3 Kenny Lofton	.75	.35	.09
☐ 4 Brian Jordan	.25	.11	.03
☐ 5 Mark McGwire	1.00	.45	.12
☐ 6 Charles Nagy	.25	.11	.03
☐ 7 Tim Salmon	.40	.18	.05
☐ 8 Cal Ripken	2.50	1.10	.30
☐ 9 Jeff Conine	.25	.11	.03
☐ 10 Paul Molitor	.60	.25	.07
☐ 11 Mariano Rivera	.25	.11	.03
☐ 12 Pedro Martinez	.25	.11	.03
☐ 13 Jeff Bagwell	1.25	.55	.16
☐ 14 Bobby Bonilla	.25	.11	.03
☐ 15 Barry Bonds	.75	.35	.09
☐ 16 Ryan Klesko	.50	.23	.06
☐ 17 Barry Larkin	.40	.18	.05
☐ 18 Jim Thome	.60	.25	.07
☐ 19 Jay Buhner	.40	.18	.05
☐ 20 Juan Gonzalez	1.50	.70	.19
☐ 21 Mike Mussina	.60	.25	.07
☐ 22 Kevin Appier	.25	.11	.03
☐ 23 Eric Karros	.25	.11	.03
☐ 24 Steve Finley	.10	.05	.01
☐ 25 Ed Sprague	.10	.05	.01
☐ 26 Bernard Gilkey	.10	.05	.01
☐ 27 Tony Phillips	.10	.05	.01
☐ 28 Henry Rodriguez	.25	.11	.03
☐ 29 John Smoltz	.50	.23	.06
☐ 30 Dante Bichette	.40	.18	.05
☐ 31 Mike Piazza	2.00	.90	.25
☐ 32 Paul O'Neill	.10	.05	.01
☐ 33 Billy Wagner	.25	.11	.03
☐ 34 Reggie Sanders	.25	.11	.03
☐ 35 John Jaha	.25	.11	.03
☐ 36 Eddie Murray	.75	.35	.09
☐ 37 Eric Young	.25	.11	.03
☐ 38 Roberto Hernandez	.10	.05	.01
☐ 39 Pat Hentgen	.25	.11	.03
☐ 40 Sammy Sosa	.50	.23	.06
☐ 41 Todd Hundley	.25	.11	.03
☐ 42 Mo Vaughn	.75	.35	.09
☐ 43 Robin Ventura	.25	.11	.03
☐ 44 Mark Grudzielanek	.10	.05	.01
☐ 45 Shane Reynolds	.10	.05	.01
☐ 46 Andy Pettitte	.10	.05	.01
☐ 47 Fred McGriff	.40	.18	.05
☐ 48 Rey Ordonez	.40	.18	.05
☐ 49 Will Clark	.40	.18	.05
☐ 50 Ken Griffey Jr.	3.00	1.35	.35
☐ 51 Todd Worrell	.10	.05	.01
☐ 52 Rusty Greer	.25	.11	.03
☐ 53 Mark Grace	.40	.18	.05
☐ 54 Tom Glavine	.40	.18	.05
☐ 55 Derek Jeter	2.00	.90	.25
☐ 56 Rafael Palmeiro	.40	.18	.05
☐ 57 Bernie Williams	.60	.25	.07
☐ 58 Marty Cordova	.25	.11	.03
☐ 59 Andres Galarraga	.40	.18	.05
☐ 60 Ken Caminiti	.50	.23	.06
☐ 61 Garret Anderson	.10	.05	.01
☐ 62 Denny Martinez	.10	.05	.01
☐ 63 Mike Greenwell	.10	.05	.01
☐ 64 David Segui	.10	.05	.01
☐ 65 Julio Franco	.10	.05	.01
☐ 66 Rickey Henderson	.40	.18	.05
☐ 67 Ozzie Guillen	.10	.05	.01
☐ 68 Pete Harnisch	.10	.05	.01
☐ 69 Chan Ho Park	.40	.18	.05
☐ 70 Harold Baines	.10	.05	.01
☐ 71 Mark Clark	.10	.05	.01
☐ 72 Steve Avery	.10	.05	.01
☐ 73 Brian Hunter	.10	.05	.01
☐ 74 Pedro Astacio	.10	.05	.01
☐ 75 Jack McDowell	.10	.05	.01
☐ 76 Gregg Jefferies	.10	.05	.01
☐ 77 Jason Kendall	.25	.11	.03
☐ 78 Todd Walker	1.25	.55	.16
☐ 79 B.J. Surhoff	.10	.05	.01
☐ 80 Moises Alou	.25	.11	.03
☐ 81 Fernando Vina	.10	.05	.01
☐ 82 Darryl Strawberry	.25	.11	.03
☐ 83 Jose Rosado	.40	.18	.05
☐ 84 Chris Gomez	.10	.05	.01
☐ 85 Chili Davis	.10	.05	.01
☐ 86 Alan Benes	.25	.11	.03
☐ 87 Todd Hollandsworth	.25	.11	.03
☐ 88 Jose Vizcaino	.10	.05	.01
☐ 89 Edgardo Alfonzo	.10	.05	.01
☐ 90 Ruben Rivera	.40	.18	.05
☐ 91 Donovan Osborne	.10	.05	.01
☐ 92 Doug Glanville	.10	.05	.01
☐ 93 Gary DiSarcina	.10	.05	.01
☐ 94 Brooks Kieschnick	.25	.11	.03
☐ 95 Bobby Jones	.10	.05	.01
☐ 96 Raul Casanova	.10	.05	.01
☐ 97 Jermaine Allensworth	.25	.11	.03
☐ 98 Kenny Rogers	.10	.05	.01
☐ 99 Mark McLemore	.10	.05	.01
☐ 100 Jeff Fassero	.10	.05	.01
☐ 101 Sandy Alomar Jr.	.10	.05	.01
☐ 102 Chuck Finley	.10	.05	.01
☐ 103 Eric Owens	.10	.05	.01
☐ 104 Billy McMillon	.10	.05	.01
☐ 105 Dwight Gooden	.25	.11	.03
☐ 106 Sterling Hitchcock	.10	.05	.01
☐ 107 Doug Drabek	.10	.05	.01
☐ 108 Paul Wilson	.25	.11	.03
☐ 109 Chris Snopek	.10	.05	.01
☐ 110 Al Leiter	.10	.05	.01
☐ 111 Bob Tewksbury	.10	.05	.01
☐ 112 Todd Greene	.10	.05	.01
☐ 113 Jose Valentin	.10	.05	.01
☐ 114 Delino DeShields	.10	.05	.01
☐ 115 Mike Bordick	.10	.05	.01
☐ 116 Pat Meares	.10	.05	.01
☐ 117 Mariano Duncan	.10	.05	.01
☐ 118 Steve Trachsel	.10	.05	.01
☐ 119 Luis Castillo	.40	.18	.05
☐ 120 Andy Benes	.10	.05	.01
☐ 121 Donne Wall	.10	.05	.01
☐ 122 Alex Gonzalez	.10	.05	.01
☐ 123 Dan Wilson	.10	.05	.01
☐ 124 Omar Vizquel	.25	.11	.03
☐ 125 Devon White	.10	.05	.01
☐ 126 Darryl Hamilton	.10	.05	.01
☐ 127 Orlando Merced	.10	.05	.01
☐ 128 Royce Clayton	.10	.05	.01
☐ 129 William VanLandingham	.10	.05	.01
☐ 130 Terry Steinbach	.10	.05	.01
☐ 131 Jeff Blauser	.10	.05	.01
☐ 132 Jeff Cirillo	.10	.05	.01
☐ 133 Roger Pavlik	.10	.05	.01
☐ 134 Danny Tartabull	.10	.05	.01
☐ 135 Jeff Montgomery	.10	.05	.01
☐ 136 Bobby Higginson	.25	.11	.03
☐ 137 Mike Grace	.10	.05	.01
☐ 138 Kevin Elster	.10	.05	.01
☐ 139 Brian Giles	.10	.05	.01
☐ 140 Rod Beck	.10	.05	.01
☐ 141 Ismael Valdes	.25	.11	.03
☐ 142 Scott Brosius	.10	.05	.01
☐ 143 Mike Fetters	.10	.05	.01
☐ 144 Gary Gaetti	.10	.05	.01
☐ 145 Mike Lansing	.10	.05	.01
☐ 146 Glenallen Hill	.10	.05	.01
☐ 147 Shawn Green	.10	.05	.01
☐ 148 Mel Rojas	.10	.05	.01
☐ 149 Joey Cora	.10	.05	.01
☐ 150 John Smiley	.10	.05	.01
☐ 151 Marvin Benard	.10	.05	.01
☐ 152 Curt Schilling	.10	.05	.01
☐ 153 Dave Nilsson	.10	.05	.01
☐ 154 Edgar Renteria	.40	.18	.05
☐ 155 Joey Hamilton	.25	.11	.03
☐ 156 Carlos Garcia	.10	.05	.01
☐ 157 Nomar Garciaparra	1.25	.55	.16
☐ 158 Kevin Ritz	.10	.05	.01
☐ 159 Keith Lockhart	.10	.05	.01
☐ 160 Justin Thompson	.25	.11	.03
☐ 161 Terry Adams	.10	.05	.01
☐ 162 Jamey Wright	.25	.11	.03
☐ 163 Otis Nixon	.10	.05	.01
☐ 164 Michael Tucker	.10	.05	.01
☐ 165 Mike Stanley	.10	.05	.01
☐ 166 Ben McDonald	.10	.05	.01
☐ 167 John Mabry	.10	.05	.01
☐ 168 Troy O'Leary	.10	.05	.01
☐ 169 Mel Nieves	.10	.05	.01
☐ 170 Bret Boone	.10	.05	.01
☐ 171 Mike Timlin	.10	.05	.01
☐ 172 Scott Rolen	1.25	.55	.16
☐ 173 Reggie Jefferson	.10	.05	.01
☐ 174 Neifi Perez	.25	.11	.03
☐ 175 Brian McRae	.10	.05	.01
☐ 176 Tom Goodwin	.10	.05	.01
☐ 177 Aaron Sele	.10	.05	.01
☐ 178 Benito Santiago	.10	.05	.01
☐ 179 Frank Rodriguez	.10	.05	.01
☐ 180 Eric Davis	.10	.05	.01
☐ 181 Andruw Jones 2000 SP	6.00	2.70	.75
☐ 182 Todd Walker 2000 SP	2.50	1.10	.30
☐ 183 Wes Helms 2000 SP	1.50	.70	.19
☐ 184 Nelson Figueroa 2000 SP	.75	.35	.09
☐ 185 Vladimir Guerrero 2000 SP	4.00	1.80	.50
☐ 186 Billy McMillon 2000	.25	.11	.03
☐ 187 Todd Helton 2000 SP	1.50	.70	.19
☐ 188 Nomar Garciaparra 2000 SP	2.50	1.10	.30
☐ 189 Katsuhiro Maeda 2000	.40	.18	.05
☐ 190 Russell Branyan 2000 SP	1.00	.45	.12
☐ 191 Glendon Rusch 2000	.40	.18	.05
☐ 192 Bartolo Colon 2000	.50	.23	.06
☐ 193 Scott Rolen 2000 SP	2.50	1.10	.30
☐ 194 Angel Echevarria 2000	.25	.11	.03
☐ 195 Bob Abreu 2000	.50	.23	.06

1997 Stadium Club Matrix

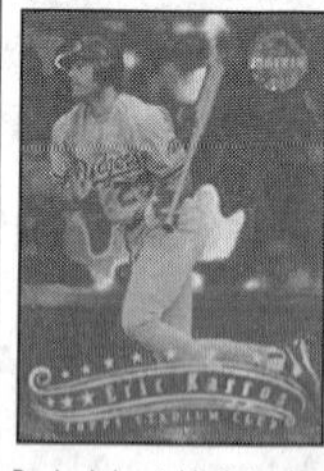
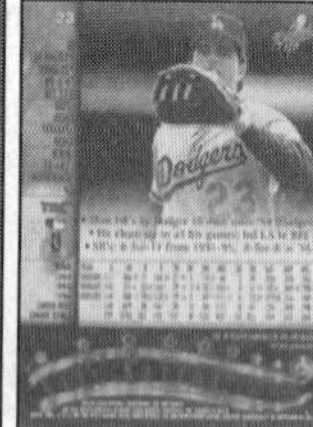

Randomly inserted in first series eight-card packs at a rate of one in 12 and first series 13-card packs at a rate of one in six, this 60-card set is parallel to the first 60 cards of the regular set. Each Matrix card was reproduced with Power Matrix technology, giving the card fronts a glittering effect.

	MINT	NRMT	EXC
COMPLETE SERIES 1 (60)	250.00	110.00	31.00
COMMON CARD (1-60)	1.25	.55	.16
*STARS: 6X TO 12X BASIC CARDS			

☐ 1 Chipper Jones	25.00	11.00	3.10
☐ 8 Cal Ripken	30.00	13.50	3.70
☐ 13 Jeff Bagwell	15.00	6.75	1.85
☐ 20 Juan Gonzalez	20.00	9.00	2.50
☐ 31 Mike Piazza	25.00	11.00	3.10
☐ 50 Ken Griffey Jr.	40.00	18.00	5.00
☐ 55 Derek Jeter	25.00	11.00	3.10

1997 Stadium Club Co-Signers

Randomly inserted in first series eight-card hobby packs at a rate of one in 168 and first series 13-card hobby collector packs at a rate of one in 96, cards (CO1-CO5) from this dual-sided, dual-player set feature color action player photos printed on 20pt. card stock with authentic signatures of two major league stand-outs per card. The last five cards (CO6-CO10) were randomly inserted in second series 10-card hobby packs with a rate of one in 168 and inserted with a rate of one in 96 hobby collector packs.

	MINT	NRMT	EXC
COMPLETE SET (10)	400.00	180.00	50.00
COMMON CARD (CO1-CO10)	60.00	27.00	7.50

☐ CO1 Andy Pettitte Derek Jeter	150.00	70.00	19.00
☐ CO2 Paul Wilson Todd Hundley	60.00	27.00	7.50
☐ CO3 Jermaine Dye Mark Wohlers	60.00	27.00	7.50
☐ CO4 Scott Rolen Gregg Jefferies	100.00	45.00	12.50
☐ CO5 Todd Hollandsworth Jason Kendall	75.00	34.00	9.50

1997 Stadium Club Firebrand Redemption

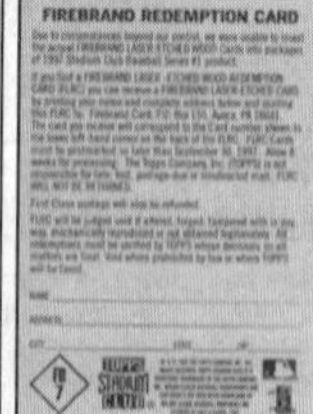

Randomly inserted exclusively into first series eight-card retail packs at a rate of one in 36, these redemption cards feature a selection of the leagues top sluggers. Due to circumstances beyond the manufacturers control, they were not able to insert the actual etched-wood cards into packs and had to resort to these redemption cards.

	MINT	NRMT	EXC
COMPLETE SET (12)	150.00	70.00	19.00
COMMON CARD (F1-F12)	4.00	1.80	.50

☐ F1 Jeff Bagwell	12.00	5.50	1.50
☐ F2 Albert Belle	12.00	5.50	1.50
☐ F3 Barry Bonds	8.00	3.60	1.00
☐ F4 Andres Galarraga	4.00	1.80	.50
☐ F5 Ken Griffey Jr.	30.00	13.50	3.70
☐ F6 Brady Anderson	4.00	1.80	.50
☐ F7 Mark McGwire	10.00	4.50	1.25
☐ F8 Chipper Jones	20.00	9.00	2.50
☐ F9 Frank Thomas	30.00	13.50	3.70
☐ F10 Mike Piazza	20.00	9.00	2.50
☐ F11 Mo Vaughn	8.00	3.60	1.00
☐ F12 Juan Gonzalez	15.00	6.75	1.85

1997 Stadium Club Instavision

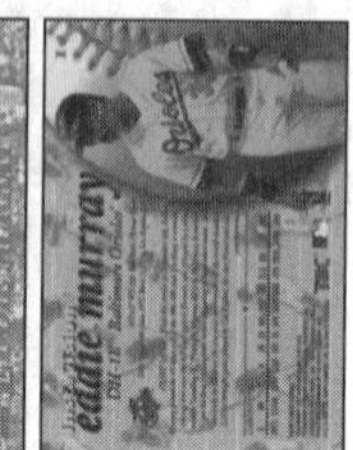

Randomly inserted in first series eight-card packs at a rate of one in 24 and first series 13-card packs at a rate of 1:12, this 10-card set highlights some of the 1996 season's most exciting moments through exclusive holographic video action.

	MINT	NRMT	EXC
COMPLETE SET (10)	40.00	18.00	5.00
COMMON CARD (I1-I10)	2.50	1.10	.30

☐ I1 Eddie Murray	6.00	2.70	.75
☐ I2 Paul Molitor	5.00	2.20	.60
☐ I3 Todd Hundley	2.50	1.10	.30
☐ I4 Roger Clemens	5.00	2.20	.60
☐ I5 Barry Bonds	6.00	2.70	.75
☐ I6 Mark McGwire	8.00	3.60	1.00
☐ I7 Brady Anderson	3.00	1.35	.35
☐ I8 Barry Larkin	3.00	1.35	.35
☐ I9 Ken Caminiti	4.00	1.80	.50
☐ I10 Hideo Nomo	6.00	2.70	.75

1997 Stadium Club Millennium

Randomly inserted in first series eight-card packs at a rate of one in 24 and first series 13-card packs at a rate of 1:12, cards from this 20-card set feature color player photos of 20 breakthrough stars of Major League Baseball reproduced using state-of-the-art advanced embossed holographic technology.

	MINT	NRMT	EXC
COMPLETE SET (20)	100.00	45.00	12.50
COMMON CARD (M1-M20)	4.00	1.80	.50

☐ M1 Derek Jeter	25.00	11.00	3.10
☐ M2 Mark Grudzielanek	4.00	1.80	.50
☐ M3 Jacob Cruz	4.00	1.80	.50
☐ M4 Ray Durham	4.00	1.80	.50
☐ M5 Tony Clark	6.00	2.70	.75
☐ M6 Chipper Jones	25.00	11.00	3.10
☐ M7 Luis Castillo	5.00	2.20	.60
☐ M8 Carlos Delgado	4.00	1.80	.50
☐ M9 Brant Brown	4.00	1.80	.50
☐ M10 Jason Kendall	4.00	1.80	.50
☐ M11 Alan Benes	4.00	1.80	.50
☐ M12 Rey Ordonez	5.00	2.20	.60
☐ M13 Justin Thompson	4.00	1.80	.50
☐ M14 Jermaine Allensworth	4.00	1.80	.50
☐ M15 Brian Hunter	4.00	1.80	.50
☐ M16 Marty Cordova	4.00	1.80	.50
☐ M17 Edgar Renteria	5.00	2.20	.60
☐ M18 Karim Garcia	6.00	2.70	.75
☐ M19 Todd Greene	4.00	1.80	.50
☐ M20 Paul Wilson	4.00	1.80	.50

1997 Stadium Club Pure Gold

Randomly inserted in first series eight-card packs at a rate of one in 72 and first series 13-card packs at a rate of one in 36, cards from this 10-card set feature color action star player photos reproduced on 20 pt. embossed gold mirror foilboard.

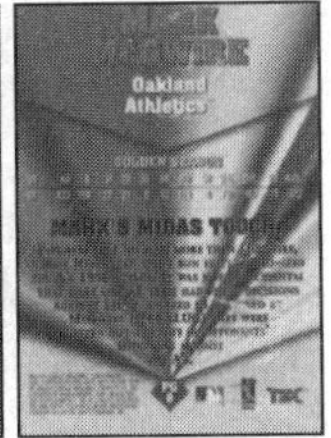

	MINT	NRMT	EXC
COMPLETE SET (10)	200.00	90.00	25.00
COMMON CARD (PG1-PG10)	8.00	3.60	1.00
☐ PG1 Brady Anderson	8.00	3.60	1.00
☐ PG2 Albert Belle	25.00	11.00	3.10
☐ PG3 Dante Bichette	8.00	3.60	1.00
☐ PG4 Barry Bonds	15.00	6.75	1.85
☐ PG5 Jay Buhner	8.00	3.60	1.00
☐ PG6 Tony Gwynn	25.00	11.00	3.10
☐ PG7 Chipper Jones	40.00	18.00	5.00
☐ PG8 Mark McGwire	20.00	9.00	2.50
☐ PG9 Gary Sheffield	10.00	4.50	1.25
☐ PG10 Frank Thomas	60.00	27.00	7.50

1997 Stadium Club Members Only

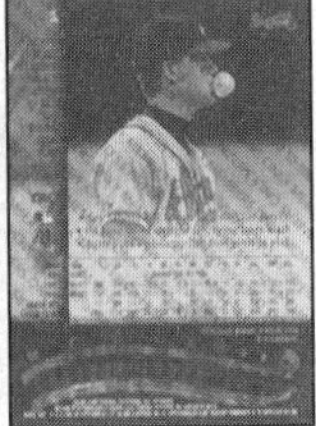

These 235 cards are a parallel issue to the 1997 Stadium Club set and the following insert sets: Millennium, Instavision and Pure Gold. No Co-SIngers or Firebrand Redemption cards are in this set. The only diffference between the regular issue cards and these inserts are the words "TSC Members Only" printed lightly in the background. The cards all come together in factory set form and one must be a member of Topps Stadium Club to order these cards.

	MINT	NRMT	EXC
COMPLETE SERIES 1 (235)	200.00	90.00	25.00
COMMON CARD (1-195)	.25	.11	.03
*MEMBERS ONLY: 6X BASIC CARDS			
☐ I1 Eddie Murray	6.00	2.70	.75
☐ I2 Paul Molitor	5.00	2.20	.60
☐ I3 Todd Hundley	2.50	1.10	.30
☐ I4 Roger Clemens	5.00	2.20	.60
☐ I5 Barry Bonds	6.00	2.70	.75
☐ I6 Mark McGwire	8.00	3.60	1.00
☐ I7 Brady Anderson	3.00	1.35	.35
☐ I8 Barry Larkin	3.00	1.35	.35
☐ I9 Ken Caminiti	4.00	1.80	.50
☐ I10 Hideo Nomo	6.00	2.70	.75
☐ M1 Derek Jeter	12.50	5.50	1.55
☐ M2 Mark Grudzielanek	2.50	1.10	.30
☐ M3 Jacob Cruz	2.00	.90	.25
☐ M4 Ray Durham	2.50	1.10	.30
☐ M5 Tony Clark	6.00	2.70	.75
☐ M6 Chipper Jones	12.50	5.50	1.55
☐ M7 Luis Castillo	2.00	.90	.25
☐ M8 Carlos Delgado	2.50	1.10	.30
☐ M9 Brant Brown	2.00	.90	.25
☐ M10 Jason Kendall	2.50	1.10	.30
☐ M11 Alan Benes	2.50	1.10	.30
☐ M12 Rey Ordonez	2.00	.90	.25
☐ M13 Justin Thompson	2.00	.90	.25
☐ M14 Jermaine Allensworth	2.50	1.10	.30
☐ M15 Brian L. Hunter	2.00	.90	.25
☐ M16 Marty Cordova	2.50	1.10	.30
☐ M17 Edgar Renteria	2.00	.90	.25
☐ M18 Karim Garcia	2.00	.90	.25
☐ M19 Todd Greene	2.00	.90	.25
☐ M20 Paul Wilson	2.00	.90	.25
☐ PG1 Brady Anderson	2.50	1.10	.30
☐ PG2 Albert Belle	8.00	3.60	1.00
☐ PG3 Dante Bichette	2.50	1.10	.30
☐ PG4 Barry Bonds	5.00	2.20	.60
☐ PG5 Jay Buhner	2.50	1.10	.30
☐ PG6 Tony Gwynn	8.00	3.60	1.00
☐ PG7 Chipper Jones	12.00	5.50	1.50
☐ PG8 Mark McGwire	7.00	3.10	.85
☐ PG9 Gary Sheffield	3.00	1.35	.35
☐ PG10 Frank Thomas	20.00	9.00	2.50

1953 Stahl Meyer

The cards in this nine-card set measure approximately 3 1/4" by 4 1/2". The 1953 Stahl Meyer set of full color, unnumbered cards includes three players from each of the three New York teams. The cards have white borders. The Lockman card is the most plentiful of any card in the set. Some batting and fielding statistics and short

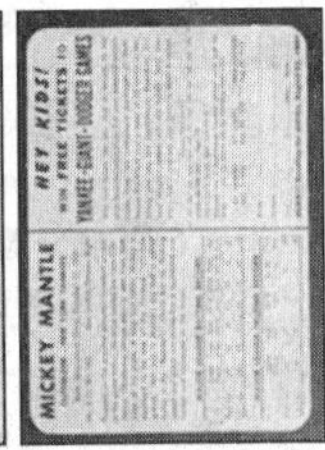

biography are included on the back. The cards are ordered in the checklist below by alphabetical order without regard to team affiliation.

	NRMT	VG-E	GOOD
COMPLETE SET	4500.00	2000.00	550.00
COMMON CARD (1-9)	125.00	55.00	15.50
☐ 1 Hank Bauer	150.00	70.00	19.00
☐ 2 Roy Campanella	600.00	275.00	75.00
☐ 3 Gil Hodges	300.00	135.00	38.00
☐ 4 Monte Irvin	200.00	90.00	25.00
☐ 5 Whitey Lockman	125.00	55.00	15.50
☐ 6 Mickey Mantle	2500.00	1100.00	300.00
☐ 7 Phil Rizzuto	300.00	135.00	38.00
☐ 8 Duke Snider	600.00	275.00	75.00
☐ 9 Bobby Thomson	150.00	70.00	19.00

1954 Stahl Meyer

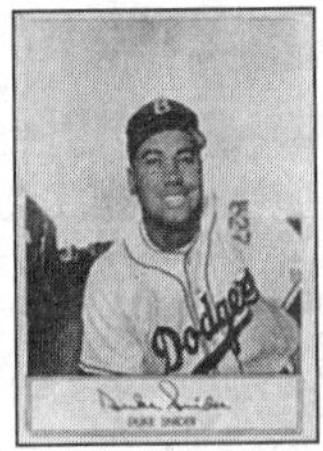

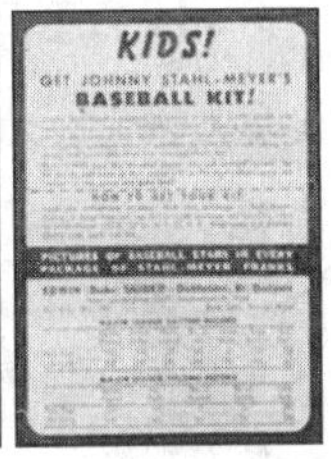

The cards in this 12-card set measure approximately 3 1/4" by 4 1/2". The 1954 Stahl Meyer set of full color, unnumbered cards includes four players from each of the three New York teams. The cards have yellow borders and the backs, oriented horizontally, include an ad for a baseball kit and the player's statistics. No player biography is included on the back. The cards are ordered in the checklist below by alphabetical order without regard to team affiliation.

	NRMT	VG-E	GOOD
COMPLETE SET	6750.00	3000.00	850.00
COMMON CARD (1-12)	150.00	70.00	19.00
☐ 1 Hank Bauer	175.00	80.00	22.00
☐ 2 Carl Erskine	175.00	80.00	22.00
☐ 3 Gil Hodges	325.00	145.00	40.00
☐ 4 Monte Irvin	225.00	100.00	28.00
☐ 5 Whitey Lockman	150.00	70.00	19.00
☐ 6 Mickey Mantle	3000.00	1350.00	375.00
☐ 7 Willie Mays	1500.00	700.00	190.00
☐ 8 Gil McDougald	175.00	80.00	22.00
☐ 9 Don Mueller	150.00	70.00	19.00
☐ 10 Don Newcombe	175.00	80.00	22.00
☐ 11 Phil Rizzuto	300.00	135.00	38.00
☐ 12 Duke Snider	600.00	275.00	75.00

1955 Stahl Meyer

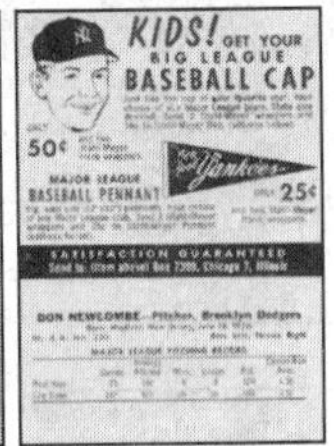

The cards in this 12-card set measure approximately 3 1/4" by 4 1/2". The 1955 Stahl Meyer set of full color, unnumbered cards contains four players each from the three New York teams. As in the 1954 set, the cards have yellow borders; however, the back of the cards contain a sketch of Mickey Mantle with an ad for a baseball cap or a pennant. The cards are ordered in the checklist below by alphabetical order without regard to team affiliation.

	NRMT	VG-E	GOOD
COMPLETE SET	5500.00	2500.00	700.00
COMMON CARD (1-12)	150.00	70.00	19.00
☐ 1 Hank Bauer	175.00	80.00	22.00
☐ 2 Carl Erskine	175.00	80.00	22.00
☐ 3 Gil Hodges	325.00	145.00	40.00
☐ 4 Monte Irvin	225.00	100.00	28.00
☐ 5 Whitey Lockman	150.00	70.00	19.00
☐ 6 Mickey Mantle	3000.00	1350.00	375.00
☐ 7 Gil McDougald	175.00	80.00	22.00
☐ 8 Don Mueller	150.00	70.00	19.00
☐ 9 Don Newcombe	175.00	80.00	22.00
☐ 10 Dusty Rhodes	150.00	70.00	19.00
☐ 11 Phil Rizzuto	325.00	145.00	40.00
☐ 12 Duke Snider	600.00	275.00	75.00

1910 Standard Caramel E93

The cards in this 30-card set measure 1 1/2" by 2 3/4". The E93 set was distributed by Standard Caramel in 1910. It consists of black and white player photos which were tinted and placed against solid color backgrounds. A checklist, starting with Ames, is printed in brown ink on the reverse. Some blank backs are known and all poses also appear in W555.

	EX-MT	VG-E	GOOD
COMPLETE SET (30)	7500.00	3400.00	950.00
COMMON CARD (1-30)	100.00	45.00	12.50
☐ 1 Red Ames	100.00	45.00	12.50
☐ 2 Chief Bender	250.00	110.00	31.00
☐ 3 Mordecai Brown	250.00	110.00	31.00
☐ 4 Frank Chance	300.00	135.00	38.00
☐ 5 Hal Chase	150.00	70.00	19.00
☐ 6 Ty Cobb	1200.00	550.00	150.00
☐ 7 Eddie Collins	300.00	135.00	38.00
☐ 8 Stan Coveleskie	250.00	110.00	31.00
☐ 9 Fred Clarke	250.00	110.00	31.00
☐ 10 Jim Delehanty	100.00	45.00	12.50
☐ 11 Bill Donovan	100.00	45.00	12.50
☐ 12 Red Dooin	100.00	45.00	12.50
☐ 13 Johnny Evers	250.00	110.00	31.00
☐ 14 George Gibson	100.00	45.00	12.50
☐ 15 Clark Griffith	250.00	110.00	31.00
☐ 16 Hugh Jennings	250.00	110.00	31.00
☐ 17 Davy Jones	100.00	45.00	12.50
☐ 18 Addie Joss	250.00	110.00	31.00
☐ 19 Napoleon Lajoie	400.00	180.00	50.00
☐ 20 Tommy Leach	125.00	55.00	15.50
☐ 21 Christy Mathewson	500.00	220.00	60.00
☐ 22 John McGraw	350.00	160.00	45.00
☐ 23 Jim Pastorius	100.00	45.00	12.50
☐ 24 Deacon Phillippe	125.00	55.00	15.50
☐ 25 Eddie Plank	350.00	160.00	45.00
☐ 26 Joe Tinker	250.00	110.00	31.00
☐ 27 Rube Waddell	250.00	110.00	31.00
☐ 28 Honus Wagner	600.00	275.00	75.00
☐ 29 Hooks Wiltse	100.00	45.00	12.50
☐ 30 Cy Young	400.00	180.00	50.00

1952 Star Cal Large

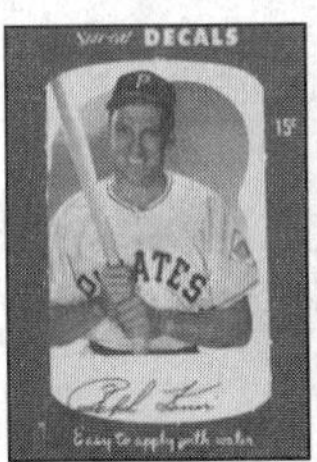

Type One of the Star Cal Decal set, issued in 1952, contains the cards listed in the checklist below. Each decal sheet measures 4 1/8" by 6 1/8". When the decal is taken from the paper wrapper, a checklist of existing decals is revealed on the wrapper. The set was issued by the Meyercord Company of Chicago and carries a catalog designation of W625-1. The asterisked decals below are somewhat tougher to find.

	NRMT	VG-E	GOOD
COMPLETE SET	4000.00	1800.00	500.00
COMMON DECAL	18.00	8.00	2.20
☐ 70A Allie Reynolds	25.00	11.00	3.10
☐ 70B Ed Lopat	25.00	11.00	3.10
☐ 70C Yogi Berra	75.00	34.00	9.50
☐ 70D Vic Raschi	20.00	9.00	2.50
☐ 70E Jerry Coleman	20.00	9.00	2.50
☐ 70F Phil Rizzuto	50.00	22.00	6.25
☐ 70G Mickey Mantle	1000.00	450.00	125.00
☐ 71A Mel Parnell	20.00	9.00	2.50
☐ 71B Ted Williams	200.00	90.00	25.00
☐ 71C Ted Williams	200.00	90.00	25.00
☐ 71D Vern Stephens	20.00	9.00	2.50
☐ 71E Billy Goodman	20.00	9.00	2.50
☐ 71F Dom DiMaggio	25.00	11.00	3.10
☐ 71G Dick Gernert	18.00	8.00	2.20
☐ 71H Hoot Evers	75.00	34.00	9.50
☐ 72A George Kell	50.00	22.00	6.25
☐ 72B Hal Newhouser	40.00	18.00	5.00
☐ 72C Hoot Evers	18.00	8.00	2.20
☐ 72D Vic Wertz	18.00	8.00	2.20
☐ 72E Fred Hutchinson	20.00	9.00	2.50
☐ 72F Johnny Groth	18.00	8.00	2.20
☐ 73A Al Zarilla	18.00	8.00	2.20
☐ 73B Billy Pierce	25.00	11.00	3.10
☐ 73C Eddie Robinson	18.00	8.00	2.20
☐ 73D Chico Carrasquel	20.00	9.00	2.50
☐ 73E Minnie Minoso	30.00	13.50	3.70
☐ 73F Jim Busby	18.00	8.00	2.20
☐ 73G Nellie Fox	40.00	18.00	5.00
☐ 73H Sam Mele	75.00	34.00	9.50
☐ 74A Larry Doby	30.00	13.50	3.70
☐ 74B Al Rosen	25.00	11.00	3.10
☐ 74C Bob Lemon	40.00	18.00	5.00
☐ 74D Jim Hegan	18.00	8.00	2.20
☐ 74E Bob Feller	75.00	34.00	9.50
☐ 74F Dale Mitchell	20.00	9.00	2.50
☐ 75A Ned Garver	18.00	8.00	2.20
☐ 76A Gus Zernial	20.00	9.00	2.50
☐ 76B Ferris Fain	18.00	8.00	2.20
☐ 76C Bobby Shantz	75.00	34.00	9.50
☐ 77A Richie Ashburn	40.00	18.00	5.00
☐ 77B Ralph Kiner	50.00	22.00	6.25
☐ 77C Curt Simmons	75.00	34.00	9.50
☐ 78A Bobby Thomson	20.00	9.00	2.50
☐ 78B Alvin Dark	20.00	9.00	2.50
☐ 78C Sal Maglie	20.00	9.00	2.50
☐ 78D Larry Jansen	20.00	9.00	2.50
☐ 78E Willie Mays	300.00	135.00	38.00
☐ 78F Monte Irvin	50.00	22.00	6.25
☐ 78G Whitey Lockman	18.00	8.00	2.20
☐ 79A Gil Hodges	50.00	22.00	6.25
☐ 79B Pee Wee Reese	60.00	27.00	7.50
☐ 79C Roy Campanella	150.00	70.00	19.00
☐ 79D Don Newcombe	30.00	13.50	3.70
☐ 79E Duke Snider	100.00	45.00	12.50
☐ 79F Preacher Roe	25.00	11.00	3.10
☐ 79G Jackie Robinson	200.00	90.00	25.00
☐ 80A Eddie Miksis	18.00	8.00	2.20
☐ 80B Dutch Leonard	18.00	8.00	2.20
☐ 80C Randy Jackson	18.00	8.00	2.20
☐ 80D Bob Rush	18.00	8.00	2.20
☐ 80E Hank Sauer	18.00	8.00	2.20
☐ 80F Phil Cavarretta	20.00	9.00	2.50
☐ 80G Warren Hacker	18.00	8.00	2.20
☐ 81A Red Schoendienst	30.00	13.50	3.70
☐ 81B Wally Westlake	18.00	8.00	2.20
☐ 81C Cliff Chambers	18.00	8.00	2.20
☐ 81D Enos Slaughter	40.00	18.00	5.00
☐ 81E Stan Musial	125.00	55.00	15.50
☐ 81F Stan Musial	125.00	55.00	15.50
☐ 81G Jerry Staley	18.00	8.00	2.20

1952 Star Cal Small

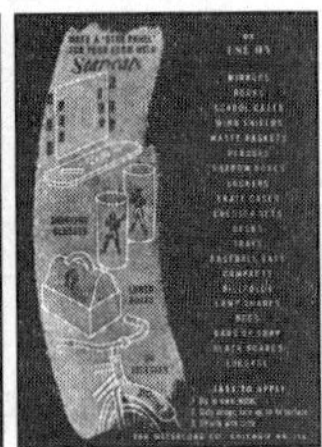

Type Two of the Star Cal Decal set features a decal package half the size of the W625-1 set, each sheet contains two decals, each of which is approximately half the size of the large decal found in the W625-1 set. Each decal package (sheet) measures 3 1/16" by 4 1/8". The set was issued by the Meyercord Company of Chicago and carries a catalog designation of W625-2. The checklist below features two players per "card".

	NRMT	VG-E	GOOD
COMPLETE SET	1300.00	575.00	160.00
COMMON DECAL	20.00	9.00	2.50
☐ 84A Allie Reynolds and Vic Raschi	25.00	11.00	3.10
☐ 84B Ed Lopat and Yogi Berra	35.00	16.00	4.40
☐ 84C Phil Rizzuto and Jerry Coleman	30.00	13.50	3.70
☐ 85A Ted Williams and Ted Williams	200.00	90.00	25.00
☐ 85B Dom DiMaggio and Mel Parnell	25.00	11.00	3.10
☐ 85C Vern Stephens and Billy Goodman	20.00	9.00	2.50
☐ 86A George Kell and Hal Newhouser	35.00	16.00	4.40
☐ 86B Hoot Evers and Vic Wertz	20.00	9.00	2.50
☐ 86C Johnny Groth and Fred Hutchinson	20.00	9.00	2.50
☐ 87A Eddie Robinson and Eddie Robinson	20.00	9.00	2.50
☐ 87B Chico Carrasquel and Minnie Minoso	25.00	11.00	3.10

☐ 87C Billy Pierce and Nellie Fox	35.00	16.00	4.40
☐ 87D Al Zarilla and Jim Busby	20.00	9.00	2.50
☐ 88A Bob Lemon and Jim Hegan	25.00	11.00	3.10
☐ 88B Larry Doby and Bob Feller	50.00	22.00	6.25
☐ 88C Dale Mitchell and Al Rosen	25.00	11.00	3.10
☐ 89A Ned Garver and Ned Garver	20.00	9.00	2.50
☐ 89B Ferris Fain and Gus Zernial	20.00	9.00	2.50
☐ 89C Richie Ashburn and Richie Ashburn	35.00	16.00	4.40
☐ 89D Ralph Kiner and Ralph Kiner	50.00	22.00	6.25
☐ 90A Willie Mays and Monty Irvin	150.00	70.00	19.00
☐ 90B Larry Jansen and Sal Maglie	25.00	11.00	3.10
☐ 90C Bobby Thomson and Al Dark	25.00	11.00	3.10
☐ 91A Gil Hodges and Pee Wee Reese	50.00	22.00	6.25
☐ 91B Roy Campanella and Jackie Robinson	150.00	70.00	19.00
☐ 91C Duke Snider and Preacher Roe	50.00	22.00	6.25
☐ 92A Phil Cavarretta and Dutch Leonard	20.00	9.00	2.50
☐ 92B Randy Jackson and Eddie Miksis	20.00	9.00	2.50
☐ 92C Bob Rush and Hank Sauer	20.00	9.00	2.50
☐ 93A Stan Musial and Stan Musial	150.00	70.00	19.00
☐ 93B Red Schoendienst and Enos Slaughter	30.00	13.50	3.70
☐ 93C Cliff Chambers and Wally Westlake	20.00	9.00	2.50

1983 Star Schmidt

This 15-card standard-size set features Phillies great Mike Schmidt. This was the first baseball set issued by the Star Company, who had the NBA contract in the mid-1980's. Star company products are usually sold in complete set form. We have, for this set, as well for all Star Company sets, listed all the cards in these sets.

	NRMT	VG-E	GOOD
COMPLETE SET	30.00	13.50	3.70
COMMON CARD	2.00	.90	.25
☐ 1 Mike Schmidt Checklist	2.00	.90	.25
☐ 2 Mike Schmidt Regular Season Stats	2.00	.90	.25
☐ 3 Mike Schmidt Post Season Stats	2.00	.90	.25
☐ 4 Mike Schmidt 1981 W.S. MVP	2.00	.90	.25
☐ 5 Mike Schmidt Seven Times A-S	2.00	.90	.25
☐ 6 Mike Schmidt 1980 N.L. MVP	2.00	.90	.25
☐ 7 Mike Schmidt 1981 N.L. MVP	2.00	.90	.25
☐ 8 Mike Schmidt ML;HR Stats	2.00	.90	.25
☐ 9 Mike Schmidt Power Stats	2.00	.90	.25
☐ 10 Mike Schmidt Four HR's In A Game	2.00	.90	.25
☐ 11 Mike Schmidt Four Cons. HR's	2.00	.90	.25
☐ 12 Mike Schmidt N.L. HR Stats	2.00	.90	.25
☐ 13 Mike Schmidt Phillies Club Records I	2.00	.90	.25
☐ 14 Mike Schmidt Phillies Club Records II	2.00	.90	.25
☐ 15 Mike Schmidt Personal Data	2.00	.90	.25

1984 Star Brett

This 24 card standard-size set features long time Kansas City Royals star George Brett. This set was issued in complete set form. However, we have listed each individual card in this set.

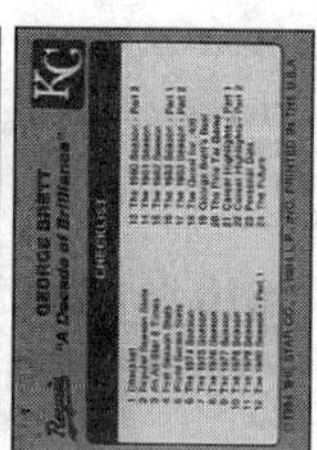

	NRMT	VG-E	GOOD
COMPLETE SET (24)	20.00	9.00	2.50
COMMON CARD (1-24)	1.00	.45	.12
☐ 1 George Brett CL	1.00	.45	.12
☐ 2 George Brett Regular Season Stats	1.00	.45	.12
☐ 3 George Brett An All-Star 8 Times	1.00	.45	.12
☐ 4 George Brett Post Season Stats	1.00	.45	.12
☐ 5 George Brett World Series Stats	1.00	.45	.12
☐ 6 George Brett The 1974 Season	1.00	.45	.12
☐ 7 George Brett The 1975 Season	1.00	.45	.12
☐ 8 George Brett The 1976 Season	1.00	.45	.12
☐ 9 George Brett The 1977 Season	1.00	.45	.12
☐ 10 George Brett The 1978 Season	1.00	.45	.12
☐ 11 George Brett The 1979 Season	1.00	.45	.12
☐ 12 George Brett The 1980 Season - Part 1	1.00	.45	.12
☐ 13 George Brett The 1980 Season - Part 2	1.00	.45	.12
☐ 14 George Brett The 1981 Season	1.00	.45	.12
☐ 15 George Brett The 1982 Season	1.00	.45	.12
☐ 16 George Brett The 1983 Season - Part 1	1.00	.45	.12
☐ 17 George Brett The 1983 Season - Part 2	1.00	.45	.12
☐ 18 George Brett The Quest For .400	1.00	.45	.12
☐ 19 George Brett George Brett's Best	1.00	.45	.12
☐ 20 George Brett The Pine Tar Game	1.00	.45	.12
☐ 21 George Brett Career Highlights - Part 1	1.00	.45	.12
☐ 22 George Brett Career Highlights - Part 2	1.00	.45	.12
☐ 23 George Brett Personal Data	1.00	.45	.12
☐ 24 George Brett The Future	1.00	.45	.12

1984 Star Carlton

This 24-card standard-size set features another Philly great, Steve Carlton. The set was issued in complete form and can be dated by the "Star 84" notation.

	NRMT	VG-E	GOOD
COMPLETE SET	20.00	9.00	2.50
COMMON CARD	1.00	.45	.12
☐ 1 Steve Carlton Checklist	1.00	.45	.12
☐ 2 Steve Carlton Regular Season Stats	1.00	.45	.12
☐ 3 Steve Carlton Career Batting	1.00	.45	.12
☐ 4 Steve Carlton The Beginning The St. Louis Years	1.00	.45	.12
☐ 5 Steve Carlton The St. Louis Years - Stats	1.00	.45	.12
☐ 6 Steve Carlton Post Season Stats	1.00	.45	.12
☐ 7 Steve Carlton W.S. Stats	1.00	.45	.12
☐ 8 Steve Carlton 1st Cy Young '72	1.00	.45	.12
☐ 9 Steve Carlton 2nd Cy Young '77	1.00	.45	.12
☐ 10 Steve Carlton 3rd Cy Young '80	1.00	.45	.12
☐ 11 Steve Carlton 4th Cy Young '82	1.00	.45	.12
☐ 12 Steve Carlton Milestone Victories	1.00	.45	.12
☐ 13 Steve Carlton All-Star Ten Times	1.00	.45	.12
☐ 14 Steve Carlton Milestone Strikeouts	1.00	.45	.12
☐ 15 Steve Carlton All-Time ML Rankings	1.00	.45	.12
☐ 16 Steve Carlton All-Time NL Rankings	1.00	.45	.12
☐ 17 Steve Carlton Phillie All-Time Rankings	1.00	.45	.12
☐ 18 Steve Carlton League Leader	1.00	.45	.12
☐ 19 Steve Carlton Steve's 1-Hitters	1.00	.45	.12
☐ 20 Steve Carlton Longest No-Hit Bid	1.00	.45	.12
☐ 21 Steve Carlton Complete Game Shutouts	1.00	.45	.12
☐ 22 Steve Carlton Other Awards, Records and Facts	1.00	.45	.12
☐ 23 Steve Carlton Personal Data	1.00	.45	.12
☐ 24 Steve Carlton The Future	1.00	.45	.12

1984 Star Garvey

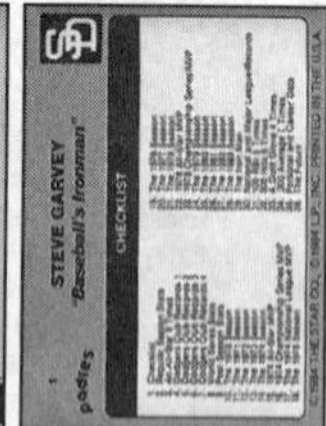

This 36 card standard-size set features San Diego and Los Angeles star Steve Garvey. Garvey, who established a consecutive game streak in the National League, led the Padres to the 1984 National League Pennant. These card trace his career.

	NRMT	VG-E	GOOD
COMPLETE SET (36)	20.00	9.00	2.50
COMMON CARD (1-36)	.60	.25	.07
☐ 1 Steve Garvey CL	.60	.25	.07
☐ 2 Steve Garvey Regular Season Stats	.60	.25	.07
☐ 3 Steve Garvey An All-Star 9 Times	.60	.25	.07
☐ 4 Steve Garvey Dodgers Club Records 1	.60	.25	.07
☐ 5 Steve Garvey Dodgers Club Records 2	.60	.25	.07
☐ 6 Steve Garvey Dodgers Club Records 3	.60	.25	.07
☐ 7 Steve Garvey Dodgers Club Records 4	.60	.25	.07
☐ 8 Steve Garvey World Series Stats	.60	.25	.07
☐ 9 Steve Garvey Post Season Stats	.60	.25	.07
☐ 10 Steve Garvey The 1970 Season	.60	.25	.07
☐ 11 Steve Garvey The 1971 Season	.60	.25	.07
☐ 12 Steve Garvey The 1972 Season	.60	.25	.07
☐ 13 Steve Garvey The 1973 Season	.60	.25	.07
☐ 14 Steve Garvey The 1974 Season	.60	.25	.07
☐ 15 Steve Garvey 1974 All-Star MVP	.60	.25	.07
☐ 16 Steve Garvey 1974 Championship Series MVP	.60	.25	.07
☐ 17 Steve Garvey The 1974 National League MVP	.60	.25	.07
☐ 18 Steve Garvey The 1975 Season	.60	.25	.07
☐ 19 Steve Garvey The 1976 Season	.60	.25	.07
☐ 20 Steve Garvey The 1977 Season	.60	.25	.07
☐ 21 Steve Garvey The 1978 Season	.60	.25	.07
☐ 22 Steve Garvey 1978 All-Star MVP	.60	.25	.07
☐ 23 Steve Garvey 1978 Championship Series MVP	.60	.25	.07
☐ 24 Steve Garvey The 1979 Season	.60	.25	.07
☐ 25 Steve Garvey The 1980 Season	.60	.25	.07
☐ 26 Steve Garvey The 1981 Season	.60	.25	.07
☐ 27 Steve Garvey The 1982 Season	.60	.25	.07
☐ 28 Steve Garvey The 1983 Season	.60	.25	.07
☐ 29 Steve Garvey The Iron Man	.60	.25	.07
☐ 30 Steve Garvey National and Major League Records	.60	.25	.07
☐ 31 Steve Garvey 100 RBI 5 Times	.60	.25	.07
☐ 32 Steve Garvey 200 Hits 6 Times	.60	.25	.07
☐ 33 Steve Garvey A Gold Glove 4 Times	.60	.25	.07
☐ 34 Steve Garvey .300 Average 7 Times	.60	.25	.07
☐ 35 Steve Garvey Personal and Career Data	.60	.25	.07
☐ 36 Steve Garvey The Future	.60	.25	.07

1984 Star Strawberry

This 12-card standard-size set features then Met phenom Darryl Strawberry. This set was issued by the Star company and takes the

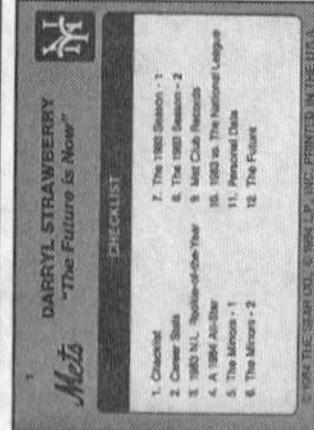

collector through the early part of Strawberry's career. The set is dated with the "Star 84" logo in the upper right corner.

	NRMT	VG-E	GOOD
COMPLETE SET (12)	8.00	3.60	1.00
COMMON CARD (1-12)	.75	.35	.09
☐ 1 Darryl Strawberry CL	.75	.35	.09
☐ 2 Darryl Strawberry Career Stats	.75	.35	.09
☐ 3 Darryl Strawberry 1983 NL Rookie of the Year	.75	.35	.09
☐ 4 Darryl Strawberry A 1984 All-Star	.75	.35	.09
☐ 5 Darryl Strawberry The Minors - 1	.75	.35	.09
☐ 6 Darryl Strawberry The Minors - 2	.75	.35	.09
☐ 7 Darryl Strawberry The 1983 Season - 1	.75	.35	.09
☐ 8 Darryl Strawberry The 1983 Season - 2	.75	.35	.09
☐ 9 Darryl Strawberry Met Club Records	.75	.35	.09
☐ 10 Darryl Strawberry 1983 vs. The National League	.75	.35	.09
☐ 11 Darryl Strawberry Personal Data	.75	.35	.09
☐ 12 Darryl Strawberry The Future	.75	.35	.09

1986 Star Boggs

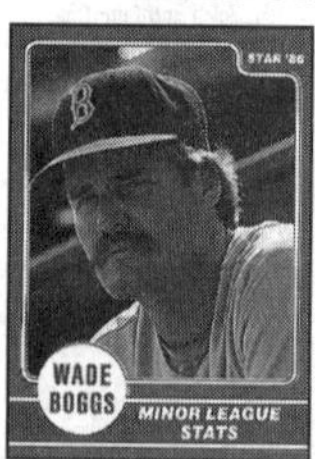

This 12-card standard-size set features then Boston Red Sox hitting star Wade Boggs. The set traces Boggs through the early part of his career. There was also a yellow sticker set issued which has the same value as these red bordered cards.

	MINT	NRMT	EXC
COMPLETE SET (12)	5.00	2.20	.60
COMMON CARD (1-12)	.50	.23	.06
☐ 1 Wade Boggs CL	.50	.23	.06
☐ 2 Wade Boggs Minor League Stats	.50	.23	.06
☐ 3 Wade Boggs Major League Stats	.50	.23	.06
☐ 4 Wade Boggs All-Stat Stats	.50	.23	.06
☐ 5 Wade Boggs 1978 AL MVP	.50	.23	.06
☐ 6 Wade Boggs ML Leaders 1976-85	.50	.23	.06
☐ 7 Wade Boggs Home Run King	.50	.23	.06
☐ 8 Wade Boggs RBI King	.50	.23	.06
☐ 9 Wade Boggs Career Highlights	.50	.23	.06
☐ 10 Wade Boggs Wade's Best	.50	.23	.06
☐ 11 Wade Boggs Personal Data	.50	.23	.06
☐ 12 Wade Boggs The Future	.50	.23	.06

1986 Star Canseco

This 15-card standard-size set was issued by the Star Company to honor young star Jose Canseco. Since many of the cards are titled "His Era Begins," we have given pose descriptions to those cards.

	MINT	NRMT	EXC
COMPLETE SET (15)	6.00	2.70	.75
COMMON CARD (1-15)	.50	.23	.06
☐ 1 Jose Canseco CL	.50	.23	.06
☐ 2 Jose Canseco Minor League Stats	.50	.23	.06

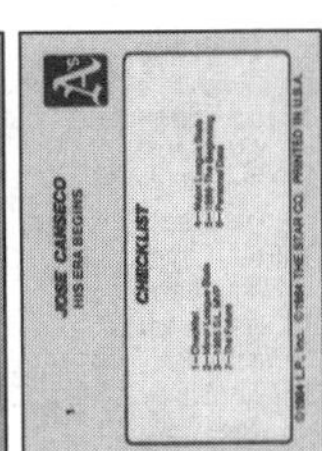

	MINT	NRMT	EXC
☐ 3 Jose Canseco 1985 SL MVP	.50	.23	.06
☐ 4 Jose Canseco Major League Stats	.50	.23	.06
☐ 5 Jose Canseco 1986 - The Beginning	.50	.23	.06
☐ 6 Jose Canseco Personal Data	.50	.23	.06
☐ 7 Jose Canseco The Future	.50	.23	.06
☐ 8 Jose Canseco Horizontal Batting Shot White Uniform	.50	.23	.06
☐ 9 Jose Canseco Running Catch in Field	.50	.23	.06
☐ 10 Jose Canseco Horizontal Batting Shot Green Uniform	.50	.23	.06
☐ 11 Jose Canseco Signing Autographs	.50	.23	.06
☐ 12 Jose Canseco Horizontal Batting Shot Yellow Uniform	.50	.23	.06
☐ 13 Jose Canseco Will Clark	.50	.23	.06
☐ 14 Jose Canseco Standing at Batting Cage	.50	.23	.06
☐ 15 Jose Canseco Follow Through	.50	.23	.06

1986 Star Joyner Red

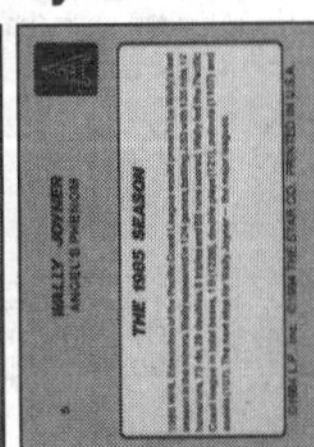

The year 1986 was a big year for young major league players. Wally Joyner, another star rookie in this class is featured in this 15-card standard-size set issued by the Star Company. We have called this the "red" set since the borders are red in color.

	MINT	NRMT	EXC
COMPLETE SET (15)	6.00	2.70	.75
COMMON CARD (1-15)	.50	.23	.06
☐ 1 Wally Joyner CL	.50	.23	.06
☐ 2 Wally Joyner Minor League Stats	.50	.23	.06
☐ 3 Wally Joyner The 1983 Season	.50	.23	.06
☐ 4 Wally Joyner The 1984 Season	.50	.23	.06
☐ 5 Wally Joyner The 1985 Season	.50	.23	.06
☐ 6 Wally Joyner Personal Data	.50	.23	.06
☐ 7 Wally Joyner The Future	.50	.23	.06
☐ 8 Wally Joyner Puzzle Piece	.50	.23	.06
☐ 9 Wally Joyner Puzzle Piece	.50	.23	.06
☐ 10 Wally Joyner Puzzle Piece	.50	.23	.06
☐ 11 Wally Joyner Puzzle Piece	.50	.23	.06
☐ 12 Wally Joyner Puzzle Piece	.50	.23	.06
☐ 13 Wally Joyner Puzzle Piece	.50	.23	.06
☐ 14 Wally Joyner Puzzle Piece	.50	.23	.06
☐ 15 Wally Joyner Puzzle Piece	.50	.23	.06

1986 Star Murphy

The Star company featured Dale Murphy, twice the National League MVP in this 12-card standard-size set. These cards trace the career of Murphy from his early days to the middle of his career.

	MINT	NRMT	EXC
COMPLETE SET (12)	5.00	2.20	.60
COMMON CARD (1-12)	.50	.23	.06

	MINT	NRMT	EXC
☐ 1 Dale Murphy CL	.50	.23	.06
☐ 2 Dale Murphy Minor League Stats	.50	.23	.06
☐ 3 Dale Murphy Regular Season Stats	.50	.23	.06
☐ 4 Dale Murphy Championship Series Stats	.50	.23	.06
☐ 5 Dale Murphy All-Star Stats	.50	.23	.06
☐ 6 Dale Murphy The League Leader	.50	.23	.06
☐ 7 Dale Murphy 1982 National League MVP	.50	.23	.06
☐ 8 Dale Murphy 1983 National League MVP	.50	.23	.06
☐ 9 Dale Murphy Member: 30-30 Club	.50	.23	.06
☐ 10 Dale Murphy Dale's Best	.50	.23	.06
☐ 11 Dale Murphy Personal Data	.50	.23	.06
☐ 12 Dale Murphy The Future	.50	.23	.06

1986 Star Rice

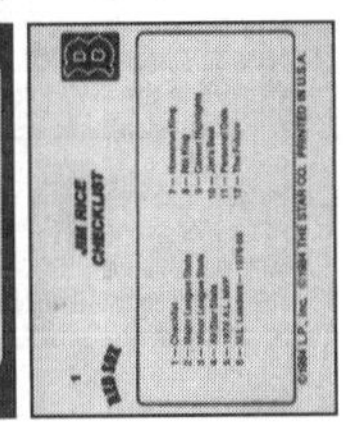

This 12-card standard-size set features Red Sox slugger Jim Rice. The set was issued by the Star company and has the traditional "Star 86" logo in the upper right corner.

	MINT	NRMT	EXC
COMPLETE SET (12)	5.00	2.20	.60
COMMON CARD (1-12)	.50	.23	.06
☐ 1 Jim Rice CL	.50	.23	.06
☐ 2 Jim Rice Major League Stats	.50	.23	.06
☐ 3 Jim Rice Minor League Stats	.50	.23	.06
☐ 4 Jim Rice All-Star Stats	.50	.23	.06
☐ 5 Jim Rice 1978 AL MVP	.50	.23	.06
☐ 6 Jim Rice M.L. Leaders - 1976-85	.50	.23	.06
☐ 7 Jim Rice Homerun King	.50	.23	.06
☐ 8 Jim Rice RBI King	.50	.23	.06
☐ 9 Jim Rice Career Highlights	.50	.23	.06
☐ 10 Jim Rice Jim's Best	.50	.23	.06
☐ 11 Jim Rice Personal Data	.50	.23	.06
☐ 12 Jim Rice The Future	.50	.23	.06

1986 Star Seaver

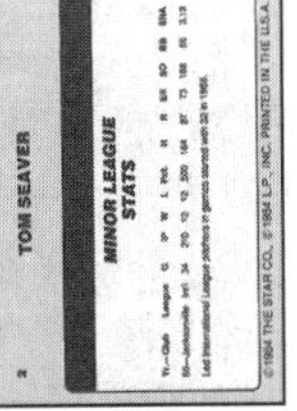

This 12-card standard-size set features Hall of Fame pitcher to be Tom Seaver. These cards trace Seaver's career from his early days in the Mets organization through the end of his career.

	MINT	NRMT	EXC
COMPLETE SET (12)	5.00	2.20	.60
COMMON CARD (1-12)	.50	.23	.06
☐ 1 Tom Seaver CL	.50	.23	.06
☐ 2 Tom Seaver Minor League Stats	.50	.23	.06
☐ 3 Tom Seaver Major League Stats	.50	.23	.06
☐ 4 Tom Seaver Championship Series Stats	.50	.23	.06
☐ 5 Tom Seaver World Series Stats	.50	.23	.06
☐ 6 Tom Seaver All-Star Stats	.50	.23	.06
☐ 7 Tom Seaver Major League Records	.50	.23	.06
☐ 8 Tom Seaver 3 Times Cy Young	.50	.23	.06
☐ 9 Tom Seaver 1967 Rookie of the Year	.50	.23	.06
☐ 10 Tom Seaver 300 Wins!	.50	.23	.06
☐ 11 Tom Seaver Tom's No-Hitter	.50	.23	.06
☐ 12 Tom Seaver The Future	.50	.23	.06

1986 Star Stickers Canseco

This 15-card standard-size set features young star Jose Canseco. This set displays the same photos as the regular Star set but these items are blank-backed.

	MINT	NRMT	EXC
COMPLETE SET (15)	6.00	2.70	.75
COMMON CARD (1-15)	.40	.18	.05
☐ 1 Jose Canseco Sticker Set/CL	.40	.18	.05
☐ 2 Jose Canseco Minor League Stats	.40	.18	.05
☐ 3 Jose Canseco 1985 S.L. MVP	.40	.18	.05
☐ 4 Jose Canseco 1986 - The Beginning	.40	.18	.05
☐ 5 Jose Canseco Major League Stats	.40	.18	.05
☐ 6 Jose Canseco Personal Data	.40	.18	.05
☐ 7 Jose Canseco The Future	.40	.18	.05
☐ 8 Jose Canseco His Era Begins	.40	.18	.05
☐ 9 Jose Canseco His Era Begins	.40	.18	.05
☐ 10 Jose Canseco His Era Begins	.40	.18	.05
☐ 11 Jose Canseco His Era Begins	.40	.18	.05
☐ 12 Jose Canseco His Era Begins	.40	.18	.05
☐ 13 Jose Canseco His Era Begins	.40	.18	.05
☐ 14 Jose Canseco His Era Begins	.40	.18	.05
☐ 15 Jose Canseco His Era Begins	.40	.18	.05

1986 Star Stickers Joyner Blue

The same photos as in the 1986 Star Joyner Red set are featured. The difference between this set and the cards are the blank backed stickers and the blue borders for these cards.

	MINT	NRMT	EXC
COMPLETE SET (15)	6.00	2.70	.75
COMMON CARD (1-15)	.40	.18	.05
☐ 1 Wally Joyner Sticker Set - Blue	.40	.18	.05
☐ 2 Wally Joyner Minor League Stats	.40	.18	.05
☐ 3 Wally Joyner The 1983 Season	.40	.18	.05
☐ 4 Wally Joyner The 1984 Season	.40	.18	.05
☐ 5 Wally Joyner The 1985 Season	.40	.18	.05
☐ 6 Wally Joyner Personal Data	.40	.18	.05
☐ 7 Wally Joyner The Future	.40	.18	.05
☐ 8 Wally Joyner Angel's Phenom	.40	.18	.05
☐ 9 Wally Joyner Angel's Phenom	.40	.18	.05
☐ 10 Wally Joyner Angel's Phenom	.40	.18	.05
☐ 11 Wally Joyner Angel's Phenom	.40	.18	.05
☐ 12 Wally Joyner Angel's Phenom	.40	.18	.05
☐ 13 Wally Joyner Angel's Phenom	.40	.18	.05
☐ 14 Wally Joyner Angel's Phenom	.40	.18	.05
☐ 15 Wally Joyner Angel's Phenom	.40	.18	.05

1987 Star Award Winners

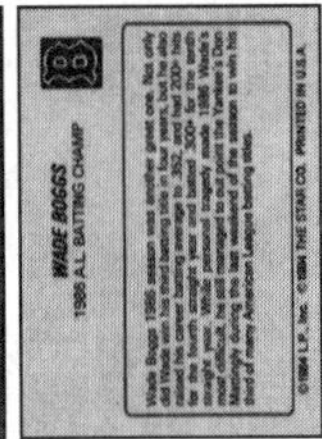

These five standard-size cards feature Jose Canseco and Wade Boggs who won various honors during the 1986 season.

	MINT	NRMT	EXC
COMPLETE SET (5)	2.00	.90	.25
COMMON CARD (1-5)	.50	.23	.06
☐ 1 Jose Canseco 1986 A.L. Top Rookie	.50	.23	.06
☐ 2 Jose Canseco 1986 Stats	.50	.23	.06
☐ 3 Jose Canseco Rookie Voting	.50	.23	.06
☐ 4 Wade Boggs 1986 A.L. Batting Champ	.50	.23	.06
☐ 5 Wade Boggs 1986 A.L. Batting Champ (Portrait)	.50	.23	.06

1987 Star Gary Carter

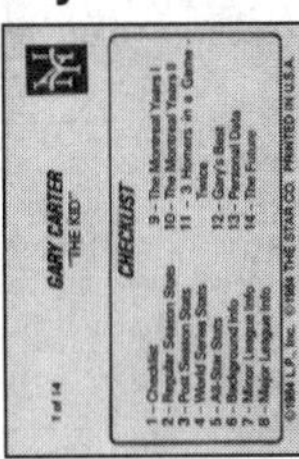

This 14-card standard-size set features long-time star catcher Gary Carter. These cards have a "Star 87" logo in the upper right corner.

	MINT	NRMT	EXC
COMPLETE SET (14)	5.00	2.20	.60
COMMON CARD (1-14)	.40	.18	.05
☐ 1 Gary Carter CL	.40	.18	.05
☐ 2 Gary Carter Regular Season Stats	.40	.18	.05
☐ 3 Gary Carter Post Season Stats	.40	.18	.05
☐ 4 Gary Carter World Series Stats	.40	.18	.05
☐ 5 Gary Carter All-Star Stats	.40	.18	.05
☐ 6 Gary Carter Background Info	.40	.18	.05
☐ 7 Gary Carter Minor League Info	.40	.18	.05
☐ 8 Gary Carter Major League Info	.40	.18	.05
☐ 9 Gary Carter The Montreal Years I	.40	.18	.05
☐ 10 Gary Carter The Montreal Years II	.40	.18	.05
☐ 11 Gary Carter	.40	.18	.05

	MINT	NRMT	EXC
3 Homers in a Game - Twice			
☐ 12 Gary Carter	.40	.18	.05
Gary's Best			
☐ 13 Gary Carter	.40	.18	.05
Personal Data			
☐ 14 Gary Carter	.40	.18	.05
The Future			

1987 Star Clemens

This 12-card standard-size set features Roger Clemens, who was in the process of winning consecutive Cy Young Awards. Clemens' career is traced from the beginning to his sensational 1986 season.

	MINT	NRMT	EXC
COMPLETE SET (12)	5.00	2.20	.60
COMMON CARD (1-12)	.50	.23	.06
☐ 1 Roger Clemens CL	.50	.23	.06
☐ 2 Roger Clemens	.50	.23	.06
Regular Season Stats			
☐ 3 Roger Clemens	.50	.23	.06
Playoff Stats			
☐ 4 Roger Clemens	.50	.23	.06
World Series Stats			
☐ 5 Roger Clemens	.50	.23	.06
1986 All-Star MVP			
☐ 6 Roger Clemens	.50	.23	.06
1986 AL Cy Young			
☐ 7 Roger Clemens	.50	.23	.06
1986 AL MVP			
☐ 8 Roger Clemens	.50	.23	.06
20 K's In 9 Innings			
☐ 9 Roger Clemens	.50	.23	.06
1986 Highlights I			
☐ 10 Roger Clemens	.50	.23	.06
1986 Highlights II			
☐ 11 Roger Clemens	.50	.23	.06
Personal Data			
☐ 12 Roger Clemens	.50	.23	.06
The Future			

1987 Star Clemens II

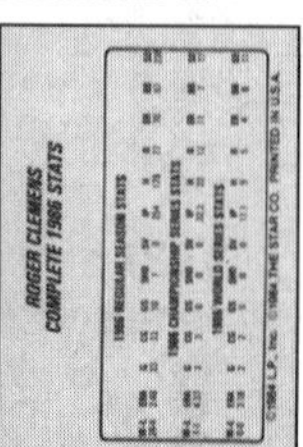

These five standard-size cards update the first Roger Clemens set issued earlier in 1987. These cards have a pink border as compared to the red border in the regular issue.

	MINT	NRMT	EXC
COMPLETE SET (5)	2.00	.90	.25
COMMON CARD (1-5)	.50	.23	.06
☐ 1 Roger Clemens	.50	.23	.06
Complete 1986 Stats			
☐ 2 Roger Clemens	.50	.23	.06
1986 Cy Young , MVP			
☐ 3 Roger Clemens	.50	.23	.06
1986 Highlights I			
☐ 4 Roger Clemens	.50	.23	.06
1986 Highlights II			
☐ 5 Roger Clemens	.50	.23	.06
1986 Highlights III			

1987 Star Hernandez

This 13-card standard-size set features Keith Hernandez. These cards trace Hernandez' career from its beginnings to the time of issue.

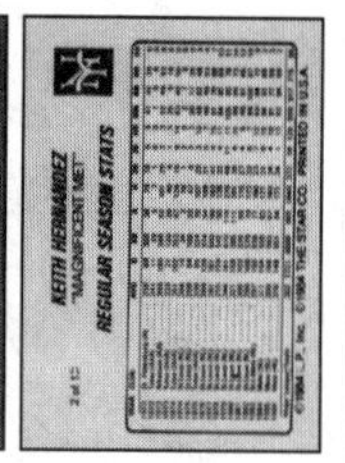

	MINT	NRMT	EXC
COMPLETE SET (13)	4.00	1.80	.50
COMMON CARD (1-13)	.35	.16	.04
☐ 1 Keith Hernandez CL	.40	.18	.05
☐ 2 Keith Hernandez	.40	.18	.05
Regular Season Stats			
☐ 3 Keith Hernandez	.40	.18	.05
Post Season Stats			
☐ 4 Keith Hernandez	.40	.18	.05
World Series Stats			
☐ 5 Keith Hernandez	.40	.18	.05
All-Star Stats			
☐ 6 Keith Hernandez	.40	.18	.05
1979 NL Co-MVP			
☐ 7 Keith Hernandez	.40	.18	.05
Background Info			
☐ 8 Keith Hernandez	.40	.18	.05
Minor League Info			
☐ 9 Keith Hernandez	.40	.18	.05
The League Leader			
☐ 10 Keith Hernandez	.40	.18	.05
Major League Info			
☐ 11 Keith Hernandez	.40	.18	.05
Keith's Best			
☐ 12 Keith Hernandez	.40	.18	.05
Personal Data			
☐ 13 Keith Hernandez	.40	.18	.05
The Future			

1987 Star Mattingly Blankback

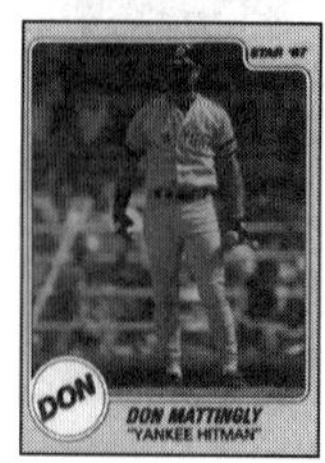

These six cards feature Yankee great Don Mattingly. These cards are differentiated from the other Mattingly cards because of the blank back

	MINT	NRMT	EXC
COMPLETE SET (6)	2.50	1.10	.30
COMMON CARD (1-6)	.50	.23	.06
☐ 1 Don Mattingly	.50	.23	.06
1986 Stats			
☐ 2 Don Mattingly	.50	.23	.06
(In fielding position)			
☐ 3 Don Mattingly	.50	.23	.06
(Talking to fans)			
☐ 4 Don Mattingly	.50	.23	.06
(Running the bases)			
☐ 5 Don Mattingly	.50	.23	.06
(Batting)			
☐ 6 Don Mattingly	.50	.23	.06
(Holding Bat)			

1987 Star Raines

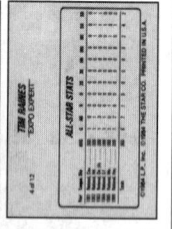

This 12-card standard-size set features baseball star Tim Raines. The "Star '87" logo in the upper right dates the set which traces his career from its beginnings to the present day.

	MINT	NRMT	EXC
COMPLETE SET (12)	4.00	1.80	.50
COMMON CARD (1-12)	.40	.18	.05
☐ 1 Tim Raines CL	.40	.18	.05
☐ 2 Tim Raines	.40	.18	.05
Regular Season Stats			
☐ 3 Tim Raines	.40	.18	.05
Playoff Stats			
☐ 4 Tim Raines	.40	.18	.05
All-Star Stats			
☐ 5 Tim Raines	.40	.18	.05
Career Highs			
☐ 6 Tim Raines	.40	.18	.05
Stolen Base King			
☐ 7 Tim Raines	.40	.18	.05
The League Leader			
☐ 8 Tim Raines	.40	.18	.05
1986 NL Batting Champ			
☐ 9 Tim Raines	.40	.18	.05
Career Highlights I			
☐ 10 Tim Raines	.40	.18	.05
Career Highlights II			
☐ 11 Tim Raines	.40	.18	.05
Personal Data			
☐ 12 Tim Raines	.40	.18	.05
The Future			

1987 Star Valenzuela

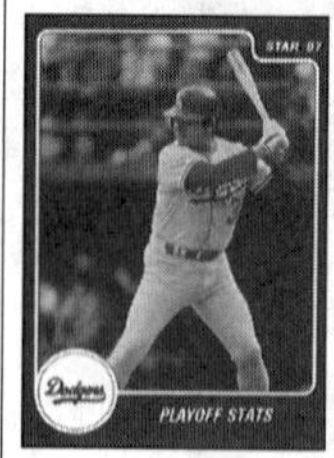

These 13 standard-size cards feature highlights in the career of Fernando Valuenzuela. These cards trace his career from its beginnings to the present day.

	MINT	NRMT	EXC
COMPLETE SET (13)	5.00	2.20	.60
COMMON CARD (1-13)	.40	.18	.05
☐ 1 Fernando Valenzuela CL	.40	.18	.05
☐ 2 Fernando Valenzuela	.40	.18	.05
Regular Season Stats			
☐ 3 Fernando Valenzuela	.40	.18	.05
Playoff Stats			
☐ 4 Fernando Valenzuela	.40	.18	.05
World Series Stats			
☐ 5 Fernando Valenzuela	.40	.18	.05
All-Star Stats			
☐ 6 Fernando Valenzuela	.40	.18	.05
Batting Stats			
☐ 7 Fernando Valenzuela	.40	.18	.05
1981 Cy Young and Top Rookie			
☐ 8 Fernando Valenzuela	.40	.18	.05
21 Wins - 1986			
☐ 9 Fernando Valenzuela	.40	.18	.05
The League Leader			
☐ 10 Fernando Valenzuela	.40	.18	.05
Fernando's Best			
☐ 11 Fernando Valenzuela	.40	.18	.05
Lifetime Won/Lost Record			
☐ 12 Fernando Valenzuela	.40	.18	.05
Personal Data			
☐ 13 Fernando Valenzuela	.40	.18	.05
The Future			

1987 Star Sticker Mattingly

These 24 standard-size stickers feature Yankee great Don Mattingly. These stickers are blank backed and trace his career from the minors to the present day.

	MINT	NRMT	EXC
COMPLETE SET (24)	10.00	4.50	1.25
COMMON CARD (1-24)	.50	.23	.06
☐ 1 Don Mattingly Sticker Set CL	.50	.23	.06
☐ 2 Don Mattingly	.50	.23	.06
Minor League Stats			
☐ 3 Don Mattingly	.50	.23	.06
Major League Stats			
☐ 4 Don Mattingly	.50	.23	.06
All-Star Stats			
☐ 5 Don Mattingly	.50	.23	.06
Career Highlights			
☐ 6 Don Mattingly	.50	.23	.06
1980 S.A.L. MVP			
☐ 7 Don Mattingly	.50	.23	.06
The 1982 Season			
☐ 8 Don Mattingly	.50	.23	.06
The 1983 Season			
☐ 9 Don Mattingly	.50	.23	.06
The 1984 Season			
☐ 10 Don Mattingly	.50	.23	.06
1985 A.L. MVP			
☐ 11 Don Mattingly	.50	.23	.06
Personal Data			
☐ 12 Don Mattingly	.50	.23	.06
The Future			
☐ 13 Don Mattingly	.50	.23	.06
Yankee Great			
☐ 14 Don Mattingly	.50	.23	.06
Yankee Great			
☐ 15 Don Mattingly	.50	.23	.06
Yankee Great			
☐ 16 Don Mattingly	.50	.23	.06
Yankee Great			
☐ 17 Don Mattingly	.50	.23	.06
Yankee Great			
☐ 18 Don Mattingly	.50	.23	.06
Yankee Great			
☐ 19 Don Mattingly	.50	.23	.06
Yankee Great			
☐ 20 Don Mattingly	.50	.23	.06
Yankee Great			
☐ 21 Don Mattingly	.50	.23	.06
Yankee Great			
☐ 22 Don Mattingly	.50	.23	.06
Yankee Great			
☐ 23 Don Mattingly	.50	.23	.06
Yankee Great			
☐ 24 Don Mattingly	.50	.23	.06
Yankee Great			

1987 Star Sticker Valenzuela

These 10 standard-size sticker set is different from the regular cards issued by Star about Valenzuela. These cards have blank backs and also feature highlights in Valenzuela's career.

	MINT	NRMT	EXC
COMPLETE SET (10)	3.50	1.55	.45
COMMON CARD (1-10)	.40	.18	.05
☐ 1 Fernando Valenzuela	.40	.18	.05
Sticker Set			
☐ 2 Fernando Valenzuela	.40	.18	.05
1274 Career K's			
☐ 3 Fernando Valenzuela	.40	.18	.05
1981 N.L. Cy Young			
☐ 4 Fernando Valenzuela	.40	.18	.05
.203 Career Hitter			
☐ 5 Fernando Valenzuela	.40	.18	.05
6 Time All-Star			
☐ 6 Fernando Valenzuela	.40	.18	.05
2.94 Career ERA			
☐ 7 Fernando Valenzuela	.40	.18	.05
21 Wins In 1986			
☐ 8 Fernando Valenzuela	.40	.18	.05
99 Career Wins			
☐ 9 Fernando Valenzuela	.40	.18	.05
1981 N.L. Top Rookie			
☐ 10 Fernando Valenzuela	.40	.18	.05
26 Career Shutouts			

1988 Star Bell

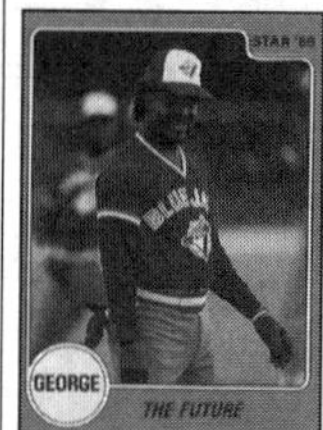
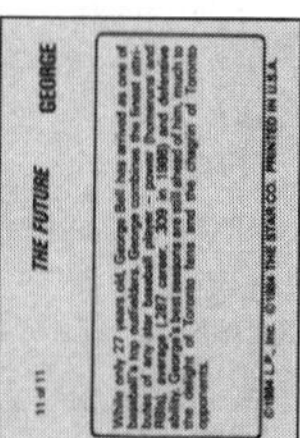

These 11 standard-size cards feature highlights in the career of George Bell, 1987 American League MVP. The cards are dated by the 1988 copyright on the back..

	MINT	NRMT	EXC
COMPLETE SET (11)	4.00	1.80	.50
COMMON CARD (1-11)	.40	.18	.05
☐ 1 George Bell CL	.40	.18	.05
☐ 2 George Bell	.40	.18	.05
Minor League Stats			
☐ 3 George Bell	.40	.18	.05
Major League Stats			
☐ 4 George Bell	.40	.18	.05
Playoff Stats			
☐ 5 George Bell	.40	.18	.05
Career Transactions			
☐ 6 George Bell	.40	.18	.05
The 1983 Season			

Card	MINT	NRMT	EXC
☐ 7 George Bell The 1984 Season	.40	.18	.05
☐ 8 George Bell The 1985 Season	.40	.18	.05
☐ 9 George Bell The 1986 Season	.40	.18	.05
☐ 10 George Bell Personal Data and Highlights	.40	.18	.05
☐ 11 George Bell The Future	.40	.18	.05

1988 Star Boggs

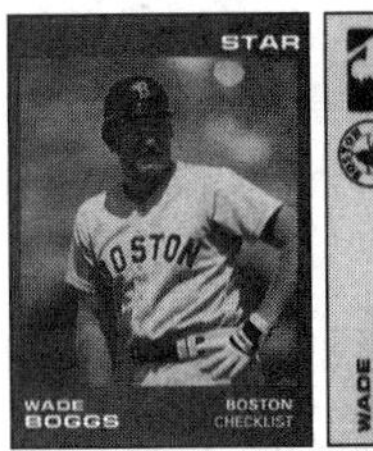

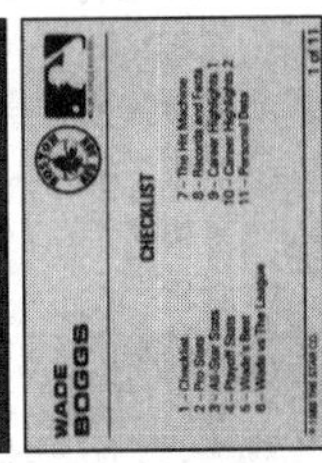

This 11-card set of Wade Boggs features color player photos in a red border. The player's name, team, and card title are printed in the bottom margin while the top contains the word, "Star," in the upper right margin. The backs carry the information indicated by the card title.

	MINT	NRMT	EXC
COMPLETE SET (11)	5.00	2.20	.60
COMMON CARD (1-11)	.50	.23	.06
☐ 1 Wade Boggs CL	.50	.23	.06
☐ 2 Wade Boggs Pro Stats	.50	.23	.06
☐ 3 Wade Boggs All-Star Stats	.50	.23	.06
☐ 4 Wade Boggs Playoff Stats	.50	.23	.06
☐ 5 Wade Boggs Wade's Best	.50	.23	.06
☐ 6 Wade Boggs Wade vs The League	.50	.23	.06
☐ 7 Wade Boggs The Hit Machine	.50	.23	.06
☐ 8 Wade Boggs Records and Facts	.50	.23	.06
☐ 9 Wade Boggs Career Highlights 1	.50	.23	.06
☐ 10 Wade Boggs Career Highlights 2	.50	.23	.06
☐ 11 Wade Boggs Personal Data	.50	.23	.06

1988 Star Boggs Hitman

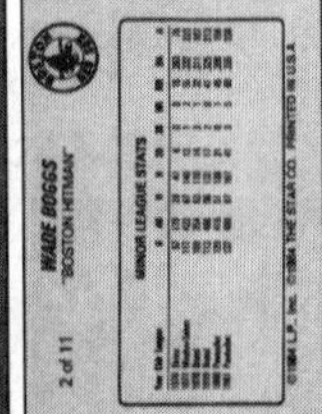

These 11 standard-size cards feature highlights in the career of Boston Red Sox hitting star, Wade Boggs. These cards are dated by the 1988 copyright on the back. Various highlights of Boggs' career are noted.

	MINT	NRMT	EXC
COMPLETE SET (11)	5.00	2.20	.60
COMMON CARD (1-11)	.50	.23	.06
☐ 1 Wade Boggs CL	.50	.23	.06
☐ 2 Wade Boggs Minor League Stats	.50	.23	.06
☐ 3 Wade Boggs Major League Stats	.50	.23	.06
☐ 4 Wade Boggs All-Star Stats	.50	.23	.06
☐ 5 Wade Boggs Post Season Stats	.50	.23	.06
☐ 6 Wade Boggs The 200+ Hit Streak	.50	.23	.06
☐ 7 Wade Boggs The .300+ Average Streak	.50	.23	.06
☐ 8 Wade Boggs 3 Time Batting Champ	.50	.23	.06
☐ 9 Wade Boggs Records	.50	.23	.06
☐ 10 Wade Boggs Personal Info	.50	.23	.06
☐ 11 Wade Boggs The Future	.50	.23	.06

1988 Star Boggs/Gwynn

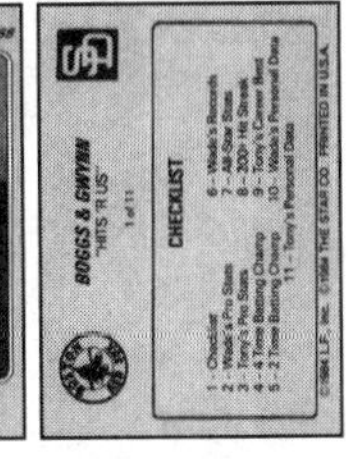

Two of baseball's best hitters: Wade Boggs and Tony Gwynn are featured in this 11-card standard-size set. Other than the checklist card on which both players are pictured, the set alternates between Boggs and Gwynn cards.

	MINT	NRMT	EXC
COMPLETE SET (11)	5.00	2.20	.60
COMMON CARD (1-11)	.50	.23	.06
☐ 1 Wade Boggs Tony Gwynn CL	.75	.35	.09
☐ 2 Wade Boggs Wade's Pro Stats	.50	.23	.06
☐ 3 Tony Gwynn Tony's Pro Stats	.75	.35	.09
☐ 4 Wade Boggs 4 Time Batting Champ	.50	.23	.06
☐ 5 Tony Gwynn 2 Time Batting Champ	.75	.35	.09
☐ 6 Wade Boggs Wade's Records	.50	.23	.06
☐ 7 Tony Gwynn All-Star Stats	.75	.35	.09
☐ 8 Wade Boggs 200+ Hit Streak	.50	.23	.06
☐ 9 Tony Gwynn Tony's Career Best	.75	.35	.09
☐ 10 Wade Boggs Wade's Personal Data	.50	.23	.06
☐ 11 Tony Gwynn Tony's Personal Data	.75	.35	.09

1988 Star Canseco

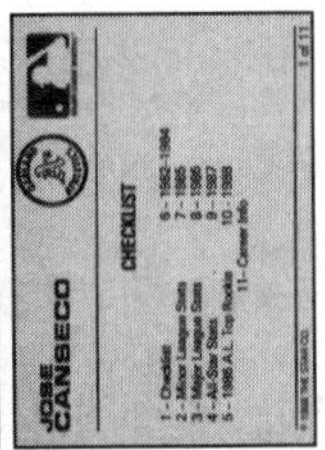

This 11-card standard-size set features highlights in the career of Jose Canseco. The set is dated to 1988 with the 1988 copyright on the back.

	MINT	NRMT	EXC
COMPLETE SET (11)	5.00	2.20	.60
COMMON CARD (1-11)	.50	.23	.06
☐ 1 Jose Canseco CL	.50	.23	.06
☐ 2 Jose Canseco Minor League Stats	.50	.23	.06
☐ 3 Jose Canseco Major League Stats	.50	.23	.06
☐ 4 Jose Canseco All-Star Stats	.50	.23	.06
☐ 5 Jose Canseco 1986 AL Top Rookie	.50	.23	.06
☐ 6 Jose Canseco 1982-1984	.50	.23	.06
☐ 7 Jose Canseco 1985	.50	.23	.06
☐ 8 Jose Canseco 1986	.50	.23	.06
☐ 9 Jose Canseco 1987	.50	.23	.06
☐ 10 Jose Canseco 1988	.50	.23	.06
☐ 11 Jose Canseco Career Info	.50	.23	.06

1988 Star Gary Carter

These 11 standard-size set, features yet again, Mets catcher Gary Carter. These cards trace his career from the beginning to the present day. The set is dated by the 1988 copyright on the back.

	MINT	NRMT	EXC
COMPLETE SET (11)	5.00	2.20	.60
COMMON CARD (1-11)	.50	.23	.06
☐ 1 Gary Carter CL	.50	.23	.06
☐ 2 Gary Carter Regular Season Stats	.50	.23	.06

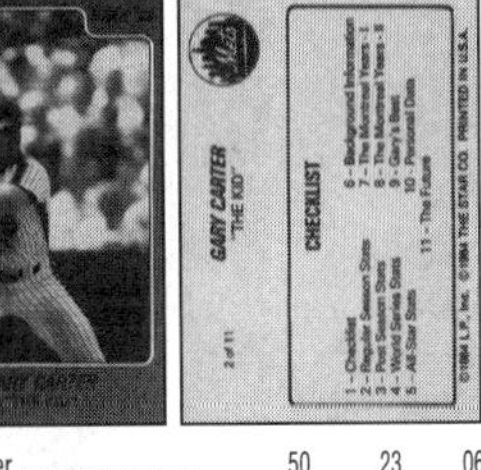

Card	MINT	NRMT	EXC
☐ 3 Gary Carter Post Season Stats	.50	.23	.06
☐ 4 Gary Carter World Series Stats	.50	.23	.06
☐ 5 Gary Carter All-Star Stats	.50	.23	.06
☐ 6 Gary Carter Background Information	.50	.23	.06
☐ 7 Gary Carter The Montreal Years - I	.50	.23	.06
☐ 8 Gary Carter The Montreal Years - II	.50	.23	.06
☐ 9 Gary Carter Gary's Best	.50	.23	.06
☐ 10 Gary Carter Personal Data	.50	.23	.06
☐ 11 Gary Carter The Future	.50	.23	.06

1988 Star Will Clark

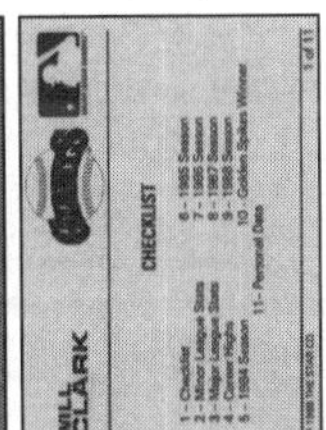

These 11 standard-size cards feature highlights in the career of former Olympian and current star, Will Clark. These cards are dated by the1988 copyright on the back.

	MINT	NRMT	EXC
COMPLETE SET (11)	5.00	2.20	.60
COMMON CARD (1-11)	.50	.23	.06
☐ 1 Will Clark CL	.50	.23	.06
☐ 2 Will Clark Minor League Stats	.50	.23	.06
☐ 3 Will Clark Major League Stats	.50	.23	.06
☐ 4 Will Clark Career Highs	.50	.23	.06
☐ 5 Will Clark 1984 Season	.50	.23	.06
☐ 6 Will Clark 1985 Season	.50	.23	.06
☐ 7 Will Clark 1986 Season	.50	.23	.06
☐ 8 Will Clark 1987 Season	.50	.23	.06
☐ 9 Will Clark 1988 Season	.50	.23	.06
☐ 10 Will Clark Golden Spikes Winner	.50	.23	.06
☐ 11 Will Clark Personal Data	.50	.23	.06

1988 Star Clemens/Gooden

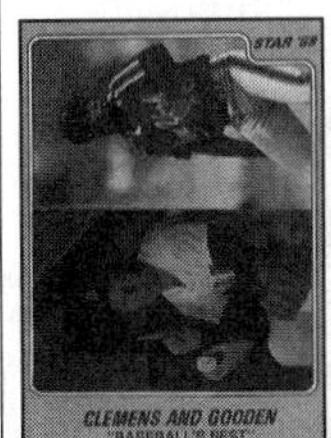

Two pitchers with very parallel careers: Dwight Gooden and Roger Clemens are featured in this set. Other than the checklist card in which pictures of both players are found, the set alternates between cards of Clemens and Gooden.

	MINT	NRMT	EXC
COMPLETE SET (11)	5.00	2.20	.60
COMMON CARD (1-11)	.50	.23	.06
☐ 1 Roger Clemens Dwight Gooden CL	.75	.35	.09
☐ 2 Roger Clemens Roger's Pro Stats	.75	.35	.09
☐ 3 Dwight Gooden Dwight's Pro Stats	.50	.23	.06
☐ 4 Roger Clemens 1986 AL MVP	.75	.35	.09
☐ 5 Dwight Gooden 1985 Cy Young	.50	.23	.06
☐ 6 Roger Clemens 1986 Cy Young	.75	.35	.09
☐ 7 Dwight Gooden 1984 NL Top Rookie	.50	.23	.06
☐ 8 Roger Clemens 1987 Cy Young	.75	.35	.09
☐ 9 Dwight Gooden Dwight's Best	.50	.23	.06
☐ 10 Roger Clemens Personal Data	.75	.35	.09
☐ 11 Dwight Gooden Personal Data	.50	.23	.06

1988 Star Cone

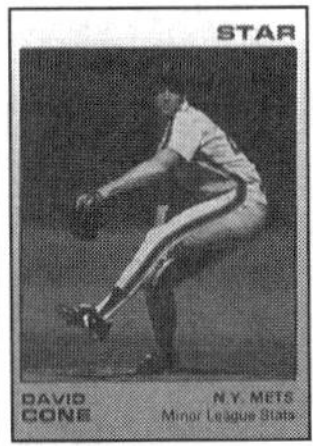

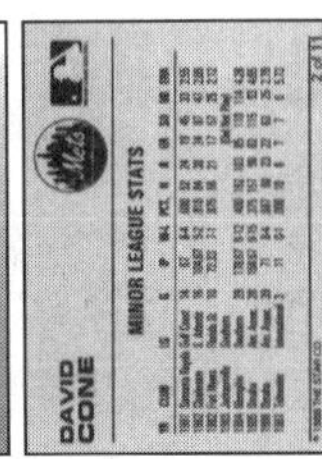

These 11 standard-size cards feature New York Mets star pitcher David Cone. These cards trace his career from the beginning through his breakthrough season in 1988.

	MINT	NRMT	EXC
COMPLETE SET (11)	4.00	1.80	.50
COMMON CARD (1-11)	.40	.18	.05
☐ 1 David Cone CL	.40	.18	.05
☐ 2 David Cone Minor League Stats	.40	.18	.05
☐ 3 David Cone Major League Stats	.40	.18	.05
☐ 4 David Cone Post Season Stats	.40	.18	.05
☐ 5 David Cone 1986 Season	.40	.18	.05
☐ 6 David Cone 1987 Season	.40	.18	.05
☐ 7 David Cone 1988 Season	.40	.18	.05
☐ 8 David Cone Personal Data	.40	.18	.05
☐ 9 David Cone The Future	.40	.18	.05
☐ 10 David Cone N.Y. Mets	.40	.18	.05
☐ 11 David Cone N.Y. Mets	.40	.18	.05

1988 Star Eric Davis

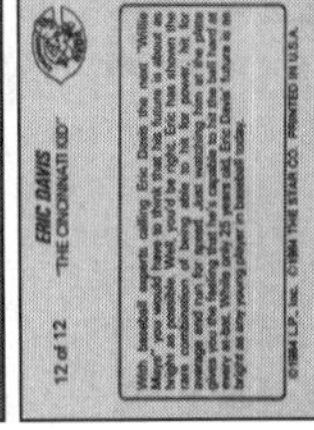

Eric Daivs is featured in this 12-card standard-size set. The cards trace his career from the minors through the present day. The set is dated by the 1988 copyright on the back.

	MINT	NRMT	EXC
COMPLETE SET (12)	4.00	1.80	.50
COMMON CARD (1-12)	.40	.18	.05
☐ 1 Eric Davis CL	.40	.18	.05
☐ 2 Eric Davis Minor League Stats	.40	.18	.05
☐ 3 Eric Davis Major League Stats	.40	.18	.05
☐ 4 Eric Davis The 1986 Season 1	.40	.18	.05
☐ 5 Eric Davis The 1986 Season 2	.40	.18	.05
☐ 6 Eric Davis Career Info 1	.40	.18	.05
☐ 7 Eric Davis Career Info 2	.40	.18	.05
☐ 8 Eric Davis The 1987 Season	.40	.18	.05
☐ 9 Eric Davis Game Highs	.40	.18	.05
☐ 10 Eric Davis	.40	.18	.05

	MINT	NRMT	EXC
1987 All-Star			
□ 11 Eric Davis Personal Data	.40	.18	.05
□ 12 Eric Davis The Future	.40	.18	.05

1988 Star Davis/McGwire

This 11-card standard-size set features cards of Eric Davis and Mark McGwire. Other than the checklist card, the set features a picture of either Davis or McGwire.

	MINT	NRMT	EXC
COMPLETE SET (11)	4.00	1.80	.50
COMMON CARD (1-11)	.40	.18	.05
□ 1 Eric Davis Mark McGwire CL	.75	.35	.09
□ 2 Eric Davis Eric's Minor Stats	.40	.18	.05
□ 3 Mark McGwire Mark's Minor Stats	.75	.35	.09
□ 4 Eric Davis Eric's Major Stats	.40	.18	.05
□ 5 Mark McGwire Mark's Major Stats	.75	.35	.09
□ 6 Eric Davis Eric: The 1987 Season	.40	.18	.05
□ 7 Mark McGwire Mark: Power King	.75	.35	.09
□ 8 Eric Davis Eric's Personal Data	.40	.18	.05
□ 9 Mark McGwire Mark's Personal Data	.75	.35	.09
□ 10 Eric Davis Eric's Future	.40	.18	.05
□ 11 Mark McGwire Mark's Future	.75	.35	.09

1988 Star Dawson

This 11-card standard-size set feature 1987 NL MVP Andre Dawson. Dawson's career is traced from its start to the time of issue. The set is dated with a 1988 copyright on the back.

	MINT	NRMT	EXC
COMPLETE SET (11)	4.00	1.80	.50
COMMON CARD (1-11)	.40	.18	.05
□ 1 Andre Dawson CL	.40	.18	.05
□ 2 Andre Dawson Minor League Stats	.40	.18	.05
□ 3 Andre Dawson Major League Stats	.40	.18	.05
□ 4 Andre Dawson Playoff Stats	.40	.18	.05
□ 5 Andre Dawson All-Star Stats	.40	.18	.05
□ 6 Andre Dawson 1977 NL Top Rookie	.40	.18	.05
□ 7 Andre Dawson 1987 NL MVP	.40	.18	.05
□ 8 Andre Dawson Records	.40	.18	.05
□ 9 Andre Dawson Career Highlights	.40	.18	.05
□ 10 Andre Dawson Personal Data	.40	.18	.05
□ 11 Andre Dawson The Future	.40	.18	.05

1988 Star Gooden Blue

This 12-card set features color photos of Dwight Gooden inside a thin white and red border surrounded by a wider blue border. The card title is printed in the bottom margin with "Star '88" in the top margin. The backs carry the information as indicated by the card title on the front.

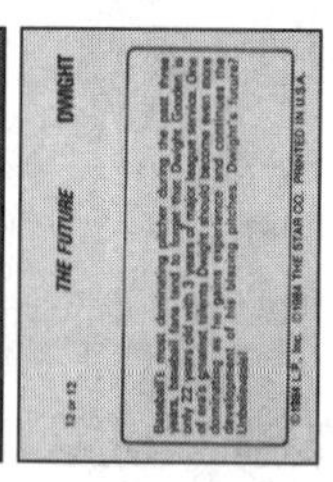

	MINT	NRMT	EXC
COMPLETE SET (12)	5.00	2.20	.60
COMMON CARD (1-12)	.50	.23	.06
□ 1 Dwight Gooden CL	.50	.23	.06
□ 2 Dwight Gooden Major League Stats	.50	.23	.06
□ 3 Dwight Gooden Playoff Stats	.50	.23	.06
□ 4 Dwight Gooden All-Star Stats	.50	.23	.06
□ 5 Dwight Gooden Dwight the Hitter	.50	.23	.06
□ 6 Dwight Gooden Minor League Stats	.50	.23	.06
□ 7 Dwight Gooden 1985 Cy Young	.50	.23	.06
□ 8 Dwight Gooden 1984 NL Top Rookie	.50	.23	.06
□ 9 Dwight Gooden Minor League Info	.50	.23	.06
□ 10 Dwight Gooden Dwight's Best	.50	.23	.06
□ 11 Dwight Gooden Personal Data	.50	.23	.06
□ 12 Dwight Gooden The Future	.50	.23	.06

1988 Star Gooden Orange

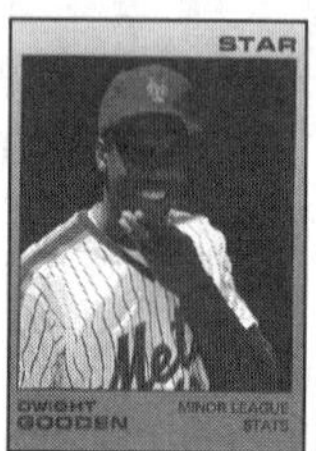

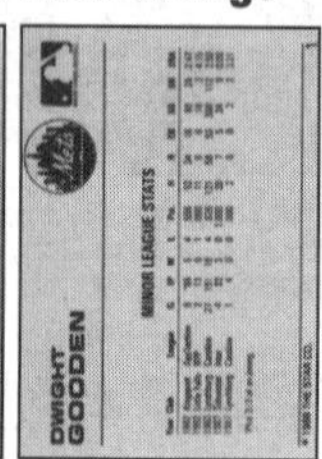

This 11-card standard-size set traces Dwight Gooden's career. These cards are dated by the 1988 copyright on the back. These cards are usually sold as a complete set but we have identified each card from this issue. The fronts feature orange-bordered color phots of Dwight Gooden with his name and card name printed in the bottom margin. The word, "Star," is printed in the top margin. The backs lists the information that identifies the card on the front.

	MINT	NRMT	EXC
COMPLETE SET (11)	5.00	2.20	.60
COMMON CARD (1-11)	.50	.23	.06
□ 1 Dwight Gooden Minor League Stats	.50	.23	.06
□ 2 Dwight Gooden Major League Stats	.50	.23	.06
□ 3 Dwight Gooden Post Season	.50	.23	.06
□ 4 Dwight Gooden All-Star Stats	.50	.23	.06
□ 5 Dwight Gooden Dwight The Hitter	.50	.23	.06
□ 6 Dwight Gooden Minor League Info	.50	.23	.06
□ 7 Dwight Gooden 1985 Cy Young	.50	.23	.06
□ 8 Dwight Gooden 1984 NL Top Rookie	.50	.23	.06
□ 9 Dwight Gooden Dwight's Best	.50	.23	.06
□ 10 Dwight Gooden Personal Data	.50	.23	.06
□ 11 Dwight Gooden The Future	.50	.23	.06

1988 Star Greenwell Purple

Mike Greenwell, Boston Red Sox outfielder, is the focus of this 11-card standard-size set. This set traces Greenwell's career from its beginnings to his breakthrough as a major leaguer. The set is dated by the 1988 copyright on the back. The fronts feature color player phots in a border of various shades of purple. The backs carry the information that the front card title indicates.

	MINT	NRMT	EXC
COMPLETE SET (11)	4.00	1.80	.50
COMMON CARD (1-11)	.40	.18	.05
□ 1 Mike Greenwell CL	.40	.18	.05
□ 2 Mike Greenwell Minor Stats	.40	.18	.05

	MINT	NRMT	EXC
□ 3 Mike Greenwell Major Stats	.40	.18	.05
□ 4 Mike Greenwell Post Season Stats	.40	.18	.05
□ 5 Mike Greenwell .300+ Streak	.40	.18	.05
□ 6 Mike Greenwell 1986 Season	.40	.18	.05
□ 7 Mike Greenwell 1987 Season	.40	.18	.05
□ 8 Mike Greenwell 1988 Season	.40	.18	.05
□ 9 Mike Greenwell Personal Data	.40	.18	.05
□ 10 Mike Greenwell The Future	.40	.18	.05
□ 11 Mike Greenwell Boston Red Sox Left Field	.40	.18	.05

1988 Star Greenwell Red

Mike Greenwell, Boston Red Sox outfielder, is the focus of this 11-card standard-size set. This set traces Greenwell's career from its beginnings to his breakthrough as a major leaguer. The set is dated by the 1988 copyright on the back. The fronts feature color player phots in a border of various shades of red. The backs carry the information that the front card title indicates.

	MINT	NRMT	EXC
COMPLETE SET (11)	4.00	1.80	.50
COMMON CARD (1-11)	.40	.18	.05
□ 1 Mike Greenwell CL	.40	.18	.05
□ 2 Mike Greenwell Minor Stats	.40	.18	.05
□ 3 Mike Greenwell Major Stats	.40	.18	.05
□ 4 Mike Greenwell Texas League MVP	.40	.18	.05
□ 5 Mike Greenwell Carolina League MVP	.40	.18	.05
□ 6 Mike Greenwell Player of the Year	.40	.18	.05
□ 7 Mike Greenwell Post Season Stats	.40	.18	.05
□ 8 Mike Greenwell Great in 1988!	.40	.18	.05
□ 9 Mike Greenwell Personal Data	.40	.18	.05
□ 10 Mike Greenwell The Future	.40	.18	.05
□ 11 Mike Greenwell Boston Red Sox	.40	.18	.05

1988 Star Gwynn

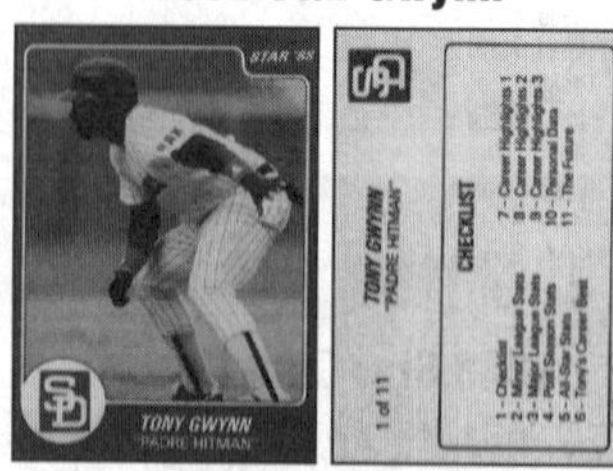

This 11-card standard-size set features highlights of Tony Gwynn's career. The set is dated with a 1988 copyright on the back.

	MINT	NRMT	EXC
COMPLETE SET (11)	5.00	2.20	.60
COMMON CARD (1-11)	.50	.23	.06
□ 1 Tony Gwynn CL	.50	.23	.06
□ 2 Tony Gwynn Minor League Stats	.50	.23	.06
□ 3 Tony Gwynn Major League Stats	.50	.23	.06
□ 4 Tony Gwynn Post Season Stats	.50	.23	.06
□ 5 Tony Gwynn All-Star Stats	.50	.23	.06
□ 6 Tony Gwynn Tony's Career Best	.50	.23	.06
□ 7 Tony Gwynn Career Highlights 1	.50	.23	.06
□ 8 Tony Gwynn Career Highlights 2	.50	.23	.06
□ 9 Tony Gwynn Career Highlights 3	.50	.23	.06
□ 10 Tony Gwynn Personal Data	.50	.23	.06
□ 11 Tony Gwynn The Future	.50	.23	.06

1988 Star Hershiser

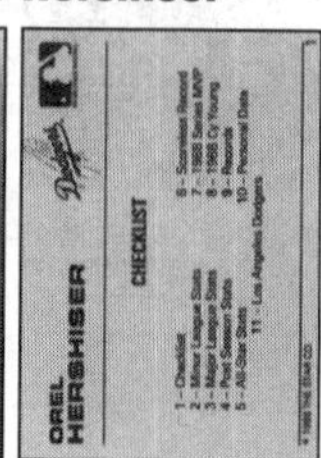

Issued after the 1988 World Series, this set focuses on Dodger star Orel Hershiser. This 11-card standard-size set includes career highlights such as his consecutive scoreless inning streak and his dominant 1988 post season.

	MINT	NRMT	EXC
COMPLETE SET (11)	4.00	1.80	.50
COMMON CARD (1-11)	.40	.18	.05
□ 1 Orel Hershiser CL	.40	.18	.05
□ 2 Orel Hershiser Minor League Stats	.40	.18	.05
□ 3 Orel Hershiser Major League Stats	.40	.18	.05
□ 4 Orel Hershiser Post Season Stats	.40	.18	.05
□ 5 Orel Hershiser All-Star Stats	.40	.18	.05
□ 6 Orel Hershiser Scoreless Record	.40	.18	.05
□ 7 Orel Hershiser 1988 Series MVP	.40	.18	.05
□ 8 Orel Hershiser 1988 Cy Young	.40	.18	.05
□ 9 Orel Hershiser Records	.40	.18	.05
□ 10 Orel Hershiser Personal Data	.40	.18	.05
□ 11 Orel Hershiser Los Angeles Dodgers	.40	.18	.05

1988 Star Horn

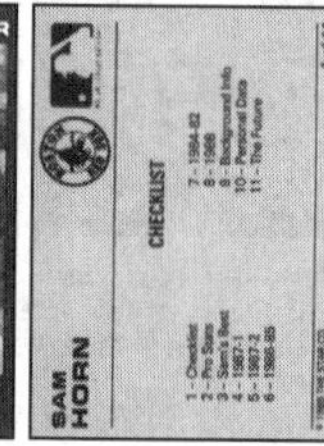

Soon to be failed Red Sox prospect, Sam Horn is featured in this set. These cards were issued after Horn tore up the American League in a late season call up in 1987. These 11 standard-size cards take the collectors through Horn's career highlights.

	MINT	NRMT	EXC
COMPLETE SET (11)	2.00	.90	.25
COMMON CARD (1-11)	.25	.11	.03
□ 1 Sam Horn CL	.25	.11	.03
□ 2 Sam Horn Pro Stats	.25	.11	.03
□ 3 Sam Horn Sam's Best	.25	.11	.03
□ 4 Sam Horn 1987 - 1	.25	.11	.03
□ 5 Sam Horn 1987 - 2	.25	.11	.03
□ 6 Sam Horn 1986-85	.25	.11	.03
□ 7 Sam Horn 1984-82	.25	.11	.03
□ 8 Sam Horn 1988	.25	.11	.03

□ 9 Sam Horn Background Info	.25	.11	.03
□ 10 Sam Horn Personal Data	.25	.11	.03
□ 11 Sam Horn The Future	.25	.11	.03

1988 Star Jefferies

Two time minor league player of the year, Gregg Jefferies is feature in this set. As the hottest prospect entering the 1988 season, this set took a person through Jefferies' minor league career. These 11 standard-size cards were issued with the 1988 copyright on the back.

	MINT	NRMT	EXC
COMPLETE SET (11)	5.00	2.20	.60
COMMON CARD (1-11)	.50	.23	.06
□ 1 Gregg Jefferies CL	.50	.23	.06
□ 2 Gregg Jefferies Minor Stats	.50	.23	.06
□ 3 Gregg Jefferies Major Stats	.50	.23	.06
□ 4 Gregg Jefferies Texas League MVP	.50	.23	.06
□ 5 Gregg Jefferies Carolina League MVP	.50	.23	.06
□ 6 Gregg Jefferies Player of the Year	.50	.23	.06
□ 7 Gregg Jefferies Post Season Stats	.50	.23	.06
□ 8 Gregg Jefferies Great in 1988!	.50	.23	.06
□ 9 Gregg Jefferies Personal Data	.50	.23	.06
□ 10 Gregg Jefferies The Future	.50	.23	.06
□ 11 Gregg Jefferies Infield	.50	.23	.06

1988 Star Jordan

After having a great rookie half season for the Philadelphia Phillies, Ricky Jordan is featured in this 11-card standard-size set. Sold in complete set form, we have described all of these cards individually.

	MINT	NRMT	EXC
COMPLETE SET (11)	2.00	.90	.25
COMMON CARD (1-11)	.25	.11	.03
□ 1 Ricky Jordan CL	.25	.11	.03
□ 2 Ricky Jordan Career Stats	.25	.11	.03
□ 3 Ricky Jordan First Hit a Homer	.25	.11	.03
□ 4 Ricky Jordan 1988 Season - 1	.25	.11	.03
□ 5 Ricky Jordan 1988 Season - 2	.25	.11	.03
□ 6 Ricky Jordan 1988 Hitting Season	.25	.11	.03
□ 7 Ricky Jordan Game Highs	.25	.11	.03
□ 8 Ricky Jordan Career Info	.25	.11	.03
□ 9 Ricky Jordan Personal Data	.25	.11	.03
□ 10 Ricky Jordan The Future	.25	.11	.03
□ 11 Ricky Jordan Philadelphia Phillies	.25	.11	.03

1988 Star Mattingly

Yankee superstar Don Mattingly is featured in this 11-card standard-size set. The 1988 copyright date is located on the back. That is how this set can be differentiated from other Mattingly Star sets.

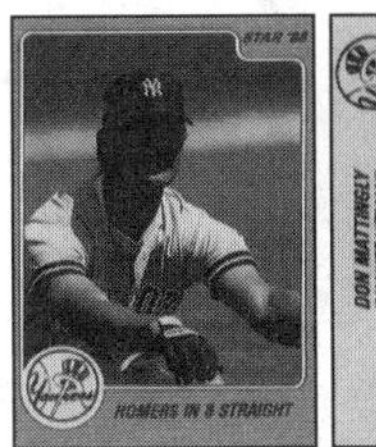

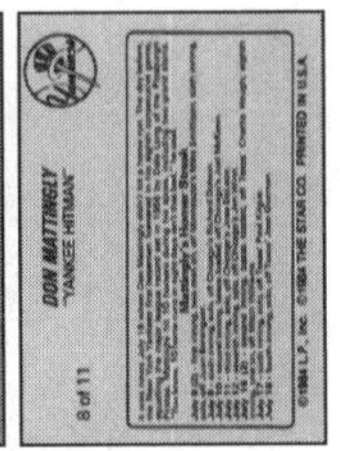

	MINT	NRMT	EXC
COMPLETE SET (11)	5.00	2.20	.60
COMMON CARD (1-11)	.50	.23	.06
□ 1 Don Mattingly CL	.50	.23	.06
□ 2 Don Mattingly Minor League Stats	.50	.23	.06
□ 3 Don Mattingly Major League Stats	.50	.23	.06
□ 4 Don Mattingly All-Star Stats	.50	.23	.06
□ 5 Don Mattingly 1985 AL MVP	.50	.23	.06
□ 6 Don Mattingly Career Highlights 1	.50	.23	.06
□ 7 Don Mattingly Career Highlights 2	.50	.23	.06
□ 8 Don Mattingly Homers in 8 Straight	.50	.23	.06
□ 9 Don Mattingly 1980 Southern League MVP	.50	.23	.06
□ 10 Don Mattingly Personal Data	.50	.23	.06
□ 11 Don Mattingly The Future	.50	.23	.06

1988 Star Mattingly/Schmidt

This 11-card standard-size set features East Coast stars: Don Mattingly and Mike Schmidt. Other than the first card in the set, either Mattingly or Schmidt is featured.

	MINT	NRMT	EXC
COMPLETE SET (11)	5.00	2.20	.60
COMMON CARD (1-11)	.50	.23	.06
□ 1 Don Mattingly Mike Schmidt Baseball's Best	.50	.23	.06
□ 2 Mike Schmidt Schmidt's Pro Stats	.50	.23	.06
□ 3 Don Mattingly Mattingly's Pro Stats	.50	.23	.06
□ 4 Mike Schmidt Schmidt The All-Star	.50	.23	.06
□ 5 Don Mattingly Mattingly The All-Star	.50	.23	.06
□ 6 Mike Schmidt Schmidt's Awards	.50	.23	.06
□ 7 Don Mattingly Mattingly The MVP	.50	.23	.06
□ 8 Mike Schmidt Schmidt's Milestone HR's	.50	.23	.06
□ 9 Don Mattingly Mattingly's Homer Streak	.50	.23	.06
□ 10 Mike Schmidt Schmidt's Personal Data	.50	.23	.06
□ 11 Don Mattingly Mattingly's Personal Data	.50	.23	.06

1988 Star McGwire

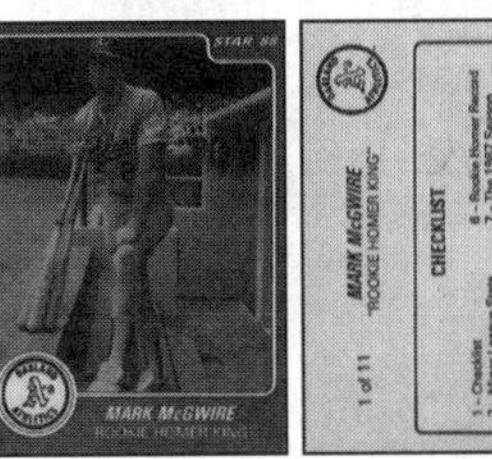

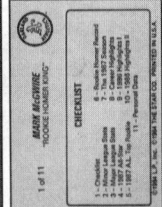

This 11-card standard-size set feature Oakland A's slugger Mark McGwire. This set is differentiated from the other Star McGwire issues by the 1988 copyright on the back.

	MINT	NRMT	EXC
COMPLETE SET (11)	5.00	2.20	.60
COMMON CARD (1-11)	.50	.23	.06
□ 1 Mark McGwire CL	.50	.23	.06
□ 2 Mark McGwire Minor League Stats	.50	.23	.06
□ 3 Mark McGwire Major League Stats	.50	.23	.06
□ 4 Mark McGwire 1987 All-Star	.50	.23	.06
□ 5 Mark McGwire 1987 A.L. Top Rookie	.50	.23	.06
□ 6 Mark McGwire Rookie Homer Record	.50	.23	.06
□ 7 Mark McGwire The 1987 Season	.50	.23	.06
□ 8 Mark McGwire Career Highlights	.50	.23	.06
□ 9 Mark McGwire 1986 Highlights I	.50	.23	.06
□ 10 Mark McGwire 1986 Highlights II	.50	.23	.06
□ 11 Mark McGwire Personal Data	.50	.23	.06

1988 Star McGwire Green

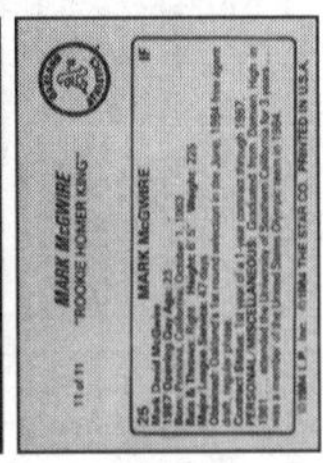

This 11-card standard-size set features Oakland A's slugger Mark McGwire. This set is differentiated from the other McGwire sets by the green borders.

	MINT	NRMT	EXC
COMPLETE SET (11)	5.00	2.20	.60
COMMON CARD (1-11)	.50	.23	.06
□ 1 Mark McGwire CL	.50	.23	.06
□ 2 Mark McGwire Minor League Stats	.50	.23	.06
□ 3 Mark McGwire Major League Stats	.50	.23	.06
□ 4 Mark McGwire 1987 All-Star	.50	.23	.06
□ 5 Mark McGwire 1987 A.L. Top Rookie	.50	.23	.06
□ 6 Mark McGwire Rookie Homer Record	.50	.23	.06
□ 7 Mark McGwire The 1987 Season	.50	.23	.06
□ 8 Mark McGwire Career Highlights	.50	.23	.06
□ 9 Mark McGwire 1986 Highlights I	.50	.23	.06
□ 10 Mark McGwire 1986 Highlights II	.50	.23	.06
□ 11 Mark McGwire Personal Data	.50	.23	.06

1988 Star McReynolds

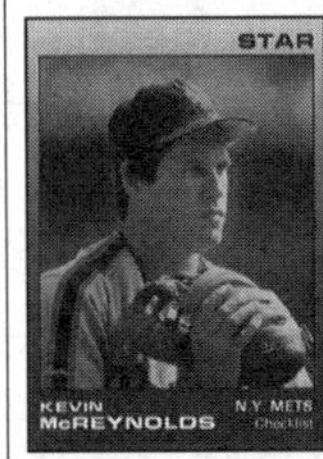

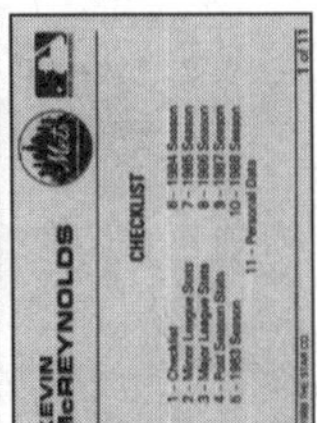

These 11 standard-size cards feature New York Mets outfielder Kevin McReynolds. These cards take McReynolds from his beginnings to the present day.

	MINT	NRMT	EXC
COMPLETE SET (11)	3.00	1.35	.35
COMMON CARD (1-11)	.30	.14	.04
□ 1 Kevin McReynolds CL	.30	.14	.04
□ 2 Kevin McReynolds Minor League Stats	.30	.14	.04
□ 3 Kevin McReynolds Major League Stats	.30	.14	.04
□ 4 Kevin McReynolds Post Season Stats	.30	.14	.04
□ 5 Kevin McReynolds 1983 Season	.30	.14	.04
□ 6 Kevin McReynolds 1984 Season	.30	.14	.04
□ 7 Kevin McReynolds 1985 Season	.30	.14	.04
□ 8 Kevin McReynolds 1986 Season	.30	.14	.04
□ 9 Kevin McReynolds 1987 Season	.30	.14	.04
□ 10 Kevin McReynolds 1988 Season	.30	.14	.04
□ 11 Kevin McReynolds Personal Data	.30	.14	.04

1988 Star Nokes

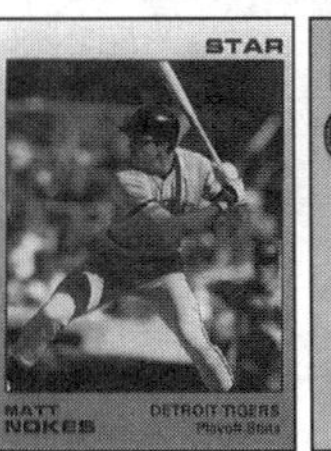

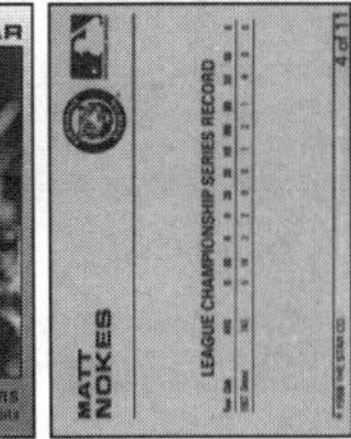

This 11-card standard-size set features Matt Nokes. These cards were printed after Nokes' 30 homer rookie season. They were designed to take advantage of Nokes' popularity.

	MINT	NRMT	EXC
COMPLETE SET (11)	3.00	1.35	.35
COMMON CARD (1-11)	.30	.14	.04
□ 1 Matt Nokes CL	.30	.14	.04
□ 2 Matt Nokes Minor League Stats	.30	.14	.04
□ 3 Matt Nokes Major League Stats	.30	.14	.04
□ 4 Matt Nokes Playoff Stats	.30	.14	.04
□ 5 Matt Nokes All Star Stats	.30	.14	.04
□ 6 Matt Nokes Matt's Best	.30	.14	.04
□ 7 Matt Nokes 1987 Season	.30	.14	.04
□ 8 Matt Nokes Career Info	.30	.14	.04
□ 9 Matt Nokes Personal Data	.30	.14	.04
□ 10 Matt Nokes Catcher	.30	.14	.04
□ 11 Matt Nokes Catcher	.30	.14	.04

1988 Star Puckett

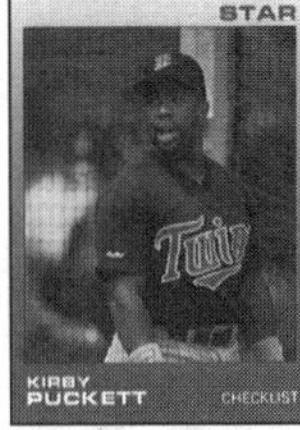

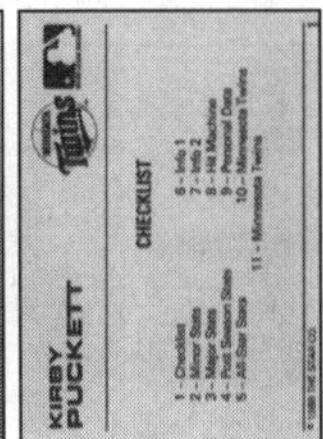

This 11-card standard-size set features Minnesota Twins superstar Kirby Puckett. The cards trace Puckett's career from the beginning through the present day.

	MINT	NRMT	EXC
COMPLETE SET (11)	5.00	2.20	.60
COMMON CARD (1-11)	.50	.23	.06
□ 1 Kirby Puckett CL	.50	.23	.06
□ 2 Kirby Puckett Minor Stats	.50	.23	.06
□ 3 Kirby Puckett Major Stats	.50	.23	.06
□ 4 Kirby Puckett Post Season Stats	.50	.23	.06
□ 5 Kirby Puckett All-Star Stats	.50	.23	.06
□ 6 Kirby Puckett Info 1	.50	.23	.06
□ 7 Kirby Puckett Info 2	.50	.23	.06
□ 8 Kirby Puckett Hit Machine	.50	.23	.06
□ 9 Kirby Puckett Personal Data	.50	.23	.06
□ 10 Kirby Puckett Minnesota Twins	.50	.23	.06
□ 11 Kirby Puckett Minnesota Twins	.50	.23	.06

1988 Star Scott

These 11 standard-size cards feature Houston Astros star pitcher Mike Scott. These cards trace Scott's career from the beginning through the present day. The cards are dated in the back by a 1988 copyright.

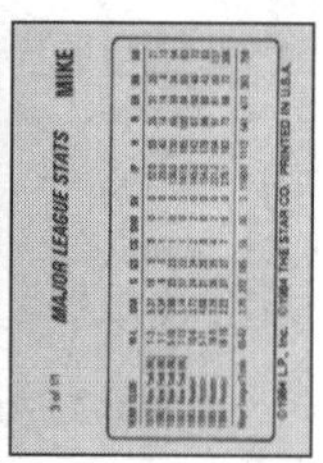

	MINT	NRMT	EXC
COMPLETE SET (11)	3.00	1.35	.35
COMMON CARD (1-11)	.30	.14	.04
□ 1 Mike Scott CL	.30	.14	.04
□ 2 Mike Scott Minor League Stats	.30	.14	.04
□ 3 Mike Scott Major League Stats	.30	.14	.04
□ 4 Mike Scott Playoff/All-Star Stats	.30	.14	.04
□ 5 Mike Scott 1986 NL	.30	.14	.04
□ 6 Mike Scott 1986 NLCS MVP	.30	.14	.04
□ 7 Mike Scott Career Transactions	.30	.14	.04
□ 8 Mike Scott No Hitter!	.30	.14	.04
□ 9 Mike Scott Game Highs	.30	.14	.04
□ 10 Mike Scott Personal Data	.30	.14	.04
□ 11 Mike Scott The Future	.30	.14	.04

1988 Star Seitzer

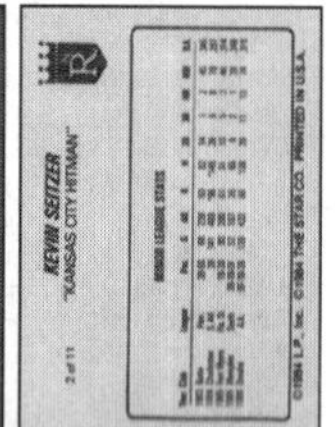

This 11-card standard-size set features young Royals player Kevin Seitzer. These cards take Seitzer's career from its beginning through the present day. The cards are notated on the back with a 1988 copyright.

	MINT	NRMT	EXC
COMPLETE SET (11)	4.00	1.80	.50
COMMON CARD (1-11)	.40	.18	.05
□ 1 Kevin Seitzer CL	.40	.18	.05
□ 2 Kevin Seitzer Minor League Stats	.40	.18	.05
□ 3 Kevin Seitzer Major League Stats	.40	.18	.05
□ 4 Kevin Seitzer Career Highlights	.40	.18	.05
□ 5 Kevin Seitzer 200 Hits!	.40	.18	.05
□ 6 Kevin Seitzer 1987 All-Star	.40	.18	.05
□ 7 Kevin Seitzer 1984 S.A.L. MVP	.40	.18	.05
□ 8 Kevin Seitzer The 1987 Season	.40	.18	.05
□ 9 Kevin Seitzer 6 for 6!	.40	.18	.05
□ 10 Kevin Seitzer Personal Data	.40	.18	.05
□ 11 Kevin Seitzer The Future	.40	.18	.05

1988 Star Snyder

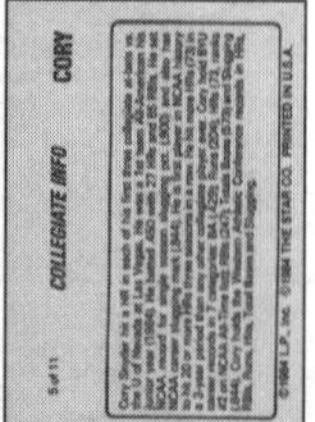

Former Olympian Cory Snyder is featured in this 11-card standard-size set. These cards trace Snyder's career from its beginnings through 1988. The cards are dated on the back with a 1988 copyright date.

	MINT	NRMT	EXC
COMPLETE SET (11)	3.00	1.35	.35
COMMON CARD (1-11)	.30	.14	.04
□ 1 Cory Snyder CL	.30	.14	.04
□ 2 Cory Snyder Minor League Stats	.30	.14	.04
□ 3 Cory Snyder Major League Stats	.30	.14	.04
□ 4 Cory Snyder 1986 Rookie Voting	.30	.14	.04
□ 5 Cory Snyder Collegiate Info	.30	.14	.04
□ 6 Cory Snyder Game Highs	.30	.14	.04
□ 7 Cory Snyder Minor League Info	.30	.14	.04
□ 8 Cory Snyder Major League Info	.30	.14	.04
□ 9 Cory Snyder Career Highlights	.30	.14	.04
□ 10 Cory Snyder Personal Data	.30	.14	.04
□ 11 Cory Snyder The Future	.30	.14	.04

1988 Star Strawberry

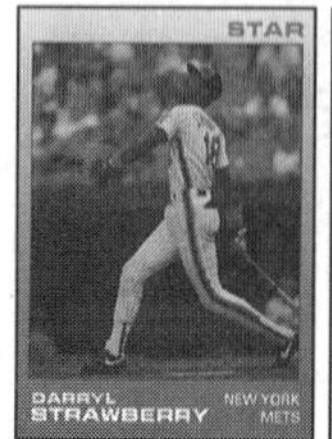

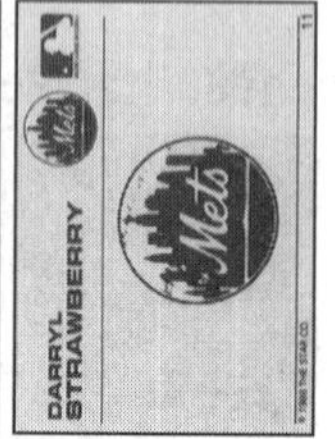

This 11-card standard-size set again features Mets player Darryl Strawberry. This set is differentiated from other Strawberry sets by the 1988 copyright date on the back and was issued with two different color borders--one violet and the other blue. The corresponding fronts of each set display different color photos of Darryl Strawberry while the backs carry the same information on the corresponding violet and blue bordered cards.

	MINT	NRMT	EXC
COMPLETE SET (11)	4.00	1.80	.50
COMMON CARD (1-11)	.40	.18	.05
□ 1 Darryl Strawberry CL	.40	.18	.05
□ 2 Darryl Strawberry Minor League Stats	.40	.18	.05
□ 3 Darryl Strawberry Major League Stats	.40	.18	.05
□ 4 Darryl Strawberry Playoff Stats	.40	.18	.05
□ 5 Darryl Strawberry All-Star Stats	.40	.18	.05
□ 6 Darryl Strawberry Career Info	.40	.18	.05
□ 7 Darryl Strawberry 1982 Texas Lg. MVP	.40	.18	.05
□ 8 Darryl Strawberry 1983 NL Top Rookie	.40	.18	.05
□ 9 Darryl Strawberry 1988 NL MVP	.40	.18	.05
□ 10 Darryl Strawberry Personal Data	.40	.18	.05
□ 11 Darryl Strawberry New York Mets	.40	.18	.05

1988 Star Trammell

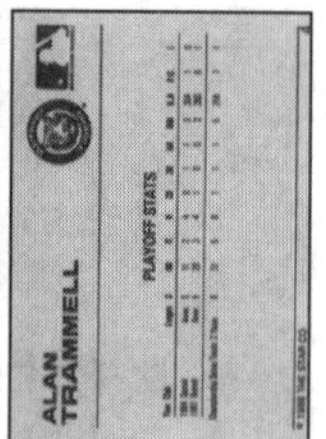

Long term Detroit Tiger star Alan Trammell is featured in this set. These 11 standard-sized cards trace his career from the minors through his major league career. These cards are dated by the 1988 copyright date on the back.

	MINT	NRMT	EXC
COMPLETE SET (11)	4.00	1.80	.50
COMMON CARD (1-11)	.40	.18	.05
□ 1 Alan Trammell CL	.40	.18	.05
□ 2 Alan Trammell Minor League Stats	.40	.18	.05
□ 3 Alan Trammell Major League Stats	.40	.18	.05
□ 4 Alan Trammell Playoff Stats	.40	.18	.05
□ 5 Alan Trammell World Series Stats	.40	.18	.05
□ 6 Alan Trammell All-Star Stats	.40	.18	.05
□ 7 Alan Trammell 1977 SL MVP	.40	.18	.05
□ 8 Alan Trammell 300+ Five Times	.40	.18	.05
□ 9 Alan Trammell Career Info	.40	.18	.05
□ 10 Alan Trammell Personal Data	.40	.18	.05
□ 11 Alan Trammell Detroit Tigers	.40	.18	.05

1988 Star Ventura

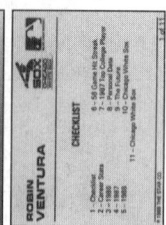

These 11 standard-size cards feature Robin Ventura. Ventura, who had established a consecutive-game hitting streak at Oklahoma State, was a highly regarded prospect. These cards feature highlights of his pre-White Sox career.

	MINT	NRMT	EXC
COMPLETE SET (11)	5.00	2.20	.60
COMMON CARD (1-11)	.50	.23	.06
□ 1 Robin Ventura CL	.50	.23	.06
□ 2 Robin Ventura Career Stats	.50	.23	.06
□ 3 Robin Ventura 1986	.50	.23	.06
□ 4 Robin Ventura 1987	.50	.23	.06
□ 5 Robin Ventura 1988	.50	.23	.06
□ 6 Robin Ventura 58 Game Hit Streak	.50	.23	.06
□ 7 Robin Ventura 1987 Top College Player	.50	.23	.06
□ 8 Robin Ventura Personal Data	.50	.23	.06
□ 9 Robin Ventura The Future	.50	.23	.06
□ 10 Robin Ventura Chicago White Sox	.50	.23	.06
□ 11 Robin Ventura Chicago White Sox	.50	.23	.06

1988 Star Winfield

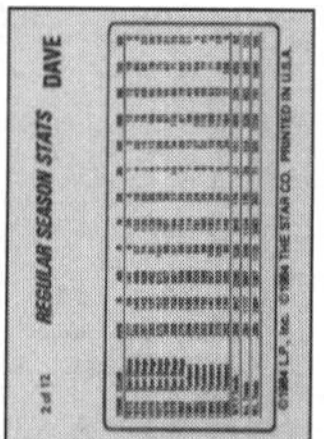

These 12 standard-size cards feature highlights in the career of Dave Winfield. These cards are dated by the 1988 copyright date on the back. Even though these issues are usually sold in complete set form we have noted all the individual cards.

	MINT	NRMT	EXC
COMPLETE SET (12)	5.00	2.20	.60
COMMON CARD (1-12)	.50	.23	.06
□ 1 Dave Winfield CL	.50	.23	.06
□ 2 Dave Winfield Regular Season Stats	.50	.23	.06
□ 3 Dave Winfield Playoff Stats	.50	.23	.06
□ 4 Dave Winfield World Series Stats	.50	.23	.06
□ 5 Dave Winfield An All-Star Ten Times	.50	.23	.06
□ 6 Dave Winfield Drafted by Four Leagues	.50	.23	.06
□ 7 Dave Winfield 300+ Career Homeruns	.50	.23	.06
□ 8 Dave Winfield 100+ RBI Six Times	.50	.23	.06
□ 9 Dave Winfield Career Highlights	.50	.23	.06
□ 10 Dave Winfield Dave's Best	.50	.23	.06
□ 11 Dave Winfield Personal Data	.50	.23	.06
□ 12 Dave Winfield The Future	.50	.23	.06

1988 Star Stickers George Bell

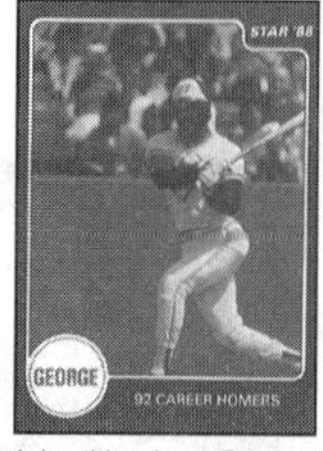

These 10 standard-size stickers feature Toronto slugging outfielder, George Bell. These stickers are blank backed and the fronts describe various career highlights.

	MINT	NRMT	EXC
COMPLETE SET (10)	2.50	1.10	.30
COMMON CARD (1-10)	.25	.11	.03
□ 1 George Bell Sticker Set	.25	.11	.03
□ 2 George Bell 31 Homeruns In 1986	.25	.11	.03
□ 3 George Bell 108 RBI's In 1986	.25	.11	.03
□ 4 George Bell .321 Playoff Average	.25	.11	.03
□ 5 George Bell 101 Runs Scored In 1986	.25	.11	.03
□ 6 George Bell Batted .309 In 1986	.25	.11	.03
□ 7 George Bell 610 Career Hits	.25	.11	.03
□ 8 George Bell .287 Lifetime Average	.25	.11	.03
□ 9 George Bell 15 Game Winning RBI-1986	.25	.11	.03
□ 10 George Bell 92 Career Homers	.25	.11	.03

1988 Star Stickers Snyder

These stickers, which are not the same as the regular card issue, feature Cleveland Indians outfielder Cory Snyder. These standard-sized stickers are blank backed and have various career highlights.

	MINT	NRMT	EXC
COMPLETE SET (8)	2.00	.90	.25
COMMON CARD (1-8)	.25	.11	.03
□ 1 Cory Snyder Sticker Set	.25	.11	.03
□ 2 Cory Snyder Member 1984 Olympic Team	.25	.11	.03
□ 3 Cory Snyder 1st Round Pick (#4)	.25	.11	.03
□ 4 Cory Snyder Hit .302 For Maine, 1986	.25	.11	.03
□ 5 Cory Snyder 69 RBI's In Rookie Debut	.25	.11	.03
□ 6 Cory Snyder Eastern League MVP - 1985	.25	.11	.03
□ 7 Cory Snyder Finished 4th In AL - Rookie Voting	.25	.11	.03
□ 8 Cory Snyder 24 Homers In Rookie Debut	.25	.11	.03

1988 Star Stickers Winfield

These 10 standard-sized stickers feature Yankee outfielder Dave Winfield. Various highlights from Winfield's career are featured in this set.

	MINT	NRMT	EXC
COMPLETE SET (10)	5.00	2.20	.60
COMMON CARD (1-10)	.50	.23	.06

	MINT	NRMT	EXC
☐ 1 Dave Winfield Sticker Set	.50	.23	.06
☐ 2 Dave Winfield Drafted By NBA, ABA and NFL	.50	.23	.06
☐ 3 Dave Winfield 10 Time All-Star	.50	.23	.06
☐ 4 Dave Winfield 305 Career Home Runs	.50	.23	.06
☐ 5 Dave Winfield 1234 Career RBI's	.50	.23	.06
☐ 6 Dave Winfield Never Played Minor League Ball	.50	.23	.06
☐ 7 Dave Winfield 2083 Career Hits	.50	.23	.06
☐ 8 Dave Winfield Batted .340 In 1984	.50	.23	.06
☐ 9 Dave Winfield 1135 Career Runs	.50	.23	.06
☐ 10 Dave Winfield 100+ RBI - '82-'86	.50	.23	.06

1989 Star Gordon

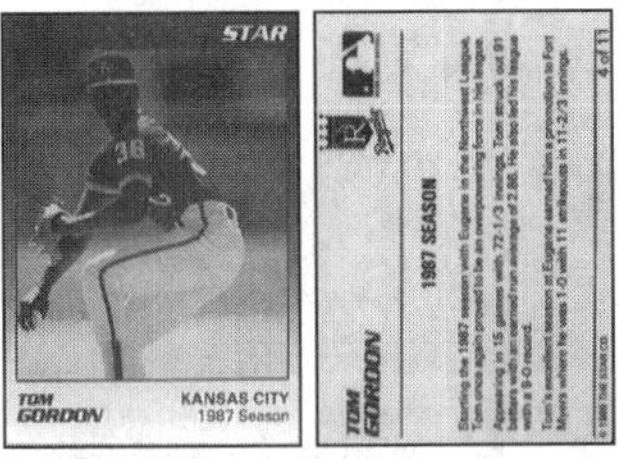

These 11 standard-sized cards feature Tom "Flash" Gordon, rookie pitcher for the Kansas City Royals. This set was issued as Gordon had an excellent rookie season and became very popular in the hobby. Issued in complete set form, these singles are rarely traded as such but are notated for informational purposes.

	MINT	NRMT	EXC
COMPLETE SET (11)	4.00	1.80	.50
COMMON CARD (1-11)	.40	.18	.05
☐ 1 Tom Gordon CL	.40	.18	.05
☐ 2 Tom Gordon Career Stats	.40	.18	.05
☐ 3 Tom Gordon 1986 Season	.40	.18	.05
☐ 4 Tom Gordon 1987 Season	.40	.18	.05
☐ 5 Tom Gordon 1988 Season - Minors	.40	.18	.05
☐ 6 Tom Gordon 1988 Season - Majors	.40	.18	.05
☐ 7 Tom Gordon 1989 Season	.40	.18	.05
☐ 8 Tom Gordon The Future	.40	.18	.05
☐ 9 Tom Gordon Personal Data	.40	.18	.05
☐ 10 Tom Gordon Kansas City	.40	.18	.05
☐ 11 Tom Gordon Kansas City	.40	.18	.05

1989 Star Mitchell

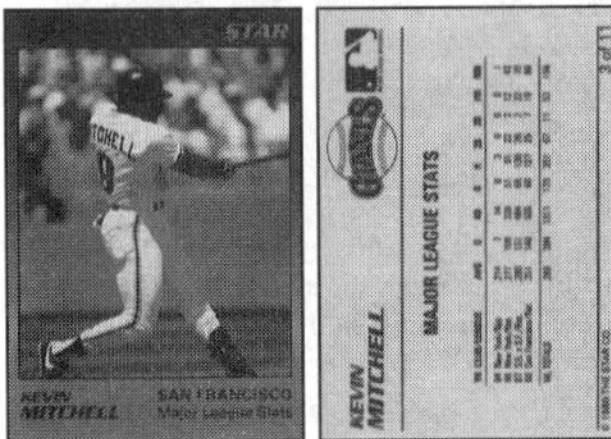

Kevin Mitchell, the 1989 NL MVP is featured in this 11 card standard-sized set. These cards trace Mitchell's career from his earliest days to the present. These cards are dated on the back and are arranged that way.

	MINT	NRMT	EXC
COMPLETE SET (11)	4.00	1.80	.50
COMMON CARD (1-11)	.40	.18	.05
☐ 1 Kevin Mitchell CL	.40	.18	.05
☐ 2 Kevin Mitchell Minor League Stats	.40	.18	.05
☐ 3 Kevin Mitchell Major League Stats	.40	.18	.05
☐ 4 Kevin Mitchell Playoff Stats	.40	.18	.05
☐ 5 Kevin Mitchell World Series Stats	.40	.18	.05
☐ 6 Kevin Mitchell 1989 A Dream Season	.40	.18	.05
☐ 7 Kevin Mitchell Career Info	.40	.18	.05
☐ 8 Kevin Mitchell Personal Data	.40	.18	.05
☐ 9 Kevin Mitchell The Future	.40	.18	.05
☐ 10 Kevin Mitchell San Francisco	.40	.18	.05
☐ 11 Kevin Mitchell San Francisco	.40	.18	.05

1989 Star Mitchell/Clark

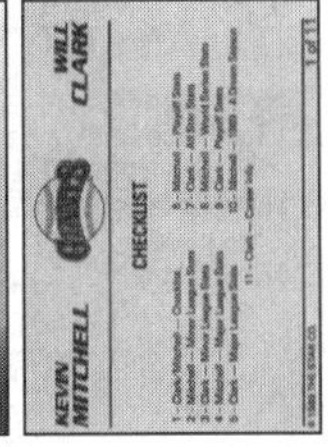

This 11 card standard-sized set features San Francisco Giant sluggers: Kevin Mitchell and Will Clark. Other than the first card, either Mitchell or Clark is pictured seperately.

	MINT	NRMT	EXC
COMPLETE SET (11)	4.00	1.80	.50
COMMON CARD (1-11)	.40	.18	.05
☐ 1 Kevin Mitchell Will Clark CL	.60	.25	.07
☐ 2 Kevin Mitchell Mitchell - Minor League Stats	.40	.18	.05
☐ 3 Will Clark Clark - Minor League Stats	.60	.25	.07
☐ 4 Kevin Mitchell Mitchell - Major League Stats	.40	.18	.05
☐ 5 Will Clark Clark - Major League Stats	.60	.25	.07
☐ 6 Kevin Mitchell Mitchell - Playoff Stats	.40	.18	.05
☐ 7 Will Clark Clark - All-Star Stats	.60	.25	.07
☐ 8 Kevin Mitchell Mitchell - World Series Stats	.40	.18	.05
☐ 9 Will Clark Clark - Playoff Stats	.60	.25	.07
☐ 10 Kevin Mitchell Mitchell - 1989-A Dream Season	.40	.18	.05
☐ 11 Will Clark Clark - Career Info	.60	.25	.07

1989 Star Santiago

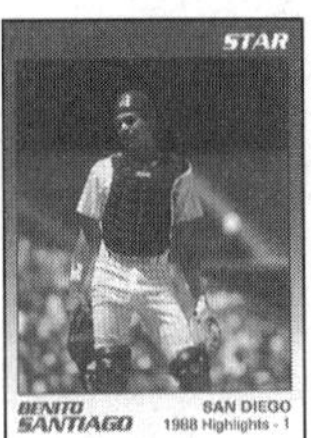

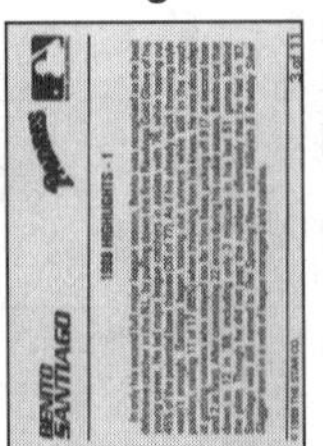

This 11 card standard-sized set features Benito Santiago. The set can be dated thanks to the 1989 copyright date on the back. This set traces Santiago's career from the earliest days through the 1988 season.

	MINT	NRMT	EXC
COMPLETE SET (11)	3.00	1.35	.35
COMMON CARD (1-11)	.30	.14	.04
☐ 1 Benito Santiago CL	.30	.14	.04
☐ 2 Benito Santiago Career Stats	.30	.14	.04
☐ 3 Benito Santiago 1988 Highlights - 1	.30	.14	.04
☐ 4 Benito Santiago 1988 Highlights - 2	.30	.14	.04
☐ 5 Benito Santiago 1987 Highlights	.30	.14	.04
☐ 6 Benito Santiago 1986 Highlights	.30	.14	.04
☐ 7 Benito Santiago 1984-85 Highlights	.30	.14	.04
☐ 8 Benito Santiago 1987 NL Top Rookie	.30	.14	.04
☐ 9 Benito Santiago Career Best	.30	.14	.04
☐ 10 Benito Santiago Personal Data	.30	.14	.04
☐ 11 Benito Santiago San Diego Padres	.30	.14	.04

1989 Star Walton

Jerome Walton is featured in this 11-card standard-size set. Walton, the 1989 NL Rookie of the Year, has his career highlighted in this set. The set is dated by the 1989 copyright on the back.

	MINT	NRMT	EXC
COMPLETE SET (11)	2.50	1.10	.30
COMMON CARD (1-11)	.25	.11	.03
☐ 1 Jerome Walton CL	.25	.11	.03
☐ 2 Jerome Walton Minor League Stats	.25	.11	.03
☐ 3 Jerome Walton 1986 Season	.25	.11	.03
☐ 4 Jerome Walton 1987 Season	.25	.11	.03
☐ 5 Jerome Walton 1988 Season - 1	.25	.11	.03
☐ 6 Jerome Walton 1988 Season - 2	.25	.11	.03
☐ 7 Jerome Walton 1989 Season	.25	.11	.03
☐ 8 Jerome Walton Personal Info	.25	.11	.03
☐ 9 Jerome Walton The Future	.25	.11	.03
☐ 10 Jerome Walton Jerome Walton	.25	.11	.03
☐ 11 Jerome Walton Jerome Walton	.25	.11	.03

1989 Star Walton/Olson

This 11 card standard-size set features Gregg Olson and Jerome Walton, the 1989 Rookies of the Year. Other than the 1st checklist card, either Walton or Olson are only featured in this set.

	MINT	NRMT	EXC
COMPLETE SET (11)	2.50	1.10	.30
COMMON CARD (1-11)	.25	.11	.03
☐ 1 Jerome Walton Gregg Olson CL	.25	.11	.03
☐ 2 Jerome Walton Walton - 1986 Season	.25	.11	.03
☐ 3 Gregg Olson Olson - Career Stats	.25	.11	.03
☐ 4 Jerome Walton Walton - 1987 Season	.25	.11	.03
☐ 5 Gregg Olson Olson - 1989 Season 1	.25	.11	.03
☐ 6 Jerome Walton Walton - 1988 Season 1	.25	.11	.03
☐ 7 Gregg Olson Olson - 1989 Season 2	.25	.11	.03
☐ 8 Jerome Walton Walton - 1988 Season 2	.25	.11	.03
☐ 9 Gregg Olson Olson - Career Info 1	.25	.11	.03
☐ 10 Jerome Walton Walton - 1989 Season	.25	.11	.03
☐ 11 Gregg Olson Olson - Career Info 2	.25	.11	.03

1990 Star Abbott

This 11-card standard-size set features highlights in the career of inspirational player, Jim Abbott. Abbott, who only has one hand, became a sucsessful major league pitcher. These cards are dated by the 1990 copyright on the back.

	MINT	NRMT	EXC
COMPLETE SET (11)	4.00	1.80	.50
COMMON CARD (1-11)	.40	.18	.05
☐ 1 Jim Abbott CL	.40	.18	.05
☐ 2 Jim Abbott 1989 Stats	.40	.18	.05
☐ 3 Jim Abbott 1989 Season - 1	.40	.18	.05
☐ 4 Jim Abbott 1989 Season - 2	.40	.18	.05
☐ 5 Jim Abbott 1989 Season - 3	.40	.18	.05
☐ 6 Jim Abbott Pro Debut	.40	.18	.05
☐ 7 Jim Abbott Career Info - 1	.40	.18	.05
☐ 8 Jim Abbott Career Info - 2	.40	.18	.05
☐ 9 Jim Abbott Career Info - 3	.40	.18	.05
☐ 10 Jim Abbott Personal Data	.40	.18	.05
☐ 11 Jim Abbott California	.40	.18	.05

1990 Star Sandy Alomar

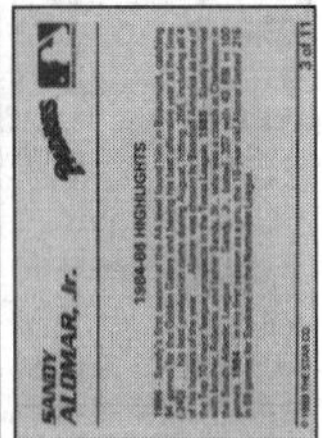

This 11-card standard-size set features Sandy Alomar Jr. While this set (as well as all Star products) are usually sold in complete set form, we have broken down this set into its individual components. The set is dated by the 1990 copyright on the back.

	MINT	NRMT	EXC
COMPLETE SET (11)	4.00	1.80	.50
COMMON CARD (1-11)	.40	.18	.05
☐ 1 Sandy Alomar, Jr. CL	.40	.18	.05
☐ 2 Sandy Alomar, Jr. Career Stats	.40	.18	.05
☐ 3 Sandy Alomar, Jr. 1984-86 Highlights	.40	.18	.05
☐ 4 Sandy Alomar, Jr. 1987 Highlights	.40	.18	.05
☐ 5 Sandy Alomar, Jr. 1988 Highlights - 1	.40	.18	.05
☐ 6 Sandy Alomar, Jr. 1988 Highlights - 2	.40	.18	.05
☐ 7 Sandy Alomar, Jr. Biography	.40	.18	.05
☐ 8 Sandy Alomar, Jr. Personal Info	.40	.18	.05
☐ 9 Sandy Alomar, Jr. The Future	.40	.18	.05
☐ 10 Sandy Alomar, Jr. San Diego	.40	.18	.05
☐ 11 Sandy Alomar, Jr. San Diego	.40	.18	.05

1990 Star Alomar Brothers

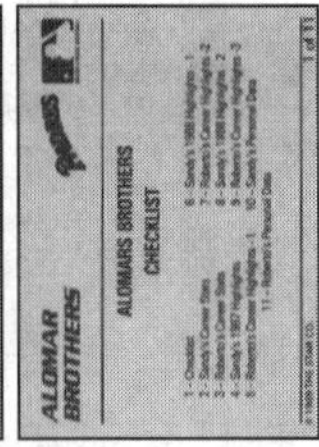

This 11-card standard-size set features the Alomar Brothers. These players, sons of former major league second basemall Sandy Alomar, each came up with the San Diego Padres. The brothers are only pictured together on card #1, otherwise we have indicated which brother is pictured on the card.

	MINT	NRMT	EXC
COMPLETE SET (11)	4.00	1.80	.50
COMMON CARD (1-11)	.40	.18	.05
☐ 1 Roberto Alomar CL Sandy Alomar Jr.	.60	.25	.07
☐ 2 Sandy Alomar Jr. Sandy's Career Stats	.40	.18	.05
☐ 3 Roberto Alomar Roberto's Career Stats	.60	.25	.07
☐ 4 Sandy Alomar Jr. Sandy's 1987 Highlights	.40	.18	.05

☐ 5 Roberto Alomar Roberto's Career Highlights - 1	.60	.25	.07
☐ 6 Sandy Alomar Jr. Sandy's 1988 Highlights - 1	.40	.18	.05
☐ 7 Roberto Alomar Roberto's Career Highlights - 2	.60	.25	.07
☐ 8 Sandy Alomar Jr. Sandy's 1988 Highlights - 2	.40	.18	.05
☐ 9 Roberto Alomar Roberto's Career Highlights - 3	.60	.25	.07
☐ 10 Sandy Alomars Jr. Sandy's Personal Data	.40	.18	.05
☐ 11 Roberto Alomar Roberto's Personal Data	.60	.25	.07

1990 Star Benes

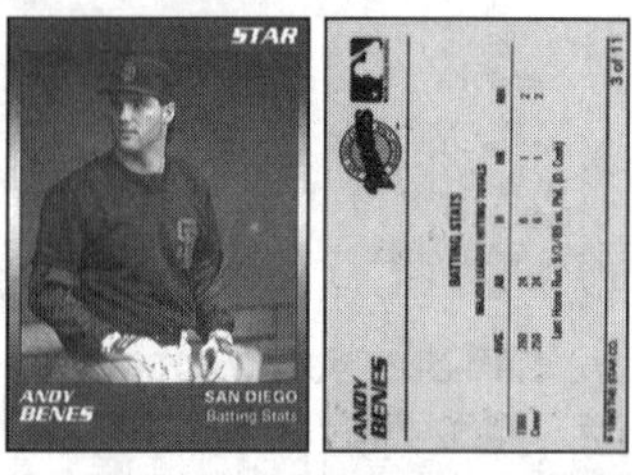

This 11-card standard-size set features former number one overall draft pick Andy Benes. These cards have highlights of Benes' career and is dated by the 1990 copyright date on the back.

	MINT	NRMT	EXC
COMPLETE SET (11)	4.00	1.80	.50
COMMON CARD (1-11)	.40	.18	.05
☐ 1 Andy Benes CL	.40	.18	.05
☐ 2 Andy Benes Career Stats	.40	.18	.05
☐ 3 Andy Benes Batting Stats	.40	.18	.05
☐ 4 Andy Benes Collegiate Info	.40	.18	.05
☐ 5 Andy Benes Olympic Info	.40	.18	.05
☐ 6 Andy Benes 1989 Highlights - 1	.40	.18	.05
☐ 7 Andy Benes 1989 Highlights - 2	.40	.18	.05
☐ 8 Andy Benes 1989 Highlights - 3	.40	.18	.05
☐ 9 Andy Benes Personal Data	.40	.18	.05
☐ 10 Andy Benes San Diego Padres	.40	.18	.05
☐ 11 Andy Benes San Diego Padres	.40	.18	.05

1990 Star Clark/Grace

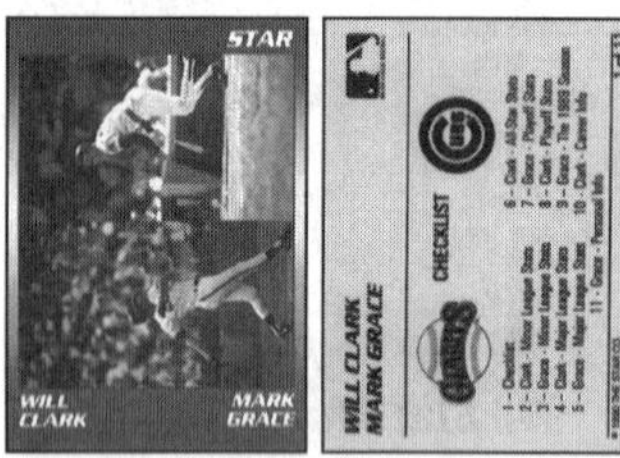

The two competing first baseman in the 1989 NL Championship series are featured in this set. These 11 standard-sized cards, other than the first card, feature either Will Clark or Mark Grace and we have identified which player is pictured.

	MINT	NRMT	EXC
COMPLETE SET (11)	5.00	2.20	.60
COMMON CARD (1-11)	.50	.23	.06
☐ 1 Will Clark Mark Grace CL	.50	.23	.06
☐ 2 Will Clark Clark - Minor League Stats	.50	.23	.06
☐ 3 Mark Grace Grace - Minor League Stats	.50	.23	.06
☐ 4 Will Clark Clark - Major League Stats	.50	.23	.06
☐ 5 Mark Grace Grace - Major League Stats	.50	.23	.06
☐ 6 Will Clark Clark - All-Star Stats	.50	.23	.06
☐ 7 Mark Grace Grace - Playoff Stats	.50	.23	.06
☐ 8 Will Clark Clark - Playoff Stats	.50	.23	.06
☐ 9 Mark Grace Grace - The 1989 Season	.50	.23	.06
☐ 10 Will Clark Clark - Career Info	.50	.23	.06
☐ 11 Mark Grace Grace - Personal Info	.50	.23	.06

1990 Star Fielder

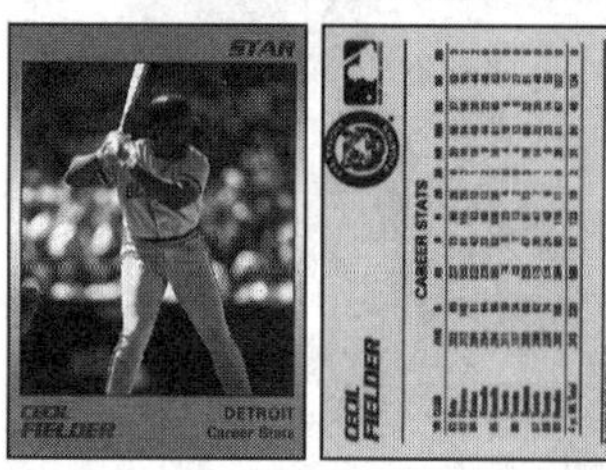

This 11-card standard-size set features homerun specialist Cecil Fielder. After playing in Japan, Fielder came back to the American League and hit 50 homers in the 1990 season. This set was issued soon after that season to take advantage of Fielder's popularity.

	MINT	NRMT	EXC
COMPLETE SET (11)	5.00	2.20	.60
COMMON CARD (1-11)	.50	.23	.06
☐ 1 Cecil Fielder CL	.50	.23	.06
☐ 2 Cecil Fielder Career Stats	.50	.23	.06
☐ 3 Cecil Fielder 1990 Season	.50	.23	.06
☐ 4 Cecil Fielder 1989 Season	.50	.23	.06
☐ 5 Cecil Fielder 1988 Season	.50	.23	.06
☐ 6 Cecil Fielder 1987 and 1986 Seasons	.50	.23	.06
☐ 7 Cecil Fielder 1985 and 1984 Seasons	.50	.23	.06
☐ 8 Cecil Fielder 1983 and 1982 Seasons	.50	.23	.06
☐ 9 Cecil Fielder HR and RBI King!	.50	.23	.06
☐ 10 Cecil Fielder Joins 50 HR Club!	.50	.23	.06
☐ 11 Cecil Fielder Personal Data	.50	.23	.06

1990 Star Griffey Jr.

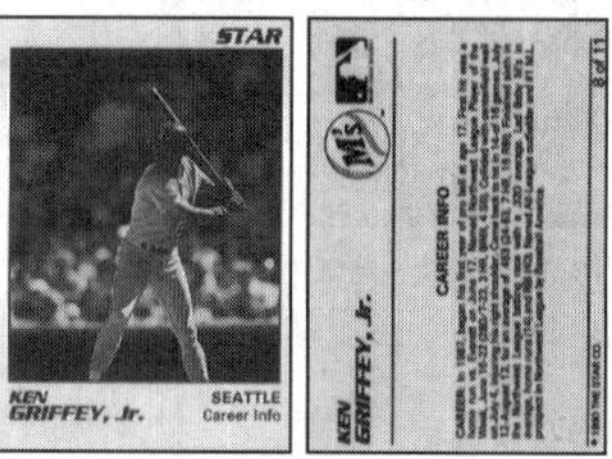

Ken Griffey Jr. is the featured player in this 11-card standard-sized set. These cards, dated by the copyright date on the back, feature highlights from the early part of his career.

	MINT	NRMT	EXC
COMPLETE SET (11)	10.00	4.50	1.25
COMMON CARD (1-11)	1.00	.45	.12
☐ 1 Ken Griffey, Jr. CL	1.00	.45	.12
☐ 2 Ken Griffey, Jr. Career Stats	1.00	.45	.12
☐ 3 Ken Griffey, Jr. 1988 Season - 1	1.00	.45	.12
☐ 4 Ken Griffey, Jr. 1988 Season - 2	1.00	.45	.12
☐ 5 Ken Griffey, Jr. 1989 Season	1.00	.45	.12
☐ 6 Ken Griffey, Jr. 1990 Season	1.00	.45	.12
☐ 7 Ken Griffey, Jr. #1 Prospect	1.00	.45	.12
☐ 8 Ken Griffey, Jr. Career Info	1.00	.45	.12
☐ 9 Ken Griffey, Jr. Ken Griffey Sr. Father/Son	1.00	.45	.12
☐ 10 Ken Griffey, Jr. Personal Data	1.00	.45	.12
☐ 11 Ken Griffey, Jr. Seattle Mariners	1.00	.45	.12

1990 Star Henderson

Rickey Henderson, perhaps the finest lead-off hitter ever, is featured in this 11-card standard-size set. These cards take the collector from the beginnings of Henderson's career to the present day.

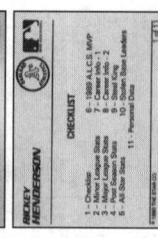

	MINT	NRMT	EXC
COMPLETE SET (11)	5.00	2.20	.60
COMMON CARD (1-11)	.50	.23	.06
☐ 2 Rickey Henderson Minor League Stats	.50	.23	.06
☐ 3 Rickey Henderson Major League Stats	.50	.23	.06
☐ 4 Rickey Henderson Post Season Stats	.50	.23	.06
☐ 5 Rickey Henderson All-Star Stats	.50	.23	.06
☐ 6 Rickey Henderson 1989 A.L.C.S. MVP	.50	.23	.06
☐ 7 Rickey Henderson Career Info - 1	.50	.23	.06
☐ 8 Rickey Henderson Career Info - 2	.50	.23	.06
☐ 9 Rickey Henderson Steal King	.50	.23	.06
☐ 10 Rickey Henderson Stolen Base Leaders	.50	.23	.06
☐ 11 Rickey Henderson Personal Data	.50	.23	.06

1990 Star Justice

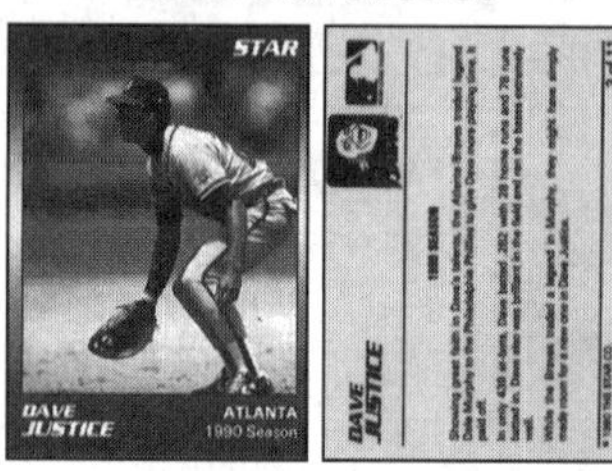

After the Atlanta Braves traded Dale Murphy, David Justice got a chance to play every day. By responding in fine fashion, collectors took notice of this young right fielder. After his rookie season, the Star Company issued this set to honor Justice. Star Company sets are usually sold in complete set form, but we have listed all the individual cards here.

	MINT	NRMT	EXC
COMPLETE SET (11)	5.00	2.20	.60
COMMON CARD (1-11)	.50	.23	.06
☐ 1 Dave Justice CL	.50	.23	.06
☐ 2 Dave Justice Career Stats	.50	.23	.06
☐ 3 Dave Justice 1990 Season	.50	.23	.06
☐ 4 Dave Justice 1989 Season	.50	.23	.06
☐ 5 Dave Justice 1988 Season	.50	.23	.06
☐ 6 Dave Justice 1987 Season	.50	.23	.06
☐ 7 Dave Justice 1986 Season	.50	.23	.06
☐ 8 Dave Justice 1985 Season	.50	.23	.06
☐ 9 Dave Justice 1990 N.L. Top Rookie	.50	.23	.06
☐ 10 Dave Justice Personal Data	.50	.23	.06
☐ 11 Dave Justice Personal Info	.50	.23	.06

1990 Star Larkin

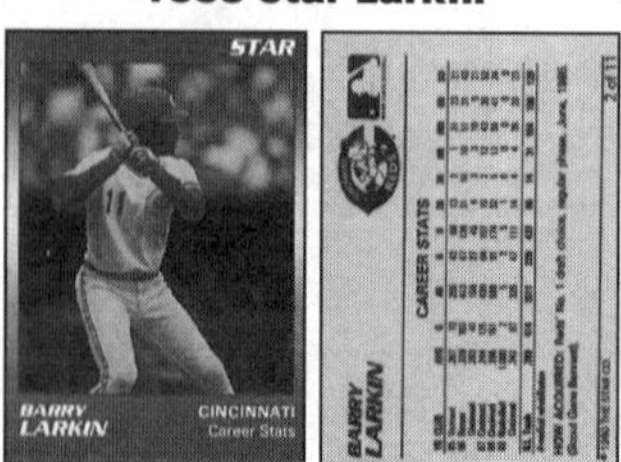

This 11-card standard-size set features highlights from the career of Cincinnati Reds shortstop Barry Larkin. These cards take the collector from the beginnings of Larkin's career to the present day.

	MINT	NRMT	EXC
COMPLETE SET (11)	5.00	2.20	.60
COMMON CARD (1-11)	.50	.23	.06
☐ 1 Barry Larkin CL	.50	.23	.06
☐ 2 Barry Larkin Career Stats	.50	.23	.06
☐ 3 Barry Larkin All-Star Stats	.50	.23	.06
☐ 4 Barry Larkin 1989 Silver Slugger	.50	.23	.06
☐ 5 Barry Larkin 1989 - 1	.50	.23	.06
☐ 6 Barry Larkin 1989 - 2	.50	.23	.06
☐ 7 Barry Larkin Career Info - 1	.50	.23	.06
☐ 8 Barry Larkin Career Info - 2	.50	.23	.06
☐ 9 Barry Larkin Game Highs	.50	.23	.06
☐ 10 Barry Larkin Personal Data	.50	.23	.06
☐ 11 Barry Larkin Cincinnati Reds	.50	.23	.06

1990 Star Maas

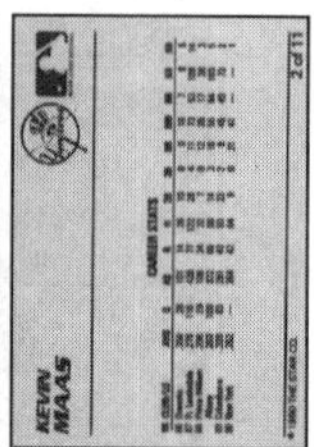

This 11-card standard-size set features highlights from the meteoric career of Yankee first baseman, Kevin Maas. Maas, who established a record for hitting his first 20 homers in the shortest number of at bats became very popular in the hobby. The Star Company issued this set to capitialize on that popularity.

	MINT	NRMT	EXC
COMPLETE SET (11)	2.50	1.10	.30
COMMON CARD (1-11)	.25	.11	.03
☐ 1 Kevin Maas CL	.25	.11	.03
☐ 2 Kevin Maas Career Stats	.25	.11	.03
☐ 3 Kevin Maas 1990 Season	.25	.11	.03
☐ 4 Kevin Maas 1989 Season	.25	.11	.03
☐ 5 Kevin Maas 1988 Season	.25	.11	.03
☐ 6 Kevin Maas 1987-86 Seasons	.25	.11	.03
☐ 7 Kevin Maas Home Run Power	.25	.11	.03
☐ 8 Kevin Maas Personal Data	.25	.11	.03
☐ 9 Kevin Maas Personal Info	.25	.11	.03
☐ 10 Kevin Maas New York Yankees	.25	.11	.03
☐ 11 Kevin Maas New York Yankees	.25	.11	.03

1990 Star Matt Williams

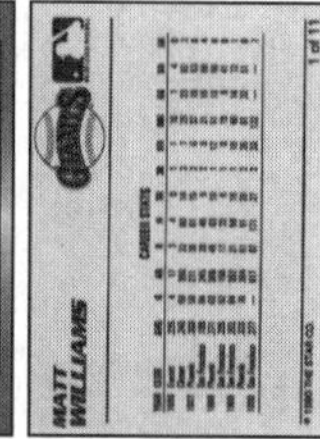

Matt Williams, slugging third baseman for the San Francisco Giants, is featured in this 11-card standard-size set. These card display various highlights (noted explicitly below) from his career.

	MINT	NRMT	EXC
COMPLETE SET (11)	5.00	2.20	.60
COMMON CARD (1-11)	.50	.23	.06
☐ 1 Matt Williams Career Stats	.50	.23	.06
☐ 2 Matt Williams Post Season Stats	.50	.23	.06
☐ 3 Matt Williams 1989 Season	.50	.23	.06
☐ 4 Matt Williams Post Season Data	.50	.23	.06
☐ 5 Matt Williams Career Info - 1	.50	.23	.06
☐ 6 Matt Williams Career Info - 2	.50	.23	.06
☐ 7 Matt Williams 1990 Season	.50	.23	.06
☐ 8 Matt Williams 1990 RBI Leader	.50	.23	.06

☐ 9 Matt Williams Career Highs	.50	.23	.06
☐ 10 Matt Williams Personal Data	.50	.23	.06
☐ 11 Matt Williams Giants	.50	.23	.06

1990 Star McDonald

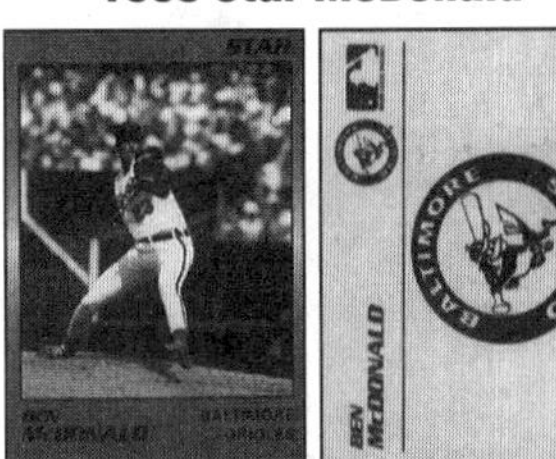

This 11-card standard-size set features young Baltimore Oriole pitcher Ben McDonald. McDonald, who was drafted first overall in 1989, has his career traced from its earliest days to the present.

	MINT	NRMT	EXC
COMPLETE SET (11)	4.00	1.80	.50
COMMON CARD (1-11)	.40	.18	.05
☐ 1 Ben McDonald Career Stats	.40	.18	.05
☐ 2 Ben McDonald High School Info	.40	.18	.05
☐ 3 Ben McDonald Collegiate Info	.40	.18	.05
☐ 4 Ben McDonald Olympic Info	.40	.18	.05
☐ 5 Ben McDonald 1989 Golden Spikes	.40	.18	.05
☐ 6 Ben McDonald #1 Pick	.40	.18	.05
☐ 7 Ben McDonald Pro Debut	.40	.18	.05
☐ 8 Ben McDonald Orioles Info	.40	.18	.05
☐ 9 Ben McDonald Personal Data	.40	.18	.05
☐ 10 Ben McDonald Baltimore Orioles	.40	.18	.05
☐ 11 Ben McDonald Baltimore Orioles	.40	.18	.05

1990 Star Mitchell/Yount

Kevin Mitchell and Robin Yount won MVP awards in 1989. This set features Mitchell and Yount on various cards. Other than the first card in the set, only one of the players is pictured.

	MINT	NRMT	EXC
COMPLETE SET (11)	4.00	1.80	.50
COMMON CARD (1-11)	.40	.18	.05
☐ 1 Kevin Mitchell Robin Yount CL	.60	.25	.07
☐ 2 Kevin Mitchell Mitchell - Major League Stats	.40	.18	.05
☐ 3 Robin Yount Yount - Career Stats	.60	.25	.07
☐ 4 Kevin Mitchell Mitchell - Playoff Stats	.40	.18	.05
☐ 5 Robin Yount Yount - World Series Stats	.60	.25	.07
☐ 6 Kevin Mitchell Mitchell - 1989 HR , RBI King	.40	.18	.05
☐ 7 Robin Yount Yount - 1982 MVP	.60	.25	.07
☐ 8 Kevin Mitchell Mitchell - 1989 MVP	.40	.18	.05
☐ 9 Robin Yount Yount - 1989 MVP	.60	.25	.07
☐ 10 Kevin Mitchell Mitchell - Career Info	.40	.18	.05
☐ 11 Robin Yount Yount - Career Info	.60	.25	.07

1990 Star Ripken

This 11-card standard-size set covers various highlights of Cal Ripken's Jr. career. These cards are usually sold in complete set form, but we have broken down and listed all the individual cards.

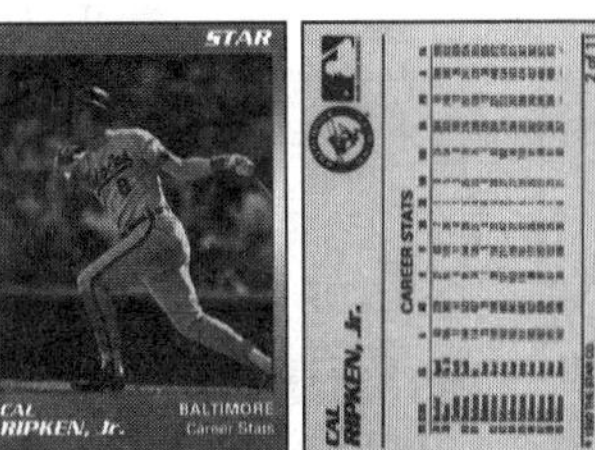

	MINT	NRMT	EXC
COMPLETE SET (11)	10.00	4.50	1.25
COMMON CARD (1-11)	1.00	.45	.12
☐ 1 Cal Ripken, Jr. CL	1.00	.45	.12
☐ 2 Cal Ripken, Jr. Career Stats	1.00	.45	.12
☐ 3 Cal Ripken, Jr. Post Season Stats	1.00	.45	.12
☐ 4 Cal Ripken, Jr. All-Star Stats	1.00	.45	.12
☐ 5 Cal Ripken, Jr. Ironman	1.00	.45	.12
☐ 6 Cal Ripken, Jr. Career Highlights - 1	1.00	.45	.12
☐ 7 Cal Ripken, Jr. Career Highlights - 2	1.00	.45	.12
☐ 8 Cal Ripken, Jr. Honors and Awards - 1	1.00	.45	.12
☐ 9 Cal Ripken, Jr. Honors and Awards - 2	1.00	.45	.12
☐ 10 Cal Ripken, Jr. Personal Data	1.00	.45	.12
☐ 11 Cal Ripken, Jr. Baltimore	1.00	.45	.12

1990 Star Ryan

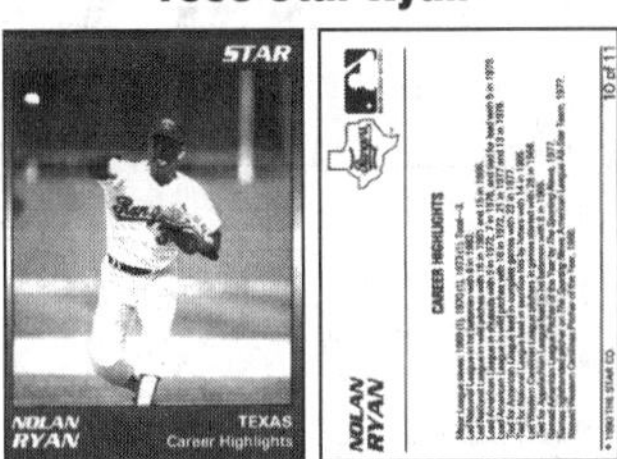

This 12-card standard-size set was issued by Star Co. in honor of Texas Rangers' pitching ace Nolan Ryan. The cards have on the fronts a mix of action and non-action color shots, with blue borders and white lettering. The horizontally oriented backs are in blue print and have player information.

	MINT	NRMT	EXC
COMPLETE SET (11)	10.00	4.50	1.25
COMMON CARD (1-11)	1.00	.45	.12
☐ 1 Nolan Ryan Checklist	1.00	.45	.12
☐ 2 Nolan Ryan Minor League Stats	1.00	.45	.12
☐ 3 Nolan Ryan Major League Stats	1.00	.45	.12
☐ 4 Nolan Ryan Post Season Stats	1.00	.45	.12
☐ 5 Nolan Ryan All-Star Stats	1.00	.45	.12
☐ 6 Nolan Ryan 6 No-Hitters!	1.00	.45	.12
☐ 7 Nolan Ryan 5000 K's!	1.00	.45	.12
☐ 8 Nolan Ryan 300 Wins!	1.00	.45	.12
☐ 9 Nolan Ryan Major League Records	1.00	.45	.12
☐ 10 Nolan Ryan Career Highlights	1.00	.45	.12
☐ 11 Nolan Ryan Personal Data	1.00	.45	.12

1990 Star Saberhagen/Davis

Bret Saberhagen and Mark Davis won their respective leagues Cy Young award in 1989. The Star Company than issued an 11-card standard-size set to honor these pitcher. Other than the first card, either Davis or Saberhagen appears on the card and we have noted who is portrayed on the card.

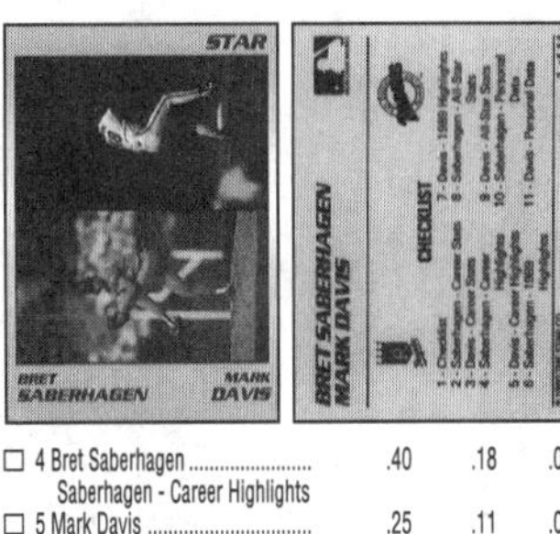

	MINT	NRMT	EXC
COMPLETE SET (11)	3.00	1.35	.35
COMMON CARD (1-11)	.25	.11	.03
☐ 1 Bret Saberhagen Mark Davis CL	.40	.18	.05
☐ 2 Bret Saberhagen Saberhagen - Career Stats	.40	.18	.05
☐ 3 Mark Davis Davis - Career Stats	.25	.11	.03
☐ 4 Bret Saberhagen Saberhagen - Career Highlights	.40	.18	.05
☐ 5 Mark Davis Davis - Career Highlights	.25	.11	.03
☐ 6 Bret Saberhagen Saberhagen - 1989 Highlights	.40	.18	.05
☐ 7 Mark Davis Davis - 1989 Highlights	.25	.11	.03
☐ 8 Bret Saberhagen Saberhagen - All-Star Stats	.40	.18	.05
☐ 9 Mark Davis Davis - All-Star Stats	.25	.11	.03
☐ 10 Bret Saberhagen Saberhagen - Personal Data	.40	.18	.05
☐ 11 Mark Davis Davis - Personal Data	.25	.11	.03

1990 Star Sandberg

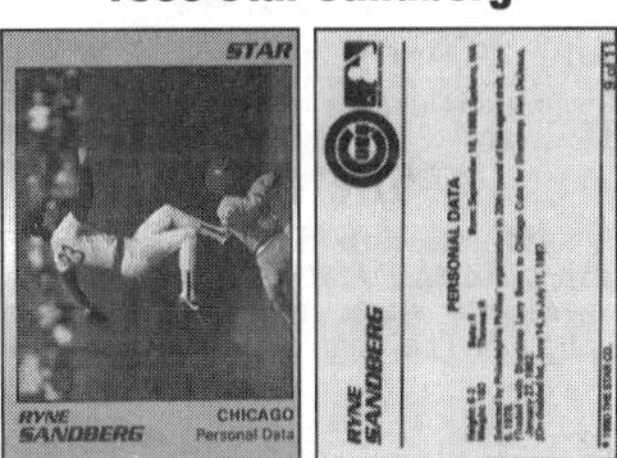

This 11-card standard-size set features highlights from the career of Chicago Cub second baseman Ryne Sandberg. These cards trace Sandberg's career from its earliest days through major league stardom.

	MINT	NRMT	EXC
COMPLETE SET (11)	5.00	2.20	.60
COMMON CARD (1-11)	.50	.23	.06
☐ 1 Ryne Sandberg CL	.50	.23	.06
☐ 2 Ryne Sandberg Minor League Stats	.50	.23	.06
☐ 3 Ryne Sandberg Major League Stats	.50	.23	.06
☐ 4 Ryne Sandberg All-Star Stats	.50	.23	.06
☐ 5 Ryne Sandberg Post Season Stats	.50	.23	.06
☐ 6 Ryne Sandberg 1984 NL MVP	.50	.23	.06
☐ 7 Ryne Sandberg Career Highlights - 1	.50	.23	.06
☐ 8 Ryne Sandberg Career Highlights - 2	.50	.23	.06
☐ 9 Ryne Sandberg Personal Data	.50	.23	.06
☐ 10 Ryne Sandberg Chicago Cubs	.50	.23	.06
☐ 11 Ryne Sandberg Chicago Cubs	.50	.23	.06

1990 Star Yount

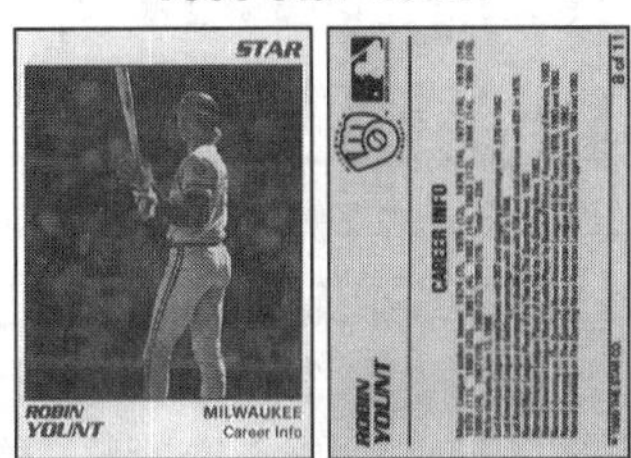

This 11-card standard-size set features highlights from the career of long-time Milwaukee Brewers star Robin Yount. These cards cover some of the best moments from his major league career. The set is dated by the 1990 copyright on the back.

	MINT	NRMT	EXC
COMPLETE SET (11)	5.00	2.20	.60
COMMON CARD (1-11)	.50	.23	.06
☐ 1 Robin Yount CL	.50	.23	.06
☐ 2 Robin Yount Career Stats	.50	.23	.06
☐ 3 Robin Yount Playoff Stats	.50	.23	.06
☐ 4 Robin Yount World Series Stats	.50	.23	.06
☐ 5 Robin Yount All-Star Stats	.50	.23	.06
☐ 6 Robin Yount 1982 MVP	.50	.23	.06
☐ 7 Robin Yount 1989 MVP	.50	.23	.06
☐ 8 Robin Yount Career Info	.50	.23	.06
☐ 9 Robin Yount Personal Data	.50	.23	.06
☐ 10 Robin Yount Milwaukee	.50	.23	.06
☐ 11 Robin Yount Milwaukee	.50	.23	.06

1991 Star Belle Rookie Guild

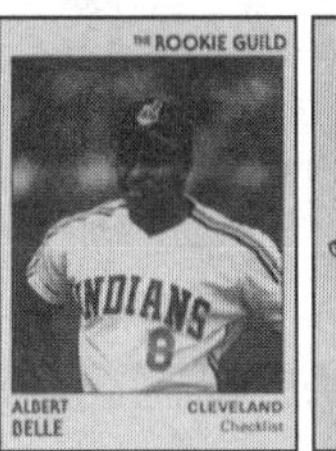
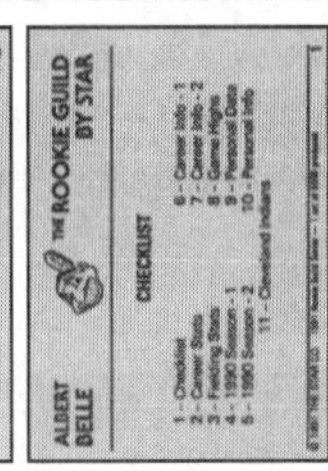

This 11-card set features Albert Belle of the Cleveland Indians. The fronts display color photos while the backs carry either statistics, career or personal information. Only 5,000 of this set were produced.

	MINT	NRMT	EXC
COMPLETE SET (11)	5.00	2.20	.60
COMMON CARD (1-11)	.50	.23	.06
☐ 1 Albert Belle CL (Squinting)	.50	.23	.06
☐ 2 Albert Belle (Stretching)	.50	.23	.06
☐ 3 Albert Belle (With batting helmet on)	.50	.23	.06
☐ 4 Albert Belle (Holding up one finger)	.50	.23	.06
☐ 5 Albert Belle (Ready to bat)	.50	.23	.06
☐ 6 Albert Belle (Hand on roof)	.50	.23	.06
☐ 7 Albert Belle (Throwing)	.50	.23	.06
☐ 8 Albert Belle (Holding bat behind him)	.50	.23	.06
☐ 9 Albert Belle (Sitting on groung)	.50	.23	.06
☐ 10 Albert Belle (Ready to run)	.50	.23	.06
☐ 11 Albert Belle (Behind net)	.50	.23	.06

1991 Star Gonzalez Rookie Guild

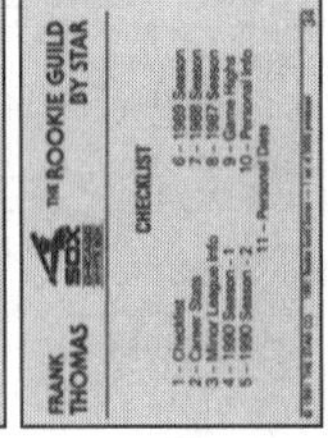

This 11-card set features Juan Gonzalez of the Texas Rangers. The fronts display color photos while the backs carry either statistics, career or personal information. Only 5,000 of this set were produced.

	MINT	NRMT	EXC
COMPLETE SET (11)	5.00	2.20	.60
COMMON CARD (1-11)	.50	.23	.06
☐ 1 Juan Gonzalez CL (Waist-up view)	.50	.23	.06
☐ 2 Juan Gonzalez (Batting)	.50	.23	.06
☐ 3 Juan Gonzalez (Throwing the ball)	.50	.23	.06
☐ 4 Juan Gonzalez (Side view with bat)	.50	.23	.06
☐ 5 Juan Gonzalez (Running with bat)	.50	.23	.06
☐ 6 Juan Gonzalez (Running in white uniform)	.50	.23	.06
☐ 7 Juan Gonzalez (Sitting and stretching)	.50	.23	.06
☐ 8 Juan Gonzalez (Waiting to bat)	.50	.23	.06
☐ 9 Juan Gonzalez	.50	.23	.06

	MINT	NRMT	EXC
(Batting)			
☐ 10 Juan Gonzalez (Back view standing)	.50	.23	.06
☐ 11 Juan Gonzalez (Fielding ball)	.50	.23	.06

1991 Star Griffeys

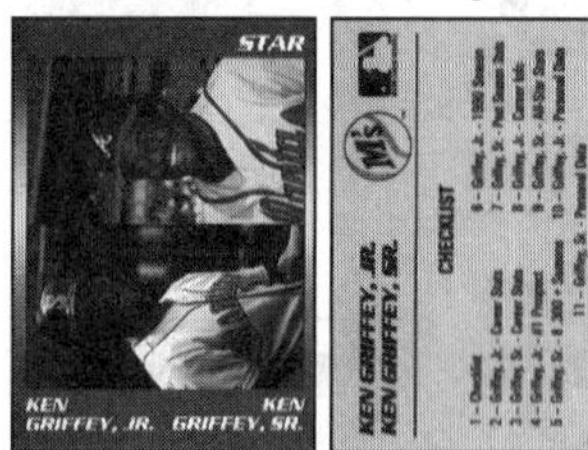

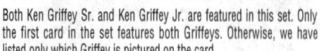

Both Ken Griffey Sr. and Ken Griffey Jr. are featured in this set. Only the first card in the set features both Griffeys. Otherwise, we have listed only which Griffey is pictured on the card.

	MINT	NRMT	EXC
COMPLETE SET (11)	7.00	3.10	.85
COMMON CARD (1-11)	.40	.18	.05
☐ 1 Ken Griffey Jr. Ken Griffey Sr. CL	1.00	.45	.12
☐ 2 Ken Griffey Jr. Griffey, Jr. - Career Stats	1.00	.45	.12
☐ 3 Ken Griffey Sr. Griffey, Sr. - Career Stats	.40	.18	.05
☐ 4 Ken Griffey Jr. Griffey, Jr. - #1 Prospect	1.00	.45	.12
☐ 5 Ken Griffey Sr. Griffey, Sr. - 8 .300 + Sea	.40	.18	.05
☐ 6 Ken Griffey Jr. Griffey, Jr. - 1990 Season	1.00	.45	.12
☐ 7 Ken Griffey Sr. Griffey, Sr. - Post Season S	.40	.18	.05
☐ 8 Ken Griffey Jr. Griffey, Jr. - Career Info	1.00	.45	.12
☐ 9 Ken Griffey Sr. Griffey, Sr. - All-Star Stat	.40	.18	.05
☐ 10 Ken Griffey Jr. Griffey, Jr. - Personal Data	1.00	.45	.12
☐ 11 Ken Griffey Sr. Griffey, Sr. - Personal Data	.40	.18	.05

1991 Star Henderson

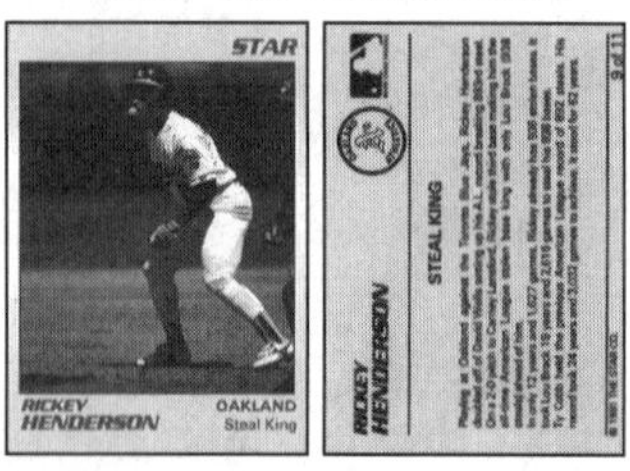

The only difference with this set as opposed to the 1990 Star Rickey Henderson set is the copyright date on the back. These cards are dated with a 1991 copyright.

	MINT	NRMT	EXC
COMPLETE SET (11)	5.00	2.20	.60
COMMON CARD (1-11)	.50	.23	.06
☐ 1 Rickey Henderson CL	.50	.23	.06
☐ 2 Rickey Henderson Minor League Stats	.50	.23	.06
☐ 3 Rickey Henderson Major League Stats	.50	.23	.06
☐ 4 Rickey Henderson Post Season Stats	.50	.23	.06
☐ 5 Rickey Henderson All-Star Stats	.50	.23	.06
☐ 6 Rickey Henderson 1989 A.L.C.S. MVP	.50	.23	.06
☐ 7 Rickey Henderson Career Info - 1	.50	.23	.06
☐ 8 Rickey Henderson Career Info - 2	.50	.23	.06
☐ 9 Rickey Henderson Steal King	.50	.23	.06
☐ 10 Rickey Henderson Stolen Base Leaders	.50	.23	.06
☐ 11 Rickey Henderson Personal Data	.50	.23	.06

1991 Star Lewis Rookie Guild

This 11-card set features Mark Lewis of the Cleveland Indians. The fronts display color photos while the backs carry either statistics, career or personal information. Only 5,000 of this set were produced.

	MINT	NRMT	EXC
COMPLETE SET (11)	4.00	1.80	.50
COMMON CARD j(1-11)	.40	.18	.05
☐ 1 Mark Lewis CL (Side head photo)	.40	.18	.05
☐ 2 Mark Lewis (Running to catch a ball)	.40	.18	.05
☐ 3 Mark Lewis (Top view throwing the ball)	.40	.18	.05
☐ 4 Mark Lewis (Batting)	.40	.18	.05
☐ 5 Mark Lewis (Sitting)	.40	.18	.05
☐ 6 Mark Lewis (Sitting on bench)	.40	.18	.05
☐ 7 Mark Lewis (Tossing the ball)	.40	.18	.05
☐ 8 Mark Lewis (Full body view throwing the ball)	.40	.18	.05
☐ 9 Mark Lewis (Top view)	.40	.18	.05
☐ 10 Mark Lewis (Top view holding ball)	.40	.18	.05
☐ 11 Mark Lewis (Throwing ball in dark blue Indians shirt)	.40	.18	.05

1991 Star Ryan

This 11-card set was issued by Star Co. in honor of Texas Rangers' pitching ace Nolan Ryan. The fronts feature a mix of action and non-action color photos, with red-and-gray borders. The backs carry player information printed in red.

	MINT	NRMT	EXC
COMPLETE SET (11)	7.50	3.40	.95
COMMON CARD (1-11)	.75	.35	.09
☐ 1 Nolan Ryan Checklist	.75	.35	.09
☐ 2 Nolan Ryan Minor League Stats	.75	.35	.09
☐ 3 Nolan Ryan Major League Stats	.75	.35	.09
☐ 4 Nolan Ryan Post Season Stats	.75	.35	.09
☐ 5 Nolan Ryan All-Star Stats	.75	.35	.09
☐ 6 Nolan Ryan 7 No-Hitters!	.75	.35	.09
☐ 7 Nolan Ryan 5000 K's!	.75	.35	.09
☐ 8 Nolan Ryan 300 Wins	.75	.35	.09
☐ 9 Nolan Ryan Major League Records	.75	.35	.09
☐ 10 Nolan Ryan Career Highlights	.75	.35	.09
☐ 11 Nolan Ryan Personal Data	.75	.35	.09

1991 Star Strawberry

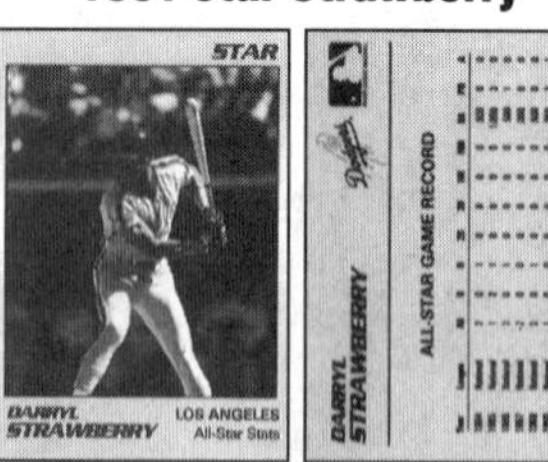

This 11-card standard-size set features outfielder Darryl Strawberry. This set can be dated to 1991 by his appearence as an Los Angeles Dodger.

	MINT	NRMT	EXC
COMPLETE SET (11)	4.00	1.80	.50
COMMON CARD (1-11)	.40	.18	.05
☐ 1 Darryl Strawberry CL	.40	.18	.05
☐ 2 Darryl Strawberry Minor League Stats	.40	.18	.05
☐ 3 Darryl Strawberry Major League Stats	.40	.18	.05
☐ 4 Darryl Strawberry Playoff Stats	.40	.18	.05
☐ 5 Darryl Strawberry All-Star Stats	.40	.18	.05
☐ 6 Darryl Strawberry 1982 Texas Lg. MVP	.40	.18	.05
☐ 7 Darryl Strawberry 1983 NL Top Rookie	.40	.18	.05
☐ 8 Darryl Strawberry Career Info	.40	.18	.05
☐ 9 Darryl Strawberry 1988 NL MVP	.40	.18	.05
☐ 10 Darryl Strawberry Personal Data	.40	.18	.05
☐ 11 Darryl Strawberry Los Angeles Dodgers	.40	.18	.05

1991 Star Thomas Rookie Guild

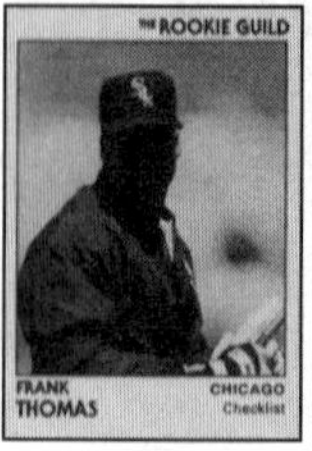

This 11-card set features Frank Thomas of the Chicago White Sox. The fronts display color photos while the backs carry either statistics, career or personal information. Only 5,000 of this set were produced.

	MINT	NRMT	EXC
COMPLETE SET (11)	7.50	3.40	.95
COMMON CARD (1-11)	.75	.35	.09
☐ 1 Frank Thomas CL (Waist-up view)	.75	.35	.09
☐ 2 Frank Thomas (Swinging)	.75	.35	.09
☐ 3 Frank Thomas (Hand on knee)	.75	.35	.09
☐ 4 Frank Thomas (Ready to bat)	.75	.35	.09
☐ 5 Frank Thomas (Top view)	.75	.35	.09
☐ 6 Frank Thomas (On base)	.75	.35	.09
☐ 7 Frank Thomas (Batting)	.75	.35	.09
☐ 8 Frank Thomas (Left side above waist view)	.75	.35	.09
☐ 9 Frank Thomas (On one knee)	.75	.35	.09
☐ 10 Frank Thomas (End of swing)	.75	.35	.09
☐ 11 Frank Thomas (Throwing)	.75	.35	.09

1992 Star Promos

These 11 standard-size cards were issued separately. The purpose of these cards was to promote some upcoming 1992 Star Company issues.

	MINT	NRMT	EXC
COMPLETE SET (11)	20.00	9.00	2.50
COMMON CARD (1-11)	1.00	.45	.12
☐ 1 Roberto Alomar	3.00	1.35	.35
☐ 2 Steve Avery	2.00	.90	.25
☐ 3 Jeff Bagwell	4.00	1.80	.50
☐ 4 Rickey Henderson	3.00	1.35	.35
☐ 5 Eric Karros	2.00	.90	.25
☐ 6 Kevin Maas	1.00	.45	.12
☐ 7 Don Mattingly	4.00	1.80	.50
☐ 8 Benito Santiago	1.00	.45	.12
☐ 9 Darryl Strawberry	2.00	.90	.25
☐ 10 Frank Thomas	6.00	2.70	.75
☐ 11 Jerome Walton	1.00	.45	.12

1992 Star Avery

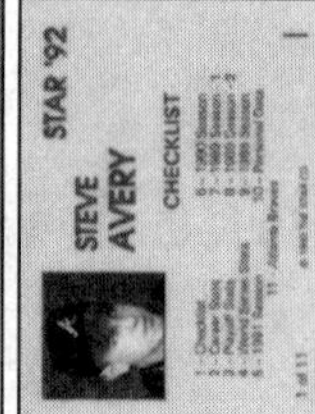

This 11-card standard-size set features Atlanta Braves pitcher Steve Avery. These cards were issued after Avery's sensational post season pitching efforts. These cards trace Avery's career from its beginnings to major league stardom.

	MINT	NRMT	EXC
COMPLETE SET (11)	4.00	1.80	.50
COMMON CARD (1-11)	.40	.18	.05
☐ 1 Steve Avery Checklist	.40	.18	.05
☐ 2 Steve Avery Career Stats	.40	.18	.05
☐ 3 Steve Avery Playoff Stats	.40	.18	.05
☐ 4 Steve Avery World Series Stats	.40	.18	.05
☐ 5 Steve Avery 1991 Season	.40	.18	.05
☐ 6 Steve Avery 1990 Season	.40	.18	.05
☐ 7 Steve Avery 1989 Season - 1	.40	.18	.05
☐ 8 Steve Avery 1989 Season - 2	.40	.18	.05
☐ 9 Steve Avery 1988 Season	.40	.18	.05
☐ 10 Steve Avery Personal Data	.40	.18	.05
☐ 11 Steve Avery Atlanta Braves	.40	.18	.05

1992 Star Bagwell

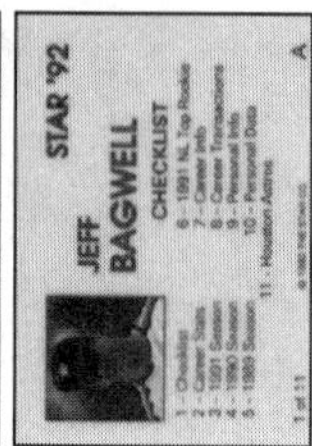

These 11 standard-size cards feature Houston Astros star player Jeff Bagwell. These cards trace Bagwell's career from his minor league days through his rookie season.

	MINT	NRMT	EXC
COMPLETE SET (11)	5.00	2.20	.60
COMMON CARD (1-11)	.50	.23	.06
☐ 1 Jeff Bagwell Checklist	.50	.23	.06
☐ 2 Jeff Bagwell Career Stats	.50	.23	.06
☐ 3 Jeff Bagwell 1991 Season	.50	.23	.06
☐ 4 Jeff Bagwell 1990 Season	.50	.23	.06
☐ 5 Jeff Bagwell 1989 Season	.50	.23	.06
☐ 6 Jeff Bagwell 1991 N.L. Top Rookie	.50	.23	.06
☐ 7 Jeff Bagwell Career Info	.50	.23	.06
☐ 8 Jeff Bagwell Career Transactions	.50	.23	.06
☐ 9 Jeff Bagwell Personal Info	.50	.23	.06
☐ 10 Jeff Bagwell Personal Data	.50	.23	.06
☐ 11 Jeff Bagwell Houston Astros	.50	.23	.06

1992 Star Belle

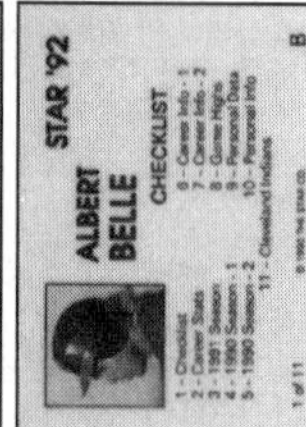

Cleveland Indians outfielder Albert Belle is featured in this 11-card standard-size set. These cards take Belle's career from his earliest days to the present day.

	MINT	NRMT	EXC
COMPLETE SET (11)	5.00	2.20	.60
COMMON CARD (1-11)	.50	.23	.06
☐ 1 Albert Belle Checklist	.50	.23	.06
☐ 2 Albert Belle Career Stats	.50	.23	.06
☐ 3 Albert Belle 1991 Season	.50	.23	.06
☐ 4 Albert Belle 1990 Season - 1	.50	.23	.06
☐ 5 Albert Belle 1990 Season - 2	.50	.23	.06
☐ 6 Albert Belle Career Info - 1	.50	.23	.06
☐ 7 Albert Belle Career Info - 2	.50	.23	.06
☐ 8 Albert Belle	.50	.23	.06

	MINT	NRMT	EXC
Game Highs			
□ 9 Albert Belle Personal Data	.50	.23	.06
□ 10 Albert Belle Personal Info	.50	.23	.06
□ 11 Albert Belle Cleveland Indians	.50	.23	.06

1992 Star Will Clark

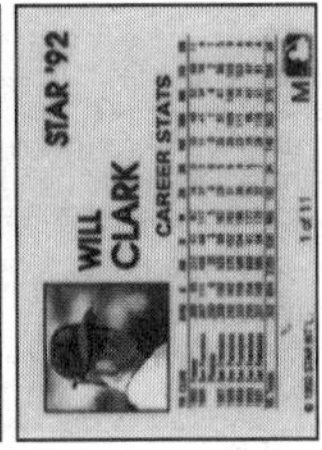

These 11 standard-size cards feature San Francisco Giants first baseman Will Clark. Clark's career is traced from its earliest days through the present day. These cards are dated by the 1992 copyright on the back.

	MINT	NRMT	EXC
COMPLETE SET (11)	5.00	2.20	.60
COMMON CARD (1-11)	.50	.23	.06
□ 1 Will Clark Career Stats	.50	.23	.06
□ 2 Will Clark Post Season Stats	.50	.23	.06
□ 3 Will Clark All-Star Stats	.50	.23	.06
□ 4 Will Clark 1991 Season - 1	.50	.23	.06
□ 5 Will Clark 1991 Season - 2	.50	.23	.06
□ 6 Will Clark 1990 Season - 1	.50	.23	.06
□ 7 Will Clark 1990 Season - 2	.50	.23	.06
□ 8 Will Clark Career Highs	.50	.23	.06
□ 9 Will Clark San Francisco vs. N.L.	.50	.23	.06
□ 10 Will Clark Personal Info	.50	.23	.06
□ 11 Will Clark Personal Data	.50	.23	.06

1992 Star Gant

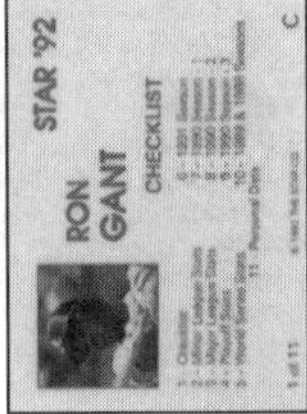

These 11 standard-sized cards feature outfielder Ron Gant. These cards are dated by the 1992 copyright on the back. These cards trace Gant's career from his minor league days to the present.

	MINT	NRMT	EXC
COMPLETE SET (11)	4.00	1.80	.50
COMMON CARD (1-11)	.40	.18	.05
□ 1 Ron Gant Checklist	.40	.18	.05
□ 2 Ron Gant Minor League Stats	.40	.18	.05
□ 3 Ron Gant Major League Sets	.40	.18	.05
□ 4 Ron Gant Playoff Stats	.40	.18	.05
□ 5 Ron Gant World Series Stats	.40	.18	.05
□ 6 Ron Gant 1991 Season	.40	.18	.05
□ 7 Ron Gant 1990 Season - 1	.40	.18	.05
□ 8 Ron Gant 1990 Season - 2	.40	.18	.05
□ 9 Ron Gant 1990 Season - 3	.40	.18	.05
□ 10 Ron Gant 1989 and 1988 Seasons	.40	.18	.05
□ 11 Ron Gant Personal Data	.40	.18	.05

1992 Star Griffey Jr.

This set, like many others issued, feature Ken Griffey Jr. These 11 standard-sized cards take the collector through various highlights of Griffey's career.

	MINT	NRMT	EXC
COMPLETE SET (11)	10.00	4.50	1.25
COMMON CARD (1-11)	1.00	.45	.12
□ 1 Ken Griffey Jr. Checklist	1.00	.45	.12
□ 2 Ken Griffey Jr. Pro Stats	1.00	.45	.12
□ 3 Ken Griffey Jr. All-Star Stats	1.00	.45	.12
□ 4 Ken Griffey Jr. 1991 Season - 1	1.00	.45	.12
□ 5 Ken Griffey Jr. 1991 Season - 2	1.00	.45	.12
□ 6 Ken Griffey Jr. 1991 Season - 3	1.00	.45	.12
□ 7 Ken Griffey Jr. Career Info	1.00	.45	.12
□ 8 Ken Griffey Jr. Personal Info	1.00	.45	.12
□ 9 Ken Griffey Jr. Personal Data	1.00	.45	.12
□ 10 Ken Griffey Jr. Seattle Mariners	1.00	.45	.12
□ 11 Ken Griffey Jr. Seattle Mariners	1.00	.45	.12

1992 Star Bo Jackson

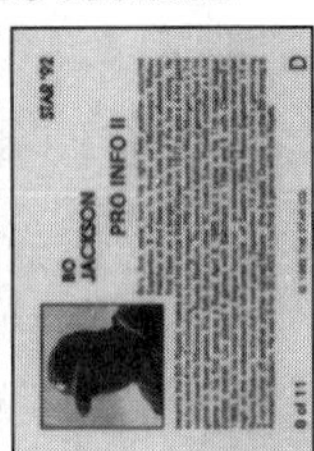

These 11 standard-size cards feature two sport star Bo Jackson. These cards basically cover only Bo's baseball career. Star company sets are usually sold in complete set form, but to provide better information we have listed each card explicitly.

	MINT	NRMT	EXC
COMPLETE SET (11)	4.00	1.80	.50
COMMON CARD (1-11)	.40	.18	.05
□ 1 Bo Jackson Checklist	.40	.18	.05
□ 2 Bo Jackson Minor League Stats	.40	.18	.05
□ 3 Bo Jackson Major League Stats	.40	.18	.05
□ 4 Bo Jackson High School Info	.40	.18	.05
□ 5 Bo Jackson Collegiate Info	.40	.18	.05
□ 6 Bo Jackson 1991 Season	.40	.18	.05
□ 7 Bo Jackson Pro Info - 1	.40	.18	.05
□ 8 Bo Jackson Pro Info - 2	.40	.18	.05
□ 9 Bo Jackson Baseball/Football	.40	.18	.05
□ 10 Bo Jackson Personal Data	.40	.18	.05
□ 11 Bo Jackson Chicago White Sox	.40	.18	.05

1992 Star Justice

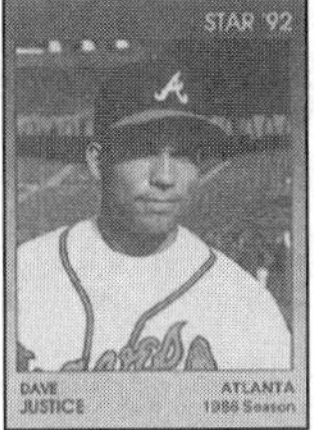

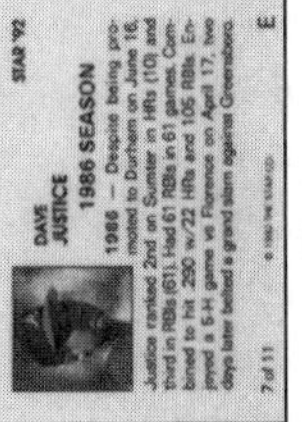

This is another set issued by Star Company about David Justice. These cards are differentiated from the first set as it had different cards as well as a 1992 copyright date.

	MINT	NRMT	EXC
COMPLETE SET (11)	4.00	1.80	.50
COMMON CARD (1-11)	.40	.18	.05
□ 1 Dave Justice Career Stats	.40	.18	.05
□ 2 Dave Justice 1991 Season	.40	.18	.05
□ 3 Dave Justice 1990 Season	.40	.18	.05
□ 4 Dave Justice 1989 Season	.40	.18	.05
□ 5 Dave Justice 1988 Season	.40	.18	.05
□ 6 Dave Justice 1987 Season	.40	.18	.05
□ 7 Dave Justice 1986 Season	.40	.18	.05
□ 8 Dave Justice 1985 Season	.40	.18	.05
□ 9 Dave Justice 1990 N.L. Top Rookie	.40	.18	.05
□ 10 Dave Justice Personal Data	.40	.18	.05
□ 11 Dave Justice Personal Info	.40	.18	.05

1992 Star Knoblauch

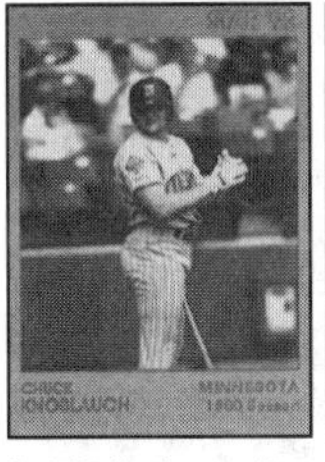

Chuck Knoblauch, second baseman for the Minnesota Twins is featured in this set. These 11 standard-size cards take the collector from his earliest playing days to the present day.

	MINT	NRMT	EXC
COMPLETE SET (11)	5.00	2.20	.60
COMMON CARD (1-11)	.50	.23	.06
□ 1 Chuck Knoblauch Checklist	.50	.23	.06
□ 2 Chuck Knoblauch Career Stats	.50	.23	.06
□ 3 Chuck Knoblauch World Series Stats	.50	.23	.06
□ 4 Chuck Knoblauch Playoff Stats	.50	.23	.06
□ 5 Chuck Knoblauch 1991 AL Top Rookie	.50	.23	.06
□ 6 Chuck Knoblauch 1991 Season	.50	.23	.06
□ 7 Chuck Knoblauch 1990 Season	.50	.23	.06
□ 8 Chuck Knoblauch 1989 Season	.50	.23	.06
□ 9 Chuck Knoblauch Pro Info	.50	.23	.06
□ 10 Chuck Knoblauch Personal Data	.50	.23	.06
□ 11 Chuck Knoblauch Personal Info	.50	.23	.06

1992 Star Palmer

Dean Palmer, young third baseman for the Texas Rangers is featured in this set. These 11 standard-size cards take Palmer's career from its beginning to the present day.

	MINT	NRMT	EXC
COMPLETE SET (11)	4.00	1.80	.50
COMMON CARD (1-11)	.40	.18	.05
□ 1 Dean Palmer Checklist	.40	.18	.05
□ 2 Dean Palmer Career Stats	.40	.18	.05
□ 3 Dean Palmer 1991 Season - 1	.40	.18	.05
□ 4 Dean Palmer 1991 Season - 2	.40	.18	.05
□ 5 Dean Palmer 1991 Season - 3	.40	.18	.05
□ 6 Dean Palmer Career Info - 1	.40	.18	.05
□ 7 Dean Palmer Career Info - 2	.40	.18	.05
□ 8 Dean Palmer Park By Park	.40	.18	.05
□ 9 Dean Palmer Career Bests	.40	.18	.05
□ 10 Dean Palmer Field Data	.40	.18	.05
□ 11 Dean Palmer Personal Info	.40	.18	.05

1992 Star Plantier

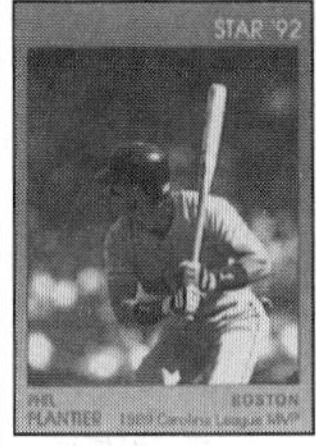

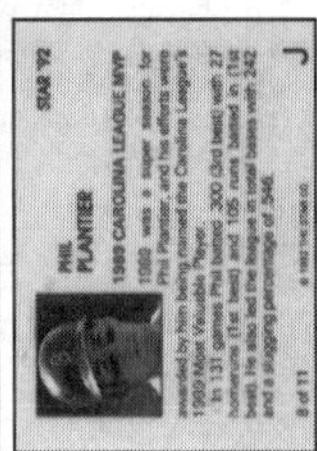

As the 1991 season ended Phil Plantier was one of the hottest players in the game. To take advantage of his popularity, Star Company issued this 11 card standard-size set featuring highlights from Plantier's career.

	MINT	NRMT	EXC
COMPLETE SET (11)	3.00	1.35	.35
COMMON CARD (1-11)	.30	.14	.04
□ 1 Phil Plantier Checklist	.30	.14	.04
□ 2 Phil Plantier Career Stats	.30	.14	.04
□ 3 Phil Plantier 1991 Season	.30	.14	.04
□ 4 Phil Plantier 1990 Season - 1	.30	.14	.04
□ 5 Phil Plantier 1990 Season - 2	.30	.14	.04
□ 6 Phil Plantier 1989 Season	.30	.14	.04
□ 7 Phil Plantier 1988 Season	.30	.14	.04
□ 8 Phil Plantier 1989 Carolina League MVP	.30	.14	.04
□ 9 Phil Plantier Personal Data	.30	.14	.04
□ 10 Phil Plantier Boston Red Sox	.30	.14	.04
□ 11 Phil Plantier Boston Red Sox	.30	.14	.04

1992 Star Puckett

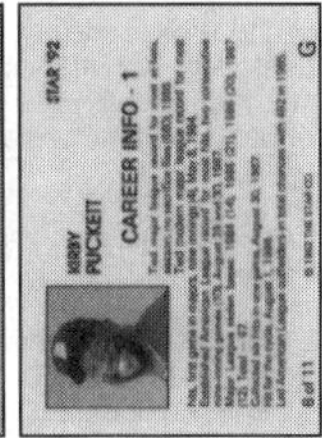

This 1992 Star Kirby Puckett set consists of 11 standard-sized cards. These cards are broken down by subject and pertain to various highlights in his career. The set is dated by the 1992 copyright on the back.

	MINT	NRMT	EXC
COMPLETE SET (11)	5.00	2.20	.60
COMMON CARD (1-11)	.50	.23	.06
□ 1 Kirby Puckett Checklist	.50	.23	.06
□ 2 Kirby Puckett Minor League Stats	.50	.23	.06
□ 3 Kirby Puckett Major League Stats	.50	.23	.06
□ 4 Kirby Puckett All-Star Stats	.50	.23	.06
□ 5 Kirby Puckett Playoff Stats	.50	.23	.06
□ 6 Kirby Puckett World Series Stats	.50	.23	.06
□ 7 Kirby Puckett Hit Machine	.50	.23	.06
□ 8 Kirby Puckett Career Info - 1	.50	.23	.06
□ 9 Kirby Puckett Career Info - 2	.50	.23	.06
□ 10 Kirby Puckett Personal Data	.50	.23	.06
□ 11 Kirby Puckett Minnesota Twins	.50	.23	.06

1992 Star Sandberg

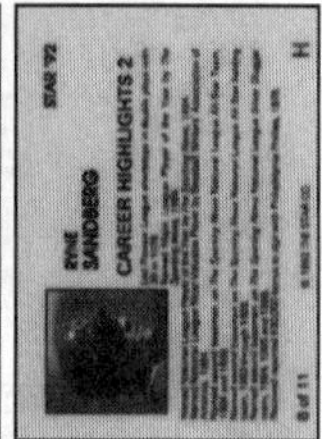

These 11 standard-size cards feature highlights in the career of Cubs second baseman Ryne Sandberg. These cards trace his career from his earliest days through the present.

	MINT	NRMT	EXC
COMPLETE SET (11)	5.00	2.20	.60
COMMON CARD (1-11)	.50	.23	.06
□ 1 Ryne Sandberg Checklist	.50	.23	.06
□ 2 Ryne Sandberg Minor League Stats	.50	.23	.06
□ 3 Ryne Sandberg Major League Stats	.50	.23	.06
□ 4 Ryne Sandberg All-Star Stats	.50	.23	.06
□ 5 Ryne Sandberg Championship Series Stats	.50	.23	.06
□ 6 Ryne Sandberg 1984 N.L. MVP	.50	.23	.06
□ 7 Ryne Sandberg Career Highlights - 1	.50	.23	.06
□ 8 Ryne Sandberg Career Highlights - 2	.50	.23	.06
□ 9 Ryne Sandberg Personal Data	.50	.23	.06
□ 10 Ryne Sandberg Chicago Cubs	.50	.23	.06
□ 11 Ryne Sandberg Chicago Cubs	.50	.23	.06

1992 Star Tartabull

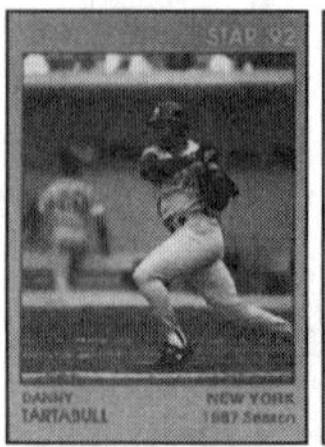

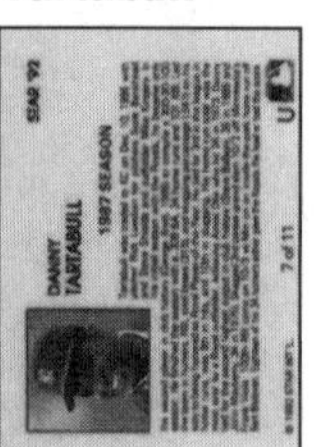

Danny Tartabull is featured in this 11-card standard-size set. These cards trace Tartabull's career from its beginnings to the present day. The set is dated by the 1992 copyright on the back. Also, Star Company sets are usually sold in complete set form. However, we have individually listed all Star cards from this set.

	MINT	NRMT	EXC
COMPLETE SET (11)	3.00	1.35	.35
COMMON CARD (1-11)	.30	.14	.04
□ 1 Danny Tartabull Career Stats	.30	.14	.04
□ 2 Danny Tartabull 1991 Season - 1	.30	.14	.04
□ 3 Danny Tartabull 1991 Season - 2	.30	.14	.04
□ 4 Danny Tartabull 1990 Season	.30	.14	.04
□ 5 Danny Tartabull 1989 Season	.30	.14	.04
□ 6 Danny Tartabull 1988 Season	.30	.14	.04
□ 7 Danny Tartabull 1987 Season	.30	.14	.04
□ 8 Danny Tartabull 1986 Season	.30	.14	.04
□ 9 Danny Tartabull Danny's Best	.30	.14	.04
□ 10 Danny Tartabull Fielding Stats	.30	.14	.04
□ 11 Danny Tartabull Personal Info	.30	.14	.04

1992 Star Van Poppel

The 1992 Star Todd Van Poppel card set consists of 11 standard-size cards. The fronts display color action shots of Van Poppel with a border that fades from green to gray. The card title is printed in green lettering at the lower right corner. The horizontal backs are yellow with green lettering. In the upper left corner is a color head shot photo of Van Poppel. The backs also contain career statistics, 1990 highlights and biography.

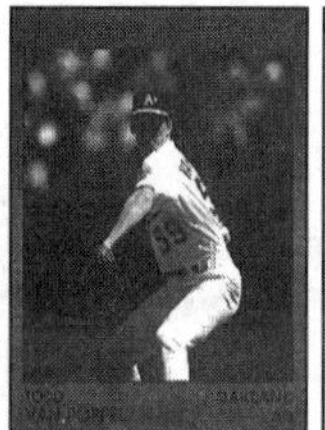

	MINT	NRMT	EXC
COMPLETE SET (10)	2.00	.90	.25
COMMON CARD (1-10)	.25	.11	.03
□ 1 Todd Van Poppel Checklist	.25	.11	.03
□ 2 Todd Van Poppel Career Stats	.25	.11	.03
□ 3 Todd Van Poppel First M.L. Start	.25	.11	.03
□ 4 Todd Van Poppel 1990 Highlights - 1	.25	.11	.03
□ 5 Todd Van Poppel 1990 Highlights - 2	.25	.11	.03
□ 6 Todd Van Poppel 1990 Highlights - 3	.25	.11	.03
□ 7 Todd Van Poppel Personal Info	.25	.11	.03
□ 8 Todd Van Poppel Personal Data	.25	.11	.03
□ 9 Todd Van Poppel What is a Rookie?	.25	.11	.03
□ 10 Todd Van Poppel Mound conference	.25	.11	.03
□ 11 Todd Van Poppel Pitching	.25	.11	.03

1995 Star Ripken

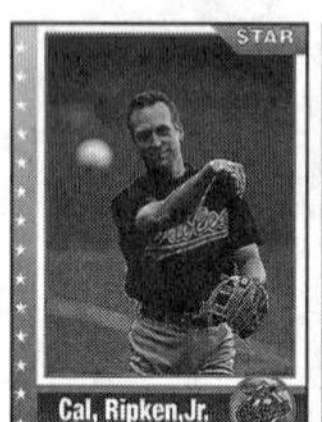

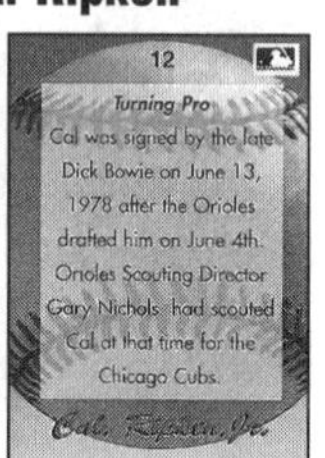

This 80-card set commemorates the 2,131 Consecutive Games Played Record set by Cal Ripken Jr. The fronts feature color action pictures of Ripken while the backs carry facts about his career.

	MINT	NRMT	EXC
COMPLETE SET (80)	20.00	9.00	2.50
COMMON CARD (1-80)	.30	.14	.04
□ 1 Cal Ripken Did you know...?	.30	.14	.04
□ 2 Cal Ripken Did you know...?	.30	.14	.04
□ 3 Cal Ripken Did you know...?	.30	.14	.04
□ 4 Cal Ripken Did you know...?	.30	.14	.04
□ 5 Cal Ripken Did you know...?	.30	.14	.04
□ 6 Cal Ripken Most homers ever...	.30	.14	.04
□ 7 Cal Ripken Did you know...?	.30	.14	.04
□ 8 Cal Ripken Did you know...?	.30	.14	.04
□ 9 Cal Ripken AL Games Leaders at SS	.30	.14	.04
□ 10 Cal Ripken Did you know...?	.30	.14	.04
□ 11 Cal Ripken Amateur Info	.30	.14	.04
□ 12 Cal Ripken Turning Pro	.30	.14	.04
□ 13 Cal Ripken Minor League Info	.30	.14	.04
□ 14 Cal Ripken 1981 Season	.30	.14	.04
□ 15 Cal Ripken 1982 Season	.30	.14	.04
□ 16 Cal Ripken 1983 Season-1	.30	.14	.04
□ 17 Cal Ripken 1983 Season-2	.30	.14	.04
□ 18 Cal Ripken 1984 Season	.30	.14	.04
□ 19 Cal Ripken 1985 Season	.30	.14	.04
□ 20 Cal Ripken 1986 Season	.30	.14	.04
□ 21 Cal Ripken 1987 Season	.30	.14	.04
□ 22 Cal Ripken 1988 Season	.30	.14	.04
□ 23 Cal Ripken#(1989 Season	.30	.14	.04
□ 24 Cal Ripken 1990 Season	.30	.14	.04
□ 25 Cal Ripken#(1991 Season-1	.30	.14	.04
□ 26 Cal Ripken 1991 Season-4	.30	.14	.04
□ 27 Cal Ripken 1991 Season-5	.30	.14	.04
□ 28 Cal Ripken 1992 Season-1	.30	.14	.04
□ 29 Cal Ripken 1992 Season-2	.30	.14	.04
□ 30 Cal Ripken 1993 Season-1	.30	.14	.04
□ 31 Cal Ripken 1993 Season-2	.30	.14	.04
□ 32 Cal Ripken 1994 Season-1	.30	.14	.04
□ 33 Cal Ripken 1994 Season-2	.30	.14	.04
□ 34 Cal Ripken 1995 Season	.30	.14	.04
□ 35 Cal Ripken 20 Homers, First 10 Years	.30	.14	.04
□ 36 Cal Ripken Single Season Club Batting Records	.30	.14	.04
□ 37 Cal Ripken Consecutive Innings Streak	.30	.14	.04
□ 38 Cal Ripken World Record	.30	.14	.04
□ 39 Cal Ripken Every Game A Start	.30	.14	.04
□ 40 Cal Ripken About the Streak-1	.30	.14	.04
□ 41 Cal Ripken About the Streak-3	.30	.14	.04
□ 42 Cal Ripken Active Hits Leaders	.30	.14	.04
□ 43 Cal Ripken Cal's Errorless Streaks	.30	.14	.04
□ 44 Cal Ripken All-Time Fielding Leaders	.30	.14	.04
□ 45 Cal Ripken Highest Fielding Percentages	.30	.14	.04
□ 46 Cal Ripken 1991 All-Star MVP-1	.30	.14	.04
□ 47 Cal Ripken Cal the All-Star-2	.30	.14	.04
□ 48 Cal Ripken The Drafting of Cal	.30	.14	.04
□ 49 Cal Ripken Hitting for the Cycle	.30	.14	.04
□ 50 Cal Ripken Cal as a Pinch Hitter	.30	.14	.04
□ 51 Cal Ripken Cal as a Pinch Runner	.30	.14	.04
□ 52 Cal Ripken They Pinch hit for Cal	.30	.14	.04
□ 53 Cal Ripken They Pinch ran for Cal	.30	.14	.04
□ 54 Cal Ripken Starting Lineup/1st major league start	.30	.14	.04
□ 55 Cal Ripken Starting Lineup/1st game of Streak	.30	.14	.04
□ 56 Cal Ripken Cal's Major League Managers	.30	.14	.04
□ 57 Cal Ripken Cal's Minor League Managers	.30	.14	.04
□ 58 Cal Ripken Cal's First Steal--Home!	.30	.14	.04
□ 59 Cal Ripken World Series Stats	.30	.14	.04
□ 60 Cal Ripken Cal Gives Back-1	.30	.14	.04
□ 61 Cal Ripken Cal Gives Back-2	.30	.14	.04
□ 62 Cal Ripken Cal Gives Back-3	.30	.14	.04
□ 63 Cal Ripken Personal Info	.30	.14	.04
□ 64 Cal Ripken Personal Stats	.30	.14	.04
□ 65 Cal Ripken The Best Excuses-1	.30	.14	.04
□ 66 Cal Ripken The Best Excuses-2	.30	.14	.04
□ 67 Cal Ripken The Best Excuses-3	.30	.14	.04
□ 68 Cal Ripken About Lou Gehrig	.30	.14	.04
□ 69 Cal Ripken Career Believe It or Not-1	.30	.14	.04
□ 70 Cal Ripken Believe It or Not-2	.30	.14	.04
□ 71 Cal Ripken Believe It or Not-3	.30	.14	.04
□ 72 Cal Ripken Close Calls	.30	.14	.04
□ 73 Cal Ripken According to Cal...	.30	.14	.04
□ 74 Cal Ripken The Tallest	.30	.14	.04
□ 75 Cal Ripken 500 Consecutive Games Played	.30	.14	.04
□ 76 Cal Ripken Cal On The Field	.30	.14	.04
□ 77 Cal Ripken Cal does Japan	.30	.14	.04
□ 78 Cal Ripken Will the Streak stop at 2,477	.30	.14	.04
□ 79 Cal Ripken All Star Stats	.30	.14	.04
□ 80 Cal Ripken Career Stats '78-'85	.30	.14	.04

1928 Star Player Candy E-Unc.

This 72-card set is presumed to have been inserts to a candy box named "Star Player Candy." The cards are sepia colored and measure approximately 1 7/8" by 2 7/8" with blank backs. The fronts feature full length action shots except for Card #1 which is a portrait. The player's name is printed in brown capital letters in the bottom border. The pictures used appear to be unique and cannot be found on other sets.

	EX-MT	VG-E	GOOD
COMPLETE SET (72)	10000.00	4500.00	1250.00
COMMON CARD (1-72)	60.00	27.00	7.50
□ 1 Dave Bancroft	75.00	34.00	9.50
□ 2 Emile Barnes	60.00	27.00	7.50
□ 3 Lu Blue	60.00	27.00	7.50
□ 4 Garland Buckeye	60.00	27.00	7.50
□ 5 George Burns	60.00	27.00	7.50
□ 6 Guy Bush	60.00	27.00	7.50
□ 7 Owen Carroll	60.00	27.00	7.50
□ 8 Bud Cissell	60.00	27.00	7.50
□ 9 Ty Cobb	1500.00	700.00	190.00
□ 10 Mickey Cochrane	150.00	70.00	19.00
□ 11 Richard Coffman	60.00	27.00	7.50
□ 12 Eddie Collins	200.00	90.00	25.00
□ 13 Stan Coveleskie	60.00	27.00	7.50
□ 14 Hugh Critz	60.00	27.00	7.50
□ 15 Kiki Cuyler	100.00	45.00	12.50
□ 16 Chuck Dressen	75.00	34.00	9.50
□ 17 Joe Dugan	75.00	34.00	9.50
□ 18 Woody English	60.00	27.00	7.50
□ 19 Bibb Falk	60.00	27.00	7.50
□ 20 Ira Flagstead	60.00	27.00	7.50
□ 21 Bob Fothergill	60.00	27.00	7.50
□ 22 Frank Frisch	150.00	70.00	19.00
□ 23 Foster Ganzel	60.00	27.00	7.50
□ 24 Lou Gehrig	1500.00	700.00	190.00
□ 25 Charley Gehringer	150.00	70.00	19.00
□ 26 George Gerken	60.00	27.00	7.50
□ 27 Grant Gillis	60.00	27.00	7.50
□ 28 Mike Gonzales	60.00	27.00	7.50
□ 29 Sam Gray	60.00	27.00	7.50
□ 30 Charlie Grimm	75.00	34.00	9.50
□ 31 Lefty Grove	250.00	110.00	31.00
□ 32 Chick Hafey	75.00	34.00	9.50
□ 33 Jesse Haines	75.00	34.00	9.50
□ 34 Gabby Hartnett	150.00	70.00	19.00
□ 35 Clifton Heathcote	60.00	27.00	7.50
□ 36 Harry Heilmann	100.00	45.00	12.50
□ 37 John Heving	60.00	27.00	7.50
□ 38 Waite Hoyt	100.00	45.00	12.50
□ 39 Charles Jamieson	60.00	27.00	7.50
□ 40 Joe Judge	60.00	27.00	7.50
□ 41 Willie Kamm	60.00	27.00	7.50
□ 42 George Kelly	75.00	34.00	9.50
□ 43 Tony Lazzeri	100.00	45.00	12.50
□ 44 Adolfo Luque	75.00	34.00	9.50
□ 45 Ted Lyons	60.00	27.00	7.50
□ 46 Hugh McMullen	60.00	27.00	7.50
□ 47 Bob Meusel	75.00	34.00	9.50
□ 48 Wilcy Moore	60.00	27.00	7.50
□ 49 Ed Morgan	60.00	27.00	7.50
□ 50 Herb Pennock	100.00	45.00	12.50
□ 51 Everett Purdy	60.00	27.00	7.50
□ 52 William Regan	60.00	27.00	7.50
□ 53 Eppa Rixey	100.00	45.00	12.50
□ 54 Charles Root	60.00	27.00	7.50
□ 55 Jack Rothrock	60.00	27.00	7.50
□ 56 Muddy Ruel	60.00	27.00	7.50
□ 57 Babe Ruth	2000.00	900.00	250.00
□ 58 Wally Schang	60.00	27.00	7.50
□ 59 Joe Sewell	100.00	45.00	12.50
□ 60 Luke Sewell	60.00	27.00	7.50
□ 61 Joe Shaute	60.00	27.00	7.50
□ 62 George Sisler	200.00	90.00	25.00
□ 63 Tris Speaker	250.00	110.00	31.00
□ 64 Riggs Stephenson	75.00	34.00	9.50
□ 65 Jack Tavener	60.00	27.00	7.50
□ 66 Al Thomas	60.00	27.00	7.50
□ 67 Pie Traynor	150.00	70.00	19.00
□ 68 George Uhle	60.00	27.00	7.50
□ 69 Dazzy Vance	100.00	45.00	12.50
□ 70 Cy Williams	60.00	27.00	7.50
□ 71 Ken Williams	60.00	27.00	7.50
□ 72 Hack Wilson	100.00	45.00	12.50

1990 Starline Long John Silver

The 1990 Starline Long John Silver set was issued over an eight-week promotion, five cards at a time within a cello pack. The set was initially available only through the Long John Silver seafood fast-food chain with one pack being given to each customer who ordered a meal with a 32-ounce Coke. This 40-card, standard-size set featured the best of today's players. There are several cards for some of the players in the set. After the promotion at Long John Silver had been completed, there were reportedly more than 100,000 sets left over that were released into the organized hobby.

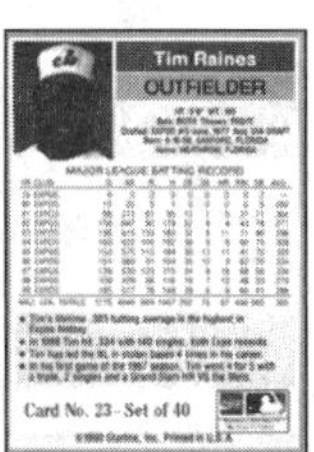

	MINT	NRMT	EXC
COMPLETE SET (40)	6.00	2.70	.75
COMMON CARD (1-40)	.10	.05	.01
☐ 1 Don Mattingly	.60	.25	.07
☐ 2 Mark Grace	.30	.14	.04
☐ 3 Eric Davis	.10	.05	.01
☐ 4 Tony Gwynn	.60	.25	.07
☐ 5 Bobby Bonilla	.20	.09	.03
☐ 6 Wade Boggs	.30	.14	.04
☐ 7 Frank Viola	.10	.05	.01
☐ 8 Ruben Sierra	.20	.09	.03
☐ 9 Mark McGwire	.50	.23	.06
☐ 10 Alan Trammell	.20	.09	.03
☐ 11 Mark McGwire	.50	.23	.06
☐ 12 Gregg Jefferies	.20	.09	.03
☐ 13 Nolan Ryan	1.00	.45	.12
☐ 14 John Smoltz	.30	.14	.04
☐ 15 Glenn Davis	.10	.05	.01
☐ 16 Mark Grace	.30	.14	.04
☐ 17 Wade Boggs	.30	.14	.04
☐ 18 Frank Viola	.10	.05	.01
☐ 19 Bret Saberhagen	.10	.05	.01
☐ 20 Chris Sabo	.10	.05	.01
☐ 21 Darryl Strawberry	.20	.09	.03
☐ 22 Wade Boggs	.30	.14	.04
☐ 23 Tim Raines	.10	.05	.01
☐ 24 Alan Trammell	.20	.09	.03
☐ 25 Chris Sabo	.10	.05	.01
☐ 26 Nolan Ryan	1.00	.45	.12
☐ 27 Mark McGwire	.50	.23	.06
☐ 28 Don Mattingly	.60	.25	.07
☐ 29 Tony Gwynn	.50	.23	.06
☐ 30 Glenn Davis	.10	.05	.01
☐ 31 Bobby Bonilla	.20	.09	.03
☐ 32 Gregg Jefferies	.20	.09	.03
☐ 33 Ruben Sierra	.10	.05	.01
☐ 34 John Smoltz	.30	.14	.04
☐ 35 Don Mattingly	.50	.23	.06
☐ 36 Bret Saberhagen	.10	.05	.01
☐ 37 Darryl Strawberry	.20	.09	.03
☐ 38 Eric Davis	.10	.05	.01
☐ 39 Tim Raines	.10	.05	.01
☐ 40 Mark Grace	.30	.14	.04

1991 Starline Prototypes

This 5-card set measures approximately 2 11/16" by 3 11/16". The fronts feature color action player photos on a black background accented by a white picture frame. The player's first name is printed across the top, while his last name is printed vertically down the right edge. The backs carry a smaller color photo, biographical information, and yearly statistics for Nolan Ryan's pitching record. Sixty of each card were produced and submitted to Major League Baseball for approval to be offered to prospective sponsors.The cards are unnumbered and checklisted below in alphabetical order.

	MINT	NRMT	EXC
COMPLETE SET (5)	250.00	110.00	31.00
COMMON CARD (1-5)	25.00	11.00	3.10
☐ 1 George Bell	25.00	11.00	3.10
☐ 2 Bobby Bonilla	50.00	22.00	6.25
☐ 3 Roger Clemens	100.00	45.00	12.50
☐ 4 Tim Raines	25.00	11.00	3.10
☐ 5 Darryl Strawberry	50.00	22.00	6.25

1991 Starshots Pinback Badges

These laminated badges were sold with 2" X 4 3/4" cardboard easels for displaying the badges. The easel is printed in red, white, and blue, and has biographical information and a five-year performance profile.The badges 2 3/16" in diameter, have a pin on the back, and feature color head and shoulders photos, encircled by a black border. The company initially issued 54 badges and planned to expand the collection to 200 or more players during the balance of the year. Both the cardboard easels and the badges are numbered on the front, but since the complete set of 200 was not issued, we have checklisted the first 54 badges below in alphabetical order.

	MINT	NRMT	EXC
COMPLETE SET (54)	75.00	34.00	9.50
COMMON PIN (1-54)	.50	.23	.06
☐ 1 Jim Abbott	.50	.23	.06
☐ 2 Sandy Alomar Jr.	1.00	.45	.12
☐ 3 Wade Boggs	2.00	.90	.25
☐ 4 Barry Bonds	2.00	.90	.25
☐ 5 Bobby Bonilla	1.00	.45	.12
☐ 6 George Brett	5.00	2.20	.60
☐ 7 Jose Canseco	2.00	.90	.25
☐ 8 Will Clark	2.00	.90	.25
☐ 9 Roger Clemens	2.00	.90	.25
☐ 10 Eric Davis	1.00	.45	.12
☐ 11 Glenn Davis	.50	.23	.06
☐ 12 Andre Dawson	1.50	.70	.19
☐ 13 Delino DeShields	.50	.23	.06
☐ 14 Doug Drabek	.50	.23	.06
☐ 15 Shawon Dunston	.50	.23	.06
☐ 16 Len Dykstra	1.00	.45	.12
☐ 17 Cecil Fielder	3.00	1.35	.35
☐ 18 Carlton Fisk	4.00	1.80	.50
☐ 19 Ron Gant	1.00	.45	.12
☐ 20 Dwight Gooden	1.00	.45	.12
☐ 21 Ken Griffey Jr.	10.00	4.50	1.25
☐ 22 Kelly Gruber	.50	.23	.06
☐ 23 Tony Gwynn	5.00	2.20	.60
☐ 24 Rickey Henderson	2.00	.90	.25
☐ 25 Orel Hershiser	1.00	.45	.12
☐ 26 Wally Joyner	.50	.23	.06
☐ 27 Dave Justice	1.50	.70	.19
☐ 28 Barry Larkin	2.00	.90	.25
☐ 29 Don Mattingly	5.00	2.20	.60
☐ 30 Mark McGwire	3.00	1.35	.35
☐ 31 Kevin McReynolds	.50	.23	.06
☐ 32 Kevin Mitchell	.50	.23	.06
☐ 33 Paul Molitor	2.50	1.10	.30
☐ 34 Eddie Murray	2.50	1.10	.30
☐ 35 Dave Parker	1.00	.45	.12
☐ 36 Kirby Puckett	5.00	2.20	.60
☐ 37 Billy Ripken	.50	.23	.06
☐ 38 Cal Ripken Jr.	8.00	3.60	1.00
☐ 39 Nolan Ryan	8.00	3.60	1.00
☐ 40 Bret Saberhagen	.50	.23	.06
☐ 41 Chris Sabo	.50	.23	.06
☐ 42 Ryne Sandberg	4.00	1.80	.50
☐ 43 Benito Santiago	.50	.23	.06
☐ 44 Steve Sax	.50	.23	.06
☐ 45 Mike Scioscia	.50	.23	.06
☐ 46 Ruben Sierra	.50	.23	.06
☐ 47 Ozzie Smith	5.00	2.20	.60
☐ 48 Dave Stieb	.50	.23	.06
☐ 49 Darryl Strawberry	1.00	.45	.12
☐ 50 Alan Trammell	1.00	.45	.12
☐ 51 Tim Wallach	.50	.23	.06
☐ 52 Bob Welch	.50	.23	.06
☐ 53 Matt Williams	2.00	.90	.25
☐ 54 Dave Winfield	3.00	1.35	.35

1988 Starting Lineup All-Stars

This set measures approximately 2 5/8" by 3" and were included in the Starting Lineup game. The fronts have a player photo while the back has recent seasonal stats and some personal information.

	MINT	NRMT	EXC
COMPLETE SET (39)	25.00	11.00	3.10
COMMON CARD (1-39)	.20	.09	.03
☐ 1 Buddy Bell	.25	.11	.03
☐ 2 George Bell	.20	.09	.03
☐ 3 Wade Boggs	.60	.25	.07
☐ 4 George Brett	2.00	.90	.25
☐ 5 Gary Carter	.40	.18	.05
☐ 6 Jack Clark	.30	.14	.04
☐ 7 Roger Clemens	1.00	.45	.12
☐ 8 Eric Davis	.25	.11	.03
☐ 9 Jody Davis	.20	.09	.03
☐ 10 Andre Dawson	.50	.23	.06
☐ 11 Carlton Fisk	.60	.25	.07
☐ 12 Dwight Gooden	.25	.11	.03
☐ 13 Tony Gwynn	2.00	.90	.25
☐ 14 Rickey Henderson	.75	.35	.09
☐ 15 Keith Hernandez	.25	.11	.03
☐ 16 Terry Kennedy	.20	.09	.03
☐ 17 Don Mattingly	3.00	1.35	.35
☐ 18 Jack Morris	.25	.11	.03
☐ 19 Dale Murphy	.40	.18	.05
☐ 20 Eddie Murray	.75	.35	.09
☐ 21 Kirby Puckett	1.50	.70	.19
☐ 22 Dan Quisenberry	.25	.11	.03
☐ 23 Tim Raines	.25	.11	.03
☐ 24 Willie Randolph	.20	.09	.03
☐ 25 Dave Righetti	.20	.09	.03
☐ 26 Cal Ripken	4.00	1.80	.50
☐ 27 Nolan Ryan	4.00	1.80	.50
☐ 28 Ryne Sandberg	1.50	.70	.19
☐ 29 Steve Sax	.20	.09	.03
☐ 30 Mike Schmidt	1.00	.45	.12
☐ 31 Mike Scott	.20	.09	.03
☐ 32 Ozzie Smith	1.00	.45	.12
☐ 33 Darryl Strawberry	.25	.11	.03
☐ 34 Fernando Valenzuela	.25	.11	.03
☐ 35 Lou Whitaker	.25	.11	.03
☐ 36 Dave Winfield	.60	.25	.07
☐ 37 Todd Worrell	.20	.09	.03
☐ 38 Robin Yount	.60	.25	.07
☐ 39 Game card and Help 2	.20	.09	.03

1988 Starting Lineup Angels

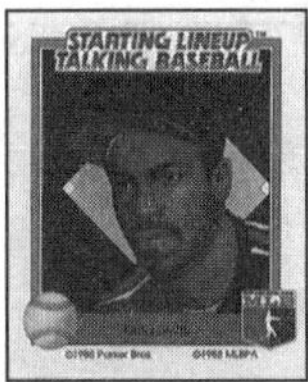

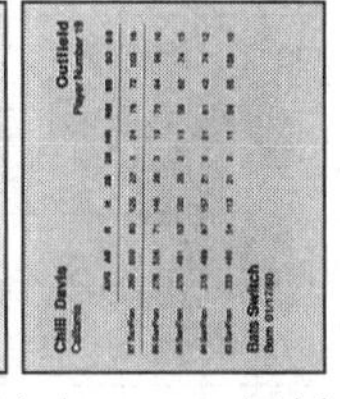

This 21-card set of the California Angels measures approximately 2 5/8" by 3" and features colored drawings of the players on the fronts while the backs carry the player's statistics. The cards are unnumbered and checklisted below in alphabetical order.

	MINT	NRMT	EXC
COMPLETE SET (21)	5.00	2.20	.60
COMMON CARD (1-21)	.20	.09	.03
☐ 1 Bob Boone	.35	.16	.04
☐ 2 Bill Buckner	.25	.11	.03
☐ 3 DeWayne Buice	.20	.09	.03
☐ 4 Chili Davis	.25	.11	.03
☐ 5 Brian Downing	.20	.09	.03
☐ 6 Chuck Finley	.35	.16	.04
☐ 7 Willie Frasier	.20	.09	.03
☐ 8 George Hendrick	.20	.09	.03
☐ 9 Jack Howell	.20	.09	.03
☐ 10 Ruppert Jones	.20	.09	.03
☐ 11 Wally Joyner	.50	.23	.06
☐ 12 Kirk McCaskill	.20	.09	.03
☐ 13 Mark McLemore	.20	.09	.03
☐ 14 Darrell Miller	.20	.09	.03
☐ 15 Greg Minton	.20	.09	.03
☐ 16 Gary Pettis	.20	.09	.03
☐ 17 Johnny Ray	.20	.09	.03
☐ 18 Dick Schofield	.20	.09	.03
☐ 19 Devon White	.50	.23	.06
☐ 20 Mike Witt	.20	.09	.03
☐ 21 Team Checklist	.20	.09	.03

1988 Starting Lineup A's

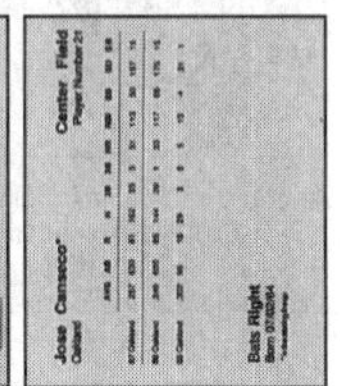

This 21-card set of the Oakland A's measures approximately 2 5/8" by 3" and features colored drawings of the players on the fronts while the backs carry the player's statistics. The cards are unnumbered and checklisted below in alphabetical order.

	MINT	NRMT	EXC
COMPLETE SET (21)	6.00	2.70	.75
COMMON CARD (1-21)	.20	.09	.03
☐ 1 Tony Bernazard	.20	.09	.03
☐ 2 Jose Canseco	1.00	.45	.12
☐ 3 Mike Davis	.20	.09	.03
☐ 4 Dennis Eckersley	.50	.23	.06
☐ 5 Mike Gallego	.20	.09	.03
☐ 6 Alfredo Griffin	.20	.09	.03
☐ 7 Dave Henderson	.20	.09	.03
☐ 8 Reggie Jackson	.75	.35	.09
☐ 9 Carney Lansford	.25	.11	.03
☐ 10 Mark McGwire	1.00	.45	.12
☐ 11 Steve Ontiveros	.20	.09	.03
☐ 12 Dave Parker	.35	.16	.04
☐ 13 Tony Phillips	.35	.16	.04
☐ 14 Luis Polonia	.20	.09	.03
☐ 15 Terry Steinbach	.50	.23	.06
☐ 16 Dave Stewart	.35	.16	.04
☐ 17 Mickey Tettleton	.25	.11	.03
☐ 18 Bob Welch	.25	.11	.03
☐ 19 Curt Young	.20	.09	.03
☐ 20 Matt Young	.20	.09	.03
☐ 21 Team Checklist	.20	.09	.03

1988 Starting Lineup Astros

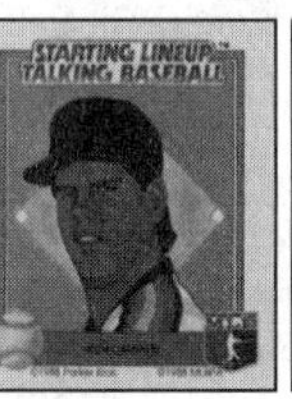

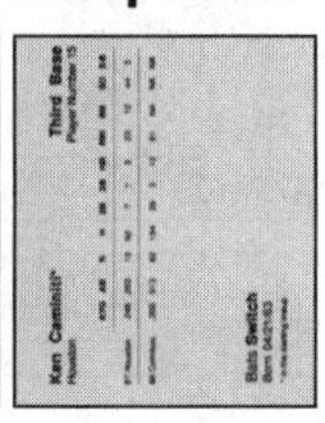

These cards feature members of the 1988 Houston Astros. These cards measure approximately 2 5/8" by 3" and have player photos on the front. The backs have recent seasonal statistics and some personal information. Ken Caminiti is featured in his Rookie Card season.

	MINT	NRMT	EXC
COMPLETE SET (21)	10.00	4.50	1.25
COMMON CARD (1-21)	.20	.09	.03
☐ 1 Juan Agosto	.20	.09	.03
☐ 2 Larry Andersen	.20	.09	.03
☐ 3 Alan Ashby	.20	.09	.03
☐ 4 Kevin Bass	.20	.09	.03
☐ 5 Ken Caminiti	1.00	.45	.12
☐ 6 Jose Cruz	.25	.11	.03
☐ 7 Danny Darwin	.20	.09	.03
☐ 8 Glenn Davis	.20	.09	.03
☐ 9 Bill Doran	.20	.09	.03
☐ 10 Billy Hatcher	.20	.09	.03
☐ 11 Jim Pankovitz	.20	.09	.03
☐ 12 Terry Puhl	.20	.09	.03
☐ 13 Rafael Ramirez	.20	.09	.03
☐ 14 Craig Reynolds	.20	.09	.03
☐ 15 Nolan Ryan	6.00	2.70	.75
☐ 16 Mike Scott	.25	.11	.03
☐ 17 Dave Smith	.20	.09	.03
☐ 18 Marc Sullivan	.20	.09	.03
☐ 19 Denny Walling	.20	.09	.03
☐ 20 Gerald Young	.20	.09	.03
☐ 21 Team Checklist	.20	.09	.03

1988 Starting Lineup Blue Jays

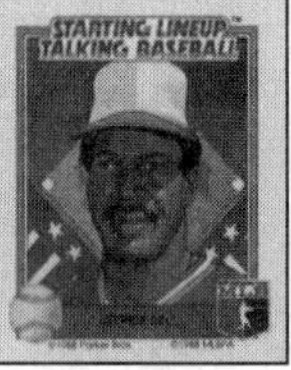

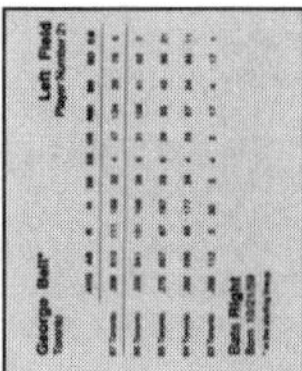

These cards feature members of the 1988 Toronto Blue Jays. These cards measure approximately 2 5/8" by 3" and have player photos on the front. The backs have recent seasonal statistics and some personal information.

	MINT	NRMT	EXC
COMPLETE SET (21)	5.00	2.20	.60
COMMON CARD (1-21)	.20	.09	.03
☐ 1 Jesse Barfield	.25	.11	.03
☐ 2 George Bell	.25	.11	.03
☐ 3 Juan Beniquez	.20	.09	.03
☐ 4 Jim Clancy	.20	.09	.03
☐ 5 Mark Eichhorn	.20	.09	.03
☐ 6 Tony Fernandez	.25	.11	.03
☐ 7 Cecil Fielder	1.00	.45	.12
☐ 8 Tom Henke	.20	.09	.03
☐ 9 Garth Iorg	.20	.09	.03
☐ 10 Jimmy Key	.50	.23	.06
☐ 11 Rick Leach	.20	.09	.03
☐ 12 Mannuel Lee	.20	.09	.03
☐ 13 Nelson Liriano	.20	.09	.03
☐ 14 Fred McGriff	1.50	.70	.19
☐ 15 Lloyd Moseby	.25	.11	.03
☐ 16 Rance Mulliniks	.20	.09	.03
☐ 17 Jeff Musselman	.20	.09	.03
☐ 18 Dave Stieb	.25	.11	.03
☐ 19 Willie Upshaw	.20	.09	.03
☐ 20 Ernie Whitt	.20	.09	.03
☐ 21 Team Checklist	.20	.09	.03

1988 Starting Lineup Braves

These cards feature members of the 1988 Atlanta Braves. These cards measure approximately 2 5/8" by 3" and have player photos on the front. The backs have recent seasonal statistics and some personal information. Jeff Blauser, Ron Gant and Tom Glavine are all featured in their Rookie Card season.

	MINT	NRMT	EXC
COMPLETE SET (21)	7.00	3.10	.85
COMMON CARD (1-21)	.20	.09	.03

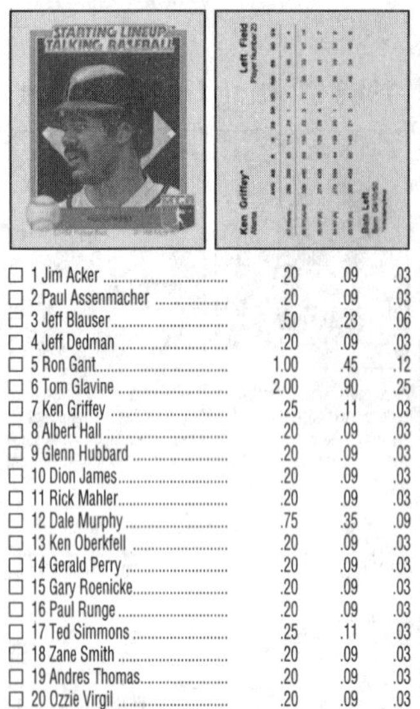

	MINT	NRMT	EXC
☐ 1 Jim Acker	.20	.09	.03
☐ 2 Paul Assenmacher	.20	.09	.03
☐ 3 Jeff Blauser	.50	.23	.06
☐ 4 Jeff Dedman	.20	.09	.03
☐ 5 Ron Gant	1.00	.45	.12
☐ 6 Tom Glavine	2.00	.90	.25
☐ 7 Ken Griffey	.25	.11	.03
☐ 8 Albert Hall	.20	.09	.03
☐ 9 Glenn Hubbard	.20	.09	.03
☐ 10 Dion James	.20	.09	.03
☐ 11 Rick Mahler	.20	.09	.03
☐ 12 Dale Murphy	.75	.35	.09
☐ 13 Ken Oberkfell	.20	.09	.03
☐ 14 Gerald Perry	.20	.09	.03
☐ 15 Gary Roenicke	.20	.09	.03
☐ 16 Paul Runge	.20	.09	.03
☐ 17 Ted Simmons	.25	.11	.03
☐ 18 Zane Smith	.20	.09	.03
☐ 19 Andres Thomas	.20	.09	.03
☐ 20 Ozzie Virgil	.20	.09	.03
☐ 21 Team Checklist	.20	.09	.03

1988 Starting Lineup Brewers

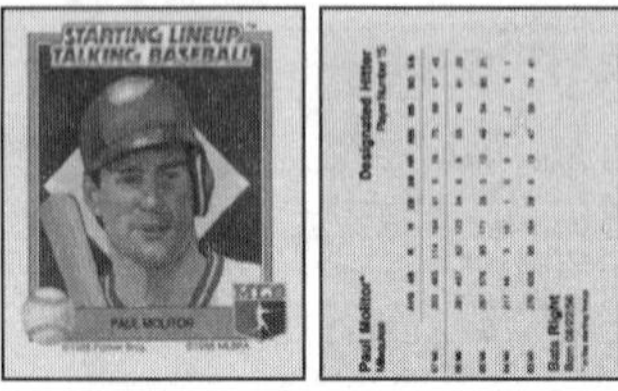

These cards feature members of the 1988 Milwaukee Brewers. These cards measure approximately 2 5/8" by 3" and have player photos on the front. The backs have recent seasonal statistics and some personal information.

	MINT	NRMT	EXC
COMPLETE SET (21)	5.00	2.20	.60
COMMON CARD (1-21)	.20	.09	.03
☐ 1 Chris Bosio	.20	.09	.03
☐ 2 Glenn Braggs	.20	.09	.03
☐ 3 Greg Brock	.20	.09	.03
☐ 4 Juan Castillo	.20	.09	.03
☐ 5 Chuck Crim	.20	.09	.03
☐ 6 Rob Deer	.20	.09	.03
☐ 7 Mike Felder	.20	.09	.03
☐ 8 Jim Gantner	.20	.09	.03
☐ 9 Ted Higuera	.20	.09	.03
☐ 10 Steve Kiefer	.20	.09	.03
☐ 11 Paul Molitor	1.00	.45	.12
☐ 12 Juan Nieves	.20	.09	.03
☐ 13 Dan Plesac	.20	.09	.03
☐ 14 Ernest Riles	.20	.09	.03
☐ 15 Billy Jo Robidoux	.20	.09	.03
☐ 16 Bill Schroeder	.20	.09	.03
☐ 17 B. J. Surhoff	.25	.11	.03
☐ 18 Dale Sveum	.20	.09	.03
☐ 19 Bill Wegman	.20	.09	.03
☐ 20 Robin Yount	.75	.35	.09
☐ 21 Team Checklist	.20	.09	.03

1988 Starting Lineup Cardinals

These cards feature members of the 1988 St. Louis Cardianals. These cards measure approximately 2 5/8" by 3" and have player photos on the front. The backs have recent seasonal statistics and some personal information.

	MINT	NRMT	EXC
COMPLETE SET (21)	5.00	2.20	.60
COMMON CARD (1-21)	.20	.09	.03
☐ 1 Rob Booker	.20	.09	.03
☐ 2 Jack Clark	.25	.11	.03
☐ 3 Vince Coleman	.25	.11	.03
☐ 4 Danny Cox	.20	.09	.03
☐ 5 Ken Dayley	.20	.09	.03
☐ 6 Curt Ford	.20	.09	.03
☐ 7 Tommy Herr	.20	.09	.03
☐ 8 Bob Horner	.25	.11	.03
☐ 9 Ricky Horton	.20	.09	.03
☐ 10 Lance Johnson	.50	.23	.06
☐ 11 Steve Lake	.20	.09	.03
☐ 12 Jim Lindeman	.20	.09	.03
☐ 13 Greg Mathews	.20	.09	.03
☐ 14 Willie McGee	.35	.16	.04
☐ 15 Jose Oquendo	.20	.09	.03
☐ 16 Tony Pena	.20	.09	.03
☐ 17 Terry Pendleton	.25	.11	.03
☐ 18 Ozzie Smith	1.50	.70	.19
☐ 19 John Tudor	.20	.09	.03
☐ 20 Todd Worrell	.25	.11	.03
☐ 21 Team Checklist	.20	.09	.03

1988 Starting Lineup Cubs

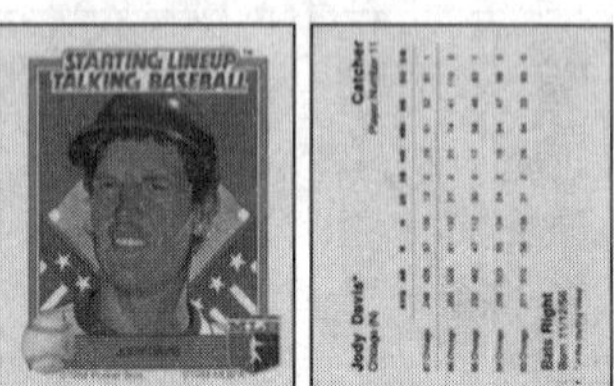

These cards feature members of the 1988 Chicago Cubs. These cards measure approximately 2 5/8" by 3" and have player photos on the front. The backs have recent seasonal statistics and some personal information.

	MINT	NRMT	EXC
COMPLETE SET (14)	4.00	1.80	.50
COMMON CARD (1-14)	.20	.09	.03
☐ 1 Andre Dawson	.75	.35	.09
☐ 2 Bob Dernier	.20	.09	.03
☐ 3 Frank DiPino	.20	.09	.03
☐ 4 Leon Durham	.20	.09	.03
☐ 5 Dave Martinez	.20	.09	.03
☐ 6 Keith Moreland	.20	.09	.03
☐ 7 Jamie Moyer	.20	.09	.03
☐ 8 Jerry Mumphrey	.20	.09	.03
☐ 9 Ryne Sandberg	1.50	.70	.19
☐ 10 Scott Sanderson	.20	.09	.03
☐ 11 Calvin Schiraldi	.20	.09	.03
☐ 12 Lee Smith	.35	.16	.04
☐ 13 Rick Sutcliffe	.25	.11	.03
☐ 14 Manny Trillo	.20	.09	.03

1988 Starting Lineup Dodgers

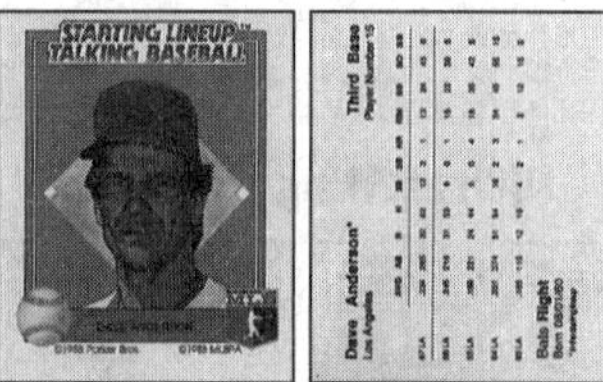

This 21-card set of the Los Angeles Dodgers measures approximately 2 5/8" by 3" and features colored drawings of the players on the fronts while the backs carry the player's statistics. The cards are unnumbered and checklisted below in alphabetical order.

	MINT	NRMT	EXC
COMPLETE SET (21)	4.00	1.80	.50
COMMON CARD (1-21)	.20	.09	.03
☐ 1 Dave Anderson	.20	.09	.03
☐ 2 Mike Davis	.20	.09	.03
☐ 3 Mariano Duncan	.20	.09	.03
☐ 4 Kirk Gibson	.35	.16	.04
☐ 5 Alfredo Griffin	.20	.09	.03
☐ 6 Pedro Guerrero	.25	.11	.03
☐ 7 Mickey Hatcher	.20	.09	.03
☐ 8 Orel Hershiser	.50	.23	.06
☐ 9 Glenn Hoffman	.20	.09	.03
☐ 10 Brian Holton	.20	.09	.03
☐ 11 Mike Marshall	.20	.09	.03
☐ 12 Jesse Orosco	.20	.09	.03
☐ 13 Alejandro Pena	.20	.09	.03
☐ 14 Steve Sax	.25	.11	.03
☐ 15 Mike Scioscia	.20	.09	.03
☐ 16 John Shelby	.20	.09	.03
☐ 17 Franklin Stubbs	.20	.09	.03
☐ 18 Don Sutton	.35	.16	.04
☐ 19 Alex Trevino	.20	.09	.03
☐ 20 Fernando Valenzuela	.25	.11	.03
☐ 21 Team Checklist	.20	.09	.03

1988 Starting Lineup Expos

This 21-card set of the Montreal Expos measures approximately 2 5/8" by 3" and features colored drawings of the players on the fronts while

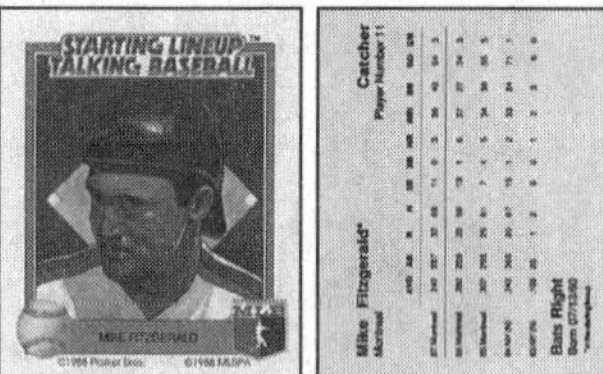

the backs carry the player's statistics. The cards are unnumbered and checklisted below in alphabetical order.

	MINT	NRMT	EXC
COMPLETE SET (21)	5.00	2.20	.60
COMMON CARD (1-21)	.20	.09	.03
☐ 1 Hubie Brooks	.20	.09	.03
☐ 2 Tim Burke	.20	.09	.03
☐ 3 Casey Candaele	.20	.09	.03
☐ 4 Mike Fitzgerald	.20	.09	.03
☐ 5 Tom Foley	.20	.09	.03
☐ 6 Andres Galarraga	.75	.35	.09
☐ 7 Neal Heaton	.20	.09	.03
☐ 8 Wallace Johnson	.20	.09	.03
☐ 9 Vance Law	.20	.09	.03
☐ 10 Bob McClure	.20	.09	.03
☐ 11 Andy McGaffigan	.20	.09	.03
☐ 12 Alonzo Powell	.20	.09	.03
☐ 13 Tim Raines	.50	.23	.06
☐ 14 Jeff Reed	.20	.09	.03
☐ 15 Luis Rivera	.20	.09	.03
☐ 16 Bryn Smith	.20	.09	.03
☐ 17 Tim Wallach	.25	.11	.03
☐ 18 Mitch Webster	.20	.09	.03
☐ 19 Herm Winningham	.20	.09	.03
☐ 20 Floyd Youmans	.20	.09	.03
☐ 21 Team Checklist	.20	.09	.03

1988 Starting Lineup Giants

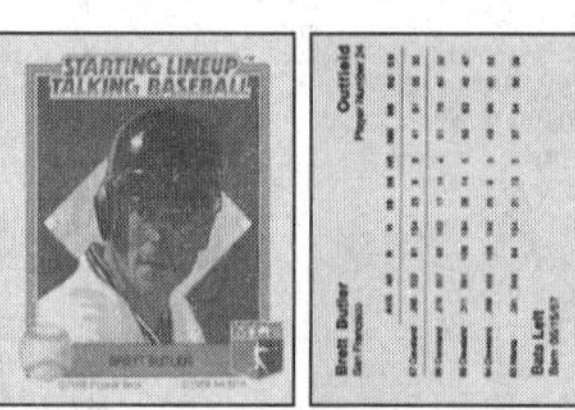

These cards feature members of the 1988 San Francisco Giants. These cards measure approximately 2 5/8" by 3" and have player photos on the front. The backs have recent seasonal statistics and some personal information. An early card of Matt Williams is included in this set.

	MINT	NRMT	EXC
COMPLETE SET (21)	8.00	3.60	1.00
COMMON CARD (1-21)	.20	.09	.03
☐ 1 Mike Aldrete	.20	.09	.03
☐ 2 Bob Brenly	.20	.09	.03
☐ 3 Brett Butler	.25	.11	.03
☐ 4 Will Clark	1.25	.55	.16
☐ 5 Chili Davis	.25	.11	.03
☐ 6 Dave Dravecky	.25	.11	.03
☐ 7 Scott Garrelts	.20	.09	.03
☐ 8 Atlee Hammaker	.20	.09	.03
☐ 9 Craig Lefferts	.20	.09	.03
☐ 10 Jeffrey Leonard	.20	.09	.03
☐ 11 Candy Maldonado	.20	.09	.03
☐ 12 Bob Melvin	.20	.09	.03
☐ 13 Kevin Mitchell	.25	.11	.03
☐ 14 Rick Reuschel	.25	.11	.03
☐ 15 Don Robinson	.20	.09	.03
☐ 16 Chris Speier	.20	.09	.03
☐ 17 Harry Spilman	.20	.09	.03
☐ 18 Robby Thompson	.20	.09	.03
☐ 19 Jose Uribe	.20	.09	.03
☐ 20 Matt Williams	3.00	1.35	.35
☐ 21 Team Checklist	.20	.09	.03

1988 Starting Lineup Indians

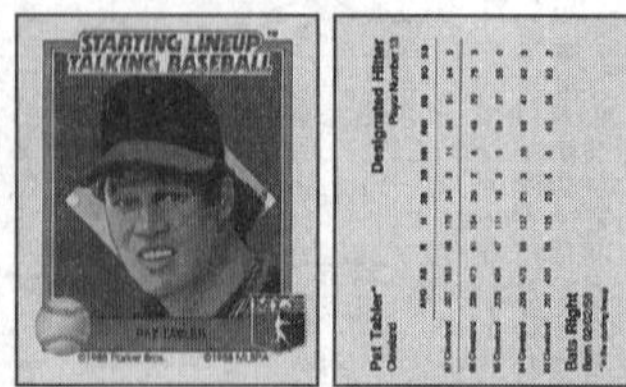

This 21-card set of the Cleveland Indians measures approximately 2 5/8" by 3" and features colored drawings of the players on the fronts while the backs carry the player's statistics. The cards are unnumbered and checklisted below in alphabetical order.

	MINT	NRMT	EXC
COMPLETE SET (21)	5.00	2.20	.60
COMMON CARD (1-21)	.20	.09	.03
☐ 1 Andy Allanson	.20	.09	.03
☐ 2 Scott Bailes	.20	.09	.03
☐ 3 Chris Bando	.20	.09	.03
☐ 4 Jay Bell	.50	.23	.06
☐ 5 Brett Butler	.25	.11	.03
☐ 6 Tom Candiotti	.20	.09	.03
☐ 7 Joe Carter	.75	.35	.09
☐ 8 Carmen Castillo	.20	.09	.03
☐ 9 Dave Clark	.20	.09	.03
☐ 10 John Farrell	.20	.09	.03
☐ 11 Julio Franco	.25	.11	.03
☐ 12 Mel Hall	.20	.09	.03
☐ 13 Tommy Hinzo	.20	.09	.03
☐ 14 Brook Jacoby	.20	.09	.03
☐ 15 Doug Jones	.20	.09	.03
☐ 16 Junior Noboa	.20	.09	.03
☐ 17 Ken Schrom	.20	.09	.03
☐ 18 Cory Snyder	.20	.09	.03
☐ 19 Greg Swindell	.20	.09	.03
☐ 20 Pat Tabler	.20	.09	.03
☐ 21 Team Checklist	.20	.09	.03

1988 Starting Lineup Mariners

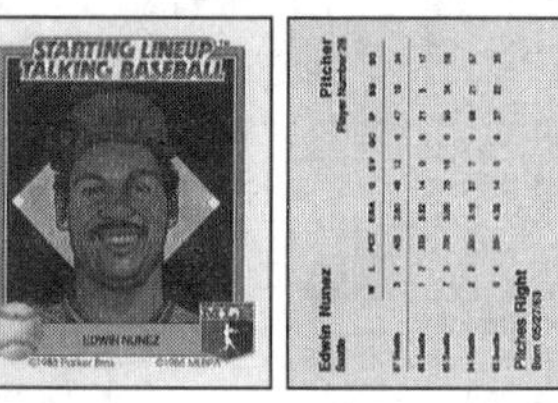

This 21-card set of the Seattle Mariners measures approximately 2 5/8" by 3" and features colored drawings of the players on the fronts while the backs carry the player's statistics. The cards are unnumbered and checklisted below in alphabetical order.

	MINT	NRMT	EXC
COMPLETE SET (21)	4.00	1.80	.50
COMMON CARD (1-21)	.20	.09	.03
☐ 1 Phil Bradley	.20	.09	.03
☐ 2 Scott Bradley	.20	.09	.03
☐ 3 Mickey Brantley	.20	.09	.03
☐ 4 Mike Campbell	.20	.09	.03
☐ 5 Henry Cotto	.20	.09	.03
☐ 6 Alvin Davis	.25	.11	.03
☐ 7 Mike Kingery	.20	.09	.03
☐ 8 Mark Langston	.35	.16	.04
☐ 9 Mike Moore	.20	.09	.03
☐ 10 John Moses	.20	.09	.03
☐ 11 Otis Nixon	.25	.11	.03
☐ 12 Edwin Nunez	.20	.09	.03
☐ 13 Ken Phelps	.20	.09	.03
☐ 14 Jim Presley	.20	.09	.03
☐ 15 Rey Quinones	.20	.09	.03
☐ 16 Jerry Reed	.20	.09	.03
☐ 17 Harold Reynolds	.25	.11	.03
☐ 18 Dave Valle	.20	.09	.03
☐ 19 Bill Wilkinson	.20	.09	.03
☐ 20 Glenn Wilson	.20	.09	.03
☐ 21 Team Checklist	.20	.09	.03

1988 Starting Lineup Mets

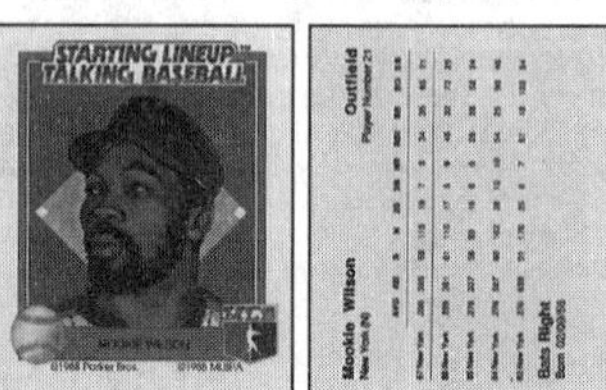

This 21-card set of the New York Mets measures approximately 2 5/8" by 3" and features colored drawings of the players on the fronts while the backs carry the player's statistics. The cards are unnumbered and checklisted below in alphabetical order.

	MINT	NRMT	EXC
COMPLETE SET (21)	5.00	2.20	.60
COMMON CARD (1-21)	.20	.09	.03
☐ 1 Bill Almon	.20	.09	.03
☐ 2 Wally Backman	.20	.09	.03
☐ 3 Gary Carter	.75	.35	.09
☐ 4 Dave Cone	.20	.09	.03
☐ 5 Ron Darling	.25	.11	.03
☐ 6 Len Dykstra	.50	.23	.06
☐ 7 Sid Fernandez	.25	.11	.03
☐ 8 Dwight Gooden	.50	.23	.06
☐ 9 Keith Hernandez	.35	.16	.04
☐ 10 Howard Johnson	.25	.11	.03
☐ 11 Barry Lyons	.20	.09	.03

□ 12 Dave Magadan	.20	.09	.03
□ 13 Lee Mazzilli	.20	.09	.03
□ 14 Roger McDowell	.20	.09	.03
□ 15 Kevin McReynolds	.25	.11	.03
□ 16 Jesse Orosco	.20	.09	.03
□ 17 Rafael Santana	.20	.09	.03
□ 18 Darryl Strawberry	.35	.16	.04
□ 19 Tim Teufel	.20	.09	.03
□ 20 Mookie Wilson	.25	.11	.03
□ 21 Team Checklist	.20	.09	.03

1988 Starting Lineup Orioles

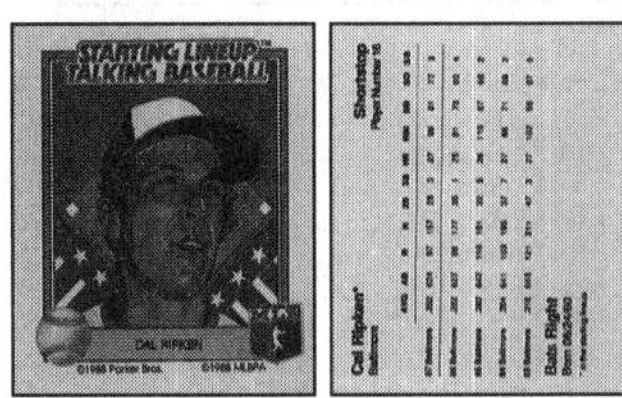

This 21-card set of the Baltimore Orioles measures approximately 2 5/8" by 3" and features colored drawings of the players on the fronts while the backs carry the player's statistics. The cards are unnumbered and checklisted below in alphabetical order.

	MINT	NRMT	EXC
COMPLETE SET (21)	10.00	4.50	1.25
COMMON CARD (1-21)	.20	.09	.03

□ 1 Eric Bell	.20	.09	.03
□ 2 Mike Boddicker	.20	.09	.03
□ 3 Jim Dwyer	.20	.09	.03
□ 4 Ken Gerhart	.20	.09	.03
□ 5 Rene Gonzales	.20	.09	.03
□ 6 Terry Kennedy	.20	.09	.03
□ 7 Ray Knight	.25	.11	.03
□ 8 Lee Lacy	.20	.09	.03
□ 9 Fred Lynn	.35	.16	.04
□ 10 Eddie Murray	1.00	.45	.12
□ 11 Tom Niedenfuer	.20	.09	.03
□ 12 Billy Ripken	.20	.09	.03
□ 13 Cal Ripken	6.00	2.70	.75
□ 14 Dave Schmidt	.20	.09	.03
□ 15 Larry Sheets	.20	.09	.03
□ 16 Steve Stanicek	.20	.09	.03
□ 17 Mark Thurmond	.20	.09	.03
□ 18 Ron Washington	.20	.09	.03
□ 19 Mark Williamson	.20	.09	.03
□ 20 Mike Young	.20	.09	.03
□ 21 Team Checklist	.20	.09	.03

1988 Starting Lineup Padres

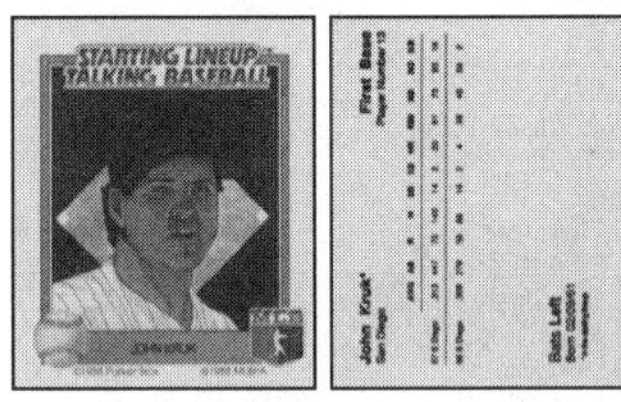

These cards feature members of the 1988 San Diego Padres. These cards measure approximately 2 5/8" by 3" and have player photos on the front. The backs have recent seasonal statistics and some personal information.

	MINT	NRMT	EXC
COMPLETE SET (14)	4.00	1.80	.50
COMMON CARD (1-14)	.20	.09	.03

□ 1 Shawn Abner	.20	.09	.03
□ 2 Mark Davis	.20	.09	.03
□ 3 Goose Gossage	.35	.16	.04
□ 4 Mark Grant	.20	.09	.03
□ 5 Tony Gwynn	2.00	.90	.25
□ 6 Stan Jefferson	.20	.09	.03
□ 7 John Kruk	.50	.23	.06
□ 8 Carmelo Martinez	.20	.09	.03
□ 9 Lance McCullers	.20	.09	.03
□ 10 Randy Ready	.20	.09	.03
□ 11 Benito Santiago	.25	.11	.03
□ 12 Eric Show	.20	.09	.03
□ 13 Ed Whitson	.20	.09	.03
□ 14 Marvell Wynne	.20	.09	.03

1988 Starting Lineup Phillies

This 21-card set of the Philadelphia Phillies measures approximately 2 5/8" by 3" and features colored drawings of the players on the fronts while the backs carry the player's statistics. The cards are unnumbered and checklisted below in alphabetical order.

	MINT	NRMT	EXC
COMPLETE SET (21)	5.00	2.20	.60
COMMON CARD (1-21)	.20	.09	.03

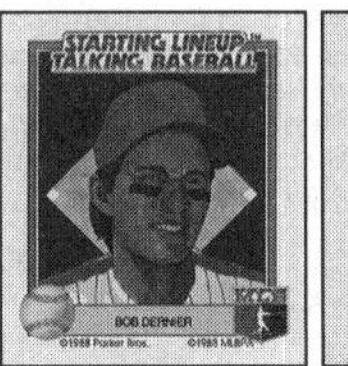

□ 1 Luis Aguayo	.20	.09	.03
□ 2 Steve Bedrosian	.20	.09	.03
□ 3 Phil Bradley	.20	.09	.03
□ 4 Jeff Calhoun	.20	.09	.03
□ 5 Don Carman	.20	.09	.03
□ 6 Darren Daulton	.50	.23	.06
□ 7 Bob Dernier	.20	.09	.03
□ 8 Greg Gross	.20	.09	.03
□ 9 Von Hayes	.20	.09	.03
□ 10 Chris James	.20	.09	.03
□ 11 Steve Jeltz	.20	.09	.03
□ 12 Lance Parrish	.25	.11	.03
□ 13 Shane Rawley	.20	.09	.03
□ 14 Bruce Ruffin	.20	.09	.03
□ 15 Juan Samuel	.20	.09	.03
□ 16 Mike Schmidt	1.50	.70	.19
□ 17 Rick Schu	.20	.09	.03
□ 18 Kent Tekulve	.20	.09	.03
□ 19 Milt Thompson	.20	.09	.03
□ 20 Glenn Wilson	.20	.09	.03
□ 21 Team Checklist	.20	.09	.03

1988 Starting Lineup Pirates

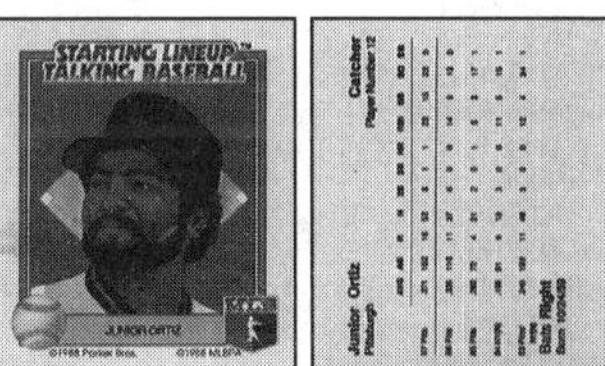

This 21-card set of the Pittsburgh Pirates measures approximately 2 5/8" by 3" and features colored drawings of the players on the fronts while the backs carry the player's statistics. The cards are unnumbered and checklisted below in alphabetical order.

	MINT	NRMT	EXC
COMPLETE SET (21)	6.00	2.70	.75
COMMON CARD (1-21)	.20	.09	.03

□ 1 Rafael Belliard	.20	.09	.03
□ 2 Barry Bonds	2.00	.90	.25
□ 3 Bobby Bonilla	.35	.16	.04
□ 4 Sid Bream	.20	.09	.03
□ 5 John Cangelosi	.20	.09	.03
□ 6 Darnell Coles	.20	.09	.03
□ 7 Mike Diaz	.20	.09	.03
□ 8 Doug Drabek	.25	.11	.03
□ 9 Mike Dunne	.20	.09	.03
□ 10 Felix Fermin	.20	.09	.03
□ 11 Brian Fisher	.20	.09	.03
□ 12 Jim Gott	.20	.09	.03
□ 13 Mike LaValliere	.20	.09	.03
□ 14 Jose Lind	.20	.09	.03
□ 15 Junior Ortiz	.20	.09	.03
□ 16 Al Pedrique	.20	.09	.03
□ 17 R.J. Reynolds	.20	.09	.03
□ 18 Jeff Robinson	.20	.09	.03
□ 19 John Smiley	.30	.14	.04
□ 20 Andy Van Slyke	.25	.11	.03
□ 21 Team Checklist	.20	.09	.03

1988 Starting Lineup Rangers

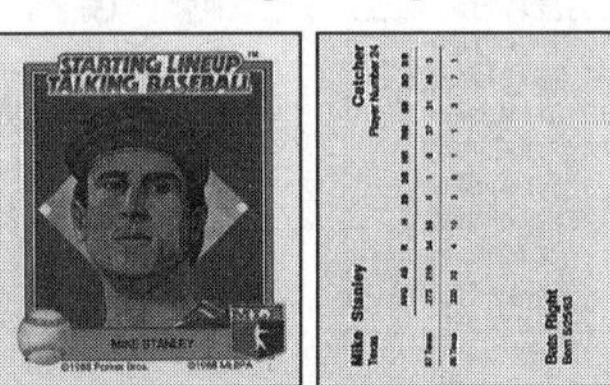

This 21-card set of the Texas Rangers measures approximately 2 5/8" by 3" and features colored drawings of the players on the fronts while the backs carry the player's statistics. The cards are unnumbered and checklisted below in alphabetical order.

	MINT	NRMT	EXC
COMPLETE SET (21)	4.00	1.80	.50
COMMON CARD (1-21)	.20	.09	.03

□ 1 Bob Brower	.20	.09	.03
□ 2 Jerry Browne	.20	.09	.03
□ 3 Steve Buechele	.20	.09	.03
□ 4 Scott Fletcher	.20	.09	.03
□ 5 Jose Guzman	.20	.09	.03
□ 6 Charlie Hough	.20	.09	.03
□ 7 Pete Incaviglia	.25	.11	.03
□ 8 Oddibe McDowell	.20	.09	.03
□ 9 Dale Mohorcic	.20	.09	.03
□ 10 Pete O'Brien	.20	.09	.03
□ 11 Tom O'Malley	.20	.09	.03
□ 12 Larry Parrish	.20	.09	.03
□ 13 Geno Petralli	.20	.09	.03
□ 14 Jeff Russell	.20	.09	.03
□ 15 Ruben Sierra	.35	.16	.04
□ 16 Don Slaught	.20	.09	.03
□ 17 Mike Stanley	.25	.11	.03
□ 18 Curt Wilkerson	.20	.09	.03
□ 19 Mitch Williams	.25	.11	.03
□ 20 Bobby Witt	.50	.23	.06
□ 21 Title Card Batting Order	.20	.09	.03

1988 Starting Lineup Red Sox

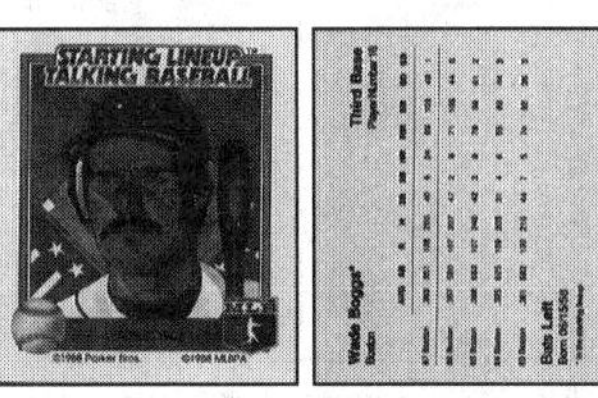

This 21-card set of the Boston Red Sox measures approximately 2 5/8" by 3" and features colored drawings of the players on the fronts while the backs carry the player's statistics. The cards are unnumbered and checklisted below in alphabetical order.

	MINT	NRMT	EXC
COMPLETE SET (21)	6.00	2.70	.75
COMMON CARD (1-21)	.20	.09	.03

□ 1 Marty Barrett	.20	.09	.03
□ 2 Todd Benzinger	.20	.09	.03
□ 3 Wade Boggs	1.00	.45	.12
□ 4 Oil Can Boyd	.20	.09	.03
□ 5 Ellis Burks	.75	.35	.09
□ 6 Roger Clemens	1.50	.70	.19
□ 7 Dwight Evans	.35	.16	.04
□ 8 Wes Gardner	.20	.09	.03
□ 9 Rich Gedman	.20	.09	.03
□ 10 Mike Greenwell	.25	.11	.03
□ 11 Sam Horn	.20	.09	.03
□ 12 Bruce Hurst	.20	.09	.03
□ 13 John Marzano	.20	.09	.03
□ 14 Spike Owen	.20	.09	.03
□ 15 Jody Reed	.20	.09	.03
□ 16 Jim Rice	.35	.16	.04
□ 17 Ed Romero	.20	.09	.03
□ 18 Kevin Romine	.20	.09	.03
□ 19 Lee Smith	.35	.16	.04
□ 20 Bob Stanley	.20	.09	.03
□ 21 Team Checklist	.20	.09	.03

1988 Starting Lineup Reds

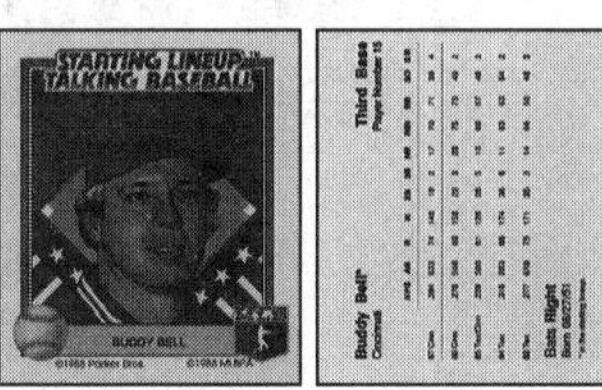

This 21-card set of the Cincinnati Reds measures approximately 2 5/8" by 3" and features colored drawings of the players on the fronts while the backs carry the player's statistics. The cards are unnumbered and checklisted below in alphabetical order.

	MINT	NRMT	EXC
COMPLETE SET (21)	5.00	2.20	.60
COMMON CARD (1-21)	.20	.09	.03

□ 1 Buddy Bell	.25	.11	.03
□ 2 Tom Browning	.20	.09	.03
□ 3 Dave Collins	.20	.09	.03
□ 4 Dave Concepcion	.25	.11	.03
□ 5 Kal Daniels	.20	.09	.03
□ 6 Eric Davis	.25	.11	.03
□ 7 Bo Diaz	.20	.09	.03
□ 8 Nick Esasky	.20	.09	.03
□ 9 John Franco	.50	.23	.06
□ 10 Terry Francona	.20	.09	.03
□ 11 Tracy Jones	.20	.09	.03
□ 12 Barry Larkin	1.00	.45	.12
□ 13 Rob Murphy	.20	.09	.03
□ 14 Paul O'Neill	.50	.23	.06
□ 15 Dave Parker	.35	.16	.04
□ 16 Ted Power	.20	.09	.03
□ 17 Dennis Rasmussen	.20	.09	.03
□ 18 Kurt Stillwell	.20	.09	.03
□ 19 Jeff Treadway	.20	.09	.03
□ 20 Frank Williams	.20	.09	.03
□ 21 Team Checklist	.20	.09	.03

1988 Starting Lineup Royals

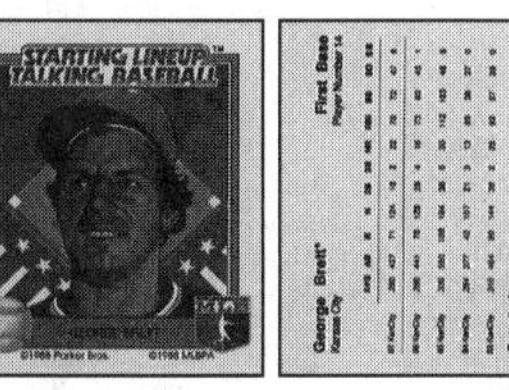

This 21-card set of the Kansas City Royals measures approximately 2 5/8" by 3" and features colored drawings of the players on the fronts while the backs carry the player's statistics. The cards are unnumbered and checklisted below in alphabetical order.

	MINT	NRMT	EXC
COMPLETE SET (21)	6.00	2.70	.75
COMMON CARD (1-21)	.20	.09	.03

□ 1 Steve Balboni	.20	.09	.03
□ 2 George Brett	2.00	.90	.25
□ 3 Jim Eisenreich	.20	.09	.03
□ 4 Gene Garber	.25	.11	.03
□ 5 Jerry Don Gleaton	.20	.09	.03
□ 6 Mark Gubicza	.20	.09	.03
□ 7 Bo Jackson	.50	.23	.06
□ 8 Charlie Leibrandt	.20	.09	.03
□ 9 Mike MacFarlane	.20	.09	.03
□ 10 Larry Owen	.20	.09	.03
□ 11 Bill Pecota	.20	.09	.03
□ 12 Jamie Quirk	.20	.09	.03
□ 13 Dan Quisenberry	.25	.11	.03
□ 14 Bret Saberhagen	.35	.16	.04
□ 15 Kevin Seitzer	.25	.11	.03
□ 16 Kurt Stillwell	.20	.09	.03
□ 17 Danny Tartabull	.35	.16	.04
□ 18 Gary Thurman	.20	.09	.03
□ 19 Frank White	.25	.11	.03
□ 20 Willie Wilson	.25	.11	.03
□ 21 Team Checklist	.20	.09	.03

1988 Starting Lineup Tigers

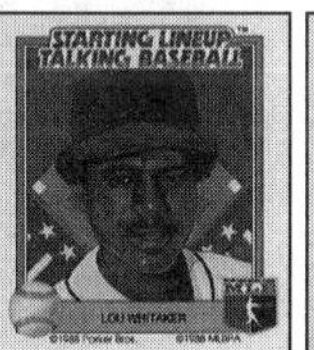
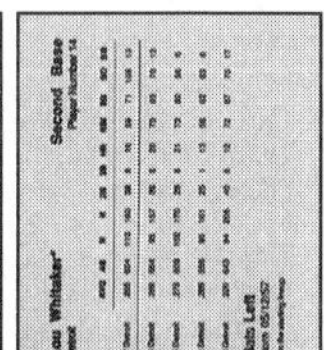

This 21-card set of the Detroit Tigers measures approximately 2 5/8" by 3" and features colored drawings of the players on the fronts while the backs carry the player's statistics. The cards are unnumbered and checklisted below in alphabetical order.

	MINT	NRMT	EXC
COMPLETE SET (21)	5.00	2.20	.60
COMMON CARD (1-21)	.20	.09	.03

□ 1 Doyle Alexander	.20	.09	.03
□ 2 Dave Bergman	.20	.09	.03
□ 3 Tom Brookens	.20	.09	.03
□ 4 Darrell Evans	.25	.11	.03
□ 5 Kirk Gibson	.35	.16	.04
□ 6 Mike Heath	.20	.09	.03
□ 7 Mike Henneman	.35	.16	.04
□ 8 Guillermo"Willie" Hernandez	.20	.09	.03
□ 9 Larry Herndon	.20	.09	.03
□ 10 Eric King	.20	.09	.03
□ 11 Ray Knight	.25	.11	.03
□ 12 Chet Lemon	.20	.09	.03
□ 13 Bill Madlock	.25	.11	.03
□ 14 Jack Morris	.35	.16	.04
□ 15 Jim Morrison	.20	.09	.03
□ 16 Matt Nokes	.35	.16	.04
□ 17 Pat Sheridan	.20	.09	.03
□ 18 Frank Tanana	.25	.11	.03
□ 19 Alan Trammell	.75	.35	.09
□ 20 Lou Whitaker	.35	.16	.04
□ 21 Team Checklist	.20	.09	.03

1988 Starting Lineup Twins

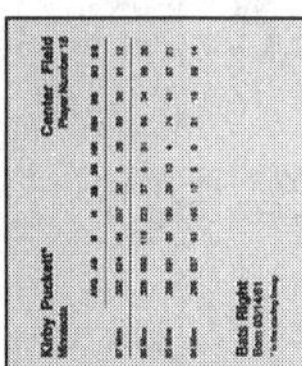

This 21-card set of the Minnesota Twins measures approximately 2 5/8" by 3" and features colored drawings of the players on the fronts while the backs carry the player's statistics. The cards are unnumbered and checklisted below in alphabetical order.

	MINT	NRMT	EXC
COMPLETE SET (21)	5.00	2.20	.60
COMMON CARD (1-21)	.20	.09	.03
☐ 1 Don Baylor	.25	.11	.03
☐ 2 Juan Berenguer	.20	.09	.03
☐ 3 Bert Blyleven	.35	.16	.04
☐ 4 Tom Brunansky	.25	.11	.03
☐ 5 Randy Bush	.20	.09	.03
☐ 6 Mark Davidson	.20	.09	.03
☐ 7 Gary Gaetti	.50	.23	.06
☐ 8 Greg Gagne	.20	.09	.03
☐ 9 Dan Gladden	.20	.09	.03
☐ 10 Kent Hrbek	.35	.16	.04
☐ 11 Gene Larkin	.20	.09	.03
☐ 12 Tim Laudner	.20	.09	.03
☐ 13 Steve Lombardozzi	.20	.09	.03
☐ 14 Al Newman	.20	.09	.03
☐ 15 Kirby Puckett	1.50	.70	.19
☐ 16 Jeff Reardon	.25	.11	.03
☐ 17 Dan Schatzeder	.20	.09	.03
☐ 18 Roy Smalley	.20	.09	.03
☐ 19 Les Straker	.20	.09	.03
☐ 20 Frank Viola	.25	.11	.03
☐ 21 Team Checklist	.20	.09	.03

1988 Starting Lineup White Sox

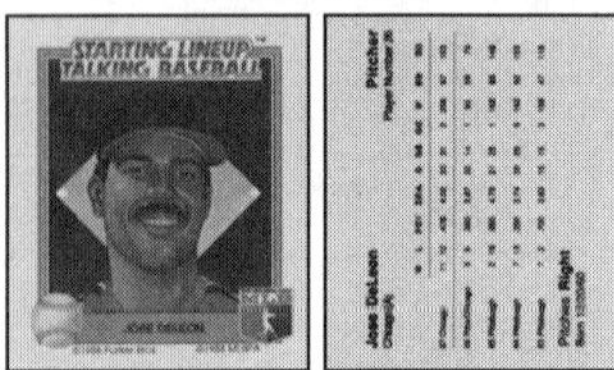

These cards feature members of the 1988 San Diego Padres. These cards measure approximately 2 5/8" by 3" and have player photos on the front. The backs have recent seasonal statistics and some personal information. The cards are unnumbered and checklisted below in alphabetical order.

	MINT	NRMT	EXC
COMPLETE SET (21)	4.00	1.80	.50
COMMON CARD (1-21)	.20	.09	.03
☐ 1 Harold Baines	.35	.16	.04
☐ 2 Floyd Bannister	.20	.09	.03
☐ 3 Daryl Boston	.20	.09	.03
☐ 4 Ivan Calderon	.20	.09	.03
☐ 5 Jose DeLeon	.20	.09	.03
☐ 6 Rich Dotson	.20	.09	.03
☐ 7 Carlton Fisk	1.00	.45	.12
☐ 8 Ozzie Guillen	.25	.11	.03
☐ 9 Jerry Hairston	.20	.09	.03
☐ 10 Donnie Hill	.20	.09	.03
☐ 11 Dave LaPoint	.20	.09	.03
☐ 12 Steve Lyons	.20	.09	.03
☐ 13 Fred Manrique	.20	.09	.03
☐ 14 Dan Pasqua	.20	.09	.03
☐ 15 Gary Redus	.20	.09	.03
☐ 16 Mark Salas	.20	.09	.03
☐ 17 Ray Searage	.20	.09	.03
☐ 18 Bobby Thigpen	.20	.09	.03
☐ 19 Greg Walker	.20	.09	.03
☐ 20 Ken Williams	.20	.09	.03
☐ 21 Team Checklist	.20	.09	.03

1988 Starting Lineup Yankees

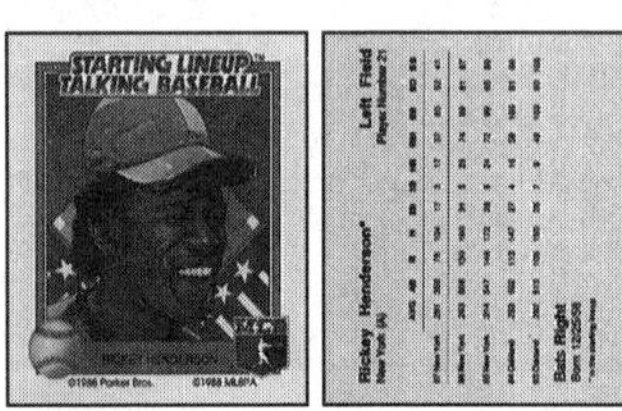

This 21-card set of the New York Yankees measures approximately 2 5/8" by 3" and features colored drawings of the players on the fronts while the backs carry the player's statistics. The cards are unnumbered and checklisted below in alphabetical order.

	MINT	NRMT	EXC
COMPLETE SET (21)	7.00	3.10	.85
COMMON CARD (1-21)	.20	.09	.03
☐ 1 Rick Cerone	.20	.09	.03
☐ 2 Jack Clark	.25	.11	.03
☐ 3 Pat Clements	.20	.09	.03
☐ 4 Mike Easler	.20	.09	.03
☐ 5 Ron Guidry	.35	.16	.04
☐ 6 Rickey Henderson	1.00	.45	.12
☐ 7 Tommy John	.35	.16	.04
☐ 8 Don Mattingly	2.00	.90	.25
☐ 9 Bobby Meacham	.20	.09	.03
☐ 10 Mike Pagliarulo	.20	.09	.03
☐ 11 Willie Randolph	.25	.11	.03
☐ 12 Rick Rhoden	.20	.09	.03
☐ 13 Dave Righetti	.25	.11	.03
☐ 14 Jerry Royster	.20	.09	.03
☐ 15 Don Slaught	.20	.09	.03
☐ 16 Tim Stoddard	.20	.09	.03
☐ 17 Wayne Tolleson	.20	.09	.03
☐ 18 Gary Ward	.20	.09	.03
☐ 19 Claudell Washington	.20	.09	.03
☐ 20 Dave Winfield	.75	.35	.09
☐ 21 Team Checklist	.20	.09	.03

1992 Sterling Dravecky

This Heroes of Life set measures the standard size. The front design features posed and action color photos of Dravecky bordered by thin black and amber lines. His name is printed horizontally in amber on celadon along the right side of the card. The words "Heroes of Life" are in a canary yellow stripe at the top. The backs feature color photos on a graded yellow background showing Dravecky in action and with fans. Some cards include player profile information, others have room for an autograph and some have quotes in amber boxes overlapping the picture. According to serious Dravecky collectors, so far only cards numbered 2 and 12 are known. If other cards are discovered, please let us know.

	MINT	NRMT	EXC
COMPLETE SET (2)	10.00	4.50	1.25
COMMON CARD (2/12)	5.00	2.20	.60
☐ 2 Dave Dravecky Profile	5.00	2.20	.60
☐ 12 Dave Dravecky Autograph	5.00	2.20	.60

1995 Stouffer Pop-ups

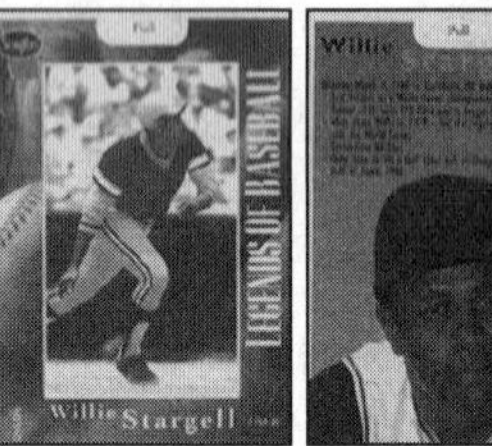

This five-card set was distributed by Stouffer's Frozen Foods and features small color photos of great baseball players set on a ball and glove background. When the tab at the top of the card is pulled, the player's image "pops" out. The backs carry another player photo with player information.

	MINT	NRMT	EXC
COMPLETE SET (5)	15.00	6.75	1.85
COMMON CARD (1-5)	2.00	.90	.25
☐ 1 Yogi Berra	5.00	2.20	.60
☐ 2 Gary Carter	2.00	.90	.25
☐ 3 Don Drysdale	4.00	1.80	.50
☐ 4 Bob Feller	4.00	1.80	.50
☐ 5 Willie Stargell	3.00	1.35	.35

1987 Stuart Panels

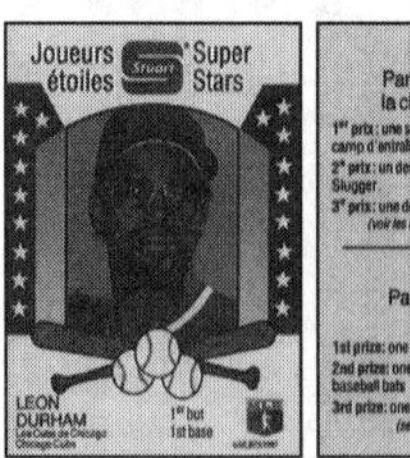

Subtitled "Super Stars" in English and French, this set consists of 28 four-part perforated panels each featuring three players from the same team and a contest entry card. All 26 teams are included at least once; the Montreal Expos and Toronto Blue Jays each have two panels. Printed on white stock, the four-part panels measure 10 1/8" by 3 7/16"; each card measures 2 1/2" by 3 7/16". The fronts feature color player headshots with white stars on a blue field on each side of the photo. The player's name, along with bilingual team name and position, appear at the bottom, below a crossed bats and baseballs icon. The plain white back carries the player's bilingual biography and 1986 statistics. Team insignias are not shown on the cards because the set was licensed only by the Major League Baseball Players Association. The set is priced below as panels because that is the way the cards are typically found and because the three player cards on each panel carry the same number (No. X de/of 28) on the back.

	MINT	NRMT	EXC
COMPLETE SET (28)	100.00	45.00	12.50
COMMON PANEL (1-28)	2.00	.90	.25
☐ 1 Darryl Strawberry Keith Hernandez Gary Carter	5.00	2.20	.60
☐ 2 Bruce Benedict Ken Griffey Sr. Dale Murphy	3.00	1.35	.35
☐ 3 Leon Durham Jody Davis Andre Dawson	3.00	1.35	.35
☐ 4 Buddy Bell Dave Parker Eric Davis	3.00	1.35	.35
☐ 5 Mike Scott Nolan Ryan Glenn Davis	10.00	4.50	1.25
☐ 6 Mike Marshall Fernando Valenzuela Pedro Guerrero	2.00	.90	.25
☐ 7 Mitch Webster Tim Wallach Tim Raines	3.00	1.35	.35
☐ 8 Bryn Smith Hubie Brooks Floyd Youmans	2.00	.90	.25
☐ 9 Juan Samuel Shane Rawley Mike Schmidt	4.00	1.80	.50
☐ 10 Jim Morrison R.J. Reynolds Johnny Ray	2.00	.90	.25
☐ 11 Ozzie Smith Vince Coleman Jack Clark	7.50	3.40	.95
☐ 12 John Kruk Tony Gwynn Steve Garvey	7.50	3.40	.95
☐ 13 Robby Thompson Jeffrey Leonard Chili Davis	3.00	1.35	.35
☐ 14 Fred Lynn Eddie Murray Cal Ripken	10.00	4.50	1.25
☐ 15 Roger Clemens Wade Boggs Don Baylor	7.50	3.40	.95
☐ 16 Mike Witt Wally Joyner Doug DeCinces	2.00	.90	.25
☐ 17 Ozzie Guillen Carlton Fisk Harold Baines	3.00	1.35	.35
☐ 18 Joe Carter Julio Franco Pat Tabler	1.50	.70	.19
☐ 19 Kirk Gibson Alan Trammell Jack Morris	4.00	1.80	.50
☐ 20 Willie Wilson Bret Saberhagen George Brett	7.50	3.40	.95
☐ 21 Paul Molitor Robin Yount Cecil Cooper	7.50	3.40	.95
☐ 22 Kirby Puckett Kent Hrbek Tom Brunansky	7.50	3.40	.95
☐ 23 Dave Winfield Don Mattingly Rickey Henderson	10.00	4.50	1.25
☐ 24 Alfredo Griffin Carney Lansford Jose Canseco	3.00	1.35	.35
☐ 25 Mark Langston Phil Bradley Alvin Davis	2.00	.90	.25
☐ 26 Larry Parrish Pete O'Brien Pete Incaviglia	2.00	.90	.25
☐ 27 George Bell Tony Fernandez Jesse Barfield	3.00	1.35	.35
☐ 28 Ernie Whitt Lloyd Moseby Dave Stieb	3.00	1.35	.35

1991 Studio Previews

This 18-card preview set was issued four at a time within 1991 Donruss retail factory sets in order to show dealers and collectors the look of their new Studio cards. The standard-size cards are exactly the same style as those in the Studio series, with black and white player photos bordered in mauve and player information on the backs.

	MINT	NRMT	EXC
COMPLETE SET (18)	20.00	9.00	2.50
COMMON CARD (1-17)	1.00	.45	.12
☐ 1 Juan Bell	1.00	.45	.12
☐ 2 Roger Clemens	6.00	2.70	.75
☐ 3 Dave Parker	1.50	.70	.19
☐ 4 Tim Raines	1.50	.70	.19
☐ 5 Kevin Seitzer	1.00	.45	.12
☐ 6 Ted Higuera	1.00	.45	.12
☐ 7 Bernie Williams	10.00	4.50	1.25
☐ 8 Harold Baines	1.50	.70	.19
☐ 9 Gary Pettis	1.00	.45	.12
☐ 10 Dave Justice	4.00	1.80	.50
☐ 11 Eric Davis	1.50	.70	.19
☐ 12 Andujar Cedeno	1.00	.45	.12
☐ 13 Tom Foley	1.00	.45	.12
☐ 14 Dwight Gooden	1.50	.70	.19
☐ 15 Doug Drabek	1.00	.45	.12
☐ 16 Steve Decker	1.00	.45	.12
☐ 17 Joe Torre MG	1.50	.70	.19
☐ NNO Title card	1.00	.45	.12

1991 Studio

The 1991 Studio set, issued by Donruss/Leaf, contains 264 standard-size cards issued in one series. Cards were distributed in foil packs each of which contained one of 21 different Rod Carew puzzle panels. The Studio card fronts feature posed black and white head-and-shoulders player photos with mauve borders. The team logo, player's name, and position appear along the bottom of the card face. The cards are ordered alphabetically within and according to teams for each league with American League teams preceding National League. Rookie Cards in the set include Jeff Bagwell, Jeff Conine and Brian McRae.

	MINT	NRMT	EXC
COMPLETE SET (264)	15.00	6.75	1.85
COMMON CARD (1-263)	.05	.02	.01
COVER CARD (NNO)	.05	.02	.01
☐ 1 Glenn Davis	.05	.02	.01
☐ 2 Dwight Evans	.15	.07	.02
☐ 3 Leo Gomez	.05	.02	.01
☐ 4 Chris Hoiles	.05	.02	.01
☐ 5 Sam Horn	.05	.02	.01
☐ 6 Ben McDonald	.15	.07	.02
☐ 7 Randy Milligan	.05	.02	.01
☐ 8 Gregg Olson	.05	.02	.01
☐ 9 Cal Ripken	1.50	.70	.19
☐ 10 David Segui	.15	.07	.02
☐ 11 Wade Boggs	.30	.14	.04
☐ 12 Ellis Burks	.15	.07	.02
☐ 13 Jack Clark	.15	.07	.02
☐ 14 Roger Clemens	.40	.18	.05
☐ 15 Mike Greenwell	.05	.02	.01
☐ 16 Tim Naehring	.15	.07	.02
☐ 17 Tony Pena	.05	.02	.01
☐ 18 Phil Plantier	.15	.07	.02
☐ 19 Jeff Reardon	.15	.07	.02
☐ 20 Mo Vaughn	1.00	.45	.12
☐ 21 Jimmy Reese CO	.15	.07	.02
☐ 22 Jim Abbott UER (Born in 1967, not 1969)	.15	.07	.02
☐ 23 Bert Blyleven	.15	.07	.02
☐ 24 Chuck Finley	.15	.07	.02
☐ 25 Gary Gaetti	.15	.07	.02
☐ 26 Wally Joyner	.15	.07	.02
☐ 27 Mark Langston	.15	.07	.02
☐ 28 Kirk McCaskill	.05	.02	.01
☐ 29 Lance Parrish	.05	.02	.01
☐ 30 Dave Winfield	.30	.14	.04
☐ 31 Alex Fernandez	.30	.14	.04
☐ 32 Carlton Fisk	.30	.14	.04
☐ 33 Scott Fletcher	.05	.02	.01
☐ 34 Greg Hibbard	.05	.02	.01
☐ 35 Charlie Hough	.05	.02	.01
☐ 36 Jack McDowell	.15	.07	.02
☐ 37 Tim Raines	.30	.14	.04
☐ 38 Sammy Sosa	.60	.25	.07
☐ 39 Bobby Thigpen	.05	.02	.01
☐ 40 Frank Thomas	4.00	1.80	.50
☐ 41 Sandy Alomar Jr.	.15	.07	.02

☐ 42 John Farrell	.05	.02	.01
☐ 43 Glenallen Hill	.05	.02	.01
☐ 44 Brook Jacoby	.05	.02	.01
☐ 45 Chris James	.05	.02	.01
☐ 46 Doug Jones	.05	.02	.01
☐ 47 Eric King	.05	.02	.01
☐ 48 Mark Lewis	.05	.02	.01
☐ 49 Greg Swindell UER (Photo actually Turner Ward)	.05	.02	.01
☐ 50 Mark Whiten	.15	.07	.02
☐ 51 Milt Cuyler	.05	.02	.01
☐ 52 Rob Deer	.05	.02	.01
☐ 53 Cecil Fielder	.15	.07	.02
☐ 54 Travis Fryman	.30	.14	.04
☐ 55 Bill Gullickson	.05	.02	.01
☐ 56 Lloyd Moseby	.05	.02	.01
☐ 57 Frank Tanana	.05	.02	.01
☐ 58 Mickey Tettleton	.15	.07	.02
☐ 59 Alan Trammell	.15	.07	.02
☐ 60 Lou Whitaker	.15	.07	.02
☐ 61 Mike Boddicker	.05	.02	.01
☐ 62 George Brett	.75	.35	.09
☐ 63 Jeff Conine	.75	.35	.09
☐ 64 Warren Cromartie	.05	.02	.01
☐ 65 Storm Davis	.05	.02	.01
☐ 66 Kirk Gibson	.15	.07	.02
☐ 67 Mark Gubicza	.05	.02	.01
☐ 68 Brian McRae	.40	.18	.05
☐ 69 Bret Saberhagen	.15	.07	.02
☐ 70 Kurt Stillwell	.05	.02	.01
☐ 71 Tim McIntosh	.05	.02	.01
☐ 72 Candy Maldonado	.05	.02	.01
☐ 73 Paul Molitor	.40	.18	.05
☐ 74 Willie Randolph	.15	.07	.02
☐ 75 Ron Robinson	.05	.02	.01
☐ 76 Gary Sheffield	.30	.14	.04
☐ 77 Franklin Stubbs	.05	.02	.01
☐ 78 B.J. Surhoff	.15	.07	.02
☐ 79 Greg Vaughn	.15	.07	.02
☐ 80 Robin Yount	.30	.14	.04
☐ 81 Rick Aguilera	.15	.07	.02
☐ 82 Steve Bedrosian	.05	.02	.01
☐ 83 Scott Erickson	.15	.07	.02
☐ 84 Greg Gagne	.05	.02	.01
☐ 85 Dan Gladden	.05	.02	.01
☐ 86 Brian Harper	.05	.02	.01
☐ 87 Kent Hrbek	.15	.07	.02
☐ 88 Shane Mack	.05	.02	.01
☐ 89 Jack Morris	.15	.07	.02
☐ 90 Kirby Puckett	.75	.35	.09
☐ 91 Jesse Barfield	.05	.02	.01
☐ 92 Steve Farr	.05	.02	.01
☐ 93 Steve Howe	.05	.02	.01
☐ 94 Roberto Kelly	.05	.02	.01
☐ 95 Tim Leary	.05	.02	.01
☐ 96 Kevin Maas	.05	.02	.01
☐ 97 Don Mattingly	1.00	.45	.12
☐ 98 Hensley Meulens	.05	.02	.01
☐ 99 Scott Sanderson	.05	.02	.01
☐ 100 Steve Sax	.05	.02	.01
☐ 101 Jose Canseco	.30	.14	.04
☐ 102 Dennis Eckersley	.15	.07	.02
☐ 103 Dave Henderson	.05	.02	.01
☐ 104 Rickey Henderson	.30	.14	.04
☐ 105 Rick Honeycutt	.05	.02	.01
☐ 106 Mark McGwire	.60	.25	.07
☐ 107 Dave Stewart UER (No-hitter against Toronto, not Texas)	.15	.07	.02
☐ 108 Eric Show	.05	.02	.01
☐ 109 Todd Van Poppel	.15	.07	.02
☐ 110 Bob Welch	.05	.02	.01
☐ 111 Alvin Davis	.05	.02	.01
☐ 112 Ken Griffey Jr.	3.00	1.35	.35
☐ 113 Ken Griffey Sr.	.05	.02	.01
☐ 114 Erik Hanson UER (Misspelled Eric)	.05	.02	.01
☐ 115 Brian Holman	.05	.02	.01
☐ 116 Randy Johnson	.30	.14	.04
☐ 117 Edgar Martinez	.15	.07	.02
☐ 118 Tino Martinez	.30	.14	.04
☐ 119 Harold Reynolds	.05	.02	.01
☐ 120 David Valle	.05	.02	.01
☐ 121 Kevin Belcher	.05	.02	.01
☐ 122 Scott Chiamparino	.05	.02	.01
☐ 123 Julio Franco	.15	.07	.02
☐ 124 Juan Gonzalez	1.50	.70	.19
☐ 125 Rich Gossage	.15	.07	.02
☐ 126 Jeff Kunkel	.05	.02	.01
☐ 127 Rafael Palmeiro	.30	.14	.04
☐ 128 Nolan Ryan	1.50	.70	.19
☐ 129 Ruben Sierra	.15	.07	.02
☐ 130 Bobby Witt	.05	.02	.01
☐ 131 Roberto Alomar	.40	.18	.05
☐ 132 Tom Candiotti	.05	.02	.01
☐ 133 Joe Carter	.15	.07	.02
☐ 134 Ken Dayley	.05	.02	.01
☐ 135 Kelly Gruber	.05	.02	.01
☐ 136 John Olerud	.15	.07	.02
☐ 137 Dave Stieb	.05	.02	.01
☐ 138 Turner Ward	.05	.02	.01
☐ 139 Devon White	.15	.07	.02
☐ 140 Mookie Wilson	.05	.02	.01
☐ 141 Steve Avery	.30	.14	.04
☐ 142 Sid Bream	.05	.02	.01
☐ 143 Nick Esasky UER (Homers abbreviated RH)	.05	.02	.01
☐ 144 Ron Gant	.15	.07	.02
☐ 145 Tom Glavine	.30	.14	.04
☐ 146 David Justice	.30	.14	.04
☐ 147 Kelly Mann	.05	.02	.01
☐ 148 Terry Pendleton	.15	.07	.02
☐ 149 John Smoltz	.30	.14	.04
☐ 150 Jeff Treadway	.05	.02	.01
☐ 151 George Bell	.05	.02	.01
☐ 152 Shawn Boskie	.05	.02	.01
☐ 153 Andre Dawson	.15	.07	.02
☐ 154 Lance Dickson	.05	.02	.01
☐ 155 Shawon Dunston	.05	.02	.01
☐ 156 Joe Girardi	.15	.07	.02
☐ 157 Mark Grace	.30	.14	.04
☐ 158 Ryne Sandberg	.50	.23	.06
☐ 159 Gary Scott	.05	.02	.01
☐ 160 Dave Smith	.05	.02	.01
☐ 161 Tom Browning	.05	.02	.01
☐ 162 Eric Davis	.15	.07	.02
☐ 163 Rob Dibble	.05	.02	.01
☐ 164 Mariano Duncan	.05	.02	.01
☐ 165 Chris Hammond	.05	.02	.01
☐ 166 Billy Hatcher	.05	.02	.01
☐ 167 Barry Larkin	.30	.14	.04
☐ 168 Hal Morris	.05	.02	.01
☐ 169 Paul O'Neill	.15	.07	.02
☐ 170 Chris Sabo	.05	.02	.01
☐ 171 Eric Anthony	.05	.02	.01
☐ 172 Jeff Bagwell	3.00	1.35	.35
☐ 173 Craig Biggio	.30	.14	.04
☐ 174 Ken Caminiti	.30	.14	.04
☐ 175 Jim Deshaies	.05	.02	.01
☐ 176 Steve Finley	.15	.07	.02
☐ 177 Pete Harnisch	.05	.02	.01
☐ 178 Darryl Kile	.05	.02	.01
☐ 179 Curt Schilling	.05	.02	.01
☐ 180 Mike Scott	.05	.02	.01
☐ 181 Brett Butler	.15	.07	.02
☐ 182 Gary Carter	.15	.07	.02
☐ 183 Orel Hershiser	.15	.07	.02
☐ 184 Ramon Martinez	.30	.14	.04
☐ 185 Eddie Murray	.50	.23	.06
☐ 186 Jose Offerman	.05	.02	.01
☐ 187 Bob Ojeda	.05	.02	.01
☐ 188 Juan Samuel	.05	.02	.01
☐ 189 Mike Scioscia	.05	.02	.01
☐ 190 Darryl Strawberry	.15	.07	.02
☐ 191 Moises Alou	.30	.14	.04
☐ 192 Brian Barnes	.05	.02	.01
☐ 193 Oil Can Boyd	.05	.02	.01
☐ 194 Ivan Calderon	.05	.02	.01
☐ 195 Delino DeShields	.05	.02	.01
☐ 196 Mike Fitzgerald	.05	.02	.01
☐ 197 Andres Galarraga	.30	.14	.04
☐ 198 Marquis Grissom	.30	.14	.04
☐ 199 Bill Sampen	.05	.02	.01
☐ 200 Tim Wallach	.05	.02	.01
☐ 201 Daryl Boston	.05	.02	.01
☐ 202 Vince Coleman	.05	.02	.01
☐ 203 John Franco	.05	.02	.01
☐ 204 Dwight Gooden	.15	.07	.02
☐ 205 Tom Herr	.05	.02	.01
☐ 206 Gregg Jefferies	.15	.07	.02
☐ 207 Howard Johnson	.05	.02	.01
☐ 208 Dave Magadan UER (Born 1862, should be 1962)	.05	.02	.01
☐ 209 Kevin McReynolds	.05	.02	.01
☐ 210 Frank Viola	.05	.02	.01
☐ 211 Wes Chamberlain	.05	.02	.01
☐ 212 Darren Daulton	.15	.07	.02
☐ 213 Len Dykstra	.15	.07	.02
☐ 214 Charlie Hayes	.05	.02	.01
☐ 215 Ricky Jordan	.05	.02	.01
☐ 216 Steve Lake (Pictured with parrot on his shoulder)	.05	.02	.01
☐ 217 Roger McDowell	.05	.02	.01
☐ 218 Mickey Morandini	.05	.02	.01
☐ 219 Terry Mulholland	.05	.02	.01
☐ 220 Dale Murphy	.30	.14	.04
☐ 221 Jay Bell	.15	.07	.02
☐ 222 Barry Bonds	.50	.23	.06
☐ 223 Bobby Bonilla	.15	.07	.02
☐ 224 Doug Drabek	.05	.02	.01
☐ 225 Bill Landrum	.05	.02	.01
☐ 226 Mike LaValliere	.05	.02	.01
☐ 227 Jose Lind	.05	.02	.01
☐ 228 Don Slaught	.05	.02	.01
☐ 229 John Smiley	.05	.02	.01
☐ 230 Andy Van Slyke	.15	.07	.02
☐ 231 Bernard Gilkey	.15	.07	.02
☐ 232 Pedro Guerrero	.05	.02	.01
☐ 233 Rex Hudler	.05	.02	.01
☐ 234 Ray Lankford	.30	.14	.04
☐ 235 Joe Magrane	.05	.02	.01
☐ 236 Jose Oquendo	.05	.02	.01
☐ 237 Lee Smith	.15	.07	.02
☐ 238 Ozzie Smith	.50	.23	.06
☐ 239 Milt Thompson	.05	.02	.01
☐ 240 Todd Zeile	.15	.07	.02
☐ 241 Larry Andersen	.05	.02	.01
☐ 242 Andy Benes	.15	.07	.02
☐ 243 Paul Faries	.05	.02	.01
☐ 244 Tony Fernandez	.05	.02	.01
☐ 245 Tony Gwynn	.75	.35	.09
☐ 246 Atlee Hammaker	.05	.02	.01
☐ 247 Fred McGriff	.30	.14	.04
☐ 248 Bip Roberts	.05	.02	.01
☐ 249 Bentio Santiago	.05	.02	.01
☐ 250 Ed Whitson	.05	.02	.01
☐ 251 Dave Anderson	.05	.02	.01
☐ 252 Mike Benjamin	.05	.02	.01
☐ 253 John Burkett UER (Front photo actually Trevor Wilson)	.15	.07	.02
☐ 254 Will Clark	.30	.14	.04
☐ 255 Scott Garrelts	.05	.02	.01
☐ 256 Willie McGee	.05	.02	.01
☐ 257 Kevin Mitchell	.15	.07	.02
☐ 258 Dave Righetti	.05	.02	.01
☐ 259 Matt Williams	.30	.14	.04
☐ 260 Bud Black Steve Decker	.05	.02	.01
☐ 261 Sparky Anderson MG CL	.15	.07	.02
☐ 262 Tom Lasorda MG CL	.15	.07	.02
☐ 263 Tony LaRussa MG CL	.15	.07	.02
☐ NNO Title Card	.05	.02	.01

1992 Studio Previews

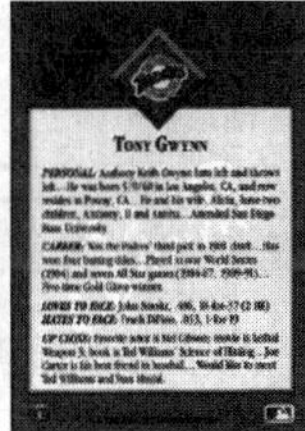

This 22-card standard-sized set was issued by Leaf to preview the design of the 1992 Leaf Studio series. A color posed player photo has been cut out and superimposed against the background of a black and white action shot of the player. These pictures are framed in black on a gold card face. The player's name and team name appear in the bottom gold border. On a white panel bordered in gold, the backs feature player information under five headings (Personal, Career, Loves to face, Hates to face, and Up Close). The cards are numbered on the back. These Preview cards were distributed on a limited basis to members of the Donruss Dealer Network to show them the new Studio design, and are among the tougher promos to obtain from the 1990s. Unlike the 1991 set of the same name, the 1992 set was not inserted in 1992 Donruss factory sets. It appears that Roberto Alomar and Ozzie Smith are a little more difficult to find than the other 20 cards; they are designated SP in the checklist below.

	MINT	NRMT	EXC
COMPLETE SET (22)	225.00	100.00	28.00
COMMON CARD (1-22)	2.50	1.10	.30
☐ 1 Ruben Sierra	2.50	1.10	.30
☐ 2 Kirby Puckett	15.00	6.75	1.85
☐ 3 Ryne Sandberg	15.00	6.75	1.85
☐ 4 John Kruk	2.50	1.10	.30
☐ 5 Cal Ripken	30.00	13.50	3.70
☐ 6 Robin Yount	6.00	2.70	.75
☐ 7 Dwight Gooden	4.00	1.80	.50
☐ 8 David Justice	4.00	1.80	.50
☐ 9 Don Mattingly	20.00	9.00	2.50
☐ 10 Wally Joyner	4.00	1.80	.50
☐ 11 Will Clark	6.00	2.70	.75
☐ 12 Rob Dibble	2.50	1.10	.30
☐ 13 Roberto Alomar SP	20.00	9.00	2.50
☐ 14 Wade Boggs	6.00	2.70	.75
☐ 15 Barry Bonds	10.00	4.50	1.25
☐ 16 Jeff Bagwell	20.00	9.00	2.50
☐ 17 Mark McGwire	12.50	5.50	1.55
☐ 18 Frank Thomas	40.00	18.00	5.00
☐ 19 Brett Butler	4.00	1.80	.50
☐ 20 Ozzie Smith SP	25.00	11.00	3.10
☐ 21 Jim Abbott	2.50	1.10	.30
☐ 22 Tony Gwynn	20.00	9.00	2.50

1992 Studio

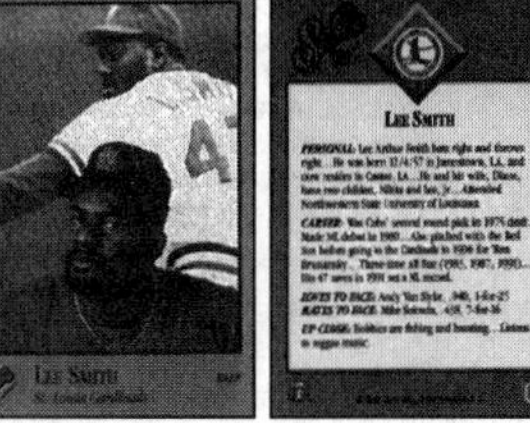
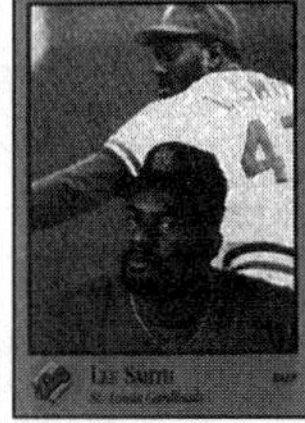
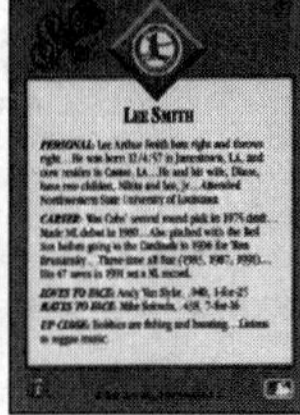

The 1992 Studio set consists of ten players from each of the 26 major league teams, three checklists, and an introduction card for a total of 264 standard-size cards. Inside champagne color metallic borders, the fronts carry a color close-up shot superimposed on a black and white action player photo. The backs focus on the personal side of each player by providing an up-close look, and unusual statistics show the batter or pitcher each player "Loves to Face" or "Hates to Face". The key Rookie Cards in this set are Chad Curtis and Brian Jordan.

	MINT	NRMT	EXC
COMPLETE SET (264)	15.00	6.75	1.85
COMMON CARD (1-264)	.05	.02	.01
☐ 1 Steve Avery	.10	.05	.01
☐ 2 Sid Bream	.05	.02	.01
☐ 3 Ron Gant	.10	.05	.01
☐ 4 Tom Glavine	.25	.11	.03
☐ 5 David Justice	.25	.11	.03
☐ 6 Mark Lemke	.05	.02	.01
☐ 7 Greg Olson	.05	.02	.01
☐ 8 Terry Pendleton	.10	.05	.01
☐ 9 Deion Sanders	.25	.11	.03
☐ 10 John Smoltz	.25	.11	.03
☐ 11 Doug Dascenzo	.05	.02	.01
☐ 12 Andre Dawson	.10	.05	.01
☐ 13 Joe Girardi	.05	.02	.01
☐ 14 Mark Grace	.25	.11	.03
☐ 15 Greg Maddux	1.25	.55	.16
☐ 16 Chuck McElroy	.05	.02	.01
☐ 17 Mike Morgan	.05	.02	.01
☐ 18 Ryne Sandberg	.40	.18	.05
☐ 19 Gary Scott	.05	.02	.01
☐ 20 Sammy Sosa	.40	.18	.05
☐ 21 Norm Charlton	.05	.02	.01
☐ 22 Rob Dibble	.05	.02	.01
☐ 23 Barry Larkin	.25	.11	.03
☐ 24 Hal Morris	.05	.02	.01
☐ 25 Paul O'Neill	.10	.05	.01
☐ 26 Jose Rijo	.05	.02	.01
☐ 27 Bip Roberts	.05	.02	.01
☐ 28 Chris Sabo	.05	.02	.01
☐ 29 Reggie Sanders	.25	.11	.03
☐ 30 Greg Swindell	.05	.02	.01
☐ 31 Jeff Bagwell	1.00	.45	.12
☐ 32 Craig Biggio	.10	.05	.01
☐ 33 Ken Caminiti	.25	.11	.03
☐ 34 Andujar Cedeno	.05	.02	.01
☐ 35 Steve Finley	.10	.05	.01
☐ 36 Pete Harnisch	.05	.02	.01
☐ 37 Butch Henry	.05	.02	.01
☐ 38 Doug Jones	.05	.02	.01
☐ 39 Darryl Kile	.05	.02	.01
☐ 40 Eddie Taubensee	.05	.02	.01
☐ 41 Brett Butler	.10	.05	.01
☐ 42 Tom Candiotti	.05	.02	.01
☐ 43 Eric Davis	.10	.05	.01
☐ 44 Orel Hershiser	.10	.05	.01
☐ 45 Eric Karros	.25	.11	.03
☐ 46 Ramon Martinez	.10	.05	.01
☐ 47 Jose Offerman	.05	.02	.01
☐ 48 Mike Scioscia	.05	.02	.01
☐ 49 Mike Sharperson	.05	.02	.01
☐ 50 Darryl Strawberry	.10	.05	.01
☐ 51 Bret Barberie	.05	.02	.01
☐ 52 Ivan Calderon	.05	.02	.01
☐ 53 Gary Carter	.25	.11	.03
☐ 54 Delino DeShields	.05	.02	.01
☐ 55 Marquis Grissom	.10	.05	.01
☐ 56 Ken Hill	.10	.05	.01
☐ 57 Dennis Martinez	.10	.05	.01
☐ 58 Spike Owen	.05	.02	.01
☐ 59 Larry Walker	.25	.11	.03
☐ 60 Tim Wallach	.05	.02	.01
☐ 61 Bobby Bonilla	.10	.05	.01
☐ 62 Tim Burke	.05	.02	.01
☐ 63 Vince Coleman	.05	.02	.01
☐ 64 John Franco	.05	.02	.01
☐ 65 Dwight Gooden	.10	.05	.01
☐ 66 Todd Hundley	.10	.05	.01
☐ 67 Howard Johnson	.05	.02	.01
☐ 68 Eddie Murray UER (He's not all-time switch homer leader, but he has most games with homers from both sides)	.40	.18	.05
☐ 69 Bret Saberhagen	.10	.05	.01
☐ 70 Anthony Young	.05	.02	.01
☐ 71 Kim Batiste	.05	.02	.01
☐ 72 Wes Chamberlain	.05	.02	.01
☐ 73 Darren Daulton	.10	.05	.01
☐ 74 Mariano Duncan	.05	.02	.01
☐ 75 Len Dykstra	.10	.05	.01
☐ 76 John Kruk	.10	.05	.01
☐ 77 Mickey Morandini	.05	.02	.01
☐ 78 Terry Mulholland	.05	.02	.01
☐ 79 Dale Murphy	.25	.11	.03
☐ 80 Mitch Williams	.05	.02	.01
☐ 81 Jay Bell	.10	.05	.01
☐ 82 Barry Bonds	.40	.18	.05
☐ 83 Steve Buechele	.05	.02	.01
☐ 84 Doug Drabek	.05	.02	.01
☐ 85 Mike LaValliere	.05	.02	.01
☐ 86 Jose Lind	.05	.02	.01
☐ 87 Denny Neagle	.25	.11	.03
☐ 88 Randy Tomlin	.05	.02	.01
☐ 89 Andy Van Slyke	.10	.05	.01
☐ 90 Gary Varsho	.05	.02	.01
☐ 91 Pedro Guerrero	.05	.02	.01
☐ 92 Rex Hudler	.05	.02	.01
☐ 93 Brian Jordan	.60	.25	.07

☐ 94 Felix Jose	.05	.02	.01
☐ 95 Donovan Osborne	.10	.05	.01
☐ 96 Tom Pagnozzi	.05	.02	.01
☐ 97 Lee Smith	.10	.05	.01
☐ 98 Ozzie Smith	.40	.18	.05
☐ 99 Todd Worrell	.05	.02	.01
☐ 100 Todd Zeile	.05	.02	.01
☐ 101 Andy Benes	.10	.05	.01
☐ 102 Jerald Clark	.05	.02	.01
☐ 103 Tony Fernandez	.05	.02	.01
☐ 104 Tony Gwynn	.60	.25	.07
☐ 105 Greg W. Harris	.05	.02	.01
☐ 106 Fred McGriff	.25	.11	.03
☐ 107 Benito Santiago	.05	.02	.01
☐ 108 Gary Sheffield	.25	.11	.03
☐ 109 Kurt Stillwell	.05	.02	.01
☐ 110 Tim Teufel	.05	.02	.01
☐ 111 Kevin Bass	.05	.02	.01
☐ 112 Jeff Brantley	.10	.05	.01
☐ 113 John Burkett	.10	.05	.01
☐ 114 Will Clark	.25	.11	.03
☐ 115 Royce Clayton	.10	.05	.01
☐ 116 Mike Jackson	.05	.02	.01
☐ 117 Darren Lewis	.05	.02	.01
☐ 118 Bill Swift	.05	.02	.01
☐ 119 Robby Thompson	.05	.02	.01
☐ 120 Matt Williams	.25	.11	.03
☐ 121 Brady Anderson	.25	.11	.03
☐ 122 Glenn Davis	.05	.02	.01
☐ 123 Mike Devereaux	.05	.02	.01
☐ 124 Chris Hoiles	.05	.02	.01
☐ 125 Sam Horn	.05	.02	.01
☐ 126 Ben McDonald	.05	.02	.01
☐ 127 Mike Mussina	.50	.23	.06
☐ 128 Gregg Olson	.05	.02	.01
☐ 129 Cal Ripken Jr.	1.25	.55	.16
☐ 130 Rick Sutcliffe	.05	.02	.01
☐ 131 Wade Boggs	.25	.11	.03
☐ 132 Roger Clemens	.30	.14	.04
☐ 133 Greg A. Harris	.05	.02	.01
☐ 134 Tim Naehring	.10	.05	.01
☐ 135 Tony Pena	.05	.02	.01
☐ 136 Phil Plantier	.10	.05	.01
☐ 137 Jeff Reardon	.10	.05	.01
☐ 138 Jody Reed	.05	.02	.01
☐ 139 Mo Vaughn	.60	.25	.07
☐ 140 Frank Viola	.05	.02	.01
☐ 141 Jim Abbott	.05	.02	.01
☐ 142 Hubie Brooks	.05	.02	.01
☐ 143 Chad Curtis	.25	.11	.03
☐ 144 Gary DiSarcina	.05	.02	.01
☐ 145 Chuck Finley	.05	.02	.01
☐ 146 Bryan Harvey	.05	.02	.01
☐ 147 Von Hayes	.05	.02	.01
☐ 148 Mark Langston	.10	.05	.01
☐ 149 Lance Parrish	.05	.02	.01
☐ 150 Lee Stevens	.05	.02	.01
☐ 151 George Bell	.05	.02	.01
☐ 152 Alex Fernandez	.25	.11	.03
☐ 153 Greg Hibbard	.05	.02	.01
☐ 154 Lance Johnson	.10	.05	.01
☐ 155 Kirk McCaskill	.05	.02	.01
☐ 156 Tim Raines	.25	.11	.03
☐ 157 Steve Sax	.05	.02	.01
☐ 158 Bobby Thigpen	.05	.02	.01
☐ 159 Frank Thomas	2.50	1.10	.30
☐ 160 Robin Ventura	.10	.05	.01
☐ 161 Sandy Alomar Jr.	.10	.05	.01
☐ 162 Jack Armstrong	.05	.02	.01
☐ 163 Carlos Baerga	.10	.05	.01
☐ 164 Albert Belle	.75	.35	.09
☐ 165 Alex Cole	.05	.02	.01
☐ 166 Glenallen Hill	.05	.02	.01
☐ 167 Mark Lewis	.05	.02	.01
☐ 168 Kenny Lofton	2.00	.90	.25
☐ 169 Paul Sorrento	.05	.02	.01
☐ 170 Mark Whiten	.10	.05	.01
☐ 171 Milt Cuyler	.05	.02	.01
☐ 172 Rob Deer	.05	.02	.01
☐ 173 Cecil Fielder	.10	.05	.01
☐ 174 Travis Fryman	.25	.11	.03
☐ 175 Mike Henneman	.05	.02	.01
☐ 176 Tony Phillips	.10	.05	.01
☐ 177 Frank Tanana	.05	.02	.01
☐ 178 Mickey Tettleton	.05	.02	.01
☐ 179 Alan Trammell	.10	.05	.01
☐ 180 Lou Whitaker	.10	.05	.01
☐ 181 George Brett	.60	.25	.07
☐ 182 Tom Gordon	.05	.02	.01
☐ 183 Mark Gubicza	.05	.02	.01
☐ 184 Gregg Jefferies	.10	.05	.01
☐ 185 Wally Joyner	.10	.05	.01
☐ 186 Brent Mayne	.05	.02	.01
☐ 187 Brian McRae	.10	.05	.01
☐ 188 Kevin McReynolds	.05	.02	.01
☐ 189 Keith Miller	.05	.02	.01
☐ 190 Jeff Montgomery	.10	.05	.01
☐ 191 Dante Bichette	.25	.11	.03
☐ 192 Ricky Bones	.05	.02	.01
☐ 193 Scott Fletcher	.05	.02	.01
☐ 194 Paul Molitor	.30	.14	.04
☐ 195 Jaime Navarro	.05	.02	.01
☐ 196 Franklin Stubbs	.05	.02	.01
☐ 197 B.J. Surhoff	.10	.05	.01
☐ 198 Greg Vaughn	.10	.05	.01
☐ 199 Bill Wegman	.05	.02	.01
☐ 200 Robin Yount	.25	.11	.03
☐ 201 Rick Aguilera	.05	.02	.01
☐ 202 Scott Erickson	.10	.05	.01
☐ 203 Greg Gagne	.05	.02	.01
☐ 204 Brian Harper	.05	.02	.01
☐ 205 Kent Hrbek	.10	.05	.01
☐ 206 Scott Leius	.05	.02	.01
☐ 207 Shane Mack	.05	.02	.01
☐ 208 Pat Mahomes	.05	.02	.01
☐ 209 Kirby Puckett	.60	.25	.07
☐ 210 John Smiley	.05	.02	.01
☐ 211 Mike Gallego	.05	.02	.01
☐ 212 Charlie Hayes	.05	.02	.01
☐ 213 Pat Kelly	.05	.02	.01
☐ 214 Roberto Kelly	.05	.02	.01
☐ 215 Kevin Maas	.05	.02	.01
☐ 216 Don Mattingly	.75	.35	.09
☐ 217 Matt Nokes	.05	.02	.01
☐ 218 Melido Perez	.05	.02	.01
☐ 219 Scott Sanderson	.05	.02	.01
☐ 220 Danny Tartabull	.05	.02	.01
☐ 221 Harold Baines	.10	.05	.01
☐ 222 Jose Canseco	.25	.11	.03
☐ 223 Dennis Eckersley	.10	.05	.01
☐ 224 Dave Henderson	.05	.02	.01
☐ 225 Carney Lansford	.10	.05	.01
☐ 226 Mark McGwire	.50	.23	.06
☐ 227 Mike Moore	.05	.02	.01
☐ 228 Randy Ready	.05	.02	.01
☐ 229 Terry Steinbach	.10	.05	.01
☐ 230 Dave Stewart	.10	.05	.01
☐ 231 Jay Buhner	.25	.11	.03
☐ 232 Ken Griffey Jr.	2.50	1.10	.30
☐ 233 Erik Hanson	.05	.02	.01
☐ 234 Randy Johnson	.25	.11	.03
☐ 235 Edgar Martinez	.10	.05	.01
☐ 236 Tino Martinez	.10	.05	.01
☐ 237 Kevin Mitchell	.10	.05	.01
☐ 238 Pete O'Brien	.05	.02	.01
☐ 239 Harold Reynolds	.05	.02	.01
☐ 240 David Valle	.05	.02	.01
☐ 241 Julio Franco	.10	.05	.01
☐ 242 Juan Gonzalez	1.00	.45	.12
☐ 243 Jose Guzman	.05	.02	.01
☐ 244 Rafael Palmeiro	.25	.11	.03
☐ 245 Dean Palmer	.10	.05	.01
☐ 246 Ivan Rodriguez	.60	.25	.07
☐ 247 Jeff Russell	.05	.02	.01
☐ 248 Nolan Ryan	1.25	.55	.16
☐ 249 Ruben Sierra	.10	.05	.01
☐ 250 Dickie Thon	.05	.02	.01
☐ 251 Roberto Alomar	.30	.14	.04
☐ 252 Derek Bell	.25	.11	.03
☐ 253 Pat Borders	.05	.02	.01
☐ 254 Joe Carter	.10	.05	.01
☐ 255 Kelly Gruber	.05	.02	.01
☐ 256 Juan Guzman	.10	.05	.01
☐ 257 Jack Morris	.10	.05	.01
☐ 258 John Olerud	.10	.05	.01
☐ 259 Devon White	.10	.05	.01
☐ 260 Dave Winfield	.25	.11	.03
☐ 261 Checklist	.05	.02	.01
☐ 262 Checklist	.05	.02	.01
☐ 263 Checklist	.05	.02	.01
☐ 264 History Card	.05	.02	.01

1992 Studio Heritage

The 1992 Studio Heritage standard-size insert set presents today's star players dressed in vintage uniforms. Cards numbered 1-8 were randomly inserted in 12-card foil packs while cards numbered 9-14 were inserted one per pack in 28-card jumbo packs. The fronts display sepia-toned portraits of the players dressed in vintage uniforms of their current teams. The pictures are bordered by dark turquoise and have bronze foil picture holders at each corner. The set title "Heritage Series" also appears in bronze foil lettering above the pictures. Within a bronze picture frame design on dark turquoise, the backs give a brief history of the team with special reference to the year of the vintage uniform. The cards are numbered on the back with a "BC" prefix.

	MINT	NRMT	EXC
COMPLETE SET (14)	25.00	11.00	3.10
COMPLETE FOIL SET (8)	15.00	6.75	1.85
COMPLETE JUMBO SET (6)	10.00	4.50	1.25
COMMON CARD (BC1-BC8)	.75	.35	.09
COMMON CARD (BC9-BC14)	.75	.35	.09
☐ BC1 Ryne Sandberg	2.00	.90	.25
☐ BC2 Carlton Fisk	1.25	.55	.16
☐ BC3 Wade Boggs	1.25	.55	.16
☐ BC4 Jose Canseco	1.25	.55	.16
☐ BC5 Don Mattingly	4.00	1.80	.50
☐ BC6 Darryl Strawberry	1.00	.45	.12
☐ BC7 Cal Ripken	8.00	3.60	1.00
☐ BC8 Will Clark	1.25	.55	.16
☐ BC9 Andre Dawson	1.00	.45	.12
☐ BC10 Andy Van Slyke	.75	.35	.09
☐ BC11 Paul Molitor	1.25	.55	.16
☐ BC12 Jeff Bagwell	5.00	2.20	.60
☐ BC13 Darren Daulton	1.00	.45	.12
☐ BC14 Kirby Puckett	3.00	1.35	.35

1993 Studio

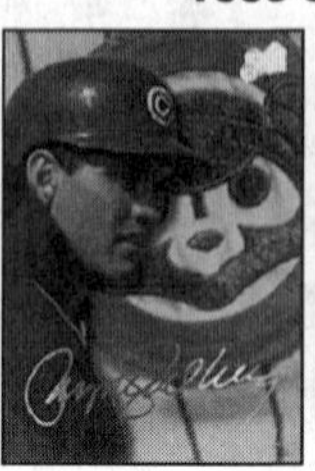

The 220 standard-size cards comprising this set feature borderless fronts with posed color player photos that are cut out and superposed upon a closeup of an embroidered team logo. A facsimile player autograph appears in prismatic gold foil across the lower portion of the photo. The borderless black backs carry another posed color player photo shunted to the right side, with the player's name, position, team, biography, and personal profile appearing in white lettering on the left side. The key Rookie Card in this set is J.T. Snow.

	MINT	NRMT	EXC
COMPLETE SET (220)	20.00	9.00	2.50
COMMON CARD (1-220)	.10	.05	.01
☐ 1 Dennis Eckersley	.20	.09	.03
☐ 2 Chad Curtis	.20	.09	.03
☐ 3 Eric Anthony	.10	.05	.01
☐ 4 Roberto Alomar	.50	.23	.06
☐ 5 Steve Avery	.20	.09	.03
☐ 6 Cal Eldred	.10	.05	.01
☐ 7 Bernard Gilkey	.20	.09	.03
☐ 8 Steve Buechele	.10	.05	.01
☐ 9 Brett Butler	.20	.09	.03
☐ 10 Terry Mulholland	.10	.05	.01
☐ 11 Moises Alou	.20	.09	.03
☐ 12 Barry Bonds	.60	.25	.07
☐ 13 Sandy Alomar Jr.	.20	.09	.03
☐ 14 Chris Bosio	.10	.05	.01
☐ 15 Scott Sanderson	.10	.05	.01
☐ 16 Bobby Bonilla	.20	.09	.03
☐ 17 Brady Anderson	.40	.18	.05
☐ 18 Derek Bell	.20	.09	.03
☐ 19 Wes Chamberlain	.10	.05	.01
☐ 20 Jay Bell	.20	.09	.03
☐ 21 Kevin Brown	.20	.09	.03
☐ 22 Roger Clemens	.50	.23	.06
☐ 23 Roberto Kelly	.10	.05	.01
☐ 24 Dante Bichette	.40	.18	.05
☐ 25 George Brett	1.00	.45	.12
☐ 26 Rob Deer	.10	.05	.01
☐ 27 Brian Harper	.10	.05	.01
☐ 28 George Bell	.10	.05	.01
☐ 29 Jim Abbott	.10	.05	.01
☐ 30 Dave Henderson	.10	.05	.01
☐ 31 Wade Boggs	.40	.18	.05
☐ 32 Chili Davis	.20	.09	.03
☐ 33 Ellis Burks	.20	.09	.03
☐ 34 Jeff Bagwell	1.00	.45	.12
☐ 35 Kent Hrbek	.20	.09	.03
☐ 36 Pat Borders	.10	.05	.01
☐ 37 Cecil Fielder	.20	.09	.03
☐ 38 Sid Bream	.10	.05	.01
☐ 39 Greg Gagne	.10	.05	.01
☐ 40 Darryl Hamilton	.10	.05	.01
☐ 41 Jerald Clark	.10	.05	.01
☐ 42 Mark Grace	.40	.18	.05
☐ 43 Barry Larkin	.40	.18	.05
☐ 44 John Burkett	.10	.05	.01
☐ 45 Scott Cooper	.10	.05	.01
☐ 46 Mike Lansing	.20	.09	.03
☐ 47 Jose Canseco	.40	.18	.05
☐ 48 Will Clark	.40	.18	.05
☐ 49 Carlos Garcia	.10	.05	.01
☐ 50 Carlos Baerga	.20	.09	.03
☐ 51 Darren Daulton	.20	.09	.03
☐ 52 Jay Buhner	.40	.18	.05
☐ 53 Andy Benes	.20	.09	.03
☐ 54 Jeff Conine	.20	.09	.03
☐ 55 Mike Devereaux	.10	.05	.01
☐ 56 Vince Coleman	.10	.05	.01
☐ 57 Terry Steinbach	.20	.09	.03
☐ 58 J.T. Snow	.40	.18	.05
☐ 59 Greg Swindell	.10	.05	.01
☐ 60 Devon White	.10	.05	.01
☐ 61 John Smoltz	.40	.18	.05
☐ 62 Todd Zeile	.10	.05	.01
☐ 63 Rick Wilkins	.10	.05	.01
☐ 64 Tim Wallach	.10	.05	.01
☐ 65 John Wetteland	.20	.09	.03
☐ 66 Matt Williams	.40	.18	.05
☐ 67 Paul Sorrento	.10	.05	.01
☐ 68 David Valle	.10	.05	.01
☐ 69 Walt Weiss	.10	.05	.01
☐ 70 John Franco	.10	.05	.01
☐ 71 Nolan Ryan	2.00	.90	.25
☐ 72 Frank Viola	.10	.05	.01
☐ 73 Chris Sabo	.10	.05	.01
☐ 74 David Nied	.10	.05	.01
☐ 75 Kevin McReynolds	.10	.05	.01
☐ 76 Lou Whitaker	.20	.09	.03
☐ 77 Dave Winfield	.40	.18	.05
☐ 78 Robin Ventura	.20	.09	.03
☐ 79 Spike Owen	.10	.05	.01
☐ 80 Cal Ripken Jr.	2.00	.90	.25
☐ 81 Dan Walters	.10	.05	.01
☐ 82 Mitch Williams	.10	.05	.01
☐ 83 Tim Wakefield	.20	.09	.03
☐ 84 Rickey Henderson	.40	.18	.05
☐ 85 Gary DiSarcina	.10	.05	.01
☐ 86 Craig Biggio	.20	.09	.03
☐ 87 Joe Carter	.20	.09	.03
☐ 88 Ron Gant	.20	.09	.03
☐ 89 John Jaha	.40	.18	.05
☐ 90 Gregg Jefferies	.20	.09	.03
☐ 91 Jose Guzman	.10	.05	.01
☐ 92 Eric Karros	.40	.18	.05
☐ 93 Wil Cordero	.20	.09	.03
☐ 94 Royce Clayton	.20	.09	.03
☐ 95 Albert Belle	1.00	.45	.12
☐ 96 Ken Griffey Jr.	2.50	1.10	.30
☐ 97 Orestes Destrade	.10	.05	.01
☐ 98 Tony Fernandez	.10	.05	.01
☐ 99 Leo Gomez	.10	.05	.01
☐ 100 Tony Gwynn	1.00	.45	.12
☐ 101 Len Dykstra	.20	.09	.03
☐ 102 Jeff King	.20	.09	.03
☐ 103 Julio Franco	.20	.09	.03
☐ 104 Andre Dawson	.20	.09	.03
☐ 105 Randy Milligan	.10	.05	.01
☐ 106 Alex Cole	.10	.05	.01
☐ 107 Phil Hiatt	.10	.05	.01
☐ 108 Travis Fryman	.20	.09	.03
☐ 109 Chuck Knoblauch	.40	.18	.05
☐ 110 Bo Jackson	.20	.09	.03
☐ 111 Pat Kelly	.10	.05	.01
☐ 112 Bret Saberhagen	.20	.09	.03
☐ 113 Ruben Sierra	.20	.09	.03
☐ 114 Tim Salmon	.60	.25	.07
☐ 115 Doug Jones	.10	.05	.01
☐ 116 Ed Sprague	.20	.09	.03
☐ 117 Terry Pendleton	.20	.09	.03
☐ 118 Robin Yount	.40	.18	.05
☐ 119 Mark Whiten	.10	.05	.01
☐ 120 Checklist 1-110	.10	.05	.01
☐ 121 Sammy Sosa	.40	.18	.05
☐ 122 Darryl Strawberry	.20	.09	.03
☐ 123 Larry Walker	.40	.18	.05
☐ 124 Robby Thompson	.10	.05	.01
☐ 125 Carlos Martinez	.10	.05	.01
☐ 126 Edgar Martinez	.20	.09	.03
☐ 127 Benito Santiago	.10	.05	.01
☐ 128 Howard Johnson	.10	.05	.01
☐ 129 Harold Reynolds	.10	.05	.01
☐ 130 Craig Shipley	.10	.05	.01
☐ 131 Curt Schilling	.10	.05	.01
☐ 132 Andy Van Slyke	.20	.09	.03
☐ 133 Ivan Rodriguez	.60	.25	.07
☐ 134 Mo Vaughn	.60	.25	.07
☐ 135 Bip Roberts	.10	.05	.01
☐ 136 Charlie Hayes	.10	.05	.01
☐ 137 Brian McRae	.20	.09	.03
☐ 138 Mickey Tettleton	.10	.05	.01
☐ 139 Frank Thomas	2.50	1.10	.30
☐ 140 Paul O'Neill	.20	.09	.03
☐ 141 Mark McGwire	.75	.35	.09
☐ 142 Damion Easley	.10	.05	.01
☐ 143 Ken Caminiti	.40	.18	.05
☐ 144 Juan Guzman	.20	.09	.03
☐ 145 Tom Glavine	.40	.18	.05
☐ 146 Pat Listach	.10	.05	.01
☐ 147 Lee Smith	.20	.09	.03
☐ 148 Derrick May	.10	.05	.01
☐ 149 Ramon Martinez	.20	.09	.03
☐ 150 Delino DeShields	.10	.05	.01
☐ 151 Kirt Manwaring	.10	.05	.01
☐ 152 Reggie Jefferson	.20	.09	.03
☐ 153 Randy Johnson	.40	.18	.05
☐ 154 Dave Magadan	.10	.05	.01
☐ 155 Dwight Gooden	.20	.09	.03
☐ 156 Chris Hoiles	.10	.05	.01
☐ 157 Fred McGriff	.40	.18	.05
☐ 158 Dave Hollins	.10	.05	.01
☐ 159 Al Martin	.20	.09	.03
☐ 160 Juan Gonzalez	1.25	.55	.16
☐ 161 Mike Greenwell	.10	.05	.01
☐ 162 Kevin Mitchell	.20	.09	.03
☐ 163 Andres Galarraga	.40	.18	.05
☐ 164 Wally Joyner	.20	.09	.03
☐ 165 Kirk Gibson	.20	.09	.03
☐ 166 Pedro Munoz	.10	.05	.01
☐ 167 Ozzie Guillen	.10	.05	.01
☐ 168 Jimmy Key	.20	.09	.03
☐ 169 Kevin Seitzer	.10	.05	.01
☐ 170 Luis Polonia	.10	.05	.01

	MINT	NRMT	EXC
☐ 171 Luis Gonzalez	.10	.05	.01
☐ 172 Paul Molitor	.50	.23	.06
☐ 173 David Justice	.40	.18	.05
☐ 174 B.J. Surhoff	.20	.09	.03
☐ 175 Ray Lankford	.20	.09	.03
☐ 176 Ryne Sandberg	.60	.25	.07
☐ 177 Jody Reed	.10	.05	.01
☐ 178 Marquis Grissom	.20	.09	.03
☐ 179 Willie McGee	.10	.05	.01
☐ 180 Kenny Lofton	1.00	.45	.12
☐ 181 Junior Felix	.10	.05	.01
☐ 182 Jose Offerman	.10	.05	.01
☐ 183 John Kruk	.20	.09	.03
☐ 184 Orlando Merced	.20	.09	.03
☐ 185 Rafael Palmeiro	.40	.18	.05
☐ 186 Billy Hatcher	.10	.05	.01
☐ 187 Joe Oliver	.10	.05	.01
☐ 188 Joe Girardi	.10	.05	.01
☐ 189 Jose Lind	.10	.05	.01
☐ 190 Harold Baines	.20	.09	.03
☐ 191 Mike Pagliarulo	.10	.05	.01
☐ 192 Lance Johnson	.20	.09	.03
☐ 193 Don Mattingly	1.25	.55	.16
☐ 194 Doug Drabek	.10	.05	.01
☐ 195 John Olerud	.10	.05	.01
☐ 196 Greg Maddux	1.50	.70	.19
☐ 197 Greg Vaughn	.20	.09	.03
☐ 198 Tom Pagnozzi	.10	.05	.01
☐ 199 Willie Wilson	.10	.05	.01
☐ 200 Jack McDowell	.20	.09	.03
☐ 201 Mike Piazza	2.50	1.10	.30
☐ 202 Mike Mussina	.50	.23	.06
☐ 203 Charles Nagy	.20	.09	.03
☐ 204 Tino Martinez	.20	.09	.03
☐ 205 Charlie Hough	.10	.05	.01
☐ 206 Todd Hundley	.20	.09	.03
☐ 207 Gary Sheffield	.40	.18	.05
☐ 208 Mickey Morandini	.10	.05	.01
☐ 209 Don Slaught	.10	.05	.01
☐ 210 Dean Palmer	.20	.09	.03
☐ 211 Jose Rijo	.10	.05	.01
☐ 212 Vinny Castilla	.40	.18	.05
☐ 213 Tony Phillips	.20	.09	.03
☐ 214 Kirby Puckett	1.00	.45	.12
☐ 215 Tim Raines	.40	.18	.05
☐ 216 Otis Nixon	.10	.05	.01
☐ 217 Ozzie Smith	.60	.25	.07
☐ 218 Jose Vizcaino	.10	.05	.01
☐ 219 Randy Tomlin	.10	.05	.01
☐ 220 Checklist 111-220	.10	.05	.01

1993 Studio Heritage

This 12-card standard-size set was randomly inserted in all 1993 Leaf Studio foil packs, and features sepia-toned portraits of current players in vintage team uniforms. The pictures are bordered in turquoise blue and have bronze-foil simulated picture holders at each corner. The set title appears in white lettering above the picture, and the player's name is printed in white below. The horizontal and turquoise-blue-bordered back shades from beige to red from top to bottom, and carries a posed sepia-toned player picture on the right within an oval set off by red and black lines. His name appears in white lettering at the top within a black arc. A brief story of the team represented by the player's vintage uniform follows below.

	MINT	NRMT	EXC
COMPLETE SET (12)	30.00	13.50	3.70
COMMON CARD (1-12)	1.00	.45	.12
☐ 1 George Brett	6.00	2.70	.75
☐ 2 Juan Gonzalez	8.00	3.60	1.00
☐ 3 Roger Clemens	3.00	1.35	.35
☐ 4 Mark McGwire	5.00	2.20	.60
☐ 5 Mark Grace	2.00	.90	.25
☐ 6 Ozzie Smith	4.00	1.80	.50
☐ 7 Barry Larkin	2.00	.90	.25
☐ 8 Frank Thomas	15.00	6.75	1.85
☐ 9 Carlos Baerga	1.00	.45	.12
☐ 10 Eric Karros	2.00	.90	.25
☐ 11 J.T. Snow	2.00	.90	.25
☐ 12 John Kruk	1.00	.45	.12

1993 Studio Silhouettes

The 1993 Studio Silhouettes 10-card standard-size set was inserted one per 20-card Studio jumbo pack. Full-bleed grayish fronts display posed color photos of star players against action silhouettes. The set's title is printed across the top and the player's name appears along the bottom in copper foil within a darker gray area. The borderless and grayish back features a color player action photo on one side and a personal profile on the other.

	MINT	NRMT	EXC
COMPLETE SET (10)	25.00	11.00	3.10
COMMON CARD (1-10)	.50	.23	.06
☐ 1 Frank Thomas	8.00	3.60	1.00
☐ 2 Barry Bonds	2.00	.90	.25
☐ 3 Jeff Bagwell	3.00	1.35	.35
☐ 4 Juan Gonzalez	4.00	1.80	.50
☐ 5 Travis Fryman	.75	.35	.09
☐ 6 J.T. Snow	1.00	.45	.12
☐ 7 John Kruk	.75	.35	.09
☐ 8 Jeff Blauser	.50	.23	.06
☐ 9 Mike Piazza	5.00	2.20	.60
☐ 10 Nolan Ryan	8.00	3.60	1.00

1993 Studio Superstars on Canvas

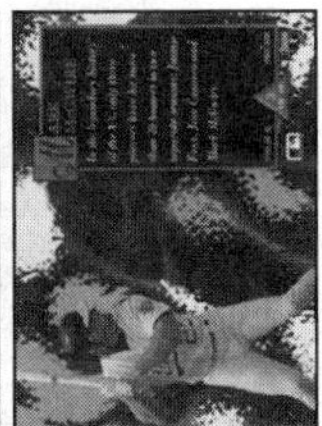

This ten-card standard-size set was randomly inserted in 1993 Studio hobby and retail foil packs. The set features players in gray-bordered portraits that blend photography and artwork. The design of each front simulates a canvas painting of a player displayed on an artist's easel. The player's name appears in copper foil across the easel's base near the bottom. The set's title appears in white lettering beneath. The horizontal back carries a cutout color action player photo on one side and the player's name and career highlights within a black rectangle on the other, all superposed upon an abstract team color-coded design.

	MINT	NRMT	EXC
COMPLETE SET (10)	35.00	16.00	4.40
COMMON CARD (1-10)	1.00	.45	.12
☐ 1 Ken Griffey Jr.	15.00	6.75	1.85
☐ 2 Jose Canseco	2.00	.90	.25
☐ 3 Mark McGwire	5.00	2.20	.60
☐ 4 Mike Mussina	3.00	1.35	.35
☐ 5 Joe Carter	1.00	.45	.12
☐ 6 Frank Thomas	15.00	6.75	1.85
☐ 7 Darren Daulton	1.00	.45	.12
☐ 8 Mark Grace	2.00	.90	.25
☐ 9 Andres Galarraga	2.00	.90	.25
☐ 10 Barry Bonds	4.00	1.80	.50

1993 Studio Thomas

The 1993 Studio Frank Thomas five-card standard-size set was randomly inserted in all 1993 Studio packs. The cards feature borderless posed black-and-white portraits of the Chicago White Sox slugging first baseman.

	MINT	NRMT	EXC
COMPLETE SET (5)	30.00	13.50	3.70
COMMON THOMAS (1-5)	7.00	3.10	.85
☐ 1 Frank Thomas Childhood	7.00	3.10	.85
☐ 2 Frank Thomas Baseball Memories	7.00	3.10	.85
☐ 3 Frank Thomas Family	7.00	3.10	.85
☐ 4 Frank Thomas Performance	7.00	3.10	.85
☐ 5 Frank Thomas Role Model	7.00	3.10	.85

1994 Studio

The 1994 Studio set consists of 220 full-bleed, standard-size cards. Card fronts offer a player photo with his jersey hanging in a locker room setting in the background. Backs contain statistics and a small photo. The set is grouped alphabetically within teams.

	MINT	NRMT	EXC
COMPLETE SET (220)	15.00	6.75	1.85
COMMON CARD (1-220)	.10	.05	.01
☐ 1 Dennis Eckersley	.25	.11	.03
☐ 2 Brent Gates	.10	.05	.01
☐ 3 Rickey Henderson	.50	.23	.06
☐ 4 Mark McGwire	1.00	.45	.12
☐ 5 Troy Neel	.10	.05	.01
☐ 6 Ruben Sierra	.25	.11	.03
☐ 7 Terry Steinbach	.25	.11	.03
☐ 8 Chad Curtis	.10	.05	.01
☐ 9 Chili Davis	.25	.11	.03
☐ 10 Gary DiSarcina	.10	.05	.01
☐ 11 Damion Easley	.10	.05	.01
☐ 12 Bo Jackson	.25	.11	.03
☐ 13 Mark Langston	.25	.11	.03
☐ 14 Eduardo Perez	.10	.05	.01
☐ 15 Tim Salmon	.50	.23	.06
☐ 16 Jeff Bagwell	1.25	.55	.16
☐ 17 Craig Biggio	.25	.11	.03
☐ 18 Ken Caminiti	.50	.23	.06
☐ 19 Andujar Cedeno	.10	.05	.01
☐ 20 Doug Drabek	.10	.05	.01
☐ 21 Steve Finley	.50	.23	.06
☐ 22 Luis Gonzalez	.10	.05	.01
☐ 23 Darryl Kile	.10	.05	.01
☐ 24 Roberto Alomar	.60	.25	.07
☐ 25 Pat Borders	.10	.05	.01
☐ 26 Joe Carter	.25	.11	.03
☐ 27 Carlos Delgado	.50	.23	.06
☐ 28 Pat Hentgen	.25	.11	.03
☐ 29 Paul Molitor	.60	.25	.07
☐ 30 John Olerud	.10	.05	.01
☐ 31 Ed Sprague	.25	.11	.03
☐ 32 Devon White	.10	.05	.01
☐ 33 Steve Avery	.25	.11	.03
☐ 34 Tom Glavine	.50	.23	.06
☐ 35 David Justice	.50	.23	.06
☐ 36 Roberto Kelly	.10	.05	.01
☐ 37 Ryan Klesko	.60	.25	.07
☐ 38 Javier Lopez	.50	.23	.06
☐ 39 Greg Maddux	2.00	.90	.25
☐ 40 Fred McGriff	.50	.23	.06
☐ 41 Terry Pendleton	.25	.11	.03
☐ 42 Ricky Bones	.10	.05	.01
☐ 43 Darryl Hamilton	.10	.05	.01
☐ 44 Brian Harper	.10	.05	.01
☐ 45 John Jaha	.25	.11	.03
☐ 46 Dave Nilsson	.25	.11	.03
☐ 47 Kevin Seitzer	.10	.05	.01
☐ 48 Greg Vaughn	.50	.23	.06
☐ 49 Turner Ward	.10	.05	.01
☐ 50 Bernard Gilkey	.25	.11	.03
☐ 51 Gregg Jefferies	.50	.23	.06
☐ 52 Ray Lankford	.25	.11	.03
☐ 53 Tom Pagnozzi	.10	.05	.01
☐ 54 Ozzie Smith	.75	.35	.09
☐ 55 Bob Tewksbury	.10	.05	.01
☐ 56 Mark Whiten	.10	.05	.01
☐ 57 Todd Zeile	.10	.05	.01
☐ 58 Steve Buechele	.10	.05	.01
☐ 59 Shawon Dunston	.10	.05	.01
☐ 60 Mark Grace	.50	.23	.06
☐ 61 Derrick May	.10	.05	.01
☐ 62 Karl Rhodes	.10	.05	.01
☐ 63 Ryne Sandberg	.75	.35	.09
☐ 64 Sammy Sosa	.50	.23	.06
☐ 65 Rick Wilkins	.10	.05	.01
☐ 66 Brett Butler	.25	.11	.03
☐ 67 Delino DeShields	.10	.05	.01
☐ 68 Orel Hershiser	.25	.11	.03
☐ 69 Eric Karros	.25	.11	.03
☐ 70 Raul Mondesi	.50	.23	.06
☐ 71 Jose Offerman	.10	.05	.01
☐ 72 Mike Piazza	2.00	.90	.25
☐ 73 Tim Wallach	.10	.05	.01
☐ 74 Moises Alou	.25	.11	.03
☐ 75 Sean Berry	.10	.05	.01
☐ 76 Wil Cordero	.25	.11	.03
☐ 77 Cliff Floyd	.50	.23	.06
☐ 78 Marquis Grissom	.25	.11	.03
☐ 79 Ken Hill	.10	.05	.01
☐ 80 Larry Walker	.50	.23	.06
☐ 81 John Wetteland	.25	.11	.03
☐ 82 Rod Beck	.25	.11	.03
☐ 83 Barry Bonds	.75	.35	.09
☐ 84 Royce Clayton	.25	.11	.03
☐ 85 Darren Lewis	.10	.05	.01
☐ 86 Willie McGee	.10	.05	.01
☐ 87 Bill Swift	.10	.05	.01
☐ 88 Robby Thompson	.10	.05	.01
☐ 89 Matt Williams	.50	.23	.06
☐ 90 Sandy Alomar Jr.	.25	.11	.03
☐ 91 Carlos Baerga	.25	.11	.03
☐ 92 Albert Belle	1.25	.55	.16
☐ 93 Kenny Lofton	1.00	.45	.12
☐ 94 Eddie Murray	.75	.35	.09
☐ 95 Manny Ramirez	1.00	.45	.12
☐ 96 Paul Sorrento	.10	.05	.01
☐ 97 Jim Thome	.75	.35	.09
☐ 98 Rich Amaral	.10	.05	.01
☐ 99 Eric Anthony	.10	.05	.01
☐ 100 Jay Buhner	.50	.23	.06
☐ 101 Ken Griffey Jr.	3.00	1.35	.35
☐ 102 Randy Johnson	.50	.23	.06
☐ 103 Edgar Martinez	.25	.11	.03
☐ 104 Tino Martinez	.25	.11	.03
☐ 105 Kurt Abbott	.25	.11	.03
☐ 106 Bret Barberie	.10	.05	.01
☐ 107 Chuck Carr	.10	.05	.01
☐ 108 Jeff Conine	.25	.11	.03
☐ 109 Chris Hammond	.10	.05	.01
☐ 110 Bryan Harvey	.10	.05	.01
☐ 111 Benito Santiago	.10	.05	.01
☐ 112 Gary Sheffield	.50	.23	.06
☐ 113 Bobby Bonilla	.25	.11	.03
☐ 114 Dwight Gooden	.25	.11	.03
☐ 115 Todd Hundley	.25	.11	.03
☐ 116 Bobby Jones	.25	.11	.03
☐ 117 Jeff Kent	.10	.05	.01
☐ 118 Kevin McReynolds	.10	.05	.01
☐ 119 Bret Saberhagen	.25	.11	.03
☐ 120 Ryan Thompson	.10	.05	.01
☐ 121 Harold Baines	.25	.11	.03
☐ 122 Mike Devereaux	.10	.05	.01
☐ 123 Jeffrey Hammonds	.25	.11	.03
☐ 124 Ben McDonald	.10	.05	.01
☐ 125 Mike Mussina	.60	.25	.07
☐ 126 Rafael Palmeiro	.50	.23	.06
☐ 127 Cal Ripken Jr.	2.50	1.10	.30
☐ 128 Lee Smith	.25	.11	.03
☐ 129 Brad Ausmus	.10	.05	.01
☐ 130 Derek Bell	.25	.11	.03
☐ 131 Andy Benes	.25	.11	.03
☐ 132 Tony Gwynn	1.25	.55	.16
☐ 133 Trevor Hoffman	.25	.11	.03
☐ 134 Scott Livingstone	.10	.05	.01
☐ 135 Phil Plantier	.10	.05	.01
☐ 136 Darren Daulton	.25	.11	.03
☐ 137 Mariano Duncan	.10	.05	.01
☐ 138 Lenny Dykstra	.25	.11	.03
☐ 139 Dave Hollins	.10	.05	.01
☐ 140 Pete Incaviglia	.10	.05	.01
☐ 141 Danny Jackson	.10	.05	.01
☐ 142 John Kruk	.25	.11	.03
☐ 143 Kevin Stocker	.10	.05	.01
☐ 144 Jay Bell	.25	.11	.03
☐ 145 Carlos Garcia	.10	.05	.01
☐ 146 Jeff King	.25	.11	.03
☐ 147 Al Martin	.10	.05	.01
☐ 148 Orlando Merced	.25	.11	.03
☐ 149 Don Slaught	.10	.05	.01
☐ 150 Andy Van Slyke	.25	.11	.03
☐ 151 Kevin Brown	.25	.11	.03
☐ 152 Jose Canseco	.50	.23	.06
☐ 153 Will Clark	.50	.23	.06
☐ 154 Juan Gonzalez	1.50	.70	.19
☐ 155 David Hulse	.10	.05	.01
☐ 156 Dean Palmer	.25	.11	.03
☐ 157 Ivan Rodriguez	.75	.35	.09
☐ 158 Kenny Rogers	.10	.05	.01
☐ 159 Roger Clemens	.60	.25	.07
☐ 160 Scott Cooper	.10	.05	.01
☐ 161 Andre Dawson	.25	.11	.03
☐ 162 Mike Greenwell	.10	.05	.01
☐ 163 Otis Nixon	.10	.05	.01
☐ 164 Aaron Sele	.25	.11	.03
☐ 165 John Valentin	.25	.11	.03
☐ 166 Mo Vaughn	.75	.35	.09
☐ 167 Bret Boone	.25	.11	.03
☐ 168 Barry Larkin	.50	.23	.06
☐ 169 Kevin Mitchell	.25	.11	.03
☐ 170 Hal Morris	.10	.05	.01
☐ 171 Jose Rijo	.10	.05	.01
☐ 172 Deion Sanders	.50	.23	.06
☐ 173 Reggie Sanders	.25	.11	.03
☐ 174 John Smiley	.10	.05	.01
☐ 175 Dante Bichette	.50	.23	.06
☐ 176 Ellis Burks	.25	.11	.03
☐ 177 Andres Galarraga	.50	.23	.06
☐ 178 Joe Girardi	.10	.05	.01
☐ 179 Charlie Hayes	.10	.05	.01
☐ 180 Roberto Mejia	.10	.05	.01
☐ 181 Walt Weiss	.10	.05	.01
☐ 182 David Cone	.25	.11	.03
☐ 183 Gary Gaetti	.25	.11	.03
☐ 184 Greg Gagne	.10	.05	.01
☐ 185 Felix Jose	.10	.05	.01
☐ 186 Wally Joyner	.25	.11	.03

☐ 187 Mike Macfarlane	.10	.05	.01
☐ 188 Brian McRae	.25	.11	.03
☐ 189 Eric Davis	.25	.11	.03
☐ 190 Cecil Fielder	.25	.11	.03
☐ 191 Travis Fryman	.25	.11	.03
☐ 192 Tony Phillips	.25	.11	.03
☐ 193 Mickey Tettleton	.10	.05	.01
☐ 194 Alan Trammell	.25	.11	.03
☐ 195 Lou Whitaker	.25	.11	.03
☐ 196 Kent Hrbek	.25	.11	.03
☐ 197 Chuck Knoblauch	.50	.23	.06
☐ 198 Shane Mack	.10	.05	.01
☐ 199 Pat Meares	.10	.05	.01
☐ 200 Kirby Puckett	1.25	.55	.16
☐ 201 Matt Walbeck	.10	.05	.01
☐ 202 Dave Winfield	.50	.23	.06
☐ 203 Wilson Alvarez	.25	.11	.03
☐ 204 Alex Fernandez	.25	.11	.03
☐ 205 Julio Franco	.25	.11	.03
☐ 206 Ozzie Guillen	.10	.05	.01
☐ 207 Jack McDowell	.25	.11	.03
☐ 208 Tim Raines	.50	.23	.06
☐ 209 Frank Thomas	3.00	1.35	.35
☐ 210 Robin Ventura	.25	.11	.03
☐ 211 Jim Abbott	.10	.05	.01
☐ 212 Wade Boggs	.50	.23	.06
☐ 213 Pat Kelly	.10	.05	.01
☐ 214 Jimmy Key	.25	.11	.03
☐ 215 Don Mattingly	1.50	.70	.19
☐ 216 Paul O'Neill	.25	.11	.03
☐ 217 Mike Stanley	.10	.05	.01
☐ 218 Danny Tartabull	.10	.05	.01
☐ 219 Checklist	.10	.05	.01
☐ 220 Checklist	.10	.05	.01

1994 Studio Editor's Choice

This eight-card standard-sized set was randomly inserted in foil packs at a rate of one in 36. These cards are acetate and were designed much like a film strip with black borders. The fronts have various stop-action shots of the player and no back.

	MINT	NRMT	EXC
COMPLETE SET (8)	40.00	18.00	5.00
COMMON CARD (1-8)	1.50	.70	.19
☐ 1 Barry Bonds	4.00	1.80	.50
☐ 2 Frank Thomas	15.00	6.75	1.85
☐ 3 Ken Griffey Jr.	15.00	6.75	1.85
☐ 4 Andres Galarraga	2.00	.90	.25
☐ 5 Juan Gonzalez	8.00	3.60	1.00
☐ 6 Tim Salmon	2.50	1.10	.30
☐ 7 Paul O'Neill	1.50	.70	.19
☐ 8 Mike Piazza	10.00	4.50	1.25

1994 Studio Heritage

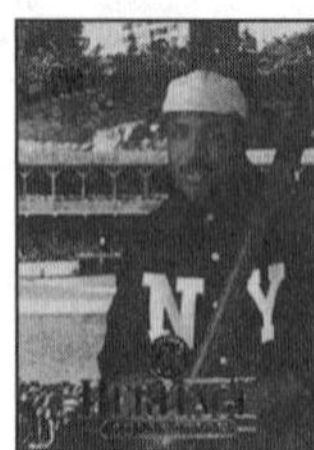

Each player in this eight-card insert set (randomly inserted in foil packs at a rate of one in nine) is modelling a vintage uniform of his team. The year of the uniform is noted in gold lettering at the top with a gold Heritage Collection logo at the bottom. A black and white photo of the stadium that the team used from the era of the depicted uniform serves as background. The back has a small photo a team highlight from that year.

	MINT	NRMT	EXC
COMPLETE SET (8)	15.00	6.75	1.85
COMMON CARD (1-8)	.50	.23	.06
☐ 1 Barry Bonds	2.00	.90	.25
☐ 2 Frank Thomas	8.00	3.60	1.00
☐ 3 Joe Carter	.75	.35	.09
☐ 4 Don Mattingly	4.00	1.80	.50
☐ 5 Ryne Sandberg	2.00	.90	.25
☐ 6 Javier Lopez	1.00	.45	.12
☐ 7 Gregg Jefferies	.50	.23	.06
☐ 8 Mike Mussina	1.50	.70	.19

1994 Studio Series Stars

This 10-card acetate set showcases top stars and was limited to 10,000 of each card. They were randomly inserted in foil packs at a rate of one in 60. The player cutout is surrounded by a small circle of stars with the player's name at the top. The team name, limited edition notation and the Series Stars logo are at the bottom. The back of the cutout contains a photo. Gold versions of this set were more difficult to obtain in packs (one in 120, 5,000 total).

	MINT	NRMT	EXC
COMPLETE SET (10)	150.00	70.00	19.00
COMMON CARD (1-10)	4.00	1.80	.50
☐ 1 Tony Gwynn	12.00	5.50	1.50
☐ 2 Barry Bonds	8.00	3.60	1.00
☐ 3 Frank Thomas	30.00	13.50	3.70
☐ 4 Ken Griffey Jr.	30.00	13.50	3.70
☐ 5 Joe Carter	4.00	1.80	.50
☐ 6 Mike Piazza	20.00	9.00	2.50
☐ 7 Cal Ripken Jr.	25.00	11.00	3.10
☐ 8 Greg Maddux	20.00	9.00	2.50
☐ 9 Juan Gonzalez	15.00	6.75	1.85
☐ 10 Don Mattingly	15.00	6.75	1.85

1995 Studio

This 200-card horizontal set was issued by Donruss for the fifth consecutive year. Using a different design than past Studio issues, these cards were designed similarly to credit cards. The cards were issued in five-card packs with a suggested retail price of $1.49. The fronts have a player photo on the right with holographic team logo in the right corner. The rest of the card has the player identified in the upper left. Underneath that information are 1994 stats as well as various vital statistics. There is also the "Studio" logo in the upper left corner. The horizontal backs have an action photo on the left. The right has the player's signature along with a pertinent fact and his career statistics. There are no Rookie Cards in this set.

	MINT	NRMT	EXC
COMPLETE SET (200)	50.00	22.00	6.25
COMMON CARD (1-200)	.15	.07	.02
☐ 1 Frank Thomas	4.00	1.80	.50
☐ 2 Jeff Bagwell	1.50	.70	.19
☐ 3 Don Mattingly	2.00	.90	.25
☐ 4 Mike Piazza	2.50	1.10	.30
☐ 5 Ken Griffey Jr.	4.00	1.80	.50
☐ 6 Greg Maddux	2.50	1.10	.30
☐ 7 Barry Bonds	1.00	.45	.12
☐ 8 Cal Ripken Jr.	3.00	1.35	.35
☐ 9 Jose Canseco	.60	.25	.07
☐ 10 Paul Molitor	.75	.35	.09
☐ 11 Kenny Lofton	1.00	.45	.12
☐ 12 Will Clark	.60	.25	.07
☐ 13 Tim Salmon	.60	.25	.07
☐ 14 Joe Carter	.30	.14	.04
☐ 15 Albert Belle	1.50	.70	.19
☐ 16 Roger Clemens	.75	.35	.09
☐ 17 Roberto Alomar	.75	.35	.09
☐ 18 Alex Rodriguez	5.00	2.20	.60
☐ 19 Raul Mondesi	.60	.25	.07
☐ 20 Deion Sanders	.60	.25	.07
☐ 21 Juan Gonzalez	2.00	.90	.25
☐ 22 Kirby Puckett	1.50	.70	.19
☐ 23 Fred McGriff	.60	.25	.07
☐ 24 Matt Williams	.60	.25	.07
☐ 25 Tony Gwynn	1.50	.70	.19
☐ 26 Cliff Floyd	.30	.14	.04
☐ 27 Travis Fryman	.30	.14	.04
☐ 28 Shawn Green	.30	.14	.04
☐ 29 Mike Mussina	.75	.35	.09
☐ 30 Bob Hamelin	.15	.07	.02
☐ 31 David Justice	.60	.25	.07
☐ 32 Manny Ramirez	1.00	.45	.12
☐ 33 David Cone	.30	.14	.04
☐ 34 Marquis Grissom	.30	.14	.04
☐ 35 Moises Alou	.30	.14	.04
☐ 36 Carlos Baerga	.30	.14	.04
☐ 37 Barry Larkin	.60	.25	.07
☐ 38 Robin Ventura	.30	.14	.04
☐ 39 Mo Vaughn	1.00	.45	.12
☐ 40 Jeffrey Hammonds	.30	.14	.04
☐ 41 Ozzie Smith	1.00	.45	.12
☐ 42 Andres Galarraga	.60	.25	.07
☐ 43 Carlos Delgado	.30	.14	.04
☐ 44 Lenny Dykstra	.30	.14	.04
☐ 45 Cecil Fielder	.30	.14	.04
☐ 46 Wade Boggs	.60	.25	.07
☐ 47 Gregg Jefferies	.30	.14	.04
☐ 48 Randy Johnson	.60	.25	.07
☐ 49 Rafael Palmeiro	.60	.25	.07
☐ 50 Craig Biggio	.30	.14	.04
☐ 51 Steve Avery	.30	.14	.04
☐ 52 Ricky Bottalico	.30	.14	.04
☐ 53 Chris Gomez	.15	.07	.02
☐ 54 Carlos Garcia	.15	.07	.02
☐ 55 Brian Anderson	.15	.07	.02
☐ 56 Wilson Alvarez	.30	.14	.04
☐ 57 Roberto Kelly	.15	.07	.02
☐ 58 Larry Walker	.60	.25	.07
☐ 59 Dean Palmer	.30	.14	.04
☐ 60 Rick Aguilera	.15	.07	.02
☐ 61 Javier Lopez	.60	.25	.07
☐ 62 Shawon Dunston	.15	.07	.02
☐ 63 Wm. VanLandingham	.15	.07	.02
☐ 64 Jeff Kent	.15	.07	.02
☐ 65 David McCarty	.15	.07	.02
☐ 66 Armando Benitez	.15	.07	.02
☐ 67 Brett Butler	.30	.14	.04
☐ 68 Bernard Gilkey	.30	.14	.04
☐ 69 Joey Hamilton	.60	.25	.07
☐ 70 Chad Curtis	.15	.07	.02
☐ 71 Dante Bichette	.60	.25	.07
☐ 72 Chuck Carr	.15	.07	.02
☐ 73 Pedro Martinez	.30	.14	.04
☐ 74 Ramon Martinez	.30	.14	.04
☐ 75 Rondell White	.30	.14	.04
☐ 76 Alex Fernandez	.30	.14	.04
☐ 77 Dennis Martinez	.30	.14	.04
☐ 78 Sammy Sosa	.60	.25	.07
☐ 79 Bernie Williams	.75	.35	.09
☐ 80 Lou Whitaker	.30	.14	.04
☐ 81 Kurt Abbott	.15	.07	.02
☐ 82 Tino Martinez	.30	.14	.04
☐ 83 Willie Greene	.15	.07	.02
☐ 84 Garret Anderson	.30	.14	.04
☐ 85 Jose Rijo	.15	.07	.02
☐ 86 Jeff Montgomery	.30	.14	.04
☐ 87 Mark Langston	.15	.07	.02
☐ 88 Reggie Sanders	.30	.14	.04
☐ 89 Rusty Greer	.60	.25	.07
☐ 90 Delino DeShields	.15	.07	.02
☐ 91 Jason Bere	.15	.07	.02
☐ 92 Lee Smith	.30	.14	.04
☐ 93 Devon White	.30	.14	.04
☐ 94 John Wetteland	.30	.14	.04
☐ 95 Luis Gonzalez	.15	.07	.02
☐ 96 Greg Vaughn	.30	.14	.04
☐ 97 Lance Johnson	.30	.14	.04
☐ 98 Alan Trammell	.30	.14	.04
☐ 99 Bret Saberhagen	.30	.14	.04
☐ 100 Jack McDowell	.30	.14	.04
☐ 101 Trevor Hoffman	.30	.14	.04
☐ 102 Dave Nilsson	.30	.14	.04
☐ 103 Bryan Harvey	.15	.07	.02
☐ 104 Chuck Knoblauch	.60	.25	.07
☐ 105 Bobby Bonilla	.30	.14	.04
☐ 106 Hal Morris	.15	.07	.02
☐ 107 Mark Whiten	.15	.07	.02
☐ 108 Phil Plantier	.15	.07	.02
☐ 109 Ryan Klesko	.60	.25	.07
☐ 110 Greg Gagne	.15	.07	.02
☐ 111 Ruben Sierra	.30	.14	.04
☐ 112 J.R. Phillips	.15	.07	.02
☐ 113 Terry Steinbach	.30	.14	.04
☐ 114 Jay Buhner	.60	.25	.07
☐ 115 Ken Caminiti	.60	.25	.07
☐ 116 Gary DiSarcina	.15	.07	.02
☐ 117 Ivan Rodriguez	1.00	.45	.12
☐ 118 Bip Roberts	.15	.07	.02
☐ 119 Jay Bell	.30	.14	.04
☐ 120 Ken Hill	.15	.07	.02
☐ 121 Mike Greenwell	.15	.07	.02
☐ 122 Rick Wilkins	.15	.07	.02
☐ 123 Rickey Henderson	.60	.25	.07
☐ 124 Dave Hollins	.15	.07	.02
☐ 125 Terry Pendleton	.30	.14	.04
☐ 126 Rich Becker	.15	.07	.02
☐ 127 Billy Ashley	.15	.07	.02
☐ 128 Derek Bell	.30	.14	.04
☐ 129 Dennis Eckersley	.30	.14	.04
☐ 130 Andujar Cedeno	.15	.07	.02
☐ 131 John Jaha	.30	.14	.04
☐ 132 Chuck Finley	.30	.14	.04
☐ 133 Steve Finley	.30	.14	.04
☐ 134 Danny Tartabull	.15	.07	.02
☐ 135 Jeff Conine	.30	.14	.04
☐ 136 Jon Lieber	.15	.07	.02
☐ 137 Jim Abbott	.15	.07	.02
☐ 138 Steve Trachsel	.15	.07	.02
☐ 139 Bret Boone	.30	.14	.04
☐ 140 Charles Johnson	.30	.14	.04
☐ 141 Mark McGwire	1.25	.55	.16
☐ 142 Eddie Murray	1.00	.45	.12
☐ 143 Doug Drabek	.15	.07	.02
☐ 144 Steve Cooke	.15	.07	.02
☐ 145 Kevin Seitzer	.15	.07	.02
☐ 146 Rod Beck	.15	.07	.02
☐ 147 Eric Karros	.30	.14	.04
☐ 148 Tim Raines	.60	.25	.07
☐ 149 Joe Girardi	.15	.07	.02
☐ 150 Aaron Sele	.30	.14	.04
☐ 151 Robby Thompson	.15	.07	.02
☐ 152 Chan Ho Park	.60	.25	.07
☐ 153 Ellis Burks	.30	.14	.04
☐ 154 Brian McRae	.30	.14	.04
☐ 155 Jimmy Key	.30	.14	.04
☐ 156 Rico Brogna	.15	.07	.02
☐ 157 Ozzie Guillen	.15	.07	.02
☐ 158 Chili Davis	.30	.14	.04
☐ 159 Darren Daulton	.30	.14	.04
☐ 160 Chipper Jones	2.50	1.10	.30
☐ 161 Walt Weiss	.15	.07	.02
☐ 162 Paul O'Neill	.30	.14	.04
☐ 163 Al Martin	.30	.14	.04
☐ 164 John Valentin	.30	.14	.04
☐ 165 Tim Wallach	.15	.07	.02
☐ 166 Scott Erickson	.15	.07	.02
☐ 167 Ryan Thompson	.15	.07	.02
☐ 168 Todd Zeile	.15	.07	.02
☐ 169 Scott Cooper	.15	.07	.02
☐ 170 Matt Mieske	.30	.14	.04
☐ 171 Allen Watson	.15	.07	.02
☐ 172 Brian L.Hunter	.30	.14	.04
☐ 173 Kevin Stocker	.15	.07	.02
☐ 174 Cal Eldred	.15	.07	.02
☐ 175 Tony Phillips	.30	.14	.04
☐ 176 Ben McDonald	.15	.07	.02
☐ 177 Mark Grace	.60	.25	.07
☐ 178 Midre Cummings	.15	.07	.02
☐ 179 Orlando Merced	.15	.07	.02
☐ 180 Jeff King	.30	.14	.04
☐ 181 Gary Sheffield	.60	.25	.07
☐ 182 Tom Glavine	.60	.25	.07
☐ 183 Edgar Martinez	.30	.14	.04
☐ 184 Steve Karsay	.15	.07	.02
☐ 185 Pat Listach	.15	.07	.02
☐ 186 Wil Cordero	.15	.07	.02
☐ 187 Brady Anderson	.60	.25	.07
☐ 188 Bobby Jones	.30	.14	.04
☐ 189 Andy Benes	.15	.07	.02
☐ 190 Ray Lankford	.30	.14	.04
☐ 191 John Doherty	.15	.07	.02
☐ 192 Wally Joyner	.30	.14	.04
☐ 193 Jim Thome	.75	.35	.09
☐ 194 Royce Clayton	.15	.07	.02
☐ 195 John Olerud	.15	.07	.02
☐ 196 Steve Buechele	.15	.07	.02
☐ 197 Harold Baines	.30	.14	.04
☐ 198 Geronimo Berroa	.15	.07	.02
☐ 199 Checklist	.15	.07	.02
☐ 200 Checklist	.15	.07	.02

1995 Studio Gold Series

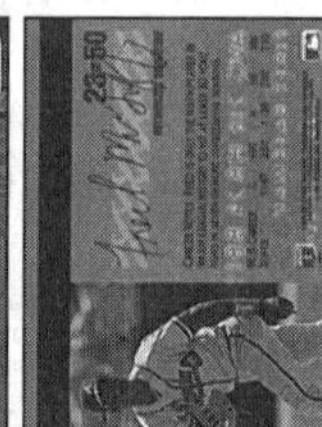

This 50-card set was inserted one per packs. This set parallels the first 50 cards of the regular studio set. The only differences between these cards and the regular issue are they were printed with a gold background and are numbered in the right corner as "X" of 50. Also the words "Studio Gold" are printed in the upper front left corner.

	MINT	NRMT	EXC
COMPLETE SET (50)	40.00	18.00	5.00
COMMON CARD (1-50)	.50	.23	.06
*GOLD: 1.5X BASIC CARDS			

1995 Studio Platinum Series

This 25-card set was randomly inserted into packs at a rate of one in 10 packs. This set parallels the first 25 cards of the regular issue. These cards are different from the regular issue in that they have a platinum background, the words "Studio Platinum" in the upper left corner and are numbered on the back as "X" of 25.

	MINT	NRMT	EXC
COMPLETE SET (25)	150.00	70.00	19.00
COMMON CARD (1-25)	2.00	.90	.25
*PLATINUM: 6X BASIC CARDS			

1996 Studio

The 1996 Studio set was issued in one series totalling 150 cards, and distributed in seven-card packs. The fronts feature color action player photos with a player portrait in the background. The backs carry another player photo, biographical information, with a head photo and vital statistics printed on the letters of the card's name.

	MINT	NRMT	EXC
COMPLETE SET (150)	15.00	6.75	1.85
COMMON CARD (1-150)	.10	.05	.01
☐ 1 Cal Ripken	2.00	.90	.25
☐ 2 Alex Gonzalez	.10	.05	.01
☐ 3 Roger Cedeno	.25	.11	.03
☐ 4 Todd Hollandsworth	.25	.11	.03
☐ 5 Gregg Jefferies	.50	.23	.06
☐ 6 Ryne Sandberg	.60	.25	.07
☐ 7 Eric Karros	.25	.11	.03
☐ 8 Jeff Conine	.25	.11	.03
☐ 9 Rafael Palmeiro	.50	.23	.06
☐ 10 Bip Roberts	.10	.05	.01
☐ 11 Roger Clemens	.50	.23	.06
☐ 12 Tom Glavine	.50	.23	.06
☐ 13 Jason Giambi	.50	.23	.06
☐ 14 Rey Ordonez	.50	.23	.06
☐ 15 Chan Ho Park	.50	.23	.06
☐ 16 Vinny Castilla	.25	.11	.03
☐ 17 Butch Huskey	.25	.11	.03
☐ 18 Greg Maddux	1.50	.70	.19
☐ 19 Bernard Gilkey	.25	.11	.03
☐ 20 Marquis Grissom	.25	.11	.03
☐ 21 Chuck Knoblauch	.50	.23	.06
☐ 22 Ozzie Smith	.60	.25	.07
☐ 23 Garret Anderson	.50	.23	.06
☐ 24 J.T. Snow	.25	.11	.03
☐ 25 John Valentin	.25	.11	.03
☐ 26 Barry Larkin	.50	.23	.06
☐ 27 Bobby Bonilla	.25	.11	.03
☐ 28 Todd Zeile	.25	.11	.03
☐ 29 Roberto Alomar	.50	.23	.06
☐ 30 Ramon Martinez	.25	.11	.03
☐ 31 Jeff King	.25	.11	.03
☐ 32 Dennis Eckersley	.25	.11	.03
☐ 33 Derek Jeter	1.50	.70	.19
☐ 34 Edgar Martinez	.25	.11	.03
☐ 35 Geronimo Berroa	.25	.11	.03
☐ 36 Hal Morris	.10	.05	.01
☐ 37 Troy Percival	.25	.11	.03
☐ 38 Jason Isringhausen	.50	.23	.06
☐ 39 Greg Vaughn	.50	.23	.06
☐ 40 Robin Ventura	.25	.11	.03
☐ 41 Craig Biggio	.25	.11	.03
☐ 42 Will Clark	.50	.23	.06
☐ 43 Sammy Sosa	.50	.23	.06
☐ 44 Bernie Williams	.50	.23	.06
☐ 45 Kenny Lofton	.60	.25	.07
☐ 46 Wade Boggs	.50	.23	.06
☐ 47 Javy Lopez	.25	.11	.03
☐ 48 Reggie Sanders	.25	.11	.03
☐ 49 Jeff Bagwell	1.00	.45	.12
☐ 50 Fred McGriff	.50	.23	.06
☐ 51 Charles Johnson	.25	.11	.03
☐ 52 Darren Daulton	.25	.11	.03
☐ 53 Jose Canseco	.50	.23	.06
☐ 54 Cecil Fielder	.25	.11	.03
☐ 55 Hideo Nomo	.60	.25	.07
☐ 56 Tim Salmon	.50	.23	.06
☐ 57 Carlos Delgado	.25	.11	.03
☐ 58 David Cone	.25	.11	.03
☐ 59 Tim Raines	.50	.23	.06
☐ 60 Lyle Mouton	.10	.05	.01
☐ 61 Wally Joyner	.10	.05	.01
☐ 62 Bret Boone	.10	.05	.01
☐ 63 Raul Mondesi	.50	.23	.06
☐ 64 Gary Sheffield	.50	.23	.06
☐ 65 Alex Rodriguez	2.50	1.10	.30
☐ 66 Russ Davis	.10	.05	.01
☐ 67 Checklist	.10	.05	.01
☐ 68 Marty Cordova	.25	.11	.03
☐ 69 Ruben Sierra	.10	.05	.01
☐ 70 Jose Mesa	.25	.11	.03
☐ 71 Matt Williams	.50	.23	.06
☐ 72 Chipper Jones	1.50	.70	.19
☐ 73 Randy Johnson	.50	.23	.06
☐ 74 Kirby Puckett	1.00	.45	.12
☐ 75 Jim Edmonds	.25	.11	.03
☐ 76 Barry Bonds	.60	.25	.07
☐ 77 David Segui	.10	.05	.01
☐ 78 Larry Walker	.50	.23	.06
☐ 79 Jason Kendall	.50	.23	.06
☐ 80 Mike Piazza	1.50	.70	.19
☐ 81 Brian L.Hunter	.25	.11	.03
☐ 82 Julio Franco	.25	.11	.03
☐ 83 Jay Bell	.25	.11	.03
☐ 84 Kevin Seitzer	.10	.05	.01
☐ 85 John Smoltz	.50	.23	.06
☐ 86 Joe Carter	.25	.11	.03
☐ 87 Ray Durham	.50	.23	.06
☐ 88 Carlos Baerga	.25	.11	.03
☐ 89 Ron Gant	.25	.11	.03
☐ 90 Orlando Merced	.10	.05	.01
☐ 91 Lee Smith	.25	.11	.03
☐ 92 Pedro Martinez	.25	.11	.03
☐ 93 Frank Thomas	2.50	1.10	.30
☐ 94 Al Martin	.10	.05	.01
☐ 95 Chad Curtis	.10	.05	.01
☐ 96 Eddie Murray	.60	.25	.07
☐ 97 Rusty Greer	.50	.23	.06
☐ 98 Jay Buhner	.50	.23	.06
☐ 99 Rico Brogna	.10	.05	.01
☐ 100 Todd Hundley	.25	.11	.03
☐ 101 Moises Alou	.25	.11	.03
☐ 102 Chili Davis	.10	.05	.01
☐ 103 Ismael Valdes	.10	.05	.01
☐ 104 Mo Vaughn	.60	.25	.07
☐ 105 Juan Gonzalez	1.25	.55	.16
☐ 106 Mark Grudzielanek	.25	.11	.03
☐ 107 Derek Bell	.25	.11	.03
☐ 108 Shawn Green	.10	.05	.01
☐ 109 David Justice	.25	.11	.03
☐ 110 Paul O'Neill	.10	.05	.01
☐ 111 Kevin Appier	.25	.11	.03
☐ 112 Ray Lankford	.25	.11	.03
☐ 113 Travis Fryman	.25	.11	.03
☐ 114 Manny Ramirez	.60	.25	.07
☐ 115 Brooks Kieschnick	.50	.23	.06
☐ 116 Ken Griffey Jr.	2.50	1.10	.30
☐ 117 Jeffrey Hammonds	.10	.05	.01
☐ 118 Mark McGwire	.75	.35	.09
☐ 119 Denny Neagle	.25	.11	.03
☐ 120 Quilvio Veras	.10	.05	.01
☐ 121 Alan Benes	.50	.23	.06
☐ 122 Rondell White	.25	.11	.03
☐ 123 Osvaldo Fernandez	.25	.11	.03
☐ 124 Andres Galarraga	.50	.23	.06
☐ 125 Johnny Damon	.25	.11	.03
☐ 126 Lenny Dykstra	.25	.11	.03
☐ 127 Jason Schmidt	.50	.23	.06
☐ 128 Mike Mussina	.50	.23	.06
☐ 129 Ken Caminiti	.50	.23	.06
☐ 130 Michael Tucker	.25	.11	.03
☐ 131 LaTroy Hawkins	.10	.05	.01
☐ 132 Checklist	.10	.05	.01
☐ 133 Delino DeShields	.10	.05	.01
☐ 134 Dave Nilsson	.25	.11	.03
☐ 135 Jack McDowell	.50	.23	.06
☐ 136 Joey Hamilton	.25	.11	.03
☐ 137 Dante Bichette	.50	.23	.06
☐ 138 Paul Molitor	.50	.23	.06
☐ 139 Ivan Rodriguez	.60	.25	.07
☐ 140 Mark Grace	.50	.23	.06
☐ 141 Paul Wilson	.25	.11	.03
☐ 142 Orel Hershiser	.25	.11	.03
☐ 143 Albert Belle	1.00	.45	.12
☐ 144 Tino Martinez	.25	.11	.03
☐ 145 Tony Gwynn	1.00	.45	.12
☐ 146 George Arias	.10	.05	.01
☐ 147 Brian Jordan	.25	.11	.03
☐ 148 Brian McRae	.10	.05	.01
☐ 149 Rickey Henderson	.50	.23	.06
☐ 150 Ryan Klesko	.50	.23	.06

1996 Studio Press Proofs Bronze

Randomly inserted in packs, this 150-card Bronze set is parallel to the regular set and is similar in design with bronze foil stamping. Only 2,000 sets were produced. Prices below refer to Bronze cards.

	MINT	NRMT	EXC
COMPLETE SET (150)	400.00	180.00	50.00
COMMON CARD (1-150)			
*STARS: 5X TO 12X BASIC CARDS			
*YOUNG STARS: 4X TO 10X BASIC CARDS			

1996 Studio Press Proofs Gold

Randomly inserted in packs, this 150-card set is parallel to the regular set and is similar in design with gold foil stamping. Only 500 sets were produced.

	MINT	NRMT	EXC
COMPLETE SET (150)	2000.00	900.00	250.00
COMMON CARD (1-150)	4.00	1.80	.50
*STARS: 25X TO 60X BASIC CARDS			
*YOUNG STARS: 20X TO 50X BASIC CARDS			

1996 Studio Press Proofs Silver

Randomly inserted in magazine packs, this 150-card set is parallel to the regular set and is similar in design with silver foil stamping. Only 100 sets were produced.

	MINT	NRMT	EXC
COMMON CARD (1-150)	10.00	4.50	1.25
*STARS: 60X TO 120X BASIC CARDS			
*YOUNG STARS: 50X TO 100X BASIC CARDS			
☐ 1 Cal Ripken	300.00	135.00	38.00
☐ 33 Derek Jeter	250.00	110.00	31.00
☐ 49 Jeff Bagwell	150.00	70.00	19.00
☐ 65 Alex Rodriguez	400.00	180.00	50.00
☐ 72 Chipper Jones	250.00	110.00	31.00
☐ 74 Kirby Puckett	150.00	70.00	19.00
☐ 80 Mike Piazza	250.00	110.00	31.00
☐ 93 Frank Thomas	400.00	180.00	50.00
☐ 105 Juan Gonzalez	200.00	90.00	25.00
☐ 116 Ken Griffey Jr.	400.00	180.00	50.00
☐ 143 Albert Belle	150.00	70.00	19.00
☐ 145 Tony Gwynn	150.00	70.00	19.00

1996 Studio Hit Parade

Randomly inserted in packs, this ten-card set features some of the Leagues's top long'ball hitters. The fronts feature color action player photos on a die-cut record design in the background. The backs carry the player's batting average breakdown.

	MINT	NRMT	EXC
COMPLETE SET (10)	100.00	45.00	12.50
COMMON CARD (1-10)	3.00	1.35	.35
☐ 1 Tony Gwynn	10.00	4.50	1.25
☐ 2 Ken Griffey Jr.	25.00	11.00	3.10
☐ 3 Frank Thomas	25.00	11.00	3.10
☐ 4 Jeff Bagwell	10.00	4.50	1.25
☐ 5 Kirby Puckett	10.00	4.50	1.25
☐ 6 Mike Piazza	15.00	6.75	1.85
☐ 7 Barry Bonds	6.00	2.70	.75
☐ 8 Albert Belle	10.00	4.50	1.25
☐ 9 Tim Salmon	3.00	1.35	.35
☐ 10 Mo Vaughn	6.00	2.70	.75

1996 Studio Masterstrokes

Randomly inserted in packs, this eight-card set features some of the League's most popular stars. Printed with brushed embossed technologies, the cards display color action player images in simulated oil painting detail. Each card from this set was also produced in a promo form.

	MINT	NRMT	EXC
COMPLETE SET (8)	150.00	70.00	19.00
COMMON CARD (1-8)	10.00	4.50	1.25
☐ 1 Tony Gwynn	15.00	6.75	1.85
☐ 2 Mike Piazza	25.00	11.00	3.10
☐ 3 Jeff Bagwell	15.00	6.75	1.85
☐ 4 Manny Ramirez	10.00	4.50	1.25
☐ 5 Cal Ripken	30.00	13.50	3.70

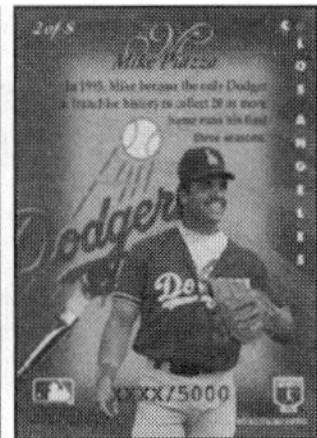

	MINT	NRMT	EXC
☐ 6 Frank Thomas	40.00	18.00	5.00
☐ 7 Ken Griffey Jr.	40.00	18.00	5.00
☐ 8 Greg Maddux	25.00	11.00	3.10

1996 Studio Stained Glass Stars

Randomly inserted in packs, this 12-card set honors some of the league's hottest superstars. The cards feature color player images on a genuine-look stained glass background and were printed with a clear plastic, die-cut technology.

	MINT	NRMT	EXC
COMPLETE SET (12)	100.00	45.00	12.50
COMMON CARD (1-12)	4.00	1.80	.50
☐ 1 Cal Ripken	12.00	5.50	1.50
☐ 2 Ken Griffey Jr.	15.00	6.75	1.85
☐ 3 Frank Thomas	15.00	6.75	1.85
☐ 4 Greg Maddux	10.00	4.50	1.25
☐ 5 Chipper Jones	10.00	4.50	1.25
☐ 6 Mike Piazza	10.00	4.50	1.25
☐ 7 Albert Belle	6.00	2.70	.75
☐ 8 Jeff Bagwell	6.00	2.70	.75
☐ 9 Hideo Nomo	4.00	1.80	.50
☐ 10 Barry Bonds	4.00	1.80	.50
☐ 11 Manny Ramirez	4.00	1.80	.50
☐ 12 Kenny Lofton	4.00	1.80	.50

1994 Sucker Saver

These sucker saver lollipops were produced by Innovative Confections. The actual discs were issued by Michael Schechter Associates, and one disc was included with each sucker. It is reported that sales of this confectionary product were so poor that it was discontinued. Each disc measures 2 5/8" in diameter. Inside a red ring, the fronts display a color player headshot within a diamond design. The player's name appears in black lettering on a yellow stripe across the top of the disc. The backs of the discs are printed in blue and are numbered "X of 20."

	MINT	NRMT	EXC
COMPLETE SET (20)	35.00	16.00	4.40
COMMON CARD (1-20)	.75	.35	.09
☐ 1 Rickey Henderson	2.00	.90	.25
☐ 2 Ken Caminiti	1.50	.70	.19
☐ 3 Terry Pendleton	.75	.35	.09
☐ 4 Tim Raines	.75	.35	.09
☐ 5 Joe Carter	1.50	.70	.19
☐ 6 Benito Santiago	.75	.35	.09
☐ 7 Jim Abbott	.75	.35	.09
☐ 8 Ozzie Smith	3.00	1.35	.35
☐ 9 Don Slaught	.75	.35	.09
☐ 10 Tony Gwynn	4.00	1.80	.50
☐ 11 Mark Langston	.75	.35	.09
☐ 12 Darryl Strawberry	1.00	.45	.12
☐ 13 Dave Justice	1.00	.45	.12
☐ 14 Cecil Fielder	1.50	.70	.19
☐ 15 Cal Ripken	6.00	2.70	.75
☐ 16 Jeff Bagwell	2.50	1.10	.30
☐ 17 Mike Piazza	3.00	1.35	.35
☐ 18 Bobby Bonilla	1.00	.45	.12
☐ 19 Barry Bonds	2.00	.90	.25
☐ 20 Roger Clemens	2.50	1.10	.30

1995 Summit Samples

This 9-card standard-sized set was issued in an 8 1/2" by 14 1/2" black portfolio. The fronts freature color action cut-out player photos on a background that is partly white and partly game action. The player's name and team logo are gold-foil stamped on a black bar below. The backs carry a color closeup photo that partially overlays a baseball diamond containing 1994 monthly statistics. The player's name, sponsors' logos and card number round out the back. The disclaimer "sample" is printed diagonally across both sides of the card.

	MINT	NRMT	EXC
COMPLETE SET (9)	15.00	6.75	1.85
COMMON CARD	.25	.11	.03
☐ 10 Barry Larkin	1.25	.55	.16
☐ 11 Albert Belle	3.00	1.35	.35
☐ 79 Cal Ripken	6.00	2.70	.75
☐ 80 David Cone	.75	.35	.09
☐ 125 Alex Gonzalez	.75	.35	.09
☐ 130 Charles Johnson	.75	.35	.09
☐ BB12 Jose Canseco	3.00	1.35	.35
☐ BB17 Fred McGriff	3.00	1.35	.35
☐ NNO Title Card	.25	.11	.03

1995 Summit

This set contains 200 standard-size cards and was sold in seven-card retail packs for a suggested price of $1.99. This set is a premium product issued by Pinnacle Brands and produced on thicker paper than the regular set. The fronts have an action photo on a white background with the player's name and team emblem at the bottom in gold-foil. The backs have a player color photo on the left side with a baseball diamond on the right that gives the player's statistics month by month for the season. Subsets featured are Rookies (112-173), Bat Speed (174-188) and Special Delivery (189-193). Notable Rookie Cards in this set include Bobby Higginson and Hideo Nomo.

	MINT	NRMT	EXC
COMPLETE SET (200)	20.00	9.00	2.50
COMMON CARD (1-200)	.10	.05	.01
☐ 1 Ken Griffey Jr.	2.50	1.10	.30
☐ 2 Alex Fernandez	.25	.11	.03
☐ 3 Fred McGriff	.50	.23	.06
☐ 4 Ben McDonald	.10	.05	.01
☐ 5 Rafael Palmeiro	.50	.23	.06
☐ 6 Tony Gwynn	1.00	.45	.12
☐ 7 Jim Thome	.50	.23	.06
☐ 8 Ken Hill	.10	.05	.01
☐ 9 Barry Bonds	.60	.25	.07
☐ 10 Barry Larkin	.50	.23	.06
☐ 11 Albert Belle	1.00	.45	.12
☐ 12 Billy Ashley	.10	.05	.01
☐ 13 Matt Williams	.50	.23	.06
☐ 14 Andy Benes	.10	.05	.01
☐ 15 Midre Cummings	.10	.05	.01
☐ 16 J.R. Phillips	.10	.05	.01
☐ 17 Edgar Martinez	.25	.11	.03
☐ 18 Manny Ramirez	.60	.25	.07
☐ 19 Jose Canseco	.50	.23	.06
☐ 20 Chili Davis	.25	.11	.03
☐ 21 Don Mattingly	1.25	.55	.16
☐ 22 Bernie Williams	.50	.23	.06
☐ 23 Tom Glavine	.50	.23	.06
☐ 24 Robin Ventura	.25	.11	.03
☐ 25 Jeff Conine	.25	.11	.03
☐ 26 Mark Grace	.50	.23	.06
☐ 27 Mark McGwire	.75	.35	.09
☐ 28 Carlos Delgado	.25	.11	.03
☐ 29 Greg Colbrunn	.10	.05	.01
☐ 30 Greg Maddux	1.50	.70	.19
☐ 31 Craig Biggio	.25	.11	.03
☐ 32 Kirby Puckett	1.00	.45	.12
☐ 33 Derek Bell	.25	.11	.03
☐ 34 Lenny Dykstra	.25	.11	.03
☐ 35 Tim Salmon	.50	.23	.06
☐ 36 Deion Sanders	.50	.23	.06
☐ 37 Moises Alou	.25	.11	.03
☐ 38 Ray Lankford	.25	.11	.03
☐ 39 Willie Greene	.10	.05	.01
☐ 40 Ozzie Smith	.60	.25	.07
☐ 41 Roger Clemens	.50	.23	.06
☐ 42 Andres Galarraga	.50	.23	.06
☐ 43 Gary Sheffield	.50	.23	.06
☐ 44 Sammy Sosa	.50	.23	.06
☐ 45 Larry Walker	.50	.23	.06
☐ 46 Kevin Appier	.25	.11	.03
☐ 47 Raul Mondesi	.50	.23	.06
☐ 48 Kenny Lofton	.60	.25	.07
☐ 49 Darryl Hamilton	.10	.05	.01
☐ 50 Roberto Alomar	.50	.23	.06
☐ 51 Hal Morris	.10	.05	.01
☐ 52 Cliff Floyd	.25	.11	.03
☐ 53 Brent Gates	.10	.05	.01
☐ 54 Rickey Henderson	.50	.23	.06
☐ 55 John Olerud	.10	.05	.01
☐ 56 Gregg Jefferies	.25	.11	.03
☐ 57 Cecil Fielder	.25	.11	.03
☐ 58 Paul Molitor	.50	.23	.06
☐ 59 Bret Boone	.25	.11	.03
☐ 60 Greg Vaughn	.25	.11	.03
☐ 61 Wally Joyner	.25	.11	.03
☐ 62 Jeffrey Hammonds	.25	.11	.03
☐ 63 James Mouton	.10	.05	.01
☐ 64 Omar Vizquel	.25	.11	.03
☐ 65 Wade Boggs	.50	.23	.06
☐ 66 Terry Steinbach	.25	.11	.03
☐ 67 Wil Cordero	.10	.05	.01
☐ 68 Joey Hamilton	.50	.23	.06
☐ 69 Rico Brogna	.10	.05	.01
☐ 70 Darren Daulton	.25	.11	.03
☐ 71 Chuck Knoblauch	.50	.23	.06
☐ 72 Bob Hamelin	.10	.05	.01
☐ 73 Carl Everett	.10	.05	.01
☐ 74 Joe Carter	.25	.11	.03
☐ 75 Dave Winfield	.50	.23	.06
☐ 76 Bobby Bonilla	.25	.11	.03
☐ 77 Paul O'Neill	.25	.11	.03
☐ 78 Javier Lopez	.50	.23	.06
☐ 79 Cal Ripken	2.00	.90	.25
☐ 80 David Cone	.25	.11	.03
☐ 81 Bernard Gilkey	.25	.11	.03
☐ 82 Ivan Rodriguez	.60	.25	.07
☐ 83 Dean Palmer	.25	.11	.03
☐ 84 Jason Bere	.10	.05	.01
☐ 85 Will Clark	.50	.23	.06
☐ 86 Scott Cooper	.10	.05	.01
☐ 87 Royce Clayton	.10	.05	.01
☐ 88 Mike Piazza	1.50	.70	.19
☐ 89 Ryan Klesko	.50	.23	.06
☐ 90 Juan Gonzalez	1.25	.55	.16
☐ 91 Travis Fryman	.25	.11	.03
☐ 92 Frank Thomas	2.50	1.10	.30
☐ 93 Eduardo Perez	.10	.05	.01
☐ 94 Mo Vaughn	.60	.25	.07
☐ 95 Jay Bell	.25	.11	.03
☐ 96 Jeff Bagwell	1.00	.45	.12
☐ 97 Randy Johnson	.50	.23	.06
☐ 98 Jimmy Key	.25	.11	.03
☐ 99 Dennis Eckersley	.25	.11	.03
☐ 100 Carlos Baerga	.25	.11	.03
☐ 101 Eddie Murray	.60	.25	.07
☐ 102 Mike Mussina	.50	.23	.06
☐ 103 Brian Anderson	.10	.05	.01
☐ 104 Jeff Cirillo	.25	.11	.03
☐ 105 Dante Bichette	.50	.23	.06
☐ 106 Bret Saberhagen	.25	.11	.03
☐ 107 Jeff Kent	.10	.05	.01
☐ 108 Ruben Sierra	.25	.11	.03
☐ 109 Kirk Gibson	.25	.11	.03
☐ 110 Steve Karsay	.10	.05	.01
☐ 111 David Justice	.50	.23	.06
☐ 112 Benji Gil	.10	.05	.01
☐ 113 Vaughn Eshelman	.10	.05	.01
☐ 114 Carlos Perez	.25	.11	.03
☐ 115 Chipper Jones	1.50	.70	.19
☐ 116 Shane Andrews	.10	.05	.01
☐ 117 Orlando Miller	.10	.05	.01
☐ 118 Scott Ruffcorn	.10	.05	.01
☐ 119 Jose Oliva	.10	.05	.01
☐ 120 Joe Vitiello	.10	.05	.01
☐ 121 Jon Nunnally	.25	.11	.03
☐ 122 Garret Anderson	.25	.11	.03
☐ 123 Curtis Goodwin	.25	.11	.03
☐ 124 Mark Grudzielanek	.60	.25	.07
☐ 125 Alex Gonzalez	.25	.11	.03
☐ 126 David Bell	.10	.05	.01
☐ 127 Dustin Hermanson	.25	.11	.03
☐ 128 Dave Nilsson	.25	.11	.03
☐ 129 Wilson Heredia	.10	.05	.01
☐ 130 Charles Johnson	.25	.11	.03
☐ 131 Frank Rodriguez	.25	.11	.03
☐ 132 Alex Ochoa	.25	.11	.03
☐ 133 Alex Rodriguez	3.00	1.35	.35
☐ 134 Bobby Higginson	.60	.25	.07
☐ 135 Edgardo Alfonzo	.25	.11	.03
☐ 136 Armando Benitez	.10	.05	.01
☐ 137 Rich Aude	.10	.05	.01
☐ 138 Tim Naehring	.10	.05	.01
☐ 139 Joe Randa	.10	.05	.01
☐ 140 Quilvio Veras	.10	.05	.01
☐ 141 Hideo Nomo	2.50	1.10	.30
☐ 142 Ray Holbert	.10	.05	.01
☐ 143 Michael Tucker	.25	.11	.03
☐ 144 Chad Mottola	.25	.11	.03
☐ 145 John Valentin	.25	.11	.03
☐ 146 James Baldwin	.25	.11	.03
☐ 147 Esteban Loaiza	.10	.05	.01
☐ 148 Marty Cordova	.50	.23	.06
☐ 149 Juan Acevedo	.10	.05	.01
☐ 150 Tim Unroe UER Cardinals logo	.25	.11	.03
☐ 151 Brad Clontz UER A's logo	.10	.05	.01
☐ 152 Steve Rodriguez UER Yankees logo	.10	.05	.01
☐ 153 Rudy Pemberton UER Dodgers logo	.10	.05	.01
☐ 154 Ozzie Timmons UER Tigers logo	.10	.05	.01
☐ 155 Ricky Otero	.10	.05	.01
☐ 156 Allen Battle	.10	.05	.01
☐ 157 Joe Rosselli	.10	.05	.01
☐ 158 Roberto Petagine	.10	.05	.01
☐ 159 Todd Hollandsworth	.50	.23	.06
☐ 160 Shannon Penn UER Cubs logo	.10	.05	.01
☐ 161 Antonio Osuna UER Tigers logo	.10	.05	.01
☐ 162 Russ Davis UER Red Sox logo	.10	.05	.01
☐ 163 Jason Giambi UER two errors: front photo actually Brent Gates also Braves logo	.50	.23	.06
☐ 164 Terry Bradshaw UER Brewers logo	.10	.05	.01
☐ 165 Ray Durham	.25	.11	.03
☐ 166 Todd Steverson	.10	.05	.01
☐ 167 Tim Belk	.10	.05	.01
☐ 168 Andy Pettitte	1.00	.45	.12
☐ 169 Roger Cedeno	.25	.11	.03
☐ 170 Jose Parra	.25	.11	.03
☐ 171 Scott Sullivan	.10	.05	.01
☐ 172 LaTroy Hawkins	.10	.05	.01
☐ 173 Jeff McCurry	.10	.05	.01
☐ 174 Ken Griffey Jr. BS	1.25	.55	.16
☐ 175 Frank Thomas BS	1.25	.55	.16
☐ 176 Cal Ripken Jr. BS	1.00	.45	.12
☐ 177 Jeff Bagwell BS	.50	.23	.06
☐ 178 Mike Piazza BS	.75	.35	.09
☐ 179 Barry Bonds BS	.50	.23	.06
☐ 180 Matt Williams BS	.50	.23	.06
☐ 181 Don Mattingly BS	.60	.25	.07
☐ 182 Will Clark BS	.50	.23	.06
☐ 183 Tony Gwynn BS	.50	.23	.06
☐ 184 Kirby Puckett BS	.50	.23	.06
☐ 185 Jose Canseco BS	.50	.23	.06
☐ 186 Paul Molitor BS	.50	.23	.06
☐ 187 Albert Belle BS	.50	.23	.06
☐ 188 Joe Carter BS	.25	.11	.03
☐ 189 Greg Maddux SD	.75	.35	.09
☐ 190 Roger Clemens SD	.50	.23	.06
☐ 191 David Cone SD	.25	.11	.03
☐ 192 Mike Mussina SD	.50	.23	.06
☐ 193 Randy Johnson SD	.50	.23	.06
☐ 194 Frank Thomas CL	1.25	.55	.16
☐ 195 Ken Griffey Jr. CL	1.25	.55	.16
☐ 196 Cal Ripken CL	1.00	.45	.12
☐ 197 Jeff Bagwell CL	.50	.23	.06
☐ 198 Mike Piazza CL	.75	.35	.09
☐ 199 Barry Bonds CL	.50	.23	.06
☐ 200 Mo Vaughn CL Matt Williams	.50	.23	.06

1995 Summit Nth Degree

This set is a parallel of the 200 regular cards from the Summit set and inserted one per four packs. The only difference between these cards and the regular set is that 'Nth degree' card fronts have a prismatic foil background.

	MINT	NRMT	EXC
COMPLETE SET (200)	400.00	180.00	50.00
COMMON CARD (1-200)	1.00	.45	.12

*STARS: 6X to 12X BASIC CARDS
*YOUNG STARS: 5X to 10X BASIC CARDS

1995 Summit Big Bang

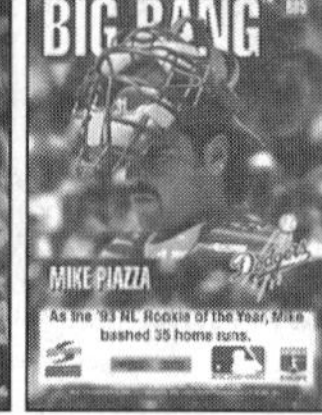

This 20-card set was randomly inserted in packs at a rate of one in 72. The set is comprised of the best home run hitters in the game. The set uses a process called "Spectrotech" which allows the card to be made of foil and have a holographic image. The fronts have an action photo with a game background which also shows the player. The backs have a player photo and information on his power exploits.

	MINT	NRMT	EXC
COMPLETE SET (20)	400.00	180.00	50.00
COMMON CARD (BB1-BB20)	6.00	2.70	.75
☐ BB1 Ken Griffey Jr.	60.00	27.00	7.50
☐ BB2 Frank Thomas	60.00	27.00	7.50
☐ BB3 Cal Ripken	50.00	22.00	6.25
☐ BB4 Jeff Bagwell	25.00	11.00	3.10
☐ BB5 Mike Piazza	40.00	18.00	5.00
☐ BB6 Barry Bonds	15.00	6.75	1.85
☐ BB7 Matt Williams	8.00	3.60	1.00
☐ BB8 Don Mattingly	30.00	13.50	3.70
☐ BB9 Will Clark	8.00	3.60	1.00
☐ BB10 Tony Gwynn	25.00	11.00	3.10
☐ BB11 Kirby Puckett	25.00	11.00	3.10
☐ BB12 Jose Canseco	8.00	3.60	1.00
☐ BB13 Paul Molitor	12.00	5.50	1.50
☐ BB14 Albert Belle	25.00	11.00	3.10
☐ BB15 Joe Carter	6.00	2.70	.75
☐ BB16 Rafael Palmeiro	8.00	3.60	1.00
☐ BB17 Fred McGriff	8.00	3.60	1.00
☐ BB18 David Justice	6.00	2.70	.75
☐ BB19 Tim Salmon	8.00	3.60	1.00
☐ BB20 Mo Vaughn	15.00	6.75	1.85

1995 Summit New Age

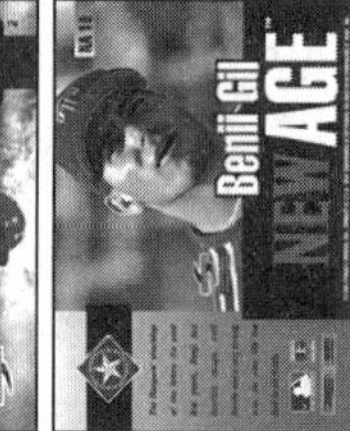

This 15-card set was randomly inserted in packs at a rate of one in 18. The set is comprised 15 of the best young players in baseball. The fronts are horizontally designed and have a color-action photo with a background of a baseball stadium with a red and gray background. The backs have a photo with player information and the words "New Age" at the bottom in red and white.

	MINT	NRMT	EXC
COMPLETE SET (15)	60.00	27.00	7.50
COMMON CARD (NA1-NA15)	1.50	.70	.19
☐ NA1 Cliff Floyd	3.00	1.35	.35
☐ NA2 Manny Ramirez	8.00	3.60	1.00
☐ NA3 Raul Mondesi	4.00	1.80	.50
☐ NA4 Alex Rodriguez	30.00	13.50	3.70
☐ NA5 Billy Ashley	1.50	.70	.19
☐ NA6 Alex Gonzalez	1.50	.70	.19
☐ NA7 Michael Tucker	1.50	.70	.19
☐ NA8 Charles Johnson	3.00	1.35	.35
☐ NA9 Carlos Delgado	4.00	1.80	.50
☐ NA10 Benji Gil	1.50	.70	.19
☐ NA11 Chipper Jones	20.00	9.00	2.50
☐ NA12 Todd Hollandsworth	4.00	1.80	.50
☐ NA13 Frankie Rodriguez	1.50	.70	.19
☐ NA14 Shawn Green	3.00	1.35	.35
☐ NA15 Ray Durham	3.00	1.35	.35

1995 Summit 21 Club

This nine-card set was randomly inserted in packs at a rate of one in 36. The set is comprised of young players with bright futures. Both sides of the card are done in foil with the front having a color photo with a gold background with "21 Club" in gray and red in the bottom right hand corner. The backs are laid out horizontally with a player head shot and information done in foil.

	MINT	NRMT	EXC
COMPLETE SET (9)	40.00	18.00	5.00
COMMON CARD (TC1-TC9)	4.00	1.80	.50
☐ TC1 Bob Abreu	10.00	4.50	1.25
☐ TC2 Pokey Reese	4.00	1.80	.50
☐ TC3 Edgardo Alfonzo	4.00	1.80	.50
☐ TC4 Jim Pittsley	4.00	1.80	.50
☐ TC5 Ruben Rivera	12.00	5.50	1.50
☐ TC6 Chan Ho Park	4.00	1.80	.50
☐ TC7 Julian Tavarez	4.00	1.80	.50
☐ TC8 Ismael Valdes	8.00	3.60	1.00
☐ TC9 Dmitri Young	6.00	2.70	.75

1996 Summit

The 1996 Summit set was issued in one series totalling 200 cards. The seven-card packs had a suggested retail of $2.99 each. The fronts feature color player photos on a gold striped black background. The backs carry another player photo with player information and statistics.

	MINT	NRMT	EXC
COMPLETE SET (200)	30.00	13.50	3.70
COMMON CARD (1-200)	.10	.05	.01

☐ 1 Mike Piazza	2.00	.90	.25
☐ 2 Matt Williams	.50	.23	.06
☐ 3 Tino Martinez	.25	.11	.03
☐ 4 Reggie Sanders	.25	.11	.03
☐ 5 Ray Durham	.50	.23	.06
☐ 6 Brad Radke	.10	.05	.01
☐ 7 Jeff Bagwell	1.25	.55	.16
☐ 8 Ron Gant	.25	.11	.03
☐ 9 Lance Johnson	.25	.11	.03
☐ 10 Kevin Seitzer	.10	.05	.01
☐ 11 Dante Bichette	.50	.23	.06
☐ 12 Ivan Rodriguez	.75	.35	.09
☐ 13 Jim Abbott	.50	.23	.06
☐ 14 Greg Colbrunn	.10	.05	.01
☐ 15 Rondell White	.25	.11	.03
☐ 16 Shawn Green	.10	.05	.01
☐ 17 Gregg Jefferies	.25	.11	.03
☐ 18 Omar Vizquel	.25	.11	.03
☐ 19 Cal Ripken	2.50	1.10	.30
☐ 20 Mark McGwire	1.00	.45	.12
☐ 21 Wally Joyner	.10	.05	.01
☐ 22 Chili Davis	.10	.05	.01
☐ 23 Jose Canseco	.50	.23	.06
☐ 24 Royce Clayton	.10	.05	.01
☐ 25 Jay Bell	.10	.05	.01
☐ 26 Travis Fryman	.25	.11	.03
☐ 27 Jeff King	.10	.05	.01
☐ 28 Todd Hundley	.25	.11	.03
☐ 29 Joe Vitiello	.10	.05	.01
☐ 30 Russ Davis	.10	.05	.01
☐ 31 Mo Vaughn	.75	.35	.09
☐ 32 Raul Mondesi	.50	.23	.06
☐ 33 Ray Lankford	.25	.11	.03
☐ 34 Mike Stanley	.10	.05	.01
☐ 35 B.J. Surhoff	.10	.05	.01
☐ 36 Greg Vaughn	.50	.23	.06
☐ 37 Todd Stottlemyre	.10	.05	.01
☐ 38 Carlos Delgado	.25	.11	.03
☐ 39 Kenny Lofton	.75	.35	.09
☐ 40 Hideo Nomo	.75	.35	.09
☐ 41 Sterling Hitchcock	.10	.05	.01
☐ 42 Pete Schourek	.10	.05	.01
☐ 43 Edgardo Alfonzo	.25	.11	.03
☐ 44 Ken Hill	.25	.11	.03
☐ 45 Ken Caminiti	.50	.23	.06
☐ 46 Bobby Higginson	.25	.11	.03
☐ 47 Michael Tucker	.25	.11	.03
☐ 48 David Cone	.25	.11	.03
☐ 49 Cecil Fielder	.25	.11	.03
☐ 50 Brian L. Hunter	.25	.11	.03
☐ 51 Charles Johnson	.25	.11	.03
☐ 52 Bobby Bonilla	.25	.11	.03
☐ 53 Eddie Murray	.75	.35	.09
☐ 54 Kenny Rogers	.10	.05	.01
☐ 55 Jim Edmonds	.25	.11	.03
☐ 56 Trevor Hoffman	.25	.11	.03
☐ 57 Kevin Mtchell UER	.10	.05	.01
☐ 58 Ruben Sierra	.10	.05	.01
☐ 59 Benji Gil	.10	.05	.01
☐ 60 Juan Gonzalez	1.50	.70	.19
☐ 61 Larry Walker	.50	.23	.06
☐ 62 Jack McDowell	.50	.23	.06
☐ 63 Shawon Dunston	.10	.05	.01
☐ 64 Andy Benes	.10	.05	.01
☐ 65 Jay Buhner	.50	.23	.06
☐ 66 Rickey Henderson	.50	.23	.06
☐ 67 Alex Gonzalez	.10	.05	.01
☐ 68 Mike Kelly	.10	.05	.01
☐ 69 Fred McGriff	.50	.23	.06
☐ 70 Ryne Sandberg	.75	.35	.09
☐ 71 Ernie Young	.10	.05	.01
☐ 72 Kevin Appier	.25	.11	.03
☐ 73 Moises Alou	.25	.11	.03
☐ 74 John Jaha	.25	.11	.03
☐ 75 J.T. Snow	.10	.05	.01
☐ 76 Jim Thome	.60	.25	.07
☐ 77 Kirby Puckett	1.25	.55	.16
☐ 78 Hal Morris	.10	.05	.01
☐ 79 Robin Ventura	.25	.11	.03
☐ 80 Ben McDonald	.10	.05	.01
☐ 81 Tim Salmon	.50	.23	.06
☐ 82 Albert Belle	1.25	.55	.16
☐ 83 Marquis Grissom	.25	.11	.03
☐ 84 Alex Rodriguez	3.00	1.35	.35
☐ 85 Manny Ramirez	.75	.35	.09
☐ 86 Ken Griffey Jr.	3.00	1.35	.35
☐ 87 Sammy Sosa	.50	.23	.06
☐ 88 Frank Thomas	3.00	1.35	.35
☐ 89 Lee Smith	.25	.11	.03
☐ 90 Marty Cordova	.25	.11	.03
☐ 91 Greg Maddux	2.00	.90	.25
☐ 92 Lenny Dykstra	.25	.11	.03
☐ 93 Butch Huskey	.25	.11	.03
☐ 94 Garret Anderson	.50	.23	.06
☐ 95 Mike Bordick	.25	.11	.03
☐ 96 Dave Justice	.25	.11	.03
☐ 97 Chad Curtis	.10	.05	.01
☐ 98 Carlos Baerga	.25	.11	.03
☐ 99 Jason Isringhausen	.50	.23	.06
☐ 100 Gary Sheffield	.50	.23	.06
☐ 101 Roger Clemens	.60	.25	.07
☐ 102 Ozzie Smith	.75	.35	.09
☐ 103 Ramon Martinez	.25	.11	.03
☐ 104 Paul O'Neill	.10	.05	.01
☐ 105 Will Clark	.50	.23	.06
☐ 106 Tom Glavine	.50	.23	.06
☐ 107 Barry Bonds	.75	.35	.09
☐ 108 Barry Larkin	.50	.23	.06
☐ 109 Derek Bell	.25	.11	.03
☐ 110 Randy Johnson	.50	.23	.06
☐ 111 Jeff Conine	.25	.11	.03
☐ 112 John Mabry	.25	.11	.03
☐ 113 Julian Tavarez	.10	.05	.01
☐ 114 Gary DiSarcina	.10	.05	.01
☐ 115 Andres Galarraga	.50	.23	.06
☐ 116 Marc Newfield	.25	.11	.03
☐ 117 Frank Rodriguez	.25	.11	.03
☐ 118 Brady Anderson	.50	.23	.06
☐ 119 Mike Mussina	.60	.25	.07
☐ 120 Orlando Merced	.25	.11	.03
☐ 121 Melvin Nieves	.25	.11	.03
☐ 122 Brian Jordan	.25	.11	.03
☐ 123 Rafael Palmeiro	.50	.23	.06
☐ 124 Johnny Damon	.25	.11	.03
☐ 125 Wil Cordero	.10	.05	.01
☐ 126 Chipper Jones	2.00	.90	.25
☐ 127 Eric Karros	.25	.11	.03
☐ 128 Darren Daulton	.25	.11	.03
☐ 129 Vinny Castilla	.25	.11	.03
☐ 130 Joe Carter	.25	.11	.03
☐ 131 Bernie Williams	.60	.25	.07
☐ 132 Bernard Gilkey	.25	.11	.03
☐ 133 Bret Boone	.10	.05	.01
☐ 134 Tony Gwynn	1.25	.55	.16
☐ 135 Dave Nilsson	.25	.11	.03
☐ 136 Ryan Klesko	.50	.23	.06
☐ 137 Paul Molitor	.60	.25	.07
☐ 138 John Olerud	.10	.05	.01
☐ 139 Craig Biggio	.25	.11	.03
☐ 140 John Valentin	.25	.11	.03
☐ 141 Chuck Knoblauch	.50	.23	.06
☐ 142 Edgar Martinez	.25	.11	.03
☐ 143 Rico Brogna	.10	.05	.01
☐ 144 Dean Palmer	.50	.23	.06
☐ 145 Mark Grace	.50	.23	.06
☐ 146 Roberto Alomar	.60	.25	.07
☐ 147 Alex Fernandez	.25	.11	.03
☐ 148 Andre Dawson	.25	.11	.03
☐ 149 Wade Boggs	.50	.23	.06
☐ 150 Mark Lewis	.10	.05	.01
☐ 151 Gary Gaetti	.25	.11	.03
☐ 152 Paul Wilson Roger Clemens	.25	.11	.03
☐ 153 Rey Ordonez Ozzie Smith	.25	.11	.03
☐ 154 Derek Jeter Cal Ripken	1.50	.70	.19
☐ 155 Andy Benes Alan Benes	.10	.05	.01
☐ 156 Jason Kendall Mike Piazza	.75	.35	.09
☐ 157 Ryan Klesko Frank Thomas	1.00	.45	.12
☐ 158 Johnny Damon Ken Griffey Jr.	1.00	.45	.12
☐ 159 Karim Garcia Sammy Sosa	.10	.05	.01
☐ 160 Raul Mondesi Tim Salmon	.10	.05	.01
☐ 161 Chipper Jones Matt Williams	.75	.35	.09
☐ 162 Rey Ordonez	.50	.23	.06
☐ 163 Bob Wolcott	.10	.05	.01
☐ 164 Brooks Kieschnick	.50	.23	.06
☐ 165 Steve Gibralter	.10	.05	.01
☐ 166 Bob Abreu	.50	.23	.06
☐ 167 Greg Zaun	.10	.05	.01
☐ 168 Tavo Alvarez	.10	.05	.01
☐ 169 Sal Fasano	.10	.05	.01
☐ 170 George Arias	.10	.05	.01
☐ 171 Derek Jeter	2.00	.90	.25
☐ 172 Livan Hernandez	.50	.23	.06
☐ 173 Alan Benes	.50	.23	.06
☐ 174 George Williams	.10	.05	.01
☐ 175 John Wasdin	.10	.05	.01
☐ 176 Chan Ho Park	.50	.23	.06
☐ 177 Paul Wilson	.25	.11	.03
☐ 178 Jeff Suppan	.50	.23	.06
☐ 179 Quinton McCracken	.10	.05	.01
☐ 180 Wilton Guerrero	1.50	.70	.19
☐ 181 Eric Owens	.10	.05	.01
☐ 182 Felipe Crespo	.10	.05	.01
☐ 183 LaTroy Hawkins	.10	.05	.01
☐ 184 Jason Schmidt	.50	.23	.06
☐ 185 Terrell Wade	.25	.11	.03
☐ 186 Mike Grace	.10	.05	.01
☐ 187 Chris Snopek	.10	.05	.01
☐ 188 Jason Kendall	.50	.23	.06
☐ 189 Todd Hollandsworth	.25	.11	.03
☐ 190 Jim Pittsley	.25	.11	.03
☐ 191 Jermaine Dye	.60	.25	.07
☐ 192 Mike Busby	.10	.05	.01
☐ 193 Richard Hidalgo	.50	.23	.06
☐ 194 Tyler Houston	.10	.05	.01
☐ 195 Jimmy Haynes	.10	.05	.01
☐ 196 Karim Garcia	.60	.25	.07
☐ 197 Ken Griffey Jr. CL	1.50	.70	.19
☐ 198 Frank Thomas CL	1.50	.70	.19
☐ 199 Greg Maddux CL	1.00	.45	.12
☐ 200 Cal Ripken CL	1.25	.55	.16

1996 Summit Above Beyond

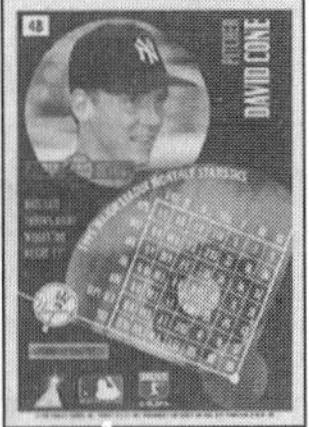

Randomly inserted in packs at a rate of one in four, this 200-card set is parallel to the regular set and is similar in design. The prismatic foil background distinguishes it from the regular set.

	MINT	NRMT	EXC
COMPLETE SET (200)	500.00	220.00	60.00
COMMON CARD (1-200)	1.50	.70	.19

*STARS: 6X to 12X BASIC CARDS
*YOUNG STARS: 5X to 10X BASIC CARDS

1996 Summit Artist's Proofs

Randomly inserted in packs at a rate of one in 36, this 200-card set is parallel to the regular set and is similar in design with the foil stamped Artist's Proof logo on the front.

	MINT	NRMT	EXC
COMPLETE SET (200)	2500.00	1100.00	300.00
COMMON CARD (1-200)	4.00	1.80	.50

*STARS: 25X TO 50X BASIC CARDS
*YOUNG STARS: 20X TO 40X BASIC CARDS

1996 Summit Foil

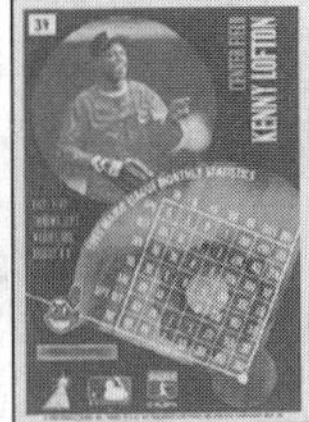

Available exclusively through seven-card retail Super Packs (SRP $2.99), these foil cards parallel the basic 200-card Summit set. The micro-etched foil card fronts distinguishes them from basic cards.

	MINT	NRMT	EXC
COMPLETE SET (200)	50.00	22.00	6.25
COMMON CARD (1-200)	.15	.07	.02

*STARS: 1.5X BASIC CARDS
*YOUNG STARS: 1.5X BASIC CARDS

1996 Summit Ballparks

Randomly inserted in packs at a rate of one in seven, this 18-card set features color action player photos on picture backgrounds of their home ballparks. The backs carry the name of the ballparks and players statistics.

	MINT	NRMT	EXC
COMPLETE SET (18)	150.00	70.00	19.00
COMMON CARD (1-18)	3.00	1.35	.35
☐ 1 Cal Ripken	20.00	9.00	2.50
☐ 2 Albert Belle	10.00	4.50	1.25
☐ 3 Dante Bichette	5.00	2.20	.60
☐ 4 Mo Vaughn	6.00	2.70	.75
☐ 5 Ken Griffey Jr.	25.00	11.00	3.10
☐ 6 Derek Jeter	15.00	6.75	1.85
☐ 7 Juan Gonzalez	12.00	5.50	1.50
☐ 8 Greg Maddux	15.00	6.75	1.85
☐ 9 Frank Thomas	25.00	11.00	3.10
☐ 10 Ryne Sandberg	6.00	2.70	.75
☐ 11 Mike Piazza	15.00	6.75	1.85
☐ 12 Johnny Damon	3.00	1.35	.35
☐ 13 Barry Bonds	6.00	2.70	.75
☐ 14 Jeff Bagwell	10.00	4.50	1.25
☐ 15 Paul Wilson	3.00	1.35	.35
☐ 16 Tim Salmon	5.00	2.20	.60
☐ 17 Kirby Puckett	10.00	4.50	1.25
☐ 18 Tony Gwynn	10.00	4.50	1.25

1996 Summit Big Bang

Randomly inserted in packs at a rate of one in 72, this 16-card set features the League's big hitters on Spectroetched backgrounds with etched foil highlights. Only 600 sets were produced and each card is individually numbered of 600 on back.The backs carry a player portrait in a diamond with a faded version of the front as a background and information about the player.

	MINT	NRMT	EXC
COMPLETE SET (16)	750.00	350.00	95.00
COMMON CARD (1-16)	10.00	4.50	1.25
☐ 1 Frank Thomas	125.00	55.00	15.50
☐ 2 Ken Griffey Jr.	125.00	55.00	15.50
☐ 3 Albert Belle	50.00	22.00	6.25
☐ 4 Mo Vaughn	30.00	13.50	3.70
☐ 5 Barry Bonds	30.00	13.50	3.70
☐ 6 Cal Ripken	100.00	45.00	12.50
☐ 7 Jeff Bagwell	50.00	22.00	6.25
☐ 8 Mike Piazza	80.00	36.00	10.00
☐ 9 Ryan Klesko	20.00	9.00	2.50
☐ 10 Manny Ramirez	30.00	13.50	3.70
☐ 11 Tim Salmon	15.00	6.75	1.85
☐ 12 Dante Bichette	15.00	6.75	1.85
☐ 13 Sammy Sosa	20.00	9.00	2.50
☐ 14 Raul Mondesi	15.00	6.75	1.85
☐ 15 Chipper Jones	80.00	36.00	10.00
☐ 16 Garret Anderson	10.00	4.50	1.25

1996 Summit Big Bang Mirage

Randomly inserted at a rate of one in 72, this 16-card set is parallel to the regular insert set and was printed with new holographic technology that created a floating background. When held in direct sunlight or an incandescent bulb, three dimensions and a floating baseball that seems to levitate could be seen in the background. Only 600 sets were produced and each card is numbered individually of 600 on the back. Collectors that managed to piece together a complete set could then send it in to Pinnacle in exchange for one box of every 1997 Pinnacle baseball product. Collectors that managed to piece together a complete set with matching print numbers could exchange that set for one box of every 1997 Pinnacle product from every sport.

	MINT	NRMT	EXC
COMPLETE SET (16)	750.00	350.00	95.00
COMMON CARD (1-16)	10.00	4.50	1.25
*MIRAGE: 1X BASIC CARDS			

1996 Summit Hitters Inc.

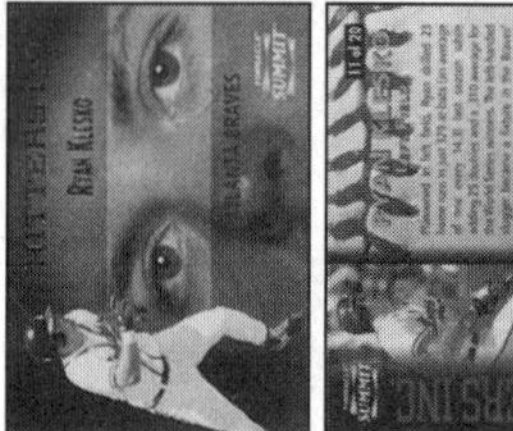

Randomly inserted in packs at a rate of one in 36, this 16-card set features color action player images with embossed highlights on an enlarged photo of the player's eyes for background. The backs carry information about the player's batting ability.

	MINT	NRMT	EXC
COMPLETE SET (16)	250.00	110.00	31.00
COMMON CARD (1-16)	5.00	2.20	.60
☐ 1 Tony Gwynn	15.00	6.75	1.85
☐ 2 Mo Vaughn	10.00	4.50	1.25
☐ 3 Tim Salmon	5.00	2.20	.60
☐ 4 Ken Griffey Jr.	40.00	18.00	5.00
☐ 5 Sammy Sosa	6.00	2.70	.75
☐ 6 Frank Thomas	40.00	18.00	5.00
☐ 7 Wade Boggs	5.00	2.20	.60
☐ 8 Albert Belle	15.00	6.75	1.85
☐ 9 Cal Ripken	30.00	13.50	3.70
☐ 10 Manny Ramirez	10.00	4.50	1.25
☐ 11 Ryan Klesko	6.00	2.70	.75
☐ 12 Dante Bichette	5.00	2.20	.60
☐ 13 Mike Piazza	25.00	11.00	3.10
☐ 14 Chipper Jones	25.00	11.00	3.10
☐ 15 Ryne Sandberg	10.00	4.50	1.25
☐ 16 Matt Williams	5.00	2.20	.60

1996 Summit Positions

Randomly inserted in Magazine packs only at the rate of one in 50, this nine-card set honors the best players at each playing position. The fronts feature color action player images on a baseball diamond background with head photos of the players at the bottom. The backs carry information about how well the players perform at their position.

	MINT	NRMT	EXC
COMPLETE SET (9)	325.00	145.00	40.00
COMMON CARD (1-9)	20.00	9.00	2.50
☐ 1 Jeff Bagwell	60.00	27.00	7.50
Mo Vaughn			
Frank Thomas			
☐ 2 Roberto Alomar	20.00	9.00	2.50
Craig Biggio			
Chuck Knoblauch			
☐ 3 Matt Williams	40.00	18.00	5.00
Jim Thome			
Chipper Jones			
☐ 4 Barry Larkin	80.00	36.00	10.00
Cal Ripken			
Alex Rodriguez			
☐ 5 Mike Piazza	40.00	18.00	5.00
Ivan Rodriguez			
Charles Johnson			
☐ 6 Hideo Nomo	40.00	18.00	5.00
Greg Maddux			
Randy Johnson			
☐ 7 Barry Bonds	30.00	13.50	3.70
Albert Belle			
Ryan Klesko			
☐ 8 Johnny Damon	50.00	22.00	6.25
Jim Edmonds			
Ken Griffey Jr.			
☐ 9 Manny Ramirez	20.00	9.00	2.50
Gary Sheffield			
Sammy Sosa			

1974 Sun-Glo Pop Kaline

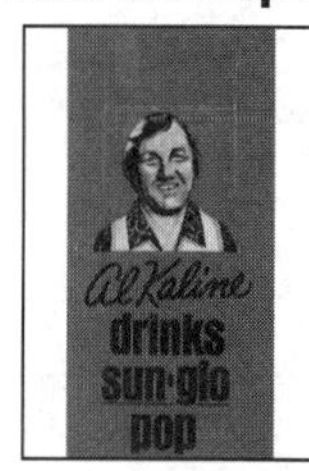

Sun-Glo Pop issued this card attached to a bottle of pop. The bright green card has a black and white portrait of Al Kaline (not in uniform) with his name printed in black script lettering below followed by the words "drinks Sun-Glo pop". The back is blank.

	NRMT	VG-E	GOOD
COMPLETE SET (1)	5.00	2.20	.60
COMMON CARD	5.00	2.20	.60
☐ 1 Al Kaline	5.00	2.20	.60

1990 Sunflower Seeds

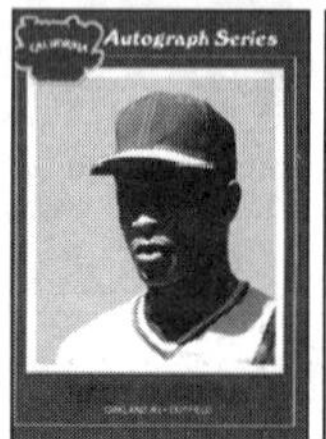

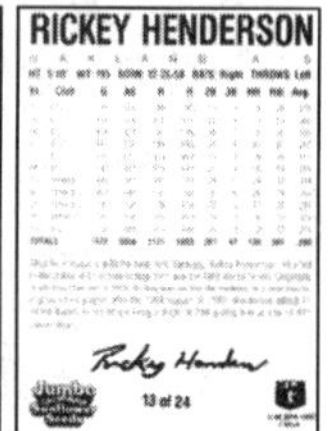

This 24-card, standard-size set is an attractive set which frames the players photo by solid blue borders. In the upper left hand of the card the description, Jumbo California Sunflower Seeds, was placed and underneath the photo is the player's name in red and the team name in very small printing in white. The back of the card features the complete major league record of the player and a short write up as well. This set was issued by Stagi and Scriven Farms Inc. with the cooperation of Michael Schechter Associates (MSA) and features some of the big-name stars in baseball at the time of printing of the set. The set was an attempt by the company to promote sunflower seeds as an alternative to chewing tobacco in the dugout. Three cards were available as an insert in each specially marked bag of Jumbo California Sunflower Seeds.

	MINT	NRMT	EXC
COMPLETE SET (24)	15.00	6.75	1.85
COMMON CARD (1-24)	.25	.11	.03
☐ 1 Kevin Mitchell	.25	.11	.03
☐ 2 Ken Griffey Jr.	5.00	2.20	.60
☐ 3 Howard Johnson	.25	.11	.03
☐ 4 Bo Jackson	.50	.23	.06
☐ 5 Kirby Puckett	3.00	1.35	.35
☐ 6 Robin Yount	.75	.35	.09
☐ 7 Dave Stieb	.25	.11	.03
☐ 8 Don Mattingly	3.00	1.35	.35
☐ 9 Barry Bonds	1.25	.55	.16
☐ 10 Pedro Guerrero	.25	.11	.03
☐ 11 Tony Gwynn	3.00	1.35	.35
☐ 12 Von Hayes	.25	.11	.03
☐ 13 Rickey Henderson	1.00	.45	.12
☐ 14 Tim Raines	.25	.11	.03
☐ 15 Alan Trammell	.50	.23	.06
☐ 16 Dave Stewart	.25	.11	.03
☐ 17 Will Clark	1.50	.70	.19
☐ 18 Roger Clemens	1.50	.70	.19
☐ 19 Wally Joyner	.50	.23	.06
☐ 20 Ryne Sandberg	2.50	1.10	.30
☐ 21 Eric Davis	.50	.23	.06
☐ 22 Mike Scott	.25	.11	.03
☐ 23 Cal Ripken	4.00	1.80	.50
☐ 24 Eddie Murray	1.25	.55	.16

1991 Sunflower Seeds

This 24-card, standard-size set was sponsored by Jumbo California Sunflower Seeds. The posed color player photos are framed by white and yellow borders on a red background. The company logo and the words "Autograph Series II" appear above the photo, with the player's name, team, and position given below the picture. A facsimile autograph is inscribed across the picture. The backs are printed in red on white and present Major League statistics and career highlights. The set was again issued by Stagi and Scriven Farms Inc. with the cooperation of Michael Schechter Associates (MSA). The set was another attempt by the company to promote sunflower seeds as an alternative to chewing tobacco in the dugout. Two cards were available as an insert in each specially marked bag of Jumbo California Sunflower Seeds.

	MINT	NRMT	EXC
COMPLETE SET (24)	10.00	4.50	1.25
COMMON CARD (1-24)	.25	.11	.03
☐ 1 Ozzie Smith	1.50	.70	.19
☐ 2 Wade Boggs	.75	.35	.09
☐ 3 Bobby Bonilla	.50	.23	.06
☐ 4 George Brett	1.50	.70	.19
☐ 5 Kal Daniels	.25	.11	.03
☐ 6 Glenn Davis	.25	.11	.03
☐ 7 Chuck Finley	.25	.11	.03
☐ 8 Cecil Fielder	.50	.23	.06
☐ 9 Len Dykstra	.50	.23	.06
☐ 10 Dwight Gooden	.50	.23	.06
☐ 11 Ken Griffey Jr.	3.00	1.35	.35
☐ 12 Kelly Gruber	.25	.11	.03
☐ 13 Kent Hrbek	.25	.11	.03
☐ 14 Andre Dawson	.50	.23	.06
☐ 15 Dave Justice	.75	.35	.09
☐ 16 Barry Larkin	.75	.35	.09
☐ 17 Ben McDonald	.50	.23	.06
☐ 18 Mark McGwire	1.00	.45	.12
☐ 19 Roberto Alomar	.75	.35	.09
☐ 20 Nolan Ryan	2.50	1.10	.30
☐ 21 Sandy Alomar Jr.	.50	.23	.06
☐ 22 Bobby Thigpen	.25	.11	.03
☐ 23 Tim Wallach	.25	.11	.03
☐ 24 Matt Williams	.75	.35	.09

1992 Sunflower Seeds

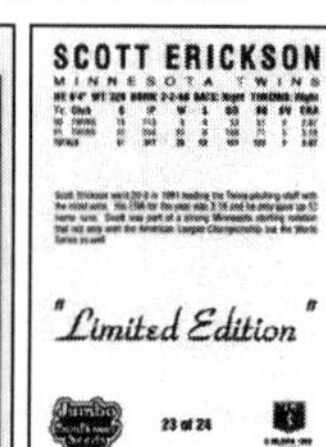

This 24-card, standard-size set was sponsored by Jumbo California Sunflower Seeds and produced by Michael Schechter Associates (MSA). The posed color player photos are framed in white and bright blue on a white background. The company log appears in the upper left corner. The words "Autograph Series III" are printed in red at the top. The player's name, team, and position are given in the blue border below the picture. A facsimile autograph is inscribed across the picture. The backs feature statistical information and career highlights printed in blue on a white background.

	MINT	NRMT	EXC
COMPLETE SET (24)	10.00	4.50	1.25
COMMON CARD (1-24)	.25	.11	.03
☐ 1 Jeff Reardon	.25	.11	.03
☐ 2 Bill Gullickson	.25	.11	.03
☐ 3 Todd Zeile	.25	.11	.03
☐ 4 Terry Mulholland	.25	.11	.03
☐ 5 Kirby Puckett	1.50	.70	.19
☐ 6 Howard Johnson	.25	.11	.03
☐ 7 Terry Pendleton	.25	.11	.03
☐ 8 Will Clark	1.00	.45	.12
☐ 9 Cal Ripken	2.50	1.10	.30
☐ 10 Chris Sabo	.25	.11	.03
☐ 11 Jim Abbott	.25	.11	.03
☐ 12 Joe Carter	.50	.23	.06
☐ 13 Paul Molitor	1.00	.45	.12
☐ 14 Ken Griffey Jr.	3.00	1.35	.35
☐ 15 Randy Johnson	1.00	.45	.12
☐ 16 Bobby Bonilla	.50	.23	.06
☐ 17 John Smiley	.25	.11	.03
☐ 18 Jose Canseco	1.00	.45	.12
☐ 19 Tom Glavine	.75	.35	.09
☐ 20 Darryl Strawberry	.50	.23	.06
☐ 21 Brett Butler	.50	.23	.06
☐ 22 Devon White	.25	.11	.03
☐ 23 Scott Erickson	.25	.11	.03
☐ 24 Willie McGee	.25	.11	.03

1970 Sunoco Pins

These pins feature members of the Chicago Cubs and Milwaukee Brewers. The pins are approximately 1 1/8" in diameter. The photo used is black and white but the border colors are either red and white (for Milwaukee Brewers players) or blue and white (for Chicago Cubs players. Since the pins are unnumbered they are ordered below in alphabetical order within team, Chicago Cubs (1-9) and Milwaukee Brewers (10-18).

	NRMT	VG-E	GOOD
COMPLETE SET (18)	100.00	45.00	12.50
COMMON PIN (1-18)	4.00	1.80	.50
☐ 1 Ernie Banks	20.00	9.00	2.50
☐ 2 Glenn Beckert	4.00	1.80	.50
☐ 3 Jim Hickman	4.00	1.80	.50
☐ 4 Randy Hundley	4.00	1.80	.50
☐ 5 Ferguson Jenkins	10.00	4.50	1.25
☐ 6 Don Kessinger	5.00	2.20	.60
☐ 7 Joe Pepitone	7.50	3.40	.95
☐ 8 Ron Santo	7.50	3.40	.95
☐ 9 Billy Williams	15.00	6.75	1.85
☐ 10 Tommy Harper	4.00	1.80	.50
☐ 11 Mike Hegan	4.00	1.80	.50
☐ 12 Lew Krausse	4.00	1.80	.50
☐ 13 Ted Kubiak	4.00	1.80	.50
☐ 14 Marty Pattin	4.00	1.80	.50
☐ 15 Phil Roof	4.00	1.80	.50
☐ 16 Ken Sanders	4.00	1.80	.50
☐ 17 Ted Savage	4.00	1.80	.50
☐ 18 Danny Walton	4.00	1.80	.50

1994 SuperSlam McDowell Promos

Gold and silver-bordered versions of 3 1/2 by 5 color cutouts of Jack McDowell beginning his pitching delivery. Measure 5 1/2 by 7 1/2 outside dimensions. Can be unfolded and stood up. The creator of this concept was also one of the founders of the Upper Deck company.

	MINT	NRMT	EXC
COMPLETE SET (2)	10.00	4.50	1.25
COMMON CARD (1-2)	5.00	2.20	.60
☐ 1 Jack McDowell	5.00	2.20	.60
Silver border			
☐ 2 Jack McDowell	5.00	2.20	.60
Gold border			

1990 Superstar Action Marbles

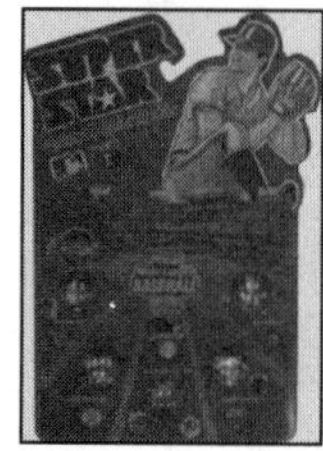

These collectible action marbles measure approximately 1" across. Each marble contains a color action player photo inside, and on the backside one finds the team logo. The marbles were issued in four sets, and each set showcases players from one of the four major divisions: 1) AL West (1-5); 2) AL East (6-10); 3) NL West (11-15); and 4) NL East (16-20). The marbles are unnumbered.

	MINT	NRMT	EXC
COMPLETE SET (20)	30.00	13.50	3.70
COMMON CARD (1-20)	1.00	.45	.12
☐ 1 Jim Abbott	1.00	.45	.12
☐ 2 Jose Canseco	3.00	1.35	.35
☐ 3 Ken Griffey Jr.	8.00	3.60	1.00
☐ 4 Kirby Puckett	4.00	1.80	.50
☐ 5 Nolan Ryan	6.00	2.70	.75
☐ 6 Robin Yount	2.00	.90	.25
☐ 7 Cecil Fielder	2.00	.90	.25
☐ 8 Cory Snyder	1.00	.45	.12
☐ 9 Fred McGriff	3.00	1.35	.35
☐ 10 Cal Ripken Jr.	6.00	2.70	.75
☐ 11 Ron Gant	1.00	.45	.12
☐ 12 Chris Sabo	1.00	.45	.12
☐ 13 Craig Biggio	2.00	.90	.25
☐ 14 Fernando Valenzuela	1.50	.70	.19
☐ 15 Benito Santiago	1.00	.45	.12
☐ 16 Tim Raines	1.00	.45	.12
☐ 17 Darryl Strawberry	1.50	.70	.19
☐ 18 Len Dykstra	1.50	.70	.19
☐ 19 Barry Bonds	2.00	.90	.25
☐ 20 Ryne Sandberg	3.00	1.35	.35

1974 Superstar Blank Backs

Little is known about this set. The biographies on the cards do not really help either, as the time frame mentioned on these cards range anywhere from the 1960's until 1972. These cards measure 2 1/4" by 3" and have color photos as well as brief biographies. The backs are blank. Hobbyists who have seen these cards believe that they are cut from record album covers. We have sequenced this set in alphabetical order.

	NRMT	VG-E	GOOD
COMPLETE SET (12)	60.00	27.00	7.50
COMMON CARD (1-12)	1.00	.45	.12
☐ 1 Ken Boyer	2.50	1.10	.30
☐ 2 Don Drysdale	6.00	2.70	.75
☐ 3 Whitey Ford	7.50	3.40	.95
☐ 4 Jim Gentile	1.00	.45	.12
☐ 5 Al Kaline	6.00	2.70	.75
☐ 6 Sandy Koufax	10.00	4.50	1.25
☐ 7 Mickey Mantle	20.00	9.00	2.50
☐ 8 Roger Maris	7.50	3.40	.95
☐ 9 Willie Mays	15.00	6.75	1.85
☐ 10 Bill Mazeroski	4.00	1.80	.50
☐ 11 Frank Robinson	7.50	3.40	.95
☐ 12 Pete Ward	1.00	.45	.12

1910 Sweet Caporal Pins P2

This unnumbered set is numbered here for convenience in alphabetical order by team, e.g., Boston Red Sox (1-7), Chicago White Sox (8-15), Cleveland Naps (16-21), Detroit Tigers (22-31), New York Yankees (32-39), Philadelphia A's (40-50), St. Louis Browns (51-56), Washington Senators (57-64), Boston Rustlers NL (65-68), Brooklyn Superbas (69-78), Chicago Cubs (79-93), Cincinnati Reds (94-105), New York Giants (106-123), Philadelphia Phillies (124-132), Pittsburgh Pirates (133-144) and St. Louis Cardinals (145-152). Pins with larger letters are worth more. Large letter variations are indicated below by LL. These pins were produced and distributed roughly between 1910 and 1912. Each pin measures approximately 7/8" in diameter. The pins are essentially brown and white. The complete set price below reflects the inclusion of all variations.

	EX-MT	VG-E	GOOD
COMPLETE SET (201)	4200.00	1900.00	525.00
COMMON PINS	10.00	4.50	1.25
COMMON LARGE LETTERS	15.00	6.75	1.85
☐ 1A Bill Carrigan	10.00	4.50	1.25
☐ 1B Bill Carrigan	15.00	6.75	1.85
☐ 2 Ed Cicotte	30.00	13.50	3.70
☐ 3A Clyde Engle	10.00	4.50	1.25
☐ 3B Clyde Engle	15.00	6.75	1.85
☐ 4 Harry Hooper	30.00	13.50	3.70
☐ 5 Ed Karger	10.00	4.50	1.25
☐ 6A Tris Speaker	50.00	22.00	6.25
☐ 6B Tris Speaker	60.00	27.00	7.50
☐ 7 Heine Wagner	10.00	4.50	1.25
☐ 8 Nixey Callahan	10.00	4.50	1.25
☐ 9 Patsy Dougherty	10.00	4.50	1.25
☐ 10A Hugh Duffy	35.00	16.00	4.40
☐ 10B Hugh Duffy	50.00	22.00	6.25
☐ 11A Harry Lord	10.00	4.50	1.25
☐ 11B Harry Lord	15.00	6.75	1.85
☐ 12A Matty McIntyre	10.00	4.50	1.25
☐ 12B Matty McIntyre	15.00	6.75	1.85
☐ 13 Fred Parent	10.00	4.50	1.25
☐ 14 Ed Walsh	30.00	13.50	3.70
☐ 15 Doc White	10.00	4.50	1.25
☐ 16 Neal Ball	10.00	4.50	1.25
☐ 17 Joe Birmingham	10.00	4.50	1.25
☐ 18 Napoleon Lajoie	60.00	27.00	7.50
☐ 19A George Stovall	10.00	4.50	1.25
☐ 19B George Stovall	25.00	11.00	3.10
☐ 20 Terry Turner	25.00	11.00	3.10
☐ 21A Cy Young	50.00	22.00	6.25
☐ 21B Cy Young Old Cy Young	60.00	27.00	7.50
☐ 22A Ty Cobb	350.00	160.00	45.00
☐ 22B Ty Cobb	400.00	180.00	50.00
☐ 23 Jim Delahanty	20.00	9.00	2.50
☐ 24 Bill Donovan	25.00	11.00	3.10
☐ 25A Hugh Jennings	30.00	13.50	3.70
☐ 25B Hugh Jennings	40.00	18.00	5.00
☐ 26 Tom Jones	25.00	11.00	3.10
☐ 27 Ed Killian	25.00	11.00	3.10
☐ 28A George Mullen (Mullin)	10.00	4.50	1.25
☐ 28B George Mullen (Mullin)	15.00	6.75	1.85
☐ 29 Charley O'Leary	10.00	4.50	1.25
☐ 30A Boss Schmidt	10.00	4.50	1.25
☐ 30B Boss Schmidt	15.00	6.75	1.85
☐ 31 Oscar Stanage	10.00	4.50	1.25
☐ 32A Hal Chase	30.00	13.50	3.70
☐ 32B Hal Chase	40.00	18.00	5.00
☐ 33 Birdie Cree	10.00	4.50	1.25
☐ 34A Russ Ford	10.00	4.50	1.25
☐ 34B Russ Ford	15.00	6.75	1.85
☐ 35 Ira Hemphill	10.00	4.50	1.25
☐ 36A Jack Knight	10.00	4.50	1.25
☐ 36B Jack Knight	15.00	6.75	1.85
☐ 37 Jack Quinn	10.00	4.50	1.25
☐ 38 Jack Warhop	25.00	11.00	3.10
☐ 39 Harry Wolter	10.00	4.50	1.25
☐ 40 Frank Baker	30.00	13.50	3.70
☐ 41 Jack Barry	10.00	4.50	1.25
☐ 42A Chief Bender	30.00	13.50	3.70
☐ 42B Chief Bender	40.00	18.00	5.00
☐ 43A Eddie Collins	35.00	16.00	4.40
☐ 43B Eddie Collins	50.00	22.00	6.25
☐ 44 Jimmy Dygert	10.00	4.50	1.25
☐ 45 Topsy Hartsel	10.00	4.50	1.25
☐ 46 Harry Krause	10.00	4.50	1.25
☐ 47 Paddy Livingston	10.00	4.50	1.25
☐ 48 Danny Murphy	10.00	4.50	1.25
☐ 49 Rube Oldring	10.00	4.50	1.25
☐ 50A Ira Thomas	10.00	4.50	1.25
☐ 50B Ira Thomas	15.00	6.75	1.85
☐ 51A Jimmy Austin	10.00	4.50	1.25
☐ 51B Jimmy Austin	15.00	6.75	1.85
☐ 52 Danny Hoffman	10.00	4.50	1.25
☐ 53A Frank LaPorte	10.00	4.50	1.25
☐ 53B Frank LaPorte	15.00	6.75	1.85
☐ 54 Barney Pelty	10.00	4.50	1.25
☐ 55 George Stone	10.00	4.50	1.25
☐ 56A Bobby Wallace	30.00	13.50	3.70
☐ 56B Bobby Wallace	50.00	22.00	6.25
☐ 57A Kid Elberfeld	10.00	4.50	1.25
☐ 57B Kid Elberfeld	15.00	6.75	1.85
☐ 58 Dolly Gray	10.00	4.50	1.25
☐ 59 Bob Groom	10.00	4.50	1.25
☐ 60A Walter Johnson	80.00	36.00	10.00
☐ 60B Walter Johnson	100.00	45.00	12.50
☐ 61 George McBride	10.00	4.50	1.25
☐ 62 Clyde Milan	15.00	6.75	1.85
☐ 63 Germany Schaefer	15.00	6.75	1.85
☐ 64A Gabby Street	10.00	4.50	1.25
☐ 64B Gabby Street	15.00	6.75	1.85
☐ 65 Ed Abbaticchio	10.00	4.50	1.25
☐ 66 Cecil Ferguson	10.00	4.50	1.25
☐ 67 Buck Herzog	10.00	4.50	1.25
☐ 68A Al Mattern	10.00	4.50	1.25
☐ 68B Al Mattern	15.00	6.75	1.85
☐ 69 Cy Barger	10.00	4.50	1.25
☐ 70A George Bell	10.00	4.50	1.25
☐ 70B George Bell	15.00	6.75	1.85
☐ 71 Bill Bergen	10.00	4.50	1.25
☐ 72 Bill Dahlen	20.00	9.00	2.50
☐ 73 Tex Erwin	10.00	4.50	1.25
☐ 74 John Hummel	10.00	4.50	1.25
☐ 75A Nap Rucker	15.00	6.75	1.85
☐ 75B Nap Rucker	20.00	9.00	2.50
☐ 76 Doc Scanlon	20.00	9.00	2.50
☐ 77 Hap Smith	10.00	4.50	1.25
☐ 78A Zach Wheat	30.00	13.50	3.70
☐ 78B Zach Wheat	40.00	18.00	5.00
☐ 79A Jimmy Archer	10.00	4.50	1.25
☐ 79B Jimmy Archer	15.00	6.75	1.85
☐ 80A Mordecai Brown	30.00	13.50	3.70
☐ 80B Mordecai Brown	40.00	18.00	5.00
☐ 81A Frank Chance	40.00	18.00	5.00
☐ 81B Frank Chance	50.00	22.00	6.25
☐ 82 Johnny Evers	40.00	18.00	5.00
☐ 83 Rube Kroh	10.00	4.50	1.25
☐ 84 Harry McIntire	10.00	4.50	1.25
☐ 85 Tom Needham	15.00	6.75	1.85
☐ 86 Orval Overall	20.00	9.00	2.50
☐ 87 Jake Pfiester	10.00	4.50	1.25
☐ 88 Ed Reulbach	15.00	6.75	1.85
☐ 89 Lew Richie	10.00	4.50	1.25
☐ 90 Wildfire Schulte	15.00	6.75	1.85
☐ 91 Jimmy Sheckard	10.00	4.50	1.25
☐ 92 Harry Steinfeldt	15.00	6.75	1.85
☐ 93A Joe Tinker	40.00	18.00	5.00
☐ 93B Joe Tinker	50.00	22.00	6.25
☐ 94 Johnny Bates	10.00	4.50	1.25
☐ 95 Fred Beebe	10.00	4.50	1.25
☐ 96 Bob Bescher	15.00	6.75	1.85
☐ 97A Tom Downey	10.00	4.50	1.25
☐ 97B Tom Downey	15.00	6.75	1.85
☐ 98 Art Fromme	10.00	4.50	1.25
☐ 99 Harry Gaspar	10.00	4.50	1.25
☐ 100 Eddie Grant	10.00	4.50	1.25
☐ 101A Clark Griffith	30.00	13.50	3.70
☐ 101B Clark Griffith	40.00	18.00	5.00
☐ 102 Dick Hoblitzell	10.00	4.50	1.25
☐ 103A Larry McLean	10.00	4.50	1.25
☐ 103B Larry McLean	15.00	6.75	1.85
☐ 104 Mike Mitchell	10.00	4.50	1.25
☐ 105 George Suggs	10.00	4.50	1.25
☐ 106 Red Ames	10.00	4.50	1.25
☐ 107 Beals Becker	10.00	4.50	1.25
☐ 108 Al Bridwell	10.00	4.50	1.25
☐ 109 Doc Crandall	10.00	4.50	1.25
☐ 110 Art Devlin	10.00	4.50	1.25
☐ 111 Josh Devore	10.00	4.50	1.25
☐ 112A Larry Doyle	15.00	6.75	1.85
☐ 112B Larry Doyle	20.00	9.00	2.50
☐ 113 Louis Drucke	10.00	4.50	1.25
☐ 114 Buck Herzog	10.00	4.50	1.25
☐ 115 Arlie Latham	10.00	4.50	1.25
☐ 116 Rube Marquard	30.00	13.50	3.70
☐ 117A Christy Mathewson	80.00	36.00	10.00
☐ 117B Christy Mathewson	110.00	50.00	14.00
☐ 118A John McGraw	40.00	18.00	5.00
☐ 118B John McGraw	60.00	27.00	7.50
☐ 119 Fred Merkle	15.00	6.75	1.85
☐ 120 Chief Meyers	15.00	6.75	1.85
☐ 121 Red Murray	10.00	4.50	1.25
☐ 122A Art Wilson	25.00	11.00	3.10
☐ 122B Art Wilson	15.00	6.75	1.85
☐ 123 Hooks Wiltse	10.00	4.50	1.25
☐ 124 Kitty Bransfield	20.00	9.00	2.50
☐ 125A Red Dooin	10.00	4.50	1.25
☐ 125B Red Dooin	15.00	6.75	1.85
☐ 126A Mickey Doolan	10.00	4.50	1.25
☐ 126B Mickey Doolan	15.00	6.75	1.85
☐ 127 Hans Lobert	10.00	4.50	1.25
☐ 128 Sherry Magee	10.00	4.50	1.25
☐ 129 Pat Moran	10.00	4.50	1.25
☐ 130A Dode Paskert	10.00	4.50	1.25
☐ 130B Dode Paskert	15.00	6.75	1.85
☐ 131 Jack Rowan	10.00	4.50	1.25
☐ 132A John Titus	10.00	4.50	1.25
☐ 132B John Titus	15.00	6.75	1.85
☐ 133 Bobby Byrne	10.00	4.50	1.25
☐ 134A Howie Camnitz	10.00	4.50	1.25
☐ 134B Howie Camnitz	15.00	6.75	1.85
☐ 135A Fred Clarke	30.00	13.50	3.70
☐ 135B Fred Clarke	40.00	18.00	5.00
☐ 136 John Flynn	10.00	4.50	1.25
☐ 137 Gepe Gibson	10.00	4.50	1.25
☐ 138 Tommy Leach	10.00	4.50	1.25
☐ 138 Tommy Leach	15.00	6.75	1.85
☐ 139 Sam Leever	10.00	4.50	1.25
☐ 140 Lefty Leifield	10.00	4.50	1.25
☐ 141 Nick Maddox	10.00	4.50	1.25
☐ 142 Dots Miller	10.00	4.50	1.25
☐ 143 Deacon Phillippe	15.00	6.75	1.85
☐ 144 Owen Wilson	10.00	4.50	1.25
☐ 145A Roger Bresnahan	30.00	13.50	3.70
☐ 145B Roger Bresnahan LL different picture	75.00	34.00	9.50
☐ 146 Steve Evans	10.00	4.50	1.25
☐ 147 Bob Harmon	10.00	4.50	1.25
☐ 148 Arnold Hauser	10.00	4.50	1.25
☐ 149A Miller Huggins	30.00	13.50	3.70
☐ 149B Miller Huggins	40.00	18.00	5.00
☐ 150 Ed Konetchy	10.00	4.50	1.25
☐ 151A Rebel Oakes	10.00	4.50	1.25
☐ 151B Rebel Oakes	15.00	6.75	1.85
☐ 152 Eddie Phelps	10.00	4.50	1.25

1948 Swell Sport Thrills

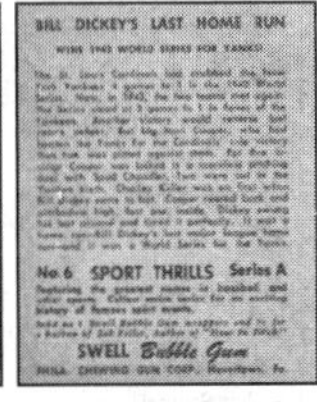

The cards in this 20-card set measure approximately 2 7/16" by 3". The 1948 Swell Gum Sports Thrills set of black and white, numbered cards highlights events from baseball history. The cards have picture framed borders with the title "Sports Thrills Highlights in the World of Sport" on the front. The backs of the cards give the story of the event pictured on the front. Cards numbered 9, 11, 16, and 20 are more difficult to obtain than the other cards in this set. The catalog designation is R448.

	NRMT	VG-E	GOOD
COMPLETE SET (20)	1000.00	450.00	125.00
COMMON CARD (1-20)	25.00	11.00	3.10
☐ 1 Greatest Single Inning Athletics' 10 Run Rally	25.00	11.00	3.10
☐ 2 Pete Reiser Amazing Record Debut With Dodgers	25.00	11.00	3.10
☐ 3 Jackie Robinson Dramatic Debut ROY	150.00	70.00	19.00
☐ 4 Walter Johnson Greatest Pitcher of Them All	60.00	27.00	7.50
☐ 5 Three Strikes Not Out: Lost Third Strike Changes Tide of 1941 World Series	25.00	11.00	3.10
☐ 6 Bill Dickey Last Home Run Wins Series	40.00	18.00	5.00
☐ 7 Hal Schumacher Never Say Die Pitcher	25.00	11.00	3.10
☐ 8 Carl Hubbell Five Strikeouts Nationals Lose All-Star Game	40.00	18.00	5.00
☐ 9 Al Gionfriddo Greatest Catch	30.00	13.50	3.70
☐ 10 Johnny VanderMeer No Hits No Runs	30.00	13.50	3.70
☐ 11 Grover C. Alexander Bases Loaded	50.00	22.00	6.25
☐ 12 Babe Ruth Points Most Dramatic Homer	200.00	90.00	25.00
☐ 13 Tommy Bridges Goose Goslin Winning Run: 1935 World Series	25.00	11.00	3.10
☐ 14 Lou Gehrig Four Homers	125.00	55.00	15.50
☐ 15 Joe DiMaggio Four Men To Stop Him Bat Streak	100.00	45.00	12.50
☐ 16 Ted Williams Three Run Homer in Ninth	175.00	80.00	22.00
☐ 17 Johnny Lindell Football Block Paves Way For Yank's Series Victory	25.00	11.00	3.10
☐ 18 Pee Wee Reese Home Run To Fame Grand Slam	50.00	22.00	6.25
☐ 19 Bob Feller Strikeout Record Whiffs Five	50.00	22.00	6.25
☐ 20 Carl Furillo Rifle Arm	35.00	16.00	4.40

1989 Swell Baseball Greats

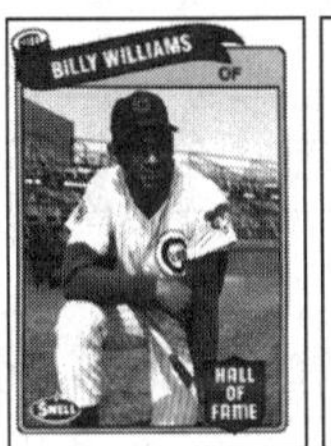

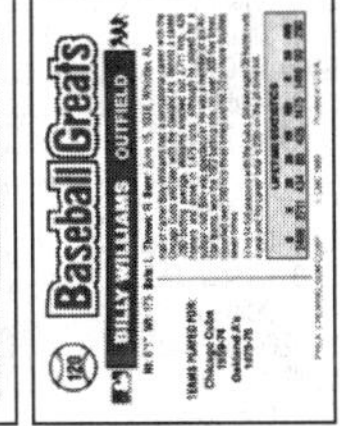

The 1989 Swell Baseball Greats set contains 135 standard-size cards. The fronts have vintage color photos with beige, red and white borders. The horizontally oriented backs are white and scarlet, and feature career highlights and lifetime stats. The set was produced by Philadelphia Chewing Gum Corporation.

	MINT	NRMT	EXC
COMPLETE SET (135)	12.00	5.50	1.50
COMMON CARD (1-135)	.05	.02	.01
☐ 1 Babe Ruth	2.50	1.10	.30
☐ 2 Ty Cobb	2.00	.90	.25
☐ 3 Walter Johnson	.50	.23	.06
☐ 4 Honus Wagner	.50	.23	.06
☐ 5 Cy Young	.50	.23	.06
☐ 6 Joe Adcock	.05	.02	.01
☐ 7 Jim Bunning	.25	.11	.03
☐ 8 Orlando Cepeda	.15	.07	.02
☐ 9 Harvey Kuenn	.05	.02	.01
☐ 10 Jim Hunter	.25	.11	.03
☐ 11 Johnny VanderMeer	.15	.07	.02
☐ 12 Tony Oliva	.15	.07	.02
☐ 13 Harvey Haddix UER (Reverse negative)	.05	.02	.01
☐ 14 Dick McAuliffe	.05	.02	.01
☐ 15 Lefty Grove	.25	.11	.03
☐ 16 Bo Belinsky	.15	.07	.02
☐ 17 Claude Osteen	.05	.02	.01
☐ 18 Doc Medich	.05	.02	.01
☐ 19 Del Ennis	.05	.02	.01
☐ 20 Rogers Hornsby	.50	.23	.06
☐ 21 Bob Buhl	.05	.02	.01
☐ 22 Phil Niekro	.25	.11	.03
☐ 23 Don Zimmer	.05	.02	.01
☐ 24 Greg Luzinski	.15	.07	.02
☐ 25 Lou Gehrig	2.00	.90	.25
☐ 26 Ken Singleton	.05	.02	.01
☐ 27 Bob Allison	.05	.02	.01
☐ 28 Ed Kranepool	.05	.02	.01
☐ 29 Manny Sanguillen	.05	.02	.01
☐ 30 Luke Appling	.25	.11	.03
☐ 31 Ralph Terry	.05	.02	.01
☐ 32 Smoky Burgess	.05	.02	.01
☐ 33 Gil Hodges	.25	.11	.03
☐ 34 Harry Walker	.05	.02	.01
☐ 35 Edd Roush	.25	.11	.03
☐ 36 Ron Santo	.15	.07	.02
☐ 37 Jim Perry	.05	.02	.01
☐ 38 Jose Morales	.05	.02	.01
☐ 39 Stan Bahnsen	.05	.02	.01
☐ 40 Al Kaline	.50	.23	.06
☐ 41 Mel Harder	.05	.02	.01
☐ 42 Ralph Houk	.05	.02	.01
☐ 43 Jack Billingham	.05	.02	.01
☐ 44 Carl Erskine	.15	.07	.02
☐ 45 Hoyt Wilhelm	.25	.11	.03
☐ 46 Dick Radatz	.05	.02	.01
☐ 47 Roy Sievers	.05	.02	.01
☐ 48 Jim Lonborg	.05	.02	.01
☐ 49 Bobby Richardson	.15	.07	.02
☐ 50 Whitey Ford	.50	.23	.06
☐ 51 Roy Face	.05	.02	.01
☐ 52 Tom Tresh	.05	.02	.01
☐ 53 Joe Nuxhall	.05	.02	.01
☐ 54 Mickey Vernon	.05	.02	.01
☐ 55 Johnny Mize	.25	.11	.03

	MINT	NRMT	EXC
☐ 56 Scott McGregor	.05	.02	.01
☐ 57 Billy Pierce	.15	.07	.02
☐ 58 Dave Giusti	.05	.02	.01
☐ 59 Minnie Minoso	.15	.07	.02
☐ 60 Early Wynn	.25	.11	.03
☐ 61 Jose Cardenal	.05	.02	.01
☐ 62 Sam Jethroe	.15	.07	.02
☐ 63 Sal Bando	.05	.02	.01
☐ 64 Elrod Hendricks	.05	.02	.01
☐ 65 Enos Slaughter	.25	.11	.03
☐ 66 Jim Bouton	.15	.07	.02
☐ 67 Bill Mazeroski	.25	.11	.03
☐ 68 Tony Kubek	.15	.07	.02
☐ 69 Joe Black	.05	.02	.01
☐ 70 Harmon Killebrew	.25	.11	.03
☐ 71 Sam McDowell	.05	.02	.01
☐ 72 Bucky Dent	.05	.02	.01
☐ 73 Virgil Trucks	.05	.02	.01
☐ 74 Andy Pafko	.05	.02	.01
☐ 75 Bob Feller	.50	.23	.06
☐ 76 Tito Francona	.05	.02	.01
☐ 77 Al Dark	.05	.02	.01
☐ 78 Larry Dierker	.15	.07	.02
☐ 79 Nellie Briles	.05	.02	.01
☐ 80 Lou Boudreau	.25	.11	.03
☐ 81 Wally Moon	.05	.02	.01
☐ 82 Hank Bauer	.15	.07	.02
☐ 83 Jim Piersall	.15	.07	.02
☐ 84 Jim Grant	.05	.02	.01
☐ 85 Richie Ashburn	.25	.11	.03
☐ 86 Bob Friend	.05	.02	.01
☐ 87 Ken Keltner	.05	.02	.01
☐ 88 Jim Kaat	.15	.07	.02
☐ 89 Dean Chance	.05	.02	.01
☐ 90 Al Lopez	.25	.11	.03
☐ 91 Dick Groat	.05	.02	.01
☐ 92 Johnny Blanchard	.05	.02	.01
☐ 93 Chuck Hinton	.05	.02	.01
☐ 94 Clete Boyer	.15	.07	.02
☐ 95 Steve Carlton	.50	.23	.06
☐ 96 Tug McGraw	.15	.07	.02
☐ 97 Mickey Lolich	.15	.07	.02
☐ 98 Earl Weaver MG	.25	.11	.03
☐ 99 Sal Maglie	.05	.02	.01
☐ 100 Ted Williams	2.00	.90	.25
☐ 101 Allie Reynolds UER (Photo actually Marius Russo)	.15	.07	.02
☐ 102 Gene Woodling UER (Photo actually Irv Noren)	.15	.07	.02
☐ 103 Moe Drabowsky	.05	.02	.01
☐ 104 Mickey Stanley	.05	.02	.01
☐ 105 Jim Palmer	.50	.23	.06
☐ 106 Bill Freehan	.15	.07	.02
☐ 107 Bob Robertson	.05	.02	.01
☐ 108 Walt Dropo	.05	.02	.01
☐ 109 Jerry Koosman	.15	.07	.02
☐ 110 Bobby Doerr	.25	.11	.03
☐ 111 Phil Rizzuto	.50	.23	.06
☐ 112 Don Kessinger	.05	.02	.01
☐ 113 Milt Pappas	.05	.02	.01
☐ 114 Herb Score	.15	.07	.02
☐ 115 Larry Doby	.15	.07	.02
☐ 116 Glenn Beckert	.05	.02	.01
☐ 117 Andre Thornton	.05	.02	.01
☐ 118 Gary Matthews	.05	.02	.01
☐ 119 Bill Virdon	.05	.02	.01
☐ 120 Billy Williams	.15	.07	.02
☐ 121 Johnny Sain	.05	.02	.01
☐ 122 Don Newcombe	.15	.07	.02
☐ 123 Rico Petrocelli	.05	.02	.01
☐ 124 Dick Bosman	.05	.02	.01
☐ 125 Roberto Clemente	2.00	.90	.25
☐ 126 Rocky Colavito	.25	.11	.03
☐ 127 Wilbur Wood	.05	.02	.01
☐ 128 Duke Sims	.05	.02	.01
☐ 129 Ken Holtzman	.05	.02	.01
☐ 130 Casey Stengel	.25	.11	.03
☐ 131 Bobby Shantz	.05	.02	.01
☐ 132 Del Crandall	.05	.02	.01
☐ 133 Bobby Thomson	.15	.07	.02
☐ 134 Brooks Robinson	.50	.23	.06
☐ 135 Checklist Card	.05	.02	.01

1990 Swell Baseball Greats

The 1990 Swell Baseball Greats set is a standard-size 135-card set. The words Baseball Greats is boldly proclaimed on the top of the card. This set was issued by Swell in both complete set form and in 10-card wax packs.

	MINT	NRMT	EXC
COMPLETE SET (135)	12.00	5.50	1.50
COMMON CARD (1-135)	.05	.02	.01
☐ 1 Tom Seaver	.50	.23	.06
☐ 2 Hank Aaron	1.50	.70	.19
☐ 3 Mickey Cochrane	.25	.11	.03
☐ 4 Rod Carew	.50	.23	.06
☐ 5 Carl Yastrzemski	.50	.23	.06
☐ 6 Dizzy Dean	.50	.23	.06
☐ 7 Sal Bando	.05	.02	.01
☐ 8 Whitey Ford	.50	.23	.06
☐ 9 Bill White	.15	.07	.02
☐ 10 Babe Ruth	2.50	1.10	.30
☐ 11 Robin Roberts	.25	.11	.03
☐ 12 Warren Spahn	.25	.11	.03
☐ 13 Billy Williams	.25	.11	.03
☐ 14 Joe Garagiola	.15	.07	.02
☐ 15 Ty Cobb	2.00	.90	.25
☐ 16 Boog Powell	.15	.07	.02
☐ 17 Tom Tresh	.05	.02	.01
☐ 18 Luke Appling	.25	.11	.03
☐ 19 Tommie Agee	.05	.02	.01
☐ 20 Roberto Clemente	2.00	.90	.25
☐ 21 Bobby Thomson	.15	.07	.02
☐ 22 Charlie Keller	.05	.02	.01
☐ 23 George Bamberger	.05	.02	.01
☐ 24 Eddie Lopat	.15	.07	.02
☐ 25 Lou Gehrig	2.00	.90	.25
☐ 26 Manny Mota	.05	.02	.01
☐ 27 Steve Stone	.05	.02	.01
☐ 28 Orlando Cepeda	.15	.07	.02
☐ 29 Al Bumbry	.05	.02	.01
☐ 30 Grover Alexander	.25	.11	.03
☐ 31 Lou Boudreau	.25	.11	.03
☐ 32 Herb Score	.15	.07	.02
☐ 33 Harry Walker	.05	.02	.01
☐ 34 Deron Johnson	.05	.02	.01
☐ 35 Edd Roush	.25	.11	.03
☐ 36 Carl Erskine	.15	.07	.02
☐ 37 Ken Forsch	.05	.02	.01
☐ 38 Sal Maglie	.05	.02	.01
☐ 39 Al Rosen	.05	.02	.01
☐ 40 Casey Stengel	.25	.11	.03
☐ 41 Cesar Cedeno	.05	.02	.01
☐ 42 Roy White	.05	.02	.01
☐ 43 Larry Doby	.25	.11	.03
☐ 44 Rod Kanehl	.05	.02	.01
☐ 45 Tris Speaker	.25	.11	.03
☐ 46 Ralph Garr	.05	.02	.01
☐ 47 Andre Thornton	.05	.02	.01
☐ 48 Frankie Crosetti	.15	.07	.02
☐ 49 Dick Groat	.15	.07	.02
☐ 50 Honus Wagner	.50	.23	.06
☐ 51 Rogers Hornsby	.50	.23	.06
☐ 52 Ken Brett	.05	.02	.01
☐ 53 Lenny Randle	.05	.02	.01
☐ 54 Enos Slaughter	.25	.11	.03
☐ 55 Mel Ott	.25	.11	.03
☐ 56 Rico Petrocelli	.05	.02	.01
☐ 57 Walt Dropo	.05	.02	.01
☐ 58 Bob Grich	.05	.02	.01
☐ 59 Billy Herman	.25	.11	.03
☐ 60 Bob Feller	.50	.23	.06
☐ 61 Davey Johnson	.15	.07	.02
☐ 62 Don Drysdale	.25	.11	.03
☐ 63 Lary Sorensen	.05	.02	.01
☐ 64 Ron Santo	.15	.07	.02
☐ 65 Eddie Mathews	.25	.11	.03
☐ 66 Gaylord Perry	.25	.11	.03
☐ 67 Lee May	.05	.02	.01
☐ 68 Johnnie LeMaster	.05	.02	.01
☐ 69 Don Kessinger	.05	.02	.01
☐ 70 Lefty Grove	.25	.11	.03
☐ 71 Lou Brock	.25	.11	.03
☐ 72 Don Cardwell	.05	.02	.01
☐ 73 Harvey Haddix	.05	.02	.01
☐ 74 Frank Torre	.05	.02	.01
☐ 75 Walter Johnson	.50	.23	.06
☐ 76 Don Newcombe	.15	.07	.02
☐ 77 Marv Throneberry	.05	.02	.01
☐ 78 Jim Northrup	.05	.02	.01
☐ 79 Fritz Peterson	.05	.02	.01
☐ 80 Ralph Kiner	.25	.11	.03
☐ 81 Mickey Lolich	.15	.07	.02
☐ 82 Donn Clendenon	.05	.02	.01
☐ 83 Pete Vuckovich	.05	.02	.01
☐ 84 Lefty Gomez	.25	.11	.03
☐ 85 Monte Irvin	.25	.11	.03
☐ 86 Rick Ferrell	.25	.11	.03
☐ 87 Tommy Hutton	.05	.02	.01
☐ 88 Julio Cruz	.05	.02	.01
☐ 89 Vida Blue	.15	.07	.02
☐ 90 Johnny Mize	.25	.11	.03
☐ 91 Rusty Staub	.15	.07	.02
☐ 92 Jimmy Piersall	.15	.07	.02
☐ 93 Bill Mazeroski	.25	.11	.03
☐ 94 Lee Lacy	.05	.02	.01
☐ 95 Ernie Banks	.50	.23	.06
☐ 96 Bobby Doerr	.25	.11	.03
☐ 97 George Foster	.15	.07	.02
☐ 98 Eric Soderholm	.05	.02	.01
☐ 99 Johnny Vander Meer	.15	.07	.02
☐ 100 Cy Young	.50	.23	.06
☐ 101 Jimmie Foxx	.50	.23	.06
☐ 102 Clete Boyer	.15	.07	.02
☐ 103 Steve Garvey	.15	.07	.02
☐ 104 Johnny Podres	.15	.07	.02
☐ 105 Yogi Berra	.50	.23	.06
☐ 106 Bill Monbouquette	.05	.02	.01
☐ 107 Milt Pappas	.05	.02	.01
☐ 108 Dave LaRoche	.05	.02	.01
☐ 109 Elliott Maddox	.05	.02	.01
☐ 110 Steve Carlton	.50	.23	.06
☐ 111 Bud Harrelson	.05	.02	.01
☐ 112 Mark Littell	.05	.02	.01
☐ 113 Frank Thomas	.05	.02	.01
☐ 114 Bill Robinson	.05	.02	.01
☐ 115 Satchel Paige	1.25	.55	.16
☐ 116 John Denny	.05	.02	.01
☐ 117 Clyde King	.05	.02	.01
☐ 118 Billy Sample	.05	.02	.01
☐ 119 Rocky Colavito	.25	.11	.03
☐ 120 Bob Gibson	.50	.23	.06
☐ 121 Bert Campaneris	.15	.07	.02
☐ 122 Mark Fidrych	.25	.11	.03
☐ 123 Ed Charles	.05	.02	.01
☐ 124 Jim Lonborg	.05	.02	.01
☐ 125 Ted Williams	2.00	.90	.25
☐ 126 Manny Sanguillen	.05	.02	.01
☐ 127 Matt Keough	.05	.02	.01
☐ 128 Vern Ruhle	.05	.02	.01
☐ 129 Bob Skinner	.05	.02	.01
☐ 130 Joe Torre	.25	.11	.03
☐ 131 Ralph Houk	.05	.02	.01
☐ 132 Gil Hodges	.25	.11	.03
☐ 133 Ralph Branca	.15	.07	.02
☐ 134 Christy Mathewson	.50	.23	.06
☐ 135 Checklist Card	.05	.02	.01

1991 Swell Baseball Greats

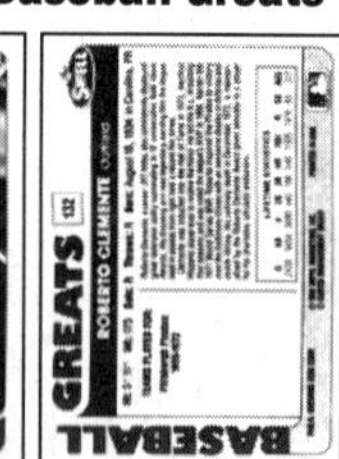

This set marks the third year Philadelphia Chewing Gum (using the Swell trade name) issued a set honoring retired players. The front of the cards feature yellow and red borders framing the full-color photo of the player(where full color was available) The cards were issued with cooperation from Impel Marketing. This 150-card standard-size set is sequenced in alphabetical orders within several seperate categories.

	MINT	NRMT	EXC
COMPLETE SET (150)	12.00	5.50	1.50
COMMON CARD (1-150)	.05	.02	.01
☐ 1 Tommie Agee	.05	.02	.01
☐ 2 Matty Alou	.05	.02	.01
☐ 3 Luke Appling	.25	.11	.03
☐ 4 Richie Ashburn	.25	.11	.03
☐ 5 Ernie Banks	.50	.23	.06
☐ 6 Don Baylor	.15	.07	.02
☐ 7 Buddy Bell	.15	.07	.02
☐ 8 Yogi Berra	.50	.23	.06
☐ 9 Joe Black	.15	.07	.02
☐ 10 Vida Blue	.15	.07	.02
☐ 11 Bobby Bonds	.15	.07	.02
☐ 12 Lou Boudreau	.25	.11	.03
☐ 13 Lou Brock	.25	.11	.03
☐ 14 Ralph Branca	.15	.07	.02
☐ 15 Bobby Brown	.15	.07	.02
☐ 16 Lou Burdette	.15	.07	.02
☐ 17 Steve Carlton	.50	.23	.06
☐ 18 Rico Carty	.15	.07	.02
☐ 19 Jerry Coleman	.15	.07	.02
☐ 20 Frankie Crosetti	.15	.07	.02
☐ 21 Julio Cruz	.05	.02	.01
☐ 22 Alvin Dark	.05	.02	.01
☐ 23 Doug DeCinces	.05	.02	.01
☐ 24 Larry Doby	.25	.11	.03
☐ 25 Bobby Doerr	.25	.11	.03
☐ 26 Don Drysdale	.25	.11	.03
☐ 27 Carl Erskine	.15	.07	.02
☐ 28 Elroy Face	.05	.02	.01
☐ 29 Rick Ferrell	.25	.11	.03
☐ 30 Rollie Fingers	.25	.11	.03
☐ 31 Joe Garagiola	.15	.07	.02
☐ 32 Steve Garvey	.15	.07	.02
☐ 33 Bob Gibson	.25	.11	.03
☐ 34 Mudcat Grant	.05	.02	.01
☐ 35 Dick Groat	.15	.07	.02
☐ 36 Jerry Grote	.05	.02	.01
☐ 37 Toby Harrah	.05	.02	.01
☐ 38 Bud Harrelson	.05	.02	.01
☐ 39 Billy Herman	.25	.11	.03
☐ 40 Ken Holtzman	.05	.02	.01
☐ 41 Willie Horton	.05	.02	.01
☐ 42 Ralph Houk	.05	.02	.01
☐ 43 Al Hrabosky	.05	.02	.01
☐ 44 Monte Irvin	.25	.11	.03
☐ 45 Fergie Jenkins	.25	.11	.03
☐ 46 Davey Johnson	.15	.07	.02
☐ 47 George Kell	.25	.11	.03
☐ 48 Charlie Keller	.15	.07	.02
☐ 49 Harmon Killebrew	.25	.11	.03
☐ 50 Ralph Kiner	.25	.11	.03
☐ 51 Clyde King	.05	.02	.01
☐ 52 Dave Kingman	.15	.07	.02
☐ 53 Al Kaline	.50	.23	.06
☐ 54 Clem Labine	.05	.02	.01
☐ 55 Vern Law	.05	.02	.01
☐ 56 Mickey Lolich	.15	.07	.02
☐ 57 Jim Lonborg	.05	.02	.01
☐ 58 Eddie Lopat	.15	.07	.02
☐ 59 Sal Maglie	.05	.02	.01
☐ 60 Bill Mazeroski	.25	.11	.03
☐ 61 Johnny VanderMeer	.15	.07	.02
☐ 62 Johnny Mize	.25	.11	.03
☐ 63 Manny Mota	.05	.02	.01
☐ 64 Wally Moon	.05	.02	.01
☐ 65 Rick Monday	.05	.02	.01
☐ 66 Tom Tresh	.15	.07	.02
☐ 67 Graig Nettles	.15	.07	.02
☐ 68 Don Newcombe	.15	.07	.02
☐ 69 Milt Pappas	.05	.02	.01
☐ 70 Gaylord Perry	.25	.11	.03
☐ 71 Rico Petrocelli	.15	.07	.02
☐ 72 Jimmy Piersall	.15	.07	.02
☐ 73 Johnny Podres	.15	.07	.02
☐ 74 Boog Powell	.15	.07	.02
☐ 75 Bobby Richardson	.15	.07	.02
☐ 76 Vern Ruhle	.05	.02	.01
☐ 77 Robin Roberts	.25	.11	.03
☐ 78 Al Rosen	.15	.07	.02
☐ 79 Billy Sample	.05	.02	.01
☐ 80 Manny Sanguillen	.05	.02	.01
☐ 81 Ron Santo	.25	.11	.03
☐ 82 Herb Score	.15	.07	.02
☐ 83 Bobby Shantz	.05	.02	.01
☐ 84 Enos Slaughter	.25	.11	.03
☐ 85 Eric Soderholm	.05	.02	.01
☐ 86 Warren Spahn	.25	.11	.03
☐ 87 Rusty Staub	.15	.07	.02
☐ 88 Bobby Thomson	.15	.07	.02
☐ 89 Marv Throneberry	.05	.02	.01
☐ 90 Luis Tiant	.15	.07	.02
☐ 91 Frank Torre	.05	.02	.01
☐ 92 Joe Torre	.25	.11	.03
☐ 93 Bill Virdon	.05	.02	.01
☐ 94 Harry Walker MG	.05	.02	.01
☐ 95 Earl Weaver	.25	.11	.03
☐ 96 Bill White	.15	.07	.02
☐ 97 Roy White	.05	.02	.01
☐ 98 Billy Williams	.25	.11	.03
☐ 99 Dick Williams	.05	.02	.01
☐ 100 Ted Williams	2.00	.90	.25
☐ 101 Gene Woodling	.05	.02	.01
☐ 102 Hank Aaron	2.00	.90	.25
☐ 103 Rod Carew	.50	.23	.06
☐ 104 Cesar Cedeno	.05	.02	.01
☐ 105 Orlando Cepeda	.25	.11	.03
☐ 106 Willie Mays	2.00	.90	.25
☐ 107 Tom Seaver	.50	.23	.06
☐ 108 Carl Yastrzemski	.50	.23	.06
☐ 109 Clete Boyer	.15	.07	.02
☐ 110 Bert Campaneris	.15	.07	.02
☐ 111 Walt Dropo	.05	.02	.01
☐ 112 George Foster	.05	.02	.01
☐ 113 Phil Garner	.05	.02	.01
☐ 114 Harvey Kuenn	.05	.02	.01
☐ 115 Don Kessinger	.05	.02	.01
☐ 116 Rocky Colavito	.25	.11	.03
☐ 117 Bobby Murcer	.15	.07	.02
☐ 118 Mel Parnell	.05	.02	.01
☐ 119 Ken Reitz	.05	.02	.01
☐ 120 Earl Wilson	.05	.02	.01
☐ 121 Wilbur Wood	.05	.02	.01
☐ 122 Ed Yost	.05	.02	.01
☐ 123 Jim Bouton	.15	.07	.02
☐ 124 Babe Ruth	2.50	1.10	.30
☐ 125 Lou Gehrig	2.00	.90	.25
☐ 126 Honus Wagner	.50	.23	.06
☐ 127 Ty Cobb	2.00	.90	.25
☐ 128 Grover C. Alexander	.50	.23	.06
☐ 129 Lefty Gomez	.25	.11	.03
☐ 130 Walter Johnson	.50	.23	.06
☐ 131 Gil Hodges	.25	.11	.03
☐ 132 Roberto Clemente	2.00	.90	.25
☐ 133 Satchel Paige	1.00	.45	.12
☐ 134 Edd Roush	.25	.11	.03
☐ 135 Cy Young	.50	.23	.06
☐ 136 Casey Stengel	.25	.11	.03
☐ 137 Rogers Hornsby	.25	.11	.03
☐ 138 Dizzy Dean	.25	.11	.03
☐ 139 Lefty Grove	.25	.11	.03
☐ 140 Tris Speaker	.25	.11	.03
☐ 141 Christy Mathewson	.50	.23	.06
☐ 142 Mickey Cochrane	.25	.11	.03
☐ 143 Jimmie Foxx	.50	.23	.06
☐ 144 Mel Ott	.25	.11	.03
☐ 145 Bob Feller	.50	.23	.06
☐ 146 Brooks Robinson	.50	.23	.06
☐ 147 Eddie Mathews	.25	.11	.03
☐ 148 Pie Traynor	.25	.11	.03
☐ 149 Thurman Munson	.25	.11	.03
☐ 150 Checklist Card	.05	.02	.01

1957 Swifts Franks

The cards in this 18-card set measure approximately 3 1/2" by 4". These full color, numbered cards issued in 1957 by the Swift Company are die-cut and have rounded corners. Each card consists of several pieces which can be punched out and assembled to form a stand-up model of the player. The cards and a game board were available directly from the company. The company-direct set consisted of three panels each containing six cards; sets found in this "uncut" state carry a value 25 percent higher than the values listed below. The catalog designation for this set is F162.

	NRMT	VG-E	GOOD
COMPLETE SET (18)	1500.00	700.00	190.00
COMMON CARD (1-18)	50.00	22.00	6.25
☐ 1 John Podres	60.00	27.00	7.50
☐ 2 Gus Triandos	50.00	22.00	6.25
☐ 3 Dale Long	50.00	22.00	6.25
☐ 4 Billy Pierce	60.00	27.00	7.50
☐ 5 Ed Bailey	50.00	22.00	6.25
☐ 6 Vic Wertz	50.00	22.00	6.25
☐ 7 Nelson Fox	150.00	70.00	19.00
☐ 8 Ken Boyer	75.00	34.00	9.50
☐ 9 Gil McDougald	60.00	27.00	7.50
☐ 10 Junior Gilliam	60.00	27.00	7.50
☐ 11 Eddie Yost	50.00	22.00	6.25
☐ 12 Johnny Logan	50.00	22.00	6.25
☐ 13 Hank Aaron	400.00	180.00	50.00
☐ 14 Bill Tuttle	50.00	22.00	6.25
☐ 15 Jackie Jensen	75.00	34.00	9.50
☐ 16 Frank Robinson	250.00	110.00	31.00
☐ 17 Richie Ashburn	150.00	70.00	19.00
☐ 18 Rocky Colavito	150.00	70.00	19.00

1988 T/M Umpires

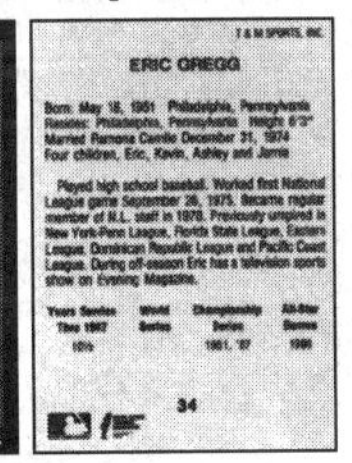

This set of 64 standard-size color cards was distributed as a small boxed set featuring Major League umpires exclusively. The box itself is blank, white, and silver. The set was produced by T and M Sports under licenses from Major League Baseball and the Major League Umpires Association. Card backs are printed in black on light blue. All the cards are black bordered, but the American Leaguers have a red thin inner border, whereas the National Leaguers have a green thin inner border. A short biographical sketch is given on the back for each umpire. The cards are numbered on the back; the number on the front of each card refers to the umpire's uniform number.

	MINT	NRMT	EXC
COMPLETE SET (64)	10.00	4.50	1.25
COMMON CARD (1-64)	.25	.11	.03
☐ 1 Doug Harvey	.50	.23	.06
☐ 2 Lee Weyer	.25	.11	.03
☐ 3 Billy Williams	.25	.11	.03
☐ 4 John Kibler	.25	.11	.03
☐ 5 Bob Engel	.50	.23	.06
☐ 6 Harry Wendelstedt	.35	.16	.04
☐ 7 Larry Barnett	.25	.11	.03
☐ 8 Don Denkinger	.35	.16	.04
☐ 9 Dave Phillips	.35	.16	.04
☐ 10 Larry McCoy	.25	.11	.03
☐ 11 Bruce Froemming	.35	.16	.04
☐ 12 John McSherry	.75	.35	.09
☐ 13 Jim Evans	.25	.11	.03
☐ 14 Frank Pulli	.25	.11	.03
☐ 15 Joe Brinkman	.25	.11	.03
☐ 16 Terry Tata	.25	.11	.03
☐ 17 Paul Runge	.25	.11	.03
☐ 18 Dutch Rennert	.25	.11	.03
☐ 19 Nick Bremigan	.25	.11	.03
☐ 20 Jim McKean	.25	.11	.03
☐ 21 Terry Cooney	.25	.11	.03
☐ 22 Rich Garcia	.35	.16	.04
☐ 23 Dale Ford	.25	.11	.03
☐ 24 Al Clark	.25	.11	.03
☐ 25 Greg Kosc	.25	.11	.03
☐ 26 Jim Quick	.25	.11	.03
☐ 27 Ed Montague	.25	.11	.03
☐ 28 Jerry Crawford	.25	.11	.03
☐ 29 Steve Palermo	1.00	.45	.12
☐ 30 Durwood Merrill	.25	.11	.03
☐ 31 Ken Kaiser	.35	.16	.04
☐ 32 Vic Voltaggio	.25	.11	.03
☐ 33 Mike Reilly	.25	.11	.03
☐ 34 Eric Gregg	.50	.23	.06
☐ 35 Ted Hendry	.25	.11	.03
☐ 36 Joe West	.25	.11	.03
☐ 37 Dave Pallone	.35	.16	.04
☐ 38 Fred Brocklander	.25	.11	.03
☐ 39 John Shulock	.25	.11	.03
☐ 40 Derryl Cousins	.25	.11	.03
☐ 41 Charlie Williams	.25	.11	.03
☐ 42 Rocky Roe	.25	.11	.03
☐ 43 Randy Marsh	.25	.11	.03
☐ 44 Bob Davidson	.25	.11	.03
☐ 45 Drew Coble	.25	.11	.03
☐ 46 Tim McClelland	.25	.11	.03
☐ 47 Dan Morrison	.25	.11	.03
☐ 48 Rick Reed	.25	.11	.03
☐ 49 Steve Rippley	.25	.11	.03
☐ 50 John Hirschbeck	.50	.23	.06
☐ 51 Mark Johnson	.25	.11	.03
☐ 52 Gerry Davis	.25	.11	.03
☐ 53 Dana DeMuth	.25	.11	.03
☐ 54 Larry Young	.25	.11	.03
☐ 55 Tim Welke	.25	.11	.03
☐ 56 Greg Bonin	.25	.11	.03
☐ 57 Tom Hallion	.25	.11	.03
☐ 58 Dale Scott	.25	.11	.03
☐ 59 Tim Tschida	.25	.11	.03
☐ 60 Dick Stello MEM	.25	.11	.03
☐ 61 All-Star Game	.25	.11	.03
☐ 62 World Series	.25	.11	.03
☐ 63 Jocko Conlan HOF	.75	.35	.09
☐ 64 Checklist Card	.25	.11	.03

1989 T/M Umpires

The 1989 Umpires set contains 63 standard-size cards. The fronts have borderless color photos with AL or NL logos. The backs are grey and include biographical information. The cards were distributed as a boxed set along with a custom album.

	MINT	NRMT	EXC
COMPLETE SET (63)	8.00	3.60	1.00
COMMON CARD (1-63)	.25	.11	.03
☐ 1 Doug Harvey	.50	.23	.06
☐ 2 John Kibler	.25	.11	.03
☐ 3 Bob Engel	.50	.23	.06
☐ 4 Harry Wendelstedt	.35	.16	.04
☐ 5 Larry Barnett	.25	.11	.03
☐ 6 Don Denkinger	.35	.16	.04
☐ 7 Dave Phillips	.35	.16	.04
☐ 8 Larry McCoy	.25	.11	.03
☐ 9 Bruce Froemming	.35	.16	.04
☐ 10 John McSherry	.50	.23	.06
☐ 11 Jim Evans	.25	.11	.03
☐ 12 Frank Pulli	.25	.11	.03
☐ 13 Joe Brinkman	.25	.11	.03
☐ 14 Terry Tata	.25	.11	.03
☐ 15 Nick Bremigan	.25	.11	.03
☐ 16 Jim McKean	.25	.11	.03
☐ 17 Paul Runge	.25	.11	.03
☐ 18 Dutch Rennert	.25	.11	.03
☐ 19 Terry Cooney	.25	.11	.03
☐ 20 Rich Garcia	.35	.16	.04
☐ 21 Dale Ford	.25	.11	.03
☐ 22 Al Clark	.25	.11	.03
☐ 23 Greg Kosc	.25	.11	.03
☐ 24 Jim Quick	.25	.11	.03
☐ 25 Eddie Montague	.25	.11	.03
☐ 26 Jerry Crawford	.25	.11	.03
☐ 27 Steve Palermo	1.00	.45	.12
☐ 28 Durwood Merrill	.25	.11	.03
☐ 29 Ken Kaiser	.35	.16	.04
☐ 30 Vic Voltaggio	.25	.11	.03
☐ 31 Mike Reilly	.25	.11	.03
☐ 32 Eric Gregg	.50	.23	.06
☐ 33 Ted Hendry	.25	.11	.03
☐ 34 Joe West	.25	.11	.03
☐ 35 Dave Pallone	.35	.16	.04
☐ 36 Fred Brocklander	.25	.11	.03
☐ 37 John Shulock	.25	.11	.03
☐ 38 Derryl Cousins	.25	.11	.03
☐ 39 Charlie Williams	.25	.11	.03
☐ 40 Rocky Roe	.25	.11	.03
☐ 41 Randy Marsh	.25	.11	.03
☐ 42 Bob Davidson	.25	.11	.03
☐ 43 Drew Coble	.25	.11	.03
☐ 44 Tim McClelland	.25	.11	.03
☐ 45 Dan Morrison	.25	.11	.03
☐ 46 Rick Reed	.25	.11	.03
☐ 47 Steve Rippley	.25	.11	.03
☐ 48 John Hirschbeck	.50	.23	.06
☐ 49 Mark Johnson	.25	.11	.03
☐ 50 Gerry Davis	.25	.11	.03
☐ 51 Dana DeMuth	.25	.11	.03
☐ 52 Larry Young	.25	.11	.03
☐ 53 Tim Welke	.25	.11	.03
☐ 54 Greg Bonin	.25	.11	.03
☐ 55 Tom Hallion	.25	.11	.03
☐ 56 Dale Scott	.25	.11	.03
☐ 57 Tim Tschida	.25	.11	.03
☐ 58 Gary Darling	.25	.11	.03
☐ 59 Mark Hirschbeck	.25	.11	.03
☐ 60 All Star Game Randy Marsh Terry Tata Frank Pulli Dan Morrison Dale Ford Larry Barnett	.25	.11	.03
☐ 61 World Series	.25	.11	.03
☐ 62 Lee Weyer	.25	.11	.03
☐ 63 Tommy Connolly and Bill Klem	.75	.35	.09

1989-90 T/M Senior League

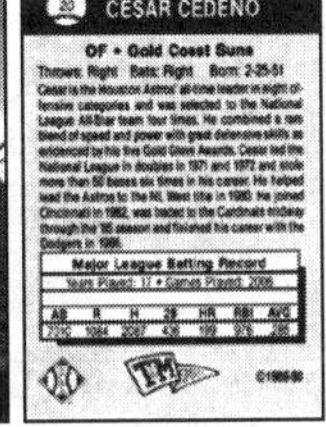

The 1989-90 T/M Senior League set contains 120 standard-size cards depicting members of the Senior League. The fronts are borderless, with full color photos and black bands at the bottom with player names and positions. The vertically oriented backs are gray and red, and show career major league totals and highlights. The cards were distributed as a boxed set with a checklist card and eight card-sized puzzle pieces. The set ordering is essentially alphabetical according to the player's name.

	MINT	NRMT	EXC
COMPLETE SET (121)	10.00	4.50	1.25
COMMON CARD (1-120)	.05	.02	.01
☐ 1 Curt Flood COMM	.35	.16	.04
☐ 2 Willie Aikens	.05	.02	.01
☐ 3 Gary Allenson	.05	.02	.01
☐ 4 Stan Bahnsen	.05	.02	.01
☐ 5 Alan Bannister	.05	.02	.01
☐ 6 Juan Beniquez	.05	.02	.01
☐ 7 Jim Bibby	.05	.02	.01
☐ 8 Paul Blair	.05	.02	.01
☐ 9 Vida Blue	.15	.07	.02
☐ 10 Bobby Bonds	.25	.11	.03
☐ 11 Pedro Borbon	.05	.02	.01
☐ 12 Clete Boyer	.15	.07	.02
☐ 13 Gates Brown	.05	.02	.01
☐ 14 Al Bumbry	.05	.02	.01
☐ 15 Sal Butera	.05	.02	.01
☐ 16 Bert Campaneris	.15	.07	.02
☐ 17 Bill Campbell	.05	.02	.01
☐ 18 Bernie Carbo	.05	.02	.01
☐ 19 Dave Cash	.05	.02	.01
☐ 20 Cesar Cedeno	.15	.07	.02
☐ 21 Gene Clines	.05	.02	.01
☐ 22 Dave Collins	.05	.02	.01
☐ 23 Cecil Cooper	.15	.07	.02
☐ 24 Doug Corbett	.05	.02	.01
☐ 25 Al Cowens	.05	.02	.01
☐ 26 Jose Cruz	.15	.07	.02
☐ 27 Mike Cuellar	.15	.07	.02
☐ 28 Pat Dobson	.05	.02	.01
☐ 29 Dick Drago	.05	.02	.01
☐ 30 Dan Driessen	.05	.02	.01
☐ 31 Jamie Easterly	.05	.02	.01
☐ 32 Juan Eichelberger	.05	.02	.01
☐ 33 Dock Ellis	.05	.02	.01
☐ 34 Ed Figueroa	.05	.02	.01
☐ 35 Rollie Fingers	.50	.23	.06
☐ 36 George Foster	.25	.11	.03
☐ 37 Oscar Gamble	.15	.07	.02
☐ 38 Wayne Garland	.05	.02	.01
☐ 39 Wayne Garrett	.05	.02	.01
☐ 40 Ross Grimsley	.05	.02	.01
☐ 41 Jerry Grote	.15	.07	.02
☐ 42 Johnny Grubb	.05	.02	.01
☐ 43 Mario Guerrero	.05	.02	.01
☐ 44 Toby Harrah	.15	.07	.02
☐ 45 Steve Henderson	.05	.02	.01
☐ 46 George Hendrick	.15	.07	.02
☐ 47 Butch Hobson	.05	.02	.01
☐ 48 Roy Howell	.05	.02	.01
☐ 49 Al Hrabosky	.15	.07	.02
☐ 50 Clint Hurdle	.05	.02	.01
☐ 51 Garth Iorg	.05	.02	.01
☐ 52 Tim Ireland	.05	.02	.01
☐ 53 Grant Jackson	.05	.02	.01
☐ 54 Ron Jackson	.05	.02	.01
☐ 55 Ferguson Jenkins	.50	.23	.06
☐ 56 Odell Jones	.05	.02	.01
☐ 57 Mike Kekich	.05	.02	.01
☐ 58 Steve Kemp	.05	.02	.01
☐ 59 Dave Kingman	.25	.11	.03
☐ 60 Bruce Kison	.05	.02	.01
☐ 61 Lee Lacy	.05	.02	.01
☐ 62 Rafael Landestoy	.05	.02	.01
☐ 63 Ken Landreaux	.05	.02	.01
☐ 64 Tito Landrum	.05	.02	.01
☐ 65 Dave LaRoche	.05	.02	.01
☐ 66 Bill Lee	.15	.07	.02
☐ 67 Ron LeFlore	.15	.07	.02
☐ 68 Dennis Leonard	.05	.02	.01
☐ 69 Bill Madlock	.25	.11	.03
☐ 70 Mickey Mahler	.05	.02	.01
☐ 71 Rich Manning	.05	.02	.01
☐ 72 Tippy Martinez	.05	.02	.01
☐ 73 Jon Matlack	.05	.02	.01
☐ 74 Bake McBride	.05	.02	.01
☐ 75 Steve McCatty	.05	.02	.01
☐ 76 Hal McRae	.15	.07	.02
☐ 77 Dan Meyer	.05	.02	.01
☐ 78 Felix Millan	.05	.02	.01
☐ 79 Paul Mirabella	.05	.02	.01
☐ 80 Omar Moreno	.05	.02	.01
☐ 81 Jim Morrison	.05	.02	.01
☐ 82 Graig Nettles	.25	.11	.03
☐ 83 Al Oliver	.25	.11	.03
☐ 84 Amos Otis	.15	.07	.02
☐ 85 Tom Paciorek	.15	.07	.02
☐ 86 Lowell Palmer	.05	.02	.01
☐ 87 Pat Putnam	.05	.02	.01
☐ 88 Lenny Randle	.05	.02	.01
☐ 89 Ken Reitz	.05	.02	.01
☐ 90 Gene Richards	.05	.02	.01
☐ 91 Mickey Rivers	.15	.07	.02
☐ 92 Leon Roberts	.05	.02	.01
☐ 93 Joe Sambito	.05	.02	.01
☐ 94 Rodney Scott	.05	.02	.01
☐ 95 Bob Shirley	.05	.02	.01
☐ 96 Jim Slaton	.05	.02	.01
☐ 97 Elias Sosa	.05	.02	.01
☐ 98 Fred Stanley	.05	.02	.01
☐ 99 Bill Stein	.05	.02	.01
☐ 100 Rennie Stennett	.05	.02	.01
☐ 101 Sammy Stewart	.05	.02	.01
☐ 102 Tim Stoddard	.05	.02	.01
☐ 103 Champ Summers	.05	.02	.01
☐ 104 Derrel Thomas	.05	.02	.01
☐ 105 Luis Tiant	.25	.11	.03
☐ 106 Bobby Tolan MG	.05	.02	.01
☐ 107 Bill Travers	.05	.02	.01
☐ 108 Tom Underwood	.05	.02	.01
☐ 109 Rick Waits	.05	.02	.01
☐ 110 Ron Washington	.05	.02	.01
☐ 111 U.L. Washington	.05	.02	.01
☐ 112 Earl Weaver MG	.50	.23	.06
☐ 113 Jerry White	.05	.02	.01
☐ 114 Milt Wilcox	.05	.02	.01
☐ 115 Dick Williams MG	.15	.07	.02
☐ 116 Walt Williams	.05	.02	.01
☐ 117 Rick Wise	.05	.02	.01
☐ 118 Favorite Suns Luis Tiant Cesar Cedeno	.15	.07	.02
☐ 119 Home Run Legends George Foster Bobby Bonds	.25	.11	.03
☐ 120 Sunshine Skippers Earl Weaver Dick Williams	.15	.07	.02
☐ NNO Checklist 1-120	.05	.02	.01

1990 T/M Umpires

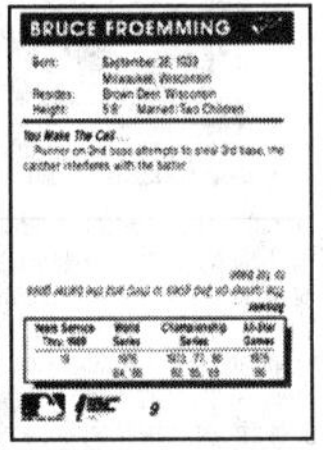

The 1990 T/M Umpires set is a standard-size set which features a picture of each umpire on the front of the card with a baseball rules question on the back of the card. The set was issued as a boxed set as well as in packs.

	MINT	NRMT	EXC
COMPLETE SET (70)	8.00	3.60	1.00
COMMON CARD (1-70)	.20	.09	.03
☐ 1 Doug Harvey	.40	.18	.05
☐ 2 John Kibler	.20	.09	.03
☐ 3 Bob Engel	.40	.18	.05
☐ 4 Harry Wendelstedt	.30	.14	.04
☐ 5 Larry Barnett	.20	.09	.03
☐ 6 Don Denkinger	.30	.14	.04

Card			
☐ 7 Dave Phillips	.30	.14	.04
☐ 8 Larry McCoy	.20	.09	.03
☐ 9 Bruce Froemming	.30	.14	.04
☐ 10 John McSherry	.40	.18	.05
☐ 11 Jim Evans	.20	.09	.03
☐ 12 Frank Pulli	.20	.09	.03
☐ 13 Joe Brinkman	.20	.09	.03
☐ 14 Terry Tata	.20	.09	.03
☐ 15 Jim McKean	.20	.09	.03
☐ 16 Dutch Rennert	.20	.09	.03
☐ 17 Paul Runge	.20	.09	.03
☐ 18 Terry Cooney	.20	.09	.03
☐ 19 Rich Garcia	.30	.14	.04
☐ 20 Dale Ford	.20	.09	.03
☐ 21 Al Clark	.20	.09	.03
☐ 22 Greg Kosc	.20	.09	.03
☐ 23 Jim Quick	.20	.09	.03
☐ 24 Eddie Montague	.20	.09	.03
☐ 25 Jerry Crawford	.20	.09	.03
☐ 26 Steve Palermo	.75	.35	.09
☐ 27 Durwood Merrill	.20	.09	.03
☐ 28 Ken Kaiser	.40	.18	.05
☐ 29 Vic Voltaggio	.20	.09	.03
☐ 30 Mike Reilly	.20	.09	.03
☐ 31 Eric Gregg	.40	.18	.05
☐ 32 Ted Hendry	.20	.09	.03
☐ 33 Joe West	.20	.09	.03
☐ 34 Fred Brocklander	.20	.09	.03
☐ 35 John Shulock	.20	.09	.03
☐ 36 Derryl Cousins	.20	.09	.03
☐ 37 Charlie Williams	.20	.09	.03
☐ 38 Rocky Roe	.20	.09	.03
☐ 39 Randy Marsh	.20	.09	.03
☐ 40 Bob Davidson	.20	.09	.03
☐ 41 Drew Coble	.20	.09	.03
☐ 42 Tim McClelland	.20	.09	.03
☐ 43 Dan Morrison	.20	.09	.03
☐ 44 Rick Reed	.20	.09	.03
☐ 45 Steve Rippley	.20	.09	.03
☐ 46 John Hirschbeck	.40	.18	.05
☐ 47 Mark Johnson	.20	.09	.03
☐ 48 Gerry Davis	.20	.09	.03
☐ 49 Dana DeMuth	.20	.09	.03
☐ 50 Larry Young	.20	.09	.03
☐ 51 Tim Welke	.20	.09	.03
☐ 52 Greg Bonin	.20	.09	.03
☐ 53 Tom Hallion	.20	.09	.03
☐ 54 Dale Scott	.20	.09	.03
☐ 55 Tim Tschida	.20	.09	.03
☐ 56 Gary Darling	.20	.09	.03
☐ 57 Mark Hirschbeck	.20	.09	.03
☐ 58 Jerry Layne	.20	.09	.03
☐ 59 Jim Joyce	.20	.09	.03
☐ 60 Bill Hohn	.20	.09	.03
☐ 61 All-Star Game	.20	.09	.03
☐ 62 World Series	.20	.09	.03
☐ 63 Nick Bremigan	.20	.09	.03
☐ 64 Ed Runge Paul Runge The Runges	.30	.14	.04
☐ 65 Bart Giamatti MEM	.50	.23	.06
☐ 66 Puzzle Piece 1	.20	.09	.03
☐ 67 Puzzle Piece 2	.20	.09	.03
☐ 68 Puzzle Piece 3	.20	.09	.03
☐ 69 Puzzle Piece 4	.20	.09	.03
☐ 70 Checklist Card	.20	.09	.03
☐ 71 Al Barlick HOF	.75	.35	.09

1911 T205 Gold Border

The cards in this 209-card set measure approximately 1 1/2" by 2 5/8". The T205 set (catalog designation), also known as the "Gold Border" set, was issued in 1911 in packages of the following cigarette brands: American Beauty, Broadleaf, Cycle, Drum, Hassan, Honest Long Cut, Piedmont, Polar Bear, Sovereign and Sweet Caporal. All the above were products of the American Tobacco Company, and the ads for the various brands appear below the biographical section on the back of each card. There are pose variations noted in the checklist (which is alphabetized and numbered for reference) and there are 12 minor league cards of a more ornate design which are somewhat scarce. The numbers below correspond to alphabetical order within category, i.e., major leaguers and minor leaguers are alphabetized separately. The gold borders of T205 cards chip easily and they are hard to find in "Mint" or even "Near Mint" condition, due to this there is a high premium on these high condition cards.

	EX-MT	VG-E	GOOD
COMPLETE SET (209)	30000.00	13500.00	3800.00
COMMON MAJORS (1-186)	70.00	32.00	8.75
COMMON MINORS (187-198)	200.00	90.00	25.00

Card	EX-MT	VG-E	GOOD
☐ 1 Ed Abbaticchio	70.00	32.00	8.75
☐ 2 Red Ames	70.00	32.00	8.75
☐ 3 Jimmy Archer	70.00	32.00	8.75
☐ 4 Jimmy Austin	70.00	32.00	8.75
☐ 5 Bill Bailey	70.00	32.00	8.75
☐ 6 Frank "Homerun" Baker	250.00	110.00	31.00
☐ 7 Neal Ball	70.00	32.00	8.75
☐ 8A Cy Barger (Full B)	70.00	32.00	8.75
☐ 8B Cy Barger Part B	300.00	135.00	38.00
☐ 9 Jack Barry	70.00	32.00	8.75
☐ 10 Johnny Bates	70.00	32.00	8.75
☐ 11 Fred Beck	70.00	32.00	8.75
☐ 12 Beals Becker	70.00	32.00	8.75
☐ 13 George Bell	70.00	32.00	8.75
☐ 14 Chief Bender	200.00	90.00	25.00
☐ 15 Bill Bergen	70.00	32.00	8.75
☐ 16 Bob Bescher	70.00	32.00	8.75
☐ 17 Joe Birmingham	70.00	32.00	8.75
☐ 18 Russ Blackburne	70.00	32.00	8.75
☐ 19 Kitty Bransfield	70.00	32.00	8.75
☐ 20A Roger Bresnahan (Mouth closed)	200.00	90.00	25.00
☐ 20B Roger Bresnahan (Mouth open)	400.00	180.00	50.00
☐ 21 Al Bridwell	70.00	32.00	8.75
☐ 22 Mordecai Brown	200.00	90.00	25.00
☐ 23 Bobby Byrne	70.00	32.00	8.75
☐ 24 Howie Camnitz	70.00	32.00	8.75
☐ 25 Bill Carrigan	70.00	32.00	8.75
☐ 26 Frank Chance	225.00	100.00	28.00
☐ 27A Hal Chase (Chase only)	350.00	160.00	45.00
☐ 27B Hal Chase (Hal Chase)	150.00	70.00	19.00
☐ 28 Eddie Cicotte	150.00	70.00	19.00
☐ 29 Fred Clarke	200.00	90.00	25.00
☐ 30 Ty Cobb	3000.00	1350.00	375.00
☐ 31A Edward T. Collins (Mouth closed)	200.00	90.00	25.00
☐ 31B Edward T. Collins (Mouth open)	400.00	180.00	50.00
☐ 32 Frank Corridon	70.00	32.00	8.75
☐ 33 Otis Crandall	70.00	32.00	8.75
☐ 34 Lou Criger	70.00	32.00	8.75
☐ 35 Bill Dahlen	200.00	90.00	25.00
☐ 36 Jake Daubert	90.00	40.00	11.00
☐ 37 Jim Delahanty	70.00	32.00	8.75
☐ 38 Art Devlin	70.00	32.00	8.75
☐ 39 Josh Devore	70.00	32.00	8.75
☐ 40 Walt Dickson	70.00	32.00	8.75
☐ 41 Jiggs Donahue UER (Misspelled Donohue on card)	225.00	100.00	28.00
☐ 42 Red Dooin	70.00	32.00	8.75
☐ 43 Mickey Doolan	70.00	32.00	8.75
☐ 44A Patsy Dougherty (White stocking)	200.00	90.00	25.00
☐ 44B Patsy Dougherty (Red stocking)	70.00	32.00	8.75
☐ 45 Tom Downey	70.00	32.00	8.75
☐ 46 Larry Doyle	90.00	40.00	11.00
☐ 47 Hugh Duffy	300.00	135.00	38.00
☐ 48 Jimmy Dygert	70.00	32.00	8.75
☐ 49 Dick Egan	70.00	32.00	8.75
☐ 50 Kid Elberfeld	70.00	32.00	8.75
☐ 51 Clyde Engle	70.00	32.00	8.75
☐ 52 Steve Evans	70.00	32.00	8.75
☐ 53 Johnny Evers	250.00	110.00	31.00
☐ 54 Bob Ewing	70.00	32.00	8.75
☐ 55 George Ferguson	70.00	32.00	8.75
☐ 56 Ray Fisher	200.00	90.00	25.00
☐ 57 Art Fletcher	70.00	32.00	8.75
☐ 58 John Flynn	70.00	32.00	8.75
☐ 59A Russell Ford (Dark cap)	70.00	32.00	8.75
☐ 59B Russell Ford (Light cap)	200.00	90.00	25.00
☐ 60 Bill Foxen	70.00	32.00	8.75
☐ 61 Art Fromme	70.00	32.00	8.75
☐ 62 Earl Gardner	70.00	32.00	8.75
☐ 63 Harry Gaspar	70.00	32.00	8.75
☐ 64 George Gibson	70.00	32.00	8.75
☐ 65 Wilbur Good	70.00	32.00	8.75
☐ 66A George F. Graham (Boston Rustlers)	70.00	32.00	8.75
☐ 66B George F. Graham (Chicago Cubs)	400.00	180.00	50.00
☐ 67 Eddie Grant	200.00	90.00	25.00
☐ 68 Dolly Gray	70.00	32.00	8.75
☐ 69 Clark Griffith	200.00	90.00	25.00
☐ 70 Bob Groom	70.00	32.00	8.75
☐ 71A Robert Harmon (Both ears)	70.00	32.00	8.75
☐ 71B Robert Harmon (Left ear only)	300.00	135.00	38.00
☐ 72 Topsy Hartsel	70.00	32.00	8.75
☐ 73 Arnold Hauser	70.00	32.00	8.75
☐ 74 Charlie Hemphill	70.00	32.00	8.75
☐ 75 Buck Herzog	70.00	32.00	8.75
☐ 76 Dick Hoblitzell	70.00	32.00	8.75
☐ 77 Danny Hoffman	70.00	32.00	8.75
☐ 78 Miller Huggins	200.00	90.00	25.00
☐ 79 John Hummell	70.00	32.00	8.75
☐ 80 Fred Jacklitsch	70.00	32.00	8.75
☐ 81 Hughie Jennings	200.00	90.00	25.00
☐ 82 Walter Johnson	1200.00	550.00	150.00
☐ 83 Davy Jones	70.00	32.00	8.75
☐ 84 Tom Jones	70.00	32.00	8.75
☐ 85 Addie Joss	600.00	275.00	75.00
☐ 86 Ed Karger	250.00	110.00	31.00
☐ 87 Ed Killian	70.00	32.00	8.75
☐ 88 Red Kleinow	250.00	110.00	31.00
☐ 89 John Kling	70.00	32.00	8.75
☐ 90 John Knight	70.00	32.00	8.75
☐ 91 Ed Konetchy	70.00	32.00	8.75
☐ 92 Harry Krause	70.00	32.00	8.75
☐ 93 Rube Kroh	70.00	32.00	8.75
☐ 94 Frank Lang	70.00	32.00	8.75
☐ 95 Frank LaPorte	70.00	32.00	8.75
☐ 96 Arlie Latham	70.00	32.00	8.75
☐ 97 Tommy Leach	70.00	32.00	8.75
☐ 98 Sam Leever	70.00	32.00	8.75
☐ 99 Lefty Leifield	70.00	32.00	8.75
☐ 100 Ed Lennox	70.00	32.00	8.75
☐ 101 Paddy Livingston	70.00	32.00	8.75
☐ 102 Hans Lobert	70.00	32.00	8.75
☐ 103 Bris Lord	70.00	32.00	8.75
☐ 104 Harry Lord	70.00	32.00	8.75
☐ 105 John Lush	70.00	32.00	8.75
☐ 106 Nick Maddox	70.00	32.00	8.75
☐ 107 Sherry Magee	70.00	32.00	8.75
☐ 108 Rube Marquard	200.00	90.00	25.00
☐ 109 Christy Mathewson	900.00	400.00	110.00
☐ 110 Al Mattern	70.00	32.00	8.75
☐ 111 George McBride	70.00	32.00	8.75
☐ 112 Amby McConnell	70.00	32.00	8.75
☐ 113 Pryor McElveen	70.00	32.00	8.75
☐ 114 John McGraw MG	300.00	135.00	38.00
☐ 115 Harry McIntire	70.00	32.00	8.75
☐ 116 Matty McIntyre	70.00	32.00	8.75
☐ 117 Larry McLean	70.00	32.00	8.75
☐ 118 Fred Merkle	90.00	40.00	11.00
☐ 119 Chief Meyers	70.00	32.00	8.75
☐ 120 Clyde Milan	90.00	40.00	11.00
☐ 121 Dots Miller	70.00	32.00	8.75
☐ 122 Mike Mitchell	70.00	32.00	8.75
☐ 123 Pat Moran	70.00	32.00	8.75
☐ 124 George Moriarty	70.00	32.00	8.75
☐ 125 George Mullin	70.00	32.00	8.75
☐ 126 Danny Murphy	70.00	32.00	8.75
☐ 127 Red Murray	70.00	32.00	8.75
☐ 128 Tom Needham	70.00	32.00	8.75
☐ 129 Rebel Oakes	70.00	32.00	8.75
☐ 130 Rube Oldring	70.00	32.00	8.75
☐ 131 Charley O'Leary	70.00	32.00	8.75
☐ 132 Fred Olmstead	70.00	32.00	8.75
☐ 133 Orval Overall	70.00	32.00	8.75
☐ 134 Freddy Parent	70.00	32.00	8.75
☐ 135 Dode Paskert	70.00	32.00	8.75
☐ 136 Fred Payne	70.00	32.00	8.75
☐ 137 Barney Pelty	70.00	32.00	8.75
☐ 138 Jack Pfiester	70.00	32.00	8.75
☐ 139 Ed Phelps	70.00	32.00	8.75
☐ 140 Decon Phillippe	90.00	40.00	11.00
☐ 141 Jack Quinn	70.00	32.00	8.75
☐ 142 Bugs Raymond	250.00	110.00	31.00
☐ 143 Ed Reulbach	70.00	32.00	8.75
☐ 144 Lewis Richie	70.00	32.00	8.75
☐ 145 Jack Rowan	200.00	90.00	25.00
☐ 146 Nap Rucker	90.00	40.00	11.00
☐ 147 Doc Scanlan	200.00	90.00	25.00
☐ 148 Germany Schaefer	70.00	32.00	8.75
☐ 149 Admiral Schlei	70.00	32.00	8.75
☐ 150 Boss Schmidt	70.00	32.00	8.75
☐ 151 Wildfire Schulte	70.00	32.00	8.75
☐ 152 Jim Scott	70.00	32.00	8.75
☐ 153 Bayard Sharpe	70.00	32.00	8.75
☐ 154A David Shean (Boston Rustlers)	70.00	32.00	8.75
☐ 154B David Shean (Chicago Cubs)	400.00	180.00	50.00
☐ 155 Jimmy Sheckard	70.00	32.00	8.75
☐ 156 Hack Simmons	70.00	32.00	8.75
☐ 157 Tony Smith	70.00	32.00	8.75
☐ 158 Fred Snodgrass	70.00	32.00	8.75
☐ 159 Tris Speaker	500.00	220.00	60.00
☐ 160 Jake Stahl	90.00	40.00	11.00
☐ 161 Oscar Stanage	70.00	32.00	8.75
☐ 162 Harry Steinfeldt	90.00	40.00	11.00
☐ 163 George Stone	70.00	32.00	8.75
☐ 164 George Stovall	70.00	32.00	8.75
☐ 165 Gabby Street	70.00	32.00	8.75
☐ 166 George Suggs	250.00	110.00	31.00
☐ 167 Ed Summers	70.00	32.00	8.75
☐ 168 Jeff Sweeney	200.00	90.00	25.00
☐ 169 Lee Tannehill	70.00	32.00	8.75
☐ 170 Ira Thomas	70.00	32.00	8.75
☐ 171 Joe Tinker	250.00	110.00	31.00
☐ 172 John Titus	70.00	32.00	8.75
☐ 173 Terry Turner	300.00	135.00	38.00
☐ 174 Hippo Vaughn	200.00	90.00	25.00
☐ 175 Heinie Wagner	200.00	90.00	25.00
☐ 176A Roderick J. Wallace (With cap)	175.00	80.00	22.00
☐ 176B Roderick J. Wallace (Without cap)	400.00	180.00	50.00
☐ 177 Ed Walsh	400.00	180.00	50.00
☐ 178 Zach Wheat	200.00	90.00	25.00
☐ 179 Doc White	70.00	32.00	8.75
☐ 180 Kirby White	200.00	90.00	25.00
☐ 181 Kaiser Wilhelm	200.00	90.00	25.00
☐ 182 Ed Willett	70.00	32.00	8.75
☐ 183A George Wiltse (Both ears)	70.00	32.00	8.75
☐ 183B George Wiltse (Right ear only)	300.00	135.00	38.00
☐ 184 Owen Wilson	70.00	32.00	8.75
☐ 185 Harry Wolter	70.00	32.00	8.75
☐ 186 Cy Young	800.00	350.00	100.00
☐ 187 Dr.Merle T. Adkins: Baltimore	200.00	90.00	25.00
☐ 188 Jack Dunn	250.00	110.00	31.00
☐ 189 George Merritt	200.00	90.00	25.00
☐ 190 Charles Hanford	200.00	90.00	25.00
☐ 191 Hick Cady	200.00	90.00	25.00
☐ 192 James Frick	200.00	90.00	25.00
☐ 193 Wyatt Lee	200.00	90.00	25.00
☐ 194 Lewis McAllister	200.00	90.00	25.00
☐ 195 John Nee	200.00	90.00	25.00
☐ 196 Jimmy Collins	450.00	200.00	55.00
☐ 197 James Phelan	200.00	90.00	25.00
☐ 198 Emil Batch	200.00	90.00	25.00

1909-11 T206 White Border

The T206 set was and is the most popular of all the tobacco issues. The set was issued from 1909 to 1911 with nineteen different brands of cigarettes: American Beauty, Broadleaf, Cycle, Carolina Brights, Coupon, Drum, El Principe de Gales, Hindu, Hustler, Lenox, Old Mill, Piedmont, Polar Bear, Red Cross, Sovereign, Sweet Caporal, Tolstoi, and Uzit. There was also a Ty Cobb back version that was a promotional issue and is very scarce. Only Cobb appears on cards with Ty Cobb backs. The minor league cards are supposedly slightly more difficult to obtain than the cards of the major leaguers, with the Southern League player cards being the most difficult. Minor League players were obtained from the American Association and the Eastern league. Southern League players were obtained from a variety of leagues including the following: South Atlantic League, Southern League, Texas League, and Virginia League. Series 150 was issued between February 1909 thru the end of May, 1909. Series 350 was issued from the end of May, 1909 thru April, 1910. The last series 350-to-406 was issued in late December 1910 thur early 1991. The set price below does not include ultra-expensive Wagner, Plank, Magie error, or Doyle variation. The Wagner card is one of the most sought after cards in the hobby. This card (#366 in the checklist below) was pulled from circulation almost immediately after being issued. While estimates of how many Wagners are in existence vary, the card is considered by many collectors the ultimate card to own. Perhaps the best conditioned example of this card was sold in a public auction in 1991 for $451,000 to hockey great Wayne Gretzky and Bruce McNall. That same card was later used in a major giveaway sponsored by most of the card companies, Treat products and Wal-Mart. That card sold for more than $600,000 in an auction in September, 1996.

	EX-MT	VG-E	GOOD
COMPLETE SET (520)	55000.00	24800.00	6900.00
COMMON MAJORS (1-389)	50.00	22.00	6.25
COMMON MINORS (390-475)	40.00	18.00	5.00
COMMON SOUTHERN(476-523)	100.00	45.00	12.50

Card	EX-MT	VG-E	GOOD
☐ 1 Ed Abbaticchio: Pitt Batting follow thru	50.00	22.00	6.25
☐ 2 Ed Abbaticchio: Pitt. Batting waiting pitch	60.00	27.00	7.50
☐ 3 Bill Abstein: Pitt.	50.00	22.00	6.25
☐ 4 Whitey Alperman: Brooklyn	60.00	27.00	7.50
☐ 5 Red Ames: N.Y. NL Portrait	60.00	27.00	7.50
☐ 6 Red Ames: N.Y. NL Hands over head	50.00	22.00	6.25
☐ 7 Red Ames: N.Y. NL Hands in front of chest	60.00	27.00	7.50
☐ 8 Frank Arellanes: Boston AL	50.00	22.00	6.25
☐ 9 Jake Atz: Chicago AL	50.00	22.00	6.25
☐ 10 Frank Baker: Phila. AL	200.00	90.00	25.00
☐ 11 Neal Ball: N.Y. AL	60.00	27.00	7.50
☐ 12 Neal Ball: Cleveland	50.00	22.00	6.25
☐ 13 Jap Barbeau: St. Louis NL	50.00	22.00	6.25
☐ 14 Jack Barry: Phila. AL	50.00	22.00	6.25
☐ 15 Johnny Bates: Boston NL	60.00	27.00	7.50
☐ 16 Ginger Beaumont: Boston NL	60.00	27.00	7.50
☐ 17 Fred Beck: Boston NL	50.00	22.00	6.25

☐ 18 Beals Becker: Boston NL 50.00 22.00 6.25

☐ 19 George Bell: Brooklyn pitching follow thru 50.00 22.00 6.25

☐ 20 George Bell: Brooklyn Hands over head 60.00 27.00 7.50

☐ 21 Chief Bender Phila. AL Portrait 225.00 100.00 28.00

☐ 22 Chief Bender Phila. AL pitching, trees 200.00 90.00 25.00

☐ 23 Chief Bender Phila AL pitching, no trees 200.00 90.00 25.00

☐ 24 Bill Bergen: Brooklyn Catching 50.00 22.00 6.25

☐ 25 Bill Bergen: Brooklyn Batting 60.00 27.00 7.50

☐ 26 Heinie Berger: Cleveland 50.00 22.00 6.25

☐ 27 Bob Bescher: Cinc. Catching fly ball 50.00 22.00 6.25

☐ 28 Bob Bescher: Cinc. Portrait 50.00 22.00 6.25

☐ 29 Joe Birmingham: Cleveland 60.00 27.00 7.50

☐ 30 Jack Bliss: St.L. NL 50.00 22.00 6.25

☐ 31 Frank Bowerman: Boston NL 60.00 27.00 7.50

☐ 32 Bill Bradley: Cleveland Portrait 60.00 27.00 7.50

☐ 33 Bill Bradley: Cleveland Batting 50.00 22.00 6.25

☐ 34 Kitty Bransfield: Phila. NL 60.00 27.00 7.50

☐ 35 Roger Bresnahan: St.L. NL Portrait 225.00 100.00 28.00

☐ 36 Roger Bresnahan: St.L. NL Batting 200.00 90.00 25.00

☐ 37 Al Bridwell: N.Y. NL Portrait 60.00 27.00 7.50

☐ 38 Al Bridwell: N.Y. NL Wearing sweater 50.00 22.00 6.25

☐ 39 George Brown: Chicago NL (Sic, Browne) 90.00 40.00 11.00

☐ 40 George Brown: Washington (Sic, Browne) 500.00 220.00 60.00

☐ 41 Mordecai Brown: Chicago NL Portrait 250.00 110.00 31.00

☐ 42 Mordecai Brown: Chicago NL Chicago down front of shirt 175.00 80.00 22.00

☐ 43 Mordecai Brown: Chicago NL Cubs across chest 300.00 135.00 38.00

☐ 44 Al Burch: Brooklyn Fielding 50.00 22.00 6.25

☐ 45 Al Burch: Brooklyn Batting 125.00 55.00 15.50

☐ 46 Bill Burns: Chicago AL 50.00 22.00 6.25

☐ 47 Donie Bush: Detroit 60.00 27.00 7.50

☐ 48 Bobby Byrne: St. Louis NL 50.00 22.00 6.25

☐ 49 Howie Camnitz: Pitt Arms folded over chest 60.00 27.00 7.50

☐ 50 Howie Camnitz: Pitt Hands over head 50.00 22.00 6.25

☐ 51 Howie Camnitz: Pitt. Throwing 50.00 22.00 6.25

☐ 52 Billy Campbell: Cincinnati 50.00 22.00 6.25

☐ 53 Bill Carrigan: Boston AL 50.00 22.00 6.25

☐ 54 Frank Chance: Chicago NL Cubs across chest 300.00 135.00 38.00

☐ 55 Frank Chance: Chicago NL Chicago down front of shirt 200.00 90.00 25.00

☐ 56 Frank Chance: Chicago NL Batting 200.00 90.00 25.00

☐ 57 Chappy Charles: St. Louis NL 50.00 22.00 6.25

☐ 58 Hal Chase: N.Y. AL Port. blue bkgd. 80.00 36.00 10.00

☐ 59 Hal Chase: N.Y. AL Port., pink bkgd. 200.00 90.00 25.00

☐ 60 Hal Chase: N.Y. AL Holding cup 75.00 34.00 9.50

☐ 61 Hal Chase: N.Y. AL Throwing, dark cap 75.00 34.00 9.50

☐ 62 Hal Chase: N.Y. AL Throwing, white cap 125.00 55.00 15.50

☐ 63 Jack Chesbro: New York AL 250.00 110.00 31.00

☐ 64 Eddie Cicotte: Boston AL 175.00 80.00 22.00

☐ 65 Fred Clarke: Pitt. Portrait 200.00 90.00 25.00

☐ 66 Fred Clarke: Pitt. 175.00 80.00 22.00

☐ 67 Josh Clarke: Cleve. 60.00 27.00 7.50

☐ 68 Ty Cobb: Detroit Port., red bkgd. 1600.00 700.00 200.00

☐ 69 Ty Cobb: Detroit Port., green background 2500.00 1100.00 300.00

☐ 70 Ty Cobb: Detroit Bat on shoulder 1600.00 700.00 200.00

☐ 71 Ty Cobb: Detroit Bat away from shoulder 1300.00 575.00 160.00

☐ 72 Eddie Collins: Phila. AL 200.00 90.00 25.00

☐ 73 Wid Conroy: Washington Fielding 60.00 27.00 7.50

☐ 74 Wid Conroy: Wash. Bat on shoulder 50.00 22.00 6.25

☐ 75 Harry Covaleski: Phila. NL 60.00 27.00 7.50

☐ 76 Doc Crandall N.Y. NL, without cap 50.00 22.00 6.25

☐ 77 Doc Crandall N.Y. NL sweater and cap 50.00 22.00 6.25

☐ 78 Sam Crawford: Detroit Batting 175.00 80.00 22.00

☐ 79 Sam Crawford: Detroit, Throwing 225.00 100.00 28.00

☐ 80 Birdie Cree: N.Y. AL 50.00 22.00 6.25

☐ 81 Lou Criger: St.L. AL 60.00 27.00 7.50

☐ 82 Dode Criss: St.L. AL 60.00 27.00 7.50

☐ 83 Bill Dahlen: Boston NL 90.00 40.00 11.00

☐ 84 Bill Dahlen: Brooklyn 225.00 100.00 28.00

☐ 85 George Davis: Chicago AL 60.00 27.00 7.50

☐ 86 Harry Davis Phila. AL Davis on card 50.00 22.00 6.25

☐ 87 Harry Davis Phila. AL H.Davis on card 60.00 27.00 7.50

☐ 88 Jim Delehanty: Wash. 60.00 27.00 7.50

☐ 89 Ray Demmitt: St.L. AL 3500.00 1600.00 450.00

☐ 90 Ray Demmitt: N.Y. AL 60.00 27.00 7.50

☐ 91 Art Devlin: N.Y. NL 60.00 27.00 7.50

☐ 92 Josh Devore: N.Y. NL 50.00 22.00 6.25

☐ 93 Bill Dineen: St. Louis AL 50.00 22.00 6.25

☐ 94 Mike Donlin N.Y. NL Fielding 125.00 55.00 15.50

☐ 95 Mike Donlin N.Y. NL Sitting 75.00 34.00 9.50

☐ 96 Mike Donlin: N.Y.NL Batting 60.00 27.00 7.50

☐ 97 Jiggs Donohue: Chicago AL 60.00 27.00 7.50

☐ 98 Bill Donovan: Detroit Portrait 60.00 27.00 7.50

☐ 99 Bill Donovan: Detroit Throwing 50.00 22.00 6.25

☐ 100 Red Dooin: Phila. NL 60.00 27.00 7.50

☐ 101 Mickey Doolan: Phila. NL Fielding 50.00 22.00 6.25

☐ 102 Mickey Doolan: Phila. NL Batting 50.00 22.00 6.25

☐ 103 Mickey Doolin (Sic, Doolan): Phila. NL 60.00 27.00 7.50

☐ 104 Patsy Dougherty: Chicago AL Portrait 60.00 27.00 7.50

☐ 105 Patsy Dougherty: Chicago AL Fielding 50.00 22.00 6.25

☐ 106 Tom Downey: Cinc. Batting 50.00 22.00 6.25

☐ 107 Tom Downey: Cinc. Fielding 50.00 22.00 6.25

☐ 108A Larry Doyle: N.Y. Hands over head 70.00 32.00 8.75

☐ 108B Larry Doyle: N.Y. NAT'L hands over head) 18000.00 8100.00 2200.00

☐ 109 Larry Doyle: N.Y. NL Sweater 60.00 27.00 7.50

☐ 110 Larry Doyle: N.Y. NL Throwing 75.00 34.00 9.50

☐ 111 Larry Doyle: N.Y. NL Bat on shoulder 60.00 27.00 7.50

☐ 112 Jean Dubuc: Cin. 50.00 22.00 6.25

☐ 113 Hugh Duffy: Chicago AL 200.00 90.00 25.00

☐ 114 Joe Dunn: Brooklyn 50.00 22.00 6.25

☐ 115 Bull Durham: N.Y. NL 60.00 27.00 7.50

☐ 116 Jimmy Dygert: Phila. AL 50.00 22.00 6.25

☐ 117 Ted Easterly: Cleveland 50.00 22.00 6.25

☐ 118 Dick Egan: Cinc. 50.00 22.00 6.25

☐ 119 Kid Elberfeld: Wash. Fielding 50.00 22.00 6.25

☐ 120 Kid Elberfeld: Wash. Portrait 1000.00 450.00 125.00

☐ 121 Kid Elberfeld: N.Y. AL Portrait 60.00 27.00 7.50

☐ 122 Clyde Engle: N.Y. AL 50.00 22.00 6.25

☐ 123 Steve Evans: St. Louis NL 50.00 22.00 6.25

☐ 124 Johnny Evers: Chicago NL Portrait 250.00 110.00 31.00

☐ 125 Johnny Evers: Chicago NL Cubs across chest 300.00 135.00 38.00

☐ 126 Johnny Evers: Chicago NL Chicago down front of shirt 200.00 90.00 25.00

☐ 127 Bob Ewing: Cinc. 60.00 27.00 7.50

☐ 128 George Ferguson: Boston NL 50.00 22.00 6.25

☐ 129 Hobe Ferris: St. Louis AL 60.00 27.00 7.50

☐ 130 Lou Fiene: Chicago AL Portrait 50.00 22.00 6.25

☐ 131 Lou Fiene: Chicago AL Throwing 50.00 22.00 6.25

☐ 132 Art Fletcher: New York NL 50.00 22.00 6.25

☐ 133 Elmer Flick: Cleveland 225.00 100.00 28.00

☐ 134 Russ Ford: N.Y. AL 50.00 22.00 6.25

☐ 135 John Frill: N.Y. AL 50.00 22.00 6.25

☐ 136 Art Fromme: Cinc. 50.00 22.00 6.25

☐ 137 Chick Gandil: Chicago AL 250.00 110.00 31.00

☐ 138 Bob Ganley: Washington 60.00 27.00 7.50

☐ 139 Harry Gasper: Cinc. (Sic, Gaspar) 50.00 22.00 6.25

☐ 140 Rube Geyer: St.L. NL 50.00 22.00 6.25

☐ 141 George Gibson: Pitt. 60.00 27.00 7.50

☐ 142 Billy Gilbert: St. Louis NL 60.00 27.00 7.50

☐ 143 Wilbur Goode (Sic, Good): Cleve. 60.00 27.00 7.50

☐ 144 Bill Graham: St. Louis AL 50.00 22.00 6.25

☐ 145 Peaches Graham: Boston NL 50.00 22.00 6.25

☐ 146 Dolly Gray: Washington 60.00 27.00 7.50

☐ 147 Clark Griffith: Cinc. Portrait 200.00 90.00 25.00

☐ 148 Clark Griffith: Cinc. Batting 150.00 70.00 19.00

☐ 149 Bob Groom: Washington 50.00 22.00 6.25

☐ 150 Ed Hahn: Chicago AL 60.00 27.00 7.50

☐ 151 Topsy Hartsel: Phila. AL 50.00 22.00 6.25

☐ 152 Charlie Hemphill: N.Y. AL 60.00 27.00 7.50

☐ 153 Buck Herzog: N.Y. NL 60.00 27.00 7.50

☐ 154 Buck Herzog: Boston NL 50.00 22.00 6.25

☐ 155 Bill Hinchman: Cleveland 60.00 27.00 7.50

☐ 156 Doc Hoblitzell: Cincinnati 50.00 22.00 6.25

☐ 157 Danny Hoffman: St. Louis AL 50.00 22.00 6.25

☐ 158 Solly Hofman: Chicago NL 50.00 22.00 6.25

☐ 159 Del Howard: Chicago NL 50.00 22.00 6.25

☐ 160 Harry Howell: St.L. AL Portrait 50.00 22.00 6.25

☐ 161 Harry Howell: St.L. AL Left hand on hip 50.00 22.00 6.25

☐ 162 Miller Huggins: Cinc. Portrait 225.00 100.00 28.00

☐ 163 Miller Huggins: Cinc. Hands to mouth 150.00 70.00 19.00

☐ 164 Rudy Hulswitt: St. Louis NL 50.00 22.00 6.25

☐ 165 John Hummel: Brooklyn 50.00 22.00 6.25

☐ 166 George Hunter: Brooklyn 50.00 22.00 6.25

☐ 167 Frank Isbell: Chicago AL 60.00 27.00 7.50

☐ 168 Fred Jacklitsch: Phila. NL 60.00 27.00 7.50

☐ 169 Hugh Jennings MG: Detroit Portrait 225.00 100.00 28.00

☐ 170 Hugh Jennings MG: Detroit Yelling 150.00 70.00 19.00

☐ 171 Hugh Jennings MG: Detroit Dancing for joy 150.00 70.00 19.00

☐ 172 Walter Johnson: Washington Portrait 900.00 400.00 110.00

☐ 173 Walter Johnson: Washington Ready to pitch 750.00 350.00 95.00

☐ 174 Tom Jones: St.L. AL 60.00 27.00 7.50

☐ 175 Tom Jones: Detroit 50.00 22.00 6.25

☐ 176 Fielder Jones: Chic. AL Portrait 60.00 27.00 7.50

☐ 177 Fielder Jones: Chic. AL Hands on hips 60.00 27.00 7.50

☐ 178 Tim Jordan: Brooklyn Portrait 60.00 27.00 7.50

☐ 179 Tim Jordan: Brooklyn Batting 50.00 22.00 6.25

☐ 180 Addie Joss: Cleveland Portrait 350.00 160.00 45.00

☐ 181 Addie Joss: Cleveland Ready to pitch 200.00 90.00 25.00

☐ 182 Ed Karger: Cinc. 60.00 27.00 7.50

☐ 183 Willie Keeler: N.Y. AL Portrait 350.00 160.00 45.00

☐ 184 Willie Keeler: N.Y. AL Batting 300.00 135.00 38.00

☐ 185 Ed Killian: Detroit Portrait 60.00 27.00 7.50

☐ 186 Ed Killian: Detroit Pitching 50.00 22.00 6.25

☐ 187 Red Kleinow: N.Y. AL Batting 60.00 27.00 7.50

☐ 188 Red Kleinow: N.Y. AL Catching 50.00 22.00 6.25

☐ 189 Red Kleinow: Boston AL Catching 300.00 135.00 38.00

☐ 190 Johnny Kling: Chicago NL 60.00 27.00 7.50

☐ 191 Otto Knabe: Phila. NL 50.00 22.00 6.25

☐ 192 John Knight: N.Y. AL Portrait 50.00 22.00 6.25

☐ 193 John Knight: N.Y. AL Batting 50.00 22.00 6.25

☐ 194 Ed Konetchy: St.L. NL Awaiting low ball 50.00 22.00 6.25

☐ 195 Ed Konetchy: St.L. NL Glove above head 60.00 27.00 7.50

☐ 196 Harry Krause: Phila. AL Portrait 50.00 22.00 6.25

☐ 197 Harry Krause: Phila. AL Pitching 50.00 22.00 6.25

☐ 198 Rube Kroh: Chicago NL 50.00 22.00 6.25

☐ 199 Nap Lajoie: Cleveland Portrait 450.00 200.00 55.00

☐ 200 Nap Lajoie: Cleveland Batting	350.00	160.00	45.00
☐ 201 Nap Lajoie: Cleveland Throwing	350.00	160.00	45.00
☐ 202 Joe Lake: N.Y. AL	60.00	27.00	7.50
☐ 203 Joe Lake: St.L. AL Hands over head	50.00	22.00	6.25
☐ 204 Joe Lake: St.L. AL Throwing	50.00	22.00	6.25
☐ 205 Frank LaPorte: N.Y. AL	50.00	22.00	6.25
☐ 206 Arlie Latham: N.Y. NL	50.00	22.00	6.25
☐ 207 Fred Leach: Pitt. Portrait	60.00	27.00	7.50
☐ 208 Fred Leach: Pitt. In fielding position	50.00	22.00	6.25
☐ 209 Lefty Leifield: Pitt. Batting	50.00	22.00	6.25
☐ 210 Lefty Leifield: Pitt. Hands behind head	60.00	27.00	7.50
☐ 211 Ed Lennox: Brooklyn	50.00	22.00	6.25
☐ 212 Glenn Liebhardt: Cleveland	60.00	27.00	7.50
☐ 213 Vive Lindaman: Boston NL	90.00	40.00	11.00
☐ 214 Paddy Livingstone: Phila. AL	50.00	22.00	6.25
☐ 215 Hans Lobert: Cinc.	60.00	27.00	7.50
☐ 216 Harry Lord: Bost. AL	50.00	22.00	6.25
☐ 217 Harry Lumley: Brooklyn	60.00	27.00	7.50
☐ 218 Carl Lundgren: Chicago NL	300.00	135.00	38.00
☐ 219 Nick Maddox: Pitt.	50.00	22.00	6.25
☐ 220 Sherry Magee: Phila. NL Portrait	75.00	34.00	9.50
☐ 221 Sherry Magee: Phila. NL Batting	50.00	22.00	6.25
☐ 222 Sherry Magie: Phila. NL, (Sic, Magee) Portrait, name misspelled	15000.00	6800.00	1900.00
☐ 223 Rube Manning: N.Y. AL Batting	60.00	27.00	7.50
☐ 224 Rube Manning: N.Y. AL Hands over head	50.00	22.00	6.25
☐ 225 Rube Marquard: N.Y. NL Portrait	225.00	100.00	28.00
☐ 226 Rube Marquard: N.Y. NL Pitching	175.00	80.00	22.00
☐ 227 Rube Marquard: N.Y. NL Standing	200.00	90.00	25.00
☐ 228 Doc Marshall: Brooklyn	50.00	22.00	6.25
☐ 229 Christy Mathewson: N.Y. NL Portrait	900.00	400.00	110.00
☐ 230 Christy Mathewson: N.Y. NL Pitching, white cap	700.00	325.00	90.00
☐ 231 Christy Mathewson: N.Y. NL Pitching, dark cap	700.00	325.00	90.00
☐ 232 Al Mattern: Boston NL	50.00	22.00	6.25
☐ 233 Jack McAleese: St. Louis AL	50.00	22.00	6.25
☐ 234 George McBride: Washington	50.00	22.00	6.25
☐ 235 Moose McCormick: N.Y. NL	50.00	22.00	6.25
☐ 236 Pryor McElveen: Brooklyn	50.00	22.00	6.25
☐ 237 John McGraw: N.Y. NL Portrait, no cap	350.00	160.00	45.00
☐ 238 John McGraw: N.Y. NL Wearing sweater	200.00	90.00	25.00
☐ 239 John McGraw: N.Y. NL pointing	225.00	100.00	28.00
☐ 240 John McGraw: N.Y. NL Glove on hip	225.00	100.00	28.00
☐ 241 Matty McIntyre: Brooklyn	60.00	27.00	7.50
☐ 242 Matty McIntyre: Brooklyn and Chicago NL	50.00	22.00	6.25
☐ 243 Mike McIntyre: Detroit	50.00	22.00	6.25
☐ 244 Larry McLean: Cinc.	50.00	22.00	6.25
☐ 245 George McQuillan: Phila. NL Throwing	60.00	27.00	7.50
☐ 246 George McQuillan: Phila. NL Batting	50.00	22.00	6.25
☐ 247 Fred Merkle: N.Y. NL Portrait	60.00	27.00	7.50
☐ 248 Fred Merkle: N.Y. NL Throwing	75.00	34.00	9.50
☐ 249 Chief Meyers: New York NL	50.00	22.00	6.25
☐ 250 Clyde Milan: Washington	50.00	22.00	6.25
☐ 251 Dots Miller: Pitt.	50.00	22.00	6.25
☐ 252 Mike Mitchell: Cinc.	50.00	22.00	6.25
☐ 253 Pat Moran: Chicago NL	50.00	22.00	6.25
☐ 254 George Moriarty: Detroit	50.00	22.00	6.25
☐ 255 Mike Mowrey: Cinc.	50.00	22.00	6.25
☐ 256 George Mullen: Detroit (Sic, Mullin)	50.00	22.00	6.25
☐ 257 George Mullin: Detroit Throwing	60.00	27.00	7.50
☐ 258 George Mullin: Detroit Batting	50.00	22.00	6.25
☐ 259 Danny Murphy: Phila. AL Throwing	60.00	27.00	7.50
☐ 260 Danny Murphy: Phila. AL Bat on shoulder	50.00	22.00	6.25
☐ 261 Red Murray: N.Y. NL Sweater	50.00	22.00	6.25
☐ 262 Red Murray: N.Y. NL Bat on shoulder	50.00	22.00	6.25
☐ 263 Chief Myers (Sic, Meyers): N.Y. NL Fielding	50.00	22.00	6.25
☐ 264 Chief Myers (Sic, Meyers): N.Y. NL Batting	50.00	22.00	6.25
☐ 265 Tom Needham: Chicago NL	50.00	22.00	6.25
☐ 266 Simon Nicholls: Phila. AL	60.00	27.00	7.50
☐ 267 Simon Nichols (Sic, Nicholls): Phila. AL	50.00	22.00	6.25
☐ 268 Harry Niles: Boston AL	60.00	27.00	7.50
☐ 269 Rebel Oakes: Cinc.	50.00	22.00	6.25
☐ 270 Bill O'Hara: N.Y. NL	50.00	22.00	6.25
☐ 271 Bill O'Hara: St. Louis NL	3500.00	1600.00	450.00
☐ 272 Rube Oldring: Phila. AL Fielding	60.00	27.00	7.50
☐ 273 Rube Oldring: Phila. AL Bat on shoulder	60.00	27.00	7.50
☐ 274 Charley O'Leary: Detroit Portrait	60.00	27.00	7.50
☐ 275 Charley O'Leary: Detroit Hands on knees	50.00	22.00	6.25
☐ 276 Orval Overall: Chicago NL Portrait	60.00	27.00	7.50
☐ 277 Orval Overall: Chicago NL Pitching follow thru	50.00	22.00	6.25
☐ 278 Orval Overall: Chicago NL, Pitching hiding ball in glove	50.00	22.00	6.25
☐ 279 Frank Owen: Chicago AL (Sic, Owens)	60.00	27.00	7.50
☐ 280 Freddy Parent: Chicago AL	60.00	27.00	7.50
☐ 281 Dode Paskert: Cinc.	50.00	22.00	6.25
☐ 282 Jim Pastorius: Brooklyn	60.00	27.00	7.50
☐ 283 Harry Pattee: Brooklyn	150.00	70.00	19.00
☐ 284 Fred Payne: Chicago AL	50.00	22.00	6.25
☐ 285 Barney Pelty: St.L. AL HOR	100.00	45.00	12.50
☐ 286 Barney Pelty: St.L. AL VERT	50.00	22.00	6.25
☐ 287 George Perring: Cleveland	50.00	22.00	6.25
☐ 288 Jeff Pfeffer: Chicago NL	50.00	22.00	6.25
☐ 289 Jack Pfeister: Chic. NL Sitting	50.00	22.00	6.25
☐ 290 Jack Pfeister: Chic. NL Pitching	50.00	22.00	6.25
☐ 291 Ed Phelps: St.L. NL	50.00	22.00	6.25
☐ 292 Deacon Phillippe: Pitt.	75.00	34.00	9.50
☐ 293 Eddie Plank: Phila. AL	25000.00	11200.00	3100.00
☐ 294 Jack Powell: St. Louis AL	60.00	27.00	7.50
☐ 295 Mike Powers: Phila. AL	125.00	55.00	15.50
☐ 296 Billy Purtell: Chicago AL	50.00	22.00	6.25
☐ 297 Jack Quinn: N.Y. AL	50.00	22.00	6.25
☐ 298 Bugs Raymond: New York NL	60.00	27.00	7.50
☐ 299 Ed Reulbach: Chicago NL Pitching	75.00	34.00	9.50
☐ 300 Ed Reulbach: Chicago NL Hands at side	125.00	55.00	15.50
☐ 301 Bob Rhoades: sic, Rhoads, Cleveland, Hand in air	50.00	22.00	6.25
☐ 302 Bob Rhoades: sic, Rhoads, Cleveland, Ready to pitch	50.00	22.00	6.25
☐ 303 Charlie Rhodes: St. Louis NL	50.00	22.00	6.25
☐ 304 Claude Ritchey: Boston NL	60.00	27.00	7.50
☐ 305 Claude Rossman: Detroit	50.00	22.00	6.25
☐ 306 Nap Rucker: Brooklyn Portrait	75.00	34.00	9.50
☐ 307 Nap Rucker: Brooklyn Pitching	60.00	27.00	7.50
☐ 308 Germany Schaefer: Washington	60.00	27.00	7.50
☐ 309 Germany Schaefer: Detroit	60.00	27.00	7.50
☐ 310 Admiral Schlei: N.Y. NL Sweater	50.00	22.00	6.25
☐ 311 Admiral Schlei: N.Y. NL Batting	50.00	22.00	6.25
☐ 312 Admiral Schlei: N.Y. NL Fielding	60.00	27.00	7.50
☐ 313 Boss Schmidt: Detroit Portrait	50.00	22.00	6.25
☐ 314 Boss Schmidt: Detroit Throwing	60.00	27.00	7.50
☐ 315 Frank Schulte: Chicago NL Batting, back turned	50.00	22.00	6.25
☐ 316 Frank Schulte: Chicago NL Batting, front pose	60.00	27.00	7.50
☐ 317 Jim Scott: Chicago AL	50.00	22.00	6.25
☐ 318 Cy Seymour: N.Y. NL Portrait	50.00	22.00	6.25
☐ 319 Cy Seymour: N.Y. NL Throwing	50.00	22.00	6.25
☐ 320 Cy Seymour: N.Y. NL Batting	60.00	27.00	7.50
☐ 321 Al Shaw: St.L. NL	60.00	27.00	7.50
☐ 322 Jimmy Sheckard: Chicago NL Throwing	50.00	22.00	6.25
☐ 323 Jimmy Sheckard: Chicago NL Side view	60.00	27.00	7.50
☐ 324 Bill Shipke: Washington	60.00	27.00	7.50
☐ 325 Frank Smith: Chicago AL, Listed as Smith	50.00	22.00	6.25
☐ 326 Frank Smith: Chicago and Boston AL	400.00	180.00	50.00
☐ 327 Frank Smith: Chicago AL (Listed as F.Smith)	60.00	27.00	7.50
☐ 328 Happy Smith: Brk.	50.00	22.00	6.25
☐ 329 Fred Snodgrass: N.Y. NL Batting	60.00	27.00	7.50
☐ 330 Fred Snodgrass: N.Y. NL Catching	60.00	27.00	7.50
☐ 331 Bob Spade: Cinc.	60.00	27.00	7.50
☐ 332 Tris Speaker: Boston AL	450.00	200.00	55.00
☐ 333 Tubby Spencer: Boston AL	60.00	27.00	7.50
☐ 334 Jake Stahl: Boston AL Catching fly ball	60.00	27.00	7.50
☐ 335 Jake Stahl: Boston AL Standing, arms down	60.00	27.00	7.50
☐ 336 Oscar Stanage: Detroit	50.00	22.00	6.25
☐ 337 Charlie Starr: Boston NL	50.00	22.00	6.25
☐ 338 Harry Steinfeldt: Chicago NL Portrait	75.00	34.00	9.50
☐ 339 Harry Steinfeldt: Chicago NL Batting	60.00	27.00	7.50
☐ 340 Jim Stephens: St.L. AL	50.00	22.00	6.25
☐ 341 George Stone: St.L. AL	60.00	27.00	7.50
☐ 342 George Stovall: Cleveland Portrait	60.00	27.00	7.50
☐ 343 George Stovall: Cleveland Batting	50.00	22.00	6.25
☐ 344 Gabby Street: Washington Portrait	60.00	27.00	7.50
☐ 345 Gabby Street: Washington Catching	50.00	22.00	6.25
☐ 346 Billy Sullivan: Chicago AL	60.00	27.00	7.50
☐ 347 Ed Summers: Detroit	50.00	22.00	6.25
☐ 348 Jeff Sweeney: New York AL	50.00	22.00	6.25
☐ 349 Bill Sweeney: Boston NL	50.00	22.00	6.25
☐ 350 Jesse Tannehill: Washington	50.00	22.00	6.25
☐ 351 Lee Tannehill: Chicago AL (Listed as L.Tannehill)	60.00	27.00	7.50
☐ 352 Lee Tannehill: Chicago AL (Listed as Tannehill)	50.00	22.00	6.25
☐ 353 Fred Tenney: N.Y. NL	60.00	27.00	7.50
☐ 354 Ira Thomas: Phila. AL	50.00	22.00	6.25
☐ 355 Joe Tinker: Chicago NL Ready to hit	175.00	80.00	22.00
☐ 356 Joe Tinker: Chicago NL Bat on shoulder	200.00	90.00	25.00
☐ 357 Joe Tinker: Chicago NL Portrait	250.00	110.00	31.00
☐ 358 Joe Tinker: Chicago NL Hands on knees	225.00	100.00	28.00
☐ 359 John Titus: Phila. NL	50.00	22.00	6.25
☐ 360 Terry Turner: Cleveland	60.00	27.00	7.50
☐ 361 Bob Unglaub: Washington	50.00	22.00	6.25
☐ 362 Rube Waddell: St.L. AL Portrait	275.00	125.00	34.00
☐ 363 Rube Waddell: St.L. AL Pitching	175.00	80.00	22.00
☐ 364 Heinie Wagner: Boston AL Bat on left shoulder	100.00	45.00	12.50
☐ 365 Heinie Wagner: Boston AL Bat on right shoulder	60.00	27.00	7.50
☐ 366 Honus Wagner: Pitt.	225000.00	100000.00	27500.00
☐ 367 Bobby Wallace: St. Louis AL	175.00	80.00	22.00
☐ 368 Ed Walsh: Chicago AL	225.00	100.00	28.00
☐ 369 Jack Warhop: N.Y. AL	50.00	22.00	6.25
☐ 370 Jake Weimer: N.Y. NL	60.00	27.00	7.50
☐ 371 Zach Wheat: Brooklyn	200.00	90.00	25.00
☐ 372 Doc White: Chicago AL Portrait	60.00	27.00	7.50
☐ 373 Doc White: Chicago AL Pitching	50.00	22.00	6.25
☐ 374 Kaiser Wilhelm: Brooklyn Batting	50.00	22.00	6.25
☐ 375 Kaiser Wilhelm: Brooklyn Hands to chest	60.00	27.00	7.50
☐ 376 Ed Willett: Detroit Batting	50.00	22.00	6.25
☐ 377 Ed Willetts (Sic, Willett): Detroit Pitching	50.00	22.00	6.25

Card	EX-MT	VG-E	GOOD
☐ 378 Jimmy Williams: St. Louis AL	60.00	27.00	7.50
☐ 379 Vic Willis: Pitt.	250.00	110.00	31.00
☐ 380 Vic Willis: St.L. NL Pitching	200.00	90.00	25.00
☐ 381 Vic Willis: St.L. NL Batting	200.00	90.00	25.00
☐ 382 Chief Wilson: Pitt.	50.00	22.00	6.25
☐ 383 Hooks Wiltse: N.Y. NL Portrait	60.00	27.00	7.50
☐ 384 Hooks Wiltse: N.Y. NL Sweater	50.00	22.00	6.25
☐ 385 Hooks Wiltse: N.Y. NL Pitching	50.00	22.00	6.25
☐ 386 Cy Young: Cleveland Portrait	700.00	325.00	90.00
☐ 387 Cy Young: Cleveland Pitch, front view	500.00	220.00	60.00
☐ 388 Cy Young: Cleveland Pitch, side view	500.00	220.00	60.00
☐ 389 Heinie Zimmerman: Chicago NL	50.00	22.00	6.25
☐ 390 Fred Abbott: Toledo	40.00	18.00	5.00
☐ 391 Merle(Doc) Adkins: Baltimore	40.00	18.00	5.00
☐ 392 John Anderson: Providence	40.00	18.00	5.00
☐ 393 Herman Armbruster: St. Paul	40.00	18.00	5.00
☐ 394 Harry Arndt: Prov.	40.00	18.00	5.00
☐ 395 Cy Barger: Rochester	50.00	22.00	6.25
☐ 396 John Barry: Milwaukee	40.00	18.00	5.00
☐ 397 Emil H. Batch: Rochester	40.00	18.00	5.00
☐ 398 Jake Beckley: K.C.	200.00	90.00	25.00
☐ 399 Russell Blackburne (Lena): Providence	40.00	18.00	5.00
☐ 400 David Brain: Buffalo	40.00	18.00	5.00
☐ 401 Roy Brashear: K.C.	40.00	18.00	5.00
☐ 402 Fred Burchell: Buffalo	40.00	18.00	5.00
☐ 403 Jimmy Burke: Ind.	40.00	18.00	5.00
☐ 404 John Butler: Roch.	40.00	18.00	5.00
☐ 405 Charles Carr: Ind.	40.00	18.00	5.00
☐ 406 James Peter Casey (Doc): Montreal	40.00	18.00	5.00
☐ 407 Peter Cassidy: Baltimore	40.00	18.00	5.00
☐ 408 Wm. Chappelle: Rochester	50.00	22.00	6.25
☐ 409 Wm. Clancy: Buffalo	40.00	18.00	5.00
☐ 410 Joshua Clark: Col.	40.00	18.00	5.00
☐ 411 William Clymer: Columbus	40.00	18.00	5.00
☐ 412 Jimmy Collins: Minneapolis	250.00	110.00	31.00
☐ 413 Bunk Congalton: Columbus	40.00	18.00	5.00
☐ 414 Gavvy Cravath: Minneapolis	60.00	27.00	7.50
☐ 415 Monte Cross: Ind.	50.00	22.00	6.25
☐ 416 Paul Davidson: Ind.	40.00	18.00	5.00
☐ 417 Frank Delehanty: Louisville	50.00	22.00	6.25
☐ 418 Rube Dessau: Balt.	40.00	18.00	5.00
☐ 419 Gus Dorner: K.C.	40.00	18.00	5.00
☐ 420 Jerome Downs: Minn.	40.00	18.00	5.00
☐ 421 Jack Dunn: Baltimore	50.00	22.00	6.25
☐ 422 James Flanagan: Buffalo	40.00	18.00	5.00
☐ 423 James Freeman: Tol.	40.00	18.00	5.00
☐ 424 John Ganzel: Roch.	40.00	18.00	5.00
☐ 425 Myron Grimshaw: Toronto	40.00	18.00	5.00
☐ 426 Robert Hall: Balt.	40.00	18.00	5.00
☐ 427 William Hallman: Kansas City	50.00	22.00	6.25
☐ 428 John Hannifan: J.C.	40.00	18.00	5.00
☐ 429 Jack Hayden: Ind.	40.00	18.00	5.00
☐ 430 Harry Hinchman: Toledo	40.00	18.00	5.00
☐ 431 Harry C. Hoffman (Izzy): Providence	40.00	18.00	5.00
☐ 432 James B. Jackson: Baltimore	50.00	22.00	6.25
☐ 433 Joe Kelley: Tor.	200.00	90.00	25.00
☐ 434 Rube Kisinger: Buffalo, (Sic) Kissinger	50.00	22.00	6.25
☐ 435 Otto Kruger: Col. (Sic) Krueger	40.00	18.00	5.00
☐ 436 Wm. Lattimore: Tol.	40.00	18.00	5.00
☐ 437 James Lavender: Providence	40.00	18.00	5.00
☐ 438 Carl Lundgren: K.C.	40.00	18.00	5.00
☐ 439 Wm. Malarkey: Buff.	50.00	22.00	6.25
☐ 440 Wm. Maloney: Roch.	40.00	18.00	5.00
☐ 441 Dennis McGann: Milwaukee	40.00	18.00	5.00
☐ 442 James McGinley: Toronto	40.00	18.00	5.00
☐ 443 Joe McGinnity: New.	225.00	100.00	28.00
☐ 444 Ulysses McGlynn: Milwaukee	40.00	18.00	5.00
☐ 445 George Merritt: Jersey City	40.00	18.00	5.00
☐ 446 Wm. Milligan: J.C.	40.00	18.00	5.00
☐ 447 Fred Mitchell: Tor.	40.00	18.00	5.00
☐ 448 Dan Moeller: J.C.	40.00	18.00	5.00
☐ 449 Joseph Herbert Moran: Providence	40.00	18.00	5.00
☐ 450 Wm. Nattress: Buffalo	40.00	18.00	5.00
☐ 451 Frank Oberlin: Minneapolis	40.00	18.00	5.00
☐ 452 Peter O'Brien: St. Paul	40.00	18.00	5.00
☐ 453 Wm. O'Neil: Minn.	40.00	18.00	5.00
☐ 454 James Phelan: Prov.	40.00	18.00	5.00
☐ 455 Oliver Pickering: Minneapolis.	40.00	18.00	5.00
☐ 456 Philip Poland: Baltimore	40.00	18.00	5.00
☐ 457 Ambrose Puttman: Louisville	40.00	18.00	5.00
☐ 458 Lee Quillen: Minn.	40.00	18.00	5.00
☐ 459 Newton Randall: Milwaukee	40.00	18.00	5.00
☐ 460 Louis Ritter: K.C.	40.00	18.00	5.00
☐ 461 Dick Rudolph: Tor.	40.00	18.00	5.00
☐ 462 George Schirm: Buffalo	40.00	18.00	5.00
☐ 463 Larry Schlafly: Newark	40.00	18.00	5.00
☐ 464 Ossie Schreck: Col. (Sic) Schreckengost	50.00	22.00	6.25
☐ 465 William Shannon: Kansas City	40.00	18.00	5.00
☐ 466 Bayard Sharpe: Newark	40.00	18.00	5.00
☐ 467 Royal Shaw: Prov.	40.00	18.00	5.00
☐ 468 James Slagle: Balt.	40.00	18.00	5.00
☐ 469 George Henry Smith: Buffalo	40.00	18.00	5.00
☐ 470 Samuel Strang: Baltimore	40.00	18.00	5.00
☐ 471 Luther Taylor: (Dummy): Buffalo	90.00	40.00	11.00
☐ 472 John Thielman: Louisville	40.00	18.00	5.00
☐ 473 John F. White: Buffalo	40.00	18.00	5.00
☐ 474 William Wright: Toledo	40.00	18.00	5.00
☐ 475 Irving M. Young: Minneapolis	50.00	22.00	6.25
☐ 476 Jack Bastian: San Antonio	100.00	45.00	12.50
☐ 477 Harry Bay: Nashv.	100.00	45.00	12.50
☐ 478 Wm. Bernhard: Nashville	100.00	45.00	12.50
☐ 479 Ted Breitenstein: New Orleans	100.00	45.00	12.50
☐ 480 George Carey: (Scoops): Memphis	100.00	45.00	12.50
☐ 481 Cad Coles: Augusta	100.00	45.00	12.50
☐ 482 Wm. Cranston: Memphis	100.00	45.00	12.50
☐ 483 Roy Ellam: Nashville	100.00	45.00	12.50
☐ 484 Edward Foster: Charleston	100.00	45.00	12.50
☐ 485 Charles Fritz: N.O.	100.00	45.00	12.50
☐ 486 Ed Greminger: Montgomery	100.00	45.00	12.50
☐ 487 Guiheen: Portsmouth	100.00	45.00	12.50
☐ 488 William F. Hart Little Rock	100.00	45.00	12.50
☐ 489 James Henry Hart: Montgomery	100.00	45.00	12.50
☐ 490 J.R. Helm: Columbus (Georgia)	100.00	45.00	12.50
☐ 491 Gordon Hickman: Mobile	100.00	45.00	12.50
☐ 492 Buck Hooker: Lynchburg	100.00	45.00	12.50
☐ 493 Ernie Howard: Sav.	100.00	45.00	12.50
☐ 494 A.O. Jordan: Atlanta	100.00	45.00	12.50
☐ 495 J.F. Kiernan: Columbia	100.00	45.00	12.50
☐ 496 Frank King: Danville	100.00	45.00	12.50
☐ 497 James LaFitte: Macon	100.00	45.00	12.50
☐ 498 Harry Lentz: Little Rock (Sic) Sentz	100.00	45.00	12.50
☐ 499 Perry Lipe: Richmond	100.00	45.00	12.50
☐ 500 George Manion: Columbia	100.00	45.00	12.50
☐ 501 McCauley: Portsmouth	100.00	45.00	12.50
☐ 502 Charles B. Miller: Dallas	100.00	45.00	12.50
☐ 503 Carlton Molesworth: Birmingham	100.00	45.00	12.50
☐ 504 Dominic Mullaney: Jacksonville	100.00	45.00	12.50
☐ 505 Albert Orth: Lynchburg	100.00	45.00	12.50
☐ 506 William Otey: Norf.	100.00	45.00	12.50
☐ 507 George Paige: Charleston	100.00	45.00	12.50
☐ 508 Hub Perdue: Nashv.	125.00	55.00	15.50
☐ 509 Archie Persons: Montgomery	100.00	45.00	12.50
☐ 510 Edward Reagan: N.O.	100.00	45.00	12.50
☐ 511 R.H. Revelle: Richmond	100.00	45.00	12.50
☐ 512 Isaac Rockenfeld: Montgomery	100.00	45.00	12.50
☐ 513 Ray Ryan: Roanoke	100.00	45.00	12.50
☐ 514 Charles Seitz: Norfolk	100.00	45.00	12.50
☐ 515 Frank Shaughnessy (Shag): Roanoke	125.00	55.00	15.50
☐ 516 Carlos Smith: Shreveport	100.00	45.00	12.50
☐ 517 Sid Smith: Atlanta	100.00	45.00	12.50
☐ 518 M.R.(Dolly) Stark: San Antonio	125.00	55.00	15.50
☐ 519 Tony Thebo: Waco	100.00	45.00	12.50
☐ 520 Woodie Thornton: Mobile	100.00	45.00	12.50
☐ 521 Juan Violat: Jacksonville: (Sic) Viola	100.00	45.00	12.50
☐ 522 James Westlake: Danville	100.00	45.00	12.50
☐ 523 Foley White: Houston	100.00	45.00	12.50

1912 T207 Brown Background

The cards in this 207-card set measure approximately 1 1/2" by 2 5/8". The T207 set, also known as the "Brown Background" set was issued beginning in May with Broadleaf, Cycle, Napoleon, Recruit and anonymous (Factories no. 2, 3 or 25) backs in 1912. Broadleaf, Cycle and anonymous backs are difficult to obtain. Although many scarcities and cards with varying degrees of difficulty to obtain exist (see prices below), the Loudermilk, Lewis (Boston NL) and Miller (Chicago NL) cards are the rarest, followed by Saier and Tyler. The cards are numbered below for reference in alphabetical order by player's name. The complete set price below does include the Lewis variation missing the Braves patch on the sleeve.

	EX-MT	VG-E	GOOD
COMPLETE SET (208)	28000.00	12600.00	3500.00
COMMON CARD (1-207)	60.00	27.00	7.50
☐ 1 Bert Adams: Cleve.	80.00	36.00	10.00
☐ 2 Eddie Ainsmith: Wash.	60.00	27.00	7.50
☐ 3 Rafael Almeida: Cinc	80.00	36.00	10.00
☐ 4 Jimmy Austin: StL AL with StL on shirt	60.00	27.00	7.50
☐ 5 Jimmy Austin: StL AL without StL on shirt	125.00	55.00	15.50
☐ 6 Neal Ball: Cleve	60.00	27.00	7.50
☐ 7 Cy Barger: Brk	60.00	27.00	7.50
☐ 8 Jack Barry: Phil AL	60.00	27.00	7.50
☐ 9 Paddy Bauman: Det	125.00	55.00	15.50
☐ 10 Beals Becker: NY NL	60.00	27.00	7.50
☐ 11 Chief Bender: Phil AL	200.00	90.00	25.00
☐ 12 Joe Benz: Chi AL	80.00	36.00	10.00
☐ 13 Bob Bescher: Cinc	60.00	27.00	7.50
☐ 14 Joe Birmingham: Cleve	80.00	36.00	10.00
☐ 15 Lena Blackburne: Chi AL	80.00	36.00	10.00
☐ 16 Fred Blanding: Cleve	80.00	36.00	10.00
☐ 17 Bruno Block: Chi AL	60.00	27.00	7.50
☐ 18 Ping Bodie: Chi AL	60.00	27.00	7.50
☐ 19 Hugh Bradley: Bos AL	60.00	27.00	7.50
☐ 20 Roger Bresnahan: StL NL	200.00	90.00	25.00
☐ 21 Jack Bushelman: Bos AL	80.00	36.00	10.00
☐ 22 Hank Butcher: Cleve	80.00	36.00	10.00
☐ 23 Bobby Byrne: Pitt	60.00	27.00	7.50
☐ 24 Nixey Callahan: Chi AL	60.00	27.00	7.50
☐ 25 Howie Camnitz: Pitt	60.00	27.00	7.50
☐ 26 Max Carey: Pitt	150.00	70.00	19.00
☐ 27 Bill Carrigan: Bos AL correct back	60.00	27.00	7.50
☐ 28 Bill Carrigan: Bos AL Wagner back	150.00	70.00	19.00
☐ 29 George Chalmers: Phil NL	60.00	27.00	7.50
☐ 30 Frank Chance: Chi NL	250.00	110.00	31.00
☐ 31 Eddie Cicotte: Bos AL	175.00	80.00	22.00
☐ 32 Tommy Clarke: Cinc	60.00	27.00	7.50
☐ 33 King Cole: Chi NL	60.00	27.00	7.50
☐ 34 Shano Collins: Chi AL	60.00	27.00	7.50
☐ 35 Bob Coulson: Brk	60.00	27.00	7.50
☐ 36 Tex Covington: Det	60.00	27.00	7.50
☐ 37 Doc Crandall: NY NL	60.00	27.00	7.50
☐ 38 Bill Cunningham: Wash	80.00	36.00	10.00
☐ 39 Dave Danforth: Phil AL	60.00	27.00	7.50
☐ 40 Bert Daniels: NY AL	60.00	27.00	7.50
☐ 41 Jake Daubert: Brk	80.00	36.00	10.00
☐ 42 Harry Davis: Cleve	60.00	27.00	7.50
☐ 43 Jim Delahanty: Det	70.00	32.00	8.75
☐ 44 Claud Derrick: Phil AL	60.00	27.00	7.50
☐ 45 Art Devlin: Bos NL	60.00	27.00	7.50
☐ 46 Josh Devore: NY NL	60.00	27.00	7.50
☐ 47 Mike Donlin: Pitt	80.00	36.00	10.00
☐ 48 Ed Donnelly: Bos NL	80.00	36.00	10.00
☐ 49 Red Dooin: Phil NL	60.00	27.00	7.50
☐ 50 Tom Downey: Phil NL	80.00	36.00	10.00
☐ 51 Larry Doyle: NY NL	70.00	32.00	8.75
☐ 52 Dellos Drake: Det	60.00	27.00	7.50
☐ 53 Ted Easterly: Cleve	60.00	27.00	7.50
☐ 54 Rube Ellis: StL NL	60.00	27.00	7.50
☐ 55 Clyde Engle: Bos AL	60.00	27.00	7.50
☐ 56 Tex Erwin: Brk	60.00	27.00	7.50
☐ 57 Steve Evans: StL NL	60.00	27.00	7.50
☐ 58 Jack Ferry: Pitt	60.00	27.00	7.50
☐ 59 Ray Fisher: NY AL white cap	150.00	70.00	19.00
☐ 60 Ray Fisher: NY AL blue cap	80.00	36.00	10.00
☐ 61 Art Fletcher: NY NL	60.00	27.00	7.50
☐ 62 Jack Fournier: Chi AL	80.00	36.00	10.00
☐ 63 Art Fromme: Cinc	60.00	27.00	7.50
☐ 64 Del Gainor: Det	60.00	27.00	7.50
☐ 65 Larry Gardner: Bos AL	60.00	27.00	7.50
☐ 66 Lefty George: Cleve	60.00	27.00	7.50
☐ 67 Roy Golden: StL NL	60.00	27.00	7.50
☐ 68 Hank Gowdy: Bos NL	70.00	32.00	8.75
☐ 69 Peaches Graham: Phil NL	80.00	36.00	10.00
☐ 70 Jack Graney: Cleve	60.00	27.00	7.50
☐ 71 Vean Gregg: Cleve	80.00	36.00	10.00
☐ 72 Casey Hageman: Bos AL	60.00	27.00	7.50
☐ 73 Sea Lion Hall: Bos AL	60.00	27.00	7.50
☐ 74 Ed Hallinan: St.L. AL	60.00	27.00	7.50
☐ 75 Earl Hamilton: St.L. AL	60.00	27.00	7.50
☐ 76 Bob Harmon: St.L. NL	60.00	27.00	7.50
☐ 77 Grover Hartley: NY NL	80.00	36.00	10.00
☐ 78 Olaf Henriksen: Bos AL	60.00	27.00	7.50
☐ 79 John Henry: Wash	80.00	36.00	10.00
☐ 80 Buck Herzog: NY NL	80.00	36.00	10.00
☐ 81 Bob Higgins: Brk	60.00	27.00	7.50
☐ 82 Red Hoff: NY AL	80.00	36.00	10.00
☐ 83 Willie Hogan: StL AL	60.00	27.00	7.50
☐ 84 Harry Hooper: Bos AL	400.00	180.00	50.00
☐ 85 Ben Houser: Bos NL	80.00	36.00	10.00
☐ 86 Ham Hyatt: Pitt	80.00	36.00	10.00
☐ 87 Walter Johnson: Wash	1000.00	450.00	125.00
☐ 88 George Kaler: Cleve	60.00	27.00	7.50
☐ 89 Billy Kelly: Pitt	80.00	36.00	10.00
☐ 90 Jay Kirke: Bos NL	80.00	36.00	10.00
☐ 91 Johnny Kling: Bos NL	60.00	27.00	7.50
☐ 92 Otto Knabe: Phil NL	60.00	27.00	7.50
☐ 93 Elmer Knetzer: Brk	60.00	27.00	7.50
☐ 94 Ed Konetchy: StL NL	60.00	27.00	7.50
☐ 95 Harry Krause: Phil AL	60.00	27.00	7.50
☐ 96 Walt Kuhn: Chi AL	80.00	36.00	10.00
☐ 97 Joe Kutina: StL AL	80.00	36.00	10.00
☐ 98 Frank Lange: Chi AL	80.00	36.00	10.00
☐ 99 Jack Lapp: Phil AL	60.00	27.00	7.50
☐ 100 Arlie Latham: NY NL	60.00	27.00	7.50
☐ 101 Tommy Leach: Pitt	60.00	27.00	7.50
☐ 102 Lefty Leifield: Pitt	60.00	27.00	7.50
☐ 103 Ed Lennox: Chi NL	60.00	27.00	7.50
☐ 104 Duffy Lewis: Bos AL	60.00	27.00	7.50
☐ 105A Irving Lewis: Bos NL Braves patch on sleeve	2000.00	900.00	250.00
☐ 105B Irving Lewis: Bos NL Nothing on sleeve	2500.00	1100.00	300.00
☐ 106 Jack Lively: Det	60.00	27.00	7.50
☐ 107 Paddy Livingston: Cleve "A" shirt	250.00	110.00	31.00
☐ 108 Paddy Livingston: Cleve "C" shirt	250.00	110.00	31.00
☐ 109 Paddy Livingston: Cleve "c" shirt	80.00	36.00	10.00
☐ 110 Bris Lord: Phil AL	60.00	27.00	7.50
☐ 111 Harry Lord: Chi AL	60.00	27.00	7.50
☐ 112 Louis Lowdermilk: StL NL	2500.00	1100.00	300.00
☐ 113 Rube Marquard: NY NL	200.00	90.00	25.00
☐ 114 Armando Marsans: Cinc	60.00	27.00	7.50
☐ 115 George McBride: Wash	60.00	27.00	7.50

☐ 116 Alex McCarthy: Pitt	150.00	70.00	19.00
☐ 117 Ed McDonald: Bos NL	60.00	27.00	7.50
☐ 118 John McGraw: NY NL	250.00	110.00	31.00
☐ 119 Harry McIntire: Chi NL	60.00	27.00	7.50
☐ 120 Matty McIntyre: Chi AL	60.00	27.00	7.50
☐ 121 Bill McKechnie: Pitt	350.00	160.00	45.00
☐ 122 Larry McLean: Cinc	60.00	27.00	7.50
☐ 123 Clyde Milan: Wash	70.00	32.00	8.75
☐ 124 Dots Miller: Pitt	60.00	27.00	7.50
☐ 125 Ward Miller: Chi NL	1500.00	700.00	190.00
☐ 126 Otto Miller: Brk	80.00	36.00	10.00
☐ 127 Doc Miller: Bos NL	80.00	36.00	10.00
☐ 128 Mike Mitchell: Cinc	60.00	27.00	7.50
☐ 129 Willie Mitchell: Cleve	80.00	36.00	10.00
☐ 130 George Mogridge: Chi AL	80.00	36.00	10.00
☐ 131 Earl Moore: Phil NL	80.00	36.00	10.00
☐ 132 Pat Moran: Phil NL	60.00	27.00	7.50
☐ 133 Cy Morgan: Phil AL	60.00	27.00	7.50
☐ 134 Ray Morgan: Wash	60.00	27.00	7.50
☐ 135 George Moriarity: Det	80.00	36.00	10.00
☐ 136 George Mullin: Det With "D" on cap)	80.00	36.00	10.00
☐ 137 George Mullin: Det Without "D" on cap	200.00	90.00	25.00
☐ 138 Tom Needham: Chi NL	60.00	27.00	7.50
☐ 139 Red Nelson: StL AL	80.00	36.00	10.00
☐ 140 Hub Northen: Brk	60.00	27.00	7.50
☐ 141 Les Nunamaker: Bos AL	60.00	27.00	7.50
☐ 142 Rebel Oakes: StL NL	60.00	27.00	7.50
☐ 143 Buck O'Brien: Bos AL	60.00	27.00	7.50
☐ 144 Rube Oldring: Phil AL	70.00	32.00	8.75
☐ 145 Ivy Olson: Cleve	60.00	27.00	7.50
☐ 146 Marty O'Toole: Pitt	60.00	27.00	7.50
☐ 147 Dode Paskert: Phil NL	60.00	27.00	7.50
☐ 148 Barney Pelty: StL AL	80.00	36.00	10.00
☐ 149 Hub Perdue: Bos NL	70.00	32.00	8.75
☐ 150 Rube Peters: Chi AL	80.00	36.00	10.00
☐ 151 Art Phelan: Cinc	80.00	36.00	10.00
☐ 152 Jack Quinn: NY AL	70.00	32.00	8.75
☐ 153 Pat Ragan: Brk	400.00	180.00	50.00
☐ 154 Rasmussen: Phil NL	350.00	160.00	45.00
☐ 155 Morrie Rath: Chi AL	80.00	36.00	10.00
☐ 156 Ed Reulbach: Chi NL	70.00	32.00	8.75
☐ 157 Nap Rucker: Brk	70.00	32.00	8.75
☐ 158 Ryan: Cleve	80.00	36.00	10.00
☐ 159 Vic Saier: Chi NL	900.00	400.00	110.00
☐ 160 Scanlon: Phil NL	60.00	27.00	7.50
☐ 161 Germany Schaefer: Wash	70.00	32.00	8.75
☐ 162 Bill Schardt: Brk	60.00	27.00	7.50
☐ 163 Frank Schulte: Chi NL	60.00	27.00	7.50
☐ 164 Jim Scott: Chi AL	60.00	27.00	7.50
☐ 165 Hank Severeid: Cinc	60.00	27.00	7.50
☐ 166 Mike Simon: Pitt NL	60.00	27.00	7.50
☐ 167 Wally Smith: StL NL	60.00	27.00	7.50
☐ 168 Frank Smith: Cinc	60.00	27.00	7.50
☐ 169 Fred Snodgrass: NY NL	80.00	36.00	10.00
☐ 170 Tris Speaker: Bos AL	1200.00	550.00	150.00
☐ 171 Harry Spratt: Bos NL	60.00	27.00	7.50
☐ 172 Eddie Stack: Brk	60.00	27.00	7.50
☐ 173 Oscar Stanage: Det	60.00	27.00	7.50
☐ 174 Bill Steele: StL NL	60.00	27.00	7.50
☐ 175 Harry Steinfeldt: StL NL	70.00	32.00	8.75
☐ 176 George Stovall: StL AL	60.00	27.00	7.50
☐ 177 Gabby Street: NY AL	70.00	32.00	8.75
☐ 178 Amos Strunk: Phil AL	60.00	27.00	7.50
☐ 179 Billy Sullivan: Chi AL	70.00	32.00	8.75
☐ 180 Bill Sweeney: Bos NL	150.00	70.00	19.00
☐ 181 Lee Tannehill: Chi AL	60.00	27.00	7.50
☐ 182 Claude Thomas: Bos AL	60.00	27.00	7.50
☐ 183 Joe Tinker: Chi NL	250.00	110.00	31.00
☐ 184 Bert Tooley: Brk	60.00	27.00	7.50
☐ 185 Terry Turner: Cleve	60.00	27.00	7.50
☐ 186 Lefty Tyler: Bos NL	600.00	275.00	75.00
☐ 187 Hippo Vaughn: NY AL	60.00	27.00	7.50
☐ 188 Heine Wagner: Bos AL correct back	80.00	36.00	10.00
☐ 189 Heine Wagner: Bos AL Carrigan back	200.00	90.00	25.00
☐ 190 Tilly Walker: Wash	60.00	27.00	7.50
☐ 191 Bobby Wallace: StL AL	175.00	80.00	22.00
☐ 192 Jack Warhop: NY AL	60.00	27.00	7.50
☐ 193 Buck Weaver: Chi AL	600.00	275.00	75.00
☐ 194 Zack Wheat: Brk	200.00	90.00	25.00
☐ 195 Doc White: Chi AL	80.00	36.00	10.00
☐ 196 Dewey Wilie: StL NL	80.00	36.00	10.00
☐ 197 Bob Williams: NY AL	60.00	27.00	7.50
☐ 198 Art Wilson: NY NL	60.00	27.00	7.50
☐ 199 Chief Wilson: Pitt	80.00	36.00	10.00
☐ 200 Hooks Wiltse: NY NL	60.00	27.00	7.50
☐ 201 Ivey Wingo: StL NL	60.00	27.00	7.50
☐ 202 Harry Wolverton: NY AL	60.00	27.00	7.50
☐ 203 Joe Wood: Bos AL	175.00	80.00	22.00
☐ 204 Gene Woodburn: StL NL	100.00	45.00	12.50
☐ 205 Ralph Works: Det	300.00	135.00	38.00
☐ 206 Steve Yerkes: Bos AL	60.00	27.00	7.50
☐ 207 Rollie Zeider: Chi AL	100.00	45.00	12.50

1912 T227 Series of Champions

The cards in this four-card set measure approximately 2 5/16" by 3 3/8". Actually these four baseball players are but a small part of a larger set featuring a total of 21 other "Champions." The set was produced in 1912. These cards are unnumbered; the players have been alphabetized and numbered for reference in the checklist below. Card backs can be found with either Miners Extra or Honest Long Cut. The complete set price refers only to the 4 subjects listed immediately below and does not include any non-baseball subjects that may be in the set.

	EX-MT	VG-E	GOOD
COMPLETE SET (4)	3500.00	1600.00	450.00
COMMON CARD (1-4)	400.00	180.00	50.00
☐ 1 Frank Baker	450.00	200.00	55.00
☐ 2 Chief Bender	400.00	180.00	50.00
☐ 3 Ty Cobb	2700.00	1200.00	350.00
☐ 4 Rube Marquard	400.00	180.00	50.00

1916 Tango Brand Eggs

This 20-card set of 1916 Tango Brand Eggs Baseball cards was issued by the L. Frank Company in New Orleans as a promotion to increase egg sales. Less than 500 examples are known to exist, with some of the cards having quantities of less than 10 copies found. The cards have a glazed finish, a process used in several other sets of this vintage (E106, D303, T213 and T216). The fronts display a player color photo in a mix of poses (portrait, throwing, fielding, and batting). The player's name, position, and team are printed below the photo. Some of the cards are off center and poorly cut. The backs carry promotional information for the Tango Brand Eggs. The cards do not carry the Federal League designation since the league dissolved in 1915 and players moved back to the National and American League teams. One irregularity is the fact that Demmitt, Dooin, Jacklitsch, and Tinker of the E106 set appear as cards of Meyer, Morgan, Meyer, and Weaver in the Tango Brand Egg set. The set can be dated 1916, as "Germany" Schaefer appears in the set as a Brooklyn player, and prior to that year he played for Neward of the Federal League. During the 1916 season he was sold to the New York Americans, making that the only year he played for Brooklyn. The cards are unnumbered and checklisted below alphabetically.

	EX-MT	VG-E	GOOD
COMPLETE SET (20)	10000.00	4500.00	1250.00
COMMON CARD (1-20)	150.00	70.00	19.00
☐ 1 Bob Bescher	150.00	70.00	19.00
☐ 2 Roger Bresnahan	250.00	110.00	31.00
☐ 3 Al Bridwell	150.00	70.00	19.00
☐ 4 Hal Chase	250.00	110.00	31.00
☐ 5 Ty Cobb	6000.00	2700.00	750.00
☐ 6 Eddie Collins	1500.00	700.00	190.00
☐ 7 Sam Crawford	1500.00	700.00	190.00
☐ 8 Red Dooin	150.00	70.00	19.00
☐ 9 Johnny Evers	300.00	135.00	38.00
☐ 10 Hap Felsch Photo of Ray Demmitt	400.00	180.00	50.00
☐ 11 Hugh Jennings	250.00	110.00	31.00
☐ 12 George McQuillen	150.00	70.00	19.00
☐ 13 Billy Meyer Photo of Fred Jacklitsch	200.00	90.00	25.00
☐ 14 Ray Morgan Photo of Red Dooin	200.00	90.00	25.00
☐ 15 Eddie Murphy	150.00	70.00	19.00
☐ 16 Germany Schaefer	200.00	90.00	25.00
☐ 17 Joe Tinker	300.00	135.00	38.00
☐ 18 Honus Wagner	500.00	220.00	60.00
☐ 19 Buck Weaver Photo of Joe Tinker	1000.00	450.00	125.00
☐ 20 Heinie Zimmerman	150.00	70.00	19.00

1934 Tarzan Thoro Bread D382

These cards measuring approximately 2 1/2"" by 3 1/8" were issued with Tarzan Thoro Bread. Since the cards are unnumbered, we have sequenced them in alphabetical order.

	EX-MT	VG-E	GOOD
COMPLETE SET	4500.00	2000.00	550.00
COMMON CARD	300.00	135.00	38.00
☐ 1 Walter Betts	300.00	135.00	38.00
☐ 2 Edward Brandt	300.00	135.00	38.00
☐ 3 Irving 'Jack' Burns	300.00	135.00	38.00
☐ 4 Bruce Campbell	300.00	135.00	38.00
☐ 5 Tex Carleton	300.00	135.00	38.00
☐ 6 Dick Coffman	300.00	135.00	38.00
☐ 7 George Connally	300.00	135.00	38.00
☐ 8 Bill Hallahan	300.00	135.00	38.00
☐ 9 Myril Hoag	300.00	135.00	38.00
☐ 10 Chief Hogsett	300.00	135.00	38.00
☐ 11 Willie Kamm	300.00	135.00	38.00
☐ 12 Dutch Leonard	300.00	135.00	38.00
☐ 13 Clyde Manion	300.00	135.00	38.00
☐ 14 Eric McNair	300.00	135.00	38.00
☐ 15 Oscar Mellilo	300.00	135.00	38.00
☐ 16 Johnny Vergez	300.00	135.00	38.00
☐ 17 Tom Zachary	300.00	135.00	38.00

1978 Tastee-Freez Discs

This set of 26 discs were given out at participating Big T and Tastee-Freez restaurants. The discs measure 3 3/8" in diameter and were produced by MSA. The front design features a black and white headshot inside a white baseball diamond pattern. Four red stars adorn the top of the discs, and the white diamond is bordered by various colors on different discs. The backs are printed in red and blue on white and provide the disc number, player's name, his batting average or won/loss record, and sponsors' advertisements. There is a multiplier for Saga Discs which is notated below.

	NRMT	VG-E	GOOD
COMPLETE SET (26)	35.00	16.00	4.40
COMMON DISC (1-26)	.50	.23	.06
*SAGA: 5X BASIC DISCS			
☐ 1 Buddy Bell	1.00	.45	.12
☐ 2 Jim Palmer	3.00	1.35	.35
☐ 3 Steve Garvey	1.50	.70	.19
☐ 4 Jeff Burroughs	.50	.23	.06
☐ 5 Greg Luzinski	1.00	.45	.12
☐ 6 Lou Brock	3.00	1.35	.35
☐ 7 Thurman Munson	2.00	.90	.25
☐ 8 Rod Carew	3.00	1.35	.35
☐ 9 George Brett	10.00	4.50	1.25
☐ 10 Tom Seaver	4.00	1.80	.50
☐ 11 Willie Stargell	3.00	1.35	.35
☐ 12 Jerry Koosman	.50	.23	.06
☐ 13 Bill North	.50	.23	.06
☐ 14 Richie Zisk	.50	.23	.06
☐ 15 Bill Madlock	1.00	.45	.12
☐ 16 Carl Yastrzemski	3.00	1.35	.35
☐ 17 Dave Cash	.50	.23	.06
☐ 18 Bob Watson	1.00	.45	.12
☐ 19 Dave Kingman	1.50	.70	.19
☐ 20 Gene Tenace	.50	.23	.06
☐ 21 Ralph Garr	.50	.23	.06
☐ 22 Mark Fidrych	2.50	1.10	.30
☐ 23 Frank Tanana	1.00	.45	.12
☐ 24 Larry Hisle	.50	.23	.06
☐ 25 Bruce Bochte	.50	.23	.06
☐ 26 Bob Bailor	.50	.23	.06

1933 Tatoo Orbit R305

The cards in this 60-card set measure 2" by 2 1/4". The 1933 Tatoo Orbit set contains unnumbered, color cards. Blaeholder and Hadley, and to a lesser degree Andrews and Hornsby are considered more difficult to obtain than the other cards in this set. The cards are ordered and numbered below alphabetically by the player's name.

	EX-MT	VG-E	GOOD
COMPLETE SET (60)	3500.00	1600.00	450.00
COMMON CARD (1-60)	40.00	18.00	5.00
☐ 1 Dale Alexander	40.00	18.00	5.00
☐ 2 Ivy Andrews	125.00	55.00	15.50
☐ 3 Earl Averill	75.00	34.00	9.50
☐ 4 Dick Bartell	40.00	18.00	5.00
☐ 5 Wally Berger	40.00	18.00	5.00
☐ 6 George Blaeholder	175.00	80.00	22.00
☐ 7 Irving Burns	40.00	18.00	5.00
☐ 8 Guy Bush	40.00	18.00	5.00
☐ 9 Bruce Campbell	40.00	18.00	5.00
☐ 10 Chalmers Cissell	40.00	18.00	5.00
☐ 11 Watson Clark	40.00	18.00	5.00
☐ 12 Mickey Cochrane	125.00	55.00	15.50
☐ 13 Phil Collins	40.00	18.00	5.00
☐ 14 Kiki Cuyler	75.00	34.00	9.50
☐ 15 Dizzy Dean	200.00	90.00	25.00
☐ 16 Jimmy Dykes	40.00	18.00	5.00
☐ 17 George Earnshaw	40.00	18.00	5.00
☐ 18 Woody English	40.00	18.00	5.00
☐ 19 Lou Fonseca	40.00	18.00	5.00
☐ 20 Jimmy Foxx	150.00	70.00	19.00
☐ 21 Burleigh Grimes	75.00	34.00	9.50
☐ 22 Charlie Grimm	50.00	22.00	6.25
☐ 23 Lefty Grove	125.00	55.00	15.50
☐ 24 Frank Grube	40.00	18.00	5.00
☐ 25 George Haas	40.00	18.00	5.00
☐ 26 Bump Hadley	175.00	80.00	22.00
☐ 27 Chick Hafey	75.00	34.00	9.50
☐ 28 Jess Haines	75.00	34.00	9.50
☐ 29 Bill Hallahan	40.00	18.00	5.00
☐ 30 Mel Harder	50.00	22.00	6.25
☐ 31 Gabby Hartnett	75.00	34.00	9.50
☐ 32 Babe Herman	50.00	22.00	6.25
☐ 33 Billy Herman	75.00	34.00	9.50
☐ 34 Rogers Hornsby	250.00	110.00	31.00
☐ 35 Roy Johnson	40.00	18.00	5.00
☐ 36 Smead Jolley	40.00	18.00	5.00
☐ 37 Billy Jurges	40.00	18.00	5.00
☐ 38 Willie Kamm	40.00	18.00	5.00
☐ 39 Mark Koenig	40.00	18.00	5.00
☐ 40 Jim Levey	40.00	18.00	5.00
☐ 41 Ernie Lombardi	75.00	34.00	9.50
☐ 42 Red Lucas	40.00	18.00	5.00
☐ 43 Ted Lyons	75.00	34.00	9.50
☐ 44 Connie Mack MG	100.00	45.00	12.50
☐ 45 Pat Malone	40.00	18.00	5.00
☐ 46 Pepper Martin	60.00	27.00	7.50
☐ 47 Marty McManus	40.00	18.00	5.00
☐ 48 Lefty O'Doul	60.00	27.00	7.50
☐ 49 Dick Porter	40.00	18.00	5.00
☐ 50 Carl N. Reynolds	40.00	18.00	5.00
☐ 51 Charlie Root	50.00	22.00	6.25
☐ 52 Bob Seeds	40.00	18.00	5.00
☐ 53 Al Simmons	75.00	34.00	9.50
☐ 54 Riggs Stephenson	50.00	22.00	6.25
☐ 55 Lyle Tinning	40.00	18.00	5.00
☐ 56 Joe Vosmik	40.00	18.00	5.00
☐ 57 Rube Walberg	40.00	18.00	5.00
☐ 58 Paul Waner	75.00	34.00	9.50
☐ 59 Lon Warneke	40.00	18.00	5.00
☐ 60 Arthur Whitney	40.00	18.00	5.00

1933 Tatoo Orbit Self Develop R308

These very small (1 1/4" by 1 7/8") and unattractive cards are very scarce. They were produced by Tatoo Orbit around 1933. The set is presumed to include the numbers between 151 and 210; a few of the numbers are still unknown at this time. Badly over exposed cards are very difficult to identify and are considered (graded) fair at best. Two types of these cards are known: A larger card (of which only very few are known) and are very rare, and a smaller type -- which is considered the normal card. We are pricing the smaller cards.

	EX-MT	VG-E	GOOD
COMPLETE SET	3800.00	1700.00	475.00
COMMON CARD (151-207)	60.00	27.00	7.50
☐ 151 Vernon Gomez	100.00	45.00	12.50
☐ 152 Kiki Cuyler	100.00	45.00	12.50
☐ 153 Jimmy Foxx	300.00	135.00	38.00
☐ 154 Al Simmons	100.00	45.00	12.50
☐ 155 Gordon Cochrane	125.00	55.00	15.50
☐ 156 Woody English	60.00	27.00	7.50
☐ 157 Chuck Klein	100.00	45.00	12.50
☐ 158 Dick Bartell	60.00	27.00	7.50
☐ 159 Pepper Martin	75.00	34.00	9.50
☐ 160 Earl Averill	80.00	36.00	10.00
☐ 161 William Dickey	125.00	55.00	15.50
☐ 162 Wesley Ferrell	60.00	27.00	7.50
☐ 163 Oral Hildebrand	60.00	27.00	7.50
☐ 164 Willie Kamm	60.00	27.00	7.50
☐ 165 Earl Whitehill	60.00	27.00	7.50
☐ 166 Charles Fullis	60.00	27.00	7.50
☐ 167 Jimmy Dykes	60.00	27.00	7.50
☐ 168 Ben Cantwell	60.00	27.00	7.50
☐ 169 George Earnshaw	60.00	27.00	7.50
☐ 170 Jackson Stephenson	75.00	34.00	9.50
☐ 171 Randy Moore	60.00	27.00	7.50
☐ 172 Ted Lyons	100.00	45.00	12.50
☐ 173 Goose Goslin	100.00	45.00	12.50
☐ 174 Evar Swanson	60.00	27.00	7.50
☐ 175 Leroy Mahaffey	60.00	27.00	7.50
☐ 176 Joe Cronin	100.00	45.00	12.50
☐ 177 Tom Bridges	60.00	27.00	7.50
☐ 178 Henry Manush	100.00	45.00	12.50
☐ 179 Walter Stewart	60.00	27.00	7.50
☐ 180 Frank Pytlak	60.00	27.00	7.50
☐ 181 Dale Alexander	60.00	27.00	7.50
☐ 182 Robert Grove	125.00	55.00	15.50
☐ 183 Charles Gehringer	100.00	45.00	12.50
☐ 184 Lewis Fonseca	60.00	27.00	7.50
☐ 185 Alvin Crowder	60.00	27.00	7.50
☐ 186 Mickey Cochrane	125.00	55.00	15.50
☐ 187 Max Bishop	60.00	27.00	7.50
☐ 188 Connie Mack	125.00	55.00	15.50
☐ 189 Guy Bush	60.00	27.00	7.50
☐ 190 Charlie Root	60.00	27.00	7.50
☐ 191 Burleigh Grimes	100.00	45.00	12.50
☐ 192 Pat Malone	60.00	27.00	7.50

☐ 193 Woody English	60.00	27.00	7.50
☐ 194 Lonnie Warneke	60.00	27.00	7.50
☐ 195 Babe Herman	75.00	34.00	9.50
☐ 200 Gabby Hartnett	100.00	45.00	12.50
☐ 201 Paul Waner	80.00	36.00	10.00
☐ 202 Dizzy Dean	300.00	135.00	38.00
☐ 205 Jim Bottomley	100.00	45.00	12.50
☐ 207 Charles Hafey	100.00	45.00	12.50

1976 Taylor/Schmierer Bowman 47

This set which measures 2 1/16" by 2 1/2" was issued by show promoters Bob Schmierer and Ted Taylor to promote what would become their long running EPSCC shows in the Philadelphia area. The set is designed in the style of the 1948 Bowman set and according to stories even some of the same paper stock was used for these sets as was used in 1948. The first series (1-49) cards sell for considerably more than the later two series.

	NRMT	VG-E	GOOD
COMPLETE SET (113)	200.00	90.00	25.00
COMMON CARD (1-49)	1.00	.45	.12
COMMON CARD (50-113)	.25	.11	.03
☐ 1 Bobby Doerr	4.00	1.80	.50
☐ 2 Stan Musial	10.00	4.50	1.25
☐ 3 Babe Ruth	20.00	9.00	2.50
☐ 4 Joe DiMaggio	15.00	6.75	1.85
☐ 5 Andy Pafko	1.00	.45	.12
☐ 6 Johnny Pesky	1.00	.45	.12
☐ 7 Gil Hodges	7.50	3.40	.95
☐ 8 Tommy Holmes	1.00	.45	.12
☐ 9 Ralph Kiner	7.50	3.40	.95
☐ 10 Yogi Berra	10.00	4.50	1.25
☐ 11 Bob Feller	1.00	.45	.12
☐ 12 Sid Gordon	1.00	.45	.12
☐ 13 Eddie Joost	1.00	.45	.12
☐ 14 Del Ennis	1.00	.45	.12
☐ 15 Johnny Mize	7.50	3.40	.95
☐ 16 Pee Wee Reese	10.00	4.50	1.25
☐ 17 Jackie Robinson	15.00	6.75	1.85
☐ 18 Enos Slaughter	4.00	1.80	.50
☐ 19 Vern Stephens	1.00	.45	.12
☐ 20 Bobby Thomson	2.00	.90	.25
☐ 21 Ted Williams	15.00	6.75	1.85
☐ 22 Bob Elliott	1.00	.45	.12
☐ 23 Mickey Vernon	1.00	.45	.12
☐ 24 Ewell Blackwell	1.00	.45	.12
☐ 25 Lou Boudreau	4.00	1.80	.50
☐ 26 Ralph Branca	1.00	.45	.12
☐ 27 Harry Breechen	1.00	.45	.12
☐ 28 Dom DiMaggio	2.00	.90	.25
☐ 29 Bruce Edwards	1.00	.45	.12
☐ 30 Sam Chapman	1.00	.45	.12
☐ 31 George Kell	4.00	1.80	.50
☐ 32 Jack Kramer	1.00	.45	.12
☐ 33 Hal Newhouser	4.00	1.80	.50
☐ 34 Charlie Keller	1.00	.45	.12
☐ 35 Ken Keltner	1.00	.45	.12
☐ 36 Hank Greenberg	7.50	3.40	.95
☐ 37 Howie Pollet	1.00	.45	.12
☐ 38 Luke Appling	4.00	1.80	.50
☐ 39 Pete Suder	1.00	.45	.12
☐ 40 Johnny Sain	2.00	.90	.25
☐ 41 Phil Cavaretta	1.00	.45	.12
☐ 42 Johnny Vander Meer	1.00	.45	.12
☐ 43 Mel Ott	7.50	3.40	.95
☐ 44 Walker Cooper	1.00	.45	.12
☐ 45 Birdie Tebbetts	1.00	.45	.12
☐ 46 Snuffy Stirnweiss	1.00	.45	.12
☐ 47 Connie Mack MG	5.00	2.20	.60
☐ 48 Jimmie Foxx	7.50	3.40	.95
☐ 49 Joe DiMaggio Babe Ruth Checklist Back	15.00	6.75	1.85
☐ 50 Schoolboy Rowe	.25	.11	.03
☐ 51 Andy Seminick	.25	.11	.03
☐ 52 Dixie Walker	.25	.11	.03
☐ 53 Virgil Trucks	.25	.11	.03
☐ 54 Dizzy Trout	.25	.11	.03
☐ 55 Hoot Evers	.25	.11	.03
☐ 56 Thurman Tucker	.25	.11	.03
☐ 57 Fritz Ostermuller	.25	.11	.03
☐ 58 Augie Galan	.25	.11	.03
☐ 59 Babe Young	.25	.11	.03
☐ 60 Skeeter Newsome	.25	.11	.03
☐ 61 Jack Lohrke	.25	.11	.03
☐ 62 Rudy York	.25	.11	.03
☐ 63 Tex Hughson	.25	.11	.03
☐ 64 Sam Mele	.25	.11	.03
☐ 65 Fred Hutchinson	.50	.23	.06
☐ 66 Don Black	.25	.11	.03
☐ 67 Les Fleming	.25	.11	.03
☐ 68 George McQuinn	.25	.11	.03
☐ 69 Mike McCormick	.25	.11	.03
☐ 70 Mickey Witek	.25	.11	.03
☐ 71 Blix Donnelly	.25	.11	.03
☐ 72 Elbie Fletcher	.25	.11	.03
☐ 73 Hal Gregg	.25	.11	.03
☐ 74 Dick Whitman	.25	.11	.03
☐ 75 Johnny Neun MG	.25	.11	.03
☐ 76 Doyle Lade	.25	.11	.03
☐ 77 Ron Northey	.25	.11	.03
☐ 78 Mort Cooper	.25	.11	.03
☐ 79 Warren Spahn	3.00	1.35	.35
☐ 80 Happy Chandler COMM	1.00	.45	.12
☐ 81 Connie Mack Roy Mack Connie Mack III Checklist Back	1.00	.45	.12
☐ 82 Earle Mack Asst MG	.25	.11	.03
☐ 83 Buddy Rosar	.25	.11	.03
☐ 84 Walt Judnich	.25	.11	.03
☐ 85 Bob Kennedy	.25	.11	.03
☐ 86 Tom Tresh	.25	.11	.03
☐ 87 Sid Hudson	.25	.11	.03
☐ 88 Gene Thompson	.25	.11	.03
☐ 89 Bill Nicholson	.25	.11	.03
☐ 90 Stan Hack	.50	.23	.06
☐ 91 Terry Moore	.50	.23	.06
☐ 92 Ted Lyons MG	1.00	.45	.12
☐ 93 Barney McCoskey	.25	.11	.03
☐ 94 Stan Spence	.25	.11	.03
☐ 95 Larry Jansen	.25	.11	.03
☐ 96 Whitey Kurowski	.25	.11	.03
☐ 97 Honus Wagner CO	4.00	1.80	.50
☐ 98 Billy Herman MG	1.00	.45	.12
☐ 99 Jim Tabor	.25	.11	.03
☐ 100 Phil Marchidon	.25	.11	.03
☐ 101 Dave Ferriss	.25	.11	.03
☐ 102 Al Zarilla	.25	.11	.03
☐ 103 Bob Dillinger	.50	.23	.06
☐ 104 Bob Lemon	2.00	.90	.25
☐ 105 Jim Hegan	.25	.11	.03
☐ 106 Johnny Lindell	.25	.11	.03
☐ 107 Williard Marshall	.25	.11	.03
☐ 108 Walt Masterson	.25	.11	.03
☐ 109 Carl Scheib	.25	.11	.03
☐ 110 Bobby Brown	1.00	.45	.12
☐ 111 Cy Block	.25	.11	.03
☐ 112 Sid Gordon	.50	.23	.06
☐ 113 Ty Cobb Babe Ruth Tris Speaker Checklist Back	7.50	3.40	.95

1975 TCMA All-Time Greats

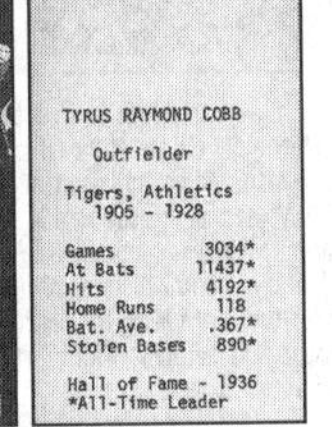

TYRUS RAYMOND COBB
Outfielder
Tigers, Athletics
1905 - 1928
Games 3034*
At Bats 11437*
Hits 4192*
Home Runs 118
Bat. Ave. .367*
Stolen Bases 890*
Hall of Fame - 1936
*All-Time Leader

This 36-card set measures approximately 2 3/8" by 3 3/4" and features blue-and white player photos. The pictures are framed in blue with a bat and ball in each top corner. The card name and player's name are in the top and bottom margins respectively. The backs carry the player's name, position, team name and career stats. The cards are unnumbered and checklisted below in alphabetical order.

	NRMT	VG-E	GOOD
COMPLETE SET (36)	50.00	22.00	6.25
COMMON CARD (1-36)	1.00	.45	.12
☐ 1 Earl Averill	1.00	.45	.12
☐ 2 Jim Bottomley	1.00	.45	.12
☐ 3 Lou Boudreau	1.00	.45	.12
☐ 4 Fred Clarke	1.00	.45	.12
☐ 5 Roberto Clemente	5.00	2.20	.60
☐ 6 Ty Cobb	5.00	2.20	.60
☐ 7 Jocko Conlon	1.00	.45	.12
☐ 8 Hugh Duffy	1.00	.45	.12
☐ 9 Red Faber	1.00	.45	.12
☐ 10 Whitey Ford	3.00	1.35	.35
☐ 11 Jimmy Foxx	2.50	1.10	.30
☐ 12 Burleigh Grimes	1.00	.45	.12
☐ 13 Lefty Grove	2.00	.90	.25
☐ 14 Bucky Harris	1.00	.45	.12
☐ 15 Billy Herman	1.00	.45	.12
☐ 16 Miller Huggins	1.00	.45	.12
☐ 17 Monte Irvin	1.00	.45	.12
☐ 18 Ralph Kiner	2.00	.90	.25
☐ 19 Sandy Koufax	3.00	1.35	.35
☐ 20 Judge Landis	1.00	.45	.12
☐ 21 Mickey Mantle	5.00	2.20	.60
☐ 22 Joe McCarthy	1.00	.45	.12
☐ 23 John McGraw	1.00	.45	.12
☐ 24 Bill McKechnie	1.00	.45	.12
☐ 25 Ducky Medwick	1.00	.45	.12
☐ 26 Hoss Radborn	1.00	.45	.12
☐ 27 Sam Rice	1.00	.45	.12
☐ 28 Jackie Robinson	5.00	2.20	.60
☐ 29 Wilbert Robinson	1.00	.45	.12
☐ 30 Babe Ruth	7.50	3.40	.95
☐ 31 Babe Ruth (Closer head photo)	7.50	3.40	.95
☐ 32 George Sisler	1.00	.45	.12
☐ 33 Tris Speaker	1.00	.45	.12
☐ 34 Zack Wheat	1.00	.45	.12
☐ 35 Ted Williams	5.00	2.20	.60
☐ 36 Ross Youngs	1.00	.45	.12

1977 TCMA The War Years

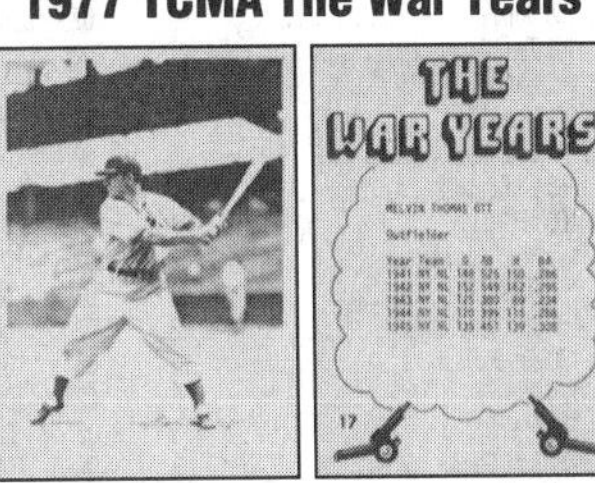

This standard-size set features players who stayed at home and played major league baseball during the Second World War.

	NRMT	VG-E	GOOD
COMPLETE SET	30.00	13.50	3.70
COMMON CARD (1-90)	.30	.14	.04
☐ 1 Sam Narron	.30	.14	.04
☐ 2 Ray Mack	.30	.14	.04
☐ 3 Mickey Owen	.30	.14	.04
☐ 4 John Gaston Peacock	.30	.14	.04
☐ 5 Dizzy Trout	.30	.14	.04
☐ 6 Birdie Tebbetts	.30	.14	.04
☐ 7 Alfred Todd	.30	.14	.04
☐ 8 Harland Clift	.30	.14	.04
☐ 9 Don Gilberto Nunez Gil Torres	.30	.14	.04
☐ 10 Al Lopez	1.00	.45	.12
☐ 11 Tony Lupien	.30	.14	.04
☐ 12 Luke Appling	1.00	.45	.12
☐ 13 Pat Seerey	.30	.14	.04
☐ 14 Phil Masi	.30	.14	.04
☐ 15 Thomas Turner	.30	.14	.04
☐ 16 Nicholas Picciuto	.30	.14	.04
☐ 17 Mel Ott	2.00	.90	.25
☐ 18 Red Treadway	.30	.14	.04
☐ 19 Samuel Naham	.30	.14	.04
☐ 20 Rip Sewell	.30	.14	.04
☐ 21 Roy Partee	.30	.14	.04
☐ 22 Richard Siebert	.30	.14	.04
☐ 23 Red Barrett	.30	.14	.04
☐ 24 Lefty O'Dea	.30	.14	.04
☐ 25 Louis Parisse	.30	.14	.04
☐ 26 Martin Marion	.75	.35	.09
☐ 27 Eugene Moore Jr.	.30	.14	.04
☐ 28 Walter "Boom Boom" Beck	.30	.14	.04
☐ 29 Donald Manno	.30	.14	.04
☐ 30 Hal Newhouser	1.00	.45	.12
☐ 31 Gus Mancuso	.30	.14	.04
☐ 32 Pinky May	.30	.14	.04
☐ 33 Gerald Priddy	.30	.14	.04
☐ 34 Herman Besse	.30	.14	.04
☐ 35 Luis Olmo	.30	.14	.04
☐ 36 Robert O'Neill	.30	.14	.04
☐ 37 John Barrett	.30	.14	.04
☐ 38 Gordon Maltzberger	.30	.14	.04
☐ 39 William Nicholson	.50	.23	.06
☐ 40 Ron Northey	.30	.14	.04
☐ 41 Howard Pollet	.30	.14	.04
☐ 42 Aloysius Piechota	.30	.14	.04
☐ 43 Robert Shepard	.30	.14	.04
☐ 44 Alfred Anderson	.30	.14	.04
☐ 45 Damon Phillips	.30	.14	.04
☐ 46 Herman Franks	.30	.14	.04
☐ 47 Aldon Wilkie	.30	.14	.04
☐ 48 Max Macon	.30	.14	.04
☐ 49 Lester Webber	.30	.14	.04
☐ 50 Robert Swift	.30	.14	.04
☐ 51 Philip Weintraub	.30	.14	.04
☐ 52 Nicholas Strincevich	.30	.14	.04
☐ 53 Michael Tresh	.30	.14	.04
☐ 54 William Trotter	.30	.14	.04
☐ 55 Frankie Crosetti Bud Metheny Billy Johnson Charley Keller Bill Dickey Nick Etten Joe Gordon Johnny Lindell Spud Chandler John Sturm 1943 New York Yankees Lineup	.75	.35	.09
☐ 57 Silas Johnson	.30	.14	.04
☐ 58 Don Kolloway	.30	.14	.04
☐ 59 Cecil Porter Vaughan	.30	.14	.04
☐ 60 George McQuinn Chet Laabs Harlond Clift Walt Judnich St. Louis Browns Bombers	.30	.14	.04
☐ 61 Harold Wagner	.30	.14	.04
☐ 62 Alva Javery	.30	.14	.04
☐ 63 George Barnicle Bob Williams Frank LaManna Art Johnson Ed Carnett Casey Stengel MG Boston Braves Rookie Pitchers	.50	.23	.06
☐ 64 Dolf Camilli	.75	.35	.09
☐ 65 Mike McCormick	.30	.14	.04
☐ 66 Dick Wakefield	.30	.14	.04
☐ 67 Mickey Vernon	.75	.35	.09
☐ 68 John Vander Meer	.75	.35	.09
☐ 69 Mack McDonnell	.30	.14	.04
☐ 70 Thomas Jordan	.30	.14	.04
☐ 71 Maurice Van Robays	.30	.14	.04
☐ 72 Charles Stanceu	.30	.14	.04
☐ 73 Samuel Zoldak	.30	.14	.04
☐ 74 Ray Starr	.30	.14	.04
☐ 75 Roger Wolff	.30	.14	.04
☐ 76 Cecil Travis	.50	.23	.06
☐ 77 Arthur Johnson	.30	.14	.04
☐ 78 Louis Riggs	.30	.14	.04
☐ 79 Peter Suder	.30	.14	.04
☐ 80 Thomas Warren	.30	.14	.04
☐ 81 John Welaj	.30	.14	.04
☐ 82 Gee Walker	.30	.14	.04
☐ 83 Dee Williams	.30	.14	.04
☐ 84 Leonard Merullo	.30	.14	.04
☐ 85 Swede Johnson	.30	.14	.04
☐ 86 Junior Thompson	.30	.14	.04
☐ 87 William Zuber	.30	.14	.04
☐ 88 Earl Johnson	.30	.14	.04
☐ 89 Babe Young	.30	.14	.04
☐ 90 Jim Wallace	.30	.14	.04

1978 TCMA 60'S I

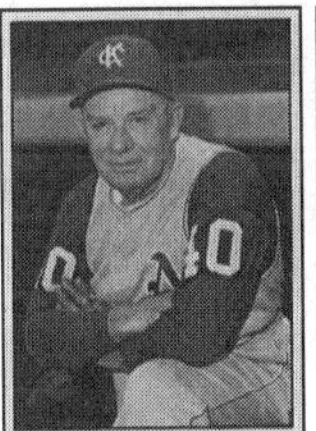

The TCMA Stars of the 60's consists of 293 standard-size cards. This set was issued through hobby dealers at the time and was TCMA's second set of retired players. The set uses many photos from Mike Aronstein's library of photos. Many of the great and not so great players of the 60's are featured. No card numbers 43 or 98 were printed.

	NRMT	VG-E	GOOD
COMPLETE SET (293)	50.00	22.00	6.25
COMMON CARD (1-293)	.05	.02	.01
☐ 1 Smoky Burgess	.10	.05	.01
☐ 2 Juan Marichal	1.00	.45	.12
☐ 3 Don Drysdale	1.00	.45	.12
☐ 4 Jim Gentile	.05	.02	.01
☐ 5 Roy Face	.10	.05	.01
☐ 6 Joe Pignatano	.10	.05	.01
☐ 7 Joe Christopher	.05	.02	.01
☐ 8 Wayne Causey	.05	.02	.01
☐ 9 Frank Bolling	.05	.02	.01
☐ 10 Jim Maloney	.10	.05	.01
☐ 11 Roger Maris	1.00	.45	.12
☐ 12 Bill White	.25	.11	.03
☐ 13 Roberto Clemente	5.00	2.20	.60
☐ 14 Bob Saverine	.05	.02	.01
☐ 15 Barney Schultz	.05	.02	.01
☐ 16 Albie Pearson	.05	.02	.01
☐ 17 Denny LeMaster	.05	.02	.01
☐ 18 Ernie Broglio	.05	.02	.01
☐ 19 Bobby Klaus	.05	.02	.01
☐ 20 Tony Cloninger	.05	.02	.01
☐ 21 Whitey Ford	1.00	.45	.12
☐ 22 Ron Santo	.50	.23	.06
☐ 23 Jim Duckworth	.05	.02	.01
☐ 24 Willie Davis	.10	.05	.01
☐ 25 Ed Charles	.05	.02	.01
☐ 26 Bob Allison	.10	.05	.01
☐ 27 Fritz Ackley	.05	.02	.01
☐ 28 Ruben Amaro	.05	.02	.01
☐ 29 Johnny Callison	.10	.05	.01
☐ 30 Greg Bollo	.05	.02	.01
☐ 31 Felix Millan	.05	.02	.01
☐ 32 Camilo Pascual	.10	.05	.01
☐ 33 Jackie Brandt	.05	.02	.01
☐ 34 Don Lock	.05	.02	.01
☐ 35 Chico Ruiz	.05	.02	.01
☐ 36 Joe Azcue	.05	.02	.01
☐ 37 Ed Bailey	.05	.02	.01

☐ 38 Pete Ramos .05 .02 .01
☐ 39 Eddie Bressoud .05 .02 .01
☐ 40 Al Kaline 2.00 .90 .25
☐ 41 Ron Brand .05 .02 .01
☐ 42 Bob Lillis .05 .02 .01
☐ 44 Buster Narum .05 .02 .01
☐ 45 Junior Gilliam .35 .16 .04
☐ 46 Claude Raymond .05 .02 .01
☐ 47 Billy Bryan .05 .02 .01
☐ 48 Marshall Bridges .05 .02 .01
☐ 49 Norm Cash .35 .16 .04
☐ 50 Orlando Cepeda .50 .23 .06
☐ 51 Lee Maye .05 .02 .01
☐ 52 Andy Rodgers .05 .02 .01
☐ 53 Ken Berry .05 .02 .01
☐ 54 Don Mincher .05 .02 .01
☐ 55 Jerry Lumpe .05 .02 .01
☐ 56 Milt Pappas .05 .02 .01
☐ 57 Steve Barber .05 .02 .01
☐ 58 Dennis Menke .05 .02 .01
☐ 59 Larry Maxie .05 .02 .01
☐ 60 Bob Gibson 1.50 .70 .19
☐ 61 Larry Bearnarth .05 .02 .01
☐ 62 Bill Mazeroski .75 .35 .09
☐ 63 Bob Rodgers .05 .02 .01
☐ 64 Jerry Arrigo .05 .02 .01
☐ 65 Joe Nuxhall .10 .05 .01
☐ 66 Dean Chance .10 .05 .01
☐ 67 Ken Boyer .35 .16 .04
☐ 68 John Odom .05 .02 .01
☐ 69 Chico Cardenas .05 .02 .01
☐ 70 Maury Wills .50 .23 .06
☐ 71 Tony Oliva .50 .23 .06
☐ 72 Don Nottebart .05 .02 .01
☐ 73 Joe Adcock .10 .05 .01
☐ 74 Felipe Alou .25 .11 .03
☐ 75 Matty Alou .10 .05 .01
☐ 76 Dick Radatz .05 .02 .01
☐ 77 Jim Bouton .25 .11 .03
☐ 78 John Blanchard .05 .02 .01
☐ 79 Juan Pizarro .05 .02 .01
☐ 80 Boog Powell .50 .23 .06
☐ 81 Earl Robinson .05 .02 .01
☐ 82 Bob Chance .05 .02 .01
☐ 83 Max Alvis .05 .02 .01
☐ 84 Don Blasingame .05 .02 .01
☐ 85 Tom Cheney .05 .02 .01
☐ 86 Jerry Arrigo .05 .02 .01
☐ 87 Tommy Davis .10 .05 .01
☐ 88 Steve Boros .05 .02 .01
☐ 89 Don Cardwell .05 .02 .01
☐ 90 Harmon Killebrew 1.00 .45 .12
☐ 91 Jim Pagliaroni .05 .02 .01
☐ 92 Jim O'Toole .05 .02 .01
☐ 93 Dennis Bennett .05 .02 .01
☐ 94 Dick McAuliffe .10 .05 .01
☐ 95 Dick Brown .05 .02 .01
☐ 96 Joe Amalfitano .05 .02 .01
☐ 97 Phil Linz .05 .02 .01
☐ 99 Dave Nicholson .05 .02 .01
☐ 100 Hoyt Wilhelm .75 .35 .09
☐ 101 Don Leppert .05 .02 .01
☐ 102 Jose Pagan .05 .02 .01
☐ 103 Sam McDowell .10 .05 .01
☐ 104 Jack Baldschun .05 .02 .01
☐ 105 Jim Perry .10 .05 .01
☐ 106 Hal Reniff .05 .02 .01
☐ 107 Lee Maye .05 .02 .01
☐ 108 Joe Adcock .10 .05 .01
☐ 109 Bob Bolin .05 .02 .01
☐ 110 Don Leppert .05 .02 .01
☐ 111 Bill Monbouquette .05 .02 .01
☐ 112 Bobby Richardson .25 .11 .03
☐ 113 Earl Battey .05 .02 .01
☐ 114 Bob Veale .05 .02 .01
☐ 115 Lou Jackson .05 .02 .01
☐ 116 Frank Kreutzer .05 .02 .01
☐ 117 Jerry Zimmerman .05 .02 .01
☐ 118 Don Schwall .05 .02 .01
☐ 119 Rich Rollins .05 .02 .01
☐ 120 Pete Ward .05 .02 .01
☐ 121 Moe Drabowsky .05 .02 .01
☐ 122 Jesse Gonder .05 .02 .01
☐ 123 Hal Woodeschick .05 .02 .01
☐ 124 John Herrnstein .05 .02 .01
☐ 125 Leon Wagner .05 .02 .01
☐ 126 Dwight Siebler .05 .02 .01
☐ 127 Gary Kroll .05 .02 .01
☐ 128 Tony Horton .05 .02 .01
☐ 129 John DeMerit .05 .02 .01
☐ 130 Sandy Koufax 3.00 1.35 .35
☐ 131 Jim Davenport .05 .02 .01
☐ 132 Wes Covington .05 .02 .01
☐ 133 Tony Taylor .10 .05 .01
☐ 134 Jack Kralick .05 .02 .01
☐ 135 Bill Pleis .05 .02 .01
☐ 136 Russ Snyder .05 .02 .01
☐ 137 Joe Torre .50 .23 .06
☐ 138 Ted Wills .05 .02 .01
☐ 139 Wes Stock .05 .02 .01
☐ 140 Frank Robinson 1.50 .70 .19
☐ 141 Dave Stenhouse .05 .02 .01
☐ 142 Ron Hansen .05 .02 .01
☐ 143 Don Elston .05 .02 .01
☐ 144 Del Crandall .05 .02 .01
☐ 145 Bennie Daniels .05 .02 .01
☐ 146 Vada Pinson .10 .05 .01
☐ 147 Bill Spanswick .05 .02 .01
☐ 148 Earl Wilson .05 .02 .01
☐ 149 Ty Cline .05 .02 .01
☐ 150 Dick Groat .10 .05 .01
☐ 151 Jim Duckworth .05 .02 .01
☐ 152 Jim Schaffer .05 .02 .01
☐ 153 George Thomas .05 .02 .01
☐ 154 Wes Stock .05 .02 .01
☐ 155 Mike White .05 .02 .01
☐ 156 John Podres .10 .05 .01
☐ 157 Willie Crawford .05 .02 .01
☐ 158 Fred Gladding .05 .02 .01
☐ 159 John Wyatt .05 .02 .01
☐ 160 Bob Friend .05 .02 .01
☐ 161 Ted Uhlaender .05 .02 .01
☐ 162 Dick Stigman .05 .02 .01
☐ 163 Don Wert .05 .02 .01
☐ 164 Eddie Bressoud .05 .02 .01
☐ 165 Ed Roebuck .05 .02 .01
☐ 166 Al Spangler .05 .02 .01
☐ 167 Bob Sadowski .05 .02 .01
☐ 168 Ralph Terry .05 .02 .01
☐ 169 Jim Schaffer .05 .02 .01
☐ 170 Jim Fregosi .10 .05 .01
☐ 170 Dick Hall .05 .02 .01
☐ 171 Al Spangler .05 .02 .01
☐ 172 Bob Tillman .05 .02 .01
☐ 173 Ed Bailey .05 .02 .01
☐ 174 Cesar Tovar .05 .02 .01
☐ 175 Morrie Stevens .05 .02 .01
☐ 176 Floyd Weaver .05 .02 .01
☐ 177 Frank Malzone .05 .02 .01
☐ 178 Norm Siebern .05 .02 .01
☐ 179 Dick Phillips .05 .02 .01
☐ 181 Bobby Wine .05 .02 .01
☐ 182 Masanori Murakami 1.50 .70 .19
☐ 183 Chuck Schilling .05 .02 .01
☐ 184 Jim Schaffer .05 .02 .01
☐ 185 John Roseboro .10 .05 .01
☐ 186 Jake Wood .05 .02 .01
☐ 187 Dallas Green .10 .05 .01
☐ 188 Tom Haller .05 .02 .01
☐ 189 Chuck Cottier .05 .02 .01
☐ 190 Brooks Robinson 1.50 .70 .19
☐ 191 Ty Cline .05 .02 .01
☐ 192 Bubba Phillips .05 .02 .01
☐ 193 Al Jackson .05 .02 .01
☐ 194 Herm Starrette .05 .02 .01
☐ 195 Dave Wickersham .05 .02 .01
☐ 196 Vic Power .05 .02 .01
☐ 197 Ray Culp .05 .02 .01
☐ 198 Don Demeter .05 .02 .01
☐ 199 Dick Schofield .05 .02 .01
☐ 200 Mudcat Grant .05 .02 .01
☐ 201 Roger Craig .10 .05 .01
☐ 202 Dick Farrell .05 .02 .01
☐ 203 Clay Dalrymple .05 .02 .01
☐ 204 Jim Duffalo .05 .02 .01
☐ 205 Tito Francona .05 .02 .01
☐ 206 Tony Conigliaro .25 .11 .03
☐ 207 Jim King .05 .02 .01
☐ 208 Joel Gibson .05 .02 .01
☐ 209 Arnold Earley .05 .02 .01
☐ 210 Denny McLain .25 .11 .03
☐ 211 Don Larsen .10 .05 .01
☐ 212 Ron Hunt .05 .02 .01
☐ 213 Deron Johnson .05 .02 .01
☐ 214 Harry Bright .05 .02 .01
☐ 215 Ernie Fazio .05 .02 .01
☐ 216 Joey Jay .05 .02 .01
☐ 217 Jim Coates .05 .02 .01
☐ 218 Jerry Kindall .05 .02 .01
☐ 219 Joe Gibbon .05 .02 .01
☐ 220 Frank Howard .35 .16 .04
☐ 221 Howie Koplitz .05 .02 .01
☐ 222 Larry Jackson .05 .02 .01
☐ 223 Dale Long .05 .02 .01
☐ 224 Jimmy Dykes MG .10 .05 .01
☐ 225 Hank Aguirre .05 .02 .01
☐ 226 Earl Francis .05 .02 .01
☐ 227 Vic Wertz .05 .02 .01
☐ 228 Larry Haney .05 .02 .01
☐ 229 Tony LaRussa .50 .23 .06
☐ 230 Moose Skowron .10 .05 .01
☐ 231 Lee Thomas .05 .02 .01
☐ 231 Tito Francona .05 .02 .01
☐ 232 Ken Johnson .05 .02 .01
☐ 233 Dick Howser .05 .02 .01
☐ 234 Bobby Knoop .05 .02 .01
☐ 236 Elston Howard .35 .16 .04
☐ 237 Donn Clendenon .05 .02 .01
☐ 238 Jesse Gonder .05 .02 .01
☐ 239 Vern Law .10 .05 .01
☐ 240 Curt Flood .25 .11 .03
☐ 241 Dal Maxvill .05 .02 .01
☐ 242 Roy Sievers .10 .05 .01
☐ 243 Jim Brewer .05 .02 .01
☐ 244 Harry Craft MG .05 .02 .01
☐ 245 Dave Eilers .05 .02 .01
☐ 246 Dave DeBusschere .35 .16 .04
☐ 247 Ken Harrelson .10 .05 .01
☐ 248 Jim Duffalo .05 .02 .01
☐ 249 Ed Kasko .05 .02 .01
☐ 250 Luis Aparicio .75 .35 .09
☐ 251 Ron Kline .05 .02 .01
☐ 252 Chuck Hinton .05 .02 .01
☐ 253 Frank Lary .05 .02 .01
☐ 254 Stu Miller .05 .02 .01
☐ 255 Ernie Banks 2.00 .90 .25
☐ 256 Dick Farrell .05 .02 .01
☐ 257 Bud Daley .05 .02 .01
☐ 258 Luis Arroyo .05 .02 .01
☐ 259 Bob Del Greco .05 .02 .01
☐ 260 Ted Williams 5.00 2.20 .60
☐ 261 Mike Epstein .05 .02 .01
☐ 262 Mickey Mantle 7.50 3.40 .95
☐ 263 Jim LeFebvre .05 .02 .01
☐ 264 Pat Jarvis .05 .02 .01
☐ 265 Chuck Hinton .05 .02 .01
☐ 266 Don Larsen .25 .11 .03
☐ 267 Jim Coates .05 .02 .01
☐ 268 Gary Kolb .05 .02 .01
☐ 269 Jim Hart .05 .02 .01
☐ 270 Dave McNally .10 .05 .01
☐ 271 Jerry Kindall .05 .02 .01
☐ 272 Hector Lopez .05 .02 .01
☐ 273 Claude Osteen .05 .02 .01
☐ 274 Jack Aker .05 .02 .01
☐ 275 Mike Shannon .10 .05 .01
☐ 276 Lew Burdette .10 .05 .01
☐ 277 Mack Jones .05 .02 .01
☐ 278 Art Shamsky .05 .02 .01
☐ 279 Bob Johnson .05 .02 .01
☐ 280 Willie Mays 4.00 1.80 .50
☐ 281 Rich Nye .05 .02 .01
☐ 282 Bill Cowan .05 .02 .01
☐ 283 Gary Kolb .05 .02 .01
☐ 284 Woody Held .05 .02 .01
☐ 285 Bill Freehan .10 .05 .01
☐ 286 Larry Jackson .05 .02 .01
☐ 287 Mike Hershberger .05 .02 .01
☐ 288 Julian Javier .05 .02 .01
☐ 289 Charley Smith .05 .02 .01
☐ 290 Hank Aaron 4.00 1.80 .50
☐ 291 John Boccabella .05 .02 .01
☐ 292 Charley James .05 .02 .01
☐ 293 Sammy Ellis .05 .02 .01

1979 TCMA 50'S

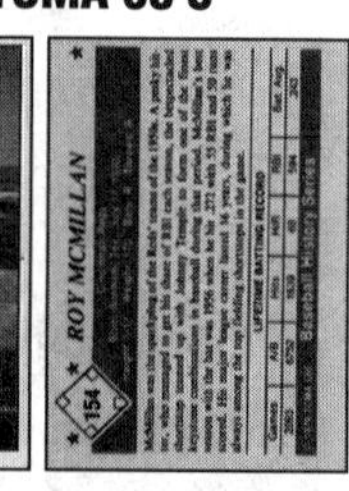

The TCMA Stars of the 50's set contains 291 standard-size cards featuring the players of the 50's. The set features a good mix of superstars and not so important players of the era. This set was TCMA's attempt at issuing cards after Topps successfully enjoined them from issuing current players. Using the style which was typical of most of the TCMA issues, the fronts are clear with an informative biography on the back. The Hutchinson and Wertz cards were also issued with the word "SAMPLE" stamped on the back. There is no extra value for these cards.

	NRMT	VG-E	GOOD
COMPLETE SET (291)	50.00	22.00	6.25
COMMON CARD (1-291)	.05	.02	.01

☐ 1 Joe DiMaggio 5.00 2.20 .60
☐ 2 Yogi Berra 2.00 .90 .25
☐ 3 Warren Spahn 1.50 .70 .19
☐ 4 Robin Roberts .75 .35 .09
☐ 5 Ernie Banks 2.50 1.10 .30
☐ 6 Willie Mays 4.00 1.80 .50
☐ 7 Mickey Mantle 7.50 3.40 .95
☐ 8 Roy Campanella 2.00 .90 .25
☐ 9 Stan Musial 2.50 1.10 .30
☐ 10 Ted Williams 5.00 2.20 .60
☐ 11 Ed Bailey .05 .02 .01
☐ 12 Ted Kluszewski .50 .23 .06
☐ 13 Ralph Kiner .75 .35 .09
☐ 14 Dick Littlefield .05 .02 .01
☐ 15 Nellie Fox .50 .23 .06
☐ 16 Billy Pierce .10 .05 .01
☐ 17 Richie Ashburn .50 .23 .06
☐ 18 Del Ennis .10 .05 .01
☐ 19 Bob Lemon .75 .35 .09
☐ 20 Early Wynn .75 .35 .09
☐ 21 Joe Collins .05 .02 .01
☐ 22 Hank Bauer .10 .05 .01
☐ 23 Roberto Clemente 5.00 2.20 .60
☐ 24 Frank Thomas .10 .05 .01
☐ 25 Alvin Dark .10 .05 .01
☐ 26 Whitey Lockman .05 .02 .01
☐ 27 Larry Doby .25 .11 .03
☐ 28 Bob Feller 2.00 .90 .25
☐ 29 Willie Jones .05 .02 .01
☐ 30 Granny Hamner .05 .02 .01
☐ 31 Clem Labine .10 .05 .01
☐ 32 Ralph Branca .10 .05 .01
☐ 33 Jack Harshman .05 .02 .01
☐ 34 Dick Donovan .05 .02 .01
☐ 35 Tommy Henrich .25 .11 .03
☐ 36 Jerry Coleman .10 .05 .01
☐ 37 Billy Hoeft .05 .02 .01
☐ 38 Johnny Groth .05 .02 .01
☐ 39 Harvey Haddix .10 .05 .01
☐ 40 Gerry Staley .05 .02 .01
☐ 41 Dale Long .05 .02 .01
☐ 42 Vernon Law .10 .05 .01
☐ 43 Duke Snider 1.00 .45 .12
Gil Hodges
Roy Campanella
Carl Furillo
Dodger Power
☐ 44 Sam Jethroe .10 .05 .01
☐ 45 Vic Wertz .10 .05 .01
☐ 46 Wes Westrum .05 .02 .01
☐ 47 Dee Fondy .05 .02 .01
☐ 48 Gene Baker .05 .02 .01
☐ 49 Sandy Koufax 2.50 1.10 .30
☐ 50 Billy Loes .05 .02 .01
☐ 51 Chuck Diering .05 .02 .01
☐ 52 Joe Ginsberg .05 .02 .01
☐ 53 Jim Konstanty .10 .05 .01
☐ 54 Curt Simmons .10 .05 .01
☐ 55 Alex Kellner .05 .02 .01
☐ 56 Charlie Dressen MG .10 .05 .01
☐ 57 Frank Sullivan .05 .02 .01
☐ 58 Mel Parnell .05 .02 .01
☐ 59 Bobby Hofman .05 .02 .01
☐ 60 Bill Connelly .05 .02 .01
☐ 61 Corky Valentine .05 .02 .01
☐ 62 Johnny Klippstein .05 .02 .01
☐ 63 Chuck Tanner .10 .05 .01
☐ 64 Dick Drott .05 .02 .01
☐ 65 Dean Stone .05 .02 .01
☐ 66 Jim Busby .05 .02 .01
☐ 67 Sid Gordon .05 .02 .01
☐ 68 Del Crandall .10 .05 .01
☐ 69 Walker Cooper .05 .02 .01
☐ 70 Hank Sauer .10 .05 .01
☐ 71 Gil Hodges .75 .35 .09
☐ 72 Duke Snider 2.00 .90 .25
☐ 73 Sherman Lollar .05 .02 .01
☐ 74 Chico Carrasquel .05 .02 .01
☐ 75 Gus Triandos .10 .05 .01
☐ 76 Bob Harrison .05 .02 .01
☐ 77 Eddie Waitkus .05 .02 .01
☐ 78 Ken Heintzelman .05 .02 .01
☐ 79 Harry Simpson .05 .02 .01
☐ 80 Luke Easter .10 .05 .01
☐ 81 Ed Dick .05 .02 .01
☐ 82 Jim DePalo .05 .02 .01
☐ 83 Billy Cox .10 .05 .01
☐ 84 Pee Wee Reese 1.50 .70 .19
☐ 85 Virgil Trucks .05 .02 .01
☐ 86 George Kell .50 .23 .06
☐ 87 Mickey Vernon .10 .05 .01
☐ 88 Eddie Yost .05 .02 .01
☐ 89 Gus Bell .05 .02 .01
☐ 90 Dick Wakefield .05 .02 .01
☐ 93 Solly Hemus .05 .02 .01
☐ 94 Red Schoendienst .50 .23 .06
☐ 95 Sammy White .05 .02 .01
☐ 96 Billy Goodman .05 .02 .01
☐ 97 Jim Hearn .05 .02 .01
☐ 98 Ruben Gomez .05 .02 .01
☐ 99 Marty Marion .10 .05 .01
☐ 100 Bill Virdon .10 .05 .01
☐ 101 Chuck Stobbs .05 .02 .01
☐ 102 Ron Samford .05 .02 .01
☐ 103 Bill Tuttle .05 .02 .01
☐ 104 Harvey Kuenn .10 .05 .01
☐ 105 Joe Cunningham .05 .02 .01
☐ 106 Bill Sarni .05 .02 .01
☐ 107 Jack Kramer .05 .02 .01
☐ 108 Eddie Stanky .10 .05 .01
☐ 109 Carmen Mauro .05 .02 .01
☐ 110 Wayne Belardi .05 .02 .01
☐ 111 Preston Ward .05 .02 .01
☐ 112 Jack Shepard .05 .02 .01
☐ 113 Buddy Kerr .05 .02 .01
☐ 114 Vern Bickford .05 .02 .01
☐ 115 Ellis Kinder .05 .02 .01
☐ 116 Walt Dropo .05 .02 .01
☐ 117 Duke Maas .05 .02 .01
☐ 118 Billy Hunter .05 .02 .01
☐ 119 Ewell Blackwell .10 .05 .01
☐ 120 Hershell Freeman .05 .02 .01
☐ 121 Freddie Martin .05 .02 .01
☐ 122 Erv Dusak .05 .02 .01
☐ 123 Roy Hartsfield .05 .02 .01
☐ 124 Willard Marshall .05 .02 .01
☐ 125 Jack Sanford .05 .02 .01
☐ 126 Herman Wehmeier .05 .02 .01
☐ 127 Hal Smith .05 .02 .01
☐ 128 Jim Finigan .05 .02 .01
☐ 129 Bob Hale .05 .02 .01
☐ 130 Jim Wilson .05 .02 .01
☐ 131 Bill Wight .05 .02 .01
☐ 132 Mike Fornieles .05 .02 .01
☐ 133 Steve Gromek .05 .02 .01
☐ 134 Herb Score .10 .05 .01

☐ 135 Ryne Duren	.10	.05	.01
☐ 136 Bob Turley	.10	.05	.01
☐ 137 Wally Moon	.10	.05	.01
☐ 138 Fred Hutchinson	.10	.05	.01
☐ 139 Jim Hegan	.05	.02	.01
☐ 140 Dale Mitchell	.05	.02	.01
☐ 141 Walt Moryn	.05	.02	.01
☐ 142 Cal Neeman	.05	.02	.01
☐ 143 Billy Martin	.75	.35	.09
☐ 144 Phil Rizzuto	1.50	.70	.19
☐ 145 Preacher Roe	.25	.11	.03
☐ 146 Carl Erskine	.25	.11	.03
☐ 147 Vic Power	.05	.02	.01
☐ 148 Elmer Valo	.05	.02	.01
☐ 149 Don Mueller	.10	.05	.01
☐ 150 Hank Thompson	.05	.02	.01
☐ 151 Stan Lopata	.05	.02	.01
☐ 152 Dick Sisler	.05	.02	.01
☐ 153 Willard Schmidt	.05	.02	.01
☐ 154 Roy McMillan	.05	.02	.01
☐ 155 Gil McDougald	.10	.05	.01
☐ 156 Gene Woodling	.10	.05	.01
☐ 157 Eddie Mathews	.75	.35	.09
☐ 158 Johnny Logan	.10	.05	.01
☐ 159 Dan Bankhead	.05	.02	.01
☐ 160 Joe Black	.10	.05	.01
☐ 161 Roger Maris	2.50	1.10	.30
☐ 162 Bob Cerv	.05	.02	.01
☐ 163 Paul Minner	.05	.02	.01
☐ 164 Bob Rush	.05	.02	.01
☐ 165 Gene Hermanski	.05	.02	.01
☐ 166 Harry Brecheen	.05	.02	.01
☐ 167 Davey Williams	.05	.02	.01
☐ 168 Monte Irvin	.50	.23	.06
☐ 169 Clint Courtney	.05	.02	.01
☐ 170 Sandy Consuegra	.05	.02	.01
☐ 171 Bobby Shantz	.10	.05	.01
☐ 172 Harry Byrd	.05	.02	.01
☐ 173 Marv Throneberry	.10	.05	.01
☐ 174 Woody Held	.05	.02	.01
☐ 175 Al Rosen	.25	.11	.03
☐ 176 Rance Pless	.05	.02	.01
☐ 177 Steve Bilko	.05	.02	.01
☐ 178 Joe Presko	.05	.02	.01
☐ 179 Ray Boone	.05	.02	.01
☐ 180 Jim Lemon	.05	.02	.01
☐ 181 Andy Pafko	.10	.05	.01
☐ 182 Don Newcombe	.25	.11	.03
☐ 183 Frank Lary	.05	.02	.01
☐ 184 Al Kaline	2.00	.90	.25
☐ 185 Allie Reynolds	.25	.11	.03
☐ 186 Vic Raschi	.10	.05	.01
☐ 187 Jake Pitler CO	.25	.11	.03
Walt Alston MG			
Joe Becker CO			
Billy Herman CO			
Dodger Braintrust			
☐ 188 Jimmy Piersall	.10	.05	.01
☐ 189 George Wilson	.05	.02	.01
☐ 190 Jim Rhodes	.05	.02	.01
☐ 191 Duane Pillette	.05	.02	.01
☐ 192 Dave Philley	.05	.02	.01
☐ 193 Bobby Morgan	.05	.02	.01
☐ 194 Russ Meyer	.05	.02	.01
☐ 195 Hector Lopez	.05	.02	.01
☐ 196 Arnie Portocarrero	.05	.02	.01
☐ 197 Joe Page	.10	.05	.01
☐ 198 Tommy Byrne	.05	.02	.01
☐ 199 Ray Monzant	.05	.02	.01
☐ 200 John McCall	.05	.02	.01
☐ 201 Leo Durocher	.50	.23	.06
☐ 202 Bobby Thomson	.25	.11	.03
☐ 203 Jack Banta	.05	.02	.01
☐ 204 Joe Pignatano	.05	.02	.01
☐ 205 Carlos Paula	.05	.02	.01
☐ 206 Roy Sievers	.10	.05	.01
☐ 207 Mickey McDermott	.05	.02	.01
☐ 208 Ray Scarborough	.05	.02	.01
☐ 209 Bill Miller	.05	.02	.01
☐ 210 Bill Skowron	.25	.11	.03
☐ 211 Bob Nieman	.05	.02	.01
☐ 212 Al Pilarcik	.05	.02	.01
☐ 213 Jerry Priddy	.05	.02	.01
☐ 214 Frank House	.05	.02	.01
☐ 215 Don Mossi	.10	.05	.01
☐ 216 Rocky Colavito	.50	.23	.06
☐ 217 Brooks Lawrence	.05	.02	.01
☐ 218 Ted Wilks	.05	.02	.01
☐ 219 Zack Monroe	.05	.02	.01
☐ 220 Art Ditmar	.05	.02	.01
☐ 221 Cal McLish	.05	.02	.01
☐ 222 Gene Bearden	.05	.02	.01
☐ 223 Norm Siebern	.05	.02	.01
☐ 224 Bob Wiesler	.05	.02	.01
☐ 225 Foster Castleman	.05	.02	.01
☐ 226 Daryl Spencer	.05	.02	.01
☐ 227 Dick Williams	.10	.05	.01
☐ 228 Don Zimmer	.10	.05	.01
☐ 229 Jackie Jensen	.10	.05	.01
☐ 230 Billy Johnson	.05	.02	.01
☐ 231 Dave Koslo	.05	.02	.01
☐ 232 Al Corwin	.05	.02	.01
☐ 233 Erv Palica	.05	.02	.01
☐ 234 Bob Milliken	.05	.02	.01
☐ 235 Ray Kaat	.05	.02	.01
☐ 236 Sammy Calderone	.05	.02	.01
☐ 237 Don Demeter	.05	.02	.01
☐ 238 Karl Spooner	.05	.02	.01
☐ 239 Preacher Roe	.10	.05	.01
Johnny Podres			
☐ 240 Enos Slaughter	.50	.23	.06
☐ 241 Dick Kryhoski	.05	.02	.01
☐ 242 Art Houtteman	.05	.02	.01
☐ 243 Andy Carey	.05	.02	.01
☐ 244 Tony Kubek	.25	.11	.03
☐ 245 Mike McCormick	.05	.02	.01
☐ 246 Bob Schmidt	.05	.02	.01
☐ 247 Nelson King	.05	.02	.01
☐ 248 Bob Skinner	.05	.02	.01
☐ 249 Dick Bokelmann	.05	.02	.01
☐ 250 Eddie Kazak	.05	.02	.01
☐ 251 Billy Klaus	.05	.02	.01
☐ 252 Norm Zauchin	.05	.02	.01
☐ 253 Art Schult	.05	.02	.01
☐ 254 Bob Martyn	.05	.02	.01
☐ 255 Larry Jansen	.05	.02	.01
☐ 256 Sal Maglie	.10	.05	.01
☐ 257 Bob Darnell	.05	.02	.01
☐ 258 Ken Lehman	.05	.02	.01
☐ 259 Jim Blackburn	.05	.02	.01
☐ 260 Bob Purkey	.05	.02	.01
☐ 261 Harry Walker	.05	.02	.01
☐ 262 Joe Garagiola	.50	.23	.06
☐ 263 Gus Zernial	.05	.02	.01
☐ 264 Walter Evers	.05	.02	.01
☐ 265 Mark Freeman	.05	.02	.01
☐ 266 Charlie Silvera	.05	.02	.01
☐ 267 Johnny Podres	.25	.11	.03
☐ 268 Jim Hughes	.05	.02	.01
☐ 269 Al Worthington	.05	.02	.01
☐ 270 Hoyt Wilhelm	.50	.23	.06
☐ 271 Elston Howard	.50	.23	.06
☐ 272 Don Larsen	.25	.11	.03
☐ 273 Don Hoak	.05	.02	.01
☐ 274 Chico Fernandez	.05	.02	.01
☐ 275 Gail Harris	.05	.02	.01
☐ 276 Valmy Thomas	.05	.02	.01
☐ 277 George Shuba	.05	.02	.01
☐ 278 Al Walker	.05	.02	.01
☐ 279 Willard Ramsdell	.05	.02	.01
☐ 280 Lindy McDaniel	.05	.02	.01
☐ 281 Bob Wilson	.05	.02	.01
☐ 282 Chuck Templeton	.05	.02	.01
☐ 283 Eddie Robinson	.05	.02	.01
☐ 284 Bob Porterfield	.05	.02	.01
☐ 285 Larry Miggins	.05	.02	.01
☐ 286 Minnie Minoso	.35	.16	.04
☐ 287 Lou Boudreau	.75	.35	.09
☐ 288 Jim Davenport	.05	.02	.01
☐ 289 Bob Miller	.05	.02	.01
☐ 290 Jim Gilliam	.35	.16	.04
☐ 291 Jackie Robinson	5.00	2.20	.60

1981 TCMA 60's II

The cards in this 189-card set measure approximately 2 1/2" by 3 1/2". This set was actually a continuation of the prior TCMA Stars of the 1960's set and includes 189 additional cards for which the numbering sequence begins at number 294. They are similar in format to the first series, however, many new and different players are featured. The set was produced in 1981 and was only issued in complete set form. No card #319 was made and there are two card numbered at 399.

	NRMT	VG-E	GOOD
COMPLETE SET (189)	35.00	16.00	4.40
COMMON CARD (294-482)	.05	.02	.01
☐ 294 Fritz Brickell	.05	.02	.01
☐ 295 Craig Anderson	.05	.02	.01
☐ 296 Cliff Cook	.05	.02	.01
☐ 297 Pumpsie Green	.05	.02	.01
☐ 298 ChooChoo Coleman	.05	.02	.01
☐ 299 Don Buford	.05	.02	.01
☐ 300 Sparky Anderson	.25	.11	.03
☐ 301 John Anderson	.05	.02	.01
☐ 302 Ted Beard	.05	.02	.01
☐ 303 Mickey Mantle	5.00	2.20	.60
Roger Maris			
☐ 304 Gene Freese	.05	.02	.01
☐ 305 Don Wilkinson	.05	.02	.01
☐ 306 Walter Alston MG	.25	.11	.03
☐ 307 George Bamberger	.05	.02	.01
☐ 308 Nelson Briles	.05	.02	.01
☐ 309 Dave Baldwin	.05	.02	.01
☐ 310 Bob Bailey	.05	.02	.01
☐ 311 Paul Blair	.05	.02	.01
☐ 312 Ken Boswell	.05	.02	.01
☐ 313 Sam Bowens	.05	.02	.01
☐ 314 Ray Barker	.05	.02	.01
☐ 315 Gil Hodges MG	.35	.16	.04
Tommie Agee			
☐ 316 Elmer Valo	.05	.02	.01
☐ 317 Ken Walters	.05	.02	.01
☐ 318 Joel Horlen	.05	.02	.01
☐ 320 Charlie Maxwell	.05	.02	.01
☐ 321 Joe Foy	.05	.02	.01
☐ 322 Cleon Jones	.05	.02	.01
Tommie Agee			
Ron Swoboda			
☐ 323 Paul Foytack	.05	.02	.01
☐ 324 Ron Fairly	.15	.07	.02
☐ 325 Wilbur Wood	.15	.07	.02
☐ 326 Don Wilson	.05	.02	.01
☐ 327 Felix Mantilla	.05	.02	.01
☐ 328 Ed Bouchee	.05	.02	.01
☐ 329 Sandy Valdespino	.05	.02	.01
☐ 330 Al Ferrara	.05	.02	.01
☐ 331 Jose Tartabull	.05	.02	.01
☐ 332 Dick Kenworthy	.05	.02	.01
☐ 333 Don Pavletich	.05	.02	.01
☐ 334 Jim Fairey	.05	.02	.01
☐ 335 Rico Petrocelli	.15	.07	.02
☐ 336 Garry Roggenburk	.05	.02	.01
☐ 337 Rick Reichardt	.05	.02	.01
☐ 338 Ken McMullen	.05	.02	.01
☐ 339 Dooley Womack	.05	.02	.01
☐ 340 Joe Moock	.05	.02	.01
☐ 341 Lou Brock	2.00	.90	.25
☐ 342 Hector Torres	.05	.02	.01
☐ 343 Ted Savage	.05	.02	.01
☐ 344 Hobie Landrith	.05	.02	.01
☐ 345 Ed Lopat MG	.15	.07	.02
☐ 346 Mel Nelson	.05	.02	.01
☐ 347 Mickey Lolich	.35	.16	.04
☐ 348 Al Lopez MG	.25	.11	.03
☐ 349 ChiChi Olivo	.05	.02	.01
☐ 350 Bob Moose	.05	.02	.01
☐ 351 Bill McCool	.05	.02	.01
☐ 352 Ernie Bowman	.05	.02	.01
☐ 353 Tommy McCraw	.05	.02	.01
☐ 354 Sam Mele MG	.05	.02	.01
☐ 355 Len Boehmer	.05	.02	.01
☐ 356 Hank Aaron	5.00	2.20	.60
☐ 357 Ron Hunt	.05	.02	.01
☐ 358 Luis Aparicio	.75	.35	.09
☐ 359 Gene Mauch MG	.15	.07	.02
☐ 360 Barry Moore	.05	.02	.01
☐ 361 John Buzhardt	.05	.02	.01
☐ 362 Solly Hemus MG	.15	.07	.02
Gussie Busch OWN			
Bill Lewis CO			
Johnny Grodzicki CO			
☐ 363 Duke Snider	2.00	.90	.25
☐ 364 Billy Martin	.75	.35	.09
☐ 365 Wes Parker	.15	.07	.02
☐ 366 Dick Stuart	.15	.07	.02
☐ 367 Glenn Beckert	.05	.02	.01
☐ 368 Ollie Brown	.05	.02	.01
☐ 369 Stan Bahnsen	.05	.02	.01
☐ 370 Wesley(Lee) Bales	.05	.02	.01
☐ 371 Johnny Keane MG	.05	.02	.01
☐ 372 Wally Moon	.15	.07	.02
☐ 373 Larry Miller	.05	.02	.01
☐ 374 Fred Newman	.05	.02	.01
☐ 375 John Orsino	.05	.02	.01
☐ 376 Joe Pactwa	.05	.02	.01
☐ 377 John O'Donoghue	.05	.02	.01
☐ 378 Jim Ollom	.05	.02	.01
☐ 379 Ray Oyler	.05	.02	.01
☐ 380 Ron Nischwitz	.05	.02	.01
☐ 381 Ron Paul	.05	.02	.01
☐ 382 Roger Maris	2.50	1.10	.30
homers on May 24, 1961			
and is greeted by			
Yogi Berra			
Johnny Blanchard			
☐ 383 Jim McKnight	.05	.02	.01
☐ 384 Gene Michael	.15	.07	.02
☐ 385 Dave May	.05	.02	.01
☐ 386 Tim McCarver	.50	.23	.06
☐ 387 Larry Mason	.05	.02	.01
☐ 388 Don Hoak	.05	.02	.01
☐ 389 Nate Oliver	.05	.02	.01
☐ 390 Phil Ortega	.05	.02	.01
☐ 391 Billy Madden	.05	.02	.01
☐ 392 John Miller	.05	.02	.01
☐ 393 Danny Murtaugh MG	.15	.07	.02
☐ 394 Nelson Mathews	.05	.02	.01
☐ 395 Red Schoendienst	.25	.11	.03
☐ 396 Roger Nelson	.05	.02	.01
☐ 397 Tom Matchick	.05	.02	.01
☐ 398 Dennis Musgraves	.05	.02	.01
☐ 399 Tommy Harper	.15	.07	.02
☐ 399 Chet Trail	.05	.02	.01
☐ 400 Francis Peters	.05	.02	.01
☐ 401 Tony Pierce	.05	.02	.01
☐ 402 Billy Williams	.75	.35	.09
☐ 403 Dave Boswell	.05	.02	.01
☐ 404 Ray Washburn	.05	.02	.01
☐ 405 Al Worthington	.05	.02	.01
☐ 406 Jesus Alou	.05	.02	.01
☐ 407 Gil Hodges MG	.50	.23	.06
Yogi Berra CO			
Eddie Yost CO			
Rube Walker CO			
Joe Pignatano CO			
☐ 408 Wally Bunker	.05	.02	.01
☐ 409 Jim Brenneman	.05	.02	.01
☐ 410 Bobby Bragan MG	.05	.02	.01
☐ 411 Cal McLish	.05	.02	.01
☐ 412 Curt Blefary	.05	.02	.01
☐ 413 Jim Bethke	.05	.02	.01
☐ 414 Bill White	.15	.07	.02
Julian Javier			
Dick Groat			
Ken Boyer			
☐ 415 Richie Allen	.25	.11	.03
☐ 416 Larry Brown	.05	.02	.01
☐ 417 Mike Andrews	.05	.02	.01
☐ 418 Don Mossi	.15	.07	.02
☐ 419 J.C. Martin	.05	.02	.01
☐ 420 Dick Rustek	.05	.02	.01
☐ 421 Elly Rodriguez	.05	.02	.01
☐ 422 Casey Stengel MG	1.50	.70	.19
☐ 423 Gil Hodges MG	.25	.11	.03
Ed Vargo UMP			
Argue Over Call			
☐ 424 Johnny Briggs	.05	.02	.01
☐ 425 Bud Harrelson	.05	.02	.01
Al Weis			
of Mets Turn a Double Play			
☐ 426 Doc Edwards	.05	.02	.01
☐ 427 Joe Hague	.05	.02	.01
☐ 428 Lee Elia	.05	.02	.01
☐ 429 Billy Moran	.05	.02	.01
☐ 430 Al Moran	.05	.02	.01
☐ 431 Pete Mikkelsen	.05	.02	.01
☐ 432 Aurelio Monteagudo	.05	.02	.01
☐ 433 Ken Mackenzie	.05	.02	.01
☐ 434 Dick Egan	.05	.02	.01
☐ 435 Al McBean	.05	.02	.01
☐ 436 Mike Ferraro	.05	.02	.01
☐ 437 Gary Wagner	.05	.02	.01
☐ 438 Jerry Grote	.05	.02	.01
J.C. Martin			
☐ 439 Ted Kluszewski	.75	.35	.09
☐ 440 Jerry Johnson	.05	.02	.01
☐ 441 Ross Moschitto	.05	.02	.01
☐ 442 Zoilo Versalles	.05	.02	.01
☐ 443 Dennis Ribant	.05	.02	.01
☐ 444 Ted Williams	5.00	2.20	.60
☐ 445 Steve Whitaker	.05	.02	.01
☐ 446 Frank Bertaina	.05	.02	.01
☐ 447 Bo Belinsky	.25	.11	.03
☐ 448 Joe Moeller	.05	.02	.01
☐ 449 Ron Taylor	.05	.02	.01
Don Shaw			
☐ 450 Al Downing	.25	.11	.03
Mel Stottlemyre			
Fritz Peterson			
Whitey Ford CO			
☐ 451 Jack Tracy	.05	.02	.01
☐ 452 Tony Curry	.05	.02	.01
☐ 453 Roy White	.15	.07	.02
☐ 454 Jim Bunning	.50	.23	.06
☐ 455 Ralph Houk MG	.15	.07	.02
☐ 456 Bobby Shantz	.15	.07	.02
☐ 457 Bill Rigney MG	.05	.02	.01
☐ 458 Roger Repoz	.05	.02	.01
☐ 459 Bob Turley	.15	.07	.02
Robin Roberts			
☐ 460 Gordon Richardson	.05	.02	.01
☐ 461 Dick Tracewski	.05	.02	.01
☐ 462 Thad Tillotson	.05	.02	.01
☐ 463 Bobo Osborne	.05	.02	.01
☐ 464 Larry Burright	.05	.02	.01
☐ 465 Alan Foster	.05	.02	.01
☐ 466 Ron Taylor	.05	.02	.01
☐ 467 Fred Talbot	.05	.02	.01
☐ 468 Bob Miller	.05	.02	.01
☐ 469 Frank Tepedino	.05	.02	.01
☐ 470 Danny Frisella	.05	.02	.01
☐ 471 Cecil Perkins	.05	.02	.01
☐ 472 Danny Napoleon	.05	.02	.01
☐ 473 John Upham	.05	.02	.01
☐ 474 Roger Maris	2.50	1.10	.30
Yogi Berra			
Mickey Mantle			
Elston Howard			
Moose Skowron			
Johnny Blanchard			
☐ 475 Al Weis	.05	.02	.01
☐ 476 Rich Beck	.05	.02	.01
☐ 477 Clete Boyer	.50	.23	.06
Tony Kubek			
Bobby Richardson			
Joe Pepitone			
☐ 478 Jack Fisher	.05	.02	.01
☐ 479 Archie Moore	.05	.02	.01
☐ 480 Ralph Terry	.05	.02	.01
☐ 481 Jim Hegan CO	.15	.07	.02
Wally Moses CO			
Ralph Houk MG			
Frank Crosetti CO			
Johnny Sain CO			
☐ 482 Gil Hodges	1.00	.45	.12
Clem Labine			
Cookie Lavagetto CO			

Roger Craig
Don Zimmer, Charlie Neal
Casey Stengel MG

1983 TCMA Playball 1942

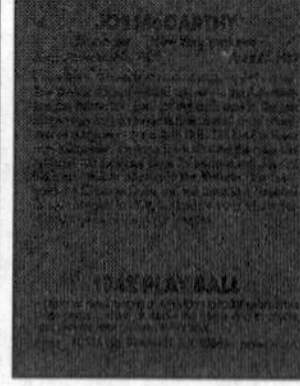

This 45-card standard-size set was printed in 1983 by TCMA and features sepia-tone posed and action player photos with white borders. A black-outline banner at the bottom contains the player's name and is accented with a baseball glove, bat, ball, and catchers mask icons. The backs are cardboard with navy blue print and display biography, player profile, and a Playball advertisement.

	NRMT	VG-E	GOOD
COMPLETE SET (45)	7.50	3.40	.95
COMMON CARD (1-45)	.10	.05	.01
☐ 1 Joe Gordon	.20	.09	.03
☐ 2 Joe DiMaggio	3.00	1.35	.35
☐ 3 Bill Dickey	.50	.23	.06
☐ 4 Joe McCarthy MG	.50	.23	.06
☐ 5 Tex Hughson	.10	.05	.01
☐ 6 Ted Williams	3.00	1.35	.35
☐ 7 Walt Judnich	.10	.05	.01
☐ 8 Vern Stephens	.20	.09	.03
☐ 9 Denny Galehouse	.10	.05	.01
☐ 10 Lou Boudreau P/MG	.50	.23	.06
☐ 11 Ken Keltner	.20	.09	.03
☐ 12 Jim Bagby	.10	.05	.01
☐ 13 Rudy York	.10	.05	.01
☐ 14 Barney McCosky	.10	.05	.01
☐ 15 Schoolboy Rowe	.10	.05	.01
☐ 16 Luke Appling	.50	.23	.06
☐ 17 Taffy Wright	.10	.05	.01
☐ 18 Ted Lyons	.50	.23	.06
☐ 19 Mickey Vernon	.20	.09	.03
☐ 20 George Case	.10	.05	.01
☐ 21 Bobo Newsom	.20	.09	.03
☐ 22 Bob Johnson	.10	.05	.01
☐ 23 Buddy Blair	.10	.05	.01
☐ 24 Pete Suder	.10	.05	.01
☐ 25 Terry Moore	.10	.05	.01
☐ 26 Stan Musial	1.50	.70	.19
☐ 27 Marty Marion	.25	.11	.03
☐ 28 Pee Wee Reese	1.00	.45	.12
☐ 29 Arky Vaughan	.50	.23	.06
☐ 30 Larry French	.10	.05	.01
☐ 31 Johnny Mize	.50	.23	.06
☐ 32 Mel Ott P/MG	.50	.23	.06
☐ 33 Willard Marshall	.10	.05	.01
☐ 34 Carl Hubbell	.50	.23	.06
☐ 35 Frank McCormick	.10	.05	.01
☐ 36 Linus Frey	.10	.05	.01
☐ 37 Bob Elliott	.20	.09	.03
☐ 38 Vince DiMaggio	.10	.05	.01
☐ 39 Al Lopez	.50	.23	.06
☐ 40 Stan Hack	.20	.09	.03
☐ 41 Lou Novikoff	.10	.05	.01
☐ 42 Casey Stengel MG	.50	.23	.06
☐ 43 Tommy Holmes	.20	.09	.03
☐ 44 Ron Northey	.10	.05	.01
☐ 45 Rube Melton	.10	.05	.01

1983 TCMA Playball 1943

This 45-card standard-size set was printed in 1983 by TCMA and features sepia-tone posed and action player photos with white borders. A black-outline banner at the bottom contains the player's name and is accented with a baseball glove, bat, ball, and catchers mask icons. The backs are cardboard with navy blue print and display biography, player profile, and a Playball advertisement.

	NRMT	VG-E	GOOD
COMPLETE SET (45)	5.00	2.20	.60
COMMON CARD (1-45)	.10	.05	.01
☐ 1 Spud Chandler	.25	.11	.03
☐ 2 Frank Crosetti	.25	.11	.03
☐ 3 Johnny Lindell	.10	.05	.01
☐ 4 Dutch Leonard	.10	.05	.01
☐ 5 Stan Spence	.10	.05	.01
☐ 6 Ray Mack	.10	.05	.01
☐ 7 Hank Edwards	.10	.05	.01
☐ 8 Al Smith	.10	.05	.01
☐ 9 Mike Tresh	.10	.05	.01
☐ 10 Don Kolloway	.10	.05	.01
☐ 11 Orval Grove	.10	.05	.01
☐ 12 Doc Cramer	.25	.11	.03
☐ 13 Mike Higgins	.10	.05	.01
☐ 14 Dick Wakefield	.10	.05	.01
☐ 15 Harland Clift	.10	.05	.01
☐ 16 Chet Laabs	.10	.05	.01
☐ 17 George McQuinn	.10	.05	.01
☐ 18 Tony Lupien	.10	.05	.01
☐ 19 Oscar Judd	.10	.05	.01
☐ 20 Roy Partee	.10	.05	.01
☐ 21 Lum Harris	.10	.05	.01
☐ 22 Roger Wolf	.10	.05	.01
☐ 23 Dick Siebert	.10	.05	.01
☐ 24 Walker Cooper	.25	.11	.03
☐ 25 Mort Cooper	.25	.11	.03
☐ 26 Whitey Kurowski	.10	.05	.01
☐ 27 Eddie Miller	.10	.05	.01
☐ 28 Elmer Riddle	.10	.05	.01
☐ 29 Bucky Walters	.25	.11	.03
☐ 30 Whitlow Wyatt	.25	.11	.03
☐ 31 Dolph Camilli	.25	.11	.03
☐ 32 Elbie Fletcher	.10	.05	.01
☐ 33 Frank Gustine	.10	.05	.01
☐ 34 Rip Sewell	.10	.05	.01
☐ 35 Phil Cavarretta	.25	.11	.03
☐ 36 Bill(Swish) Nicholson	.25	.11	.03
☐ 37 Peanuts Lowery	.10	.05	.01
☐ 38 Phil Masi	.10	.05	.01
☐ 39 Al Javery	.10	.05	.01
☐ 40 Jim Tobin	.10	.05	.01
☐ 41 Glen Stewart	.10	.05	.01
☐ 42 Mickey Livingston	.10	.05	.01
☐ 43 Ace Adams	.10	.05	.01
☐ 44 Joe Medwick	.50	.23	.06
☐ 45 Sid Gordon	.25	.11	.03

1983 TCMA Playball 1944

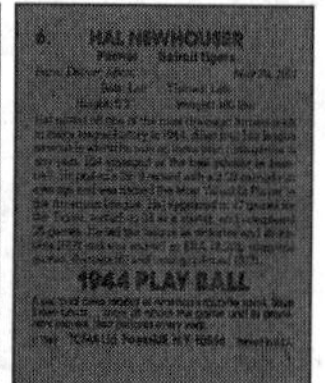

This 45-card standard-size set was printed in 1983 by TCMA and features black and white posed and action player photos with white borders. A blue-outline banner at the bottom contains the player's name and is accented with a baseball glove, bat, ball and catchers mask icons. The backs are cardboard with black print and display biography, player profile, and a Playball advertisement.

	NRMT	VG-E	GOOD
COMPLETE SET (45)	5.00	2.20	.60
COMMON CARD (1-45)	.10	.05	.01
☐ 1 Don Gutteridge	.10	.05	.01
☐ 2 Mark Christman	.10	.05	.01
☐ 3 Mike Kreevich	.10	.05	.01
☐ 4 Jimmy Outlaw	.10	.05	.01
☐ 5 Paul Richards	.25	.11	.03
☐ 6 Hal Newhouser	.50	.23	.06
☐ 7 Bud Metheny	.10	.05	.01
☐ 8 Mike Garbark	.10	.05	.01
☐ 9 Hersh Martin	.10	.05	.01
☐ 10 Bob Johnson	.10	.05	.01
☐ 11 Mike Ryba	.10	.05	.01
☐ 12 Oris Hockett	.10	.05	.01
☐ 13 Ed Klieman	.10	.05	.01
☐ 14 Ford Garrison	.10	.05	.01
☐ 15 Irv Hall	.10	.05	.01
☐ 16 Ed Busch	.10	.05	.01
☐ 17 Ralph Hogdin	.10	.05	.01
☐ 18 Thurman Tucker	.10	.05	.01
☐ 19 Bill Dietrich	.10	.05	.01
☐ 20 Rick Ferrell	.50	.23	.06
☐ 21 John Sullivan	.10	.05	.01
☐ 22 Mickey Haefner	.10	.05	.01
☐ 23 Ray Sanders	.10	.05	.01
☐ 24 Johnny Hopp	.10	.05	.01
☐ 25 Ted Wilks	.10	.05	.01
☐ 26 John Barrett	.10	.05	.01
☐ 27 Jim Russell	.10	.05	.01
☐ 28 Nick Strincevich	.10	.05	.01
☐ 29 Eric Tipton	.10	.05	.01
☐ 30 Jim Konstanty	.25	.11	.03
☐ 31 Gee Walker	.10	.05	.01
☐ 32 Dom Dellessandro	.10	.05	.01
☐ 33 Bob Chipman	.10	.05	.01
☐ 34 Hank Wyse	.10	.05	.01
☐ 35 Phil Weintraub	.10	.05	.01
☐ 36 George Hausmann	.10	.05	.01
☐ 37 Bill Voiselle	.10	.05	.01
☐ 38 Whitey Wietelman	.10	.05	.01
☐ 39 Clyde Kluttz	.10	.05	.01
☐ 40 Connie Ryan	.10	.05	.01
☐ 41 Eddie Stanky	.25	.11	.03
☐ 42 Augie Galan	.25	.11	.03
☐ 43 Mickey Owen	.10	.05	.01
☐ 44 Charlie Schanz	.10	.05	.01
☐ 45 Bob Finley	.10	.05	.01

1983 TCMA Playball 1945

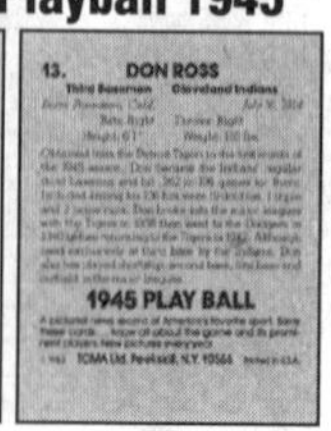

This 45-card standard-size set was printed in 1983 by TCMA and features black and white posed and action player photos with white borders. A blue-outline banner at the bottom contains the player's name and is accented with a baseball glove, bat, ball, and catchers mask icons. The backs are cardboard with black print and display biography, player profile, and a Playball advertisement.

	NRMT	VG-E	GOOD
COMPLETE SET (45)	5.00	2.20	.60
COMMON CARD (1-45)	.10	.05	.01
☐ 1 Eddie Mayo	.10	.05	.01
☐ 2 Dizzy Trout	.25	.11	.03
☐ 3 Roy Cullenbine	.10	.05	.01
☐ 4 Joe Kuhel	.10	.05	.01
☐ 5 George Binks	.10	.05	.01
☐ 6 Roger Wolff	.10	.05	.01
☐ 7 Gene Moore	.10	.05	.01
☐ 8 Frank Mancuso	.10	.05	.01
☐ 9 Bob Muncrief	.10	.05	.01
☐ 10 Tuck Stainback	.10	.05	.01
☐ 11 Bill Bevens	.10	.05	.01
☐ 12 Snuffy Stirnweiss	.25	.11	.03
☐ 13 Don Ross	.10	.05	.01
☐ 14 Felix Mackiewicz	.10	.05	.01
☐ 15 Jeff Heath	.25	.11	.03
☐ 16 Johnny Dickshot	.10	.05	.01
☐ 17 Ed Lopat	.40	.18	.05
☐ 18 Skeeter Newsom	.10	.05	.01
☐ 19 Eddie Lake	.10	.05	.01
☐ 20 John Lazor	.10	.05	.01
☐ 21 Hal Peck	.10	.05	.01
☐ 22 Al Brancato	.10	.05	.01
☐ 23 Paul Derringer	.25	.11	.03
☐ 24 x	.10	.05	.01
☐ 25 Lenny Merullo	.10	.05	.01
☐ 26 Emil Verban	.10	.05	.01
☐ 27 Ken O'Dea	.10	.05	.01
☐ 28 Red Barrett	.10	.05	.01
☐ 29 Eddie Basinski	.10	.05	.01
☐ 30 Dixie Walker	.25	.11	.03
☐ 31 Goody Rosen	.10	.05	.01
☐ 32 Preacher Roe	.25	.11	.03
☐ 33 Pete Coscarart	.10	.05	.01
☐ 34 Frankie Frisch MG	.50	.23	.06
☐ 35 Nap Reyes	.10	.05	.01
☐ 36 Danny Gardella	.10	.05	.01
☐ 37 Buddy Kerr	.10	.05	.01
☐ 38 Dick Culler	.10	.05	.01
☐ 39 Tommy Holmes	.25	.11	.03
☐ 40 Al Libke	.10	.05	.01
☐ 41 Howie Fox	.10	.05	.01
☐ 42 Johnny Riddle	.10	.05	.01
☐ 43 Andy Seminick	.25	.11	.03
☐ 44 Andy Karl	.10	.05	.01
☐ 45 Rene Monteguedo	.10	.05	.01

1984 TCMA Playball 1946

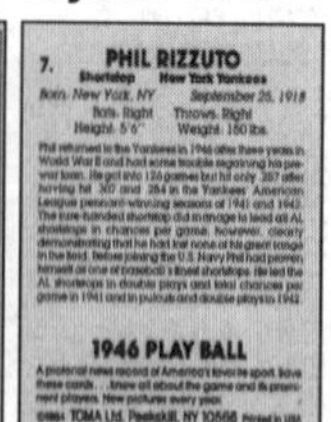

This 45-card standard-size set was printed in 1984 by TCMA and features black and white posed and action player photos with white borders. A green-outline banner at the bottom contains the player's name and is accented with a baseball glove, bat, ball, and catchers mask icons. The backs are cardboard with black print and display biography, player profile, and a Playball advertisement.

	NRMT	VG-E	GOOD
COMPLETE SET (45)	6.00	2.70	.75
COMMON CARD (1-45)	.10	.05	.01
☐ 1 Dom DiMaggio	.35	.16	.04
☐ 2 Boo Ferriss	.10	.05	.01
☐ 3 Johnny Pesky	.25	.11	.03
☐ 4 Hank Greenberg	.75	.35	.09
☐ 5 George Kell	.50	.23	.06
☐ 6 Virgil Trucks	.10	.05	.01
☐ 7 Phil Rizzuto	.75	.35	.09
☐ 8 Charlie Keller	.25	.11	.03
☐ 9 Tommy Henrich	.25	.11	.03
☐ 10 Cecil Travis	.10	.05	.01
☐ 11 Al Evans	.10	.05	.01
☐ 12 Buddy Lewis	.10	.05	.01
☐ 13 Edgar Smith	.10	.05	.01
☐ 14 Dario Lodigiani	.10	.05	.01
☐ 15 Earl Caldwell	.10	.05	.01
☐ 16 Jim Hegan	.10	.05	.01
☐ 17 Bob Feller	.75	.35	.09
☐ 18 John Berardino	.25	.11	.03
☐ 19 Jack Kramer	.10	.05	.01
☐ 20 John Lucadello	.10	.05	.01
☐ 21 Hank Majeski	.10	.05	.01
☐ 22 Elmer Valo	.10	.05	.01
☐ 23 Buddy Rosar	.10	.05	.01
☐ 24 Red Schoendienst	.50	.23	.06
☐ 25 Dick Sisler	.10	.05	.01
☐ 26 Johnny Beazley	.10	.05	.01
☐ 27 Vic Lombardi	.10	.05	.01
☐ 28 Dick Whitman	.10	.05	.01
☐ 29 Carl Furillo	.35	.16	.04
☐ 30 Billy Jurges	.10	.05	.01
☐ 31 Marv Rickert	.10	.05	.01
☐ 32 Clyde McCullough	.10	.05	.01
☐ 33 Johnny Hopp	.10	.05	.01
☐ 34 Mort Cooper	.10	.05	.01
☐ 35 Johnny Sain	.25	.11	.03
☐ 36 Del Ennis	.25	.11	.03
☐ 37 Roy Hughes	.10	.05	.01
☐ 38 Bert Haas	.10	.05	.01
☐ 39 Grady Hatton	.10	.05	.01
☐ 40 Ed Bahr	.10	.05	.01
☐ 41 Billy Cox	.25	.11	.03
☐ 42 Lee Handley	.10	.05	.01
☐ 43 Bill Rigney	.10	.05	.01
☐ 44 Babe Young	.10	.05	.01
☐ 45 Buddy Blattner	.10	.05	.01

1985 TCMA Playball 1947

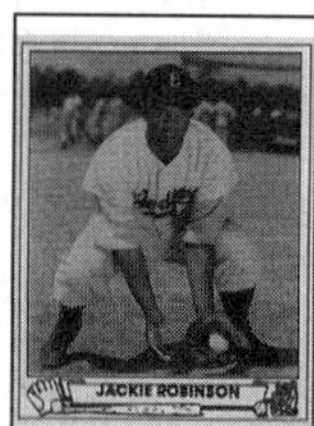

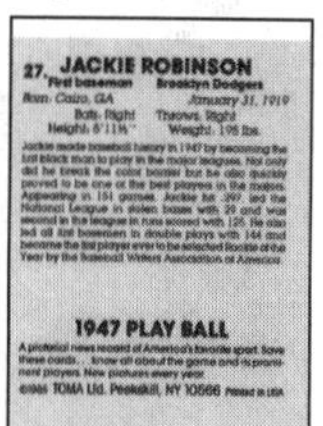

This 45-card standard-size set was printed in 1985 by TCMA and features black and white posed and action player photos with white borders. A blue-outline banner at the bottom contains the player's name and is accented with a baseball glove, bat, ball, and catchers mask icons. The backs are cardboard with black print and display biography, player profile, and a Playball advertisement.

	NRMT	VG-E	GOOD
COMPLETE SET (45)	6.00	2.70	.75
COMMON CARD (1-45)	.10	.05	.01
☐ 1 Hal Wagner	.10	.05	.01
☐ 2 Jake Jones	.10	.05	.01
☐ 3 Bobby Doerr	.50	.23	.06
☐ 4 Fred Hutchinson	.25	.11	.03
☐ 5 Bob Swift	.10	.05	.01
☐ 6 Pat Mullin	.10	.05	.01
☐ 7 Joe Page	.25	.11	.03
☐ 8 Allie Reynolds	.25	.11	.03
☐ 9 Billy Johnson	.10	.05	.01
☐ 10 Early Wynn	.50	.23	.06
☐ 11 Eddie Yost	.10	.05	.01
☐ 12 Floyd Baker	.10	.05	.01
☐ 13 Dave Philley	.10	.05	.01
☐ 14 George Dickey	.10	.05	.01
☐ 15 Dale Mitchell	.25	.11	.03
☐ 16 Bob Lemon	.50	.23	.06
☐ 17 Jerry Witte	.10	.05	.01
☐ 18 Paul Lehner	.10	.05	.01
☐ 19 Sam Zoldak	.10	.05	.01
☐ 20 Sam Chapman	.10	.05	.01
☐ 21 Eddie Joost	.25	.11	.03
☐ 22 Ferris Fain	.25	.11	.03
☐ 23 Erv Dusak	.10	.05	.01
☐ 24 Joe Garagiola	.35	.16	.04
☐ 25 Vernal "Nippy" Jones	.10	.05	.01
☐ 26 Bobby Bragan	.10	.05	.01
☐ 27 Jackie Robinson	3.00	1.35	.35
☐ 28 Spider Jorgensen	.10	.05	.01
☐ 29 Bob Scheffing	.10	.05	.01
☐ 30 Johnny Schmitz	.10	.05	.01
☐ 31 Doyle Lade	.10	.05	.01
☐ 32 Earl Torgeson	.10	.05	.01

	MINT	NRMT	EXC
☐ 33 Warren Spahn	.50	.23	.06
☐ 34 Walt Lanfranconi	.10	.05	.01
☐ 35 Johnny Wyrostek	.10	.05	.01
☐ 36 Oscar Judd	.10	.05	.01
☐ 37 Ewell Blackwell	.25	.11	.03
☐ 38 Eddie Lukon	.10	.05	.01
☐ 39 Benny Zientara	.10	.05	.01
☐ 40 Gene Woodling	.25	.11	.03
☐ 41 Ernie Bonham	.10	.05	.01
☐ 42 Hank Greenberg	.50	.23	.06
☐ 43 Bobby Thomson	.35	.16	.04
☐ 44 Jack "Lucky" Lohrke	.10	.05	.01
☐ 45 Dave Koslo	.10	.05	.01

1986 TCMA

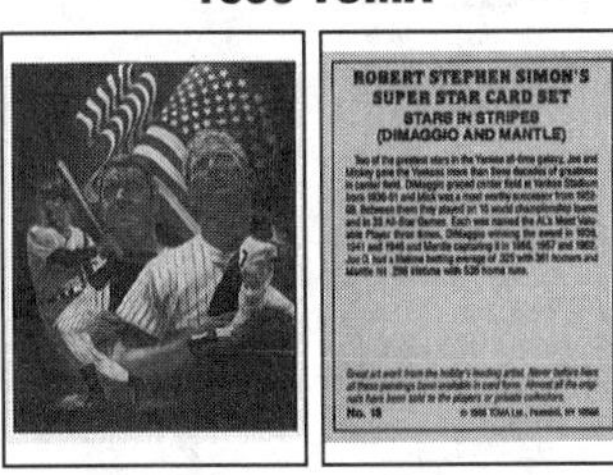
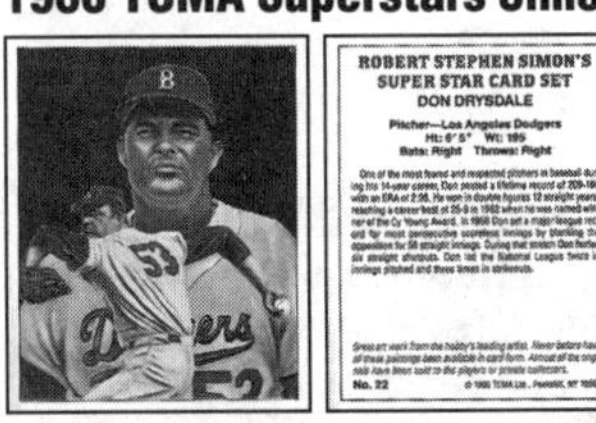

The 1986 TCMA set is comprised of 20 cards measure 2 5/16" by 3 1/2". The cards were styled after the 1953 Bowman Black and White set. The fronts feature posed and action black-and-white photos within a white outer border and an inner fine black line. The player's name does not appear on the front. The horizontal white backs contain biography within a red stripe, player profile and lifetime statistics are printed below. The card number appears in the top left corner on a diamond icon. The cards are numbered on the back.

	MINT	NRMT	EXC
COMPLETE SET (20)	15.00	6.75	1.85
COMMON CARD (1-20)	.50	.23	.06
☐ 1 Roberto Clemente	2.00	.90	.25
☐ 2 Duke Snider	1.00	.45	.12
☐ 3 Sandy Koufax	1.50	.70	.19
☐ 4 Carl Hubbell	.50	.23	.06
☐ 5 Ty Cobb	2.00	.90	.25
☐ 6 Willie Mays	2.00	.90	.25
☐ 7 Jackie Robinson	2.00	.90	.25
☐ 8 Joe DiMaggio	2.00	.90	.25
☐ 9 Stan Musial	1.00	.45	.12
☐ 10 Pie Traynor	.50	.23	.06
☐ 11 Yogi Berra	1.00	.45	.12
☐ 12 Babe Ruth	2.50	1.10	.30
☐ 13 Brooks Robinson	.50	.23	.06
☐ 14 Walter Johnson	1.00	.45	.12
☐ 15 Ted Williams	1.50	.70	.19
☐ 16 Bill Dickey	.50	.23	.06
☐ 17 Lou Gehrig	2.00	.90	.25
☐ 18 Hank Aaron	1.50	.70	.19
☐ 19 Eddie Mathews	.50	.23	.06
☐ 20 Mickey Mantle	2.50	1.10	.30

1986 TCMA Superstars Simon

These 50 cards mesaure 2 3/4" by 3 1/2". The cards feature drawings from sports artist Robert Stephen Simon on the front. The backs have vital statistics and biographical information.

	MINT	NRMT	EXC
COMPLETE SET (50)	15.00	6.75	1.85
COMMON CARD (1-50)	.25	.11	.03
☐ 1 Carl Erskine	.25	.11	.03
☐ 2 Babe Ruth Hank Aaron	1.25	.55	.16
☐ 3 Ted Williams	2.00	.90	.25
☐ 4 Mickey Mantle	2.50	1.10	.30
☐ 5 Gil Hodges	.50	.23	.06
☐ 6 Roberto Clemente	2.00	.90	.25
☐ 7 Mickey Mantle	2.50	1.10	.30
☐ 8 Walter Johnson	.50	.23	.06
☐ 9 Joe DiMaggio Mickey Mantle Whitey Ford Phil Rizzuto Roger Maris Casey Stengel MG Babe Ruth Lou Gehrig Yogi Berra	1.50	.70	.19
☐ 10 Carl Yatrzemski Ted Williams	.50	.23	.06
☐ 11 Mickey Mantle	2.50	1.10	.30
☐ 12 Harmon Killebrew	.50	.23	.06
☐ 13 Warren Spahn	.50	.23	.06
☐ 14 Ralph Kiner Babe Ruth	1.25	.55	.16
☐ 15 Bob Gibson	.50	.23	.06
☐ 16 Pee Wee Reese	.50	.23	.06
☐ 17 Billy Martin	.35	.16	.04
☐ 18 Joe DiMaggio Mickey Mantle	2.00	.90	.25
☐ 19 Phil Rizzuto	.50	.23	.06
☐ 20 Sandy Koufax	1.00	.45	.12
☐ 21 Jackie Robinson	2.00	.90	.25
☐ 22 Don Drysdale	.75	.35	.09
☐ 23 Mickey Mantle	2.50	1.10	.30
☐ 24 Mickey Mantle	2.50	1.10	.30
☐ 25 Joe DiMaggio	2.00	.90	.25
☐ 26 Robin Roberts	.50	.23	.06
☐ 27 Lou Brock	.50	.23	.06
☐ 28 Lou Gehrig	2.00	.90	.25
☐ 29 Willie Mays	1.50	.70	.19
☐ 30 Brooks Robinson	.50	.23	.06
☐ 31 Thurman Munson	.50	.23	.06
☐ 32 Roger Maris	1.00	.45	.12
☐ 33 Jim Palmer	.50	.23	.06
☐ 34 Stan Musial	1.00	.45	.12
☐ 35 Roy Campanella	1.00	.45	.12
☐ 36 Joe Pepitone	.25	.11	.03
☐ 37 Ebbetts Field	.25	.11	.03
☐ 38 Honus Wagner	.75	.35	.09
☐ 39 Yogi Berra	1.00	.45	.12
☐ 40 Eddie Mathews	.50	.23	.06
☐ 41 Carl Yastrzemski	.75	.35	.09
☐ 42 Babe Ruth	2.50	1.10	.30
☐ 43 Babe Ruth	2.50	1.10	.30
☐ 44 Pete Reiser	.25	.11	.03
☐ 45 Don Larsen	.25	.11	.03
☐ 46 Ernie Banks	.75	.35	.09
☐ 47 Casey Stengel	1.00	.45	.12
☐ 48 Jackie Robinson	2.00	.90	.25
☐ 49 Duke Snider	1.00	.45	.12
☐ 50 Duke Snider CL	.75	.35	.09

1996 Team Out

This 101-card set makes up a Baseball card game and is distributed in boxes of 60-card decks with a suggested retail of $12.95 a box. Each deck contains 37 player photo cards and 23 cartoon player cards. A total of 91 different player cards and 10 cartoon cards are available. The backs carry the name of the card game printed on a picture of a section of a baseball. The cards are unnumbered and checklisted below in alphabetical order with the last 10 cards being the cartoon cards and listed with a "C" prefix.

	MINT	NRMT	EXC
COMPLETE SET (101)	75.00	34.00	9.50
COMMON CARD (1-91)	.25	.11	.03
COMMON CARTOON (C92-C101)	.10	.05	.01
☐ 1 Roberto Alomar	.25	.11	.03
☐ 2 Brady Anderson	.75	.35	.09
☐ 3 Kevin Appier	.50	.23	.06
☐ 4 Carlos Baerga	.50	.23	.06
☐ 5 Jeff Bagwell	2.50	1.10	.30
☐ 6 Albert Belle	2.50	1.10	.30
☐ 7 Dante Bichette	.75	.35	.09
☐ 8 Craig Biggio	.50	.23	.06
☐ 9 Wade Boggs	1.00	.45	.12
☐ 10 Barry Bonds	1.25	.55	.16
☐ 11 Kevin Brown	.50	.23	.06
☐ 12 Jay Buhner	.75	.35	.09
☐ 13 Ellis Burks	.50	.23	.06
☐ 14 Ken Caminiti	.75	.35	.09
☐ 15 Joe Carter	.50	.23	.06
☐ 16 Vinny Castilla	.50	.23	.06
☐ 17 Jeff Cirillo	.25	.11	.03
☐ 18 Will Clark	1.00	.45	.12
☐ 19 Jeff Conine	.50	.23	.06
☐ 20 Joey Cora	.25	.11	.03
☐ 21 Marty Cordova	.50	.23	.06
☐ 22 Eric Davis	.25	.11	.03
☐ 23 Ray Durham	.25	.11	.03
☐ 24 Jim Edmonds	.50	.23	.06
☐ 25 Cecil Fielder	.50	.23	.06
☐ 26 Travis Fryman	.50	.23	.06
☐ 27 Jason Giambi	.75	.35	.09
☐ 28 Bernard Gilkey	.25	.11	.03
☐ 29 Tom Glavine	.75	.35	.09
☐ 30 Juan Gonzalez	2.50	1.10	.30
☐ 31 Mark Grace	1.25	.55	.16
☐ 32 Ken Griffey Jr.	5.00	2.20	.60
☐ 33 Marquis Grissom	.50	.23	.06
☐ 34 Mark Grudzielanek	.50	.23	.06
☐ 35 Ozzie Guillen	.25	.11	.03
☐ 36 Tony Gwynn	2.00	.90	.25
☐ 37 Bobby Higginson	.50	.23	.06
☐ 38 Todd Hundley	.50	.23	.06
☐ 39 Derek Jeter	3.00	1.35	.35
☐ 40 Lance Johnson	.25	.11	.03
☐ 41 Randy Johnson	.75	.35	.09
☐ 42 Chipper Jones	3.00	1.35	.35
☐ 43 Brian Jordan	.50	.23	.06
☐ 44 Wally Joyner	.25	.11	.03
☐ 45 Jason Kendall	.25	.11	.03
☐ 46 Chuck Knoblauch	1.00	.45	.12
☐ 47 Ray Lankford	.50	.23	.06
☐ 48 Mike Lansing	.25	.11	.03
☐ 49 Barry Larkin	1.00	.45	.12
☐ 50 Kenny Lofton	1.50	.70	.19
☐ 51 Javier Lopez	.50	.23	.06
☐ 52 Mike Macfarlane	.25	.11	.03
☐ 53 Greg Maddux	3.00	1.35	.35
☐ 54 Al Martin	.25	.11	.03
☐ 55 Mark McGwire	1.50	.70	.19
☐ 56 Brian McRae	.25	.11	.03
☐ 57 Raul Mondesi	1.00	.45	.12
☐ 58 Denny Neagle	.25	.11	.03
☐ 59 Hideo Nomo	2.00	.90	.25
☐ 60 John Olerud	.50	.23	.06
☐ 61 Rey Ordonez	.75	.35	.09
☐ 62 Troy Percival	.25	.11	.03
☐ 63 Andy Pettitte	1.25	.55	.16
☐ 64 Mike Piazza	3.00	1.35	.35
☐ 65 Manny Ramirez	1.25	.55	.16
☐ 66 Cal Ripken	3.00	1.35	.35
☐ 67 Alex Rodriguez	5.00	2.20	.60
☐ 68 Ivan Rodriguez	1.25	.55	.16
☐ 69 Tim Salmon	.75	.35	.09
☐ 70 Ryne Sandberg	2.00	.90	.25
☐ 71 Benito Santiago	.25	.11	.03
☐ 72 Kevin Seitzer	.25	.11	.03
☐ 73 Scott Servais	.25	.11	.03
☐ 74 Gary Sheffield	1.25	.55	.16
☐ 75 Ozzie Smith	2.00	.90	.25
☐ 76 John Smoltz	.75	.35	.09
☐ 77 Sammy Sosa	.75	.35	.09
☐ 78 Mike Stanley	.25	.11	.03
☐ 79 Terry Steinbach	.25	.11	.03
☐ 80 Frank Thomas	5.00	2.20	.60
☐ 81 Steve Trachsel	.25	.11	.03
☐ 82 Jose Valentin	.25	.11	.03
☐ 83 Mo Vaughn	1.25	.55	.16
☐ 84 Robin Ventura	.50	.23	.06
☐ 85 Jose Vizciano	.25	.11	.03
☐ 86 Larry Walker	.75	.35	.09
☐ 87 Walt Weiss	.25	.11	.03
☐ 88 Bernie Williams	1.25	.55	.16
☐ 89 Matt Williams	.75	.35	.09
☐ 90 Eric Young	.50	.23	.06
☐ 91 Todd Zeile	.25	.11	.03
☐ C92 Roberto Alomar	.25	.11	.03
☐ C93 Albert Belle Raul Mondesi	.25	.11	.03
☐ C94 Barry Bonds	.25	.11	.03
☐ C95 Ken Griffey Sammy Sosa	1.25	.55	.16
☐ C96 Greg Maddux	1.00	.45	.12
☐ C97 Mark McGwire Ozzie Smith MO Vaughn	.75	.35	.09
☐ C98 Mike Piazza Matt Williams	.50	.23	.06
☐ C99 Alex Rodriguez Cal Ripken	1.50	.70	.19
☐ C100 Frank Thomas	2.50	1.10	.30
☐ C101 G.T. Roped	.10	.05	.01

1993 Ted Williams Promos

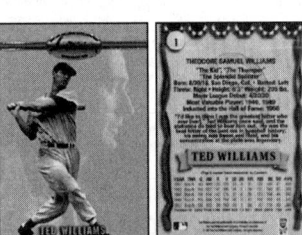

These three standard-size promo cards were issued to preview the design of the forthcoming 1993 Ted Williams baseball set. Though the cards differ from the corresponding numbered cards in the regular series, the promos are not marked as such. Promo card 1 features a different action photo on its front as well as a different ghosted background picture. Also the lettering of Ted Williams' name differs slightly in color, lime green on the promo, orange on the regular issue card. The layout of the backs is identical, but close inspection reveals that the career summaries on each card are slightly different. The promo is easily distinguished by the fact that the career summary begins with a quote by Williams himself. Promo cards 115 and 160 are easily distinguished from their counterparts in the regular issue; in the promo set, player cards have replaced the checklist cards from the regular series. The cards are unnumbered and checklisted below in alphabetical order.

	MINT	NRMT	EXC
COMPLETE SET (3)	30.00	13.50	3.70
COMMON CARD	6.00	2.70	.75
☐ 1 Ted Williams	15.00	6.75	1.85
☐ 115 Satchell Paige	6.00	2.70	.75
☐ 160 Juan Gonzalez The Measure of a Hitter	10.00	4.50	1.25

1993 Ted Williams

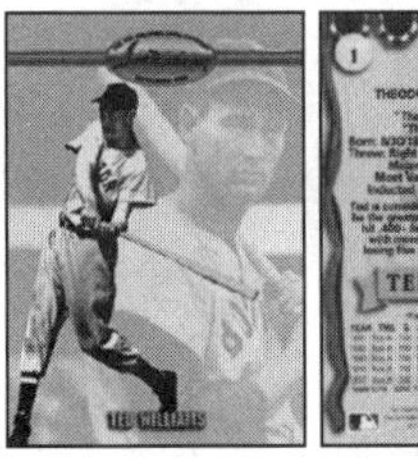
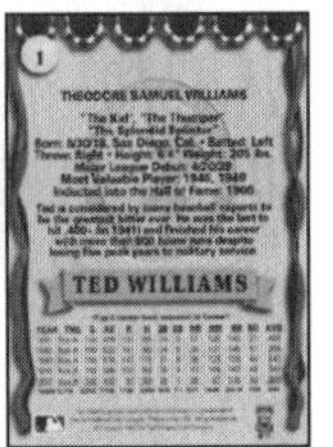

This set of 160 cards marks the inaugural effort of the Ted Williams Card Company. The standard-size cards are UV-coated, and bear the company's embossed logo. The card designs vary from subset to subset, and since the borderless cards feature players of the past (with only two exceptions), some of the photos on the fronts are black-and-white, some are color, and still others are sepia-toned. Generally, the backs carry Williams' comments on each player's abilities and career highlights. All the cards are numbered on the back and are grouped according to team and subset as follows: Boston Red Sox (1-7), Brooklyn/Los Angeles Dodgers (8-17), California Angels (18, 19), Chicago Cubs (20-24), Chicago White Sox (25-27), Cincinnati Reds (28-30), Cleveland Indians (31-35), Detroit Tigers (36-40), Houston Astros (41), Kansas City/Oakland Athletics (42-45), Milwaukee/Atlanta Braves (46-48), Milwaukee Brewers (49), Minnesota Twins (50), New York/San Francisco Giants (51-55), New York Mets (56, 57), New York Yankees (58-69), Philadelphia Phillies (70-73), Pittsburgh Pirates (74-81), Baltimore Orioles (82-85), St. Louis Cardinals (86-93), San Diego Padres (94), The Negro Leagues (97-115), All-American Girls' Professional Baseball League (116-120), Ted's Greatest Hitters (121-130), Barrier Breakers (131-140), Goin' North (141-150), and Dawning of a Legacy (151-160), which features cards of Juan Gonzalez and Jeff Bagwell, the only two current players in the set. Ted Williams personally signed 406 of his Locklear Collection insert card for this set and Juan Gonzalez signed 172 cards (43 each of his four different regular cards in this set) as well. Also, two POGs, or milk bottle caps, were inserted in each pack. These feature illustrations of former major and Negro league players, logos of their teams, and reproductions of selected signatures of former major league players.

	MINT	NRMT	EXC
COMPLETE SET (160)	15.00	6.75	1.85
COMMON CARD (1-160)	.05	.02	.01
☐ 1 Ted Williams	2.00	.90	.25
☐ 2 Rick Ferrell	.20	.09	.03
☐ 3 Jim Lonborg	.05	.02	.01
☐ 4 Mel Parnell	.05	.02	.01
☐ 5 Jim Piersall	.10	.05	.01
☐ 6 Luis Tiant	.10	.05	.01
☐ 7 Carl Yastrzemski	.50	.23	.06
☐ 8 Ralph Branca	.10	.05	.01
☐ 9 Roy Campanella	.75	.35	.09
☐ 10 Ron Cey	.10	.05	.01
☐ 11 Tommy Davis	.10	.05	.01
☐ 12 Don Drysdale	.35	.16	.04
☐ 13 Carl Erskine	.10	.05	.01
☐ 14 Steve Garvey	.25	.11	.03
☐ 15 Don Newcombe	.15	.07	.02
☐ 16 Duke Snider	.75	.35	.09
☐ 17 Maury Wills	.20	.09	.03
☐ 18 Jim Fregosi	.10	.05	.01
☐ 19 Bobby Grich	.10	.05	.01
☐ 20 Bill Buckner	.10	.05	.01
☐ 21 Billy Herman UER (Ted Williams stats on back)	.25	.11	.03
☐ 22 Ferguson Jenkins	.25	.11	.03
☐ 23 Ron Santo	.15	.07	.02
☐ 24 Billy Williams	.25	.11	.03
☐ 25 Luis Aparicio	.25	.11	.03
☐ 26 Luke Appling	.20	.09	.03
☐ 27 Minnie Minoso	.15	.07	.02
☐ 28 Johnny Bench	.50	.23	.06
☐ 29 George Foster	.10	.05	.01
☐ 30 Joe Morgan	.25	.11	.03
☐ 31 Buddy Bell	.10	.05	.01
☐ 32 Lou Boudreau	.20	.09	.03
☐ 33 Rocky Colavito	.25	.11	.03
☐ 34 Jim(Mudcat) Grant	.05	.02	.01
☐ 35 Tris Speaker	.25	.11	.03
☐ 36 Ray Boone	.05	.02	.01
☐ 37 Darrell Evans	.10	.05	.01
☐ 38 Al Kaline	.50	.23	.06
☐ 39 George Kell	.25	.11	.03
☐ 40 Mickey Lolich	.15	.07	.02
☐ 41 Cesar Cedeno	.10	.05	.01
☐ 42 Sal Bando	.05	.02	.01
☐ 43 Vida Blue	.10	.05	.01
☐ 44 Bert Campaneris	.05	.02	.01
☐ 45 Ken Holtzman	.05	.02	.01

☐ 46 Lew Burdette	.10	.05	.01
☐ 47 Bob Horner	.05	.02	.01
☐ 48 Warren Spahn	.25	.11	.03
☐ 49 Cecil Cooper	.10	.05	.01
☐ 50 Tony Oliva	.15	.07	.02
☐ 51 Bobby Bonds	.15	.07	.02
☐ 52 Alvin Dark	.05	.02	.01
☐ 53 Dave Dravecky	.10	.05	.01
☐ 54 Monte Irvin	.25	.11	.03
☐ 55 Willie Mays	1.00	.45	.12
☐ 56 Bud Harrelson	.10	.05	.01
☐ 57 Dave Kingman UER (Darrell Evans has 414 homers and is not in HOF)	.10	.05	.01
☐ 58 Yogi Berra	.50	.23	.06
☐ 59 Don Baylor	.15	.07	.02
☐ 60 Jim Bouton	.10	.05	.01
☐ 61 Bobby Brown	.10	.05	.01
☐ 62 Whitey Ford	.50	.23	.06
☐ 63 Lou Gehrig	1.50	.70	.19
☐ 64 Charlie Keller	.10	.05	.01
☐ 65 Eddie Lopat	.10	.05	.01
☐ 66 Johnny Mize	.25	.11	.03
☐ 67 Bobby Murcer	.10	.05	.01
☐ 68 Graig Nettles	.10	.05	.01
☐ 69 Bobby Shantz	.05	.02	.01
☐ 70 Richie Ashburn	.25	.11	.03
☐ 71 Larry Bowa	.10	.05	.01
☐ 72 Steve Carlton	.40	.18	.05
☐ 73 Robin Roberts	.25	.11	.03
☐ 74 Matty Alou	.05	.02	.01
☐ 75 Harvey Haddix	.05	.02	.01
☐ 76 Ralph Kiner	.25	.11	.03
☐ 77 Bill Madlock	.10	.05	.01
☐ 78 Bill Mazeroski	.15	.07	.02
☐ 79 Al Oliver	.10	.05	.01
☐ 80 Manny Sanguillen	.05	.02	.01
☐ 81 Willie Stargell	.25	.11	.03
☐ 82 Al Bumbry	.05	.02	.01
☐ 83 Davey Johnson	.10	.05	.01
☐ 84 Boog Powell	.15	.07	.02
☐ 85 Earl Weaver MG	.15	.07	.02
☐ 86 Lou Brock	.25	.11	.03
☐ 87 Orlando Cepeda UER (Born in Puerto Rico, not Dominican Republic)	.20	.09	.03
☐ 88 Curt Flood	.10	.05	.01
☐ 89 Joe Garagiola	.15	.07	.02
☐ 90 Bob Gibson	.25	.11	.03
☐ 91 Rogers Hornsby UER (Misspelled Rodgers on card front)	.25	.11	.03
☐ 92 Enos Slaughter	.20	.09	.03
☐ 93 Joe Torre	.15	.07	.02
☐ 94 Gaylord Perry	.20	.09	.03
☐ 95 Checklist	.05	.02	.01
☐ 96 Checklist	.05	.02	.01
☐ 97 Cool Papa Bell	.30	.14	.04
☐ 98 Garnett Blair	.10	.05	.01
☐ 99 Gene Benson	.15	.07	.02
☐ 100 Lyman Bostock Sr.	.10	.05	.01
☐ 101 Marlin Carter	.10	.05	.01
☐ 102 Oscar Charleston	.25	.11	.03
☐ 103 Ray Dandridge	.25	.11	.03
☐ 104 Mahlon Duckett	.10	.05	.01
☐ 105 Josh Gibson	.75	.35	.09
☐ 106 Cowan(Bubber) Hyde	.10	.05	.01
☐ 107 William(Judy) Johnson	.25	.11	.03
☐ 108 Buck Leonard	.25	.11	.03
☐ 109 John Henry Lloyd	.25	.11	.03
☐ 110 Lester Lockett	.10	.05	.01
☐ 111 Max Manning	.10	.05	.01
☐ 112 Satchel Paige	.75	.35	.09
☐ 113 Armando Vazquez	.10	.05	.01
☐ 114 Joe(Smokey) Williams	.20	.09	.03
☐ 115 Checklist	.05	.02	.01
☐ 116 Alice(Lefty) Hohlmeyer	.25	.11	.03
☐ 117 Dotty Kamenshek	.25	.11	.03
☐ 118 Lavonne(Pepper) Davis	.25	.11	.03
☐ 119 Marge Wenzell	.25	.11	.03
☐ 120 Checklist	.05	.02	.01
☐ 121 Babe Ruth	2.50	1.10	.30
☐ 122 Lou Gehrig	1.50	.70	.19
☐ 123 Jimmie Foxx	.50	.23	.06
☐ 124 Rogers Hornsby	.50	.23	.06
☐ 125 Ty Cobb	1.50	.70	.19
☐ 126 Willie Mays	1.00	.45	.12
☐ 127 Ralph Kiner	.40	.18	.05
☐ 128 Tris Speaker	.40	.18	.05
☐ 129 Johnny Mize	.35	.16	.04
☐ 130 Checklist	.05	.02	.01
☐ 131 Satchel Paige	.50	.23	.06
☐ 132 Joe Black	.15	.07	.02
☐ 133 Roy Campanella	.50	.23	.06
☐ 134 Larry Doby UER (Misspelled Dolby on card back)	.25	.11	.03
☐ 135 Jim Gilliam	.15	.07	.02
☐ 136 Monte Irvin	.40	.18	.05
☐ 137 Sam Jethroe	.15	.07	.02
☐ 138 Willie Mays	1.00	.45	.12
☐ 139 Don Newcombe	.15	.07	.02
☐ 140 Checklist	.05	.02	.01
☐ 141 Roy Campanella	.50	.23	.06
☐ 142 Bob Gibson	.25	.11	.03
☐ 143 Boog Powell	.15	.07	.02
☐ 144 Willie Mays	1.00	.45	.12
☐ 145 Johnny Mize	.25	.11	.03
☐ 146 Monte Irvin	.25	.11	.03
☐ 147 Earl Weaver MG	.15	.07	.02
☐ 148 Ted Williams	1.50	.70	.19
☐ 149 Jim Gilliam	.10	.05	.01
☐ 150 Checklist	.05	.02	.01
☐ 151 Juan Gonzalez Footsteps to Greatness	.75	.35	.09
☐ 152 Juan Gonzalez Sign 'em Up	.75	.35	.09
☐ 153 Juan Gonzalez The Road to Success	.75	.35	.09
☐ 154 Juan Gonzalez Looking Ahead	.75	.35	.09
☐ 155 Checklist 151-155	.05	.02	.01
☐ 156 Jeff Bagwell Born with Red Sox Blood	.50	.23	.06
☐ 157 Jeff Bagwell Movin' Up Then Out	.50	.23	.06
☐ 158 Jeff Bagwell Year 1	.50	.23	.06
☐ 159 Jeff Bagwell Year 2	.50	.23	.06
☐ 160 Checklist 156-160	.05	.02	.01
☐ AU151 Juan Gonzalez AU (Certified autograph) Footsteps to Greatness	250.00	110.00	31.00
☐ AU152 Juan Gonzalez AU (Certified autograph) Sign 'em Up	250.00	110.00	31.00
☐ AU153 Juan Gonzalez AU (Certified autograph) The Road to Success	250.00	110.00	31.00
☐ AU154 Juan Gonzalez AU (Certified autograph) Looking Ahead	250.00	110.00	31.00

1993 Ted Williams Brooks Robinson

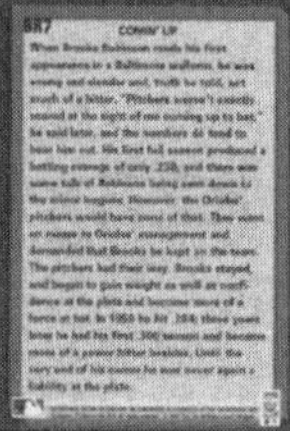

Randomly inserted in retail packs, this ten-card standard-size set features on its fronts borderless photos of Brooks Robinson. His name is stamped in gold foil, the set's logo appears in one corner, and the embossed company logo appears in another. The back carries Williams' comments on Robinson's outstanding career within a simulated embroidery panel. Autographed cards of Robinson were randomly inserted into retail packs. These cards are certified but have been rarely seen in the marketplace

	MINT	NRMT	EXC
COMPLETE SET (10)	15.00	6.75	1.85
COMMON CARD (1-10)	1.50	.70	.19
☐ 1 Brooks Robinson Salad Days	1.50	.70	.19
☐ 2 Brooks Robinson Brooks Calbert Robinson	1.50	.70	.19
☐ 3 Brooks Robinson '66 Series	1.50	.70	.19
☐ 4 Brooks Robinson Fielding Stats	1.50	.70	.19
☐ 5 Brooks Robinson '70 Series 2	1.50	.70	.19
☐ 6 Brooks Robinson '70 Series 1	1.50	.70	.19
☐ 7 Brooks Robinson Comin' Up	1.50	.70	.19
☐ 8 Brooks Robinson All-Star Games	1.50	.70	.19
☐ 9 Brooks Robinson 1964	1.50	.70	.19
☐ 10 Checklist Card	1.50	.70	.19

1993 Ted Williams Locklear Collection

This ten-card standard-size set features the artwork of noted artist and former major league player Gene Locklear. The set includes famous players from the past. The white-edged fronts carry the player's name, vertically presented along the left edge, in blue print. A logo for Gene Locklear is overlaid on the lower right corner. The backs have descriptive career summaries superimposed over a ghosted collage of all the players in the set. The cards are numbered on the back with an "LC" prefix with the order of players being alphabetical.

	MINT	NRMT	EXC
COMPLETE SET (10)	35.00	16.00	4.40
COMMON CARD (1-10)	3.00	1.35	.35

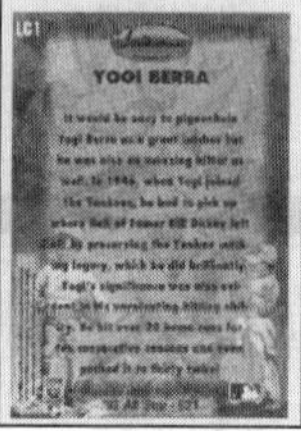

☐ 1 Yogi Berra	6.00	2.70	.75
☐ 2 Lou Brock	3.00	1.35	.35
☐ 3 Willie Mays	7.50	3.40	.95
☐ 4 Johnny Mize	3.00	1.35	.35
☐ 5 Satchel Paige	6.00	2.70	.75
☐ 6 Babe Ruth	10.00	4.50	1.25
☐ 7 Enos Slaughter	3.00	1.35	.35
☐ 8 Carl Yastrzemski	5.00	2.20	.60
☐ 9 Ted Williams	8.00	3.60	1.00
☐ 10 Checklist	3.00	1.35	.35
☐ AU9 Ted Williams AU (Certified autograph)	500.00	220.00	60.00

1993 Ted Williams Memories

Individual cards from this special 20-card standard-size set were regionally but otherwise randomly inserted in foil hobby packs. For example, the 1973 Oakland A's cards were randomly inserted only in packs destined for shipment to the West Coast while the 1955 Brooklyn Dodgers cards were available only on the East Coast. The fronts feature borderless action player photos that have dimmed edges. The player's name appears in white lettering at the bottom and the embossed company logo is displayed in an upper corner. The set logo, along with the year, rests in the lower left. Ted Williams' comments on each player are printed obliquely within a ragged-edged white rectangle that resembles a newspaper article cutout. This is superposed upon text that resembles a newspaper article. The cards are numbered on the back with an "M" prefix.

	MINT	NRMT	EXC
COMPLETE SET (20)	40.00	18.00	5.00
COMMON CARD (1-20)	1.75	.80	.22
☐ 1 Roy Campanella	5.00	2.20	.60
☐ 2 Jim Gilliam	1.75	.80	.22
☐ 3 Gil Hodges	4.00	1.80	.50
☐ 4 Duke Snider	5.00	2.20	.60
☐ 5 1955 Brooklyn Dodgers Checklist	1.75	.80	.22
☐ 6 Don Drysdale	4.00	1.80	.50
☐ 7 Tommy Davis	1.75	.80	.22
☐ 8 Johnny Podres	1.75	.80	.22
☐ 9 Maury Wills	2.50	1.10	.30
☐ 10 1963 Los Angeles Dodgers Checklist	1.75	.80	.22
☐ 11 Roberto Clemente	7.00	3.10	.85
☐ 12 Al Oliver	1.75	.80	.22
☐ 13 Manny Sanguillen	1.75	.80	.22
☐ 14 Willie Stargell	3.00	1.35	.35
☐ 15 1971 Pittsburgh Pirates Checklist	1.75	.80	.22
☐ 16 Johnny Bench	3.00	1.35	.35
☐ 17 George Foster	1.75	.80	.22
☐ 18 Joe Morgan	3.00	1.35	.35
☐ 19 Tony Perez	3.00	1.35	.35
☐ 20 1975 Cincinnati Reds Checklist	1.75	.80	.22

1993 Ted Williams POG Cards

This set of 52 POGs was issued in pairs on 26 cards. The cards measure approximately 2 9/16" by 3 9/16" and are printed on a thick cardboard stock. Each POG measures 1 5/8" in diameter and is perforated for punch out. The fronts of the cards are black and the backs are white. The POGs consist of team logos, various special logos, and some players. The POGs are unnumbered and checklisted below alphabetically according to non-player cards (1-20) and cards which feature at least one player (21-26).

	MINT	NRMT	EXC
COMPLETE SET (26)	6.00	2.70	.75
COMMON CARD (1-26)	.25	.11	.03
☐ 1 Atlanta Black Crackers Baltimore Elite Giants	.25	.11	.03
☐ 2 Atlanta Braves New York Mets	.25	.11	.03
☐ 3 Baltimore Orioles 1993 All-Star Game 1993 World Series	.25	.11	.03
☐ 4 Birmingham Black Barons New York Cuban Stars	.25	.11	.03
☐ 5 Chicago Cubs Detroit Tigers	.25	.11	.03
☐ 6 Cincinnati Reds Kansas City Royals 1969-1993	.25	.11	.03
☐ 7 Classic Teams The Negro Leagues Negro League Baseball Players Assoc.	.25	.11	.03
☐ 8 Cleveland Buckeyes Detroit Stars	.25	.11	.03
☐ 9 Cleveland Indians Kansas City Athletics	.25	.11	.03
☐ 10 Houston Colt .45s New York Yankees	.25	.11	.03
☐ 11 Florida Marlins 1993 Inaugural Year Colorado Rockies 1993 Inaugural Year	.25	.11	.03
☐ 12 Indianapolis ABCs New York Harlem Stars	.25	.11	.03
☐ 13 Louisville Black Caps Philadelphia Stars	.25	.11	.03
☐ 14 Minnesota Twins Boston Red Sox	.25	.11	.03
☐ 15 Montreal Expos 1969-1993 San Diego Padres 1969-1993	.25	.11	.03
☐ 16 New York Black Yankees Homestead Grays	.25	.11	.03
☐ 17 New York Giants Milwaukee Braves	.25	.11	.03
☐ 18 Oakland A's 21 (Clemente's number)	.25	.11	.03
☐ 19 Pittsburgh Pirates St. Louis Cardinals	.25	.11	.03
☐ 20 St. Louis Browns Brooklyn Dodgers	.25	.11	.03
☐ 21 Yogi Berra Roy Campanella	1.00	.45	.12
☐ 22 Brooklyn Dodgers Roy Campanella	.75	.35	.09
☐ 23 Lou Gehrig Ted Williams	2.00	.90	.25
☐ 24 Lou Gehrig New York Yankees	1.50	.70	.19
☐ 25 Tommy Davis George Foster	.40	.18	.05
☐ 26 Ted Williams 1941 - .406 Ted Williams	1.50	.70	.19

1993 Ted Williams Roberto Clemente

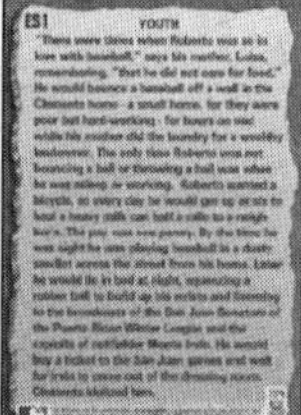

Randomly inserted in foil packs and subtitled "Etched in Stone," this ten-card standard-size set features on its fronts borderless photos of Roberto Clemente. His name and the set subtitle are "graven" in the upper right, and the company logo, along with the words "Tribute '93" within gold foil bars, are embossed in the lower left. On the back, Ted Williams' comments on Clemente's illustrious career appear within a simulated glazed stone tablet. The cards are numbered on the back with an "ES" prefix. The card numbering follows chronological order.

	MINT	NRMT	EXC
COMPLETE SET (10)	20.00	9.00	2.50
COMMON CARD (1-10)	2.00	.90	.25
☐ 1 Roberto Clemente Youth	2.00	.90	.25
☐ 2 Roberto Clemente Sign Up	2.00	.90	.25
☐ 3 Roberto Clemente Try-Out	2.00	.90	.25

Card	MINT	NRMT	EXC
☐ 4 Roberto Clemente Playing Mad	2.00	.90	.25
☐ 5 Roberto Clemente Minor Leagues	2.00	.90	.25
☐ 6 Roberto Clemente 1955-1959	2.00	.90	.25
☐ 7 Roberto Clemente 1960	2.00	.90	.25
☐ 8 Roberto Clemente 1963	2.00	.90	.25
☐ 9 Roberto Clemente 1970	2.00	.90	.25
☐ 10 Roberto Clemente Checklist	2.00	.90	.25

1994 Ted Williams

The 1994 Ted Williams set comprises 162 standard-size cards distributed in 12-card packs. The series features former major league baseball players, players from the All-American Girls Professional Baseball League, 17 Negro League stars, and 17 current top prospects. The fronts feature color action player photos that are full-bleed, except at the right where a rugged and textured rock edges the picture. The backs have a similar design, only that the photo is replaced by biography, player profile, and statistics superposed on a wooden simulation of the team's logo. Topical subsets featured are Women in Baseball (93-99), The Negro League (100-117), The Campaign (118-135), Goin' North (136-144), Swinging for the Fences (145-153), and Dawning of a Legacy (154-162).The cards are numbered on the back. A red foil version of the Ted Williams (LP1) and Larry Bird (LP2) insert cards were produced. The values are the same as those listed below. Leon Day signed some cards for release in the packs.

	MINT	NRMT	EXC
COMPLETE SET (162)	10.00	4.50	1.25
COMMON CARD (1-162)	.05	.02	.01
☐ 1 Ted Williams	1.00	.45	.12
☐ 2 Bernie Carbo	.05	.02	.01
☐ 3 Bobby Doerr	.15	.07	.02
☐ 4 Fred Lynn	.10	.05	.01
☐ 5 John Pesky	.10	.05	.01
☐ 6 Rico Petrocelli	.10	.05	.01
☐ 7 Cy Young	.25	.11	.03
☐ 8 Paul Blair	.05	.02	.01
☐ 9 Andy Etchebarren	.05	.02	.01
☐ 10 Brooks Robinson	.25	.11	.03
☐ 11 Gil Hodges	.15	.07	.02
☐ 12 Tommy John	.10	.05	.01
☐ 13 Rick Monday	.05	.02	.01
☐ 14 Dean Chance	.05	.02	.01
☐ 15 Doug DeCinces	.05	.02	.01
☐ 16 Gabby Hartnett	.10	.05	.01
☐ 17 Don Kessinger	.05	.02	.01
☐ 18 Bruce Sutter	.10	.05	.01
☐ 19 Eddie Collins Sr.	.10	.05	.01
☐ 20 Nellie Fox	.10	.05	.01
☐ 21 Carlos May	.05	.02	.01
☐ 22 Ted Kluszewski	.10	.05	.01
☐ 23 Vada Pinson	.10	.05	.01
☐ 24 Johnny Vander Meer	.10	.05	.01
☐ 25 Bob Feller	.20	.09	.03
☐ 26 Mike Garcia	.05	.02	.01
☐ 27 Sam McDowell	.05	.02	.01
☐ 28 Al Rosen	.10	.05	.01
☐ 29 Norm Cash	.10	.05	.01
☐ 30 Ty Cobb	.75	.35	.09
☐ 31 Mark Fidrych	.10	.05	.01
☐ 32 Hank Greenberg	.20	.09	.03
☐ 33 Dennis McLain	.10	.05	.01
☐ 34 Virgil Trucks	.05	.02	.01
☐ 35 Enos Cabell	.05	.02	.01
☐ 36 Mike Scott	.05	.02	.01
☐ 37 Bob Watson	.10	.05	.01
☐ 38 Amos Otis	.05	.02	.01
☐ 39 Frank White	.05	.02	.01
☐ 40 Joe Adcock	.10	.05	.01
☐ 41 Rico Carty	.05	.02	.01
☐ 42 Ralph Garr	.05	.02	.01
☐ 43 Ed Mathews	.10	.05	.01
☐ 44 Ben Oglivie	.05	.02	.01
☐ 45 Gorman Thomas	.05	.02	.01
☐ 46 Earl Battey	.05	.02	.01
☐ 47 Rod Carew	.20	.09	.03
☐ 48 Jim Kaat	.10	.05	.01
☐ 49 Harmon Killebrew	.20	.09	.03
☐ 50 Gary Carter	.10	.05	.01
☐ 51 Steve Rogers	.05	.02	.01
☐ 52 Rusty Staub	.10	.05	.01
☐ 53 Sal Maglie	.10	.05	.01
☐ 54 Juan Marichal	.10	.05	.01
☐ 55 Mel Ott	.15	.07	.02
☐ 56 Bobby Thomson	.10	.05	.01
☐ 57 Tommie Agee	.05	.02	.01
☐ 58 Tug McGraw	.10	.05	.01
☐ 59 Elston Howard	.10	.05	.01
☐ 60 Sparky Lyle	.10	.05	.01
☐ 61 Billy Martin	.10	.05	.01
☐ 62 Thurman Munson	.10	.05	.01
☐ 63 Bobby Richardson	.10	.05	.01
☐ 64 Bill Skowron	.10	.05	.01
☐ 65 Mickey Cochrane	.10	.05	.01
☐ 66 Rollie Fingers	.10	.05	.01
☐ 67 Lefty Grove	.10	.05	.01
☐ 68 James Hunter	.15	.07	.02
☐ 69 Connie Mack MG	.15	.07	.02
☐ 70 Al Simmons	.10	.05	.01
☐ 71 Dick Allen	.10	.05	.01
☐ 72 Bob Boone	.10	.05	.01
☐ 73 Del Ennis	.05	.02	.01
☐ 74 Chuck Klein	.10	.05	.01
☐ 75 Mike Schmidt	.35	.16	.04
☐ 76 Dock Ellis	.05	.02	.01
☐ 77 Elroy Face	.05	.02	.01
☐ 78 Phil Garner	.05	.02	.01
☐ 79 Bill Mazeroski	.10	.05	.01
☐ 80 Pie Traynor	.10	.05	.01
☐ 81 Honus Wagner	.35	.16	.04
☐ 82 Dizzy Dean	.10	.05	.01
☐ 83 Red Schoendienst	.10	.05	.01
☐ 84 Randy Jones	.05	.02	.01
☐ 85 Nate Colbert	.05	.02	.01
☐ 86 Jeff Burroughs	.05	.02	.01
☐ 87 Jim Sundberg	.05	.02	.01
☐ 88 Frank Howard	.10	.05	.01
☐ 89 Walter Johnson	.20	.09	.03
☐ 90 Eddie Yost	.05	.02	.01
☐ 91 Checklist 1	.05	.02	.01
☐ 92 Checklist 2	.05	.02	.01
☐ 93 Faye Dancer	.15	.07	.02
☐ 94 Snookie Dayle	.10	.05	.01
☐ 95 Maddy English	.10	.05	.01
☐ 96 Nickie Fox	.10	.05	.01
☐ 97 Sophie Kurys	.25	.11	.03
☐ 98 Alma Ziegler	.10	.05	.01
☐ 99 Checklist	.05	.02	.01
☐ 100 Newton Allen	.10	.05	.01
☐ 101 Willard Brown	.10	.05	.01
☐ 102 Larry Brown	.10	.05	.01
☐ 103 Leon Day	.20	.09	.03
☐ 104 John Donaldson	.10	.05	.01
☐ 105 Rube Foster	.15	.07	.02
☐ 106 John Fowler	.10	.05	.01
☐ 107 Elander Harris	.10	.05	.01
☐ 108 Webster McDonald	.10	.05	.01
☐ 109 Buck O'Neil	.20	.09	.03
☐ 110 Ted "Double Duty" Radcliffe	.15	.07	.02
☐ 111 Wilber Rogan	.10	.05	.01
☐ 112 Marcenia Stone	.10	.05	.01
☐ 113 James Taylor	.10	.05	.01
☐ 114 Fleetwood Walker	.15	.07	.02
☐ 115 George Wilson	.10	.05	.01
☐ 116 Judson Wilson	.10	.05	.01
☐ 117 Checklist	.05	.02	.01
☐ 118 Howard Battle	.10	.05	.01
☐ 119 John Burke	.10	.05	.01
☐ 120 Brian Dubose	.10	.05	.01
☐ 121 Alex Gonzalez	.25	.11	.03
☐ 122 Jose Herrera	.10	.05	.01
☐ 123 Jason Giambi	.25	.11	.03
☐ 124 Derek Jeter	1.00	.45	.12
☐ 125 Charles Johnson	.50	.23	.06
☐ 126 Daron Kirkreit	.10	.05	.01
☐ 127 Jason Moler	.10	.05	.01
☐ 128 Vince Moore	.10	.05	.01
☐ 129 Chad Mottola	.10	.05	.01
☐ 130 Jose Silva	.20	.09	.03
☐ 131 Mac Suzuki	.15	.07	.02
☐ 132 Brien Taylor	.10	.05	.01
☐ 133 Michael Tucker	.20	.09	.03
☐ 134 Billy Wagner	.25	.11	.03
☐ 135 Checklist	.05	.02	.01
☐ 136 Gary Carter	.10	.05	.01
☐ 137 Tony Conigliaro	.10	.05	.01
☐ 138 Sparky Lyle	.10	.05	.01
☐ 139 Roger Maris	.25	.11	.03
☐ 140 Vada Pinson	.10	.05	.01
☐ 141 Mike Schmidt	.25	.11	.03
☐ 142 Frank White	.05	.02	.01
☐ 143 Ted Williams	.75	.35	.09
☐ 144 Checklist	.05	.02	.01
☐ 145 Joe Adcock	.05	.02	.01
☐ 146 Rocky Colavito	.10	.05	.01
☐ 147 Lou Gehrig	1.00	.45	.12
☐ 148 Gil Hodges	.10	.05	.01
☐ 149 Bob Horner	.05	.02	.01
☐ 150 Willie Mays	1.00	.45	.12
☐ 151 Mike Schmidt	.20	.09	.03
☐ 152 Pat Seerey	.05	.02	.01
☐ 153 Checklist	.05	.02	.01
☐ 154 Cliff Floyd The Honors Begin	.20	.09	.03
☐ 155 Cliff Floyd The Top Polecat	.20	.09	.03
☐ 156 Cliff Floyd Minor League Team of the Year	.20	.09	.03
☐ 157 Cliff Floyd Major League Debut	.20	.09	.03
☐ 158 Tim Salmon Award Winner	.25	.11	.03
☐ 159 Tim Salmon Early Professional Career	.25	.11	.03
☐ 160 Tim Salmon An MVP Season	.25	.11	.03
☐ 161 Tim Salmon Rookie of the Year	.25	.11	.03
☐ 162 Checklist	.05	.02	.01
☐ P1 Ted Williams Promo	2.00	.90	.25
☐ LP1 Larry Bird	5.00	2.20	.60
☐ LP2 Ted Williams	5.00	2.20	.60
☐ NNO Leon Day AU Certified Autograph	25.00	11.00	3.10

1994 Ted Williams 500 Club

Randomly inserted in foil packs, this nine-card standard-size set profiles members of baseball's elite 500 home run club. The fronts display full-bleed color action shots that have a ribbed appearance. The words "The 500 Club" appear on a sign in the lower left corner, with the player's name following the curve of the sign. On a wood plaque hung on a simulated wooden wall, the backs summarize the player's outstanding achievement. Cards numbers are prefixed with a "5C." A red foil version of this set was produced. The values are the same as those listed below.

	MINT	NRMT	EXC
COMPLETE SET (9)	20.00	9.00	2.50
COMMON CARD (1-8)	1.00	.45	.12
☐ 1 Hank Aaron	4.00	1.80	.50
☐ 2 Reggie Jackson	3.00	1.35	.35
☐ 3 Harmon Killebrew	1.25	.55	.16
☐ 4 Mickey Mantle	8.00	3.60	1.00
☐ 5 Jimmie Foxx	3.00	1.35	.35
☐ 6 Babe Ruth	6.00	2.70	.75
☐ 7 Mike Schmidt	5.00	2.20	.60
☐ 8 Ted Williams	6.00	2.70	.75
☐ 9 Checklist	1.00	.45	.12

1994 Ted Williams Dan Gardiner Collection

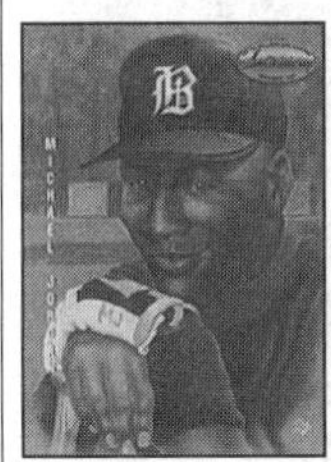

Randomly inserted in foil packs, this nine-card standard-size set presents top minor league prospects. Both sides display color paintings by noted artist Dan Gardiner. The backs also include a brief player profile.

	MINT	NRMT	EXC
COMPLETE SET (9)	20.00	9.00	2.50
COMMON CARD (DG1-DG9)	.75	.35	.09
☐ DG1 Michael Jordan	15.00	6.75	1.85
☐ DG2 Michael Tucker	2.50	1.10	.30
☐ DG3 Derek Jeter	8.00	3.60	1.00
☐ DG4 Charles Johnson	3.00	1.35	.35
☐ DG5 Howard Battle	1.50	.70	.19
☐ DG6 Quilvio Veras	1.50	.70	.19
☐ DG7 Brian L. Hunter	1.25	.55	.16
☐ DG8 Brien Taylor	.75	.35	.09
☐ DG9 Checklist	2.00	.90	.25

1994 Ted Williams Locklear Collection

Randomly inserted in foil packs, this nine-card standard-size set again features the work of noted artist Gene Locklear. Inside white borders, the fronts display full-color paintings of former major league greats. The player's name is printed vertically along the left edge. The backs have descriptive career summaries superposed over a collage of all the players portrayed in the set. The numbering on the backs is in continuation of last year's Locklear Collection insert series.

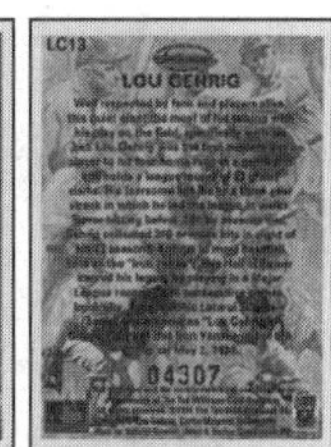

	MINT	NRMT	EXC
COMPLETE SET (9)	20.00	9.00	2.50
COMMON CARD (LC11-LC19)	1.50	.70	.19
☐ LC11 Ty Cobb	5.00	2.20	.60
☐ LC12 Bob Feller	2.50	1.10	.30
☐ LC13 Lou Gehrig	8.00	3.60	1.00
☐ LC14 Josh Gibson	3.00	1.35	.35
☐ LC15 Walter Johnson	3.00	1.35	.35
☐ LC16 Casey Stengel	3.00	1.35	.35
☐ LC17 Honus Wagner	6.00	2.70	.75
☐ LC18 Cy Young	4.00	1.80	.50
☐ LC19 Checklist	1.50	.70	.19

1994 Ted Williams Memories

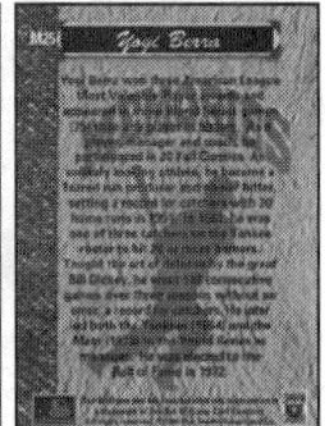

Randomly inserted only in hobby packs, this special regional insert set was sold on a regional basis, highlighting four great teams of the past. This year's set captures the 1954 New York Giants (M21-M24), the 1961 New York Yankees (M25-M28), the 1968 Detroit Tigers (M29-M32), and the 1975 Boston Red Sox (M33-M36). The numbering on the backs is in continuation of last year's Memories insert series.

	MINT	NRMT	EXC
COMPLETE SET (17)	40.00	18.00	5.00
COMMON CARD (M21-M37)	1.00	.45	.12
☐ M21 Monte Irvin	3.00	1.35	.35
☐ M22 Sal Maglie	2.50	1.10	.30
☐ M23 Dusty Rhodes	1.50	.70	.19
☐ M24 Hank Thompson	1.50	.70	.19
☐ M25 Yogi Berra	5.00	2.20	.60
☐ M26 Elston Howard	4.00	1.80	.50
☐ M27 Roger Maris	6.00	2.70	.75
☐ M28 Bobby Richardson	2.50	1.10	.30
☐ M29 Norm Cash	2.50	1.10	.30
☐ M30 Al Kaline	6.00	2.70	.75
☐ M31 Mickey Lolich	2.50	1.10	.30
☐ M32 Denny McLain	2.50	1.10	.30
☐ M33 Bernie Carbo	1.50	.70	.19
☐ M34 Fred Lynn	2.50	1.10	.30
☐ M35 Rico Petrocelli	2.50	1.10	.30
☐ M36 Luis Tiant	2.50	1.10	.30
☐ M37 Checklist	1.00	.45	.12

1994 Ted Williams Mike Schmidt

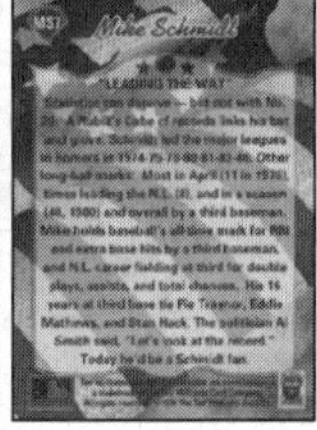

Randomly inserted one per jumbo pack, this nine-card standard-size set highlights the career of Mike Schmidt. The fronts display full-bleed color player photos that have a textured appearance. On a background consisting of a red, white, and blue flag, a ghosted panel summarizes his career by presenting various highlights.

	MINT	NRMT	EXC
COMPLETE SET (9)	6.00	2.70	.75
COMMON CARD (MS1-MS9)	.50	.23	.06
☐ MS1 Mike Schmidt Mike	.75	.35	.09
☐ MS2 Mike Schmidt The White House	.75	.35	.09
☐ MS3 Mike Schmidt Soaping Up	.75	.35	.09

☐ MS4 Mike Schmidt The Promised Land	.75	.35	.09
☐ MS5 Mike Schmidt Who is Who	.75	.35	.09
☐ MS6 Mike Schmidt The Call	.75	.35	.09
☐ MS7 Mike Schmidt Leading The Way	.75	.35	.09
☐ MS8 Mike Schmidt Award Winner	.75	.35	.09
☐ MS9 Checklist	.50	.23	.06

1994 Ted Williams Roger Maris

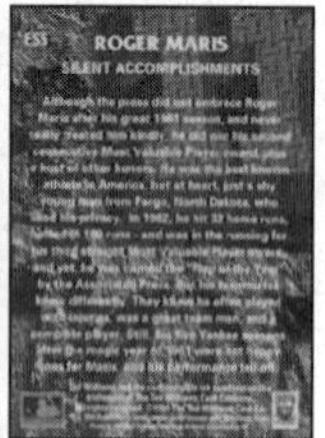

Randomly inserted in foil packs, this nine-card standard-size set highlights the career of Roger Maris. The full-color photos on the fronts are partly full-bleed and partly edged by jagged bronze borders. When placed in a 9-card plastic sheet, the background on the backs form a composite "Etched in Stone" logo. The text overprinted on the backs summarize Maris' career from amateur baseball until his untimely death in 1985. A red foil version of this set was also produced. The values are the same as those listed below.

	MINT	NRMT	EXC
COMPLETE SET (9)	12.00	5.50	1.50
COMMON CARD (ES1-ES9)	1.00	.45	.12
☐ ES1 Roger Maris Scouting Report	1.50	.70	.19
☐ ES2 Roger Maris Traded	1.50	.70	.19
☐ ES3 Roger Maris Career Year	1.50	.70	.19
☐ ES4 Roger Maris 1961	1.50	.70	.19
☐ ES5 Roger Maris Silent Accomplishments	1.50	.70	.19
☐ ES6 Roger Maris Team Player	1.50	.70	.19
☐ ES7 Roger Maris Reborn	1.50	.70	.19
☐ ES8 Roger Maris Hero's Welcome	1.50	.70	.19
☐ ES9 Roger Maris Checklist	1.00	.45	.12

1994 Ted Williams Trade for Babe

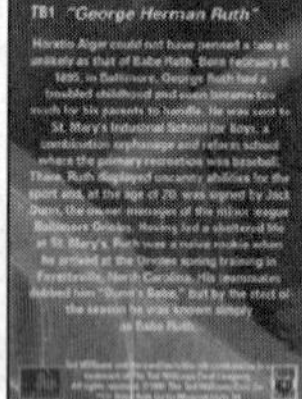

A special "Trade for Babe" chase card was randomly inserted throughout the packs. By mailing in the trade card plus 4.50 for shipping and handling, the collector received this nine-card standard-size set. The fronts display full-bleed colorized photos while the text on the backs highlight various turning points in his career or aspects of his personality.

	MINT	NRMT	EXC
COMPLETE SET (9)	40.00	18.00	5.00
COMMON CARD (T1-T9)	4.00	1.80	.50
☐ T1 Babe Ruth German Herman Ruth	5.00	2.20	.60
☐ T2 Babe Ruth King of the Hill	5.00	2.20	.60
☐ T3 Babe Ruth On to New York	5.00	2.20	.60
☐ T4 Babe Ruth Called Shot?	5.00	2.20	.60
☐ T5 Babe Ruth The Bambino and The Iron Horse	5.00	2.20	.60
☐ T6 Babe Ruth Larger Than Life	5.00	2.20	.60
☐ T7 Babe Ruth Always a Yankee	5.00	2.20	.60
☐ T8 Babe Ruth The Babe	5.00	2.20	.60
☐ T9 Babe Ruth Checklist	4.00	1.80	.50
☐ NNO0 Trade Card	4.00	1.80	.50

1993 Texas Supermarket Ryan Stickers

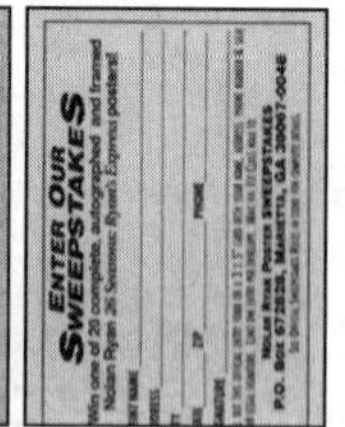

These stickers featured reprints of Nolan Ryan Topps cards. They were regionally issued in various Texas Supermarkets: Minyards, Super S, Brookshire Borthers and Budget Chopper. over a period of ten weeks. Each sticker sheet contained three "reprint" cards. These stickers were issued by Big League Collectibles and measure 98 percent of the regular card size.

	MINT	NRMT	EXC
COMPLETE SET (30)	10.00	4.50	1.25
COMMON STICKER (1-30)	.50	.23	.06
☐ 1 Nolan Ryan 1968 Topps	.50	.23	.06
☐ 2 Nolan Ryan 1969 Topps	.50	.23	.06
☐ 3 Nolan Ryan 1970 Topps	.50	.23	.06
☐ 4 Nolan Ryan 1971 Topps	.50	.23	.06
☐ 5 Nolan Ryan 1972 Topps	.50	.23	.06
☐ 6 Nolan Ryan 1973 Topps	.50	.23	.06
☐ 7 Nolan Ryan 1974 Topps	.50	.23	.06
☐ 8 Nolan Ryan 1975 Topps	.50	.23	.06
☐ 9 Nolan Ryan 1976 Topps	.50	.23	.06
☐ 10 Nolan Ryan 1977 Topps	.50	.23	.06
☐ 11 Nolan Ryan 1978 Topps	.50	.23	.06
☐ 12 Nolan Ryan 1979 Topps	.50	.23	.06
☐ 13 Nolan Ryan 1980 Topps	.50	.23	.06
☐ 14 Nolan Ryan 1981 Topps	.50	.23	.06
☐ 15 Nolan Ryan 1982 Topps	.50	.23	.06
☐ 16 Nolan Ryan 1983 Topps	.50	.23	.06
☐ 17 Nolan Ryan 1984 Topps	.50	.23	.06
☐ 18 Nolan Ryan 1985 Topps	.50	.23	.06
☐ 19 Nolan Ryan 1986 Topps	.50	.23	.06
☐ 20 Nolan Ryan 1987 Topps	.50	.23	.06
☐ 21 Nolan Ryan 1988 Topps	.50	.23	.06
☐ 22 Nolan Ryan 1989 Topps	.50	.23	.06
☐ 23 Nolan Ryan 1990 Topps	.50	.23	.06
☐ 24 Nolan Ryan 1991 Topps	.50	.23	.06
☐ 25 Nolan Ryan 1992 Topps	.50	.23	.06
☐ 26 Nolan Ryan 1993 Topps	.50	.23	.06
☐ 27 Nolan Ryan 1994 Topps	.50	.23	.06
☐ 28 Nolan Ryan 1982 Topps Astros Team Leaders	.50	.23	.06
☐ 29 Nolan Ryan 1990 Topps Rangers Special	.50	.23	.06
☐ 30 Nolan Ryan 1991 Topps Record Breaker	.50	.23	.06

1914 Texas Tommy E224

There are two types of these cards:Type I are 1-50 and Type II are 51-64. The type one cards measure 2 3/8" by 3 1/2" while the type two cards measure 1 7/8" by 3". The type one cards have stats on the back while the type 2 cards have blank backs. Harry Hooper and Rube Marquard only exist in type two fashion.

	EX-MT	VG-E	GOOD
COMPLETE SET (62)	32000.00	14400.00	4000.00
COMMON CARD (1-62)	275.00	125.00	34.00
☐ 1 Jimmy Archer	275.00	125.00	34.00
☐ 2 Jimmy Austin	275.00	125.00	34.00
☐ 3 Frank Baker	600.00	275.00	75.00
☐ 4 Chief Bender	600.00	275.00	75.00
☐ 5 Bob Bescher	275.00	125.00	34.00
☐ 6 Ping Bodie	350.00	160.00	45.00
☐ 7 Donie Bush	275.00	125.00	34.00
☐ 8 Bobby Byrne	275.00	125.00	34.00
☐ 9 Nixey Callahan	275.00	125.00	34.00
☐ 10 Howie Camnitz	275.00	125.00	34.00
☐ 11 Frank Chance	600.00	275.00	75.00
☐ 12 Hal Chase	500.00	220.00	60.00
☐ 13 Ty Cobb	3500.00	1600.00	450.00
☐ 14 Jack Coombs	350.00	160.00	45.00
☐ 15 Sam Crawford	600.00	275.00	75.00
☐ 16 Birdie Cree	275.00	125.00	34.00
☐ 17 Al Demaree	275.00	125.00	34.00
☐ 18 Red Dooin	275.00	125.00	34.00
☐ 19 Larry Doyle	500.00	220.00	60.00
☐ 20 Johnny Evers	600.00	275.00	75.00
☐ 21 Vean Gregg	275.00	125.00	34.00
☐ 22 Bob Harmon	275.00	125.00	34.00
☐ 23 Joe Jackson	4000.00	1800.00	500.00
☐ 24 Walter Johnson	750.00	350.00	95.00
☐ 25 Otto Knabe	275.00	125.00	34.00
☐ 26 Nap Lajoie	600.00	275.00	75.00
☐ 27 Bris Lord	275.00	125.00	34.00
☐ 28 Connie Mack MG	600.00	275.00	75.00
☐ 29 Armando Marsans	275.00	125.00	34.00
☐ 30 Christy Mathewson	750.00	350.00	95.00
☐ 31 George McBride	275.00	125.00	34.00
☐ 32 John McGraw MG	900.00	400.00	110.00
☐ 33 Snuffy McInnis	300.00	135.00	38.00
☐ 34 Chief Meyers	275.00	125.00	34.00
☐ 35 Earl Moore	275.00	125.00	34.00
☐ 36 Mike Mowrey	275.00	125.00	34.00
☐ 37 Marty O'Toole	275.00	125.00	34.00
☐ 38 Eddle Plank	600.00	275.00	75.00
☐ 39 Jack Ryan	275.00	125.00	34.00
☐ 40 Tris Speaker	750.00	350.00	95.00
☐ 41 Jake Stahl	275.00	125.00	34.00
☐ 42 Oscar Stanage	275.00	125.00	34.00
☐ 43 Bill Sweeney	275.00	125.00	34.00
☐ 44 Honus Wagner	2000.00	900.00	250.00
☐ 45 Ed Walsh	600.00	275.00	75.00
☐ 47 Harry Wolter	275.00	125.00	34.00
☐ 48 Joe Wood	500.00	220.00	60.00
☐ 49 Steve Yerkes	350.00	160.00	45.00
☐ 50 Heinie Zimmerman	275.00	125.00	34.00
☐ 51 Ping Bodie	275.00	125.00	34.00
☐ 52 Larry Doyle	500.00	220.00	60.00
☐ 53 Vean Gregg	350.00	160.00	45.00
☐ 54 Harry Hooper	750.00	350.00	95.00
☐ 55 Walter Johnson	1000.00	450.00	125.00
☐ 56 Connie Mack MG	750.00	350.00	95.00
☐ 57 Rube Marquard	750.00	350.00	95.00
☐ 58 Christy Mathewson	750.00	350.00	95.00
☐ 59 Walter Johnson	1000.00	450.00	125.00
☐ 60 John McGraw MG	600.00	275.00	75.00
☐ 61 Chief Meyers	275.00	125.00	34.00
☐ 62 Jake Stahl	350.00	160.00	45.00
☐ 63 Steve Yerkes	275.00	125.00	34.00
☐ 63 Honus Wagner	1600.00	700.00	200.00
☐ 64 Joe Wood	300.00	135.00	38.00

1948 Thom McAn Feller

This one-card set was distributed by Thom McAn Shoe Stores and features a black-and-white picture of Bob Feller of the Cleveland Indians with a facsimile autograph. The back carrys a Baseball Quiz with the answers to the questions at the bottom.

	NRMT	VG-E	GOOD
COMPLETE SET (1)	10.00	4.50	1.25
COMMON CARD (1)	10.00	4.50	1.25
☐ 1 Bob Feller	10.00	4.50	1.25

1985 Thom McAn Discs

MSA (Michael Schechter Associates) produced this 46-disc set for Thom McAn to promote a specially developed line of boys' and young men's JOX all-turf cleat shoes. The give-away consisted of a set of 10 discs with every pair of shoes purchased. The production of the discs was discontinued when a decision was made to replace this line of shoes with a newer one. The discs measure 2 3/4" in diameter. The front design resembles a baseball, with a black and white headshot sandwiched between the two rows of stitching. Four stars appear above the player's picture, and the two ovals created by the stitching are colored yellow, green, red, or mustard. In addition, at least 8 players (Cedeno, Cooper, Cowens, Hargrove, Leonard, Valenzuela, Walker, and Zahn) had their photo and information printed in two different colors. The back of the discs are printed in black on white and have a Thom McAn advertisement. The discs are unnumbered and checklisted below alphabetically according to AL (1-24) and NL players (25-46). The same checklist was used for discs with the Subway sandwich chain. Please see multiplier tables below for values.

	NRMT	VG-E	GOOD
COMPLETE SET (46)	350.00	160.00	45.00
COMMON DISC (1-46)	1.00	.45	.12
*SUBWAY DISCS: .3X BASIC DISCS ..			
☐ 1 Benny Ayala	1.00	.45	.12
☐ 2 Buddy Bell	2.00	.90	.25
☐ 3 Juan Beniquez	1.00	.45	.12
☐ 4 Tony Bernazard	1.00	.45	.12
☐ 5 Mike Boddicker	1.00	.45	.12
☐ 6 Bill Buckner	1.00	.45	.12
☐ 7 Rod Carew	35.00	16.00	4.40
☐ 8 Onix Concepcion	1.00	.45	.12
☐ 9 Cecil Cooper	2.00	.90	.25
☐ 10 Al Cowens	1.00	.45	.12
☐ 11 Ron Guidry	2.00	.90	.25
☐ 12 Mike Hargrove	2.00	.90	.25
☐ 13 Kent Hrbek	2.00	.90	.25
☐ 14 Rick Langford	1.00	.45	.12
☐ 15 Jack Morris	2.00	.90	.25
☐ 16 Dan Quisenberry	1.00	.45	.12
☐ 17 Cal Ripken	75.00	34.00	9.50
☐ 18 Ed Romero	1.00	.45	.12
☐ 19 Tom Seaver	35.00	16.00	4.40
☐ 20 Alan Trammell	4.00	1.80	.50
☐ 21 Greg Walker	1.00	.45	.12
☐ 22 Willie Wilson	1.00	.45	.12
☐ 23 Dave Winfield	35.00	16.00	4.40
☐ 24 Geoff Zahn	1.00	.45	.12
☐ 25 Steve Carlton	35.00	16.00	4.40
☐ 26 Cesar Cedeno	1.00	.45	.12
☐ 27 Jose Cruz	1.00	.45	.12
☐ 28 Ivan DeJesus	1.00	.45	.12
☐ 29 Luis DeLeon	1.00	.45	.12
☐ 30 Rich Gossage	2.00	.90	.25
☐ 31 Pedro Guerrero	1.00	.45	.12
☐ 32 Tony Gwynn	50.00	22.00	6.25
☐ 33 Keith Hernandez	2.00	.90	.25
☐ 34 Bob Horner	1.00	.45	.12
☐ 35 Jeff Leonard	1.00	.45	.12
☐ 36 Willie McGee	2.00	.90	.25
☐ 37 Jesse Orosco	1.00	.45	.12
☐ 38 Junior Ortiz	1.00	.45	.12
☐ 39 Terry Puhl	1.00	.45	.12
☐ 40 Johnny Ray	1.00	.45	.12
☐ 41 Ryne Sandberg	50.00	22.00	6.25
☐ 42 Mike Schmidt	35.00	16.00	4.40
☐ 43 Rick Sutcliffe	1.00	.45	.12
☐ 44 Bruce Sutter	1.00	.45	.12
☐ 45 Fernando Valenzuela	2.00	.90	.25
☐ 46 Ozzie Virgil	1.00	.45	.12

1907-09 Tigers A.C. Dietsche Postcards PC765

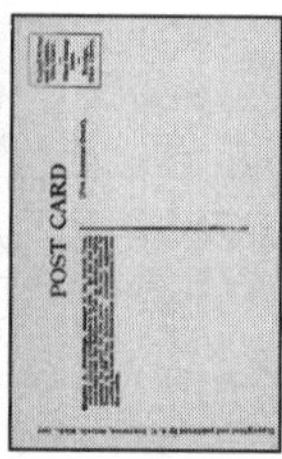

The team card is oversized and has not had its existence verified. The date next to the player's name is the copyright date. Cards are unnumbered; in the list below they are ordered alphabetically within series. Cards numbered 1-15 below are known as series I and have a 1907 copyright. Cards numbered 16-29 are known as series II and have 1908 or 1909 copyrights. Those cards in series II only produced in one year are noted by the last two digits of the year.

	EX-MT	VG-E	GOOD
COMPLETE SET (29)	2000.00	900.00	250.00
COMMON CARD (1-29)	75.00	34.00	9.50
☐ 1 Ty Cobb	350.00	160.00	45.00
☐ 2 William Coughlin	75.00	34.00	9.50
☐ 3 Sam Crawford	125.00	55.00	15.50
☐ 4 Bill Donovan	75.00	34.00	9.50
☐ 5 Jerome W. Downs	75.00	34.00	9.50
☐ 6 Hugh Jennings MG	125.00	55.00	15.50
☐ 7 Davy Jones	75.00	34.00	9.50
☐ 8 Ed Killian	75.00	34.00	9.50
☐ 9 George Mullin	75.00	34.00	9.50
☐ 10 Charles O'Leary	75.00	34.00	9.50
☐ 11 Fred T. Payne	75.00	34.00	9.50
☐ 12 Claude Rossman	75.00	34.00	9.50
☐ 13 Germany Schaefer	75.00	34.00	9.50
☐ 14 Boss Schmidt	75.00	34.00	9.50
☐ 15 Edward Siever	75.00	34.00	9.50
☐ 16 Henry Beckendorf 08	75.00	34.00	9.50
☐ 17 Owen Bush 08	75.00	34.00	9.50
☐ 18 Ty Cobb 08 (batting)	350.00	160.00	45.00

☐ 19 James Delehanty 09	75.00	34.00	9.50
☐ 20 Bill Donovan 08	75.00	34.00	9.50
☐ 21 Hugh Jennings MG 08	125.00	55.00	15.50
☐ 22 Tom Jones 09	75.00	34.00	9.50
☐ 23 Matthew McIntrye 08	75.00	34.00	9.50
☐ 24 George Moriarty 08	75.00	34.00	9.50
☐ 25 Oscar Stanage 08	75.00	34.00	9.50
☐ 26 Oren Edgar Summers 08	75.00	34.00	9.50
☐ 27 Edgar Willett 08	75.00	34.00	9.50
☐ 28 Ralph Works 09	75.00	34.00	9.50
☐ 29 Team Picture 09	125.00	34.00	9.50

1908 Tigers Fred G.Wright Postcards

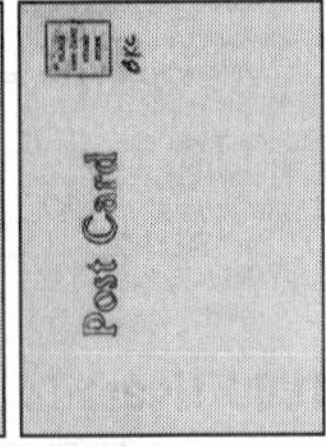

Fred G. Wright was the photographer for several cards including the Detroit Tigers set produced by H.M. Taylor, established his own company. The only card positively identified is one of "Wild Bill" Donovan, a star pitcher for the Tigers. All additions to this checklist are appreciated.

	EX-MT	VG-E	GOOD
COMPLETE SET	200.00	90.00	25.00
COMMON CARD	200.00	90.00	25.00
☐ 1 Bill Donovan	200.00	90.00	25.00

1909-11 Tigers H.M. Taylor PC773-2

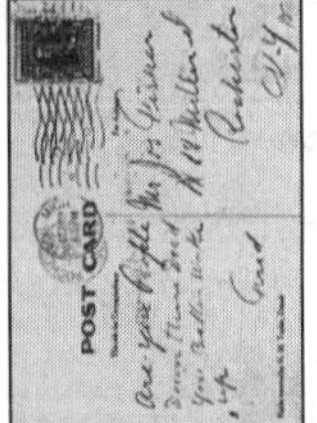

The H.M. Taylor postcard set measures 3 1/2" by 5 1/2" and was issued during the 1909-11 time period and features Detroit Tigers players only. The cards are black and white with a rather large border around the card. The H.M Taylor identification is presented on the back of the card.

	EX-MT	VG-E	GOOD
COMPLETE SET (9)	2750.00	1250.00	350.00
COMMON CARD (1-9)	150.00	70.00	19.00
☐ 1 Ty Cobb	1200.00	550.00	150.00
At Bat			
☐ 2 Bill Coughlin	150.00	70.00	19.00
Batting			
☐ 3 Sam Crawford	250.00	110.00	31.00
Ready for the ball			
☐ 4 Detroit Team Card	500.00	220.00	60.00
☐ 5 Wild Bill Donovan	150.00	70.00	19.00
Floral Horseshoe prented at Philadelphia			
☐ 6 Wild Bill Donovan	150.00	70.00	19.00
Batting			
☐ 7 Hugh Jennings	300.00	135.00	38.00
Wee Ah; Yours Truly			
☐ 8 Wild Bill Donovan	150.00	70.00	19.00
Hugh Jennings			
Frank Chance			
In Dugout			
☐ 9 Hugh Jennings MG	250.00	110.00	31.00
and his Tigers			
Caraciture			

1909-10 Tigers Topping and Company PC773-1

This set of Detroit Tiger stars is believed to have been issued in late 1909 and early 1910. This distinctive set features yellow bands at the top and bottom and a face shot of the player in a center of a six-pointed star, which also contains a yellow outline. The words "Tiger Stars" are printed in the upper yellow band whereas the player's name and position appears in the lower band. Topping and Publishers Company, Detroit, is identified on the reverse.

	EX-MT	VG-E	GOOD
COMPLETE SET (20)	4000.00	1800.00	500.00
COMMON CARD (1-20)	150.00	70.00	19.00
☐ 1 Henry Beckendorf	150.00	70.00	19.00
☐ 2 Donie Bush	150.00	70.00	19.00
☐ 3 Ty Cobb	1500.00	700.00	190.00
☐ 4 Sam Crawford	300.00	135.00	38.00
☐ 5 Jim Delahanty	150.00	70.00	19.00
☐ 6 Bill Donovan	150.00	70.00	19.00
☐ 7 Hugh Jennings MG	300.00	135.00	38.00
☐ 8 Davy Jones	150.00	70.00	19.00
☐ 9 Tom Jones	150.00	70.00	19.00
☐ 10 Ed Killian	150.00	70.00	19.00
☐ 11 Matty McIntyre	150.00	70.00	19.00
☐ 12 George Moriarty	150.00	70.00	19.00
☐ 13 George Mullin	150.00	70.00	19.00
☐ 14 Charlie O'Leary	150.00	70.00	19.00
☐ 15 Charlie Schmidt	150.00	70.00	19.00
☐ 16 George Speer	150.00	70.00	19.00
☐ 17 Oscar Stanage	150.00	70.00	19.00
☐ 18 Eddie Summers	150.00	70.00	19.00
☐ 19 Edgar Willet	150.00	70.00	19.00
☐ 20 Ralph Works	150.00	70.00	19.00

1909 Tigers Wolverine News Postcards PC773-3

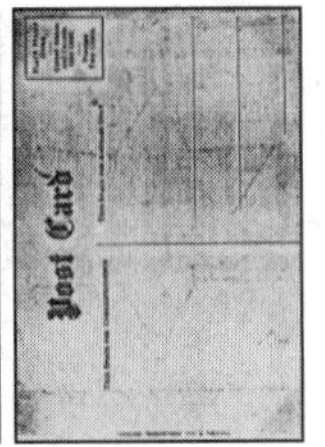

The Wolverine News Company features Detroit Tigers. Two poses each of Ty Cobb and Sam Crawford highlight this black and white set. The Wolverine News Company identification is printed on the back of the card.

	EX-MT	VG-E	GOOD
COMPLETE SET	2000.00	900.00	250.00
COMMON CARD	60.00	27.00	7.50
☐ 1 Ty Cobb at bat	500.00	220.00	60.00
☐ 2 Ty Cobb Portrait	500.00	220.00	60.00
☐ 3 Bill Coughlin Capt.	60.00	27.00	7.50
and Third Baseman			
☐ 4 Sam Crawford	125.00	55.00	15.50
Bunting			
☐ 5 Sam Crawford	125.00	55.00	15.50
☐ 6 Wild Bill Donovan	75.00	34.00	9.50
Pitcher			
☐ 7 Jerry Downs	60.00	27.00	7.50
Utility			
☐ 8 Hugh Jennings MG	125.00	55.00	15.50
On the Coaching Line HOR			
☐ 9 Davy Jones	60.00	27.00	7.50
Left Fielder			
☐ 10 Ed Killian	60.00	27.00	7.50
Pitcher			
☐ 11 George Mullin	60.00	27.00	7.50
Pitcher			
☐ 12 Charlie O'Leary	60.00	27.00	7.50
Short Stop			
☐ 13 Fred Payne	60.00	27.00	7.50
Catcher			
☐ 14 Claude Rossman	60.00	27.00	7.50
1st Baseman			
☐ 15 Herman Schaefer	60.00	27.00	7.50
2d. Baseman			
☐ 16 Germany Schaefer	75.00	34.00	9.50
Charlie O'Leary			
working double play HOR			
☐ 17 Charlie Schmidt	60.00	27.00	7.50
Catcher			
☐ 18 Eddie Siever	60.00	27.00	7.50
Pitcher			
☐ 19 Wild Bill Donovan	75.00	34.00	9.50
At the Water Wagon			

1935 Tigers Free Press

This 21-card newsprint set of the 1935 Detroit Tigers measures approximately 9" by 11" and was within the "The Detroit Free Press." The cards are unnumbered and checklisted below in alphabetical order.

	EX-MT	VG-E	GOOD
COMPLETE SET (21)	225.00	100.00	28.00
COMMON CARD (1-21)	10.00	4.50	1.25
☐ 1 Eldon Auker	10.00	4.50	1.25
☐ 2 Del Baker	10.00	4.50	1.25
☐ 3 Mickey Cochrane	25.00	11.00	3.10
☐ 4 Frank Deljack	10.00	4.50	1.25
☐ 5 Carl Fischer	10.00	4.50	1.25
☐ 6 Pete Fox	10.00	4.50	1.25
☐ 7 Charlie Gehringer	20.00	9.00	2.50
☐ 8 Goose Goslin	20.00	9.00	2.50
☐ 9 Hank Greenberg	25.00	11.00	3.10
☐ 10 Luke Hamlin	10.00	4.50	1.25
☐ 11 Ray Hayworth	10.00	4.50	1.25
☐ 12 Chief Hogsett	10.00	4.50	1.25
☐ 13 Firpo Marberry	10.00	4.50	1.25
☐ 14 Marvin Owen	10.00	4.50	1.25
☐ 15 Cy Perkins	10.00	4.50	1.25
☐ 16 Billie Rogell	10.00	4.50	1.25
☐ 17 Schoolboy Rowe	15.00	6.75	1.85
☐ 18 Geinie Schuble	10.00	4.50	1.25
☐ 19 Victor Sorrell	10.00	4.50	1.25
☐ 20 Jerry Walker	10.00	4.50	1.25
☐ 21 Jo-Jo White	10.00	4.50	1.25

1953 Tigers Glendale

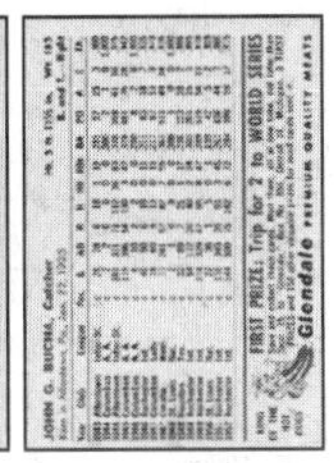

The cards in this 28-card set measure approximately 2 5/8" by 3 3/4". The 1953 Glendale Meats set of full-color, unnumbered cards features Detroit Tiger ballplayers exclusively and was distributed one per package of Glendale Meats in the Detroit area. The back contains the complete major and minor league record through the 1952 season. The scarcer cards of the set command higher prices, with the Houtteman card being the most difficult to find. There is an album associated with the set (which also is quite scarce now). The catalog designation for this scarce regional set is F151. Since the cards are unnumbered, they are ordered below alphabetically.

	NRMT	VG-E	GOOD
COMPLETE SET (28)	5000.00	2200.00	600.00
COMMON CARD (1-28)	150.00	70.00	19.00
☐ 1 Matt Batts	150.00	70.00	19.00
☐ 2 Johnny Bucha	150.00	70.00	19.00
☐ 3 Frank Carswell	150.00	70.00	19.00
☐ 4 Jim Delsing	175.00	80.00	22.00
☐ 5 Walt Dropo	175.00	80.00	22.00
☐ 6 Hal Erickson	150.00	70.00	19.00
☐ 7 Paul Foytack	150.00	70.00	19.00
☐ 8 Owen Friend	150.00	70.00	19.00
☐ 9 Ned Garver	175.00	80.00	22.00
☐ 10 Joe Ginsberg SP	350.00	160.00	45.00
☐ 11 Ted Gray	150.00	70.00	19.00
☐ 12 Fred Hatfield	150.00	70.00	19.00
☐ 13 Ray Herbert	150.00	70.00	19.00
☐ 14 Billy Hitchcock	150.00	70.00	19.00
☐ 15 Billy Hoeft SP	250.00	110.00	31.00
☐ 16 Art Houtteman SP	2000.00	900.00	250.00
☐ 17 Milt Jordan	150.00	70.00	19.00
☐ 18 Harvey Kuenn	450.00	200.00	55.00
☐ 19 Don Lund	150.00	70.00	19.00
☐ 20 Dave Madison	150.00	70.00	19.00
☐ 21 Dick Marlowe	150.00	70.00	19.00
☐ 22 Pat Mullin	150.00	70.00	19.00
☐ 23 Bob Nieman	150.00	70.00	19.00
☐ 24 Johnny Pesky	175.00	80.00	22.00
☐ 25 Jerry Priddy	150.00	70.00	19.00
☐ 26 Steve Souchock	150.00	70.00	19.00
☐ 27 Russ Sullivan	150.00	70.00	19.00
☐ 28 Bill Wight	150.00	70.00	19.00

1959 Tigers Graphic Arts Service PC749

The Graphic Art Service postcards were issued in the late 1950's and early 60's in Cincinnati, Ohio. Despite being issued in Cincinnati, the players featured are all Detroit Tigers. These black and white, unnumbered cards feature facsimile autographs on the front. Two poses of Reno Bertoia exist.

	NRMT	VG-E	GOOD
COMPLETE SET (16)	75.00	34.00	9.50
COMMON CARD (1-16)	3.50	1.55	.45
☐ 1 Al Aber	3.50	1.55	.45
☐ 2 Hank Aguirre	5.00	2.20	.60
☐ 3 Reno Bertoia	3.50	1.55	.45
☐ 4 Frank Bolling	3.50	1.55	.45
☐ 5 Jim Bunning	15.00	6.75	1.85
☐ 6 Paul Foytack	3.50	1.55	.45
☐ 7 Jim Hegan	3.50	1.55	.45
☐ 8 Tom Heinrich CO	10.00	4.50	1.25
☐ 9 Bill Hoeft	3.50	1.55	.45
☐ 10 Frank House	3.50	1.55	.45
☐ 11 Harvey Kuenn	5.00	2.20	.60
☐ 12 Billy Martin	10.00	4.50	1.25
☐ 13 Tom Morgan	5.00	2.20	.60
☐ 14 Bob Shaw	3.50	1.55	.45
☐ 15 Lou Slater	3.50	1.55	.45
☐ 16 Tim Thompson	3.50	1.55	.45

1960 Tigers Jay Publishing

This 12-card set of the Detroit Tigers measures approximately 5" by 7" and features black-and-white player photos in a white border. These cards were packaged 12 to a packet. The backs are blank. The cards are unnumbered and checklisted below in alphabetical order.

	NRMT	VG-E	GOOD
COMPLETE SET (12)	35.00	16.00	4.40
COMMON CARD (1-12)	2.00	.90	.25
☐ 1 Lou Berberet	2.00	.90	.25
☐ 2 Frank Bolling	2.00	.90	.25
☐ 3 Rocky Bridges	3.00	1.35	.35
☐ 4 Jim Bunning	7.50	3.40	.95
☐ 5 Rocky Colavito	5.00	2.20	.60
☐ 6 Paul Foytack	2.00	.90	.25
☐ 7 Al Kaline	10.00	4.50	1.25
☐ 8 Frank Lary	2.00	.90	.25
☐ 9 Charlie Maxwell	2.00	.90	.25
☐ 10 Don Mossi	2.00	.90	.25
☐ 11 Ray Narleski	2.00	.90	.25
☐ 12 Eddie Yost	2.00	.90	.25

1961 Tigers Jay Publishing

This 12-card set of the Detroit Tigers measures approximately 5" by 7". The fronts feature black-and-white posed player photos with the player's and team name printed below in the white border. These cards were packaged 12 in a packet. The backs are blank. The cards are unnumbered and checklisted below in alphabetical order.

	NRMT	VG-E	GOOD
COMPLETE SET (12)	35.00	16.00	4.40
COMMON CARD (1-12)	2.50	1.10	.30
☐ 1 Steve Boros	2.50	1.10	.30
☐ 2 Dick Brown	2.50	1.10	.30
☐ 3 Bill Bruton	2.50	1.10	.30
☐ 4 Jim Bunning	6.00	2.70	.75
☐ 5 Norm Cash	3.50	1.55	.45
☐ 6 Rocky Colavito	6.00	2.70	.75
☐ 7 Chuck Cottier	2.50	1.10	.30
☐ 8 Dick Gernert	2.50	1.10	.30
☐ 9 Al Kaline	10.00	4.50	1.25
☐ 10 Frank Lary	2.50	1.10	.30
☐ 11 Charlie Maxwell	2.50	1.10	.30
☐ 12 Bob Sheffing MG	2.50	1.10	.30

1962 Tigers Jay Publishing

This 12-card set of the Detroit Tigers measures approximately 5" by 7". The fronts feature black-and-white posed player photos with the player's and team name printed below in the white border. These cards were packaged 12 in a packet. The backs are blank. The cards are unnumbered and checklisted below in alphabetical order.

	NRMT	VG-E	GOOD
COMPLETE SET (12)	30.00	13.50	3.70
COMMON CARD (1-12)	2.50	1.10	.30
☐ 1 Steve Boros	3.50	1.55	.45
☐ 2 Dick Brown	2.50	1.10	.30
☐ 3 JIm Bunning	7.50	3.40	.95
☐ 4 Norm Cash	5.00	2.20	.60
☐ 5 Rocky Colavito	7.50	3.40	.95
☐ 6 Chico Fernandez	2.50	1.10	.30
☐ 7 Al Kaline	12.50	5.50	1.55
☐ 8 Frank Lary	2.50	1.10	.30
☐ 9 Charley Maxwell	2.50	1.10	.30
☐ 10 Don Mossi	2.50	1.10	.30
☐ 11 Bob Scheffing MG	2.50	1.10	.30
☐ 12 Jake Wood	2.50	1.10	.30

1962 Tiger Post Cards Ford

These postcards feature members of the 1962 Detroit Tigers. They are unnumbered and we have sequenced them in alphabetical order.

	NRMT	VG-E	GOOD
COMPLETE SET	850.00	375.00	105.00
COMMON CARD	50.00	22.00	6.25
☐ 1 Hank Aguirre	75.00	34.00	9.50
☐ 2 Steve Boros	65.00	29.00	8.00
☐ 3 Dick Brown	50.00	22.00	6.25
☐ 4 Jim Bunning	125.00	55.00	15.50
☐ 5 Phil Cavarretta CO	75.00	34.00	9.50
☐ 6 Rocky Colavito	100.00	45.00	12.50
☐ 7 Terry Fox	50.00	22.00	6.25
☐ 8 Purnal Goldy	50.00	22.00	6.25
☐ 9 Homel TR	50.00	22.00	6.25
☐ 10 Ron Kline	50.00	22.00	6.25
☐ 11 Don Mossi	65.00	29.00	8.00
☐ 12 George Myatt CO	65.00	29.00	8.00
☐ 13 Ron Nischwitz	50.00	22.00	6.25
☐ 14 Larry Osborne	50.00	22.00	6.25
☐ 15 Phil Regan	50.00	22.00	6.25
☐ 16 Mike Roarke	50.00	22.00	6.25

1963 Tigers Jay Publishing

This 12-card set of the Detroit Tigers measures approximately 5" by 7". The fronts feature black-and-white posed player photos with the player's and team name printed below in the white border. These cards were packaged 12 in a packet. The backs are blank. The cards are unnumbered and checklisted below in alphabetical order.

	NRMT	VG-E	GOOD
COMPLETE SET (12)	35.00	16.00	4.40
COMMON CARD (1-12)	2.00	.90	.25
☐ 1 Hank Aguirre	3.50	1.55	.45
☐ 2 Bill Bruton	2.00	.90	.25
☐ 3 Jim Bunning	7.50	3.40	.95
☐ 4 Norm Cash	4.00	1.80	.50
☐ 5 Rocky Colavito	7.50	3.40	.95
☐ 6 Chico Fernandez	2.00	.90	.25
☐ 7 Paul Foytack	2.00	.90	.25
☐ 8 Al Kaline	12.50	5.50	1.55
☐ 9 Frank Lary	3.50	1.55	.45
☐ 10 Bob Sheffing MG	2.00	.90	.25
☐ 11 Gus Triandos	3.50	1.55	.45
☐ 12 Jake Wood	2.00	.90	.25

1964 Tigers Jay Publishing

This 12-card set of the Detroit Tigers measures approximately 5" by 7". The fronts feature black-and-white posed player photos with the player's and team name printed below in the white border. These cards were packaged 12 in a packet. The backs are blank. The cards are unnumbered and checklisted below in alphabetical order.

	NRMT	VG-E	GOOD
COMPLETE SET (12)	30.00	13.50	3.70
COMMON CARD (1-12)	2.00	.90	.25
☐ 1 Hank Aguirre	3.00	1.35	.35
☐ 2 Bill Bruton	2.00	.90	.25
☐ 3 Norm Cash	3.50	1.55	.45
☐ 4 Chuck Dressen MG	2.50	1.10	.30
☐ 5 Bill Freehan	3.50	1.55	.45
☐ 6 Al Kaline	7.50	3.40	.95
☐ 7 Frank Lary	2.00	.90	.25
☐ 8 Jerry Lumpe	2.00	.90	.25
☐ 9 Ed Rakow	2.00	.90	.25
☐ 10 Phil Regan	2.00	.90	.25
☐ 11 Mike Roarke	2.00	.90	.25
☐ 12 Jake Wood	2.00	.90	.25

1964 Tiger Lids

This set of 14 lids was produced in 1964 and features members of the Detroit Tigers. The catalog designation for this set is F96-5. These lids are actually milk bottle caps. Each lid is blank backed and measures approximately 1 1/4" in diameter. Since the lids are unnumbered, they are ordered below in alphabetical order. The players are drawn on the lids in blue and the player's name is written in orange. The lids say "Visit Tiger Stadium" at the top and "See the Tigers More in '64" at the bottom of every lid.

	NRMT	VG-E	GOOD
COMPLETE SET	90.00	40.00	11.00
COMMON LID (1-14)	5.00	2.20	.60
☐ 1 Hank Aguirre	5.00	2.20	.60
☐ 2 Billy Bruton	5.00	2.20	.60
☐ 3 Norm Cash	10.00	4.50	1.25
☐ 4 Don Demeter	5.00	2.20	.60
☐ 5 Chuck Dressen MG	6.00	2.70	.75
☐ 6 Bill Freehan	10.00	4.50	1.25
☐ 7 Al Kaline	45.00	20.00	5.50
☐ 8 Frank Lary	6.00	2.70	.75
☐ 9 Jerry Lumpe	5.00	2.20	.60
☐ 10 Dick McAuliffe	6.00	2.70	.75
☐ 11 Bubba Phillips	5.00	2.20	.60
☐ 12 Ed Rakow	5.00	2.20	.60
☐ 13 Phil Regan	6.00	2.70	.75
☐ 14 Dave Wickersham	5.00	2.20	.60

1965 Tigers Jay Publishing

These 11 blank-backed photos measure approximately 5" by 7" and feature white-bordered black-and-white posed player photos. The photos are printed on thin paper stock. The player's name and team appear below the photo within the bottom margin. The cards are unnumbered and checklisted below in alphabetical order.

	NRMT	VG-E	GOOD
COMPLETE SET (11)	25.00	11.00	3.10
COMMON CARD (1-11)	2.00	.90	.25
☐ 1 Hank Aguirre	2.00	.90	.25
☐ 2 Gates Brown	2.50	1.10	.30
☐ 3 Norm Cash	3.00	1.35	.35
☐ 4 Don Demeter	2.00	.90	.25
☐ 5 Charlie Dressen MG	2.50	1.10	.30
☐ 6 Bill Freehan	3.00	1.35	.35
☐ 7 Mickey Lolich	2.00	.90	.25
☐ 8 Jerry Lumpe	2.00	.90	.25
☐ 9 Dick McAuliffe	2.50	1.10	.30
☐ 10 Don Wert	2.00	.90	.25
☐ 11 Dave Wickersham	2.00	.90	.25

1967 Tigers Dexter Press

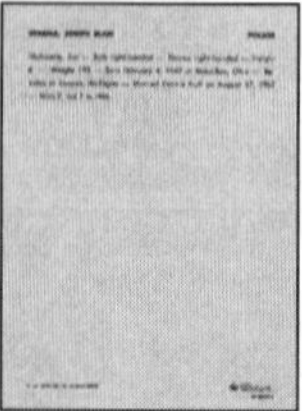

This set, which features 11 photo cards that measure approximately 5 1/2" by 7", has white-bordered posed color player photos on its fronts. The set was produced by Dexter Press located in West Nyack, New York and features Detroit Tigers' players. A facsimile autograph is printed across the top of the picture. The white backs carry a short biography printed in blue ink, with only one line providing statistics for the 1966 season. The cards are unnumbered and checklisted below in alphabetical order.

	NRMT	VG-E	GOOD
COMPLETE SET (11)	30.00	13.50	3.70
COMMON CARD (1-11)	2.50	1.10	.30
☐ 1 Norm Cash	3.50	1.55	.45
☐ 2 Bill Freehan	3.50	1.55	.45
☐ 3 Willie Horton	3.00	1.35	.35
☐ 4 Al Kaline	7.50	3.40	.95
☐ 5 Jerry Lumpe	2.50	1.10	.30
☐ 6 Dick McAullife	3.00	1.35	.35
☐ 7 Johnny Podres	3.00	1.35	.35
☐ 8 Joe Sparma	2.50	1.10	.30
☐ 9 Don Wert	2.50	1.10	.30
☐ 10 Dave Wickersham	2.50	1.10	.30
☐ 11 Earl Wilson	2.50	1.10	.30

1968 Tigers Detroit Free Press Bubblegumless

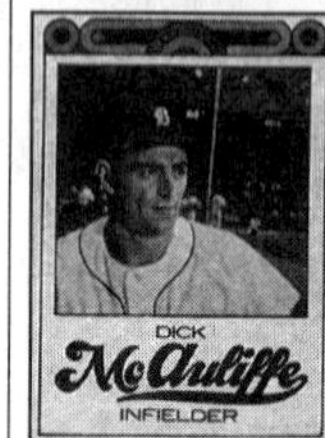

This set features members of the World Champion 1968 Detroit Tigers. The cards are unnumbered so we have sequenced them in alphabetical order.

	NRMT	VG-E	GOOD
COMPLETE SET	60.00	27.00	7.50
COMMON CARD	1.50	.70	.19
☐ 1 Gates Brown	2.50	1.10	.30
☐ 2 Norm Cash	5.00	2.20	.60
☐ 3 Tony Cuccinello CO	1.50	.70	.19
☐ 4 Pat Dobson	1.50	.70	.19
☐ 5 Bill Freehan	5.00	2.20	.60
☐ 6 John Hiller	1.50	.70	.19
☐ 7 Willie Horton	3.50	1.55	.45
☐ 8 Al Kaline	10.00	4.50	1.25
☐ 9 Fred Lasher	1.50	.70	.19
☐ 10 Mickey Lolich	5.00	2.20	.60
☐ 11 Dick McAuliffe	2.50	1.10	.30
☐ 12 Denny McLain	5.00	2.20	.60
☐ 13 Don McMahon	1.50	.70	.19
☐ 14 Tom Matchick	1.50	.70	.19
☐ 15 Wally Moses CO	1.50	.70	.19
☐ 16 Jim Northrup	3.50	1.55	.45
☐ 17 Ray Oyler	1.50	.70	.19
☐ 18 Jim Price	1.50	.70	.19
☐ 19 Daryl Patterson	1.50	.70	.19
☐ 20 Johnny Sain CO	2.50	1.10	.30
☐ 21 Mayo Smith MG	2.50	1.10	.30
☐ 22 Joe Sparma	1.50	.70	.19
☐ 23 Mickey Stanley	2.50	1.10	.30
☐ 24 Dick Tracewski	1.50	.70	.19
☐ 25 Jon Warden	1.50	.70	.19
☐ 26 Don Wert	1.50	.70	.19
☐ 27 Earl Wilson	1.50	.70	.19
☐ 28 John Wyatt	1.50	.70	.19

1969 Tigers Farmer Jack

This set features six-inch iron-on transfers of player faces of the 1969 Detroit Tigers team and was distributed by Farmer Jack's Supermarket. An iron-on facsimile autograph is printed below the head. The transfers are unnumbered and checklisted below in alphabetical order. The checklist is incomplete and additions are welcomed.

	NRMT	VG-E	GOOD
COMPLETE SET	7.50	3.40	.95
COMMON CARD	3.00	1.35	.35
☐ 1 Jim Northrup	5.00	2.20	.60
☐ 2 Joe Sparma	3.00	1.35	.35

1969 Tigers Team Issue

This 12-card set of the Detroit Tigers measures approximately 4 1/4" by 7". The fronts display black-and-white player portraits bordered in white. The player's name and team are printed in the top margin. The backs are blank. The cards are unnumbered and checklisted below in alphabetical order.

	NRMT	VG-E	GOOD
COMPLETE SET (12)	25.00	11.00	3.10
COMMON CARD (1-12)	1.50	.70	.19
☐ 1 Norm Cash	3.50	1.55	.45
☐ 2 Bill Freehan	3.50	1.55	.45
☐ 3 Willie Horton	3.50	1.55	.45
☐ 4 Al Kaline	5.00	2.20	.60
☐ 5 Mike Kilkenny	1.50	.70	.19
☐ 6 Mickey Lolich	3.50	1.55	.45
☐ 7 Dick McAuliffe	2.00	.90	.25
☐ 8 Denny McLain	3.50	1.55	.45
☐ 9 Jim Northrup	2.50	1.10	.30
☐ 10 Mayo Smith MG	2.00	.90	.25
☐ 11 Mickey Stanley	2.00	.90	.25
☐ 12 Don Wert	1.50	.70	.19

1969 Tigers Team Issue Color

This 10-card set of the Detroit Tigers measures approximately 7" by 8 3/4" with the fronts featuring white-bordered color player photos. The player's name and team is printed in black in the white margin below the picture. The backs are blank. The cards are unnumbered and checklisted below in alphabetical order.

	NRMT	VG-E	GOOD
COMPLETE SET (10)	25.00	11.00	3.10
COMMON CARD (20)	2.00	.90	.25
☐ 1 Norm Cash	4.00	1.80	.50
☐ 2 Pat Dobson	2.00	.90	.25
☐ 3 Bill Freehan	4.00	1.80	.50
☐ 4 John Hiller	2.00	.90	.25
☐ 5 Willie Horton	4.00	1.80	.50
☐ 6 Mickey Lolich	4.00	1.80	.50
☐ 7 Denny McLain	5.00	2.20	.60
☐ 8 Joe Sparma	2.00	.90	.25
☐ 9 Mickey Stanley	3.00	1.35	.35
☐ 10 Dick Tracewski	2.00	.90	.25

1973 Tigers Jewel

This 20-card set of the Detroit Tigers was produced by Jewel Food Stores and was issued in two series of ten cards each. Measuring approximately 7" by 8 3/4", the set features color posed player photos in white borders with blank backs. The cards are unnumbered and checklisted below in alphabetical order.

	NRMT	VG-E	GOOD
COMPLETE SET (20)	75.00	34.00	9.50
COMMON CARD (1-20)	4.00	1.80	.50
☐ 1 Ed Brinkman	4.00	1.80	.50
☐ 2 Gates Brown	5.00	2.20	.60
☐ 3 Ike Brown	4.00	1.80	.50
☐ 4 Les Cain	4.00	1.80	.50
☐ 5 Norman Cash	7.50	3.40	.95
☐ 6 Joe Coleman	4.00	1.80	.50
☐ 7 Bill Freehan	7.50	3.40	.95
☐ 8 Tom Haller	4.00	1.80	.50
☐ 9 Willie Horton	7.50	3.40	.95
☐ 10 Al Kaline	15.00	6.75	1.85
☐ 11 Mickey Lolich	7.50	3.40	.95
☐ 12 Billy Martin	7.50	3.40	.95
☐ 13 Dick McAuliffe	4.00	1.80	.50
☐ 14 Joe Niekro	5.00	2.20	.60
☐ 15 Jim Northrup	5.00	2.20	.60
☐ 16 Aurelio Rodriguez	4.00	1.80	.50
☐ 17 Red Scherman	4.00	1.80	.50
☐ 18 Mickey Stanley	5.00	2.20	.60
☐ 19 Tony Taylor	4.00	1.80	.50
☐ 20 Tom Timmerman	4.00	1.80	.50

1974 Tigers

This 12-piece set of photos are blank-backed, white-bordered and 7" X 8 3/4". The player's name and team in black are within lower margin. The photos are unnumbered and checklisted below in alphabetical order.

	NRMT	VG-E	GOOD
COMPLETE SET (12)	20.00	9.00	2.50
COMMON CARD (1-12)	1.50	.70	.19
☐ 1 Gates Brown	2.00	.90	.25
☐ 2 Ron Cash	1.50	.70	.19
☐ 3 Joe Coleman	1.50	.70	.19
☐ 4 Bill Freehan	2.00	.90	.25
☐ 5 John Hiller	1.50	.70	.19
☐ 6 Al Kaline	5.00	2.20	.60
☐ 7 John Knox	1.50	.70	.19
☐ 8 Jim Northrup	2.00	.90	.25
☐ 9 Ben Oglivie	2.00	.90	.25
☐ 10 Jim Ray	1.50	.70	.19
☐ 11 Chuck Seelbach	1.50	.70	.19
☐ 12 Dick Sharon	1.50	.70	.19

1976 Tigers Old-Timers Troy Show

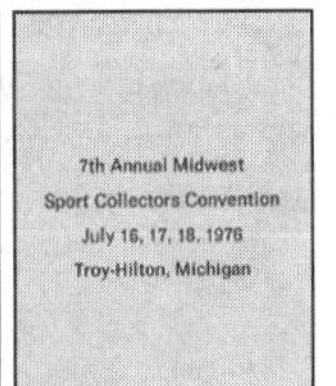

This 23-card set was available at the 7th Annual Midwest Sports Collectors Convention held July 16-18, 1976 in Troy-Hilton, Michigan. The cards measure 2 3/8" by 2 7/8" and feature portrait and action black-and-white illustrations of players. The player's name is near the top as is a small paragraph giving career history. A box at the bottom contains unusual personal facts. The backs carry information about the card show. The cards are unnumbered and checklisted below in alphabetical order.

	NRMT	VG-E	GOOD
COMPLETE SET (23)	12.50	5.50	1.55
COMMON CARD (1-23)	.25	.11	.03
☐ 1 Elden Auker	.25	.11	.03
☐ 2 Tommy Bridges	.75	.35	.09
☐ 3 Flea Clifton	.25	.11	.03
☐ 4 Mickey Cochrane	1.50	.70	.19
☐ 5 General Crowder	.25	.11	.03
☐ 6 Frank Doljack	.25	.11	.03
☐ 7 Carl Fischer	.25	.11	.03
☐ 8 Pete Fox	.25	.11	.03
☐ 9 Charles Gehringer	1.00	.45	.12
☐ 10 Goose Goslin	1.00	.45	.12
☐ 11 Hank Greenberg	1.50	.70	.19
☐ 12 Luke Hamlin	.25	.11	.03
☐ 13 Ray Hayworth	.25	.11	.03
☐ 14 Chief Hogsett	.25	.11	.03
☐ 15 Firpo Marberry	.25	.11	.03
☐ 16 Marvin Owen	.75	.35	.09
☐ 17 Cy Perkins	.25	.11	.03
☐ 18 Bill Rogell	.25	.11	.03
☐ 19 Schoolboy Rowe	1.00	.45	.12
☐ 20 Heinie Schuble	.25	.11	.03
☐ 21 Vic Sorrell	.25	.11	.03
☐ 22 Gerald Walker	.25	.11	.03
☐ 23 Jo Jo White	.25	.11	.03

1977 Tigers Burger King

This four-card set was issued in 1977 by Burger King and features Detroit Tigers. The photo cards measure approximately 8" by 10" and carry posed player color portraits. The backs are blank and the set is checklisted below in alphabetical order.

	NRMT	VG-E	GOOD
COMPLETE SET (4)	10.00	4.50	1.25
COMMON CARD (1-4)	2.00	.90	.25
☐ 1 Mark Fidyrich	5.00	2.20	.60
☐ 2 Ron LeFlore	2.50	1.10	.30
☐ 3 Dave Rozema	2.00	.90	.25
☐ 4 Mickey Stanley	2.50	1.10	.30

1978 Tigers Burger King

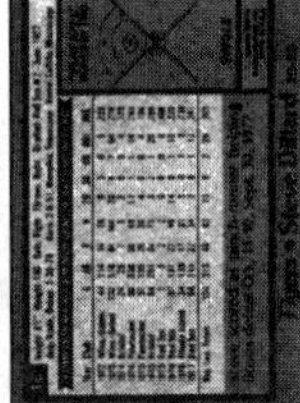

The cards in this 23-card set measure 2 1/2" by 3 1/2". Twenty-three color cards, 22 players and one numbered checklist, comprise the 1978 Burger King Tigers set issued in the Detroit area. The cards marked with an asterisk contain photos different from those appearing on the Topps regular issue cards of that year. For example, Jack Morris, Alan Trammell, and Lou Whitaker (in the 1978 Topps regular issue cards) each appear on rookie prospect cards with three other young players; whereas in this Burger King set, each has his own individual card.

	NRMT	VG-E	GOOD
COMPLETE SET (23)	50.00	22.00	6.25
COMMON CARD (1-22)	.25	.11	.03
☐ 1 Ralph Houk MG	.75	.35	.09
☐ 2 Milt May	.25	.11	.03
☐ 3 John Wockenfuss	.25	.11	.03
☐ 4 Mark Fidrych	.75	.35	.09
☐ 5 Dave Rozema	.25	.11	.03
☐ 6 Jack Billingham *	.25	.11	.03
☐ 7 Jim Slaton *	.25	.11	.03
☐ 8 Jack Morris *	7.50	3.40	.95
☐ 9 John Hiller	.50	.23	.06
☐ 10 Steve Foucault	.25	.11	.03
☐ 11 Milt Wilcox	.25	.11	.03
☐ 12 Jason Thompson	.75	.35	.09
☐ 13 Lou Whitaker *	12.50	5.50	1.55
☐ 14 Aurelio Rodriguez	.25	.11	.03
☐ 15 Alan Trammell *	25.00	11.00	3.10
☐ 16 Steve Dillard *	.25	.11	.03
☐ 17 Phil Mankowski	.25	.11	.03
☐ 18 Steve Kemp	.50	.23	.06
☐ 19 Ron LeFlore	.75	.35	.09
☐ 20 Tim Corcoran	.25	.11	.03
☐ 21 Mickey Stanley	.75	.35	.09
☐ 22 Rusty Staub	1.25	.55	.16
☐ NNO Checklist Card TP	.15	.07	.02

1978 Tigers Dearborn Card Show

These cards were issued in conjuction with the annual Detroit area Dearborn card show. They feature Tiger greats from the past.

	NRMT	VG-E	GOOD
COMPLETE SET (18)	15.00	6.75	1.85
COMMON CARD (18)	.75	.35	.09
☐ 1 Rocky Colavito	1.50	.70	.19
☐ 2 Ervin Fox	.75	.35	.09
☐ 3 Schoolboy Rowe	.75	.35	.09
☐ 4 Gerald Walker	.75	.35	.09
☐ 5 Leon Goslin	1.25	.55	.16
☐ 6 Harvey Kuenn	1.00	.45	.12
☐ 7 Frank Howard	1.00	.45	.12
☐ 8 Woodie Fryman	.75	.35	.09
☐ 9 Don Wert	.75	.35	.09
☐ 10 Jim Perry	1.00	.45	.12
☐ 11 Mayo Smith MG	.75	.35	.09
☐ 12 Al Kaline	2.50	1.10	.30
☐ 13 Norm Cash	1.50	.70	.19
☐ 14 Mickey Cochrane	1.25	.55	.16
☐ 15 Fred Marberry	.75	.35	.09
☐ 16 Bill Freehan	1.00	.45	.12
☐ 17 Charley Gehringer	1.25	.55	.16
☐ 18 Jim Northrup	.75	.35	.09

1979 Tigers Free Press

This 10" by 15" poster was published in the Detroit Free Press Newspaper and displays a black-and-white player photo with player information and statistics including a printed feature on the player with his career highlights. There may be more posters and all additions to the checklist are welcomed.

	NRMT	VG-E	GOOD
COMPLETE SET	3.00	1.35	.35
COMMON CARD	3.00	1.35	.35
☐ 1 Jason Thompson	3.00	1.35	.35

1980 Tigers Greats TCMA

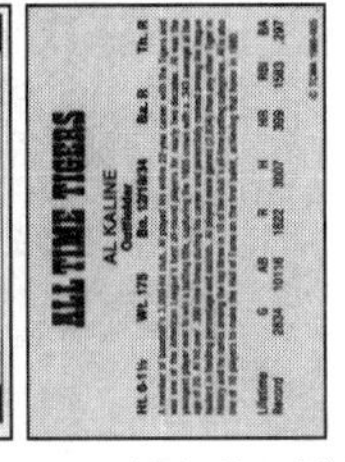

This 12-card standard-size set features some of the best Tigers of all time. The fronts have a player photo while the horizontal backs have vital statistics, a biography and career statistics.

	NRMT	VG-E	GOOD
COMPLETE SET (12)	6.00	2.70	.75
COMMON CARD (1-12)	.25	.11	.03
☐ 1 George Kell	.50	.23	.06
☐ 2 Billy Rogell	.25	.11	.03
☐ 3 Ty Cobb	1.50	.70	.19
☐ 4 Hank Greenberg	1.00	.45	.12
☐ 5 Al Kaline	1.00	.45	.12
☐ 6 Charlie Gehringer	.75	.35	.09
☐ 7 Harry Heilmann	.75	.35	.09
☐ 8 Hal Newhouser	.50	.23	.06
☐ 9 Steve O'Neill MG	.25	.11	.03
☐ 10 Denny McLain	.50	.23	.06
☐ 11 Mickey Cochrane	.75	.35	.09
☐ 12 John Hiller	.25	.11	.03

1981 Tigers Detroit News

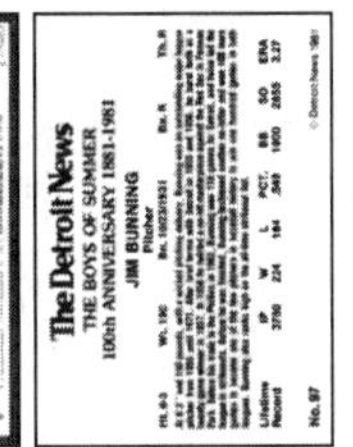

This 135-card, standard-size set was issued in 1981 to celebrate the centennial of professional baseball in Detroit. This set features black and white photos surrounded by solid red borders, while the back provides information about either the player or event featured on the front of the card. This set was issued by the Detroit newspaper, the Detroit News and covered players from the nineteenth century right up to players and other personnel active at the time of issue.

	NRMT	VG-E	GOOD
COMPLETE SET (135)	20.00	9.00	2.50
COMMON CARD (1-135)	.10	.05	.01
☐ 1 Detroit's Boys of Summer 100th Anniversary	.50	.23	.06
☐ 2 Charles W. Bennett	.10	.05	.01
☐ 3 Mickey Cochrane	.75	.35	.09
☐ 4 Harry Heilmann	.50	.23	.06
☐ 5 Walter O. Briggs OWN	.10	.05	.01
☐ 6 Mark Fidrych	.50	.23	.06
☐ 7 1887 Tigers	.10	.05	.01
☐ 8 Tiger Stadium	.10	.05	.01
☐ 9 Rudy York	.10	.05	.01
☐ 10 George Kell	.50	.23	.06
☐ 11 Steve O'Neill MG	.10	.05	.01
☐ 12 John Hiller	.10	.05	.01
☐ 13 1934 Tigers	.10	.05	.01
☐ 14 Charlie Gehringer	.75	.35	.09
☐ 15 Denny McLain	.50	.23	.06
☐ 16 Billy Rogell	.10	.05	.01
☐ 17 Ty Cobb	3.00	1.35	.35
☐ 18 Sparky Anderson MG	.50	.23	.06
☐ 19 Davy Jones	.10	.05	.01
☐ 20 Kirk Gibson	.50	.23	.06
☐ 21 Pat Mullin	.10	.05	.01
☐ 22 1972 Tigers	.10	.05	.01
☐ 23 What A Night	.10	.05	.01
☐ 24 Doc Cramer	.10	.05	.01
☐ 25 Mickey Stanley	.10	.05	.01
☐ 26 John Lipon	.10	.05	.01
☐ 27 Jo Jo White	.10	.05	.01
☐ 28 Recreation Park	.10	.05	.01
☐ 29 Wild Bill Donovan	.10	.05	.01
☐ 30 Ray Oyler	.10	.05	.01
☐ 31 Earl Whitehill	.10	.05	.01
☐ 32 Billy Hoeft	.10	.05	.01
☐ 33 Johnny Groth	.10	.05	.01
☐ 34 Hughie Jennings P/MG	.50	.23	.06
☐ 35 Mayo Smith MG	.10	.05	.01
☐ 36 Bennett Park	.10	.05	.01
☐ 37 Tigers Win	.10	.05	.01
☐ 38 Donie Bush P/MG	.10	.05	.01
☐ 39 Harry Coveleski	.10	.05	.01
☐ 40 Paul Richards	.10	.05	.01
☐ 41 Jonathon Stone	.10	.05	.01
☐ 42 Bob Swift	.10	.05	.01
☐ 43 Roy Cullenbine	.10	.05	.01
☐ 44 Hoot Evers	.10	.05	.01
☐ 45 Tigers Win Series	.10	.05	.01
☐ 46 Art Houtteman	.10	.05	.01
☐ 47 Aurelio Rodriguez	.10	.05	.01
☐ 48 Fred Hutchinson P/MG	.10	.05	.01
☐ 49 Don Mossi	.25	.11	.03
☐ 50 Lou Gehrig Streak Ends in Detroit At 2130 Games	.75	.35	.09
☐ 51 Earl Wilson	.10	.05	.01
☐ 52 Jim Northrup	.10	.05	.01
☐ 53 1907 Tigers	.10	.05	.01
☐ 54 Hank Greenberg Hits 2 Homers to Draw Even With Ruth	.75	.35	.09
☐ 55 Mickey Lolich	.50	.23	.06
☐ 56 Tommy Bridges	.10	.05	.01
☐ 57 Al Benton	.10	.05	.01
☐ 58 Del Baker MG	.10	.05	.01
☐ 59 Lou Whitaker	.75	.35	.09
☐ 60 Navin Field	.10	.05	.01
☐ 61 1945 Tigers	.10	.05	.01
☐ 62 Ernie Harwell ANN	.50	.23	.06
☐ 63 Tigers League Champs	.10	.05	.01
☐ 64 Bobo Newsom	.25	.11	.03
☐ 65 Don Wert	.10	.05	.01
☐ 66 Ed Summers	.10	.05	.01
☐ 67 Billy Martin MG	.75	.35	.09
☐ 68 Alan Trammell	1.25	.55	.16
☐ 69 Dale Alexander	.10	.05	.01
☐ 70 Ed Brinkman	.10	.05	.01
☐ 71 Right Man in Right Place in Right Park Wins Game	.10	.05	.01
☐ 72 Bill Freehan	.25	.11	.03
☐ 73A Norm Cash (Red border)	.50	.23	.06
☐ 73B Norm Cash (Black border)	.50	.23	.06
☐ 74 George Dauss	.10	.05	.01
☐ 75 Aurelio Lopez	.10	.05	.01
☐ 76 Charlie Maxwell	.10	.05	.01
☐ 77 Ed Barrow MG	.25	.11	.03
☐ 78 Willie Horton	.25	.11	.03
☐ 79 Denny McLain Sets Record 31 Wins	.50	.23	.06
☐ 80 Dan Brouthers	.75	.35	.09
☐ 81 John E. Fetzer OWN	.10	.05	.01
☐ 82A Heinie Manush (Red border)	.50	.23	.06
☐ 82B Heinie Manush (Black border)	.50	.23	.06
☐ 83 1935 Tigers	.10	.05	.01
☐ 84 Ray Boone	.25	.11	.03
☐ 85 Bob Fothergill	.10	.05	.01
☐ 86 Steve Kemp	.10	.05	.01
☐ 87 Ed Killian	.10	.05	.01
☐ 88 Floyd Giebell Ineligible for Series, But ...	.10	.05	.01
☐ 89 Pinky Higgins	.10	.05	.01
☐ 90 Lance Parrish	.25	.11	.03
☐ 91 Eldon Auker	.10	.05	.01
☐ 92 Birdie Tebbetts	.10	.05	.01
☐ 93 Schoolboy Rowe	.25	.11	.03
☐ 94 Tiger Rally Gives Denny McLain 30	.50	.23	.06
☐ 95 1909 Tigers	.10	.05	.01
☐ 96 Harvey Kuenn	.50	.23	.06
☐ 97 Jim Bunning	.50	.23	.06
☐ 98 1940 Tigers	.10	.05	.01
☐ 99 Rocky Colavito	.50	.23	.06
☐ 100 Al Kaline Enters Hall Of Fame	1.25	.55	.16
☐ 101 Billy Bruton	.10	.05	.01
☐ 102 Germany Schaefer	.25	.11	.03
☐ 103 Frank Bolling	.10	.05	.01
☐ 104 Briggs Stadium	.10	.05	.01
☐ 105 Bucky Harris P/MG	.25	.11	.03
☐ 106 Gates Brown	.10	.05	.01
☐ 107 Billy Martin Made the Difference	.50	.23	.06
☐ 108 1908 Tigers	.10	.05	.01
☐ 109 Gee Walker	.10	.05	.01

☐ 110 Pete Fox	.10	.05	.01
☐ 111 Virgil Trucks	.10	.05	.01
☐ 112 1968 Tigers	.25	.11	.03
☐ 113 Dizzy Trout	.10	.05	.01
☐ 114 Barney McCosky	.10	.05	.01
☐ 115 Lu Blue	.10	.05	.01
☐ 116 Hal Newhouser	.75	.35	.09
☐ 117 Tigers Are Home To Prepare For World's Championship Series	.10	.05	.01
☐ 118 Bobby Veach	.10	.05	.01
☐ 119 George Mullin	.10	.05	.01
☐ 120 Reggie Jackson Super Homer Ignites A.L.	.75	.35	.09
☐ 121 Sam Crawford	.50	.23	.06
☐ 122 Hank Aguirre	.10	.05	.01
☐ 123 Vic Wertz	.25	.11	.03
☐ 124 Goose Goslin	.50	.23	.06
☐ 125 Frank Lary	.25	.11	.03
☐ 126 Joe Coleman	.10	.05	.01
☐ 127 Ed Katalinas Scout	.10	.05	.01
☐ 128 Jack Morris	.75	.35	.09
☐ 129 Tigers Picked As Winners Of Pirate Battle	.10	.05	.01
☐ 130 James A. Campbell GM	.25	.11	.03
☐ 131 Ted Gray	.10	.05	.01
☐ 132 Al Kaline	2.50	1.10	.30
☐ 133 Hank Greenberg	.75	.35	.09
☐ 134 Dick McAuliffe	.25	.11	.03
☐ 135 Ozzie Virgil	.10	.05	.01

1981 Tigers Pepsi Trammell

This one-card set produced by Pepsi-Cola features a small color photo of Detroit Tigers player, Alan Trammell, and was an invitation to kids to join the Pepsi-Tiger Fan Club. The back displays the official application form.

	NRMT	VG-E	GOOD
COMPLETE SET (1)	5.00	2.20	.60
COMMON CARD (1)	5.00	2.20	.60
☐ 1 Alan Trammell	5.00	2.20	.60

1981 Tigers Second National Plymouth

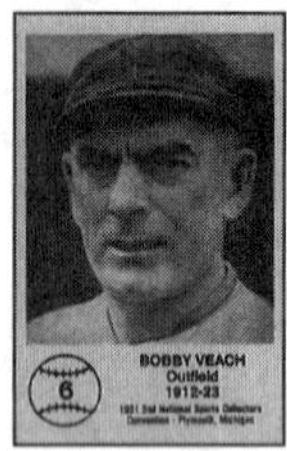

This set was issued in conjuction with the Second National Sports Collectors Convention held in Plymouth, Michigan. The fronts have a photo, the player's name and his years as a Tiger. The backs are blank.

	NRMT	VG-E	GOOD
COMPLETE SET (32)	20.00	9.00	2.50
COMMON CARD (1-32)	.50	.23	.06
☐ 1 Ty Cobb	3.00	1.35	.35
☐ 2 Hughie Jennings MG	1.50	.70	.19
☐ 3 Heinie Manush	1.50	.70	.19
☐ 4 George Mullin	.50	.23	.06
☐ 5 Donie Bush	.50	.23	.06
☐ 6 Bobby Veach	.50	.23	.06
☐ 7 Wild Bill Donovan	.50	.23	.06
☐ 8 Harry Heilmann	1.00	.45	.12
☐ 9 Sam Crawford	1.00	.45	.12
☐ 10 Lu Blue	.50	.23	.06
☐ 11 Bob Fothergill	.50	.23	.06
☐ 12 Harry Coveleski	.50	.23	.06
☐ 13 Dale Alexander	.50	.23	.06
☐ 14 Charlie Gehringer	1.50	.70	.19
☐ 15 Tommy Bridges	.75	.35	.09
☐ 16 Detroit Tigers 1935 Team Photo	.50	.23	.06
☐ 17 Hank Greenberg	2.00	.90	.25
☐ 18 Goose Goslin	1.00	.45	.12
☐ 19 Firpo Marberry	.50	.23	.06
☐ 20 Hal Newhouser	1.00	.45	.12
☐ 21 Schoolboy Rowe	.75	.35	.09
☐ 22 Mickey Cochrane	1.00	.45	.12
☐ 23 Gee Walker	.50	.23	.06
☐ 24 Marv Owen	.50	.23	.06
☐ 25 Barney McCosky	.50	.23	.06
☐ 26 Rudy York	.75	.35	.09
☐ 27 Pete Fox	.50	.23	.06
☐ 28 Al Benton	.50	.23	.06
☐ 29 Billy Rogell	.50	.23	.06
☐ 30 JoJo White	.50	.23	.06
☐ 31 Dizzy Trout	.50	.23	.06
☐ 32 Detroit Tigers 1945 Team Photo	.50	.23	.06

1983 Tigers

This set features members of the 1983 Detroit Tigers. Since these cards are unnumbered we have checklisted them below in alphabetical order.

	NRMT	VG-E	GOOD
COMPLETE SET (32)	10.00	4.50	1.25
COMMON CARD (1-32)	.25	.11	.03
☐ 1 Sparky Anderson MG	.75	.35	.09
☐ 2 Sal Butera	.25	.11	.03
☐ 3 Howard Bailey	.25	.11	.03
☐ 4 Juan Berenguer	.25	.11	.03
☐ 5 Tom Brookens	.25	.11	.03
☐ 6 Gates Brown CO	.25	.11	.03
☐ 7 Enos Cabell	.25	.11	.03
☐ 8 Bill Consolo CO	.25	.11	.03
☐ 9 Roger Craig CO	.25	.11	.03
☐ 10 Bill Fahey	.25	.11	.03
☐ 11 Kirk Gibson	2.00	.90	.25
☐ 12 Alex Grammas CO	.25	.11	.03
☐ 13 John Grubb	.25	.11	.03
☐ 14 Larry Herndon	.25	.11	.03
☐ 15 Howard Johnson	1.00	.45	.12
☐ 16 Lynn Jones	.25	.11	.03
☐ 17 Rick Leach	.25	.11	.03
☐ 18 Chet Lemon	.50	.23	.06
☐ 19 Aurelio Lopez	.25	.11	.03
☐ 20 Jack Morris	1.25	.55	.16
☐ 21 Lance Parrish	.75	.35	.09
☐ 22 Larry Pashnick	.25	.11	.03
☐ 23 Dan Petry	.25	.11	.03
☐ 24 Dave Rozema	.25	.11	.03
☐ 25 Dave Rucker	.25	.11	.03
☐ 26 Dick Tracewski CO	.25	.11	.03
☐ 27 Alan Trammell	2.00	.90	.25
☐ 28 Jerry Ujdur	.25	.11	.03
☐ 29 Lou Whitaker	1.25	.55	.16
☐ 30 Milt Wilcox	.25	.11	.03
☐ 31 Glenn Wilson	.25	.11	.03
☐ 32 John Wockenfuss	.25	.11	.03

1983 Tigers Al Kaline Story

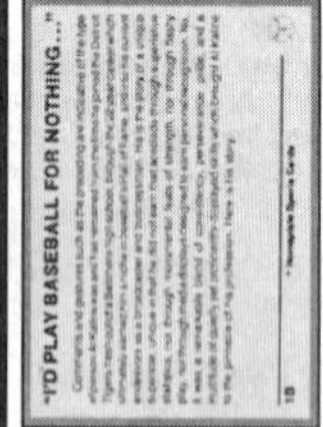

This 72-card set was issued in 1983 to celebrate Al Kaline's thirtieth year of association with the Detroit Tigers. The set was issued in its own orange box and most of the cards in the series have orange borders. There are some cards which have black borders and those cards are the cards in the set which feature color photos. The set is basically in chronological order and covers events crucial to Kaline's career and the backs of the cards give further details about the picture on the front. The set was produced by Homeplate Sports Cards.

	NRMT	VG-E	GOOD
COMPLETE SET (73)	20.00	9.00	2.50
COMMON CARD (1-72)	.25	.11	.03
COMMON CARD COLOR	.35	.16	.04
☐ 1A Autographed Title Card (Color)	10.00	4.50	1.25
☐ 1B Al Kaline I'd play for nothing (Color)	.50	.23	.06
☐ 2 Al Kaline Sandlot Days	.25	.11	.03
☐ 3 Al Kaline Prep MVP	.25	.11	.03
☐ 4 Al Kaline Learning the Ropes	.25	.11	.03
☐ 5 Al Kaline Working for a Living	.25	.11	.03
☐ 6 Al Kaline Pleasing a Young Fan	.25	.11	.03
☐ 7 Al Kaline Louise Kaline	.35	.16	.04
☐ 8 Al Kaline Pat Mullin	.25	.11	.03
☐ 9 Al Kaline How Al Does It, 1	.25	.11	.03
☐ 10 Al Kaline How Al Does It, 2	.25	.11	.03
☐ 11 Al Kaline Silver Bat 1955	.35	.16	.04
☐ 12 Al Kaline George Stark	.25	.11	.03
☐ 13 Al Kaline Gordie Howe Howe taking batting practice	1.50	.70	.19
☐ 14 Al Kaline Mickey Mantle	2.50	1.10	.30
☐ 15 Jim Hegan Billy Martin Ray Boone Harvey Kuenn Jim Bunning Al Kaline	.50	.23	.06
☐ 16 Billy Martin Al Kaline Harvey Kuenn Mickey Mantle Whitey Ford (color)	1.50	.70	.19
☐ 17 Al Kaline Crossing the Plate	.25	.11	.03
☐ 18 Bill Skowron Al Kaline	.50	.23	.06
☐ 19 Norm Cash Rocky Colavito Al Kaline	.75	.35	.09
☐ 20 Al Kaline Nellie Fox Kaline Slides Under Fox	.75	.35	.09
☐ 21 Al Kaline 1961 Gold Glove	.35	.16	.04
☐ 22 Al Kaline Jim Campbell GM Norm Cash	.50	.23	.06
☐ 23 Al Kaline Costly Catch	.25	.11	.03
☐ 24 Jim Bunning Al Kaline Norm Cash and others Japan Tour, 1962	.50	.23	.06
☐ 25 Al Kaline Perfect Form	.25	.11	.03
☐ 26 Ernie Harwell ANN Al Kaline George Kell ANN	.75	.35	.09
☐ 27 Al Kaline Life Isn't Always Easy	.25	.11	.03
☐ 28 Al Kaline Michael Kaline Mark Kaline	.25	.11	.03
☐ 29 Al Kaline Charlie Dressen MG	.25	.11	.03
☐ 30 George Kell Al Kaline	.60	.25	.07
☐ 31 Al Kaline Hal Newhouser	.60	.25	.07
☐ 32 Michael Kaline Louise Kaline Al Kaline Mark Kaline	.25	.11	.03
☐ 33 Al Kaline Charlie Gehringer Bill Freehan	.75	.35	.09
☐ 34 Al Kaline Rapping a Hit, 1967 Color	.50	.23	.06
☐ 35 Mickey Mantle Al Kaline	2.50	1.10	.30
☐ 36 Al Kaline Homers vs. Boston	.25	.11	.03
☐ 37 Al Kaline 1968 World Series Homer	.25	.11	.03
☐ 38 Al Kaline Premier Fielder	.25	.11	.03
☐ 39 Hank Greenberg Hal Newhouser Billy Rogell Al Kaline John Fetzer OWN Dennis McLain George Kell Charlie Gehringer	.60	.25	.07
☐ 40 Al Kaline Part of the Game	.25	.11	.03
☐ 41 Al Kaline Family Portrait, Color	.50	.23	.06
☐ 42 Al Kaline Spring Training Tribute	.25	.11	.03
☐ 43 Billy Martin Al Kaline	.60	.25	.07
☐ 44 Al Kaline John Fetzer OWN Jim Campbell GM	.35	.16	.04
☐ 45 Al Kaline On Deck, 1972; Color	.50	.23	.06
☐ 46 Al Kaline A Close Call	.25	.11	.03
☐ 47 Al Kaline On Deck in Baltimore	.25	.11	.03
☐ 48 Al Kaline Hit Number 3,000	.35	.16	.04
☐ 49 Al Kaline April 17, 1955; Three Homers	.25	.11	.03
☐ 50 Al Kaline All-Star Game Record	.25	.11	.03
☐ 51 Al Kaline Orlando Cepeda	.60	.25	.07
☐ 52 Al Kaline John Hiller Jim Northrup	.35	.16	.04
☐ 53 Al Kaline Day; Color	.60	.25	.07
☐ 54 Al Kaline Lee McPhail PRES Jim Campbell GM Nicholas Kaline Naomi Kaline	.35	.16	.04
☐ 55 Al Kaline September 29, 1974; Thank You	.25	.11	.03
☐ 56 Al Kaline Silver Salute	.25	.11	.03
☐ 57 Al Kaline George Kell Color	.75	.35	.09
☐ 58 Al Kaline George Kell	.50	.23	.06
☐ 59 Al Kaline Tiger Record Setter; Color	.50	.23	.06
☐ 60 Al Kaline Last All-Star Team; Color	.50	.23	.06
☐ 61 Pat Mullin Al Kaline	.25	.11	.03
☐ 62 Al Kaline Mickey Lolich Color	.50	.23	.06
☐ 63 Al Kaline Hall of Fame Plaque	.25	.11	.03
☐ 64 Al Kaline Bowie Kuhn COMM Color	.50	.23	.06
☐ 65 Al Kaline Nicholas Kaline Naomi Kaline) (color)	.35	.16	.04
☐ 66 Al Kaline Kaline Family at Hall; color	.35	.16	.04
☐ 67 Stan Musial Al Kaline	1.00	.45	.12
☐ 68 Ted Williams Al Kaline	1.50	.70	.19
☐ 69 Al Kaline Brooks Robinson color	.75	.35	.09
☐ 70 Al Kaline Pat Underwood	.25	.11	.03
☐ 71 Al Kaline at Batting Cage	.25	.11	.03
☐ 72 Al Kaline A Tiger Forever; Color	.75	.35	.09

1984 Tigers Farmer Jack

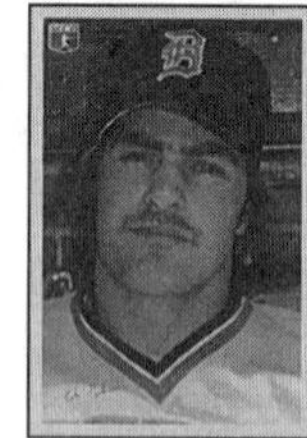

These 16 photo cards were sponsored by the Farmer Jack grocery store chain in the upper Midwest in 1984, to honor the 1984 World Champion Detroit Tigers. The photos were a promotional item given away singly with a purchase. The cards measure approximately 6" by 9" and are printed on photographic paper stock. The white bordered fronts feature color player portraits with an autograph facsimile superimposed on the photo. The backs are blank. The cards are unnumbered and are checklisted alphabetically below.

	NRMT	VG-E	GOOD
COMPLETE SET (16)	12.50	5.50	1.55
COMMON CARD (1-16)	.50	.23	.06
☐ 1 Dave Bergman	.50	.23	.06
☐ 2 Darrell Evans	1.00	.45	.12
☐ 3 Barbaro Garbey	.50	.23	.06
☐ 4 Kirk Gibson	1.50	.70	.19

☐ 5 John Grubb	.50	.23	.06
☐ 6 Willie Hernandez	.75	.35	.09
☐ 7 Larry Herndon	.50	.23	.06
☐ 8 Howard Johnson	1.00	.45	.12
☐ 9 Chet Lemon	.50	.23	.06
☐ 10 Jack Morris	1.50	.70	.19
☐ 11 Lance Parrish	1.00	.45	.12
☐ 12 Dan Petry	.75	.35	.09
☐ 13 Dave Rozema	.50	.23	.06
☐ 14 Alan Trammell	3.00	1.35	.35
☐ 15 Lou Whitaker	2.50	1.10	.30
☐ 16 Milt Wilcox	.50	.23	.06

1984 Tigers Wave Postcards

During the 1984 Tigers World Championship season, these post cards were issued. These cards are unnumbered and we have sequenced them in alphabetical order.

	NRMT	VG-E	GOOD
COMPLETE SET (35)	15.00	6.75	1.85
COMMON CARD (1-35)	.50	.23	.06
☐ 1 Sparky Anderson MG	1.00	.45	.12
☐ 2 Glenn Abbott	.50	.23	.06
☐ 3 Doug Bair	.50	.23	.06
☐ 4 Doug Baker	.50	.23	.06
☐ 5 Bill Behm	.50	.23	.06
☐ 6 Juan Berenguer	.50	.23	.06
☐ 7 Dave Bergman	.50	.23	.06
☐ 8 Tom Brookens	.50	.23	.06
☐ 9 Gates Brown CO	.50	.23	.06
☐ 10 Marty Castillo	.50	.23	.06
☐ 11 Billy Consolo CO	.50	.23	.06
☐ 12 Roger Craig CO	.75	.35	.09
☐ 13 Pio DiSalvo	.50	.23	.06
☐ 14 Darrell Evans	.75	.35	.09
☐ 15 Barbaro Garbey	.50	.23	.06
☐ 16 Kirk Gibson	2.00	.90	.25
☐ 17 Alex Grammas CO	.50	.23	.06
☐ 18 John Grubb	.50	.23	.06
☐ 19 Willie Hernandez	.75	.35	.09
☐ 20 Larry Herndon	.50	.23	.06
☐ 21 Howard Johnson	1.00	.45	.12
☐ 22 Ruppert Jones	.50	.23	.06
☐ 23 Chet Lemon	.50	.23	.06
☐ 24 Rusty Kuntz	.50	.23	.06
☐ 25 Aurelio Lopez	.50	.23	.06
☐ 26 Sid Monge	.50	.23	.06
☐ 27 Jack Morris	2.00	.90	.25
☐ 28 Lance Parrish	.75	.35	.09
☐ 29 Dan Petry	.50	.23	.06
☐ 30 Dave Rozema	.50	.23	.06
☐ 31 Jim Schmakel	.50	.23	.06
☐ 32 Dick Tracewski CO	.50	.23	.06
☐ 33 Alan Trammell	3.00	1.35	.35
☐ 34 Lou Whitaker	2.00	.90	.25
☐ 35 Milt Wilcox	.50	.23	.06

1985 Tigers Cain's Discs

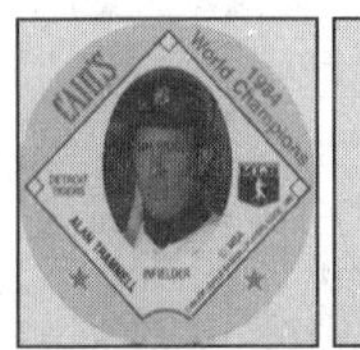

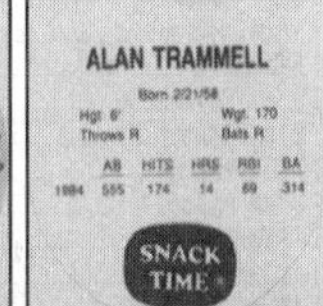

This set of discs was distributed by Cain's Potato Chips in 1985 to commemorate the Tigers' World Championship in 1984. Each disc measures 2 3/4" in diameter. Each disc has a distinctive yellow border on the front. Inside this yellow border is a full color photo of the player with his hat on. The statistics on back of the disc give the player's 1984 pitching or hitting record as well as his vital statistics. The discs are not numbered; hence they are listed below in alphabetical order.

	NRMT	VG-E	GOOD
COMPLETE SET (20)	35.00	16.00	4.40
COMMON DISC (1-20)	1.25	.55	.16
☐ 1 Doug Bair	1.25	.55	.16
☐ 2 Juan Berenguer	1.25	.55	.16
☐ 3 Dave Bergman	1.25	.55	.16
☐ 4 Tom Brookens	1.25	.55	.16
☐ 5 Marty Castillo	1.25	.55	.16
☐ 6 Darrell Evans	2.50	1.10	.30
☐ 7 Barbaro Garbey	1.25	.55	.16
☐ 8 Kirk Gibson	5.00	2.20	.60
☐ 9 John Grubb	1.25	.55	.16
☐ 10 Willie Hernandez	2.50	1.10	.30
☐ 11 Larry Herndon	1.25	.55	.16
☐ 12 Chet Lemon	2.50	1.10	.30
☐ 13 Aurelio Lopez	1.25	.55	.16
☐ 14 Jack Morris	4.00	1.80	.50
☐ 15 Lance Parrish	3.00	1.35	.35
☐ 16 Dan Petry	1.25	.55	.16
☐ 17 Bill Scherrer	1.25	.55	.16
☐ 18 Alan Trammell	6.00	2.70	.75
☐ 19 Lou Whitaker	5.00	2.20	.60
☐ 20 Milt Wilcox	1.25	.55	.16

1985 Tigers Wendy's/Coke

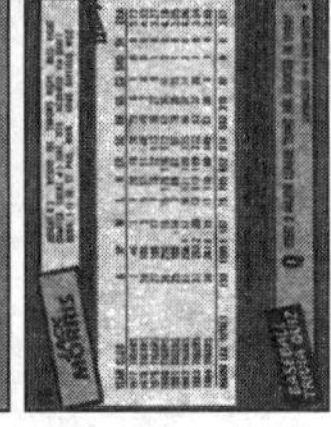

This 22-card standard-size set features Detroit Tigers. The set was co-sponsored by Wendy's and Coca-Cola and was distributed in the Detroit metropolitan area. Coca-Cola purchasers were given a pack which contained three Tiger cards plus a header card. The orange-bordered player photos are different from those used by Topps in their regular set. The cards were produced by Topps as evidenced by the similarity of the card backs with the Topps regular set backs. The set is numbered on the back; the order corresponds to the alphabetical order of the player's names.

	NRMT	VG-E	GOOD
COMPLETE SET (22)	6.00	2.70	.75
COMMON CARD (1-22)	.10	.05	.01
☐ 1 Sparky Anderson MG (Checklist back)	.50	.23	.06
☐ 2 Doug Bair	.10	.05	.01
☐ 3 Juan Berenguer	.10	.05	.01
☐ 4 Dave Bergman	.10	.05	.01
☐ 5 Tom Brookens	.10	.05	.01
☐ 6 Marty Castillo	.10	.05	.01
☐ 7 Darrell Evans	.35	.16	.04
☐ 8 Barbaro Garbey	.10	.05	.01
☐ 9 Kirk Gibson	1.25	.55	.16
☐ 10 Johnny Grubb	.10	.05	.01
☐ 11 Willie Hernandez	.25	.11	.03
☐ 12 Larry Herndon	.10	.05	.01
☐ 13 Rusty Kuntz	.10	.05	.01
☐ 14 Chet Lemon	.25	.11	.03
☐ 15 Aurelio Lopez	.10	.05	.01
☐ 16 Jack Morris	1.25	.55	.16
☐ 17 Lance Parrish	.50	.23	.06
☐ 18 Dan Petry	.25	.11	.03
☐ 19 Bill Scherrer	.10	.05	.01
☐ 20 Alan Trammell	2.50	1.10	.30
☐ 21 Lou Whitaker	1.50	.70	.19
☐ 22 Milt Wilcox	.10	.05	.01

1986 Tigers Cain's Discs

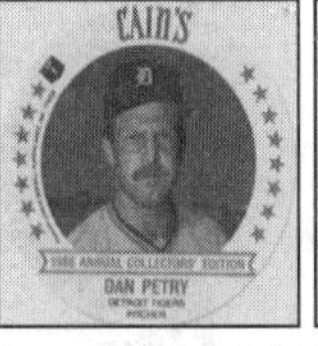

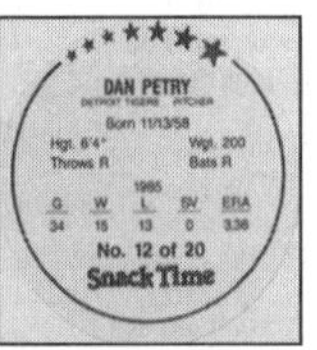

This set of 20 discs was distributed by Cain's Potato Chips in 1986 and consists solely of Detroit Tigers. Each disc measures 2 3/4" in diameter. The statistics on back of the disc give the player's 1985 pitching or hitting record as well as his vital statistics. The discs are not numbered; hence they are listed below in alphabetical order.

	MINT	NRMT	EXC
COMPLETE SET (20)	35.00	16.00	4.40
COMMON DISC (1-20)	1.25	.55	.16
☐ 1 Dave Bergman	1.25	.55	.16
☐ 2 Tom Brookens	1.25	.55	.16
☐ 3 Dave Collins	1.25	.55	.16
☐ 4 Darrell Evans	2.50	1.10	.30
☐ 5 Doug Flynn	1.25	.55	.16
☐ 6 Kirk Gibson	5.00	2.20	.60
☐ 7 John Grubb	1.25	.55	.16
☐ 8 Willie Hernandez	2.50	1.10	.30
☐ 9 Larry Herndon	1.25	.55	.16
☐ 10 Dave LaPoint	1.25	.55	.16
☐ 11 Chet Lemon	1.25	.55	.16
☐ 12 Jack Morris	4.00	1.80	.50
☐ 13 Randy O'Neal	1.25	.55	.16
☐ 14 Lance Parrish	3.00	1.35	.35
☐ 15 Dan Petry	1.25	.55	.16
☐ 16 Nelson Simmons	1.25	.55	.16
☐ 17 Frank Tanana	2.50	1.10	.30
☐ 18 Walt Terrell	1.25	.55	.16
☐ 19 Alan Trammell	6.00	2.70	.75
☐ 20 Lou Whitaker	5.00	2.20	.60

1986 Tigers Sports Design

This 22-card standard-size set displays an unknown artist's portrait of "All-Time Great Tigers." The fronts are bordered in white with an inner black border. The player's name is printed across the bottom with a blue line above and below. The horizontal backs are printed in blue over a light gray background with a ghosted design that includes several bats and balls. Player statistics, biography and career summary are included.

	MINT	NRMT	EXC
COMPLETE SET (22)	7.50	3.40	.95
COMMON CARD (1-22)	.25	.11	.03
☐ 1 Ty Cobb	1.50	.70	.19
☐ 2 Hughie Jennings	.50	.23	.06
☐ 3 Harry Heilmann	.50	.23	.06
☐ 4 Charlie Gehringer	.75	.35	.09
☐ 5 Mickey Cochrane	.50	.23	.06
☐ 6 Hank Greenberg	.75	.35	.09
☐ 7 Billy Rogell	.25	.11	.03
☐ 8 Schoolboy Rowe	.25	.11	.03
☐ 9 Hal Newhouser	.75	.35	.09
☐ 10 George Kell	.50	.23	.06
☐ 11 Harvey Kuenn	.35	.16	.04
☐ 12 Al Kaline	1.00	.45	.12
☐ 13 Jim Bunning	.50	.23	.06
☐ 14 Norm Cash	.35	.16	.04
☐ 15 Mickey Stanley	.25	.11	.03
☐ 16 Jim Northrup	.25	.11	.03
☐ 17 Bill Freehan	.35	.16	.04
☐ 18 Gates Brown	.25	.11	.03
☐ 19 Willie Horton	.35	.16	.04
☐ 20 Mickey Lolich	.35	.16	.04
☐ 21 Denny McLain	.35	.16	.04
☐ 22 John Hiller	.25	.11	.03

1987 Tigers Cain's Discs

This set of 20 discs was distributed by Cain's Potato Chips in 1987 and consists solely of Detroit Tigers. Each disc measures 2 3/4" in diameter. The statistics on back of the disc give the player's 1986 pitching or hitting record as well as his vital statistics. The discs are numbered on the back and have a distinctive orange border on the front of the disc.

	MINT	NRMT	EXC
COMPLETE SET (20)	25.00	11.00	3.10
COMMON DISC (1-20)	1.00	.45	.12
☐ 1 Tom Brookens	1.00	.45	.12
☐ 2 Darnell Coles	1.00	.45	.12
☐ 3 Mike Heath	1.00	.45	.12
☐ 4 Dave Bergman	1.00	.45	.12
☐ 5 Dwight Lowry	1.00	.45	.12
☐ 6 Darrell Evans	2.00	.90	.25
☐ 7 Alan Trammell	5.00	2.20	.60
☐ 8 Lou Whitaker	4.00	1.80	.50
☐ 9 Kirk Gibson	4.00	1.80	.50
☐ 10 Chet Lemon	1.00	.45	.12
☐ 11 Larry Herndon	1.00	.45	.12
☐ 12 John Grubb	1.00	.45	.12
☐ 13 Willie Hernandez	2.00	.90	.25
☐ 14 Jack Morris	3.00	1.35	.35
☐ 15 Dan Petry	1.00	.45	.12
☐ 16 Walt Terrell	1.00	.45	.12
☐ 17 Mark Thurmond	1.00	.45	.12
☐ 18 Pat Sheridan	1.00	.45	.12
☐ 19 Eric King	1.00	.45	.12
☐ 20 Frank Tanana	2.00	.90	.25

1987 Tigers Coke

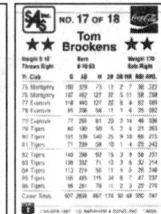

Coca-Cola, in collaboration with S. Abraham and Sons, issued a set of 18 cards featuring the Detroit Tigers. The cards are numbered on the back. The cards are distinguished by the bright yellow border framing the full-color picture of the player on the front. The cards were issued in panels of four: three player cards and a team logo card. The cards measure the standard size and were produced by MSA, Mike Schechter Associates.

	MINT	NRMT	EXC
COMPLETE SET (18)	6.00	2.70	.75
COMMON CARD (1-18)	.10	.05	.01
☐ 1 Kirk Gibson	1.25	.55	.16
☐ 2 Larry Herndon	.10	.05	.01
☐ 3 Walt Terrell	.10	.05	.01
☐ 4 Alan Trammell	2.00	.90	.25
☐ 5 Frank Tanana	.25	.11	.03
☐ 6 Pat Sheridan	.10	.05	.01
☐ 7 Jack Morris	1.25	.55	.16
☐ 8 Mike Heath	.10	.05	.01
☐ 9 Dave Bergman	.10	.05	.01
☐ 10 Chet Lemon	.25	.11	.03
☐ 11 Dwight Lowry	.10	.05	.01
☐ 12 Dan Petry	.10	.05	.01
☐ 13 Darrell Evans	.50	.23	.06
☐ 14 Darnell Coles	.10	.05	.01
☐ 15 Willie Hernandez	.25	.11	.03
☐ 16 Lou Whitaker	1.50	.70	.19
☐ 17 Tom Brookens	.10	.05	.01
☐ 18 John Grubb	.10	.05	.01

1988 Tigers Domino's

This rather unattractive set commemorates the 20th anniversary of the Detroit Tigers' World Championship season in 1968. The card stock used is rather thin. The cards measure approximately 2 1/2" by 3 1/2". There are a number of errors in the set including biographical errors, misspellings, and photo misidentifications. Players are pictured in black and white inside a red and blue horseshoe. The numerous factual errors in the set detract from the set's collectibility in the eyes of many collectors. The set numbering is in alphabetical order by player's name.

	MINT	NRMT	EXC
COMPLETE SET (28)	4.00	1.80	.50
COMMON CARD (1-28)	.10	.05	.01
☐ 1 Gates Brown	.25	.11	.03
☐ 2 Norm Cash	.50	.23	.06
☐ 3 Wayne Comer	.10	.05	.01
☐ 4 Pat Dobson	.25	.11	.03
☐ 5 Bill Freehan	.50	.23	.06
☐ 6 Ernie Harwell ANN	.50	.23	.06
☐ 7 John Hiller	.25	.11	.03
☐ 8 Willie Horton	.25	.11	.03
☐ 9 Al Kaline	1.25	.55	.16
☐ 10 Fred Lasher	.10	.05	.01
☐ 11 Mickey Lolich	.50	.23	.06
☐ 12 Tom Matchick	.10	.05	.01
☐ 13 Ed Mathews	.75	.35	.09
☐ 14 Dick McAuliffe	.25	.11	.03
☐ 15 Denny McLain	.50	.23	.06
☐ 16 Don McMahon	.10	.05	.01
☐ 17 Jim Northrup	.25	.11	.03
☐ 18 Ray Oyler	.10	.05	.01
☐ 19 Daryl Patterson	.10	.05	.01
☐ 20 Jim Price	.10	.05	.01
☐ 21 Joe Sparma	.10	.05	.01
☐ 22 Mickey Stanley	.25	.11	.03
☐ 23 Dick Tracewski	.10	.05	.01
☐ 24 Jon Warden	.10	.05	.01
☐ 25 Don Wert	.10	.05	.01
☐ 26 Earl Wilson	.10	.05	.01
☐ 27 Pizza Buck Coupon	.10	.05	.01
☐ 28 Title Card Old Timers Game 1988	.10	.05	.01

1988 Tigers Pepsi/Kroger

This set of 25 cards features members of the Detroit Tigers and was sponsored by Pepsi Cola and Kroger. The cards are in full color on the fronts and measure approximately 2 7/8" by 4 1/4". The card backs contain complete Major and Minor League season-by-season statistics. The cards are unnumbered so they are listed below by uniform number, which is given on the card.

	MINT	NRMT	EXC
COMPLETE SET (25)	12.00	5.50	1.50
COMMON CARD	.25	.11	.03
☐ 1 Lou Whitaker	2.00	.90	.25
☐ 2 Alan Trammell	3.00	1.35	.35
☐ 8 Mike Heath	.25	.11	.03
☐ 11 Sparky Anderson MG	1.00	.45	.12
☐ 12 Luis Salazar	.25	.11	.03
☐ 14 Dave Bergman	.25	.11	.03
☐ 15 Pat Sheridan	.25	.11	.03
☐ 16 Tom Brookens	.25	.11	.03
☐ 19 Doyle Alexander	.50	.23	.06
☐ 21 Willie Hernandez	.50	.23	.06
☐ 22 Ray Knight	.50	.23	.06
☐ 24 Gary Pettis	.25	.11	.03
☐ 25 Eric King	.25	.11	.03
☐ 26 Frank Tanana	.50	.23	.06
☐ 31 Larry Herndon	.25	.11	.03
☐ 32 Jim Walewander	.25	.11	.03
☐ 33 Matt Nokes	.75	.35	.09
☐ 34 Chet Lemon	.50	.23	.06
☐ 35 Walt Terrell	.25	.11	.03
☐ 39 Mike Henneman	1.00	.45	.12
☐ 41 Darrell Evans	.50	.23	.06
☐ 44 Jeff M. Robinson	.25	.11	.03
☐ 47 Jack Morris	1.50	.70	.19
☐ 48 Paul Gibson	.25	.11	.03
☐ NNO Tigers Coaches	.25	.11	.03
Billy Consolo			
Alex Grammas			
Billy Muffett			
Vada Pinson			
Dick Tracewski			

1988 Tigers Police

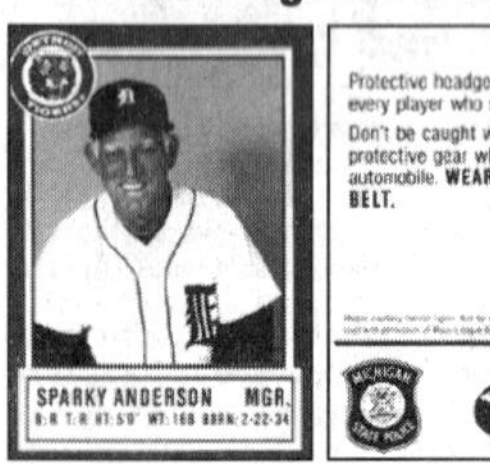

This set was sponsored by the Michigan State Police and the Detroit Tigers organization. There are 14 blue-bordered cards in the set; each card measures approximately 2 1/2" by 3 1/2". The cards are completely unnumbered as there is not even any reference to uniform numbers on the cards; the cards are listed below in alphabetical order.

	MINT	NRMT	EXC
COMPLETE SET (14)	30.00	13.50	3.70
COMMON CARD (1-14)	1.50	.70	.19
☐ 1 Doyle Alexander	2.00	.90	.25
☐ 2 Sparky Anderson MG	5.00	2.20	.60
☐ 3 Dave Bergman	1.50	.70	.19
☐ 4 Tom Brookens	1.50	.70	.19
☐ 5 Darrell Evans	2.50	1.10	.30
☐ 6 Larry Herndon	1.50	.70	.19
☐ 7 Chet Lemon	2.00	.90	.25
☐ 8 Jack Morris	7.50	3.40	.95
☐ 9 Matt Nokes	3.00	1.35	.35
☐ 10 Jeff M. Robinson	1.50	.70	.19
☐ 11 Frank Tanana	2.00	.90	.25
☐ 12 Walt Terrell	1.50	.70	.19
☐ 13 Alan Trammell	12.50	5.50	1.55
☐ 14 Lou Whitaker	7.50	3.40	.95

1989 Tigers Marathon

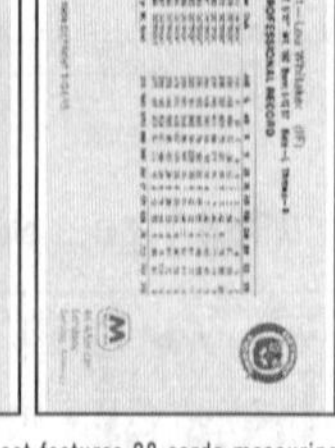

The 1989 Marathon Tigers set features 28 cards measuring approximately 2 3/4" by 4 1/2". The set features color photos surrounded by blue borders and a white background. The Tigers logo is featured prominently under the photo and then the players uniform number name and position is underneath the Tiger logo. The horizontally oriented backs show career stats. The set was given away at the July 15, 1989 Tigers home game against the Seattle Mariners. The cards are numbered by the players' uniform numbers.

	MINT	NRMT	EXC
COMPLETE SET (28)	10.00	4.50	1.25
COMMON CARD	.25	.11	.03
☐ 1 Lou Whitaker	2.00	.90	.25
☐ 3 Alan Trammell	2.50	1.10	.30
☐ 8 Mike Heath	.25	.11	.03
☐ 9 Fred Lynn	.50	.23	.06
☐ 10 Keith Moreland	.25	.11	.03
☐ 11 Sparky Anderson MG	.75	.35	.09
☐ 12 Mike Brumley	.25	.11	.03
☐ 14 Dave Bergman	.25	.11	.03
☐ 15 Pat Sheridan	.25	.11	.03
☐ 17 Al Pedrique	.25	.11	.03
☐ 18 Ramon Pena	.25	.11	.03
☐ 19 Doyle Alexander	.50	.23	.06
☐ 21 Willie Hernandez	.50	.23	.06
☐ 23 Torey Lovullo	.25	.11	.03
☐ 24 Gary Pettis	.25	.11	.03
☐ 25 Ken Williams	.25	.11	.03
☐ 26 Frank Tanana	.75	.35	.09
☐ 27 Charles Hudson	.25	.11	.03
☐ 32 Gary Ward	.25	.11	.03
☐ 33 Matt Nokes	.75	.35	.09
☐ 34 Chet Lemon	.50	.23	.06
☐ 35 Rick Schu	.25	.11	.03
☐ 36 Frank Williams	.25	.11	.03
☐ 39 Mike Henneman	.75	.35	.09
☐ 44 Jeff M. Robinson	.25	.11	.03
☐ 47 Jack Morris	1.50	.70	.19
☐ 48 Paul Gibson	.25	.11	.03
☐ NNO Tiger Coaches	.25	.11	.03
Billy Consolo			
Alex Grammas			
Billy Muffett			
Vada Pinson			
Dick Tracewski			

1989 Tigers Police

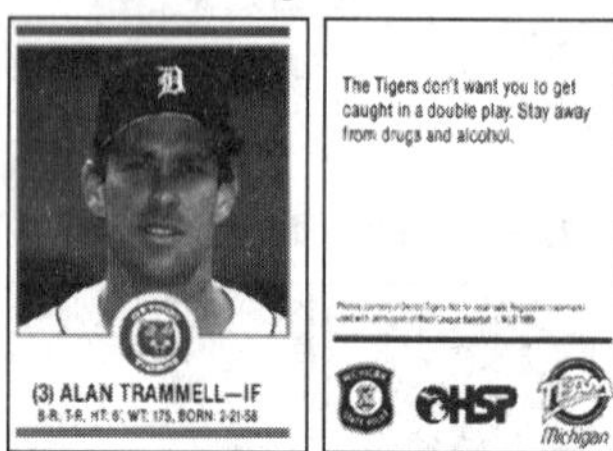

The Tigers don't want you to get caught in a double play. Stay away from drugs and alcohol.
(3) ALAN TRAMMELL—IF
OHSP

The 1989 Police Detroit Tigers set contains 14 standard-size cards. The fronts have color photos with blue and orange borders; the backs feature safety tips. These unnumbered cards were given away by the Michigan state police. The cards are numbered below according to uniform number.

	MINT	NRMT	EXC
COMPLETE SET (14)	12.00	5.50	1.50
COMMON CARD	.50	.23	.06
☐ 1 Lou Whitaker	3.00	1.35	.35
☐ 3 Alan Trammell	4.00	1.80	.50
☐ 9 Fred Lynn	1.00	.45	.12
☐ 14 Dave Bergman	.50	.23	.06
☐ 15 Pat Sheridan	.50	.23	.06
☐ 19 Doyle Alexander	.50	.23	.06
☐ 21 Willie Hernandez	.75	.35	.09
☐ 26 Frank Tanana	1.00	.45	.12
☐ 33 Matt Nokes	.75	.35	.09
☐ 34 Chet Lemon	.75	.35	.09
☐ 39 Mike Henneman	1.00	.45	.12
☐ 44 Jeff M. Robinson	.50	.23	.06
☐ 47 Jack Morris	2.00	.90	.25
☐ NNO Sparky Anderson MG	1.50	.70	.19

1990 Tigers Coke/Kroger

The 1990 Coke/Kroger Detroit Tigers set contains 28 cards, measuring approximately 2 7/8" by 4 1/4", which was used as a giveaway at the July 14th Detroit Tigers home game. The player photo is surrounded by green borders with complete career statistical information printed on the back of each card. This set is checklisted alphabetically in the listings below.

	MINT	NRMT	EXC
COMPLETE SET (28)	8.00	3.60	1.00
COMMON CARD (1-28)	.25	.11	.03
☐ 1 Sparky Anderson MG	.75	.35	.09
☐ 2 Dave Bergman	.25	.11	.03
☐ 3 Brian DuBois	.25	.11	.03
☐ 4 Cecil Fielder	.50	.23	.06
☐ 5 Paul Gibson	.25	.11	.03
☐ 6 Jerry Don Gleaton	.25	.11	.03
☐ 7 Mike Heath	.25	.11	.03
☐ 8 Mike Henneman	.50	.23	.06
☐ 9 Tracy Jones	.25	.11	.03
☐ 10 Chet Lemon	.50	.23	.06
☐ 11 Urbano Lugo	.25	.11	.03
☐ 12 Jack Morris	1.25	.55	.16
☐ 13 Lloyd Moseby	.25	.11	.03
☐ 14 Matt Nokes	.50	.23	.06
☐ 15 Edwin Nunez	.25	.11	.03
☐ 16 Dan Petry	.25	.11	.03
☐ 17 Tony Phillips	.75	.35	.09
☐ 18 Kevin Ritz	1.00	.45	.12
☐ 19 Jeff M. Robinson	.25	.11	.03
☐ 20 Ed Romero	.25	.11	.03
☐ 21 Mark Salas	.25	.11	.03
☐ 22 Larry Sheets	.25	.11	.03
☐ 23 Frank Tanana	.75	.35	.09
☐ 24 Alan Trammell	2.00	.90	.25
☐ 25 Gary Ward	.25	.11	.03
☐ 26 Lou Whitaker	1.50	.70	.19
☐ 27 Ken Williams	.25	.11	.03
☐ 28 Tigers Coaches	.50	.23	.06
Billy Consolo			
Alex Grammas			
Billy Muffett			
UER (Sic, Muffett)			
Vada Pinson			
Dick Tracewski			

1990 Tigers Milk Henneman

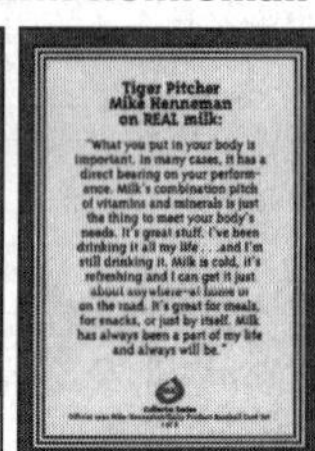

This eight-card standard-size set was a collector series issued by Real Milk Co. The set includes a title card and a membership card that enabled the consumer to mail in the card and become a Tiger Clubhouse Member. The fronts have an irregular red border on the top, orange border on the right, white border at the bottom and blue border on the left. The words "Get in the Game With Milk" are superimposed on the photo. All the cards picture Mike Henneman and a carton of Real milk. The backs are bordered in red and contain promotional comments by Henneman on milk, Henneman's biography, career highlights and statistics. The cards are numbered on the back and front.

	MINT	NRMT	EXC
COMPLETE SET (8)	7.50	3.40	.95
COMMON CARD (1-6)	.75	.35	.09
☐ 1 Mike Henneman (Drinking milk from carton)	2.00	.90	.25
☐ 2 Mike Henneman (Throwing)	2.00	.90	.25
☐ 3 Mike Henneman (Blue uniform jacket)	2.00	.90	.25
☐ 4 Mike Henneman (Transferring ball from left to right hand)	2.00	.90	.25
☐ 5 Half Gallon Milk	.75	.35	.09
☐ 6 Half Gallon Milk (With Mike Henneman's hand also shown)	.75	.35	.09
☐ NNO Title card	.75	.35	.09
☐ NNO Membership card	.75	.35	.09

1991 Tigers Coke/Kroger

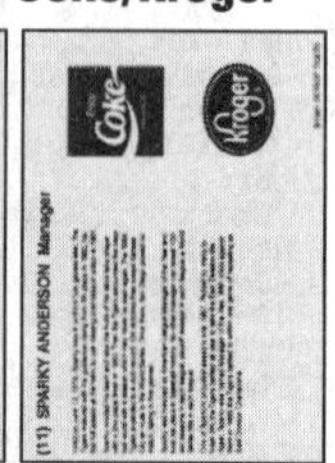

The 1991 Coke/Kroger Tigers set contains 27 cards measuring approximately 2 7/8" by 4 1/4". The fronts feature a mix of action or posed color player photos with white borders. The player's name is written vertically in a purple stripe on the right side of the picture, and the player's number appears in an inverted orange triangle toward the bottom of the stripe. In a horizontal format the back has the sponsors' logos and presents complete statistical information. The set is skip-numbered by uniform number and checklisted below accordingly.

	MINT	NRMT	EXC
COMPLETE SET (27)	10.00	4.50	1.25
COMMON CARD	.25	.11	.03
☐ 1 Lou Whitaker	1.50	.70	.19
☐ 3 Alan Trammell	2.00	.90	.25
☐ 4 Tony Phillips	.75	.35	.09
☐ 10 Andy Allanson	.25	.11	.03
☐ 11 Sparky Anderson MG	.75	.35	.09
☐ 14 Dave Bergman	.25	.11	.03
☐ 15 Lloyd Moseby	.25	.11	.03
☐ 19 Jerry Don Gleaton	.25	.11	.03
☐ 20 Mickey Tettleton	1.00	.45	.12
☐ 22 Milt Cuyler	.25	.11	.03
☐ 23 Mark Leiter	.25	.11	.03
☐ 24 Travis Fryman	.75	.35	.09
☐ 25 John Shelby	.25	.11	.03
☐ 26 Frank Tanana	.75	.35	.09
☐ 27 Mark Salas	.25	.11	.03
☐ 29 Pete Incaviglia	.75	.35	.09
☐ 31 Kevin Ritz	1.00	.45	.12
☐ 35 Walt Terrell	.25	.11	.03
☐ 36 Bill Gullickson	.25	.11	.03
☐ 39 Mike Henneman	.50	.23	.06
☐ 44 Rob Deer	.25	.11	.03
☐ 45 Cecil Fielder	2.00	.90	.25
☐ 46 Dan Petry	.25	.11	.03
☐ 48 Paul Gibson	.25	.11	.03
☐ 49 Steve Searcy	.25	.11	.03
☐ 55 John Cerutti	.25	.11	.03
☐ NNO Coaches Card	.25	.11	.03
Billy Consolo			
Jim Davenport			
Alex Grammas			
Billy Muffett			
Vada Pinson			
Dick Tracewski			

1991 Tigers Police

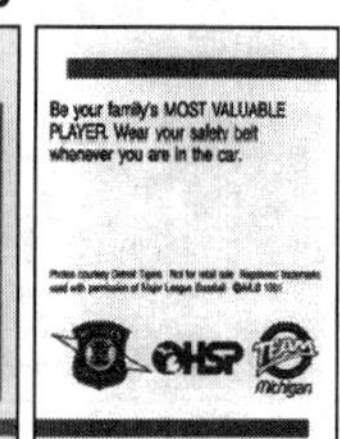

This 14-card standard-sized set was sponsored by the Michigan State Police, HSP, and Team Michigan, and their sponsor logos appear on the backs. The cards feature a mix of posed and action color player photos. The player's name appears in blue lettering in an orange stripe above the picture, while a second orange stripe below the picture intersects the team logo at the lower right corner. The backs contain safety tips. The cards are unnumbered and checklisted below in alphabetical order.

	MINT	NRMT	EXC
COMPLETE SET (14)	25.00	11.00	3.10
COMMON CARD (1-14)	1.25	.55	.16
☐ 1 Sparky Anderson MG	2.50	1.10	.30
☐ 2 Dave Bergman	1.25	.55	.16
☐ 3 Cecil Fielder	1.50	.70	.19
☐ 4 Travis Fryman	10.00	4.50	1.25
☐ 5 Paul Gibson	1.25	.55	.16
☐ 6 Jerry Don Gleaton	1.25	.55	.16
☐ 7 Lloyd Moseby	1.25	.55	.16
☐ 8 Dan Petry	1.25	.55	.16
☐ 9 Tony Phillips	2.00	.90	.25
☐ 10 Mark Salas	1.25	.55	.16
☐ 11 John Shelby	1.25	.55	.16
☐ 12 Frank Tanana	1.50	.70	.19
☐ 13 Alan Trammell	7.50	3.40	.95
☐ 14 Lou Whitaker	1.50	.70	.19

1993 Tigers Gatorade

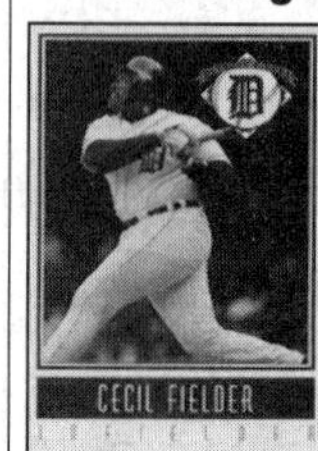

Sponsored by Gatorade, this 28-card set measures approximately 2 7/8" by 4 1/4". The fronts feature color player photos inside two team color-coded inner border stripes and a white outer border. The player's name appears in a blue bar beneath the picture, with his position printed in orange lettering immediately below on the white border. The team logo at the upper right corner of the picture rounds out the front. The horizontal backs carry the sponsor logo, biography, and complete statistical information. The cards are unnumbered and checklisted below in alphabetical order.

	MINT	NRMT	EXC
COMPLETE SET (28)	8.00	3.60	1.00
COMMON CARD (1-28)	.25	.11	.03
☐ 1 Sparky Anderson MG	.75	.35	.09
☐ 2 Skeeter Barnes	.25	.11	.03

☐ 3 Tom Bolton	.25	.11	.03
☐ 4 Milt Cuyler	.25	.11	.03
☐ 5 Rob Deer	.25	.11	.03
☐ 6 John Doherty	.25	.11	.03
☐ 7 Cecil Fielder	1.50	.70	.19
☐ 8 Travis Fryman	1.50	.70	.19
☐ 9 Kirk Gibson	.75	.35	.09
☐ 10 Dan Gladden	.25	.11	.03
☐ 11 Buddy Groom	.25	.11	.03
☐ 12 Bill Gullickson	.25	.11	.03
☐ 13 David Haas	.25	.11	.03
☐ 14 Mike Henneman	.50	.23	.06
☐ 15 Kurt Knudsen	.25	.11	.03
☐ 16 Chad Kreuter	.25	.11	.03
☐ 17 Bill Krueger	.25	.11	.03
☐ 18 Mark Leiter	.50	.23	.06
☐ 19 Scott Livingstone	.25	.11	.03
☐ 20 Bob MacDonald	.25	.11	.03
☐ 21 Mike Moore	.25	.11	.03
☐ 22 Tony Phillips	.75	.35	.09
☐ 23 Mickey Tettleton	.75	.35	.09
☐ 24 Gary Thurman	.25	.11	.03
☐ 25 Alan Trammell	1.50	.70	.19
☐ 26 David Wells	.50	.23	.06
☐ 27 Lou Whitaker	1.00	.45	.12
☐ 28 Coaches Card Dick Tracewski Billy Muffett Larry Herndon Gene Roof Dan Whitmer	.25	.11	.03

1993 Tigers Little Caesars

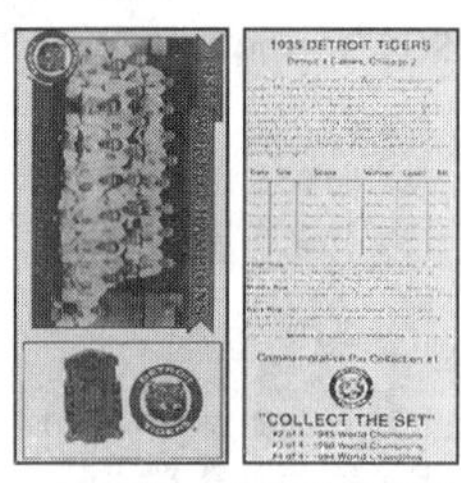

Issued as a seven-card/pin set, the '93 Tigers Little Caesars set spotlights the Tigers' World Series victories. The cards measure 2 1/2" by 5 1/4", are printed on thin white card stock, and have black-and-white or color photos on their fronts. The backs carry information regarding the particular Tigers team that won that World Series. The brass pins are affixed to the cards near the bottom. Cards 1-4 are numbered as such on their backs; cards 5-7 are unnumbered and so are checklisted below in chronological order.

	MINT	NRMT	EXC
COMPLETE SET (7)	10.00	4.50	1.25
COMMON CARD (1-7)	1.50	.70	.19
☐ 1 1935 World Champions	1.50	.70	.19
☐ 2 1945 World Champions	1.50	.70	.19
☐ 3 1968 World Champions	1.50	.70	.19
☐ 4 1984 World Champions	1.50	.70	.19
☐ 5 Denny McLain 31 Win Season	4.00	1.80	.50
☐ 6 1968 Tigers Celebration	1.50	.70	.19
☐ 7 Mickey Lolich World Series MVP	3.00	1.35	.35

1947 Tip Top

The cards in this 163-card set measure approximately 2 1/4" by 3". The 1947 Tip Top Bread issue contains unnumbered cards with black and white player photos. The set is of interest to baseball historians in that it contains cards of many players not appearing in any other card sets. The cards were issued locally for the eleven following teams: Red Sox (1-15), White Sox (16-30), Tigers (31-45), Yankees (46-60), Browns (61-75), Braves (76-90), Dodgers (91-104), Cubs (105-119), Giants (120-135), Pirates (136-149), and Cardinals (150-164). Players of the Red Sox, Tigers, White Sox, Braves, and the Cubs are scarcer than those of the other teams; players from these tougher teams are marked by SP below to indicate their scarcity. The catalog designation is D323. These unnumbered cards are listed in alphabetical order within teams (with teams also alphabetized within league) for convenience.

	EX-MT	VG-E	GOOD
COMPLETE SET (163)	9000.00	4000.00	1100.00
COMMON CARD (1-164)	25.00	11.00	3.10
COMMON SP PLAYER	75.00	34.00	9.50
☐ 1 Leon Culberson SP	75.00	34.00	9.50
☐ 2 Dom DiMaggio SP	150.00	70.00	19.00
☐ 3 Joe Dobson SP	75.00	34.00	9.50
☐ 4 Bob Doerr SP	300.00	135.00	38.00
☐ 5 Dave(Boo) Ferris SP	75.00	34.00	9.50
☐ 6 Mickey Harris SP	75.00	34.00	9.50
☐ 7 Frank Hayes SP	75.00	34.00	9.50
☐ 8 Cecil Hughson SP	75.00	34.00	9.50
☐ 9 Earl Johnson SP	75.00	34.00	9.50
☐ 10 Roy Partee SP	75.00	34.00	9.50
☐ 11 Johnny Pesky SP	90.00	40.00	11.00
☐ 12 Rip Russell SP	75.00	34.00	9.50
☐ 13 Hal Wagner SP	75.00	34.00	9.50
☐ 14 Rudy York SP	90.00	40.00	11.00
☐ 15 Bill Zuber SP	75.00	34.00	9.50
☐ 16 Floyd Baker SP	75.00	34.00	9.50
☐ 17 Earl Caldwell SP	75.00	34.00	9.50
☐ 18 Loyd Christopher SP	75.00	34.00	9.50
☐ 19 George Dickey SP	75.00	34.00	9.50
☐ 20 Ralph Hodgin SP	75.00	34.00	9.50
☐ 21 Bob Kennedy SP	75.00	34.00	9.50
☐ 22 Joe Kuhel SP	75.00	34.00	9.50
☐ 23 Thornton Lee SP	75.00	34.00	9.50
☐ 24 Ed Lopat SP	125.00	55.00	15.50
☐ 25 Cass Michaels SP	75.00	34.00	9.50
☐ 26 John Rigney SP	75.00	34.00	9.50
☐ 27 Mike Tresh SP	75.00	34.00	9.50
☐ 28 Thurman Tucker SP	75.00	34.00	9.50
☐ 29 Jack Wallasca SP	75.00	34.00	9.50
☐ 30 Taft Wright SP	75.00	34.00	9.50
☐ 31 Walter(Hoot)Evers SP	75.00	34.00	9.50
☐ 32 John Gorsica SP	75.00	34.00	9.50
☐ 33 Fred Hutchinson SP	90.00	40.00	11.00
☐ 34 George Kell SP	400.00	180.00	50.00
☐ 35 Eddie Lake SP	75.00	34.00	9.50
☐ 36 Ed Mayo SP	75.00	34.00	9.50
☐ 37 Arthur Mills SP	75.00	34.00	9.50
☐ 38 Pat Mullin SP	75.00	34.00	9.50
☐ 39 James Outlaw SP	75.00	34.00	9.50
☐ 40 Frank Overmire SP	75.00	34.00	9.50
☐ 41 Bob Swift SP	75.00	34.00	9.50
☐ 42 Birdie Tebbetts SP	75.00	34.00	9.50
☐ 43 Dizzy Trout SP	90.00	40.00	11.00
☐ 44 Virgil Trucks SP	90.00	40.00	11.00
☐ 45 Dick Wakefield SP	75.00	34.00	9.50
☐ 46 Yogi Berra (Listed as Larry on card)	400.00	180.00	50.00
☐ 47 Floyd(Bill) Bevans	25.00	11.00	3.10
☐ 48 Bobby Brown	30.00	13.50	3.70
☐ 49 Thomas Byrne	25.00	11.00	3.10
☐ 50 Frank Crosetti	35.00	16.00	4.40
☐ 51 Tom Henrich	35.00	16.00	4.40
☐ 52 Charlie Keller	35.00	16.00	4.40
☐ 53 Johnny Lindell	25.00	11.00	3.10
☐ 54 Joe Page	30.00	13.50	3.70
☐ 55 Mel Queen	25.00	11.00	3.10
☐ 56 Allie Reynolds	35.00	16.00	4.40
☐ 57 Phil Rizzuto	150.00	70.00	19.00
☐ 58 Aaron Robinson	25.00	11.00	3.10
☐ 59 George Stirnweiss	25.00	11.00	3.10
☐ 60 Charles Wensloff	25.00	11.00	3.10
☐ 61 John Berardino	35.00	16.00	4.40
☐ 62 Clifford Fannin	25.00	11.00	3.10
☐ 63 Dennis Galehouse	25.00	11.00	3.10
☐ 64 Jeff Heath	25.00	11.00	3.10
☐ 65 Walter Judnich	25.00	11.00	3.10
☐ 66 Jack Kramer	25.00	11.00	3.10
☐ 67 Paul Lehner	25.00	11.00	3.10
☐ 68 Lester Moss	25.00	11.00	3.10
☐ 69 Bob Muncrief	25.00	11.00	3.10
☐ 70 Nelson Potter	25.00	11.00	3.10
☐ 71 Fred Sanford	25.00	11.00	3.10
☐ 72 Joe Schultz	25.00	11.00	3.10
☐ 73 Vern Stephens	30.00	13.50	3.70
☐ 74 Jerry Witte	25.00	11.00	3.10
☐ 75 Al Zarilla	25.00	11.00	3.10
☐ 76 Charles Barrett SP	75.00	34.00	9.50
☐ 77 Hank Camelli SP	75.00	34.00	9.50
☐ 78 Dick Culler SP	75.00	34.00	9.50
☐ 79 Nanny Fernandez SP	75.00	34.00	9.50
☐ 80 Si Johnson SP	75.00	34.00	9.50
☐ 81 Danny Litwhiler SP	75.00	34.00	9.50
☐ 82 Phil Masi SP	75.00	34.00	9.50
☐ 83 Carvel Rowell SP	75.00	34.00	9.50
☐ 84 Connie Ryan SP	75.00	34.00	9.50
☐ 85 John Sain SP	125.00	55.00	15.50
☐ 86 Ray Sanders SP	75.00	34.00	9.50
☐ 87 Sibby Sisti SP	75.00	34.00	9.50
☐ 88 Billy Southworth SP MG	90.00	40.00	11.00
☐ 89 Warren Spahn SP	500.00	220.00	60.00
☐ 90 Ed Wright SP	75.00	34.00	9.50
☐ 91 Bob Bragan	30.00	13.50	3.70
☐ 92 Ralph Branca	30.00	13.50	3.70
☐ 93 Hugh Casey	25.00	11.00	3.10
☐ 94 Bruce Edwards	25.00	11.00	3.10
☐ 95 Hal Gregg	25.00	11.00	3.10
☐ 96 Joe Hatten	25.00	11.00	3.10
☐ 97 Gene Hermanski	25.00	11.00	3.10
☐ 98 John Jorgensen	25.00	11.00	3.10
☐ 99 Harry Lavagetto	30.00	13.50	3.70
☐ 100 Vic Lombardi	25.00	11.00	3.10
☐ 101 Frank Melton	25.00	11.00	3.10
☐ 102 Ed Miksis	25.00	11.00	3.10
☐ 103 Marv Rackley	25.00	11.00	3.10
☐ 104 Ed Stevens	25.00	11.00	3.10
☐ 105 Phil Cavarretta SP	125.00	55.00	15.50
☐ 106 Bob Chipman SP	75.00	34.00	9.50
☐ 107 Stan Hack SP	90.00	40.00	11.00
☐ 108 Don Johnson SP	75.00	34.00	9.50
☐ 109 Emil Kush SP	75.00	34.00	9.50
☐ 110 Bill Lee SP	90.00	40.00	11.00
☐ 111 Mickey Livingston SP	75.00	34.00	9.50
☐ 112 Harry Lowrey SP	75.00	34.00	9.50
☐ 113 Clyde McCullough SP	75.00	34.00	9.50
☐ 114 Andy Pafko SP	90.00	40.00	11.00
☐ 115 Marv Rickert SP	75.00	34.00	9.50
☐ 116 John Schmitz SP	75.00	34.00	9.50
☐ 117 Bobby Sturgeon SP	75.00	34.00	9.50
☐ 118 Ed Waitkus SP	90.00	40.00	11.00
☐ 119 Henry Wyse SP	75.00	34.00	9.50
☐ 120 Bill Ayers	25.00	11.00	3.10
☐ 121 Buddy Blattner	25.00	11.00	3.10
☐ 122 Mike Budnick	25.00	11.00	3.10
☐ 123 Sid Gordon	25.00	11.00	3.10
☐ 124 Clint Hartung	25.00	11.00	3.10
☐ 125 Monte Kennedy	25.00	11.00	3.10
☐ 126 Dave Koslo	25.00	11.00	3.10
☐ 127 Whitey Lockman	30.00	13.50	3.70
☐ 128 Jack Lohrke	25.00	11.00	3.10
☐ 129 Ernie Lombardi	75.00	34.00	9.50
☐ 130 Willard Marshall	25.00	11.00	3.10
☐ 131 John Mize	125.00	55.00	15.50
☐ 132 Eugene Thompson (Does not exist)			
☐ 133 Ken Trinkle	25.00	11.00	3.10
☐ 134 Bill Voiselle	25.00	11.00	3.10
☐ 135 Mickey Witek	25.00	11.00	3.10
☐ 136 Eddie Basinski	25.00	11.00	3.10
☐ 137 Ernie Bonham	25.00	11.00	3.10
☐ 138 Billy Cox	30.00	13.50	3.70
☐ 139 Elbie Fletcher	25.00	11.00	3.10
☐ 140 Frank Gustine	25.00	11.00	3.10
☐ 141 Kirby Higbe	25.00	11.00	3.10
☐ 142 Leroy Jarvis	25.00	11.00	3.10
☐ 143 Ralph Kiner	125.00	55.00	15.50
☐ 144 Fred Ostermueller	25.00	11.00	3.10
☐ 145 Preacher Roe	35.00	16.00	4.40
☐ 146 Jim Russell	25.00	11.00	3.10
☐ 147 Rip Sewell	25.00	11.00	3.10
☐ 148 Nick Strincevich	25.00	11.00	3.10
☐ 149 Honus Wagner CO	125.00	55.00	15.50
☐ 150 Alpha Brazle	25.00	11.00	3.10
☐ 151 Ken Burkhart	25.00	11.00	3.10
☐ 152 Bernard Creger	25.00	11.00	3.10
☐ 153 Joffre Cross	25.00	11.00	3.10
☐ 154 Chuck Diering	25.00	11.00	3.10
☐ 155 Ervin Dusak	25.00	11.00	3.10
☐ 156 Joe Garagiola	75.00	34.00	9.50
☐ 157 Tony Kaufmann	25.00	11.00	3.10
☐ 158 Whitey Kurowski	25.00	11.00	3.10
☐ 159 Marty Marion	35.00	16.00	4.40
☐ 160 George Munger	25.00	11.00	3.10
☐ 161 Del Rice	25.00	11.00	3.10
☐ 162 Dick Sisler	30.00	13.50	3.70
☐ 163 Enos Slaughter	125.00	55.00	15.50
☐ 164 Ted Wilks	25.00	11.00	3.10

1952 Tip Top Labels

This set of 48 bread end-labels was issued by Tip Top in 1952. The labels measure 2 3/4" by 2 1/2". An album distributed with the labels names 47 ball players and has one blank slot with advertising. A second pose of Rizzuto -- which appears "cropped" from the first photo -- suggests either a last minute substitution for another player, or simply his popularity in the market area. These labels are unnumbered so we have sequenced them in alphabetical order. The catalog designation is D290-1.

	NRMT	VG-E	GOOD
COMPLETE SET (48)	5500.00	2500.00	700.00
COMMON LABEL (1-48)	60.00	27.00	7.50
☐ 1 Hank Bauer	100.00	45.00	12.50
☐ 2 Yogi Berra	225.00	100.00	28.00
☐ 3 Ralph Branca	75.00	34.00	9.50
☐ 4 Lou Brissie	60.00	27.00	7.50
☐ 5 Roy Campanella	225.00	100.00	28.00
☐ 6 Phil Cavarretta	75.00	34.00	9.50
☐ 7 Murray Dickson	60.00	27.00	7.50
☐ 8 Ferris Fain	60.00	27.00	7.50
☐ 9 Carl Furillo	100.00	45.00	12.50
☐ 10 Ned Garver	60.00	27.00	7.50
☐ 11 Sid Gordon	75.00	34.00	9.50
☐ 12 Johnny Groth	60.00	27.00	7.50
☐ 13 Granny Hamner	60.00	27.00	7.50
☐ 14 Jim Hearn	60.00	27.00	7.50
☐ 15 Gene Hermanski	60.00	27.00	7.50
☐ 16 Gil Hodges	175.00	80.00	22.00
☐ 17 Larry Jansen	75.00	34.00	9.50
☐ 18 Eddie Joost	60.00	27.00	7.50
☐ 19 George Kell	150.00	70.00	19.00
☐ 20 Dutch Leonard	60.00	27.00	7.50
☐ 21 Whitey Lockman	60.00	27.00	7.50
☐ 22 Eddie Lopat	100.00	45.00	12.50
☐ 23 Sal Maglie	100.00	45.00	12.50
☐ 24 Mickey Mantle	1750.00	800.00	220.00
☐ 25 Gil McDougald	100.00	45.00	12.50
☐ 26 Dale Mitchell	75.00	34.00	9.50
☐ 27 Don Mueller	60.00	27.00	7.50
☐ 28 Andy Pafko	60.00	27.00	7.50
☐ 29 Bob Porterfield	60.00	27.00	7.50
☐ 30 Ken Raffensberger	60.00	27.00	7.50
☐ 31 Allie Reynolds	100.00	45.00	12.50
☐ 32 Phil Rizzuto (large)	125.00	55.00	15.50
☐ 33 Phil Rizzuto (small)	125.00	55.00	15.50
☐ 34 Robin Roberts	175.00	80.00	22.00
☐ 35 Saul Rogovin	60.00	27.00	7.50
☐ 36 Ray Scarborough	60.00	27.00	7.50
☐ 37 Red Schoendienst	100.00	45.00	12.50
☐ 38 Dick Sisler	60.00	27.00	7.50
☐ 39 Enos Slaughter	150.00	70.00	19.00
☐ 40 Duke Snider	250.00	110.00	31.00
☐ 41 Warren Spahn	200.00	90.00	25.00
☐ 42 Vern Stephens	60.00	27.00	7.50
☐ 43 Earl Torgeson	60.00	27.00	7.50
☐ 44 Mickey Vernon	75.00	34.00	9.50
☐ 45 Eddie Waitkus	60.00	27.00	7.50
☐ 46 Wes Westrum	60.00	27.00	7.50
☐ 47 Eddie Yost	60.00	27.00	7.50
☐ 48 Al Zarilla	60.00	27.00	7.50

1913 Tom Barker WG6

These cards were distributed as part of a baseball game produced in 1913 as indicated by the patent date on the backs of the cards. The cards each measure approximately 2 7/16" by 3 7/16" and have rounded corners. The card fronts show a sepia photo of the player, his name, his team, and the game outcome associated with that particular card. The card backs are all the same, each showing an ornate red and white design with "Tom Barker Baseball Card Game" at the bottom under a drawing of a lefthanded batter all surrounded by a thick white outer border. Since the cards are unnumbered, they are listed below in alphabetical order. Some of the card photos are oriented horizontally (HOR). There are a number of cards without player identification. These action scenes are not explicitly listed in the checklist below and are valued as a "common" card unless a positive identification can be made of a major Hall of Famer in the action scene on the card.

	EX-MT	VG-E	GOOD
COMPLETE SET	3000.00	1350.00	375.00
COMMON CARD (1-42)	30.00	13.50	3.70
COMMON ACTION CARD	15.00	6.75	1.85
☐ 1 Grover Alexander	100.00	45.00	12.50
☐ 2 Chief Bender	75.00	34.00	9.50
☐ 3 Bob Bescher	30.00	13.50	3.70
☐ 4 Joe Birmingham	30.00	13.50	3.70
☐ 5 Roger Bresnahan	75.00	34.00	9.50
☐ 6 Nixey Callahan	30.00	13.50	3.70
☐ 7 Bill Carrigan	30.00	13.50	3.70
☐ 8 Frank Chance	75.00	34.00	9.50
☐ 9 Hal Chase	50.00	22.00	6.25
☐ 10 Fred Clarke	75.00	34.00	9.50
☐ 11 Ty Cobb	300.00	135.00	38.00
☐ 12 Sam Crawford	75.00	34.00	9.50
☐ 13 Jake Daubert	35.00	16.00	4.40
☐ 14 Red Dooin	30.00	13.50	3.70
☐ 15 Johnny Evers	75.00	34.00	9.50
☐ 16 Vean Gregg	30.00	13.50	3.70
☐ 17 Clark Griffith MG	75.00	34.00	9.50
☐ 18 Dick Hoblitzel	30.00	13.50	3.70
☐ 19 Miller Huggins	75.00	34.00	9.50
☐ 20 Joe Jackson	500.00	220.00	60.00
☐ 21 Hugh Jennings MG	75.00	34.00	9.50
☐ 22 Walter Johnson	150.00	70.00	19.00
☐ 23 Ed Konetchy	30.00	13.50	3.70
☐ 24 Nap Lajoie	125.00	55.00	15.50
☐ 25 Connie Mack MG	125.00	55.00	15.50
☐ 26 Rube Marquard	75.00	34.00	9.50
☐ 27 Christy Mathewson	150.00	70.00	19.00
☐ 28 John McGraw MG	125.00	55.00	15.50
☐ 29 Chief Meyers	30.00	13.50	3.70
☐ 30 Clyde Milan	30.00	13.50	3.70
☐ 31 Marty O'Toole	30.00	13.50	3.70
☐ 32 Nap Rucker	30.00	13.50	3.70
☐ 33 Tris Speaker	125.00	55.00	15.50
☐ 34 George Stallings MG	30.00	13.50	3.70
☐ 35 Bill Sweeney	30.00	13.50	3.70
☐ 36 Joe Tinker	75.00	34.00	9.50
☐ 37 Honus Wagner	150.00	70.00	19.00

☐ 38 Ed Walsh	75.00	34.00	9.50
☐ 39 Zack Wheat	75.00	34.00	9.50
☐ 40 Ivy Wingo	30.00	13.50	3.70
☐ 41 Joe Wood	50.00	22.00	6.25
☐ 42 Cy Young	125.00	55.00	15.50

1994 Tombstone Pizza

Produced by Michael Schlechter Associates for Pinnacle and sponsored by Tombstone Pizza, this 30-card standard-size set showcases 15 of the hottest players from the National (1-15) and American (16-30) Leagues. The promotion ran from May 15 to July 4, 1994, or while supplies lasted. One card was packaged in each Tombstone pizza. Collectors could obtain the complete set by sending in five proofs-of-purchase and 1.00 for shipping and handling. The fronts feature color action player photos on a black background with thin green borders. The words "94 Tombstone Super-Pro Series" are printed in orange letters above the picture, while the player's name and team name along with the sponsor's logo appear under the picture. The horizontal backs carry a color player portrait with the player's name and position, biography and statistics, and a facsimile autograph. Like most MSA sets, the team logos have been airbrushed away. The cards are arranged alphabetically within each league.

	MINT	NRMT	EXC
COMPLETE SET (30)	18.00	8.00	2.20
COMMON CARD (1-30)	.15	.07	.02
☐ 1 Jeff Bagwell	1.25	.55	.16
☐ 2 Jay Bell	.15	.07	.02
☐ 3 Barry Bonds	.75	.35	.09
☐ 4 Bobby Bonilla	.30	.14	.04
☐ 5 Andres Galarraga	.40	.18	.05
☐ 6 Mark Grace	.50	.23	.06
☐ 7 Marquis Grissom	.30	.14	.04
☐ 8 Tony Gwynn	1.50	.70	.19
☐ 9 Bryan Harvey	.15	.07	.02
☐ 10 Gregg Jefferies	.15	.07	.02
☐ 11 David Justice	.50	.23	.06
☐ 12 John Kruk	.30	.14	.04
☐ 13 Barry Larkin	.50	.23	.06
☐ 14 Greg Maddux	1.75	.80	.22
☐ 15 Mike Piazza	1.75	.80	.22
☐ 16 Jim Abbott	.15	.07	.02
☐ 17 Albert Belle	1.50	.70	.19
☐ 18 Cecil Fielder	.30	.14	.04
☐ 19 Juan Gonzalez	1.50	.70	.19
☐ 20 Mike Greenwell	.15	.07	.02
☐ 21 Ken Griffey Jr.	3.00	1.35	.35
☐ 22 Jack McDowell	.15	.07	.02
☐ 23 Jeff Montgomery	.15	.07	.02
☐ 24 John Olerud	.30	.14	.04
☐ 25 Kirby Puckett	1.50	.70	.19
☐ 26 Cal Ripken	3.00	1.35	.35
☐ 27 Tim Salmon	.75	.35	.09
☐ 28 Ruben Sierra	.15	.07	.02
☐ 29 Frank Thomas	3.00	1.35	.35
☐ 30 Robin Yount	.50	.23	.06

1995 Tombstone Pizza

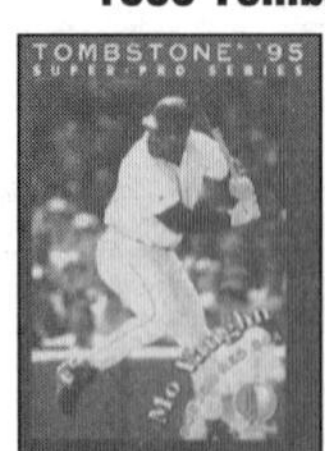

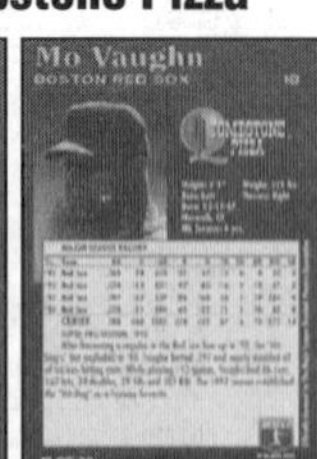

This 30-card standard-size set features 15 of the hottest players each from the National and the American Leagues. One card was packaged in each Tombstone Pizza. Six thousand classic player cards, autographed by Johnny Bench, George Brett or Bob Gibson, were randomly packed. Collectors who pulled one of these autograph cards could receive an 8 1/2" by 11" certificate of authenticity through a mail-in offer. Also collectors could obtain the complete set by sending in five proofs-of-purchase. The limit was two sets per family or address, and the offer expired December 31, 1995, or while supplies lasted. The cards are numbered on the back "X of 30."

	MINT	NRMT	EXC
COMPLETE SET (30)	15.00	6.75	1.85
COMMON CARD (1-30)	.15	.07	.02
☐ 1 Frank Thomas	3.00	1.35	.35
☐ 2 David Cone	.30	.14	.04
☐ 3 Bob Hamelin	.15	.07	.02
☐ 4 Jeff Bagwell	1.25	.55	.16
☐ 5 Greg Maddux	1.75	.80	.22
☐ 6 Raul Mondesi	.60	.25	.07
☐ 7 Chili Davis	.15	.07	.02
☐ 8 Cecil Fielder	.30	.14	.04
☐ 9 Ken Griffey Jr.	3.00	1.35	.35
☐ 10 Jimmy Key	.15	.07	.02
☐ 11 Kenny Lofton	.75	.35	.09
☐ 12 Paul Molitor	.60	.25	.07
☐ 13 Kirby Puckett	1.50	.70	.19
☐ 14 Cal Ripken	2.50	1.10	.30
☐ 15 Ivan Rodriguez	.75	.35	.09
☐ 16 Kevin Seitzer	.15	.07	.02
☐ 17 Ruben Sierra	.15	.07	.02
☐ 18 Mo Vaughn	.75	.35	.09
☐ 19 Moises Alou	.30	.14	.04
☐ 20 Barry Bonds	.75	.35	.09
☐ 21 Jeff Conine	.30	.14	.04
☐ 22 Lenny Dykstra	.30	.14	.04
☐ 23 Andres Galarraga	.40	.18	.05
☐ 24 Tony Gwynn	1.25	.55	.16
☐ 25 Barry Larkin	.40	.18	.05
☐ 26 Fred McGriff	.50	.23	.06
☐ 27 Orlando Merced	.15	.07	.02
☐ 28 Bret Saberhagen	.15	.07	.02
☐ 29 Ozzie Smith	1.00	.45	.12
☐ 30 Sammy Sosa	.50	.23	.06

1951 Topps Blue Backs

The cards in this 52-card set measure approximately 2" by 2 5/8". The 1951 Topps series of blue-backed baseball cards could be used to play a baseball game by shuffling the cards and drawing them from a pile. These cards (packaged two adjoined in a penny pack) were marketed with a piece of caramel candy, which often melted or was squashed in such a way as to damage the card and wrapper (despite the fact that a paper shield was inserted between candy and card). Blue Backs are more difficult to obtain than the similarly styled Red Backs. The set is denoted on the cards as "Set B" and the Red Back set is correspondingly Set A. The only notable Rookie Card in the set is Billy Pierce.

	NRMT	VG-E	GOOD
COMPLETE SET (52)	1700.00	750.00	210.00
COMMON CARD (1-52)	30.00	13.50	3.70
WRAPPER (1-CENT)	200.00	90.00	25.00
☐ 1 Eddie Yost	60.00	18.00	6.00
☐ 2 Hank Majeski	30.00	13.50	3.70
☐ 3 Richie Ashburn	225.00	100.00	28.00
☐ 4 Del Ennis	35.00	16.00	4.40
☐ 5 Johnny Pesky	35.00	16.00	4.40
☐ 6 Red Schoendienst	100.00	45.00	12.50
☐ 7 Gerry Staley	30.00	13.50	3.70
☐ 8 Dick Sisler	30.00	13.50	3.70
☐ 9 Johnny Sain	50.00	22.00	6.25
☐ 10 Joe Page	35.00	16.00	4.40
☐ 11 Johnny Groth	30.00	13.50	3.70
☐ 12 Sam Jethroe	35.00	16.00	4.40
☐ 13 Mickey Vernon	35.00	16.00	4.40
☐ 14 Red Munger	30.00	13.50	3.70
☐ 15 Eddie Joost	30.00	13.50	3.70
☐ 16 Murry Dickson	30.00	13.50	3.70
☐ 17 Roy Smalley	30.00	13.50	3.70
☐ 18 Ned Garver	30.00	13.50	3.70
☐ 19 Phil Masi	30.00	13.50	3.70
☐ 20 Ralph Branca	50.00	22.00	6.25
☐ 21 Billy Johnson	30.00	13.50	3.70
☐ 22 Bob Kuzava	30.00	13.50	3.70
☐ 23 Dizzy Trout	35.00	16.00	4.40
☐ 24 Sherman Lollar	35.00	16.00	4.40
☐ 25 Sam Mele	30.00	13.50	3.70
☐ 26 Chico Carrasquel	35.00	16.00	4.40
☐ 27 Andy Pafko	35.00	16.00	4.40
☐ 28 Harry Brecheen	35.00	16.00	4.40
☐ 29 Granville Hamner	30.00	13.50	3.70
☐ 30 Enos Slaughter	100.00	45.00	12.50
☐ 31 Lou Brissie	30.00	13.50	3.70
☐ 32 Bob Elliott	35.00	16.00	4.40
☐ 33 Don Lenhardt	30.00	13.50	3.70
☐ 34 Earl Torgeson	30.00	13.50	3.70
☐ 35 Tommy Byrne	30.00	13.50	3.70
☐ 36 Cliff Fannin	30.00	13.50	3.70
☐ 37 Bobby Doerr	90.00	40.00	11.00
☐ 38 Irv Noren	35.00	16.00	4.40
☐ 39 Ed Lopat	45.00	20.00	5.50
☐ 40 Vic Wertz	35.00	16.00	4.40
☐ 41 Johnny Schmitz	30.00	13.50	3.70
☐ 42 Bruce Edwards	30.00	13.50	3.70
☐ 43 Willie Jones	30.00	13.50	3.70
☐ 44 Johnny Wyrostek	30.00	13.50	3.70
☐ 45 Billy Pierce	50.00	22.00	6.25
☐ 46 Gerry Priddy	30.00	13.50	3.70
☐ 47 Herman Wehmeier	30.00	13.50	3.70
☐ 48 Billy Cox	30.00	13.50	3.70
☐ 49 Hank Sauer	35.00	16.00	4.40
☐ 50 Johnny Mize	100.00	45.00	12.50
☐ 51 Eddie Waitkus	35.00	16.00	4.40
☐ 52 Sam Chapman	40.00	13.50	5.00

1951 Topps Red Backs

The cards in this 52-card set measure approximately 2" by 2 5/8". The 1951 Topps Red Back set is identical in style to the Blue Back set of the same year. The cards have rounded corners and were designed to be used as a baseball game. Zernial, number 36, is listed with either the White Sox or Athletics, and Holmes, number 52, with either the Braves or Hartford. The set is denoted on the cards as "Set A" and the Blue Back set is correspondingly Set B. The cards were packaged as two connected cards along with a piece of caramel in a penny pack. The most notable Rookie Card in the set is Monte Irvin.

	NRMT	VG-E	GOOD
COMPLETE SET (54)	850.00	375.00	105.00
COMMON CARD (1-52)	10.00	4.50	1.25
WRAPPER (1-CENT)	5.00	2.20	.60
☐ 1 Yogi Berra	125.00	45.00	12.50
☐ 2 Sid Gordon	10.00	4.50	1.25
☐ 3 Ferris Fain	12.00	5.50	1.50
☐ 4 Vern Stephens	12.00	5.50	1.50
☐ 5 Phil Rizzuto	60.00	27.00	7.50
☐ 6 Allie Reynolds	18.00	8.00	2.20
☐ 7 Howie Pollet	10.00	4.50	1.25
☐ 8 Early Wynn	25.00	11.00	3.10
☐ 9 Roy Sievers	12.00	5.50	1.50
☐ 10 Mel Parnell	12.00	5.50	1.50
☐ 11 Gene Hermanski	10.00	4.50	1.25
☐ 12 Jim Hegan	12.00	5.50	1.50
☐ 13 Dale Mitchell	12.00	5.50	1.50
☐ 14 Wayne Terwilliger	10.00	4.50	1.25
☐ 15 Ralph Kiner	25.00	11.00	3.10
☐ 16 Preacher Roe	12.00	5.50	1.50
☐ 17 Gus Bell	15.00	6.75	1.85
☐ 18 Jerry Coleman	15.00	6.75	1.85
☐ 19 Dick Kokos	10.00	4.50	1.25
☐ 20 Dom DiMaggio	18.00	8.00	2.20
☐ 21 Larry Jansen	12.00	5.50	1.50
☐ 22 Bob Feller	60.00	27.00	7.50
☐ 23 Ray Boone	15.00	6.75	1.85
☐ 24 Hank Bauer	18.00	8.00	2.20
☐ 25 Cliff Chambers	10.00	4.50	1.25
☐ 26 Luke Easter	12.00	5.50	1.50
☐ 27 Wally Westlake	10.00	4.50	1.25
☐ 28 Elmer Valo	10.00	4.50	1.25
☐ 29 Bob Kennedy	12.00	5.50	1.50
☐ 30 Warren Spahn	60.00	27.00	7.50
☐ 31 Gil Hodges	40.00	18.00	5.00
☐ 32 Henry Thompson	12.00	5.50	1.50
☐ 33 William Werle	10.00	4.50	1.25
☐ 34 Grady Hatton	10.00	4.50	1.25
☐ 35 Al Rosen	12.00	5.50	1.50
☐ 36A Gus Zernial (Chicago)	40.00	18.00	5.00
☐ 36B Gus Zernial (Philadelphia)	20.00	9.00	2.50
☐ 37 Wes Westrum	12.00	5.50	1.50
☐ 38 Duke Snider	60.00	27.00	7.50
☐ 39 Ted Kluszewski	20.00	9.00	2.50
☐ 40 Mike Garcia	12.00	5.50	1.50
☐ 41 Whitey Lockman	12.00	5.50	1.50
☐ 42 Ray Scarborough	10.00	4.50	1.25
☐ 43 Maurice McDermott	10.00	4.50	1.25
☐ 44 Sid Hudson	10.00	4.50	1.25
☐ 45 Andy Seminick	10.00	4.50	1.25
☐ 46 Billy Goodman	12.00	5.50	1.50
☐ 47 Tommy Glaviano	10.00	4.50	1.25
☐ 48 Eddie Stanky	12.00	5.50	1.50
☐ 49 Al Zarilla	10.00	4.50	1.25
☐ 50 Monte Irvin	40.00	18.00	5.00
☐ 51 Eddie Robinson	10.00	4.50	1.25
☐ 52A Tommy Holmes (Boston)	40.00	10.00	4.00
☐ 52B Tommy Holmes (Hartford)	25.00	6.25	2.50

1951 Topps Connie Mack AS

The cards in this 11-card set measure approximately 2 1/16" by 5 1/4". The series of die-cut cards which comprise the set entitled Connie Mack All-Stars was one of Topps' most distinctive and fragile card designs. Printed on thin cardboard, these elegant cards were protected in the wrapper by panels of accompanying Red Backs, but once removed were easily damaged (after all, they were intended to

be folded and used as toy figures). Cards without tops have a value less than one-half of that listed below. The cards are unnumbered and are listed below in alphabetical order.

	NRMT	VG-E	GOOD
COMPLETE SET (11)	7000.00	3200.00	900.00
COMMON CARD (1-11)	150.00	70.00	19.00
WRAPPER (1-CENT)	350.00	160.00	45.00
☐ 1 Grover C. Alexander	400.00	180.00	50.00
☐ 2 Mickey Cochrane	300.00	135.00	38.00
☐ 3 Eddie Collins	150.00	70.00	19.00
☐ 4 Jimmy Collins	150.00	70.00	19.00
☐ 5 Lou Gehrig	2000.00	900.00	250.00
☐ 6 Walter Johnson	650.00	300.00	80.00
☐ 7 Connie Mack	350.00	160.00	45.00
☐ 8 Christy Mathewson	425.00	190.00	52.50
☐ 9 Babe Ruth	2500.00	1100.00	300.00
☐ 10 Tris Speaker	150.00	70.00	19.00
☐ 11 Honus Wagner	400.00	180.00	50.00

1951 Topps Current AS

The cards in this 11-card set measure approximately 2 1/16" by 5 1/4". The 1951 Topps Current All-Star series is probably the rarest of all legitimate, nationally issued, post war baseball issues. The set price listed below does not include the prices for the cards of Konstanty, Roberts and Stanky, which likely never were released to the public in gum packs. These three cards (SP in the checklist below) were probably obtained directly from the company and exist in extremely limited numbers. As with the Connie Mack set, cards without the die-cut background are worth half of the value listed below. The cards are unnumbered and are listed below in alphabetical order. These cards were issued in two card packs (one being a Current AS the other being a Topps Team card).

	NRMT	VG-E	GOOD
COMPLETE SET (8)	4500.00	2000.00	550.00
COMMON CARD (1-11)	250.00	110.00	31.00
WRAPPER (1-CENT)	500.00	220.00	60.00
☐ 1 Yogi Berra	1500.00	700.00	190.00
☐ 2 Larry Doby	300.00	135.00	38.00
☐ 3 Walt Dropo	250.00	110.00	31.00
☐ 4 Hoot Evers	250.00	110.00	31.00
☐ 5 George Kell	600.00	275.00	75.00
☐ 6 Ralph Kiner	750.00	350.00	95.00
☐ 7 Jim Konstanty SP	12500.00	5600.00	1600.00
☐ 8 Bob Lemon	600.00	275.00	75.00
☐ 9 Phil Rizzuto	750.00	350.00	95.00
☐ 10 Robin Roberts SP	15000.00	6800.00	1900.00
☐ 11 Eddie Stanky SP	12500.00	5600.00	1600.00

1951 Topps Teams

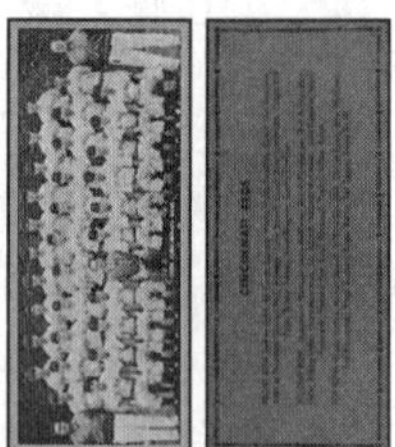

The cards in this nine-card set measure approximately 2 1/16" by 5 1/4". These unnumbered team cards issued by Topps in 1951 carry black and white photographs framed by a yellow border. These cards were issued in the same five-cent wrapper as the Connie Mack and Current All Stars. They have been assigned reference numbers in the checklist alphabetically by team city and team name. They are found with or without "1950" printed in the name panel before the team name. Although the dated variations are slightly more difficult to find, there is usually no difference in value.

	NRMT	VG-E	GOOD
COMPLETE SET (9)	2250.00	1000.00	275.00
COMMON TEAM (1-9)	200.00	90.00	25.00
☐ 1 Boston Red Sox	400.00	180.00	50.00
☐ 2 Brooklyn Dodgers	375.00	170.00	47.50
☐ 3 Chicago White Sox	200.00	90.00	25.00
☐ 4 Cincinnati Reds	200.00	90.00	25.00
☐ 5 New York Giants	250.00	110.00	31.00
☐ 6 Phila. Athletics	200.00	90.00	25.00
☐ 7 Phila. Phillies	200.00	90.00	25.00
☐ 8 St. Louis Cardinals	350.00	160.00	45.00
☐ 9 Washington Senators	200.00	90.00	25.00

1952 Topps

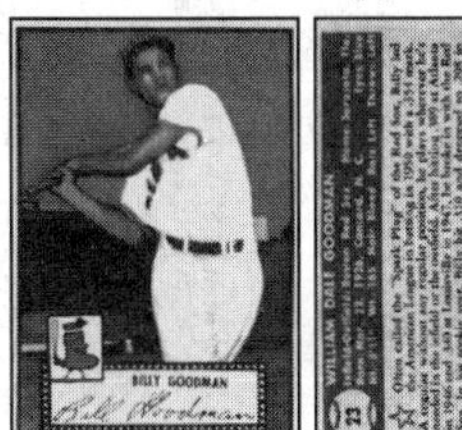

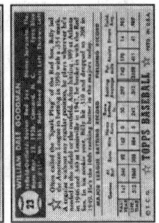

The cards in this 407-card set measure approximately 2 5/8" by 3 3/4". The 1952 Topps set is Topps' first truly major set. Card numbers 1 to 80 were issued with red or black backs, both of which are less plentiful than card numbers 81 to 250. In fact, the first series is considered the most difficult with respect to finding perfect condition cards. Card number 48 (Joe Page) and number 49 (Johnny Sain) can be found with each other's write-up on their back. However, many dealers today believe that all cards numbered 1-250 are valued the same. Card numbers 251 to 310 are somewhat scarce and numbers 311 to 407 are quite scarce. Cards 281-300 were single printed compared to the other cards in the next to last series. Cards 311-313 were double printed on the last high number printing sheet. The key card in the set is obviously Mickey Mantle, number 311, Mickey's first of many Topps cards. A really obscure variation on cards from 311 through 313 is that they exist with the stitching on the number circle in the back either clockwise or counter clockwise. There is no price differential for either variation. Card #307, Frank Campos has been discovered to have a black star next to the words "Topps Baseball" on the back. This card is very scarce but since it is rarely traded in the secondary market -- no value can be established at this time. Many collectors are not aware of this variation. In the early 1980's, Topps issued a standard-size reprint set of the 52 Topps set. These cards were issued only as a factory set and have a current market value of between two and three hundred dollars. Five people portrayed in the regular set: Billy Loes (#20), Dom DiMaggio (#22), Saul Rogovin (#159), Solly Hemus (#196) and Tommy Holmes (#289) are not in the reprint set. Although rarely seen, there exist salesman sample panels of three cards containing the fronts of regular cards with ad information on the back. Two such panels seen are Bob Mahoney/Robin Roberts/Sid Hudson and Wally Westlake/Dizzy Trout/Irv Noren. The cards were issued in one-card penny packs and six-card nickle packs. The key Rookie Cards in this set are Billy Martin, Eddie Mathews (the last card in the set), and Hoyt Wilhelm.

	NRMT	VG-E	GOOD
COMPLETE SET (407)	65000.00	29200.00	8100.00
COMMON CARD (1-80)	35.00	16.00	4.40
COMMON CARD (81-250)	35.00	16.00	4.40
COMMON CARD (251-310)	50.00	22.00	6.25
COMMON CARD (311-407)	250.00	110.00	31.00
*RED/BLACK BACKS 1-80 SAME VALUE			
WRAPPER (1-cent)	250.00	110.00	31.00
WRAPPER (5-cent)	100.00	45.00	12.50

	NRMT	VG-E	GOOD
☐ 1 Andy Pafko	1200.00	120.00	40.00
☐ 2 Pete Runnels	90.00	40.00	11.00
☐ 3 Hank Thompson	40.00	18.00	5.00
☐ 4 Don Lenhardt	35.00	16.00	4.40
☐ 5 Larry Jansen	35.00	16.00	4.40
☐ 6 Grady Hatton	35.00	16.00	4.40
☐ 7 Wayne Terwilliger	40.00	18.00	5.00
☐ 8 Fred Marsh	35.00	16.00	4.40
☐ 9 Robert Hogue	35.00	16.00	4.40
☐ 10 Al Rosen	40.00	18.00	5.00
☐ 11 Phil Rizzuto	200.00	90.00	25.00
☐ 12 Monty Basgall	35.00	16.00	4.40
☐ 13 Johnny Wyrostek	35.00	16.00	4.40
☐ 14 Bob Elliott	40.00	18.00	5.00
☐ 15 Johnny Pesky	35.00	16.00	4.40
☐ 16 Gene Hermanski	35.00	16.00	4.40
☐ 17 Jim Hegan	40.00	18.00	5.00
☐ 18 Merrill Combs	35.00	16.00	4.40
☐ 19 Johnny Bucha	35.00	16.00	4.40
☐ 20 Billy Loes	100.00	45.00	12.50
☐ 21 Ferris Fain	40.00	18.00	5.00
☐ 22 Dom DiMaggio	90.00	40.00	11.00
☐ 23 Billy Goodman	40.00	18.00	5.00
☐ 24 Luke Easter	35.00	16.00	4.40
☐ 25 Johnny Groth	35.00	16.00	4.40
☐ 26 Monte Irvin	90.00	40.00	11.00
☐ 27 Sam Jethroe	50.00	22.00	6.25
☐ 28 Jerry Priddy	35.00	16.00	4.40
☐ 29 Ted Kluszewski	90.00	40.00	11.00
☐ 30 Mel Parnell	40.00	18.00	5.00
☐ 31 Gus Zernial	80.00	36.00	10.00
☐ 32 Eddie Robinson	35.00	16.00	4.40
☐ 33 Warren Spahn	200.00	90.00	25.00
☐ 34 Elmer Valo	35.00	16.00	4.40
☐ 35 Hank Sauer	40.00	18.00	5.00
☐ 36 Gil Hodges	160.00	70.00	20.00
☐ 37 Duke Snider	250.00	110.00	31.00
☐ 38 Wally Westlake	35.00	16.00	4.40
☐ 39 Dizzy Trout	40.00	18.00	5.00
☐ 40 Irv Noren	40.00	18.00	5.00
☐ 41 Bob Wellman	35.00	16.00	4.40
☐ 42 Lou Kretlow	35.00	16.00	4.40
☐ 43 Ray Scarborough	35.00	16.00	4.40
☐ 44 Con Dempsey	35.00	16.00	4.40
☐ 45 Eddie Joost	35.00	16.00	4.40
☐ 46 Gordon Goldsberry	35.00	16.00	4.40
☐ 47 Willie Jones	40.00	18.00	5.00
☐ 48A Joe Page COR	75.00	34.00	9.50
☐ 48B Joe Page ERR (Bio for Sain)	275.00	125.00	34.00
☐ 49A Johnny Sain COR	75.00	34.00	9.50
☐ 49B Johnny Sain ERR (Bio for Page)	275.00	125.00	34.00
☐ 50 Marv Rickert	35.00	16.00	4.40
☐ 51 Jim Russell	35.00	16.00	4.40
☐ 52 Don Mueller	40.00	18.00	5.00
☐ 53 Chris Van Cuyk	35.00	16.00	4.40
☐ 54 Leo Kiely	35.00	16.00	4.40
☐ 55 Ray Boone	35.00	16.00	4.40
☐ 56 Tommy Glaviano	35.00	16.00	4.40
☐ 57 Ed Lopat	90.00	40.00	11.00
☐ 58 Bob Mahoney	35.00	16.00	4.40
☐ 59 Robin Roberts	150.00	70.00	19.00
☐ 60 Sid Hudson	35.00	16.00	4.40
☐ 61 Tookie Gilbert	35.00	16.00	4.40
☐ 62 Chuck Stobbs	35.00	16.00	4.40
☐ 63 Howie Pollet	35.00	16.00	4.40
☐ 64 Roy Sievers	35.00	16.00	4.40
☐ 65 Enos Slaughter	150.00	70.00	19.00
☐ 66 Preacher Roe	90.00	40.00	11.00
☐ 67 Allie Reynolds	90.00	40.00	11.00
☐ 68 Cliff Chambers	35.00	16.00	4.40
☐ 69 Virgil Stallcup	35.00	16.00	4.40
☐ 70 Al Zarilla	35.00	16.00	4.40
☐ 71 Tom Upton	35.00	16.00	4.40
☐ 72 Karl Olson	35.00	16.00	4.40
☐ 73 Bill Werle	35.00	16.00	4.40
☐ 74 Andy Hansen	35.00	16.00	4.40
☐ 75 Wes Westrum	40.00	18.00	5.00
☐ 76 Eddie Stanky	35.00	16.00	4.40
☐ 77 Bob Kennedy	40.00	18.00	5.00
☐ 78 Ellis Kinder	35.00	16.00	4.40
☐ 79 Gerry Staley	35.00	16.00	4.40
☐ 80 Herman Wehmeier	35.00	16.00	4.40
☐ 81 Vernon Law	40.00	18.00	5.00
☐ 82 Duane Pillette	35.00	16.00	4.40
☐ 83 Billy Johnson	35.00	16.00	4.40
☐ 84 Vern Stephens	40.00	18.00	5.00
☐ 85 Bob Kuzava	40.00	18.00	5.00
☐ 86 Ted Gray	35.00	16.00	4.40
☐ 87 Dale Coogan	35.00	16.00	4.40
☐ 88 Bob Feller	200.00	90.00	25.00
☐ 89 Johnny Lipon	35.00	16.00	4.40
☐ 90 Mickey Grasso	35.00	16.00	4.40
☐ 91 Red Schoendienst	75.00	34.00	9.50
☐ 92 Dale Mitchell	40.00	18.00	5.00
☐ 93 Al Sima	35.00	16.00	4.40
☐ 94 Sam Mele	35.00	16.00	4.40
☐ 95 Ken Holcombe	35.00	16.00	4.40
☐ 96 Willard Marshall	35.00	16.00	4.40
☐ 97 Earl Torgeson	35.00	16.00	4.40
☐ 98 Billy Pierce	40.00	18.00	5.00
☐ 99 Gene Woodling	50.00	22.00	6.25
☐ 100 Del Rice	35.00	16.00	4.40
☐ 101 Max Lanier	35.00	16.00	4.40
☐ 102 Bill Kennedy	35.00	16.00	4.40
☐ 103 Cliff Mapes	35.00	16.00	4.40
☐ 104 Don Kolloway	35.00	16.00	4.40
☐ 105 Johnny Pramesa	35.00	16.00	4.40
☐ 106 Mickey Vernon	40.00	18.00	5.00
☐ 107 Connie Ryan	35.00	16.00	4.40
☐ 108 Jim Konstanty	50.00	22.00	6.25
☐ 109 Ted Wilks	35.00	16.00	4.40
☐ 110 Dutch Leonard	35.00	16.00	4.40
☐ 111 Peanuts Lowrey	35.00	16.00	4.40
☐ 112 Hank Majeski	35.00	16.00	4.40
☐ 113 Dick Sisler	40.00	18.00	5.00
☐ 114 Willard Ramsdell	35.00	16.00	4.40
☐ 115 Red Munger	35.00	16.00	4.40
☐ 116 Carl Scheib	35.00	16.00	4.40
☐ 117 Sherm Lollar	40.00	18.00	5.00
☐ 118 Ken Raffensberger	35.00	16.00	4.40
☐ 119 Mickey McDermott	35.00	16.00	4.40
☐ 120 Bob Chakales	35.00	16.00	4.40
☐ 121 Gus Niarhos	35.00	16.00	4.40
☐ 122 Jackie Jensen	70.00	32.00	8.75
☐ 123 Eddie Yost	40.00	18.00	5.00
☐ 124 Monte Kennedy	35.00	16.00	4.40
☐ 125 Bill Rigney	35.00	16.00	4.40
☐ 126 Fred Hutchinson	40.00	18.00	5.00
☐ 127 Paul Minner	35.00	16.00	4.40
☐ 128 Don Bollweg	35.00	16.00	4.40
☐ 129 Johnny Mize	90.00	40.00	11.00
☐ 130 Sheldon Jones	35.00	16.00	4.40
☐ 131 Morrie Martin	35.00	16.00	4.40
☐ 132 Clyde Kluttz	35.00	16.00	4.40
☐ 133 Al Widmar	35.00	16.00	4.40
☐ 134 Joe Tipton	35.00	16.00	4.40
☐ 135 Dixie Howell	35.00	16.00	4.40
☐ 136 Johnny Schmitz	35.00	16.00	4.40
☐ 137 Roy McMillan	40.00	18.00	5.00
☐ 138 Bill MacDonald	35.00	16.00	4.40
☐ 139 Ken Wood	35.00	16.00	4.40
☐ 140 Johnny Antonelli	40.00	18.00	5.00
☐ 141 Clint Hartung	35.00	16.00	4.40
☐ 142 Harry Perkowski	35.00	16.00	4.40
☐ 143 Les Moss	35.00	16.00	4.40
☐ 144 Ed Blake	35.00	16.00	4.40
☐ 145 Joe Haynes	35.00	16.00	4.40
☐ 146 Frank House	35.00	16.00	4.40
☐ 147 Bob Young	35.00	16.00	4.40
☐ 148 Johnny Klippstein	35.00	16.00	4.40
☐ 149 Dick Kryhoski	35.00	16.00	4.40
☐ 150 Ted Beard	35.00	16.00	4.40
☐ 151 Wally Post	40.00	18.00	5.00
☐ 152 Al Evans	35.00	16.00	4.40
☐ 153 Bob Rush	35.00	16.00	4.40
☐ 154 Joe Muir	35.00	16.00	4.40
☐ 155 Frank Overmire	35.00	16.00	4.40
☐ 156 Frank Hiller	35.00	16.00	4.40
☐ 157 Bob Usher	35.00	16.00	4.40
☐ 158 Eddie Waitkus	35.00	16.00	4.40
☐ 159 Saul Rogovin	35.00	16.00	4.40
☐ 160 Owen Friend	35.00	16.00	4.40
☐ 161 Bud Byerly	35.00	16.00	4.40
☐ 162 Del Crandall	40.00	18.00	5.00
☐ 163 Stan Rojek	35.00	16.00	4.40
☐ 164 Walt Dubiel	35.00	16.00	4.40
☐ 165 Eddie Kazak	35.00	16.00	4.40
☐ 166 Paul LaPalme	35.00	16.00	4.40
☐ 167 Bill Howerton	35.00	16.00	4.40
☐ 168 Charlie Silvera	50.00	22.00	6.25
☐ 169 Howie Judson	35.00	16.00	4.40
☐ 170 Gus Bell	40.00	18.00	5.00
☐ 171 Ed Erautt	35.00	16.00	4.40
☐ 172 Eddie Miksis	35.00	16.00	4.40
☐ 173 Roy Smalley	35.00	16.00	4.40
☐ 174 Clarence Marshall	35.00	16.00	4.40
☐ 175 Billy Martin	300.00	135.00	38.00
☐ 176 Hank Edwards	35.00	16.00	4.40
☐ 177 Bill Wight	35.00	16.00	4.40
☐ 178 Cass Michaels	35.00	16.00	4.40
☐ 179 Frank Smith	35.00	16.00	4.40
☐ 180 Charlie Maxwell	40.00	18.00	5.00
☐ 181 Bob Swift	35.00	16.00	4.40
☐ 182 Billy Hitchcock	35.00	16.00	4.40
☐ 183 Erv Dusak	35.00	16.00	4.40
☐ 184 Bob Ramazzotti	35.00	16.00	4.40
☐ 185 Bill Nicholson	40.00	18.00	5.00
☐ 186 Walt Masterson	35.00	16.00	4.40
☐ 187 Bob Miller	35.00	16.00	4.40
☐ 188 Clarence Podbielan	35.00	16.00	4.40
☐ 189 Pete Reiser	40.00	18.00	5.00
☐ 190 Don Johnson	35.00	16.00	4.40
☐ 191 Yogi Berra	350.00	160.00	45.00
☐ 192 Myron Ginsberg	35.00	16.00	4.40
☐ 193 Harry Simpson	40.00	18.00	5.00
☐ 194 Joe Hatton	35.00	16.00	4.40
☐ 195 Minnie Minoso	150.00	70.00	19.00
☐ 196 Solly Hemus	40.00	18.00	5.00
☐ 197 George Strickland	35.00	16.00	4.40
☐ 198 Phil Haugstad	35.00	16.00	4.40
☐ 199 George Zuverink	35.00	16.00	4.40
☐ 200 Ralph Houk	70.00	32.00	8.75
☐ 201 Alex Kellner	35.00	16.00	4.40
☐ 202 Joe Collins	50.00	22.00	6.25
☐ 203 Curt Simmons	50.00	22.00	6.25
☐ 204 Ron Northey	35.00	16.00	4.40
☐ 205 Clyde King	50.00	22.00	6.25
☐ 206 Joe Ostrowski	35.00	16.00	4.40
☐ 207 Mickey Harris	35.00	16.00	4.40
☐ 208 Marlin Stuart	35.00	16.00	4.40
☐ 209 Howie Fox	35.00	16.00	4.40
☐ 210 Dick Fowler	35.00	16.00	4.40
☐ 211 Ray Coleman	35.00	16.00	4.40
☐ 212 Ned Garver	35.00	16.00	4.40
☐ 213 Nippy Jones	35.00	16.00	4.40
☐ 214 Johnny Hopp	40.00	18.00	5.00
☐ 215 Hank Bauer	50.00	22.00	6.25
☐ 216 Richie Ashburn	175.00	80.00	22.00
☐ 217 Snuffy Stirnweiss	40.00	18.00	5.00
☐ 218 Clyde McCullough	35.00	16.00	4.40
☐ 219 Bobby Shantz	50.00	22.00	6.25
☐ 220 Joe Presko	35.00	16.00	4.40
☐ 221 Granny Hamner	35.00	16.00	4.40
☐ 222 Hoot Evers	35.00	16.00	4.40
☐ 223 Del Ennis	40.00	18.00	5.00
☐ 224 Bruce Edwards	35.00	16.00	4.40
☐ 225 Frank Baumholtz	35.00	16.00	4.40
☐ 226 Dave Philley	35.00	16.00	4.40
☐ 227 Joe Garagiola	80.00	36.00	10.00
☐ 228 Al Brazle	35.00	16.00	4.40
☐ 229 Gene Bearden UER (Misspelled Beardon)	35.00	16.00	4.40
☐ 230 Matt Batts	35.00	16.00	4.40
☐ 231 Sam Zoldak	35.00	16.00	4.40
☐ 232 Billy Cox	40.00	18.00	5.00
☐ 233 Bob Friend	50.00	22.00	6.25
☐ 234 Steve Souchock	35.00	16.00	4.40
☐ 235 Walt Dropo	35.00	16.00	4.40
☐ 236 Ed Fitzgerald	35.00	16.00	4.40
☐ 237 Jerry Coleman	50.00	22.00	6.25
☐ 238 Art Houtteman	35.00	16.00	4.40
☐ 239 Rocky Bridges	40.00	18.00	5.00
☐ 240 Jack Phillips	35.00	16.00	4.40
☐ 241 Tommy Byrne	35.00	16.00	4.40
☐ 242 Tom Poholsky	35.00	16.00	4.40
☐ 243 Larry Doby	70.00	32.00	8.75
☐ 244 Vic Wertz	40.00	18.00	5.00
☐ 245 Sherry Robertson	35.00	16.00	4.40
☐ 246 George Kell	75.00	34.00	9.50
☐ 247 Randy Gumpert	35.00	16.00	4.40
☐ 248 Frank Shea	35.00	16.00	4.40
☐ 249 Bobby Adams	35.00	16.00	4.40
☐ 250 Carl Erskine	80.00	36.00	10.00
☐ 251 Chico Carrasquel	50.00	22.00	6.25
☐ 252 Vern Bickford	50.00	22.00	6.25
☐ 253 Johnny Berardino	55.00	25.00	7.00
☐ 254 Joe Dobson	50.00	22.00	6.25
☐ 255 Clyde Vollmer	50.00	22.00	6.25
☐ 256 Pete Suder	50.00	22.00	6.25
☐ 257 Bobby Avila	55.00	25.00	7.00
☐ 258 Steve Gromek	50.00	22.00	6.25
☐ 259 Bob Addis	50.00	22.00	6.25
☐ 260 Pete Castiglione	50.00	22.00	6.25
☐ 261 Willie Mays	2500.00	1100.00	300.00
☐ 262 Virgil Trucks	55.00	25.00	7.00
☐ 263 Harry Brecheen	55.00	25.00	7.00
☐ 264 Roy Hartsfield	50.00	22.00	6.25
☐ 265 Chuck Diering	50.00	22.00	6.25
☐ 266 Murry Dickson	50.00	22.00	6.25
☐ 267 Sid Gordon	55.00	25.00	7.00
☐ 268 Bob Lemon	150.00	70.00	19.00
☐ 269 Willard Nixon	50.00	22.00	6.25
☐ 270 Lou Brissie	50.00	22.00	6.25
☐ 271 Jim Delsing	50.00	22.00	6.25
☐ 272 Mike Garcia	55.00	25.00	7.00
☐ 273 Erv Palica	50.00	22.00	6.25
☐ 274 Ralph Branca	100.00	45.00	12.50
☐ 275 Pat Mullin	50.00	22.00	6.25
☐ 276 Jim Wilson	50.00	22.00	6.25
☐ 277 Early Wynn	150.00	70.00	19.00
☐ 278 Allie Clark	50.00	22.00	6.25
☐ 279 Eddie Stewart	50.00	22.00	6.25
☐ 280 Cloyd Boyer	40.00	18.00	5.00
☐ 281 Tommy Brown SP	50.00	22.00	6.25
☐ 282 Birdie Tebbetts SP	55.00	25.00	7.00
☐ 283 Phil Masi SP	50.00	22.00	6.25
☐ 284 Hank Arft SP	50.00	22.00	6.25
☐ 285 Cliff Fannin SP	50.00	22.00	6.25
☐ 286 Joe DeMaestri SP	50.00	22.00	6.25
☐ 287 Steve Bilko SP	50.00	22.00	6.25
☐ 288 Chet Nichols SP	50.00	22.00	6.25
☐ 289 Tommy Holmes SP	55.00	25.00	7.00
☐ 290 Joe Astroth SP	50.00	22.00	6.25
☐ 291 Gil Coan SP	50.00	22.00	6.25
☐ 292 Floyd Baker SP	50.00	22.00	6.25
☐ 293 Sibby Sisti SP	50.00	22.00	6.25
☐ 294 Walker Cooper SP	50.00	22.00	6.25
☐ 295 Phil Cavarretta SP	55.00	25.00	7.00
☐ 296 Red Rolfe MG SP	55.00	25.00	7.00
☐ 297 Andy Seminick SP	50.00	22.00	6.25
☐ 298 Bob Ross SP	50.00	22.00	6.25
☐ 299 Ray Murray SP	50.00	22.00	6.25
☐ 300 Barney McCosky SP	50.00	22.00	6.25
☐ 301 Bob Porterfield	50.00	22.00	6.25
☐ 302 Max Surkont	50.00	22.00	6.25
☐ 303 Harry Dorish	50.00	22.00	6.25
☐ 304 Sam Dente	50.00	22.00	6.25
☐ 305 Paul Richards MG	55.00	25.00	7.00
☐ 306 Lou Sleater	50.00	22.00	6.25
☐ 307 Frank Campos	50.00	22.00	6.25
☐ 308 Luis Aloma	50.00	22.00	6.25
☐ 309 Jim Busby	50.00	22.00	6.25
☐ 310 George Metkovich	55.00	25.00	7.00
☐ 311 Mickey Mantle	24000.00	10800.00	3000.00
☐ 312 Jackie Robinson DP	1400.00	650.00	180.00
☐ 313 Bobby Thomson DP	300.00	135.00	38.00
☐ 314 Roy Campanella	2000.00	900.00	250.00
☐ 315 Leo Durocher MG	375.00	170.00	47.50
☐ 316 Dave Williams	275.00	125.00	34.00
☐ 317 Conrado Marrero	275.00	125.00	34.00
☐ 318 Harold Gregg	250.00	110.00	31.00
☐ 319 Al Walker	250.00	110.00	31.00
☐ 320 John Rutherford	275.00	125.00	34.00
☐ 321 Joe Black	350.00	160.00	45.00
☐ 322 Randy Jackson	250.00	110.00	31.00
☐ 323 Bubba Church	250.00	110.00	31.00
☐ 324 Warren Hacker	250.00	110.00	31.00
☐ 325 Bill Serena	250.00	110.00	31.00
☐ 326 George Shuba	400.00	180.00	50.00
☐ 327 Al Wilson	250.00	110.00	31.00
☐ 328 Bob Borkowski	250.00	110.00	31.00
☐ 329 Ike Delock	250.00	110.00	31.00
☐ 330 Turk Lown	250.00	110.00	31.00
☐ 331 Tom Morgan	250.00	110.00	31.00
☐ 332 Anthony Bartirome	250.00	110.00	31.00
☐ 333 Pee Wee Reese	1400.00	650.00	180.00
☐ 334 Wilmer Mizell	300.00	135.00	38.00
☐ 335 Ted Lepcio	250.00	110.00	31.00
☐ 336 Dave Koslo	250.00	110.00	31.00
☐ 337 Jim Hearn	250.00	110.00	31.00
☐ 338 Sal Yvars	250.00	110.00	31.00
☐ 339 Russ Meyer	250.00	110.00	31.00
☐ 340 Bob Hooper	250.00	110.00	31.00
☐ 341 Hal Jeffcoat	250.00	110.00	31.00
☐ 342 Clem Labine	400.00	180.00	50.00

☐ 343 Dick Gernert	250.00	110.00	31.00
☐ 344 Ewell Blackwell	300.00	135.00	38.00
☐ 345 Sammy White	250.00	110.00	31.00
☐ 346 George Spencer	250.00	110.00	31.00
☐ 347 Joe Adcock	300.00	135.00	38.00
☐ 348 Robert Kelly	250.00	110.00	31.00
☐ 349 Bob Cain	250.00	110.00	31.00
☐ 350 Cal Abrams	250.00	110.00	31.00
☐ 351 Alvin Dark	300.00	135.00	38.00
☐ 352 Karl Drews	250.00	110.00	31.00
☐ 353 Bobby Del Greco	250.00	110.00	31.00
☐ 354 Fred Hatfield	250.00	110.00	31.00
☐ 355 Bobby Morgan	250.00	110.00	31.00
☐ 356 Toby Atwell	250.00	110.00	31.00
☐ 357 Smoky Burgess	300.00	135.00	38.00
☐ 358 John Kucab	250.00	110.00	31.00
☐ 359 Dee Fondy	250.00	110.00	31.00
☐ 360 George Crowe	275.00	125.00	34.00
☐ 361 William Posedel CO	250.00	110.00	31.00
☐ 362 Ken Heintzelman	250.00	110.00	31.00
☐ 363 Dick Rozek	250.00	110.00	31.00
☐ 364 Clyde Sukeforth CO	250.00	110.00	31.00
☐ 365 Cookie Lavagetto CO	375.00	170.00	47.50
☐ 366 Dave Madison	250.00	110.00	31.00
☐ 367 Ben Thorpe	250.00	110.00	31.00
☐ 368 Ed Wright	250.00	110.00	31.00
☐ 369 Dick Groat	350.00	160.00	45.00
☐ 370 Billy Hoeft	275.00	125.00	34.00
☐ 371 Bobby Hofman	250.00	110.00	31.00
☐ 372 Gil McDougald	375.00	170.00	47.50
☐ 373 Jim Turner CO	400.00	180.00	50.00
☐ 374 John Benton	250.00	110.00	31.00
☐ 375 John Merson	250.00	110.00	31.00
☐ 376 Faye Throneberry	250.00	110.00	31.00
☐ 377 Chuck Dressen MG	375.00	170.00	47.50
☐ 378 Leroy Fusselman	250.00	110.00	31.00
☐ 379 Joe Rossi	250.00	110.00	31.00
☐ 380 Clem Koshorek	250.00	110.00	31.00
☐ 381 Milton Stock CO	250.00	110.00	31.00
☐ 382 Sam Jones	350.00	160.00	45.00
☐ 383 Del Wilber	250.00	110.00	31.00
☐ 384 Frank Crosetti CO	400.00	180.00	50.00
☐ 385 Herman Franks CO	250.00	110.00	31.00
☐ 386 John Yuhas	250.00	110.00	31.00
☐ 387 Billy Meyer MG	250.00	110.00	31.00
☐ 388 Bob Chipman	250.00	110.00	31.00
☐ 389 Ben Wade	250.00	110.00	31.00
☐ 390 Glenn Nelson	250.00	110.00	31.00
☐ 391 Ben Chapman UER CO (Photo actually Sam Chapman)	250.00	110.00	31.00
☐ 392 Hoyt Wilhelm	700.00	325.00	90.00
☐ 393 Ebba St.Claire	250.00	110.00	31.00
☐ 394 Billy Herman CO	400.00	180.00	50.00
☐ 395 Jake Pitler CO	375.00	170.00	47.50
☐ 396 Dick Williams	400.00	180.00	50.00
☐ 397 Forrest Main	250.00	110.00	31.00
☐ 398 Hal Rice	250.00	110.00	31.00
☐ 399 Jim Fridley	250.00	110.00	31.00
☐ 400 Bill Dickey CO	800.00	350.00	100.00
☐ 401 Bob Schultz	250.00	110.00	31.00
☐ 402 Earl Harrist	250.00	110.00	31.00
☐ 403 Bill Miller	250.00	110.00	31.00
☐ 404 Dick Brodowski	250.00	110.00	31.00
☐ 405 Eddie Pellagrini	250.00	110.00	31.00
☐ 406 Joe Nuxhall	350.00	160.00	45.00
☐ 407 Eddie Mathews	3400.00	850.00	350.00

1953 Topps

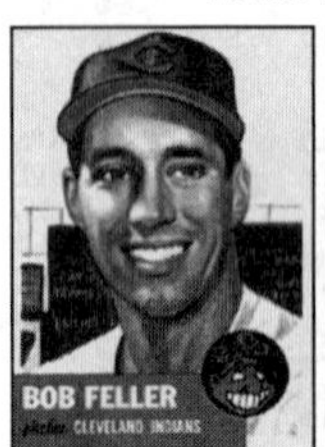

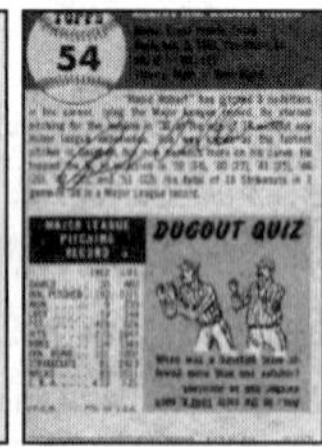

The cards in this 274-card set measure 2 5/8" by 3 3/4". Although the last card is numbered 280, there are only 274 cards in the set since numbers 253, 261, 267, 268, 271, and 275 were never issued. The 1953 Topps series contains line drawings of players in full color. The name and team panel at the card base is easily damaged, making it very difficult to complete a mint set. The high number series, 221 to 280, was produced in shorter supply late in the year and hence is more difficult to complete than the lower numbers. The key cards in the set are Mickey Mantle (82) and Willie Mays (244). The key Rookie Cards in this set are Roy Face, Jim Gilliam, and Johnny Podres, all from the last series. There are a number of double-printed cards (actually not double but 50 percent more of each of these numbers were printed compared to the other cards in the series) indicated by DP in the checklist below. There were five players (10 Smoky Burgess, 44 Ellis Kinder, 61 Early Wynn, 72 Fred Hutchinson, and 81 Joe Black) held out of the first run of 1-85 (but printed in with numbers 86-165), who are each marked by SP in the checklist below. In addition, there are five numbers which were printed with the more plentiful series 166-220; these cards (94, 107, 131, 145, and 156) are also indicated by DP in the checklist below. The cards were issued in one-card penny packs or six-card nickle packs. There were some three-card advertising panels produced by Topps; the players include Johnny Mize/Clem Koshorek/Toby Atwell and Mickey Mantle/Johnny Wyrostek/Sal Yvars. When cut apart, these advertising cards are distinguished by the non-standard card back, i.e., part of an advertisement for the 1953 Topps set instead of the typical statistics and biographical information about the player pictured.

	NRMT	VG-E	GOOD
COMPLETE SET (274)	13500.00	6100.00	1700.00
COMMON CARD (1-165)	30.00	13.50	3.70
COMMON CARD (166-220)	25.00	11.00	3.10
COMMON CARD (221-280)	100.00	45.00	12.50
WRAPPER (1-cent, dated)	200.00	90.00	25.00
WRAPPER (1-cent, undated)	300.00	135.00	38.00
WRAPPER (5-cent, dated)	400.00	180.00	50.00
WRAPPER (5-cent, undated)	350.00	160.00	45.00
☐ 1 Jackie Robinson DP	450.00	125.00	45.00
☐ 2 Luke Easter DP	20.00	9.00	2.50
☐ 3 George Crowe	30.00	13.50	3.70
☐ 4 Ben Wade	30.00	13.50	3.70
☐ 5 Joe Dobson	30.00	13.50	3.70
☐ 6 Sam Jones	35.00	16.00	4.40
☐ 7 Bob Borkowski DP	15.00	6.75	1.85
☐ 8 Clem Koshorek DP	15.00	6.75	1.85
☐ 9 Joe Collins	35.00	16.00	4.40
☐ 10 Smoky Burgess SP	70.00	32.00	8.75
☐ 11 Sal Yvars	30.00	13.50	3.70
☐ 12 Howie Judson DP	15.00	6.75	1.85
☐ 13 Conrado Marrero DP	15.00	6.75	1.85
☐ 14 Clem Labine DP	20.00	9.00	2.50
☐ 15 Bobo Newsom DP	20.00	9.00	2.50
☐ 16 Peanuts Lowrey DP	15.00	6.75	1.85
☐ 17 Billy Hitchcock	30.00	13.50	3.70
☐ 18 Ted Lepcio DP	15.00	6.75	1.85
☐ 19 Mel Parnell DP	20.00	9.00	2.50
☐ 20 Hank Thompson	35.00	16.00	4.40
☐ 21 Billy Johnson	30.00	13.50	3.70
☐ 22 Howie Fox	30.00	13.50	3.70
☐ 23 Toby Atwell DP	15.00	6.75	1.85
☐ 24 Ferris Fain	35.00	16.00	4.40
☐ 25 Ray Boone	35.00	16.00	4.40
☐ 26 Dale Mitchell DP	20.00	9.00	2.50
☐ 27 Roy Campanella DP	175.00	80.00	22.00
☐ 28 Eddie Pellagrini	30.00	13.50	3.70
☐ 29 Hal Jeffcoat	30.00	13.50	3.70
☐ 30 Willard Nixon	30.00	13.50	3.70
☐ 31 Ewell Blackwell	50.00	22.00	6.25
☐ 32 Clyde Vollmer	30.00	13.50	3.70
☐ 33 Bob Kennedy DP	20.00	9.00	2.50
☐ 34 George Shuba	35.00	16.00	4.40
☐ 35 Irv Noren DP	20.00	9.00	2.50
☐ 36 Johnny Groth DP	15.00	6.75	1.85
☐ 37 Eddie Mathews DP	100.00	45.00	12.50
☐ 38 Jim Hearn DP	15.00	6.75	1.85
☐ 39 Eddie Miksis	30.00	13.50	3.70
☐ 40 John Lipon	30.00	13.50	3.70
☐ 41 Enos Slaughter	80.00	36.00	10.00
☐ 42 Gus Zernial DP	20.00	9.00	2.50
☐ 43 Gil McDougald	50.00	22.00	6.25
☐ 44 Ellis Kinder SP	35.00	16.00	4.40
☐ 45 Grady Hatton DP	15.00	6.75	1.85
☐ 46 Johnny Klippstein DP	15.00	6.75	1.85
☐ 47 Bubba Church DP	15.00	6.75	1.85
☐ 48 Bob Del Greco DP	15.00	6.75	1.85
☐ 49 Faye Throneberry DP	15.00	6.75	1.85
☐ 50 Chuck Dressen MG DP	22.50	10.00	2.80
☐ 51 Frank Campos DP	15.00	6.75	1.85
☐ 52 Ted Gray DP	15.00	6.75	1.85
☐ 53 Sherm Lollar DP	20.00	9.00	2.50
☐ 54 Bob Feller DP	100.00	45.00	12.50
☐ 55 Maurice McDermott DP	15.00	6.75	1.85
☐ 56 Gerry Staley DP	15.00	6.75	1.85
☐ 57 Carl Scheib	30.00	13.50	3.70
☐ 58 George Metkovich	30.00	13.50	3.70
☐ 59 Karl Drews DP	15.00	6.75	1.85
☐ 60 Cloyd Boyer DP	15.00	6.75	1.85
☐ 61 Early Wynn SP	90.00	40.00	11.00
☐ 62 Monte Irvin DP	35.00	16.00	4.40
☐ 63 Gus Niarhos DP	15.00	6.75	1.85
☐ 64 Dave Philley	30.00	13.50	3.70
☐ 65 Earl Harrist	30.00	13.50	3.70
☐ 66 Minnie Minoso	50.00	22.00	6.25
☐ 67 Roy Sievers DP	20.00	9.00	2.50
☐ 68 Del Rice	30.00	13.50	3.70
☐ 69 Dick Brodowski	30.00	13.50	3.70
☐ 70 Ed Yuhas	30.00	13.50	3.70
☐ 71 Tony Bartirome	30.00	13.50	3.70
☐ 72 Fred Hutchinson MG SP	50.00	22.00	6.25
☐ 73 Eddie Robinson	30.00	13.50	3.70
☐ 74 Joe Rossi	30.00	13.50	3.70
☐ 75 Mike Garcia	35.00	16.00	4.40
☐ 76 Pee Wee Reese	150.00	70.00	19.00
☐ 77 Johnny Mize DP	50.00	22.00	6.25
☐ 78 Red Schoendienst	60.00	27.00	7.50
☐ 79 Johnny Wyrostek	30.00	13.50	3.70
☐ 80 Jim Hegan	35.00	16.00	4.40
☐ 81 Joe Black SP	70.00	32.00	8.75
☐ 82 Mickey Mantle	3000.00	1350.00	375.00
☐ 83 Howie Pollet	30.00	13.50	3.70
☐ 84 Bob Hooper DP	15.00	6.75	1.85
☐ 85 Bobby Morgan DP	15.00	6.75	1.85
☐ 86 Billy Martin	125.00	55.00	15.50
☐ 87 Ed Lopat	50.00	22.00	6.25
☐ 88 Willie Jones DP	15.00	6.75	1.85
☐ 89 Chuck Stobbs DP	15.00	6.75	1.85
☐ 90 Hank Edwards DP	15.00	6.75	1.85
☐ 91 Ebba St.Claire DP	15.00	6.75	1.85
☐ 92 Paul Minner DP	15.00	6.75	1.85
☐ 93 Hal Rice DP	15.00	6.75	1.85
☐ 94 Bill Kennedy DP	15.00	6.75	1.85
☐ 95 Willard Marshall DP	15.00	6.75	1.85
☐ 96 Virgil Trucks	35.00	16.00	4.40
☐ 97 Don Kolloway DP	15.00	6.75	1.85
☐ 98 Cal Abrams DP	15.00	6.75	1.85
☐ 99 Dave Madison	30.00	13.50	3.70
☐ 100 Bill Miller	30.00	13.50	3.70
☐ 101 Ted Wilks	30.00	13.50	3.70
☐ 102 Connie Ryan DP	15.00	6.75	1.85
☐ 103 Joe Astroth DP	15.00	6.75	1.85
☐ 104 Yogi Berra	200.00	90.00	25.00
☐ 105 Joe Nuxhall DP	20.00	9.00	2.50
☐ 106 Johnny Antonelli	35.00	16.00	4.40
☐ 107 Danny O'Connell DP	15.00	6.75	1.85
☐ 108 Bob Porterfield DP	15.00	6.75	1.85
☐ 109 Alvin Dark	35.00	16.00	4.40
☐ 110 Herman Wehmeier DP	15.00	6.75	1.85
☐ 111 Hank Sauer DP	20.00	9.00	2.50
☐ 112 Ned Garver DP	15.00	6.75	1.85
☐ 113 Jerry Priddy	30.00	13.50	3.70
☐ 114 Phil Rizzuto	150.00	70.00	19.00
☐ 115 George Spencer	30.00	13.50	3.70
☐ 116 Frank Smith DP	15.00	6.75	1.85
☐ 117 Sid Gordon DP	15.00	6.75	1.85
☐ 118 Gus Bell DP	20.00	9.00	2.50
☐ 119 Johnny Sain SP	50.00	22.00	6.25
☐ 120 Davey Williams	35.00	16.00	4.40
☐ 121 Walt Dropo	35.00	16.00	4.40
☐ 122 Elmer Valo	30.00	13.50	3.70
☐ 123 Tommy Byrne DP	15.00	6.75	1.85
☐ 124 Sibby Sisti DP	15.00	6.75	1.85
☐ 125 Dick Williams DP	22.50	10.00	2.80
☐ 126 Bill Connelly DP	15.00	6.75	1.85
☐ 127 Clint Courtney DP	15.00	6.75	1.85
☐ 128 Wilmer Mizell DP (Inconsistent design, logo on front with black birds)	20.00	9.00	2.50
☐ 129 Keith Thomas	30.00	13.50	3.70
☐ 130 Turk Lown DP	15.00	6.75	1.85
☐ 131 Harry Byrd DP	15.00	6.75	1.85
☐ 132 Tom Morgan	30.00	13.50	3.70
☐ 133 Gil Coan	30.00	13.50	3.70
☐ 134 Rube Walker	35.00	16.00	4.40
☐ 135 Al Rosen DP	25.00	11.00	3.10
☐ 136 Ken Heintzelman DP	15.00	6.75	1.85
☐ 137 John Rutherford DP	15.00	6.75	1.85
☐ 138 George Kell	60.00	27.00	7.50
☐ 139 Sammy White	30.00	13.50	3.70
☐ 140 Tommy Glaviano	30.00	13.50	3.70
☐ 141 Allie Reynolds DP	25.00	11.00	3.10
☐ 142 Vic Wertz	35.00	16.00	4.40
☐ 143 Billy Pierce !	50.00	22.00	6.25
☐ 144 Bob Schultz DP	15.00	6.75	1.85
☐ 145 Harry Dorish DP	15.00	6.75	1.85
☐ 146 Granny Hamner	30.00	13.50	3.70
☐ 147 Warren Spahn	150.00	70.00	19.00
☐ 148 Mickey Grasso	30.00	13.50	3.70
☐ 149 Dom DiMaggio DP	35.00	16.00	4.40
☐ 150 Harry Simpson DP	15.00	6.75	1.85
☐ 151 Hoyt Wilhelm	80.00	36.00	10.00
☐ 152 Bob Adams DP	15.00	6.75	1.85
☐ 153 Andy Seminick DP	15.00	6.75	1.85
☐ 154 Dick Groat	35.00	16.00	4.40
☐ 155 Dutch Leonard	30.00	13.50	3.70
☐ 156 Jim Rivera DP	20.00	9.00	2.50
☐ 157 Bob Addis DP	15.00	6.75	1.85
☐ 158 Johnny Logan	35.00	16.00	4.40
☐ 159 Wayne Terwilliger DP	15.00	6.75	1.85
☐ 160 Bob Young	30.00	13.50	3.70
☐ 161 Vern Bickford DP	15.00	6.75	1.85
☐ 162 Ted Kluszewski	50.00	22.00	6.25
☐ 163 Fred Hatfield DP	15.00	6.75	1.85
☐ 164 Frank Shea DP	15.00	6.75	1.85
☐ 165 Billy Hoeft	30.00	13.50	3.70
☐ 166 Billy Hunter	25.00	11.00	3.10
☐ 167 Art Schult	25.00	11.00	3.10
☐ 168 Willard Schmidt	25.00	11.00	3.10
☐ 169 Dizzy Trout	30.00	13.50	3.70
☐ 170 Bill Werle	25.00	11.00	3.10
☐ 171 Bill Glynn	25.00	11.00	3.10
☐ 172 Rip Repulski	25.00	11.00	3.10
☐ 173 Preston Ward	25.00	11.00	3.10
☐ 174 Billy Loes	40.00	18.00	5.00
☐ 175 Ron Kline	25.00	11.00	3.10
☐ 176 Don Hoak	40.00	18.00	5.00
☐ 177 Jim Dyck	25.00	11.00	3.10
☐ 178 Jim Waugh	25.00	11.00	3.10
☐ 179 Gene Hermanski	25.00	11.00	3.10
☐ 180 Virgil Stallcup	25.00	11.00	3.10
☐ 181 Al Zarilla	25.00	11.00	3.10
☐ 182 Bobby Hofman	25.00	11.00	3.10
☐ 183 Stu Miller	30.00	13.50	3.70
☐ 184 Hal Brown	25.00	11.00	3.10
☐ 185 Jim Pendleton	25.00	11.00	3.10
☐ 186 Charlie Bishop	25.00	11.00	3.10
☐ 187 Jim Fridley	25.00	11.00	3.10
☐ 188 Andy Carey	40.00	18.00	5.00
☐ 189 Ray Jablonski	25.00	11.00	3.10
☐ 190 Dixie Walker CO	30.00	13.50	3.70
☐ 191 Ralph Kiner	80.00	36.00	10.00
☐ 192 Wally Westlake	25.00	11.00	3.10
☐ 193 Mike Clark	25.00	11.00	3.10
☐ 194 Eddie Kazak	25.00	11.00	3.10
☐ 195 Ed McGhee	25.00	11.00	3.10
☐ 196 Bob Keegan	25.00	11.00	3.10
☐ 197 Del Crandall	30.00	13.50	3.70
☐ 198 Forrest Main	25.00	11.00	3.10
☐ 199 Marion Fricano	25.00	11.00	3.10
☐ 200 Gordon Goldsberry	25.00	11.00	3.10
☐ 201 Paul LaPalme	25.00	11.00	3.10
☐ 202 Carl Sawatski	25.00	11.00	3.10
☐ 203 Cliff Fannin	25.00	11.00	3.10
☐ 204 Dick Bokelman	25.00	11.00	3.10
☐ 205 Vern Benson	25.00	11.00	3.10
☐ 206 Ed Bailey	25.00	11.00	3.10
☐ 207 Whitey Ford	150.00	70.00	19.00
☐ 208 Jim Wilson	25.00	11.00	3.10
☐ 209 Jim Greengrass	25.00	11.00	3.10
☐ 210 Bob Cerv	40.00	18.00	5.00
☐ 211 J.W. Porter	25.00	11.00	3.10
☐ 212 Jack Dittmer	25.00	11.00	3.10
☐ 213 Ray Scarborough	25.00	11.00	3.10
☐ 214 Bill Bruton	30.00	13.50	3.70
☐ 215 Gene Conley	30.00	13.50	3.70
☐ 216 Jim Hughes	25.00	11.00	3.10
☐ 217 Murray Wall	25.00	11.00	3.10
☐ 218 Les Fusselman	25.00	11.00	3.10
☐ 219 Pete Runnels UER (Photo actually Don Johnson)	30.00	13.50	3.70
☐ 220 Satchel Paige UER (Misspelled Satchell on card front)	450.00	200.00	55.00
☐ 221 Bob Milliken	100.00	45.00	12.50
☐ 222 Vic Janowicz DP	60.00	27.00	7.50
☐ 223 Johnny O'Brien DP	60.00	27.00	7.50
☐ 224 Lou Sleater DP	50.00	22.00	6.25
☐ 225 Bobby Shantz	110.00	50.00	14.00
☐ 226 Ed Erautt	100.00	45.00	12.50
☐ 227 Morrie Martin	100.00	45.00	12.50
☐ 228 Hal Newhouser	150.00	70.00	19.00
☐ 229 Rocky Krsnich	100.00	45.00	12.50
☐ 230 Johnny Lindell DP	50.00	22.00	6.25
☐ 231 Solly Hemus DP	50.00	22.00	6.25
☐ 232 Dick Kokos	100.00	45.00	12.50
☐ 233 Al Aber	100.00	45.00	12.50
☐ 234 Ray Murray DP	50.00	22.00	6.25
☐ 235 John Hetki DP	50.00	22.00	6.25
☐ 236 Harry Perkowski DP	50.00	22.00	6.25
☐ 237 Bud Podbielan DP	50.00	22.00	6.25
☐ 238 Cal Hogue DP	50.00	22.00	6.25
☐ 239 Jim Delsing	100.00	45.00	12.50
☐ 240 Fred Marsh	100.00	45.00	12.50
☐ 241 Al Sima DP	50.00	22.00	6.25
☐ 242 Charlie Silvera	110.00	50.00	14.00
☐ 243 Carlos Bernier DP	50.00	22.00	6.25
☐ 244 Willie Mays	2700.00	1200.00	350.00
☐ 245 Bill Norman CO	100.00	45.00	12.50
☐ 246 Roy Face DP	80.00	36.00	10.00
☐ 247 Mike Sandlock DP	50.00	22.00	6.25
☐ 248 Gene Stephens DP	50.00	22.00	6.25
☐ 249 Eddie O'Brien	100.00	45.00	12.50
☐ 250 Bob Wilson	100.00	45.00	12.50
☐ 251 Sid Hudson	100.00	45.00	12.50
☐ 252 Hank Foiles	100.00	45.00	12.50
☐ 253 Does not exist			
☐ 254 Preacher Roe DP	80.00	36.00	10.00
☐ 255 Dixie Howell	100.00	45.00	12.50
☐ 256 Les Peden	100.00	45.00	12.50
☐ 257 Bob Boyd	100.00	45.00	12.50
☐ 258 Jim Gilliam	300.00	135.00	38.00
☐ 259 Roy McMillan DP	60.00	27.00	7.50
☐ 260 Sam Calderone	100.00	45.00	12.50
☐ 261 Does not exist			
☐ 262 Bob Oldis	100.00	45.00	12.50
☐ 263 Johnny Podres	275.00	125.00	34.00
☐ 264 Gene Woodling DP	60.00	27.00	7.50
☐ 265 Jackie Jensen	125.00	55.00	15.50
☐ 266 Bob Cain	100.00	45.00	12.50
☐ 267 Does not exist			
☐ 268 Does not exist			
☐ 269 Duane Pillette	100.00	45.00	12.50
☐ 270 Vern Stephens	110.00	50.00	14.00
☐ 271 Does not exist			
☐ 272 Bill Antonello	100.00	45.00	12.50
☐ 273 Harvey Haddix	125.00	55.00	15.50
☐ 274 John Riddle CO	100.00	45.00	12.50
☐ 275 Does not exist			
☐ 276 Ken Raffensberger	100.00	45.00	12.50
☐ 277 Don Lund	100.00	45.00	12.50
☐ 278 Willie Miranda	100.00	45.00	12.50
☐ 279 Joe Coleman DP	50.00	22.00	6.25
☐ 280 Milt Bolling	300.00	50.00	20.00

1954 Topps

The cards in this 250-card set measure approximately 2 5/8" by 3 3/4". Each of the cards in the 1954 Topps set contains a large "head" shot of the player in color plus a smaller full-length photo in black and white set against a color background. The cards were issued in one-card penny packs or five-card nickle packs. This set contains the Rookie Cards of Hank Aaron, Ernie Banks, and Al Kaline and two separate cards of Ted Williams (number 1 and number 250). Conspicuous by his absence is Mickey Mantle who apparently was the exclusive property of Bowman during 1954 (and 1955). The first two issues of Sports Illustrated magazine contained "card" inserts on regular paper stock. The first issue showed actual cards in the set in

color, while the second issue showed some created cards of New York Yankees players in black and white, including Mickey Mantle.

	NRMT	VG-E	GOOD
COMPLETE SET (250)	7500.00	3400.00	950.00
COMMON CARD (1-50)	15.00	6.75	1.85
COMMON CARD (51-75)	25.00	11.00	3.10
COMMON CARD (76-250)	15.00	6.75	1.85
WRAPPER (1-CENT, DATED)	200.00	90.00	25.00
WRAPPER (1-CENT, UNDATED)	150.00	70.00	19.00
WRAPPER (5-CENT, DATED)	300.00	135.00	38.00
WRAPPER (5-CENT, UNDATED)	250.00	110.00	31.00
☐ 1 Ted Williams	650.00	230.00	65.00
☐ 2 Gus Zernial	20.00	9.00	2.50
☐ 3 Monte Irvin	40.00	18.00	5.00
☐ 4 Hank Sauer	25.00	11.00	3.10
☐ 5 Ed Lopat	25.00	11.00	3.10
☐ 6 Pete Runnels	20.00	9.00	2.50
☐ 7 Ted Kluszewski	40.00	18.00	5.00
☐ 8 Bob Young	15.00	6.75	1.85
☐ 9 Harvey Haddix	25.00	11.00	3.10
☐ 10 Jackie Robinson	300.00	135.00	38.00
☐ 11 Paul Leslie Smith	15.00	6.75	1.85
☐ 12 Del Crandall	25.00	11.00	3.10
☐ 13 Billy Martin	50.00	22.00	6.25
☐ 14 Preacher Roe	25.00	11.00	3.10
☐ 15 Al Rosen	25.00	11.00	3.10
☐ 16 Vic Janowicz	20.00	9.00	2.50
☐ 17 Phil Rizzuto	75.00	34.00	9.50
☐ 18 Walt Dropo	20.00	9.00	2.50
☐ 19 Johnny Lipon	15.00	6.75	1.85
☐ 20 Warren Spahn	75.00	34.00	9.50
☐ 21 Bobby Shantz	20.00	9.00	2.50
☐ 22 Jim Greengrass	15.00	6.75	1.85
☐ 23 Luke Easter	25.00	11.00	3.10
☐ 24 Granny Hamner	15.00	6.75	1.85
☐ 25 Harvey Kuenn	40.00	18.00	5.00
☐ 26 Ray Jablonski	15.00	6.75	1.85
☐ 27 Ferris Fain	20.00	9.00	2.50
☐ 28 Paul Minner	15.00	6.75	1.85
☐ 29 Jim Hegan	20.00	9.00	2.50
☐ 30 Eddie Mathews	75.00	34.00	9.50
☐ 31 Johnny Klippstein	15.00	6.75	1.85
☐ 32 Duke Snider	125.00	55.00	15.50
☐ 33 Johnny Schmitz	15.00	6.75	1.85
☐ 34 Jim Rivera	15.00	6.75	1.85
☐ 35 Jim Gilliam	40.00	18.00	5.00
☐ 36 Hoyt Wilhelm	50.00	22.00	6.25
☐ 37 Whitey Ford	100.00	45.00	12.50
☐ 38 Eddie Stanky MG	25.00	11.00	3.10
☐ 39 Sherm Lollar	20.00	9.00	2.50
☐ 40 Mel Parnell	20.00	9.00	2.50
☐ 41 Willie Jones	15.00	6.75	1.85
☐ 42 Don Mueller	20.00	9.00	2.50
☐ 43 Dick Groat	25.00	11.00	3.10
☐ 44 Ned Garver	15.00	6.75	1.85
☐ 45 Richie Ashburn	70.00	32.00	8.75
☐ 46 Ken Raffensberger	15.00	6.75	1.85
☐ 47 Ellis Kinder	15.00	6.75	1.85
☐ 48 Billy Hunter	20.00	9.00	2.50
☐ 49 Ray Murray	15.00	6.75	1.85
☐ 50 Yogi Berra	150.00	70.00	19.00
☐ 51 Johnny Lindell	25.00	11.00	3.10
☐ 52 Vic Power	35.00	16.00	4.40
☐ 53 Jack Dittmer	25.00	11.00	3.10
☐ 54 Vern Stephens	30.00	13.50	3.70
☐ 55 Phil Cavarretta MG	30.00	13.50	3.70
☐ 56 Willie Miranda	25.00	11.00	3.10
☐ 57 Luis Aloma	25.00	11.00	3.10
☐ 58 Bob Wilson	25.00	11.00	3.10
☐ 59 Gene Conley	30.00	13.50	3.70
☐ 60 Frank Baumholtz	25.00	11.00	3.10
☐ 61 Bob Cain	25.00	11.00	3.10
☐ 62 Eddie Robinson	25.00	11.00	3.10
☐ 63 Johnny Pesky	30.00	13.50	3.70
☐ 64 Hank Thompson	25.00	11.00	3.10
☐ 65 Bob Swift CO	25.00	11.00	3.10
☐ 66 Ted Lepcio	25.00	11.00	3.10
☐ 67 Jim Willis	25.00	11.00	3.10
☐ 68 Sam Calderone	25.00	11.00	3.10
☐ 69 Bud Podbielan	25.00	11.00	3.10
☐ 70 Larry Doby	50.00	22.00	6.25
☐ 71 Frank Smith	25.00	11.00	3.10
☐ 72 Preston Ward	25.00	11.00	3.10
☐ 73 Wayne Terwilliger	25.00	11.00	3.10
☐ 74 Bill Taylor	25.00	11.00	3.10
☐ 75 Fred Haney MG	25.00	11.00	3.10
☐ 76 Bob Scheffing CO	15.00	6.75	1.85
☐ 77 Ray Boone	20.00	9.00	2.50
☐ 78 Ted Kazanski	15.00	6.75	1.85
☐ 79 Andy Pafko	25.00	11.00	3.10
☐ 80 Jackie Jensen	25.00	11.00	3.10
☐ 81 Dave Hoskins	15.00	6.75	1.85
☐ 82 Milt Bolling	15.00	6.75	1.85
☐ 83 Joe Collins	22.50	10.00	2.80
☐ 84 Dick Cole	15.00	6.75	1.85
☐ 85 Bob Turley	30.00	13.50	3.70
☐ 86 Billy Herman CO	25.00	11.00	3.10
☐ 87 Roy Face	25.00	11.00	3.10
☐ 88 Matt Batts	15.00	6.75	1.85
☐ 89 Howie Pollet	15.00	6.75	1.85
☐ 90 Willie Mays	500.00	220.00	60.00
☐ 91 Bob Oldis	15.00	6.75	1.85
☐ 92 Wally Westlake	15.00	6.75	1.85
☐ 93 Sid Hudson	15.00	6.75	1.85
☐ 94 Ernie Banks	750.00	350.00	95.00
☐ 95 Hal Rice	15.00	6.75	1.85
☐ 96 Charlie Silvera	25.00	11.00	3.10
☐ 97 Jerald Hal Lane	15.00	6.75	1.85
☐ 98 Joe Black	30.00	13.50	3.70
☐ 99 Bobby Hofman	15.00	6.75	1.85
☐ 100 Bob Keegan	15.00	6.75	1.85
☐ 101 Gene Woodling	25.00	11.00	3.10
☐ 102 Gil Hodges	70.00	32.00	8.75
☐ 103 Jim Lemon	15.00	6.75	1.85
☐ 104 Mike Sandlock	15.00	6.75	1.85
☐ 105 Andy Carey	25.00	11.00	3.10
☐ 106 Dick Kokos	15.00	6.75	1.85
☐ 107 Duane Pillette	15.00	6.75	1.85
☐ 108 Thornton Kipper	15.00	6.75	1.85
☐ 109 Bill Bruton	20.00	9.00	2.50
☐ 110 Harry Dorish	15.00	6.75	1.85
☐ 111 Jim Delsing	15.00	6.75	1.85
☐ 112 Bill Renna	15.00	6.75	1.85
☐ 113 Bob Boyd	15.00	6.75	1.85
☐ 114 Dean Stone	15.00	6.75	1.85
☐ 115 Rip Repulski	15.00	6.75	1.85
☐ 116 Steve Bilko	15.00	6.75	1.85
☐ 117 Solly Hemus	15.00	6.75	1.85
☐ 118 Carl Scheib	15.00	6.75	1.85
☐ 119 Johnny Antonelli	20.00	9.00	2.50
☐ 120 Roy McMillan	20.00	9.00	2.50
☐ 121 Clem Labine	22.50	10.00	2.80
☐ 122 Johnny Logan	20.00	9.00	2.50
☐ 123 Bobby Adams	15.00	6.75	1.85
☐ 124 Marion Fricano	15.00	6.75	1.85
☐ 125 Harry Perkowski	15.00	6.75	1.85
☐ 126 Ben Wade	15.00	6.75	1.85
☐ 127 Steve O'Neill MG	15.00	6.75	1.85
☐ 128 Hank Aaron	1500.00	700.00	190.00
☐ 129 Forrest Jacobs	15.00	6.75	1.85
☐ 130 Hank Bauer	25.00	11.00	3.10
☐ 131 Reno Bertoia	15.00	6.75	1.85
☐ 132 Tom Lasorda	150.00	70.00	19.00
☐ 133 Dave Baker CO	15.00	6.75	1.85
☐ 134 Cal Hogue	15.00	6.75	1.85
☐ 135 Joe Presko	15.00	6.75	1.85
☐ 136 Connie Ryan	15.00	6.75	1.85
☐ 137 Wally Moon	30.00	13.50	3.70
☐ 138 Bob Borkowski	15.00	6.75	1.85
☐ 139 The O'Briens Johnny O'Brien Eddie O'Brien	40.00	18.00	5.00
☐ 140 Tom Wright	15.00	6.75	1.85
☐ 141 Joey Jay	20.00	9.00	2.50
☐ 142 Tom Poholsky	15.00	6.75	1.85
☐ 143 Rollie Hemsley CO	15.00	6.75	1.85
☐ 144 Bill Werle	15.00	6.75	1.85
☐ 145 Elmer Valo	15.00	6.75	1.85
☐ 146 Don Johnson	15.00	6.75	1.85
☐ 147 Johnny Riddle CO	15.00	6.75	1.85
☐ 148 Bob Trice	15.00	6.75	1.85
☐ 149 Al Robertson	15.00	6.75	1.85
☐ 150 Dick Kryhoski	15.00	6.75	1.85
☐ 151 Alex Grammas	15.00	6.75	1.85
☐ 152 Michael Blyzka	15.00	6.75	1.85
☐ 153 Al Walker	15.00	6.75	1.85
☐ 154 Mike Fornieles	15.00	6.75	1.85
☐ 155 Bob Kennedy	20.00	9.00	2.50
☐ 156 Joe Coleman	15.00	6.75	1.85
☐ 157 Don Lenhardt	15.00	6.75	1.85
☐ 158 Peanuts Lowrey	15.00	6.75	1.85
☐ 159 Dave Philley	15.00	6.75	1.85
☐ 160 Ralph Kress CO	15.00	6.75	1.85
☐ 161 John Hetki	15.00	6.75	1.85
☐ 162 Herman Wehmeier	15.00	6.75	1.85
☐ 163 Frank House	15.00	6.75	1.85
☐ 164 Stu Miller	20.00	9.00	2.50
☐ 165 Jim Pendleton	15.00	6.75	1.85
☐ 166 Johnny Podres	30.00	13.50	3.70
☐ 167 Don Lund	15.00	6.75	1.85
☐ 168 Morrie Martin	15.00	6.75	1.85
☐ 169 Jim Hughes	25.00	11.00	3.10
☐ 170 James(Dusty) Rhodes	25.00	11.00	3.10
☐ 171 Leo Kiely	15.00	6.75	1.85
☐ 172 Harold Brown	15.00	6.75	1.85
☐ 173 Jack Harshman	15.00	6.75	1.85
☐ 174 Tom Qualters	15.00	6.75	1.85
☐ 175 Frank Leja	20.00	9.00	2.50
☐ 176 Robert Keely CO	15.00	6.75	1.85
☐ 177 Bob Milliken	15.00	6.75	1.85
☐ 178 Bill Glynn	15.00	6.75	1.85
☐ 179 Gair Allie	15.00	6.75	1.85
☐ 180 Wes Westrum	20.00	9.00	2.50
☐ 181 Mel Roach	15.00	6.75	1.85
☐ 182 Chuck Harmon	15.00	6.75	1.85
☐ 183 Earle Combs CO	25.00	11.00	3.10
☐ 184 Ed Bailey	15.00	6.75	1.85
☐ 185 Chuck Stobbs	15.00	6.75	1.85
☐ 186 Karl Olson	15.00	6.75	1.85
☐ 187 Heinie Manush CO	25.00	11.00	3.10
☐ 188 Dave Jolly	15.00	6.75	1.85
☐ 189 Bob Ross	15.00	6.75	1.85
☐ 190 Ray Herbert	15.00	6.75	1.85
☐ 191 John(Dick) Schofield	20.00	9.00	2.50
☐ 192 Ellis Deal CO	15.00	6.75	1.85
☐ 193 Johnny Hopp CO	20.00	9.00	2.50
☐ 194 Bill Sarni	15.00	6.75	1.85
☐ 195 Billy Consolo	15.00	6.75	1.85
☐ 196 Stan Jok	15.00	6.75	1.85
☐ 197 Lynwood Rowe CO ("Schoolboy")	20.00	9.00	2.50
☐ 198 Carl Sawatski	15.00	6.75	1.85
☐ 199 Glenn(Rocky) Nelson	15.00	6.75	1.85
☐ 200 Larry Jansen	20.00	9.00	2.50
☐ 201 Al Kaline	750.00	350.00	95.00
☐ 202 Bob Purkey	20.00	9.00	2.50
☐ 203 Harry Brecheen CO	20.00	9.00	2.50
☐ 204 Angel Scull	15.00	6.75	1.85
☐ 205 Johnny Sain	30.00	13.50	3.70
☐ 206 Ray Crone	15.00	6.75	1.85
☐ 207 Tom Oliver CO	15.00	6.75	1.85
☐ 208 Grady Hatton	15.00	6.75	1.85
☐ 209 Chuck Thompson	15.00	6.75	1.85
☐ 210 Bob Buhl	25.00	11.00	3.10
☐ 211 Don Hoak	20.00	9.00	2.50
☐ 212 Bob Micelotta	15.00	6.75	1.85
☐ 213 Johnny Fitzpatrick CO	15.00	6.75	1.85
☐ 214 Arnie Portocarrero	15.00	6.75	1.85
☐ 215 Ed McGhee	15.00	6.75	1.85
☐ 216 Al Sima	15.00	6.75	1.85
☐ 217 Paul Schreiber CO	15.00	6.75	1.85
☐ 218 Fred Marsh	15.00	6.75	1.85
☐ 219 Chuck Kress	15.00	6.75	1.85
☐ 220 Ruben Gomez	20.00	9.00	2.50
☐ 221 Dick Brodowski	15.00	6.75	1.85
☐ 222 Bill Wilson	15.00	6.75	1.85
☐ 223 Joe Haynes CO	15.00	6.75	1.85
☐ 224 Dick Weik	15.00	6.75	1.85
☐ 225 Don Liddle	15.00	6.75	1.85
☐ 226 Jehosie Heard	15.00	6.75	1.85
☐ 227 Colonel Mills CO	15.00	6.75	1.85
☐ 228 Gene Hermanski	15.00	6.75	1.85
☐ 229 Bob Talbot	15.00	6.75	1.85
☐ 230 Bob Kuzava	25.00	11.00	3.10
☐ 231 Roy Smalley	15.00	6.75	1.85
☐ 232 Lou Limmer	15.00	6.75	1.85
☐ 233 Augie Galan CO	15.00	6.75	1.85
☐ 234 Jerry Lynch	15.00	6.75	1.85
☐ 235 Vernon Law	20.00	9.00	2.50
☐ 236 Paul Penson	15.00	6.75	1.85
☐ 237 Mike Ryba CO	15.00	6.75	1.85
☐ 238 Al Aber	15.00	6.75	1.85
☐ 239 Bill Skowron	100.00	45.00	12.50
☐ 240 Sam Mele	20.00	9.00	2.50
☐ 241 Robert Miller	15.00	6.75	1.85
☐ 242 Curt Roberts	15.00	6.75	1.85
☐ 243 Ray Blades CO	15.00	6.75	1.85
☐ 244 Leroy Wheat	15.00	6.75	1.85
☐ 245 Roy Sievers	20.00	9.00	2.50
☐ 246 Howie Fox	15.00	6.75	1.85
☐ 247 Ed Mayo CO	15.00	6.75	1.85
☐ 248 Al Smith	20.00	9.00	2.50
☐ 249 Wilmer Mizell	20.00	9.00	2.50
☐ 250 Ted Williams	750.00	300.00	75.00

1955 Topps

The cards in this 206-card set measure approximately 2 5/8" by 3 3/4". Both the large "head" shot and the smaller full-length photos used on each card of the 1955 Topps set are in color. The card fronts were designed horizontally for the first time in Topps' history. The first card features Dusty Rhodes, hitting star and MVP in the New York Giants' 1954 World Series sweep over the Cleveland Indians. A "high" series, 161 to 210, is more difficult to find than cards 1 to 160. Numbers 175, 186, 203, and 209 were never issued. To fill in for the four cards not issued in the high number series, Topps double printed four players, those appearing on cards 170, 172, 184, and 188. Cards were issued in one-card penny packs or six-card nickle packs. Although rarely seen, there exist salesman sample panels of three cards containing the fronts of regular cards with ad information for the 1955 Topps regular and the 1955 Topps Doubleheaders on the back. One such ad panel depicts (from top to bottom) Danny Schell, Jake Thies, and Howie Pollet. The key Rookie Cards in this set are Ken Boyer, Roberto Clemente, Harmon Killebrew, and Sandy Koufax.

	NRMT	VG-E	GOOD
COMPLETE SET (206)	7200.00	3200.00	900.00
COMMON CARD (1-150)	12.00	5.50	1.50
COMMON CARD (151-160)	20.00	9.00	2.50
COMMON CARD (161-210)	30.00	13.50	3.70
WRAPPER (1-CENT, DATED)	150.00	70.00	19.00
WRAPPER (1-CENT, UNDATED)	75.00	34.00	9.50
WRAPPER (5-CENT, DATED)	150.00	70.00	19.00
WRAPPER (5-CENT, DATED)	100.00	45.00	12.50
☐ 1 Dusty Rhodes	50.00	10.00	3.30
☐ 2 Ted Williams	450.00	200.00	55.00
☐ 3 Art Fowler	16.00	7.25	2.00
☐ 4 Al Kaline	175.00	80.00	22.00
☐ 5 Jim Gilliam	25.00	11.00	3.10
☐ 6 Stan Hack MG	18.00	8.00	2.20
☐ 7 Jim Hegan	16.00	7.25	2.00
☐ 8 Harold Smith	12.00	5.50	1.50
☐ 9 Robert Miller	12.00	5.50	1.50
☐ 10 Bob Keegan	12.00	5.50	1.50
☐ 11 Ferris Fain	16.00	7.25	2.00
☐ 12 Vernon(Jake) Thies	12.00	5.50	1.50
☐ 13 Fred Marsh	12.00	5.50	1.50
☐ 14 Jim Finigan	12.00	5.50	1.50
☐ 15 Jim Pendleton	12.00	5.50	1.50
☐ 16 Roy Sievers	16.00	7.25	2.00
☐ 17 Bobby Hofman	12.00	5.50	1.50
☐ 18 Russ Kemmerer	12.00	5.50	1.50
☐ 19 Billy Herman CO	18.00	8.00	2.20
☐ 20 Andy Carey	18.00	8.00	2.20
☐ 21 Alex Grammas	12.00	5.50	1.50
☐ 22 Bill Skowron	20.00	9.00	2.50
☐ 23 Jack Parks	12.00	5.50	1.50
☐ 24 Hal Newhouser	18.00	8.00	2.20
☐ 25 Johnny Podres	20.00	9.00	2.50
☐ 26 Dick Groat	18.00	8.00	2.20
☐ 27 Billy Gardner	16.00	7.25	2.00
☐ 28 Ernie Banks	175.00	80.00	22.00
☐ 29 Herman Wehmeier	12.00	5.50	1.50
☐ 30 Vic Power	16.00	7.25	2.00
☐ 31 Warren Spahn	90.00	40.00	11.00
☐ 32 Warren McGhee	12.00	5.50	1.50
☐ 33 Tom Qualters	12.00	5.50	1.50
☐ 34 Wayne Terwilliger	12.00	5.50	1.50
☐ 35 Dave Jolly	12.00	5.50	1.50
☐ 36 Leo Kiely	12.00	5.50	1.50
☐ 37 Joe Cunningham	16.00	7.25	2.00
☐ 38 Bob Turley	18.00	8.00	2.20
☐ 39 Bill Glynn	12.00	5.50	1.50
☐ 40 Don Hoak	18.00	8.00	2.20
☐ 41 Chuck Stobbs	12.00	5.50	1.50
☐ 42 John(Windy) McCall	12.00	5.50	1.50
☐ 43 Harvey Haddix	18.00	8.00	2.20
☐ 44 Harold Valentine	12.00	5.50	1.50
☐ 45 Hank Sauer	18.00	8.00	2.20
☐ 46 Ted Kazanski	12.00	5.50	1.50
☐ 47 Hank Aaron UER (Birth incorrectly listed as 2/10)	350.00	160.00	45.00
☐ 48 Bob Kennedy	16.00	7.25	2.00
☐ 49 J.W. Porter	12.00	5.50	1.50
☐ 50 Jackie Robinson	300.00	135.00	38.00
☐ 51 Jim Hughes	18.00	8.00	2.20
☐ 52 Bill Tremel	12.00	5.50	1.50
☐ 53 Bill Taylor	12.00	5.50	1.50
☐ 54 Lou Limmer	12.00	5.50	1.50
☐ 55 Rip Repulski	12.00	5.50	1.50
☐ 56 Ray Jablonski	12.00	5.50	1.50
☐ 57 Billy O'Dell	12.00	5.50	1.50
☐ 58 Jim Rivera	12.00	5.50	1.50
☐ 59 Gair Allie	12.00	5.50	1.50
☐ 60 Dean Stone	12.00	5.50	1.50
☐ 61 Forrest Jacobs	12.00	5.50	1.50
☐ 62 Thornton Kipper	12.00	5.50	1.50
☐ 63 Joe Collins	18.00	8.00	2.20
☐ 64 Gus Triandos	18.00	8.00	2.20
☐ 65 Ray Boone	18.00	8.00	2.20
☐ 66 Ron Jackson	12.00	5.50	1.50
☐ 67 Wally Moon	18.00	8.00	2.20
☐ 68 Jim Davis	12.00	5.50	1.50
☐ 69 Ed Bailey	16.00	7.25	2.00
☐ 70 Al Rosen	18.00	8.00	2.20
☐ 71 Ruben Gomez	12.00	5.50	1.50
☐ 72 Karl Olson	12.00	5.50	1.50
☐ 73 Jack Shepard	12.00	5.50	1.50
☐ 74 Bob Borkowski	12.00	5.50	1.50
☐ 75 Sandy Amoros	30.00	13.50	3.70
☐ 76 Howie Pollet	12.00	5.50	1.50
☐ 77 Arnie Portocarrero	12.00	5.50	1.50
☐ 78 Gordon Jones	12.00	5.50	1.50
☐ 79 Clyde(Danny) Schell	12.00	5.50	1.50
☐ 80 Bob Grim	18.00	8.00	2.20
☐ 81 Gene Conley	16.00	7.25	2.00
☐ 82 Chuck Harmon	12.00	5.50	1.50
☐ 83 Tom Brewer	12.00	5.50	1.50
☐ 84 Camilo Pascual	18.00	8.00	2.20
☐ 85 Don Mossi	18.00	8.00	2.20
☐ 86 Bill Wilson	12.00	5.50	1.50
☐ 87 Frank House	12.00	5.50	1.50
☐ 88 Bob Skinner	18.00	8.00	2.20
☐ 89 Joe Frazier	16.00	7.25	2.00
☐ 90 Karl Spooner	18.00	8.00	2.20
☐ 91 Milt Bolling	12.00	5.50	1.50
☐ 92 Don Zimmer	30.00	13.50	3.70
☐ 93 Steve Bilko	12.00	5.50	1.50
☐ 94 Reno Bertoia	12.00	5.50	1.50
☐ 95 Preston Ward	12.00	5.50	1.50
☐ 96 Chuck Bishop	12.00	5.50	1.50
☐ 97 Carlos Paula	12.00	5.50	1.50

☐ 98 John Riddle CO	12.00	5.50	1.50
☐ 99 Frank Leja	12.00	5.50	1.50
☐ 100 Monte Irvin	35.00	16.00	4.40
☐ 101 Johnny Gray	12.00	5.50	1.50
☐ 102 Wally Westlake	12.00	5.50	1.50
☐ 103 Chuck White	12.00	5.50	1.50
☐ 104 Jack Harshman	12.00	5.50	1.50
☐ 105 Chuck Diering	12.00	5.50	1.50
☐ 106 Frank Sullivan	12.00	5.50	1.50
☐ 107 Curt Roberts	12.00	5.50	1.50
☐ 108 Al Walker	16.00	7.25	2.00
☐ 109 Ed Lopat	18.00	8.00	2.20
☐ 110 Gus Zernial	16.00	7.25	2.00
☐ 111 Bob Milliken	16.00	7.25	2.00
☐ 112 Nelson King	12.00	5.50	1.50
☐ 113 Harry Brecheen CO	16.00	7.25	2.00
☐ 114 Louis Ortiz	12.00	5.50	1.50
☐ 115 Ellis Kinder	12.00	5.50	1.50
☐ 116 Tom Hurd	12.00	5.50	1.50
☐ 117 Mel Roach	12.00	5.50	1.50
☐ 118 Bob Purkey	12.00	5.50	1.50
☐ 119 Bob Lennon	12.00	5.50	1.50
☐ 120 Ted Kluszewski	40.00	18.00	5.00
☐ 121 Bill Renna	12.00	5.50	1.50
☐ 122 Carl Sawatski	12.00	5.50	1.50
☐ 123 Sandy Koufax	900.00	400.00	110.00
☐ 124 Harmon Killebrew	250.00	110.00	31.00
☐ 125 Ken Boyer	60.00	27.00	7.50
☐ 126 Dick Hall	12.00	5.50	1.50
☐ 127 Dale Long	18.00	8.00	2.20
☐ 128 Ted Lepcio	12.00	5.50	1.50
☐ 129 Elvin Tappe	12.00	5.50	1.50
☐ 130 Mayo Smith MG	12.00	5.50	1.50
☐ 131 Grady Hatton	12.00	5.50	1.50
☐ 132 Bob Trice	12.00	5.50	1.50
☐ 133 Dave Hoskins	12.00	5.50	1.50
☐ 134 Joey Jay	16.00	7.25	2.00
☐ 135 Johnny O'Brien	16.00	7.25	2.00
☐ 136 Veston(Bunky) Stewart	12.00	5.50	1.50
☐ 137 Harry Elliott	12.00	5.50	1.50
☐ 138 Ray Herbert	12.00	5.50	1.50
☐ 139 Steve Kraly	12.00	5.50	1.50
☐ 140 Mel Parnell	16.00	7.25	2.00
☐ 141 Tom Wright	12.00	5.50	1.50
☐ 142 Jerry Lynch	16.00	7.25	2.00
☐ 143 John(Dick) Schofield	16.00	7.25	2.00
☐ 144 John(Joe) Amalfitano	12.00	5.50	1.50
☐ 145 Elmer Valo	12.00	5.50	1.50
☐ 146 Dick Donovan	12.00	5.50	1.50
☐ 147 Hugh Pepper	12.00	5.50	1.50
☐ 148 Hector Brown	12.00	5.50	1.50
☐ 149 Ray Crone	12.00	5.50	1.50
☐ 150 Mike Higgins MG	12.00	5.50	1.50
☐ 151 Ralph Kress CO	20.00	9.00	2.50
☐ 152 Harry Agganis	70.00	32.00	8.75
☐ 153 Bud Podbielan	20.00	9.00	2.50
☐ 154 Willie Miranda	20.00	9.00	2.50
☐ 155 Eddie Mathews	90.00	40.00	11.00
☐ 156 Joe Black	35.00	16.00	4.40
☐ 157 Robert Miller	20.00	9.00	2.50
☐ 158 Tommy Carroll	20.00	9.00	2.50
☐ 159 Johnny Schmitz	20.00	9.00	2.50
☐ 160 Ray Narleski	20.00	9.00	2.50
☐ 161 Chuck Tanner	35.00	16.00	4.40
☐ 162 Joe Coleman	30.00	13.50	3.70
☐ 163 Faye Throneberry	30.00	13.50	3.70
☐ 164 Roberto Clemente	2200.00	1000.00	275.00
☐ 165 Don Johnson	30.00	13.50	3.70
☐ 166 Hank Bauer	45.00	20.00	5.50
☐ 167 Thomas Casagrande	30.00	13.50	3.70
☐ 168 Duane Pillette	30.00	13.50	3.70
☐ 169 Bob Oldis	30.00	13.50	3.70
☐ 170 Jim Pearce DP	15.00	6.75	1.85
☐ 171 Dick Brodowski	30.00	13.50	3.70
☐ 172 Frank Baumholtz DP	15.00	6.75	1.85
☐ 173 Bob Kline	30.00	13.50	3.70
☐ 174 Rudy Minarcin	30.00	13.50	3.70
☐ 175 Does not exist			
☐ 176 Norm Zauchin	30.00	13.50	3.70
☐ 177 Al Robertson	30.00	13.50	3.70
☐ 178 Bobby Adams	30.00	13.50	3.70
☐ 179 Jim Bolger	30.00	13.50	3.70
☐ 180 Clem Labine	45.00	20.00	5.50
☐ 181 Roy McMillan	35.00	16.00	4.40
☐ 182 Humberto Robinson	30.00	13.50	3.70
☐ 183 Anthony Jacobs	30.00	13.50	3.70
☐ 184 Harry Perkowski DP	15.00	6.75	1.85
☐ 185 Don Ferrarese	30.00	13.50	3.70
☐ 186 Does not exist			
☐ 187 Gil Hodges	125.00	55.00	15.50
☐ 188 Charlie Silvera DP	15.00	6.75	1.85
☐ 189 Phil Rizzuto	125.00	55.00	15.50
☐ 190 Gene Woodling	45.00	20.00	5.50
☐ 191 Eddie Stanky MG	30.00	13.50	3.70
☐ 192 Jim Delsing	30.00	13.50	3.70
☐ 193 Johnny Sain	45.00	20.00	5.50
☐ 194 Willie Mays	400.00	180.00	50.00
☐ 195 Ed Roebuck	45.00	20.00	5.50
☐ 196 Gale Wade	30.00	13.50	3.70
☐ 197 Al Smith	35.00	16.00	4.40
☐ 198 Yogi Berra	200.00	90.00	25.00
☐ 199 Odbert Hamric	35.00	16.00	4.40
☐ 200 Jackie Jensen	35.00	16.00	4.40
☐ 201 Sherman Lollar !	20.00	9.00	2.50
☐ 202 Jim Owens	30.00	13.50	3.70
☐ 203 Does not exist			
☐ 204 Frank Smith	30.00	13.50	3.70
☐ 205 Gene Freese	30.00	13.50	3.70
☐ 206 Pete Daley	30.00	13.50	3.70
☐ 207 Billy Consolo	30.00	13.50	3.70
☐ 208 Ray Moore	30.00	13.50	3.70
☐ 209 Does not exist			
☐ 210 Duke Snider	450.00	135.00	45.00

1955 Topps Double Header

The cards in this 66-card set measure approximately 2 1/16" by 4 7/8". Borrowing a design from the T201 Mecca series, Topps issued a 132-player "Double Header" set in a separate wrapper in 1955. Each player is numbered in the biographical section on the reverse. When open, with perforated flap up, one player is revealed; when the flap is lowered, or closed, the player design on top incorporates a portion of the inside player artwork. When the cards are placed side by side, a continuous ballpark background is formed. Some cards have been found without perforations, and all players pictured appear in the low series of the 1955 regular issue. The cards were issued in one-card penny packs with a piece of bubble gum.

	NRMT	VG-E	GOOD
COMPLETE SET (66)	4000.00	1800.00	500.00
COMMON PAIR (1-132)	40.00	18.00	5.00
WRAPPER (1-CENT)	200.00	90.00	25.00
☐ 1 Al Rosen and 2 Chuck Diering	50.00	22.00	6.25
☐ 3 Monte Irvin and 4 Russ Kemmerer	75.00	34.00	9.50
☐ 5 Ted Kazanski and 6 Gordon Jones	40.00	18.00	5.00
☐ 7 Bill Taylor and 8 Billy O'Dell	40.00	18.00	5.00
☐ 9 J.W. Porter and 10 Thornton Kipper	40.00	18.00	5.00
☐ 11 Curt Roberts and 12 Arnie Portocarrero	40.00	18.00	5.00
☐ 13 Wally Westlake and 14 Frank House	40.00	18.00	5.00
☐ 15 Rube Walker and 16 Lou Limmer	40.00	18.00	5.00
☐ 17 Dean Stone and 18 Charlie White	40.00	18.00	5.00
☐ 19 Karl Spooner and 20 Jim Hughes	40.00	18.00	5.00
☐ 21 Bill Skowron and 22 Frank Sullivan	50.00	22.00	6.25
☐ 23 Jack Shepard and 24 Stan Hack MG	40.00	18.00	5.00
☐ 25 Jackie Robinson and 26 Don Hoak	300.00	135.00	38.00
☐ 27 Dusty Rhodes and 28 Jim Davis	40.00	18.00	5.00
☐ 29 Vic Power and 30 Ed Bailey	40.00	18.00	5.00
☐ 31 Howie Pollet and 32 Ernie Banks	225.00	100.00	28.00
☐ 33 Jim Pendleton and 34 Gene Conley	40.00	18.00	5.00
☐ 35 Karl Olson and 36 Andy Carey	40.00	18.00	5.00
☐ 37 Wally Moon and 38 Joe Cunningham	50.00	22.00	6.25
☐ 39 Freddie Marsh and 40 Vernon Thies	40.00	18.00	5.00
☐ 41 Eddie Lopat and 42 Harvey Haddix	50.00	22.00	6.25
☐ 43 Leo Kiely and 44 Chuck Stobbs	40.00	18.00	5.00
☐ 45 Al Kaline and 46 Harold Valentine	225.00	100.00	28.00
☐ 47 Forrest Jacobs and 48 Johnny Gray	40.00	18.00	5.00
☐ 49 Ron Jackson and 50 Jim Finigan	40.00	18.00	5.00
☐ 51 Ray Jablonski and 52 Bob Keegan	40.00	18.00	5.00
☐ 53 Billy Herman CO and 54 Sandy Amoros	75.00	34.00	9.50
☐ 55 Chuck Harmon and 56 Bob Skinner	40.00	18.00	5.00
☐ 57 Dick Hall and 58 Bob Grim	40.00	18.00	5.00
☐ 59 Billy Glynn and 60 Bob Miller	40.00	18.00	5.00
☐ 61 Billy Gardner and 62 John Hetki	40.00	18.00	5.00
☐ 63 Bob Borkowski and 64 Bob Turley	40.00	18.00	5.00
☐ 65 Joe Collins and 66 Jack Harshman	40.00	18.00	5.00
☐ 67 Jim Hegan and 68 Jack Parks	40.00	18.00	5.00
☐ 69 Ted Williams and 70 Mayo Smith MG	400.00	180.00	50.00
☐ 71 Gair Allie and 72 Grady Hatton	40.00	18.00	5.00
☐ 73 Jerry Lynch and 74 Harry Brecheen CO	40.00	18.00	5.00
☐ 75 Tom Wright and 76 Vernon Stewart	40.00	18.00	5.00
☐ 77 Dave Hoskins and 78 Warren McGhee	40.00	18.00	5.00
☐ 79 Roy Sievers and 80 Art Fowler	40.00	18.00	5.00
☐ 81 Danny Schell and 82 Gus Triandos	40.00	18.00	5.00
☐ 83 Joe Frazier and 84 Don Mossi	40.00	18.00	5.00
☐ 85 Elmer Valo and 86 Hector Brown	40.00	18.00	5.00
☐ 87 Bob Kennedy and 88 Windy McCall	40.00	18.00	5.00
☐ 89 Ruben Gomez and 90 Jim Rivera	40.00	18.00	5.00
☐ 91 Louis Ortiz and 92 Milt Bolling	40.00	18.00	5.00
☐ 93 Carl Sawatski and 94 El Tappe	40.00	18.00	5.00
☐ 95 Dave Jolly and 96 Bobby Hofman	40.00	18.00	5.00
☐ 97 Preston Ward and 98 Don Zimmer	50.00	22.00	6.25
☐ 99 Bill Renna and 100 Dick Groat	50.00	22.00	6.25
☐ 101 Bill Wilson and 102 Bill Tremel	40.00	18.00	5.00
☐ 103 Hank Sauer and 104 Camilo Pascual	50.00	22.00	6.25
☐ 105 Hank Aaron and 106 Ray Herbert	500.00	220.00	60.00
☐ 107 Alex Grammas and 108 Tom Qualters	40.00	18.00	5.00
☐ 109 Hal Newhouser and 110 Chuck Bishop	75.00	34.00	9.50
☐ 111 Harmon Killebrew and 112 John Podres	200.00	90.00	25.00
☐ 113 Ray Boone and 114 Bob Purkey	40.00	18.00	5.00
☐ 115 Dale Long and 116 Ferris Fain	40.00	18.00	5.00
☐ 117 Steve Bilko and 118 Bob Milliken	40.00	18.00	5.00
☐ 119 Mel Parnell and 120 Tom Hurd	40.00	18.00	5.00
☐ 121 Ted Kluszewski and 122 Jim Owens	75.00	34.00	9.50
☐ 123 Gus Zernial and 124 Bob Trice	40.00	18.00	5.00
☐ 125 Rip Repulski and 126 Ted Lepcio	40.00	18.00	5.00
☐ 127 Warren Spahn and 128 Tom Brewer	200.00	90.00	25.00
☐ 129 Jim Gilliam and 130 Ellis Kinder	75.00	34.00	9.50
☐ 131 Herm Wehmeier and 132 Wayne Terwilliger	40.00	18.00	5.00

1955 Topps Test Stamps

These test issues stamps "are full-size versions of regular first series cards, but with blank, gummed backs and perforated edges." These stamps are listed in alphabetical order with their corresponding card number listed immediately after their name. Since these "stamps" show up very infrequently in the hobby -- any additions to this checklist are appreciated.

	NRMT	VG-E	GOOD
COMPLETE SET	3000.00	1350.00	375.00
COMMON CARD	300.00	135.00	38.00
☐ 1 Jim Davis Card number 68	300.00	135.00	38.00
☐ 2 Stan Hack MG Card number 6	350.00	160.00	45.00
☐ 3 Harvey Haddix Card number 43	300.00	135.00	38.00
☐ 4 Bobby Hofman Card number 17	300.00	135.00	38.00
☐ 5 Dave Jolly Card number 35	300.00	135.00	38.00
☐ 6 Don Mossi Card number 85	400.00	180.00	50.00
☐ 7 Jim Pendleton Card number 15	300.00	135.00	38.00
☐ 8 Karl Spooner Card number 90	350.00	160.00	45.00
☐ 9 Rube Walker Card number 108	350.00	160.00	45.00
☐ 10 Charlie White Card number 103	300.00	135.00	38.00

1956 Topps

The cards in this 340-card set measure approximately 2 5/8" by 3 3/4". Following up with another horizontally oriented card in 1956, Topps improved the format by layering the color "head" shot onto an actual action sequence involving the player. Cards 1 to 180 come with either white or gray backs: in the 1 to 100 sequence, gray backs are less common (worth about 10 percent more) and in the 101 to 180 sequence, white backs are less common (worth 30 percent more). The team cards, used for the first time in a regular set by Topps, are found dated 1955, or undated, with the team name appearing on either side. The dated team cards in the first series were not printed on the gray stock. The two unnumbered checklist cards are highly prized (must be unmarked to qualify as excellent or mint). The complete set price below does not include the unnumbered checklist cards or any of the variations. The set was issued in one-card penny packs or six-card nickle packs. Both types of packs included a piece of bubble gum. The key Rookie Cards in this set are Walt Alston, Luis Aparicio, and Roger Craig. There are ten double-printed cards in the first series as evidenced by the discovery of an uncut sheet of 110 cards (10 by 11); these DP's are listed below.

	NRMT	VG-E	GOOD
COMPLETE SET (340)	7000.00	3200.00	900.00
COMMON CARD (1-100)	10.00	4.50	1.25
COMMON CARD (101-180)	12.00	5.50	1.50
COMMON CARD (181-260)	15.00	6.75	1.85
COMMON CARD (261-340)	12.00	5.50	1.50
WRAPPER (1-CENT)	250.00	110.00	31.00
WRAPPER (1-CENT, REPEAT)	100.00	45.00	12.50
WRAPPER (5-CENT)	200.00	90.00	25.00
☐ 1 William Harridge (AL President)	100.00	28.00	10.00
☐ 2 Warren Giles (NL President)	25.00	11.00	3.10
☐ 3 Elmer Valo	10.00	4.50	1.25
☐ 4 Carlos Paula	10.00	4.50	1.25
☐ 5 Ted Williams	325.00	145.00	40.00
☐ 6 Ray Boone	16.00	7.25	2.00
☐ 7 Ron Negray	10.00	4.50	1.25
☐ 8 Walter Alston MG	40.00	18.00	5.00
☐ 9 Ruben Gomez DP	9.00	4.00	1.10
☐ 10 Warren Spahn	70.00	32.00	8.75
☐ 11A Chicago Cubs (Centered)	30.00	13.50	3.70
☐ 11B Cubs Team (Dated 1955)	75.00	34.00	9.50
☐ 11C Cubs Team (Name at far left)	30.00	13.50	3.70
☐ 12 Andy Carey	16.00	7.25	2.00
☐ 13 Roy Face	16.00	7.25	2.00
☐ 14 Ken Boyer DP	16.00	7.25	2.00
☐ 15 Ernie Banks DP	80.00	36.00	10.00
☐ 16 Hector Lopez	16.00	7.25	2.00
☐ 17 Gene Conley	12.00	5.50	1.50
☐ 18 Dick Donovan	10.00	4.50	1.25
☐ 19 Chuck Diering	10.00	4.50	1.25
☐ 20 Al Kaline	90.00	40.00	11.00
☐ 21 Joe Collins DP	14.00	6.25	1.75
☐ 22 Jim Finigan	10.00	4.50	1.25
☐ 23 Fred Marsh	10.00	4.50	1.25
☐ 24 Dick Groat	16.00	7.25	2.00
☐ 25 Ted Kluszewski	35.00	16.00	4.40
☐ 26 Grady Hatton	10.00	4.50	1.25
☐ 27 Nelson Burbrink	10.00	4.50	1.25
☐ 28 Bobby Hofman	10.00	4.50	1.25
☐ 29 Jack Harshman	10.00	4.50	1.25
☐ 30 Jackie Robinson DP	175.00	80.00	22.00
☐ 31 Hank Aaron UER (Small photo actually Willie Mays)	275.00	125.00	34.00
☐ 32 Frank House	10.00	4.50	1.25
☐ 33 Roberto Clemente	450.00	200.00	55.00
☐ 34 Tom Brewer	10.00	4.50	1.25
☐ 35 Al Rosen	16.00	7.25	2.00
☐ 36 Rudy Minarcin	10.00	4.50	1.25
☐ 37 Alex Grammas	10.00	4.50	1.25
☐ 38 Bob Kennedy	12.00	5.50	1.50
☐ 39 Don Mossi	12.00	5.50	1.50
☐ 40 Bob Turley	16.00	7.25	2.00
☐ 41 Hank Sauer	16.00	7.25	2.00
☐ 42 Sandy Amoros	16.00	7.25	2.00
☐ 43 Ray Moore	10.00	4.50	1.25
☐ 44 Windy McCall	10.00	4.50	1.25
☐ 45 Gus Zernial	12.00	5.50	1.50
☐ 46 Gene Freese DP	9.00	4.00	1.10
☐ 47 Art Fowler	10.00	4.50	1.25
☐ 48 Jim Hegan	12.00	5.50	1.50
☐ 49 Pedro Ramos	10.00	4.50	1.25
☐ 50 Dusty Rhodes	16.00	7.25	2.00
☐ 51 Ernie Oravetz	10.00	4.50	1.25

☐ 52 Bob Grim	16.00	7.25	2.00
☐ 53 Arnie Portocarrero	10.00	4.50	1.25
☐ 54 Bob Keegan	10.00	4.50	1.25
☐ 55 Wally Moon	16.00	7.25	2.00
☐ 56 Dale Long	16.00	7.25	2.00
☐ 57 Duke Maas	10.00	4.50	1.25
☐ 58 Ed Roebuck	16.00	7.25	2.00
☐ 59 Jose Santiago	10.00	4.50	1.25
☐ 60 Mayo Smith MG DP	9.00	4.00	1.10
☐ 61 Bill Skowron	16.00	7.25	2.00
☐ 62 Hal Smith	10.00	4.50	1.25
☐ 63 Roger Craig	16.00	7.25	2.00
☐ 64 Luis Arroyo	10.00	4.50	1.25
☐ 65 Johnny O'Brien	12.00	5.50	1.50
☐ 66 Bob Speake	10.00	4.50	1.25
☐ 67 Vic Power	12.00	5.50	1.50
☐ 68 Chuck Stobbs	10.00	4.50	1.25
☐ 69 Chuck Tanner	16.00	7.25	2.00
☐ 70 Jim Rivera	10.00	4.50	1.25
☐ 71 Frank Sullivan	10.00	4.50	1.25
☐ 72A Phillies Team (Centered)	30.00	13.50	3.70
☐ 72B Phillies Team (Dated 1955)	75.00	34.00	9.50
☐ 72C Phillies Team (Name at far left)	30.00	13.50	3.70
☐ 73 Wayne Terwilliger	10.00	4.50	1.25
☐ 74 Jim King	10.00	4.50	1.25
☐ 75 Roy Sievers DP	12.00	5.50	1.50
☐ 76 Ray Crone	10.00	4.50	1.25
☐ 77 Harvey Haddix	16.00	7.25	2.00
☐ 78 Herman Wehmeier	10.00	4.50	1.25
☐ 79 Sandy Koufax	350.00	160.00	45.00
☐ 80 Gus Triandos DP	10.00	4.50	1.25
☐ 81 Wally Westlake	10.00	4.50	1.25
☐ 82 Bill Renna	10.00	4.50	1.25
☐ 83 Karl Spooner	16.00	7.25	2.00
☐ 84 Babe Birrer	10.00	4.50	1.25
☐ 85A Cleveland Indians (Centered)	30.00	13.50	3.70
☐ 85B Indians Team (Dated 1955)	75.00	34.00	9.50
☐ 85C Indians Team (Name at far left)	30.00	13.50	3.70
☐ 86 Ray Jablonski DP	9.00	4.00	1.10
☐ 87 Dean Stone	10.00	4.50	1.25
☐ 88 Johnny Kucks	16.00	7.25	2.00
☐ 89 Norm Zauchin	10.00	4.50	1.25
☐ 90A Cincinnati Redlegs Team (Centered)	30.00	13.50	3.70
☐ 90B Reds Team (Dated 1955)	75.00	34.00	9.50
☐ 90C Reds Team (Name at far left)	30.00	13.50	3.70
☐ 91 Gail Harris	10.00	4.50	1.25
☐ 92 Bob(Red) Wilson	10.00	4.50	1.25
☐ 93 George Susce	10.00	4.50	1.25
☐ 94 Ron Kline	10.00	4.50	1.25
☐ 95A Milwaukee Braves Team (Centered)	42.00	19.00	5.25
☐ 95B Braves Team (Dated 1955)	75.00	34.00	9.50
☐ 95C Braves Team (Name at far left)	42.00	19.00	5.25
☐ 96 Bill Tremel	10.00	4.50	1.25
☐ 97 Jerry Lynch	12.00	5.50	1.50
☐ 98 Camilo Pascual	12.00	5.50	1.50
☐ 99 Don Zimmer	12.00	5.50	1.50
☐ 100A Baltimore Orioles Team (centered)	35.00	16.00	4.40
☐ 100B Orioles Team (Dated 1955)	75.00	34.00	9.50
☐ 100C Orioles Team (Name at far left)	35.00	16.00	4.40
☐ 101 Roy Campanella	150.00	70.00	19.00
☐ 102 Jim Davis	12.00	5.50	1.50
☐ 103 Willie Miranda	12.00	5.50	1.50
☐ 104 Bob Lennon	12.00	5.50	1.50
☐ 105 Al Smith	12.00	5.50	1.50
☐ 106 Joe Astroth	12.00	5.50	1.50
☐ 107 Eddie Mathews	60.00	27.00	7.50
☐ 108 Laurin Pepper	12.00	5.50	1.50
☐ 109 Enos Slaughter	35.00	16.00	4.40
☐ 110 Yogi Berra	125.00	55.00	15.50
☐ 111 Boston Red Sox Team Card	35.00	16.00	4.40
☐ 112 Dee Fondy	12.00	5.50	1.50
☐ 113 Phil Rizzuto	90.00	40.00	11.00
☐ 114 Jim Owens	12.00	5.50	1.50
☐ 115 Jackie Jensen	16.00	7.25	2.00
☐ 116 Eddie O'Brien	12.00	5.50	1.50
☐ 117 Virgil Trucks	14.00	6.25	1.75
☐ 118 Nellie Fox	50.00	22.00	6.25
☐ 119 Larry Jackson	14.00	6.25	1.75
☐ 120 Richie Ashburn	50.00	22.00	6.25
☐ 121 Pittsburgh Pirates Team Card	35.00	16.00	4.40
☐ 122 Willard Nixon	12.00	5.50	1.50
☐ 123 Roy McMillan	14.00	6.25	1.75
☐ 124 Don Kaiser	12.00	5.50	1.50
☐ 125 Minnie Minoso	35.00	16.00	4.40
☐ 126 Jim Brady	12.00	5.50	1.50
☐ 127 Willie Jones	14.00	6.25	1.75
☐ 128 Eddie Yost	14.00	6.25	1.75
☐ 129 Jake Martin	12.00	5.50	1.50
☐ 130 Willie Mays	300.00	135.00	38.00
☐ 131 Bob Roselli	12.00	5.50	1.50
☐ 132 Bobby Avila	12.00	5.50	1.50
☐ 133 Ray Narleski	12.00	5.50	1.50
☐ 134 St. Louis Cardinals Team Card	35.00	16.00	4.40
☐ 135 Mickey Mantle	1400.00	650.00	180.00
☐ 136 Johnny Logan	14.00	6.25	1.75
☐ 137 Al Silvera	12.00	5.50	1.50
☐ 138 Johnny Antonelli	14.00	6.25	1.75
☐ 139 Tommy Carroll	12.00	5.50	1.50
☐ 140 Herb Score	60.00	27.00	7.50
☐ 141 Joe Frazier	12.00	5.50	1.50
☐ 142 Gene Baker	12.00	5.50	1.50
☐ 143 Jim Piersall	16.00	7.25	2.00
☐ 144 Leroy Powell	12.00	5.50	1.50
☐ 145 Gil Hodges	50.00	22.00	6.25
☐ 146 Washington Nationals Team Card	35.00	16.00	4.40
☐ 147 Earl Torgeson	12.00	5.50	1.50
☐ 148 Alvin Dark	16.00	7.25	2.00
☐ 149 Dixie Howell	12.00	5.50	1.50
☐ 150 Duke Snider	90.00	40.00	11.00
☐ 151 Spook Jacobs	14.00	6.25	1.75
☐ 152 Billy Hoeft	14.00	6.25	1.75
☐ 153 Frank Thomas	14.00	6.25	1.75
☐ 154 Dave Pope	12.00	5.50	1.50
☐ 155 Harvey Kuenn	16.00	7.25	2.00
☐ 156 Wes Westrum	14.00	6.25	1.75
☐ 157 Dick Brodowski	12.00	5.50	1.50
☐ 158 Wally Post	14.00	6.25	1.75
☐ 159 Clint Courtney	12.00	5.50	1.50
☐ 160 Billy Pierce	16.00	7.25	2.00
☐ 161 Joe DeMaestri	12.00	5.50	1.50
☐ 162 Dave(Gus) Bell	14.00	6.25	1.75
☐ 163 Gene Woodling	14.00	6.25	1.75
☐ 164 Harmon Killebrew	100.00	45.00	12.50
☐ 165 Red Schoendienst	35.00	16.00	4.40
☐ 166 Brooklyn Dodgers Team Card	250.00	110.00	31.00
☐ 167 Harry Dorish	12.00	5.50	1.50
☐ 168 Sammy White	12.00	5.50	1.50
☐ 169 Bob Nelson	12.00	5.50	1.50
☐ 170 Bill Virdon	14.00	6.25	1.75
☐ 171 Jim Wilson	12.00	5.50	1.50
☐ 172 Frank Torre	14.00	6.25	1.75
☐ 173 Johnny Podres	22.50	10.00	2.80
☐ 174 Glen Gorbous	12.00	5.50	1.50
☐ 175 Del Crandall	14.00	6.25	1.75
☐ 176 Alex Kellner	12.00	5.50	1.50
☐ 177 Hank Bauer	22.50	10.00	2.80
☐ 178 Joe Black	16.00	7.25	2.00
☐ 179 Harry Chiti	12.00	5.50	1.50
☐ 180 Robin Roberts	40.00	18.00	5.00
☐ 181 Billy Martin	50.00	22.00	6.25
☐ 182 Paul Minner	15.00	6.75	1.85
☐ 183 Stan Lopata	15.00	6.75	1.85
☐ 184 Don Bessent	15.00	6.75	1.85
☐ 185 Bill Bruton	18.00	8.00	2.20
☐ 186 Ron Jackson	15.00	6.75	1.85
☐ 187 Early Wynn	40.00	18.00	5.00
☐ 188 Chicago White Sox Team Card	40.00	18.00	5.00
☐ 189 Ned Garver	15.00	6.75	1.85
☐ 190 Carl Furillo	35.00	16.00	4.40
☐ 191 Frank Lary	18.00	8.00	2.20
☐ 192 Smoky Burgess	18.00	8.00	2.20
☐ 193 Wilmer Mizell	18.00	8.00	2.20
☐ 194 Monte Irvin	35.00	16.00	4.40
☐ 195 George Kell	35.00	16.00	4.40
☐ 196 Tom Poholsky	15.00	6.75	1.85
☐ 197 Granny Hamner	15.00	6.75	1.85
☐ 198 Ed Fitzgerald	15.00	6.75	1.85
☐ 199 Hank Thompson	18.00	8.00	2.20
☐ 200 Bob Feller	100.00	45.00	12.50
☐ 201 Rip Repulski	15.00	6.75	1.85
☐ 202 Jim Hearn	15.00	6.75	1.85
☐ 203 Bill Tuttle	15.00	6.75	1.85
☐ 204 Art Swanson	15.00	6.75	1.85
☐ 205 Whitey Lockman	18.00	8.00	2.20
☐ 206 Erv Palica	15.00	6.75	1.85
☐ 207 Jim Small	15.00	6.75	1.85
☐ 208 Elston Howard	50.00	22.00	6.25
☐ 209 Max Surkont	15.00	6.75	1.85
☐ 210 Mike Garcia	18.00	8.00	2.20
☐ 211 Murry Dickson	15.00	6.75	1.85
☐ 212 Johnny Temple	15.00	6.75	1.85
☐ 213 Detroit Tigers Team Card	55.00	25.00	7.00
☐ 214 Bob Rush	15.00	6.75	1.85
☐ 215 Tommy Byrne	22.50	10.00	2.80
☐ 216 Jerry Schoonmaker	15.00	6.75	1.85
☐ 217 Billy Klaus	15.00	6.75	1.85
☐ 218 Joe Nuxhall UER (Misspelled Nuxall)	18.00	8.00	2.20
☐ 219 Lew Burdette	20.00	9.00	2.50
☐ 220 Del Ennis	18.00	8.00	2.20
☐ 221 Bob Friend	20.00	9.00	2.50
☐ 222 Dave Philley	15.00	6.75	1.85
☐ 223 Randy Jackson	15.00	6.75	1.85
☐ 224 Bud Podbielan	15.00	6.75	1.85
☐ 225 Gil McDougald	30.00	13.50	3.70
☐ 226 New York Giants Team Card	75.00	34.00	9.50
☐ 227 Russ Meyer	15.00	6.75	1.85
☐ 228 Mickey Vernon	20.00	9.00	2.50
☐ 229 Harry Brecheen CO	18.00	8.00	2.20
☐ 230 Chico Carrasquel	15.00	6.75	1.85
☐ 231 Bob Hale	15.00	6.75	1.85
☐ 232 Toby Atwell	15.00	6.75	1.85
☐ 233 Carl Erskine	35.00	16.00	4.40
☐ 234 Pete Runnels	18.00	8.00	2.20
☐ 235 Don Newcombe	50.00	22.00	6.25
☐ 236 Kansas City Athletics Team Card	35.00	16.00	4.40
☐ 237 Jose Valdivielso	15.00	6.75	1.85
☐ 238 Walt Dropo	18.00	8.00	2.20
☐ 239 Harry Simpson	15.00	6.75	1.85
☐ 240 Whitey Ford	100.00	45.00	12.50
☐ 241 Don Mueller UER (6" tall)	18.00	8.00	2.20
☐ 242 Hershell Freeman	15.00	6.75	1.85
☐ 243 Sherm Lollar	18.00	8.00	2.20
☐ 244 Bob Buhl	18.00	8.00	2.20
☐ 245 Billy Goodman	18.00	8.00	2.20
☐ 246 Tom Gorman	15.00	6.75	1.85
☐ 247 Bill Sarni	15.00	6.75	1.85
☐ 248 Bob Porterfield	15.00	6.75	1.85
☐ 249 Johnny Klippstein	15.00	6.75	1.85
☐ 250 Larry Doby	35.00	16.00	4.40
☐ 251 New York Yankees Team Card UER (Don Larsen misspelled as Larson on front)	275.00	125.00	34.00
☐ 252 Vern Law	18.00	8.00	2.20
☐ 253 Irv Noren	15.00	6.75	1.85
☐ 254 George Crowe	15.00	6.75	1.85
☐ 255 Bob Lemon	35.00	16.00	4.40
☐ 256 Tom Hurd	15.00	6.75	1.85
☐ 257 Bobby Thomson	35.00	16.00	4.40
☐ 258 Art Ditmar	15.00	6.75	1.85
☐ 259 Sam Jones	18.00	8.00	2.20
☐ 260 Pee Wee Reese	120.00	55.00	15.00
☐ 261 Bobby Shantz	14.00	6.25	1.75
☐ 262 Howie Pollet	12.00	5.50	1.50
☐ 263 Bob Miller	12.00	5.50	1.50
☐ 264 Ray Monzant	12.00	5.50	1.50
☐ 265 Sandy Consuegra	12.00	5.50	1.50
☐ 266 Don Ferrarese	12.00	5.50	1.50
☐ 267 Bob Nieman	12.00	5.50	1.50
☐ 268 Dale Mitchell	16.00	7.25	2.00
☐ 269 Jack Meyer	12.00	5.50	1.50
☐ 270 Billy Loes	14.00	6.25	1.75
☐ 271 Foster Castleman	12.00	5.50	1.50
☐ 272 Danny O'Connell	12.00	5.50	1.50
☐ 273 Walker Cooper	12.00	5.50	1.50
☐ 274 Frank Baumholtz	12.00	5.50	1.50
☐ 275 Jim Greengrass	12.00	5.50	1.50
☐ 276 George Zuverink	12.00	5.50	1.50
☐ 277 Daryl Spencer	12.00	5.50	1.50
☐ 278 Chet Nichols	12.00	5.50	1.50
☐ 279 Johnny Groth	12.00	5.50	1.50
☐ 280 Jim Gilliam	35.00	16.00	4.40
☐ 281 Art Houtteman	12.00	5.50	1.50
☐ 282 Warren Hacker	12.00	5.50	1.50
☐ 283 Hal Smith	12.00	5.50	1.50
☐ 284 Ike Delock	12.00	5.50	1.50
☐ 285 Eddie Miksis	12.00	5.50	1.50
☐ 286 Bill Wight	12.00	5.50	1.50
☐ 287 Bobby Adams	12.00	5.50	1.50
☐ 288 Bob Cerv	40.00	18.00	5.00
☐ 289 Hal Jeffcoat	12.00	5.50	1.50
☐ 290 Curt Simmons	14.00	6.25	1.75
☐ 291 Frank Kellert	12.00	5.50	1.50
☐ 292 Luis Aparicio	125.00	55.00	15.50
☐ 293 Stu Miller	14.00	6.25	1.75
☐ 294 Ernie Johnson	14.00	6.25	1.75
☐ 295 Clem Labine	18.00	8.00	2.20
☐ 296 Andy Seminick	12.00	5.50	1.50
☐ 297 Bob Skinner	14.00	6.25	1.75
☐ 298 Johnny Schmitz	12.00	5.50	1.50
☐ 299 Charlie Neal	35.00	16.00	4.40
☐ 300 Vic Wertz	16.00	7.25	2.00
☐ 301 Marv Grissom	12.00	5.50	1.50
☐ 302 Eddie Robinson	12.00	5.50	1.50
☐ 303 Jim Dyck	12.00	5.50	1.50
☐ 304 Frank Malzone	16.00	7.25	2.00
☐ 305 Brooks Lawrence	12.00	5.50	1.50
☐ 306 Curt Roberts	12.00	5.50	1.50
☐ 307 Hoyt Wilhelm	35.00	16.00	4.40
☐ 308 Chuck Harmon	12.00	5.50	1.50
☐ 309 Don Blasingame	16.00	7.25	2.00
☐ 310 Steve Gromek	12.00	5.50	1.50
☐ 311 Hal Naragon	12.00	5.50	1.50
☐ 312 Andy Pafko	16.00	7.25	2.00
☐ 313 Gene Stephens	12.00	5.50	1.50
☐ 314 Hobie Landrith	12.00	5.50	1.50
☐ 315 Milt Bolling	12.00	5.50	1.50
☐ 316 Jerry Coleman	18.00	8.00	2.20
☐ 317 Al Aber	12.00	5.50	1.50
☐ 318 Fred Hatfield	12.00	5.50	1.50
☐ 319 Jack Crimian	12.00	5.50	1.50
☐ 320 Joe Adcock	16.00	7.25	2.00
☐ 321 Jim Konstanty	16.00	7.25	2.00
☐ 322 Karl Olson	12.00	5.50	1.50
☐ 323 Willard Schmidt	12.00	5.50	1.50
☐ 324 Rocky Bridges	14.00	6.25	1.75
☐ 325 Don Liddle	12.00	5.50	1.50
☐ 326 Connie Johnson	12.00	5.50	1.50
☐ 327 Bob Wiesler	12.00	5.50	1.50
☐ 328 Preston Ward	12.00	5.50	1.50
☐ 329 Lou Berberet	12.00	5.50	1.50
☐ 330 Jim Busby	12.00	5.50	1.50
☐ 331 Dick Hall	12.00	5.50	1.50
☐ 332 Don Larsen	60.00	27.00	7.50
☐ 333 Rube Walker	12.00	5.50	1.50
☐ 334 Bob Miller	12.00	5.50	1.50
☐ 335 Don Hoak	14.00	6.25	1.75
☐ 336 Ellis Kinder	12.00	5.50	1.50
☐ 337 Bobby Morgan	12.00	5.50	1.50
☐ 338 Jim Delsing	12.00	5.50	1.50
☐ 339 Rance Pless	12.00	5.50	1.50
☐ 340 Mickey McDermott	60.00	12.00	3.60
☐ NNO Checklist 2/4	300.00	95.00	45.00
☐ NNO Checklist 1/3	300.00	95.00	45.00

1956 Topps Hocus Focus

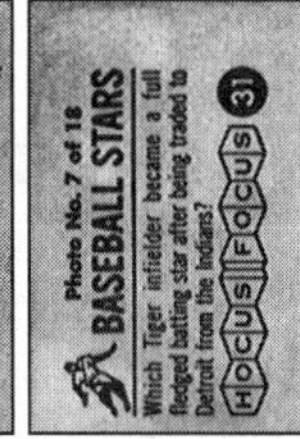

This 1956 Topps issue is often confused with the Magic Photos issue of 1950. The R714-26 (catalog designation) set comes in two types, which we have arbitrarily labeled A and B. Style A, the larger size (1" by 1 5/8"), contains 18 baseball subjects with the ones known checklisted below. Type B, the smaller size (7/8" by 1 3/8"), is reported to contain baseball subjects, those known are checklisted below. Like the Magic Photo set, these cards were "developed" by sunlight. The baseball players in these sets are but a portion of the total cards in the set. Dogs, personalities and other subjects were also featured.

	NRMT	VG-E	GOOD
COMPLETE BASEBALL PLAYERS	2000.00	900.00	250.00
COMMON A CARD	30.00	13.50	3.70
COMMON B CARD	40.00	18.00	5.00
☐ A9 Mayo Smith MG 51	30.00	13.50	3.70
☐ A1 Dick Groat 43	40.00	18.00	5.00
☐ A2 Ed Lopat 44	50.00	22.00	6.25
☐ A3 Hank Sauer 30	40.00	18.00	5.00
☐ A4 Dusty Rhodes 86	30.00	13.50	3.70
☐ A5 Ted Williams 5	200.00	90.00	25.00
☐ A6 Harvey Haddix 26	30.00	13.50	3.70
☐ A7 Ray Boone 31	30.00	13.50	3.70
☐ A8 Al Rosen 69	40.00	18.00	5.00
☐ A10 Warren Spahn 87	100.00	45.00	12.50
☐ A11 Jim Rivera 67	30.00	13.50	3.70
☐ A12 Ted Kluszewski 79	50.00	22.00	6.25
☐ A13 Gus Zernial 49	30.00	13.50	3.70
☐ A14 Jackie Robinson 13	200.00	90.00	25.00
☐ A15 Hal Smith 42	30.00	13.50	3.70
☐ A16 Johnny Schmitz 84	30.00	13.50	3.70
☐ A17 Spook Jacobs 60	30.00	13.50	3.70
☐ A18 Mel Parnell 18	40.00	18.00	5.00
☐ B1 Babe Ruth 117	400.00	180.00	50.00
☐ B3 Dick Groat 43	50.00	22.00	6.25
☐ B6 Dusty Rhodes 86	50.00	22.00	6.25
☐ B7 Ted Williams 5	250.00	110.00	31.00
☐ B8 Harvey Haddix 26	40.00	18.00	5.00
☐ B9 Ray Boone 31	40.00	18.00	5.00
☐ B12 Warren Spahn 87	125.00	55.00	15.50
☐ B13 Jim Rivera 67	40.00	18.00	5.00
☐ B14 Ted Kluszewski 79	60.00	27.00	7.50
☐ B15 Gus Zernial 49	40.00	18.00	5.00
☐ B18 Johnny Schmitz 84	40.00	18.00	5.00
☐ B20 Karl Spooner 122	40.00	18.00	5.00
☐ B21 Ed Mathews 109	125.00	55.00	15.50

1956 Topps Pins

This set of 60 full-color pins was Topps first and only baseball player pin set. Each pin measures 1 3/16" in diameter. Although the set was advertised to contain 90 pins, only 60 were issued. The checklist below lists the players in alphabetical order within team, e.g., Baltimore Orioles (1-4), Chicago Cubs (5-7), Cleveland Indians (8-11), Kansas City A's (12-15), Milwaukee Braves (16-19), Philadelphia Phillies (20-22), Boston Red Sox (23-26), New York Yankees (27-31), Chicago White Sox (32-35), Detroit Tigers (36-38), New York Giants (39-41), Pittsburgh Pirates (42-44), St. Louis Cardinals (45-48), Brooklyn Dodgers (49-53), Cincinnati Redlegs (54-57) and Washington Senators (58-60). Chuck Diering, Hector Lopez and Chuck Stobbs (noted below with SP) are more difficult to obtain than other pins in the set.

	NRMT	VG-E	GOOD
COMPLETE SET (60)	2250.00	1000.00	275.00
COMMON PIN (1-60)	15.00	6.75	1.85
PIN BOX	200.00	90.00	25.00
☐ 1 Chuck Diering SP	250.00	110.00	31.00
☐ 2 Willie Miranda	15.00	6.75	1.85
☐ 3 Hal Smith	15.00	6.75	1.85
☐ 4 Gus Triandos	20.00	9.00	2.50
☐ 5 Ernie Banks	75.00	34.00	9.50
☐ 6 Hank Sauer	20.00	9.00	2.50
☐ 7 Bill Tremel	15.00	6.75	1.85
☐ 8 Jim Hegan	15.00	6.75	1.85
☐ 9 Don Mossi	15.00	6.75	1.85
☐ 10 Al Rosen	25.00	11.00	3.10
☐ 11 Al Smith	15.00	6.75	1.85
☐ 12 Jim Finigan	15.00	6.75	1.85
☐ 13 Hector Lopez SP	200.00	90.00	25.00
☐ 14 Vic Power	15.00	6.75	1.85
☐ 15 Gus Zernial	20.00	9.00	2.50
☐ 16 Hank Aaron	125.00	55.00	15.50
☐ 17 Gene Conley	15.00	6.75	1.85
☐ 18 Ed Mathews	75.00	34.00	9.50
☐ 19 Warren Spahn	75.00	34.00	9.50
☐ 20 Ron Negray	15.00	6.75	1.85
☐ 21 Mayo Smith MG	15.00	6.75	1.85
☐ 22 Herman Wehmeier	15.00	6.75	1.85
☐ 23 Grady Hatton	15.00	6.75	1.85
☐ 24 Jackie Jensen	25.00	11.00	3.10
☐ 25 Frank Sullivan	15.00	6.75	1.85
☐ 26 Ted Williams	150.00	70.00	19.00
☐ 27 Yogi Berra	100.00	45.00	12.50
☐ 28 Joe Collins	20.00	9.00	2.50
☐ 29 Phil Rizzuto	50.00	22.00	6.25
☐ 30 Bill Skowron	25.00	11.00	3.10
☐ 31 Bob Turley	25.00	11.00	3.10
☐ 32 Dick Donovan	15.00	6.75	1.85
☐ 33 Jack Harshman	15.00	6.75	1.85
☐ 34 Bob Kennedy	15.00	6.75	1.85
☐ 35 Jim Rivera	15.00	6.75	1.85
☐ 36 Ray Boone	20.00	9.00	2.50
☐ 37 Frank House	15.00	6.75	1.85
☐ 38 Al Kaline	75.00	34.00	9.50
☐ 39 Ruben Gomez	15.00	6.75	1.85
☐ 40 Bobby Hofman	15.00	6.75	1.85
☐ 41 Willie Mays	125.00	55.00	15.50
☐ 42 Dick Groat	25.00	11.00	3.10
☐ 43 Dale Long	20.00	9.00	2.50
☐ 44 Johnny O'Brien	15.00	6.75	1.85
☐ 45 Luis Arroyo	15.00	6.75	1.85
☐ 46 Ken Boyer	25.00	11.00	3.10
☐ 47 Harvey Haddix	15.00	6.75	1.85
☐ 48 Wally Moon	15.00	6.75	1.85
☐ 49 Sandy Amoros	15.00	6.75	1.85
☐ 50 Gil Hodges	50.00	22.00	6.25
☐ 51 Jackie Robinson	135.00	60.00	17.00
☐ 52 Duke Snider	75.00	34.00	9.50
☐ 53 Karl Spooner	15.00	6.75	1.85
☐ 54 Joe Black	25.00	11.00	3.10
☐ 55 Art Fowler	15.00	6.75	1.85
☐ 56 Ted Kluszewski	30.00	13.50	3.70
☐ 57 Roy McMillan	15.00	6.75	1.85
☐ 58 Carlos Paula	15.00	6.75	1.85
☐ 59 Roy Sievers	15.00	6.75	1.85
☐ 60 Chuck Stobbs SP	200.00	90.00	25.00

1957 Topps

The cards in this 407-card set measure 2 1/2" by 3 1/2". In 1957, Topps returned to the vertical obverse, adopted what we now call the standard card size, and used a large, uncluttered color photo for the first time since 1952. Cards in the series 265 to 352 and the unnumbered checklist cards are scarcer than other cards in the set. However within this scarce series (265-352) there are 22 cards which were printed in double the quantity of the other cards in the series; these 22 double prints are indicated by DP in the checklist below. The first star combination cards, cards 400 and 407, are quite popular with collectors. They feature the big stars of the previous season's World Series teams, the Dodgers (Furillo, Hodges, Campanella, and Snider) and Yankees (Berra and Mantle). The complete set price below does not include the unnumbered checklist cards. Confirmed packaging includes one-cent penny packs and six-card nickle packs. Cello packs are definately known to exist and some collectors remember buyikng rack packs of 57's as well. The key Rookie Cards in this set are Jim Bunning, Rocky Colavito, Don Drysdale, Whitey Herzog, Tony Kubek, Bill Mazeroski, Bobby Richardson, Brooks Robinson, and Frank Robinson.

	NRMT	VG-E	GOOD
COMPLETE SET (407)	7000.00	3200.00	900.00
COMMON CARD (1-88)	10.00	4.50	1.25
COMMON CARD (89-176)	8.00	3.60	1.00
COMMON CARD (177-264)	8.00	3.60	1.00
COMMON CARD (265-352)	20.00	9.00	2.50
COMMON CARD (353-407)	8.00	3.60	1.00
WRAPPER (1-CENT)	300.00	135.00	38.00
WRAPPER (5-CENT)	200.00	90.00	25.00
☐ 1 Ted Williams	500.00	150.00	50.00
☐ 2 Yogi Berra	125.00	55.00	15.50
☐ 3 Dale Long	12.00	5.50	1.50
☐ 4 Johnny Logan	12.00	5.50	1.50
☐ 5 Sal Maglie	15.00	6.75	1.85
☐ 6 Hector Lopez	12.00	5.50	1.50
☐ 7 Luis Aparicio	35.00	16.00	4.40
☐ 8 Don Mossi	12.00	5.50	1.50
☐ 9 Johnny Temple	12.00	5.50	1.50
☐ 10 Willie Mays	225.00	100.00	28.00
☐ 11 George Zuverink	10.00	4.50	1.25
☐ 12 Dick Groat	12.00	5.50	1.50
☐ 13 Wally Burnette	10.00	4.50	1.25
☐ 14 Bob Nieman	10.00	4.50	1.25
☐ 15 Robin Roberts	35.00	16.00	4.40
☐ 16 Walt Moryn	10.00	4.50	1.25
☐ 17 Billy Gardner	10.00	4.50	1.25
☐ 18 Don Drysdale	180.00	80.00	22.00
☐ 19 Bob Wilson	10.00	4.50	1.25
☐ 20 Hank Aaron UER (Reverse negative photo on front)	200.00	90.00	25.00
☐ 21 Frank Sullivan	10.00	4.50	1.25
☐ 22 Jerry Snyder UER (Photo actually Ed Fitzgerald)	10.00	4.50	1.25
☐ 23 Sherm Lollar	12.00	5.50	1.50
☐ 24 Bill Mazeroski	75.00	34.00	9.50
☐ 25 Whitey Ford	70.00	32.00	8.75
☐ 26 Bob Boyd	10.00	4.50	1.25
☐ 27 Ted Kazanski	10.00	4.50	1.25
☐ 28 Gene Conley	12.00	5.50	1.50
☐ 29 Whitey Herzog	25.00	11.00	3.10
☐ 30 Pee Wee Reese	65.00	29.00	8.00
☐ 31 Ron Northey	10.00	4.50	1.25
☐ 32 Hershell Freeman	10.00	4.50	1.25
☐ 33 Jim Small	10.00	4.50	1.25
☐ 34 Tom Sturdivant	15.00	6.75	1.85
☐ 35 Frank Robinson	180.00	80.00	22.00
☐ 36 Bob Grim	10.00	4.50	1.25
☐ 37 Frank Torre	12.00	5.50	1.50
☐ 38 Nellie Fox	45.00	20.00	5.50
☐ 39 Al Worthington	10.00	4.50	1.25
☐ 40 Early Wynn	30.00	13.50	3.70
☐ 41 Hal W. Smith	10.00	4.50	1.25
☐ 42 Dee Fondy	10.00	4.50	1.25
☐ 43 Connie Johnson	10.00	4.50	1.25
☐ 44 Joe DeMaestri	10.00	4.50	1.25
☐ 45 Carl Furillo	20.00	9.00	2.50
☐ 46 Robert J. Miller	10.00	4.50	1.25
☐ 47 Don Blasingame	10.00	4.50	1.25
☐ 48 Bill Bruton	12.00	5.50	1.50
☐ 49 Daryl Spencer	10.00	4.50	1.25
☐ 50 Herb Score	20.00	9.00	2.50
☐ 51 Clint Courtney	10.00	4.50	1.25
☐ 52 Lee Walls	10.00	4.50	1.25
☐ 53 Clem Labine	15.00	6.75	1.85
☐ 54 Elmer Valo	10.00	4.50	1.25
☐ 55 Ernie Banks	120.00	55.00	15.00
☐ 56 Dave Sisler	10.00	4.50	1.25
☐ 57 Jim Lemon	12.00	5.50	1.50
☐ 58 Ruben Gomez	10.00	4.50	1.25
☐ 59 Dick Williams	12.00	5.50	1.50
☐ 60 Billy Hoeft	12.00	5.50	1.50
☐ 61 James(Dusty) Rhodes	12.00	5.50	1.50
☐ 62 Billy Martin	35.00	16.00	4.40
☐ 63 Ike Delock	10.00	4.50	1.25
☐ 64 Pete Runnels	12.00	5.50	1.50
☐ 65 Wally Moon	12.00	5.50	1.50
☐ 66 Brooks Lawrence	10.00	4.50	1.25
☐ 67 Chico Carrasquel	10.00	4.50	1.25
☐ 68 Ray Crone	10.00	4.50	1.25
☐ 69 Roy McMillan	12.00	5.50	1.50
☐ 70 Richie Ashburn	45.00	20.00	5.50
☐ 71 Murry Dickson	10.00	4.50	1.25
☐ 72 Bill Tuttle	10.00	4.50	1.25
☐ 73 George Crowe	10.00	4.50	1.25
☐ 74 Vito Valentinetti	10.00	4.50	1.25
☐ 75 Jim Piersall	12.00	5.50	1.50
☐ 76 Roberto Clemente	300.00	135.00	38.00
☐ 77 Paul Foytack	10.00	4.50	1.25
☐ 78 Vic Wertz	12.00	5.50	1.50
☐ 79 Lindy McDaniel	12.00	5.50	1.50
☐ 80 Gil Hodges	45.00	20.00	5.50
☐ 81 Herman Wehmeier	10.00	4.50	1.25
☐ 82 Elston Howard	20.00	9.00	2.50
☐ 83 Lou Skizas	10.00	4.50	1.25
☐ 84 Moe Drabowsky	12.00	5.50	1.50
☐ 85 Larry Doby	20.00	9.00	2.50
☐ 86 Bill Sarni	10.00	4.50	1.25
☐ 87 Tom Gorman	10.00	4.50	1.25
☐ 88 Harvey Kuenn	12.00	5.50	1.50
☐ 89 Roy Sievers	10.00	4.50	1.25
☐ 90 Warren Spahn	70.00	32.00	8.75
☐ 91 Mack Burk	8.00	3.60	1.00
☐ 92 Mickey Vernon	12.00	5.50	1.50
☐ 93 Hal Jeffcoat	8.00	3.60	1.00
☐ 94 Bobby Del Greco	8.00	3.60	1.00
☐ 95 Mickey Mantle	1000.00	450.00	125.00
☐ 96 Hank Aguirre	8.00	3.60	1.00
☐ 97 New York Yankees Team Card	80.00	36.00	10.00
☐ 98 Alvin Dark	12.00	5.50	1.50
☐ 99 Bob Keegan	8.00	3.60	1.00
☐ 100 League Presidents Warren Giles Will Harridge	12.00	5.50	1.50
☐ 101 Chuck Stobbs	8.00	3.60	1.00
☐ 102 Ray Boone	12.00	5.50	1.50
☐ 103 Joe Nuxhall	12.00	5.50	1.50
☐ 104 Hank Foiles	8.00	3.60	1.00
☐ 105 Johnny Antonelli	12.00	5.50	1.50
☐ 106 Ray Moore	8.00	3.60	1.00
☐ 107 Jim Rivera	8.00	3.60	1.00
☐ 108 Tommy Byrne	12.00	5.50	1.50
☐ 109 Hank Thompson	8.00	3.60	1.00
☐ 110 Bill Virdon	10.00	4.50	1.25
☐ 111 Hal R. Smith	8.00	3.60	1.00
☐ 112 Tom Brewer	8.00	3.60	1.00
☐ 113 Wilmer Mizell	10.00	4.50	1.25
☐ 114 Milwaukee Braves Team Card	22.00	10.00	2.70
☐ 115 Jim Gilliam	12.00	5.50	1.50
☐ 116 Mike Fornieles	8.00	3.60	1.00
☐ 117 Joe Adcock	12.00	5.50	1.50
☐ 118 Bob Porterfield	8.00	3.60	1.00
☐ 119 Stan Lopata	8.00	3.60	1.00
☐ 120 Bob Lemon	25.00	11.00	3.10
☐ 121 Clete Boyer	20.00	9.00	2.50
☐ 122 Ken Boyer	15.00	6.75	1.85
☐ 123 Steve Ridzik	8.00	3.60	1.00
☐ 124 Dave Philley	8.00	3.60	1.00
☐ 125 Al Kaline	100.00	45.00	12.50
☐ 126 Bob Wiesler	8.00	3.60	1.00
☐ 127 Bob Buhl	10.00	4.50	1.25
☐ 128 Ed Bailey	10.00	4.50	1.25
☐ 129 Saul Rogovin	8.00	3.60	1.00
☐ 130 Don Newcombe	20.00	9.00	2.50
☐ 131 Milt Bolling	8.00	3.60	1.00
☐ 132 Art Ditmar	10.00	4.50	1.25
☐ 133 Del Crandall	10.00	4.50	1.25
☐ 134 Don Kaiser	8.00	3.60	1.00
☐ 135 Bill Skowron	15.00	6.75	1.85
☐ 136 Jim Hegan	10.00	4.50	1.25
☐ 137 Bob Rush	8.00	3.60	1.00
☐ 138 Minnie Minoso	20.00	9.00	2.50
☐ 139 Lou Kretlow	8.00	3.60	1.00
☐ 140 Frank Thomas	10.00	4.50	1.25
☐ 141 Al Aber	8.00	3.60	1.00
☐ 142 Charley Thompson	8.00	3.60	1.00
☐ 143 Andy Pafko	12.00	5.50	1.50
☐ 144 Ray Narleski	8.00	3.60	1.00
☐ 145 Al Smith	8.00	3.60	1.00
☐ 146 Don Ferrarese	8.00	3.60	1.00
☐ 147 Al Walker	8.00	3.60	1.00
☐ 148 Don Mueller	10.00	4.50	1.25
☐ 149 Bob Kennedy	10.00	4.50	1.25
☐ 150 Bob Friend	12.00	5.50	1.50
☐ 151 Willie Miranda	8.00	3.60	1.00
☐ 152 Jack Harshman	8.00	3.60	1.00
☐ 153 Karl Olson	8.00	3.60	1.00
☐ 154 Red Schoendienst	25.00	11.00	3.10
☐ 155 Jim Brosnan	10.00	4.50	1.25
☐ 156 Gus Triandos	10.00	4.50	1.25
☐ 157 Wally Post	10.00	4.50	1.25
☐ 158 Curt Simmons	10.00	4.50	1.25
☐ 159 Solly Drake	8.00	3.60	1.00
☐ 160 Billy Pierce	8.00	3.60	1.00
☐ 161 Pittsburgh Pirates Team Card	18.00	8.00	2.20
☐ 162 Jack Meyer	8.00	3.60	1.00
☐ 163 Sammy White	8.00	3.60	1.00
☐ 164 Tommy Carroll	8.00	3.60	1.00
☐ 165 Ted Kluszewski	50.00	22.00	6.25
☐ 166 Roy Face	10.00	4.50	1.25
☐ 167 Vic Power	10.00	4.50	1.25
☐ 168 Frank Lary	10.00	4.50	1.25
☐ 169 Herb Plews	8.00	3.60	1.00
☐ 170 Duke Snider	100.00	45.00	12.50
☐ 171 Boston Red Sox Team Card	18.00	8.00	2.20
☐ 172 Gene Woodling	10.00	4.50	1.25
☐ 173 Roger Craig	12.00	5.50	1.50
☐ 174 Willie Jones	8.00	3.60	1.00
☐ 175 Don Larsen	25.00	11.00	3.10
☐ 176A Gene Baker ERR (Misspelled Bakep on card back)	350.00	160.00	45.00
☐ 176B Gene Baker COR	10.00	4.50	1.25
☐ 177 Eddie Yost	10.00	4.50	1.25
☐ 178 Don Bessent	8.00	3.60	1.00
☐ 179 Ernie Oravetz	8.00	3.60	1.00
☐ 180 Gus Bell	10.00	4.50	1.25
☐ 181 Dick Donovan	8.00	3.60	1.00
☐ 182 Hobie Landrith	8.00	3.60	1.00
☐ 183 Chicago Cubs Team Card	18.00	8.00	2.20
☐ 184 Tito Francona	8.00	3.60	1.00
☐ 185 Johnny Kucks	12.00	5.50	1.50
☐ 186 Jim King	8.00	3.60	1.00
☐ 187 Virgil Trucks	10.00	4.50	1.25
☐ 188 Felix Mantilla	10.00	4.50	1.25
☐ 189 Willard Nixon	8.00	3.60	1.00
☐ 190 Randy Jackson	8.00	3.60	1.00
☐ 191 Joe Margoneri	8.00	3.60	1.00
☐ 192 Jerry Coleman	12.00	5.50	1.50
☐ 193 Del Rice	8.00	3.60	1.00
☐ 194 Hal Brown	8.00	3.60	1.00
☐ 195 Bobby Avila	8.00	3.60	1.00
☐ 196 Larry Jackson	10.00	4.50	1.25
☐ 197 Hank Sauer	10.00	4.50	1.25
☐ 198 Detroit Tigers Team Card	18.00	8.00	2.20
☐ 199 Vern Law	10.00	4.50	1.25
☐ 200 Gil McDougald	15.00	6.75	1.85
☐ 201 Sandy Amoros	12.00	5.50	1.50
☐ 202 Dick Gernert	8.00	3.60	1.00
☐ 203 Hoyt Wilhelm	25.00	11.00	3.10
☐ 204 Kansas City Athletics Team Card	18.00	8.00	2.20
☐ 205 Charlie Maxwell	10.00	4.50	1.25
☐ 206 Willard Schmidt	8.00	3.60	1.00
☐ 207 Gordon(Billy) Hunter	8.00	3.60	1.00
☐ 208 Lou Burdette	12.00	5.50	1.50
☐ 209 Bob Skinner	10.00	4.50	1.25
☐ 210 Roy Campanella	125.00	55.00	15.50
☐ 211 Camilo Pascual	10.00	4.50	1.25
☐ 212 Rocky Colavito	160.00	70.00	20.00
☐ 213 Les Moss	8.00	3.60	1.00
☐ 214 Philadelphia Phillies Team Card	18.00	8.00	2.20
☐ 215 Enos Slaughter	25.00	11.00	3.10
☐ 216 Marv Grissom	8.00	3.60	1.00
☐ 217 Gene Stephens	8.00	3.60	1.00
☐ 218 Ray Jablonski	8.00	3.60	1.00
☐ 219 Tom Acker	8.00	3.60	1.00
☐ 220 Jackie Jensen	10.00	4.50	1.25
☐ 221 Dixie Howell	8.00	3.60	1.00
☐ 222 Alex Grammas	8.00	3.60	1.00
☐ 223 Frank House	8.00	3.60	1.00
☐ 224 Marv Blaylock	8.00	3.60	1.00
☐ 225 Harry Simpson	8.00	3.60	1.00
☐ 226 Preston Ward	8.00	3.60	1.00
☐ 227 Gerry Staley	8.00	3.60	1.00
☐ 228 Smoky Burgess UER (Misspelled Smokey on card back)	10.00	4.50	1.25
☐ 229 George Susce	8.00	3.60	1.00
☐ 230 George Kell	25.00	11.00	3.10
☐ 231 Solly Hemus	8.00	3.60	1.00
☐ 232 Whitey Lockman	10.00	4.50	1.25
☐ 233 Art Fowler	8.00	3.60	1.00
☐ 234 Dick Cole	8.00	3.60	1.00
☐ 235 Tom Poholsky	8.00	3.60	1.00
☐ 236 Joe Ginsberg	8.00	3.60	1.00
☐ 237 Foster Castleman	8.00	3.60	1.00
☐ 238 Eddie Robinson	8.00	3.60	1.00
☐ 239 Tom Morgan	8.00	3.60	1.00
☐ 240 Hank Bauer	12.00	5.50	1.50
☐ 241 Joe Lonnett	8.00	3.60	1.00
☐ 242 Charlie Neal	12.00	5.50	1.50
☐ 243 St. Louis Cardinals Team Card	18.00	8.00	2.20
☐ 244 Billy Loes	10.00	4.50	1.25
☐ 245 Rip Repulski	8.00	3.60	1.00
☐ 246 Jose Valdivielso	8.00	3.60	1.00
☐ 247 Turk Lown	8.00	3.60	1.00
☐ 248 Jim Finigan	8.00	3.60	1.00
☐ 249 Dave Pope	8.00	3.60	1.00
☐ 250 Eddie Mathews	45.00	20.00	5.50
☐ 251 Baltimore Orioles Team Card	18.00	8.00	2.20
☐ 252 Carl Erskine	12.00	5.50	1.50
☐ 253 Gus Zernial	10.00	4.50	1.25
☐ 254 Ron Negray	8.00	3.60	1.00
☐ 255 Charlie Silvera	10.00	4.50	1.25
☐ 256 Ron Kline	8.00	3.60	1.00
☐ 257 Walt Dropo	8.00	3.60	1.00
☐ 258 Steve Gromek	8.00	3.60	1.00
☐ 259 Eddie O'Brien	8.00	3.60	1.00
☐ 260 Del Ennis	10.00	4.50	1.25
☐ 261 Bob Chakales	8.00	3.60	1.00
☐ 262 Bobby Thomson	10.00	4.50	1.25
☐ 263 George Strickland	8.00	3.60	1.00
☐ 264 Bob Turley	12.00	5.50	1.50
☐ 265 Harvey Haddix DP	14.00	6.25	1.75
☐ 266 Ken Kuhn DP	14.00	6.25	1.75
☐ 267 Danny Kravitz	20.00	9.00	2.50
☐ 268 Jack Collum	20.00	9.00	2.50
☐ 269 Bob Cerv	22.50	10.00	2.80
☐ 270 Washington Senators Team Card	60.00	27.00	7.50
☐ 271 Danny O'Connell DP	14.00	6.25	1.75
☐ 272 Bobby Shantz	25.00	11.00	3.10
☐ 273 Jim Davis	20.00	9.00	2.50
☐ 274 Don Hoak	20.00	9.00	2.50
☐ 275 Cleveland Indians Team Card UER (Text on back credits Tribe with winning AL title in '28. The Yankees won that year.)	60.00	27.00	7.50
☐ 276 Jim Pyburn	20.00	9.00	2.50
☐ 277 Johnny Podres DP	45.00	20.00	5.50
☐ 278 Fred Hatfield DP	14.00	6.25	1.75
☐ 279 Bob Thurman	20.00	9.00	2.50
☐ 280 Alex Kellner	20.00	9.00	2.50
☐ 281 Gail Harris	20.00	9.00	2.50
☐ 282 Jack Dittmer DP	14.00	6.25	1.75
☐ 283 Wes Covington DP	17.50	8.00	2.20
☐ 284 Don Zimmer	35.00	16.00	4.40
☐ 285 Ned Garver	20.00	9.00	2.50
☐ 286 Bobby Richardson	120.00	55.00	15.00

☐ 287 Sam Jones	20.00	9.00	2.50
☐ 288 Ted Lepcio	20.00	9.00	2.50
☐ 289 Jim Bolger DP	14.00	6.25	1.75
☐ 290 Andy Carey DP	20.00	9.00	2.50
☐ 291 Windy McCall	20.00	9.00	2.50
☐ 292 Billy Klaus	20.00	9.00	2.50
☐ 293 Ted Abernathy	20.00	9.00	2.50
☐ 294 Rocky Bridges DP	14.00	6.25	1.75
☐ 295 Joe Collins DP	20.00	9.00	2.50
☐ 296 Johnny Klippstein	20.00	9.00	2.50
☐ 297 Jack Crimian	20.00	9.00	2.50
☐ 298 Irv Noren DP	14.00	6.25	1.75
☐ 299 Chuck Harmon	20.00	9.00	2.50
☐ 300 Mike Garcia	22.50	10.00	2.80
☐ 301 Sammy Esposito DP	14.00	6.25	1.75
☐ 302 Sandy Koufax DP	250.00	110.00	31.00
☐ 303 Billy Goodman	22.50	10.00	2.80
☐ 304 Joe Cunningham	22.50	10.00	2.80
☐ 305 Chico Fernandez	20.00	9.00	2.50
☐ 306 Darrell Johnson DP	14.00	6.25	1.75
☐ 307 Jack D. Phillips DP	14.00	6.25	1.75
☐ 308 Dick Hall	20.00	9.00	2.50
☐ 309 Jim Busby DP	14.00	6.25	1.75
☐ 310 Max Surkont DP	14.00	6.25	1.75
☐ 311 Al Pilarcik DP	14.00	6.25	1.75
☐ 312 Tony Kubek DP	65.00	29.00	8.00
☐ 313 Mel Parnell	22.50	10.00	2.80
☐ 314 Ed Bouchee DP	14.00	6.25	1.75
☐ 315 Lou Berberet DP	14.00	6.25	1.75
☐ 316 Billy O'Dell	20.00	9.00	2.50
☐ 317 New York Giants Team Card	70.00	32.00	8.75
☐ 318 Mickey McDermott	20.00	9.00	2.50
☐ 319 Gino Cimoli	20.00	9.00	2.50
☐ 320 Neil Chrisley	20.00	9.00	2.50
☐ 321 John(Red) Murff	20.00	9.00	2.50
☐ 322 Cincinnati Reds Team Card	70.00	32.00	8.75
☐ 323 Wes Westrum	22.50	10.00	2.80
☐ 324 Brooklyn Dodgers Team Card	125.00	55.00	15.50
☐ 325 Frank Bolling	20.00	9.00	2.50
☐ 326 Pedro Ramos	20.00	9.00	2.50
☐ 327 Jim Pendleton	20.00	9.00	2.50
☐ 328 Brooks Robinson	400.00	180.00	50.00
☐ 329 Chicago White Sox Team Card	60.00	27.00	7.50
☐ 330 Jim Wilson	20.00	9.00	2.50
☐ 331 Ray Katt	20.00	9.00	2.50
☐ 332 Bob Bowman	20.00	9.00	2.50
☐ 333 Ernie Johnson	20.00	9.00	2.50
☐ 334 Jerry Schoonmaker	20.00	9.00	2.50
☐ 335 Granny Hamner	20.00	9.00	2.50
☐ 336 Haywood Sullivan	22.50	10.00	2.80
☐ 337 Rene Valdes	20.00	9.00	2.50
☐ 338 Jim Bunning	130.00	57.50	16.00
☐ 339 Bob Speake	20.00	9.00	2.50
☐ 340 Bill Wight	20.00	9.00	2.50
☐ 341 Don Gross	20.00	9.00	2.50
☐ 342 Gene Mauch	22.50	10.00	2.80
☐ 343 Taylor Phillips	20.00	9.00	2.50
☐ 344 Paul LaPalme	20.00	9.00	2.50
☐ 345 Paul Smith	20.00	9.00	2.50
☐ 346 Dick Littlefield	20.00	9.00	2.50
☐ 347 Hal Naragon	20.00	9.00	2.50
☐ 348 Jim Hearn	20.00	9.00	2.50
☐ 349 Nellie King	20.00	9.00	2.50
☐ 350 Eddie Miksis	20.00	9.00	2.50
☐ 351 Dave Hillman	20.00	9.00	2.50
☐ 352 Ellis Kinder	20.00	9.00	2.50
☐ 353 Cal Neeman	8.00	3.60	1.00
☐ 354 W. (Rip) Coleman	8.00	3.60	1.00
☐ 355 Frank Malzone	10.00	4.50	1.25
☐ 356 Faye Throneberry	8.00	3.60	1.00
☐ 357 Earl Torgeson	8.00	3.60	1.00
☐ 358 Jerry Lynch	10.00	4.50	1.25
☐ 359 Tom Cheney	10.00	4.50	1.25
☐ 360 Johnny Groth	8.00	3.60	1.00
☐ 361 Curt Barclay	8.00	3.60	1.00
☐ 362 Roman Mejias	10.00	4.50	1.25
☐ 363 Eddie Kasko	8.00	3.60	1.00
☐ 364 Cal McLish	10.00	4.50	1.25
☐ 365 Ozzie Virgil	8.00	3.60	1.00
☐ 366 Ken Lehman	8.00	3.60	1.00
☐ 367 Ed Fitzgerald	8.00	3.60	1.00
☐ 368 Bob Purkey	8.00	3.60	1.00
☐ 369 Milt Graff	8.00	3.60	1.00
☐ 370 Warren Hacker	8.00	3.60	1.00
☐ 371 Bob Lennon	8.00	3.60	1.00
☐ 372 Norm Zauchin	8.00	3.60	1.00
☐ 373 Pete Whisenant	8.00	3.60	1.00
☐ 374 Don Cardwell	8.00	3.60	1.00
☐ 375 Jim Landis	10.00	4.50	1.25
☐ 376 Don Elston	8.00	3.60	1.00
☐ 377 Andre Rodgers	8.00	3.60	1.00
☐ 378 Elmer Singleton	8.00	3.60	1.00
☐ 379 Don Lee	8.00	3.60	1.00
☐ 380 Walker Cooper	8.00	3.60	1.00
☐ 381 Dean Stone	8.00	3.60	1.00
☐ 382 Jim Bridewester	8.00	3.60	1.00
☐ 383 Juan Pizarro	8.00	3.60	1.00
☐ 384 Bobby G. Smith	8.00	3.60	1.00
☐ 385 Art Houtteman	8.00	3.60	1.00
☐ 386 Lyle Luttrell	8.00	3.60	1.00
☐ 387 Jack Sanford	10.00	4.50	1.25
☐ 388 Pete Daley	8.00	3.60	1.00
☐ 389 Dave Jolly	8.00	3.60	1.00
☐ 390 Reno Bertoia	8.00	3.60	1.00
☐ 391 Ralph Terry	10.00	4.50	1.25
☐ 392 Chuck Tanner	12.00	5.50	1.50
☐ 393 Raul Sanchez	8.00	3.60	1.00
☐ 394 Luis Arroyo	10.00	4.50	1.25
☐ 395 Bubba Phillips	8.00	3.60	1.00
☐ 396 Casey Wise	8.00	3.60	1.00
☐ 397 Roy Smalley	8.00	3.60	1.00
☐ 398 Al Cicotte	10.00	4.50	1.25
☐ 399 Billy Consolo	8.00	3.60	1.00
☐ 400 Dodgers' Sluggers Carl Furillo Gil Hodges Roy Campanella Duke Snider	250.00	110.00	31.00
☐ 401 Earl Battey	14.00	6.25	1.75
☐ 402 Jim Pisoni	8.00	3.60	1.00
☐ 403 Dick Hyde	8.00	3.60	1.00
☐ 404 Harry Anderson	8.00	3.60	1.00
☐ 405 Duke Maas	8.00	3.60	1.00
☐ 406 Bob Hale	8.00	3.60	1.00
☐ 407 Yankee Power Hitters Mickey Mantle Yogi Berra	500.00	150.00	50.00
☐ NNO1 Checklist 1/2	250.00	75.00	25.00
☐ NNO2 Checklist 2/3	400.00	100.00	40.00
☐ NNO3 Checklist 3/4	750.00	170.00	75.00
☐ NNO4 Checklist 4/5	900.00	200.00	90.00
☐ NNO5 Saturday, May 4th Boston Red Sox vs. Cleveland Indians Cincinnati Redlegs vs. New York Giants	80.00	20.00	8.00
☐ NNO6 Saturday, May 25th Detroit Tigers vs. Kansas City Athletics Pittsburgh Pirates vs. Philadelphia Phillies	80.00	20.00	8.00
☐ NNO7 Saturday, June 22nd Brooklyn Dodgers vs. St. Louis Cardinals Chicago White Sox vs. New York Yankees	100.00	25.00	10.00
☐ NNO8 Saturday, July 19th Milwaukee Braves vs. New York Giants Baltimore Orioles vs. Kansas City Athletics	100.00	25.00	10.00
☐ NNO9 Lucky Penny Charm and Key Chain offer card	70.00	32.00	8.75

1958 Topps

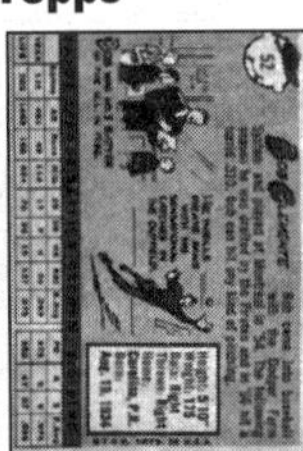

This is a 494-card standard-size set. Card number 145, which was supposedly to be Ed Bouchee, was not issued. The 1958 Topps set contains the first Sport Magazine All-Star Selection series (475-495) and expanded use of combination cards. For the first time team cards carried series checklists on back (Milwaukee, Detroit, Baltimore, and Cincinnati are also found with players listed alphabetically). In the first series some name (YL) or team (YT) lettering, as opposed to the common white lettering. They are explicity noted below. Cards were issued in one-card penny packs or six-card nickle packs. In the last series, All-Star cards of Stan Musial and Mickey Mantle were triple printed; the cards they replaced (443, 446, 450, and 462) on the printing sheet were hence printed in shorter supply than other cards in the last series and are marked with an SP in the list below. The All-Star card of Musial marked his first appearence on a Topps card. Technically the New York Giants team card (19) is an error as the Giants had already moved to San Francisco. The key Rookie Cards in this set are Orlando Cepeda, Curt Flood, Roger Maris, and Vada Pinson.

	NRMT	VG-E	GOOD
COMPLETE SET (494)	4800.00	2200.00	600.00
COMMON CARD (1-110)	12.00	5.50	1.50
COMMON CARD (111-198)	8.00	3.60	1.00
COMMON CARD (199-352)	8.00	3.60	1.00
COMMON CARD (353-440)	8.00	3.60	1.00
COMMON CARD (441-474)	8.00	3.60	1.00
COMMON AS (475-495)	8.00	3.60	1.00
WRAPPER (1-CENT)	100.00	45.00	12.50
WRAPPER (5-CENT)	125.00	55.00	15.50

☐ 1 Ted Williams	425.00	150.00	42.50
☐ 2A Bob Lemon	35.00	16.00	4.40
☐ 2B Bob Lemon YT	60.00	27.00	7.50
☐ 3 Alex Kellner	12.00	5.50	1.50
☐ 4 Hank Foiles	12.00	5.50	1.50
☐ 5 Willie Mays	225.00	100.00	28.00
☐ 6 George Zuverink	12.00	5.50	1.50
☐ 7 Dale Long	14.00	6.25	1.75
☐ 8A Eddie Kasko	12.00	5.50	1.50
☐ 8B Eddie Kasko YL	45.00	20.00	5.50
☐ 9 Hank Bauer	15.00	6.75	1.85
☐ 10 Lou Burdette	14.00	6.25	1.75
☐ 11A Jim Rivera	12.00	5.50	1.50
☐ 11B Jim Rivera YT	45.00	20.00	5.50
☐ 12 George Crowe	12.00	5.50	1.50
☐ 13A Billy Hoeft	12.00	5.50	1.50
☐ 13B Billy Hoeft YL	45.00	20.00	5.50
☐ 14 Rip Repulski	12.00	5.50	1.50
☐ 15 Jim Lemon	14.00	6.25	1.75
☐ 16 Charlie Neal	14.00	6.25	1.75
☐ 17 Felix Mantilla	12.00	5.50	1.50
☐ 18 Frank Sullivan	12.00	5.50	1.50
☐ 19 New York Giants Team Card (Checklist on back)	40.00	8.00	4.00
☐ 20A Gil McDougald	18.00	8.00	2.20
☐ 20B Gil McDougald YL	60.00	27.00	7.50
☐ 21 Curt Barclay	12.00	5.50	1.50
☐ 22 Hal Naragon	12.00	5.50	1.50
☐ 23A Bill Tuttle	12.00	5.50	1.50
☐ 23B Bill Tuttle YL	45.00	20.00	5.50
☐ 24A Hobie Landrith	12.00	5.50	1.50
☐ 24B Hobie Landrith YL	45.00	20.00	5.50
☐ 25 Don Drysdale	85.00	38.00	10.50
☐ 26 Ron Jackson	12.00	5.50	1.50
☐ 27 Bud Freeman	12.00	5.50	1.50
☐ 28 Jim Busby	12.00	5.50	1.50
☐ 29 Ted Lepcio	12.00	5.50	1.50
☐ 30A Hank Aaron	200.00	90.00	25.00
☐ 30B Hank Aaron YL	425.00	190.00	52.50
☐ 31 Tex Clevenger	12.00	5.50	1.50
☐ 32A J.W. Porter	12.00	5.50	1.50
☐ 32B J.W. Porter YL	45.00	20.00	5.50
☐ 33A Cal Neeman	12.00	5.50	1.50
☐ 33B Cal Neeman YT	45.00	20.00	5.50
☐ 34 Bob Thurman	12.00	5.50	1.50
☐ 35A Don Mossi	14.00	6.25	1.75
☐ 35B Don Mossi YT	45.00	20.00	5.50
☐ 36 Ted Kazanski	12.00	5.50	1.50
☐ 37 Mike McCormick UER (Photo actually Ray Monzant)	15.00	6.75	1.85
☐ 38 Dick Gernert	12.00	5.50	1.50
☐ 39 Bob Martyn	12.00	5.50	1.50
☐ 40 George Kell	18.00	8.00	2.20
☐ 41 Dave Hillman	12.00	5.50	1.50
☐ 42 John Roseboro	24.00	11.00	3.00
☐ 43 Sal Maglie	15.00	6.75	1.85
☐ 44 Washington Senators Team Card (Checklist on back)	20.00	4.00	2.00
☐ 45 Dick Groat	14.00	6.25	1.75
☐ 46A Lou Sleater	12.00	5.50	1.50
☐ 46B Lou Sleater YL	45.00	20.00	5.50
☐ 47 Roger Maris	400.00	180.00	50.00
☐ 48 Chuck Harmon	12.00	5.50	1.50
☐ 49 Smoky Burgess	14.00	6.25	1.75
☐ 50A Billy Pierce	14.00	6.25	1.75
☐ 50B Billy Pierce YT	50.00	22.00	6.25
☐ 51 Del Rice	12.00	5.50	1.50
☐ 52A Bob Clemente	275.00	125.00	34.00
☐ 52B Bob Clemente YT	450.00	200.00	55.00
☐ 53A Morrie Martin	12.00	5.50	1.50
☐ 53B Morrie Martin YL	45.00	20.00	5.50
☐ 54 Norm Siebern	18.00	8.00	2.20
☐ 55 Chico Carrasquel	12.00	5.50	1.50
☐ 56 Bill Fischer	12.00	5.50	1.50
☐ 57A Tim Thompson	12.00	5.50	1.50
☐ 57B Tim Thompson YL	45.00	20.00	5.50
☐ 58A Art Schult	12.00	5.50	1.50
☐ 58B Art Schult YT	45.00	20.00	5.50
☐ 59 Dave Sisler	12.00	5.50	1.50
☐ 60A Del Ennis	14.00	6.25	1.75
☐ 60B Del Ennis YL	50.00	22.00	6.25
☐ 61A Darrell Johnson	12.00	5.50	1.50
☐ 61B Darrell Johnson YL	45.00	20.00	5.50
☐ 62 Joe DeMaestri	12.00	5.50	1.50
☐ 63 Joe Nuxhall	14.00	6.25	1.75
☐ 64 Joe Lonnett	12.00	5.50	1.50
☐ 65A Von McDaniel	12.00	5.50	1.50
☐ 65B Von McDaniel YL	45.00	20.00	5.50
☐ 66 Lee Walls	12.00	5.50	1.50
☐ 67 Joe Ginsberg	12.00	5.50	1.50
☐ 68 Daryl Spencer	12.00	5.50	1.50
☐ 69 Wally Burnette	12.00	5.50	1.50
☐ 70A Al Kaline	100.00	45.00	12.50
☐ 70B Al Kaline YL	180.00	80.00	22.00
☐ 71 Dodgers Team (Checklist on back)	60.00	12.00	6.00
☐ 72 Bud Byerly	12.00	5.50	1.50
☐ 73 Pete Daley	12.00	5.50	1.50
☐ 74 Roy Face	14.00	6.25	1.75
☐ 75 Gus Bell	14.00	6.25	1.75
☐ 76A Dick Farrell	12.00	5.50	1.50
☐ 76B Dick Farrell YT	45.00	20.00	5.50
☐ 77A Don Zimmer	14.00	6.25	1.75
☐ 77B Don Zimmer YT	50.00	22.00	6.25
☐ 78A Ernie Johnson	14.00	6.25	1.75
☐ 78B Ernie Johnson YL	50.00	22.00	6.25
☐ 79A Dick Williams	14.00	6.25	1.75
☐ 79B Dick Williams YT	50.00	22.00	6.25
☐ 80 Dick Drott	12.00	5.50	1.50
☐ 81A Steve Boros	12.00	5.50	1.50
☐ 81B Steve Boros YT	45.00	20.00	5.50
☐ 82 Ron Kline	12.00	5.50	1.50
☐ 83 Bob Hazle	12.00	5.50	1.50
☐ 84 Billy O'Dell	12.00	5.50	1.50
☐ 85A Luis Aparicio	30.00	13.50	3.70
☐ 85B Luis Aparicio YT	70.00	32.00	8.75
☐ 86 Valmy Thomas	12.00	5.50	1.50
☐ 87 Johnny Kucks	12.00	5.50	1.50
☐ 88 Duke Snider	75.00	34.00	9.50
☐ 89 Billy Klaus	12.00	5.50	1.50
☐ 90 Robin Roberts	30.00	13.50	3.70
☐ 91 Chuck Tanner	14.00	6.25	1.75
☐ 92A Clint Courtney	12.00	5.50	1.50
☐ 92B Clint Courtney YL	45.00	20.00	5.50
☐ 93 Sandy Amoros	15.00	6.75	1.85
☐ 94 Bob Skinner	14.00	6.25	1.75
☐ 95 Frank Bolling	12.00	5.50	1.50
☐ 96 Joe Durham	12.00	5.50	1.50
☐ 97A Larry Jackson	12.00	5.50	1.50
☐ 97B Larry Jackson YL	45.00	20.00	5.50
☐ 98A Billy Hunter	12.00	5.50	1.50
☐ 98B Billy Hunter YL	45.00	20.00	5.50
☐ 99 Bobby Adams	12.00	5.50	1.50
☐ 100A Early Wynn	25.00	11.00	3.10
☐ 100B Early Wynn YT	60.00	27.00	7.50
☐ 101A Bobby Richardson	24.00	11.00	3.00
☐ 101B Bobby Richardson YL	55.00	25.00	7.00
☐ 102 George Strickland	12.00	5.50	1.50
☐ 103 Jerry Lynch	14.00	6.25	1.75
☐ 104 Jim Pendleton	12.00	5.50	1.50
☐ 105 Billy Gardner	12.00	5.50	1.50
☐ 106 Dick Schofield	14.00	6.25	1.75
☐ 107 Ossie Virgil	12.00	5.50	1.50
☐ 108A Jim Landis	12.00	5.50	1.50
☐ 108B Jim Landis YT	45.00	20.00	5.50
☐ 109 Herb Plews	12.00	5.50	1.50
☐ 110 Johnny Logan	14.00	6.25	1.75
☐ 111 Stu Miller	9.00	4.00	1.10
☐ 112 Gus Zernial	9.00	4.00	1.10
☐ 113 Jerry Walker	8.00	3.60	1.00
☐ 114 Irv Noren	9.00	4.00	1.10
☐ 115 Jim Bunning	25.00	11.00	3.10
☐ 116 Dave Philley	8.00	3.60	1.00
☐ 117 Frank Torre	9.00	4.00	1.10
☐ 118 Harvey Haddix	9.00	4.00	1.10
☐ 119 Harry Chiti	8.00	3.60	1.00
☐ 120 Johnny Podres	10.00	4.50	1.25
☐ 121 Eddie Miksis	8.00	3.60	1.00
☐ 122 Walt Moryn	8.00	3.60	1.00
☐ 123 Dick Tomanek	8.00	3.60	1.00
☐ 124 Bobby Usher	8.00	3.60	1.00
☐ 125 Alvin Dark	9.00	4.00	1.10
☐ 126 Stan Palys	8.00	3.60	1.00
☐ 127 Tom Sturdivant	10.00	4.50	1.25
☐ 128 Willie Kirkland	9.00	4.00	1.10
☐ 129 Jim Derrington	8.00	3.60	1.00
☐ 130 Jackie Jensen	10.00	4.50	1.25
☐ 131 Bob Henrich	8.00	3.60	1.00
☐ 132 Vern Law	9.00	4.00	1.10
☐ 133 Russ Nixon	8.00	3.60	1.00
☐ 134 Philadelphia Phillies Team Card (Checklist on back)	15.00	3.00	1.50
☐ 135 Mike(Moe) Drabowsky	9.00	4.00	1.10
☐ 136 Jim Finigan	8.00	3.60	1.00
☐ 137 Russ Kemmerer	8.00	3.60	1.00
☐ 138 Earl Torgeson	8.00	3.60	1.00
☐ 139 George Brunet	8.00	3.60	1.00
☐ 140 Wes Covington	9.00	4.00	1.10
☐ 141 Ken Lehman	8.00	3.60	1.00
☐ 142 Enos Slaughter	25.00	11.00	3.10
☐ 143 Billy Muffett	8.00	3.60	1.00
☐ 144 Bobby Morgan	8.00	3.60	1.00
☐ 145 Never issued			
☐ 146 Dick Gray	8.00	3.60	1.00
☐ 147 Don McMahon	8.00	3.60	1.00
☐ 148 Billy Consolo	8.00	3.60	1.00
☐ 149 Tom Acker	8.00	3.60	1.00
☐ 150 Mickey Mantle	800.00	350.00	100.00
☐ 151 Buddy Pritchard	8.00	3.60	1.00
☐ 152 Johnny Antonelli	9.00	4.00	1.10
☐ 153 Les Moss	8.00	3.60	1.00
☐ 154 Harry Byrd	8.00	3.60	1.00
☐ 155 Hector Lopez	9.00	4.00	1.10
☐ 156 Dick Hyde	8.00	3.60	1.00
☐ 157 Dee Fondy	8.00	3.60	1.00
☐ 158 Cleveland Indians Team Card (Checklist on back)	15.00	3.00	1.50
☐ 159 Taylor Phillips	8.00	3.60	1.00
☐ 160 Don Hoak	9.00	4.00	1.10
☐ 161 Don Larsen	14.00	6.25	1.75
☐ 162 Gil Hodges	25.00	11.00	3.10
☐ 163 Jim Wilson	8.00	3.60	1.00
☐ 164 Bob Taylor	8.00	3.60	1.00
☐ 165 Bob Nieman	8.00	3.60	1.00
☐ 166 Danny O'Connell	8.00	3.60	1.00
☐ 167 Frank Baumann	8.00	3.60	1.00
☐ 168 Joe Cunningham	8.00	3.60	1.00
☐ 169 Ralph Terry	9.00	4.00	1.10
☐ 170 Vic Wertz	9.00	4.00	1.10
☐ 171 Harry Anderson	8.00	3.60	1.00
☐ 172 Don Gross	8.00	3.60	1.00

- ☐ 173 Eddie Yost 9.00 4.00 1.10
- ☐ 174 Athletics Team 15.00 3.00 1.50
  (Checklist on back)
- ☐ 175 Marv Throneberry 16.00 7.25 2.00
- ☐ 176 Bob Buhl 9.00 4.00 1.10
- ☐ 177 Al Smith 8.00 3.60 1.00
- ☐ 178 Ted Kluszewski 16.00 7.25 2.00
- ☐ 179 Willie Miranda 8.00 3.60 1.00
- ☐ 180 Lindy McDaniel 9.00 4.00 1.10
- ☐ 181 Willie Jones 8.00 3.60 1.00
- ☐ 182 Joe Caffie 8.00 3.60 1.00
- ☐ 183 Dave Jolly 8.00 3.60 1.00
- ☐ 184 Elvin Tappe 8.00 3.60 1.00
- ☐ 185 Ray Boone 9.00 4.00 1.10
- ☐ 186 Jack Meyer 8.00 3.60 1.00
- ☐ 187 Sandy Koufax 225.00 100.00 28.00
- ☐ 188 Milt Bolling UER 8.00 3.60 1.00
  (Photo actually
  Lou Berberet)
- ☐ 189 George Susce 8.00 3.60 1.00
- ☐ 190 Red Schoendienst 18.00 8.00 2.20
- ☐ 191 Art Ceccarelli 8.00 3.60 1.00
- ☐ 192 Milt Graff 8.00 3.60 1.00
- ☐ 193 Jerry Lumpe 8.00 3.60 1.00
- ☐ 194 Roger Craig 9.00 4.00 1.10
- ☐ 195 Whitey Lockman 9.00 4.00 1.10
- ☐ 196 Mike Garcia 9.00 4.00 1.10
- ☐ 197 Haywood Sullivan 9.00 4.00 1.10
- ☐ 198 Bill Virdon 9.00 4.00 1.10
- ☐ 199 Don Blasingame 8.00 3.60 1.00
- ☐ 200 Bob Keegan 8.00 3.60 1.00
- ☐ 201 Jim Bolger 8.00 3.60 1.00
- ☐ 202 Woody Held 8.00 3.60 1.00
- ☐ 203 Al Walker 8.00 3.60 1.00
- ☐ 204 Leo Kiely 8.00 3.60 1.00
- ☐ 205 Johnny Temple 9.00 4.00 1.10
- ☐ 206 Bob Shaw 8.00 3.60 1.00
- ☐ 207 Solly Hemus 8.00 3.60 1.00
- ☐ 208 Cal McLish 8.00 3.60 1.00
- ☐ 209 Bob Anderson 8.00 3.60 1.00
- ☐ 210 Wally Moon 9.00 4.00 1.10
- ☐ 211 Pete Burnside 8.00 3.60 1.00
- ☐ 212 Bubba Phillips 8.00 3.60 1.00
- ☐ 213 Red Wilson 8.00 3.60 1.00
- ☐ 214 Willard Schmidt 8.00 3.60 1.00
- ☐ 215 Jim Gilliam 14.00 6.25 1.75
- ☐ 216 St. Louis Cardinals 15.00 3.00 1.50
  Team Card
  (Checklist on back)
- ☐ 217 Jack Harshman 8.00 3.60 1.00
- ☐ 218 Dick Rand 8.00 3.60 1.00
- ☐ 219 Camilo Pascual 9.00 4.00 1.10
- ☐ 220 Tom Brewer 8.00 3.60 1.00
- ☐ 221 Jerry Kindall 8.00 3.60 1.00
- ☐ 222 Bud Daley 8.00 3.60 1.00
- ☐ 223 Andy Pafko 9.00 4.00 1.10
- ☐ 224 Bob Grim 9.00 4.00 1.10
- ☐ 225 Billy Goodman 9.00 4.00 1.10
- ☐ 226 Bob Smith 8.00 3.60 1.00
- ☐ 227 Gene Stephens 8.00 3.60 1.00
- ☐ 228 Duke Maas 8.00 3.60 1.00
- ☐ 229 Frank Zupo 8.00 3.60 1.00
- ☐ 230 Richie Ashburn 30.00 13.50 3.70
- ☐ 231 Lloyd Merritt 8.00 3.60 1.00
- ☐ 232 Reno Bertoia 8.00 3.60 1.00
- ☐ 233 Mickey Vernon 9.00 4.00 1.10
- ☐ 234 Carl Sawatski 8.00 3.60 1.00
- ☐ 235 Tom Gorman 8.00 3.60 1.00
- ☐ 236 Ed Fitzgerald 8.00 3.60 1.00
- ☐ 237 Bill Wight 8.00 3.60 1.00
- ☐ 238 Bill Mazeroski 24.00 11.00 3.00
- ☐ 239 Chuck Stobbs 8.00 3.60 1.00
- ☐ 240 Bill Skowron 16.00 7.25 2.00
- ☐ 241 Dick Littlefield 8.00 3.60 1.00
- ☐ 242 Johnny Klippstein 8.00 3.60 1.00
- ☐ 243 Larry Raines 8.00 3.60 1.00
- ☐ 244 Don Demeter 8.00 3.60 1.00
- ☐ 245 Frank Lary 9.00 4.00 1.10
- ☐ 246 New York Yankees 80.00 16.00 8.00
  Team Card
  (Checklist on back)
- ☐ 247 Casey Wise 8.00 3.60 1.00
- ☐ 248 Herman Wehmeier 8.00 3.60 1.00
- ☐ 249 Ray Moore 8.00 3.60 1.00
- ☐ 250 Roy Sievers 9.00 4.00 1.10
- ☐ 251 Warren Hacker 8.00 3.60 1.00
- ☐ 252 Bob Trowbridge 8.00 3.60 1.00
- ☐ 253 Don Mueller 9.00 4.00 1.10
- ☐ 254 Alex Grammas 8.00 3.60 1.00
- ☐ 255 Bob Turley 10.00 4.50 1.25
- ☐ 256 Chicago White Sox 15.00 3.00 1.50
  Team Card
  (Checklist on back)
- ☐ 257 Hal Smith 8.00 3.60 1.00
- ☐ 258 Carl Erskine 14.00 6.25 1.75
- ☐ 259 Al Pilarcik 8.00 3.60 1.00
- ☐ 260 Frank Malzone 9.00 4.00 1.10
- ☐ 261 Turk Lown 8.00 3.60 1.00
- ☐ 262 Johnny Groth 8.00 3.60 1.00
- ☐ 263 Eddie Bressoud 9.00 4.00 1.10
- ☐ 264 Jack Sanford 9.00 4.00 1.10
- ☐ 265 Pete Runnels 9.00 4.00 1.10
- ☐ 266 Connie Johnson 8.00 3.60 1.00
- ☐ 267 Sherm Lollar 9.00 4.00 1.10
- ☐ 268 Granny Hamner 8.00 3.60 1.00
- ☐ 269 Paul Smith 8.00 3.60 1.00
- ☐ 270 Warren Spahn 50.00 22.00 6.25
- ☐ 271 Billy Martin 20.00 9.00 2.50
- ☐ 272 Ray Crone 8.00 3.60 1.00
- ☐ 273 Hal Smith 8.00 3.60 1.00
- ☐ 274 Rocky Bridges 8.00 3.60 1.00
- ☐ 275 Elston Howard 16.00 7.25 2.00
- ☐ 276 Bobby Avila 8.00 3.60 1.00
- ☐ 277 Virgil Trucks 9.00 4.00 1.10
- ☐ 278 Mack Burk 8.00 3.60 1.00
- ☐ 279 Bob Boyd 8.00 3.60 1.00
- ☐ 280 Jim Piersall 10.00 4.50 1.25
- ☐ 281 Sammy Taylor 8.00 3.60 1.00
- ☐ 282 Paul Foytack 8.00 3.60 1.00
- ☐ 283 Ray Shearer 8.00 3.60 1.00
- ☐ 284 Ray Katt 8.00 3.60 1.00
- ☐ 285 Frank Robinson 100.00 45.00 12.50
- ☐ 286 Gino Cimoli 8.00 3.60 1.00
- ☐ 287 Sam Jones 9.00 4.00 1.10
- ☐ 288 Harmon Killebrew 85.00 38.00 10.50
- ☐ 289 Series Hurling Rivals 9.00 4.00 1.10
  Lou Burdette
  Bobby Shantz
- ☐ 290 Dick Donovan 8.00 3.60 1.00
- ☐ 291 Don Landrum 8.00 3.60 1.00
- ☐ 292 Ned Garver 8.00 3.60 1.00
- ☐ 293 Gene Freese 8.00 3.60 1.00
- ☐ 294 Hal Jeffcoat 8.00 3.60 1.00
- ☐ 295 Minnie Minoso 14.00 6.25 1.75
- ☐ 296 Ryne Duren 16.00 7.25 2.00
- ☐ 297 Don Buddin 8.00 3.60 1.00
- ☐ 298 Jim Hearn 8.00 3.60 1.00
- ☐ 299 Harry Simpson 8.00 3.60 1.00
- ☐ 300 League Presidents 14.00 6.25 1.75
  Will Harridge
  Warren Giles
- ☐ 301 Randy Jackson 8.00 3.60 1.00
- ☐ 302 Mike Baxes 8.00 3.60 1.00
- ☐ 303 Neil Chrisley 8.00 3.60 1.00
- ☐ 304 Tigers' Big Bats 20.00 9.00 2.50
  Harvey Kuenn
  Al Kaline
- ☐ 305 Clem Labine 10.00 4.50 1.25
- ☐ 306 Whammy Douglas 8.00 3.60 1.00
- ☐ 307 Brooks Robinson 100.00 45.00 12.50
- ☐ 308 Paul Giel 9.00 4.00 1.10
- ☐ 309 Gail Harris 8.00 3.60 1.00
- ☐ 310 Ernie Banks 100.00 45.00 12.50
- ☐ 311 Bob Purkey 8.00 3.60 1.00
- ☐ 312 Boston Red Sox 15.00 3.00 1.50
  Team Card
  (Checklist on back)
- ☐ 313 Bob Rush 8.00 3.60 1.00
- ☐ 314 Dodgers' Boss and 25.00 11.00 3.10
  Power: Duke Snider
  Walt Alston MG
- ☐ 315 Bob Friend 9.00 4.00 1.10
- ☐ 316 Tito Francona 9.00 4.00 1.10
- ☐ 317 Albie Pearson 9.00 4.00 1.10
- ☐ 318 Frank House 8.00 3.60 1.00
- ☐ 319 Lou Skizas 8.00 3.60 1.00
- ☐ 320 Whitey Ford 50.00 22.00 6.25
- ☐ 321 Sluggers Supreme 70.00 32.00 8.75
  Ted Kluszewski
  Ted Williams
- ☐ 322 Harding Peterson 9.00 4.00 1.10
- ☐ 323 Elmer Valo 8.00 3.60 1.00
- ☐ 324 Hoyt Wilhelm 18.00 8.00 2.20
- ☐ 325 Joe Adcock 9.00 4.00 1.10
- ☐ 326 Bob Miller 8.00 3.60 1.00
- ☐ 327 Chicago Cubs 15.00 3.00 1.50
  Team Card
  (Checklist on back)
- ☐ 328 Ike Delock 8.00 3.60 1.00
- ☐ 329 Bob Cerv 9.00 4.00 1.10
- ☐ 330 Ed Bailey 9.00 4.00 1.10
- ☐ 331 Pedro Ramos 8.00 3.60 1.00
- ☐ 332 Jim King 8.00 3.60 1.00
- ☐ 333 Andy Carey 10.00 4.50 1.25
- ☐ 334 Mound Aces 9.00 4.00 1.10
  Bob Friend
  Billy Pierce
- ☐ 335 Ruben Gomez 8.00 3.60 1.00
- ☐ 336 Bert Hamric 8.00 3.60 1.00
- ☐ 337 Hank Aguirre 8.00 3.60 1.00
- ☐ 338 Walt Dropo 9.00 4.00 1.10
- ☐ 339 Fred Hatfield 8.00 3.60 1.00
- ☐ 340 Don Newcombe 14.00 6.25 1.75
- ☐ 341 Pittsburgh Pirates 15.00 3.00 1.50
  Team Card
  (Checklist on back)
- ☐ 342 Jim Brosnan 9.00 4.00 1.10
- ☐ 343 Orlando Cepeda 90.00 40.00 11.00
- ☐ 344 Bob Porterfield 8.00 3.60 1.00
- ☐ 345 Jim Hegan 9.00 4.00 1.10
- ☐ 346 Steve Bilko 8.00 3.60 1.00
- ☐ 347 Don Rudolph 8.00 3.60 1.00
- ☐ 348 Chico Fernandez 8.00 3.60 1.00
- ☐ 349 Murry Dickson 8.00 3.60 1.00
- ☐ 350 Ken Boyer 16.00 7.25 2.00
- ☐ 351 Braves Fence Busters 35.00 16.00 4.40
  Del Crandall
  Eddie Mathews
  Hank Aaron
  Joe Adcock
- ☐ 352 Herb Score 14.00 6.25 1.75
- ☐ 353 Stan Lopata 8.00 3.60 1.00
- ☐ 354 Art Ditmar 10.00 4.50 1.25
- ☐ 355 Bill Bruton 9.00 4.00 1.10
- ☐ 356 Bob Malkmus 8.00 3.60 1.00
- ☐ 357 Danny McDevitt 8.00 3.60 1.00
- ☐ 358 Gene Baker 8.00 3.60 1.00
- ☐ 359 Billy Loes 9.00 4.00 1.10
- ☐ 360 Roy McMillan 9.00 4.00 1.10
- ☐ 361 Mike Fornieles 8.00 3.60 1.00
- ☐ 362 Ray Jablonski 8.00 3.60 1.00
- ☐ 363 Don Elston 8.00 3.60 1.00
- ☐ 364 Earl Battey 8.00 3.60 1.00
- ☐ 365 Tom Morgan 8.00 3.60 1.00
- ☐ 366 Gene Green 8.00 3.60 1.00
- ☐ 367 Jack Urban 8.00 3.60 1.00
- ☐ 368 Rocky Colavito 50.00 22.00 6.25
- ☐ 369 Ralph Lumenti 8.00 3.60 1.00
- ☐ 370 Yogi Berra 90.00 40.00 11.00
- ☐ 371 Marty Keough 8.00 3.60 1.00
- ☐ 372 Don Cardwell 8.00 3.60 1.00
- ☐ 373 Joe Pignatano 8.00 3.60 1.00
- ☐ 374 Brooks Lawrence 8.00 3.60 1.00
- ☐ 375 Pee Wee Reese 50.00 22.00 6.25
- ☐ 376 Charley Rabe 8.00 3.60 1.00
- ☐ 377A Milwaukee Braves 15.00 6.75 1.85
  Team Card
  (Alphabetical)
- ☐ 377B Milwaukee Team 100.00 20.00 10.00
  numerical checklist
- ☐ 378 Hank Sauer 9.00 4.00 1.10
- ☐ 379 Ray Herbert 8.00 3.60 1.00
- ☐ 380 Charlie Maxwell 9.00 4.00 1.10
- ☐ 381 Hal Brown 8.00 3.60 1.00
- ☐ 382 Al Cicotte 8.00 3.60 1.00
- ☐ 383 Lou Berberet 8.00 3.60 1.00
- ☐ 384 John Goryl 8.00 3.60 1.00
- ☐ 385 Wilmer Mizell 9.00 4.00 1.10
- ☐ 386 Birdie's Sluggers 14.00 6.25 1.75
  Ed Bailey
  Birdie Tebbetts MG
  Frank Robinson
- ☐ 387 Wally Post 9.00 4.00 1.10
- ☐ 388 Billy Moran 8.00 3.60 1.00
- ☐ 389 Bill Taylor 8.00 3.60 1.00
- ☐ 390 Del Crandall 9.00 4.00 1.10
- ☐ 391 Dave Melton 8.00 3.60 1.00
- ☐ 392 Bennie Daniels 8.00 3.60 1.00
- ☐ 393 Tony Kubek 18.00 8.00 2.20
- ☐ 394 Jim Grant 8.00 3.60 1.00
- ☐ 395 Willard Nixon 8.00 3.60 1.00
- ☐ 396 Dutch Dotterer 8.00 3.60 1.00
- ☐ 397A Detroit Tigers 15.00 6.75 1.85
  Team Card
  (Alphabetical)
- ☐ 397B Detroit Team 100.00 20.00 10.00
  numerical checklist
- ☐ 398 Gene Woodling 9.00 4.00 1.10
- ☐ 399 Marv Grissom 8.00 3.60 1.00
- ☐ 400 Nellie Fox 25.00 11.00 3.10
- ☐ 401 Don Bessent 8.00 3.60 1.00
- ☐ 402 Bobby Gene Smith 8.00 3.60 1.00
- ☐ 403 Steve Korcheck 8.00 3.60 1.00
- ☐ 404 Curt Simmons 9.00 4.00 1.10
- ☐ 405 Ken Aspromonte 8.00 3.60 1.00
- ☐ 406 Vic Power 9.00 4.00 1.10
- ☐ 407 Carlton Willey 9.00 4.00 1.10
- ☐ 408A Baltimore Orioles 15.00 6.75 1.85
  Team Card
  (Alphabetical)
- ☐ 408B Baltimore Team 100.00 20.00 10.00
  numerical checklist
- ☐ 409 Frank Thomas 9.00 4.00 1.10
- ☐ 410 Murray Wall 8.00 3.60 1.00
- ☐ 411 Tony Taylor 9.00 4.00 1.10
- ☐ 412 Gerry Staley 8.00 3.60 1.00
- ☐ 413 Jim Davenport 8.00 3.60 1.00
- ☐ 414 Sammy White 8.00 3.60 1.00
- ☐ 415 Bob Bowman 8.00 3.60 1.00
- ☐ 416 Foster Castleman 8.00 3.60 1.00
- ☐ 417 Carl Furillo 14.00 6.25 1.75
- ☐ 418 World Series Batting 275.00 125.00 34.00
  Foes: Mickey Mantle
  Hank Aaron
- ☐ 419 Bobby Shantz 9.00 4.00 1.10
- ☐ 420 Vada Pinson 40.00 18.00 5.00
- ☐ 421 Dixie Howell 8.00 3.60 1.00
- ☐ 422 Norm Zauchin 8.00 3.60 1.00
- ☐ 423 Phil Clark 8.00 3.60 1.00
- ☐ 424 Larry Doby 14.00 6.25 1.75
- ☐ 425 Sammy Esposito 8.00 3.60 1.00
- ☐ 426 Johnny O'Brien 9.00 4.00 1.10
- ☐ 427 Al Worthington 8.00 3.60 1.00
- ☐ 428A Cincinnati Reds 15.00 6.75 1.85
  Team Card
  (Alphabetical)
- ☐ 428B Cincinnati Team 100.00 20.00 10.00
  numerical checklist
- ☐ 429 Gus Triandos 9.00 4.00 1.10
- ☐ 430 Bobby Thomson 10.00 4.50 1.25
- ☐ 431 Gene Conley 9.00 4.00 1.10
- ☐ 432 John Powers 8.00 3.60 1.00
- ☐ 433A Pancho Herrer ERR 650.00 300.00 80.00
- ☐ 433B Pancho Herrera COR 9.00 4.00 1.10
- ☐ 434 Harvey Kuenn 9.00 4.00 1.10
- ☐ 435 Ed Roebuck 9.00 4.00 1.10
- ☐ 436 Rival Fence Busters 75.00 34.00 9.50
  Willie Mays
  Duke Snider
- ☐ 437 Bob Speake 8.00 3.60 1.00
- ☐ 438 Whitey Herzog 9.00 4.00 1.10
- ☐ 439 Ray Narleski 8.00 3.60 1.00
- ☐ 440 Eddie Mathews 40.00 18.00 5.00
- ☐ 441 Jim Marshall 9.00 4.00 1.10
- ☐ 442 Phil Paine 8.00 3.60 1.00
- ☐ 443 Billy Harrell SP 18.00 8.00 2.20
- ☐ 444 Danny Kravitz 8.00 3.60 1.00
- ☐ 445 Bob Smith 8.00 3.60 1.00
- ☐ 446 Carroll Hardy SP 18.00 8.00 2.20
- ☐ 447 Ray Monzant 8.00 3.60 1.00
- ☐ 448 Charlie Lau 8.00 3.60 1.00
- ☐ 449 Gene Fodge 8.00 3.60 1.00
- ☐ 450 Preston Ward SP 18.00 8.00 2.20
- ☐ 451 Joe Taylor 8.00 3.60 1.00
- ☐ 452 Roman Mejias 8.00 3.60 1.00
- ☐ 453 Tom Qualters 8.00 3.60 1.00
- ☐ 454 Harry Hanebrink 8.00 3.60 1.00
- ☐ 455 Hal Griggs 8.00 3.60 1.00
- ☐ 456 Dick Brown 8.00 3.60 1.00
- ☐ 457 Milt Pappas 8.00 3.60 1.00
- ☐ 458 Julio Becquer 8.00 3.60 1.00
- ☐ 459 Ron Blackburn 8.00 3.60 1.00
- ☐ 460 Chuck Essegian 8.00 3.60 1.00
- ☐ 461 Ed Mayer 8.00 3.60 1.00
- ☐ 462 Gary Geiger SP 18.00 8.00 2.20
- ☐ 463 Vito Valentinetti 8.00 3.60 1.00
- ☐ 464 Curt Flood 30.00 13.50 3.70
- ☐ 465 Arnie Portocarrero 8.00 3.60 1.00
- ☐ 466 Pete Whisenant 8.00 3.60 1.00
- ☐ 467 Glen Hobbie 8.00 3.60 1.00
- ☐ 468 Bob Schmidt 8.00 3.60 1.00
- ☐ 469 Don Ferrarese 8.00 3.60 1.00
- ☐ 470 R.C. Stevens 8.00 3.60 1.00
- ☐ 471 Lenny Green 8.00 3.60 1.00
- ☐ 472 Joey Jay 9.00 4.00 1.10
- ☐ 473 Bill Renna 8.00 3.60 1.00
- ☐ 474 Roman Semproch 8.00 3.60 1.00
- ☐ 475 Fred Haney AS MG and 20.00 9.00 2.50
  Casey Stengel AS MG
  (Checklist back)
- ☐ 476 Stan Musial AS TP 40.00 18.00 5.00
- ☐ 478 Johnny Temple AS 8.00 3.60 1.00
- ☐ 479 Nellie Fox AS 18.00 8.00 2.20
- ☐ 480 Eddie Mathews AS 20.00 9.00 2.50
- ☐ 481 Frank Malzone AS 8.00 3.60 1.00
- ☐ 482 Ernie Banks AS 35.00 16.00 4.40
- ☐ 483 Luis Aparicio AS 18.00 8.00 2.20
- ☐ 484 Frank Robinson AS 24.00 11.00 3.00
- ☐ 485 Ted Williams AS 125.00 55.00 15.50
- ☐ 486 Willie Mays AS 50.00 22.00 6.25
- ☐ 487 Mickey Mantle AS TP 200.00 90.00 25.00
- ☐ 488 Hank Aaron AS 50.00 22.00 6.25
- ☐ 489 Jackie Jensen AS 9.00 4.00 1.10
- ☐ 490 Ed Bailey AS 8.00 3.60 1.00
- ☐ 491 Sherm Lollar AS 8.00 3.60 1.00
- ☐ 492 Bob Friend AS 8.00 3.60 1.00
- ☐ 493 Bob Turley AS 9.00 4.00 1.10
- ☐ 494 Warren Spahn AS 24.00 11.00 3.00
- ☐ 495 Herb Score AS 16.00 3.20 1.05
- ☐ xx Contest Cards 50.00 22.00 6.25

1959 Topps

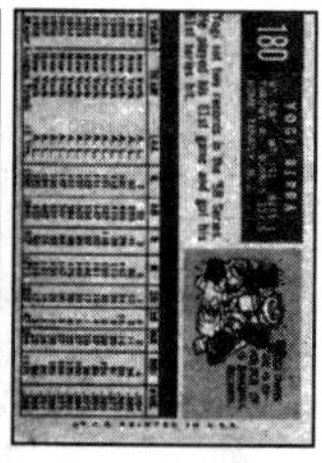

The cards in this 572-card set measure 2 1/2" by 3 1/2". The 1959 Topps set contains bust pictures of the players in a colored circle. Card numbers 551 to 572 are Sporting News All-Star Selections. High numbers 507 to 572 have the card number in a black background on the reverse rather than a green background as in the lower numbers. The high numbers are more difficult to obtain. Several cards in the 300s exist with or without an extra traded or option line on the back of the card. Cards 199 to 286 exist with either white or gray backs. There is no price differential for either colored back. Cards 461 to 470 contain "Highlights" while cards 116 to 146 give an alphabetically ordered listing of "Rookie Prospects." These Rookie Prospects (RP) were Topps' first organized inclusion of untested "Rookie" cards. Card 440 features Lew Burdette erroneously posing as a left-handed pitcher. Cards were issued in one-card penny packs or six-card nickle packs. There were some three-card advertising panels produced by Topps; the players included are from the first series. One advertising panel shows Don McMahon, Red Wilson and Bob Boyd on the front with Ted Kluszewski's card back on the back of the panel. Other panels are: Joe Pignatano, Sam Jones and Jack Urban also with Kluszewski's card back on back, Billy Hunter, Chuck Stobbs and Carl Sawatski on the front with the back of Nellie Fox's card on the back, Vito Valentinetti, Ken Lehman and Ed Bouchee on the front with Fox's card back on back and Mel Roach, Brooks Lawrence and Warren Spahn also with Fox on back. When separated, these advertising cards are distinguished by the non-standard card back, i.e., part of an advertisement for the 1959 Topps set instead of the typical statistics and biographical information about the player pictured. The key Rookie Cards in this set are Felipe Alou, Sparky Anderson (called George on the card), Norm Cash, Bob Gibson, and Bill White.

	NRMT	VG-E	GOOD
COMPLETE SET (572)	4500.00	2000.00	550.00
COMMON CARD (1-110)	6.00	2.70	.75
COMMON CARD (111-506)	4.00	1.80	.50
COMMON CARD (507-550)	16.00	7.25	2.00
COMMON AS (551-572)	16.00	7.25	2.00
WRAPPER (1-CENT)	125.00	55.00	15.50
WRAPPER (5-CENT)	100.00	45.00	12.50
□ 1 Ford Frick COMM	50.00	13.50	4.50
□ 2 Eddie Yost	7.00	3.10	.85
□ 3 Don McMahon	7.00	3.10	.85
□ 4 Albie Pearson	7.00	3.10	.85
□ 5 Dick Donovan	7.00	3.10	.85
□ 6 Alex Grammas	6.00	2.70	.75
□ 7 Al Pilarcik	6.00	2.70	.75
□ 8 Phillies Team	65.00	13.00	6.50
(Checklist on back)			
□ 9 Paul Giel	7.00	3.10	.85
□ 10 Mickey Mantle	600.00	275.00	75.00
□ 11 Billy Hunter	7.00	3.10	.85
□ 12 Vern Law	7.00	3.10	.85
□ 13 Dick Gernert	6.00	2.70	.75
□ 14 Pete Whisenant	6.00	2.70	.75
□ 15 Dick Drott	6.00	2.70	.75
□ 16 Joe Pignatano	6.00	2.70	.75
□ 17 Danny's Stars	7.00	3.10	.85
Frank Thomas			
Danny Murtaugh MG			
Ted Kluszewski			
□ 18 Jack Urban	6.00	2.70	.75
□ 19 Eddie Bressoud	6.00	2.70	.75
□ 20 Duke Snider	50.00	22.00	6.25
□ 21 Connie Johnson	6.00	2.70	.75
□ 22 Al Smith	7.00	3.10	.85
□ 23 Murry Dickson	7.00	3.10	.85
□ 24 Red Wilson	6.00	2.70	.75
□ 25 Don Hoak	7.00	3.10	.85
□ 26 Chuck Stobbs	6.00	2.70	.75
□ 27 Andy Pafko	7.00	3.10	.85
□ 28 Al Worthington	6.00	2.70	.75
□ 29 Jim Bolger	6.00	2.70	.75
□ 30 Nellie Fox	25.00	11.00	3.10
□ 31 Ken Lehman	6.00	2.70	.75
□ 32 Don Buddin	6.00	2.70	.75
□ 33 Ed Fitzgerald	6.00	2.70	.75
□ 34 Pitchers Beware	20.00	9.00	2.50
Al Kaline			
Charley Maxwell			
□ 35 Ted Kluszewski	16.00	7.25	2.00
□ 36 Hank Aguirre	6.00	2.70	.75
□ 37 Gene Green	6.00	2.70	.75
□ 38 Morrie Martin	6.00	2.70	.75
□ 39 Ed Bouchee	6.00	2.70	.75
□ 40A Warren Spahn ERR	75.00	34.00	9.50
(Born 1931)			
□ 40B Warren Spahn ERR	100.00	45.00	12.50
(Born 1931, but three			
is partially obscured)			
□ 40C Warren Spahn COR	50.00	22.00	6.25
(Born 1921)			
□ 41 Bob Martyn	6.00	2.70	.75
□ 42 Murray Wall	6.00	2.70	.75
□ 43 Steve Bilko	6.00	2.70	.75
□ 44 Vito Valentinetti	6.00	2.70	.75
□ 45 Andy Carey	7.00	3.10	.85
□ 46 Bill R. Henry	6.00	2.70	.75
□ 47 Jim Finigan	6.00	2.70	.75
□ 48 Orioles Team	24.00	4.80	2.40
(Checklist on back)			
□ 49 Bill Hall	6.00	2.70	.75
□ 50 Willie Mays	125.00	55.00	15.50
□ 51 Rip Coleman	6.00	2.70	.75
□ 52 Coot Veal	6.00	2.70	.75
□ 53 Stan Williams	7.00	3.10	.85
□ 54 Mel Roach	6.00	2.70	.75
□ 55 Tom Brewer	6.00	2.70	.75
□ 56 Carl Sawatski	6.00	2.70	.75
□ 57 Al Cicotte	6.00	2.70	.75
□ 58 Eddie Miksis	6.00	2.70	.75
□ 59 Irv Noren	7.00	3.10	.85
□ 60 Bob Turley	7.00	3.10	.85
□ 61 Dick Brown	6.00	2.70	.75
□ 62 Tony Taylor	7.00	3.10	.85
□ 63 Jim Hearn	6.00	2.70	.75
□ 64 Joe DeMaestri	6.00	2.70	.75
□ 65 Frank Torre	7.00	3.10	.85
□ 66 Joe Ginsberg	6.00	2.70	.75
□ 67 Brooks Lawrence	6.00	2.70	.75
□ 68 Dick Schofield	7.00	3.10	.85
□ 69 Giants Team	24.00	4.80	2.40
(Checklist on back)			
□ 70 Harvey Kuenn	8.00	3.60	1.00
□ 71 Don Bessent	6.00	2.70	.75
□ 72 Bill Renna	6.00	2.70	.75
□ 73 Ron Jackson	7.00	3.10	.85
□ 74 Directing Power	7.00	3.10	.85
Jim Lemon			
Cookie Lavagetto MG			
Roy Sievers			
□ 75 Sam Jones	7.00	3.10	.85
□ 76 Bobby Richardson	20.00	9.00	2.50
□ 77 John Goryl	6.00	2.70	.75
□ 78 Pedro Ramos	6.00	2.70	.75
□ 79 Harry Chiti	6.00	2.70	.75
□ 80 Minnie Minoso	10.00	4.50	1.25
□ 81 Hal Jeffcoat	6.00	2.70	.75
□ 82 Bob Boyd	6.00	2.70	.75
□ 83 Bob Smith	6.00	2.70	.75
□ 84 Reno Bertoia	6.00	2.70	.75
□ 85 Harry Anderson	6.00	2.70	.75
□ 86 Bob Keegan	7.00	3.10	.85
□ 87 Danny O'Connell	6.00	2.70	.75
□ 88 Herb Score	10.00	4.50	1.25
□ 89 Billy Gardner	6.00	2.70	.75
□ 90 Bill Skowron	16.00	7.25	2.00
□ 91 Herb Moford	6.00	2.70	.75
□ 92 Dave Philley	6.00	2.70	.75
□ 93 Julio Becquer	6.00	2.70	.75
□ 94 White Sox Team	40.00	8.00	4.00
(Checklist on back)			
□ 95 Carl Willey	6.00	2.70	.75
□ 96 Lou Berberet	6.00	2.70	.75
□ 97 Jerry Lynch	7.00	3.10	.85
□ 98 Arnie Portocarrero	6.00	2.70	.75
□ 99 Ted Kazanski	6.00	2.70	.75
□ 100 Bob Cerv	7.00	3.10	.85
□ 101 Alex Kellner	6.00	2.70	.75
□ 102 Felipe Alou	30.00	13.50	3.70
□ 103 Billy Goodman	7.00	3.10	.85
□ 104 Del Rice	7.00	3.10	.85
□ 105 Lee Walls	6.00	2.70	.75
□ 106 Hal Woodeshick	6.00	2.70	.75
□ 107 Norm Larker	7.00	3.10	.85
□ 108 Zack Monroe	7.00	3.10	.85
□ 109 Bob Schmidt	6.00	2.70	.75
□ 110 George Witt	7.00	3.10	.85
□ 111 Redlegs Team	15.00	3.00	1.50
(Checklist on back)			
□ 112 Billy Consolo	4.00	1.80	.50
□ 113 Taylor Phillips	4.00	1.80	.50
□ 114 Earl Battey	5.00	2.20	.60
□ 115 Mickey Vernon	5.00	2.20	.60
□ 116 Bob Allison RP	12.00	5.50	1.50
□ 117 John Blanchard RP	7.00	3.10	.85
□ 118 John Buzhardt RP	5.00	2.20	.60
□ 119 John Callison RP	12.00	5.50	1.50
□ 120 Chuck Coles RP	5.00	2.20	.60
□ 121 Bob Conley RP	5.00	2.20	.60
□ 122 Bennie Daniels RP	5.00	2.20	.60
□ 123 Don Dillard RP	5.00	2.20	.60
□ 124 Dan Dobbek RP	5.00	2.20	.60
□ 125 Ron Fairly RP	7.00	3.10	.85
□ 126 Ed Haas RP	5.00	2.20	.60
□ 127 Kent Hadley RP	5.00	2.20	.60
□ 128 Bob Hartman RP	5.00	2.20	.60
□ 129 Frank Herrera RP	5.00	2.20	.60
□ 130 Lou Jackson RP	5.00	2.20	.60
□ 131 Deron Johnson RP	7.00	3.10	.85
□ 132 Don Lee RP	5.00	2.20	.60
□ 133 Bob Lillis RP	5.00	2.20	.60
□ 134 Jim McDaniel RP	5.00	2.20	.60
□ 135 Gene Oliver RP	5.00	2.20	.60
□ 136 Jim O'Toole RP	5.00	2.20	.60
□ 137 Dick Ricketts RP	5.00	2.20	.60
□ 138 John Romano RP	5.00	2.20	.60
□ 139 Ed Sadowski RP	5.00	2.20	.60
□ 140 Charlie Secrest RP	5.00	2.20	.60
□ 141 Joe Shipley RP	5.00	2.20	.60
□ 142 Dick Stigman RP	5.00	2.20	.60
□ 143 Willie Tasby RP	5.00	2.20	.60
□ 144 Jerry Walker RP	5.00	2.20	.60
□ 145 Dom Zanni RP	5.00	2.20	.60
□ 146 Jerry Zimmerman RP	5.00	2.20	.60
□ 147 Cubs Clubbers	25.00	11.00	3.10
Dale Long			
Ernie Banks			
Walt Moryn			
□ 148 Mike McCormick	5.00	2.20	.60
□ 149 Jim Bunning	20.00	9.00	2.50
□ 150 Stan Musial	125.00	55.00	15.50
□ 151 Bob Malkmus	4.00	1.80	.50
□ 152 Johnny Klippstein	4.00	1.80	.50
□ 153 Jim Marshall	4.00	1.80	.50
□ 154 Ray Herbert	4.00	1.80	.50
□ 155 Enos Slaughter	20.00	9.00	2.50
□ 156 Ace Hurlers	12.00	5.50	1.50
Billy Pierce			
Robin Roberts			
□ 157 Felix Mantilla	4.00	1.80	.50
□ 158 Walt Dropo	4.00	1.80	.50
□ 159 Bob Shaw	5.00	2.20	.60
□ 160 Dick Groat	5.00	2.20	.60
□ 161 Frank Baumann	4.00	1.80	.50
□ 162 Bobby G. Smith	4.00	1.80	.50
□ 163 Sandy Koufax	150.00	70.00	19.00
□ 164 Johnny Groth	4.00	1.80	.50
□ 165 Bill Bruton	4.00	1.80	.50
□ 166 Destruction Crew	20.00	9.00	2.50
Minnie Minoso			
Rocky Colavito			
(Misspelled Colovito			
on card back)			
Larry Doby			
□ 167 Duke Maas	4.00	1.80	.50
□ 168 Carroll Hardy	4.00	1.80	.50
□ 169 Ted Abernathy	4.00	1.80	.50
□ 170 Gene Woodling	5.00	2.20	.60
□ 171 Willard Schmidt	4.00	1.80	.50
□ 172 Athletics Team	15.00	3.00	1.50
(Checklist on back)			
□ 173 Bill Monbouquette	5.00	2.20	.60
□ 174 Jim Pendleton	4.00	1.80	.50
□ 175 Dick Farrell	5.00	2.20	.60
□ 176 Preston Ward	4.00	1.80	.50
□ 177 John Briggs	4.00	1.80	.50
□ 178 Ruben Amaro	5.00	2.20	.60
□ 179 Don Rudolph	4.00	1.80	.50
□ 180 Yogi Berra	75.00	34.00	9.50
□ 181 Bob Porterfield	4.00	1.80	.50
□ 182 Milt Graff	4.00	1.80	.50
□ 183 Stu Miller	5.00	2.20	.60
□ 184 Harvey Haddix	5.00	2.20	.60
□ 185 Jim Busby	4.00	1.80	.50
□ 186 Mudcat Grant	5.00	2.20	.60
□ 187 Bubba Phillips	5.00	2.20	.60
□ 188 Juan Pizarro	4.00	1.80	.50
□ 189 Neil Chrisley	4.00	1.80	.50
□ 190 Bill Virdon	5.00	2.20	.60
□ 191 Russ Kemmerer	4.00	1.80	.50
□ 192 Charlie Beamon	4.00	1.80	.50
□ 193 Sammy Taylor	4.00	1.80	.50
□ 194 Jim Brosnan	5.00	2.20	.60
□ 195 Rip Repulski	4.00	1.80	.50
□ 196 Billy Moran	4.00	1.80	.50
□ 197 Ray Semproch	4.00	1.80	.50
□ 198 Jim Davenport	5.00	2.20	.60
□ 199 Leo Kiely	4.00	1.80	.50
□ 200 Warren Giles	8.00	3.60	1.00
(NL President)			
□ 201 Tom Acker	4.00	1.80	.50
□ 202 Roger Maris	90.00	40.00	11.00
□ 203 Ossie Virgil	4.00	1.80	.50
□ 204 Casey Wise	4.00	1.80	.50
□ 205 Don Larsen	8.00	3.60	1.00
□ 206 Carl Furillo	8.00	3.60	1.00
□ 207 George Strickland	4.00	1.80	.50
□ 208 Willie Jones	4.00	1.80	.50
□ 209 Lenny Green	4.00	1.80	.50
□ 210 Ed Bailey	4.00	1.80	.50
□ 211 Bob Blaylock	4.00	1.80	.50
□ 212 Fence Busters	75.00	34.00	9.50
Hank Aaron			
Eddie Mathews			
□ 213 Jim Rivera	5.00	2.20	.60
□ 214 Marcelino Solis	4.00	1.80	.50
□ 215 Jim Lemon	5.00	2.20	.60
□ 216 Andre Rodgers	4.00	1.80	.50
□ 217 Carl Erskine	5.00	2.20	.60
□ 218 Roman Mejias	4.00	1.80	.50
□ 219 George Zuverink	4.00	1.80	.50
□ 220 Frank Malzone	5.00	2.20	.60
□ 221 Bob Bowman	4.00	1.80	.50
□ 222 Bobby Shantz	4.00	1.80	.50
□ 223 Cardinals Team	15.00	3.00	1.50
(Checklist on back)			
□ 224 Claude Osteen	5.00	2.20	.60
□ 225 Johnny Logan	5.00	2.20	.60
□ 226 Art Ceccarelli	4.00	1.80	.50
□ 227 Hal W. Smith	4.00	1.80	.50
□ 228 Don Gross	4.00	1.80	.50
□ 229 Vic Power	5.00	2.20	.60
□ 230 Bill Fischer	4.00	1.80	.50
□ 231 Ellis Burton	4.00	1.80	.50
□ 232 Eddie Kasko	4.00	1.80	.50
□ 233 Paul Foytack	4.00	1.80	.50
□ 234 Chuck Tanner	5.00	2.20	.60
□ 235 Valmy Thomas	4.00	1.80	.50
□ 236 Ted Bowsfield	4.00	1.80	.50
□ 237 Run Preventers	12.00	5 50	1.50
Gil McDougald			
Bob Turley			
Bobby Richardson			
□ 238 Gene Baker	4.00	1.80	.50
□ 239 Bob Trowbridge	4.00	1.80	.50
□ 240 Hank Bauer	5.00	2.20	.60
□ 241 Billy Muffett	4.00	1.80	.50
□ 242 Ron Samford	4.00	1.80	.50
□ 243 Marv Grissom	4.00	1.80	.50
□ 244 Ted Gray	4.00	1.80	.50
□ 245 Ned Garver	4.00	1.80	.50
□ 246 J.W. Porter	4.00	1.80	.50
□ 247 Don Ferrarese	4.00	1.80	.50
□ 248 Red Sox Team	15.00	3.00	1.50
(Checklist on back)			
□ 249 Bobby Adams	4.00	1.80	.50
□ 250 Billy O'Dell	4.00	1.80	.50
□ 251 Clete Boyer	5.00	2.20	.60
□ 252 Ray Boone	5.00	2.20	.60
□ 253 Seth Morehead	4.00	1.80	.50
□ 254 Zeke Bella	4.00	1.80	.50
□ 255 Del Ennis	5.00	2.20	.60
□ 256 Jerry Davie	4.00	1.80	.50
□ 257 Leon Wagner	5.00	2.20	.60
□ 258 Fred Kipp	4.00	1.80	.50
□ 259 Jim Pisoni	4.00	1.80	.50
□ 260 Early Wynn UER	16.00	7.25	2.00
(1957 Cleevland)			
□ 261 Gene Stephens	4.00	1.80	.50
□ 262 Hitters' Foes	16.00	7.25	2.00
Johnny Podres			
Clem Labine			
Don Drysdale			
□ 263 Bud Daley	4.00	1.80	.50
□ 264 Chico Carrasquel	4.00	1.80	.50
□ 265 Ron Kline	4.00	1.80	.50
□ 266 Woody Held	4.00	1.80	.50
□ 267 John Romonosky	4.00	1.80	.50
□ 268 Tito Francona	5.00	2.20	.60
□ 269 Jack Meyer	4.00	1.80	.50
□ 270 Gil Hodges	25.00	11.00	3.10
□ 271 Orlando Pena	4.00	1.80	.50
□ 272 Jerry Lumpe	4.00	1.80	.50
□ 273 Joey Jay	5.00	2.20	.60
□ 274 Jerry Kindall	5.00	2.20	.60
□ 275 Jack Sanford	5.00	2.20	.60
□ 276 Pete Daley	4.00	1.80	.50
□ 277 Turk Lown	5.00	2.20	.60
□ 278 Chuck Essegian	4.00	1.80	.50
□ 279 Ernie Johnson	5.00	2.20	.60
□ 280 Frank Bolling	4.00	1.80	.50
□ 281 Walt Craddock	4.00	1.80	.50
□ 282 R.C. Stevens	4.00	1.80	.50
□ 283 Russ Heman	4.00	1.80	.50
□ 284 Steve Korcheck	4.00	1.80	.50
□ 285 Joe Cunningham	4.00	1.80	.50
□ 286 Dean Stone	4.00	1.80	.50
□ 287 Don Zimmer	5.00	2.20	.60
□ 288 Dutch Dotterer	4.00	1.80	.50
□ 289 Johnny Kucks	8.00	3.60	1.00
□ 290 Wes Covington	5.00	2.20	.60
□ 291 Pitching Partners	5.00	2.20	.60
Pedro Ramos			
Camilo Pascual			
□ 292 Dick Williams	5.00	2.20	.60
□ 293 Ray Moore	4.00	1.80	.50
□ 294 Hank Foiles	4.00	1.80	.50
□ 295 Billy Martin	20.00	9.00	2.50
□ 296 Ernie Broglio	4.00	1.80	.50
□ 297 Jackie Brandt	4.00	1.80	.50
□ 298 Tex Clevenger	4.00	1.80	.50
□ 299 Billy Klaus	4.00	1.80	.50
□ 300 Richie Ashburn	25.00	11.00	3.10
□ 301 Earl Averill	4.00	1.80	.50
□ 302 Don Mossi	5.00	2.20	.60
□ 303 Marty Keough	4.00	1.80	.50
□ 304 Cubs Team	15.00	3.00	1.50
(Checklist on back)			
□ 305 Curt Raydon	4.00	1.80	.50
□ 306 Jim Gilliam	5.00	2.20	.60
□ 307 Curt Barclay	4.00	1.80	.50
□ 308 Norm Siebern	4.00	1.80	.50
□ 309 Sal Maglie	5.00	2.20	.60
□ 310 Luis Aparicio	20.00	9.00	2.50
□ 311 Norm Zauchin	4.00	1.80	.50
□ 312 Don Newcombe	5.00	2.20	.60
□ 313 Frank House	4.00	1.80	.50
□ 314 Don Cardwell	4.00	1.80	.50
□ 315 Joe Adcock	5.00	2.20	.60
□ 316A Ralph Lumenti UER	4.00	1.80	.50
(Option)			
(Photo actually			
Camilo Pascual)			
□ 316B Ralph Lumenti UER	80.00	36.00	10.00
(No option)			
(Photo actually			
Camilo Pascual)			
□ 317 Hitting Kings	65.00	29.00	8.00
Willie Mays			
Richie Ashburn			
□ 318 Rocky Bridges	4.00	1.80	.50
□ 319 Dave Hillman	4.00	1.80	.50
□ 320 Bob Skinner	5.00	2.20	.60
□ 321A Bob Giallombardo	4.00	1.80	.50
(Option)			
□ 321B Bob Giallombardo	80.00	36.00	10.00
(No option)			
□ 322A Harry Hanebrink	4.00	1.80	.50
(Traded)			
□ 322B Harry Hanebrink	80.00	36.00	10.00
(No trade)			
□ 323 Frank Sullivan	4.00	1.80	.50
□ 324 Don Demeter	4.00	1.80	.50
□ 325 Ken Boyer	10.00	4.50	1.25
□ 326 Marv Throneberry	5.00	2.20	.60
□ 327 Gary Bell	4.00	1.80	.50
□ 328 Lou Skizas	4.00	1.80	.50
□ 329 Tigers Team	15.00	3.00	1.50
(Checklist on back)			
□ 330 Gus Triandos	5.00	2.20	.60
□ 331 Steve Boros	4.00	1.80	.50
□ 332 Ray Monzant	4.00	1.80	.50
□ 333 Harry Simpson	4.00	1.80	.50
□ 334 Glen Hobbie	4.00	1.80	.50
□ 335 Johnny Temple	5.00	2.20	.60
□ 336A Billy Loes	5.00	2.20	.60
(With traded line)			
□ 336B Billy Loes	80.00	36.00	10.00
(No trade)			
□ 337 George Crowe	4.00	1.80	.50
□ 338 Sparky Anderson	75.00	34.00	9.50
□ 339 Roy Face	5.00	2.20	.60
□ 340 Roy Sievers	5.00	2.20	.60
□ 341 Tom Qualters	4.00	1.80	.50
□ 342 Ray Jablonski	4.00	1.80	.50
□ 343 Billy Hoeft	4.00	1.80	.50

☐ 344 Russ Nixon 4.00 1.80 .50
☐ 345 Gil McDougald 8.00 3.60 1.00
☐ 346 Batter Bafflers 4.00 1.80 .50
Dave Sisler
Tom Brewer
☐ 347 Bob Buhl 5.00 2.20 .60
☐ 348 Ted Lepcio 4.00 1.80 .50
☐ 349 Hoyt Wilhelm 16.00 7.25 2.00
☐ 350 Ernie Banks 75.00 34.00 9.50
☐ 351 Earl Torgeson 4.00 1.80 .50
☐ 352 Robin Roberts 20.00 9.00 2.50
☐ 353 Curt Flood 5.00 2.20 .60
☐ 354 Pete Burnside 4.00 1.80 .50
☐ 355 Jim Piersall 5.00 2.20 .60
☐ 356 Bob Mabe 4.00 1.80 .50
☐ 357 Dick Stuart 5.00 2.20 .60
☐ 358 Ralph Terry 5.00 2.20 .60
☐ 359 Bill White 25.00 11.00 3.10
☐ 360 Al Kaline 65.00 29.00 8.00
☐ 361 Willard Nixon 4.00 1.80 .50
☐ 362A Dolan Nichols 4.00 1.80 .50
(With option line)
☐ 362B Dolan Nichols 80.00 36.00 10.00
(No option)
☐ 363 Bobby Avila 4.00 1.80 .50
☐ 364 Danny McDevitt 4.00 1.80 .50
☐ 365 Gus Bell 5.00 2.20 .60
☐ 366 Humberto Robinson 4.00 1.80 .50
☐ 367 Cal Neeman 4.00 1.80 .50
☐ 368 Don Mueller 5.00 2.20 .60
☐ 369 Dick Tomanek 4.00 1.80 .50
☐ 370 Pete Runnels 5.00 2.20 .60
☐ 371 Dick Brodowski 4.00 1.80 .50
☐ 372 Jim Hegan 5.00 2.20 .60
☐ 373 Herb Plews 4.00 1.80 .50
☐ 374 Art Ditmar 5.00 2.20 .60
☐ 375 Bob Nieman 4.00 1.80 .50
☐ 376 Hal Naragon 4.00 1.80 .50
☐ 377 John Antonelli 5.00 2.20 .60
☐ 378 Gail Harris 4.00 1.80 .50
☐ 379 Bob Miller 4.00 1.80 .50
☐ 380 Hank Aaron 125.00 55.00 15.50
☐ 381 Mike Baxes 4.00 1.80 .50
☐ 382 Curt Simmons 5.00 2.20 .60
☐ 383 Words of Wisdom 14.00 6.25 1.75
Don Larsen
Casey Stengel MG
☐ 384 Dave Sisler 4.00 1.80 .50
☐ 385 Sherm Lollar 5.00 2.20 .60
☐ 386 Jim Delsing 4.00 1.80 .50
☐ 387 Don Drysdale 35.00 16.00 4.40
☐ 388 Bob Will 4.00 1.80 .50
☐ 389 Joe Nuxhall 5.00 2.20 .60
☐ 390 Orlando Cepeda 16.00 7.25 2.00
☐ 391 Milt Pappas 5.00 2.20 .60
☐ 392 Whitey Herzog 5.00 2.20 .60
☐ 393 Frank Lary 5.00 2.20 .60
☐ 394 Randy Jackson 4.00 1.80 .50
☐ 395 Elston Howard 10.00 4.50 1.25
☐ 396 Bob Rush 4.00 1.80 .50
☐ 397 Senators Team 15.00 3.00 1.50
(Checklist on back)
☐ 398 Wally Post 5.00 2.20 .60
☐ 399 Larry Jackson 4.00 1.80 .50
☐ 400 Jackie Jensen 5.00 2.20 .60
☐ 401 Ron Blackburn 4.00 1.80 .50
☐ 402 Hector Lopez 5.00 2.20 .60
☐ 403 Clem Labine 5.00 2.20 .60
☐ 404 Hank Sauer 5.00 2.20 .60
☐ 405 Roy McMillan 5.00 2.20 .60
☐ 406 Solly Drake 4.00 1.80 .50
☐ 407 Moe Drabowsky 5.00 2.20 .60
☐ 408 Keystone Combo 25.00 11.00 3.10
Nellie Fox
Luis Aparicio
☐ 409 Gus Zernial 5.00 2.20 .60
☐ 410 Billy Pierce 5.00 2.20 .60
☐ 411 Whitey Lockman 5.00 2.20 .60
☐ 412 Stan Lopata 4.00 1.80 .50
☐ 413 Camilo Pascual UER 5.00 2.20 .60
(Listed as Camillo
on front and Pasqual
on back)
☐ 414 Dale Long 5.00 2.20 .60
☐ 415 Bill Mazeroski 12.00 5.50 1.50
☐ 416 Haywood Sullivan 5.00 2.20 .60
☐ 417 Virgil Trucks 5.00 2.20 .60
☐ 418 Gino Cimoli 4.00 1.80 .50
☐ 419 Braves Team 15.00 3.00 1.50
(Checklist on back)
☐ 420 Rocky Colavito 30.00 13.50 3.70
☐ 421 Herman Wehmeier 4.00 1.80 .50
☐ 422 Hobie Landrith 4.00 1.80 .50
☐ 423 Bob Grim 5.00 2.20 .60
☐ 424 Ken Aspromonte 4.00 1.80 .50
☐ 425 Del Crandall 5.00 2.20 .60
☐ 426 Gerry Staley 5.00 2.20 .60
☐ 427 Charlie Neal 5.00 2.20 .60
☐ 428 Buc Hill Aces 5.00 2.20 .60
Ron Kline
Bob Friend
Vernon Law
Roy Face
☐ 429 Bobby Thomson 5.00 2.20 .60
☐ 430 Whitey Ford 50.00 22.00 6.25
☐ 431 Whammy Douglas 4.00 1.80 .50
☐ 432 Smoky Burgess 5.00 2.20 .60
☐ 433 Billy Harrell 4.00 1.80 .50
☐ 434 Hal Griggs 4.00 1.80 .50
☐ 435 Frank Robinson 50.00 22.00 6.25
☐ 436 Granny Hamner 4.00 1.80 .50
☐ 437 Ike Delock 4.00 1.80 .50
☐ 438 Sammy Esposito 4.00 1.80 .50
☐ 439 Brooks Robinson 50.00 22.00 6.25
☐ 440 Lou Burdette 8.00 3.60 1.00
(Posing as if
lefthanded)
☐ 441 John Roseboro 5.00 2.20 .60
☐ 442 Ray Narleski 4.00 1.80 .50
☐ 443 Daryl Spencer 4.00 1.80 .50
☐ 444 Ron Hansen 5.00 2.20 .60
☐ 445 Cal McLish 4.00 1.80 .50
☐ 446 Rocky Nelson 4.00 1.80 .50
☐ 447 Bob Anderson 4.00 1.80 .50
☐ 448 Vada Pinson UER 10.00 4.50 1.25
(Born: 8/8/38
should be 8/11/38)
☐ 449 Tom Gorman 4.00 1.80 .50
☐ 450 Eddie Mathews 35.00 16.00 4.40
☐ 451 Jimmy Constable 4.00 1.80 .50
☐ 452 Chico Fernandez 4.00 1.80 .50
☐ 453 Les Moss 4.00 1.80 .50
☐ 454 Phil Clark 4.00 1.80 .50
☐ 455 Larry Doby 5.00 2.20 .60
☐ 456 Jerry Casale 4.00 1.80 .50
☐ 457 Dodgers Team 30.00 6.00 3.00
(Checklist on back)
☐ 458 Gordon Jones 4.00 1.80 .50
☐ 459 Bill Tuttle 4.00 1.80 .50
☐ 460 Bob Friend 5.00 2.20 .60
☐ 461 Mickey Mantle HL 130.00 57.50 16.00
☐ 462 Rocky Colavito HL 16.00 7.25 2.00
☐ 463 Al Kaline HL 20.00 9.00 2.50
☐ 464 Willie Mays HL 40.00 18.00 5.00
54 World Series Catch
☐ 465 Roy Sievers HL 5.00 2.20 .60
☐ 466 Billy Pierce HL 5.00 2.20 .60
☐ 467 Hank Aaron HL 30.00 13.50 3.70
☐ 468 Duke Snider HL 18.00 8.00 2.20
☐ 469 Ernie Banks HL 18.00 8.00 2.20
☐ 470 Stan Musial HL 25.00 11.00 3.10
3,000 Hits
☐ 471 Tom Sturdivant 4.00 1.80 .50
☐ 472 Gene Freese 4.00 1.80 .50
☐ 473 Mike Fornieles 4.00 1.80 .50
☐ 474 Moe Thacker 4.00 1.80 .50
☐ 475 Jack Harshman 4.00 1.80 .50
☐ 476 Indians Team 15.00 3.00 1.50
(Checklist on back)
☐ 477 Barry Latman 4.00 1.80 .50
☐ 478 Bob Clemente 225.00 100.00 28.00
☐ 479 Lindy McDaniel 5.00 2.20 .60
☐ 480 Red Schoendienst 16.00 7.25 2.00
☐ 481 Charlie Maxwell 5.00 2.20 .60
☐ 482 Russ Meyer 4.00 1.80 .50
☐ 483 Clint Courtney 4.00 1.80 .50
☐ 484 Willie Kirkland 4.00 1.80 .50
☐ 485 Ryne Duren 8.00 3.60 1.00
☐ 486 Sammy White 4.00 1.80 .50
☐ 487 Hal Brown 4.00 1.80 .50
☐ 488 Walt Moryn 4.00 1.80 .50
☐ 489 John Powers 4.00 1.80 .50
☐ 490 Frank Thomas 5.00 2.20 .60
☐ 491 Don Blasingame 4.00 1.80 .50
☐ 492 Gene Conley 5.00 2.20 .60
☐ 493 Jim Landis 5.00 2.20 .60
☐ 494 Don Pavletich 4.00 1.80 .50
☐ 495 Johnny Podres 5.00 2.20 .60
☐ 496 Wayne Terwilliger UER 4.00 1.80 .50
(Athlftics on front)
☐ 497 Hal R. Smith 4.00 1.80 .50
☐ 498 Dick Hyde 4.00 1.80 .50
☐ 499 Johnny O'Brien 5.00 2.20 .60
☐ 500 Vic Wertz 5.00 2.20 .60
☐ 501 Bob Tiefenauer 4.00 1.80 .50
☐ 502 Alvin Dark 5.00 2.20 .60
☐ 503 Jim Owens 4.00 1.80 .50
☐ 504 Ossie Alvarez 4.00 1.80 .50
☐ 505 Tony Kubek 12.00 5.50 1.50
☐ 506 Bob Purkey 4.00 1.80 .50
☐ 507 Bob Hale 16.00 7.25 2.00
☐ 508 Art Fowler 16.00 7.25 2.00
☐ 509 Norm Cash 65.00 29.00 8.00
☐ 510 Yankees Team 125.00 25.00 12.50
(Checklist on back)
☐ 511 George Susce 16.00 7.25 2.00
☐ 512 George Altman 16.00 7.25 2.00
☐ 513 Tommy Carroll 16.00 7.25 2.00
☐ 514 Bob Gibson 250.00 110.00 31.00
☐ 515 Harmon Killebrew 125.00 55.00 15.50
☐ 516 Mike Garcia 18.00 8.00 2.20
☐ 517 Joe Koppe 16.00 7.25 2.00
☐ 518 Mike Cueller UER 30.00 13.50 3.70
(Sic, Cuellar)
☐ 519 Infield Power 18.00 8.00 2.20
Pete Runnels
Dick Gernert
Frank Malzone
☐ 520 Don Elston 16.00 7.25 2.00
☐ 521 Gary Geiger 16.00 7.25 2.00
☐ 522 Gene Snyder 16.00 7.25 2.00
☐ 523 Harry Bright 16.00 7.25 2.00
☐ 524 Larry Osborne 16.00 7.25 2.00
☐ 525 Jim Coates 20.00 9.00 2.50
☐ 526 Bob Speake 16.00 7.25 2.00
☐ 527 Solly Hemus 16.00 7.25 2.00
☐ 528 Pirates Team 65.00 13.00 6.50
(Checklist on back)
☐ 529 George Bamberger 20.00 9.00 2.50
☐ 530 Wally Moon 20.00 9.00 2.50
☐ 531 Ray Webster 16.00 7.25 2.00
☐ 532 Mark Freeman 16.00 7.25 2.00
☐ 533 Darrell Johnson 20.00 9.00 2.50
☐ 534 Faye Throneberry 16.00 7.25 2.00
☐ 535 Ruben Gomez 16.00 7.25 2.00
☐ 536 Danny Kravitz 16.00 7.25 2.00
☐ 537 Rudolph Arias 16.00 7.25 2.00
☐ 538 Chick King 16.00 7.25 2.00
☐ 539 Gary Blaylock 16.00 7.25 2.00
☐ 540 Willie Miranda 16.00 7.25 2.00
☐ 541 Bob Thurman 16.00 7.25 2.00
☐ 542 Jim Perry 30.00 13.50 3.70
☐ 543 Corsair Trio 175.00 80.00 22.00
Bob Skinner
Bill Virdon
Roberto Clemente
☐ 544 Lee Tate 16.00 7.25 2.00
☐ 545 Tom Morgan 16.00 7.25 2.00
☐ 546 Al Schroll 16.00 7.25 2.00
☐ 547 Jim Baxes 16.00 7.25 2.00
☐ 548 Elmer Singleton 16.00 7.25 2.00
☐ 549 Howie Nunn 16.00 7.25 2.00
☐ 550 Roy Campanella 160.00 70.00 20.00
(Symbol of Courage)
☐ 551 Fred Haney AS MG 16.00 7.25 2.00
☐ 552 Casey Stengel AS MG 35.00 16.00 4.40
☐ 553 Orlando Cepeda AS 25.00 11.00 3.10
☐ 554 Bill Skowron AS 25.00 11.00 3.10
☐ 555 Bill Mazeroski AS 25.00 11.00 3.10
☐ 556 Nellie Fox AS 35.00 16.00 4.40
☐ 557 Ken Boyer AS 25.00 11.00 3.10
☐ 558 Frank Malzone AS 16.00 7.25 2.00
☐ 559 Ernie Banks AS 65.00 29.00 8.00
☐ 560 Luis Aparicio AS 35.00 16.00 4.40
☐ 561 Hank Aaron AS 125.00 55.00 15.50
☐ 562 Al Kaline AS 65.00 29.00 8.00
☐ 563 Willie Mays AS 125.00 55.00 15.50
☐ 564 Mickey Mantle AS 300.00 135.00 38.00
☐ 565 Wes Covington AS 16.00 7.25 2.00
☐ 566 Roy Sievers AS 16.00 7.25 2.00
☐ 567 Del Crandall AS 16.00 7.25 2.00
☐ 568 Gus Triandos AS 16.00 7.25 2.00
☐ 569 Bob Friend AS 16.00 7.25 2.00
☐ 570 Bob Turley AS 16.00 7.25 2.00
☐ 571 Warren Spahn AS 40.00 18.00 5.00
☐ 572 Billy Pierce AS 35.00 11.00 3.50

1959 Topps Venezuelan

This set is a parallel version of the first 196 cards of the regular 1959 Topps set and is similar in design. The difference is found in the words "Impreso en Venezuela por Benco Co." printed on thebottom of the card back. The cards were issued for the Venezuelan market.

	NRMT	VG-E	GOOD
COMPLETED SET (196)	5000.00	2200.00	600.00
COMMON CARD (1-196)	10.00	4.50	1.25

☐ 1 Ford Frick COMM 100.00 45.00 12.50
☐ 2 Eddie Yost 10.00 4.50 1.25
☐ 3 Don McMahon 10.00 4.50 1.25
☐ 4 Albie Pearson 10.00 4.50 1.25
☐ 5 Dick Donovan 10.00 4.50 1.25
☐ 6 Alex Grammas 10.00 4.50 1.25
☐ 7 Al Pilarcik 10.00 4.50 1.25
☐ 8 Phillies Team 125.00 55.00 15.50
(Checklist on back)
☐ 9 Paul Giel 10.00 4.50 1.25
☐ 10 Mickey Mantle 1500.00 700.00 190.00
☐ 11 Billy Hunter 10.00 4.50 1.25
☐ 12 Vern Law 10.00 4.50 1.25
☐ 13 Dick Gernert 10.00 4.50 1.25
☐ 14 Pete Whisenant 10.00 4.50 1.25
☐ 15 Dick Drott 10.00 4.50 1.25
☐ 16 Joe Pignatano 10.00 4.50 1.25
☐ 17 Danny's Stars 15.00 6.75 1.85
Frank Thomas
Danny Murtaugh MG
Ted Kluszewski
☐ 18 Jack Urban 10.00 4.50 1.25
☐ 19 Eddie Bressoud 10.00 4.50 1.25
☐ 20 Duke Snider 150.00 70.00 19.00
☐ 21 Connie Johnson 10.00 4.50 1.25
☐ 22 Al Smith 10.00 4.50 1.25
☐ 23 Murry Dickson 10.00 4.50 1.25
☐ 24 Red Wilson 10.00 4.50 1.25
☐ 25 Don Hoak 10.00 4.50 1.25
☐ 26 Chuck Stobbs 10.00 4.50 1.25
☐ 27 Andy Pafko 10.00 4.50 1.25
☐ 28 Al Worthington 10.00 4.50 1.25
☐ 29 Jim Bolger 10.00 4.50 1.25
☐ 30 Nellie Fox 50.00 22.00 6.25
☐ 31 Ken Lehman 10.00 4.50 1.25
☐ 32 Don Buddin 10.00 4.50 1.25
☐ 33 Ed Fitzgerald 10.00 4.50 1.25
☐ 34 Pitchers Beware 40.00 18.00 5.00
Al Kaline
Charley Maxwell
☐ 35 Ted Kluszewski 50.00 22.00 6.25
☐ 36 Hank Aguirre 10.00 4.50 1.25
☐ 37 Gene Green 10.00 4.50 1.25
☐ 38 Morrie Martin 10.00 4.50 1.25
☐ 39 Ed Bouchee 10.00 4.50 1.25
☐ 40 Warren Spahn 125.00 55.00 15.50
☐ 41 Bob Martyn 10.00 4.50 1.25
☐ 42 Murray Wall 10.00 4.50 1.25
☐ 43 Steve Bilko 10.00 4.50 1.25
☐ 44 Vito Valentinetti 10.00 4.50 1.25
☐ 45 Andy Carey 10.00 4.50 1.25
☐ 46 Bill R. Henry 10.00 4.50 1.25
☐ 47 Jim Finigan 10.00 4.50 1.25
☐ 48 Orioles Team 50.00 22.00 6.25
(Checklist on back)
☐ 49 Bill Hall 10.00 4.50 1.25
☐ 50 Willie Mays 300.00 135.00 38.00
☐ 51 Rip Coleman 10.00 4.50 1.25
☐ 52 Coot Veal 10.00 4.50 1.25
☐ 53 Stan Williams 10.00 4.50 1.25
☐ 54 Mel Roach 10.00 4.50 1.25
☐ 55 Tom Brewer 10.00 4.50 1.25
☐ 56 Carl Sawatski 10.00 4.50 1.25
☐ 57 Al Cicotte 10.00 4.50 1.25
☐ 58 Eddie Miksis 10.00 4.50 1.25
☐ 59 Irv Noren 10.00 4.50 1.25
☐ 60 Bob Turley 15.00 6.75 1.85
☐ 61 Dick Brown 10.00 4.50 1.25
☐ 62 Tony Taylor 10.00 4.50 1.25
☐ 63 Jim Hearn 10.00 4.50 1.25
☐ 64 Joe DeMaestri 10.00 4.50 1.25
☐ 65 Frank Torre 10.00 4.50 1.25
☐ 66 Joe Ginsberg 10.00 4.50 1.25
☐ 67 Brooks Lawrence 10.00 4.50 1.25
☐ 68 Dick Schofield 10.00 4.50 1.25
☐ 69 Giants Team 50.00 22.00 6.25
(Checklist on back)
☐ 70 Harvey Kuenn 15.00 6.75 1.85
☐ 71 Don Bessent 10.00 4.50 1.25
☐ 72 Bill Renna 10.00 4.50 1.25
☐ 73 Ron Jackson 10.00 4.50 1.25
☐ 74 Directing Power 10.00 4.50 1.25
Jim Lemon
Cookie Lavagetto MG
Roy Sievers
☐ 75 Sam Jones 10.00 4.50 1.25
☐ 76 Bobby Richardson 60.00 27.00 7.50
☐ 77 John Goryl 10.00 4.50 1.25
☐ 78 Pedro Ramos 10.00 4.50 1.25
☐ 79 Harry Chiti 10.00 4.50 1.25
☐ 80 Minnie Minoso 30.00 13.50 3.70
☐ 81 Hal Jeffcoat 10.00 4.50 1.25
☐ 82 Bob Boyd 10.00 4.50 1.25
☐ 83 Bob Smith 10.00 4.50 1.25
☐ 84 Reno Bertoia 10.00 4.50 1.25
☐ 85 Harry Anderson 10.00 4.50 1.25
☐ 86 Bob Keegan 10.00 4.50 1.25
☐ 87 Danny O'Connell 10.00 4.50 1.25
☐ 88 Herb Score 25.00 11.00 3.10
☐ 89 Billy Gardner 10.00 4.50 1.25
☐ 90 Bill Skowron 40.00 18.00 5.00
☐ 91 Herb Moford 10.00 4.50 1.25
☐ 92 Dave Philley 10.00 4.50 1.25
☐ 93 Julio Becquer 10.00 4.50 1.25
☐ 94 White Sox Team 75.00 34.00 9.50
(Checklist on back)
☐ 95 Carl Willey 10.00 4.50 1.25
☐ 96 Lou Berberet 10.00 4.50 1.25
☐ 97 Jerry Lynch 10.00 4.50 1.25
☐ 98 Arnie Portocarrero 10.00 4.50 1.25
☐ 99 Ted Kazanski 10.00 4.50 1.25
☐ 100 Bob Cerv 10.00 4.50 1.25
☐ 101 Alex Kellner 10.00 4.50 1.25
☐ 102 Felipe Alou 75.00 34.00 9.50
☐ 103 Billy Goodman 10.00 4.50 1.25
☐ 104 Del Rice 10.00 4.50 1.25
☐ 105 Lee Walls 10.00 4.50 1.25
☐ 106 Hal Woodeshick 10.00 4.50 1.25
☐ 107 Norm Larker 10.00 4.50 1.25
☐ 108 'Zack Monroe 10.00 4.50 1.25
☐ 109 Bob Schmidt 10.00 4.50 1.25
☐ 110 George Witt 10.00 4.50 1.25
☐ 111 Redlegs Team 30.00 13.50 3.70
(Checklist on back)
☐ 112 Billy Consolo 10.00 4.50 1.25
☐ 113 Taylor Phillips 10.00 4.50 1.25
☐ 114 Earl Battey 10.00 4.50 1.25
☐ 115 Mickey Vernon 15.00 6.75 1.85
☐ 116 Bob Allison RP 20.00 9.00 2.50

Card	NRMT	VG-E	GOOD
☐ 117 John Blanchard RP	10.00	4.50	1.25
☐ 118 John Buzhardt RP	10.00	4.50	1.25
☐ 119 John Callison RP	25.00	11.00	3.10
☐ 120 Chuck Coles RP	10.00	4.50	1.25
☐ 121 Bob Conley RP	10.00	4.50	1.25
☐ 122 Bennie Daniels RP	10.00	4.50	1.25
☐ 123 Don Dillard RP	10.00	4.50	1.25
☐ 124 Dan Dobbek RP	10.00	4.50	1.25
☐ 125 Ron Fairly RP	20.00	9.00	2.50
☐ 126 Ed Haas RP	10.00	4.50	1.25
☐ 127 Kent Hadley RP	10.00	4.50	1.25
☐ 128 Bob Hartman RP	10.00	4.50	1.25
☐ 129 Frank Herrera RP	10.00	4.50	1.25
☐ 130 Lou Jackson RP	10.00	4.50	1.25
☐ 131 Deron Johnson RP	10.00	4.50	1.25
☐ 132 Don Lee RP	10.00	4.50	1.25
☐ 133 Bob Lillis RP	10.00	4.50	1.25
☐ 134 Jim McDaniel RP	10.00	4.50	1.25
☐ 135 Gene Oliver RP	10.00	4.50	1.25
☐ 136 Jim O'Toole RP	10.00	4.50	1.25
☐ 137 Dick Ricketts RP	10.00	4.50	1.25
☐ 138 John Romano RP	10.00	4.50	1.25
☐ 139 Ed Sadowski RP	10.00	4.50	1.25
☐ 140 Charlie Secrest RP	10.00	4.50	1.25
☐ 141 Joe Shipley RP	10.00	4.50	1.25
☐ 142 Dick Stigman RP	10.00	4.50	1.25
☐ 143 Willie Tasby RP	10.00	4.50	1.25
☐ 144 Jerry Walker RP	10.00	4.50	1.25
☐ 145 Dom Zanni RP	10.00	4.50	1.25
☐ 146 Jerry Zimmerman RP	10.00	4.50	1.25
☐ 147 Cubs Clubbers	60.00	27.00	7.50
Dale Long			
Ernie Banks			
Walt Moryn			
☐ 148 Mike McCormick	15.00	6.75	1.85
☐ 149 Jim Bunning	50.00	22.00	6.25
☐ 150 Stan Musial	300.00	135.00	38.00
☐ 151 Bob Malkmus	10.00	4.50	1.25
☐ 152 Johnny Klippstein	10.00	4.50	1.25
☐ 153 Jim Marshall	10.00	4.50	1.25
☐ 154 Ray Herbert	10.00	4.50	1.25
☐ 155 Enos Slaughter	50.00	22.00	6.25
☐ 156 Ace Hurlers	25.00	11.00	3.10
Billy Pierce			
Robin Roberts			
☐ 157 Felix Mantilla	10.00	4.50	1.25
☐ 158 Walt Dropo	10.00	4.50	1.25
☐ 159 Bob Shaw	10.00	4.50	1.25
☐ 160 Dick Groat	15.00	6.75	1.85
☐ 161 Frank Baumann	10.00	4.50	1.25
☐ 162 Bobby G. Smith	10.00	4.50	1.25
☐ 163 Sandy Koufax	375.00	170.00	47.50
☐ 164 Johnny Groth	10.00	4.50	1.25
☐ 165 Bill Bruton	10.00	4.50	1.25
☐ 166 Destruction Crew	50.00	22.00	6.25
Minnie Minoso			
Rocky Colavito			
Misspelled Colovito on card back			
Larry Doby			
☐ 167 Duke Maas	10.00	4.50	1.25
☐ 168 Carroll Hardy	10.00	4.50	1.25
☐ 169 Ted Abernathy	10.00	4.50	1.25
☐ 170 Gene Woodling	10.00	4.50	1.25
☐ 171 Willard Schmidt	10.00	4.50	1.25
☐ 172 Athletics Team	30.00	13.50	3.70
(Checklist on back)			
☐ 173 Bill Monbouquette	10.00	4.50	1.25
☐ 174 Jim Pendleton	10.00	4.50	1.25
☐ 175 Dick Farrell	10.00	4.50	1.25
☐ 176 Preston Ward	10.00	4.50	1.25
☐ 177 John Briggs	10.00	4.50	1.25
☐ 178 Ruben Amaro	10.00	4.50	1.25
☐ 179 Don Rudolph	10.00	4.50	1.25
☐ 180 Yogi Berra	200.00	90.00	25.00
☐ 181 Bob Porterfield	10.00	4.50	1.25
☐ 182 Milt Graff	10.00	4.50	1.25
☐ 183 Stu Miller	10.00	4.50	1.25
☐ 184 Harvey Haddix	10.00	4.50	1.25
☐ 185 Jim Busby	10.00	4.50	1.25
☐ 186 Mudcat Grant	10.00	4.50	1.25
☐ 187 Bubba Phillips	10.00	4.50	1.25
☐ 188 Juan Pizarro	10.00	4.50	1.25
☐ 189 Neil Chrisley	10.00	4.50	1.25
☐ 190 Bill Virdon	10.00	4.50	1.25
☐ 191 Russ Kemmerer	10.00	4.50	1.25
☐ 192 Charlie Beamon	10.00	4.50	1.25
☐ 193 Sammy Taylor	10.00	4.50	1.25
☐ 194 Jim Brosnan	10.00	4.50	1.25
☐ 195 Rip Repulski	10.00	4.50	1.25
☐ 196 Billy Moran	10.00	4.50	1.25

1960 Topps

The cards in this 572-card set measure 2 1/2" by 3 1/2". The 1960 Topps set is the only Topps standard size issue to use a horizontally oriented front. World Series cards appeared for the first time (385 to 391), and there is a Rookie Prospect (RP) series (117-148), the most famous of which is Carl Yastrzemski, and a Sport Magazine All-Star Selection (AS) series (553-572). There are 16 manager cards listed alphabetically from 212 through 227. The 1959 Topps All-Rookie team is featured on cards 316-325. The coaching staff of each team was also afforded their own card in a 16-card subset (455-470). Cards 375 to 440 come with either gray or white backs. There is no price differential for either color back. The high series (507-572) were printed on a more limited basis than the rest of the set. The team cards have series checklists on the reverse. Cards were issued in one-

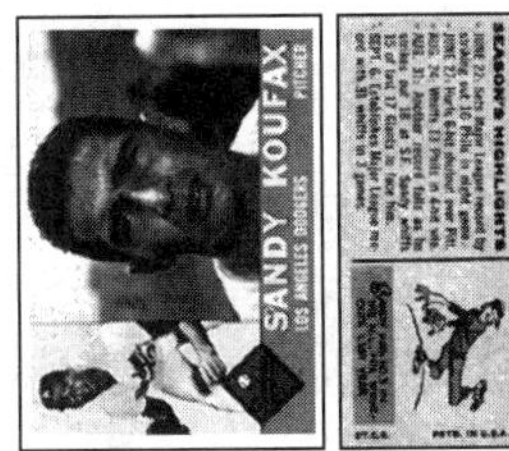

card penny packs and six-card nickle packs. The key Rookie Cards in this set are Jim Kaat, Willie McCovey and Carl Yastrzemski.

	NRMT	VG-E	GOOD
COMPLETE SET (572)	3500.00	1600.00	450.00
COMMON CARD (1-440)	4.00	1.80	.50
COMMON CARD (441-506)	7.00	3.10	.85
COMMON CARD (507-552)	16.00	7.25	2.00
COMMON AS (553-572)	16.00	7.25	2.00
WRAPPER (1-CENT)	500.00	220.00	60.00
WRAPPER (5-CENT)	40.00	18.00	5.00

Card	NRMT	VG-E	GOOD
☐ 1 Early Wynn	30.00	7.50	3.00
☐ 2 Roman Mejias	4.00	1.80	.50
☐ 3 Joe Adcock	5.00	2.20	.60
☐ 4 Bob Purkey	4.00	1.80	.50
☐ 5 Wally Moon	5.00	2.20	.60
☐ 6 Lou Berberet	4.00	1.80	.50
☐ 7 Master and Mentor	25.00	11.00	3.10
Willie Mays			
Bill Rigney MG			
☐ 8 Bud Daley	4.00	1.80	.50
☐ 9 Faye Throneberry	4.00	1.80	.50
☐ 10 Ernie Banks	50.00	22.00	6.25
☐ 11 Norm Siebern	4.00	1.80	.50
☐ 12 Milt Pappas	5.00	2.20	.60
☐ 13 Wally Post	5.00	2.20	.60
☐ 14 Jim Grant	5.00	2.20	.60
☐ 15 Pete Runnels	5.00	2.20	.60
☐ 16 Ernie Broglio	5.00	2.20	.60
☐ 17 Johnny Callison	5.00	2.20	.60
☐ 18 Dodgers Team	50.00	10.00	5.00
(Checklist on back)			
☐ 19 Felix Mantilla	4.00	1.80	.50
☐ 20 Roy Face	5.00	2.20	.60
☐ 21 Dutch Dotterer	4.00	1.80	.50
☐ 22 Rocky Bridges	4.00	1.80	.50
☐ 23 Eddie Fisher	4.00	1.80	.50
☐ 24 Dick Gray	4.00	1.80	.50
☐ 25 Roy Sievers	5.00	2.20	.60
☐ 26 Wayne Terwilliger	4.00	1.80	.50
☐ 27 Dick Drott	4.00	1.80	.50
☐ 28 Brooks Robinson	50.00	22.00	6.25
☐ 29 Clem Labine	5.00	2.20	.60
☐ 30 Tito Francona	4.00	1.80	.50
☐ 31 Sammy Esposito	4.00	1.80	.50
☐ 32 Sophomore Stalwarts	4.00	1.80	.50
Jim O'Toole			
Vada Pinson			
☐ 33 Tom Morgan	4.00	1.80	.50
☐ 34 Sparky Anderson	14.00	6.25	1.75
☐ 35 Whitey Ford	50.00	22.00	6.25
☐ 36 Russ Nixon	4.00	1.80	.50
☐ 37 Bill Bruton	4.00	1.80	.50
☐ 38 Jerry Casale	4.00	1.80	.50
☐ 39 Earl Averill	4.00	1.80	.50
☐ 40 Joe Cunningham	4.00	1.80	.50
☐ 41 Barry Latman	4.00	1.80	.50
☐ 42 Hobie Landrith	4.00	1.80	.50
☐ 43 Senators Team	10.00	2.00	1.00
(Checklist on back)			
☐ 44 Bobby Locke	4.00	1.80	.50
☐ 45 Roy McMillan	5.00	2.20	.60
☐ 46 Jerry Fisher	4.00	1.80	.50
☐ 47 Don Zimmer	5.00	2.20	.60
☐ 48 Hal W. Smith	4.00	1.80	.50
☐ 49 Curt Raydon	4.00	1.80	.50
☐ 50 Al Kaline	50.00	22.00	6.25
☐ 51 Jim Coates	5.00	2.20	.60
☐ 52 Dave Philley	4.00	1.80	.50
☐ 53 Jackie Brandt	4.00	1.80	.50
☐ 54 Mike Fornieles	4.00	1.80	.50
☐ 55 Bill Mazeroski	10.00	4.50	1.25
☐ 56 Steve Korcheck	4.00	1.80	.50
☐ 57 Win Savers	4.00	1.80	.50
Turk Lown			
Gerry Staley			
☐ 58 Gino Cimoli	4.00	1.80	.50
☐ 59 Juan Pizarro	4.00	1.80	.50
☐ 60 Gus Triandos	5.00	2.20	.60
☐ 61 Eddie Kasko	4.00	1.80	.50
☐ 62 Roger Craig	5.00	2.20	.60
☐ 63 George Strickland	4.00	1.80	.50
☐ 64 Jack Meyer	4.00	1.80	.50
☐ 65 Elston Howard	6.00	2.70	.75
☐ 66 Bob Trowbridge	4.00	1.80	.50
☐ 67 Jose Pagan	4.00	1.80	.50
☐ 68 Dave Hillman	4.00	1.80	.50
☐ 69 Billy Goodman	5.00	2.20	.60
☐ 70 Lew Burdette	5.00	2.20	.60
☐ 71 Marty Keough	4.00	1.80	.50
☐ 72 Tigers Team	20.00	4.00	2.00
(Checklist on back)			
☐ 73 Bob Gibson	50.00	22.00	6.25
☐ 74 Walt Moryn	4.00	1.80	.50
☐ 75 Vic Power	5.00	2.20	.60
☐ 76 Bill Fischer	4.00	1.80	.50
☐ 77 Hank Foiles	4.00	1.80	.50
☐ 78 Bob Grim	4.00	1.80	.50
☐ 79 Walt Dropo	4.00	1.80	.50
☐ 80 Johnny Antonelli	5.00	2.20	.60
☐ 81 Russ Snyder	4.00	1.80	.50
☐ 82 Ruben Gomez	4.00	1.80	.50
☐ 83 Tony Kubek	6.00	2.70	.75
☐ 84 Hal R. Smith	4.00	1.80	.50
☐ 85 Frank Lary	5.00	2.20	.60
☐ 86 Dick Gernert	4.00	1.80	.50
☐ 87 John Romonosky	4.00	1.80	.50
☐ 88 John Roseboro	5.00	2.20	.60
☐ 89 Hal Brown	4.00	1.80	.50
☐ 90 Bobby Avila	4.00	1.80	.50
☐ 91 Bennie Daniels	4.00	1.80	.50
☐ 92 Whitey Herzog	5.00	2.20	.60
☐ 93 Art Schult	4.00	1.80	.50
☐ 94 Leo Kiely	4.00	1.80	.50
☐ 95 Frank Thomas	5.00	2.20	.60
☐ 96 Ralph Terry	5.00	2.20	.60
☐ 97 Ted Lepcio	4.00	1.80	.50
☐ 98 Gordon Jones	4.00	1.80	.50
☐ 99 Lenny Green	4.00	1.80	.50
☐ 100 Nellie Fox	16.00	7.25	2.00
☐ 101 Bob Miller	4.00	1.80	.50
☐ 102 Kent Hadley	4.00	1.80	.50
☐ 103 Dick Farrell	5.00	2.20	.60
☐ 104 Dick Schofield	5.00	2.20	.60
☐ 105 Larry Sherry	5.00	2.20	.60
☐ 106 Billy Gardner	4.00	1.80	.50
☐ 107 Carlton Willey	4.00	1.80	.50
☐ 108 Pete Daley	4.00	1.80	.50
☐ 109 Clete Boyer	5.00	2.20	.60
☐ 110 Cal McLish	4.00	1.80	.50
☐ 111 Vic Wertz	5.00	2.20	.60
☐ 112 Jack Harshman	4.00	1.80	.50
☐ 113 Bob Skinner	4.00	1.80	.50
☐ 114 Ken Aspromonte	4.00	1.80	.50
☐ 115 Fork and Knuckler	6.00	2.70	.75
Roy Face			
Hoyt Wilhelm			
☐ 116 Jim Rivera	4.00	1.80	.50
☐ 117 Tom Borland RP	4.00	1.80	.50
☐ 118 Bob Bruce RP	4.00	1.80	.50
☐ 119 Chico Cardenas RP	5.00	2.20	.60
☐ 120 Duke Carmel RP	4.00	1.80	.50
☐ 121 Camilo Carreon RP	4.00	1.80	.50
☐ 122 Don Dillard RP	4.00	1.80	.50
☐ 123 Dan Dobbek RP	4.00	1.80	.50
☐ 124 Jim Donohue RP	4.00	1.80	.50
☐ 125 Dick Ellsworth RP	5.00	2.20	.60
☐ 126 Chuck Estrada RP	4.00	1.80	.50
☐ 127 Ron Hansen RP	5.00	2.20	.60
☐ 128 Bill Harris RP	4.00	1.80	.50
☐ 129 Bob Hartman RP	4.00	1.80	.50
☐ 130 Frank Herrera RP	4.00	1.80	.50
☐ 131 Ed Hobaugh RP	4.00	1.80	.50
☐ 132 Frank Howard RP	20.00	9.00	2.50
☐ 133 Manuel Javier RP	5.00	2.20	.60
(Sic, Julian)			
☐ 134 Deron Johnson RP	5.00	2.20	.60
☐ 135 Ken Johnson RP	4.00	1.80	.50
☐ 136 Jim Kaat RP	40.00	18.00	5.00
☐ 137 Lou Klimchock RP	4.00	1.80	.50
☐ 138 Art Mahaffey RP	5.00	2.20	.60
☐ 139 Carl Mathias RP	4.00	1.80	.50
☐ 140 Julio Navarro RP	4.00	1.80	.50
☐ 141 Jim Proctor RP	4.00	1.80	.50
☐ 142 Bill Short RP	4.00	1.80	.50
☐ 143 Al Spangler RP	4.00	1.80	.50
☐ 144 Al Stieglitz RP	4.00	1.80	.50
☐ 145 Jim Umbricht RP	4.00	1.80	.50
☐ 146 Ted Wieand RP	4.00	1.80	.50
☐ 147 Bob Will RP	4.00	1.80	.50
☐ 148 Carl Yastrzemski RP	125.00	55.00	15.50
☐ 149 Bob Nieman	4.00	1.80	.50
☐ 150 Billy Pierce	5.00	2.20	.60
☐ 151 Giants Team	10.00	2.00	1.00
(Checklist on back)			
☐ 152 Gail Harris	4.00	1.80	.50
☐ 153 Bobby Thomson	5.00	2.20	.60
☐ 154 Jim Davenport	5.00	2.20	.60
☐ 155 Charlie Neal	5.00	2.20	.60
☐ 156 Art Ceccarelli	4.00	1.80	.50
☐ 157 Rocky Nelson	5.00	2.20	.60
☐ 158 Wes Covington	5.00	2.20	.60
☐ 159 Jim Piersall	5.00	2.20	.60
☐ 160 Rival All-Stars	140.00	65.00	17.50
Mickey Mantle			
Ken Boyer			
☐ 161 Ray Narleski	4.00	1.80	.50
☐ 162 Sammy Taylor	4.00	1.80	.50
☐ 163 Hector Lopez	5.00	2.20	.60
☐ 164 Reds Team	10.00	2.00	1.00
(Checklist on back)			
☐ 165 Jack Sanford	5.00	2.20	.60
☐ 166 Chuck Essegian	4.00	1.80	.50
☐ 167 Valmy Thomas	4.00	1.80	.50
☐ 168 Alex Grammas	4.00	1.80	.50
☐ 169 Jake Striker	4.00	1.80	.50
☐ 170 Del Crandall	5.00	2.20	.60
☐ 171 Johnny Groth	4.00	1.80	.50
☐ 172 Willie Kirkland	4.00	1.80	.50
☐ 173 Billy Martin	14.00	6.25	1.75
☐ 174 Indians Team	10.00	2.00	1.00
(Checklist on back)			
☐ 175 Pedro Ramos	4.00	1.80	.50
☐ 176 Vada Pinson	5.00	2.20	.60
☐ 177 Johnny Kucks	4.00	1.80	.50
☐ 178 Woody Held	4.00	1.80	.50
☐ 179 Rip Coleman	4.00	1.80	.50
☐ 180 Harry Simpson	4.00	1.80	.50
☐ 181 Billy Loes	5.00	2.20	.60
☐ 182 Glen Hobbie	4.00	1.80	.50
☐ 183 Eli Grba	4.00	1.80	.50
☐ 184 Gary Geiger	4.00	1.80	.50
☐ 185 Jim Owens	4.00	1.80	.50
☐ 186 Dave Sisler	4.00	1.80	.50
☐ 187 Jay Hook	4.00	1.80	.50
☐ 188 Dick Williams	5.00	2.20	.60
☐ 189 Don McMahon	4.00	1.80	.50
☐ 190 Gene Woodling	5.00	2.20	.60
☐ 191 Johnny Klippstein	4.00	1.80	.50
☐ 192 Danny O'Connell	4.00	1.80	.50
☐ 193 Dick Hyde	4.00	1.80	.50
☐ 194 Bobby Gene Smith	4.00	1.80	.50
☐ 195 Lindy McDaniel	5.00	2.20	.60
☐ 196 Andy Carey	5.00	2.20	.60
☐ 197 Ron Kline	4.00	1.80	.50
☐ 198 Jerry Lynch	5.00	2.20	.60
☐ 199 Dick Donovan	5.00	2.20	.60
☐ 200 Willie Mays	90.00	40.00	11.00
☐ 201 Larry Osborne	4.00	1.80	.50
☐ 202 Fred Kipp	4.00	1.80	.50
☐ 203 Sammy White	4.00	1.80	.50
☐ 204 Ryne Duren	5.00	2.20	.60
☐ 205 Johnny Logan	5.00	2.20	.60
☐ 206 Claude Osteen	5.00	2.20	.60
☐ 207 Bob Boyd	4.00	1.80	.50
☐ 208 White Sox Team	10.00	2.00	1.00
(Checklist on back)			
☐ 209 Ron Blackburn	4.00	1.80	.50
☐ 210 Harmon Killebrew	25.00	11.00	3.10
☐ 211 Taylor Phillips	4.00	1.80	.50
☐ 212 Walt Alston MG	12.00	5.50	1.50
☐ 213 Chuck Dressen MG	5.00	2.20	.60
☐ 214 Jimmy Dykes MG	5.00	2.20	.60
☐ 215 Bob Elliott MG	5.00	2.20	.60
☐ 216 Joe Gordon MG	5.00	2.20	.60
☐ 217 Charlie Grimm MG	5.00	2.20	.60
☐ 218 Solly Hemus MG	4.00	1.80	.50
☐ 219 Fred Hutchinson MG	5.00	2.20	.60
☐ 220 Billy Jurges MG	4.00	1.80	.50
☐ 221 Cookie Lavagetto MG	4.00	1.80	.50
☐ 222 Al Lopez MG	5.00	2.20	.60
☐ 223 Danny Murtaugh MG	5.00	2.20	.60
☐ 224 Paul Richards MG	5.00	2.20	.60
☐ 225 Bill Rigney MG	4.00	1.80	.50
☐ 226 Eddie Sawyer MG	4.00	1.80	.50
☐ 227 Casey Stengel MG	16.00	7.25	2.00
☐ 228 Ernie Johnson	5.00	2.20	.60
☐ 229 Joe M. Morgan	4.00	1.80	.50
☐ 230 Mound Magicians	12.00	5.50	1.50
Lou Burdette			
Warren Spahn			
Bob Buhl			
☐ 231 Hal Naragon	4.00	1.80	.50
☐ 232 Jim Busby	4.00	1.80	.50
☐ 233 Don Elston	4.00	1.80	.50
☐ 234 Don Demeter	4.00	1.80	.50
☐ 235 Gus Bell	5.00	2.20	.60
☐ 236 Dick Ricketts	4.00	1.80	.50
☐ 237 Elmer Valo	4.00	1.80	.50
☐ 238 Danny Kravitz	4.00	1.80	.50
☐ 239 Joe Shipley	4.00	1.80	.50
☐ 240 Luis Aparicio	16.00	7.25	2.00
☐ 241 Albie Pearson	5.00	2.20	.60
☐ 242 Cardinals Team	10.00	2.00	1.00
(Checklist on back)			
☐ 243 Bubba Phillips	4.00	1.80	.50
☐ 244 Hal Griggs	4.00	1.80	.50
☐ 245 Eddie Yost	5.00	2.20	.60
☐ 246 Lee Maye	5.00	2.20	.60
☐ 247 Gil McDougald	5.00	2.20	.60
☐ 248 Del Rice	4.00	1.80	.50
☐ 249 Earl Wilson	5.00	2.20	.60
☐ 250 Stan Musial	80.00	36.00	10.00
☐ 251 Bob Malkmus	4.00	1.80	.50
☐ 252 Ray Herbert	4.00	1.80	.50
☐ 253 Eddie Bressoud	4.00	1.80	.50
☐ 254 Arnie Portocarrero	4.00	1.80	.50
☐ 255 Jim Gilliam	5.00	2.20	.60
☐ 256 Dick Brown	4.00	1.80	.50
☐ 257 Gordy Coleman	4.00	1.80	.50
☐ 258 Dick Groat	5.00	2.20	.60
☐ 259 George Altman	4.00	1.80	.50
☐ 260 Power Plus	14.00	6.25	1.75
Rocky Colavito			
Tito Francona			
☐ 261 Pete Burnside	4.00	1.80	.50
☐ 262 Hank Bauer	5.00	2.20	.60
☐ 263 Darrell Johnson	4.00	1.80	.50
☐ 264 Robin Roberts	14.00	6.25	1.75
☐ 265 Rip Repulski	4.00	1.80	.50
☐ 266 Joey Jay	5.00	2.20	.60
☐ 267 Jim Marshall	4.00	1.80	.50

☐ 268 Al Worthington	4.00	1.80	.50
☐ 269 Gene Green	4.00	1.80	.50
☐ 270 Bob Turley	5.00	2.20	.60
☐ 271 Julio Becquer	4.00	1.80	.50
☐ 272 Fred Green	5.00	2.20	.60
☐ 273 Neil Chrisley	4.00	1.80	.50
☐ 274 Tom Acker	4.00	1.80	.50
☐ 275 Curt Flood	5.00	2.20	.60
☐ 276 Ken McBride	4.00	1.80	.50
☐ 277 Harry Bright	4.00	1.80	.50
☐ 278 Stan Williams	5.00	2.20	.60
☐ 279 Chuck Tanner	5.00	2.20	.60
☐ 280 Frank Sullivan	4.00	1.80	.50
☐ 281 Ray Boone	5.00	2.20	.60
☐ 282 Joe Nuxhall	5.00	2.20	.60
☐ 283 John Blanchard	5.00	2.20	.60
☐ 284 Don Gross	4.00	1.80	.50
☐ 285 Harry Anderson	4.00	1.80	.50
☐ 286 Ray Semproch	4.00	1.80	.50
☐ 287 Felipe Alou	5.00	2.20	.60
☐ 288 Bob Mabe	4.00	1.80	.50
☐ 289 Willie Jones	4.00	1.80	.50
☐ 290 Jerry Lumpe	4.00	1.80	.50
☐ 291 Bob Keegan	4.00	1.80	.50
☐ 292 Dodger Backstops	5.00	2.20	.60
Joe Pignatano			
John Roseboro			
☐ 293 Gene Conley	5.00	2.20	.60
☐ 294 Tony Taylor	5.00	2.20	.60
☐ 295 Gil Hodges	20.00	9.00	2.50
☐ 296 Nelson Chittum	4.00	1.80	.50
☐ 297 Reno Bertoia	4.00	1.80	.50
☐ 298 George Witt	4.00	1.80	.50
☐ 299 Earl Torgeson	4.00	1.80	.50
☐ 300 Hank Aaron	80.00	36.00	10.00
☐ 301 Jerry Davie	4.00	1.80	.50
☐ 302 Phillies Team	10.00	2.00	1.00
(Checklist on back)			
☐ 303 Billy O'Dell	4.00	1.80	.50
☐ 304 Joe Ginsberg	4.00	1.80	.50
☐ 305 Richie Ashburn	20.00	9.00	2.50
☐ 306 Frank Baumann	4.00	1.80	.50
☐ 307 Gene Oliver	4.00	1.80	.50
☐ 308 Dick Hall	4.00	1.80	.50
☐ 309 Bob Hale	4.00	1.80	.50
☐ 310 Frank Malzone	5.00	2.20	.60
☐ 311 Raul Sanchez	4.00	1.80	.50
☐ 312 Charley Lau	5.00	2.20	.60
☐ 313 Turk Lown	4.00	1.80	.50
☐ 314 Chico Fernandez	4.00	1.80	.50
☐ 315 Bobby Shantz	5.00	2.20	.60
☐ 316 Willie McCovey	115.00	52.50	14.50
☐ 317 Pumpsie Green	5.00	2.20	.60
☐ 318 Jim Baxes	5.00	2.20	.60
☐ 319 Joe Koppe	5.00	2.20	.60
☐ 320 Bob Allison	5.00	2.20	.60
☐ 321 Ron Fairly	5.00	2.20	.60
☐ 322 Willie Tasby	5.00	2.20	.60
☐ 323 John Romano	5.00	2.20	.60
☐ 324 Jim Perry	5.00	2.20	.60
☐ 325 Jim O'Toole	5.00	2.20	.60
☐ 326 Bob Clemente	225.00	100.00	28.00
☐ 327 Ray Sadecki	4.00	1.80	.50
☐ 328 Earl Battey	4.00	1.80	.50
☐ 329 Zack Monroe	4.00	1.80	.50
☐ 330 Harvey Kuenn	5.00	2.20	.60
☐ 331 Henry Mason	4.00	1.80	.50
☐ 332 Yankees Team	80.00	16.00	8.00
(Checklist on back)			
☐ 333 Danny McDevitt	4.00	1.80	.50
☐ 334 Ted Abernathy	4.00	1.80	.50
☐ 335 Red Schoendienst	12.00	5.50	1.50
☐ 336 Ike Delock	4.00	1.80	.50
☐ 337 Cal Neeman	4.00	1.80	.50
☐ 338 Ray Monzant	4.00	1.80	.50
☐ 339 Harry Chiti	4.00	1.80	.50
☐ 340 Harvey Haddix	5.00	2.20	.60
☐ 341 Carroll Hardy	4.00	1.80	.50
☐ 342 Casey Wise	4.00	1.80	.50
☐ 343 Sandy Koufax	160.00	70.00	20.00
☐ 344 Clint Courtney	4.00	1.80	.50
☐ 345 Don Newcombe	5.00	2.20	.60
☐ 346 J.C. Martin UER	5.00	2.20	.60
(Face actually			
Gary Peters)			
☐ 347 Ed Bouchee	4.00	1.80	.50
☐ 348 Barry Shetrone	4.00	1.80	.50
☐ 349 Moe Drabowsky	5.00	2.20	.60
☐ 350 Mickey Mantle	475.00	210.00	60.00
☐ 351 Don Nottebart	4.00	1.80	.50
☐ 352 Cincy Clouters	8.00	3.60	1.00
Gus Bell			
Frank Robinson			
Jerry Lynch			
☐ 353 Don Larsen	5.00	2.20	.60
☐ 354 Bob Lillis	4.00	1.80	.50
☐ 355 Bill White	5.00	2.20	.60
☐ 356 Joe Amalfitano	4.00	1.80	.50
☐ 357 Al Schroll	4.00	1.80	.50
☐ 358 Joe DeMaestri	4.00	1.80	.50
☐ 359 Buddy Gilbert	4.00	1.80	.50
☐ 360 Herb Score	5.00	2.20	.60
☐ 361 Bob Oldis	4.00	1.80	.50
☐ 362 Russ Kemmerer	4.00	1.80	.50
☐ 363 Gene Stephens	4.00	1.80	.50
☐ 364 Paul Foytack	4.00	1.80	.50
☐ 365 Minnie Minoso	6.00	2.70	.75
☐ 366 Dallas Green	8.00	3.60	1.00
☐ 367 Bill Tuttle	4.00	1.80	.50
☐ 368 Daryl Spencer	4.00	1.80	.50
☐ 369 Billy Hoeft	4.00	1.80	.50
☐ 370 Bill Skowron	6.00	2.70	.75
☐ 371 Bud Byerly	4.00	1.80	.50
☐ 372 Frank House	4.00	1.80	.50
☐ 373 Don Hoak	5.00	2.20	.60
☐ 374 Bob Buhl	5.00	2.20	.60
☐ 375 Dale Long	5.00	2.20	.60
☐ 376 John Briggs	4.00	1.80	.50
☐ 377 Roger Maris	80.00	36.00	10.00
☐ 378 Stu Miller	5.00	2.20	.60
☐ 379 Red Wilson	4.00	1.80	.50
☐ 380 Bob Shaw	4.00	1.80	.50
☐ 381 Braves Team	10.00	2.00	1.00
(Checklist on back)			
☐ 382 Ted Bowsfield	4.00	1.80	.50
☐ 383 Leon Wagner	4.00	1.80	.50
☐ 384 Don Cardwell	4.00	1.80	.50
☐ 385 Charlie Neal WS	7.00	3.10	.85
☐ 386 Charlie Neal WS	7.00	3.10	.85
☐ 387 Carl Furillo WS	7.00	3.10	.85
☐ 388 Gil Hodges WS	10.00	4.50	1.25
☐ 389 Luis Aparicio WS	12.00	5.50	1.50
Maury Wills			
☐ 390 World Series Game 6	7.00	3.10	.85
☐ 391 World Series Summary	7.00	3.10	.85
The Champs Celebrate			
☐ 392 Tex Clevenger	4.00	1.80	.50
☐ 393 Smoky Burgess	5.00	2.20	.60
☐ 394 Norm Larker	5.00	2.20	.60
☐ 395 Hoyt Wilhelm	14.00	6.25	1.75
☐ 396 Steve Bilko	4.00	1.80	.50
☐ 397 Don Blasingame	4.00	1.80	.50
☐ 398 Mike Cuellar	5.00	2.20	.60
☐ 399 Young Hill Stars	5.00	2.20	.60
Milt Pappas			
Jack Fisher			
Jerry Walker			
☐ 400 Rocky Colavito	20.00	9.00	2.50
☐ 401 Bob Duliba	4.00	1.80	.50
☐ 402 Dick Stuart	5.00	2.20	.60
☐ 403 Ed Sadowski	4.00	1.80	.50
☐ 404 Bob Rush	4.00	1.80	.50
☐ 405 Bobby Richardson	14.00	6.25	1.75
☐ 406 Billy Klaus	4.00	1.80	.50
☐ 407 Gary Peters UER	5.00	2.20	.60
(Face actually			
J.C. Martin)			
☐ 408 Carl Furillo	5.00	2.20	.60
☐ 409 Ron Samford	4.00	1.80	.50
☐ 410 Sam Jones	5.00	2.20	.60
☐ 411 Ed Bailey	4.00	1.80	.50
☐ 412 Bob Anderson	4.00	1.80	.50
☐ 413 Athletics Team			
(Checklist on back)			
☐ 414 Don Williams	4.00	1.80	.50
☐ 415 Bob Cerv	4.00	1.80	.50
☐ 416 Humberto Robinson	4.00	1.80	.50
☐ 417 Chuck Cottier	4.00	1.80	.50
☐ 418 Don Mossi	5.00	2.20	.60
☐ 419 George Crowe	4.00	1.80	.50
☐ 420 Eddie Mathews	30.00	13.50	3.70
☐ 421 Duke Maas	4.00	1.80	.50
☐ 422 John Powers	4.00	1.80	.50
☐ 423 Ed Fitzgerald	4.00	1.80	.50
☐ 424 Pete Whisenant	4.00	1.80	.50
☐ 425 Johnny Podres	5.00	2.20	.60
☐ 426 Ron Jackson	4.00	1.80	.50
☐ 427 Al Grunwald	4.00	1.80	.50
☐ 428 Al Smith	4.00	1.80	.50
☐ 429 AL Kings	12.00	5.50	1.50
Nellie Fox			
Harvey Kuenn			
☐ 430 Art Ditmar	4.00	1.80	.50
☐ 431 Andre Rodgers	4.00	1.80	.50
☐ 432 Chuck Stobbs	4.00	1.80	.50
☐ 433 Irv Noren	4.00	1.80	.50
☐ 434 Brooks Lawrence	4.00	1.80	.50
☐ 435 Gene Freese	4.00	1.80	.50
☐ 436 Marv Throneberry	5.00	2.20	.60
☐ 437 Bob Friend	5.00	2.20	.60
☐ 438 Jim Coker	4.00	1.80	.50
☐ 439 Tom Brewer	4.00	1.80	.50
☐ 440 Jim Lemon	5.00	2.20	.60
☐ 441 Gary Bell	7.00	3.10	.85
☐ 442 Joe Pignatano	7.00	3.10	.85
☐ 443 Charlie Maxwell	7.00	3.10	.85
☐ 444 Jerry Kindall	7.00	3.10	.85
☐ 445 Warren Spahn	50.00	22.00	6.25
☐ 446 Ellis Burton	7.00	3.10	.85
☐ 447 Ray Moore	7.00	3.10	.85
☐ 448 Jim Gentile	20.00	9.00	2.50
☐ 449 Jim Brosnan	7.50	3.40	.95
☐ 450 Orlando Cepeda	18.00	8.00	2.20
☐ 451 Curt Simmons	7.50	3.40	.95
☐ 452 Ray Webster	7.00	3.10	.85
☐ 453 Vern Law	8.00	3.60	1.00
☐ 454 Hal Woodeshick	7.00	3.10	.85
☐ 455 Baltimore Coaches	7.00	3.10	.85
Eddie Robinson			
Harry Brecheen			
Luman Harris			
☐ 456 Red Sox Coaches	8.00	3.60	1.00
Rudy York			
Billy Herman			
Sal Maglie			
Del Baker			
☐ 457 Cubs Coaches	7.00	3.10	.85
Charlie Root			
Lou Klein			
Elvin Tappe			
☐ 458 White Sox Coaches	7.00	3.10	.85
Johnny Cooney			
Don Gutteridge			
Tony Cuccinello			
Ray Berres			
☐ 459 Reds Coaches	7.00	3.10	.85
Reggie Otero			
Cot Deal			
Wally Moses			
☐ 460 Indians Coaches	8.00	3.60	1.00
Mel Harder			
Jo-Jo White			
Bob Lemon			
Ralph(Red) Kress			
☐ 461 Tigers Coaches	8.00	3.60	1.00
Tom Ferrick			
Luke Appling			
Billy Hitchcock			
☐ 462 Athletics Coaches	7.00	3.10	.85
Fred Fitzsimmons			
Don Heffner			
Walker Cooper			
☐ 463 Dodgers Coaches	7.00	3.10	.85
Bobby Bragan			
Pete Reiser			
Joe Becker			
Greg Mulleavy			
☐ 464 Braves Coaches	7.00	3.10	.85
Bob Scheffing			
Whitlow Wyatt			
Andy Pafko			
George Myatt			
☐ 465 Yankees Coaches	12.00	5.50	1.50
Bill Dickey			
Ralph Houk			
Frank Crosetti			
Ed Lopat			
☐ 466 Phillies Coaches	7.00	3.10	.85
Ken Silvestri			
Dick Carter			
Andy Cohen			
☐ 467 Pirates Coaches	7.00	3.10	.85
Mickey Vernon			
Frank Oceak			
Sam Narron			
Bill Burwell			
☐ 468 Cardinals Coaches	7.00	3.10	.85
Johnny Keane			
Howie Pollet			
Ray Katt			
Harry Walker			
☐ 469 Giants Coaches	7.00	3.10	.85
Wes Westrum			
Salty Parker			
Bill Posedel			
☐ 470 Senators Coaches	7.00	3.10	.85
Bob Swift			
Ellis Clary			
Sam Mele			
☐ 471 Ned Garver	7.00	3.10	.85
☐ 472 Alvin Dark	7.50	3.40	.95
☐ 473 Al Cicotte	7.00	3.10	.85
☐ 474 Haywood Sullivan	7.00	3.10	.85
☐ 475 Don Drysdale	35.00	16.00	4.40
☐ 476 Lou Johnson	7.00	3.10	.85
☐ 477 Don Ferrarese	7.00	3.10	.85
☐ 478 Frank Torre	7.50	3.40	.95
☐ 479 Georges Maranda	7.00	3.10	.85
☐ 480 Yogi Berra	70.00	32.00	8.75
☐ 481 Wes Stock	7.00	3.10	.85
☐ 482 Frank Bolling	7.00	3.10	.85
☐ 483 Camilo Pascual	7.00	3.10	.85
☐ 484 Pirates Team	50.00	10.00	5.00
(Checklist on back)			
☐ 485 Ken Boyer	14.00	6.25	1.75
☐ 486 Bobby Del Greco	7.00	3.10	.85
☐ 487 Tom Sturdivant	7.00	3.10	.85
☐ 488 Norm Cash	20.00	9.00	2.50
☐ 489 Steve Ridzik	7.00	3.10	.85
☐ 490 Frank Robinson	50.00	22.00	6.25
☐ 491 Mel Roach	7.00	3.10	.85
☐ 492 Larry Jackson	7.00	3.10	.85
☐ 493 Duke Snider	50.00	22.00	6.25
☐ 494 Orioles Team	25.00	5.00	2.50
(Checklist on back)			
☐ 495 Sherm Lollar	7.50	3.40	.95
☐ 496 Bill Virdon	8.00	3.60	1.00
☐ 497 John Tsitouris	7.00	3.10	.85
☐ 498 Al Pilarcik	7.00	3.10	.85
☐ 499 Johnny James	8.00	3.60	1.00
☐ 500 Johnny Temple	7.50	3.40	.95
☐ 501 Bob Schmidt	7.00	3.10	.85
☐ 502 Jim Bunning	20.00	9.00	2.50
☐ 503 Don Lee	7.00	3.10	.85
☐ 504 Seth Morehead	7.00	3.10	.85
☐ 505 Ted Kluszewski	20.00	9.00	2.50
☐ 506 Lee Walls	7.00	3.10	.85
☐ 507 Dick Stigman	18.00	8.00	2.20
☐ 508 Billy Consolo	16.00	7.25	2.00
☐ 509 Tommy Davis	25.00	11.00	3.10
☐ 510 Gerry Staley	16.00	7.25	2.00
☐ 511 Ken Walters	16.00	7.25	2.00
☐ 512 Joe Gibbon	16.00	7.25	2.00
☐ 513 Chicago Cubs	30.00	6.00	3.00
Team Card			
(Checklist on back)			
☐ 514 Steve Barber	18.00	8.00	2.20
☐ 515 Stan Lopata	16.00	7.25	2.00
☐ 516 Marty Kutyna	16.00	7.25	2.00
☐ 517 Charlie James	16.00	7.25	2.00
☐ 518 Tony Gonzalez	18.00	8.00	2.20
☐ 519 Ed Roebuck	16.00	7.25	2.00
☐ 520 Don Buddin	16.00	7.25	2.00
☐ 521 Mike Lee	16.00	7.25	2.00
☐ 522 Ken Hunt	20.00	9.00	2.50
☐ 523 Clay Dalrymple	16.00	7.25	2.00
☐ 524 Bill Henry	16.00	7.25	2.00
☐ 525 Marv Breeding	16.00	7.25	2.00
☐ 526 Paul Giel	16.00	7.25	2.00
☐ 527 Jose Valdivielso	16.00	7.25	2.00
☐ 528 Ben Johnson	16.00	7.25	2.00
☐ 529 Norm Sherry	20.00	9.00	2.50
☐ 530 Mike McCormick	18.00	8.00	2.20
☐ 531 Sandy Amoros	18.00	8.00	2.20
☐ 532 Mike Garcia	18.00	8.00	2.20
☐ 533 Lu Clinton	16.00	7.25	2.00
☐ 534 Ken MacKenzie	16.00	7.25	2.00
☐ 535 Whitey Lockman	18.00	8.00	2.20
☐ 536 Wynn Hawkins	16.00	7.25	2.00
☐ 537 Boston Red Sox	30.00	6.00	3.00
Team Card			
(Checklist on back)			
☐ 538 Frank Barnes	16.00	7.25	2.00
☐ 539 Gene Baker	16.00	7.25	2.00
☐ 540 Jerry Walker	16.00	7.25	2.00
☐ 541 Tony Curry	16.00	7.25	2.00
☐ 542 Ken Hamlin	16.00	7.25	2.00
☐ 543 Elio Chacon	16.00	7.25	2.00
☐ 544 Bill Monbouquette	16.00	7.25	2.00
☐ 545 Carl Sawatski	16.00	7.25	2.00
☐ 546 Hank Aguirre	16.00	7.25	2.00
☐ 547 Bob Aspromonte	16.00	7.25	2.00
☐ 548 Don Mincher	18.00	8.00	2.20
☐ 549 John Buzhardt	16.00	7.25	2.00
☐ 550 Jim Landis	16.00	7.25	2.00
☐ 551 Ed Rakow	16.00	7.25	2.00
☐ 552 Walt Bond	16.00	7.25	2.00
☐ 553 Bill Skowron AS	18.00	8.00	2.20
☐ 554 Willie McCovey AS	30.00	13.50	3.70
☐ 555 Nellie Fox AS	30.00	13.50	3.70
☐ 556 Charlie Neal AS	16.00	7.25	2.00
☐ 557 Frank Malzone AS	16.00	7.25	2.00
☐ 558 Eddie Mathews AS	30.00	13.50	3.70
☐ 559 Luis Aparicio AS	30.00	13.50	3.70
☐ 560 Ernie Banks AS	60.00	27.00	7.50
☐ 561 Al Kaline AS	60.00	27.00	7.50
☐ 562 Joe Cunningham AS	16.00	7.25	2.00
☐ 563 Mickey Mantle AS	325.00	145.00	40.00
☐ 564 Willie Mays AS	125.00	55.00	15.50
☐ 565 Roger Maris AS	80.00	36.00	10.00
☐ 566 Hank Aaron AS	115.00	52.50	14.50
☐ 567 Sherm Lollar AS	16.00	7.25	2.00
☐ 568 Del Crandall AS	16.00	7.25	2.00
☐ 569 Camilo Pascual AS	16.00	7.25	2.00
☐ 570 Don Drysdale AS	30.00	13.50	3.70
☐ 571 Billy Pierce AS	18.00	8.00	2.20
☐ 572 Johnny Antonelli AS	30.00	9.00	3.00
☐ NNO Iron-on team transfer	4.00	1.80	.50

1960 Topps Tattoos

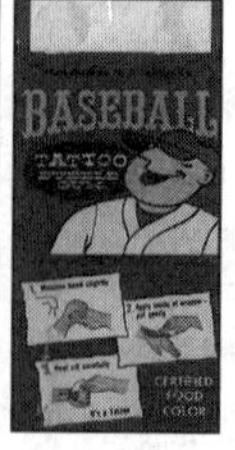

In 1960 this tattoo set was issued separately by both Topps and O-Pee-Chee. They are actually the reverses (inside surfaces) of the wrappers in which the (one cent) product "Tattoo Bubble Gum" was packaged. The dimensions given (1 9/16" by 3 1/2") are for the entire wrapper. The wrapper lists instructions on how to apply the tattoo. The "tattoos" were to be applied by moistening the skin and then pressing the tattoo to the moistened spot. The tattoos are unnumbered and are colored. There are 96 tattoos in the set: 55 players, 16 team logos, 15 action shots and ten autographed balls. In the checklist below the player tattoos are numbered 1-55 in alphabetical order, the team tattoos (56-71) are numbered in alphabetical team order (within league), the action photos (72-86) are numbered in alphabetical order by title and the facsimile autographed ball tattoos (87-96) are numbered in alphabetical order according to the autographing player.

	NRMT	VG-E	GOOD
COMPLETE SET (96)	1800.00	800.00	220.00
COMMON TATTOO (1-55)	7.00	3.10	.85
COMMON TEAM (56-71)	5.00	2.20	.60
COMMON ACTION (72-86)	2.50	1.10	.30
COMMON BALL (87-96)	2.50	1.10	.30
WRAPPER	10.00	4.50	1.25
□ 1 Hank Aaron	125.00	55.00	15.50
□ 2 Bob Allison	8.50	3.80	1.05
□ 3 Johnny Antonelli	8.50	3.80	1.05
□ 4 Richie Ashburn	30.00	13.50	3.70
□ 5 Ernie Banks	50.00	22.00	6.25
□ 6 Yogi Berra	100.00	45.00	12.50
□ 7 Lew Burdette	8.50	3.80	1.05
□ 8 Orlando Cepeda	20.00	9.00	2.50
□ 9 Rocky Colavito	20.00	9.00	2.50
□ 10 Joe Cunningham	8.50	3.80	1.05
□ 11 Bud Daley	7.00	3.10	.85
□ 12 Don Drysdale	40.00	18.00	5.00
□ 13 Ryne Duren	10.00	4.50	1.25
□ 14 Roy Face	10.00	4.50	1.25
□ 15 Whitey Ford	40.00	18.00	5.00
□ 16 Nellie Fox	30.00	13.50	3.70
□ 17 Tito Francona	7.00	3.10	.85
□ 18 Gene Freese	7.00	3.10	.85
□ 19 Jim Gilliam	15.00	6.75	1.85
□ 20 Dick Groat	10.00	4.50	1.25
□ 21 Ray Herbert	7.00	3.10	.85
□ 22 Glen Hobbie	7.00	3.10	.85
□ 23 Jackie Jensen	15.00	6.75	1.85
□ 24 Sam Jones	7.00	3.10	.85
□ 25 Al Kaline	50.00	22.00	6.25
□ 26 Harmon Killebrew	35.00	16.00	4.40
□ 27 Harvey Kuenn	15.00	6.75	1.85
□ 28 Frank Lary	8.50	3.80	1.05
□ 29 Vern Law	10.00	4.50	1.25
□ 30 Frank Malzone	8.50	3.80	1.05
□ 31 Mickey Mantle	400.00	180.00	50.00
□ 32 Roger Maris	50.00	22.00	6.25
□ 33 Eddie Mathews	35.00	16.00	4.40
□ 34 Willie Mays	135.00	60.00	17.00
□ 35 Cal McLish	7.00	3.10	.85
□ 36 Wally Moon	8.50	3.80	1.05
□ 37 Walt Moryn	7.00	3.10	.85
□ 38 Don Mossi	8.50	3.80	1.05
□ 39 Stan Musial	75.00	34.00	9.50
□ 40 Charley Neal	8.50	3.80	1.05
□ 41 Don Newcombe	10.00	4.50	1.25
□ 42 Milt Pappas	8.50	3.80	1.05
□ 43 Camilo Pascual	8.50	3.80	1.05
□ 44 Billy Pierce	8.50	3.80	1.05
□ 45 Robin Roberts	30.00	13.50	3.70
□ 46 Frank Robinson	35.00	16.00	4.40
□ 47 Pete Runnels	8.50	3.80	1.05
□ 48 Herb Score	10.00	4.50	1.25
□ 49 Warren Spahn	40.00	18.00	5.00
□ 50 Johnny Temple	8.50	3.80	1.05
□ 51 Gus Triandos	8.50	3.80	1.05
□ 52 Jerry Walker	7.00	3.10	.85
□ 53 Bill White	15.00	6.75	1.85
□ 54 Gene Woodling	8.50	3.80	1.05
□ 55 Early Wynn	30.00	13.50	3.70
□ 56 Chicago Cubs	5.00	2.20	.60
□ 57 Cincinnati Reds	5.00	2.20	.60
□ 58 Los Angeles Dodgers	5.00	2.20	.60
□ 59 Milwaukee Braves	5.00	2.20	.60
□ 60 Philadelphia Phillies	5.00	2.20	.60
□ 61 Pittsburgh Pirates	5.00	2.20	.60
□ 62 St. Louis Cardinals	5.00	2.20	.60
□ 63 San Francisco Giants	5.00	2.20	.60
□ 64 Baltimore Orioles	5.00	2.20	.60
□ 65 Boston Red Sox	7.00	3.10	.85
□ 66 Chicago White Sox	5.00	2.20	.60
□ 67 Cleveland Indians	5.00	2.20	.60
□ 68 Detroit Tigers	5.00	2.20	.60
□ 69 Kansas City Athletics	5.00	2.20	.60
□ 70 New York Yankees	8.50	3.80	1.05
□ 71 Washington Senators	5.00	2.20	.60
□ 72 Circus Catch	2.50	1.10	.30
□ 73 Double Play	2.50	1.10	.30
□ 74 Grand Slam Homer	2.50	1.10	.30
□ 75 Great Catch	2.50	1.10	.30
□ 76 Left Hand Batter	2.50	1.10	.30
□ 77 Left Hand Pitcher	2.50	1.10	.30
□ 78 Out at First	2.50	1.10	.30
□ 79 Out at Home	2.50	1.10	.30
□ 80 Right Hand Batter	2.50	1.10	.30
□ 81 Right Hand Pitcher	2.50	1.10	.30
□ 82 Right Hand Pitcher	2.50	1.10	.30
(Different pose)			
□ 83 Run Down	2.50	1.10	.30
□ 84 Stolen Base	2.50	1.10	.30
□ 85 The Final Word	2.50	1.10	.30
□ 86 Twisting Foul	2.50	1.10	.30
□ 87 Richie Ashburn	8.50	3.80	1.05
(Autographed ball)			
□ 88 Rocky Colavito	8.50	3.80	1.05
(Autographed ball)			
□ 89 Roy Face	2.50	1.10	.30
(Autographed ball)			
□ 90 Jackie Jensen	4.00	1.80	.50
(Autographed ball)			
□ 91 Harmon Killebrew	10.00	4.50	1.25
(Autographed ball)			
□ 92 Mickey Mantle	175.00	80.00	22.00
(Autographed ball)			
□ 93 Willie Mays	35.00	16.00	4.40
(Autographed ball)			
□ 94 Stan Musial	25.00	11.00	3.10
(Autographed ball)			
□ 95 Billy Pierce	4.00	1.80	.50
(Autographed ball)			
□ 96 Jerry Walker	2.50	1.10	.30
(Autographed ball)			

1960 Topps Venezuelan

This set is a parallel version of the first 196 cards of the regular 1960 Topps set and are similar in design. The cards were issued for the Venezuelan market. Although the cards were printed in the United States, they are faded compared to the American issued cards.

	NRMT	VG-E	GOOD
COMPLETE SET (196)	3500.00	1600.00	450.00
COMMON CARD (1-196)	10.00	4.50	1.25
□ 1 Early Wynn	75.00	34.00	9.50
□ 2 Roman Mejias	10.00	4.50	1.25
□ 3 Joe Adcock	15.00	6.75	1.85
□ 4 Bob Purkey	10.00	4.50	1.25
□ 5 Wally Moon	10.00	4.50	1.25
□ 6 Lou Berberet	10.00	4.50	1.25
□ 7 Master and Mentor	60.00	27.00	7.50
Willie Mays			
Bill Rigney MG			
□ 8 Bud Daley	10.00	4.50	1.25
□ 9 Faye Throneberry	10.00	4.50	1.25
□ 10 Ernie Banks	125.00	55.00	15.50
□ 11 Norm Siebern	10.00	4.50	1.25
□ 12 Milt Pappas	10.00	4.50	1.25
□ 13 Wally Post	10.00	4.50	1.25
□ 14 Jim Grant	10.00	4.50	1.25
□ 15 Pete Runnels	10.00	4.50	1.25
□ 16 Ernie Broglio	10.00	4.50	1.25
□ 17 Johnny Callison	10.00	4.50	1.25
□ 18 Dodgers Team	100.00	45.00	12.50
(Checklist on back)			
□ 19 Felix Mantilla	10.00	4.50	1.25
□ 20 Roy Face	10.00	4.50	1.25
□ 21 Dutch Dotterer	10.00	4.50	1.25
□ 22 Rocky Bridges	10.00	4.50	1.25
□ 23 Eddie Fisher	10.00	4.50	1.25
□ 24 Dick Gray	10.00	4.50	1.25
□ 25 Roy Sievers	10.00	4.50	1.25
□ 26 Wayne Terwilliger	10.00	4.50	1.25
□ 27 Dick Drott	10.00	4.50	1.25
□ 28 Brooks Robinson	125.00	55.00	15.50
□ 29 Clem Labine	10.00	4.50	1.25
□ 30 Tito Francona	10.00	4.50	1.25
□ 31 Sammy Esposito	10.00	4.50	1.25
□ 32 Sophomore Stalwarts	10.00	4.50	1.25
Jim O'Toole			
Vada Pinson			
□ 33 Tom Morgan	10.00	4.50	1.25
□ 34 Sparky Anderson	35.00	16.00	4.40
□ 35 Whitey Ford	125.00	55.00	15.50
□ 36 Russ Nixon	10.00	4.50	1.25
□ 37 Bill Bruton	10.00	4.50	1.25
□ 38 Jerry Casale	10.00	4.50	1.25
□ 39 Earl Averill	10.00	4.50	1.25
□ 40 Joe Cunningham	10.00	4.50	1.25
□ 41 Barry Latman	10.00	4.50	1.25
□ 42 Hobie Landrith	10.00	4.50	1.25
□ 43 Senators Team	20.00	9.00	2.50
(Checklist on back)			
□ 44 Bobby Locke	10.00	4.50	1.25
□ 45 Roy McMillan	10.00	4.50	1.25
□ 46 Jerry Fisher	10.00	4.50	1.25
□ 47 Don Zimmer	10.00	4.50	1.25
□ 48 Hal W. Smith	10.00	4.50	1.25
□ 49 Curt Raydon	10.00	4.50	1.25
□ 50 Al Kaline	125.00	55.00	15.50
□ 51 Jim Coates	10.00	4.50	1.25
□ 52 Dave Philley	10.00	4.50	1.25
□ 53 Jackie Brandt	10.00	4.50	1.25
□ 54 Mike Fornieles	10.00	4.50	1.25
□ 55 Bill Mazeroski	25.00	11.00	3.10
□ 56 Steve Korcheck	10.00	4.50	1.25
□ 57 Win Savers	10.00	4.50	1.25
Turk Lown			
Gerry Staley			
□ 58 Gino Cimoli	10.00	4.50	1.25
□ 59 Juan Pizarro	10.00	4.50	1.25
□ 60 Gus Triandos	10.00	4.50	1.25
□ 61 Eddie Kasko	10.00	4.50	1.25
□ 62 Roger Craig	10.00	4.50	1.25
□ 63 George Strickland	10.00	4.50	1.25
□ 64 Jack Meyer	10.00	4.50	1.25
□ 65 Elston Howard	15.00	6.75	1.85
□ 66 Bob Trowbridge	10.00	4.50	1.25
□ 67 Jose Pagan	10.00	4.50	1.25
□ 68 Dave Hillman	10.00	4.50	1.25
□ 69 Billy Goodman	10.00	4.50	1.25
□ 70 Lew Burdette	15.00	6.75	1.85
□ 71 Marty Keough	10.00	4.50	1.25
□ 72 Tigers Team	40.00	18.00	5.00
(Checklist on back)			
□ 73 Bob Gibson	125.00	55.00	15.50
□ 74 Walt Moryn	10.00	4.50	1.25
□ 75 Vic Power	10.00	4.50	1.25
□ 76 Bill Fischer	10.00	4.50	1.25
□ 77 Hank Foiles	10.00	4.50	1.25
□ 78 Bob Grim	10.00	4.50	1.25
□ 79 Walt Dropo	10.00	4.50	1.25
□ 80 Johnny Antonelli	10.00	4.50	1.25
□ 81 Russ Snyder	10.00	4.50	1.25
□ 82 Ruben Gomez	10.00	4.50	1.25
□ 83 Tony Kubek	15.00	6.75	1.85
□ 84 Hal R. Smith	10.00	4.50	1.25
□ 85 Frank Lary	10.00	4.50	1.25
□ 86 Dick Gernert	10.00	4.50	1.25
□ 87 John Romonosky	10.00	4.50	1.25
□ 88 John Roseboro	10.00	4.50	1.25
□ 89 Hal Brown	10.00	4.50	1.25
□ 90 Bobby Avila	10.00	4.50	1.25
□ 91 Bennie Daniels	10.00	4.50	1.25
□ 92 Whitey Herzog	10.00	4.50	1.25
□ 93 Art Schult	10.00	4.50	1.25
□ 94 Leo Kiely	10.00	4.50	1.25
□ 95 Frank Thomas	10.00	4.50	1.25
□ 96 Ralph Terry	10.00	4.50	1.25
□ 97 Ted Lepcio	10.00	4.50	1.25
□ 98 Gordon Jones	10.00	4.50	1.25
□ 99 Lenny Green	10.00	4.50	1.25
□ 100 Nellie Fox	30.00	13.50	3.70
□ 101 Bob Miller	10.00	4.50	1.25
□ 102 Kent Hadley	10.00	4.50	1.25
□ 103 Dick Farrell	10.00	4.50	1.25
□ 104 Dick Schofield	10.00	4.50	1.25
□ 105 Larry Sherry	10.00	4.50	1.25
□ 106 Billy Gardner	10.00	4.50	1.25
□ 107 Carlton Willey	10.00	4.50	1.25
□ 108 Pete Daley	10.00	4.50	1.25
□ 109 Clete Boyer	10.00	4.50	1.25
□ 110 Cal McLish	10.00	4.50	1.25
□ 111 Vic Wertz	10.00	4.50	1.25
□ 112 Jack Harshman	10.00	4.50	1.25
□ 113 Bob Skinner	10.00	4.50	1.25
□ 114 Ken Aspromonte	10.00	4.50	1.25
□ 115 Fork and Knuckler	15.00	6.75	1.85
Roy Face			
Hoyt Wilhelm			
□ 116 Jim Rivera	10.00	4.50	1.25
□ 117 Tom Borland RP	10.00	4.50	1.25
□ 118 Bob Bruce RP	10.00	4.50	1.25
□ 119 Chico Cardenas RP	10.00	4.50	1.25
□ 120 Duke Carmel RP	10.00	4.50	1.25
□ 121 Camilo Carreon RP	10.00	4.50	1.25
□ 122 Don Dillard RP	10.00	4.50	1.25
□ 123 Dan Dobbek RP	10.00	4.50	1.25
□ 124 Jim Donohue RP	10.00	4.50	1.25
□ 125 Dick Ellsworth RP	10.00	4.50	1.25
□ 126 Chuck Estrada RP	10.00	4.50	1.25
□ 127 Ron Hansen RP	10.00	4.50	1.25
□ 128 Bill Harris RP	10.00	4.50	1.25
□ 129 Bob Hartman RP	10.00	4.50	1.25
□ 130 Frank Herrera RP	10.00	4.50	1.25
□ 131 Ed Hobaugh RP	10.00	4.50	1.25
□ 132 Frank Howard RP	50.00	22.00	6.25
□ 133 Manuel Javier RP	10.00	4.50	1.25
(Sic, Julian)			
□ 134 Deron Johnson RP	10.00	4.50	1.25
□ 135 Ken Johnson RP	10.00	4.50	1.25
□ 136 Jim Kaat RP	100.00	45.00	12.50
□ 137 Lou Klimchock RP	10.00	4.50	1.25
□ 138 Art Mahaffey RP	10.00	4.50	1.25
□ 139 Carl Mathias RP	10.00	4.50	1.25
□ 140 Julio Navarro RP	10.00	4.50	1.25
□ 141 Jim Proctor RP	10.00	4.50	1.25
□ 142 Bill Short RP	10.00	4.50	1.25
□ 143 Al Spangler RP	10.00	4.50	1.25
□ 144 Al Stieglitz RP	10.00	4.50	1.25
□ 145 Jim Umbricht RP	10.00	4.50	1.25
□ 146 Ted Wieand RP	10.00	4.50	1.25
□ 147 Bob Will RP	10.00	4.50	1.25
□ 148 Carl Yastrzemski RP	300.00	135.00	38.00
□ 149 Bob Nieman	10.00	4.50	1.25
□ 150 Billy Pierce	15.00	6.75	1.85
□ 151 Giants Team	20.00	9.00	2.50
(Checklist on back)			
□ 152 Gail Harris	10.00	4.50	1.25
□ 153 Bobby Thomson	15.00	6.75	1.85
□ 154 Jim Davenport	10.00	4.50	1.25
□ 155 Charlie Neal	10.00	4.50	1.25
□ 156 Art Ceccarelli	10.00	4.50	1.25
□ 157 Rocky Nelson	10.00	4.50	1.25
□ 158 Wes Covington	10.00	4.50	1.25
□ 159 Jim Piersall	15.00	6.75	1.85
□ 160 Rival All-Stars	350.00	160.00	45.00
Mickey Mantle			
Ken Boyer			
□ 161 Ray Narleski	10.00	4.50	1.25
□ 162 Sammy Taylor	10.00	4.50	1.25
□ 163 Hector Lopez	10.00	4.50	1.25
□ 164 Reds Team	20.00	9.00	2.50
(Checklist on back)			
□ 165 Jack Sanford	10.00	4.50	1.25
□ 166 Chuck Essegian	10.00	4.50	1.25
□ 167 Valmy Thomas	10.00	4.50	1.25
□ 168 Alex Grammas	10.00	4.50	1.25
□ 169 Jake Striker	10.00	4.50	1.25
□ 170 Del Crandall	10.00	4.50	1.25
□ 171 Johnny Groth	10.00	4.50	1.25
□ 172 Willie Kirkland	10.00	4.50	1.25
□ 173 Billy Martin	35.00	16.00	4.40
□ 174 Indians Team	20.00	9.00	2.50
(Checklist on back)			
□ 175 Pedro Ramos	10.00	4.50	1.25
□ 176 Vada Pinson	15.00	6.75	1.85
□ 177 Johnny Kucks	10.00	4.50	1.25
□ 178 Woody Held	10.00	4.50	1.25
□ 179 Rip Coleman	10.00	4.50	1.25
□ 180 Harry Simpson	10.00	4.50	1.25
□ 181 Billy Loes	10.00	4.50	1.25
□ 182 Glen Hobbie	10.00	4.50	1.25
□ 183 Eli Grba	10.00	4.50	1.25
□ 184 Gary Geiger	10.00	4.50	1.25
□ 185 Jim Owens	10.00	4.50	1.25
□ 186 Dave Sisler	10.00	4.50	1.25
□ 187 Jay Hook	10.00	4.50	1.25
□ 188 Dick Williams	10.00	4.50	1.25
□ 189 Don McMahon	10.00	4.50	1.25
□ 190 Gene Woodling	10.00	4.50	1.25
□ 191 Johnny Klippstein	10.00	4.50	1.25
□ 192 Danny O'Connell	10.00	4.50	1.25
□ 193 Dick Hyde	10.00	4.50	1.25
□ 194 Bobby Gene Smith	10.00	4.50	1.25
□ 195 Lindy McDaniel	10.00	4.50	1.25
□ 196 Andy Carey	10.00	4.50	1.25

1961 Topps

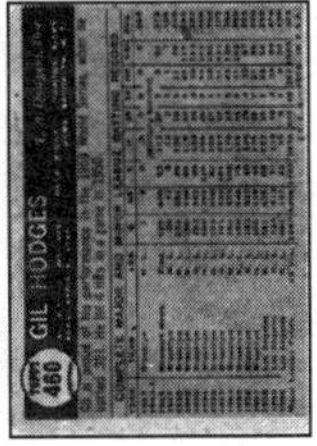

The cards in this 587-card set measure 2 1/2" by 3 1/2". In 1961, Topps returned to the vertical obverse format. Introduced for the first time were "League Leaders" (41-50) and separate, numbered checklist cards. Two number 463s exist: the Braves team card carrying that number was meant to be number 426. There are three versions of the second series checklist card number 98; the variations are distinguished by the color of the "CHECKLIST" headline on the front of the card, the color of the printing of the card number on the bottom of the reverse, and the presence of the copyright notice running vertically on the card back. There are two groups of managers (131-139/219-226) as well as separate subsets of World Series cards (306-313), Baseball Thrills (401-410), MVP's of the 1950's (AL 471-478/NL 479-486) and Sporting News All-Stars (566-589). The usual last series scarcity (523-589) exists. Some collectors believe that 61 high numbers are the toughest of all the Topps hi numbers. The set actually totals 587 cards since numbers 587 and 588 were never issued. Cards were issued in one-card penny packs as well as five-card nickle packs. The key Rookie Cards in this set are Juan Marichal, Ron Santo and Billy Williams.

	NRMT	VG-E	GOOD
COMPLETE SET (587)	4800.00	2200.00	600.00
COMMON CARD (1-370)	3.00	1.35	.35
COMMON CARD (371-446)	4.00	1.80	.50
COMMON CARD (447-522)	7.00	3.10	.85
COMMON CARD (523-565)	30.00	13.50	3.70
COMMON AS (566-589)	30.00	13.50	3.70
NOT ISSUED (587/588)	30.00		
WRAPPER (1-CENT)	200.00	90.00	25.00
WRAPPER (1-CENT, REPEAT)	200.00	90.00	25.00
WRAPPER (5-CENT)	40.00	18.00	5.00
□ 1 Dick Groat	30.00	6.00	3.00
□ 2 Roger Maris	140.00	65.00	17.50
□ 3 John Buzhardt	3.00	1.35	.35
□ 4 Lenny Green	3.00	1.35	.35
□ 5 John Romano	3.00	1.35	.35
□ 6 Ed Roebuck	3.00	1.35	.35
□ 7 White Sox Team	9.00	4.00	1.10
□ 8 Dick Williams	5.00	2.20	.60
□ 9 Bob Purkey	3.00	1.35	.35
□ 10 Brooks Robinson	40.00	18.00	5.00
□ 11 Curt Simmons	5.00	2.20	.60
□ 12 Moe Thacker	3.00	1.35	.35
□ 13 Chuck Cottier	3.00	1.35	.35
□ 14 Don Mossi	5.00	2.20	.60
□ 15 Willie Kirkland	3.00	1.35	.35
□ 16 Billy Muffett	3.00	1.35	.35
□ 17 Checklist 1	10.00	2.00	1.00
□ 18 Jim Grant	5.00	2.20	.60
□ 19 Clete Boyer	5.00	2.20	.60
□ 20 Robin Roberts	14.00	6.25	1.75

☐ 21 Zorro Versalles UER 5.00 2.20 .60
(First name should
be Zoilo)
☐ 22 Clem Labine 5.00 2.20 .60
☐ 23 Don Demeter 3.00 1.35 .35
☐ 24 Ken Johnson 3.00 1.35 .35
☐ 25 Reds' Heavy Artillery 8.00 3.60 1.00
Vada Pinson
Gus Bell
Frank Robinson
☐ 26 Wes Stock 3.00 1.35 .35
☐ 27 Jerry Kindall 3.00 1.35 .35
☐ 28 Hector Lopez 5.00 2.20 .60
☐ 29 Don Nottebart 3.00 1.35 .35
☐ 30 Nellie Fox 16.00 7.25 2.00
☐ 31 Bob Schmidt 3.00 1.35 .35
☐ 32 Ray Sadecki 3.00 1.35 .35
☐ 33 Gary Geiger 3.00 1.35 .35
☐ 34 Wynn Hawkins 3.00 1.35 .35
☐ 35 Ron Santo 45.00 20.00 5.50
☐ 36 Jack Kralick 3.00 1.35 .35
☐ 37 Charley Maxwell 5.00 2.20 .60
☐ 38 Bob Lillis 3.00 1.35 .35
☐ 39 Leo Posada 3.00 1.35 .35
☐ 40 Bob Turley 5.00 2.20 .60
☐ 41 NL Batting Leaders 35.00 16.00 4.40
Dick Groat
Norm Larker
Willie Mays
Roberto Clemente
☐ 42 AL Batting Leaders 7.00 3.10 .85
Pete Runnels
Al Smith
Minnie Minoso
Bill Skowron
☐ 43 NL Home Run Leaders 30.00 13.50 3.70
Ernie Banks
Hank Aaron
Ed Mathews
Ken Boyer
☐ 44 AL Home Run Leaders 120.00 55.00 15.00
Mickey Mantle
Roger Maris
Jim Lemon
Rocky Colavito
☐ 45 NL ERA Leaders 7.00 3.10 .85
Mike McCormick
Ernie Broglio
Don Drysdale
Bob Friend
Stan Williams
☐ 46 AL ERA Leaders 7.00 3.10 .85
Frank Baumann
Jim Bunning
Art Ditmar
Hal Brown
☐ 47 NL Pitching Leaders 7.00 3.10 .85
Ernie Broglio
Warren Spahn
Vern Law
Lou Burdette
☐ 48 AL Pitching Leaders 7.00 3.10 .85
Chuck Estrada
Jim Perry UER
(Listed as an Oriole)
Bud Daley
Art Ditmar
Frank Lary
Milt Pappas
☐ 49 NL Strikeout Leaders 20.00 9.00 2.50
Don Drysdale
Sandy Koufax
Sam Jones
Ernie Broglio
☐ 50 AL Strikeout Leaders 7.00 3.10 .85
Jim Bunning
Pedro Ramos
Early Wynn
Frank Lary
☐ 51 Detroit Tigers 9.00 4.00 1.10
Team Card
☐ 52 George Crowe 3.00 1.35 .35
☐ 53 Russ Nixon 3.00 1.35 .35
☐ 54 Earl Francis 3.00 1.35 .35
☐ 55 Jim Davenport 5.00 2.20 .60
☐ 56 Russ Kemmerer 3.00 1.35 .35
☐ 57 Marv Throneberry 5.00 2.20 .60
☐ 58 Joe Schaffernoth 3.00 1.35 .35
☐ 59 Jim Woods 3.00 1.35 .35
☐ 60 Woody Held 3.00 1.35 .35
☐ 61 Ron Piche 3.00 1.35 .35
☐ 62 Al Pilarcik 3.00 1.35 .35
☐ 63 Jim Kaat 8.00 3.60 1.00
☐ 64 Alex Grammas 3.00 1.35 .35
☐ 65 Ted Kluszewski 8.00 3.60 1.00
☐ 66 Bill Henry 3.00 1.35 .35
☐ 67 Ossie Virgil 3.00 1.35 .35
☐ 68 Deron Johnson 5.00 2.20 .60
☐ 69 Earl Wilson 5.00 2.20 .60
☐ 70 Bill Virdon 5.00 2.20 .60
☐ 71 Jerry Adair 3.00 1.35 .35
☐ 72 Stu Miller 5.00 2.20 .60
☐ 73 Al Spangler 3.00 1.35 .35
☐ 74 Joe Pignatano 3.00 1.35 .35
☐ 75 Lindy Shows Larry 5.00 2.20 .60
Lindy McDaniel
Larry Jackson
☐ 76 Harry Anderson 3.00 1.35 .35
☐ 77 Dick Stigman 3.00 1.35 .35
☐ 78 Lee Walls 3.00 1.35 .35
☐ 79 Joe Ginsberg 3.00 1.35 .35
☐ 80 Harmon Killebrew 20.00 9.00 2.50
☐ 81 Tracy Stallard 3.00 1.35 .35
☐ 82 Joe Christopher 3.00 1.35 .35
☐ 83 Bob Bruce 3.00 1.35 .35
☐ 84 Lee Maye 3.00 1.35 .35
☐ 85 Jerry Walker 3.00 1.35 .35
☐ 86 Los Angeles Dodgers 9.00 4.00 1.10
Team Card
☐ 87 Joe Amalfitano 3.00 1.35 .35
☐ 88 Richie Ashburn 16.00 7.25 2.00
☐ 89 Billy Martin 16.00 7.25 2.00
☐ 90 Gerry Staley 3.00 1.35 .35
☐ 91 Walt Moryn 3.00 1.35 .35
☐ 92 Hal Naragon 3.00 1.35 .35
☐ 93 Tony Gonzalez 3.00 1.35 .35
☐ 94 Johnny Kucks 3.00 1.35 .35
☐ 95 Norm Cash 5.00 2.20 .60
☐ 96 Billy O'Dell 3.00 1.35 .35
☐ 97 Jerry Lynch 5.00 2.20 .60
☐ 98A Checklist 2 10.00 2.00 1.00
(Red "Checklist"
98 black on white)
☐ 98B Checklist 2 10.00 2.00 1.00
(Yellow "Checklist"
98 black on white)
☐ 98C Checklist 2 10.00 2.00 1.00
(Yellow "Checklist"
98 white on black
no copyright)
☐ 99 Don Buddin UER 3.00 1.35 .35
(66 HR's)
☐ 100 Harvey Haddix 5.00 2.20 .60
☐ 101 Bubba Phillips 3.00 1.35 .35
☐ 102 Gene Stephens 3.00 1.35 .35
☐ 103 Ruben Amaro 3.00 1.35 .35
☐ 104 John Blanchard 5.00 2.20 .60
☐ 105 Carl Willey 3.00 1.35 .35
☐ 106 Whitey Herzog 3.00 1.35 .35
☐ 107 Seth Morehead 3.00 1.35 .35
☐ 108 Dan Dobbek 3.00 1.35 .35
☐ 109 Johnny Podres 5.00 2.20 .60
☐ 110 Vada Pinson 5.00 2.20 .60
☐ 111 Jack Meyer 3.00 1.35 .35
☐ 112 Chico Fernandez 3.00 1.35 .35
☐ 113 Mike Fornieles 3.00 1.35 .35
☐ 114 Hobie Landrith 3.00 1.35 .35
☐ 115 Johnny Antonelli 5.00 2.20 .60
☐ 116 Joe DeMaestri 3.00 1.35 .35
☐ 117 Dale Long 5.00 2.20 .60
☐ 118 Chris Cannizzaro 3.00 1.35 .35
☐ 119 A's Big Armor 5.00 2.20 .60
Norm Siebern
Hank Bauer
Jerry Lumpe
☐ 120 Eddie Mathews 30.00 13.50 3.70
☐ 121 Eli Grba 5.00 2.20 .60
☐ 122 Chicago Cubs 9.00 4.00 1.10
Team Card
☐ 123 Billy Gardner 3.00 1.35 .35
☐ 124 J.C. Martin 3.00 1.35 .35
☐ 125 Steve Barber 3.00 1.35 .35
☐ 126 Dick Stuart 5.00 2.20 .60
☐ 127 Ron Kline 3.00 1.35 .35
☐ 128 Rip Repulski 3.00 1.35 .35
☐ 129 Ed Hobaugh 3.00 1.35 .35
☐ 130 Norm Larker 3.00 1.35 .35
☐ 131 Paul Richards MG 5.00 2.20 .60
☐ 132 Al Lopez MG 5.00 2.20 .60
☐ 133 Ralph Houk MG 5.00 2.20 .60
☐ 134 Mickey Vernon MG 5.00 2.20 .60
☐ 135 Fred Hutchinson MG 5.00 2.20 .60
☐ 136 Walt Alston MG 6.00 2.70 .75
☐ 137 Chuck Dressen MG 5.00 2.20 .60
☐ 138 Danny Murtaugh MG 5.00 2.20 .60
☐ 139 Solly Hemus MG 5.00 2.20 .60
☐ 140 Gus Triandos 5.00 2.20 .60
☐ 141 Billy Williams 60.00 27.00 7.50
☐ 142 Luis Arroyo 5.00 2.20 .60
☐ 143 Russ Snyder 3.00 1.35 .35
☐ 144 Jim Coker 3.00 1.35 .35
☐ 145 Bob Buhl 5.00 2.20 .60
☐ 146 Marty Keough 3.00 1.35 .35
☐ 147 Ed Rakow 3.00 1.35 .35
☐ 148 Julian Javier 5.00 2.20 .60
☐ 149 Bob Oldis 3.00 1.35 .35
☐ 150 Willie Mays 100.00 45.00 12.50
☐ 151 Jim Donohue 3.00 1.35 .35
☐ 152 Earl Torgeson 3.00 1.35 .35
☐ 153 Don Lee 3.00 1.35 .35
☐ 154 Bobby Del Greco 3.00 1.35 .35
☐ 155 Johnny Temple 5.00 2.20 .60
☐ 156 Ken Hunt 5.00 2.20 .60
☐ 157 Cal McLish 3.00 1.35 .35
☐ 158 Pete Daley 3.00 1.35 .35
☐ 159 Orioles Team 9.00 4.00 1.10
☐ 160 Whitey Ford UER 40.00 18.00 5.00
(Incorrectly listed
as 5'0" tall)
☐ 161 Sherman Jones UER 3.00 1.35 .35
(Photo actually
Eddie Fisher)
☐ 162 Jay Hook 3.00 1.35 .35
☐ 163 Ed Sadowski 3.00 1.35 .35
☐ 164 Felix Mantilla 3.00 1.35 .35
☐ 165 Gino Cimoli 3.00 1.35 .35
☐ 166 Danny Kravitz 3.00 1.35 .35
☐ 167 San Francisco Giants 9.00 4.00 1.10
Team Card
☐ 168 Tommy Davis 5.00 2.20 .60
☐ 169 Don Elston 3.00 1.35 .35
☐ 170 Al Smith 3.00 1.35 .35
☐ 171 Paul Foytack 3.00 1.35 .35
☐ 172 Don Dillard 3.00 1.35 .35
☐ 173 Beantown Bombers 5.00 2.20 .60
Frank Malzone
Vic Wertz
Jackie Jensen
☐ 174 Ray Semproch 3.00 1.35 .35
☐ 175 Gene Freese 3.00 1.35 .35
☐ 176 Ken Aspromonte 3.00 1.35 .35
☐ 177 Don Larsen 5.00 2.20 .60
☐ 178 Bob Nieman 3.00 1.35 .35
☐ 179 Joe Koppe 3.00 1.35 .35
☐ 180 Bobby Richardson 12.00 5.50 1.50
☐ 181 Fred Green 3.00 1.35 .35
☐ 182 Dave Nicholson 3.00 1.35 .35
☐ 183 Andre Rodgers 3.00 1.35 .35
☐ 184 Steve Bilko 5.00 2.20 .60
☐ 185 Herb Score 5.00 2.20 .60
☐ 186 Elmer Valo 5.00 2.20 .60
☐ 187 Billy Klaus 3.00 1.35 .35
☐ 188 Jim Marshall 3.00 1.35 .35
☐ 189A Checklist 3 10.00 2.00 1.00
(Copyright symbol
almost adjacent to
263 Ken Hamlin)
☐ 189B Checklist 3 10.00 2.00 1.00
(Copyright symbol
adjacent to
264 Glen Hobbie)
☐ 190 Stan Williams 5.00 2.20 .60
☐ 191 Mike de la Hoz 3.00 1.35 .35
☐ 192 Dick Brown 3.00 1.35 .35
☐ 193 Gene Conley 5.00 2.20 .60
☐ 194 Gordy Coleman 5.00 2.20 .60
☐ 195 Jerry Casale 3.00 1.35 .35
☐ 196 Ed Bouchee 3.00 1.35 .35
☐ 197 Dick Hall 3.00 1.35 .35
☐ 198 Carl Sawatski 3.00 1.35 .35
☐ 199 Bob Boyd 3.00 1.35 .35
☐ 200 Warren Spahn 30.00 13.50 3.70
☐ 201 Pete Whisenant 3.00 1.35 .35
☐ 202 Al Neiger 3.00 1.35 .35
☐ 203 Eddie Bressoud 3.00 1.35 .35
☐ 204 Bob Skinner 5.00 2.20 .60
☐ 205 Billy Pierce 5.00 2.20 .60
☐ 206 Gene Green 3.00 1.35 .35
☐ 207 Dodger Southpaws 30.00 13.50 3.70
Sandy Koufax
Johnny Podres
☐ 208 Larry Osborne 3.00 1.35 .35
☐ 209 Ken McBride 3.00 1.35 .35
☐ 210 Pete Runnels 5.00 2.20 .60
☐ 211 Bob Gibson 40.00 18.00 5.00
☐ 212 Haywood Sullivan 5.00 2.20 .60
☐ 213 Bill Stafford 3.00 1.35 .35
☐ 214 Danny Murphy 3.00 1.35 .35
☐ 215 Gus Bell 5.00 2.20 .60
☐ 216 Ted Bowsfield 3.00 1.35 .35
☐ 217 Mel Roach 3.00 1.35 .35
☐ 218 Hal Brown 3.00 1.35 .35
☐ 219 Gene Mauch MG 5.00 2.20 .60
☐ 220 Alvin Dark MG 5.00 2.20 .60
☐ 221 Mike Higgins MG 3.00 1.35 .35
☐ 222 Jimmy Dykes MG 5.00 2.20 .60
☐ 223 Bob Scheffing MG 3.00 1.35 .35
☐ 224 Joe Gordon MG 5.00 2.20 .60
☐ 225 Bill Rigney MG 5.00 2.20 .60
☐ 226 Cookie Lavagetto MG 5.00 2.20 .60
☐ 227 Juan Pizarro 3.00 1.35 .35
☐ 228 New York Yankees 70.00 32.00 8.75
Team Card
☐ 229 Rudy Hernandez 3.00 1.35 .35
☐ 230 Don Hoak 5.00 2.20 .60
☐ 231 Dick Drott 3.00 1.35 .35
☐ 232 Bill White 5.00 2.20 .60
☐ 233 Joey Jay 5.00 2.20 .60
☐ 234 Ted Lepcio 3.00 1.35 .35
☐ 235 Camilo Pascual 5.00 2.20 .60
☐ 236 Don Gile 3.00 1.35 .35
☐ 237 Billy Loes 5.00 2.20 .60
☐ 238 Jim Gilliam 5.00 2.20 .60
☐ 239 Dave Sisler 3.00 1.35 .35
☐ 240 Ron Hansen 3.00 1.35 .35
☐ 241 Al Cicotte 3.00 1.35 .35
☐ 242 Hal Smith 3.00 1.35 .35
☐ 243 Frank Lary 5.00 2.20 .60
☐ 244 Chico Cardenas 5.00 2.20 .60
☐ 245 Joe Adcock 5.00 2.20 .60
☐ 246 Bob Davis 3.00 1.35 .35
☐ 247 Billy Goodman 5.00 2.20 .60
☐ 248 Ed Keegan 3.00 1.35 .35
☐ 249 Cincinnati Reds 9.00 4.00 1.10
Team Card
☐ 250 Buc Hill Aces 5.00 2.20 .60
Vern Law
Roy Face
☐ 251 Bill Bruton 3.00 1.35 .35
☐ 252 Bill Short 3.00 1.35 .35
☐ 253 Sammy Taylor 3.00 1.35 .35
☐ 254 Ted Sadowski 3.00 1.35 .35
☐ 255 Vic Power 5.00 2.20 .60
☐ 256 Billy Hoeft 3.00 1.35 .35
☐ 257 Carroll Hardy 3.00 1.35 .35
☐ 258 Jack Sanford 5.00 2.20 .60
☐ 259 John Schaive 3.00 1.35 .35
☐ 260 Don Drysdale 30.00 13.50 3.70
☐ 261 Charlie Lau 5.00 2.20 .60
☐ 262 Tony Curry 3.00 1.35 .35
☐ 263 Ken Hamlin 3.00 1.35 .35
☐ 264 Glen Hobbie 3.00 1.35 .35
☐ 265 Tony Kubek 8.00 3.60 1.00
☐ 266 Lindy McDaniel 5.00 2.20 .60
☐ 267 Norm Siebern 3.00 1.35 .35
☐ 268 Ike Delock 3.00 1.35 .35
☐ 269 Harry Chiti 3.00 1.35 .35
☐ 270 Bob Friend 5.00 2.20 .60
☐ 271 Jim Landis 3.00 1.35 .35
☐ 272 Tom Morgan 3.00 1.35 .35
☐ 273A Checklist 4 15.00 3.00 1.50
(Copyright symbol
adjacent to
336 Don Mincher)
☐ 273B Checklist 4 10.00 2.00 1.00
(Copyright symbol
adjacent to
339 Gene Baker)
☐ 274 Gary Bell 3.00 1.35 .35
☐ 275 Gene Woodling 5.00 2.20 .60
☐ 276 Ray Rippelmeyer 3.00 1.35 .35
☐ 277 Hank Foiles 3.00 1.35 .35
☐ 278 Don McMahon 3.00 1.35 .35
☐ 279 Jose Pagan 3.00 1.35 .35
☐ 280 Frank Howard 8.00 3.60 1.00
☐ 281 Frank Sullivan 3.00 1.35 .35
☐ 282 Faye Throneberry 3.00 1.35 .35
☐ 283 Bob Anderson 3.00 1.35 .35
☐ 284 Dick Gernert 3.00 1.35 .35
☐ 285 Sherm Lollar 5.00 2.20 .60
☐ 286 George Witt 3.00 1.35 .35
☐ 287 Carl Yastrzemski 50.00 22.00 6.25
☐ 288 Albie Pearson 5.00 2.20 .60
☐ 289 Ray Moore 3.00 1.35 .35
☐ 290 Stan Musial 100.00 45.00 12.50
☐ 291 Tex Clevenger 3.00 1.35 .35
☐ 292 Jim Baumer 3.00 1.35 .35
☐ 293 Tom Sturdivant 3.00 1.35 .35
☐ 294 Don Blasingame 3.00 1.35 .35
☐ 295 Milt Pappas 5.00 2.20 .60
☐ 296 Wes Covington 5.00 2.20 .60
☐ 297 Athletics Team 9.00 4.00 1.10
☐ 298 Jim Golden 3.00 1.35 .35
☐ 299 Clay Dalrymple 3.00 1.35 .35
☐ 300 Mickey Mantle 475.00 210.00 60.00
☐ 301 Chet Nichols 3.00 1.35 .35
☐ 302 Al Heist 3.00 1.35 .35
☐ 303 Gary Peters 5.00 2.20 .60
☐ 304 Rocky Nelson 3.00 1.35 .35
☐ 305 Mike McCormick 5.00 2.20 .60
☐ 306 Bill Virdon WS 8.00 3.60 1.00
☐ 307 Mickey Mantle WS 100.00 45.00 12.50
☐ 308 Bobby Richardson WS 10.00 4.50 1.25
☐ 309 Gino Cimoli WS 8.00 3.60 1.00
☐ 310 Roy Face WS 8.00 3.60 1.00
☐ 311 Whitey Ford WS 16.00 7.25 2.00
☐ 312 Bill Mazeroski WS 20.00 9.00 2.50
Mazeroski Homer Wins it
☐ 313 World Series Summary 16.00 7.25 2.00
Pirates Celebrate
☐ 314 Bob Miller 3.00 1.35 .35
☐ 315 Earl Battey 5.00 2.20 .60
☐ 316 Bobby Gene Smith 3.00 1.35 .35
☐ 317 Jim Brewer 3.00 1.35 .35
☐ 318 Danny O'Connell 3.00 1.35 .35
☐ 319 Valmy Thomas 3.00 1.35 .35
☐ 320 Lou Burdette 5.00 2.20 .60
☐ 321 Marv Breeding 3.00 1.35 .35
☐ 322 Bill Kunkel 5.00 2.20 .60
☐ 323 Sammy Esposito 3.00 1.35 .35
☐ 324 Hank Aguirre 3.00 1.35 .35
☐ 325 Wally Moon 5.00 2.20 .60
☐ 326 Dave Hillman 3.00 1.35 .35
☐ 327 Matty Alou 10.00 4.50 1.25
☐ 328 Jim O'Toole 5.00 2.20 .60
☐ 329 Julio Becquer 3.00 1.35 .35
☐ 330 Rocky Colavito 20.00 9.00 2.50
☐ 331 Ned Garver 3.00 1.35 .35
☐ 332 Dutch Dotterer UER 3.00 1.35 .35
(Photo actually
Tommy Dotterer
Dutch's brother)
☐ 333 Fritz Brickell 3.00 1.35 .35
☐ 334 Walt Bond 3.00 1.35 .35
☐ 335 Frank Bolling 3.00 1.35 .35
☐ 336 Don Mincher 5.00 2.20 .60
☐ 337 Al's Aces 6.00 2.70 .75
Early Wynn
Al Lopez
Herb Score
☐ 338 Don Landrum 3.00 1.35 .35
☐ 339 Gene Baker 3.00 1.35 .35
☐ 340 Vic Wertz 5.00 2.20 .60

☐ 341 Jim Owens	3.00	1.35	.35
☐ 342 Clint Courtney	3.00	1.35	.35
☐ 343 Earl Robinson	3.00	1.35	.35
☐ 344 Sandy Koufax	120.00	55.00	15.00
☐ 345 Jim Piersall	5.00	2.20	.60
☐ 346 Howie Nunn	3.00	1.35	.35
☐ 347 St. Louis Cardinals Team Card	9.00	4.00	1.10
☐ 348 Steve Boros	3.00	1.35	.35
☐ 349 Danny McDevitt	3.00	1.35	.35
☐ 350 Ernie Banks	45.00	20.00	5.50
☐ 351 Jim King	3.00	1.35	.35
☐ 352 Bob Shaw	3.00	1.35	.35
☐ 353 Howie Bedell	3.00	1.35	.35
☐ 354 Billy Harrell	3.00	1.35	.35
☐ 355 Bob Allison	5.00	2.20	.60
☐ 356 Ryne Duren	3.00	1.35	.35
☐ 357 Daryl Spencer	3.00	1.35	.35
☐ 358 Earl Averill	5.00	2.20	.60
☐ 359 Dallas Green	3.00	1.35	.35
☐ 360 Frank Robinson	40.00	18.00	5.00
☐ 361A Checklist 5 (No ad on back)	10.00	2.00	1.00
☐ 361B Checklist 5 (Special Feature ad on back)	15.00	3.00	1.50
☐ 362 Frank Funk	3.00	1.35	.35
☐ 363 John Roseboro	5.00	2.20	.60
☐ 364 Moe Drabowsky	5.00	2.20	.60
☐ 365 Jerry Lumpe	3.00	1.35	.35
☐ 366 Eddie Fisher	3.00	1.35	.35
☐ 367 Jim Rivera	3.00	1.35	.35
☐ 368 Bennie Daniels	3.00	1.35	.35
☐ 369 Dave Philley	3.00	1.35	.35
☐ 370 Roy Face	5.00	2.20	.60
☐ 371 Bill Skowron SP	60.00	27.00	7.50
☐ 372 Bob Hendley	4.00	1.80	.50
☐ 373 Boston Red Sox Team Card	10.00	4.50	1.25
☐ 374 Paul Giel	4.00	1.80	.50
☐ 375 Ken Boyer	10.00	4.50	1.25
☐ 376 Mike Roarke	4.00	1.80	.50
☐ 377 Ruben Gomez	4.00	1.80	.50
☐ 378 Wally Post	6.00	2.70	.75
☐ 379 Bobby Shantz	4.00	1.80	.50
☐ 380 Minnie Minoso	7.00	3.10	.85
☐ 381 Dave Wickersham	4.00	1.80	.50
☐ 382 Frank Thomas	6.00	2.70	.75
☐ 383 Frisco First Liners Mike McCormick Jack Sanford Billy O'Dell	6.00	2.70	.75
☐ 384 Chuck Essegian	4.00	1.80	.50
☐ 385 Jim Perry	6.00	2.70	.75
☐ 386 Joe Hicks	4.00	1.80	.50
☐ 387 Duke Maas	4.00	1.80	.50
☐ 388 Bob Clemente	160.00	70.00	20.00
☐ 389 Ralph Terry	6.00	2.70	.75
☐ 390 Del Crandall	6.00	2.70	.75
☐ 391 Winston Brown	4.00	1.80	.50
☐ 392 Reno Bertoia	4.00	1.80	.50
☐ 393 Batter Bafflers Don Cardwell Glen Hobbie	4.00	1.80	.50
☐ 394 Ken Walters	4.00	1.80	.50
☐ 395 Chuck Estrada	6.00	2.70	.75
☐ 396 Bob Aspromonte	4.00	1.80	.50
☐ 397 Hal Woodeshick	4.00	1.80	.50
☐ 398 Hank Bauer	6.00	2.70	.75
☐ 399 Cliff Cook	4.00	1.80	.50
☐ 400 Vern Law	6.00	2.70	.75
☐ 401 Babe Ruth HL 60th HR	50.00	22.00	6.25
☐ 402 Don Larsen HL SP WS Perfect Game	30.00	13.50	3.70
☐ 403 Joe Oeschger HL Leon Cadore 26 Inning Tie	6.00	2.70	.75
☐ 404 Rogers Hornsby HL .424 Season BA	10.00	4.50	1.25
☐ 405 Lou Gehrig HL Consecutive Game Streak	80.00	36.00	10.00
☐ 406 Mickey Mantle HL 565 foot HR	100.00	45.00	12.50
☐ 407 Jack Chesbro HL 41 victories	6.00	2.70	.75
☐ 408 Christy Mathewson HL SP 267 Strikeouts	20.00	9.00	2.50
☐ 409 Walter Johnson SL 3 Shutouts in 4 days	12.00	5.50	1.50
☐ 410 Harvey Haddix HL 12 Perfect Innings	6.00	2.70	.75
☐ 411 Tony Taylor	6.00	2.70	.75
☐ 412 Larry Sherry	6.00	2.70	.75
☐ 413 Eddie Yost	6.00	2.70	.75
☐ 414 Dick Donovan	6.00	2.70	.75
☐ 415 Hank Aaron	90.00	40.00	11.00
☐ 416 Dick Howser	10.00	4.50	1.25
☐ 417 Juan Marichal SP	125.00	55.00	15.50
☐ 418 Ed Bailey	6.00	2.70	.75
☐ 419 Tom Borland	4.00	1.80	.50
☐ 420 Ernie Broglio	6.00	2.70	.75
☐ 421 Ty Cline SP	18.00	8.00	2.20
☐ 422 Bud Daley	4.00	1.80	.50
☐ 423 Charlie Neal SP	18.00	8.00	2.20
☐ 424 Turk Lown	4.00	1.80	.50
☐ 425 Yogi Berra	70.00	32.00	8.75
☐ 426 Milwaukee Braves Team Card (Back numbered 463)	12.00	5.50	1.50
☐ 427 Dick Ellsworth	6.00	2.70	.75
☐ 428 Ray Barker SP	18.00	8.00	2.20
☐ 429 Al Kaline	45.00	20.00	5.50
☐ 430 Bill Mazeroski SP	60.00	27.00	7.50
☐ 431 Chuck Stobbs	4.00	1.80	.50
☐ 432 Coot Veal	6.00	2.70	.75
☐ 433 Art Mahaffey	4.00	1.80	.50
☐ 434 Tom Brewer	4.00	1.80	.50
☐ 435 Orlando Cepeda UER (San Francis on card front)	14.00	6.25	1.75
☐ 436 Jim Maloney SP	20.00	9.00	2.50
☐ 437A Checklist 6 440 Louis Aparicio	15.00	3.00	1.50
☐ 437B Checklist 6 440 Luis Aparicio	15.00	3.00	1.50
☐ 438 Curt Flood	7.00	3.10	.85
☐ 439 Phil Regan	6.00	2.70	.75
☐ 440 Luis Aparicio	16.00	7.25	2.00
☐ 441 Dick Bertell	4.00	1.80	.50
☐ 442 Gordon Jones	4.00	1.80	.50
☐ 443 Duke Snider	40.00	18.00	5.00
☐ 444 Joe Nuxhall	6.00	2.70	.75
☐ 445 Frank Malzone	6.00	2.70	.75
☐ 446 Bob Taylor	4.00	1.80	.50
☐ 447 Harry Bright	7.00	3.10	.85
☐ 448 Del Rice	7.00	3.10	.85
☐ 449 Bob Bolin	7.00	3.10	.85
☐ 450 Jim Lemon	7.00	3.10	.85
☐ 451 Power for Ernie Daryl Spencer Bill White Ernie Broglio	7.00	3.10	.85
☐ 452 Bob Allen	7.00	3.10	.85
☐ 453 Dick Schofield	7.00	3.10	.85
☐ 454 Pumpsie Green	7.00	3.10	.85
☐ 455 Early Wynn	16.00	7.25	2.00
☐ 456 Hal Bevan	7.00	3.10	.85
☐ 457 Johnny James (Listed as Angel, but wearing Yankee uniform and cap)	7.00	3.10	.85
☐ 458 Willie Tasby	7.00	3.10	.85
☐ 459 Terry Fox	7.00	3.10	.85
☐ 460 Gil Hodges	16.00	7.25	2.00
☐ 461 Smoky Burgess	8.00	3.60	1.00
☐ 462 Lou Klimchock	7.00	3.10	.85
☐ 463 Jack Fisher (See also 426)	7.00	3.10	.85
☐ 464 Lee Thomas (Pictured with Yankee cap but listed as Los Angeles Angel)	8.00	3.60	1.00
☐ 465 Roy McMillan	7.00	3.10	.85
☐ 466 Ron Moeller	7.00	3.10	.85
☐ 467 Cleveland Indians Team Card	12.00	5.50	1.50
☐ 468 John Callison	10.00	4.50	1.25
☐ 469 Ralph Lumenti	7.00	3.10	.85
☐ 470 Roy Sievers	10.00	4.50	1.25
☐ 471 Phil Rizzuto MVP	20.00	9.00	2.50
☐ 472 Yogi Berra MVP	60.00	27.00	7.50
☐ 473 Bob Shantz MVP	7.00	3.10	.85
☐ 474 Al Rosen MVP	10.00	4.50	1.25
☐ 475 Mickey Mantle MVP	200.00	90.00	25.00
☐ 476 Jackie Jensen MVP	10.00	4.50	1.25
☐ 477 Nellie Fox MVP	18.00	8.00	2.20
☐ 478 Roger Maris MVP	45.00	20.00	5.50
☐ 479 Jim Konstanty MVP	7.00	3.10	.85
☐ 480 Roy Campanella MVP	35.00	16.00	4.40
☐ 481 Hank Sauer MVP	7.00	3.10	.85
☐ 482 Willie Mays MVP	50.00	22.00	6.25
☐ 483 Don Newcombe MVP	10.00	4.50	1.25
☐ 484 Hank Aaron MVP	50.00	22.00	6.25
☐ 485 Ernie Banks MVP	35.00	16.00	4.40
☐ 486 Dick Groat MVP	10.00	4.50	1.25
☐ 487 Gene Oliver	7.00	3.10	.85
☐ 488 Joe McClain	8.00	3.60	1.00
☐ 489 Walt Dropo	7.00	3.10	.85
☐ 490 Jim Bunning	16.00	7.25	2.00
☐ 491 Philadelphia Phillies Team Card	12.00	5.50	1.50
☐ 492 Ron Fairly	8.00	3.60	1.00
☐ 493 Don Zimmer UER (Brooklyn A.L.)	8.00	3.60	1.00
☐ 494 Tom Cheney	7.00	3.10	.85
☐ 495 Elston Howard	12.00	5.50	1.50
☐ 496 Ken MacKenzie	7.00	3.10	.85
☐ 497 Willie Jones	7.00	3.10	.85
☐ 498 Ray Herbert	7.00	3.10	.85
☐ 499 Chuck Schilling	7.00	3.10	.85
☐ 500 Harvey Kuenn	8.00	3.60	1.00
☐ 501 John DeMerit	7.00	3.10	.85
☐ 502 Clarence Coleman	8.00	3.60	1.00
☐ 503 Tito Francona	7.00	3.10	.85
☐ 504 Billy Consolo	7.00	3.10	.85
☐ 505 Red Schoendienst	14.00	6.25	1.75
☐ 506 Willie Davis	16.00	7.25	2.00
☐ 507 Pete Burnside	8.00	3.60	1.00
☐ 508 Rocky Bridges	8.00	3.60	1.00
☐ 509 Camilo Carreon	7.00	3.10	.85
☐ 510 Art Ditmar	7.00	3.10	.85
☐ 511 Joe M. Morgan	7.00	3.10	.85
☐ 512 Bob Will	7.00	3.10	.85
☐ 513 Jim Brosnan	8.00	3.60	1.00
☐ 514 Jake Wood	7.00	3.10	.85
☐ 515 Jackie Brandt	7.00	3.10	.85
☐ 516 Checklist 7	15.00	3.00	1.50
☐ 517 Willie McCovey	50.00	22.00	6.25
☐ 518 Andy Carey	8.00	3.60	1.00
☐ 519 Jim Pagliaroni	8.00	3.60	1.00
☐ 520 Joe Cunningham	7.00	3.10	.85
☐ 521 Brother Battery Norm Sherry Larry Sherry	8.00	3.60	1.00
☐ 522 Dick Farrell UER (Phillies cap but listed on Dodgers)	8.00	3.60	1.00
☐ 523 Joe Gibbon	30.00	13.50	3.70
☐ 524 Johnny Logan	30.00	13.50	3.70
☐ 525 Ron Perranoski	35.00	16.00	4.40
☐ 526 R.C. Stevens	30.00	13.50	3.70
☐ 527 Gene Leek	30.00	13.50	3.70
☐ 528 Pedro Ramos	30.00	13.50	3.70
☐ 529 Bob Roselli	30.00	13.50	3.70
☐ 530 Bob Malkmus	30.00	13.50	3.70
☐ 531 Jim Coates	35.00	16.00	4.40
☐ 532 Bob Hale	30.00	13.50	3.70
☐ 533 Jack Curtis	30.00	13.50	3.70
☐ 534 Eddie Kasko	30.00	13.50	3.70
☐ 535 Larry Jackson	30.00	13.50	3.70
☐ 536 Bill Tuttle	30.00	13.50	3.70
☐ 537 Bobby Locke	30.00	13.50	3.70
☐ 538 Chuck Hiller	30.00	13.50	3.70
☐ 539 Johnny Klippstein	30.00	13.50	3.70
☐ 540 Jackie Jensen	35.00	16.00	4.40
☐ 541 Roland Sheldon	40.00	18.00	5.00
☐ 542 Minnesota Twins Team Card	70.00	32.00	8.75
☐ 543 Roger Craig	32.50	14.50	4.10
☐ 544 George Thomas	30.00	13.50	3.70
☐ 545 Hoyt Wilhelm	50.00	22.00	6.25
☐ 546 Marty Kutyna	30.00	13.50	3.70
☐ 547 Leon Wagner	30.00	13.50	3.70
☐ 548 Ted Wills	30.00	13.50	3.70
☐ 549 Hal R. Smith	30.00	13.50	3.70
☐ 550 Frank Baumann	30.00	13.50	3.70
☐ 551 George Altman	30.00	13.50	3.70
☐ 552 Jim Archer	30.00	13.50	3.70
☐ 553 Bill Fischer	30.00	13.50	3.70
☐ 554 Pittsburgh Pirates Team Card	70.00	32.00	8.75
☐ 555 Sam Jones	30.00	13.50	3.70
☐ 556 Ken R. Hunt	30.00	13.50	3.70
☐ 557 Jose Valdivielso	30.00	13.50	3.70
☐ 558 Don Ferrarese	30.00	13.50	3.70
☐ 559 Jim Gentile	55.00	25.00	7.00
☐ 560 Barry Latman	30.00	13.50	3.70
☐ 561 Charley James	30.00	13.50	3.70
☐ 562 Bill Monbouquette	30.00	13.50	3.70
☐ 563 Bob Cerv	45.00	20.00	5.50
☐ 564 Don Cardwell	30.00	13.50	3.70
☐ 565 Felipe Alou	32.50	14.50	4.10
☐ 566 Paul Richards AS MG	30.00	13.50	3.70
☐ 567 Danny Murtaugh AS MG	30.00	13.50	3.70
☐ 568 Bill Skowron AS	40.00	18.00	5.00
☐ 569 Frank Herrera AS	30.00	13.50	3.70
☐ 570 Nellie Fox AS	45.00	20.00	5.50
☐ 571 Bill Mazeroski AS	40.00	18.00	5.00
☐ 572 Brooks Robinson AS	90.00	40.00	11.00
☐ 573 Ken Boyer AS	40.00	18.00	5.00
☐ 574 Luis Aparicio AS	45.00	20.00	5.50
☐ 575 Ernie Banks AS	90.00	40.00	11.00
☐ 576 Roger Maris AS	160.00	70.00	20.00
☐ 577 Hank Aaron AS	160.00	70.00	20.00
☐ 578 Mickey Mantle AS	425.00	190.00	52.50
☐ 579 Willie Mays AS	160.00	70.00	20.00
☐ 580 Al Kaline AS	90.00	40.00	11.00
☐ 581 Frank Robinson AS	90.00	40.00	11.00
☐ 582 Earl Battey AS	30.00	13.50	3.70
☐ 583 Del Crandall AS	30.00	13.50	3.70
☐ 584 Jim Perry AS	30.00	13.50	3.70
☐ 585 Bob Friend AS	30.00	13.50	3.70
☐ 586 Whitey Ford AS	90.00	40.00	11.00
☐ 589 Warren Spahn AS	100.00	30.00	10.00

1961 Topps Magic Rub-Offs

There are 36 "Magic Rub-Offs" in this set of inserts also marketed in packages of 1961 Topps baseball cards. Each rub off measures 2 1/16" by 3 1/16". Of this number, 18 are team designs (numbered 1-18 below), while the remaining 18 depict players (numbered 19-36 below). The latter, one from each team, were apparently selected for their unusual nicknames. Note: The Duke Maas insert is misspelled "Mass".

	NRMT	VG-E	GOOD
COMPLETE SET (36)	140.00	65.00	17.50
COMMON RUB-OFF (1-18)	2.00	.90	.25
COMMON CARD (19-36)	4.00	1.80	.50
☐ 1 Detroit Tigers	3.00	1.35	.35
☐ 2 New York Yankees	4.00	1.80	.50
☐ 3 Minnesota Twins	2.00	.90	.25
☐ 4 Washington Senators	2.00	.90	.25
☐ 5 Boston Red Sox	3.00	1.35	.35
☐ 6 Los Angeles Angels	2.00	.90	.25
☐ 7 Kansas City A's	2.00	.90	.25
☐ 8 Baltimore Orioles	2.00	.90	.25
☐ 9 Chicago White Sox	2.00	.90	.25
☐ 10 Cleveland Indians	2.00	.90	.25
☐ 11 Pittsburgh Pirates	2.00	.90	.25
☐ 12 San Francisco Giants	2.00	.90	.25
☐ 13 Los Angeles Dodgers	4.00	1.80	.50
☐ 14 Philadelphia Phillies	2.00	.90	.25
☐ 15 Cincinnati Redlegs	2.00	.90	.25
☐ 16 St. Louis Cardinals	2.00	.90	.25
☐ 17 Chicago Cubs	2.00	.90	.25
☐ 18 Milwaukee Braves	2.00	.90	.25
☐ 19 John Romano	2.00	.90	.25
☐ 20 Ray Moore	2.00	.90	.25
☐ 21 Ernie Banks	25.00	11.00	3.10
☐ 22 Charlie Maxwell	4.00	1.80	.50
☐ 23 Yogi Berra	25.00	11.00	3.10
☐ 24 Henry "Dutch" Dotterer	4.00	1.80	.50
☐ 25 Jim Brosnan	4.00	1.80	.50
☐ 26 Billy Martin	10.00	4.50	1.25
☐ 27 Jackie Brandt	4.00	1.80	.50
☐ 28 Duke Maas UER (sic, Mass)	5.00	2.20	.60
☐ 29 Pete Runnels	5.00	2.20	.60
☐ 30 Joe Gordon MG	5.00	2.20	.60
☐ 31 Sam Jones	4.00	1.80	.50
☐ 32 Walt Moryn	4.00	1.80	.50
☐ 33 Harvey Haddix	5.00	2.20	.60
☐ 34 Frank Howard	6.00	2.70	.75
☐ 35 Turk Lown	4.00	1.80	.50
☐ 36 Frank Herrera	4.00	1.80	.50

1961 Topps Stamps

There are 207 different baseball players depicted in this stamp series, which was issued as an insert in packages of the regular Topps cards of 1961. The set is actually comprised of 208 stamps: 104 players are pictured on brown stamps and 104 players appear on green stamps, with Kaline found in both colors. The stamps were issued in attached pairs and an album was sold separately (10 cents) at retail outlets. Each stamp measures 1 3/8" by 1 3/16". Stamps are unnumbered but are presented here in alphabetical order by team, Chicago Cubs (1-12), Cincinnati Reds (13-24), Los Angeles Dodgers (25-36), Milwaukee Braves (37-48), Philadelphia Phillies (49-60), Pittsburgh Pirates (61-72), San Francisco Giants (73-84), St. Louis Cardinals (85-96), Baltimore Orioles AL (97-107), Boston Red Sox (108-119), Chicago White Sox (120-131), Cleveland Indians (132-143), Detroit Tigers (144-155), Kansas City A's (156-168), Los Angeles Angels (169-175), Minnesota Twins (176-187), New York Yankees (188-200) and Washington Senators (201-207).

	NRMT	VG-E	GOOD
COMPLETE SET (207)	350.00	160.00	45.00
COMMON STAMP (1-207)	.80	.35	.10
☐ 1 George Altman	.80	.35	.10
☐ 2 Bob Anderson (brown)	.80	.35	.10
☐ 3 Richie Ashburn	5.00	2.20	.60
☐ 4 Ernie Banks	8.00	3.60	1.00
☐ 5 Ed Bouchee	.80	.35	.10
☐ 6 Jim Brewer	.80	.35	.10
☐ 7 Dick Ellsworth	.80	.35	.10
☐ 8 Don Elston	.80	.35	.10
☐ 10 Sammy Taylor	.80	.35	.10
☐ 11 Bob Will	.80	.35	.10
☐ 12 Billy Williams	5.00	2.20	.60
☐ 13 Ed Bailey	.80	.35	.10
☐ 14 Gus Bell	.80	.35	.10
☐ 15 Jim Brosnan (brown)	.80	.35	.10
☐ 16 Chico Cardenas	.80	.35	.10
☐ 17 Gene Freese	.80	.35	.10
☐ 18 Eddie Kasko	.80	.35	.10
☐ 19 Jerry Lynch	.80	.35	.10
☐ 21 Jim O'Toole	.80	.35	.10
☐ 22 Vada Pinson	1.50	.70	.19
☐ 23 Wally Post	.80	.35	.10
☐ 24 Frank Robinson	8.00	3.60	1.00
☐ 25 Tommy Davis	1.50	.70	.19
☐ 26 Don Drysdale	6.00	2.70	.75
☐ 27 Frank Howard (brown)	2.00	.90	.25
☐ 28 Norm Larker	.80	.35	.10
☐ 29 Wally Moon	1.00	.45	.12
☐ 31 Johnny Podres	2.00	.90	.25
☐ 32 Ed Roebuck	.80	.35	.10
☐ 33 Johnny Roseboro	.80	.35	.10
☐ 34 Larry Sherry	.80	.35	.10
☐ 37 Hank Aaron	15.00	6.75	1.85
☐ 38 Joe Adcock	1.00	.45	.12
☐ 39 Bill Bruton	.80	.35	.10
☐ 40 Bob Buhl	.80	.35	.10

☐ 41 Wes Covington	.80	.35	.10
(brown)			
☐ 42 Del Crandall	1.00	.45	.12
☐ 43 Joey Jay	.80	.35	.10
☐ 44 Felix Mantilla	.80	.35	.10
☐ 45 Eddie Mathews	6.00	2.70	.75
☐ 46 Roy McMillan	.80	.35	.10
☐ 47 Warren Spahn	8.00	3.60	1.00
☐ 48 Carlton Willey	.80	.35	.10
☐ 49 John Buzhardt	.80	.35	.10
☐ 50 Johnny Callison	1.00	.45	.12
☐ 51 Tony Curry	.80	.35	.10
☐ 52 Clay Dalrymple	.80	.35	.10
(brown)			
☐ 53 Bobby Del Greco	.80	.35	.10
☐ 54 Dick Farrell	.80	.35	.10
☐ 55 Tony Gonzalez	.80	.35	.10
☐ 56 Pancho Herrera	.80	.35	.10
☐ 57 Art Mahaffey	.80	.35	.10
☐ 58 Robin Roberts	5.00	2.20	.60
☐ 59 Tony Taylor	1.00	.45	.12
☐ 60 Lee Walls	.80	.35	.10
☐ 61 Smoky Burgess	1.00	.45	.12
☐ 62 Elroy Face (brown)	1.50	.70	.19
☐ 64 Dick Groat	1.50	.70	.19
☐ 65 Don Hoak	.80	.35	.10
☐ 66 Vernon Law	1.50	.70	.19
☐ 67 Bill Mazeroski	2.00	.90	.25
☐ 68 Rocky Nelson	.80	.35	.10
☐ 69 Bob Skinner	.80	.35	.10
☐ 70 Hal Smith	.80	.35	.10
☐ 71 Dick Stuart	1.00	.45	.12
☐ 72 Bill Virdon	1.50	.70	.19
☐ 73 Don Blasingame	.80	.35	.10
☐ 74 Eddie Bressoud	.80	.35	.10
(brown)			
☐ 75 Orlando Cepeda	2.50	1.10	.30
☐ 76 Jim Davenport	.80	.35	.10
☐ 77 Harvey Kuenn	2.00	.90	.25
☐ 78 Hobie Landrith	.80	.35	.10
☐ 79 Juan Marichal	6.00	2.70	.75
☐ 81 Mike McCormick	1.00	.45	.12
☐ 82 Willie McCovey	8.00	3.60	1.00
☐ 83 Billy O'Dell	.80	.35	.10
☐ 84 Jack Sanford	.80	.35	.10
☐ 85 Ken Boyer	2.00	.90	.25
☐ 86 Curt Flood	1.50	.70	.19
☐ 87 Alex Grammas (brown)	.80	.35	.10
☐ 88 Larry Jackson	.80	.35	.10
☐ 89 Julian Javier	.80	.35	.10
☐ 90 Ron Kline	.80	.35	.10
☐ 91 Lindy McDaniel	.80	.35	.10
☐ 92 Stan Musial	15.00	6.75	1.85
☐ 93 Curt Simmons	.80	.35	.10
☐ 94 Hal Smith	.80	.35	.10
☐ 95 Daryl Spencer	.80	.35	.10
☐ 96 Bill White	1.50	.70	.19
☐ 97 Steve Barber	.80	.35	.10
☐ 98 Jackie Brandt	.80	.35	.10
(brown)			
☐ 99 Marv Breeding	.80	.35	.10
☐ 100 Chuck Estrada	.80	.35	.10
☐ 101 Jim Gentile	1.50	.70	.19
☐ 102 Ron Hansen	.80	.35	.10
☐ 103 Milt Pappas	1.00	.45	.12
☐ 104 Brooks Robinson	8.00	3.60	1.00
☐ 105 Gene Stephens	.80	.35	.10
☐ 106 Gus Triandos	1.00	.45	.12
☐ 107 Hoyt Wilhelm	5.00	2.20	.60
☐ 108 Tom Brewer	.80	.35	.10
☐ 110 Ike Delock	.80	.35	.10
☐ 111 Gary Geiger	.80	.35	.10
☐ 112 Jackie Jensen	2.00	.90	.25
☐ 113 Frank Malzone	1.00	.45	.12
☐ 114 Bill Monbouquette	.80	.35	.10
☐ 115 Russ Nixon	.80	.35	.10
☐ 116 Pete Runnels	1.00	.45	.12
☐ 117 Willie Tasby	.80	.35	.10
☐ 118 Vic Wertz	1.00	.45	.12
☐ 119 Gene Conley (brown)	.80	.35	.10
☐ 119 Carl Yastrzemski	12.50	5.50	1.55
☐ 120 Luis Aparicio	5.00	2.20	.60
☐ 121 Russ Kemmerer	.80	.35	.10
(brown)			
☐ 122 Jim Landis	.80	.35	.10
☐ 123 Sherm Lollar	.80	.35	.10
☐ 124 J.C. Martin	.80	.35	.10
☐ 125 Minnie Minoso	2.00	.90	.25
☐ 126 Billy Pierce	1.50	.70	.19
☐ 127 Bob Shaw	.80	.35	.10
☐ 128 Roy Sievers	1.50	.70	.19
☐ 129 Al Smith	.80	.35	.10
☐ 130 Gerry Staley	.80	.35	.10
☐ 131 Early Wynn	5.00	2.20	.60
☐ 132 Johnny Antonelli	1.00	.45	.12
(brown)			
☐ 133 Ken Aspromonte	.80	.35	.10
☐ 134 Tito Francona	.80	.35	.10
☐ 135 Jim Grant	.80	.35	.10
☐ 136 Woody Held	.80	.35	.10
☐ 137 Barry Latman	.80	.35	.10
☐ 138 Jim Perry	1.00	.45	.12
☐ 139 Jimmy Piersall	2.00	.90	.25
☐ 140 Bubba Phillips	.80	.35	.10
☐ 142 John Romano	.80	.35	.10
☐ 143 Johnny Temple	.80	.35	.10
☐ 144 Hank Aguirre (brown)	.80	.35	.10
☐ 145 Frank Bolling	.80	.35	.10
☐ 146 Steve Boros	1.00	.45	.12
☐ 147 Jim Bunning	5.00	2.20	.60
☐ 148 Norm Cash	2.00	.90	.25
☐ 149 Harry Chiti	.80	.35	.10
☐ 150 Chico Fernandez	.80	.35	.10
☐ 151 Dick Gernert	.80	.35	.10
☐ 152A Al Kaline (green)	8.00	3.60	1.00
☐ 152B Al Kaline (brown)	8.00	3.60	1.00
☐ 153 Frank Lary	1.00	.45	.12
☐ 154 Charlie Maxwell	.80	.35	.10
☐ 155 Dave Sisler	.80	.35	.10
☐ 156 Hank Bauer	1.00	.45	.12
☐ 157 Bob Boyd (brown)	.80	.35	.10
☐ 158 Andy Carey	.80	.35	.10
☐ 159 Bud Daley	.80	.35	.10
☐ 160 Dick Hall	.80	.35	.10
☐ 161 J.C. Hartman	.80	.35	.10
☐ 162 Ray Herbert	.80	.35	.10
☐ 163 Whitey Herzog	2.00	.90	.25
☐ 164 Jerry Lumpe	.80	.35	.10
☐ 165 Norm Siebern	.80	.35	.10
☐ 166 Marv Throneberry	2.00	.90	.25
☐ 167 Bill Tuttle	.80	.35	.10
☐ 168 Dick Williams	1.50	.70	.19
☐ 169 Jerry Casale (brown)	.80	.35	.10
☐ 170 Bob Cerv	1.00	.45	.12
☐ 171 Ned Garver	.80	.35	.10
☐ 172 Ron Hunt	.80	.35	.10
☐ 173 Ted Kluszewski	2.50	1.10	.30
☐ 174 Bob Sadowski	.80	.35	.10
☐ 175 Eddie Yost	.80	.35	.10
☐ 176 Bob Allison	1.50	.70	.19
☐ 177 Earl Battey (brown)	.80	.35	.10
☐ 178 Reno Bertoia	.80	.35	.10
☐ 179 Billy Gardner	1.00	.45	.12
☐ 180 Jim Kaat	2.50	1.10	.30
☐ 181 Harmon Killebrew	6.00	2.70	.75
☐ 182 Jim Lemon	1.00	.45	.12
☐ 183 Camilo Pascual	1.00	.45	.12
☐ 184 Pedro Ramos	.80	.35	.10
☐ 185 Chuck Stobbs	.80	.35	.10
☐ 186 Zoilo Versalles	.80	.35	.10
☐ 187 Pete Whisenant	.80	.35	.10
☐ 188 Luis Arroyo (brown)	1.00	.45	.12
☐ 189 Yogi Berra	12.50	5.50	1.55
☐ 190 John Blanchard	1.00	.45	.12
☐ 191 Clete Boyer	1.50	.70	.19
☐ 192 Art Ditmar	.80	.35	.10
☐ 193 Whitey Ford	12.50	5.50	1.55
☐ 194 Elston Howard	2.50	1.10	.30
☐ 195 Tony Kubek	2.50	1.10	.30
☐ 196 Mickey Mantle	60.00	27.00	7.50
☐ 197 Roger Maris	15.00	6.75	1.85
☐ 198 Bobby Shantz	1.00	.45	.12
☐ 199 Bill Stafford	.80	.35	.10
☐ 200 Bob Turley	1.00	.45	.12
☐ 201 Bud Daley (brown)	.80	.35	.10
☐ 202 Dick Donovan	.80	.35	.10
☐ 203 Bobby Klaus	.80	.35	.10
☐ 204 Johnny Klippstein	.80	.35	.10
☐ 205 Dale Long	1.00	.45	.12
☐ 206 Ray Semproch	.80	.35	.10
☐ 207 Gene Woodling	1.00	.45	.12
☐ XX Stamp Album	20.00	9.00	2.50

1961 Topps Dice Game

This 18-card standard-size set may never have been issued by Topps; it is considered a very obscure "test" issue and is quite scarce. The cards are printed completely in black and white on white card stock. There is no reference to Topps anywhere on the front or back of the card. The card back lays out the batter's outcome depending on the type of pitch thrown and the sum of two dice rolled. The cards are unnumbered and hence they are ordered below and assigned numbers alphabetically.

	NRMT	VG-E	GOOD
COMPLETE SET (18)	7000.00	3200.00	900.00
COMMON CARD (1-18)	100.00	45.00	12.50
☐ 1 Earl Battey	100.00	45.00	12.50
☐ 2 Del Crandall	100.00	45.00	12.50
☐ 3 Jim Davenport	100.00	45.00	12.50
☐ 4 Don Drysdale	300.00	135.00	38.00
☐ 5 Dick Groat	125.00	55.00	15.50
☐ 6 Al Kaline	450.00	200.00	55.00
☐ 7 Tony Kubek	150.00	70.00	19.00
☐ 8 Mickey Mantle	3000.00	1350.00	375.00
☐ 9 Willie Mays	1000.00	450.00	125.00
☐ 10 Bill Mazeroski	150.00	70.00	19.00
☐ 11 Stan Musial	750.00	350.00	95.00
☐ 12 Camilo Pascual	100.00	45.00	12.50
☐ 13 Bobby Richardson	150.00	70.00	19.00
☐ 14 Brooks Robinson	450.00	200.00	55.00
☐ 15 Frank Robinson	400.00	180.00	50.00
☐ 16 Norm Siebern	100.00	45.00	12.50
☐ 17 Leon Wagner	100.00	45.00	12.50
☐ 18 Bill White	125.00	55.00	15.50

1962 Topps

The cards in this 598-card set measure 2 1/2" by 3 1/2". The 1962 Topps set contains a mini-series spotlighting Babe Ruth (135-144). Other subsets in the set include League Leaders (51-60), World Series cards (232-237), In Action cards (311-319), NL All Stars (390-399), AL All Stars (466-475), and Rookie Prospects (591-598). The All-Star selections were again provided by Sport Magazine, as in 1958 and 1960. The second series had two distinct printings which are distinguishable by numerous color and pose variations. Those cards with a distinctive "green tint" are valued at a slight premuim as they are basically the result of a flawed printing process occurring early in the second series run. Card number 139 exists as A: Babe Ruth Special card, B: Hal Reniff with arms over head, or C: Hal Reniff in the same pose as card number 159. In addition, two poses exist for these cards: 129, 132, 134, 147, 174, 176, and 190. The high number series, 523 to 598, is somewhat more difficult to obtain than other cards in the set. Within the last series (523-598) there are 43 cards which were printed in lesser quantities; these are marked SP in the checklist below. In particular, the Rookie Parade subset (591-598) of this last series is even more difficult. This was the first year Topps produced multi-player Rookie Cards. The set price listed does not include the pose variations (see checklist below for individual values). Cards were issued in one-card penny packs as well as five-card nickle packs. The key Rookie Cards in this set are Lou Brock, Tim McCarver, Gaylord Perry, and Bob Uecker.

	NRMT	VG-E	GOOD
COMPLETE SET (598)	4600.00	2100.00	575.00
COMMON CARD (1-370)	5.00	2.20	.60
COMMON CARD (371-446)	6.00	2.70	.75
COMMON CARD (447-522)	12.00	5.50	1.50
COMMON CARD (523-590)	20.00	9.00	2.50
COMMON ROOKIES (591-598)	45.00	20.00	5.50
WRAPPER (1-CENT)	100.00	45.00	12.50
WRAPPER (5-CENT)	40.00	18.00	5.00
☐ 1 Roger Maris	200.00	50.00	20.00
☐ 2 Jim Brosnan	5.00	2.20	.60
☐ 3 Pete Runnels	5.00	2.20	.60
☐ 4 John DeMerit	5.50	2.50	.70
☐ 5 Sandy Koufax UER	175.00	80.00	22.00
(Struck ou 18)			
☐ 6 Marv Breeding	5.00	2.20	.60
☐ 7 Frank Thomas	6.00	2.70	.75
☐ 8 Ray Herbert	5.00	2.20	.60
☐ 9 Jim Davenport	5.50	2.50	.70
☐ 10 Bob Clemente	225.00	100.00	28.00
☐ 11 Tom Morgan	5.00	2.20	.60
☐ 12 Harry Craft MG	5.50	2.50	.70
☐ 13 Dick Howser	5.50	2.50	.70
☐ 14 Bill White	5.50	2.50	.70
☐ 15 Dick Donovan	5.00	2.20	.60
☐ 16 Darrell Johnson	5.00	2.20	.60
☐ 17 John Callison	5.50	2.50	.70
☐ 18 Managers' Dream	200.00	90.00	25.00
Mickey Mantle			
Willie Mays			
☐ 19 Ray Washburn	5.00	2.20	.60
☐ 20 Rocky Colavito	15.00	6.75	1.85
☐ 21 Jim Kaat	8.00	3.60	1.00
☐ 22A Checklist 1 ERR	12.00	2.40	1.20
(121-176 on back)			
☐ 22B Checklist 1 COR	12.00	2.40	1.20
☐ 23 Norm Larker	5.00	2.20	.60
☐ 24 Tigers Team	8.00	3.60	1.00
☐ 25 Ernie Banks	45.00	20.00	5.50
☐ 26 Chris Cannizzaro	6.00	2.70	.75
☐ 27 Chuck Cottier	5.00	2.20	.60
☐ 28 Minnie Minoso	7.00	3.10	.85
☐ 29 Casey Stengel MG	20.00	9.00	2.50
☐ 30 Eddie Mathews	25.00	11.00	3.10
☐ 31 Tom Tresh	20.00	9.00	2.50
☐ 32 John Roseboro	6.00	2.70	.75
☐ 33 Don Larsen	5.50	2.50	.70
☐ 34 Johnny Temple	5.50	2.50	.70
☐ 35 Don Schwall	5.50	2.50	.70
☐ 36 Don Leppert	5.00	2.20	.60
☐ 37 Tribe Hill Trio	5.00	2.20	.60
Barry Latman			
Dick Stigman			
Jim Perry			
☐ 38 Gene Stephens	5.00	2.20	.60
☐ 39 Joe Koppe	5.00	2.20	.60
☐ 40 Orlando Cepeda	14.00	6.25	1.75
☐ 41 Cliff Cook	5.00	2.20	.60
☐ 42 Jim King	5.00	2.20	.60
☐ 43 Los Angeles Dodgers	8.00	3.60	1.00
Team Card			
☐ 44 Don Taussig	5.00	2.20	.60
☐ 45 Brooks Robinson	45.00	20.00	5.50
☐ 46 Jack Daldschun	5.00	2.20	.60
☐ 47 Bob Will	5.00	2.20	.60
☐ 48 Ralph Terry	6.00	2.70	.75
☐ 49 Hal Jones	5.00	2.20	.60
☐ 50 Stan Musial	100.00	45.00	12.50
☐ 51 AL Batting Leaders	8.00	3.60	1.00
Norm Cash			
Jim Piersall			
Al Kaline			
Elston Howard			
☐ 52 NL Batting Leaders	15.00	6.75	1.85
Bob Clemente			
Vada Pinson			
Ken Boyer			
Wally Moon			
☐ 53 AL Home Run Leaders	110.00	50.00	14.00
Roger Maris			
Mickey Mantle			
Jim Gentile			
Harmon Killebrew			
☐ 54 NL Home Run Leaders	14.00	6.25	1.75
Orlando Cepeda			
Willie Mays			
Frank Robinson			
☐ 55 AL ERA Leaders	7.00	3.10	.85
Dick Donovan			
Bill Stafford			
Don Mossi			
Milt Pappas			
☐ 56 NL ERA Leaders	8.00	3.60	1.00
Warren Spahn			
Jim O'Toole			
Curt Simmons			
Mike McCormick			
☐ 57 AL Wins Leaders	8.00	3.60	1.00
Whitey Ford			
Frank Lary			
Steve Barber			
Jim Bunning			
☐ 58 NL Wins Leaders	8.00	3.60	1.00
Warren Spahn			
Joe Jay			
Jim O'Toole			
☐ 59 AL Strikeout Leaders	8.00	3.60	1.00
Camilo Pascual			
Whitey Ford			
Jim Bunning			
Juan Pizzaro			
☐ 60 NL Strikeout Leaders	12.00	5.50	1.50
Sandy Koufax			
Stan Williams			
Don Drysdale			
Jim O'Toole			
☐ 61 Cardinals Team	8.00	3.60	1.00
☐ 62 Steve Boros	5.00	2.20	.60
☐ 63 Tony Cloninger	5.50	2.50	.70
☐ 64 Russ Snyder	5.00	2.20	.60
☐ 65 Bobby Richardson	12.00	5.50	1.50
☐ 66 Cuno Barragan	5.00	2.20	.60
☐ 67 Harvey Haddix	5.50	2.50	.70
☐ 68 Ken Hunt	5.00	2.20	.60
☐ 69 Phil Ortega	5.00	2.20	.60
☐ 70 Harmon Killebrew	25.00	11.00	3.10
☐ 71 Dick LeMay	5.00	2.20	.60
☐ 72 Bob's Pupils	5.00	2.20	.60
Steve Boros			
Bob Scheffing MG			
Jake Wood			
☐ 73 Nellie Fox	16.00	7.25	2.00
☐ 74 Bob Lillis	5.50	2.50	.70
☐ 75 Milt Pappas	5.50	2.50	.70
☐ 76 Howie Bedell	5.00	2.20	.60
☐ 77 Tony Taylor	5.50	2.50	.70
☐ 78 Gene Green	5.00	2.20	.60
☐ 79 Ed Hobaugh	5.00	2.20	.60
☐ 80 Vada Pinson	7.00	3.10	.85
☐ 81 Jim Pagliaroni	5.00	2.20	.60
☐ 82 Deron Johnson	5.50	2.50	.70
☐ 83 Larry Jackson	5.00	2.20	.60
☐ 84 Lenny Green	5.00	2.20	.60
☐ 85 Gil Hodges	15.00	6.75	1.85
☐ 86 Donn Clendenon	5.50	2.50	.70
☐ 87 Mike Roarke	5.00	2.20	.60
☐ 88 Ralph Houk MG	5.50	2.50	.70
(Berra in background)			
☐ 89 Barney Schultz	5.00	2.20	.60
☐ 90 Jim Piersall	5.50	2.50	.70
☐ 91 J.C. Martin	5.00	2.20	.60
☐ 92 Sam Jones	5.00	2.20	.60
☐ 93 John Blanchard	6.00	2.70	.75
☐ 94 Jay Hook	6.00	2.70	.75
☐ 95 Don Hoak	5.50	2.50	.70
☐ 96 Eli Grba	5.00	2.20	.60
☐ 97 Tito Francona	5.00	2.20	.60
☐ 98 Checklist 2	12.00	2.40	1.20
☐ 99 John (Boog) Powell	30.00	13.50	3.70

☐ 100 Warren Spahn 30.00 13.50 3.70
☐ 101 Carroll Hardy 5.00 2.20 .60
☐ 102 Al Schroll 5.00 2.20 .60
☐ 103 Don Blasingame 5.00 2.20 .60
☐ 104 Ted Savage 5.00 2.20 .60
☐ 105 Don Mossi 5.50 2.50 .70
☐ 106 Carl Sawatski 5.00 2.20 .60
☐ 107 Mike McCormick 5.50 2.50 .70
☐ 108 Willie Davis 6.00 2.70 .75
☐ 109 Bob Shaw 5.00 2.20 .60
☐ 110 Bill Skowron 7.00 3.10 .85
☐ 111 Dallas Green 5.50 2.50 .70
☐ 112 Hank Foiles 5.00 2.20 .60
☐ 113 Chicago White Sox 8.00 3.60 1.00
Team Card
☐ 114 Howie Koplitz 5.00 2.20 .60
☐ 115 Bob Skinner 5.50 2.50 .70
☐ 116 Herb Score 5.50 2.50 .70
☐ 117 Gary Geiger 5.00 2.20 .60
☐ 118 Julian Javier 5.50 2.50 .70
☐ 119 Danny Murphy 5.00 2.20 .60
☐ 120 Bob Purkey 5.00 2.20 .60
☐ 121 Billy Hitchcock MG 5.00 2.20 .60
☐ 122 Norm Bass 5.00 2.20 .60
☐ 123 Mike de la Hoz 5.00 2.20 .60
☐ 124 Bill Pleis 5.00 2.20 .60
☐ 125 Gene Woodling 5.50 2.50 .70
☐ 126 Al Cicotte 5.00 2.20 .60
☐ 127 Pride of A's 5.00 2.20 .60
Norm Siebern
Hank Bauer MG
Jerry Lumpe
☐ 128 Art Fowler 5.00 2.20 .60
☐ 129A Lee Walls 5.00 2.20 .60
(Facing right)
☐ 129B Lee Walls 25.00 11.00 3.10
(Facing left)
☐ 130 Frank Bolling 5.00 2.20 .60
☐ 131 Pete Richert 5.00 2.20 .60
☐ 132A Angels Team 8.00 3.60 1.00
(Without photo)
☐ 132B Angels Team 25.00 11.00 3.10
(With photo)
☐ 133 Felipe Alou 5.50 2.50 .70
☐ 134A Billy Hoeft 5.00 2.20 .60
(Facing right)
☐ 134B Billy Hoeft 25.00 11.00 3.10
(Facing straight)
☐ 135 Babe Ruth Special 1 20.00 9.00 2.50
Babe as a Boy
☐ 136 Babe Ruth Special 2 20.00 9.00 2.50
Babe Joins Yanks
☐ 137 Babe Ruth Special 3 20.00 9.00 2.50
With Miller Huggins
☐ 138 Babe Ruth Special 4 20.00 9.00 2.50
Famous Slugger
☐ 139A Babe Ruth Special 5 30.00 13.50 3.70
Babe Hits 60
☐ 139B Hal Reniff PORT 12.00 5.50 1.50
☐ 139C Hal Reniff 65.00 29.00 8.00
(Pitching)
☐ 140 Babe Ruth Special 6 50.00 22.00 6.25
With Lou Gehrig
☐ 141 Babe Ruth Special 7 20.00 9.00 2.50
Twilight Years
☐ 142 Babe Ruth Special 8 20.00 9.00 2.50
Coaching Dodgers
☐ 143 Babe Ruth Special 9 20.00 9.00 2.50
Greatest Sports Hero
☐ 144 Babe Ruth Special 10 20.00 9.00 2.50
Farewell Speech
☐ 145 Barry Latman 5.00 2.20 .60
☐ 146 Don Demeter 5.00 2.20 .60
☐ 147A Bill Kunkel PORT 5.00 2.20 .60
☐ 147B Bill Kunkel 25.00 11.00 3.10
(Pitching pose)
☐ 148 Wally Post 5.00 2.20 .60
☐ 149 Bob Duliba 5.00 2.20 .60
☐ 150 Al Kaline 45.00 20.00 5.50
☐ 151 Johnny Klippstein 5.00 2.20 .60
☐ 152 Mickey Vernon MG 5.50 2.50 .70
☐ 153 Pumpsie Green 5.50 2.50 .70
☐ 154 Lee Thomas 5.50 2.50 .70
☐ 155 Stu Miller 5.50 2.50 .70
☐ 156 Merritt Ranew 5.00 2.20 .60
☐ 157 Wes Covington 5.50 2.50 .70
☐ 158 Braves Team 8.00 3.60 1.00
☐ 159 Hal Reniff 5.50 2.50 .70
☐ 160 Dick Stuart 5.50 2.50 .70
☐ 161 Frank Baumann 5.00 2.20 .60
☐ 162 Sammy Drake 5.00 2.20 .60
☐ 163 Hot Corner Guard 6.00 2.70 .75
Billy Gardner
Cletis Boyer
☐ 164 Hal Naragon 5.00 2.20 .60
☐ 165 Jackie Brandt 5.00 2.20 .60
☐ 166 Don Lee 5.00 2.20 .60
☐ 167 Tim McCarver 30.00 13.50 3.70
☐ 168 Leo Posada 5.00 2.20 .60
☐ 169 Bob Cerv 5.50 2.50 .70
☐ 170 Ron Santo 14.00 6.25 1.75
☐ 171 Dave Sisler 5.00 2.20 .60
☐ 172 Fred Hutchinson MG 5.50 2.50 .70
☐ 173 Chico Fernandez 5.00 2.20 .60
☐ 174A Carl Willey 5.00 2.20 .60
(Capless)
☐ 174B Carl Willey 25.00 11.00 3.10
(With cap)
☐ 175 Frank Howard 6.00 2.70 .75
☐ 176A Eddie Yost PORT 5.00 2.20 .60
☐ 176B Eddie Yost BATTING 28.00 12.50 3.50
☐ 177 Bobby Shantz 5.50 2.50 .70
☐ 178 Camilo Carreon 5.00 2.20 .60
☐ 179 Tom Sturdivant 5.00 2.20 .60
☐ 180 Bob Allison 5.50 2.50 .70
☐ 181 Paul Brown 5.00 2.20 .60
☐ 182 Bob Nieman 5.00 2.20 .60
☐ 183 Roger Craig 6.00 2.70 .75
☐ 184 Haywood Sullivan 5.50 2.50 .70
☐ 185 Roland Sheldon 6.00 2.70 .75
☐ 186 Mack Jones 5.00 2.20 .60
☐ 187 Gene Conley 5.00 2.20 .60
☐ 188 Chuck Hiller 5.00 2.20 .60
☐ 189 Dick Hall 5.00 2.20 .60
☐ 190A Wally Moon PORT 5.00 2.20 .60
☐ 190B Wally Moon BATTING 28.00 12.50 3.50
☐ 191 Jim Brewer 5.00 2.20 .60
☐ 192A Checklist 3 12.00 2.40 1.20
(Without comma)
☐ 192B Checklist 3 12.00 2.40 1.20
(Comma after Checklist)
☐ 193 Eddie Kasko 5.00 2.20 .60
☐ 194 Dean Chance 5.50 2.50 .70
☐ 195 Joe Cunningham 5.00 2.20 .60
☐ 196 Terry Fox 5.00 2.20 .60
☐ 197 Daryl Spencer 5.00 2.20 .60
☐ 198 Johnny Keane MG 5.00 2.20 .60
☐ 199 Gaylord Perry 80.00 36.00 10.00
☐ 200 Mickey Mantle 450.00 200.00 55.00
☐ 201 Ike Delock 5.00 2.20 .60
☐ 202 Carl Warwick 5.00 2.20 .60
☐ 203 Jack Fisher 5.00 2.20 .60
☐ 204 Johnny Weekly 5.00 2.20 .60
☐ 205 Gene Freese 5.00 2.20 .60
☐ 206 Senators Team 8.00 3.60 1.00
☐ 207 Pete Burnside 5.00 2.20 .60
☐ 208 Billy Martin 14.00 6.25 1.75
☐ 209 Jim Fregosi 14.00 6.25 1.75
☐ 210 Roy Face 5.50 2.50 .70
☐ 211 Midway Masters 5.00 2.20 .60
Frank Bolling
Roy McMillan
☐ 212 Jim Owens 5.00 2.20 .60
☐ 213 Richie Ashburn 20.00 9.00 2.50
☐ 214 Dom Zanni 5.00 2.20 .60
☐ 215 Woody Held 5.00 2.20 .60
☐ 216 Ron Kline 5.00 2.20 .60
☐ 217 Walt Alston MG 7.00 3.10 .85
☐ 218 Joe Torre 40.00 18.00 5.00
☐ 219 Al Downing 6.00 2.70 .75
☐ 220 Roy Sievers 5.50 2.50 .70
☐ 221 Bill Short 5.00 2.20 .60
☐ 222 Jerry Zimmerman 5.00 2.20 .60
☐ 223 Alex Grammas 5.00 2.20 .60
☐ 224 Don Rudolph 5.00 2.20 .60
☐ 225 Frank Malzone 5.50 2.50 .70
☐ 226 San Francisco Giants 8.00 3.60 1.00
Team Card
☐ 227 Bob Tiefenauer 5.00 2.20 .60
☐ 228 Dale Long 5.50 2.50 .70
☐ 229 Jesus McFarlane 5.00 2.20 .60
☐ 230 Camilo Pascual 5.50 2.50 .70
☐ 231 Ernie Bowman 5.00 2.20 .60
☐ 232 World Series Game 1 7.00 3.10 .85
Yanks win opener
☐ 233 Joey Jay WS 7.00 3.10 .85
☐ 234 Roger Maris WS 20.00 9.00 2.50
☐ 235 Whitey Ford WS 10.00 4.50 1.25
sets new mark
☐ 236 World Series Game 5 7.00 3.10 .85
Yanks crush Reds
☐ 237 World Series Summary 7.00 3.10 .85
Yanks celebrate
☐ 238 Norm Sherry 5.00 2.20 .60
☐ 239 Cecil Butler 5.00 2.20 .60
☐ 240 George Altman 5.00 2.20 .60
☐ 241 Johnny Kucks 5.00 2.20 .60
☐ 242 Mel McGaha MG 5.00 2.20 .60
☐ 243 Robin Roberts 16.00 7.25 2.00
☐ 244 Don Gile 5.00 2.20 .60
☐ 245 Ron Hansen 5.00 2.20 .60
☐ 246 Art Ditmar 5.00 2.20 .60
☐ 247 Joe Pignatano 5.00 2.20 .60
☐ 248 Bob Aspromonte 5.50 2.50 .70
☐ 249 Ed Keegan 5.00 2.20 .60
☐ 250 Norm Cash 8.00 3.60 1.00
☐ 251 New York Yankees 60.00 27.00 7.50
Team Card
☐ 252 Earl Francis 5.00 2.20 .60
☐ 253 Harry Chiti MG 5.00 2.20 .60
☐ 254 Gordon Windhorn 5.00 2.20 .60
☐ 255 Juan Pizarro 5.00 2.20 .60
☐ 256 Elio Chacon 6.00 2.70 .75
☐ 257 Jack Spring 5.00 2.20 .60
☐ 258 Marty Keough 5.00 2.20 .60
☐ 259 Lou Klimchock 5.00 2.20 .60
☐ 260 Billy Pierce 5.50 2.50 .70
☐ 261 George Alusik 5.00 2.20 .60
☐ 262 Bob Schmidt 5.00 2.20 .60
☐ 263 The Right Pitch 5.00 2.20 .60
Bob Purkey
Jim Turner CO
Joe Jay
☐ 264 Dick Ellsworth 5.50 2.50 .70
☐ 265 Joe Adcock 5.50 2.50 .70
☐ 266 John Anderson 5.00 2.20 .60
☐ 267 Dan Dobbek 5.00 2.20 .60
☐ 268 Ken McBride 5.00 2.20 .60
☐ 269 Bob Oldis 5.00 2.20 .60
☐ 270 Dick Groat 5.50 2.50 .70
☐ 271 Ray Rippelmeyer 5.00 2.20 .60
☐ 272 Earl Robinson 5.00 2.20 .60
☐ 273 Gary Bell 5.00 2.20 .60
☐ 274 Sammy Taylor 5.00 2.20 .60
☐ 275 Norm Siebern 5.00 2.20 .60
☐ 276 Hal Kolstad 5.00 2.20 .60
☐ 277 Checklist 4 12.00 2.40 1.20
☐ 278 Ken Johnson 5.50 2.50 .70
☐ 279 Hobie Landrith UER 5.50 2.50 .70
(Wrong birthdate)
☐ 280 Johnny Podres 6.00 2.70 .75
☐ 281 Jake Gibbs 6.00 2.70 .75
☐ 282 Dave Hillman 5.00 2.20 .60
☐ 283 Charlie Smith 5.00 2.20 .60
☐ 284 Ruben Amaro 5.00 2.20 .60
☐ 285 Curt Simmons 5.50 2.50 .70
☐ 286 Al Lopez MG 6.00 2.70 .75
☐ 287 George Witt 5.00 2.20 .60
☐ 288 Billy Williams 30.00 13.50 3.70
☐ 289 Mike Krsnich 5.00 2.20 .60
☐ 290 Jim Gentile 5.50 2.50 .70
☐ 291 Hal Stowe 5.00 2.20 .60
☐ 292 Jerry Kindall 5.00 2.20 .60
☐ 293 Bob Miller 5.50 2.50 .70
☐ 294 Phillies Team 9.00 4.00 1.10
☐ 295 Vern Law 5.50 2.50 .70
☐ 296 Ken Hamlin 5.00 2.20 .60
☐ 297 Ron Perranoski 5.50 2.50 .70
☐ 298 Bill Tuttle 5.00 2.20 .60
☐ 299 Don Wert 5.00 2.20 .60
☐ 300 Willie Mays 150.00 70.00 19.00
☐ 301 Galen Cisco 5.00 2.20 .60
☐ 302 Johnny Edwards 5.00 2.20 .60
☐ 303 Frank Torre 5.50 2.50 .70
☐ 304 Dick Farrell 5.50 2.50 .70
☐ 305 Jerry Lumpe 5.00 2.20 .60
☐ 306 Redbird Rippers 5.00 2.20 .60
Lindy McDaniel
Larry Jackson
☐ 307 Jim Grant 5.50 2.50 .70
☐ 308 Neil Chrisley 5.50 2.50 .70
☐ 309 Moe Morhardt 5.00 2.20 .60
☐ 310 Whitey Ford 45.00 20.00 5.50
☐ 311 Tony Kubek IA 7.00 3.10 .85
☐ 312 Warren Spahn IA 14.00 6.25 1.75
☐ 313 Roger Maris IA 35.00 16.00 4.40
Blasts 61th
☐ 314 Rocky Colavito IA 12.00 5.50 1.50
☐ 315 Whitey Ford IA 15.00 6.75 1.85
☐ 316 Harmon Killebrew IA 15.00 6.75 1.85
☐ 317 Stan Musial IA 20.00 9.00 2.50
☐ 318 Mickey Mantle IA 175.00 80.00 22.00
☐ 319 Mike McCormick IA 5.00 2.20 .60
☐ 320 Hank Aaron 140.00 65.00 17.50
☐ 321 Lee Stange 5.00 2.20 .60
☐ 322 Alvin Dark MG 5.50 2.50 .70
☐ 323 Don Landrum 5.00 2.20 .60
☐ 324 Joe McClain 5.00 2.20 .60
☐ 325 Luis Aparicio 16.00 7.25 2.00
☐ 326 Tom Parsons 5.00 2.20 .60
☐ 327 Ozzie Virgil 5.00 2.20 .60
☐ 328 Ken Walters 5.00 2.20 .60
☐ 329 Bob Bolin 5.00 2.20 .60
☐ 330 John Romano 5.00 2.20 .60
☐ 331 Moe Drabowsky 5.50 2.50 .70
☐ 332 Don Buddin 5.00 2.20 .60
☐ 333 Frank Cipriani 5.00 2.20 .60
☐ 334 Boston Red Sox 9.00 4.00 1.10
Team Card
☐ 335 Bill Bruton 5.00 2.20 .60
☐ 336 Billy Muffett 5.00 2.20 .60
☐ 337 Jim Marshall 6.00 2.70 .75
☐ 338 Billy Gardner 5.00 2.20 .60
☐ 339 Jose Valdivielso 5.00 2.20 .60
☐ 340 Don Drysdale 35.00 16.00 4.40
☐ 341 Mike Hershberger 5.00 2.20 .60
☐ 342 Ed Rakow 5.00 2.20 .60
☐ 343 Albie Pearson 5.50 2.50 .70
☐ 344 Ed Bauta 5.00 2.20 .60
☐ 345 Chuck Schilling 5.00 2.20 .60
☐ 346 Jack Kralick 5.00 2.20 .60
☐ 347 Chuck Hinton 5.00 2.20 .60
☐ 348 Larry Burright 6.00 2.70 .75
☐ 349 Paul Foytack 5.00 2.20 .60
☐ 350 Frank Robinson 45.00 20.00 5.50
☐ 351 Braves' Backstops 8.00 3.60 1.00
Joe Torre
Del Crandall
☐ 352 Frank Sullivan 5.00 2.20 .60
☐ 353 Bill Mazeroski 10.00 4.50 1.25
☐ 354 Roman Mejias 5.50 2.50 .70
☐ 355 Steve Barber 5.00 2.20 .60
☐ 356 Tom Haller 5.00 2.20 .60
☐ 357 Jerry Walker 5.00 2.20 .60
☐ 358 Tommy Davis 6.00 2.70 .75
☐ 359 Bobby Locke 5.00 2.20 .60
☐ 360 Yogi Berra 75.00 34.00 9.50
☐ 361 Bob Hendley 5.00 2.20 .60
☐ 362 Ty Cline 5.00 2.20 .60
☐ 363 Bob Roselli 5.00 2.20 .60
☐ 364 Ken Hunt 5.00 2.20 .60
☐ 365 Charlie Neal 6.00 2.70 .75
☐ 366 Phil Regan 6.00 2.70 .75
☐ 367 Checklist 5 12.00 2.40 1.20
☐ 368 Bob Tillman 5.00 2.20 .60
☐ 369 Ted Bowsfield 5.00 2.20 .60
☐ 370 Ken Boyer 5.50 2.50 .70
☐ 371 Earl Battey 6.00 2.70 .75
☐ 372 Jack Curtis 6.00 2.70 .75
☐ 373 Al Heist 6.00 2.70 .75
☐ 374 Gene Mauch MG 7.00 3.10 .85
☐ 375 Ron Fairly 7.50 3.40 .95
☐ 376 Bud Daley 7.50 3.40 .95
☐ 377 John Orsino 6.00 2.70 .75
☐ 378 Bennie Daniels 6.00 2.70 .75
☐ 379 Chuck Essegian 6.00 2.70 .75
☐ 380 Lou Burdette 7.00 3.10 .85
☐ 381 Chico Cardenas 7.00 3.10 .85
☐ 382 Dick Williams 7.00 3.10 .85
☐ 383 Ray Sadecki 6.00 2.70 .75
☐ 384 K.C. Athletics 12.00 5.50 1.50
Team Card
☐ 385 Early Wynn 18.00 8.00 2.20
☐ 386 Don Mincher 7.00 3.10 .85
☐ 387 Lou Brock 125.00 55.00 15.50
☐ 388 Ryne Duren 7.00 3.10 .85
☐ 389 Smoky Burgess 7.00 3.10 .85
☐ 390 Orlando Cepeda AS 10.00 4.50 1.25
☐ 391 Bill Mazeroski AS 10.00 4.50 1.25
☐ 392 Ken Boyer AS 7.00 3.10 .85
☐ 393 Roy McMillan AS 6.00 2.70 .75
☐ 394 Hank Aaron AS 45.00 20.00 5.50
☐ 395 Willie Mays AS 50.00 22.00 6.25
☐ 396 Frank Robinson AS 16.00 7.25 2.00
☐ 397 John Roseboro AS 6.00 2.70 .75
☐ 398 Don Drysdale AS 16.00 7.25 2.00
☐ 399 Warren Spahn AS 16.00 7.25 2.00
☐ 400 Elston Howard 10.00 4.50 1.25
☐ 401 AL/NL Homer Kings 60.00 27.00 7.50
Roger Maris
Orlando Cepeda
☐ 402 Gino Cimoli 6.00 2.70 .75
☐ 403 Chet Nichols 6.00 2.70 .75
☐ 404 Tim Harkness 7.50 3.40 .95
☐ 405 Jim Perry 7.00 3.10 .85
☐ 406 Bob Taylor 6.00 2.70 .75
☐ 407 Hank Aguirre 6.00 2.70 .75
☐ 408 Gus Bell 7.00 3.10 .85
☐ 409 Pittsburgh Pirates 12.00 5.50 1.50
Team Card
☐ 410 Al Smith 6.00 2.70 .75
☐ 411 Danny O'Connell 6.00 2.70 .75
☐ 412 Charlie James 6.00 2.70 .75
☐ 413 Matty Alou 7.00 3.10 .85
☐ 414 Joe Gaines 6.00 2.70 .75
☐ 415 Bill Virdon 7.00 3.10 .85
☐ 416 Bob Scheffing MG 6.00 2.70 .75
☐ 417 Joe Azcue 6.00 2.70 .75
☐ 418 Andy Carey 6.00 2.70 .75
☐ 419 Bob Bruce 7.00 3.10 .85
☐ 420 Gus Triandos 7.00 3.10 .85
☐ 421 Ken MacKenzie 7.50 3.40 .95
☐ 422 Steve Bilko 6.00 2.70 .75
☐ 423 Rival League 8.00 3.60 1.00
Relief Aces:
Roy Face
Hoyt Wilhelm
☐ 424 Al McBean 6.00 2.70 .75
☐ 425 Carl Yastrzemski 125.00 55.00 15.50
☐ 426 Bob Farley 6.00 2.70 .75
☐ 427 Jake Wood 6.00 2.70 .75
☐ 428 Joe Hicks 6.00 2.70 .75
☐ 429 Billy O'Dell 6.00 2.70 .75
☐ 430 Tony Kubek 10.00 4.50 1.25
☐ 431 Bob Rodgers 7.00 3.10 .85
☐ 432 Jim Pendleton 6.00 2.70 .75
☐ 433 Jim Archer 6.00 2.70 .75
☐ 434 Clay Dalrymple 6.00 2.70 .75
☐ 435 Larry Sherry 7.00 3.10 .85
☐ 436 Felix Mantilla 7.50 3.40 .95
☐ 437 Ray Moore 6.00 2.70 .75
☐ 438 Dick Brown 6.00 2.70 .75
☐ 439 Jerry Buchek 6.00 2.70 .75
☐ 440 Joey Jay 6.00 2.70 .75
☐ 441 Checklist 6 16.00 7.25 2.00
☐ 442 Wes Stock 6.00 2.70 .75
☐ 443 Del Crandall 7.00 3.10 .85
☐ 444 Ted Wills 6.00 2.70 .75
☐ 445 Vic Power 7.00 3.10 .85
☐ 446 Don Elston 6.00 2.70 .75
☐ 447 Willie Kirkland 12.00 5.50 1.50
☐ 448 Joe Gibbon 12.00 5.50 1.50
☐ 449 Jerry Adair 12.00 5.50 1.50
☐ 450 Jim O'Toole 13.00 5.75 1.60
☐ 451 Jose Tartabull 15.00 6.75 1.85
☐ 452 Earl Averill Jr. 12.00 5.50 1.50
☐ 453 Cal McLish 12.00 5.50 1.50
☐ 454 Floyd Robinson 12.00 5.50 1.50
☐ 455 Luis Arroyo 15.00 6.75 1.85
☐ 456 Joe Amalfitano 13.00 5.75 1.60
☐ 457 Lou Clinton 12.00 5.50 1.50

☐ 458A Bob Buhl (Braves emblem on cap)	13.00	5.75	1.60
☐ 458B Bob Buhl (No emblem on cap)	50.00	22.00	6.25
☐ 459 Ed Bailey	12.00	5.50	1.50
☐ 460 Jim Bunning	18.00	8.00	2.20
☐ 461 Ken Hubbs	35.00	16.00	4.40
☐ 462A Willie Tasby (Senators emblem on cap)	12.00	5.50	1.50
☐ 462B Willie Tasby (No emblem on cap)	50.00	22.00	6.25
☐ 463 Hank Bauer MG	15.00	6.75	1.85
☐ 464 Al Jackson	15.00	6.75	1.85
☐ 465 Reds Team	16.00	7.25	2.00
☐ 466 Norm Cash AS	13.00	5.75	1.60
☐ 467 Chuck Schilling AS	12.00	5.50	1.50
☐ 468 Brooks Robinson AS	25.00	11.00	3.10
☐ 469 Luis Aparicio AS	16.00	7.25	2.00
☐ 470 Al Kaline AS	25.00	11.00	3.10
☐ 471 Mickey Mantle AS	200.00	90.00	25.00
☐ 472 Rocky Colavito AS	16.00	7.25	2.00
☐ 473 Elston Howard AS	15.00	6.75	1.85
☐ 474 Frank Lary AS	12.00	5.50	1.50
☐ 475 Whitey Ford AS	16.00	7.25	2.00
☐ 476 Orioles Team	16.00	7.25	2.00
☐ 477 Andre Rodgers	12.00	5.50	1.50
☐ 478 Don Zimmer (Shown with Mets cap, but listed as with Cincinnati)	15.00	6.75	1.85
☐ 479 Joel Horlen	12.00	5.50	1.50
☐ 480 Harvey Kuenn	15.00	6.75	1.85
☐ 481 Vic Wertz	15.00	6.75	1.85
☐ 482 Sam Mele MG	12.00	5.50	1.50
☐ 483 Don McMahon	12.00	5.50	1.50
☐ 484 Dick Schofield	12.00	5.50	1.50
☐ 485 Pedro Ramos	12.00	5.50	1.50
☐ 486 Jim Gilliam	15.00	6.75	1.85
☐ 487 Jerry Lynch	12.00	5.50	1.50
☐ 488 Hal Brown	12.00	5.50	1.50
☐ 489 Julio Gotay	12.00	5.50	1.50
☐ 490 Clete Boyer	15.00	6.75	1.85
☐ 491 Leon Wagner	12.00	5.50	1.50
☐ 492 Hal W. Smith	13.00	5.75	1.60
☐ 493 Danny McDevitt	12.00	5.50	1.50
☐ 494 Sammy White	12.00	5.50	1.50
☐ 495 Don Cardwell	12.00	5.50	1.50
☐ 496 Wayne Causey	12.00	5.50	1.50
☐ 497 Ed Bouchee	15.00	6.75	1.85
☐ 498 Jim Donohue	12.00	5.50	1.50
☐ 499 Zoilo Versalles	13.00	5.75	1.60
☐ 500 Duke Snider	50.00	22.00	6.25
☐ 501 Claude Osteen	13.00	5.75	1.60
☐ 502 Hector Lopez	15.00	6.75	1.85
☐ 503 Danny Murtaugh MG	13.00	5.75	1.60
☐ 504 Eddie Bressoud	12.00	5.50	1.50
☐ 505 Juan Marichal	45.00	20.00	5.50
☐ 506 Charlie Maxwell	13.00	5.75	1.60
☐ 507 Ernie Broglio	13.00	5.75	1.60
☐ 508 Gordy Coleman	13.00	5.75	1.60
☐ 509 Dave Giusti	15.00	6.75	1.85
☐ 510 Jim Lemon	12.00	5.50	1.50
☐ 511 Bubba Phillips	12.00	5.50	1.50
☐ 512 Mike Fornieles	12.00	5.50	1.50
☐ 513 Whitey Herzog	15.00	6.75	1.85
☐ 514 Sherm Lollar	13.00	5.75	1.60
☐ 515 Stan Williams	15.00	6.75	1.85
☐ 516 Checklist 7	16.00	3.20	1.60
☐ 517 Dave Wickersham	12.00	5.50	1.50
☐ 518 Lee Maye	12.00	5.50	1.50
☐ 519 Bob Johnson	12.00	5.50	1.50
☐ 520 Bob Friend	15.00	6.75	1.85
☐ 521 Jacke Davis UER (Listed as OF on front and P on back)	12.00	5.50	1.50
☐ 522 Lindy McDaniel	13.00	5.75	1.60
☐ 523 Russ Nixon SP	32.00	14.50	4.00
☐ 524 Howie Nunn SP	32.00	14.50	4.00
☐ 525 George Thomas	20.00	9.00	2.50
☐ 526 Hal Woodeshick SP	32.00	14.50	4.00
☐ 527 Dick McAuliffe	25.00	11.00	3.10
☐ 528 Turk Lown	20.00	9.00	2.50
☐ 529 John Schaive SP	32.00	14.50	4.00
☐ 530 Bob Gibson SP	150.00	70.00	19.00
☐ 531 Bobby G. Smith	20.00	9.00	2.50
☐ 532 Dick Stigman	20.00	9.00	2.50
☐ 533 Charley Lau SP	35.00	16.00	4.40
☐ 534 Tony Gonzalez SP	32.00	14.50	4.00
☐ 535 Ed Roebuck	20.00	9.00	2.50
☐ 536 Dick Gernert	20.00	9.00	2.50
☐ 537 Cleveland Indians Team Card	50.00	22.00	6.25
☐ 538 Jack Sanford	20.00	9.00	2.50
☐ 539 Billy Moran	20.00	9.00	2.50
☐ 540 Jim Landis SP	32.00	14.50	4.00
☐ 541 Don Nottebart SP	32.00	14.50	4.00
☐ 542 Dave Philley	20.00	9.00	2.50
☐ 543 Bob Allen SP	32.00	14.50	4.00
☐ 544 Willie McCovey SP	115.00	52.50	14.50
☐ 545 Hoyt Wilhelm SP	50.00	22.00	6.25
☐ 546 Moe Thacker SP	32.00	14.50	4.00
☐ 547 Don Ferrarese	20.00	9.00	2.50
☐ 548 Bobby Del Greco	20.00	9.00	2.50
☐ 549 Bill Rigney MG SP	32.00	14.50	4.00
☐ 550 Art Mahaffey SP	32.00	14.50	4.00
☐ 551 Harry Bright	20.00	9.00	2.50
☐ 552 Chicago Cubs SP Team Card	55.00	25.00	7.00
☐ 553 Jim Coates	25.00	11.00	3.10
☐ 554 Bubba Morton SP	32.00	14.50	4.00
☐ 555 John Buzhardt SP	32.00	14.50	4.00
☐ 556 Al Spangler	20.00	9.00	2.50
☐ 557 Bob Anderson SP	32.00	14.50	4.00
☐ 558 John Goryl	20.00	9.00	2.50
☐ 559 Mike Higgins MG	20.00	9.00	2.50
☐ 560 Chuck Estrada SP	32.00	14.50	4.00
☐ 561 Gene Oliver SP	32.00	14.50	4.00
☐ 562 Bill Henry	20.00	9.00	2.50
☐ 563 Ken Aspromonte	20.00	9.00	2.50
☐ 564 Bob Grim	20.00	9.00	2.50
☐ 565 Jose Pagan	20.00	9.00	2.50
☐ 566 Marty Kutyna SP	32.00	14.50	4.00
☐ 567 Tracy Stallard SP	32.00	14.50	4.00
☐ 568 Jim Golden	20.00	9.00	2.50
☐ 569 Ed Sadowski SP	32.00	14.50	4.00
☐ 570 Bill Stafford SP	32.00	14.50	4.00
☐ 571 Billy Klaus SP	32.00	14.50	4.00
☐ 572 Bob G. Miller SP	35.00	16.00	4.40
☐ 573 Johnny Logan	20.00	9.00	2.50
☐ 574 Dean Stone	20.00	9.00	2.50
☐ 575 Red Schoendienst SP	45.00	20.00	5.50
☐ 576 Russ Kemmerer SP	32.00	14.50	4.00
☐ 577 Dave Nicholson SP	32.00	14.50	4.00
☐ 578 Jim Duffalo	20.00	9.00	2.50
☐ 579 Jim Schaffer SP	32.00	14.50	4.00
☐ 580 Bill Monbouquette	20.00	9.00	2.50
☐ 581 Mel Roach	20.00	9.00	2.50
☐ 582 Ron Piche	20.00	9.00	2.50
☐ 583 Larry Osborne	20.00	9.00	2.50
☐ 584 Minnesota Twins SP Team Card	55.00	25.00	7.00
☐ 585 Glen Hobbie SP	32.00	14.50	4.00
☐ 586 Sammy Esposito SP	32.00	14.50	4.00
☐ 587 Frank Funk SP	32.00	14.50	4.00
☐ 588 Birdie Tebbetts MG	20.00	9.00	2.50
☐ 589 Bob Turley	25.00	11.00	3.10
☐ 590 Curt Flood	30.00	13.50	3.70
☐ 591 Rookie Pitchers SP Sam McDowell Ron Taylor Ron Nischwitz Art Quirk Dick Radatz	70.00	32.00	8.75
☐ 592 Rookie Pitchers SP Dan Pfister Bo Belinsky Dave Stenhouse Jim Bouton Joe Bonikowski	70.00	32.00	8.75
☐ 593 Rookie Pitchers SP Jack Lamabe Craig Anderson Jack Hamilton Bob Moorhead Bob Veale	45.00	20.00	5.50
☐ 594 Rookie Catchers SP Doc Edwards Ken Retzer Bob Uecker Doug Camilli Don Pavletich	75.00	34.00	9.50
☐ 595 Rookie Infielders SP Bob Sadowski Felix Torres Marlan Coughtry Ed Charles	45.00	20.00	5.50
☐ 596 Rookie Infielders SP Bernie Allen Joe Pepitone Phil Linz Rich Rollins	70.00	32.00	8.75
☐ 597 Rookie Infielders SP Jim McKnight Rod Kanehl Amado Samuel Denis Menke	45.00	20.00	5.50
☐ 598 Rookie Outfielders SP Al Luplow Manny Jimenez Howie Goss Jim Hickman Ed Olivares	80.00	23.00	8.00

1962 Topps Bucks

There are 96 "Baseball Bucks" in this unusual set released in its own one-cent package in 1962. Each "buck" measures 1 3/4" by 4 1/8". Each depicts a player with accompanying biography and facsimile autograph to the left. To the right is found a drawing of the player's home stadium. His team and position are listed under the ribbon design containing his name. The team affiliation and league are also indicated within circles on the reverse.

	NRMT	VG-E	GOOD
COMPLETE SET (96)	1250.00	550.00	160.00
COMMON BUCK (1-96)	4.50	2.00	.55
WRAPPER (5-CENT)	60.00	27.00	7.50

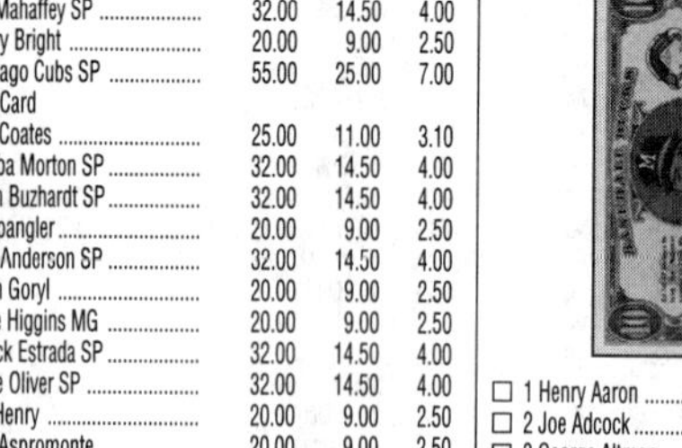

☐ 1 Henry Aaron	60.00	27.00	7.50
☐ 2 Joe Adcock	6.00	2.70	.75
☐ 3 George Altman	4.50	2.00	.55
☐ 4 Jim Archer	4.50	2.00	.55
☐ 5 Richie Ashburn	25.00	11.00	3.10
☐ 6 Ernie Banks	35.00	16.00	4.40
☐ 7 Earl Battey	4.50	2.00	.55
☐ 8 Gus Bell	4.50	2.00	.55
☐ 9 Yogi Berra	40.00	18.00	5.00
☐ 10 Ken Boyer	8.00	3.60	1.00
☐ 11 Jackie Brandt	4.50	2.00	.55
☐ 12 Jim Bunning	25.00	11.00	3.10
☐ 13 Lew Burdette	6.00	2.70	.75
☐ 14 Don Cardwell	4.50	2.00	.55
☐ 15 Norm Cash	8.00	3.60	1.00
☐ 16 Orlando Cepeda	15.00	6.75	1.85
☐ 17 Bob Clemente	100.00	45.00	12.50
☐ 18 Rocky Colavito	15.00	6.75	1.85
☐ 19 Chuck Cottier	4.50	2.00	.55
☐ 20 Roger Craig	6.00	2.70	.75
☐ 21 Bennie Daniels	4.50	2.00	.55
☐ 22 Don Demeter	4.50	2.00	.55
☐ 23 Don Drysdale	25.00	11.00	3.10
☐ 24 Chuck Estrada	4.50	2.00	.55
☐ 25 Dick Farrell	4.50	2.00	.55
☐ 26 Whitey Ford	40.00	18.00	5.00
☐ 27 Nellie Fox	25.00	11.00	3.10
☐ 27 Nelson Fox	25.00	11.00	3.10
☐ 28 Tito Francona	4.50	2.00	.55
☐ 29 Bob Friend	4.50	2.00	.55
☐ 30 Jim Gentile	6.00	2.70	.75
☐ 31 Dick Gernert	4.50	2.00	.55
☐ 32 Lenny Green	4.50	2.00	.55
☐ 33 Dick Groat	6.00	2.70	.75
☐ 34 Woodie Held	4.50	2.00	.55
☐ 35 Don Hoak	4.50	2.00	.55
☐ 36 Gil Hodges	25.00	11.00	3.10
☐ 37 Elston Howard	15.00	6.75	1.85
☐ 38 Frank Howard	8.00	3.60	1.00
☐ 39 Dick Howser	6.00	2.70	.75
☐ 40 Ken Hunt	4.50	2.00	.55
☐ 41 Larry Jackson	4.50	2.00	.55
☐ 42 Joey Jay	4.50	2.00	.55
☐ 43 Al Kaline	35.00	16.00	4.40
☐ 44 Harmon Killebrew	25.00	11.00	3.10
☐ 45 Sandy Koufax	50.00	22.00	6.25
☐ 46 Harvey Kuenn	6.00	2.70	.75
☐ 47 Jim Landis	4.50	2.00	.55
☐ 48 Norm Larker	4.50	2.00	.55
☐ 49 Frank Lary	4.50	2.00	.55
☐ 50 Jerry Lumpe	4.50	2.00	.55
☐ 51 Art Mahaffey	4.50	2.00	.55
☐ 52 Frank Malzone	4.50	2.00	.55
☐ 53 Felix Mantilla	4.50	2.00	.55
☐ 54 Mickey Mantle	200.00	90.00	25.00
☐ 55 Roger Maris	50.00	22.00	6.25
☐ 56 Eddie Mathews	25.00	11.00	3.10
☐ 57 Willie Mays	60.00	27.00	7.50
☐ 58 Ken McBride	4.50	2.00	.55
☐ 59 Mike McCormick	4.50	2.00	.55
☐ 60 Stu Miller	4.50	2.00	.55
☐ 61 Minnie Minoso	10.00	4.50	1.25
☐ 62 Wally Moon	6.00	2.70	.75
☐ 63 Stan Musial	60.00	27.00	7.50
☐ 64 Danny O'Connell	4.50	2.00	.55
☐ 65 Jim O'Toole	4.50	2.00	.55
☐ 66 Camilo Pascual	4.50	2.00	.55
☐ 67 Jim Perry	6.00	2.70	.75
☐ 68 Jimmy Piersall	6.00	2.70	.75
☐ 69 Vada Pinson	10.00	4.50	1.25
☐ 70 Juan Pizarro	4.50	2.00	.55
☐ 71 Johnny Podres	6.00	2.70	.75
☐ 72 Vic Power	4.50	2.00	.55
☐ 73 Bob Purkey	4.50	2.00	.55
☐ 74 Pedro Ramos	4.50	2.00	.55
☐ 75 Brooks Robinson	35.00	16.00	4.40
☐ 76 Floyd Robinson	4.50	2.00	.55
☐ 77 Frank Robinson	35.00	16.00	4.40
☐ 78 John Romano	4.50	2.00	.55
☐ 79 Pete Runnels	4.50	2.00	.55
☐ 80 Don Schwall	4.50	2.00	.55
☐ 81 Bobby Shantz	4.50	2.00	.55
☐ 82 Norm Siebern	4.50	2.00	.55
☐ 83 Roy Sievers	4.50	2.00	.55
☐ 84 Hal Smith	4.50	2.00	.55
☐ 85 Warren Spahn	25.00	11.00	3.10
☐ 86 Dick Stuart	6.00	2.70	.75
☐ 87 Tony Taylor	4.50	2.00	.55
☐ 88 Leroy Thomas	6.00	2.70	.75
☐ 89 Gus Triandos	4.50	2.00	.55
☐ 90 Leon Wagner	4.50	2.00	.55
☐ 91 Jerry Walker	4.50	2.00	.55
☐ 92 Bill White	8.00	3.60	1.00
☐ 93 Billy Williams	25.00	11.00	3.10
☐ 94 Gene Woodling	6.00	2.70	.75
☐ 95 Early Wynn	25.00	11.00	3.10
☐ 96 Carl Yastrzemski	35.00	16.00	4.40

1962 Topps Stamps

The 201 baseball player stamps inserted into the Topps regular issue of 1962 are color photos set upon red or yellow backgrounds (100 players for each color). They came in two-stamp panels with a small additional strip which contained advertising for an album. Roy Sievers appears with Kansas City or Philadelphia; the set price includes both versions. Each stamp measures 1 3/8" by 1 7/8". Stamps are unnumbered but are presented here in alphabetical order by team, Baltimore Orioles AL (1-10), Boston Red Sox (11-20), Chicago White Sox (21-30), Cleveland Indians (31-40), Detroit Tigers (41-50), Kansas City A's (51-61), Los Angeles Angels (62-71), Minnesota Twins (72-81), New York Yankees (82-91), Washington Senators (92-101), Chicago Cubs NL (102-111), Cincinnati Reds (112-121), Houston Colt .45's (122-131), Los Angeles Dodgers (132-141), Milwaukee Braves (142-151), New York Mets (152-161), Philadelphia Phillies (162-171), Pittsburgh Pirates (172-181), St. Louis Cardinals (182-191) and San Francisco Giants (192-201).

	NRMT	VG-E	GOOD
COMPLETE SET (201)	350.00	160.00	45.00
COMMON STAMP (1-201)	.80	.35	.10
☐ 1 Baltimore Emblem	.80	.35	.10
☐ 2 Jerry Adair	.80	.35	.10
☐ 3 Jackie Brandt	.80	.35	.10
☐ 4 Chuck Estrada	.80	.35	.10
☐ 5 Jim Gentile	1.00	.45	.12
☐ 6 Ron Hansen	.80	.35	.10
☐ 7 Milt Pappas	1.00	.45	.12
☐ 8 Brooks Robinson	8.00	3.60	1.00
☐ 9 Gus Triandos	1.00	.45	.12
☐ 10 Hoyt Wilhelm	5.00	2.20	.60
☐ 11 Boston Emblem	.80	.35	.10
☐ 12 Mike Fornieles	.80	.35	.10
☐ 13 Gary Geiger	.80	.35	.10
☐ 14 Frank Malzone	1.00	.45	.12
☐ 15 Bill Monbouquette	.80	.35	.10
☐ 16 Russ Nixon	.80	.35	.10
☐ 17 Pete Runnels	1.00	.45	.12
☐ 18 Chuck Schilling	.80	.35	.10
☐ 19 Don Schwall	.80	.35	.10
☐ 20 Carl Yastrzemski	12.50	5.50	1.55
☐ 21 Chicago Emblem	.80	.35	.10
☐ 22 Luis Aparicio	5.00	2.20	.60
☐ 23 Camilo Carreon	.80	.35	.10
☐ 24 Nellie Fox	5.00	2.20	.60
☐ 25 Ray Herbert	.80	.35	.10
☐ 26 Jim Landis	.80	.35	.10
☐ 27 J.C. Martin	.80	.35	.10
☐ 28 Juan Pizarro	.80	.35	.10
☐ 29 Floyd Robinson	.80	.35	.10
☐ 30 Early Wynn	5.00	2.20	.60
☐ 31 Cleveland Emblem	.80	.35	.10
☐ 32 Ty Cline	.80	.35	.10
☐ 33 Dick Donovan	.80	.35	.10
☐ 34 Tito Francona	.80	.35	.10
☐ 35 Woody Held	.80	.35	.10
☐ 36 Barry Latman	.80	.35	.10
☐ 37 Jim Perry	1.00	.45	.12
☐ 38 Bubba Phillips	.80	.35	.10
☐ 39 Vic Power	.80	.35	.10
☐ 40 Johnny Romano	.80	.35	.10
☐ 41 Detroit Emblem	.80	.35	.10
☐ 42 Steve Boros	1.00	.45	.12
☐ 43 Bill Bruton	.80	.35	.10
☐ 44 Jim Bunning	5.00	2.20	.60
☐ 45 Norm Cash	1.50	.70	.19
☐ 46 Rocky Colavito	4.00	1.80	.50
☐ 47 Al Kaline	8.00	3.60	1.00
☐ 48 Frank Lary	1.00	.45	.12
☐ 49 Don Mossi	1.00	.45	.12
☐ 50 Jake Wood	.80	.35	.10
☐ 51 Kansas City Emblem	.80	.35	.10
☐ 52 Jim Archer	.80	.35	.10
☐ 53 Dick Howser	1.50	.70	.19
☐ 54 Jerry Lumpe	.80	.35	.10
☐ 55 Leo Posada	.80	.35	.10
☐ 56 Bob Shaw	.80	.35	.10
☐ 57 Norm Siebern	.80	.35	.10
☐ 58 Roy Sievers (see also 169)	1.50	.70	.19
☐ 59 Gene Stephens	.80	.35	.10
☐ 60 Haywood Sullivan	.80	.35	.10
☐ 61 Jerry Walker	.80	.35	.10
☐ 62 Los Angeles Emblem	.80	.35	.10

☐ 63 Steve Bilko	.80	.35	.10
☐ 64 Ted Bowsfield	.80	.35	.10
☐ 65 Ken Hunt	.80	.35	.10
☐ 66 Ken McBride	.80	.35	.10
☐ 67 Albie Pearson	.80	.35	.10
☐ 68 Bob Rodgers	1.50	.70	.19
☐ 69 George Thomas	.80	.35	.10
☐ 70 Lee Thomas	1.00	.45	.12
☐ 71 Leon Wagner	.80	.35	.10
☐ 72 Minnesota Emblem	.80	.35	.10
☐ 73 Bob Allison	1.00	.45	.12
☐ 74 Earl Battey	.80	.35	.10
☐ 75 Lenny Green	.80	.35	.10
☐ 76 Harmon Killebrew	6.00	2.70	.75
☐ 77 Jack Kralick	.80	.35	.10
☐ 78 Camilo Pascual	1.00	.45	.12
☐ 79 Pedro Ramos	.80	.35	.10
☐ 80 Bill Tuttle	.80	.35	.10
☐ 81 Zoilo Versailles	.80	.35	.10
☐ 82 New York Emblem	1.00	.45	.12
☐ 83 Yogi Berra	12.50	5.50	1.55
☐ 84 Clete Boyer	1.50	.70	.19
☐ 85 Whitey Ford	10.00	4.50	1.25
☐ 86 Elston Howard	2.00	.90	.25
☐ 87 Tony Kubek	2.50	1.10	.30
☐ 88 Mickey Mantle	60.00	27.00	7.50
☐ 89 Roger Maris	20.00	9.00	2.50
☐ 90 Bobby Richardson	2.50	1.10	.30
☐ 91 Bill Skowron	1.50	.70	.19
☐ 92 Washington Emblem	.80	.35	.10
☐ 93 Chuck Cottier	.80	.35	.10
☐ 94 Pete Daley	.80	.35	.10
☐ 95 Bennie Daniels	.80	.35	.10
☐ 96 Chuck Hinton	.80	.35	.10
☐ 97 Bob Johnson	.80	.35	.10
☐ 98 Joe McClain	.80	.35	.10
☐ 99 Danny O'Connell	.80	.35	.10
☐ 100 Jimmy Piersall	1.50	.70	.19
☐ 101 Gene Woodling	1.00	.45	.12
☐ 102 Chicago Emblem	.80	.35	.10
☐ 103 George Altman	.80	.35	.10
☐ 104 Ernie Banks	8.00	3.60	1.00
☐ 105 Dick Bertell	.80	.35	.10
☐ 106 Don Cardwell	.80	.35	.10
☐ 107 Dick Ellsworth	.80	.35	.10
☐ 108 Glen Hobbie	.80	.35	.10
☐ 109 Ron Santo	1.50	.70	.19
☐ 110 Barney Schultz	.80	.35	.10
☐ 111 Billy Williams	4.00	1.80	.50
☐ 112 Cincinnati Emblem	.80	.35	.10
☐ 113 Gordon Coleman	.80	.35	.10
☐ 114 John Edwards	.80	.35	.10
☐ 115 Gene Freese	.80	.35	.10
☐ 116 Joe Jay	.80	.35	.10
☐ 117 Eddie Kasko	.80	.35	.10
☐ 118 Jim O'Toole	.80	.35	.10
☐ 119 Vada Pinson	1.50	.70	.19
☐ 120 Bob Purkey	.80	.35	.10
☐ 121 Frank Robinson	8.00	3.60	1.00
☐ 122 Houston Emblem	.80	.35	.10
☐ 123 Joe Amalfitano	.80	.35	.10
☐ 124 Bob Aspromonte	.80	.35	.10
☐ 125 Dick Farrell	.80	.35	.10
☐ 126 Al Heist	.80	.35	.10
☐ 127 Sam Jones	.80	.35	.10
☐ 128 Bobby Shantz	1.00	.45	.12
☐ 129 Hal W. Smith	.80	.35	.10
☐ 130 Al Spangler	.80	.35	.10
☐ 131 Bob Tiefenauer	.80	.35	.10
☐ 132 Los Angeles Emblem	.80	.35	.10
☐ 133 Don Drysdale	6.00	2.70	.75
☐ 134 Ron Fairly	1.00	.45	.12
☐ 135 Frank Howard	1.50	.70	.19
☐ 136 Sandy Koufax	18.00	8.00	2.20
☐ 137 Wally Moon	1.00	.45	.12
☐ 138 Johnny Podres	1.50	.70	.19
☐ 139 John Roseboro	.80	.35	.10
☐ 140 Duke Snider	10.00	4.50	1.25
☐ 141 Daryl Spencer	.80	.35	.10
☐ 142 Milwaukee Emblem	.80	.35	.10
☐ 143 Hank Aaron	15.00	6.75	1.85
☐ 144 Joe Adcock	1.00	.45	.12
☐ 145 Frank Bolling	.80	.35	.10
☐ 146 Lou Burdette	1.50	.70	.19
☐ 147 Del Crandall	1.00	.45	.12
☐ 148 Ed Mathews	6.00	2.70	.75
☐ 149 Roy McMillan	.80	.35	.10
☐ 150 Warren Spahn	8.00	3.60	1.00
☐ 151 Joe Torre	1.50	.70	.19
☐ 152 New York Emblem	1.00	.45	.12
☐ 153 Gus Bell	1.00	.45	.12
☐ 154 Roger Craig	1.50	.70	.19
☐ 155 Gil Hodges	6.00	2.70	.75
☐ 156 Jay Hook	1.00	.45	.12
☐ 157 Hobie Landrith	1.00	.45	.12
☐ 158 Felix Mantilla	1.00	.45	.12
☐ 159 Bob L. Miller	1.00	.45	.12
☐ 160 Lee Walls	1.00	.45	.12
☐ 161 Don Zimmer	1.50	.70	.19
☐ 162 Philadelphia Emblem	.80	.35	.10
☐ 163 Ruben Amaro	.80	.35	.10
☐ 164 Jack Baldschun	.80	.35	.10
☐ 165 Johnny Callison UER	1.00	.45	.12
Name spelled Callizon			
☐ 166 Clay Dalrymple	.80	.35	.10
☐ 167 Don Demeter	.80	.35	.10
☐ 168 Tony Gonzalez	.80	.35	.10
☐ 169 Roy Sievers	1.50	.70	.19
(see also 58)			
☐ 170 Tony Taylor	1.00	.45	.12
☐ 171 Art Mahaffey	.80	.35	.10
☐ 172 Pittsburgh Emblem	.80	.35	.10
☐ 173 Smoky Burgess	1.00	.45	.12
☐ 174 Bob Clemente	40.00	18.00	5.00
☐ 175 Roy Face	1.50	.70	.19
☐ 176 Bob Friend	1.00	.45	.12
☐ 177 Dick Groat	1.50	.70	.19
☐ 178 Don Hoak	.80	.35	.10
☐ 179 Bill Mazeroski	1.50	.70	.19
☐ 180 Dick Stuart	1.00	.45	.12
☐ 181 Bill Virdon	1.50	.70	.19
☐ 182 St. Louis Emblem	.80	.35	.10
☐ 183 Ken Boyer	1.50	.70	.19
☐ 184 Larry Jackson	.80	.35	.10
☐ 185 Julian Javier	.80	.35	.10
☐ 186 Tim McCarver	2.00	.90	.25
☐ 187 Lindy McDaniel	.80	.35	.10
☐ 188 Minnie Minoso	1.50	.70	.19
☐ 189 Stan Musial	15.00	6.75	1.85
☐ 190 Ray Sadecki	.80	.35	.10
☐ 191 Bill White	1.50	.70	.19
☐ 192 San Francisco Emblem	.80	.35	.10
☐ 193 Felipe Alou	1.25	.55	.16
☐ 194 Ed Bailey	.80	.35	.10
☐ 195 Orlando Cepeda	2.00	.90	.25
☐ 196 Jim Davenport	.80	.35	.10
☐ 197 Harvey Kuenn	1.50	.70	.19
☐ 198 Juan Marichal	5.00	2.20	.60
☐ 199 Willie Mays	18.00	8.00	2.20
☐ 200 Mike McCormick	1.00	.45	.12
☐ 201 Stu Miller	.80	.35	.10
☐ XX Stamp Album	20.00	9.00	2.50

1962 Topps Venezuelan

These 198 cards are parallel to the first 198 cards of the regular 1962 Topps set. They were issued for the Venezuelan market and are printed in Spanish. Also note this is not quite an exact parallel as cards #197 and #198 were not printed but were replaced by Elio Chacon and Luis Aparicio as cards #199 and #200. Both Chacon and Aparicio were natives of Venezuela.

	NRMT	VG-E	GOOD
COMPLETE SET (198)	5500.00	2500.00	700.00
COMMON CARD (1-200)	10.00	4.50	1.25
☐ 1 Roger Maris	500.00	125.00	50.00
☐ 2 Jim Brosnan	10.00	4.50	1.25
☐ 3 Pete Runnels	10.00	4.50	1.25
☐ 4 John DeMerit	10.00	4.50	1.25
☐ 5 Sandy Koufax UER	450.00	200.00	55.00
(Struck ou 18)			
☐ 6 Marv Breeding	10.00	4.50	1.25
☐ 7 Frank Thomas	10.00	4.50	1.25
☐ 8 Ray Herbert	10.00	4.50	1.25
☐ 9 Jim Davenport	10.00	4.50	1.25
☐ 10 Bob Clemente	600.00	275.00	75.00
☐ 11 Tom Morgan	10.00	4.50	1.25
☐ 12 Harry Craft MG	10.00	4.50	1.25
☐ 13 Dick Howser	10.00	4.50	1.25
☐ 14 Bill White	15.00	6.75	1.85
☐ 15 Dick Donovan	10.00	4.50	1.25
☐ 16 Darrell Johnson	10.00	4.50	1.25
☐ 17 John Callison	10.00	4.50	1.25
☐ 18 Managers' Dream	500.00	220.00	60.00
Mickey Mantle			
Willie Mays			
☐ 19 Ray Washburn	10.00	4.50	1.25
☐ 20 Rocky Colavito	50.00	22.00	6.25
☐ 21 Jim Kaat	30.00	13.50	3.70
☐ 22 Checklist 1	25.00	5.00	2.50
☐ 23 Norm Larker	10.00	4.50	1.25
☐ 24 Tigers Team	15.00	6.75	1.85
☐ 25 Ernie Banks	125.00	55.00	15.50
☐ 26 Chris Cannizzaro	10.00	4.50	1.25
☐ 27 Chuck Cottier	10.00	4.50	1.25
☐ 28 Minnie Minoso	20.00	9.00	2.50
☐ 29 Casey Stengel MG	50.00	22.00	6.25
☐ 30 Eddie Mathews	60.00	27.00	7.50
☐ 31 Tom Tresh	40.00	18.00	5.00
☐ 32 John Roseboro	10.00	4.50	1.25
☐ 33 Don Larsen	10.00	4.50	1.25
☐ 34 Johnny Temple	10.00	4.50	1.25
☐ 35 Don Schwall	10.00	4.50	1.25
☐ 36 Don Leppert	10.00	4.50	1.25
☐ 37 Tribe Hill Trio	10.00	4.50	1.25
Barry Latman			
Dick Stigman			
Jim Perry			
☐ 38 Gene Stephens	10.00	4.50	1.25
☐ 39 Joe Koppe	10.00	4.50	1.25
☐ 40 Orlando Cepeda	35.00	16.00	4.40
☐ 41 Cliff Cook	10.00	4.50	1.25
☐ 42 Jim King	10.00	4.50	1.25
☐ 43 Los Angeles Dodgers	15.00	6.75	1.85
Team Card			
☐ 44 Don Taussig	10.00	4.50	1.25
☐ 45 Brooks Robinson	125.00	55.00	15.50
☐ 46 Jack Baldschun	10.00	4.50	1.25
☐ 47 Bob Will	10.00	4.50	1.25
☐ 48 Ralph Terry	10.00	4.50	1.25
☐ 49 Hal Jones	10.00	4.50	1.25
☐ 50 Stan Musial	250.00	110.00	31.00
☐ 51 AL Batting Leaders	15.00	6.75	1.85
Norm Cash			
Jim Piersall			
Al Kaline			
Elston Howard			
☐ 52 NL Batting Leaders	30.00	13.50	3.70
Bob Clemente			
Vada Pinson			
Ken Boyer			
Wally Moon			
☐ 53 AL Home Run Leaders	250.00	110.00	31.00
Roger Maris			
Mickey Mantle			
Jim Gentile			
Harmon Killebrew			
☐ 54 NL Home Run Leaders	35.00	16.00	4.40
Orlando Cepeda			
Willie Mays			
Frank Robinson			
☐ 55 AL ERA Leaders	15.00	6.75	1.85
Dick Donovan			
Bill Stafford			
Don Mossi			
Milt Pappas			
☐ 56 NL ERA Leaders	15.00	6.75	1.85
Warren Spahn			
Jim O'Toole			
Curt Simmons			
Mike McCormick			
☐ 57 AL Wins Leaders	15.00	6.75	1.85
Whitey Ford			
Frank Lary			
Steve Barber			
Jim Bunning			
☐ 58 NL Wins Leaders	15.00	6.75	1.85
Warren Spahn			
Joe Jay			
Jim O'Toole			
☐ 59 AL Strikeout Leaders	15.00	6.75	1.85
Camilo Pascual			
Whitey Ford			
Jim Bunning			
Juan Pizzaro			
☐ 60 NL Strikeout Leaders	25.00	11.00	3.10
Sandy Koufax			
Stan Williams			
Don Drysdale			
Jim O'Toole			
☐ 61 Cardinals Team	20.00	9.00	2.50
☐ 62 Steve Boros	10.00	4.50	1.25
☐ 63 Tony Cloninger	10.00	4.50	1.25
☐ 64 Russ Snyder	10.00	4.50	1.25
☐ 65 Bobby Richardson	30.00	13.50	3.70
☐ 66 Cuno Barragan	10.00	4.50	1.25
☐ 67 Harvey Haddix	10.00	4.50	1.25
☐ 68 Ken Hunt	10.00	4.50	1.25
☐ 69 Phil Ortega	10.00	4.50	1.25
☐ 70 Harmon Killebrew	60.00	27.00	7.50
☐ 71 Dick LeMay	10.00	4.50	1.25
☐ 72 Bob's Pupils	10.00	4.50	1.25
Steve Boros			
Bob Scheffing MG			
Jake Wood			
☐ 73 Nellie Fox	25.00	11.00	3.10
☐ 74 Bob Lillis	10.00	4.50	1.25
☐ 75 Milt Pappas	15.00	6.75	1.85
☐ 76 Howie Bedell	10.00	4.50	1.25
☐ 77 Tony Taylor	10.00	4.50	1.25
☐ 78 Gene Green	10.00	4.50	1.25
☐ 79 Ed Hobaugh	10.00	4.50	1.25
☐ 80 Vada Pinson	15.00	6.75	1.85
☐ 81 Jim Pagliaroni	10.00	4.50	1.25
☐ 82 Deron Johnson	10.00	4.50	1.25
☐ 83 Larry Jackson	10.00	4.50	1.25
☐ 84 Lenny Green	10.00	4.50	1.25
☐ 85 Gil Hodges	35.00	16.00	4.40
☐ 86 Donn Clendenon	10.00	4.50	1.25
☐ 87 Mike Roarke	10.00	4.50	1.25
☐ 88 Ralph Houk MG	10.00	4.50	1.25
(Berra in background)			
☐ 89 Barney Schultz	10.00	4.50	1.25
☐ 90 Jim Piersall	10.00	4.50	1.25
☐ 91 J.C. Martin	10.00	4.50	1.25
☐ 92 Sam Jones	10.00	4.50	1.25
☐ 93 John Blanchard	10.00	4.50	1.25
☐ 94 Jay Hook	10.00	4.50	1.25
☐ 95 Don Hoak	10.00	4.50	1.25
☐ 96 Eli Grba	10.00	4.50	1.25
☐ 97 Tito Francona	10.00	4.50	1.25
☐ 98 Checklist 2	25.00	5.00	2.50
☐ 99 John (Boog) Powell	75.00	34.00	9.50
☐ 100 Warren Spahn	75.00	34.00	9.50
☐ 101 Carroll Hardy	10.00	4.50	1.25
☐ 102 Al Schroll	10.00	4.50	1.25
☐ 103 Don Blasingame	10.00	4.50	1.25
☐ 104 Ted Savage	10.00	4.50	1.25
☐ 105 Don Mossi	10.00	4.50	1.25
☐ 106 Carl Sawatski	10.00	4.50	1.25
☐ 107 Mike McCormick	10.00	4.50	1.25
☐ 108 Willie Davis	10.00	4.50	1.25
☐ 109 Bob Shaw	10.00	4.50	1.25
☐ 110 Bill Skowron	15.00	6.75	1.85
☐ 111 Dallas Green	10.00	4.50	1.25
☐ 112 Hank Foiles	10.00	4.50	1.25
☐ 113 Chicago White Sox	15.00	6.75	1.85
Team Card			
☐ 114 Howie Koplitz	10.00	4.50	1.25
☐ 115 Bob Skinner	10.00	4.50	1.25
☐ 116 Herb Score	15.00	6.75	1.85
☐ 117 Gary Geiger	10.00	4.50	1.25
☐ 118 Julian Javier	10.00	4.50	1.25
☐ 119 Danny Murphy	10.00	4.50	1.25
☐ 120 Bob Purkey	10.00	4.50	1.25
☐ 121 Billy Hitchcock MG	10.00	4.50	1.25
☐ 122 Norm Bass	10.00	4.50	1.25
☐ 123 Mike de la Hoz	10.00	4.50	1.25
☐ 124 Bill Pleis	10.00	4.50	1.25
☐ 125 Gene Woodling	10.00	4.50	1.25
☐ 126 Al Cicotte	10.00	4.50	1.25
☐ 127 Pride of A's	10.00	4.50	1.25
Norm Siebern			
Hank Bauer MG			
Jerry Lumpe			
☐ 128 Art Fowler	10.00	4.50	1.25
☐ 129 Lee Walls	10.00	4.50	1.25
☐ 130 Frank Bolling	10.00	4.50	1.25
☐ 131 Pete Richert	10.00	4.50	1.25
☐ 132 Angels Team	15.00	6.75	1.85
☐ 133 Felipe Alou	15.00	6.75	1.85
☐ 134 Billy Hoeft	10.00	4.50	1.25
☐ 135 Babe Ruth Special 1	50.00	22.00	6.25
Babe as a Boy			
☐ 136 Babe Ruth Special 2	50.00	22.00	6.25
Babe Joins Yanks			
☐ 137 Babe Ruth Special 3	50.00	22.00	6.25
With Miller Huggins			
☐ 138 Babe Ruth Special 4	50.00	22.00	6.25
Famous Slugger			
☐ 139 Babe Ruth Special 5	60.00	27.00	7.50
Babe Hits 60			
☐ 140 Babe Ruth Special 6	50.00	22.00	6.25
With Lou Gehrig			
☐ 141 Babe Ruth Special 7	50.00	22.00	6.25
Twilight Years			
☐ 142 Babe Ruth Special 8	50.00	22.00	6.25
Coaching Dodgers			
☐ 143 Babe Ruth Special 9	50.00	22.00	6.25
Greatest Sports Hero			
☐ 144 Babe Ruth Special 10	50.00	22.00	6.25
Farewell Speech			
☐ 145 Barry Latman	10.00	4.50	1.25
☐ 146 Don Demeter	10.00	4.50	1.25
☐ 147 Bill Kunkel	10.00	4.50	1.25
☐ 148 Wally Post	10.00	4.50	1.25
☐ 149 Bob Duliba	10.00	4.50	1.25
☐ 150 Al Kaline	125.00	55.00	15.50
☐ 151 Johnny Klippstein	10.00	4.50	1.25
☐ 152 Mickey Vernon MG	10.00	4.50	1.25
☐ 153 Pumpsie Green	10.00	4.50	1.25
☐ 154 Lee Thomas	10.00	4.50	1.25
☐ 155 Stu Miller	10.00	4.50	1.25
☐ 156 Merritt Ranew	10.00	4.50	1.25
☐ 157 Wes Covington	15.00	6.75	1.85
☐ 158 Braves Team	15.00	6.75	1.85
☐ 159 Hal Reniff	10.00	4.50	1.25
☐ 160 Dick Stuart	10.00	4.50	1.25
☐ 161 Frank Baumann	10.00	4.50	1.25
☐ 162 Sammy Drake	10.00	4.50	1.25
☐ 163 Hot Corner Guard	10.00	4.50	1.25
Billy Gardner			
Cletis Boyer			
☐ 164 Hal Naragon	10.00	4.50	1.25
☐ 165 Jackie Brandt	10.00	4.50	1.25
☐ 166 Don Lee	10.00	4.50	1.25
☐ 167 Tim McCarver	75.00	34.00	9.50
☐ 168 Leo Posada	10.00	4.50	1.25
☐ 169 Bob Cerv	10.00	4.50	1.25
☐ 170 Ron Santo	35.00	16.00	4.40
☐ 171 Dave Sisler	10.00	4.50	1.25
☐ 172 Fred Hutchinson MG	10.00	4.50	1.25
☐ 173 Chico Fernandez	10.00	4.50	1.25
☐ 174 Carl Willey	10.00	4.50	1.25
☐ 175 Frank Howard	15.00	6.75	1.85
☐ 176 Eddie Yost	10.00	4.50	1.25
☐ 177 Bobby Shantz	10.00	4.50	1.25
☐ 178 Camilo Carreon	10.00	4.50	1.25
☐ 179 Tom Sturdivant	10.00	4.50	1.25
☐ 180 Bob Allison	10.00	4.50	1.25
☐ 181 Paul Brown	10.00	4.50	1.25
☐ 182 Bob Nieman	10.00	4.50	1.25
☐ 183 Roger Craig	10.00	4.50	1.25
☐ 184 Haywood Sullivan	10.00	4.50	1.25
☐ 185 Roland Sheldon	10.00	4.50	1.25
☐ 186 Mack Jones	10.00	4.50	1.25

□ 187 Gene Conley	10.00	4.50	1.25
□ 188 Chuck Hiller	10.00	4.50	1.25
□ 189 Dick Hall	10.00	4.50	1.25
□ 190 Wally Moon	10.00	4.50	1.25
□ 191 Jim Brewer	10.00	4.50	1.25
□ 192 Checklist 3	25.00	5.00	2.50
□ 193 Eddie Kasko	10.00	4.50	1.25
□ 194 Dean Chance	10.00	4.50	1.25
□ 195 Joe Cunningham	10.00	4.50	1.25
□ 196 Terry Fox	10.00	4.50	1.25
□ 199 Elio Chacon	20.00	9.00	2.50
□ 200 Luis Aparicio	50.00	22.00	6.25

1963 Topps

The cards in this 576-card set measure 2 1/2" by 3 1/2". The sharp color photographs of the 1963 set are a vivid contrast to the drab pictures of 1962. In addition to the "League Leaders" series (1-10) and World Series cards (142-148), the seventh and last series of cards (523-576) contains seven rookie cards (each depicting four players). Cards were issued, among other ways, in one-card penny packs and five-card nickle packs. There were some three-card advertising panels produced by Topps; the players included are from the first series; one panel shows Hoyt Wilhelm, Don Lock, and Bob Duliba on the front with a Stan Musial ad/endorsement on one of the backs. Key Rookie Cards in this set are Bill Freehan, Tony Oliva, Pete Rose, Willie Stargell and Rusty Staub.

	NRMT	VG-E	GOOD
COMPLETE SET (576)	5000.00	2200.00	600.00
COMMON CARD (1-196)	4.00	1.80	.50
COMMON CARD (197-283)	5.00	2.20	.60
COMMON CARD (284-370)	5.00	2.20	.60
COMMON CARD (371-446)	5.00	2.20	.60
COMMON CARD (447-522)	25.00	11.00	3.10
COMMON CARD (523-576)	15.00	6.75	1.85
WRAPPER (1-CENT)	50.00	22.00	6.25
WRAPPER (5-CENT)	40.00	18.00	5.00

	NRMT	VG-E	GOOD
□ 1 NL Batting Leaders	40.00	8.00	4.00
Tommy Davis			
Frank Robinson			
Stan Musial			
Hank Aaron			
Bill White			
□ 2 AL Batting Leaders	50.00	22.00	6.25
Pete Runnels			
Mickey Mantle			
Floyd Robinson			
Norm Siebern			
Chuck Hinton			
□ 3 NL Home Run Leaders	30.00	13.50	3.70
Willie Mays			
Hank Aaron			
Frank Robinson			
Orlando Cepeda			
Ernie Banks			
□ 4 AL Home Run Leaders	16.00	7.25	2.00
Harmon Killebrew			
Norm Cash			
Rocky Colavito			
Roger Maris			
Jim Gentile			
Leon Wagner			
□ 5 NL ERA Leaders	20.00	9.00	2.50
Sandy Koufax			
Bob Shaw			
Bob Purkey			
Bob Gibson			
Don Drysdale			
□ 6 AL ERA Leaders	8.00	3.60	1.00
Hank Aguirre			
Robin Roberts			
Whitey Ford			
Eddie Fisher			
Dean Chance			
□ 7 NL Pitching Leaders	8.00	3.60	1.00
Don Drysdale			
Jack Sanford			
Bob Purkey			
Billy O'Dell			
Art Mahaffey			
Joe Jay			
□ 8 AL Pitching Leaders	8.00	3.60	1.00
Ralph Terry			
Dick Donovan			
Ray Herbert			
Jim Bunning			
Camilo Pascual			
□ 9 NL Strikeout Leaders	16.00	7.25	2.00
Don Drysdale			
Sandy Koufax			
Bob Gibson			
Billy O'Dell			
Dick Farrell			
□ 10 AL Strikeout Leaders	8.00	3.60	1.00
Camilo Pascual			
Jim Bunning			
Ralph Terry			
Juan Pizarro			
Jim Kaat			
□ 11 Lee Walls	4.00	1.80	.50
□ 12 Steve Barber	4.00	1.80	.50
□ 13 Philadelphia Phillies	6.00	2.70	.75
Team Card			
□ 14 Pedro Ramos	4.00	1.80	.50
□ 15 Ken Hubbs UER	6.00	2.70	.75
(No position listed			
on front of card)			
□ 16 Al Smith	4.00	1.80	.50
□ 17 Ryne Duren	4.50	2.00	.55
□ 18 Buc Blasters	70.00	32.00	8.75
Smoky Burgess			
Dick Stuart			
Bob Clemente			
Bob Skinner			
□ 19 Pete Burnside	4.00	1.80	.50
□ 20 Tony Kubek	6.00	2.70	.75
□ 21 Marty Keough	4.00	1.80	.50
□ 22 Curt Simmons	4.50	2.00	.55
□ 23 Ed Lopat MG	4.50	2.00	.55
□ 24 Bob Bruce	4.00	1.80	.50
□ 25 Al Kaline	45.00	20.00	5.50
□ 26 Ray Moore	4.00	1.80	.50
□ 27 Choo Choo Coleman	4.50	2.00	.55
□ 28 Mike Fornieles	4.00	1.80	.50
□ 29A 1962 Rookie Stars	7.00	3.10	.85
Sammy Ellis			
Ray Culp			
John Boozer			
Jesse Gonder			
□ 29B 1963 Rookie Stars	4.00	1.80	.50
Sammy Ellis			
Ray Culp			
John Boozer			
Jesse Gonder			
□ 30 Harvey Kuenn	4.50	2.00	.55
□ 31 Cal Koonce	4.00	1.80	.50
□ 32 Tony Gonzalez	4.00	1.80	.50
□ 33 Bo Belinsky	4.50	2.00	.55
□ 34 Dick Schofield	4.00	1.80	.50
□ 35 John Buzhardt	4.00	1.80	.50
□ 36 Jerry Kindall	4.00	1.80	.50
□ 37 Jerry Lynch	4.00	1.80	.50
□ 38 Bud Daley	5.00	2.20	.60
□ 39 Angels Team	6.00	2.70	.75
□ 40 Vic Power	4.50	2.00	.55
□ 41 Charley Lau	4.50	2.00	.55
□ 42 Stan Williams	4.50	2.00	.55
(Listed as Yankee on			
card but LA cap)			
□ 43 Veteran Masters	4.50	2.00	.55
Casey Stengel MG			
Gene Woodling			
□ 44 Terry Fox	4.00	1.80	.50
□ 45 Bob Aspromonte	4.00	1.80	.50
□ 46 Tommie Aaron	4.50	2.00	.55
□ 47 Don Lock	4.00	1.80	.50
□ 48 Birdie Tebbetts MG	4.50	2.00	.55
□ 49 Dal Maxvill	4.50	2.00	.55
□ 50 Billy Pierce	4.50	2.00	.55
□ 51 George Alusik	4.00	1.80	.50
□ 52 Chuck Schilling	4.00	1.80	.50
□ 53 Joe Moeller	5.00	2.20	.60
□ 54A 1962 Rookie Stars	16.00	7.25	2.00
Nelson Mathews			
Harry Fanok			
Jack Cullen			
Dave DeBusschere			
□ 54B 1963 Rookie Stars	8.00	3.60	1.00
Nelson Mathews			
Harry Fanok			
Jack Cullen			
Dave DeBusschere			
□ 55 Bill Virdon	4.50	2.00	.55
□ 56 Dennis Bennett	4.00	1.80	.50
□ 57 Billy Moran	4.00	1.80	.50
□ 58 Bob Will	4.00	1.80	.50
□ 59 Craig Anderson	4.00	1.80	.50
□ 60 Elston Howard	6.00	2.70	.75
□ 61 Ernie Bowman	4.00	1.80	.50
□ 62 Bob Hendley	4.00	1.80	.50
□ 63 Reds Team	6.00	2.70	.75
□ 64 Dick McAuliffe	4.50	2.00	.55
□ 65 Jackie Brandt	4.00	1.80	.50
□ 66 Mike Joyce	4.00	1.80	.50
□ 67 Ed Charles	4.00	1.80	.50
□ 68 Friendly Foes	25.00	11.00	3.10
Duke Snider			
Gil Hodges			
□ 69 Bud Zipfel	4.00	1.80	.50
□ 70 Jim O'Toole	4.50	2.00	.55
□ 71 Bobby Wine	4.50	2.00	.55
□ 72 Johnny Romano	4.00	1.80	.50
□ 73 Bobby Bragan MG	4.50	2.00	.55
□ 74 Denny Lemaster	4.00	1.80	.50
□ 75 Bob Allison	4.50	2.00	.55
□ 76 Earl Wilson	4.50	2.00	.55
□ 77 Al Spangler	4.00	1.80	.50
□ 78 Marv Throneberry	4.50	2.00	.55
□ 79 Checklist 1	12.00	2.40	1.20
□ 80 Jim Gilliam	5.00	2.20	.60
□ 81 Jim Schaffer	4.00	1.80	.50
□ 82 Ed Rakow	4.00	1.80	.50
□ 83 Charley James	4.00	1.80	.50
□ 84 Ron Kline	4.00	1.80	.50
□ 85 Tom Haller	4.50	2.00	.55
□ 86 Charley Maxwell	4.50	2.00	.55
□ 87 Bob Veale	4.50	2.00	.55
□ 88 Ron Hansen	4.00	1.80	.50
□ 89 Dick Stigman	4.00	1.80	.50
□ 90 Gordy Coleman	4.50	2.00	.55
□ 91 Dallas Green	4.50	2.00	.55
□ 92 Hector Lopez	5.00	2.20	.60
□ 93 Galen Cisco	4.00	1.80	.50
□ 94 Bob Schmidt	4.00	1.80	.50
□ 95 Larry Jackson	4.00	1.80	.50
□ 96 Lou Clinton	4.00	1.80	.50
□ 97 Bob Duliba	4.00	1.80	.50
□ 98 George Thomas	4.00	1.80	.50
□ 99 Jim Umbricht	4.00	1.80	.50
□ 100 Joe Cunningham	4.00	1.80	.50
□ 101 Joe Gibbon	4.00	1.80	.50
□ 102A Checklist 2	12.00	2.40	1.20
(Red on yellow)			
□ 102B Checklist 2	12.00	2.40	1.20
(White on red)			
□ 103 Chuck Essegian	4.00	1.80	.50
□ 104 Lew Krausse	4.00	1.80	.50
□ 105 Ron Fairly	5.00	2.20	.60
□ 106 Bobby Bolin	4.00	1.80	.50
□ 107 Jim Hickman	4.50	2.00	.55
□ 108 Hoyt Wilhelm	10.00	4.50	1.25
□ 109 Lee Maye	4.00	1.80	.50
□ 110 Rich Rollins	4.50	2.00	.55
□ 111 Al Jackson	4.00	1.80	.50
□ 112 Dick Brown	4.00	1.80	.50
□ 113 Don Landrum UER	4.00	1.80	.50
(Photo actually			
Ron Santo)			
□ 114 Dan Osinski	4.00	1.80	.50
□ 115 Carl Yastrzemski	40.00	18.00	5.00
□ 116 Jim Brosnan	4.50	2.00	.55
□ 117 Jacke Davis	4.00	1.80	.50
□ 118 Sherm Lollar	4.00	1.80	.50
□ 119 Bob Lillis	4.00	1.80	.50
□ 120 Roger Maris	45.00	20.00	5.50
□ 121 Jim Hannan	4.00	1.80	.50
□ 122 Julio Gotay	4.00	1.80	.50
□ 123 Frank Howard	6.00	2.70	.75
□ 124 Dick Howser	4.50	2.00	.55
□ 125 Robin Roberts	14.00	6.25	1.75
□ 126 Bob Uecker	14.00	6.25	1.75
□ 127 Bill Tuttle	4.00	1.80	.50
□ 128 Matty Alou	4.50	2.00	.55
□ 129 Gary Bell	4.00	1.80	.50
□ 130 Dick Groat	4.50	2.00	.55
□ 131 Washington Senators	6.00	2.70	.75
Team Card			
□ 132 Jack Hamilton	4.00	1.80	.50
□ 133 Gene Freese	4.00	1.80	.50
□ 134 Bob Scheffing MG	4.00	1.80	.50
□ 135 Richie Ashburn	20.00	9.00	2.50
□ 136 Ike Delock	4.00	1.80	.50
□ 137 Mack Jones	4.00	1.80	.50
□ 138 Pride of NL	70.00	32.00	8.75
Willie Mays			
Stan Musial			
□ 139 Earl Averill	4.00	1.80	.50
□ 140 Frank Lary	4.50	2.00	.55
□ 141 Manny Mota	7.00	3.10	.85
□ 142 Whitey Ford WS	8.00	3.60	1.00
□ 143 Jack Sanford WS	6.00	2.70	.75
□ 144 Roger Maris WS	12.00	5.50	1.50
□ 145 Chuck Hiller WS	6.00	2.70	.75
□ 146 Tom Tresh WS	6.00	2.70	.75
□ 147 Billy Pierce WS	6.00	2.70	.75
□ 148 Ralph Terry WS	6.00	2.70	.75
□ 149 Marv Breeding	4.00	1.80	.50
□ 150 Johnny Podres	5.00	2.20	.60
□ 151 Pirates Team	6.00	2.70	.75
□ 152 Ron Nischwitz	4.00	1.80	.50
□ 153 Hal Smith	4.00	1.80	.50
□ 154 Walt Alston MG	6.00	2.70	.75
□ 155 Bill Stafford	4.00	1.80	.50
□ 156 Roy McMillan	4.50	2.00	.55
□ 157 Diego Segui	4.50	2.00	.55
□ 158 Rookie Stars	4.50	2.00	.55
Rogelio Alvares			
Dave Roberts			
Tommy Harper			
Bob Saverine			
□ 159 Jim Pagliaroni	4.00	1.80	.50
□ 160 Juan Pizarro	4.00	1.80	.50
□ 161 Frank Torre	4.50	2.00	.55
□ 162 Twins Team	6.00	2.70	.75
□ 163 Don Larsen	4.50	2.00	.55
□ 164 Bubba Morton	4.00	1.80	.50
□ 165 Jim Kaat	6.00	2.70	.75
□ 166 Johnny Keane MG	4.00	1.80	.50
□ 167 Jim Fregosi	4.50	2.00	.55
□ 168 Russ Nixon	4.00	1.80	.50
□ 169 Rookie Stars	25.00	11.00	3.10
Dick Egan			
Julio Navarro			
Tommie Sisk			
Gaylord Perry			
□ 170 Joe Adcock	4.50	2.00	.55
□ 171 Steve Hamilton	4.00	1.80	.50
□ 172 Gene Oliver	4.00	1.80	.50
□ 173 Bombers' Best	200.00	90.00	25.00
Tom Tresh			
Mickey Mantle			
Bobby Richardson			
□ 174 Larry Burright	4.00	1.80	.50
□ 175 Bob Buhl	4.50	2.00	.55
□ 176 Jim King	4.00	1.80	.50
□ 177 Bubba Phillips	4.00	1.80	.50
□ 178 Johnny Edwards	4.00	1.80	.50
□ 179 Ron Piche	4.00	1.80	.50
□ 180 Bill Skowron	5.00	2.20	.60
□ 181 Sammy Esposito	4.00	1.80	.50
□ 182 Albie Pearson	4.50	2.00	.55
□ 183 Joe Pepitone	6.00	2.70	.75
□ 184 Vern Law	4.50	2.00	.55
□ 185 Chuck Hiller	4.00	1.80	.50
□ 186 Jerry Zimmerman	4.00	1.80	.50
□ 187 Willie Kirkland	4.00	1.80	.50
□ 188 Eddie Bressoud	4.00	1.80	.50
□ 189 Dave Giusti	4.50	2.00	.55
□ 190 Minnie Minoso	6.00	2.70	.75
□ 191 Checklist 3	12.00	2.40	1.20
□ 192 Clay Dalrymple	4.00	1.80	.50
□ 193 Andre Rodgers	4.00	1.80	.50
□ 194 Joe Nuxhall	4.50	2.00	.55
□ 195 Manny Jimenez	4.00	1.80	.50
□ 196 Doug Camilli	4.00	1.80	.50
□ 197 Roger Craig	5.50	2.50	.70
□ 198 Lenny Green	5.00	2.20	.60
□ 199 Joe Amalfitano	5.00	2.20	.60
□ 200 Mickey Mantle	550.00	250.00	70.00
□ 201 Cecil Butler	5.00	2.20	.60
□ 202 Boston Red Sox	7.00	3.10	.85
Team Card			
□ 203 Chico Cardenas	5.50	2.50	.70
□ 204 Don Nottebart	5.00	2.20	.60
□ 205 Luis Aparicio	16.00	7.25	2.00
□ 206 Ray Washburn	5.00	2.20	.60
□ 207 Ken Hunt	5.00	2.20	.60
□ 208 Rookie Stars	5.00	2.20	.60
Ron Herbel			
John Miller			
Wally Wolf			
Ron Taylor			
□ 209 Hobie Landrith	5.00	2.20	.60
□ 210 Sandy Koufax !	175.00	80.00	22.00
□ 211 Fred Whitfield	5.00	2.20	.60
□ 212 Glen Hobbie	5.00	2.20	.60
□ 213 Billy Hitchcock MG	5.00	2.20	.60
□ 214 Orlando Pena	5.00	2.20	.60
□ 215 Bob Skinner	5.50	2.50	.70
□ 216 Gene Conley	5.50	2.50	.70
□ 217 Joe Christopher	5.00	2.20	.60
□ 218 Tiger Twirlers	5.50	2.50	.70
Frank Lary			
Don Mossi			
Jim Bunning			
□ 219 Chuck Cottier	5.00	2.20	.60
□ 220 Camilo Pascual	5.50	2.50	.70
□ 221 Cookie Rojas	5.50	2.50	.70
□ 222 Cubs Team	7.00	3.10	.85
□ 223 Eddie Fisher	5.00	2.20	.60
□ 224 Mike Roarke	5.00	2.20	.60
□ 225 Joey Jay	5.00	2.20	.60
□ 226 Julian Javier	5.50	2.50	.70
□ 227 Jim Grant	5.50	2.50	.70
□ 228 Rookie Stars	40.00	18.00	5.00
Max Alvis			
Bob Bailey			
Tony Oliva			
(Listed as Pedro)			
Ed Kranepool			
□ 229 Willie Davis	6.00	2.70	.75
□ 230 Pete Runnels	5.50	2.50	.70
□ 231 Eli Grba UER	5.00	2.20	.60
(Large photo is			
Ryne Duren)			
□ 232 Frank Malzone	5.50	2.50	.70
□ 233 Casey Stengel MG	20.00	9.00	2.50
□ 234 Dave Nicholson	5.00	2.20	.60
□ 235 Billy O'Dell	5.00	2.20	.60
□ 236 Bill Bryan	5.00	2.20	.60
□ 237 Jim Coates	6.00	2.70	.75
□ 238 Lou Johnson	5.00	2.20	.60
□ 239 Harvey Haddix	5.50	2.50	.70
□ 240 Rocky Colavito	16.00	7.25	2.00
□ 241 Bob Smith	5.00	2.20	.60
□ 242 Power Plus	60.00	27.00	7.50
Ernie Banks			
Hank Aaron			
□ 243 Don Leppert	5.00	2.20	.60
□ 244 John Tsitouris	5.00	2.20	.60
□ 245 Gil Hodges	20.00	9.00	2.50
□ 246 Lee Stange	5.00	2.20	.60
□ 247 Yankees Team	40.00	18.00	5.00
□ 248 Tito Francona	5.00	2.20	.60
□ 249 Leo Burke	5.00	2.20	.60
□ 250 Stan Musial	125.00	55.00	15.50
□ 251 Jack Lamabe	5.00	2.20	.60

☐ 252 Ron Santo 10.00 4.50 1.25
☐ 253 Rookie Stars 5.00 2.20 .60
Len Gabrielson
Pete Jernigan
John Wojcik
Deacon Jones
☐ 254 Mike Hershberger 5.00 2.20 .60
☐ 255 Bob Shaw 5.00 2.20 .60
☐ 256 Jerry Lumpe 5.00 2.20 .60
☐ 257 Hank Aguirre 5.00 2.20 .60
☐ 258 Alvin Dark MG 5.50 2.50 .70
☐ 259 Johnny Logan 5.50 2.50 .70
☐ 260 Jim Gentile 5.50 2.50 .70
☐ 261 Bob Miller 5.00 2.20 .60
☐ 262 Ellis Burton 5.00 2.20 .60
☐ 263 Dave Stenhouse 5.00 2.20 .60
☐ 264 Phil Linz 5.00 2.20 .60
☐ 265 Vada Pinson 5.50 2.50 .70
☐ 266 Bob Allen 5.00 2.20 .60
☐ 267 Carl Sawatski 5.00 2.20 .60
☐ 268 Don Demeter 5.00 2.20 .60
☐ 269 Don Mincher 5.00 2.20 .60
☐ 270 Felipe Alou 5.50 2.50 .70
☐ 271 Dean Stone 5.00 2.20 .60
☐ 272 Danny Murphy 5.00 2.20 .60
☐ 273 Sammy Taylor 5.00 2.20 .60
☐ 274 Checklist 4 12.00 2.40 1.20
☐ 275 Eddie Mathews 20.00 9.00 2.50
☐ 276 Barry Shetrone 5.00 2.20 .60
☐ 277 Dick Farrell 5.00 2.20 .60
☐ 278 Chico Fernandez 5.00 2.20 .60
☐ 279 Wally Moon 6.00 2.70 .75
☐ 280 Bob Rodgers 5.00 2.20 .60
☐ 281 Tom Sturdivant 5.00 2.20 .60
☐ 282 Bobby Del Greco 5.00 2.20 .60
☐ 283 Roy Sievers 5.50 2.50 .70
☐ 284 Dave Sisler 5.00 2.20 .60
☐ 285 Dick Stuart 5.50 2.50 .70
☐ 286 Stu Miller 5.50 2.50 .70
☐ 287 Dick Bertell 5.00 2.20 .60
☐ 288 Chicago White Sox 10.00 4.50 1.25
Team Card
☐ 289 Hal Brown 5.00 2.20 .60
☐ 290 Bill White 6.00 2.70 .75
☐ 291 Don Rudolph 5.00 2.20 .60
☐ 292 Pumpsie Green 5.50 2.50 .70
☐ 293 Bill Pleis 5.00 2.20 .60
☐ 294 Bill Rigney MG 5.00 2.20 .60
☐ 295 Ed Roebuck 5.00 2.20 .60
☐ 296 Doc Edwards 5.00 2.20 .60
☐ 297 Jim Golden 5.00 2.20 .60
☐ 298 Don Dillard 5.00 2.20 .60
☐ 299 Rookie Stars 5.50 2.50 .70
Dave Morehead
Bob Dustal
Tom Butters
Dan Schneider
☐ 300 Willie Mays 135.00 60.00 17.00
☐ 301 Bill Fischer 5.00 2.20 .60
☐ 302 Whitey Herzog 5.50 2.50 .70
☐ 303 Earl Francis 5.00 2.20 .60
☐ 304 Harry Bright 5.00 2.20 .60
☐ 305 Don Hoak 5.00 2.20 .60
☐ 306 Star Receivers 7.00 3.10 .85
Earl Battey
Elston Howard
☐ 307 Chet Nichols 5.00 2.20 .60
☐ 308 Camilo Carreon 5.00 2.20 .60
☐ 309 Jim Brewer 5.00 2.20 .60
☐ 310 Tommy Davis 6.00 2.70 .75
☐ 311 Joe McClain 5.00 2.20 .60
☐ 312 Houston Colts 25.00 11.00 3.10
Team Card
☐ 313 Ernie Broglio 5.00 2.20 .60
☐ 314 John Goryl 5.00 2.20 .60
☐ 315 Ralph Terry 6.00 2.70 .75
☐ 316 Norm Sherry 5.50 2.50 .70
☐ 317 Sam McDowell 8.00 3.60 1.00
☐ 318 Gene Mauch MG 5.50 2.50 .70
☐ 319 Joe Gaines 5.00 2.20 .60
☐ 320 Warren Spahn 40.00 18.00 5.00
☐ 321 Gino Cimoli 5.00 2.20 .60
☐ 322 Bob Turley 5.50 2.50 .70
☐ 323 Bill Mazeroski 8.00 3.60 1.00
☐ 324 Rookie Stars 6.00 2.70 .75
George Williams
Pete Ward
Phil Roof
Vic Davalillo
☐ 325 Jack Sanford 5.00 2.20 .60
☐ 326 Hank Foiles 5.00 2.20 .60
☐ 327 Paul Foytack 5.00 2.20 .60
☐ 328 Dick Williams 5.50 2.50 .70
☐ 329 Lindy McDaniel 5.50 2.50 .70
☐ 330 Chuck Hinton 5.00 2.20 .60
☐ 331 Series Foes 5.50 2.50 .70
Bill Stafford
Bill Pierce
☐ 332 Joel Horlen 5.50 2.50 .70
☐ 333 Carl Warwick 5.00 2.20 .60
☐ 334 Wynn Hawkins 5.00 2.20 .60
☐ 335 Leon Wagner 5.00 2.20 .60
☐ 336 Ed Bauta 5.00 2.20 .60
☐ 337 Dodgers Team 25.00 11.00 3.10
☐ 338 Russ Kemmerer 5.00 2.20 .60
☐ 339 Ted Bowsfield 5.00 2.20 .60
☐ 340 Yogi Berra P/CO 70.00 32.00 8.75
☐ 341 Jack Baldschun 5.00 2.20 .60
☐ 342 Gene Woodling 5.50 2.50 .70
☐ 343 Johnny Pesky MG 5.50 2.50 .70
☐ 344 Don Schwall 5.00 2.20 .60
☐ 345 Brooks Robinson 60.00 27.00 7.50
☐ 346 Billy Hoeft 5.00 2.20 .60
☐ 347 Joe Torre 14.00 6.25 1.75
☐ 348 Vic Wertz 5.50 2.50 .70
☐ 349 Zoilo Versalles 5.50 2.50 .70
☐ 350 Bob Purkey 5.00 2.20 .60
☐ 351 Al Luplow 5.00 2.20 .60
☐ 352 Ken Johnson 5.00 2.20 .60
☐ 353 Billy Williams 30.00 13.50 3.70
☐ 354 Dom Zanni 5.00 2.20 .60
☐ 355 Dean Chance 5.50 2.50 .70
☐ 356 John Schaive 5.00 2.20 .60
☐ 357 George Altman 5.00 2.20 .60
☐ 358 Milt Pappas 5.50 2.50 .70
☐ 359 Haywood Sullivan 5.50 2.50 .70
☐ 360 Don Drysdale 40.00 18.00 5.00
☐ 361 Clete Boyer 7.00 3.10 .85
☐ 362 Checklist 5 12.00 2.40 1.20
☐ 363 Dick Radatz 5.50 2.50 .70
☐ 364 Howie Goss 5.00 2.20 .60
☐ 365 Jim Bunning 16.00 7.25 2.00
☐ 366 Tony Taylor 5.50 2.50 .70
☐ 367 Tony Cloninger 5.00 2.20 .60
☐ 368 Ed Bailey 5.00 2.20 .60
☐ 369 Jim Lemon 5.00 2.20 .60
☐ 370 Dick Donovan 5.00 2.20 .60
☐ 371 Rod Kanehl 6.00 2.70 .75
☐ 372 Don Lee 5.00 2.20 .60
☐ 373 Jim Campbell 5.00 2.20 .60
☐ 374 Claude Osteen 5.50 2.50 .70
☐ 375 Ken Boyer 8.00 3.60 1.00
☐ 376 John Wyatt 5.00 2.20 .60
☐ 377 Baltimore Orioles 10.00 4.50 1.25
Team Card
☐ 378 Bill Henry 5.00 2.20 .60
☐ 379 Bob Anderson 5.00 2.20 .60
☐ 380 Ernie Banks UER 75.00 34.00 9.50
(Back has career Major
and Minor, but he
never played in Minors)
☐ 381 Frank Baumann 5.00 2.20 .60
☐ 382 Ralph Houk MG 6.00 2.70 .75
☐ 383 Pete Richert 5.00 2.20 .60
☐ 384 Bob Tillman 5.00 2.20 .60
☐ 385 Art Mahaffey 5.00 2.20 .60
☐ 386 Rookie Stars 5.00 2.20 .60
Ed Kirkpatrick
John Bateman
Larry Bearnarth
Garry Roggenburk
☐ 387 Al McBean 5.00 2.20 .60
☐ 388 Jim Davenport 5.50 2.50 .70
☐ 389 Frank Sullivan 5.00 2.20 .60
☐ 390 Hank Aaron 125.00 55.00 15.50
☐ 391 Bill Dailey 5.00 2.20 .60
☐ 392 Tribe Thumpers 5.00 2.20 .60
Johnny Romano
Tito Francona
☐ 393 Ken MacKenzie 5.50 2.50 .70
☐ 394 Tim McCarver 14.00 6.25 1.75
☐ 395 Don McMahon 5.00 2.20 .60
☐ 396 Joe Koppe 5.00 2.20 .60
☐ 397 Kansas City Athletics 10.00 4.50 1.25
Team Card
☐ 398 Boog Powell 25.00 11.00 3.10
☐ 399 Dick Ellsworth 5.50 2.50 .70
☐ 400 Frank Robinson 60.00 27.00 7.50
☐ 401 Jim Bouton 14.00 6.25 1.75
☐ 402 Mickey Vernon MG 5.50 2.50 .70
☐ 403 Ron Perranoski 6.00 2.70 .75
☐ 404 Bob Oldis 5.00 2.20 .60
☐ 405 Floyd Robinson 5.00 2.20 .60
☐ 406 Howie Koplitz 5.00 2.20 .60
☐ 407 Rookie Stars 5.00 2.20 .60
Frank Kostro
Chico Ruiz
Larry Elliot
Dick Simpson
☐ 408 Billy Gardner 5.00 2.20 .60
☐ 409 Roy Face 5.50 2.50 .70
☐ 410 Earl Battey 5.00 2.20 .60
☐ 411 Jim Constable 5.00 2.20 .60
☐ 412 Dodger Big Three 40.00 18.00 5.00
Johnny Podres
Don Drysdale
Sandy Koufax
☐ 413 Jerry Walker 5.00 2.20 .60
☐ 414 Ty Cline 5.00 2.20 .60
☐ 415 Bob Gibson 60.00 27.00 7.50
☐ 416 Alex Grammas 5.00 2.20 .60
☐ 417 Giants Team 10.00 4.50 1.25
☐ 418 John Orsino 5.00 2.20 .60
☐ 419 Tracy Stallard 5.00 2.20 .60
☐ 420 Bobby Richardson 14.00 6.25 1.75
☐ 421 Tom Morgan 5.00 2.20 .60
☐ 422 Fred Hutchinson MG 5.50 2.50 .70
☐ 423 Ed Hobaugh 5.00 2.20 .60
☐ 424 Charlie Smith 5.00 2.20 .60
☐ 425 Smoky Burgess 5.50 2.50 .70
☐ 426 Barry Latman 5.00 2.20 .60
☐ 427 Bernie Allen 5.00 2.20 .60
☐ 428 Carl Boles 5.00 2.20 .60
☐ 429 Lou Burdette 5.50 2.50 .70
☐ 430 Norm Siebern 5.00 2.20 .60
☐ 431A Checklist 6 12.00 2.40 1.20
(White on red)
☐ 431B Checklist 6 30.00 6.00 3.00
(Black on orange)
☐ 432 Roman Mejias 5.00 2.20 .60
☐ 433 Denis Menke 5.00 2.20 .60
☐ 434 John Callison 5.50 2.50 .70
☐ 435 Woody Held 5.00 2.20 .60
☐ 436 Tim Harkness 6.00 2.70 .75
☐ 437 Bill Bruton 5.00 2.20 .60
☐ 438 Wes Stock 5.00 2.20 .60
☐ 439 Don Zimmer 5.50 2.50 .70
☐ 440 Juan Marichal 30.00 13.50 3.70
☐ 441 Lee Thomas 5.50 2.50 .70
☐ 442 J.C. Hartman 5.00 2.20 .60
☐ 443 Jim Piersall 5.50 2.50 .70
☐ 444 Jim Maloney 5.50 2.50 .70
☐ 445 Norm Cash 7.00 3.10 .85
☐ 446 Whitey Ford 40.00 18.00 5.00
☐ 447 Felix Mantilla 25.00 11.00 3.10
☐ 448 Jack Kralick 25.00 11.00 3.10
☐ 449 Jose Tartabull 25.00 11.00 3.10
☐ 450 Bob Friend 25.00 11.00 3.10
☐ 451 Indians Team 40.00 18.00 5.00
☐ 452 Barney Schultz 25.00 11.00 3.10
☐ 453 Jake Wood 25.00 11.00 3.10
☐ 454A Art Fowler 25.00 11.00 3.10
(Card number on
white background)
☐ 454B Art Fowler 30.00 13.50 3.70
(Card number on
orange background)
☐ 455 Ruben Amaro 25.00 11.00 3.10
☐ 456 Jim Coker 25.00 11.00 3.10
☐ 457 Tex Clevenger 25.00 11.00 3.10
☐ 458 Al Lopez MG 25.00 11.00 3.10
☐ 459 Dick LeMay 25.00 11.00 3.10
☐ 460 Del Crandall 25.00 11.00 3.10
☐ 461 Norm Bass 25.00 11.00 3.10
☐ 462 Wally Post 25.00 11.00 3.10
☐ 463 Joe Schaffernoth 25.00 11.00 3.10
☐ 464 Ken Aspromonte 25.00 11.00 3.10
☐ 465 Chuck Estrada 25.00 11.00 3.10
☐ 466 Rookie Stars SP 60.00 27.00 7.50
Nate Oliver
Tony Martinez
Bill Freehan
Jerry Robinson
☐ 467 Phil Ortega 25.00 11.00 3.10
☐ 468 Carroll Hardy 25.00 11.00 3.10
☐ 469 Jay Hook 25.00 11.00 3.10
☐ 470 Tom Tresh SP 60.00 27.00 7.50
☐ 471 Ken Retzer 25.00 11.00 3.10
☐ 472 Lou Brock 100.00 45.00 12.50
☐ 473 New York Mets 100.00 45.00 12.50
Team Card
☐ 474 Jack Fisher 25.00 11.00 3.10
☐ 475 Gus Triandos 25.00 11.00 3.10
☐ 476 Frank Funk 25.00 11.00 3.10
☐ 477 Donn Clendenon 25.00 11.00 3.10
☐ 478 Paul Brown 25.00 11.00 3.10
☐ 479 Ed Brinkman 25.00 11.00 3.10
☐ 480 Bill Monbouquette 25.00 11.00 3.10
☐ 481 Bob Taylor 25.00 11.00 3.10
☐ 482 Felix Torres 25.00 11.00 3.10
☐ 483 Jim Owens UER 25.00 11.00 3.10
(Stat column for Wins
has an R instead)
☐ 484 Dale Long SP 30.00 13.50 3.70
☐ 485 Jim Landis 25.00 11.00 3.10
☐ 486 Ray Sadecki 25.00 11.00 3.10
☐ 487 John Roseboro 25.00 11.00 3.10
☐ 488 Jerry Adair 25.00 11.00 3.10
☐ 489 Paul Toth 25.00 11.00 3.10
☐ 490 Willie McCovey 125.00 55.00 15.50
☐ 491 Harry Craft MG 25.00 11.00 3.10
☐ 492 Dave Wickersham 25.00 11.00 3.10
☐ 493 Walt Bond 25.00 11.00 3.10
☐ 494 Phil Regan 25.00 11.00 3.10
☐ 495 Frank Thomas SP 30.00 13.50 3.70
☐ 496 Rookie Stars 25.00 11.00 3.10
Steve Dalkowski
Fred Newman
Jack Smith
Carl Bouldin
☐ 497 Bennie Daniels 25.00 11.00 3.10
☐ 498 Eddie Kasko 25.00 11.00 3.10
☐ 499 J.C. Martin 25.00 11.00 3.10
☐ 500 Harmon Killebrew SP 150.00 70.00 19.00
☐ 501 Joe Azcue 25.00 11.00 3.10
☐ 502 Daryl Spencer 25.00 11.00 3.10
☐ 503 Braves Team 40.00 18.00 5.00
☐ 504 Bob Johnson 25.00 11.00 3.10
☐ 505 Curt Flood 25.00 11.00 3.10
☐ 506 Gene Green 25.00 11.00 3.10
☐ 507 Roland Sheldon 30.00 13.50 3.70
☐ 508 Ted Savage 25.00 11.00 3.10
☐ 509A Checklist 7 30.00 6.00 3.00
(Copyright centered)
☐ 509B Checklist 7 30.00 6.00 3.00
(Copyright to right)
☐ 510 Ken McBride 25.00 11.00 3.10
☐ 511 Charlie Neal 25.00 11.00 3.10
☐ 512 Cal McLish 25.00 11.00 3.10
☐ 513 Gary Geiger 25.00 11.00 3.10
☐ 514 Larry Osborne 25.00 11.00 3.10
☐ 515 Don Elston 25.00 11.00 3.10
☐ 516 Purnell Goldy 25.00 11.00 3.10
☐ 517 Hal Woodeshick 25.00 11.00 3.10
☐ 518 Don Blasingame 25.00 11.00 3.10
☐ 519 Claude Raymond 25.00 11.00 3.10
☐ 520 Orlando Cepeda 30.00 13.50 3.70
☐ 521 Dan Pfister 25.00 11.00 3.10
☐ 522 Rookie Stars 25.00 11.00 3.10
Mel Nelson
Gary Peters
Jim Roland
Art Quirk
☐ 523 Bill Kunkel 15.00 6.75 1.85
☐ 524 Cardinals Team 30.00 13.50 3.70
☐ 525 Nellie Fox 40.00 18.00 5.00
☐ 526 Dick Hall 15.00 6.75 1.85
☐ 527 Ed Sadowski 15.00 6.75 1.85
☐ 528 Carl Willey 15.00 6.75 1.85
☐ 529 Wes Covington 15.00 6.75 1.85
☐ 530 Don Mossi 17.50 8.00 2.20
☐ 531 Sam Mele MG 15.00 6.75 1.85
☐ 532 Steve Boros 15.00 6.75 1.85
☐ 533 Bobby Shantz 17.50 8.00 2.20
☐ 534 Ken Walters 15.00 6.75 1.85
☐ 535 Jim Perry 17.50 8.00 2.20
☐ 536 Norm Larker 15.00 6.75 1.85
☐ 537 Rookie Stars 1000.00 450.00 125.00
Pedro Gonzalez
Ken McMullen
Al Weis
Pete Rose
☐ 538 George Brunet 15.00 6.75 1.85
☐ 539 Wayne Causey 15.00 6.75 1.85
☐ 540 Bob Clemente 375.00 170.00 47.50
☐ 541 Ron Moeller 15.00 6.75 1.85
☐ 542 Lou Klimchock 15.00 6.75 1.85
☐ 543 Russ Snyder 15.00 6.75 1.85
☐ 544 Rookie Stars 40.00 18.00 5.00
Duke Carmel
Bill Haas
Rusty Staub
Dick Phillips
☐ 545 Jose Pagan 15.00 6.75 1.85
☐ 546 Hal Reniff 17.50 8.00 2.20
☐ 547 Gus Bell 15.00 6.75 1.85
☐ 548 Tom Satriano 15.00 6.75 1.85
☐ 549 Rookie Stars 15.00 6.75 1.85
Marcelino Lopez
Pete Lovrich
Paul Ratliff
Elmo Plaskett
☐ 550 Duke Snider 75.00 34.00 9.50
☐ 551 Billy Klaus 15.00 6.75 1.85
☐ 552 Detroit Tigers 45.00 20.00 5.50
Team Card
☐ 553 Rookie Stars 125.00 55.00 15.50
Brock Davis
Jim Gosger
Willie Stargell
John Herrnstein
☐ 554 Hank Fischer 15.00 6.75 1.85
☐ 555 John Blanchard 17.50 8.00 2.20
☐ 556 Al Worthington 15.00 6.75 1.85
☐ 557 Cuno Barragan 15.00 6.75 1.85
☐ 558 Rookie Stars 18.00 8.00 2.20
Bill Faul
Ron Hunt
Al Moran
Bob Lipski
☐ 559 Danny Murtaugh MG 15.00 6.75 1.85
☐ 560 Ray Herbert 15.00 6.75 1.85
☐ 561 Mike De La Hoz 15.00 6.75 1.85
☐ 562 Rookie Stars 25.00 11.00 3.10
Randy Cardinal
Dave McNally
Ken Rowe
Don Rowe
☐ 563 Mike McCormick 15.00 6.75 1.85
☐ 564 George Banks 15.00 6.75 1.85
☐ 565 Larry Sherry 15.00 6.75 1.85
☐ 566 Cliff Cook 15.00 6.75 1.85
☐ 567 Jim Duffalo 15.00 6.75 1.85
☐ 568 Bob Sadowski 15.00 6.75 1.85
☐ 569 Luis Arroyo 17.50 8.00 2.20
☐ 570 Frank Bolling 15.00 6.75 1.85
☐ 571 Johnny Klippstein 15.00 6.75 1.85
☐ 572 Jack Spring 15.00 6.75 1.85
☐ 573 Coot Veal 15.00 6.75 1.85
☐ 574 Hal Kolstad 15.00 6.75 1.85
☐ 575 Don Cardwell 15.00 6.75 1.85
☐ 576 Johnny Temple 25.00 9.50 2.60

1963 Topps Stick-On Inserts

Stick-on inserts were found in several series of the 1963 Topps cards. Each sticker measures 1 1/4" by 2 3/4". They are found either with blank backs or with instructions on the reverse. Stick-ons with the instruction backs are a little tougher to find. The player photo is in color inside an oval with name, team and postion below. Since these inserts were unnumbered, they are ordered below alphabetically.

	NRMT	VG-E	GOOD
COMPLETE SET (46)	300.00	135.00	38.00
COMMON STICKER(1-46)	2.50	1.10	.30
□ 1 Hank Aaron	30.00	13.50	3.70
□ 2 Luis Aparicio	10.00	4.50	1.25
□ 3 Richie Ashburn	10.00	4.50	1.25
□ 4 Bob Aspromonte	2.50	1.10	.30
□ 5 Ernie Banks	15.00	6.75	1.85
□ 6 Ken Boyer	5.00	2.20	.60
□ 7 Jim Bunning	10.00	4.50	1.25
□ 8 Johnny Callison	2.50	1.10	.30
□ 9 Bob Clemente	50.00	22.00	6.25
□ 10 Orlando Cepeda	7.50	3.40	.95
□ 11 Rocky Colavito	7.50	3.40	.95
□ 12 Tommy Davis	3.50	1.55	.45
□ 13 Dick Donovan	2.50	1.10	.30
□ 14 Don Drysdale	10.00	4.50	1.25
□ 15 Dick Farrell	2.50	1.10	.30
□ 16 Jim Gentile	3.50	1.55	.45
□ 17 Ray Herbert	2.50	1.10	.30
□ 18 Chuck Hinton	2.50	1.10	.30
□ 19 Ken Hubbs	3.50	1.55	.45
□ 20 Al Jackson	2.50	1.10	.30
□ 21 Al Kaline	15.00	6.75	1.85
□ 22 Harmon Killebrew	10.00	4.50	1.25
□ 23 Sandy Koufax	25.00	11.00	3.10
□ 24 Jerry Lumpe	2.50	1.10	.30
□ 25 Art Mahaffey	2.50	1.10	.30
□ 26 Mickey Mantle	80.00	36.00	10.00
□ 27 Willie Mays	35.00	16.00	4.40
□ 28 Bill Mazeroski	5.00	2.20	.60
□ 29 Bill Monbouquette	2.50	1.10	.30
□ 30 Stan Musial	25.00	11.00	3.10
□ 31 Camilo Pascual	2.50	1.10	.30
□ 32 Bob Purkey	2.50	1.10	.30
□ 33 Bobby Richardson	5.00	2.20	.60
□ 34 Brooks Robinson	15.00	6.75	1.85
□ 35 Floyd Robinson	2.50	1.10	.30
□ 36 Frank Robinson	15.00	6.75	1.85
□ 37 Bob Rodgers	2.50	1.10	.30
□ 38 Johnny Romano	2.50	1.10	.30
□ 39 Jack Sanford	2.50	1.10	.30
□ 40 Norm Siebern	2.50	1.10	.30
□ 41 Warren Spahn	10.00	4.50	1.25
□ 42 Dave Stenhouse	2.50	1.10	.30
□ 43 Ralph Terry	2.50	1.10	.30
□ 44 Lee Thomas	3.50	1.55	.45
□ 45 Bill White	5.00	2.20	.60
□ 46 Carl Yastrzemski	20.00	9.00	2.50

1964 Topps

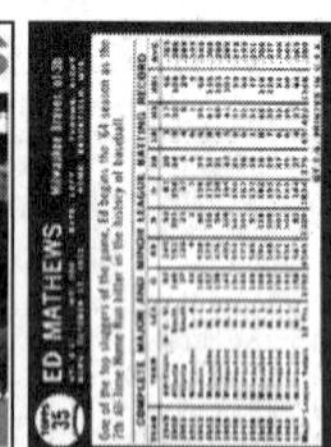

The cards in this 587-card set measure 2 1/2" by 3 1/2". Players in the 1964 Topps baseball series were easy to sort by team due to the giant block lettering found at the top of each card. The name and position of the player are found underneath the picture, and the card is numbered in a ball design on the orange-colored back. The usual last series scarcity holds for this set (523 to 587). Subsets within this set include League Leaders (1-12) and World Series cards (136-140). Among other vehicles, cards were issued in one-card penny packs as well as five-card nickle packs. There were some three-card advertising panels produced by Topps; the players included are from the first series; one panel shows Walt Alston, Bill Henry, and Vada Pinson on the front with a Mickey Mantle card back on one of the backs. Another panel shows Carl Willey, White Sox Rookies, and Bob Friend on the front with a Mickey Mantle card back on one of the backs. The key Rookie Cards in this set are Richie Allen, Tony Conigliaro, Tommy John, Tony LaRussa, Phil Niekro and Lou Piniella.

	NRMT	VG-E	GOOD
COMPLETE SET (587)	3000.00	1350.00	375.00
COMMON CARD (1-196)	3.00	1.35	.35
COMMON CARD (197-370)	4.00	1.80	.50
COMMON CARD (371-522)	7.00	3.10	.85
COMMON CARD (523-587)	16.00	7.25	2.00
WRAPPER (1-CENT)	100.00	45.00	12.50
WRAPPER (1-CENT, REPEAT)	125.00	55.00	15.50
WRAPPER (5-CENT)	30.00	13.50	3.70
WRAPPER (5-CENT, COIN)	40.00	18.00	5.00
□ 1 NL ERA Leaders	30.00	9.00	3.00
Sandy Koufax			
Dick Ellsworth			
Bob Friend			
□ 2 AL ERA Leaders	6.00	2.70	.75
Gary Peters			
Juan Pizarro			
Camilo Pascual			
□ 3 NL Pitching Leaders	18.00	8.00	2.20
Sandy Koufax			
Juan Marichal			
Warren Spahn			
Jim Maloney			
□ 4 AL Pitching Leaders	10.00	4.50	1.25
Whitey Ford			
Camilo Pascual			
Jim Bouton			
□ 5 NL Strikeout Leaders	14.00	6.25	1.75
Sandy Koufax			
Jim Maloney			
Don Drysdale			
□ 6 AL Strikeout Leaders	6.00	2.70	.75
Camilo Pascual			
Jim Bunning			
Dick Stigman			
□ 7 NL Batting Leaders	20.00	9.00	2.50
Tommy Davis			
Bob Clemente			
Dick Groat			
Hank Aaron			
□ 8 AL Batting Leaders	12.00	5.50	1.50
Carl Yastrzemski			
Al Kaline			
Rich Rollins			
□ 9 NL Home Run Leaders	30.00	13.50	3.70
Hank Aaron			
Willie McCovey			
Willie Mays			
Orlando Cepeda			
□ 10 AL Home Run Leaders	10.00	4.50	1.25
Harmon Killebrew			
Dick Stuart			
Bob Allison			
□ 11 NL RBI Leaders	12.00	5.50	1.50
Hank Aaron			
Ken Boyer			
Bill White			
□ 12 AL RBI Leaders	10.00	4.50	1.25
Dick Stuart			
Al Kaline			
Harmon Killebrew			
□ 13 Hoyt Wilhelm	10.00	4.50	1.25
□ 14 Dodgers Rookies	3.00	1.35	.35
Dick Nen			
Nick Willhite			
□ 15 Zoilo Versalles	4.00	1.80	.50
□ 16 John Boozer	3.00	1.35	.35
□ 17 Willie Kirkland	3.00	1.35	.35
□ 18 Billy O'Dell	3.00	1.35	.35
□ 19 Don Wert	3.00	1.35	.35
□ 20 Bob Friend	4.00	1.80	.50
□ 21 Yogi Berra MG	30.00	13.50	3.70
□ 22 Jerry Adair	3.00	1.35	.35
□ 23 Chris Zachary	3.00	1.35	.35
□ 24 Carl Sawatski	3.00	1.35	.35
□ 25 Bill Monbouquette	3.00	1.35	.35
□ 26 Gino Cimoli	3.00	1.35	.35
□ 27 New York Mets	8.00	3.60	1.00
Team Card			
□ 28 Claude Osteen	4.00	1.80	.50
□ 29 Lou Brock	35.00	16.00	4.40
□ 30 Ron Perranoski	4.00	1.80	.50
□ 31 Dave Nicholson	3.00	1.35	.35
□ 32 Dean Chance	4.00	1.80	.50
□ 33 Reds Rookies	4.00	1.80	.50
Sammy Ellis			
Mel Queen			
□ 34 Jim Perry	4.00	1.80	.50
□ 35 Eddie Mathews	20.00	9.00	2.50
□ 36 Hal Reniff	3.00	1.35	.35
□ 37 Smoky Burgess	4.00	1.80	.50
□ 38 Jim Wynn	7.00	3.10	.85
□ 39 Hank Aguirre	3.00	1.35	.35
□ 40 Dick Groat	4.00	1.80	.50
□ 41 Friendly Foes	8.00	3.60	1.00
Willie McCovey			
Leon Wagner			
□ 42 Moe Drabowsky	4.00	1.80	.50
□ 43 Roy Sievers	4.00	1.80	.50
□ 44 Duke Carmel	3.00	1.35	.35
□ 45 Milt Pappas	4.00	1.80	.50
□ 46 Ed Brinkman	3.00	1.35	.35
□ 47 Giants Rookies	5.00	2.20	.60
Jesus Alou			
Ron Herbel			
□ 48 Bob Perry	3.00	1.35	.35
□ 49 Bill Henry	3.00	1.35	.35
□ 50 Mickey Mantle	300.00	135.00	38.00
□ 51 Pete Richert	3.00	1.35	.35
□ 52 Chuck Hinton	3.00	1.35	.35
□ 53 Denis Menke	3.00	1.35	.35
□ 54 Sam Mele MG	3.00	1.35	.35
□ 55 Ernie Banks	35.00	16.00	4.40
□ 56 Hal Brown	3.00	1.35	.35
□ 57 Tim Harkness	3.00	1.35	.35
□ 58 Don Demeter	3.00	1.35	.35
□ 59 Ernie Broglio	3.00	1.35	.35
□ 60 Frank Malzone	4.00	1.80	.50
□ 61 Angel Backstops	4.00	1.80	.50
Bob Rodgers			
Ed Sadowski			
□ 62 Ted Savage	3.00	1.35	.35
□ 63 John Orsino	3.00	1.35	.35
□ 64 Ted Abernathy	3.00	1.35	.35
□ 65 Felipe Alou	4.00	1.80	.50
□ 66 Eddie Fisher	3.00	1.35	.35
□ 67 Tigers Team	6.00	2.70	.75
□ 68 Willie Davis	4.00	1.80	.50
□ 69 Clete Boyer	4.00	1.80	.50
□ 70 Joe Torre	8.00	3.60	1.00
□ 71 Jack Spring	3.00	1.35	.35
□ 72 Chico Cardenas	4.00	1.80	.50
□ 73 Jimmie Hall	4.00	1.80	.50
□ 74 Pirates Rookies	3.00	1.35	.35
Bob Priddy			
Tom Butters			
□ 75 Wayne Causey	3.00	1.35	.35
□ 76 Checklist 1	10.00	2.00	1.00
□ 77 Jerry Walker	3.00	1.35	.35
□ 78 Merritt Ranew	3.00	1.35	.35
□ 79 Bob Heffner	3.00	1.35	.35
□ 80 Vada Pinson	4.00	1.80	.50
□ 81 All-Star Vets	10.00	4.50	1.25
Nellie Fox			
Harmon Killebrew			
□ 82 Jim Davenport	4.00	1.80	.50
□ 83 Gus Triandos	4.00	1.80	.50
□ 84 Carl Willey	3.00	1.35	.35
□ 85 Pete Ward	3.00	1.35	.35
□ 86 Al Downing	4.00	1.80	.50
□ 87 St. Louis Cardinals	6.00	2.70	.75
Team Card			
□ 88 John Roseboro	4.00	1.80	.50
□ 89 Boog Powell	6.00	2.70	.75
□ 90 Earl Battey	3.00	1.35	.35
□ 91 Bob Bailey	4.00	1.80	.50
□ 92 Steve Ridzik	3.00	1.35	.35
□ 93 Gary Geiger	3.00	1.35	.35
□ 94 Braves Rookies	3.00	1.35	.35
Jim Britton			
Larry Maxie			
□ 95 George Altman	3.00	1.35	.35
□ 96 Bob Buhl	4.00	1.80	.50
□ 97 Jim Fregosi	4.00	1.80	.50
□ 98 Bill Bruton	3.00	1.35	.35
□ 99 Al Stanek	3.00	1.35	.35
□ 100 Elston Howard	4.00	1.80	.50
□ 101 Walt Alston MG	4.00	1.80	.50
□ 102 Checklist 2	10.00	2.00	1.00
□ 103 Curt Flood	4.00	1.80	.50
□ 104 Art Mahaffey	4.00	1.80	.50
□ 105 Woody Held	3.00	1.35	.35
□ 106 Joe Nuxhall	4.00	1.80	.50
□ 107 White Sox Rookies	3.00	1.35	.35
Bruce Howard			
Frank Kreutzer			
□ 108 John Wyatt	3.00	1.35	.35
□ 109 Rusty Staub	5.00	2.20	.60
□ 110 Albie Pearson	4.00	1.80	.50
□ 111 Don Elston	3.00	1.35	.35
□ 112 Bob Tillman	3.00	1.35	.35
□ 113 Grover Powell	3.00	1.35	.35
□ 114 Don Lock	3.00	1.35	.35
□ 115 Frank Bolling	3.00	1.35	.35
□ 116 Twins Rookies	12.00	5.50	1.50
Jay Ward			
Tony Oliva			
□ 117 Earl Francis	3.00	1.35	.35
□ 118 John Blanchard	4.00	1.80	.50
□ 119 Gary Kolb	3.00	1.35	.35
□ 120 Don Drysdale	20.00	9.00	2.50
□ 121 Pete Runnels	4.00	1.80	.50
□ 122 Don McMahon	3.00	1.35	.35
□ 123 Jose Pagan	3.00	1.35	.35
□ 124 Orlando Pena	3.00	1.35	.35
□ 125 Pete Rose	150.00	70.00	19.00
□ 126 Russ Snyder	3.00	1.35	.35
□ 127 Angels Rookies	3.00	1.35	.35
Aubrey Gatewood			
Dick Simpson			
□ 128 Mickey Lolich	20.00	9.00	2.50
□ 129 Amado Samuel	3.00	1.35	.35
□ 130 Gary Peters	4.00	1.80	.50
□ 131 Steve Boros	3.00	1.35	.35
□ 132 Braves Team	6.00	2.70	.75
□ 133 Jim Grant	4.00	1.80	.50
□ 134 Don Zimmer	4.00	1.80	.50
□ 135 Johnny Callison	4.00	1.80	.50
□ 136 Sandy Koufax WS	16.00	7.25	2.00
strikes out 15			
□ 137 Tommy Davis WS	6.00	2.70	.75
□ 138 Ron Fairly WS	6.00	2.70	.75
□ 139 Frank Howard WS	6.00	2.70	.75
□ 140 World Series Summary	6.00	2.70	.75
Dodgers celebrate			
□ 141 Danny Murtaugh MG	4.00	1.80	.50
□ 142 John Bateman	3.00	1.35	.35
□ 143 Bubba Phillips	3.00	1.35	.35
□ 144 Al Worthington	3.00	1.35	.35
□ 145 Norm Siebern	3.00	1.35	.35
□ 146 Indians Rookies	30.00	13.50	3.70
Tommy John			
Bob Chance			
□ 147 Ray Sadecki	3.00	1.35	.35
□ 148 J.C. Martin	3.00	1.35	.35
□ 149 Paul Foytack	3.00	1.35	.35
□ 150 Willie Mays	100.00	45.00	12.50
□ 151 Athletics Team	6.00	2.70	.75
□ 152 Denny Lemaster	3.00	1.35	.35
□ 153 Dick Williams	4.00	1.80	.50
□ 154 Dick Tracewski	4.00	1.80	.50
□ 155 Duke Snider	30.00	13.50	3.70
□ 156 Bill Dailey	3.00	1.35	.35
□ 157 Gene Mauch MG	4.00	1.80	.50
□ 158 Ken Johnson	3.00	1.35	.35
□ 159 Charlie Dees	3.00	1.35	.35
□ 160 Ken Boyer	4.00	1.80	.50
□ 161 Dave McNally	4.00	1.80	.50
□ 162 Hitting Area	4.00	1.80	.50
Dick Sisler CO			
Vada Pinson			
□ 163 Donn Clendenon	4.00	1.80	.50
□ 164 Bud Daley	3.00	1.35	.35
□ 165 Jerry Lumpe	3.00	1.35	.35
□ 166 Marty Keough	3.00	1.35	.35
□ 167 Senators Rookies	30.00	13.50	3.70
Mike Brumley			
Lou Piniella			
□ 168 Al Weis	3.00	1.35	.35
□ 169 Del Crandall	4.00	1.80	.50
□ 170 Dick Radatz	4.00	1.80	.50
□ 171 Ty Cline	3.00	1.35	.35
□ 172 Indians Team	6.00	2.70	.75
□ 173 Ryne Duren	4.00	1.80	.50
□ 174 Doc Edwards	3.00	1.35	.35
□ 175 Billy Williams	14.00	6.25	1.75
□ 176 Tracy Stallard	3.00	1.35	.35
□ 177 Harmon Killebrew	20.00	9.00	2.50
□ 178 Hank Bauer MG	4.00	1.80	.50
□ 179 Carl Warwick	3.00	1.35	.35
□ 180 Tommy Davis	4.00	1.80	.50
□ 181 Dave Wickersham	3.00	1.35	.35
□ 182 Sox Sockers	14.00	6.25	1.75
Carl Yastrzemski			
Chuck Schilling			
□ 183 Ron Taylor	3.00	1.35	.35
□ 184 Al Luplow	3.00	1.35	.35
□ 185 Jim O'Toole	4.00	1.80	.50
□ 186 Roman Mejias	3.00	1.35	.35
□ 187 Ed Roebuck	3.00	1.35	.35
□ 188 Checklist 3	10.00	2.00	1.00
□ 189 Bob Hendley	3.00	1.35	.35
□ 190 Bobby Richardson	8.00	3.60	1.00
□ 191 Clay Dalrymple	4.00	1.80	.50
□ 192 Cubs Rookies	3.00	1.35	.35
John Boccabella			
Billy Cowan			
□ 193 Jerry Lynch	3.00	1.35	.35
□ 194 John Goryl	3.00	1.35	.35
□ 195 Floyd Robinson	3.00	1.35	.35
□ 196 Jim Gentile	3.00	1.35	.35
□ 197 Frank Lary	5.00	2.20	.60
□ 198 Len Gabrielson	4.00	1.80	.50
□ 199 Joe Azcue	4.00	1.80	.50
□ 200 Sandy Koufax	100.00	45.00	12.50
□ 201 Orioles Rookies	5.00	2.20	.60
Sam Bowens			
Wally Bunker			
□ 202 Galen Cisco	5.00	2.20	.60
□ 203 John Kennedy	5.00	2.20	.60
□ 204 Matty Alou	5.00	2.20	.60
□ 205 Nellie Fox	14.00	6.25	1.75
□ 206 Steve Hamilton	5.00	2.20	.60
□ 207 Fred Hutchinson MG	5.00	2.20	.60
□ 208 Wes Covington	5.00	2.20	.60
□ 209 Bob Allen	4.00	1.80	.50
□ 210 Carl Yastrzemski	35.00	16.00	4.40
□ 211 Jim Coker	4.00	1.80	.50
□ 212 Pete Lovrich	4.00	1.80	.50
□ 213 Angels Team	7.00	3.10	.85
□ 214 Ken McMullen	5.00	2.20	.60
□ 215 Ray Herbert	4.00	1.80	.50
□ 216 Mike de la Hoz	4.00	1.80	.50
□ 217 Jim King	4.00	1.80	.50
□ 218 Hank Fischer	4.00	1.80	.50
□ 219 Young Aces	5.00	2.20	.60
Al Downing			
Jim Bouton			
□ 220 Dick Ellsworth	5.00	2.20	.60
□ 221 Bob Saverine	4.00	1.80	.50
□ 222 Billy Pierce	5.00	2.20	.60
□ 223 George Banks	4.00	1.80	.50
□ 224 Tommie Sisk	4.00	1.80	.50
□ 225 Roger Maris	50.00	22.00	6.25
□ 226 Colts Rookies	7.00	3.10	.85
Jerry Grote			
Larry Yellen			
□ 227 Barry Latman	4.00	1.80	.50
□ 228 Felix Mantilla	4.00	1.80	.50
□ 229 Charley Lau	5.00	2.20	.60
□ 230 Brooks Robinson	35.00	16.00	4.40
□ 231 Dick Calmus	4.00	1.80	.50
□ 232 Al Lopez MG	5.00	2.20	.60

☐ 233 Hal Smith 4.00 1.80 .50
☐ 234 Gary Bell 4.00 1.80 .50
☐ 235 Ron Hunt 4.00 1.80 .50
☐ 236 Bill Faul 4.00 1.80 .50
☐ 237 Cubs Team 7.00 3.10 .85
☐ 238 Roy McMillan 5.00 2.20 .60
☐ 239 Herm Starrette 4.00 1.80 .50
☐ 240 Bill White 5.00 2.20 .60
☐ 241 Jim Owens 4.00 1.80 .50
☐ 242 Harvey Kuenn 5.00 2.20 .60
☐ 243 Phillies Rookies 30.00 13.50 3.70
Richie Allen
John Herrnstein
☐ 244 Tony LaRussa 30.00 13.50 3.70
☐ 245 Dick Stigman 4.00 1.80 .50
☐ 246 Manny Mota 5.00 2.20 .60
☐ 247 Dave DeBusschere 6.00 2.70 .75
☐ 248 Johnny Pesky MG 5.00 2.20 .60
☐ 249 Doug Camilli 4.00 1.80 .50
☐ 250 Al Kaline 40.00 18.00 5.00
☐ 251 Choo Choo Coleman 5.00 2.20 .60
☐ 252 Ken Aspromonte 4.00 1.80 .50
☐ 253 Wally Post 5.00 2.20 .60
☐ 254 Don Hoak 5.00 2.20 .60
☐ 255 Lee Thomas 5.00 2.20 .60
☐ 256 Johnny Weekly 4.00 1.80 .50
☐ 257 San Francisco Giants 7.00 3.10 .85
Team Card
☐ 258 Garry Roggenburk 4.00 1.80 .50
☐ 259 Harry Bright 4.00 1.80 .50
☐ 260 Frank Robinson 35.00 16.00 4.40
☐ 261 Jim Hannan 4.00 1.80 .50
☐ 262 Cards Rookies 8.00 3.60 1.00
Mike Shannon
Harry Fanok
☐ 263 Chuck Estrada 4.00 1.80 .50
☐ 264 Jim Landis 4.00 1.80 .50
☐ 265 Jim Bunning 14.00 6.25 1.75
☐ 266 Gene Freese 4.00 1.80 .50
☐ 267 Wilbur Wood 7.00 3.10 .85
☐ 268 Bill's Got It 5.00 2.20 .60
Danny Murtaugh MG
Bill Virdon
☐ 269 Ellis Burton 4.00 1.80 .50
☐ 270 Rich Rollins 5.00 2.20 .60
☐ 271 Bob Sadowski 4.00 1.80 .50
☐ 272 Jake Wood 4.00 1.80 .50
☐ 273 Mel Nelson 4.00 1.80 .50
☐ 274 Checklist 4 10.00 2.00 1.00
☐ 275 John Tsitouris 4.00 1.80 .50
☐ 276 Jose Tartabull 5.00 2.20 .60
☐ 277 Ken Retzer 4.00 1.80 .50
☐ 278 Bobby Shantz 5.00 2.20 .60
☐ 279 Joe Koppe UER 4.00 1.80 .50
(Glove on wrong hand)
☐ 280 Juan Marichal 14.00 6.25 1.75
☐ 281 Yankees Rookies 5.00 2.20 .60
Jake Gibbs
Tom Metcalf
☐ 282 Bob Bruce 4.00 1.80 .50
☐ 283 Tom McCraw 4.00 1.80 .50
☐ 284 Dick Schofield 4.00 1.80 .50
☐ 285 Robin Roberts 14.00 6.25 1.75
☐ 286 Don Landrum 4.00 1.80 .50
☐ 287 Red Sox Rookies 50.00 22.00 6.25
Tony Conigliaro
Bill Spanswick
☐ 288 Al Moran 4.00 1.80 .50
☐ 289 Frank Funk 4.00 1.80 .50
☐ 290 Bob Allison 5.00 2.20 .60
☐ 291 Phil Ortega 4.00 1.80 .50
☐ 292 Mike Roarke 4.00 1.80 .50
☐ 293 Phillies Team 7.00 3.10 .85
☐ 294 Ken L. Hunt 4.00 1.80 .50
☐ 295 Roger Craig 5.00 2.20 .60
☐ 296 Ed Kirkpatrick 4.00 1.80 .50
☐ 297 Ken MacKenzie 4.00 1.80 .50
☐ 298 Harry Craft MG 4.00 1.80 .50
☐ 299 Bill Stafford 4.00 1.80 .50
☐ 300 Hank Aaron 90.00 40.00 11.00
☐ 301 Larry Brown 4.00 1.80 .50
☐ 302 Dan Pfister 4.00 1.80 .50
☐ 303 Jim Campbell 4.00 1.80 .50
☐ 304 Bob Johnson 4.00 1.80 .50
☐ 305 Jack Lamabe 4.00 1.80 .50
☐ 306 Giant Gunners 35.00 16.00 4.40
Willie Mays
Orlando Cepeda
☐ 307 Joe Gibbon 4.00 1.80 .50
☐ 308 Gene Stephens 4.00 1.80 .50
☐ 309 Paul Toth 4.00 1.80 .50
☐ 310 Jim Gilliam 5.00 2.20 .60
☐ 311 Tom Brown 5.00 2.20 .60
☐ 312 Tigers Rookies 4.00 1.80 .50
Fritz Fisher
Fred Gladding
☐ 313 Chuck Hiller 4.00 1.80 .50
☐ 314 Jerry Buchek 4.00 1.80 .50
☐ 315 Bo Belinsky 5.00 2.20 .60
☐ 316 Gene Oliver 4.00 1.80 .50
☐ 317 Al Smith 4.00 1.80 .50
☐ 318 Minnesota Twins 7.00 3.10 .85
Team Card
☐ 319 Paul Brown 4.00 1.80 .50
☐ 320 Rocky Colavito 14.00 6.25 1.75

☐ 321 Bob Lillis 4.00 1.80 .50
☐ 322 George Brunet 4.00 1.80 .50
☐ 323 John Buzhardt 4.00 1.80 .50
☐ 324 Casey Stengel MG 16.00 7.25 2.00
☐ 325 Hector Lopez 5.00 2.20 .60
☐ 326 Ron Brand 4.00 1.80 .50
☐ 327 Don Blasingame 4.00 1.80 .50
☐ 328 Bob Shaw 4.00 1.80 .50
☐ 329 Russ Nixon 4.00 1.80 .50
☐ 330 Tommy Harper 5.00 2.20 .60
☐ 331 AL Bombers 175.00 80.00 22.00
Roger Maris
Norm Cash
Mickey Mantle
Al Kaline
☐ 332 Ray Washburn 4.00 1.80 .50
☐ 333 Billy Moran 4.00 1.80 .50
☐ 334 Lew Krausse 4.00 1.80 .50
☐ 335 Don Mossi 5.00 2.20 .60
☐ 336 Andre Rodgers 4.00 1.80 .50
☐ 337 Dodgers Rookies 5.00 2.20 .60
Al Ferrara
Jeff Torborg
☐ 338 Jack Kralick 4.00 1.80 .50
☐ 339 Walt Bond 4.00 1.80 .50
☐ 340 Joe Cunningham 4.00 1.80 .50
☐ 341 Jim Roland 4.00 1.80 .50
☐ 342 Willie Stargell 30.00 13.50 3.70
☐ 343 Senators Team 7.00 3.10 .85
☐ 344 Phil Linz 5.00 2.20 .60
☐ 345 Frank Thomas 5.00 2.20 .60
☐ 346 Joey Jay 4.00 1.80 .50
☐ 347 Bobby Wine 5.00 2.20 .60
☐ 348 Ed Lopat MG 5.00 2.20 .60
☐ 349 Art Fowler 4.00 1.80 .50
☐ 350 Willie McCovey 20.00 9.00 2.50
☐ 351 Dan Schneider 4.00 1.80 .50
☐ 352 Eddie Bressoud 4.00 1.80 .50
☐ 353 Wally Moon 5.00 2.20 .60
☐ 354 Dave Giusti 4.00 1.80 .50
☐ 355 Vic Power 5.00 2.20 .60
☐ 356 Reds Rookies 5.00 2.20 .60
Bill McCool
Chico Ruiz
☐ 357 Charley James 4.00 1.80 .50
☐ 358 Ron Kline 4.00 1.80 .50
☐ 359 Jim Schaffer 4.00 1.80 .50
☐ 360 Joe Pepitone 7.00 3.10 .85
☐ 361 Jay Hook 4.00 1.80 .50
☐ 362 Checklist 5 10.00 2.00 1.00
☐ 363 Dick McAuliffe 5.00 2.20 .60
☐ 364 Joe Gaines 4.00 1.80 .50
☐ 365 Cal McLish 5.00 2.20 .60
☐ 366 Nelson Mathews 4.00 1.80 .50
☐ 367 Fred Whitfield 4.00 1.80 .50
☐ 368 White Sox Rookies 5.00 2.20 .60
Fritz Ackley
Don Buford
☐ 369 Jerry Zimmerman 4.00 1.80 .50
☐ 370 Hal Woodeshick 4.00 1.80 .50
☐ 371 Frank Howard 8.00 3.60 1.00
☐ 372 Howie Koplitz 7.00 3.10 .85
☐ 373 Pirates Team 12.00 5.50 1.50
☐ 374 Bobby Bolin 7.00 3.10 .85
☐ 375 Ron Santo 10.00 4.50 1.25
☐ 376 Dave Morehead 7.00 3.10 .85
☐ 377 Bob Skinner 7.50 3.40 .95
☐ 378 Braves Rookies 8.00 3.60 1.00
Woody Woodward
Jack Smith
☐ 379 Tony Gonzalez 7.50 3.40 .95
☐ 380 Whitey Ford 35.00 16.00 4.40
☐ 381 Bob Taylor 7.00 3.10 .85
☐ 382 Wes Stock 7.00 3.10 .85
☐ 383 Bill Rigney MG 7.00 3.10 .85
☐ 384 Ron Hansen 7.00 3.10 .85
☐ 385 Curt Simmons 8.00 3.60 1.00
☐ 386 Lenny Green 7.00 3.10 .85
☐ 387 Terry Fox 7.00 3.10 .85
☐ 388 A's Rookies 7.50 3.40 .95
John O'Donoghue
George Williams
☐ 389 Jim Umbricht 7.50 3.40 .95
(Card back mentions
his death)
☐ 390 Orlando Cepeda 8.00 3.60 1.00
☐ 391 Sam McDowell 7.50 3.40 .95
☐ 392 Jim Pagliaroni 7.00 3.10 .85
☐ 393 Casey Teaches 10.00 4.50 1.25
Casey Stengel MG
Ed Kranepool
☐ 394 Bob Miller 7.00 3.10 .85
☐ 395 Tom Tresh 9.00 4.00 1.10
☐ 396 Dennis Bennett 7.00 3.10 .85
☐ 397 Chuck Cottier 7.00 3.10 .85
☐ 398 Mets Rookies 7.00 3.10 .85
Bill Haas
Dick Smith
☐ 399 Jackie Brandt 7.00 3.10 .85
☐ 400 Warren Spahn 40.00 18.00 5.00
☐ 401 Charlie Maxwell 7.50 3.40 .95
☐ 402 Tom Sturdivant 7.00 3.10 .85
☐ 403 Reds Team 12.00 5.50 1.50
☐ 404 Tony Martinez 7.00 3.10 .85
☐ 405 Ken McBride 7.00 3.10 .85

☐ 406 Al Spangler 7.00 3.10 .85
☐ 407 Bill Freehan 8.00 3.60 1.00
☐ 408 Cubs Rookies 7.00 3.10 .85
Jim Stewart
Fred Burdette
☐ 409 Bill Fischer 7.00 3.10 .85
☐ 410 Dick Stuart 7.50 3.40 .95
☐ 411 Lee Walls 7.00 3.10 .85
☐ 412 Ray Culp 7.50 3.40 .95
☐ 413 Johnny Keane MG 7.00 3.10 .85
☐ 414 Jack Sanford 7.00 3.10 .85
☐ 415 Tony Kubek 10.00 4.50 1.25
☐ 416 Lee Maye 7.00 3.10 .85
☐ 417 Don Cardwell 7.00 3.10 .85
☐ 418 Orioles Rookies 7.50 3.40 .95
Darold Knowles
Les Narum
☐ 419 Ken Harrelson 14.00 6.25 1.75
☐ 420 Jim Maloney 7.50 3.40 .95
☐ 421 Camilo Carreon 7.00 3.10 .85
☐ 422 Jack Fisher 7.00 3.10 .85
☐ 423 Tops in NL 125.00 55.00 15.50
Hank Aaron
Willie Mays
☐ 424 Dick Bertell 7.00 3.10 .85
☐ 425 Norm Cash 8.00 3.60 1.00
☐ 426 Bob Rodgers 7.50 3.40 .95
☐ 427 Don Rudolph 7.00 3.10 .85
☐ 428 Red Sox Rookies 7.00 3.10 .85
Archie Skeen
Pete Smith
(Back states Archie
has retired)
☐ 429 Tim McCarver 10.00 4.50 1.25
☐ 430 Juan Pizarro 7.00 3.10 .85
☐ 431 George Alusik 7.00 3.10 .85
☐ 432 Ruben Amaro 7.50 3.40 .95
☐ 433 Yankees Team 35.00 16.00 4.40
☐ 434 Don Nottebart 7.00 3.10 .85
☐ 435 Vic Davalillo 7.00 3.10 .85
☐ 436 Charlie Neal 7.50 3.40 .95
☐ 437 Ed Bailey 7.00 3.10 .85
☐ 438 Checklist 6 16.00 3.20 1.60
☐ 439 Harvey Haddix 7.50 3.40 .95
☐ 440 Bob Clemente UER 250.00 110.00 31.00
(1960 Pittsbufh)
☐ 441 Bob Duliba 7.00 3.10 .85
☐ 442 Pumpsie Green 7.50 3.40 .95
☐ 443 Chuck Dressen MG 7.50 3.40 .95
☐ 444 Larry Jackson 7.00 3.10 .85
☐ 445 Bill Skowron 9.00 4.00 1.10
☐ 446 Julian Javier 7.50 3.40 .95
☐ 447 Ted Bowsfield 7.00 3.10 .85
☐ 448 Cookie Rojas 7.50 3.40 .95
☐ 449 Deron Johnson 7.50 3.40 .95
☐ 450 Steve Barber 7.00 3.10 .85
☐ 451 Joe Amalfitano 7.00 3.10 .85
☐ 452 Giants Rookies 8.00 3.60 1.00
Gil Garrido
Jim Ray Hart
☐ 453 Frank Baumann 7.00 3.10 .85
☐ 454 Tommie Aaron 7.50 3.40 .95
☐ 455 Bernie Allen 7.00 3.10 .85
☐ 456 Dodgers Rookies 10.00 4.50 1.25
Wes Parker
John Werhas
☐ 457 Jesse Gonder 7.00 3.10 .85
☐ 458 Ralph Terry 7.50 3.40 .95
☐ 459 Red Sox Rookies 7.00 3.10 .85
Pete Charton
Dalton Jones
☐ 460 Bob Gibson 35.00 16.00 4.40
☐ 461 George Thomas 7.00 3.10 .85
☐ 462 Birdie Tebbetts MG 7.50 3.40 .95
☐ 463 Don Leppert 7.00 3.10 .85
☐ 464 Dallas Green 8.00 3.60 1.00
☐ 465 Mike Hershberger 7.00 3.10 .85
☐ 466 A's Rookies 7.50 3.40 .95
Dick Green
Aurelio Monteagudo
☐ 467 Bob Aspromonte 7.00 3.10 .85
☐ 468 Gaylord Perry 40.00 18.00 5.00
☐ 469 Cubs Rookies 7.50 3.40 .95
Fred Norman
Sterling Slaughter
☐ 470 Jim Bouton 10.00 4.50 1.25
☐ 471 Gates Brown 10.00 4.50 1.25
☐ 472 Vern Law 7.50 3.40 .95
☐ 473 Baltimore Orioles 12.00 5.50 1.50
Team Card
☐ 474 Larry Sherry 7.50 3.40 .95
☐ 475 Ed Charles 7.00 3.10 .85
☐ 476 Braves Rookies 14.00 6.25 1.75
Rico Carty
Dick Kelley
☐ 477 Mike Joyce 7.00 3.10 .85
☐ 478 Dick Howser 7.50 3.40 .95
☐ 479 Cardinals Rookies 7.00 3.10 .85
Dave Bakenhaster
Johnny Lewis
☐ 480 Bob Purkey 7.00 3.10 .85
☐ 481 Chuck Schilling 7.00 3.10 .85
☐ 482 Phillies Rookies 7.50 3.40 .95
John Briggs
Danny Cater

☐ 483 Fred Valentine 7.00 3.10 .85
☐ 484 Bill Pleis 7.00 3.10 .85
☐ 485 Tom Haller 7.50 3.40 .95
☐ 486 Bob Kennedy MG 7.50 3.40 .95
☐ 487 Mike McCormick 7.50 3.40 .95
☐ 488 Yankees Rookies 8.00 3.60 1.00
Pete Mikkelsen
Bob Meyer
☐ 489 Julio Navarro 7.00 3.10 .85
☐ 490 Ron Fairly 9.00 4.00 1.10
☐ 491 Ed Rakow 7.00 3.10 .85
☐ 492 Colts Rookies 7.00 3.10 .85
Jim Beauchamp
Mike White
☐ 493 Don Lee 7.00 3.10 .85
☐ 494 Al Jackson 7.00 3.10 .85
☐ 495 Bill Virdon 7.50 3.40 .95
☐ 496 White Sox Team 12.00 5.50 1.50
☐ 497 Jeoff Long 7.00 3.10 .85
☐ 498 Dave Stenhouse 7.00 3.10 .85
☐ 499 Indians Rookies 7.50 3.40 .95
Chico Salmon
Gordon Seyfried
☐ 500 Camilo Pascual 7.50 3.40 .95
☐ 501 Bob Veale 7.50 3.40 .95
☐ 502 Angels Rookies 7.00 3.10 .85
Bobby Knoop
Bob Lee
☐ 503 Earl Wilson 7.50 3.40 .95
☐ 504 Claude Raymond 7.50 3.40 .95
☐ 505 Stan Williams 7.50 3.40 .95
☐ 506 Bobby Bragan MG 7.00 3.10 .85
☐ 507 Johnny Edwards 7.00 3.10 .85
☐ 508 Diego Segui 7.00 3.10 .85
☐ 509 Pirates Rookies 8.00 3.60 1.00
Gene Alley
Orlando McFarlane
☐ 510 Lindy McDaniel 7.50 3.40 .95
☐ 511 Lou Jackson 7.50 3.40 .95
☐ 512 Tigers Rookies 14.00 6.25 1.75
Willie Horton
Joe Sparma
☐ 513 Don Larsen 7.50 3.40 .95
☐ 514 Jim Hickman 7.50 3.40 .95
☐ 515 Johnny Romano 7.00 3.10 .85
☐ 516 Twins Rookies 7.00 3.10 .85
Jerry Arrigo
Dwight Siebler
☐ 517A Checklist 7 ERR 25.00 5.00 2.50
(Incorrect numbering
sequence on back)
☐ 517B Checklist 7 COR 16.00 3.20 1.60
(Correct numbering
on back)
☐ 518 Carl Bouldin 7.00 3.10 .85
☐ 519 Charlie Smith 7.00 3.10 .85
☐ 520 Jack Baldschun 7.50 3.40 .95
☐ 521 Tom Satriano 7.00 3.10 .85
☐ 522 Bob Tiefenauer 7.00 3.10 .85
☐ 523 Lou Burdette UER 17.00 7.75 2.10
(Pitching lefty)
☐ 524 Reds Rookies 16.00 7.25 2.00
Jim Dickson
Bobby Klaus
☐ 525 Al McBean 16.00 7.25 2.00
☐ 526 Lou Clinton 16.00 7.25 2.00
☐ 527 Larry Bearnarth 16.00 7.25 2.00
☐ 528 A's Rookies 17.00 7.75 2.10
Dave Duncan
Tommie Reynolds
☐ 529 Alvin Dark MG 17.00 7.75 2.10
☐ 530 Leon Wagner 16.00 7.25 2.00
☐ 531 Los Angeles Dodgers 25.00 11.00 3.10
Team Card
☐ 532 Twins Rookies 16.00 7.25 2.00
Bud Bloomfield
(Bloomfield photo
actually Jay Ward)
Joe Nossek
☐ 533 Johnny Klippstein 16.00 7.25 2.00
☐ 534 Gus Bell 16.00 7.25 2.00
☐ 535 Phil Regan 16.00 7.25 2.00
☐ 536 Mets Rookies 16.00 7.25 2.00
Larry Elliot
John Stephenson
☐ 537 Dan Osinski 16.00 7.25 2.00
☐ 538 Minnie Minoso 17.00 7.75 2.10
☐ 539 Roy Face 17.00 7.75 2.10
☐ 540 Luis Aparicio 25.00 11.00 3.10
☐ 541 Braves Rookies 100.00 45.00 12.50
Phil Roof
Phil Niekro
☐ 542 Don Mincher 16.00 7.25 2.00
☐ 543 Bob Uecker 40.00 18.00 5.00
☐ 544 Colts Rookies 16.00 7.25 2.00
Steve Hertz
Joe Hoerner
☐ 545 Max Alvis 16.00 7.25 2.00
☐ 546 Joe Christopher 16.00 7.25 2.00
☐ 547 Gil Hodges MG 25.00 11.00 3.10
☐ 548 NL Rookies 16.00 7.25 2.00
Wayne Schurr
Paul Speckenbach
☐ 549 Joe Moeller 16.00 7.25 2.00
☐ 550 Ken Hubbs MEM 35.00 16.00 4.40

☐ 551 Billy Hoeft	16.00	7.25	2.00
☐ 552 Indians Rookies	16.00	7.25	2.00
Tom Kelley			
Sonny Siebert			
☐ 553 Jim Brewer	16.00	7.25	2.00
☐ 554 Hank Foiles	16.00	7.25	2.00
☐ 555 Lee Stange	16.00	7.25	2.00
☐ 556 Mets Rookies	16.00	7.25	2.00
Steve Dillon			
Ron Locke			
☐ 557 Leo Burke	16.00	7.25	2.00
☐ 558 Don Schwall	16.00	7.25	2.00
☐ 559 Dick Phillips	16.00	7.25	2.00
☐ 560 Dick Farrell	16.00	7.25	2.00
☐ 561 Phillies Rookies UER	20.00	9.00	2.50
Dave Bennett			
(19 ... is 18)			
Rick Wise			
☐ 562 Pedro Ramos	16.00	7.25	2.00
☐ 563 Dal Maxvill	16.00	7.25	2.00
☐ 564 AL Rookies	16.00	7.25	2.00
Joe McCabe			
Jerry McNertney			
☐ 565 Stu Miller	16.00	7.25	2.00
☐ 566 Ed Kranepool	17.00	7.75	2.10
☐ 567 Jim Kaat	18.00	8.00	2.20
☐ 568 NL Rookies	16.00	7.25	2.00
Phil Gagliano			
Cap Peterson			
☐ 569 Fred Newman	16.00	7.25	2.00
☐ 570 Bill Mazeroski	18.00	8.00	2.20
☐ 571 Gene Conley	16.00	7.25	2.00
☐ 572 AL Rookies	16.00	7.25	2.00
Dave Gray			
Dick Egan			
☐ 573 Jim Duffalo	16.00	7.25	2.00
☐ 574 Manny Jimenez	16.00	7.25	2.00
☐ 575 Tony Cloninger	16.00	7.25	2.00
☐ 576 Mets Rookies	16.00	7.25	2.00
Jerry Hinsley			
Bill Wakefield			
☐ 577 Gordy Coleman	16.00	7.25	2.00
☐ 578 Glen Hobbie	16.00	7.25	2.00
☐ 579 Red Sox Team	25.00	11.00	3.10
☐ 580 Johnny Podres	20.00	9.00	2.50
☐ 581 Yankees Rookies	18.00	8.00	2.20
Pedro Gonzalez			
Archie Moore			
☐ 582 Rod Kanehl	17.00	7.75	2.10
☐ 583 Tito Francona	16.00	7.25	2.00
☐ 584 Joel Horlen	16.00	7.25	2.00
☐ 585 Tony Taylor	17.00	7.75	2.10
☐ 586 Jim Piersall	17.00	7.75	2.10
☐ 587 Bennie Daniels	20.00	8.00	2.20

1964 Topps Coins

This set of 164 unnumbered coins issued in 1964 is sometimes divided into two sets -- the regular series (1-120) and the all-star series (121-164). Each metal coin is approximately 1 1/2" in diameter. The regular series features gold and silver coins with a full color photo of the player, including the background of the photo. The player's name, team and position are delineated on the coin front. The back includes the line "Collect the entire set of 120 all-stars". The all-star series (denoted AS in the checklist below) contains a full color cutout photo of the player on a solid background. The fronts feature the line "1964 All-stars" along with the name only of the player. The backs contain the line "Collect all 44 special stars". Mantle, Causey and Hinton appear in two variations each. The complete set price below includes all variations.

	NRMT	VG-E	GOOD
COMPLETE SET (167)	600.00	275.00	75.00
COMMON COIN (1-164)	1.00	.45	.12
☐ 1 Don Zimmer	1.50	.70	.19
☐ 2 Jim Wynn	1.50	.70	.19
☐ 3 Johnny Orsino	1.00	.45	.12
☐ 4 Jim Bouton	1.50	.70	.19
☐ 5 Dick Groat	1.50	.70	.19
☐ 6 Leon Wagner	1.00	.45	.12
☐ 7 Frank Malzone	1.00	.45	.12
☐ 8 Steve Barber	1.00	.45	.12
☐ 9 Johnny Romano	1.00	.45	.12
☐ 10 Tom Tresh	1.50	.70	.19
☐ 11 Felipe Alou	1.50	.70	.19
☐ 12 Dick Stuart	1.50	.70	.19
☐ 13 Claude Osteen	1.00	.45	.12
☐ 14 Juan Pizarro	1.00	.45	.12
☐ 15 Donn Clendenon	1.00	.45	.12
☐ 16 Jimmie Hall	1.00	.45	.12
☐ 17 Al Jackson	1.00	.45	.12
☐ 18 Brooks Robinson	15.00	6.75	1.85
☐ 19 Bob Allison	1.50	.70	.19
☐ 20 Ed Roebuck	1.00	.45	.12
☐ 21 Pete Ward	1.00	.45	.12
☐ 22 Willie McCovey	8.00	3.60	1.00
☐ 23 Elston Howard	2.00	.90	.25
☐ 24 Diego Segui	1.00	.45	.12
☐ 25 Ken Boyer	1.50	.70	.19
☐ 26 Carl Yastrzemski	15.00	6.75	1.85
☐ 27 Bill Mazeroski	2.00	.90	.25
☐ 28 Jerry Lumpe	1.00	.45	.12
☐ 29 Woody Held	1.00	.45	.12
☐ 30 Dick Radatz	1.00	.45	.12
☐ 31 Luis Aparicio	6.00	2.70	.75
☐ 32 Dave Nicholson	1.00	.45	.12
☐ 33 Eddie Mathews	10.00	4.50	1.25
☐ 34 Don Drysdale	10.00	4.50	1.25
☐ 35 Ray Culp	1.00	.45	.12
☐ 36 Juan Marichal	8.00	3.60	1.00
☐ 37 Frank Robinson	15.00	6.75	1.85
☐ 38 Chuck Hinton	1.00	.45	.12
☐ 39 Floyd Robinson	1.00	.45	.12
☐ 40 Tommy Harper	1.50	.70	.19
☐ 41 Ron Hansen	1.00	.45	.12
☐ 42 Ernie Banks	15.00	6.75	1.85
☐ 43 Jesse Gonder	1.00	.45	.12
☐ 44 Billy Williams	5.00	2.20	.60
☐ 45 Vada Pinson	2.00	.90	.25
☐ 46 Rocky Colavito	3.00	1.35	.35
☐ 47 Bill Monbouquette	1.00	.45	.12
☐ 48 Max Alvis	1.00	.45	.12
☐ 49 Norm Siebern	1.00	.45	.12
☐ 50 John Callison	1.50	.70	.19
☐ 51 Rich Rollins	1.00	.45	.12
☐ 52 Ken McBride	1.00	.45	.12
☐ 53 Don Lock	1.00	.45	.12
☐ 54 Ron Fairly	1.50	.70	.19
☐ 55 Bob Clemente	40.00	18.00	5.00
☐ 56 Dick Ellsworth	1.00	.45	.12
☐ 57 Tommy Davis	1.50	.70	.19
☐ 58 Tony Gonzalez	1.00	.45	.12
☐ 59 Bob Gibson	8.00	3.60	1.00
☐ 60 Jim Maloney	1.50	.70	.19
☐ 61 Frank Howard	2.00	.90	.25
☐ 62 Jim Pagliaroni	1.00	.45	.12
☐ 63 Orlando Cepeda	3.00	1.35	.35
☐ 64 Ron Perranoski	1.00	.45	.12
☐ 65 Curt Flood	2.00	.90	.25
☐ 66 Alvin McBean	1.00	.45	.12
☐ 67 Dean Chance	1.00	.45	.12
☐ 68 Ron Santo	3.00	1.35	.35
☐ 69 Jack Baldschun	1.00	.45	.12
☐ 70 Milt Pappas	1.50	.70	.19
☐ 71 Gary Peters	1.00	.45	.12
☐ 72 Bobby Richardson	2.00	.90	.25
☐ 73 Frank Thomas	1.00	.45	.12
☐ 74 Hank Aguirre	1.00	.45	.12
☐ 75 Carlton Willey	1.00	.45	.12
☐ 76 Camilo Pascual	1.00	.45	.12
☐ 77 Bob Friend	1.00	.45	.12
☐ 78 Bill White	1.50	.70	.19
☐ 79 Norm Cash	2.00	.90	.25
☐ 80 Willie Mays	30.00	13.50	3.70
☐ 81 Leon Carmel	1.00	.45	.12
☐ 82 Pete Rose	25.00	11.00	3.10
☐ 83 Henry Aaron	25.00	11.00	3.10
☐ 84 Bob Aspromonte	1.00	.45	.12
☐ 85 Jim O'Toole	1.00	.45	.12
☐ 86 Vic Davalillo	1.00	.45	.12
☐ 87 Bill Freehan	1.50	.70	.19
☐ 88 Warren Spahn	10.00	4.50	1.25
☐ 89 Ken Hunt	1.00	.45	.12
☐ 90 Denis Menke	1.00	.45	.12
☐ 91 Dick Farrell	1.00	.45	.12
☐ 92 Jim Hickman	1.00	.45	.12
☐ 93 Jim Bunning	5.00	2.20	.60
☐ 94 Bob Hendley	1.00	.45	.12
☐ 95 Ernie Broglio	1.00	.45	.12
☐ 96 Rusty Staub	2.00	.90	.25
☐ 97 Lou Brock	8.00	3.60	1.00
☐ 98 Jim Fregosi	2.00	.90	.25
☐ 99 Jim Grant	1.00	.45	.12
☐ 100 Al Kaline	10.00	4.50	1.25
☐ 101 Earl Battey	1.00	.45	.12
☐ 102 Wayne Causey	1.00	.45	.12
☐ 103 Chuck Schilling	1.00	.45	.12
☐ 104 Boog Powell	2.00	.90	.25
☐ 105 Dave Wickersham	1.00	.45	.12
☐ 106 Sandy Koufax	20.00	9.00	2.50
☐ 107 John Bateman	1.00	.45	.12
☐ 108 Ed Brinkman	1.00	.45	.12
☐ 109 Al Downing	1.00	.45	.12
☐ 110 Joe Azcue	1.00	.45	.12
☐ 111 Albie Pearson	1.00	.45	.12
☐ 112 Harmon Killebrew	8.00	3.60	1.00
☐ 113 Tony Taylor	1.50	.70	.19
☐ 114 Larry Jackson	1.00	.45	.12
☐ 115 Billy O'Dell	1.00	.45	.12
☐ 116 Don Demeter	1.00	.45	.12
☐ 117 Ed Charles	1.00	.45	.12
☐ 118 Joe Torre	2.00	.90	.25
☐ 119 Don Nottebart	1.00	.45	.12
☐ 120 Mickey Mantle	80.00	36.00	10.00
☐ 121 Joe Pepitone AS	1.50	.70	.19
☐ 122 Dick Stuart AS	1.00	.45	.12
☐ 123 Bobby Richardson AS	2.00	.90	.25
☐ 124 Jerry Lumpe AS	1.00	.45	.12
☐ 125 Brooks Robinson AS	10.00	4.50	1.25
☐ 126 Frank Malzone AS	1.00	.45	.12
☐ 127 Luis Aparicio AS	5.00	2.20	.60
☐ 128 Jim Fregosi AS	1.50	.70	.19
☐ 129 Al Kaline AS	10.00	4.50	1.25
☐ 130 Leon Wagner AS	1.00	.45	.12
☐ 131A Mickey Mantle AS	60.00	27.00	7.50
(right handed)			
☐ 131B Mickey Mantle AS	60.00	27.00	7.50
(left handed)			
☐ 132 Albie Pearson AS	1.00	.45	.12
☐ 133 Harmon Killebrew AS	10.00	4.50	1.25
☐ 134 Carl Yastrzemski AS	10.00	4.50	1.25
☐ 135 Elston Howard AS	2.00	.90	.25
☐ 136 Earl Battey AS	1.00	.45	.12
☐ 137 Camilo Pascual AS	1.00	.45	.12
☐ 138 Jim Bouton AS	1.50	.70	.19
☐ 139 Whitey Ford AS	10.00	4.50	1.25
☐ 140 Gary Peters AS	1.00	.45	.12
☐ 141 Bill White AS	1.50	.70	.19
☐ 142 Orlando Cepeda AS	2.00	.90	.25
☐ 143 Bill Mazeroski AS	2.00	.90	.25
☐ 144 Tony Taylor AS	1.00	.45	.12
☐ 145 Ken Boyer AS	2.00	.90	.25
☐ 146 Ron Santo AS	2.00	.90	.25
☐ 147 Dick Groat AS	1.50	.70	.19
☐ 148 Roy McMillan AS	1.00	.45	.12
☐ 149 Henry Aaron AS	20.00	9.00	2.50
☐ 150 Bob Clemente AS	30.00	13.50	3.70
☐ 151 Willie Mays AS	25.00	11.00	3.10
☐ 152 Vada Pinson AS	1.50	.70	.19
☐ 153 Tommy Davis AS	1.50	.70	.19
☐ 154 Frank Robinson AS	10.00	4.50	1.25
☐ 155 Joe Torre AS	2.00	.90	.25
☐ 156 Tim McCarver AS	3.00	1.35	.35
☐ 157 Juan Marichal AS	5.00	2.20	.60
☐ 158 Jim Maloney AS	1.50	.70	.19
☐ 159 Sandy Koufax AS	15.00	6.75	1.85
☐ 160 Warren Spahn AS	6.00	2.70	.75
☐ 161A Wayne Causey AS	10.00	4.50	1.25
National League			
☐ 161B Wayne Causey AS	1.50	.70	.19
American League			
☐ 162A Chuck Hinton AS	10.00	4.50	1.25
National League			
☐ 162B Chuck Hinton AS	1.50	.70	.19
American League			
☐ 163 Bob Aspromonte AS	1.00	.45	.12
☐ 164 Ron Hunt AS	1.00	.45	.12

1964 Topps Stamps

Many of the 100 color portraits of baseball players featured in this 1964 Topps stamp series show players without caps. Each small stamp is 1" by 1 1/2". The subject's name, team and position are found in a colored rectangle beneath the picture area. Each sheet is numbered in the upper left hand corner outside the picture area. The sheet number is given after the player's name in the checklist below with the prefix S. The stamps were issued in sheets of 10 but an album to hold this particular set has not yet been seen.

	NRMT	VG-E	GOOD
COMPLETE SET (100)	450.00	200.00	55.00
COMMON STAMP (1-100)	1.00	.45	.12
☐ 1 Ed Charles S1	1.00	.45	.12
☐ 2 Vada Pinson S1	2.00	.90	.25
☐ 3 Jimmy Hall S1	1.00	.45	.12
☐ 4 Milt Pappas S1	1.50	.70	.19
☐ 5 Dick Ellsworth S1	1.00	.45	.12
☐ 6 Frank Malzone S1	1.50	.70	.19
☐ 7 Max Alvis S1	1.00	.45	.12
☐ 8 Pete Ward S1	1.00	.45	.12
☐ 9 Tony Taylor S1	1.50	.70	.19
☐ 10 Bill White S1	2.50	1.10	.30
☐ 11 Don Zimmer S2	2.00	.90	.25
☐ 12 Bobby Richardson S2	5.00	2.20	.60
☐ 13 Larry Jackson S2	1.00	.45	.12
☐ 14 Norm Siebern S2	1.00	.45	.12
☐ 15 Frank Robinson S2	15.00	6.75	1.85
☐ 16 Bob Aspromonte S2	1.00	.45	.12
☐ 17 Al McBean S2	1.00	.45	.12
☐ 18 Floyd Robinson S2	1.00	.45	.12
☐ 19 Bill Monbouquette S2	1.00	.45	.12
☐ 20 Willie Mays S2	40.00	18.00	5.00
☐ 21 Brooks Robinson S3	20.00	9.00	2.50
☐ 22 Joe Pepitone S3	2.50	1.10	.30
☐ 23 Carl Yastrzemski S3	20.00	9.00	2.50
☐ 24 Don Lock S3	1.00	.45	.12
☐ 25 Ernie Banks S3	20.00	9.00	2.50
☐ 26 Dave Nicholson S3	1.00	.45	.12
☐ 27 Bob Clemente S3	50.00	22.00	6.25
☐ 28 Curt Flood S3	2.50	1.10	.30
☐ 29 Woody Held S3	1.00	.45	.12
☐ 30 Jesse Gonder S3	1.00	.45	.12
☐ 31 Juan Pizarro S4	1.00	.45	.12
☐ 32 Jim Maloney S4	1.50	.70	.19
☐ 33 Ron Santo S4	2.50	1.10	.30
☐ 34 Harmon Killebrew S4	10.00	4.50	1.25
☐ 35 Ed Roebuck S4	1.00	.45	.12
☐ 36 Boog Powell S4	2.50	1.10	.30
☐ 37 Jim Grant S4	1.00	.45	.12
☐ 38 Hank Aguirre S4	1.00	.45	.12
☐ 39 Juan Marichal S4	10.00	4.50	1.25
☐ 40 Bill Mazeroski S4	2.50	1.10	.30
☐ 41 Dick Radatz S5	1.00	.45	.12
☐ 42 Albie Pearson S5	1.00	.45	.12
☐ 43 Tommy Harper S5	1.50	.70	.19
☐ 44 Carl Willey S5	1.00	.45	.12
☐ 45 Jim Bouton S5	2.50	1.10	.30
☐ 46 Ron Perranoski S5	1.00	.45	.12
☐ 47 Chuck Hinton S5	1.00	.45	.12
☐ 48 John Romano S5	1.00	.45	.12
☐ 49 Norm Cash S5	2.50	1.10	.30
☐ 50 Orlando Cepeda S5	5.00	2.20	.60
☐ 51 Dick Stuart S6	1.00	.45	.12
☐ 52 Rich Rollins S6	1.00	.45	.12
☐ 53 Mickey Mantle S6	75.00	34.00	9.50
☐ 54 Steve Barber S6	1.00	.45	.12
☐ 55 Jim O'Toole S6	1.00	.45	.12
☐ 56 Gary Peters S6	1.00	.45	.12
☐ 57 Warren Spahn S6	12.50	5.50	1.55
☐ 58 Tony Gonzalez S6	1.00	.45	.12
☐ 59 Joe Torre S6	2.50	1.10	.30
☐ 60 Jim Fregosi S6	2.00	.90	.25
☐ 61 Ken Boyer S7	2.50	1.10	.30
☐ 62 Felipe Alou S7	2.00	.90	.25
☐ 63 Jim Davenport S7	1.00	.45	.12
☐ 64 Tommy Davis S7	2.00	.90	.25
☐ 65 Rocky Colavito S7	4.00	1.80	.50
☐ 66 Bob Friend S7	1.50	.70	.19
☐ 67 Billy Moran S7	1.00	.45	.12
☐ 68 Bill Freehan S7	2.00	.90	.25
☐ 69 George Altman S7	1.00	.45	.12
☐ 70 Ken Johnson S7	1.00	.45	.12
☐ 71 Earl Battey S8	1.00	.45	.12
☐ 72 Elston Howard S8	2.50	1.10	.30
☐ 73 Billy Williams S8	10.00	4.50	1.25
☐ 74 Claude Osteen S8	1.50	.70	.19
☐ 75 Jim Gentile S8	1.50	.70	.19
☐ 76 Donn Clendenon S8	1.50	.70	.19
☐ 77 Ernie Broglio S8	1.00	.45	.12
☐ 78 Hal Woodeshick S8	1.00	.45	.12
☐ 79 Don Drysdale S8	10.00	4.50	1.25
☐ 80 John Callison S8	1.50	.70	.19
☐ 81 Dick Groat S9	1.00	.45	.12
☐ 82 Moe Drabowsky S9	1.00	.45	.12
☐ 83 Frank Howard S9	1.50	.70	.19
☐ 84 Hank Aaron S9	40.00	18.00	5.00
☐ 85 Al Jackson S9	1.00	.45	.12
☐ 86 Jerry Lumpe S9	1.00	.45	.12
☐ 87 Wayne Causey S9	1.00	.45	.12
☐ 88 Rusty Staub S9	2.50	1.10	.30
☐ 89 Ken McBride S9	1.00	.45	.12
☐ 90 Jack Baldschun S9	1.00	.45	.12
☐ 91 Sandy Koufax S10	25.00	11.00	3.10
☐ 92 Camilo Pascual S10	1.00	.45	.12
☐ 93 Ron Hunt S10	1.00	.45	.12
☐ 94 Willie McCovey S10	12.50	5.50	1.55
☐ 95 Al Kaline S10	15.00	6.75	1.85
☐ 96 Ray Culp S10	1.00	.45	.12
☐ 97 Ed Mathews S10	12.50	5.50	1.55
☐ 98 Dick Farrell S10	1.00	.45	.12
☐ 99 Lee Thomas S10	1.50	.70	.19
☐ 100 Vic Davalillo S10	1.00	.45	.12

1964 Topps Giants

The cards in this 60-card set measure approximately 3 1/8" by 5 1/4". The 1964 Topps Giants are postcard size cards containing color player photographs. They are numbered on the backs, which also contain biographical information presented in a newspaper format. These "giant size" cards were distributed in both cellophane and waxed gum packs apart from the Topps regular issue of 1964. The gum packs contain three cards. The Cards 3, 28, 42, 45, 47, 51 and 60 are more difficult to find and are indicated by SP in the checklist below.

	NRMT	VG-E	GOOD
COMPLETE SET (60)	200.00	90.00	25.00
COMMON CARD (1-60)	.50	.23	.06
☐ 1 Gary Peters	.75	.35	.09
☐ 2 Ken Johnson	.50	.23	.06

☐ 3 Sandy Koufax SP	40.00	18.00	5.00
☐ 4 Bob Bailey	.50	.23	.06
☐ 5 Milt Pappas	.75	.35	.09
☐ 6 Ron Hunt	.50	.23	.06
☐ 7 Whitey Ford	4.00	1.80	.50
☐ 8 Roy McMillan	.50	.23	.06
☐ 9 Rocky Colavito	1.25	.55	.16
☐ 10 Jim Bunning	3.00	1.35	.35
☐ 11 Bob Clemente	15.00	6.75	1.85
☐ 12 Al Kaline	5.00	2.20	.60
☐ 13 Nellie Fox	3.00	1.35	.35
☐ 14 Tony Gonzalez	.50	.23	.06
☐ 15 Jim Gentile	.50	.23	.06
☐ 16 Dean Chance	.75	.35	.09
☐ 17 Dick Ellsworth	.75	.35	.09
☐ 18 Jim Fregosi	.75	.35	.09
☐ 19 Dick Groat	.75	.35	.09
☐ 20 Chuck Hinton	.50	.23	.06
☐ 21 Elston Howard	.75	.35	.09
☐ 22 Dick Farrell	.50	.23	.06
☐ 23 Albie Pearson	.50	.23	.06
☐ 24 Frank Howard	.75	.35	.09
☐ 25 Mickey Mantle	30.00	13.50	3.70
☐ 26 Joe Torre	1.25	.55	.16
☐ 27 Eddie Brinkman	.50	.23	.06
☐ 28 Bob Friend SP	10.00	4.50	1.25
☐ 29 Frank Robinson	5.00	2.20	.60
☐ 30 Bill Freehan	.75	.35	.09
☐ 31 Warren Spahn	4.00	1.80	.50
☐ 32 Camilo Pascual	.75	.35	.09
☐ 33 Pete Ward	.50	.23	.06
☐ 34 Jim Maloney	.75	.35	.09
☐ 35 Dave Wickersham	.50	.23	.06
☐ 36 Johnny Callison	.75	.35	.09
☐ 37 Juan Marichal	4.00	1.80	.50
☐ 38 Harmon Killebrew	4.00	1.80	.50
☐ 39 Luis Aparicio	3.00	1.35	.35
☐ 40 Dick Radatz	.50	.23	.06
☐ 41 Bob Gibson	4.00	1.80	.50
☐ 42 Dick Stuart SP	10.00	4.50	1.25
☐ 43 Tommy Davis	.75	.35	.09
☐ 44 Tony Oliva	1.25	.55	.16
☐ 45 Wayne Causey SP	10.00	4.50	1.25
☐ 46 Max Alvis	.50	.23	.06
☐ 47 Galen Cisco SP	10.00	4.50	1.25
☐ 48 Carl Yastrzemski	5.00	2.20	.60
☐ 49 Hank Aaron	10.00	4.50	1.25
☐ 50 Brooks Robinson	5.00	2.20	.60
☐ 51 Willie Mays SP	50.00	22.00	6.25
☐ 52 Billy Williams	3.00	1.35	.35
☐ 53 Juan Pizarro	.50	.23	.06
☐ 54 Leon Wagner	.50	.23	.06
☐ 55 Orlando Cepeda	1.25	.55	.16
☐ 56 Vada Pinson	.75	.35	.09
☐ 57 Ken Boyer	.75	.35	.09
☐ 58 Ron Santo	1.25	.55	.16
☐ 59 John Romano	.50	.23	.06
☐ 60 Bill Skowron SP	15.00	6.75	1.85

1964 Topps Stand Ups

In 1964 Topps produced a die-cut "Stand-Up" card design for the first time since their Connie Mack and Current All Stars of 1951. The cards have full-length, color player photos set against a green and yellow background. Of the 77 cards in the set, 22 were single printed and these are marked in the checklist below with an SP. These unnumbered cards are standard-size (2 1/2" by 3 1/2"), blank backed, and have been numbered here for reference in alphabetical order of players.

	NRMT	VG-E	GOOD
COMPLETE SET (77)	2500.00	1100.00	300.00
COMMON CARD (1-77)	7.50	3.40	.95
COMMON CARD SP	30.00	13.50	3.70
WRAPPER (1-CENT)	150.00	70.00	19.00
WRAPPER (5-CENT)	200.00	90.00	25.00

☐ 1 Hank Aaron	150.00	70.00	19.00
☐ 2 Hank Aguirre	7.50	3.40	.95
☐ 3 George Altman	7.50	3.40	.95
☐ 4 Max Alvis	7.50	3.40	.95
☐ 5 Bob Aspromonte	7.50	3.40	.95
☐ 6 Jack Baldschun SP	30.00	13.50	3.70
☐ 7 Ernie Banks	60.00	27.00	7.50
☐ 8 Steve Barber	7.50	3.40	.95
☐ 9 Earl Battey	7.50	3.40	.95
☐ 10 Ken Boyer	10.00	4.50	1.25
☐ 11 Ernie Broglio	7.50	3.40	.95
☐ 12 John Callison	10.00	4.50	1.25
☐ 13 Norm Cash SP	35.00	16.00	4.40
☐ 14 Wayne Causey	7.50	3.40	.95
☐ 15 Orlando Cepeda	15.00	6.75	1.85
☐ 16 Ed Charles	7.50	3.40	.95
☐ 17 Bob Clemente	225.00	100.00	28.00
☐ 18 Donn Clendenon SP	30.00	13.50	3.70
☐ 19 Rocky Colavito	20.00	9.00	2.50
☐ 20 Ray Culp SP	30.00	13.50	3.70
☐ 21 Tommy Davis	10.00	4.50	1.25
☐ 22 Don Drysdale SP	100.00	45.00	12.50
☐ 23 Dick Ellsworth	7.50	3.40	.95
☐ 24 Dick Farrell	7.50	3.40	.95
☐ 25 Jim Fregosi	10.00	4.50	1.25
☐ 26 Bob Friend	7.50	3.40	.95
☐ 27 Jim Gentile	10.00	4.50	1.25
☐ 28 Jesse Gonder SP	30.00	13.50	3.70
☐ 29 Tony Gonzalez SP	30.00	13.50	3.70
☐ 30 Dick Groat	10.00	4.50	1.25
☐ 31 Woody Held	7.50	3.40	.95
☐ 32 Chuck Hinton	7.50	3.40	.95
☐ 33 Elston Howard	10.00	4.50	1.25
☐ 34 Frank Howard SP	35.00	16.00	4.40
☐ 35 Ron Hunt	7.50	3.40	.95
☐ 36 Al Jackson	7.50	3.40	.95
☐ 37 Ken Johnson	7.50	3.40	.95
☐ 38 Al Kaline	60.00	27.00	7.50
☐ 39 Harmon Killebrew	40.00	18.00	5.00
☐ 40 Sandy Koufax	100.00	45.00	12.50
☐ 41 Don Lock SP	30.00	13.50	3.70
☐ 42 Jerry Lumpe SP	30.00	13.50	3.70
☐ 43 Jim Maloney	10.00	4.50	1.25
☐ 44 Frank Malzone	7.50	3.40	.95
☐ 45 Mickey Mantle	550.00	250.00	70.00
☐ 46 Juan Marichal SP	100.00	45.00	12.50
☐ 47 Eddie Mathews SP	100.00	45.00	12.50
☐ 48 Willie Mays	150.00	70.00	19.00
☐ 49 Bill Mazeroski	15.00	6.75	1.85
☐ 50 Ken McBride	7.50	3.40	.95
☐ 51 Willie McCovey SP	100.00	45.00	12.50
☐ 52 Claude Osteen	10.00	4.50	1.25
☐ 53 Jim O'Toole	7.50	3.40	.95
☐ 54 Camilo Pascual	10.00	4.50	1.25
☐ 55 Albie Pearson SP	30.00	13.50	3.70
☐ 56 Gary Peters	7.50	3.40	.95
☐ 57 Vada Pinson	10.00	4.50	1.25
☐ 58 Juan Pizarro	7.50	3.40	.95
☐ 59 Boog Powell	12.00	5.50	1.50
☐ 60 Bobby Richardson	10.00	4.50	1.25
☐ 61 Brooks Robinson	60.00	27.00	7.50
☐ 62 Floyd Robinson	7.50	3.40	.95
☐ 63 Frank Robinson	60.00	27.00	7.50
☐ 64 Ed Roebuck SP	30.00	13.50	3.70
☐ 65 Rich Rollins	7.50	3.40	.95
☐ 66 John Romano	7.50	3.40	.95
☐ 67 Ron Santo SP	35.00	16.00	4.40
☐ 68 Norm Siebern	7.50	3.40	.95
☐ 69 Warren Spahn SP	100.00	45.00	12.50
☐ 70 Dick Stuart SP	30.00	13.50	3.70
☐ 71 Lee Thomas	7.50	3.40	.95
☐ 72 Joe Torre	12.00	5.50	1.50
☐ 73 Pete Ward	7.50	3.40	.95
☐ 74 Bill White SP	35.00	16.00	4.40
☐ 75 Billy Williams SP	75.00	34.00	9.50
☐ 76 Hal Woodeshick SP	30.00	13.50	3.70
☐ 77 Carl Yastrzemski SP	400.00	180.00	50.00

1964 Topps Tattoos

These tattoos measure 1 9/16" by 3 1/2" and are printed in color on very thin paper. One side gives instructions for applying the tattoo. The picture side gives either the team logo and name (on tattoos numbered 1-20 below) or the player's face, name and team (21-75 below). The tattoos are unnumbered and are presented below in alphabetical order within type for convenience.

	NRMT	VG-E	GOOD
COMPLETE SET (75)	1350.00	600.00	170.00
COMMON TEAM (1-20)	4.00	1.80	.50
COMMON TATTOO (21-75)	8.00	3.60	1.00

☐ 1 Baltimore Orioles	4.00	1.80	.50
☐ 2 Boston Red Sox	4.00	1.80	.50
☐ 3 California Angels	4.00	1.80	.50
☐ 4 Chicago Cubs	4.00	1.80	.50
☐ 5 Chicago White Sox	4.00	1.80	.50
☐ 6 Cincinnati Reds	4.00	1.80	.50
☐ 7 Cleveland Indians	4.00	1.80	.50
☐ 8 Detroit Tigers	5.00	2.20	.60
☐ 9 Houston Astros	4.00	1.80	.50
☐ 10 Kansas City Athletics	4.00	1.80	.50
☐ 11 Los Angeles Dodgers	7.50	3.40	.95
☐ 12 Milwaukee Braves	4.00	1.80	.50
☐ 13 Minnesota Twins	4.00	1.80	.50
☐ 14 New York Mets	5.00	2.20	.60
☐ 15 New York Yankees	7.50	3.40	.95
☐ 16 Philadelphia Phillies	4.00	1.80	.50
☐ 17 Pittsburgh Pirates	4.00	1.80	.50
☐ 18 St. Louis Cardinals	4.00	1.80	.50
☐ 19 San Francisco Giants	4.00	1.80	.50
☐ 20 Washington Senators	4.00	1.80	.50
☐ 21 Hank Aaron	100.00	45.00	12.50
☐ 22 Max Alvis	8.00	3.60	1.00
☐ 23 Hank Aguirre	8.00	3.60	1.00
☐ 24 Ernie Banks	60.00	27.00	7.50
☐ 25 Steve Barber	8.00	3.60	1.00
☐ 26 Ken Boyer	15.00	6.75	1.85
☐ 27 John Callison	8.00	3.60	1.00
☐ 28 Norm Cash	10.00	4.50	1.25
☐ 29 Wayne Causey	8.00	3.60	1.00
☐ 30 Orlando Cepeda	15.00	6.75	1.85
☐ 31 Rocky Colavito	20.00	9.00	2.50
☐ 32 Ray Culp	8.00	3.60	1.00
☐ 33 Vic Davalillo	8.00	3.60	1.00
☐ 34 Moe Drabowsky	8.00	3.60	1.00
☐ 35 Dick Ellsworth	8.00	3.60	1.00
☐ 36 Curt Flood	12.00	5.50	1.50
☐ 37 Bill Freehan	10.00	4.50	1.25
☐ 38 Jim Fregosi	10.00	4.50	1.25
☐ 39 Bob Friend	8.00	3.60	1.00
☐ 40 Dick Groat	12.00	5.50	1.50
☐ 41 Woody Held	8.00	3.60	1.00
☐ 42 Frank Howard	12.00	5.50	1.50
☐ 43 Al Jackson	8.00	3.60	1.00
☐ 44 Larry Jackson	8.00	3.60	1.00
☐ 45 Ken Johnson	8.00	3.60	1.00
☐ 46 Al Kaline	60.00	27.00	7.50
☐ 47 Harmon Killebrew	50.00	22.00	6.25
☐ 48 Sandy Koufax	100.00	45.00	12.50
☐ 49 Don Lock	8.00	3.60	1.00
☐ 50 Frank Malzone	10.00	4.50	1.25
☐ 51 Mickey Mantle	250.00	110.00	31.00
☐ 52 Eddie Mathews	50.00	22.00	6.25
☐ 53 Willie Mays	100.00	45.00	12.50
☐ 54 Bill Mazeroski	12.00	5.50	1.50
☐ 55 Ken McBride	8.00	3.60	1.00
☐ 56 Bill Monbouquette	8.00	3.60	1.00
☐ 57 Dave Nicholson	8.00	3.60	1.00
☐ 58 Claude Osteen	8.00	3.60	1.00
☐ 59 Milt Pappas	10.00	4.50	1.25
☐ 60 Camilo Pascual	8.00	3.60	1.00
☐ 61 Albie Pearson	8.00	3.60	1.00
☐ 62 Ron Perranoski	8.00	3.60	1.00
☐ 63 Gary Peters	8.00	3.60	1.00
☐ 64 Boog Powell	12.00	5.50	1.50
☐ 65 Frank Robinson	50.00	22.00	6.25
☐ 66 Johnny Romano	8.00	3.60	1.00
☐ 67 Norm Siebern	8.00	3.60	1.00
☐ 68 Warren Spahn	50.00	22.00	6.25
☐ 69 Dick Stuart	10.00	4.50	1.25
☐ 70 Lee Thomas	10.00	4.50	1.25
☐ 71 Joe Torre	15.00	6.75	1.85
☐ 72 Pete Ward	8.00	3.60	1.00
☐ 73 Carlton Willey	8.00	3.60	1.00
☐ 74 Billy Williams	40.00	18.00	5.00
☐ 75 Carl Yastrzemski	75.00	34.00	9.50

1964 Topps Venezuelan

This set is a parallel version of the first 370 cards in the regular 1964 Topps set and is similar in design. The major difference is the black margin featured on the card back. The cards were issued for the Venezuelan market.

	NRMT	VG-E	GOOD
COMPLETE SET (370)	6500.00	2900.00	800.00
COMMON CARD (1-370)	7.50	3.40	.95

☐ 1 NL ERA Leaders	60.00	27.00	7.50
Sandy Koufax			
Dick Ellsworth			
Bob Friend			
☐ 2 AL ERA Leaders	10.00	4.50	1.25
Gary Peters			
Juan Pizarro			
Camilo Pascual			
☐ 3 NL Pitching Leaders	45.00	20.00	5.50
Sandy Koufax			
Juan Marichal			
Warren Spahn			
Jim Maloney			
☐ 4 AL Pitching Leaders	25.00	11.00	3.10
Whitey Ford			
Camilo Pascual			
Jim Bouton			
☐ 5 NL Strikeout Leaders	35.00	16.00	4.40
Sandy Koufax			
Jim Maloney			
Don Drysdale			
☐ 6 AL Strikeout Leaders	10.00	4.50	1.25
Camilo Pascual			
Jim Bunning			
Dick Stigman			
☐ 7 NL Batting Leaders	50.00	22.00	6.25
Tommy Davis			
Bob Clemente			
Dick Groat			
Hank Aaron			
☐ 8 AL Batting Leaders	30.00	13.50	3.70
Carl Yastrzemski			
Al Kaline			
Rich Rollins			
☐ 9 NL Home Run Leaders	75.00	34.00	9.50
Hank Aaron			
Willie McCovey			
Willie Mays			
Orlando Cepeda			
☐ 10 AL Home Run Leaders	25.00	11.00	3.10
Harmon Killebrew			
Dick Stuart			
Bob Allison			
☐ 11 NL RBI Leaders	30.00	13.50	3.70
Hank Aaron			
Ken Boyer			
Bill White			
☐ 12 AL RBI Leaders	25.00	11.00	3.10
Dick Stuart			
Al Kaline			
Harmon Killebrew			
☐ 13 Hoyt Wilhelm	25.00	11.00	3.10
☐ 14 Dodgers Rookies	7.50	3.40	.95
Dick Nen			
Nick Willhite			
☐ 15 Zoilo Versalles	7.50	3.40	.95
☐ 16 John Boozer	7.50	3.40	.95
☐ 17 Willie Kirkland	7.50	3.40	.95
☐ 18 Billy O'Dell	7.50	3.40	.95
☐ 19 Don Wert	7.50	3.40	.95
☐ 20 Bob Friend	7.50	3.40	.95
☐ 21 Yogi Berra MG	75.00	34.00	9.50
☐ 22 Jerry Adair	7.50	3.40	.95
☐ 23 Chris Zachary	7.50	3.40	.95
☐ 24 Carl Sawatski	7.50	3.40	.95
☐ 25 Bill Monbouquette	7.50	3.40	.95
☐ 26 Gino Cimoli	7.50	3.40	.95
☐ 27 New York Mets	15.00	6.75	1.85
Team Card			
☐ 28 Claude Osteen	7.50	3.40	.95
☐ 29 Lou Brock	80.00	36.00	10.00
☐ 30 Ron Perranoski	7.50	3.40	.95
☐ 31 Dave Nicholson	7.50	3.40	.95
☐ 32 Dean Chance	7.50	3.40	.95
☐ 33 Reds Rookies	7.50	3.40	.95
Sammy Ellis			
Mel Queen			
☐ 34 Jim Perry	7.50	3.40	.95
☐ 35 Eddie Mathews	7.50	3.40	.95
☐ 36 Hal Reniff	7.50	3.40	.95
☐ 37 Smoky Burgess	7.50	3.40	.95
☐ 38 Jim Wynn	15.00	6.75	1.85
☐ 39 Hank Aguirre	7.50	3.40	.95
☐ 40 Dick Groat	7.50	3.40	.95
☐ 41 Friendly Foes	15.00	6.75	1.85
Willie McCovey			
Leon Wagner			
☐ 42 Moe Drabowsky	7.50	3.40	.95
☐ 43 Roy Sievers	7.50	3.40	.95
☐ 44 Duke Carmel	7.50	3.40	.95
☐ 45 Milt Pappas	7.50	3.40	.95
☐ 46 Ed Brinkman	7.50	3.40	.95
☐ 47 Giants Rookies	7.50	3.40	.95
Jesus Alou			
Ron Herbel			
☐ 48 Bob Perry	7.50	3.40	.95
☐ 49 Bill Henry	7.50	3.40	.95
☐ 50 Mickey Mantle	750.00	350.00	95.00
☐ 51 Pete Richert	7.50	3.40	.95
☐ 52 Chuck Hinton	7.50	3.40	.95
☐ 53 Denis Menke	7.50	3.40	.95
☐ 54 Sam Mele MG	7.50	3.40	.95
☐ 55 Ernie Banks	80.00	36.00	10.00
☐ 56 Hal Brown	7.50	3.40	.95
☐ 57 Tim Harkness	7.50	3.40	.95
☐ 58 Don Demeter	7.50	3.40	.95
☐ 59 Ernie Broglio	7.50	3.40	.95
☐ 60 Frank Malzone	7.50	3.40	.95
☐ 61 Angel Backstops	7.50	3.40	.95
Bob Rodgers			
Ed Sadowski			
☐ 62 Ted Savage	7.50	3.40	.95
☐ 63 John Orsino	7.50	3.40	.95
☐ 64 Ted Abernathy	7.50	3.40	.95
☐ 65 Felipe Alou	7.50	3.40	.95
☐ 66 Eddie Fisher	7.50	3.40	.95
☐ 67 Tigers Team	10.00	4.50	1.25
☐ 68 Willie Davis	7.50	3.40	.95
☐ 69 Clete Boyer	7.50	3.40	.95
☐ 70 Joe Torre	10.00	4.50	1.25
☐ 71 Jack Spring	7.50	3.40	.95
☐ 72 Chico Cardenas	7.50	3.40	.95
☐ 73 Jimmie Hall	7.50	3.40	.95
☐ 74 Pirates Rookies	7.50	3.40	.95
Bob Priddy			
Tom Butters			
☐ 75 Wayne Causey	7.50	3.40	.95
☐ 76 Checklist 1	20.00	9.00	2.50
☐ 77 Jerry Walker	7.50	3.40	.95
☐ 78 Merritt Ranew	7.50	3.40	.95
☐ 79 Bob Heffner	7.50	3.40	.95
☐ 80 Vada Pinson	10.00	4.50	1.25
☐ 81 All-Star Vets	20.00	9.00	2.50
Nellie Fox			
Harmon Killebrew			
☐ 82 Jim Davenport	7.50	3.40	.95
☐ 83 Gus Triandos	7.50	3.40	.95
☐ 84 Carl Willey	7.50	3.40	.95
☐ 85 Pete Ward	7.50	3.40	.95
☐ 86 Al Downing	7.50	3.40	.95
☐ 87 St. Louis Cardinals	10.00	4.50	1.25
Team Card			
☐ 88 John Roseboro	7.50	3.40	.95
☐ 89 Boog Powell	15.00	6.75	1.85
☐ 90 Earl Battey	7.50	3.40	.95
☐ 91 Bob Bailey	7.50	3.40	.95
☐ 92 Steve Ridzik	7.50	3.40	.95
☐ 93 Gary Geiger	7.50	3.40	.95
☐ 94 Braves Rookies	7.50	3.40	.95
Jim Britton			
Larry Maxie			
☐ 95 George Altman	7.50	3.40	.95

□ 96 Bob Buhl 7.50 3.40 .95
□ 97 Jim Fregosi 7.50 3.40 .95
□ 98 Bill Bruton 7.50 3.40 .95
□ 99 Al Stanek 7.50 3.40 .95
□ 100 Elston Howard 10.00 4.50 1.25
□ 101 Walt Alston MG 10.00 4.50 1.25
□ 102 Checklist 2 20.00 9.00 2.50
□ 103 Curt Flood 10.00 4.50 1.25
□ 104 Art Mahaffey 7.50 3.40 .95
□ 105 Woody Helkd 7.50 3.40 .95
□ 106 Joe Nuxhall 7.50 3.40 .95
□ 107 White Sox Rookies 7.50 3.40 .95
Bruce Howard
Frank Kreutzer
□ 108 John Wyatt 7.50 3.40 .95
□ 109 Rusty Staub 10.00 4.50 1.25
□ 110 Albie Pearson 7.50 3.40 .95
□ 111 Don Elston 7.50 3.40 .95
□ 112 Bob Tillman 7.50 3.40 .95
□ 113 Grover Powell 7.50 3.40 .95
□ 114 Don Lock 7.50 3.40 .95
□ 115 Frank Bolling 7.50 3.40 .95
□ 116 Twins Rookies 30.00 13.50 3.70
Jay Ward
Tony Oliva
□ 117 Earl Francis 7.50 3.40 .95
□ 118 John Blanchard 7.50 3.40 .95
□ 119 Gary Kolb 7.50 3.40 .95
□ 120 Don Drysdale 50.00 22.00 6.25
□ 121 Pete Runnels 7.50 3.40 .95
□ 122 Don McMahon 7.50 3.40 .95
□ 123 Jose Pagan 7.50 3.40 .95
□ 124 Orlando Pena 7.50 3.40 .95
□ 125 Pete Rose 375.00 170.00 47.50
□ 126 Russ Snyder 7.50 3.40 .95
□ 127 Angels Rookies 7.50 3.40 .95
Aubrey Gatewood
Dick Simpson
□ 128 Mickey Lolich 50.00 22.00 6.25
□ 129 Amado Samuel 7.50 3.40 .95
□ 130 Gary Peters 7.50 3.40 .95
□ 131 Steve Boros 7.50 3.40 .95
□ 132 Braves Team 10.00 4.50 1.25
□ 133 Jim Grant 7.50 3.40 .95
□ 134 Don Zimmer 7.50 3.40 .95
□ 135 Johnny Callison 7.50 3.40 .95
□ 136 Sandy Koufax WS 40.00 18.00 5.00
Strikes out 15
□ 137 Tommy Davis WS 10.00 4.50 1.25
□ 138 Ron Fairly WS 10.00 4.50 1.25
□ 139 Frank Howard WS 10.00 4.50 1.25
□ 140 World Series Summary 10.00 4.50 1.25
Dodgers celebrate
□ 141 Danny Murtaugh MG 7.50 3.40 .95
□ 142 John Bateman 7.50 3.40 .95
□ 143 Bubba Phillips 7.50 3.40 .95
□ 144 Al Worthington 7.50 3.40 .95
□ 145 Norm Siebern 7.50 3.40 .95
□ 146 Indians Rookies 75.00 34.00 9.50
Tommy John
Bob Chance
□ 147 Ray Sadecki 7.50 3.40 .95
□ 148 J.C. Martin 7.50 3.40 .95
□ 149 Paul Foytack 7.50 3.40 .95
□ 150 Willie Mays 250.00 110.00 31.00
□ 151 Athletics Team 10.00 4.50 1.25
□ 152 Denny Lemaster 7.50 3.40 .95
□ 153 Dick Williams 7.50 3.40 .95
□ 154 Dick Tracewski 7.50 3.40 .95
□ 155 Duke Snider 75.00 34.00 9.50
□ 156 Bill Dailey 7.50 3.40 .95
□ 157 Gene Mauch MG 7.50 3.40 .95
□ 158 Ken Johnson 7.50 3.40 .95
□ 159 Charlie Dees 7.50 3.40 .95
□ 160 Ken Boyer 10.00 4.50 1.25
□ 161 Dave McNally 7.50 3.40 .95
□ 162 Hitting Area 7.50 3.40 .95
Dick Sisler CO
Vada Pinson
□ 163 Donn Clendenon 7.50 3.40 .95
□ 164 Bud Daley 7.50 3.40 .95
□ 165 Jerry Lumpe 7.50 3.40 .95
□ 166 Marty Keough 7.50 3.40 .95
□ 167 Senators Rookies 75.00 34.00 9.50
Mike Brumley
Lou Piniella
□ 168 Al Weis 7.50 3.40 .95
□ 169 Del Crandall 7.50 3.40 .95
□ 170 Dick Radatz 7.50 3.40 .95
□ 171 Ty Cline 7.50 3.40 .95
□ 172 Indians Team 10.00 4.50 1.25
□ 173 Ryne Duren 7.50 3.40 .95
□ 174 Doc Edwards 7.50 3.40 .95
□ 175 Billy Williams 35.00 16.00 4.40
□ 176 Tracy Stallard 7.50 3.40 .95
□ 177 Harmon Killebrew 50.00 22.00 6.25
□ 178 Hank Bauer MG 7.50 3.40 .95
□ 179 Carl Warwick 7.50 3.40 .95
□ 180 Tommy Davis 7.50 3.40 .95
□ 181 Dave Wickersham 7.50 3.40 .95
□ 182 Sox Sockers 35.00 16.00 4.40
Carl Yastrzemski
Chuck Schilling
□ 183 Ron Taylor 7.50 3.40 .95
□ 184 Al Luplow 7.50 3.40 .95
□ 185 Jim O'Toole 7.50 3.40 .95
□ 186 Roman Mejias 7.50 3.40 .95
□ 187 Ed Roebuck 7.50 3.40 .95
□ 188 Checklist 3 20.00 9.00 2.50
□ 189 Bob Hendley 7.50 3.40 .95
□ 190 Bobby Richardson 20.00 9.00 2.50
□ 191 Clay Dalrymple 7.50 3.40 .95
□ 192 Cubs Rookies 7.50 3.40 .95
John Boccabella
Billy Cowan
□ 193 Jerry Lynch 7.50 3.40 .95
□ 194 John Goryl 7.50 3.40 .95
□ 195 Floyd Robinson 7.50 3.40 .95
□ 196 Jim Gentile 7.50 3.40 .95
□ 197 Frank Lary 7.50 3.40 .95
□ 198 Len Gabrielson 7.50 3.40 .95
□ 199 Joe Azcue 7.50 3.40 .95
□ 200 Sandy Koufax 250.00 110.00 31.00
□ 201 Orioles Rookies 7.50 3.40 .95
Sam Bowens
Wally Bunker
□ 202 Galen Cisco 7.50 3.40 .95
□ 203 John Kennedy 7.50 3.40 .95
□ 204 Matty Alou 10.00 4.50 1.25
□ 205 Nellie Fox 25.00 11.00 3.10
□ 206 Steve Hamilton 7.50 3.40 .95
□ 207 Fred Hutchinson MG 7.50 3.40 .95
□ 208 Wes Covington 7.50 3.40 .95
□ 209 Bob Allen 7.50 3.40 .95
□ 210 Carl Yastrzemski 80.00 36.00 10.00
□ 211 Jim Coker 7.50 3.40 .95
□ 212 Pete Lovrich 7.50 3.40 .95
□ 213 Angels Team 10.00 4.50 1.25
□ 214 Ken McMullen 7.50 3.40 .95
□ 215 Ray Herbert 7.50 3.40 .95
□ 216 Mike de la Hoz 7.50 3.40 .95
□ 217 Jim King 7.50 3.40 .95
□ 218 Hank Fischer 7.50 3.40 .95
□ 219 Young Aces 7.50 3.40 .95
Al Downing
Jim Bouton
□ 220 Dick Ellsworth 7.50 3.40 .95
□ 221 Bob Saverine 7.50 3.40 .95
□ 222 Billy Pierce 10.00 4.50 1.25
□ 223 George Banks 7.50 3.40 .95
□ 224 Tommie Sisk 7.50 3.40 .95
□ 225 Roger Maris 125.00 55.00 15.50
□ 226 Colts Rookies 10.00 4.50 1.25
Jerry Grote
Larry Yellen
□ 227 Barry Latman 7.50 3.40 .95
□ 228 Felix Mantilla 7.50 3.40 .95
□ 229 Charley Lau 7.50 3.40 .95
□ 230 Brooks Robinson 80.00 36.00 10.00
□ 231 Dick Calmus 7.50 3.40 .95
□ 232 Al Lopez MG 10.00 4.50 1.25
□ 233 Hal Smith 7.50 3.40 .95
□ 234 Gary Bell 7.50 3.40 .95
□ 235 Ron Hunt 7.50 3.40 .95
□ 236 Bill Faul 7.50 3.40 .95
□ 237 Cubs Team 10.00 4.50 1.25
□ 238 Roy McMillan 7.50 3.40 .95
□ 239 Herm Starrette 7.50 3.40 .95
□ 240 Bill White 10.00 4.50 1.25
□ 241 Jim Owens 7.50 3.40 .95
□ 242 Harvey Kuenn 7.50 3.40 .95
□ 243 Phillies Rookies 75.00 34.00 9.50
Richie Allen
John Herrnstein
□ 244 Tony LaRussa 75.00 34.00 9.50
□ 245 Dick Stigman 7.50 3.40 .95
□ 246 Manny Mota 10.00 4.50 1.25
□ 247 Dave DeBusschere 12.00 5.50 1.50
□ 248 Johnny Pesky MG 7.50 3.40 .95
□ 249 Doug Camilli 7.50 3.40 .95
□ 250 Al Kaline 100.00 45.00 12.50
□ 251 Choo Choo Coleman 7.50 3.40 .95
□ 252 Ken Aspromonte 7.50 3.40 .95
□ 253 Wally Post 7.50 3.40 .95
□ 254 Don Hoak 7.50 3.40 .95
□ 255 Lee Thomas 7.50 3.40 .95
□ 256 Johnny Weekly 7.50 3.40 .95
□ 257 San Francisco Giants 10.00 4.50 1.25
Team Card
□ 258 Garry Roggenburk 7.50 3.40 .95
□ 259 Harry Bright 7.50 3.40 .95
□ 260 Frank Robinson 80.00 36.00 10.00
□ 261 Jim Hannan 7.50 3.40 .95
□ 262 Cards Rookies 20.00 9.00 2.50
Mike Shannon
Harry Fanok
□ 263 Chuck Estrada 7.50 3.40 .95
□ 264 Jim Landis 7.50 3.40 .95
□ 265 Jim Bunning 35.00 16.00 4.40
□ 266 Gene Freese 7.50 3.40 .95
□ 267 Wilbur Wood 10.00 4.50 1.25
□ 268 Bill's Got It 7.50 3.40 .95
Danny Murtaugh
Bill Virdon MG
□ 269 Ellis Burton 7.50 3.40 .95
□ 270 Rich Rollins 7.50 3.40 .95
□ 271 Bob Sadowski 7.50 3.40 .95
□ 272 Jake Wood 7.50 3.40 .95
□ 273 Mel Nelson 7.50 3.40 .95
□ 274 Checklist 4 20.00 9.00 2.50
□ 275 John Tsitouris 7.50 3.40 .95
□ 276 Jose Tartabull 7.50 3.40 .95
□ 277 Ken Retzer 7.50 3.40 .95
□ 278 Bobby Shantz 7.50 3.40 .95
□ 279 Joe Koppe UER 7.50 3.40 .95
(Glove on wrong hand)
□ 280 Juan Marichal 35.00 16.00 4.40
□ 281 Yankees Rookies 7.50 3.40 .95
Jake Gibbs
Tom Metcalf
□ 282 Bob Bruce 7.50 3.40 .95
□ 283 Tom McCraw 7.50 3.40 .95
□ 284 Dick Schofield 7.50 3.40 .95
□ 285 Robin Roberts 35.00 16.00 4.40
□ 286 Don Landrum 7.50 3.40 .95
□ 287 Red Sox Rookies 125.00 55.00 15.50
Tony Conigliaro
Bill Spanswick
□ 288 Al Moran 7.50 3.40 .95
□ 289 Frank Funk 7.50 3.40 .95
□ 290 Bob Allison 7.50 3.40 .95
□ 291 Phil Ortega 7.50 3.40 .95
□ 292 Mike Roarke 7.50 3.40 .95
□ 293 Phillies Team 7.50 3.40 .95
□ 294 Ken L. Hunt 7.50 3.40 .95
□ 295 Roger Craig 7.50 3.40 .95
□ 296 Ed Kirkpatrick 7.50 3.40 .95
□ 297 Ken MacKenzie 7.50 3.40 .95
□ 298 Harry Craft MG 7.50 3.40 .95
□ 299 Bill Stafford 7.50 3.40 .95
□ 300 Hank Aaron 225.00 100.00 28.00
□ 301 Larry Brown 7.50 3.40 .95
□ 302 Dan Pfister 7.50 3.40 .95
□ 303 Jim Campbell 7.50 3.40 .95
□ 304 Bob Johnson 7.50 3.40 .95
□ 305 Jack Lamabe 7.50 3.40 .95
□ 306 Giant Gunners 80.00 36.00 10.00
Willie Mays
Orlando Cepeda
□ 307 Joe Gibbon 7.50 3.40 .95
□ 308 Gene Stephens 7.50 3.40 .95
□ 309 Paul Toth 7.50 3.40 .95
□ 310 Jim Gilliam 10.00 4.50 1.25
□ 311 Tom Brown 7.50 3.40 .95
□ 312 Tigers Rookies 7.50 3.40 .95
Fritz Fisher
Fred Gladding
□ 313 Chuck Hiller 7.50 3.40 .95
□ 314 Jerry Buchek 7.50 3.40 .95
□ 315 Bo Belinsky 7.50 3.40 .95
□ 316 Gene Oliver 7.50 3.40 .95
□ 317 Al Smith 7.50 3.40 .95
□ 318 Minnesota Twins 7.50 3.40 .95
Team Card
□ 319 Paul Brown 7.50 3.40 .95
□ 320 Rocky Colavito 35.00 16.00 4.40
□ 321 Bob Lillis 7.50 3.40 .95
□ 322 George Brunet 7.50 3.40 .95
□ 323 John Buzhardt 7.50 3.40 .95
□ 324 Casey Stengel MG 40.00 18.00 5.00
□ 325 Hector Lopez 7.50 3.40 .95
□ 326 Ron Brand 7.50 3.40 .95
□ 327 Don Blasingame 7.50 3.40 .95
□ 328 Bob Shaw 7.50 3.40 .95
□ 329 Russ Nixon 7.50 3.40 .95
□ 330 Tommy Harper 7.50 3.40 .95
□ 331 AL Bombers 450.00 200.00 55.00
Roger Maris
Norm Cash
Mickey Mantle
Al Kaline
□ 332 Ray Washburn 7.50 3.40 .95
□ 333 Billy Moran 7.50 3.40 .95
□ 334 Lew Krausse 7.50 3.40 .95
□ 335 Don Mossi 7.50 3.40 .95
□ 336 Andre Rodgers 7.50 3.40 .95
□ 337 Dodgers Rookies 7.50 3.40 .95
Al Ferrara
Jeff Torborg
□ 338 Jack Kralick 7.50 3.40 .95
□ 339 Walt Bond 7.50 3.40 .95
□ 340 Joe Cuningham 7.50 3.40 .95
□ 341 Jim Roland 7.50 3.40 .95
□ 342 Willie Stargell 75.00 34.00 9.50
□ 343 Senators Team 10.00 4.50 1.25
□ 344 Phil Linz 7.50 3.40 .95
□ 345 Frank Thomas 7.50 3.40 .95
□ 346 Joey Jay 7.50 3.40 .95
□ 347 Bobby Wine 7.50 3.40 .95
□ 348 Ed Lopat MG 7.50 3.40 .95
□ 349 Art Fowler 7.50 3.40 .95
□ 350 Willie McCovey 50.00 22.00 6.25
□ 351 Dan Schneider 7.50 3.40 .95
□ 352 Eddie Bressoud 7.50 3.40 .95
□ 353 Wally Moon 7.50 3.40 .95
□ 354 Dave Giusti 7.50 3.40 .95
□ 355 Vic Power 7.50 3.40 .95
□ 356 Reds Rookies 7.50 3.40 .95
Bill McCool
Chico Ruiz
□ 357 Charley James 7.50 3.40 .95
□ 358 Ron Kline 7.50 3.40 .95
□ 359 Jim Schaffer 7.50 3.40 .95
□ 360 Joe Pepitone 7.50 3.40 .95
□ 361 Jay Hook 7.50 3.40 .95
□ 362 Checklist 5 7.50 3.40 .95
□ 363 Dick McAuliffe 7.50 3.40 .95
□ 364 Joe Gaines 7.50 3.40 .95
□ 365 Cal McLish 7.50 3.40 .95
□ 366 Nelson Mathews 7.50 3.40 .95
□ 367 Fred Whitfield 7.50 3.40 .95
□ 368 White Sox Rookies 7.50 3.40 .95
Fritz Ackley
Don Buford
□ 369 Jerry Zimmerman 7.50 3.40 .95
□ 370 Hal Woodeshick 7.50 3.40 .95

1965 Topps

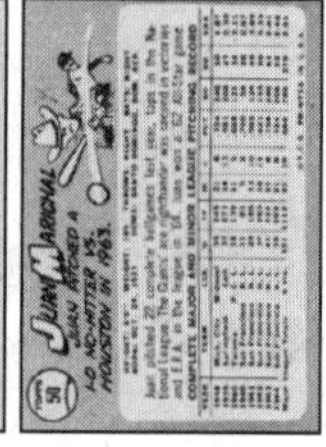

The cards in this 598-card set measure 2 1/2" by 3 1/2". The cards comprising the 1965 Topps set have team names located within a distinctive pennant design below the picture. The cards have blue borders on the reverse and were issued by series. Within this last series (523-598) there are 44 cards that were printed in lesser quantities than the other cards in that series; these shorter-printed cards are marked by SP in the checklist below. Featured subsets within this set include League Leaders (1-12) and World Series cards (132-139). This was the last year Topps issued one-card penny packs. Card were also issued in five-card nickle packs. The key Rookie Cards in this set are Steve Carlton, Jim "Catfish" Hunter, Joe Morgan, Mansori Murakami and Tony Perez.

	NRMT	VG-E	GOOD
COMPLETE SET (598)	3500.00	1600.00	450.00
COMMON CARD (1-196)	2.00	.90	.25
COMMON CARD (197-283)	2.50	1.10	.30
COMMON CARD (284-370)	4.00	1.80	.50
COMMON CARD (371-598)	7.00	3.10	.85
WRAPPER (1-CENT)	125.00	55.00	15.50
WRAPPER (5-CENT)	100.00	45.00	12.50

□ 1 AL Batting Leaders 20.00 6.00 2.00
Tony Oliva
Elston Howard
Brooks Robinson
□ 2 NL Batting Leaders 24.00 11.00 3.00
Bob Clemente
Hank Aaron
Rico Carty
□ 3 AL Home Run Leaders 40.00 18.00 5.00
Harmon Killebrew
Mickey Mantle
Boog Powell
□ 4 NL Home Run Leaders 14.00 6.25 1.75
Willie Mays
Billy Williams
Jim Ray Hart
Orlando Cepeda
Johnny Callison
□ 5 AL RBI Leaders 40.00 18.00 5.00
Brooks Robinson
Harmon Killebrew
Mickey Mantle
Dick Stuart
□ 6 NL RBI Leaders 8.00 3.60 1.00
Ken Boyer
Willie Mays
Ron Santo
□ 7 AL ERA Leaders 4.00 1.80 .50
Dean Chance
Joel Horlen
□ 8 NL ERA Leaders 20.00 9.00 2.50
Sandy Koufax
Don Drysdale
□ 9 AL Pitching Leaders 4.00 1.80 .50
Dean Chance
Gary Peters
Dave Wickersham
Juan Pizarro
Wally Bunker
□ 10 NL Pitching Leaders 4.00 1.80 .50
Larry Jackson
Ray Sadecki
Juan Marichal
□ 11 AL Strikeout Leaders 4.00 1.80 .50
Al Downing
Dean Chance
Camilo Pascual
□ 12 NL Strikeout Leaders 8.00 3.60 1.00
Bob Veale
Don Drysdale
Bob Gibson
□ 13 Pedro Ramos 2.50 1.10 .30
□ 14 Len Gabrielson 2.00 .90 .25

□ 15 Robin Roberts 10.00 4.50 1.25
□ 16 Houston Rookie DP 70.00 32.00 8.75
(Joe Morgan
Sonny Jackson
□ 17 Johnny Romano 2.00 .90 .25
□ 18 Bill McCool 2.00 .90 .25
□ 19 Gates Brown 2.50 1.10 .30
□ 20 Jim Bunning 10.00 4.50 1.25
□ 21 Don Blasingame 2.00 .90 .25
□ 22 Charlie Smith 2.00 .90 .25
□ 23 Bob Tiefenauer 2.00 .90 .25
□ 24 Minnesota Twins 4.00 1.80 .50
Team Card
□ 25 Al McBean 2.00 .90 .25
□ 26 Bobby Knoop 2.00 .90 .25
□ 27 Dick Bertell 2.00 .90 .25
□ 28 Barney Schultz 2.00 .90 .25
□ 29 Felix Mantilla 2.00 .90 .25
□ 30 Jim Bouton 5.00 2.20 .60
□ 31 Mike White 2.00 .90 .25
□ 32 Herman Franks MG 2.00 .90 .25
□ 33 Jackie Brandt 2.00 .90 .25
□ 34 Cal Koonce 2.00 .90 .25
□ 35 Ed Charles 2.00 .90 .25
□ 36 Bobby Wine 2.00 .90 .25
□ 37 Fred Gladding 2.00 .90 .25
□ 38 Jim King 2.00 .90 .25
□ 39 Gerry Arrigo 2.00 .90 .25
□ 40 Frank Howard 2.50 1.10 .30
□ 41 White Sox Rookies 2.00 .90 .25
Bruce Howard
Marv Staehle
□ 42 Earl Wilson 2.50 1.10 .30
□ 43 Mike Shannon 2.50 1.10 .30
(Name in red, other
Cardinals in yellow)
□ 44 Wade Blasingame 2.00 .90 .25
□ 45 Roy McMillan 2.50 1.10 .30
□ 46 Bob Lee 2.00 .90 .25
□ 47 Tommy Harper 2.50 1.10 .30
□ 48 Claude Raymond 2.50 1.10 .30
□ 49 Orioles Rookies 2.50 1.10 .30
Curt Blefary
John Miller
□ 50 Juan Marichal 10.00 4.50 1.25
□ 51 Bill Bryan 2.00 .90 .25
□ 52 Ed Roebuck 2.00 .90 .25
□ 53 Dick McAuliffe 2.50 1.10 .30
□ 54 Joe Gibbon 2.00 .90 .25
□ 55 Tony Conigliaro 15.00 6.75 1.85
□ 56 Ron Kline 2.00 .90 .25
□ 57 Cardinals Team 4.00 1.80 .50
□ 58 Fred Talbot 2.00 .90 .25
□ 59 Nate Oliver 2.00 .90 .25
□ 60 Jim O'Toole 2.50 1.10 .30
□ 61 Chris Cannizzaro 2.00 .90 .25
□ 62 Jim Kaat UER DP 5.00 2.20 .60
(Misspelled Katt)
□ 63 Ty Cline 2.00 .90 .25
□ 64 Lou Burdette 2.50 1.10 .30
□ 65 Tony Kubek 4.00 1.80 .50
□ 66 Bill Rigney MG 2.00 .90 .25
□ 67 Harvey Haddix 2.50 1.10 .30
□ 68 Del Crandall 2.50 1.10 .30
□ 69 Bill Virdon 2.50 1.10 .30
□ 70 Bill Skowron 2.50 1.10 .30
□ 71 John O'Donoghue 2.00 .90 .25
□ 72 Tony Gonzalez 2.00 .90 .25
□ 73 Dennis Ribant 2.00 .90 .25
□ 74 Red Sox Rookies 12.00 5.50 1.50
Rico Petrocelli
Jerry Stephenson
□ 75 Deron Johnson 2.50 1.10 .30
□ 76 Sam McDowell 2.50 1.10 .30
□ 77 Doug Camilli 2.00 .90 .25
□ 78 Dal Maxvill 2.00 .90 .25
□ 79A Checklist 1 10.00 2.00 1.00
(61 Cannizzaro)
□ 79B Checklist 1 10.00 2.00 1.00
(61 C.Cannizzaro)
□ 80 Turk Farrell 2.00 .90 .25
□ 81 Don Buford 2.50 1.10 .30
□ 82 Braves Rookies 6.00 2.70 .75
Santos Alomar
John Braun
□ 83 George Thomas 2.00 .90 .25
□ 84 Ron Herbel 2.00 .90 .25
□ 85 Willie Smith 2.00 .90 .25
□ 86 Les Narum 2.00 .90 .25
□ 87 Nelson Mathews 2.00 .90 .25
□ 88 Jack Lamabe 2.00 .90 .25
□ 89 Mike Hershberger 2.00 .90 .25
□ 90 Rich Rollins 2.50 1.10 .30
□ 91 Cubs Team 4.00 1.80 .50
□ 92 Dick Howser 2.50 1.10 .30
□ 93 Jack Fisher 2.00 .90 .25
□ 94 Charlie Lau 2.50 1.10 .30
□ 95 Bill Mazeroski DP 4.00 1.80 .50
□ 96 Sonny Siebert 2.50 1.10 .30
□ 97 Pedro Gonzalez 2.00 .90 .25
□ 98 Bob Miller 2.00 .90 .25
□ 99 Gil Hodges MG 7.00 3.10 .85
□ 100 Ken Boyer 2.50 1.10 .30
□ 101 Fred Newman 2.00 .90 .25
□ 102 Steve Boros 2.00 .90 .25
□ 103 Harvey Kuenn 2.50 1.10 .30
□ 104 Checklist 2 10.00 2.00 1.00
□ 105 Chico Salmon 2.00 .90 .25
□ 106 Gene Oliver 2.00 .90 .25
□ 107 Phillies Rookies 2.50 1.10 .30
Pat Corrales
Costen Shockley
□ 108 Don Mincher 2.00 .90 .25
□ 109 Walt Bond 2.00 .90 .25
□ 110 Ron Santo 5.00 2.20 .60
□ 111 Lee Thomas 2.50 1.10 .30
□ 112 Derrell Griffith 2.00 .90 .25
□ 113 Steve Barber 2.00 .90 .25
□ 114 Jim Hickman 2.50 1.10 .30
□ 115 Bobby Richardson 5.00 2.20 .60
□ 116 Cardinals Rookies 2.50 1.10 .30
Dave Dowling
Bob Tolan
□ 117 Wes Stock 2.00 .90 .25
□ 118 Hal Lanier 2.50 1.10 .30
□ 119 John Kennedy 2.00 .90 .25
□ 120 Frank Robinson 35.00 16.00 4.40
□ 121 Gene Alley 2.50 1.10 .30
□ 122 Bill Pleis 2.00 .90 .25
□ 123 Frank Thomas 2.50 1.10 .30
□ 124 Tom Satriano 2.00 .90 .25
□ 125 Juan Pizarro 2.00 .90 .25
□ 126 Dodgers Team 5.00 2.20 .60
□ 127 Frank Lary 2.00 .90 .25
□ 128 Vic Davalillo 2.00 .90 .25
□ 129 Bennie Daniels 2.00 .90 .25
□ 130 Al Kaline 35.00 16.00 4.40
□ 131 Johnny Keane MG 2.00 .90 .25
□ 132 Mike Shannon WS 4.00 1.80 .50
□ 133 Mel Stottlemyre WS 4.00 1.80 .50
□ 134 Mickey Mantle WS 75.00 34.00 9.50
Mantle's Clutch HR
□ 135 Ken Boyer WS 4.00 1.80 .50
□ 136 Tim McCarver WS 4.00 1.80 .50
□ 137 Jim Bouton WS 4.00 1.80 .50
□ 138 Bob Gibson WS 12.00 5.50 1.50
□ 139 World Series Summary 4.00 1.80 .50
Cards celebrate
□ 140 Dean Chance 2.50 1.10 .30
□ 141 Charlie James 2.00 .90 .25
□ 142 Bill Monbouquette 2.00 .90 .25
□ 143 Pirates Rookies 2.00 .90 .25
John Gelnar
Jerry May
□ 144 Ed Kranepool 2.50 1.10 .30
□ 145 Luis Tiant 18.00 8.00 2.20
□ 146 Ron Hansen 2.00 .90 .25
□ 147 Dennis Bennett 2.00 .90 .25
□ 148 Willie Kirkland 2.00 .90 .25
□ 149 Wayne Schurr 2.00 .90 .25
□ 150 Brooks Robinson 35.00 16.00 4.40
□ 151 Athletics Team 4.00 1.80 .50
□ 152 Phil Ortega 2.00 .90 .25
□ 153 Norm Cash 2.50 1.10 .30
□ 154 Bob Humphreys 2.00 .90 .25
□ 155 Roger Maris 40.00 18.00 5.00
□ 156 Bob Sadowski 2.00 .90 .25
□ 157 Zoilo Versalles 2.50 1.10 .30
□ 158 Dick Sisler 2.00 .90 .25
□ 159 Jim Duffalo 2.00 .90 .25
□ 160 Bob Clemente UER 160.00 70.00 20.00
(1960 Pittsburfh)
□ 161 Frank Baumann 2.00 .90 .25
□ 162 Russ Nixon 2.00 .90 .25
□ 163 Johnny Briggs 2.00 .90 .25
□ 164 Al Spangler 2.00 .90 .25
□ 165 Dick Ellsworth 2.00 .90 .25
□ 166 Indians Rookies 2.50 1.10 .30
George Culver
Tommie Agee
□ 167 Bill Wakefield 2.00 .90 .25
□ 168 Dick Green 2.00 .90 .25
□ 169 Dave Vineyard 2.00 .90 .25
□ 170 Hank Aaron 90.00 40.00 11.00
□ 171 Jim Roland 2.00 .90 .25
□ 172 Jim Piersall 2.50 1.10 .30
□ 173 Detroit Tigers 4.00 1.80 .50
Team Card
□ 174 Joey Jay 2.00 .90 .25
□ 175 Bob Aspromonte 2.00 .90 .25
□ 176 Willie McCovey 20.00 9.00 2.50
□ 177 Pete Mikkelsen 2.00 .90 .25
□ 178 Dalton Jones 2.00 .90 .25
□ 179 Hal Woodeshick 2.00 .90 .25
□ 180 Bob Allison 2.50 1.10 .30
□ 181 Senators Rookies 2.00 .90 .25
Don Loun
Joe McCabe
□ 182 Mike de la Hoz 2.00 .90 .25
□ 183 Dave Nicholson 2.00 .90 .25
□ 184 John Boozer 2.00 .90 .25
□ 185 Max Alvis 2.00 .90 .25
□ 186 Billy Cowan 2.00 .90 .25
□ 187 Casey Stengel MG 15.00 6.75 1.85
□ 188 Sam Bowens 2.00 .90 .25
□ 189 Checklist 3 10.00 2.00 1.00
□ 190 Bill White 2.50 1.10 .30
□ 191 Phil Regan 2.50 1.10 .30
□ 192 Jim Coker 2.00 .90 .25
□ 193 Gaylord Perry 18.00 8.00 2.20
□ 194 Rookie Stars 2.00 .90 .25
Bill Kelso
Rick Reichardt
□ 195 Bob Veale 2.50 1.10 .30
□ 196 Ron Fairly 2.50 1.10 .30
□ 197 Diego Segui 2.50 1.10 .30
□ 198 Smoky Burgess 3.00 1.35 .35
□ 199 Bob Heffner 2.50 1.10 .30
□ 200 Joe Torre 5.00 2.20 .60
□ 201 Twins Rookies 3.00 1.35 .35
Sandy Valdespino
Cesar Tovar
□ 202 Leo Burke 2.50 1.10 .30
□ 203 Dallas Green 3.00 1.35 .35
□ 204 Russ Snyder 2.50 1.10 .30
□ 205 Warren Spahn 30.00 13.50 3.70
□ 206 Willie Horton 3.00 1.35 .35
□ 207 Pete Rose 150.00 70.00 19.00
□ 208 Tommy John 8.00 3.60 1.00
□ 209 Pirates Team 5.00 2.20 .60
□ 210 Jim Fregosi 3.00 1.35 .35
□ 211 Steve Ridzik 2.50 1.10 .30
□ 212 Ron Brand 2.50 1.10 .30
□ 213 Jim Davenport 2.50 1.10 .30
□ 214 Bob Purkey 2.50 1.10 .30
□ 215 Pete Ward 2.50 1.10 .30
□ 216 Al Worthington 2.50 1.10 .30
□ 217 Walt Alston MG 4.00 1.80 .50
□ 218 Dick Schofield 2.50 1.10 .30
□ 219 Bob Meyer 2.50 1.10 .30
□ 220 Billy Williams 10.00 4.50 1.25
□ 221 John Tsitouris 2.50 1.10 .30
□ 222 Bob Tillman 2.50 1.10 .30
□ 223 Dan Osinski 2.50 1.10 .30
□ 224 Bob Chance 2.50 1.10 .30
□ 225 Bo Belinsky 3.00 1.35 .35
□ 226 Yankees Rookies 3.00 1.35 .35
Elvio Jimenez
Jake Gibbs
□ 227 Bobby Klaus 2.50 1.10 .30
□ 228 Jack Sanford 2.50 1.10 .30
□ 229 Lou Clinton 2.50 1.10 .30
□ 230 Ray Sadecki 2.50 1.10 .30
□ 231 Jerry Adair 2.50 1.10 .30
□ 232 Steve Blass 3.00 1.35 .35
□ 233 Don Zimmer 3.00 1.35 .35
□ 234 White Sox Team 5.00 2.20 .60
□ 235 Chuck Hinton 2.50 1.10 .30
□ 236 Denny McLain 30.00 13.50 3.70
□ 237 Bernie Allen 2.50 1.10 .30
□ 238 Joe Moeller 2.50 1.10 .30
□ 239 Doc Edwards 2.50 1.10 .30
□ 240 Bob Bruce 2.50 1.10 .30
□ 241 Mack Jones 2.50 1.10 .30
□ 242 George Brunet 2.50 1.10 .30
□ 243 Reds Rookies 3.00 1.35 .35
Ted Davidson
Tommy Helms
□ 244 Lindy McDaniel 3.00 1.35 .35
□ 245 Joe Pepitone 3.50 1.55 .45
□ 246 Tom Butters 3.00 1.35 .35
□ 247 Wally Moon 3.00 1.35 .35
□ 248 Gus Triandos 3.00 1.35 .35
□ 249 Dave McNally 3.00 1.35 .35
□ 250 Willie Mays 100.00 45.00 12.50
□ 251 Billy Herman MG 4.00 1.80 .50
□ 252 Pete Richert 2.50 1.10 .30
□ 253 Danny Cater 2.50 1.10 .30
□ 254 Roland Sheldon 2.50 1.10 .30
□ 255 Camilo Pascual 3.00 1.35 .35
□ 256 Tito Francona 2.50 1.10 .30
□ 257 Jim Wynn 3.00 1.35 .35
□ 258 Larry Bearnarth 2.50 1.10 .30
□ 259 Tigers Rookies 7.00 3.10 .85
Jim Northrup
Ray Oyler
□ 260 Don Drysdale 20.00 9.00 2.50
□ 261 Duke Carmel 2.50 1.10 .30
□ 262 Bud Daley 2.50 1.10 .30
□ 263 Marty Keough 2.50 1.10 .30
□ 264 Bob Buhl 3.00 1.35 .35
□ 265 Jim Pagliaroni 2.50 1.10 .30
□ 266 Bert Campaneris 10.00 4.50 1.25
□ 267 Senators Team 5.00 2.20 .60
□ 268 Ken McBride 2.50 1.10 .30
□ 269 Frank Bolling 2.50 1.10 .30
□ 270 Milt Pappas 3.00 1.35 .35
□ 271 Don Wert 2.50 1.10 .30
□ 272 Chuck Schilling 2.50 1.10 .30
□ 273 Checklist 4 10.00 2.00 1.00
□ 274 Lum Harris MG 2.50 1.10 .30
□ 275 Dick Groat 3.00 1.35 .35
□ 276 Hoyt Wilhelm 10.00 4.50 1.25
□ 277 Johnny Lewis 2.50 1.10 .30
□ 278 Ken Retzer 2.50 1.10 .30
□ 279 Dick Tracewski 2.50 1.10 .30
□ 280 Dick Stuart 3.00 1.35 .35
□ 281 Bill Stafford 2.50 1.10 .30
□ 282 Giants Rookies 35.00 16.00 4.40
Dick Estelle
Masanori Murakami
□ 283 Fred Whitfield 2.50 1.10 .30
□ 284 Nick Willhite 4.00 1.80 .50
□ 285 Ron Hunt 4.00 1.80 .50
□ 286 Athletics Rookies 4.00 1.80 .50
Jim Dickson
Aurelio Monteagudo
□ 287 Gary Kolb 4.00 1.80 .50
□ 288 Jack Hamilton 4.00 1.80 .50
□ 289 Gordy Coleman 4.50 2.00 .55
□ 290 Wally Bunker 4.50 2.00 .55
□ 291 Jerry Lynch 4.00 1.80 .50
□ 292 Larry Yellen 4.00 1.80 .50
□ 293 Angels Team 7.00 3.10 .85
□ 294 Tim McCarver 7.00 3.10 .85
□ 295 Dick Radatz 4.50 2.00 .55
□ 296 Tony Taylor 4.50 2.00 .55
□ 297 Dave DeBusschere 6.00 2.70 .75
□ 298 Jim Stewart 4.00 1.80 .50
□ 299 Jerry Zimmerman 4.00 1.80 .50
□ 300 Sandy Koufax 120.00 55.00 15.00
□ 301 Birdie Tebbetts MG 4.50 2.00 .55
□ 302 Al Stanek 4.00 1.80 .50
□ 303 John Orsino 4.00 1.80 .50
□ 304 Dave Stenhouse 4.00 1.80 .50
□ 305 Rico Carty 4.50 2.00 .55
□ 306 Bubba Phillips 4.00 1.80 .50
□ 307 Barry Latman 4.00 1.80 .50
□ 308 Mets Rookies 4.50 2.00 .55
Cleon Jones
Tom Parsons
□ 309 Steve Hamilton 4.50 2.00 .55
□ 310 Johnny Callison 4.50 2.00 .55
□ 311 Orlando Pena 4.00 1.80 .50
□ 312 Joe Nuxhall 4.50 2.00 .55
□ 313 Jim Schaffer 4.00 1.80 .50
□ 314 Sterling Slaughter 4.00 1.80 .50
□ 315 Frank Malzone 4.50 2.00 .55
□ 316 Reds Team 7.00 3.10 .85
□ 317 Don McMahon 4.00 1.80 .50
□ 318 Matty Alou 4.50 2.00 .55
□ 319 Ken McMullen 4.00 1.80 .50
□ 320 Bob Gibson 40.00 18.00 5.00
□ 321 Rusty Staub 5.00 2.20 .60
□ 322 Rick Wise 4.50 2.00 .55
□ 323 Hank Bauer MG 4.50 2.00 .55
□ 324 Bobby Locke 4.00 1.80 .50
□ 325 Donn Clendenon 4.50 2.00 .55
□ 326 Dwight Siebler 4.00 1.80 .50
□ 327 Denis Menke 4.00 1.80 .50
□ 328 Eddie Fisher 4.00 1.80 .50
□ 329 Hawk Taylor 4.00 1.80 .50
□ 330 Whitey Ford 35.00 16.00 4.40
□ 331 Dodgers Rookies 4.50 2.00 .55
Al Ferrara
John Purdin
□ 332 Ted Abernathy 4.00 1.80 .50
□ 333 Tom Reynolds 4.00 1.80 .50
□ 334 Vic Roznovsky 4.00 1.80 .50
□ 335 Mickey Lolich 8.00 3.60 1.00
□ 336 Woody Held 4.00 1.80 .50
□ 337 Mike Cuellar 4.50 2.00 .55
□ 338 Philadelphia Phillies 7.00 3.10 .85
Team Card
□ 339 Ryne Duren 4.50 2.00 .55
□ 340 Tony Oliva 18.00 8.00 2.20
□ 341 Bob Bolin 4.00 1.80 .50
□ 342 Bob Rodgers 4.50 2.00 .55
□ 343 Mike McCormick 4.50 2.00 .55
□ 344 Wes Parker 4.50 2.00 .55
□ 345 Floyd Robinson 4.00 1.80 .50
□ 346 Bobby Bragan MG 4.00 1.80 .50
□ 347 Roy Face 4.50 2.00 .55
□ 348 George Banks 4.00 1.80 .50
□ 349 Larry Miller 4.00 1.80 .50
□ 350 Mickey Mantle 550.00 250.00 70.00
□ 351 Jim Perry 4.50 2.00 .55
□ 352 Alex Johnson 4.50 2.00 .55
□ 353 Jerry Lumpe 4.00 1.80 .50
□ 354 Cubs Rookies 4.00 1.80 .50
Billy Ott
Jack Warner
□ 355 Vada Pinson 4.50 2.00 .55
□ 356 Bill Spanswick 4.00 1.80 .50
□ 357 Carl Warwick 4.00 1.80 .50
□ 358 Albie Pearson 4.50 2.00 .55
□ 359 Ken Johnson 4.00 1.80 .50
□ 360 Orlando Cepeda 8.00 3.60 1.00
□ 361 Checklist 5 12.00 2.40 1.20
□ 362 Don Schwall 4.00 1.80 .50
□ 363 Bob Johnson 4.00 1.80 .50
□ 364 Galen Cisco 4.00 1.80 .50
□ 365 Jim Gentile 4.50 2.00 .55
□ 366 Dan Schneider 4.00 1.80 .50
□ 367 Leon Wagner 4.00 1.80 .50
□ 368 White Sox Rookies 4.50 2.00 .55
Ken Berry
Joel Gibson
□ 369 Phil Linz 4.50 2.00 .55
□ 370 Tommy Davis 4.50 2.00 .55
□ 371 Frank Kreutzer 7.00 3.10 .85
□ 372 Clay Dalrymple 7.00 3.10 .85
□ 373 Curt Simmons 7.50 3.40 .95
□ 374 Angels Rookies 8.00 3.60 1.00
Jose Cardenal
Dick Simpson
□ 375 Dave Wickersham 7.00 3.10 .85
□ 376 Jim Landis 7.00 3.10 .85
□ 377 Willie Stargell 30.00 13.50 3.70
□ 378 Chuck Estrada 7.00 3.10 .85
□ 379 Giants Team 10.00 4.50 1.25

Card	NRMT	VG-E	GOOD
☐ 380 Rocky Colavito	18.00	8.00	2.20
☐ 381 Al Jackson	7.00	3.10	.85
☐ 382 J.C. Martin	7.00	3.10	.85
☐ 383 Felipe Alou	8.00	3.60	1.00
☐ 384 Johnny Klippstein	7.00	3.10	.85
☐ 385 Carl Yastrzemski	70.00	32.00	8.75
☐ 386 Cubs Rookies	7.00	3.10	.85
Paul Jaeckel			
Fred Norman			
☐ 387 Johnny Podres	8.00	3.60	1.00
☐ 388 John Blanchard	8.00	3.60	1.00
☐ 389 Don Larsen	8.00	3.60	1.00
☐ 390 Bill Freehan	8.00	3.60	1.00
☐ 391 Mel McGaha MG	7.00	3.10	.85
☐ 392 Bob Friend	7.50	3.40	.95
☐ 393 Ed Kirkpatrick	7.00	3.10	.85
☐ 394 Jim Hannan	7.00	3.10	.85
☐ 395 Jim Ray Hart	7.50	3.40	.95
☐ 396 Frank Bertaina	7.00	3.10	.85
☐ 397 Jerry Buchek	7.00	3.10	.85
☐ 398 Reds Rookies	7.50	3.40	.95
Dan Neville			
Art Shamsky			
☐ 399 Ray Herbert	7.00	3.10	.85
☐ 400 Harmon Killebrew	40.00	18.00	5.00
☐ 401 Carl Willey	7.00	3.10	.85
☐ 402 Joe Amalfitano	7.00	3.10	.85
☐ 403 Boston Red Sox	10.00	4.50	1.25
Team Card			
☐ 404 Stan Williams	7.50	3.40	.95
(Listed as Indian			
but Yankee cap)			
☐ 405 John Roseboro	7.50	3.40	.95
☐ 406 Ralph Terry	7.50	3.40	.95
☐ 407 Lee Maye	7.00	3.10	.85
☐ 408 Larry Sherry	7.50	3.40	.95
☐ 409 Astros Rookies	8.00	3.60	1.00
Jim Beauchamp			
Larry Dierker			
☐ 410 Luis Aparicio	12.00	5.50	1.50
☐ 411 Roger Craig	7.50	3.40	.95
☐ 412 Bob Bailey	7.50	3.40	.95
☐ 413 Hal Reniff	7.00	3.10	.85
☐ 414 Al Lopez MG	8.00	3.60	1.00
☐ 415 Curt Flood	10.00	4.50	1.25
☐ 416 Jim Brewer	7.00	3.10	.85
☐ 417 Ed Brinkman	7.00	3.10	.85
☐ 418 Johnny Edwards	7.00	3.10	.85
☐ 419 Ruben Amaro	7.00	3.10	.85
☐ 420 Larry Jackson	7.00	3.10	.85
☐ 421 Twins Rookies	7.00	3.10	.85
Gary Dotter			
Jay Ward			
☐ 422 Aubrey Gatewood	7.00	3.10	.85
☐ 423 Jesse Gonder	7.00	3.10	.85
☐ 424 Gary Bell	7.00	3.10	.85
☐ 425 Wayne Causey	7.00	3.10	.85
☐ 426 Braves Team	10.00	4.50	1.25
☐ 427 Bob Saverine	7.00	3.10	.85
☐ 428 Bob Shaw	7.00	3.10	.85
☐ 429 Don Demeter	7.00	3.10	.85
☐ 430 Gary Peters	7.00	3.10	.85
☐ 431 Cards Rookies	8.00	3.60	1.00
Nelson Briles			
Wayne Spiezio			
☐ 432 Jim Grant	7.50	3.40	.95
☐ 433 John Bateman	7.00	3.10	.85
☐ 434 Dave Morehead	7.00	3.10	.85
☐ 435 Willie Davis	9.00	4.00	1.10
☐ 436 Don Elston	7.00	3.10	.85
☐ 437 Chico Cardenas	7.50	3.40	.95
☐ 438 Harry Walker MG	7.00	3.10	.85
☐ 439 Moe Drabowsky	7.50	3.40	.95
☐ 440 Tom Tresh	9.00	4.00	1.10
☐ 441 Denny Lemaster	7.00	3.10	.85
☐ 442 Vic Power	7.50	3.40	.95
☐ 443 Checklist 6	12.00	2.40	1.20
☐ 444 Bob Hendley	7.00	3.10	.85
☐ 445 Don Lock	7.00	3.10	.85
☐ 446 Art Mahaffey	7.00	3.10	.85
☐ 447 Julian Javier	7.50	3.40	.95
☐ 448 Lee Stange	7.00	3.10	.85
☐ 449 Mets Rookies	7.00	3.10	.85
Jerry Hinsley			
Gary Kroll			
☐ 450 Elston Howard	10.00	4.50	1.25
☐ 451 Jim Owens	7.00	3.10	.85
☐ 452 Gary Geiger	7.00	3.10	.85
☐ 453 Dodgers Rookies	7.50	3.40	.95
Willie Crawford			
John Werhas			
☐ 454 Ed Rakow	7.00	3.10	.85
☐ 455 Norm Siebern	7.00	3.10	.85
☐ 456 Bill Henry	7.00	3.10	.85
☐ 457 Bob Kennedy MG	7.50	3.40	.95
☐ 458 John Buzhardt	7.00	3.10	.85
☐ 459 Frank Kostro	7.00	3.10	.85
☐ 460 Richie Allen	40.00	18.00	5.00
☐ 461 Braves Rookies	60.00	27.00	7.50
Clay Carroll			
Phil Niekro			
☐ 462 Lew Krausse UER	7.50	3.40	.95
(Photo actually			
Pete Lovrich)			
☐ 463 Manny Mota	8.00	3.60	1.00

Card	NRMT	VG-E	GOOD
☐ 464 Ron Piche	7.00	3.10	.85
☐ 465 Tom Haller	7.50	3.40	.95
☐ 466 Senators Rookies	7.00	3.10	.85
Pete Craig			
Dick Nen			
☐ 467 Ray Washburn	7.00	3.10	.85
☐ 468 Larry Brown	7.00	3.10	.85
☐ 469 Don Nottebart	7.00	3.10	.85
☐ 470 Yogi Berra P/CO	50.00	22.00	6.25
☐ 471 Billy Hoeft	7.00	3.10	.85
☐ 472 Don Pavletich UER	7.00	3.10	.85
Listed as a pitcher			
☐ 473 Orioles Rookies	16.00	7.25	2.00
Paul Blair			
Dave Johnson			
☐ 474 Cookie Rojas	7.50	3.40	.95
☐ 475 Clete Boyer	9.00	4.00	1.10
☐ 476 Billy O'Dell	7.00	3.10	.85
☐ 477 Cards Rookies	250.00	110.00	31.00
Fritz Ackley			
Steve Carlton			
☐ 478 Wilbur Wood	8.00	3.60	1.00
☐ 479 Ken Harrelson	8.00	3.60	1.00
☐ 480 Joel Horlen	7.00	3.10	.85
☐ 481 Cleveland Indians	12.00	5.50	1.50
Team Card			
☐ 482 Bob Priddy	7.00	3.10	.85
☐ 483 George Smith	7.00	3.10	.85
☐ 484 Ron Perranoski	9.00	4.00	1.10
☐ 485 Nellie Fox P/CO	16.00	7.25	2.00
☐ 486 Angels Rookies	7.00	3.10	.85
Tom Egan			
Pat Rogan			
☐ 487 Woody Woodward	7.50	3.40	.95
☐ 488 Ted Wills	7.00	3.10	.85
☐ 489 Gene Mauch MG	7.50	3.40	.95
☐ 490 Earl Battey	7.00	3.10	.85
☐ 491 Tracy Stallard	7.00	3.10	.85
☐ 492 Gene Freese	7.00	3.10	.85
☐ 493 Tigers Rookies	7.00	3.10	.85
Bill Roman			
Bruce Brubaker			
☐ 494 Jay Ritchie	7.00	3.10	.85
☐ 495 Joe Christopher	7.00	3.10	.85
☐ 496 Joe Cunningham	7.00	3.10	.85
☐ 497 Giants Rookies	7.50	3.40	.95
Ken Henderson			
Jack Hiatt			
☐ 498 Gene Stephens	7.00	3.10	.85
☐ 499 Stu Miller	7.50	3.40	.95
☐ 500 Eddie Mathews	35.00	16.00	4.40
☐ 501 Indians Rookies	7.00	3.10	.85
Ralph Gagliano			
Jim Rittwage			
☐ 502 Don Cardwell	7.00	3.10	.85
☐ 503 Phil Gagliano	7.00	3.10	.85
☐ 504 Jerry Grote	7.50	3.40	.95
☐ 505 Ray Culp	7.00	3.10	.85
☐ 506 Sam Mele MG	7.00	3.10	.85
☐ 507 Sammy Ellis	7.00	3.10	.85
☐ 508 Checklist 7	12.00	2.40	1.20
☐ 509 Red Sox Rookies	7.00	3.10	.85
Bob Guindon			
Gerry Vezendy			
☐ 510 Ernie Banks	80.00	36.00	10.00
☐ 511 Ron Locke	7.00	3.10	.85
☐ 512 Cap Peterson	7.00	3.10	.85
☐ 513 New York Yankees	40.00	18.00	5.00
Team Card			
☐ 514 Joe Azcue	7.00	3.10	.85
☐ 515 Vern Law	7.50	3.40	.95
☐ 516 Al Weis	7.00	3.10	.85
☐ 517 Angels Rookies	7.50	3.40	.95
Paul Schaal			
Jack Warner			
☐ 518 Ken Rowe	7.00	3.10	.85
☐ 519 Bob Uecker UER	30.00	13.50	3.70
(Posing as a left-			
handed batter)			
☐ 520 Tony Cloninger	7.00	3.10	.85
☐ 521 Phillies Rookies	7.00	3.10	.85
Dave Bennett			
Morrie Stevens			
☐ 522 Hank Aguirre	7.00	3.10	.85
☐ 523 Mike Brumley SP	12.00	5.50	1.50
☐ 524 Dave Giusti SP	12.00	5.50	1.50
☐ 525 Eddie Bressoud	7.00	3.10	.85
☐ 526 Athletics Rookies SP	80.00	36.00	10.00
Rene Lachemann			
Johnny Odom			
Jim Hunter UER			
(Tim on back)			
Skip Lockwood			
☐ 527 Jeff Torborg SP	16.00	7.25	2.00
☐ 528 George Altman	7.00	3.10	.85
☐ 529 Jerry Fosnow SP	12.00	5.50	1.50
☐ 530 Jim Maloney	7.50	3.40	.95
☐ 531 Chuck Hiller	7.00	3.10	.85
☐ 532 Hector Lopez	8.00	3.60	1.00
☐ 533 Mets Rookies SP	25.00	11.00	3.10
Dan Napoleon			
Ron Swoboda			
Tug McGraw			
Jim Bethke			
☐ 534 John Herrnstein	7.00	3.10	.85

Card	NRMT	VG-E	GOOD
☐ 535 Jack Kralick SP	12.00	5.50	1.50
☐ 536 Andre Rodgers SP	12.00	5.50	1.50
☐ 537 Angels Rookies	7.00	3.10	.85
Marcelino Lopez			
Phil Roof			
Rudy May			
☐ 538 Chuck Dressen SP MG	14.00	6.25	1.75
☐ 539 Herm Starrette	7.00	3.10	.85
☐ 540 Lou Brock SP	50.00	22.00	6.25
☐ 541 White Sox Rookies	7.00	3.10	.85
Greg Bollo			
Bob Locker			
☐ 542 Lou Klimchock	7.00	3.10	.85
☐ 543 Ed Connolly SP	12.00	5.50	1.50
☐ 544 Howie Reed	8.00	3.60	1.00
☐ 545 Jesus Alou SP	14.00	6.25	1.75
☐ 546 Indians Rookies	7.00	3.10	.85
Bill Davis			
Mike Hedlund			
Ray Barker			
Floyd Weaver			
☐ 547 Jake Wood SP	12.00	5.50	1.50
☐ 548 Dick Stigman	7.00	3.10	.85
☐ 549 Cubs Rookies SP	20.00	9.00	2.50
Roberto Pena			
Glenn Beckert			
☐ 550 Mel Stottlemyre SP	30.00	13.50	3.70
☐ 551 New York Mets SP	30.00	13.50	3.70
Team Card			
☐ 552 Julio Gotay	7.00	3.10	.85
☐ 553 Astros Rookies	7.00	3.10	.85
Dan Coombs			
Gene Ratliff			
Jack McClure			
☐ 554 Chico Ruiz SP	12.00	5.50	1.50
☐ 555 Jack Baldschun SP	12.00	5.50	1.50
☐ 556 Red Schoendienst	24.00	11.00	3.00
SP MG			
☐ 557 Jose Santiago	7.00	3.10	.85
☐ 558 Tommie Sisk	7.00	3.10	.85
☐ 559 Ed Bailey SP	12.00	5.50	1.50
☐ 560 Boog Powell SP	24.00	11.00	3.00
☐ 561 Dodgers Rookies	10.00	4.50	1.25
Dennis Daboll			
Mike Kekich			
Hector Valle			
Jim Lefebvre			
☐ 562 Billy Moran	7.00	3.10	.85
☐ 563 Julio Navarro	7.00	3.10	.85
☐ 564 Mel Nelson	7.00	3.10	.85
☐ 565 Ernie Broglio SP	12.00	5.50	1.50
☐ 566 Yankees Rookies SP	14.00	6.25	1.75
Gil Blanco			
Ross Moschitto			
Art Lopez			
☐ 567 Tommie Aaron	7.50	3.40	.95
☐ 568 Ron Taylor SP	12.00	5.50	1.50
☐ 569 Gino Cimoli SP	12.00	5.50	1.50
☐ 570 Claude Osteen SP	14.00	6.25	1.75
☐ 571 Ossie Virgil SP	12.00	5.50	1.50
☐ 572 Baltimore Orioles SP	30.00	13.50	3.70
Team Card			
☐ 573 Red Sox Rookies SP	24.00	11.00	3.00
Jim Lonborg			
Gerry Moses			
Bill Schlesinger			
Mike Ryan			
☐ 574 Roy Sievers	7.50	3.40	.95
☐ 575 Jose Pagan	7.00	3.10	.85
☐ 576 Terry Fox SP	12.00	5.50	1.50
☐ 577 AL Rookie Stars SP	14.00	6.25	1.75
Darold Knowles			
Don Buschhorn			
Richie Scheinblum			
☐ 578 Camilo Carreon SP	12.00	5.50	1.50
☐ 579 Dick Smith SP	12.00	5.50	1.50
☐ 580 Jimmie Hall SP	12.00	5.50	1.50
☐ 581 NL Rookie Stars SP	90.00	40.00	11.00
Tony Perez			
Dave Ricketts			
Kevin Collins			
☐ 582 Bob Schmidt SP	12.00	5.50	1.50
☐ 583 Wes Covington SP	12.00	5.50	1.50
☐ 584 Harry Bright	8.00	3.60	1.00
☐ 585 Hank Fischer	7.00	3.10	.85
☐ 586 Tom McCraw SP	12.00	5.50	1.50
☐ 587 Joe Sparma	7.00	3.10	.85
☐ 588 Lenny Green	7.00	3.10	.85
☐ 589 Giants Rookies SP	12.00	5.50	1.50
Frank Linzy			
Bob Schroder			
☐ 590 John Wyatt	7.00	3.10	.85
☐ 591 Bob Skinner SP	14.00	6.25	1.75
☐ 592 Frank Bork SP	12.00	5.50	1.50
☐ 593 Tigers Rookies SP	12.00	5.50	1.50
Jackie Moore			
John Sullivan			
☐ 594 Joe Gaines	7.00	3.10	.85
☐ 595 Don Lee	7.00	3.10	.85
☐ 596 Don Landrum SP	12.00	5.50	1.50
☐ 597 Twins Rookies	7.00	3.10	.85
Joe Nossek			
John Sevcik			
Dick Reese			
☐ 598 Al Downing SP	24.00	7.25	2.40

1965 Topps Embossed

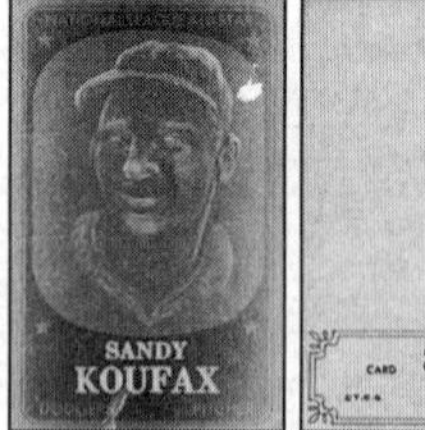

The cards in this 72-card set measure approximately 2 1/8" by 3 1/2". The 1965 Topps Embossed set contains gold foil cameo player portraits. Each league had 36 representatives set on blue backgrounds for the AL and red backgrounds for the NL. The Topps embossed set was distributed as inserts in packages of the regular 1965 baseball series.

	NRMT	VG-E	GOOD
COMPLETE SET (72)	150.00	70.00	19.00
COMMON CARD (1-72)	.50	.23	.06
☐ 1 Carl Yastrzemski	6.00	2.70	.75
☐ 2 Ron Fairly	.50	.23	.06
☐ 3 Max Alvis	.50	.23	.06
☐ 4 Jim Ray Hart	.50	.23	.06
☐ 5 Bill Skowron	1.00	.45	.12
☐ 6 Ed Kranepool	.75	.35	.09
☐ 7 Tim McCarver	1.00	.45	.12
☐ 8 Sandy Koufax	12.00	5.50	1.50
☐ 9 Donn Clendenon	.75	.35	.09
☐ 10 John Romano	.50	.23	.06
☐ 11 Mickey Mantle	60.00	27.00	7.50
☐ 12 Joe Torre	1.00	.45	.12
☐ 13 Al Kaline	6.00	2.70	.75
☐ 14 Al McBean	.50	.23	.06
☐ 15 Don Drysdale	3.00	1.35	.35
☐ 16 Brooks Robinson	6.00	2.70	.75
☐ 17 Jim Bunning	3.00	1.35	.35
☐ 18 Gary Peters	.50	.23	.06
☐ 19 Bob Clemente	25.00	11.00	3.10
☐ 20 Milt Pappas	.50	.23	.06
☐ 21 Wayne Causey	.50	.23	.06
☐ 22 Frank Robinson	6.00	2.70	.75
☐ 23 Bill Mazeroski	1.00	.45	.12
☐ 24 Diego Segui	.50	.23	.06
☐ 25 Jim Bouton	1.00	.45	.12
☐ 26 Ed Mathews	3.00	1.35	.35
☐ 27 Willie Mays	18.00	8.00	2.20
☐ 28 Ron Santo	1.00	.45	.12
☐ 29 Boog Powell	1.00	.45	.12
☐ 30 Ken McBride	.50	.23	.06
☐ 31 Leon Wagner	.50	.23	.06
☐ 32 John Callison	.75	.35	.09
☐ 33 Zoilo Versalles	.75	.35	.09
☐ 34 Jack Baldschun	.50	.23	.06
☐ 35 Ron Hunt	.50	.23	.06
☐ 36 Richie Allen	1.00	.45	.12
☐ 37 Frank Malzone	.50	.23	.06
☐ 38 Bob Allison	.75	.35	.09
☐ 39 Jim Fregosi	1.00	.45	.12
☐ 40 Billy Williams	2.00	.90	.25
☐ 41 Bill Freehan	1.00	.45	.12
☐ 42 Vada Pinson	1.00	.45	.12
☐ 43 Bill White	1.00	.45	.12
☐ 44 Roy McMillan	.50	.23	.06
☐ 45 Orlando Cepeda	2.00	.90	.25
☐ 46 Rocky Colavito	2.00	.90	.25
☐ 47 Ken Boyer	1.00	.45	.12
☐ 48 Dick Radatz	.50	.23	.06
☐ 49 Tommy Davis	.75	.35	.09
☐ 50 Walt Bond	.75	.35	.09
☐ 51 John Orsino	.50	.23	.06
☐ 52 Joe Christopher	.50	.23	.06
☐ 53 Al Spangler	.50	.23	.06
☐ 54 Jim King	.50	.23	.06
☐ 55 Mickey Lolich	1.00	.45	.12
☐ 56 Harmon Killebrew	3.00	1.35	.35
☐ 57 Bob Shaw	.50	.23	.06
☐ 58 Ernie Banks	6.00	2.70	.75
☐ 59 Hank Aaron	15.00	6.75	1.85
☐ 60 Chuck Hinton	.50	.23	.06
☐ 61 Bob Aspromonte	.50	.23	.06
☐ 62 Lee Maye	.50	.23	.06
☐ 63 Joe Cunningham	.50	.23	.06
☐ 64 Pete Ward	.50	.23	.06
☐ 65 Bobby Richardson	1.00	.45	.12
☐ 66 Dean Chance	.75	.35	.09
☐ 67 Dick Ellsworth	.50	.23	.06
☐ 68 Jim Maloney	.75	.35	.09
☐ 69 Bob Gibson	3.00	1.35	.35
☐ 70 Earl Battey	.50	.23	.06
☐ 71 Tony Kubek	1.00	.45	.12
☐ 72 Jack Kralick	.50	.23	.06

1965 Topps Transfers

The 1965 Topps transfers (2" by 3") were issued in series of 24 each as inserts in three of the regular 1965 Topps cards series. Thirty-six of the transfers feature blue bands at the top and bottom while 36 feature red bands at the top and bottom. The team name and position

are listed in the top band while the player's name is listed in the bottom band. Transfers 1-36 have blue panels whereas 37-72 have red panels. These unnumbered transfers are ordered below alphabetically by player's name within each color group. Transfers of Bob Veale and Carl Yastrzemski are supposedly tougher to find than the others in the set; they are marked below by SP.

	NRMT	VG-E	GOOD
COMPLETE SET (72)	400.00	180.00	50.00
COMMON TRANSFER (1-72)	1.50	.70	.19
☐ 1 Bob Allison	1.50	.70	.19
☐ 2 Max Alvis	1.50	.70	.19
☐ 3 Luis Aparicio	6.00	2.70	.75
☐ 4 Walt Bond	1.50	.70	.19
☐ 5 Jim Bouton	2.00	.90	.25
☐ 6 Jim Bunning	6.00	2.70	.75
☐ 7 Rico Carty	2.00	.90	.25
☐ 8 Wayne Causey	1.50	.70	.19
☐ 9 Orlando Cepeda	4.00	1.80	.50
☐ 10 Dean Chance	1.50	.70	.19
☐ 11 Tony Conigliaro	2.00	.90	.25
☐ 12 Bill Freehan	2.00	.90	.25
☐ 13 Jim Fregosi	2.00	.90	.25
☐ 14 Bob Gibson	10.00	4.50	1.25
☐ 15 Dick Groat	2.00	.90	.25
☐ 16 Tom Haller	1.50	.70	.19
☐ 17 Al Jackson	1.50	.70	.19
☐ 18 Bobby Knoop	1.50	.70	.19
☐ 19 Jim Maloney	2.00	.90	.25
☐ 20 Juan Marichal	6.00	2.70	.75
☐ 21 Lee Maye	1.50	.70	.19
☐ 22 Jim O'Toole	1.50	.70	.19
☐ 23 Camilo Pascual	1.50	.70	.19
☐ 24 Vada Pinson	2.00	.90	.25
☐ 25 Juan Pizarro	1.50	.70	.19
☐ 26 Bobby Richardson	3.00	1.35	.35
☐ 27 Bob Rodgers	1.50	.70	.19
☐ 28 John Roseboro	1.50	.70	.19
☐ 29 Dick Stuart	2.00	.90	.25
☐ 30 Luis Tiant	2.00	.90	.25
☐ 31 Joe Torre	2.00	.90	.25
☐ 32 Bob Veale SP	10.00	4.50	1.25
☐ 33 Leon Wagner	1.50	.70	.19
☐ 34 Dave Wickersham	1.50	.70	.19
☐ 35 Billy Williams	6.00	2.70	.75
☐ 36 Carl Yastrzemski SP	40.00	18.00	5.00
☐ 37 Henry Aaron	30.00	13.50	3.70
☐ 38 Richie Allen	2.00	.90	.25
☐ 39 Ken Aspromonte	1.50	.70	.19
☐ 40 Ken Boyer	3.00	1.35	.35
☐ 41 Johnny Callison	2.00	.90	.25
☐ 42 Dean Chance	1.50	.70	.19
☐ 43 Joe Christopher	1.50	.70	.19
☐ 44 Bob Clemente	50.00	22.00	6.25
☐ 45 Rocky Colavito	6.00	2.70	.75
☐ 46 Tommy Davis	2.00	.90	.25
☐ 47 Don Drysdale	10.00	4.50	1.25
☐ 48 Chuck Hinton	1.50	.70	.19
☐ 49 Frank Howard	2.00	.90	.25
☐ 50 Ron Hunt	1.50	.70	.19
☐ 51 Al Kaline	15.00	6.75	1.85
☐ 52 Harmon Killebrew	10.00	4.50	1.25
☐ 53 Jim King	1.50	.70	.19
☐ 54 Ron Kline	1.50	.70	.19
☐ 55 Sandy Koufax	25.00	11.00	3.10
☐ 56 Ed Kranepool	1.50	.70	.19
☐ 57 Mickey Mantle	100.00	45.00	12.50
☐ 58 Willie Mays	35.00	16.00	4.40
☐ 59 Bill Mazeroski	3.00	1.35	.35
☐ 60 Tony Oliva	4.00	1.80	.50
☐ 61 Milt Pappas	1.50	.70	.19
☐ 62 Gary Peters	1.50	.70	.19
☐ 63 Boog Powell	3.00	1.35	.35
☐ 64 Dick Radatz	1.50	.70	.19
☐ 65 Brooks Robinson	15.00	6.75	1.85
☐ 66 Frank Robinson	15.00	6.75	1.85
☐ 67 Ron Santo	3.00	1.35	.35
☐ 68 Diego Segui	1.50	.70	.19
☐ 69 Bill Skowron	2.00	.90	.25
☐ 70 Al Spangler	1.50	.70	.19
☐ 71 Pete Ward	1.50	.70	.19
☐ 72 Bill White	2.00	.90	.25

1966 Topps

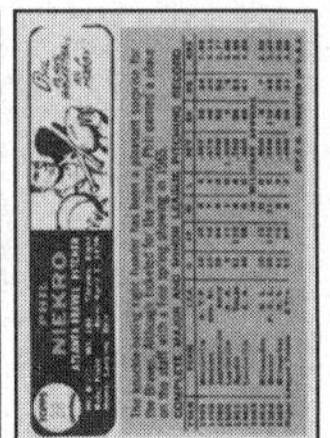

The cards in this 598-card set measure 2 1/2" by 3 1/2". There are the same number of cards as in the 1965 set. Once again, the seventh series cards (523 to 598) are considered more difficult to obtain than the cards of any other series in the set. Within this last series there are 43 cards that were printed in lesser quantities than the other cards in that series; these shorter-printed cards are marked by SP in the checklist below. Among other ways, cards were issued in five-card nickle packs. The only featured subset within this set is League Leaders (215-226). Noteworthy Rookie Cards in the set include Jim Palmer (126), Ferguson Jenkins (254), and Don Sutton (288). Jim Palmer is described in the bio (on his card back) as a left-hander.

	NRMT	VG-E	GOOD
COMPLETE SET (598)	4000.00	1800.00	500.00
COMMON CARD (1-109)	1.50	.70	.19
COMMON CARD (110-283)	2.00	.90	.25
COMMON CARD (284-370)	3.00	1.35	.35
COMMON CARD (371-446)	5.00	2.20	.60
COMMON CARD (447-522)	9.00	4.00	1.10
COMMON CARD (523-598)	15.00	6.75	1.85
WRAPPER (5-CENT)	25.00	11.00	3.10
☐ 1 Willie Mays	135.00	42.50	16.00
☐ 2 Ted Abernathy	1.50	.70	.19
☐ 3 Sam Mele MG	1.50	.70	.19
☐ 4 Ray Culp	1.50	.70	.19
☐ 5 Jim Fregosi	2.50	1.10	.30
☐ 6 Chuck Schilling	1.50	.70	.19
☐ 7 Tracy Stallard	1.50	.70	.19
☐ 8 Floyd Robinson	1.50	.70	.19
☐ 9 Clete Boyer	2.50	1.10	.30
☐ 10 Tony Cloninger	1.50	.70	.19
☐ 11 Senators Rookies	1.50	.70	.19
Brant Alyea			
Pete Craig			
☐ 12 John Tsitouris	1.50	.70	.19
☐ 13 Lou Johnson	2.50	1.10	.30
☐ 14 Norm Siebern	1.50	.70	.19
☐ 15 Vern Law	2.50	1.10	.30
☐ 16 Larry Brown	1.50	.70	.19
☐ 17 John Stephenson	1.50	.70	.19
☐ 18 Roland Sheldon	1.50	.70	.19
☐ 19 San Francisco Giants	4.00	1.80	.50
Team Card			
☐ 20 Willie Horton	2.50	1.10	.30
☐ 21 Don Nottebart	1.50	.70	.19
☐ 22 Joe Nossek	1.50	.70	.19
☐ 23 Jack Sanford	1.50	.70	.19
☐ 24 Don Kessinger	6.00	2.70	.75
☐ 25 Pete Ward	1.50	.70	.19
☐ 26 Ray Sadecki	1.50	.70	.19
☐ 27 Orioles Rookies	1.50	.70	.19
Darold Knowles			
Andy Etchebarren			
☐ 28 Phil Niekro	20.00	9.00	2.50
☐ 29 Mike Brumley	1.50	.70	.19
☐ 30 Pete Rose DP	35.00	16.00	4.40
☐ 31 Jack Cullen	2.50	1.10	.30
☐ 32 Adolfo Phillips	1.50	.70	.19
☐ 33 Jim Pagliaroni	1.50	.70	.19
☐ 34 Checklist 1	8.00	1.60	.80
☐ 35 Ron Swoboda	2.50	1.10	.30
☐ 36 Jim Hunter UER	20.00	9.00	2.50
(Stats say 1963 and 1964, should be 1964 and 1965)			
☐ 37 Billy Herman MG	2.50	1.10	.30
☐ 38 Ron Nischwitz	1.50	.70	.19
☐ 39 Ken Henderson	1.50	.70	.19
☐ 40 Jim Grant	1.50	.70	.19
☐ 41 Don LeJohn	1.50	.70	.19
☐ 42 Aubrey Gatewood	1.50	.70	.19
☐ 43A Don Landrum	2.00	.90	.25
(Dark button on pants showing)			
☐ 43B Don Landrum	20.00	9.00	2.50
(Button on pants partially airbrushed)			
☐ 43C Don Landrum	2.00	.90	.25
(Button on pants not showing)			
☐ 44 Indians Rookies	1.50	.70	.19
Bill Davis			
Tom Kelley			
☐ 45 Jim Gentile	2.50	1.10	.30
☐ 46 Howie Koplitz	1.50	.70	.19
☐ 47 J.C. Martin	1.50	.70	.19
☐ 48 Paul Blair	2.50	1.10	.30
☐ 49 Woody Woodward	2.50	1.10	.30
☐ 50 Mickey Mantle DP	200.00	90.00	25.00
☐ 51 Gordon Richardson	1.50	.70	.19
☐ 52 Power Plus	2.50	1.10	.30
Wes Covington			
Johnny Callison			
☐ 53 Bob Duliba	1.50	.70	.19
☐ 54 Jose Pagan	1.50	.70	.19
☐ 55 Ken Harrelson	2.50	1.10	.30
☐ 56 Sandy Valdespino	1.50	.70	.19
☐ 57 Jim Lefebvre	2.50	1.10	.30
☐ 58 Dave Wickersham	1.50	.70	.19
☐ 59 Reds Team	4.00	1.80	.50
☐ 60 Curt Flood	2.50	1.10	.30
☐ 61 Bob Bolin	1.50	.70	.19
☐ 62A Merritt Ranew	1.50	.70	.19
(With sold line)			
☐ 62B Merritt Ranew	40.00	18.00	5.00
(Without sold line)			
☐ 63 Jim Stewart	1.50	.70	.19
☐ 64 Bob Bruce	1.50	.70	.19
☐ 65 Leon Wagner	1.50	.70	.19
☐ 66 Al Weis	1.50	.70	.19
☐ 67 Mets Rookies	2.50	1.10	.30
Cleon Jones			
Dick Selma			
☐ 68 Hal Reniff	1.50	.70	.19
☐ 69 Ken Hamlin	1.50	.70	.19
☐ 70 Carl Yastrzemski	25.00	11.00	3.10
☐ 71 Frank Carpin	1.50	.70	.19
☐ 72 Tony Perez	25.00	11.00	3.10
☐ 73 Jerry Zimmerman	1.50	.70	.19
☐ 74 Don Mossi	2.50	1.10	.30
☐ 75 Tommy Davis	2.50	1.10	.30
☐ 76 Red Schoendienst MG	4.00	1.80	.50
☐ 77 John Orsino	1.50	.70	.19
☐ 78 Frank Linzy	1.50	.70	.19
☐ 79 Joe Pepitone	2.50	1.10	.30
☐ 80 Richie Allen	5.00	2.20	.60
☐ 81 Ray Oyler	1.50	.70	.19
☐ 82 Bob Hendley	1.50	.70	.19
☐ 83 Albie Pearson	2.50	1.10	.30
☐ 84 Braves Rookies	1.50	.70	.19
Jim Beauchamp			
Dick Kelley			
☐ 85 Eddie Fisher	1.50	.70	.19
☐ 86 John Bateman	1.50	.70	.19
☐ 87 Dan Napoleon	1.50	.70	.19
☐ 88 Fred Whitfield	1.50	.70	.19
☐ 89 Ted Davidson	1.50	.70	.19
☐ 90 Luis Aparicio	7.00	3.10	.85
☐ 91A Bob Uecker TR	12.00	5.50	1.50
☐ 91B Bob Uecker NTR	40.00	18.00	5.00
☐ 92 Yankees Team	14.00	6.25	1.75
☐ 93 Jim Lonborg	2.50	1.10	.30
☐ 94 Matty Alou	2.50	1.10	.30
☐ 95 Pete Richert	1.50	.70	.19
☐ 96 Felipe Alou	2.50	1.10	.30
☐ 97 Jim Merritt	1.50	.70	.19
☐ 98 Don Demeter	1.50	.70	.19
☐ 99 Buc Belters	6.00	2.70	.75
Willie Stargell			
Donn Clendenon			
☐ 100 Sandy Koufax	75.00	34.00	9.50
☐ 101A Checklist 2	16.00	3.20	1.60
(115 W. Spahn) ERR			
☐ 101B Checklist 2	10.00	2.00	1.00
(115 Bill Henry) COR			
☐ 102 Ed Kirkpatrick	1.50	.70	.19
☐ 103A Dick Groat TR	2.50	1.10	.30
☐ 103B Dick Groat NTR	40.00	18.00	5.00
☐ 104A Alex Johnson TR	2.50	1.10	.30
☐ 104B Alex Johnson NTR	40.00	18.00	5.00
☐ 105 Milt Pappas	2.50	1.10	.30
☐ 106 Rusty Staub	4.00	1.80	.50
☐ 107 A's Rookies	1.50	.70	.19
Larry Stahl			
Ron Tompkins			
☐ 108 Bobby Klaus	1.50	.70	.19
☐ 109 Ralph Terry	2.50	1.10	.30
☐ 110 Ernie Banks	30.00	13.50	3.70
☐ 111 Gary Peters	2.00	.90	.25
☐ 112 Manny Mota	3.00	1.35	.35
☐ 113 Hank Aguirre	2.00	.90	.25
☐ 114 Jim Gosger	2.00	.90	.25
☐ 115 Bill Henry	2.00	.90	.25
☐ 116 Walt Alston MG	4.00	1.80	.50
☐ 117 Jake Gibbs	3.00	1.35	.35
☐ 118 Mike McCormick	3.00	1.35	.35
☐ 119 Art Shamsky	2.00	.90	.25
☐ 120 Harmon Killebrew	16.00	7.25	2.00
☐ 121 Ray Herbert	2.00	.90	.25
☐ 122 Joe Gaines	2.00	.90	.25
☐ 123 Pirates Rookies	2.00	.90	.25
Frank Bork			
Jerry May			
☐ 124 Tug McGraw	4.00	1.80	.50
☐ 125 Lou Brock	20.00	9.00	2.50
☐ 126 Jim Palmer UER	100.00	45.00	12.50
(Described as a lefthander on card back)			
☐ 127 Ken Berry	2.00	.90	.25
☐ 128 Jim Landis	2.00	.90	.25
☐ 129 Jack Kralick	2.00	.90	.25
☐ 130 Joe Torre	4.00	1.80	.50
☐ 131 Angels Team	5.00	2.20	.60
☐ 132 Orlando Cepeda	5.00	2.20	.60
☐ 133 Don McMahon	2.00	.90	.25
☐ 134 Wes Parker	3.00	1.35	.35
☐ 135 Dave Morehead	2.00	.90	.25
☐ 136 Woody Held	2.00	.90	.25
☐ 137 Pat Corrales	3.00	1.35	.35
☐ 138 Roger Repoz	2.00	.90	.25
☐ 139 Cubs Rookies	2.00	.90	.25
Byron Browne			
Don Young			
☐ 140 Jim Maloney	3.00	1.35	.35
☐ 141 Tom McCraw	2.00	.90	.25
☐ 142 Don Dennis	2.00	.90	.25
☐ 143 Jose Tartabull	3.00	1.35	.35
☐ 144 Don Schwall	2.00	.90	.25
☐ 145 Bill Freehan	3.00	1.35	.35
☐ 146 George Altman	2.00	.90	.25
☐ 147 Lum Harris MG	2.00	.90	.25
☐ 148 Bob Johnson	2.00	.90	.25
☐ 149 Dick Nen	2.00	.90	.25
☐ 150 Rocky Colavito	8.00	3.60	1.00
☐ 151 Gary Wagner	2.00	.90	.25
☐ 152 Frank Malzone	3.00	1.35	.35
☐ 153 Rico Carty	3.00	1.35	.35
☐ 154 Chuck Hiller	2.00	.90	.25
☐ 155 Marcelino Lopez	2.00	.90	.25
☐ 156 Double Play Combo	2.00	.90	.25
Dick Schofield			
Hal Lanier			
☐ 157 Rene Lachemann	2.00	.90	.25
☐ 158 Jim Brewer	2.00	.90	.25
☐ 159 Chico Ruiz	2.00	.90	.25
☐ 160 Whitey Ford	25.00	11.00	3.10
☐ 161 Jerry Lumpe	2.00	.90	.25
☐ 162 Lee Maye	2.00	.90	.25
☐ 163 Tito Francona	2.00	.90	.25
☐ 164 White Sox Rookies	3.00	1.35	.35
Tommie Agee			
Marv Staehle			
☐ 165 Don Lock	2.00	.90	.25
☐ 166 Chris Krug	2.00	.90	.25
☐ 167 Boog Powell	5.00	2.20	.60
☐ 168 Dan Osinski	2.00	.90	.25
☐ 169 Duke Sims	2.00	.90	.25
☐ 170 Cookie Rojas	3.00	1.35	.35
☐ 171 Nick Willhite	2.00	.90	.25
☐ 172 Mets Team	5.00	2.20	.60
☐ 173 Al Spangler	2.00	.90	.25
☐ 174 Ron Taylor	2.00	.90	.25
☐ 175 Bert Campaneris	3.00	1.35	.35
☐ 176 Jim Davenport	2.00	.90	.25
☐ 177 Hector Lopez	2.00	.90	.25
☐ 178 Bob Tillman	2.00	.90	.25
☐ 179 Cards Rookies	3.00	1.35	.35
Dennis Aust			
Bob Tolan			
☐ 180 Vada Pinson	3.00	1.35	.35
☐ 181 Al Worthington	2.00	.90	.25
☐ 182 Jerry Lynch	2.00	.90	.25
☐ 183A Checklist 3	8.00	1.60	.80
(Large print on front)			
☐ 183B Checklist 3	8.00	1.60	.80
(Small print on front)			
☐ 184 Denis Menke	2.00	.90	.25
☐ 185 Bob Buhl	3.00	1.35	.35
☐ 186 Ruben Amaro	2.00	.90	.25
☐ 187 Chuck Dressen MG	3.00	1.35	.35
☐ 188 Al Luplow	2.00	.90	.25
☐ 189 John Roseboro	3.00	1.35	.35
☐ 190 Jimmie Hall	2.00	.90	.25
☐ 191 Darrell Sutherland	2.00	.90	.25
☐ 192 Vic Power	3.00	1.35	.35
☐ 193 Dave McNally	3.00	1.35	.35
☐ 194 Senators Team	5.00	2.20	.60
☐ 195 Joe Morgan	14.00	6.25	1.75
☐ 196 Don Pavletich	2.00	.90	.25
☐ 197 Sonny Siebert	2.00	.90	.25
☐ 198 Mickey Stanley	4.00	1.80	.50
☐ 199 Chisox Clubbers	3.00	1.35	.35
Bill Skowron			
Johnny Romano			
Floyd Robinson			
☐ 200 Eddie Mathews	14.00	6.25	1.75
☐ 201 Jim Dickson	2.00	.90	.25
☐ 202 Clay Dalrymple	2.00	.90	.25
☐ 203 Jose Santiago	2.00	.90	.25
☐ 204 Cubs Team	5.00	2.20	.60
☐ 205 Tom Tresh	3.00	1.35	.35
☐ 206 Al Jackson	2.00	.90	.25
☐ 207 Frank Quilici	2.00	.90	.25
☐ 208 Bob Miller	2.00	.90	.25
☐ 209 Tigers Rookies	3.00	1.35	.35
Fritz Fisher			
John Hiller			
☐ 210 Bill Mazeroski	5.00	2.20	.60
☐ 211 Frank Kreutzer	2.00	.90	.25
☐ 212 Ed Kranepool	3.00	1.35	.35
☐ 213 Fred Newman	2.00	.90	.25
☐ 214 Tommy Harper	3.00	1.35	.35
☐ 215 NL Batting Leaders	50.00	22.00	6.25
Bob Clemente			
Hank Aaron			
Willie Mays			
☐ 216 AL Batting Leaders	6.00	2.70	.75
Tony Oliva			
Carl Yastrzemski			
Vic Davalillo			
☐ 217 NL Home Run Leaders	20.00	9.00	2.50
Willie Mays			
Willie McCovey			
Billy Williams			
☐ 218 AL Home Run Leaders	5.00	2.20	.60

Tony Conigliaro
Norm Cash
Willie Horton
☐ 219 NL RBI Leaders 12.00 5.50 1.50
Deron Johnson
Frank Robinson
Willie Mays
☐ 220 AL RBI Leaders .... 5.00 2.20 .60
Rocky Colavito
Willie Horton
Tony Oliva
☐ 221 NL ERA Leaders 12.00 5.50 1.50
Sandy Koufax
Juan Marichal
Vern Law
☐ 222 AL ERA Leaders .... 5.00 2.20 .60
Sam McDowell
Eddie Fisher
Sonny Siebert
☐ 223 NL Pitching Leaders 12.00 5.50 1.50
Sandy Koufax
Tony Cloninger
Don Drysdale
☐ 224 AL Pitching Leaders .... 5.00 2.20 .60
Jim Grant
Mel Stottlemyre
Jim Kaat
☐ 225 NL Strikeout Leaders 12.00 5.50 1.50
Sandy Koufax
Bob Veale
Bob Gibson
☐ 226 AL Strikeout Leaders .... 5.00 2.20 .60
Sam McDowell
Mickey Lolich
Dennis McLain
Sonny Siebert
☐ 227 Russ Nixon .... 2.00 .90 .25
☐ 228 Larry Dierker .... 3.00 1.35 .35
☐ 229 Hank Bauer MG .... 3.00 1.35 .35
☐ 230 Johnny Callison .... 3.00 1.35 .35
☐ 231 Floyd Weaver .... 2.00 .90 .25
☐ 232 Glenn Beckert .... 3.00 1.35 .35
☐ 233 Dom Zanni .... 2.00 .90 .25
☐ 234 Yankees Rookies 8.00 3.60 1.00
Rich Beck
Roy White
☐ 235 Don Cardwell .... 2.00 .90 .25
☐ 236 Mike Hershberger .... 2.00 .90 .25
☐ 237 Billy O'Dell .... 2.00 .90 .25
☐ 238 Dodgers Team .... 5.00 2.20 .60
☐ 239 Orlando Pena .... 2.00 .90 .25
☐ 240 Earl Battey .... 2.00 .90 .25
☐ 241 Dennis Ribant .... 2.00 .90 .25
☐ 242 Jesus Alou .... 2.00 .90 .25
☐ 243 Nelson Briles .... 3.00 1.35 .35
☐ 244 Astros Rookies .... 2.00 .90 .25
Chuck Harrison
Sonny Jackson
☐ 245 John Buzhardt .... 2.00 .90 .25
☐ 246 Ed Bailey .... 2.00 .90 .25
☐ 247 Carl Warwick .... 2.00 .90 .25
☐ 248 Pete Mikkelsen .... 2.00 .90 .25
☐ 249 Bill Rigney MG .... 2.00 .90 .25
☐ 250 Sammy Ellis .... 2.00 .90 .25
☐ 251 Ed Brinkman .... 2.00 .90 .25
☐ 252 Denny Lemaster .... 2.00 .90 .25
☐ 253 Don Wert .... 2.00 .90 .25
☐ 254 Phillies Rookies 80.00 36.00 10.00
Ferguson Jenkins
Bill Sorrell
☐ 255 Willie Stargell 20.00 9.00 2.50
☐ 256 Lew Krausse .... 2.00 .90 .25
☐ 257 Jeff Torborg .... 3.00 1.35 .35
☐ 258 Dave Giusti .... 2.00 .90 .25
☐ 259 Boston Red Sox .... 5.00 2.20 .60
Team Card
☐ 260 Bob Shaw .... 2.00 .90 .25
☐ 261 Ron Hansen .... 2.00 .90 .25
☐ 262 Jack Hamilton .... 2.00 .90 .25
☐ 263 Tom Egan .... 2.00 .90 .25
☐ 264 Twins Rookies .... 2.00 .90 .25
Andy Kosco
Ted Uhlaender
☐ 265 Stu Miller .... 3.00 1.35 .35
☐ 266 Pedro Gonzalez UER .... 2.00 .90 .25
(Misspelled Gonzales
on card back)
☐ 267 Joe Sparma .... 2.00 .90 .25
☐ 268 John Blanchard .... 2.00 .90 .25
☐ 269 Don Heffner MG .... 2.00 .90 .25
☐ 270 Claude Osteen .... 3.00 1.35 .35
☐ 271 Hal Lanier .... 2.00 .90 .25
☐ 272 Jack Baldschun .... 2.00 .90 .25
☐ 273 Astro Aces .... 3.00 1.35 .35
Bob Aspromonte
Rusty Staub
☐ 274 Buster Narum .... 2.00 .90 .25
☐ 275 Tim McCarver .... 4.00 1.80 .50
☐ 276 Jim Bouton .... 4.00 1.80 .50
☐ 277 George Thomas .... 2.00 .90 .25
☐ 278 Cal Koonce .... 2.00 .90 .25
☐ 279A Checklist 4 .... 8.00 1.60 .80
(Player's cap black)
☐ 279B Checklist 4 .... 8.00 1.60 .80
(Player's cap red)
☐ 280 Bobby Knoop .... 2.00 .90 .25
☐ 281 Bruce Howard .... 2.00 .90 .25
☐ 282 Johnny Lewis .... 2.00 .90 .25
☐ 283 Jim Perry .... 3.00 1.35 .35
☐ 284 Bobby Wine .... 3.50 1.55 .45
☐ 285 Luis Tiant .... 3.50 1.55 .45
☐ 286 Gary Geiger .... 3.00 1.35 .35
☐ 287 Jack Aker .... 3.00 1.35 .35
☐ 288 Dodgers Rookies 45.00 20.00 5.50
Bill Singer
Don Sutton
☐ 289 Larry Sherry .... 3.50 1.55 .45
☐ 290 Ron Santo .... 5.00 2.20 .60
☐ 291 Moe Drabowsky .... 3.50 1.55 .45
☐ 292 Jim Coker .... 3.00 1.35 .35
☐ 293 Mike Shannon .... 3.50 1.55 .45
☐ 294 Steve Ridzik .... 3.00 1.35 .35
☐ 295 Jim Ray Hart .... 3.50 1.55 .45
☐ 296 Johnny Keane MG .... 3.50 1.55 .45
☐ 297 Jim Owens .... 3.00 1.35 .35
☐ 298 Rico Petrocelli .... 3.50 1.55 .45
☐ 299 Lou Burdette .... 3.50 1.55 .45
☐ 300 Bob Clemente 150.00 70.00 19.00
☐ 301 Greg Bollo .... 3.00 1.35 .35
☐ 302 Ernie Bowman .... 3.00 1.35 .35
☐ 303 Cleveland Indians .... 5.00 2.20 .60
Team Card
☐ 304 John Herrnstein .... 3.00 1.35 .35
☐ 305 Camilo Pascual .... 3.50 1.55 .45
☐ 306 Ty Cline .... 3.00 1.35 .35
☐ 307 Clay Carroll .... 3.50 1.55 .45
☐ 308 Tom Haller .... 3.50 1.55 .45
☐ 309 Diego Segui .... 3.00 1.35 .35
☐ 310 Frank Robinson 30.00 13.50 3.70
☐ 311 Reds Rookies .... 3.50 1.55 .45
Tommy Helms
Dick Simpson
☐ 312 Bob Saverine .... 3.00 1.35 .35
☐ 313 Chris Zachary .... 3.00 1.35 .35
☐ 314 Hector Valle .... 3.00 1.35 .35
☐ 315 Norm Cash .... 3.50 1.55 .45
☐ 316 Jack Fisher .... 3.00 1.35 .35
☐ 317 Dalton Jones .... 3.00 1.35 .35
☐ 318 Harry Walker MG .... 3.00 1.35 .35
☐ 319 Gene Freese .... 3.00 1.35 .35
☐ 320 Bob Gibson 25.00 11.00 3.10
☐ 321 Rick Reichardt .... 3.00 1.35 .35
☐ 322 Bill Faul .... 3.00 1.35 .35
☐ 323 Ray Barker .... 3.00 1.35 .35
☐ 324 John Boozer .... 3.00 1.35 .35
☐ 325 Vic Davalillo .... 3.00 1.35 .35
☐ 326 Braves Team .... 5.00 2.20 .60
☐ 327 Bernie Allen .... 3.00 1.35 .35
☐ 328 Jerry Grote .... 3.50 1.55 .45
☐ 329 Pete Charton .... 3.00 1.35 .35
☐ 330 Ron Fairly .... 3.50 1.55 .45
☐ 331 Ron Herbel .... 3.00 1.35 .35
☐ 332 Bill Bryan .... 3.00 1.35 .35
☐ 333 Senators Rookies .... 3.00 1.35 .35
Joe Coleman
Jim French
☐ 334 Marty Keough .... 3.00 1.35 .35
☐ 335 Juan Pizarro .... 3.00 1.35 .35
☐ 336 Gene Alley .... 3.50 1.55 .45
☐ 337 Fred Gladding .... 3.00 1.35 .35
☐ 338 Dal Maxvill .... 3.00 1.35 .35
☐ 339 Del Crandall .... 3.50 1.55 .45
☐ 340 Dean Chance .... 3.50 1.55 .45
☐ 341 Wes Westrum MG .... 3.50 1.55 .45
☐ 342 Bob Humphreys .... 3.00 1.35 .35
☐ 343 Joe Christopher .... 3.00 1.35 .35
☐ 344 Steve Blass .... 3.50 1.55 .45
☐ 345 Bob Allison .... 3.50 1.55 .45
☐ 346 Mike de la Hoz .... 3.00 1.35 .35
☐ 347 Phil Regan .... 3.50 1.55 .45
☐ 348 Orioles Team 8.00 3.60 1.00
☐ 349 Cap Peterson .... 3.00 1.35 .35
☐ 350 Mel Stottlemyre .... 5.00 2.20 .60
☐ 351 Fred Valentine .... 3.00 1.35 .35
☐ 352 Bob Aspromonte .... 3.00 1.35 .35
☐ 353 Al McBean .... 3.00 1.35 .35
☐ 354 Smoky Burgess .... 3.50 1.55 .45
☐ 355 Wade Blasingame .... 3.00 1.35 .35
☐ 356 Red Sox Rookies .... 3.00 1.35 .35
Owen Johnson
Ken Sanders
☐ 357 Gerry Arrigo .... 3.00 1.35 .35
☐ 358 Charlie Smith .... 3.00 1.35 .35
☐ 359 Johnny Briggs .... 3.00 1.35 .35
☐ 360 Ron Hunt .... 3.00 1.35 .35
☐ 361 Tom Satriano .... 3.00 1.35 .35
☐ 362 Gates Brown .... 3.50 1.55 .45
☐ 363 Checklist 5 .... 10.00 2.00 1.00
☐ 364 Nate Oliver .... 3.00 1.35 .35
☐ 365 Roger Maris 35.00 16.00 4.40
☐ 366 Wayne Causey .... 3.00 1.35 .35
☐ 367 Mel Nelson .... 3.00 1.35 .35
☐ 368 Charlie Lau .... 3.50 1.55 .45
☐ 369 Jim King .... 3.00 1.35 .35
☐ 370 Chico Cardenas .... 3.00 1.35 .35
☐ 371 Lee Stange .... 5.00 2.20 .60
☐ 372 Harvey Kuenn .... 5.50 2.50 .70
☐ 373 Giants Rookies .... 5.50 2.50 .70
Jack Hiatt
Dick Estelle
☐ 374 Bob Locker .... 5.00 2.20 .60
☐ 375 Donn Clendenon .... 5.50 2.50 .70
☐ 376 Paul Schaal .... 5.00 2.20 .60
☐ 377 Turk Farrell .... 5.00 2.20 .60
☐ 378 Dick Tracewski .... 5.00 2.20 .60
☐ 379 Cardinal Team 10.00 4.50 1.25
☐ 380 Tony Conigliaro 10.00 4.50 1.25
☐ 381 Hank Fischer .... 5.00 2.20 .60
☐ 382 Phil Roof .... 5.00 2.20 .60
☐ 383 Jackie Brandt .... 5.00 2.20 .60
☐ 384 Al Downing .... 5.50 2.50 .70
☐ 385 Ken Boyer .... 5.50 2.50 .70
☐ 386 Gil Hodges MG 8.00 3.60 1.00
☐ 387 Howie Reed .... 5.00 2.20 .60
☐ 388 Don Mincher .... 5.00 2.20 .60
☐ 389 Jim O'Toole .... 5.50 2.50 .70
☐ 390 Brooks Robinson 45.00 20.00 5.50
☐ 391 Chuck Hinton .... 5.00 2.20 .60
☐ 392 Cubs Rookies .... 7.00 3.10 .85
Bill Hands
Randy Hundley
☐ 393 George Brunet .... 5.00 2.20 .60
☐ 394 Ron Brand .... 5.00 2.20 .60
☐ 395 Len Gabrielson .... 5.00 2.20 .60
☐ 396 Jerry Stephenson .... 5.00 2.20 .60
☐ 397 Bill White .... 5.50 2.50 .70
☐ 398 Danny Cater .... 5.00 2.20 .60
☐ 399 Ray Washburn .... 5.00 2.20 .60
☐ 400 Zoilo Versalles .... 5.50 2.50 .70
☐ 401 Ken McMullen .... 5.00 2.20 .60
☐ 402 Jim Hickman .... 5.00 2.20 .60
☐ 403 Fred Talbot .... 5.00 2.20 .60
☐ 404 Pittsburgh Pirates 10.00 4.50 1.25
Team Card
☐ 405 Elston Howard .... 6.00 2.70 .75
☐ 406 Joey Jay .... 5.00 2.20 .60
☐ 407 John Kennedy .... 5.00 2.20 .60
☐ 408 Lee Thomas .... 5.50 2.50 .70
☐ 409 Billy Hoeft .... 5.00 2.20 .60
☐ 410 Al Kaline 35.00 16.00 4.40
☐ 411 Gene Mauch MG .... 5.00 2.20 .60
☐ 412 Sam Bowens .... 5.00 2.20 .60
☐ 413 Johnny Romano .... 5.00 2.20 .60
☐ 414 Dan Coombs .... 5.00 2.20 .60
☐ 415 Max Alvis .... 5.00 2.20 .60
☐ 416 Phil Ortega .... 5.00 2.20 .60
☐ 417 Angels Rookies .... 5.00 2.20 .60
Jim McGlothlin
Ed Sukla
☐ 418 Phil Gagliano .... 5.00 2.20 .60
☐ 419 Mike Ryan .... 5.00 2.20 .60
☐ 420 Juan Marichal 14.00 6.25 1.75
☐ 421 Roy McMillan .... 5.50 2.50 .70
☐ 422 Ed Charles .... 5.00 2.20 .60
☐ 423 Ernie Broglio .... 5.00 2.20 .60
☐ 424 Reds Rookies 10.00 4.50 1.25
Lee May
Darrell Osteen
☐ 425 Bob Veale .... 5.50 2.50 .70
☐ 426 White Sox Team 10.00 4.50 1.25
☐ 427 John Miller .... 5.00 2.20 .60
☐ 428 Sandy Alomar .... 5.50 2.50 .70
☐ 429 Bill Monbouquette .... 5.00 2.20 .60
☐ 430 Don Drysdale 20.00 9.00 2.50
☐ 431 Walt Bond .... 5.00 2.20 .60
☐ 432 Bob Heffner .... 5.00 2.20 .60
☐ 433 Alvin Dark MG .... 5.50 2.50 .70
☐ 434 Willie Kirkland .... 5.00 2.20 .60
☐ 435 Jim Bunning 14.00 6.25 1.75
☐ 436 Julian Javier .... 5.50 2.50 .70
☐ 437 Al Stanek .... 5.00 2.20 .60
☐ 438 Willie Smith .... 5.00 2.20 .60
☐ 439 Pedro Ramos .... 5.00 2.20 .60
☐ 440 Deron Johnson .... 5.50 2.50 .70
☐ 441 Tommie Sisk .... 5.00 2.20 .60
☐ 442 Orioles Rookies .... 5.00 2.20 .60
Ed Barnowski
Eddie Watt
☐ 443 Bill Wakefield .... 5.00 2.20 .60
☐ 444 Checklist 6 .... 10.00 2.00 1.00
☐ 445 Jim Kaat 10.00 4.50 1.25
☐ 446 Mack Jones .... 5.00 2.20 .60
☐ 447 Dick Ellsworth UER 12.00 5.50 1.50
(Photo actually
Ken Hubbs)
☐ 448 Eddie Stanky MG 9.00 4.00 1.10
☐ 449 Joe Moeller 9.00 4.00 1.10
☐ 450 Tony Oliva 10.00 4.50 1.25
☐ 451 Barry Latman 9.00 4.00 1.10
☐ 452 Joe Azcue 9.00 4.00 1.10
☐ 453 Ron Kline 9.00 4.00 1.10
☐ 454 Jerry Buchek 9.00 4.00 1.10
☐ 455 Mickey Lolich 10.00 4.50 1.25
☐ 456 Red Sox Rookies 9.00 4.00 1.10
Darrell Brandon
Joe Foy
☐ 457 Joe Gibbon 9.00 4.00 1.10
☐ 458 Manny Jiminez 9.00 4.00 1.10
☐ 459 Bill McCool 9.00 4.00 1.10
☐ 460 Curt Blefary 9.00 4.00 1.10
☐ 461 Roy Face 9.50 4.30 1.20
☐ 462 Bob Rodgers 9.00 4.00 1.10
☐ 463 Philadelphia Phillies 14.00 6.25 1.75
Team Card
☐ 464 Larry Bearnarth 9.00 4.00 1.10
☐ 465 Don Buford 9.00 4.00 1.10
☐ 466 Ken Johnson 9.00 4.00 1.10
☐ 467 Vic Roznovsky 9.00 4.00 1.10
☐ 468 Johnny Podres 11.00 4.90 1.35
☐ 469 Yankees Rookies 25.00 11.00 3.10
Bobby Murcer
Dooley Womack
☐ 470 Sam McDowell 9.50 4.30 1.20
☐ 471 Bob Skinner 9.00 4.00 1.10
☐ 472 Terry Fox 9.00 4.00 1.10
☐ 473 Rich Rollins 9.00 4.00 1.10
☐ 474 Dick Schofield 9.00 4.00 1.10
☐ 475 Dick Radatz 9.00 4.00 1.10
☐ 476 Bobby Bragan MG 9.00 4.00 1.10
☐ 477 Steve Barber 9.00 4.00 1.10
☐ 478 Tony Gonzalez 9.00 4.00 1.10
☐ 479 Jim Hannan 9.00 4.00 1.10
☐ 480 Dick Stuart 9.00 4.00 1.10
☐ 481 Bob Lee 9.00 4.00 1.10
☐ 482 Cubs Rookies 9.00 4.00 1.10
John Boccabella
Dave Dowling
☐ 483 Joe Nuxhall 9.00 4.00 1.10
☐ 484 Wes Covington 9.00 4.00 1.10
☐ 485 Bob Bailey 9.00 4.00 1.10
☐ 486 Tommy John 10.00 4.50 1.25
☐ 487 Al Ferrara 9.00 4.00 1.10
☐ 488 George Banks 9.00 4.00 1.10
☐ 489 Curt Simmons 9.00 4.00 1.10
☐ 490 Bobby Richardson 12.00 5.50 1.50
☐ 491 Dennis Bennett 9.00 4.00 1.10
☐ 492 Athletics Team 14.00 6.25 1.75
☐ 493 Johnny Klippstein 9.00 4.00 1.10
☐ 494 Gordy Coleman 9.00 4.00 1.10
☐ 495 Dick McAuliffe 9.00 4.00 1.10
☐ 496 Lindy McDaniel 9.00 4.00 1.10
☐ 497 Chris Cannizzaro 9.00 4.00 1.10
☐ 498 Pirates Rookies 9.00 4.00 1.10
Luke Walker
Woody Fryman
☐ 499 Wally Bunker 9.00 4.00 1.10
☐ 500 Hank Aaron 125.00 55.00 15.50
☐ 501 John O'Donoghue 9.00 4.00 1.10
☐ 502 Lenny Green UER 9.00 4.00 1.10
(Born: aJn. 6, 1933)
☐ 503 Steve Hamilton 10.00 4.50 1.25
☐ 504 Grady Hatton MG 9.00 4.00 1.10
☐ 505 Jose Cardenal 9.00 4.00 1.10
☐ 506 Bo Belinsky 9.50 4.30 1.20
☐ 507 Johnny Edwards 9.00 4.00 1.10
☐ 508 Steve Hargan 9.00 4.00 1.10
☐ 509 Jake Wood 9.00 4.00 1.10
☐ 510 Hoyt Wilhelm 16.00 7.25 2.00
☐ 511 Giants Rookies 9.00 4.00 1.10
Bob Barton
Tito Fuentes
☐ 512 Dick Stigman 9.00 4.00 1.10
☐ 513 Camilo Carreon 9.00 4.00 1.10
☐ 514 Hal Woodeshick 9.00 4.00 1.10
☐ 515 Frank Howard 14.00 6.25 1.75
☐ 516 Eddie Bressoud 9.00 4.00 1.10
☐ 517A Checklist 7 .... 16.00 3.20 1.60
529 White Sox Rookies
544 Cardinals Rookies
☐ 517B Checklist 7 .... 16.00 3.20 1.60
529 W. Sox Rookies
544 Cards Rookies
☐ 518 Braves Rookies 9.00 4.00 1.10
Herb Hippauf
Arnie Umbach
☐ 519 Bob Friend 10.00 4.50 1.25
☐ 520 Jim Wynn 9.50 4.30 1.20
☐ 521 John Wyatt 9.00 4.00 1.10
☐ 522 Phil Linz 9.00 4.00 1.10
☐ 523 Bob Sadowski 17.50 8.00 2.20
☐ 524 Giants Rookies SP 30.00 13.50 3.70
Ollie Brown
Don Mason
☐ 525 Gary Bell SP 30.00 13.50 3.70
☐ 526 Twins Team SP 100.00 45.00 12.50
☐ 527 Julio Navarro 15.00 6.75 1.85
☐ 528 Jesse Gonder SP 30.00 13.50 3.70
☐ 529 White Sox Rookies 17.50 8.00 2.20
Lee Elia
Dennis Higgins
Bill Voss
☐ 530 Robin Roberts 60.00 27.00 7.50
☐ 531 Joe Cunningham 15.00 6.75 1.85
☐ 532 Aurelio Monteagudo SP 30.00 13.50 3.70
☐ 533 Jerry Adair SP 30.00 13.50 3.70
☐ 534 Mets Rookies 15.00 6.75 1.85
Dave Eilers
Rob Gardner
☐ 535 Willie Davis SP 40.00 18.00 5.00
☐ 536 Dick Egan 15.00 6.75 1.85
☐ 537 Herman Franks MG 15.00 6.75 1.85
☐ 538 Bob Allen SP 30.00 13.50 3.70
☐ 539 Astros Rookies 15.00 6.75 1.85
Bill Heath
Carroll Sembera
☐ 540 Denny McLain SP 80.00 36.00 10.00
☐ 541 Gene Oliver SP 30.00 13.50 3.70
☐ 542 George Smith 15.00 6.75 1.85
☐ 543 Roger Craig SP 35.00 16.00 4.40
☐ 544 Cardinals Rookies SP 30.00 13.50 3.70
Joe Hoerner

George Kernek			
Jimy Williams UER			
(Misspelled Jimmy			
on card)			
☐ 545 Dick Green SP	30.00	13.50	3.70
☐ 546 Dwight Siebler	15.00	6.75	1.85
☐ 547 Horace Clarke SP	40.00	18.00	5.00
☐ 548 Gary Kroll SP	30.00	13.50	3.70
☐ 549 Senators Rookies	15.00	6.75	1.85
Al Closter			
Casey Cox			
☐ 550 Willie McCovey SP	90.00	40.00	11.00
☐ 551 Bob Purkey SP	30.00	13.50	3.70
☐ 552 Birdie Tebbetts	30.00	13.50	3.70
MG SP			
☐ 553 Rookie Stars	15.00	6.75	1.85
Pat Garrett			
Jackie Warner			
☐ 554 Jim Northrup SP	30.00	13.50	3.70
☐ 555 Ron Perranoski SP	30.00	13.50	3.70
☐ 556 Mel Queen SP	30.00	13.50	3.70
☐ 557 Felix Mantilla SP	30.00	13.50	3.70
☐ 558 Red Sox Rookies	20.00	9.00	2.50
Guido Grilli			
Pete Magrini			
George Scott			
☐ 559 Roberto Pena SP	30.00	13.50	3.70
☐ 560 Joel Horlen	15.00	6.75	1.85
☐ 561 ChooChoo Coleman SP	35.00	16.00	4.40
☐ 562 Russ Snyder	15.00	6.75	1.85
☐ 563 Twins Rookies	15.00	6.75	1.85
Pete Cimino			
Cesar Tovar			
☐ 564 Bob Chance SP	30.00	13.50	3.70
☐ 565 Jim Piersall SP	40.00	18.00	5.00
☐ 566 Mike Cuellar SP	35.00	16.00	4.40
☐ 567 Dick Howser SP	40.00	18.00	5.00
☐ 568 Athletics Rookies	15.00	6.75	1.85
Paul Lindblad			
Ron Stone			
☐ 569 Orlando McFarlane SP	30.00	13.50	3.70
☐ 570 Art Mahaffey SP	30.00	13.50	3.70
☐ 571 Dave Roberts SP	30.00	13.50	3.70
☐ 572 Bob Priddy	15.00	6.75	1.85
☐ 573 Derrell Griffith	15.00	6.75	1.85
☐ 574 Mets Rookies	15.00	6.75	1.85
Bill Hepler			
Bill Murphy			
☐ 575 Earl Wilson	17.50	8.00	2.20
☐ 576 Dave Nicholson SP	30.00	13.50	3.70
☐ 577 Jack Lamabe SP	30.00	13.50	3.70
☐ 578 Chi Chi Olivo SP	30.00	13.50	3.70
☐ 579 Orioles Rookies	20.00	9.00	2.50
Frank Bertaina			
Gene Brabender			
Dave Johnson			
☐ 580 Billy Williams SP	70.00	32.00	8.75
☐ 581 Tony Martinez	15.00	6.75	1.85
☐ 582 Garry Roggenburk	15.00	6.75	1.85
☐ 583 Tigers Team SP UER	125.00	55.00	15.50
(Text on back states Tigers			
finished third in 1966 instead			
of fourth.)			
☐ 584 Yankees Rookies	15.00	6.75	1.85
Frank Fernandez			
Fritz Peterson			
☐ 585 Tony Taylor	17.50	8.00	2.20
☐ 586 Claude Raymond SP	30.00	13.50	3.70
☐ 587 Dick Bertell	15.00	6.75	1.85
☐ 588 Athletics Rookies	15.00	6.75	1.85
Chuck Dobson			
Ken Suarez			
☐ 589 Lou Klimchock SP	35.00	16.00	4.40
☐ 590 Bill Skowron SP	40.00	18.00	5.00
☐ 591 NL Rookies SP	40.00	18.00	5.00
Bart Shirley			
Grant Jackson			
☐ 592 Andre Rodgers	15.00	6.75	1.85
☐ 593 Doug Camilli SP	30.00	13.50	3.70
☐ 594 Chico Salmon	15.00	6.75	1.85
☐ 595 Larry Jackson	15.00	6.75	1.85
☐ 596 Astros Rookies SP	35.00	16.00	4.40
Nate Colbert			
Greg Sims			
☐ 597 John Sullivan	15.00	6.75	1.85
☐ 598 Gaylord Perry SP	190.00	55.00	16.00

1966 Topps Rub-Offs

There are 120 "rub-offs" in the Topps insert set of 1966, of which 100 depict players and the remaining 20 show team pennants. Each rub off measures 2 1/16" by 3". The color player photos are vertical while the team pennants are horizontal; both types of transfer have a large black printer's mark. These rub-offs were originally printed in rolls of 20 and are frequently still found this way. Since these rub-offs are unnumbered, they are ordered below alphabetically within type, players (1-100) and team pennants (101-120).

	NRMT	VG-E	GOOD
COMPLETE SET (120)	375.00	170.00	47.50
COMMON RUB-OFF (1-100)	1.00	.45	.12
COMMON PENNANT (101-120)	.75	.35	.09
☐ 1 Henry Aaron	15.00	6.75	1.85
☐ 2 Jerry Adair	1.00	.45	.12
☐ 3 Richie Allen	2.00	.90	.25
☐ 4 Jesus Alou	1.50	.70	.19
☐ 5 Max Alvis	1.00	.45	.12
☐ 6 Bob Aspromonte	1.00	.45	.12
☐ 7 Ernie Banks	10.00	4.50	1.25
☐ 8 Earl Battey	1.00	.45	.12
☐ 9 Curt Blefary	1.00	.45	.12
☐ 10 Ken Boyer	1.50	.70	.19
☐ 11 Bob Bruce	1.00	.45	.12
☐ 12 Jim Bunning	5.00	2.20	.60
☐ 13 Johnny Callison	1.50	.70	.19
☐ 14 Bert Campaneris	1.50	.70	.19
☐ 15 Jose Cardenal	1.00	.45	.12
☐ 16 Dean Chance	1.50	.70	.19
☐ 17 Ed Charles	1.00	.45	.12
☐ 18 Bob Clemente	50.00	22.00	6.25
☐ 19 Tony Cloninger	1.00	.45	.12
☐ 20 Rocky Colavito	3.00	1.35	.35
☐ 21 Tony Conigliaro	2.00	.90	.25
☐ 22 Vic Davalillo	1.00	.45	.12
☐ 23 Willie Davis	1.50	.70	.19
☐ 24 Don Drysdale	6.00	2.70	.75
☐ 25 Sammy Ellis	1.00	.45	.12
☐ 26 Dick Ellsworth	1.00	.45	.12
☐ 27 Ron Fairly	1.50	.70	.19
☐ 28 Dick Farrell	1.00	.45	.12
☐ 29 Eddie Fisher	1.00	.45	.12
☐ 30 Jack Fisher	1.00	.45	.12
☐ 31 Curt Flood	2.00	.90	.25
☐ 32 Whitey Ford	6.00	2.70	.75
☐ 33 Bill Freehan	1.50	.70	.19
☐ 34 Jim Fregosi	1.50	.70	.19
☐ 35 Bob Gibson	5.00	2.20	.60
☐ 36 Jim Grant	1.00	.45	.12
☐ 37 Jimmie Hall	1.00	.45	.12
☐ 38 Ken Harrelson	1.50	.70	.19
☐ 39 Jim Ray Hart	1.00	.45	.12
☐ 40 Joel Horlen	1.00	.45	.12
☐ 41 Willie Horton	1.50	.70	.19
☐ 42 Frank Howard	2.00	.90	.25
☐ 43 Deron Johnson	1.00	.45	.12
☐ 44 Al Kaline	10.00	4.50	1.25
☐ 45 Harmon Killebrew	6.00	2.70	.75
☐ 46 Bobby Knoop	1.00	.45	.12
☐ 47 Sandy Koufax	15.00	6.75	1.85
☐ 48 Ed Kranepool	1.00	.45	.12
☐ 49 Gary Kroll	1.00	.45	.12
☐ 50 Don Landrum	1.00	.45	.12
☐ 51 Vern Law	1.50	.70	.19
☐ 52 Johnny Lewis	1.00	.45	.12
☐ 53 Don Lock	1.00	.45	.12
☐ 54 Mickey Lolich	2.00	.90	.25
☐ 55 Jim Maloney	1.50	.70	.19
☐ 56 Felix Mantilla	1.00	.45	.12
☐ 57 Mickey Mantle	75.00	34.00	9.50
☐ 58 Juan Marichal	5.00	2.20	.60
☐ 59 Eddie Mathews	5.00	2.20	.60
☐ 60 Willie Mays	18.00	8.00	2.20
☐ 61 Bill Mazeroski	2.00	.90	.25
☐ 62 Dick McAuliffe	1.00	.45	.12
☐ 63 Tim McCarver	2.00	.90	.25
☐ 64 Willie McCovey	5.00	2.20	.60
☐ 65 Sam McDowell	1.50	.70	.19
☐ 66 Ken McMullen	1.00	.45	.12
☐ 67 Denis Menke	1.00	.45	.12
☐ 68 Bill Monbouquette	1.00	.45	.12
☐ 69 Joe Morgan	6.00	2.70	.75
☐ 70 Fred Newman	1.00	.45	.12
☐ 71 John O'Donoghue	1.00	.45	.12
☐ 72 Tony Oliva	3.00	1.35	.35
☐ 73 Johnny Orsino	1.00	.45	.12
☐ 74 Phil Ortega	1.00	.45	.12
☐ 75 Milt Pappas	1.50	.70	.19
☐ 76 Dick Radatz	1.50	.70	.19
☐ 77 Bobby Richardson	2.00	.90	.25
☐ 78 Pete Richert	1.00	.45	.12
☐ 79 Brooks Robinson	10.00	4.50	1.25
☐ 80 Floyd Robinson	1.00	.45	.12
☐ 81 Frank Robinson	10.00	4.50	1.25
☐ 82 Cookie Rojas	2.00	.90	.25
☐ 83 Pete Rose	30.00	13.50	3.70
☐ 84 John Roseboro	1.50	.70	.19
☐ 85 Ron Santo	2.00	.90	.25
☐ 86 Bill Skowron	1.50	.70	.19
☐ 87 Willie Stargell	6.00	2.70	.75
☐ 88 Mel Stottlemyre	1.50	.70	.19
☐ 89 Dick Stuart	1.00	.45	.12
☐ 90 Ron Swoboda	1.50	.70	.19
☐ 91 Fred Talbot	1.00	.45	.12
☐ 92 Ralph Terry	1.50	.70	.19
☐ 93 Joe Torre	2.00	.90	.25
☐ 94 Tom Tresh	1.50	.70	.19
☐ 95 Bob Veale	1.00	.45	.12
☐ 96 Pete Ward	1.00	.45	.12
☐ 97 Bill White	1.50	.70	.19
☐ 98 Billy Williams	5.00	2.20	.60
☐ 99 Jim Wynn	1.50	.70	.19
☐ 100 Carl Yastrzemski	10.00	4.50	1.25
☐ 101 Baltimore Orioles	1.50	.70	.19
☐ 102 Boston Red Sox	1.50	.70	.19
☐ 103 California Angels	.75	.35	.09
☐ 104 Chicago Cubs	.75	.35	.09
☐ 105 Chicago White Sox	.75	.35	.09
☐ 106 Cincinnati Reds	.75	.35	.09
☐ 107 Cleveland Indians	.75	.35	.09
☐ 108 Detroit Tigers	1.50	.70	.19
☐ 109 Houston Astros	.75	.35	.09
☐ 110 Kansas City Athletics	.75	.35	.09
☐ 111 Los Angeles Dodgers	1.50	.70	.19
☐ 112 Milwaukee Braves	.75	.35	.09
☐ 113 Minnesota Twins	.75	.35	.09
☐ 114 New York Mets	1.50	.70	.19
☐ 115 New York Yankees	2.00	.90	.25
☐ 116 Philadelphia Phillies	.75	.35	.09
☐ 117 Pittsburgh Pirates	.75	.35	.09
☐ 118 San Francisco Giants	.75	.35	.09
☐ 119 St. Louis Cardinals	.75	.35	.09
☐ 120 Washington Senators	1.50	.70	.19

1966 Topps Venezuelan

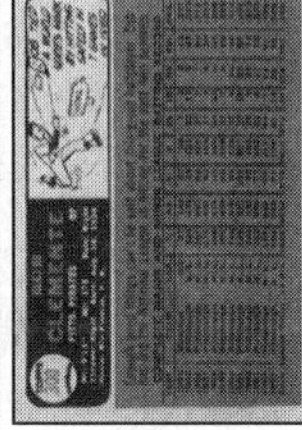

This set is a parallel version of the first 370 cards of the regular 1966 Topps set and is similar in design. The cards were issued for the Venezuelan market.

	NRMT	VG-E	GOOD
COMPLETE SET (378)	4500.00	2000.00	550.00
COMMON CARD (1-370)	5.00	2.20	.60
☐ 1 Willie Mays	325.00	145.00	40.00
☐ 2 Ted Abernathy	5.00	2.20	.60
☐ 3 Sam Mele MG	5.00	2.20	.60
☐ 4 Ray Culp	5.00	2.20	.60
☐ 5 Jim Fregosi	5.00	2.20	.60
☐ 6 Chuck Schilling	5.00	2.20	.60
☐ 7 Tracy Stallard	5.00	2.20	.60
☐ 8 Floyd Robinson	5.00	2.20	.60
☐ 9 Clete Boyer	5.00	2.20	.60
☐ 10 Tony Cloninger	5.00	2.20	.60
☐ 11 Senators Rookies	5.00	2.20	.60
Brant Alyea			
Pete Craig			
☐ 12 John Tsitouris	5.00	2.20	.60
☐ 13 Lou Johnson	5.00	2.20	.60
☐ 14 Norm Siebern	5.00	2.20	.60
☐ 15 Vern Law	5.00	2.20	.60
☐ 16 Larry Brown	5.00	2.20	.60
☐ 17 John Stephenson	5.00	2.20	.60
☐ 18 Roland Sheldon	5.00	2.20	.60
☐ 19 San Francisco Giants	7.50	3.40	.95
Team Card			
☐ 20 Willie Horton	7.50	3.40	.95
☐ 21 Don Nottebart	5.00	2.20	.60
☐ 22 Joe Nossek	5.00	2.20	.60
☐ 23 Jack Sanford	5.00	2.20	.60
☐ 24 Don Kessinger	7.50	3.40	.95
☐ 25 Pete Ward	5.00	2.20	.60
☐ 26 Ray Sadecki	5.00	2.20	.60
☐ 27 Orioles Rookies	5.00	2.20	.60
Darold Knowles			
Andy Etchebarren			
☐ 28 Phil Niekro	50.00	22.00	6.25
☐ 29 Mike Brumley	5.00	2.20	.60
☐ 30 Pete Rose	80.00	36.00	10.00
☐ 31 Jack Cullen	5.00	2.20	.60
☐ 32 Adolfo Phillips	5.00	2.20	.60
☐ 33 Jim Pagliaroni	5.00	2.20	.60
☐ 34 Checklist 1	15.00	6.75	1.85
☐ 35 Ron Swoboda	5.00	2.20	.60
☐ 36 Jim Hunter UER	50.00	22.00	6.25
(Stats say 1963 and 1964, should be 1964 and 1965)			
☐ 37 Billy Herman MG	7.50	3.40	.95
☐ 38 Ron Nischwitz	5.00	2.20	.60
☐ 39 Ken Henderson	5.00	2.20	.60
☐ 40 Jim Grant	5.00	2.20	.60
☐ 41 Don LeJohn	5.00	2.20	.60
☐ 42 Aubrey Gatewood	5.00	2.20	.60
☐ 43 Don Landrum	5.00	2.20	.60
☐ 44 Indians Rookies	5.00	2.20	.60
Bill Davis			
Tom Kelley			
☐ 45 Jim Gentile	5.00	2.20	.60
☐ 46 Howie Koplitz	5.00	2.20	.60
☐ 47 J.C. Martin	5.00	2.20	.60
☐ 48 Paul Blair	5.00	2.20	.60
☐ 49 Woody Woodward	5.00	2.20	.60
☐ 50 Mickey Mantle DP	500.00	220.00	60.00
☐ 51 Gordon Richardson	5.00	2.20	.60
☐ 52 Power Plus	5.00	2.20	.60
Wes Covington			
Johnny Callison			
☐ 53 Bob Duliba	5.00	2.20	.60
☐ 54 Jose Pagan	5.00	2.20	.60
☐ 55 Ken Harrelson	5.00	2.20	.60
☐ 56 Sandy Valdespino	5.00	2.20	.60
☐ 57 Jim Lefebvre	5.00	2.20	.60
☐ 58 Dave Wickersham	5.00	2.20	.60
☐ 59 Reds Team	5.00	2.20	.60
☐ 60 Curt Flood	7.50	3.40	.95
☐ 61 Bob Bolin	5.00	2.20	.60
☐ 62 Merritt Ranew	5.00	2.20	.60
☐ 63 Jim Stewart	5.00	2.20	.60
☐ 64 Bob Bruce	5.00	2.20	.60
☐ 65 Leon Wagner	5.00	2.20	.60
☐ 66 Al Weis	5.00	2.20	.60
☐ 67 Mets Rookies	5.00	2.20	.60
Cleon Jones			
Dick Selma			
☐ 68 Hal Reniff	5.00	2.20	.60
☐ 69 Ken Hamlin	5.00	2.20	.60
☐ 70 Carl Yastrzemski	60.00	27.00	7.50
☐ 71 Frank Carpin	5.00	2.20	.60
☐ 72 Tony Perez	60.00	27.00	7.50
☐ 73 Jerry Zimmerman	5.00	2.20	.60
☐ 74 Don Mossi	5.00	2.20	.60
☐ 75 Tommy Davis	7.50	3.40	.95
☐ 76 Red Schoendienst MG	7.50	3.40	.95
☐ 77 John Orsino	5.00	2.20	.60
☐ 78 Frank Linzy	5.00	2.20	.60
☐ 79 Joe Pepitone	5.00	2.20	.60
☐ 80 Richie Allen	12.50	5.50	1.55
☐ 81 Ray Oyler	5.00	2.20	.60
☐ 82 Bob Hendley	5.00	2.20	.60
☐ 83 Albie Pearson	5.00	2.20	.60
☐ 84 Braves Rookies	5.00	2.20	.60
Jim Beauchamp			
Dick Kelley			
☐ 85 Eddie Fisher	5.00	2.20	.60
☐ 86 John Bateman	5.00	2.20	.60
☐ 87 Dan Napoleon	5.00	2.20	.60
☐ 88 Fred Whitfield	5.00	2.20	.60
☐ 89 Ted Davidson	5.00	2.20	.60
☐ 90 Luis Aparicio	20.00	9.00	2.50
☐ 91 Bob Uecker	25.00	11.00	3.10
☐ 92 Yankes Team	30.00	13.50	3.70
☐ 93 Jim Lonborg	5.00	2.20	.60
☐ 94 Matty Alou	7.50	3.40	.95
☐ 95 Pete Richert	5.00	2.20	.60
☐ 96 Felipe Alou	7.50	3.40	.95
☐ 97 Jim Merritt	5.00	2.20	.60
☐ 98 Don Demeter	5.00	2.20	.60
☐ 99 Buc Belters	15.00	6.75	1.85
Willie Stargell			
Donn Clendenon			
☐ 100 Sandy Koufax	175.00	80.00	22.00
☐ 101 Checklist 2	20.00	9.00	2.50
☐ 102 Ed Kirkpatrick	5.00	2.20	.60
☐ 103 Dick Groat	5.00	2.20	.60
☐ 104 Alex Johnson	5.00	2.20	.60
☐ 105 Milt Pappas	5.00	2.20	.60
☐ 106 Rusty Staub	7.50	3.40	.95
☐ 107 A's Rookies	5.00	2.20	.60
Larry Stahl			
Ron Tompkins			
☐ 108 Bobby Klaus	5.00	2.20	.60
☐ 109 Ralph Terry	5.00	2.20	.60
☐ 110 Ernie Banks	75.00	34.00	9.50
☐ 111 Gary Peters	5.00	2.20	.60
☐ 112 Manny Mota	7.50	3.40	.95
☐ 113 Hank Aguirre	5.00	2.20	.60
☐ 114 Jim Gosger	5.00	2.20	.60
☐ 115 Bill Henry	5.00	2.20	.60
☐ 116 Walt Alston MG	7.50	3.40	.95
☐ 117 Jake Gibbs	5.00	2.20	.60
☐ 118 Mike McCormick	5.00	2.20	.60
☐ 119 Art Shamsky	5.00	2.20	.60
☐ 120 Harmon Killebrew	40.00	18.00	5.00
☐ 121 Ray Herbert	5.00	2.20	.60
☐ 122 Joe Gaines	5.00	2.20	.60
☐ 123 Pirates Rookies	5.00	2.20	.60
Frank Bork			
Jerry May			
☐ 124 Tug McGraw	7.50	3.40	.95
☐ 125 Lou Brock	50.00	22.00	6.25
☐ 126 Jim Palmer UER	250.00	110.00	31.00
(Described as a lefthander on card back)			
☐ 127 Ken Berry	5.00	2.20	.60
☐ 128 Jim Landis	5.00	2.20	.60
☐ 129 Jack Kralick	5.00	2.20	.60
☐ 130 Joe Torre	7.50	3.40	.95
☐ 131 Angels Team	7.50	3.40	.95
☐ 132 Orlando Cepeda	10.00	4.50	1.25
☐ 133 Don McMahon	5.00	2.20	.60
☐ 134 Wes Parker	5.00	2.20	.60
☐ 135 Dave Morehead	5.00	2.20	.60
☐ 136 Woody Held	5.00	2.20	.60
☐ 137 Pat Corrales	5.00	2.20	.60
☐ 138 Roger Repoz	5.00	2.20	.60
☐ 139 Cubs Rookies	5.00	2.20	.60
Byron Browne			
Don Young			

☐ 140 Jim Maloney	5.00	2.20	.60
☐ 141 Tom McCraw	5.00	2.20	.60
☐ 142 Don Dennis	5.00	2.20	.60
☐ 143 Jose Tartabull	5.00	2.20	.60
☐ 144 Don Schwall	5.00	2.20	.60
☐ 145 Bill Freehan	5.00	2.20	.60
☐ 146 George Altman	5.00	2.20	.60
☐ 147 Lum Harris MG	5.00	2.20	.60
☐ 148 Bob Johnson	5.00	2.20	.60
☐ 149 Dick Nen	5.00	2.20	.60
☐ 150 Rocky Colavito	20.00	9.00	2.50
☐ 151 Gary Wagner	5.00	2.20	.60
☐ 152 Frank Malzone	5.00	2.20	.60
☐ 153 Rico Carty	5.00	2.20	.60
☐ 154 Chuck Hiller	5.00	2.20	.60
☐ 155 Marcelino Lopez	5.00	2.20	.60
☐ 156 Double Play Combo	5.00	2.20	.60
Dick Schofield			
Hal Lanier			
☐ 157 Rene Lachemann	5.00	2.20	.60
☐ 158 Jim Brewer	5.00	2.20	.60
☐ 159 Chico Ruiz	5.00	2.20	.60
☐ 160 Whitey Ford	60.00	27.00	7.50
☐ 161 Jerry Lumpe	5.00	2.20	.60
☐ 162 Lee Maye	5.00	2.20	.60
☐ 163 Tito Francona	5.00	2.20	.60
☐ 164 White Sox Rookies	5.00	2.20	.60
Tommie Agee			
Marv Staehle			
☐ 165 Don Lock	5.00	2.20	.60
☐ 166 Chris Krug	5.00	2.20	.60
☐ 167 Boog Powell	12.50	5.50	1.55
☐ 168 Dan Osinski	5.00	2.20	.60
☐ 169 Duke Sims	5.00	2.20	.60
☐ 170 Cookie Rojas	5.00	2.20	.60
☐ 171 Nick Willhite	5.00	2.20	.60
☐ 172 Mets Team	10.00	4.50	1.25
☐ 173 Al Spangler	5.00	2.20	.60
☐ 174 Ron Taylor	5.00	2.20	.60
☐ 175 Bert Campaneris	5.00	2.20	.60
☐ 176 Jim Davenport	5.00	2.20	.60
☐ 177 Hector Lopez	5.00	2.20	.60
☐ 178 Bob Tillman	5.00	2.20	.60
☐ 179 Cards Rookies	5.00	2.20	.60
Dennis Aust			
Bob Tolan			
☐ 180 Vada Pinson	5.00	2.20	.60
☐ 181 Al Worthington	5.00	2.20	.60
☐ 182 Jerry Lynch	5.00	2.20	.60
☐ 183 Checklist 3	15.00	6.75	1.85
☐ 184 Denis Menke	5.00	2.20	.60
☐ 185 Bob Buhl	5.00	2.20	.60
☐ 186 Ruben Amaro	5.00	2.20	.60
☐ 187 Chuck Dressen MG	5.00	2.20	.60
☐ 188 Al Luplow	5.00	2.20	.60
☐ 189 John Roseboro	5.00	2.20	.60
☐ 190 Jimmie Hall	5.00	2.20	.60
☐ 191 Darrell Sutherland	5.00	2.20	.60
☐ 192 Vic Power	5.00	2.20	.60
☐ 193 Dave McNally	5.00	2.20	.60
☐ 194 Senators Team	5.00	2.20	.60
☐ 195 Joe Morgan	35.00	16.00	4.40
☐ 196 Don Pavletich	5.00	2.20	.60
☐ 197 Sonny Siebert	5.00	2.20	.60
☐ 198 Mickey Stanley	5.00	2.20	.60
☐ 199 Chisox Clubbers	5.00	2.20	.60
Bill Skowron			
Johnny Romano			
Floyd Robinson			
☐ 200 Eddie Mathews	35.00	16.00	4.40
☐ 201 Jim Dickson	5.00	2.20	.60
☐ 202 Clay Dalrymple	5.00	2.20	.60
☐ 203 Jose Santiago	5.00	2.20	.60
☐ 204 Cubs Team	5.00	2.20	.60
☐ 205 Tom Tresh	5.00	2.20	.60
☐ 206 Al Jackson	5.00	2.20	.60
☐ 207 Frank Quilici	5.00	2.20	.60
☐ 208 Bob Miller	5.00	2.20	.60
☐ 209 Tigers Rookies	5.00	2.20	.60
Fritz Fisher			
John Hiller			
☐ 210 Bill Mazeroski	5.00	2.20	.60
☐ 211 Frank Kreutzer	5.00	2.20	.60
☐ 212 Ed Kranepool	5.00	2.20	.60
☐ 213 Fred Newman	5.00	2.20	.60
☐ 214 Tommy Harper	5.00	2.20	.60
☐ 215 NL Batting Leaders	125.00	55.00	15.50
Bob Clemente			
Hank Aaron			
Willie Mays			
☐ 216 AL Batting Leaders	12.50	5.50	1.55
Tony Oliva			
Carl Yastrzemski			
Vic Davalillo			
☐ 217 NL Home Run Leaders	50.00	22.00	6.25
Willie Mays			
Willie McCovey			
☐ 218 Al Home Run Leaders	10.00	4.50	1.25
Tony Conigliaro			
Norm Cash			
Willie Horton			
☐ 219 NL RBI Leaders	25.00	11.00	3.10
Deron Johnson			
Frank Robinson			
Willie Mays			
☐ 220 AL RBI Leaders	10.00	4.50	1.25
Rocky Colavito			
Willie Horton			
Tony Oliva			
☐ 221 NL ERA Leaders	25.00	11.00	3.10
Sandy Koufax			
Juan Marichal			
Vern Law			
☐ 222 AL ERA Leaders	10.00	4.50	1.25
Sam McDowell			
Eddie Fisher			
Sonny Siebert			
☐ 223 NL Pitching Leaders	25.00	11.00	3.10
Sandy Koufax			
Tony Cloninger			
Don Drysdale			
☐ 224 AL Pitching Leaders	10.00	4.50	1.25
Jim Grant			
Mel Stottlemyre			
Jim Kaat			
☐ 225 NL Strikeout Leaders	25.00	11.00	3.10
Sandy Koufax			
Bob Veale			
Bob Gibson			
☐ 226 AL Strikeout Leaders	10.00	4.50	1.25
Sam McDowell			
Mickey Lolich			
Dennis McLain			
Sonny Siebert			
☐ 227 Russ Nixon	5.00	2.20	.60
☐ 228 Larry Dierker	7.50	3.40	.95
☐ 229 Hank Bauer MG	5.00	2.20	.60
☐ 230 Johnny Callison	5.00	2.20	.60
☐ 231 Floyd Weaver	5.00	2.20	.60
☐ 232 Glenn Beckert	5.00	2.20	.60
☐ 233 Dom Zanni	5.00	2.20	.60
☐ 234 Yankees Rookies	5.00	2.20	.60
Rich Beck			
Roy White			
☐ 235 Don Cardwell	5.00	2.20	.60
☐ 236 Mike Hershberger	5.00	2.20	.60
☐ 237 Billy O'Dell	5.00	2.20	.60
☐ 238 Dodgers Team	10.00	4.50	1.25
☐ 239 Orlando Pena	5.00	2.20	.60
☐ 240 Earl Battey	5.00	2.20	.60
☐ 241 Dennis Ribant	5.00	2.20	.60
☐ 242 Jesus Alou	5.00	2.20	.60
☐ 243 Nelson Briles	5.00	2.20	.60
☐ 244 Astros Rookies	5.00	2.20	.60
Chuck Harrison			
Sonny Jackson			
☐ 245 John Buzhardt	5.00	2.20	.60
☐ 246 Ed Bailey	5.00	2.20	.60
☐ 247 Carl Warwick	5.00	2.20	.60
☐ 248 Pete Mikkelsen	5.00	2.20	.60
☐ 249 Bill Rigney MG	5.00	2.20	.60
☐ 250 Sammy Ellis	5.00	2.20	.60
☐ 251 Ed Brinkman	5.00	2.20	.60
☐ 252 Denny Lemaster	5.00	2.20	.60
☐ 253 Don Wert	5.00	2.20	.60
☐ 254 Phillies Rookies	200.00	90.00	25.00
Ferguson Jenkins			
Bill Sorrell			
☐ 255 Willie Stargell	50.00	22.00	6.25
☐ 256 Lew Krausse	5.00	2.20	.60
☐ 257 Jeff Torborg	5.00	2.20	.60
☐ 258 Dave Giusti	5.00	2.20	.60
☐ 259 Boston Red Sox	10.00	4.50	1.25
Team Card			
☐ 260 Bob Shaw	5.00	2.20	.60
☐ 261 Ron Hansen	5.00	2.20	.60
☐ 262 Jack Hamilton	5.00	2.20	.60
☐ 263 Tom Egan	5.00	2.20	.60
☐ 264 Twins Rookies	5.00	2.20	.60
Andy Kosco			
Ted Uhlaender			
☐ 265 Stu Miller	5.00	2.20	.60
☐ 266 Pedro Gonzalez UER	5.00	2.20	.60
Misspelled Gonzales on card ba			
☐ 267 Joe Sparma	5.00	2.20	.60
☐ 268 John Blanchard	5.00	2.20	.60
☐ 269 Don Heffner MG	5.00	2.20	.60
☐ 270 Claude Osteen	5.00	2.20	.60
☐ 271 Hal Lanier	5.00	2.20	.60
☐ 272 Jack Bladschun	5.00	2.20	.60
☐ 273 Astro Aces	5.00	2.20	.60
Bob Aspromonte			
Rusty Staub			
☐ 274 Buster Narum	5.00	2.20	.60
☐ 275 Tim McCarver	10.00	4.50	1.25
☐ 276 Jim Bouton	7.50	3.40	.95
☐ 277 George Thomas	5.00	2.20	.60
☐ 278 Cal Koonce	5.00	2.20	.60
☐ 279 Checklist 4	5.00	2.20	.60
☐ 280 Bobby Knoop	5.00	2.20	.60
☐ 281 Bruce Howard	5.00	2.20	.60
☐ 282 Johnny Lewis	5.00	2.20	.60
☐ 283 Jim Perry	5.00	2.20	.60
☐ 284 Bobby Wine	5.00	2.20	.60
☐ 285 Luis Tiant	5.00	2.20	.60
☐ 286 Gary Geiger	5.00	2.20	.60
☐ 287 Jack Aker	5.00	2.20	.60
☐ 288 Dodgers Rookies	100.00	45.00	12.50
Bill Singer			
Don Sutton			
☐ 289 Larry Sherry	5.00	2.20	.60
☐ 290 Ron Santo	12.50	5.50	1.55
☐ 291 Moe Drabowsky	5.00	2.20	.60
☐ 292 Jim Coker	5.00	2.20	.60
☐ 293 Mike Shannon	5.00	2.20	.60
☐ 294 Steve Ridzik	5.00	2.20	.60
☐ 295 Jim Ray Hart	5.00	2.20	.60
☐ 296 Johnny Keane MG	5.00	2.20	.60
☐ 297 Jim Owens	5.00	2.20	.60
☐ 298 Rico Petrocelli	5.00	2.20	.60
☐ 299 Lou Burdette	5.00	2.20	.60
☐ 300 Bob Clemente	375.00	170.00	47.50
☐ 301 Greg Bollo	5.00	2.20	.60
☐ 302 Ernie Bowman	5.00	2.20	.60
☐ 303 Cleveland Indians	5.00	2.20	.60
Team Card			
☐ 304 John Herrnstein	5.00	2.20	.60
☐ 305 Camilo Pascual	5.00	2.20	.60
☐ 306 Ty Cline	5.00	2.20	.60
☐ 307 Clay Carroll	5.00	2.20	.60
☐ 308 Tom Haller	5.00	2.20	.60
☐ 309 Diego Segui	5.00	2.20	.60
☐ 310 Frank Robinson	75.00	34.00	9.50
☐ 311 Reds Rookies	5.00	2.20	.60
Tommy Helms			
Dick Simpson			
☐ 312 Bob Saverine	5.00	2.20	.60
☐ 313 Chris Zachary	5.00	2.20	.60
☐ 314 Hector Valle	5.00	2.20	.60
☐ 315 Norm Cash	7.50	3.40	.95
☐ 316 Jack Fisher	5.00	2.20	.60
☐ 317 Dalton Jones	5.00	2.20	.60
☐ 318 Harry Walker MG	5.00	2.20	.60
☐ 319 Gene Freese	5.00	2.20	.60
☐ 320 Bob Gibson	60.00	27.00	7.50
☐ 321 Rick Reichardt	5.00	2.20	.60
☐ 322 Bill Faul	5.00	2.20	.60
☐ 323 Ray Barker	5.00	2.20	.60
☐ 324 John Boozer	5.00	2.20	.60
☐ 325 Vic Davalillo	5.00	2.20	.60
☐ 326 Braves Team	5.00	2.20	.60
☐ 327 Bernie Allen	5.00	2.20	.60
☐ 328 Jerry Grote	5.00	2.20	.60
☐ 329 Pete Charton	5.00	2.20	.60
☐ 330 Ron Fairly	5.00	2.20	.60
☐ 331 Ron Herbel	5.00	2.20	.60
☐ 332 Bill Bryan	5.00	2.20	.60
☐ 333 Senators Rookies	5.00	2.20	.60
Joe Coleman			
Jim French			
☐ 334 Marty Keough	5.00	2.20	.60
☐ 335 Juan Pizarro	5.00	2.20	.60
☐ 336 Gene Alley	5.00	2.20	.60
☐ 337 Fred Gladding	5.00	2.20	.60
☐ 338 Dal Maxvill	5.00	2.20	.60
☐ 339 Del Crandall	5.00	2.20	.60
☐ 340 Dean Chance	5.00	2.20	.60
☐ 341 Wes Westrum MG	5.00	2.20	.60
☐ 342 Bob Humphreys	5.00	2.20	.60
☐ 343 Joe Christopher	5.00	2.20	.60
☐ 344 Steve Blass	5.00	2.20	.60
☐ 345 Bob Allison	5.00	2.20	.60
☐ 346 Mike de la Hoz	5.00	2.20	.60
☐ 347 Phil Regan	5.00	2.20	.60
☐ 348 Orioles Team	15.00	6.75	1.85
☐ 349 Cap Peterson	5.00	2.20	.60
☐ 350 Mel Stottlemyre	5.00	2.20	.60
☐ 351 Fred Valentine	5.00	2.20	.60
☐ 352 Bob Aspromonte	5.00	2.20	.60
☐ 353 Al McBean	5.00	2.20	.60
☐ 354 Smoky Burgess	5.00	2.20	.60
☐ 355 Wade Blasingame	5.00	2.20	.60
☐ 356 Red Sox Rookies	5.00	2.20	.60
Owen Johnson			
Ken Sanders			
☐ 357 Gerry Arrigo	5.00	2.20	.60
☐ 358 Charlie Smith	5.00	2.20	.60
☐ 359 Johnny Briggs	5.00	2.20	.60
☐ 360 Ron Hunt	5.00	2.20	.60
☐ 361 Tom Satriano	5.00	2.20	.60
☐ 362 Gates Brown	5.00	2.20	.60
☐ 363 Checklist 5	20.00	9.00	2.50
☐ 364 Nate Oliver	5.00	2.20	.60
☐ 365 Roger Maris	80.00	36.00	10.00
☐ 366 Wayne Causey	5.00	2.20	.60
☐ 367 Mel Nelson	5.00	2.20	.60
☐ 368 Charlie Lau	5.00	2.20	.60
☐ 369 Jim King	5.00	2.20	.60
☐ 370 Chico Cardenas	5.00	2.20	.60

1967 Topps

The cards in this 609-card set measure 2 1/2" by 3 1/2". The 1967 Topps series is considered by some collectors to be one of the company's finest accomplishments in baseball card production. Excellent color photographs are combined with easy-to-read backs. Cards 458 to 533 are slightly harder to find than numbers 1 to 457, and the inevitable high series (534 to 609) exists. Each checklist card features a small circular picture of a popular player included in that series. Printing discrepancies resulted in some high series cards being in shorter supply. The checklist below identifies (by DP) 22 double-printed high numbers; of the 76 cards in the last series, 54 cards were short printed and the other 22 cards are much more plentiful. Featured subsets within this set include World Series cards (151-155) and League Leaders (233-244). A limited number of "proof" Roger Maris cards were produced. These cards are blank backed and

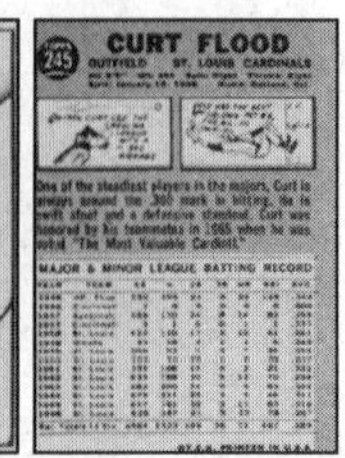

Maris is listed as a New York Yankee on it. The Maris card is currently valued between $500 and $1000. Some Bob Bolin cards: #252 have a white smear in between his names. Another tough variation that has been recently discovered is a variation on card #58 Paul Schaal. The tough version has a green bat above his name. The key Rookie Cards in the set are high number cards of Rod Carew and Tom Seaver. Confirmed methods of selling these cards include five-card nickle wax packs. Although rarely seen, there exists a salesman's sample panel of three cards that pictures Earl Battey, Manny Mota, and Gene Brabender with ad information on the back about the "new" Topps cards.

	NRMT	VG-E	GOOD
COMPLETE SET (609)	4600.00	2100.00	575.00
COMMON CARD (1-109)	1.50	.70	.19
COMMON CARD (110-283)	2.00	.90	.25
COMMON CARD (284-370)	2.50	1.10	.30
COMMON CARD (371-457)	4.00	1.80	.50
COMMON CARD (458-533)	6.00	2.70	.75
COMMON CARD (534-609)	16.00	7.25	2.00
WRAPPER (5-CENT)	25.00	11.00	3.10
☐ 1 The Champs DP	20.00	6.00	2.00
Frank Robinson			
Hank Bauer MG			
Brooks Robinson			
☐ 2 Jack Hamilton	1.50	.70	.19
☐ 3 Duke Sims	1.50	.70	.19
☐ 4 Hal Lanier	1.50	.70	.19
☐ 5 Whitey Ford UER	20.00	9.00	2.50
(1953 listed as			
1933 in stats on back)			
☐ 6 Dick Simpson	1.50	.70	.19
☐ 7 Don McMahon	1.50	.70	.19
☐ 8 Chuck Harrison	1.50	.70	.19
☐ 9 Ron Hansen	1.50	.70	.19
☐ 10 Matty Alou	2.50	1.10	.30
☐ 11 Barry Moore	1.50	.70	.19
☐ 12 Dodgers Rookies	2.50	1.10	.30
Jim Campanis			
Bill Singer			
☐ 13 Joe Sparma	1.50	.70	.19
☐ 14 Phil Linz	2.50	1.10	.30
☐ 15 Earl Battey	1.50	.70	.19
☐ 16 Bill Hands	1.50	.70	.19
☐ 17 Jim Gosger	1.50	.70	.19
☐ 18 Gene Oliver	1.50	.70	.19
☐ 19 Jim McGlothlin	1.50	.70	.19
☐ 20 Orlando Cepeda	6.00	2.70	.75
☐ 21 Dave Bristol MG	1.50	.70	.19
☐ 22 Gene Brabender	1.50	.70	.19
☐ 23 Larry Elliot	1.50	.70	.19
☐ 24 Bob Allen	1.50	.70	.19
☐ 25 Elston Howard	4.00	1.80	.50
☐ 26A Bob Priddy NTR	30.00	13.50	3.70
☐ 26B Bob Priddy TR	1.50	.70	.19
☐ 27 Bob Saverine	1.50	.70	.19
☐ 28 Barry Latman	1.50	.70	.19
☐ 29 Tom McCraw	1.50	.70	.19
☐ 30 Al Kaline DP	16.00	7.25	2.00
☐ 31 Jim Brewer	1.50	.70	.19
☐ 32 Bob Bailey	2.50	1.10	.30
☐ 33 Athletic Rookies	5.00	2.20	.60
Sal Bando			
Randy Schwartz			
☐ 34 Pete Cimino	1.50	.70	.19
☐ 35 Rico Carty	2.50	1.10	.30
☐ 36 Bob Tillman	1.50	.70	.19
☐ 37 Rick Wise	2.50	1.10	.30
☐ 38 Bob Johnson	1.50	.70	.19
☐ 39 Curt Simmons	2.50	1.10	.30
☐ 40 Rick Reichardt	1.50	.70	.19
☐ 41 Joe Hoerner	1.50	.70	.19
☐ 42 Mets Team	10.00	4.50	1.25
☐ 43 Chico Salmon	1.50	.70	.19
☐ 44 Joe Nuxhall	2.50	1.10	.30
☐ 45 Roger Maris	30.00	13.50	3.70
☐ 46 Lindy McDaniel	2.50	1.10	.30
☐ 47 Ken McMullen	1.50	.70	.19
☐ 48 Bill Freehan	2.50	1.10	.30
☐ 49 Roy Face	2.50	1.10	.30
☐ 50 Tony Oliva	6.00	2.70	.75
☐ 51 Astros Rookies	1.50	.70	.19
Dave Adlesh			
Wes Bales			
☐ 52 Dennis Higgins	1.50	.70	.19
☐ 53 Clay Dalrymple	1.50	.70	.19
☐ 54 Dick Green	1.50	.70	.19
☐ 55 Don Drysdale	16.00	7.25	2.00
☐ 56 Jose Tartabull	2.50	1.10	.30
☐ 57 Pat Jarvis	1.50	.70	.19
☐ 58 Paul Schaal	1.50	.70	.19

Card			
☐ 59 Ralph Terry	2.50	1.10	.30
☐ 60 Luis Aparicio	6.00	2.70	.75
☐ 61 Gordy Coleman	2.50	1.10	.30
☐ 62 Checklist 1	7.00	1.40	.70
Frank Robinson			
☐ 63 Cards' Clubbers	10.00	4.50	1.25
Lou Brock			
Curt Flood			
☐ 64 Fred Valentine	1.50	.70	.19
☐ 65 Tom Haller	2.50	1.10	.30
☐ 66 Manny Mota	2.50	1.10	.30
☐ 67 Ken Berry	1.50	.70	.19
☐ 68 Bob Buhl	2.50	1.10	.30
☐ 69 Vic Davalillo	1.50	.70	.19
☐ 70 Ron Santo	4.00	1.80	.50
☐ 71 Camilo Pascual	2.50	1.10	.30
☐ 72 Tigers Rookies	1.50	.70	.19
George Korince			
(Photo actually			
James Murray Brown)			
John (Tom) Matchick			
☐ 73 Rusty Staub	4.00	1.80	.50
☐ 74 Wes Stock	1.50	.70	.19
☐ 75 George Scott	2.50	1.10	.30
☐ 76 Jim Barbieri	1.50	.70	.19
☐ 77 Dooley Womack	2.50	1.10	.30
☐ 78 Pat Corrales	2.50	1.10	.30
☐ 79 Bubba Morton	1.50	.70	.19
☐ 80 Jim Maloney	2.50	1.10	.30
☐ 81 Eddie Stanky MG	2.50	1.10	.30
☐ 82 Steve Barber	1.50	.70	.19
☐ 83 Ollie Brown	1.50	.70	.19
☐ 84 Tommie Sisk	1.50	.70	.19
☐ 85 Johnny Callison	2.50	1.10	.30
☐ 86A Mike McCormick NTR	30.00	13.50	3.70
(Senators on front			
and Senators on back)			
☐ 86B Mike McCormick TR	2.50	1.10	.30
(Traded line			
at end of bio;			
Senators on front,			
but Giants on back)			
☐ 87 George Altman	1.50	.70	.19
☐ 88 Mickey Lolich	4.00	1.80	.50
☐ 89 Felix Millan	2.50	1.10	.30
☐ 90 Jim Nash	1.50	.70	.19
☐ 91 Johnny Lewis	1.50	.70	.19
☐ 92 Ray Washburn	1.50	.70	.19
☐ 93 Yankees Rookies	4.00	1.80	.50
Stan Bahnsen			
Bobby Murcer			
☐ 94 Ron Fairly	2.50	1.10	.30
☐ 95 Sonny Siebert	1.50	.70	.19
☐ 96 Art Shamsky	1.50	.70	.19
☐ 97 Mike Cuellar	2.50	1.10	.30
☐ 98 Rich Rollins	1.50	.70	.19
☐ 99 Lee Stange	1.50	.70	.19
☐ 100 Frank Robinson DP	14.00	6.25	1.75
☐ 101 Ken Johnson	1.50	.70	.19
☐ 102 Philadelphia Phillies	3.00	1.35	.35
Team Card			
☐ 103 Checklist 2	16.00	3.20	1.60
Mickey Mantle			
☐ 104 Minnie Rojas	1.50	.70	.19
☐ 105 Ken Boyer	2.50	1.10	.30
☐ 106 Randy Hundley	2.50	1.10	.30
☐ 107 Joel Horlen	1.50	.70	.19
☐ 108 Alex Johnson	2.50	1.10	.30
☐ 109 Tribe Thumpers	5.00	2.20	.60
Rocky Colavito			
Leon Wagner			
☐ 110 Jack Aker	3.00	1.35	.35
☐ 111 John Kennedy	2.00	.90	.25
☐ 112 Dave Wickersham	2.00	.90	.25
☐ 113 Dave Nicholson	2.00	.90	.25
☐ 114 Jack Baldschun	2.00	.90	.25
☐ 115 Paul Casanova	2.00	.90	.25
☐ 116 Herman Franks MG	2.00	.90	.25
☐ 117 Darrell Brandon	2.00	.90	.25
☐ 118 Bernie Allen	2.00	.90	.25
☐ 119 Wade Blasingame	2.00	.90	.25
☐ 120 Floyd Robinson	2.00	.90	.25
☐ 121 Eddie Bressoud	2.00	.90	.25
☐ 122 George Brunet	2.00	.90	.25
☐ 123 Pirates Rookies	2.00	.90	.25
Jim Price			
Luke Walker			
☐ 124 Jim Stewart	2.00	.90	.25
☐ 125 Moe Drabowsky	3.00	1.35	.35
☐ 126 Tony Taylor	2.00	.90	.25
☐ 127 John O'Donoghue	2.00	.90	.25
☐ 128 Ed Spiezio	2.00	.90	.25
☐ 129 Phil Roof	2.00	.90	.25
☐ 130 Phil Regan	3.00	1.35	.35
☐ 131 Yankees Team	10.00	4.50	1.25
☐ 132 Ozzie Virgil	2.00	.90	.25
☐ 133 Ron Kline	2.00	.90	.25
☐ 134 Gates Brown	3.00	1.35	.35
☐ 135 Deron Johnson	3.00	1.35	.35
☐ 136 Carroll Sembera	2.00	.90	.25
☐ 137 Twins Rookies	2.00	.90	.25
Ron Clark			
Jim Ollum			
☐ 138 Dick Kelley	2.00	.90	.25
☐ 139 Dalton Jones	3.00	1.35	.35
☐ 140 Willie Stargell	20.00	9.00	2.50
☐ 141 John Miller	2.00	.90	.25
☐ 142 Jackie Brandt	2.00	.90	.25
☐ 143 Sox Sockers	2.00	.90	.25
Pete Ward			
Don Buford			
☐ 144 Bill Hepler	2.00	.90	.25
☐ 145 Larry Brown	2.00	.90	.25
☐ 146 Steve Carlton	70.00	32.00	8.75
☐ 147 Tom Egan	2.00	.90	.25
☐ 148 Adolfo Phillips	2.00	.90	.25
☐ 149 Joe Moeller	2.00	.90	.25
☐ 150 Mickey Mantle	300.00	135.00	38.00
☐ 151 Moe Drabowsky WS	4.00	1.80	.50
☐ 152 Jim Palmer WS	8.00	3.60	1.00
☐ 153 Paul Blair WS	4.00	1.80	.50
☐ 154 Brooks Robinson WS	4.00	1.80	.50
Dave McNally			
☐ 155 World Series Summary	4.00	1.80	.50
Winners celebrate			
☐ 156 Ron Herbel	2.00	.90	.25
☐ 157 Danny Cater	2.00	.90	.25
☐ 158 Jimmie Coker	2.00	.90	.25
☐ 159 Bruce Howard	2.00	.90	.25
☐ 160 Willie Davis	3.00	1.35	.35
☐ 161 Dick Williams MG	3.00	1.35	.35
☐ 162 Billy O'Dell	2.00	.90	.25
☐ 163 Vic Roznovsky	2.00	.90	.25
☐ 164 Dwight Siebler UER	2.00	.90	.25
(Last line of stats			
shows 1960 Minnesota)			
☐ 165 Cleon Jones	3.00	1.35	.35
☐ 166 Eddie Mathews	16.00	7.25	2.00
☐ 167 Senators Rookies	2.00	.90	.25
Joe Coleman			
Tim Cullen			
☐ 168 Ray Culp	2.00	.90	.25
☐ 169 Horace Clarke	3.00	1.35	.35
☐ 170 Dick McAuliffe	3.00	1.35	.35
☐ 171 Cal Koonce	2.00	.90	.25
☐ 172 Bill Heath	2.00	.90	.25
☐ 173 St. Louis Cardinals	4.00	1.80	.50
Team Card			
☐ 174 Dick Radatz	3.00	1.35	.35
☐ 175 Bobby Knoop	2.00	.90	.25
☐ 176 Sammy Ellis	2.00	.90	.25
☐ 177 Tito Fuentes	2.00	.90	.25
☐ 178 John Buzhardt	2.00	.90	.25
☐ 179 Braves Rookies	2.00	.90	.25
Charles Vaughan			
Cecil Upshaw			
☐ 180 Curt Blefary	2.00	.90	.25
☐ 181 Terry Fox	2.00	.90	.25
☐ 182 Ed Charles	2.00	.90	.25
☐ 183 Jim Pagliaroni	2.00	.90	.25
☐ 184 George Thomas	2.00	.90	.25
☐ 185 Ken Holtzman	3.00	1.35	.35
☐ 186 Mets Maulers	3.00	1.35	.35
Ed Kranepool			
Ron Swoboda			
☐ 187 Pedro Ramos	2.00	.90	.25
☐ 188 Ken Harrelson	3.00	1.35	.35
☐ 189 Chuck Hinton	2.00	.90	.25
☐ 190 Turk Farrell	2.00	.90	.25
☐ 191A Checklist 3	8.00	1.60	.80
(214 Tom Kelley)			
(Willie Mays)			
☐ 191B Checklist 3	12.00	2.40	1.20
(214 Dick Kelley)			
(Willie Mays)			
☐ 192 Fred Gladding	2.00	.90	.25
☐ 193 Jose Cardenal	3.00	1.35	.35
☐ 194 Bob Allison	3.00	1.35	.35
☐ 195 Al Jackson	2.00	.90	.25
☐ 196 Johnny Romano	2.00	.90	.25
☐ 197 Ron Perranoski	3.00	1.35	.35
☐ 198 Chuck Hiller	2.00	.90	.25
☐ 199 Billy Hitchcock MG	2.00	.90	.25
☐ 200 Willie Mays UER	85.00	38.00	10.50
('63 Sna Francisco			
on card back stats)			
☐ 201 Hal Reniff	3.00	1.35	.35
☐ 202 Johnny Edwards	2.00	.90	.25
☐ 203 Al McBean	2.00	.90	.25
☐ 204 Orioles Rookies	3.00	1.35	.35
Mike Epstein			
Tom Phoebus			
☐ 205 Dick Groat	3.00	1.35	.35
☐ 206 Dennis Bennett	2.00	.90	.25
☐ 207 John Orsino	2.00	.90	.25
☐ 208 Jack Lamabe	2.00	.90	.25
☐ 209 Joe Nossek	2.00	.90	.25
☐ 210 Bob Gibson	20.00	9.00	2.50
☐ 211 Twins Team	4.00	1.80	.50
☐ 212 Chris Zachary	2.00	.90	.25
☐ 213 Jay Johnstone	3.00	1.35	.35
☐ 214 Dick Kelley	2.00	.90	.25
☐ 215 Ernie Banks	20.00	9.00	2.50
☐ 216 Bengal Belters	10.00	4.50	1.25
Norm Cash			
Al Kaline			
☐ 217 Rob Gardner	2.00	.90	.25
☐ 218 Wes Parker	3.00	1.35	.35
☐ 219 Clay Carroll	3.00	1.35	.35
☐ 220 Jim Ray Hart	3.00	1.35	.35
☐ 221 Woody Fryman	3.00	1.35	.35
☐ 222 Reds Rookies	3.00	1.35	.35
Darrell Osteen			
Lee May			
☐ 223 Mike Ryan	3.00	1.35	.35
☐ 224 Walt Bond	2.00	.90	.25
☐ 225 Mel Stottlemyre	3.00	1.35	.35
☐ 226 Julian Javier	3.00	1.35	.35
☐ 227 Paul Lindblad	2.00	.90	.25
☐ 228 Gil Hodges MG	5.00	2.20	.60
☐ 229 Larry Jackson	2.00	.90	.25
☐ 230 Boog Powell	6.00	2.70	.75
☐ 231 John Bateman	2.00	.90	.25
☐ 232 Don Buford	2.00	.90	.25
☐ 233 AL ERA Leaders	4.00	1.80	.50
Gary Peters			
Joel Horlen			
Steve Hargan			
☐ 234 NL ERA Leaders	15.00	6.75	1.85
Sandy Koufax			
Mike Cuellar			
Juan Marichal			
☐ 235 AL Pitching Leaders	6.00	2.70	.75
Jim Kaat			
Denny McLain			
Earl Wilson			
☐ 236 NL Pitching Leaders	25.00	11.00	3.10
Sandy Koufax			
Juan Marichal			
Bob Gibson			
Gaylord Perry			
☐ 237 AL Strikeout Leaders	6.00	2.70	.75
Sam McDowell			
Jim Kaat			
Earl Wilson			
☐ 238 NL Strikeout Leaders	12.00	5.50	1.50
Sandy Koufax			
Jim Bunning			
Bob Veale			
☐ 239 AL Batting Leaders	9.00	4.00	1.10
Frank Robinson			
Tony Oliva			
Al Kaline			
☐ 240 NL Batting Leaders	6.00	2.70	.75
Matty Alou			
Felipe Alou			
Rico Carty			
☐ 241 AL RBI Leaders	9.00	4.00	1.10
Frank Robinson			
Harmon Killebrew			
Boog Powell			
☐ 242 NL RBI Leaders	24.00	11.00	3.00
Hank Aaron			
Bob Clemente			
Richie Allen			
☐ 243 AL Home Run Leaders	9.00	4.00	1.10
Frank Robinson			
Harmon Killebrew			
Boog Powell			
☐ 244 NL Home Run Leaders	20.00	9.00	2.50
Hank Aaron			
Richie Allen			
Willie Mays			
☐ 245 Curt Flood	3.00	1.35	.35
☐ 246 Jim Perry	3.00	1.35	.35
☐ 247 Jerry Lumpe	2.00	.90	.25
☐ 248 Gene Mauch MG	3.00	1.35	.35
☐ 249 Nick Willhite	2.00	.90	.25
☐ 250 Hank Aaron UER	80.00	36.00	10.00
(Second 1961 in stats			
should be 1962)			
☐ 251 Woody Held	2.00	.90	.25
☐ 252 Bob Bolin	2.00	.90	.25
☐ 253 Indians Rookies	2.00	.90	.25
Bill Davis			
Gus Gil			
☐ 254 Milt Pappas	3.00	1.35	.35
(No facsimile auto-			
graph on card front)			
☐ 255 Frank Howard	4.00	1.80	.50
☐ 256 Bob Hendley	2.00	.90	.25
☐ 257 Charlie Smith	2.00	.90	.25
☐ 258 Lee Maye	2.00	.90	.25
☐ 259 Don Dennis	2.00	.90	.25
☐ 260 Jim Lefebvre	3.00	1.35	.35
☐ 261 John Wyatt	2.00	.90	.25
☐ 262 Athletics Team	4.00	1.80	.50
☐ 263 Hank Aguirre	2.00	.90	.25
☐ 264 Ron Swoboda	3.00	1.35	.35
☐ 265 Lou Burdette	3.00	1.35	.35
☐ 266 Pitt Power	5.00	2.20	.60
Willie Stargell			
Donn Clendenon			
☐ 267 Don Schwall	2.00	.90	.25
☐ 268 Johnny Briggs	2.00	.90	.25
☐ 269 Don Nottebart	2.00	.90	.25
☐ 270 Zoilo Versalles	2.00	.90	.25
☐ 271 Eddie Watt	2.00	.90	.25
☐ 272 Cubs Rookies	3.00	1.35	.35
Bill Connors			
Dave Dowling			
☐ 273 Dick Lines	2.00	.90	.25
☐ 274 Bob Aspromonte	2.00	.90	.25
☐ 275 Fred Whitfield	2.00	.90	.25
☐ 276 Bruce Brubaker	2.00	.90	.25
☐ 277 Steve Whitaker	3.00	1.35	.35
☐ 278 Checklist 4	7.00	1.40	.70
Jim Kaat			
☐ 279 Frank Linzy	2.00	.90	.25
☐ 280 Tony Conigliaro	10.00	4.50	1.25
☐ 281 Bob Rodgers	2.00	.90	.25
☐ 282 John Odom	2.00	.90	.25
☐ 283 Gene Alley	3.00	1.35	.35
☐ 284 Johnny Podres	3.00	1.35	.35
☐ 285 Lou Brock	20.00	9.00	2.50
☐ 286 Wayne Causey	2.50	1.10	.30
☐ 287 Mets Rookies	2.50	1.10	.30
Greg Goossen			
Bart Shirley			
☐ 288 Denny Lemaster	2.50	1.10	.30
☐ 289 Tom Tresh	3.50	1.55	.45
☐ 290 Bill White	3.00	1.35	.35
☐ 291 Jim Hannan	2.50	1.10	.30
☐ 292 Don Pavletich	2.50	1.10	.30
☐ 293 Ed Kirkpatrick	2.50	1.10	.30
☐ 294 Walt Alston MG	4.00	1.80	.50
☐ 295 Sam McDowell	3.00	1.35	.35
☐ 296 Glenn Beckert	3.00	1.35	.35
☐ 297 Dave Morehead	3.00	1.35	.35
☐ 298 Ron Davis	2.50	1.10	.30
☐ 299 Norm Siebern	2.50	1.10	.30
☐ 300 Jim Kaat	6.00	2.70	.75
☐ 301 Jesse Gonder	2.50	1.10	.30
☐ 302 Orioles Team	6.00	2.70	.75
☐ 303 Gil Blanco	2.50	1.10	.30
☐ 304 Phil Gagliano	2.50	1.10	.30
☐ 305 Earl Wilson	3.00	1.35	.35
☐ 306 Bud Harrelson	6.00	2.70	.75
☐ 307 Jim Beauchamp	2.50	1.10	.30
☐ 308 Al Downing	3.00	1.35	.35
☐ 309 Hurlers Beware	3.00	1.35	.35
Johnny Callison			
Richie Allen			
☐ 310 Gary Peters	2.50	1.10	.30
☐ 311 Ed Brinkman	2.50	1.10	.30
☐ 312 Don Mincher	2.50	1.10	.30
☐ 313 Bob Lee	2.50	1.10	.30
☐ 314 Red Sox Rookies	8.00	3.60	1.00
Mike Andrews			
Reggie Smith			
☐ 315 Billy Williams	10.00	4.50	1.25
☐ 316 Jack Kralick	2.50	1.10	.30
☐ 317 Cesar Tovar	3.00	1.35	.35
☐ 318 Dave Giusti	2.50	1.10	.30
☐ 319 Paul Blair	3.00	1.35	.35
☐ 320 Gaylord Perry	14.00	6.25	1.75
☐ 321 Mayo Smith MG	2.50	1.10	.30
☐ 322 Jose Pagan	2.50	1.10	.30
☐ 323 Mike Hershberger	2.50	1.10	.30
☐ 324 Hal Woodeshick	2.50	1.10	.30
☐ 325 Chico Cardenas	3.00	1.35	.35
☐ 326 Bob Uecker	10.00	4.50	1.25
☐ 327 California Angels	6.00	2.70	.75
Team Card			
☐ 328 Clete Boyer UER	3.00	1.35	.35
(Stats only go up			
through 1965)			
☐ 329 Charlie Lau	3.00	1.35	.35
☐ 330 Claude Osteen	3.00	1.35	.35
☐ 331 Joe Foy	3.00	1.35	.35
☐ 332 Jesus Alou	2.50	1.10	.30
☐ 333 Fergie Jenkins	18.00	8.00	2.20
☐ 334 Twin Terrors	6.00	2.70	.75
Bob Allison			
Harmon Killebrew			
☐ 335 Bob Veale	3.00	1.35	.35
☐ 336 Joe Azcue	2.50	1.10	.30
☐ 337 Joe Morgan	14.00	6.25	1.75
☐ 338 Bob Locker	2.50	1.10	.30
☐ 339 Chico Ruiz	2.50	1.10	.30
☐ 340 Joe Pepitone	3.50	1.55	.45
☐ 341 Giants Rookies	2.50	1.10	.30
Dick Dietz			
Bill Sorrell			
☐ 342 Hank Fischer	2.50	1.10	.30
☐ 343 Tom Satriano	2.50	1.10	.30
☐ 344 Ossie Chavarria	2.50	1.10	.30
☐ 345 Stu Miller	3.00	1.35	.35
☐ 346 Jim Hickman	2.50	1.10	.30
☐ 347 Grady Hatton MG	2.50	1.10	.30
☐ 348 Tug McGraw	3.00	1.35	.35
☐ 349 Bob Chance	2.50	1.10	.30
☐ 350 Joe Torre	5.00	2.20	.60
☐ 351 Vern Law	3.00	1.35	.35
☐ 352 Ray Oyler	2.50	1.10	.30
☐ 353 Bill McCool	2.50	1.10	.30
☐ 354 Cubs Team	6.00	2.70	.75
☐ 355 Carl Yastrzemski	50.00	22.00	6.25
☐ 356 Larry Jaster	2.50	1.10	.30
☐ 357 Bill Skowron	3.00	1.35	.35
☐ 358 Ruben Amaro	2.50	1.10	.30
☐ 359 Dick Ellsworth	2.50	1.10	.30
☐ 360 Leon Wagner	2.50	1.10	.30
☐ 361 Checklist 5	14.00	2.80	1.40
Roberto Clemente			
☐ 362 Darold Knowles	2.50	1.10	.30
☐ 363 Dave Johnson	3.00	1.35	.35
☐ 364 Claude Raymond	2.50	1.10	.30
☐ 365 John Roseboro	3.00	1.35	.35
☐ 366 Andy Kosco	2.50	1.10	.30

Card	NRMT	VG-E	GOOD
☐ 367 Angels Rookies	2.50	1.10	.30
Bill Kelso			
Don Wallace			
☐ 368 Jack Hiatt	2.50	1.10	.30
☐ 369 Jim Hunter	18.00	8.00	2.20
☐ 370 Tommy Davis	3.00	1.35	.35
☐ 371 Jim Lonborg	6.00	2.70	.75
☐ 372 Mike de la Hoz	4.00	1.80	.50
☐ 373 White Sox Rookies DP	4.00	1.80	.50
Duane Josephson			
Fred Klages			
☐ 374A Mel Queen ERR DP	20.00	9.00	2.50
(Incomplete stat			
line on back)			
☐ 374B Mel Queen COR DP	4.00	1.80	.50
(Complete stat			
line on back)			
☐ 375 Jake Gibbs	5.00	2.20	.60
☐ 376 Don Lock DP	4.00	1.80	.50
☐ 377 Luis Tiant	5.00	2.20	.60
☐ 378 Detroit Tigers	8.00	3.60	1.00
Team Card UER			
(Willie Horton with			
262 RBI's in 1966)			
☐ 379 Jerry May DP	4.00	1.80	.50
☐ 380 Dean Chance DP	4.00	1.80	.50
☐ 381 Dick Schofield DP	4.00	1.80	.50
☐ 382 Dave McNally	5.00	2.20	.60
☐ 383 Ken Henderson DP	4.00	1.80	.50
☐ 384 Cardinals Rookies	4.00	1.80	.50
Jim Cosman			
Dick Hughes			
☐ 385 Jim Fregosi	5.00	2.20	.60
(Batting wrong)			
☐ 386 Dick Selma DP	4.00	1.80	.50
☐ 387 Cap Peterson DP	4.00	1.80	.50
☐ 388 Arnold Earley DP	4.00	1.80	.50
☐ 389 Alvin Dark MG DP	5.00	2.20	.60
☐ 390 Jim Wynn DP	5.00	2.20	.60
☐ 391 Wilbur Wood DP	5.00	2.20	.60
☐ 392 Tommy Harper DP	5.00	2.20	.60
☐ 393 Jim Bouton DP	5.00	2.20	.60
☐ 394 Jake Wood DP	4.00	1.80	.50
☐ 395 Chris Short	5.00	2.20	.60
☐ 396 Atlanta Aces	4.00	1.80	.50
Denis Menke			
Tony Cloninger			
☐ 397 Willie Smith DP	4.00	1.80	.50
☐ 398 Jeff Torborg	5.00	2.20	.60
☐ 399 Al Worthington DP	4.00	1.80	.50
☐ 400 Bob Clemente DP	100.00	45.00	12.50
☐ 401 Jim Coates	4.00	1.80	.50
☐ 402A Phillies Rookies DP	20.00	9.00	2.50
Grant Jackson			
Billy Wilson			
Incomplete stat line			
☐ 402B Phillies Rookies DP	5.00	2.20	.60
Grant Jackson			
Billy Wilson			
☐ 403 Dick Nen	4.00	1.80	.50
☐ 404 Nelson Briles	5.00	2.20	.60
☐ 405 Russ Snyder	4.00	1.80	.50
☐ 406 Lee Elia DP	4.00	1.80	.50
☐ 407 Reds Team	8.00	3.60	1.00
☐ 408 Jim Northrup DP	5.00	2.20	.60
☐ 409 Ray Sadecki	4.00	1.80	.50
☐ 410 Lou Johnson DP	4.00	1.80	.50
☐ 411 Dick Howser DP	5.00	2.20	.60
☐ 412 Astros Rookies	5.00	2.20	.60
Norm Miller			
Doug Rader			
☐ 413 Jerry Grote	4.00	1.80	.50
☐ 414 Casey Cox	4.00	1.80	.50
☐ 415 Sonny Jackson	4.00	1.80	.50
☐ 416 Roger Repoz	4.00	1.80	.50
☐ 417A Bob Bruce ERR DP	30.00	13.50	3.70
(RBAVES on back)			
☐ 417B Bob Bruce COR DP	4.00	1.80	.50
☐ 418 Sam Mele MG	4.00	1.80	.50
☐ 419 Don Kessinger DP	5.00	2.20	.60
☐ 420 Denny McLain	6.00	2.70	.75
☐ 421 Dal Maxvill DP	4.00	1.80	.50
☐ 422 Hoyt Wilhelm	10.00	4.50	1.25
☐ 423 Fence Busters DP	25.00	11.00	3.10
Willie Mays			
Willie McCovey			
☐ 424 Pedro Gonzalez	4.00	1.80	.50
☐ 425 Pete Mikkelsen	4.00	1.80	.50
☐ 426 Lou Clinton	4.00	1.80	.50
☐ 427A Ruben Gomez ERR DP	20.00	9.00	2.50
(Incomplete stat			
line on back)			
☐ 427B Ruben Gomez COR DP	4.00	1.80	.50
(Complete stat			
line on back)			
☐ 428 Dodgers Rookies DP	5.00	2.20	.60
Tom Hutton			
Gene Michael			
☐ 429 Garry Roggenburk DP	4.00	1.80	.50
☐ 430 Pete Rose	80.00	36.00	10.00
☐ 431 Ted Uhlaender	4.00	1.80	.50
☐ 432 Jimmie Hall DP	4.00	1.80	.50
☐ 433 Al Luplow DP	4.00	1.80	.50
☐ 434 Eddie Fisher DP	4.00	1.80	.50
☐ 435 Mack Jones DP	4.00	1.80	.50
☐ 436 Pete Ward	4.00	1.80	.50
☐ 437 Senators Team	8.00	3.60	1.00
☐ 438 Chuck Dobson	4.00	1.80	.50
☐ 439 Byron Browne	4.00	1.80	.50
☐ 440 Steve Hargan	4.00	1.80	.50
☐ 441 Jim Davenport	4.00	1.80	.50
☐ 442 Yankees Rookies DP	5.00	2.20	.60
Bill Robinson			
Joe Verbanic			
☐ 443 Tito Francona DP	4.00	1.80	.50
☐ 444 George Smith	4.00	1.80	.50
☐ 445 Don Sutton	25.00	11.00	3.10
☐ 446 Russ Nixon DP	4.00	1.80	.50
☐ 447A Bo Belinsky ERR DP	5.00	2.20	.60
(Incomplete stat			
line on back)			
☐ 447B Bo Belinsky COR DP	5.00	2.20	.60
(Complete stat			
line on back)			
☐ 448 Harry Walker DP MG	4.00	1.80	.50
☐ 449 Orlando Pena	4.00	1.80	.50
☐ 450 Richie Allen	9.00	4.00	1.10
☐ 451 Fred Newman DP	4.00	1.80	.50
☐ 452 Ed Kranepool	5.00	2.20	.60
☐ 453 Aurelio Monteagudo DP	4.00	1.80	.50
☐ 454A Checklist 6 DP	8.00	1.60	.80
Juan Marichal			
(Missing left ear)			
☐ 454B Checklist 6 DP	8.00	1.60	.80
Juan Marichal			
(left ear showing)			
☐ 455 Tommie Agee	5.00	2.20	.60
☐ 456 Phil Niekro	16.00	7.25	2.00
☐ 457 Andy Etchebarren DP	5.00	2.20	.60
☐ 458 Lee Thomas	7.50	3.40	.95
☐ 459 Senators Rookies	6.00	2.70	.75
Dick Bosman			
Pete Craig			
☐ 460 Harmon Killebrew	60.00	27.00	7.50
☐ 461 Bob Miller	6.00	2.70	.75
☐ 462 Bob Barton	6.00	2.70	.75
☐ 463 Hill Aces	7.50	3.40	.95
Sam McDowell			
Sonny Siebert			
☐ 464 Dan Coombs	6.00	2.70	.75
☐ 465 Willie Horton	7.50	3.40	.95
☐ 466 Bobby Wine	6.00	2.70	.75
☐ 467 Jim O'Toole	7.50	3.40	.95
☐ 468 Ralph Houk MG	7.50	3.40	.95
☐ 469 Len Gabrielson	6.00	2.70	.75
☐ 470 Bob Shaw	7.50	3.40	.95
☐ 471 Rene Lachemann	7.50	3.40	.95
☐ 472 Rookies Pirates	6.00	2.70	.75
John Gelnar			
George Spriggs			
☐ 473 Jose Santiago	7.50	3.40	.95
☐ 474 Bob Tolan	7.50	3.40	.95
☐ 475 Jim Palmer	85.00	38.00	10.50
☐ 476 Tony Perez SP	70.00	32.00	8.75
☐ 477 Braves Team	15.00	6.75	1.85
☐ 478 Bob Humphreys	6.00	2.70	.75
☐ 479 Gary Bell	6.00	2.70	.75
☐ 480 Willie McCovey	35.00	16.00	4.40
☐ 481 Leo Durocher MG	15.00	6.75	1.85
☐ 482 Bill Monbouquette	6.00	2.70	.75
☐ 483 Jim Landis	6.00	2.70	.75
☐ 484 Jerry Adair	6.00	2.70	.75
☐ 485 Tim McCarver	20.00	9.00	2.50
☐ 486 Twins Rookies	6.00	2.70	.75
Rich Reese			
Bill Whitby			
☐ 487 Tommie Reynolds	6.00	2.70	.75
☐ 488 Gerry Arrigo	6.00	2.70	.75
☐ 489 Doug Clemens	6.00	2.70	.75
☐ 490 Tony Cloninger	6.00	2.70	.75
☐ 491 Sam Bowens	6.00	2.70	.75
☐ 492 Pittsburgh Pirates	15.00	6.75	1.85
Team Card			
☐ 493 Phil Ortega	6.00	2.70	.75
☐ 494 Bill Rigney MG	6.00	2.70	.75
☐ 495 Fritz Peterson	7.50	3.40	.95
☐ 496 Orlando McFarlane	6.00	2.70	.75
☐ 497 Ron Campbell	6.00	2.70	.75
☐ 498 Larry Dierker	7.50	3.40	.95
☐ 499 Indians Rookies	6.00	2.70	.75
George Culver			
Jose Vidal			
☐ 500 Juan Marichal	25.00	11.00	3.10
☐ 501 Jerry Zimmerman	6.00	2.70	.75
☐ 502 Derrell Griffith	6.00	2.70	.75
☐ 503 Los Angeles Dodgers	15.00	6.75	1.85
Team Card			
☐ 504 Orlando Martinez	6.00	2.70	.75
☐ 505 Tommy Helms	7.50	3.40	.95
☐ 506 Smoky Burgess	7.50	3.40	.95
☐ 507 Orioles Rookies	6.00	2.70	.75
Ed Barnowski			
Larry Haney			
☐ 508 Dick Hall	6.00	2.70	.75
☐ 509 Jim King	6.00	2.70	.75
☐ 510 Bill Mazeroski	15.00	6.75	1.85
☐ 511 Don Wert	6.00	2.70	.75
☐ 512 Red Schoendienst MG	15.00	6.75	1.85
☐ 513 Marcelino Lopez	6.00	2.70	.75
☐ 514 John Werhas	6.00	2.70	.75
☐ 515 Bert Campaneris	9.00	4.00	1.10
☐ 516 Giants Team	15.00	6.75	1.85
☐ 517 Fred Talbot	6.00	2.70	.75
☐ 518 Denis Menke	6.00	2.70	.75
☐ 519 Ted Davidson	6.00	2.70	.75
☐ 520 Max Alvis	6.00	2.70	.75
☐ 521 Bird Bombers	7.50	3.40	.95
Boog Powell			
Curt Blefary			
☐ 522 John Stephenson	6.00	2.70	.75
☐ 523 Jim Merritt	6.00	2.70	.75
☐ 524 Felix Mantilla	6.00	2.70	.75
☐ 525 Ron Hunt	6.00	2.70	.75
☐ 526 Tigers Rookies	6.00	2.70	.75
Pat Dobson			
George Korince			
(See 67T-72)			
☐ 527 Dennis Ribant	6.00	2.70	.75
☐ 528 Rico Petrocelli	10.00	4.50	1.25
☐ 529 Gary Wagner	6.00	2.70	.75
☐ 530 Felipe Alou	7.50	3.40	.95
☐ 531 Checklist 7	14.00	2.80	1.40
Brooks Robinson			
☐ 532 Jim Hicks	6.00	2.70	.75
☐ 533 Jack Fisher	6.00	2.70	.75
☐ 534 Hank Bauer MG DP	10.00	4.50	1.25
☐ 535 Donn Clendenon	18.00	8.00	2.20
☐ 536 Cubs Rookies	35.00	16.00	4.40
Joe Niekro			
Paul Popovich			
☐ 537 Chuck Estrada DP	9.00	4.00	1.10
☐ 538 J.C. Martin	16.00	7.25	2.00
☐ 539 Dick Egan DP	9.00	4.00	1.10
☐ 540 Norm Cash	35.00	16.00	4.40
☐ 541 Joe Gibbon	16.00	7.25	2.00
☐ 542 Athletics Rookies DP	15.00	6.75	1.85
Rick Monday			
Tony Pierce			
☐ 543 Dan Schneider	16.00	7.25	2.00
☐ 544 Cleveland Indians	30.00	13.50	3.70
Team Card			
☐ 545 Jim Grant	16.00	7.25	2.00
☐ 546 Woody Woodward	18.00	8.00	2.20
☐ 547 Red Sox Rookies DP	9.00	4.00	1.10
Russ Gibson			
Bill Rohr			
☐ 548 Tony Gonzalez DP	9.00	4.00	1.10
☐ 549 Jack Sanford	16.00	7.25	2.00
☐ 550 Vada Pinson DP	10.00	4.50	1.25
☐ 551 Doug Camilli DP	9.00	4.00	1.10
☐ 552 Ted Savage	16.00	7.25	2.00
☐ 553 Yankees Rookies	30.00	13.50	3.70
Mike Hegan			
Thad Tillotson			
☐ 554 Andre Rodgers DP	9.00	4.00	1.10
☐ 555 Don Cardwell	18.00	8.00	2.20
☐ 556 Al Weis DP	9.00	4.00	1.10
☐ 557 Al Ferrara	16.00	7.25	2.00
☐ 558 Orioles Rookies	50.00	22.00	6.25
Mark Belanger			
Bill Dillman			
☐ 559 Dick Tracewski DP	9.00	4.00	1.10
☐ 560 Jim Bunning	70.00	32.00	8.75
☐ 561 Sandy Alomar	20.00	9.00	2.50
☐ 562 Steve Blass DP	10.00	4.50	1.25
☐ 563 Joe Adcock	20.00	9.00	2.50
☐ 564 Astros Rookies DP	9.00	4.00	1.10
Alonzo Harris			
Aaron Pointer			
☐ 565 Lew Krausse	16.00	7.25	2.00
☐ 566 Gary Geiger DP	9.00	4.00	1.10
☐ 567 Steve Hamilton	18.00	8.00	2.20
☐ 568 John Sullivan	16.00	7.25	2.00
☐ 569 AL Rookies DP	250.00	110.00	31.00
Rod Carew			
Hank Allen			
☐ 570 Maury Wills	85.00	38.00	10.50
☐ 571 Larry Sherry	16.00	7.25	2.00
☐ 572 Don Demeter	16.00	7.25	2.00
☐ 573 Chicago White Sox	30.00	13.50	3.70
Team Card UER			
(Indians team			
stats on back)			
☐ 574 Jerry Buchek	18.00	8.00	2.20
☐ 575 Dave Boswell	16.00	7.25	2.00
☐ 576 NL Rookies	18.00	8.00	2.20
Ramon Hernandez			
Norm Gigon			
☐ 577 Bill Short	16.00	7.25	2.00
☐ 578 John Boccabella	16.00	7.25	2.00
☐ 579 Bill Henry	16.00	7.25	2.00
☐ 580 Rocky Colavito	90.00	40.00	11.00
☐ 581 Mets Rookies	850.00	375.00	105.00
Bill Denehy			
Tom Seaver			
☐ 582 Jim Owens DP	9.00	4.00	1.10
☐ 583 Ray Barker	18.00	8.00	2.20
☐ 584 Jim Piersall	35.00	16.00	4.40
☐ 585 Wally Bunker	16.00	7.25	2.00
☐ 586 Manny Jimenez	16.00	7.25	2.00
☐ 587 NL Rookies	35.00	16.00	4.40
Don Shaw			
Gary Sutherland			
☐ 588 Johnny Klippstein DP	9.00	4.00	1.10
☐ 589 Dave Ricketts DP	9.00	4.00	1.10
☐ 590 Pete Richert	16.00	7.25	2.00
☐ 591 Ty Cline	16.00	7.25	2.00
☐ 592 NL Rookies	18.00	8.00	2.20
Jim Shellenback			
Ron Willis			
☐ 593 Wes Westrum MG	18.00	8.00	2.20
☐ 594 Dan Osinski	18.00	8.00	2.20
☐ 595 Cookie Rojas	18.00	8.00	2.20
☐ 596 Galen Cisco DP	10.00	4.50	1.25
☐ 597 Ted Abernathy	16.00	7.25	2.00
☐ 598 White Sox Rookies	18.00	8.00	2.20
Walt Williams			
Ed Stroud			
☐ 599 Bob Duliba DP	9.00	4.00	1.10
☐ 600 Brooks Robinson	275.00	125.00	34.00
☐ 601 Bill Bryan DP	9.00	4.00	1.10
☐ 602 Juan Pizarro	16.00	7.25	2.00
☐ 603 Athletics Rookies	16.00	7.25	2.00
Tim Talton			
Ramon Webster			
☐ 604 Red Sox Team	125.00	55.00	15.50
☐ 605 Mike Shannon	50.00	22.00	6.25
☐ 606 Ron Taylor	18.00	8.00	2.20
☐ 607 Mickey Stanley	40.00	18.00	5.00
☐ 608 Cubs Rookies DP	9.00	4.00	1.10
Rich Nye			
John Upham			
☐ 609 Tommy John	70.00	23.00	8.25

1967 Topps Posters

The wrappers of the 1967 Topps cards have this 32-card set advertised as follows: 'Extra -- All Star Pin-Up Inside.' Printed on (5" by 7") paper in full color, these "All-Star" inserts have fold lines which are generally not very noticeable when stored carefully. They are numbered, blank-backed, and carry a facsimile autograph.

	NRMT	VG-E	GOOD
COMPLETE SET (32)	60.00	27.00	7.50
COMMON CARD (1-32)	.50	.23	.06
☐ 1 Boog Powell	1.00	.45	.12
☐ 2 Bert Campaneris	.50	.23	.06
☐ 3 Brooks Robinson	4.00	1.80	.50
☐ 4 Tommie Agee	.50	.23	.06
☐ 5 Carl Yastrzemski	3.00	1.35	.35
☐ 6 Mickey Mantle	20.00	9.00	2.50
☐ 7 Frank Howard	1.00	.45	.12
☐ 8 Sam McDowell	.50	.23	.06
☐ 9 Orlando Cepeda	1.00	.45	.12
☐ 10 Chico Cardenas	.50	.23	.06
☐ 11 Roberto Clemente	10.00	4.50	1.25
☐ 12 Willie Mays	8.00	3.60	1.00
☐ 13 Cleon Jones	.50	.23	.06
☐ 14 John Callison	1.00	.45	.12
☐ 15 Hank Aaron	6.00	2.70	.75
☐ 16 Don Drysdale	3.00	1.35	.35
☐ 17 Bobby Knoop	.50	.23	.06
☐ 18 Tony Oliva	1.00	.45	.12
☐ 19 Frank Robinson	3.00	1.35	.35
☐ 20 Denny McLain	1.00	.45	.12
☐ 21 Al Kaline	4.00	1.80	.50
☐ 22 Joe Pepitone	1.00	.45	.12
☐ 23 Harmon Killebrew	3.00	1.35	.35
☐ 24 Leon Wagner	.50	.23	.06
☐ 25 Joe Morgan	2.50	1.10	.30
☐ 26 Ron Santo	1.00	.45	.12
☐ 27 Joe Torre	1.50	.70	.19
☐ 28 Juan Marichal	3.00	1.35	.35
☐ 29 Matty Alou	.50	.23	.06
☐ 30 Felipe Alou	1.00	.45	.12
☐ 31 Ron Hunt	.75	.35	.09
☐ 32 Willie McCovey	2.50	1.10	.30

1967 Topps Pirate Stickers

This was a limited production "test" issue for Topps. It is very similar to the Red Sox "test" issue following. The stickers are blank backed and measure 2 1/2" by 3 1/2". The stickers look like cards from the front and are somewhat attractive in spite of the "no neck" presentation of many of the players' photos. The cards are numbered on the front.

	NRMT	VG-E	GOOD
COMPLETE SET (33)	450.00	200.00	55.00
COMMON STICKER (1-33)	6.00	2.70	.75
WRAPPER (5-CENT)	50.00	22.00	6.25
☐ 1 Gene Alley	7.50	3.40	.95
☐ 2 Matty Alou	7.50	3.40	.95
☐ 3 Dennis Ribant	6.00	2.70	.75
☐ 4 Steve Blass	7.50	3.40	.95
☐ 5 Juan Pizarro	6.00	2.70	.75
☐ 6 Roberto Clemente	150.00	70.00	19.00
☐ 7 Donn Clendenon	7.50	3.40	.95
☐ 8 Elroy Face	10.00	4.50	1.25
☐ 9 Woodie Fryman	6.00	2.70	.75
☐ 10 Jesse Gonder	6.00	2.70	.75
☐ 11 Vern Law	7.50	3.40	.95
☐ 12 Al McBean	6.00	2.70	.75
☐ 13 Jerry May	6.00	2.70	.75
☐ 14 Bill Mazeroski	15.00	6.75	1.85
☐ 15 Pete Mikkelsen	6.00	2.70	.75
☐ 16 Manny Mota	7.50	3.40	.95
☐ 17 Bill O'Dell	6.00	2.70	.75
☐ 18 Jose Pagan	6.00	2.70	.75
☐ 19 Jim Pagliaroni	6.00	2.70	.75
☐ 20 Johnny Pesky CO	6.00	2.70	.75
☐ 21 Tommie Sisk	6.00	2.70	.75
☐ 22 Willie Stargell	50.00	22.00	6.25
☐ 23 Bob Veale	7.50	3.40	.95
☐ 24 Harry Walker MG	6.00	2.70	.75
☐ 25 I Love the Pirates	6.00	2.70	.75
☐ 26 Let's Go Pirates	6.00	2.70	.75
☐ 27 Bob Clemente for Mayor	75.00	34.00	9.50
☐ 28 Matty Alou NL Batting Champ	7.50	3.40	.95
☐ 29 Happiness is a Pirate Win	6.00	2.70	.75
☐ 30 Donn Clendenon is my Hero	7.50	3.40	.95
☐ 31 Willie Stargell Pirates HR Champ	40.00	18.00	5.00
☐ 32 Pirates Logo	6.00	2.70	.75
☐ 33 Pirates Pennant	6.00	2.70	.75

1967 Topps Red Sox Stickers

This was a limited production "test" issue for Topps. It is very similar to the Pirates "test" issue preceding. The stickers are blank backed and measure 2 1/2" by 3 1/2". The stickers look like cards from the front and are somewhat attractive in spite of the "no neck" presentation of many of the players' photos. The cards are numbered on the front.

	NRMT	VG-E	GOOD
COMPLETE SET (33)	250.00	110.00	31.00
COMMON STICKER (1-33)	4.00	1.80	.50
WRAPPER (5-CENT)	4.00	1.80	.50
☐ 1 Dennis Bennett	4.00	1.80	.50
☐ 2 Darrell Brandon	4.00	1.80	.50
☐ 3 Tony Conigliaro	10.00	4.50	1.25
☐ 4 Don Demeter	4.00	1.80	.50
☐ 5 Hank Fischer	4.00	1.80	.50
☐ 6 Joe Foy	4.00	1.80	.50
☐ 7 Mike Andrews	4.00	1.80	.50
☐ 8 Dalton Jones	4.00	1.80	.50
☐ 9 Jim Lonborg	7.50	3.40	.95
☐ 10 Don McMahon	4.00	1.80	.50
☐ 11 Dave Morehead	4.00	1.80	.50
☐ 12 Reggie Smith	10.00	4.50	1.25
☐ 13 Rico Petrocelli	7.50	3.40	.95
☐ 14 Mike Ryan	4.00	1.80	.50
☐ 15 Jose Santiago	4.00	1.80	.50
☐ 16 George Scott	7.50	3.40	.95
☐ 17 Sal Maglie CO	7.50	3.40	.95
☐ 18 George Smith	4.00	1.80	.50
☐ 19 Lee Stange	4.00	1.80	.50
☐ 20 Jerry Stephenson	4.00	1.80	.50
☐ 21 Jose Tartabull	4.00	1.80	.50
☐ 22 George Thomas	4.00	1.80	.50
☐ 23 Bob Tillman	4.00	1.80	.50
☐ 24 John Wyatt	4.00	1.80	.50
☐ 25 Carl Yastrzemski	75.00	34.00	9.50
☐ 26 Dick Williams MG	10.00	4.50	1.25
☐ 27 I Love the Red Sox	4.00	1.80	.50
☐ 28 Let's Go Red Sox	4.00	1.80	.50
☐ 29 Carl Yastrzemski for Mayor	40.00	18.00	5.00
☐ 30 Tony Conigliaro is my Hero	10.00	4.50	1.25
☐ 31 Happiness is a Boston Win	4.00	1.80	.50
☐ 32 Red Sox Logo	4.00	1.80	.50
☐ 33 Red Sox Pennant	4.00	1.80	.50

1967 Topps Venezuelan

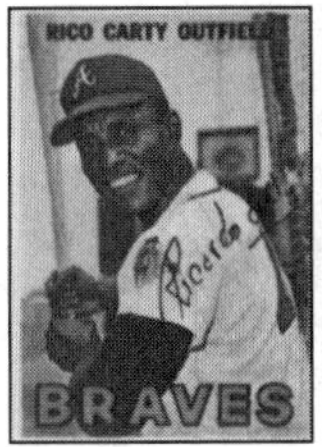
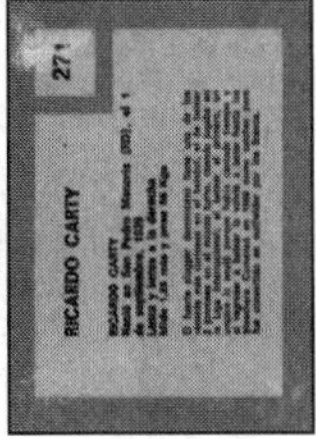

This 200-card set features color player photos in a white border on the fronts. The horizontal backs carry player information. The cards are printed in Spanish and were issued for the Venezuelan market.

	NRMT	VG-E	GOOD
COMPLETE SET (139-338)	10000.00	4500.00	1250.00
COMMON CARD (139-188)	40.00	18.00	5.00
COMMON CARD (189-338)	5.00	2.20	.60
☐ 139 Walter Johnson	200.00	90.00	25.00
☐ 140 Bill Dickey	100.00	45.00	12.50
☐ 141 Lou Gehrig	400.00	180.00	50.00
☐ 142 Rogers Hornsby	200.00	90.00	25.00
☐ 143 Honus Wagner	250.00	110.00	31.00
☐ 144 Pie Traynor	100.00	45.00	12.50
☐ 145 Joe DiMaggio	400.00	180.00	50.00
☐ 146 Ty Cobb	400.00	180.00	50.00
☐ 147 Babe Ruth	500.00	220.00	60.00
☐ 148 Ted Williams	400.00	180.00	50.00
☐ 149 Mel Ott	125.00	55.00	15.50
☐ 150 Cy Young	200.00	90.00	25.00
☐ 151 Christy Matthewson	200.00	90.00	25.00
☐ 152 Warren Spahn	125.00	55.00	15.50
☐ 153 Mickey Cochrane	100.00	45.00	12.50
☐ 154 George Sisler	75.00	34.00	9.50
☐ 155 Jimmy Collins	60.00	27.00	7.50
☐ 156 Tris Speaker	150.00	70.00	19.00
☐ 157 Stan Musial	200.00	90.00	25.00
☐ 158 Luke Appling	75.00	34.00	9.50
☐ 159 Nap Lajoie	150.00	70.00	19.00
☐ 160 Bob Feller	200.00	90.00	25.00
☐ 161 Bill Terry	60.00	27.00	7.50
☐ 162 Sandy Koufax	250.00	110.00	31.00
☐ 163 Jimmy Foxx	200.00	90.00	25.00
☐ 164 Joe Cronin	75.00	34.00	9.50
☐ 165 Frank Frisch	75.00	34.00	9.50
☐ 166 Paul Waner	100.00	45.00	12.50
☐ 167 Lloyd Waner	75.00	34.00	9.50
☐ 168 Lefty Grove	150.00	70.00	19.00
☐ 169 Bobby Doerr	60.00	27.00	7.50
☐ 170 Al Simmons	75.00	34.00	9.50
☐ 171 Grover Alexander	200.00	90.00	25.00
☐ 172 Carl Hubbell	200.00	90.00	25.00
☐ 173 Mordecai Brown	150.00	70.00	19.00
☐ 174 Ted Lyons	75.00	34.00	9.50
☐ 175 Johnny Vander Meer	60.00	27.00	7.50
☐ 176 Alex Carrasquel	40.00	18.00	5.00
☐ 177 Satchel Paige	300.00	135.00	38.00
☐ 178 Whitey Ford	150.00	70.00	19.00
☐ 179 Yogi Berra	150.00	70.00	19.00
☐ 180 Roy Campanella	150.00	70.00	19.00
☐ 181 Chico Carrasquel	40.00	18.00	5.00
☐ 182 Johnny Mize	75.00	34.00	9.50
☐ 183 Ted Kluszewski Ray Herbert	40.00	18.00	5.00
☐ 184 Jackie Robinson	400.00	180.00	50.00
☐ 185 Beto Avila	40.00	18.00	5.00
☐ 186 Phil Rizzuto	150.00	70.00	19.00
☐ 187 Minnie Minoso	75.00	34.00	9.50
☐ 188 Conrado Marrero	40.00	18.00	5.00
☐ 189 Luis Aparicio	15.00	6.75	1.85
☐ 190 Vic Davalillo	5.00	2.20	.60
☐ 191 Cesar Tovar	5.00	2.20	.60
☐ 192 Mickey Mantle	750.00	350.00	95.00
☐ 193 Carl Yastrzemski	125.00	55.00	15.50
☐ 194 Frank Robinson	35.00	16.00	4.40
☐ 195 Willie Horton	7.50	3.40	.95
☐ 196 Gary Peters	5.00	2.20	.60
☐ 197 Bert Campaneris	5.00	2.20	.60
☐ 198 Norm Cash	7.50	3.40	.95
☐ 199 Boog Powell	15.00	6.75	1.85
☐ 200 George Scott	5.00	2.20	.60
☐ 201 Frank Howard	7.50	3.40	.95
☐ 202 Rick Reichardt	5.00	2.20	.60
☐ 203 Jose Cardenal	5.00	2.20	.60
☐ 204 Rico Petrocelli	5.00	2.20	.60
☐ 205 Lew Krausse	5.00	2.20	.60
☐ 206 Harmon Killebrew	40.00	18.00	5.00
☐ 207 Leon Wagner	5.00	2.20	.60
☐ 208 Joe Foy	5.00	2.20	.60
☐ 209 Joe Pepitone	5.00	2.20	.60
☐ 210 Al Kaline	40.00	18.00	5.00
☐ 211 Brooks Robinson	50.00	22.00	6.25
☐ 212 Bill Freehan	5.00	2.20	.60
☐ 213 Jim Lonborg	5.00	2.20	.60
☐ 214 Ed Mathews	40.00	18.00	5.00
☐ 215 Dick Green	5.00	2.20	.60
☐ 216 Tom Tresh	5.00	2.20	.60
☐ 217 Dean Chance	5.00	2.20	.60
☐ 218 Paul Blair	5.00	2.20	.60
☐ 219 Larry Brown	5.00	2.20	.60
☐ 220 Fred Valentine	5.00	2.20	.60
☐ 221 Al Downing	5.00	2.20	.60
☐ 222 Earl Battey	5.00	2.20	.60
☐ 223 Don Mincher	5.00	2.20	.60
☐ 224 Tommie Agee	5.00	2.20	.60
☐ 225 Jim McGlothlin	5.00	2.20	.60
☐ 226 Zolio Versalles	5.00	2.20	.60
☐ 227 Curt Blefary	5.00	2.20	.60
☐ 228 Joel Horlen	5.00	2.20	.60
☐ 229 Stu Miller	5.00	2.20	.60
☐ 230 Tony Oliva	7.50	3.40	.95
☐ 231 Paul Casanova	5.00	2.20	.60
☐ 232 Orlando Pena	5.00	2.20	.60
☐ 233 Ron Hansen	5.00	2.20	.60
☐ 234 Earl Wilson	5.00	2.20	.60
☐ 235 Ken Boyer	7.50	3.40	.95
☐ 236 Jim Kaat	7.50	3.40	.95
☐ 237 Dalton Jones	5.00	2.20	.60
☐ 238 Pete Ward	5.00	2.20	.60
☐ 239 Mickey Lolich	7.50	3.40	.95
☐ 240 Jose Santiago	5.00	2.20	.60
☐ 241 Dick McAuliffe	5.00	2.20	.60
☐ 242 Mel Stottlemyre	5.00	2.20	.60
☐ 243 Camilo Pascual	5.00	2.20	.60
☐ 244 Jim Fregosi	5.00	2.20	.60
☐ 245 Tony Conigliaro	25.00	11.00	3.10
☐ 246 Sonny Siebert	5.00	2.20	.60
☐ 247 Jim Perry	5.00	2.20	.60
☐ 248 Dave McNally	5.00	2.20	.60
☐ 249 Fred Whitfield	5.00	2.20	.60
☐ 250 Ken Berry	5.00	2.20	.60
☐ 251 Jim Grant	5.00	2.20	.60
☐ 252 Hank Aguirre	5.00	2.20	.60
☐ 253 Don Wert	5.00	2.20	.60
☐ 254 Wally Bunker	5.00	2.20	.60
☐ 255 Elston Howard	7.50	3.40	.95
☐ 256 Dave Johnson	5.00	2.20	.60
☐ 257 Hoyt Wilhelm	25.00	11.00	3.10
☐ 258 Dick Buford	5.00	2.20	.60
☐ 259 Sam McDowell	5.00	2.20	.60
☐ 260 Bobby Knoop	5.00	2.20	.60
☐ 261 Denny McLain	15.00	6.75	1.85
☐ 262 Steve Hargan	5.00	2.20	.60
☐ 263 Jim Nash	5.00	2.20	.60
☐ 264 Jerry Adair	5.00	2.20	.60
☐ 265 Tony Gonzalez	5.00	2.20	.60
☐ 266 Mike Shannon	5.00	2.20	.60
☐ 267 Bob Gibson	50.00	22.00	6.25
☐ 268 John Roseboro	5.00	2.20	.60
☐ 269 Bob Aspromonte	5.00	2.20	.60
☐ 270 Pete Rose	200.00	90.00	25.00
☐ 271 Rico Carty	5.00	2.20	.60
☐ 272 Juan Pizarro	5.00	2.20	.60
☐ 273 Willie Mays	225.00	100.00	28.00
☐ 274 Jim Bunning	75.00	34.00	9.50
☐ 275 Ernie Banks	50.00	22.00	6.25
☐ 276 Curt Flood	5.00	2.20	.60
☐ 277 Mack Jones	5.00	2.20	.60
☐ 278 Roberto Clemente	250.00	110.00	31.00
☐ 279 Sammy Ellis	5.00	2.20	.60
☐ 280 Willie Stargell	50.00	22.00	6.25
☐ 281 Felipe Alou	7.50	3.40	.95
☐ 282 Ed Kranepool	5.00	2.20	.60
☐ 283 Nelson Briles	5.00	2.20	.60
☐ 284 Hank Aaron	200.00	90.00	25.00
☐ 285 Vada Pinson	7.50	3.40	.95
☐ 286 Jim LeFebvre	5.00	2.20	.60
☐ 287 Hal Lanier	5.00	2.20	.60
☐ 288 Ron Swoboda	5.00	2.20	.60
☐ 289 Mike McCormick	5.00	2.20	.60
☐ 290 Lou Johnson	5.00	2.20	.60
☐ 291 Orlando Cepeda	15.00	6.75	1.85
☐ 292 Rusty Staub	7.50	3.40	.95
☐ 293 Manny Mota	7.50	3.40	.95
☐ 294 Tommy Harper	5.00	2.20	.60
☐ 295 Don Drysdale	40.00	18.00	5.00
☐ 296 Mel Queen	5.00	2.20	.60
☐ 297 Red Schoendienst MG	20.00	9.00	2.50
☐ 298 Matty Alou	7.50	3.40	.95
☐ 299 Johnny Callison	5.00	2.20	.60
☐ 300 Juan Marichal	40.00	18.00	5.00
☐ 301 Al McBean	5.00	2.20	.60
☐ 302 Claude Osteen	5.00	2.20	.60
☐ 303 Willie McCovey	50.00	22.00	6.25
☐ 304 Jim Owens	5.00	2.20	.60
☐ 305 Chico Ruiz	5.00	2.20	.60
☐ 306 Ferguson Jenkins	40.00	18.00	5.00
☐ 307 Lou Brock	50.00	22.00	6.25
☐ 308 Joe Morgan	35.00	16.00	4.40
☐ 309 Ron Santo	7.50	3.40	.95
☐ 310 Chico Cardenas	5.00	2.20	.60
☐ 311 Richie Allen	7.50	3.40	.95
☐ 312 Gaylord Perry	35.00	16.00	4.40
☐ 313 Bill Mazeroski	20.00	9.00	2.50
☐ 314 Tony Taylor	5.00	2.20	.60
☐ 315 Tommy Helms	5.00	2.20	.60
☐ 316 Jim Wynn	5.00	2.20	.60
☐ 317 Don Sutton	40.00	18.00	5.00
☐ 318 Mike Cuellar	7.50	3.40	.95
☐ 319 Willie Davis	5.00	2.20	.60
☐ 320 Julian Javier	5.00	2.20	.60
☐ 321 Maury Willis	7.50	3.40	.95
☐ 322 Gene Alley	5.00	2.20	.60
☐ 323 Ray Sadecki	5.00	2.20	.60
☐ 324 Joe Torre	7.50	3.40	.95
☐ 325 Jim Maloney	5.00	2.20	.60
☐ 326 Jim Davenport	5.00	2.20	.60
☐ 327 Tony Perez	30.00	13.50	3.70
☐ 328 Roger Maris	75.00	34.00	9.50
☐ 329 Chris Short	5.00	2.20	.60
☐ 330 Jesus Alou	5.00	2.20	.60
☐ 331 Deron Johnson	5.00	2.20	.60
☐ 332 Tommy Davis	5.00	2.20	.60
☐ 333 Bob Veale	5.00	2.20	.60
☐ 334 Bill McCool	5.00	2.20	.60
☐ 335 Jim Hart	5.00	2.20	.60
☐ 336 Roy Face	5.00	2.20	.60
☐ 337 Billy Williams	25.00	11.00	3.10
☐ 338 Dick Groat	7.50	3.40	.95

1968 Topps

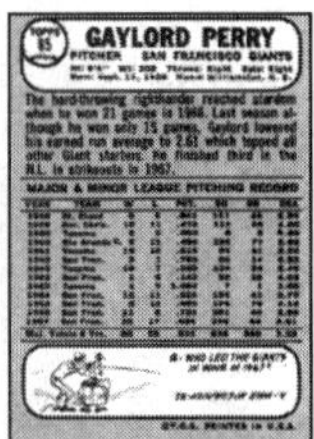

The cards in this 598-card set measure 2 1/2" by 3 1/2". The 1968 Topps set includes Sporting News All-Star Selections as card numbers 361 to 380. Other subsets in the set include League Leaders (1-12) and World Series cards (151-158). The front of each checklist card features a picture of a popular player inside a circle. Higher numbers 458 to 598 are slightly more difficult to obtain. The first series looks different from the other series, as it has a lighter, wider mesh background on the card front. The later series all had a much darker, finer mesh pattern. Among other fashions, cards were issued in five-card nickle packs. The key Rookie Cards in the set are Johnny Bench and Nolan Ryan.

	NRMT	VG-E	GOOD
COMPLETE SET (598)	3000.00	1350.00	375.00
COMMON CARD (1-457)	1.75	.80	.22
COMMON CARD (458-598)	3.50	1.55	.45
WRAPPER (5-CENT)	25.00	11.00	3.10
☐ 1 NL Batting Leaders Bob Clemente Tony Gonzalez Matty Alou	30.00	12.00	6.00
☐ 2 AL Batting Leaders Carl Yastrzemski Frank Robinson Al Kaline	14.00	6.25	1.75
☐ 3 NL RBI Leaders Orlando Cepeda Bob Clemente Hank Aaron	20.00	9.00	2.50
☐ 4 AL RBI Leaders Carl Yastrzemski Harmon Killebrew Frank Robinson	12.00	5.50	1.50
☐ 5 NL Home Run Leaders Hank Aaron Jim Wynn Ron Santo Willie McCovey	8.00	3.60	1.00
☐ 6 AL Home Run Leaders Carl Yastrzemski Harmon Killebrew Frank Howard	8.00	3.60	1.00
☐ 7 NL ERA Leaders Phil Niekro Jim Bunning Chris Short	3.50	1.55	.45
☐ 8 AL ERA Leaders Joel Horlen Gary Peters Sonny Siebert	3.50	1.55	.45
☐ 9 NL Pitching Leaders Mike McCormick Ferguson Jenkins Jim Bunning Claude Osteen	4.00	1.80	.50
☐ 10A AL Pitching Leaders Jim Lonborg ERR (Misspelled Lonberg on card back) Earl Wilson Dean Chance	4.00	1.80	.50
☐ 10B AL Pitching Leaders Jim Lonborg COR Earl Wilson Dean Chance	4.00	1.80	.50
☐ 11 NL Strikeout Leaders Jim Bunning Ferguson Jenkins	5.00	2.20	.60

Gaylord Perry
☐ 12 AL Strikeout Leaders 3.50 1.55 .45
Jim Lonborg UER
(Misspelled Longberg
on card back)
Sam McDowell
Dean Chance
☐ 13 Chuck Hartenstein 1.75 .80 .22
☐ 14 Jerry McNertney 1.75 .80 .22
☐ 15 Ron Hunt 1.75 .80 .22
☐ 16 Indians Rookies 4.00 1.80 .50
Lou Piniella
Richie Scheinblum
☐ 17 Dick Hall 1.75 .80 .22
☐ 18 Mike Hershberger 1.75 .80 .22
☐ 19 Juan Pizarro 1.75 .80 .22
☐ 20 Brooks Robinson 25.00 11.00 3.10
☐ 21 Ron Davis 1.75 .80 .22
☐ 22 Pat Dobson 2.50 1.10 .30
☐ 23 Chico Cardenas 2.00 .90 .25
☐ 24 Bobby Locke 1.75 .80 .22
☐ 25 Julian Javier 2.00 .90 .25
☐ 26 Darrell Brandon 1.75 .80 .22
☐ 27 Gil Hodges MG 8.00 3.60 1.00
☐ 28 Ted Uhlaender 1.75 .80 .22
☐ 29 Joe Verbanic 1.75 .80 .22
☐ 30 Joe Torre 4.00 1.80 .50
☐ 31 Ed Stroud 1.75 .80 .22
☐ 32 Joe Gibbon 1.75 .80 .22
☐ 33 Pete Ward 1.75 .80 .22
☐ 34 Al Ferrara 1.75 .80 .22
☐ 35 Steve Hargan 1.75 .80 .22
☐ 36 Pirates Rookies 2.00 .90 .25
Bob Moose
Bob Robertson
☐ 37 Billy Williams 10.00 4.50 1.25
☐ 38 Tony Pierce 1.75 .80 .22
☐ 39 Cookie Rojas 2.00 .90 .25
☐ 40 Denny McLain 10.00 4.50 1.25
☐ 41 Julio Gotay 1.75 .80 .22
☐ 42 Larry Haney 1.75 .80 .22
☐ 43 Gary Bell 1.75 .80 .22
☐ 44 Frank Kostro 1.75 .80 .22
☐ 45 Tom Seaver 50.00 22.00 6.25
☐ 46 Dave Ricketts 1.75 .80 .22
☐ 47 Ralph Houk MG 2.50 1.10 .30
☐ 48 Ted Davidson 1.75 .80 .22
☐ 49A Eddie Brinkman 1.75 .80 .22
(White team name)
☐ 49B Eddie Brinkman 50.00 22.00 6.25
(Yellow team name)
☐ 50 Willie Mays 65.00 29.00 8.00
☐ 51 Bob Locker 1.75 .80 .22
☐ 52 Hawk Taylor 1.75 .80 .22
☐ 53 Gene Alley 2.00 .90 .25
☐ 54 Stan Williams 2.00 .90 .25
☐ 55 Felipe Alou 3.00 1.35 .35
☐ 56 Orioles Rookies 1.75 .80 .22
Dave Leonhard
Dave May
☐ 57 Dan Schneider 1.75 .80 .22
☐ 58 Eddie Mathews 16.00 7.25 2.00
☐ 59 Don Lock 1.75 .80 .22
☐ 60 Ken Holtzman 2.00 .90 .25
☐ 61 Reggie Smith 3.00 1.35 .35
☐ 62 Chuck Dobson 1.75 .80 .22
☐ 63 Dick Kenworthy 1.75 .80 .22
☐ 64 Jim Merritt 1.75 .80 .22
☐ 65 John Roseboro 2.00 .90 .25
☐ 66A Casey Cox 1.75 .80 .22
(White team name)
☐ 66B Casey Cox 100.00 45.00 12.50
(Yellow team name)
☐ 67 Checklist 1 6.00 1.20 .60
Jim Kaat
☐ 68 Ron Willis 1.75 .80 .22
☐ 69 Tom Tresh 2.50 1.10 .30
☐ 70 Bob Veale 2.00 .90 .25
☐ 71 Vern Fuller 1.75 .80 .22
☐ 72 Tommy John 5.00 2.20 .60
☐ 73 Jim Ray Hart 2.00 .90 .25
☐ 74 Milt Pappas 2.00 .90 .25
☐ 75 Don Mincher 1.75 .80 .22
☐ 76 Braves Rookies 2.00 .90 .25
Jim Britton
Ron Reed
☐ 77 Don Wilson 2.00 .90 .25
☐ 78 Jim Northrup 2.50 1.10 .30
☐ 79 Ted Kubiak 1.75 .80 .22
☐ 80 Rod Carew 50.00 22.00 6.25
☐ 81 Larry Jackson 1.75 .80 .22
☐ 82 Sam Bowens 1.75 .80 .22
☐ 83 John Stephenson 1.75 .80 .22
☐ 84 Bob Tolan 2.00 .90 .25
☐ 85 Gaylord Perry 8.00 3.60 1.00
☐ 86 Willie Stargell 8.00 3.60 1.00
☐ 87 Dick Williams MG 2.00 .90 .25
☐ 88 Phil Regan 2.00 .90 .25
☐ 89 Jake Gibbs 2.50 1.10 .30
☐ 90 Vada Pinson 3.00 1.35 .35
☐ 91 Jim Ollom 1.75 .80 .22
☐ 92 Ed Kranepool 2.00 .90 .25
☐ 93 Tony Cloninger 1.75 .80 .22
☐ 94 Lee Maye 1.75 .80 .22
☐ 95 Bob Aspromonte 1.75 .80 .22
☐ 96 Senator Rookies 1.75 .80 .22
Frank Coggins
Dick Nold
☐ 97 Tom Phoebus 1.75 .80 .22
☐ 98 Gary Sutherland 1.75 .80 .22
☐ 99 Rocky Colavito 8.00 3.60 1.00
☐ 100 Bob Gibson 25.00 11.00 3.10
☐ 101 Glenn Beckert 2.00 .90 .25
☐ 102 Jose Cardenal 2.00 .90 .25
☐ 103 Don Sutton 6.00 2.70 .75
☐ 104 Dick Dietz 1.75 .80 .22
☐ 105 Al Downing 2.50 1.10 .30
☐ 106 Dalton Jones 1.75 .80 .22
☐ 107A Checklist 2 6.00 1.20 .60
Juan Marichal
(Tan wide mesh)
☐ 107B Checklist 2 6.00 1.20 .60
Juan Marichal
(Brown fine mesh)
☐ 108 Don Pavletich 1.75 .80 .22
☐ 109 Bert Campaneris 2.00 .90 .25
☐ 110 Hank Aaron 60.00 27.00 7.50
☐ 111 Rich Reese 1.75 .80 .22
☐ 112 Woody Fryman 1.75 .80 .22
☐ 113 Tigers Rookies 2.50 1.10 .30
Tom Matchick
Daryl Patterson
☐ 114 Ron Swoboda 2.00 .90 .25
☐ 115 Sam McDowell 2.00 .90 .25
☐ 116 Ken McMullen 1.75 .80 .22
☐ 117 Larry Jaster 1.75 .80 .22
☐ 118 Mark Belanger 2.00 .90 .25
☐ 119 Ted Savage 1.75 .80 .22
☐ 120 Mel Stottlemyre 3.00 1.35 .35
☐ 121 Jimmie Hall 1.75 .80 .22
☐ 122 Gene Mauch MG 2.00 .90 .25
☐ 123 Jose Santiago 1.75 .80 .22
☐ 124 Nate Oliver 1.75 .80 .22
☐ 125 Joel Horlen 1.75 .80 .22
☐ 126 Bobby Etheridge 1.75 .80 .22
☐ 127 Paul Lindblad 1.75 .80 .22
☐ 128 Astros Rookies 1.75 .80 .22
Tom Dukes
Alonzo Harris
☐ 129 Mickey Stanley 3.00 1.35 .35
☐ 130 Tony Perez 8.00 3.60 1.00
☐ 131 Frank Bertaina 1.75 .80 .22
☐ 132 Bud Harrelson 2.00 .90 .25
☐ 133 Fred Whitfield 1.75 .80 .22
☐ 134 Pat Jarvis 1.75 .80 .22
☐ 135 Paul Blair 2.00 .90 .25
☐ 136 Randy Hundley 2.00 .90 .25
☐ 137 Twins Team 3.50 1.55 .45
☐ 138 Ruben Amaro 1.75 .80 .22
☐ 139 Chris Short 1.75 .80 .22
☐ 140 Tony Conigliaro 8.00 3.60 1.00
☐ 141 Dal Maxvill 1.75 .80 .22
☐ 142 White Sox Rookies 1.75 .80 .22
Buddy Bradford
Bill Voss
☐ 143 Pete Cimino 1.75 .80 .22
☐ 144 Joe Morgan 12.00 5.50 1.50
☐ 145 Don Drysdale 12.00 5.50 1.50
☐ 146 Sal Bando 2.00 .90 .25
☐ 147 Frank Linzy 1.75 .80 .22
☐ 148 Dave Bristol MG 1.75 .80 .22
☐ 149 Bob Saverine 1.75 .80 .22
☐ 150 Bob Clemente 70.00 32.00 8.75
☐ 151 Lou Brock WS 10.00 4.50 1.25
☐ 152 Carl Yastrzemski WS 10.00 4.50 1.25
☐ 153 Nellie Briles WS 4.50 2.00 .55
☐ 154 Bob Gibson WS 8.00 3.60 1.00
☐ 155 Jim Lonborg WS 4.50 2.00 .55
☐ 156 Rico Petrocelli WS 4.50 2.00 .55
☐ 157 World Series Game 7 4.50 2.00 .55
St. Louis wins it
☐ 158 World Series Summary 4.50 2.00 .55
Cardinals celebrate
☐ 159 Don Kessinger 2.00 .90 .25
☐ 160 Earl Wilson 2.00 .90 .25
☐ 161 Norm Miller 1.75 .80 .22
☐ 162 Cards Rookies 2.00 .90 .25
Hal Gilson
Mike Torrez
☐ 163 Gene Brabender 1.75 .80 .22
☐ 164 Ramon Webster 1.75 .80 .22
☐ 165 Tony Oliva 3.00 1.35 .35
☐ 166 Claude Raymond 1.75 .80 .22
☐ 167 Elston Howard 3.00 1.35 .35
☐ 168 Dodgers Team 3.50 1.55 .45
☐ 169 Bob Bolin 1.75 .80 .22
☐ 170 Jim Fregosi 2.00 .90 .25
☐ 171 Don Nottebart 1.75 .80 .22
☐ 172 Walt Williams 1.75 .80 .22
☐ 173 John Boozer 1.75 .80 .22
☐ 174 Bob Tillman 1.75 .80 .22
☐ 175 Maury Wills 5.00 2.20 .60
☐ 176 Bob Allen 1.75 .80 .22
☐ 177 Mets Rookies 900.00 400.00 110.00
Jerry Koosman
Nolan Ryan
☐ 178 Don Wert 2.00 .90 .25
☐ 179 Bill Stoneman 1.75 .80 .22
☐ 180 Curt Flood 3.00 1.35 .35
☐ 181 Jerry Zimmerman 1.75 .80 .22
☐ 182 Dave Giusti 1.75 .80 .22
☐ 183 Bob Kennedy MG 2.00 .90 .25
☐ 184 Lou Johnson 2.00 .90 .25
☐ 185 Tom Haller 1.75 .80 .22
☐ 186 Eddie Watt 1.75 .80 .22
☐ 187 Sonny Jackson 1.75 .80 .22
☐ 188 Cap Peterson 1.75 .80 .22
☐ 189 Bill Landis 1.75 .80 .22
☐ 190 Bill White 3.00 1.35 .35
☐ 191 Dan Frisella 1.75 .80 .22
☐ 192A Checklist 3 7.50 1.50 .75
Carl Yastrzemski
(Special Baseball
Playing Card)
☐ 192B Checklist 3 7.50 1.50 .75
Carl Yastrzemski
(Special Baseball
Playing Card Game)
☐ 193 Jack Hamilton 1.75 .80 .22
☐ 194 Don Buford 1.75 .80 .22
☐ 195 Joe Pepitone 2.50 1.10 .30
☐ 196 Gary Nolan 2.00 .90 .25
☐ 197 Larry Brown 1.75 .80 .22
☐ 198 Roy Face 2.00 .90 .25
☐ 199 A's Rookies 1.75 .80 .22
Roberto Rodriquez
Darrell Osteen
☐ 200 Orlando Cepeda 5.00 2.20 .60
☐ 201 Mike Marshall 3.00 1.35 .35
☐ 202 Adolfo Phillips 1.75 .80 .22
☐ 203 Dick Kelley 1.75 .80 .22
☐ 204 Andy Etchebarren 1.75 .80 .22
☐ 205 Juan Marichal 8.00 3.60 1.00
☐ 206 Cal Ermer MG 1.75 .80 .22
☐ 207 Carroll Sembera 1.75 .80 .22
☐ 208 Willie Davis 2.50 1.10 .30
☐ 209 Tim Cullen 1.75 .80 .22
☐ 210 Gary Peters 1.75 .80 .22
☐ 211 J.C. Martin 1.75 .80 .22
☐ 212 Dave Morehead 1.75 .80 .22
☐ 213 Chico Ruiz 1.75 .80 .22
☐ 214 Yankees Rookies 2.00 .90 .25
Stan Bahnsen
Frank Fernandez
☐ 215 Jim Bunning 7.00 3.10 .85
☐ 216 Bubba Morton 1.75 .80 .22
☐ 217 Dick Farrell 1.75 .80 .22
☐ 218 Ken Suarez 1.75 .80 .22
☐ 219 Rob Gardner 1.75 .80 .22
☐ 220 Harmon Killebrew 14.00 6.25 1.75
☐ 221 Braves Team 3.50 1.55 .45
☐ 222 Jim Hardin 1.75 .80 .22
☐ 223 Ollie Brown 1.75 .80 .22
☐ 224 Jack Aker 1.75 .80 .22
☐ 225 Richie Allen 5.00 2.20 .60
☐ 226 Jimmie Price 1.75 .80 .22
☐ 227 Joe Hoerner 1.75 .80 .22
☐ 228 Dodgers Rookies 2.50 1.10 .30
Jack Billingham
Jim Fairey
☐ 229 Fred Klages 1.75 .80 .22
☐ 230 Pete Rose 40.00 18.00 5.00
☐ 231 Dave Baldwin 1.75 .80 .22
☐ 232 Denis Menke 1.75 .80 .22
☐ 233 George Scott 2.00 .90 .25
☐ 234 Bill Monbouquette 1.75 .80 .22
☐ 235 Ron Santo 5.00 2.20 .60
☐ 236 Tug McGraw 3.00 1.35 .35
☐ 237 Alvin Dark MG 2.00 .90 .25
☐ 238 Tom Satriano 1.75 .80 .22
☐ 239 Bill Henry 1.75 .80 .22
☐ 240 Al Kaline 25.00 11.00 3.10
☐ 241 Felix Millan 1.75 .80 .22
☐ 242 Moe Drabowsky 2.00 .90 .25
☐ 243 Rich Rollins 1.75 .80 .22
☐ 244 John Donaldson 1.75 .80 .22
☐ 245 Tony Gonzalez 1.75 .80 .22
☐ 246 Fritz Peterson 2.50 1.10 .30
☐ 247 Reds Rookies 125.00 55.00 15.50
Johnny Bench
Ron Tompkins
☐ 248 Fred Valentine 1.75 .80 .22
☐ 249 Bill Singer 1.75 .80 .22
☐ 250 Carl Yastrzemski 25.00 11.00 3.10
☐ 251 Manny Sanguillen 6.00 2.70 .75
☐ 252 Angels Team 3.50 1.55 .45
☐ 253 Dick Hughes 1.75 .80 .22
☐ 254 Cleon Jones 2.00 .90 .25
☐ 255 Dean Chance 2.00 .90 .25
☐ 256 Norm Cash 6.00 2.70 .75
☐ 257 Phil Niekro 8.00 3.60 1.00
☐ 258 Cubs Rookies 1.75 .80 .22
Jose Arcia
Bill Schlesinger
☐ 259 Ken Boyer 3.00 1.35 .35
☐ 260 Jim Wynn 2.00 .90 .25
☐ 261 Dave Duncan 2.00 .90 .25
☐ 262 Rick Wise 2.00 .90 .25
☐ 263 Horace Clarke 2.50 1.10 .30
☐ 264 Ted Abernathy 1.75 .80 .22
☐ 265 Tommy Davis 2.00 .90 .25
☐ 266 Paul Popovich 1.75 .80 .22
☐ 267 Herman Franks MG 1.75 .80 .22
☐ 268 Bob Humphreys 1.75 .80 .22
☐ 269 Bob Tiefenauer 1.75 .80 .22
☐ 270 Matty Alou 2.00 .90 .25
☐ 271 Bobby Knoop 1.75 .80 .22
☐ 272 Ray Culp 1.75 .80 .22
☐ 273 Dave Johnson 2.00 .90 .25
☐ 274 Mike Cuellar 2.00 .90 .25
☐ 275 Tim McCarver 4.00 1.80 .50
☐ 276 Jim Roland 1.75 .80 .22
☐ 277 Jerry Buchek 1.75 .80 .22
☐ 278 Checklist 4 6.00 1.20 .60
Orlando Cepeda
☐ 279 Bill Hands 1.75 .80 .22
☐ 280 Mickey Mantle 250.00 110.00 31.00
☐ 281 Jim Campanis 1.75 .80 .22
☐ 282 Rick Monday 2.00 .90 .25
☐ 283 Mel Queen 1.75 .80 .22
☐ 284 Johnny Briggs 1.75 .80 .22
☐ 285 Dick McAuliffe 2.00 .90 .25
☐ 286 Cecil Upshaw 1.75 .80 .22
☐ 287 White Sox Rookies 1.75 .80 .22
Mickey Abarbanel
Cisco Carlos
☐ 288 Dave Wickersham 1.75 .80 .22
☐ 289 Woody Held 1.75 .80 .22
☐ 290 Willie McCovey 12.00 5.50 1.50
☐ 291 Dick Lines 1.75 .80 .22
☐ 292 Art Shamsky 1.75 .80 .22
☐ 293 Bruce Howard 1.75 .80 .22
☐ 294 Red Schoendienst MG 4.00 1.80 .50
☐ 295 Sonny Siebert 1.75 .80 .22
☐ 296 Byron Browne 1.75 .80 .22
☐ 297 Russ Gibson 1.75 .80 .22
☐ 298 Jim Brewer 1.75 .80 .22
☐ 299 Gene Michael 2.50 1.10 .30
☐ 300 Rusty Staub 3.00 1.35 .35
☐ 301 Twins Rookies 1.75 .80 .22
George Mitterwald
Rick Renick
☐ 302 Gerry Arrigo 1.75 .80 .22
☐ 303 Dick Green 2.00 .90 .25
☐ 304 Sandy Valdespino 1.75 .80 .22
☐ 305 Minnie Rojas 1.75 .80 .22
☐ 306 Mike Ryan 1.75 .80 .22
☐ 307 John Hiller 2.00 .90 .25
☐ 308 Pirates Team 3.50 1.55 .45
☐ 309 Ken Henderson 1.75 .80 .22
☐ 310 Luis Aparicio 7.00 3.10 .85
☐ 311 Jack Lamabe 1.75 .80 .22
☐ 312 Curt Blefary 1.75 .80 .22
☐ 313 Al Weis 1.75 .80 .22
☐ 314 Red Sox Rookies 1.75 .80 .22
Bill Rohr
George Spriggs
☐ 315 Zoilo Versalles 1.75 .80 .22
☐ 316 Steve Barber 1.75 .80 .22
☐ 317 Ron Brand 1.75 .80 .22
☐ 318 Chico Salmon 1.75 .80 .22
☐ 319 George Culver 1.75 .80 .22
☐ 320 Frank Howard 3.00 1.35 .35
☐ 321 Leo Durocher MG 4.00 1.80 .50
☐ 322 Dave Boswell 1.75 .80 .22
☐ 323 Deron Johnson 2.00 .90 .25
☐ 324 Jim Nash 1.75 .80 .22
☐ 325 Manny Mota 2.00 .90 .25
☐ 326 Dennis Ribant 1.75 .80 .22
☐ 327 Tony Taylor 2.00 .90 .25
☐ 328 Angels Rookies 1.75 .80 .22
Chuck Vinson
Jim Weaver
☐ 329 Duane Josephson 1.75 .80 .22
☐ 330 Roger Maris 30.00 13.50 3.70
☐ 331 Dan Osinski 1.75 .80 .22
☐ 332 Doug Rader 2.00 .90 .25
☐ 333 Ron Herbel 1.75 .80 .22
☐ 334 Orioles Team 3.50 1.55 .45
☐ 335 Bob Allison 2.00 .90 .25
☐ 336 John Purdin 1.75 .80 .22
☐ 337 Bill Robinson 2.50 1.10 .30
☐ 338 Bob Johnson 1.75 .80 .22
☐ 339 Rich Nye 1.75 .80 .22
☐ 340 Max Alvis 1.75 .80 .22
☐ 341 Jim Lemon MG 1.75 .80 .22
☐ 342 Ken Johnson 1.75 .80 .22
☐ 343 Jim Gosger 1.75 .80 .22
☐ 344 Donn Clendenon 2.00 .90 .25
☐ 345 Bob Hendley 1.75 .80 .22
☐ 346 Jerry Adair 1.75 .80 .22
☐ 347 George Brunet 1.75 .80 .22
☐ 348 Phillies Rookies 1.75 .80 .22
Larry Colton
Dick Thoenen
☐ 349 Ed Spiezio 1.75 .80 .22
☐ 350 Hoyt Wilhelm 7.00 3.10 .85
☐ 351 Bob Barton 1.75 .80 .22
☐ 352 Jackie Hernandez 1.75 .80 .22
☐ 353 Mack Jones 1.75 .80 .22
☐ 354 Pete Richert 1.75 .80 .22
☐ 355 Ernie Banks 25.00 11.00 3.10
☐ 356A Checklist 5 6.00 1.20 .60
Ken Holtzman
(Head centered
within circle)
☐ 356B Checklist 5 6.00 1.20 .60
Ken Holtzman
(Head shifted right
within circle)
☐ 357 Len Gabrielson 1.75 .80 .22
☐ 358 Mike Epstein 1.75 .80 .22

☐ 359 Joe Moeller	1.75	.80	.22
☐ 360 Willie Horton	3.00	1.35	.35
☐ 361 Harmon Killebrew AS	8.00	3.60	1.00
☐ 362 Orlando Cepeda AS	4.00	1.80	.50
☐ 363 Rod Carew AS	8.00	3.60	1.00
☐ 364 Joe Morgan AS	8.00	3.60	1.00
☐ 365 Brooks Robinson AS	8.00	3.60	1.00
☐ 366 Ron Santo AS	3.00	1.35	.35
☐ 367 Jim Fregosi AS	2.50	1.10	.30
☐ 368 Gene Alley AS	2.50	1.10	.30
☐ 369 Carl Yastrzemski AS	10.00	4.50	1.25
☐ 370 Hank Aaron AS	20.00	9.00	2.50
☐ 371 Tony Oliva AS	3.00	1.35	.35
☐ 372 Lou Brock AS	8.00	3.60	1.00
☐ 373 Frank Robinson AS	8.00	3.60	1.00
☐ 374 Bob Clemente AS	30.00	13.50	3.70
☐ 375 Bill Freehan AS	3.00	1.35	.35
☐ 376 Tim McCarver AS	3.00	1.35	.35
☐ 377 Joel Horlen AS	2.50	1.10	.30
☐ 378 Bob Gibson AS	8.00	3.60	1.00
☐ 379 Gary Peters AS	2.50	1.10	.30
☐ 380 Ken Holtzman AS	2.50	1.10	.30
☐ 381 Boog Powell	4.00	1.80	.50
☐ 382 Ramon Hernandez	1.75	.80	.22
☐ 383 Steve Whitaker	1.75	.80	.22
☐ 384 Reds Rookies	6.00	2.70	.75
Bill Henry			
Hal McRae			
☐ 385 Jim Hunter	12.00	5.50	1.50
☐ 386 Greg Goossen	1.75	.80	.22
☐ 387 Joe Foy	1.75	.80	.22
☐ 388 Ray Washburn	1.75	.80	.22
☐ 389 Jay Johnstone	2.00	.90	.25
☐ 390 Bill Mazeroski	4.00	1.80	.50
☐ 391 Bob Priddy	1.75	.80	.22
☐ 392 Grady Hatton MG	1.75	.80	.22
☐ 393 Jim Perry	2.00	.90	.25
☐ 394 Tommie Aaron	2.00	.90	.25
☐ 395 Camilo Pascual	2.00	.90	.25
☐ 396 Bobby Wine	1.75	.80	.22
☐ 397 Vic Davalillo	1.75	.80	.22
☐ 398 Jim Grant	1.75	.80	.22
☐ 399 Ray Oyler	2.00	.90	.25
☐ 400A Mike McCormick	2.00	.90	.25
(Yellow letters)			
☐ 400B Mike McCormick	125.00	55.00	15.50
(Team name in			
white letters)			
☐ 401 Mets Team	3.50	1.55	.45
☐ 402 Mike Hegan	2.00	.90	.25
☐ 403 John Buzhardt	1.75	.80	.22
☐ 404 Floyd Robinson	1.75	.80	.22
☐ 405 Tommy Helms	2.00	.90	.25
☐ 406 Dick Ellsworth	1.75	.80	.22
☐ 407 Gary Kolb	1.75	.80	.22
☐ 408 Steve Carlton	30.00	13.50	3.70
☐ 409 Orioles Rookies	1.75	.80	.22
Frank Peters			
Ron Stone			
☐ 410 Fergie Jenkins	12.00	5.50	1.50
☐ 411 Ron Hansen	1.75	.80	.22
☐ 412 Clay Carroll	2.00	.90	.25
☐ 413 Tom McCraw	1.75	.80	.22
☐ 414 Mickey Lolich	8.00	3.60	1.00
☐ 415 Johnny Callison	2.00	.90	.25
☐ 416 Bill Rigney MG	1.75	.80	.22
☐ 417 Willie Crawford	1.75	.80	.22
☐ 418 Eddie Fisher	1.75	.80	.22
☐ 419 Jack Hiatt	1.75	.80	.22
☐ 420 Cesar Tovar	1.75	.80	.22
☐ 421 Ron Taylor	1.75	.80	.22
☐ 422 Rene Lachemann	1.75	.80	.22
☐ 423 Fred Gladding	1.75	.80	.22
☐ 424 Chicago White Sox	3.50	1.55	.45
Team Card			
☐ 425 Jim Maloney	2.00	.90	.25
☐ 426 Hank Allen	1.75	.80	.22
☐ 427 Dick Calmus	1.75	.80	.22
☐ 428 Vic Roznovsky	1.75	.80	.22
☐ 429 Tommie Sisk	1.75	.80	.22
☐ 430 Rico Petrocelli	2.00	.90	.25
☐ 431 Dooley Womack	1.75	.80	.22
☐ 432 Indians Rookies	1.75	.80	.22
Bill Davis			
Jose Vidal			
☐ 433 Bob Rodgers	1.75	.80	.22
☐ 434 Ricardo Joseph	1.75	.80	.22
☐ 435 Ron Perranoski	2.00	.90	.25
☐ 436 Hal Lanier	1.75	.80	.22
☐ 437 Don Cardwell	1.75	.80	.22
☐ 438 Lee Thomas	2.00	.90	.25
☐ 439 Lum Harris MG	1.75	.80	.22
☐ 440 Claude Osteen	2.00	.90	.25
☐ 441 Alex Johnson	2.00	.90	.25
☐ 442 Dick Bosman	1.75	.80	.22
☐ 443 Joe Azcue	1.75	.80	.22
☐ 444 Jack Fisher	1.75	.80	.22
☐ 445 Mike Shannon	2.00	.90	.25
☐ 446 Ron Kline	1.75	.80	.22
☐ 447 Tigers Rookies	2.50	1.10	.30
George Korince			
Fred Lasher			
☐ 448 Gary Wagner	1.75	.80	.22
☐ 449 Gene Oliver	1.75	.80	.22
☐ 450 Jim Kaat	5.00	2.20	.60
☐ 451 Al Spangler	1.75	.80	.22
☐ 452 Jesus Alou	1.75	.80	.22
☐ 453 Sammy Ellis	1.75	.80	.22
☐ 454A Checklist 6	7.50	1.50	.75
Frank Robinson			
(Cap complete			
within circle)			
☐ 454B Checklist 6	7.50	1.50	.75
Frank Robinson			
(Cap partially			
within circle)			
☐ 455 Rico Carty	2.00	.90	.25
☐ 456 John O'Donoghue	1.75	.80	.22
☐ 457 Jim Lefebvre	2.00	.90	.25
☐ 458 Lew Krausse	4.00	1.80	.50
☐ 459 Dick Simpson	3.50	1.55	.45
☐ 460 Jim Lonborg	4.00	1.80	.50
☐ 461 Chuck Hiller	3.50	1.55	.45
☐ 462 Barry Moore	3.50	1.55	.45
☐ 463 Jim Schaffer	3.50	1.55	.45
☐ 464 Don McMahon	3.50	1.55	.45
☐ 465 Tommie Agee	4.00	1.80	.50
☐ 466 Bill Dillman	3.50	1.55	.45
☐ 467 Dick Howser	4.00	1.80	.50
☐ 468 Larry Sherry	3.50	1.55	.45
☐ 469 Ty Cline	3.50	1.55	.45
☐ 470 Bill Freehan	5.00	2.20	.60
☐ 471 Orlando Pena	3.50	1.55	.45
☐ 472 Walt Alston MG	5.00	2.20	.60
☐ 473 Al Worthington	3.50	1.55	.45
☐ 474 Paul Schaal	3.50	1.55	.45
☐ 475 Joe Niekro	5.00	2.20	.60
☐ 476 Woody Woodward	4.00	1.80	.50
☐ 477 Philadelphia Phillies	7.00	3.10	.85
Team Card			
☐ 478 Dave McNally	4.00	1.80	.50
☐ 479 Phil Gagliano	3.50	1.55	.45
☐ 480 Manager's Dream	80.00	36.00	10.00
Tony Oliva			
Chico Cardenas			
Bob Clemente			
☐ 481 John Wyatt	3.50	1.55	.45
☐ 482 Jose Pagan	3.50	1.55	.45
☐ 483 Darold Knowles	3.50	1.55	.45
☐ 484 Phil Roof	3.50	1.55	.45
☐ 485 Ken Berry	3.50	1.55	.45
☐ 486 Cal Koonce	3.50	1.55	.45
☐ 487 Lee May	4.00	1.80	.50
☐ 488 Dick Tracewski	4.50	2.00	.55
☐ 489 Wally Bunker	3.50	1.55	.45
☐ 490 Super Stars	175.00	80.00	22.00
Harmon Killebrew			
Willie Mays			
Mickey Mantle			
☐ 491 Denny Lemaster	3.50	1.55	.45
☐ 492 Jeff Torborg	4.00	1.80	.50
☐ 493 Jim McGlothlin	3.50	1.55	.45
☐ 494 Ray Sadecki	3.50	1.55	.45
☐ 495 Leon Wagner	3.50	1.55	.45
☐ 496 Steve Hamilton	4.50	2.00	.55
☐ 497 Cardinals Team	7.00	3.10	.85
☐ 498 Bill Bryan	3.50	1.55	.45
☐ 499 Steve Blass	4.00	1.80	.50
☐ 500 Frank Robinson	30.00	13.50	3.70
☐ 501 John Odom	4.00	1.80	.50
☐ 502 Mike Andrews	3.50	1.55	.45
☐ 503 Al Jackson	3.50	1.55	.45
☐ 504 Russ Snyder	3.50	1.55	.45
☐ 505 Joe Sparma	10.00	4.50	1.25
☐ 506 Clarence Jones	4.00	1.80	.50
☐ 507 Wade Blasingame	3.50	1.55	.45
☐ 508 Duke Sims	3.50	1.55	.45
☐ 509 Dennis Higgins	3.50	1.55	.45
☐ 510 Ron Fairly	4.00	1.80	.50
☐ 511 Bill Kelso	3.50	1.55	.45
☐ 512 Grant Jackson	3.50	1.55	.45
☐ 513 Hank Bauer MG	4.00	1.80	.50
☐ 514 Al McBean	3.50	1.55	.45
☐ 515 Russ Nixon	3.50	1.55	.45
☐ 516 Pete Mikkelsen	3.50	1.55	.45
☐ 517 Diego Segui	4.00	1.80	.50
☐ 518A Checklist 7 ERR	12.00	2.40	1.20
(539 AL Rookies)			
(Clete Boyer)			
☐ 518B Checklist 7 COR	12.00	2.40	1.20
(539 ML Rookies)			
(Clete Boyer)			
☐ 519 Jerry Stephenson	3.50	1.55	.45
☐ 520 Lou Brock	25.00	11.00	3.10
☐ 521 Don Shaw	3.50	1.55	.45
☐ 522 Wayne Causey	3.50	1.55	.45
☐ 523 John Tsitouris	3.50	1.55	.45
☐ 524 Andy Kosco	3.50	1.55	.45
☐ 525 Jim Davenport	3.50	1.55	.45
☐ 526 Bill Denehy	3.50	1.55	.45
☐ 527 Tito Francona	3.50	1.55	.45
☐ 528 Tigers Team	70.00	32.00	8.75
☐ 529 Bruce Von Hoff	3.50	1.55	.45
☐ 530 Bird Belters	40.00	18.00	5.00
Brooks Robinson			
Frank Robinson			
☐ 531 Chuck Hinton	3.50	1.55	.45
☐ 532 Luis Tiant	5.00	2.20	.60
☐ 533 Wes Parker	4.50	2.00	.55
☐ 534 Bob Miller	3.50	1.55	.45
☐ 535 Danny Cater	4.00	1.80	.50
☐ 536 Bill Short	3.50	1.55	.45
☐ 537 Norm Siebern	3.50	1.55	.45
☐ 538 Manny Jimenez	3.50	1.55	.45
☐ 539 Major League Rookies	3.50	1.55	.45
Jim Ray			
Mike Ferraro			
☐ 540 Nelson Briles	4.00	1.80	.50
☐ 541 Sandy Alomar	4.00	1.80	.50
☐ 542 John Boccabella	3.50	1.55	.45
☐ 543 Bob Lee	3.50	1.55	.45
☐ 544 Mayo Smith MG	8.00	3.60	1.00
☐ 545 Lindy McDaniel	4.00	1.80	.50
☐ 546 Roy White	4.50	2.00	.55
☐ 547 Dan Coombs	3.50	1.55	.45
☐ 548 Bernie Allen	3.50	1.55	.45
☐ 549 Orioles Rookies	3.50	1.55	.45
Curt Motton			
Roger Nelson			
☐ 550 Clete Boyer	4.00	1.80	.50
☐ 551 Darrell Sutherland	3.50	1.55	.45
☐ 552 Ed Kirkpatrick	3.50	1.55	.45
☐ 553 Hank Aguirre	3.50	1.55	.45
☐ 554 A's Team	8.00	3.60	1.00
☐ 555 Jose Tartabull	4.00	1.80	.50
☐ 556 Dick Selma	3.50	1.55	.45
☐ 557 Frank Quilici	3.50	1.55	.45
☐ 558 Johnny Edwards	3.50	1.55	.45
☐ 559 Pirates Rookies	3.50	1.55	.45
Carl Taylor			
Luke Walker			
☐ 560 Paul Casanova	3.50	1.55	.45
☐ 561 Lee Elia	3.50	1.55	.45
☐ 562 Jim Bouton	5.00	2.20	.60
☐ 563 Ed Charles	3.50	1.55	.45
☐ 564 Eddie Stanky MG	4.00	1.80	.50
☐ 565 Larry Dierker	4.00	1.80	.50
☐ 566 Ken Harrelson	4.00	1.80	.50
☐ 567 Clay Dalrymple	3.50	1.55	.45
☐ 568 Willie Smith	3.50	1.55	.45
☐ 569 NL Rookies	3.50	1.55	.45
Ivan Murrell			
Les Rohr			
☐ 570 Rick Reichardt	3.50	1.55	.45
☐ 571 Tony LaRussa	12.00	5.50	1.50
☐ 572 Don Bosch	3.50	1.55	.45
☐ 573 Joe Coleman	3.50	1.55	.45
☐ 574 Cincinnati Reds	8.00	3.60	1.00
Team Card			
☐ 575 Jim Palmer	35.00	16.00	4.40
☐ 576 Dave Adlesh	3.50	1.55	.45
☐ 577 Fred Talbot	3.50	1.55	.45
☐ 578 Orlando Martinez	3.50	1.55	.45
☐ 579 NL Rookies	5.00	2.20	.60
Larry Hisle			
Mike Lum			
☐ 580 Bob Bailey	3.50	1.55	.45
☐ 581 Garry Roggenburk	3.50	1.55	.45
☐ 582 Jerry Grote	4.00	1.80	.50
☐ 583 Gates Brown	8.00	3.60	1.00
☐ 584 Larry Shepard MG	3.50	1.55	.45
☐ 585 Wilbur Wood	4.00	1.80	.50
☐ 586 Jim Pagliaroni	4.00	1.80	.50
☐ 587 Roger Repoz	3.50	1.55	.45
☐ 588 Dick Schofield	3.50	1.55	.45
☐ 589 Twins Rookies	3.50	1.55	.45
Ron Clark			
Moe Ogier			
☐ 590 Tommy Harper	4.00	1.80	.50
☐ 591 Dick Nen	3.50	1.55	.45
☐ 592 John Bateman	3.50	1.55	.45
☐ 593 Lee Stange	3.50	1.55	.45
☐ 594 Phil Linz	4.00	1.80	.50
☐ 595 Phil Ortega	3.50	1.55	.45
☐ 596 Charlie Smith	3.50	1.55	.45
☐ 597 Bill McCool	3.50	1.55	.45
☐ 598 Jerry May	7.00	2.20	.65

1968 Topps Game

The cards in this 33-card set measure approximately 2 1/4" by 3 1/4". This "Game" card set of players, issued as inserts with the regular third series 1968 Topps baseball cards, was patterned directly after the Red Back and Blue Back sets of 1951. Each card has a color player photo set upon a pure white background, with a facsimile autograph underneath the picture. The cards have blue backs, and were also sold in boxed sets on a limited basis.

	NRMT	VG-E	GOOD
COMPLETE SET (33)	125.00	55.00	15.50
COMMON CARD (1-33)	.80	.35	.10

☐ 1 Matty Alou	1.00	.45	.12
☐ 2 Mickey Mantle	40.00	18.00	5.00
☐ 3 Carl Yastrzemski	4.00	1.80	.50
☐ 4 Hank Aaron	15.00	6.75	1.85
☐ 5 Harmon Killebrew	3.00	1.35	.35
☐ 6 Roberto Clemente	25.00	11.00	3.10
☐ 7 Frank Robinson	5.00	2.20	.60
☐ 8 Willie Mays	18.00	8.00	2.20
☐ 9 Brooks Robinson	5.00	2.20	.60
☐ 10 Tommy Davis	.80	.35	.10
☐ 11 Bill Freehan	1.00	.45	.12
☐ 12 Claude Osteen	.80	.35	.10
☐ 13 Gary Peters	.80	.35	.10
☐ 14 Jim Lonborg	.80	.35	.10
☐ 15 Steve Hargan	.80	.35	.10
☐ 16 Dean Chance	.80	.35	.10
☐ 17 Mike McCormick	.80	.35	.10
☐ 18 Tim McCarver	1.00	.45	.12
☐ 19 Ron Santo	1.00	.45	.12
☐ 20 Tony Gonzalez	.80	.35	.10
☐ 21 Frank Howard	1.00	.45	.12
☐ 22 George Scott	.80	.35	.10
☐ 23 Rich Allen	1.00	.45	.12
☐ 24 Jim Wynn	1.00	.45	.12
☐ 25 Gene Alley	.80	.35	.10
☐ 26 Rick Monday	.80	.35	.10
☐ 27 Al Kaline	5.00	2.20	.60
☐ 28 Rusty Staub	1.00	.45	.12
☐ 29 Rod Carew	5.00	2.20	.60
☐ 30 Pete Rose	15.00	6.75	1.85
☐ 31 Joe Torre	1.50	.70	.19
☐ 32 Orlando Cepeda	1.50	.70	.19
☐ 33 Jim Fregosi	1.00	.45	.12

1968 Topps 3-D

The cards in this 12-card set measure 2 1/4" by 3 1/2". Topps' experiment with "3-D" cards came two years before Kellogg's inaugural set. These cards are considered to be quite rare. This was a "test set" sold in a plain white wrapper with a sticker attached as a design, a device used by Topps for limited marketing. The cards employ a sharp foreground picture set against an indistinct background, covered by a layer of plastic to produce the "3-D" effect. The checklist below is ordered alphabetically.

	NRMT	VG-E	GOOD
COMPLETE SET (12)	12500.00	5600.00	1600.00
COMMON CARD (1-12)	750.00	350.00	95.00
WRAPPERS (10-CENTS)	1000.00	450.00	125.00

☐ 1 Roberto Clemente	6000.00	2700.00	750.00
☐ 2 Willie Davis	1200.00	550.00	150.00
☐ 3 Ron Fairly	750.00	350.00	95.00
☐ 4 Curt Flood	1200.00	550.00	150.00
☐ 5 Jim Lonborg	1200.00	550.00	150.00
☐ 6 Jim Maloney	1200.00	550.00	150.00
☐ 7 Tony Perez	2000.00	900.00	250.00
☐ 8 Boog Powell	1200.00	550.00	150.00
☐ 9 Bill Robinson	750.00	350.00	95.00
☐ 10 Rusty Staub	1200.00	550.00	150.00
☐ 11 Mel Stottlemyre	1200.00	550.00	150.00
☐ 12 Ron Swoboda	750.00	350.00	95.00

1968 Topps Action Stickers

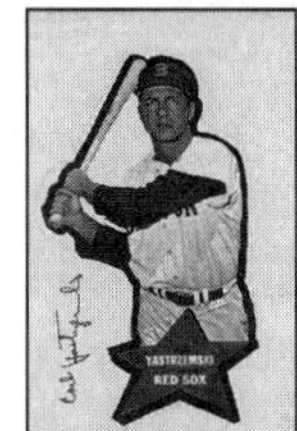

This test issue is a set of 16 long stickers which is perforated and can be divided into three stickers. The middle sticker features a large sticker depicting only one player, whereas the top and bottom stickers feature three smaller stickers. These stickers are attractive and colorful.

	NRMT	VG-E	GOOD
COMPLETE SET (48)	1800.00	800.00	220.00
COMMON INDIV. PANEL	7.50	3.40	.95
COMMON TRIPLE PANEL	30.00	13.50	3.70
WRAPPER (10-CENT)	400.00	180.00	50.00

☐ 1A Joel Horlen	7.50	3.40	.95
Orlando Cepeda			
Bill Mazeroski			

☐ 1B Carl Yastrzemski	125.00	55.00	15.50
☐ 1C Mel Stottlemyre	20.00	9.00	2.50
Al Kaline			
Claude Osteen			
☐ 2A Pete Ward	7.50	3.40	.95
Mike McCormick			
Ron Swoboda			
☐ 2B Harmon Killebrew	60.00	27.00	7.50
☐ 2C George Scott	15.00	6.75	1.85
Tom Phoebus			
Don Drysdale			
☐ 3A Jim Maloney	20.00	9.00	2.50
Joe Pepitone			
Henry Aaron			
☐ 3B Frank Robinson	75.00	34.00	9.50
☐ 3C Paul Casanova	20.00	9.00	2.50
Rick Reichardt			
Tom Seaver			
☐ 4A Frank Robinson	15.00	6.75	1.85
Jim Lefebvre			
Dean Chance			
☐ 4B Ron Santo	20.00	9.00	2.50
☐ 4C Johnny Callison	7.50	3.40	.95
Jim Lonborg			
Bob Aspromonte			
☐ 5A Bert Campaneris	7.50	3.40	.95
Ron Santo			
Al Downing			
☐ 5B Willie Mays	160.00	70.00	20.00
☐ 5C Pete Rose	75.00	34.00	9.50
Ed Kranepool			
Willie Horton			
☐ 6A Carl Yastrzemski	35.00	16.00	4.40
Max Alvis			
Walt Williams			
☐ 6B Al Kaline	100.00	45.00	12.50
☐ 6C Ernie Banks	35.00	16.00	4.40
Tim McCarver			
Rusty Staub			
☐ 7A Willie McCovey	20.00	9.00	2.50
Rick Monday			
Steve Hargan			
☐ 7B Mickey Mantle	350.00	160.00	45.00
☐ 7C Rod Carew	25.00	11.00	3.10
Tony Gonzalez			
Billy Williams			
☐ 8A Ken Boyer	15.00	6.75	1.85
Don Mincher			
Jim Bunning			
☐ 8B Joel Horlen	20.00	9.00	2.50
☐ 8C Tony Conigliaro	7.50	3.40	.95
Ken McMullen			
Mike Cuellar			
☐ 9A Harmon Killebrew	15.00	6.75	1.85
Jim Fregosi			
Earl Wilson			
☐ 9B Orlando Cepeda	35.00	16.00	4.40
☐ 9C Roberto Clemente	125.00	55.00	15.50
Willie Mays			
Chris Short			
☐ 10A Mickey Mantle	100.00	45.00	12.50
Jim Hunter			
Vada Pinson			
☐ 10B Hank Aaron	150.00	70.00	19.00
☐ 10C Gary Peters	15.00	6.75	1.85
Bob Gibson			
Ken Harrelson			
☐ 11A Tony Oliva	7.50	3.40	.95
Bob Veale			
Bill Freehan			
☐ 11B Don Drysdale	60.00	27.00	7.50
☐ 11C Frank Howard	7.50	3.40	.95
Fergie Jenkins			
Jim Wynn			
☐ 12A Joe Torre	7.50	3.40	.95
Dick Allen			
Jim McGlothlin			
☐ 12B Roberto Clemente	225.00	100.00	28.00
☐ 12C Brooks Robinson	25.00	11.00	3.10
Tony Perez			
Sam McDowell			
☐ 13A Frank Robinson	20.00	9.00	2.50
Jim Lefebvre			
Dean Chance			
☐ 13B Carl Yastrzemski	125.00	55.00	15.50
☐ 13C Tom Phoebus	15.00	6.75	1.85
George Scott			
Don Drysdale			
☐ 14A Joel Horlen	7.50	3.40	.95
Orlando Cepeda			
Bill Mazeroski			
☐ 14B Harmon Killebrew	60.00	27.00	7.50
☐ 14C Paul Casanova	20.00	9.00	2.50
Rick Reichardt			
Tom Seaver			
☐ 15A Pete Ward	7.50	3.40	.95
Mike McCormick			
Ron Swoboda			
☐ 15B Frank Robinson	100.00	45.00	12.50
☐ 15C Johnny Callison	7.50	3.40	.95
Jim Lonborg			
Bob Aspromonte			
☐ 16A Jim Maloney	20.00	9.00	2.50
Joe Pepitone			
Henry Aaron			
☐ 16B Ron Santo	20.00	9.00	2.50
☐ 16C Mel Stottlemyre	20.00	9.00	2.50
Al Kaline			
Claude Osteen			

1968 Topps Plaks

These brown plastic "busts," measue roughly 1" by 2". Checklists are cards measuring 2 1/8 by 4. The set is sequenced and therefore checklisted in alphabetical order within each league.

	NRMT	VG-E	GOOD
COMPLETE SET (26)	6500.00	2900.00	800.00
COMMON PLAYER	75.00	34.00	9.50
*WRAPPER (10-CENT)	600.00	275.00	75.00
☐ 1 Max Alvis	75.00	34.00	9.50
☐ 2 Dean Chance	125.00	55.00	15.50
☐ 3 Jim Fregosi	125.00	55.00	15.50
☐ 4 Frank Howard	125.00	55.00	15.50
☐ 5 Jim Hunter	200.00	90.00	25.00
☐ 6 Al Kaline	350.00	160.00	45.00
☐ 7 Harmon Killebrew	250.00	110.00	31.00
☐ 8 Jim Lonborg	125.00	55.00	15.50
☐ 9 Mickey Mantle	1500.00	700.00	190.00
☐ 10 Gary Peters	75.00	34.00	9.50
☐ 11 Frank Robinson	250.00	110.00	31.00
☐ 12 Carl Yastrzemski	300.00	135.00	38.00
☐ 13 Hank Aaron	750.00	350.00	95.00
☐ 14 Richie Allen	125.00	55.00	15.50
☐ 15 Orlando Cepeda	175.00	80.00	22.00
☐ 16 Roberto Clemente	900.00	400.00	110.00
☐ 17 Tommy Davis	125.00	55.00	15.50
☐ 18 Don Drysdale	250.00	110.00	31.00
☐ 19 Willie Mays	800.00	350.00	100.00
☐ 20 Tim McCarver	125.00	55.00	15.50
☐ 21 Pete Rose	750.00	350.00	95.00
☐ 22 Ron Santo	125.00	55.00	15.50
☐ 23 Rusty Staub	125.00	55.00	15.50
☐ 24 Jim Wynn	125.00	55.00	15.50
☐ NNO Checklist Card 1-12	75.00	34.00	9.50
☐ NNO Checklist Card 13-24	75.00	34.00	9.50

1968 Topps Posters

This 1968 color poster set is not an "insert" but was issued separately with a piece of gum and in its own wrapper. The posters are numbered at the lower left and the player's name and team appear in a large star. The poster was folded six times to fit into the package, so fold lines are a factor in grading. Each poster measures 9 3/4" by 18 1/8".

	NRMT	VG-E	GOOD
COMPLETE SET (24)	300.00	135.00	38.00
COMMON CARD (1-24)	2.50	1.10	.30
☐ 1 Dean Chance	3.50	1.55	.45
☐ 2 Max Alvis	2.50	1.10	.30
☐ 3 Frank Howard	3.50	1.55	.45
☐ 4 Jim Fregosi	3.50	1.55	.45
☐ 5 Jim Hunter	10.00	4.50	1.25
☐ 6 Bob Clemente	60.00	27.00	7.50
☐ 7 Don Drysdale	10.00	4.50	1.25
☐ 8 Jim Wynn	2.50	1.10	.30
☐ 9 Al Kaline	15.00	6.75	1.85
☐ 10 Harmon Killebrew	12.00	5.50	1.50
☐ 11 Jim Lonborg	3.50	1.55	.45
☐ 12 Orlando Cepeda	5.00	2.20	.60
☐ 13 Gary Peters	2.50	1.10	.30
☐ 14 Hank Aaron	20.00	9.00	2.50
☐ 15 Richie Allen	3.50	1.55	.45
☐ 16 Carl Yastrzemski	15.00	6.75	1.85
☐ 17 Ron Swoboda	2.50	1.10	.30
☐ 18 Mickey Mantle	75.00	34.00	9.50
☐ 19 Tim McCarver	3.50	1.55	.45
☐ 20 Willie Mays	20.00	9.00	2.50
☐ 21 Ron Santo	3.50	1.55	.45
☐ 22 Rusty Staub	3.50	1.55	.45
☐ 23 Pete Rose	40.00	18.00	5.00
☐ 24 Frank Robinson	15.00	6.75	1.85

1968 Topps Venezuelan

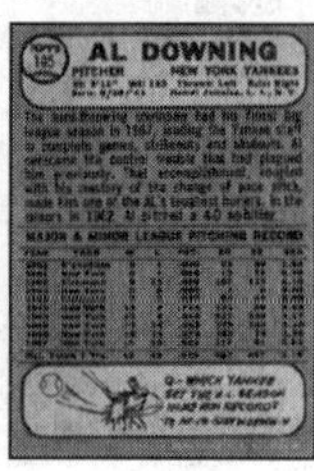

This set is a parallel version of the first 370 cards of the regular 1968 Topps set and is similar in design. The difference is the line "Hecho en Venezuela - C. A. Litoven" printed at the bottom on the back of the card.

	NRMT	VG-E	GOOD
COMPLETE SET (376)	7000.00	3200.00	900.00
COMMON CARD (1-370)	4.00	1.80	.50
☐ 1 NL Batting Leaders	60.00	27.00	7.50
Bob Clemente			
Tony Gonzalez			
Matty Alou			
☐ 2 AL Batting Leaders	30.00	13.50	3.70
Carl Yastrzemski			
Frank Robinson			
Al Kaline			
☐ 3 NL RBI Leaders	40.00	18.00	5.00
Orlando Cepeda			
Bob Clemente			
Hank Aaron			
☐ 4 AL RBI Leaders	25.00	11.00	3.10
Carl Yastrzemski			
Harmon Killebrew			
Frank Robinson			
☐ 5 NL Home Run Leaders	15.00	6.75	1.85
Hank Aaron			
John Wynn			
Ron Santo			
Willie McCovey			
☐ 6 AL Home Run Leaders	15.00	6.75	1.85
Carl Yastrzemski			
Harmon Killebrew			
Frank Howard			
☐ 7 NL ERA Leaders	7.50	3.40	.95
Phil Neikro			
Jim Bunning			
Chris Short			
☐ 8 AL ERA Leaders	7.50	3.40	.95
Joel Horlen			
Gary Peters			
Sonny Siebert			
☐ 9 NL Pitching Leaders	7.50	3.40	.95
Mike McCormick			
Ferguson Jenkins			
Jim Bunning			
Claude Osteen			
☐ 10 AL Pitching Leaders	7.50	3.40	.95
Jim Lonborg			
Earl Wilson			
Dean Chance			
☐ 11 NL Strikeout Leaders	10.00	4.50	1.25
Jim Bunning			
Ferguson Jenkins			
Gaylor Perry			
☐ 12 AL Strikeout Leaders	10.00	4.50	1.25
Jim Lonborg UER			
(Misspelled Longberg on card back)			
Sam McDowell			
Dean Chance			
☐ 13 Chuck Hartenstein	4.00	1.80	.50
☐ 14 Jerry McNertney	4.00	1.80	.50
☐ 15 Ron Hunt	4.00	1.80	.50
☐ 16 Indians Rookies	7.50	3.40	.95
Lou Piniella			
Richie Scheinblum			
☐ 17 Dick Hall	4.00	1.80	.50
☐ 18 Mike Hershberger	4.00	1.80	.50
☐ 19 Juan Pizarro	4.00	1.80	.50
☐ 20 Brooks Robinson	60.00	27.00	7.50
☐ 21 Ron Davis	4.00	1.80	.50
☐ 22 Pat Dobson	4.00	1.80	.50
☐ 23 Chico Cardenas	4.00	1.80	.50
☐ 24 Bobby Locke	4.00	1.80	.50
☐ 25 Julian Javier	4.00	1.80	.50
☐ 26 Darrell Brandon	4.00	1.80	.50
☐ 27 Gil Hodges MG	20.00	9.00	2.50
☐ 28 Ted Uhlaender	4.00	1.80	.50
☐ 29 Joe Verbanic	4.00	1.80	.50
☐ 30 Joe Torre	10.00	4.50	1.25
☐ 31 Ed Stroud	4.00	1.80	.50
☐ 32 Joe Gibbon	4.00	1.80	.50
☐ 33 Pete Ward	4.00	1.80	.50
☐ 34 Al Ferrara	4.00	1.80	.50
☐ 35 Steve Hargan	4.00	1.80	.50
☐ 36 Piarates Rookies	4.00	1.80	.50
Bob Moose			
Bob Robertson			
☐ 37 Billy Williams	25.00	11.00	3.10
☐ 38 Tony Pierce	4.00	1.80	.50
☐ 39 Cookie Rojas	4.00	1.80	.50
☐ 40 Denny McLain	25.00	11.00	3.10
☐ 41 Julio Gotay	4.00	1.80	.50
☐ 42 Larry Haney	4.00	1.80	.50
☐ 43 Gary Bell	4.00	1.80	.50
☐ 44 Frank Kostro	4.00	1.80	.50
☐ 45 Tom Seaver	125.00	55.00	15.50
☐ 46 Dave Ricketts	4.00	1.80	.50
☐ 47 Ralph Houk MG	4.00	1.80	.50
☐ 48 Ted Davidson	4.00	1.80	.50
☐ 49 Eddie Brinkman	4.00	1.80	.50
☐ 50 Willie Mays	150.00	70.00	19.00
☐ 51 Bob Locker	4.00	1.80	.50
☐ 52 Hawk Taylor	4.00	1.80	.50
☐ 53 Gene Alley	4.00	1.80	.50
☐ 54 Stan Williams	4.00	1.80	.50
☐ 55 Felipe Alou	7.50	3.40	.95
☐ 56 Orioles Rookies	4.00	1.80	.50
Dave Leonhard			
Dave May			
☐ 57 Dan Schneider	4.00	1.80	.50
☐ 58 Eddie Mathews	40.00	18.00	5.00
☐ 59 Don Lock	4.00	1.80	.50
☐ 60 Ken Holtzman	4.00	1.80	.50
☐ 61 Reggie Smith	7.50	3.40	.95
☐ 62 Chuck Dobson	4.00	1.80	.50
☐ 63 Dick Kenworthy	4.00	1.80	.50
☐ 64 Jim Merritt	4.00	1.80	.50
☐ 65 John Roseboro	4.00	1.80	.50
☐ 66 Casey Cox	4.00	1.80	.50
☐ 67 Checklist 1	12.00	5.50	1.50
Jim Kaat			
☐ 68 Ron Willis	4.00	1.80	.50
☐ 69 Tom Tresh	4.00	1.80	.50
☐ 70 Bob Veale	4.00	1.80	.50
☐ 71 Vern Fuller	4.00	1.80	.50
☐ 72 Tommy John	10.00	4.50	1.25
☐ 73 Jim Ray Hart	4.00	1.80	.50
☐ 74 Milt Pappas	4.00	1.80	.50
☐ 75 Don Mincher	4.00	1.80	.50
☐ 76 Braves Rookies	4.00	1.80	.50
Jim Britton			
Ron Reed			
☐ 77 Don Wilson	4.00	1.80	.50
☐ 78 Jim Northrup	4.00	1.80	.50
☐ 79 Ted Kubiak	4.00	1.80	.50
☐ 80 Rod Carew	125.00	55.00	15.50
☐ 81 Larry Jackson	4.00	1.80	.50
☐ 83 John Stephenson	4.00	1.80	.50
☐ 83 Sam Bowens	4.00	1.80	.50
☐ 84 Bob Tolan	4.00	1.80	.50
☐ 85 Gaylord Perry	20.00	9.00	2.50
☐ 86 Willie Stargell	20.00	9.00	2.50
☐ 87 Dick Williams MG	4.00	1.80	.50
☐ 88 Phil Regan	4.00	1.80	.50
☐ 89 Jake Gibbs	4.00	1.80	.50
☐ 90 Vada Pinson	10.00	4.50	1.25
☐ 91 Jim Ollom	4.00	1.80	.50
☐ 92 Ed Kranepool	4.00	1.80	.50
☐ 93 Tony Cloninger	4.00	1.80	.50
☐ 94 Lee Maye	4.00	1.80	.50
☐ 95 Bob Aspromonte	4.00	1.80	.50
☐ 96 Senator Rookies	4.00	1.80	.50
Frank Coggins			
Dick Nold			
☐ 97 Tom Phoebus	4.00	1.80	.50
☐ 98 Gary Sutherland	4.00	1.80	.50
☐ 99 Rocky Colavito	20.00	9.00	2.50
☐ 100 Bob Gibson	60.00	27.00	7.50
☐ 101 Glenn Beckert	4.00	1.80	.50
☐ 102 Jose Cardenal	4.00	1.80	.50
☐ 103 Don Sutton	15.00	6.75	1.85
☐ 104 Dick Dietz	4.00	1.80	.50
☐ 105 Al Downing	4.00	1.80	.50
☐ 106 Dalton Jones	4.00	1.80	.50
☐ 107 Checklist 2	12.00	5.50	1.50
Juan Marichal			
☐ 108 Don Pavletich	4.00	1.80	.50
☐ 109 Bert Campaneris	4.00	1.80	.50
☐ 110 Hank Aaron	150.00	70.00	19.00
☐ 111 Rich Reese	4.00	1.80	.50
☐ 112 Woody Fryman	4.00	1.80	.50
☐ 113 Tigers Rookies	4.00	1.80	.50
Tom Matchick			
Daryl Patterson			
☐ 114 Ron Swoboda	4.00	1.80	.50
☐ 115 Sam McDowell	4.00	1.80	.50
☐ 116 Ken McMullen	4.00	1.80	.50
☐ 117 Larry Jaster	4.00	1.80	.50
☐ 118 Mark Belanger	4.00	1.80	.50
☐ 119 Ted Savage	4.00	1.80	.50
☐ 120 Mel Stottlemyre	4.00	1.80	.50
☐ 121 Jimmie Hall	4.00	1.80	.50
☐ 122 Gene Mauch MG	4.00	1.80	.50
☐ 123 Jose Santiago	4.00	1.80	.50
☐ 124 Nate Oliver	4.00	1.80	.50
☐ 125 Joel Horlen	4.00	1.80	.50
☐ 126 Bobby Etheridge	4.00	1.80	.50
☐ 127 Paul Lindblad	4.00	1.80	.50
☐ 128 Astros Rookies	4.00	1.80	.50
Tom Dukes			
Alonzo Harris			
☐ 129 Mickey Stanley	4.00	1.80	.50
☐ 130 Tony Perez	20.00	9.00	2.50
☐ 131 Frank Bertaina	4.00	1.80	.50

☐ 132 Bud Harrelson 4.00 1.80 .50
☐ 133 Fred Whitfield 4.00 1.80 .50
☐ 134 Pat Jarvis 4.00 1.80 .50
☐ 135 Paul Blair 4.00 1.80 .50
☐ 136 Randy Hundley 4.00 1.80 .50
☐ 137 Twins Team 4.00 1.80 .50
☐ 138 Ruben Amaro 4.00 1.80 .50
☐ 139 Chris Short 4.00 1.80 .50
☐ 140 Tony Conigliaro 20.00 9.00 2.50
☐ 141 Dal Maxvill 4.00 1.80 .50
☐ 142 White Sox Rookies 4.00 1.80 .50
Buddy Bradford
Bill Voss
☐ 143 Pete Cimino 4.00 1.80 .50
☐ 144 Joe Morgan 30.00 13.50 3.70
☐ 145 Don Drysdale 30.00 13.50 3.70
☐ 146 Sal Bando 4.00 1.80 .50
☐ 147 Frank Linzy 4.00 1.80 .50
☐ 148 Dave Bristol MG 4.00 1.80 .50
☐ 149 Bob Saverine 4.00 1.80 .50
☐ 150 Bob Clemente 175.00 80.00 22.00
☐ 151 Lou Brock WS 25.00 11.00 3.10
☐ 152 Carl Yastrzemski WS 25.00 11.00 3.10
☐ 153 Nellie Briles WS 10.00 4.50 1.25
☐ 154 Bob Gibson WS 20.00 9.00 2.50
☐ 155 Jim Lonborg WS 10.00 4.50 1.25
☐ 156 Rico Petrocelli WS 10.00 4.50 1.25
☐ 157 World Series Game 7 10.00 4.50 1.25
St. Louis wins it
☐ 158 World Series Summary 10.00 4.50 1.25
Cardinals celebrate
☐ 159 Don Kessinger 4.00 1.80 .50
☐ 160 Earl Wilson 4.00 1.80 .50
☐ 161 Norm Miller 4.00 1.80 .50
☐ 162 Cards Rookies 4.00 1.80 .50
Hal Gibson
Mike Torrez
☐ 163 Gene Brabender 4.00 1.80 .50
☐ 164 Ramon Webster 4.00 1.80 .50
☐ 165 Tony Oliva 10.00 4.50 1.25
☐ 166 Claude Raymond 4.00 1.80 .50
☐ 167 Elston Howard 10.00 4.50 1.25
☐ 168 Dodgers Team 4.00 1.80 .50
☐ 169 Bob Bolin 4.00 1.80 .50
☐ 170 Jim Fregosi 4.00 1.80 .50
☐ 171 Don Nottebart 4.00 1.80 .50
☐ 172 Walt Williams 4.00 1.80 .50
☐ 173 John Boozer 4.00 1.80 .50
☐ 174 Bob Tillman 4.00 1.80 .50
☐ 175 Maury Wills 10.00 4.50 1.25
☐ 176 Bob Allen 4.00 1.80 .50
☐ 177 Mets Rookies 3000.00 1350.00 375.00
Jerry Koosman
Nolan Ryan
☐ 178 Don Wert 4.00 1.80 .50
☐ 179 Bill Stoneman 4.00 1.80 .50
☐ 180 Curt Flood 10.00 4.50 1.25
☐ 181 Jerry Zimmerman 4.00 1.80 .50
☐ 182 Dave Giusti 4.00 1.80 .50
☐ 183 Bob Kennedy MG 4.00 1.80 .50
☐ 184 Lou Johnson 4.00 1.80 .50
☐ 185 Tom Haller 4.00 1.80 .50
☐ 186 Eddie Watt 4.00 1.80 .50
☐ 187 Sonny Jackson 4.00 1.80 .50
☐ 188 Cap Peterson 4.00 1.80 .50
☐ 189 Bill Landis 4.00 1.80 .50
☐ 190 Bill White 10.00 4.50 1.25
☐ 191 Dan Frisella 4.00 1.80 .50
☐ 192 Checklist 3 20.00 9.00 2.50
Carl Yastrzemski
☐ 193 Jack Hamilton 4.00 1.80 .50
☐ 194 Don Buford 4.00 1.80 .50
☐ 195 Joe Pepitone 4.00 1.80 .50
☐ 196 Gary Nolan 4.00 1.80 .50
☐ 197 Larry Brown 4.00 1.80 .50
☐ 198 Roy Face 4.00 1.80 .50
☐ 199 A's Rookies 4.00 1.80 .50
Roberto Rodriguez
Darrell f0steen
☐ 200 Orlando Cepeda 12.50 5.50 1.55
☐ 201 Mike Marshall 4.00 1.80 .50
☐ 202 Adolfo Phillips 4.00 1.80 .50
☐ 203 Dick Kelley 4.00 1.80 .50
☐ 204 Andy Etchebarren 4.00 1.80 .50
☐ 205 Juan Marichal 20.00 9.00 2.50
☐ 206 Cal Ermer MG 4.00 1.80 .50
☐ 207 Carroll Sembera 4.00 1.80 .50
☐ 208 Willie Davis 4.00 1.80 .50
☐ 209 Tim Cullen 4.00 1.80 .50
☐ 210 Gary Peters 4.00 1.80 .50
☐ 211 J.C. Martin 4.00 1.80 .50
☐ 212 Dave Morehead 4.00 1.80 .50
☐ 213 Chico Ruiz 4.00 1.80 .50
☐ 214 Yankees Rookies 4.00 1.80 .50
Stan Bahnsen
Frank Fernandez
☐ 215 Jim Bunning 20.00 9.00 2.50
☐ 216 Bubba Morton 4.00 1.80 .50
☐ 217 Dick Farrell 4.00 1.80 .50
☐ 218 Ken Suarez 4.00 1.80 .50
☐ 219 Rob Gardner 4.00 1.80 .50
☐ 220 Harmon Killebrew 35.00 16.00 4.40
☐ 221 Braves Team 7.50 3.40 .95
☐ 222 Jim Hardin 4.00 1.80 .50
☐ 223 Ollie Brown 4.00 1.80 .50
☐ 224 Jack Aker 4.00 1.80 .50
☐ 225 Richie Allen 15.00 6.75 1.85
☐ 226 Jimmie Price 4.00 1.80 .50
☐ 227 Joe Hoerner 4.00 1.80 .50
☐ 228 Dodgers Rookies 4.00 1.80 .50
Jack Billingham
Jim Fairey
☐ 229 Fred Klages 4.00 1.80 .50
☐ 230 Pete Rose 100.00 45.00 12.50
☐ 231 Dave Baldwin 4.00 1.80 .50
☐ 232 Denis Manke 4.00 1.80 .50
☐ 233 George Scott 4.00 1.80 .50
☐ 234 Bill Monbouquette 4.00 1.80 .50
☐ 235 Ron Santo 12.50 5.50 1.55
☐ 236 Tug McGraw 10.00 4.50 1.25
☐ 237 Alvin Dark MG 7.50 3.40 .95
☐ 238 Tom Satriano 4.00 1.80 .50
☐ 239 Bill Henry 4.00 1.80 .50
☐ 240 Al Kaline 60.00 27.00 7.50
☐ 241 Felix Millan 4.00 1.80 .50
☐ 242 Moe Drabowsky 4.00 1.80 .50
☐ 243 Rich Rollins 4.00 1.80 .50
☐ 244 John Donaldson 4.00 1.80 .50
☐ 245 Tony Gonzalez 4.00 1.80 .50
☐ 246 Fritz Peterson 4.00 1.80 .50
☐ 247 Reds Rookies 300.00 135.00 38.00
Johnny Bench
Ron Tompkins
☐ 248 Fred Valentine 4.00 1.80 .50
☐ 249 Bill Singer 4.00 1.80 .50
☐ 250 Carl Yastrzemski 60.00 27.00 7.50
☐ 251 Manny Sanguillen 12.00 5.50 1.50
☐ 252 Angels Team 7.50 3.40 .95
☐ 253 Dick Hughes 4.00 1.80 .50
☐ 254 Cleon Jones 4.00 1.80 .50
☐ 255 Dean Chance 4.00 1.80 .50
☐ 256 Norm Cash 15.00 6.75 1.85
☐ 257 Phil Niekro 20.00 9.00 2.50
☐ 258 Cubs Rookies 4.00 1.80 .50
Jose Arcia
Bill Schlesinger
☐ 259 Ken Boyer 7.50 3.40 .95
☐ 260 Jim Wynn 4.00 1.80 .50
☐ 261 Dave Duncan 4.00 1.80 .50
☐ 262 Rick Wise 4.00 1.80 .50
☐ 263 Horace Clarke 4.00 1.80 .50
☐ 264 Ted Abernathy 4.00 1.80 .50
☐ 265 Tommy Davis 4.00 1.80 .50
☐ 266 Paul Popovich 4.00 1.80 .50
☐ 267 Herman Franks MG 4.00 1.80 .50
☐ 268 Bob Humphreys 4.00 1.80 .50
☐ 269 Bob Tiefenauer 4.00 1.80 .50
☐ 270 Matty Alou 7.50 3.40 .95
☐ 271 Bobby Knoop 4.00 1.80 .50
☐ 272 Ray Culp 4.00 1.80 .50
☐ 273 Dave Johnson 7.50 3.40 .95
☐ 274 Mike Cuellar 7.50 3.40 .95
☐ 275 Tim McCarver 10.00 4.50 1.25
☐ 276 Jim Roland 4.00 1.80 .50
☐ 277 Jerry Buchek 4.00 1.80 .50
☐ 278 Checklist 4 12.00 5.50 1.50
Orlando Cepeda
☐ 279 Bill Hands 4.00 1.80 .50
☐ 280 Mickey Mantle 600.00 275.00 75.00
☐ 281 Jim Campanis 4.00 1.80 .50
☐ 282 Rick Monday 4.00 1.80 .50
☐ 283 Mel Queen 4.00 1.80 .50
☐ 284 Johnny Briggs 4.00 1.80 .50
☐ 285 Dick McAuliffe 4.00 1.80 .50
☐ 286 Cecil Upshaw 4.00 1.80 .50
☐ 287 White Sox Rookies 4.00 1.80 .50
Mickey Abarbanel
Cisco Carlos
☐ 288 Dave Wickersham 4.00 1.80 .50
☐ 289 Woody Held 4.00 1.80 .50
☐ 290 Willie McCovey 30.00 13.50 3.70
☐ 291 Dick Lines 4.00 1.80 .50
☐ 292 Art Shamsky 4.00 1.80 .50
☐ 293 Bruce Howard 4.00 1.80 .50
☐ 294 Red Schoendienst MG 10.00 4.50 1.25
☐ 295 Sonny Siebert 4.00 1.80 .50
☐ 296 Byron Browne 4.00 1.80 .50
☐ 297 Russ Gibson 4.00 1.80 .50
☐ 298 Jim Brewer 4.00 1.80 .50
☐ 299 Gene Michael 4.00 1.80 .50
☐ 300 Rusty Staub 7.50 3.40 .95
☐ 301 Twins Rookies 4.00 1.80 .50
George Mitterwald
Rick Renick
☐ 302 Gerry Arrigo 4.00 1.80 .50
☐ 303 Dick Green 4.00 1.80 .50
☐ 304 Sandy Valdespino 4.00 1.80 .50
☐ 305 Minnie Rojas 4.00 1.80 .50
☐ 306 Mike Ryan 4.00 1.80 .50
☐ 307 John Hiller 4.00 1.80 .50
☐ 308 Pirates Team 7.50 3.40 .95
☐ 309 Ken Henderson 4.00 1.80 .50
☐ 310 Luis Aparicio 17.50 8.00 2.20
☐ 311 Jack Lamabe 4.00 1.80 .50
☐ 312 Curt Blefary 4.00 1.80 .50
☐ 313 Al Weis 4.00 1.80 .50
☐ 314 Red Sox Rookies 4.00 1.80 .50
Bill Rohr
George Spriggs
☐ 315 Zoilo Versalles 4.00 1.80 .50
☐ 316 Steve Barber 4.00 1.80 .50
☐ 317 Ron Brand 4.00 1.80 .50
☐ 318 Chico Salmon 4.00 1.80 .50
☐ 319 George Culver 4.00 1.80 .50
☐ 320 Frank Howard 7.50 3.40 .95
☐ 321 Leo Durocher MG 10.00 4.50 1.25
☐ 322 Dave Boswell 4.00 1.80 .50
☐ 323 Deron Johnson 4.00 1.80 .50
☐ 324 Jim Nash 4.00 1.80 .50
☐ 325 Manny Mota 7.50 3.40 .95
☐ 326 Dennis Ribant 4.00 1.80 .50
☐ 327 Tony Taylor 4.00 1.80 .50
☐ 328 Angels Rookies 4.00 1.80 .50
Chuck Vinson
Jim Weaver
☐ 329 Duane Josephson 4.00 1.80 .50
☐ 330 Roger Maris 75.00 34.00 9.50
☐ 331 Dan Osinski 4.00 1.80 .50
☐ 332 Doug Rader 4.00 1.80 .50
☐ 333 Ron Herbel 4.00 1.80 .50
☐ 334 Orioles Team 4.00 1.80 .50
☐ 335 Bob Allison 4.00 1.80 .50
☐ 336 John Purdin 4.00 1.80 .50
☐ 337 Bill Robinson 4.00 1.80 .50
☐ 338 Bob Johnson 4.00 1.80 .50
☐ 339 Rich Nye 4.00 1.80 .50
☐ 340 Max Alvis 4.00 1.80 .50
☐ 341 Jim Lemon MG 4.00 1.80 .50
☐ 342 Ken Johnson 4.00 1.80 .50
☐ 343 Jim Gosger 4.00 1.80 .50
☐ 344 Donn Clendenon 4.00 1.80 .50
☐ 345 Bob Hendley 4.00 1.80 .50
☐ 346 Jerry Adair 4.00 1.80 .50
☐ 347 George Brunet 4.00 1.80 .50
☐ 348 Phillies Rookies 4.00 1.80 .50
Larry Colton
Dick Thoenen
☐ 349 Ed Spiezio 4.00 1.80 .50
☐ 350 Hoyt Wilhelm 15.00 6.75 1.85
☐ 351 Bob Barton 4.00 1.80 .50
☐ 352 Jackie Hernandez 4.00 1.80 .50
☐ 353 Mack Jones 4.00 1.80 .50
☐ 354 Pete Richert 4.00 1.80 .50
☐ 355 Ernie Banks 60.00 27.00 7.50
☐ 356 Checklist 5 12.00 5.50 1.50
Ken Holtzman
☐ 357 Len Gabrielson 4.00 1.80 .50
☐ 358 Mike Epstein 4.00 1.80 .50
☐ 359 Joe Moeller 4.00 1.80 .50
☐ 360 Willie Horton 7.50 3.40 .95
☐ 361 Harmon Killebrew AS 15.00 6.75 1.85
☐ 362 Orlando Cepeda AS 10.00 4.50 1.25
☐ 363 Rod Carew AS 15.00 6.75 1.85
☐ 364 Joe Morgan AS 15.00 6.75 1.85
☐ 365 Brooks Robinson AS 15.00 6.75 1.85
☐ 366 Ron Santo AS 7.50 3.40 .95
☐ 367 Jim Fregosi AS 4.00 1.80 .50
☐ 368 Gene Alley AS 4.00 1.80 .50
☐ 369 Carl Yastrzemski AS 25.00 11.00 3.10
☐ 370 Hank Aaron AS 50.00 22.00 6.25

1969 Topps

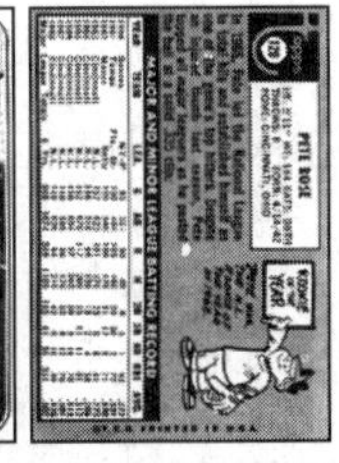

The cards in this 664-card set measure 2 1/2" by 3 1/2". The 1969 Topps set includes Sporting News All-Star Selections as card numbers 416 to 435. Other popular subsets within this set include League Leaders (1-12) and World Series cards (162-169). The fifth series contains several variations; the more difficult variety consists of cards with the player's first name, last name, and/or position in white letters instead of lettering in some other color. These are designated in the checklist below by WL (white letters). Each checklist card features a different popular player's picture inside a circle on the front of the checklist card. Two different team identifications of Clay Dalrymple and Donn Clendenon exist, as indicated in the checklist. The key Rookie Cards in this set are Rollie Fingers, Reggie Jackson, and Graig Nettles. This was the last year that Topps issued multi-player special star cards, ending a 13-year tradition, which they had begun in 1957. There were cropping differences in checklist cards 57, 214, and 412, due to their each being printed with two different series. The differences are difficult to explain and have not been greatly sought by collectors; hence they are not listed explicitly in the list below. The All-Star cards 426-435, when turned over and placed together, form a puzzle back of Pete Rose. This would turn out to be the final year that Topps issued cards in five-card nickle wax packs.

	NRMT	VG-E	GOOD
COMPLETE SET (664)	2200.00	1000.00	275.00
COMMON CARD (1-218)	1.50	.70	.19
COMMON CARD (219-327)	2.50	1.10	.30
COMMON CARD (328-512)	1.50	.70	.19
COMMON CARD (513-588)	2.00	.90	.25
COMMON CARD (589-664)	3.00	1.35	.35
WRAPPER (5-CENT)	20.00	9.00	2.50

☐ 1 AL Batting Leaders 14.00 5.00 2.00
Carl Yastrzemski
Danny Cater
Tony Oliva
☐ 2 NL Batting Leaders 7.00 3.10 .85
Pete Rose
Matty Alou
Felipe Alou
☐ 3 AL RBI Leaders 3.50 1.55 .45
Ken Harrelson
Frank Howard
Jim Northrup
☐ 4 NL RBI Leaders 6.00 2.70 .75
Willie McCovey
Ron Santo
Billy Williams
☐ 5 AL Home Run Leaders 3.50 1.55 .45
Frank Howard
Willie Horton
Ken Harrelson
☐ 6 NL Home Run Leaders 6.00 2.70 .75
Willie McCovey
Richie Allen
Ernie Banks
☐ 7 AL ERA Leaders 3.50 1.55 .45
Luis Tiant
Sam McDowell
Dave McNally
☐ 8 NL ERA Leaders 5.00 2.20 .60
Bob Gibson
Bobby Bolin
Bob Veale
☐ 9 AL Pitching Leaders 3.50 1.55 .45
Denny McLain
Dave McNally
Luis Tiant
Mel Stottlemyre
☐ 10 NL Pitching Leaders 7.00 3.10 .85
Juan Marichal
Bob Gibson
Fergie Jenkins
☐ 11 AL Strikeout Leaders 3.50 1.55 .45
Sam McDowell
Denny McLain
Luis Tiant
☐ 12 NL Strikeout Leaders 4.00 1.80 .50
Bob Gibson
Fergie Jenkins
Bill Singer
☐ 13 Mickey Stanley 2.00 .90 .25
☐ 14 Al McBean 1.50 .70 .19
☐ 15 Boog Powell 3.50 1.55 .45
☐ 16 Giants Rookies 1.50 .70 .19
Cesar Gutierrez
Rich Robertson
☐ 17 Mike Marshall 2.00 .90 .25
☐ 18 Dick Schofield 1.50 .70 .19
☐ 19 Ken Suarez 1.50 .70 .19
☐ 20 Ernie Banks 18.00 8.00 2.20
☐ 21 Jose Santiago 1.50 .70 .19
☐ 22 Jesus Alou 2.00 .90 .25
☐ 23 Lew Krausse 1.50 .70 .19
☐ 24 Walt Alston MG 2.50 1.10 .30
☐ 25 Roy White 2.00 .90 .25
☐ 26 Clay Carroll 2.00 .90 .25
☐ 27 Bernie Allen 1.50 .70 .19
☐ 28 Mike Ryan 1.50 .70 .19
☐ 29 Dave Morehead 1.50 .70 .19
☐ 30 Bob Allison 2.00 .90 .25
☐ 31 Mets Rookies 2.50 1.10 .30
Gary Gentry
Amos Otis
☐ 32 Sammy Ellis 1.50 .70 .19
☐ 33 Wayne Causey 1.50 .70 .19
☐ 34 Gary Peters 1.50 .70 .19
☐ 35 Joe Morgan 10.00 4.50 1.25
☐ 36 Luke Walker 1.50 .70 .19
☐ 37 Curt Motton 1.50 .70 .19
☐ 38 Zoilo Versalles 2.00 .90 .25
☐ 39 Dick Hughes 1.50 .70 .19
☐ 40 Mayo Smith MG 1.50 .70 .19
☐ 41 Bob Barton 1.50 .70 .19
☐ 42 Tommy Harper 2.00 .90 .25
☐ 43 Joe Niekro 2.00 .90 .25
☐ 44 Danny Cater 1.50 .70 .19
☐ 45 Maury Wills 3.00 1.35 .35
☐ 46 Fritz Peterson 2.00 .90 .25
☐ 47A Paul Popovich 1.50 .70 .19
(No helmet emblem)
☐ 47B Paul Popovich 25.00 11.00 3.10
(C emblem on helmet)
☐ 48 Brant Alyea 1.50 .70 .19
☐ 49A Royals Rookies ERR 25.00 11.00 3.10
Steve Jones
E. Rodriquez
☐ 49B Royals Rookies COR 1.50 .70 .19
Steve Jones
E. Rodriguez
☐ 50 Bob Clemente UER 50.00 22.00 6.25
(Bats Right
listed twice)
☐ 51 Woody Fryman 1.50 .70 .19
☐ 52 Mike Andrews 1.50 .70 .19
☐ 53 Sonny Jackson 1.50 .70 .19

☐ 54 Cisco Carlos 1.50 .70 .19
☐ 55 Jerry Grote 2.00 .90 .25
☐ 56 Rich Reese 1.50 .70 .19
☐ 57 Checklist 1 6.00 1.20 .60
Denny McLain
☐ 58 Fred Gladding 1.50 .70 .19
☐ 59 Jay Johnstone 2.00 .90 .25
☐ 60 Nelson Briles 2.00 .90 .25
☐ 61 Jimmie Hall 1.50 .70 .19
☐ 62 Chico Salmon 1.50 .70 .19
☐ 63 Jim Hickman 2.00 .90 .25
☐ 64 Bill Monbouquette 1.50 .70 .19
☐ 65 Willie Davis 2.00 .90 .25
☐ 66 Orioles Rookies 1.50 .70 .19
Mike Adamson
Merv Rettenmund
☐ 67 Bill Stoneman 2.00 .90 .25
☐ 68 Dave Duncan 2.00 .90 .25
☐ 69 Steve Hamilton 2.00 .90 .25
☐ 70 Tommy Helms 2.00 .90 .25
☐ 71 Steve Whitaker 2.00 .90 .25
☐ 72 Ron Taylor 1.50 .70 .19
☐ 73 Johnny Briggs 1.50 .70 .19
☐ 74 Preston Gomez MG 2.00 .90 .25
☐ 75 Luis Aparicio 5.00 2.20 .60
☐ 76 Norm Miller 1.50 .70 .19
☐ 77A Ron Perranoski 2.00 .90 .25
(No emblem on cap)
☐ 77B Ron Perranoski 25.00 11.00 3.10
(LA on cap)
☐ 78 Tom Satriano 1.50 .70 .19
☐ 79 Milt Pappas 2.00 .90 .25
☐ 80 Norm Cash 2.50 1.10 .30
☐ 81 Mel Queen 1.50 .70 .19
☐ 82 Pirates Rookies 10.00 4.50 1.25
Rich Hebner
Al Oliver
☐ 83 Mike Ferraro 2.00 .90 .25
☐ 84 Bob Humphreys 1.50 .70 .19
☐ 85 Lou Brock 18.00 8.00 2.20
☐ 86 Pete Richert 1.50 .70 .19
☐ 87 Horace Clarke 2.00 .90 .25
☐ 88 Rich Nye 1.50 .70 .19
☐ 89 Russ Gibson 1.50 .70 .19
☐ 90 Jerry Koosman 2.50 1.10 .30
☐ 91 Alvin Dark MG 2.00 .90 .25
☐ 92 Jack Billingham 2.00 .90 .25
☐ 93 Joe Foy 2.00 .90 .25
☐ 94 Hank Aguirre 1.50 .70 .19
☐ 95 Johnny Bench 45.00 20.00 5.50
☐ 96 Denny Lemaster 1.50 .70 .19
☐ 97 Buddy Bradford 1.50 .70 .19
☐ 98 Dave Giusti 1.50 .70 .19
☐ 99A Twins Rookies 16.00 7.25 2.00
Danny Morris
Graig Nettles
(No loop)
☐ 99B Twins Rookies 16.00 7.25 2.00
Danny Morris
Graig Nettles
(Errant loop in
upper left corner
of obverse)
☐ 100 Hank Aaron 35.00 16.00 4.40
☐ 101 Daryl Patterson 1.50 .70 .19
☐ 102 Jim Davenport 1.50 .70 .19
☐ 103 Roger Repoz 1.50 .70 .19
☐ 104 Steve Blass 2.00 .90 .25
☐ 105 Rick Monday 2.00 .90 .25
☐ 106 Jim Hannan 1.50 .70 .19
☐ 107A Checklist 2 ERR 6.00 1.20 .60
(161 Jim Purdin)
(Bob Gibson)
☐ 107B Checklist 2 COR 7.50 1.50 .75
(161 John Purdin)
(Bob Gibson)
☐ 108 Tony Taylor 2.00 .90 .25
☐ 109 Jim Lonborg 2.00 .90 .25
☐ 110 Mike Shannon 2.00 .90 .25
☐ 111 Johnny Morris 1.50 .70 .19
☐ 112 J.C. Martin 2.00 .90 .25
☐ 113 Dave May 1.50 .70 .19
☐ 114 Yankees Rookies 2.00 .90 .25
Alan Closter
John Cumberland
☐ 115 Bill Hands 1.50 .70 .19
☐ 116 Chuck Harrison 1.50 .70 .19
☐ 117 Jim Fairey 1.50 .70 .19
☐ 118 Stan Williams 1.50 .70 .19
☐ 119 Doug Rader 2.00 .90 .25
☐ 120 Pete Rose 25.00 11.00 3.10
☐ 121 Joe Grzenda 1.50 .70 .19
☐ 122 Ron Fairly 2.00 .90 .25
☐ 123 Wilbur Wood 2.00 .90 .25
☐ 124 Hank Bauer MG 2.00 .90 .25
☐ 125 Ray Sadecki 1.50 .70 .19
☐ 126 Dick Tracewski 1.50 .70 .19
☐ 127 Kevin Collins 2.00 .90 .25
☐ 128 Tommie Aaron 2.00 .90 .25
☐ 129 Bill McCool 1.50 .70 .19
☐ 130 Carl Yastrzemski 18.00 8.00 2.20
☐ 131 Chris Cannizzaro 1.50 .70 .19
☐ 132 Dave Baldwin 1.50 .70 .19
☐ 133 Johnny Callison 2.00 .90 .25
☐ 134 Jim Weaver 1.50 .70 .19
☐ 135 Tommy Davis 2.00 .90 .25
☐ 136 Cards Rookies 1.50 .70 .19
Steve Huntz
Mike Torrez
☐ 137 Wally Bunker 1.50 .70 .19
☐ 138 John Bateman 1.50 .70 .19
☐ 139 Andy Kosco 1.50 .70 .19
☐ 140 Jim Lefebvre 2.00 .90 .25
☐ 141 Bill Dillman 1.50 .70 .19
☐ 142 Woody Woodward 2.00 .90 .25
☐ 143 Joe Nossek 1.50 .70 .19
☐ 144 Bob Hendley 2.00 .90 .25
☐ 145 Max Alvis 1.50 .70 .19
☐ 146 Jim Perry 2.00 .90 .25
☐ 147 Leo Durocher MG 4.00 1.80 .50
☐ 148 Lee Stange 1.50 .70 .19
☐ 149 Ollie Brown 2.00 .90 .25
☐ 150 Denny McLain 4.00 1.80 .50
☐ 151A Clay Dalrymple 1.50 .70 .19
(Portrait, Orioles)
☐ 151B Clay Dalrymple 16.00 7.25 2.00
(Catching, Phillies)
☐ 152 Tommie Sisk 1.50 .70 .19
☐ 153 Ed Brinkman 1.50 .70 .19
☐ 154 Jim Britton 1.50 .70 .19
☐ 155 Pete Ward 1.50 .70 .19
☐ 156 Houston Rookies 1.50 .70 .19
Hal Gilson
Leon McFadden
☐ 157 Bob Rodgers 2.00 .90 .25
☐ 158 Joe Gibbon 1.50 .70 .19
☐ 159 Jerry Adair 1.50 .70 .19
☐ 160 Vada Pinson 2.50 1.10 .30
☐ 161 John Purdin 1.50 .70 .19
☐ 162 Bob Gibson WS 8.00 3.60 1.00
Fans 17
☐ 163 Willie Horton WS 5.00 2.20 .60
☐ 164 Tim McCarver WS 7.00 3.10 .85
☐ 165 Lou Brock WS 8.00 3.60 1.00
☐ 166 Al Kaline WS 8.00 3.60 1.00
☐ 167 Jim Northrup WS 5.00 2.20 .60
☐ 168 Mickey Lolich WS 8.00 3.60 1.00
Bob Gibson
☐ 169 Dick McAuliffe WS 5.00 2.20 .60
Denny McLain
Willie Horton
☐ 170 Frank Howard 3.00 1.35 .35
☐ 171 Glenn Beckert 2.00 .90 .25
☐ 172 Jerry Stephenson 1.50 .70 .19
☐ 173 White Sox Rookies 1.50 .70 .19
Bob Christian
Gerry Nyman
☐ 174 Grant Jackson 1.50 .70 .19
☐ 175 Jim Bunning 7.00 3.10 .85
☐ 176 Joe Azcue 1.50 .70 .19
☐ 177 Ron Reed 1.50 .70 .19
☐ 178 Ray Oyler 2.00 .90 .25
☐ 179 Don Pavletich 1.50 .70 .19
☐ 180 Willie Horton 2.00 .90 .25
☐ 181 Mel Nelson 1.50 .70 .19
☐ 182 Bill Rigney MG 1.50 .70 .19
☐ 183 Don Shaw 1.50 .70 .19
☐ 184 Roberto Pena 1.50 .70 .19
☐ 185 Tom Phoebus 1.50 .70 .19
☐ 186 Johnny Edwards 1.50 .70 .19
☐ 187 Leon Wagner 1.50 .70 .19
☐ 188 Rick Wise 2.00 .90 .25
☐ 189 Red Sox Rookies 1.50 .70 .19
Joe Lahoud
John Thibodeau
☐ 190 Willie Mays 45.00 20.00 5.50
☐ 191 Lindy McDaniel 2.00 .90 .25
☐ 192 Jose Pagan 1.50 .70 .19
☐ 193 Don Cardwell 2.00 .90 .25
☐ 194 Ted Uhlaender 1.50 .70 .19
☐ 195 John Odom 1.50 .70 .19
☐ 196 Lum Harris MG 1.50 .70 .19
☐ 197 Dick Selma 1.50 .70 .19
☐ 198 Willie Smith 1.50 .70 .19
☐ 199 Jim French 1.50 .70 .19
☐ 200 Bob Gibson 12.00 5.50 1.50
☐ 201 Russ Snyder 1.50 .70 .19
☐ 202 Don Wilson 2.00 .90 .25
☐ 203 Dave Johnson 2.00 .90 .25
☐ 204 Jack Hiatt 1.50 .70 .19
☐ 205 Rick Reichardt 1.50 .70 .19
☐ 206 Phillies Rookies 2.00 .90 .25
Larry Hisle
Barry Lersch
☐ 207 Roy Face 2.00 .90 .25
☐ 208A Donn Clendenon 2.00 .90 .25
(Houston)
☐ 208B Donn Clendenon 16.00 7.25 2.00
(Expos)
☐ 209 Larry Haney UER 1.50 .70 .19
(Reverse negative)
☐ 210 Felix Millan 1.50 .70 .19
☐ 211 Galen Cisco 1.50 .70 .19
☐ 212 Tom Tresh 2.00 .90 .25
☐ 213 Gerry Arrigo 1.50 .70 .19
☐ 214 Checklist 3 6.00 1.20 .60
With 69T deckle CL
on back (no player)
☐ 215 Rico Petrocelli 2.00 .90 .25
☐ 216 Don Sutton 6.00 2.70 .75
☐ 217 John Donaldson 1.50 .70 .19
☐ 218 John Roseboro 2.00 .90 .25
☐ 219 Freddie Patek 3.00 1.35 .35
☐ 220 Sam McDowell 3.00 1.35 .35
☐ 221 Art Shamsky 3.00 1.35 .35
☐ 222 Duane Josephson 2.50 1.10 .30
☐ 223 Tom Dukes 3.00 1.35 .35
☐ 224 Angels Rookies 2.50 1.10 .30
Bill Harrelson
Steve Kealey
☐ 225 Don Kessinger 3.00 1.35 .35
☐ 226 Bruce Howard 2.50 1.10 .30
☐ 227 Frank Johnson 2.50 1.10 .30
☐ 228 Dave Leonhard 2.50 1.10 .30
☐ 229 Don Lock 2.50 1.10 .30
☐ 230 Rusty Staub UER 4.00 1.80 .50
For 1966 stats, Houston spelled Huoston
☐ 231 Pat Dobson 3.00 1.35 .35
☐ 232 Dave Ricketts 2.50 1.10 .30
☐ 233 Steve Barber 3.00 1.35 .35
☐ 234 Dave Bristol MG 2.50 1.10 .30
☐ 235 Jim Hunter 10.00 4.50 1.25
☐ 236 Manny Mota 3.00 1.35 .35
☐ 237 Bobby Cox 10.00 4.50 1.25
☐ 238 Ken Johnson 2.50 1.10 .30
☐ 239 Bob Taylor 3.00 1.35 .35
☐ 240 Ken Harrelson 3.00 1.35 .35
☐ 241 Jim Brewer 2.50 1.10 .30
☐ 242 Frank Kostro 2.50 1.10 .30
☐ 243 Ron Kline 2.50 1.10 .30
☐ 244 Indians Rookies 3.00 1.35 .35
Ray Fosse
George Woodson
☐ 245 Ed Charles 3.00 1.35 .35
☐ 246 Joe Coleman 2.50 1.10 .30
☐ 247 Gene Oliver 2.50 1.10 .30
☐ 248 Bob Priddy 2.50 1.10 .30
☐ 249 Ed Spiezio 3.00 1.35 .35
☐ 250 Frank Robinson 20.00 9.00 2.50
☐ 251 Ron Herbel 2.50 1.10 .30
☐ 252 Chuck Cottier 2.50 1.10 .30
☐ 253 Jerry Johnson 2.50 1.10 .30
☐ 254 Joe Schultz MG 3.00 1.35 .35
☐ 255 Steve Carlton 30.00 13.50 3.70
☐ 256 Gates Brown 3.00 1.35 .35
☐ 257 Jim Ray 2.50 1.10 .30
☐ 258 Jackie Hernandez 3.00 1.35 .35
☐ 259 Bill Short 2.50 1.10 .30
☐ 260 Reggie Jackson 350.00 160.00 45.00
☐ 261 Bob Johnson 2.50 1.10 .30
☐ 262 Mike Kekich 3.00 1.35 .35
☐ 263 Jerry May 2.50 1.10 .30
☐ 264 Bill Landis 2.50 1.10 .30
☐ 265 Chico Cardenas 3.00 1.35 .35
☐ 266 Dodger Rookies 3.00 1.35 .35
Tom Hutton
Alan Foster
☐ 267 Vicente Romo 2.50 1.10 .30
☐ 268 Al Spangler 2.50 1.10 .30
☐ 269 Al Weis 3.00 1.35 .35
☐ 270 Mickey Lolich 3.00 1.35 .35
☐ 271 Larry Stahl 3.00 1.35 .35
☐ 272 Ed Stroud 2.50 1.10 .30
☐ 273 Ron Willis 2.50 1.10 .30
☐ 274 Clyde King MG 2.50 1.10 .30
☐ 275 Vic Davalillo 2.50 1.10 .30
☐ 276 Gary Wagner 2.50 1.10 .30
☐ 277 Elrod Hendricks 2.50 1.10 .30
☐ 278 Gary Geiger UER 2.50 1.10 .30
(Batting wrong)
☐ 279 Roger Nelson 3.00 1.35 .35
☐ 280 Alex Johnson 3.00 1.35 .35
☐ 281 Ted Kubiak 2.50 1.10 .30
☐ 282 Pat Jarvis 2.50 1.10 .30
☐ 283 Sandy Alomar 3.00 1.35 .35
☐ 284 Expos Rookies 3.00 1.35 .35
Jerry Robertson
Mike Wegener
☐ 285 Don Mincher 3.00 1.35 .35
☐ 286 Dock Ellis 3.00 1.35 .35
☐ 287 Jose Tartabull 3.00 1.35 .35
☐ 288 Ken Holtzman 3.00 1.35 .35
☐ 289 Bart Shirley 2.50 1.10 .30
☐ 290 Jim Kaat 4.00 1.80 .50
☐ 291 Vern Fuller 2.50 1.10 .30
☐ 292 Al Downing 3.00 1.35 .35
☐ 293 Dick Dietz 2.50 1.10 .30
☐ 294 Jim Lemon MG 2.50 1.10 .30
☐ 295 Tony Perez 12.00 5.50 1.50
☐ 296 Andy Messersmith 4.00 1.80 .50
☐ 297 Deron Johnson 2.50 1.10 .30
☐ 298 Dave Nicholson 3.00 1.35 .35
☐ 299 Mark Belanger 3.00 1.35 .35
☐ 300 Felipe Alou 3.00 1.35 .35
☐ 301 Darrell Brandon 3.00 1.35 .35
☐ 302 Jim Pagliaroni 2.50 1.10 .30
☐ 303 Cal Koonce 3.00 1.35 .35
☐ 304 Padres Rookies 8.00 3.60 1.00
Bill Davis
Clarence Gaston
☐ 305 Dick McAuliffe 3.00 1.35 .35
☐ 306 Jim Grant 3.00 1.35 .35
☐ 307 Gary Kolb 2.50 1.10 .30
☐ 308 Wade Blasingame 2.50 1.10 .30
☐ 309 Walt Williams 2.50 1.10 .30
☐ 310 Tom Haller 2.50 1.10 .30
☐ 311 Sparky Lyle 8.00 3.60 1.00
☐ 312 Lee Elia 2.50 1.10 .30
☐ 313 Bill Robinson 3.00 1.35 .35
☐ 314 Checklist 4 6.00 1.20 .60
Don Drysdale
☐ 315 Eddie Fisher 2.50 1.10 .30
☐ 316 Hal Lanier 2.50 1.10 .30
☐ 317 Bruce Look 2.50 1.10 .30
☐ 318 Jack Fisher 2.50 1.10 .30
☐ 319 Ken McMullen UER 2.50 1.10 .30
(Headings on back
are for a pitcher)
☐ 320 Dal Maxvill 2.50 1.10 .30
☐ 321 Jim McAndrew 3.00 1.35 .35
☐ 322 Jose Vidal 3.00 1.35 .35
☐ 323 Larry Miller 2.50 1.10 .30
☐ 324 Tiger Rookies 4.00 1.80 .50
Les Cain
Dave Campbell
☐ 325 Jose Cardenal 3.00 1.35 .35
☐ 326 Gary Sutherland 3.00 1.35 .35
☐ 327 Willie Crawford 2.50 1.10 .30
☐ 328 Joel Horlen 1.50 .70 .19
☐ 329 Rick Joseph 1.50 .70 .19
☐ 330 Tony Conigliaro 5.00 2.20 .60
☐ 331 Braves Rookies 2.50 1.10 .30
Gil Garrido
Tom House
☐ 332 Fred Talbot 1.50 .70 .19
☐ 333 Ivan Murrell 1.50 .70 .19
☐ 334 Phil Roof 1.50 .70 .19
☐ 335 Bill Mazeroski 3.00 1.35 .35
☐ 336 Jim Roland 1.50 .70 .19
☐ 337 Marty Martinez 1.50 .70 .19
☐ 338 Del Unser 1.50 .70 .19
☐ 339 Reds Rookies 1.50 .70 .19
Steve Mingori
Jose Pena
☐ 340 Dave McNally 2.00 .90 .25
☐ 341 Dave Adlesh 1.50 .70 .19
☐ 342 Bubba Morton 1.50 .70 .19
☐ 343 Dan Frisella 1.50 .70 .19
☐ 344 Tom Matchick 1.50 .70 .19
☐ 345 Frank Linzy 1.50 .70 .19
☐ 346 Wayne Comer 1.50 .70 .19
☐ 347 Randy Hundley 2.00 .90 .25
☐ 348 Steve Hargan 1.50 .70 .19
☐ 349 Dick Williams MG 2.00 .90 .25
☐ 350 Richie Allen 4.00 1.80 .50
☐ 351 Carroll Sembera 1.50 .70 .19
☐ 352 Paul Schaal 2.00 .90 .25
☐ 353 Jeff Torborg 2.00 .90 .25
☐ 354 Nate Oliver 1.50 .70 .19
☐ 355 Phil Niekro 7.00 3.10 .85
☐ 356 Frank Quilici 1.50 .70 .19
☐ 357 Carl Taylor 1.50 .70 .19
☐ 358 Athletics Rookies 1.50 .70 .19
George Lauzerique
Roberto Rodriquez
☐ 359 Dick Kelley 1.50 .70 .19
☐ 360 Jim Wynn 2.00 .90 .25
☐ 361 Gary Holman 1.50 .70 .19
☐ 362 Jim Maloney 2.00 .90 .25
☐ 363 Russ Nixon 1.50 .70 .19
☐ 364 Tommie Agee 2.50 1.10 .30
☐ 365 Jim Fregosi 2.00 .90 .25
☐ 366 Bo Belinsky 2.00 .90 .25
☐ 367 Lou Johnson 2.00 .90 .25
☐ 368 Vic Roznovsky 1.50 .70 .19
☐ 369 Bob Skinner MG 2.00 .90 .25
☐ 370 Juan Marichal 8.00 3.60 1.00
☐ 371 Sal Bando 2.00 .90 .25
☐ 372 Adolfo Phillips 1.50 .70 .19
☐ 373 Fred Lasher 1.50 .70 .19
☐ 374 Bob Tillman 1.50 .70 .19
☐ 375 Harmon Killebrew 16.00 7.25 2.00
☐ 376 Royals Rookies 1.50 .70 .19
Mike Fiore
Jim Rooker
☐ 377 Gary Bell 2.00 .90 .25
☐ 378 Jose Herrera 1.50 .70 .19
☐ 379 Ken Boyer 2.50 1.10 .30
☐ 380 Stan Bahnsen 2.00 .90 .25
☐ 381 Ed Kranepool 2.00 .90 .25
☐ 382 Pat Corrales 2.00 .90 .25
☐ 383 Casey Cox 1.50 .70 .19
☐ 384 Larry Shepard MG 1.50 .70 .19
☐ 385 Orlando Cepeda 3.50 1.55 .45
☐ 386 Jim McGlothlin 1.50 .70 .19
☐ 387 Bobby Klaus 1.50 .70 .19
☐ 388 Tom McCraw 1.50 .70 .19
☐ 389 Dan Coombs 1.50 .70 .19
☐ 390 Bill Freehan 2.50 1.10 .30
☐ 391 Ray Culp 1.50 .70 .19
☐ 392 Bob Burda 1.50 .70 .19
☐ 393 Gene Brabender 2.00 .90 .25
☐ 394 Pilots Rookies 5.00 2.20 .60
Lou Piniella
Marv Staehle
☐ 395 Chris Short 1.50 .70 .19
☐ 396 Jim Campanis 1.50 .70 .19
☐ 397 Chuck Dobson 1.50 .70 .19
☐ 398 Tito Francona 1.50 .70 .19
☐ 399 Bob Bailey 2.00 .90 .25

☐ 400 Don Drysdale	15.00	6.75	1.85
☐ 401 Jake Gibbs	2.00	.90	.25
☐ 402 Ken Boswell	2.00	.90	.25
☐ 403 Bob Miller	1.50	.70	.19
☐ 404 Cubs Rookies	2.00	.90	.25
Vic LaRose			
Gary Ross			
☐ 405 Lee May	2.00	.90	.25
☐ 406 Phil Ortega	1.50	.70	.19
☐ 407 Tom Egan	1.50	.70	.19
☐ 408 Nate Colbert	1.50	.70	.19
☐ 409 Bob Moose	1.50	.70	.19
☐ 410 Al Kaline	25.00	11.00	3.10
☐ 411 Larry Dierker	2.00	.90	.25
☐ 412 Checklist 5 DP	12.00	2.40	1.20
Mickey Mantle			
☐ 413 Roland Sheldon	2.00	.90	.25
☐ 414 Duke Sims	1.50	.70	.19
☐ 415 Ray Washburn	1.50	.70	.19
☐ 416 Willie McCovey AS	7.00	3.10	.85
☐ 417 Ken Harrelson AS	2.50	1.10	.30
☐ 418 Tommy Helms AS	2.50	1.10	.30
☐ 419 Rod Carew AS	10.00	4.50	1.25
☐ 420 Ron Santo AS	3.00	1.35	.35
☐ 421 Brooks Robinson AS	7.00	3.10	.85
☐ 422 Don Kessinger AS	2.50	1.10	.30
☐ 423 Bert Campaneris AS	2.50	1.10	.30
☐ 424 Pete Rose AS	15.00	6.75	1.85
☐ 425 Carl Yastrzemski AS	10.00	4.50	1.25
☐ 426 Curt Flood AS	3.00	1.35	.35
☐ 427 Tony Oliva AS	3.00	1.35	.35
☐ 428 Lou Brock AS	6.00	2.70	.75
☐ 429 Willie Horton AS	2.50	1.10	.30
☐ 430 Johnny Bench AS	10.00	4.50	1.25
☐ 431 Bill Freehan AS	3.00	1.35	.35
☐ 432 Bob Gibson AS	6.00	2.70	.75
☐ 433 Denny McLain AS	2.50	1.10	.30
☐ 434 Jerry Koosman AS	3.00	1.35	.35
☐ 435 Sam McDowell AS	2.50	1.10	.30
☐ 436 Gene Alley	2.00	.90	.25
☐ 437 Luis Alcaraz	1.50	.70	.19
☐ 438 Gary Waslewski	1.50	.70	.19
☐ 439 White Sox Rookies	1.50	.70	.19
Ed Herrmann			
Dan Lazar			
☐ 440A Willie McCovey	18.00	8.00	2.20
☐ 440B Willie McCovey WL	100.00	45.00	12.50
(McCovey white)			
☐ 441A Dennis Higgins	1.50	.70	.19
☐ 441B Dennis Higgins WL	20.00	9.00	2.50
(Higgins white)			
☐ 442 Ty Cline	1.50	.70	.19
☐ 443 Don Wert	1.50	.70	.19
☐ 444A Joe Moeller	1.50	.70	.19
☐ 444B Joe Moeller WL	20.00	9.00	2.50
(Moeller white)			
☐ 445 Bobby Knoop	1.50	.70	.19
☐ 446 Claude Raymond	1.50	.70	.19
☐ 447A Ralph Houk MG	2.00	.90	.25
☐ 447B Ralph Houk WL	22.00	10.00	2.70
MG (Houk white)			
☐ 448 Bob Tolan	2.00	.90	.25
☐ 449 Paul Lindblad	1.50	.70	.19
☐ 450 Billy Williams	7.00	3.10	.85
☐ 451A Rich Rollins	2.00	.90	.25
☐ 451B Rich Rollins WL	20.00	9.00	2.50
(Rich and 3B white)			
☐ 452A Al Ferrara	1.50	.70	.19
☐ 452B Al Ferrara WL	20.00	9.00	2.50
(Al and OF white)			
☐ 453 Mike Cuellar	2.50	1.10	.30
☐ 454A Phillies Rookies	2.00	.90	.25
Larry Colton			
Don Money			
☐ 454B Phillies Rookies WL	22.00	10.00	2.70
Larry Colton			
Don Money			
(Names in white)			
☐ 455 Sonny Siebert	1.50	.70	.19
☐ 456 Bud Harrelson	2.00	.90	.25
☐ 457 Dalton Jones	1.50	.70	.19
☐ 458 Curt Blefary	1.50	.70	.19
☐ 459 Dave Boswell	1.50	.70	.19
☐ 460 Joe Torre	3.50	1.55	.45
☐ 461A Mike Epstein	1.50	.70	.19
☐ 461B Mike Epstein WL	20.00	9.00	2.50
(Epstein white)			
☐ 462 Red Schoendienst	2.50	1.10	.30
MG			
☐ 463 Dennis Ribant	1.50	.70	.19
☐ 464A Dave Marshall	1.50	.70	.19
☐ 464B Dave Marshall WL	20.00	9.00	2.50
(Marshall white)			
☐ 465 Tommy John	4.00	1.80	.50
☐ 466 John Boccabella	2.00	.90	.25
☐ 467 Tommie Reynolds	1.50	.70	.19
☐ 468A Pirates Rookies	1.50	.70	.19
Bruce Dal Canton			
Bob Robertson			
☐ 468B Pirates Rookies WL	20.00	9.00	2.50
Bruce Dal Canton			
Bob Robertson			
(Names in white)			
☐ 469 Chico Ruiz	1.50	.70	.19
☐ 470A Mel Stottlemyre	2.50	1.10	.30
☐ 470B Mel Stottlemyre WL	30.00	13.50	3.70
(Stottlemyre white)			
☐ 471A Ted Savage	1.50	.70	.19
☐ 471B Ted Savage WL	20.00	9.00	2.50
(Savage white)			
☐ 472 Jim Price	1.50	.70	.19
☐ 473A Jose Arcia	1.50	.70	.19
☐ 473B Jose Arcia WL	20.00	9.00	2.50
(Jose and 2B white)			
☐ 474 Tom Murphy	1.50	.70	.19
☐ 475 Tim McCarver	3.00	1.35	.35
☐ 476A Boston Rookies	3.00	1.35	.35
Ken Brett			
Gerry Moses			
☐ 476B Boston Rookies WL	30.00	13.50	3.70
Ken Brett			
Gerry Moses			
(Names in white)			
☐ 477 Jeff James	1.50	.70	.19
☐ 478 Don Buford	1.50	.70	.19
☐ 479 Richie Scheinblum	1.50	.70	.19
☐ 480 Tom Seaver	80.00	36.00	10.00
☐ 481 Bill Melton	2.00	.90	.25
☐ 482A Jim Gosger	1.50	.70	.19
☐ 482B Jim Gosger WL	20.00	9.00	2.50
(Jim and OF white)			
☐ 483 Ted Abernathy	1.50	.70	.19
☐ 484 Joe Gordon MG	2.00	.90	.25
☐ 485A Gaylord Perry	10.00	4.50	1.25
☐ 485B Gaylord Perry WL	85.00	38.00	10.50
(Perry white)			
☐ 486A Paul Casanova	1.50	.70	.19
☐ 486B Paul Casanova WL	20.00	9.00	2.50
(Casanova white)			
☐ 487 Denis Menke	1.50	.70	.19
☐ 488 Joe Sparma	1.50	.70	.19
☐ 489 Clete Boyer	2.00	.90	.25
☐ 490 Matty Alou	2.00	.90	.25
☐ 491A Twins Rookies	1.50	.70	.19
Jerry Crider			
George Mitterwald			
☐ 491B Twins Rookies WL	20.00	9.00	2.50
Jerry Crider			
George Mitterwald			
(Names in white)			
☐ 492 Tony Cloninger	1.50	.70	.19
☐ 493A Wes Parker	2.00	.90	.25
☐ 493B Wes Parker WL	22.00	10.00	2.70
(Parker white)			
☐ 494 Ken Berry	1.50	.70	.19
☐ 495 Bert Campaneris	2.00	.90	.25
☐ 496 Larry Jaster	1.50	.70	.19
☐ 497 Julian Javier	2.00	.90	.25
☐ 498 Juan Pizarro	2.00	.90	.25
☐ 499 Astro Rookies	1.50	.70	.19
Don Bryant			
Steve Shea			
☐ 500A Mickey Mantle UER	350.00	160.00	45.00
(No Topps copy-			
right on card back)			
☐ 500B Mickey Mantle WL	1000.00	450.00	125.00
(Mantle in white;			
no Topps copyright			
on card back) UER			
☐ 501A Tony Gonzalez	2.00	.90	.25
☐ 501B Tony Gonzalez WL	22.00	10.00	2.70
(Tony and OF white)			
☐ 502 Minnie Rojas	1.50	.70	.19
☐ 503 Larry Brown	1.50	.70	.19
☐ 504 Checklist 6	7.00	1.40	.70
Brooks Robinson			
☐ 505A Bobby Bolin	1.50	.70	.19
☐ 505B Bobby Bolin WL	22.00	10.00	2.70
(Bolin white)			
☐ 506 Paul Blair	2.00	.90	.25
☐ 507 Cookie Rojas	2.00	.90	.25
☐ 508 Moe Drabowsky	2.00	.90	.25
☐ 509 Manny Sanguillen	2.00	.90	.25
☐ 510 Rod Carew	35.00	16.00	4.40
☐ 511A Diego Segui	2.00	.90	.25
☐ 511B Diego Segui WL	22.00	10.00	2.70
(Diego and P white)			
☐ 512 Cleon Jones	2.00	.90	.25
☐ 513 Camilo Pascual	3.00	1.35	.35
☐ 514 Mike Lum	2.00	.90	.25
☐ 515 Dick Green	2.00	.90	.25
☐ 516 Earl Weaver MG	18.00	8.00	2.20
☐ 517 Mike McCormick	3.00	1.35	.35
☐ 518 Fred Whitfield	2.00	.90	.25
☐ 519 Yankees Rookies	2.00	.90	.25
Jerry Kenney			
Len Boehmer			
☐ 520 Bob Veale	3.00	1.35	.35
☐ 521 George Thomas	2.00	.90	.25
☐ 522 Joe Hoerner	2.00	.90	.25
☐ 523 Bob Chance	2.00	.90	.25
☐ 524 Expos Rookies	3.00	1.35	.35
Jose Laboy			
Floyd Wicker			
☐ 525 Earl Wilson	3.00	1.35	.35
☐ 526 Hector Torres	2.00	.90	.25
☐ 527 Al Lopez MG	4.00	1.80	.50
☐ 528 Claude Osteen	3.00	1.35	.35
☐ 529 Ed Kirkpatrick	3.00	1.35	.35
☐ 530 Cesar Tovar	2.00	.90	.25
☐ 531 Dick Farrell	2.00	.90	.25
☐ 532 Bird Hill Aces	3.00	1.35	.35
Tom Phoebus			
Jim Hardin			
Dave McNally			
Mike Cuellar			
☐ 533 Nolan Ryan	425.00	190.00	52.50
☐ 534 Jerry McNertney	3.00	1.35	.35
☐ 535 Phil Regan	3.00	1.35	.35
☐ 536 Padres Rookies	2.00	.90	.25
Danny Breeden			
Dave Roberts			
☐ 537 Mike Paul	2.00	.90	.25
☐ 538 Charlie Smith	2.00	.90	.25
☐ 539 Ted Shows How	8.00	3.60	1.00
Mike Epstein			
Ted Williams MG			
☐ 540 Curt Flood	3.00	1.35	.35
☐ 541 Joe Verbanic	2.00	.90	.25
☐ 542 Bob Aspromonte	2.00	.90	.25
☐ 543 Fred Newman	2.00	.90	.25
☐ 544 Tigers Rookies	2.00	.90	.25
Mike Kilkenny			
Ron Woods			
☐ 545 Willie Stargell	12.00	5.50	1.50
☐ 546 Jim Nash	2.00	.90	.25
☐ 547 Billy Martin MG	6.00	2.70	.75
☐ 548 Bob Locker	2.00	.90	.25
☐ 549 Ron Brand	2.00	.90	.25
☐ 550 Brooks Robinson	30.00	13.50	3.70
☐ 551 Wayne Granger	2.00	.90	.25
☐ 552 Dodgers Rookies	3.00	1.35	.35
Ted Sizemore			
Bill Sudakis			
☐ 553 Ron Davis	2.00	.90	.25
☐ 554 Frank Bertaina	2.00	.90	.25
☐ 555 Jim Ray Hart	3.00	1.35	.35
☐ 556 A's Stars	3.00	1.35	.35
Sal Bando			
Bert Campaneris			
Danny Cater			
☐ 557 Frank Fernandez	2.00	.90	.25
☐ 558 Tom Burgmeier	3.00	1.35	.35
☐ 559 Cardinals Rookies	2.00	.90	.25
Joe Hague			
Jim Hicks			
☐ 560 Luis Tiant	3.00	1.35	.35
☐ 561 Ron Clark	2.00	.90	.25
☐ 562 Bob Watson	7.00	3.10	.85
☐ 563 Marty Pattin	3.00	1.35	.35
☐ 564 Gil Hodges MG	10.00	4.50	1.25
☐ 565 Hoyt Wilhelm	7.00	3.10	.85
☐ 566 Ron Hansen	2.00	.90	.25
☐ 567 Pirates Rookies	2.00	.90	.25
Elvio Jimenez			
Jim Shellenback			
☐ 568 Cecil Upshaw	2.00	.90	.25
☐ 569 Billy Harris	2.00	.90	.25
☐ 570 Ron Santo	7.00	3.10	.85
☐ 571 Cap Peterson	2.00	.90	.25
☐ 572 Giants Heroes	16.00	7.25	2.00
Willie McCovey			
Juan Marichal			
☐ 573 Jim Palmer	35.00	16.00	4.40
☐ 574 George Scott	3.00	1.35	.35
☐ 575 Bill Singer	3.00	1.35	.35
☐ 576 Phillies Rookies	2.00	.90	.25
Ron Stone			
Bill Wilson			
☐ 577 Mike Hegan	3.00	1.35	.35
☐ 578 Don Bosch	2.00	.90	.25
☐ 579 Dave Nelson	2.00	.90	.25
☐ 580 Jim Northrup	3.00	1.35	.35
☐ 581 Gary Nolan	3.00	1.35	.35
☐ 582A Checklist 7	6.00	1 20	.60
(White circle on back)			
(Tony Oliva)			
☐ 582B Checklist 7	7.50	1.50	.75
(Red circle on back)			
(Tony Oliva)			
☐ 583 Clyde Wright	2.00	.90	.25
☐ 584 Don Mason	2.00	.90	.25
☐ 585 Ron Swoboda	3.00	1.35	.35
☐ 586 Tim Cullen	2.00	.90	.25
☐ 587 Joe Rudi	7.00	3.10	.85
☐ 588 Bill White	3.00	1.35	.35
☐ 589 Joe Pepitone	4.00	1.80	.50
☐ 590 Rico Carty	4.00	1.80	.50
☐ 591 Mike Hedlund	3.00	1.35	.35
☐ 592 Padres Rookies	4.00	1.80	.50
Rafael Robles			
Al Santorini			
☐ 593 Don Nottebart	3.00	1.35	.35
☐ 594 Dooley Womack	3.00	1.35	.35
☐ 595 Lee Maye	3.00	1.35	.35
☐ 596 Chuck Hartenstein	3.00	1.35	.35
☐ 597 A.L. Rookies	45.00	20.00	5.50
Bob Floyd			
Larry Burchart			
Rollie Fingers			
☐ 598 Ruben Amaro	3.00	1.35	.35
☐ 599 John Boozer	3.00	1.35	.35
☐ 600 Tony Oliva	6.00	2.70	.75
☐ 601 Tug McGraw	7.00	3.10	.85
☐ 602 Cubs Rookies	4.00	1.80	.50
Alec Distaso			
Don Young			
Jim Qualls			
☐ 603 Joe Keough	3.00	1.35	.35
☐ 604 Bobby Etheridge	3.00	1.35	.35
☐ 605 Dick Ellsworth	3.00	1.35	.35
☐ 606 Gene Mauch MG	4.00	1.80	.50
☐ 607 Dick Bosman	3.00	1.35	.35
☐ 608 Dick Simpson	3.00	1.35	.35
☐ 609 Phil Gagliano	3.00	1.35	.35
☐ 610 Jim Hardin	3.00	1.35	.35
☐ 611 Braves Rookies	4.00	1.80	.50
Bob Didier			
Walt Hriniak			
Gary Neibauer			
☐ 612 Jack Aker	4.00	1.80	.50
☐ 613 Jim Beauchamp	3.00	1.35	.35
☐ 614 Houston Rookies	3.00	1.35	.35
Tom Griffin			
Skip Guinn			
☐ 615 Len Gabrielson	3.00	1.35	.35
☐ 616 Don McMahon	3.00	1.35	.35
☐ 617 Jesse Gonder	3.00	1.35	.35
☐ 618 Ramon Webster	3.00	1.35	.35
☐ 619 Royals Rookies	4.00	1.80	.50
Bill Butler			
Pat Kelly			
Juan Rios			
☐ 620 Dean Chance	4.00	1.80	.50
☐ 621 Bill Voss	3.00	1.35	.35
☐ 622 Dan Osinski	3.00	1.35	.35
☐ 623 Hank Allen	3.00	1.35	.35
☐ 624 NL Rookies	4.00	1.80	.50
Darrel Chaney			
Duffy Dyer			
Terry Harmon			
☐ 625 Mack Jones UER	4.00	1.80	.50
(Batting wrong)			
☐ 626 Gene Michael	4.00	1.80	.50
☐ 627 George Stone	3.00	1.35	.35
☐ 628 Red Sox Rookies	4.00	1.80	.50
Bill Conigliaro			
Syd O'Brien			
Fred Wenz			
☐ 629 Jack Hamilton	3.00	1.35	.35
☐ 630 Bobby Bonds	35.00	16.00	4.40
☐ 631 John Kennedy	4.00	1.80	.50
☐ 632 Jon Warden	3.00	1.35	.35
☐ 633 Harry Walker MG	3.00	1.35	.35
☐ 634 Andy Etchebarren	3.00	1.35	.35
☐ 635 George Culver	3.00	1.35	.35
☐ 636 Woody Held	3.00	1.35	.35
☐ 637 Padres Rookies	4.00	1.80	.50
Jerry DaVanon			
Frank Reberger			
Clay Kirby			
☐ 638 Ed Sprague	3.00	1.35	.35
☐ 639 Barry Moore	3.00	1.35	.35
☐ 640 Fergie Jenkins	20.00	9.00	2.50
☐ 641 NL Rookies	4.00	1.80	.50
Bobby Darwin			
John Miller			
Tommy Dean			
☐ 642 John Hiller	3.00	1.35	.35
☐ 643 Billy Cowan	3.00	1.35	.35
☐ 644 Chuck Hinton	3.00	1.35	.35
☐ 645 George Brunet	3.00	1.35	.35
☐ 646 Expos Rookies	4.00	1.80	.50
Dan McGinn			
Carl Morton			
☐ 647 Dave Wickersham	3.00	1.35	.35
☐ 648 Bobby Wine	4.00	1.80	.50
☐ 649 Al Jackson	3.00	1.35	.35
☐ 650 Ted Williams MG	16.00	7.25	2.00
☐ 651 Gus Gil	4.00	1.80	.50
☐ 652 Eddie Watt	3.00	1.35	.35
☐ 653 Aurelio Rodriguez UER	5.00	2.20	.60
(Photo actually			
Angels' batboy)			
☐ 654 White Sox Rookies	4.00	1.80	.50
Carlos May			
Don Secrist			
Rich Morales			
☐ 655 Mike Hershberger	3.00	1.35	.35
☐ 656 Dan Schneider	3.00	1.35	.35
☐ 657 Bobby Murcer	6.00	2.70	.75
☐ 658 AL Rookies	3.00	1.35	.35
Tom Hall			
Bill Burbach			
Jim Miles			
☐ 659 Johnny Podres	4.00	1.80	.50
☐ 660 Reggie Smith	6.00	2.70	.75
☐ 661 Jim Merritt	3.00	1.35	.35
☐ 662 Royals Rookies	4.00	1.80	.50
Dick Drago			
George Spriggs			
Bob Oliver			
☐ 663 Dick Radatz	4.00	1.80	.50
☐ 664 Ron Hunt	5.00	1.35	.40

1969 Topps Decal Inserts

The 1969 Topps Decal Inserts are a set of 48 unnumbered decals issued as inserts in packages of 1969 Topps regular issue cards. Each decal is approximately 1" by 1 1/2" although including the plain backing the measurement is 1 3/4" by 2 1/8". The decals appear to be

miniature versions of the Topps regular issue of that year. The copyright notice on the side indicates that these decals were produced in the United Kingdom. Most of the players on the decals are stars.

	NRMT	VG-E	GOOD
COMPLETE SET (48)	450.00	200.00	55.00
COMMON DECAL (1-48)	2.50	1.10	.30
☐ 1 Hank Aaron	50.00	22.00	6.25
☐ 2 Richie Allen	5.00	2.20	.60
☐ 3 Felipe Alou	3.00	1.35	.35
☐ 4 Matty Alou	3.00	1.35	.35
☐ 5 Luis Aparicio	7.50	3.40	.95
☐ 6 Bob Clemente	60.00	27.00	7.50
☐ 7 Donn Clendenon	2.50	1.10	.30
☐ 8 Tommy Davis	3.00	1.35	.35
☐ 9 Don Drysdale	12.50	5.50	1.55
☐ 10 Joe Foy	2.50	1.10	.30
☐ 11 Jim Fregosi	3.00	1.35	.35
☐ 12 Bob Gibson	12.50	5.50	1.55
☐ 13 Tony Gonzalez	2.50	1.10	.30
☐ 14 Tom Haller	2.50	1.10	.30
☐ 15 Ken Harrelson	3.00	1.35	.35
☐ 16 Tommy Helms	2.50	1.10	.30
☐ 17 Willie Horton	3.00	1.35	.35
☐ 18 Frank Howard	3.00	1.35	.35
☐ 19 Reggie Jackson	50.00	22.00	6.25
☐ 20 Fergie Jenkins	7.50	3.40	.95
☐ 21 Harmon Killebrew	7.50	3.40	.95
☐ 22 Jerry Koosman	3.00	1.35	.35
☐ 23 Mickey Mantle	125.00	55.00	15.50
☐ 24 Willie Mays	50.00	22.00	6.25
☐ 25 Tim McCarver	5.00	2.20	.60
☐ 26 Willie McCovey	12.50	5.50	1.55
☐ 27 Sam McDowell	3.00	1.35	.35
☐ 28 Denny McLain	3.00	1.35	.35
☐ 29 Dave McNally	3.00	1.35	.35
☐ 30 Don Mincher	2.50	1.10	.30
☐ 31 Rick Monday	3.00	1.35	.35
☐ 32 Tony Oliva	3.50	1.55	.45
☐ 33 Camilo Pascual	2.50	1.10	.30
☐ 34 Rick Reichardt	2.50	1.10	.30
☐ 35 Frank Robinson	15.00	6.75	1.85
☐ 36 Pete Rose	35.00	16.00	4.40
☐ 37 Ron Santo	5.00	2.20	.60
☐ 38 Tom Seaver	25.00	11.00	3.10
☐ 39 Dick Selma	2.50	1.10	.30
☐ 40 Chris Short	2.50	1.10	.30
☐ 41 Rusty Staub	3.50	1.55	.45
☐ 42 Mel Stottlemyre	3.00	1.35	.35
☐ 43 Luis Tiant	3.00	1.35	.35
☐ 44 Pete Ward	2.50	1.10	.30
☐ 45 Hoyt Wilhelm	7.50	3.40	.95
☐ 46 Maury Wills	5.00	2.20	.60
☐ 47 Jim Wynn	1.25	.55	.16
☐ 48 Carl Yastrzemski	20.00	9.00	2.50

1969 Topps Deckle

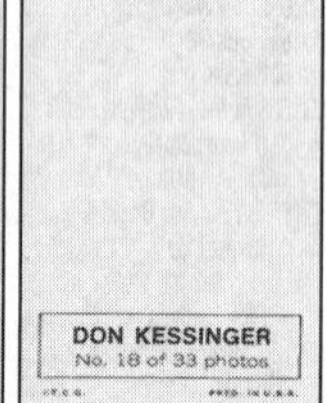

The cards in this 33-card set measure approximately 2 1/4" by 3 1/4". This unusual black and white insert set derives its name from the serrated border, or edge, of the cards. The cards were included as inserts in the regularly issued Topps baseball third series of 1969. Card number 11 is found with either Hoyt Wilhelm or Jim Wynn, and number 22 with either Rusty Staub or Joe Foy. The set price below does include all variations. The set numbering is arranged in team order by league except for cards 11 and 22.

	NRMT	VG-E	GOOD
COMPLETE SET (35)	100.00	45.00	12.50
COMMON CARD (1-33)	.50	.23	.06
☐ 1 Brooks Robinson	7.50	3.40	.95
☐ 2 Boog Powell	1.50	.70	.19
☐ 3 Ken Harrelson	.50	.23	.06
☐ 4 Carl Yastrzemski	6.00	2.70	.75
☐ 5 Jim Fregosi	.75	.35	.09
☐ 6 Luis Aparicio	3.00	1.35	.35
☐ 7 Luis Tiant	.75	.35	.09
☐ 8 Denny McLain	.75	.35	.09
☐ 9 Willie Horton	.75	.35	.09
☐ 10 Bill Freehan	.75	.35	.09
☐ 11A Hoyt Wilhelm	7.50	3.40	.95
☐ 11B Jim Wynn	12.00	5.50	1.50
☐ 12 Rod Carew	5.00	2.20	.60
☐ 13 Mel Stottlemyre	.75	.35	.09
☐ 14 Rick Monday	.50	.23	.06
☐ 15 Tommy Davis	.75	.35	.09
☐ 16 Frank Howard	.75	.35	.09
☐ 17 Felipe Alou	.75	.35	.09
☐ 18 Don Kessinger	.50	.23	.06
☐ 19 Ron Santo	1.50	.70	.19
☐ 20 Tommy Helms	.50	.23	.06
☐ 21 Pete Rose	10.00	4.50	1.25
☐ 22A Rusty Staub	3.00	1.35	.35
☐ 22B Joe Foy	12.00	5.50	1.50
☐ 23 Tom Haller	.50	.23	.06
☐ 24 Maury Wills	.75	.35	.09
☐ 25 Jerry Koosman	.75	.35	.09
☐ 26 Richie Allen	1.50	.70	.19
☐ 27 Bob Clemente	20.00	9.00	2.50
☐ 28 Curt Flood	.75	.35	.09
☐ 29 Bob Gibson	5.00	2.20	.60
☐ 30 Al Ferrara	.50	.23	.06
☐ 31 Willie McCovey	4.00	1.80	.50
☐ 32 Juan Marichal	4.00	1.80	.50
☐ 33 Willie Mays	12.00	5.50	1.50

1969 Topps Four-in-One

This was a test issue consisting of 25 sticker cards (blank back). Each card measures 2 1/2" by 3 1/2" and features four mini-stickers. These unnumbered stickers are ordered in the checklist below alphabetically by the upper left player's name on each card. Each mini-card featured is from the 1969 Topps second series. Five of the cards were double printed (technically 50 percent more were printed) compared to the others in the set; these are marked below by DP.

	NRMT	VG-E	GOOD
COMPLETE SET (25)	900.00	400.00	110.00
COMMON CARD (1-25)	12.00	5.50	1.50
☐ 1 Jerry Adair	100.00	45.00	12.50
Don Wilson			
Willie Mays			
Johnny Morris			
☐ 2 Astros Rookies	12.00	5.50	1.50
(Gilson/McFadden)			
Wally Bunker			
Joe Gibbon			
Don Cardwell			
☐ 3 Donn Clendenon	12.00	5.50	1.50
Woody Woodward			
Tommie Aaron			
Jim Britton			
☐ 4 Tommy Davis	20.00	9.00	2.50
Don Pavletich			
W.S. Game 4			
(Brock homer)			
Vada Pinson			
☐ 5 Ron Fairly	12.00	5.50	1.50
Rick Wise			
Max Alvis			
Glenn Beckert			
☐ 6 Jim French	12.00	5.50	1.50
Dick Selma			
Johnny Callison			
Lum Harris MG			
☐ 7 Bob Gibson DP	40.00	18.00	5.00
W.S. Game 3			
(McCarver homer)			
Rick Reichardt			
Larry Haney			
☐ 8 Andy Kosco	15.00	6.75	1.85
Ron Reed			
Jim Bunning			
Ollie Brown			
☐ 9 Jim Lefebvre	12.00	5.50	1.50
John Purdin			
Bill Dillman			
John Roseboro			
☐ 10 Felix Millan DP	12.00	5.50	1.50
Bill Hands			
Lindy McDaniel			
Chuck Harrison			
☐ 11 Mel Nelson	15.00	6.75	1.85
Dave Johnson			
Jack Hiatt			
Tommie Sisk			
☐ 12 John Odom	15.00	6.75	1.85
Leo Durocher MG			
Wilbur Wood			
Clay Dalrymple			
☐ 13 Ray Oyler DP	12.00	5.50	1.50
Hank Bauer MG			
Kevin Collins			
Russ Snyder			
☐ 14 Jim Perry	15.00	6.75	1.85
W.S. Game 7			
(Lolich/B.Gibson)			
Gerry Arrigo			
Red Sox Rookies			
(Lahoud/Thibodeau)			
☐ 15 Doug Rader	12.00	5.50	1.50
Bill McCool			
Roberto Pena			
W.S. Game 2			
(Tiger homers)			
☐ 16 Bob Rodgers	15.00	6.75	1.85
Willie Horton			
Roy Face			
Ed Brinkman			
☐ 17 Ray Sadecki	12.00	5.50	1.50
Dave Baldwin			
J.C. Martin			
Dave May			
☐ 18 Mike Shannon DP	15.00	6.75	1.85
W.S. Game 1			
(Gibson fans 17)			
Jose Pagan			
Tom Phoebus			
☐ 19 Lee Stange	300.00	135.00	38.00
Don Sutton			
Ted Uhlaender			
Pete Rose			
☐ 20 Jim Weaver	12.00	5.50	1.50
Dick Tracewski			
Joe Grzenda			
Frank Howard			
☐ 21 White Sox Rookies	15.00	6.75	1.85
(Christian/Nyman)			
Denny McLain			
Grant Jackson			
Joe Azcue			
☐ 22 Stan Williams	12.00	5.50	1.50
John Edwards			
Jim Fairey			
Phillies Rookies			
(Hisle/Lersch)			
☐ 23 W.S. Celebration	12.00	5.50	1.50
(Tigers celebrate)			
Leon Wagner			
John Bateman			
Willie Smith			
☐ 24 Yankees Rookies	12.00	5.50	1.50
(Closter/Cumberland)			
Chris Cannizzaro			
W.S. Game 5			
(Kaline's hit)			
Bob Hendley			
☐ 25 Carl Yastrzemski DP	175.00	80.00	22.00
Rico Petrocelli			
Joe Nossek			
Cards Rookies			
(Huntz/Torrez)			

1969 Topps Bowie Kuhn

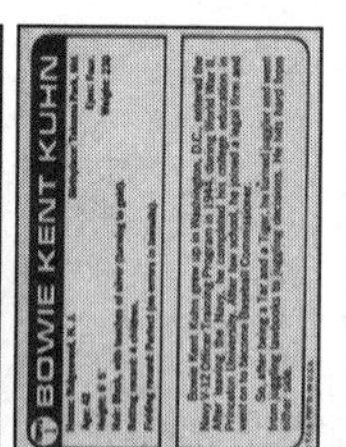

This one-card standard-size set was issued soon after Bowie Kuhn's elevation to Baseball Commissioner. The front features a superimposed photo of Kuhn in regal wear sitting on a base. The horizontal back features vital statistics as well as a brief biography.

	NRMT	VG-E	GOOD
COMPLETE SET (1)	40.00	18.00	5.00
COMMON CARD	40.00	18.00	5.00
☐ 1 Bowie Kuhn	40.00	18.00	5.00

1969 Topps Super

The cards in this 66-card set measure approximately 2 1/4" by 3 1/4". This beautiful Topps set was released independently of the regular baseball series of 1969. It is referred to as "Super Baseball" on the back of the card, a title which was also used for the postcard-size cards issued in 1970 and 1971. Complete sheets, and cards with square corners cut from these sheets, are sometimes encountered. The set numbering is in alphabetical order by teams within league. Cards from the far right of each row are usually found with a white line on the right edge. Although rarely seen, this set was issued in 3-card cello packs. The set features Reggie Jackson in his Rookie Card year.

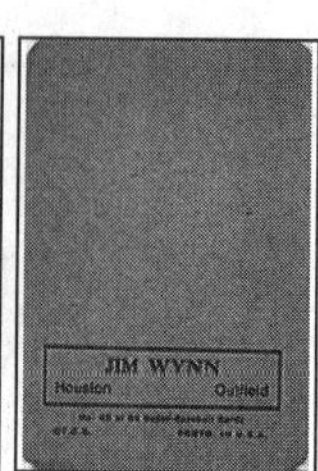

	NRMT	VG-E	GOOD
COMPLETE SET (66)	5500.00	2500.00	700.00
COMMON CARD (1-66)	12.00	5.50	1.50
☐ 1 Dave McNally	12.00	5.50	1.50
☐ 2 Frank Robinson	200.00	90.00	25.00
☐ 3 Brooks Robinson	200.00	90.00	25.00
☐ 4 Ken Harrelson	15.00	6.75	1.85
☐ 5 Carl Yastrzemski	250.00	110.00	31.00
☐ 6 Ray Culp	12.00	5.50	1.50
☐ 7 Jim Fregosi	15.00	6.75	1.85
☐ 8 Rick Reichardt	12.00	5.50	1.50
☐ 9 Vic Davalillo	12.00	5.50	1.50
☐ 10 Luis Aparicio	75.00	34.00	9.50
☐ 11 Pete Ward	12.00	5.50	1.50
☐ 12 Joel Horlen	12.00	5.50	1.50
☐ 13 Luis Tiant	15.00	6.75	1.85
☐ 14 Sam McDowell	12.00	5.50	1.50
☐ 15 Jose Cardenal	12.00	5.50	1.50
☐ 16 Willie Horton	15.00	6.75	1.85
☐ 17 Denny McLain	20.00	9.00	2.50
☐ 18 Bill Freehan	15.00	6.75	1.85
☐ 19 Harmon Killebrew	150.00	70.00	19.00
☐ 20 Tony Oliva	30.00	13.50	3.70
☐ 21 Dean Chance	12.00	5.50	1.50
☐ 22 Joe Foy	12.00	5.50	1.50
☐ 23 Roger Nelson	12.00	5.50	1.50
☐ 24 Mickey Mantle	1000.00	450.00	125.00
☐ 25 Mel Stottlemyre	15.00	6.75	1.85
☐ 26 Roy White	15.00	6.75	1.85
☐ 27 Rick Monday	12.00	5.50	1.50
☐ 28 Reggie Jackson	450.00	200.00	55.00
☐ 29 Bert Campaneris	15.00	6.75	1.85
☐ 30 Frank Howard	20.00	9.00	2.50
☐ 31 Camilo Pascual	12.00	5.50	1.50
☐ 32 Tommy Davis	15.00	6.75	1.85
☐ 33 Don Mincher	12.00	5.50	1.50
☐ 34 Hank Aaron	450.00	200.00	55.00
☐ 35 Felipe Alou	20.00	9.00	2.50
☐ 36 Joe Torre	40.00	18.00	5.00
☐ 37 Fergie Jenkins	75.00	34.00	9.50
☐ 38 Ron Santo	30.00	13.50	3.70
☐ 39 Billy Williams	75.00	34.00	9.50
☐ 40 Tommy Helms	12.00	5.50	1.50
☐ 41 Pete Rose	400.00	180.00	50.00
☐ 42 Joe Morgan	125.00	55.00	15.50
☐ 43 Jim Wynn	12.00	5.50	1.50
☐ 44 Curt Blefary	12.00	5.50	1.50
☐ 45 Willie Davis	12.00	5.50	1.50
☐ 46 Don Drysdale	100.00	45.00	12.50
☐ 47 Tom Haller	12.00	5.50	1.50
☐ 48 Rusty Staub	20.00	9.00	2.50
☐ 49 Maury Wills	25.00	11.00	3.10
☐ 50 Cleon Jones	12.00	5.50	1.50
☐ 51 Jerry Koosman	20.00	9.00	2.50
☐ 52 Tom Seaver	400.00	180.00	50.00
☐ 53 Richie Allen	20.00	9.00	2.50
☐ 54 Chris Short	12.00	5.50	1.50
☐ 55 Cookie Rojas	12.00	5.50	1.50
☐ 56 Matty Alou	12.00	5.50	1.50
☐ 57 Steve Blass	12.00	5.50	1.50
☐ 58 Roberto Clemente	600.00	275.00	75.00
☐ 59 Curt Flood	20.00	9.00	2.50
☐ 60 Bob Gibson	150.00	70.00	19.00
☐ 61 Tim McCarver	25.00	11.00	3.10
☐ 62 Dick Selma	12.00	5.50	1.50
☐ 63 Ollie Brown	12.00	5.50	1.50
☐ 64 Juan Marichal	100.00	45.00	12.50
☐ 65 Willie Mays	475.00	210.00	60.00
☐ 66 Willie McCovey	100.00	45.00	12.50

1969 Topps Stamps

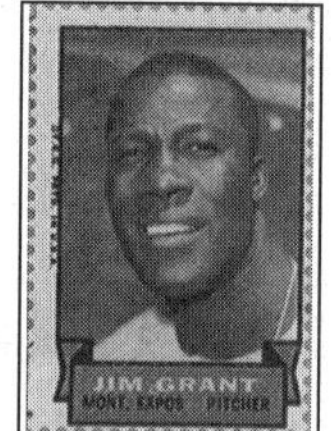

The 1969 Topps set of baseball player stamps contains 240 individual stamps and 24 separate albums, 10 stamps and one album per major league team. The stamps were issued in strips of 12 and have gummed backs. Each stamp measures 1" by 1 7/16". The eight-page albums are bright orange and have an autograph feature on the back cover. The stamps are numbered here alphabetically within each team and the teams are listed in alphabetical order within league, e.g., Atlanta Braves NL (1-10), Chicago Cubs (11-20), Cincinnati Reds (21-30), Houston Astros (31-40), Los Angeles Dodgers (41-50), Montreal Expos (51-60), New York Mets (61-70), Philadelphia Phillies (71-80), Pittsburgh Pirates (81-90), San Diego Padres (91-100), San Francisco Giants (101-110), St. Louis Cardinals (111-120), Baltimore Orioles AL (121-130), Boston Red Sox (131-140), California Angels (141-150), Chicago White Sox (151-160), Cleveland Indians (161-170), Detroit Tigers (171-180), Kansas City Royals (181-190), Minnesota Twins (191-200), New York Yankees (201-210), Oakland A's (211-220), Seattle Pilots (221-230) and Washington Senators (231-240).

	NRMT	VG-E	GOOD
COMPLETE SET (240)	175.00	80.00	22.00
COMMON STAMP (1-240)	.25	.11	.03
☐ 1 Hank Aaron	12.50	5.50	1.55
☐ 2 Felipe Alou	.50	.23	.06
☐ 3 Clete Boyer	.50	.23	.06
☐ 4 Tito Francona	.25	.11	.03
☐ 5 Sonny Jackson	.25	.11	.03
☐ 6 Pat Jarvis	.25	.11	.03
☐ 7 Felix Millan	.25	.11	.03
☐ 8 Milt Pappas	.50	.23	.06
☐ 9 Ron Reed	.25	.11	.03
☐ 10 Joe Torre	1.25	.55	.16
☐ 11 Ernie Banks	4.00	1.80	.50
☐ 12 Glenn Beckert	.25	.11	.03
☐ 13 Bill Hands	.25	.11	.03
☐ 14 Randy Hundley	.25	.11	.03
☐ 15 Ferguson Jenkins	2.50	1.10	.30
☐ 16 Don Kessinger	.50	.23	.06
☐ 17 Adolpho Phillips	.25	.11	.03
☐ 18 Phil Regan	.25	.11	.03
☐ 19 Ron Santo	1.25	.55	.16
☐ 20 Billy Williams	2.50	1.10	.30
☐ 21 Ted Abernathy	.25	.11	.03
☐ 22 Gerry Arrigo	.25	.11	.03
☐ 23 Johnny Bench	5.00	2.20	.60
☐ 24 Tommy Helms	.25	.11	.03
☐ 25 Alex Johnson	.25	.11	.03
☐ 26 Jim Maloney	.50	.23	.06
☐ 27 Lee May	.50	.23	.06
☐ 28 Tony Perez	1.50	.70	.19
☐ 29 Pete Rose	15.00	6.75	1.85
☐ 30 Bobby Tolan	.25	.11	.03
☐ 31 Bob Aspromonte	.25	.11	.03
☐ 32 Larry Dierker	.25	.11	.03
☐ 33 Johnny Edwards	.25	.11	.03
☐ 34 Denver Lemaster	.25	.11	.03
☐ 35 Denis Menke	.25	.11	.03
☐ 36 Joe Morgan	3.00	1.35	.35
☐ 37 Doug Rader	.25	.11	.03
☐ 38 Rusty Staub	1.00	.45	.12
☐ 39 Don Wilson	.25	.11	.03
☐ 40 Jim Wynn	.50	.23	.06
☐ 41 Willie Davis	.50	.23	.06
☐ 42 Don Drysdale	.25	.11	.03
☐ 43 Ron Fairly	.25	.11	.03
☐ 44 Len Gabrielson	.25	.11	.03
☐ 45 Tom Haller	.25	.11	.03
☐ 46 Jim LeFebvre	.25	.11	.03
☐ 47 Claude Osteen	.50	.23	.06
☐ 48 Paul Popovich	.25	.11	.03
☐ 49 Bill Singer	.25	.11	.03
☐ 50 Don Sutton	2.00	.90	.25
☐ 51 Jesus Alou	.25	.11	.03
☐ 52 Bob Bailey	.25	.11	.03
☐ 53 John Bateman	.25	.11	.03
☐ 54 Donn Clendenon	.25	.11	.03
☐ 55 Jim Grant	.25	.11	.03
☐ 56 Larry Jaster	.25	.11	.03
☐ 57 Mack Jones	.25	.11	.03
☐ 58 Manny Mota	.50	.23	.06
☐ 59 Gary Sutherland	.25	.11	.03
☐ 60 Maury Wills	1.50	.70	.19
☐ 61 Tommy Agee	.25	.11	.03
☐ 62 Ed Charles	.25	.11	.03
☐ 63 Jerry Grote	.25	.11	.03
☐ 64 Bud Harrelson	.25	.11	.03
☐ 65 Cleon Jones	.25	.11	.03
☐ 66 Jerry Koosman	.50	.23	.06
☐ 67 Ed Kranepool	.25	.11	.03
☐ 68 Tom Seaver	8.00	3.60	1.00
☐ 69 Art Shamsky	.25	.11	.03
☐ 70 Ron Swoboda	.25	.11	.03
☐ 71 Richie Allen	1.00	.45	.12
☐ 72 John Briggs	.25	.11	.03
☐ 73 John Callison	.50	.23	.06
☐ 74 Clay Dalrymple	.25	.11	.03
☐ 75 Woody Fryman	.25	.11	.03
☐ 76 Don Lock	.25	.11	.03
☐ 77 Cookie Rojas	.50	.23	.06
☐ 78 Chris Short	.25	.11	.03
☐ 79 Ron Taylor	.25	.11	.03
☐ 80 Rick Wise	.25	.11	.03
☐ 81 Gene Alley	.25	.11	.03
☐ 82 Matty Alou	.50	.23	.06
☐ 83 Steve Blass	.50	.23	.06
☐ 84 Jim Bunning	2.50	1.10	.30
☐ 85 Roberto Clemente	20.00	9.00	2.50
☐ 86 Ron Kline	.25	.11	.03
☐ 87 Jerry May	.25	.11	.03
☐ 88 Bill Mazeroski	2.00	.90	.25
☐ 89 Willie Stargell	3.00	1.35	.35
☐ 90 Bob Veale	.25	.11	.03
☐ 91 Jose Arcia	.25	.11	.03
☐ 92 Ollie Brown	.25	.11	.03
☐ 93 Al Ferrara	.25	.11	.03
☐ 94 Tony Gonzalez	.25	.11	.03
☐ 95 Dave Giusti	.25	.11	.03
☐ 96 Alvin McBean	.25	.11	.03
☐ 97 Orlando Pena	.25	.11	.03
☐ 98 Dick Selma	.25	.11	.03
☐ 99 Larry Stahl	.25	.11	.03
☐ 100 Zoilo Versalles	.25	.11	.03
☐ 101 Bobby Bolin	.25	.11	.03
☐ 102 Jim Davenport	.25	.11	.03
☐ 103 Dick Dietz	.25	.11	.03
☐ 104 Jim Ray Hart	.25	.11	.03
☐ 105 Ron Hunt	.25	.11	.03
☐ 106 Hal Lanier	.50	.23	.06
☐ 107 Juan Marichal	3.00	1.35	.35
☐ 108 Willie Mays	10.00	4.50	1.25
☐ 109 Willie McCovey	3.00	1.35	.35
☐ 110 Gaylord Perry	2.50	1.10	.30
☐ 111 Nelson Briles	.25	.11	.03
☐ 112 Lou Brock	4.00	1.80	.50
☐ 113 Orlando Cepeda	2.00	.90	.25
☐ 114 Curt Flood	1.00	.45	.12
☐ 115 Bob Gibson	3.00	1.35	.35
☐ 116 Julian Javier	.25	.11	.03
☐ 117 Dal Maxvill	.25	.11	.03
☐ 118 Tim McCarver	1.00	.45	.12
☐ 119 Vada Pinson	1.00	.45	.12
☐ 120 Mike Shannon	.50	.23	.06
☐ 121 Mark Belanger	.50	.23	.06
☐ 122 Curt Blefary	.25	.11	.03
☐ 123 Don Buford	.25	.11	.03
☐ 124 Jim Hardin	.25	.11	.03
☐ 125 Dave Johnson	1.00	.45	.12
☐ 126 Dave McNally	.50	.23	.06
☐ 127 Tom Phoebus	.25	.11	.03
☐ 128 Boog Powell	1.25	.55	.16
☐ 129 Brooks Robinson	4.00	1.80	.50
☐ 130 Frank Robinson	4.00	1.80	.50
☐ 131 Mike Andrews	.25	.11	.03
☐ 132 Ray Culp	.25	.11	.03
☐ 133 Russ Gibson	.25	.11	.03
☐ 134 Ken Harrelson	1.00	.45	.12
☐ 135 Jim Lonborg	.50	.23	.06
☐ 136 Rico Petrocelli	.50	.23	.06
☐ 137 Jose Santiago	.25	.11	.03
☐ 138 George Scott	.50	.23	.06
☐ 139 Reggie Smith	1.00	.45	.12
☐ 140 Carl Yastrzemski	5.00	2.20	.60
☐ 141 George Brunet	.25	.11	.03
☐ 142 Vic Davalillo	.25	.11	.03
☐ 143 Eddie Fisher	.25	.11	.03
☐ 144 Jim Fregosi	.50	.23	.06
☐ 145 Bobby Knoop	.25	.11	.03
☐ 146 Jim McGlothlin	.25	.11	.03
☐ 147 Rick Reichardt	.25	.11	.03
☐ 148 Roger Repoz	.25	.11	.03
☐ 149 Bob Rodgers	.50	.23	.06
☐ 150 Tom Satriano	.25	.11	.03
☐ 151 Sandy Alomar	.25	.11	.03
☐ 152 Luis Aparicio	2.50	1.10	.30
☐ 153 Ken Berry	.25	.11	.03
☐ 154 Joel Horlen	.25	.11	.03
☐ 155 Tommy John	1.50	.70	.19
☐ 156 Duane Josephson	.25	.11	.03
☐ 157 Gary Peters	.25	.11	.03
☐ 158 Gary Wagner	.25	.11	.03
☐ 159 Pete Ward	.25	.11	.03
☐ 160 Wilbur Wood	.25	.11	.03
☐ 161 Max Alvis	.25	.11	.03
☐ 162 Joe Azcue	.25	.11	.03
☐ 163 Larry Brown	.25	.11	.03
☐ 164 Jose Cardenal	.25	.11	.03
☐ 165 Lee Maye	.25	.11	.03
☐ 166 Sam McDowell	.50	.23	.06
☐ 167 Sonny Siebert	.25	.11	.03
☐ 168 Duke Sims	.25	.11	.03
☐ 169 Luis Tiant	1.00	.45	.12
☐ 170 Stan Williams	.25	.11	.03
☐ 171 Norm Cash	1.00	.45	.12
☐ 172 Bill Freehan	.50	.23	.06
☐ 173 Willie Horton	.50	.23	.06
☐ 174 Al Kaline	4.00	1.80	.50
☐ 175 Mickey Lolich	1.00	.45	.12
☐ 176 Dick McAuliffe	.25	.11	.03
☐ 177 Denny McLain	1.00	.45	.12
☐ 178 Jim Northrup	.25	.11	.03
☐ 179 Mickey Stanley	.25	.11	.03
☐ 180 Don Wert	.25	.11	.03
☐ 181 Jerry Adair	.25	.11	.03
☐ 182 Wally Bunker	.25	.11	.03
☐ 183 Moe Drabowsky	.25	.11	.03
☐ 184 Joe Foy	.25	.11	.03
☐ 185 Jackie Hernandez	.25	.11	.03
☐ 186 Roger Nelson	.25	.11	.03
☐ 187 Bob Oliver	.25	.11	.03
☐ 188 Paul Schaal	.25	.11	.03
☐ 189 Steve Whitaker	.25	.11	.03
☐ 190 Hoyt Wilhelm	2.50	1.10	.30
☐ 191 Bob Allison	.50	.23	.06
☐ 192 Rod Carew	4.00	1.80	.50
☐ 193 Dean Chance	.50	.23	.06
☐ 194 Jim Kaat	1.25	.55	.16
☐ 195 Harmon Killebrew	3.00	1.35	.35
☐ 196 Tony Oliva	1.50	.70	.19
☐ 197 Ron Perranoski	.25	.11	.03
☐ 198 John Roseboro	.25	.11	.03
☐ 199 Cesar Tovar	.25	.11	.03
☐ 200 Ted Uhlaender	.25	.11	.03
☐ 201 Stan Bahnsen	.25	.11	.03
☐ 202 Horace Clarke	.25	.11	.03
☐ 203 Jake Gibbs	.25	.11	.03
☐ 204 Andy Kosco	.25	.11	.03
☐ 205 Mickey Mantle	35.00	16.00	4.40
☐ 206 Joe Pepitone	.50	.23	.06
☐ 207 Bill Robinson	.50	.23	.06
☐ 208 Mel Stottlemyre	.50	.23	.06
☐ 209 Tom Tresh	.50	.23	.06
☐ 210 Roy White	.50	.23	.06
☐ 211 Sal Bando	.50	.23	.06
☐ 212 Bert Campaneris	.50	.23	.06
☐ 213 Danny Cater	.25	.11	.03
☐ 214 Dave Duncan	.25	.11	.03
☐ 215 Dick Green	.25	.11	.03
☐ 216 Jim Hunter	2.50	1.10	.30
☐ 217 Lew Krausse	.25	.11	.03
☐ 218 Rick Monday	.50	.23	.06
☐ 219 Jim Nash	.25	.11	.03
☐ 220 John Odom	.25	.11	.03
☐ 221 Jack Aker	.25	.11	.03
☐ 222 Steve Barber	.25	.11	.03
☐ 223 Gary Bell	.25	.11	.03
☐ 224 Tommy Davis	.50	.23	.06
☐ 225 Tommy Harper	.25	.11	.03
☐ 226 Jerry McNertney	.25	.11	.03
☐ 227 Don Mincher	.25	.11	.03
☐ 228 Ray Oyler	.25	.11	.03
☐ 229 Rich Rollins	.25	.11	.03
☐ 230 Chico Salmon	.25	.11	.03
☐ 231 Bernie Allen	.25	.11	.03
☐ 232 Ed Brinkman	.25	.11	.03
☐ 233 Paul Casanova	.25	.11	.03
☐ 234 Joe Coleman	.25	.11	.03
☐ 235 Mike Epstein	.25	.11	.03
☐ 236 Jim Hannan	.25	.11	.03
☐ 237 Dennis Higgins	.25	.11	.03
☐ 238 Frank Howard	1.00	.45	.12
☐ 239 Ken McMullen	.25	.11	.03
☐ 240 Camilo Pascual	.25	.11	.03

1969 Topps Stamp Albums

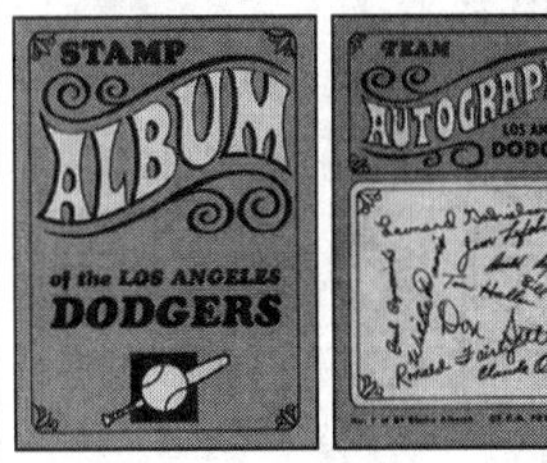

The 1969 Topps stamp set of baseball player stamps was intended to be mounted in 24 separate team albums, 10 stamps for that team's players going into that team's album. The eight-page albums are bright orange and have an autograph feature on the back cover. The albums measure approximately 2 1/2" by 3 1/2".

	NRMT	VG-E	GOOD
COMPLETE SET (24)	30.00	13.50	3.70
COMMON TEAM (1-24)	1.50	.70	.19
☐ 1 Atlanta Braves	1.50	.70	.19
☐ 2 Baltimore Orioles	1.50	.70	.19
☐ 3 Boston Red Sox	1.50	.70	.19
☐ 4 California Angels	1.50	.70	.19
☐ 5 Chicago Cubs	1.50	.70	.19
☐ 6 Chicago White Sox	1.50	.70	.19
☐ 7 Cincinnati Reds	1.50	.70	.19
☐ 8 Cleveland Indians	1.50	.70	.19
☐ 9 Detroit Tigers	1.50	.70	.19
☐ 10 Houston Astros	1.50	.70	.19
☐ 11 Kansas City Royals	1.50	.70	.19
☐ 12 Los Angeles Dodgers	1.50	.70	.19
☐ 13 Minnesota Twins	1.50	.70	.19
☐ 15 New York Mets	1.50	.70	.19
☐ 16 New York Yankees	1.50	.70	.19
☐ 17 Oakland A's	1.50	.70	.19
☐ 18 Philadelphia Phillies	1.50	.70	.19
☐ 19 Pittsburgh Pirates	1.50	.70	.19
☐ 20 St. Louis Cardinals	1.50	.70	.19
☐ 21 San Diego Padres	1.50	.70	.19
☐ 22 San Francisco Giants	1.50	.70	.19
☐ 23 Seattle Pilots	2.50	1.10	.30
☐ 24 Washington Senators	1.50	.70	.19

1969 Topps Team Posters

This set was issued as a separate set by Topps, but was apparently not widely distributed. It was folded many times to fit the packaging and hence is typically found with relatively heavy fold creases. Each team poster measures approximately 12" by 20". These posters are in full color with a blank back. Each team features nine or ten individual players; a complete list is listed in the checklist below. Each player photo is accompanied by a facsimile autograph. The posters are numbered in the bottom left corner.

	NRMT	VG-E	GOOD
COMPLETE SET (24)	1200.00	550.00	150.00
COMMON TEAM (1-24)	20.00	9.00	2.50
☐ 1 Detroit Tigers	40.00	18.00	5.00
Norm Cash			
Al Kaline			
Mickey Lolich			
Denny McLain			
Bill Freehan			
Willie Horton			
Dick McAuliffe			
Jim Northrup			
Mickey Stanley			
Don Wert			
Earl Wilson			
☐ 2 Atlanta Braves	60.00	27.00	7.50
Hank Aaron			
Phil Niekro			
Joe Torre			
Felipe Alou			
Clete Boyer			
Rico Carty			
Tito Francona			
Sonny Jackson			
Pat Jarvis			
Felix Millan			
Milt Pappas			
☐ 3 Boston Red Sox	60.00	27.00	7.50
Carl Yastrzemski			
Mike Andrews			
Tony Conigliaro			
Ray Culp			
Russ Gibson			
Ken Harrelson			
Jim Lonborg			
Rico Petrocelli			
Jose Santiago			
George Scott			
Reggie Smith			
☐ 4 Chicago Cubs	50.00	22.00	6.25
Ernie Banks			
Billy Williams			
Glenn Beckert			
Bill Hands			
Jim Hickman			
Ken Holtzman			
Randy Hundley			
Fergie Jenkins			
Don Kessinger			
Adolpho Phillips			
Ron Santo			
☐ 5 Baltimore Orioles	60.00	27.00	7.50
Boog Powell			
Brooks Robinson			
Frank Robinson			
Mark Belanger			
Paul Blair			
Don Buford			
Andy Etchebarren			
Jim Hardin			
Dave Johnson			
Dave McNally			
Tom Phoebus			
☐ 6 Houston Astros	20.00	9.00	2.50
Joe Morgan			
Curt Blefary			
Donn Clendenon			
Larry Dierker			
John Edwards			
Denny Lemaster			
Denis Menke			
Norm Miller			
Doug Rader			
Don Wilson			
Jim Wynn			
☐ 7 Kansas City Royals	20.00	9.00	2.50
Wally Bunker			
Jerry Adair			
Mike Fiore			
Joe Foy			
Jackie Hernandez			
Pat Kelly			
Dave Morehead			
Roger Nelson			
Dave Nicholson			
Ellie Rodriguez			
Steve Whitaker			
☐ 8 Philadelphia Phillies	20.00	9.00	2.50
Richie Allen			
John Callison			
Woodie Fryman			

Larry Hisle
Don Money
Cookie Rojas
Mike Ryan
Chris Short
Tony Taylor
Bill White
Rick Wise

☐ 9 Seattle Pilots 40.00 18.00 5.00
Tommy Davis
Jack Aker
Steve Barber
Gary Bell
Jim Gosger
Tommy Harper
Jerry McNertney
Don Mincher
Ray Oyler
Rich Rollins
Chico Salmon

☐ 10 Montreal Expos 20.00 9.00 2.50
Rusty Staub
Maury Wills
Bob Bailey
John Bateman
Jack Billingham
Jim Grant
Larry Jaster
Mack Jones
Manny Mota
Gary Sutherland
Jimy Williams

☐ 11 Chicago White Sox 20.00 9.00 2.50
Luis Aparicio
Tommy John
Sandy Alomar
Ken Berry
Buddy Bradford
Joe Horlen
Duane Josephson
Tom McCraw
Bill Melton
Pete Ward
Wilbur Wood

☐ 12 San Diego Padres 20.00 9.00 2.50
Ollie Brown
Jose Arcia
Danny Breeden
Bill Davis
Ron Davis
Tony Gonzalez
Dick Kelley
Al McBean
Roberto Pena
Dick Selma
Ed Spiezio

☐ 13 Cleveland Indians 20.00 9.00 2.50
Luis Tiant
Max Alvis
Joe Azcue
Jose Cardenal
Vern Fuller
Lou Johnson
Sam McDowell
Sonny Siebert
Duke Sims
Russ Snyder
Zoilo Versalles

☐ 14 San Francisco Giants 50.00 22.00 6.25
Juan Marichal
Willie Mays
Willie McCovey
Gaylord Perry
Bobby Bolin
Jim Davenport
Dick Dietz
Jim Ray Hart
Ron Hunt
Hal Lanier
Charley Smith

☐ 15 Minnesota Twins 30.00 13.50 3.70
Rod Carew
Harmon Killebrew
Bob Allison
Chico Cardenas
Dean Chance
Jim Kaat
Tony Oliva
Jim Perry
John Roseboro
Cesar Tovar
Ted Uhlaender

☐ 16 Pittsburgh Pirates 125.00 55.00 15.50
Roberto Clemente
Willie Stargell
Gene Alley
Matty Alou
Steve Blass
Jim Bunning
Richie Hebner
Jerry May
Bill Mazeroski
Bob Robertson
Bob Veale

☐ 17 California Angels 20.00 9.00 2.50
Hoyt Wilhelm
Ruben Amaro
George Brunet
Bob Chance
Vic Davalillo
Jim Fregosi
Bobby Knoop
Jim McGlothlin
Rick Reichardt
Roger Repoz
Bob Rodgers

☐ 18 St. Louis Cardinals 40.00 18.00 5.00
Lou Brock
Orlando Cepeda
Curt Flood
Bob Gibson
Nellie Briles
Julian Javier
Dal Maxvill
Tim McCarver
Vada Pinson
Mike Shannon
Ray Washburn

☐ 19 New York Yankees 175.00 80.00 22.00
Mickey Mantle
Mel Stottlemyre
Tom Tresh
Stan Bahnsen
Horace Clarke
Bobby Cox
Jake Gibbs
Joe Pepitone
Fritz Peterson
Bill Robinson
Roy White

☐ 20 Cincinnati Reds 100.00 45.00 12.50
Johnny Bench
Tony Perez
Pete Rose
Gerry Arrigo
Tommy Helms
Alex Johnson
Jim Maloney
Lee May
Gary Nolan
Bob Tolan
Woody Woodward

☐ 21 Oakland A's 100.00 45.00 12.50
Jim Hunter
Reggie Jackson
Sal Bando
Bert Campaneris
Danny Cater
Dick Green
Mike Hershberger
Rick Monday
Jim Nash
John Odom
Jim Pagliaroni

☐ 22 Los Angeles Dodgers 30.00 13.50 3.70
Don Drysdale
Willie Crawford
Willie Davis
Ron Fairly
Tom Haller
Andy Kosco
Jim Lefevre
Claude Osteen
Paul Popovich
Bill Singer
Bill Sudakis

☐ 23 Washington Senators 20.00 9.00 2.50
Frank Howard
Bernie Allen
Brant Alyea
Ed Brinkman
Paul Casanova
Joe Coleman
Mike Epstein
Jim Hannan
Ken McMullen
Camilo Pascual
Del Unser

☐ 24 New York Mets 100.00 45.00 12.50
Tom Seaver
Tommie Agee
Ken Boswell
Ed Charles
Jerry Grote
Bud Harrelson
Cleon Jones
Jerry Koosman
Ed Kranepool
Jim McAndrew
Ron Swoboda

1970 Topps

The cards in this 720-card set measure 2 1/2" by 3 1/2". The Topps set for 1970 has color photos surrounded by white frame lines and gray borders. The backs have a blue biographical section and a yellow record section. All-Star selections are featured on cards 450 to 469. Other topical subsets within this set include League Leaders (61-72), Playoffs cards (195-202), and World Series cards (305-310). There are graduations of scarcity, terminating in the high series (634-720), which are outlined in the value summary. Cards were issued in ten-card dime packs as well as thirty-three card cello packs encased in a small Topps box. The key Rookie Card in this set is Thurman Munson.

	NRMT	VG-E	GOOD
COMPLETE SET (720)	1800.00	800.00	220.00
COMMON CARD (1-372)	1.00	.45	.12
COMMON CARD (373-459)	1.50	.70	.19
COMMON CARD (460-546)	2.00	.90	.25
COMMON CARD (547-633)	4.00	1.80	.50
COMMON CARD (634-720)	10.00	4.50	1.25
WRAPPER (10-CENT)	1.00	.45	.12
☐ 1 New York Mets Team Card	16.00	5.00	1.50
☐ 2 Diego Segui	1.50	.70	.19
☐ 3 Darrel Chaney	1.00	.45	.12
☐ 4 Tom Egan	1.00	.45	.12
☐ 5 Wes Parker	1.50	.70	.19
☐ 6 Grant Jackson	1.00	.45	.12
☐ 7 Indians Rookies	1.00	.45	.12
Gary Boyd			
Russ Nagelson			
☐ 8 Jose Martinez	1.00	.45	.12
☐ 9 Checklist 1	12.00	2.40	1.20
☐ 10 Carl Yastrzemski	14.00	6.25	1.75
☐ 11 Nate Colbert	1.00	.45	.12
☐ 12 John Hiller	1.50	.70	.19
☐ 13 Jack Hiatt	1.00	.45	.12
☐ 14 Hank Allen	1.00	.45	.12
☐ 15 Larry Dierker	1.50	.70	.19
☐ 16 Charlie Metro MG	1.00	.45	.12
☐ 17 Hoyt Wilhelm	5.00	2.20	.60
☐ 18 Carlos May	1.50	.70	.19
☐ 19 John Boccabella	1.00	.45	.12
☐ 20 Dave McNally	1.50	.70	.19
☐ 21 A's Rookies	6.00	2.70	.75
Vida Blue			
Gene Tenace			
☐ 22 Ray Washburn	1.00	.45	.12
☐ 23 Bill Robinson	1.50	.70	.19
☐ 24 Dick Selma	1.00	.45	.12
☐ 25 Cesar Tovar	1.00	.45	.12
☐ 26 Tug McGraw	1.50	.70	.19
☐ 27 Chuck Hinton	1.00	.45	.12
☐ 28 Billy Wilson	1.00	.45	.12
☐ 29 Sandy Alomar	1.50	.70	.19
☐ 30 Matty Alou	1.50	.70	.19
☐ 31 Marty Pattin	1.50	.70	.19
☐ 32 Harry Walker MG	1.00	.45	.12
☐ 33 Don Wert	1.00	.45	.12
☐ 34 Willie Crawford	1.00	.45	.12
☐ 35 Joel Horlen	1.00	.45	.12
☐ 36 Red Rookies	2.00	.90	.25
Danny Breeden			
Bernie Carbo			
☐ 37 Dick Drago	1.00	.45	.12
☐ 38 Mack Jones	1.00	.45	.12
☐ 39 Mike Nagy	1.00	.45	.12
☐ 40 Rich Allen	2.00	.90	.25
☐ 41 George Lauzerique	1.00	.45	.12
☐ 42 Tito Fuentes	1.00	.45	.12
☐ 43 Jack Aker	1.00	.45	.12
☐ 44 Roberto Pena	1.00	.45	.12
☐ 45 Dave Johnson	2.00	.90	.25
☐ 46 Ken Rudolph	1.00	.45	.12
☐ 47 Bob Miller	1.00	.45	.12
☐ 48 Gil Garrido	1.00	.45	.12
☐ 49 Tim Cullen	1.00	.45	.12
☐ 50 Tommie Agee	1.50	.70	.19
☐ 51 Bob Christian	1.00	.45	.12
☐ 52 Bruce Dal Canton	1.00	.45	.12
☐ 53 John Kennedy	1.00	.45	.12
☐ 54 Jeff Torborg	1.50	.70	.19
☐ 55 John Odom	1.00	.45	.12
☐ 56 Phillies Rookies	1.00	.45	.12
Joe Lis			
Scott Reid			
☐ 57 Pat Kelly	1.00	.45	.12
☐ 58 Dave Marshall	1.00	.45	.12
☐ 59 Dick Ellsworth	1.00	.45	.12
☐ 60 Jim Wynn	1.50	.70	.19
☐ 61 NL Batting Leaders	12.00	5.50	1.50
Pete Rose			
Bob Clemente			
Cleon Jones			
☐ 62 AL Batting Leaders	3.50	1.55	.45
Rod Carew			
Reggie Smith			
Tony Oliva			
☐ 63 NL RBI Leaders	4.00	1.80	.50
Willie McCovey			
Ron Santo			
Tony Perez			
☐ 64 AL RBI Leaders	6.00	2.70	.75
Harmon Killebrew			
Boog Powell			
Reggie Jackson			
☐ 65 NL Home Run Leaders	6.00	2.70	.75
Willie McCovey			
Hank Aaron			
Lee May			
☐ 66 AL Home Run Leaders	6.00	2.70	.75
Harmon Killebrew			
Frank Howard			
Reggie Jackson			
☐ 67 NL ERA Leaders	7.00	3.10	.85
Juan Marichal			
Steve Carlton			
Bob Gibson			
☐ 68 AL ERA Leaders	3.00	1.35	.35
Dick Bosman			
Jim Palmer			
Mike Cuellar			
☐ 69 NL Pitching Leaders	7.00	3.10	.85
Tom Seaver			
Phil Niekro			
Fergie Jenkins			
Juan Marichal			
☐ 70 AL Pitching Leaders	2.00	.90	.25
Dennis McLain			
Mike Cuellar			
Dave Boswell			
Dave McNally			
Jim Perry			
Mel Stottlemyre			
☐ 71 NL Strikeout Leaders	4.00	1.80	.50
Fergie Jenkins			
Bob Gibson			
Bill Singer			
☐ 72 AL Strikeout Leaders	2.00	.90	.25
Sam McDowell			
Mickey Lolich			
Andy Messersmith			
☐ 73 Wayne Granger	1.00	.45	.12
☐ 74 Angels Rookies	1.00	.45	.12
Greg Washburn			
Wally Wolf			
☐ 75 Jim Kaat	2.00	.90	.25
☐ 76 Carl Taylor	1.00	.45	.12
☐ 77 Frank Linzy	1.00	.45	.12
☐ 78 Joe Lahoud	1.00	.45	.12
☐ 79 Clay Kirby	1.00	.45	.12
☐ 80 Don Kessinger	1.50	.70	.19
☐ 81 Dave May	1.00	.45	.12
☐ 82 Frank Fernandez	1.00	.45	.12
☐ 83 Don Cardwell	1.00	.45	.12
☐ 84 Paul Casanova	1.00	.45	.12
☐ 85 Max Alvis	1.00	.45	.12
☐ 86 Lum Harris MG	1.00	.45	.12
☐ 87 Steve Renko	1.00	.45	.12
☐ 88 Pilots Rookies	1.50	.70	.19
Miguel Fuentes			
Dick Baney			
☐ 89 Juan Rios	1.00	.45	.12
☐ 90 Tim McCarver	1.50	.70	.19
☐ 91 Rich Morales	1.00	.45	.12
☐ 92 George Culver	1.00	.45	.12
☐ 93 Rick Renick	1.00	.45	.12
☐ 94 Freddie Patek	1.50	.70	.19
☐ 95 Earl Wilson	1.50	.70	.19
☐ 96 Cardinals Rookies	2.00	.90	.25
Leron Lee			
Jerry Reuss			
☐ 97 Joe Moeller	1.00	.45	.12
☐ 98 Gates Brown	1.50	.70	.19
☐ 99 Bobby Pfeil	1.00	.45	.12
☐ 100 Mel Stottlemyre	2.00	.90	.25
☐ 101 Bobby Floyd	1.00	.45	.12
☐ 102 Joe Rudi	1.50	.70	.19
☐ 103 Frank Reberger	1.00	.45	.12
☐ 104 Gerry Moses	1.00	.45	.12
☐ 105 Tony Gonzalez	1.00	.45	.12
☐ 106 Darold Knowles	1.00	.45	.12
☐ 107 Bobby Etheridge	1.00	.45	.12
☐ 108 Tom Burgmeier	1.00	.45	.12
☐ 109 Expos Rookies	1.00	.45	.12
Garry Jestadt			
Carl Morton			
☐ 110 Bob Moose	1.00	.45	.12
☐ 111 Mike Hegan	1.50	.70	.19
☐ 112 Dave Nelson	1.00	.45	.12
☐ 113 Jim Ray	1.00	.45	.12
☐ 114 Gene Michael	1.50	.70	.19
☐ 115 Alex Johnson	1.50	.70	.19
☐ 116 Sparky Lyle	2.00	.90	.25
☐ 117 Don Young	1.00	.45	.12
☐ 118 George Mitterwald	1.00	.45	.12
☐ 119 Chuck Taylor	1.00	.45	.12
☐ 120 Sal Bando	2.00	.90	.25
☐ 121 Orioles Rookies	1.00	.45	.12
Fred Beene			
Terry Crowley			
☐ 122 George Stone	1.00	.45	.12
☐ 123 Don Gutteridge MG	1.00	.45	.12
☐ 124 Larry Jaster	1.00	.45	.12
☐ 125 Deron Johnson	1.00	.45	.12
☐ 126 Marty Martinez	1.00	.45	.12
☐ 127 Joe Coleman	1.00	.45	.12

Card			
☐ 128A Checklist 2 ERR	6.00	1.20	.60
(226 R Perranoski)			
☐ 128B Checklist 2 COR	6.00	1.20	.60
(226 R. Perranoski)			
☐ 129 Jimmie Price	1.00	.45	.12
☐ 130 Ollie Brown	1.00	.45	.12
☐ 131 Dodgers Rookies	1.00	.45	.12
Ray Lamb			
Bob Stinson			
☐ 132 Jim McGlothlin	1.00	.45	.12
☐ 133 Clay Carroll	1.00	.45	.12
☐ 134 Danny Walton	1.00	.45	.12
☐ 135 Dick Dietz	1.00	.45	.12
☐ 136 Steve Hargan	1.00	.45	.12
☐ 137 Art Shamsky	1.00	.45	.12
☐ 138 Joe Foy	1.00	.45	.12
☐ 139 Rich Nye	1.00	.45	.12
☐ 140 Reggie Jackson	50.00	22.00	6.25
☐ 141 Pirates Rookies	1.50	.70	.19
Dave Cash			
Johnny Jeter			
☐ 142 Fritz Peterson	1.00	.45	.12
☐ 143 Phil Gagliano	1.00	.45	.12
☐ 144 Ray Culp	1.00	.45	.12
☐ 145 Rico Carty	1.50	.70	.19
☐ 146 Danny Murphy	1.00	.45	.12
☐ 147 Angel Hermoso	1.00	.45	.12
☐ 148 Earl Weaver MG	3.00	1.35	.35
☐ 149 Billy Champion	1.00	.45	.12
☐ 150 Harmon Killebrew	8.00	3.60	1.00
☐ 151 Dave Roberts	1.00	.45	.12
☐ 152 Ike Brown	1.00	.45	.12
☐ 153 Gary Gentry	1.00	.45	.12
☐ 154 Senators Rookies	1.00	.45	.12
Jim Miles			
Jan Dukes			
☐ 155 Denis Menke	1.00	.45	.12
☐ 156 Eddie Fisher	1.00	.45	.12
☐ 157 Manny Mota	1.50	.70	.19
☐ 158 Jerry McNertney	1.50	.70	.19
☐ 159 Tommy Helms	1.50	.70	.19
☐ 160 Phil Niekro	5.00	2.20	.60
☐ 161 Richie Scheinblum	1.00	.45	.12
☐ 162 Jerry Johnson	1.00	.45	.12
☐ 163 Syd O'Brien	1.00	.45	.12
☐ 164 Ty Cline	1.00	.45	.12
☐ 165 Ed Kirkpatrick	1.00	.45	.12
☐ 166 Al Oliver	2.00	.90	.25
☐ 167 Bill Burbach	1.00	.45	.12
☐ 168 Dave Watkins	1.00	.45	.12
☐ 169 Tom Hall	1.00	.45	.12
☐ 170 Billy Williams	7.00	3.10	.85
☐ 171 Jim Nash	1.00	.45	.12
☐ 172 Braves Rookies	2.00	.90	.25
Garry Hill			
Ralph Garr			
☐ 173 Jim Hicks	1.00	.45	.12
☐ 174 Ted Sizemore	1.50	.70	.19
☐ 175 Dick Bosman	1.00	.45	.12
☐ 176 Jim Ray Hart	1.50	.70	.19
☐ 177 Jim Northrup	1.50	.70	.19
☐ 178 Denny Lemaster	1.00	.45	.12
☐ 179 Ivan Murrell	1.00	.45	.12
☐ 180 Tommy John	2.00	.90	.25
☐ 181 Sparky Anderson MG	5.00	2.20	.60
☐ 182 Dick Hall	1.00	.45	.12
☐ 183 Jerry Grote	1.00	.45	.12
☐ 184 Ray Fosse	1.00	.45	.12
☐ 185 Don Mincher	1.50	.70	.19
☐ 186 Rick Joseph	1.00	.45	.12
☐ 187 Mike Hedlund	1.00	.45	.12
☐ 188 Manny Sanguillen	1.50	.70	.19
☐ 189 Yankees Rookies	50.00	22.00	6.25
Thurman Munson			
Dave McDonald			
☐ 190 Joe Torre	2.00	.90	.25
☐ 191 Vicente Romo	1.00	.45	.12
☐ 192 Jim Qualls	1.00	.45	.12
☐ 193 Mike Wegener	1.00	.45	.12
☐ 194 Chuck Manuel	1.00	.45	.12
☐ 195 Tom Seaver NLCS	15.00	6.75	1.85
☐ 196 Ken Boswell NLCS	2.50	1.10	.30
☐ 197 Nolan Ryan NLCS	30.00	13.50	3.70
☐ 198 NL Playoff Summary	15.00	6.75	1.85
Mets celebrate			
(Nolan Ryan)			
☐ 199 Mike Cuellar ALCS	2.50	1.10	.30
☐ 200 Boog Powell ALCS	3.50	1.55	.45
☐ 201 Boog Powell ALCS	2.50	1.10	.30
Andy Etchebarren)			
☐ 202 AL Playoff Summary	2.50	1.10	.30
Orioles celebrate			
☐ 203 Rudy May	1.00	.45	.12
☐ 204 Len Gabrielson	1.00	.45	.12
☐ 205 Bert Campaneris	2.00	.90	.25
☐ 206 Clete Boyer	1.50	.70	.19
☐ 207 Tigers Rookies	1.00	.45	.12
Norman McRae			
Bob Reed			
☐ 208 Fred Gladding	1.00	.45	.12
☐ 209 Ken Suarez	1.00	.45	.12
☐ 210 Juan Marichal	7.00	3.10	.85
☐ 211 Ted Williams MG	12.00	5.50	1.50
☐ 212 Al Santorini	1.00	.45	.12
☐ 213 Andy Etchebarren	1.00	.45	.12
☐ 214 Ken Boswell	1.00	.45	.12
☐ 215 Reggie Smith	2.00	.90	.25
☐ 216 Chuck Hartenstein	1.00	.45	.12
☐ 217 Ron Hansen	1.00	.45	.12
☐ 218 Ron Stone	1.00	.45	.12
☐ 219 Jerry Kenney	1.00	.45	.12
☐ 220 Steve Carlton	15.00	6.75	1.85
☐ 221 Ron Brand	1.00	.45	.12
☐ 222 Jim Rooker	1.50	.70	.19
☐ 223 Nate Oliver	1.00	.45	.12
☐ 224 Steve Barber	1.50	.70	.19
☐ 225 Lee May	1.50	.70	.19
☐ 226 Ron Perranoski	1.50	.70	.19
☐ 227 Astros Rookies	1.50	.70	.19
John Mayberry			
Bob Watkins			
☐ 228 Aurelio Rodriguez	1.50	.70	.19
☐ 229 Rich Robertson	1.00	.45	.12
☐ 230 Brooks Robinson	14.00	6.25	1.75
☐ 231 Luis Tiant	1.50	.70	.19
☐ 232 Bob Didier	1.00	.45	.12
☐ 233 Lew Krausse	1.00	.45	.12
☐ 234 Tommy Dean	1.00	.45	.12
☐ 235 Mike Epstein	1.00	.45	.12
☐ 236 Bob Veale	1.50	.70	.19
☐ 237 Russ Gibson	1.00	.45	.12
☐ 238 Jose Laboy	1.00	.45	.12
☐ 239 Ken Berry	1.00	.45	.12
☐ 240 Fergie Jenkins	7.00	3.10	.85
☐ 241 Royals Rookies	1.00	.45	.12
Al Fitzmorris			
Scott Northey			
☐ 242 Walter Alston MG	2.00	.90	.25
☐ 243 Joe Sparma	1.00	.45	.12
☐ 244A Checklist 3	6.00	1.20	.60
(Red bat on front)			
☐ 244B Checklist 3	6.00	1.20	.60
(Brown bat on front)			
☐ 245 Leo Cardenas	1.00	.45	.12
☐ 246 Jim McAndrew	1.00	.45	.12
☐ 247 Lou Klimchock	1.00	.45	.12
☐ 248 Jesus Alou	1.00	.45	.12
☐ 249 Bob Locker	1.00	.45	.12
☐ 250 Willie McCovey UER	10.00	4.50	1.25
(1963 San Francisci)			
☐ 251 Dick Schofield	1.00	.45	.12
☐ 252 Lowell Palmer	1.00	.45	.12
☐ 253 Ron Woods	1.00	.45	.12
☐ 254 Camilo Pascual	1.50	.70	.19
☐ 255 Jim Spencer	1.00	.45	.12
☐ 256 Vic Davalillo	1.00	.45	.12
☐ 257 Dennis Higgins	1.00	.45	.12
☐ 258 Paul Popovich	1.00	.45	.12
☐ 259 Tommie Reynolds	1.00	.45	.12
☐ 260 Claude Osteen	1.50	.70	.19
☐ 261 Curt Motton	1.00	.45	.12
☐ 262 Padres Rookies	1.00	.45	.12
Jerry Morales			
Jim Williams			
☐ 263 Duane Josephson	1.50	.70	.19
☐ 264 Rich Hebner	1.50	.70	.19
☐ 265 Randy Hundley	1.00	.45	.12
☐ 266 Wally Bunker	1.00	.45	.12
☐ 267 Twins Rookies	1.00	.45	.12
Herman Hill			
Paul Ratliff			
☐ 268 Claude Raymond	1.00	.45	.12
☐ 269 Cesar Gutierrez	1.00	.45	.12
☐ 270 Chris Short	1.00	.45	.12
☐ 271 Greg Goossen	1.00	.45	.12
☐ 272 Hector Torres	1.00	.45	.12
☐ 273 Ralph Houk MG	1.50	.70	.19
☐ 274 Gerry Arrigo	1.00	.45	.12
☐ 275 Duke Sims	1.00	.45	.12
☐ 276 Ron Hunt	1.00	.45	.12
☐ 277 Paul Doyle	1.00	.45	.12
☐ 278 Tommie Aaron	1.50	.70	.19
☐ 279 Bill Lee	2.00	.90	.25
☐ 280 Donn Clendenon	1.50	.70	.19
☐ 281 Casey Cox	1.00	.45	.12
☐ 282 Steve Huntz	1.00	.45	.12
☐ 283 Angel Bravo	1.00	.45	.12
☐ 284 Jack Baldschun	1.00	.45	.12
☐ 285 Paul Blair	1.50	.70	.19
☐ 286 Dodgers Rookies	6.00	2.70	.75
Jack Jenkins			
Bill Buckner			
☐ 287 Fred Talbot	1.00	.45	.12
☐ 288 Larry Hisle	1.50	.70	.19
☐ 289 Gene Brabender	1.00	.45	.12
☐ 290 Rod Carew	18.00	8.00	2.20
☐ 291 Leo Durocher MG	3.00	1.35	.35
☐ 292 Eddie Leon	1.00	.45	.12
☐ 293 Bob Bailey	1.00	.45	.12
☐ 294 Jose Azcue	1.00	.45	.12
☐ 295 Cecil Upshaw	1.00	.45	.12
☐ 296 Woody Woodward	1.50	.70	.19
☐ 297 Curt Blefary	1.00	.45	.12
☐ 298 Ken Henderson	1.00	.45	.12
☐ 299 Buddy Bradford	1.00	.45	.12
☐ 300 Tom Seaver	40.00	18.00	5.00
☐ 301 Chico Salmon	1.00	.45	.12
☐ 302 Jeff James	1.00	.45	.12
☐ 303 Brant Alyea	1.00	.45	.12
☐ 304 Bill Russell	6.00	2.70	.75
☐ 305 Don Buford WS	3.00	1.35	.35
☐ 306 Donn Clendenon WS	3.00	1.35	.35
☐ 307 Tommie Agee WS	3.00	1.35	.35
☐ 308 J.C. Martin WS	3.00	1.35	.35
☐ 309 Jerry Koosman WS	3.50	1.55	.45
☐ 310 World Series Summary	5.00	2.20	.60
Mets whoop it up			
☐ 311 Dick Green	1.00	.45	.12
☐ 312 Mike Torrez	1.50	.70	.19
☐ 313 Mayo Smith MG	1.00	.45	.12
☐ 314 Bill McCool	1.00	.45	.12
☐ 315 Luis Aparicio	5.00	2.20	.60
☐ 316 Skip Guinn	1.00	.45	.12
☐ 317 Red Sox Rookies	1.50	.70	.19
Billy Conigliaro			
Luis Alvarado			
☐ 318 Willie Smith	1.00	.45	.12
☐ 319 Clay Dalrymple	1.00	.45	.12
☐ 320 Jim Maloney	1.50	.70	.19
☐ 321 Lou Piniella	2.00	.90	.25
☐ 322 Luke Walker	1.00	.45	.12
☐ 323 Wayne Comer	1.00	.45	.12
☐ 324 Tony Taylor	1.50	.70	.19
☐ 325 Dave Boswell	1.00	.45	.12
☐ 326 Bill Voss	1.00	.45	.12
☐ 327 Hal King	1.00	.45	.12
☐ 328 George Brunet	1.00	.45	.12
☐ 329 Chris Cannizzaro	1.00	.45	.12
☐ 330 Lou Brock	10.00	4.50	1.25
☐ 331 Chuck Dobson	1.00	.45	.12
☐ 332 Bobby Wine	1.00	.45	.12
☐ 333 Bobby Murcer	2.00	.90	.25
☐ 334 Phil Regan	1.50	.70	.19
☐ 335 Bill Freehan	2.00	.90	.25
☐ 336 Del Unser	1.00	.45	.12
☐ 337 Mike McCormick	1.50	.70	.19
☐ 338 Paul Schaal	1.00	.45	.12
☐ 339 Johnny Edwards	1.00	.45	.12
☐ 340 Tony Conigliaro	3.00	1.35	.35
☐ 341 Bill Sudakis	1.00	.45	.12
☐ 342 Wilbur Wood	1.50	.70	.19
☐ 343A Checklist 4	6.00	1.20	.60
(Red bat on front)			
☐ 343B Checklist 4	6.00	1.20	.60
(Brown bat on front)			
☐ 344 Marcelino Lopez	1.00	.45	.12
☐ 345 Al Ferrara	1.00	.45	.12
☐ 346 Red Schoendienst MG	2.00	.90	.25
☐ 347 Russ Snyder	1.00	.45	.12
☐ 348 Mets Rookies	1.50	.70	.19
Mike Jorgensen			
Jesse Hudson			
☐ 349 Steve Hamilton	1.00	.45	.12
☐ 350 Roberto Clemente	70.00	32.00	8.75
☐ 351 Tom Murphy	1.00	.45	.12
☐ 352 Bob Barton	1.00	.45	.12
☐ 353 Stan Williams	1.00	.45	.12
☐ 354 Amos Otis	1.50	.70	.19
☐ 355 Doug Rader	1.50	.70	.19
☐ 356 Fred Lasher	1.00	.45	.12
☐ 357 Bob Burda	1.00	.45	.12
☐ 358 Pedro Borbon	1.50	.70	.19
☐ 359 Phil Roof	1.00	.45	.12
☐ 360 Curt Flood	2.00	.90	.25
☐ 361 Ray Jarvis	1.00	.45	.12
☐ 362 Joe Hague	1.00	.45	.12
☐ 363 Tom Shopay	1.00	.45	.12
☐ 364 Dan McGinn	1.00	.45	.12
☐ 365 Zoilo Versalles	1.00	.45	.12
☐ 366 Barry Moore	1.00	.45	.12
☐ 367 Mike Lum	1.00	.45	.12
☐ 368 Ed Herrmann	1.00	.45	.12
☐ 369 Alan Foster	1.00	.45	.12
☐ 370 Tommy Harper	1.50	.70	.19
☐ 371 Rod Gaspar	1.00	.45	.12
☐ 372 Dave Giusti	1.50	.70	.19
☐ 373 Roy White	2.00	.90	.25
☐ 374 Tommie Sisk	1.50	.70	.19
☐ 375 Johnny Callison	2.00	.90	.25
☐ 376 Lefty Phillips MG	1.50	.70	.19
☐ 377 Bill Butler	1.50	.70	.19
☐ 378 Jim Davenport	1.50	.70	.19
☐ 379 Tom Tischinski	1.50	.70	.19
☐ 380 Tony Perez	7.00	3.10	.85
☐ 381 Athletics Rookies	1.50	.70	.19
Bobby Brooks			
Mike Olivo			
☐ 382 Jack DiLauro	1.50	.70	.19
☐ 383 Mickey Stanley	2.00	.90	.25
☐ 384 Gary Neibauer	1.50	.70	.19
☐ 385 George Scott	2.00	.90	.25
☐ 386 Bill Dillman	1.50	.70	.19
☐ 387 Baltimore Orioles	3.00	1.35	.35
Team Card			
☐ 388 Byron Browne	1.50	.70	.19
☐ 389 Jim Shellenback	1.50	.70	.19
☐ 390 Willie Davis	2.00	.90	.25
☐ 391 Larry Brown	1.50	.70	.19
☐ 392 Walt Hriniak	2.00	.90	.25
☐ 393 John Gelnar	1.50	.70	.19
☐ 394 Gil Hodges MG	5.00	2.20	.60
☐ 395 Walt Williams	1.50	.70	.19
☐ 396 Steve Blass	2.00	.90	.25
☐ 397 Roger Repoz	1.50	.70	.19
☐ 398 Bill Stoneman	1.50	.70	.19
☐ 399 New York Yankees	3.00	1.35	.35
Team Card			
☐ 400 Denny McLain	2.50	1.10	.30
☐ 401 Giants Rookies	1.50	.70	.19
John Harrell			
Bernie Williams			
☐ 402 Ellie Rodriguez	1.50	.70	.19
☐ 403 Jim Bunning	5.00	2.20	.60
☐ 404 Rich Reese	1.50	.70	.19
☐ 405 Bill Hands	1.50	.70	.19
☐ 406 Mike Andrews	1.50	.70	.19
☐ 407 Bob Watson	2.50	1.10	.30
☐ 408 Paul Lindblad	1.50	.70	.19
☐ 409 Bob Tolan	2.00	.90	.25
☐ 410 Boog Powell	2.50	1.10	.30
☐ 411 Los Angeles Dodgers	3.00	1.35	.35
Team Card			
☐ 412 Larry Burchart	1.50	.70	.19
☐ 413 Sonny Jackson	1.50	.70	.19
☐ 414 Paul Edmondson	1.50	.70	.19
☐ 415 Julian Javier	2.00	.90	.25
☐ 416 Joe Verbanic	1.50	.70	.19
☐ 417 John Bateman	1.50	.70	.19
☐ 418 John Donaldson	1.50	.70	.19
☐ 419 Ron Taylor	1.50	.70	.19
☐ 420 Ken McMullen	2.00	.90	.25
☐ 421 Pat Dobson	2.00	.90	.25
☐ 422 Royals Team	3.00	1.35	.35
☐ 423 Jerry May	1.50	.70	.19
☐ 424 Mike Kilkenny	1.50	.70	.19
(Inconsistent design			
card number in			
white circle)			
☐ 425 Bobby Bonds	6.00	2.70	.75
☐ 426 Bill Rigney MG	1.50	.70	.19
☐ 427 Fred Norman	1.50	.70	.19
☐ 428 Don Buford	1.50	.70	.19
☐ 429 Cubs Rookies	1.50	.70	.19
Randy Bobb			
Jim Cosman			
☐ 430 Andy Messersmith	2.00	.90	.25
☐ 431 Ron Swoboda	2.00	.90	.25
☐ 432A Checklist 5	6.00	1.20	.60
(Baseball in			
yellow letters)			
☐ 432B Checklist 5	6.00	1.20	.60
(Baseball in			
white letters)			
☐ 433 Ron Bryant	1.50	.70	.19
☐ 434 Felipe Alou	2.00	.90	.25
☐ 435 Nelson Briles	2.00	.90	.25
☐ 436 Philadelphia Phillies	3.00	1.35	.35
Team Card			
☐ 437 Danny Cater	1.50	.70	.19
☐ 438 Pat Jarvis	1.50	.70	.19
☐ 439 Lee Maye	1.50	.70	.19
☐ 440 Bill Mazeroski	3.00	1.35	.35
☐ 441 John O'Donoghue	1.50	.70	.19
☐ 442 Gene Mauch MG	2.00	.90	.25
☐ 443 Al Jackson	1.50	.70	.19
☐ 444 White Sox Rookies	1.50	.70	.19
Billy Farmer			
John Matias			
☐ 445 Vada Pinson	2.00	.90	.25
☐ 446 Billy Grabarkewitz	1.50	.70	.19
☐ 447 Lee Stange	1.50	.70	.19
☐ 448 Houston Astros	3.00	1.35	.35
Team Card			
☐ 449 Jim Palmer	12.00	5.50	1.50
☐ 450 Willie McCovey AS	7.00	3.10	.85
☐ 451 Boog Powell AS	2.50	1.10	.30
☐ 452 Felix Millan AS	2.00	.90	.25
☐ 453 Rod Carew AS	7.00	3.10	.85
☐ 454 Ron Santo AS	2.50	1.10	.30
☐ 455 Brooks Robinson AS	7.00	3.10	.85
☐ 456 Don Kessinger AS	2.00	.90	.25
☐ 457 Rico Petrocelli AS	2.50	1.10	.30
☐ 458 Pete Rose AS	14.00	6.25	1.75
☐ 459 Reggie Jackson AS	14.00	6.25	1.75
☐ 460 Matty Alou AS	2.50	1.10	.30
☐ 461 Carl Yastrzemski AS	10.00	4.50	1.25
☐ 462 Hank Aaron AS	15.00	6.75	1.85
☐ 463 Frank Robinson AS	7.00	3.10	.85
☐ 464 Johnny Bench AS	14.00	6.25	1.75
☐ 465 Bill Freehan AS	3.00	1.35	.35
☐ 466 Juan Marichal AS	4.00	1.80	.50
☐ 467 Denny McLain AS	3.00	1.35	.35
☐ 468 Jerry Koosman AS	3.00	1.35	.35
☐ 469 Sam McDowell AS	2.50	1.10	.30
☐ 470 Willie Stargell	10.00	4.50	1.25
☐ 471 Chris Zachary	2.00	.90	.25
☐ 472 Braves Team	3.50	1.55	.45
☐ 473 Don Bryant	2.00	.90	.25
☐ 474 Dick Kelley	2.00	.90	.25
☐ 475 Dick McAuliffe	2.50	1.10	.30
☐ 476 Don Shaw	2.00	.90	.25
☐ 477 Orioles Rookies	2.00	.90	.25
Al Severinsen			
Roger Freed			
☐ 478 Bobby Heise	2.00	.90	.25
☐ 479 Dick Woodson	2.00	.90	.25
☐ 480 Glenn Beckert	2.50	1.10	.30
☐ 481 Jose Tartabull	2.50	1.10	.30
☐ 482 Tom Hilgendorf	2.00	.90	.25
☐ 483 Gail Hopkins	2.00	.90	.25

☐ 484 Gary Nolan	2.50	1.10	.30
☐ 485 Jay Johnstone	2.50	1.10	.30
☐ 486 Terry Harmon	2.00	.90	.25
☐ 487 Cisco Carlos	2.00	.90	.25
☐ 488 J.C. Martin	2.00	.90	.25
☐ 489 Eddie Kasko MG	2.00	.90	.25
☐ 490 Bill Singer	2.50	1.10	.30
☐ 491 Graig Nettles	6.00	2.70	.75
☐ 492 Astros Rookies	2.00	.90	.25
Keith Lampard			
Scipio Spinks			
☐ 493 Lindy McDaniel	2.50	1.10	.30
☐ 494 Larry Stahl	2.00	.90	.25
☐ 495 Dave Morehead	2.00	.90	.25
☐ 496 Steve Whitaker	2.00	.90	.25
☐ 497 Eddie Watt	2.00	.90	.25
☐ 498 Al Weis	2.00	.90	.25
☐ 499 Skip Lockwood	2.50	1.10	.30
☐ 500 Hank Aaron	50.00	22.00	6.25
☐ 501 Chicago White Sox	3.50	1.55	.45
Team Card			
☐ 502 Rollie Fingers	10.00	4.50	1.25
☐ 503 Dal Maxvill	2.00	.90	.25
☐ 504 Don Pavletich	2.00	.90	.25
☐ 505 Ken Holtzman	2.50	1.10	.30
☐ 506 Ed Stroud	2.00	.90	.25
☐ 507 Pat Corrales	2.50	1.10	.30
☐ 508 Joe Niekro	3.00	1.35	.35
☐ 509 Montreal Expos	3.50	1.55	.45
Team Card			
☐ 510 Tony Oliva	3.00	1.35	.35
☐ 511 Joe Hoerner	2.00	.90	.25
☐ 512 Billy Harris	2.00	.90	.25
☐ 513 Preston Gomez MG	2.00	.90	.25
☐ 514 Steve Hovley	2.00	.90	.25
☐ 515 Don Wilson	2.50	1.10	.30
☐ 516 Yankees Rookies	2.00	.90	.25
John Ellis			
Jim Lyttle			
☐ 517 Joe Gibbon	2.00	.90	.25
☐ 518 Bill Melton	2.00	.90	.25
☐ 519 Don McMahon	2.00	.90	.25
☐ 520 Willie Horton	3.00	1.35	.35
☐ 521 Cal Koonce	2.00	.90	.25
☐ 522 Angels Team	3.50	1.55	.45
☐ 523 Jose Pena	2.00	.90	.25
☐ 524 Alvin Dark MG	2.50	1.10	.30
☐ 525 Jerry Adair	2.00	.90	.25
☐ 526 Ron Herbel	2.00	.90	.25
☐ 527 Don Bosch	2.00	.90	.25
☐ 528 Elrod Hendricks	2.00	.90	.25
☐ 529 Bob Aspromonte	2.00	.90	.25
☐ 530 Bob Gibson	14.00	6.25	1.75
☐ 531 Ron Clark	2.00	.90	.25
☐ 532 Danny Murtaugh MG	2.50	1.10	.30
☐ 533 Buzz Stephen	2.00	.90	.25
☐ 534 Minnesota Twins	3.50	1.55	.45
Team Card			
☐ 535 Andy Kosco	2.00	.90	.25
☐ 536 Mike Kekich	2.00	.90	.25
☐ 537 Joe Morgan	10.00	4.50	1.25
☐ 538 Bob Humphreys	2.00	.90	.25
☐ 539 Phillies Rookies	6.00	2.70	.75
Denny Doyle			
Larry Bowa			
☐ 540 Gary Peters	2.00	.90	.25
☐ 541 Bill Heath	2.00	.90	.25
☐ 542 Checklist 6	6.00	1.20	.60
☐ 543 Clyde Wright	2.00	.90	.25
☐ 544 Cincinnati Reds	3.50	1.55	.45
Team Card			
☐ 545 Ken Harrelson	2.50	1.10	.30
☐ 546 Ron Reed	2.00	.90	.25
☐ 547 Rick Monday	4.50	2.00	.55
☐ 548 Howie Reed	4.00	1.80	.50
☐ 549 St. Louis Cardinals	6.00	2.70	.75
Team Card			
☐ 550 Frank Howard	5.00	2.20	.60
☐ 551 Dock Ellis	4.50	2.00	.55
☐ 552 Royals Rookies	4.00	1.80	.50
Don O'Riley			
Dennis Paepke			
Fred Rico			
☐ 553 Jim Lefebvre	4.50	2.00	.55
☐ 554 Tom Timmermann	4.00	1.80	.50
☐ 555 Orlando Cepeda	6.00	2.70	.75
☐ 556 Dave Bristol MG	4.50	2.00	.55
☐ 557 Ed Kranepool	4.50	2.00	.55
☐ 558 Vern Fuller	4.00	1.80	.50
☐ 559 Tommy Davis	4.50	2.00	.55
☐ 560 Gaylord Perry	10.00	4.50	1.25
☐ 561 Tom McCraw	4.00	1.80	.50
☐ 562 Ted Abernathy	4.00	1.80	.50
☐ 563 Boston Red Sox	6.00	2.70	.75
Team Card			
☐ 564 Johnny Briggs	4.00	1.80	.50
☐ 565 Jim Hunter	10.00	4.50	1.25
☐ 566 Gene Alley	4.50	2.00	.55
☐ 567 Bob Oliver	4.00	1.80	.50
☐ 568 Stan Bahnsen	4.50	2.00	.55
☐ 569 Cookie Rojas	4.50	2.00	.55
☐ 570 Jim Fregosi	5.00	2.20	.60
☐ 571 Jim Brewer	4.00	1.80	.50
☐ 572 Frank Quilici MG	4.00	1.80	.50
☐ 573 Padres Rookies	4.00	1.80	.50
Mike Corkins			
Rafael Robles			
Ron Slocum			
☐ 574 Bobby Bolin	4.50	2.00	.55
☐ 575 Cleon Jones	4.50	2.00	.55
☐ 576 Milt Pappas	4.50	2.00	.55
☐ 577 Bernie Allen	4.00	1.80	.50
☐ 578 Tom Griffin	4.00	1.80	.50
☐ 579 Detroit Tigers	6.00	2.70	.75
Team Card			
☐ 580 Pete Rose	50.00	22.00	6.25
☐ 581 Tom Satriano	4.00	1.80	.50
☐ 582 Mike Paul	4.00	1.80	.50
☐ 583 Hal Lanier	4.00	1.80	.50
☐ 584 Al Downing	4.50	2.00	.55
☐ 585 Rusty Staub	5.00	2.20	.60
☐ 586 Rickey Clark	4.00	1.80	.50
☐ 587 Jose Arcia	4.00	1.80	.50
☐ 588A Checklist 7 ERR	8.00	1.60	.80
(666 Adolfo)			
☐ 588B Checklist 7 COR	6.00	1.20	.60
(666 Adolpho)			
☐ 589 Joe Keough	4.00	1.80	.50
☐ 590 Mike Cuellar	5.00	2.20	.60
☐ 591 Mike Ryan UER	4.00	1.80	.50
(Pitching Record			
header on card back)			
☐ 592 Daryl Patterson	4.00	1.80	.50
☐ 593 Chicago Cubs	6.00	2.70	.75
Team Card			
☐ 594 Jake Gibbs	4.00	1.80	.50
☐ 595 Maury Wills	5.00	2.20	.60
☐ 596 Mike Hershberger	4.50	2.00	.55
☐ 597 Sonny Siebert	4.00	1.80	.50
☐ 598 Joe Pepitone	4.50	2.00	.55
☐ 599 Senators Rookies	4.00	1.80	.50
Dick Stelmaszek			
Gene Martin			
Dick Such			
☐ 600 Willie Mays	70.00	32.00	8.75
☐ 601 Pete Richert	4.00	1.80	.50
☐ 602 Ted Savage	4.00	1.80	.50
☐ 603 Ray Oyler	4.00	1.80	.50
☐ 604 Clarence Gaston	5.00	2.20	.60
☐ 605 Rick Wise	4.50	2.00	.55
☐ 606 Chico Ruiz	4.00	1.80	.50
☐ 607 Gary Waslewski	4.00	1.80	.50
☐ 608 Pittsburgh Pirates	6.00	2.70	.75
Team Card			
☐ 609 Buck Martinez	5.00	2.20	.60
(Inconsistent design			
card number in			
white circle)			
☐ 610 Jerry Koosman	5.00	2.20	.60
☐ 611 Norm Cash	5.00	2.20	.60
☐ 612 Jim Hickman	4.50	2.00	.55
☐ 613 Dave Baldwin	4.50	2.00	.55
☐ 614 Mike Shannon	4.50	2.00	.55
☐ 615 Mark Belanger	4.50	2.00	.55
☐ 616 Jim Merritt	4.00	1.80	.50
☐ 617 Jim French	4.00	1.80	.50
☐ 618 Billy Wynne	4.00	1.80	.50
☐ 619 Norm Miller	4.00	1.80	.50
☐ 620 Jim Perry	5.00	2.20	.60
☐ 621 Braves Rookies	10.00	4.50	1.25
Mike McQueen			
Darrell Evans			
Rick Kester			
☐ 622 Don Sutton	10.00	4.50	1.25
☐ 623 Horace Clarke	4.50	2.00	.55
☐ 624 Clyde King MG	4.00	1.80	.50
☐ 625 Dean Chance	4.00	1.80	.50
☐ 626 Dave Ricketts	4.00	1.80	.50
☐ 627 Gary Wagner	4.00	1.80	.50
☐ 628 Wayne Garrett	4.00	1.80	.50
☐ 629 Merv Rettenmund	4.00	1.80	.50
☐ 630 Ernie Banks	50.00	22.00	6.25
☐ 631 Oakland Athletics	6.00	2.70	.75
Team Card			
☐ 632 Gary Sutherland	4.00	1.80	.50
☐ 633 Roger Nelson	4.00	1.80	.50
☐ 634 Bud Harrelson	11.00	4.90	1.35
☐ 635 Bob Allison	11.00	4.90	1.35
☐ 636 Jim Stewart	10.00	4.50	1.25
☐ 637 Cleveland Indians	12.00	5.50	1.50
Team Card			
☐ 638 Frank Bertaina	10.00	4.50	1.25
☐ 639 Dave Campbell	10.00	4.50	1.25
☐ 640 Al Kaline	50.00	22.00	6.25
☐ 641 Al McBean	10.00	4.50	1.25
☐ 642 Angels Rookies	10.00	4.50	1.25
Greg Garrett			
Gordon Lund			
Jarvis Tatum			
☐ 643 Jose Pagan	10.00	4.50	1.25
☐ 644 Gerry Nyman	10.00	4.50	1.25
☐ 645 Don Money	11.00	4.90	1.35
☐ 646 Jim Britton	10.00	4.50	1.25
☐ 647 Tom Matchick	10.00	4.50	1.25
☐ 648 Larry Haney	10.00	4.50	1.25
☐ 649 Jimmie Hall	10.00	4.50	1.25
☐ 650 Sam McDowell	11.00	4.90	1.35
☐ 651 Jim Gosger	10.00	4.50	1.25
☐ 652 Rich Rollins	11.00	4.90	1.35
☐ 653 Moe Drabowsky	10.00	4.50	1.25
☐ 654 NL Rookies	12.00	5.50	1.50
Oscar Gamble			
Boots Day			
Angel Mangual			
☐ 655 John Roseboro	11.00	4.90	1.35
☐ 656 Jim Hardin	10.00	4.50	1.25
☐ 657 San Diego Padres	12.00	5.50	1.50
Team Card			
☐ 658 Ken Tatum	10.00	4.50	1.25
☐ 659 Pete Ward	10.00	4.50	1.25
☐ 660 Johnny Bench	100.00	45.00	12.50
☐ 661 Jerry Robertson	10.00	4.50	1.25
☐ 662 Frank Lucchesi MG	10.00	4.50	1.25
☐ 663 Tito Francona	10.00	4.50	1.25
☐ 664 Bob Robertson	10.00	4.50	1.25
☐ 665 Jim Lonborg	11.00	4.90	1.35
☐ 666 Adolpho Phillips	10.00	4.50	1.25
☐ 667 Bob Meyer	11.00	4.90	1.35
☐ 668 Bob Tillman	10.00	4.50	1.25
☐ 669 White Sox Rookies	10.00	4.50	1.25
Bart Johnson			
Dan Lazar			
Mickey Scott			
☐ 670 Ron Santo	12.00	5.50	1.50
☐ 671 Jim Campanis	10.00	4.50	1.25
☐ 672 Leon McFadden	10.00	4.50	1.25
☐ 673 Ted Uhlaender	10.00	4.50	1.25
☐ 674 Dave Leonhard	10.00	4.50	1.25
☐ 675 Jose Cardenal	11.00	4.90	1.35
☐ 676 Washington Senators	12.00	5.50	1.50
Team Card			
☐ 677 Woodie Fryman	10.00	4.50	1.25
☐ 678 Dave Duncan	11.00	4.90	1.35
☐ 679 Ray Sadecki	10.00	4.50	1.25
☐ 680 Rico Petrocelli	11.00	4.90	1.35
☐ 681 Bob Garibaldi	10.00	4.50	1.25
☐ 682 Dalton Jones	10.00	4.50	1.25
☐ 683 Reds Rookies	11.00	4.90	1.35
Vern Geishert			
Hal McRae			
Wayne Simpson			
☐ 684 Jack Fisher	10.00	4.50	1.25
☐ 685 Tom Haller	10.00	4.50	1.25
☐ 686 Jackie Hernandez	10.00	4.50	1.25
☐ 687 Bob Priddy	10.00	4.50	1.25
☐ 688 Ted Kubiak	11.00	4.90	1.35
☐ 689 Frank Tepedino	10.00	4.50	1.25
☐ 690 Ron Fairly	11.00	4.90	1.35
☐ 691 Joe Grzenda	10.00	4.50	1.25
☐ 692 Duffy Dyer	10.00	4.50	1.25
☐ 693 Bob Johnson	10.00	4.50	1.25
☐ 694 Gary Ross	10.00	4.50	1.25
☐ 695 Bobby Knoop	10.00	4.50	1.25
☐ 696 San Francisco Giants	12.00	5.50	1.50
Team Card			
☐ 697 Jim Hannan	10.00	4.50	1.25
☐ 698 Tom Tresh	11.00	4.90	1.35
☐ 699 Hank Aguirre	10.00	4.50	1.25
☐ 700 Frank Robinson	50.00	22.00	6.25
☐ 701 Jack Billingham	10.00	4.50	1.25
☐ 702 AL Rookies	10.00	4.50	1.25
Bob Johnson			
Ron Klimkowski			
Bill Zepp			
☐ 703 Lou Marone	10.00	4.50	1.25
☐ 704 Frank Baker	10.00	4.50	1.25
☐ 705 Tony Cloninger UER	10.00	4.50	1.25
(Batter headings			
on card back)			
☐ 706 John McNamara MG	10.00	4.50	1.25
☐ 707 Kevin Collins	10.00	4.50	1.25
☐ 708 Jose Santiago	10.00	4.50	1.25
☐ 709 Mike Fiore	10.00	4.50	1.25
☐ 710 Felix Millan	10.00	4.50	1.25
☐ 711 Ed Brinkman	10.00	4.50	1.25
☐ 712 Nolan Ryan	375.00	170.00	47.50
☐ 713 Seattle Pilots	25.00	11.00	3.10
Team Card			
☐ 714 Al Spangler	10.00	4.50	1.25
☐ 715 Mickey Lolich	11.00	4.90	1.35
☐ 716 Cardinals Rookies	11.00	4.90	1.35
Sal Campisi			
Reggie Cleveland			
Santiago Guzman			
☐ 717 Tom Phoebus	10.00	4.50	1.25
☐ 718 Ed Spiezio	10.00	4.50	1.25
☐ 719 Jim Roland	10.00	4.50	1.25
☐ 720 Rick Reichardt	14.00	4.70	1.35

1970 Topps Booklets

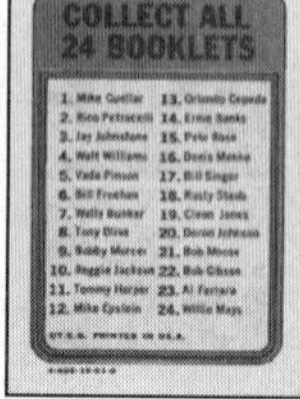

Inserted into packages of the 1970 Topps (and O-Pee-Chee) regular issue of cards, there are 24 miniature biographies of ballplayers in the set. Each numbered paper booklet contains six pages of comic book style story and a checklist of the booklet is available on the back page. These little booklets measure approximately 2 1/2" by 3 7/16".

	NRMT	VG-E	GOOD
COMPLETE SET (24)	40.00	18.00	5.00
COMMON CARD (1-16)	.50	.23	.06
COMMON CARD (17-24)	.60	.25	.07
☐ 1 Mike Cuellar	.50	.23	.06
☐ 2 Rico Petrocelli	.60	.25	.07
☐ 3 Jay Johnstone	.60	.25	.07
☐ 4 Walt Williams	.50	.23	.06
☐ 5 Vada Pinson	.75	.35	.09
☐ 6 Bill Freehan	.75	.35	.09
☐ 7 Wally Bunker	.50	.23	.06
☐ 8 Tony Oliva	1.00	.45	.12
☐ 9 Bobby Murcer	.75	.35	.09
☐ 10 Reggie Jackson	6.00	2.70	.75
☐ 11 Tommy Harper	.50	.23	.06
☐ 12 Mike Epstein	.50	.23	.06
☐ 13 Orlando Cepeda	1.50	.70	.19
☐ 14 Ernie Banks	5.00	2.20	.60
☐ 15 Pete Rose	6.00	2.70	.75
☐ 16 Denis Menke	.50	.23	.06
☐ 17 Bill Singer	.60	.25	.07
☐ 18 Rusty Staub	1.00	.45	.12
☐ 19 Cleon Jones	.60	.25	.07
☐ 20 Deron Johnson	.60	.25	.07
☐ 21 Bob Moose	.60	.25	.07
☐ 22 Bob Gibson	5.00	2.20	.60
☐ 23 Al Ferrara	.60	.25	.07
☐ 24 Willie Mays	7.50	3.40	.95

1970 Topps Posters

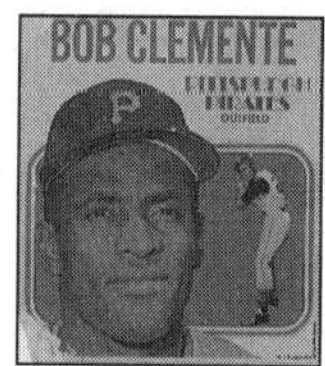

In 1970 Topps raised its price per package of cards to ten cents, and a series of 24 color posters was included as a bonus to the collector. Each thin-paper poster is numbered and features a large portrait and a smaller black and white action pose. It was folded five times to fit in the packaging. Each poster measures 8 11/16" by 9 5/8".

	NRMT	VG-E	GOOD
COMPLETE SET (24)	50.00	22.00	6.25
COMMON CARD (1-24)	.75	.35	.09
☐ 1 Joe Horlen	.75	.35	.09
☐ 2 Phil Niekro	3.00	1.35	.35
☐ 3 Willie Davis	1.00	.45	.12
☐ 4 Lou Brock	4.00	1.80	.50
☐ 5 Ron Santo	1.00	.45	.12
☐ 6 Ken Harrelson	1.00	.45	.12
☐ 7 Willie McCovey	4.00	1.80	.50
☐ 8 Rick Wise	.75	.35	.09
☐ 9 Andy Messersmith	.75	.35	.09
☐ 10 Ron Fairly	.75	.35	.09
☐ 11 Johnny Bench	6.00	2.70	.75
☐ 12 Frank Robinson	4.00	1.80	.50
☐ 13 Tommie Agee	.75	.35	.09
☐ 14 Roy White	.75	.35	.09
☐ 15 Larry Dierker	.75	.35	.09
☐ 16 Rod Carew	4.00	1.80	.50
☐ 17 Don Mincher	.75	.35	.09
☐ 18 Ollie Brown	.75	.35	.09
☐ 19 Ed Kirkpatrick	.75	.35	.09
☐ 20 Reggie Smith	1.00	.45	.12
☐ 21 Bob Clemente	15.00	6.75	1.85
☐ 22 Frank Howard	1.00	.45	.12
☐ 23 Bert Campaneris	.75	.35	.09
☐ 24 Denny McLain	1.00	.45	.12

1970-71 Topps Scratchoffs

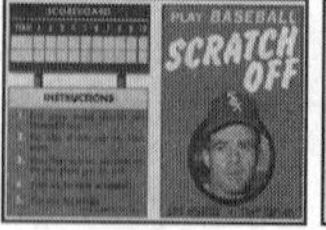

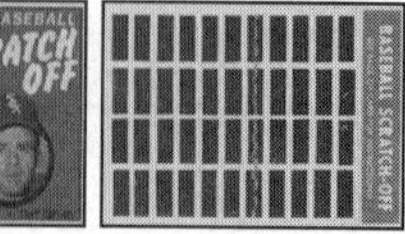

The 1970-71 Topps Scratch-off inserts are heavy cardboard, folded inserts issued with the regular card series of those years. Unfolded, they form a game board upon which a baseball game is played by means of rubbing off black ink from the playing squares to reveal moves. Inserts with white centers were issued in 1970 and inserts with red centers in 1971. Unfolded, these inserts measure 3 3/8" by 5".

	NRMT	VG-E	GOOD
COMPLETE SET (24)	40.00	18.00	5.00
COMMON CARD (1-24)	.60	.25	.07
☐ 1 Hank Aaron	6.00	2.70	.75
☐ 2 Rich Allen	1.25	.55	.16

☐ 3 Luis Aparicio	3.00	1.35	.35
☐ 4 Sal Bando	.60	.25	.07
☐ 5 Glenn Beckert	.60	.25	.07
☐ 6 Dick Bosman	.60	.25	.07
☐ 7 Nate Colbert	.60	.25	.07
☐ 8 Mike Hegan	.60	.25	.07
☐ 9 Mack Jones	.60	.25	.07
☐ 10 Al Kaline	4.00	1.80	.50
☐ 11 Harmon Killebrew	4.00	1.80	.50
☐ 12 Juan Marichal	3.00	1.35	.35
☐ 13 Tim McCarver	1.25	.55	.16
☐ 14 Sam McDowell	.75	.35	.09
☐ 15 Claude Osteen	.60	.25	.07
☐ 16 Tony Perez	2.00	.90	.25
☐ 17 Lou Piniella	1.25	.55	.16
☐ 18 Boog Powell	1.25	.55	.16
☐ 19 Tom Seaver	5.00	2.20	.60
☐ 20 Jim Spencer	.60	.25	.07
☐ 21 Willie Stargell	4.00	1.80	.50
☐ 22 Mel Stottlemyre	.75	.35	.09
☐ 23 Jim Wynn	.75	.35	.09
☐ 24 Carl Yastrzemski	4.00	1.80	.50

1970 Topps Super

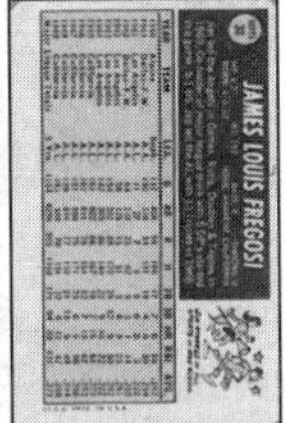

The cards in this 42-card set measure approximately 3 1/8" by 5 1/4". The 1970 Topps Super set was a separate Topps issue printed on heavy stock and marketed in its own wrapper with gum. The blue and yellow backs are identical to the respective player's backs in the 1970 Topps regular issue. Cards 38, Boog Powell, is the key card of the set; other short print run cards are listed in the checklist with SP. The obverse pictures are borderless and contain a facsimile autograph. The set was issued in three-card wax packs.

	NRMT	VG-E	GOOD
COMPLETE SET (42)	200.00	90.00	25.00
COMMON CARD (1-42)	1.00	.45	.12
☐ 1 Claude Osteen SP	3.00	1.35	.35
☐ 2 Sal Bando SP	3.00	1.35	.35
☐ 3 Luis Aparicio	3.00	1.35	.35
☐ 4 Harmon Killebrew	5.00	2.20	.60
☐ 5 Tom Seaver SP	20.00	9.00	2.50
☐ 6 Larry Dierker	1.25	.55	.16
☐ 7 Bill Freehan	1.25	.55	.16
☐ 8 Johnny Bench	10.00	4.50	1.25
☐ 9 Tommy Harper	1.00	.45	.12
☐ 10 Sam McDowell	1.00	.45	.12
☐ 11 Lou Brock	5.00	2.20	.60
☐ 12 Roberto Clemente	30.00	13.50	3.70
☐ 13 Willie McCovey	5.00	2.20	.60
☐ 14 Rico Petrocelli	1.00	.45	.12
☐ 15 Phil Niekro	4.00	1.80	.50
☐ 16 Frank Howard	1.25	.55	.16
☐ 17 Denny McLain	1.25	.55	.16
☐ 18 Willie Mays	15.00	6.75	1.85
☐ 19 Willie Stargell	5.00	2.20	.60
☐ 20 Joel Horlen	1.00	.45	.12
☐ 21 Ron Santo	1.50	.70	.19
☐ 22 Dick Bosman	1.00	.45	.12
☐ 23 Tim McCarver	1.50	.70	.19
☐ 24 Hank Aaron	15.00	6.75	1.85
☐ 25 Andy Messersmith	1.00	.45	.12
☐ 26 Tony Oliva	1.50	.70	.19
☐ 27 Mel Stottlemyre	1.25	.55	.16
☐ 28 Reggie Jackson	15.00	6.75	1.85
☐ 29 Carl Yastrzemski	7.50	3.40	.95
☐ 30 Jim Fregosi	1.25	.55	.16
☐ 31 Vada Pinson	1.25	.55	.16
☐ 32 Lou Piniella	1.50	.70	.19
☐ 33 Bob Gibson	4.00	1.80	.50
☐ 34 Pete Rose	15.00	6.75	1.85
☐ 35 Jim Wynn	1.25	.55	.16
☐ 36 Ollie Brown SP	6.00	2.70	.75
☐ 37 Frank Robinson SP	20.00	9.00	2.50
☐ 38 Boog Powell SP	50.00	22.00	6.25
☐ 39 Willie Davis SP	3.00	1.35	.35
☐ 40 Billy Williams SP	7.50	3.40	.95
☐ 41 Rusty Staub	1.50	.70	.19
☐ 42 Tommie Agee	1.00	.45	.12

1971 Topps

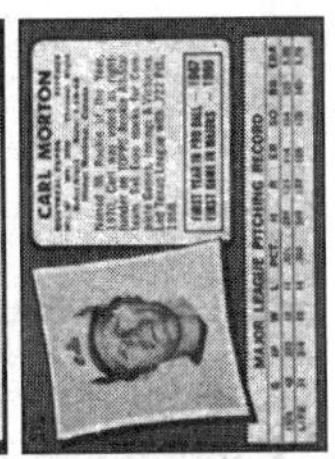

The cards in this 752-card set measure 2 1/2" by 3 1/2". The 1971 Topps set is a challenge to complete in strict mint condition because the black obverse border is easily scratched and damaged. An unusual feature of this set is that the player is also pictured in black and white on the back of the card. Featured subsets within this set include League Leaders (61-72), Playoffs cards (195-202), and World Series cards (327-332). Cards 524-643 and the last series (644-752) are somewhat scarce. The last series was printed in two sheets of 132. On the printing sheets 44 cards were printed in 50 percent greater quantity than the other 66 cards. These 66 (slightly) shorter-printed numbers are identified in the checklist below by SP. The key Rookie Cards in this set are the multi-player Rookie Card of Dusty Baker and Don Baylor and the individual cards of Bert Blyleven, Dave Concepcion, Steve Garvey, and Ted Simmons.

	NRMT	VG-E	GOOD
COMPLETE SET (752)	2000.00	900.00	250.00
COMMON CARD (1-393)	1.75	.80	.22
COMMON CARD (394-523)	2.50	1.10	.30
COMMON CARD (524-643)	4.00	1.80	.50
COMMON CARD (644-752)	8.00	3.60	1.00
WRAPPER (10-CENT)	15.00	6.75	1.85
☐ 1 Baltimore Orioles	15.00	5.00	2.00
Team Card			
☐ 2 Dock Ellis	2.00	.90	.25
☐ 3 Dick McAuliffe	2.00	.90	.25
☐ 4 Vic Davalillo	1.75	.80	.22
☐ 5 Thurman Munson	18.00	8.00	2.20
☐ 6 Ed Spiezio	1.75	.80	.22
☐ 7 Jim Holt	1.75	.80	.22
☐ 8 Mike McQueen	1.75	.80	.22
☐ 9 George Scott	2.00	.90	.25
☐ 10 Claude Osteen	2.00	.90	.25
☐ 11 Elliott Maddox	2.00	.90	.25
☐ 12 Johnny Callison	2.00	.90	.25
☐ 13 White Sox Rookies	1.75	.80	.22
Charlie Brinkman			
Dick Moloney			
☐ 14 Dave Concepcion	18.00	8.00	2.20
☐ 15 Andy Messersmith	2.00	.90	.25
☐ 16 Ken Singleton	4.00	1.80	.50
☐ 17 Billy Sorrell	1.75	.80	.22
☐ 18 Norm Miller	1.75	.80	.22
☐ 19 Skip Pitlock	1.75	.80	.22
☐ 20 Reggie Jackson	30.00	13.50	3.70
☐ 21 Dan McGinn	1.75	.80	.22
☐ 22 Phil Roof	1.75	.80	.22
☐ 23 Oscar Gamble	2.00	.90	.25
☐ 24 Rich Hand	1.75	.80	.22
☐ 25 Clarence Gaston	2.50	1.10	.30
☐ 26 Bert Blyleven	6.00	2.70	.75
☐ 27 Pirates Rookies	1.75	.80	.22
Fred Cambria			
Gene Clines			
☐ 28 Ron Klimkowski	1.75	.80	.22
☐ 29 Don Buford	1.75	.80	.22
☐ 30 Phil Niekro	5.00	2.20	.60
☐ 31 Eddie Kasko MG	1.75	.80	.22
☐ 32 Jerry DaVanon	1.75	.80	.22
☐ 33 Del Unser	1.75	.80	.22
☐ 34 Sandy Vance	1.75	.80	.22
☐ 35 Lou Piniella	2.50	1.10	.30
☐ 36 Dean Chance	1.75	.80	.22
☐ 37 Rich McKinney	1.75	.80	.22
☐ 38 Jim Colborn	1.75	.80	.22
☐ 39 Tiger Rookies	1.75	.80	.22
Lerrin LaGrow			
Gene Lamont			
☐ 40 Lee May	2.50	1.10	.30
☐ 41 Rick Austin	1.75	.80	.22
☐ 42 Boots Day	1.75	.80	.22
☐ 43 Steve Kealey	1.75	.80	.22
☐ 44 Johnny Edwards	1.75	.80	.22
☐ 45 Jim Hunter	7.00	3.10	.85
☐ 46 Dave Campbell	1.75	.80	.22
☐ 47 Johnny Jeter	1.75	.80	.22
☐ 48 Dave Baldwin	1.75	.80	.22
☐ 49 Don Money	1.75	.80	.22
☐ 50 Willie McCovey	8.00	3.60	1.00
☐ 51 Steve Kline	1.75	.80	.22
☐ 52 Braves Rookies	1.75	.80	.22
Oscar Brown			
Earl Williams			
☐ 53 Paul Blair	2.00	.90	.25
☐ 54 Checklist 1	6.00	1.20	.60
☐ 55 Steve Carlton	15.00	6.75	1.85
☐ 56 Duane Josephson	1.75	.80	.22
☐ 57 Von Joshua	1.75	.80	.22
☐ 58 Bill Lee	2.00	.90	.25
☐ 59 Gene Mauch MG	2.00	.90	.25
☐ 60 Dick Bosman	1.75	.80	.22
☐ 61 AL Batting Leaders	3.50	1.55	.45
Alex Johnson			
Carl Yastrzemski			
Tony Oliva			
☐ 62 NL Batting Leaders	2.50	1.10	.30
Rico Carty			
Joe Torre			
Manny Sanguillen			
☐ 63 AL RBI Leaders	2.50	1.10	.30
Frank Howard			
Tony Conigliaro			
Boog Powell			
☐ 64 NL RBI Leaders	5.00	2.20	.60
Johnny Bench			
Tony Perez			
Billy Williams			
☐ 65 AL HR Leaders	4.00	1.80	.50
Frank Howard			
Harmon Killebrew			
Carl Yastrzemski			
☐ 66 NL HR Leaders	6.00	2.70	.75
Johnny Bench			
Billy Williams			
Tony Perez			
☐ 67 AL ERA Leaders	3.50	1.55	.45
Diego Segui			
Jim Palmer			
Clyde Wright			
☐ 68 NL ERA Leaders	3.50	1.55	.45
Tom Seaver			
Wayne Simpson			
Luke Walker			
☐ 69 AL Pitching Leaders	2.50	1.10	.30
Mike Cuellar			
Dave McNally			
Jim Perry			
☐ 70 NL Pitching Leaders	6.00	2.70	.75
Bob Gibson			
Gaylord Perry			
Fergie Jenkins			
☐ 71 AL Strikeout Leaders	2.50	1.10	.30
Sam McDowell			
Mickey Lolich			
Bob Johnson			
☐ 72 NL Strikeout Leaders	7.00	3.10	.85
Tom Seaver			
Bob Gibson			
Fergie Jenkins			
☐ 73 George Brunet	1.75	.80	.22
☐ 74 Twins Rookies	1.75	.80	.22
Pete Hamm			
Jim Nettles			
☐ 75 Gary Nolan	2.00	.90	.25
☐ 76 Ted Savage	1.75	.80	.22
☐ 77 Mike Compton	1.75	.80	.22
☐ 78 Jim Spencer	1.75	.80	.22
☐ 79 Wade Blasingame	1.75	.80	.22
☐ 80 Bill Melton	1.75	.80	.22
☐ 81 Felix Millan	1.75	.80	.22
☐ 82 Casey Cox	1.75	.80	.22
☐ 83 Met Rookies	2.00	.90	.25
Tim Foli			
Randy Bobb			
☐ 84 Marcel Lachemann	1.75	.80	.22
☐ 85 Billy Grabarkewitz	1.75	.80	.22
☐ 86 Mike Kilkenny	1.75	.80	.22
☐ 87 Jack Heidemann	1.75	.80	.22
☐ 88 Hal King	1.75	.80	.22
☐ 89 Ken Brett	1.75	.80	.22
☐ 90 Joe Pepitone	2.50	1.10	.30
☐ 91 Bob Lemon MG	2.50	1.10	.30
☐ 92 Fred Wenz	1.75	.80	.22
☐ 93 Senators Rookies	1.75	.80	.22
Norm McRae			
Denny Riddleberger			
☐ 94 Don Hahn	1.75	.80	.22
☐ 95 Luis Tiant	2.50	1.10	.30
☐ 96 Joe Hague	1.75	.80	.22
☐ 97 Floyd Wicker	1.75	.80	.22
☐ 98 Joe Decker	1.75	.80	.22
☐ 99 Mark Belanger	2.00	.90	.25
☐ 100 Pete Rose	35.00	16.00	4.40
☐ 101 Les Cain	1.75	.80	.22
☐ 102 Astros Rookies	2.50	1.10	.30
Ken Forsch			
Larry Howard			
☐ 103 Rich Severson	1.75	.80	.22
☐ 104 Dan Frisella	1.75	.80	.22
☐ 105 Tony Conigliaro	2.50	1.10	.30
☐ 106 Tom Dukes	1.75	.80	.22
☐ 107 Roy Foster	1.75	.80	.22
☐ 108 John Cumberland	1.75	.80	.22
☐ 109 Steve Hovley	1.75	.80	.22
☐ 110 Bill Mazeroski	2.50	1.10	.30
☐ 111 Yankee Rookies	1.75	.80	.22
Loyd Colson			
Bobby Mitchell			
☐ 112 Manny Mota	2.50	1.10	.30
☐ 113 Jerry Crider	1.75	.80	.22
☐ 114 Billy Conigliaro	2.00	.90	.25
☐ 115 Donn Clendenon	2.00	.90	.25
☐ 116 Ken Sanders	1.75	.80	.22
☐ 117 Ted Simmons	10.00	4.50	1.25
☐ 118 Cookie Rojas	2.50	1.10	.30
☐ 119 Frank Lucchesi MG	1.75	.80	.22
☐ 120 Willie Horton	2.50	1.10	.30
☐ 121 Cubs Rookies	1.75	.80	.22
Jim Dunegan			
Roe Skidmore			
☐ 122 Eddie Watt	1.75	.80	.22
☐ 123A Checklist 2	6.00	1.20	.60
(Card number			
at bottom right)			
☐ 123B Checklist 2	6.00	1.20	.60
(Card number			
centered)			
☐ 124 Don Gullett	2.50	1.10	.30
☐ 125 Ray Fosse	2.00	.90	.25
☐ 126 Danny Coombs	1.75	.80	.22
☐ 127 Danny Thompson	2.50	1.10	.30
☐ 128 Frank Johnson	1.75	.80	.22
☐ 129 Aurelio Monteagudo	1.75	.80	.22
☐ 130 Denis Menke	1.75	.80	.22
☐ 131 Curt Blefary	1.75	.80	.22
☐ 132 Jose Laboy	1.75	.80	.22
☐ 133 Mickey Lolich	2.50	1.10	.30
☐ 134 Jose Arcia	1.75	.80	.22
☐ 135 Rick Monday	2.50	1.10	.30
☐ 136 Duffy Dyer	1.75	.80	.22
☐ 137 Marcelino Lopez	1.75	.80	.22
☐ 138 Phillies Rookies	2.50	1.10	.30
Joe Lis			
Willie Montanez			
☐ 139 Paul Casanova	1.75	.80	.22
☐ 140 Gaylord Perry	7.00	3.10	.85
☐ 141 Frank Quilici	1.75	.80	.22
☐ 142 Mack Jones	1.75	.80	.22
☐ 143 Steve Blass	2.50	1.10	.30
☐ 144 Jackie Hernandez	1.75	.80	.22
☐ 145 Bill Singer	2.00	.90	.25
☐ 146 Ralph Houk MG	2.50	1.10	.30
☐ 147 Bob Priddy	1.75	.80	.22
☐ 148 John Mayberry	2.50	1.10	.30
☐ 149 Mike Hershberger	1.75	.80	.22
☐ 150 Sam McDowell	2.50	1.10	.30
☐ 151 Tommy Davis	2.00	.90	.25
☐ 152 Angels Rookies	1.75	.80	.22
Lloyd Allen			
Winston Llenas			
☐ 153 Gary Ross	1.75	.80	.22
☐ 154 Cesar Gutierrez	1.75	.80	.22
☐ 155 Ken Henderson	1.75	.80	.22
☐ 156 Bart Johnson	1.75	.80	.22
☐ 157 Bob Bailey	1.75	.80	.22
☐ 158 Jerry Reuss	2.50	1.10	.30
☐ 159 Jarvis Tatum	1.75	.80	.22
☐ 160 Tom Seaver	18.00	8.00	2.20
☐ 161 Coin Checklist	6.00	1.20	.60
☐ 162 Jack Billingham	1.75	.80	.22
☐ 163 Buck Martinez	2.00	.90	.25
☐ 164 Reds Rookies	2.50	1.10	.30
Frank Duffy			
Milt Wilcox			
☐ 165 Cesar Tovar	1.75	.80	.22
☐ 166 Joe Hoerner	1.75	.80	.22
☐ 167 Tom Grieve	2.50	1.10	.30
☐ 168 Bruce Dal Canton	1.75	.80	.22
☐ 169 Ed Herrmann	1.75	.80	.22
☐ 170 Mike Cuellar	2.50	1.10	.30
☐ 171 Bobby Wine	1.75	.80	.22
☐ 172 Duke Sims	1.75	.80	.22
☐ 173 Gil Garrido	1.75	.80	.22
☐ 174 Dave LaRoche	1.75	.80	.22
☐ 175 Jim Hickman	1.75	.80	.22
☐ 176 Red Sox Rookies	2.50	1.10	.30
Bob Montgomery			
Doug Griffin			
☐ 177 Hal McRae	2.50	1.10	.30
☐ 178 Dave Duncan	1.75	.80	.22
☐ 179 Mike Corkins	1.75	.80	.22
☐ 180 Al Kaline UER	18.00	8.00	2.20
(Home instead			
of Birth)			
☐ 181 Hal Lanier	1.75	.80	.22
☐ 182 Al Downing	2.50	1.10	.30
☐ 183 Gil Hodges MG	4.00	1.80	.50
☐ 184 Stan Bahnsen	1.75	.80	.22
☐ 185 Julian Javier	2.00	.90	.25
☐ 186 Bob Spence	1.75	.80	.22
☐ 187 Ted Abernathy	1.75	.80	.22
☐ 188 Dodgers Rookies	3.00	1.35	.35
Bob Valentine			
Mike Strahler			
☐ 189 George Mitterwald	1.75	.80	.22
☐ 190 Bob Tolan	2.00	.90	.25
☐ 191 Mike Andrews	1.75	.80	.22
☐ 192 Billy Wilson	1.75	.80	.22
☐ 193 Bob Grich	4.00	1.80	.50
☐ 194 Mike Lum	1.75	.80	.22
☐ 195 Boog Powell ALCS	3.00	1.35	.35
☐ 196 Dave McNally ALCS	3.00	1.35	.35
☐ 197 Jim Palmer ALCS	5.00	2.20	.60
☐ 198 AL Playoff Summary	2.50	1.10	.30
Orioles celebrate			
☐ 199 Ty Cline NLCS	2.50	1.10	.30
☐ 200 Bobby Tolan NLCS	2.50	1.10	.30
☐ 201 Ty Cline NLCS	2.50	1.10	.30
☐ 202 NL Playoff Summary	2.50	1.10	.30
Reds celebrate			
☐ 203 Larry Gura	2.50	1.10	.30
☐ 204 Brewers Rookies	1.75	.80	.22
Bernie Smith			
George Kopacz			
☐ 205 Gerry Moses	1.75	.80	.22
☐ 206 Checklist 3	6.00	1.20	.60
☐ 207 Alan Foster	1.75	.80	.22
☐ 208 Billy Martin MG	4.00	1.80	.50
☐ 209 Steve Renko	1.75	.80	.22
☐ 210 Rod Carew	18.00	8.00	2.20
☐ 211 Phil Hennigan	1.75	.80	.22
☐ 212 Rich Hebner	2.00	.90	.25

☐ 213 Frank Baker 1.75 .80 .22
☐ 214 Al Ferrara 1.75 .80 .22
☐ 215 Diego Segui 1.75 .80 .22
☐ 216 Cards Rookies 1.75 .80 .22
Reggie Cleveland
Luis Melendez
☐ 217 Ed Stroud 1.75 .80 .22
☐ 218 Tony Cloninger 1.75 .80 .22
☐ 219 Elrod Hendricks 1.75 .80 .22
☐ 220 Ron Santo 2.50 1.10 .30
☐ 221 Dave Morehead 1.75 .80 .22
☐ 222 Bob Watson 2.50 1.10 .30
☐ 223 Cecil Upshaw 1.75 .80 .22
☐ 224 Alan Gallagher 1.75 .80 .22
☐ 225 Gary Peters 1.75 .80 .22
☐ 226 Bill Russell 2.50 1.10 .30
☐ 227 Floyd Weaver 1.75 .80 .22
☐ 228 Wayne Garrett 1.75 .80 .22
☐ 229 Jim Hannan 1.75 .80 .22
☐ 230 Willie Stargell 8.00 3.60 1.00
☐ 231 Indians Rookies 1.75 .80 .22
Vince Colbert
John Lowenstein
☐ 232 John Strohmayer 1.75 .80 .22
☐ 233 Larry Bowa 2.50 1.10 .30
☐ 234 Jim Lyttle 1.75 .80 .22
☐ 235 Nate Colbert 1.75 .80 .22
☐ 236 Bob Humphreys 1.75 .80 .22
☐ 237 Cesar Cedeno 3.00 1.35 .35
☐ 238 Chuck Dobson 1.75 .80 .22
☐ 239 Red Schoendienst MG 2.50 1.10 .30
☐ 240 Clyde Wright 1.75 .80 .22
☐ 241 Dave Nelson 1.75 .80 .22
☐ 242 Jim Ray 1.75 .80 .22
☐ 243 Carlos May 2.00 .90 .25
☐ 244 Bob Tillman 1.75 .80 .22
☐ 245 Jim Kaat 2.50 1.10 .30
☐ 246 Tony Taylor 2.00 .90 .25
☐ 247 Royals Rookies 2.00 .90 .25
Jerry Cram
Paul Splittorff
☐ 248 Hoyt Wilhelm 4.00 1.80 .50
☐ 249 Chico Salmon 1.75 .80 .22
☐ 250 Johnny Bench 18.00 8.00 2.20
☐ 251 Frank Reberger 1.75 .80 .22
☐ 252 Eddie Leon 1.75 .80 .22
☐ 253 Bill Sudakis 1.75 .80 .22
☐ 254 Cal Koonce 1.75 .80 .22
☐ 255 Bob Robertson 2.50 1.10 .30
☐ 256 Tony Gonzalez 1.75 .80 .22
☐ 257 Nelson Briles 1.75 .80 .22
☐ 258 Dick Green 1.75 .80 .22
☐ 259 Dave Marshall 1.75 .80 .22
☐ 260 Tommy Harper 2.00 .90 .25
☐ 261 Darold Knowles 1.75 .80 .22
☐ 262 Padres Rookies 1.75 .80 .22
Jim Williams
Dave Robinson
☐ 263 John Ellis 1.75 .80 .22
☐ 264 Joe Morgan 7.00 3.10 .85
☐ 265 Jim Northrup 2.00 .90 .25
☐ 266 Bill Stoneman 1.75 .80 .22
☐ 267 Rich Morales 1.75 .80 .22
☐ 268 Philadelphia Phillies 3.00 1.35 .35
Team Card
☐ 269 Gail Hopkins 1.75 .80 .22
☐ 270 Rico Carty 2.50 1.10 .30
☐ 271 Bill Zepp 1.75 .80 .22
☐ 272 Tommy Helms 2.00 .90 .25
☐ 273 Pete Richert 1.75 .80 .22
☐ 274 Ron Slocum 1.75 .80 .22
☐ 275 Vada Pinson 2.50 1.10 .30
☐ 276 Giants Rookies 8.00 3.60 1.00
Mike Davison
George Foster
☐ 277 Gary Waslewski 1.75 .80 .22
☐ 278 Jerry Grote 1.75 .80 .22
☐ 279 Lefty Phillips MG 1.75 .80 .22
☐ 280 Fergie Jenkins 7.00 3.10 .85
☐ 281 Danny Walton 1.75 .80 .22
☐ 282 Jose Pagan 1.75 .80 .22
☐ 283 Dick Such 1.75 .80 .22
☐ 284 Jim Gosger 1.75 .80 .22
☐ 285 Sal Bando 2.50 1.10 .30
☐ 286 Jerry McNertney 1.75 .80 .22
☐ 287 Mike Fiore 1.75 .80 .22
☐ 288 Joe Moeller 1.75 .80 .22
☐ 289 Chicago White Sox 3.00 1.35 .35
Team Card
☐ 290 Tony Oliva 2.50 1.10 .30
☐ 291 George Culver 1.75 .80 .22
☐ 292 Jay Johnstone 2.00 .90 .25
☐ 293 Pat Corrales 2.00 .90 .25
☐ 294 Steve Dunning 1.75 .80 .22
☐ 295 Bobby Bonds 5.00 2.20 .60
☐ 296 Tom Timmermann 1.75 .80 .22
☐ 297 Johnny Briggs 1.75 .80 .22
☐ 298 Jim Nelson 1.75 .80 .22
☐ 299 Ed Kirkpatrick 1.75 .80 .22
☐ 300 Brooks Robinson 18.00 8.00 2.20
☐ 301 Earl Wilson 1.75 .80 .22
☐ 302 Phil Gagliano 1.75 .80 .22
☐ 303 Lindy McDaniel 2.00 .90 .25
☐ 304 Ron Brand 1.75 .80 .22
☐ 305 Reggie Smith 2.50 1.10 .30
☐ 306 Jim Nash 1.75 .80 .22
☐ 307 Don Wert 1.75 .80 .22
☐ 308 St. Louis Cardinals 3.00 1.35 .35
Team Card
☐ 309 Dick Ellsworth 1.75 .80 .22
☐ 310 Tommie Agee 2.50 1.10 .30
☐ 311 Lee Stange 1.75 .80 .22
☐ 312 Harry Walker MG 1.75 .80 .22
☐ 313 Tom Hall 1.75 .80 .22
☐ 314 Jeff Torborg 2.00 .90 .25
☐ 315 Ron Fairly 2.50 1.10 .30
☐ 316 Fred Scherman 1.75 .80 .22
☐ 317 Athletic Rookies 1.75 .80 .22
Jim Driscoll
Angel Mangual
☐ 318 Rudy May 1.75 .80 .22
☐ 319 Ty Cline 1.75 .80 .22
☐ 320 Dave McNally 2.50 1.10 .30
☐ 321 Tom Matchick 1.75 .80 .22
☐ 322 Jim Beauchamp 1.75 .80 .22
☐ 323 Billy Champion 1.75 .80 .22
☐ 324 Graig Nettles 2.50 1.10 .30
☐ 325 Juan Marichal 7.00 3.10 .85
☐ 326 Richie Scheinblum 1.75 .80 .22
☐ 327 Boog Powell WS 2.50 1.10 .30
☐ 328 Don Buford WS 2.50 1.10 .30
☐ 329 Frank Robinson WS 5.00 2.20 .60
☐ 330 World Series Game 4 2.50 1.10 .30
Reds stay alive
☐ 331 Brooks Robinson WS 6.00 2.70 .75
commits robbery
☐ 332 World Series Summary 2.50 1.10 .30
Orioles celebrate
☐ 333 Clay Kirby 1.75 .80 .22
☐ 334 Roberto Pena 1.75 .80 .22
☐ 335 Jerry Koosman 2.50 1.10 .30
☐ 336 Detroit Tigers 3.00 1.35 .35
Team Card
☐ 337 Jesus Alou 1.75 .80 .22
☐ 338 Gene Tenace 2.50 1.10 .30
☐ 339 Wayne Simpson 1.75 .80 .22
☐ 340 Rico Petrocelli 2.50 1.10 .30
☐ 341 Steve Garvey 25.00 11.00 3.10
☐ 342 Frank Tepedino 1.75 .80 .22
☐ 343 Pirates Rookies 1.75 .80 .22
Ed Acosta
Milt May
☐ 344 Ellie Rodriguez 1.75 .80 .22
☐ 345 Joel Horlen 1.75 .80 .22
☐ 346 Lum Harris MG 1.75 .80 .22
☐ 347 Ted Uhlaender 1.75 .80 .22
☐ 348 Fred Norman 1.75 .80 .22
☐ 349 Rich Reese 1.75 .80 .22
☐ 350 Billy Williams 7.00 3.10 .85
☐ 351 Jim Shellenback 1.75 .80 .22
☐ 352 Denny Doyle 1.75 .80 .22
☐ 353 Carl Taylor 1.75 .80 .22
☐ 354 Don McMahon 1.75 .80 .22
☐ 355 Bud Harrelson 3.50 1.55 .45
(Nolan Ryan in photo)
☐ 356 Bob Locker 1.75 .80 .22
☐ 357 Cincinnati Reds 3.00 1.35 .35
Team Card
☐ 358 Danny Cater 1.75 .80 .22
☐ 359 Ron Reed 1.75 .80 .22
☐ 360 Jim Fregosi 2.00 .90 .25
☐ 361 Don Sutton 7.00 3.10 .85
☐ 362 Orioles Rookies 1.75 .80 .22
Mike Adamson
Roger Freed
☐ 363 Mike Nagy 1.75 .80 .22
☐ 364 Tommy Dean 1.75 .80 .22
☐ 365 Bob Johnson 1.75 .80 .22
☐ 366 Ron Stone 1.75 .80 .22
☐ 367 Dalton Jones 1.75 .80 .22
☐ 368 Bob Veale 2.00 .90 .25
☐ 369 Checklist 4 6.00 1.20 .60
☐ 370 Joe Torre 2.50 1.10 .30
☐ 371 Jack Hiatt 1.75 .80 .22
☐ 372 Lew Krausse 1.75 .80 .22
☐ 373 Tom McCraw 1.75 .80 .22
☐ 374 Clete Boyer 2.00 .90 .25
☐ 375 Steve Hargan 1.75 .80 .22
☐ 376 Expos Rookies 1.75 .80 .22
Clyde Mashore
Ernie McAnally
☐ 377 Greg Garrett 1.75 .80 .22
☐ 378 Tito Fuentes 1.75 .80 .22
☐ 379 Wayne Granger 1.75 .80 .22
☐ 380 Ted Williams MG 10.00 4.50 1.25
☐ 381 Fred Gladding 1.75 .80 .22
☐ 382 Jake Gibbs 1.75 .80 .22
☐ 383 Rod Gaspar 1.75 .80 .22
☐ 384 Rollie Fingers 6.00 2.70 .75
☐ 385 Maury Wills 2.50 1.10 .30
☐ 386 Boston Red Sox 3.00 1.35 .35
Team Card
☐ 387 Ron Herbel 1.75 .80 .22
☐ 388 Al Oliver 2.50 1.10 .30
☐ 389 Ed Brinkman 1.75 .80 .22
☐ 390 Glenn Beckert 2.50 1.10 .30
☐ 391 Twins Rookies 2.00 .90 .25
Steve Brye
Cotton Nash
☐ 392 Grant Jackson 1.75 .80 .22
☐ 393 Merv Rettenmund 2.50 1.10 .30
☐ 394 Clay Carroll 2.50 1.10 .30
☐ 395 Roy White 3.00 1.35 .35
☐ 396 Dick Schofield 2.50 1.10 .30
☐ 397 Alvin Dark MG 3.00 1.35 .35
☐ 398 Howie Reed 2.50 1.10 .30
☐ 399 Jim French 2.50 1.10 .30
☐ 400 Hank Aaron 50.00 22.00 6.25
☐ 401 Tom Murphy 2.50 1.10 .30
☐ 402 Los Angeles Dodgers 5.00 2.20 .60
Team Card
☐ 403 Joe Coleman 2.50 1.10 .30
☐ 404 Astros Rookies 2.50 1.10 .30
Buddy Harris
Roger Metzger
☐ 405 Leo Cardenas 2.50 1.10 .30
☐ 406 Ray Sadecki 2.50 1.10 .30
☐ 407 Joe Rudi 3.00 1.35 .35
☐ 408 Rafael Robles 2.50 1.10 .30
☐ 409 Don Pavletich 2.50 1.10 .30
☐ 410 Ken Holtzman 3.00 1.35 .35
☐ 411 George Spriggs 2.50 1.10 .30
☐ 412 Jerry Johnson 2.50 1.10 .30
☐ 413 Pat Kelly 2.50 1.10 .30
☐ 414 Woodie Fryman 2.50 1.10 .30
☐ 415 Mike Hegan 2.50 1.10 .30
☐ 416 Gene Alley 2.50 1.10 .30
☐ 417 Dick Hall 2.50 1.10 .30
☐ 418 Adolfo Phillips 2.50 1.10 .30
☐ 419 Ron Hansen 2.50 1.10 .30
☐ 420 Jim Merritt 2.50 1.10 .30
☐ 421 John Stephenson 2.50 1.10 .30
☐ 422 Frank Bertaina 2.50 1.10 .30
☐ 423 Tigers Rookies 2.50 1.10 .30
Dennis Saunders
Tim Marting
☐ 424 Roberto Rodriquez 2.50 1.10 .30
☐ 425 Doug Rader 2.50 1.10 .30
☐ 426 Chris Cannizzaro 2.50 1.10 .30
☐ 427 Bernie Allen 2.50 1.10 .30
☐ 428 Jim McAndrew 2.50 1.10 .30
☐ 429 Chuck Hinton 2.50 1.10 .30
☐ 430 Wes Parker 2.50 1.10 .30
☐ 431 Tom Burgmeier 2.50 1.10 .30
☐ 432 Bob Didier 2.50 1.10 .30
☐ 433 Skip Lockwood 2.50 1.10 .30
☐ 434 Gary Sutherland 2.50 1.10 .30
☐ 435 Jose Cardenal 3.00 1.35 .35
☐ 436 Wilbur Wood 2.50 1.10 .30
☐ 437 Danny Murtaugh MG 3.00 1.35 .35
☐ 438 Mike McCormick 3.00 1.35 .35
☐ 439 Phillies Rookies 6.00 2.70 .75
Greg Luzinski
Scott Reid
☐ 440 Bert Campaneris 3.00 1.35 .35
☐ 441 Milt Pappas 4.00 1.80 .50
☐ 442 California Angels 5.00 2.20 .60
Team Card
☐ 443 Rich Robertson 2.50 1.10 .30
☐ 444 Jimmie Price 2.50 1.10 .30
☐ 445 Art Shamsky 2.50 1.10 .30
☐ 446 Bobby Bolin 2.50 1.10 .30
☐ 447 Cesar Geronimo 3.00 1.35 .35
☐ 448 Dave Roberts 2.50 1.10 .30
☐ 449 Brant Alyea 2.50 1.10 .30
☐ 450 Bob Gibson 18.00 8.00 2.20
☐ 451 Joe Keough 2.50 1.10 .30
☐ 452 John Boccabella 2.50 1.10 .30
☐ 453 Terry Crowley 2.50 1.10 .30
☐ 454 Mike Paul 2.50 1.10 .30
☐ 455 Don Kessinger 3.00 1.35 .35
☐ 456 Bob Meyer 2.50 1.10 .30
☐ 457 Willie Smith 2.50 1.10 .30
☐ 458 White Sox Rookies 2.50 1.10 .30
Ron Lolich
Dave Lemonds
☐ 459 Jim Lefebvre 2.50 1.10 .30
☐ 460 Fritz Peterson 2.50 1.10 .30
☐ 461 Jim Ray Hart 2.50 1.10 .30
☐ 462 Washington Senators 5.00 2.20 .60
Team Card
☐ 463 Tom Kelley 2.50 1.10 .30
☐ 464 Aurelio Rodriguez 2.50 1.10 .30
☐ 465 Tim McCarver 4.00 1.80 .50
☐ 466 Ken Berry 2.50 1.10 .30
☐ 467 Al Santorini 2.50 1.10 .30
☐ 468 Frank Fernandez 2.50 1.10 .30
☐ 469 Bob Aspromonte 2.50 1.10 .30
☐ 470 Bob Oliver 2.50 1.10 .30
☐ 471 Tom Griffin 2.50 1.10 .30
☐ 472 Ken Rudolph 2.50 1.10 .30
☐ 473 Gary Wagner 2.50 1.10 .30
☐ 474 Jim Fairey 2.50 1.10 .30
☐ 475 Ron Perranoski 2.50 1.10 .30
☐ 476 Dal Maxvill 2.50 1.10 .30
☐ 477 Earl Weaver MG 4.00 1.80 .50
☐ 478 Bernie Carbo 2.50 1.10 .30
☐ 479 Dennis Higgins 2.50 1.10 .30
☐ 480 Manny Sanguillen 3.00 1.35 .35
☐ 481 Daryl Patterson 2.50 1.10 .30
☐ 482 San Diego Padres 5.00 2.20 .60
Team Card
☐ 483 Gene Michael 3.00 1.35 .35
☐ 484 Don Wilson 2.50 1.10 .30
☐ 485 Ken McMullen 2.50 1.10 .30
☐ 486 Steve Huntz 2.50 1.10 .30
☐ 487 Paul Schaal 2.50 1.10 .30
☐ 488 Jerry Stephenson 2.50 1.10 .30
☐ 489 Luis Alvarado 2.50 1.10 .30
☐ 490 Deron Johnson 3.00 1.35 .35
☐ 491 Jim Hardin 2.50 1.10 .30
☐ 492 Ken Boswell 2.50 1.10 .30
☐ 493 Dave May 2.50 1.10 .30
☐ 494 Braves Rookies 3.00 1.35 .35
Ralph Garr
Rick Kester
☐ 495 Felipe Alou 4.00 1.80 .50
☐ 496 Woody Woodward 2.50 1.10 .30
☐ 497 Horacio Pina 2.50 1.10 .30
☐ 498 John Kennedy 2.50 1.10 .30
☐ 499 Checklist 5 6.00 1.20 .60
☐ 500 Jim Perry 4.00 1.80 .50
☐ 501 Andy Etchebarren 2.50 1.10 .30
☐ 502 Chicago Cubs 5.00 2.20 .60
Team Card
☐ 503 Gates Brown 3.00 1.35 .35
☐ 504 Ken Wright 2.50 1.10 .30
☐ 505 Ollie Brown 2.50 1.10 .30
☐ 506 Bobby Knoop 2.50 1.10 .30
☐ 507 George Stone 2.50 1.10 .30
☐ 508 Roger Repoz 2.50 1.10 .30
☐ 509 Jim Grant 2.50 1.10 .30
☐ 510 Ken Harrelson 3.00 1.35 .35
☐ 511 Chris Short 4.00 1.80 .50
(Pete Rose leading off second)
☐ 512 Red Sox Rookies 2.50 1.10 .30
Dick Mills
Mike Garman
☐ 513 Nolan Ryan 250.00 110.00 31.00
☐ 514 Ron Woods 2.50 1.10 .30
☐ 515 Carl Morton 2.50 1.10 .30
☐ 516 Ted Kubiak 2.50 1.10 .30
☐ 517 Charlie Fox MG 2.50 1.10 .30
☐ 518 Joe Grzenda 2.50 1.10 .30
☐ 519 Willie Crawford 2.50 1.10 .30
☐ 520 Tommy John 5.00 2.20 .60
☐ 521 Leron Lee 2.50 1.10 .30
☐ 522 Minnesota Twins 5.00 2.20 .60
Team Card
☐ 523 John Odom 2.50 1.10 .30
☐ 524 Mickey Stanley 5.00 2.20 .60
☐ 525 Ernie Banks 50.00 22.00 6.25
☐ 526 Ray Jarvis 4.00 1.80 .50
☐ 527 Cleon Jones 5.00 2.20 .60
☐ 528 Wally Bunker 4.00 1.80 .50
☐ 529 NL Rookie Infielders 5.00 2.20 .60
Enzo Hernandez
Bill Buckner
Marty Perez
☐ 530 Carl Yastrzemski 40.00 18.00 5.00
☐ 531 Mike Torrez 5.00 2.20 .60
☐ 532 Bill Rigney MG 4.00 1.80 .50
☐ 533 Mike Ryan 4.00 1.80 .50
☐ 534 Luke Walker 4.00 1.80 .50
☐ 535 Curt Flood 5.00 2.20 .60
☐ 536 Claude Raymond 5.00 2.20 .60
☐ 537 Tom Egan 4.00 1.80 .50
☐ 538 Angel Bravo 4.00 1.80 .50
☐ 539 Larry Brown 4.00 1.80 .50
☐ 540 Larry Dierker 5.00 2.20 .60
☐ 541 Bob Burda 4.00 1.80 .50
☐ 542 Bob Miller 4.00 1.80 .50
☐ 543 New York Yankees 10.00 4.50 1.25
Team Card
☐ 544 Vida Blue 6.00 2.70 .75
☐ 545 Dick Dietz 4.00 1.80 .50
☐ 546 John Matias 4.00 1.80 .50
☐ 547 Pat Dobson 5.00 2.20 .60
☐ 548 Don Mason 4.00 1.80 .50
☐ 549 Jim Brewer 5.00 2.20 .60
☐ 550 Harmon Killebrew 25.00 11.00 3.10
☐ 551 Frank Linzy 4.00 1.80 .50
☐ 552 Buddy Bradford 4.00 1.80 .50
☐ 553 Kevin Collins 4.00 1.80 .50
☐ 554 Lowell Palmer 4.00 1.80 .50
☐ 555 Walt Williams 4.00 1.80 .50
☐ 556 Jim McGlothlin 4.00 1.80 .50
☐ 557 Tom Satriano 4.00 1.80 .50
☐ 558 Hector Torres 4.00 1.80 .50
☐ 559 AL Rookie Pitchers 4.00 1.80 .50
Terry Cox
Bill Gogolewski
Gary Jones
☐ 560 Rusty Staub 5.00 2.20 .60
☐ 561 Syd O'Brien 4.00 1.80 .50
☐ 562 Dave Giusti 4.00 1.80 .50
☐ 563 San Francisco Giants 8.00 3.60 1.00
Team Card
☐ 564 Al Fitzmorris 4.00 1.80 .50
☐ 565 Jim Wynn 5.00 2.20 .60
☐ 566 Tim Cullen 4.00 1.80 .50
☐ 567 Walt Alston MG 6.00 2.70 .75
☐ 568 Sal Campisi 4.00 1.80 .50
☐ 569 Ivan Murrell 4.00 1.80 .50
☐ 570 Jim Palmer 30.00 13.50 3.70
☐ 571 Ted Sizemore 4.00 1.80 .50
☐ 572 Jerry Kenney 4.00 1.80 .50
☐ 573 Ed Kranepool 5.00 2.20 .60
☐ 574 Jim Bunning 7.00 3.10 .85
☐ 575 Bill Freehan 5.00 2.20 .60

□ 576 Cubs Rookies	4.00	1.80	.50
Adrian Garrett			
Brock Davis			
Garry Jestadt			
□ 577 Jim Lonborg	5.00	2.20	.60
□ 578 Ron Hunt	4.00	1.80	.50
□ 579 Marty Pattin	4.00	1.80	.50
□ 580 Tony Perez	18.00	8.00	2.20
□ 581 Roger Nelson	4.00	1.80	.50
□ 582 Dave Cash	5.00	2.20	.60
□ 583 Ron Cook	4.00	1.80	.50
□ 584 Cleveland Indians Team Card	8.00	3.60	1.00
□ 585 Willie Davis	5.00	2.20	.60
□ 586 Dick Woodson	4.00	1.80	.50
□ 587 Sonny Jackson	4.00	1.80	.50
□ 588 Tom Bradley	4.00	1.80	.50
□ 589 Bob Barton	4.00	1.80	.50
□ 590 Alex Johnson	5.00	2.20	.60
□ 591 Jackie Brown	4.00	1.80	.50
□ 592 Randy Hundley	5.00	2.20	.60
□ 593 Jack Aker	4.00	1.80	.50
□ 594 Cards Rookies	5.00	2.20	.60
Bob Chlupsa			
Bob Stinson			
Al Hrabosky			
□ 595 Dave Johnson	5.00	2.20	.60
□ 596 Mike Jorgensen	4.00	1.80	.50
□ 597 Ken Suarez	4.00	1.80	.50
□ 598 Rick Wise	5.00	2.20	.60
□ 599 Norm Cash	5.00	2.20	.60
□ 600 Willie Mays	90.00	40.00	11.00
□ 601 Ken Tatum	4.00	1.80	.50
□ 602 Marty Martinez	4.00	1.80	.50
□ 603 Pittsburgh Pirates Team Card	8.00	3.60	1.00
□ 604 John Gelnar	4.00	1.80	.50
□ 605 Orlando Cepeda	6.00	2.70	.75
□ 606 Chuck Taylor	4.00	1.80	.50
□ 607 Paul Ratliff	4.00	1.80	.50
□ 608 Mike Wegener	4.00	1.80	.50
□ 609 Leo Durocher MG	7.00	3.10	.85
□ 610 Amos Otis	5.00	2.20	.60
□ 611 Tom Phoebus	4.00	1.80	.50
□ 612 Indians Rookies	4.00	1.80	.50
Lou Camilli			
Ted Ford			
Steve Mingori			
□ 613 Pedro Borbon	4.00	1.80	.50
□ 614 Billy Cowan	4.00	1.80	.50
□ 615 Mel Stottlemyre	5.00	2.20	.60
□ 616 Larry Hisle	5.00	2.20	.60
□ 617 Clay Dalrymple	4.00	1.80	.50
□ 618 Tug McGraw	5.00	2.20	.60
□ 619A Checklist 6 ERR (No copyright)	6.00	1.20	.60
□ 619B Checklist 6 COR (Copyright on back)	10.00	2.00	1.00
□ 620 Frank Howard	5.00	2.20	.60
□ 621 Ron Bryant	4.00	1.80	.50
□ 622 Joe Lahoud	4.00	1.80	.50
□ 623 Pat Jarvis	4.00	1.80	.50
□ 624 Oakland Athletics Team Card	8.00	3.60	1.00
□ 625 Lou Brock	30.00	13.50	3.70
□ 626 Freddie Patek	5.00	2.20	.60
□ 627 Steve Hamilton	4.00	1.80	.50
□ 628 John Bateman	4.00	1.80	.50
□ 629 John Hiller	5.00	2.20	.60
□ 630 Roberto Clemente	110.00	50.00	14.00
□ 631 Eddie Fisher	4.00	1.80	.50
□ 632 Darrel Chaney	4.00	1.80	.50
□ 633 AL Rookie Outfielders	4.00	1.80	.50
Bobby Brooks			
Pete Koegel			
Scott Northey			
□ 634 Phil Regan	5.00	2.20	.60
□ 635 Bobby Murcer	5.00	2.20	.60
□ 636 Denny Lemaster	4.00	1.80	.50
□ 637 Dave Bristol MG	4.00	1.80	.50
□ 638 Stan Williams	4.00	1.80	.50
□ 639 Tom Haller	4.00	1.80	.50
□ 640 Frank Robinson	40.00	18.00	5.00
□ 641 New York Mets Team Card	14.00	6.25	1.75
□ 642 Jim Roland	4.00	1.80	.50
□ 643 Rick Reichardt	5.00	2.20	.60
□ 644 Jim Stewart SP	12.00	5.50	1.50
□ 645 Jim Maloney SP	14.00	6.25	1.75
□ 646 Bobby Floyd SP	12.00	5.50	1.50
□ 647 Juan Pizarro	8.00	3.60	1.00
□ 648 Mets Rookies SP	25.00	11.00	3.10
Rich Folkers			
Ted Martinez			
John Matlack			
□ 649 Sparky Lyle SP	18.00	8.00	2.20
□ 650 Rich Allen SP	40.00	18.00	5.00
□ 651 Jerry Robertson SP	12.00	5.50	1.50
□ 652 Atlanta Braves Team Card	12.00	5.50	1.50
□ 653 Russ Snyder SP	12.00	5.50	1.50
□ 654 Don Shaw SP	12.00	5.50	1.50
□ 655 Mike Epstein SP	12.00	5.50	1.50
□ 656 Gerry Nyman SP	12.00	5.50	1.50
□ 657 Jose Azcue	8.00	3.60	1.00
□ 658 Paul Lindblad SP	12.00	5.50	1.50
□ 659 Byron Browne SP	12.00	5.50	1.50
□ 660 Ray Culp	8.00	3.60	1.00
□ 661 Chuck Tanner MG SP	14.00	6.25	1.75
□ 662 Mike Hedlund SP	12.00	5.50	1.50
□ 663 Marv Staehle	8.00	3.60	1.00
□ 664 Rookie Pitchers SP	14.00	6.25	1.75
Archie Reynolds			
Bob Reynolds			
Ken Reynolds			
□ 665 Ron Swoboda SP	18.00	8.00	2.20
□ 666 Gene Brabender SP	12.00	5.50	1.50
□ 667 Pete Ward	8.00	3.60	1.00
□ 668 Gary Neibauer	8.00	3.60	1.00
□ 669 Ike Brown SP	14.00	6.25	1.75
□ 670 Bill Hands	8.00	3.60	1.00
□ 671 Bill Voss SP	12.00	5.50	1.50
□ 672 Ed Crosby SP	12.00	5.50	1.50
□ 673 Gerry Janeski SP	12.00	5.50	1.50
□ 674 Montreal Expos Team Card	12.00	5.50	1.50
□ 675 Dave Boswell	8.00	3.60	1.00
□ 676 Tommie Reynolds	8.00	3.60	1.00
□ 677 Jack DiLauro SP	12.00	5.50	1.50
□ 678 George Thomas	8.00	3.60	1.00
□ 679 Don O'Riley	8.00	3.60	1.00
□ 680 Don Mincher SP	12.00	5.50	1.50
□ 681 Bill Butler	8.00	3.60	1.00
□ 682 Terry Harmon	8.00	3.60	1.00
□ 683 Bill Burbach SP	12.00	5.50	1.50
□ 684 Curt Motton	8.00	3.60	1.00
□ 685 Moe Drabowsky	8.00	3.60	1.00
□ 686 Chico Ruiz SP	12.00	5.50	1.50
□ 687 Ron Taylor SP	12.00	5.50	1.50
□ 688 Sparky Anderson MG SP	40.00	18.00	5.00
□ 689 Frank Baker	8.00	3.60	1.00
□ 690 Bob Moose	8.00	3.60	1.00
□ 691 Bobby Heise	8.00	3.60	1.00
□ 692 AL Rookie Pitchers SP	12.00	5.50	1.50
Hal Haydel			
Rogelio Moret			
Wayne Twitchell			
□ 693 Jose Pena SP	12.00	5.50	1.50
□ 694 Rick Renick SP	12.00	5.50	1.50
□ 695 Joe Niekro	9.00	4.00	1.10
□ 696 Jerry Morales	8.00	3.60	1.00
□ 697 Rickey Clark SP	12.00	5.50	1.50
□ 698 Milwaukee Brewers SP Team Card	20.00	9.00	2.50
□ 699 Jim Britton	8.00	3.60	1.00
□ 700 Boog Powell SP	30.00	13.50	3.70
□ 701 Bob Garibaldi	8.00	3.60	1.00
□ 702 Milt Ramirez	8.00	3.60	1.00
□ 703 Mike Kekich	8.00	3.60	1.00
□ 704 J.C. Martin SP	12.00	5.50	1.50
□ 705 Dick Selma SP	12.00	5.50	1.50
□ 706 Joe Foy SP	12.00	5.50	1.50
□ 707 Fred Lasher	8.00	3.60	1.00
□ 708 Russ Nagelson SP	12.00	5.50	1.50
□ 709 Rookie Outfielders SP	90.00	40.00	11.00
Dusty Baker			
Don Baylor			
Tom Paciorek			
□ 710 Sonny Siebert	8.00	3.60	1.00
□ 711 Larry Stahl SP	12.00	5.50	1.50
□ 712 Jose Martinez	8.00	3.60	1.00
□ 713 Mike Marshall SP	14.00	6.25	1.75
□ 714 Dick Williams MG SP	14.00	6.25	1.75
□ 715 Horace Clarke SP	14.00	6.25	1.75
□ 716 Dave Leonhard	8.00	3.60	1.00
□ 717 Tommie Aaron SP	12.00	5.50	1.50
□ 718 Billy Wynne	8.00	3.60	1.00
□ 719 Jerry May SP	12.00	5.50	1.50
□ 720 Matty Alou	9.00	4.00	1.10
□ 721 John Morris	8.00	3.60	1.00
□ 722 Houston Astros SP Team Card	20.00	9.00	2.50
□ 723 Vicente Romo SP	12.00	5.50	1.50
□ 724 Tom Tischinski SP	12.00	5.50	1.50
□ 725 Gary Gentry SP	12.00	5.50	1.50
□ 726 Paul Popovich	8.00	3.60	1.00
□ 727 Ray Lamb SP	12.00	5.50	1.50
□ 728 NL Rookie Outfielders	8.00	3.60	1.00
Wayne Redmond			
Keith Lampard			
Bernie Williams			
□ 729 Dick Billings	8.00	3.60	1.00
□ 730 Jim Rooker	8.00	3.60	1.00
□ 731 Jim Qualls SP	12.00	5.50	1.50
□ 732 Bob Reed	8.00	3.60	1.00
□ 733 Lee Maye SP	12.00	5.50	1.50
□ 734 Rob Gardner SP	12.00	5.50	1.50
□ 735 Mike Shannon SP	14.00	6.25	1.75
□ 736 Mel Queen SP	12.00	5.50	1.50
□ 737 Preston Gomez SP MG	12.00	5.50	1.50
□ 738 Russ Gibson SP	12.00	5.50	1.50
□ 739 Barry Lersch SP	12.00	5.50	1.50
□ 740 Luis Aparicio SP UER (Led AL in steals from 1965 to 1964, should be 1956 to 1964)	30.00	13.50	3.70
□ 741 Skip Guinn	8.00	3.60	1.00
□ 742 Kansas City Royals Team Card	12.00	5.50	1.50
□ 743 John O'Donoghue SP	12.00	5.50	1.50
□ 744 Chuck Manuel SP	12.00	5.50	1.50
□ 745 Sandy Alomar SP	12.00	5.50	1.50
□ 746 Andy Kosco	8.00	3.60	1.00
□ 747 NL Rookie Pitchers	8.00	3.60	1.00
Al Severinsen			
Scipio Spinks			
Balor Moore			
□ 748 John Purdin SP	12.00	5.50	1.50
□ 749 Ken Szotkiewicz	8.00	3.60	1.00
□ 750 Denny McLain SP	25.00	11.00	3.10
□ 751 Al Weis SP	15.00	6.75	1.85
□ 752 Dick Drago	12.00	2.90	.95

1971 Topps Coins

This full-color set of 153 coins, which were inserted into packs, contains the photo of the player surrounded by a colored band, which contains the player's name, his team, his position and several stars. The backs contain the coin number, short biographical data and the line "Collect the entire set of 153 coins." The set was evidently produced in three groups of 51 as coins 1-51 have brass backs, coins 52-102 have chrome backs and coins 103-153 have blue backs. In fact it has been verified that the coins were printed in three sheets of 51 coins comprised of three rows of 17 coins. Each coin measures approximately 1 1/2" in diameter.

	NRMT	VG-E	GOOD
COMPLETE SET (153)	300.00	135.00	38.00
COMMON COIN (1-153)	.75	.35	.09
□ 1 Clarence Gaston	1.00	.45	.12
□ 2 Dave Johnson	1.00	.45	.12
□ 3 Jim Bunning	4.00	1.80	.50
□ 4 Jim Spencer	.75	.35	.09
□ 5 Felix Millan	.75	.35	.09
□ 6 Gerry Moses	.75	.35	.09
□ 7 Fergie Jenkins	4.00	1.80	.50
□ 8 Felipe Alou	1.00	.45	.12
□ 9 Jim McGlothlin	.75	.35	.09
□ 10 Dick McAuliffe	.75	.35	.09
□ 11 Joe Torre	3.00	1.35	.35
□ 12 Jim Perry	1.00	.45	.12
□ 13 Bobby Bonds	2.00	.90	.25
□ 14 Danny Cater	.75	.35	.09
□ 15 Bill Mazeroski	1.50	.70	.19
□ 16 Luis Aparicio	4.00	1.80	.50
□ 17 Doug Rader	.75	.35	.09
□ 18 Vada Pinson	1.50	.70	.19
□ 19 John Bateman	.75	.35	.09
□ 20 Lew Krausse	.75	.35	.09
□ 21 Billy Grabarkewitz	.75	.35	.09
□ 22 Frank Howard	1.50	.70	.19
□ 23 Jerry Koosman	1.50	.70	.19
□ 24 Rod Carew	6.00	2.70	.75
□ 25 Al Ferrara	.75	.35	.09
□ 26 Dave McNally	1.00	.45	.12
□ 27 Jim Hickman	.75	.35	.09
□ 28 Sandy Alomar	1.00	.45	.12
□ 29 Lee May	1.00	.45	.12
□ 30 Rico Petrocelli	1.00	.45	.12
□ 31 Don Money	.75	.35	.09
□ 32 Jim Rooker	.75	.35	.09
□ 33 Dick Dietz	.75	.35	.09
□ 34 Roy White	1.00	.45	.12
□ 35 Carl Morton	.75	.35	.09
□ 36 Walt Williams	.75	.35	.09
□ 37 Phil Niekro	4.00	1.80	.50
□ 38 Bill Freehan	1.00	.45	.12
□ 39 Julian Javier	.75	.35	.09
□ 40 Rick Monday	1.00	.45	.12
□ 41 Don Wilson	.75	.35	.09
□ 42 Ray Fosse	1.00	.45	.12
□ 43 Art Shamsky	.75	.35	.09
□ 44 Ted Savage	.75	.35	.09
□ 45 Claude Osteen	1.00	.45	.12
□ 46 Ed Brinkman	.75	.35	.09
□ 47 Matty Alou	1.00	.45	.12
□ 48 Bob Oliver	.75	.35	.09
□ 49 Danny Coombs	.75	.35	.09
□ 50 Frank Robinson	8.00	3.60	1.00
□ 51 Randy Hundley	.75	.35	.09
□ 52 Cesar Tovar	1.00	.45	.12
□ 53 Wayne Simpson	.75	.35	.09
□ 54 Bobby Murcer	1.50	.70	.19
□ 55 Carl Taylor	.75	.35	.09
□ 56 Tommy John	2.00	.90	.25
□ 57 Willie McCovey	6.00	2.70	.75
□ 58 Carl Yastrzemski	8.00	3.60	1.00
□ 59 Bob Bailey	.75	.35	.09
□ 60 Clyde Wright	.75	.35	.09
□ 61 Orlando Cepeda	2.00	.90	.25
□ 62 Al Kaline	8.00	3.60	1.00
□ 63 Bob Gibson	8.00	3.60	1.00
□ 64 Bert Campaneris	1.00	.45	.12
□ 65 Ted Sizemore	.75	.35	.09
□ 66 Duke Sims	.75	.35	.09
□ 67 Bud Harrelson	.75	.35	.09
□ 68 Gerald McNertney	.75	.35	.09
□ 69 Jim Wynn	1.00	.45	.12
□ 70 Dick Bosman	.75	.35	.09
□ 71 Roberto Clemente	20.00	9.00	2.50
□ 72 Rich Reese	.75	.35	.09
□ 73 Gaylord Perry	4.00	1.80	.50
□ 74 Boog Powell	2.00	.90	.25
□ 75 Billy Williams	4.00	1.80	.50
□ 76 Bill Melton	.75	.35	.09
□ 77 Nate Colbert	.75	.35	.09
□ 78 Reggie Smith	1.00	.45	.12
□ 79 Deron Johnson	.75	.35	.09
□ 80 Jim Hunter	4.00	1.80	.50
□ 81 Bobby Tolan	1.00	.45	.12
□ 82 Jim Northrup	.75	.35	.09
□ 83 Ron Fairly	1.00	.45	.12
□ 84 Alex Johnson	.75	.35	.09
□ 85 Pat Jarvis	.75	.35	.09
□ 86 Sam McDowell	1.00	.45	.12
□ 87 Lou Brock	6.00	2.70	.75
□ 88 Danny Walton	.75	.35	.09
□ 89 Denis Menke	.75	.35	.09
□ 90 Jim Palmer	6.00	2.70	.75
□ 91 Tommy Agee	1.00	.45	.12
□ 92 Duane Josephson	.75	.35	.09
□ 93 Willie Davis	1.00	.45	.12
□ 94 Mel Stottlemyre	1.00	.45	.12
□ 95 Ron Santo	1.50	.70	.19
□ 96 Amos Otis	1.00	.45	.12
□ 97 Ken Henderson	.75	.35	.09
□ 98 George Scott	1.00	.45	.12
□ 99 Dock Ellis	1.00	.45	.12
□ 100 Harmon Killebrew	6.00	2.70	.75
□ 101 Pete Rose	10.00	4.50	1.25
□ 102 Rick Reichardt	.75	.35	.09
□ 103 Cleon Jones	.75	.35	.09
□ 104 Ron Perranoski	.75	.35	.09
□ 105 Tony Perez	2.00	.90	.25
□ 106 Mickey Lolich	2.00	.90	.25
□ 107 Tim McCarver	1.50	.70	.19
□ 108 Reggie Jackson	10.00	4.50	1.25
□ 109 Chris Cannizzaro	.75	.35	.09
□ 110 Steve Hargan	.75	.35	.09
□ 111 Rusty Staub	2.00	.90	.25
□ 112 Andy Messersmith	1.00	.45	.12
□ 113 Rico Carty	1.00	.45	.12
□ 114 Brooks Robinson	8.00	3.60	1.00
□ 115 Steve Carlton	8.00	3.60	1.00
□ 116 Mike Hegan	.75	.35	.09
□ 117 Joe Morgan	6.00	2.70	.75
□ 118 Thurman Munson	6.00	2.70	.75
□ 119 Don Kessinger	.75	.35	.09
□ 120 Joel Horlen	.75	.35	.09
□ 121 Wes Parker	1.00	.45	.12
□ 122 Sonny Siebert	.75	.35	.09
□ 123 Willie Stargell	6.00	2.70	.75
□ 124 Aurelio Rodriguez	.75	.35	.09
□ 125 Juan Marichal	6.00	2.70	.75
□ 126 Mike Epstein	.75	.35	.09
□ 127 Tom Seaver	10.00	4.50	1.25
□ 128 Tony Oliva	2.00	.90	.25
□ 129 Jim Merritt	.75	.35	.09
□ 130 Willie Horton	1.00	.45	.12
□ 131 Rick Wise	.75	.35	.09
□ 132 Sal Bando	1.00	.45	.12
□ 133 Ollie Brown	.75	.35	.09
□ 134 Ken Harrelson	1.00	.45	.12
□ 135 Mack Jones	.75	.35	.09
□ 136 Jim Fregosi	1.00	.45	.12
□ 137 Hank Aaron	12.50	5.50	1.55
□ 138 Fritz Peterson	.75	.35	.09
□ 139 Joe Hague	.75	.35	.09
□ 140 Tommy Harper	.75	.35	.09
□ 141 Larry Dierker	.75	.35	.09
□ 142 Tony Conigliaro	1.50	.70	.19
□ 143 Glenn Beckert	.75	.35	.09
□ 144 Carlos May	.75	.35	.09
□ 145 Don Sutton	3.00	1.35	.35
□ 146 Paul Casanova	.75	.35	.09
□ 147 Bob Moose	.75	.35	.09
□ 148 Chico Cardenas	.75	.35	.09
□ 149 Johnny Bench	10.00	4.50	1.25
□ 150 Mike Cuellar	1.00	.45	.12
□ 151 Donn Clendenon	.75	.35	.09
□ 152 Lou Piniella	2.00	.90	.25
□ 153 Willie Mays	15.00	6.75	1.85

1971 Topps Greatest Moments

The cards in this 55-card set measure 2 1/2" by 4 3/4". The 1971 Topps Greatest Moments set contains numbered cards depicting specific career highlights of current players. The obverses are black bordered and contain a small cameo picture of the left side; a deckle-bordered black and white action photo dominates the rest of the card. The backs are designed in newspaper style. Sometimes found in uncut sheets, this test set was retailed in gum packs on a very limited basis. Double prints (DP) are listed in the checklist below; there were 22 double prints and 33 single prints.

	NRMT	VG-E	GOOD
COMPLETE SET (55)	1350.00	600.00	170.00
COMMON CARD (1-55)	20.00	9.00	2.50
COMMON DP	5.00	2.20	.60

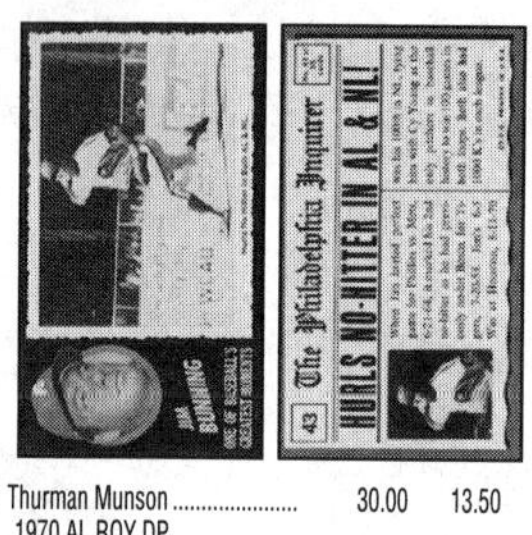

	NRMT	VG-E	GOOD
☐ 1 Thurman Munson 1970 AL ROY DP	30.00	13.50	3.70
☐ 2 Hoyt Wilhelm Hurls 1000th Game	30.00	13.50	3.70
☐ 3 Rico Carty: Leads ML .366 in 1970	20.00	9.00	2.50
☐ 4 Carl Morton 1970 NL ROY DP	5.00	2.20	.60
☐ 5 Sal Bando: Plays All A's Games 1st 2 years DP	5.00	2.20	.60
☐ 6 Bert Campaneris Hits 2 HRs in First ML Game DP	5.00	2.20	.60
☐ 7 Jim Kaat: Gold Glove 9 Straight Years	25.00	11.00	3.10
☐ 8 Harmon Killebrew: Tops 40 Homers 8th Time	50.00	22.00	6.25
☐ 9 Brooks Robinson MVP 1970 W.S.	75.00	34.00	9.50
☐ 10 Jim Perry AL Cy Young 1970	20.00	9.00	2.50
☐ 11 Tony Oliva Leads AL in Batting 1st 2 Full Years	25.00	11.00	3.10
☐ 12 Vada Pinson Tops 200 Hits 1st Full Year in ML	25.00	11.00	3.10
☐ 13 Johnny Bench 1970 ML Player of the Year	125.00	55.00	15.50
☐ 14 Tony Perez 15th Inning Homer Wins A-S Game	30.00	13.50	3.70
☐ 15 Pete Rose: Leads ML Batting 2nd Cons. year. DP	75.00	34.00	9.50
☐ 16 Jim Fregosi: Hits for cycle twice DP	5.00	2.20	.60
☐ 17 Alex Johnson: Leads AL batting 1st year in league DP	5.00	2.20	.60
☐ 18 Clyde Wright: No-Hitter vs. A's DP	5.00	2.20	.60
☐ 19 Al Kaline: Youngest player to win AL batting crown DP	30.00	13.50	3.70
☐ 20 Denny McLain: 1st AL Pitcher to win 30 in 37 years	25.00	11.00	3.10
☐ 21 Jim Northrup Hits Three Grand-Slams in One Week	20.00	9.00	2.50
☐ 22 Bill Freehan: Leads AL Catchers in fielding 6 cons. years	20.00	9.00	2.50
☐ 23 Mickey Lolich: Wins 3 in 1968 W.S.	25.00	11.00	3.10
☐ 24 Bob Gibson: Lowest ERA ever 300 or more innings DP	20.00	9.00	2.50
☐ 25 Tim McCarver 1st catcher to lead ML in triples DP	5.00	2.20	.60
☐ 26 Orlando Cepeda 1967 NL player of the year DP	7.50	3.40	.95
☐ 27 Lou Brock: 50 SB's 6th straight year DP	20.00	9.00	2.50
☐ 28 Nate Colbert: New Club Mark with 38 HR's DP	5.00	2.20	.60
☐ 29 Maury Wills Sets Modern Mark with 104 SB's	25.00	11.00	3.10
☐ 30 Wes Parker: Leads ML with 47 Doubles	20.00	9.00	2.50
☐ 31 Jim Wynn: 1 of 2 Astro Grand Slams Same Inning	20.00	9.00	2.50
☐ 32 Larry Dierker Makes ML Debut on 18th Birthday	20.00	9.00	2.50
☐ 33 Bill Melton 1st Chisox to Hit 30 HR's	20.00	9.00	2.50
☐ 34 Joe Morgan Ties Record 6 Hits in 6 AB's	35.00	16.00	4.40
☐ 35 Rusty Staub Leads ML 44 2B's	25.00	11.00	3.10
☐ 36 Ernie Banks: Sets ML Record with 5 Grand Slams. DP	30.00	13.50	3.70
☐ 37 Billy Williams 1117 Cons. Games	35.00	16.00	4.40
☐ 38 Lou Piniella 1969 AL ROY	25.00	11.00	3.10
☐ 39 Rico Petrocelli: AL HR Mark for SS's DP	5.00	2.20	.60
☐ 40 Carl Yastrzemski AL Triple Crown DP	50.00	22.00	6.25
☐ 41 Willie Mays: 3000th Career Hit DP	75.00	34.00	9.50
☐ 42 Tommy Harper Leads ML 73 SB's	20.00	9.00	2.50
☐ 43 Jim Bunning: No-Hitter Both AL and NL DP	15.00	6.75	1.85
☐ 44 Fritz Peterson Wins 20th on Last Day of 1970	20.00	9.00	2.50
☐ 45 Roy White: Hits HR's Lefty and Righty	20.00	9.00	2.50
☐ 46 Bobby Murcer Hits 4 Cons. HR's in a Twinbill	20.00	9.00	2.50
☐ 47 Reggie Jackson 10 RBI's One Game	125.00	55.00	15.50
☐ 48 Frank Howard New Record, 10 HR's in One Week	25.00	11.00	3.10
☐ 49 Dick Bosman Leads AL in ERA	20.00	9.00	2.50
☐ 50 Sam McDowell Hurls Two Cons. One-Hitters DP	5.00	2.20	.60
☐ 51 Luis Aparicio Leads AL SB's 9 cons. years DP	15.00	6.75	1.85
☐ 52 Willie McCovey Four Hits in His First Game DP	20.00	9.00	2.50
☐ 53 Joe Pepitone 2 HR's One Inning	20.00	9.00	2.50
☐ 54 Jerry Grote: 20 PO's in 9 Inning Game	20.00	9.00	2.50
☐ 55 Bud Harrelson 54 Consecutive Errorless Games, SS	20.00	9.00	2.50

1971 Topps Super

The cards in this 63-card set measure 3 1/8" by 5 1/4". The obverse format of the Topps Super set of 1971 is identical to that of the 1970 set, that is, a borderless color photograph with a facsimile autograph printed on it. The backs are enlargements of the respective player's cards of the 1971 regular baseball issue. There are no reported scarcities in the set. Just as in 1970, this set was issued in three-card wax packs.

	NRMT	VG-E	GOOD
COMPLETE SET (63)	200.00	90.00	25.00
COMMON CARD (1-63)	1.00	.45	.12
☐ 1 Reggie Smith	1.50	.70	.19
☐ 2 Gaylord Perry	3.00	1.35	.35
☐ 3 Ted Savage	1.00	.45	.12
☐ 4 Donn Clendenon	1.00	.45	.12
☐ 5 Boog Powell	2.00	.90	.25
☐ 6 Tony Perez	3.00	1.35	.35
☐ 7 Dick Bosman	1.00	.45	.12
☐ 8 Alex Johnson	1.00	.45	.12
☐ 9 Rusty Staub	2.00	.90	.25
☐ 10 Mel Stottlemyre	1.25	.55	.16
☐ 11 Tony Oliva	2.00	.90	.25
☐ 12 Bill Freehan	1.50	.70	.19
☐ 13 Fritz Peterson	1.00	.45	.12
☐ 14 Wes Parker	1.25	.55	.16
☐ 15 Cesar Cedeno	1.25	.55	.16
☐ 16 Sam McDowell	1.00	.45	.12
☐ 17 Frank Howard	1.50	.70	.19
☐ 18 Dave McNally	1.25	.55	.16
☐ 19 Rico Petrocelli	1.25	.55	.16
☐ 20 Pete Rose	25.00	11.00	3.10
☐ 21 Luke Walker	1.00	.45	.12
☐ 22 Nate Colbert	1.00	.45	.12
☐ 23 Luis Aparicio	3.00	1.35	.35
☐ 24 Jim Perry	1.25	.55	.16
☐ 25 Lou Brock	5.00	2.20	.60
☐ 26 Roy White	1.00	.45	.12
☐ 27 Claude Osteen	1.00	.45	.12
☐ 28 Carl Morton	1.00	.45	.12
☐ 29 Rico Carty	1.25	.55	.16
☐ 30 Larry Dierker	1.00	.45	.12
☐ 31 Bert Campaneris	1.00	.45	.12
☐ 32 Johnny Bench	10.00	4.50	1.25
☐ 33 Felix Millan	1.00	.45	.12
☐ 34 Tim McCarver	2.00	.90	.25
☐ 35 Ron Santo	2.00	.90	.25
☐ 36 Tommie Agee	1.00	.45	.12
☐ 37 Roberto Clemente	35.00	16.00	4.40
☐ 38 Reggie Jackson	15.00	6.75	1.85
☐ 39 Clyde Wright	1.00	.45	.12
☐ 40 Rich Allen	2.00	.90	.25
☐ 41 Curt Flood	1.25	.55	.16
☐ 42 Fergie Jenkins	3.00	1.35	.35
☐ 43 Willie Stargell	4.00	1.80	.50
☐ 44 Hank Aaron	15.00	6.75	1.85
☐ 45 Amos Otis	1.25	.55	.16
☐ 46 Willie McCovey	4.00	1.80	.50
☐ 47 Bill Melton	1.00	.45	.12
☐ 48 Bob Gibson	4.00	1.80	.50
☐ 49 Carl Yastrzemski	10.00	4.50	1.25
☐ 50 Glenn Beckert	1.00	.45	.12
☐ 51 Ray Fosse	1.00	.45	.12
☐ 52 Cito Gaston	1.50	.70	.19
☐ 53 Tom Seaver	10.00	4.50	1.25
☐ 54 Al Kaline	8.00	3.60	1.00
☐ 55 Jim Northrup	1.00	.45	.12
☐ 56 Willie Mays	18.00	8.00	2.20
☐ 57 Sal Bando	1.00	.45	.12
☐ 58 Deron Johnson	1.00	.45	.12
☐ 59 Brooks Robinson	8.00	3.60	1.00
☐ 60 Harmon Killebrew	4.00	1.80	.50
☐ 61 Joe Torre	3.00	1.35	.35
☐ 62 Lou Piniella	1.50	.70	.19
☐ 63 Tommy Harper	1.00	.45	.12

1971 Topps Tattoos

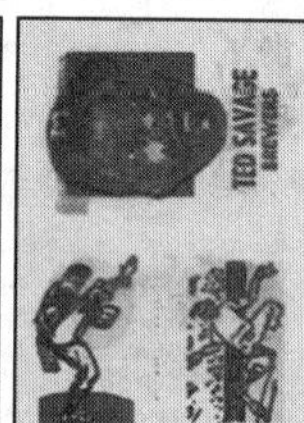

There are 16 different sheets (3 1/2" X 14 1/4") of baseball tattoos issued by Topps in 1971. Each contains two distinct sizes (1 3/4" by 2 3/8" and 1 3/16" by 1 3/4") of tattoos; those of players feature flesh-tone faces on red or yellow backgrounds; those of baseball figures, facsimile autographs (these are denoted by AU in the checklist) and team pennants are one-half the player tattoo size. The "Baseball Tattoos" logo panel at the top of each sheet contains the sheet number; the sheet number is given (with an S prefix) in the checklist below after the name. The small baseball figures are not priced in the checklist. The complete tattoo panel prices can be figured as the sum of the individual (player, team and autograph) tatoos.

	NRMT	VG-E	GOOD
COMPLETE SET (134)	175.00	80.00	22.00
COMMON TATTOO (1-134)	.75	.35	.09
☐ 1 Sal Bando S1	1.00	.45	.12
☐ 2 Dick Bosman S1	.75	.35	.09
☐ 3 Nate Colbert S1	.75	.35	.09
☐ 4 Cleon Jones S1	.75	.35	.09
☐ 5 Juan Marichal S1	4.00	1.80	.50
☐ 6 Brooks Robinson S1	6.00	2.70	.75
☐ 7 Brooks Robinson AU S1	1.50	.70	.19
☐ 8 Montreal Expos S1	.75	.35	.09
☐ 9 San Fran. Giants S1	.75	.35	.09
☐ 10 Glenn Beckert S2	.75	.35	.09
☐ 11 Tommy Harper S2	.75	.35	.09
☐ 12 Ken Henderson S2	.75	.35	.09
☐ 13 Carl Yastrzemski S2	6.00	2.70	.75
☐ 14 Carl Yastrzemski AU S2	1.50	.70	.19
☐ 15 Boston Red Sox S2	.75	.35	.09
☐ 16 New York Mets S2	.75	.35	.09
☐ 17 Orlando Cepeda S3	1.50	.70	.19
☐ 18 Jim Fregosi S3	.75	.35	.09
☐ 19 Jim Fregosi AU S3	1.00	.45	.12
☐ 20 Randy Hundley S3	.75	.35	.09
☐ 21 Reggie Jackson S3	8.00	3.60	1.00
☐ 22 Jerry Koosman S3	1.50	.70	.19
☐ 23 Jim Palmer S3	4.00	1.80	.50
☐ 24 Phila. Phillies S3	.75	.35	.09
☐ 25 New York Yankees S3	1.00	.45	.12
☐ 26 Dick Dietz S4	.75	.35	.09
☐ 27 Clarence Gaston S4	1.50	.70	.19
☐ 28 Dave Johnson S4	1.00	.45	.12
☐ 29 Sam McDowell S4	.75	.35	.09
☐ 30 Sam McDowell AU S4	.75	.35	.09
☐ 31 Gary Nolan S4	.75	.35	.09
☐ 32 Amos Otis S4	.75	.35	.09
☐ 33 Kansas City Royals S4	.75	.35	.09
☐ 34 Oakland A's S4	.75	.35	.09
☐ 35 Billy Grabarkewitz S5	.75	.35	.09
☐ 36 Al Kaline S5	6.00	2.70	.75
☐ 37 Al Kaline AU S5	1.50	.70	.19
☐ 38 Lee May S5	1.00	.45	.12
☐ 39 Tom Murphy S5	.75	.35	.09
☐ 40 Vada Pinson S5	1.50	.70	.19
☐ 41 Manny Sanguillen S5	.75	.35	.09
☐ 42 Atlanta Braves S5	.75	.35	.09
☐ 43 Los Angeles Dodgers S5	.75	.35	.09
☐ 44 Luis Aparicio S6	4.00	1.80	.50
☐ 45 Paul Blair S6	.75	.35	.09
☐ 46 Chris Cannizzaro S6	.75	.35	.09
☐ 47 Donn Clendenon S6	.75	.35	.09
☐ 48 Larry Dierker S6	.75	.35	.09
☐ 49 Harmon Killebrew S6	4.00	1.80	.50
☐ 50 Harmon Killebrew AU S6	1.50	.70	.19
☐ 51 Chicago Cubs S6	.75	.35	.09
☐ 52 Cincinnati Reds S6	.75	.35	.09
☐ 53 Rich Allen S7	1.50	.70	.19
☐ 54 Bert Campaneris S7	1.00	.45	.12
☐ 55 Don Money S7	.75	.35	.09
☐ 56 Boog Powell S7	2.00	.90	.25
☐ 57 Boog Powell AU S7	1.00	.45	.12
☐ 58 Ted Savage S7	.75	.35	.09
☐ 59 Rusty Staub S7	1.50	.70	.19
☐ 60 Cleveland Indians S7	.75	.35	.09
☐ 61 Milwaukee Brewers S7	.75	.35	.09
☐ 62 Leo Cardenas S8	.75	.35	.09
☐ 63 Bill Hands S8	.75	.35	.09
☐ 64 Frank Howard S8	1.50	.70	.19
☐ 65 Frank Howard AU S8	1.00	.45	.12
☐ 66 Wes Parker S8	.75	.35	.09
☐ 67 Reggie Smith S8	1.00	.45	.12
☐ 68 Willie Stargell S8	4.00	1.80	.50
☐ 69 Chicago White Sox S8	.75	.35	.09
☐ 70 San Diego Padres S8	.75	.35	.09
☐ 71 Hank Aaron S9	10.00	4.50	1.25
☐ 72 Hank Aaron AU S9	2.00	.90	.25
☐ 73 Tommy Agee S9	.75	.35	.09
☐ 74 Jim Hunter S9	4.00	1.80	.50
☐ 75 Dick McAuliffe S9	.75	.35	.09
☐ 76 Tony Perez S9	2.50	1.10	.30
☐ 77 Lou Piniella S9	1.50	.70	.19
☐ 78 Detroit Tigers S9	.75	.35	.09
☐ 79 Roberto Clemente S10	15.00	6.75	1.85
☐ 80 Tony Conigliaro S10	1.00	.45	.12
☐ 81 Fergie Jenkins S10	4.00	1.80	.50
☐ 82 Fergie Jenkins AU S10	1.50	.70	.19
☐ 83 Thurman Munson S10	5.00	2.20	.60
☐ 84 Gary Peters S10	.75	.35	.09
☐ 85 Joe Torre S10	1.50	.70	.19
☐ 86 Baltimore Orioles S10	.75	.35	.09
☐ 87 Johnny Bench S11	6.00	2.70	.75
☐ 88 Johnny Bench AU S11	1.50	.70	.19
☐ 89 Rico Carty S11	1.00	.45	.12
☐ 90 Bill Mazeroski S11	2.00	.90	.25
☐ 91 Bob Oliver S11	.75	.35	.09
☐ 92 Rico Petrocelli S11	1.00	.45	.12
☐ 93 Frank Robinson S11	.75	.35	.09
☐ 94 Washington Senators S11	.75	.35	.09
☐ 95 Bill Freehan S12	1.00	.45	.12
☐ 96 Dave McNally S12	.75	.35	.09
☐ 97 Felix Millan S12	.75	.35	.09
☐ 98 Mel Stottlemyre S12	1.00	.45	.12
☐ 99 Bob Tolan S12	.75	.35	.09
☐ 100 Billy Williams S12	4.00	1.80	.50
☐ 101 Billy Williams AU S12	1.50	.70	.19
☐ 102 Houston Astros S12	.75	.35	.09
☐ 103 Ray Culp S13	.75	.35	.09
☐ 104 Bud Harrelson S13	.75	.35	.09
☐ 105 Mickey Lolich S13	1.50	.70	.19
☐ 106 Willie McCovey S13	4.00	1.80	.50
☐ 107 Willie McCovey AU S13	1.50	.70	.19
☐ 108 Ron Santo S13	2.00	.90	.25
☐ 109 Roy White S13	1.00	.45	.12
☐ 110 Pittsburgh Pirates S13	.75	.35	.09
☐ 111 Bill Melton S14	.75	.35	.09
☐ 112 Jim Perry S14	1.00	.45	.12
☐ 113 Pete Rose S14	10.00	4.50	1.25
☐ 114 Tom Seaver S14	8.00	3.60	1.00
☐ 115 Tom Seaver AU S14	1.50	.70	.19
☐ 116 Maury Wills S14	1.50	.70	.19
☐ 117 Clyde Wright S14	.75	.35	.09
☐ 118 Minnesota Twins S14	.75	.35	.09
☐ 119 Rod Carew S15	6.00	2.70	.75
☐ 120 Bob Gibson S15	6.00	2.70	.75
☐ 121 Bob Gibson AU S15	1.50	.70	.19
☐ 122 Alex Johnson S15	.75	.35	.09
☐ 123 Don Kessinger S15	.75	.35	.09
☐ 124 Jim Merritt S15	.75	.35	.09
☐ 125 Rick Monday S15	.75	.35	.09
☐ 126 St. Louis Cardinals S15	.75	.35	.09
☐ 127 Larry Bowa S16	1.00	.45	.12
☐ 128 Mike Cuellar S16	1.00	.45	.12
☐ 129 Ray Fosse S16	.75	.35	.09
☐ 130 Willie Mays S16	12.00	5.50	1.50
☐ 131 Willie Mays AU S16	2.00	.90	.25
☐ 132 Carl Morton S16	.75	.35	.09
☐ 133 Tony Oliva S16	2.50	1.10	.30
☐ 134 California Angels S16	.75	.35	.09

1972 Topps

The cards in this 787-card set measure 2 1/2" by 3 1/2". The 1972 Topps set contained the most cards ever for a Topps set to that point in time. Features appearing for the first time were "Boyhood Photos"

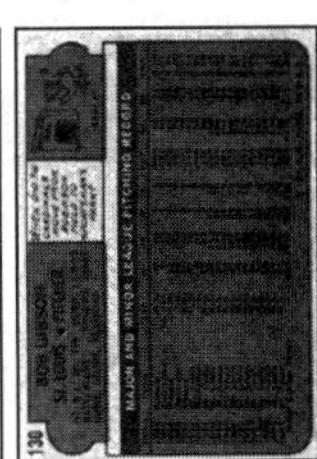

(341-348/491-498), Awards and Trophy cards (621-626), "In Action" (distributed throughout the set), and "Traded Cards" (751-757). Other subsets included League Leaders (85-96), Playoffs cards (221-222), and World Series cards (223-230). The curved lines of the color picture are a departure from the rectangular designs of other years. There is a series of intermediate scarcity (526-656) and the usual high numbers (657-787). The backs of cards 692, 694, 696, 700, 706 and 710 form a picture back of Tom Seaver. The backs of cards 698, 702, 704, 708, 712, 714 form a picture back of Tony Oliva. As in previous years, cards were issued in a variety of ways including ten-card dime wax packs. The key Rookie Card in this set is Carlton Fisk.

	NRMT	VG-E	GOOD
COMPLETE SET (787)	1700.00	750.00	210.00
COMMON CARD (1-132)	.60	.25	.07
COMMON CARD (133-263)	1.00	.45	.12
COMMON CARD (264-394)	1.25	.55	.16
COMMON CARD (395-525)	1.50	.70	.19
COMMON CARD (526-656)	4.00	1.80	.50
COMMON CARD (657-787)	12.00	5.50	1.50
WRAPPER (10-CENT)	15.00	6.75	1.85
☐ 1 Pittsburgh Pirates	7.00	2.50	1.00
Team Card			
☐ 2 Ray Culp	.60	.25	.07
☐ 3 Bob Tolan	.60	.25	.07
☐ 4 Checklist 1-132	4.00	.80	.40
☐ 5 John Bateman	.60	.25	.07
☐ 6 Fred Scherman	.60	.25	.07
☐ 7 Enzo Hernandez	.60	.25	.07
☐ 8 Ron Swoboda	1.00	.45	.12
☐ 9 Stan Williams	.60	.25	.07
☐ 10 Amos Otis	1.00	.45	.12
☐ 11 Bobby Valentine	1.00	.45	.12
☐ 12 Jose Cardenal	.60	.25	.07
☐ 13 Joe Grzenda	.60	.25	.07
☐ 14 Phillies Rookies	.60	.25	.07
Pete Koegel			
Mike Anderson			
Wayne Twitchell			
☐ 15 Walt Williams	.60	.25	.07
☐ 16 Mike Jorgensen	.60	.25	.07
☐ 17 Dave Duncan	.60	.25	.07
☐ 18A Juan Pizarro	.60	.25	.07
(Yellow underline			
C and S of Cubs)			
☐ 18B Juan Pizarro	5.00	2.20	.60
(Green underline			
C and S of Cubs)			
☐ 19 Billy Cowan	.60	.25	.07
☐ 20 Don Wilson	.60	.25	.07
☐ 21 Atlanta Braves	1.50	.70	.19
Team Card			
☐ 22 Rob Gardner	.60	.25	.07
☐ 23 Ted Kubiak	.60	.25	.07
☐ 24 Ted Ford	.60	.25	.07
☐ 25 Bill Singer	.60	.25	.07
☐ 26 Andy Etchebarren	.60	.25	.07
☐ 27 Bob Johnson	.60	.25	.07
☐ 28 Twins Rookies	.60	.25	.07
Bob Gebhard			
Steve Brye			
Hal Haydel			
☐ 29A Bill Bonham	.60	.25	.07
(Yellow underline			
C and S of Cubs)			
☐ 29B Bill Bonham	5.00	2.20	.60
(Green underline			
C and S of Cubs)			
☐ 30 Rico Petrocelli	1.00	.45	.12
☐ 31 Cleon Jones	1.00	.45	.12
☐ 32 Cleon Jones IA	.60	.25	.07
☐ 33 Billy Martin MG	4.00	1.80	.50
☐ 34 Billy Martin IA	2.00	.90	.25
☐ 35 Jerry Johnson	.60	.25	.07
☐ 36 Jerry Johnson IA	.60	.25	.07
☐ 37 Carl Yastrzemski	10.00	4.50	1.25
☐ 38 Carl Yastrzemski IA	6.00	2.70	.75
☐ 39 Bob Barton	.60	.25	.07
☐ 40 Bob Barton IA	.60	.25	.07
☐ 41 Tommy Davis	1.00	.45	.12
☐ 42 Tommy Davis IA	.60	.25	.07
☐ 43 Rick Wise	1.00	.45	.12
☐ 44 Rick Wise IA	.60	.25	.07
☐ 45A Glenn Beckert	1.00	.45	.12
(Yellow underline			
C and S of Cubs)			
☐ 45B Glenn Beckert	5.00	2.20	.60
(Green underline			
C and S of Cubs)			
☐ 46 Glenn Beckert IA	.60	.25	.07
☐ 47 John Ellis	.60	.25	.07
☐ 48 John Ellis IA	.60	.25	.07
☐ 49 Willie Mays	25.00	11.00	3.10
☐ 50 Willie Mays IA	12.00	5.50	1.50
☐ 51 Harmon Killebrew	7.00	3.10	.85
☐ 52 Harmon Killebrew IA	3.50	1.55	.45
☐ 53 Bud Harrelson	1.00	.45	.12
☐ 54 Bud Harrelson IA	.60	.25	.07
☐ 55 Clyde Wright	.60	.25	.07
☐ 56 Rich Chiles	.60	.25	.07
☐ 57 Bob Oliver	.60	.25	.07
☐ 58 Ernie McAnally	.60	.25	.07
☐ 59 Fred Stanley	.60	.25	.07
☐ 60 Manny Sanguillen	1.00	.45	.12
☐ 61 Cubs Rookies	1.00	.45	.12
Burt Hooton			
Gene Hiser			
Earl Stephenson			
☐ 62 Angel Mangual	.60	.25	.07
☐ 63 Duke Sims	.60	.25	.07
☐ 64 Pete Broberg	.60	.25	.07
☐ 65 Cesar Cedeno	1.00	.45	.12
☐ 66 Ray Corbin	.60	.25	.07
☐ 67 Red Schoendienst MG	1.00	.45	.12
☐ 68 Jim York	.60	.25	.07
☐ 69 Roger Freed	.60	.25	.07
☐ 70 Mike Cuellar	1.00	.45	.12
☐ 71 California Angels	1.50	.70	.19
Team Card			
☐ 72 Bruce Kison	.60	.25	.07
☐ 73 Steve Huntz	.60	.25	.07
☐ 74 Cecil Upshaw	.60	.25	.07
☐ 75 Bert Campaneris	1.00	.45	.12
☐ 76 Don Carrithers	.60	.25	.07
☐ 77 Ron Theobald	.60	.25	.07
☐ 78 Steve Arlin	.60	.25	.07
☐ 79 Red Sox Rookies	60.00	27.00	7.50
Mike Garman			
Cecil Cooper			
Carlton Fisk			
☐ 80 Tony Perez	4.00	1.80	.50
☐ 81 Mike Hedlund	.60	.25	.07
☐ 82 Ron Woods	.60	.25	.07
☐ 83 Dalton Jones	.60	.25	.07
☐ 84 Vince Colbert	.60	.25	.07
☐ 85 NL Batting Leaders	1.75	.80	.22
Joe Torre			
Ralph Garr			
Glenn Beckert			
☐ 86 AL Batting Leaders	1.75	.80	.22
Tony Oliva			
Bobby Murcer			
Merv Rettenmund			
☐ 87 NL RBI Leaders	3.50	1.55	.45
Joe Torre			
Willie Stargell			
Hank Aaron			
☐ 88 AL RBI Leaders	3.00	1.35	.35
Harmon Killebrew			
Frank Robinson			
Reggie Smith			
☐ 89 NL Home Run Leaders	3.00	1.35	.35
Willie Stargell			
Hank Aaron			
Lee May			
☐ 90 AL Home Run Leaders	2.50	1.10	.30
Bill Melton			
Norm Cash			
Reggie Jackson			
☐ 91 NL ERA Leaders	2.50	1.10	.30
Tom Seaver			
Dave Roberts UER			
(Photo actually			
Danny Coombs)			
Don Wilson			
☐ 92 AL ERA Leaders	2.50	1.10	.30
Vida Blue			
Wilbur Wood			
Jim Palmer			
☐ 93 NL Pitching Leaders	4.00	1.80	.50
Fergie Jenkins			
Steve Carlton			
Al Downing			
Tom Seaver			
☐ 94 AL Pitching Leaders	1.75	.80	.22
Mickey Lolich			
Vida Blue			
Wilbur Wood			
☐ 95 NL Strikeout Leaders	3.00	1.35	.35
Tom Seaver			
Fergie Jenkins			
Bill Stoneman			
☐ 96 AL Strikeout Leaders	1.75	.80	.22
Mickey Lolich			
Vida Blue			
Joe Coleman			
☐ 97 Tom Kelley	.60	.25	.07
☐ 98 Chuck Tanner MG	1.00	.45	.12
☐ 99 Ross Grimsley	.60	.25	.07
☐ 100 Frank Robinson	8.00	3.60	1.00
☐ 101 Astros Rookies	1.50	.70	.19
Bill Greif			
J.R. Richard			
Ray Busse			
☐ 102 Lloyd Allen	.60	.25	.07
☐ 103 Checklist 133-263	4.00	.80	.40
☐ 104 Toby Harrah	1.50	.70	.19
☐ 105 Gary Gentry	.60	.25	.07
☐ 106 Milwaukee Brewers	1.50	.70	.19
Team Card			
☐ 107 Jose Cruz	1.50	.70	.19
☐ 108 Gary Waslewski	.60	.25	.07
☐ 109 Jerry May	.60	.25	.07
☐ 110 Ron Hunt	.60	.25	.07
☐ 111 Jim Grant	.60	.25	.07
☐ 112 Greg Luzinski	1.50	.70	.19
☐ 113 Rogelio Moret	.60	.25	.07
☐ 114 Bill Buckner	1.50	.70	.19
☐ 115 Jim Fregosi	1.00	.45	.12
☐ 116 Ed Farmer	.60	.25	.07
☐ 117A Cleo James	.60	.25	.07
(Yellow underline			
C and S of Cubs)			
☐ 117B Cleo James	5.00	2.20	.60
(Green underline			
C and S of Cubs)			
☐ 118 Skip Lockwood	.60	.25	.07
☐ 119 Marty Perez	.60	.25	.07
☐ 120 Bill Freehan	1.00	.45	.12
☐ 121 Ed Sprague	.60	.25	.07
☐ 122 Larry Biittner	.60	.25	.07
☐ 123 Ed Acosta	.60	.25	.07
☐ 124 Yankees Rookies	.60	.25	.07
Alan Closter			
Rusty Torres			
Roger Hambright			
☐ 125 Dave Cash	1.00	.45	.12
☐ 126 Bart Johnson	.60	.25	.07
☐ 127 Duffy Dyer	.60	.25	.07
☐ 128 Eddie Watt	.60	.25	.07
☐ 129 Charlie Fox MG	.60	.25	.07
☐ 130 Bob Gibson	8.00	3.60	1.00
☐ 131 Jim Nettles	.60	.25	.07
☐ 132 Joe Morgan	6.00	2.70	.75
☐ 133 Joe Keough	1.00	.45	.12
☐ 134 Carl Morton	1.00	.45	.12
☐ 135 Vada Pinson	1.50	.70	.19
☐ 136 Darrel Chaney	1.00	.45	.12
☐ 137 Dick Williams MG	1.50	.70	.19
☐ 138 Mike Kekich	1.00	.45	.12
☐ 139 Tim McCarver	1.50	.70	.19
☐ 140 Pat Dobson	1.50	.70	.19
☐ 141 Mets Rookies	1.50	.70	.19
Buzz Capra			
Lee Stanton			
Jon Matlack			
☐ 142 Chris Chambliss	4.00	1.80	.50
☐ 143 Garry Jestadt	1.00	.45	.12
☐ 144 Marty Pattin	1.00	.45	.12
☐ 145 Don Kessinger	1.50	.70	.19
☐ 146 Steve Kealey	1.00	.45	.12
☐ 147 Dave Kingman	5.00	2.20	.60
☐ 148 Dick Billings	1.00	.45	.12
☐ 149 Gary Neibauer	1.00	.45	.12
☐ 150 Norm Cash	1.50	.70	.19
☐ 151 Jim Brewer	1.00	.45	.12
☐ 152 Gene Clines	1.00	.45	.12
☐ 153 Rick Auerbach	1.00	.45	.12
☐ 154 Ted Simmons	3.00	1.35	.35
☐ 155 Larry Dierker	1.50	.70	.19
☐ 156 Minnesota Twins	1.50	.70	.19
Team Card			
☐ 157 Don Gullett	1.00	.45	.12
☐ 158 Jerry Kenney	1.00	.45	.12
☐ 159 John Boccabella	1.00	.45	.12
☐ 160 Andy Messersmith	1.50	.70	.19
☐ 161 Brock Davis	1.00	.45	.12
☐ 162 Brewers Rookies UER	2.00	.90	.25
Jerry Bell			
Darrell Porter			
Bob Reynolds			
(Porter and Bell			
photos switched)			
☐ 163 Tug McGraw	2.00	.90	.25
☐ 164 Tug McGraw IA	1.50	.70	.19
☐ 165 Chris Speier	2.00	.90	.25
☐ 166 Chris Speier IA	1.50	.70	.19
☐ 167 Deron Johnson	1.00	.45	.12
☐ 168 Deron Johnson IA	1.00	.45	.12
☐ 169 Vida Blue	2.00	.90	.25
☐ 170 Vida Blue IA	1.50	.70	.19
☐ 171 Darrell Evans	2.00	.90	.25
☐ 172 Darrell Evans IA	1.50	.70	.19
☐ 173 Clay Kirby	1.00	.45	.12
☐ 174 Clay Kirby IA	1.00	.45	.12
☐ 175 Tom Haller	1.00	.45	.12
☐ 176 Tom Haller IA	1.00	.45	.12
☐ 177 Paul Schaal	1.00	.45	.12
☐ 178 Paul Schaal IA	1.00	.45	.12
☐ 179 Dock Ellis	1.00	.45	.12
☐ 180 Dock Ellis IA	1.00	.45	.12
☐ 181 Ed Kranepool	1.00	.45	.12
☐ 182 Ed Kranepool IA	1.00	.45	.12
☐ 183 Bill Melton	1.00	.45	.12
☐ 184 Bill Melton IA	1.00	.45	.12
☐ 185 Ron Bryant	1.00	.45	.12
☐ 186 Ron Bryant IA	1.00	.45	.12
☐ 187 Gates Brown	1.00	.45	.12
☐ 188 Frank Lucchesi MG	1.00	.45	.12
☐ 189 Gene Tenace	1.50	.70	.19
☐ 190 Dave Giusti	1.00	.45	.12
☐ 191 Jeff Burroughs	2.00	.90	.25
☐ 192 Chicago Cubs	1.50	.70	.19
Team Card			
☐ 193 Kurt Bevacqua	1.00	.45	.12
☐ 194 Fred Norman	1.00	.45	.12
☐ 195 Orlando Cepeda	2.00	.90	.25
☐ 196 Mel Queen	1.00	.45	.12
☐ 197 Johnny Briggs	1.00	.45	.12
☐ 198 Dodgers Rookies	4.00	1.80	.50
Charlie Hough			
Bob O'Brien			
Mike Strahler			
☐ 199 Mike Fiore	1.00	.45	.12
☐ 200 Lou Brock	7.00	3.10	.85
☐ 201 Phil Roof	1.00	.45	.12
☐ 202 Scipio Spinks	1.00	.45	.12
☐ 203 Ron Blomberg	1.00	.45	.12
☐ 204 Tommy Helms	1.00	.45	.12
☐ 205 Dick Drago	1.00	.45	.12
☐ 206 Dal Maxvill	1.00	.45	.12
☐ 207 Tom Egan	1.00	.45	.12
☐ 208 Milt Pappas	1.50	.70	.19
☐ 209 Joe Rudi	1.50	.70	.19
☐ 210 Denny McLain	1.50	.70	.19
☐ 211 Gary Sutherland	1.00	.45	.12
☐ 212 Grant Jackson	1.00	.45	.12
☐ 213 Angels Rookies	1.00	.45	.12
Billy Parker			
Art Kusnyer			
Tom Silverio			
☐ 214 Mike McQueen	1.00	.45	.12
☐ 215 Alex Johnson	1.50	.70	.19
☐ 216 Joe Niekro	1.50	.70	.19
☐ 217 Roger Metzger	1.00	.45	.12
☐ 218 Eddie Kasko MG	1.00	.45	.12
☐ 219 Rennie Stennett	1.50	.70	.19
☐ 220 Jim Perry	1.50	.70	.19
☐ 221 NL Playoffs	1.50	.70	.19
Bucs champs			
☐ 222 Brooks Robinson ALCS	3.00	1.35	.35
☐ 223 Dave McNally WS	1.75	.80	.22
☐ 224 Dave Johnson WS	1.75	.80	.22
Mark Belanger			
☐ 225 Manny Sanguillen WS	1.75	.80	.22
☐ 226 Roberto Clemente WS	6.00	2.70	.75
☐ 227 Nellie Briles WS	1.75	.80	.22
☐ 228 Frank Robinson WS	2.50	1.10	.30
Manny Sanguillen			
☐ 229 Steve Blass WS	1.75	.80	.22
☐ 230 World Series Summary	1.75	.80	.22
(Pirates celebrate)			
☐ 231 Casey Cox	1.00	.45	.12
☐ 232 Giants Rookies	1.00	.45	.12
Chris Arnold			
Jim Barr			
Dave Rader			
☐ 233 Jay Johnstone	1.50	.70	.19
☐ 234 Ron Taylor	1.00	.45	.12
☐ 235 Merv Rettenmund	1.00	.45	.12
☐ 236 Jim McGlothlin	1.00	.45	.12
☐ 237 New York Yankees	1.50	.70	.19
Team Card			
☐ 238 Leron Lee	1.00	.45	.12
☐ 239 Tom Timmermann	1.00	.45	.12
☐ 240 Rich Allen	2.00	.90	.25
☐ 241 Rollie Fingers	5.00	2.20	.60
☐ 242 Don Mincher	1.50	.70	.19
☐ 243 Frank Linzy	1.00	.45	.12
☐ 244 Steve Braun	1.00	.45	.12
☐ 245 Tommie Agee	1.50	.70	.19
☐ 246 Tom Burgmeier	1.00	.45	.12
☐ 247 Milt May	1.00	.45	.12
☐ 248 Tom Bradley	1.00	.45	.12
☐ 249 Harry Walker MG	1.00	.45	.12
☐ 250 Boog Powell	2.00	.90	.25
☐ 251 Checklist 264-394	4.00	.80	.40
☐ 252 Ken Reynolds	1.00	.45	.12
☐ 253 Sandy Alomar	1.50	.70	.19
☐ 254 Boots Day	1.00	.45	.12
☐ 255 Jim Lonborg	1.50	.70	.19
☐ 256 George Foster	2.50	1.10	.30
☐ 257 Tigers Rookies	1.00	.45	.12
Jim Foor			
Tim Hosley			
Paul Jata			
☐ 258 Randy Hundley	1.50	.70	.19
☐ 259 Sparky Lyle	2.00	.90	.25
☐ 260 Ralph Garr	1.50	.70	.19
☐ 261 Steve Mingori	1.00	.45	.12
☐ 262 San Diego Padres	1.50	.70	.19
Team Card			
☐ 263 Felipe Alou	1.50	.70	.19
☐ 264 Tommy John	1.50	.70	.19
☐ 265 Wes Parker	1.50	.70	.19
☐ 266 Bobby Bolin	1.25	.55	.16
☐ 267 Dave Concepcion	3.00	1.35	.35
☐ 268 A's Rookies	1.25	.55	.16
Dwain Anderson			
Chris Floethe			
☐ 269 Don Hahn	1.25	.55	.16
☐ 270 Jim Palmer	8.00	3.60	1.00
☐ 271 Ken Rudolph	1.25	.55	.16
☐ 272 Mickey Rivers	1.50	.70	.19
☐ 273 Bobby Floyd	1.25	.55	.16
☐ 274 Al Severinsen	1.25	.55	.16

☐ 275 Cesar Tovar 1.25 .55 .16
☐ 276 Gene Mauch MG 1.50 .70 .19
☐ 277 Elliott Maddox 1.25 .55 .16
☐ 278 Dennis Higgins 1.25 .55 .16
☐ 279 Larry Brown 1.25 .55 .16
☐ 280 Willie McCovey 7.00 3.10 .85
☐ 281 Bill Parsons 1.25 .55 .16
☐ 282 Houston Astros 2.00 .90 .25
Team Card
☐ 283 Darrell Brandon 1.25 .55 .16
☐ 284 Ike Brown 1.25 .55 .16
☐ 285 Gaylord Perry 6.00 2.70 .75
☐ 286 Gene Alley 1.50 .70 .19
☐ 287 Jim Hardin 1.25 .55 .16
☐ 288 Johnny Jeter 1.25 .55 .16
☐ 289 Syd O'Brien 1.25 .55 .16
☐ 290 Sonny Siebert 1.25 .55 .16
☐ 291 Hal McRae 1.50 .70 .19
☐ 292 Hal McRae IA 1.50 .70 .19
☐ 293 Dan Frisella 1.25 .55 .16
☐ 294 Dan Frisella IA 1.25 .55 .16
☐ 295 Dick Dietz 1.25 .55 .16
☐ 296 Dick Dietz IA 1.25 .55 .16
☐ 297 Claude Osteen 1.50 .70 .19
☐ 298 Claude Osteen IA 1.25 .55 .16
☐ 299 Hank Aaron 40.00 18.00 5.00
☐ 300 Hank Aaron IA 20.00 9.00 2.50
☐ 301 George Mitterwald 1.25 .55 .16
☐ 302 George Mitterwald IA 1.25 .55 .16
☐ 303 Joe Pepitone 1.50 .70 .19
☐ 304 Joe Pepitone IA 1.25 .55 .16
☐ 305 Ken Boswell 1.25 .55 .16
☐ 306 Ken Boswell IA 1.25 .55 .16
☐ 307 Steve Renko 1.25 .55 .16
☐ 308 Steve Renko IA 1.25 .55 .16
☐ 309 Roberto Clemente 50.00 22.00 6.25
☐ 310 Roberto Clemente IA 25.00 11.00 3.10
☐ 311 Clay Carroll 1.25 .55 .16
☐ 312 Clay Carroll IA 1.25 .55 .16
☐ 313 Luis Aparicio 4.00 1.80 .50
☐ 314 Luis Aparicio IA 1.75 .80 .22
☐ 315 Paul Splittorff 1.25 .55 .16
☐ 316 Cardinals Rookies 1.50 .70 .19
Jim Bibby
Jorge Roque
Santiago Guzman
☐ 317 Rich Hand 1.25 .55 .16
☐ 318 Sonny Jackson 1.25 .55 .16
☐ 319 Aurelio Rodriguez 1.25 .55 .16
☐ 320 Steve Blass 1.50 .70 .19
☐ 321 Joe Lahoud 1.25 .55 .16
☐ 322 Jose Pena 1.25 .55 .16
☐ 323 Earl Weaver MG 1.50 .70 .19
☐ 324 Mike Ryan 1.25 .55 .16
☐ 325 Mel Stottlemyre 1.50 .70 .19
☐ 326 Pat Kelly 1.25 .55 .16
☐ 327 Steve Stone 1.50 .70 .19
☐ 328 Boston Red Sox 2.00 .90 .25
Team Card
☐ 329 Roy Foster 1.25 .55 .16
☐ 330 Jim Hunter 4.00 1.80 .50
☐ 331 Stan Swanson 1.25 .55 .16
☐ 332 Buck Martinez 1.25 .55 .16
☐ 333 Steve Barber 1.25 .55 .16
☐ 334 Rangers Rookies 1.25 .55 .16
Bill Fahey
Jim Mason
Tom Ragland
☐ 335 Bill Hands 1.25 .55 .16
☐ 336 Marty Martinez 1.25 .55 .16
☐ 337 Mike Kilkenny 1.25 .55 .16
☐ 338 Bob Grich 1.50 .70 .19
☐ 339 Ron Cook 1.25 .55 .16
☐ 340 Roy White 1.50 .70 .19
☐ 341 Joe Torre KP 1.25 .55 .16
☐ 342 Wilbur Wood KP 1.25 .55 .16
☐ 343 Willie Stargell KP 1.50 .70 .19
☐ 344 Dave McNally KP 1.25 .55 .16
☐ 345 Rick Wise KP 1.25 .55 .16
☐ 346 Jim Fregosi KP 1.25 .55 .16
☐ 347 Tom Seaver KP 3.00 1.35 .35
☐ 348 Sal Bando KP 1.25 .55 .16
☐ 349 Al Fitzmorris 1.25 .55 .16
☐ 350 Frank Howard 1.50 .70 .19
☐ 351 Braves Rookies 1.50 .70 .19
Tom House
Rick Kester
Jimmy Britton
☐ 352 Dave LaRoche 1.25 .55 .16
☐ 353 Art Shamsky 1.25 .55 .16
☐ 354 Tom Murphy 1.25 .55 .16
☐ 355 Bob Watson 1.50 .70 .19
☐ 356 Gerry Moses 1.25 .55 .16
☐ 357 Woody Fryman 1.25 .55 .16
☐ 358 Sparky Anderson MG 3.00 1.35 .35
☐ 359 Don Pavletich 1.25 .55 .16
☐ 360 Dave Roberts 1.25 .55 .16
☐ 361 Mike Andrews 1.25 .55 .16
☐ 362 New York Mets 2.00 .90 .25
Team Card
☐ 363 Ron Klimkowski 1.25 .55 .16
☐ 364 Johnny Callison 1.50 .70 .19
☐ 365 Dick Bosman 1.50 .70 .19
☐ 366 Jimmy Rosario 1.25 .55 .16
☐ 367 Ron Perranoski 1.50 .70 .19
☐ 368 Danny Thompson 1.25 .55 .16
☐ 369 Jim Lefebvre 1.50 .70 .19
☐ 370 Don Buford 1.25 .55 .16
☐ 371 Denny Lemaster 1.25 .55 .16
☐ 372 Royals Rookies 1.25 .55 .16
Lance Clemons
Monty Montgomery
☐ 373 John Mayberry 1.50 .70 .19
☐ 374 Jack Heidemann 1.25 .55 .16
☐ 375 Reggie Cleveland 1.25 .55 .16
☐ 376 Andy Kosco 1.25 .55 .16
☐ 377 Terry Harmon 1.25 .55 .16
☐ 378 Checklist 395-525 4.00 .80 .40
☐ 379 Ken Berry 1.25 .55 .16
☐ 380 Earl Williams 1.25 .55 .16
☐ 381 Chicago White Sox 2.00 .90 .25
Team Card
☐ 382 Joe Gibbon 1.25 .55 .16
☐ 383 Brant Alyea 1.25 .55 .16
☐ 384 Dave Campbell 1.50 .70 .19
☐ 385 Mickey Stanley 1.50 .70 .19
☐ 386 Jim Colborn 1.25 .55 .16
☐ 387 Horace Clarke 1.50 .70 .19
☐ 388 Charlie Williams 1.25 .55 .16
☐ 389 Bill Rigney MG 1.25 .55 .16
☐ 390 Willie Davis 1.50 .70 .19
☐ 391 Ken Sanders 1.25 .55 .16
☐ 392 Pirates Rookies 1.50 .70 .19
Fred Cambria
Richie Zisk
☐ 393 Curt Motton 1.25 .55 .16
☐ 394 Ken Forsch 1.50 .70 .19
☐ 395 Matty Alou 1.75 .80 .22
☐ 396 Paul Lindblad 1.50 .70 .19
☐ 397 Philadelphia Phillies 3.00 1.35 .35
Team Card
☐ 398 Larry Hisle 1.75 .80 .22
☐ 399 Milt Wilcox 1.50 .70 .19
☐ 400 Tony Oliva 1.75 .80 .22
☐ 401 Jim Nash 1.50 .70 .19
☐ 402 Bobby Heise 1.50 .70 .19
☐ 403 John Cumberland 1.50 .70 .19
☐ 404 Jeff Torborg 1.75 .80 .22
☐ 405 Ron Fairly 1.75 .80 .22
☐ 406 George Hendrick 1.75 .80 .22
☐ 407 Chuck Taylor 1.50 .70 .19
☐ 408 Jim Northrup 1.75 .80 .22
☐ 409 Frank Baker 1.50 .70 .19
☐ 410 Fergie Jenkins 6.00 2.70 .75
☐ 411 Bob Montgomery 1.50 .70 .19
☐ 412 Dick Kelley 1.50 .70 .19
☐ 413 White Sox Rookies 1.50 .70 .19
Don Eddy
Dave Lemonds
☐ 414 Bob Miller 1.50 .70 .19
☐ 415 Cookie Rojas 1.75 .80 .22
☐ 416 Johnny Edwards 1.50 .70 .19
☐ 417 Tom Hall 1.50 .70 .19
☐ 418 Tom Shopay 1.50 .70 .19
☐ 419 Jim Spencer 1.50 .70 .19
☐ 420 Steve Carlton 18.00 8.00 2.20
☐ 421 Ellie Rodriguez 1.50 .70 .19
☐ 422 Ray Lamb 1.50 .70 .19
☐ 423 Oscar Gamble 1.75 .80 .22
☐ 424 Bill Gogolewski 1.50 .70 .19
☐ 425 Ken Singleton 1.75 .80 .22
☐ 426 Ken Singleton IA 1.50 .70 .19
☐ 427 Tito Fuentes 1.50 .70 .19
☐ 428 Tito Fuentes IA 1.50 .70 .19
☐ 429 Bob Robertson 1.50 .70 .19
☐ 430 Bob Robertson IA 1.50 .70 .19
☐ 431 Clarence Gaston 1.75 .80 .22
☐ 432 Clarence Gaston IA 1.75 .80 .22
☐ 433 Johnny Bench 25.00 11.00 3.10
☐ 434 Johnny Bench IA 14.00 6.25 1.75
☐ 435 Reggie Jackson 25.00 11.00 3.10
☐ 436 Reggie Jackson IA 14.00 6.25 1.75
☐ 437 Maury Wills 1.75 .80 .22
☐ 438 Maury Wills IA 1.75 .80 .22
☐ 439 Billy Williams 6.00 2.70 .75
☐ 440 Billy Williams IA 3.00 1.35 .35
☐ 441 Thurman Munson 14.00 6.25 1.75
☐ 442 Thurman Munson IA 7.00 3.10 .85
☐ 443 Ken Henderson 1.50 .70 .19
☐ 444 Ken Henderson IA 1.50 .70 .19
☐ 445 Tom Seaver 30.00 13.50 3.70
☐ 446 Tom Seaver IA 15.00 6.75 1.85
☐ 447 Willie Stargell 6.00 2.70 .75
☐ 448 Willie Stargell IA 3.00 1.35 .35
☐ 449 Bob Lemon MG 1.75 .80 .22
☐ 450 Mickey Lolich 1.75 .80 .22
☐ 451 Tony LaRussa 3.00 1.35 .35
☐ 452 Ed Herrmann 1.50 .70 .19
☐ 453 Barry Lersch 1.50 .70 .19
☐ 454 Oakland A's 3.00 1.35 .35
Team Card
☐ 455 Tommy Harper 1.75 .80 .22
☐ 456 Mark Belanger 1.75 .80 .22
☐ 457 Padres Rookies 1.50 .70 .19
Darcy Fast
Derrel Thomas
Mike Ivie
☐ 458 Aurelio Monteagudo 1.50 .70 .19
☐ 459 Rick Renick 1.50 .70 .19
☐ 460 Al Downing 1.50 .70 .19
☐ 461 Tim Cullen 1.50 .70 .19
☐ 462 Rickey Clark 1.50 .70 .19
☐ 463 Bernie Carbo 1.50 .70 .19
☐ 464 Jim Roland 1.50 .70 .19
☐ 465 Gil Hodges MG 4.00 1.80 .50
☐ 466 Norm Miller 1.50 .70 .19
☐ 467 Steve Kline 1.50 .70 .19
☐ 468 Richie Scheinblum 1.50 .70 .19
☐ 469 Ron Herbel 1.50 .70 .19
☐ 470 Ray Fosse 1.50 .70 .19
☐ 471 Luke Walker 1.50 .70 .19
☐ 472 Phil Gagliano 1.50 .70 .19
☐ 473 Dan McGinn 1.50 .70 .19
☐ 474 Orioles Rookies 15.00 6.75 1.85
Don Baylor
Roric Harrison
Johnny Oates
☐ 475 Gary Nolan 1.75 .80 .22
☐ 476 Lee Richard 1.50 .70 .19
☐ 477 Tom Phoebus 1.50 .70 .19
☐ 478 Checklist 526-656 4.00 .80 .40
☐ 479 Don Shaw 1.50 .70 .19
☐ 480 Lee May 1.75 .80 .22
☐ 481 Billy Conigliaro 1.75 .80 .22
☐ 482 Joe Hoerner 1.50 .70 .19
☐ 483 Ken Suarez 1.50 .70 .19
☐ 484 Lum Harris MG 1.50 .70 .19
☐ 485 Phil Regan 1.75 .80 .22
☐ 486 John Lowenstein 1.50 .70 .19
☐ 487 Detroit Tigers 3.00 1.35 .35
Team Card
☐ 488 Mike Nagy 1.50 .70 .19
☐ 489 Expos Rookies 1.50 .70 .19
Terry Humphrey
Keith Lampard
☐ 490 Dave McNally 1.75 .80 .22
☐ 491 Lou Piniella KP 1.75 .80 .22
☐ 492 Mel Stottlemyre KP 1.75 .80 .22
☐ 493 Bob Bailey KP 1.75 .80 .22
☐ 494 Willie Horton KP 1.75 .80 .22
☐ 495 Bill Melton KP 1.75 .80 .22
☐ 496 Bud Harrelson KP 1.75 .80 .22
☐ 497 Jim Perry KP 1.75 .80 .22
☐ 498 Brooks Robinson KP 3.00 1.35 .35
☐ 499 Vicente Romo 1.50 .70 .19
☐ 500 Joe Torre 1.75 .80 .22
☐ 501 Pete Hamm 1.50 .70 .19
☐ 502 Jackie Hernandez 1.50 .70 .19
☐ 503 Gary Peters 1.50 .70 .19
☐ 504 Ed Spiezio 1.50 .70 .19
☐ 505 Mike Marshall 1.75 .80 .22
☐ 506 Indians Rookies 1.50 .70 .19
Terry Ley
Jim Moyer
Dick Tidrow
☐ 507 Fred Gladding 1.50 .70 .19
☐ 508 Elrod Hendricks 1.50 .70 .19
☐ 509 Don McMahon 1.50 .70 .19
☐ 510 Ted Williams MG 10.00 4.50 1.25
☐ 511 Tony Taylor 1.75 .80 .22
☐ 512 Paul Popovich 1.50 .70 .19
☐ 513 Lindy McDaniel 1.75 .80 .22
☐ 514 Ted Sizemore 1.50 .70 .19
☐ 515 Bert Blyleven 3.00 1.35 .35
☐ 516 Oscar Brown 1.50 .70 .19
☐ 517 Ken Brett 1.50 .70 .19
☐ 518 Wayne Garrett 1.50 .70 .19
☐ 519 Ted Abernathy 1.50 .70 .19
☐ 520 Larry Bowa 1.75 .80 .22
☐ 521 Alan Foster 1.50 .70 .19
☐ 522 Los Angeles Dodgers 3.00 1.35 .35
Team Card
☐ 523 Chuck Dobson 1.50 .70 .19
☐ 524 Reds Rookies 1.50 .70 .19
Ed Armbrister
Mel Behney
☐ 525 Carlos May 1.75 .80 .22
☐ 526 Bob Bailey 4.50 2.00 .55
☐ 527 Dave Leonhard 4.00 1.80 .50
☐ 528 Ron Stone 4.00 1.80 .50
☐ 529 Dave Nelson 4.50 2.00 .55
☐ 530 Don Sutton 7.00 3.10 .85
☐ 531 Freddie Patek 4.50 2.00 .55
☐ 532 Fred Kendall 4.00 1.80 .50
☐ 533 Ralph Houk MG 4.50 2.00 .55
☐ 534 Jim Hickman 4.50 2.00 .55
☐ 535 Ed Brinkman 4.00 1.80 .50
☐ 536 Doug Rader 4.50 2.00 .55
☐ 537 Bob Locker 4.00 1.80 .50
☐ 538 Charlie Sands 4.00 1.80 .50
☐ 539 Terry Forster 4.50 2.00 .55
☐ 540 Felix Millan 4.00 1.80 .50
☐ 541 Roger Repoz 4.00 1.80 .50
☐ 542 Jack Billingham 4.00 1.80 .50
☐ 543 Duane Josephson 4.00 1.80 .50
☐ 544 Ted Martinez 4.00 1.80 .50
☐ 545 Wayne Granger 4.00 1.80 .50
☐ 546 Joe Hague 4.00 1.80 .50
☐ 547 Cleveland Indians 7.00 3.10 .85
Team Card
☐ 548 Frank Reberger 4.00 1.80 .50
☐ 549 Dave May 4.00 1.80 .50
☐ 550 Brooks Robinson 25.00 11.00 3.10
☐ 551 Ollie Brown 4.00 1.80 .50
☐ 552 Ollie Brown IA 4.00 1.80 .50
☐ 553 Wilbur Wood 4.50 2.00 .55
☐ 554 Wilbur Wood IA 4.00 1.80 .50
☐ 555 Ron Santo 4.50 2.00 .55
☐ 556 Ron Santo IA 4.50 2.00 .55
☐ 557 John Odom 4.00 1.80 .50
☐ 558 John Odom IA 4.00 1.80 .50
☐ 559 Pete Rose 40.00 18.00 5.00
☐ 560 Pete Rose IA 20.00 9.00 2.50
☐ 561 Leo Cardenas 4.00 1.80 .50
☐ 562 Leo Cardenas IA 4.00 1.80 .50
☐ 563 Ray Sadecki 4.00 1.80 .50
☐ 564 Ray Sadecki IA 4.00 1.80 .50
☐ 565 Reggie Smith 4.50 2.00 .55
☐ 566 Reggie Smith IA 4.00 1.80 .50
☐ 567 Juan Marichal 12.00 5.50 1.50
☐ 568 Juan Marichal IA 6.00 2.70 .75
☐ 569 Ed Kirkpatrick 4.00 1.80 .50
☐ 570 Ed Kirkpatrick IA 4.00 1.80 .50
☐ 571 Nate Colbert 4.00 1.80 .50
☐ 572 Nate Colbert IA 4.00 1.80 .50
☐ 573 Fritz Peterson 4.00 1.80 .50
☐ 574 Fritz Peterson IA 4.00 1.80 .50
☐ 575 Al Oliver 4.50 2.00 .55
☐ 576 Leo Durocher MG 5.00 2.20 .60
☐ 577 Mike Paul 4.50 2.00 .55
☐ 578 Billy Grabarkewitz 4.00 1.80 .50
☐ 579 Doyle Alexander 4.50 2.00 .55
☐ 580 Lou Piniella 5.00 2.20 .60
☐ 581 Wade Blasingame 4.00 1.80 .50
☐ 582 Montreal Expos 7.00 3.10 .85
Team Card
☐ 583 Darold Knowles 4.00 1.80 .50
☐ 584 Jerry McNertney 4.00 1.80 .50
☐ 585 George Scott 4.50 2.00 .55
☐ 586 Denis Menke 4.00 1.80 .50
☐ 587 Billy Wilson 4.00 1.80 .50
☐ 588 Jim Holt 4.00 1.80 .50
☐ 589 Hal Lanier 4.00 1.80 .50
☐ 590 Graig Nettles 4.50 2.00 .55
☐ 591 Paul Casanova 4.00 1.80 .50
☐ 592 Lew Krausse 4.00 1.80 .50
☐ 593 Rich Morales 4.00 1.80 .50
☐ 594 Jim Beauchamp 4.00 1.80 .50
☐ 595 Nolan Ryan 225.00 100.00 28.00
☐ 596 Manny Mota 4.50 2.00 .55
☐ 597 Jim Magnuson 4.00 1.80 .50
☐ 598 Hal King 4.50 2.00 .55
☐ 599 Billy Champion 4.00 1.80 .50
☐ 600 Al Kaline 25.00 11.00 3.10
☐ 601 George Stone 4.00 1.80 .50
☐ 602 Dave Bristol MG 4.00 1.80 .50
☐ 603 Jim Ray 4.00 1.80 .50
☐ 604A Checklist 657-787 10.00 2.00 1.00
(Copyright on back
bottom right)
☐ 604B Checklist 657-787 10.00 2.00 1.00
(Copyright on back
bottom left)
☐ 605 Nelson Briles 4.50 2.00 .55
☐ 606 Luis Melendez 4.00 1.80 .50
☐ 607 Frank Duffy 4.00 1.80 .50
☐ 608 Mike Corkins 4.00 1.80 .50
☐ 609 Tom Grieve 4.50 2.00 .55
☐ 610 Bill Stoneman 4.50 2.00 .55
☐ 611 Rich Reese 4.00 1.80 .50
☐ 612 Joe Decker 4.00 1.80 .50
☐ 613 Mike Ferraro 4.00 1.80 .50
☐ 614 Ted Uhlaender 4.00 1.80 .50
☐ 615 Steve Hargan 4.00 1.80 .50
☐ 616 Joe Ferguson 4.50 2.00 .55
☐ 617 Kansas City Royals 7.00 3.10 .85
Team Card
☐ 618 Rich Robertson 4.00 1.80 .50
☐ 619 Rich McKinney 4.00 1.80 .50
☐ 620 Phil Niekro 10.00 4.50 1.25
☐ 621 Commissioners Award 5.00 2.20 .60
☐ 622 MVP Award 5.00 2.20 .60
☐ 623 Cy Young Award 5.00 2.20 .60
☐ 624 Minor League Player 5.00 2.20 .60
of the Year
☐ 625 Rookie of the Year 5.00 2.20 .60
☐ 626 Babe Ruth Award 5.00 2.20 .60
☐ 627 Moe Drabowsky 4.00 1.80 .50
☐ 628 Terry Crowley 4.00 1.80 .50
☐ 629 Paul Doyle 4.00 1.80 .50
☐ 630 Rich Hebner 4.50 2.00 .55
☐ 631 John Strohmayer 4.00 1.80 .50
☐ 632 Mike Hegan 4.00 1.80 .50
☐ 633 Jack Hiatt 4.00 1.80 .50
☐ 634 Dick Woodson 4.00 1.80 .50
☐ 635 Don Money 4.50 2.00 .55
☐ 636 Bill Lee 4.50 2.00 .55
☐ 637 Preston Gomez MG 4.00 1.80 .50
☐ 638 Ken Wright 4.00 1.80 .50
☐ 639 J.C. Martin 4.00 1.80 .50
☐ 640 Joe Coleman 4.00 1.80 .50
☐ 641 Mike Lum 4.00 1.80 .50
☐ 642 Dennis Riddleberger 4.00 1.80 .50
☐ 643 Russ Gibson 4.00 1.80 .50
☐ 644 Bernie Allen 4.00 1.80 .50
☐ 645 Jim Maloney 4.50 2.00 .55
☐ 646 Chico Salmon 4.00 1.80 .50
☐ 647 Bob Moose 4.00 1.80 .50
☐ 648 Jim Lyttle 4.00 1.80 .50
☐ 649 Pete Richert 4.00 1.80 .50

Card	NRMT	VG-E	GOOD
☐ 650 Sal Bando	4.50	2.00	.55
☐ 651 Cincinnati Reds	7.00	3.10	.85
Team Card			
☐ 652 Marcelino Lopez	4.00	1.80	.50
☐ 653 Jim Fairey	4.00	1.80	.50
☐ 654 Horacio Pina	4.50	2.00	.55
☐ 655 Jerry Grote	4.00	1.80	.50
☐ 656 Rudy May	4.00	1.80	.50
☐ 657 Bobby Wine	12.00	5.50	1.50
☐ 658 Steve Dunning	12.00	5.50	1.50
☐ 659 Bob Aspromonte	12.00	5.50	1.50
☐ 660 Paul Blair	13.00	5.75	1.60
☐ 661 Bill Virdon MG	13.00	5.75	1.60
☐ 662 Stan Bahnsen	12.00	5.50	1.50
☐ 663 Fran Healy	13.00	5.75	1.60
☐ 664 Bobby Knoop	12.00	5.50	1.50
☐ 665 Chris Short	12.00	5.50	1.50
☐ 666 Hector Torres	12.00	5.50	1.50
☐ 667 Ray Newman	12.00	5.50	1.50
☐ 668 Texas Rangers	30.00	13.50	3.70
Team Card			
☐ 669 Willie Crawford	12.00	5.50	1.50
☐ 670 Ken Holtzman	13.00	5.75	1.60
☐ 671 Donn Clendenon	13.00	5.75	1.60
☐ 672 Archie Reynolds	12.00	5.50	1.50
☐ 673 Dave Marshall	12.00	5.50	1.50
☐ 674 John Kennedy	12.00	5.50	1.50
☐ 675 Pat Jarvis	12.00	5.50	1.50
☐ 676 Danny Cater	12.00	5.50	1.50
☐ 677 Ivan Murrell	12.00	5.50	1.50
☐ 678 Steve Luebber	12.00	5.50	1.50
☐ 679 Astros Rookies	12.00	5.50	1.50
Bob Fenwick			
Bob Stinson			
☐ 680 Dave Johnson	13.00	5.75	1.60
☐ 681 Bobby Pfeil	12.00	5.50	1.50
☐ 682 Mike McCormick	13.00	5.75	1.60
☐ 683 Steve Hovley	12.00	5.50	1.50
☐ 684 Hal Breeden	12.00	5.50	1.50
☐ 685 Joel Horlen	12.00	5.50	1.50
☐ 686 Steve Garvey	40.00	18.00	5.00
☐ 687 Del Unser	12.00	5.50	1.50
☐ 688 St. Louis Cardinals	20.00	9.00	2.50
Team Card			
☐ 689 Eddie Fisher	12.00	5.50	1.50
☐ 690 Willie Montanez	13.00	5.75	1.60
☐ 691 Curt Blefary	12.00	5.50	1.50
☐ 692 Curt Blefary IA	12.00	5.50	1.50
☐ 693 Alan Gallagher	12.00	5.50	1.50
☐ 694 Alan Gallagher IA	12.00	5.50	1.50
☐ 695 Rod Carew	75.00	34.00	9.50
☐ 696 Rod Carew IA	35.00	16.00	4.40
☐ 697 Jerry Koosman	15.00	6.75	1.85
☐ 698 Jerry Koosman IA	13.00	5.75	1.60
☐ 699 Bobby Murcer	15.00	6.75	1.85
☐ 700 Bobby Murcer IA	13.00	5.75	1.60
☐ 701 Jose Pagan	12.00	5.50	1.50
☐ 702 Jose Pagan IA	12.00	5.50	1.50
☐ 703 Doug Griffin	12.00	5.50	1.50
☐ 704 Doug Griffin IA	12.00	5.50	1.50
☐ 705 Pat Corrales	13.00	5.75	1.60
☐ 706 Pat Corrales IA	12.00	5.50	1.50
☐ 707 Tim Foli	12.00	5.50	1.50
☐ 708 Tim Foli IA	12.00	5.50	1.50
☐ 709 Jim Kaat	16.00	7.25	2.00
☐ 710 Jim Kaat IA	14.00	6.25	1.75
☐ 711 Bobby Bonds	20.00	9.00	2.50
☐ 712 Bobby Bonds IA	14.00	6.25	1.75
☐ 713 Gene Michael	12.00	5.50	1.50
☐ 714 Gene Michael IA	12.00	5.50	1.50
☐ 715 Mike Epstein	12.00	5.50	1.50
☐ 716 Jesus Alou	12.00	5.50	1.50
☐ 717 Bruce Dal Canton	12.00	5.50	1.50
☐ 718 Del Rice MG	12.00	5.50	1.50
☐ 719 Cesar Geronimo	12.00	5.50	1.50
☐ 720 Sam McDowell	13.00	5.75	1.60
☐ 721 Eddie Leon	12.00	5.50	1.50
☐ 722 Bill Sudakis	12.00	5.50	1.50
☐ 723 Al Santorini	12.00	5.50	1.50
☐ 724 AL Rookie Pitchers	12.00	5.50	1.50
John Curtis			
Rich Hinton			
Mickey Scott			
☐ 725 Dick McAuliffe	13.00	5.75	1.60
☐ 726 Dick Selma	12.00	5.50	1.50
☐ 727 Jose Laboy	12.00	5.50	1.50
☐ 728 Gail Hopkins	12.00	5.50	1.50
☐ 729 Bob Veale	13.00	5.75	1.60
☐ 730 Rick Monday	13.00	5.75	1.60
☐ 731 Baltimore Orioles	20.00	9.00	2.50
Team Card			
☐ 732 George Culver	12.00	5.50	1.50
☐ 733 Jim Ray Hart	13.00	5.75	1.60
☐ 734 Bob Burda	12.00	5.50	1.50
☐ 735 Diego Segui	12.00	5.50	1.50
☐ 736 Bill Russell	13.00	5.75	1.60
☐ 737 Len Randle	13.00	5.75	1.60
☐ 738 Jim Merritt	12.00	5.50	1.50
☐ 739 Don Mason	12.00	5.50	1.50
☐ 740 Rico Carty	13.00	5.75	1.60
☐ 741 Rookie First Basemen	13.00	5.75	1.60
Tom Hutton			
John Milner			
Rick Miller			
☐ 742 Jim Rooker	12.00	5.50	1.50
☐ 743 Cesar Gutierrez	12.00	5.50	1.50
☐ 744 Jim Slaton	12.00	5.50	1.50
☐ 745 Julian Javier	13.00	5.75	1.60
☐ 746 Lowell Palmer	12.00	5.50	1.50
☐ 747 Jim Stewart	12.00	5.50	1.50
☐ 748 Phil Hennigan	12.00	5.50	1.50
☐ 749 Walter Alston MG	14.00	6.25	1.75
☐ 750 Willie Horton	13.00	5.75	1.60
☐ 751 Steve Carlton TR	50.00	22.00	6.25
☐ 752 Joe Morgan TR	45.00	20.00	5.50
☐ 753 Denny McLain TR	20.00	9.00	2.50
☐ 754 Frank Robinson TR	45.00	20.00	5.50
☐ 755 Jim Fregosi TR	13.00	5.75	1.60
☐ 756 Rick Wise TR	13.00	5.75	1.60
☐ 757 Jose Cardenal TR	13.00	5.75	1.60
☐ 758 Gil Garrido	12.00	5.50	1.50
☐ 759 Chris Cannizzaro	12.00	5.50	1.50
☐ 760 Bill Mazeroski	18.00	8.00	2.20
☐ 761 Rookie Outfielders	25.00	11.00	3.10
Ben Oglivie			
Ron Cey			
Bernie Williams			
☐ 762 Wayne Simpson	12.00	5.50	1.50
☐ 763 Ron Hansen	12.00	5.50	1.50
☐ 764 Dusty Baker	20.00	9.00	2.50
☐ 765 Ken McMullen	12.00	5.50	1.50
☐ 766 Steve Hamilton	12.00	5.50	1.50
☐ 767 Tom McCraw	13.00	5.75	1.60
☐ 768 Denny Doyle	12.00	5.50	1.50
☐ 769 Jack Aker	12.00	5.50	1.50
☐ 770 Jim Wynn	13.00	5.75	1.60
☐ 771 San Francisco Giants	20.00	9.00	2.50
Team Card			
☐ 772 Ken Tatum	12.00	5.50	1.50
☐ 773 Ron Brand	12.00	5.50	1.50
☐ 774 Luis Alvarado	12.00	5.50	1.50
☐ 775 Jerry Reuss	13.00	5.75	1.60
☐ 776 Bill Voss	12.00	5.50	1.50
☐ 777 Hoyt Wilhelm	25.00	11.00	3.10
☐ 778 Twins Rookies	18.00	8.00	2.20
Vic Albury			
Rick Dempsey			
Jim Strickland			
☐ 779 Tony Cloninger	12.00	5.50	1.50
☐ 780 Dick Green	12.00	5.50	1.50
☐ 781 Jim McAndrew	12.00	5.50	1.50
☐ 782 Larry Stahl	12.00	5.50	1.50
☐ 783 Les Cain	12.00	5.50	1.50
☐ 784 Ken Aspromonte	12.00	5.50	1.50
☐ 785 Vic Davalillo	12.00	5.50	1.50
☐ 786 Chuck Brinkman	12.00	5.50	1.50
☐ 787 Ron Reed	16.00	5.50	1.50

1972 Topps Posters

This giant (9 7/16" by 18"), full-color series of 24 paper-thin posters was issued as a separate set in 1972. The posters are individually numbered and unlike other Topps posters described in this book, are borderless. They are printed on thin paper and were folded five times to facilitate packaging.

	NRMT	VG-E	GOOD
COMPLETE SET (24)	500.00	220.00	60.00
COMMON CARD (1-24)	7.50	3.40	.95
☐ 1 Dave McNally	7.50	3.40	.95
☐ 2 Carl Yastrzemski	75.00	34.00	9.50
☐ 3 Bill Melton	7.50	3.40	.95
☐ 4 Ray Fosse	7.50	3.40	.95
☐ 5 Mickey Lolich	10.00	4.50	1.25
☐ 6 Amos Otis	10.00	4.50	1.25
☐ 7 Tony Oliva	10.00	4.50	1.25
☐ 8 Vida Blue	10.00	4.50	1.25
☐ 9 Hank Aaron	110.00	50.00	14.00
☐ 10 Fergie Jenkins	20.00	9.00	2.50
☐ 11 Pete Rose	100.00	45.00	12.50
☐ 12 Willie Davis	10.00	4.50	1.25
☐ 13 Tom Seaver	75.00	34.00	9.50
☐ 14 Rick Wise	7.50	3.40	.95
☐ 15 Willie Stargell	40.00	18.00	5.00
☐ 16 Joe Torre	10.00	4.50	1.25
☐ 17 Willie Mays	100.00	45.00	12.50
☐ 18 Andy Messersmith	10.00	4.50	1.25
☐ 19 Wilbur Wood	10.00	4.50	1.25
☐ 20 Harmon Killebrew	40.00	18.00	5.00
☐ 21 Billy Williams	40.00	18.00	5.00
☐ 22 Bud Harrelson	7.50	3.40	.95
☐ 23 Roberto Clemente	150.00	70.00	19.00
☐ 24 Willie McCovey	40.00	18.00	5.00

1972 Topps Cloth Test

These "test" issue cards look like 1972 Topps cards except that they are on a "cloth sticker". Each card measures 2 1/2" by 3 1/2". The "cards" in this set are all taken from the third series of the 1972 Topps regular issue. Cards are blank backed and unnumbered. They are listed below in alphabetical order.

	NRMT	VG-E	GOOD
COMPLETE SET (33)	600.00	275.00	75.00
COMMON CARD (1-33)	15.00	6.75	1.85
☐ 1 Hank Aaron	100.00	45.00	12.50
☐ 2 Luis Aparicio IA	30.00	13.50	3.70
☐ 3 Ike Brown	15.00	6.75	1.85
☐ 4 Johnny Callison	20.00	9.00	2.50
☐ 5 Checklist 264-319	15.00	6.75	1.85
☐ 6 Roberto Clemente	150.00	70.00	19.00
☐ 7 Dave Concepcion	25.00	11.00	3.10
☐ 8 Ron Cook	15.00	6.75	1.85
☐ 9 Willie Davis	20.00	9.00	2.50
☐ 10 Al Fitzmorris	15.00	6.75	1.85
☐ 11 Bobby Floyd	15.00	6.75	1.85
☐ 12 Roy Foster	15.00	6.75	1.85
☐ 13 Jim Fregosi KP	20.00	9.00	2.50
☐ 14 Danny Frisella IA	15.00	6.75	1.85
☐ 15 Woody Fryman	15.00	6.75	1.85
☐ 16 Terry Harmon	15.00	6.75	1.85
☐ 17 Frank Howard	20.00	9.00	2.50
☐ 18 Ron Klimkowski	15.00	6.75	1.85
☐ 19 Joe Lahoud	15.00	6.75	1.85
☐ 20 Jim Lefebvre	15.00	6.75	1.85
☐ 21 Elliott Maddox	15.00	6.75	1.85
☐ 22 Marty Martinez	15.00	6.75	1.85
☐ 23 Willie McCovey	60.00	27.00	7.50
☐ 24 Hal McRae	20.00	9.00	2.50
☐ 25 Syd O'Brien	15.00	6.75	1.85
☐ 26 Red Sox Team	20.00	9.00	2.50
☐ 27 Aurelio Rodriguez	15.00	6.75	1.85
☐ 28 Al Severinsen	15.00	6.75	1.85
☐ 29 Art Shamsky	15.00	6.75	1.85
☐ 30 Steve Stone	20.00	9.00	2.50
☐ 31 Stan Swanson	15.00	6.75	1.85
☐ 32 Bob Watson	20.00	9.00	2.50
☐ 33 Roy White	20.00	9.00	2.50

1972 Topps Test 53

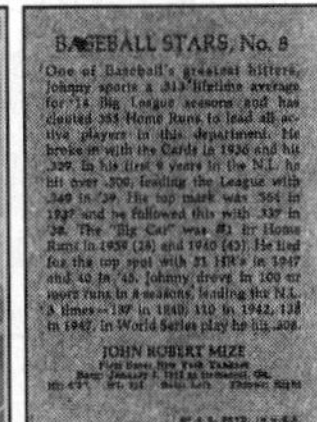

These "test" issue cards were made to look like 1953 Topps cards as the cards show drawings rather than photos. The card number of the corresponding art from the 1953 Topps set is given in parentheses after the name of the player. For three of the cards in this set the player pictured in the art is not the same player as listed on the card; in these cases the actual player pictured is alos listed parenthetically in the checklist below. Each card measures 2 1/2" by 3 1/2". Printing on the back is in blue ink on gray card stock.

	NRMT	VG-E	GOOD
COMPLETE SET (8)	600.00	275.00	75.00
COMMON CARD (1-8)	40.00	18.00	5.00
☐ 1 Satchel Paige UER	150.00	70.00	19.00
(53 Topps 220, spelled Satchell)			
☐ 2 Jackie Robinson	150.00	70.00	19.00
(53 Topps 1)			
☐ 3 Carl Furillo	60.00	27.00	7.50
(53 Topps 272)			
(picture actually			
Bill Antonello)			
☐ 4 Al Rosen	60.00	27.00	7.50
(53 Topps 187)			
(picture actually			
Jim Fridley)			
☐ 5 Hal Newhouser	60.00	27.00	7.50
(53 Topps 228)			
☐ 6 Clyde McCullough	40.00	18.00	5.00
(53 Topps 222)			
(picture actually			
Vic Janowicz)			
☐ 7 Peanuts Lowrey	40.00	18.00	5.00
(53 Topps 16)			
☐ 8 Johnny Mize	100.00	45.00	12.50
(53 Topps 77)			

1973 Topps

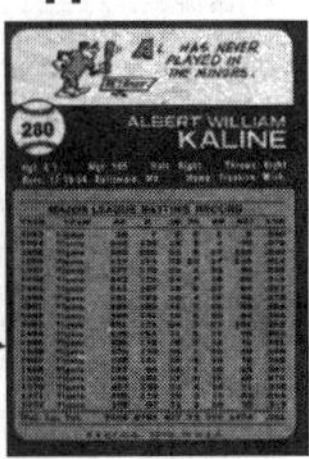

The cards in this 660-card set measure 2 1/2" by 3 1/2". The 1973 Topps set marked the last year in which Topps marketed baseball cards in consecutive series. The last series (529-660) is more difficult to obtain. In some parts of the country, however, all five series were distributed together. Beginning in 1974, all Topps cards were printed at the same time, thus eliminating the "high number" factor. The set features team leader cards with small individual pictures of the coaching staff members and a larger picture of the manager. The "background" variations below with respect to these leader cards are subtle and are best understood after a side-by-side comparison of the two varieties. An "All-Time Leaders" series (471-478) appeared for the first time in this set. Kid Pictures appeared again for the second year in a row (341-346). Other topical subsets within the set included League Leaders (61-68), Playoffs cards (201-202), World Series cards (203-210), and Rookie Prospects (601-616). For the fourth and final time, cards were issued in ten-card dime packs, cards were also released in 54-card rack packs. The key Rookie Cards in this set are all in the Rookie Prospect series: Bob Boone, Dwight Evans, and Mike Schmidt.

	NRMT	VG-E	GOOD
COMPLETE SET (660)	750.00	350.00	95.00
COMMON CARD (1-264)	.50	.23	.06
COMMON CARD (265-396)	.75	.35	.09
COMMON CARD (397-528)	1.25	.55	.16
COMMON CARD (529-660)	3.50	1.55	.45
WRAPPER (10-CENT, BATTER)	15.00	6.75	1.85
WRAPPER (10-CENT, ALL 660 CARDS)		15.00	6.75
1.85			
☐ 1 All-Time HR Leaders	40.00	11.50	4.00
Babe Ruth 714			
Hank Aaron 673			
Willie Mays 654			
☐ 2 Rich Hebner	.75	.35	.09
☐ 3 Jim Lonborg	.75	.35	.09
☐ 4 John Milner	.50	.23	.06
☐ 5 Ed Brinkman	.50	.23	.06
☐ 6 Mac Scarce	.50	.23	.06
☐ 7 Texas Rangers	1.25	.55	.16
Team Card			
☐ 8 Tom Hall	.50	.23	.06
☐ 9 Johnny Oates	.50	.23	.06
☐ 10 Don Sutton	1.00	.45	.12
☐ 11 Chris Chambliss	.75	.35	.09
☐ 12A Padres Leaders	.75	.35	.09
Don Zimmer MG			
Dave Garcia CO			
Johnny Podres CO			
Bob Skinner CO			
Whitey Wietelmann CO			
(Podres no right ear)			
☐ 12B Padres Leaders	1.50	.70	.19
(Podres has right ear)			
☐ 13 George Hendrick	.75	.35	.09
☐ 14 Sonny Siebert	.50	.23	.06
☐ 15 Ralph Garr	.75	.35	.09
☐ 16 Steve Braun	.50	.23	.06
☐ 17 Fred Gladding	.50	.23	.06
☐ 18 Leroy Stanton	.50	.23	.06
☐ 19 Tim Foli	.50	.23	.06
☐ 20 Stan Bahnsen	.50	.23	.06
☐ 21 Randy Hundley	.75	.35	.09
☐ 22 Ted Abernathy	.50	.23	.06
☐ 23 Dave Kingman	1.00	.45	.12
☐ 24 Al Santorini	.50	.23	.06
☐ 25 Roy White	.75	.35	.09
☐ 26 Pittsburgh Pirates	1.25	.55	.16
Team Card			
☐ 27 Bill Gogolewski	.50	.23	.06
☐ 28 Hal McRae	1.00	.45	.12
☐ 29 Tony Taylor	.75	.35	.09
☐ 30 Tug McGraw	.75	.35	.09
☐ 31 Buddy Bell	3.00	1.35	.35
☐ 32 Fred Norman	.50	.23	.06
☐ 33 Jim Breazeale	.50	.23	.06
☐ 34 Pat Dobson	.75	.35	.09
☐ 35 Willie Davis	.75	.35	.09
☐ 36 Steve Barber	.50	.23	.06
☐ 37 Bill Robinson	.75	.35	.09
☐ 38 Mike Epstein	.50	.23	.06
☐ 39 Dave Roberts	.50	.23	.06
☐ 40 Reggie Smith	.75	.35	.09
☐ 41 Tom Walker	.50	.23	.06
☐ 42 Mike Andrews	.50	.23	.06

☐ 43 Randy Moffitt .50 .23 .06
☐ 44 Rick Monday .75 .35 .09
☐ 45 Ellie Rodriguez UER .50 .23 .06
(Photo actually
John Felske)
☐ 46 Lindy McDaniel .75 .35 .09
☐ 47 Luis Melendez .50 .23 .06
☐ 48 Paul Splittorff .50 .23 .06
☐ 49A Twins Leaders .75 .35 .09
Frank Quilici MG
Vern Morgan CO
Bob Rodgers CO
Ralph Rowe CO
Al Worthington CO
(Solid backgrounds)
☐ 49B Twins Leaders 1.50 .70 .19
(Natural backgrounds)
☐ 50 Roberto Clemente 60.00 27.00 7.50
☐ 51 Chuck Seelbach .50 .23 .06
☐ 52 Denis Menke .50 .23 .06
☐ 53 Steve Dunning .50 .23 .06
☐ 54 Checklist 1-132 3.00 .60 .30
☐ 55 Jon Matlack .75 .35 .09
☐ 56 Merv Rettenmund .50 .23 .06
☐ 57 Derrel Thomas .50 .23 .06
☐ 58 Mike Paul .50 .23 .06
☐ 59 Steve Yeager 1.00 .45 .12
☐ 60 Ken Holtzman .75 .35 .09
☐ 61 Batting Leaders 3.00 1.35 .35
Billy Williams
Rod Carew
☐ 62 Home Run Leaders 2.50 1.10 .30
Johnny Bench
Dick Allen
☐ 63 RBI Leaders 2.50 1.10 .30
Johnny Bench
Dick Allen
☐ 64 Stolen Base Leaders 2.00 .90 .25
Lou Brock
Bert Campaneris
☐ 65 ERA Leaders 2.00 .90 .25
Steve Carlton
Luis Tiant
☐ 66 Victory Leaders 2.00 .90 .25
Steve Carlton
Gaylord Perry
Wilbur Wood
☐ 67 Strikeout Leaders 30.00 13.50 3.70
Steve Carlton
Nolan Ryan
☐ 68 Leading Firemen 1.00 .45 .12
Clay Carroll
Sparky Lyle
☐ 69 Phil Gagliano .50 .23 .06
☐ 70 Milt Pappas .75 .35 .09
☐ 71 Johnny Briggs .50 .23 .06
☐ 72 Ron Reed .50 .23 .06
☐ 73 Ed Herrmann .50 .23 .06
☐ 74 Billy Champion .50 .23 .06
☐ 75 Vada Pinson 1.00 .45 .12
☐ 76 Doug Rader .50 .23 .06
☐ 77 Mike Torrez .75 .35 .09
☐ 78 Richie Scheinblum .50 .23 .06
☐ 79 Jim Willoughby .50 .23 .06
☐ 80 Tony Oliva UER 1.00 .45 .12
(Minnseota on front)
☐ 81A Cubs Leaders 1.50 .70 .19
Whitey Lockman MG
Hank Aguirre CO
Ernie Banks CO
Larry Jansen CO
Pete Reiser CO
(Solid backgrounds)
☐ 81B Cubs Leaders 2.00 .90 .25
(Natural backgrounds)
☐ 82 Fritz Peterson .50 .23 .06
☐ 83 Leron Lee .50 .23 .06
☐ 84 Rollie Fingers 5.00 2.20 .60
☐ 85 Ted Simmons 1.00 .45 .12
☐ 86 Tom McCraw .50 .23 .06
☐ 87 Ken Boswell .50 .23 .06
☐ 88 Mickey Stanley .75 .35 .09
☐ 89 Jack Billingham .50 .23 .06
☐ 90 Brooks Robinson 7.00 3.10 .85
☐ 91 Los Angeles Dodgers 1.25 .55 .16
Team Card
☐ 92 Jerry Bell .50 .23 .06
☐ 93 Jesus Alou .50 .23 .06
☐ 94 Dick Billings .50 .23 .06
☐ 95 Steve Blass .75 .35 .09
☐ 96 Doug Griffin .50 .23 .06
☐ 97 Willie Montanez .75 .35 .09
☐ 98 Dick Woodson .50 .23 .06
☐ 99 Carl Taylor .50 .23 .06
☐ 100 Hank Aaron 30.00 13.50 3.70
☐ 101 Ken Henderson .50 .23 .06
☐ 102 Rudy May .50 .23 .06
☐ 103 Celerino Sanchez .50 .23 .06
☐ 104 Reggie Cleveland .50 .23 .06
☐ 105 Carlos May .50 .23 .06
☐ 106 Terry Humphrey .50 .23 .06
☐ 107 Phil Hennigan .50 .23 .06
☐ 108 Bill Russell .75 .35 .09
☐ 109 Doyle Alexander .75 .35 .09
☐ 110 Bob Watson 1.00 .45 .12
☐ 111 Dave Nelson .50 .23 .06
☐ 112 Gary Ross .50 .23 .06
☐ 113 Jerry Grote .50 .23 .06
☐ 114 Lynn McGlothen .50 .23 .06
☐ 115 Ron Santo 1.00 .45 .12
☐ 116A Yankees Leaders .75 .35 .09
Ralph Houk MG
Jim Hegan CO
Elston Howard CO
Dick Howser CO
Jim Turner CO
(Solid backgrounds)
☐ 116B Yankees Leaders 1.50 .70 .19
(Natural backgrounds)
☐ 117 Ramon Hernandez .50 .23 .06
☐ 118 John Mayberry .75 .35 .09
☐ 119 Larry Bowa .75 .35 .09
☐ 120 Joe Coleman .50 .23 .06
☐ 121 Dave Rader .50 .23 .06
☐ 122 Jim Strickland .50 .23 .06
☐ 123 Sandy Alomar .75 .35 .09
☐ 124 Jim Hardin .50 .23 .06
☐ 125 Ron Fairly .75 .35 .09
☐ 126 Jim Brewer .50 .23 .06
☐ 127 Milwaukee Brewers 1.25 .55 .16
Team Card
☐ 128 Ted Sizemore .50 .23 .06
☐ 129 Terry Forster .75 .35 .09
☐ 130 Pete Rose 18.00 8.00 2.20
☐ 131A Red Sox Leaders .75 .35 .09
Eddie Kasko MG
Doug Camilli CO
Don Lenhardt CO
Eddie Popowski CO
(No right ear)
Lee Stange CO
☐ 131B Red Sox Leaders 1.50 .70 .19
(Popowski has right
ear showing)
☐ 132 Matty Alou .75 .35 .09
☐ 133 Dave Roberts .50 .23 .06
☐ 134 Milt Wilcox .50 .23 .06
☐ 135 Lee May UER .75 .35 .09
(Career average .000)
☐ 136A Orioles Leaders 2.00 .90 .25
Earl Weaver MG
George Bamberger CO
Jim Frey CO
Billy Hunter CO
George Staller CO
(Orange backgrounds)
☐ 136B Orioles Leaders 3.00 1.35 .35
(Dark pale
backgrounds)
☐ 137 Jim Beauchamp .50 .23 .06
☐ 138 Horacio Pina .50 .23 .06
☐ 139 Carmen Fanzone .50 .23 .06
☐ 140 Lou Piniella 1.00 .45 .12
☐ 141 Bruce Kison .50 .23 .06
☐ 142 Thurman Munson 6.00 2.70 .75
☐ 143 John Curtis .50 .23 .06
☐ 144 Marty Perez .50 .23 .06
☐ 145 Bobby Bonds 1.00 .45 .12
☐ 146 Woodie Fryman .50 .23 .06
☐ 147 Mike Anderson .50 .23 .06
☐ 148 Dave Goltz .50 .23 .06
☐ 149 Ron Hunt .50 .23 .06
☐ 150 Wilbur Wood .75 .35 .09
☐ 151 Wes Parker .75 .35 .09
☐ 152 Dave May .50 .23 .06
☐ 153 Al Hrabosky .75 .35 .09
☐ 154 Jeff Torborg .75 .35 .09
☐ 155 Sal Bando .75 .35 .09
☐ 156 Cesar Geronimo .50 .23 .06
☐ 157 Denny Riddleberger .50 .23 .06
☐ 158 Houston Astros 1.25 .55 .16
Team Card
☐ 159 Clarence Gaston 1.00 .45 .12
☐ 160 Jim Palmer 7.00 3.10 .85
☐ 161 Ted Martinez .50 .23 .06
☐ 162 Pete Broberg .50 .23 .06
☐ 163 Vic Davalillo .50 .23 .06
☐ 164 Monty Montgomery .50 .23 .06
☐ 165 Luis Aparicio 3.00 1.35 .35
☐ 166 Terry Harmon .50 .23 .06
☐ 167 Steve Stone .75 .35 .09
☐ 168 Jim Northrup .75 .35 .09
☐ 169 Ron Schueler .50 .23 .06
☐ 170 Harmon Killebrew 5.00 2.20 .60
☐ 171 Bernie Carbo .50 .23 .06
☐ 172 Steve Kline .50 .23 .06
☐ 173 Hal Breeden .50 .23 .06
☐ 174 Rich Gossage 8.00 3.60 1.00
☐ 175 Frank Robinson 7.00 3.10 .85
☐ 176 Chuck Taylor .50 .23 .06
☐ 177 Bill Plummer .50 .23 .06
☐ 178 Don Rose .50 .23 .06
☐ 179A A's Leaders .75 .35 .09
Dick Williams MG
Jerry Adair CO
Vern Hoscheit CO
Irv Noren CO
Wes Stock CO
(Hoscheit left ear
showing)
☐ 179B A's Leaders 1.50 .70 .19
(Hoscheit left ear
not showing)
☐ 180 Fergie Jenkins 5.00 2.20 .60
☐ 181 Jack Brohamer .50 .23 .06
☐ 182 Mike Caldwell .75 .35 .09
☐ 183 Don Buford .50 .23 .06
☐ 184 Jerry Koosman 1.00 .45 .12
☐ 185 Jim Wynn .75 .35 .09
☐ 186 Bill Fahey .50 .23 .06
☐ 187 Luke Walker .50 .23 .06
☐ 188 Cookie Rojas .75 .35 .09
☐ 189 Greg Luzinski 1.00 .45 .12
☐ 190 Bob Gibson 7.00 3.10 .85
☐ 191 Detroit Tigers 1.25 .55 .16
Team Card
☐ 192 Pat Jarvis .50 .23 .06
☐ 193 Carlton Fisk 10.00 4.50 1.25
☐ 194 Jorge Orta .50 .23 .06
☐ 195 Clay Carroll .50 .23 .06
☐ 196 Ken McMullen .50 .23 .06
☐ 197 Ed Goodson .50 .23 .06
☐ 198 Horace Clarke .50 .23 .06
☐ 199 Bert Blyleven 1.00 .45 .12
☐ 200 Billy Williams 5.00 2.20 .60
☐ 201 George Hendrick ALCS 1.00 .45 .12
☐ 202 George Foster NLCS 1.50 .70 .19
☐ 203 Gene Tenace WS 1.50 .70 .19
☐ 204 World Series Game 2 1.00 .45 .12
A's two straight
☐ 205 Tony Perez WS 2.00 .90 .25
☐ 206 Gene Tenace WS 1.50 .70 .19
☐ 207 John "Blue Moon" Odom WS 1.00 .45 .12
☐ 208 Johnny Bench WS6 4.00 1.80 .50
☐ 209 Bert Campaneris WS 1.50 .70 .19
☐ 210 World Series Summary 1.00 .45 .12
World champions:
A's Win
☐ 211 Balor Moore .50 .23 .06
☐ 212 Joe Lahoud .50 .23 .06
☐ 213 Steve Garvey 6.00 2.70 .75
☐ 214 Steve Hamilton .50 .23 .06
☐ 215 Dusty Baker 1.00 .45 .12
☐ 216 Toby Harrah .75 .35 .09
☐ 217 Don Wilson .50 .23 .06
☐ 218 Aurelio Rodriguez .50 .23 .06
☐ 219 St. Louis Cardinals 1.25 .55 .16
Team Card
☐ 220 Nolan Ryan 100.00 45.00 12.50
☐ 221 Fred Kendall .50 .23 .06
☐ 222 Rob Gardner .50 .23 .06
☐ 223 Bud Harrelson .75 .35 .09
☐ 224 Bill Lee .75 .35 .09
☐ 225 Al Oliver 1.00 .45 .12
☐ 226 Ray Fosse .50 .23 .06
☐ 227 Wayne Twitchell .50 .23 .06
☐ 228 Bobby Darwin .50 .23 .06
☐ 229 Roric Harrison .50 .23 .06
☐ 230 Joe Morgan 6.00 2.70 .75
☐ 231 Bill Parsons .50 .23 .06
☐ 232 Ken Singleton .75 .35 .09
☐ 233 Ed Kirkpatrick .50 .23 .06
☐ 234 Bill North .50 .23 .06
☐ 235 Jim Hunter 4.00 1.80 .50
☐ 236 Tito Fuentes .50 .23 .06
☐ 237A Braves Leaders 1.50 .70 .19
Eddie Mathews MG
Lew Burdette CO
Jim Busby CO
Roy Hartsfield CO
Ken Silvestri CO
(Burdette right ear
showing)
☐ 237B Braves Leaders 3.00 1.35 .35
(Burdette right ear
not showing)
☐ 238 Tony Muser .50 .23 .06
☐ 239 Pete Richert .50 .23 .06
☐ 240 Bobby Murcer .75 .35 .09
☐ 241 Dwain Anderson .50 .23 .06
☐ 242 George Culver .50 .23 .06
☐ 243 California Angels 1.25 .55 .16
Team Card
☐ 244 Ed Acosta .50 .23 .06
☐ 245 Carl Yastrzemski 10.00 4.50 1.25
☐ 246 Ken Sanders .50 .23 .06
☐ 247 Del Unser .50 .23 .06
☐ 248 Jerry Johnson .50 .23 .06
☐ 249 Larry Biittner .50 .23 .06
☐ 250 Manny Sanguillen .75 .35 .09
☐ 251 Roger Nelson .50 .23 .06
☐ 252A Giants Leaders .75 .35 .09
Charlie Fox MG
Joe Amalfitano CO
Andy Gilbert CO
Don McMahon CO
John McNamara CO
(Orange backgrounds)
☐ 252B Giants Leaders 1.50 .70 .19
(Dark pale
backgrounds)
☐ 253 Mark Belanger .75 .35 .09
☐ 254 Bill Stoneman .50 .23 .06
☐ 255 Reggie Jackson 16.00 7.25 2.00
☐ 256 Chris Zachary .50 .23 .06
☐ 257A Mets Leaders 2.50 1.10 .30
Yogi Berra MG
Roy McMillan CO
Joe Pignatano CO
Rube Walker CO
Eddie Yost CO
(Orange backgrounds)
☐ 257B Mets Leaders 5.00 2.20 .60
(Dark pale
backgrounds)
☐ 258 Tommy John 1.00 .45 .12
☐ 259 Jim Holt .50 .23 .06
☐ 260 Gary Nolan .75 .35 .09
☐ 261 Pat Kelly .50 .23 .06
☐ 262 Jack Aker .50 .23 .06
☐ 263 George Scott .75 .35 .09
☐ 264 Checklist 133-264 3.00 .60 .30
☐ 265 Gene Michael .75 .35 .09
☐ 266 Mike Lum .75 .35 .09
☐ 267 Lloyd Allen .75 .35 .09
☐ 268 Jerry Morales .75 .35 .09
☐ 269 Tim McCarver 1.00 .45 .12
☐ 270 Luis Tiant 1.00 .45 .12
☐ 271 Tom Hutton .75 .35 .09
☐ 272 Ed Farmer .75 .35 .09
☐ 273 Chris Speier .75 .35 .09
☐ 274 Darold Knowles .75 .35 .09
☐ 275 Tony Perez 4.00 1.80 .50
☐ 276 Joe Lovitto .75 .35 .09
☐ 277 Bob Miller .75 .35 .09
☐ 278 Baltimore Orioles 1.50 .70 .19
Team Card
☐ 279 Mike Strahler .75 .35 .09
☐ 280 Al Kaline 7.00 3.10 .85
☐ 281 Mike Jorgensen .75 .35 .09
☐ 282 Steve Hovley .75 .35 .09
☐ 283 Ray Sadecki .75 .35 .09
☐ 284 Glenn Borgmann .75 .35 .09
☐ 285 Don Kessinger .75 .35 .09
☐ 286 Frank Linzy .75 .35 .09
☐ 287 Eddie Leon .75 .35 .09
☐ 288 Gary Gentry .75 .35 .09
☐ 289 Bob Oliver .75 .35 .09
☐ 290 Cesar Cedeno 1.00 .45 .12
☐ 291 Rogelio Moret .75 .35 .09
☐ 292 Jose Cruz 1.00 .45 .12
☐ 293 Bernie Allen .75 .35 .09
☐ 294 Steve Arlin .75 .35 .09
☐ 295 Bert Campaneris 1.00 .45 .12
☐ 296 Reds Leaders 2.50 1.10 .30
Sparky Anderson MG
Alex Grammas CO
Ted Kluszewski CO
George Scherger CO
Larry Shepard CO
☐ 297 Walt Williams .75 .35 .09
☐ 298 Ron Bryant .75 .35 .09
☐ 299 Ted Ford .75 .35 .09
☐ 300 Steve Carlton 10.00 4.50 1.25
☐ 301 Billy Grabarkewitz .75 .35 .09
☐ 302 Terry Crowley .75 .35 .09
☐ 303 Nelson Briles .75 .35 .09
☐ 304 Duke Sims .75 .35 .09
☐ 305 Willie Mays 40.00 18.00 5.00
☐ 306 Tom Burgmeier .75 .35 .09
☐ 307 Boots Day .75 .35 .09
☐ 308 Skip Lockwood .75 .35 .09
☐ 309 Paul Popovich .75 .35 .09
☐ 310 Dick Allen 1.50 .70 .19
☐ 311 Joe Decker .75 .35 .09
☐ 312 Oscar Brown .75 .35 .09
☐ 313 Jim Ray .75 .35 .09
☐ 314 Ron Swoboda .75 .35 .09
☐ 315 John Odom .75 .35 .09
☐ 316 San Diego Padres 1.50 .70 .19
Team Card
☐ 317 Danny Cater .75 .35 .09
☐ 318 Jim McGlothlin .75 .35 .09
☐ 319 Jim Spencer .75 .35 .09
☐ 320 Lou Brock 6.00 2.70 .75
☐ 321 Rich Hinton .75 .35 .09
☐ 322 Garry Maddox 1.00 .45 .12
☐ 323 Tigers Leaders 1.50 .70 .19
Billy Martin MG
Art Fowler CO
Charlie Silvera CO
Dick Tracewski CO
☐ 324 Al Downing .75 .35 .09
☐ 325 Boog Powell 1.00 .45 .12
☐ 326 Darrell Brandon .75 .35 .09
☐ 327 John Lowenstein .75 .35 .09
☐ 328 Bill Bonham .75 .35 .09
☐ 329 Ed Kranepool .75 .35 .09
☐ 330 Rod Carew 7.00 3.10 .85
☐ 331 Carl Morton .75 .35 .09
☐ 332 John Felske .75 .35 .09
☐ 333 Gene Clines .75 .35 .09
☐ 334 Freddie Patek .75 .35 .09
☐ 335 Bob Tolan .75 .35 .09
☐ 336 Tom Bradley .75 .35 .09
☐ 337 Dave Duncan .75 .35 .09
☐ 338 Checklist 265-396 3.00 .60 .30
☐ 339 Dick Tidrow .75 .35 .09
☐ 340 Nate Colbert .75 .35 .09
☐ 341 Jim Palmer KP 1.50 .70 .19

☐ 342 Sam McDowell KP .75 .35 .09
☐ 343 Bobby Murcer KP .75 .35 .09
☐ 344 Jim Hunter KP 1.50 .70 .19
☐ 345 Chris Speier KP .75 .35 .09
☐ 346 Gaylord Perry KP 1.50 .70 .19
☐ 347 Kansas City Royals 1.50 .70 .19
Team Card
☐ 348 Rennie Stennett .75 .35 .09
☐ 349 Dick McAuliffe .75 .35 .09
☐ 350 Tom Seaver 14.00 6.25 1.75
☐ 351 Jimmy Stewart .75 .35 .09
☐ 352 Don Stanhouse .75 .35 .09
☐ 353 Steve Brye .75 .35 .09
☐ 354 Billy Parker .75 .35 .09
☐ 355 Mike Marshall 1.00 .45 .12
☐ 356 White Sox Leaders .75 .35 .09
Chuck Tanner MG
Joe Lonnett CO
Jim Mahoney CO
Al Monchak CO
Johnny Sain CO
☐ 357 Ross Grimsley .75 .35 .09
☐ 358 Jim Nettles .75 .35 .09
☐ 359 Cecil Upshaw .75 .35 .09
☐ 360 Joe Rudi UER 1.00 .45 .12
(Photo actually
Gene Tenace)
☐ 361 Fran Healy .75 .35 .09
☐ 362 Eddie Watt .75 .35 .09
☐ 363 Jackie Hernandez .75 .35 .09
☐ 364 Rick Wise .75 .35 .09
☐ 365 Rico Petrocelli 1.00 .45 .12
☐ 366 Brock Davis .75 .35 .09
☐ 367 Burt Hooton .75 .35 .09
☐ 368 Bill Buckner 1.00 .45 .12
☐ 369 Lerrin LaGrow .75 .35 .09
☐ 370 Willie Stargell 5.00 2.20 .60
☐ 371 Mike Kekich .75 .35 .09
☐ 372 Oscar Gamble .75 .35 .09
☐ 373 Clyde Wright .75 .35 .09
☐ 374 Darrell Evans 1.00 .45 .12
☐ 375 Larry Dierker 1.00 .45 .12
☐ 376 Frank Duffy .75 .35 .09
☐ 377 Expos Leaders .75 .35 .09
Gene Mauch MG
Dave Bristol CO
Larry Doby CO
Cal McLish CO
Jerry Zimmerman CO
☐ 378 Len Randle .75 .35 .09
☐ 379 Cy Acosta .75 .35 .09
☐ 380 Johnny Bench 8.00 3.60 1.00
☐ 381 Vicente Romo .75 .35 .09
☐ 382 Mike Hegan .75 .35 .09
☐ 383 Diego Segui .75 .35 .09
☐ 384 Don Baylor 4.00 1.80 .50
☐ 385 Jim Perry 1.00 .45 .12
☐ 386 Don Money .75 .35 .09
☐ 387 Jim Barr .75 .35 .09
☐ 388 Ben Oglivie 1.00 .45 .12
☐ 389 New York Mets 3.00 1.35 .35
Team Card
☐ 390 Mickey Lolich 1.00 .45 .12
☐ 391 Lee Lacy .75 .35 .09
☐ 392 Dick Drago .75 .35 .09
☐ 393 Jose Cardenal .75 .35 .09
☐ 394 Sparky Lyle 1.00 .45 .12
☐ 395 Roger Metzger .75 .35 .09
☐ 396 Grant Jackson .75 .35 .09
☐ 397 Dave Cash 1.25 .55 .16
☐ 398 Rich Hand 1.25 .55 .16
☐ 399 George Foster 2.00 .90 .25
☐ 400 Gaylord Perry 5.00 2.20 .60
☐ 401 Clyde Mashore 1.25 .55 .16
☐ 402 Jack Hiatt 1.25 .55 .16
☐ 403 Sonny Jackson 1.25 .55 .16
☐ 404 Chuck Brinkman 1.25 .55 .16
☐ 405 Cesar Tovar 1.25 .55 .16
☐ 406 Paul Lindblad 1.25 .55 .16
☐ 407 Felix Millan 1.25 .55 .16
☐ 408 Jim Colborn 1.25 .55 .16
☐ 409 Ivan Murrell 1.25 .55 .16
☐ 410 Willie McCovey 6.00 2.70 .75
(Bench behind plate)
☐ 411 Ray Corbin 1.25 .55 .16
☐ 412 Manny Mota 2.00 .90 .25
☐ 413 Tom Timmermann 1.25 .55 .16
☐ 414 Ken Rudolph 1.25 .55 .16
☐ 415 Marty Pattin 1.25 .55 .16
☐ 416 Paul Schaal 1.25 .55 .16
☐ 417 Scipio Spinks 1.25 .55 .16
☐ 418 Bob Grich 2.00 .90 .25
☐ 419 Casey Cox 1.25 .55 .16
☐ 420 Tommie Agee 1.25 .55 .16
☐ 421A Angels Leaders 1.50 .70 .19
Bobby Winkles MG
Tom Morgan CO
Salty Parker CO
Jimmie Reese CO
John Roseboro CO
(Orange backgrounds)
☐ 421B Angels Leaders 3.00 1.35 .35
(Dark pale
backgrounds)
☐ 422 Bob Robertson 1.25 .55 .16
☐ 423 Johnny Jeter 1.25 .55 .16
☐ 424 Denny Doyle 1.25 .55 .16
☐ 425 Alex Johnson 1.25 .55 .16
☐ 426 Dave LaRoche 1.25 .55 .16
☐ 427 Rick Auerbach 1.25 .55 .16
☐ 428 Wayne Simpson 1.25 .55 .16
☐ 429 Jim Fairey 1.25 .55 .16
☐ 430 Vida Blue 2.00 .90 .25
☐ 431 Gerry Moses 1.25 .55 .16
☐ 432 Dan Frisella 1.25 .55 .16
☐ 433 Willie Horton 2.00 .90 .25
☐ 434 San Francisco Giants 2.50 1.10 .30
Team Card
☐ 435 Rico Carty 2.00 .90 .25
☐ 436 Jim McAndrew 1.25 .55 .16
☐ 437 John Kennedy 1.25 .55 .16
☐ 438 Enzo Hernandez 1.25 .55 .16
☐ 439 Eddie Fisher 1.25 .55 .16
☐ 440 Glenn Beckert 1.25 .55 .16
☐ 441 Gail Hopkins 1.25 .55 .16
☐ 442 Dick Dietz 1.25 .55 .16
☐ 443 Danny Thompson 1.25 .55 .16
☐ 444 Ken Brett 1.25 .55 .16
☐ 445 Ken Berry 1.25 .55 .16
☐ 446 Jerry Reuss 2.00 .90 .25
☐ 447 Joe Hague 1.25 .55 .16
☐ 448 John Hiller 1.25 .55 .16
☐ 449A Indians Leaders 4.00 1.80 .50
Ken Aspromonte MG
Rocky Colavito CO
Joe Lutz CO
Warren Spahn CO
(Spahn's right
ear pointed)
☐ 449B Indians Leaders 4.00 1.80 .50
(Spahn's right
ear round)
☐ 450 Joe Torre 2.00 .90 .25
☐ 451 John Vukovich 1.25 .55 .16
☐ 452 Paul Casanova 1.25 .55 .16
☐ 453 Checklist 397-528 3.00 .60 .30
☐ 454 Tom Haller 1.25 .55 .16
☐ 455 Bill Melton 1.25 .55 .16
☐ 456 Dick Green 1.25 .55 .16
☐ 457 John Strohmayer 1.25 .55 .16
☐ 458 Jim Mason 1.25 .55 .16
☐ 459 Jimmy Howarth 1.25 .55 .16
☐ 460 Bill Freehan 2.00 .90 .25
☐ 461 Mike Corkins 1.25 .55 .16
☐ 462 Ron Blomberg 1.25 .55 .16
☐ 463 Ken Tatum 1.25 .55 .16
☐ 464 Chicago Cubs 2.50 1.10 .30
Team Card
☐ 465 Dave Giusti 1.25 .55 .16
☐ 466 Jose Arcia 1.25 .55 .16
☐ 467 Mike Ryan 1.25 .55 .16
☐ 468 Tom Griffin 1.25 .55 .16
☐ 469 Dan Monzon 1.25 .55 .16
☐ 470 Mike Cuellar 2.00 .90 .25
☐ 471 Ty Cobb ATL 8.00 3.60 1.00
4191 Hits
☐ 472 Lou Gehrig ATL 14.00 6.25 1.75
23 Grand Slams
☐ 473 Hank Aaron ATL 10.00 4.50 1.25
6172 Total Bases
☐ 474 Babe Ruth ATL 16.00 7.25 2.00
2209 RBI
☐ 475 Ty Cobb ATL 8.00 3.60 1.00
.367 Batting Average
☐ 476 Walter Johnson ATL 3.00 1.35 .35
113 Shutouts
☐ 477 Cy Young ATL 3.00 1.35 .35
511 Victories
☐ 478 Walter Johnson ATL 3.00 1.35 .35
3508 Strikeouts
☐ 479 Hal Lanier 1.25 .55 .16
☐ 480 Juan Marichal 5.00 2.20 .60
☐ 481 Chicago White Sox 2.50 1.10 .30
Team Card
☐ 482 Rick Reuschel 3.00 1.35 .35
☐ 483 Dal Maxvill 1.25 .55 .16
☐ 484 Ernie McAnally 1.25 .55 .16
☐ 485 Norm Cash 2.00 .90 .25
☐ 486A Phillies Leaders 1.50 .70 .19
Danny Ozark MG
Carroll Beringer CO
Billy DeMars CO
Ray Rippelmeyer CO
Bobby Wine CO
(Orange backgrounds)
☐ 486B Phillies Leaders 3.00 1.35 .35
(Dark pale
backgrounds)
☐ 487 Bruce Dal Canton 1.25 .55 .16
☐ 488 Dave Campbell 2.00 .90 .25
☐ 489 Jeff Burroughs 2.00 .90 .25
☐ 490 Claude Osteen 1.25 .55 .16
☐ 491 Bob Montgomery 1.25 .55 .16
☐ 492 Pedro Borbon 1.25 .55 .16
☐ 493 Duffy Dyer 1.25 .55 .16
☐ 494 Rich Morales 1.25 .55 .16
☐ 495 Tommy Helms 1.25 .55 .16
☐ 496 Ray Lamb 1.25 .55 .16
☐ 497A Cardinals Leaders 2.00 .90 .25
Red Schoendienst MG
Vern Benson CO
George Kissell CO
Barney Schultz CO
(Orange backgrounds)
☐ 497B Cardinals Leaders 3.00 1.35 .35
(Dark pale
backgrounds)
☐ 498 Graig Nettles 3.00 1.35 .35
☐ 499 Bob Moose 1.25 .55 .16
☐ 500 Oakland A's 2.50 1.10 .30
Team Card
☐ 501 Larry Gura 1.25 .55 .16
☐ 502 Bobby Valentine 2.00 .90 .25
☐ 503 Phil Niekro 5.00 2.20 .60
☐ 504 Earl Williams 1.25 .55 .16
☐ 505 Bob Bailey 1.25 .55 .16
☐ 506 Bart Johnson 1.25 .55 .16
☐ 507 Darrel Chaney 1.25 .55 .16
☐ 508 Gates Brown 1.25 .55 .16
☐ 509 Jim Nash 1.25 .55 .16
☐ 510 Amos Otis 2.00 .90 .25
☐ 511 Sam McDowell 2.00 .90 .25
☐ 512 Dalton Jones 1.25 .55 .16
☐ 513 Dave Marshall 1.25 .55 .16
☐ 514 Jerry Kenney 1.25 .55 .16
☐ 515 Andy Messersmith 2.00 .90 .25
☐ 516 Danny Walton 1.25 .55 .16
☐ 517A Pirates Leaders 1.50 .70 .19
Bill Virdon MG
Don Leppert CO
Bill Mazeroski CO
Dave Ricketts CO
Mel Wright CO
(Mazeroski has
no right ear)
☐ 517B Pirates Leaders 3.00 1.35 .35
(Mazeroski has
right ear)
☐ 518 Bob Veale 1.25 .55 .16
☐ 519 Johnny Edwards 1.25 .55 .16
☐ 520 Mel Stottlemyre 2.00 .90 .25
☐ 521 Atlanta Braves 2.50 1.10 .30
Team Card
☐ 522 Leo Cardenas 1.25 .55 .16
☐ 523 Wayne Granger 1.25 .55 .16
☐ 524 Gene Tenace 2.00 .90 .25
☐ 525 Jim Fregosi 2.00 .90 .25
☐ 526 Ollie Brown 1.25 .55 .16
☐ 527 Dan McGinn 1.25 .55 .16
☐ 528 Paul Blair 1.25 .55 .16
☐ 529 Milt May 3.50 1.55 .45
☐ 530 Jim Kaat 5.00 2.20 .60
☐ 531 Ron Woods 3.50 1.55 .45
☐ 532 Steve Mingori 3.50 1.55 .45
☐ 533 Larry Stahl 3.50 1.55 .45
☐ 534 Dave Lemonds 3.50 1.55 .45
☐ 535 Johnny Callison 4.00 1.80 .50
☐ 536 Philadelphia Phillies 6.00 2.70 .75
Team Card
☐ 537 Bill Slayback 3.50 1.55 .45
☐ 538 Jim Ray Hart 4.00 1.80 .50
☐ 539 Tom Murphy 3.50 1.55 .45
☐ 540 Cleon Jones 4.00 1.80 .50
☐ 541 Bob Bolin 3.50 1.55 .45
☐ 542 Pat Corrales 4.00 1.80 .50
☐ 543 Alan Foster 3.50 1.55 .45
☐ 544 Von Joshua 3.50 1.55 .45
☐ 545 Orlando Cepeda 5.00 2.20 .60
☐ 546 Jim York 3.50 1.55 .45
☐ 547 Bobby Heise 3.50 1.55 .45
☐ 548 Don Durham 3.50 1.55 .45
☐ 549 Rangers Leaders 5.00 2.20 .60
Whitey Herzog MG
Chuck Estrada CO
Chuck Hiller CO
Jackie Moore CO
☐ 550 Dave Johnson 4.00 1.80 .50
☐ 551 Mike Kilkenny 3.50 1.55 .45
☐ 552 J.C. Martin 3.50 1.55 .45
☐ 553 Mickey Scott 3.50 1.55 .45
☐ 554 Dave Concepcion 5.00 2.20 .60
☐ 555 Bill Hands 3.50 1.55 .45
☐ 556 New York Yankees 8.00 3.60 1.00
Team Card
☐ 557 Bernie Williams 3.50 1.55 .45
☐ 558 Jerry May 3.50 1.55 .45
☐ 559 Barry Lersch 3.50 1.55 .45
☐ 560 Frank Howard 4.00 1.80 .50
☐ 561 Jim Geddes 3.50 1.55 .45
☐ 562 Wayne Garrett 3.50 1.55 .45
☐ 563 Larry Haney 3.50 1.55 .45
☐ 564 Mike Thompson 3.50 1.55 .45
☐ 565 Jim Hickman 3.50 1.55 .45
☐ 566 Lew Krausse 3.50 1.55 .45
☐ 567 Bob Fenwick 3.50 1.55 .45
☐ 568 Ray Newman 3.50 1.55 .45
☐ 569 Dodgers Leaders 5.00 2.20 .60
Walt Alston MG
Red Adams CO
Monty Basgall CO
Jim Gilliam CO
Tom Lasorda CO
☐ 570 Bill Singer 4.00 1.80 .50
☐ 571 Rusty Torres 3.50 1.55 .45
☐ 572 Gary Sutherland 3.50 1.55 .45
☐ 573 Fred Beene 3.50 1.55 .45
☐ 574 Bob Didier 3.50 1.55 .45
☐ 575 Dock Ellis 3.50 1.55 .45
☐ 576 Montreal Expos 6.00 2.70 .75
Team Card
☐ 577 Eric Soderholm 3.50 1.55 .45
☐ 578 Ken Wright 3.50 1.55 .45
☐ 579 Tom Grieve 4.00 1.80 .50
☐ 580 Joe Pepitone 4.00 1.80 .50
☐ 581 Steve Kealey 3.50 1.55 .45
☐ 582 Darrell Porter 4.00 1.80 .50
☐ 583 Bill Grief 3.50 1.55 .45
☐ 584 Chris Arnold 3.50 1.55 .45
☐ 585 Joe Niekro 4.00 1.80 .50
☐ 586 Bill Sudakis 3.50 1.55 .45
☐ 587 Rich McKinney 3.50 1.55 .45
☐ 588 Checklist 529-660 24.00 4.80 2.40
☐ 589 Ken Forsch 3.50 1.55 .45
☐ 590 Deron Johnson 4.00 1.80 .50
☐ 591 Mike Hedlund 3.50 1.55 .45
☐ 592 John Boccabella 3.50 1.55 .45
☐ 593 Royals Leaders 3.50 1.55 .45
Jack McKeon MG
Galen Cisco CO
Harry Dunlop CO
Charlie Lau CO
☐ 594 Vic Harris 3.50 1.55 .45
☐ 595 Don Gullett 4.00 1.80 .50
☐ 596 Boston Red Sox 6.00 2.70 .75
Team Card
☐ 597 Mickey Rivers 4.00 1.80 .50
☐ 598 Phil Roof 3.50 1.55 .45
☐ 599 Ed Crosby 3.50 1.55 .45
☐ 600 Dave McNally 4.00 1.80 .50
☐ 601 Rookie Catchers 4.00 1.80 .50
Sergio Robles
George Pena
Rick Stelmaszek
☐ 602 Rookie Pitchers 4.00 1.80 .50
Mel Behney
Ralph Garcia
Doug Rau
☐ 603 Rookie 3rd Basemen 4.00 1.80 .50
Terry Hughes
Bill McNulty
Ken Reitz
☐ 604 Rookie Pitchers 4.00 1.80 .50
Jesse Jefferson
Dennis O'Toole
Bob Strampe
☐ 605 Rookie 1st Basemen 5.00 2.20 .60
Enos Cabell
Pat Bourque
Gonzalo Marquez
☐ 606 Rookie Outfielders 5.00 2.20 .60
Gary Matthews
Tom Paciorek
Jorge Roque
☐ 607 Rookie Shortstops 4.00 1.80 .50
Pepe Frias
Ray Busse
Mario Guerrero
☐ 608 Rookie Pitchers 5.00 2.20 .60
Steve Busby
Dick Colpaert
George Medich
☐ 609 Rookie 2nd Basemen 6.00 2.70 .75
Larvell Blanks
Pedro Garcia
Dave Lopes
☐ 610 Rookie Pitchers 5.00 2.20 .60
Jimmy Freeman
Charlie Hough
Hank Webb
☐ 611 Rookie Outfielders 4.00 1.80 .50
Rich Coggins
Jim Wohlford
Richie Zisk
☐ 612 Rookie Pitchers 4.00 1.80 .50
Steve Lawson
Bob Reynolds
Brent Strom
☐ 613 Rookie Catchers 25.00 11.00 3.10
Bob Boone
Skip Jutze
Mike Ivie
☐ 614 Rookie Outfielders 25.00 11.00 3.10
Al Bumbry
Dwight Evans
Charlie Spikes
☐ 615 Rookie 3rd Basemen 300.00 135.00 38.00
Ron Cey
John Hilton
Mike Schmidt
☐ 616 Rookie Pitchers 4.00 1.80 .50
Norm Angelini
Steve Blateric
Mike Garman
☐ 617 Rich Chiles 3.50 1.55 .45
☐ 618 Andy Etchebarren 3.50 1.55 .45
☐ 619 Billy Wilson 3.50 1.55 .45
☐ 620 Tommy Harper 4.00 1.80 .50
☐ 621 Joe Ferguson 4.00 1.80 .50
☐ 622 Larry Hisle 4.00 1.80 .50
☐ 623 Steve Renko 3.50 1.55 .45
☐ 624 Astros Leaders 6.00 2.70 .75

Leo Durocher MG			
Preston Gomez CO			
Grady Hatton CO			
Hub Kittle CO			
Jim Owens CO			
☐ 625 Angel Mangual	3.50	1.55	.45
☐ 626 Bob Barton	3.50	1.55	.45
☐ 627 Luis Alvarado	3.50	1.55	.45
☐ 628 Jim Slaton	3.50	1.55	.45
☐ 629 Cleveland Indians	6.00	2.70	.75
Team Card			
☐ 630 Denny McLain	5.00	2.20	.60
☐ 631 Tom Matchick	3.50	1.55	.45
☐ 632 Dick Selma	3.50	1.55	.45
☐ 633 Ike Brown	3.50	1.55	.45
☐ 634 Alan Closter	3.50	1.55	.45
☐ 635 Gene Alley	4.00	1.80	.50
☐ 636 Rickey Clark	3.50	1.55	.45
☐ 637 Norm Miller	3.50	1.55	.45
☐ 638 Ken Reynolds	3.50	1.55	.45
☐ 639 Willie Crawford	3.50	1.55	.45
☐ 640 Dick Bosman	3.50	1.55	.45
☐ 641 Cincinnati Reds	6.00	2.70	.75
Team Card			
☐ 642 Jose Laboy	3.50	1.55	.45
☐ 643 Al Fitzmorris	3.50	1.55	.45
☐ 644 Jack Heidemann	3.50	1.55	.45
☐ 645 Bob Locker	3.50	1.55	.45
☐ 646 Brewers Leaders	3.50	1.55	.45
Del Crandall MG			
Harvey Kuenn CO			
Joe Nossek CO			
Bob Shaw CO			
Jim Walton CO			
☐ 647 George Stone	3.50	1.55	.45
☐ 648 Tom Egan	3.50	1.55	.45
☐ 649 Rich Folkers	3.50	1.55	.45
☐ 650 Felipe Alou	4.00	1.80	.50
☐ 651 Don Carrithers	3.50	1.55	.45
☐ 652 Ted Kubiak	3.50	1.55	.45
☐ 653 Joe Hoerner	3.50	1.55	.45
☐ 654 Minnesota Twins	6.00	2.70	.75
Team Card			
☐ 655 Clay Kirby	3.50	1.55	.45
☐ 656 John Ellis	3.50	1.55	.45
☐ 657 Bob Johnson	3.50	1.55	.45
☐ 658 Elliott Maddox	3.50	1.55	.45
☐ 659 Jose Pagan	3.50	1.55	.45
☐ 660 Fred Scherman	4.00	1.55	.45

1973 Topps Blue Team Checklists

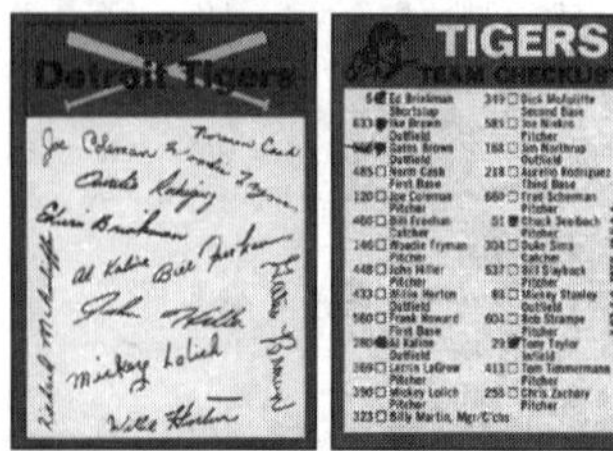

This 24-card standard-size set is rather difficult to find. These blue-bordered team checklist cards are very similar in design to the mass produced red trim team checklist cards issued by Topps the next year. Reportedly these were inserts only found in the test packs that included all series.

	NRMT	VG-E	GOOD
COMPLETE SET (24)	175.00	80.00	22.00
COMMON TEAM (1-24)	8.00	3.60	1.00
☐ 1 Atlanta Braves	8.00	3.60	1.00
☐ 2 Baltimore Orioles	8.00	3.60	1.00
☐ 3 Boston Red Sox	8.00	3.60	1.00
☐ 4 California Angels	8.00	3.60	1.00
☐ 5 Chicago Cubs	8.00	3.60	1.00
☐ 6 Chicago White Sox	8.00	3.60	1.00
☐ 7 Cincinnati Reds	8.00	3.60	1.00
☐ 8 Cleveland Indians	8.00	3.60	1.00
☐ 9 Detroit Tigers	8.00	3.60	1.00
☐ 10 Houston Astros	8.00	3.60	1.00
☐ 11 Kansas City Royals	8.00	3.60	1.00
☐ 12 Los Angeles Dodgers	8.00	3.60	1.00
☐ 13 Milwaukee Brewers	8.00	3.60	1.00
☐ 14 Minnesota Twins	8.00	3.60	1.00
☐ 15 Montreal Expos	8.00	3.60	1.00
☐ 16 New York Mets	10.00	4.50	1.25
☐ 17 New York Yankees	10.00	4.50	1.25
☐ 18 Oakland A's	8.00	3.60	1.00
☐ 19 Philadelphia Phillies	8.00	3.60	1.00
☐ 20 Pittsburgh Pirates	8.00	3.60	1.00
☐ 21 San Diego Padres	8.00	3.60	1.00
☐ 22 San Francisco Giants	8.00	3.60	1.00
☐ 23 St. Louis Cardinals	8.00	3.60	1.00
☐ 24 Texas Rangers	8.00	3.60	1.00

1973 Topps Pin-Ups

This test issue of 24 pin-ups is quite scarce. Each pin-up measures approximately 3 7/16" by 4 5/8" and is very colorful with a thick white border. The thin-paper pin-ups contain a facsimile autograph on the front of the card. The set shares the same checklist with the 1973 Topps Comics. The set is unnumbered and hence is ordered below alphabetically. The team insignia and logos on the cards have been airbrushed away, which is contra-indicative of a Topps issue.

	NRMT	VG-E	GOOD
COMPLETE SET (24)	3000.00	1350.00	375.00
COMMON CARD (1-24)	50.00	22.00	6.25
☐ 1 Hank Aaron	250.00	110.00	31.00
☐ 2 Dick Allen	75.00	34.00	9.50
☐ 3 Johnny Bench	200.00	90.00	25.00
☐ 4 Steve Carlton	175.00	80.00	22.00
☐ 5 Nate Colbert	50.00	22.00	6.25
☐ 6 Willie Davis	50.00	22.00	6.25
☐ 7 Bill Freehan	50.00	22.00	6.25
☐ 8 Reggie Jackson	225.00	100.00	28.00
☐ 9 Harmon Killebrew	125.00	55.00	15.50
☐ 10 Mickey Lolich	75.00	34.00	9.50
☐ 11 Willie McCovey	125.00	55.00	15.50
☐ 12 Bobby Murcer	75.00	34.00	9.50
☐ 13 Jim Palmer	175.00	80.00	22.00
☐ 14 Gaylord Perry	125.00	55.00	15.50
☐ 15 Lou Piniella	75.00	34.00	9.50
☐ 16 Brooks Robinson	175.00	80.00	22.00
☐ 17 Nolan Ryan	375.00	170.00	47.50
☐ 18 George Scott	50.00	22.00	6.25
☐ 19 Tom Seaver	225.00	100.00	28.00
☐ 20 Willie Stargell	125.00	55.00	15.50
☐ 21 Don Sutton	100.00	45.00	12.50
☐ 22 Joe Torre	75.00	34.00	9.50
☐ 23 Billy Williams	125.00	55.00	15.50
☐ 24 Carl Yastrzemski	250.00	110.00	31.00

1973 Topps Candy Lids

One of Topps' most unusual test sets is this series of 55 color portraits of baseball players printed on the bottom of candy lids. These lids measure 1 7/8" in diameter. The product was called "Baseball Stars Bubble Gum" and consisted of a small tub of candy-coated gum kernels. Issued in 1973, the lids are unnumbered and each has a small tab. Underneath the picture is a small ribbon design which contains the player's name, team and position.

	NRMT	VG-E	GOOD
COMPLETE SET (55)	600.00	275.00	75.00
COMMON LID (1-55)	3.00	1.35	.35
☐ 1 Hank Aaron	35.00	16.00	4.40
☐ 2 Dick Allen	5.00	2.20	.60
☐ 3 Dusty Baker	5.00	2.20	.60
☐ 4 Sal Bando	3.00	1.35	.35
☐ 5 Johnny Bench	25.00	11.00	3.10
☐ 6 Bobby Bonds	5.00	2.20	.60
☐ 7 Dick Bosman	3.00	1.35	.35
☐ 8 Lou Brock	15.00	6.75	1.85
☐ 9 Rod Carew	15.00	6.75	1.85
☐ 10 Steve Carlton	15.00	6.75	1.85
☐ 11 Nate Colbert	3.00	1.35	.35
☐ 12 Willie Davis	3.00	1.35	.35
☐ 13 Larry Dierker	3.00	1.35	.35
☐ 14 Mike Epstein	3.00	1.35	.35
☐ 15 Carlton Fisk	15.00	6.75	1.85
☐ 16 Tim Foli	3.00	1.35	.35
☐ 17 Ray Fosse	3.00	1.35	.35
☐ 18 Bill Freehan	3.00	1.35	.35
☐ 19 Bob Gibson	15.00	6.75	1.85
☐ 20 Bud Harrelson	3.00	1.35	.35
☐ 21 Jim Hunter	10.00	4.50	1.25
☐ 22 Reggie Jackson	25.00	11.00	3.10
☐ 23 Fergie Jenkins	10.00	4.50	1.25
☐ 24 Al Kaline	15.00	6.75	1.85
☐ 25 Harmon Killebrew	15.00	6.75	1.85
☐ 26 Clay Kirby	3.00	1.35	.35
☐ 27 Mickey Lolich	5.00	2.20	.60
☐ 28 Greg Luzinski	5.00	2.20	.60
☐ 29 Willie McCovey	15.00	6.75	1.85
☐ 30 Mike Marshall	3.00	1.35	.35
☐ 31 Lee May	3.00	1.35	.35
☐ 32 John Mayberry	3.00	1.35	.35
☐ 33 Willie Mays	35.00	16.00	4.40
☐ 34 Thurman Munson	10.00	4.50	1.25
☐ 35 Bobby Murcer	5.00	2.20	.60
☐ 36 Gary Nolan	3.00	1.35	.35
☐ 37 Amos Otis	3.00	1.35	.35
☐ 38 Jim Palmer	15.00	6.75	1.85
☐ 39 Gaylord Perry	10.00	4.50	1.25
☐ 40 Lou Piniella	5.00	2.20	.60
☐ 41 Brooks Robinson	15.00	6.75	1.85
☐ 42 Frank Robinson	15.00	6.75	1.85
☐ 43 Ellie Rodriguez	3.00	1.35	.35
☐ 44 Pete Rose	35.00	16.00	4.40
☐ 45 Nolan Ryan	100.00	45.00	12.50
☐ 46 Manny Sanguillen	3.00	1.35	.35
☐ 47 George Scott	3.00	1.35	.35
☐ 48 Tom Seaver	25.00	11.00	3.10
☐ 49 Chris Speier	3.00	1.35	.35
☐ 50 Willie Stargell	15.00	6.75	1.85
☐ 51 Don Sutton	10.00	4.50	1.25
☐ 52 Joe Torre	5.00	2.20	.60
☐ 53 Billy Williams	10.00	4.50	1.25
☐ 54 Wilbur Wood	3.00	1.35	.35
☐ 55 Carl Yastrzemski	25.00	11.00	3.10

1973 Topps Comics

This test issue of 24 comics is quite scarce. Each comic measures approximately 4 5/8" by 3 7/16" and is very colorful. The comics are subtitled "Career Highlights of ..." and feature six or seven panels of information about the particular player. The set shares the same checklist with the 1973 Topps Pin-Ups. The set is unnumbered and hence is ordered below alphabetically. The team insignia and logos on the cards have been airbrushed away, which is contra-indicative of a Topps issue.

	NRMT	VG-E	GOOD
COMPLETE SET (24)	2500.00	1100.00	300.00
COMMON CARD (1-24)	40.00	18.00	5.00
☐ 1 Hank Aaron	200.00	90.00	25.00
☐ 2 Dick Allen	75.00	34.00	9.50
☐ 3 Johnny Bench	150.00	70.00	19.00
☐ 4 Steve Carlton	150.00	70.00	19.00
☐ 5 Nate Colbert	40.00	18.00	5.00
☐ 6 Willie Davis	40.00	18.00	5.00
☐ 7 Bill Freehan	75.00	34.00	9.50
☐ 8 Reggie Jackson	175.00	80.00	22.00
☐ 9 Harmon Killebrew	125.00	55.00	15.50
☐ 10 Mickey Lolich	75.00	34.00	9.50
☐ 11 Willie McCovey	125.00	55.00	15.50
☐ 12 Bobby Murcer	75.00	34.00	9.50
☐ 13 Jim Palmer	150.00	70.00	19.00
☐ 14 Gaylord Perry	125.00	55.00	15.50
☐ 15 Lou Piniella	75.00	34.00	9.50
☐ 16 Brooks Robinson	150.00	70.00	19.00
☐ 17 Nolan Ryan	275.00	125.00	34.00
☐ 18 George Scott	40.00	18.00	5.00
☐ 19 Tom Seaver	175.00	80.00	22.00
☐ 20 Willie Stargell	125.00	55.00	15.50
☐ 21 Don Sutton	100.00	45.00	12.50
☐ 22 Joe Torre	75.00	34.00	9.50
☐ 23 Billy Williams	125.00	55.00	15.50
☐ 24 Carl Yastrzemski	200.00	90.00	25.00

1974 Topps

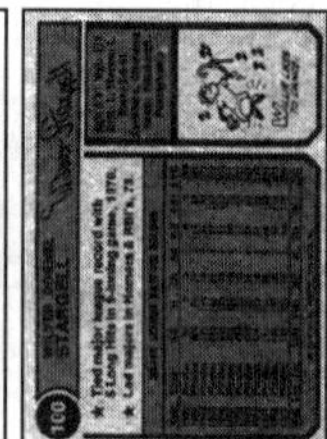

The cards in this 660-card set measure 2 1/2" by 3 1/2". This year marked the first time Topps issued all the cards of its baseball set at the same time rather than in series. Among other methods, cards were issued in eight-card dime wax packs and 42 card rack packs. For the first time, factory sets were issued through the JC Penny's catalog. Sales were probably disappointing for it would be several years before factory sets were issued again. Some interesting variations were created by the rumored move of the San Diego Padres to Washington. Fifteen cards (13 players, the team card, and the rookie card (599) of the Padres were printed either as "San Diego" (SD) or "Washington." The latter are the scarcer variety and are denoted in the checklist below by WAS. Each team's manager and his coaches again have a combined card with small pictures of each coach below the larger photo of the team's manager. The first six cards in the set (1-6) feature Hank Aaron and his illustrious career. Other topical subsets included in the set are League Leaders (201-208), All-Star selections (331-339), Playoffs cards (470-471), World Series cards (472-479), and Rookie Prospects (596-608). The card backs for the All-Stars (331-339) have no statistics, but form a picture puzzle of Bobby Bonds, the 1973 All-Star Game MVP. The key Rookie Cards in this set are Ken Griffey Sr., Dave Parker, and Dave Winfield.

	NRMT	VG-E	GOOD
COMPLETE SET (660)	600.00	275.00	75.00
COMPLETE FACT.SET (660)	625.00	275.00	80.00
COMMON CARD (1-660)	.50	.23	.06
WRAPPERS (10-CENTS)	10.00	4.50	1.25
☐ 1 Hank Aaron	40.00	12.00	5.00
All-Time Home Run King			
(Complete ML record)			
☐ 2 Aaron Special 54-57	7.00	3.10	.85
(Records on back)			
☐ 3 Aaron Special 58-61	7.00	3.10	.85
(Memorable homers)			
☐ 4 Aaron Special 62-65	7.00	3.10	.85
(Life in ML's 1954-63)			
☐ 5 Aaron Special 66-69	7.00	3.10	.85
(Life in ML's 1964-73)			
☐ 6 Aaron Special 70-73	7.00	3.10	.85
(Milestone homers)			
☐ 7 Jim Hunter	3.00	1.35	.35
☐ 8 George Theodore	.50	.23	.06
☐ 9 Mickey Lolich	.75	.35	.09
☐ 10 Johnny Bench	12.00	5.50	1.50
☐ 11 Jim Bibby	.50	.23	.06
☐ 12 Dave May	.50	.23	.06
☐ 13 Tom Hilgendorf	.50	.23	.06
☐ 14 Paul Popovich	.50	.23	.06
☐ 15 Joe Torre	1.00	.45	.12
☐ 16 Baltimore Orioles	1.50	.70	.19
Team Card			
☐ 17 Doug Bird	.50	.23	.06
☐ 18 Gary Thomasson	.50	.23	.06
☐ 19 Gerry Moses	.50	.23	.06
☐ 20 Nolan Ryan	70.00	32.00	8.75
☐ 21 Bob Gallagher	.50	.23	.06
☐ 22 Cy Acosta	.50	.23	.06
☐ 23 Craig Robinson	.50	.23	.06
☐ 24 John Hiller	.75	.35	.09
☐ 25 Ken Singleton	.75	.35	.09
☐ 26 Bill Campbell	.50	.23	.06
☐ 27 George Scott	.75	.35	.09
☐ 28 Manny Sanguillen	.75	.35	.09
☐ 29 Phil Niekro	2.50	1.10	.30
☐ 30 Bobby Bonds	1.50	.70	.19
☐ 31 Astros Leaders	.75	.35	.09
Preston Gomez MG			
Roger Craig CO			
Hub Kittle CO			
Grady Hatton CO			
Bob Lillis CO			
☐ 32A Johnny Grubb SD	.75	.35	.09
☐ 32B Johnny Grubb WAS	7.00	3.10	.85
☐ 33 Don Newhauser	.50	.23	.06
☐ 34 Andy Kosco	.50	.23	.06
☐ 35 Gaylord Perry	3.00	1.35	.35
☐ 36 St. Louis Cardinals	1.50	.70	.19
Team Card			
☐ 37 Dave Sells	.50	.23	.06
☐ 38 Don Kessinger	.75	.35	.09
☐ 39 Ken Suarez	.50	.23	.06
☐ 40 Jim Palmer	5.00	2.20	.60
☐ 41 Bobby Floyd	.50	.23	.06
☐ 42 Claude Osteen	.75	.35	.09
☐ 43 Jim Wynn	.75	.35	.09
☐ 44 Mel Stottlemyre	.75	.35	.09
☐ 45 Dave Johnson	.75	.35	.09
☐ 46 Pat Kelly	.50	.23	.06
☐ 47 Dick Ruthven	.50	.23	.06
☐ 48 Dick Sharon	.50	.23	.06
☐ 49 Steve Renko	.50	.23	.06
☐ 50 Rod Carew	5.00	2.20	.60
☐ 51 Bobby Heise	.50	.23	.06
☐ 52 Al Oliver	.50	.23	.06
☐ 53A Fred Kendall SD	.75	.35	.09
☐ 53B Fred Kendall WAS	7.00	3.10	.85
☐ 54 Elias Sosa	.50	.23	.06
☐ 55 Frank Robinson	7.00	3.10	.85
☐ 56 New York Mets	1.50	.70	.19
Team Card			
☐ 57 Darold Knowles	.50	.23	.06
☐ 58 Charlie Spikes	.50	.23	.06
☐ 59 Ross Grimsley	.50	.23	.06
☐ 60 Lou Brock	5.00	2.20	.60
☐ 61 Luis Aparicio	3.00	1.35	.35
☐ 62 Bob Locker	.50	.23	.06
☐ 63 Bill Sudakis	.50	.23	.06
☐ 64 Doug Rau	.50	.23	.06
☐ 65 Amos Otis	.75	.35	.09
☐ 66 Sparky Lyle	.75	.35	.09
☐ 67 Tommy Helms	.50	.23	.06
☐ 68 Grant Jackson	.50	.23	.06
☐ 69 Del Unser	.50	.23	.06
☐ 70 Dick Allen	1.00	.45	.12
☐ 71 Dan Frisella	.50	.23	.06
☐ 72 Aurelio Rodriguez	.50	.23	.06
☐ 73 Mike Marshall	1.00	.45	.12
☐ 74 Minnesota Twins	1.50	.70	.19
Team Card			
☐ 75 Jim Colborn	.50	.23	.06
☐ 76 Mickey Rivers	.75	.35	.09
☐ 77A Rich Troedson SD	.75	.35	.09
☐ 77B Rich Troedson WAS	7.00	3.10	.85
☐ 78 Giants Leaders	.75	.35	.09
Charlie Fox MG			
John McNamara CO			
Joe Amalfitano CO			
Andy Gilbert CO			
Don McMahon CO			
☐ 79 Gene Tenace	.75	.35	.09

□ 80 Tom Seaver 14.00 6.25 1.75
□ 81 Frank Duffy .50 .23 .06
□ 82 Dave Giusti .50 .23 .06
□ 83 Orlando Cepeda 1.50 .70 .19
□ 84 Rick Wise .50 .23 .06
□ 85 Joe Morgan 5.00 2.20 .60
□ 86 Joe Ferguson .75 .35 .09
□ 87 Fergie Jenkins 3.00 1.35 .35
□ 88 Freddie Patek .75 .35 .09
□ 89 Jackie Brown .50 .23 .06
□ 90 Bobby Murcer .75 .35 .09
□ 91 Ken Forsch .50 .23 .06
□ 92 Paul Blair .75 .35 .09
□ 93 Rod Gilbreath .50 .23 .06
□ 94 Detroit Tigers 1.50 .70 .19
Team Card
□ 95 Steve Carlton 7.00 3.10 .85
□ 96 Jerry Hairston .50 .23 .06
□ 97 Bob Bailey .50 .23 .06
□ 98 Bert Blyleven 1.00 .45 .12
□ 99 Brewers Leaders .75 .35 .09
Del Crandall MG
Harvey Kuenn CO
Joe Nossek CO
Jim Walton CO
Al Widmar CO
□ 100 Willie Stargell 4.00 1.80 .50
□ 101 Bobby Valentine .75 .35 .09
□ 102A Bill Greif SD .75 .35 .09
□ 102B Bill Greif WAS 7.00 3.10 .85
□ 103 Sal Bando .75 .35 .09
□ 104 Ron Bryant .50 .23 .06
□ 105 Carlton Fisk 14.00 6.25 1.75
□ 106 Harry Parker .50 .23 .06
□ 107 Alex Johnson .50 .23 .06
□ 108 Al Hrabosky .75 .35 .09
□ 109 Bob Grich .75 .35 .09
□ 110 Billy Williams 4.00 1.80 .50
□ 111 Clay Carroll .50 .23 .06
□ 112 Dave Lopes 1.00 .45 .12
□ 113 Dick Drago .50 .23 .06
□ 114 Angels Team 1.50 .70 .19
□ 115 Willie Horton .75 .35 .09
□ 116 Jerry Reuss .75 .35 .09
□ 117 Ron Blomberg .50 .23 .06
□ 118 Bill Lee .75 .35 .09
□ 119 Phillies Leaders .75 .35 .09
Danny Ozark MG
Ray Ripplemeyer CO
Bobby Wine CO
Carroll Beringer CO
Billy DeMars CO
□ 120 Wilbur Wood .50 .23 .06
□ 121 Larry Lintz .50 .23 .06
□ 122 Jim Holt .50 .23 .06
□ 123 Nelson Briles .75 .35 .09
□ 124 Bobby Coluccio .50 .23 .06
□ 125A Nate Colbert SD .75 .35 .09
□ 125B Nate Colbert WAS 7.00 3.10 .85
□ 126 Checklist 1-132 2.50 .50 .25
□ 127 Tom Paciorek .75 .35 .09
□ 128 John Ellis .50 .23 .06
□ 129 Chris Speier .50 .23 .06
□ 130 Reggie Jackson 18.00 8.00 2.20
□ 131 Bob Boone 1.50 .70 .19
□ 132 Felix Millan .50 .23 .06
□ 133 David Clyde .75 .35 .09
□ 134 Denis Menke .50 .23 .06
□ 135 Roy White .75 .35 .09
□ 136 Rick Reuschel 1.00 .45 .12
□ 137 Al Bumbry .75 .35 .09
□ 138 Eddie Brinkman .50 .23 .06
□ 139 Aurelio Monteagudo .50 .23 .06
□ 140 Darrell Evans 1.00 .45 .12
□ 141 Pat Bourque .50 .23 .06
□ 142 Pedro Garcia .50 .23 .06
□ 143 Dick Woodson .50 .23 .06
□ 144 Dodgers Leaders 1.50 .70 .19
Walter Alston MG
Tom Lasorda CO
Jim Gilliam CO
Red Adams CO
Monty Basgall CO
□ 145 Dock Ellis .50 .23 .06
□ 146 Ron Fairly .75 .35 .09
□ 147 Bart Johnson .50 .23 .06
□ 148A Dave Hilton SD .75 .35 .09
□ 148B Dave Hilton WAS 7.00 3.10 .85
□ 149 Mac Scarce .50 .23 .06
□ 150 John Mayberry .75 .35 .09
□ 151 Diego Segui .50 .23 .06
□ 152 Oscar Gamble .75 .35 .09
□ 153 Jon Matlack .75 .35 .09
□ 154 Houston Astros 1.50 .70 .19
Team Card
□ 155 Bert Campaneris .75 .35 .09
□ 156 Randy Moffitt .50 .23 .06
□ 157 Vic Harris .50 .23 .06
□ 158 Jack Billingham .50 .23 .06
□ 159 Jim Ray Hart .75 .35 .09
□ 160 Brooks Robinson 7.00 3.10 .85
□ 161 Ray Burris UER .75 .35 .09
(Card number is
printed sideways)
□ 162 Bill Freehan .75 .35 .09
□ 163 Ken Berry .50 .23 .06
□ 164 Tom House .50 .23 .06
□ 165 Willie Davis .75 .35 .09
□ 166 Royals Leaders .75 .35 .09
Jack McKeon MG
Charlie Lau CO
Harry Dunlop CO
Galen Cisco CO
□ 167 Luis Tiant 1.00 .45 .12
□ 168 Danny Thompson .50 .23 .06
□ 169 Steve Rogers 1.00 .45 .12
□ 170 Bill Melton .50 .23 .06
□ 171 Eduardo Rodriguez .50 .23 .06
□ 172 Gene Clines .50 .23 .06
□ 173A Randy Jones SD 1.00 .45 .12
□ 173B Randy Jones WAS 10.00 4.50 1.25
□ 174 Bill Robinson .75 .35 .09
□ 175 Reggie Cleveland .50 .23 .06
□ 176 John Lowenstein .50 .23 .06
□ 177 Dave Roberts .50 .23 .06
□ 178 Garry Maddox .75 .35 .09
□ 179 Mets Leaders 2.00 .90 .25
Yogi Berra MG
Rube Walker CO
Eddie Yost CO
Roy McMillan CO
Joe Pignatano CO
□ 180 Ken Holtzman .75 .35 .09
□ 181 Cesar Geronimo .50 .23 .06
□ 182 Lindy McDaniel .75 .35 .09
□ 183 Johnny Oates .75 .35 .09
□ 184 Texas Rangers 1.50 .70 .19
Team Card
□ 185 Jose Cardenal .50 .23 .06
□ 186 Fred Scherman .50 .23 .06
□ 187 Don Baylor 1.50 .70 .19
□ 188 Rudy Meoli .50 .23 .06
□ 189 Jim Brewer .50 .23 .06
□ 190 Tony Oliva 1.00 .45 .12
□ 191 Al Fitzmorris .50 .23 .06
□ 192 Mario Guerrero .50 .23 .06
□ 193 Tom Walker .50 .23 .06
□ 194 Darrell Porter .75 .35 .09
□ 195 Carlos May .50 .23 .06
□ 196 Jim Fregosi .75 .35 .09
□ 197A Vicente Romo SD .75 .35 .09
□ 197B Vicente Romo WAS 7.00 3.10 .85
□ 198 Dave Cash .50 .23 .06
□ 199 Mike Kekich .50 .23 .06
□ 200 Cesar Cedeno .75 .35 .09
□ 201 Batting Leaders 5.00 2.20 .60
Rod Carew
Pete Rose
□ 202 Home Run Leaders 5.00 2.20 .60
Reggie Jackson
Willie Stargell
□ 203 RBI Leaders 5.00 2.20 .60
Reggie Jackson
Willie Stargell
□ 204 Stolen Base Leaders 1.50 .70 .19
Tommy Harper
Lou Brock
□ 205 Victory Leaders 1.00 .45 .12
Wilbur Wood
Ron Bryant
□ 206 ERA Leaders 5.00 2.20 .60
Jim Palmer
Tom Seaver
□ 207 Strikeout Leaders 20.00 9.00 2.50
Nolan Ryan
Tom Seaver
□ 208 Leading Firemen 1.00 .45 .12
John Hiller
Mike Marshall
□ 209 Ted Sizemore .50 .23 .06
□ 210 Bill Singer .50 .23 .06
□ 211 Chicago Cubs Team 1.50 .70 .19
□ 212 Rollie Fingers 3.00 1.35 .35
□ 213 Dave Rader .50 .23 .06
□ 214 Billy Grabarkewitz .50 .23 .06
□ 215 Al Kaline UER 5.00 2.20 .60
(No copyright on back)
□ 216 Ray Sadecki .50 .23 .06
□ 217 Tim Foli .50 .23 .06
□ 218 Johnny Briggs .50 .23 .06
□ 219 Doug Griffin .50 .23 .06
□ 220 Don Sutton 1.50 .70 .19
□ 221 White Sox Leaders .75 .35 .09
Chuck Tanner MG
Jim Mahoney CO
Alex Monchak CO
Johnny Sain CO
Joe Lonnett CO
□ 222 Ramon Hernandez .50 .23 .06
□ 223 Jeff Burroughs 1.00 .45 .12
□ 224 Roger Metzger .50 .23 .06
□ 225 Paul Splittorff .50 .23 .06
□ 226A Padres Team SD 1.50 .70 .19
□ 226B Padres Team WAS 9.00 4.00 1.10
□ 227 Mike Lum .50 .23 .06
□ 228 Ted Kubiak .50 .23 .06
□ 229 Fritz Peterson .50 .23 .06
□ 230 Tony Perez 3.00 1.35 .35
□ 231 Dick Tidrow .50 .23 .06
□ 232 Steve Brye .50 .23 .06
□ 233 Jim Barr .50 .23 .06
□ 234 John Milner .50 .23 .06
□ 235 Dave McNally .75 .35 .09
□ 236 Cardinals Leaders 1.00 .45 .12
Red Schoendienst MG
Barney Schultz CO
George Kissell CO
Johnny Lewis CO
Vern Benson CO
□ 237 Ken Brett .50 .23 .06
□ 238 Fran Healy HOR .75 .35 .09
(Munson sliding
in background)
□ 239 Bill Russell .75 .35 .09
□ 240 Joe Coleman .50 .23 .06
□ 241A Glenn Beckert SD .75 .35 .09
□ 241B Glenn Beckert WAS 7.00 3.10 .85
□ 242 Bill Gogolewski .50 .23 .06
□ 243 Bob Oliver .50 .23 .06
□ 244 Carl Morton .50 .23 .06
□ 245 Cleon Jones .75 .35 .09
□ 246 Oakland Athletics 1.50 .70 .19
Team Card
□ 247 Rick Miller .50 .23 .06
□ 248 Tom Hall .50 .23 .06
□ 249 George Mitterwald .50 .23 .06
□ 250A Willie McCovey SD 6.00 2.70 .75
□ 250B Willie McCovey WAS 30.00 13.50 3.70
□ 251 Graig Nettles 1.50 .70 .19
□ 252 Dave Parker 10.00 4.50 1.25
□ 253 John Boccabella .50 .23 .06
□ 254 Stan Bahnsen .50 .23 .06
□ 255 Larry Bowa .75 .35 .09
□ 256 Tom Griffin .50 .23 .06
□ 257 Buddy Bell 1.00 .45 .12
□ 258 Jerry Morales .50 .23 .06
□ 259 Bob Reynolds .50 .23 .06
□ 260 Ted Simmons 1.50 .70 .19
□ 261 Jerry Bell .50 .23 .06
□ 262 Ed Kirkpatrick .50 .23 .06
□ 263 Checklist 133-264 2.50 .50 .25
□ 264 Joe Rudi .75 .35 .09
□ 265 Tug McGraw 1.00 .45 .12
□ 266 Jim Northrup .75 .35 .09
□ 267 Andy Messersmith .75 .35 .09
□ 268 Tom Grieve .75 .35 .09
□ 269 Bob Johnson .50 .23 .06
□ 270 Ron Santo 1.00 .45 .12
□ 271 Bill Hands .50 .23 .06
□ 272 Paul Casanova .50 .23 .06
□ 273 Checklist 265-396 2.50 .50 .25
□ 274 Fred Beene .50 .23 .06
□ 275 Ron Hunt .50 .23 .06
□ 276 Angels Leaders .75 .35 .09
Bobby Winkles MG
John Roseboro CO
Tom Morgan CO
Jimmie Reese CO
Salty Parker CO
□ 277 Gary Nolan .75 .35 .09
□ 278 Cookie Rojas .75 .35 .09
□ 279 Jim Crawford .50 .23 .06
□ 280 Carl Yastrzemski 6.00 2.70 .75
□ 281 San Francisco Giants 1.50 .70 .19
Team Card
□ 282 Doyle Alexander .75 .35 .09
□ 283 Mike Schmidt 50.00 22.00 6.25
□ 284 Dave Duncan .50 .23 .06
□ 285 Reggie Smith .75 .35 .09
□ 286 Tony Muser .50 .23 .06
□ 287 Clay Kirby .50 .23 .06
□ 288 Gorman Thomas 1.50 .70 .19
□ 289 Rick Auerbach .50 .23 .06
□ 290 Vida Blue .75 .35 .09
□ 291 Don Hahn .50 .23 .06
□ 292 Chuck Seelbach .50 .23 .06
□ 293 Milt May .50 .23 .06
□ 294 Steve Foucault .50 .23 .06
□ 295 Rick Monday .75 .35 .09
□ 296 Ray Corbin .50 .23 .06
□ 297 Hal Breeden .50 .23 .06
□ 298 Roric Harrison .50 .23 .06
□ 299 Gene Michael .75 .35 .09
□ 300 Pete Rose 16.00 7.25 2.00
□ 301 Bob Montgomery .50 .23 .06
□ 302 Rudy May .50 .23 .06
□ 303 George Hendrick .75 .35 .09
□ 304 Don Wilson .50 .23 .06
□ 305 Tito Fuentes .50 .23 .06
□ 306 Orioles Leaders 1.50 .70 .19
Earl Weaver MG
Jim Frey CO
George Bamberger CO
Billy Hunter CO
George Staller CO
□ 307 Luis Melendez .50 .23 .06
□ 308 Bruce Dal Canton .50 .23 .06
□ 309A Dave Roberts SD .75 .35 .09
□ 309B Dave Roberts WAS 9.00 4.00 1.10
□ 310 Terry Forster .75 .35 .09
□ 311 Jerry Grote .50 .23 .06
□ 312 Deron Johnson .75 .35 .09
□ 313 Barry Lersch .50 .23 .06
□ 314 Milwaukee Brewers 1.50 .70 .19
Team Card
□ 315 Ron Cey 1.00 .45 .12
□ 316 Jim Perry .75 .35 .09
□ 317 Richie Zisk .75 .35 .09
□ 318 Jim Merritt .50 .23 .06
□ 319 Randy Hundley .75 .35 .09
□ 320 Dusty Baker 1.50 .70 .19
□ 321 Steve Braun .50 .23 .06
□ 322 Ernie McAnally .50 .23 .06
□ 323 Richie Scheinblum .50 .23 .06
□ 324 Steve Kline .50 .23 .06
□ 325 Tommy Harper .75 .35 .09
□ 326 Reds Leaders 2.50 1.10 .30
Sparky Anderson MG
Larry Shepard CO
George Scherger CO
Alex Grammas CO
Ted Kluszewski CO
□ 327 Tom Timmermann .50 .23 .06
□ 328 Skip Jutze .50 .23 .06
□ 329 Mark Belanger .75 .35 .09
□ 330 Juan Marichal 3.00 1.35 .35
□ 331 All-Star Catchers 5.00 2.20 .60
Carlton Fisk
Johnny Bench
□ 332 All-Star 1B 5.00 2.20 .60
Dick Allen
Hank Aaron
□ 333 All-Star 2B 2.50 1.10 .30
Rod Carew
Joe Morgan
□ 334 All-Star 3B 2.50 1.10 .30
Brooks Robinson
Ron Santo
□ 335 All-Star SS .75 .35 .09
Bert Campaneris
Chris Speier
□ 336 All-Star LF 3.00 1.35 .35
Bobby Murcer
Pete Rose
□ 337 All-Star CF 1.00 .45 .12
Amos Otis
Cesar Cedeno
□ 338 All-Star RF 5.00 2.20 .60
Reggie Jackson
Billy Williams
□ 339 All-Star Pitchers 1.50 .70 .19
Jim Hunter
Rick Wise
□ 340 Thurman Munson 6.00 2.70 .75
□ 341 Dan Driessen 1.00 .45 .12
□ 342 Jim Lonborg .75 .35 .09
□ 343 Royals Team 1.50 .70 .19
□ 344 Mike Caldwell .50 .23 .06
□ 345 Bill North .50 .23 .06
□ 346 Ron Reed .50 .23 .06
□ 347 Sandy Alomar .75 .35 .09
□ 348 Pete Richert .50 .23 .06
□ 349 John Vukovich .50 .23 .06
□ 350 Bob Gibson 5.00 2.20 .60
□ 351 Dwight Evans 3.00 1.35 .35
□ 352 Bill Stoneman .50 .23 .06
□ 353 Rich Coggins .50 .23 .06
□ 354 Cubs Leaders .75 .35 .09
Whitey Lockman MG
J.C. Martin CO
Hank Aguirre CO
Al Spangler CO
Jim Marshall CO
□ 355 Dave Nelson .50 .23 .06
□ 356 Jerry Koosman .75 .35 .09
□ 357 Buddy Bradford .50 .23 .06
□ 358 Dal Maxvill .50 .23 .06
□ 359 Brent Strom .50 .23 .06
□ 360 Greg Luzinski 1.00 .45 .12
□ 361 Don Carrithers .50 .23 .06
□ 362 Hal King .50 .23 .06
□ 363 New York Yankees 1.50 .70 .19
Team Card
□ 364A Cito Gaston SD 1.50 .70 .19
□ 364B Cito Gaston WAS 10.00 4.50 1.25
□ 365 Steve Busby .75 .35 .09
□ 366 Larry Hisle .75 .35 .09
□ 367 Norm Cash 1.00 .45 .12
□ 368 Manny Mota .75 .35 .09
□ 369 Paul Lindblad .50 .23 .06
□ 370 Bob Watson .75 .35 .09
□ 371 Jim Slaton .50 .23 .06
□ 372 Ken Reitz .50 .23 .06
□ 373 John Curtis .50 .23 .06
□ 374 Marty Perez .50 .23 .06
□ 375 Earl Williams .50 .23 .06
□ 376 Jorge Orta .50 .23 .06
□ 377 Ron Woods .50 .23 .06
□ 378 Burt Hooton .75 .35 .09
□ 379 Rangers Leaders 1.00 .45 .12
Billy Martin MG
Frank Lucchesi CO
Art Fowler CO
Charlie Silvera CO
Jackie Moore CO
□ 380 Bud Harrelson .75 .35 .09
□ 381 Charlie Sands .50 .23 .06
□ 382 Bob Moose .50 .23 .06
□ 383 Philadelphia Phillies 1.50 .70 .19
Team Card

Card	NRMT	VG-E	GOOD
☐ 384 Chris Chambliss	.75	.35	.09
☐ 385 Don Gullett	.75	.35	.09
☐ 386 Gary Matthews	.75	.35	.09
☐ 387A Rich Morales SD	.75	.35	.09
☐ 387B Rich Morales WAS	9.00	4.00	1.10
☐ 388 Phil Roof	.50	.23	.06
☐ 389 Gates Brown	.50	.23	.06
☐ 390 Lou Piniella	1.50	.70	.19
☐ 391 Billy Champion	.50	.23	.06
☐ 392 Dick Green	.50	.23	.06
☐ 393 Orlando Pena	.50	.23	.06
☐ 394 Ken Henderson	.50	.23	.06
☐ 395 Doug Rader	.50	.23	.06
☐ 396 Tommy Davis	.75	.35	.09
☐ 397 George Stone	.50	.23	.06
☐ 398 Duke Sims	.50	.23	.06
☐ 399 Mike Paul	.50	.23	.06
☐ 400 Harmon Killebrew	5.00	2.20	.60
☐ 401 Elliott Maddox	.50	.23	.06
☐ 402 Jim Rooker	.50	.23	.06
☐ 403 Red Sox Leaders	.75	.35	.09
Darrell Johnson MG			
Eddie Popowski CO			
Lee Stange CO			
Don Zimmer CO			
Don Bryant CO			
☐ 404 Jim Howarth	.50	.23	.06
☐ 405 Ellie Rodriguez	.50	.23	.06
☐ 406 Steve Arlin	.50	.23	.06
☐ 407 Jim Wohlford	.50	.23	.06
☐ 408 Charlie Hough	1.00	.45	.12
☐ 409 Ike Brown	.50	.23	.06
☐ 410 Pedro Borbon	.50	.23	.06
☐ 411 Frank Baker	.50	.23	.06
☐ 412 Chuck Taylor	.50	.23	.06
☐ 413 Don Money	.75	.35	.09
☐ 414 Checklist 397-528	2.50	.50	.25
☐ 415 Gary Gentry	.50	.23	.06
☐ 416 Chicago White Sox	1.50	.70	.19
Team Card			
☐ 417 Rich Folkers	.50	.23	.06
☐ 418 Walt Williams	.50	.23	.06
☐ 419 Wayne Twitchell	.50	.23	.06
☐ 420 Ray Fosse	.50	.23	.06
☐ 421 Dan Fife	.50	.23	.06
☐ 422 Gonzalo Marquez	.50	.23	.06
☐ 423 Fred Stanley	.50	.23	.06
☐ 424 Jim Beauchamp	.50	.23	.06
☐ 425 Pete Broberg	.50	.23	.06
☐ 426 Rennie Stennett	.50	.23	.06
☐ 427 Bobby Bolin	.50	.23	.06
☐ 428 Gary Sutherland	.50	.23	.06
☐ 429 Dick Lange	.50	.23	.06
☐ 430 Matty Alou	.75	.35	.09
☐ 431 Gene Garber	1.00	.45	.12
☐ 432 Chris Arnold	.50	.23	.06
☐ 433 Lerrin LaGrow	.50	.23	.06
☐ 434 Ken McMullen	.50	.23	.06
☐ 435 Dave Concepcion	1.50	.70	.19
☐ 436 Don Hood	.50	.23	.06
☐ 437 Jim Lyttle	.50	.23	.06
☐ 438 Ed Herrmann	.50	.23	.06
☐ 439 Norm Miller	.50	.23	.06
☐ 440 Jim Kaat	1.50	.70	.19
☐ 441 Tom Ragland	.50	.23	.06
☐ 442 Alan Foster	.50	.23	.06
☐ 443 Tom Hutton	.50	.23	.06
☐ 444 Vic Davalillo	.50	.23	.06
☐ 445 George Medich	.50	.23	.06
☐ 446 Len Randle	.50	.23	.06
☐ 447 Twins Leaders	.75	.35	.09
Frank Quilici MG			
Ralph Rowe CO			
Bob Rodgers CO			
Vern Morgan CO			
☐ 448 Ron Hodges	.50	.23	.06
☐ 449 Tom McCraw	.50	.23	.06
☐ 450 Rich Hebner	.75	.35	.09
☐ 451 Tommy John	1.50	.70	.19
☐ 452 Gene Hiser	.50	.23	.06
☐ 453 Balor Moore	.50	.23	.06
☐ 454 Kurt Bevacqua	.50	.23	.06
☐ 455 Tom Bradley	.50	.23	.06
☐ 456 Dave Winfield	125.00	55.00	15.50
☐ 457 Chuck Goggin	.50	.23	.06
☐ 458 Jim Ray	.50	.23	.06
☐ 459 Cincinnati Reds	1.50	.70	.19
Team Card			
☐ 460 Boog Powell	1.00	.45	.12
☐ 461 John Odom	.50	.23	.06
☐ 462 Luis Alvarado	.50	.23	.06
☐ 463 Pat Dobson	.50	.23	.06
☐ 464 Jose Cruz	.75	.35	.09
☐ 465 Dick Bosman	.50	.23	.06
☐ 466 Dick Billings	.50	.23	.06
☐ 467 Winston Llenas	.50	.23	.06
☐ 468 Pepe Frias	.50	.23	.06
☐ 469 Joe Decker	.50	.23	.06
☐ 470 Reggie Jackson ALCS	6.00	2.70	.75
☐ 471 Jon Matlack NLCS	1.00	.45	.12
☐ 472 Darold Knowles WS	1.00	.45	.12
☐ 473 Willie Mays WS	7.00	3.10	.85
☐ 474 Bert Campaneris WS	1.00	.45	.12
☐ 475 Rusty Staub WS	1.00	.45	.12
☐ 476 Cleon Jones WS	1.00	.45	.12
☐ 477 Reggie Jackson WS	6.00	2.70	.75
☐ 478 Bert Campaneris WS	1.00	.45	.12
☐ 479 World Series Summary	1.00	.45	.12
A's celebrate; win			
2nd consecutive			
championship			
☐ 480 Willie Crawford	.50	.23	.06
☐ 481 Jerry Terrell	.50	.23	.06
☐ 482 Bob Didier	.50	.23	.06
☐ 483 Atlanta Braves	1.50	.70	.19
Team Card			
☐ 484 Carmen Fanzone	.50	.23	.06
☐ 485 Felipe Alou	1.00	.45	.12
☐ 486 Steve Stone	.75	.35	.09
☐ 487 Ted Martinez	.50	.23	.06
☐ 488 Andy Etchebarren	.50	.23	.06
☐ 489 Pirates Leaders	1.00	.45	.12
Danny Murtaugh MG			
Don Osborn CO			
Don Leppert CO			
Bill Mazeroski CO			
Bob Skinner CO			
☐ 490 Vada Pinson	1.00	.45	.12
☐ 491 Roger Nelson	.50	.23	.06
☐ 492 Mike Rogodzinski	.50	.23	.06
☐ 493 Joe Hoerner	.50	.23	.06
☐ 494 Ed Goodson	.50	.23	.06
☐ 495 Dick McAuliffe	.75	.35	.09
☐ 496 Tom Murphy	.50	.23	.06
☐ 497 Bobby Mitchell	.50	.23	.06
☐ 498 Pat Corrales	.75	.35	.09
☐ 499 Rusty Torres	.50	.23	.06
☐ 500 Lee May	.75	.35	.09
☐ 501 Eddie Leon	.50	.23	.06
☐ 502 Dave LaRoche	.50	.23	.06
☐ 503 Eric Soderholm	.50	.23	.06
☐ 504 Joe Niekro	.75	.35	.09
☐ 505 Bill Buckner	1.00	.45	.12
☐ 506 Ed Farmer	.50	.23	.06
☐ 507 Larry Stahl	.50	.23	.06
☐ 508 Montreal Expos	1.50	.70	.19
Team Card			
☐ 509 Jesse Jefferson	.50	.23	.06
☐ 510 Wayne Garrett	.50	.23	.06
☐ 511 Toby Harrah	.75	.35	.09
☐ 512 Joe Lahoud	.50	.23	.06
☐ 513 Jim Campanis	.50	.23	.06
☐ 514 Paul Schaal	.50	.23	.06
☐ 515 Willie Montanez	.50	.23	.06
☐ 516 Horacio Pina	.50	.23	.06
☐ 517 Mike Hegan	.50	.23	.06
☐ 518 Derrel Thomas	.50	.23	.06
☐ 519 Bill Sharp	.50	.23	.06
☐ 520 Tim McCarver	1.00	.45	.12
☐ 521 Indians Leaders	.75	.35	.09
Ken Aspromonte MG			
Clay Bryant CO			
Tony Pacheco CO			
☐ 522 J.R. Richard	1.00	.45	.12
☐ 523 Cecil Cooper	1.00	.45	.12
☐ 524 Bill Plummer	.50	.23	.06
☐ 525 Clyde Wright	.50	.23	.06
☐ 526 Frank Tepedino	.50	.23	.06
☐ 527 Bobby Darwin	.50	.23	.06
☐ 528 Bill Bonham	.50	.23	.06
☐ 529 Horace Clarke	.75	.35	.09
☐ 530 Mickey Stanley	.75	.35	.09
☐ 531 Expos Leaders	.75	.35	.09
Gene Mauch MG			
Dave Bristol CO			
Cal McLish CO			
Larry Doby CO			
Jerry Zimmerman CO			
☐ 532 Skip Lockwood	.50	.23	.06
☐ 533 Mike Phillips	.50	.23	.06
☐ 534 Eddie Watt	.50	.23	.06
☐ 535 Bob Tolan	.50	.23	.06
☐ 536 Duffy Dyer	.50	.23	.06
☐ 537 Steve Mingori	.50	.23	.06
☐ 538 Cesar Tovar	.50	.23	.06
☐ 539 Lloyd Allen	.50	.23	.06
☐ 540 Bob Robertson	.50	.23	.06
☐ 541 Cleveland Indians	1.50	.70	.19
Team Card			
☐ 542 Rich Gossage	1.50	.70	.19
☐ 543 Danny Cater	.50	.23	.06
☐ 544 Ron Schueler	.50	.23	.06
☐ 545 Billy Conigliaro	.75	.35	.09
☐ 546 Mike Corkins	.50	.23	.06
☐ 547 Glenn Borgmann	.50	.23	.06
☐ 548 Sonny Siebert	.50	.23	.06
☐ 549 Mike Jorgensen	.50	.23	.06
☐ 550 Sam McDowell	.75	.35	.09
☐ 551 Von Joshua	.50	.23	.06
☐ 552 Denny Doyle	.50	.23	.06
☐ 553 Jim Willoughby	.50	.23	.06
☐ 554 Tim Johnson	.50	.23	.06
☐ 555 Woodie Fryman	.50	.23	.06
☐ 556 Dave Campbell	.50	.23	.06
☐ 557 Jim McGlothlin	.50	.23	.06
☐ 558 Bill Fahey	.50	.23	.06
☐ 559 Darrel Chaney	.50	.23	.06
☐ 560 Mike Cuellar	1.00	.45	.12
☐ 561 Ed Kranepool	.75	.35	.09
☐ 562 Jack Aker	.50	.23	.06
☐ 563 Hal McRae	1.00	.45	.12
☐ 564 Mike Ryan	.50	.23	.06
☐ 565 Milt Wilcox	.50	.23	.06
☐ 566 Jackie Hernandez	.50	.23	.06
☐ 567 Boston Red Sox	1.50	.70	.19
Team Card			
☐ 568 Mike Torrez	.75	.35	.09
☐ 569 Rick Dempsey	.75	.35	.09
☐ 570 Ralph Garr	.75	.35	.09
☐ 571 Rich Hand	.50	.23	.06
☐ 572 Enzo Hernandez	.50	.23	.06
☐ 573 Mike Adams	.50	.23	.06
☐ 574 Bill Parsons	.50	.23	.06
☐ 575 Steve Garvey	4.00	1.80	.50
☐ 576 Scipio Spinks	.50	.23	.06
☐ 577 Mike Sadek	.50	.23	.06
☐ 578 Ralph Houk MG	.75	.35	.09
☐ 579 Cecil Upshaw	.50	.23	.06
☐ 580 Jim Spencer	.50	.23	.06
☐ 581 Fred Norman	.50	.23	.06
☐ 582 Bucky Dent	3.00	1.35	.35
☐ 583 Marty Pattin	.50	.23	.06
☐ 584 Ken Rudolph	.50	.23	.06
☐ 585 Merv Rettenmund	.50	.23	.06
☐ 586 Jack Brohamer	.50	.23	.06
☐ 587 Larry Christenson	.50	.23	.06
☐ 588 Hal Lanier	.50	.23	.06
☐ 589 Boots Day	.50	.23	.06
☐ 590 Roger Moret	.50	.23	.06
☐ 591 Sonny Jackson	.50	.23	.06
☐ 592 Ed Bane	.50	.23	.06
☐ 593 Steve Yeager	.75	.35	.09
☐ 594 Leroy Stanton	.50	.23	.06
☐ 595 Steve Blass	.75	.35	.09
☐ 596 Rookie Pitchers	.50	.23	.06
Wayne Garland			
Fred Holdsworth			
Mark Littell			
Dick Pole			
☐ 597 Rookie Shortstops	.75	.35	.09
Dave Chalk			
John Gamble			
Pete MacKanin			
Manny Trillo			
☐ 598 Rookie Outfielders	12.00	5.50	1.50
Dave Augustine			
Ken Griffey			
Steve Ontiveros			
Jim Tyrone			
☐ 599A Rookie Pitchers WAS	1.50	.70	.19
Ron Diorio			
Dave Freisleben			
Frank Riccelli			
Greg Shanahan			
☐ 599B Rookie Pitchers SD	4.00	1.80	.50
(SD in large print)			
☐ 599C Rookie Pitchers SD	6.00	2.70	.75
(SD in small print)			
☐ 600 Rookie Infielders	5.00	2.20	.60
Ron Cash			
Jim Cox			
Bill Madlock			
Reggie Sanders			
☐ 601 Rookie Outfielders	2.50	1.10	.30
Ed Armbrister			
Rich Bladt			
Brian Downing			
Bake McBride			
☐ 602 Rookie Pitchers	.75	.35	.09
Glen Abbott			
Rick Henninger			
Craig Swan			
Dan Vossler			
☐ 603 Rookie Catchers	.75	.35	.09
Barry Foote			
Tom Lundstedt			
Charlie Moore			
Sergio Robles			
☐ 604 Rookie Infielders	5.00	2.20	.60
Terry Hughes			
John Knox			
Andre Thornton			
Frank White			
☐ 605 Rookie Pitchers	4.00	1.80	.50
Vic Albury			
Ken Frailing			
Kevin Kobel			
Frank Tanana			
☐ 606 Rookie Outfielders	.75	.35	.09
Jim Fuller			
Wilbur Howard			
Tommy Smith			
Otto Velez			
☐ 607 Rookie Shortstops	.75	.35	.09
Leo Foster			
Tom Heintzelman			
Dave Rosello			
Frank Taveras			
☐ 608A Rookie Pitchers: ERR	1.50	.70	.19
Bob Apodaco (sic)			
Dick Baney			
John D'Acquisto			
Mike Wallace			
☐ 608B Rookie Pitchers: COR	.75	.35	.09
Bob Apodaca			
Dick Baney			
John D'Acquisto			
Mike Wallace			
☐ 609 Rico Petrocelli	.75	.35	.09
☐ 610 Dave Kingman	1.00	.45	.12
☐ 611 Rich Stelmaszek	.50	.23	.06
☐ 612 Luke Walker	.50	.23	.06
☐ 613 Dan Monzon	.50	.23	.06
☐ 614 Adrian Devine	.50	.23	.06
☐ 615 Johnny Jeter UER	.50	.23	.06
(Misspelled Johnnie			
on card back)			
☐ 616 Larry Gura	.50	.23	.06
☐ 617 Ted Ford	.50	.23	.06
☐ 618 Jim Mason	.50	.23	.06
☐ 619 Mike Anderson	.50	.23	.06
☐ 620 Al Downing	.50	.23	.06
☐ 621 Bernie Carbo	.50	.23	.06
☐ 622 Phil Gagliano	.50	.23	.06
☐ 623 Celerino Sanchez	.50	.23	.06
☐ 624 Bob Miller	.50	.23	.06
☐ 625 Ollie Brown	.50	.23	.06
☐ 626 Pittsburgh Pirates	1.50	.70	.19
Team Card			
☐ 627 Carl Taylor	.50	.23	.06
☐ 628 Ivan Murrell	.50	.23	.06
☐ 629 Rusty Staub	1.00	.45	.12
☐ 630 Tommie Agee	.75	.35	.09
☐ 631 Steve Barber	.50	.23	.06
☐ 632 George Culver	.50	.23	.06
☐ 633 Dave Hamilton	.50	.23	.06
☐ 634 Braves Leaders	1.00	.45	.12
Eddie Mathews MG			
Herm Starrette CO			
Connie Ryan CO			
Jim Busby CO			
Ken Silvestri CO			
☐ 635 Johnny Edwards	.50	.23	.06
☐ 636 Dave Goltz	.50	.23	.06
☐ 637 Checklist 529-660	2.50	.50	.25
☐ 638 Ken Sanders	.50	.23	.06
☐ 639 Joe Lovitto	.50	.23	.06
☐ 640 Milt Pappas	.75	.35	.09
☐ 641 Chuck Brinkman	.50	.23	.06
☐ 642 Terry Harmon	.50	.23	.06
☐ 643 Dodgers Team	1.50	.70	.19
☐ 644 Wayne Granger	.50	.23	.06
☐ 645 Ken Boswell	.50	.23	.06
☐ 646 George Foster	1.50	.70	.19
☐ 647 Juan Beniquez	.50	.23	.06
☐ 648 Terry Crowley	.50	.23	.06
☐ 649 Fernando Gonzalez	.50	.23	.06
☐ 650 Mike Epstein	.50	.23	.06
☐ 651 Leron Lee	.50	.23	.06
☐ 652 Gail Hopkins	.50	.23	.06
☐ 653 Bob Stinson	.50	.23	.06
☐ 654A Jesus Alou ERR	.75	.35	.09
(No position)			
☐ 654B Jesus Alou COR	7.00	3.10	.85
(Outfield)			
☐ 655 Mike Tyson	.50	.23	.06
☐ 656 Adrian Garrett	.50	.23	.06
☐ 657 Jim Shellenback	.50	.23	.06
☐ 658 Lee Lacy	.50	.23	.06
☐ 659 Joe Lis	.50	.23	.06
☐ 660 Larry Dierker	1.00	.23	.06

1974 Topps Traded

The cards in this 44-card set measure 2 1/2" by 3 1/2". The 1974 Topps Traded set contains 43 player cards and one unnumbered checklist card. The fronts have the word "traded" in block letters and the backs are designed in newspaper style. Card numbers are the same as in the regular set except they are followed by a "T." No known scarcities exist for this set. The cards were inserted in all packs toward the end of the production run. They were produced in large enough quantity that they are no scarcer than the regular Topps cards.

	NRMT	VG-E	GOOD
COMPLETE SET (44)	15.00	6.75	1.85
COMMON CARD	.50	.23	.06
☐ 23T Craig Robinson	.50	.23	.06
☐ 42T Claude Osteen	.75	.35	.09
☐ 43T Jim Wynn	.75	.35	.09
☐ 51T Bobby Heise	.50	.23	.06
☐ 59T Ross Grimsley	.50	.23	.06
☐ 62T Bob Locker	.50	.23	.06
☐ 63T Bill Sudakis	.50	.23	.06
☐ 73T Mike Marshall	.75	.35	.09
☐ 123T Nelson Briles	.75	.35	.09

☐ 139T Aurelio Monteagudo	.50	.23	.06
☐ 151T Diego Segui	.50	.23	.06
☐ 165T Willie Davis	.75	.35	.09
☐ 175T Reggie Cleveland	.50	.23	.06
☐ 182T Lindy McDaniel	.75	.35	.09
☐ 186T Fred Scherman	.50	.23	.06
☐ 249T George Mitterwald	.50	.23	.06
☐ 262T Ed Kirkpatrick	.50	.23	.06
☐ 269T Bob Johnson	.50	.23	.06
☐ 270T Ron Santo	1.00	.45	.12
☐ 313T Barry Lersch	.50	.23	.06
☐ 319T Randy Hundley	.75	.35	.09
☐ 330T Juan Marichal	2.00	.90	.25
☐ 348T Pete Richert	.50	.23	.06
☐ 373T John Curtis	.50	.23	.06
☐ 390T Lou Piniella	1.00	.45	.12
☐ 428T Gary Sutherland	.50	.23	.06
☐ 454T Kurt Bevacqua	.50	.23	.06
☐ 458T Jim Ray	.50	.23	.06
☐ 485T Felipe Alou	1.00	.45	.12
☐ 486T Steve Stone	.75	.35	.09
☐ 496T Tom Murphy	.50	.23	.06
☐ 516T Horacio Pina	.50	.23	.06
☐ 534T Eddie Watt	.50	.23	.06
☐ 538T Cesar Tovar	.50	.23	.06
☐ 544T Ron Schueler	.50	.23	.06
☐ 579T Cecil Upshaw	.50	.23	.06
☐ 585T Merv Rettenmund	.50	.23	.06
☐ 612T Luke Walker	.50	.23	.06
☐ 616T Larry Gura	.75	.35	.09
☐ 618T Jim Mason	.50	.23	.06
☐ 630T Tommie Agee	.75	.35	.09
☐ 648T Terry Crowley	.50	.23	.06
☐ 649T Fernando Gonzalez	.50	.23	.06
☐ NNO Traded Checklist	1.50	.30	.15

1974 Topps Team Checklists

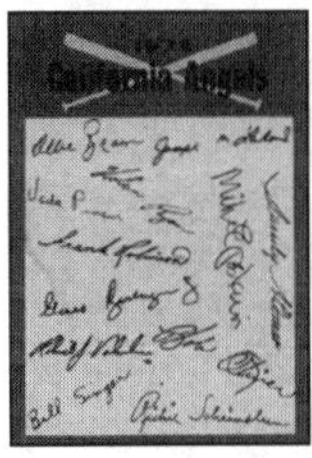

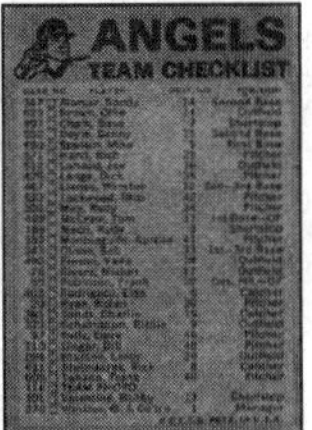

The cards in this 24-card set measure 2 1/2" by 3 1/2". The 1974 series of checklists was issued in packs with the regular cards for that year. The cards are unnumbered (arbitrarily numbered below alphabetically by team name) and have bright red borders. The year and team name appear in a green panel decorated by a crossed bats design, below which is a white area containing facsimile autographs of various players. The mustard-yellow and gray-colored backs list team members alphabetically, along with their card number, uniform number and position. Uncut sheets of these cards were also available through a wrapper mail-in offer. The uncut sheet value in NR/Mt or better condition is approximately $150.

	NRMT	VG-E	GOOD
COMPLETE SET (24)	20.00	9.00	2.50
COMMON TEAM (1-24)	1.00	.30	.10
☐ 1 Atlanta Braves	1.00	.30	.10
☐ 2 Baltimore Orioles	1.00	.30	.10
☐ 3 Boston Red Sox	1.00	.30	.10
☐ 4 California Angels	1.00	.30	.10
☐ 5 Chicago Cubs	1.00	.30	.10
☐ 6 Chicago White Sox	1.00	.30	.10
☐ 7 Cincinnati Reds	1.00	.30	.10
☐ 8 Cleveland Indians	1.00	.30	.10
☐ 9 Detroit Tigers	1.00	.30	.10
☐ 10 Houston Astros	1.00	.30	.10
☐ 11 Kansas City Royals	1.00	.30	.10
☐ 12 Los Angeles Dodgers	1.00	.30	.10
☐ 13 Milwaukee Brewers	1.00	.30	.10
☐ 14 Minnesota Twins	1.00	.30	.10
☐ 15 Montreal Expos	1.00	.30	.10
☐ 16 New York Mets	1.00	.30	.10
☐ 17 New York Yankees	1.00	.30	.10
☐ 18 Oakland A's	1.00	.30	.10
☐ 19 Philadelphia Phillies	1.00	.30	.10
☐ 20 Pittsburgh Pirates	1.00	.30	.10
☐ 21 San Diego Padres	1.00	.30	.10
☐ 22 San Francisco Giants	1.00	.30	.10
☐ 23 St. Louis Cardinals	1.00	.30	.10
☐ 24 Texas Rangers	1.00	.30	.10

1974 Topps Deckle Edge

The cards in this 72-card set measure 2 7/8" by 5". Returning to a format first used in 1969, Topps produced a set of black and white photo cards in 1974 bearing an unusual serrated or "deckle" border. A facsimile autograph appears on the obverse while the backs contain the card number and a "newspaper-clipping" design detailing a milestone in the player's career. This was a test set and uncut sheets are sometimes found. Card backs are either white or gray; the white back cards are slightly tougher to obtain. The wrapper is also considered collectible. Wrappers featured either Reggie Jackson or Tom Seaver and come with or without the phrase "With gum". Wrappers with the usual folds which are in Nr Mt condition have an approximate value of $20.

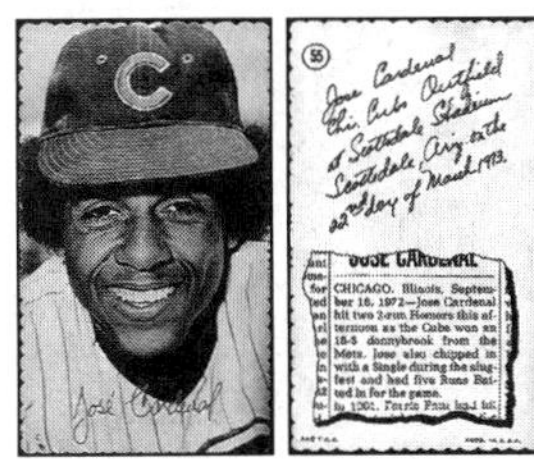

	NRMT	VG-E	GOOD
COMPLETE SET (72)	3000.00	1350.00	375.00
COMMON CARD (1-72)	15.00	6.75	1.85
☐ 1 Amos Otis	25.00	11.00	3.10
☐ 2 Darrell Evans	25.00	11.00	3.10
☐ 3 Bob Gibson	100.00	45.00	12.50
☐ 4 Dave Nelson	15.00	6.75	1.85
☐ 5 Steve Carlton	125.00	55.00	15.50
☐ 6 Jim Hunter	100.00	45.00	12.50
☐ 7 Thurman Munson	150.00	70.00	19.00
☐ 8 Bob Grich	25.00	11.00	3.10
☐ 9 Tom Seaver	200.00	90.00	25.00
☐ 10 Ted Simmons	25.00	11.00	3.10
☐ 11 Bobby Valentine	25.00	11.00	3.10
☐ 12 Don Sutton	50.00	22.00	6.25
☐ 13 Wilbur Wood	15.00	6.75	1.85
☐ 14 Doug Rader	15.00	6.75	1.85
☐ 15 Chris Chambliss	15.00	6.75	1.85
☐ 16 Pete Rose	175.00	80.00	22.00
☐ 17 John Hiller	15.00	6.75	1.85
☐ 18 Burt Hooton	15.00	6.75	1.85
☐ 19 Tim Foli	15.00	6.75	1.85
☐ 20 Lou Brock	100.00	45.00	12.50
☐ 21 Ron Bryant	15.00	6.75	1.85
☐ 22 Manny Sanguillen	15.00	6.75	1.85
☐ 23 Bob Tolan	15.00	6.75	1.85
☐ 24 Greg Luzinski	25.00	11.00	3.10
☐ 25 Brooks Robinson	125.00	55.00	15.50
☐ 26 Felix Millan	15.00	6.75	1.85
☐ 27 Luis Tiant	25.00	11.00	3.10
☐ 28 Willie McCovey	100.00	45.00	12.50
☐ 29 Chris Speier	15.00	6.75	1.85
☐ 30 George Scott	15.00	6.75	1.85
☐ 31 Willie Stargell	75.00	34.00	9.50
☐ 32 Rod Carew	125.00	55.00	15.50
☐ 33 Charlie Spikes	15.00	6.75	1.85
☐ 34 Nate Colbert	15.00	6.75	1.85
☐ 35 Rich Hebner	15.00	6.75	1.85
☐ 36 Bobby Bonds	25.00	11.00	3.10
☐ 37 Buddy Bell	25.00	11.00	3.10
☐ 38 Claude Osteen	15.00	6.75	1.85
☐ 39 Dick Allen	25.00	11.00	3.10
☐ 40 Bill Russell	15.00	6.75	1.85
☐ 41 Nolan Ryan	1000.00	450.00	125.00
☐ 42 Willie Davis	15.00	6.75	1.85
☐ 43 Carl Yastrzemski	125.00	55.00	15.50
☐ 44 Jon Matlack	15.00	6.75	1.85
☐ 45 Jim Palmer	100.00	45.00	12.50
☐ 46 Bert Campaneris	15.00	6.75	1.85
☐ 47 Bert Blyleven	25.00	11.00	3.10
☐ 48 Jeff Burroughs	15.00	6.75	1.85
☐ 49 Jim Colborn	15.00	6.75	1.85
☐ 50 Dave Johnson	25.00	11.00	3.10
☐ 51 John Mayberry	15.00	6.75	1.85
☐ 52 Don Kessinger	15.00	6.75	1.85
☐ 53 Joe Coleman	15.00	6.75	1.85
☐ 54 Tony Perez	60.00	27.00	7.50
☐ 55 Jose Cardenal	15.00	6.75	1.85
☐ 56 Paul Splittorff	15.00	6.75	1.85
☐ 57 Hank Aaron	150.00	70.00	19.00
☐ 58 Dave May	15.00	6.75	1.85
☐ 59 Fergie Jenkins	100.00	45.00	12.50
☐ 60 Ron Blomberg	15.00	6.75	1.85
☐ 61 Reggie Jackson	175.00	80.00	22.00
☐ 62 Tony Oliva	25.00	11.00	3.10
☐ 63 Bobby Murcer	25.00	11.00	3.10
☐ 64 Carlton Fisk	100.00	45.00	12.50
☐ 65 Steve Rogers	15.00	6.75	1.85
☐ 66 Frank Robinson	125.00	55.00	15.50
☐ 67 Joe Ferguson	15.00	6.75	1.85
☐ 68 Bill Melton	15.00	6.75	1.85
☐ 69 Bob Watson	15.00	6.75	1.85
☐ 70 Larry Bowa	25.00	11.00	3.10
☐ 71 Johnny Bench	150.00	70.00	19.00
☐ 72 Willie Horton	15.00	6.75	1.85

1974 Topps Puzzles

This set of 12 jigsaw puzzles was supposedly distributed by Topps in 1974 as a test issue. Each puzzle measures approximately 5" by 7 1/8" and shows a colorful picture of the player inside a white border. Puzzles contained 40 pieces. The wrapper for the puzzles is also collectible as it shows a picture of Tom Seaver. The wrapper comes 2 ways: either with a pre-printed price of 29 cents or 25 cents. The 29 cent wrapper is valued at about $20 while the 25 cent wrapper is valued at approximately $75.The puzzles are blank backed and unnumbered; they are listed below alphabetically.

	NRMT	VG-E	GOOD
COMPLETE SET (12)	1250.00	550.00	160.00
COMMON CARD (1-12)	35.00	16.00	4.40
☐ 1 Hank Aaron	150.00	70.00	19.00
☐ 2 Dick Allen	35.00	16.00	4.40
☐ 3 Johnny Bench	125.00	55.00	15.50
☐ 4 Bobby Bonds	35.00	16.00	4.40
☐ 5 Bob Gibson	75.00	34.00	9.50
☐ 6 Reggie Jackson	175.00	80.00	22.00
☐ 7 Bobby Murcer	35.00	16.00	4.40
☐ 8 Jim Palmer	75.00	34.00	9.50
☐ 9 Nolan Ryan	600.00	275.00	75.00
☐ 10 Tom Seaver	125.00	55.00	15.50
☐ 11 Willie Stargell	75.00	34.00	9.50
☐ 12 Carl Yastrzemski	100.00	45.00	12.50

1974 Topps Stamps

The 240 color portraits depicted on stamps in this 1974 Topps series have the player's name, team and position inside an oval below the picture area. Each stamp measures 1" by 1 1/2". The stamps were marketed in strips of six, along with an album, in their own wrapper. The booklets have eight pages and measure 2 1/2" by 3 7/8". There are 24 albums, one for each team, designed to hold 10 stamps apiece. The stamps are numbered here alphabetically within each team and the teams are listed in alphabetical order within league, e.g., Atlanta Braves NL (1-10), Chicago Cubs (11-20), Cincinnati Reds (21-30), Houston Astros (31-40), Los Angeles Dodgers (41-50), Montreal Expos (51-60), New York Mets (61-70), Philadelphia Phillies (71-80), Pittsburgh Pirates (81-90), San Diego Padres (91-100), San Francisco Giants (101-110), St. Louis Cardinals (111-120), Baltimore Orioles AL (121-130), Boston Red Sox (131-140), California Angels (141-150), Chicago White Sox (151-160), Cleveland Indians (161-170), Detroit Tigers (171-180), Kansas City Royals (181-190), Milwaukee Brewers (191-200), Minnesota Twins (201-210), New York Yankees (211-220), Oakland A's (221-230) and Texas Rangers (231-240).

	NRMT	VG-E	GOOD
COMPLETE SET (240)	125.00	55.00	15.50
COMMON STAMP (1-240)	.15	.07	.02
☐ 1 Hank Aaron	10.00	4.50	1.25
☐ 2 Dusty Baker	.25	.11	.03
☐ 3 Darrell Evans	.50	.23	.06
☐ 4 Ralph Garr	.25	.11	.03
☐ 5 Roric Harrison	.15	.07	.02
☐ 6 Dave Johnson	.75	.35	.09
☐ 7 Mike Lum	.15	.07	.02
☐ 8 Carl Morton	.15	.07	.02
☐ 9 Phil Niekro	3.00	1.35	.35
☐ 10 Johnny Oates	.15	.07	.02
☐ 11 Glenn Beckert	.15	.07	.02
☐ 12 Jose Cardenal	.15	.07	.02
☐ 13 Vic Harris	.15	.07	.02
☐ 14 Burt Hooton	.15	.07	.02
☐ 15 Randy Hundley	.15	.07	.02
☐ 16 Don Kessinger	.25	.11	.03
☐ 17 Rick Monday	.25	.11	.03
☐ 18 Rick Reuschel	.75	.35	.09
☐ 19 Ron Santo	1.00	.45	.12
☐ 20 Billy Williams	3.00	1.35	.35
☐ 21 Johnny Bench	6.00	2.70	.75
☐ 22 Jack Billingham	.15	.07	.02
☐ 23 Pedro Borbon	.15	.07	.02
☐ 24 Dave Concepcion	1.00	.45	.12
☐ 25 Dan Driessen	.25	.11	.03
☐ 26 Cesar Geronimo	.15	.07	.02
☐ 27 Don Gullett	.25	.11	.03
☐ 28 Joe Morgan	4.00	1.80	.50
☐ 29 Tony Perez	1.00	.45	.12
☐ 30 Pete Rose	10.00	4.50	1.25
☐ 31 Cesar Cedeno	.25	.11	.03
☐ 32 Tommy Helms	.15	.07	.02
☐ 33 Lee May	.25	.11	.03
☐ 34 Roger Metzger	.15	.07	.02
☐ 35 Doug Rader	.15	.07	.02
☐ 36 J.R. Richard	.25	.11	.03
☐ 37 Dave Roberts	.15	.07	.02
☐ 38 Jerry Reuss	.25	.11	.03
☐ 39 Bob Watson	.25	.11	.03
☐ 40 Jim Wynn	.25	.11	.03
☐ 41 Bill Buckner	.50	.23	.06
☐ 42 Ron Cey	.50	.23	.06
☐ 43 Willie Crawford	.15	.07	.02
☐ 44 Willie Davis	.25	.11	.03
☐ 45 Joe Ferguson	.15	.07	.02
☐ 46 Davey Lopes	.25	.11	.03
☐ 47 Andy Messersmith	.25	.11	.03
☐ 48 Claude Osteen	.25	.11	.03
☐ 49 Bill Russell	.25	.11	.03
☐ 50 Don Sutton	2.00	.90	.25
☐ 51 Bob Bailey	.15	.07	.02
☐ 52 John Boccabella	.15	.07	.02
☐ 53 Ron Fairly	.25	.11	.03
☐ 54 Tim Foli	.15	.07	.02
☐ 55 Ron Hunt	.15	.07	.02
☐ 56 Mike Jorgensen	.15	.07	.02
☐ 57 Mike Marshall	.25	.11	.03
☐ 58 Steve Renko	.15	.07	.02
☐ 59 Steve Rogers	.25	.11	.03
☐ 60 Ken Singleton	.50	.23	.06
☐ 61 Wayne Garrett	.15	.07	.02
☐ 62 Jerry Grote	.15	.07	.02
☐ 63 Bud Harrelson	.25	.11	.03
☐ 64 Cleon Jones	.15	.07	.02
☐ 65 Jerry Koosman	.75	.35	.09
☐ 66 Jon Matlack	.25	.11	.03
☐ 67 Tug McGraw	.75	.35	.09
☐ 68 Felix Millan	.15	.07	.02
☐ 69 John Milner	.15	.07	.02
☐ 70 Tom Seaver	6.00	2.70	.75
☐ 71 Bob Boone	.75	.35	.09
☐ 72 Larry Bowa	.50	.23	.06
☐ 73 Steve Carlton	6.00	2.70	.75
☐ 74 Bill Grabarkewitz	.15	.07	.02
☐ 75 Jim Lonborg	.25	.11	.03
☐ 76 Greg Luzinski	.50	.23	.06
☐ 77 Willie Montanez	.15	.07	.02
☐ 78 Bill Robinson	.25	.11	.03
☐ 79 Wayne Twitchell	.15	.07	.02
☐ 80 Del Unser	.15	.07	.02
☐ 81 Nelson Briles	.25	.11	.03
☐ 82 Dock Ellis	.15	.07	.02
☐ 83 Dave Giusti	.15	.07	.02
☐ 84 Richie Hebner	.15	.07	.02
☐ 85 Al Oliver	.50	.23	.06
☐ 86 Dave Parker	3.00	1.35	.35
☐ 87 Manny Sanguillen	.25	.11	.03
☐ 88 Willie Stargell	4.00	1.80	.50
☐ 89 Rennie Stennett	.15	.07	.02
☐ 90 Richie Zisk	.25	.11	.03
☐ 91 Nate Colbert	.15	.07	.02
☐ 92 Bill Grief	.15	.07	.02
☐ 93 Johnny Grubb	.15	.07	.02
☐ 94 Randy Jones	.25	.11	.03
☐ 95 Fred Kendall	.15	.07	.02
☐ 96 Clay Kirby	.15	.07	.02
☐ 97 Willie McCovey	4.00	1.80	.50
☐ 98 Jerry Morales	.15	.07	.02
☐ 99 Dave Roberts	.15	.07	.02
☐ 100 Dave Winfield	10.00	4.50	1.25
☐ 101 Bobby Bonds	.75	.35	.09
☐ 102 Tom Bradley	.15	.07	.02
☐ 103 Ron Bryant	.15	.07	.02
☐ 104 Tito Fuentes	.15	.07	.02
☐ 105 Ed Goodson	.15	.07	.02
☐ 106 Dave Kingman	1.00	.45	.12
☐ 107 Garry Maddox	.25	.11	.03
☐ 108 Dave Rader	.15	.07	.02
☐ 109 Elias Sosa	.15	.07	.02
☐ 110 Chris Speier	.25	.11	.03
☐ 111 Lou Brock	4.00	1.80	.50
☐ 112 Reggie Cleveland	.15	.07	.02
☐ 113 Jose Cruz	.50	.23	.06
☐ 114 Bob Gibson	4.00	1.80	.50
☐ 115 Tim McCarver	.50	.23	.06
☐ 116 Ted Simmons	.50	.23	.06
☐ 117 Ted Sizemore	.15	.07	.02
☐ 118 Reggie Smith	.25	.11	.03
☐ 119 Joe Torre	.75	.35	.09
☐ 120 Mike Tyson	.15	.07	.02
☐ 121 Don Baylor	.75	.35	.09
☐ 122 Mark Belanger	.25	.11	.03
☐ 123 Paul Blair	.15	.07	.02
☐ 124 Tommy Davis	.25	.11	.03
☐ 125 Bobby Grich	.25	.11	.03
☐ 126 Grant Jackson	.15	.07	.02
☐ 127 Dave McNally	.25	.11	.03
☐ 128 Jim Palmer	3.00	1.35	.35
☐ 129 Brooks Robinson	5.00	2.20	.60
☐ 130 Earl Williams	.15	.07	.02
☐ 131 Luis Aparicio	3.00	1.35	.35
☐ 132 Orlando Cepeda	2.00	.90	.25
☐ 133 Carlton Fisk	5.00	2.20	.60
☐ 134 Tommy Harper	.15	.07	.02
☐ 135 Bill Lee	.25	.11	.03
☐ 136 Rick Miller	.15	.07	.02
☐ 137 Roger Moret	.15	.07	.02
☐ 138 Luis Tiant	.75	.35	.09
☐ 139 Rick Wise	.15	.07	.02
☐ 140 Carl Yastrzemski	6.00	2.70	.75
☐ 141 Sandy Alomar	.15	.07	.02
☐ 142 Mike Epstein	.15	.07	.02
☐ 143 Bob Oliver	.15	.07	.02
☐ 144 Vada Pinson	.50	.23	.06
☐ 145 Frank Robinson	5.00	2.20	.60
☐ 146 Ellie Rodriguez	.15	.07	.02
☐ 147 Nolan Ryan	20.00	9.00	2.50
☐ 148 Richie Scheinblum	.15	.07	.02
☐ 149 Bill Singer	.15	.07	.02
☐ 150 Bobby Valentine	.75	.35	.09
☐ 151 Dick Allen	.75	.35	.09
☐ 152 Stan Bahnsen	.15	.07	.02
☐ 153 Terry Forster	.25	.11	.03
☐ 154 Ken Henderson	.15	.07	.02
☐ 155 Ed Herrmann	.15	.07	.02
☐ 156 Pat Kelly	.15	.07	.02
☐ 157 Carlos May	.15	.07	.02
☐ 158 Bill Melton	.15	.07	.02
☐ 159 Jorge Orta	.15	.07	.02

160 Wilbur Wood	.25	.11	.03
161 Buddy Bell	.75	.35	.09
162 Chris Chambliss	.50	.23	.06
163 Frank Duffy	.15	.07	.02
164 Dave Duncan	.15	.07	.02
165 John Ellis	.15	.07	.02
166 Oscar Gamble	.25	.11	.03
167 George Hendrick	.25	.11	.03
168 Gaylord Perry	3.00	1.35	.35
169 Charlie Spikes	.15	.07	.02
170 Dick Tidrow	.15	.07	.02
171 Ed Brinkman	.15	.07	.02
172 Norm Cash	.75	.35	.09
173 Joe Coleman	.15	.07	.02
174 Bill Freehan	.50	.23	.06
175 John Hiller	.25	.11	.03
176 Willie Horton	.25	.11	.03
177 Al Kaline	6.00	2.70	.75
178 Mickey Lolich	.75	.35	.09
179 Aurelio Rodriguez	.15	.07	.02
180 Mickey Stanley	.15	.07	.02
181 Steve Busby	.25	.11	.03
182 Fran Healy	.15	.07	.02
183 Ed Kirkpatrick	.15	.07	.02
184 John Mayberry	.25	.11	.03
185 Amos Otis	.50	.23	.06
186 Fred Patek	.15	.07	.02
187 Marty Pattin	.15	.07	.02
188 Lou Piniella	.75	.35	.09
189 Cookie Rojas	.15	.07	.02
190 Paul Splittorff	.15	.07	.02
191 Jerry Bell	.15	.07	.02
192 Johnny Briggs	.15	.07	.02
193 Jim Colborn	.15	.07	.02
194 Bob Collucio	.15	.07	.02
195 Pedro Garcia	.15	.07	.02
196 Dave May	.15	.07	.02
197 Don Money	.15	.07	.02
198 Darrell Porter	.25	.11	.03
199 George Scott	.25	.11	.03
200 Jim Slaton	.15	.07	.02
201 Bert Blyleven	.75	.35	.09
202 Steve Braun	.15	.07	.02
203 Rod Carew	6.00	2.70	.75
204 Ray Corbin	.15	.07	.02
205 Bobby Darwin	.15	.07	.02
206 Joe Decker	.15	.07	.02
207 Jim Holt	.15	.07	.02
208 Harmon Killebrew	4.00	1.80	.50
209 George Mitterwald	.15	.07	.02
210 Tony Oliva	1.00	.45	.12
211 Ron Blomberg	.15	.07	.02
212 Sparky Lyle	.50	.23	.06
213 George Medich	.15	.07	.02
214 Gene Michael	.15	.07	.02
215 Thurman Munson	5.00	2.20	.60
216 Bobby Murcer	.50	.23	.06
217 Graig Nettles	.75	.35	.09
218 Mel Stottlemyre	.50	.23	.06
219 Otto Velez	.15	.07	.02
220 Roy White	.25	.11	.03
221 Sal Bando	.25	.11	.03
222 Vida Blue	.75	.35	.09
223 Bert Campaneris	.25	.11	.03
224 Ken Holtzman	.25	.11	.03
225 Jim Hunter	3.00	1.35	.35
226 Reggie Jackson	8.00	3.60	1.00
227 Deron Johnson	.15	.07	.02
228 Bill North	.15	.07	.02
229 Joe Rudi	.25	.11	.03
230 Gene Tenace	.25	.11	.03
231 Jim Bibby	.15	.07	.02
232 Jeff Burroughs	.25	.11	.03
233 David Clyde	.15	.07	.02
234 Jim Fregosi	.50	.23	.06
235 Toby Harrah	.25	.11	.03
236 Ferguson Jenkins	3.00	1.35	.35
237 Alex Johnson	.15	.07	.02
238 Dave Nelson	.15	.07	.02
239 Jim Spencer	.15	.07	.02
240 Bill Sudakis	.15	.07	.02

1974 Topps Stamp Albums

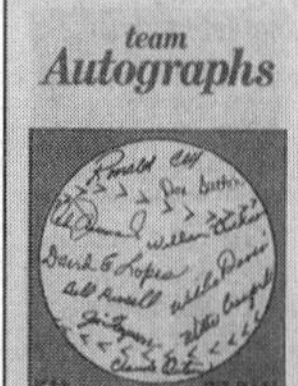

The 1974 Topps stamp set of baseball player stamps was intended to be mounted in 24 separate team albums, 10 stamps for that team's players going into that team's album. The albums measure approximately 2 1/2" by 3 1/2".

	NRMT	VG-E	GOOD
COMPLETE SET (24)	120.00	55.00	15.00
COMMON TEAM (1-24)	5.00	2.20	.60
1 Atlanta Braves	5.00	2.20	.60
2 Baltimore Orioles	5.00	2.20	.60
3 Boston Red Sox	5.00	2.20	.60
4 California Angels	5.00	2.20	.60
5 Chicago Cubs	5.00	2.20	.60
6 Chicago White Sox	5.00	2.20	.60
7 Cincinnati Reds	5.00	2.20	.60
8 Cleveland Indians	5.00	2.20	.60
9 Detroit Tigers	5.00	2.20	.60
10 Houston Astros	5.00	2.20	.60
11 Kansas City Royals	5.00	2.20	.60
12 Los Angeles Dodgers	5.00	2.20	.60
13 Milwaukee Brewers	5.00	2.20	.60
14 Minnesota Twins	5.00	2.20	.60
15 Montreal Expos	5.00	2.20	.60
16 New York Mets	5.00	2.20	.60
17 New York Yankees	6.00	2.70	.75
18 Oakland A's	5.00	2.20	.60
19 Philadelphia Phillies	5.00	2.20	.60
20 Pittsburgh Pirates	5.00	2.20	.60
21 San Diego Padres	5.00	2.20	.60
22 San Francisco Giants	5.00	2.20	.60
23 St. Louis Cardinals	5.00	2.20	.60
24 Texas Rangers	5.00	2.20	.60

1975 Topps

The cards in the 1975 Topps set were issued in two different sizes: a regular standard size (2 1/2" by 3 1/2") and a mini size (2 1/2" by 3 1/8") which was issued as a test in certain areas of the country. The 660-card Topps baseball set for 1975 was radically different in appearance from sets of the preceding years. The most prominent change was the use of a two-color frame surrounding the picture area rather than a single, subdued color. A facsimile autograph appears on the picture, and the backs are printed in red and green on gray. Cards were released in ten-card wax packs as well as in 42-card rack packs. Cards 189-212 depict the MVP's of both leagues from 1951 through 1974. The first seven cards (1-7) feature players (listed in alphabetical order) breaking records or achieving milestones during the previous season. Cards 306-313 picture league leaders in various statistical categories. Cards 459-466 depict the results of post-season action. Team cards feature a checklist back for players on that team and show a small inset photo of the manager on the front. The following players' regular issue cards are explicitly denoted as All-Stars, 1, 50, 80, 140, 170, 180, 260, 320, 350, 390, 400, 420, 440, 470, 530, 570, and 600. This set is quite popular with collectors, at least in part due to the fact that the Rookie Cards of George Brett, Gary Carter, Keith Hernandez, Fred Lynn, Jim Rice and Robin Yount are all in the set. Topps minis have the same checklist and are valued approximately 1.5 times the prices listed below.

	NRMT	VG-E	GOOD
COMPLETE SET (660)	800.00	350.00	100.00
COMMON CARD (1-660)	.50	.23	.06
WRAPPER (15-CENT)	10.00	4.50	1.25
1 Hank Aaron RB Sets Homer Mark	30.00	10.00	5.00
2 Lou Brock RB 118 Stolen Bases	3.50	1.55	.45
3 Bob Gibson RB 3000th Strikeout	3.50	1.55	.45
4 Al Kaline RB 3000 Hit Club	4.00	1.80	.50
5 Nolan Ryan RB Fans 300 for 3rd Year in a Row	30.00	13.50	3.70
6 Mike Marshall RB Hurls 106 Games	.75	.35	.09
7 Steve Busby HL Dick Bosman Nolan Ryan	12.00	5.50	1.50
8 Rogelio Moret	.50	.23	.06
9 Frank Tepedino	.50	.23	.06
10 Willie Davis	.75	.35	.09
11 Bill Melton	.50	.23	.06
12 David Clyde	.50	.23	.06
13 Gene Locklear	.75	.35	.09
14 Milt Wilcox	.50	.23	.06
15 Jose Cardenal	.75	.35	.09
16 Frank Tanana	1.50	.70	.19
17 Dave Concepcion	1.50	.70	.19
18 Tigers: Team/Mgr. Ralph Houk (Checklist back)	2.00	.40	.20
19 Jerry Koosman	.75	.35	.09
20 Thurman Munson	6.00	2.70	.75
21 Rollie Fingers	3.00	1.35	.35
22 Dave Cash	.50	.23	.06
23 Bill Russell	.75	.35	.09
24 Al Fitzmorris	.50	.23	.06
25 Lee May	.75	.35	.09
26 Dave McNally	.75	.35	.09
27 Ken Reitz	.50	.23	.06
28 Tom Murphy	.50	.23	.06
29 Dave Parker	4.00	1.80	.50
30 Bert Blyleven	1.00	.45	.12
31 Dave Rader	.50	.23	.06
32 Reggie Cleveland	.50	.23	.06
33 Dusty Baker	1.50	.70	.19
34 Steve Renko	.50	.23	.06
35 Ron Santo	1.00	.45	.12
36 Joe Lovitto	.50	.23	.06
37 Dave Freisleben	.50	.23	.06
38 Buddy Bell	1.00	.45	.12
39 Andre Thornton	.75	.35	.09
40 Bill Singer	.50	.23	.06
41 Cesar Geronimo	.75	.35	.09
42 Joe Coleman	.50	.23	.06
43 Cleon Jones	.75	.35	.09
44 Pat Dobson	.50	.23	.06
45 Joe Rudi	.75	.35	.09
46 Phillies: Team/Mgr. Danny Ozark UER (Checklist back) (Terry Harmon listed as 339 instead of 399)	2.00	.40	.20
47 Tommy John	1.50	.70	.19
48 Freddie Patek	.75	.35	.09
49 Larry Dierker	.50	.23	.06
50 Brooks Robinson	6.00	2.70	.75
51 Bob Forsch	.50	.23	.06
52 Darrell Porter	.75	.35	.09
53 Dave Giusti	.50	.23	.06
54 Eric Soderholm	.50	.23	.06
55 Bobby Bonds	1.50	.70	.19
56 Rick Wise	.75	.35	.09
57 Dave Johnson	.75	.35	.09
58 Chuck Taylor	.50	.23	.06
59 Ken Henderson	.50	.23	.06
60 Fergie Jenkins	3.00	1.35	.35
61 Dave Winfield	50.00	22.00	6.25
62 Fritz Peterson	.50	.23	.06
63 Steve Swisher	.50	.23	.06
64 Dave Chalk	.50	.23	.06
65 Don Gullett	.75	.35	.09
66 Willie Horton	.75	.35	.09
67 Tug McGraw	.75	.35	.09
68 Ron Blomberg	.50	.23	.06
69 John Odom	.50	.23	.06
70 Mike Schmidt	50.00	22.00	6.25
71 Charlie Hough	1.00	.45	.12
72 Royals: Team/Mgr. Jack McKeon (Checklist back)	2.00	.40	.20
73 J.R. Richard	.75	.35	.09
74 Mark Belanger	.75	.35	.09
75 Ted Simmons	1.00	.45	.12
76 Ed Sprague	.50	.23	.06
77 Richie Zisk	.75	.35	.09
78 Ray Corbin	.50	.23	.06
79 Gary Matthews	.75	.35	.09
80 Carlton Fisk	12.00	5.50	1.50
81 Ron Reed	.50	.23	.06
82 Pat Kelly	.50	.23	.06
83 Jim Merritt	.50	.23	.06
84 Enzo Hernandez	.50	.23	.06
85 Bill Bonham	.50	.23	.06
86 Joe Lis	.50	.23	.06
87 George Foster	1.50	.70	.19
88 Tom Egan	.50	.23	.06
89 Jim Ray	.50	.23	.06
90 Rusty Staub	1.00	.45	.12
91 Dick Green	.50	.23	.06
92 Cecil Upshaw	.50	.23	.06
93 Dave Lopes	1.00	.45	.12
94 Jim Lonborg	.75	.35	.09
95 John Mayberry	.75	.35	.09
96 Mike Cosgrove	.50	.23	.06
97 Earl Williams	.50	.23	.06
98 Rich Folkers	.50	.23	.06
99 Mike Hegan	.50	.23	.06
100 Willie Stargell	4.00	1.80	.50
101 Expos: Team/Mgr. Gene Mauch (Checklist back)	2.00	.40	.20
102 Joe Decker	.50	.23	.06
103 Rick Miller	.50	.23	.06
104 Bill Madlock	1.00	.45	.12
105 Buzz Capra	.50	.23	.06
106 Mike Hargrove	3.00	1.35	.35
107 Jim Barr	.50	.23	.06
108 Tom Hall	.50	.23	.06
109 George Hendrick	.75	.35	.09
110 Wilbur Wood	.50	.23	.06
111 Wayne Garrett	.50	.23	.06
112 Larry Hardy	.50	.23	.06
113 Elliott Maddox	.50	.23	.06
114 Dick Lange	.50	.23	.06
115 Joe Ferguson	.50	.23	.06
116 Lerrin LaGrow	.50	.23	.06
117 Orioles: Team/Mgr. Earl Weaver (Checklist back)	2.00	.40	.20
118 Mike Anderson	.50	.23	.06
119 Tommy Helms	.50	.23	.06
120 Steve Busby UER (Photo actually Fran Healy)	.75	.35	.09
121 Bill North	.50	.23	.06
122 Al Hrabosky	.75	.35	.09
123 Johnny Briggs	.50	.23	.06
124 Jerry Reuss	.75	.35	.09
125 Ken Singleton	.75	.35	.09
126 Checklist 1-132	2.00	.40	.20
127 Glenn Borgmann	.50	.23	.06
128 Bill Lee	.75	.35	.09
129 Rick Monday	.75	.35	.09
130 Phil Niekro	2.50	1.10	.30
131 Toby Harrah	.75	.35	.09
132 Randy Moffitt	.50	.23	.06
133 Dan Driessen	.75	.35	.09
134 Ron Hodges	.50	.23	.06
135 Charlie Spikes	.50	.23	.06
136 Jim Mason	.50	.23	.06
137 Terry Forster	.75	.35	.09
138 Del Unser	.50	.23	.06
139 Horacio Pina	.50	.23	.06
140 Steve Garvey	5.00	2.20	.60
141 Mickey Stanley	.75	.35	.09
142 Bob Reynolds	.50	.23	.06
143 Cliff Johnson	.75	.35	.09
144 Jim Wohlford	.50	.23	.06
145 Ken Holtzman	.75	.35	.09
146 Padres: Team/Mgr. John McNamara (Checklist back)	2.00	.40	.20
147 Pedro Garcia	.50	.23	.06
148 Jim Rooker	.50	.23	.06
149 Tim Foli	.50	.23	.06
150 Bob Gibson	5.00	2.20	.60
151 Steve Brye	.50	.23	.06
152 Mario Guerrero	.50	.23	.06
153 Rick Reuschel	.75	.35	.09
154 Mike Lum	.50	.23	.06
155 Jim Bibby	.50	.23	.06
156 Dave Kingman	1.00	.45	.12
157 Pedro Borbon	.75	.35	.09
158 Jerry Grote	.50	.23	.06
159 Steve Arlin	.50	.23	.06
160 Graig Nettles	1.50	.70	.19
161 Stan Bahnsen	.50	.23	.06
162 Willie Montanez	.50	.23	.06
163 Jim Brewer	.50	.23	.06
164 Mickey Rivers	.75	.35	.09
165 Doug Rader	.75	.35	.09
166 Woodie Fryman	.50	.23	.06
167 Rich Coggins	.50	.23	.06
168 Bill Greif	.50	.23	.06
169 Cookie Rojas	.75	.35	.09
170 Bert Campaneris	.75	.35	.09
171 Ed Kirkpatrick	.50	.23	.06
172 Red Sox: Team/Mgr. Darrell Johnson (Checklist back)	2.00	.40	.20
173 Steve Rogers	.75	.35	.09
174 Bake McBride	.75	.35	.09
175 Don Money	.75	.35	.09
176 Burt Hooton	.75	.35	.09
177 Vic Correll	.50	.23	.06
178 Cesar Tovar	.50	.23	.06
179 Tom Bradley	.50	.23	.06
180 Joe Morgan	5.00	2.20	.60
181 Fred Beene	.50	.23	.06
182 Don Hahn	.50	.23	.06
183 Mel Stottlemyre	.75	.35	.09
184 Jorge Orta	.50	.23	.06
185 Steve Carlton	6.00	2.70	.75
186 Willie Crawford	.50	.23	.06
187 Denny Doyle	.50	.23	.06
188 Tom Griffin	.50	.23	.06
189 1951 MVP's Larry (Yogi) Berra Roy Campanella (Campy never issued)	3.50	1.55	.45
190 1952 MVP's Bobby Shantz Hank Sauer	1.50	.70	.19
191 1953 MVP's Al Rosen Roy Campanella	2.00	.90	.25
192 1954 MVP's Yogi Berra Willie Mays	4.00	1.80	.50
193 1955 MVP's UER Yogi Berra Roy Campanella (Campy card never issued, pictured with LA cap)	3.50	1.55	.45
194 1956 MVP's Mickey Mantle Don Newcombe	14.00	6.25	1.75
195 1957 MVP's Mickey Mantle Hank Aaron	25.00	11.00	3.10
196 1958 MVP's Jackie Jensen Ernie Banks	1.50	.70	.19
197 1959 MVP's Nellie Fox	1.50	.70	.19

Ernie Banks			
☐ 198 1960 MVP's	1.50	.70	.19
Roger Maris			
Dick Groat			
☐ 199 1961 MVP's	3.00	1.35	.35
Roger Maris			
Frank Robinson			
☐ 200 1962 MVP's	14.00	6.25	1.75
Mickey Mantle			
Maury Wills			
(Wills never issued)			
☐ 201 1963 MVP's	1.50	.70	.19
Elston Howard			
Sandy Koufax			
☐ 202 1964 MVP's	1.50	.70	.19
Brooks Robinson			
Ken Boyer			
☐ 203 1965 MVP's	1.50	.70	.19
Zoilo Versalles			
Willie Mays			
☐ 204 1966 MVP's	6.00	2.70	.75
Frank Robinson			
Bob Clemente			
☐ 205 1967 MVP's	1.50	.70	.19
Carl Yastrzemski			
Orlando Cepeda			
☐ 206 1968 MVP's	1.50	.70	.19
Denny McLain			
Bob Gibson			
☐ 207 1969 MVP's	1.50	.70	.19
Harmon Killebrew			
Willie McCovey			
☐ 208 1970 MVP's	1.50	.70	.19
Boog Powell			
Johnny Bench			
☐ 209 1971 MVP's	1.50	.70	.19
Vida Blue			
Joe Torre			
☐ 210 1972 MVP's	1.50	.70	.19
Rich Allen			
Johnny Bench			
☐ 211 1973 MVP's	6.00	2.70	.75
Reggie Jackson			
Pete Rose			
☐ 212 1974 MVP's	1.50	.70	.19
Jeff Burroughs			
Steve Garvey			
☐ 213 Oscar Gamble	.75	.35	.09
☐ 214 Harry Parker	.50	.23	.06
☐ 215 Bobby Valentine	.75	.35	.09
☐ 216 Giants: Team/Mgr.	2.00	.40	.20
Wes Westrum			
(Checklist back)			
☐ 217 Lou Piniella	1.50	.70	.19
☐ 218 Jerry Johnson	.50	.23	.06
☐ 219 Ed Herrmann	.50	.23	.06
☐ 220 Don Sutton	1.50	.70	.19
☐ 221 Aurelio Rodriguez	.50	.23	.06
☐ 222 Dan Spillner	.50	.23	.06
☐ 223 Robin Yount	110.00	50.00	14.00
☐ 224 Ramon Hernandez	.50	.23	.06
☐ 225 Bob Grich	.75	.35	.09
☐ 226 Bill Campbell	.50	.23	.06
☐ 227 Bob Watson	.75	.35	.09
☐ 228 George Brett	200.00	90.00	25.00
☐ 229 Barry Foote	.50	.23	.06
☐ 230 Jim Hunter	3.00	1.35	.35
☐ 231 Mike Tyson	.50	.23	.06
☐ 232 Diego Segui	.50	.23	.06
☐ 233 Billy Grabarkewitz	.50	.23	.06
☐ 234 Tom Grieve	.75	.35	.09
☐ 235 Jack Billingham	.75	.35	.09
☐ 236 Angels: Team/Mgr.	2.00	.40	.20
Dick Williams			
(Checklist back)			
☐ 237 Carl Morton	.50	.23	.06
☐ 238 Dave Duncan	.50	.23	.06
☐ 239 George Stone	.50	.23	.06
☐ 240 Garry Maddox	.75	.35	.09
☐ 241 Dick Tidrow	.50	.23	.06
☐ 242 Jay Johnstone	.75	.35	.09
☐ 243 Jim Kaat	1.00	.45	.12
☐ 244 Bill Buckner	.75	.35	.09
☐ 245 Mickey Lolich	.75	.35	.09
☐ 246 Cardinals: Team/Mgr.	2.00	.40	.20
Red Schoendienst			
(Checklist back)			
☐ 247 Enos Cabell	.50	.23	.06
☐ 248 Randy Jones	.75	.35	.09
☐ 249 Danny Thompson	.50	.23	.06
☐ 250 Ken Brett	.50	.23	.06
☐ 251 Fran Healy	.50	.23	.06
☐ 252 Fred Scherman	.50	.23	.06
☐ 253 Jesus Alou	.50	.23	.06
☐ 254 Mike Torrez	.75	.35	.09
☐ 255 Dwight Evans	1.50	.70	.19
☐ 256 Billy Champion	.50	.23	.06
☐ 257 Checklist: 133-264	2.00	.40	.20
☐ 258 Dave LaRoche	.50	.23	.06
☐ 259 Len Randle	.50	.23	.06
☐ 260 Johnny Bench	12.00	5.50	1.50
☐ 261 Andy Hassler	.50	.23	.06
☐ 262 Rowland Office	.50	.23	.06
☐ 263 Jim Perry	.75	.35	.09
☐ 264 John Milner	.50	.23	.06
☐ 265 Ron Bryant	.50	.23	.06
☐ 266 Sandy Alomar	.75	.35	.09
☐ 267 Dick Ruthven	.50	.23	.06
☐ 268 Hal McRae	1.00	.45	.12
☐ 269 Doug Rau	.50	.23	.06
☐ 270 Ron Fairly	.75	.35	.09
☐ 271 Gerry Moses	.50	.23	.06
☐ 272 Lynn McGlothen	.50	.23	.06
☐ 273 Steve Braun	.50	.23	.06
☐ 274 Vicente Romo	.50	.23	.06
☐ 275 Paul Blair	.75	.35	.09
☐ 276 White Sox Team/Mgr.	2.00	.40	.20
Chuck Tanner			
(Checklist back)			
☐ 277 Frank Taveras	.50	.23	.06
☐ 278 Paul Lindblad	.50	.23	.06
☐ 279 Milt May	.50	.23	.06
☐ 280 Carl Yastrzemski	6.00	2.70	.75
☐ 281 Jim Slaton	.50	.23	.06
☐ 282 Jerry Morales	.50	.23	.06
☐ 283 Steve Foucault	.50	.23	.06
☐ 284 Ken Griffey	5.00	2.20	.60
☐ 285 Ellie Rodriguez	.50	.23	.06
☐ 286 Mike Jorgensen	.50	.23	.06
☐ 287 Roric Harrison	.50	.23	.06
☐ 288 Bruce Ellingsen	.50	.23	.06
☐ 289 Ken Rudolph	.50	.23	.06
☐ 290 Jon Matlack	.50	.23	.06
☐ 291 Bill Sudakis	.50	.23	.06
☐ 292 Ron Schueler	.50	.23	.06
☐ 293 Dick Sharon	.50	.23	.06
☐ 294 Geoff Zahn	.50	.23	.06
☐ 295 Vada Pinson	1.00	.45	.12
☐ 296 Alan Foster	.50	.23	.06
☐ 297 Craig Kusick	.50	.23	.06
☐ 298 Johnny Grubb	.50	.23	.06
☐ 299 Bucky Dent	1.00	.45	.12
☐ 300 Reggie Jackson	20.00	9.00	2.50
☐ 301 Dave Roberts	.50	.23	.06
☐ 302 Rick Burleson	1.00	.45	.12
☐ 303 Grant Jackson	.50	.23	.06
☐ 304 Pirates: Team/Mgr.	2.00	.40	.20
Danny Murtaugh			
(Checklist back)			
☐ 305 Jim Colborn	.50	.23	.06
☐ 306 Batting Leaders	1.50	.70	.19
Rod Carew			
Ralph Garr			
☐ 307 Home Run Leaders	3.50	1.55	.45
Dick Allen			
Mike Schmidt			
☐ 308 RBI Leaders	1.50	.70	.19
Jeff Burroughs			
Johnny Bench			
☐ 309 Stolen Base Leaders	1.50	.70	.19
Bill North			
Lou Brock			
☐ 310 Victory Leaders	1.50	.70	.19
Jim Hunter			
Fergie Jenkins			
Andy Messersmith			
Phil Niekro			
☐ 311 ERA Leaders	1.50	.70	.19
Jim Hunter			
Buzz Capra			
☐ 312 Strikeout Leaders	20.00	9.00	2.50
Nolan Ryan			
Steve Carlton			
☐ 313 Leading Firemen	.75	.35	.09
Terry Forster			
Mike Marshall			
☐ 314 Buck Martinez	.50	.23	.06
☐ 315 Don Kessinger	.75	.35	.09
☐ 316 Jackie Brown	.50	.23	.06
☐ 317 Joe Lahoud	.50	.23	.06
☐ 318 Ernie McAnally	.50	.23	.06
☐ 319 Johnny Oates	.75	.35	.09
☐ 320 Pete Rose	20.00	9.00	2.50
☐ 321 Rudy May	.50	.23	.06
☐ 322 Ed Goodson	.50	.23	.06
☐ 323 Fred Holdsworth	.50	.23	.06
☐ 324 Ed Kranepool	.75	.35	.09
☐ 325 Tony Oliva	1.00	.45	.12
☐ 326 Wayne Twitchell	.50	.23	.06
☐ 327 Jerry Hairston	.50	.23	.06
☐ 328 Sonny Siebert	.50	.23	.06
☐ 329 Ted Kubiak	.50	.23	.06
☐ 330 Mike Marshall	.75	.35	.09
☐ 331 Indians: Team/Mgr.	2.00	.40	.20
Frank Robinson			
(Checklist back)			
☐ 332 Fred Kendall	.50	.23	.06
☐ 333 Dick Drago	.50	.23	.06
☐ 334 Greg Gross	.50	.23	.06
☐ 335 Jim Palmer	5.00	2.20	.60
☐ 336 Rennie Stennett	.50	.23	.06
☐ 337 Kevin Kobel	.50	.23	.06
☐ 338 Rich Stelmaszek	.50	.23	.06
☐ 339 Jim Fregosi	.75	.35	.09
☐ 340 Paul Splittorff	.50	.23	.06
☐ 341 Hal Breeden	.50	.23	.06
☐ 342 Leroy Stanton	.50	.23	.06
☐ 343 Danny Frisella	.50	.23	.06
☐ 344 Ben Oglivie	.75	.35	.09
☐ 345 Clay Carroll	.75	.35	.09
☐ 346 Bobby Darwin	.50	.23	.06
☐ 347 Mike Caldwell	.50	.23	.06
☐ 348 Tony Muser	.50	.23	.06
☐ 349 Ray Sadecki	.50	.23	.06
☐ 350 Bobby Murcer	1.00	.45	.12
☐ 351 Bob Boone	1.50	.70	.19
☐ 352 Darold Knowles	.50	.23	.06
☐ 353 Luis Melendez	.50	.23	.06
☐ 354 Dick Bosman	.50	.23	.06
☐ 355 Chris Cannizzaro	.50	.23	.06
☐ 356 Rico Petrocelli	.75	.35	.09
☐ 357 Ken Forsch	.50	.23	.06
☐ 358 Al Bumbry	.75	.35	.09
☐ 359 Paul Popovich	.50	.23	.06
☐ 360 George Scott	.75	.35	.09
☐ 361 Dodgers: Team/Mgr.	2.00	.40	.20
Walter Alston			
(Checklist back)			
☐ 362 Steve Hargan	.50	.23	.06
☐ 363 Carmen Fanzone	.50	.23	.06
☐ 364 Doug Bird	.50	.23	.06
☐ 365 Bob Bailey	.50	.23	.06
☐ 366 Ken Sanders	.50	.23	.06
☐ 367 Craig Robinson	.50	.23	.06
☐ 368 Vic Albury	.50	.23	.06
☐ 369 Merv Rettenmund	.50	.23	.06
☐ 370 Tom Seaver	14.00	6.25	1.75
☐ 371 Gates Brown	.50	.23	.06
☐ 372 John D'Acquisto	.50	.23	.06
☐ 373 Bill Sharp	.50	.23	.06
☐ 374 Eddie Watt	.50	.23	.06
☐ 375 Roy White	.75	.35	.09
☐ 376 Steve Yeager	.75	.35	.09
☐ 377 Tom Hilgendorf	.50	.23	.06
☐ 378 Derrel Thomas	.50	.23	.06
☐ 379 Bernie Carbo	.50	.23	.06
☐ 380 Sal Bando	.75	.35	.09
☐ 381 John Curtis	.50	.23	.06
☐ 382 Don Baylor	1.50	.70	.19
☐ 383 Jim York	.50	.23	.06
☐ 384 Brewers: Team/Mgr.	2.00	.40	.20
Del Crandall			
(Checklist back)			
☐ 385 Dock Ellis	.50	.23	.06
☐ 386 Checklist: 265-396	2.00	.40	.20
☐ 387 Jim Spencer	.50	.23	.06
☐ 388 Steve Stone	.75	.35	.09
☐ 389 Tony Solaita	.50	.23	.06
☐ 390 Ron Cey	1.00	.45	.12
☐ 391 Don DeMola	.50	.23	.06
☐ 392 Bruce Bochte	.75	.35	.09
☐ 393 Gary Gentry	.50	.23	.06
☐ 394 Larvell Blanks	.50	.23	.06
☐ 395 Bud Harrelson	.75	.35	.09
☐ 396 Fred Norman	.75	.35	.09
☐ 397 Bill Freehan	.75	.35	.09
☐ 398 Elias Sosa	.50	.23	.06
☐ 399 Terry Harmon	.50	.23	.06
☐ 400 Dick Allen	1.00	.45	.12
☐ 401 Mike Wallace	.50	.23	.06
☐ 402 Bob Tolan	.50	.23	.06
☐ 403 Tom Buskey	.50	.23	.06
☐ 404 Ted Sizemore	.50	.23	.06
☐ 405 John Montague	.50	.23	.06
☐ 406 Bob Gallagher	.50	.23	.06
☐ 407 Herb Washington	1.50	.70	.19
☐ 408 Clyde Wright	.50	.23	.06
☐ 409 Bob Robertson	.50	.23	.06
☐ 410 Mike Cueller UER	.75	.35	.09
(Sic, Cuellar)			
☐ 411 George Mitterwald	.50	.23	.06
☐ 412 Bill Hands	.50	.23	.06
☐ 413 Marty Pattin	.50	.23	.06
☐ 414 Manny Mota	.75	.35	.09
☐ 415 John Hiller	.75	.35	.09
☐ 416 Larry Lintz	.50	.23	.06
☐ 417 Skip Lockwood	.50	.23	.06
☐ 418 Leo Foster	.50	.23	.06
☐ 419 Dave Goltz	.50	.23	.06
☐ 420 Larry Bowa	1.00	.45	.12
☐ 421 Mets: Team/Mgr.	2.00	.40	.20
Yogi Berra			
(Checklist back)			
☐ 422 Brian Downing	.75	.35	.09
☐ 423 Clay Kirby	.50	.23	.06
☐ 424 John Lowenstein	.50	.23	.06
☐ 425 Tito Fuentes	.50	.23	.06
☐ 426 George Medich	.50	.23	.06
☐ 427 Clarence Gaston	.75	.35	.09
☐ 428 Dave Hamilton	.50	.23	.06
☐ 429 Jim Dwyer	.50	.23	.06
☐ 430 Luis Tiant	1.00	.45	.12
☐ 431 Rod Gilbreath	.50	.23	.06
☐ 432 Ken Berry	.50	.23	.06
☐ 433 Larry Demery	.50	.23	.06
☐ 434 Bob Locker	.50	.23	.06
☐ 435 Dave Nelson	.50	.23	.06
☐ 436 Ken Frailing	.50	.23	.06
☐ 437 Al Cowens	.75	.35	.09
☐ 438 Don Carrithers	.50	.23	.06
☐ 439 Ed Brinkman	.50	.23	.06
☐ 440 Andy Messersmith	.75	.35	.09
☐ 441 Bobby Heise	.50	.23	.06
☐ 442 Maximino Leon	.50	.23	.06
☐ 443 Twins: Team/Mgr.	2.00	.40	.20
Frank Quilici			
(Checklist back)			
☐ 444 Gene Garber	.75	.35	.09
☐ 445 Felix Millan	.50	.23	.06
☐ 446 Bart Johnson	.50	.23	.06
☐ 447 Terry Crowley	.50	.23	.06
☐ 448 Frank Duffy	.50	.23	.06
☐ 449 Charlie Williams	.50	.23	.06
☐ 450 Willie McCovey	5.00	2.20	.60
☐ 451 Rick Dempsey	.75	.35	.09
☐ 452 Angel Mangual	.50	.23	.06
☐ 453 Claude Osteen	.75	.35	.09
☐ 454 Doug Griffin	.50	.23	.06
☐ 455 Don Wilson	.50	.23	.06
☐ 456 Bob Coluccio	.50	.23	.06
☐ 457 Mario Mendoza	.50	.23	.06
☐ 458 Ross Grimsley	.50	.23	.06
☐ 459 1974 AL Champs	1.00	.45	.12
A's over Orioles			
(Second base action			
pictured)			
☐ 460 Frank Taveras NLCS	1.50	.70	.19
Steve Garvey			
☐ 461 Reggie Jackson WS	4.00	1.80	.50
☐ 462 World Series Game 2	1.00	.45	.12
(Dodger dugout)			
☐ 463 Rollie Fingers WS	1.50	.70	.19
☐ 464 World Series Game 4	1.00	.45	.12
(A's batter)			
☐ 465 Joe Rudi WS	1.00	.45	.12
☐ 466 World Series Summary	1.50	.70	.19
A's do it again;			
win third straight			
(A's group picture)			
☐ 467 Ed Halicki	.50	.23	.06
☐ 468 Bobby Mitchell	.50	.23	.06
☐ 469 Tom Dettore	.50	.23	.06
☐ 470 Jeff Burroughs	.75	.35	.09
☐ 471 Bob Stinson	.50	.23	.06
☐ 472 Bruce Dal Canton	.50	.23	.06
☐ 473 Ken McMullen	.50	.23	.06
☐ 474 Luke Walker	.50	.23	.06
☐ 475 Darrell Evans	.75	.35	.09
☐ 476 Ed Figueroa	.50	.23	.06
☐ 477 Tom Hutton	.50	.23	.06
☐ 478 Tom Burgmeier	.50	.23	.06
☐ 479 Ken Boswell	.50	.23	.06
☐ 480 Carlos May	.50	.23	.06
☐ 481 Will McEnaney	.75	.35	.09
☐ 482 Tom McCraw	.50	.23	.06
☐ 483 Steve Ontiveros	.50	.23	.06
☐ 484 Glenn Beckert	.75	.35	.09
☐ 485 Sparky Lyle	1.00	.45	.12
☐ 486 Ray Fosse	.50	.23	.06
☐ 487 Astros: Team/Mgr.	2.00	.40	.20
Preston Gomez			
(Checklist back)			
☐ 488 Bill Travers	.50	.23	.06
☐ 489 Cecil Cooper	1.00	.45	.12
☐ 490 Reggie Smith	.75	.35	.09
☐ 491 Doyle Alexander	.75	.35	.09
☐ 492 Rich Hebner	.75	.35	.09
☐ 493 Don Stanhouse	.50	.23	.06
☐ 494 Pete LaCock	.50	.23	.06
☐ 495 Nelson Briles	.75	.35	.09
☐ 496 Pepe Frias	.50	.23	.06
☐ 497 Jim Nettles	.50	.23	.06
☐ 498 Al Downing	.50	.23	.06
☐ 499 Marty Perez	.50	.23	.06
☐ 500 Nolan Ryan	75.00	34.00	9.50
☐ 501 Bill Robinson	.75	.35	.09
☐ 502 Pat Bourque	.50	.23	.06
☐ 503 Fred Stanley	.50	.23	.06
☐ 504 Buddy Bradford	.50	.23	.06
☐ 505 Chris Speier	.50	.23	.06
☐ 506 Leron Lee	.50	.23	.06
☐ 507 Tom Carroll	.50	.23	.06
☐ 508 Bob Hansen	.50	.23	.06
☐ 509 Dave Hilton	.50	.23	.06
☐ 510 Vida Blue	.75	.35	.09
☐ 511 Rangers: Team/Mgr.	2.00	.40	.20
Billy Martin			
(Checklist back)			
☐ 512 Larry Milbourne	.50	.23	.06
☐ 513 Dick Pole	.50	.23	.06
☐ 514 Jose Cruz	.75	.35	.09
☐ 515 Manny Sanguillen	.75	.35	.09
☐ 516 Don Hood	.50	.23	.06
☐ 517 Checklist: 397-528	2.00	.40	.20
☐ 518 Leo Cardenas	.50	.23	.06
☐ 519 Jim Todd	.50	.23	.06
☐ 520 Amos Otis	.75	.35	.09
☐ 521 Dennis Blair	.50	.23	.06
☐ 522 Gary Sutherland	.50	.23	.06
☐ 523 Tom Paciorek	.75	.35	.09
☐ 524 John Doherty	.50	.23	.06
☐ 525 Tom House	.50	.23	.06
☐ 526 Larry Hisle	.75	.35	.09
☐ 527 Mac Scarce	.50	.23	.06
☐ 528 Eddie Leon	.50	.23	.06
☐ 529 Gary Thomasson	.50	.23	.06
☐ 530 Gaylord Perry	3.00	1.35	.35
☐ 531 Reds: Team/Mgr.	4.00	.80	.40
Sparky Anderson			
(Checklist back)			
☐ 532 Gorman Thomas	.75	.35	.09
☐ 533 Rudy Meoli	.50	.23	.06

Card	NRMT	VG-E	GOOD
☐ 534 Alex Johnson	.50	.23	.06
☐ 535 Gene Tenace	.75	.35	.09
☐ 536 Bob Moose	.50	.23	.06
☐ 537 Tommy Harper	.75	.35	.09
☐ 538 Duffy Dyer	.50	.23	.06
☐ 539 Jesse Jefferson	.50	.23	.06
☐ 540 Lou Brock	5.00	2.20	.60
☐ 541 Roger Metzger	.50	.23	.06
☐ 542 Pete Broberg	.50	.23	.06
☐ 543 Larry Biittner	.50	.23	.06
☐ 544 Steve Mingori	.50	.23	.06
☐ 545 Billy Williams	3.50	1.55	.45
☐ 546 John Knox	.50	.23	.06
☐ 547 Von Joshua	.50	.23	.06
☐ 548 Charlie Sands	.50	.23	.06
☐ 549 Bill Butler	.50	.23	.06
☐ 550 Ralph Garr	.75	.35	.09
☐ 551 Larry Christenson	.50	.23	.06
☐ 552 Jack Brohamer	.50	.23	.06
☐ 553 John Boccabella	.50	.23	.06
☐ 554 Rich Gossage	1.50	.70	.19
☐ 555 Al Oliver	1.00	.45	.12
☐ 556 Tim Johnson	.50	.23	.06
☐ 557 Larry Gura	.50	.23	.06
☐ 558 Dave Roberts	.50	.23	.06
☐ 559 Bob Montgomery	.50	.23	.06
☐ 560 Tony Perez	3.00	1.35	.35
☐ 561 A's: Team/Mgr.	2.00	.40	.20
Alvin Dark			
(Checklist back)			
☐ 562 Gary Nolan	.75	.35	.09
☐ 563 Wilbur Howard	.50	.23	.06
☐ 564 Tommy Davis	.75	.35	.09
☐ 565 Joe Torre	1.00	.45	.12
☐ 566 Ray Burris	.50	.23	.06
☐ 567 Jim Sundberg	1.50	.70	.19
☐ 568 Dale Murray	.50	.23	.06
☐ 569 Frank White	.75	.35	.09
☐ 570 Jim Wynn	.75	.35	.09
☐ 571 Dave Lemanczyk	.50	.23	.06
☐ 572 Roger Nelson	.50	.23	.06
☐ 573 Orlando Pena	.50	.23	.06
☐ 574 Tony Taylor	.75	.35	.09
☐ 575 Gene Clines	.50	.23	.06
☐ 576 Phil Roof	.50	.23	.06
☐ 577 John Morris	.50	.23	.06
☐ 578 Dave Tomlin	.50	.23	.06
☐ 579 Skip Pitlock	.50	.23	.06
☐ 580 Frank Robinson	6.00	2.70	.75
☐ 581 Darrel Chaney	.50	.23	.06
☐ 582 Eduardo Rodriguez	.50	.23	.06
☐ 583 Andy Etchebarren	.50	.23	.06
☐ 584 Mike Garman	.50	.23	.06
☐ 585 Chris Chambliss	.75	.35	.09
☐ 586 Tim McCarver	1.00	.45	.12
☐ 587 Chris Ward	.50	.23	.06
☐ 588 Rick Auerbach	.50	.23	.06
☐ 589 Braves: Team/Mgr.	2.00	.40	.20
Clyde King			
(Checklist back)			
☐ 590 Cesar Cedeno	.75	.35	.09
☐ 591 Glenn Abbott	.50	.23	.06
☐ 592 Balor Moore	.50	.23	.06
☐ 593 Gene Lamont	.50	.23	.06
☐ 594 Jim Fuller	.50	.23	.06
☐ 595 Joe Niekro	.75	.35	.09
☐ 596 Ollie Brown	.50	.23	.06
☐ 597 Winston Llenas	.50	.23	.06
☐ 598 Bruce Kison	.50	.23	.06
☐ 599 Nate Colbert	.50	.23	.06
☐ 600 Rod Carew	5.00	2.20	.60
☐ 601 Juan Beniquez	.50	.23	.06
☐ 602 John Vukovich	.50	.23	.06
☐ 603 Lew Krausse	.50	.23	.06
☐ 604 Oscar Zamora	.50	.23	.06
☐ 605 John Ellis	.50	.23	.06
☐ 606 Bruce Miller	.50	.23	.06
☐ 607 Jim Holt	.50	.23	.06
☐ 608 Gene Michael	.75	.35	.09
☐ 609 Elrod Hendricks	.50	.23	.06
☐ 610 Ron Hunt	.50	.23	.06
☐ 611 Yankees: Team/Mgr.	2.00	.40	.20
Bill Virdon			
(Checklist back)			
☐ 612 Terry Hughes	.50	.23	.06
☐ 613 Bill Parsons	.50	.23	.06
☐ 614 Rookie Pitchers	.75	.35	.09
Jack Kucek			
Dyar Miller			
Vern Ruhle			
Paul Siebert			
☐ 615 Rookie Pitchers	1.00	.45	.12
Pat Darcy			
Dennis Leonard			
Tom Underwood			
Hank Webb			
☐ 616 Rookie Outfielders	14.00	6.25	1.75
Dave Augustine			
Pepe Mangual			
Jim Rice			
John Scott			
☐ 617 Rookie Infielders	1.50	.70	.19
Mike Cubbage			
Doug DeCinces			
Reggie Sanders			
Manny Trillo			
☐ 618 Rookie Pitchers	1.00	.45	.12
Jamie Easterly			
Tom Johnson			
Scott McGregor			
Rick Rhoden			
☐ 619 Rookie Outfielders	.75	.35	.09
Benny Ayala			
Nyls Nyman			
Tommy Smith			
Jerry Turner			
☐ 620 Rookie Catcher/OF	20.00	9.00	2.50
Gary Carter			
Marc Hill			
Danny Meyer			
Leon Roberts			
☐ 621 Rookie Pitchers	1.00	.45	.12
John Denny			
Rawly Eastwick			
Jim Kern			
Juan Veintidos			
☐ 622 Rookie Outfielders	6.00	2.70	.75
Ed Armbrister			
Fred Lynn			
Tom Poquette			
Terry Whitfield UER			
(Listed as Ney York)			
☐ 623 Rookie Infielders	6.00	2.70	.75
Phil Garner			
Keith Hernandez UER			
(Sic, bats right)			
Bob Sheldon			
Tom Veryzer			
☐ 624 Rookie Pitchers	.75	.35	.09
Doug Konieczny			
Gary Lavelle			
Jim Otten			
Eddie Solomon			
☐ 625 Boog Powell	1.00	.45	.12
☐ 626 Larry Haney UER	.50	.23	.06
(Photo actually			
Dave Duncan)			
☐ 627 Tom Walker	.50	.23	.06
☐ 628 Ron LeFlore	1.00	.45	.12
☐ 629 Joe Hoerner	.50	.23	.06
☐ 630 Greg Luzinski	1.00	.45	.12
☐ 631 Lee Lacy	.50	.23	.06
☐ 632 Morris Nettles	.50	.23	.06
☐ 633 Paul Casanova	.50	.23	.06
☐ 634 Cy Acosta	.50	.23	.06
☐ 635 Chuck Dobson	.50	.23	.06
☐ 636 Charlie Moore	.50	.23	.06
☐ 637 Ted Martinez	.50	.23	.06
☐ 638 Cubs: Team/Mgr.	2.00	.40	.20
Jim Marshall			
(Checklist back)			
☐ 639 Steve Kline	.50	.23	.06
☐ 640 Harmon Killebrew	5.00	2.20	.60
☐ 641 Jim Northrup	.50	.23	.06
☐ 642 Mike Phillips	.50	.23	.06
☐ 643 Brent Strom	.50	.23	.06
☐ 644 Bill Fahey	.50	.23	.06
☐ 645 Danny Cater	.50	.23	.06
☐ 646 Checklist: 529-660	2.00	.40	.20
☐ 647 Claudell Washington	1.00	.45	.12
☐ 648 Dave Pagan	.50	.23	.06
☐ 649 Jack Heidemann	.50	.23	.06
☐ 650 Dave May	.50	.23	.06
☐ 651 John Morlan	.50	.23	.06
☐ 652 Lindy McDaniel	.75	.35	.09
☐ 653 Lee Richard UER	.50	.23	.06
(Listed as Richards			
on card front)			
☐ 654 Jerry Terrell	.50	.23	.06
☐ 655 Rico Carty	.75	.35	.09
☐ 656 Bill Plummer	.50	.23	.06
☐ 657 Bob Oliver	.50	.23	.06
☐ 658 Vic Harris	.50	.23	.06
☐ 659 Bob Apodaca	.50	.23	.06
☐ 660 Hank Aaron	35.00	10.50	7.00

1975 Topps Team Checklist Sheet

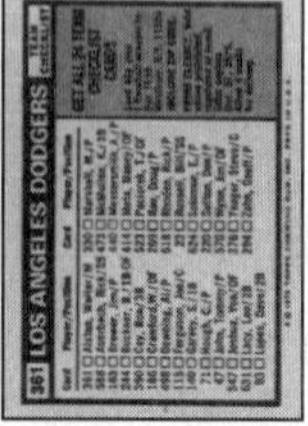

This uncut sheet of the 24 1975 Topps team checklists measures 10 1/2" by 20 1/8". The sheet was obtained by sending 40 cents plus one wrapper to Topps. When cut, each card measures the standard size.

	NRMT	VG-E	GOOD
COMPLETE SET (1)	20.00	9.00	2.50
COMMON CARD	20.00	9.00	2.50
☐ 1 Topps Team CL Sheet	20.00	9.00	2.50

1975 Topps Photographers

This standard-size set was issued to feature various photographers. This set was a test issued and little other information is known.

	NRMT	VG-E	GOOD
COMPLETE SET (11)	20.00	9.00	2.50
COMMON CARD	2.00	.90	.25
☐ 18 Harry Callahan	2.00	.90	.25
☐ 24 Mike Mandel	2.50	1.10	.30
☐ 30 Micheal Simon	2.00	.90	.25
☐ 52 Fred McDarrah	2.00	.90	.25
☐ 75 M.J. Walker	2.00	.90	.25
☐ 85 Anne Noggle	2.00	.90	.25
☐ 104 Wynn Bullock	2.00	.90	.25
☐ 117 Lionel Suntop	2.00	.90	.25
☐ 119 Doug Prince	2.00	.90	.25
☐ 123 Scott Hyde	2.00	.90	.25
☐ 128 Bob Fichter	2.00	.90	.25

1976 Topps

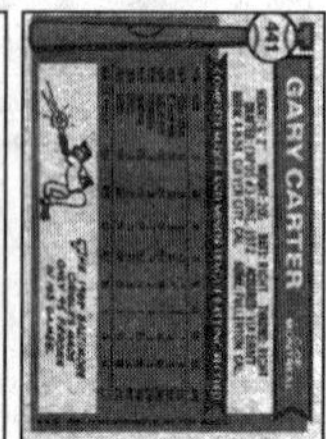

The 1976 Topps set of 660 standard-size cards is known for its sharp color photographs and interesting presentation of subjects. Team cards feature a checklist back for players on that team and show a small inset photo of the manager on the front. A "Father and Son" series (66-70) spotlights five Major Leaguers whose fathers also made the "Big Show." Other subseries include "All Time All Stars" (341-350), "Record Breakers" from the previous season (1-6), League Leaders (191-205), Post-season cards (461-462), and Rookie Prospects (589-599). The following players' regular issue cards are explicitly denoted as All-Stars, 10, 48, 60, 140, 150, 165, 169, 240, 300, 370, 380, 395, 400, 420, 475, 500, 580, and 650. Cards were issued in ten-card wax packs, 42-card rack packs as well as cello packs and other options. The key Rookie Cards in this set are Dennis Eckersley, Ron Guidry, and Willie Randolph.

	NRMT	VG-E	GOOD
COMPLETE SET (660)	400.00	180.00	50.00
COMMON CARD (1-660)	.25	.11	.03
☐ 1 Hank Aaron RB	16.00	5.00	2.00
2262 Career RBIs			
☐ 2 Bobby Bonds RB	1.00	.45	.12
Most leadoff HR's 32;			
plus three seasons			
30 homers/30 steals			
☐ 3 Mickey Lolich RB	.75	.35	.09
Most Lefthanded Strikeouts: 2679			
☐ 4 Dave Lopes RB	.75	.35	.09
Most Consecutive SB's: 38			
☐ 5 Tom Seaver RB	4.00	1.80	.50
Most Consecutive seasons			
with 200 Strikeouts			
☐ 6 Rennie Stennett RB	.50	.23	.06
7 Hits in a 9 inning game			
☐ 7 Jim Umbarger	.25	.11	.03
☐ 8 Tito Fuentes	.25	.11	.03
☐ 9 Paul Lindblad	.25	.11	.03
☐ 10 Lou Brock	4.00	1.80	.50
☐ 11 Jim Hughes	.25	.11	.03
☐ 12 Richie Zisk	.50	.23	.06
☐ 13 John Wockenfuss	.25	.11	.03
☐ 14 Gene Garber	.50	.23	.06
☐ 15 George Scott	.50	.23	.06
☐ 16 Bob Apodaca	.25	.11	.03
☐ 17 New York Yankees	1.50	.30	.15
Team Card;			
Billy Martin MG			
(Checklist back)			
☐ 18 Dale Murray	.25	.11	.03
☐ 19 George Brett	60.00	27.00	7.50
☐ 20 Bob Watson	.50	.23	.06
☐ 21 Dave LaRoche	.25	.11	.03
☐ 22 Bill Russell	.50	.23	.06
☐ 23 Brian Downing	.25	.11	.03
☐ 24 Cesar Geronimo	.50	.23	.06
☐ 25 Mike Torrez	.50	.23	.06
☐ 26 Andre Thornton	.50	.23	.06
☐ 27 Ed Figueroa	.25	.11	.03
☐ 28 Dusty Baker	1.00	.45	.12
☐ 29 Rick Burleson	.50	.23	.06
☐ 30 John Montefusco	.50	.23	.06
☐ 31 Len Randle	.25	.11	.03
☐ 32 Danny Frisella	.25	.11	.03
☐ 33 Bill North	.25	.11	.03
☐ 34 Mike Garman	.25	.11	.03
☐ 35 Tony Oliva	.75	.35	.09
☐ 36 Frank Taveras	.25	.11	.03
☐ 37 John Hiller	.50	.23	.06
☐ 38 Garry Maddox	.50	.23	.06
☐ 39 Pete Broberg	.25	.11	.03
☐ 40 Dave Kingman	.75	.35	.09
☐ 41 Tippy Martinez	.75	.35	.09
☐ 42 Barry Foote	.25	.11	.03
☐ 43 Paul Splittorff	.25	.11	.03
☐ 44 Doug Rader	.50	.23	.06
☐ 45 Boog Powell	.75	.35	.09
☐ 46 Los Angeles Dodgers	1.50	.30	.15
Team Card;			
Walter Alston MG			
(Checklist back)			
☐ 47 Jesse Jefferson	.25	.11	.03
☐ 48 Dave Concepcion	1.00	.45	.12
☐ 49 Dave Duncan	.25	.11	.03
☐ 50 Fred Lynn	1.50	.70	.19
☐ 51 Ray Burris	.25	.11	.03
☐ 52 Dave Chalk	.25	.11	.03
☐ 53 Mike Beard	.25	.11	.03
☐ 54 Dave Rader	.25	.11	.03
☐ 55 Gaylord Perry	2.50	1.10	.30
☐ 56 Bob Tolan	.25	.11	.03
☐ 57 Phil Garner	.50	.23	.06
☐ 58 Ron Reed	.25	.11	.03
☐ 59 Larry Hisle	.50	.23	.06
☐ 60 Jerry Reuss	.50	.23	.06
☐ 61 Ron LeFlore	.50	.23	.06
☐ 62 Johnny Oates	.50	.23	.06
☐ 63 Bobby Darwin	.25	.11	.03
☐ 64 Jerry Koosman	.50	.23	.06
☐ 65 Chris Chambliss	.50	.23	.06
☐ 66 Gus Bell FS	.50	.23	.06
Buddy Bell			
☐ 67 Ray Boone FS	.50	.23	.06
Bob Boone			
☐ 68 Joe Coleman FS	.25	.11	.03
Joe Coleman Jr.			
☐ 69 Jim Hegan FS	.25	.11	.03
Mike Hegan			
☐ 70 Roy Smalley FS	.50	.23	.06
Roy Smalley Jr.			
☐ 71 Steve Rogers	.50	.23	.06
☐ 72 Hal McRae	.75	.35	.09
☐ 73 Baltimore Orioles	1.50	.30	.15
Team Card;			
Earl Weaver MG			
(Checklist back)			
☐ 74 Oscar Gamble	.50	.23	.06
☐ 75 Larry Dierker	.25	.11	.03
☐ 76 Willie Crawford	.25	.11	.03
☐ 77 Pedro Borbon	.50	.23	.06
☐ 78 Cecil Cooper	.50	.23	.06
☐ 79 Jerry Morales	.25	.11	.03
☐ 80 Jim Kaat	.75	.35	.09
☐ 81 Darrell Evans	.50	.23	.06
☐ 82 Von Joshua	.25	.11	.03
☐ 83 Jim Spencer	.25	.11	.03
☐ 84 Brent Strom	.25	.11	.03
☐ 85 Mickey Rivers	.50	.23	.06
☐ 86 Mike Tyson	.25	.11	.03
☐ 87 Tom Burgmeier	.25	.11	.03
☐ 88 Duffy Dyer	.25	.11	.03
☐ 89 Vern Ruhle	.25	.11	.03
☐ 90 Sal Bando	.50	.23	.06
☐ 91 Tom Hutton	.25	.11	.03
☐ 92 Eduardo Rodriguez	.25	.11	.03
☐ 93 Mike Phillips	.25	.11	.03
☐ 94 Jim Dwyer	.25	.11	.03
☐ 95 Brooks Robinson	6.00	2.70	.75
☐ 96 Doug Bird	.25	.11	.03
☐ 97 Wilbur Howard	.25	.11	.03
☐ 98 Dennis Eckersley	40.00	18.00	5.00
☐ 99 Lee Lacy	.25	.11	.03
☐ 100 Jim Hunter	2.50	1.10	.30
☐ 101 Pete LaCock	.25	.11	.03
☐ 102 Jim Willoughby	.25	.11	.03
☐ 103 Biff Pocoroba	.25	.11	.03
☐ 104 Cincinnati Reds	3.00	.60	.30
Team Card;			
Sparky Anderson MG			
(Checklist back)			
☐ 105 Gary Lavelle	.25	.11	.03
☐ 106 Tom Grieve	.50	.23	.06
☐ 107 Dave Roberts	.25	.11	.03
☐ 108 Don Kirkwood	.25	.11	.03
☐ 109 Larry Lintz	.25	.11	.03
☐ 110 Carlos May	.25	.11	.03
☐ 111 Danny Thompson	.25	.11	.03
☐ 112 Kent Tekulve	1.00	.45	.12
☐ 113 Gary Sutherland	.25	.11	.03
☐ 114 Jay Johnstone	.50	.23	.06
☐ 115 Ken Holtzman	.50	.23	.06
☐ 116 Charlie Moore	.25	.11	.03
☐ 117 Mike Jorgensen	.25	.11	.03
☐ 118 Boston Red Sox	1.50	.30	.15
Team Card;			
Darrell Johnson MG			
(Checklist back)			
☐ 119 Checklist 1-132	1.50	.30	.15
☐ 120 Rusty Staub	.50	.23	.06
☐ 121 Tony Solaita	.25	.11	.03
☐ 122 Mike Cosgrove	.25	.11	.03
☐ 123 Walt Williams	.25	.11	.03
☐ 124 Doug Rau	.25	.11	.03
☐ 125 Don Baylor	1.50	.70	.19
☐ 126 Tom Dettore	.25	.11	.03

☐ 127 Larvell Blanks	.25	.11	.03
☐ 128 Ken Griffey	2.50	1.10	.30
☐ 129 Andy Etchebarren	.25	.11	.03
☐ 130 Luis Tiant	.75	.35	.09
☐ 131 Bill Stein	.25	.11	.03
☐ 132 Don Hood	.25	.11	.03
☐ 133 Gary Matthews	.50	.23	.06
☐ 134 Mike Ivie	.25	.11	.03
☐ 135 Bake McBride	.50	.23	.06
☐ 136 Dave Goltz	.25	.11	.03
☐ 137 Bill Robinson	.50	.23	.06
☐ 138 Lerrin LaGrow	.25	.11	.03
☐ 139 Gorman Thomas	.50	.23	.06
☐ 140 Vida Blue	.50	.23	.06
☐ 141 Larry Parrish	.75	.35	.09
☐ 142 Dick Drago	.25	.11	.03
☐ 143 Jerry Grote	.25	.11	.03
☐ 144 Al Fitzmorris	.25	.11	.03
☐ 145 Larry Bowa	.50	.23	.06
☐ 146 George Medich	.25	.11	.03
☐ 147 Houston Astros	1.50	.30	.15
Team Card;			
Bill Virdon MG			
(Checklist back)			
☐ 148 Stan Thomas	.25	.11	.03
☐ 149 Tommy Davis	.50	.23	.06
☐ 150 Steve Garvey	4.00	1.80	.50
☐ 151 Bill Bonham	.25	.11	.03
☐ 152 Leroy Stanton	.25	.11	.03
☐ 153 Buzz Capra	.25	.11	.03
☐ 154 Bucky Dent	.50	.23	.06
☐ 155 Jack Billingham	.50	.23	.06
☐ 156 Rico Carty	.50	.23	.06
☐ 157 Mike Caldwell	.25	.11	.03
☐ 158 Ken Reitz	.25	.11	.03
☐ 159 Jerry Terrell	.25	.11	.03
☐ 160 Dave Winfield	25.00	11.00	3.10
☐ 161 Bruce Kison	.25	.11	.03
☐ 162 Jack Pierce	.25	.11	.03
☐ 163 Jim Slaton	.25	.11	.03
☐ 164 Pepe Mangual	.25	.11	.03
☐ 165 Gene Tenace	.50	.23	.06
☐ 166 Skip Lockwood	.25	.11	.03
☐ 167 Freddie Patek	.50	.23	.06
☐ 168 Tom Hilgendorf	.25	.11	.03
☐ 169 Graig Nettles	.75	.35	.09
☐ 170 Rick Wise	.25	.11	.03
☐ 171 Greg Gross	.25	.11	.03
☐ 172 Texas Rangers	1.50	.30	.15
Team Card;			
Frank Lucchesi MG			
(Checklist back)			
☐ 173 Steve Swisher	.25	.11	.03
☐ 174 Charlie Hough	.75	.35	.09
☐ 175 Ken Singleton	.50	.23	.06
☐ 176 Dick Lange	.25	.11	.03
☐ 177 Marty Perez	.25	.11	.03
☐ 178 Tom Buskey	.25	.11	.03
☐ 179 George Foster	.75	.35	.09
☐ 180 Rich Gossage	1.50	.70	.19
☐ 181 Willie Montanez	.25	.11	.03
☐ 182 Harry Rasmussen	.25	.11	.03
☐ 183 Steve Braun	.25	.11	.03
☐ 184 Bill Greif	.25	.11	.03
☐ 185 Dave Parker	2.00	.90	.25
☐ 186 Tom Walker	.25	.11	.03
☐ 187 Pedro Garcia	.25	.11	.03
☐ 188 Fred Scherman	.25	.11	.03
☐ 189 Claudell Washington	.50	.23	.06
☐ 190 Jon Matlack	.25	.11	.03
☐ 191 NL Batting Leaders	.75	.35	.09
Bill Madlock			
Ted Simmons			
Manny Sanguillen			
☐ 192 AL Batting Leaders	2.00	.90	.25
Rod Carew			
Fred Lynn			
Thurman Munson			
☐ 193 NL Home Run Leaders	3.00	1.35	.35
Mike Schmidt			
Dave Kingman			
Greg Luzinski			
☐ 194 AL Home Run Leaders	2.50	1.10	.30
Reggie Jackson			
George Scott			
John Mayberry			
☐ 195 NL RBI Leaders	1.50	.70	.19
Greg Luzinski			
Johnny Bench			
Tony Perez			
☐ 196 AL RBI Leaders	.75	.35	.09
George Scott			
John Mayberry			
Fred Lynn			
☐ 197 NL Steals Leaders	1.50	.70	.19
Dave Lopes			
Joe Morgan			
Lou Brock			
☐ 198 AL Steals Leaders	.75	.35	.09
Mickey Rivers			
Claudell Washington			
Amos Otis			
☐ 199 NL Victory Leaders	1.50	.70	.19
Tom Seaver			
Randy Jones			
Andy Messersmith			
☐ 200 AL Victory Leaders	1.50	.70	.19
Jim Hunter			
Jim Palmer			
Vida Blue			
☐ 201 NL ERA Leaders	1.50	.70	.19
Randy Jones			
Andy Messersmith			
Tom Seaver			
☐ 202 AL ERA Leaders	5.00	2.20	.60
Jim Palmer			
Jim Hunter			
Dennis Eckersley			
☐ 203 NL Strikeout Leaders	1.50	.70	.19
Tom Seaver			
John Montefusco			
Andy Messersmith			
☐ 204 AL Strikeout Leaders	1.00	.45	.12
Frank Tanana			
Bert Blyleven			
Gaylord Perry			
☐ 205 Leading Firemen	.75	.35	.09
Al Hrabosky			
Rich Gossage			
☐ 206 Manny Trillo	.25	.11	.03
☐ 207 Andy Hassler	.25	.11	.03
☐ 208 Mike Lum	.25	.11	.03
☐ 209 Alan Ashby	.50	.23	.06
☐ 210 Lee May	.50	.23	.06
☐ 211 Clay Carroll	.50	.23	.06
☐ 212 Pat Kelly	.25	.11	.03
☐ 213 Dave Heaverlo	.25	.11	.03
☐ 214 Eric Soderholm	.25	.11	.03
☐ 215 Reggie Smith	.50	.23	.06
☐ 216 Montreal Expos	1.50	.30	.15
Team Card;			
Karl Kuehl MG			
(Checklist back)			
☐ 217 Dave Freisleben	.25	.11	.03
☐ 218 John Knox	.25	.11	.03
☐ 219 Tom Murphy	.25	.11	.03
☐ 220 Manny Sanguillen	.50	.23	.06
☐ 221 Jim Todd	.25	.11	.03
☐ 222 Wayne Garrett	.25	.11	.03
☐ 223 Ollie Brown	.25	.11	.03
☐ 224 Jim York	.25	.11	.03
☐ 225 Roy White	.50	.23	.06
☐ 226 Jim Sundberg	.50	.23	.06
☐ 227 Oscar Zamora	.25	.11	.03
☐ 228 John Hale	.25	.11	.03
☐ 229 Jerry Remy	.25	.11	.03
☐ 230 Carl Yastrzemski	5.00	2.20	.60
☐ 231 Tom House	.25	.11	.03
☐ 232 Frank Duffy	.25	.11	.03
☐ 233 Grant Jackson	.25	.11	.03
☐ 234 Mike Sadek	.25	.11	.03
☐ 235 Bert Blyleven	.75	.35	.09
☐ 236 Kansas City Royals	1.50	.30	.15
Team Card;			
Whitey Herzog MG			
(Checklist back)			
☐ 237 Dave Hamilton	.25	.11	.03
☐ 238 Larry Biittner	.25	.11	.03
☐ 239 John Curtis	.25	.11	.03
☐ 240 Pete Rose	12.00	5.50	1.50
☐ 241 Hector Torres	.25	.11	.03
☐ 242 Dan Meyer	.25	.11	.03
☐ 243 Jim Rooker	.25	.11	.03
☐ 244 Bill Sharp	.25	.11	.03
☐ 245 Felix Millan	.25	.11	.03
☐ 246 Cesar Tovar	.25	.11	.03
☐ 247 Terry Harmon	.25	.11	.03
☐ 248 Dick Tidrow	.25	.11	.03
☐ 249 Cliff Johnson	.50	.23	.06
☐ 250 Fergie Jenkins	2.50	1.10	.30
☐ 251 Rick Monday	.50	.23	.06
☐ 252 Tim Nordbrook	.25	.11	.03
☐ 253 Bill Buckner	.50	.23	.06
☐ 254 Rudy Meoli	.25	.11	.03
☐ 255 Fritz Peterson	.25	.11	.03
☐ 256 Rowland Office	.25	.11	.03
☐ 257 Ross Grimsley	.25	.11	.03
☐ 258 Nyls Nyman	.25	.11	.03
☐ 259 Darrel Chaney	.25	.11	.03
☐ 260 Steve Busby	.25	.11	.03
☐ 261 Gary Thomasson	.25	.11	.03
☐ 262 Checklist 133-264	1.50	.30	.15
☐ 263 Lyman Bostock	1.00	.45	.12
☐ 264 Steve Renko	.25	.11	.03
☐ 265 Willie Davis	.50	.23	.06
☐ 266 Alan Foster	.25	.11	.03
☐ 267 Aurelio Rodriguez	.25	.11	.03
☐ 268 Del Unser	.25	.11	.03
☐ 269 Rick Austin	.25	.11	.03
☐ 270 Willie Stargell	3.00	1.35	.35
☐ 271 Jim Lonborg	.50	.23	.06
☐ 272 Rick Dempsey	.50	.23	.06
☐ 273 Joe Niekro	.50	.23	.06
☐ 274 Tommy Harper	.50	.23	.06
☐ 275 Rick Manning	.25	.11	.03
☐ 276 Mickey Scott	.25	.11	.03
☐ 277 Chicago Cubs	1.50	.30	.15
Team Card;			
Jim Marshall MG			
(Checklist back)			
☐ 278 Bernie Carbo	.25	.11	.03
☐ 279 Roy Howell	.25	.11	.03
☐ 280 Burt Hooton	.50	.23	.06
☐ 281 Dave May	.25	.11	.03
☐ 282 Dan Osborn	.25	.11	.03
☐ 283 Merv Rettenmund	.25	.11	.03
☐ 284 Steve Ontiveros	.25	.11	.03
☐ 285 Mike Cuellar	.50	.23	.06
☐ 286 Jim Wohlford	.25	.11	.03
☐ 287 Pete Mackanin	.25	.11	.03
☐ 288 Bill Campbell	.25	.11	.03
☐ 289 Enzo Hernandez	.25	.11	.03
☐ 290 Ted Simmons	.75	.35	.09
☐ 291 Ken Sanders	.25	.11	.03
☐ 292 Leon Roberts	.25	.11	.03
☐ 293 Bill Castro	.25	.11	.03
☐ 294 Ed Kirkpatrick	.25	.11	.03
☐ 295 Dave Cash	.25	.11	.03
☐ 296 Pat Dobson	.25	.11	.03
☐ 297 Roger Metzger	.25	.11	.03
☐ 298 Dick Bosman	.25	.11	.03
☐ 299 Champ Summers	.25	.11	.03
☐ 300 Johnny Bench	7.00	3.10	.85
☐ 301 Jackie Brown	.25	.11	.03
☐ 302 Rick Miller	.25	.11	.03
☐ 303 Steve Foucault	.25	.11	.03
☐ 304 California Angels	1.50	.30	.15
Team Card;			
Dick Williams MG			
(Checklist back)			
☐ 305 Andy Messersmith	.50	.23	.06
☐ 306 Rod Gilbreath	.25	.11	.03
☐ 307 Al Bumbry	.50	.23	.06
☐ 308 Jim Barr	.25	.11	.03
☐ 309 Bill Melton	.25	.11	.03
☐ 310 Randy Jones	.50	.23	.06
☐ 311 Cookie Rojas	.50	.23	.06
☐ 312 Don Carrithers	.25	.11	.03
☐ 313 Dan Ford	.25	.11	.03
☐ 314 Ed Kranepool	.25	.11	.03
☐ 315 Al Hrabosky	.50	.23	.06
☐ 316 Robin Yount	30.00	13.50	3.70
☐ 317 John Candelaria	1.50	.70	.19
☐ 318 Bob Boone	.75	.35	.09
☐ 319 Larry Gura	.25	.11	.03
☐ 320 Willie Horton	.50	.23	.06
☐ 321 Jose Cruz	.50	.23	.06
☐ 322 Glenn Abbott	.25	.11	.03
☐ 323 Rob Sperring	.25	.11	.03
☐ 324 Jim Bibby	.25	.11	.03
☐ 325 Tony Perez	2.00	.90	.25
☐ 326 Dick Pole	.25	.11	.03
☐ 327 Dave Moates	.25	.11	.03
☐ 328 Carl Morton	.25	.11	.03
☐ 329 Joe Ferguson	.25	.11	.03
☐ 330 Nolan Ryan	65.00	29.00	8.00
☐ 331 San Diego Padres	1.50	.30	.15
Team Card;			
John McNamara MG			
(Checklist back)			
☐ 332 Charlie Williams	.25	.11	.03
☐ 333 Bob Coluccio	.25	.11	.03
☐ 334 Dennis Leonard	.50	.23	.06
☐ 335 Bob Grich	.50	.23	.06
☐ 336 Vic Albury	.25	.11	.03
☐ 337 Bud Harrelson	.50	.23	.06
☐ 338 Bob Bailey	.25	.11	.03
☐ 339 John Denny	.50	.23	.06
☐ 340 Jim Rice	5.00	2.20	.60
☐ 341 Lou Gehrig ATG	12.00	5.50	1.50
☐ 342 Rogers Hornsby ATG	3.00	1.35	.35
☐ 343 Pie Traynor ATG	1.00	.45	.12
☐ 344 Honus Wagner ATG	5.00	2.20	.60
☐ 345 Babe Ruth ATG	15.00	6.75	1.85
☐ 346 Ty Cobb ATG	8.00	3.60	1.00
☐ 347 Ted Williams ATG	10.00	4.50	1.25
☐ 348 Mickey Cochrane ATG	1.00	.45	.12
☐ 349 Walter Johnson ATG	3.00	1.35	.35
☐ 350 Lefty Grove ATG	1.00	.45	.12
☐ 351 Randy Hundley	.50	.23	.06
☐ 352 Dave Giusti	.25	.11	.03
☐ 353 Sixto Lezcano	.50	.23	.06
☐ 354 Ron Blomberg	.25	.11	.03
☐ 355 Steve Carlton	6.00	2.70	.75
☐ 356 Ted Martinez	.25	.11	.03
☐ 357 Ken Forsch	.25	.11	.03
☐ 358 Buddy Bell	.50	.23	.06
☐ 359 Rick Reuschel	.50	.23	.06
☐ 360 Jeff Burroughs	.50	.23	.06
☐ 361 Detroit Tigers	1.50	.30	.15
Team Card;			
Ralph Houk MG			
(Checklist back)			
☐ 362 Will McEnaney	.50	.23	.06
☐ 363 Dave Collins	.50	.23	.06
☐ 364 Elias Sosa	.25	.11	.03
☐ 365 Carlton Fisk	7.00	3.10	.85
☐ 366 Bobby Valentine	.50	.23	.06
☐ 367 Bruce Miller	.25	.11	.03
☐ 368 Wilbur Wood	.25	.11	.03
☐ 369 Frank White	.50	.23	.06
☐ 370 Ron Cey	.50	.23	.06
☐ 371 Elrod Hendricks	.25	.11	.03
☐ 372 Rick Baldwin	.25	.11	.03
☐ 373 Johnny Briggs	.25	.11	.03
☐ 374 Dan Warthen	.25	.11	.03
☐ 375 Ron Fairly	.50	.23	.06
☐ 376 Rich Hebner	.50	.23	.06
☐ 377 Mike Hegan	.25	.11	.03
☐ 378 Steve Stone	.50	.23	.06
☐ 379 Ken Boswell	.25	.11	.03
☐ 380 Bobby Bonds	1.50	.70	.19
☐ 381 Denny Doyle	.25	.11	.03
☐ 382 Matt Alexander	.25	.11	.03
☐ 383 John Ellis	.25	.11	.03
☐ 384 Philadelphia Phillies	1.50	.30	.15
Team Card;			
Danny Ozark MG			
(Checklist back)			
☐ 385 Mickey Lolich	.50	.23	.06
☐ 386 Ed Goodson	.25	.11	.03
☐ 387 Mike Miley	.25	.11	.03
☐ 388 Stan Perzanowski	.25	.11	.03
☐ 389 Glenn Adams	.25	.11	.03
☐ 390 Don Gullett	.50	.23	.06
☐ 391 Jerry Hairston	.25	.11	.03
☐ 392 Checklist 265-396	1.50	.30	.15
☐ 393 Paul Mitchell	.25	.11	.03
☐ 394 Fran Healy	.25	.11	.03
☐ 395 Jim Wynn	.50	.23	.06
☐ 396 Bill Lee	.25	.11	.03
☐ 397 Tim Foli	.25	.11	.03
☐ 398 Dave Tomlin	.25	.11	.03
☐ 399 Luis Melendez	.25	.11	.03
☐ 400 Rod Carew	4.00	1.80	.50
☐ 401 Ken Brett	.25	.11	.03
☐ 402 Don Money	.50	.23	.06
☐ 403 Geoff Zahn	.25	.11	.03
☐ 404 Enos Cabell	.25	.11	.03
☐ 405 Rollie Fingers	2.50	1.10	.30
☐ 406 Ed Herrmann	.25	.11	.03
☐ 407 Tom Underwood	.25	.11	.03
☐ 408 Charlie Spikes	.25	.11	.03
☐ 409 Dave Lemanczyk	.25	.11	.03
☐ 410 Ralph Garr	.50	.23	.06
☐ 411 Bill Singer	.25	.11	.03
☐ 412 Toby Harrah	.50	.23	.06
☐ 413 Pete Varney	.25	.11	.03
☐ 414 Wayne Garland	.25	.11	.03
☐ 415 Vada Pinson	.75	.35	.09
☐ 416 Tommy John	.75	.35	.09
☐ 417 Gene Clines	.25	.11	.03
☐ 418 Jose Morales	.25	.11	.03
☐ 419 Reggie Cleveland	.25	.11	.03
☐ 420 Joe Morgan	4.00	1.80	.50
☐ 421 Oakland A's	1.50	.30	.15
Team Card;			
(No MG on front;			
checklist back)			
☐ 422 Johnny Grubb	.25	.11	.03
☐ 423 Ed Halicki	.25	.11	.03
☐ 424 Phil Roof	.25	.11	.03
☐ 425 Rennie Stennett	.25	.11	.03
☐ 426 Bob Forsch	.25	.11	.03
☐ 427 Kurt Bevacqua	.25	.11	.03
☐ 428 Jim Crawford	.25	.11	.03
☐ 429 Fred Stanley	.25	.11	.03
☐ 430 Jose Cardenal	.50	.23	.06
☐ 431 Dick Ruthven	.25	.11	.03
☐ 432 Tom Veryzer	.25	.11	.03
☐ 433 Rick Waits	.25	.11	.03
☐ 434 Morris Nettles	.25	.11	.03
☐ 435 Phil Niekro	2.00	.90	.25
☐ 436 Bill Fahey	.25	.11	.03
☐ 437 Terry Forster	.25	.11	.03
☐ 438 Doug DeCinces	.50	.23	.06
☐ 439 Rick Rhoden	.50	.23	.06
☐ 440 John Mayberry	.50	.23	.06
☐ 441 Gary Carter	7.00	3.10	.85
☐ 442 Hank Webb	.25	.11	.03
☐ 443 San Francisco Giants	1.50	.30	.15
Team Card;			
(No MG on front;			
checklist back)			
☐ 444 Gary Nolan	.50	.23	.06
☐ 445 Rico Petrocelli	.50	.23	.06
☐ 446 Larry Haney	.25	.11	.03
☐ 447 Gene Locklear	.50	.23	.06
☐ 448 Tom Johnson	.25	.11	.03
☐ 449 Bob Robertson	.25	.11	.03
☐ 450 Jim Palmer	4.00	1.80	.50
☐ 451 Buddy Bradford	.25	.11	.03
☐ 452 Tom Hausman	.25	.11	.03
☐ 453 Lou Piniella	1.50	.70	.19
☐ 454 Tom Griffin	.25	.11	.03
☐ 455 Dick Allen	.75	.35	.09
☐ 456 Joe Coleman	.25	.11	.03
☐ 457 Ed Crosby	.25	.11	.03
☐ 458 Earl Williams	.25	.11	.03
☐ 459 Jim Brewer	.25	.11	.03
☐ 460 Cesar Cedeno	.50	.23	.06
☐ 461 NL and AL Champs	.75	.35	.09
Reds sweep Bucs,			
Bosox surprise A's			
☐ 462 '75 World Series	.75	.35	.09
Reds Champs			
☐ 463 Steve Hargan	.25	.11	.03
☐ 464 Ken Henderson	.25	.11	.03
☐ 465 Mike Marshall	.50	.23	.06
☐ 466 Bob Stinson	.25	.11	.03
☐ 467 Woodie Fryman	.25	.11	.03

☐ 468 Jesus Alou .25 .11 .03
☐ 469 Rawly Eastwick .50 .23 .06
☐ 470 Bobby Murcer .50 .23 .06
☐ 471 Jim Burton .25 .11 .03
☐ 472 Bob Davis .25 .11 .03
☐ 473 Paul Blair .50 .23 .06
☐ 474 Ray Corbin .25 .11 .03
☐ 475 Joe Rudi .50 .23 .06
☐ 476 Bob Moose .25 .11 .03
☐ 477 Cleveland Indians 1.50 .30 .15
Team Card;
Frank Robinson MG
(Checklist back)
☐ 478 Lynn McGlothen .25 .11 .03
☐ 479 Bobby Mitchell .25 .11 .03
☐ 480 Mike Schmidt 25.00 11.00 3.10
☐ 481 Rudy May .25 .11 .03
☐ 482 Tim Hosley .25 .11 .03
☐ 483 Mickey Stanley .25 .11 .03
☐ 484 Eric Raich .25 .11 .03
☐ 485 Mike Hargrove .50 .23 .06
☐ 486 Bruce Dal Canton .25 .11 .03
☐ 487 Leron Lee .25 .11 .03
☐ 488 Claude Osteen .50 .23 .06
☐ 489 Skip Jutze .25 .11 .03
☐ 490 Frank Tanana .75 .35 .09
☐ 491 Terry Crowley .25 .11 .03
☐ 492 Marty Pattin .25 .11 .03
☐ 493 Derrel Thomas .25 .11 .03
☐ 494 Craig Swan .50 .23 .06
☐ 495 Nate Colbert .25 .11 .03
☐ 496 Juan Beniquez .25 .11 .03
☐ 497 Joe McIntosh .25 .11 .03
☐ 498 Glenn Borgmann .25 .11 .03
☐ 499 Mario Guerrero .25 .11 .03
☐ 500 Reggie Jackson 14.00 6.25 1.75
☐ 501 Billy Champion .25 .11 .03
☐ 502 Tim McCarver .50 .23 .06
☐ 503 Elliott Maddox .25 .11 .03
☐ 504 Pittsburgh Pirates 1.50 .30 .15
Team Card;
Danny Murtaugh MG
(Checklist back)
☐ 505 Mark Belanger .50 .23 .06
☐ 506 George Mitterwald .25 .11 .03
☐ 507 Ray Bare .25 .11 .03
☐ 508 Duane Kuiper .25 .11 .03
☐ 509 Bill Hands .25 .11 .03
☐ 510 Amos Otis .50 .23 .06
☐ 511 Jamie Easterley .25 .11 .03
☐ 512 Ellie Rodriguez .25 .11 .03
☐ 513 Bart Johnson .25 .11 .03
☐ 514 Dan Driessen .50 .23 .06
☐ 515 Steve Yeager .50 .23 .06
☐ 516 Wayne Granger .25 .11 .03
☐ 517 John Milner .25 .11 .03
☐ 518 Doug Flynn .25 .11 .03
☐ 519 Steve Brye .25 .11 .03
☐ 520 Willie McCovey 4.00 1.80 .50
☐ 521 Jim Colborn .25 .11 .03
☐ 522 Ted Sizemore .25 .11 .03
☐ 523 Bob Montgomery .25 .11 .03
☐ 524 Pete Falcone .25 .11 .03
☐ 525 Billy Williams 2.50 1.10 .30
☐ 526 Checklist 397-528 1.50 .30 .15
☐ 527 Mike Anderson .25 .11 .03
☐ 528 Dock Ellis .25 .11 .03
☐ 529 Deron Johnson .50 .23 .06
☐ 530 Don Sutton 1.50 .70 .19
☐ 531 New York Mets 1.50 .30 .15
Team Card;
Joe Frazier MG
(Checklist back)
☐ 532 Milt May .25 .11 .03
☐ 533 Lee Richard .25 .11 .03
☐ 534 Stan Bahnsen .25 .11 .03
☐ 535 Dave Nelson .25 .11 .03
☐ 536 Mike Thompson .25 .11 .03
☐ 537 Tony Muser .25 .11 .03
☐ 538 Pat Darcy .25 .11 .03
☐ 539 John Balaz .50 .23 .06
☐ 540 Bill Freehan .50 .23 .06
☐ 541 Steve Mingori .25 .11 .03
☐ 542 Keith Hernandez 1.50 .70 .19
☐ 543 Wayne Twitchell .25 .11 .03
☐ 544 Pepe Frias .25 .11 .03
☐ 545 Sparky Lyle .50 .23 .06
☐ 546 Dave Rosello .25 .11 .03
☐ 547 Roric Harrison .25 .11 .03
☐ 548 Manny Mota .50 .23 .06
☐ 549 Randy Tate .25 .11 .03
☐ 550 Hank Aaron 25.00 11.00 3.10
☐ 551 Jerry DaVanon .25 .11 .03
☐ 552 Terry Humphrey .25 .11 .03
☐ 553 Randy Moffitt .25 .11 .03
☐ 554 Ray Fosse .25 .11 .03
☐ 555 Dyar Miller .25 .11 .03
☐ 556 Minnesota Twins 1.50 .30 .15
Team Card;
Gene Mauch MG
(Checklist back)
☐ 557 Dan Spillner .25 .11 .03
☐ 558 Clarence Gaston .50 .23 .06
☐ 559 Clyde Wright .25 .11 .03
☐ 560 Jorge Orta .25 .11 .03
☐ 561 Tom Carroll .25 .11 .03
☐ 562 Adrian Garrett .25 .11 .03
☐ 563 Larry Demery .25 .11 .03
☐ 564 Bubble Gum Champ 1.50 .70 .19
Kurt Bevacqua
☐ 565 Tug McGraw .50 .23 .06
☐ 566 Ken McMullen .25 .11 .03
☐ 567 George Stone .25 .11 .03
☐ 568 Rob Andrews .25 .11 .03
☐ 569 Nelson Briles .50 .23 .06
☐ 570 George Hendrick .50 .23 .06
☐ 571 Don DeMola .25 .11 .03
☐ 572 Rich Coggins .25 .11 .03
☐ 573 Bill Travers .25 .11 .03
☐ 574 Don Kessinger .50 .23 .06
☐ 575 Dwight Evans 1.50 .70 .19
☐ 576 Maximino Leon .25 .11 .03
☐ 577 Marc Hill .25 .11 .03
☐ 578 Ted Kubiak .25 .11 .03
☐ 579 Clay Kirby .25 .11 .03
☐ 580 Bert Campaneris .50 .23 .06
☐ 581 St. Louis Cardinals 1.50 .30 .15
Team Card;
Red Schoendienst MG
(Checklist back)
☐ 582 Mike Kekich .25 .11 .03
☐ 583 Tommy Helms .25 .11 .03
☐ 584 Stan Wall .25 .11 .03
☐ 585 Joe Torre .75 .35 .09
☐ 586 Ron Schueler .25 .11 .03
☐ 587 Leo Cardenas .25 .11 .03
☐ 588 Kevin Kobel .25 .11 .03
☐ 589 Rookie Pitchers 1.50 .70 .19
Santo Alcala
Mike Flanagan
Joe Pactwa
Pablo Torrealba
☐ 590 Rookie Outfielders .75 .35 .09
Henry Cruz
Chet Lemon
Ellis Valentine
Terry Whitfield
☐ 591 Rookie Pitchers .50 .23 .06
Steve Grilli
Craig Mitchell
Jose Sosa
George Throop
☐ 592 Rookie Infielders 6.00 2.70 .75
Willie Randolph
Dave McKay
Jerry Royster
Roy Staiger
☐ 593 Rookie Pitchers .50 .23 .06
Larry Anderson
Ken Crosby
Mark Littell
Butch Metzger
☐ 594 Rookie Catchers/OF .50 .23 .06
Andy Merchant
Ed Ott
Royle Stillman
Jerry White
☐ 595 Rookie Pitchers .50 .23 .06
Art DeFillipis
Randy Lerch
Sid Monge
Steve Barr
☐ 596 Rookie Infielders .50 .23 .06
Craig Reynolds
Lamar Johnson
Johnnie LeMaster
Jerry Manuel
☐ 597 Rookie Pitchers .50 .23 .06
Don Aase
Jack Kucek
Frank LaCorte
Mike Pazik
☐ 598 Rookie Outfielders .50 .23 .06
Hector Cruz
Jamie Quirk
Jerry Turner
Joe Wallis
☐ 599 Rookie Pitchers 6.00 2.70 .75
Rob Dressler
Ron Guidry
Bob McClure
Pat Zachry
☐ 600 Tom Seaver 7.00 3.10 .85
☐ 601 Ken Rudolph .25 .11 .03
☐ 602 Doug Konieczny .25 .11 .03
☐ 603 Jim Holt .25 .11 .03
☐ 604 Joe Lovitto .25 .11 .03
☐ 605 Al Downing .25 .11 .03
☐ 606 Milwaukee Brewers 1.50 .30 .15
Team Card;
Alex Grammas MG
(Checklist back)
☐ 607 Rich Hinton .25 .11 .03
☐ 608 Vic Correll .25 .11 .03
☐ 609 Fred Norman .50 .23 .06
☐ 610 Greg Luzinski .75 .35 .09
☐ 611 Rich Folkers .25 .11 .03
☐ 612 Joe Lahoud .25 .11 .03
☐ 613 Tim Johnson .25 .11 .03
☐ 614 Fernando Arroyo .25 .11 .03
☐ 615 Mike Cubbage .25 .11 .03
☐ 616 Buck Martinez .25 .11 .03
☐ 617 Darold Knowles .25 .11 .03
☐ 618 Jack Brohamer .25 .11 .03
☐ 619 Bill Butler .25 .11 .03
☐ 620 Al Oliver .50 .23 .06
☐ 621 Tom Hall .25 .11 .03
☐ 622 Rick Auerbach .25 .11 .03
☐ 623 Bob Allietta .25 .11 .03
☐ 624 Tony Taylor .50 .23 .06
☐ 625 J.R. Richard .50 .23 .06
☐ 626 Bob Sheldon .25 .11 .03
☐ 627 Bill Plummer .25 .11 .03
☐ 628 John D'Acquisto .25 .11 .03
☐ 629 Sandy Alomar .50 .23 .06
☐ 630 Chris Speier .25 .11 .03
☐ 631 Atlanta Braves 1.50 .30 .15
Team Card;
Dave Bristol MG
(Checklist back)
☐ 632 Rogelio Moret .25 .11 .03
☐ 633 John Stearns .50 .23 .06
☐ 634 Larry Christenson .25 .11 .03
☐ 635 Jim Fregosi .50 .23 .06
☐ 636 Joe Decker .25 .11 .03
☐ 637 Bruce Bochte .25 .11 .03
☐ 638 Doyle Alexander .50 .23 .06
☐ 639 Fred Kendall .25 .11 .03
☐ 640 Bill Madlock .75 .35 .09
☐ 641 Tom Paciorek .50 .23 .06
☐ 642 Dennis Blair .25 .11 .03
☐ 643 Checklist 529-660 1.50 .30 .15
☐ 644 Tom Bradley .25 .11 .03
☐ 645 Darrell Porter .50 .23 .06
☐ 646 John Lowenstein .25 .11 .03
☐ 647 Ramon Hernandez .25 .11 .03
☐ 648 Al Cowens .25 .11 .03
☐ 649 Dave Roberts .25 .11 .03
☐ 650 Thurman Munson 4.00 1.80 .50
☐ 651 John Odom .25 .11 .03
☐ 652 Ed Armbrister .25 .11 .03
☐ 653 Mike Norris .50 .23 .06
☐ 654 Doug Griffin .25 .11 .03
☐ 655 Mike Vail .25 .11 .03
☐ 656 Chicago White Sox 1.50 .30 .15
Team Card;
Chuck Tanner MG
(Checklist back)
☐ 657 Roy Smalley .50 .23 .06
☐ 658 Jerry Johnson .25 .11 .03
☐ 659 Ben Oglivie .50 .23 .06
☐ 660 Dave Lopes 1.00 .45 .12

1976 Topps Traded

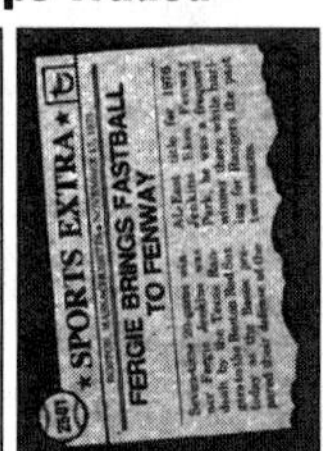

The cards in this 44-card set measure 2 1/2" by 3 1/2". The 1976 Topps Traded set contains 43 players and one unnumbered checklist card. The individuals pictured were traded after the Topps regular set was printed. A "Sports Extra" heading design is found on each picture and is also used to introduce the biographical section of the reverse. Each card is numbered according to the player's regular 1976 card with the addition of "T" to indicate his new status. As in 1974, the cards were inserted in all packs toward the end of the production run. Because they were produced in large quantities, they are no scarcer than the basic cards.

	NRMT	VG-E	GOOD
COMPLETE SET (44)	20.00	9.00	2.50
COMMON CARD	.25	.11	.03

☐ 27T Ed Figueroa .25 .11 .03
☐ 28T Dusty Baker 1.00 .45 .12
☐ 44T Doug Rader .50 .23 .06
☐ 58T Ron Reed .25 .11 .03
☐ 74T Oscar Gamble .75 .35 .09
☐ 80T Jim Kaat .75 .35 .09
☐ 83T Jim Spencer .25 .11 .03
☐ 85T Mickey Rivers .50 .23 .06
☐ 99T Lee Lacy .25 .11 .03
☐ 120T Rusty Staub .50 .23 .06
☐ 127T Larvell Blanks .25 .11 .03
☐ 146T George Medich .25 .11 .03
☐ 158T Ken Reitz .25 .11 .03
☐ 208T Mike Lum .25 .11 .03
☐ 211T Clay Carroll .25 .11 .03
☐ 231T Tom House .25 .11 .03
☐ 250T Fergie Jenkins 2.50 1.10 .30
☐ 259T Darrel Chaney .25 .11 .03
☐ 292T Leon Roberts .25 .11 .03
☐ 296T Pat Dobson .25 .11 .03
☐ 309T Bill Melton .25 .11 .03
☐ 338T Bob Bailey .25 .11 .03
☐ 380T Bobby Bonds 1.00 .45 .12
☐ 383T John Ellis .25 .11 .03
☐ 385T Mickey Lolich .50 .23 .06
☐ 401T Ken Brett .25 .11 .03
☐ 410T Ralph Garr .50 .23 .06
☐ 411T Bill Singer .25 .11 .03
☐ 428T Jim Crawford .25 .11 .03
☐ 434T Morris Nettles .25 .11 .03
☐ 464T Ken Henderson .25 .11 .03
☐ 497T Joe McIntosh .25 .11 .03
☐ 524T Pete Falcone .25 .11 .03
☐ 527T Mike Anderson .25 .11 .03
☐ 528T Dock Ellis .25 .11 .03
☐ 532T Milt May .25 .11 .03
☐ 554T Ray Fosse .25 .11 .03
☐ 579T Clay Kirby .25 .11 .03
☐ 583T Tommy Helms .25 .11 .03
☐ 592T Willie Randolph 4.00 1.80 .50
☐ 618T Jack Brohamer .25 .11 .03
☐ 632T Rogelio Moret .25 .11 .03
☐ 649T Dave Roberts .25 .11 .03
☐ NNO Traded Checklist 1.25 .25 .12

1976 Topps Team Checklist Sheet

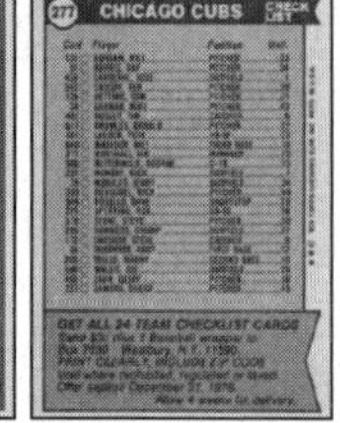

This uncut sheet of the 24 1976 Topps team checklists measures 10" by 21". The sheet was obtained by sending 50 cents plus one wrapper to Topps. When seperated, these cards measure the standard-size.

	NRMT	VG-E	GOOD
COMPLETE SET (1)	15.00	6.75	1.85
COMMON CARD	15.00	6.75	1.85

☐ 1 Topps Team CL Sheet 15.00 6.75 1.85

1977 Topps

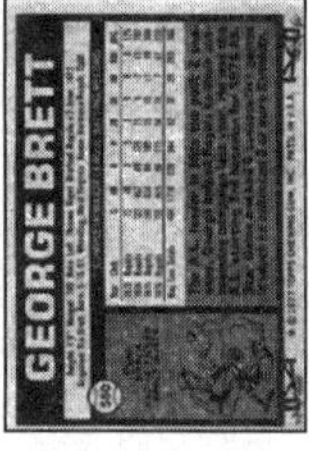

In 1977 for the fifth consecutive year, Topps produced a 660-card standard-size baseball set. Among other fashions, this set was released in 10-card wax packs as well as thirty-nine card rack packs. The player's name, team affiliation, and his position are compactly arranged over the picture area and a facsimile autograph appears on the photo. Team cards feature a checklist of that team's players in the set and a small picture of the manager on the front of the card. Appearing for the first time are the series "Brothers" (631-634) and "Turn Back the Clock" (433-437). Other subseries in the set are League Leaders (1-8), Record Breakers (231-234), Playoffs cards (276-277), World Series cards (411-413), and Rookie Prospects (472-479/487-494). The following players' regular issue cards are explicitly denoted as All-Stars, 30, 70, 100, 120, 170, 210, 240, 265, 301, 347, 400, 420, 450, 500, 521, 550, 560, and 580. The key Rookie Cards in the set are Jack Clark, Andre Dawson, Mark "The Bird" Fidrych, Dennis Martinez and Dale Murphy. Cards numbered 23 or lower, that feature Yankees and do not follow the numbering checklisted below, are not necessarily error cards. They are undoubtedly Burger King cards, a separate set with its own pricing and mass distribution. Burger King cards are indistinguishable from the corresponding Topps cards except for the card numbering difference and the fact that Burger King cards do not have a printing sheet designation (such as A through F like the regular Topps) anywhere on the card back in very small print. There was an aluminum version of the Dale Murphy rookie card number 476 produced (legally) in the early '80s; proceeds from the sales originally priced at 10.00) of this "card" went to the Huntington's Disease Foundation.

	NRMT	VG-E	GOOD
COMPLETE SET (660)	375.00	170.00	47.50
COMMON CARD (1-660)	.25	.11	.03

☐ 1 Batting Leaders 7.00 2.00 .75
George Brett
Bill Madlock
☐ 2 Home Run Leaders 1.75 .80 .22
Graig Nettles
Mike Schmidt
☐ 3 RBI Leaders .75 .35 .09

Lee May			
George Foster			
☐ 4 Stolen Base Leaders	.40	.18	.05
Bill North			
Dave Lopes			
☐ 5 Victory Leaders	.75	.35	.09
Jim Palmer			
Randy Jones			
☐ 6 Strikeout Leaders	15.00	6.75	1.85
Nolan Ryan			
Tom Seaver			
☐ 7 ERA Leaders	.40	.18	.05
Mark Fidrych			
John Denny			
☐ 8 Leading Firemen	.40	.18	.05
Bill Campbell			
Rawly Eastwick			
☐ 9 Doug Rader	.25	.11	.03
☐ 10 Reggie Jackson	10.00	4.50	1.25
☐ 11 Rob Dressler	.25	.11	.03
☐ 12 Larry Haney	.25	.11	.03
☐ 13 Luis Gomez	.25	.11	.03
☐ 14 Tommy Smith	.25	.11	.03
☐ 15 Don Gullett	.40	.18	.05
☐ 16 Bob Jones	.25	.11	.03
☐ 17 Steve Stone	.40	.18	.05
☐ 18 Indians Team/Mgr.	1.25	.25	.12
Frank Robinson			
(Checklist back)			
☐ 19 John D'Acquisto	.25	.11	.03
☐ 20 Graig Nettles	.75	.35	.09
☐ 21 Ken Forsch	.25	.11	.03
☐ 22 Bill Freehan	.40	.18	.05
☐ 23 Dan Driessen	.25	.11	.03
☐ 24 Carl Morton	.25	.11	.03
☐ 25 Dwight Evans	.75	.35	.09
☐ 26 Ray Sadecki	.25	.11	.03
☐ 27 Bill Buckner	.40	.18	.05
☐ 28 Woodie Fryman	.25	.11	.03
☐ 29 Bucky Dent	.40	.18	.05
☐ 30 Greg Luzinski	.75	.35	.09
☐ 31 Jim Todd	.25	.11	.03
☐ 32 Checklist 1-132	1.25	.25	.12
☐ 33 Wayne Garland	.25	.11	.03
☐ 34 Angels Team/Mgr.	1.25	.25	.12
Norm Sherry			
(Checklist back)			
☐ 35 Rennie Stennett	.25	.11	.03
☐ 36 John Ellis	.25	.11	.03
☐ 37 Steve Hargan	.25	.11	.03
☐ 38 Craig Kusick	.25	.11	.03
☐ 39 Tom Griffin	.25	.11	.03
☐ 40 Bobby Murcer	.40	.18	.05
☐ 41 Jim Kern	.25	.11	.03
☐ 42 Jose Cruz	.40	.18	.05
☐ 43 Ray Bare	.25	.11	.03
☐ 44 Bud Harrelson	.40	.18	.05
☐ 45 Rawly Eastwick	.25	.11	.03
☐ 46 Buck Martinez	.25	.11	.03
☐ 47 Lynn McGlothen	.25	.11	.03
☐ 48 Tom Paciorek	.40	.18	.05
☐ 49 Grant Jackson	.25	.11	.03
☐ 50 Ron Cey	.40	.18	.05
☐ 51 Brewers Team/Mgr.	1.25	.25	.12
Alex Grammas			
(Checklist back)			
☐ 52 Ellis Valentine	.25	.11	.03
☐ 53 Paul Mitchell	.25	.11	.03
☐ 54 Sandy Alomar	.40	.18	.05
☐ 55 Jeff Burroughs	.40	.18	.05
☐ 56 Rudy May	.25	.11	.03
☐ 57 Marc Hill	.25	.11	.03
☐ 58 Chet Lemon	.40	.18	.05
☐ 59 Larry Christenson	.25	.11	.03
☐ 60 Jim Rice	2.50	1.10	.30
☐ 61 Manny Sanguillen	.40	.18	.05
☐ 62 Eric Raich	.25	.11	.03
☐ 63 Tito Fuentes	.25	.11	.03
☐ 64 Larry Biittner	.25	.11	.03
☐ 65 Skip Lockwood	.25	.11	.03
☐ 66 Roy Smalley	.40	.18	.05
☐ 67 Joaquin Andujar	.40	.18	.05
☐ 68 Bruce Bochte	.25	.11	.03
☐ 69 Jim Crawford	.25	.11	.03
☐ 70 Johnny Bench	6.00	2.70	.75
☐ 71 Dock Ellis	.25	.11	.03
☐ 72 Mike Anderson	.25	.11	.03
☐ 73 Charlie Williams	.25	.11	.03
☐ 74 A's Team/Mgr.	1.25	.25	.12
Jack McKeon			
(Checklist back)			
☐ 75 Dennis Leonard	.40	.18	.05
☐ 76 Tim Foli	.25	.11	.03
☐ 77 Dyar Miller	.25	.11	.03
☐ 78 Bob Davis	.25	.11	.03
☐ 79 Don Money	.40	.18	.05
☐ 80 Andy Messersmith	.40	.18	.05
☐ 81 Juan Beniquez	.25	.11	.03
☐ 82 Jim Rooker	.25	.11	.03
☐ 83 Kevin Bell	.25	.11	.03
☐ 84 Ollie Brown	.25	.11	.03
☐ 85 Duane Kuiper	.25	.11	.03
☐ 86 Pat Zachry	.25	.11	.03
☐ 87 Glenn Borgmann	.25	.11	.03
☐ 88 Stan Wall	.25	.11	.03
☐ 89 Butch Hobson	.75	.35	.09

☐ 90 Cesar Cedeno	.40	.18	.05
☐ 91 John Verhoeven	.25	.11	.03
☐ 92 Dave Rosello	.25	.11	.03
☐ 93 Tom Poquette	.25	.11	.03
☐ 94 Craig Swan	.25	.11	.03
☐ 95 Keith Hernandez	.40	.18	.05
☐ 96 Lou Piniella	.75	.35	.09
☐ 97 Dave Heaverlo	.25	.11	.03
☐ 98 Milt May	.25	.11	.03
☐ 99 Tom Hausman	.25	.11	.03
☐ 100 Joe Morgan	3.00	1.35	.35
☐ 101 Dick Bosman	.25	.11	.03
☐ 102 Jose Morales	.25	.11	.03
☐ 103 Mike Bacsik	.25	.11	.03
☐ 104 Omar Moreno	.40	.18	.05
☐ 105 Steve Yeager	.40	.18	.05
☐ 106 Mike Flanagan	.40	.18	.05
☐ 107 Bill Melton	.25	.11	.03
☐ 108 Alan Foster	.25	.11	.03
☐ 109 Jorge Orta	.25	.11	.03
☐ 110 Steve Carlton	5.00	2.20	.60
☐ 111 Rico Petrocelli	.40	.18	.05
☐ 112 Bill Greif	.25	.11	.03
☐ 113 Blue Jays Leaders	1.25	.25	.12
Roy Hartsfield MG			
Don Leppert CO			
Bob Miller CO			
Jackie Moore CO			
Harry Warner CO			
(Checklist back)			
☐ 114 Bruce Dal Canton	.25	.11	.03
☐ 115 Rick Manning	.25	.11	.03
☐ 116 Joe Niekro	.40	.18	.05
☐ 117 Frank White	.40	.18	.05
☐ 118 Rick Jones	.25	.11	.03
☐ 119 John Stearns	.25	.11	.03
☐ 120 Rod Carew	3.00	1.35	.35
☐ 121 Gary Nolan	.25	.11	.03
☐ 122 Ben Oglivie	.40	.18	.05
☐ 123 Fred Stanley	.25	.11	.03
☐ 124 George Mitterwald	.25	.11	.03
☐ 125 Bill Travers	.25	.11	.03
☐ 126 Rod Gilbreath	.25	.11	.03
☐ 127 Ron Fairly	.40	.18	.05
☐ 128 Tommy John	.75	.35	.09
☐ 129 Mike Sadek	.25	.11	.03
☐ 130 Al Oliver	.40	.18	.05
☐ 131 Orlando Ramirez	.25	.11	.03
☐ 132 Chip Lang	.25	.11	.03
☐ 133 Ralph Garr	.40	.18	.05
☐ 134 Padres Team/Mgr.	1.25	.25	.12
John McNamara			
(Checklist back)			
☐ 135 Mark Belanger	.40	.18	.05
☐ 136 Jerry Mumphrey	.40	.18	.05
☐ 137 Jeff Terpko	.25	.11	.03
☐ 138 Bob Stinson	.25	.11	.03
☐ 139 Fred Norman	.25	.11	.03
☐ 140 Mike Schmidt	16.00	7.25	2.00
☐ 141 Mark Littell	.25	.11	.03
☐ 142 Steve Dillard	.25	.11	.03
☐ 143 Ed Herrmann	.25	.11	.03
☐ 144 Bruce Sutter	2.50	1.10	.30
☐ 145 Tom Veryzer	.25	.11	.03
☐ 146 Dusty Baker	.75	.35	.09
☐ 147 Jackie Brown	.25	.11	.03
☐ 148 Fran Healy	.25	.11	.03
☐ 149 Mike Cubbage	.25	.11	.03
☐ 150 Tom Seaver	5.00	2.20	.60
☐ 151 Johnny LeMaster	.25	.11	.03
☐ 152 Gaylord Perry	2.00	.90	.25
☐ 153 Ron Jackson	.25	.11	.03
☐ 154 Dave Giusti	.25	.11	.03
☐ 155 Joe Rudi	.40	.18	.05
☐ 156 Pete Mackanin	.25	.11	.03
☐ 157 Ken Brett	.25	.11	.03
☐ 158 Ted Kubiak	.25	.11	.03
☐ 159 Bernie Carbo	.25	.11	.03
☐ 160 Will McEnaney	.25	.11	.03
☐ 161 Garry Templeton	1.25	.55	.16
☐ 162 Mike Cuellar	.40	.18	.05
☐ 163 Dave Hilton	.25	.11	.03
☐ 164 Tug McGraw	.40	.18	.05
☐ 165 Jim Wynn	.40	.18	.05
☐ 166 Bill Campbell	.25	.11	.03
☐ 167 Rich Hebner	.40	.18	.05
☐ 168 Charlie Spikes	.25	.11	.03
☐ 169 Darold Knowles	.25	.11	.03
☐ 170 Thurman Munson	4.00	1.80	.50
☐ 171 Ken Sanders	.25	.11	.03
☐ 172 John Milner	.25	.11	.03
☐ 173 Chuck Scrivener	.25	.11	.03
☐ 174 Nelson Briles	.40	.18	.05
☐ 175 Butch Wynegar	.40	.18	.05
☐ 176 Bob Robertson	.25	.11	.03
☐ 177 Bart Johnson	.25	.11	.03
☐ 178 Bombo Rivera	.25	.11	.03
☐ 179 Paul Hartzell	.25	.11	.03
☐ 180 Dave Lopes	.40	.18	.05
☐ 181 Ken McMullen	.25	.11	.03
☐ 182 Dan Spillner	.25	.11	.03
☐ 183 Cardinals Team/Mgr.	1.25	.25	.12
Vern Rapp			
(Checklist back)			
☐ 184 Bo McLaughlin	.25	.11	.03

☐ 185 Sixto Lezcano	.25	.11	.03
☐ 186 Doug Flynn	.25	.11	.03
☐ 187 Dick Pole	.25	.11	.03
☐ 188 Bob Tolan	.25	.11	.03
☐ 189 Rick Dempsey	.40	.18	.05
☐ 190 Ray Burris	.25	.11	.03
☐ 191 Doug Griffin	.25	.11	.03
☐ 192 Clarence Gaston	.40	.18	.05
☐ 193 Larry Gura	.25	.11	.03
☐ 194 Gary Matthews	.40	.18	.05
☐ 195 Ed Figueroa	.25	.11	.03
☐ 196 Len Randle	.25	.11	.03
☐ 197 Ed Ott	.25	.11	.03
☐ 198 Wilbur Wood	.25	.11	.03
☐ 199 Pepe Frias	.25	.11	.03
☐ 200 Frank Tanana	.75	.35	.09
☐ 201 Ed Kranepool	.25	.11	.03
☐ 202 Tom Johnson	.25	.11	.03
☐ 203 Ed Armbrister	.25	.11	.03
☐ 204 Jeff Newman	.25	.11	.03
☐ 205 Pete Falcone	.25	.11	.03
☐ 206 Boog Powell	.40	.18	.05
☐ 207 Glenn Abbott	.25	.11	.03
☐ 208 Checklist 133-264	1.25	.25	.12
☐ 209 Rob Andrews	.25	.11	.03
☐ 210 Fred Lynn	.40	.08	.04
☐ 211 Giants Team/Mgr.	1.25	.55	.16
Joe Altobelli			
(Checklist back)			
☐ 212 Jim Mason	.25	.11	.03
☐ 213 Maximino Leon	.25	.11	.03
☐ 214 Darrell Porter	.40	.18	.05
☐ 215 Butch Metzger	.25	.11	.03
☐ 216 Doug DeCinces	.40	.18	.05
☐ 217 Tom Underwood	.25	.11	.03
☐ 218 John Wathan	.25	.11	.03
☐ 219 Joe Coleman	.25	.11	.03
☐ 220 Chris Chambliss	.40	.18	.05
☐ 221 Bob Bailey	.25	.11	.03
☐ 222 Francisco Barrios	.25	.11	.03
☐ 223 Earl Williams	.25	.11	.03
☐ 224 Rusty Torres	.25	.11	.03
☐ 225 Bob Apodaca	.25	.11	.03
☐ 226 Leroy Stanton	.40	.18	.05
☐ 227 Joe Sambito	.25	.11	.03
☐ 228 Twins Team/Mgr.	1.25	.25	.12
Gene Mauch			
(Checklist back)			
☐ 229 Don Kessinger	.40	.18	.05
☐ 230 Vida Blue	.40	.18	.05
☐ 231 George Brett RB	12.00	5.50	1.50
Most consecutive games			
3 or more hits			
☐ 232 Minnie Minoso RB	.40	.18	.05
Oldest to hit safely			
☐ 233 Jose Morales RB	.25	.11	.03
Most pinch-hits season			
☐ 234 Nolan Ryan RB	18.00	8.00	2.20
Most seasons, 300 strikeouts			
☐ 235 Cecil Cooper	.40	.18	.05
☐ 236 Tom Buskey	.25	.11	.03
☐ 237 Gene Clines	.25	.11	.03
☐ 238 Tippy Martinez	.40	.18	.05
☐ 239 Bill Plummer	.25	.11	.03
☐ 240 Ron LeFlore	.40	.18	.05
☐ 241 Dave Tomlin	.25	.11	.03
☐ 242 Ken Henderson	.25	.11	.03
☐ 243 Ron Reed	.25	.11	.03
☐ 244 John Mayberry	.75	.35	.09
(Cartoon mentions			
T206 Wagner)			
☐ 245 Rick Rhoden	.40	.18	.05
☐ 246 Mike Vail	.25	.11	.03
☐ 247 Chris Knapp	.25	.11	.03
☐ 248 Wilbur Howard	.25	.11	.03
☐ 249 Pete Redfern	.25	.11	.03
☐ 250 Bill Madlock	.40	.18	.05
☐ 251 Tony Muser	.25	.11	.03
☐ 252 Dale Murray	.25	.11	.03
☐ 253 John Hale	.25	.11	.03
☐ 254 Doyle Alexander	.25	.11	.03
☐ 255 George Scott	.40	.18	.05
☐ 256 Joe Hoerner	.25	.11	.03
☐ 257 Mike Miley	.25	.11	.03
☐ 258 Luis Tiant	.40	.18	.05
☐ 259 Mets Team/Mgr.	1.25	.25	.12
Joe Frazier			
(Checklist back)			
☐ 260 J.R. Richard	.40	.18	.05
☐ 261 Phil Garner	.40	.18	.05
☐ 262 Al Cowens	.25	.11	.03
☐ 263 Mike Marshall	.40	.18	.05
☐ 264 Tom Hutton	.25	.11	.03
☐ 265 Mark Fidrych	5.00	2.20	.60
☐ 266 Derrel Thomas	.25	.11	.03
☐ 267 Ray Fosse	.25	.11	.03
☐ 268 Rick Sawyer	.25	.11	.03
☐ 269 Joe Lis	.25	.11	.03
☐ 270 Dave Parker	.75	.35	.09
☐ 271 Terry Forster	.25	.11	.03
☐ 272 Lee Lacy	.25	.11	.03
☐ 273 Eric Soderholm	.25	.11	.03
☐ 274 Don Stanhouse	.25	.11	.03
☐ 275 Mike Hargrove	.40	.18	.05
☐ 276 Chris Chambliss ALCS	.75	.35	.09

homer decides it			
☐ 277 Pete Rose NLCS	2.00	.90	.25
☐ 278 Danny Frisella	.25	.11	.03
☐ 279 Joe Wallis	.25	.11	.03
☐ 280 Jim Hunter	2.00	.90	.25
☐ 281 Roy Staiger	.25	.11	.03
☐ 282 Sid Monge	.25	.11	.03
☐ 283 Jerry DaVanon	.25	.11	.03
☐ 284 Mike Norris	.25	.11	.03
☐ 285 Brooks Robinson	4.00	1.80	.50
☐ 286 Johnny Grubb	.25	.05	.03
☐ 287 Reds Team/Mgr.	1.25	.55	.16
Sparky Anderson			
(Checklist back)			
☐ 288 Bob Montgomery	.25	.11	.03
☐ 289 Gene Garber	.40	.18	.05
☐ 290 Amos Otis	.40	.18	.05
☐ 291 Jason Thompson	.40	.18	.05
☐ 292 Rogelio Moret	.25	.11	.03
☐ 293 Jack Brohamer	.25	.11	.03
☐ 294 George Medich	.25	.11	.03
☐ 295 Gary Carter	4.00	1.80	.50
☐ 296 Don Hood	.25	.11	.03
☐ 297 Ken Reitz	.25	.11	.03
☐ 298 Charlie Hough	.75	.35	.09
☐ 299 Otto Velez	.40	.18	.05
☐ 300 Jerry Koosman	.40	.18	.05
☐ 301 Toby Harrah	.40	.18	.05
☐ 302 Mike Garman	.25	.11	.03
☐ 303 Gene Tenace	.40	.18	.05
☐ 304 Jim Hughes	.25	.11	.03
☐ 305 Mickey Rivers	.40	.18	.05
☐ 306 Rick Waits	.25	.11	.03
☐ 307 Gary Sutherland	.25	.11	.03
☐ 308 Gene Pentz	.25	.11	.03
☐ 309 Red Sox Team/Mgr.	1.25	.25	.12
Don Zimmer			
(Checklist back)			
☐ 310 Larry Bowa	.75	.35	.09
☐ 311 Vern Ruhle	.25	.11	.03
☐ 312 Rob Belloir	.25	.11	.03
☐ 313 Paul Blair	.40	.18	.05
☐ 314 Steve Mingori	.25	.11	.03
☐ 315 Dave Chalk	.25	.11	.03
☐ 316 Steve Rogers	.25	.11	.03
☐ 317 Kurt Bevacqua	.25	.11	.03
☐ 318 Duffy Dyer	.25	.11	.03
☐ 319 Rich Gossage	1.25	.55	.16
☐ 320 Ken Griffey	.75	.35	.09
☐ 321 Dave Goltz	.25	.11	.03
☐ 322 Bill Russell	.40	.18	.05
☐ 323 Larry Lintz	.25	.11	.03
☐ 324 John Curtis	.25	.11	.03
☐ 325 Mike Ivie	.25	.11	.03
☐ 326 Jesse Jefferson	.25	.11	.03
☐ 327 Astros Team/Mgr.	1.25	.25	.12
Bill Virdon			
(Checklist back)			
☐ 328 Tommy Boggs	.25	.11	.03
☐ 329 Ron Hodges	.25	.11	.03
☐ 330 George Hendrick	.40	.18	.05
☐ 331 Jim Colborn	.25	.11	.03
☐ 332 Elliott Maddox	.25	.11	.03
☐ 333 Paul Reuschel	.25	.11	.03
☐ 334 Bill Stein	.25	.11	.03
☐ 335 Bill Robinson	.40	.18	.05
☐ 336 Denny Doyle	.25	.11	.03
☐ 337 Ron Schueler	.25	.11	.03
☐ 338 Dave Duncan	.25	.11	.03
☐ 339 Adrian Devine	.25	.11	.03
☐ 340 Hal McRae	.75	.35	.09
☐ 341 Joe Kerrigan	.25	.11	.03
☐ 342 Jerry Remy	.25	.11	.03
☐ 343 Ed Halicki	.25	.11	.03
☐ 344 Brian Downing	.40	.18	.05
☐ 345 Reggie Smith	.40	.18	.05
☐ 346 Bill Singer	.25	.11	.03
☐ 347 George Foster	.75	.35	.09
☐ 348 Brent Strom	.25	.11	.03
☐ 349 Jim Holt	.25	.11	.03
☐ 350 Larry Dierker	.40	.18	.05
☐ 351 Jim Sundberg	.40	.18	.05
☐ 352 Mike Phillips	.25	.11	.03
☐ 353 Stan Thomas	.25	.11	.03
☐ 354 Pirates Team/Mgr.	1.25	.25	.12
Chuck Tanner			
(Checklist back)			
☐ 355 Lou Brock	3.00	1.35	.35
☐ 356 Checklist 265-396	1.25	.25	.12
☐ 357 Tim McCarver	.40	.18	.05
☐ 358 Tom House	.25	.11	.03
☐ 359 Willie Randolph	.75	.35	.09
☐ 360 Rick Monday	.40	.18	.05
☐ 361 Eduardo Rodriguez	.25	.11	.03
☐ 362 Tommy Davis	.40	.18	.05
☐ 363 Dave Roberts	.25	.11	.03
☐ 364 Vic Correll	.25	.11	.03
☐ 365 Mike Torrez	.40	.18	.05
☐ 366 Ted Sizemore	.25	.11	.03
☐ 367 Dave Hamilton	.25	.11	.03
☐ 368 Mike Jorgensen	.25	.11	.03
☐ 369 Terry Humphrey	.25	.11	.03
☐ 370 John Montefusco	.25	.11	.03
☐ 371 Royals Team/Mgr.	1.25	.25	.12
Whitey Herzog			
(Checklist back)			

☐ 372 Rich Folkers .25 .11 .03
☐ 373 Bert Campaneris .40 .18 .05
☐ 374 Kent Tekulve .75 .35 .09
☐ 375 Larry Hisle .40 .18 .05
☐ 376 Nino Espinosa .25 .11 .03
☐ 377 Dave McKay .25 .11 .03
☐ 378 Jim Umbarger .25 .11 .03
☐ 379 Larry Cox .25 .11 .03
☐ 380 Lee May .40 .18 .05
☐ 381 Bob Forsch .25 .11 .03
☐ 382 Charlie Moore .25 .11 .03
☐ 383 Stan Bahnsen .25 .11 .03
☐ 384 Darrel Chaney .25 .11 .03
☐ 385 Dave LaRoche .25 .11 .03
☐ 386 Manny Mota .40 .18 .05
☐ 387 Yankees Team/Mgr. 1.75 .35 .17
Billy Martin
(Checklist back)
☐ 388 Terry Harmon .25 .11 .03
☐ 389 Ken Kravec .25 .11 .03
☐ 390 Dave Winfield 16.00 7.25 2.00
☐ 391 Dan Warthen .25 .11 .03
☐ 392 Phil Roof .25 .11 .03
☐ 393 John Lowenstein .25 .11 .03
☐ 394 Bill Laxton .25 .11 .03
☐ 395 Manny Trillo .25 .11 .03
☐ 396 Tom Murphy .25 .11 .03
☐ 397 Larry Herndon .40 .18 .05
☐ 398 Tom Burgmeier .25 .11 .03
☐ 399 Bruce Boisclair .25 .11 .03
☐ 400 Steve Garvey 2.50 1.10 .30
☐ 401 Mickey Scott .25 .11 .03
☐ 402 Tommy Helms .25 .11 .03
☐ 403 Tom Grieve .40 .18 .05
☐ 404 Eric Rasmussen .25 .11 .03
☐ 405 Claudell Washington .40 .18 .05
☐ 406 Tim Johnson .25 .11 .03
☐ 407 Dave Freisleben .25 .11 .03
☐ 408 Cesar Tovar .25 .11 .03
☐ 409 Pete Broberg .25 .11 .03
☐ 410 Willie Montanez .25 .11 .03
☐ 411 Joe Morgan WS 1.75 .80 .22
Johnny Bench
☐ 412 Johnny Bench WS 1.75 .80 .22
☐ 413 World Series Summary .75 .35 .09
Cincy wins 2nd
straight series
☐ 414 Tommy Harper .40 .18 .05
☐ 415 Jay Johnstone .40 .18 .05
☐ 416 Chuck Hartenstein .25 .11 .03
☐ 417 Wayne Garrett .25 .11 .03
☐ 418 White Sox Team/Mgr. 1.25 .25 .12
Bob Lemon
(Checklist back)
☐ 419 Steve Swisher .25 .11 .03
☐ 420 Rusty Staub .75 .35 .09
☐ 421 Doug Rau .25 .11 .03
☐ 422 Freddie Patek .40 .18 .05
☐ 423 Gary Lavelle .25 .11 .03
☐ 424 Steve Brye .25 .11 .03
☐ 425 Joe Torre .40 .18 .05
☐ 426 Dick Drago .25 .11 .03
☐ 427 Dave Rader .25 .11 .03
☐ 428 Rangers Team/Mgr. 1.25 .25 .12
Frank Lucchesi
(Checklist back)
☐ 429 Ken Boswell .25 .11 .03
☐ 430 Fergie Jenkins 2.00 .90 .25
☐ 431 Dave Collins UER .40 .18 .05
(Photo actually
Bobby Jones)
☐ 432 Buzz Capra .25 .11 .03
☐ 433 Nate Colbert TBC .25 .11 .03
(5 HR, 13 RBI)
☐ 434 Carl Yastrzemski TBC 1.50 .70 .19
'67 Triple Crown
☐ 435 Maury Wills TBC .40 .18 .05
104 steals
☐ 436 Bob Keegan TBC .25 .11 .03
Majors' only no-hitter
☐ 437 Ralph Kiner TBC .75 .35 .09
Leads NL in HR's
7th straight year
☐ 438 Marty Perez .25 .11 .03
☐ 439 Gorman Thomas .40 .18 .05
☐ 440 Jon Matlack .25 .11 .03
☐ 441 Larvell Blanks .25 .11 .03
☐ 442 Braves Team/Mgr. 1.25 .25 .12
Dave Bristol
(Checklist back)
☐ 443 Lamar Johnson .25 .11 .03
☐ 444 Wayne Twitchell .25 .11 .03
☐ 445 Ken Singleton .40 .18 .05
☐ 446 Bill Bonham .25 .11 .03
☐ 447 Jerry Turner .25 .11 .03
☐ 448 Ellie Rodriguez .25 .11 .03
☐ 449 Al Fitzmorris .25 .11 .03
☐ 450 Pete Rose 10.00 4.50 1.25
☐ 451 Checklist 397-528 1.25 .25 .12
☐ 452 Mike Caldwell .25 .11 .03
☐ 453 Pedro Garcia .25 .11 .03
☐ 454 Andy Etchebarren .25 .11 .03
☐ 455 Rick Wise .25 .11 .03
☐ 456 Leon Roberts .25 .11 .03
☐ 457 Steve Luebber .25 .11 .03
☐ 458 Leo Foster .25 .11 .03
☐ 459 Steve Foucault .25 .11 .03
☐ 460 Willie Stargell 2.50 1.10 .30
☐ 461 Dick Tidrow .25 .11 .03
☐ 462 Don Baylor 1.25 .55 .16
☐ 463 Jamie Quirk .25 .11 .03
☐ 464 Randy Moffitt .25 .11 .03
☐ 465 Rico Carty .40 .18 .05
☐ 466 Fred Holdsworth .25 .11 .03
☐ 467 Phillies Team/Mgr. 1.25 .25 .12
Danny Ozark
(Checklist back)
☐ 468 Ramon Hernandez .25 .11 .03
☐ 469 Pat Kelly .25 .11 .03
☐ 470 Ted Simmons .40 .18 .05
☐ 471 Del Unser .25 .11 .03
☐ 472 Rookie Pitchers .25 .11 .03
Don Aase
Bob McClure
Gil Patterson
Dave Wehrmeister
☐ 473 Rookie Outfielders 60.00 27.00 7.50
Andre Dawson
Gene Richards
John Scott
Denny Walling
☐ 474 Rookie Shortstops .40 .18 .05
Bob Bailor
Kiko Garcia
Craig Reynolds
Alex Taveras
☐ 475 Rookie Pitchers .75 .35 .09
Chris Batton
Rick Camp
Scott McGregor
Manny Sarmiento
☐ 476 Rookie Catchers 20.00 9.00 2.50
Gary Alexander
Rick Cerone
Dale Murphy
Kevin Pasley
☐ 477 Rookie Infielders .75 .35 .09
Doug Ault
Rich Dauer
Orlando Gonzalez
Phil Mankowski
☐ 478 Rookie Pitchers .40 .18 .05
Jim Gideon
Leon Hooten
Dave Johnson
Mark Lemongello
☐ 479 Rookie Outfielders .75 .35 .09
Brian Asselstine
Wayne Gross
Sam Mejias
Alvis Woods
☐ 480 Carl Yastrzemski 4.00 1.80 .50
☐ 481 Roger Metzger .25 .11 .03
☐ 482 Tony Solaita .25 .11 .03
☐ 483 Richie Zisk .25 .11 .03
☐ 484 Burt Hooton .40 .18 .05
☐ 485 Roy White .40 .18 .05
☐ 486 Ed Bane .25 .11 .03
☐ 487 Rookie Pitchers .40 .18 .05
Larry Anderson
Ed Glynn
Joe Henderson
Greg Terlecky
☐ 488 Rookie Outfielders 5.00 2.20 .60
Jack Clark
Ruppert Jones
Lee Mazzilli
Dan Thomas
☐ 489 Rookie Pitchers .75 .35 .09
Len Barker
Randy Lerch
Greg Minton
Mike Overy
☐ 490 Rookie Shortstops .40 .18 .05
Billy Almon
Mickey Klutts
Tommy McMillan
Mark Wagner
☐ 491 Rookie Pitchers 6.00 2.70 .75
Mike Dupree
Dennis Martinez
Craig Mitchell
Bob Sykes
☐ 492 Rookie Outfielders .75 .35 .09
Tony Armas
Steve Kemp
Carlos Lopez
Gary Woods
☐ 493 Rookie Pitchers .40 .18 .05
Mike Krukow
Jim Otten
Gary Wheelock
Mike Willis
☐ 494 Rookie Infielders 1.25 .55 .16
Juan Bernhardt
Mike Champion
Jim Gantner
Bump Wills
☐ 495 Al Hrabosky .25 .11 .03
☐ 496 Gary Thomasson .25 .11 .03
☐ 497 Clay Carroll .25 .11 .03
☐ 498 Sal Bando .40 .18 .05
☐ 499 Pablo Torrealba .25 .11 .03
☐ 500 Dave Kingman .40 .18 .05
☐ 501 Jim Bibby .25 .11 .03
☐ 502 Randy Hundley .25 .11 .03
☐ 503 Bill Lee .25 .11 .03
☐ 504 Dodgers Team/Mgr. 1.25 .25 .12
Tom Lasorda
(Checklist back)
☐ 505 Oscar Gamble .40 .18 .05
☐ 506 Steve Grilli .25 .11 .03
☐ 507 Mike Hegan .25 .11 .03
☐ 508 Dave Pagan .25 .11 .03
☐ 509 Cookie Rojas .40 .18 .05
☐ 510 John Candelaria .25 .11 .03
☐ 511 Bill Fahey .25 .11 .03
☐ 512 Jack Billingham .25 .11 .03
☐ 513 Jerry Terrell .25 .11 .03
☐ 514 Cliff Johnson .25 .11 .03
☐ 515 Chris Speier .25 .11 .03
☐ 516 Bake McBride .40 .18 .05
☐ 517 Pete Vuckovich .40 .18 .05
☐ 518 Cubs Team/Mgr. 1.25 .25 .12
Herman Franks
(Checklist back)
☐ 519 Don Kirkwood .25 .11 .03
☐ 520 Garry Maddox .25 .11 .03
☐ 521 Bob Grich .40 .18 .05
☐ 522 Enzo Hernandez .25 .11 .03
☐ 523 Rollie Fingers 2.00 .90 .25
☐ 524 Rowland Office .25 .11 .03
☐ 525 Dennis Eckersley 6.00 2.70 .75
☐ 526 Larry Parrish .40 .18 .05
☐ 527 Dan Meyer .40 .18 .05
☐ 528 Bill Castro .25 .11 .03
☐ 529 Jim Essian .25 .11 .03
☐ 530 Rick Reuschel .40 .18 .05
☐ 531 Lyman Bostock .40 .18 .05
☐ 532 Jim Willoughby .25 .11 .03
☐ 533 Mickey Stanley .25 .11 .03
☐ 534 Paul Splittorff .25 .11 .03
☐ 535 Cesar Geronimo .25 .11 .03
☐ 536 Vic Albury .25 .11 .03
☐ 537 Dave Roberts .25 .11 .03
☐ 538 Frank Taveras .25 .11 .03
☐ 539 Mike Wallace .25 .11 .03
☐ 540 Bob Watson .40 .18 .05
☐ 541 John Denny .40 .18 .05
☐ 542 Frank Duffy .25 .11 .03
☐ 543 Ron Blomberg .25 .11 .03
☐ 544 Gary Ross .25 .11 .03
☐ 545 Bob Boone .75 .35 .09
☐ 546 Orioles Team/Mgr. 1.25 .25 .12
Earl Weaver
(Checklist back)
☐ 547 Willie McCovey 3.00 1.35 .35
☐ 548 Joel Youngblood .25 .11 .03
☐ 549 Jerry Royster .25 .11 .03
☐ 550 Randy Jones .25 .11 .03
☐ 551 Bill North .25 .11 .03
☐ 552 Pepe Mangual .25 .11 .03
☐ 553 Jack Heidemann .25 .11 .03
☐ 554 Bruce Kimm .25 .11 .03
☐ 555 Dan Ford .25 .11 .03
☐ 556 Doug Bird .25 .11 .03
☐ 557 Jerry White .25 .11 .03
☐ 558 Elias Sosa .25 .11 .03
☐ 559 Alan Bannister .25 .11 .03
☐ 560 Dave Concepcion .75 .35 .09
☐ 561 Pete LaCock .25 .11 .03
☐ 562 Checklist 529-660 1.25 .25 .12
☐ 563 Bruce Kison .25 .11 .03
☐ 564 Alan Ashby .40 .18 .05
☐ 565 Mickey Lolich .40 .18 .05
☐ 566 Rick Miller .25 .11 .03
☐ 567 Enos Cabell .25 .11 .03
☐ 568 Carlos May .25 .11 .03
☐ 569 Jim Lonborg .40 .18 .05
☐ 570 Bobby Bonds .75 .35 .09
☐ 571 Darrell Evans .40 .18 .05
☐ 572 Ross Grimsley .25 .11 .03
☐ 573 Joe Ferguson .25 .11 .03
☐ 574 Aurelio Rodriguez .25 .11 .03
☐ 575 Dick Ruthven .25 .11 .03
☐ 576 Fred Kendall .25 .11 .03
☐ 577 Jerry Augustine .25 .11 .03
☐ 578 Bob Randall .25 .11 .03
☐ 579 Don Carrithers .25 .11 .03
☐ 580 George Brett 35.00 16.00 4.40
☐ 581 Pedro Borbon .25 .11 .03
☐ 582 Ed Kirkpatrick .25 .11 .03
☐ 583 Paul Lindblad .25 .11 .03
☐ 584 Ed Goodson .25 .11 .03
☐ 585 Rick Burleson .40 .18 .05
☐ 586 Steve Renko .25 .11 .03
☐ 587 Rick Baldwin .25 .11 .03
☐ 588 Dave Moates .25 .11 .03
☐ 589 Mike Cosgrove .25 .11 .03
☐ 590 Buddy Bell .40 .18 .05
☐ 591 Chris Arnold .25 .11 .03
☐ 592 Dan Briggs .25 .11 .03
☐ 593 Dennis Blair .25 .11 .03
☐ 594 Biff Pocoroba .25 .11 .03
☐ 595 John Hiller .25 .11 .03
☐ 596 Jerry Martin .25 .11 .03
☐ 597 Mariners Leaders 1.25 .25 .12
Darrell Johnson MG
Don Bryant CO
Jim Busby CO
Vada Pinson CO
Wes Stock CO
(Checklist back)
☐ 598 Sparky Lyle .40 .18 .05
☐ 599 Mike Tyson .25 .11 .03
☐ 600 Jim Palmer 3.00 1.35 .35
☐ 601 Mike Lum .25 .11 .03
☐ 602 Andy Hassler .25 .11 .03
☐ 603 Willie Davis .40 .18 .05
☐ 604 Jim Slaton .25 .11 .03
☐ 605 Felix Millan .25 .11 .03
☐ 606 Steve Braun .25 .11 .03
☐ 607 Larry Demery .25 .11 .03
☐ 608 Roy Howell .25 .11 .03
☐ 609 Jim Barr .25 .11 .03
☐ 610 Jose Cardenal .40 .18 .05
☐ 611 Dave Lemanczyk .25 .11 .03
☐ 612 Barry Foote .25 .11 .03
☐ 613 Reggie Cleveland .25 .11 .03
☐ 614 Greg Gross .25 .11 .03
☐ 615 Phil Niekro 1.50 .70 .19
☐ 616 Tommy Sandt .25 .11 .03
☐ 617 Bobby Darwin .25 .11 .03
☐ 618 Pat Dobson .25 .11 .03
☐ 619 Johnny Oates .40 .18 .05
☐ 620 Don Sutton 1.25 .55 .16
☐ 621 Tigers Team/Mgr. 1.25 .25 .12
Ralph Houk
(Checklist back)
☐ 622 Jim Wohlford .25 .11 .03
☐ 623 Jack Kucek .25 .11 .03
☐ 624 Hector Cruz .25 .11 .03
☐ 625 Ken Holtzman .40 .18 .05
☐ 626 Al Bumbry .40 .18 .05
☐ 627 Bob Myrick .25 .11 .03
☐ 628 Mario Guerrero .25 .11 .03
☐ 629 Bobby Valentine .25 .11 .03
☐ 630 Bert Blyleven .75 .35 .09
☐ 631 George Brett 8.00 3.60 1.00
Ken Brett
☐ 632 Bob Forsch .40 .18 .05
Ken Forsch
☐ 633 Lee May .40 .18 .05
Carlos May
☐ 634 Paul Reuschel .40 .18 .05
Rick Reuschel UER
(Photos switched)
☐ 635 Robin Yount 20.00 9.00 2.50
☐ 636 Santo Alcala .25 .11 .03
☐ 637 Alex Johnson .25 .11 .03
☐ 638 Jim Kaat .75 .35 .09
☐ 639 Jerry Morales .25 .11 .03
☐ 640 Carlton Fisk 5.00 2.20 .60
☐ 641 Dan Larson .25 .11 .03
☐ 642 Willie Crawford .25 .11 .03
☐ 643 Mike Pazik .25 .11 .03
☐ 644 Matt Alexander .25 .11 .03
☐ 645 Jerry Reuss .40 .18 .05
☐ 646 Andres Mora .25 .11 .03
☐ 647 Expos Team/Mgr. 1.25 .25 .12
Dick Williams
(Checklist back)
☐ 648 Jim Spencer .25 .11 .03
☐ 649 Dave Cash .25 .11 .03
☐ 650 Nolan Ryan 45.00 20.00 5.50
☐ 651 Von Joshua .25 .11 .03
☐ 652 Tom Walker .25 .11 .03
☐ 653 Diego Segui .40 .18 .05
☐ 654 Ron Pruitt .25 .11 .03
☐ 655 Tony Perez 1.50 .70 .19
☐ 656 Ron Guidry .75 .35 .09
☐ 657 Mick Kelleher .25 .11 .03
☐ 658 Marty Pattin .25 .11 .03
☐ 659 Merv Rettenmund .25 .11 .03
☐ 660 Willie Horton .75 .35 .09

1977 Topps Cloth Stickers

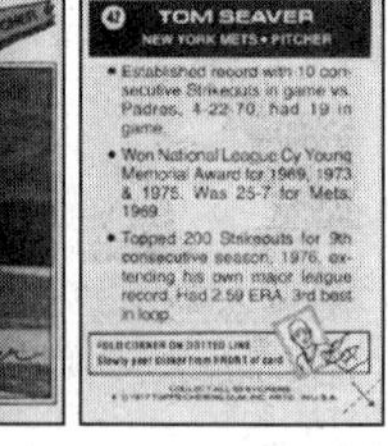

The "cards" in this 73-card set measure 2 1/2" by 3 1/2". The 1977 Cloth Stickers series was issued as a test set separately from the regular baseball series of that year. The packs of these cards contained two stickers as well as one "checklist puzzle" piece. The obverse pictures are identical to those appearing in the regular set, but the backs are completely different. There are 55 player cards and

18 unnumbered checklists, the latter bearing the title "Baseball Patches". The player cards are sequenced in alphabetical order. The checklists are puzzle pieces which, when properly arranged, form pictures of the A.L. and N.L. All-Star teams. Puzzle pieces are coded below by U (Upper), M (Middle), B (Bottom), L (left), C (Center), and R (Right). Cards marked with an SP in the checklist are in shorter supply than all others in the set.

	NRMT	VG-E	GOOD
COMPLETE SET (73)	200.00	90.00	25.00
COMMON CARD (1-55)	.50	.23	.06
COMMON SP PLAYER (1-55)	1.00	.45	.12
COMMON PUZZLE (56-73)	.15	.07	.02
☐ 1 Alan Ashby	.50	.23	.06
☐ 2 Buddy Bell SP	1.50	.70	.19
☐ 3 Johnny Bench	8.00	3.60	1.00
☐ 4 Vida Blue	1.00	.45	.12
☐ 5 Bert Blyleven	1.00	.45	.12
☐ 6 Steve Braun SP	1.00	.45	.12
☐ 7 George Brett	25.00	11.00	3.10
☐ 8 Lou Brock	5.00	2.20	.60
☐ 9 Jose Cardenal	.50	.23	.06
☐ 10 Rod Carew SP	10.00	4.50	1.25
☐ 11 Steve Carlton	7.00	3.10	.85
☐ 12 Dave Cash	1.00	.45	.12
☐ 13 Cesar Cedeno SP	1.50	.70	.19
☐ 14 Ron Cey	1.00	.45	.12
☐ 15 Mark Fidrych	1.00	.45	.12
☐ 16 Dan Ford	.50	.23	.06
☐ 17 Wayne Garland	.50	.23	.06
☐ 18 Ralph Garr	.75	.35	.09
☐ 19 Steve Garvey	4.00	1.80	.50
☐ 20 Mike Hargrove	1.00	.45	.12
☐ 21 Jim Hunter	3.00	1.35	.35
☐ 22 Reggie Jackson	12.00	5.50	1.50
☐ 23 Randy Jones	.50	.23	.06
☐ 24 Dave Kingman SP	1.50	.70	.19
☐ 25 Bill Madlock	1.00	.45	.12
☐ 26 Lee May SP	1.50	.70	.19
☐ 27 John Mayberry	.50	.23	.06
☐ 28 John(Andy)Messersmith	.50	.23	.06
☐ 29 Willie Montanez	.50	.23	.06
☐ 30 John Montefusco SP	1.00	.45	.12
☐ 31 Joe Morgan	5.00	2.20	.60
☐ 32 Thurman Munson	3.00	1.35	.35
☐ 33 Bobby Murcer	1.00	.45	.12
☐ 34 Al Oliver SP	1.50	.70	.19
☐ 35 Dave Pagan	.50	.23	.06
☐ 36 Jim Palmer SP	10.00	4.50	1.25
☐ 37 Tony Perez	1.00	.45	.12
☐ 38 Pete Rose SP	15.00	6.75	1.85
☐ 39 Joe Rudi	.75	.35	.09
☐ 40 Nolan Ryan SP	60.00	27.00	7.50
☐ 41 Mike Schmidt	20.00	9.00	2.50
☐ 42 Tom Seaver	10.00	4.50	1.25
☐ 43 Ted Simmons	1.00	.45	.12
☐ 44 Bill Singer	.50	.23	.06
☐ 45 Willie Stargell	4.00	1.80	.50
☐ 46 Rusty Staub	1.00	.45	.12
☐ 47 Don Sutton	2.00	.90	.25
☐ 48 Luis Tiant	1.00	.45	.12
☐ 49 Bill Travers	.50	.23	.06
☐ 50 Claudell Washington	1.00	.45	.12
☐ 51 Bob Watson	1.00	.45	.12
☐ 52 Dave Winfield	12.00	5.50	1.50
☐ 53 Carl Yastrzemski	6.00	2.70	.75
☐ 54 Robin Yount	12.00	5.50	1.50
☐ 55 Richie Zisk	.50	.23	.06
☐ 56 AL Puzzle UL (unnumbered)	.15	.07	.02
☐ 57 AL Puzzle UC (unnumbered)	.15	.07	.02
☐ 58 AL Puzzle UR (unnumbered)	.15	.07	.02
☐ 59 AL Puzzle ML (unnumbered)	.15	.07	.02
☐ 60 AL Puzzle MC (unnumbered)	.15	.07	.02
☐ 61 AL Puzzle MR (unnumbered)	.15	.07	.02
☐ 62 AL Puzzle BL SP (unnumbered)	.25	.11	.03
☐ 63 AL Puzzle BC SP (unnumbered)	.25	.11	.03
☐ 64 AL Puzzle BR SP (unnumbered)	.25	.11	.03
☐ 65 NL Puzzle UL (unnumbered)	.15	.07	.02
☐ 66 NL Puzzle UC (unnumbered)	.15	.07	.02
☐ 67 NL Puzzle UR (unnumbered)	.15	.07	.02
☐ 68 NL Puzzle ML (unnumbered)	.15	.07	.02
☐ 69 NL Puzzle MC (unnumbered)	.15	.07	.02
☐ 70 NL Puzzle MR (unnumbered)	.15	.07	.02
☐ 71 NL Puzzle BL (unnumbered)	.15	.07	.02
☐ 72 NL Puzzle BC (unnumbered)	.15	.07	.02
☐ 73 NL Puzzle BR (unnumbered)	.15	.07	.02

1978 Topps

The cards in this 726-card set measure 2 1/2" by 3 1/2". The 1978 Topps set experienced an increase in number of cards from the previous five regular issue sets of 660. Card numbers 1 through 7 feature Record Breakers (RB) of the 1977 season. Other subsets within this set include League Leaders (201-208), Post-season cards (411-413), and Rookie Prospects (701-711). The key Rookie Cards in this set are the multi-player Rookie Card of Paul Molitor and Alan Trammell, Jack Morris, Eddie Murray, Lance Parrish, and Lou Whitaker. Almost all of the Molitor/Trammell cards are found with black printing smudges. The manager cards in the set feature a "then and now" format on the card front showing the manager as he looked during his playing days. While no scarcities exist, 66 of the cards are more abundant in supply, as they were "double printed." These 66 double-printed cards are noted in the checklist by DP. Team cards again feature a checklist of that team's players in the set on the back. As in previous years, this set was issued in many different ways: some of them include 14-card wax packs and 39-card rack packs. Cards numbered 23 or lower, that feature Astros, Rangers, Tigers, or Yankees and do not follow the numbering checklisted below, are not necessarily error cards. They are undoubtedly Burger King cards, a separate set with its own pricing and mass distribution. Burger King cards are indistinguishable from the corresponding Topps cards except for the card numbering difference and the fact that Burger King cards do not have a printing sheet designation (such as A through F like the regular Topps) anywhere on the card back in very small print.

	NRMT	VG-E	GOOD
COMPLETE SET (726)	275.00	125.00	34.00
COMMON CARD (1-726)	.25	.11	.03
COMMON CARD DP	.15	.07	.02
☐ 1 Lou Brock RB Most lifetime steals	2.50	.75	.25
☐ 2 Sparky Lyle RB Most career games pure relief	.40	.18	.05
☐ 3 Willie McCovey RB Most times 2 HR's in inning	1.50	.70	.19
☐ 4 Brooks Robinson RB Most consecutive seasons with one club	2.00	.90	.25
☐ 5 Pete Rose RB Most lifetime switch-hitter hits	3.50	1.55	.45
☐ 6 Nolan Ryan RB Most games 10 or more strikeouts	15.00	6.75	1.85
☐ 7 Reggie Jackson RB Most homers, one World Series	3.50	1.55	.45
☐ 8 Mike Sadek	.25	.11	.03
☐ 9 Doug DeCinces	.40	.18	.05
☐ 10 Phil Niekro	1.00	.45	.12
☐ 11 Rick Manning	.25	.11	.03
☐ 12 Don Aase	.25	.11	.03
☐ 13 Art Howe	.40	.18	.05
☐ 14 Lerrin LaGrow	.25	.11	.03
☐ 15 Tony Perez DP	.75	.35	.09
☐ 16 Roy White	.40	.18	.05
☐ 17 Mike Krukow	.25	.11	.03
☐ 18 Bob Grich	.40	.18	.05
☐ 19 Darrell Porter	.40	.18	.05
☐ 20 Pete Rose DP	5.00	2.20	.60
☐ 21 Steve Kemp	.25	.11	.03
☐ 22 Charlie Hough	.40	.18	.05
☐ 23 Bump Wills	.25	.11	.03
☐ 24 Don Money DP	.15	.07	.02
☐ 25 Jon Matlack	.25	.11	.03
☐ 26 Rich Hebner	.40	.18	.05
☐ 27 Geoff Zahn	.25	.11	.03
☐ 28 Ed Ott	.25	.11	.03
☐ 29 Bob Lacey	.25	.11	.03
☐ 30 George Hendrick	.40	.18	.05
☐ 31 Glenn Abbott	.25	.11	.03
☐ 32 Garry Templeton	.75	.35	.09
☐ 33 Dave Lemanczyk	.25	.11	.03
☐ 34 Willie McCovey	2.50	1.10	.30
☐ 35 Sparky Lyle	.40	.18	.05
☐ 36 Eddie Murray	125.00	55.00	15.50
☐ 37 Rick Waits	.25	.11	.03
☐ 38 Willie Montanez	.25	.11	.03
☐ 39 Floyd Bannister	.25	.11	.03
☐ 40 Carl Yastrzemski	3.00	1.35	.35
☐ 41 Burt Hooton	.40	.18	.05
☐ 42 Jorge Orta	.25	.11	.03
☐ 43 Bill Atkinson	.25	.11	.03
☐ 44 Toby Harrah	.40	.18	.05
☐ 45 Mark Fidrych	.75	.35	.09
☐ 46 Al Cowens	.25	.11	.03
☐ 47 Jack Billingham	.25	.11	.03
☐ 48 Don Baylor	.75	.35	.09
☐ 49 Ed Kranepool	.40	.18	.05
☐ 50 Rick Reuschel	.40	.18	.05
☐ 51 Charlie Moore DP	.15	.07	.02
☐ 52 Jim Lonborg	.25	.11	.03
☐ 53 Phil Garner DP	.25	.11	.03
☐ 54 Tom Johnson	.25	.11	.03
☐ 55 Mitchell Page	.25	.11	.03
☐ 56 Randy Jones	.25	.11	.03
☐ 57 Dan Meyer	.25	.11	.03
☐ 58 Bob Forsch	.25	.11	.03
☐ 59 Otto Velez	.25	.11	.03
☐ 60 Thurman Munson	3.00	1.35	.35
☐ 61 Larvell Blanks	.25	.11	.03
☐ 62 Jim Barr	.25	.11	.03
☐ 63 Don Zimmer MG	.40	.18	.05
☐ 64 Gene Pentz	.25	.11	.03
☐ 65 Ken Singleton	.40	.18	.05
☐ 66 Chicago White Sox Team Card (Checklist back)	1.25	.25	.12
☐ 67 Claudell Washington	.40	.18	.05
☐ 68 Steve Foucault DP	.15	.07	.02
☐ 69 Mike Vail	.25	.11	.03
☐ 70 Rich Gossage	.75	.35	.09
☐ 71 Terry Humphrey	.25	.11	.03
☐ 72 Andre Dawson	15.00	6.75	1.85
☐ 73 Andy Hassler	.25	.11	.03
☐ 74 Checklist 1-121	1.25	.25	.12
☐ 75 Dick Ruthven	.25	.11	.03
☐ 76 Steve Ontiveros	.25	.11	.03
☐ 77 Ed Kirkpatrick	.25	.11	.03
☐ 78 Pablo Torrealba	.25	.11	.03
☐ 79 Darrell Johnson DP MG	.15	.07	.02
☐ 80 Ken Griffey	.75	.35	.09
☐ 81 Pete Redfern	.25	.11	.03
☐ 82 San Francisco Giants Team Card (Checklist back)	1.25	.25	.12
☐ 83 Bob Montgomery	.25	.11	.03
☐ 84 Kent Tekulve	.40	.18	.05
☐ 85 Ron Fairly	.40	.18	.05
☐ 86 Dave Tomlin	.25	.11	.03
☐ 87 John Lowenstein	.25	.11	.03
☐ 88 Mike Phillips	.25	.11	.03
☐ 89 Ken Clay	.25	.11	.03
☐ 90 Larry Bowa	.75	.35	.09
☐ 91 Oscar Zamora	.25	.11	.03
☐ 92 Adrian Devine	.25	.11	.03
☐ 93 Bobby Cox DP	.25	.11	.03
☐ 94 Chuck Scrivener	.25	.11	.03
☐ 95 Jamie Quirk	.25	.11	.03
☐ 96 Baltimore Orioles Team Card (Checklist back)	1.25	.25	.12
☐ 97 Stan Bahnsen	.25	.11	.03
☐ 98 Jim Essian	.40	.18	.05
☐ 99 Willie Hernandez	.75	.35	.09
☐ 100 George Brett	22.00	10.00	2.70
☐ 101 Sid Monge	.25	.11	.03
☐ 102 Matt Alexander	.25	.11	.03
☐ 103 Tom Murphy	.25	.11	.03
☐ 104 Lee Lacy	.25	.11	.03
☐ 105 Reggie Cleveland	.25	.11	.03
☐ 106 Bill Plummer	.25	.11	.03
☐ 107 Ed Halicki	.25	.11	.03
☐ 108 Von Joshua	.25	.11	.03
☐ 109 Joe Torre MG	.40	.18	.05
☐ 110 Richie Zisk	.25	.11	.03
☐ 111 Mike Tyson	.25	.11	.03
☐ 112 Houston Astros Team Card (Checklist back)	1.25	.25	.12
☐ 113 Don Carrithers	.25	.11	.03
☐ 114 Paul Blair	.40	.18	.05
☐ 115 Gary Nolan	.25	.11	.03
☐ 116 Tucker Ashford	.25	.11	.03
☐ 117 John Montague	.25	.11	.03
☐ 118 Terry Harmon	.25	.11	.03
☐ 119 Dennis Martinez	2.00	.90	.25
☐ 120 Gary Carter	.75	.35	.09
☐ 121 Alvis Woods	.25	.11	.03
☐ 122 Dennis Eckersley	4.00	1.80	.50
☐ 123 Manny Trillo	.25	.11	.03
☐ 124 Dave Rozema	.25	.11	.03
☐ 125 George Scott	.40	.18	.05
☐ 126 Paul Moskau	.25	.11	.03
☐ 127 Chet Lemon	.40	.18	.05
☐ 128 Bill Russell	.40	.18	.05
☐ 129 Jim Colborn	.25	.11	.03
☐ 130 Jeff Burroughs	.40	.18	.05
☐ 131 Bert Blyleven	.75	.35	.09
☐ 132 Enos Cabell	.25	.11	.03
☐ 133 Jerry Augustine	.25	.11	.03
☐ 134 Steve Henderson	.25	.11	.03
☐ 135 Ron Guidry DP	.75	.35	.09
☐ 136 Ted Sizemore	.25	.11	.03
☐ 137 Craig Kusick	.25	.11	.03
☐ 138 Larry Demery	.25	.11	.03
☐ 139 Wayne Gross	.25	.11	.03
☐ 140 Rollie Fingers	1.50	.70	.19
☐ 141 Ruppert Jones	.25	.11	.03
☐ 142 John Montefusco	.25	.11	.03
☐ 143 Keith Hernandez	.40	.18	.05
☐ 144 Jesse Jefferson	.25	.11	.03
☐ 145 Rick Monday	.40	.18	.05
☐ 146 Doyle Alexander	.25	.11	.03
☐ 147 Lee Mazzilli	.25	.11	.03
☐ 148 Andre Thornton	.40	.18	.05
☐ 149 Dale Murray	.25	.11	.03
☐ 150 Bobby Bonds	.75	.35	.09
☐ 151 Milt Wilcox	.25	.11	.03
☐ 152 Ivan DeJesus	.25	.11	.03
☐ 153 Steve Stone	.40	.18	.05
☐ 154 Cecil Cooper DP	.25	.11	.03
☐ 155 Butch Hobson	.25	.11	.03
☐ 156 Andy Messersmith	.40	.18	.05
☐ 157 Pete LaCock DP	.15	.07	.02
☐ 158 Joaquin Andujar	.40	.18	.05
☐ 159 Lou Piniella	.25	.11	.03
☐ 160 Jim Palmer	2.50	1.10	.30
☐ 161 Bob Boone	.75	.35	.09
☐ 162 Paul Thormodsgard	.25	.11	.03
☐ 163 Bill North	.25	.11	.03
☐ 164 Bob Owchinko	.25	.11	.03
☐ 165 Rennie Stennett	.25	.11	.03
☐ 166 Carlos Lopez	.25	.11	.03
☐ 167 Tim Foli	.25	.11	.03
☐ 168 Reggie Smith	.40	.18	.05
☐ 169 Jerry Johnson	.25	.11	.03
☐ 170 Lou Brock	2.50	1.10	.30
☐ 171 Pat Zachry	.25	.11	.03
☐ 172 Mike Hargrove	.40	.18	.05
☐ 173 Robin Yount UER (Played for Newark in 1973, not 1971)	14.00	6.25	1.75
☐ 174 Wayne Garland	.25	.11	.03
☐ 175 Jerry Morales	.25	.11	.03
☐ 176 Milt May	.25	.11	.03
☐ 177 Gene Garber DP	.25	.11	.03
☐ 178 Dave Chalk	.25	.11	.03
☐ 179 Dick Tidrow	.25	.11	.03
☐ 180 Dave Concepcion	.75	.35	.09
☐ 181 Ken Forsch	.25	.11	.03
☐ 182 Jim Spencer	.25	.11	.03
☐ 183 Doug Bird	.25	.11	.03
☐ 184 Checklist 122-242	1.25	.25	.12
☐ 185 Ellis Valentine	.25	.11	.03
☐ 186 Bob Stanley DP	.25	.11	.03
☐ 187 Jerry Royster DP	.15	.07	.02
☐ 188 Al Bumbry	.40	.18	.05
☐ 189 Tom Lasorda MG	1.00	.45	.12
☐ 190 John Candelaria	.40	.18	.05
☐ 191 Rodney Scott	.25	.11	.03
☐ 192 San Diego Padres Team Card (Checklist back)	1.25	.25	.12
☐ 193 Rich Chiles	.25	.11	.03
☐ 194 Derrel Thomas	.25	.11	.03
☐ 195 Larry Dierker	.40	.18	.05
☐ 196 Bob Bailor	.25	.11	.03
☐ 197 Nino Espinosa	.25	.11	.03
☐ 198 Ron Pruitt	.25	.11	.03
☐ 199 Craig Reynolds	.25	.11	.03
☐ 200 Reggie Jackson	8.00	3.60	1.00
☐ 201 Batting Leaders Dave Parker Rod Carew	1.00	.45	.12
☐ 202 Home Run Leaders DP George Foster Jim Rice	.40	.18	.05
☐ 203 RBI Leaders George Foster Larry Hisle	.40	.18	.05
☐ 204 Steals Leaders DP Frank Taveras Freddie Patek	.25	.11	.03
☐ 205 Victory Leaders Steve Carlton Dave Goltz Dennis Leonard Jim Palmer	1.50	.70	.19
☐ 206 Strikeout Leaders DP Phil Niekro Nolan Ryan	5.00	2.20	.60
☐ 207 ERA Leaders DP John Candelaria Frank Tanana	.40	.18	.05
☐ 208 Top Firemen Rollie Fingers Bill Campbell	.75	.35	.09
☐ 209 Dock Ellis	.25	.11	.03
☐ 210 Jose Cardenal	.25	.11	.03
☐ 211 Earl Weaver MG DP	.40	.18	.05
☐ 212 Mike Caldwell	.25	.11	.03
☐ 213 Alan Bannister	.25	.11	.03
☐ 214 California Angels Team Card (Checklist back)	1.25	.25	.12
☐ 215 Darrell Evans	.75	.35	.09
☐ 216 Mike Paxton	.25	.11	.03
☐ 217 Rod Gilbreath	.25	.11	.03
☐ 218 Marty Pattin	.25	.11	.03
☐ 219 Mike Cubbage	.25	.11	.03
☐ 220 Pedro Borbon	.25	.11	.03
☐ 221 Chris Speier	.25	.11	.03
☐ 222 Jerry Martin	.25	.11	.03
☐ 223 Bruce Kison	.25	.11	.03
☐ 224 Jerry Tabb	.25	.11	.03
☐ 225 Don Gullett DP	.40	.18	.05
☐ 226 Joe Ferguson	.25	.11	.03
☐ 227 Al Fitzmorris	.25	.11	.03
☐ 228 Manny Mota DP	.25	.11	.03

Card			
☐ 229 Leo Foster	.25	.11	.03
☐ 230 Al Hrabosky	.25	.11	.03
☐ 231 Wayne Nordhagen	.25	.11	.03
☐ 232 Mickey Stanley	.25	.11	.03
☐ 233 Dick Pole	.25	.11	.03
☐ 234 Herman Franks MG	.25	.11	.03
☐ 235 Tim McCarver	.40	.18	.05
☐ 236 Terry Whitfield	.25	.11	.03
☐ 237 Rich Dauer	.25	.11	.03
☐ 238 Juan Beniquez	.25	.11	.03
☐ 239 Dyar Miller	.25	.11	.03
☐ 240 Gene Tenace	.40	.18	.05
☐ 241 Pete Vuckovich	.40	.18	.05
☐ 242 Barry Bonnell DP	.15	.07	.02
☐ 243 Bob McClure	.25	.11	.03
☐ 244 Montreal Expos Team Card DP (Checklist back)	.50	.10	.05
☐ 245 Rick Burleson	.40	.18	.05
☐ 246 Dan Driessen	.25	.11	.03
☐ 247 Larry Christenson	.25	.11	.03
☐ 248 Frank White DP	.40	.18	.05
☐ 249 Dave Goltz DP	.15	.07	.02
☐ 250 Graig Nettles DP	.40	.18	.05
☐ 251 Don Kirkwood	.25	.11	.03
☐ 252 Steve Swisher DP	.15	.07	.02
☐ 253 Jim Kern	.25	.11	.03
☐ 254 Dave Collins	.40	.18	.05
☐ 255 Jerry Reuss	.40	.18	.05
☐ 256 Joe Altobelli MG	.25	.11	.03
☐ 257 Hector Cruz	.25	.11	.03
☐ 258 John Hiller	.25	.11	.03
☐ 259 Los Angeles Dodgers Team Card (Checklist back)	1.25	.25	.12
☐ 260 Bert Campaneris	.40	.18	.05
☐ 261 Tim Hosley	.25	.11	.03
☐ 262 Rudy May	.25	.11	.03
☐ 263 Danny Walton	.25	.11	.03
☐ 264 Jamie Easterly	.25	.11	.03
☐ 265 Sal Bando DP	.40	.18	.05
☐ 266 Bob Shirley	.25	.11	.03
☐ 267 Doug Ault	.25	.11	.03
☐ 268 Gil Flores	.25	.11	.03
☐ 269 Wayne Twitchell	.25	.11	.03
☐ 270 Carlton Fisk	3.00	1.35	.35
☐ 271 Randy Lerch DP	.15	.07	.02
☐ 272 Royle Stillman	.25	.11	.03
☐ 273 Fred Norman	.25	.11	.03
☐ 274 Freddie Patek	.40	.18	.05
☐ 275 Dan Ford	.25	.11	.03
☐ 276 Bill Bonham DP	.15	.07	.02
☐ 277 Bruce Boisclair	.25	.11	.03
☐ 278 Enrique Romo	.25	.11	.03
☐ 279 Bill Virdon MG	.25	.11	.03
☐ 280 Buddy Bell	.40	.18	.05
☐ 281 Eric Rasmussen DP	.15	.07	.02
☐ 282 New York Yankees Team Card (Checklist back)	1.50	.30	.15
☐ 283 Omar Moreno	.25	.11	.03
☐ 284 Randy Moffitt	.25	.11	.03
☐ 285 Steve Yeager DP	.40	.18	.05
☐ 286 Ben Oglivie	.40	.18	.05
☐ 287 Kiko Garcia	.25	.11	.03
☐ 288 Dave Hamilton	.25	.11	.03
☐ 289 Checklist 243-363	1.25	.25	.12
☐ 290 Willie Horton	.40	.18	.05
☐ 291 Gary Ross	.25	.11	.03
☐ 292 Gene Richards	.25	.11	.03
☐ 293 Mike Willis	.25	.11	.03
☐ 294 Larry Parrish	.40	.18	.05
☐ 295 Bill Lee	.25	.11	.03
☐ 296 Biff Pocoroba	.25	.11	.03
☐ 297 Warren Brusstar DP	.15	.07	.02
☐ 298 Tony Armas	.40	.18	.05
☐ 299 Whitey Herzog MG	.40	.18	.05
☐ 300 Joe Morgan	2.50	1.10	.30
☐ 301 Buddy Schultz	.25	.11	.03
☐ 302 Chicago Cubs Team Card (Checklist back)	1.25	.25	.12
☐ 303 Sam Hinds	.25	.11	.03
☐ 304 John Milner	.25	.11	.03
☐ 305 Rico Carty	.40	.18	.05
☐ 306 Joe Niekro	.40	.18	.05
☐ 307 Glenn Borgmann	.25	.11	.03
☐ 308 Jim Rooker	.25	.11	.03
☐ 309 Cliff Johnson	.25	.11	.03
☐ 310 Don Sutton	.75	.35	.09
☐ 311 Jose Baez DP	.15	.07	.02
☐ 312 Greg Minton	.25	.11	.03
☐ 313 Andy Etchebarren	.25	.11	.03
☐ 314 Paul Lindblad	.25	.11	.03
☐ 315 Mark Belanger	.40	.18	.05
☐ 316 Henry Cruz DP	.15	.07	.02
☐ 317 Dave Johnson	.25	.11	.03
☐ 318 Tom Griffin	.25	.11	.03
☐ 319 Alan Ashby	.25	.11	.03
☐ 320 Fred Lynn	.40	.18	.05
☐ 321 Santo Alcala	.25	.11	.03
☐ 322 Tom Paciorek	.40	.18	.05
☐ 323 Jim Fregosi DP	.25	.11	.03
☐ 324 Vern Rapp MG	.25	.11	.03
☐ 325 Bruce Sutter	.75	.35	.09
☐ 326 Mike Lum DP	.15	.07	.02
☐ 327 Rick Langford DP	.15	.07	.02
☐ 328 Milwaukee Brewers Team Card (Checklist back)	1.25	.25	.12
☐ 329 John Verhoeven	.25	.11	.03
☐ 330 Bob Watson	.40	.18	.05
☐ 331 Mark Littell	.25	.11	.03
☐ 332 Duane Kuiper	.25	.11	.03
☐ 333 Jim Todd	.25	.11	.03
☐ 334 John Stearns	.25	.11	.03
☐ 335 Bucky Dent	.40	.18	.05
☐ 336 Steve Busby	.25	.11	.03
☐ 337 Tom Grieve	.40	.18	.05
☐ 338 Dave Heaverlo	.25	.11	.03
☐ 339 Mario Guerrero	.25	.11	.03
☐ 340 Bake McBride	.40	.18	.05
☐ 341 Mike Flanagan	.40	.18	.05
☐ 342 Aurelio Rodriguez	.25	.11	.03
☐ 343 John Wathan DP	.15	.07	.02
☐ 344 Sam Ewing	.25	.11	.03
☐ 345 Luis Tiant	.40	.18	.05
☐ 346 Larry Biittner	.25	.11	.03
☐ 347 Terry Forster	.25	.11	.03
☐ 348 Del Unser	.25	.11	.03
☐ 349 Rick Camp DP	.15	.07	.02
☐ 350 Steve Garvey	1.25	.55	.16
☐ 351 Jeff Torborg	.40	.18	.05
☐ 352 Tony Scott	.25	.11	.03
☐ 353 Doug Bair	.25	.11	.03
☐ 354 Cesar Geronimo	.25	.11	.03
☐ 355 Bill Travers	.25	.11	.03
☐ 356 New York Mets Team Card (Checklist back)	1.25	.25	.12
☐ 357 Tom Poquette	.25	.11	.03
☐ 358 Mark Lemongello	.25	.11	.03
☐ 359 Marc Hill	.25	.11	.03
☐ 360 Mike Schmidt	12.00	5.50	1.50
☐ 361 Chris Knapp	.25	.11	.03
☐ 362 Dave May	.25	.11	.03
☐ 363 Bob Randall	.25	.11	.03
☐ 364 Jerry Turner	.25	.11	.03
☐ 365 Ed Figueroa	.25	.11	.03
☐ 366 Larry Milbourne DP	.15	.07	.02
☐ 367 Rick Dempsey	.40	.18	.05
☐ 368 Balor Moore	.25	.11	.03
☐ 369 Tim Nordbrook	.25	.11	.03
☐ 370 Rusty Staub	.75	.35	.09
☐ 371 Ray Burris	.25	.11	.03
☐ 372 Brian Asselstine	.25	.11	.03
☐ 373 Jim Willoughby	.25	.11	.03
☐ 374 Jose Morales	.25	.11	.03
☐ 375 Tommy John	.75	.35	.09
☐ 376 Jim Wohlford	.25	.11	.03
☐ 377 Manny Sarmiento	.25	.11	.03
☐ 378 Bobby Winkles MG	.25	.11	.03
☐ 379 Skip Lockwood	.25	.11	.03
☐ 380 Ted Simmons	.40	.18	.05
☐ 381 Philadelphia Phillies Team Card (Checklist back)	1.25	.25	.12
☐ 382 Joe Lahoud	.25	.11	.03
☐ 383 Mario Mendoza	.25	.11	.03
☐ 384 Jack Clark	.75	.35	.09
☐ 385 Tito Fuentes	.25	.11	.03
☐ 386 Bob Gorinski	.25	.11	.03
☐ 387 Ken Holtzman	.40	.18	.05
☐ 388 Bill Fahey DP	.15	.07	.02
☐ 389 Julio Gonzalez	.25	.11	.03
☐ 390 Oscar Gamble	.40	.18	.05
☐ 391 Larry Haney	.25	.11	.03
☐ 392 Billy Almon	.25	.11	.03
☐ 393 Tippy Martinez	.40	.18	.05
☐ 394 Roy Howell DP	.15	.07	.02
☐ 395 Jim Hughes	.25	.11	.03
☐ 396 Bob Stinson DP	.15	.07	.02
☐ 397 Greg Gross	.25	.11	.03
☐ 398 Don Hood	.25	.11	.03
☐ 399 Pete Mackanin	.25	.11	.03
☐ 400 Nolan Ryan	35.00	16.00	4.40
☐ 401 Sparky Anderson MG	.40	.18	.05
☐ 402 Dave Campbell	.25	.11	.03
☐ 403 Bud Harrelson	.40	.18	.05
☐ 404 Detroit Tigers Team Card (Checklist back)	1.25	.25	.12
☐ 405 Rawly Eastwick	.25	.11	.03
☐ 406 Mike Jorgensen	.25	.11	.03
☐ 407 Odell Jones	.25	.11	.03
☐ 408 Joe Zdeb	.25	.11	.03
☐ 409 Ron Schueler	.25	.11	.03
☐ 410 Bill Madlock	.40	.18	.05
☐ 411 Willie Randolph ALCS	.40	.18	.05
☐ 412 Davey Lopes NLCS	.40	.18	.05
☐ 413 Reggie Jackson WS	3.00	1.35	.35
☐ 414 Darold Knowles DP	.15	.07	.02
☐ 415 Ray Fosse	.25	.11	.03
☐ 416 Jack Brohamer	.25	.11	.03
☐ 417 Mike Garman DP	.15	.07	.02
☐ 418 Tony Muser	.25	.11	.03
☐ 419 Jerry Garvin	.25	.11	.03
☐ 420 Greg Luzinski	.75	.35	.09
☐ 421 Junior Moore	.25	.11	.03
☐ 422 Steve Braun	.25	.11	.03
☐ 423 Dave Rosello	.25	.11	.03
☐ 424 Boston Red Sox Team Card (Checklist back)	1.25	.25	.12
☐ 425 Steve Rogers DP	.20	.09	.03
☐ 426 Fred Kendall	.25	.11	.03
☐ 427 Mario Soto	.40	.18	.05
☐ 428 Joel Youngblood	.25	.11	.03
☐ 429 Mike Barlow	.25	.11	.03
☐ 430 Al Oliver	.40	.18	.05
☐ 431 Butch Metzger	.25	.11	.03
☐ 432 Terry Bulling	.25	.11	.03
☐ 433 Fernando Gonzalez	.25	.11	.03
☐ 434 Mike Norris	.25	.11	.03
☐ 435 Checklist 364-484	1.25	.25	.12
☐ 436 Vic Harris DP	.15	.07	.02
☐ 437 Bo McLaughlin	.25	.11	.03
☐ 438 John Ellis	.25	.11	.03
☐ 439 Ken Kravec	.25	.11	.03
☐ 440 Dave Lopes	.40	.18	.05
☐ 441 Larry Gura	.25	.11	.03
☐ 442 Elliott Maddox	.25	.11	.03
☐ 443 Darrel Chaney	.25	.11	.03
☐ 444 Roy Hartsfield MG	.25	.11	.03
☐ 445 Mike Ivie	.25	.11	.03
☐ 446 Tug McGraw	.40	.18	.05
☐ 447 Leroy Stanton	.25	.11	.03
☐ 448 Bill Castro	.25	.11	.03
☐ 449 Tim Blackwell DP	.15	.07	.02
☐ 450 Tom Seaver	4.00	1.80	.50
☐ 451 Minnesota Twins Team Card (Checklist back)	1.25	.25	.12
☐ 452 Jerry Mumphrey	.25	.11	.03
☐ 453 Doug Flynn	.25	.11	.03
☐ 454 Dave LaRoche	.25	.11	.03
☐ 455 Bill Robinson	.40	.18	.05
☐ 456 Vern Ruhle	.25	.11	.03
☐ 457 Bob Bailey	.25	.11	.03
☐ 458 Jeff Newman	.25	.11	.03
☐ 459 Charlie Spikes	.25	.11	.03
☐ 460 Jim Hunter	1.50	.70	.19
☐ 461 Rob Andrews DP	.15	.07	.02
☐ 462 Rogelio Moret	.25	.11	.03
☐ 463 Kevin Bell	.25	.11	.03
☐ 464 Jerry Grote	.25	.11	.03
☐ 465 Hal McRae	.75	.35	.09
☐ 466 Dennis Blair	.25	.11	.03
☐ 467 Alvin Dark MG	.40	.18	.05
☐ 468 Warren Cromartie	.40	.18	.05
☐ 469 Rick Cerone	.40	.18	.05
☐ 470 J.R. Richard	.40	.18	.05
☐ 471 Roy Smalley	.40	.18	.05
☐ 472 Ron Reed	.25	.11	.03
☐ 473 Bill Buckner	.75	.35	.09
☐ 474 Jim Slaton	.25	.11	.03
☐ 475 Gary Matthews	.40	.18	.05
☐ 476 Bill Stein	.25	.11	.03
☐ 477 Doug Capilla	.25	.11	.03
☐ 478 Jerry Remy	.25	.11	.03
☐ 479 St. Louis Cardinals Team Card (Checklist back)	1.25	.25	.12
☐ 480 Ron LeFlore	.40	.18	.05
☐ 481 Jackson Todd	.25	.11	.03
☐ 482 Rick Miller	.25	.11	.03
☐ 483 Ken Macha	.25	.11	.03
☐ 484 Jim Norris	.25	.11	.03
☐ 485 Chris Chambliss	.40	.18	.05
☐ 486 John Curtis	.25	.11	.03
☐ 487 Jim Tyrone	.25	.11	.03
☐ 488 Dan Spillner	.25	.11	.03
☐ 489 Rudy Meoli	.25	.11	.03
☐ 490 Amos Otis	.40	.18	.05
☐ 491 Scott McGregor	.40	.18	.05
☐ 492 Jim Sundberg	.40	.18	.05
☐ 493 Steve Renko	.25	.11	.03
☐ 494 Chuck Tanner MG	.40	.18	.05
☐ 495 Dave Cash	.25	.11	.03
☐ 496 Jim Clancy DP	.15	.07	.02
☐ 497 Glenn Adams	.25	.11	.03
☐ 498 Joe Sambito	.25	.11	.03
☐ 499 Seattle Mariners Team Card (Checklist back)	1.25	.25	.12
☐ 500 George Foster	.75	.35	.09
☐ 501 Dave Roberts	.25	.11	.03
☐ 502 Pat Rockett	.25	.11	.03
☐ 503 Ike Hampton	.25	.11	.03
☐ 504 Roger Freed	.25	.11	.03
☐ 505 Felix Millan	.25	.11	.03
☐ 506 Ron Blomberg	.25	.11	.03
☐ 507 Willie Crawford	.25	.11	.03
☐ 508 Johnny Oates	.40	.18	.05
☐ 509 Brent Strom	.25	.11	.03
☐ 510 Willie Stargell	2.00	.90	.25
☐ 511 Frank Duffy	.25	.11	.03
☐ 512 Larry Herndon	.25	.11	.03
☐ 513 Barry Foote	.25	.11	.03
☐ 514 Rob Sperring	.25	.11	.03
☐ 515 Tim Corcoran	.25	.11	.03
☐ 516 Gary Beare	.25	.11	.03
☐ 517 Andres Mora	.25	.11	.03
☐ 518 Tommy Boggs DP	.15	.07	.02
☐ 519 Brian Downing	.40	.18	.05
☐ 520 Larry Hisle	.25	.11	.03
☐ 521 Steve Staggs	.25	.11	.03
☐ 522 Dick Williams MG	.40	.18	.05
☐ 523 Donnie Moore	.25	.11	.03
☐ 524 Bernie Carbo	.25	.11	.03
☐ 525 Jerry Terrell	.25	.11	.03
☐ 526 Cincinnati Reds Team Card (Checklist back)	1.25	.25	.12
☐ 527 Vic Correll	.25	.11	.03
☐ 528 Rob Picciolo	.25	.11	.03
☐ 529 Paul Hartzell	.25	.11	.03
☐ 530 Dave Winfield	12.00	5.50	1.50
☐ 531 Tom Underwood	.25	.11	.03
☐ 532 Skip Jutze	.25	.11	.03
☐ 533 Sandy Alomar	.40	.18	.05
☐ 534 Wilbur Howard	.25	.11	.03
☐ 535 Checklist 485-605	1.25	.25	.12
☐ 536 Roric Harrison	.25	.11	.03
☐ 537 Bruce Bochte	.25	.11	.03
☐ 538 Johnny LeMaster	.25	.11	.03
☐ 539 Vic Davalillo DP	.15	.07	.02
☐ 540 Steve Carlton	3.00	1.35	.35
☐ 541 Larry Cox	.25	.11	.03
☐ 542 Tim Johnson	.25	.11	.03
☐ 543 Larry Harlow DP	.15	.07	.02
☐ 544 Len Randle DP	.15	.07	.02
☐ 545 Bill Campbell	.25	.11	.03
☐ 546 Ted Martinez	.25	.11	.03
☐ 547 John Scott	.25	.11	.03
☐ 548 Billy Hunter DP MG	.15	.07	.02
☐ 549 Joe Kerrigan	.25	.11	.03
☐ 550 John Mayberry	.40	.18	.05
☐ 551 Atlanta Braves Team Card (Checklist back)	1.25	.25	.12
☐ 552 Francisco Barrios	.25	.11	.03
☐ 553 Terry Puhl	.75	.35	.09
☐ 554 Joe Coleman	.25	.11	.03
☐ 555 Butch Wynegar	.25	.11	.03
☐ 556 Ed Armbrister	.25	.11	.03
☐ 557 Tony Solaita	.25	.11	.03
☐ 558 Paul Mitchell	.25	.11	.03
☐ 559 Phil Mankowski	.25	.11	.03
☐ 560 Dave Parker	.75	.35	.09
☐ 561 Charlie Williams	.25	.11	.03
☐ 562 Glenn Burke	.25	.11	.03
☐ 563 Dave Rader	.25	.11	.03
☐ 564 Mick Kelleher	.25	.11	.03
☐ 565 Jerry Koosman	.40	.18	.05
☐ 566 Merv Rettenmund	.25	.11	.03
☐ 567 Dick Drago	.25	.11	.03
☐ 568 Tom Hutton	.25	.11	.03
☐ 569 Lary Sorensen	.25	.11	.03
☐ 570 Dave Kingman	.40	.18	.05
☐ 571 Buck Martinez	.25	.11	.03
☐ 572 Rick Wise	.25	.11	.03
☐ 573 Luis Gomez	.25	.11	.03
☐ 574 Bob Lemon MG	.40	.18	.05
☐ 575 Pat Dobson	.25	.11	.03
☐ 576 Sam Mejias	.25	.11	.03
☐ 577 Oakland A's Team Card (Checklist back)	1.25	.25	.12
☐ 578 Buzz Capra	.25	.11	.03
☐ 579 Rance Mulliniks	.25	.11	.03
☐ 580 Rod Carew	2.50	1.10	.30
☐ 581 Lynn McGlothen	.25	.11	.03
☐ 582 Fran Healy	.25	.11	.03
☐ 583 George Medich	.25	.11	.03
☐ 584 John Hale	.25	.11	.03
☐ 585 Woodie Fryman DP	.15	.07	.02
☐ 586 Ed Goodson	.25	.11	.03
☐ 587 John Urrea	.25	.11	.03
☐ 588 Jim Mason	.25	.11	.03
☐ 589 Bob Knepper	.25	.11	.03
☐ 590 Bobby Murcer	.40	.18	.05
☐ 591 George Zeber	.25	.11	.03
☐ 592 Bob Apodaca	.25	.11	.03
☐ 593 Dave Skaggs	.25	.11	.03
☐ 594 Dave Freisleben	.25	.11	.03
☐ 595 Sixto Lezcano	.25	.11	.03
☐ 596 Gary Wheelock	.25	.11	.03
☐ 597 Steve Dillard	.25	.11	.03
☐ 598 Eddie Solomon	.25	.11	.03
☐ 599 Gary Woods	.25	.11	.03
☐ 600 Frank Tanana	.40	.18	.05
☐ 601 Gene Mauch MG	.40	.18	.05
☐ 602 Eric Soderholm	.25	.11	.03
☐ 603 Will McEnaney	.25	.11	.03
☐ 604 Earl Williams	.25	.11	.03
☐ 605 Rick Rhoden	.40	.18	.05
☐ 606 Pittsburgh Pirates Team Card (Checklist back)	1.25	.25	.12
☐ 607 Fernando Arroyo	.25	.11	.03
☐ 608 Johnny Grubb	.25	.11	.03
☐ 609 John Denny	.25	.11	.03
☐ 610 Garry Maddox	.40	.18	.05
☐ 611 Pat Scanlon	.25	.11	.03
☐ 612 Ken Henderson	.25	.11	.03
☐ 613 Marty Perez	.25	.11	.03
☐ 614 Joe Wallis	.25	.11	.03
☐ 615 Clay Carroll	.25	.11	.03
☐ 616 Pat Kelly	.25	.11	.03

	NRMT	VG-E	GOOD
□ 617 Joe Nolan	.25	.11	.03
□ 618 Tommy Helms	.25	.11	.03
□ 619 Thad Bosley DP	.15	.07	.02
□ 620 Willie Randolph	.75	.35	.09
□ 621 Craig Swan DP	.15	.07	.02
□ 622 Champ Summers	.25	.11	.03
□ 623 Eduardo Rodriguez	.25	.11	.03
□ 624 Gary Alexander DP	.15	.07	.02
□ 625 Jose Cruz	.40	.18	.05
□ 626 Toronto Blue Jays	.50	.10	.05
Team Card DP			
(Checklist back)			
□ 627 David Johnson	.25	.11	.03
□ 628 Ralph Garr	.40	.18	.05
□ 629 Don Stanhouse	.25	.11	.03
□ 630 Ron Cey	.75	.35	.09
□ 631 Danny Ozark MG	.25	.11	.03
□ 632 Rowland Office	.25	.11	.03
□ 633 Tom Veryzer	.25	.11	.03
□ 634 Len Barker	.25	.11	.03
□ 635 Joe Rudi	.40	.18	.05
□ 636 Jim Bibby	.25	.11	.03
□ 637 Duffy Dyer	.25	.11	.03
□ 638 Paul Splittorff	.25	.11	.03
□ 639 Gene Clines	.25	.11	.03
□ 640 Lee May DP	.25	.11	.03
□ 641 Doug Rau	.25	.11	.03
□ 642 Denny Doyle	.25	.11	.03
□ 643 Tom House	.25	.11	.03
□ 644 Jim Dwyer	.25	.11	.03
□ 645 Mike Torrez	.40	.18	.05
□ 646 Rick Auerbach DP	.15	.07	.02
□ 647 Steve Dunning	.25	.11	.03
□ 648 Gary Thomasson	.25	.11	.03
□ 649 Moose Haas	.25	.11	.03
□ 650 Cesar Cedeno	.40	.18	.05
□ 651 Doug Rader	.25	.11	.03
□ 652 Checklist 606-726	1.25	.25	.12
□ 653 Ron Hodges DP	.15	.07	.02
□ 654 Pepe Frias	.25	.11	.03
□ 655 Lyman Bostock	.40	.18	.05
□ 656 Dave Garcia MG	.25	.11	.03
□ 657 Bombo Rivera	.25	.11	.03
□ 658 Manny Sanguillen	.40	.18	.05
□ 659 Texas Rangers	1.25	.25	.12
Team Card			
(Checklist back)			
□ 660 Jason Thompson	.40	.18	.05
□ 661 Grant Jackson	.25	.11	.03
□ 662 Paul Dade	.25	.11	.03
□ 663 Paul Reuschel	.25	.11	.03
□ 664 Fred Stanley	.25	.11	.03
□ 665 Dennis Leonard	.40	.18	.05
□ 666 Billy Smith	.25	.11	.03
□ 667 Jeff Byrd	.25	.11	.03
□ 668 Dusty Baker	.75	.35	.09
□ 669 Pete Falcone	.25	.11	.03
□ 670 Jim Rice	.75	.35	.09
□ 671 Gary Lavelle	.25	.11	.03
□ 672 Don Kessinger	.40	.18	.05
□ 673 Steve Brye	.25	.11	.03
□ 674 Ray Knight	2.50	1.10	.30
□ 675 Jay Johnstone	.75	.35	.09
□ 676 Bob Myrick	.25	.11	.03
□ 677 Ed Herrmann	.25	.11	.03
□ 678 Tom Burgmeier	.25	.11	.03
□ 679 Wayne Garrett	.25	.11	.03
□ 680 Vida Blue	.40	.18	.05
□ 681 Rob Belloir	.25	.11	.03
□ 682 Ken Brett	.25	.11	.03
□ 683 Mike Champion	.25	.11	.03
□ 684 Ralph Houk MG	.40	.18	.05
□ 685 Frank Taveras	.25	.11	.03
□ 686 Gaylord Perry	1.50	.70	.19
□ 687 Julio Cruz	.25	.11	.03
□ 688 George Mitterwald	.25	.11	.03
□ 689 Cleveland Indians	1.25	.25	.12
Team Card			
(Checklist back)			
□ 690 Mickey Rivers	.40	.18	.05
□ 691 Ross Grimsley	.25	.11	.03
□ 692 Ken Reitz	.25	.11	.03
□ 693 Lamar Johnson	.25	.11	.03
□ 694 Elias Sosa	.25	.11	.03
□ 695 Dwight Evans	.75	.35	.09
□ 696 Steve Mingori	.25	.11	.03
□ 697 Roger Metzger	.25	.11	.03
□ 698 Juan Bernhardt	.25	.11	.03
□ 699 Jackie Brown	.25	.11	.03
□ 700 Johnny Bench	3.00	1.35	.35
□ 701 Rookie Pitchers	.40	.18	.05
Tom Hume			
Larry Landreth			
Steve McCatty			
Bruce Taylor			
□ 702 Rookie Catchers	.40	.18	.05
Bill Nahorodny			
Kevin Pasley			
Rick Sweet			
Don Werner			
□ 703 Rookie Pitchers DP	5.00	2.20	.60
Larry Andersen			
Tim Jones			
Mickey Mahler			
Jack Morris			
□ 704 Rookie 2nd Basemen	20.00	9.00	2.50
Garth Iorg			
Dave Oliver			
Sam Perlozzo			
Lou Whitaker			
□ 705 Rookie Outfielders	.75	.35	.09
Dave Bergman			
Miguel Dilone			
Clint Hurdle			
Willie Norwood			
□ 706 Rookie 1st Basemen	.40	.18	.05
Wayne Cage			
Ted Cox			
Pat Putnam			
Dave Revering			
□ 707 Rookie Shortstops	100.00	45.00	12.50
Mickey Klutts			
Paul Molitor			
Alan Trammell			
U.L. Washington			
□ 708 Rookie Catchers	8.00	3.60	1.00
Bo Diaz			
Dale Murphy			
Lance Parrish			
Ernie Whitt			
□ 709 Rookie Pitchers	.40	.18	.05
Steve Burke			
Matt Keough			
Lance Rautzhan			
Dan Schatzeder			
□ 710 Rookie Outfielders	.75	.35	.09
Dell Alston			
Rick Bosetti			
Mike Easler			
Keith Smith			
□ 711 Rookie Pitchers DP	.25	.11	.03
Cardell Camper			
Dennis Lamp			
Craig Mitchell			
Roy Thomas			
□ 712 Bobby Valentine	.40	.18	.05
□ 713 Bob Davis	.25	.11	.03
□ 714 Mike Anderson	.25	.11	.03
□ 715 Jim Kaat	.75	.35	.09
□ 716 Clarence Gaston	.40	.18	.05
□ 717 Nelson Briles	.25	.11	.03
□ 718 Ron Jackson	.25	.11	.03
□ 719 Randy Elliott	.25	.11	.03
□ 720 Fergie Jenkins	1.50	.70	.19
□ 721 Billy Martin MG	.75	.35	.09
□ 722 Pete Broberg	.25	.11	.03
□ 723 John Wockenfuss	.25	.11	.03
□ 724 Kansas City Royals	1.25	.25	.12
Team Card			
(Checklist back)			
□ 725 Kurt Bevacqua	.25	.11	.03
□ 726 Wilbur Wood	.75	.17	.04

1978 Topps Team Checklist Sheet

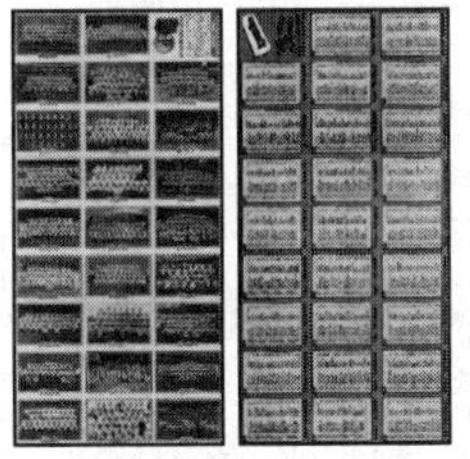

As part of a mail-away offer, Topps offered all 26 team checklist cards on an uncut sheet. These cards enabled the collector to have an easy reference for which card(s) he/she needed to finish their sets. When cut from the sheet, all cards measure the standard size.

	NRMT	VG-E	GOOD
COMPLETE SET (1)	15.00	6.75	1.85
COMMON SHEET (1)	15.00	6.75	1.85
□ 1 Team Checklist Sheet	15.00	6.75	1.85

1978 Topps Zest

This set of five standard-size cards is very similar to the 1978 Topps regular issue. Although the cards were produced by Topps, they were used in a promotion for Zest Soap. The sponsor of the set, Zest Soap, is not mentioned anywhere on the cards. The card numbers are different and the backs are written in English and Spanish. By the choice of players in this small set, Zest appears to have been targeting the Hispanic community. Each player's card number in the regular 1978 Topps set is also given. A different photo was used for Montanez, showing his head and shoulders as a New York Met rather than as an Atlanta Brave in a batting stance as shown on Willie's Topps regular card.

	NRMT	VG-E	GOOD
COMPLETE SET (5)	6.00	2.70	.75
COMMON CARD (1-5)	1.00	.45	.12
□ 1 Joaquin Andujar	1.50	.70	.19
78T-158			
□ 2 Bert Campaneris	2.00	.90	.25
78T-260			
□ 3 Ed Figueroa	1.00	.45	.12
78T-365			
□ 4 Willie Montanez	1.50	.70	.19
78T-38			
(different pose)			
(New York Mets)			
□ 5 Manny Mota	1.50	.70	.19
78T-228			

1979 Topps

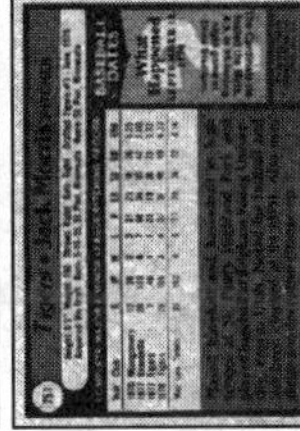

The cards in this 726-card set measure 2 1/2" by 3 1/2". Topps continued with the same number of cards as in 1978. Various series spotlight League Leaders (1-8), "Season and Career Record Holders" (411-418), "Record Breakers" (201-206), and one "Prospects" card for each team (701-726). Team cards feature a checklist on back of that team's players in the set and a small picture of the manager on the front of the card. There are 66 cards that were double printed and these are noted in the checklist by the abbreviation DP. Bump Wills (369) was initially depicted in a Ranger uniform but with a Blue Jays affiliation; later printings correctly labeled him with Texas. The set price includes either Wills card. The key Rookie Cards in this set are Pedro Guerrero, Carney Lansford, Ozzie Smith, Bob Welch and Willie Wilson. As in previous years, this set was released in many different formats, among them are 12-card wax packs and 39-card rack packs. Cards numbered 23 or lower, which feature Phillies or Yankees and do not follow the numbering checklisted below, are not necessarily error cards. They are undoubtedly Burger King cards, separate sets for each team each with its own pricing and mass distribution. Burger King cards are indistinguishable from the corresponding Topps cards except for the card numbering difference and the fact that Burger King cards do not have a printing sheet designation (such as A through F like the regular Topps) anywhere on the card back in very small print.

	NRMT	VG-E	GOOD
COMPLETE SET (726)	200.00	90.00	25.00
COMMON CARD (1-726)	.20	.09	.03
COMMON CARD DP	.10	.05	.01
□ 1 Batting Leaders	2.50	.50	.25
Rod Carew			
Dave Parker			
□ 2 Home Run Leaders	.50	.23	.06
Jim Rice			
George Foster			
□ 3 RBI Leaders	.50	.23	.06
Jim Rice			
George Foster			
□ 4 Stolen Base Leaders	.35	.16	.04
Ron LeFlore			
Omar Moreno			
□ 5 Victory Leaders	.35	.16	.04
Ron Guidry			
Gaylord Perry			
□ 6 Strikeout Leaders	6.00	2.70	.75
Nolan Ryan			
J.R. Richard			
□ 7 ERA Leaders	.35	.16	.04
Ron Guidry			
Craig Swan			
□ 8 Leading Firemen	.50	.23	.06
Rich Gossage			
Rollie Fingers			
□ 9 Dave Campbell	.20	.09	.03
□ 10 Lee May	.35	.16	.04
□ 11 Marc Hill	.20	.09	.03
□ 12 Dick Drago	.20	.09	.03
□ 13 Paul Dade	.20	.09	.03
□ 14 Rafael Landestoy	.20	.09	.03
□ 15 Ross Grimsley	.20	.09	.03
□ 16 Fred Stanley	.20	.09	.03
□ 17 Donnie Moore	.20	.09	.03
□ 18 Tony Solaita	.20	.09	.03
□ 19 Larry Gura DP	.10	.05	.01
□ 20 Joe Morgan DP	1.00	.45	.12
□ 21 Kevin Kobel	.20	.09	.03
□ 22 Mike Jorgensen	.20	.09	.03
□ 23 Terry Forster	.20	.09	.03
□ 24 Paul Molitor	20.00	9.00	2.50
□ 25 Steve Carlton	2.50	1.10	.30
□ 26 Jamie Quirk	.20	.09	.03
□ 27 Dave Goltz	.20	.09	.03
□ 28 Steve Brye	.20	.09	.03
□ 29 Rick Langford	.20	.09	.03
□ 30 Dave Winfield	8.00	3.60	1.00
□ 31 Tom House DP	.10	.05	.01
□ 32 Jerry Mumphrey	.20	.09	.03
□ 33 Dave Rozema	.20	.09	.03
□ 34 Rob Andrews	.20	.09	.03
□ 35 Ed Figueroa	.20	.09	.03
□ 36 Alan Ashby	.20	.09	.03
□ 37 Joe Kerrigan DP	.10	.05	.01
□ 38 Bernie Carbo	.20	.09	.03
□ 39 Dale Murphy	5.00	2.20	.60
□ 40 Dennis Eckersley	2.00	.90	.25
□ 41 Twins Team/Mgr.	1.00	.20	.10
Gene Mauch			
(Checklist back)			
□ 42 Ron Blomberg	.20	.09	.03
□ 43 Wayne Twitchell	.20	.09	.03
□ 44 Kurt Bevacqua	.20	.09	.03
□ 45 Al Hrabosky	.20	.09	.03
□ 46 Ron Hodges	.20	.09	.03
□ 47 Fred Norman	.20	.09	.03
□ 48 Merv Rettenmund	.20	.09	.03
□ 49 Vern Ruhle	.20	.09	.03
□ 50 Steve Garvey DP	.75	.35	.09
□ 51 Ray Fosse DP	.10	.05	.01
□ 52 Randy Lerch	.20	.09	.03
□ 53 Mick Kelleher	.20	.09	.03
□ 54 Dell Alston DP	.10	.05	.01
□ 55 Willie Stargell	1.50	.70	.19
□ 56 John Hale	.20	.09	.03
□ 57 Eric Rasmussen	.20	.09	.03
□ 58 Bob Randall DP	.10	.05	.01
□ 59 John Denny DP	.15	.07	.02
□ 60 Mickey Rivers	.35	.16	.04
□ 61 Bo Diaz	.20	.09	.03
□ 62 Randy Moffitt	.20	.09	.03
□ 63 Jack Brohamer	.20	.09	.03
□ 64 Tom Underwood	.20	.09	.03
□ 65 Mark Belanger	.35	.16	.04
□ 66 Tigers Team/Mgr.	1.00	.20	.10
Les Moss			
(Checklist back)			
□ 67 Jim Mason DP	.10	.05	.01
□ 68 Joe Niekro DP	.20	.09	.03
□ 69 Elliott Maddox	.20	.09	.03
□ 70 John Candelaria	.35	.16	.04
□ 71 Brian Downing	.35	.16	.04
□ 72 Steve Mingori	.20	.09	.03
□ 73 Ken Henderson	.20	.09	.03
□ 74 Shane Rawley	.20	.09	.03
□ 75 Steve Yeager	.35	.16	.04
□ 76 Warren Cromartie	.35	.16	.04
□ 77 Dan Briggs DP	.10	.05	.01
□ 78 Elias Sosa	.20	.09	.03
□ 79 Ted Cox	.20	.09	.03
□ 80 Jason Thompson	.35	.16	.04
□ 81 Roger Erickson	.20	.09	.03
□ 82 Mets Team/Mgr.	1.00	.20	.10
Joe Torre			
(Checklist back)			
□ 83 Fred Kendall	.20	.09	.03
□ 84 Greg Minton	.20	.09	.03
□ 85 Gary Matthews	.35	.16	.04
□ 86 Rodney Scott	.20	.09	.03
□ 87 Pete Falcone	.20	.09	.03
□ 88 Bob Molinaro	.20	.09	.03
□ 89 Dick Tidrow	.20	.09	.03
□ 90 Bob Boone	.50	.23	.06
□ 91 Terry Crowley	.20	.09	.03
□ 92 Jim Bibby	.20	.09	.03
□ 93 Phil Mankowski	.20	.09	.03
□ 94 Len Barker	.20	.09	.03
□ 95 Robin Yount	10.00	4.50	1.25
□ 96 Indians Team/Mgr.	1.00	.20	.10
Jeff Torborg			
(Checklist back)			
□ 97 Sam Mejias	.20	.09	.03
□ 98 Ray Burris	.20	.09	.03
□ 99 John Wathan	.35	.16	.04
□ 100 Tom Seaver DP	2.00	.90	.25
□ 101 Roy Howell	.20	.09	.03
□ 102 Mike Anderson	.20	.09	.03
□ 103 Jim Todd	.20	.09	.03
□ 104 Johnny Oates DP	.20	.09	.03
□ 105 Rick Camp DP	.10	.05	.01
□ 106 Frank Duffy	.20	.09	.03
□ 107 Jesus Alou DP	.10	.05	.01
□ 108 Eduardo Rodriguez	.20	.09	.03
□ 109 Joel Youngblood	.20	.09	.03
□ 110 Vida Blue	.35	.16	.04
□ 111 Roger Freed	.20	.09	.03
□ 112 Phillies Team/Mgr.	1.00	.20	.10
Danny Ozark			
(Checklist back)			
□ 113 Pete Redfern	.20	.09	.03
□ 114 Cliff Johnson	.20	.09	.03
□ 115 Nolan Ryan	30.00	13.50	3.70
□ 116 Ozzie Smith	100.00	45.00	12.50

☐ 117 Grant Jackson .20 .09 .03
☐ 118 Bud Harrelson .35 .16 .04
☐ 119 Don Stanhouse .20 .09 .03
☐ 120 Jim Sundberg .35 .16 .04
☐ 121 Checklist 1-121 DP .60 .12 .06
☐ 122 Mike Paxton .20 .09 .03
☐ 123 Lou Whitaker 10.00 4.50 1.25
☐ 124 Dan Schatzeder .20 .09 .03
☐ 125 Rick Burleson .20 .09 .03
☐ 126 Doug Bair .20 .09 .03
☐ 127 Thad Bosley .20 .09 .03
☐ 128 Ted Martinez .20 .09 .03
☐ 129 Marty Pattin DP .10 .05 .01
☐ 130 Bob Watson DP .20 .09 .03
☐ 131 Jim Clancy .20 .09 .03
☐ 132 Rowland Office .20 .09 .03
☐ 133 Bill Castro .20 .09 .03
☐ 134 Alan Bannister .20 .09 .03
☐ 135 Bobby Murcer .35 .16 .04
☐ 136 Jim Kaat .35 .16 .04
☐ 137 Larry Wolfe DP .10 .05 .01
☐ 138 Mark Lee .20 .09 .03
☐ 139 Luis Pujols .20 .09 .03
☐ 140 Don Gullett .35 .16 .04
☐ 141 Tom Paciorek .35 .16 .04
☐ 142 Charlie Williams .20 .09 .03
☐ 143 Tony Scott .20 .09 .03
☐ 144 Sandy Alomar .35 .16 .04
☐ 145 Rick Rhoden .20 .09 .03
☐ 146 Duane Kuiper .20 .09 .03
☐ 147 Dave Hamilton .20 .09 .03
☐ 148 Bruce Boisclair .20 .09 .03
☐ 149 Manny Sarmiento .20 .09 .03
☐ 150 Wayne Cage .20 .09 .03
☐ 151 John Hiller .20 .09 .03
☐ 152 Rick Cerone .20 .09 .03
☐ 153 Dennis Lamp .20 .09 .03
☐ 154 Jim Gantner DP .20 .09 .03
☐ 155 Dwight Evans .50 .23 .06
☐ 156 Buddy Solomon .20 .09 .03
☐ 157 U.L. Washington UER .20 .09 .03
(Sic, bats left,
should be right)
☐ 158 Joe Sambito .20 .09 .03
☐ 159 Roy White .35 .16 .04
☐ 160 Mike Flanagan .50 .23 .06
☐ 161 Barry Foote .20 .09 .03
☐ 162 Tom Johnson .20 .09 .03
☐ 163 Glenn Burke .20 .09 .03
☐ 164 Mickey Lolich .35 .16 .04
☐ 165 Frank Taveras .20 .09 .03
☐ 166 Leon Roberts .20 .09 .03
☐ 167 Roger Metzger DP .10 .05 .01
☐ 168 Dave Freisleben .20 .09 .03
☐ 169 Bill Nahorodny .20 .09 .03
☐ 170 Don Sutton .50 .23 .06
☐ 171 Gene Clines .20 .09 .03
☐ 172 Mike Bruhert .20 .09 .03
☐ 173 John Lowenstein .20 .09 .03
☐ 174 Rick Auerbach .20 .09 .03
☐ 175 George Hendrick .35 .16 .04
☐ 176 Aurelio Rodriguez .20 .09 .03
☐ 177 Ron Reed .20 .09 .03
☐ 178 Alvis Woods .20 .09 .03
☐ 179 Jim Beattie DP .20 .09 .03
☐ 180 Larry Hisle .20 .09 .03
☐ 181 Mike Garman .20 .09 .03
☐ 182 Tim Johnson .20 .09 .03
☐ 183 Paul Splittorff .20 .09 .03
☐ 184 Darrel Chaney .20 .09 .03
☐ 185 Mike Torrez .35 .16 .04
☐ 186 Eric Soderholm .20 .09 .03
☐ 187 Mark Lemongello .20 .09 .03
☐ 188 Pat Kelly .20 .09 .03
☐ 189 Eddie Whitson .20 .09 .03
☐ 190 Ron Cey .35 .16 .04
☐ 191 Mike Norris .20 .09 .03
☐ 192 Cardinals Team/Mgr. 1.00 .20 .10
Ken Boyer
(Checklist back)
☐ 193 Glenn Adams .20 .09 .03
☐ 194 Randy Jones .20 .09 .03
☐ 195 Bill Madlock .35 .16 .04
☐ 196 Steve Kemp DP .15 .07 .02
☐ 197 Bob Apodaca .20 .09 .03
☐ 198 Johnny Grubb .20 .09 .03
☐ 199 Larry Milbourne .20 .09 .03
☐ 200 Johnny Bench DP 2.00 .90 .25
☐ 201 Mike Edwards RB .20 .09 .03
☐ 202 Ron Guidry RB .50 .23 .06
☐ 203 J.R. Richard RB .20 .09 .03
☐ 204 Pete Rose RB 2.00 .90 .25
☐ 205 John Stearns RB .20 .09 .03
☐ 206 Sammy Stewart RB .20 .09 .03
☐ 207 Dave Lemanczyk .20 .09 .03
☐ 208 Clarence Gaston .35 .16 .04
☐ 209 Reggie Cleveland .20 .09 .03
☐ 210 Larry Bowa .35 .16 .04
☐ 211 Denny Martinez 1.50 .70 .19
☐ 212 Carney Lansford 1.50 .70 .19
☐ 213 Bill Travers .20 .09 .03
☐ 214 Red Sox Team/Mgr. 1.00 .20 .10
Don Zimmer
(Checklist back)
☐ 215 Willie McCovey 2.00 .90 .25
☐ 216 Wilbur Wood .20 .09 .03
☐ 217 Steve Dillard .20 .09 .03
☐ 218 Dennis Leonard .35 .16 .04
☐ 219 Roy Smalley .35 .16 .04
☐ 220 Cesar Geronimo .20 .09 .03
☐ 221 Jesse Jefferson .20 .09 .03
☐ 222 Bob Beall .20 .09 .03
☐ 223 Kent Tekulve .35 .16 .04
☐ 224 Dave Revering .20 .09 .03
☐ 225 Rich Gossage .50 .23 .06
☐ 226 Ron Pruitt .20 .09 .03
☐ 227 Steve Stone .35 .16 .04
☐ 228 Vic Davalillo .20 .09 .03
☐ 229 Doug Flynn .20 .09 .03
☐ 230 Bob Forsch .20 .09 .03
☐ 231 John Wockenfuss .20 .09 .03
☐ 232 Jimmy Sexton .20 .09 .03
☐ 233 Paul Mitchell .20 .09 .03
☐ 234 Toby Harrah .35 .16 .04
☐ 235 Steve Rogers .20 .09 .03
☐ 236 Jim Dwyer .20 .09 .03
☐ 237 Billy Smith .20 .09 .03
☐ 238 Balor Moore .20 .09 .03
☐ 239 Willie Horton .35 .16 .04
☐ 240 Rick Reuschel .35 .16 .04
☐ 241 Checklist 122-242 DP .60 .12 .06
☐ 242 Pablo Torrealba .20 .09 .03
☐ 243 Buck Martinez DP .10 .05 .01
☐ 244 Pirates Team/Mgr. .50 .10 .05
Chuck Tanner
(Checklist back)
☐ 245 Jeff Burroughs .35 .16 .04
☐ 246 Darrell Jackson .20 .09 .03
☐ 247 Tucker Ashford DP .10 .05 .01
☐ 248 Pete LaCock .20 .09 .03
☐ 249 Paul Thormodsgard .20 .09 .03
☐ 250 Willie Randolph .35 .16 .04
☐ 251 Jack Morris 2.00 .90 .25
☐ 252 Bob Stinson .20 .09 .03
☐ 253 Rick Wise .20 .09 .03
☐ 254 Luis Gomez .20 .09 .03
☐ 255 Tommy John .50 .23 .06
☐ 256 Mike Sadek .20 .09 .03
☐ 257 Adrian Devine .20 .09 .03
☐ 258 Mike Phillips .20 .09 .03
☐ 259 Reds Team/Mgr. 1.00 .20 .10
Sparky Anderson
(Checklist back)
☐ 260 Richie Zisk .20 .09 .03
☐ 261 Mario Guerrero .20 .09 .03
☐ 262 Nelson Briles .20 .09 .03
☐ 263 Oscar Gamble .35 .16 .04
☐ 264 Don Robinson .20 .09 .03
☐ 265 Don Money .20 .09 .03
☐ 266 Jim Willoughby .20 .09 .03
☐ 267 Joe Rudi .35 .16 .04
☐ 268 Julio Gonzalez .20 .09 .03
☐ 269 Woodie Fryman .20 .09 .03
☐ 270 Butch Hobson .35 .16 .04
☐ 271 Rawly Eastwick .20 .09 .03
☐ 272 Tim Corcoran .20 .09 .03
☐ 273 Jerry Terrell .20 .09 .03
☐ 274 Willie Norwood .20 .09 .03
☐ 275 Junior Moore .20 .09 .03
☐ 276 Jim Colborn .20 .09 .03
☐ 277 Tom Grieve .35 .16 .04
☐ 278 Andy Messersmith .35 .16 .04
☐ 279 Jerry Grote DP .10 .05 .01
☐ 280 Andre Thornton .35 .16 .04
☐ 281 Vic Correll DP .10 .05 .01
☐ 282 Blue Jays Team/Mgr. 1.00 .20 .10
Roy Hartsfield
(Checklist back)
☐ 283 Ken Kravec .20 .09 .03
☐ 284 Johnnie LeMaster .20 .09 .03
☐ 285 Bobby Bonds .50 .23 .06
☐ 286 Duffy Dyer .20 .09 .03
☐ 287 Andres Mora .20 .09 .03
☐ 288 Milt Wilcox .20 .09 .03
☐ 289 Jose Cruz .35 .16 .04
☐ 290 Dave Lopes .35 .16 .04
☐ 291 Tom Griffin .20 .09 .03
☐ 292 Don Reynolds .20 .09 .03
☐ 293 Jerry Garvin .20 .09 .03
☐ 294 Pepe Frias .20 .09 .03
☐ 295 Mitchell Page .20 .09 .03
☐ 296 Preston Hanna .20 .09 .03
☐ 297 Ted Sizemore .20 .09 .03
☐ 298 Rich Gale .20 .09 .03
☐ 299 Steve Ontiveros .20 .09 .03
☐ 300 Rod Carew 2.00 .90 .25
☐ 301 Tom Hume .20 .09 .03
☐ 302 Braves Team/Mgr. 1.00 .20 .10
Bobby Cox
(Checklist back)
☐ 303 Lary Sorensen DP .10 .05 .01
☐ 304 Steve Swisher .20 .09 .03
☐ 305 Willie Montanez .20 .09 .03
☐ 306 Floyd Bannister .20 .09 .03
☐ 307 Larvell Blanks .20 .09 .03
☐ 308 Bert Blyleven .50 .23 .06
☐ 309 Ralph Garr .35 .16 .04
☐ 310 Thurman Munson 2.00 .90 .25
☐ 311 Gary Lavelle .20 .09 .03
☐ 312 Bob Robertson .20 .09 .03
☐ 313 Dyar Miller .20 .09 .03
☐ 314 Larry Harlow .20 .09 .03
☐ 315 Jon Matlack .20 .09 .03
☐ 316 Milt May .20 .09 .03
☐ 317 Jose Cardenal .35 .16 .04
☐ 318 Bob Welch 2.00 .90 .25
☐ 319 Wayne Garrett .20 .09 .03
☐ 320 Carl Yastrzemski 2.50 1.10 .30
☐ 321 Gaylord Perry 1.00 .45 .12
☐ 322 Danny Goodwin .20 .09 .03
☐ 323 Lynn McGlothen .20 .09 .03
☐ 324 Mike Tyson .20 .09 .03
☐ 325 Cecil Cooper .35 .16 .04
☐ 326 Pedro Borbon .20 .09 .03
☐ 327 Art Howe DP .20 .09 .03
☐ 328 Oakland A's Team/Mgr. 1.00 .20 .10
Jack McKeon
(Checklist back)
☐ 329 Joe Coleman .20 .09 .03
☐ 330 George Brett 18.00 8.00 2.20
☐ 331 Mickey Mahler .20 .09 .03
☐ 332 Gary Alexander .20 .09 .03
☐ 333 Chet Lemon .35 .16 .04
☐ 334 Craig Swan .20 .09 .03
☐ 335 Chris Chambliss .35 .16 .04
☐ 336 Bobby Thompson .20 .09 .03
☐ 337 John Montague .20 .09 .03
☐ 338 Vic Harris .20 .09 .03
☐ 339 Ron Jackson .20 .09 .03
☐ 340 Jim Palmer 2.00 .90 .25
☐ 341 Willie Upshaw .35 .16 .04
☐ 342 Dave Roberts .20 .09 .03
☐ 343 Ed Glynn .20 .09 .03
☐ 344 Jerry Royster .20 .09 .03
☐ 345 Tug McGraw .35 .16 .04
☐ 346 Bill Buckner .35 .16 .04
☐ 347 Doug Rau .20 .09 .03
☐ 348 Andre Dawson 8.00 3.60 1.00
☐ 349 Jim Wright .20 .09 .03
☐ 350 Garry Templeton .35 .16 .04
☐ 351 Wayne Nordhagen DP .10 .05 .01
☐ 352 Steve Renko .20 .09 .03
☐ 353 Checklist 243-363 1.00 .20 .10
☐ 354 Bill Bonham .20 .09 .03
☐ 355 Lee Mazzilli .20 .09 .03
☐ 356 Giants Team/Mgr. 1.00 .20 .10
Joe Altobelli
(Checklist back)
☐ 357 Jerry Augustine .20 .09 .03
☐ 358 Alan Trammell 12.00 5.50 1.50
☐ 359 Dan Spillner DP .10 .05 .01
☐ 360 Amos Otis .35 .16 .04
☐ 361 Tom Dixon .20 .09 .03
☐ 362 Mike Cubbage .20 .09 .03
☐ 363 Craig Skok .20 .09 .03
☐ 364 Gene Richards .20 .09 .03
☐ 365 Sparky Lyle .35 .16 .04
☐ 366 Juan Bernhardt .20 .09 .03
☐ 367 Dave Skaggs .20 .09 .03
☐ 368 Don Aase .20 .09 .03
☐ 369A Bump Wills ERR 3.00 1.35 .35
(Blue Jays)
☐ 369B Bump Wills COR 3.00 1.35 .35
(Rangers)
☐ 370 Dave Kingman .35 .16 .04
☐ 371 Jeff Holly .20 .09 .03
☐ 372 Lamar Johnson .20 .09 .03
☐ 373 Lance Rautzhan .20 .09 .03
☐ 374 Ed Herrmann .20 .09 .03
☐ 375 Bill Campbell .20 .09 .03
☐ 376 Gorman Thomas .35 .16 .04
☐ 377 Paul Moskau .20 .09 .03
☐ 378 Rob Picciolo DP .10 .05 .01
☐ 379 Dale Murray .20 .09 .03
☐ 380 John Mayberry .35 .16 .04
☐ 381 Astros Team/Mgr. 1.00 .20 .10
Bill Virdon
(Checklist back)
☐ 382 Jerry Martin .20 .09 .03
☐ 383 Phil Garner .35 .16 .04
☐ 384 Tommy Boggs .20 .09 .03
☐ 385 Dan Ford .20 .09 .03
☐ 386 Francisco Barrios .20 .09 .03
☐ 387 Gary Thomasson .20 .09 .03
☐ 388 Jack Billingham .20 .09 .03
☐ 389 Joe Zdeb .20 .09 .03
☐ 390 Rollie Fingers 1.00 .45 .12
☐ 391 Al Oliver .35 .16 .04
☐ 392 Doug Ault .20 .09 .03
☐ 393 Scott McGregor .35 .16 .04
☐ 394 Randy Stein .20 .09 .03
☐ 395 Dave Cash .20 .09 .03
☐ 396 Bill Plummer .20 .09 .03
☐ 397 Sergio Ferrer .20 .09 .03
☐ 398 Ivan DeJesus .20 .09 .03
☐ 399 David Clyde .20 .09 .03
☐ 400 Jim Rice .35 .16 .04
☐ 401 Ray Knight .35 .16 .04
☐ 402 Paul Hartzell .20 .09 .03
☐ 403 Tim Foli .20 .09 .03
☐ 404 White Sox Team/Mgr 1.00 .20 .10
Don Kessinger
(Checklist back)
☐ 405 Butch Wynegar DP .10 .05 .01
☐ 406 Joe Wallis DP .10 .05 .01
☐ 407 Pete Vuckovich .35 .16 .04
☐ 408 Charlie Moore DP .10 .05 .01
☐ 409 Willie Wilson 1.50 .70 .19
☐ 410 Darrell Evans .50 .23 .06
☐ 411 George Sisler ATL 1.00 .45 .12
Ty Cobb
☐ 412 Hack Wilson ATL 1.00 .45 .12
Hank Aaron
☐ 413 Roger Maris ATL 1.50 .70 .19
Hank Aaron
☐ 414 Rogers Hornsby ATL 1.00 .45 .12
Ty Cobb
☐ 415 Lou Brock ATL .50 .23 .06
☐ 416 Jack Chesbro ATL .35 .16 .04
Cy Young
☐ 417 Nolan Ryan ATL DP 4.00 1.80 .50
Walter Johnson
☐ 418 Dutch Leonard ATL DP .25 .11 .03
Walter Johnson
☐ 419 Dick Ruthven .20 .09 .03
☐ 420 Ken Griffey .35 .16 .04
☐ 421 Doug DeCinces .35 .16 .04
☐ 422 Ruppert Jones .20 .09 .03
☐ 423 Bob Montgomery .20 .09 .03
☐ 424 Angels Team/Mgr. 1.00 .20 .10
Jim Fregosi
(Checklist back)
☐ 425 Rick Manning .20 .09 .03
☐ 426 Chris Speier .20 .09 .03
☐ 427 Andy Replogle .20 .09 .03
☐ 428 Bobby Valentine .35 .16 .04
☐ 429 John Urrea DP .10 .05 .01
☐ 430 Dave Parker .35 .16 .04
☐ 431 Glenn Borgmann .20 .09 .03
☐ 432 Dave Heaverlo .20 .09 .03
☐ 433 Larry Biittner .20 .09 .03
☐ 434 Ken Clay .20 .09 .03
☐ 435 Gene Tenace .35 .16 .04
☐ 436 Hector Cruz .20 .09 .03
☐ 437 Rick Williams .20 .09 .03
☐ 438 Horace Speed .20 .09 .03
☐ 439 Frank White .35 .16 .04
☐ 440 Rusty Staub .50 .23 .06
☐ 441 Lee Lacy .20 .09 .03
☐ 442 Doyle Alexander .20 .09 .03
☐ 443 Bruce Bochte .20 .09 .03
☐ 444 Aurelio Lopez .20 .09 .03
☐ 445 Steve Henderson .20 .09 .03
☐ 446 Jim Lonborg .35 .16 .04
☐ 447 Manny Sanguillen .35 .16 .04
☐ 448 Moose Haas .20 .09 .03
☐ 449 Bombo Rivera .20 .09 .03
☐ 450 Dave Concepcion .50 .23 .06
☐ 451 Royals Team/Mgr. 1.00 .20 .10
Whitey Herzog
(Checklist back)
☐ 452 Jerry Morales .20 .09 .03
☐ 453 Chris Knapp .20 .09 .03
☐ 454 Len Randle .20 .09 .03
☐ 455 Bill Lee DP .10 .05 .01
☐ 456 Chuck Baker .20 .09 .03
☐ 457 Bruce Sutter .35 .16 .04
☐ 458 Jim Essian .20 .09 .03
☐ 459 Sid Monge .20 .09 .03
☐ 460 Graig Nettles .35 .16 .04
☐ 461 Jim Barr DP .10 .05 .01
☐ 462 Otto Velez .20 .09 .03
☐ 463 Steve Comer .20 .09 .03
☐ 464 Joe Nolan .20 .09 .03
☐ 465 Reggie Smith .35 .16 .04
☐ 466 Mark Littell .20 .09 .03
☐ 467 Don Kessinger DP .15 .07 .02
☐ 468 Stan Bahnsen DP .10 .05 .01
☐ 469 Lance Parrish .50 .23 .06
☐ 470 Garry Maddox DP .20 .09 .03
☐ 471 Joaquin Andujar .35 .16 .04
☐ 472 Craig Kusick .20 .09 .03
☐ 473 Dave Roberts .20 .09 .03
☐ 474 Dick Davis .20 .09 .03
☐ 475 Dan Driessen .20 .09 .03
☐ 476 Tom Poquette .20 .09 .03
☐ 477 Bob Grich .35 .16 .04
☐ 478 Juan Beniquez .20 .09 .03
☐ 479 Padres Team/Mgr. 1.00 .20 .10
Roger Craig
(Checklist back)
☐ 480 Fred Lynn .35 .16 .04
☐ 481 Skip Lockwood .20 .09 .03
☐ 482 Craig Reynolds .20 .09 .03
☐ 483 Checklist 364-484 DP .60 .12 .06
☐ 484 Rick Waits .20 .09 .03
☐ 485 Bucky Dent .35 .16 .04
☐ 486 Bob Knepper .20 .09 .03
☐ 487 Miguel Dilone .20 .09 .03
☐ 488 Bob Owchinko .20 .09 .03
☐ 489 Larry Cox UER .20 .09 .03
(Photo actually
Dave Rader)
☐ 490 Al Cowens .20 .09 .03
☐ 491 Tippy Martinez .35 .16 .04
☐ 492 Bob Bailor .20 .09 .03
☐ 493 Larry Christenson .20 .09 .03
☐ 494 Jerry White .20 .09 .03
☐ 495 Tony Perez 1.00 .45 .12
☐ 496 Barry Bonnell DP .20 .09 .03

☐ 497 Glenn Abbott .20 .09 .03
☐ 498 Rich Chiles .20 .04 .02
☐ 499 Rangers Team/Mgr. 1.00 .45 .12
Pat Corrales
(Checklist back)
☐ 500 Ron Guidry .35 .16 .04
☐ 501 Junior Kennedy .20 .09 .03
☐ 502 Steve Braun .20 .09 .03
☐ 503 Terry Humphrey .20 .09 .03
☐ 504 Larry McWilliams .20 .09 .03
☐ 505 Ed Kranepool .35 .16 .04
☐ 506 John D'Acquisto .20 .09 .03
☐ 507 Tony Armas .35 .16 .04
☐ 508 Charlie Hough .35 .16 .04
☐ 509 Mario Mendoza UER .20 .09 .03
(Career BA .278,
should say .204)
☐ 510 Ted Simmons .20 .09 .03
☐ 511 Paul Reuschel DP .10 .05 .01
☐ 512 Jack Clark .35 .16 .04
☐ 513 Dave Johnson .35 .16 .04
☐ 514 Mike Proly .20 .09 .03
☐ 515 Enos Cabell .20 .09 .03
☐ 516 Champ Summers DP .10 .05 .01
☐ 517 Al Bumbry .35 .16 .04
☐ 518 Jim Umbarger .20 .09 .03
☐ 519 Ben Oglivie .35 .16 .04
☐ 520 Gary Carter .35 .16 .04
☐ 521 Sam Ewing .20 .09 .03
☐ 522 Ken Holtzman .35 .16 .04
☐ 523 John Milner .20 .09 .03
☐ 524 Tom Burgmeier .20 .09 .03
☐ 525 Freddie Patek .20 .09 .03
☐ 526 Dodgers Team/Mgr. 1.00 .20 .10
Tom Lasorda
(Checklist back)
☐ 527 Lerrin LaGrow .20 .09 .03
☐ 528 Wayne Gross DP .10 .05 .01
☐ 529 Brian Asselstine .20 .09 .03
☐ 530 Frank Tanana .35 .16 .04
☐ 531 Fernando Gonzalez .20 .09 .03
☐ 532 Buddy Schultz .20 .09 .03
☐ 533 Leroy Stanton .20 .09 .03
☐ 534 Ken Forsch .20 .09 .03
☐ 535 Ellis Valentine .20 .09 .03
☐ 536 Jerry Reuss .35 .16 .04
☐ 537 Tom Veryzer .20 .09 .03
☐ 538 Mike Ivie DP .10 .05 .01
☐ 539 John Ellis .20 .09 .03
☐ 540 Greg Luzinski .35 .16 .04
☐ 541 Jim Slaton .20 .09 .03
☐ 542 Rick Bosetti .20 .09 .03
☐ 543 Kiko Garcia .20 .09 .03
☐ 544 Fergie Jenkins 1.00 .45 .12
☐ 545 John Stearns .20 .09 .03
☐ 546 Bill Russell .35 .16 .04
☐ 547 Clint Hurdle .20 .09 .03
☐ 548 Enrique Romo .20 .09 .03
☐ 549 Bob Bailey .20 .09 .03
☐ 550 Sal Bando .35 .16 .04
☐ 551 Cubs Team/Mgr. 1.00 .20 .10
Herman Franks
(Checklist back)
☐ 552 Jose Morales .20 .09 .03
☐ 553 Denny Walling .20 .09 .03
☐ 554 Matt Keough .20 .09 .03
☐ 555 Biff Pocoroba .20 .09 .03
☐ 556 Mike Lum .20 .09 .03
☐ 557 Ken Brett .20 .09 .03
☐ 558 Jay Johnstone .35 .16 .04
☐ 559 Greg Pryor .20 .09 .03
☐ 560 John Montefusco .20 .09 .03
☐ 561 Ed Ott .20 .09 .03
☐ 562 Dusty Baker .50 .23 .06
☐ 563 Roy Thomas .20 .09 .03
☐ 564 Jerry Turner .20 .09 .03
☐ 565 Rico Carty .35 .16 .04
☐ 566 Nino Espinosa .20 .09 .03
☐ 567 Richie Hebner .35 .16 .04
☐ 568 Carlos Lopez .20 .09 .03
☐ 569 Bob Sykes .20 .09 .03
☐ 570 Cesar Cedeno .35 .16 .04
☐ 571 Darrell Porter .35 .16 .04
☐ 572 Rod Gilbreath .20 .09 .03
☐ 573 Jim Kern .20 .09 .03
☐ 574 Claudell Washington .35 .16 .04
☐ 575 Luis Tiant .35 .16 .04
☐ 576 Mike Parrott .20 .09 .03
☐ 577 Brewers Team/Mgr. 1.00 .20 .10
George Bamberger
(Checklist back)
☐ 578 Pete Broberg .20 .09 .03
☐ 579 Greg Gross .20 .09 .03
☐ 580 Ron Fairly .35 .16 .04
☐ 581 Darold Knowles .20 .09 .03
☐ 582 Paul Blair .35 .16 .04
☐ 583 Julio Cruz .20 .09 .03
☐ 584 Jim Rooker .20 .09 .03
☐ 585 Hal McRae .50 .23 .06
☐ 586 Bob Horner .50 .23 .06
☐ 587 Ken Reitz .20 .09 .03
☐ 588 Tom Murphy .20 .09 .03
☐ 589 Terry Whitfield .20 .09 .03
☐ 590 J.R. Richard .35 .16 .04
☐ 591 Mike Hargrove .35 .16 .04
☐ 592 Mike Krukow .20 .09 .03
☐ 593 Rick Dempsey .35 .16 .04
☐ 594 Bob Shirley .20 .09 .03
☐ 595 Phil Niekro .75 .35 .09
☐ 596 Jim Wohlford .20 .09 .03
☐ 597 Bob Stanley .20 .09 .03
☐ 598 Mark Wagner .20 .09 .03
☐ 599 Jim Spencer .20 .09 .03
☐ 600 George Foster .35 .16 .04
☐ 601 Dave LaRoche .20 .09 .03
☐ 602 Checklist 485-605 1.00 .20 .10
☐ 603 Rudy May .20 .09 .03
☐ 604 Jeff Newman .20 .09 .03
☐ 605 Rick Monday DP .15 .07 .02
☐ 606 Expos Team/Mgr. 1.00 .20 .10
Dick Williams
(Checklist back)
☐ 607 Omar Moreno .20 .09 .03
☐ 608 Dave McKay .20 .09 .03
☐ 609 Silvio Martinez .20 .09 .03
☐ 610 Mike Schmidt 8.00 3.60 1.00
☐ 611 Jim Norris .20 .09 .03
☐ 612 Rick Honeycutt .35 .16 .04
☐ 613 Mike Edwards .20 .09 .03
☐ 614 Willie Hernandez .35 .16 .04
☐ 615 Ken Singleton .35 .16 .04
☐ 616 Billy Almon .20 .09 .03
☐ 617 Terry Puhl .35 .16 .04
☐ 618 Jerry Remy .20 .09 .03
☐ 619 Ken Landreaux .35 .16 .04
☐ 620 Bert Campaneris .35 .16 .04
☐ 621 Pat Zachry .20 .09 .03
☐ 622 Dave Collins .35 .16 .04
☐ 623 Bob McClure .20 .09 .03
☐ 624 Larry Herndon .20 .09 .03
☐ 625 Mark Fidrych .35 .16 .04
☐ 626 Yankees Team/Mgr. 1.00 .20 .10
Bob Lemon
(Checklist back)
☐ 627 Gary Serum .20 .09 .03
☐ 628 Del Unser .20 .09 .03
☐ 629 Gene Garber .35 .16 .04
☐ 630 Bake McBride .35 .16 .04
☐ 631 Jorge Orta .20 .09 .03
☐ 632 Don Kirkwood .20 .09 .03
☐ 633 Rob Wilfong DP .10 .05 .01
☐ 634 Paul Lindblad .20 .09 .03
☐ 635 Don Baylor .75 .35 .09
☐ 636 Wayne Garland .20 .09 .03
☐ 637 Bill Robinson .35 .16 .04
☐ 638 Al Fitzmorris .20 .09 .03
☐ 639 Manny Trillo .20 .09 .03
☐ 640 Eddie Murray 30.00 13.50 3.70
☐ 641 Bobby Castillo .20 .09 .03
☐ 642 Wilbur Howard DP .10 .05 .01
☐ 643 Tom Hausman .20 .09 .03
☐ 644 Manny Mota .35 .16 .04
☐ 645 George Scott DP .15 .07 .02
☐ 646 Rick Sweet .20 .09 .03
☐ 647 Bob Lacey .20 .09 .03
☐ 648 Lou Piniella .35 .16 .04
☐ 649 John Curtis .20 .09 .03
☐ 650 Pete Rose 5.00 2.20 .60
☐ 651 Mike Caldwell .20 .09 .03
☐ 652 Stan Papi .20 .09 .03
☐ 653 Warren Brusstar DP .10 .05 .01
☐ 654 Rick Miller .20 .09 .03
☐ 655 Jerry Koosman .35 .16 .04
☐ 656 Hosken Powell .20 .09 .03
☐ 657 George Medich .20 .09 .03
☐ 658 Taylor Duncan .20 .09 .03
☐ 659 Mariners Team/Mgr. 1.00 .20 .10
Darrell Johnson
(Checklist back)
☐ 660 Ron LeFlore DP .20 .09 .03
☐ 661 Bruce Kison .20 .09 .03
☐ 662 Kevin Bell .20 .09 .03
☐ 663 Mike Vail .20 .09 .03
☐ 664 Doug Bird .20 .09 .03
☐ 665 Lou Brock 2.00 .90 .25
☐ 666 Rich Dauer .20 .09 .03
☐ 667 Don Hood .20 .09 .03
☐ 668 Bill North .20 .09 .03
☐ 669 Checklist 606-726 1.00 .20 .10
☐ 670 Jim Hunter DP .75 .35 .09
☐ 671 Joe Ferguson DP .10 .05 .01
☐ 672 Ed Halicki .20 .09 .03
☐ 673 Tom Hutton .20 .09 .03
☐ 674 Dave Tomlin .20 .09 .03
☐ 675 Tim McCarver .35 .16 .04
☐ 676 Johnny Sutton .20 .09 .03
☐ 677 Larry Parrish .35 .16 .04
☐ 678 Geoff Zahn .20 .09 .03
☐ 679 Derrel Thomas .20 .09 .03
☐ 680 Carlton Fisk 2.50 1.10 .30
☐ 681 John Henry Johnson .20 .09 .03
☐ 682 Dave Chalk .20 .09 .03
☐ 683 Dan Meyer DP .10 .05 .01
☐ 684 Jamie Easterly DP .10 .05 .01
☐ 685 Sixto Lezcano .20 .09 .03
☐ 686 Ron Schueler DP .10 .05 .01
☐ 687 Rennie Stennett .20 .09 .03
☐ 688 Mike Willis .20 .09 .03
☐ 689 Orioles Team/Mgr. 1.00 .20 .10
Earl Weaver
(Checklist back)
☐ 690 Buddy Bell DP .20 .09 .03
☐ 691 Dock Ellis DP .10 .05 .01
☐ 692 Mickey Stanley .20 .09 .03
☐ 693 Dave Rader .20 .09 .03
☐ 694 Burt Hooton .35 .16 .04
☐ 695 Keith Hernandez .35 .16 .04
☐ 696 Andy Hassler .20 .09 .03
☐ 697 Dave Bergman .20 .09 .03
☐ 698 Bill Stein .20 .09 .03
☐ 699 Hal Dues .20 .09 .03
☐ 700 Reggie Jackson DP 2.00 .90 .25
☐ 701 Orioles Prospects .35 .16 .04
Mark Corey
John Flinn
Sammy Stewart
☐ 702 Red Sox Prospects .35 .16 .04
Joel Finch
Garry Hancock
Allen Ripley
☐ 703 Angels Prospects .35 .16 .04
Jim Anderson
Dave Frost
Bob Slater
☐ 704 White Sox Prospects .35 .16 .04
Ross Baumgarten
Mike Colbern
Mike Squires
☐ 705 Indians Prospects .50 .23 .06
Alfredo Griffin
Tim Norrid
Dave Oliver
☐ 706 Tigers Prospects .35 .16 .04
Dave Stegman
Dave Tobik
Kip Young
☐ 707 Royals Prospects .50 .23 .06
Randy Bass
Jim Gaudet
Randy McGilberry
☐ 708 Brewers Prospects .75 .35 .09
Kevin Bass
Eddie Romero
Ned Yost
☐ 709 Twins Prospects .35 .16 .04
Sam Perlozzo
Rick Sofield
Kevin Stanfield
☐ 710 Yankees Prospects .35 .16 .04
Brian Doyle
Mike Heath
Dave Rajsich
☐ 711 A's Prospects .50 .23 .06
Dwayne Murphy
Bruce Robinson
Alan Wirth
☐ 712 Mariners Prospects .35 .16 .04
Bud Anderson
Greg Biercevicz
Byron McLaughlin
☐ 713 Rangers Prospects .50 .23 .06
Danny Darwin
Pat Putnam
Billy Sample
☐ 714 Blue Jays Prospects .35 .16 .04
Victor Cruz
Pat Kelly
Ernie Whitt
☐ 715 Braves Prospects .50 .23 .06
Bruce Benedict
Glenn Hubbard
Larry Whisenton
☐ 716 Cubs Prospects .35 .16 .04
Dave Geisel
Karl Pagel
Scot Thompson
☐ 717 Reds Prospects .35 .16 .04
Mike LaCoss
Ron Oester
Harry Spilman
☐ 718 Astros Prospects .35 .16 .04
Bruce Bochy
Mike Fischlin
Don Pisker
☐ 719 Dodgers Prospects 1.50 .70 .19
Pedro Guerrero
Rudy Law
Joe Simpson
☐ 720 Expos Prospects .50 .23 .06
Jerry Fry
Jerry Pirtle
Scott Sanderson
☐ 721 Mets Prospects .35 .16 .04
Juan Berenguer
Dwight Bernard
Dan Norman
☐ 722 Phillies Prospects .50 .23 .06
Jim Morrison
Lonnie Smith
Jim Wright
☐ 723 Pirates Prospects .35 .16 .04
Dale Berra
Eugenio Cotes
Ben Wiltbank
☐ 724 Cardinals Prospects .50 .23 .06
Tom Bruno
George Frazier
Terry Kennedy
☐ 725 Padres Prospects .35 .16 .04
Jim Beswick
Steve Mura
Broderick Perkins
☐ 726 Giants Prospects .35 .07 .03
Greg Johnston
Joe Strain
John Tamargo

1979 Topps Comics

This 33 card (comic) set, which measures approximately 3" by 3 1/4", is rather plentiful in spite of the fact that it was originally touted as a limited edition "test" issue. This flimsy set has never been very popular with collectors. These waxy comics are numbered and are blank backed. Each comic also features an "Inside Baseball" tip in the lower right corner.

	NRMT	VG-E	GOOD
COMPLETE SET (33)	20.00	9.00	2.50
COMMON CARD (1-33)	.15	.07	.02
☐ 1 Eddie Murray	1.50	.70	.19
☐ 2 Jim Rice	.50	.23	.06
☐ 3 Carl Yastrzemski	.75	.35	.09
☐ 4 Nolan Ryan	4.00	1.80	.50
☐ 5 Chet Lemon	.15	.07	.02
☐ 6 Andre Thornton	.15	.07	.02
☐ 7 Rusty Staub	.25	.11	.03
☐ 8 Ron LeFlore	.15	.07	.02
☐ 9 George Brett	3.00	1.35	.35
☐ 10 Larry Hisle	.15	.07	.02
☐ 11 Rod Carew	1.00	.45	.12
☐ 12 Reggie Jackson	2.00	.90	.25
☐ 13 Ron Guidry	.25	.11	.03
☐ 14 Mitchell Page	.15	.07	.02
☐ 15 Leon Roberts	.15	.07	.02
☐ 16 Al Oliver	.25	.11	.03
☐ 17 John Mayberry	.15	.07	.02
☐ 18 Bob Horner	.25	.11	.03
☐ 19 Phil Niekro	.75	.35	.09
☐ 20 Dave Kingman	.25	.11	.03
☐ 21 Johnny Bench	1.00	.45	.12
☐ 22 Tom Seaver	1.00	.45	.12
☐ 23 J.R. Richard	.15	.07	.02
☐ 24 Steve Garvey	.50	.23	.06
☐ 25 Reggie Smith	.15	.07	.02
☐ 26 Ross Grimsley	.15	.07	.02
☐ 27 Craig Swan	.15	.07	.02
☐ 28 Pete Rose	1.50	.70	.19
☐ 29 Dave Parker	.25	.11	.03
☐ 30 Ted Simmons	.25	.11	.03
☐ 31 Dave Winfield	1.00	.45	.12
☐ 32 Jack Clark	.25	.11	.03
☐ 33 Vida Blue	.15	.07	.02

1979 Topps Team Checklist Sheet

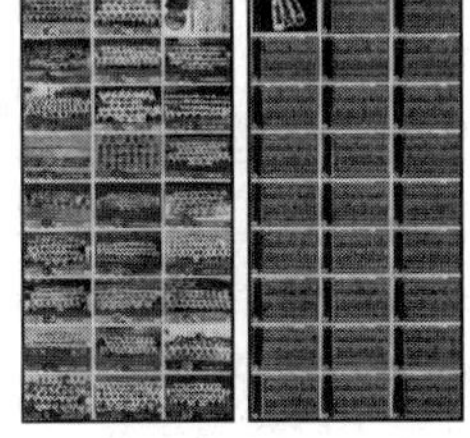

As part of a mail-away offer, Topps offered all 26 1979 team cards checklist cards on an uncut sheet. These cards enabled the collector to have an easy reference for which card(s) he/she needed to finish their sets. When cut from the sheet, all cards measure the standard size.

	NRMT	VG-E	GOOD
COMPLETE SET (1)	15.00	6.75	1.85
COMMON SHEET (1)	15.00	6.75	1.85
☐ 1 Team Checklist Sheet	15.00	6.75	1.85

1980 Topps

The cards in this 726-card set measure the standard size. In 1980 Topps released another set of the same size and number of cards as the previous two years. As with those sets, Topps again produced 66 double-printed cards in the set; they are noted by DP in the checklist below. The player's name appears over the picture and his position and team are found in pennant design. Every card carries a facsimile

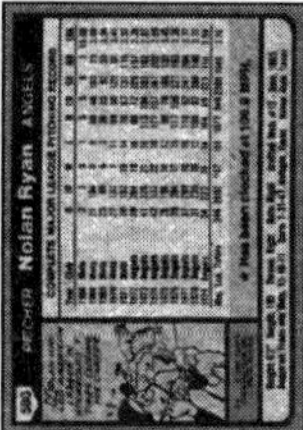

autograph. Team cards feature a team checklist of players in the set on the back and the manager's name on the front. Cards 1-6 show Highlights (HL) of the 1979 season, cards 201-207 are League Leaders, and cards 661-686 feature American and National League rookie "Future Stars," one card for each team showing three young prospects. Ways this set was released include 15-card wax packs as well as 42-card rack packs. A special experiment in 1980 was the issuance of a 28-card cello pack with a three-pack of gum at the bottom so no cards would be damaged. The key Rookie Card in this set is Rickey Henderson; other Rookie Cards included in this set are Dan Quisenberry, Dave Stieb and Rick Sutcliffe.

	NRMT	VG-E	GOOD
COMPLETE SET (726)	150.00	70.00	19.00
COMMON CARD (1-726)	.20	.09	.03
COMMON CARD DP	.10	.05	.01
☐ 1 Lou Brock HL	3.00	.60	.30
Carl Yastrzemski			
Enter 3000 hit circle			
☐ 2 Willie McCovey HL	.75	.35	.09
512th homer sets new			
mark for NL lefties			
☐ 3 Manny Mota HL	.35	.16	.04
All-time pinch-hits, 145			
☐ 4 Pete Rose HL	2.00	.90	.25
Career Record 10th season			
with 200 or more hits			
☐ 5 Garry Templeton HL	.35	.16	.04
First with 100 hits			
from each side of plate			
☐ 6 Del Unser HL	.35	.16	.04
3 consecutive			
pinch homers			
☐ 7 Mike Lum	.20	.09	.03
☐ 8 Craig Swan	.20	.09	.03
☐ 9 Steve Braun	.20	.09	.03
☐ 10 Dennis Martinez	.50	.23	.06
☐ 11 Jimmy Sexton	.20	.09	.03
☐ 12 John Curtis DP	.10	.05	.01
☐ 13 Ron Pruitt	.20	.09	.03
☐ 14 Dave Cash	.20	.09	.03
☐ 15 Bill Campbell	.20	.09	.03
☐ 16 Jerry Narron	.20	.09	.03
☐ 17 Bruce Sutter	.35	.16	.04
☐ 18 Ron Jackson	.20	.09	.03
☐ 19 Balor Moore	.20	.09	.03
☐ 20 Dan Ford	.20	.09	.03
☐ 21 Manny Sarmiento	.20	.09	.03
☐ 22 Pat Putnam	.20	.09	.03
☐ 23 Derrel Thomas	.20	.09	.03
☐ 24 Jim Slaton	.20	.09	.03
☐ 25 Lee Mazzilli	.35	.16	.04
☐ 26 Marty Pattin	.20	.09	.03
☐ 27 Del Unser	.20	.09	.03
☐ 28 Bruce Kison	.20	.09	.03
☐ 29 Mark Wagner	.20	.09	.03
☐ 30 Vida Blue	.50	.23	.06
☐ 31 Jay Johnstone	.35	.16	.04
☐ 32 Julio Cruz DP	.10	.05	.01
☐ 33 Tony Scott	.20	.09	.03
☐ 34 Jeff Newman DP	.10	.05	.01
☐ 35 Luis Tiant	.35	.16	.04
☐ 36 Rusty Torres	.20	.09	.03
☐ 37 Kiko Garcia	.20	.09	.03
☐ 38 Dan Spillner DP	.10	.05	.01
☐ 39 Rowland Office	.20	.09	.03
☐ 40 Carlton Fisk	2.00	.90	.25
☐ 41 Rangers Team/Mgr.	.75	.15	.07
Pat Corrales			
(Checklist back)			
☐ 42 David Palmer	.20	.09	.03
☐ 43 Bombo Rivera	.20	.09	.03
☐ 44 Bill Fahey	.20	.09	.03
☐ 45 Frank White	.50	.23	.06
☐ 46 Rico Carty	.35	.16	.04
☐ 47 Bill Bonham DP	.10	.05	.01
☐ 48 Rick Miller	.20	.09	.03
☐ 49 Mario Guerrero	.20	.09	.03
☐ 50 J.R. Richard	.35	.16	.04
☐ 51 Joe Ferguson DP	.10	.05	.01
☐ 52 Warren Brusstar	.20	.09	.03
☐ 53 Ben Oglivie	.35	.16	.04
☐ 54 Dennis Lamp	.20	.09	.03
☐ 55 Bill Madlock	.35	.16	.04
☐ 56 Bobby Valentine	.20	.09	.03
☐ 57 Pete Vuckovich	.20	.09	.03
☐ 58 Doug Flynn	.20	.09	.03
☐ 59 Eddy Putman	.20	.09	.03
☐ 60 Bucky Dent	.35	.16	.04
☐ 61 Gary Serum	.20	.09	.03
☐ 62 Mike Ivie	.20	.09	.03
☐ 63 Bob Stanley	.20	.09	.03
☐ 64 Joe Nolan	.20	.09	.03
☐ 65 Al Bumbry	.35	.16	.04
☐ 66 Royals Team/Mgr.	.75	.15	.07
Jim Frey			
(Checklist back)			
☐ 67 Doyle Alexander	.20	.09	.03
☐ 68 Larry Harlow	.20	.09	.03
☐ 69 Rick Williams	.20	.09	.03
☐ 70 Gary Carter	.35	.16	.04
☐ 71 John Milner DP	.10	.05	.01
☐ 72 Fred Howard DP	.10	.05	.01
☐ 73 Dave Collins	.20	.09	.03
☐ 74 Sid Monge	.20	.09	.03
☐ 75 Bill Russell	.35	.16	.04
☐ 76 John Stearns	.20	.09	.03
☐ 77 Dave Stieb	1.50	.70	.19
☐ 78 Ruppert Jones	.20	.09	.03
☐ 79 Bob Owchinko	.20	.09	.03
☐ 80 Ron LeFlore	.35	.16	.04
☐ 81 Ted Sizemore	.20	.09	.03
☐ 82 Astros Team/Mgr.	.75	.15	.07
Bill Virdon			
(Checklist back)			
☐ 83 Steve Trout	.20	.09	.03
☐ 84 Gary Lavelle	.20	.09	.03
☐ 85 Ted Simmons	.35	.16	.04
☐ 86 Dave Hamilton	.20	.09	.03
☐ 87 Pepe Frias	.20	.09	.03
☐ 88 Ken Landreaux	.20	.09	.03
☐ 89 Don Hood	.20	.09	.03
☐ 90 Manny Trillo	.35	.16	.04
☐ 91 Rick Dempsey	.35	.16	.04
☐ 92 Rick Rhoden	.20	.09	.03
☐ 93 Dave Roberts DP	.10	.05	.01
☐ 94 Neil Allen	.35	.16	.04
☐ 95 Cecil Cooper	.35	.16	.04
☐ 96 A's Team/Mgr.	.75	.15	.07
Jim Marshall			
(Checklist back)			
☐ 97 Bill Lee	.35	.16	.04
☐ 98 Jerry Terrell	.20	.09	.03
☐ 99 Victor Cruz	.20	.09	.03
☐ 100 Johnny Bench	3.00	1.35	.35
☐ 101 Aurelio Lopez	.20	.09	.03
☐ 102 Rich Dauer	.20	.09	.03
☐ 103 Bill Caudill	.20	.09	.03
☐ 104 Manny Mota	.35	.16	.04
☐ 105 Frank Tanana	.35	.16	.04
☐ 106 Jeff Leonard	.50	.23	.06
☐ 107 Francisco Barrios	.20	.09	.03
☐ 108 Bob Horner	.35	.16	.04
☐ 109 Bill Travers	.20	.09	.03
☐ 110 Fred Lynn DP	.35	.16	.04
☐ 111 Bob Knepper	.20	.09	.03
☐ 112 White Sox Team/Mgr.	.75	.15	.07
Tony LaRussa			
(Checklist back)			
☐ 113 Geoff Zahn	.20	.09	.03
☐ 114 Juan Beniquez	.20	.09	.03
☐ 115 Sparky Lyle	.35	.16	.04
☐ 116 Larry Cox	.20	.09	.03
☐ 117 Dock Ellis	.20	.09	.03
☐ 118 Phil Garner	.35	.16	.04
☐ 119 Sammy Stewart	.20	.09	.03
☐ 120 Greg Luzinski	.35	.16	.04
☐ 121 Checklist 1-121	.75	.15	.07
☐ 122 Dave Rosello DP	.10	.05	.01
☐ 123 Lynn Jones	.20	.09	.03
☐ 124 Dave Lemanczyk	.20	.09	.03
☐ 125 Tony Perez	.60	.25	.07
☐ 126 Dave Tomlin	.20	.09	.03
☐ 127 Gary Thomasson	.20	.09	.03
☐ 128 Tom Burgmeier	.20	.09	.03
☐ 129 Craig Reynolds	.20	.09	.03
☐ 130 Amos Otis	.35	.16	.04
☐ 131 Paul Mitchell	.20	.09	.03
☐ 132 Biff Pocoroba	.20	.09	.03
☐ 133 Jerry Turner	.20	.09	.03
☐ 134 Matt Keough	.20	.09	.03
☐ 135 Bill Buckner	.35	.16	.04
☐ 136 Dick Ruthven	.20	.09	.03
☐ 137 John Castino	.20	.09	.03
☐ 138 Ross Baumgarten	.20	.09	.03
☐ 139 Dane Iorg	.20	.09	.03
☐ 140 Rich Gossage	.60	.25	.07
☐ 141 Gary Alexander	.20	.09	.03
☐ 142 Phil Huffman	.20	.09	.03
☐ 143 Bruce Bochte DP	.10	.05	.01
☐ 144 Steve Comer	.20	.09	.03
☐ 145 Darrell Evans	.35	.16	.04
☐ 146 Bob Welch	.35	.16	.04
☐ 147 Terry Puhl	.20	.09	.03
☐ 148 Manny Sanguillen	.35	.16	.04
☐ 149 Tom Hume	.20	.09	.03
☐ 150 Jason Thompson	.20	.09	.03
☐ 151 Tom Hausman DP	.10	.05	.01
☐ 152 John Fulgham	.20	.09	.03
☐ 153 Tim Blackwell	.20	.09	.03
☐ 154 Lary Sorensen	.20	.09	.03
☐ 155 Jerry Remy	.20	.09	.03
☐ 156 Tony Brizzolara	.20	.09	.03
☐ 157 Willie Wilson DP	.35	.16	.04
☐ 158 Rob Picciolo DP	.10	.05	.01
☐ 159 Ken Clay	.20	.09	.03
☐ 160 Eddie Murray	16.00	7.25	2.00
☐ 161 Larry Christenson	.20	.09	.03
☐ 162 Bob Randall	.20	.09	.03
☐ 163 Steve Swisher	.20	.09	.03
☐ 164 Greg Pryor	.20	.09	.03
☐ 165 Omar Moreno	.20	.09	.03
☐ 166 Glenn Abbott	.20	.09	.03
☐ 167 Jack Clark	.35	.16	.04
☐ 168 Rick Waits	.20	.09	.03
☐ 169 Luis Gomez	.20	.09	.03
☐ 170 Burt Hooton	.35	.16	.04
☐ 171 Fernando Gonzalez	.20	.09	.03
☐ 172 Ron Hodges	.20	.09	.03
☐ 173 John Henry Johnson	.20	.09	.03
☐ 174 Ray Knight	.35	.16	.04
☐ 175 Rick Reuschel	.35	.16	.04
☐ 176 Champ Summers	.20	.09	.03
☐ 177 Dave Heaverlo	.20	.09	.03
☐ 178 Tim McCarver	.50	.23	.06
☐ 179 Ron Davis	.20	.09	.03
☐ 180 Warren Cromartie	.20	.09	.03
☐ 181 Moose Haas	.20	.09	.03
☐ 182 Ken Reitz	.20	.09	.03
☐ 183 Jim Anderson DP	.10	.05	.01
☐ 184 Steve Renko DP	.10	.05	.01
☐ 185 Hal McRae	.50	.23	.06
☐ 186 Junior Moore	.20	.09	.03
☐ 187 Alan Ashby	.20	.09	.03
☐ 188 Terry Crowley	.20	.09	.03
☐ 189 Kevin Kobel	.20	.09	.03
☐ 190 Buddy Bell	.35	.16	.04
☐ 191 Ted Martinez	.20	.09	.03
☐ 192 Braves Team/Mgr.	.75	.15	.07
Bobby Cox			
(Checklist back)			
☐ 193 Dave Goltz	.20	.09	.03
☐ 194 Mike Easler	.20	.09	.03
☐ 195 John Montefusco	.35	.16	.04
☐ 196 Lance Parrish	.35	.16	.04
☐ 197 Byron McLaughlin	.20	.09	.03
☐ 198 Dell Alston DP	.10	.05	.01
☐ 199 Mike LaCoss	.20	.09	.03
☐ 200 Jim Rice	.35	.16	.04
☐ 201 Batting Leaders	.50	.23	.06
Keith Hernandez			
Fred Lynn			
☐ 202 Home Run Leaders	.50	.23	.06
Dave Kingman			
Gorman Thomas			
☐ 203 RBI Leaders	1.00	.45	.12
Dave Winfield			
Don Baylor			
☐ 204 Stolen Base Leaders	.35	.16	.04
Omar Moreno			
Willie Wilson			
☐ 205 Victory Leaders	.50	.23	.06
Joe Niekro			
Phil Niekro			
Mike Flanagan			
☐ 206 Strikeout Leaders	4.00	1.80	.50
J.R. Richard			
Nolan Ryan			
☐ 207 ERA Leaders	.50	.23	.06
J.R. Richard			
Ron Guidry			
☐ 208 Wayne Cage	.20	.09	.03
☐ 209 Von Joshua	.20	.09	.03
☐ 210 Steve Carlton	2.00	.90	.25
☐ 211 Dave Skaggs DP	.10	.05	.01
☐ 212 Dave Roberts	.20	.09	.03
☐ 213 Mike Jorgensen DP	.10	.05	.01
☐ 214 Angels Team/Mgr.	.75	.15	.07
Jim Fregosi			
(Checklist back)			
☐ 215 Sixto Lezcano	.20	.09	.03
☐ 216 Phil Mankowski	.20	.09	.03
☐ 217 Ed Halicki	.20	.09	.03
☐ 218 Jose Morales	.20	.09	.03
☐ 219 Steve Mingori	.20	.09	.03
☐ 220 Dave Concepcion	.50	.23	.06
☐ 221 Joe Cannon	.20	.09	.03
☐ 222 Ron Hassey	.20	.09	.03
☐ 223 Bob Sykes	.20	.09	.03
☐ 224 Willie Montanez	.20	.09	.03
☐ 225 Lou Piniella	.50	.23	.06
☐ 226 Bill Stein	.20	.09	.03
☐ 227 Len Barker	.20	.09	.03
☐ 228 Johnny Oates	.35	.16	.04
☐ 229 Jim Bibby	.20	.09	.03
☐ 230 Dave Winfield	6.00	2.70	.75
☐ 231 Steve McCatty	.20	.09	.03
☐ 232 Alan Trammell	6.00	2.70	.75
☐ 233 LaRue Washington	.20	.09	.03
☐ 234 Vern Ruhle	.20	.09	.03
☐ 235 Andre Dawson	5.00	2.20	.60
☐ 236 Marc Hill	.20	.09	.03
☐ 237 Scott McGregor	.35	.16	.04
☐ 238 Rob Wilfong	.20	.09	.03
☐ 239 Don Aase	.20	.09	.03
☐ 240 Dave Kingman	.35	.16	.04
☐ 241 Checklist 122-242	.75	.15	.07
☐ 242 Lamar Johnson	.20	.09	.03
☐ 243 Jerry Augustine	.20	.09	.03
☐ 244 Cardinals Team/Mgr.	.75	.15	.07
Ken Boyer			
(Checklist back)			
☐ 245 Phil Niekro	.50	.23	.06
☐ 246 Tim Foli DP	.10	.05	.01
☐ 247 Frank Riccelli	.20	.09	.03
☐ 248 Jamie Quirk	.20	.09	.03
☐ 249 Jim Clancy	.20	.09	.03
☐ 250 Jim Kaat	.50	.23	.06
☐ 251 Kip Young	.20	.09	.03
☐ 252 Ted Cox	.20	.09	.03
☐ 253 John Montague	.20	.09	.03
☐ 254 Paul Dade DP	.10	.05	.01
☐ 255 Dusty Baker DP	.20	.09	.03
☐ 256 Roger Erickson	.20	.09	.03
☐ 257 Larry Herndon	.20	.09	.03
☐ 258 Paul Moskau	.20	.09	.03
☐ 259 Mets Team/Mgr.	.75	.15	.07
Joe Torre			
(Checklist back)			
☐ 260 Al Oliver	.50	.23	.06
☐ 261 Dave Chalk	.20	.09	.03
☐ 262 Benny Ayala	.20	.09	.03
☐ 263 Dave LaRoche DP	.10	.05	.01
☐ 264 Bill Robinson	.20	.09	.03
☐ 265 Robin Yount	8.00	3.60	1.00
☐ 266 Bernie Carbo	.20	.09	.03
☐ 267 Dan Schatzeder	.20	.09	.03
☐ 268 Rafael Landestoy	.20	.09	.03
☐ 269 Dave Tobik	.20	.09	.03
☐ 270 Mike Schmidt DP	3.00	1.35	.35
☐ 271 Dick Drago DP	.10	.05	.01
☐ 272 Ralph Garr	.35	.16	.04
☐ 273 Eduardo Rodriguez	.20	.09	.03
☐ 274 Dale Murphy	2.50	1.10	.30
☐ 275 Jerry Koosman	.35	.16	.04
☐ 276 Tom Veryzer	.20	.09	.03
☐ 277 Rick Bosetti	.20	.09	.03
☐ 278 Jim Spencer	.20	.09	.03
☐ 279 Rob Andrews	.20	.09	.03
☐ 280 Gaylord Perry	.75	.35	.09
☐ 281 Paul Blair	.35	.16	.04
☐ 282 Mariners Team/Mgr.	.75	.15	.07
Darrell Johnson			
(Checklist back)			
☐ 283 John Ellis	.20	.09	.03
☐ 284 Larry Murray DP	.10	.05	.01
☐ 285 Don Baylor	.50	.23	.06
☐ 286 Darold Knowles DP	.10	.05	.01
☐ 287 John Lowenstein	.20	.09	.03
☐ 288 Dave Rozema	.20	.09	.03
☐ 289 Bruce Bochy	.20	.09	.03
☐ 290 Steve Garvey	.60	.25	.07
☐ 291 Randy Scarberry	.20	.09	.03
☐ 292 Dale Berra	.20	.09	.03
☐ 293 Elias Sosa	.20	.09	.03
☐ 294 Charlie Spikes	.20	.09	.03
☐ 295 Larry Gura	.20	.09	.03
☐ 296 Dave Rader	.20	.09	.03
☐ 297 Tim Johnson	.20	.09	.03
☐ 298 Ken Holtzman	.35	.16	.04
☐ 299 Steve Henderson	.20	.09	.03
☐ 300 Ron Guidry	.35	.16	.04
☐ 301 Mike Edwards	.20	.09	.03
☐ 302 Dodgers Team/Mgr.	.75	.15	.07
Tom Lasorda			
(Checklist back)			
☐ 303 Bill Castro	.20	.09	.03
☐ 304 Butch Wynegar	.20	.09	.03
☐ 305 Randy Jones	.20	.09	.03
☐ 306 Denny Walling	.20	.09	.03
☐ 307 Rick Honeycutt	.35	.16	.04
☐ 308 Mike Hargrove	.35	.16	.04
☐ 309 Larry McWilliams	.20	.09	.03
☐ 310 Dave Parker	.35	.16	.04
☐ 311 Roger Metzger	.20	.09	.03
☐ 312 Mike Barlow	.20	.09	.03
☐ 313 Johnny Grubb	.20	.09	.03
☐ 314 Tim Stoddard	.20	.09	.03
☐ 315 Steve Kemp	.20	.09	.03
☐ 316 Bob Lacey	.20	.09	.03
☐ 317 Mike Anderson DP	.10	.05	.01
☐ 318 Jerry Reuss	.35	.16	.04
☐ 319 Chris Speier	.20	.09	.03
☐ 320 Dennis Eckersley	1.50	.70	.19
☐ 321 Keith Hernandez	.35	.16	.04
☐ 322 Claudell Washington	.35	.16	.04
☐ 323 Mick Kelleher	.20	.09	.03
☐ 324 Tom Underwood	.20	.09	.03
☐ 325 Dan Driessen	.20	.09	.03
☐ 326 Bo McLaughlin	.20	.09	.03
☐ 327 Ray Fosse DP	.10	.05	.01
☐ 328 Twins Team/Mgr.	.75	.15	.07
Gene Mauch			
(Checklist back)			
☐ 329 Bert Roberge	.20	.09	.03
☐ 330 Al Cowens	.20	.09	.03
☐ 331 Richie Hebner	.35	.16	.04
☐ 332 Enrique Romo	.20	.09	.03
☐ 333 Jim Norris DP	.10	.05	.01
☐ 334 Jim Beattie	.20	.09	.03
☐ 335 Willie McCovey	1.50	.70	.19
☐ 336 George Medich	.20	.09	.03
☐ 337 Carney Lansford	.35	.16	.04
☐ 338 John Wockenfuss	.20	.09	.03
☐ 339 John D'Acquisto	.20	.09	.03
☐ 340 Ken Singleton	.35	.16	.04
☐ 341 Jim Essian	.20	.09	.03

☐ 342 Odell Jones .20 .09 .03
☐ 343 Mike Vail .20 .09 .03
☐ 344 Randy Lerch .20 .09 .03
☐ 345 Larry Parrish .35 .16 .04
☐ 346 Buddy Solomon .20 .09 .03
☐ 347 Harry Chappas .20 .09 .03
☐ 348 Checklist 243-363 .75 .15 .07
☐ 349 Jack Brohamer .20 .09 .03
☐ 350 George Hendrick .35 .16 .04
☐ 351 Bob Davis .20 .09 .03
☐ 352 Dan Briggs .20 .09 .03
☐ 353 Andy Hassler .20 .09 .03
☐ 354 Rick Auerbach .20 .09 .03
☐ 355 Gary Matthews .35 .16 .04
☐ 356 Padres Team/Mgr. .75 .15 .07
Jerry Coleman
(Checklist back)
☐ 357 Bob McClure .20 .09 .03
☐ 358 Lou Whitaker 5.00 2.20 .60
☐ 359 Randy Moffitt .20 .09 .03
☐ 360 Darrell Porter DP .20 .09 .03
☐ 361 Wayne Garland .20 .09 .03
☐ 362 Danny Goodwin .20 .09 .03
☐ 363 Wayne Gross .20 .09 .03
☐ 364 Ray Burris .20 .09 .03
☐ 365 Bobby Murcer .35 .16 .04
☐ 366 Rob Dressler .20 .09 .03
☐ 367 Billy Smith .20 .09 .03
☐ 368 Willie Aikens .20 .09 .03
☐ 369 Jim Kern .20 .09 .03
☐ 370 Cesar Cedeno .35 .16 .04
☐ 371 Jack Morris .50 .23 .06
☐ 372 Joel Youngblood .20 .09 .03
☐ 373 Dan Petry DP .35 .16 .04
☐ 374 Jim Gantner .35 .16 .04
☐ 375 Ross Grimsley .20 .09 .03
☐ 376 Gary Allenson .20 .09 .03
☐ 377 Junior Kennedy .20 .09 .03
☐ 378 Jerry Mumphrey .20 .09 .03
☐ 379 Kevin Bell .20 .09 .03
☐ 380 Garry Maddox .35 .16 .04
☐ 381 Cubs Team/Mgr. .75 .15 .07
Preston Gomez
(Checklist back)
☐ 382 Dave Freisleben .20 .09 .03
☐ 383 Ed Ott .20 .09 .03
☐ 384 Joey McLaughlin .20 .09 .03
☐ 385 Enos Cabell .20 .09 .03
☐ 386 Darrell Jackson .20 .09 .03
☐ 387A Fred Stanley YL 2.00 .90 .25
☐ 387B Fred Stanley .20 .09 .03
(Red name on front)
☐ 388 Mike Paxton .20 .09 .03
☐ 389 Pete LaCock .20 .09 .03
☐ 390 Fergie Jenkins .75 .35 .09
☐ 391 Tony Armas DP .20 .09 .03
☐ 392 Milt Wilcox .20 .09 .03
☐ 393 Ozzie Smith 18.00 8.00 2.20
☐ 394 Reggie Cleveland .20 .09 .03
☐ 395 Ellis Valentine .20 .09 .03
☐ 396 Dan Meyer .20 .09 .03
☐ 397 Roy Thomas DP .10 .05 .01
☐ 398 Barry Foote .20 .09 .03
☐ 399 Mike Proly DP .10 .05 .01
☐ 400 George Foster .35 .16 .04
☐ 401 Pete Falcone .20 .09 .03
☐ 402 Merv Rettenmund .20 .09 .03
☐ 403 Pete Redfern DP .10 .05 .01
☐ 404 Orioles Team/Mgr. .75 .15 .07
Earl Weaver
(Checklist back)
☐ 405 Dwight Evans .35 .16 .04
☐ 406 Paul Molitor 14.00 6.25 1.75
☐ 407 Tony Solaita .20 .09 .03
☐ 408 Bill North .20 .09 .03
☐ 409 Paul Splittorff .20 .09 .03
☐ 410 Bobby Bonds .50 .23 .06
☐ 411 Frank LaCorte .20 .09 .03
☐ 412 Thad Bosley .20 .09 .03
☐ 413 Allen Ripley .20 .09 .03
☐ 414 George Scott .35 .16 .04
☐ 415 Bill Atkinson .20 .09 .03
☐ 416 Tom Brookens .20 .09 .03
☐ 417 Craig Chamberlain DP .10 .05 .01
☐ 418 Roger Freed DP .10 .05 .01
☐ 419 Vic Correll .20 .09 .03
☐ 420 Butch Hobson .35 .16 .04
☐ 421 Doug Bird .20 .09 .03
☐ 422 Larry Milbourne .20 .09 .03
☐ 423 Dave Frost .20 .09 .03
☐ 424 Yankees Team/Mgr. .75 .15 .07
Dick Howser
(Checklist back)
☐ 425 Mark Belanger .35 .16 .04
☐ 426 Grant Jackson .20 .09 .03
☐ 427 Tom Hutton DP .10 .05 .01
☐ 428 Pat Zachry .20 .09 .03
☐ 429 Duane Kuiper .20 .09 .03
☐ 430 Larry Hisle DP .10 .05 .01
☐ 431 Mike Krukow .20 .09 .03
☐ 432 Willie Norwood .20 .09 .03
☐ 433 Rich Gale .20 .09 .03
☐ 434 Johnnie LeMaster .20 .09 .03
☐ 435 Don Gullett .35 .16 .04
☐ 436 Billy Almon .20 .09 .03
☐ 437 Joe Niekro .35 .16 .04
☐ 438 Dave Revering .20 .09 .03
☐ 439 Mike Phillips .20 .09 .03
☐ 440 Don Sutton .60 .25 .07
☐ 441 Eric Soderholm .20 .09 .03
☐ 442 Jorge Orta .20 .09 .03
☐ 443 Mike Parrott .20 .09 .03
☐ 444 Alvis Woods .20 .09 .03
☐ 445 Mark Fidrych .35 .16 .04
☐ 446 Duffy Dyer .20 .09 .03
☐ 447 Nino Espinosa .20 .09 .03
☐ 448 Jim Wohlford .20 .09 .03
☐ 449 Doug Bair .20 .09 .03
☐ 450 George Brett 16.00 7.25 2.00
☐ 451 Indians Team/Mgr. .75 .15 .07
Dave Garcia
(Checklist back)
☐ 452 Steve Dillard .20 .09 .03
☐ 453 Mike Bacsik .20 .09 .03
☐ 454 Tom Donohue .20 .09 .03
☐ 455 Mike Torrez .20 .09 .03
☐ 456 Frank Taveras .20 .09 .03
☐ 457 Bert Blyleven .50 .23 .06
☐ 458 Billy Sample .20 .09 .03
☐ 459 Mickey Lolich DP .20 .09 .03
☐ 460 Willie Randolph .35 .16 .04
☐ 461 Dwayne Murphy .20 .09 .03
☐ 462 Mike Sadek DP .10 .05 .01
☐ 463 Jerry Royster .20 .09 .03
☐ 464 John Denny .20 .09 .03
☐ 465 Rick Monday .20 .09 .03
☐ 466 Mike Squires .20 .09 .03
☐ 467 Jesse Jefferson .20 .09 .03
☐ 468 Aurelio Rodriguez .20 .09 .03
☐ 469 Randy Niemann DP .10 .05 .01
☐ 470 Bob Boone .50 .23 .06
☐ 471 Hosken Powell DP .10 .05 .01
☐ 472 Willie Hernandez .35 .16 .04
☐ 473 Bump Wills .20 .09 .03
☐ 474 Steve Busby .20 .09 .03
☐ 475 Cesar Geronimo .20 .09 .03
☐ 476 Bob Shirley .20 .09 .03
☐ 477 Buck Martinez .20 .09 .03
☐ 478 Gil Flores .20 .09 .03
☐ 479 Expos Team/Mgr. .75 .15 .07
Dick Williams
(Checklist back)
☐ 480 Bob Watson .35 .16 .04
☐ 481 Tom Paciorek .35 .16 .04
☐ 482 Rickey Henderson UER 40.00 18.00 5.00
(7 steals at Modesto,
should be at Fresno)
☐ 483 Bo Diaz .20 .09 .03
☐ 484 Checklist 364-484 .75 .15 .07
☐ 485 Mickey Rivers .35 .16 .04
☐ 486 Mike Tyson DP .10 .05 .01
☐ 487 Wayne Nordhagen .20 .09 .03
☐ 488 Roy Howell .20 .09 .03
☐ 489 Preston Hanna DP .10 .05 .01
☐ 490 Lee May .35 .16 .04
☐ 491 Steve Mura DP .10 .05 .01
☐ 492 Todd Cruz .20 .09 .03
☐ 493 Jerry Martin .20 .09 .03
☐ 494 Craig Minetto .20 .09 .03
☐ 495 Bake McBride .20 .09 .03
☐ 496 Silvio Martinez .20 .09 .03
☐ 497 Jim Mason .20 .09 .03
☐ 498 Danny Darwin .20 .09 .03
☐ 499 Giants Team/Mgr. .75 .15 .07
Dave Bristol
(Checklist back)
☐ 500 Tom Seaver 3.00 1.35 .35
☐ 501 Rennie Stennett .20 .09 .03
☐ 502 Rich Wortham DP .10 .05 .01
☐ 503 Mike Cubbage .20 .09 .03
☐ 504 Gene Garber .20 .09 .03
☐ 505 Bert Campaneris .35 .16 .04
☐ 506 Tom Buskey .20 .09 .03
☐ 507 Leon Roberts .20 .09 .03
☐ 508 U.L. Washington .20 .09 .03
☐ 509 Ed Glynn .20 .09 .03
☐ 510 Ron Cey .35 .16 .04
☐ 511 Eric Wilkins .20 .09 .03
☐ 512 Jose Cardenal .20 .09 .03
☐ 513 Tom Dixon DP .10 .05 .01
☐ 514 Steve Ontiveros .20 .09 .03
☐ 515 Mike Caldwell UER .20 .09 .03
1979 loss total reads
96 instead of 6#
☐ 516 Hector Cruz .20 .09 .03
☐ 517 Don Stanhouse .20 .09 .03
☐ 518 Nelson Norman .20 .09 .03
☐ 519 Steve Nicosia .20 .09 .03
☐ 520 Steve Rogers .20 .09 .03
☐ 521 Ken Brett .20 .09 .03
☐ 522 Jim Morrison .20 .09 .03
☐ 523 Ken Henderson .20 .09 .03
☐ 524 Jim Wright DP .10 .05 .01
☐ 525 Clint Hurdle .20 .09 .03
☐ 526 Phillies Team/Mgr. .75 .15 .07
Dallas Green
(Checklist back)
☐ 527 Doug Rau DP .10 .05 .01
☐ 528 Adrian Devine .20 .09 .03
☐ 529 Jim Barr .20 .09 .03
☐ 530 Jim Sundberg DP .35 .16 .04
☐ 531 Eric Rasmussen .20 .09 .03
☐ 532 Willie Horton .35 .16 .04
☐ 533 Checklist 485-605 .75 .15 .07
☐ 534 Andre Thornton .20 .09 .03
☐ 535 Bob Forsch .20 .09 .03
☐ 536 Lee Lacy .20 .09 .03
☐ 537 Alex Trevino .20 .09 .03
☐ 538 Joe Strain .20 .09 .03
☐ 539 Rudy May .20 .09 .03
☐ 540 Pete Rose 4.00 1.80 .50
☐ 541 Miguel Dilone .20 .09 .03
☐ 542 Joe Coleman .20 .09 .03
☐ 543 Pat Kelly .20 .09 .03
☐ 544 Rick Sutcliffe 2.00 .90 .25
☐ 545 Jeff Burroughs .35 .16 .04
☐ 546 Rick Langford .20 .09 .03
☐ 547 John Wathan .20 .09 .03
☐ 548 Dave Rajsich .20 .09 .03
☐ 549 Larry Wolfe .20 .09 .03
☐ 550 Ken Griffey .35 .16 .04
☐ 551 Pirates Team/Mgr. .75 .15 .07
Chuck Tanner
(Checklist back)
☐ 552 Bill Nahorodny .20 .09 .03
☐ 553 Dick Davis .20 .09 .03
☐ 554 Art Howe .35 .16 .04
☐ 555 Ed Figueroa .20 .09 .03
☐ 556 Joe Rudi .35 .16 .04
☐ 557 Mark Lee .20 .09 .03
☐ 558 Alfredo Griffin .20 .09 .03
☐ 559 Dale Murray .20 .09 .03
☐ 560 Dave Lopes .35 .16 .04
☐ 561 Eddie Whitson .20 .09 .03
☐ 562 Joe Wallis .20 .09 .03
☐ 563 Will McEnaney .20 .09 .03
☐ 564 Rick Manning .20 .09 .03
☐ 565 Dennis Leonard .35 .16 .04
☐ 566 Bud Harrelson .35 .16 .04
☐ 567 Skip Lockwood .20 .09 .03
☐ 568 Gary Roenicke .35 .16 .04
☐ 569 Terry Kennedy .35 .16 .04
☐ 570 Roy Smalley .20 .09 .03
☐ 571 Joe Sambito .20 .09 .03
☐ 572 Jerry Morales DP .10 .05 .01
☐ 573 Kent Tekulve .35 .16 .04
☐ 574 Scot Thompson .20 .09 .03
☐ 575 Ken Kravec .20 .09 .03
☐ 576 Jim Dwyer .20 .09 .03
☐ 577 Blue Jays Team/Mgr. .75 .15 .07
Bobby Mattick
(Checklist back)
☐ 578 Scott Sanderson .35 .16 .04
☐ 579 Charlie Moore .20 .09 .03
☐ 580 Nolan Ryan 20.00 9.00 2.50
☐ 581 Bob Bailor .20 .09 .03
☐ 582 Brian Doyle .20 .09 .03
☐ 583 Bob Stinson .20 .09 .03
☐ 584 Kurt Bevacqua .20 .09 .03
☐ 585 Al Hrabosky .20 .09 .03
☐ 586 Mitchell Page .20 .09 .03
☐ 587 Garry Templeton .20 .09 .03
☐ 588 Greg Minton .20 .09 .03
☐ 589 Chet Lemon .35 .16 .04
☐ 590 Jim Palmer 1.50 .70 .19
☐ 591 Rick Cerone .20 .09 .03
☐ 592 Jon Matlack .20 .09 .03
☐ 593 Jesus Alou .20 .09 .03
☐ 594 Dick Tidrow .20 .09 .03
☐ 595 Don Money .20 .09 .03
☐ 596 Rick Matula .20 .09 .03
☐ 597 Tom Poquette .20 .09 .03
☐ 598 Fred Kendall DP .10 .05 .01
☐ 599 Mike Norris .20 .09 .03
☐ 600 Reggie Jackson 4.00 1.80 .50
☐ 601 Buddy Schultz .20 .09 .03
☐ 602 Brian Downing .20 .09 .03
☐ 603 Jack Billingham DP .10 .05 .01
☐ 604 Glenn Adams .20 .09 .03
☐ 605 Terry Forster .20 .09 .03
☐ 606 Reds Team/Mgr. .75 .15 .07
John McNamara
(Checklist back)
☐ 607 Woodie Fryman .20 .09 .03
☐ 608 Alan Bannister .20 .09 .03
☐ 609 Ron Reed .20 .09 .03
☐ 610 Willie Stargell 1.25 .55 .16
☐ 611 Jerry Garvin DP .10 .05 .01
☐ 612 Cliff Johnson .20 .09 .03
☐ 613 Randy Stein .20 .09 .03
☐ 614 John Hiller .20 .09 .03
☐ 615 Doug DeCinces .35 .16 .04
☐ 616 Gene Richards .20 .09 .03
☐ 617 Joaquin Andujar .35 .16 .04
☐ 618 Bob Montgomery DP .10 .05 .01
☐ 619 Sergio Ferrer .20 .09 .03
☐ 620 Richie Zisk .20 .09 .03
☐ 621 Bob Grich .35 .16 .04
☐ 622 Mario Soto .20 .09 .03
☐ 623 Gorman Thomas .35 .16 .04
☐ 624 Lerrin LaGrow .20 .09 .03
☐ 625 Chris Chambliss .35 .16 .04
☐ 626 Tigers Team/Mgr. .75 .15 .07
Sparky Anderson
(Checklist back)
☐ 627 Pedro Borbon .20 .09 .03
☐ 628 Doug Capilla .20 .09 .03
☐ 629 Jim Todd .20 .09 .03
☐ 630 Larry Bowa .35 .16 .04
☐ 631 Mark Littell .20 .09 .03
☐ 632 Barry Bonnell .20 .09 .03
☐ 633 Bob Apodaca .20 .09 .03
☐ 634 Glenn Borgmann DP .10 .05 .01
☐ 635 John Candelaria .35 .16 .04
☐ 636 Toby Harrah .35 .16 .04
☐ 637 Joe Simpson .20 .09 .03
☐ 638 Mark Clear .20 .09 .03
☐ 639 Larry Biittner .20 .09 .03
☐ 640 Mike Flanagan .35 .16 .04
☐ 641 Ed Kranepool .20 .09 .03
☐ 642 Ken Forsch DP .10 .05 .01
☐ 643 John Mayberry .35 .16 .04
☐ 644 Charlie Hough .35 .16 .04
☐ 645 Rick Burleson .20 .09 .03
☐ 646 Checklist 606-726 .75 .15 .07
☐ 647 Milt May .20 .09 .03
☐ 648 Roy White .20 .09 .03
☐ 649 Tom Griffin .20 .09 .03
☐ 650 Joe Morgan 1.50 .70 .19
☐ 651 Rollie Fingers .75 .35 .09
☐ 652 Mario Mendoza .20 .09 .03
☐ 653 Stan Bahnsen .20 .09 .03
☐ 654 Bruce Boisclair DP .10 .05 .01
☐ 655 Tug McGraw .35 .16 .04
☐ 656 Larvell Blanks .20 .09 .03
☐ 657 Dave Edwards .20 .09 .03
☐ 658 Chris Knapp .20 .09 .03
☐ 659 Brewers Team/Mgr. .75 .15 .07
George Bamberger
(Checklist back)
☐ 660 Rusty Staub .35 .16 .04
☐ 661 Orioles Rookies .35 .16 .04
Mark Corey
Dave Ford
Wayne Krenchicki
☐ 662 Red Sox Rookies .35 .16 .04
Joel Finch
Mike O'Berry
Chuck Rainey
☐ 663 Angels Rookies .50 .23 .06
Ralph Botting
Bob Clark
Dickie Thon
☐ 664 White Sox Rookies .35 .16 .04
Mike Colbern
Guy Hoffman
Dewey Robinson
☐ 665 Indians Rookies .50 .23 .06
Larry Andersen
Bobby Cuellar
Sandy Wihtol
☐ 666 Tigers Rookies .35 .16 .04
Mike Chris
Al Greene
Bruce Robbins
☐ 667 Royals Rookies 2.00 .90 .25
Renie Martin
Bill Paschall
Dan Quisenberry
☐ 668 Brewers Rookies .35 .16 .04
Danny Boitano
Willie Mueller
Lenn Sakata
☐ 669 Twins Rookies .35 .16 .04
Dan Graham
Rick Sofield
Gary Ward
☐ 670 Yankees Rookies .35 .16 .04
Bobby Brown
Brad Gulden
Darryl Jones
☐ 671 A's Rookies .60 .25 .07
Derek Bryant
Brian Kingman
Mike Morgan
☐ 672 Mariners Rookies .35 .16 .04
Charlie Beamon
Rodney Craig
Rafael Vasquez
☐ 673 Rangers Rookies .35 .16 .04
Brian Allard
Jerry Don Gleaton
Greg Mahlberg
☐ 674 Blue Jays Rookies .35 .16 .04
Butch Edge
Pat Kelly
Ted Wilborn
☐ 675 Braves Rookies .35 .16 .04
Bruce Benedict
Larry Bradford
Eddie Miller
☐ 676 Cubs Rookies .35 .16 .04
Dave Geisel
Steve Macko
Karl Pagel
☐ 677 Reds Rookies .35 .16 .04
Art DeFreites
Frank Pastore
Harry Spilman
☐ 678 Astros Rookies .35 .16 .04

	NRMT	VG-E	GOOD
Reggie Baldwin			
Alan Knicely			
Pete Ladd			
☐ 679 Dodgers Rookies	.50	.23	.06
Joe Beckwith			
Mickey Hatcher			
Dave Patterson			
☐ 680 Expos Rookies	.50	.23	.06
Tony Bernazard			
Randy Miller			
John Tamargo			
☐ 681 Mets Rookies	.60	.25	.07
Dan Norman			
Jesse Orosco			
Mike Scott			
☐ 682 Phillies Rookies	.35	.16	.04
Ramon Aviles			
Dickie Noles			
Kevin Saucier			
☐ 683 Pirates Rookies	.35	.16	.04
Dorian Boyland			
Alberto Lois			
Harry Saferight			
☐ 684 Cardinals Rookies	.50	.23	.06
George Frazier			
Tom Herr			
Dan O'Brien			
☐ 685 Padres Rookies	.35	.16	.04
Tim Flannery			
Brian Greer			
Jim Wilhelm			
☐ 686 Giants Rookies	.35	.16	.04
Greg Johnston			
Dennis Littlejohn			
Phil Nastu			
☐ 687 Mike Heath DP	.10	.05	.01
☐ 688 Steve Stone	.35	.16	.04
☐ 689 Red Sox Team/Mgr.	.75	.15	.07
Don Zimmer			
(Checklist back)			
☐ 690 Tommy John	.50	.23	.06
☐ 691 Ivan DeJesus	.20	.09	.03
☐ 692 Rawly Eastwick DP	.10	.05	.01
☐ 693 Craig Kusick	.20	.09	.03
☐ 694 Jim Rooker	.20	.09	.03
☐ 695 Reggie Smith	.35	.16	.04
☐ 696 Julio Gonzalez	.20	.09	.03
☐ 697 David Clyde	.20	.09	.03
☐ 698 Oscar Gamble	.35	.16	.04
☐ 699 Floyd Bannister	.20	.09	.03
☐ 700 Rod Carew DP	1.00	.45	.12
☐ 701 Ken Oberkfell	.20	.09	.03
☐ 702 Ed Farmer	.20	.09	.03
☐ 703 Otto Velez	.20	.09	.03
☐ 704 Gene Tenace	.35	.16	.04
☐ 705 Freddie Patek	.20	.09	.03
☐ 706 Tippy Martinez	.35	.16	.04
☐ 707 Elliott Maddox	.20	.09	.03
☐ 708 Bob Tolan	.20	.09	.03
☐ 709 Pat Underwood	.20	.09	.03
☐ 710 Graig Nettles	.35	.16	.04
☐ 711 Bob Galasso	.20	.09	.03
☐ 712 Rodney Scott	.20	.09	.03
☐ 713 Terry Whitfield	.20	.09	.03
☐ 714 Fred Norman	.20	.09	.03
☐ 715 Sal Bando	.35	.16	.04
☐ 716 Lynn McGlothen	.20	.09	.03
☐ 717 Mickey Klutts DP	.10	.05	.01
☐ 718 Greg Gross	.20	.09	.03
☐ 719 Don Robinson	.35	.16	.04
☐ 720 Carl Yastrzemski DP	1.50	.70	.19
☐ 721 Paul Hartzell	.20	.09	.03
☐ 722 Jose Cruz	.35	.16	.04
☐ 723 Shane Rawley	.20	.09	.03
☐ 724 Jerry White	.20	.09	.03
☐ 725 Rick Wise	.20	.09	.03
☐ 726 Steve Yeager	.35	.07	.03

1980 Topps Super

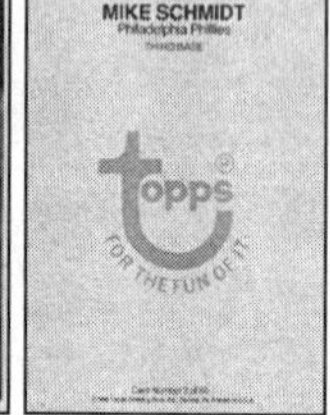

This 60-card set, measuring 4 7/8" by 6 7/8", consists primarily of star players. A player photo comprises the entire front with a facsimile signature at the lower portion of the photo. The backs contain a large Topps logo and the player's name. The cards were issued with either white or gray backs. The white backs have thicker card stock than the gray. White back cards were issued in three-card cellophane packs and gray back cards were issued through various promotional means. The prices below reflect those of the gray back. White backs are valued at 2.5 times these prices. There are a number of cards that were Triple Printed. They are indicated by below (TP).

	NRMT	VG-E	GOOD
COMPLETE SET (60)	20.00	9.00	2.50
COMMON CARD (1-60)	.10	.05	.01
☐ 1 Willie Stargell	.50	.23	.06
☐ 2 Mike Schmidt TP	.75	.35	.09
☐ 3 Johnny Bench	.75	.35	.09
☐ 4 Jim Palmer	.50	.23	.06
☐ 5 Jim Rice	.25	.11	.03
☐ 6 Reggie Jackson TP	.75	.35	.09
☐ 7 Ron Guidry	.25	.11	.03
☐ 8 Lee Mazzilli	.25	.11	.03
☐ 9 Don Baylor	.50	.23	.06
☐ 10 Fred Lynn	.25	.11	.03
☐ 11 Ken Singleton	.25	.11	.03
☐ 12 Rod Carew TP	.50	.23	.06
☐ 13 Steve Garvey TP	.30	.14	.04
☐ 14 George Brett TP	1.50	.70	.19
☐ 15 Tom Seaver	.75	.35	.09
☐ 16 Dave Kingman	.25	.11	.03
☐ 17 Dave Parker TP	.25	.11	.03
☐ 18 Dave Winfield	.75	.35	.09
☐ 19 Pete Rose	1.00	.45	.12
☐ 20 Nolan Ryan	3.00	1.35	.35
☐ 21 Graig Nettles	.25	.11	.03
☐ 22 Carl Yastrzemski	.75	.35	.09
☐ 23 Tommy John	.50	.23	.06
☐ 24 George Foster	.25	.11	.03
☐ 25 J.R. Richard	.10	.05	.01
☐ 26 Keith Hernandez	.25	.11	.03
☐ 27 Bob Horner	.10	.05	.01
☐ 28 Eddie Murray	2.00	.90	.25
☐ 29 Steve Kemp	.10	.05	.01
☐ 30 Gorman Thomas	.10	.05	.01
☐ 31 Sixto Lezcano	.10	.05	.01
☐ 32 Bruce Sutter	.25	.11	.03
☐ 33 Cecil Cooper	.25	.11	.03
☐ 34 Larry Bowa	.25	.11	.03
☐ 35 Al Oliver	.50	.23	.06
☐ 36 Ted Simmons	.25	.11	.03
☐ 37 Garry Templeton	.10	.05	.01
☐ 38 Jerry Koosman	.25	.11	.03
☐ 39 Darrell Porter	.10	.05	.01
☐ 40 Roy Smalley	.10	.05	.01
☐ 41 Craig Swan	.10	.05	.01
☐ 42 Jason Thompson	.10	.05	.01
☐ 43 Andre Thornton	.10	.05	.01
☐ 44 Rick Manning	.10	.05	.01
☐ 45 Kent Tekulve	.10	.05	.01
☐ 46 Phil Niekro	.75	.35	.09
☐ 47 Buddy Bell	.25	.11	.03
☐ 48 Randy Jones	.10	.05	.01
☐ 49 Brian Downing	.10	.05	.01
☐ 50 Amos Otis	.10	.05	.01
☐ 51 Rick Bosetti	.10	.05	.01
☐ 52 Gary Carter	.50	.23	.06
☐ 53 Larry Parrish	.25	.11	.03
☐ 54 Jack Clark	.25	.11	.03
☐ 55 Bruce Bochte	.10	.05	.01
☐ 56 Cesar Cedeno	.10	.05	.01
☐ 57 Chet Lemon	.10	.05	.01
☐ 58 Dave Revering	.10	.05	.01
☐ 59 Vida Blue	.25	.11	.03
☐ 60 Dave Lopes	.25	.11	.03

1980 Topps Team Checklist Sheet

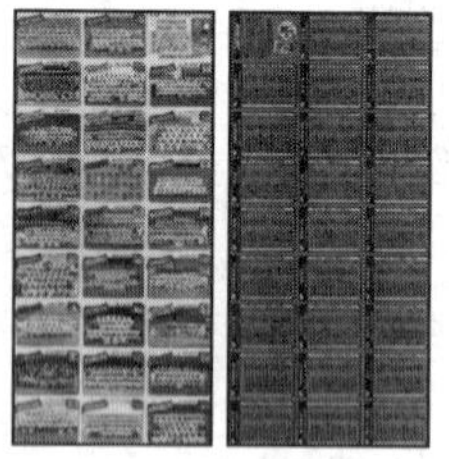

As part of a mail-away offer, Topps offered all 26 1980 team checklist cards on an uncut sheet. These cards enabled the collector to have an easy reference for which card(s) he/she needed to finish their sets. When cut from the sheet, all cards measure the standard size.

	NRMT	VG-E	GOOD
COMPLETE SET (1)	15.00	6.75	1.85
COMMON SHEET (1)	15.00	6.75	1.85
☐ 1 Team Checklist Sheet	15.00	6.75	1.85

1981 Topps

The cards in this 726-card set measure the standard size. League Leaders (1-8), Record Breakers (201-208), and Post-season cards (401-404) are the topical subsets. The team cards are all grouped together (661-686) and feature team checklist backs and a very small photo of the team's manager in the upper right corner of the obverse. The obverses carry the player's position and team in a baseball cap design, and the company name is printed in a small baseball. The backs are red and gray. The 66 double-printed cards are noted in the checklist by DP. This set was issued primarily in 15-card wax packs and 50-card rack packs. Notable Rookie Cards in the set include Harold Baines, Kirk Gibson, Tim Raines, Jeff Reardon, and Fernando Valenzuela.

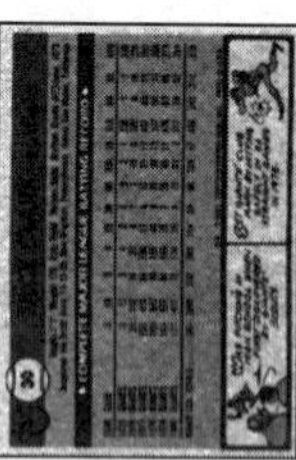

	NRMT	VG-E	GOOD
COMPLETE SET (726)	50.00	22.00	6.25
COMMON CARD (1-726)	.15	.07	.02
COMMON CARD DP	.07	.03	.01
☐ 1 Batting Leaders	2.50	1.10	.30
George Brett			
Bill Buckner			
☐ 2 Home Run Leaders	1.00	.45	.12
Reggie Jackson			
Ben Oglivie			
Mike Schmidt			
☐ 3 RBI Leaders	.75	.35	.09
Cecil Cooper			
Mike Schmidt			
☐ 4 Stolen Base Leaders	1.50	.70	.19
Rickey Henderson			
Ron LeFlore			
☐ 5 Victory Leaders	.75	.35	.09
Steve Stone			
Steve Carlton			
☐ 6 Strikeout Leaders	.75	.35	.09
Len Barker			
Steve Carlton			
☐ 7 ERA Leaders	.40	.18	.05
Rudy May			
Don Sutton			
☐ 8 Leading Firemen	.40	.18	.05
Dan Quisenberry			
Rollie Fingers			
Tom Hume			
☐ 9 Pete LaCock DP	.07	.03	.01
☐ 10 Mike Flanagan	.25	.11	.03
☐ 11 Jim Wohlford DP	.07	.03	.01
☐ 12 Mark Clear	.15	.07	.02
☐ 13 Joe Charboneau	.25	.11	.03
☐ 14 John Tudor	.25	.11	.03
☐ 15 Larry Parrish	.15	.07	.02
☐ 16 Ron Davis	.15	.07	.02
☐ 17 Cliff Johnson	.15	.07	.02
☐ 18 Glenn Adams	.15	.07	.02
☐ 19 Jim Clancy	.15	.07	.02
☐ 20 Jeff Burroughs	.15	.07	.02
☐ 21 Ron Oester	.15	.07	.02
☐ 22 Danny Darwin	.25	.11	.03
☐ 23 Alex Trevino	.15	.07	.02
☐ 24 Don Stanhouse	.15	.07	.02
☐ 25 Sixto Lezcano	.15	.07	.02
☐ 26 U.L. Washington	.15	.07	.02
☐ 27 Champ Summers DP	.07	.03	.01
☐ 28 Enrique Romo	.15	.07	.02
☐ 29 Gene Tenace	.25	.11	.03
☐ 30 Jack Clark	.25	.11	.03
☐ 31 Checklist 1-121 DP	.15	.07	.02
☐ 32 Ken Oberkfell	.15	.07	.02
☐ 33 Rick Honeycutt	.15	.07	.02
☐ 34 Aurelio Rodriguez	.15	.07	.02
☐ 35 Mitchell Page	.15	.07	.02
☐ 36 Ed Farmer	.15	.07	.02
☐ 37 Gary Roenicke	.15	.07	.02
☐ 38 Win Remmerswaal	.15	.07	.02
☐ 39 Tom Veryzer	.15	.07	.02
☐ 40 Tug McGraw	.25	.11	.03
☐ 41 Ranger Rookies	.15	.07	.02
Bob Babcock			
John Butcher			
Jerry Don Gleaton			
☐ 42 Jerry White DP	.07	.03	.01
☐ 43 Jose Morales	.15	.07	.02
☐ 44 Larry McWilliams	.15	.07	.02
☐ 45 Enos Cabell	.15	.07	.02
☐ 46 Rick Bosetti	.15	.07	.02
☐ 47 Ken Brett	.15	.07	.02
☐ 48 Dave Skaggs	.15	.07	.02
☐ 49 Bob Shirley	.15	.07	.02
☐ 50 Dave Lopes	.25	.11	.03
☐ 51 Bill Robinson DP	.15	.07	.02
☐ 52 Hector Cruz	.15	.07	.02
☐ 53 Kevin Saucier	.15	.07	.02
☐ 54 Ivan DeJesus	.15	.07	.02
☐ 55 Mike Norris	.15	.07	.02
☐ 56 Buck Martinez	.15	.07	.02
☐ 57 Dave Roberts	.15	.07	.02
☐ 58 Joel Youngblood	.15	.07	.02
☐ 59 Dan Petry	.25	.11	.03
☐ 60 Willie Randolph	.25	.11	.03
☐ 61 Butch Wynegar	.15	.07	.02
☐ 62 Joe Pettini	.15	.07	.02
☐ 63 Steve Renko DP	.07	.03	.01
☐ 64 Brian Asselstine	.15	.07	.02
☐ 65 Scott McGregor	.15	.07	.02
☐ 66 Royals Rookies	.15	.07	.02
Manny Castillo			
Tim Ireland			
Mike Jones			
☐ 67 Ken Kravec	.15	.07	.02
☐ 68 Matt Alexander DP	.07	.03	.01
☐ 69 Ed Halicki	.15	.07	.02
☐ 70 Al Oliver DP	.25	.11	.03
☐ 71 Hal Dues	.15	.07	.02
☐ 72 Barry Evans DP	.07	.03	.01
☐ 73 Doug Bair	.15	.07	.02
☐ 74 Mike Hargrove	.25	.11	.03
☐ 75 Reggie Smith	.25	.11	.03
☐ 76 Mario Mendoza	.15	.07	.02
☐ 77 Mike Barlow	.15	.07	.02
☐ 78 Steve Dillard	.15	.07	.02
☐ 79 Bruce Robbins	.15	.07	.02
☐ 80 Rusty Staub	.25	.11	.03
☐ 81 Dave Stapleton	.15	.07	.02
☐ 82 Astros Rookies DP	.15	.07	.02
Danny Heep			
Alan Knicely			
Bobby Sprowl			
☐ 83 Mike Proly	.15	.07	.02
☐ 84 Johnnie LeMaster	.15	.07	.02
☐ 85 Mike Caldwell	.15	.07	.02
☐ 86 Wayne Gross	.15	.07	.02
☐ 87 Rick Camp	.15	.07	.02
☐ 88 Joe Lefebvre	.15	.07	.02
☐ 89 Darrell Jackson	.15	.07	.02
☐ 90 Bake McBride	.15	.07	.02
☐ 91 Tim Stoddard DP	.07	.03	.01
☐ 92 Mike Easler	.15	.07	.02
☐ 93 Ed Glynn DP	.15	.07	.02
☐ 94 Harry Spilman DP	.07	.03	.01
☐ 95 Jim Sundberg	.25	.11	.03
☐ 96 A's Rookies	.15	.07	.02
Dave Beard			
Ernie Camacho			
Pat Dempsey			
☐ 97 Chris Speier	.15	.07	.02
☐ 98 Clint Hurdle	.15	.07	.02
☐ 99 Eric Wilkins	.15	.07	.02
☐ 100 Rod Carew	1.25	.55	.16
☐ 101 Benny Ayala	.15	.07	.02
☐ 102 Dave Tobik	.15	.07	.02
☐ 103 Jerry Martin	.15	.07	.02
☐ 104 Terry Forster	.15	.07	.02
☐ 105 Jose Cruz	.25	.11	.03
☐ 106 Don Money	.15	.07	.02
☐ 107 Rich Wortham	.15	.07	.02
☐ 108 Bruce Benedict	.15	.07	.02
☐ 109 Mike Scott	.25	.11	.03
☐ 110 Carl Yastrzemski	1.50	.70	.19
☐ 111 Greg Minton	.15	.07	.02
☐ 112 White Sox Rookies	.15	.07	.02
Rusty Kuntz			
Fran Mullins			
Leo Sutherland			
☐ 113 Mike Phillips	.15	.07	.02
☐ 114 Tom Underwood	.15	.07	.02
☐ 115 Roy Smalley	.15	.07	.02
☐ 116 Joe Simpson	.15	.07	.02
☐ 117 Pete Falcone	.15	.07	.02
☐ 118 Kurt Bevacqua	.15	.07	.02
☐ 119 Tippy Martinez	.15	.07	.02
☐ 120 Larry Bowa	.25	.11	.03
☐ 121 Larry Harlow	.15	.07	.02
☐ 122 John Denny	.15	.07	.02
☐ 123 Al Cowens	.15	.07	.02
☐ 124 Jerry Garvin	.15	.07	.02
☐ 125 Andre Dawson	2.00	.90	.25
☐ 126 Charlie Leibrandt	.40	.18	.05
☐ 127 Rudy Law	.15	.07	.02
☐ 128 Gary Allenson DP	.07	.03	.01
☐ 129 Art Howe	.15	.07	.02
☐ 130 Larry Gura	.15	.07	.02
☐ 131 Keith Moreland	.25	.11	.03
☐ 132 Tommy Boggs	.15	.07	.02
☐ 133 Jeff Cox	.15	.07	.02
☐ 134 Steve Mura	.15	.07	.02
☐ 135 Gorman Thomas	.25	.11	.03
☐ 136 Doug Capilla	.15	.07	.02
☐ 137 Hosken Powell	.15	.07	.02
☐ 138 Rich Dotson DP	.15	.07	.02
☐ 139 Oscar Gamble	.15	.07	.02
☐ 140 Bob Forsch	.15	.07	.02
☐ 141 Miguel Dilone	.15	.07	.02
☐ 142 Jackson Todd	.15	.07	.02
☐ 143 Dan Meyer	.15	.07	.02
☐ 144 Allen Ripley	.15	.07	.02
☐ 145 Mickey Rivers	.25	.11	.03
☐ 146 Bobby Castillo	.15	.07	.02
☐ 147 Dale Berra	.15	.07	.02
☐ 148 Randy Niemann	.15	.07	.02
☐ 149 Joe Nolan	.15	.07	.02
☐ 150 Mark Fidrych	.40	.18	.05
☐ 151 Claudell Washington	.15	.07	.02
☐ 152 John Urrea	.15	.07	.02
☐ 153 Tom Poquette	.15	.07	.02
☐ 154 Rick Langford	.15	.07	.02
☐ 155 Chris Chambliss	.25	.11	.03
☐ 156 Bob McClure	.15	.07	.02
☐ 157 John Wathan	.15	.07	.02
☐ 158 Fergie Jenkins	.75	.35	.09
☐ 159 Brian Doyle	.15	.07	.02
☐ 160 Garry Maddox	.15	.07	.02

☐ 161 Dan Graham	.15	.07	.02
☐ 162 Doug Corbett	.15	.07	.02
☐ 163 Bill Almon	.15	.07	.02
☐ 164 LaMarr Hoyt	.25	.11	.03
☐ 165 Tony Scott	.15	.07	.02
☐ 166 Floyd Bannister	.15	.07	.02
☐ 167 Terry Whitfield	.15	.07	.02
☐ 168 Don Robinson DP	.07	.03	.01
☐ 169 John Mayberry	.15	.07	.02
☐ 170 Ross Grimsley	.15	.07	.02
☐ 171 Gene Richards	.15	.07	.02
☐ 172 Gary Woods	.15	.07	.02
☐ 173 Bump Wills	.15	.07	.02
☐ 174 Doug Rau	.15	.07	.02
☐ 175 Dave Collins	.15	.07	.02
☐ 176 Mike Krukow	.15	.07	.02
☐ 177 Rick Peters	.15	.07	.02
☐ 178 Jim Essian DP	.07	.03	.01
☐ 179 Rudy May	.15	.07	.02
☐ 180 Pete Rose	2.50	1.10	.30
☐ 181 Elias Sosa	.15	.07	.02
☐ 182 Bob Grich	.25	.11	.03
☐ 183 Dick Davis DP	.07	.03	.01
☐ 184 Jim Dwyer	.15	.07	.02
☐ 185 Dennis Leonard	.15	.07	.02
☐ 186 Wayne Nordhagen	.15	.07	.02
☐ 187 Mike Parrott	.15	.07	.02
☐ 188 Doug DeCinces	.25	.11	.03
☐ 189 Craig Swan	.15	.07	.02
☐ 190 Cesar Cedeno	.25	.11	.03
☐ 191 Rick Sutcliffe	.25	.11	.03
☐ 192 Braves Rookies	.25	.11	.03
Terry Harper			
Ed Miller			
Rafael Ramirez			
☐ 193 Pete Vuckovich	.25	.11	.03
☐ 194 Rod Scurry	.15	.07	.02
☐ 195 Rich Murray	.15	.07	.02
☐ 196 Duffy Dyer	.15	.07	.02
☐ 197 Jim Kern	.15	.07	.02
☐ 198 Jerry Dybzinski	.15	.07	.02
☐ 199 Chuck Rainey	.15	.07	.02
☐ 200 George Foster	.25	.11	.03
☐ 201 Johnny Bench RB	.75	.35	.09
Most homers catchers			
☐ 202 Steve Carlton RB	.75	.35	.09
Most strikeouts,			
lefthander, lifetime			
☐ 203 Bill Gullickson RB	.40	.18	.05
Most SO's, game, rookie			
☐ 204 Ron LeFlore RB	.25	.11	.03
Rodney Scott RB			
Most stolen bases			
teammates, season			
☐ 205 Pete Rose RB	1.50	.70	.19
Most cons. seasons			
600 or more at-bats			
☐ 206 Mike Schmidt RB	1.50	.70	.19
Most homers, 3rd baseman, season			
☐ 207 Ozzie Smith RB	2.00	.90	.25
Most assists,			
season, shortstop			
☐ 208 Willie Wilson RB	.25	.11	.03
Most AB's season			
☐ 209 Dickie Thon DP	.25	.11	.03
☐ 210 Jim Palmer	1.00	.45	.12
☐ 211 Derrel Thomas	.15	.07	.02
☐ 212 Steve Nicosia	.15	.07	.02
☐ 213 Al Holland	.15	.07	.02
☐ 214 Angels Rookies	.15	.07	.02
Ralph Botting			
Jim Dorsey			
John Harris			
☐ 215 Larry Hisle	.15	.07	.02
☐ 216 John Henry Johnson	.15	.07	.02
☐ 217 Rich Hebner	.15	.07	.02
☐ 218 Paul Splittorff	.15	.07	.02
☐ 219 Ken Landreaux	.15	.07	.02
☐ 220 Tom Seaver	2.00	.90	.25
☐ 221 Bob Davis	.15	.07	.02
☐ 222 Jorge Orta	.15	.07	.02
☐ 223 Roy Lee Jackson	.15	.07	.02
☐ 224 Pat Zachry	.15	.07	.02
☐ 225 Ruppert Jones	.15	.07	.02
☐ 226 Manny Sanguillen DP	.07	.03	.01
☐ 227 Fred Martinez	.15	.07	.02
☐ 228 Tom Paciorek	.15	.07	.02
☐ 229 Rollie Fingers	.40	.18	.05
☐ 230 George Hendrick	.15	.07	.02
☐ 231 Joe Beckwith	.15	.07	.02
☐ 232 Mickey Klutts	.15	.07	.02
☐ 233 Skip Lockwood	.15	.07	.02
☐ 234 Lou Whitaker	1.50	.70	.19
☐ 235 Scott Sanderson	.15	.07	.02
☐ 236 Mike Ivie	.15	.07	.02
☐ 237 Charlie Moore	.15	.07	.02
☐ 238 Willie Hernandez	.25	.11	.03
☐ 239 Rick Miller DP	.07	.03	.01
☐ 240 Nolan Ryan	8.00	3.60	1.00
☐ 241 Checklist 122-242 DP	.15	.07	.02
☐ 242 Chet Lemon	.15	.07	.02
☐ 243 Sal Butera	.15	.07	.02
☐ 244 Cardinals Rookies	.15	.07	.02
Tito Landrum			
Al Olmsted			
Andy Rincon			
☐ 245 Ed Figueroa	.15	.07	.02
☐ 246 Ed Ott DP	.07	.03	.01
☐ 247 Glenn Hubbard DP	.07	.03	.01
☐ 248 Joey McLaughlin	.15	.07	.02
☐ 249 Larry Cox	.15	.07	.02
☐ 250 Ron Guidry	.25	.11	.03
☐ 251 Tom Brookens	.15	.07	.02
☐ 252 Victor Cruz	.15	.07	.02
☐ 253 Dave Bergman	.15	.07	.02
☐ 254 Ozzie Smith	6.00	2.70	.75
☐ 255 Mark Littell	.15	.07	.02
☐ 256 Bombo Rivera	.15	.07	.02
☐ 257 Rennie Stennett	.15	.07	.02
☐ 258 Joe Price	.15	.07	.02
☐ 259 Mets Rookies	.75	.35	.09
Juan Berenguer			
Hubie Brooks			
Mookie Wilson			
☐ 260 Ron Cey	.25	.11	.03
☐ 261 Rickey Henderson	5.00	2.20	.60
☐ 262 Sammy Stewart	.15	.07	.02
☐ 263 Brian Downing	.15	.07	.02
☐ 264 Jim Norris	.15	.07	.02
☐ 265 John Candelaria	.25	.11	.03
☐ 266 Tom Herr	.25	.11	.03
☐ 267 Stan Bahnsen	.15	.07	.02
☐ 268 Jerry Royster	.15	.07	.02
☐ 269 Ken Forsch	.15	.07	.02
☐ 270 Greg Luzinski	.25	.11	.03
☐ 271 Bill Castro	.15	.07	.02
☐ 272 Bruce Kimm	.15	.07	.02
☐ 273 Stan Papi	.15	.07	.02
☐ 274 Craig Chamberlain	.15	.07	.02
☐ 275 Dwight Evans	.40	.18	.05
☐ 276 Dan Spillner	.15	.07	.02
☐ 277 Alfredo Griffin	.15	.07	.02
☐ 278 Rick Sofield	.15	.07	.02
☐ 279 Bob Knepper	.15	.07	.02
☐ 280 Ken Griffey	.25	.11	.03
☐ 281 Fred Stanley	.15	.07	.02
☐ 282 Mariners Rookies	.15	.07	.02
Rick Anderson			
Greg Biercevicz			
Rodney Craig			
☐ 283 Billy Sample	.15	.07	.02
☐ 284 Brian Kingman	.15	.07	.02
☐ 285 Jerry Turner	.15	.07	.02
☐ 286 Dave Frost	.15	.07	.02
☐ 287 Lenn Sakata	.15	.07	.02
☐ 288 Bob Clark	.15	.07	.02
☐ 289 Mickey Hatcher	.25	.11	.03
☐ 290 Bob Boone DP	.25	.11	.03
☐ 291 Aurelio Lopez	.15	.07	.02
☐ 292 Mike Squires	.15	.07	.02
☐ 293 Charlie Lea	.15	.07	.02
☐ 294 Mike Tyson DP	.07	.03	.01
☐ 295 Hal McRae	.40	.18	.05
☐ 296 Bill Nahorodny DP	.07	.03	.01
☐ 297 Bob Bailor	.15	.07	.02
☐ 298 Buddy Solomon	.15	.07	.02
☐ 299 Elliott Maddox	.15	.07	.02
☐ 300 Paul Molitor	4.00	1.80	.50
☐ 301 Matt Keough	.15	.07	.02
☐ 302 Dodgers Rookies	4.00	1.80	.50
Jack Perconte			
Mike Scioscia			
Fernando Valenzuela			
☐ 303 Johnny Oates	.25	.11	.03
☐ 304 John Castino	.15	.07	.02
☐ 305 Ken Clay	.15	.07	.02
☐ 306 Juan Beniquez DP	.07	.03	.01
☐ 307 Gene Garber	.15	.07	.02
☐ 308 Rick Manning	.15	.07	.02
☐ 309 Luis Salazar	.15	.07	.02
☐ 310 Vida Blue DP	.15	.07	.02
☐ 311 Freddie Patek	.15	.07	.02
☐ 312 Rick Rhoden	.15	.07	.02
☐ 313 Luis Pujols	.15	.07	.02
☐ 314 Rich Dauer	.15	.07	.02
☐ 315 Kirk Gibson	4.00	1.80	.50
☐ 316 Craig Minetto	.15	.07	.02
☐ 317 Lonnie Smith	.25	.11	.03
☐ 318 Steve Yeager	.15	.07	.02
☐ 319 Rowland Office	.15	.07	.02
☐ 320 Tom Burgmeier	.15	.07	.02
☐ 321 Leon Durham	.25	.11	.03
☐ 322 Neil Allen	.15	.07	.02
☐ 323 Jim Morrison DP	.07	.03	.01
☐ 324 Mike Willis	.15	.07	.02
☐ 325 Ray Knight	.25	.11	.03
☐ 326 Biff Pocoroba	.15	.07	.02
☐ 327 Moose Haas	.15	.07	.02
☐ 328 Twins Rookies	.15	.07	.02
Dave Engle			
Greg Johnston			
Gary Ward			
☐ 329 Joaquin Andujar	.25	.11	.03
☐ 330 Frank White	.25	.11	.03
☐ 331 Dennis Lamp	.15	.07	.02
☐ 332 Lee Lacy DP	.07	.03	.01
☐ 333 Sid Monge	.15	.07	.02
☐ 334 Dane Iorg	.15	.07	.02
☐ 335 Rick Cerone	.15	.07	.02
☐ 336 Eddie Whitson	.15	.07	.02
☐ 337 Lynn Jones	.15	.07	.02
☐ 338 Checklist 243-363	.40	.18	.05
☐ 339 John Ellis	.15	.07	.02
☐ 340 Bruce Kison	.15	.07	.02
☐ 341 Dwayne Murphy	.15	.07	.02
☐ 342 Eric Rasmussen DP	.07	.03	.01
☐ 343 Frank Taveras	.15	.07	.02
☐ 344 Byron McLaughlin	.15	.07	.02
☐ 345 Warren Cromartie	.15	.07	.02
☐ 346 Larry Christenson DP	.07	.03	.01
☐ 347 Harold Baines	4.00	1.80	.50
☐ 348 Bob Sykes	.15	.07	.02
☐ 349 Glenn Hoffman	.15	.07	.02
☐ 350 J.R. Richard	.25	.11	.03
☐ 351 Otto Velez	.15	.07	.02
☐ 352 Dick Tidrow DP	.07	.03	.01
☐ 353 Terry Kennedy	.15	.07	.02
☐ 354 Mario Soto	.15	.07	.02
☐ 355 Bob Horner	.25	.11	.03
☐ 356 Padres Rookies	.15	.07	.02
George Stablein			
Craig Stimac			
Tom Tellmann			
☐ 357 Jim Slaton	.15	.07	.02
☐ 358 Mark Wagner	.15	.07	.02
☐ 359 Tom Hausman	.15	.07	.02
☐ 360 Willie Wilson	.25	.11	.03
☐ 361 Joe Strain	.15	.07	.02
☐ 362 Bo Diaz	.15	.07	.02
☐ 363 Geoff Zahn	.15	.07	.02
☐ 364 Mike Davis	.15	.07	.02
☐ 365 Graig Nettles DP	.25	.11	.03
☐ 366 Mike Ramsey	.15	.07	.02
☐ 367 Dennis Martinez	.40	.18	.05
☐ 368 Leon Roberts	.15	.07	.02
☐ 369 Frank Tanana	.25	.11	.03
☐ 370 Dave Winfield	2.50	1.10	.30
☐ 371 Charlie Hough	.25	.11	.03
☐ 372 Jay Johnstone	.25	.11	.03
☐ 373 Pat Underwood	.15	.07	.02
☐ 374 Tommy Hutton	.15	.07	.02
☐ 375 Dave Concepcion	.25	.11	.03
☐ 376 Ron Reed	.15	.07	.02
☐ 377 Jerry Morales	.15	.07	.02
☐ 378 Dave Rader	.15	.07	.02
☐ 379 Lary Sorensen	.15	.07	.02
☐ 380 Willie Stargell	1.00	.45	.12
☐ 381 Cubs Rookies	.15	.07	.02
Carlos Lezcano			
Steve Macko			
Randy Martz			
☐ 382 Paul Mirabella	.15	.07	.02
☐ 383 Eric Soderholm DP	.07	.03	.01
☐ 384 Mike Sadek	.15	.07	.02
☐ 385 Joe Sambito	.15	.07	.02
☐ 386 Dave Edwards	.15	.07	.02
☐ 387 Phil Niekro	.60	.25	.07
☐ 388 Andre Thornton	.25	.11	.03
☐ 389 Marty Pattin	.15	.07	.02
☐ 390 Cesar Geronimo	.15	.07	.02
☐ 391 Dave Lemanczyk DP	.07	.03	.01
☐ 392 Lance Parrish	.25	.11	.03
☐ 393 Broderick Perkins	.15	.07	.02
☐ 394 Woodie Fryman	.15	.07	.02
☐ 395 Scot Thompson	.15	.07	.02
☐ 396 Bill Campbell	.15	.07	.02
☐ 397 Julio Cruz	.15	.07	.02
☐ 398 Ross Baumgarten	.15	.07	.02
☐ 399 Orioles Rookies	.40	.18	.05
Mike Boddicker			
Mark Corey			
Floyd Rayford			
☐ 400 Reggie Jackson	2.00	.90	.25
☐ 401 George Brett ALCS	2.00	.90	.25
☐ 402 NL Champs	.40	.18	.05
Phillies squeak			
past Astros			
(Phillies celebrating)			
☐ 403 Larry Bowa WS	.40	.18	.05
☐ 404 Tug McGraw WS	.40	.18	.05
☐ 405 Nino Espinosa	.15	.07	.02
☐ 406 Dickie Noles	.15	.07	.02
☐ 407 Ernie Whitt	.15	.07	.02
☐ 408 Fernando Arroyo	.15	.07	.02
☐ 409 Larry Herndon	.15	.07	.02
☐ 410 Bert Campaneris	.25	.11	.03
☐ 411 Terry Puhl	.15	.07	.02
☐ 412 Britt Burns	.15	.07	.02
☐ 413 Tony Bernazard	.15	.07	.02
☐ 414 John Pacella DP	.07	.03	.01
☐ 415 Ben Oglivie	.25	.11	.03
☐ 416 Gary Alexander	.15	.07	.02
☐ 417 Dan Schatzeder	.15	.07	.02
☐ 418 Bobby Brown	.15	.07	.02
☐ 419 Tom Hume	.15	.07	.02
☐ 420 Keith Hernandez	.25	.11	.03
☐ 421 Bob Stanley	.15	.07	.02
☐ 422 Dan Ford	.15	.07	.02
☐ 423 Shane Rawley	.15	.07	.02
☐ 424 Yankees Rookies	.15	.07	.02
Tim Lollar			
Bruce Robinson			
Dennis Werth			
☐ 425 Al Bumbry	.25	.11	.03
☐ 426 Warren Brusstar	.15	.07	.02
☐ 427 John D'Acquisto	.15	.07	.02
☐ 428 John Stearns	.15	.07	.02
☐ 429 Mick Kelleher	.15	.07	.02
☐ 430 Jim Bibby	.15	.07	.02
☐ 431 Dave Roberts	.15	.07	.02
☐ 432 Len Barker	.15	.07	.02
☐ 433 Rance Mulliniks	.15	.07	.02
☐ 434 Roger Erickson	.15	.07	.02
☐ 435 Jim Spencer	.15	.07	.02
☐ 436 Gary Lucas	.15	.07	.02
☐ 437 Mike Heath DP	.07	.03	.01
☐ 438 John Montefusco	.15	.07	.02
☐ 439 Denny Walling	.15	.07	.02
☐ 440 Jerry Reuss	.25	.11	.03
☐ 441 Ken Reitz	.15	.07	.02
☐ 442 Ron Pruitt	.15	.07	.02
☐ 443 Jim Beattie DP	.15	.07	.02
☐ 444 Garth Iorg	.15	.07	.02
☐ 445 Ellis Valentine	.15	.07	.02
☐ 446 Checklist 364-484	.40	.18	.05
☐ 447 Junior Kennedy DP	.07	.03	.01
☐ 448 Tim Corcoran	.15	.07	.02
☐ 449 Paul Mitchell	.15	.07	.02
☐ 450 Dave Kingman DP	.25	.11	.03
☐ 451 Indians Rookies	.15	.07	.02
Chris Bando			
Tom Brennan			
Sandy Wihtol			
☐ 452 Renie Martin	.15	.07	.02
☐ 453 Rob Wilfong DP	.07	.03	.01
☐ 454 Andy Hassler	.15	.07	.02
☐ 455 Rick Burleson	.15	.07	.02
☐ 456 Jeff Reardon	2.00	.90	.25
☐ 457 Mike Lum	.15	.07	.02
☐ 458 Randy Jones	.15	.07	.02
☐ 459 Greg Gross	.15	.07	.02
☐ 460 Rich Gossage	.40	.18	.05
☐ 461 Dave McKay	.15	.07	.02
☐ 462 Jack Brohamer	.15	.07	.02
☐ 463 Milt May	.15	.07	.02
☐ 464 Adrian Devine	.15	.07	.02
☐ 465 Bill Russell	.25	.11	.03
☐ 466 Bob Molinaro	.15	.07	.02
☐ 467 Dave Stieb	.25	.11	.03
☐ 468 John Wockenfuss	.15	.07	.02
☐ 469 Jeff Leonard	.25	.11	.03
☐ 470 Manny Trillo	.15	.07	.02
☐ 471 Mike Vail	.15	.07	.02
☐ 472 Dyar Miller DP	.07	.03	.01
☐ 473 Jose Cardenal	.15	.07	.02
☐ 474 Mike LaCoss	.15	.07	.02
☐ 475 Buddy Bell	.25	.11	.03
☐ 476 Jerry Koosman	.25	.11	.03
☐ 477 Luis Gomez	.15	.07	.02
☐ 478 Juan Eichelberger	.15	.07	.02
☐ 479 Expos Rookies	6.00	2.70	.75
Tim Raines			
Roberto Ramos			
Bobby Pate			
☐ 480 Carlton Fisk	2.00	.90	.25
☐ 481 Bob Lacey DP	.07	.03	.01
☐ 482 Jim Gantner	.25	.11	.03
☐ 483 Mike Griffin	.15	.07	.02
☐ 484 Max Venable DP	.07	.03	.01
☐ 485 Garry Templeton	.15	.07	.02
☐ 486 Marc Hill	.15	.07	.02
☐ 487 Dewey Robinson	.15	.07	.02
☐ 488 Damaso Garcia	.15	.07	.02
☐ 489 John Littlefield	.15	.07	.02
☐ 490 Eddie Murray	6.00	2.70	.75
☐ 491 Gordy Pladson	.15	.07	.02
☐ 492 Barry Foote	.15	.07	.02
☐ 493 Dan Quisenberry	.25	.11	.03
☐ 494 Bob Walk	.25	.11	.03
☐ 495 Dusty Baker	.40	.18	.05
☐ 496 Paul Dade	.15	.07	.02
☐ 497 Fred Norman	.15	.07	.02
☐ 498 Pat Putnam	.15	.07	.02
☐ 499 Frank Pastore	.15	.07	.02
☐ 500 Jim Rice	.25	.11	.03
☐ 501 Tim Foli DP	.07	.03	.01
☐ 502 Giants Rookies	.15	.07	.02
Chris Bourjos			
Al Hargesheimer			
Mike Rowland			
☐ 503 Steve McCatty	.15	.07	.02
☐ 504 Dale Murphy	1.25	.55	.16
☐ 505 Jason Thompson	.15	.07	.02
☐ 506 Phil Huffman	.15	.07	.02
☐ 507 Jamie Quirk	.15	.07	.02
☐ 508 Rob Dressler	.15	.07	.02
☐ 509 Pete Mackanin	.15	.07	.02
☐ 510 Lee Mazzilli	.15	.07	.02
☐ 511 Wayne Garland	.15	.07	.02
☐ 512 Gary Thomasson	.15	.07	.02
☐ 513 Frank LaCorte	.15	.07	.02
☐ 514 George Riley	.15	.07	.02
☐ 515 Robin Yount	2.50	1.10	.30
☐ 516 Doug Bird	.15	.07	.02
☐ 517 Richie Zisk	.15	.07	.02
☐ 518 Grant Jackson	.15	.07	.02
☐ 519 John Tamargo DP	.07	.03	.01
☐ 520 Steve Stone	.25	.11	.03
☐ 521 Sam Mejias	.15	.07	.02
☐ 522 Mike Colbern	.15	.07	.02
☐ 523 John Fulgham	.15	.07	.02

☐ 524 Willie Aikens .15 .07 .02
☐ 525 Mike Torrez .15 .07 .02
☐ 526 Phillies Rookies .15 .07 .02
Marty Bystrom
Jay Loviglio
Jim Wright
☐ 527 Danny Goodwin .15 .07 .02
☐ 528 Gary Matthews .25 .11 .03
☐ 529 Dave LaRoche .15 .07 .02
☐ 530 Steve Garvey .40 .18 .05
☐ 531 John Curtis .15 .07 .02
☐ 532 Bill Stein .15 .07 .02
☐ 533 Jesus Figueroa .15 .07 .02
☐ 534 Dave Smith .25 .11 .03
☐ 535 Omar Moreno .15 .07 .02
☐ 536 Bob Owchinko DP .07 .03 .01
☐ 537 Ron Hodges .15 .07 .02
☐ 538 Tom Griffin .15 .07 .02
☐ 539 Rodney Scott .15 .07 .02
☐ 540 Mike Schmidt DP 2.00 .90 .25
☐ 541 Steve Swisher .15 .07 .02
☐ 542 Larry Bradford DP .07 .03 .01
☐ 543 Terry Crowley .15 .07 .02
☐ 544 Rich Gale .15 .07 .02
☐ 545 Johnny Grubb .15 .07 .02
☐ 546 Paul Moskau .15 .07 .02
☐ 547 Mario Guerrero .15 .07 .02
☐ 548 Dave Goltz .15 .07 .02
☐ 549 Jerry Remy .15 .07 .02
☐ 550 Tommy John .40 .18 .05
☐ 551 Pirates Rookies .75 .35 .09
Vance Law
Tony Pena
Pascual Perez
☐ 552 Steve Trout .15 .07 .02
☐ 553 Tim Blackwell .15 .07 .02
☐ 554 Bert Blyleven UER .40 .18 .05
(1 is missing from
1980 on card back)
☐ 555 Cecil Cooper .25 .11 .03
☐ 556 Jerry Mumphrey .15 .07 .02
☐ 557 Chris Knapp .15 .07 .02
☐ 558 Barry Bonnell .15 .07 .02
☐ 559 Willie Montanez .15 .07 .02
☐ 560 Joe Morgan 1.00 .45 .12
☐ 561 Dennis Littlejohn .15 .07 .02
☐ 562 Checklist 485-605 .40 .18 .05
☐ 563 Jim Kaat .25 .11 .03
☐ 564 Ron Hassey DP .07 .03 .01
☐ 565 Burt Hooton .15 .07 .02
☐ 566 Del Unser .15 .07 .02
☐ 567 Mark Bomback .15 .07 .02
☐ 568 Dave Revering .15 .07 .02
☐ 569 Al Williams DP .07 .03 .01
☐ 570 Ken Singleton .25 .11 .03
☐ 571 Todd Cruz .15 .07 .02
☐ 572 Jack Morris .40 .18 .05
☐ 573 Phil Garner .25 .11 .03
☐ 574 Bill Caudill .15 .07 .02
☐ 575 Tony Perez .75 .35 .09
☐ 576 Reggie Cleveland .15 .07 .02
☐ 577 Blue Jays Rookies .15 .07 .02
Luis Leal
Brian Milner
Ken Schrom
☐ 578 Bill Gullickson .40 .18 .05
☐ 579 Tim Flannery .15 .07 .02
☐ 580 Don Baylor .40 .18 .05
☐ 581 Roy Howell .15 .07 .02
☐ 582 Gaylord Perry .75 .35 .09
☐ 583 Larry Milbourne .15 .07 .02
☐ 584 Randy Lerch .15 .07 .02
☐ 585 Amos Otis .25 .11 .03
☐ 586 Silvio Martinez .15 .07 .02
☐ 587 Jeff Newman .15 .07 .02
☐ 588 Gary Lavelle .15 .07 .02
☐ 589 Lamar Johnson .15 .07 .02
☐ 590 Bruce Sutter .25 .11 .03
☐ 591 John Lowenstein .15 .07 .02
☐ 592 Steve Comer .15 .07 .02
☐ 593 Steve Kemp .15 .07 .02
☐ 594 Preston Hanna DP .07 .03 .01
☐ 595 Butch Hobson .15 .07 .02
☐ 596 Jerry Augustine .15 .07 .02
☐ 597 Rafael Landestoy .15 .07 .02
☐ 598 George Vukovich DP .07 .03 .01
☐ 599 Dennis Kinney .15 .07 .02
☐ 600 Johnny Bench 2.00 .90 .25
☐ 601 Don Aase .15 .07 .02
☐ 602 Bobby Murcer .25 .11 .03
☐ 603 John Verhoeven .15 .07 .02
☐ 604 Rob Picciolo .15 .07 .02
☐ 605 Don Sutton .75 .35 .09
☐ 606 Reds Rookies DP .15 .07 .02
Bruce Berenyi
Geoff Combe
Paul Householder
☐ 607 David Palmer .15 .07 .02
☐ 608 Greg Pryor .15 .07 .02
☐ 609 Lynn McGlothen .15 .07 .02
☐ 610 Darrell Porter .15 .07 .02
☐ 611 Rick Matula DP .07 .03 .01
☐ 612 Duane Kuiper .15 .07 .02
☐ 613 Jim Anderson .15 .07 .02
☐ 614 Dave Rozema .15 .07 .02
☐ 615 Rick Dempsey .25 .11 .03
☐ 616 Rick Wise .15 .07 .02
☐ 617 Craig Reynolds .15 .07 .02
☐ 618 John Milner .15 .07 .02
☐ 619 Steve Henderson .15 .07 .02
☐ 620 Dennis Eckersley 1.25 .55 .16
☐ 621 Tom Donohue .15 .07 .02
☐ 622 Randy Moffitt .15 .07 .02
☐ 623 Sal Bando .25 .11 .03
☐ 624 Bob Welch .25 .11 .03
☐ 625 Bill Buckner .25 .11 .03
☐ 626 Tigers Rookies .15 .07 .02
Dave Steffen
Jerry Ujdur
Roger Weaver
☐ 627 Luis Tiant .25 .11 .03
☐ 628 Vic Correll .15 .07 .02
☐ 629 Tony Armas .25 .11 .03
☐ 630 Steve Carlton 1.50 .70 .19
☐ 631 Ron Jackson .15 .07 .02
☐ 632 Alan Bannister .15 .07 .02
☐ 633 Bill Lee .25 .11 .03
☐ 634 Doug Flynn .15 .07 .02
☐ 635 Bobby Bonds .25 .11 .03
☐ 636 Al Hrabosky .15 .07 .02
☐ 637 Jerry Narron .15 .07 .02
☐ 638 Checklist 606-726 .40 .18 .05
☐ 639 Carney Lansford .25 .11 .03
☐ 640 Dave Parker .25 .11 .03
☐ 641 Mark Belanger .25 .11 .03
☐ 642 Vern Ruhle .15 .07 .02
☐ 643 Lloyd Moseby .25 .11 .03
☐ 644 Ramon Aviles DP .07 .03 .01
☐ 645 Rick Reuschel .25 .11 .03
☐ 646 Marvis Foley .15 .07 .02
☐ 647 Dick Drago .15 .07 .02
☐ 648 Darrell Evans .25 .11 .03
☐ 649 Manny Sarmiento .15 .07 .02
☐ 650 Bucky Dent .25 .11 .03
☐ 651 Pedro Guerrero .40 .18 .05
☐ 652 John Montague .15 .07 .02
☐ 653 Bill Fahey .15 .07 .02
☐ 654 Ray Burris .15 .07 .02
☐ 655 Dan Driessen .15 .07 .02
☐ 656 Jon Matlack .15 .07 .02
☐ 657 Mike Cubbage DP .07 .03 .01
☐ 658 Milt Wilcox .15 .07 .02
☐ 659 Brewers Rookies .15 .07 .02
John Flinn
Ed Romero
Ned Yost
☐ 660 Gary Carter .25 .11 .03
☐ 661 Orioles Team/Mgr. .40 .18 .05
Earl Weaver
(Checklist back)
☐ 662 Red Sox Team/Mgr. .40 .18 .05
Ralph Houk
(Checklist back)
☐ 663 Angels Team/Mgr. .40 .18 .05
Jim Fregosi
(Checklist back)
☐ 664 White Sox Team/Mgr. .40 .18 .05
Tony LaRussa
(Checklist back)
☐ 665 Indians Team/Mgr. .40 .18 .05
Dave Garcia
(Checklist back)
☐ 666 Tigers Team/Mgr. .40 .18 .05
Sparky Anderson
(Checklist back)
☐ 667 Royals Team/Mgr. .40 .18 .05
Jim Frey
(Checklist back)
☐ 668 Brewers Team/Mgr. .40 .18 .05
Bob Rodgers
(Checklist back)
☐ 669 Twins Team/Mgr. .40 .18 .05
John Goryl
(Checklist back)
☐ 670 Yankees Team/Mgr. .40 .18 .05
Gene Michael
(Checklist back)
☐ 671 A's Team/Mgr. .40 .18 .05
Billy Martin
(Checklist back)
☐ 672 Mariners Team/Mgr. .40 .18 .05
Maury Wills
(Checklist back)
☐ 673 Rangers Team/Mgr. .40 .18 .05
Don Zimmer
(Checklist back)
☐ 674 Blue Jays Team/Mgr. .40 .18 .05
Bobby Mattick
(Checklist back)
☐ 675 Braves Team/Mgr. .40 .18 .05
Bobby Cox
(Checklist back)
☐ 676 Cubs Team/Mgr. .40 .18 .05
Joe Amalfitano
(Checklist back)
☐ 677 Reds Team/Mgr. .40 .18 .05
John McNamara
(Checklist back)
☐ 678 Astros Team/Mgr. .40 .18 .05
Bill Virdon
(Checklist back)
☐ 679 Dodgers Team/Mgr. .40 .18 .05
Tom Lasorda
(Checklist back)
☐ 680 Expos Team/Mgr. .40 .18 .05
Dick Williams
(Checklist back)
☐ 681 Mets Team/Mgr. .40 .18 .05
Joe Torre
(Checklist back)
☐ 682 Phillies Team/Mgr. .40 .18 .05
Dallas Green
(Checklist back)
☐ 683 Pirates Team/Mgr. .40 .18 .05
Chuck Tanner
(Checklist back)
☐ 684 Cardinals Team/Mgr. .40 .18 .05
Whitey Herzog
(Checklist back)
☐ 685 Padres Team/Mgr. .40 .18 .05
Frank Howard
(Checklist back)
☐ 686 Giants Team/Mgr. .40 .18 .05
Dave Bristol
(Checklist back)
☐ 687 Jeff Jones .15 .07 .02
☐ 688 Kiko Garcia .15 .07 .02
☐ 689 Red Sox Rookies .75 .35 .09
Bruce Hurst
Keith MacWhorter
Reid Nichols
☐ 690 Bob Watson .25 .11 .03
☐ 691 Dick Ruthven .15 .07 .02
☐ 692 Lenny Randle .15 .07 .02
☐ 693 Steve Howe .15 .07 .02
☐ 694 Bud Harrelson DP .07 .03 .01
☐ 695 Kent Tekulve .25 .11 .03
☐ 696 Alan Ashby .15 .07 .02
☐ 697 Rick Waits .15 .07 .02
☐ 698 Mike Jorgensen .15 .07 .02
☐ 699 Glenn Abbott .15 .07 .02
☐ 700 George Brett 6.00 2.70 .75
☐ 701 Joe Rudi .25 .11 .03
☐ 702 George Medich .15 .07 .02
☐ 703 Alvis Woods .15 .07 .02
☐ 704 Bill Travers DP .07 .03 .01
☐ 705 Ted Simmons .25 .11 .03
☐ 706 Dave Ford .15 .07 .02
☐ 707 Dave Cash .15 .07 .02
☐ 708 Doyle Alexander .15 .07 .02
☐ 709 Alan Trammell DP 1.50 .70 .19
☐ 710 Ron LeFlore DP .07 .03 .01
☐ 711 Joe Ferguson .15 .07 .02
☐ 712 Bill Bonham .15 .07 .02
☐ 713 Bill North .15 .07 .02
☐ 714 Pete Redfern .15 .07 .02
☐ 715 Bill Madlock .25 .11 .03
☐ 716 Glenn Borgmann .15 .07 .02
☐ 717 Jim Barr DP .07 .03 .01
☐ 718 Larry Biittner .15 .07 .02
☐ 719 Sparky Lyle .25 .11 .03
☐ 720 Fred Lynn .25 .11 .03
☐ 721 Toby Harrah .25 .11 .03
☐ 722 Joe Niekro .25 .11 .03
☐ 723 Bruce Bochte .15 .07 .02
☐ 724 Lou Piniella .25 .11 .03
☐ 725 Steve Rogers .15 .07 .02
☐ 726 Rick Monday .25 .11 .03

1981 Topps Traded

For the first time since 1976, Topps issued a 132-card factory boxed "traded" set in 1981, issued exclusively through hobby dealers. This set was sequentially numbered, alphabetically, from 727 to 858 and carries the same design as the regular issue 1981 Topps set. There are no key Rookie Cards in this set although Tim Raines, Jeff Reardon, and Fernando Valenzuela are depicted in their rookie year for cards. The key extended Rookie Card in the set is Danny Ainge.

	NRMT	VG-E	GOOD
COMPLETE SET (132)	30.00	13.50	3.70
COMPLETE FACT.SET (132)	30.00	13.50	3.70
COMMON CARD (727-858)	.25	.11	.03

☐ 727 Danny Ainge 5.00 2.20 .60
☐ 728 Doyle Alexander .25 .11 .03
☐ 729 Gary Alexander .25 .11 .03
☐ 730 Bill Almon .25 .11 .03
☐ 731 Joaquin Andujar .50 .23 .06
☐ 732 Bob Bailor .25 .11 .03
☐ 733 Juan Beniquez .25 .11 .03
☐ 734 Dave Bergman .25 .11 .03
☐ 735 Tony Bernazard .25 .11 .03
☐ 736 Larry Biittner .25 .11 .03
☐ 737 Doug Bird .25 .11 .03
☐ 738 Bert Blyleven 1.00 .45 .12
☐ 739 Mark Bomback .25 .11 .03
☐ 740 Bobby Bonds .50 .23 .06
☐ 741 Rick Bosetti .25 .11 .03
☐ 742 Hubie Brooks .50 .23 .06
☐ 743 Rick Burleson .25 .11 .03
☐ 744 Ray Burris .25 .11 .03
☐ 745 Jeff Burroughs .25 .11 .03
☐ 746 Enos Cabell .25 .11 .03
☐ 747 Ken Clay .25 .11 .03
☐ 748 Mark Clear .25 .11 .03
☐ 749 Larry Cox .25 .11 .03
☐ 750 Hector Cruz .25 .11 .03
☐ 751 Victor Cruz .25 .11 .03
☐ 752 Mike Cubbage .25 .11 .03
☐ 753 Dick Davis .25 .11 .03
☐ 754 Brian Doyle .25 .11 .03
☐ 755 Dick Drago .25 .11 .03
☐ 756 Leon Durham .50 .23 .06
☐ 757 Jim Dwyer .25 .11 .03
☐ 758 Dave Edwards UER .25 .11 .03
No birthdate on card
☐ 759 Jim Essian .25 .11 .03
☐ 760 Bill Fahey .25 .11 .03
☐ 761 Rollie Fingers 1.00 .45 .12
☐ 762 Carlton Fisk 4.00 1.80 .50
☐ 763 Barry Foote .25 .11 .03
☐ 764 Ken Forsch .25 .11 .03
☐ 765 Kiko Garcia .25 .11 .03
☐ 766 Cesar Geronimo .25 .11 .03
☐ 767 Gary Gray .25 .11 .03
☐ 768 Mickey Hatcher .50 .23 .06
☐ 769 Steve Henderson .25 .11 .03
☐ 770 Marc Hill .25 .11 .03
☐ 771 Butch Hobson .25 .11 .03
☐ 772 Rick Honeycutt .25 .11 .03
☐ 773 Roy Howell .25 .11 .03
☐ 774 Mike Ivie .25 .11 .03
☐ 775 Roy Lee Jackson .25 .11 .03
☐ 776 Cliff Johnson .25 .11 .03
☐ 777 Randy Jones .25 .11 .03
☐ 778 Ruppert Jones .25 .11 .03
☐ 779 Mick Kelleher .25 .11 .03
☐ 780 Terry Kennedy .25 .11 .03
☐ 781 Dave Kingman .50 .23 .06
☐ 782 Bob Knepper .25 .11 .03
☐ 783 Ken Kravec .25 .11 .03
☐ 784 Bob Lacey .25 .11 .03
☐ 785 Dennis Lamp .25 .11 .03
☐ 786 Rafael Landestoy .25 .11 .03
☐ 787 Ken Landreaux .25 .11 .03
☐ 788 Carney Lansford .50 .23 .06
☐ 789 Dave LaRoche .25 .11 .03
☐ 790 Joe Lefebvre .25 .11 .03
☐ 791 Ron LeFlore .50 .23 .06
☐ 792 Randy Lerch .25 .11 .03
☐ 793 Sixto Lezcano .25 .11 .03
☐ 794 John Littlefield .25 .11 .03
☐ 795 Mike Lum .25 .11 .03
☐ 796 Greg Luzinski .50 .23 .06
☐ 797 Fred Lynn .50 .23 .06
☐ 798 Jerry Martin .25 .11 .03
☐ 799 Buck Martinez .25 .11 .03
☐ 800 Gary Matthews .50 .23 .06
☐ 801 Mario Mendoza .25 .11 .03
☐ 802 Larry Milbourne .25 .11 .03
☐ 803 Rick Miller .25 .11 .03
☐ 804 John Montefusco .25 .11 .03
☐ 805 Jerry Morales .25 .11 .03
☐ 806 Jose Morales .25 .11 .03
☐ 807 Joe Morgan 3.00 1.35 .35
☐ 808 Jerry Mumphrey .25 .11 .03
☐ 809 Gene Nelson .25 .11 .03
☐ 810 Ed Ott .25 .11 .03
☐ 811 Bob Owchinko .25 .11 .03
☐ 812 Gaylord Perry 1.00 .45 .12
☐ 813 Mike Phillips .25 .11 .03
☐ 814 Darrell Porter .25 .11 .03
☐ 815 Mike Proly .25 .11 .03
☐ 816 Tim Raines 10.00 4.50 1.25
☐ 817 Lenny Randle .25 .11 .03
☐ 818 Doug Rau .25 .11 .03
☐ 819 Jeff Reardon 3.00 1.35 .35
☐ 820 Ken Reitz .25 .11 .03
☐ 821 Steve Renko .25 .11 .03
☐ 822 Rick Reuschel .50 .23 .06
☐ 823 Dave Revering .25 .11 .03
☐ 824 Dave Roberts .25 .11 .03
☐ 825 Leon Roberts .25 .11 .03
☐ 826 Joe Rudi .50 .23 .06
☐ 827 Kevin Saucier .25 .11 .03
☐ 828 Tony Scott .25 .11 .03
☐ 829 Bob Shirley .25 .11 .03
☐ 830 Ted Simmons .50 .23 .06
☐ 831 Lary Sorensen .25 .11 .03
☐ 832 Jim Spencer .25 .11 .03
☐ 833 Harry Spilman .25 .11 .03
☐ 834 Fred Stanley .25 .11 .03
☐ 835 Rusty Staub .50 .23 .06
☐ 836 Bill Stein .25 .11 .03
☐ 837 Joe Strain .25 .11 .03
☐ 838 Bruce Sutter .50 .23 .06

Card	NRMT	VG-E	GOOD
☐ 839 Don Sutton	1.00	.45	.12
☐ 840 Steve Swisher	.25	.11	.03
☐ 841 Frank Tanana	.50	.23	.06
☐ 842 Gene Tenace	.50	.23	.06
☐ 843 Jason Thompson	.25	.11	.03
☐ 844 Dickie Thon	.50	.23	.06
☐ 845 Bill Travers	.25	.11	.03
☐ 846 Tom Underwood	.25	.11	.03
☐ 847 John Urrea	.25	.11	.03
☐ 848 Mike Vail	.25	.11	.03
☐ 849 Ellis Valentine	.25	.11	.03
☐ 850 Fernando Valenzuela	3.00	1.35	.35
☐ 851 Pete Vuckovich	.50	.23	.06
☐ 852 Mark Wagner	.25	.11	.03
☐ 853 Bob Walk	.50	.23	.06
☐ 854 Claudell Washington	.25	.11	.03
☐ 855 Dave Winfield	8.00	3.60	1.00
☐ 856 Geoff Zahn	.25	.11	.03
☐ 857 Richie Zisk	.25	.11	.03
☐ 858 Checklist 727-858	.25	.11	.03

1981 Topps Scratchoffs

The cards in this 108-card set measure 1 13/16" by 3 1/4" in a three-card panel measuring 3 1/4" by 5 1/4". The 1981 Topps Scratch-Offs were issued in their own wrapper with bubble gum. The title "Scratch-Off" refers to the black dots of each card which, when rubbed or scraped with a hard edge, reveal a baseball game. While there are only 108 possible individual cards in the set, there are 144 possible panels combinations. The N.L. players appear with green backgrounds and A.L. players with red backgrounds. The numbering of the cards in the set is according to league with American Leaguers (1-54) and National Leaguers (55-108). Some cards are found without dots. An intact panel is worth 20 percent more than the sum of its individual cards.

	NRMT	VG-E	GOOD
COMPLETE SET (108)	6.00	2.70	.75
COMMON CARD (1-108)	.05	.02	.01
☐ 1 George Brett	.75	.35	.09
☐ 2 Cecil Cooper	.10	.05	.01
☐ 3 Reggie Jackson	.35	.16	.04
☐ 4 Al Oliver	.10	.05	.01
☐ 5 Fred Lynn	.10	.05	.01
☐ 6 Tony Armas	.10	.05	.01
☐ 7 Ben Oglivie	.10	.05	.01
☐ 8 Tony Perez	.20	.09	.03
☐ 9 Eddie Murray	.35	.16	.04
☐ 10 Robin Yount	.25	.11	.03
☐ 11 Steve Kemp	.05	.02	.01
☐ 12 Joe Charboneau	.10	.05	.01
☐ 13 Jim Rice	.15	.07	.02
☐ 14 Lance Parrish	.10	.05	.01
☐ 15 John Mayberry	.05	.02	.01
☐ 16 Richie Zisk	.05	.02	.01
☐ 17 Ken Singleton	.10	.05	.01
☐ 18 Rod Carew	.25	.11	.03
☐ 19 Rick Manning	.05	.02	.01
☐ 20 Willie Wilson	.10	.05	.01
☐ 21 Buddy Bell	.10	.05	.01
☐ 22 Dave Revering	.05	.02	.01
☐ 23 Tom Paciorek	.05	.02	.01
☐ 24 Champ Summers	.05	.02	.01
☐ 25 Carney Lansford	.10	.05	.01
☐ 26 Lamar Johnson	.05	.02	.01
☐ 27 Willie Aikens	.05	.02	.01
☐ 28 Rick Cerone	.05	.02	.01
☐ 29 Al Bumbry	.05	.02	.01
☐ 30 Bruce Bochte	.05	.02	.01
☐ 31 Mickey Rivers	.10	.05	.01
☐ 32 Mike Hargrove	.10	.05	.01
☐ 33 John Castino	.05	.02	.01
☐ 34 Chet Lemon	.05	.02	.01
☐ 35 Paul Molitor	.40	.18	.05
☐ 36 Willie Randolph	.10	.05	.01
☐ 37 Rick Burleson	.05	.02	.01
☐ 38 Alan Trammell	.30	.14	.04
☐ 39 Rickey Henderson	.40	.18	.05
☐ 40 Dan Meyer	.05	.02	.01
☐ 41 Ken Landreaux	.05	.02	.01
☐ 42 Damaso Garcia	.05	.02	.01
☐ 43 Roy Smalley	.05	.02	.01
☐ 44 Otto Velez	.05	.02	.01
☐ 45 Sixto Lezcano	.05	.02	.01
☐ 46 Toby Harrah	.10	.05	.01
☐ 47 Frank White	.10	.05	.01
☐ 48 Dave Stapleton	.05	.02	.01
☐ 49 Steve Stone	.05	.02	.01
☐ 50 Jim Palmer	.25	.11	.03
☐ 51 Larry Gura	.05	.02	.01
☐ 52 Tommy John	.15	.07	.02
☐ 53 Mike Norris	.05	.02	.01
☐ 54 Ed Farmer	.05	.02	.01
☐ 55 Bill Buckner	.10	.05	.01
☐ 56 Steve Garvey	.15	.07	.02
☐ 57 Reggie Smith	.10	.05	.01
☐ 58 Bake McBride	.05	.02	.01
☐ 59 Dave Parker	.10	.05	.01
☐ 60 Mike Schmidt	.35	.16	.04
☐ 61 Bob Horner	.10	.05	.01
☐ 62 Pete Rose	.35	.16	.04
☐ 63 Ted Simmons	.10	.05	.01
☐ 64 Johnny Bench	.25	.11	.03
☐ 65 George Foster	.10	.05	.01
☐ 66 Gary Carter	.15	.07	.02
☐ 67 Keith Hernandez	.10	.05	.01
☐ 68 Ozzie Smith	.50	.23	.06
☐ 69 Dave Kingman	.10	.05	.01
☐ 70 Jack Clark	.10	.05	.01
☐ 71 Dusty Baker	.10	.05	.01
☐ 72 Dale Murphy	.25	.11	.03
☐ 73 Ron Cey	.10	.05	.01
☐ 74 Greg Luzinski	.10	.05	.01
☐ 75 Lee Mazzilli	.05	.02	.01
☐ 76 Gary Matthews	.05	.02	.01
☐ 77 Cesar Cedeno	.05	.02	.01
☐ 78 Warren Cromartie	.05	.02	.01
☐ 79 Steve Henderson	.05	.02	.01
☐ 80 Ellis Valentine	.05	.02	.01
☐ 81 Mike Easler	.05	.02	.01
☐ 82 Garry Templeton	.05	.02	.01
☐ 83 Jose Cruz	.10	.05	.01
☐ 84 Dave Collins	.05	.02	.01
☐ 85 George Hendrick	.05	.02	.01
☐ 86 Gene Richards	.05	.02	.01
☐ 87 Terry Whitfield	.05	.02	.01
☐ 88 Terry Puhl	.05	.02	.01
☐ 89 Larry Parrish	.05	.02	.01
☐ 90 Andre Dawson	.25	.11	.03
☐ 91 Ken Griffey	.10	.05	.01
☐ 92 Dave Lopes	.10	.05	.01
☐ 93 Doug Flynn	.05	.02	.01
☐ 94 Ivan DeJesus	.05	.02	.01
☐ 95 Dave Concepcion	.10	.05	.01
☐ 96 John Stearns	.05	.02	.01
☐ 97 Jerry Mumphrey	.05	.02	.01
☐ 98 Jerry Martin	.05	.02	.01
☐ 99 Art Howe	.10	.05	.01
☐ 100 Omar Moreno	.05	.02	.01
☐ 101 Ken Reitz	.05	.02	.01
☐ 102 Phil Garner	.10	.05	.01
☐ 103 Jerry Reuss	.10	.05	.01
☐ 104 Steve Carlton	.25	.11	.03
☐ 105 Jim Bibby	.05	.02	.01
☐ 106 Steve Rogers	.05	.02	.01
☐ 107 Tom Seaver	.25	.11	.03
☐ 108 Vida Blue	.10	.05	.01

1981 Topps Stickers

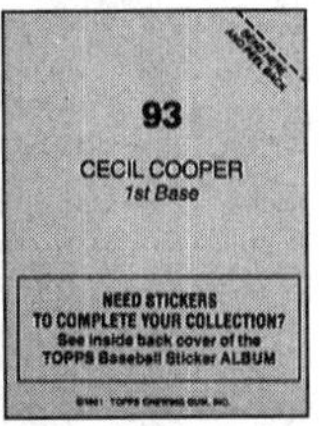

93
CECIL COOPER
1st Base
NEED STICKERS TO COMPLETE YOUR COLLECTION?
See inside back cover of the TOPPS Baseball Sticker ALBUM

Made for Topps by Panini, an Italian company, these 262 stickers measure 1 15/16" by 2 9/16" and are numbered on both front and back. The set was the first of the Topps/O-Pee-Chee/Panini genre of sticker sets. The fronts feature white-bordered color player action shots. The backs carry the player's name and position. Team affiliations are not shown. An album onto which the stickers could be affixed was available at retail stores. The first 32 stickers depict 1980 major league pitching and batting leaders. Stickers 33-240 are arranged by teams as follows: Baltimore Orioles (33-40), Boston Red Sox (41-48), California Angels (49-56), Chicago White Sox (57-64), Cleveland Indians (65-72), Detroit Tigers (73-80), Kansas City Royals (81-88), Milwaukee Brewers (91-98), Minnesota Twins (99-106), New York Yankees (107-114), Oakland A's (115-122), Seattle Mariners (123-130), Texas Rangers (130-136), Toronto Blue Jays (137-143), Atlanta Braves (144-150), Chicago Cubs (151-158), Cincinnati Reds (159-166), Houston Astros (167-174), Los Angeles Dodgers (175-182), Montreal Expos (183-190), New York Mets (191-198), Philadelphia Phillies (199-208), Pittsburgh Pirates (209-216), St. Louis Cardinals (217-224), San Diego Padres (225-232) and San Francisco Giants (233-240). Stickers 241-262 have color photos of "All-Star" players printed on silver (AL) or gold (NL) foil.

	NRMT	VG-E	GOOD
COMPLETE SET (262)	25.00	11.00	3.10
COMMON STICKER (1-240)	.05	.02	.01
COMMON FOIL (241-262)	.10	.05	.01
☐ 1 Steve Stone	.05	.02	.01
☐ 2 Tommy John Mike Norris	.15	.07	.02
☐ 3 Rudy May	.05	.02	.01
☐ 4 Mike Norris	.05	.02	.01
☐ 5 Len Barker	.05	.02	.01
☐ 6 Mike Norris	.05	.02	.01
☐ 7 Dan Quisenberry	.15	.07	.02
☐ 8 Rich Gossage	.25	.11	.03
☐ 9 George Brett	2.50	1.10	.30
☐ 10 Cecil Cooper	.15	.07	.02
☐ 11 Reggie Jackson Ben Oglivie	.40	.18	.05
☐ 12 Gorman Thomas	.05	.02	.01
☐ 13 Cecil Cooper	.15	.07	.02
☐ 14 George Brett Ben Oglivie	1.25	.55	.16
☐ 15 Rickey Henderson	2.50	1.10	.30
☐ 16 Willie Wilson	.15	.07	.02
☐ 17 Bill Buckner	.15	.07	.02
☐ 18 Keith Hernandez	.15	.07	.02
☐ 19 Mike Schmidt	1.50	.70	.19
☐ 20 Bob Horner	.05	.02	.01
☐ 21 Mike Schmidt	1.50	.70	.19
☐ 22 George Hendrick	.05	.02	.01
☐ 23 Ron LeFlore	.15	.07	.02
☐ 24 Omar Moreno	.05	.02	.01
☐ 25 Steve Carlton	.60	.25	.07
☐ 26 Joe Niekro	.15	.07	.02
☐ 27 Don Sutton	.25	.11	.03
☐ 28 Steve Carlton	.60	.25	.07
☐ 29 Steve Carlton	.60	.25	.07
☐ 30 Nolan Ryan	3.00	1.35	.35
☐ 31 Rollie Fingers Tom Hume	.15	.07	.02
☐ 32 Bruce Sutter	.15	.07	.02
☐ 33 Ken Singleton	.05	.02	.01
☐ 34 Eddie Murray	2.00	.90	.25
☐ 35 Al Bumbry	.05	.02	.01
☐ 36 Rich Dauer	.05	.02	.01
☐ 37 Scott McGregor	.05	.02	.01
☐ 38 Rick Dempsey	.15	.07	.02
☐ 39 Jim Palmer	.40	.18	.05
☐ 40 Steve Stone	.05	.02	.01
☐ 41 Jim Rice	.25	.11	.03
☐ 42 Fred Lynn	.15	.07	.02
☐ 43 Carney Lansford	.15	.07	.02
☐ 44 Tony Perez	.25	.11	.03
☐ 45 Carl Yastrzemski	.60	.25	.07
☐ 46 Carlton Fisk	.75	.35	.09
☐ 47 Dave Stapleton	.05	.02	.01
☐ 48 Dennis Eckersley	.30	.14	.04
☐ 49 Rod Carew	.60	.25	.07
☐ 50 Brian Downing	.15	.07	.02
☐ 51 Don Baylor	.25	.11	.03
☐ 52 Rick Burleson	.05	.02	.01
☐ 53 Bobby Grich	.15	.07	.02
☐ 54 Butch Hobson	.05	.02	.01
☐ 55 Andy Hassler	.05	.02	.01
☐ 56 Frank Tanana	.15	.07	.02
☐ 57 Chet Lemon	.05	.02	.01
☐ 58 Lamar Johnson	.05	.02	.01
☐ 59 Wayne Nordhagen	.05	.02	.01
☐ 60 Jim Morrison	.05	.02	.01
☐ 61 Bob Molinaro	.05	.02	.01
☐ 62 Rich Dotson	.05	.02	.01
☐ 63 Britt Burns	.05	.02	.01
☐ 64 Ed Farmer	.05	.02	.01
☐ 65 Toby Harrah	.15	.07	.02
☐ 66 Joe Charboneau	.25	.11	.03
☐ 67 Miguel Dilone	.05	.02	.01
☐ 68 Mike Hargrove	.15	.07	.02
☐ 69 Rick Manning	.05	.02	.01
☐ 70 Andre Thornton	.15	.07	.02
☐ 71 Ron Hassey	.05	.02	.01
☐ 72 Len Barker	.05	.02	.01
☐ 73 Lance Parrish	.15	.07	.02
☐ 74 Steve Kemp	.05	.02	.01
☐ 75 Alan Trammell	.75	.35	.09
☐ 76 Champ Summers	.05	.02	.01
☐ 77 Rick Peters	.05	.02	.01
☐ 78 Kirk Gibson	1.25	.55	.16
☐ 79 Johnny Wockenfuss	.05	.02	.01
☐ 80 Jack Morris	.25	.11	.03
☐ 81 Willie Wilson	.15	.07	.02
☐ 82 George Brett	2.50	1.10	.30
☐ 83 Frank White	.15	.07	.02
☐ 84 Willie Aikens	.05	.02	.01
☐ 85 Clint Hurdle	.05	.02	.01
☐ 86 Hal McRae	.15	.07	.02
☐ 87 Dennis Leonard	.05	.02	.01
☐ 88 Larry Gura	.05	.02	.01
☐ 89 AL Pennant Winner	.05	.02	.01
☐ 90 AL Pennant Winner	.05	.02	.01
☐ 91 Paul Molitor	1.50	.70	.19
☐ 92 Ben Oglivie	.15	.07	.02
☐ 93 Cecil Cooper	.15	.07	.02
☐ 94 Ted Simmons	.15	.07	.02
☐ 95 Robin Yount	.75	.35	.09
☐ 96 Gorman Thomas	.05	.02	.01
☐ 97 Mike Caldwell	.05	.02	.01
☐ 98 Moose Haas	.05	.02	.01
☐ 99 John Castino	.05	.02	.01
☐ 100 Roy Smalley	.05	.02	.01
☐ 101 Ken Landreaux	.05	.02	.01
☐ 102 Butch Wynegar	.05	.02	.01
☐ 103 Ron Jackson	.05	.02	.01
☐ 104 Jerry Koosman	.15	.07	.02
☐ 105 Roger Erickson	.05	.02	.01
☐ 106 Doug Corbett	.05	.02	.01
☐ 107 Reggie Jackson	.75	.35	.09
☐ 108 Willie Randolph	.15	.07	.02
☐ 109 Rick Cerone	.05	.02	.01
☐ 110 Bucky Dent	.15	.07	.02
☐ 111 Dave Winfield	.75	.35	.09
☐ 112 Ron Guidry	.15	.07	.02
☐ 113 Rich Gossage	.25	.11	.03
☐ 114 Tommy John	.25	.11	.03
☐ 115 Rickey Henderson	2.50	1.10	.30
☐ 116 Tony Armas	.05	.02	.01
☐ 117 Dave Revering	.05	.02	.01
☐ 118 Wayne Gross	.05	.02	.01
☐ 119 Dwayne Murphy	.05	.02	.01
☐ 120 Jeff Newman	.05	.02	.01
☐ 121 Rick Langford	.05	.02	.01
☐ 122 Mike Norris	.05	.02	.01
☐ 123 Bruce Bochte	.05	.02	.01
☐ 124 Tom Paciorek	.05	.02	.01
☐ 125 Dan Meyer	.05	.02	.01
☐ 126 Julio Cruz	.05	.02	.01
☐ 127 Richie Zisk	.05	.02	.01
☐ 128 Floyd Bannister	.05	.02	.01
☐ 129 Shane Rawley	.05	.02	.01
☐ 130 Buddy Bell	.15	.07	.02
☐ 131 Al Oliver	.15	.07	.02
☐ 132 Mickey Rivers	.15	.07	.02
☐ 133 Jim Sundberg	.15	.07	.02
☐ 134 Bump Wills	.05	.02	.01
☐ 135 Jon Matlack	.05	.02	.01
☐ 136 Danny Darwin	.15	.07	.02
☐ 137 Damaso Garcia	.05	.02	.01
☐ 138 Otto Velez	.05	.02	.01
☐ 139 John Mayberry	.05	.02	.01
☐ 140 Alfredo Griffin	.05	.02	.01
☐ 141 Alvis Woods	.05	.02	.01
☐ 142 Dave Stieb	.15	.07	.02
☐ 143 Jim Clancy	.05	.02	.01
☐ 144 Gary Matthews	.15	.07	.02
☐ 145 Bob Horner	.15	.07	.02
☐ 146 Dale Murphy	.50	.23	.06
☐ 147 Chris Chambliss	.15	.07	.02
☐ 148 Phil Niekro	.25	.11	.03
☐ 149 Glenn Hubbard	.05	.02	.01
☐ 150 Rick Camp	.05	.02	.01
☐ 151 Dave Kingman	.15	.07	.02
☐ 152 Bill Caudill	.05	.02	.01
☐ 153 Bill Buckner	.15	.07	.02
☐ 154 Barry Foote	.05	.02	.01
☐ 155 Mike Tyson	.05	.02	.01
☐ 156 Ivan DeJesus	.05	.02	.01
☐ 157 Rick Reuschel	.15	.07	.02
☐ 158 Ken Reitz	.05	.02	.01
☐ 159 George Foster	.15	.07	.02
☐ 160 Johnny Bench	.75	.35	.09
☐ 161 Dave Concepcion	.15	.07	.02
☐ 162 Dave Collins	.05	.02	.01
☐ 163 Ken Griffey	.15	.07	.02
☐ 164 Dan Driessen	.05	.02	.01
☐ 165 Tom Seaver	.75	.35	.09
☐ 166 Tom Hume	.05	.02	.01
☐ 167 Cesar Cedeno	.15	.07	.02
☐ 168 Rafael Landestoy	.05	.02	.01
☐ 169 Jose Cruz	.15	.07	.02
☐ 170 Art Howe	.05	.02	.01
☐ 171 Terry Puhl	.05	.02	.01
☐ 172 Joe Sambito	.05	.02	.01
☐ 173 Nolan Ryan	3.00	1.35	.35
☐ 174 Joe Niekro	.15	.07	.02
☐ 175 Dave Lopes	.15	.07	.02
☐ 176 Steve Garvey	.25	.11	.03
☐ 177 Ron Cey	.15	.07	.02
☐ 178 Reggie Smith	.15	.07	.02
☐ 179 Bill Russell	.15	.07	.02
☐ 180 Burt Hooton	.05	.02	.01
☐ 181 Jerry Reuss	.15	.07	.02
☐ 182 Dusty Baker	.15	.07	.02
☐ 183 Larry Parrish	.05	.02	.01
☐ 184 Gary Carter	.30	.14	.04
☐ 185 Rodney Scott	.05	.02	.01
☐ 186 Ellis Valentine	.05	.02	.01
☐ 187 Andre Dawson	.75	.35	.09
☐ 188 Warren Cromartie	.05	.02	.01
☐ 189 Chris Speier	.05	.02	.01
☐ 190 Steve Rogers	.05	.02	.01
☐ 191 Lee Mazzilli	.05	.02	.01
☐ 192 Doug Flynn	.05	.02	.01
☐ 193 Steve Henderson	.05	.02	.01
☐ 194 John Stearns	.05	.02	.01
☐ 195 Joel Youngblood	.05	.02	.01
☐ 196 Frank Taveras	.05	.02	.01
☐ 197 Pat Zachry	.05	.02	.01
☐ 198 Neil Allen	.05	.02	.01
☐ 199 Mike Schmidt	1.50	.70	.19
☐ 200 Pete Rose	1.25	.55	.16
☐ 201 Larry Bowa	.15	.07	.02
☐ 202 Bake McBride	.05	.02	.01
☐ 203 Bob Boone	.15	.07	.02
☐ 204 Garry Maddox	.05	.02	.01
☐ 205 Tug McGraw	.15	.07	.02
☐ 206 Steve Carlton	.50	.23	.06
☐ 207 NL Pennant Winner (World Champions)	.05	.02	.01
☐ 208 NL Pennant Winner (World Champions)	.05	.02	.01
☐ 209 Phil Garner	.15	.07	.02
☐ 210 Dave Parker	.15	.07	.02
☐ 211 Omar Moreno	.05	.02	.01

☐ 212 Mike Easler	.05	.02	.01
☐ 213 Bill Madlock	.15	.07	.02
☐ 214 Ed Ott	.05	.02	.01
☐ 215 Willie Stargell	.40	.18	.05
☐ 216 Jim Bibby	.05	.02	.01
☐ 217 Garry Templeton	.05	.02	.01
☐ 218 Sixto Lezcano	.05	.02	.01
☐ 219 Keith Hernandez	.15	.07	.02
☐ 220 George Hendrick	.05	.02	.01
☐ 221 Bruce Sutter	15	.07	.02
☐ 222 Ken Oberkfell	.05	.02	.01
☐ 223 Tony Scott	.05	.02	.01
☐ 224 Darrell Porter	.15	.07	.02
☐ 225 Gene Richards	.05	.02	.01
☐ 226 Broderick Perkins	.05	.02	.01
☐ 227 Jerry Mumphrey	.05	.02	.01
☐ 228 Luis Salazar	.05	.02	.01
☐ 229 Jerry Turner	.05	.02	.01
☐ 230 Ozzie Smith	2.50	1.10	.30
☐ 231 John Curtis	.05	.02	.01
☐ 232 Rick Wise	.05	.02	.01
☐ 233 Terry Whitfield	.05	.02	.01
☐ 234 Jack Clark	.15	.07	.02
☐ 235 Darrell Evans	.15	.07	.02
☐ 236 Larry Herndon	.05	.02	.01
☐ 237 Milt May	.05	.02	.01
☐ 238 Greg Minton	.05	.02	.01
☐ 239 Vida Blue	.15	.07	.02
☐ 240 Eddie Whitson	.05	.02	.01
☐ 241 Cecil Cooper FOIL	.25	.11	.03
☐ 242 Willie Randolph FOIL	.15	.07	.02
☐ 243 George Brett FOIL	3.00	1.35	.35
☐ 244 Robin Yount FOIL	1.00	.45	.12
☐ 245 Reggie Jackson FOIL	1.00	.45	.12
☐ 246 Al Oliver FOIL	.25	.11	.03
☐ 247 Willie Wilson FOIL	.25	.11	.03
☐ 248 Rick Cerone FOIL	.10	.05	.01
☐ 249 Steve Stone FOIL	.10	.05	.01
☐ 250 Tommy John FOIL	.25	.11	.03
☐ 251 Rich Gossage FOIL	.25	.11	.03
☐ 252 Steve Garvey FOIL	.25	.11	.03
☐ 253 Phil Garner FOIL	.25	.11	.03
☐ 254 Mike Schmidt FOIL	2.00	.90	.25
☐ 255 Garry Templeton FOIL	.10	.05	.01
☐ 256 George Hendrick FOIL	.10	.05	.01
☐ 257 Dave Parker FOIL	.25	.11	.03
☐ 258 Cesar Cedeno FOIL	.25	.11	.03
☐ 259 Gary Carter FOIL	.40	.18	.05
☐ 260 Jim Bibby FOIL	.10	.05	.01
☐ 261 Steve Carlton FOIL	.75	.35	.09
☐ 262 Tug McGraw FOIL	.25	.11	.03
☐ xx Album	1.00	.45	.12

1981 Topps Super Home Team

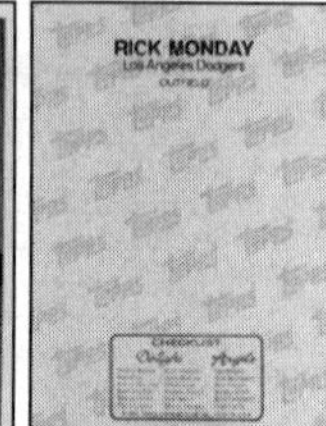

The cards in this 102-card set measure 4 7/8" by 6 7/8". In 1981 Topps issued an attractive series of photos of players from eleven AL and NL teams. The Phillies, Red Sox and Reds each were marketed in twelve-player subsets. Eighteen-player subsets were issued for the following areas: Chicago (nine White Sox and nine Cubs); New York (twelve Yankees and six Mets); Los Angeles (twelve Dodgers and six Angels); and Texas (six Rangers and six Astros). The cards of each subset contain a subset checklist on the reverse. Team sets could be obtained via a mail offer printed on the wrapper. These cards are often sold by the team or team pair. The checklist below is organized alphabetically by team(s); Boston (1-12), Chicago (13-30), Cincinnati (31-42), Los Angeles (43-60), New York (61-78), Philadelphia (79-90) and Texas (91-102).

	NRMT	VG-E	GOOD
COMPLETE SET (102)	35.00	16.00	4.40
COMMON CARD (1-102)	.15	.07	.02
☐ 1 Tom Burgmeier	.15	.07	.02
☐ 2 Dennis Eckersley	.60	.25	.07
☐ 3 Dwight Evans	.50	.23	.06
☐ 4 Carlton Fisk	.75	.35	.09
☐ 5 Glenn Hoffman	.15	.07	.02
☐ 6 Carney Lansford	.30	.14	.04
☐ 7 Tony Perez	.60	.25	.07
☐ 8 Jim Rice	.75	.35	.09
☐ 9 Bob Stanley	.15	.07	.02
☐ 10 Dave Stapleton	.15	.07	.02
☐ 11 Frank Tanana	.30	.14	.04
☐ 12 Carl Yastrzemski	1.00	.45	.12
☐ 13 Britt Burns	.15	.07	.02
☐ 14 Rich Dotson	.15	.07	.02
☐ 15 Ed Farmer	.15	.07	.02
☐ 16 Lamar Johnson	.15	.07	.02
☐ 17 Ron LeFlore	.30	.14	.04
☐ 18 Chet Lemon	.15	.07	.02
☐ 19 Bob Molinaro	.15	.07	.02
☐ 20 Jim Morrison	.15	.07	.02
☐ 21 Wayne Nordhagen	.15	.07	.02
☐ 22 Tim Blackwell	.15	.07	.02
☐ 23 Bill Buckner	.30	.14	.04
☐ 24 Ivan DeJesus	.15	.07	.02
☐ 25 Leon Durham	.30	.14	.04
☐ 26 Dave Kingman	.50	.23	.06
☐ 27 Mike Krukow	.15	.07	.02
☐ 28 Ken Reitz	.15	.07	.02
☐ 29 Rick Reuschel	.30	.14	.04
☐ 30 Mike Tyson	.15	.07	.02
☐ 31 Johnny Bench	1.00	.45	.12
☐ 32 Dave Collins	.15	.07	.02
☐ 33 Dave Concepcion	.30	.14	.04
☐ 34 Dan Driessen	.15	.07	.02
☐ 35 George Foster	.30	.14	.04
☐ 36 Ken Griffey	.30	.14	.04
☐ 37 Tom Hume	.15	.07	.02
☐ 38 Ray Knight	.30	.14	.04
☐ 39 Joe Nolan	.15	.07	.02
☐ 40 Ron Oester	.15	.07	.02
☐ 41 Tom Seaver	1.00	.45	.12
☐ 42 Mario Soto	.15	.07	.02
☐ 43 Dusty Baker	.30	.14	.04
☐ 44 Ron Cey	.30	.14	.04
☐ 45 Steve Garvey	.60	.25	.07
☐ 46 Burt Hooton	.15	.07	.02
☐ 47 Steve Howe	.15	.07	.02
☐ 48 Davey Lopes	.30	.14	.04
☐ 49 Rick Monday	.30	.14	.04
☐ 50 Jerry Reuss	.30	.14	.04
☐ 51 Bill Russell	.30	.14	.04
☐ 52 Reggie Smith	.30	.14	.04
☐ 53 Bob Welch	.30	.14	.04
☐ 54 Steve Yeager	.15	.07	.02
☐ 55 Don Baylor	.50	.23	.06
☐ 56 Rick Burleson	.15	.07	.02
☐ 57 Rod Carew	1.00	.45	.12
☐ 58 Bobby Grich	.30	.14	.04
☐ 59 Butch Hobson	.15	.07	.02
☐ 60 Fred Lynn	.30	.14	.04
☐ 61 Rick Cerone	.15	.07	.02
☐ 62 Bucky Dent	.30	.14	.04
☐ 63 Rich Gossage	.50	.23	.06
☐ 64 Ron Guidry	.30	.14	.04
☐ 65 Reggie Jackson	1.00	.45	.12
☐ 66 Tommy John	.50	.23	.06
☐ 67 Ruppert Jones	.15	.07	.02
☐ 68 Rudy May	.15	.07	.02
☐ 69 Graig Nettles	.50	.23	.06
☐ 70 Willie Randolph	.30	.14	.04
☐ 71 Bob Watson	.50	.23	.06
☐ 72 Dave Winfield	1.00	.45	.12
☐ 73 Neil Allen	.15	.07	.02
☐ 74 Doug Flynn	.15	.07	.02
☐ 75 Lee Mazzilli	.15	.07	.02
☐ 76 Rusty Staub	.30	.14	.04
☐ 77 Frank Taveras	.15	.07	.02
☐ 78 Alex Trevino	.15	.07	.02
☐ 79 Bob Boone	.30	.14	.04
☐ 80 Larry Bowa	.30	.14	.04
☐ 81 Steve Carlton	1.00	.45	.12
☐ 82 Greg Luzinski	.30	.14	.04
☐ 83 Garry Maddox	.15	.07	.02
☐ 84 Bake McBride	.15	.07	.02
☐ 85 Tug McGraw	.30	.14	.04
☐ 86 Pete Rose	1.25	.55	.16
☐ 87 Dick Ruthven	.15	.07	.02
☐ 88 Mike Schmidt	1.25	.55	.16
☐ 89 Manny Trillo	.15	.07	.02
☐ 90 Del Unser	.15	.07	.02
☐ 91 Buddy Bell	.30	.14	.04
☐ 92 Jon Matlack	.15	.07	.02
☐ 93 Al Oliver	.30	.14	.04
☐ 94 Mickey Rivers	.30	.14	.04
☐ 95 Jim Sundberg	.30	.14	.04
☐ 96 Bump Wills	.15	.07	.02
☐ 97 Cesar Cedeno	.30	.14	.04
☐ 98 Jose Cruz	.50	.23	.06
☐ 99 Art Howe	.30	.14	.04
☐ 100 Terry Puhl	.15	.07	.02
☐ 101 Nolan Ryan	3.00	1.35	.35
☐ 102 Don Sutton	.50	.23	.06

1981 Topps Super National

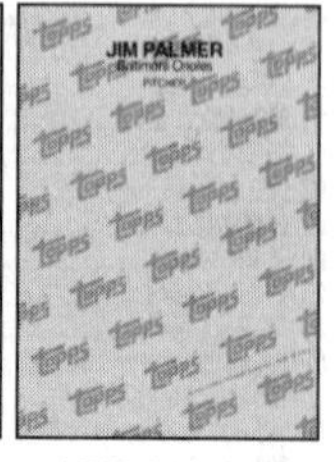

The cards in this 15-card set measure 4 7/8" by 6 7/8". In a format similar to the Home Team series of 1981 and the Super Star Photo set of 1980, these cards feature excellent photos of the top stars of 1981. The pictures of players appearing in both the regional Home Team and National sets are identical, but Brett, Cooper, Palmer, Parker and Simmons are unique to the latter and are indicated in the checklist below with an asterisk. The backs of the cards contain the player's name, team and position and a single copyright line.

	NRMT	VG-E	GOOD
COMPLETE SET (15)	4.00	1.80	.50
COMMON CARD (1-15)	.15	.07	.02
☐ 1 Buddy Bell	.15	.07	.02
☐ 2 Johnny Bench	.50	.23	.06
☐ 3 George Brett	1.00	.45	.12
☐ 4 Rod Carew	.40	.18	.05
☐ 5 Cecil Cooper	.15	.07	.02
☐ 6 Steve Garvey	.30	.14	.04
☐ 7 Rich Gossage	.25	.11	.03
☐ 8 Reggie Jackson	.50	.23	.06
☐ 9 Jim Palmer	.40	.18	.05
☐ 10 Dave Parker	.25	.11	.03
☐ 11 Jim Rice	.25	.11	.03
☐ 12 Pete Rose	.75	.35	.09
☐ 13 Mike Schmidt	.75	.35	.09
☐ 14 Tom Seaver	.50	.23	.06
☐ 15 Ted Simmons	.15	.07	.02

1981 Topps Team Checklist Sheet

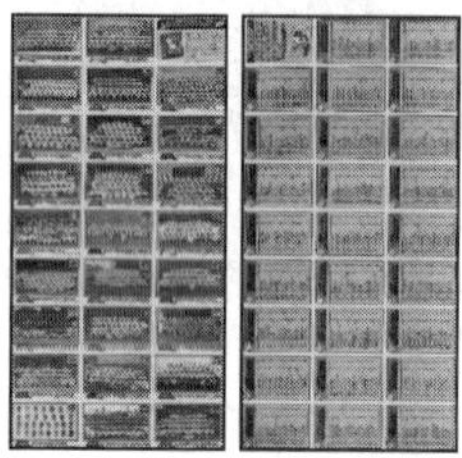

As part of a mail-away offer, Topps offered all 26 1981 team checklist cards on an uncut sheet. These cards enabled the collector to have an easy reference for which card(s) he/she needed to finish their sets. When cut form the sheet, all cards measure the standard size.

	NRMT	VG-E	GOOD
COMPLETE SET (1)	15.00	6.75	1.85
COMMON SHEET (1)	15.00	6.75	1.85
☐ 1 Team Checklist Sheet	15.00	6.75	1.85

1982 Topps

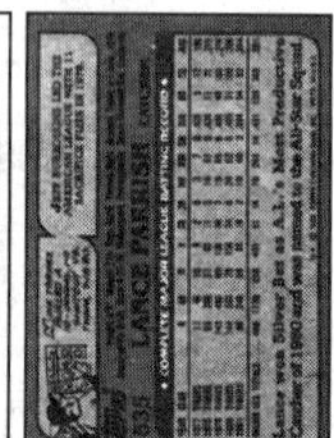

The cards in this 792-card set measure the standard size. The 1982 baseball series was the first of the largest sets Topps issued at one printing. The 66-card increase from the previous year's total eliminated the "double print" practice, that had occurred in every regular issue since 1978. Cards 1-6 depict Highlights of the strike-shortened 1981 season, cards 161-168 picture League Leaders, and there are subsets of AL (547-557) and NL (337-347) All-Stars (AS). The abbreviation "SA" in the checklist is given for the 40 "Super Action" cards introduced in this set. The team cards are actually Team Leader (TL) cards picturing the batting average and ERA leader for that team with a checklist back. All 26 of these cards were available from Topps on a perforated sheet through an offer on wax pack wrappers. Cards were primarily distributed in 15-card wax packs and 51-card rack packs. Notable Rookie Cards include Brett Butler, Chili Davis, Cal Ripken Jr., Lee Smith, and Dave Stewart. Be careful when purchasing blank-back Cal Ripken Jr. Rookie Cards. Those cards are undoubtedly counterfeit.

	NRMT	VG-E	GOOD
COMPLETE SET (792)	125.00	55.00	15.50
COMMON CARD (1-792)	.10	.05	.01
☐ 1 Steve Carlton HL	1.00	.45	.12
Sets new NL strikeout record			
☐ 2 Ron Davis HL	.25	.11	.03
Fans 8 straight in relief			
☐ 3 Tim Raines HL	.50	.23	.06
71 steals as rookie			
☐ 4 Pete Rose HL	1.00	.45	.12
Sets NL hit mark			
☐ 5 Nolan Ryan HL	3.00	1.35	.35
Pitches fifth no-hitter			
☐ 6 Fernando Valenzuela HL	.25	.11	.03
8 shutouts as rookie			
☐ 7 Scott Sanderson	.10	.05	.01
☐ 8 Rich Dauer	.10	.05	.01
☐ 9 Ron Guidry	.25	.11	.03
☐ 10 Ron Guidry SA	.25	.11	.03
☐ 11 Gary Alexander	.10	.05	.01
☐ 12 Moose Haas	.10	.05	.01
☐ 13 Lamar Johnson	.10	.05	.01
☐ 14 Steve Howe	.10	.05	.01
☐ 15 Ellis Valentine	.10	.05	.01
☐ 16 Steve Comer	.10	.05	.01
☐ 17 Darrell Evans	.25	.11	.03
☐ 18 Fernando Arroyo	.10	.05	.01
☐ 19 Ernie Whitt	.10	.05	.01
☐ 20 Garry Maddox	.10	.05	.01
☐ 21 Orioles Rookies	75.00	34.00	9.50
Bob Bonner			
Cal Ripken			
Jeff Schneider			
☐ 22 Jim Beattie	.10	.05	.01
☐ 23 Willie Hernandez	.25	.11	.03
☐ 24 Dave Frost	.10	.05	.01
☐ 25 Jerry Remy	.10	.05	.01
☐ 26 Jorge Orta	.10	.05	.01
☐ 27 Tom Herr	.25	.11	.03
☐ 28 John Urrea	.10	.05	.01
☐ 29 Dwayne Murphy	.10	.05	.01
☐ 30 Tom Seaver	1.25	.55	.16
☐ 31 Tom Seaver SA	.60	.25	.07
☐ 32 Gene Garber	.10	.05	.01
☐ 33 Jerry Morales	.10	.05	.01
☐ 34 Joe Sambito	.10	.05	.01
☐ 35 Willie Aikens	.10	.05	.01
☐ 36 Rangers TL	.50	.23	.06
BA: Al Oliver			
Pitching: Doc Medich			
(Checklist on back)			
☐ 37 Dan Graham	.10	.05	.01
☐ 38 Charlie Lea	.10	.05	.01
☐ 39 Lou Whitaker	.50	.23	.06
☐ 40 Dave Parker	.25	.11	.03
☐ 41 Dave Parker SA	.25	.11	.03
☐ 42 Rick Sofield	.10	.05	.01
☐ 43 Mike Cubbage	.10	.05	.01
☐ 44 Britt Burns	.10	.05	.01
☐ 45 Rick Cerone	.10	.05	.01
☐ 46 Jerry Augustine	.10	.05	.01
☐ 47 Jeff Leonard	.10	.05	.01
☐ 48 Bobby Castillo	.10	.05	.01
☐ 49 Alvis Woods	.10	.05	.01
☐ 50 Buddy Bell	.25	.11	.03
☐ 51 Cubs Rookies	.50	.23	.06
Jay Howell			
Carlos Lezcano			
Ty Waller			
☐ 52 Larry Andersen	.10	.05	.01
☐ 53 Greg Gross	.10	.05	.01
☐ 54 Ron Hassey	.10	.05	.01
☐ 55 Rick Burleson	.10	.05	.01
☐ 56 Mark Littell	.10	.05	.01
☐ 57 Craig Reynolds	.10	.05	.01
☐ 58 John D'Acquisto	.10	.05	.01
☐ 59 Rich Gedman	.25	.11	.03
☐ 60 Tony Armas	.10	.05	.01
☐ 61 Tommy Boggs	.10	.05	.01
☐ 62 Mike Tyson	.10	.05	.01
☐ 63 Mario Soto	.10	.05	.01
☐ 64 Lynn Jones	.10	.05	.01
☐ 65 Terry Kennedy	.10	.05	.01
☐ 66 Astros TL	2.00	.90	.25
BA: Art Howe			
Pitching: Nolan Ryan			
(Checklist on back)			
☐ 67 Rich Gale	.10	.05	.01
☐ 68 Roy Howell	.10	.05	.01
☐ 69 Al Williams	.10	.05	.01
☐ 70 Tim Raines	1.50	.70	.19
☐ 71 Roy Lee Jackson	.10	.05	.01
☐ 72 Rick Auerbach	.10	.05	.01
☐ 73 Buddy Solomon	.10	.05	.01
☐ 74 Bob Clark	.10	.05	.01
☐ 75 Tommy John	.50	.23	.06
☐ 76 Greg Pryor	.10	.05	.01
☐ 77 Miguel Dilone	.10	.05	.01
☐ 78 George Medich	.10	.05	.01
☐ 79 Bob Bailor	.10	.05	.01
☐ 80 Jim Palmer	.75	.35	.09
☐ 81 Jim Palmer SA	.50	.23	.06
☐ 82 Bob Welch	.25	.11	.03
☐ 83 Yankees Rookies	.50	.23	.06
Steve Balboni			
Andy McGaffigan			
Andre Robertson			
☐ 84 Rennie Stennett	.10	.05	.01
☐ 85 Lynn McGlothen	.10	.05	.01
☐ 86 Dane Iorg	.10	.05	.01
☐ 87 Matt Keough	.10	.05	.01
☐ 88 Biff Pocoroba	.10	.05	.01
☐ 89 Steve Henderson	.10	.05	.01
☐ 90 Nolan Ryan	6.00	2.70	.75
☐ 91 Carney Lansford	.25	.11	.03
☐ 92 Brad Havens	.10	.05	.01
☐ 93 Larry Hisle	.10	.05	.01
☐ 94 Andy Hassler	.10	.05	.01
☐ 95 Ozzie Smith	4.00	1.80	.50
☐ 96 Royals TL	.75	.35	.09
BA: George Brett			
Pitching: Larry Gura			
(Checklist on back)			
☐ 97 Paul Moskau	.10	.05	.01
☐ 98 Terry Bulling	.10	.05	.01

□ 99 Barry Bonnell .10 .05 .01
□ 100 Mike Schmidt 2.50 1.10 .30
□ 101 Mike Schmidt SA 1.50 .70 .19
□ 102 Dan Briggs .10 .05 .01
□ 103 Bob Lacey .10 .05 .01
□ 104 Rance Mulliniks .10 .05 .01
□ 105 Kirk Gibson 1.00 .45 .12
□ 106 Enrique Romo .10 .05 .01
□ 107 Wayne Krenchicki .10 .05 .01
□ 108 Bob Sykes .10 .05 .01
□ 109 Dave Revering .10 .05 .01
□ 110 Carlton Fisk 1.50 .70 .19
□ 111 Carlton Fisk SA .75 .35 .09
□ 112 Billy Sample .10 .05 .01
□ 113 Steve McCatty .10 .05 .01
□ 114 Ken Landreaux .10 .05 .01
□ 115 Gaylord Perry .50 .23 .06
□ 116 Jim Wohlford .10 .05 .01
□ 117 Rawly Eastwick .10 .05 .01
□ 118 Expos Rookies .25 .11 .03
Terry Francona
Brad Mills
Bryn Smith
□ 119 Joe Pittman .10 .05 .01
□ 120 Gary Lucas .10 .05 .01
□ 121 Ed Lynch .10 .05 .01
□ 122 Jamie Easterly UER .10 .05 .01
(Photo actually
Reggie Cleveland)
□ 123 Danny Goodwin .10 .05 .01
□ 124 Reid Nichols .10 .05 .01
□ 125 Danny Ainge 2.00 .90 .25
□ 126 Braves TL .50 .23 .06
BA: Claudell Washington
Pitching: Rick Mahler
(Checklist on back)
□ 127 Lonnie Smith .25 .11 .03
□ 128 Frank Pastore .10 .05 .01
□ 129 Checklist 1-132 .50 .23 .06
□ 130 Julio Cruz .10 .05 .01
□ 131 Stan Bahnsen .10 .05 .01
□ 132 Lee May .25 .11 .03
□ 133 Pat Underwood .10 .05 .01
□ 134 Dan Ford .10 .05 .01
□ 135 Andy Rincon .10 .05 .01
□ 136 Lenn Sakata .10 .05 .01
□ 137 George Cappuzzello .10 .05 .01
□ 138 Tony Pena .25 .11 .03
□ 139 Jeff Jones .10 .05 .01
□ 140 Ron LeFlore .25 .11 .03
□ 141 Indians Rookies .25 .11 .03
Chris Bando
Tom Brennan
Von Hayes
□ 142 Dave LaRoche .10 .05 .01
□ 143 Mookie Wilson .25 .11 .03
□ 144 Fred Breining .10 .05 .01
□ 145 Bob Horner .25 .11 .03
□ 146 Mike Griffin .10 .05 .01
□ 147 Denny Walling .10 .05 .01
□ 148 Mickey Klutts .10 .05 .01
□ 149 Pat Putnam .10 .05 .01
□ 150 Ted Simmons .25 .11 .03
□ 151 Dave Edwards .10 .05 .01
□ 152 Ramon Aviles .10 .05 .01
□ 153 Roger Erickson .10 .05 .01
□ 154 Dennis Werth .10 .05 .01
□ 155 Otto Velez .10 .05 .01
□ 156 Oakland A's TL .75 .35 .09
BA: Rickey Henderson
Pitching: Steve McCatty
(Checklist on back)
□ 157 Steve Crawford .10 .05 .01
□ 158 Brian Downing .10 .05 .01
□ 159 Larry Biittner .10 .05 .01
□ 160 Luis Tiant .25 .11 .03
□ 161 Batting Leaders .25 .11 .03
Bill Madlock
Carney Lansford
□ 162 Home Run Leaders .75 .35 .09
Mike Schmidt
Tony Armas
Dwight Evans
Bobby Grich
Eddie Murray
□ 163 RBI Leaders .75 .35 .09
Mike Schmidt
Eddie Murray
□ 164 Stolen Base Leaders 1.00 .45 .12
Tim Raines
Rickey Henderson
□ 165 Victory Leaders .50 .23 .06
Tom Seaver
Denny Martinez
Steve McCatty
Jack Morris
Pete Vuckovich
□ 166 Strikeout Leaders .25 .11 .03
Fernando Valenzuela
Len Barker
□ 167 ERA Leaders 2.00 .90 .25
Nolan Ryan
Steve McCatty
□ 168 Leading Firemen .50 .23 .06
Bruce Sutter
Rollie Fingers
□ 169 Charlie Leibrandt .10 .05 .01
□ 170 Jim Bibby .10 .05 .01
□ 171 Giants Rookies 2.50 1.10 .30
Bob Brenly
Chili Davis
Bob Tufts
□ 172 Bill Gullickson .10 .05 .01
□ 173 Jamie Quirk .10 .05 .01
□ 174 Dave Ford .10 .05 .01
□ 175 Jerry Mumphrey .10 .05 .01
□ 176 Dewey Robinson .10 .05 .01
□ 177 John Ellis .10 .05 .01
□ 178 Dyar Miller .10 .05 .01
□ 179 Steve Garvey .50 .23 .06
□ 180 Steve Garvey SA .25 .11 .03
□ 181 Silvio Martinez .10 .05 .01
□ 182 Larry Herndon .10 .05 .01
□ 183 Mike Proly .10 .05 .01
□ 184 Mick Kelleher .10 .05 .01
□ 185 Phil Niekro .50 .23 .06
□ 186 Cardinals TL .50 .23 .06
BA: Keith Hernandez
Pitching: Bob Forsch
(Checklist on back)
□ 187 Jeff Newman .10 .05 .01
□ 188 Randy Martz .10 .05 .01
□ 189 Glenn Hoffman .10 .05 .01
□ 190 J.R. Richard .25 .11 .03
□ 191 Tim Wallach 1.00 .45 .12
□ 192 Broderick Perkins .10 .05 .01
□ 193 Darrell Jackson .10 .05 .01
□ 194 Mike Vail .10 .05 .01
□ 195 Paul Molitor 2.50 1.10 .30
□ 196 Willie Upshaw .10 .05 .01
□ 197 Shane Rawley .10 .05 .01
□ 198 Chris Speier .10 .05 .01
□ 199 Don Aase .10 .05 .01
□ 200 George Brett 5.00 2.20 .60
□ 201 George Brett SA 2.50 1.10 .30
□ 202 Rick Manning .10 .05 .01
□ 203 Blue Jays Rookies .50 .23 .06
Jesse Barfield
Brian Milner
Boomer Wells
□ 204 Gary Roenicke .10 .05 .01
□ 205 Neil Allen .10 .05 .01
□ 206 Tony Bernazard .10 .05 .01
□ 207 Rod Scurry .10 .05 .01
□ 208 Bobby Murcer .25 .11 .03
□ 209 Gary Lavelle .10 .05 .01
□ 210 Keith Hernandez .25 .11 .03
□ 211 Dan Petry .10 .05 .01
□ 212 Mario Mendoza .10 .05 .01
□ 213 Dave Stewart 2.50 1.10 .30
□ 214 Brian Asselstine .10 .05 .01
□ 215 Mike Krukow .10 .05 .01
□ 216 White Sox TL .50 .23 .06
BA: Chet Lemon
Pitching: Dennis Lamp
(Checklist on back)
□ 217 Bo McLaughlin .10 .05 .01
□ 218 Dave Roberts .10 .05 .01
□ 219 John Curtis .10 .05 .01
□ 220 Manny Trillo .10 .05 .01
□ 221 Jim Slaton .10 .05 .01
□ 222 Butch Wynegar .10 .05 .01
□ 223 Lloyd Moseby .10 .05 .01
□ 224 Bruce Bochte .10 .05 .01
□ 225 Mike Torrez .10 .05 .01
□ 226 Checklist 133-264 .50 .23 .06
□ 227 Ray Burris .10 .05 .01
□ 228 Sam Mejias .10 .05 .01
□ 229 Geoff Zahn .10 .05 .01
□ 230 Willie Wilson .25 .11 .03
□ 231 Phillies Rookies .50 .23 .06
Mark Davis
Bob Dernier
Ozzie Virgil
□ 232 Terry Crowley .10 .05 .01
□ 233 Duane Kuiper .10 .05 .01
□ 234 Ron Hodges .10 .05 .01
□ 235 Mike Easler .10 .05 .01
□ 236 John Martin .10 .05 .01
□ 237 Rusty Kuntz .10 .05 .01
□ 238 Kevin Saucier .10 .05 .01
□ 239 Jon Matlack .10 .05 .01
□ 240 Bucky Dent .25 .11 .03
□ 241 Bucky Dent SA .10 .05 .01
□ 242 Milt May .10 .05 .01
□ 243 Bob Owchinko .10 .05 .01
□ 244 Rufino Linares .10 .05 .01
□ 245 Ken Reitz .10 .05 .01
□ 246 New York Mets TL .50 .23 .06
BA: Hubie Brooks
Pitching: Mike Scott
(Checklist on back)
□ 247 Pedro Guerrero .25 .11 .03
□ 248 Frank LaCorte .10 .05 .01
□ 249 Tim Flannery .10 .05 .01
□ 250 Tug McGraw .25 .11 .03
□ 251 Fred Lynn .25 .11 .03
□ 252 Fred Lynn SA .25 .11 .03
□ 253 Chuck Baker .10 .05 .01
□ 254 Jorge Bell 1.00 .45 .12
□ 255 Tony Perez .50 .23 .06
□ 256 Tony Perez SA .25 .11 .03
□ 257 Larry Harlow .10 .05 .01
□ 258 Bo Diaz .10 .05 .01
□ 259 Rodney Scott .10 .05 .01
□ 260 Bruce Sutter .25 .11 .03
□ 261 Tigers Rookies UER .10 .05 .01
Howard Bailey
Marty Castillo
Dave Rucker
(Rucker photo act-
ally Roger Weaver)
□ 262 Doug Bair .10 .05 .01
□ 263 Victor Cruz .10 .05 .01
□ 264 Dan Quisenberry .25 .11 .03
□ 265 Al Bumbry .25 .11 .03
□ 266 Rick Leach .10 .05 .01
□ 267 Kurt Bevacqua .10 .05 .01
□ 268 Rickey Keeton .10 .05 .01
□ 269 Jim Essian .10 .05 .01
□ 270 Rusty Staub .25 .11 .03
□ 271 Larry Bradford .10 .05 .01
□ 272 Bump Wills .10 .05 .01
□ 273 Doug Bird .10 .05 .01
□ 274 Bob Ojeda .50 .23 .06
□ 275 Bob Watson .25 .11 .03
□ 276 Angels TL .50 .23 .06
BA: Rod Carew
Pitching: Ken Forsch
(Checklist on back)
□ 277 Terry Puhl .10 .05 .01
□ 278 John Littlefield .10 .05 .01
□ 279 Bill Russell .25 .11 .03
□ 280 Ben Oglivie .25 .11 .03
□ 281 John Verhoeven .10 .05 .01
□ 282 Ken Macha .10 .05 .01
□ 283 Brian Allard .10 .05 .01
□ 284 Bob Grich .25 .11 .03
□ 285 Sparky Lyle .25 .11 .03
□ 286 Bill Fahey .10 .05 .01
□ 287 Alan Bannister .10 .05 .01
□ 288 Garry Templeton .10 .05 .01
□ 289 Bob Stanley .10 .05 .01
□ 290 Ken Singleton .25 .11 .03
□ 291 Pirates Rookies .25 .11 .03
Vance Law
Bob Long
Johnny Ray
□ 292 David Palmer .10 .05 .01
□ 293 Rob Picciolo .10 .05 .01
□ 294 Mike LaCoss .10 .05 .01
□ 295 Jason Thompson .10 .05 .01
□ 296 Bob Walk .10 .05 .01
□ 297 Clint Hurdle .10 .05 .01
□ 298 Danny Darwin .10 .05 .01
□ 299 Steve Trout .10 .05 .01
□ 300 Reggie Jackson 1.50 .70 .19
□ 301 Reggie Jackson SA .75 .35 .09
□ 302 Doug Flynn .10 .05 .01
□ 303 Bill Caudill .10 .05 .01
□ 304 Johnnie LeMaster .10 .05 .01
□ 305 Don Sutton .50 .23 .06
□ 306 Don Sutton SA .25 .11 .03
□ 307 Randy Bass .25 .11 .03
□ 308 Charlie Moore .10 .05 .01
□ 309 Pete Redfern .10 .05 .01
□ 310 Mike Hargrove .25 .11 .03
□ 311 Dodgers TL .50 .23 .06
BA: Dusty Baker
Pitching: Burt Hooton
(Checklist on back)
□ 312 Lenny Randle .10 .05 .01
□ 313 John Harris .10 .05 .01
□ 314 Buck Martinez .10 .05 .01
□ 315 Burt Hooton .10 .05 .01
□ 316 Steve Braun .10 .05 .01
□ 317 Dick Ruthven .10 .05 .01
□ 318 Mike Heath .10 .05 .01
□ 319 Dave Rozema .10 .05 .01
□ 320 Chris Chambliss .25 .11 .03
□ 321 Chris Chambliss SA .10 .05 .01
□ 322 Garry Hancock .10 .05 .01
□ 323 Bill Lee .25 .11 .03
□ 324 Steve Dillard .10 .05 .01
□ 325 Jose Cruz .25 .11 .03
□ 326 Pete Falcone .10 .05 .01
□ 327 Joe Nolan .10 .05 .01
□ 328 Ed Farmer .10 .05 .01
□ 329 U.L. Washington .10 .05 .01
□ 330 Rick Wise .10 .05 .01
□ 331 Benny Ayala .10 .05 .01
□ 332 Don Robinson .10 .05 .01
□ 333 Brewers Rookies .10 .05 .01
Frank DiPino
Marshall Edwards
Chuck Porter
□ 334 Aurelio Rodriguez .10 .05 .01
□ 335 Jim Sundberg .25 .11 .03
□ 336 Mariners TL .50 .23 .06
BA: Tom Paciorek
Pitching: Glenn Abbott
(Checklist on back)
□ 337 Pete Rose AS 1.00 .45 .12
□ 338 Dave Lopes AS .25 .11 .03
□ 339 Mike Schmidt AS .75 .35 .09
□ 340 Dave Concepcion AS .25 .11 .03
□ 341 Andre Dawson AS .50 .23 .06
□ 342A George Foster AS .25 .11 .03
(With autograph)
□ 342B George Foster AS 1.00 .45 .12
(W/o autograph)
□ 343 Dave Parker AS .25 .11 .03
□ 344 Gary Carter AS .25 .11 .03
□ 345 Fernando Valenzuela AS .25 .11 .03
□ 346 Tom Seaver AS ERR 1.25 .55 .16
("t ed")
□ 346B Tom Seaver AS COR 1.25 .55 .16
("tied")
□ 347 Bruce Sutter AS .25 .11 .03
□ 348 Derrel Thomas .10 .05 .01
□ 349 George Frazier .10 .05 .01
□ 350 Thad Bosley .10 .05 .01
□ 351 Reds Rookies .10 .05 .01
Scott Brown
Geoff Combe
Paul Householder
□ 352 Dick Davis .10 .05 .01
□ 353 Jack O'Connor .10 .05 .01
□ 354 Roberto Ramos .10 .05 .01
□ 355 Dwight Evans .50 .23 .06
□ 356 Denny Lewallyn .10 .05 .01
□ 357 Butch Hobson .10 .05 .01
□ 358 Mike Parrott .10 .05 .01
□ 359 Jim Dwyer .10 .05 .01
□ 360 Len Barker .10 .05 .01
□ 361 Rafael Landestoy .10 .05 .01
□ 362 Jim Wright UER .10 .05 .01
(Wrong Jim Wright
pictured)
□ 363 Bob Molinaro .10 .05 .01
□ 364 Doyle Alexander .10 .05 .01
□ 365 Bill Madlock .25 .11 .03
□ 366 Padres TL .50 .23 .06
BA: Luis Salazar
Pitching: Juan
Eichelberger
(Checklist on back)
□ 367 Jim Kaat .25 .11 .03
□ 368 Alex Trevino .10 .05 .01
□ 369 Champ Summers .10 .05 .01
□ 370 Mike Norris .10 .05 .01
□ 371 Jerry Don Gleaton .10 .05 .01
□ 372 Luis Gomez .10 .05 .01
□ 373 Gene Nelson .10 .05 .01
□ 374 Tim Blackwell .10 .05 .01
□ 375 Dusty Baker .50 .23 .06
□ 376 Chris Welsh .10 .05 .01
□ 377 Kiko Garcia .10 .05 .01
□ 378 Mike Caldwell .10 .05 .01
□ 379 Rob Wilfong .10 .05 .01
□ 380 Dave Stieb .25 .11 .03
□ 381 Red Sox Rookies .25 .11 .03
Bruce Hurst
Dave Schmidt
Julio Valdez
□ 382 Joe Simpson .10 .05 .01
□ 383A Pascual Perez ERR 10.00 4.50 1.25
(No position
on front)
□ 383B Pascual Perez COR .25 .11 .03
□ 384 Keith Moreland .10 .05 .01
□ 385 Ken Forsch .10 .05 .01
□ 386 Jerry White .10 .05 .01
□ 387 Tom Veryzer .10 .05 .01
□ 388 Joe Rudi .10 .05 .01
□ 389 George Vukovich .10 .05 .01
□ 390 Eddie Murray 4.00 1.80 .50
□ 391 Dave Tobik .10 .05 .01
□ 392 Rick Bosetti .10 .05 .01
□ 393 Al Hrabosky .10 .05 .01
□ 394 Checklist 265-396 .50 .23 .06
□ 395 Omar Moreno .10 .05 .01
□ 396 Twins TL .50 .23 .06
BA: John Castino
Pitching: Fernando
Arroyo
(Checklist on back)
□ 397 Ken Brett .10 .05 .01
□ 398 Mike Squires .10 .05 .01
□ 399 Pat Zachry .10 .05 .01
□ 400 Johnny Bench 1.25 .55 .16
□ 401 Johnny Bench SA .60 .25 .07
□ 402 Bill Stein .10 .05 .01
□ 403 Jim Tracy .10 .05 .01
□ 404 Dickie Thon .10 .05 .01
□ 405 Rick Reuschel .25 .11 .03
□ 406 Al Holland .10 .05 .01
□ 407 Danny Boone .10 .05 .01
□ 408 Ed Romero .10 .05 .01
□ 409 Don Cooper .10 .05 .01
□ 410 Ron Cey .25 .11 .03
□ 411 Ron Cey SA .10 .05 .01
□ 412 Luis Leal .10 .05 .01
□ 413 Dan Meyer .10 .05 .01
□ 414 Elias Sosa .10 .05 .01
□ 415 Don Baylor .50 .23 .06
□ 416 Marty Bystrom .10 .05 .01
□ 417 Pat Kelly .10 .05 .01
□ 418 Rangers Rookies .10 .05 .01
John Butcher
Bobby Johnson

Dave Schmidt
☐ 419 Steve Stone .25 .11 .03
☐ 420 George Hendrick .10 .05 .01
☐ 421 Mark Clear .10 .05 .01
☐ 422 Cliff Johnson .10 .05 .01
☐ 423 Stan Papi .10 .05 .01
☐ 424 Bruce Benedict .10 .05 .01
☐ 425 John Candelaria .10 .05 .01
☐ 426 Orioles TL .50 .23 .06
BA: Eddie Murray
Pitching: Sammy Stewart
(Checklist on back)
☐ 427 Ron Oester .10 .05 .01
☐ 428 LaMarr Hoyt .10 .05 .01
☐ 429 John Wathan .10 .05 .01
☐ 430 Vida Blue .25 .11 .03
☐ 431 Vida Blue SA .10 .05 .01
☐ 432 Mike Scott .25 .11 .03
☐ 433 Alan Ashby .10 .05 .01
☐ 434 Joe Lefebvre .10 .05 .01
☐ 435 Robin Yount 2.00 .90 .25
☐ 436 Joe Strain .10 .05 .01
☐ 437 Juan Berenguer .10 .05 .01
☐ 438 Pete Mackanin .10 .05 .01
☐ 439 Dave Righetti .50 .23 .06
☐ 440 Jeff Burroughs .10 .05 .01
☐ 441 Astros Rookies .10 .05 .01
Danny Heep
Billy Smith
Bobby Sprowl
☐ 442 Bruce Kison .10 .05 .01
☐ 443 Mark Wagner .10 .05 .01
☐ 444 Terry Forster .10 .05 .01
☐ 445 Larry Parrish .10 .05 .01
☐ 446 Wayne Garland .10 .05 .01
☐ 447 Darrell Porter .25 .11 .03
☐ 448 Darrell Porter SA .10 .05 .01
☐ 449 Luis Aguayo .10 .05 .01
☐ 450 Jack Morris .25 .11 .03
☐ 451 Ed Miller .10 .05 .01
☐ 452 Lee Smith 8.00 3.60 1.00
☐ 453 Art Howe .10 .05 .01
☐ 454 Rick Langford .10 .05 .01
☐ 455 Tom Burgmeier .10 .05 .01
☐ 456 Chicago Cubs TL .50 .23 .06
BA: Bill Buckner
Pitching: Randy Martz
(Checklist on back)
☐ 457 Tim Stoddard .10 .05 .01
☐ 458 Willie Montanez .10 .05 .01
☐ 459 Bruce Berenyi .10 .05 .01
☐ 460 Jack Clark .25 .11 .03
☐ 461 Rich Dotson .10 .05 .01
☐ 462 Dave Chalk .10 .05 .01
☐ 463 Jim Kern .10 .05 .01
☐ 464 Juan Bonilla .10 .05 .01
☐ 465 Lee Mazzilli .10 .05 .01
☐ 466 Randy Lerch .10 .05 .01
☐ 467 Mickey Hatcher .10 .05 .01
☐ 468 Floyd Bannister .10 .05 .01
☐ 469 Ed Ott .10 .05 .01
☐ 470 John Mayberry .10 .05 .01
☐ 471 Royals Rookies .10 .05 .01
Atlee Hammaker
Mike Jones
Darryl Motley
☐ 472 Oscar Gamble .10 .05 .01
☐ 473 Mike Stanton .10 .05 .01
☐ 474 Ken Oberkfell .10 .05 .01
☐ 475 Alan Trammell 1.25 .55 .16
☐ 476 Brian Kingman .10 .05 .01
☐ 477 Steve Yeager .10 .05 .01
☐ 478 Ray Searage .10 .05 .01
☐ 479 Rowland Office .10 .05 .01
☐ 480 Steve Carlton 1.25 .55 .16
☐ 481 Steve Carlton SA .50 .23 .06
☐ 482 Glenn Hubbard .10 .05 .01
☐ 483 Gary Woods .10 .05 .01
☐ 484 Ivan DeJesus .10 .05 .01
☐ 485 Kent Tekulve .25 .11 .03
☐ 486 Yankees TL .25 .11 .03
BA: Jerry Mumphrey
Pitching: Tommy John
(Checklist on back)
☐ 487 Bob McClure .10 .05 .01
☐ 488 Ron Jackson .10 .05 .01
☐ 489 Rick Dempsey .25 .11 .03
☐ 490 Dennis Eckersley .50 .23 .06
☐ 491 Checklist 397-528 .50 .23 .06
☐ 492 Joe Price .10 .05 .01
☐ 493 Chet Lemon .10 .05 .01
☐ 494 Hubie Brooks .25 .11 .03
☐ 495 Dennis Leonard .10 .05 .01
☐ 496 Johnny Grubb .10 .05 .01
☐ 497 Jim Anderson .10 .05 .01
☐ 498 Dave Bergman .10 .05 .01
☐ 499 Paul Mirabella .10 .05 .01
☐ 500 Rod Carew 1.00 .45 .12
☐ 501 Rod Carew SA .50 .23 .06
☐ 502 Braves Rookies 3.00 1.35 .35
Steve Bedrosian UER
(Photo actually
Larry Owen)
Brett Butler
Larry Owen
☐ 503 Julio Gonzalez .10 .05 .01
☐ 504 Rick Peters .10 .05 .01
☐ 505 Graig Nettles .25 .11 .03
☐ 506 Graig Nettles SA .10 .05 .01
☐ 507 Terry Harper .10 .05 .01
☐ 508 Jody Davis .10 .05 .01
☐ 509 Harry Spilman .10 .05 .01
☐ 510 Fernando Valenzuela .50 .23 .06
☐ 511 Ruppert Jones .10 .05 .01
☐ 512 Jerry Dybzinski .10 .05 .01
☐ 513 Rick Rhoden .10 .05 .01
☐ 514 Joe Ferguson .10 .05 .01
☐ 515 Larry Bowa .25 .11 .03
☐ 516 Larry Bowa SA .10 .05 .01
☐ 517 Mark Brouhard .10 .05 .01
☐ 518 Garth Iorg .10 .05 .01
☐ 519 Glenn Adams .10 .05 .01
☐ 520 Mike Flanagan .25 .11 .03
☐ 521 Bill Almon .10 .05 .01
☐ 522 Chuck Rainey .10 .05 .01
☐ 523 Gary Gray .10 .05 .01
☐ 524 Tom Hausman .10 .05 .01
☐ 525 Ray Knight .25 .11 .03
☐ 526 Expos TL .50 .23 .06
BA: Warren Cromartie
Pitching: Bill Gullickson
(Checklist on back)
☐ 527 John Henry Johnson .10 .05 .01
☐ 528 Matt Alexander .10 .05 .01
☐ 529 Allen Ripley .10 .05 .01
☐ 530 Dickie Noles .10 .05 .01
☐ 531 A's Rookies .10 .05 .01
Rich Bordi
Mark Budaska
Kelvin Moore
☐ 532 Toby Harrah .25 .11 .03
☐ 533 Joaquin Andujar .25 .11 .03
☐ 534 Dave McKay .10 .05 .01
☐ 535 Lance Parrish .50 .23 .06
☐ 536 Rafael Ramirez .10 .05 .01
☐ 537 Doug Capilla .10 .05 .01
☐ 538 Lou Piniella .25 .11 .03
☐ 539 Vern Ruhle .10 .05 .01
☐ 540 Andre Dawson 1.50 .70 .19
☐ 541 Barry Evans .10 .05 .01
☐ 542 Ned Yost .10 .05 .01
☐ 543 Bill Robinson .10 .05 .01
☐ 544 Larry Christenson .10 .05 .01
☐ 545 Reggie Smith .25 .11 .03
☐ 546 Reggie Smith SA .10 .05 .01
☐ 547 Rod Carew AS .50 .23 .06
☐ 548 Willie Randolph AS .25 .11 .03
☐ 549 George Brett AS 2.50 1.10 .30
☐ 550 Bucky Dent AS .25 .11 .03
☐ 551 Reggie Jackson AS .75 .35 .09
☐ 552 Ken Singleton AS .25 .11 .03
☐ 553 Dave Winfield AS 1.25 .55 .16
☐ 554 Carlton Fisk AS .50 .23 .06
☐ 555 Scott McGregor AS .10 .05 .01
☐ 556 Jack Morris AS .25 .11 .03
☐ 557 Rich Gossage AS .25 .11 .03
☐ 558 John Tudor .25 .11 .03
☐ 559 Indians TL .25 .11 .03
BA: Mike Hargrove
Pitching: Bert Blyleven
(Checklist on back)
☐ 560 Doug Corbett .10 .05 .01
☐ 561 Cardinals Rookies .10 .05 .01
Glenn Brummer
Luis DeLeon
Gene Roof
☐ 562 Mike O'Berry .10 .05 .01
☐ 563 Ross Baumgarten .10 .05 .01
☐ 564 Doug DeCinces .25 .11 .03
☐ 565 Jackson Todd .10 .05 .01
☐ 566 Mike Jorgensen .10 .05 .01
☐ 567 Bob Babcock .10 .05 .01
☐ 568 Joe Pettini .10 .05 .01
☐ 569 Willie Randolph .25 .11 .03
☐ 570 Willie Randolph SA .25 .11 .03
☐ 571 Glenn Abbott .10 .05 .01
☐ 572 Juan Beniquez .10 .05 .01
☐ 573 Rick Waits .10 .05 .01
☐ 574 Mike Ramsey .10 .05 .01
☐ 575 Al Cowens .10 .05 .01
☐ 576 Giants TL .50 .23 .06
BA: Milt May
Pitching: Vida Blue
(Checklist on back)
☐ 577 Rick Monday .10 .05 .01
☐ 578 Shooty Babitt .10 .05 .01
☐ 579 Rick Mahler .10 .05 .01
☐ 580 Bobby Bonds .25 .11 .03
☐ 581 Ron Reed .10 .05 .01
☐ 582 Luis Pujols .10 .05 .01
☐ 583 Tippy Martinez .10 .05 .01
☐ 584 Hosken Powell .10 .05 .01
☐ 585 Rollie Fingers .50 .23 .06
☐ 586 Rollie Fingers SA .25 .11 .03
☐ 587 Tim Lollar .10 .05 .01
☐ 588 Dale Berra .10 .05 .01
☐ 589 Dave Stapleton .10 .05 .01
☐ 590 Al Oliver .25 .11 .03
☐ 591 Al Oliver SA .10 .05 .01
☐ 592 Craig Swan .10 .05 .01
☐ 593 Billy Smith .10 .05 .01
☐ 594 Renie Martin .10 .05 .01
☐ 595 Dave Collins .10 .05 .01
☐ 596 Damaso Garcia .10 .05 .01
☐ 597 Wayne Nordhagen .10 .05 .01
☐ 598 Bob Galasso .10 .05 .01
☐ 599 White Sox Rookies .10 .05 .01
Jay Loviglio
Reggie Patterson
Leo Sutherland
☐ 600 Dave Winfield 2.00 .90 .25
☐ 601 Sid Monge .10 .05 .01
☐ 602 Freddie Patek .10 .05 .01
☐ 603 Rich Hebner .25 .11 .03
☐ 604 Orlando Sanchez .10 .05 .01
☐ 605 Steve Rogers .10 .05 .01
☐ 606 Blue Jays TL .50 .23 .06
BA: John Mayberry
Pitching: Dave Stieb
(Checklist on back)
☐ 607 Leon Durham .25 .11 .03
☐ 608 Jerry Royster .10 .05 .01
☐ 609 Rick Sutcliffe .25 .11 .03
☐ 610 Rickey Henderson 3.00 1.35 .35
☐ 611 Joe Niekro .25 .11 .03
☐ 612 Gary Ward .10 .05 .01
☐ 613 Jim Gantner .25 .11 .03
☐ 614 Juan Eichelberger .10 .05 .01
☐ 615 Bob Boone .25 .11 .03
☐ 616 Bob Boone SA .10 .05 .01
☐ 617 Scott McGregor .10 .05 .01
☐ 618 Tim Foli .10 .05 .01
☐ 619 Bill Campbell .10 .05 .01
☐ 620 Ken Griffey .25 .11 .03
☐ 621 Ken Griffey SA .25 .11 .03
☐ 622 Dennis Lamp .10 .05 .01
☐ 623 Mets Rookies .50 .23 .06
Ron Gardenhire
Terry Leach
Tim Leary
☐ 624 Fergie Jenkins .50 .23 .06
☐ 625 Hal McRae .25 .11 .03
☐ 626 Randy Jones .10 .05 .01
☐ 627 Enos Cabell .10 .05 .01
☐ 628 Bill Travers .10 .05 .01
☐ 629 John Wockenfuss .10 .05 .01
☐ 630 Joe Charboneau .10 .05 .01
☐ 631 Gene Tenace .25 .11 .03
☐ 632 Bryan Clark .10 .05 .01
☐ 633 Mitchell Page .10 .05 .01
☐ 634 Checklist 529-660 .50 .23 .06
☐ 635 Ron Davis .10 .05 .01
☐ 636 Phillies TL .50 .23 .06
BA: Pete Rose
Pitching: Steve Carlton
(Checklist on back)
☐ 637 Rick Camp .10 .05 .01
☐ 638 John Milner .10 .05 .01
☐ 639 Ken Kravec .10 .05 .01
☐ 640 Cesar Cedeno .25 .11 .03
☐ 641 Steve Mura .10 .05 .01
☐ 642 Mike Scioscia .25 .11 .03
☐ 643 Pete Vuckovich .10 .05 .01
☐ 644 John Castino .10 .05 .01
☐ 645 Frank White .25 .11 .03
☐ 646 Frank White SA .10 .05 .01
☐ 647 Warren Brusstar .10 .05 .01
☐ 648 Jose Morales .10 .05 .01
☐ 649 Ken Clay .10 .05 .01
☐ 650 Carl Yastrzemski 1.25 .55 .16
☐ 651 Carl Yastrzemski SA .50 .23 .06
☐ 652 Steve Nicosia .10 .05 .01
☐ 653 Angels Rookies .50 .23 .06
Tom Brunansky
Luis Sanchez
Daryl Sconiers
☐ 654 Jim Morrison .10 .05 .01
☐ 655 Joel Youngblood .10 .05 .01
☐ 656 Eddie Whitson .10 .05 .01
☐ 657 Tom Poquette .10 .05 .01
☐ 658 Tito Landrum .10 .05 .01
☐ 659 Fred Martinez .10 .05 .01
☐ 660 Dave Concepcion .25 .11 .03
☐ 661 Dave Concepcion SA .10 .05 .01
☐ 662 Luis Salazar .10 .05 .01
☐ 663 Hector Cruz .10 .05 .01
☐ 664 Dan Spillner .10 .05 .01
☐ 665 Jim Clancy .10 .05 .01
☐ 666 Tigers TL .50 .23 .06
BA: Steve Kemp
Pitching: Dan Petry
(Checklist on back)
☐ 667 Jeff Reardon .50 .23 .06
☐ 668 Dale Murphy .50 .23 .06
☐ 669 Larry Milbourne .10 .05 .01
☐ 670 Steve Kemp .10 .05 .01
☐ 671 Mike Davis .10 .05 .01
☐ 672 Bob Knepper .10 .05 .01
☐ 673 Keith Drumwright .10 .05 .01
☐ 674 Dave Goltz .10 .05 .01
☐ 675 Cecil Cooper .25 .11 .03
☐ 676 Sal Butera .10 .05 .01
☐ 677 Alfredo Griffin .10 .05 .01
☐ 678 Tom Paciorek .10 .05 .01
☐ 679 Sammy Stewart .10 .05 .01
☐ 680 Gary Matthews .25 .11 .03
☐ 681 Dodgers Rookies .50 .23 .06
Mike Marshall
Ron Roenicke
Steve Sax
☐ 682 Jesse Jefferson .10 .05 .01
☐ 683 Phil Garner .25 .11 .03
☐ 684 Harold Baines .50 .23 .06
☐ 685 Bert Blyleven .50 .23 .06
☐ 686 Gary Allenson .10 .05 .01
☐ 687 Greg Minton .10 .05 .01
☐ 688 Leon Roberts .10 .05 .01
☐ 689 Lary Sorensen .10 .05 .01
☐ 690 Dave Kingman .25 .11 .03
☐ 691 Dan Schatzeder .10 .05 .01
☐ 692 Wayne Gross .10 .05 .01
☐ 693 Cesar Geronimo .10 .05 .01
☐ 694 Dave Wehrmeister .10 .05 .01
☐ 695 Warren Cromartie .10 .05 .01
☐ 696 Pirates TL .50 .23 .06
BA: Bill Madlock
Pitching: Eddie Solomon
(Checklist on back)
☐ 697 John Montefusco .10 .05 .01
☐ 698 Tony Scott .10 .05 .01
☐ 699 Dick Tidrow .10 .05 .01
☐ 700 George Foster .25 .11 .03
☐ 701 George Foster SA .10 .05 .01
☐ 702 Steve Renko .10 .05 .01
☐ 703 Brewers TL .50 .23 .06
BA: Cecil Cooper
Pitching: Pete Vuckovich
(Checklist on back)
☐ 704 Mickey Rivers .10 .05 .01
☐ 705 Mickey Rivers SA .10 .05 .01
☐ 706 Barry Foote .10 .05 .01
☐ 707 Mark Bomback .10 .05 .01
☐ 708 Gene Richards .10 .05 .01
☐ 709 Don Money .10 .05 .01
☐ 710 Jerry Reuss .25 .11 .03
☐ 711 Mariners Rookies .50 .23 .06
Dave Edler
Dave Henderson
Reggie Walton
☐ 712 Dennis Martinez .25 .11 .03
☐ 713 Del Unser .10 .05 .01
☐ 714 Jerry Koosman .25 .11 .03
☐ 715 Willie Stargell .50 .23 .06
☐ 716 Willie Stargell SA .25 .11 .03
☐ 717 Rick Miller .10 .05 .01
☐ 718 Charlie Hough .25 .11 .03
☐ 719 Jerry Narron .10 .05 .01
☐ 720 Greg Luzinski .25 .11 .03
☐ 721 Greg Luzinski SA .10 .05 .01
☐ 722 Jerry Martin .10 .05 .01
☐ 723 Junior Kennedy .10 .05 .01
☐ 724 Dave Rosello .10 .05 .01
☐ 725 Amos Otis .25 .11 .03
☐ 726 Amos Otis SA .10 .05 .01
☐ 727 Sixto Lezcano .10 .05 .01
☐ 728 Aurelio Lopez .10 .05 .01
☐ 729 Jim Spencer .10 .05 .01
☐ 730 Gary Carter .25 .11 .03
☐ 731 Padres Rookies .10 .05 .01
Mike Armstrong
Doug Gwosdz
Fred Kuhaulua
☐ 732 Mike Lum .10 .05 .01
☐ 733 Larry McWilliams .10 .05 .01
☐ 734 Mike Ivie .10 .05 .01
☐ 735 Rudy May .10 .05 .01
☐ 736 Jerry Turner .10 .05 .01
☐ 737 Reggie Cleveland .10 .05 .01
☐ 738 Dave Engle .10 .05 .01
☐ 739 Joey McLaughlin .10 .05 .01
☐ 740 Dave Lopes .25 .11 .03
☐ 741 Dave Lopes SA .10 .05 .01
☐ 742 Dick Drago .10 .05 .01
☐ 743 John Stearns .10 .05 .01
☐ 744 Mike Witt .25 .11 .03
☐ 745 Bake McBride .10 .05 .01
☐ 746 Andre Thornton .10 .05 .01
☐ 747 John Lowenstein .10 .05 .01
☐ 748 Marc Hill .10 .05 .01
☐ 749 Bob Shirley .10 .05 .01
☐ 750 Jim Rice .25 .11 .03
☐ 751 Rick Honeycutt .10 .05 .01
☐ 752 Lee Lacy .10 .05 .01
☐ 753 Tom Brookens .10 .05 .01
☐ 754 Joe Morgan .75 .35 .09
☐ 755 Joe Morgan SA .25 .11 .03
☐ 756 Reds TL .50 .23 .06
BA: Ken Griffey
Pitching: Tom Seaver
(Checklist on back)
☐ 757 Tom Underwood .10 .05 .01
☐ 758 Claudell Washington .10 .05 .01
☐ 759 Paul Splittorff .10 .05 .01
☐ 760 Bill Buckner .25 .11 .03
☐ 761 Dave Smith .10 .05 .01
☐ 762 Mike Phillips .10 .05 .01
☐ 763 Tom Hume .10 .05 .01
☐ 764 Steve Swisher .10 .05 .01
☐ 765 Gorman Thomas .25 .11 .03
☐ 766 Twins Rookies 3.00 1.35 .35
Lenny Faedo

	NRMT	VG-E	GOOD
Kent Hrbek			
Tim Laudner			
☐ 767 Roy Smalley	.10	.05	.01
☐ 768 Jerry Garvin	.10	.05	.01
☐ 769 Richie Zisk	.10	.05	.01
☐ 770 Rich Gossage	.50	.23	.06
☐ 771 Rich Gossage SA	.25	.11	.03
☐ 772 Bert Campaneris	.25	.11	.03
☐ 773 John Denny	.10	.05	.01
☐ 774 Jay Johnstone	.25	.11	.03
☐ 775 Bob Forsch	.10	.05	.01
☐ 776 Mark Belanger	.25	.11	.03
☐ 777 Tom Griffin	.10	.05	.01
☐ 778 Kevin Hickey	.10	.05	.01
☐ 779 Grant Jackson	.10	.05	.01
☐ 780 Pete Rose	2.00	.90	.25
☐ 781 Pete Rose SA	1.00	.45	.12
☐ 782 Frank Taveras	.10	.05	.01
☐ 783 Greg Harris	.10	.05	.01
☐ 784 Milt Wilcox	.10	.05	.01
☐ 785 Dan Driessen	.10	.05	.01
☐ 786 Red Sox TL	.50	.23	.06
BA: Carney Lansford			
Pitching: Mike Torrez			
(Checklist on back)			
☐ 787 Fred Stanley	.10	.05	.01
☐ 788 Woodie Fryman	.10	.05	.01
☐ 789 Checklist 661-792	.50	.23	.06
☐ 790 Larry Gura	.10	.05	.01
☐ 791 Bobby Brown	.10	.05	.01
☐ 792 Frank Tanana	.25	.11	.03

1982 Topps Sticker Variations

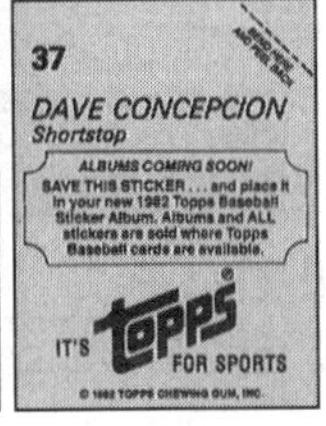

This 48-card (skip-numbered) set is actually a slightly different version of the 1982 Topps stickers. They are the same size (1 15/16" by 2 9/16") and are easily confused. They were produced for insertion into the regular packs of cards that year. They are distinguishable from the "other" sticker set by the fact that on their backs these say the Topps sticker album is "Coming Soon." There are no foils in this set. All of the stickers in this set depict a single player. Colored borders surround the posed color player photos on the fronts, blue for the NL and red for the AL. The player's name and position appear on the back. The stickers are numbered on the front and back. Choice of players for this small set appears to have been systematic, i.e., taking every fourth player between number 17 and number 109 and every fifth player between number 151 and number 251.

	NRMT	VG-E	GOOD
COMPLETE SET (48)	4.00	1.80	.50
COMMON STICKER	.05	.02	.01
☐ 17 Chris Chambliss	.05	.02	.01
☐ 21 Bruce Benedict	.05	.02	.01
☐ 25 Leon Durham	.10	.05	.01
☐ 29 Bill Buckner	.10	.05	.01
☐ 33 Dave Collins	.05	.02	.01
☐ 37 Dave Concepcion	.10	.05	.01
☐ 41 Nolan Ryan	2.00	.90	.25
☐ 45 Bob Knepper	.05	.02	.01
☐ 49 Ken Landreaux	.05	.02	.01
☐ 53 Burt Hooton	.05	.02	.01
☐ 57 Andre Dawson	.40	.18	.05
☐ 61 Gary Carter	.15	.07	.02
☐ 65 Joel Youngblood	.05	.02	.01
☐ 69 Ellis Valentine	.05	.02	.01
☐ 73 Garry Maddox	.05	.02	.01
☐ 77 Bob Boone	.10	.05	.01
☐ 81 Omar Moreno	.05	.02	.01
☐ 85 Willie Stargell	.25	.11	.03
☐ 89 Ken Oberkfell	.05	.02	.01
☐ 93 Darrell Porter	.05	.02	.01
☐ 97 Juan Eichelberger	.05	.02	.01
☐ 101 Luis Salazar	.05	.02	.01
☐ 105 Enos Cabell	.05	.02	.01
☐ 109 Larry Herndon	.05	.02	.01
☐ 143 Scott McGregor	.05	.02	.01
☐ 148 Mike Flanagan	.10	.05	.01
☐ 151 Mike Torrez	.05	.02	.01
☐ 156 Carney Lansford	.10	.05	.01
☐ 161 Fred Lynn	.10	.05	.01
☐ 166 Rich Dotson	.05	.02	.01
☐ 171 Tony Bernazard	.05	.02	.01
☐ 176 Bo Diaz	.05	.02	.01
☐ 181 Alan Trammell	.25	.11	.03
☐ 186 Milt Wilcox	.05	.02	.01
☐ 191 Dennis Leonard	.05	.02	.01
☐ 196 Willie Aikens	.05	.02	.01
☐ 201 Ted Simmons	.10	.05	.01
☐ 206 Hosken Powell	.05	.02	.01
☐ 211 Roger Erickson	.05	.02	.01
☐ 215 Graig Nettles	.10	.05	.01
☐ 216 Reggie Jackson	.50	.23	.06
☐ 221 Rickey Henderson	.75	.35	.09
☐ 226 Cliff Johnson	.05	.02	.01
☐ 231 Jeff Burroughs	.05	.02	.01
☐ 236 Tom Paciorek	.05	.02	.01
☐ 241 Pat Putnam	.05	.02	.01
☐ 246 Lloyd Moseby	.05	.02	.01
☐ 251 Barry Bonnell	.05	.02	.01

1982 Topps Team Checklist Sheet

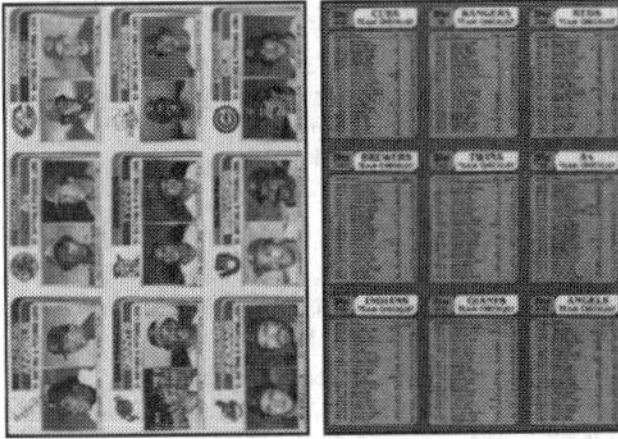

As part of a mail-away offer, Topps offered all 26 1982 team checklist cards on an uncut sheet. These cards enabled the collector to have an easy reference for which card(s) he/she needed to finish their sets. When cut from the sheet, all cards measure the standard-size.

	NRMT	VG-E	GOOD
COMPLETE SET (1)	15.00	6.75	1.85
COMMON SHEET (1)	15.00	6.75	1.85
☐ 1 Team Checklist Sheet	15.00	6.75	1.85

1982 Topps Traded

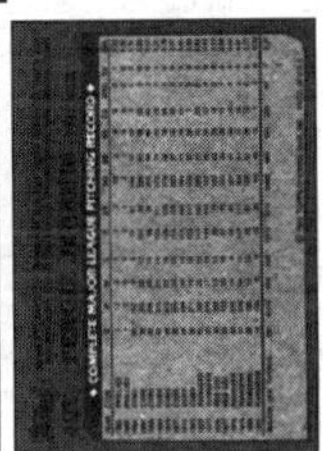

The cards in this 132-card set measure the standard size. The 1982 Topps Traded or extended series is distinguished by a "T" printed after the number (located on the reverse). This was the first time Topps began a tradition of newly numbering (and alphabetizing) their traded series from 1T to 132T. All 131 player photos used in the set are completely new. Of this total, 112 individuals are seen in the uniform of their new team, 11 youngsters have been elevated to single card status from multi-player "Future Stars" cards, and eight more are entirely new to the 1982 Topps lineup. The backs are almost completely red in color with black print. There are no key Rookie Cards in this set. Although the Cal Ripken card is this set's most valuable card, it is not his Rookie Card since he had already been included in the 1982 regular set, albeit on a multi-player card.

	NRMT	VG-E	GOOD
COMPLETE FACT.SET (132)	300.00	135.00	38.00
COMMON CARD (1T-132T)	.25	.11	.03
☐ 1T Doyle Alexander	.25	.11	.03
☐ 2T Jesse Barfield	.50	.23	.06
☐ 3T Ross Baumgarten	.25	.11	.03
☐ 4T Steve Bedrosian	.50	.23	.06
☐ 5T Mark Belanger	.50	.23	.06
☐ 6T Kurt Bevacqua	.25	.11	.03
☐ 7T Tim Blackwell	.25	.11	.03
☐ 8T Vida Blue	.50	.23	.06
☐ 9T Bob Boone	.50	.23	.06
☐ 10T Larry Bowa	.50	.23	.06
☐ 11T Dan Briggs	.25	.11	.03
☐ 12T Bobby Brown	.25	.11	.03
☐ 13T Tom Brunansky	.50	.23	.06
☐ 14T Jeff Burroughs	.25	.11	.03
☐ 15T Enos Cabell	.25	.11	.03
☐ 16T Bill Campbell	.25	.11	.03
☐ 17T Bobby Castillo	.25	.11	.03
☐ 18T Bill Caudill	.25	.11	.03
☐ 19T Cesar Cedeno	.50	.23	.06
☐ 20T Dave Collins	.25	.11	.03
☐ 21T Doug Corbett	.25	.11	.03
☐ 22T Al Cowens	.25	.11	.03
☐ 23T Chili Davis	3.00	1.35	.35
☐ 24T Dick Davis	.25	.11	.03
☐ 25T Ron Davis	.25	.11	.03
☐ 26T Doug DeCinces	.50	.23	.06
☐ 27T Ivan DeJesus	.25	.11	.03
☐ 28T Bob Dernier	.25	.11	.03
☐ 29T Bo Diaz	.25	.11	.03
☐ 30T Roger Erickson	.25	.11	.03
☐ 31T Jim Essian	.25	.11	.03
☐ 32T Ed Farmer	.25	.11	.03
☐ 33T Doug Flynn	.25	.11	.03
☐ 34T Tim Foli	.25	.11	.03

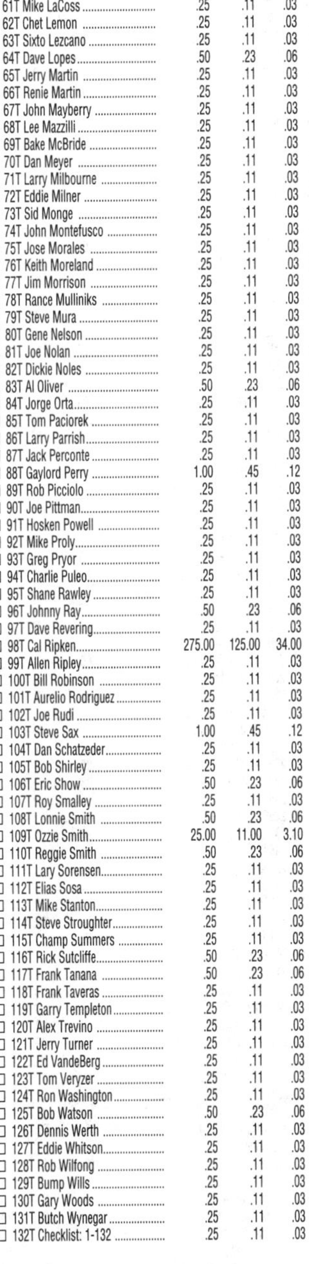

	NRMT	VG-E	GOOD
☐ 35T Dan Ford	.25	.11	.03
☐ 36T George Foster	.50	.23	.06
☐ 37T Dave Frost	.25	.11	.03
☐ 38T Rich Gale	.25	.11	.03
☐ 39T Ron Gardenhire	.25	.11	.03
☐ 40T Ken Griffey	.50	.23	.06
☐ 41T Greg Harris	.25	.11	.03
☐ 42T Von Hayes	.50	.23	.06
☐ 43T Larry Herndon	.25	.11	.03
☐ 44T Kent Hrbek	2.00	.90	.25
☐ 45T Mike Ivie	.25	.11	.03
☐ 46T Grant Jackson	.25	.11	.03
☐ 47T Reggie Jackson	10.00	4.50	1.25
☐ 48T Ron Jackson	.25	.11	.03
☐ 49T Fergie Jenkins	1.00	.45	.12
☐ 50T Lamar Johnson	.25	.11	.03
☐ 51T Randy Johnson	.25	.11	.03
☐ 52T Jay Johnstone	.50	.23	.06
☐ 53T Mick Kelleher	.25	.11	.03
☐ 54T Steve Kemp	.25	.11	.03
☐ 55T Junior Kennedy	.25	.11	.03
☐ 56T Jim Kern	.25	.11	.03
☐ 57T Ray Knight	.50	.23	.06
☐ 58T Wayne Krenchicki	.25	.11	.03
☐ 59T Mike Krukow	.25	.11	.03
☐ 60T Duane Kuiper	.25	.11	.03
☐ 61T Mike LaCoss	.25	.11	.03
☐ 62T Chet Lemon	.25	.11	.03
☐ 63T Sixto Lezcano	.25	.11	.03
☐ 64T Dave Lopes	.50	.23	.06
☐ 65T Jerry Martin	.25	.11	.03
☐ 66T Renie Martin	.25	.11	.03
☐ 67T John Mayberry	.25	.11	.03
☐ 68T Lee Mazzilli	.25	.11	.03
☐ 69T Bake McBride	.25	.11	.03
☐ 70T Dan Meyer	.25	.11	.03
☐ 71T Larry Milbourne	.25	.11	.03
☐ 72T Eddie Milner	.25	.11	.03
☐ 73T Sid Monge	.25	.11	.03
☐ 74T John Montefusco	.25	.11	.03
☐ 75T Jose Morales	.25	.11	.03
☐ 76T Keith Moreland	.25	.11	.03
☐ 77T Jim Morrison	.25	.11	.03
☐ 78T Rance Mulliniks	.25	.11	.03
☐ 79T Steve Mura	.25	.11	.03
☐ 80T Gene Nelson	.25	.11	.03
☐ 81T Joe Nolan	.25	.11	.03
☐ 82T Dickie Noles	.25	.11	.03
☐ 83T Al Oliver	.50	.23	.06
☐ 84T Jorge Orta	.25	.11	.03
☐ 85T Tom Paciorek	.25	.11	.03
☐ 86T Larry Parrish	.25	.11	.03
☐ 87T Jack Perconte	.25	.11	.03
☐ 88T Gaylord Perry	1.00	.45	.12
☐ 89T Rob Picciolo	.25	.11	.03
☐ 90T Joe Pittman	.25	.11	.03
☐ 91T Hosken Powell	.25	.11	.03
☐ 92T Mike Proly	.25	.11	.03
☐ 93T Greg Pryor	.25	.11	.03
☐ 94T Charlie Puleo	.25	.11	.03
☐ 95T Shane Rawley	.25	.11	.03
☐ 96T Johnny Ray	.50	.23	.06
☐ 97T Dave Revering	.25	.11	.03
☐ 98T Cal Ripken	275.00	125.00	34.00
☐ 99T Allen Ripley	.25	.11	.03
☐ 100T Bill Robinson	.25	.11	.03
☐ 101T Aurelio Rodriguez	.25	.11	.03
☐ 102T Joe Rudi	.25	.11	.03
☐ 103T Steve Sax	1.00	.45	.12
☐ 104T Dan Schatzeder	.25	.11	.03
☐ 105T Bob Shirley	.25	.11	.03
☐ 106T Eric Show	.50	.23	.06
☐ 107T Roy Smalley	.25	.11	.03
☐ 108T Lonnie Smith	.50	.23	.06
☐ 109T Ozzie Smith	25.00	11.00	3.10
☐ 110T Reggie Smith	.50	.23	.06
☐ 111T Lary Sorensen	.25	.11	.03
☐ 112T Elias Sosa	.25	.11	.03
☐ 113T Mike Stanton	.25	.11	.03
☐ 114T Steve Stroughter	.25	.11	.03
☐ 115T Champ Summers	.25	.11	.03
☐ 116T Rick Sutcliffe	.50	.23	.06
☐ 117T Frank Tanana	.50	.23	.06
☐ 118T Frank Taveras	.25	.11	.03
☐ 119T Garry Templeton	.25	.11	.03
☐ 120T Alex Trevino	.25	.11	.03
☐ 121T Jerry Turner	.25	.11	.03
☐ 122T Ed VandeBerg	.25	.11	.03
☐ 123T Tom Veryzer	.25	.11	.03
☐ 124T Ron Washington	.25	.11	.03
☐ 125T Bob Watson	.50	.23	.06
☐ 126T Dennis Werth	.25	.11	.03
☐ 127T Eddie Whitson	.25	.11	.03
☐ 128T Rob Wilfong	.25	.11	.03
☐ 129T Bump Wills	.25	.11	.03
☐ 130T Gary Woods	.25	.11	.03
☐ 131T Butch Wynegar	.25	.11	.03
☐ 132T Checklist: 1-132	.25	.11	.03

1982 Topps/O-Pee-Chee Stickers

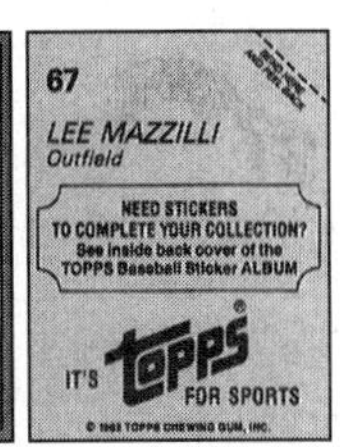

67
LEE MAZZILLI
Outfield
NEED STICKERS TO COMPLETE YOUR COLLECTION? See inside back cover of the TOPPS Baseball Sticker ALBUM
IT'S
topps
FOR SPORTS

Made for Topps and O-Pee-Chee by Panini, an Italian company, these 260 stickers measure 1 15/16" by 2 9/16" and are numbered on both front and back. The fronts feature color player photos with color borders, blue for the NL and red for the AL. The backs carry the player's name and position and a bilingual ad for O-Pee-Chee. Team affiliations are not shown. The stickers were issued both as inserts in the regular 1982 issue and in individual gumless packs. An album onto which the stickers could be affixed was available at retail stores. The album and the sticker numbering are organized as follows: League Leaders (1-16), Atlanta Braves (17-24), Chicago Cubs (25-32), Cincinnati Reds (33-40), Houston Astros (41-48), Los Angeles Dodgers (49-56), Montreal Expos (57-65), New York Mets (66-72), Philadelphia Phillies (73-80), Pittsburgh Pirates (81-88), St. Louis Cardinals (89-96), San Diego Padres (97-104), San Francisco Giants (105-112), Highlights (113-120), NL Foil All-Stars (121-130), AL Foil All-Stars (131-140), Baltimore Orioles (141-148), Boston Red Sox (149-156), California Angels (157-164), Chicago White Sox (165-172) Cleveland Indians (173-180), Detroit Tigers (181-188), Kansas City Royals (189-196), Milwaukee Brewers (197-204), Minnesota Twins (205-212), New York Yankees (213-221), Oakland A's (222-228), Seattle Mariners (229-236), Texas Rangers (237-244), Toronto Blue Jays (245-252) and postseason games (253-260).

	NRMT	VG-E	GOOD
COMPLETE SET (260)	15.00	6.75	1.85
COMMON STICKER (1-120)	.05	.02	.01
COMMON FOIL (121-140)	.10	.05	.01
COMMON STICKER (141-260)	.05	.02	.01
*TOPPS AND OPC: SAME VALUE			
☐ 1 Bill Madlock LL	.10	.05	.01
☐ 2 Carney Lansford LL	.10	.05	.01
☐ 3 Mike Schmidt LL	.60	.25	.07
☐ 4 Tony Armas LL	.30	.14	.04
Bobby Grich			
Dwight Evans			
Eddie Murray			
☐ 5 Mike Schmidt LL	.60	.25	.07
☐ 6 Eddie Murray LL	.60	.25	.07
☐ 7 Tim Raines LL	.15	.07	.02
☐ 8 Rickey Henderson LL	.60	.25	.07
☐ 9 Tom Seaver LL	.40	.18	.05
☐ 10 Steve McCatty LL	.05	.02	.01
Dennis Martinez			
Pete Vuckovich			
Jack Morris			
☐ 11 Fernando Valenzuela LL	.15	.07	.02
☐ 12 Len Barker LL	.05	.02	.01
☐ 13 Nolan Ryan LL	1.50	.70	.19
☐ 14 Steve McCatty LL	.05	.02	.01
☐ 15 Bruce Sutter LL	.10	.05	.01
☐ 16 Rollie Fingers LL	.15	.07	.02
☐ 17 Chris Chambliss	.05	.02	.01
☐ 18 Bob Horner	.10	.05	.01
☐ 19 Dale Murphy	.40	.18	.05
☐ 20 Phil Niekro	.15	.07	.02
☐ 21 Bruce Benedict	.05	.02	.01
☐ 22 Claudell Washington	.05	.02	.01
☐ 23 Glenn Hubbard	.05	.02	.01
☐ 24 Rick Camp	.05	.02	.01
☐ 25 Leon Durham	.10	.05	.01
☐ 26 Ken Reitz	.05	.02	.01
☐ 27 Dick Tidrow	.05	.02	.01
☐ 28 Tim Blackwell	.05	.02	.01
☐ 29 Bill Buckner	.10	.05	.01
☐ 30 Steve Henderson	.05	.02	.01
☐ 31 Mike Krukow	.05	.02	.01
☐ 32 Ivan DeJesus	.05	.02	.01
☐ 33 Dave Collins	.05	.02	.01
☐ 34 Ron Oester	.05	.02	.01
☐ 35 Johnny Bench	.75	.35	.09
☐ 36 Tom Seaver	.75	.35	.09
☐ 37 Dave Concepcion	.10	.05	.01
☐ 38 Tom Hume	.05	.02	.01
☐ 39 Ray Knight	.10	.05	.01
☐ 40 George Foster	.10	.05	.01
☐ 41 Nolan Ryan	3.00	1.35	.35
☐ 42 Terry Puhl	.05	.02	.01
☐ 43 Art Howe	.10	.05	.01
☐ 44 Jose Cruz	.10	.05	.01
☐ 45 Bob Knepper	.05	.02	.01
☐ 46 Craig Reynolds	.05	.02	.01
☐ 47 Cesar Cedeno	.10	.05	.01
☐ 48 Alan Ashby	.05	.02	.01
☐ 49 Ken Landreaux	.05	.02	.01
☐ 50 Fernando Valenzuela	.40	.18	.05
☐ 51 Ron Cey	.10	.05	.01
☐ 52 Dusty Baker	.10	.05	.01
☐ 53 Burt Hooton	.05	.02	.01
☐ 54 Steve Garvey	.15	.07	.02
☐ 55 Pedro Guerrero	.10	.05	.01
☐ 56 Jerry Reuss	.10	.05	.01
☐ 57 Andre Dawson	.60	.25	.07

☐ 58 Chris Speier	.05	.02	.01
☐ 59 Steve Rogers	.05	.02	.01
☐ 60 Warren Cromartie	.05	.02	.01
☐ 61 Gary Carter	.25	.11	.03
☐ 62 Tim Raines	.40	.18	.05
☐ 63 Scott Sanderson	.05	.02	.01
☐ 64 Larry Parrish	.05	.02	.01
☐ 65 Joel Youngblood	.05	.02	.01
☐ 66 Neil Allen	.05	.02	.01
☐ 67 Lee Mazzilli	.05	.02	.01
☐ 68 Hubie Brooks	.10	.05	.01
☐ 69 Ellis Valentine	.05	.02	.01
☐ 70 Doug Flynn	.05	.02	.01
☐ 71 Pat Zachry	.05	.02	.01
☐ 72 Dave Kingman	.10	.05	.01
☐ 73 Garry Maddox	.05	.02	.01
☐ 74 Mike Schmidt	1.25	.55	.16
☐ 75 Steve Carlton	.60	.25	.07
☐ 76 Manny Trillo	.05	.02	.01
☐ 77 Bob Boone	.10	.05	.01
☐ 78 Pete Rose	1.25	.55	.16
☐ 79 Gary Matthews	.10	.05	.01
☐ 80 Larry Bowa	.10	.05	.01
☐ 81 Omar Moreno	.05	.02	.01
☐ 82 Rick Rhoden	.05	.02	.01
☐ 83 Bill Madlock	.10	.05	.01
☐ 84 Mike Easler	.05	.02	.01
☐ 85 Willie Stargell	.40	.18	.05
☐ 86 Jim Bibby	.05	.02	.01
☐ 87 Dave Parker	.10	.05	.01
☐ 88 Tim Foli	.05	.02	.01
☐ 89 Ken Oberkfell	.05	.02	.01
☐ 90 Bob Forsch	.05	.02	.01
☐ 91 George Hendrick	.05	.02	.01
☐ 92 Keith Hernandez	.10	.05	.01
☐ 93 Darrell Porter	.05	.02	.01
☐ 94 Bruce Sutter	.10	.05	.01
☐ 95 Sixto Lezcano	.05	.02	.01
☐ 96 Garry Templeton	.05	.02	.01
☐ 97 Juan Eichelberger	.05	.02	.01
☐ 98 Broderick Perkins	.05	.02	.01
☐ 99 Ruppert Jones	.05	.02	.01
☐ 100 Terry Kennedy	.05	.02	.01
☐ 101 Luis Salazar	.05	.02	.01
☐ 102 Gary Lucas	.05	.02	.01
☐ 103 Gene Richards	.05	.02	.01
☐ 104 Ozzie Smith	2.00	.90	.25
☐ 105 Enos Cabell	.05	.02	.01
☐ 106 Jack Clark	.10	.05	.01
☐ 107 Greg Minton	.05	.02	.01
☐ 108 Johnnie LeMaster	.05	.02	.01
☐ 109 Larry Herndon	.05	.02	.01
☐ 110 Milt May	.05	.02	.01
☐ 111 Vida Blue	.10	.05	.01
☐ 112 Darrell Evans	.10	.05	.01
☐ 113 Len Barker HL	.05	.02	.01
☐ 114 Julio Cruz HL	.05	.02	.01
☐ 115 Billy Martin MG HL	.10	.05	.01
☐ 116 Tim Raines HL	.15	.07	.02
☐ 117 Pete Rose HL	.60	.25	.07
☐ 118 Bill Stein HL	.05	.02	.01
☐ 119 Fern.Valenzuela HL	.15	.07	.02
☐ 120 Carl Yastrzemski HL	.30	.14	.04
☐ 121 Pete Rose FOIL	1.50	.70	.19
☐ 122 Manny Trillo FOIL	.10	.05	.01
☐ 123 Mike Schmidt FOIL	1.50	.70	.19
☐ 124 Dave Concepcion FOIL	.15	.07	.02
☐ 125 Andre Dawson FOIL	.75	.35	.09
☐ 126 George Foster FOIL	.15	.07	.02
☐ 127 Dave Parker FOIL	.25	.11	.03
☐ 128 Gary Carter FOIL	.30	.14	.04
☐ 129 Steve Carlton FOIL	.75	.35	.09
☐ 130 Bruce Sutter FOIL	.15	.07	.02
☐ 131 Rod Carew FOIL	.75	.35	.09
☐ 132 Jerry Remy FOIL	.10	.05	.01
☐ 133 George Brett FOIL	2.50	1.10	.30
☐ 134 Rick Burleson FOIL	.10	.05	.01
☐ 135 Dwight Evans FOIL	.15	.07	.02
☐ 136 Ken Singleton FOIL	.10	.05	.01
☐ 137 Dave Winfield FOIL	.75	.35	.09
☐ 138 Carlton Fisk FOIL	.75	.35	.09
☐ 139 Jack Morris FOIL	.25	.11	.03
☐ 140 Rich Gossage FOIL	.15	.07	.02
☐ 141 Al Bumbry	.10	.05	.01
☐ 142 Doug DeCinces	.05	.02	.01
☐ 143 Scott McGregor	.05	.02	.01
☐ 144 Ken Singleton	.05	.02	.01
☐ 145 Eddie Murray	1.50	.70	.19
☐ 146 Jim Palmer	.40	.18	.05
☐ 147 Rich Dauer	.05	.02	.01
☐ 148 Mike Flanagan	.10	.05	.01
☐ 149 Jerry Remy	.05	.02	.01
☐ 150 Jim Rice	.10	.05	.01
☐ 151 Mike Torrez	.05	.02	.01
☐ 152 Tony Perez	.15	.07	.02
☐ 153 Dwight Evans	.10	.05	.01
☐ 154 Mark Clear	.05	.02	.01
☐ 155 Carl Yastrzemski	.60	.25	.07
☐ 156 Carney Lansford	.10	.05	.01
☐ 157 Rick Burleson	.05	.02	.01
☐ 158 Don Baylor	.15	.07	.02
☐ 159 Ken Forsch	.05	.02	.01
☐ 160 Rod Carew	.60	.25	.07
☐ 161 Fred Lynn	.10	.05	.01
☐ 162 Bob Grich	.10	.05	.01
☐ 163 Dan Ford	.05	.02	.01
☐ 164 Butch Hobson	.05	.02	.01
☐ 165 Greg Luzinski	.10	.05	.01
☐ 166 Rich Dotson	.05	.02	.01
☐ 167 Billy Almon	.05	.02	.01
☐ 168 Chet Lemon	.05	.02	.01
☐ 169 Steve Trout	.05	.02	.01
☐ 170 Carlton Fisk	.60	.25	.07
☐ 171 Tony Bernazard	.05	.02	.01
☐ 172 Ron LeFlore	.10	.05	.01
☐ 173 Bert Blyleven	.15	.07	.02
☐ 174 Andre Thornton	.05	.02	.01
☐ 175 Jorge Orta	.05	.02	.01
☐ 176 Bo Diaz	.05	.02	.01
☐ 177 Toby Harrah	.10	.05	.01
☐ 178 Len Barker	.05	.02	.01
☐ 179 Rick Manning	.05	.02	.01
☐ 180 Mike Hargrove	.10	.05	.01
☐ 181 Alan Trammell	.40	.18	.05
☐ 182 Al Cowens	.05	.02	.01
☐ 183 Jack Morris	.10	.05	.01
☐ 184 Kirk Gibson	.30	.14	.04
☐ 185 Steve Kemp	.05	.02	.01
☐ 186 Milt Wilcox	.05	.02	.01
☐ 187 Lou Whitaker	.30	.14	.04
☐ 188 Lance Parrish	.15	.07	.02
☐ 189 Willie Wilson	.05	.02	.01
☐ 190 George Brett	2.00	.90	.25
☐ 191 Dennis Leonard	.05	.02	.01
☐ 192 John Wathan	.05	.02	.01
☐ 193 Frank White	.10	.05	.01
☐ 194 Amos Otis	.10	.05	.01
☐ 195 Larry Gura	.05	.02	.01
☐ 196 Willie Aikens	.05	.02	.01
☐ 197 Ben Oglivie	.10	.05	.01
☐ 198 Rollie Fingers	.30	.14	.04
☐ 199 Cecil Cooper	.10	.05	.01
☐ 200 Paul Molitor	.75	.35	.09
☐ 201 Ted Simmons	.10	.05	.01
☐ 202 Pete Vuckovich	.05	.02	.01
☐ 203 Robin Yount	.60	.25	.07
☐ 204 Gorman Thomas	.10	.05	.01
☐ 205 Rob Wilfong	.05	.02	.01
☐ 206 Hosken Powell	.05	.02	.01
☐ 207 Roy Smalley	.05	.02	.01
☐ 208 Butch Wynegar	.05	.02	.01
☐ 209 John Castino	.05	.02	.01
☐ 210 Doug Corbett	.05	.02	.01
☐ 211 Roger Erickson	.05	.02	.01
☐ 212 Mickey Hatcher	.05	.02	.01
☐ 213 Dave Winfield	.60	.25	.07
☐ 214 Tommy John	.15	.07	.02
☐ 215 Graig Nettles	.10	.05	.01
☐ 216 Reggie Jackson	.75	.35	.09
☐ 217 Rich Gossage	.15	.07	.02
☐ 218 Rick Cerone	.05	.02	.01
☐ 219 Willie Randolph	.10	.05	.01
☐ 220 Jerry Mumphrey	.05	.02	.01
☐ 221 Rickey Henderson	1.25	.55	.16
☐ 222 Mike Norris	.05	.02	.01
☐ 223 Jim Spencer	.05	.02	.01
☐ 224 Tony Armas	.05	.02	.01
☐ 225 Matt Keough	.05	.02	.01
☐ 226 Cliff Johnson	.05	.02	.01
☐ 227 Dwayne Murphy	.05	.02	.01
☐ 228 Steve McCatty	.05	.02	.01
☐ 229 Richie Zisk	.05	.02	.01
☐ 230 Lenny Randle	.05	.02	.01
☐ 231 Jeff Burroughs	.05	.02	.01
☐ 232 Bruce Bochte	.05	.02	.01
☐ 233 Gary Gray	.05	.02	.01
☐ 234 Floyd Bannister	.05	.02	.01
☐ 235 Julio Cruz	.05	.02	.01
☐ 236 Tom Paciorek	.05	.02	.01
☐ 237 Danny Darwin	.10	.05	.01
☐ 238 Buddy Bell	.10	.05	.01
☐ 239 Al Oliver	.10	.05	.01
☐ 240 Jim Sundberg	.10	.05	.01
☐ 241 Pat Putnam	.05	.02	.01
☐ 242 Steve Comer	.05	.02	.01
☐ 243 Mickey Rivers	.05	.02	.01
☐ 244 Bump Wills	.05	.02	.01
☐ 245 Damaso Garcia	.05	.02	.01
☐ 246 Lloyd Moseby	.05	.02	.01
☐ 247 Ernie Whitt	.05	.02	.01
☐ 248 John Mayberry	.05	.02	.01
☐ 249 Otto Velez	.05	.02	.01
☐ 250 Dave Stieb	.10	.05	.01
☐ 251 Barry Bonnell	.05	.02	.01
☐ 252 Alfredo Griffin	.05	.02	.01
☐ 253 Gary Carter PLAY	.10	.05	.01
☐ 254 1981 AL Playoffs	.05	.02	.01
(Action at plate)			
☐ 255 Dodgers Team	.10	.05	.01
World Champions			
(Left half photo)			
☐ 256 Dodgers Team	.10	.05	.01
World Champions			
(Right half photo)			
☐ 257 Fernando Valenzuela WS	.15	.07	.02
☐ 258 Steve Garvey WS	.10	.05	.01
☐ 259 Jerry Reuss WS	.10	.05	.01
Steve Yeager			
☐ 260 Pedro Guerrero WS	.10	.05	.01
☐ xx Album	1.00	.45	.12

1983 Topps

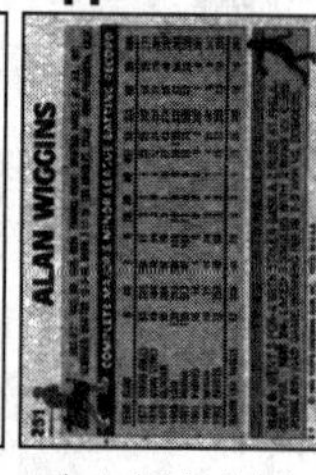

The cards in this 792-card set measure the standard size. Each player card front features a large action shot with a small cameo portrait at bottom right. There are special series for AL and NL All Stars (386-407), League Leaders (701-708), and Record Breakers (1-6). In addition, there are 34 "Super Veteran" (SV) cards and six numbered checklist cards. The Super Veteran cards are oriented horizontally and show two pictures of the featured player, a recent picture and a picture showing the player as a rookie. The team cards are actually Team Leader (TL) cards picturing the batting and pitching leader for that team with a checklist back. Cards were primarily issued in 15-card wax packs and 51-card rack packs. Notable Rookie Cards include Wade Boggs, Tony Gwynn and Ryne Sandberg.

	NRMT	VG-E	GOOD
COMPLETE SET (792)	125.00	55.00	15.50
COMMON CARD (1-792)	.10	.05	.01
☐ 1 Tony Armas RB	.50	.23	.06
☐ 2 Rickey Henderson RB	1.00	.45	.12
Sets modern SB record			
☐ 3 Greg Minton RB	.10	.05	.01
269 1/3 homerless			
innings streak			
☐ 4 Lance Parrish RB	.25	.11	.03
☐ 5 Manny Trillo RB	.25	.11	.03
479 consecutive			
errorless chances,			
second baseman			
☐ 6 John Wathan RB	.10	.05	.01
ML catcher steals, season			
☐ 7 Gene Richards	.10	.05	.01
☐ 8 Steve Balboni	.10	.05	.01
☐ 9 Joey McLaughlin	.10	.05	.01
☐ 10 Gorman Thomas	.10	.05	.01
☐ 11 Billy Gardner MG	.10	.05	.01
☐ 12 Paul Mirabella	.10	.05	.01
☐ 13 Larry Herndon	.10	.05	.01
☐ 14 Frank LaCorte	.10	.05	.01
☐ 15 Ron Cey	.25	.11	.03
☐ 16 George Vukovich	.10	.05	.01
☐ 17 Kent Tekulve	.25	.11	.03
☐ 18 Kent Tekulve SV	.10	.05	.01
☐ 19 Oscar Gamble	.10	.05	.01
☐ 20 Carlton Fisk	1.00	.45	.12
☐ 21 Baltimore Orioles TL	.50	.23	.06
BA: Eddie Murray			
ERA: Jim Palmer			
(Checklist on back)			
☐ 22 Randy Martz	.10	.05	.01
☐ 23 Mike Heath	.10	.05	.01
☐ 24 Steve Mura	.10	.05	.01
☐ 25 Hal McRae	.25	.11	.03
☐ 26 Jerry Royster	.10	.05	.01
☐ 27 Doug Corbett	.10	.05	.01
☐ 28 Bruce Bochte	.10	.05	.01
☐ 29 Randy Jones	.10	.05	.01
☐ 30 Jim Rice	.25	.11	.03
☐ 31 Bill Gullickson	.25	.11	.03
☐ 32 Dave Bergman	.10	.05	.01
☐ 33 Jack O'Connor	.10	.05	.01
☐ 34 Paul Householder	.10	.05	.01
☐ 35 Rollie Fingers	.50	.23	.06
☐ 36 Rollie Fingers SV	.25	.11	.03
☐ 37 Darrell Johnson MG	.10	.05	.01
☐ 38 Tim Flannery	.10	.05	.01
☐ 39 Terry Puhl	.10	.05	.01
☐ 40 Fernando Valenzuela	.50	.23	.06
☐ 41 Jerry Turner	.10	.05	.01
☐ 42 Dale Murray	.50	.23	.06
☐ 43 Bob Dernier	.10	.05	.01
☐ 44 Don Robinson	.10	.05	.01
☐ 45 John Mayberry	.10	.05	.01
☐ 46 Richard Dotson	.10	.05	.01
☐ 47 Dave McKay	.10	.05	.01
☐ 48 Lary Sorensen	.10	.05	.01
☐ 49 Willie McGee	.50	.23	.06
☐ 50 Bob Horner UER	.10	.05	.01
('82 RBI total 7)			
☐ 51 Chicago Cubs TL	.25	.11	.03
BA: Leon Durham			
ERA: Fergie Jenkins			
(Checklist on back)			
☐ 52 Onix Concepcion	.10	.05	.01
☐ 53 Mike Witt	.10	.05	.01
☐ 54 Jim Maler	.10	.05	.01
☐ 55 Mookie Wilson	.25	.11	.03
☐ 56 Chuck Rainey	.10	.05	.01
☐ 57 Tim Blackwell	.10	.05	.01
☐ 58 Al Holland	.10	.05	.01
☐ 59 Benny Ayala	.10	.05	.01
☐ 60 Johnny Bench	1.00	.45	.12
☐ 61 Johnny Bench SV	.50	.23	.06
☐ 62 Bob McClure	.10	.05	.01
☐ 63 Rick Monday	.10	.05	.01
☐ 64 Bill Stein	.10	.05	.01
☐ 65 Jack Morris	.25	.11	.03
☐ 66 Bob Lillis MG	.10	.05	.01
☐ 67 Sal Butera	.10	.05	.01
☐ 68 Eric Show	.10	.05	.01
☐ 69 Lee Lacy	.10	.05	.01
☐ 70 Steve Carlton	1.00	.45	.12
☐ 71 Steve Carlton SV	.50	.23	.06
☐ 72 Tom Paciorek	.10	.05	.01
☐ 73 Allen Ripley	.10	.05	.01
☐ 74 Julio Gonzalez	.10	.05	.01
☐ 75 Amos Otis	.25	.11	.03
☐ 76 Rick Mahler	.10	.05	.01
☐ 77 Hosken Powell	.10	.05	.01
☐ 78 Bill Caudill	.10	.05	.01
☐ 79 Mick Kelleher	.10	.05	.01
☐ 80 George Foster	.25	.11	.03
☐ 81 Yankees TL	.25	.11	.03
BA: Jerry Mumphrey			
ERA: Dave Righetti			
(Checklist on back)			
☐ 82 Bruce Hurst	.25	.11	.03
☐ 83 Ryne Sandberg	25.00	11.00	3.10
☐ 84 Milt May	.10	.05	.01
☐ 85 Ken Singleton	.25	.11	.03
☐ 86 Tom Hume	.10	.05	.01
☐ 87 Joe Rudi	.10	.05	.01
☐ 88 Jim Gantner	.25	.11	.03
☐ 89 Leon Roberts	.10	.05	.01
☐ 90 Jerry Reuss	.25	.11	.03
☐ 91 Larry Milbourne	.10	.05	.01
☐ 92 Mike LaCoss	.10	.05	.01
☐ 93 John Castino	.10	.05	.01
☐ 94 Dave Edwards	.10	.05	.01
☐ 95 Alan Trammell	.50	.23	.06
☐ 96 Dick Howser MG	.25	.11	.03
☐ 97 Ross Baumgarten	.10	.05	.01
☐ 98 Vance Law	.10	.05	.01
☐ 99 Dickie Noles	.10	.05	.01
☐ 100 Pete Rose	2.00	.90	.25
☐ 101 Pete Rose SV	1.00	.45	.12
☐ 102 Dave Beard	.10	.05	.01
☐ 103 Darrell Porter	.10	.05	.01
☐ 104 Bob Walk	.10	.05	.01
☐ 105 Don Baylor	.50	.23	.06
☐ 106 Gene Nelson	.10	.05	.01
☐ 107 Mike Jorgensen	.10	.05	.01
☐ 108 Glenn Hoffman	.10	.05	.01
☐ 109 Luis Leal	.10	.05	.01
☐ 110 Ken Griffey	.25	.11	.03
☐ 111 Montreal Expos TL	.25	.11	.03
BA: Al Oliver			
ERA: Steve Rogers			
(Checklist on back)			
☐ 112 Bob Shirley	.10	.05	.01
☐ 113 Ron Roenicke	.10	.05	.01
☐ 114 Jim Slaton	.10	.05	.01
☐ 115 Chili Davis	.25	.11	.03
☐ 116 Dave Schmidt	.10	.05	.01
☐ 117 Alan Knicely	.10	.05	.01
☐ 118 Chris Welsh	.10	.05	.01
☐ 119 Tom Brookens	.10	.05	.01
☐ 120 Len Barker	.10	.05	.01
☐ 121 Mickey Hatcher	.10	.05	.01
☐ 122 Jimmy Smith	.10	.05	.01
☐ 123 George Frazier	.10	.05	.01
☐ 124 Marc Hill	.10	.05	.01
☐ 125 Leon Durham	.10	.05	.01
☐ 126 Joe Torre MG	.25	.11	.03
☐ 127 Preston Hanna	.10	.05	.01
☐ 128 Mike Ramsey	.10	.05	.01
☐ 129 Checklist: 1-132	.25	.11	.03
☐ 130 Dave Stieb	.25	.11	.03
☐ 131 Ed Ott	.10	.05	.01
☐ 132 Todd Cruz	.10	.05	.01
☐ 133 Jim Barr	.10	.05	.01
☐ 134 Hubie Brooks	.25	.11	.03
☐ 135 Dwight Evans	.25	.11	.03
☐ 136 Willie Aikens	.10	.05	.01
☐ 137 Woodie Fryman	.10	.05	.01
☐ 138 Rick Dempsey	.25	.11	.03
☐ 139 Bruce Berenyi	.10	.05	.01
☐ 140 Willie Randolph	.25	.11	.03
☐ 141 Indians TL	.25	.11	.03
BA: Toby Harrah			
ERA: Rick Sutcliffe			
(Checklist on back)			
☐ 142 Mike Caldwell	.10	.05	.01
☐ 143 Joe Pettini	.10	.05	.01
☐ 144 Mark Wagner	.10	.05	.01
☐ 145 Don Sutton	.50	.23	.06
☐ 146 Don Sutton SV	.25	.11	.03
☐ 147 Rick Leach	.10	.05	.01
☐ 148 Dave Roberts	.10	.05	.01
☐ 149 Johnny Ray	.10	.05	.01
☐ 150 Bruce Sutter	.25	.11	.03
☐ 151 Bruce Sutter SV	.10	.05	.01
☐ 152 Jay Johnstone	.25	.11	.03
☐ 153 Jerry Koosman	.25	.11	.03
☐ 154 Johnnie LeMaster	.10	.05	.01
☐ 155 Dan Quisenberry	.25	.11	.03
☐ 156 Billy Martin MG	.25	.11	.03

☐ 157 Steve Bedrosian .25 .11 .03
☐ 158 Rob Wilfong .10 .05 .01
☐ 159 Mike Stanton .10 .05 .01
☐ 160 Dave Kingman .25 .11 .03
☐ 161 Dave Kingman SV .10 .05 .01
☐ 162 Mark Clear .10 .05 .01
☐ 163 Cal Ripken 20.00 9.00 2.50
☐ 164 David Palmer .10 .05 .01
☐ 165 Dan Driessen .10 .05 .01
☐ 166 John Pacella .10 .05 .01
☐ 167 Mark Brouhard .10 .05 .01
☐ 168 Juan Eichelberger .10 .05 .01
☐ 169 Doug Flynn .10 .05 .01
☐ 170 Steve Howe .10 .05 .01
☐ 171 Giants TL .50 .23 .06
BA: Joe Morgan
ERA: Bill Laskey
(Checklist on back)
☐ 172 Vern Ruhle .10 .05 .01
☐ 173 Jim Morrison .10 .05 .01
☐ 174 Jerry Ujdur .10 .05 .01
☐ 175 Bo Diaz .10 .05 .01
☐ 176 Dave Righetti .25 .11 .03
☐ 177 Harold Baines .25 .11 .03
☐ 178 Luis Tiant .25 .11 .03
☐ 179 Luis Tiant SV .10 .05 .01
☐ 180 Rickey Henderson 2.00 .90 .25
☐ 181 Terry Felton .10 .05 .01
☐ 182 Mike Fischlin .10 .05 .01
☐ 183 Ed VandeBerg .10 .05 .01
☐ 184 Bob Clark .10 .05 .01
☐ 185 Tim Lollar .10 .05 .01
☐ 186 Whitey Herzog MG .25 .11 .03
☐ 187 Terry Leach .10 .05 .01
☐ 188 Rick Miller .10 .05 .01
☐ 189 Dan Schatzeder .10 .05 .01
☐ 190 Cecil Cooper .25 .11 .03
☐ 191 Joe Price .10 .05 .01
☐ 192 Floyd Rayford .10 .05 .01
☐ 193 Harry Spilman .10 .05 .01
☐ 194 Cesar Geronimo .10 .05 .01
☐ 195 Bob Stoddard .10 .05 .01
☐ 196 Bill Fahey .10 .05 .01
☐ 197 Jim Eisenreich 1.00 .45 .12
☐ 198 Kiko Garcia .10 .05 .01
☐ 199 Marty Bystrom .10 .05 .01
☐ 200 Rod Carew .75 .35 .09
☐ 201 Rod Carew SV .50 .23 .06
☐ 202 Blue Jays TL .25 .11 .03
BA: Damaso Garcia
ERA: Dave Stieb
(Checklist on back)
☐ 203 Mike Morgan .10 .05 .01
☐ 204 Junior Kennedy .10 .05 .01
☐ 205 Dave Parker .25 .11 .03
☐ 206 Ken Oberkfell .10 .05 .01
☐ 207 Rick Camp .10 .05 .01
☐ 208 Dan Meyer .10 .05 .01
☐ 209 Mike Moore .25 .11 .03
☐ 210 Jack Clark .25 .11 .03
☐ 211 John Denny .10 .05 .01
☐ 212 John Stearns .10 .05 .01
☐ 213 Tom Burgmeier .10 .05 .01
☐ 214 Jerry White .10 .05 .01
☐ 215 Mario Soto .10 .05 .01
☐ 216 Tony LaRussa MG .25 .11 .03
☐ 217 Tim Stoddard .10 .05 .01
☐ 218 Roy Howell .10 .05 .01
☐ 219 Mike Armstrong .10 .05 .01
☐ 220 Dusty Baker .25 .11 .03
☐ 221 Joe Niekro .25 .11 .03
☐ 222 Damaso Garcia .10 .05 .01
☐ 223 John Montefusco .10 .05 .01
☐ 224 Mickey Rivers .10 .05 .01
☐ 225 Enos Cabell .10 .05 .01
☐ 226 Enrique Romo .10 .05 .01
☐ 227 Chris Bando .10 .05 .01
☐ 228 Joaquin Andujar .10 .05 .01
☐ 229 Phillies TL .50 .23 .06
BA: Bo Diaz
ERA: Steve Carlton
(Checklist on back)
☐ 230 Fergie Jenkins .50 .23 .06
☐ 231 Fergie Jenkins SV .25 .11 .03
☐ 232 Tom Brunansky .25 .11 .03
☐ 233 Wayne Gross .10 .05 .01
☐ 234 Larry Andersen .10 .05 .01
☐ 235 Claudell Washington .10 .05 .01
☐ 236 Steve Renko .10 .05 .01
☐ 237 Dan Norman .10 .05 .01
☐ 238 Bud Black .25 .11 .03
☐ 239 Dave Stapleton .10 .05 .01
☐ 240 Rich Gossage .50 .23 .06
☐ 241 Rich Gossage SV .25 .11 .03
☐ 242 Joe Nolan .10 .05 .01
☐ 243 Duane Walker .10 .05 .01
☐ 244 Dwight Bernard .10 .05 .01
☐ 245 Steve Sax .25 .11 .03
☐ 246 George Bamberger MG .10 .05 .01
☐ 247 Dave Smith .10 .05 .01
☐ 248 Bake McBride .10 .05 .01
☐ 249 Checklist: 133-264 .25 .11 .03
☐ 250 Bill Buckner .25 .11 .03
☐ 251 Alan Wiggins .10 .05 .01
☐ 252 Luis Aguayo .10 .05 .01
☐ 253 Larry McWilliams .10 .05 .01
☐ 254 Rick Cerone .10 .05 .01
☐ 255 Gene Garber .10 .05 .01
☐ 256 Gene Garber SV .10 .05 .01
☐ 257 Jesse Barfield .25 .11 .03
☐ 258 Manny Castillo .10 .05 .01
☐ 259 Jeff Jones .10 .05 .01
☐ 260 Steve Kemp .10 .05 .01
☐ 261 Tigers TL .25 .11 .03
BA: Larry Herndon
ERA: Dan Petry
(Checklist on back)
☐ 262 Ron Jackson .10 .05 .01
☐ 263 Renie Martin .10 .05 .01
☐ 264 Jamie Quirk .10 .05 .01
☐ 265 Joel Youngblood .10 .05 .01
☐ 266 Paul Boris .10 .05 .01
☐ 267 Terry Francona .10 .05 .01
☐ 268 Storm Davis .10 .05 .01
☐ 269 Ron Oester .10 .05 .01
☐ 270 Dennis Eckersley .50 .23 .06
☐ 271 Ed Romero .10 .05 .01
☐ 272 Frank Tanana .25 .11 .03
☐ 273 Mark Belanger .10 .05 .01
☐ 274 Terry Kennedy .10 .05 .01
☐ 275 Ray Knight .25 .11 .03
☐ 276 Gene Mauch MG .10 .05 .01
☐ 277 Rance Mulliniks .10 .05 .01
☐ 278 Kevin Hickey .10 .05 .01
☐ 279 Greg Gross .10 .05 .01
☐ 280 Bert Blyleven .50 .23 .06
☐ 281 Andre Robertson .10 .05 .01
☐ 282 Reggie Smith .50 .23 .06
(Ryne Sandberg
ducking back)
☐ 283 Reggie Smith SV .10 .05 .01
☐ 284 Jeff Lahti .10 .05 .01
☐ 285 Lance Parrish .25 .11 .03
☐ 286 Rick Langford .10 .05 .01
☐ 287 Bobby Brown .10 .05 .01
☐ 288 Joe Cowley .10 .05 .01
☐ 289 Jerry Dybzinski .10 .05 .01
☐ 290 Jeff Reardon .25 .11 .03
☐ 291 Pirates TL .25 .11 .03
BA: Bill Madlock
ERA: John Candelaria
(Checklist on back)
☐ 292 Craig Swan .10 .05 .01
☐ 293 Glenn Gulliver .10 .05 .01
☐ 294 Dave Engle .10 .05 .01
☐ 295 Jerry Remy .10 .05 .01
☐ 296 Greg Harris .10 .05 .01
☐ 297 Ned Yost .10 .05 .01
☐ 298 Floyd Chiffer .10 .05 .01
☐ 299 George Wright .10 .05 .01
☐ 300 Mike Schmidt 2.00 .90 .25
☐ 301 Mike Schmidt SV 1.00 .45 .12
☐ 302 Ernie Whitt .10 .05 .01
☐ 303 Miguel Dilone .10 .05 .01
☐ 304 Dave Rucker .10 .05 .01
☐ 305 Larry Bowa .25 .11 .03
☐ 306 Tom Lasorda MG .25 .11 .03
☐ 307 Lou Piniella .25 .11 .03
☐ 308 Jesus Vega .10 .05 .01
☐ 309 Jeff Leonard .10 .05 .01
☐ 310 Greg Luzinski .25 .11 .03
☐ 311 Glenn Brummer .10 .05 .01
☐ 312 Brian Kingman .10 .05 .01
☐ 313 Gary Gray .10 .05 .01
☐ 314 Ken Dayley .10 .05 .01
☐ 315 Rick Burleson .10 .05 .01
☐ 316 Paul Splittorff .10 .05 .01
☐ 317 Gary Rajsich .10 .05 .01
☐ 318 John Tudor .10 .05 .01
☐ 319 Lenn Sakata .10 .05 .01
☐ 320 Steve Rogers .10 .05 .01
☐ 321 Brewers TL .50 .23 .06
BA: Robin Yount
ERA: Pete Vuckovich
(Checklist on back)
☐ 322 Dave Van Gorder .10 .05 .01
☐ 323 Luis DeLeon .10 .05 .01
☐ 324 Mike Marshall .10 .05 .01
☐ 325 Von Hayes .25 .11 .03
☐ 326 Garth Iorg .10 .05 .01
☐ 327 Bobby Castillo .10 .05 .01
☐ 328 Craig Reynolds .10 .05 .01
☐ 329 Randy Niemann .10 .05 .01
☐ 330 Buddy Bell .25 .11 .03
☐ 331 Mike Krukow .10 .05 .01
☐ 332 Glenn Wilson .25 .11 .03
☐ 333 Dave LaRoche .10 .05 .01
☐ 334 Dave LaRoche SV .10 .05 .01
☐ 335 Steve Henderson .10 .05 .01
☐ 336 Rene Lachemann MG .10 .05 .01
☐ 337 Tito Landrum .10 .05 .01
☐ 338 Bob Owchinko .10 .05 .01
☐ 339 Terry Harper .10 .05 .01
☐ 340 Larry Gura .10 .05 .01
☐ 341 Doug DeCinces .25 .11 .03
☐ 342 Atlee Hammaker .10 .05 .01
☐ 343 Bob Bailor .10 .05 .01
☐ 344 Roger LaFrancois .10 .05 .01
☐ 345 Jim Clancy .10 .05 .01
☐ 346 Joe Pittman .10 .05 .01
☐ 347 Sammy Stewart .10 .05 .01
☐ 348 Alan Bannister .10 .05 .01
☐ 349 Checklist: 265-396 .25 .11 .03
☐ 350 Robin Yount 2.00 .90 .25
☐ 351 Reds TL .25 .11 .03
BA: Cesar Cedeno
ERA: Mario Soto
(Checklist on back)
☐ 352 Mike Scioscia .25 .11 .03
☐ 353 Steve Comer .10 .05 .01
☐ 354 Randy Johnson .10 .05 .01
☐ 355 Jim Bibby .10 .05 .01
☐ 356 Gary Woods .10 .05 .01
☐ 357 Len Matuszek .10 .05 .01
☐ 358 Jerry Garvin .10 .05 .01
☐ 359 Dave Collins .10 .05 .01
☐ 360 Nolan Ryan 6.00 2.70 .75
☐ 361 Nolan Ryan SV 4.00 1.80 .50
☐ 362 Bill Almon .10 .05 .01
☐ 363 John Stuper .10 .05 .01
☐ 364 Brett Butler .50 .23 .06
☐ 365 Dave Lopes .25 .11 .03
☐ 366 Dick Williams MG .10 .05 .01
☐ 367 Bud Anderson .10 .05 .01
☐ 368 Richie Zisk .10 .05 .01
☐ 369 Jesse Orosco .10 .05 .01
☐ 370 Gary Carter .25 .11 .03
☐ 371 Mike Richardt .10 .05 .01
☐ 372 Terry Crowley .10 .05 .01
☐ 373 Kevin Saucier .10 .05 .01
☐ 374 Wayne Krenchicki .10 .05 .01
☐ 375 Pete Vuckovich .10 .05 .01
☐ 376 Ken Landreaux .10 .05 .01
☐ 377 Lee May .25 .11 .03
☐ 378 Lee May SV .10 .05 .01
☐ 379 Guy Sularz .10 .05 .01
☐ 380 Ron Davis .10 .05 .01
☐ 381 Red Sox TL .25 .11 .03
BA: Jim Rice
ERA: Bob Stanley
(Checklist on back)
☐ 382 Bob Knepper .10 .05 .01
☐ 383 Ozzie Virgil .10 .05 .01
☐ 384 Dave Dravecky .50 .23 .06
☐ 385 Mike Easler .10 .05 .01
☐ 386 Rod Carew AS .50 .23 .06
☐ 387 Bob Grich AS .25 .11 .03
☐ 388 George Brett AS 2.00 .90 .25
☐ 389 Robin Yount AS 1.25 .55 .16
☐ 390 Reggie Jackson AS .75 .35 .09
☐ 391 Rickey Henderson AS 1.00 .45 .12
☐ 392 Fred Lynn AS .25 .11 .03
☐ 393 Carlton Fisk AS .50 .23 .06
☐ 394 Pete Vuckovich AS .10 .05 .01
☐ 395 Larry Gura AS .10 .05 .01
☐ 396 Dan Quisenberry AS .25 .11 .03
☐ 397 Pete Rose AS 1.00 .45 .12
☐ 398 Manny Trillo AS .10 .05 .01
☐ 399 Mike Schmidt AS 1.00 .45 .12
☐ 400 Dave Concepcion AS .25 .11 .03
☐ 401 Dale Murphy AS .50 .23 .06
☐ 402 Andre Dawson AS .50 .23 .06
☐ 403 Tim Raines AS .50 .23 .06
☐ 404 Gary Carter AS .25 .11 .03
☐ 405 Steve Rogers AS .10 .05 .01
☐ 406 Steve Carlton AS .50 .23 .06
☐ 407 Bruce Sutter AS .25 .11 .03
☐ 408 Rudy May .10 .05 .01
☐ 409 Marvis Foley .10 .05 .01
☐ 410 Phil Niekro .50 .23 .06
☐ 411 Phil Niekro SV .25 .11 .03
☐ 412 Rangers TL .25 .11 .03
BA: Buddy Bell
ERA: Charlie Hough
(Checklist on back)
☐ 413 Matt Keough .10 .05 .01
☐ 414 Julio Cruz .10 .05 .01
☐ 415 Bob Forsch .10 .05 .01
☐ 416 Joe Ferguson .10 .05 .01
☐ 417 Tom Hausman .10 .05 .01
☐ 418 Greg Pryor .10 .05 .01
☐ 419 Steve Crawford .10 .05 .01
☐ 420 Al Oliver .25 .11 .03
☐ 421 Al Oliver SV .10 .05 .01
☐ 422 George Cappuzzello .10 .05 .01
☐ 423 Tom Lawless .10 .05 .01
☐ 424 Jerry Augustine .10 .05 .01
☐ 425 Pedro Guerrero .25 .11 .03
☐ 426 Earl Weaver MG .50 .23 .06
☐ 427 Roy Lee Jackson .10 .05 .01
☐ 428 Champ Summers .10 .05 .01
☐ 429 Eddie Whitson .10 .05 .01
☐ 430 Kirk Gibson .50 .23 .06
☐ 431 Gary Gaetti 1.00 .45 .12
☐ 432 Porfirio Altamirano .10 .05 .01
☐ 433 Dale Berra .10 .05 .01
☐ 434 Dennis Lamp .10 .05 .01
☐ 435 Tony Armas .10 .05 .01
☐ 436 Bill Campbell .10 .05 .01
☐ 437 Rick Sweet .10 .05 .01
☐ 438 Dave LaPoint .10 .05 .01
☐ 439 Rafael Ramirez .10 .05 .01
☐ 440 Ron Guidry .25 .11 .03
☐ 441 Astros TL .25 .11 .03
BA: Ray Knight
ERA: Joe Niekro
(Checklist on back)
☐ 442 Brian Downing .10 .05 .01
☐ 443 Don Hood .10 .05 .01
☐ 444 Wally Backman .10 .05 .01
☐ 445 Mike Flanagan .25 .11 .03
☐ 446 Reid Nichols .10 .05 .01
☐ 447 Bryn Smith .10 .05 .01
☐ 448 Darrell Evans .25 .11 .03
☐ 449 Eddie Milner .10 .05 .01
☐ 450 Ted Simmons .25 .11 .03
☐ 451 Ted Simmons SV .10 .05 .01
☐ 452 Lloyd Moseby .10 .05 .01
☐ 453 Lamar Johnson .10 .05 .01
☐ 454 Bob Welch .25 .11 .03
☐ 455 Sixto Lezcano .10 .05 .01
☐ 456 Lee Elia MG .10 .05 .01
☐ 457 Milt Wilcox .10 .05 .01
☐ 458 Ron Washington .10 .05 .01
☐ 459 Ed Farmer .10 .05 .01
☐ 460 Roy Smalley .10 .05 .01
☐ 461 Steve Trout .10 .05 .01
☐ 462 Steve Nicosia .10 .05 .01
☐ 463 Gaylord Perry .50 .23 .06
☐ 464 Gaylord Perry SV .25 .11 .03
☐ 465 Lonnie Smith .10 .05 .01
☐ 466 Tom Underwood .10 .05 .01
☐ 467 Rufino Linares .10 .05 .01
☐ 468 Dave Goltz .10 .05 .01
☐ 469 Ron Gardenhire .10 .05 .01
☐ 470 Greg Minton .10 .05 .01
☐ 471 Kansas City Royals TL .25 .11 .03
BA: Willie Wilson
ERA: Vida Blue
(Checklist on back)
☐ 472 Gary Allenson .10 .05 .01
☐ 473 John Lowenstein .10 .05 .01
☐ 474 Ray Burris .10 .05 .01
☐ 475 Cesar Cedeno .25 .11 .03
☐ 476 Rob Picciolo .10 .05 .01
☐ 477 Tom Niedenfuer .10 .05 .01
☐ 478 Phil Garner .25 .11 .03
☐ 479 Charlie Hough .25 .11 .03
☐ 480 Toby Harrah .10 .05 .01
☐ 481 Scot Thompson .10 .05 .01
☐ 482 Tony Gwynn UER 35.00 16.00 4.40
(No Topps logo under
card number on back)
☐ 483 Lynn Jones .10 .05 .01
☐ 484 Dick Ruthven .10 .05 .01
☐ 485 Omar Moreno .10 .05 .01
☐ 486 Clyde King MG .10 .05 .01
☐ 487 Jerry Hairston .10 .05 .01
☐ 488 Alfredo Griffin .10 .05 .01
☐ 489 Tom Herr .25 .11 .03
☐ 490 Jim Palmer .60 .25 .07
☐ 491 Jim Palmer SV .50 .23 .06
☐ 492 Paul Serna .10 .05 .01
☐ 493 Steve McCatty .10 .05 .01
☐ 494 Bob Brenly .10 .05 .01
☐ 495 Warren Cromartie .10 .05 .01
☐ 496 Tom Veryzer .10 .05 .01
☐ 497 Rick Sutcliffe .25 .11 .03
☐ 498 Wade Boggs 16.00 7.25 2.00
☐ 499 Jeff Little .10 .05 .01
☐ 500 Reggie Jackson 1.25 .55 .16
☐ 501 Reggie Jackson SV .75 .35 .09
☐ 502 Atlanta Braves TL .25 .11 .03
BA: Dale Murphy
ERA: Phil Niekro
(Checklist on back)
☐ 503 Moose Haas .10 .05 .01
☐ 504 Don Werner .10 .05 .01
☐ 505 Garry Templeton .10 .05 .01
☐ 506 Jim Gott .10 .05 .01
☐ 507 Tony Scott .10 .05 .01
☐ 508 Tom Filer .10 .05 .01
☐ 509 Lou Whitaker .25 .11 .03
☐ 510 Tug McGraw .25 .11 .03
☐ 511 Tug McGraw SV .10 .05 .01
☐ 512 Doyle Alexander .10 .05 .01
☐ 513 Fred Stanley .10 .05 .01
☐ 514 Rudy Law .10 .05 .01
☐ 515 Gene Tenace .25 .11 .03
☐ 516 Bill Virdon MG .10 .05 .01
☐ 517 Gary Ward .10 .05 .01
☐ 518 Bill Laskey .10 .05 .01
☐ 519 Terry Bulling .10 .05 .01
☐ 520 Fred Lynn .25 .11 .03
☐ 521 Bruce Benedict .10 .05 .01
☐ 522 Pat Zachry .10 .05 .01
☐ 523 Carney Lansford .25 .11 .03
☐ 524 Tom Brennan .10 .05 .01
☐ 525 Frank White .25 .11 .03
☐ 526 Checklist: 397-528 .25 .11 .03
☐ 527 Larry Biittner .10 .05 .01
☐ 528 Jamie Easterly .10 .05 .01
☐ 529 Tim Laudner .10 .05 .01
☐ 530 Eddie Murray 3.00 1.35 .35
☐ 531 Oakland A's TL .50 .23 .06
BA: Rickey Henderson
ERA: Rick Langford
(Checklist on back)
☐ 532 Dave Stewart .25 .11 .03
☐ 533 Luis Salazar .10 .05 .01
☐ 534 John Butcher .10 .05 .01

Card	NRMT	VG-E	GOOD
☐ 535 Manny Trillo	.10	.05	.01
☐ 536 John Wockenfuss	.10	.05	.01
☐ 537 Rod Scurry	.10	.05	.01
☐ 538 Danny Heep	.10	.05	.01
☐ 539 Roger Erickson	.10	.05	.01
☐ 540 Ozzie Smith	3.00	1.35	.35
☐ 541 Britt Burns	.10	.05	.01
☐ 542 Jody Davis	.10	.05	.01
☐ 543 Alan Fowlkes	.10	.05	.01
☐ 544 Larry Whisenton	.10	.05	.01
☐ 545 Floyd Bannister	.10	.05	.01
☐ 546 Dave Garcia MG	.10	.05	.01
☐ 547 Geoff Zahn	.10	.05	.01
☐ 548 Brian Giles	.10	.05	.01
☐ 549 Charlie Puleo	.10	.05	.01
☐ 550 Carl Yastrzemski	1.00	.45	.12
☐ 551 Carl Yastrzemski SV	.50	.23	.06
☐ 552 Tim Wallach	.25	.11	.03
☐ 553 Dennis Martinez	.25	.11	.03
☐ 554 Mike Vail	.10	.05	.01
☐ 555 Steve Yeager	.10	.05	.01
☐ 556 Willie Upshaw	.10	.05	.01
☐ 557 Rick Honeycutt	.10	.05	.01
☐ 558 Dickie Thon	.10	.05	.01
☐ 559 Pete Redfern	.10	.05	.01
☐ 560 Ron LeFlore	.25	.11	.03
☐ 561 Cardinals TL	.25	.11	.03
BA: Lonnie Smith			
ERA: Joaquin Andujar			
(Checklist on back)			
☐ 562 Dave Rozema	.10	.05	.01
☐ 563 Juan Bonilla	.10	.05	.01
☐ 564 Sid Monge	.10	.05	.01
☐ 565 Bucky Dent	.25	.11	.03
☐ 566 Manny Sarmiento	.10	.05	.01
☐ 567 Joe Simpson	.10	.05	.01
☐ 568 Willie Hernandez	.25	.11	.03
☐ 569 Jack Perconte	.10	.05	.01
☐ 570 Vida Blue	.25	.11	.03
☐ 571 Mickey Klutts	.10	.05	.01
☐ 572 Bob Watson	.25	.11	.03
☐ 573 Andy Hassler	.10	.05	.01
☐ 574 Glenn Adams	.10	.05	.01
☐ 575 Neil Allen	.10	.05	.01
☐ 576 Frank Robinson MG	.50	.23	.06
☐ 577 Luis Aponte	.10	.05	.01
☐ 578 David Green	.10	.05	.01
☐ 579 Rich Dauer	.10	.05	.01
☐ 580 Tom Seaver	1.00	.45	.12
☐ 581 Tom Seaver SV	.50	.23	.06
☐ 582 Marshall Edwards	.10	.05	.01
☐ 583 Terry Forster	.10	.05	.01
☐ 584 Dave Hostetler	.10	.05	.01
☐ 585 Jose Cruz	.25	.11	.03
☐ 586 Frank Viola	1.00	.45	.12
☐ 587 Ivan DeJesus	.10	.05	.01
☐ 588 Pat Underwood	.10	.05	.01
☐ 589 Alvis Woods	.10	.05	.01
☐ 590 Tony Pena	.25	.11	.03
☐ 591 White Sox TL	.25	.11	.03
BA: Greg Luzinski			
ERA: LaMarr Hoyt			
(Checklist on back)			
☐ 592 Shane Rawley	.10	.05	.01
☐ 593 Broderick Perkins	.10	.05	.01
☐ 594 Eric Rasmussen	.10	.05	.01
☐ 595 Tim Raines	.50	.23	.06
☐ 596 Randy Johnson	.10	.05	.01
☐ 597 Mike Proly	.10	.05	.01
☐ 598 Dwayne Murphy	.10	.05	.01
☐ 599 Don Aase	.10	.05	.01
☐ 600 George Brett	4.00	1.80	.50
☐ 601 Ed Lynch	.10	.05	.01
☐ 602 Rich Gedman	.10	.05	.01
☐ 603 Joe Morgan	.50	.23	.06
☐ 604 Joe Morgan SV	.50	.23	.06
☐ 605 Gary Roenicke	.10	.05	.01
☐ 606 Bobby Cox MG	.25	.11	.03
☐ 607 Charlie Leibrandt	.10	.05	.01
☐ 608 Don Money	.10	.05	.01
☐ 609 Danny Darwin	.10	.05	.01
☐ 610 Steve Garvey	.50	.23	.06
☐ 611 Bert Roberge	.10	.05	.01
☐ 612 Steve Swisher	.10	.05	.01
☐ 613 Mike Ivie	.10	.05	.01
☐ 614 Ed Glynn	.10	.05	.01
☐ 615 Garry Maddox	.10	.05	.01
☐ 616 Bill Nahorodny	.10	.05	.01
☐ 617 Butch Wynegar	.10	.05	.01
☐ 618 LaMarr Hoyt	.25	.11	.03
☐ 619 Keith Moreland	.10	.05	.01
☐ 620 Mike Norris	.10	.05	.01
☐ 621 New York Mets TL	.25	.11	.03
BA: Mookie Wilson			
ERA: Craig Swan			
(Checklist on back)			
☐ 622 Dave Edler	.10	.05	.01
☐ 623 Luis Sanchez	.10	.05	.01
☐ 624 Glenn Hubbard	.10	.05	.01
☐ 625 Ken Forsch	.10	.05	.01
☐ 626 Jerry Martin	.10	.05	.01
☐ 627 Doug Bair	.10	.05	.01
☐ 628 Julio Valdez	.10	.05	.01
☐ 629 Charlie Lea	.10	.05	.01
☐ 630 Paul Molitor	2.00	.90	.25
☐ 631 Tippy Martinez	.10	.05	.01
☐ 632 Alex Trevino	.10	.05	.01
☐ 633 Vicente Romo	.10	.05	.01
☐ 634 Max Venable	.10	.05	.01
☐ 635 Graig Nettles	.25	.11	.03
☐ 636 Graig Nettles SV	.10	.05	.01
☐ 637 Pat Corrales MG	.10	.05	.01
☐ 638 Dan Petry	.10	.05	.01
☐ 639 Art Howe	.10	.05	.01
☐ 640 Andre Thornton	.10	.05	.01
☐ 641 Billy Sample	.10	.05	.01
☐ 642 Checklist: 529-660	.25	.11	.03
☐ 643 Bump Wills	.10	.05	.01
☐ 644 Joe Lefebvre	.10	.05	.01
☐ 645 Bill Madlock	.25	.11	.03
☐ 646 Jim Essian	.10	.05	.01
☐ 647 Bobby Mitchell	.10	.05	.01
☐ 648 Jeff Burroughs	.10	.05	.01
☐ 649 Tommy Boggs	.10	.05	.01
☐ 650 George Hendrick	.10	.05	.01
☐ 651 Angels TL	.50	.23	.06
BA: Rod Carew			
ERA: Mike Witt			
(Checklist on back)			
☐ 652 Butch Hobson	.10	.05	.01
☐ 653 Ellis Valentine	.10	.05	.01
☐ 654 Bob Ojeda	.10	.05	.01
☐ 655 Al Bumbry	.25	.11	.03
☐ 656 Dave Frost	.10	.05	.01
☐ 657 Mike Gates	.10	.05	.01
☐ 658 Frank Pastore	.10	.05	.01
☐ 659 Charlie Moore	.10	.05	.01
☐ 660 Mike Hargrove	.25	.11	.03
☐ 661 Bill Russell	.25	.11	.03
☐ 662 Joe Sambito	.10	.05	.01
☐ 663 Tom O'Malley	.10	.05	.01
☐ 664 Bob Molinaro	.10	.05	.01
☐ 665 Jim Sundberg	.25	.11	.03
☐ 666 Sparky Anderson MG	.25	.11	.03
☐ 667 Dick Davis	.10	.05	.01
☐ 668 Larry Christenson	.10	.05	.01
☐ 669 Mike Squires	.10	.05	.01
☐ 670 Jerry Mumphrey	.10	.05	.01
☐ 671 Lenny Faedo	.10	.05	.01
☐ 672 Jim Kaat	.25	.11	.03
☐ 673 Jim Kaat SV	.10	.05	.01
☐ 674 Kurt Bevacqua	.10	.05	.01
☐ 675 Jim Beattie	.10	.05	.01
☐ 676 Biff Pocoroba	.10	.05	.01
☐ 677 Dave Revering	.10	.05	.01
☐ 678 Juan Beniquez	.10	.05	.01
☐ 679 Mike Scott	.25	.11	.03
☐ 680 Andre Dawson	1.00	.45	.12
☐ 681 Dodgers Leaders	.25	.11	.03
BA: Pedro Guerrero			
ERA: Fernando Valenzuela			
(Checklist on back)			
☐ 682 Bob Stanley	.10	.05	.01
☐ 683 Dan Ford	.10	.05	.01
☐ 684 Rafael Landestoy	.10	.05	.01
☐ 685 Lee Mazzilli	.10	.05	.01
☐ 686 Randy Lerch	.10	.05	.01
☐ 687 U.L. Washington	.10	.05	.01
☐ 688 Jim Wohlford	.10	.05	.01
☐ 689 Ron Hassey	.10	.05	.01
☐ 690 Kent Hrbek	.25	.11	.03
☐ 691 Dave Tobik	.10	.05	.01
☐ 692 Denny Walling	.10	.05	.01
☐ 693 Sparky Lyle	.25	.11	.03
☐ 694 Sparky Lyle SV	.10	.05	.01
☐ 695 Ruppert Jones	.10	.05	.01
☐ 696 Chuck Tanner MG	.25	.11	.03
☐ 697 Barry Foote	.10	.05	.01
☐ 698 Tony Bernazard	.10	.05	.01
☐ 699 Lee Smith	2.50	1.10	.30
☐ 700 Keith Hernandez	.25	.11	.03
☐ 701 Batting Leaders	.25	.11	.03
AL: Willie Wilson			
NL: Al Oliver			
☐ 702 Home Run Leaders	.50	.23	.06
AL: Reggie Jackson			
AL: Gorman Thomas			
NL: Dave Kingman			
☐ 703 RBI Leaders	.25	.11	.03
AL: Hal McRae			
NL: Dale Murphy			
NL: Al Oliver			
☐ 704 SB Leaders	1.00	.45	.12
AL: Rickey Henderson			
NL: Tim Raines			
☐ 705 Victory Leaders	.50	.23	.06
AL: LaMarr Hoyt			
NL: Steve Carlton			
☐ 706 Strikeout Leaders	.50	.23	.06
AL: Floyd Bannister			
NL: Steve Carlton			
☐ 707 ERA Leaders	.25	.11	.03
AL: Rick Sutcliffe			
NL: Steve Rogers			
☐ 708 Leading Firemen	.25	.11	.03
AL: Dan Quisenberry			
NL: Bruce Sutter			
☐ 709 Jimmy Sexton	.10	.05	.01
☐ 710 Willie Wilson	.25	.11	.03
☐ 711 Mariners TL	.25	.11	.03
BA: Bruce Bochte			
ERA: Jim Beattie			
(Checklist on back)			
☐ 712 Bruce Kison	.10	.05	.01
☐ 713 Ron Hodges	.10	.05	.01
☐ 714 Wayne Nordhagen	.10	.05	.01
☐ 715 Tony Perez	.50	.23	.06
☐ 716 Tony Perez SV	.25	.11	.03
☐ 717 Scott Sanderson	.10	.05	.01
☐ 718 Jim Dwyer	.10	.05	.01
☐ 719 Rich Gale	.10	.05	.01
☐ 720 Dave Concepcion	.25	.11	.03
☐ 721 John Martin	.10	.05	.01
☐ 722 Jorge Orta	.10	.05	.01
☐ 723 Randy Moffitt	.10	.05	.01
☐ 724 Johnny Grubb	.10	.05	.01
☐ 725 Dan Spillner	.10	.05	.01
☐ 726 Harvey Kuenn MG	.25	.11	.03
☐ 727 Chet Lemon	.10	.05	.01
☐ 728 Ron Reed	.10	.05	.01
☐ 729 Jerry Morales	.10	.05	.01
☐ 730 Jason Thompson	.10	.05	.01
☐ 731 Al Williams	.10	.05	.01
☐ 732 Dave Henderson	.25	.11	.03
☐ 733 Buck Martinez	.10	.05	.01
☐ 734 Steve Braun	.10	.05	.01
☐ 735 Tommy John	.50	.23	.06
☐ 736 Tommy John SV	.25	.11	.03
☐ 737 Mitchell Page	.10	.05	.01
☐ 738 Tim Foli	.10	.05	.01
☐ 739 Rick Ownbey	.10	.05	.01
☐ 740 Rusty Staub	.25	.11	.03
☐ 741 Rusty Staub SV	.10	.05	.01
☐ 742 Padres TL	.25	.11	.03
BA: Terry Kennedy			
ERA: Tim Lollar			
(Checklist on back)			
☐ 743 Mike Torrez	.10	.05	.01
☐ 744 Brad Mills	.10	.05	.01
☐ 745 Scott McGregor	.10	.05	.01
☐ 746 John Wathan	.10	.05	.01
☐ 747 Fred Breining	.10	.05	.01
☐ 748 Derrel Thomas	.10	.05	.01
☐ 749 Jon Matlack	.10	.05	.01
☐ 750 Ben Oglivie	.10	.05	.01
☐ 751 Brad Havens	.10	.05	.01
☐ 752 Luis Pujols	.10	.05	.01
☐ 753 Elias Sosa	.10	.05	.01
☐ 754 Bill Robinson	.10	.05	.01
☐ 755 John Candelaria	.10	.05	.01
☐ 756 Russ Nixon MG	.10	.05	.01
☐ 757 Rick Manning	.10	.05	.01
☐ 758 Aurelio Rodriguez	.10	.05	.01
☐ 759 Doug Bird	.10	.05	.01
☐ 760 Dale Murphy	.50	.23	.06
☐ 761 Gary Lucas	.10	.05	.01
☐ 762 Cliff Johnson	.10	.05	.01
☐ 763 Al Cowens	.10	.05	.01
☐ 764 Pete Falcone	.10	.05	.01
☐ 765 Bob Boone	.25	.11	.03
☐ 766 Barry Bonnell	.10	.05	.01
☐ 767 Duane Kuiper	.10	.05	.01
☐ 768 Chris Speier	.10	.05	.01
☐ 769 Checklist: 661-792	.25	.11	.03
☐ 770 Dave Winfield	2.00	.90	.25
☐ 771 Twins TL	.25	.11	.03
BA: Kent Hrbek			
ERA: Bobby Castillo			
(Checklist on back)			
☐ 772 Jim Kern	.10	.05	.01
☐ 773 Larry Hisle	.10	.05	.01
☐ 774 Alan Ashby	.10	.05	.01
☐ 775 Burt Hooton	.10	.05	.01
☐ 776 Larry Parrish	.10	.05	.01
☐ 777 John Curtis	.10	.05	.01
☐ 778 Rich Hebner	.25	.11	.03
☐ 779 Rick Waits	.10	.05	.01
☐ 780 Gary Matthews	.25	.11	.03
☐ 781 Rick Rhoden	.10	.05	.01
☐ 782 Bobby Murcer	.25	.11	.03
☐ 783 Bobby Murcer SV	.10	.05	.01
☐ 784 Jeff Newman	.10	.05	.01
☐ 785 Dennis Leonard	.10	.05	.01
☐ 786 Ralph Houk MG	.10	.05	.01
☐ 787 Dick Tidrow	.10	.05	.01
☐ 788 Dane Iorg	.10	.05	.01
☐ 789 Bryan Clark	.10	.05	.01
☐ 790 Bob Grich	.25	.11	.03
☐ 791 Gary Lavelle	.10	.05	.01
☐ 792 Chris Chambliss	.25	.11	.03

1983 Topps Glossy Send-Ins

The cards in this 40-card set measure the standard size. The 1983 Topps "Collector's Edition" or "All-Star Set" (popularly known as "Glossies") consists of color ballplayer picture cards with shiny, glazed surfaces. The player's name appears in small print outside the frame line at bottom left. The backs contain no biography or record and list only the set titles, the player's name, team, position, and the card number.

	NRMT	VG-E	GOOD
COMPLETE SET (40)	15.00	6.75	1.85
COMMON CARD (1-40)	.10	.05	.01

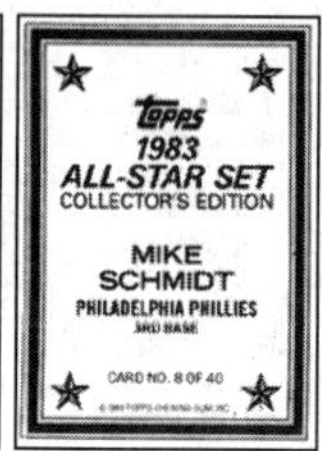

Card	NRMT	VG-E	GOOD
☐ 1 Carl Yastrzemski	1.00	.45	.12
☐ 2 Mookie Wilson	.10	.05	.01
☐ 3 Andre Thornton	.10	.05	.01
☐ 4 Keith Hernandez	.25	.11	.03
☐ 5 Robin Yount	1.00	.45	.12
☐ 6 Terry Kennedy	.10	.05	.01
☐ 7 Dave Winfield	1.00	.45	.12
☐ 8 Mike Schmidt	2.00	.90	.25
☐ 9 Buddy Bell	.25	.11	.03
☐ 10 Fernando Valenzuela	.35	.16	.04
☐ 11 Rich Gossage	.25	.11	.03
☐ 12 Bob Horner	.10	.05	.01
☐ 13 Toby Harrah	.10	.05	.01
☐ 14 Pete Rose	2.00	.90	.25
☐ 15 Cecil Cooper	.25	.11	.03
☐ 16 Dale Murphy	.50	.23	.06
☐ 17 Carlton Fisk	1.00	.45	.12
☐ 18 Ray Knight	.10	.05	.01
☐ 19 Jim Palmer	.75	.35	.09
☐ 20 Gary Carter	.35	.16	.04
☐ 21 Richie Zisk	.10	.05	.01
☐ 22 Dusty Baker	.25	.11	.03
☐ 23 Willie Wilson	.10	.05	.01
☐ 24 Bill Buckner	.25	.11	.03
☐ 25 Dave Stieb	.10	.05	.01
☐ 26 Bill Madlock	.10	.05	.01
☐ 27 Lance Parrish	.25	.11	.03
☐ 28 Nolan Ryan	5.00	2.20	.60
☐ 29 Rod Carew	1.00	.45	.12
☐ 30 Al Oliver	.25	.11	.03
☐ 31 George Brett	2.50	1.10	.30
☐ 32 Jack Clark	.10	.05	.01
☐ 33 Rickey Henderson	1.25	.55	.16
☐ 34 Dave Concepcion	.25	.11	.03
☐ 35 Kent Hrbek	.25	.11	.03
☐ 36 Steve Carlton	.75	.35	.09
☐ 37 Eddie Murray	1.50	.70	.19
☐ 38 Ruppert Jones	.10	.05	.01
☐ 39 Reggie Jackson	1.00	.45	.12
☐ 40 Bruce Sutter	.25	.11	.03

1983 Topps Traded

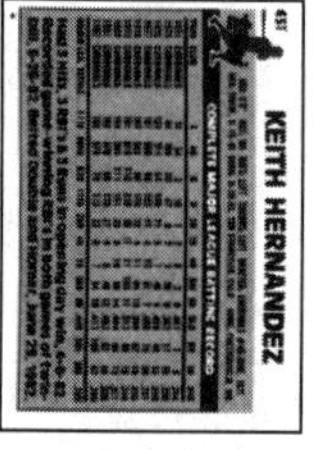

For the third year in a row, Topps issued a 132-card standard-size Traded (or extended) set featuring some of the year's top rookies and players who had changed teams during the year. The cards were available through hobby dealers only in factory set form and were printed in Ireland by the Topps affiliate in that country. The set is numbered alphabetically by player. The Darryl Strawberry card number 108 can be found with either one or two asterisks (in the lower left corner of the reverse). There is no difference in value for either version. The key (extended) Rookie Cards in this set include Julio Franco, Tony Phillips and Darryl Strawberry.

	NRMT	VG-E	GOOD
COMPLETE FACT.SET (132)	40.00	18.00	5.00
COMMON CARD (1T-132T)	.25	.11	.03

Card	NRMT	VG-E	GOOD
☐ 1T Neil Allen	.25	.11	.03
☐ 2T Bill Almon	.25	.11	.03
☐ 3T Joe Altobelli MG	.25	.11	.03
☐ 4T Tony Armas	.25	.11	.03
☐ 5T Doug Bair	.25	.11	.03
☐ 6T Steve Baker	.25	.11	.03
☐ 7T Floyd Bannister	.25	.11	.03
☐ 8T Don Baylor	1.00	.45	.12
☐ 9T Tony Bernazard	.25	.11	.03
☐ 10T Larry Biittner	.25	.11	.03
☐ 11T Dann Bilardello	.25	.11	.03
☐ 12T Doug Bird	.25	.11	.03
☐ 13T Steve Boros MG	.25	.11	.03
☐ 14T Greg Brock	.25	.11	.03
☐ 15T Mike C. Brown	.25	.11	.03
☐ 16T Tom Burgmeier	.25	.11	.03
☐ 17T Randy Bush	.25	.11	.03
☐ 18T Bert Campaneris	.50	.23	.06
☐ 19T Ron Cey	.50	.23	.06
☐ 20T Chris Codiroli	.25	.11	.03
☐ 21T Dave Collins	.25	.11	.03

☐ 22T Terry Crowley	.25	.11	.03
☐ 23T Julio Cruz	.25	.11	.03
☐ 24T Mike Davis	.25	.11	.03
☐ 25T Frank DiPino	.25	.11	.03
☐ 26T Bill Doran	.50	.23	.06
☐ 27T Jerry Dybzinski	.25	.11	.03
☐ 28T Jamie Easterly	.25	.11	.03
☐ 29T Juan Eichelberger	.25	.11	.03
☐ 30T Jim Essian	.25	.11	.03
☐ 31T Pete Falcone	.25	.11	.03
☐ 32T Mike Ferraro MG	.25	.11	.03
☐ 33T Terry Forster	.25	.11	.03
☐ 34T Julio Franco	3.00	1.35	.35
☐ 35T Rich Gale	.25	.11	.03
☐ 36T Kiko Garcia	.25	.11	.03
☐ 37T Steve Garvey	1.00	.45	.12
☐ 38T Johnny Grubb	.25	.11	.03
☐ 39T Mel Hall	.50	.23	.06
☐ 40T Von Hayes	.50	.23	.06
☐ 41T Danny Heep	.25	.11	.03
☐ 42T Steve Henderson	.25	.11	.03
☐ 43T Keith Hernandez	.50	.23	.06
☐ 44T Leo Hernandez	.25	.11	.03
☐ 45T Willie Hernandez	.50	.23	.06
☐ 46T Al Holland	.25	.11	.03
☐ 47T Frank Howard MG	.50	.23	.06
☐ 48T Bobby Johnson	.25	.11	.03
☐ 49T Cliff Johnson	.25	.11	.03
☐ 50T Odell Jones	.25	.11	.03
☐ 51T Mike Jorgensen	.25	.11	.03
☐ 52T Bob Kearney	.25	.11	.03
☐ 53T Steve Kemp	.25	.11	.03
☐ 54T Matt Keough	.25	.11	.03
☐ 55T Ron Kittle	.50	.23	.06
☐ 56T Mickey Klutts	.25	.11	.03
☐ 57T Alan Knicely	.25	.11	.03
☐ 58T Mike Krukow	.25	.11	.03
☐ 59T Rafael Landestoy	.25	.11	.03
☐ 60T Carney Lansford	.50	.23	.06
☐ 61T Joe Lefebvre	.25	.11	.03
☐ 62T Bryan Little	.25	.11	.03
☐ 63T Aurelio Lopez	.25	.11	.03
☐ 64T Mike Madden	.25	.11	.03
☐ 65T Rick Manning	.25	.11	.03
☐ 66T Billy Martin MG	.50	.23	.06
☐ 67T Lee Mazzilli	.25	.11	.03
☐ 68T Andy McGaffigan	.25	.11	.03
☐ 69T Craig McMurtry	.25	.11	.03
☐ 70T John McNamara MG	.25	.11	.03
☐ 71T Orlando Mercado	.25	.11	.03
☐ 72T Larry Milbourne	.25	.11	.03
☐ 73T Randy Moffitt	.25	.11	.03
☐ 74T Sid Monge	.25	.11	.03
☐ 75T Jose Morales	.25	.11	.03
☐ 76T Omar Moreno	.25	.11	.03
☐ 77T Joe Morgan	2.00	.90	.25
☐ 78T Mike Morgan	.25	.11	.03
☐ 79T Dale Murray	1.00	.45	.12
☐ 80T Jeff Newman	.25	.11	.03
☐ 81T Pete O'Brien	.50	.23	.06
☐ 82T Jorge Orta	.25	.11	.03
☐ 83T Alejandro Pena	.50	.23	.06
☐ 84T Pascual Perez	.25	.11	.03
☐ 85T Tony Perez	1.00	.45	.12
☐ 86T Broderick Perkins	.25	.11	.03
☐ 87T Tony Phillips	6.00	2.70	.75
☐ 88T Charlie Puleo	.25	.11	.03
☐ 89T Pat Putnam	.25	.11	.03
☐ 90T Jamie Quirk	.25	.11	.03
☐ 91T Doug Rader MG	.25	.11	.03
☐ 92T Chuck Rainey	.25	.11	.03
☐ 93T Bobby Ramos	.25	.11	.03
☐ 94T Gary Redus	.50	.23	.06
☐ 95T Steve Renko	.25	.11	.03
☐ 96T Leon Roberts	.25	.11	.03
☐ 97T Aurelio Rodriguez	.25	.11	.03
☐ 98T Dick Ruthven	.25	.11	.03
☐ 99T Daryl Sconiers	.25	.11	.03
☐ 100T Mike Scott	.50	.23	.06
☐ 101T Tom Seaver	5.00	2.20	.60
☐ 102T John Shelby	.25	.11	.03
☐ 103T Bob Shirley	.25	.11	.03
☐ 104T Joe Simpson	.25	.11	.03
☐ 105T Doug Sisk	.25	.11	.03
☐ 106T Mike Smithson	.25	.11	.03
☐ 107T Elias Sosa	.25	.11	.03
☐ 108T Darryl Strawberry	25.00	11.00	3.10
☐ 109T Tom Tellmann	.25	.11	.03
☐ 110T Gene Tenace	.50	.23	.06
☐ 111T Gorman Thomas	.25	.11	.03
☐ 112T Dick Tidrow	.25	.11	.03
☐ 113T Dave Tobik	.25	.11	.03
☐ 114T Wayne Tolleson	.25	.11	.03
☐ 115T Mike Torrez	.25	.11	.03
☐ 116T Manny Trillo	.25	.11	.03
☐ 117T Steve Trout	.25	.11	.03
☐ 118T Lee Tunnell	.25	.11	.03
☐ 119T Mike Vail	.25	.11	.03
☐ 120T Ellis Valentine	.25	.11	.03
☐ 121T Tom Veryzer	.25	.11	.03
☐ 122T George Vukovich	.25	.11	.03
☐ 123T Rick Waits	.25	.11	.03
☐ 124T Greg Walker	.50	.23	.06
☐ 125T Chris Welsh	.25	.11	.03
☐ 126T Len Whitehouse	.25	.11	.03
☐ 127T Eddie Whitson	.25	.11	.03
☐ 128T Jim Wohlford	.25	.11	.03
☐ 129T Matt Young	.25	.11	.03
☐ 130T Joel Youngblood	.25	.11	.03
☐ 131T Pat Zachry	.25	.11	.03
☐ 132T Checklist 1T-132T	.25	.11	.03

1983 Topps Foldouts

The cards in this 85-card (five folders with 17 photos in each folder) set measure 3 1/2" by 5 5/16". The 1983 Fold-Outs were an innovation by Topps featuring five sets of 17 postcard-size photos each. Each of the five sets had a theme of career leaders in a particular category. The five catagories -- batting leaders, home run leaders, stolen base leaders, pitching leaders and relief aces -- featured the 17 top active players in their respective categories. If a player were a leader in more than one category, he is pictured in more than one of the five sets. These foldout booklets are typically sold intact and are priced below at one price per complete panel. Each picture contains a facsimile autograph as well. The quality of the photos is very good. In the checklist below the leaders are listed in order of their career standing as shown on each foldout.

	NRMT	VG-E	GOOD
COMPLETE SET (5)	5.00	2.20	.60
COMMON PANEL (1-5)	1.00	.45	.12
☐ 1 Career Wins Gaylord Perry, 307 Steve Carlton Jim Kaat Fergie Jenkins Tom Seaver Jim Palmer Don Sutton Phil Niekro Tommy John Nolan Ryan Vida Blue Jerry Koosman Mike Torrez Bert Blyleven Joe Niekro Jerry Reuss Paul Splittorff	1.25	.55	.16
☐ 2 Home Run Leaders Reggie Jackson, 464 Carl Yastrzemski Johnny Bench Tony Perez Mike Schmidt Dave Kingman Graig Nettles Rusty Staub Greg Luzinski George Foster John Mayberry Bobby Murcer Joe Morgan Jim Rice Rick Monday Darrell Evans Ron Cey	1.50	.70	.19
☐ 3 Batting Leaders Rod Carew, .331 George Brett Bill Madlock Lonnie Smith Willie Wilson Pete Rose Dave Parker Cecil Cooper Jim Rice Al Oliver Pedro Guerrero Ken Griffey Fred Lynn Steve Garvey Bake McBride Keith Hernandez Dane Iorg	1.50	.70	.19
☐ 4 Relief Aces Rollie Fingers, 301 Bruce Sutter Rich Gossage Tug McGraw Gene Garber Kent Tekulve Bill Campbell Terry Forster Tom Burgmeier Greg Lavelle Dan Quisenberry Jim Kern Randy Moffitt Ron Reed EliasSosa Ed Farmer Greg Minton	1.00	.45	.12
☐ 5 Steals Leaders Joe Morgan, 663 Cesar Cedeno Ron LeFlore Davey Lopes Omar Moreno Rod Carew Amos Otis Rickey Henderson Larry Bowa Willie Wilson Don Baylor Julio Cruz Mickey Rivers Dave Concepcion Jose Cruz Garry Maddox Al Bumbry	1.00	.45	.12

1983 Topps Leader Sheet

The cards in this 8-player sheet measure 2 1/2" by 3 1/2". The full sheet is 7 1/2" by 10 1/2". The full sheet is typically kept intact as it has not been perforated. The cards are blank backed and feature the league statistical leaders from the previous season. The cards are unnumbered and are listed below in left to right order of appearance on the sheet.

	NRMT	VG-E	GOOD
COMPLETE SHEET	2.00	.90	.25
COMMON CARD	.25	.11	.03
☐ 1 Willie Wilson AL Batting .332 Batting Average	.25	.11	.03
☐ 2 Reggie Jackson and Gorman Thomas AL Home Runs 39 Home Runs	.50	.23	.06
☐ 3 Al Oliver NL Batting .331 Batting Average	.25	.11	.03
☐ 4 LaMarr Hoyt AL Victories 19 Victories	.25	.11	.03
☐ 5 Steve Carlton NL Victories 23 Victories	.50	.23	.06
☐ 6 Dan Quisenberry AL Saves 35 Saves	.25	.11	.03
☐ 7 Dave Kingman NL Home Runs 37 Home Runs	.25	.11	.03
☐ 8 Bruce Sutter NL Saves 36 Saves	.25	.11	.03

1983 Topps/O-Pee-Chee Stickers

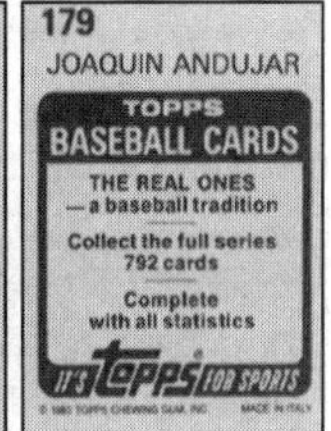

Made for Topps and O-Pee-Chee by Panini, an Italian company, these 330 stickers measure approximately 1 15/16" by 2 9/16" and are numbered on both front and back. The fronts feature white-bordered color player photos framed with a colored and a black line. The colored line is red for AL players and blue for NL players. The backs carry player names and a bilingual ad for the O-Pee-Chee sticker album. The album, onto which the stickers could be affixed, was available at retail stores. The album and the sticker numbering are organized as follows: Home Run Kings (1-14), AL Pitching and Batting Leaders (15-22), Baltimore Orioles (23-30), Boston Red Sox (31-38), California Angels (39-46), Chicago White Sox (47-54), Cleveland Indians (55-62), Detroit Tigers (63-70), Kansas City Royals (71-78), Milwaukee Brewers (79-86), Minnesota Twins (87-94), New York Yankees (95-102), Oakland A's (103-110), Seattle Mariners (111-118), Texas Rangers (119-126), Toronto Blue Jays (127-134), 1982 Record Breakers (135-146), 1982 Championship Series (147-158), AL and NL All-Stars (159-178), 1982 World Series (179-190), 1982 Record Breakers (191-202), NL Pitching and Batting Leaders (203-210), Atlanta Braves (211-218), Chicago Cubs (219-226), Cincinnati Reds (227-234), Houston Astros (235-242), Los Angeles Dodgers (243-250), Montreal Expos (251-258), New York Mets (259-266), Philadelphia Phillies (267-274), Pittsburgh Pirates (275-282), St. Louis Cardinals (283-290), San Diego Padres (291-298), San Francisco Giants (299-306), and Stars of the Future (307-330). Wade Boggs and Ryne Sandberg are featured during their Rookie Card year.

	NRMT	VG-E	GOOD
COMPLETE SET (330)	15.00	6.75	1.85
COMMON STICKER (1-330)	.05	.02	.01
COMMON FOIL	.10	.05	.01
*OPC: 2X VALUES BELOW			
☐ 1 Hank Aaron FOIL	1.25	.55	.16
☐ 2 Babe Ruth FOIL	3.00	1.35	.35
☐ 3 Willie Mays FOIL	1.50	.70	.19
☐ 4 Frank Robinson FOIL	.30	.14	.04
☐ 5 Reggie Jackson	.50	.23	.06
☐ 6 Carl Yastrzemski	.40	.18	.05
☐ 7 Johnny Bench	.50	.23	.06
☐ 8 Tony Perez	.15	.07	.02
☐ 9 Lee May	.10	.05	.01
☐ 10 Mike Schmidt	.60	.25	.07
☐ 11 Dave Kingman	.10	.05	.01
☐ 12 Reggie Smith	.10	.05	.01
☐ 13 Graig Nettles	.10	.05	.01
☐ 14 Rusty Staub	.10	.05	.01
☐ 15 Willie Wilson	.05	.02	.01
☐ 16 LaMarr Hoyt	.05	.02	.01
☐ 17 Reggie Jackson and Gorman Thomas	.15	.07	.02
☐ 18 Floyd Bannister	.05	.02	.01
☐ 19 Hal McRae	.10	.05	.01
☐ 20 Rick Sutcliffe	.05	.02	.01
☐ 21 Rickey Henderson	.50	.23	.06
☐ 22 Dan Quisenberry	.05	.02	.01
☐ 23 Jim Palmer FOIL	.40	.18	.05
☐ 24 John Lowenstein	.05	.02	.01
☐ 25 Mike Flanagan	.10	.05	.01
☐ 26 Cal Ripken	4.00	1.80	.50
☐ 27 Rich Dauer	.05	.02	.01
☐ 28 Ken Singleton	.10	.05	.01
☐ 29 Eddie Murray	.50	.23	.06
☐ 30 Rick Dempsey	.10	.05	.01
☐ 31 Carl Yastrzemski FOIL	.60	.25	.07
☐ 32 Carney Lansford	.10	.05	.01
☐ 33 Jerry Remy	.05	.02	.01
☐ 34 Dennis Eckersley	.15	.07	.02
☐ 35 Dave Stapleton	.05	.02	.01
☐ 36 Mark Clear	.05	.02	.01
☐ 37 Jim Rice	.10	.05	.01
☐ 38 Dwight Evans	.10	.05	.01
☐ 39 Rod Carew	.40	.18	.05
☐ 40 Don Baylor	.10	.05	.01
☐ 41 Reggie Jackson FOIL	.75	.35	.09
☐ 42 Geoff Zahn	.05	.02	.01
☐ 43 Bobby Grich	.10	.05	.01
☐ 44 Fred Lynn	.10	.05	.01
☐ 45 Bob Boone	.10	.05	.01
☐ 46 Doug DeCinces	.05	.02	.01
☐ 47 Tom Paciorek	.05	.02	.01
☐ 48 Britt Burns	.05	.02	.01
☐ 49 Tony Bernazard	.05	.02	.01
☐ 50 Steve Kemp	.05	.02	.01
☐ 51 Greg Luzinski FOIL	.15	.07	.02
☐ 52 Harold Baines	.10	.05	.01
☐ 53 LaMarr Hoyt	.05	.02	.01
☐ 54 Carlton Fisk	.30	.14	.04
☐ 55 Andre Thornton FOIL	.10	.05	.01
☐ 56 Mike Hargrove	.10	.05	.01
☐ 57 Len Barker	.05	.02	.01
☐ 58 Toby Harrah	.05	.02	.01
☐ 59 Dan Spillner	.05	.02	.01
☐ 60 Rick Manning	.05	.02	.01
☐ 61 Rick Sutcliffe	.05	.02	.01
☐ 62 Ron Hassey	.05	.02	.01
☐ 63 Lance Parrish FOIL	.15	.07	.02
☐ 64 John Wockenfuss	.05	.02	.01
☐ 65 Lou Whitaker	.10	.05	.01
☐ 66 Alan Trammell	.15	.07	.02
☐ 67 Kirk Gibson	.15	.07	.02
☐ 68 Larry Herndon	.05	.02	.01
☐ 69 Jack Morris	.10	.05	.01
☐ 70 Dan Petry	.05	.02	.01
☐ 71 Frank White	.10	.05	.01
☐ 72 Amos Otis	.10	.05	.01
☐ 73 Willie Wilson FOIL	.10	.05	.01
☐ 74 Dan Quisenberry	.05	.02	.01
☐ 75 Hal McRae	.10	.05	.01
☐ 76 George Brett	1.50	.70	.19
☐ 77 Larry Gura	.05	.02	.01
☐ 78 John Wathan	.05	.02	.01
☐ 79 Rollie Fingers	.15	.07	.02
☐ 80 Cecil Cooper	.10	.05	.01
☐ 81 Robin Yount FOIL	.50	.23	.06
☐ 82 Ben Oglivie	.05	.02	.01
☐ 83 Paul Molitor	.40	.18	.05
☐ 84 Gorman Thomas	.05	.02	.01

☐ 85 Ted Simmons .10 .05 .01
☐ 86 Pete Vuckovich .05 .02 .01
☐ 87 Gary Gaetti .25 .11 .03
☐ 88 Kent Hrbek FOIL .30 .14 .04
☐ 89 John Castino .05 .02 .01
☐ 90 Tom Brunansky .05 .02 .01
☐ 91 Bobby Mitchell .05 .02 .01
☐ 92 Gary Ward .05 .02 .01
☐ 93 Tim Laudner .05 .02 .01
☐ 94 Ron Davis .05 .02 .01
☐ 95 Willie Randolph .10 .05 .01
☐ 96 Roy Smalley .05 .02 .01
☐ 97 Jerry Mumphrey .05 .02 .01
☐ 98 Ken Griffey .10 .05 .01
☐ 99 Dave Winfield FOIL .50 .23 .06
☐ 100 Rich Gossage .10 .05 .01
☐ 101 Butch Wynegar .05 .02 .01
☐ 102 Ron Guidry .10 .05 .01
☐ 103 Rickey Henderson FOIL .75 .35 .09
☐ 104 Mike Heath .05 .02 .01
☐ 105 Dave Lopes .10 .05 .01
☐ 106 Rick Langford .05 .02 .01
☐ 107 Dwayne Murphy .05 .02 .01
☐ 108 Tony Armas .05 .02 .01
☐ 109 Matt Keough .05 .02 .01
☐ 110 Danny Meyer .05 .02 .01
☐ 111 Bruce Bochte .05 .02 .01
☐ 112 Julio Cruz .05 .02 .01
☐ 113 Floyd Bannister .05 .02 .01
☐ 114 Gaylord Perry FOIL .30 .14 .04
☐ 115 Al Cowens .05 .02 .01
☐ 116 Richie Zisk .05 .02 .01
☐ 117 Jim Essian .05 .02 .01
☐ 118 Bill Caudill .05 .02 .01
☐ 119 Buddy Bell FOIL .15 .07 .02
☐ 120 Larry Parrish .05 .02 .01
☐ 121 Danny Darwin .05 .02 .01
☐ 122 Bucky Dent .10 .05 .01
☐ 123 Johnny Grubb .05 .02 .01
☐ 124 George Wright .05 .02 .01
☐ 125 Charlie Hough .10 .05 .01
☐ 126 Jim Sundberg .05 .02 .01
☐ 127 Dave Stieb FOIL .10 .05 .01
☐ 128 Willie Upshaw .05 .02 .01
☐ 129 Alfredo Griffin .05 .02 .01
☐ 130 Lloyd Moseby .05 .02 .01
☐ 131 Ernie Whitt .05 .02 .01
☐ 132 Jim Clancy .05 .02 .01
☐ 133 Barry Bonnell .05 .02 .01
☐ 134 Damaso Garcia .05 .02 .01
☐ 135 Jim Kaat RB .10 .05 .01
☐ 136 Jim Kaat RB .10 .05 .01
☐ 137 Greg Minton RB .05 .02 .01
☐ 138 Greg Minton RB .05 .02 .01
☐ 139 Paul Molitor RB .15 .07 .02
☐ 140 Paul Molitor RB .15 .07 .02
☐ 141 Manny Trillo RB .05 .02 .01
☐ 142 Manny Trillo RB .05 .02 .01
☐ 143 Joel Youngblood RB .05 .02 .01
☐ 144 Joel Youngblood RB .05 .02 .01
☐ 145 Robin Yount RB .15 .07 .02
☐ 146 Robin Yount RB .15 .07 .02
☐ 147 Willie McGee LCS .10 .05 .01
☐ 148 Darrell Porter LCS .05 .02 .01
☐ 149 Darrell Porter LCS .05 .02 .01
☐ 150 Robin Yount LCS .15 .07 .02
☐ 151 Bruce Benedict LCS .05 .02 .01
☐ 152 Bruce Benedict LCS .05 .02 .01
☐ 153 George Hendrick LCS .05 .02 .01
☐ 154 Bruce Benedict LCS .05 .02 .01
☐ 155 Doug DeCinces LCS .05 .02 .01
☐ 156 Paul Molitor LCS .15 .07 .02
☐ 157 Charlie Moore LCS .05 .02 .01
☐ 158 Fred Lynn LCS .10 .05 .01
☐ 159 Rickey Henderson .50 .23 .06
☐ 160 Dale Murphy .15 .07 .02
☐ 161 Willie Wilson .05 .02 .01
☐ 162 Jack Clark .10 .05 .01
☐ 163 Reggie Jackson .50 .23 .06
☐ 164 Andre Dawson .25 .11 .03
☐ 165 Dan Quisenberry .05 .02 .01
☐ 166 Bruce Sutter .10 .05 .01
☐ 167 Robin Yount .30 .14 .04
☐ 168 Ozzie Smith .75 .35 .09
☐ 169 Frank White .10 .05 .01
☐ 170 Phil Garner .10 .05 .01
☐ 171 Doug DeCinces .05 .02 .01
☐ 172 Mike Schmidt .60 .25 .07
☐ 173 Cecil Cooper .10 .05 .01
☐ 174 Al Oliver .10 .05 .01
☐ 175 Jim Palmer .25 .11 .03
☐ 176 Steve Carlton .40 .18 .05
☐ 177 Carlton Fisk .30 .14 .04
☐ 178 Gary Carter .10 .05 .01
☐ 179 Joaquin Andujar WS .05 .02 .01
☐ 180 Ozzie Smith WS .25 .11 .03
☐ 181 Cecil Cooper WS .10 .05 .01
☐ 182 Darrell Porter WS .05 .02 .01
☐ 183 Darrell Porter WS .05 .02 .01
☐ 184 Mike Caldwell WS .05 .02 .01
☐ 185 Mike Caldwell WS .05 .02 .01
☐ 186 Ozzie Smith WS .25 .11 .03
☐ 187 Bruce Sutter WS .10 .05 .01
☐ 188 Keith Hernandez WS .10 .05 .01
☐ 189 Dane Iorg WS .05 .02 .01
☐ 190 Dane Iorg WS .05 .02 .01
☐ 191 Tony Armas RB .05 .02 .01
☐ 192 Tony Armas RB .05 .02 .01
☐ 193 Lance Parrish RB .10 .05 .01
☐ 194 Lance Parrish RB .10 .05 .01
☐ 195 John Wathan RB .05 .02 .01
☐ 196 John Wathan RB .05 .02 .01
☐ 197 Rickey Henderson RB .25 .11 .03
☐ 198 Rickey Henderson RB .25 .11 .03
☐ 199 Rickey Henderson RB .25 .11 .03
☐ 200 Rickey Henderson RB .25 .11 .03
☐ 201 Rickey Henderson RB .25 .11 .03
☐ 202 Rickey Henderson RB .25 .11 .03
☐ 203 Steve Carlton .40 .18 .05
☐ 204 Steve Carlton .40 .18 .05
☐ 205 Al Oliver .10 .05 .01
☐ 206 Dale Murphy and Al Oliver .15 .07 .02
☐ 207 Dave Kingman .10 .05 .01
☐ 208 Steve Rogers .05 .02 .01
☐ 209 Bruce Sutter .10 .05 .01
☐ 210 Tim Raines .15 .07 .02
☐ 211 Dale Murphy FOIL .30 .14 .04
☐ 212 Chris Chambliss .10 .05 .01
☐ 213 Gene Garber .05 .02 .01
☐ 214 Bob Horner .05 .02 .01
☐ 215 Glenn Hubbard .05 .02 .01
☐ 216 Claudell Washington .05 .02 .01
☐ 217 Bruce Benedict .05 .02 .01
☐ 218 Phil Niekro .15 .07 .02
☐ 219 Leon Durham FOIL .10 .05 .01
☐ 220 Jay Johnstone .10 .05 .01
☐ 221 Larry Bowa .10 .05 .01
☐ 222 Keith Moreland .05 .02 .01
☐ 223 Bill Buckner .10 .05 .01
☐ 224 Fergie Jenkins .15 .07 .02
☐ 225 Dick Tidrow .05 .02 .01
☐ 226 Jody Davis .05 .02 .01
☐ 227 Dave Concepcion .10 .05 .01
☐ 228 Dan Driessen .05 .02 .01
☐ 229 Johnny Bench .50 .23 .06
☐ 230 Ron Oester .05 .02 .01
☐ 231 Cesar Cedeno .10 .05 .01
☐ 232 Alex Trevino .05 .02 .01
☐ 233 Tom Seaver .50 .23 .06
☐ 234 Mario Soto .05 .02 .01
☐ 235 Nolan Ryan FOIL 3.00 1.35 .35
☐ 236 Art Howe .10 .05 .01
☐ 237 Phil Garner .10 .05 .01
☐ 238 Ray Knight .10 .05 .01
☐ 239 Terry Puhl .05 .02 .01
☐ 240 Joe Niekro .10 .05 .01
☐ 241 Alan Ashby .05 .02 .01
☐ 242 Jose Cruz .10 .05 .01
☐ 243 Steve Garvey .15 .07 .02
☐ 244 Ron Cey .10 .05 .01
☐ 245 Dusty Baker .10 .05 .01
☐ 246 Ken Landreaux .05 .02 .01
☐ 247 Jerry Reuss .10 .05 .01
☐ 248 Pedro Guerrero .10 .05 .01
☐ 249 Bill Russell .10 .05 .01
☐ 250 Fern.Valenzuela FOIL .15 .07 .02
☐ 251 Al Oliver FOIL .15 .07 .02
☐ 252 Andre Dawson .25 .11 .03
☐ 253 Tim Raines .15 .07 .02
☐ 254 Jeff Reardon .10 .05 .01
☐ 255 Gary Carter .10 .05 .01
☐ 256 Steve Rogers .05 .02 .01
☐ 257 Tim Wallach .10 .05 .01
☐ 258 Chris Speier .05 .02 .01
☐ 259 Dave Kingman .10 .05 .01
☐ 260 Bob Bailor .05 .02 .01
☐ 261 Hubie Brooks .10 .05 .01
☐ 262 Craig Swan .05 .02 .01
☐ 263 George Foster .10 .05 .01
☐ 264 John Stearns .05 .02 .01
☐ 265 Neil Allen .05 .02 .01
☐ 266 Mookie Wilson FOIL .25 .11 .03
☐ 267 Steve Carlton FOIL .60 .25 .07
☐ 268 Manny Trillo .05 .02 .01
☐ 269 Gary Matthews .05 .02 .01
☐ 270 Mike Schmidt .60 .25 .07
☐ 271 Ivan DeJesus .05 .02 .01
☐ 272 Pete Rose .75 .35 .09
☐ 273 Bo Diaz .05 .02 .01
☐ 274 Sid Monge .05 .02 .01
☐ 275 Bill Madlock FOIL .15 .07 .02
☐ 276 Jason Thompson .05 .02 .01
☐ 277 Don Robinson .05 .02 .01
☐ 278 Omar Moreno .05 .02 .01
☐ 279 Dale Berra .05 .02 .01
☐ 280 Dave Parker .10 .05 .01
☐ 281 Tony Pena .05 .02 .01
☐ 282 John Candelaria .05 .02 .01
☐ 283 Lonnie Smith .05 .02 .01
☐ 284 Bruce Sutter FOIL .15 .07 .02
☐ 285 George Hendrick .05 .02 .01
☐ 286 Tom Herr .10 .05 .01
☐ 287 Ken Oberkfell .05 .02 .01
☐ 288 Ozzie Smith .75 .35 .09
☐ 289 Bob Forsch .05 .02 .01
☐ 290 Keith Hernandez .10 .05 .01
☐ 291 Garry Templeton .05 .02 .01
☐ 292 Broderick Perkins .05 .02 .01
☐ 293 Terry Kennedy FOIL .10 .05 .01
☐ 294 Gene Richards .05 .02 .01
☐ 295 Ruppert Jones .05 .02 .01
☐ 296 Tim Lollar .05 .02 .01
☐ 297 John Montefusco .05 .02 .01
☐ 298 Sixto Lezcano .05 .02 .01
☐ 299 Greg Minton .05 .02 .01
☐ 300 Jack Clark FOIL .15 .07 .02
☐ 301 Milt May .05 .02 .01
☐ 302 Reggie Smith .10 .05 .01
☐ 303 Joe Morgan .25 .11 .03
☐ 304 John LeMaster .05 .02 .01
☐ 305 Darrell Evans .10 .05 .01
☐ 306 Al Holland .05 .02 .01
☐ 307 Jesse Barfield .10 .05 .01
☐ 308 Wade Boggs 3.00 1.35 .35
☐ 309 Tom Brunansky .05 .02 .01
☐ 310 Storm Davis .05 .02 .01
☐ 311 Von Hayes .05 .02 .01
☐ 312 Dave Hostetler .05 .02 .01
☐ 313 Kent Hrbek .10 .05 .01
☐ 314 Tim Laudner .05 .02 .01
☐ 315 Cal Ripken 4.00 1.80 .50
☐ 316 Andre Robertson .05 .02 .01
☐ 317 Ed VandeBerg .05 .02 .01
☐ 318 Glenn Wilson .10 .05 .01
☐ 319 Chili Davis .10 .05 .01
☐ 320 Bob Dernier .05 .02 .01
☐ 321 Terry Francona .05 .02 .01
☐ 322 Brian Giles .05 .02 .01
☐ 323 David Green .05 .02 .01
☐ 324 Atlee Hammaker .05 .02 .01
☐ 325 Bill Laskey .05 .02 .01
☐ 326 Willie McGee .25 .11 .03
☐ 327 Johnny Ray .05 .02 .01
☐ 328 Ryne Sandberg 4.00 1.80 .50
☐ 329 Steve Sax .10 .05 .01
☐ 330 Eric Show .05 .02 .01
☐ xx Album 1.00 .45 .12

1983 Topps Sticker Boxes

The cards in this eight (box) card set measure the standard size. The 1983 Topps baseball stickers were distributed in boxes which themselves contained a baseball card. In all there were eight different boxes each originally containing 30 stickers but no foils; hence, eight blank-backed cards comprise the box set. The box itself contained an offer for the sticker album and featured a Reggie Jackson photo. Stickers in the boxes came in six strips of five. The prices below reflect the value of the cards on the outside of the box only.

	NRMT	VG-E	GOOD
COMPLETE SET (8)	5.00	2.20	.60
COMMON CARD (1-8)	.40	.18	.05
☐ 1 Fernando Valenzuela	.40	.18	.05
☐ 2 Gary Carter	.40	.18	.05
☐ 3 Mike Schmidt	1.25	.55	.16
☐ 4 Reggie Jackson	1.00	.45	.12
☐ 5 Jim Palmer	.50	.23	.06
☐ 6 Rollie Fingers	.40	.18	.05
☐ 7 Pete Rose	1.50	.70	.19
☐ 8 Rickey Henderson	1.00	.45	.12

1983 Topps Gaylord Perry

This six-card, standard-size, set depicts Gaylord Perry during various parts of his career. These cards have the looks of Topps cards and were produced by Topps but have no Topps logo on either the front or the back of the card.

	NRMT	VG-E	GOOD
COMPLETE SET (6)	15.00	6.75	1.85
COMMON CARD (1-6)	3.00	1.35	.35
☐ 1 Gaylord Perry San Francisco Giants (Perry wins first game in 1962)	3.00	1.35	.35
☐ 2 Gaylord Perry San Francisco Giants (Perry pitches no- hitter in 1968)	3.00	1.35	.35
☐ 3 Gaylord Perry Cleveland Indians (Perry wins Cy Young Award in 1972)	3.00	1.35	.35
☐ 4 Gaylord Perry Texas Rangers (Perry strikes out 2,500th in 1975)	3.00	1.35	.35
☐ 5 Gaylord Perry San Diego Padres (Perry wins second Cy Young and strikes out 3,000th in 1978)	3.00	1.35	.35
☐ 6 Gaylord Perry Seattle Mariners (Perry wins 300th game in 1982)	3.00	1.35	.35

1983 Topps Reprint 52

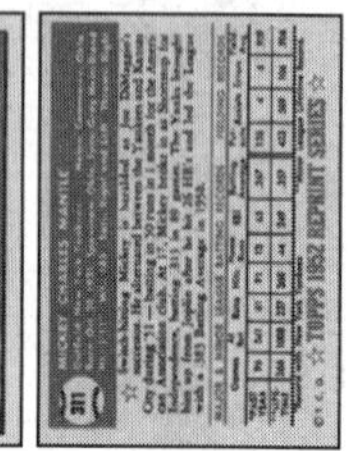

This 402 card standard-size set feature reprinted versions of the cards in the 52 Topps set. These sets were issued in complete form only available from Topps. Five players did not agree to be in this set, that is why the set only contains 402 cards.

	NRMT	VG-E	GOOD
COMP. SET (402)	225.00	100.00	28.00
COMP. FACTORY SET (402)	275.00	125.00	34.00
COMMON CARD (1-407)	.50	.23	.06
SEMISTARS	1.00	.45	.12
STARS	2.00	.90	.25
☐ 1 Andy Pafko	3.00	1.35	.35
☐ 11 Phil Rizzuto	10.00	4.50	1.25
☐ 20 Billy Loes	3.00	1.35	.35
☐ 22 Dom DiMaggio	5.00	2.20	.60
☐ 26 Monte Irvin	7.50	3.40	.95
☐ 29 Ted Kluszewski	7.50	3.40	.95
☐ 33 Warren Spahn	10.00	4.50	1.25
☐ 36 Gil Hodges	10.00	4.50	1.25
☐ 37 Duke Snider	15.00	6.75	1.85
☐ 59 Robin Roberts	10.00	4.50	1.25
☐ 65 Enos Slaughter	10.00	4.50	1.25
☐ 88 Bob Feller	15.00	6.75	1.85
☐ 91 Red Schoendienst	7.50	3.40	.95
☐ 122 Jackie Jensen	5.00	2.20	.60
☐ 129 Johnny Mize	7.50	3.40	.95
☐ 175 Billy Martin	10.00	4.50	1.25
☐ 191 Yogi Berra	15.00	6.75	1.85
☐ 195 Minnie Minoso	7.50	3.40	.95
☐ 216 Richie Ashburn	10.00	4.50	1.25
☐ 227 Joe Garagiola	5.00	2.20	.60
☐ 243 Larry Doby	5.00	2.20	.60
☐ 246 George Kell	7.50	3.40	.95
☐ 261 Willie Mays	25.00	11.00	3.10
☐ 268 Bob Lemon	7.50	3.40	.95
☐ 277 Early Wynn	7.50	3.40	.95
☐ 311 Mickey Mantle	50.00	22.00	6.25
☐ 312 Jackie Robinson	25.00	11.00	3.10
☐ 313 Bobby Thomson	5.00	2.20	.60
☐ 314 Roy Campanella	10.00	4.50	1.25
☐ 315 Leo Durocher MG	7.50	3.40	.95
☐ 321 Joe Black	5.00	2.20	.60
☐ 333 Pee Wee Reese	10.00	4.50	1.25
☐ 342 Clem Labine	5.00	2.20	.60
☐ 369 Dick Groat	5.00	2.20	.60
☐ 372 Gil McDougald	5.00	2.20	.60
☐ 384 Frank Crosetti CO	5.00	2.20	.60
☐ 392 Hoyt Wilhelm	7.50	3.40	.95
☐ 394 Billy Herman CO	5.00	2.20	.60
☐ 396 Dick Williams	5.00	2.20	.60
☐ 400 Bill Dickey CO	7.50	3.40	.95
☐ 407 Eddie Mathews	10.00	4.50	1.25

1983-91 Topps Traded Bronze Premiums

Dealers who ordered Topps Traded cases received these bronze replica cards as bonuses. These cards which measure approximately 1 1/4" by 1 3/4" started off by featuring current players but later switched to retired stars. We have sequenced this set by year of release.

	NRMT	VG-E	GOOD
COMPLETE SET (9)	200.00	90.00	25.00
COMMON CARDS (1-9)	15.00	6.75	1.85
☐ 1 Steve Carlton	40.00	18.00	5.00
☐ 2 Darryl Strawberry	15.00	6.75	1.85

☐ 3 Pete Rose	15.00	6.75	1.85
☐ 4 Mickey Mantle	50.00	22.00	6.25
☐ 5 Willie Mays	25.00	11.00	3.10
☐ 6 Duke Snider	15.00	6.75	1.85
☐ 7 Hank Aaron	20.00	9.00	2.50
☐ 8 Jackie Robinson	20.00	9.00	2.50
☐ 9 Brooks Robinson	20.00	9.00	2.50

1984 Topps

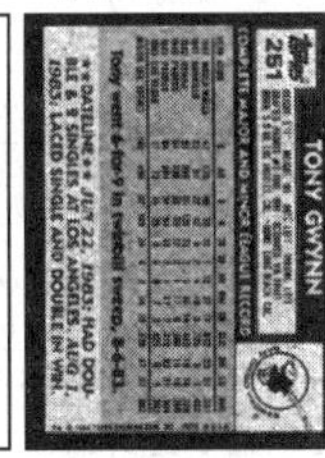

The cards in this 792-card set measure the standard size. For the second year in a row, Topps utilized a dual picture on the front of the card. A portrait is shown in a square insert and an action shot is featured in the main photo. Card numbers 1-6 feature 1983 Highlights (HL), cards 131-138 depict League Leaders, card numbers 386-407 feature All-Stars, and card numbers 701-718 feature active Major League career leaders in various statistical categories. Each team leader (TL) card features the team's leading hitter and pitcher pictured on the front with a team checklist back. There are six numerical checklist cards in the set. The player cards feature team logos in the upper right corner of the reverse. Cards were primarily distributed in 15-card wax packs and 54-card rack packs. The key Rookie Cards in this set are Don Mattingly and Darryl Strawberry. Topps tested a special send-in offer in Michigan and a few other states whereby collectors could obtain direct from Topps ten cards of their choice. Needless to say most people ordered the key (most valuable) players necessitating the printing of a special sheet to keep up with the demand. The special sheet had five cards of Darryl Strawberry, three cards of Don Mattingly, etc. The test was apparently a failure in Topps' eyes as they have never tried it again.

	NRMT	VG-E	GOOD
COMPLETE SET (792)	50.00	22.00	6.25
COMMON CARD (1-792)	.08	.04	.01
☐ 1 Steve Carlton HL	.50	.23	.06
300th win and			
all-time SO king			
☐ 2 Rickey Henderson HL	.75	.35	.09
100 stolen bases			
three times			
☐ 3 Dan Quisenberry HL	.08	.04	.01
Sets save record			
☐ 4 Nolan Ryan HL	1.00	.45	.12
Steve Carlton			
Gaylord Perry			
All surpass Johnson			
☐ 5 Dave Righetti HL	.15	.07	.02
Bob Forsch			
Mike Warren			
All pitch no-hitters			
☐ 6 Johnny Bench HL	.40	.18	.05
Gaylord Perry			
Carl Yastrzemski			
Superstars retire			
☐ 7 Gary Lucas	.08	.04	.01
☐ 8 Don Mattingly	12.00	5.50	1.50
☐ 9 Jim Gott	.08	.04	.01
☐ 10 Robin Yount	1.00	.45	.12
☐ 11 Minnesota Twins TL	.15	.07	.02
Kent Hrbek			
Ken Schrom			
(Checklist on back)			
☐ 12 Billy Sample	.08	.04	.01
☐ 13 Scott Holman	.08	.04	.01
☐ 14 Tom Brookens	.15	.07	.02
☐ 15 Burt Hooton	.08	.04	.01
☐ 16 Omar Moreno	.08	.04	.01
☐ 17 John Denny	.08	.04	.01
☐ 18 Dale Berra	.08	.04	.01
☐ 19 Ray Fontenot	.08	.04	.01
☐ 20 Greg Luzinski	.15	.07	.02
☐ 21 Joe Altobelli MG	.08	.04	.01
☐ 22 Bryan Clark	.08	.04	.01
☐ 23 Keith Moreland	.08	.04	.01
☐ 24 John Martin	.08	.04	.01
☐ 25 Glenn Hubbard	.08	.04	.01
☐ 26 Bud Black	.08	.04	.01
☐ 27 Daryl Sconiers	.08	.04	.01
☐ 28 Frank Viola	.40	.18	.05
☐ 29 Danny Heep	.08	.04	.01
☐ 30 Wade Boggs	1.25	.55	.16
☐ 31 Andy McGaffigan	.08	.04	.01
☐ 32 Bobby Ramos	.08	.04	.01
☐ 33 Tom Burgmeier	.08	.04	.01
☐ 34 Eddie Milner	.08	.04	.01
☐ 35 Don Sutton	.40	.18	.05
☐ 36 Denny Walling	.08	.04	.01
☐ 37 Texas Rangers TL	.15	.07	.02
Buddy Bell			
Rick Honeycutt			
(Checklist on back)			
☐ 38 Luis DeLeon	.08	.04	.01
☐ 39 Garth Iorg	.08	.04	.01
☐ 40 Dusty Baker	.40	.18	.05
☐ 41 Tony Bernazard	.08	.04	.01
☐ 42 Johnny Grubb	.08	.04	.01
☐ 43 Ron Reed	.08	.04	.01
☐ 44 Jim Morrison	.08	.04	.01
☐ 45 Jerry Mumphrey	.08	.04	.01
☐ 46 Ray Smith	.08	.04	.01
☐ 47 Rudy Law	.08	.04	.01
☐ 48 Julio Franco	.40	.18	.05
☐ 49 John Stuper	.08	.04	.01
☐ 50 Chris Chambliss	.08	.04	.01
☐ 51 Jim Frey MG	.08	.04	.01
☐ 52 Paul Splittorff	.08	.04	.01
☐ 53 Juan Beniquez	.08	.04	.01
☐ 54 Jesse Orosco	.08	.04	.01
☐ 55 Dave Concepcion	.15	.07	.02
☐ 56 Gary Allenson	.08	.04	.01
☐ 57 Dan Schatzeder	.08	.04	.01
☐ 58 Max Venable	.08	.04	.01
☐ 59 Sammy Stewart	.08	.04	.01
☐ 60 Paul Molitor UER	1.00	.45	.12
('83 stats .272, 613,			
167; should be .270,			
608, 164)			
☐ 61 Chris Codiroli	.08	.04	.01
☐ 62 Dave Hostetler	.08	.04	.01
☐ 63 Ed VandeBerg	.08	.04	.01
☐ 64 Mike Scioscia	.08	.04	.01
☐ 65 Kirk Gibson	.40	.18	.05
☐ 66 Houston Astros TL	.75	.35	.09
Jose Cruz			
Nolan Ryan			
(Checklist on back)			
☐ 67 Gary Ward	.08	.04	.01
☐ 68 Luis Salazar	.08	.04	.01
☐ 69 Rod Scurry	.08	.04	.01
☐ 70 Gary Matthews	.08	.04	.01
☐ 71 Leo Hernandez	.08	.04	.01
☐ 72 Mike Squires	.08	.04	.01
☐ 73 Jody Davis	.08	.04	.01
☐ 74 Jerry Martin	.08	.04	.01
☐ 75 Bob Forsch	.08	.04	.01
☐ 76 Alfredo Griffin	.08	.04	.01
☐ 77 Brett Butler	.40	.18	.05
☐ 78 Mike Torrez	.08	.04	.01
☐ 79 Rob Wilfong	.08	.04	.01
☐ 80 Steve Rogers	.08	.04	.01
☐ 81 Billy Martin MG	.15	.07	.02
☐ 82 Doug Bird	.08	.04	.01
☐ 83 Richie Zisk	.08	.04	.01
☐ 84 Lenny Faedo	.08	.04	.01
☐ 85 Atlee Hammaker	.08	.04	.01
☐ 86 John Shelby	.08	.04	.01
☐ 87 Frank Pastore	.08	.04	.01
☐ 88 Rob Picciolo	.08	.04	.01
☐ 89 Mike Smithson	.08	.04	.01
☐ 90 Pedro Guerrero	.15	.07	.02
☐ 91 Dan Spillner	.08	.04	.01
☐ 92 Lloyd Moseby	.08	.04	.01
☐ 93 Bob Knepper	.08	.04	.01
☐ 94 Mario Ramirez	.08	.04	.01
☐ 95 Aurelio Lopez	.15	.07	.02
☐ 96 Kansas City Royals TL	.40	.18	.05
Hal McRae			
Larry Gura			
(Checklist on back)			
☐ 97 LaMarr Hoyt	.08	.04	.01
☐ 98 Steve Nicosia	.08	.04	.01
☐ 99 Craig Lefferts	.08	.04	.01
☐ 100 Reggie Jackson	.75	.35	.09
☐ 101 Porfirio Altamirano	.08	.04	.01
☐ 102 Ken Oberkfell	.08	.04	.01
☐ 103 Dwayne Murphy	.08	.04	.01
☐ 104 Ken Dayley	.08	.04	.01
☐ 105 Tony Armas	.08	.04	.01
☐ 106 Tim Stoddard	.08	.04	.01
☐ 107 Ned Yost	.08	.04	.01
☐ 108 Randy Moffitt	.08	.04	.01
☐ 109 Brad Wellman	.08	.04	.01
☐ 110 Ron Guidry	.15	.07	.02
☐ 111 Bill Virdon MG	.08	.04	.01
☐ 112 Tom Niedenfuer	.08	.04	.01
☐ 113 Kelly Paris	.08	.04	.01
☐ 114 Checklist 1-132	.15	.07	.02
☐ 115 Andre Thornton	.08	.04	.01
☐ 116 George Bjorkman	.08	.04	.01
☐ 117 Tom Veryzer	.08	.04	.01
☐ 118 Charlie Hough	.15	.07	.02
☐ 119 John Wockenfuss	.08	.04	.01
☐ 120 Keith Hernandez	.15	.07	.02
☐ 121 Pat Sheridan	.08	.04	.01
☐ 122 Cecilio Guante	.08	.04	.01
☐ 123 Butch Wynegar	.08	.04	.01
☐ 124 Damaso Garcia	.08	.04	.01
☐ 125 Britt Burns	.08	.04	.01
☐ 126 Atlanta Braves TL	.40	.18	.05
Dale Murphy			
Craig McMurtry			
(Checklist on back)			
☐ 127 Mike Madden	.08	.04	.01
☐ 128 Rick Manning	.08	.04	.01
☐ 129 Bill Laskey	.08	.04	.01
☐ 130 Ozzie Smith	1.50	.70	.19
☐ 131 Batting Leaders	.50	.23	.06
Bill Madlock			
Wade Boggs			
☐ 132 Home Run Leaders	.40	.18	.05
Mike Schmidt			
Jim Rice			
☐ 133 RBI Leaders	.40	.18	.05
Dale Murphy			
Cecil Cooper			
Jim Rice			
☐ 134 Stolen Base Leaders	.75	.35	.09
Tim Raines			
Rickey Henderson			
☐ 135 Victory Leaders	.40	.18	.05
John Denny			
LaMarr Hoyt			
☐ 136 Strikeout Leaders	.40	.18	.05
Steve Carlton			
Jack Morris			
☐ 137 ERA Leaders	.40	.18	.05
Atlee Hammaker			
Rick Honeycutt			
☐ 138 Leading Firemen	.40	.18	.05
Al Holland			
Dan Quisenberry			
☐ 139 Bert Campaneris	.15	.07	.02
☐ 140 Storm Davis	.08	.04	.01
☐ 141 Pat Corrales MG	.08	.04	.01
☐ 142 Rich Gale	.08	.04	.01
☐ 143 Jose Morales	.08	.04	.01
☐ 144 Brian Harper	.40	.18	.05
☐ 145 Gary Lavelle	.08	.04	.01
☐ 146 Ed Romero	.08	.04	.01
☐ 147 Dan Petry	.15	.07	.02
☐ 148 Joe Lefebvre	.08	.04	.01
☐ 149 Jon Matlack	.08	.04	.01
☐ 150 Dale Murphy	.40	.18	.05
☐ 151 Steve Trout	.08	.04	.01
☐ 152 Glenn Brummer	.08	.04	.01
☐ 153 Dick Tidrow	.08	.04	.01
☐ 154 Dave Henderson	.15	.07	.02
☐ 155 Frank White	.15	.07	.02
☐ 156 Oakland A's TL	.40	.18	.05
Rickey Henderson			
Tim Conroy			
(Checklist on back)			
☐ 157 Gary Gaetti	.40	.18	.05
☐ 158 John Curtis	.08	.04	.01
☐ 159 Darryl Cias	.08	.04	.01
☐ 160 Mario Soto	.08	.04	.01
☐ 161 Junior Ortiz	.08	.04	.01
☐ 162 Bob Ojeda	.08	.04	.01
☐ 163 Lorenzo Gray	.08	.04	.01
☐ 164 Scott Sanderson	.08	.04	.01
☐ 165 Ken Singleton	.08	.04	.01
☐ 166 Jamie Nelson	.08	.04	.01
☐ 167 Marshall Edwards	.08	.04	.01
☐ 168 Juan Bonilla	.08	.04	.01
☐ 169 Larry Parrish	.08	.04	.01
☐ 170 Jerry Reuss	.08	.04	.01
☐ 171 Frank Robinson MG	.40	.18	.05
☐ 172 Frank DiPino	.08	.04	.01
☐ 173 Marvell Wynne	.08	.04	.01
☐ 174 Juan Berenguer	.08	.04	.01
☐ 175 Graig Nettles	.15	.07	.02
☐ 176 Lee Smith	.75	.35	.09
☐ 177 Jerry Hairston	.08	.04	.01
☐ 178 Bill Krueger	.08	.04	.01
☐ 179 Buck Martinez	.08	.04	.01
☐ 180 Manny Trillo	.08	.04	.01
☐ 181 Roy Thomas	.08	.04	.01
☐ 182 Darryl Strawberry	3.00	1.35	.35
☐ 183 Al Williams	.08	.04	.01
☐ 184 Mike O'Berry	.08	.04	.01
☐ 185 Sixto Lezcano	.08	.04	.01
☐ 186 Cardinal TL	.15	.07	.02
Lonnie Smith			
John Stuper			
(Checklist on back)			
☐ 187 Luis Aponte	.08	.04	.01
☐ 188 Bryan Little	.08	.04	.01
☐ 189 Tim Conroy	.08	.04	.01
☐ 190 Ben Oglivie	.08	.04	.01
☐ 191 Mike Boddicker	.08	.04	.01
☐ 192 Nick Esasky	.08	.04	.01
☐ 193 Darrell Brown	.08	.04	.01
☐ 194 Domingo Ramos	.08	.04	.01
☐ 195 Jack Morris	.15	.07	.02
☐ 196 Don Slaught	.15	.07	.02
☐ 197 Garry Hancock	.08	.04	.01
☐ 198 Bill Doran	.15	.07	.02
☐ 199 Willie Hernandez	.15	.07	.02
☐ 200 Andre Dawson	.75	.35	.09
☐ 201 Bruce Kison	.08	.04	.01
☐ 202 Bobby Cox MG	.15	.07	.02
☐ 203 Matt Keough	.08	.04	.01
☐ 204 Bobby Meacham	.08	.04	.01
☐ 205 Greg Minton	.08	.04	.01
☐ 206 Andy Van Slyke	.60	.25	.07
☐ 207 Donnie Moore	.08	.04	.01
☐ 208 Jose Oquendo	.15	.07	.02
☐ 209 Manny Sarmiento	.08	.04	.01
☐ 210 Joe Morgan	.40	.18	.05
☐ 211 Rick Sweet	.08	.04	.01
☐ 212 Broderick Perkins	.08	.04	.01
☐ 213 Bruce Hurst	.08	.04	.01
☐ 214 Paul Householder	.08	.04	.01
☐ 215 Tippy Martinez	.08	.04	.01
☐ 216 White Sox TL	.40	.18	.05
Carlton Fisk			
Richard Dotson			
(Checklist on back)			
☐ 217 Alan Ashby	.08	.04	.01
☐ 218 Rick Waits	.08	.04	.01
☐ 219 Joe Simpson	.08	.04	.01
☐ 220 Fernando Valenzuela	.15	.07	.02
☐ 221 Cliff Johnson	.08	.04	.01
☐ 222 Rick Honeycutt	.08	.04	.01
☐ 223 Wayne Krenchicki	.08	.04	.01
☐ 224 Sid Monge	.08	.04	.01
☐ 225 Lee Mazzilli	.08	.04	.01
☐ 226 Juan Eichelberger	.08	.04	.01
☐ 227 Steve Braun	.08	.04	.01
☐ 228 John Rabb	.08	.04	.01
☐ 229 Paul Owens MG	.08	.04	.01
☐ 230 Rickey Henderson	1.00	.45	.12
☐ 231 Gary Woods	.08	.04	.01
☐ 232 Tim Wallach	.15	.07	.02
☐ 233 Checklist 133-264	.15	.07	.02
☐ 234 Rafael Ramirez	.08	.04	.01
☐ 235 Matt Young	.08	.04	.01
☐ 236 Ellis Valentine	.08	.04	.01
☐ 237 John Castino	.08	.04	.01
☐ 238 Reid Nichols	.08	.04	.01
☐ 239 Jay Howell	.08	.04	.01
☐ 240 Eddie Murray	1.50	.70	.19
☐ 241 Bill Almon	.08	.04	.01
☐ 242 Alex Trevino	.08	.04	.01
☐ 243 Pete Ladd	.08	.04	.01
☐ 244 Candy Maldonado	.08	.04	.01
☐ 245 Rick Sutcliffe	.15	.07	.02
☐ 246 New York Mets TL	.40	.18	.05
Mookie Wilson			
Tom Seaver			
(Checklist on back)			
☐ 247 Onix Concepcion	.08	.04	.01
☐ 248 Bill Dawley	.08	.04	.01
☐ 249 Jay Johnstone	.15	.07	.02
☐ 250 Bill Madlock	.08	.04	.01
☐ 251 Tony Gwynn	5.00	2.20	.60
☐ 252 Larry Christenson	.08	.04	.01
☐ 253 Jim Wohlford	.08	.04	.01
☐ 254 Shane Rawley	.08	.04	.01
☐ 255 Bruce Benedict	.08	.04	.01
☐ 256 Dave Geisel	.08	.04	.01
☐ 257 Julio Cruz	.08	.04	.01
☐ 258 Luis Sanchez	.08	.04	.01
☐ 259 Sparky Anderson MG	.15	.07	.02
☐ 260 Scott McGregor	.08	.04	.01
☐ 261 Bobby Brown	.08	.04	.01
☐ 262 Tom Candiotti	.40	.18	.05
☐ 263 Jack Fimple	.08	.04	.01
☐ 264 Doug Frobel	.08	.04	.01
☐ 265 Donnie Hill	.08	.04	.01
☐ 266 Steve Lubratich	.08	.04	.01
☐ 267 Carmelo Martinez	.08	.04	.01
☐ 268 Jack O'Connor	.08	.04	.01
☐ 269 Aurelio Rodriguez	.08	.04	.01
☐ 270 Jeff Russell	.40	.18	.05
☐ 271 Moose Haas	.08	.04	.01
☐ 272 Rick Dempsey	.08	.04	.01
☐ 273 Charlie Puleo	.08	.04	.01
☐ 274 Rick Monday	.08	.04	.01
☐ 275 Len Matuszek	.08	.04	.01
☐ 276 Angels TL	.40	.18	.05
Rod Carew			
Geoff Zahn			
(Checklist on back)			
☐ 277 Eddie Whitson	.08	.04	.01
☐ 278 Jorge Bell	.15	.07	.02
☐ 279 Ivan DeJesus	.08	.04	.01
☐ 280 Floyd Bannister	.08	.04	.01
☐ 281 Larry Milbourne	.08	.04	.01
☐ 282 Jim Barr	.08	.04	.01
☐ 283 Larry Biittner	.08	.04	.01
☐ 284 Howard Bailey	.08	.04	.01
☐ 285 Darrell Porter	.08	.04	.01
☐ 286 Lary Sorensen	.08	.04	.01
☐ 287 Warren Cromartie	.08	.04	.01
☐ 288 Jim Beattie	.08	.04	.01
☐ 289 Randy Johnson	.08	.04	.01
☐ 290 Dave Dravecky	.15	.07	.02
☐ 291 Chuck Tanner MG	.08	.04	.01
☐ 292 Tony Scott	.08	.04	.01
☐ 293 Ed Lynch	.08	.04	.01
☐ 294 U.L. Washington	.08	.04	.01
☐ 295 Mike Flanagan	.08	.04	.01
☐ 296 Jeff Newman	.08	.04	.01
☐ 297 Bruce Berenyi	.08	.04	.01
☐ 298 Jim Gantner	.15	.07	.02
☐ 299 John Butcher	.08	.04	.01
☐ 300 Pete Rose	1.00	.45	.12
☐ 301 Frank LaCorte	.08	.04	.01
☐ 302 Barry Bonnell	.08	.04	.01
☐ 303 Marty Castillo	.08	.04	.01
☐ 304 Warren Brusstar	.08	.04	.01
☐ 305 Roy Smalley	.08	.04	.01
☐ 306 Dodgers TL	.15	.07	.02
Pedro Guerrero			
Bob Welch			

(Checklist on back)			
☐ 307 Bobby Mitchell	.08	.04	.01
☐ 308 Ron Hassey	.08	.04	.01
☐ 309 Tony Phillips	1.00	.45	.12
☐ 310 Willie McGee	.40	.18	.05
☐ 311 Jerry Koosman	.15	.07	.02
☐ 312 Jorge Orta	.08	.04	.01
☐ 313 Mike Jorgensen	.08	.04	.01
☐ 314 Orlando Mercado	.08	.04	.01
☐ 315 Bob Grich	.15	.07	.02
☐ 316 Mark Bradley	.08	.04	.01
☐ 317 Greg Pryor	.08	.04	.01
☐ 318 Bill Gullickson	.08	.04	.01
☐ 319 Al Bumbry	.15	.07	.02
☐ 320 Bob Stanley	.08	.04	.01
☐ 321 Harvey Kuenn MG	.15	.07	.02
☐ 322 Ken Schrom	.08	.04	.01
☐ 323 Alan Knicely	.08	.04	.01
☐ 324 Alejandro Pena	.15	.07	.02
☐ 325 Darrell Evans	.15	.07	.02
☐ 326 Bob Kearney	.08	.04	.01
☐ 327 Ruppert Jones	.08	.04	.01
☐ 328 Vern Ruhle	.08	.04	.01
☐ 329 Pat Tabler	.08	.04	.01
☐ 330 John Candelaria	.08	.04	.01
☐ 331 Bucky Dent	.15	.07	.02
☐ 332 Kevin Gross	.15	.07	.02
☐ 333 Larry Herndon	.15	.07	.02
☐ 334 Chuck Rainey	.08	.04	.01
☐ 335 Don Baylor	.40	.18	.05
☐ 336 Seattle Mariners TL	.15	.07	.02
Pat Putnam			
Matt Young			
(Checklist on back)			
☐ 337 Kevin Hagen	.08	.04	.01
☐ 338 Mike Warren	.08	.04	.01
☐ 339 Roy Lee Jackson	.08	.04	.01
☐ 340 Hal McRae	.15	.07	.02
☐ 341 Dave Tobik	.08	.04	.01
☐ 342 Tim Foli	.08	.04	.01
☐ 343 Mark Davis	.08	.04	.01
☐ 344 Rick Miller	.08	.04	.01
☐ 345 Kent Hrbek	.15	.07	.02
☐ 346 Kurt Bevacqua	.08	.04	.01
☐ 347 Allan Ramirez	.08	.04	.01
☐ 348 Toby Harrah	.15	.07	.02
☐ 349 Bob L. Gibson	.08	.04	.01
☐ 350 George Foster	.15	.07	.02
☐ 351 Russ Nixon MG	.08	.04	.01
☐ 352 Dave Stewart	.15	.07	.02
☐ 353 Jim Anderson	.08	.04	.01
☐ 354 Jeff Burroughs	.08	.04	.01
☐ 355 Jason Thompson	.08	.04	.01
☐ 356 Glenn Abbott	.08	.04	.01
☐ 357 Ron Cey	.15	.07	.02
☐ 358 Bob Dernier	.08	.04	.01
☐ 359 Jim Acker	.08	.04	.01
☐ 360 Willie Randolph	.15	.07	.02
☐ 361 Dave Smith	.08	.04	.01
☐ 362 David Green	.08	.04	.01
☐ 363 Tim Laudner	.08	.04	.01
☐ 364 Scott Fletcher	.08	.04	.01
☐ 365 Steve Bedrosian	.08	.04	.01
☐ 366 Padres TL	.15	.07	.02
Terry Kennedy			
Dave Dravecky			
(Checklist on back)			
☐ 367 Jamie Easterly	.08	.04	.01
☐ 368 Hubie Brooks	.08	.04	.01
☐ 369 Steve McCatty	.08	.04	.01
☐ 370 Tim Raines	.40	.18	.05
☐ 371 Dave Gumpert	.08	.04	.01
☐ 372 Gary Roenicke	.08	.04	.01
☐ 373 Bill Scherrer	.08	.04	.01
☐ 374 Don Money	.08	.04	.01
☐ 375 Dennis Leonard	.08	.04	.01
☐ 376 Dave Anderson	.08	.04	.01
☐ 377 Danny Darwin	.08	.04	.01
☐ 378 Bob Brenly	.08	.04	.01
☐ 379 Checklist 265-396	.15	.07	.02
☐ 380 Steve Garvey	.40	.18	.05
☐ 381 Ralph Houk MG	.15	.07	.02
☐ 382 Chris Nyman	.08	.04	.01
☐ 383 Terry Puhl	.08	.04	.01
☐ 384 Lee Tunnell	.08	.04	.01
☐ 385 Tony Perez	.40	.18	.05
☐ 386 George Hendrick AS	.08	.04	.01
☐ 387 Johnny Ray AS	.08	.04	.01
☐ 388 Mike Schmidt AS	.50	.23	.06
☐ 389 Ozzie Smith AS	.75	.35	.09
☐ 390 Tim Raines AS	.40	.18	.05
☐ 391 Dale Murphy AS	.40	.18	.05
☐ 392 Andre Dawson AS	.40	.18	.05
☐ 393 Gary Carter AS	.15	.07	.02
☐ 394 Steve Rogers AS	.08	.04	.01
☐ 395 Steve Carlton AS	.40	.18	.05
☐ 396 Jesse Orosco AS	.08	.04	.01
☐ 397 Eddie Murray AS	.75	.35	.09
☐ 398 Lou Whitaker AS	.15	.07	.02
☐ 399 George Brett AS	1.00	.45	.12
☐ 400 Cal Ripken AS	2.00	.90	.25
☐ 401 Jim Rice AS	.15	.07	.02
☐ 402 Dave Winfield AS	.60	.25	.07
☐ 403 Lloyd Moseby AS	.08	.04	.01
☐ 404 Ted Simmons AS	.15	.07	.02
☐ 405 LaMarr Hoyt AS	.08	.04	.01
☐ 406 Ron Guidry AS	.15	.07	.02
☐ 407 Dan Quisenberry AS	.08	.04	.01
☐ 408 Lou Piniella	.15	.07	.02
☐ 409 Juan Agosto	.08	.04	.01
☐ 410 Claudell Washington	.08	.04	.01
☐ 411 Houston Jimenez	.08	.04	.01
☐ 412 Doug Rader MG	.08	.04	.01
☐ 413 Spike Owen	.15	.07	.02
☐ 414 Mitchell Page	.08	.04	.01
☐ 415 Tommy John	.40	.18	.05
☐ 416 Dane Iorg	.08	.04	.01
☐ 417 Mike Armstrong	.08	.04	.01
☐ 418 Ron Hodges	.08	.04	.01
☐ 419 John Henry Johnson	.08	.04	.01
☐ 420 Cecil Cooper	.15	.07	.02
☐ 421 Charlie Lea	.08	.04	.01
☐ 422 Jose Cruz	.15	.07	.02
☐ 423 Mike Morgan	.15	.07	.02
☐ 424 Dann Bilardello	.08	.04	.01
☐ 425 Steve Howe	.08	.04	.01
☐ 426 Orioles TL	1.50	.70	.19
Cal Ripken			
Mike Boddicker			
(Checklist on back)			
☐ 427 Rick Leach	.08	.04	.01
☐ 428 Fred Breining	.08	.04	.01
☐ 429 Randy Bush	.08	.04	.01
☐ 430 Rusty Staub	.15	.07	.02
☐ 431 Chris Bando	.08	.04	.01
☐ 432 Charles Hudson	.08	.04	.01
☐ 433 Rich Hebner	.08	.04	.01
☐ 434 Harold Baines	.15	.07	.02
☐ 435 Neil Allen	.08	.04	.01
☐ 436 Rick Peters	.08	.04	.01
☐ 437 Mike Proly	.08	.04	.01
☐ 438 Biff Pocoroba	.08	.04	.01
☐ 439 Bob Stoddard	.08	.04	.01
☐ 440 Steve Kemp	.08	.04	.01
☐ 441 Bob Lillis MG	.08	.04	.01
☐ 442 Byron McLaughlin	.08	.04	.01
☐ 443 Benny Ayala	.08	.04	.01
☐ 444 Steve Renko	.08	.04	.01
☐ 445 Jerry Remy	.08	.04	.01
☐ 446 Luis Pujols	.08	.04	.01
☐ 447 Tom Brunansky	.15	.07	.02
☐ 448 Ben Hayes	.08	.04	.01
☐ 449 Joe Pettini	.08	.04	.01
☐ 450 Gary Carter	.15	.07	.02
☐ 451 Bob Jones	.08	.04	.01
☐ 452 Chuck Porter	.08	.04	.01
☐ 453 Willie Upshaw	.08	.04	.01
☐ 454 Joe Beckwith	.08	.04	.01
☐ 455 Terry Kennedy	.08	.04	.01
☐ 456 Chicago Cubs TL	.40	.18	.05
Keith Moreland			
Fergie Jenkins			
(Checklist on back)			
☐ 457 Dave Rozema	.08	.04	.01
☐ 458 Kiko Garcia	.08	.04	.01
☐ 459 Kevin Hickey	.08	.04	.01
☐ 460 Dave Winfield	1.00	.45	.12
☐ 461 Jim Maler	.08	.04	.01
☐ 462 Lee Lacy	.08	.04	.01
☐ 463 Dave Engle	.08	.04	.01
☐ 464 Jeff A. Jones	.08	.04	.01
☐ 465 Mookie Wilson	.15	.07	.02
☐ 466 Gene Garber	.08	.04	.01
☐ 467 Mike Ramsey	.08	.04	.01
☐ 468 Geoff Zahn	.08	.04	.01
☐ 469 Tom O'Malley	.08	.04	.01
☐ 470 Nolan Ryan	4.00	1.80	.50
☐ 471 Dick Howser MG	.08	.04	.01
☐ 472 Mike G. Brown	.08	.04	.01
☐ 473 Jim Dwyer	.08	.04	.01
☐ 474 Greg Bargar	.08	.04	.01
☐ 475 Gary Redus	.08	.04	.01
☐ 476 Tom Tellmann	.08	.04	.01
☐ 477 Rafael Landestoy	.08	.04	.01
☐ 478 Alan Bannister	.08	.04	.01
☐ 479 Frank Tanana	.15	.07	.02
☐ 480 Ron Kittle	.08	.04	.01
☐ 481 Mark Thurmond	.08	.04	.01
☐ 482 Enos Cabell	.08	.04	.01
☐ 483 Fergie Jenkins	.40	.18	.05
☐ 484 Ozzie Virgil	.08	.04	.01
☐ 485 Rick Rhoden	.08	.04	.01
☐ 486 N.Y. Yankees TL	.40	.18	.05
Don Baylor			
Ron Guidry			
(Checklist on back)			
☐ 487 Ricky Adams	.08	.04	.01
☐ 488 Jesse Barfield	.15	.07	.02
☐ 489 Dave Von Ohlen	.08	.04	.01
☐ 490 Cal Ripken	6.00	2.70	.75
☐ 491 Bobby Castillo	.08	.04	.01
☐ 492 Tucker Ashford	.08	.04	.01
☐ 493 Mike Norris	.08	.04	.01
☐ 494 Chili Davis	.15	.07	.02
☐ 495 Rollie Fingers	.40	.18	.05
☐ 496 Terry Francona	.08	.04	.01
☐ 497 Bud Anderson	.08	.04	.01
☐ 498 Rich Gedman	.08	.04	.01
☐ 499 Mike Witt	.08	.04	.01
☐ 500 George Brett	2.00	.90	.25
☐ 501 Steve Henderson	.08	.04	.01
☐ 502 Joe Torre MG	.15	.07	.02
☐ 503 Elias Sosa	.08	.04	.01
☐ 504 Mickey Rivers	.08	.04	.01
☐ 505 Pete Vuckovich	.08	.04	.01
☐ 506 Ernie Whitt	.08	.04	.01
☐ 507 Mike LaCoss	.08	.04	.01
☐ 508 Mel Hall	.15	.07	.02
☐ 509 Brad Havens	.08	.04	.01
☐ 510 Alan Trammell	.40	.18	.05
☐ 511 Marty Bystrom	.08	.04	.01
☐ 512 Oscar Gamble	.08	.04	.01
☐ 513 Dave Beard	.08	.04	.01
☐ 514 Floyd Rayford	.08	.04	.01
☐ 515 Gorman Thomas	.08	.04	.01
☐ 516 Montreal Expos TL	.15	.07	.02
Al Oliver			
Charlie Lea			
(Checklist on back)			
☐ 517 John Moses	.08	.04	.01
☐ 518 Greg Walker	.15	.07	.02
☐ 519 Ron Davis	.08	.04	.01
☐ 520 Bob Boone	.15	.07	.02
☐ 521 Pete Falcone	.08	.04	.01
☐ 522 Dave Bergman	.08	.04	.01
☐ 523 Glenn Hoffman	.08	.04	.01
☐ 524 Carlos Diaz	.08	.04	.01
☐ 525 Willie Wilson	.08	.04	.01
☐ 526 Ron Oester	.08	.04	.01
☐ 527 Checklist 397-528	.15	.07	.02
☐ 528 Mark Brouhard	.08	.04	.01
☐ 529 Keith Atherton	.08	.04	.01
☐ 530 Dan Ford	.08	.04	.01
☐ 531 Steve Boros MG	.08	.04	.01
☐ 532 Eric Show	.08	.04	.01
☐ 533 Ken Landreaux	.08	.04	.01
☐ 534 Pete O'Brien	.40	.18	.05
☐ 535 Bo Diaz	.08	.04	.01
☐ 536 Doug Bair	.08	.04	.01
☐ 537 Johnny Ray	.08	.04	.01
☐ 538 Kevin Bass	.08	.04	.01
☐ 539 George Frazier	.08	.04	.01
☐ 540 George Hendrick	.08	.04	.01
☐ 541 Dennis Lamp	.08	.04	.01
☐ 542 Duane Kuiper	.08	.04	.01
☐ 543 Craig McMurtry	.08	.04	.01
☐ 544 Cesar Geronimo	.08	.04	.01
☐ 545 Bill Buckner	.15	.07	.02
☐ 546 Indians TL	.15	.07	.02
Mike Hargrove			
Lary Sorensen			
(Checklist on back)			
☐ 547 Mike Moore	.15	.07	.02
☐ 548 Ron Jackson	.08	.04	.01
☐ 549 Walt Terrell	.08	.04	.01
☐ 550 Jim Rice	.15	.07	.02
☐ 551 Scott Ullger	.08	.04	.01
☐ 552 Ray Burris	.08	.04	.01
☐ 553 Joe Nolan	.08	.04	.01
☐ 554 Ted Power	.08	.04	.01
☐ 555 Greg Brock	.08	.04	.01
☐ 556 Joey McLaughlin	.08	.04	.01
☐ 557 Wayne Tolleson	.08	.04	.01
☐ 558 Mike Davis	.08	.04	.01
☐ 559 Mike Scott	.15	.07	.02
☐ 560 Carlton Fisk	.75	.35	.09
☐ 561 Whitey Herzog MG	.15	.07	.02
☐ 562 Manny Castillo	.08	.04	.01
☐ 563 Glenn Wilson	.15	.07	.02
☐ 564 Al Holland	.08	.04	.01
☐ 565 Leon Durham	.08	.04	.01
☐ 566 Jim Bibby	.08	.04	.01
☐ 567 Mike Heath	.08	.04	.01
☐ 568 Pete Filson	.08	.04	.01
☐ 569 Bake McBride	.08	.04	.01
☐ 570 Dan Quisenberry	.08	.04	.01
☐ 571 Bruce Bochy	.08	.04	.01
☐ 572 Jerry Royster	.08	.04	.01
☐ 573 Dave Kingman	.15	.07	.02
☐ 574 Brian Downing	.08	.04	.01
☐ 575 Jim Clancy	.08	.04	.01
☐ 576 Giants TL	.15	.07	.02
Jeff Leonard			
Atlee Hammaker			
(Checklist on back)			
☐ 577 Mark Clear	.08	.04	.01
☐ 578 Lenn Sakata	.08	.04	.01
☐ 579 Bob James	.08	.04	.01
☐ 580 Lonnie Smith	.08	.04	.01
☐ 581 Jose DeLeon	.08	.04	.01
☐ 582 Bob McClure	.08	.04	.01
☐ 583 Derrel Thomas	.08	.04	.01
☐ 584 Dave Schmidt	.08	.04	.01
☐ 585 Dan Driessen	.08	.04	.01
☐ 586 Joe Niekro	.15	.07	.02
☐ 587 Von Hayes	.08	.04	.01
☐ 588 Milt Wilcox	.08	.04	.01
☐ 589 Mike Easler	.08	.04	.01
☐ 590 Dave Stieb	.08	.04	.01
☐ 591 Tony LaRussa MG	.15	.07	.02
☐ 592 Andre Robertson	.08	.04	.01
☐ 593 Jeff Lahti	.08	.04	.01
☐ 594 Gene Richards	.08	.04	.01
☐ 595 Jeff Reardon	.15	.07	.02
☐ 596 Ryne Sandberg	4.00	1.80	.50
☐ 597 Rick Camp	.08	.04	.01
☐ 598 Rusty Kuntz	.08	.04	.01
☐ 599 Doug Sisk	.08	.04	.01
☐ 600 Rod Carew	.60	.25	.07
☐ 601 John Tudor	.08	.04	.01
☐ 602 John Wathan	.08	.04	.01
☐ 603 Renie Martin	.08	.04	.01
☐ 604 John Lowenstein	.08	.04	.01
☐ 605 Mike Caldwell	.08	.04	.01
☐ 606 Blue Jays TL	.15	.07	.02
Lloyd Moseby			
Dave Stieb			
(Checklist on back)			
☐ 607 Tom Hume	.08	.04	.01
☐ 608 Bobby Johnson	.08	.04	.01
☐ 609 Dan Meyer	.08	.04	.01
☐ 610 Steve Sax	.15	.07	.02
☐ 611 Chet Lemon	.15	.07	.02
☐ 612 Harry Spilman	.08	.04	.01
☐ 613 Greg Gross	.08	.04	.01
☐ 614 Len Barker	.08	.04	.01
☐ 615 Garry Templeton	.08	.04	.01
☐ 616 Don Robinson	.08	.04	.01
☐ 617 Rick Cerone	.08	.04	.01
☐ 618 Dickie Noles	.08	.04	.01
☐ 619 Jerry Dybzinski	.08	.04	.01
☐ 620 Al Oliver	.15	.07	.02
☐ 621 Frank Howard MG	.15	.07	.02
☐ 622 Al Cowens	.08	.04	.01
☐ 623 Ron Washington	.08	.04	.01
☐ 624 Terry Harper	.08	.04	.01
☐ 625 Larry Gura	.08	.04	.01
☐ 626 Bob Clark	.08	.04	.01
☐ 627 Dave LaPoint	.08	.04	.01
☐ 628 Ed Jurak	.08	.04	.01
☐ 629 Rick Langford	.08	.04	.01
☐ 630 Ted Simmons	.15	.07	.02
☐ 631 Dennis Martinez	.15	.07	.02
☐ 632 Tom Foley	.08	.04	.01
☐ 633 Mike Krukow	.08	.04	.01
☐ 634 Mike Marshall	.08	.04	.01
☐ 635 Dave Righetti	.15	.07	.02
☐ 636 Pat Putnam	.08	.04	.01
☐ 637 Phillies TL	.15	.07	.02
Gary Matthews			
John Denny			
(Checklist on back)			
☐ 638 George Vukovich	.08	.04	.01
☐ 639 Rick Lysander	.08	.04	.01
☐ 640 Lance Parrish	.15	.07	.02
☐ 641 Mike Richardt	.08	.04	.01
☐ 642 Tom Underwood	.08	.04	.01
☐ 643 Mike C. Brown	.08	.04	.01
☐ 644 Tim Lollar	.08	.04	.01
☐ 645 Tony Pena	.08	.04	.01
☐ 646 Checklist 529-660	.15	.07	.02
☐ 647 Ron Roenicke	.08	.04	.01
☐ 648 Len Whitehouse	.08	.04	.01
☐ 649 Tom Herr	.15	.07	.02
☐ 650 Phil Niekro	.40	.18	.05
☐ 651 John McNamara MG	.08	.04	.01
☐ 652 Rudy May	.08	.04	.01
☐ 653 Dave Stapleton	.08	.04	.01
☐ 654 Bob Bailor	.08	.04	.01
☐ 655 Amos Otis	.15	.07	.02
☐ 656 Bryn Smith	.08	.04	.01
☐ 657 Thad Bosley	.08	.04	.01
☐ 658 Jerry Augustine	.08	.04	.01
☐ 659 Duane Walker	.08	.04	.01
☐ 660 Ray Knight	.15	.07	.02
☐ 661 Steve Yeager	.08	.04	.01
☐ 662 Tom Brennan	.08	.04	.01
☐ 663 Johnnie LeMaster	.08	.04	.01
☐ 664 Dave Stegman	.08	.04	.01
☐ 665 Buddy Bell	.15	.07	.02
☐ 666 Detroit Tigers TL	.40	.18	.05
Lou Whitaker			
Jack Morris			
(Checklist on back)			
☐ 667 Vance Law	.08	.04	.01
☐ 668 Larry McWilliams	.08	.04	.01
☐ 669 Dave Lopes	.15	.07	.02
☐ 670 Rich Gossage	.40	.18	.05
☐ 671 Jamie Quirk	.08	.04	.01
☐ 672 Ricky Nelson	.08	.04	.01
☐ 673 Mike Walters	.08	.04	.01
☐ 674 Tim Flannery	.08	.04	.01
☐ 675 Pascual Perez	.08	.04	.01
☐ 676 Brian Giles	.08	.04	.01
☐ 677 Doyle Alexander	.08	.04	.01
☐ 678 Chris Speier	.08	.04	.01
☐ 679 Art Howe	.08	.04	.01
☐ 680 Fred Lynn	.15	.07	.02
☐ 681 Tom Lasorda MG	.15	.07	.02
☐ 682 Dan Morogiello	.08	.04	.01
☐ 683 Marty Barrett	.15	.07	.02
☐ 684 Bob Shirley	.08	.04	.01
☐ 685 Willie Aikens	.08	.04	.01
☐ 686 Joe Price	.08	.04	.01
☐ 687 Roy Howell	.08	.04	.01
☐ 688 George Wright	.08	.04	.01
☐ 689 Mike Fischlin	.08	.04	.01
☐ 690 Jack Clark	.15	.07	.02
☐ 691 Steve Lake	.08	.04	.01
☐ 692 Dickie Thon	.08	.04	.01
☐ 693 Alan Wiggins	.08	.04	.01

☐ 694 Mike Stanton	.08	.04	.01
☐ 695 Lou Whitaker	.15	.07	.02
☐ 696 Pirates TL	.15	.07	.02
Bill Madlock			
Rick Rhoden			
(Checklist on back)			
☐ 697 Dale Murray	.08	.04	.01
☐ 698 Marc Hill	.08	.04	.01
☐ 699 Dave Rucker	.08	.04	.01
☐ 700 Mike Schmidt	1.50	.70	.19
☐ 701 NL Active Batting	.40	.18	.05
Bill Madlock			
Pete Rose			
Dave Parker			
☐ 702 NL Active Hits	.40	.18	.05
Pete Rose			
Rusty Staub			
Tony Perez			
☐ 703 NL Active Home Run	.40	.18	.05
Mike Schmidt			
Tony Perez			
Dave Kingman			
☐ 704 NL Active RBI	.40	.18	.05
Tony Perez			
Rusty Staub			
Al Oliver			
☐ 705 NL Active Steals	.40	.18	.05
Joe Morgan			
Cesar Cedeno			
Larry Bowa			
☐ 706 NL Active Victory	.40	.18	.05
Steve Carlton			
Fergie Jenkins			
Tom Seaver			
☐ 707 NL Active Strikeout	1.50	.70	.19
Steve Carlton			
Nolan Ryan			
Tom Seaver			
☐ 708 NL Active ERA	.40	.18	.05
Tom Seaver			
Steve Carlton			
Steve Rogers			
☐ 709 NL Active Save	.15	.07	.02
Bruce Sutter			
Tug McGraw			
Gene Garber			
☐ 710 AL Active Batting	.40	.18	.05
Rod Carew			
George Brett			
Cecil Cooper			
☐ 711 AL Active Hits	.40	.18	.05
Rod Carew			
Bert Campaneris			
Reggie Jackson			
☐ 712 AL Active Home Run	.40	.18	.05
Reggie Jackson			
Graig Nettles			
Greg Luzinski			
☐ 713 AL Active RBI	.40	.18	.05
Reggie Jackson			
Ted Simmons			
Graig Nettles			
☐ 714 AL Active Steals	.15	.07	.02
Bert Campaneris			
Dave Lopes			
Omar Moreno			
☐ 715 AL Active Victory	.40	.18	.05
Jim Palmer			
Don Sutton			
Tommy John			
☐ 716 AL Active Strikeout	.40	.18	.05
Don Sutton			
Bert Blyleven			
Jerry Koosman			
☐ 717 AL Active ERA	.40	.18	.05
Jim Palmer			
Rollie Fingers			
Ron Guidry			
☐ 718 AL Active Save	.40	.18	.05
Rollie Fingers			
Rich Gossage			
Dan Quisenberry			
☐ 719 Andy Hassler	.08	.04	.01
☐ 720 Dwight Evans	.15	.07	.02
☐ 721 Del Crandall MG	.08	.04	.01
☐ 722 Bob Welch	.08	.04	.01
☐ 723 Rich Dauer	.08	.04	.01
☐ 724 Eric Rasmussen	.08	.04	.01
☐ 725 Cesar Cedeno	.15	.07	.02
☐ 726 Brewers TL	.15	.07	.02
Ted Simmons			
Moose Haas			
(Checklist on back)			
☐ 727 Joel Youngblood	.08	.04	.01
☐ 728 Tug McGraw	.15	.07	.02
☐ 729 Gene Tenace	.15	.07	.02
☐ 730 Bruce Sutter	.15	.07	.02
☐ 731 Lynn Jones	.08	.04	.01
☐ 732 Terry Crowley	.08	.04	.01
☐ 733 Dave Collins	.08	.04	.01
☐ 734 Odell Jones	.08	.04	.01
☐ 735 Rick Burleson	.08	.04	.01
☐ 736 Dick Ruthven	.08	.04	.01
☐ 737 Jim Essian	.08	.04	.01
☐ 738 Bill Schroeder	.08	.04	.01
☐ 739 Bob Watson	.15	.07	.02
☐ 740 Tom Seaver	.75	.35	.09
☐ 741 Wayne Gross	.08	.04	.01
☐ 742 Dick Williams MG	.15	.07	.02
☐ 743 Don Hood	.08	.04	.01
☐ 744 Jamie Allen	.08	.04	.01
☐ 745 Dennis Eckersley	.50	.23	.06
☐ 746 Mickey Hatcher	.08	.04	.01
☐ 747 Pat Zachry	.08	.04	.01
☐ 748 Jeff Leonard	.08	.04	.01
☐ 749 Doug Flynn	.08	.04	.01
☐ 750 Jim Palmer	.60	.25	.07
☐ 751 Charlie Moore	.08	.04	.01
☐ 752 Phil Garner	.15	.07	.02
☐ 753 Doug Gwosdz	.08	.04	.01
☐ 754 Kent Tekulve	.15	.07	.02
☐ 755 Garry Maddox	.08	.04	.01
☐ 756 Reds TL	.15	.07	.02
Ron Oester			
Mario Soto			
(Checklist on back)			
☐ 757 Larry Bowa	.15	.07	.02
☐ 758 Bill Stein	.08	.04	.01
☐ 759 Richard Dotson	.08	.04	.01
☐ 760 Bob Horner	.08	.04	.01
☐ 761 John Montefusco	.08	.04	.01
☐ 762 Rance Mulliniks	.08	.04	.01
☐ 763 Craig Swan	.08	.04	.01
☐ 764 Mike Hargrove	.15	.07	.02
☐ 765 Ken Forsch	.08	.04	.01
☐ 766 Mike Vail	.08	.04	.01
☐ 767 Carney Lansford	.15	.07	.02
☐ 768 Champ Summers	.08	.04	.01
☐ 769 Bill Caudill	.08	.04	.01
☐ 770 Ken Griffey	.15	.07	.02
☐ 771 Billy Gardner MG	.08	.04	.01
☐ 772 Jim Slaton	.08	.04	.01
☐ 773 Todd Cruz	.08	.04	.01
☐ 774 Tom Gorman	.08	.04	.01
☐ 775 Dave Parker	.15	.07	.02
☐ 776 Craig Reynolds	.08	.04	.01
☐ 777 Tom Paciorek	.08	.04	.01
☐ 778 Andy Hawkins	.08	.04	.01
☐ 779 Jim Sundberg	.15	.07	.02
☐ 780 Steve Carlton	.75	.35	.09
☐ 781 Checklist 661-792	.15	.07	.02
☐ 782 Steve Balboni	.08	.04	.01
☐ 783 Luis Leal	.08	.04	.01
☐ 784 Leon Roberts	.08	.04	.01
☐ 785 Joaquin Andujar	.08	.04	.01
☐ 786 Red Sox TL	.40	.18	.05
Wade Boggs			
Bob Ojeda			
(Checklist on back)			
☐ 787 Bill Campbell	.08	.04	.01
☐ 788 Milt May	.08	.04	.01
☐ 789 Bert Blyleven	.15	.07	.02
☐ 790 Doug DeCinces	.08	.04	.01
☐ 791 Terry Forster	.08	.04	.01
☐ 792 Bill Russell	.08	.04	.01

1984 Topps Tiffany

This 792 card standard-size set was issued by Topps as a parallel to their regular issue. Printed in their Ireland facility, these cards are differentiated from the regular cards by the glossy fronts and pure white stock. These sets were available only through Topps' dealer network and sold only in factory set form.

	NRMT	VG-E	GOOD
COMPLETE SET (792)	200.00	90.00	25.00
COMMON CARD (1-792)	.25	.11	.03
*STARS: 6X to 10X BASIC CARDS			
*ROOKIES: 4X to 8X BASIC CARDS			

1984 Topps Glossy All-Stars

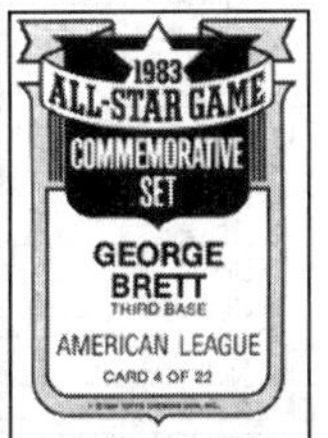

The cards in this 22-card set measure the standard size. Unlike the 1983 Topps Glossy set which was not distributed with its regular baseball cards, the 1984 Topps Glossy set was distributed as inserts in Topps Rak-Paks. The set features the nine American and National League All-Stars who started in the 1983 All Star game in Chicago. The managers and team captains (Yastrzemski and Bench) complete the set. The cards are numbered on the back and are ordered by position within league (AL: 1-11 and NL: 12-22).

	NRMT	VG-E	GOOD
COMPLETE SET (22)	5.00	2.20	.60
COMMON CARD (1-22)	.05	.02	.01
☐ 1 Harvey Kuenn MG	.05	.02	.01
☐ 2 Rod Carew	.50	.23	.06
☐ 3 Manny Trillo	.05	.02	.01
☐ 4 George Brett	1.00	.45	.12
☐ 5 Robin Yount	.50	.23	.06
☐ 6 Jim Rice	.10	.05	.01
☐ 7 Fred Lynn	.10	.05	.01
☐ 8 Dave Winfield	.50	.23	.06
☐ 9 Ted Simmons	.10	.05	.01
☐ 10 Dave Stieb	.05	.02	.01
☐ 11 Carl Yastrzemski CAPT	.50	.23	.06
☐ 12 Whitey Herzog MG	.05	.02	.01
☐ 13 Al Oliver	.10	.05	.01
☐ 14 Steve Sax	.10	.05	.01
☐ 15 Mike Schmidt	.75	.35	.09
☐ 16 Ozzie Smith	1.00	.45	.12
☐ 17 Tim Raines	.20	.09	.03
☐ 18 Andre Dawson	.20	.09	.03
☐ 19 Dale Murphy	.25	.11	.03
☐ 20 Gary Carter	.20	.09	.03
☐ 21 Mario Soto	.05	.02	.01
☐ 22 Johnny Bench CAPT	.50	.23	.06

1984 Topps Glossy Send-Ins

The cards in this 40-card set measure the standard size. Similar to last year's glossy set, this set was issued as a bonus prize to Topps All-Star Baseball Game cards found in wax packs. Twenty-five bonus runs from the game cards were necessary to obtain a five card subset of the series. There were eight different subsets of five cards. The cards are numbered and the set contains 20 stars from each league.

	NRMT	VG-E	GOOD
COMPLETE SET (40)	12.50	5.50	1.55
COMMON CARD (1-40)	.10	.05	.01
☐ 1 Pete Rose	2.00	.90	.25
☐ 2 Lance Parrish	.25	.11	.03
☐ 3 Steve Rogers	.10	.05	.01
☐ 4 Eddie Murray	1.50	.70	.19
☐ 5 Johnny Ray	.10	.05	.01
☐ 6 Rickey Henderson	1.25	.55	.16
☐ 7 Atlee Hammaker	.10	.05	.01
☐ 8 Wade Boggs	1.50	.70	.19
☐ 9 Gary Carter	.25	.11	.03
☐ 10 Jack Morris	.25	.11	.03
☐ 11 Darrell Evans	.25	.11	.03
☐ 12 George Brett	2.50	1.10	.30
☐ 13 Bob Horner	.10	.05	.01
☐ 14 Ron Guidry	.25	.11	.03
☐ 15 Nolan Ryan	5.00	2.20	.60
☐ 16 Dave Winfield	1.00	.45	.12
☐ 17 Ozzie Smith	2.50	1.10	.30
☐ 18 Ted Simmons	.25	.11	.03
☐ 19 Bill Madlock	.10	.05	.01
☐ 20 Tony Armas	.10	.05	.01
☐ 21 Al Oliver	.25	.11	.03
☐ 22 Jim Rice	.25	.11	.03
☐ 23 George Hendrick	.10	.05	.01
☐ 24 Dave Stieb	.10	.05	.01
☐ 25 Pedro Guerrero	.25	.11	.03
☐ 26 Rod Carew	1.00	.45	.12
☐ 27 Steve Carlton	.75	.35	.09
☐ 28 Dave Righetti	.10	.05	.01
☐ 29 Darryl Strawberry	.50	.23	.06
☐ 30 Lou Whitaker	.25	.11	.03
☐ 31 Dale Murphy	.50	.23	.06
☐ 32 LaMarr Hoyt	.10	.05	.01
☐ 33 Jesse Orosco	.10	.05	.01
☐ 34 Cecil Cooper	.25	.11	.03
☐ 35 Andre Dawson	.50	.23	.06
☐ 36 Robin Yount	1.00	.45	.12
☐ 37 Tim Raines	.35	.16	.04
☐ 38 Dan Quisenberry	.10	.05	.01
☐ 39 Mike Schmidt	2.00	.90	.25
☐ 40 Carlton Fisk	1.00	.45	.12

1984 Topps Traded

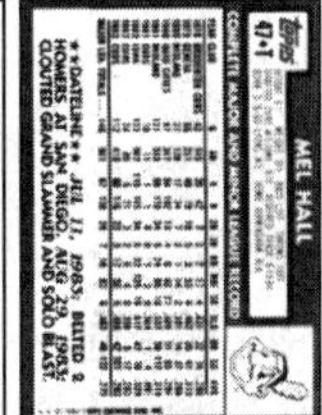

In now standard procedure, Topps issued its standard-size Traded (or extended) set for the fourth year in a row. Several of 1984's top rookies not contained in the regular set are pictured in the Traded set. Extended Rookie Cards in this set include Dwight Gooden, Jimmy Key, Mark Langston, Jose Rijo, and Bret Saberhagen. Again this year, the Topps affiliate in Ireland printed the cards, and the cards were available through hobby channels only in factory set form. The set numbering is in alphabetical order by player's name.

	NRMT	VG-E	GOOD
COMPLETE FACT.SET (132)	50.00	22.00	6.25
COMMON CARD (1T-132T)	.25	.11	.03
☐ 1T Willie Aikens	.25	.11	.03
☐ 2T Luis Aponte	.25	.11	.03
☐ 3T Mike Armstrong	.25	.11	.03
☐ 4T Bob Bailor	.25	.11	.03
☐ 5T Dusty Baker	.75	.35	.09
☐ 6T Steve Balboni	.25	.11	.03
☐ 7T Alan Bannister	.25	.11	.03
☐ 8T Dave Beard	.25	.11	.03
☐ 9T Joe Beckwith	.25	.11	.03
☐ 10T Bruce Berenyi	.25	.11	.03
☐ 11T Dave Bergman	.25	.11	.03
☐ 12T Tony Bernazard	.25	.11	.03
☐ 13T Yogi Berra MG	1.00	.45	.12
☐ 14T Barry Bonnell	.25	.11	.03
☐ 15T Phil Bradley	.40	.18	.05
☐ 16T Fred Breining	.25	.11	.03
☐ 17T Bill Buckner	.40	.18	.05
☐ 18T Ray Burris	.25	.11	.03
☐ 19T John Butcher	.25	.11	.03
☐ 20T Brett Butler	.75	.35	.09
☐ 21T Enos Cabell	.25	.11	.03
☐ 22T Bill Campbell	.25	.11	.03
☐ 23T Bill Caudill	.25	.11	.03
☐ 24T Bob Clark	.25	.11	.03
☐ 25T Bryan Clark	.25	.11	.03
☐ 26T Jaime Cocanower	.25	.11	.03
☐ 27T Ron Darling	.75	.35	.09
☐ 28T Alvin Davis	.40	.18	.05
☐ 29T Ken Dayley	.25	.11	.03
☐ 30T Jeff Dedmon	.25	.11	.03
☐ 31T Bob Dernier	.25	.11	.03
☐ 32T Carlos Diaz	.25	.11	.03
☐ 33T Mike Easler	.25	.11	.03
☐ 34T Dennis Eckersley	3.00	1.35	.35
☐ 35T Jim Essian	.25	.11	.03
☐ 36T Darrell Evans	.40	.18	.05
☐ 37T Mike Fitzgerald	.25	.11	.03
☐ 38T Tim Foli	.25	.11	.03
☐ 39T George Frazier	.25	.11	.03
☐ 40T Rich Gale	.25	.11	.03
☐ 41T Barbaro Garbey	.25	.11	.03
☐ 42T Dwight Gooden	10.00	4.50	1.25
☐ 43T Rich Gossage	.75	.35	.09
☐ 44T Wayne Gross	.25	.11	.03
☐ 45T Mark Gubicza	.75	.35	.09
☐ 46T Jackie Gutierrez	.25	.11	.03
☐ 47T Mel Hall	.40	.18	.05
☐ 48T Toby Harrah	.40	.18	.05
☐ 49T Ron Hassey	.25	.11	.03
☐ 50T Rich Hebner	.25	.11	.03
☐ 51T Willie Hernandez	.40	.18	.05
☐ 52T Ricky Horton	.25	.11	.03
☐ 53T Art Howe	.25	.11	.03
☐ 54T Dane Iorg	.25	.11	.03
☐ 55T Brook Jacoby	.40	.18	.05
☐ 56T Mike Jeffcoat	.25	.11	.03
☐ 57T Dave Johnson MG	.40	.18	.05
☐ 58T Lynn Jones	.25	.11	.03
☐ 59T Ruppert Jones	.25	.11	.03
☐ 60T Mike Jorgensen	.25	.11	.03
☐ 61T Bob Kearney	.25	.11	.03
☐ 62T Jimmy Key	2.50	1.10	.30
☐ 63T Dave Kingman	.40	.18	.05
☐ 64T Jerry Koosman	.40	.18	.05
☐ 65T Wayne Krenchicki	.25	.11	.03
☐ 66T Rusty Kuntz	.25	.11	.03
☐ 67T Rene Lachemann MG	.25	.11	.03
☐ 68T Frank LaCorte	.25	.11	.03
☐ 69T Dennis Lamp	.25	.11	.03
☐ 70T Mark Langston	3.00	1.35	.35
☐ 71T Rick Leach	.25	.11	.03
☐ 72T Craig Lefferts	.40	.18	.05
☐ 73T Gary Lucas	.25	.11	.03
☐ 74T Jerry Martin	.25	.11	.03
☐ 75T Carmelo Martinez	.25	.11	.03
☐ 76T Mike Mason	.25	.11	.03
☐ 77T Gary Matthews	.25	.11	.03
☐ 78T Andy McGaffigan	.25	.11	.03
☐ 79T Larry Milbourne	.25	.11	.03
☐ 80T Sid Monge	.25	.11	.03
☐ 81T Jackie Moore MG	.25	.11	.03
☐ 82T Joe Morgan	2.00	.90	.25
☐ 83T Graig Nettles	.40	.18	.05
☐ 84T Phil Niekro	.75	.35	.09
☐ 85T Ken Oberkfell	.25	.11	.03
☐ 86T Mike O'Berry	.25	.11	.03
☐ 87T Al Oliver	.40	.18	.05
☐ 88T Jorge Orta	.25	.11	.03
☐ 89T Amos Otis	.40	.18	.05
☐ 90T Dave Parker	.40	.18	.05
☐ 91T Tony Perez	.75	.35	.09
☐ 92T Gerald Perry	.40	.18	.05
☐ 93T Gary Pettis	.25	.11	.03
☐ 94T Rob Picciolo	.25	.11	.03
☐ 95T Vern Rapp MG	.25	.11	.03

Card	NRMT	VG-E	GOOD
☐ 96T Floyd Rayford	.25	.11	.03
☐ 97T Randy Ready	.40	.18	.05
☐ 98T Ron Reed	.25	.11	.03
☐ 99T Gene Richards	.25	.11	.03
☐ 100T Jose Rijo	3.00	1.35	.35
☐ 101T Jeff D. Robinson	.25	.11	.03
☐ 102T Ron Romanick	.25	.11	.03
☐ 103T Pete Rose	8.00	3.60	1.00
☐ 104T Bret Saberhagen	3.00	1.35	.35
☐ 105T Juan Samuel	.75	.35	.09
☐ 106T Scott Sanderson	.25	.11	.03
☐ 107T Dick Schofield	.40	.18	.05
☐ 108T Tom Seaver	4.00	1.80	.50
☐ 109T Jim Slaton	.25	.11	.03
☐ 110T Mike Smithson	.25	.11	.03
☐ 111T Lary Sorensen	.25	.11	.03
☐ 112T Tim Stoddard	.25	.11	.03
☐ 113T Champ Summers	.25	.11	.03
☐ 114T Jim Sundberg	.40	.18	.05
☐ 115T Rick Sutcliffe	.40	.18	.05
☐ 116T Craig Swan	.25	.11	.03
☐ 117T Tim Teufel	.25	.11	.03
☐ 118T Derrel Thomas	.25	.11	.03
☐ 119T Gorman Thomas	.25	.11	.03
☐ 120T Alex Trevino	.25	.11	.03
☐ 121T Manny Trillo	.25	.11	.03
☐ 122T John Tudor	.25	.11	.03
☐ 123T Tom Underwood	.25	.11	.03
☐ 124T Mike Vail	.25	.11	.03
☐ 125T Tom Waddell	.25	.11	.03
☐ 126T Gary Ward	.25	.11	.03
☐ 127T Curt Wilkerson	.25	.11	.03
☐ 128T Frank Williams	.25	.11	.03
☐ 129T Glenn Wilson	.40	.18	.05
☐ 130T John Wockenfuss	.25	.11	.03
☐ 131T Ned Yost	.25	.11	.03
☐ 132T Checklist 1T-132T	.25	.11	.03

1984 Topps Traded Tiffany

This 132-card standard-size set was issued by Topps as a premium parallel to their regular issue. This set was printed in the Topps Ireland factory and are differentiated from the regular cards by their glossy sheen and clean backs. These sets were only available through the Topps hobby distribution system.

	NRMT	VG-E	GOOD
COMPLETE FACT.SET (132)	75.00	34.00	9.50
COMMON CARD (1T-132T)	.40	.18	.05
*STARS: 1.5X BASIC CARDS			
*ROOKIES: 1.5X BASIC CARDS			

1984 Topps Cereal

The cards in this 33-card set measure the standard size. The cards are numbered both on the front and the back. The 1984 Topps Cereal Series is exactly the same as the Ralston-Purina issue of this year except for a Topps logo and the words "Cereal Series" on the tops of the fronts of the cards in place of the Ralston checkerboard background. The checkerboard background is absent from the reverse, and a Topps logo is on the reverse of the cereal cards. These cards were distributed in unmarked boxes of Ralston-Purina cereal with a pack of four cards (three players and a checklist) being inside random cereal boxes. The back of the checklist details an offer to obtain any twelve cards direct from the issuer for only 1.50.

Card	NRMT	VG-E	GOOD
COMPLETE SET (34)	12.50	5.50	1.55
COMMON CARD (1-33)	.10	.05	.01
☐ 1 Eddie Murray	2.00	.90	.25
☐ 2 Ozzie Smith	2.50	1.10	.30
☐ 3 Ted Simmons	.25	.11	.03
☐ 4 Pete Rose	1.50	.70	.19
☐ 5 Greg Luzinski	.25	.11	.03
☐ 6 Andre Dawson	.50	.23	.06
☐ 7 Dave Winfield	1.00	.45	.12
☐ 8 Tom Seaver	1.00	.45	.12
☐ 9 Jim Rice	.25	.11	.03
☐ 10 Fernando Valenzuela	.25	.11	.03
☐ 11 Wade Boggs	1.25	.55	.16
☐ 12 Dale Murphy	.50	.23	.06
☐ 13 George Brett	2.50	1.10	.30
☐ 14 Nolan Ryan	4.00	1.80	.50
☐ 15 Rickey Henderson	1.00	.45	.12
☐ 16 Steve Carlton	1.00	.45	.12
☐ 17 Rod Carew	1.00	.45	.12
☐ 18 Steve Garvey	.25	.11	.03
☐ 19 Reggie Jackson	1.00	.45	.12
☐ 20 Dave Concepcion	.25	.11	.03
☐ 21 Robin Yount	1.00	.45	.12
☐ 22 Mike Schmidt	1.50	.70	.19
☐ 23 Jim Palmer	1.00	.45	.12
☐ 24 Bruce Sutter	.25	.11	.03
☐ 25 Dan Quisenberry	.10	.05	.01
☐ 26 Bill Madlock	.10	.05	.01
☐ 27 Cecil Cooper	.25	.11	.03
☐ 28 Gary Carter	.50	.23	.06
☐ 29 Fred Lynn	.25	.11	.03
☐ 30 Pedro Guerrero	.25	.11	.03
☐ 31 Ron Guidry	.25	.11	.03
☐ 32 Keith Hernandez	.25	.11	.03
☐ 33 Carlton Fisk	1.00	.45	.12
☐ NNO Checklist Card	.10	.05	.01

1984 Topps Gallery of Champions

These 12 "mini" cards were issued in set form only. These "Cards" measure approximately 1 1/4" by 1 3/4" and have the same design as the regular Topps cards from that year. In 1984 and 1985 no aluminum sets were issued. We have sequenced this set in alphabetical order. These cards were issued in bronze and silver versions. We have priced the bronze version. The silver versions are valued at approximately 2.5 times the values listed below.

Card	NRMT	VG-E	GOOD
COMPLETE SET (12)	450.00	200.00	55.00
COMMON CARD (1-12)	10.00	4.50	1.25
☐ 1 George Brett	65.00	29.00	8.00
☐ 2 Rod Carew	25.00	11.00	3.10
☐ 3 Steve Carlton	25.00	11.00	3.10
☐ 4 Rollie Fingers	10.00	4.50	1.25
☐ 5 Steve Garvey	25.00	11.00	3.10
☐ 6 Reggie Jackson	35.00	16.00	4.40
☐ 7 Joe Morgan	15.00	6.75	1.85
☐ 8 Jim Palmer	15.00	6.75	1.85
☐ 9 Pete Rose	45.00	20.00	5.50
☐ 10 Nolan Ryan	175.00	80.00	22.00
☐ 11 Mike Schmidt	50.00	22.00	6.25
☐ 12 Tom Seaver	40.00	18.00	5.00

1984 Topps/O-Pee-Chee Stickers

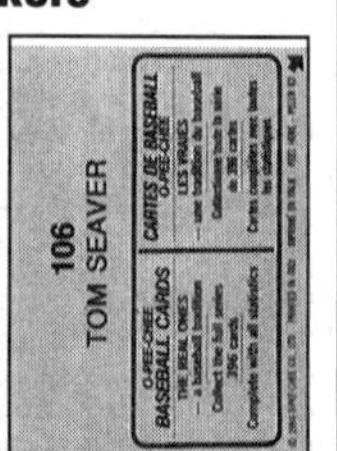

Made in Italy for Topps and O-Pee-Chee by Panini, these 386 stickers measure approximately 1 15/16" by 2 9/16" and are numbered on both front and back. The fronts feature white-bordered color player photos. The horizontal back carries the player's name and a bilingual ad for O-Pee-Chee in red lettering. The stickers were also issued boxes of seven strips of five stickers each. An album onto which the stickers could be affixed was available at retail stores. The album and the sticker numbering are organized as follows: 1983 Highlights (1-10), 1983 Championship Series (11-18), World Series (19-26), Atlanta Braves (27-38), Chicago Cubs (39-50), Cincinnati Reds (51-62), Houston Astros (63-74), Los Angeles Dodgers (75-86), Montreal Expos (87-98), 1983 Stat Leaders (99-102), New York Mets (103-114), Philadelphia Phillies (115-126), Pittsburgh Pirates (127-138), St. Louis Cardinals (139-150), San Diego Padres (151-162), San Francisco Giants (163-174), 1983 Stat Leaders (175-178), Foil All-Stars (179-198), 1983 Stat Leaders (199-202), Baltimore Orioles (203-214), Boston Red Sox (215-226), California Angels (227-238), Chicago White Sox (239-250), Cleveland Indians (251-262), Detroit Tigers (263-274), Kansas City Royals (275-286), 1983 Stat Leaders (287-290), Milwaukee Brewers (291-302), Minnesota Twins (303-314), New York Yankees (315-326), Oakland A's (327-338), Seattle Mariners (339-350), Texas Rangers (351-362), Toronto Blue Jays (363-374), and Stars of the Future (375-386). There were stickers issued which corresponded with Don Mattingly and Darryl Strawberry Rookie Year for cards.

Card	NRMT	VG-E	GOOD
COMPLETE SET (386)	15.00	6.75	1.85
COMMON STICKER (1-178)	.05	.02	.01
COMMON FOIL (179-198)	.10	.05	.01
COMMON STICKER (199-386)	.05	.02	.01
*TOPPS AND OPC: SAME VALUE			
☐ 1 Steve Carlton (Top half)	.15	.07	.02
☐ 2 Steve Carlton (Bottom half)	.15	.07	.02
☐ 3 Rickey Henderson (Top half)	.15	.07	.02
☐ 4 Rickey Henderson (Bottom half)	.15	.07	.02
☐ 5 Fred Lynn (Top half)	.10	.05	.01
☐ 6 Fred Lynn (Bottom half)	.10	.05	.01
☐ 7 Greg Luzinski (Top half)	.10	.05	.01
☐ 8 Greg Luzinski (Bottom half)	.10	.05	.01
☐ 9 Dan Quisenberry (Top half)	.05	.02	.01
☐ 10 Dan Quisenberry (Bottom half)	.05	.02	.01
☐ 11 LaMarr Hoyt LCS	.05	.02	.01
☐ 12 Mike Flanagan LCS	.05	.02	.01
☐ 13 Mike Boddicker LCS	.05	.02	.01
☐ 14 Tito Landrum LCS	.05	.02	.01
☐ 15 Steve Carlton LCS	.15	.07	.02
☐ 16 Fern.Valenzuela LCS	.10	.05	.01
☐ 17 Charlie Hudson LCS	.05	.02	.01
☐ 18 Gary Matthews LCS	.05	.02	.01
☐ 19 John Denny WS	.05	.02	.01
☐ 20 John Lowenstein WS	.05	.02	.01
☐ 21 Jim Palmer WS	.15	.07	.02
☐ 22 Benny Ayala WS	.05	.02	.01
☐ 23 Rick Dempsey WS	.05	.02	.01
☐ 24 Cal Ripken WS	1.25	.55	.16
☐ 25 Sammy Stewart WS	.05	.02	.01
☐ 26 Eddie Murray WS	.15	.07	.02
☐ 27 Dale Murphy	.15	.07	.02
☐ 28 Chris Chambliss	.05	.02	.01
☐ 29 Glenn Hubbard	.05	.02	.01
☐ 30 Bob Horner	.05	.02	.01
☐ 31 Phil Niekro	.15	.07	.02
☐ 32 Claudell Washington	.05	.02	.01
☐ 33 Rafael Ramirez (135)	.05	.02	.01
☐ 34 Bruce Benedict (82)	.05	.02	.01
☐ 35 Gene Garber (59)	.05	.02	.01
☐ 36 Pascual Perez (347)	.05	.02	.01
☐ 37 Jerry Royster (281)	.05	.02	.01
☐ 38 Steve Bedrosian(283)	.05	.02	.01
☐ 39 Keith Moreland	.05	.02	.01
☐ 40 Leon Durham	.05	.02	.01
☐ 41 Ron Cey	.10	.05	.01
☐ 42 Bill Buckner	.10	.05	.01
☐ 43 Jody Davis	.05	.02	.01
☐ 44 Lee Smith	.30	.14	.04
☐ 45 Ryne Sandberg (70)	1.25	.55	.16
☐ 46 Larry Bowa (301)	.10	.05	.01
☐ 47 Chuck Rainey (247)	.05	.02	.01
☐ 48 Fergie Jenkins (170)	.15	.07	.02
☐ 49 Dick Ruthven (333)	.05	.02	.01
☐ 50 Jay Johnstone (298)	.05	.02	.01
☐ 51 Mario Soto	.05	.02	.01
☐ 52 Gary Redus	.05	.02	.01
☐ 53 Ron Oester	.05	.02	.01
☐ 54 Cesar Cedeno	.10	.05	.01
☐ 55 Dan Driessen	.05	.02	.01
☐ 56 Dave Concepcion	.10	.05	.01
☐ 57 Dann Bilardello(147)	.05	.02	.01
☐ 58 Joe Price (98)	.05	.02	.01
☐ 59 Tom Hume (35)	.05	.02	.01
☐ 60 Eddie Milner (84)	.05	.02	.01
☐ 61 Paul Householder (226)	.05	.02	.01
☐ 62 Bill Scherrer (269)	.05	.02	.01
☐ 63 Phil Garner	.10	.05	.01
☐ 64 Dickie Thon	.05	.02	.01
☐ 65 Jose Cruz	.10	.05	.01
☐ 66 Nolan Ryan	2.00	.90	.25
☐ 67 Terry Puhl	.05	.02	.01
☐ 68 Ray Knight	.10	.05	.01
☐ 69 Joe Niekro (312)	.10	.05	.01
☐ 70 Jerry Mumphrey (45)	.05	.02	.01
☐ 71 Bill Dawley (314)	.05	.02	.01
☐ 72 Alan Ashby (162)	.05	.02	.01
☐ 73 Denny Walling (81)	.05	.02	.01
☐ 74 Frank DiPino (360)	.05	.02	.01
☐ 75 Pedro Guerrero	.10	.05	.01
☐ 76 Ken Landreaux	.05	.02	.01
☐ 77 Bill Russell	.10	.05	.01
☐ 78 Steve Sax	.10	.05	.01
☐ 79 Fernando Valenzuela	.10	.05	.01
☐ 80 Dusty Baker	.10	.05	.01
☐ 81 Jerry Reuss (73)	.05	.02	.01
☐ 82 Alejandro Pena (34)	.10	.05	.01
☐ 83 Rick Monday	.05	.02	.01
☐ 84 Rick Honeycutt (60)	.05	.02	.01
☐ 85 Mike Marshall (245)	.05	.02	.01
☐ 86 Steve Yeager (284)	.05	.02	.01
☐ 87 Al Oliver	.10	.05	.01
☐ 88 Steve Rogers	.05	.02	.01
☐ 89 Jeff Reardon	.10	.05	.01
☐ 90 Gary Carter	.10	.05	.01
☐ 91 Tim Raines	.15	.07	.02
☐ 92 Andre Dawson	.15	.07	.02
☐ 93 Manny Trillo (137)	.05	.02	.01
☐ 94 Tim Wallach (348)	.10	.05	.01
☐ 95 Chris Speier (172)	.05	.02	.01
☐ 96 Bill Gullickson(134)	.05	.02	.01
☐ 97 Doug Flynn (271)	.05	.02	.01
☐ 98 Charlie Lea (58)	.05	.02	.01
☐ 99 Bill Madlock (102B/288B)	.10	.05	.01
☐ 100 Wade Boggs (200B/287B)	.60	.25	.07
☐ 101 Mike Schmidt (176)	.60	.25	.07
☐ 102A Jim Rice (287A/177)	.10	.05	.01
☐ 102B Reggie Jackson (99/288B)	.50	.23	.06
☐ 103 Hubie Brooks	.05	.02	.01
☐ 104 Jesse Orosco	.05	.02	.01
☐ 105 George Foster	.10	.05	.01
☐ 106 Tom Seaver	.50	.23	.06
☐ 107 Keith Hernandez	.10	.05	.01
☐ 108 Mookie Wilson	.10	.05	.01
☐ 109 Bob Bailor (122)	.05	.02	.01
☐ 110 Walt Terrell (209)	.05	.02	.01
☐ 111 Brian Giles (126)	.05	.02	.01
☐ 112 Jose Oquendo (372)	.05	.02	.01
☐ 113 Mike Torrez (258)	.05	.02	.01
☐ 114 Junior Ortiz (371)	.05	.02	.01
☐ 115 Pete Rose	.75	.35	.09
☐ 116 Joe Morgan	.25	.11	.03
☐ 117 Mike Schmidt	.60	.25	.07
☐ 118 Gary Matthews	.05	.02	.01
☐ 119 Steve Carlton	.40	.18	.05
☐ 120 Bo Diaz	.05	.02	.01
☐ 121 Ivan DeJesus (210)	.05	.02	.01
☐ 122 John Denny (109)	.05	.02	.01
☐ 123 Garry Maddox (335)	.05	.02	.01
☐ 124 Von Hayes (224)	.05	.02	.01
☐ 125 Al Holland (158)	.05	.02	.01
☐ 126 Tony Perez (111)	.15	.07	.02
☐ 127 John Candelaria	.05	.02	.01
☐ 128 Jason Thompson	.05	.02	.01
☐ 129 Tony Pena	.05	.02	.01
☐ 130 Dave Parker	.10	.05	.01
☐ 131 Bill Madlock	.05	.02	.01
☐ 132 Kent Tekulve	.10	.05	.01
☐ 133 Larry McWilliams (146)	.05	.02	.01
☐ 134 Johnny Ray (96)	.05	.02	.01
☐ 135 Marvell Wynne (33)	.05	.02	.01
☐ 136 Dale Berra (299)	.05	.02	.01
☐ 137 Mike Easler (93)	.05	.02	.01
☐ 138 Lee Lacy (233)	.05	.02	.01
☐ 139 George Hendrick	.05	.02	.01
☐ 140 Lonnie Smith	.05	.02	.01
☐ 141 Willie McGee	.15	.07	.02
☐ 142 Tom Herr	.10	.05	.01
☐ 143 Darrell Porter	.05	.02	.01
☐ 144 Ozzie Smith	.40	.18	.05
☐ 145 Bruce Sutter (221)	.10	.05	.01
☐ 146 Dave LaPoint (133)	.05	.02	.01
☐ 147 Neil Allen (57)	.05	.02	.01
☐ 148 Ken Oberkfell (238)	.05	.02	.01
☐ 149 David Green (324)	.05	.02	.01
☐ 150 Andy Van Slyke (235)	.25	.11	.03
☐ 151 Garry Templeton	.05	.02	.01
☐ 152 Juan Bonilla	.05	.02	.01
☐ 153 Alan Wiggins	.05	.02	.01
☐ 154 Terry Kennedy	.05	.02	.01
☐ 155 Dave Dravecky	.10	.05	.01
☐ 156 Steve Garvey	.15	.07	.02
☐ 157 Bobby Brown (361)	.05	.02	.01
☐ 158 Ruppert Jones (125)	.05	.02	.01
☐ 159 Luis Salazar (214)	.05	.02	.01
☐ 160 Tony Gwynn (212)	2.50	1.10	.30
☐ 161 Gary Lucas (211)	.05	.02	.01
☐ 162 Eric Show (72)	.05	.02	.01
☐ 163 Darrell Evans	.10	.05	.01
☐ 164 Gary Lavelle	.05	.02	.01
☐ 165 Atlee Hammaker	.05	.02	.01
☐ 166 Jeff Leonard	.05	.02	.01
☐ 167 Jack Clark	.10	.05	.01
☐ 168 Johnny LeMaster	.05	.02	.01
☐ 169 Duane Kuiper (260)	.05	.02	.01
☐ 170 Tom O'Malley (48)	.05	.02	.01
☐ 171 Chili Davis (311)	.10	.05	.01
☐ 172 Bill Laskey (95)	.05	.02	.01
☐ 173 Joel Youngblood(300)	.05	.02	.01
☐ 174 Bob Brenly (225)	.05	.02	.01
☐ 175 Atlee Hammaker(202)	.05	.02	.01
☐ 176 Rick Honeycutt (101)	.05	.02	.01
☐ 177 John Denny (102A/287A)	.05	.02	.01
☐ 178 LaMarr Hoyt (200A/288A)	.05	.02	.01
☐ 179 Tim Raines FOIL	.15	.07	.02
☐ 180 Dale Murphy FOIL	.25	.11	.03
☐ 181 Andre Dawson FOIL	.25	.11	.03
☐ 182 Steve Rogers FOIL	.10	.05	.01
☐ 183 Gary Carter FOIL	.10	.05	.01
☐ 184 Steve Carlton FOIL	.50	.23	.06
☐ 185 George Hendrick FOIL	.10	.05	.01
☐ 186 Johnny Ray FOIL	.10	.05	.01
☐ 187 Ozzie Smith FOIL	.50	.23	.06
☐ 188 Mike Schmidt FOIL	.75	.35	.09
☐ 189 Jim Rice FOIL	.10	.05	.01
☐ 190 Dave Winfield FOIL	.40	.18	.05
☐ 191 Lloyd Moseby FOIL	.10	.05	.01
☐ 192 LaMarr Hoyt FOIL	.10	.05	.01
☐ 193 Ted Simmons FOIL	.10	.05	.01
☐ 194 Ron Guidry FOIL	.10	.05	.01
☐ 195 Eddie Murray FOIL	.50	.23	.06
☐ 196 Lou Whitaker FOIL	.10	.05	.01
☐ 197 Cal Ripken FOIL	3.00	1.35	.35
☐ 198 George Brett FOIL	1.25	.55	.16
☐ 199 Dale Murphy (290)	.15	.07	.02
☐ 200A Cecil Cooper (288A/178)	.10	.05	.01
☐ 200B Jim Rice (287B/100)	.10	.05	.01
☐ 201 Tim Raines (289)	.15	.07	.02
☐ 202 Rickey Henderson (175)	.40	.18	.05
☐ 203 Eddie Murray	.40	.18	.05

☐ 204 Cal Ripken	2.50	1.10	.30
☐ 205 Gary Roenicke	.05	.02	.01
☐ 206 Ken Singleton	.05	.02	.01
☐ 207 Scott McGregor	.05	.02	.01
☐ 208 Tippy Martinez	.05	.02	.01
☐ 209 John Lowenstein(110)	.05	.02	.01
☐ 210 Mike Flanagan (121)	.05	.02	.01
☐ 211 Jim Palmer (161)	.25	.11	.03
☐ 212 Dan Ford (160)	.05	.02	.01
☐ 213 Rick Dempsey (234)	.05	.02	.01
☐ 214 Rich Dauer (159)	.05	.02	.01
☐ 215 Jerry Remy	.05	.02	.01
☐ 216 Wade Boggs	.60	.25	.07
☐ 217 Jim Rice	.10	.05	.01
☐ 218 Tony Armas	.05	.02	.01
☐ 219 Dwight Evans	.10	.05	.01
☐ 220 Bob Stanley (370)	.05	.02	.01
☐ 221 Dave Stapleton (145)	.05	.02	.01
☐ 222 Rich Gedman	.05	.02	.01
☐ 223 Glenn Hoffman (272)	.05	.02	.01
☐ 224 Dennis Eckersley (124)	.15	.07	.02
☐ 225 John Tudor (174)	.05	.02	.01
☐ 226 Bruce Hurst (61)	.05	.02	.01
☐ 227 Rod Carew	.40	.18	.05
☐ 228 Bobby Grich	.10	.05	.01
☐ 229 Doug DeCinces	.05	.02	.01
☐ 230 Fred Lynn	.10	.05	.01
☐ 231 Reggie Jackson	.50	.23	.06
☐ 232 Tommy John	.10	.05	.01
☐ 233 Luis Sanchez (138)	.05	.02	.01
☐ 234 Bob Boone (213)	.10	.05	.01
☐ 235 Bruce Kison (150)	.05	.02	.01
☐ 236 Brian Downing (262)	.05	.02	.01
☐ 237 Ken Forsch (246)	.05	.02	.01
☐ 238 Rick Burleson (148)	.05	.02	.01
☐ 239 Dennis Lamp	.05	.02	.01
☐ 240 LaMarr Hoyt	.05	.02	.01
☐ 241 Richard Dotson	.05	.02	.01
☐ 242 Harold Baines	.10	.05	.01
☐ 243 Carlton Fisk	.30	.14	.04
☐ 244 Greg Luzinski	.10	.05	.01
☐ 245 Rudy Law (85)	.05	.02	.01
☐ 246 Tom Paciorek (237)	.05	.02	.01
☐ 247 Floyd Bannister(47)	.05	.02	.01
☐ 248 Julio Cruz (369)	.05	.02	.01
☐ 249 Vance Law (358)	.05	.02	.01
☐ 250 Scott Fletcher(270)	.05	.02	.01
☐ 251 Toby Harrah	.10	.05	.01
☐ 252 Pat Tabler	.05	.02	.01
☐ 253 Gorman Thomas	.05	.02	.01
☐ 254 Rick Sutcliffe	.10	.05	.01
☐ 255 Andre Thornton	.05	.02	.01
☐ 256 Bake McBride	.05	.02	.01
☐ 257 Alan Bannister(313)	.05	.02	.01
☐ 258 Jamie Easterly(113)	.05	.02	.01
☐ 259 Lary Sorensen (285)	.05	.02	.01
☐ 260 Mike Hargrove (169)	.10	.05	.01
☐ 261 Bert Blyleven (346)	.10	.05	.01
☐ 262 Ron Hassey (236)	.05	.02	.01
☐ 263 Jack Morris	.10	.05	.01
☐ 264 Larry Herndon	.05	.02	.01
☐ 265 Lance Parrish	.10	.05	.01
☐ 266 Alan Trammell	.15	.07	.02
☐ 267 Lou Whitaker	.10	.05	.01
☐ 268 Aurelio Lopez	.05	.02	.01
☐ 269 Dan Petry (62)	.05	.02	.01
☐ 270 Glenn Wilson (250)	.10	.05	.01
☐ 271 Chet Lemon (97)	.05	.02	.01
☐ 272 Kirk Gibson (223)	.15	.07	.02
☐ 273 Enos Cabell (338)	.05	.02	.01
☐ 274 John Wockenfuss(321)	.05	.02	.01
☐ 275 George Brett	1.00	.45	.12
☐ 276 Willie Aikens	.05	.02	.01
☐ 277 Frank White	.10	.05	.01
☐ 278 Hal McRae	.10	.05	.01
☐ 279 Dan Quisenberry	.05	.02	.01
☐ 280 Willie Wilson	.05	.02	.01
☐ 281 Paul Splittorff(281)	.05	.02	.01
☐ 282 U.L. Washington(322)	.05	.02	.01
☐ 283 Bud Black (38)	.05	.02	.01
☐ 284 John Wathan (86)	.05	.02	.01
☐ 285 Larry Gura (259)	.05	.02	.01
☐ 286 Pat Sheridan (323)	.05	.02	.01
☐ 287A Rusty Staub (102A/177)	.10	.05	.01
☐ 287B Dave Righetti (100/200B)	.05	.02	.01
☐ 288A Bob Forsch (178/200A)	.05	.02	.01
☐ 288B Mike Warren (99/102B)	.05	.02	.01
☐ 289 Al Holland (201)	.05	.02	.01
☐ 290 Dan Quisenberry(199)	.05	.02	.01
☐ 291 Cecil Cooper	.10	.05	.01
☐ 292 Moose Haas	.05	.02	.01
☐ 293 Ted Simmons	.10	.05	.01
☐ 294 Paul Molitor	.30	.14	.04
☐ 295 Robin Yount	.30	.14	.04
☐ 296 Ben Oglivie	.05	.02	.01
☐ 297 Tom Tellman (325)	.05	.02	.01
☐ 298 Jim Gantner (50)	.10	.05	.01
☐ 299 Rick Manning (136)	.05	.02	.01
☐ 300 Don Sutton (173)	.15	.07	.02
☐ 301 Charlie Moore (46)	.05	.02	.01
☐ 302 Jim Slaton (337)	.05	.02	.01
☐ 303 Gary Ward	.05	.02	.01
☐ 304 Tom Brunansky	.10	.05	.01
☐ 305 Kent Hrbek	.10	.05	.01
☐ 306 Gary Gaetti	.15	.07	.02
☐ 307 John Castino	.05	.02	.01
☐ 308 Ken Schrom	.05	.02	.01
☐ 309 Ron Davis (334)	.05	.02	.01
☐ 310 Lenny Faedo (336)	.05	.02	.01
☐ 311 Darrell Brown (171)	.05	.02	.01
☐ 312 Frank Viola (69)	.15	.07	.02
☐ 313 Dave Engle (257)	.05	.02	.01
☐ 314 Randy Bush (71)	.05	.02	.01
☐ 315 Dave Righetti	.05	.02	.01
☐ 316 Rich Gossage	.10	.05	.01
☐ 317 Ken Griffey	.10	.05	.01
☐ 318 Ron Guidry	.10	.05	.01
☐ 319 Dave Winfield	.30	.14	.04
☐ 320 Don Baylor	.10	.05	.01
☐ 321 Butch Wynegar (274)	.05	.02	.01
☐ 322 Omar Moreno (282)	.05	.02	.01
☐ 323 Andre Robertson(286)	.05	.02	.01
☐ 324 Willie Randolph(149)	.10	.05	.01
☐ 325 Don Mattingly (297)	5.00	2.20	.60
☐ 326 Graig Nettles	.10	.05	.01
☐ 327 Rickey Henderson	.40	.18	.05
☐ 328 Carney Lansford	.10	.05	.01
☐ 329 Jeff Burroughs	.05	.02	.01
☐ 330 Chris Codiroli	.05	.02	.01
☐ 331 Dave Lopes	.10	.05	.01
☐ 332 Dwayne Murphy	.05	.02	.01
☐ 333 Wayne Gross (49)	.05	.02	.01
☐ 334 Bill Almon (309)	.05	.02	.01
☐ 335 Tom Underwood (123)	.05	.02	.01
☐ 336 Dave Beard (310)	.05	.02	.01
☐ 337 Mike Heath (302)	.05	.02	.01
☐ 338 Mike Davis (273)	.05	.02	.01
☐ 339 Pat Putnam	.05	.02	.01
☐ 340 Tony Bernazard	.05	.02	.01
☐ 341 Steve Henderson	.05	.02	.01
☐ 342 Richie Zisk	.05	.02	.01
☐ 343 Dave Henderson	.10	.05	.01
☐ 344 Al Cowens	.05	.02	.01
☐ 345 Bill Caudill (359)	.05	.02	.01
☐ 346 Jim Beattie (261)	.05	.02	.01
☐ 347 Rick Nelson (36)	.05	.02	.01
☐ 348 Roy Thomas (94)	.05	.02	.01
☐ 349 Spike Owen (362)	.10	.05	.01
☐ 350 Jamie Allen (373)	.05	.02	.01
☐ 351 Buddy Bell	.10	.05	.01
☐ 352 Billy Sample	.05	.02	.01
☐ 353 George Wright	.05	.02	.01
☐ 354 Larry Parrish	.05	.02	.01
☐ 355 Jim Sundberg	.10	.05	.01
☐ 356 Charlie Hough	.10	.05	.01
☐ 357 Pete O'Brien	.05	.02	.01
☐ 358 Wayne Tolleson(249)	.05	.02	.01
☐ 359 Danny Darwin (345)	.05	.02	.01
☐ 360 Dave Stewart (74)	.10	.05	.01
☐ 361 Mickey Rivers (157)	.05	.02	.01
☐ 362 Bucky Dent (349)	.10	.05	.01
☐ 363 Willie Upshaw	.05	.02	.01
☐ 364 Damaso Garcia	.05	.02	.01
☐ 365 Lloyd Moseby	.05	.02	.01
☐ 366 Cliff Johnson	.05	.02	.01
☐ 367 Jim Clancy	.05	.02	.01
☐ 368 Dave Stieb	.05	.02	.01
☐ 369 Alfredo Griffin(248)	.05	.02	.01
☐ 370 Barry Bonnell (222)	.05	.02	.01
☐ 371 Luis Leal (114)	.05	.02	.01
☐ 372 Jesse Barfield(112)	.05	.02	.01
☐ 373 Ernie Whitt (350)	.05	.02	.01
☐ 374 Rance Mulliniks(326)	.05	.02	.01
☐ 375 Mike Boddicker	.05	.02	.01
☐ 376 Greg Brock	.05	.02	.01
☐ 377 Bill Doran	.10	.05	.01
☐ 378 Nick Esasky	.05	.02	.01
☐ 379 Julio Franco	.25	.11	.03
☐ 380 Mel Hall	.05	.02	.01
☐ 381 Bob Kearney	.05	.02	.01
☐ 382 Ron Kittle	.05	.02	.01
☐ 383 Carmelo Martinez	.05	.02	.01
☐ 384 Craig McMurtry	.05	.02	.01
☐ 385 Darryl Strawberry	1.25	.55	.16
☐ 386 Matt Young	.05	.02	.01
☐ xx Album	1.00	.45	.12

1984 Topps Sticker Boxes

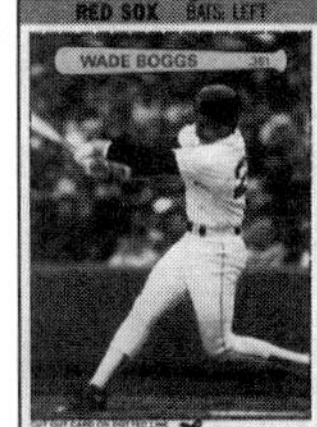

The 24 cards in this set measure 2 1/2" by 3 1/2". For the second straight year, Topps issued blank-backed baseball cards on the boxes containing its stickers. Two cards per box were issued featuring "24 Leaders in Batting Average in 1983 -- Righties, Lefties and Switch Hitters." Officially called Super Bats Picture Cards, the player's name and 1983 batting average were featured within the dotted line cut-out around the card. The team name and batting side(s) of the player were on the outside of the dotted line. The price below includes only the cards on the box. Box 10 was not issued.

	NRMT	VG-E	GOOD
COMPLETE SET (12)	6.00	2.70	.75
COMMON PAIR (1-13)	.10	.05	.01
☐ 1 Al Oliver Lou Whitaker	.40	.18	.05
☐ 2 Ken Oberkfell Ted Simmons	.10	.05	.01
☐ 3 Alan Wiggins Hal McRae	.20	.09	.03
☐ 4 Tim Raines Lloyd Moseby	.40	.18	.05
☐ 5 Lonnie Smith Willie Wilson	.10	.05	.01
☐ 6 Keith Hernandez Robin Yount	.20	.09	.03
☐ 7 Johnny Ray Wade Boggs	1.00	.45	.12
☐ 8 Willie McGee Ken Singleton	.40	.18	.05
☐ 9 Ray Knight Alan Trammell	.40	.18	.05
☐ 11 George Hendrick Rod Carew	.60	.25	.07
☐ 12 Bill Madlock Eddie Murray	.60	.25	.07
☐ 13 Jose Cruz Cal Ripken	4.00	1.80	.50

1984 Topps Rub Downs

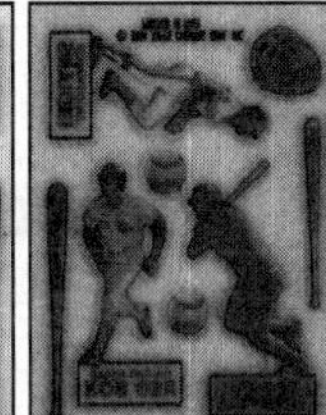

The cards in this 112-player (32 different sheets) set measure 2 3/8" by 3 5/16". The Topps Rub Downs set was actually similar to earlier Topps tatoo or decal-type offerings. The full color photo could be transfered from the rub down to another surface by rubbing a coin over the paper backing. Distributed in packages of two rub down sheets, some contained two or three player action poses, others head shots and various pieces of player equipment. Players from all teams were included in the set. Although the sheets are unnumbered, they are numbered here in alphabetical order based on each card first being placed in alphabetical order.

	NRMT	VG-E	GOOD
COMPLETE SET (32)	8.00	3.60	1.00
COMMON SHEET (1-32)	.10	.05	.01
☐ 1 Tony Armas Harold Baines Lonnie Smith	.10	.05	.01
☐ 2 Don Baylor George Hendrick Ron Kittle Johnnie LeMaster	.10	.05	.01
☐ 3 Buddy Bell Ray Knight Lloyd Moseby	.15	.07	.02
☐ 4 Bruce Benedict Atlee Hammaker Frank White	.10	.05	.01
☐ 5 Wade Boggs Rick Dempsey Keith Hernandez	.75	.35	.09
☐ 6 George Brett Andre Dawson Paul Molitor Alan Wiggins	1.50	.70	.19
☐ 7 Tom Brunansky Pedro Guerrero Darryl Strawberry	.75	.35	.09
☐ 8 Bill Buckner Rich Gossage Dave Stieb Rick Sutcliffe	.15	.07	.02
☐ 9 Rod Carew Carlton Fisk Johnny Ray Matt Young	.75	.35	.09
☐ 10 Steve Carlton Bob Horner Dan Quisenberry	.40	.18	.05
☐ 11 Gary Carter Phil Garner Ron Guidry	.15	.07	.02
☐ 12 Ron Cey Steve Kemp Greg Luzinski Kent Tekulve	.15	.07	.02
☐ 13 Chris Chambliss Dwight Evans Julio Franco	.40	.18	.05
☐ 14 Jack Clark Damaso Garcia Hal McRae Lance Parrish	.25	.11	.03
☐ 15 Dave Concepcion Cecil Cooper Fred Lynn Jesse Orosco	.25	.11	.03
☐ 16 Jose Cruz Gary Matthews Jack Morris Jim Rice	.25	.11	.03
☐ 17 Ron Davis Kent Hrbek Tom Seaver	.60	.25	.07
☐ 18 John Denny Carney Lansford Mario Soto Lou Whitaker	.15	.07	.02
☐ 19 Leon Durham Dave Lopes Steve Sax	.10	.05	.01
☐ 20 George Foster Gary Gaetti Bobby Grich Gary Redus	.25	.11	.03
☐ 21 Steve Garvey Jerry Remy Bill Russell George Wright	.15	.07	.02
☐ 22 Moose Haas Bruce Sutter Dickie Thon Andre Thornton	.10	.05	.01
☐ 23 Toby Harrah Pat Putnam Tim Raines Mike Schmidt	.75	.35	.09
☐ 24 Rickey Henderson Dave Righetti Pete Rose	1.25	.55	.16
☐ 25 Steve Henderson Bill Madlock Alan Trammell	.25	.11	.03
☐ 26 LaMarr Hoyt Larry Parrish Nolan Ryan	2.00	.90	.25
☐ 27 Reggie Jackson Eric Show Jason Thompson	.50	.23	.06
☐ 28 Tommy John Terry Kennedy Eddie Murray Ozzie Smith	1.00	.45	.12
☐ 29 Jeff Leonard Dale Murphy Ken Singleton Dave Winfield	.50	.23	.06
☐ 30 Craig McMurtry Cal Ripken Steve Rogers Willie Upshaw	2.50	1.10	.30
☐ 31 Ben Oglivie Jim Palmer Darrell Porter	.25	.11	.03
☐ 32 Tony Pena Fernando Valenzuela Robin Yount	.40	.18	.05

1984 Topps Super

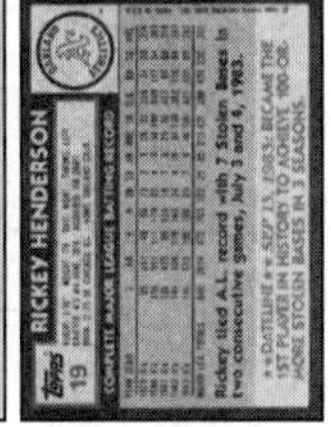

The cards in this 30-card set measure 4 7/8" by 6 7/8". The 1984 Topps Supers feature enlargements from the 1984 regular set. The cards differ from the corresponding cards of the regular set in size and number only. As one would expect, only those considered stars and superstars appear in this set.

	NRMT	VG-E	GOOD
COMPLETE SET (30)	10.00	4.50	1.25
COMMON CARD (1-30)	.10	.05	.01
☐ 1 Cal Ripken	4.00	1.80	.50
☐ 2 Dale Murphy	1.00	.45	.12
☐ 3 LaMarr Hoyt	.10	.05	.01
☐ 4 John Denny	.10	.05	.01
☐ 5 Jim Rice	.25	.11	.03
☐ 6 Mike Schmidt	1.25	.55	.16
☐ 7 Wade Boggs	1.50	.70	.19

Card	NRMT	VG-E	GOOD
☐ 8 Bill Madlock	.10	.05	.01
☐ 9 Dan Quisenberry	.10	.05	.01
☐ 10 Al Holland	.10	.05	.01
☐ 11 Ron Kittle	.10	.05	.01
☐ 12 Darryl Strawberry	1.00	.45	.12
☐ 13 George Brett	1.50	.70	.19
☐ 14 Bill Buckner	.25	.11	.03
☐ 15 Carlton Fisk	.50	.23	.06
☐ 16 Steve Carlton	.60	.25	.07
☐ 17 Ron Guidry	.25	.11	.03
☐ 18 Gary Carter	.50	.23	.06
☐ 19 Rickey Henderson	.75	.35	.09
☐ 20 Andre Dawson	.50	.23	.06
☐ 21 Reggie Jackson	1.00	.45	.12
☐ 22 Steve Garvey	.25	.11	.03
☐ 23 Fred Lynn	.25	.11	.03
☐ 24 Pedro Guerrero	.25	.11	.03
☐ 25 Eddie Murray	1.25	.55	.16
☐ 26 Keith Hernandez	.25	.11	.03
☐ 27 Dave Winfield	.60	.25	.07
☐ 28 Nolan Ryan	3.00	1.35	.35
☐ 29 Robin Yount	.50	.23	.06
☐ 30 Fernando Valenzuela	.25	.11	.03

1984-91 Topps Pewter Bonuses

During the eight year period that Topps issued their Gallery of Champions set, various other metal cards were issued as well. During that period, Topps issued Pewter cards as a premium. From 1984 to 1987 these Pewters were issued as a bonus for ordering "Tiffany" cases. From 1988-91, these Pewters were issued as bonuses for Gallery of Champion cases. The cards are sequenced in year order. A different Jose Canseco card was issued in 1987 and 1989.

	NRMT	VG-E	GOOD
COMPLETE SET (8)	800.00	350.00	100.00
COMMON CARD (1-8)	35.00	16.00	4.40
☐ 1 Tom Seaver '84	350.00	160.00	45.00
☐ 2 Dwight Gooden '85	50.00	22.00	6.25
☐ 3 Don Mattingly '86	100.00	45.00	12.50
☐ 4 Jose Canseco '87	50.00	22.00	6.25
☐ 5 Mark McGwire '88	50.00	22.00	6.25
☐ 6 Jose Canseco '89	35.00	16.00	4.40
☐ 7 Nolan Ryan '90	200.00	90.00	25.00
☐ 8 Rickey Henderson '91	50.00	22.00	6.25

1985 Topps

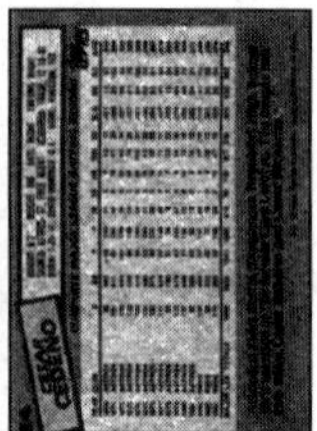

The 1985 Topps set contains 792 standard-size full-color cards. Cards were primarily distributed in 15-card wax packs and 51-card rack packs. Full color card fronts feature both the Topps and team logos along with the team name, player's name, and his position. The first ten cards (1-10) are Record Breakers, cards 131-143 are Father and Sons, and cards 701 to 722 portray All-Star selections. Cards 271-282 represent "First Draft Picks" still active in professional baseball and cards 389-404 feature selected members of the 1984 U.S. Olympic Baseball Team. Rookie Cards include Roger Clemens, Eric Davis, Shawon Dunston, Dwight Gooden, Orel Hershiser, Jimmy Key, Mark Langston, Mark McGwire, Terry Pendleton, Kirby Puckett, Jose Rijo and Bret Saberhagen.

Card	NRMT	VG-E	GOOD
COMPLETE SET (792)	50.00	22.00	6.25
COMMON CARD (1-792)	.08	.04	.01
☐ 1 Carlton Fisk RB	.30	.14	.04
Longest game by catcher			
☐ 2 Steve Garvey RB	.30	.14	.04
Consecutive error-less games, 1B			
☐ 3 Dwight Gooden RB	.50	.23	.06
Most rookie strikeouts			
☐ 4 Cliff Johnson RB	.08	.04	.01
Most pinch-hit homers			
☐ 5 Joe Morgan RB	.30	.14	.04
Most homers 2B, lifetime			
☐ 6 Pete Rose RB	.40	.18	.05
Most career singles			
☐ 7 Nolan Ryan RB	1.50	.70	.19
Most career strikeouts			
☐ 8 Juan Samuel RB	.08	.04	.01
Most SB's, rookie season			
☐ 9 Bruce Sutter RB	.15	.07	.02
Most NL season saves			
☐ 10 Don Sutton RB	.15	.07	.02
Most seasons 100 or more K's			
☐ 11 Ralph Houk MG	.08	.04	.01
(Checklist back)			
☐ 12 Dave Lopes	.15	.07	.02
(Now with Cubs on card front)			
☐ 13 Tim Lollar	.08	.04	.01
☐ 14 Chris Bando	.08	.04	.01
☐ 15 Jerry Koosman	.08	.04	.01
☐ 16 Bobby Meacham	.08	.04	.01
☐ 17 Mike Scott	.08	.04	.01
☐ 18 Mickey Hatcher	.08	.04	.01
☐ 19 George Frazier	.08	.04	.01
☐ 20 Chet Lemon	.08	.04	.01
☐ 21 Lee Tunnell	.08	.04	.01
☐ 22 Duane Kuiper	.08	.04	.01
☐ 23 Bret Saberhagen	.60	.25	.07
☐ 24 Jesse Barfield	.08	.04	.01
☐ 25 Steve Bedrosian	.08	.04	.01
☐ 26 Roy Smalley	.08	.04	.01
☐ 27 Bruce Berenyi	.08	.04	.01
☐ 28 Dann Bilardello	.08	.04	.01
☐ 29 Odell Jones	.08	.04	.01
☐ 30 Cal Ripken	3.00	1.35	.35
☐ 31 Terry Whitfield	.08	.04	.01
☐ 32 Chuck Porter	.08	.04	.01
☐ 33 Tito Landrum	.08	.04	.01
☐ 34 Ed Nunez	.08	.04	.01
☐ 35 Graig Nettles	.15	.07	.02
☐ 36 Fred Breining	.08	.04	.01
☐ 37 Reid Nichols	.08	.04	.01
☐ 38 Jackie Moore MG	.08	.04	.01
(Checklist back)			
☐ 39 John Wockenfuss	.08	.04	.01
☐ 40 Phil Niekro	.30	.14	.04
☐ 41 Mike Fischlin	.08	.04	.01
☐ 42 Luis Sanchez	.08	.04	.01
☐ 43 Andre David	.08	.04	.01
☐ 44 Dickie Thon	.08	.04	.01
☐ 45 Greg Minton	.08	.04	.01
☐ 46 Gary Woods	.08	.04	.01
☐ 47 Dave Rozema	.08	.04	.01
☐ 48 Tony Fernandez	.15	.07	.02
☐ 49 Butch Davis	.08	.04	.01
☐ 50 John Candelaria	.08	.04	.01
☐ 51 Bob Watson	.15	.07	.02
☐ 52 Jerry Dybzinski	.08	.04	.01
☐ 53 Tom Gorman	.08	.04	.01
☐ 54 Cesar Cedeno	.15	.07	.02
☐ 55 Frank Tanana	.08	.04	.01
☐ 56 Jim Dwyer	.08	.04	.01
☐ 57 Pat Zachry	.08	.04	.01
☐ 58 Orlando Mercado	.08	.04	.01
☐ 59 Rick Waits	.08	.04	.01
☐ 60 George Hendrick	.08	.04	.01
☐ 61 Curt Kaufman	.08	.04	.01
☐ 62 Mike Ramsey	.08	.04	.01
☐ 63 Steve McCatty	.08	.04	.01
☐ 64 Mark Bailey	.08	.04	.01
☐ 65 Bill Buckner	.15	.07	.02
☐ 66 Dick Williams MG	.15	.07	.02
(Checklist back)			
☐ 67 Rafael Santana	.08	.04	.01
☐ 68 Von Hayes	.08	.04	.01
☐ 69 Jim Winn	.08	.04	.01
☐ 70 Don Baylor	.30	.14	.04
☐ 71 Tim Laudner	.08	.04	.01
☐ 72 Rick Sutcliffe	.08	.04	.01
☐ 73 Rusty Kuntz	.08	.04	.01
☐ 74 Mike Krukow	.08	.04	.01
☐ 75 Willie Upshaw	.08	.04	.01
☐ 76 Alan Bannister	.08	.04	.01
☐ 77 Joe Beckwith	.08	.04	.01
☐ 78 Scott Fletcher	.08	.04	.01
☐ 79 Rick Mahler	.08	.04	.01
☐ 80 Keith Hernandez	.15	.07	.02
☐ 81 Lenn Sakata	.08	.04	.01
☐ 82 Joe Price	.08	.04	.01
☐ 83 Charlie Moore	.08	.04	.01
☐ 84 Spike Owen	.08	.04	.01
☐ 85 Mike Marshall	.08	.04	.01
☐ 86 Don Aase	.08	.04	.01
☐ 87 David Green	.08	.04	.01
☐ 88 Bryn Smith	.08	.04	.01
☐ 89 Jackie Gutierrez	.08	.04	.01
☐ 90 Rich Gossage	.30	.14	.04
☐ 91 Jeff Burroughs	.08	.04	.01
☐ 92 Paul Owens MG	.08	.04	.01
(Checklist back)			
☐ 93 Don Schulze	.08	.04	.01
☐ 94 Toby Harrah	.08	.04	.01
☐ 95 Jose Cruz	.15	.07	.02
☐ 96 Johnny Ray	.08	.04	.01
☐ 97 Pete Filson	.08	.04	.01
☐ 98 Steve Lake	.08	.04	.01
☐ 99 Milt Wilcox	.08	.04	.01
☐ 100 George Brett	1.50	.70	.19
☐ 101 Jim Acker	.08	.04	.01
☐ 102 Tommy Dunbar	.08	.04	.01
☐ 103 Randy Lerch	.08	.04	.01
☐ 104 Mike Fitzgerald	.08	.04	.01
☐ 105 Ron Kittle	.08	.04	.01
☐ 106 Pascual Perez	.08	.04	.01
☐ 107 Tom Foley	.08	.04	.01
☐ 108 Darnell Coles	.08	.04	.01
☐ 109 Gary Roenicke	.08	.04	.01
☐ 110 Alejandro Pena	.08	.04	.01
☐ 111 Doug DeCinces	.08	.04	.01
☐ 112 Tom Tellmann	.08	.04	.01
☐ 113 Tom Herr	.15	.07	.02
☐ 114 Bob James	.08	.04	.01
☐ 115 Rickey Henderson	.60	.25	.07
☐ 116 Dennis Boyd	.08	.04	.01
☐ 117 Greg Gross	.08	.04	.01
☐ 118 Eric Show	.08	.04	.01
☐ 119 Pat Corrales MG	.08	.04	.01
(Checklist back)			
☐ 120 Steve Kemp	.08	.04	.01
☐ 121 Checklist: 1-132	.15	.07	.02
☐ 122 Tom Brunansky	.15	.07	.02
☐ 123 Dave Smith	.08	.04	.01
☐ 124 Rich Hebner	.08	.04	.01
☐ 125 Kent Tekulve	.08	.04	.01
☐ 126 Ruppert Jones	.08	.04	.01
☐ 127 Mark Gubicza	.30	.14	.04
☐ 128 Ernie Whitt	.08	.04	.01
☐ 129 Gene Garber	.08	.04	.01
☐ 130 Al Oliver	.15	.07	.02
☐ 131 Buddy Bell FS	.15	.07	.02
Gus Bell			
☐ 132 Dale Berra FS	.15	.07	.02
Yogi Berra			
☐ 133 Bob Boone FS	.15	.07	.02
Ray Boone			
☐ 134 Terry Francona FS	.15	.07	.02
Tito Francona			
☐ 135 Terry Kennedy FS	.15	.07	.02
Bob Kennedy			
☐ 136 Jeff Kunkel FS	.08	.04	.01
Bill Kunkel			
☐ 137 Vance Law FS	.15	.07	.02
Vern Law			
☐ 138 Dick Schofield FS	.08	.04	.01
Dick Schofield			
☐ 139 Joel Skinner FS	.08	.04	.01
Bob Skinner			
☐ 140 Roy Smalley Jr. FS	.15	.07	.02
Roy Smalley			
☐ 141 Mike Stenhouse FS	.08	.04	.01
Dave Stenhouse			
☐ 142 Steve Trout FS	.15	.07	.02
Dizzy Trout			
☐ 143 Ozzie Virgil FS	.08	.04	.01
Ossie Virgil			
☐ 144 Ron Gardenhire	.08	.04	.01
☐ 145 Alvin Davis	.15	.07	.02
☐ 146 Gary Redus	.08	.04	.01
☐ 147 Bill Swaggerty	.08	.04	.01
☐ 148 Steve Yeager	.08	.04	.01
☐ 149 Dickie Noles	.08	.04	.01
☐ 150 Jim Rice	.15	.07	.02
☐ 151 Moose Haas	.08	.04	.01
☐ 152 Steve Braun	.08	.04	.01
☐ 153 Frank LaCorte	.08	.04	.01
☐ 154 Argenis Salazar	.08	.04	.01
☐ 155 Yogi Berra MG	.30	.14	.04
(Checklist back)			
☐ 156 Craig Reynolds	.08	.04	.01
☐ 157 Tug McGraw	.15	.07	.02
☐ 158 Pat Tabler	.08	.04	.01
☐ 159 Carlos Diaz	.08	.04	.01
☐ 160 Lance Parrish	.15	.07	.02
☐ 161 Ken Schrom	.08	.04	.01
☐ 162 Benny Distefano	.08	.04	.01
☐ 163 Dennis Eckersley	.30	.14	.04
☐ 164 Jorge Orta	.08	.04	.01
☐ 165 Dusty Baker	.15	.07	.02
☐ 166 Keith Atherton	.08	.04	.01
☐ 167 Rufino Linares	.08	.04	.01
☐ 168 Garth Iorg	.08	.04	.01
☐ 169 Dan Spillner	.08	.04	.01
☐ 170 George Foster	.15	.07	.02
☐ 171 Bill Stein	.08	.04	.01
☐ 172 Jack Perconte	.08	.04	.01
☐ 173 Mike Young	.08	.04	.01
☐ 174 Rick Honeycutt	.08	.04	.01
☐ 175 Dave Parker	.15	.07	.02
☐ 176 Bill Schroeder	.08	.04	.01
☐ 177 Dave Von Ohlen	.08	.04	.01
☐ 178 Miguel Dilone	.08	.04	.01
☐ 179 Tommy John	.30	.14	.04
☐ 180 Dave Winfield	.60	.25	.07
☐ 181 Roger Clemens	7.00	3.10	.85
☐ 182 Tim Flannery	.08	.04	.01
☐ 183 Larry McWilliams	.08	.04	.01
☐ 184 Carmen Castillo	.08	.04	.01
☐ 185 Al Holland	.08	.04	.01
☐ 186 Bob Lillis MG	.08	.04	.01
(Checklist back)			
☐ 187 Mike Walters	.08	.04	.01
☐ 188 Greg Pryor	.08	.04	.01
☐ 189 Warren Brusstar	.08	.04	.01
☐ 190 Rusty Staub	.15	.07	.02
☐ 191 Steve Nicosia	.08	.04	.01
☐ 192 Howard Johnson	.15	.07	.02
☐ 193 Jimmy Key	.40	.18	.05
☐ 194 Dave Stegman	.08	.04	.01
☐ 195 Glenn Hubbard	.08	.04	.01
☐ 196 Pete O'Brien	.08	.04	.01
☐ 197 Mike Warren	.08	.04	.01
☐ 198 Eddie Milner	.08	.04	.01
☐ 199 Dennis Martinez	.15	.07	.02
☐ 200 Reggie Jackson	.60	.25	.07
☐ 201 Burt Hooton	.08	.04	.01
☐ 202 Gorman Thomas	.08	.04	.01
☐ 203 Bob McClure	.08	.04	.01
☐ 204 Art Howe	.08	.04	.01
☐ 205 Steve Rogers	.08	.04	.01
☐ 206 Phil Garner	.08	.04	.01
☐ 207 Mark Clear	.08	.04	.01
☐ 208 Champ Summers	.08	.04	.01
☐ 209 Bill Campbell	.08	.04	.01
☐ 210 Gary Matthews	.08	.04	.01
☐ 211 Clay Christiansen	.08	.04	.01
☐ 212 George Vukovich	.08	.04	.01
☐ 213 Billy Gardner MG	.15	.07	.02
(Checklist back)			
☐ 214 John Tudor	.08	.04	.01
☐ 215 Bob Brenly	.08	.04	.01
☐ 216 Jerry Don Gleaton	.08	.04	.01
☐ 217 Leon Roberts	.08	.04	.01
☐ 218 Doyle Alexander	.08	.04	.01
☐ 219 Gerald Perry	.08	.04	.01
☐ 220 Fred Lynn	.15	.07	.02
☐ 221 Ron Reed	.08	.04	.01
☐ 222 Hubie Brooks	.08	.04	.01
☐ 223 Tom Hume	.08	.04	.01
☐ 224 Al Cowens	.08	.04	.01
☐ 225 Mike Boddicker	.08	.04	.01
☐ 226 Juan Beniquez	.08	.04	.01
☐ 227 Danny Darwin	.08	.04	.01
☐ 228 Dion James	.08	.04	.01
☐ 229 Dave LaPoint	.08	.04	.01
☐ 230 Gary Carter	.15	.07	.02
☐ 231 Dwayne Murphy	.08	.04	.01
☐ 232 Dave Beard	.08	.04	.01
☐ 233 Ed Jurak	.08	.04	.01
☐ 234 Jerry Narron	.08	.04	.01
☐ 235 Garry Maddox	.08	.04	.01
☐ 236 Mark Thurmond	.08	.04	.01
☐ 237 Julio Franco	.30	.14	.04
☐ 238 Jose Rijo	.40	.18	.05
☐ 239 Tim Teufel	.08	.04	.01
☐ 240 Dave Stieb	.15	.07	.02
☐ 241 Jim Frey MG	.08	.04	.01
(Checklist back)			
☐ 242 Greg Harris	.08	.04	.01
☐ 243 Barbaro Garbey	.08	.04	.01
☐ 244 Mike Jones	.08	.04	.01
☐ 245 Chili Davis	.15	.07	.02
☐ 246 Mike Norris	.08	.04	.01
☐ 247 Wayne Tolleson	.08	.04	.01
☐ 248 Terry Forster	.08	.04	.01
☐ 249 Harold Baines	.15	.07	.02
☐ 250 Jesse Orosco	.08	.04	.01
☐ 251 Brad Gulden	.08	.04	.01
☐ 252 Dan Ford	.08	.04	.01
☐ 253 Sid Bream	.30	.14	.04
☐ 254 Pete Vuckovich	.08	.04	.01
☐ 255 Lonnie Smith	.08	.04	.01
☐ 256 Mike Stanton	.08	.04	.01
☐ 257 Bryan Little UER	.08	.04	.01
Name spelled Brian on front			
☐ 258 Mike C. Brown	.08	.04	.01
☐ 259 Gary Allenson	.08	.04	.01
☐ 260 Dave Righetti	.15	.07	.02
☐ 261 Checklist: 133-264	.15	.07	.02
☐ 262 Greg Booker	.08	.04	.01
☐ 263 Mel Hall	.08	.04	.01
☐ 264 Joe Sambito	.08	.04	.01
☐ 265 Juan Samuel	.08	.04	.01
☐ 266 Frank Viola	.15	.07	.02
☐ 267 Henry Cotto	.08	.04	.01
☐ 268 Chuck Tanner MG	.15	.07	.02
(Checklist back)			
☐ 269 Doug Baker	.08	.04	.01
☐ 270 Dan Quisenberry	.15	.07	.02
☐ 271 Tim Foli FDP68	.08	.04	.01
☐ 272 Jeff Burroughs FDP69	.08	.04	.01
☐ 273 Bill Almon FDP74	.08	.04	.01
☐ 274 Floyd Bannister FDP76	.08	.04	.01
☐ 275 Harold Baines FDP77	.15	.07	.02
☐ 276 Bob Horner FDP78	.08	.04	.01
☐ 277 Al Chambers FDP79	.08	.04	.01
☐ 278 Darryl Strawberry FDP80	.30	.14	.04
☐ 279 Mike Moore FDP81	.08	.04	.01
☐ 280 Shawon Dunston FDP82	.40	.18	.05
☐ 281 Tim Belcher FDP83	.30	.14	.04
☐ 282 Shawn Abner FDP84	.08	.04	.01
☐ 283 Fran Mullins	.08	.04	.01
☐ 284 Marty Bystrom	.08	.04	.01
☐ 285 Dan Driessen	.08	.04	.01
☐ 286 Rudy Law	.08	.04	.01
☐ 287 Walt Terrell	.08	.04	.01
☐ 288 Jeff Kunkel	.08	.04	.01
☐ 289 Tom Underwood	.08	.04	.01
☐ 290 Cecil Cooper	.15	.07	.02
☐ 291 Bob Welch	.08	.04	.01
☐ 292 Brad Komminsk	.08	.04	.01
☐ 293 Curt Young	.08	.04	.01
☐ 294 Tom Nieto	.08	.04	.01
☐ 295 Joe Niekro	.08	.04	.01
☐ 296 Ricky Nelson	.08	.04	.01
☐ 297 Gary Lucas	.08	.04	.01
☐ 298 Marty Barrett	.08	.04	.01
☐ 299 Andy Hawkins	.08	.04	.01
☐ 300 Rod Carew	.50	.23	.06
☐ 301 John Montefusco	.08	.04	.01
☐ 302 Tim Corcoran	.08	.04	.01

☐ 303 Mike Jeffcoat .08 .04 .01
☐ 304 Gary Gaetti .15 .07 .02
☐ 305 Dale Berra .08 .04 .01
☐ 306 Rick Reuschel .08 .04 .01
☐ 307 Sparky Anderson MG .15 .07 .02
(Checklist back)
☐ 308 John Wathan .08 .04 .01
☐ 309 Mike Witt .08 .04 .01
☐ 310 Manny Trillo .08 .04 .01
☐ 311 Jim Gott .08 .04 .01
☐ 312 Marc Hill .08 .04 .01
☐ 313 Dave Schmidt .08 .04 .01
☐ 314 Ron Oester .08 .04 .01
☐ 315 Doug Sisk .08 .04 .01
☐ 316 John Lowenstein .08 .04 .01
☐ 317 Jack Lazorko .08 .04 .01
☐ 318 Ted Simmons .15 .07 .02
☐ 319 Jeff Jones .08 .04 .01
☐ 320 Dale Murphy .30 .14 .04
☐ 321 Ricky Horton .08 .04 .01
☐ 322 Dave Stapleton .08 .04 .01
☐ 323 Andy McGaffigan .08 .04 .01
☐ 324 Bruce Bochy .08 .04 .01
☐ 325 John Denny .08 .04 .01
☐ 326 Kevin Bass .08 .04 .01
☐ 327 Brook Jacoby .08 .04 .01
☐ 328 Bob Shirley .08 .04 .01
☐ 329 Ron Washington .08 .04 .01
☐ 330 Leon Durham .08 .04 .01
☐ 331 Bill Laskey .08 .04 .01
☐ 332 Brian Harper .15 .07 .02
☐ 333 Willie Hernandez .08 .04 .01
☐ 334 Dick Howser MG .15 .07 .02
(Checklist back)
☐ 335 Bruce Benedict .08 .04 .01
☐ 336 Rance Mulliniks .08 .04 .01
☐ 337 Billy Sample .08 .04 .01
☐ 338 Britt Burns .08 .04 .01
☐ 339 Danny Heep .08 .04 .01
☐ 340 Robin Yount .75 .35 .09
☐ 341 Floyd Rayford .08 .04 .01
☐ 342 Ted Power .08 .04 .01
☐ 343 Bill Russell .08 .04 .01
☐ 344 Dave Henderson .15 .07 .02
☐ 345 Charlie Lea .08 .04 .01
☐ 346 Terry Pendleton .60 .25 .07
☐ 347 Rick Langford .08 .04 .01
☐ 348 Bob Boone .15 .07 .02
☐ 349 Domingo Ramos .08 .04 .01
☐ 350 Wade Boggs 1.00 .45 .12
☐ 351 Juan Agosto .08 .04 .01
☐ 352 Joe Morgan .30 .14 .04
☐ 353 Julio Solano .08 .04 .01
☐ 354 Andre Robertson .08 .04 .01
☐ 355 Bert Blyleven .30 .14 .04
☐ 356 Dave Meier .08 .04 .01
☐ 357 Rich Bordi .08 .04 .01
☐ 358 Tony Pena .08 .04 .01
☐ 359 Pat Sheridan .08 .04 .01
☐ 360 Steve Carlton .40 .18 .05
☐ 361 Alfredo Griffin .08 .04 .01
☐ 362 Craig McMurtry .08 .04 .01
☐ 363 Ron Hodges .08 .04 .01
☐ 364 Richard Dotson .08 .04 .01
☐ 365 Danny Ozark MG .08 .04 .01
(Checklist back)
☐ 366 Todd Cruz .08 .04 .01
☐ 367 Keefe Cato .08 .04 .01
☐ 368 Dave Bergman .08 .04 .01
☐ 369 R.J. Reynolds .08 .04 .01
☐ 370 Bruce Sutter .15 .07 .02
☐ 371 Mickey Rivers .08 .04 .01
☐ 372 Roy Howell .08 .04 .01
☐ 373 Mike Moore .08 .04 .01
☐ 374 Brian Downing .08 .04 .01
☐ 375 Jeff Reardon .15 .07 .02
☐ 376 Jeff Newman .08 .04 .01
☐ 377 Checklist: 265-396 .15 .07 .02
☐ 378 Alan Wiggins .08 .04 .01
☐ 379 Charles Hudson .08 .04 .01
☐ 380 Ken Griffey .15 .07 .02
☐ 381 Roy Smith .08 .04 .01
☐ 382 Denny Walling .08 .04 .01
☐ 383 Rick Lysander .08 .04 .01
☐ 384 Jody Davis .08 .04 .01
☐ 385 Jose DeLeon .08 .04 .01
☐ 386 Dan Gladden .15 .07 .02
☐ 387 Buddy Biancalana .08 .04 .01
☐ 388 Bert Roberge .08 .04 .01
☐ 389 Rod Dedeaux OLY CO .15 .07 .02
☐ 390 Sid Akins OLY .15 .07 .02
☐ 391 Flavio Alfaro OLY .15 .07 .02
☐ 392 Don August OLY .15 .07 .02
☐ 393 Scott Bankhead OLY .15 .07 .02
☐ 394 Bob Caffrey OLY .08 .04 .01
☐ 395 Mike Dunne OLY .15 .07 .02
☐ 396 Gary Green OLY .15 .07 .02
☐ 397 John Hoover OLY .08 .04 .01
☐ 398 Shane Mack OLY .30 .14 .04
☐ 399 John Marzano OLY .15 .07 .02
☐ 400 Oddibe McDowell OLY .15 .07 .02
☐ 401 Mark McGwire OLY 20.00 9.00 2.50
☐ 402 Pat Pacillo OLY .15 .07 .02
☐ 403 Cory Snyder OLY .15 .07 .02
☐ 404 Billy Swift OLY .50 .23 .06

☐ 405 Tom Veryzer .08 .04 .01
☐ 406 Len Whitehouse .08 .04 .01
☐ 407 Bobby Ramos .08 .04 .01
☐ 408 Sid Monge .08 .04 .01
☐ 409 Brad Wellman .08 .04 .01
☐ 410 Bob Horner .08 .04 .01
☐ 411 Bobby Cox MG .15 .07 .02
(Checklist back)
☐ 412 Bud Black .08 .04 .01
☐ 413 Vance Law .08 .04 .01
☐ 414 Gary Ward .08 .04 .01
☐ 415 Ron Darling UER .15 .07 .02
(No trivia answer)
☐ 416 Wayne Gross .08 .04 .01
☐ 417 John Franco .40 .18 .05
☐ 418 Ken Landreaux .08 .04 .01
☐ 419 Mike Caldwell .08 .04 .01
☐ 420 Andre Dawson .30 .14 .04
☐ 421 Dave Rucker .08 .04 .01
☐ 422 Carney Lansford .15 .07 .02
☐ 423 Barry Bonnell .08 .04 .01
☐ 424 Al Nipper .08 .04 .01
☐ 425 Mike Hargrove .15 .07 .02
☐ 426 Vern Ruhle .08 .04 .01
☐ 427 Mario Ramirez .08 .04 .01
☐ 428 Larry Andersen .08 .04 .01
☐ 429 Rick Cerone .08 .04 .01
☐ 430 Ron Davis .08 .04 .01
☐ 431 U.L. Washington .08 .04 .01
☐ 432 Thad Bosley .08 .04 .01
☐ 433 Jim Morrison .08 .04 .01
☐ 434 Gene Richards .08 .04 .01
☐ 435 Dan Petry .08 .04 .01
☐ 436 Willie Aikens .08 .04 .01
☐ 437 Al Jones .08 .04 .01
☐ 438 Joe Torre MG .30 .14 .04
(Checklist back)
☐ 439 Junior Ortiz .08 .04 .01
☐ 440 Fernando Valenzuela .15 .07 .02
☐ 441 Duane Walker .08 .04 .01
☐ 442 Ken Forsch .08 .04 .01
☐ 443 George Wright .08 .04 .01
☐ 444 Tony Phillips .30 .14 .04
☐ 445 Tippy Martinez .08 .04 .01
☐ 446 Jim Sundberg .08 .04 .01
☐ 447 Jeff Lahti .08 .04 .01
☐ 448 Derrel Thomas .08 .04 .01
☐ 449 Phil Bradley .15 .07 .02
☐ 450 Steve Garvey .30 .14 .04
☐ 451 Bruce Hurst .08 .04 .01
☐ 452 John Castino .08 .04 .01
☐ 453 Tom Waddell .08 .04 .01
☐ 454 Glenn Wilson .08 .04 .01
☐ 455 Bob Knepper .08 .04 .01
☐ 456 Tim Foli .08 .04 .01
☐ 457 Cecilio Guante .08 .04 .01
☐ 458 Randy Johnson .08 .04 .01
☐ 459 Charlie Leibrandt .08 .04 .01
☐ 460 Ryne Sandberg 1.50 .70 .19
☐ 461 Marty Castillo .08 .04 .01
☐ 462 Gary Lavelle .08 .04 .01
☐ 463 Dave Collins .08 .04 .01
☐ 464 Mike Mason .08 .04 .01
☐ 465 Bob Grich .15 .07 .02
☐ 466 Tony LaRussa MG .15 .07 .02
(Checklist back)
☐ 467 Ed Lynch .08 .04 .01
☐ 468 Wayne Krenchicki .08 .04 .01
☐ 469 Sammy Stewart .08 .04 .01
☐ 470 Steve Sax .15 .07 .02
☐ 471 Pete Ladd .08 .04 .01
☐ 472 Jim Essian .08 .04 .01
☐ 473 Tim Wallach .15 .07 .02
☐ 474 Kurt Kepshire .08 .04 .01
☐ 475 Andre Thornton .08 .04 .01
☐ 476 Jeff Stone .08 .04 .01
☐ 477 Bob Ojeda .08 .04 .01
☐ 478 Kurt Bevacqua .08 .04 .01
☐ 479 Mike Madden .08 .04 .01
☐ 480 Lou Whitaker .30 .14 .04
☐ 481 Dale Murray .08 .04 .01
☐ 482 Harry Spilman .08 .04 .01
☐ 483 Mike Smithson .08 .04 .01
☐ 484 Larry Bowa .15 .07 .02
☐ 485 Matt Young .08 .04 .01
☐ 486 Steve Balboni .08 .04 .01
☐ 487 Frank Williams .08 .04 .01
☐ 488 Joel Skinner .08 .04 .01
☐ 489 Bryan Clark .08 .04 .01
☐ 490 Jason Thompson .08 .04 .01
☐ 491 Rick Camp .08 .04 .01
☐ 492 Dave Johnson MG .15 .07 .02
(Checklist back)
☐ 493 Orel Hershiser 1.00 .45 .12
☐ 494 Rich Dauer .08 .04 .01
☐ 495 Mario Soto .08 .04 .01
☐ 496 Donnie Scott .08 .04 .01
☐ 497 Gary Pettis UER .08 .04 .01
(Photo actually
Gary's little
brother Lynn)
☐ 498 Ed Romero .08 .04 .01
☐ 499 Danny Cox .08 .04 .01
☐ 500 Mike Schmidt 1.00 .45 .12
☐ 501 Dan Schatzeder .08 .04 .01

☐ 502 Rick Miller .08 .04 .01
☐ 503 Tim Conroy .08 .04 .01
☐ 504 Jerry Willard .08 .04 .01
☐ 505 Jim Beattie .08 .04 .01
☐ 506 Franklin Stubbs .08 .04 .01
☐ 507 Ray Fontenot .08 .04 .01
☐ 508 John Shelby .08 .04 .01
☐ 509 Milt May .08 .04 .01
☐ 510 Kent Hrbek .30 .14 .04
☐ 511 Lee Smith .30 .14 .04
☐ 512 Tom Brookens .08 .04 .01
☐ 513 Lynn Jones .08 .04 .01
☐ 514 Jeff Cornell .08 .04 .01
☐ 515 Dave Concepcion .15 .07 .02
☐ 516 Roy Lee Jackson .08 .04 .01
☐ 517 Jerry Martin .08 .04 .01
☐ 518 Chris Chambliss .08 .04 .01
☐ 519 Doug Rader MG .08 .04 .01
(Checklist back)
☐ 520 LaMarr Hoyt .08 .04 .01
☐ 521 Rick Dempsey .08 .04 .01
☐ 522 Paul Molitor .75 .35 .09
☐ 523 Candy Maldonado .08 .04 .01
☐ 524 Rob Wilfong .08 .04 .01
☐ 525 Darrell Porter .08 .04 .01
☐ 526 David Palmer .08 .04 .01
☐ 527 Checklist: 397-528 .15 .07 .02
☐ 528 Bill Krueger .08 .04 .01
☐ 529 Rich Gedman .08 .04 .01
☐ 530 Dave Dravecky .15 .07 .02
☐ 531 Joe Lefebvre .08 .04 .01
☐ 532 Frank DiPino .08 .04 .01
☐ 533 Tony Bernazard .08 .04 .01
☐ 534 Brian Dayett .08 .04 .01
☐ 535 Pat Putnam .08 .04 .01
☐ 536 Kirby Puckett 12.00 5.50 1.50
☐ 537 Don Robinson .08 .04 .01
☐ 538 Keith Moreland .08 .04 .01
☐ 539 Aurelio Lopez .08 .04 .01
☐ 540 Claudell Washington .08 .04 .01
☐ 541 Mark Davis .08 .04 .01
☐ 542 Don Slaught .08 .04 .01
☐ 543 Mike Squires .08 .04 .01
☐ 544 Bruce Kison .08 .04 .01
☐ 545 Lloyd Moseby .08 .04 .01
☐ 546 Brent Gaff .08 .04 .01
☐ 547 Pete Rose MG .50 .23 .06
(Checklist back)
☐ 548 Larry Parrish .08 .04 .01
☐ 549 Mike Scioscia .08 .04 .01
☐ 550 Scott McGregor .08 .04 .01
☐ 551 Andy Van Slyke .30 .14 .04
☐ 552 Chris Codiroli .08 .04 .01
☐ 553 Bob Clark .08 .04 .01
☐ 554 Doug Flynn .08 .04 .01
☐ 555 Bob Stanley .08 .04 .01
☐ 556 Sixto Lezcano .08 .04 .01
☐ 557 Len Barker .08 .04 .01
☐ 558 Carmelo Martinez .08 .04 .01
☐ 559 Jay Howell .08 .04 .01
☐ 560 Bill Madlock .08 .04 .01
☐ 561 Darryl Motley .08 .04 .01
☐ 562 Houston Jimenez .08 .04 .01
☐ 563 Dick Ruthven .08 .04 .01
☐ 564 Alan Ashby .08 .04 .01
☐ 565 Kirk Gibson .15 .07 .02
☐ 566 Ed VandeBerg .08 .04 .01
☐ 567 Joel Youngblood .08 .04 .01
☐ 568 Cliff Johnson .08 .04 .01
☐ 569 Ken Oberkfell .08 .04 .01
☐ 570 Darryl Strawberry .30 .14 .04
☐ 571 Charlie Hough .15 .07 .02
☐ 572 Tom Paciorek .08 .04 .01
☐ 573 Jay Tibbs .08 .04 .01
☐ 574 Joe Altobelli MG .08 .04 .01
(Checklist back)
☐ 575 Pedro Guerrero .15 .07 .02
☐ 576 Jaime Cocanower .08 .04 .01
☐ 577 Chris Speier .08 .04 .01
☐ 578 Terry Francona .08 .04 .01
☐ 579 Ron Romanick .08 .04 .01
☐ 580 Dwight Evans .15 .07 .02
☐ 581 Mark Wagner .08 .04 .01
☐ 582 Ken Phelps .08 .04 .01
☐ 583 Bobby Brown .08 .04 .01
☐ 584 Kevin Gross .08 .04 .01
☐ 585 Butch Wynegar .08 .04 .01
☐ 586 Bill Scherrer .08 .04 .01
☐ 587 Doug Frobel .08 .04 .01
☐ 588 Bobby Castillo .08 .04 .01
☐ 589 Bob Dernier .08 .04 .01
☐ 590 Ray Knight .15 .07 .02
☐ 591 Larry Herndon .08 .04 .01
☐ 592 Jeff D. Robinson .08 .04 .01
☐ 593 Rick Leach .08 .04 .01
☐ 594 Curt Wilkerson .08 .04 .01
☐ 595 Larry Gura .08 .04 .01
☐ 596 Jerry Hairston .08 .04 .01
☐ 597 Brad Lesley .08 .04 .01
☐ 598 Jose Oquendo .08 .04 .01
☐ 599 Storm Davis .08 .04 .01
☐ 600 Pete Rose .75 .35 .09
☐ 601 Tom Lasorda MG .30 .14 .04
(Checklist back)
☐ 602 Jeff Dedmon .08 .04 .01

☐ 603 Rick Manning .08 .04 .01
☐ 604 Daryl Sconiers .08 .04 .01
☐ 605 Ozzie Smith 1.00 .45 .12
☐ 606 Rich Gale .08 .04 .01
☐ 607 Bill Almon .08 .04 .01
☐ 608 Craig Lefferts .08 .04 .01
☐ 609 Broderick Perkins .08 .04 .01
☐ 610 Jack Morris .15 .07 .02
☐ 611 Ozzie Virgil .08 .04 .01
☐ 612 Mike Armstrong .08 .04 .01
☐ 613 Terry Puhl .08 .04 .01
☐ 614 Al Williams .08 .04 .01
☐ 615 Marvell Wynne .08 .04 .01
☐ 616 Scott Sanderson .08 .04 .01
☐ 617 Willie Wilson .08 .04 .01
☐ 618 Pete Falcone .08 .04 .01
☐ 619 Jeff Leonard .08 .04 .01
☐ 620 Dwight Gooden 2.00 .90 .25
☐ 621 Marvis Foley .08 .04 .01
☐ 622 Luis Leal .08 .04 .01
☐ 623 Greg Walker .08 .04 .01
☐ 624 Benny Ayala .08 .04 .01
☐ 625 Mark Langston .50 .23 .06
☐ 626 German Rivera .08 .04 .01
☐ 627 Eric Davis .60 .25 .07
☐ 628 Rene Lachemann MG .08 .04 .01
(Checklist back)
☐ 629 Dick Schofield .08 .04 .01
☐ 630 Tim Raines .15 .07 .02
☐ 631 Bob Forsch .08 .04 .01
☐ 632 Bruce Bochte .08 .04 .01
☐ 633 Glenn Hoffman .08 .04 .01
☐ 634 Bill Dawley .08 .04 .01
☐ 635 Terry Kennedy .08 .04 .01
☐ 636 Shane Rawley .08 .04 .01
☐ 637 Brett Butler .15 .07 .02
☐ 638 Mike Pagliarulo .08 .04 .01
☐ 639 Ed Hodge .08 .04 .01
☐ 640 Steve Henderson .08 .04 .01
☐ 641 Rod Scurry .08 .04 .01
☐ 642 Dave Owen .08 .04 .01
☐ 643 Johnny Grubb .08 .04 .01
☐ 644 Mark Huismann .08 .04 .01
☐ 645 Damaso Garcia .08 .04 .01
☐ 646 Scot Thompson .08 .04 .01
☐ 647 Rafael Ramirez .08 .04 .01
☐ 648 Bob Jones .08 .04 .01
☐ 649 Sid Fernandez .30 .14 .04
☐ 650 Greg Luzinski .15 .07 .02
☐ 651 Jeff Russell .15 .07 .02
☐ 652 Joe Nolan .08 .04 .01
☐ 653 Mark Brouhard .08 .04 .01
☐ 654 Dave Anderson .08 .04 .01
☐ 655 Joaquin Andujar .08 .04 .01
☐ 656 Chuck Cottier MG .08 .04 .01
(Checklist back)
☐ 657 Jim Slaton .08 .04 .01
☐ 658 Mike Stenhouse .08 .04 .01
☐ 659 Checklist: 529-660 .15 .07 .02
☐ 660 Tony Gwynn 2.00 .90 .25
☐ 661 Steve Crawford .08 .04 .01
☐ 662 Mike Heath .08 .04 .01
☐ 663 Luis Aguayo .08 .04 .01
☐ 664 Steve Farr .15 .07 .02
☐ 665 Don Mattingly 3.00 1.35 .35
☐ 666 Mike LaCoss .08 .04 .01
☐ 667 Dave Engle .08 .04 .01
☐ 668 Steve Trout .08 .04 .01
☐ 669 Lee Lacy .08 .04 .01
☐ 670 Tom Seaver .40 .18 .05
☐ 671 Dane Iorg .08 .04 .01
☐ 672 Juan Berenguer .08 .04 .01
☐ 673 Buck Martinez .08 .04 .01
☐ 674 Atlee Hammaker .08 .04 .01
☐ 675 Tony Perez .30 .14 .04
☐ 676 Albert Hall .08 .04 .01
☐ 677 Wally Backman .08 .04 .01
☐ 678 Joey McLaughlin .08 .04 .01
☐ 679 Bob Kearney .08 .04 .01
☐ 680 Jerry Reuss .08 .04 .01
☐ 681 Ben Oglivie .08 .04 .01
☐ 682 Doug Corbett .08 .04 .01
☐ 683 Whitey Herzog MG .15 .07 .02
(Checklist back)
☐ 684 Bill Doran .08 .04 .01
☐ 685 Bill Caudill .08 .04 .01
☐ 686 Mike Easler .08 .04 .01
☐ 687 Bill Gullickson .08 .04 .01
☐ 688 Len Matuszek .08 .04 .01
☐ 689 Luis DeLeon .08 .04 .01
☐ 690 Alan Trammell .30 .14 .04
☐ 691 Dennis Rasmussen .08 .04 .01
☐ 692 Randy Bush .08 .04 .01
☐ 693 Tim Stoddard .08 .04 .01
☐ 694 Joe Carter 2.00 .90 .25
☐ 695 Rick Rhoden .08 .04 .01
☐ 696 John Rabb .08 .04 .01
☐ 697 Onix Concepcion .08 .04 .01
☐ 698 Jorge Bell .15 .07 .02
☐ 699 Donnie Moore .08 .04 .01
☐ 700 Eddie Murray 1.00 .45 .12
☐ 701 Eddie Murray AS .30 .14 .04
☐ 702 Damaso Garcia AS .08 .04 .01
☐ 703 George Brett AS .75 .35 .09
☐ 704 Cal Ripken AS 1.50 .70 .19

Card			
☐ 705 Dave Winfield AS	.30	.14	.04
☐ 706 Rickey Henderson AS	.30	.14	.04
☐ 707 Tony Armas AS	.08	.04	.01
☐ 708 Lance Parrish AS	.15	.07	.02
☐ 709 Mike Boddicker AS	.08	.04	.01
☐ 710 Frank Viola AS	.15	.07	.02
☐ 711 Dan Quisenberry AS	.08	.04	.01
☐ 712 Keith Hernandez AS	.15	.07	.02
☐ 713 Ryne Sandberg AS	.60	.25	.07
☐ 714 Mike Schmidt AS	.40	.18	.05
☐ 715 Ozzie Smith AS	.50	.23	.06
☐ 716 Dale Murphy AS	.30	.14	.04
☐ 717 Tony Gwynn AS	.75	.35	.09
☐ 718 Jeff Leonard AS	.08	.04	.01
☐ 719 Gary Carter AS	.15	.07	.02
☐ 720 Rick Sutcliffe AS	.08	.04	.01
☐ 721 Bob Knepper AS	.08	.04	.01
☐ 722 Bruce Sutter AS	.15	.07	.02
☐ 723 Dave Stewart	.15	.07	.02
☐ 724 Oscar Gamble	.08	.04	.01
☐ 725 Floyd Bannister	.08	.04	.01
☐ 726 Al Bumbry	.08	.04	.01
☐ 727 Frank Pastore	.08	.04	.01
☐ 728 Bob Bailor	.08	.04	.01
☐ 729 Don Sutton	.30	.14	.04
☐ 730 Dave Kingman	.15	.07	.02
☐ 731 Neil Allen	.08	.04	.01
☐ 732 John McNamara MG (Checklist back)	.08	.04	.01
☐ 733 Tony Scott	.08	.04	.01
☐ 734 John Henry Johnson	.08	.04	.01
☐ 735 Garry Templeton	.08	.04	.01
☐ 736 Jerry Mumphrey	.08	.04	.01
☐ 737 Bo Diaz	.08	.04	.01
☐ 738 Omar Moreno	.08	.04	.01
☐ 739 Ernie Camacho	.08	.04	.01
☐ 740 Jack Clark	.15	.07	.02
☐ 741 John Butcher	.08	.04	.01
☐ 742 Ron Hassey	.08	.04	.01
☐ 743 Frank White	.15	.07	.02
☐ 744 Doug Bair	.08	.04	.01
☐ 745 Buddy Bell	.15	.07	.02
☐ 746 Jim Clancy	.08	.04	.01
☐ 747 Alex Trevino	.08	.04	.01
☐ 748 Lee Mazzilli	.08	.04	.01
☐ 749 Julio Cruz	.08	.04	.01
☐ 750 Rollie Fingers	.30	.14	.04
☐ 751 Kelvin Chapman	.08	.04	.01
☐ 752 Bob Owchinko	.08	.04	.01
☐ 753 Greg Brock	.08	.04	.01
☐ 754 Larry Milbourne	.08	.04	.01
☐ 755 Ken Singleton	.08	.04	.01
☐ 756 Rob Picciolo	.08	.04	.01
☐ 757 Willie McGee	.15	.07	.02
☐ 758 Ray Burris	.08	.04	.01
☐ 759 Jim Fanning MG (Checklist back)	.08	.04	.01
☐ 760 Nolan Ryan	3.00	1.35	.35
☐ 761 Jerry Remy	.08	.04	.01
☐ 762 Eddie Whitson	.08	.04	.01
☐ 763 Kiko Garcia	.08	.04	.01
☐ 764 Jamie Easterly	.08	.04	.01
☐ 765 Willie Randolph	.15	.07	.02
☐ 766 Paul Mirabella	.08	.04	.01
☐ 767 Darrell Brown	.08	.04	.01
☐ 768 Ron Cey	.15	.07	.02
☐ 769 Joe Cowley	.08	.04	.01
☐ 770 Carlton Fisk	.40	.18	.05
☐ 771 Geoff Zahn	.08	.04	.01
☐ 772 Johnnie LeMaster	.08	.04	.01
☐ 773 Hal McRae	.15	.07	.02
☐ 774 Dennis Lamp	.08	.04	.01
☐ 775 Mookie Wilson	.15	.07	.02
☐ 776 Jerry Royster	.08	.04	.01
☐ 777 Ned Yost	.08	.04	.01
☐ 778 Mike Davis	.08	.04	.01
☐ 779 Nick Esasky	.08	.04	.01
☐ 780 Mike Flanagan	.08	.04	.01
☐ 781 Jim Gantner	.08	.04	.01
☐ 782 Tom Niedenfuer	.08	.04	.01
☐ 783 Mike Jorgensen	.08	.04	.01
☐ 784 Checklist: 661-792	.15	.07	.02
☐ 785 Tony Armas	.08	.04	.01
☐ 786 Enos Cabell	.08	.04	.01
☐ 787 Jim Wohlford	.08	.04	.01
☐ 788 Steve Comer	.08	.04	.01
☐ 789 Luis Salazar	.08	.04	.01
☐ 790 Ron Guidry	.15	.07	.02
☐ 791 Ivan DeJesus	.08	.04	.01
☐ 792 Darrell Evans	.15	.07	.02

1985 Topps Tiffany

For the second year, Topps issued a special glossy set through their hobby dealers. This set is a direct parallel to the regular Topps issue. These 792 cards are differentiated from the regular issue by their glossy fronts and very clear backs. These sets were only available through Topps' hobby dealers. Within the hobby, it is highly believed that 10,000 of these sets were made by Topps.

	NRMT	VG-E	GOOD
COMPLETE FACT.SET (792)	225.00	100.00	28.00
COMMON CARD (1-792)	.25	.11	.03

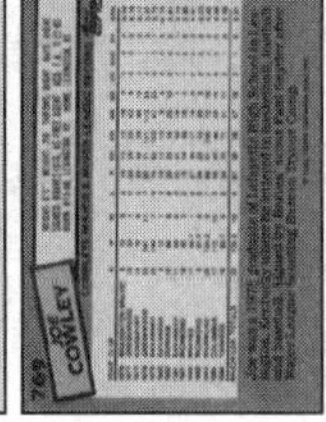

*STARS: 4X to 8X BASIC CARDS
*ROOKIES: 3X to 6X BASIC CARDS

1985 Topps Glossy All-Stars

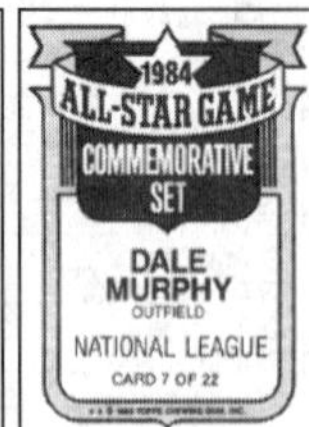

The cards in this 22-card set the standard size. Similar in design, both front and back, to last year's Glossy set, this edition features the managers, starting nine players and honorary captains of the National and American League teams in the 1984 All-Star game. The set is numbered on the reverse with players essentially ordered by position within league, NL: 1-11 and AL: 12-22.

	NRMT	VG-E	GOOD
COMPLETE SET (22)	5.00	2.20	.60
COMMON CARD (1-22)	.05	.02	.01
☐ 1 Paul Owens MG	.05	.02	.01
☐ 2 Steve Garvey	.10	.05	.01
☐ 3 Ryne Sandberg	1.00	.45	.12
☐ 4 Mike Schmidt	.75	.35	.09
☐ 5 Ozzie Smith	1.00	.45	.12
☐ 6 Tony Gwynn	1.25	.55	.16
☐ 7 Dale Murphy	.25	.11	.03
☐ 8 Darryl Strawberry	.10	.05	.01
☐ 9 Gary Carter	.20	.09	.03
☐ 10 Charlie Lea	.05	.02	.01
☐ 11 Willie McCovey CAPT	.10	.05	.01
☐ 12 Joe Altobelli MG	.05	.02	.01
☐ 13 Rod Carew	.50	.23	.06
☐ 14 Lou Whitaker	.10	.05	.01
☐ 15 George Brett	1.00	.45	.12
☐ 16 Cal Ripken	2.00	.90	.25
☐ 17 Dave Winfield	.50	.23	.06
☐ 18 Chet Lemon	.05	.02	.01
☐ 19 Reggie Jackson	.50	.23	.06
☐ 20 Lance Parrish	.05	.02	.01
☐ 21 Dave Stieb	.05	.02	.01
☐ 22 Hank Greenberg CAPT	.10	.05	.01

1985 Topps Glossy Send-Ins

The cards in this 40-card set measure the standard size. Similar to last year's glossy set, this set was issued as a bonus prize to Topps All-Star Baseball Game cards found in wax packs. The set could be obtained by sending in the "Bonus Runs" from the "Winning Pitch" game insert cards. For 25 runs and 75 cents, a collector could send in for one of the eight different five card series plus automatically be entered in the Grand Prize Sweepstakes for a chance at a free trip to the All-Star game. The cards are numbered and contain 20 stars from each league.

	NRMT	VG-E	GOOD
COMPLETE SET (40)	10.00	4.50	1.25
COMMON CARD (1-40)	.10	.05	.01
☐ 1 Dale Murphy	.50	.23	.06
☐ 2 Jesse Orosco	.10	.05	.01
☐ 3 Bob Brenly	.10	.05	.01
☐ 4 Mike Boddicker	.10	.05	.01
☐ 5 Dave Kingman	.10	.05	.01
☐ 6 Jim Rice	.25	.11	.03
☐ 7 Frank Viola	.25	.11	.03
☐ 8 Alvin Davis	.10	.05	.01
☐ 9 Rick Sutcliffe	.10	.05	.01
☐ 10 Pete Rose	1.50	.70	.19
☐ 11 Leon Durham	.10	.05	.01
☐ 12 Joaquin Andujar	.10	.05	.01
☐ 13 Keith Hernandez	.25	.11	.03
☐ 14 Dave Winfield	.75	.35	.09
☐ 15 Reggie Jackson	.75	.35	.09
☐ 16 Alan Trammell	.50	.23	.06
☐ 17 Bert Blyleven	.25	.11	.03
☐ 18 Tony Armas	.10	.05	.01
☐ 19 Rich Gossage	.25	.11	.03
☐ 20 Jose Cruz	.10	.05	.01
☐ 21 Ryne Sandberg	2.50	1.10	.30
☐ 22 Bruce Sutter	.10	.05	.01
☐ 23 Mike Schmidt	1.50	.70	.19
☐ 24 Cal Ripken	5.00	2.20	.60
☐ 25 Dan Petry	.10	.05	.01
☐ 26 Jack Morris	.25	.11	.03
☐ 27 Don Mattingly	3.00	1.35	.35
☐ 28 Eddie Murray	1.50	.70	.19
☐ 29 Tony Gwynn	3.00	1.35	.35
☐ 30 Charlie Lea	.10	.05	.01
☐ 31 Juan Samuel	.10	.05	.01
☐ 32 Phil Niekro	.50	.23	.06
☐ 33 Alejandro Pena	.10	.05	.01
☐ 34 Harold Baines	.25	.11	.03
☐ 35 Dan Quisenberry	.10	.05	.01
☐ 36 Gary Carter	.50	.23	.06
☐ 37 Mario Soto	.10	.05	.01
☐ 38 Dwight Gooden	.75	.35	.09
☐ 39 Tom Brunansky	.25	.11	.03
☐ 40 Dave Stieb	.10	.05	.01

1985 Topps Traded

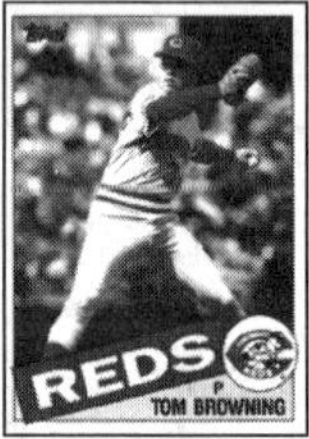

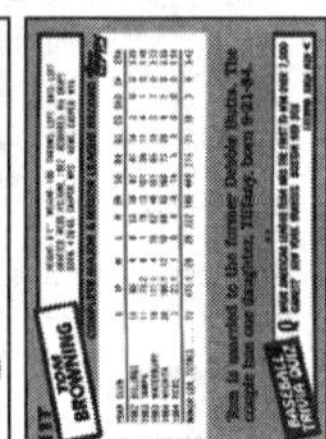

In its now standard procedure, Topps issued its standard-size Traded (or extended) set for the fifth year in a row. In addition to the typical factory set hobby distribution, Topps tested the limited issuance of these Traded cards in wax packs. Card design is identical to the regular-issue 1985 Topps set except for whiter card stock and T-suffixed numbering on back. The set numbering is in alphabetical order by player's name. The key extended Rookie Cards in this set include Vince Coleman, Mariano Duncan, Ozzie Guillen, and Mickey Tettleton.

	NRMT	VG-E	GOOD
COMPLETE FACT.SET (132)	15.00	6.75	1.85
COMMON CARD (1T-132T)	.15	.07	.02
☐ 1T Don Aase	.15	.07	.02
☐ 2T Bill Almon	.15	.07	.02
☐ 3T Benny Ayala	.15	.07	.02
☐ 4T Dusty Baker	.40	.18	.05
☐ 5T George Bamberger MG	.15	.07	.02
☐ 6T Dale Berra	.15	.07	.02
☐ 7T Rich Bordi	.15	.07	.02
☐ 8T Daryl Boston	.15	.07	.02
☐ 9T Hubie Brooks	.15	.07	.02
☐ 10T Chris Brown	.15	.07	.02
☐ 11T Tom Browning	.75	.35	.09
☐ 12T Al Bumbry	.15	.07	.02
☐ 13T Ray Burris	.15	.07	.02
☐ 14T Jeff Burroughs	.15	.07	.02
☐ 15T Bill Campbell	.15	.07	.02
☐ 16T Don Carman	.15	.07	.02
☐ 17T Gary Carter	.40	.18	.05
☐ 18T Bobby Castillo	.15	.07	.02
☐ 19T Bill Caudill	.15	.07	.02
☐ 20T Rick Cerone	.15	.07	.02
☐ 21T Bryan Clark	.15	.07	.02
☐ 22T Jack Clark	.40	.18	.05
☐ 23T Pat Clements	.15	.07	.02
☐ 24T Vince Coleman	1.00	.45	.12
☐ 25T Dave Collins	.15	.07	.02
☐ 26T Danny Darwin	.15	.07	.02
☐ 27T Jim Davenport MG	.15	.07	.02
☐ 28T Jerry Davis	.15	.07	.02
☐ 29T Brian Dayett	.15	.07	.02
☐ 30T Ivan DeJesus	.15	.07	.02
☐ 31T Ken Dixon	.15	.07	.02
☐ 32T Mariano Duncan	.75	.35	.09
☐ 33T John Felske MG	.15	.07	.02
☐ 34T Mike Fitzgerald	.15	.07	.02
☐ 35T Ray Fontenot	.15	.07	.02
☐ 36T Greg Gagne	.40	.18	.05
☐ 37T Oscar Gamble	.15	.07	.02
☐ 38T Scott Garrelts	.15	.07	.02
☐ 39T Bob L. Gibson	.15	.07	.02
☐ 40T Jim Gott	.15	.07	.02
☐ 41T David Green	.15	.07	.02
☐ 42T Alfredo Griffin	.15	.07	.02
☐ 43T Ozzie Guillen	1.50	.70	.19
☐ 44T Eddie Haas MG	.15	.07	.02
☐ 45T Terry Harper	.15	.07	.02
☐ 46T Toby Harrah	.15	.07	.02
☐ 47T Greg Harris	.15	.07	.02
☐ 48T Ron Hassey	.15	.07	.02
☐ 49T Rickey Henderson	1.50	.70	.19
☐ 50T Steve Henderson	.15	.07	.02
☐ 51T George Hendrick	.15	.07	.02
☐ 52T Joe Hesketh	.15	.07	.02
☐ 53T Teddy Higuera	.40	.18	.05
☐ 54T Donnie Hill	.15	.07	.02
☐ 55T Al Holland	.15	.07	.02
☐ 56T Burt Hooton	.15	.07	.02
☐ 57T Jay Howell	.15	.07	.02
☐ 58T Ken Howell	.15	.07	.02
☐ 59T LaMarr Hoyt	.15	.07	.02
☐ 60T Tim Hulett	.15	.07	.02
☐ 61T Bob James	.15	.07	.02
☐ 62T Steve Jeltz	.15	.07	.02
☐ 63T Cliff Johnson	.15	.07	.02
☐ 64T Howard Johnson	.40	.18	.05
☐ 65T Ruppert Jones	.15	.07	.02
☐ 66T Steve Kemp	.15	.07	.02
☐ 67T Bruce Kison	.15	.07	.02
☐ 68T Alan Knicely	.15	.07	.02
☐ 69T Mike LaCoss	.15	.07	.02
☐ 70T Lee Lacy	.15	.07	.02
☐ 71T Dave LaPoint	.15	.07	.02
☐ 72T Gary Lavelle	.15	.07	.02
☐ 73T Vance Law	.15	.07	.02
☐ 74T Johnnie LeMaster	.15	.07	.02
☐ 75T Sixto Lezcano	.15	.07	.02
☐ 76T Tim Lollar	.15	.07	.02
☐ 77T Fred Lynn	.40	.18	.05
☐ 78T Billy Martin MG	.40	.18	.05
☐ 79T Ron Mathis	.15	.07	.02
☐ 80T Len Matuszek	.15	.07	.02
☐ 81T Gene Mauch MG	.40	.18	.05
☐ 82T Oddibe McDowell	.40	.18	.05
☐ 83T Roger McDowell	.40	.18	.05
☐ 84T John McNamara MG	.15	.07	.02
☐ 85T Donnie Moore	.15	.07	.02
☐ 86T Gene Nelson	.15	.07	.02
☐ 87T Steve Nicosia	.15	.07	.02
☐ 88T Al Oliver	.40	.18	.05
☐ 89T Joe Orsulak	.40	.18	.05
☐ 90T Rob Picciolo	.15	.07	.02
☐ 91T Chris Pittaro	.15	.07	.02
☐ 92T Jim Presley	.40	.18	.05
☐ 93T Rick Reuschel	.15	.07	.02
☐ 94T Bert Roberge	.15	.07	.02
☐ 95T Bob Rodgers MG	.15	.07	.02
☐ 96T Jerry Royster	.15	.07	.02
☐ 97T Dave Rozema	.15	.07	.02
☐ 98T Dave Rucker	.15	.07	.02
☐ 99T Vern Ruhle	.15	.07	.02
☐ 100T Paul Runge	.15	.07	.02
☐ 101T Mark Salas	.15	.07	.02
☐ 102T Luis Salazar	.15	.07	.02
☐ 103T Joe Sambito	.15	.07	.02
☐ 104T Rick Schu	.15	.07	.02
☐ 105T Donnie Scott	.15	.07	.02
☐ 106T Larry Sheets	.15	.07	.02
☐ 107T Don Slaught	.15	.07	.02
☐ 108T Roy Smalley	.15	.07	.02
☐ 109T Lonnie Smith	.15	.07	.02
☐ 110T Nate Snell UER (Headings on back for a batter)	.15	.07	.02
☐ 111T Chris Speier	.15	.07	.02
☐ 112T Mike Stenhouse	.15	.07	.02
☐ 113T Tim Stoddard	.15	.07	.02
☐ 114T Jim Sundberg	.15	.07	.02
☐ 115T Bruce Sutter	.40	.18	.05
☐ 116T Don Sutton	.75	.35	.09
☐ 117T Kent Tekulve	.15	.07	.02
☐ 118T Tom Tellmann	.15	.07	.02
☐ 119T Walt Terrell	.15	.07	.02
☐ 120T Mickey Tettleton	4.00	1.80	.50
☐ 121T Derrel Thomas	.15	.07	.02
☐ 122T Rich Thompson	.15	.07	.02
☐ 123T Alex Trevino	.15	.07	.02
☐ 124T John Tudor	.15	.07	.02
☐ 125T Jose Uribe	.15	.07	.02
☐ 126T Bobby Valentine MG	.15	.07	.02
☐ 127T Dave Von Ohlen	.15	.07	.02
☐ 128T U.L. Washington	.15	.07	.02
☐ 129T Earl Weaver MG	.75	.35	.09
☐ 130T Eddie Whitson	.15	.07	.02
☐ 131T Herm Winningham	.15	.07	.02
☐ 132T Checklist 1-132	.15	.07	.02

1985 Topps Traded Tiffany

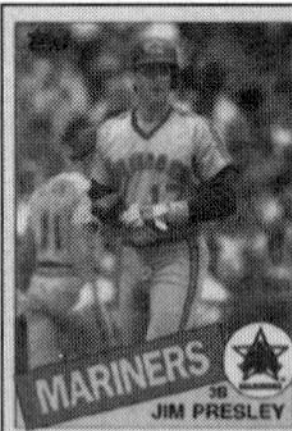

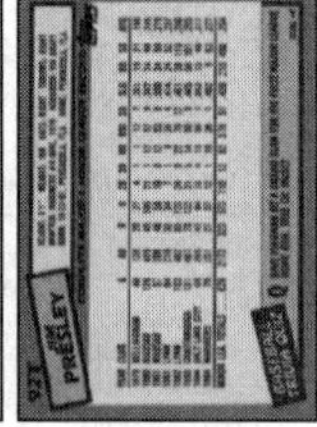

Just as in 1984, Topps issued an glossy update set. The 132-card standard-size set is a parallel to the Topps update issue. These sets were issued to the hobby through Topps dealer network and were printed in Ireland,

	NRMT	VG-E	GOOD
COMPLETE FACT.SET (132)	50.00	22.00	6.25
COMMON CARD (1T-132T)	.40	.18	.05
*STARS: 3X TO 6X BASIC CARDS			
*ROOKIES: 1.5X TO 3X BASIC CARDS			

1985 Topps 3-D

This innovative 30-card set was issued in packs of one. These large cards are very difficult to store (due to the 3-D effect) as they are not really stackable and are crumpled if placed in an album using plastic sheets. The cards are blank-backed except for two covered adhesive strips and measure approximately 4 1/4" by 5 7/8". Cards are numbered on the front and feature a prominent team logo on the front as well.

	NRMT	VG-E	GOOD
COMPLETE SET (30)	15.00	6.75	1.85
COMMON CARD (1-30)	.10	.05	.01
☐ 1 Mike Schmidt	1.25	.55	.16
☐ 2 Eddie Murray	1.25	.55	.16
☐ 3 Dale Murphy	.50	.23	.06
☐ 4 George Brett	2.50	1.10	.30
☐ 5 Pete Rose	1.00	.45	.12
☐ 6 Jim Rice	.25	.11	.03
☐ 7 Ryne Sandberg	2.50	1.10	.30
☐ 8 Don Mattingly	3.00	1.35	.35
☐ 9 Darryl Strawberry	.25	.11	.03
☐ 10 Rickey Henderson	.75	.35	.09
☐ 11 Keith Hernandez	.25	.11	.03
☐ 12 Dave Kingman	.10	.05	.01
☐ 13 Tony Gwynn	2.50	1.10	.30
☐ 14 Reggie Jackson	.75	.35	.09
☐ 15 Gary Carter	.50	.23	.06
☐ 16 Cal Ripken	4.00	1.80	.50
☐ 17 Tim Raines	.25	.11	.03
☐ 18 Dave Winfield	.75	.35	.09
☐ 19 Dwight Gooden	.60	.25	.07
☐ 20 Dave Stieb	.10	.05	.01
☐ 21 Fernando Valenzuela	.25	.11	.03
☐ 22 Mark Langston	.25	.11	.03
☐ 23 Bruce Sutter	.10	.05	.01
☐ 24 Dan Quisenberry	.10	.05	.01
☐ 25 Steve Carlton	.60	.25	.07
☐ 26 Mike Boddicker	.10	.05	.01
☐ 27 Rich Gossage	.25	.11	.03
☐ 28 Jack Morris	.25	.11	.03
☐ 29 Rick Sutcliffe	.10	.05	.01
☐ 30 Tom Seaver	.60	.25	.07

1985 Topps Gallery of Champions

This would be the second year that Topps issued a 12-card set featuring baseball stars. These "cards" were made of either silver or bronze and measure approximately 1 1/4" by 1 3/4". Since the cards are replicas of the 1985 Topps cards and would be skip-numbered, we have sequenced these cards in alphabetical order. This would be the last year that no aluminum cards were produced. The silver cards are valued at 2.5X the bronze versions.

	NRMT	VG-E	GOOD
COMPLETE SET (12)	350.00	160.00	45.00
COMMON CARD (1-12)	10.00	4.50	1.25
☐ 1 Tony Armas	10.00	4.50	1.25
☐ 2 Alvin Davis	10.00	4.50	1.25
☐ 3 Dwight Gooden	35.00	16.00	4.40
☐ 4 Tony Gwynn	65.00	29.00	8.00
☐ 5 Willie Hernandez	10.00	4.50	1.25
☐ 6 Don Matttingly	65.00	29.00	8.00
☐ 7 Dale Murphy	40.00	18.00	5.00
☐ 8 Dan Quisenberry	10.00	4.50	1.25
☐ 9 Ryne Sandberg	65.00	29.00	8.00
☐ 10 Mike Schmidt	40.00	18.00	5.00
☐ 11 Rick Sutcliffe	10.00	4.50	1.25
☐ 12 Bruce Sutter	10.00	4.50	1.25

1985 Topps/O-Pee-Chee Stickers

Made in Italy for Topps and O-Pee-Chee by Panini, these 376 stickers measure approximately 2 1/8" by 3" and are numbered on both front and back. Some stickers are player cutouts. The fronts feature white-bordered color player photos. The horizontal backs carry a bilingual ad for O-Pee-Chee in blue lettering. An album onto which the stickers could be affixed was available at retail stores. The album and the sticker numbering are organized as follows: 1984 Record Breakers (1-8), 1984 Championship Series (9-14), 1984 World Series (15-21), Atlanta Braves (22-33), Chicago Cubs (34-45), Cincinnati Reds (46-57), Houston Astros (58-69), Los Angeles Dodgers (70-81), Montreal Expos (82-93), 1984 Stat Leaders (94-97), New York Mets (98-109),

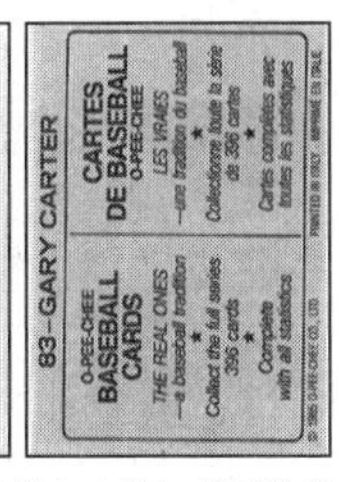

Philadelphia Phillies (110-121), Pittsburgh Pirates (122-133), St. Louis Cardinals (134-145), San Diego Padres (146-157), San Francisco Giants (158-169), 1984 Stat Leaders (170-173), Foil All-Stars (174-191), 1984 Stat Leaders (192-195), Baltimore Orioles (196-207), Boston Red Sox (208-219), California Angels (220-231), Chicago White Sox (232-243), Cleveland Indians (244-255), Detroit Tigers (256-267), Kansas City Royals (268-279), 1984 Stat Leaders (280-283), Milwaukee Brewers (284-295), Minnesota Twins (296-307), New York Yankees (308-319), Oakland A's (320-331), Seattle Mariners (332-343), Texas Rangers (344-355), Toronto Blue Jays (356-367) and Future Stars (368-376). For those stickers featuring more than one player, the other numbers on that sticker are given below in parentheses. Kirby Puckett, Mark Langston and Dwight Gooden are featured in their Rookie Card year.

	NRMT	VG-E	GOOD
COMPLETE SET (376)	15.00	6.75	1.85
COMMON STICKERS (1-376)	.05	.02	.01
COMMON FOIL	.10	.05	.01
*TOPPS AND OPC: SAME VALUE			
☐ 1 Steve Garvey FOIL (Top half)	.15	.07	.02
☐ 2 Steve Garvey FOIL (Bottom half)	.15	.07	.02
☐ 3 Dwight Gooden (Top half)	.50	.23	.06
☐ 4 Dwight Gooden (Bottom half)	.50	.23	.06
☐ 5 Joe Morgan (Top half)	.10	.05	.01
☐ 6 Joe Morgan (Bottom half)	.10	.05	.01
☐ 7 Don Sutton (Top half)	.10	.05	.01
☐ 8 Don Sutton (Bottom half)	.10	.05	.01
☐ 9 AL Championships (Jack Morris)	.10	.05	.01
☐ 10 AL Championships (Milt Wilcox)	.05	.02	.01
☐ 11 AL Championships (Kirk Gibson)	.10	.05	.01
☐ 12 NL Championships (Cubs at plate)	.05	.02	.01
☐ 13 NL Championships (Steve Garvey swings)	.10	.05	.01
☐ 14 NL Championships (Steve Garvey)	.10	.05	.01
☐ 15 World Series (Jack Morris)	.10	.05	.01
☐ 16 World Series (Kurt Bevacqua)	.05	.02	.01
☐ 17 World Series (Milt Wilcox)	.05	.02	.01
☐ 18 World Series (Alan Trammell ready to throw)	.10	.05	.01
☐ 19 World Series (Kirk Gibson)	.10	.05	.01
☐ 20 World Series (Alan Trammell)	.10	.05	.01
☐ 21 World Series (Chet Lemon back)	.05	.02	.01
☐ 22 Dale Murphy	.15	.07	.02
☐ 23 Steve Bedrosian	.05	.02	.01
☐ 24 Bob Horner	.05	.02	.01
☐ 25 Claudell Washington	.05	.02	.01
☐ 26 Rick Mahler (212)	.05	.02	.01
☐ 27 Rafael Ramirez (213)	.05	.02	.01
☐ 28 Craig McMurtry (214)	.05	.02	.01
☐ 29 Chris Chambliss(215)	.10	.05	.01
☐ 30 Alex Trevino (216)	.05	.02	.01
☐ 31 Bruce Benedict (217)	.05	.02	.01
☐ 32 Ken Oberkfell (218)	.05	.02	.01
☐ 33 Glenn Hubbard (219)	.05	.02	.01
☐ 34 Ryne Sandberg	1.25	.55	.16
☐ 35 Rick Sutcliffe	.05	.02	.01
☐ 36 Leon Durham	.05	.02	.01
☐ 37 Jody Davis	.05	.02	.01
☐ 38 Bob Dernier (224)	.05	.02	.01
☐ 39 Keith Moreland(225)	.05	.02	.01
☐ 40 Scott Sanderson(226)	.05	.02	.01
☐ 41 Lee Smith (227)	.25	.11	.03
☐ 42 Ron Cey (228)	.10	.05	.01
☐ 43 Steve Trout (229)	.05	.02	.01
☐ 44 Gary Matthews(230)	.05	.02	.01
☐ 45 Larry Bowa (231)	.10	.05	.01
☐ 46 Mario Soto	.05	.02	.01
☐ 47 Dave Parker	.10	.05	.01
☐ 48 Dave Concepcion	.10	.05	.01
☐ 49 Gary Redus	.05	.02	.01
☐ 50 Ted Power (236)	.05	.02	.01
☐ 51 Nick Esasky (237)	.05	.02	.01
☐ 52 Duane Walker (238)	.05	.02	.01
☐ 53 Eddie Milner (239)	.05	.02	.01
☐ 54 Ron Oester (240)	.05	.02	.01
☐ 55 Cesar Cedeno (241)	.10	.05	.01
☐ 56 Joe Price (242)	.05	.02	.01
☐ 57 Pete Rose (243)	.75	.35	.09
☐ 58 Nolan Ryan	2.50	1.10	.30
☐ 59 Jose Cruz	.10	.05	.01
☐ 60 Jerry Mumphrey	.05	.02	.01
☐ 61 Enos Cabell	.05	.02	.01
☐ 62 Bob Knepper (248)	.05	.02	.01
☐ 63 Dickie Thon (249)	.05	.02	.01
☐ 64 Phil Garner (250)	.10	.05	.01
☐ 65 Craig Reynolds (251)	.05	.02	.01
☐ 66 Frank DiPino (252)	.05	.02	.01
☐ 67 Terry Puhl (253)	.05	.02	.01
☐ 68 Bill Doran (254)	.05	.02	.01
☐ 69 Joe Niekro (255)	.05	.02	.01
☐ 70 Pedro Guerrero	.10	.05	.01
☐ 71 Fernando Valenzuela	.10	.05	.01
☐ 72 Mike Marshall	.05	.02	.01
☐ 73 Alejandro Pena	.05	.02	.01
☐ 74 Orel Hershiser(260)	.75	.35	.09
☐ 75 Ken Landreaux (261)	.05	.02	.01
☐ 76 Bill Russell (262)	.10	.05	.01
☐ 77 Steve Sax (263)	.10	.05	.01
☐ 78 Rick Honeycutt(264)	.05	.02	.01
☐ 79 Mike Scioscia (265)	.05	.02	.01
☐ 80 Tom Niedenfuer(266)	.05	.02	.01
☐ 81 Candy Maldonado(267)	.05	.02	.01
☐ 82 Tim Raines	.10	.05	.01
☐ 83 Gary Carter	.10	.05	.01
☐ 84 Charlie Lea	.05	.02	.01
☐ 85 Jeff Reardon	.10	.05	.01
☐ 86 Andre Dawson (272)	.15	.07	.02
☐ 87 Tim Wallach (273)	.10	.05	.01
☐ 88 Terry Francona (274)	.05	.02	.01
☐ 89 Steve Rogers (275)	.05	.02	.01
☐ 90 Bryn Smith (276)	.05	.02	.01
☐ 91 Bill Gullickson(277)	.05	.02	.01
☐ 92 Dan Driessen (278)	.05	.02	.01
☐ 93 Doug Flynn (279)	.05	.02	.01
☐ 94 Mike Schmidt (170/192/280)	.60	.25	.07
☐ 95 Tony Armas (171/193/281)	.05	.02	.01
☐ 96 Dale Murphy (172/194/282)	.15	.07	.02
☐ 97 Rick Sutcliffe (173/195/283)	.05	.02	.01
☐ 98 Keith Hernandez	.10	.05	.01
☐ 99 George Foster	.10	.05	.01
☐ 100 Darryl Strawberry	.30	.14	.04
☐ 101 Jesse Orosco	.05	.02	.01
☐ 102 Mookie Wilson (288)	.10	.05	.01
☐ 103 Doug Sisk (289)	.05	.02	.01
☐ 104 Hubie Brooks (290)	.05	.02	.01
☐ 105 Ron Darling (291)	.10	.05	.01
☐ 106 Wally Backman (292)	.05	.02	.01
☐ 107 Dwight Gooden (293)	.75	.35	.09
☐ 108 Mike Fitzgerald(294)	.05	.02	.01
☐ 109 Walt Terrell (295)	.05	.02	.01
☐ 110 Ozzie Virgil	.05	.02	.01
☐ 111 Mike Schmidt	.60	.25	.07
☐ 112 Steve Carlton	.40	.18	.05
☐ 113 Al Holland	.05	.02	.01
☐ 114 Juan Samuel (300)	.05	.02	.01
☐ 115 Von Hayes (301)	.05	.02	.01
☐ 116 Jeff Stone (302)	.05	.02	.01
☐ 117 Jerry Koosman (303)	.10	.05	.01
☐ 118 Al Oliver (304)	.10	.05	.01
☐ 119 John Denny (305)	.05	.02	.01
☐ 120 Charles Hudson (306)	.05	.02	.01
☐ 121 Garry Maddox (307)	.05	.02	.01
☐ 122 Bill Madlock	.10	.05	.01
☐ 123 John Candelaria	.05	.02	.01
☐ 124 Tony Pena	.05	.02	.01
☐ 125 Jason Thompson	.05	.02	.01
☐ 126 Lee Lacy (312)	.05	.02	.01
☐ 127 Rick Rhoden (313)	.05	.02	.01
☐ 128 Doug Frobel (314)	.05	.02	.01
☐ 129 Kent Tekulve (315)	.05	.02	.01
☐ 130 Johnny Ray (316)	.05	.02	.01
☐ 131 Marvell Wynne (317)	.05	.02	.01
☐ 132 Larry McWilliams (318)	.05	.02	.01
☐ 133 Dale Berra (319)	.05	.02	.01
☐ 134 George Hendrick	.05	.02	.01
☐ 135 Bruce Sutter	.10	.05	.01
☐ 136 Joaquin Andujar	.05	.02	.01
☐ 137 Ozzie Smith	.40	.18	.05
☐ 138 Andy Van Slyke (324)	.15	.07	.02
☐ 139 Lonnie Smith (325)	.05	.02	.01
☐ 140 Darrell Porter (326)	.05	.02	.01
☐ 141 Willie McGee (327)	.10	.05	.01
☐ 142 Tom Herr (328)	.10	.05	.01
☐ 143 Dave LaPoint (329)	.05	.02	.01
☐ 144 Neil Allen (330)	.05	.02	.01
☐ 145 David Green (331)	.05	.02	.01
☐ 146 Tony Gwynn	2.00	.90	.25
☐ 147 Rich Gossage	.10	.05	.01
☐ 148 Terry Kennedy	.05	.02	.01
☐ 149 Steve Garvey	.15	.07	.02
☐ 150 Alan Wiggins (336)	.05	.02	.01
☐ 151 Garry Templeton(337)	.05	.02	.01
☐ 152 Ed Whitson (338)	.05	.02	.01
☐ 153 Tim Lollar (339)	.05	.02	.01
☐ 154 Dave Dravecky (340)	.10	.05	.01
☐ 155 Graig Nettles (341)	.10	.05	.01
☐ 156 Eric Show (342)	.05	.02	.01
☐ 157 Carmelo Martinez (343)	.05	.02	.01
☐ 158 Bob Brenly	.05	.02	.01
☐ 159 Gary Lavelle	.05	.02	.01
☐ 160 Jack Clark	.10	.05	.01
☐ 161 Jeff Leonard	.05	.02	.01
☐ 162 Chili Davis (348)	.10	.05	.01
☐ 163 Mike Krukow (349)	.05	.02	.01
☐ 164 Johnnie LeMaster (350)	.05	.02	.01
☐ 165 Atlee Hammaker (351)	.05	.02	.01
☐ 166 Dan Gladden (352)	.05	.02	.01
☐ 167 Greg Minton (353)	.05	.02	.01
☐ 168 Joel Youngblood(354)	.05	.02	.01
☐ 169 Frank Williams (355)	.05	.02	.01
☐ 170 Tony Gwynn (94/192/280)	1.50	.70	.19
☐ 171 Don Mattingly (95/193/281)	2.00	.90	.25
☐ 172 Bruce Sutter (96/194/282)	.10	.05	.01
☐ 173 Dan Quisenberry (97/195/283)	.05	.02	.01
☐ 174 Tony Gwynn FOIL	2.50	1.10	.30
☐ 175 Ryne Sandberg FOIL	1.50	.70	.19
☐ 176 Steve Garvey FOIL	.30	.14	.04
☐ 177 Dale Murphy FOIL	.30	.14	.04
☐ 179 Darryl Strawberry FOIL	.50	.23	.06
☐ 180 Gary Carter FOIL	.30	.14	.04
☐ 181 Ozzie Smith FOIL	.60	.25	.07
☐ 182 Charlie Lea FOIL	.10	.05	.01
☐ 183 Lou Whitaker FOIL	.15	.07	.02
☐ 184 Rod Carew FOIL	.60	.25	.07
☐ 185 Cal Ripken FOIL	3.00	1.35	.35
☐ 186 Dave Winfield FOIL	.50	.23	.06
☐ 187 Reggie Jackson FOIL	.75	.35	.09
☐ 188 George Brett FOIL	1.25	.55	.16
☐ 189 Lance Parrish FOIL	.15	.07	.02
☐ 190 Chet Lemon FOIL	.10	.05	.01
☐ 191 Dave Stieb FOIL	.10	.05	.01
☐ 192 Gary Carter (94/170/280)	.10	.05	.01
☐ 193 Mike Schmidt (95/171/281)	.60	.25	.07
☐ 194 Tony Armas (96/172/282)	.05	.02	.01
☐ 195 Mike Witt (97/173/283)	.05	.02	.01
☐ 196 Eddie Murray	.40	.18	.05
☐ 197 Cal Ripken	2.50	1.10	.30
☐ 198 Scott McGregor	.05	.02	.01
☐ 199 Rick Dempsey	.05	.02	.01
☐ 200 Tippy Martinez (360)	.05	.02	.01
☐ 201 Ken Singleton (361)	.05	.02	.01
☐ 202 Mike Boddicker (362)	.05	.02	.01
☐ 203 Rich Dauer (363)	.05	.02	.01
☐ 204 John Shelby (364)	.05	.02	.01
☐ 205 Al Bumbry (365)	.05	.02	.01
☐ 206 John Lowenstein(366)	.05	.02	.01
☐ 207 Mike Flanagan (367)	.05	.02	.01
☐ 208 Jim Rice	.10	.05	.01
☐ 209 Tony Armas	.05	.02	.01
☐ 210 Wade Boggs	.50	.23	.06
☐ 211 Bruce Hurst	.05	.02	.01
☐ 212 Dwight Evans (26)	.10	.05	.01
☐ 213 Mike Easler (27)	.05	.02	.01
☐ 214 Bill Buckner (28)	.10	.05	.01
☐ 215 Bob Stanley (29)	.05	.02	.01
☐ 216 Jackie Gutierrez(30)	.05	.02	.01
☐ 217 Rich Gedman (31)	.05	.02	.01
☐ 218 Jerry Remy (32)	.05	.02	.01
☐ 219 Marty Barrett (33)	.05	.02	.01
☐ 220 Reggie Jackson	.50	.23	.06
☐ 221 Geoff Zahn	.05	.02	.01
☐ 222 Doug DeCinces	.05	.02	.01
☐ 223 Rod Carew	.40	.18	.05
☐ 224 Brian Downing (38)	.10	.05	.01
☐ 225 Fred Lynn (39)	.10	.05	.01
☐ 226 Gary Pettis (40)	.05	.02	.01
☐ 227 Mike Witt (41)	.05	.02	.01
☐ 228 Bob Boone (42)	.10	.05	.01
☐ 229 Tommy John (43)	.15	.07	.02
☐ 230 Bobby Grich (44)	.10	.05	.01
☐ 231 Ron Romanick (45)	.05	.02	.01
☐ 232 Ron Kittle	.05	.02	.01
☐ 233 Richard Dotson	.05	.02	.01
☐ 234 Harold Baines	.10	.05	.01
☐ 235 Tom Seaver	.50	.23	.06
☐ 236 Greg Walker (50)	.05	.02	.01
☐ 237 Roy Smalley (51)	.05	.02	.01
☐ 238 Greg Luzinski (52)	.10	.05	.01
☐ 239 Julio Cruz (53)	.05	.02	.01
☐ 240 Scott Fletcher (54)	.05	.02	.01
☐ 241 Rudy Law (55)	.05	.02	.01
☐ 242 Vance Law (56)	.05	.02	.01
☐ 243 Carlton Fisk (57)	.30	.14	.04
☐ 244 Andre Thornton	.05	.02	.01
☐ 245 Julio Franco	.15	.07	.02

☐ 246 Brett Butler	.10	.05	.01
☐ 247 Bert Blyleven	.10	.05	.01
☐ 248 Mike Hargrove (62)	.10	.05	.01
☐ 249 George Vukovich(63)	.05	.02	.01
☐ 250 Pat Tabler (64)	.05	.02	.01
☐ 251 Brook Jacoby (65)	.05	.02	.01
☐ 252 Tony Bernazard (66)	.05	.02	.01
☐ 253 Ernie Camacho (67)	.05	.02	.01
☐ 254 Mel Hall (68)	.05	.02	.01
☐ 255 Carmen Castillo (69)	.05	.02	.01
☐ 256 Jack Morris	.10	.05	.01
☐ 257 Willie Hernandez	.05	.02	.01
☐ 258 Alan Trammell	.15	.07	.02
☐ 259 Lance Parrish	.10	.05	.01
☐ 260 Chet Lemon (74)	.05	.02	.01
☐ 261 Lou Whitaker (75)	.15	.07	.02
☐ 262 Howard Johnson (76)	.10	.05	.01
☐ 263 Barbaro Garbey (77)	.05	.02	.01
☐ 264 Dan Petry (78)	.05	.02	.01
☐ 265 Aurelio Lopez (79)	.05	.02	.01
☐ 266 Larry Herndon (80)	.05	.02	.01
☐ 267 Kirk Gibson (81)	.10	.05	.01
☐ 268 George Brett	.75	.35	.09
☐ 269 Dan Quisenberry	.05	.02	.01
☐ 270 Hal McRae	.10	.05	.01
☐ 271 Steve Balboni	.05	.02	.01
☐ 272 Pat Sheridan (86)	.05	.02	.01
☐ 273 Jorge Orta (87)	.05	.02	.01
☐ 274 Frank White (88)	.10	.05	.01
☐ 275 Bud Black (89)	.05	.02	.01
☐ 276 Darryl Motley (90)	.05	.02	.01
☐ 277 Willie Wilson (91)	.05	.02	.01
☐ 278 Larry Gura (92)	.05	.02	.01
☐ 279 Don Slaught (93)	.05	.02	.01
☐ 280 Dwight Gooden (94/170/192)	1.50	.70	.19
☐ 281 Mark Langston (95/171/193)	.25	.11	.03
☐ 282 Tim Raines (96/172/194)	.10	.05	.01
☐ 283 Rickey Henderson (97/173/195/283)	.30	.14	.04
☐ 284 Robin Yount	.30	.14	.04
☐ 285 Rollie Fingers	.25	.11	.03
☐ 286 Jim Sundberg	.05	.02	.01
☐ 287 Cecil Cooper	.10	.05	.01
☐ 288 Jamie Cocanower(102)	.05	.02	.01
☐ 289 Mike Caldwell (103)	.05	.02	.01
☐ 290 Don Sutton (104)	.15	.07	.02
☐ 291 Rick Manning (105)	.05	.02	.01
☐ 292 Ben Oglivie (106)	.05	.02	.01
☐ 293 Moose Haas (107)	.05	.02	.01
☐ 294 Ted Simmons (108)	.10	.05	.01
☐ 295 Jim Gantner (109)	.05	.02	.01
☐ 296 Kent Hrbek	.10	.05	.01
☐ 297 Ron Davis	.05	.02	.01
☐ 298 Dave Engle	.05	.02	.01
☐ 299 Tom Brunansky	.10	.05	.01
☐ 300 Frank Viola (114)	.10	.05	.01
☐ 301 Mike Smithson (115)	.05	.02	.01
☐ 302 Gary Gaetti (116)	.10	.05	.01
☐ 303 Tim Teufel (117)	.05	.02	.01
☐ 304 Mickey Hatcher(118)	.05	.02	.01
☐ 305 John Butcher (119)	.05	.02	.01
☐ 306 Darrell Brown (120)	.05	.02	.01
☐ 307 Kirby Puckett (121)	5.00	2.20	.60
☐ 308 Dave Winfield	.30	.14	.04
☐ 309 Phil Niekro	.15	.07	.02
☐ 310 Don Mattingly	2.00	.90	.25
☐ 311 Don Baylor	.10	.05	.01
☐ 312 Willie Randolph(126)	.10	.05	.01
☐ 313 Ron Guidry (127)	.10	.05	.01
☐ 314 Dave Righetti (128)	.10	.05	.01
☐ 315 Bobby Meacham (129)	.05	.02	.01
☐ 316 Butch Wynegar (130)	.05	.02	.01
☐ 317 Mike Pagliarulo(131)	.05	.02	.01
☐ 318 Joe Cowley (132)	.05	.02	.01
☐ 319 John Montefusco(133)	.05	.02	.01
☐ 320 Dave Kingman	.10	.05	.01
☐ 321 Rickey Henderson	.30	.14	.04
☐ 322 Bill Caudill	.05	.02	.01
☐ 323 Dwayne Murphy	.05	.02	.01
☐ 324 Steve McCatty (138)	.05	.02	.01
☐ 325 Joe Morgan (139)	.25	.11	.03
☐ 326 Mike Heath (140)	.05	.02	.01
☐ 327 Chris Codiroli (141)	.05	.02	.01
☐ 328 Ray Burris (142)	.05	.02	.01
☐ 329 Tony Phillips (143)	.15	.07	.02
☐ 330 Carney Lansford(144)	.10	.05	.01
☐ 331 Bruce Bochte (145)	.05	.02	.01
☐ 332 Alvin Davis	.10	.05	.01
☐ 333 Al Cowens	.05	.02	.01
☐ 334 Jim Beattie	.05	.02	.01
☐ 335 Bob Kearney	.05	.02	.01
☐ 336 Ed VandeBerg (150)	.05	.02	.01
☐ 337 Mark Langston (151)	.25	.11	.03
☐ 338 Dave Henderson (152)	.10	.05	.01
☐ 339 Spike Owen (153)	.05	.02	.01
☐ 340 Matt Young (154)	.05	.02	.01
☐ 341 Jack Perconte (155)	.05	.02	.01
☐ 342 Barry Bonnell (156)	.05	.02	.01
☐ 343 Mike Stanton (157)	.05	.02	.01
☐ 344 Pete O'Brien	.05	.02	.01
☐ 345 Charlie Hough	.10	.05	.01
☐ 346 Larry Parrish	.05	.02	.01
☐ 347 Buddy Bell	.10	.05	.01
☐ 348 Frank Tanana (162)	.05	.02	.01
☐ 349 Curt Wilkerson (163)	.05	.02	.01
☐ 350 Jeff Kunkel (164)	.05	.02	.01
☐ 351 Billy Sample (165)	.05	.02	.01
☐ 352 Danny Darwin (166)	.05	.02	.01
☐ 353 Gary Ward (167)	.05	.02	.01
☐ 354 Mike Mason (168)	.05	.02	.01
☐ 355 Mickey Rivers (169)	.05	.02	.01
☐ 356 Dave Stieb	.05	.02	.01
☐ 357 Damaso Garcia	.05	.02	.01
☐ 358 Willie Upshaw	.05	.02	.01
☐ 359 Lloyd Moseby	.05	.02	.01
☐ 360 George Bell (200)	.10	.05	.01
☐ 361 Luis Leal (201)	.05	.02	.01
☐ 362 Jesse Barfield (202)	.05	.02	.01
☐ 363 Dave Collins (203)	.05	.02	.01
☐ 364 Roy Lee Jackson(204)	.05	.02	.01
☐ 365 Doyle Alexander(205)	.05	.02	.01
☐ 366 Alfredo Griffin(206)	.05	.02	.01
☐ 367 Cliff Johnson (207)	.05	.02	.01
☐ 368 Alvin Davis	.10	.05	.01
☐ 369 Juan Samuel	.05	.02	.01
☐ 370 Brook Jacoby	.05	.02	.01
☐ 371 Mark Langston and Dwight Gooden	.25	.11	.03
☐ 372 Mike Fitzgerald	.05	.02	.01
☐ 373 Jackie Gutierrez	.05	.02	.01
☐ 374 Dan Gladden	.05	.02	.01
☐ 375 Carmelo Martinez	.05	.02	.01
☐ 376 Kirby Puckett	5.00	2.20	.60
☐ xx Album	1.00	.45	.12

1985 Topps/OPC Minis

This 132 card test set looks exactly like their 1985 Topps standard-size counterparts, but measure a smaller 2 3/8" by 3 9/32". These cards were never distributed, are extremely limited but some doubt exists to their authenticity as a test issue. Supposedly, only about 100 of each card exists. Of these 100 cards, approximately 2/3 of them are fully printed with the complete back while the others are blank backed. Values for the blank back cards are from the same value to 1.5 times the prices listed below. Card numbering matches the 1985 Topps issues; therefore we have listed the cards in skip numbered fashion below.

	NRMT	VG-E	GOOD
COMPLETE SET (132)	2000.00	900.00	250.00
COMMON CARD	10.00	4.50	1.25
☐ 12 Davey Lopes	20.00	9.00	2.50
☐ 15 Jerry Koosman	20.00	9.00	2.50
☐ 17 Mike Scott	20.00	9.00	2.50
☐ 25 Steve Bedrosian	10.00	4.50	1.25
☐ 44 Dickie Thon	10.00	4.50	1.25
☐ 65 Bill Buckner	20.00	9.00	2.50
☐ 68 Von Hayes	10.00	4.50	1.25
☐ 72 Rick Sutcliffe	20.00	9.00	2.50
☐ 75 Willie Upshaw	10.00	4.50	1.25
☐ 82 Joe Price	10.00	4.50	1.25
☐ 88 Bryn Smith	10.00	4.50	1.25
☐ 91 Jeff Burroughs	10.00	4.50	1.25
☐ 95 Jose Cruz	20.00	9.00	2.50
☐ 96 Johnny Ray	10.00	4.50	1.25
☐ 109 Gary Roenicke	10.00	4.50	1.25
☐ 113 Tom Herr	10.00	4.50	1.25
☐ 114 Bob James	10.00	4.50	1.25
☐ 117 Greg Gross	10.00	4.50	1.25
☐ 120 Steve Kemp	10.00	4.50	1.25
☐ 121 Checklist	10.00	4.50	1.25
☐ 128 Ernie Whitt	10.00	4.50	1.25
☐ 148 Steve Yeager	10.00	4.50	1.25
☐ 150 Jim Rice	40.00	18.00	5.00
☐ 151 Moose Haas	10.00	4.50	1.25
☐ 154 Argenis Salazar	10.00	4.50	1.25
☐ 156 Craig Reynolds	10.00	4.50	1.25
☐ 160 Lance Parrish	20.00	9.00	2.50
☐ 165 Dusty Baker	20.00	9.00	2.50
☐ 170 George Foster	20.00	9.00	2.50
☐ 178 Miguel Dilone	10.00	4.50	1.25
☐ 185 Al Holland	10.00	4.50	1.25
☐ 190 Rusty Staub	20.00	9.00	2.50
☐ 198 Eddie Milner	10.00	4.50	1.25
☐ 201 Burt Hooton	10.00	4.50	1.25
☐ 205 Steve Rogers	10.00	4.50	1.25
☐ 209 Bill Campbell	10.00	4.50	1.25
☐ 210 Gary Matthews	10.00	4.50	1.25
☐ 218 Doyle Alexander	10.00	4.50	1.25
☐ 222 Hubie Brooks	10.00	4.50	1.25
☐ 223 Tom Hume	10.00	4.50	1.25
☐ 225 Mike Boddicker	10.00	4.50	1.25
☐ 229 Dave LaPoint	10.00	4.50	1.25
☐ 230 Gary Carter	40.00	18.00	5.00
☐ 235 Garry Maddox	10.00	4.50	1.25
☐ 236 Mark Thurmond	10.00	4.50	1.25
☐ 237 Julio Franco	20.00	9.00	2.50
☐ 239 Tim Teufel	10.00	4.50	1.25
☐ 248 Terry Forster	10.00	4.50	1.25
☐ 250 Jesse Orosco	10.00	4.50	1.25
☐ 251 Brad Gulden	10.00	4.50	1.25
☐ 255 Lonnie Smith	10.00	4.50	1.25
☐ 261 Checklist	10.00	4.50	1.25
☐ 263 Mel Hall	10.00	4.50	1.25
☐ 266 Frank Voila	20.00	9.00	2.50
☐ 287 Walt Terrell	10.00	4.50	1.25
☐ 306 Rick Reuschel	10.00	4.50	1.25
☐ 310 Manny Trillo	10.00	4.50	1.25
☐ 313 Dave Schmidt	10.00	4.50	1.25
☐ 325 John Denny	10.00	4.50	1.25
☐ 330 Leon Durham	10.00	4.50	1.25
☐ 333 Willie Hernandez	10.00	4.50	1.25
☐ 340 Robin Yount	60.00	27.00	7.50
☐ 343 Bill Russell	10.00	4.50	1.25
☐ 345 Charlie Lea	10.00	4.50	1.25
☐ 352 Joe Morgan	75.00	34.00	9.50
☐ 355 Bert Blyleven	40.00	18.00	5.00
☐ 358 Tony Pena	10.00	4.50	1.25
☐ 360 Steve Carlton	100.00	45.00	12.50
☐ 362 Craig McMurtry	10.00	4.50	1.25
☐ 375 Jeff Reardon	20.00	9.00	2.50
☐ 379 Charles Hudson	10.00	4.50	1.25
☐ 415 Ron Darling	10.00	4.50	1.25
☐ 445 Tippy Martinez	10.00	4.50	1.25
☐ 446 Jim Sundberg	10.00	4.50	1.25
☐ 450 Steve Garvey	40.00	18.00	5.00
☐ 452 John Castino	10.00	4.50	1.25
☐ 464 Mike Mason	10.00	4.50	1.25
☐ 470 Steve Sax	10.00	4.50	1.25
☐ 485 Matt Young	10.00	4.50	1.25
☐ 487 Frank Williams	10.00	4.50	1.25
☐ 489 Bryan Clark	10.00	4.50	1.25
☐ 491 Rick Camp	10.00	4.50	1.25
☐ 495 Mario Soto	10.00	4.50	1.25
☐ 500 Mike Schmidt	150.00	70.00	19.00
☐ 501 Dan Schatzeder	10.00	4.50	1.25
☐ 504 Jerry Williard	10.00	4.50	1.25
☐ 511 Lee Smith	40.00	18.00	5.00
☐ 515 Dave Concepcion	20.00	9.00	2.50
☐ 520 LaMarr Hoyt	10.00	4.50	1.25
☐ 526 Dave Palmer	10.00	4.50	1.25
☐ 530 Dave Dravecky	20.00	9.00	2.50
☐ 538 Keith Moreland	10.00	4.50	1.25
☐ 545 Lloyd Moseby	10.00	4.50	1.25
☐ 551 Andy Van Slyke	40.00	18.00	5.00
☐ 554 Doug Flynn	10.00	4.50	1.25
☐ 556 Sixto Lezcano	10.00	4.50	1.25
☐ 560 Bill Madlock	20.00	9.00	2.50
☐ 563 Dick Ruthven	10.00	4.50	1.25
☐ 566 Ed Vande Berg	10.00	4.50	1.25
☐ 568 Cliff Johnson	10.00	4.50	1.25
☐ 569 Ken Oberkfell	10.00	4.50	1.25
☐ 575 Pedro Guerrero	20.00	9.00	2.50
☐ 580 Dwight Evans	40.00	18.00	5.00
☐ 589 Bob Dernier	10.00	4.50	1.25
☐ 592 Jeff D. Robinson	10.00	4.50	1.25
☐ 603 Rick Manning	10.00	4.50	1.25
☐ 608 Craig Lefferts	10.00	4.50	1.25
☐ 610 Jack Morris	40.00	18.00	5.00
☐ 613 Terry Puhl	10.00	4.50	1.25
☐ 615 Marvell Wynne	10.00	4.50	1.25
☐ 619 Jeffrey Leonard	10.00	4.50	1.25
☐ 625 Mark Langston	40.00	18.00	5.00
☐ 630 Tim Raines	40.00	18.00	5.00
☐ 634 Bill Dawley	10.00	4.50	1.25
☐ 670 Tom Seaver	150.00	70.00	19.00
☐ 673 Buck Martinez	10.00	4.50	1.25
☐ 674 Atlee Hammaker	10.00	4.50	1.25
☐ 685 Bill Caudill	10.00	4.50	1.25
☐ 700 Eddie Murray	175.00	80.00	22.00
☐ 725 Floyd Bannister	10.00	4.50	1.25
☐ 729 Don Sutton	50.00	22.00	6.25
☐ 731 Neil Allen	10.00	4.50	1.25
☐ 736 Jerry Mumphrey	10.00	4.50	1.25
☐ 748 Lee Mazzilli	20.00	9.00	2.50
☐ 753 Greg Brock	10.00	4.50	1.25
☐ 755 Ken Singleton	10.00	4.50	1.25
☐ 757 Willie McGee	40.00	18.00	5.00
☐ 760 Nolan Ryan	300.00	135.00	38.00
☐ 762 Eddie Whitson	10.00	4.50	1.25
☐ 775 Mookie Wilson	10.00	4.50	1.25
☐ 780 Mike Flanagan	10.00	4.50	1.25
☐ 782 Tom Neidenfuer	10.00	4.50	1.25

1985 Topps Rub Downs

The cards in this 112 player (32 different sheets) set measure 2 3/8" by 3 5/16". The full color photo could be transfered from the rub down to another surface by rubbing a coin over the paper backing. Distributed in packages of two rub down sheets, some contained two or three player action poses, others head shots and various pieces of player equipment. Players from all teams were included in the set. Although the sheets are unnumbered, they are numbered here in alphabetical order based on each card first being placed in alphabetical order.

	NRMT	VG-E	GOOD
COMPLETE SET (32)	10.00	4.50	1.25
COMMON SHEET (1-32)	.10	.05	.01
☐ 1 Tony Armas Harold Baines Lonnie Smith	.10	.05	.01
☐ 2 Don Baylor George Hendrick Ron Kittle Johnnie LeMaster	.10	.05	.01
☐ 3 Buddy Bell Tony Gwynn Lloyd Moseby	1.50	.70	.19
☐ 4 Bruce Benedict Atlee Hammaker Frank White	.10	.05	.01
☐ 5 Mike Boddicker Rod Carew Carlton Fisk Johnny Ray	.75	.35	.09
☐ 6 Wade Boggs Rick Dempsey Keith Hernandez	.60	.25	.07
☐ 7 George Brett Andre Dawson Paul Molitor Alan Wiggins	1.25	.55	.16
☐ 8 Tom Brunansky Pedro Guerrero Darryl Strawberry	.25	.11	.03
☐ 9 Bill Buckner Tim Raines Ryne Sandberg Mike Schmidt	1.50	.70	.19
☐ 10 Steve Carlton Bob Horner Dan Quisenberry	.40	.18	.05
☐ 11 Gary Carter Phil Garner Ron Guidry	.15	.07	.02
☐ 12 Jack Clark Damaso Garcia Hal McRae Lance Parrish	.15	.07	.02
☐ 13 Dave Concepcion Cecil Cooper Fred Lynn Jesse Orosco	.15	.07	.02
☐ 14 Jose Cruz Jack Morris Jim Rice Rick Sutcliffe	.25	.11	.03
☐ 15 Alvin Davis Steve Kemp Greg Luzinski Kent Tekulve	.15	.07	.02
☐ 16 Ron Davis Kent Hrbek Juan Samuel	.10	.05	.01
☐ 17 John Denny Carney Lansford Mario Soto Lou Whitaker	.10	.05	.01
☐ 18 Leon Durham Willie Hernandez Steve Sax	.10	.05	.01
☐ 19 Dwight Evans Julio Franco Dwight Gooden	1.00	.45	.12
☐ 20 George Foster Gary Gaetti Bobby Grich Gary Redus	.15	.07	.02
☐ 21 Steve Garvey Jerry Remy Bill Russell George Wright	.15	.07	.02
☐ 22 Kirk Gibson Rich Gossage Don Mattingly Dave Stieb	2.00	.90	.25
☐ 23 Moose Haas Bruce Sutter Dickie Thon Andre Thornton	.10	.05	.01
☐ 24 Rickey Henderson Dave Righetti Pete Rose	1.00	.45	.12
☐ 25 Steve Henderson Bill Madlock Alan Trammell	.15	.07	.02
☐ 26 LaMarr Hoyt Larry Parrish Nolan Ryan	2.00	.90	.25
☐ 27 Reggie Jackson Eric Show Jason Thompson	.50	.23	.06
☐ 28 Terry Kennedy Eddie Murray Tom Seaver Ozzie Smith	1.25	.55	.16
☐ 29 Mark Langston Ben Oglivie Darrell Porter	.50	.23	.06
☐ 30 Jeff Leonard Gary Matthews Dale Murphy Dave Winfield	.50	.23	.06

□ 31 Craig McMurtry	2.00	.90	.25
Cal Ripken			
Steve Rogers			
Willie Upshaw			
□ 32 Tony Pena	.40	.18	.05
Fernando Valenzuela			
Robin Yount			

1985 Topps Super

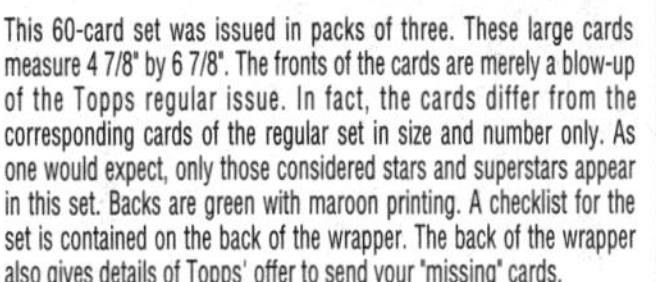

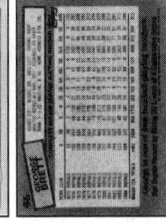

This 60-card set was issued in packs of three. These large cards measure 4 7/8" by 6 7/8". The fronts of the cards are merely a blow-up of the Topps regular issue. In fact, the cards differ from the corresponding cards of the regular set in size and number only. As one would expect, only those considered stars and superstars appear in this set. Backs are green with maroon printing. A checklist for the set is contained on the back of the wrapper. The back of the wrapper also gives details of Topps' offer to send your "missing" cards.

	NRMT	VG-E	GOOD
COMPLETE SET (60)	10.00	4.50	1.25
COMMON CARD (1-60)	.10	.05	.01
□ 1 Ryne Sandberg	2.00	.90	.25
□ 2 Willie Hernandez	.10	.05	.01
□ 3 Rick Sutcliffe	.10	.05	.01
□ 4 Don Mattingly	3.00	1.35	.35
□ 5 Tony Gwynn	2.00	.90	.25
□ 6 Alvin Davis	.10	.05	.01
□ 7 Dwight Gooden	.60	.25	.07
□ 8 Dan Quisenberry	.10	.05	.01
□ 9 Bruce Sutter	.10	.05	.01
□ 10 Tony Armas	.10	.05	.01
□ 11 Dale Murphy	.50	.23	.06
□ 12 Mike Schmidt	.75	.35	.09
□ 13 Gary Carter	.50	.23	.06
□ 14 Rickey Henderson	.60	.25	.07
□ 15 Tim Raines	.25	.11	.03
□ 16 Mike Boddicker	.10	.05	.01
□ 17 Alejandro Pena	.10	.05	.01
□ 18 Eddie Murray	.75	.35	.09
□ 19 Gary Matthews	.10	.05	.01
□ 20 Mark Langston	.25	.11	.03
□ 21 Mario Soto	.10	.05	.01
□ 22 Dave Stieb	.10	.05	.01
□ 23 Nolan Ryan	3.00	1.35	.35
□ 24 Steve Carlton	.60	.25	.07
□ 25 Alan Trammell	.50	.23	.06
□ 26 Steve Garvey	.50	.23	.06
□ 27 Kirk Gibson	.25	.11	.03
□ 28 Juan Samuel	.10	.05	.01
□ 29 Reggie Jackson	.60	.25	.07
□ 30 Darryl Strawberry	.25	.11	.03
□ 31 Tom Seaver	.60	.25	.07
□ 32 Pete Rose	.75	.35	.09
□ 33 Dwight Evans	.25	.11	.03
□ 34 Jose Cruz	.25	.11	.03
□ 35 Bert Blyleven	.25	.11	.03
□ 36 Keith Hernandez	.25	.11	.03
□ 37 Robin Yount	.50	.23	.06
□ 38 Joaquin Andujar	.10	.05	.01
□ 39 Lloyd Moseby	.10	.05	.01
□ 40 Chili Davis	.25	.11	.03
□ 41 Kent Hrbek	.25	.11	.03
□ 42 Dave Parker	.25	.11	.03
□ 43 Jack Morris	.25	.11	.03
□ 44 Pedro Guerrero	.10	.05	.01
□ 45 Mike Witt	.10	.05	.01
□ 46 George Brett	1.50	.70	.19
□ 47 Ozzie Smith	1.50	.70	.19
□ 48 Cal Ripken	3.00	1.35	.35
□ 49 Rich Gossage	.25	.11	.03
□ 50 Jim Rice	.25	.11	.03
□ 51 Harold Baines	.25	.11	.03
□ 52 Fernando Valenzuela	.25	.11	.03
□ 53 Buddy Bell	.10	.05	.01
□ 54 Jesse Orosco	.10	.05	.01
□ 55 Lance Parrish	.10	.05	.01
□ 56 Jason Thompson	.10	.05	.01
□ 57 Tom Brunansky	.10	.05	.01
□ 58 Dave Righetti	.10	.05	.01
□ 59 Dave Kingman	.10	.05	.01
□ 60 Dave Winfield	.60	.25	.07

1986 Topps

This set consists of 792 standard-size cards. Cards were primarily distributed in 15-card wax packs and 48-card rack packs. This was also the first year Topps offered a factory set to hobby dealers. Standard card fronts feature a black and white split border framing a color photo with team name on top and player name on bottom. Subsets include Pete Rose tribute (1-7), Record Breakers (201-207),

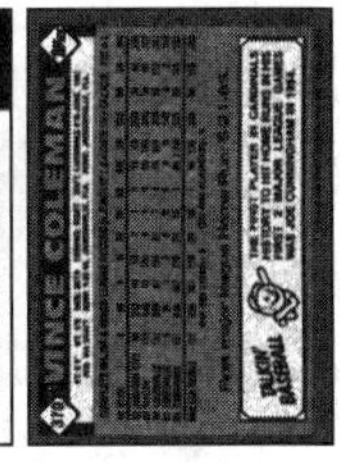

Turn Back the Clock (401-405), All-Stars (701-722) and Team Leaders (seeded throughout the set). Manager cards feature the team checklist on the reverse. There are two uncorrected errors involving misnumbered cards; see card numbers 51, 57, 141, and 171 in the checklist below. The key Rookie Cards in this set are Darren Daulton, Len Dykstra, Cecil Fielder, and Mickey Tettleton.

	MINT	NRMT	EXC
COMPLETE SET (792)	25.00	11.00	3.10
COMPLETE FACT.SET (792)	30.00	13.50	3.70
COMMON CARD (1-792)	.05	.02	.01
□ 1 Pete Rose	.75	.35	.09
□ 2 Rose Special: '63-'66	.30	.14	.04
□ 3 Rose Special: '67-'70	.30	.14	.04
□ 4 Rose Special: '71-'74	.30	.14	.04
□ 5 Rose Special: '75-'78	.30	.14	.04
□ 6 Rose Special: '79-'82	.30	.14	.04
□ 7 Rose Special: '83-'85	.30	.14	.04
□ 8 Dwayne Murphy	.05	.02	.01
□ 9 Roy Smith	.05	.02	.01
□ 10 Tony Gwynn	1.00	.45	.12
□ 11 Bob Ojeda	.05	.02	.01
□ 12 Jose Uribe	.05	.02	.01
□ 13 Bob Kearney	.05	.02	.01
□ 14 Julio Cruz	.05	.02	.01
□ 15 Eddie Whitson	.05	.02	.01
□ 16 Rick Schu	.05	.02	.01
□ 17 Mike Stenhouse	.05	.02	.01
□ 18 Brent Gaff	.05	.02	.01
□ 19 Rich Hebner	.05	.02	.01
□ 20 Lou Whitaker	.10	.05	.01
□ 21 George Bamberger MG	.05	.02	.01
(Checklist back)			
□ 22 Duane Walker	.05	.02	.01
□ 23 Manny Lee	.05	.02	.01
□ 24 Len Barker	.05	.02	.01
□ 25 Willie Wilson	.05	.02	.01
□ 26 Frank DiPino	.05	.02	.01
□ 27 Ray Knight	.10	.05	.01
□ 28 Eric Davis	.10	.05	.01
□ 29 Tony Phillips	.10	.05	.01
□ 30 Eddie Murray	.50	.23	.06
□ 31 Jamie Easterly	.05	.02	.01
□ 32 Steve Yeager	.05	.02	.01
□ 33 Jeff Lahti	.05	.02	.01
□ 34 Ken Phelps	.05	.02	.01
□ 35 Jeff Reardon	.10	.05	.01
□ 36 Lance Parrish TL	.05	.02	.01
□ 37 Mark Thurmond	.05	.02	.01
□ 38 Glenn Hoffman	.05	.02	.01
□ 39 Dave Rucker	.05	.02	.01
□ 40 Ken Griffey	.10	.05	.01
□ 41 Brad Wellman	.05	.02	.01
□ 42 Geoff Zahn	.05	.02	.01
□ 43 Dave Engle	.05	.02	.01
□ 44 Lance McCullers	.05	.02	.01
□ 45 Damaso Garcia	.05	.02	.01
□ 46 Billy Hatcher	.10	.05	.01
□ 47 Juan Berenguer	.05	.02	.01
□ 48 Bill Almon	.05	.02	.01
□ 49 Rick Manning	.05	.02	.01
□ 50 Dan Quisenberry	.05	.02	.01
□ 51 Bobby Wine MG ERR	.10	.05	.01
(Checklist back)			
(Number of card on			
back is actually 57)			
□ 52 Chris Welsh	.05	.02	.01
□ 53 Len Dykstra	.75	.35	.09
□ 54 John Franco	.15	.07	.02
□ 55 Fred Lynn	.10	.05	.01
□ 56 Tom Niedenfuer	.05	.02	.01
□ 57 Bill Doran	.05	.02	.01
(See also 51)			
□ 58 Bill Krueger	.05	.02	.01
□ 59 Andre Thornton	.05	.02	.01
□ 60 Dwight Evans	.10	.05	.01
□ 61 Karl Best	.05	.02	.01
□ 62 Bob Boone	.10	.05	.01
□ 63 Ron Roenicke	.05	.02	.01
□ 64 Floyd Bannister	.05	.02	.01
□ 65 Dan Driessen	.05	.02	.01
□ 66 Bob Forsch TL	.10	.05	.01
□ 67 Carmelo Martinez	.05	.02	.01
□ 68 Ed Lynch	.05	.02	.01
□ 69 Luis Aguayo	.05	.02	.01
□ 70 Dave Winfield	.25	.11	.03
□ 71 Ken Schrom	.05	.02	.01
□ 72 Shawon Dunston	.10	.05	.01
□ 73 Randy O'Neal	.05	.02	.01
□ 74 Rance Mulliniks	.05	.02	.01
□ 75 Jose DeLeon	.05	.02	.01
□ 76 Dion James	.05	.02	.01
□ 77 Charlie Leibrandt	.05	.02	.01
□ 78 Bruce Benedict	.05	.02	.01
□ 79 Dave Schmidt	.05	.02	.01
□ 80 Darryl Strawberry	.15	.07	.02
□ 81 Gene Mauch MG	.10	.05	.01
(Checklist back)			
□ 82 Tippy Martinez	.05	.02	.01
□ 83 Phil Garner	.05	.02	.01
□ 84 Curt Young	.05	.02	.01
□ 85 Tony Perez	.15	.07	.02
(Eric Davis also			
shown on card)			
□ 86 Tom Waddell	.05	.02	.01
□ 87 Candy Maldonado	.05	.02	.01
□ 88 Tom Nieto	.05	.02	.01
□ 89 Randy St.Claire	.05	.02	.01
□ 90 Garry Templeton	.05	.02	.01
□ 91 Steve Crawford	.05	.02	.01
□ 92 Al Cowens	.05	.02	.01
□ 93 Scot Thompson	.05	.02	.01
□ 94 Rich Bordi	.05	.02	.01
□ 95 Ozzie Virgil	.05	.02	.01
□ 96 Jim Clancy TL	.10	.05	.01
□ 97 Gary Gaetti	.10	.05	.01
□ 98 Dick Ruthven	.05	.02	.01
□ 99 Buddy Biancalana	.05	.02	.01
□ 100 Nolan Ryan	1.50	.70	.19
□ 101 Dave Bergman	.05	.02	.01
□ 102 Joe Orsulak	.05	.02	.01
□ 103 Luis Salazar	.05	.02	.01
□ 104 Sid Fernandez	.10	.05	.01
□ 105 Gary Ward	.05	.02	.01
□ 106 Ray Burris	.05	.02	.01
□ 107 Rafael Ramirez	.05	.02	.01
□ 108 Ted Power	.05	.02	.01
□ 109 Len Matuszek	.05	.02	.01
□ 110 Scott McGregor	.05	.02	.01
□ 111 Roger Craig MG	.10	.05	.01
(Checklist back)			
□ 112 Bill Campbell	.05	.02	.01
□ 113 U.L. Washington	.05	.02	.01
□ 114 Mike C. Brown	.05	.02	.01
□ 115 Jay Howell	.05	.02	.01
□ 116 Brook Jacoby	.05	.02	.01
□ 117 Bruce Kison	.05	.02	.01
□ 118 Jerry Royster	.05	.02	.01
□ 119 Barry Bonnell	.05	.02	.01
□ 120 Steve Carlton	.20	.09	.03
□ 121 Nelson Simmons	.05	.02	.01
□ 122 Pete Filson	.05	.02	.01
□ 123 Greg Walker	.05	.02	.01
□ 124 Luis Sanchez	.05	.02	.01
□ 125 Dave Lopes	.10	.05	.01
□ 126 Mookie Wilson TL	.10	.05	.01
□ 127 Jack Howell	.05	.02	.01
□ 128 John Wathan	.05	.02	.01
□ 129 Jeff Dedmon	.05	.02	.01
□ 130 Alan Trammell	.15	.07	.02
□ 131 Checklist: 1-132	.10	.05	.01
□ 132 Razor Shines	.05	.02	.01
□ 133 Andy McGaffigan	.05	.02	.01
□ 134 Carney Lansford	.10	.05	.01
□ 135 Joe Niekro	.05	.02	.01
□ 136 Mike Hargrove	.10	.05	.01
□ 137 Charlie Moore	.05	.02	.01
□ 138 Mark Davis	.05	.02	.01
□ 139 Daryl Boston	.05	.02	.01
□ 140 John Candelaria	.05	.02	.01
□ 141 Chuck Cottier MG	.05	.02	.01
(Checklist back)			
(See also 171)			
□ 142 Bob Jones	.05	.02	.01
□ 143 Dave Van Gorder	.05	.02	.01
□ 144 Doug Sisk	.05	.02	.01
□ 145 Pedro Guerrero	.10	.05	.01
□ 146 Jack Perconte	.05	.02	.01
□ 147 Larry Sheets	.05	.02	.01
□ 148 Mike Heath	.05	.02	.01
□ 149 Brett Butler	.10	.05	.01
□ 150 Joaquin Andujar	.05	.02	.01
□ 151 Dave Stapleton	.05	.02	.01
□ 152 Mike Morgan	.05	.02	.01
□ 153 Ricky Adams	.05	.02	.01
□ 154 Bert Roberge	.05	.02	.01
□ 155 Bob Grich	.10	.05	.01
□ 156 Richard Dotson TL	.05	.02	.01
□ 157 Ron Hassey	.05	.02	.01
□ 158 Derrel Thomas	.05	.02	.01
□ 159 Orel Hershiser UER	.15	.07	.02
(82 Alburquerque)			
□ 160 Chet Lemon	.05	.02	.01
□ 161 Lee Tunnell	.05	.02	.01
□ 162 Greg Gagne	.10	.05	.01
□ 163 Pete Ladd	.05	.02	.01
□ 164 Steve Balboni	.05	.02	.01
□ 165 Mike Davis	.05	.02	.01
□ 166 Dickie Thon	.05	.02	.01
□ 167 Zane Smith	.05	.02	.01
□ 168 Jeff Burroughs	.05	.02	.01
□ 169 George Wright	.05	.02	.01
□ 170 Gary Carter	.10	.05	.01
□ 171 Bob Rodgers MG ERR	.05	.02	.01
(Checklist back)			
(Number of card on			
back actually 141)			
□ 172 Jerry Reed	.05	.02	.01
□ 173 Wayne Gross	.05	.02	.01
□ 174 Brian Snyder	.05	.02	.01
□ 175 Steve Sax	.05	.02	.01
□ 176 Jay Tibbs	.05	.02	.01
□ 177 Joel Youngblood	.05	.02	.01
□ 178 Ivan DeJesus	.05	.02	.01
□ 179 Stu Cliburn	.05	.02	.01
□ 180 Don Mattingly	1.25	.55	.16
□ 181 Al Nipper	.05	.02	.01
□ 182 Bobby Brown	.05	.02	.01
□ 183 Larry Andersen	.05	.02	.01
□ 184 Tim Laudner	.05	.02	.01
□ 185 Rollie Fingers	.15	.07	.02
□ 186 Jose Cruz TL	.10	.05	.01
□ 187 Scott Fletcher	.05	.02	.01
□ 188 Bob Dernier	.05	.02	.01
□ 189 Mike Mason	.05	.02	.01
□ 190 George Hendrick	.05	.02	.01
□ 191 Wally Backman	.05	.02	.01
□ 192 Milt Wilcox	.05	.02	.01
□ 193 Daryl Sconiers	.05	.02	.01
□ 194 Craig McMurtry	.05	.02	.01
□ 195 Dave Concepcion	.10	.05	.01
□ 196 Doyle Alexander	.05	.02	.01
□ 197 Enos Cabell	.05	.02	.01
□ 198 Ken Dixon	.05	.02	.01
□ 199 Dick Howser MG	.10	.05	.01
(Checklist back)			
□ 200 Mike Schmidt	.40	.18	.05
□ 201 Vince Coleman RB	.10	.05	.01
Most SB's rookie season			
□ 202 Dwight Gooden RB	.15	.07	.02
Youngest 20 game			
winner			
□ 203 Keith Hernandez RB	.10	.05	.01
Most game-winning RBI's			
□ 204 Phil Niekro RB	.15	.07	.02
Oldest shutout pitcher			
□ 205 Tony Perez RB	.10	.05	.01
Oldest grand slammer			
□ 206 Pete Rose RB	.30	.14	.04
Most lifetime hits			
□ 207 Fernando Valenzuela RB	.10	.05	.01
Most cons. innings			
start of season,			
no earned runs			
□ 208 Ramon Romero	.05	.02	.01
□ 209 Randy Ready	.05	.02	.01
□ 210 Calvin Schiraldi	.05	.02	.01
□ 211 Ed Wojna	.05	.02	.01
□ 212 Chris Speier	.05	.02	.01
□ 213 Bob Shirley	.05	.02	.01
□ 214 Randy Bush	.05	.02	.01
□ 215 Frank White	.10	.05	.01
□ 216 Dwayne Murphy TL	.10	.05	.01
□ 217 Bill Scherrer	.05	.02	.01
□ 218 Randy Hunt	.05	.02	.01
□ 219 Dennis Lamp	.05	.02	.01
□ 220 Bob Horner	.05	.02	.01
□ 221 Dave Henderson	.05	.02	.01
□ 222 Craig Gerber	.05	.02	.01
□ 223 Atlee Hammaker	.05	.02	.01
□ 224 Cesar Cedeno	.10	.05	.01
□ 225 Ron Darling	.05	.02	.01
□ 226 Lee Lacy	.05	.02	.01
□ 227 Al Jones	.05	.02	.01
□ 228 Tom Lawless	.05	.02	.01
□ 229 Bill Gullickson	.05	.02	.01
□ 230 Terry Kennedy	.05	.02	.01
□ 231 Jim Frey MG	.10	.05	.01
(Checklist back)			
□ 232 Rick Rhoden	.05	.02	.01
□ 233 Steve Lyons	.05	.02	.01
□ 234 Doug Corbett	.05	.02	.01
□ 235 Butch Wynegar	.05	.02	.01
□ 236 Frank Eufemia	.05	.02	.01
□ 237 Ted Simmons	.10	.05	.01
□ 238 Larry Parrish	.05	.02	.01
□ 239 Joel Skinner	.05	.02	.01
□ 240 Tommy John	.15	.07	.02
□ 241 Tony Fernandez	.05	.02	.01
□ 242 Rich Thompson	.05	.02	.01
□ 243 Johnny Grubb	.05	.02	.01
□ 244 Craig Lefferts	.05	.02	.01
□ 245 Jim Sundberg	.05	.02	.01
□ 246 Steve Carlton TL	.10	.05	.01
□ 247 Terry Harper	.05	.02	.01
□ 248 Spike Owen	.05	.02	.01
□ 249 Rob Deer	.10	.05	.01
□ 250 Dwight Gooden	.20	.09	.03
□ 251 Rich Dauer	.05	.02	.01
□ 252 Bobby Castillo	.05	.02	.01
□ 253 Dann Bilardello	.05	.02	.01
□ 254 Ozzie Guillen	.15	.07	.02
□ 255 Tony Armas	.05	.02	.01
□ 256 Kurt Kepshire	.05	.02	.01
□ 257 Doug DeCinces	.05	.02	.01
□ 258 Tim Burke	.05	.02	.01
□ 259 Dan Pasqua	.05	.02	.01
□ 260 Tony Pena	.05	.02	.01
□ 261 Bobby Valentine MG	.10	.05	.01
(Checklist back)			
□ 262 Mario Ramirez	.05	.02	.01
□ 263 Checklist: 133-264	.10	.05	.01

☐ 264 Darren Daulton .75 .35 .09
☐ 265 Ron Davis .05 .02 .01
☐ 266 Keith Moreland .05 .02 .01
☐ 267 Paul Molitor .40 .18 .05
☐ 268 Mike Scott .05 .02 .01
☐ 269 Dane Iorg .05 .02 .01
☐ 270 Jack Morris .10 .05 .01
☐ 271 Dave Collins .05 .02 .01
☐ 272 Tim Tolman .05 .02 .01
☐ 273 Jerry Willard .05 .02 .01
☐ 274 Ron Gardenhire .05 .02 .01
☐ 275 Charlie Hough .10 .05 .01
☐ 276 Willie Randolph TL .10 .05 .01
☐ 277 Jaime Cocanower .05 .02 .01
☐ 278 Sixto Lezcano .05 .02 .01
☐ 279 Al Pardo .05 .02 .01
☐ 280 Tim Raines .10 .05 .01
☐ 281 Steve Mura .05 .02 .01
☐ 282 Jerry Mumphrey .05 .02 .01
☐ 283 Mike Fischlin .05 .02 .01
☐ 284 Brian Dayett .05 .02 .01
☐ 285 Buddy Bell .10 .05 .01
☐ 286 Luis DeLeon .05 .02 .01
☐ 287 John Christensen .05 .02 .01
☐ 288 Don Aase .05 .02 .01
☐ 289 Johnnie LeMaster .05 .02 .01
☐ 290 Carlton Fisk .15 .07 .02
☐ 291 Tom Lasorda MG .10 .05 .01
(Checklist back)
☐ 292 Chuck Porter .05 .02 .01
☐ 293 Chris Chambliss .10 .05 .01
☐ 294 Danny Cox .05 .02 .01
☐ 295 Kirk Gibson .10 .05 .01
☐ 296 Geno Petralli .05 .02 .01
☐ 297 Tim Lollar .05 .02 .01
☐ 298 Craig Reynolds .05 .02 .01
☐ 299 Bryn Smith .05 .02 .01
☐ 300 George Brett .75 .35 .09
☐ 301 Dennis Rasmussen .05 .02 .01
☐ 302 Greg Gross .05 .02 .01
☐ 303 Curt Wardle .05 .02 .01
☐ 304 Mike Gallego .10 .05 .01
☐ 305 Phil Bradley .05 .02 .01
☐ 306 Terry Kennedy TL .05 .02 .01
☐ 307 Dave Sax .05 .02 .01
☐ 308 Ray Fontenot .05 .02 .01
☐ 309 John Shelby .05 .02 .01
☐ 310 Greg Minton .05 .02 .01
☐ 311 Dick Schofield .05 .02 .01
☐ 312 Tom Filer .05 .02 .01
☐ 313 Joe DeSa .05 .02 .01
☐ 314 Frank Pastore .05 .02 .01
☐ 315 Mookie Wilson .10 .05 .01
☐ 316 Sammy Khalifa .05 .02 .01
☐ 317 Ed Romero .05 .02 .01
☐ 318 Terry Whitfield .05 .02 .01
☐ 319 Rick Camp .05 .02 .01
☐ 320 Jim Rice .10 .05 .01
☐ 321 Earl Weaver MG .15 .07 .02
(Checklist back)
☐ 322 Bob Forsch .05 .02 .01
☐ 323 Jerry Davis .05 .02 .01
☐ 324 Dan Schatzeder .05 .02 .01
☐ 325 Juan Beniquez .05 .02 .01
☐ 326 Kent Tekulve .05 .02 .01
☐ 327 Mike Pagliarulo .05 .02 .01
☐ 328 Pete O'Brien .05 .02 .01
☐ 329 Kirby Puckett 2.00 .90 .25
☐ 330 Rick Sutcliffe .05 .02 .01
☐ 331 Alan Ashby .05 .02 .01
☐ 332 Darryl Motley .05 .02 .01
☐ 333 Tom Henke .10 .05 .01
☐ 334 Ken Oberkfell .05 .02 .01
☐ 335 Don Sutton .15 .07 .02
☐ 336 Andre Thornton TL .05 .02 .01
☐ 337 Darnell Coles .05 .02 .01
☐ 338 Jorge Bell .10 .05 .01
☐ 339 Bruce Berenyi .05 .02 .01
☐ 340 Cal Ripken 1.50 .70 .19
☐ 341 Frank Williams .05 .02 .01
☐ 342 Gary Redus .05 .02 .01
☐ 343 Carlos Diaz .05 .02 .01
☐ 344 Jim Wohlford .05 .02 .01
☐ 345 Donnie Moore .05 .02 .01
☐ 346 Bryan Little .05 .02 .01
☐ 347 Teddy Higuera .10 .05 .01
☐ 348 Cliff Johnson .05 .02 .01
☐ 349 Mark Clear .05 .02 .01
☐ 350 Jack Clark .10 .05 .01
☐ 351 Chuck Tanner MG .10 .05 .01
(Checklist back)
☐ 352 Harry Spilman .05 .02 .01
☐ 353 Keith Atherton .05 .02 .01
☐ 354 Tony Bernazard .05 .02 .01
☐ 355 Lee Smith .15 .07 .02
☐ 356 Mickey Hatcher .05 .02 .01
☐ 357 Ed VandeBerg .05 .02 .01
☐ 358 Rick Dempsey .05 .02 .01
☐ 359 Mike LaCoss .05 .02 .01
☐ 360 Lloyd Moseby .05 .02 .01
☐ 361 Shane Rawley .05 .02 .01
☐ 362 Tom Paciorek .05 .02 .01
☐ 363 Terry Forster .05 .02 .01
☐ 364 Reid Nichols .05 .02 .01
☐ 365 Mike Flanagan .05 .02 .01
☐ 366 Dave Concepcion TL .10 .05 .01
☐ 367 Aurelio Lopez .05 .02 .01
☐ 368 Greg Brock .05 .02 .01
☐ 369 Al Holland .05 .02 .01
☐ 370 Vince Coleman .15 .07 .02
☐ 371 Bill Stein .05 .02 .01
☐ 372 Ben Oglivie .05 .02 .01
☐ 373 Urbano Lugo .05 .02 .01
☐ 374 Terry Francona .05 .02 .01
☐ 375 Rich Gedman .05 .02 .01
☐ 376 Bill Dawley .05 .02 .01
☐ 377 Joe Carter 1.00 .45 .12
☐ 378 Bruce Bochte .05 .02 .01
☐ 379 Bobby Meacham .05 .02 .01
☐ 380 LaMarr Hoyt .05 .02 .01
☐ 381 Ray Miller MG .05 .02 .01
(Checklist back)
☐ 382 Ivan Calderon .10 .05 .01
☐ 383 Chris Brown .05 .02 .01
☐ 384 Steve Trout .05 .02 .01
☐ 385 Cecil Cooper .10 .05 .01
☐ 386 Cecil Fielder 1.50 .70 .19
☐ 387 Steve Kemp .05 .02 .01
☐ 388 Dickie Noles .05 .02 .01
☐ 389 Glenn Davis .10 .05 .01
☐ 390 Tom Seaver .20 .09 .03
☐ 391 Julio Franco .15 .07 .02
☐ 392 John Russell .05 .02 .01
☐ 393 Chris Pittaro .05 .02 .01
☐ 394 Checklist: 265-396 .10 .05 .01
☐ 395 Scott Garrelts .05 .02 .01
☐ 396 Dwight Evans TL .10 .05 .01
☐ 397 Steve Buechele .10 .05 .01
☐ 398 Earnie Riles .05 .02 .01
☐ 399 Bill Swift .10 .05 .01
☐ 400 Rod Carew .20 .09 .03
☐ 401 Fernando Valenzuela .10 .05 .01
TBC '81
☐ 402 Tom Seaver TBC '76 .15 .07 .02
☐ 403 Willie Mays TBC '71 .15 .07 .02
☐ 404 Frank Robinson .15 .07 .02
TBC '66
☐ 405 Roger Maris TBC '61 .15 .07 .02
☐ 406 Scott Sanderson .05 .02 .01
☐ 407 Sal Butera .05 .02 .01
☐ 408 Dave Smith .05 .02 .01
☐ 409 Paul Runge .05 .02 .01
☐ 410 Dave Kingman .10 .05 .01
☐ 411 Sparky Anderson MG .10 .05 .01
(Checklist back)
☐ 412 Jim Clancy .05 .02 .01
☐ 413 Tim Flannery .05 .02 .01
☐ 414 Tom Gorman .05 .02 .01
☐ 415 Hal McRae .10 .05 .01
☐ 416 Dennis Martinez .10 .05 .01
☐ 417 R.J. Reynolds .05 .02 .01
☐ 418 Alan Knicely .05 .02 .01
☐ 419 Frank Wills .05 .02 .01
☐ 420 Von Hayes .05 .02 .01
☐ 421 David Palmer .05 .02 .01
☐ 422 Mike Jorgensen .05 .02 .01
☐ 423 Dan Spillner .05 .02 .01
☐ 424 Rick Miller .05 .02 .01
☐ 425 Larry McWilliams .05 .02 .01
☐ 426 Charlie Moore TL .10 .05 .01
☐ 427 Joe Cowley .05 .02 .01
☐ 428 Max Venable .05 .02 .01
☐ 429 Greg Booker .05 .02 .01
☐ 430 Kent Hrbek .10 .05 .01
☐ 431 George Frazier .05 .02 .01
☐ 432 Mark Bailey .05 .02 .01
☐ 433 Chris Codiroli .05 .02 .01
☐ 434 Curt Wilkerson .05 .02 .01
☐ 435 Bill Caudill .05 .02 .01
☐ 436 Doug Flynn .05 .02 .01
☐ 437 Rick Mahler .05 .02 .01
☐ 438 Clint Hurdle .05 .02 .01
☐ 439 Rick Honeycutt .05 .02 .01
☐ 440 Alvin Davis .05 .02 .01
☐ 441 Whitey Herzog MG .10 .05 .01
(Checklist back)
☐ 442 Ron Robinson .05 .02 .01
☐ 443 Bill Buckner .10 .05 .01
☐ 444 Alex Trevino .05 .02 .01
☐ 445 Bert Blyleven .15 .07 .02
☐ 446 Lenn Sakata .05 .02 .01
☐ 447 Jerry Don Gleaton .05 .02 .01
☐ 448 Herm Winningham .05 .02 .01
☐ 449 Rod Scurry .05 .02 .01
☐ 450 Graig Nettles .10 .05 .01
☐ 451 Mark Brown .05 .02 .01
☐ 452 Bob Clark .05 .02 .01
☐ 453 Steve Jeltz .05 .02 .01
☐ 454 Burt Hooton .05 .02 .01
☐ 455 Willie Randolph .10 .05 .01
☐ 456 Dale Murphy TL .10 .05 .01
☐ 457 Mickey Tettleton .60 .25 .07
☐ 458 Kevin Bass .05 .02 .01
☐ 459 Luis Leal .05 .02 .01
☐ 460 Leon Durham .05 .02 .01
☐ 461 Walt Terrell .05 .02 .01
☐ 462 Domingo Ramos .05 .02 .01
☐ 463 Jim Gott .05 .02 .01
☐ 464 Ruppert Jones .05 .02 .01
☐ 465 Jesse Orosco .05 .02 .01
☐ 466 Tom Foley .05 .02 .01
☐ 467 Bob James .05 .02 .01
☐ 468 Mike Scioscia .05 .02 .01
☐ 469 Storm Davis .05 .02 .01
☐ 470 Bill Madlock .05 .02 .01
☐ 471 Bobby Cox MG .10 .05 .01
(Checklist back)
☐ 472 Joe Hesketh .05 .02 .01
☐ 473 Mark Brouhard .05 .02 .01
☐ 474 John Tudor .05 .02 .01
☐ 475 Juan Samuel .05 .02 .01
☐ 476 Ron Mathis .05 .02 .01
☐ 477 Mike Easler .05 .02 .01
☐ 478 Andy Hawkins .05 .02 .01
☐ 479 Bob Melvin .05 .02 .01
☐ 480 Oddibe McDowell .05 .02 .01
☐ 481 Scott Bradley .05 .02 .01
☐ 482 Rick Lysander .05 .02 .01
☐ 483 George Vukovich .05 .02 .01
☐ 484 Donnie Hill .05 .02 .01
☐ 485 Gary Matthews .05 .02 .01
☐ 486 Bobby Grich TL .10 .05 .01
☐ 487 Bret Saberhagen .15 .07 .02
☐ 488 Lou Thornton .05 .02 .01
☐ 489 Jim Winn .05 .02 .01
☐ 490 Jeff Leonard .05 .02 .01
☐ 491 Pascual Perez .05 .02 .01
☐ 492 Kelvin Chapman .05 .02 .01
☐ 493 Gene Nelson .05 .02 .01
☐ 494 Gary Roenicke .05 .02 .01
☐ 495 Mark Langston .10 .05 .01
☐ 496 Jay Johnstone .10 .05 .01
☐ 497 John Stuper .05 .02 .01
☐ 498 Tito Landrum .05 .02 .01
☐ 499 Bob L. Gibson .05 .02 .01
☐ 500 Rickey Henderson .30 .14 .04
☐ 501 Dave Johnson MG .10 .05 .01
(Checklist back)
☐ 502 Glen Cook .05 .02 .01
☐ 503 Mike Fitzgerald .05 .02 .01
☐ 504 Denny Walling .05 .02 .01
☐ 505 Jerry Koosman .10 .05 .01
☐ 506 Bill Russell .05 .02 .01
☐ 507 Steve Ontiveros .10 .05 .01
☐ 508 Alan Wiggins .05 .02 .01
☐ 509 Ernie Camacho .05 .02 .01
☐ 510 Wade Boggs .40 .18 .05
☐ 511 Ed Nunez .05 .02 .01
☐ 512 Thad Bosley .05 .02 .01
☐ 513 Ron Washington .05 .02 .01
☐ 514 Mike Jones .05 .02 .01
☐ 515 Darrell Evans .10 .05 .01
☐ 516 Greg Minton TL .05 .02 .01
☐ 517 Milt Thompson .10 .05 .01
☐ 518 Buck Martinez .05 .02 .01
☐ 519 Danny Darwin .05 .02 .01
☐ 520 Keith Hernandez .10 .05 .01
☐ 521 Nate Snell .05 .02 .01
☐ 522 Bob Bailor .05 .02 .01
☐ 523 Joe Price .05 .02 .01
☐ 524 Darrell Miller .05 .02 .01
☐ 525 Marvell Wynne .05 .02 .01
☐ 526 Charlie Lea .05 .02 .01
☐ 527 Checklist: 397-528 .10 .05 .01
☐ 528 Terry Pendleton .15 .07 .02
☐ 529 Marc Sullivan .05 .02 .01
☐ 530 Rich Gossage .15 .07 .02
☐ 531 Tony LaRussa MG .10 .05 .01
(Checklist back)
☐ 532 Don Carman .05 .02 .01
☐ 533 Billy Sample .05 .02 .01
☐ 534 Jeff Calhoun .05 .02 .01
☐ 535 Toby Harrah .05 .02 .01
☐ 536 Jose Rijo .10 .05 .01
☐ 537 Mark Salas .05 .02 .01
☐ 538 Dennis Eckersley .15 .07 .02
☐ 539 Glenn Hubbard .05 .02 .01
☐ 540 Dan Petry .05 .02 .01
☐ 541 Jorge Orta .05 .02 .01
☐ 542 Don Schulze .05 .02 .01
☐ 543 Jerry Narron .05 .02 .01
☐ 544 Eddie Milner .05 .02 .01
☐ 545 Jimmy Key .15 .07 .02
☐ 546 Dave Henderson TL .10 .05 .01
☐ 547 Roger McDowell .10 .05 .01
☐ 548 Mike Young .05 .02 .01
☐ 549 Bob Welch .05 .02 .01
☐ 550 Tom Herr .05 .02 .01
☐ 551 Dave LaPoint .05 .02 .01
☐ 552 Marc Hill .05 .02 .01
☐ 553 Jim Morrison .05 .02 .01
☐ 554 Paul Householder .05 .02 .01
☐ 555 Hubie Brooks .05 .02 .01
☐ 556 John Denny .05 .02 .01
☐ 557 Gerald Perry .05 .02 .01
☐ 558 Tim Stoddard .05 .02 .01
☐ 559 Tommy Dunbar .05 .02 .01
☐ 560 Dave Righetti .05 .02 .01
☐ 561 Bob Lillis MG .05 .02 .01
(Checklist back)
☐ 562 Joe Beckwith .05 .02 .01
☐ 563 Alejandro Sanchez .05 .02 .01
☐ 564 Warren Brusstar .05 .02 .01
☐ 565 Tom Brunansky .05 .02 .01
☐ 566 Alfredo Griffin .05 .02 .01
☐ 567 Jeff Barkley .05 .02 .01
☐ 568 Donnie Scott .05 .02 .01
☐ 569 Jim Acker .05 .02 .01
☐ 570 Rusty Staub .10 .05 .01
☐ 571 Mike Jeffcoat .05 .02 .01
☐ 572 Paul Zuvella .05 .02 .01
☐ 573 Tom Hume .05 .02 .01
☐ 574 Ron Kittle .05 .02 .01
☐ 575 Mike Boddicker .05 .02 .01
☐ 576 Andre Dawson TL .15 .07 .02
☐ 577 Jerry Reuss .05 .02 .01
☐ 578 Lee Mazzilli .05 .02 .01
☐ 579 Jim Slaton .05 .02 .01
☐ 580 Willie McGee .10 .05 .01
☐ 581 Bruce Hurst .05 .02 .01
☐ 582 Jim Gantner .05 .02 .01
☐ 583 Al Bumbry .05 .02 .01
☐ 584 Brian Fisher .05 .02 .01
☐ 585 Garry Maddox .05 .02 .01
☐ 586 Greg Harris .05 .02 .01
☐ 587 Rafael Santana .05 .02 .01
☐ 588 Steve Lake .05 .02 .01
☐ 589 Sid Bream .05 .02 .01
☐ 590 Bob Knepper .05 .02 .01
☐ 591 Jackie Moore MG .05 .02 .01
(Checklist back)
☐ 592 Frank Tanana .05 .02 .01
☐ 593 Jesse Barfield .05 .02 .01
☐ 594 Chris Bando .05 .02 .01
☐ 595 Dave Parker .10 .05 .01
☐ 596 Onix Concepcion .05 .02 .01
☐ 597 Sammy Stewart .05 .02 .01
☐ 598 Jim Presley .05 .02 .01
☐ 599 Rick Aguilera .15 .07 .02
☐ 600 Dale Murphy .15 .07 .02
☐ 601 Gary Lucas .05 .02 .01
☐ 602 Mariano Duncan .15 .07 .02
☐ 603 Bill Laskey .05 .02 .01
☐ 604 Gary Pettis .05 .02 .01
☐ 605 Dennis Boyd .05 .02 .01
☐ 606 Hal McRae TL .05 .02 .01
☐ 607 Ken Dayley .05 .02 .01
☐ 608 Bruce Bochy .05 .02 .01
☐ 609 Barbaro Garbey .05 .02 .01
☐ 610 Ron Guidry .10 .05 .01
☐ 611 Gary Woods .05 .02 .01
☐ 612 Richard Dotson .05 .02 .01
☐ 613 Roy Smalley .05 .02 .01
☐ 614 Rick Waits .05 .02 .01
☐ 615 Johnny Ray .05 .02 .01
☐ 616 Glenn Brummer .05 .02 .01
☐ 617 Lonnie Smith .05 .02 .01
☐ 618 Jim Pankovits .05 .02 .01
☐ 619 Danny Heep .05 .02 .01
☐ 620 Bruce Sutter .10 .05 .01
☐ 621 John Felske MG .05 .02 .01
(Checklist back)
☐ 622 Gary Lavelle .05 .02 .01
☐ 623 Floyd Rayford .05 .02 .01
☐ 624 Steve McCatty .05 .02 .01
☐ 625 Bob Brenly .05 .02 .01
☐ 626 Roy Thomas .05 .02 .01
☐ 627 Ron Oester .05 .02 .01
☐ 628 Kirk McCaskill .10 .05 .01
☐ 629 Mitch Webster .05 .02 .01
☐ 630 Fernando Valenzuela .10 .05 .01
☐ 631 Steve Braun .05 .02 .01
☐ 632 Dave Von Ohlen .05 .02 .01
☐ 633 Jackie Gutierrez .05 .02 .01
☐ 634 Roy Lee Jackson .05 .02 .01
☐ 635 Jason Thompson .05 .02 .01
☐ 636 Lee Smith TL .15 .07 .02
☐ 637 Rudy Law .05 .02 .01
☐ 638 John Butcher .05 .02 .01
☐ 639 Bo Diaz .05 .02 .01
☐ 640 Jose Cruz .05 .02 .01
☐ 641 Wayne Tolleson .05 .02 .01
☐ 642 Ray Searage .05 .02 .01
☐ 643 Tom Brookens .05 .02 .01
☐ 644 Mark Gubicza .10 .05 .01
☐ 645 Dusty Baker .10 .05 .01
☐ 646 Mike Moore .05 .02 .01
☐ 647 Mel Hall .05 .02 .01
☐ 648 Steve Bedrosian .05 .02 .01
☐ 649 Ronn Reynolds .05 .02 .01
☐ 650 Dave Stieb .05 .02 .01
☐ 651 Billy Martin MG .10 .05 .01
(Checklist back)
☐ 652 Tom Browning .05 .02 .01
☐ 653 Jim Dwyer .05 .02 .01
☐ 654 Ken Howell .05 .02 .01
☐ 655 Manny Trillo .05 .02 .01
☐ 656 Brian Harper .05 .02 .01
☐ 657 Juan Agosto .05 .02 .01
☐ 658 Rob Wilfong .05 .02 .01
☐ 659 Checklist: 529-660 .10 .05 .01
☐ 660 Steve Garvey .15 .07 .02
☐ 661 Roger Clemens 1.00 .45 .12
☐ 662 Bill Schroeder .05 .02 .01
☐ 663 Neil Allen .05 .02 .01
☐ 664 Tim Corcoran .05 .02 .01
☐ 665 Alejandro Pena .05 .02 .01
☐ 666 Rangers Leaders .10 .05 .01
Charlie Hough
☐ 667 Tim Teufel .05 .02 .01

Card	MINT	NRMT	EXC
☐ 668 Cecilio Guante	.05	.02	.01
☐ 669 Ron Cey	.10	.05	.01
☐ 670 Willie Hernandez	.05	.02	.01
☐ 671 Lynn Jones	.05	.02	.01
☐ 672 Rob Picciolo	.05	.02	.01
☐ 673 Ernie Whitt	.05	.02	.01
☐ 674 Pat Tabler	.05	.02	.01
☐ 675 Claudell Washington	.05	.02	.01
☐ 676 Matt Young	.05	.02	.01
☐ 677 Nick Esasky	.05	.02	.01
☐ 678 Dan Gladden	.05	.02	.01
☐ 679 Britt Burns	.05	.02	.01
☐ 680 George Foster	.10	.05	.01
☐ 681 Dick Williams MG (Checklist back)	.10	.05	.01
☐ 682 Junior Ortiz	.05	.02	.01
☐ 683 Andy Van Slyke	.10	.05	.01
☐ 684 Bob McClure	.05	.02	.01
☐ 685 Tim Wallach	.05	.02	.01
☐ 686 Jeff Stone	.05	.02	.01
☐ 687 Mike Trujillo	.05	.02	.01
☐ 688 Larry Herndon	.05	.02	.01
☐ 689 Dave Stewart	.10	.05	.01
☐ 690 Ryne Sandberg UER (No Topps logo on front)	.75	.35	.09
☐ 691 Mike Madden	.05	.02	.01
☐ 692 Dale Berra	.05	.02	.01
☐ 693 Tom Tellmann	.05	.02	.01
☐ 694 Garth Iorg	.05	.02	.01
☐ 695 Mike Smithson	.05	.02	.01
☐ 696 Bill Russell TL	.10	.05	.01
☐ 697 Bud Black	.05	.02	.01
☐ 698 Brad Komminsk	.05	.02	.01
☐ 699 Pat Corrales MG (Checklist back)	.05	.02	.01
☐ 700 Reggie Jackson	.30	.14	.04
☐ 701 Keith Hernandez AS	.10	.05	.01
☐ 702 Tom Herr AS	.05	.02	.01
☐ 703 Tim Wallach AS	.05	.02	.01
☐ 704 Ozzie Smith AS	.15	.07	.02
☐ 705 Dale Murphy AS	.15	.07	.02
☐ 706 Pedro Guerrero AS	.10	.05	.01
☐ 707 Willie McGee AS	.10	.05	.01
☐ 708 Gary Carter AS	.10	.05	.01
☐ 709 Dwight Gooden AS	.15	.07	.02
☐ 710 John Tudor AS	.05	.02	.01
☐ 711 Jeff Reardon AS	.10	.05	.01
☐ 712 Don Mattingly AS	.50	.23	.06
☐ 713 Damaso Garcia AS	.05	.02	.01
☐ 714 George Brett AS	.50	.23	.06
☐ 715 Cal Ripken AS	1.00	.45	.12
☐ 716 Rickey Henderson AS	.15	.07	.02
☐ 717 Dave Winfield AS	.15	.07	.02
☐ 718 George Bell AS	.05	.02	.01
☐ 719 Carlton Fisk AS	.10	.05	.01
☐ 720 Bret Saberhagen AS	.15	.07	.02
☐ 721 Ron Guidry AS	.10	.05	.01
☐ 722 Dan Quisenberry AS	.05	.02	.01
☐ 723 Marty Bystrom	.05	.02	.01
☐ 724 Tim Hulett	.05	.02	.01
☐ 725 Mario Soto	.05	.02	.01
☐ 726 Rick Dempsey TL	.10	.05	.01
☐ 727 David Green	.05	.02	.01
☐ 728 Mike Marshall	.05	.02	.01
☐ 729 Jim Beattie	.05	.02	.01
☐ 730 Ozzie Smith	.50	.23	.06
☐ 731 Don Robinson	.05	.02	.01
☐ 732 Floyd Youmans	.05	.02	.01
☐ 733 Ron Romanick	.05	.02	.01
☐ 734 Marty Barrett	.05	.02	.01
☐ 735 Dave Dravecky	.10	.05	.01
☐ 736 Glenn Wilson	.05	.02	.01
☐ 737 Pete Vuckovich	.05	.02	.01
☐ 738 Andre Robertson	.05	.02	.01
☐ 739 Dave Rozema	.05	.02	.01
☐ 740 Lance Parrish	.10	.05	.01
☐ 741 Pete Rose MG (Checklist back)	.20	.09	.03
☐ 742 Frank Viola	.10	.05	.01
☐ 743 Pat Sheridan	.05	.02	.01
☐ 744 Lary Sorensen	.05	.02	.01
☐ 745 Willie Upshaw	.05	.02	.01
☐ 746 Denny Gonzalez	.05	.02	.01
☐ 747 Rick Cerone	.05	.02	.01
☐ 748 Steve Henderson	.05	.02	.01
☐ 749 Ed Jurak	.05	.02	.01
☐ 750 Gorman Thomas	.05	.02	.01
☐ 751 Howard Johnson	.10	.05	.01
☐ 752 Mike Krukow	.05	.02	.01
☐ 753 Dan Ford	.05	.02	.01
☐ 754 Pat Clements	.05	.02	.01
☐ 755 Harold Baines	.15	.07	.02
☐ 756 Rick Rhoden TL	.05	.02	.01
☐ 757 Darrell Porter	.05	.02	.01
☐ 758 Dave Anderson	.05	.02	.01
☐ 759 Moose Haas	.05	.02	.01
☐ 760 Andre Dawson	.15	.07	.02
☐ 761 Don Slaught	.05	.02	.01
☐ 762 Eric Show	.05	.02	.01
☐ 763 Terry Puhl	.05	.02	.01
☐ 764 Kevin Gross	.05	.02	.01
☐ 765 Don Baylor	.15	.07	.02
☐ 766 Rick Langford	.05	.02	.01
☐ 767 Jody Davis	.05	.02	.01
☐ 768 Vern Ruhle	.05	.02	.01
☐ 769 Harold Reynolds	.20	.09	.03
☐ 770 Vida Blue	.10	.05	.01
☐ 771 John McNamara MG (Checklist back)	.05	.02	.01
☐ 772 Brian Downing	.05	.02	.01
☐ 773 Greg Pryor	.05	.02	.01
☐ 774 Terry Leach	.05	.02	.01
☐ 775 Al Oliver	.10	.05	.01
☐ 776 Gene Garber	.05	.02	.01
☐ 777 Wayne Krenchicki	.05	.02	.01
☐ 778 Jerry Hairston	.05	.02	.01
☐ 779 Rick Reuschel	.05	.02	.01
☐ 780 Robin Yount	.30	.14	.04
☐ 781 Joe Nolan	.05	.02	.01
☐ 782 Ken Landreaux	.05	.02	.01
☐ 783 Ricky Horton	.05	.02	.01
☐ 784 Alan Bannister	.05	.02	.01
☐ 785 Bob Stanley	.05	.02	.01
☐ 786 Mickey Hatcher TL	.05	.02	.01
☐ 787 Vance Law	.05	.02	.01
☐ 788 Marty Castillo	.05	.02	.01
☐ 789 Kurt Bevacqua	.05	.02	.01
☐ 790 Phil Niekro	.15	.07	.02
☐ 791 Checklist: 661-792	.10	.05	.01
☐ 792 Charles Hudson	.05	.02	.01

1986 Topps Tiffany

These 792 cards form a parallel to the regular Topps set. These cards, available only through the Topps dealer network were issued in factory sealed boxes. These cards have a "glossy" front and a very clear back. These cards were printed in the Topps Ireland plant. Reports within the hobby indicate that it is believed that 5,000 of these sets were produced.

	MINT	NRMT	EXC
COMPLETE FACT.SET (792)	150.00	70.00	19.00
COMMON CARD (1-792)	.15	.07	.02
*STARS: 5X to 10 X BASIC CARDS			
*ROOKIES: 4X to 8X BASIC CARDS			

1986 Topps Glossy All-Stars

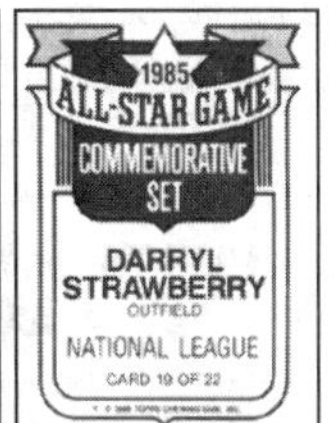

This 22-card standard-size set was distributed as an insert, one card per rak pack. The players featured are the starting lineups of the 1985 All-Star Game played in Minnesota. The cards are very colorful and have a high gloss finish.

	MINT	NRMT	EXC
COMPLETE SET (22)	5.00	2.20	.60
COMMON CARD (1-22)	.05	.02	.01
☐ 1 Sparky Anderson MG	.05	.02	.01
☐ 2 Eddie Murray	.75	.35	.09
☐ 3 Lou Whitaker	.10	.05	.01
☐ 4 George Brett	1.00	.45	.12
☐ 5 Cal Ripken	2.00	.90	.25
☐ 6 Jim Rice	.10	.05	.01
☐ 7 Rickey Henderson	.40	.18	.05
☐ 8 Dave Winfield	.50	.23	.06
☐ 9 Carlton Fisk	.40	.18	.05
☐ 10 Jack Morris	.10	.05	.01
☐ 11 AL Team Photo	.05	.02	.01
☐ 12 Dick Williams MG	.05	.02	.01
☐ 13 Steve Garvey	.10	.05	.01
☐ 14 Tom Herr	.05	.02	.01
☐ 15 Graig Nettles	.05	.02	.01
☐ 16 Ozzie Smith	1.00	.45	.12
☐ 17 Tony Gwynn	1.25	.55	.16
☐ 18 Dale Murphy	.20	.09	.03
☐ 19 Darryl Strawberry	.10	.05	.01
☐ 20 Terry Kennedy	.05	.02	.01
☐ 21 LaMarr Hoyt	.05	.02	.01
☐ 22 NL Team Photo	.05	.02	.01

1986 Topps Glossy Send-Ins

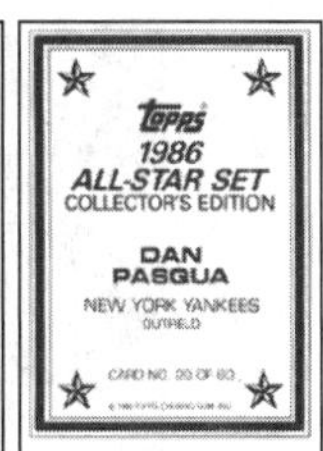

This 60-card glossy standard-size set was produced by Topps and distributed ten cards at a time based on the offer found on the wax packs. Each series of ten cards was available by sending in 1.00 plus six "special offer" cards inserted one per wax pack. The card backs are printed in red and blue on white card stock. The card fronts feature a white border and a green frame surrounding a full-color photo of the player.

	MINT	NRMT	EXC
COMPLETE SET (60)	12.50	5.50	1.55
COMMON CARD (1-60)	.10	.05	.01
☐ 1 Oddibe McDowell	.10	.05	.01
☐ 2 Reggie Jackson	.75	.35	.09
☐ 3 Fernando Valenzuela	.25	.11	.03
☐ 4 Jack Clark	.10	.05	.01
☐ 5 Rickey Henderson	.60	.25	.07
☐ 6 Steve Balboni	.10	.05	.01
☐ 7 Keith Hernandez	.25	.11	.03
☐ 8 Lance Parrish	.25	.11	.03
☐ 9 Willie McGee	.25	.11	.03
☐ 10 Chris Brown	.10	.05	.01
☐ 11 Darryl Strawberry	.35	.16	.04
☐ 12 Ron Guidry	.25	.11	.03
☐ 13 Dave Parker	.25	.11	.03
☐ 14 Cal Ripken	4.00	1.80	.50
☐ 15 Tim Raines	.25	.11	.03
☐ 16 Rod Carew	.75	.35	.09
☐ 17 Mike Schmidt	1.25	.55	.16
☐ 18 George Brett	2.00	.90	.25
☐ 19 Joe Hesketh	.10	.05	.01
☐ 20 Dan Pasqua	.10	.05	.01
☐ 21 Vince Coleman	.25	.11	.03
☐ 22 Tom Seaver	.50	.23	.06
☐ 23 Gary Carter	.35	.16	.04
☐ 24 Orel Hershiser	.35	.16	.04
☐ 25 Pedro Guerrero	.10	.05	.01
☐ 26 Wade Boggs	.75	.35	.09
☐ 27 Bret Saberhagen	.25	.11	.03
☐ 28 Carlton Fisk	.75	.35	.09
☐ 29 Kirk Gibson	.25	.11	.03
☐ 30 Brian Fisher	.10	.05	.01
☐ 31 Don Mattingly	2.50	1.10	.30
☐ 32 Tom Herr	.10	.05	.01
☐ 33 Eddie Murray	1.25	.55	.16
☐ 34 Ryne Sandberg	2.00	.90	.25
☐ 35 Dan Quisenberry	.10	.05	.01
☐ 36 Jim Rice	.25	.11	.03
☐ 37 Dale Murphy	.35	.16	.04
☐ 38 Steve Garvey	.25	.11	.03
☐ 39 Roger McDowell	.10	.05	.01
☐ 40 Earnie Riles	.10	.05	.01
☐ 41 Dwight Gooden	.35	.16	.04
☐ 42 Dave Winfield	.60	.25	.07
☐ 43 Dave Stieb	.10	.05	.01
☐ 44 Bob Horner	.10	.05	.01
☐ 45 Nolan Ryan	4.00	1.80	.50
☐ 46 Ozzie Smith	2.00	.90	.25
☐ 47 George Bell	.10	.05	.01
☐ 48 Gorman Thomas	.10	.05	.01
☐ 49 Tom Browning	.10	.05	.01
☐ 50 Larry Sheets	.10	.05	.01
☐ 51 Pete Rose	1.25	.55	.16
☐ 52 Brett Butler	.25	.11	.03
☐ 53 John Tudor	.10	.05	.01
☐ 54 Phil Bradley	.10	.05	.01
☐ 55 Jeff Reardon	.25	.11	.03
☐ 56 Rich Gossage	.25	.11	.03
☐ 57 Tony Gwynn	2.50	1.10	.30
☐ 58 Ozzie Guillen	.25	.11	.03
☐ 59 Glenn Davis	.10	.05	.01
☐ 60 Darrell Evans	.10	.05	.01

1986 Topps Wax Box Cards

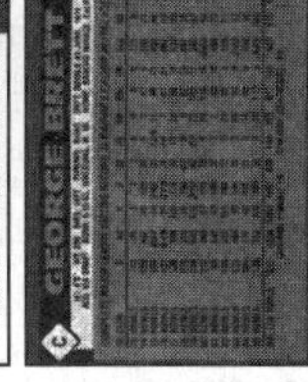

Topps printed cards (each measuring the standard 2 1/2" by 3 1/2") on the bottoms of their wax pack boxes for their regular issue cards; there are four different boxes, each with four cards. These sixteen cards ("numbered" A through P) are listed below; they are not considered an integral part of the regular set but are considered a separate set. The order of the set is alphabetical by player's name. These wax box cards are styled almost exactly like the 1986 Topps regular issue cards. Complete boxes would be worth an additional 25 percent premium over the prices below. The card lettering is sequenced in alphabetical order.

	MINT	NRMT	EXC
COMPLETE SET (16)	8.00	3.60	1.00
COMMON CARD (A-P)	.25	.11	.03
☐ A George Bell	.25	.11	.03
☐ B Wade Boggs	1.00	.45	.12
☐ C George Brett	2.00	.90	.25
☐ D Vince Coleman	.40	.18	.05
☐ E Carlton Fisk	.75	.35	.09
☐ F Dwight Gooden	.60	.25	.07
☐ G Pedro Guerrero	.40	.18	.05
☐ H Ron Guidry	.40	.18	.05
☐ I Reggie Jackson	1.00	.45	.12
☐ J Don Mattingly	2.00	.90	.25
☐ K Oddibe McDowell	.25	.11	.03
☐ L Willie McGee	.40	.18	.05
☐ M Dale Murphy	.60	.25	.07
☐ N Pete Rose	1.50	.70	.19
☐ O Bret Saberhagen	.40	.18	.05
☐ P Fernando Valenzuela	.40	.18	.05

1986 Topps Traded

This 132-card standard-size Traded set was distributed in factory set form in a red and white box through hobby dealers. The cards are identical in style to regular-issue 1986 Topps cards except for whiter stock and t-suffixed numbering. The key extended Rookie Cards in this set are Barry Bonds, Bobby Bonilla, Jose Canseco, Will Clark, Andres Galarraga, Bo Jackson, Wally Joyner, John Kruk, and Kevin Mitchell.

	MINT	NRMT	EXC
COMPLETE FACT.SET (132)	12.00	5.50	1.50
COMMON CARD (1T-132T)	.05	.02	.01
☐ 1T Andy Allanson	.05	.02	.01
☐ 2T Neil Allen	.05	.02	.01
☐ 3T Joaquin Andujar	.05	.02	.01
☐ 4T Paul Assenmacher	.05	.02	.01
☐ 5T Scott Bailes	.05	.02	.01
☐ 6T Don Baylor	.15	.07	.02
☐ 7T Steve Bedrosian	.05	.02	.01
☐ 8T Juan Beniquez	.05	.02	.01
☐ 9T Juan Berenguer	.05	.02	.01
☐ 10T Mike Bielecki	.05	.02	.01
☐ 11T Barry Bonds	3.00	1.35	.35
☐ 12T Bobby Bonilla	.50	.23	.06
☐ 13T Juan Bonilla	.05	.02	.01
☐ 14T Rich Bordi	.05	.02	.01
☐ 15T Steve Boros MG	.05	.02	.01
☐ 16T Rick Burleson	.05	.02	.01
☐ 17T Bill Campbell	.05	.02	.01
☐ 18T Tom Candiotti	.05	.02	.01
☐ 19T John Cangelosi	.05	.02	.01
☐ 20T Jose Canseco	2.00	.90	.25
☐ 21T Carmen Castillo	.05	.02	.01
☐ 22T Rick Cerone	.05	.02	.01
☐ 23T John Cerutti	.05	.02	.01
☐ 24T Will Clark	1.50	.70	.19
☐ 25T Mark Clear	.05	.02	.01
☐ 26T Darnell Coles	.05	.02	.01
☐ 27T Dave Collins	.05	.02	.01
☐ 28T Tim Conroy	.05	.02	.01
☐ 29T Joe Cowley	.05	.02	.01
☐ 30T Joel Davis	.05	.02	.01
☐ 31T Rob Deer	.10	.05	.01
☐ 32T John Denny	.05	.02	.01
☐ 33T Mike Easler	.05	.02	.01
☐ 34T Mark Eichhorn	.05	.02	.01
☐ 35T Steve Farr	.05	.02	.01
☐ 36T Scott Fletcher	.05	.02	.01
☐ 37T Terry Forster	.05	.02	.01
☐ 38T Terry Francona	.05	.02	.01
☐ 39T Jim Fregosi MG	.05	.02	.01
☐ 40T Andres Galarraga	1.50	.70	.19
☐ 41T Ken Griffey	.10	.05	.01
☐ 42T Bill Gullickson	.05	.02	.01
☐ 43T Jose Guzman	.05	.02	.01
☐ 44T Moose Haas	.05	.02	.01
☐ 45T Billy Hatcher	.10	.05	.01
☐ 46T Mike Heath	.05	.02	.01
☐ 47T Tom Hume	.05	.02	.01
☐ 48T Pete Incaviglia	.15	.07	.02
☐ 49T Dane Iorg	.05	.02	.01
☐ 50T Bo Jackson	.75	.35	.09
☐ 51T Wally Joyner	.40	.18	.05
☐ 52T Charlie Kerfeld	.05	.02	.01

Card	MINT	NRMT	EXC
☐ 53T Eric King	.05	.02	.01
☐ 54T Bob Kipper	.05	.02	.01
☐ 55T Wayne Krenchicki	.05	.02	.01
☐ 56T John Kruk	.15	.07	.02
☐ 57T Mike LaCoss	.05	.02	.01
☐ 58T Pete Ladd	.05	.02	.01
☐ 59T Mike Laga	.05	.02	.01
☐ 60T Hal Lanier MG	.05	.02	.01
☐ 61T Dave LaPoint	.05	.02	.01
☐ 62T Rudy Law	.05	.02	.01
☐ 63T Rick Leach	.05	.02	.01
☐ 64T Tim Leary	.05	.02	.01
☐ 65T Dennis Leonard	.05	.02	.01
☐ 66T Jim Leyland MG	.05	.02	.01
☐ 67T Steve Lyons	.05	.02	.01
☐ 68T Mickey Mahler	.05	.02	.01
☐ 69T Candy Maldonado	.05	.02	.01
☐ 70T Roger Mason	.05	.02	.01
☐ 71T Bob McClure	.05	.02	.01
☐ 72T Andy McGaffigan	.05	.02	.01
☐ 73T Gene Michael MG	.05	.02	.01
☐ 74T Kevin Mitchell	.15	.07	.02
☐ 75T Omar Moreno	.05	.02	.01
☐ 76T Jerry Mumphrey	.05	.02	.01
☐ 77T Phil Niekro	.15	.07	.02
☐ 78T Randy Niemann	.05	.02	.01
☐ 79T Juan Nieves	.05	.02	.01
☐ 80T Otis Nixon	.15	.07	.02
☐ 81T Bob Ojeda	.05	.02	.01
☐ 82T Jose Oquendo	.05	.02	.01
☐ 83T Tom Paciorek	.05	.02	.01
☐ 84T David Palmer	.05	.02	.01
☐ 85T Frank Pastore	.05	.02	.01
☐ 86T Lou Piniella MG	.10	.05	.01
☐ 87T Dan Plesac	.05	.02	.01
☐ 88T Darrell Porter	.05	.02	.01
☐ 89T Rey Quinones	.05	.02	.01
☐ 90T Gary Redus	.05	.02	.01
☐ 91T Bip Roberts	.15	.07	.02
☐ 92T Billy Joe Robidoux	.05	.02	.01
☐ 93T Jeff D. Robinson	.05	.02	.01
☐ 94T Gary Roenicke	.05	.02	.01
☐ 95T Ed Romero	.05	.02	.01
☐ 96T Argenis Salazar	.05	.02	.01
☐ 97T Joe Sambito	.05	.02	.01
☐ 98T Billy Sample	.05	.02	.01
☐ 99T Dave Schmidt	.05	.02	.01
☐ 100T Ken Schrom	.05	.02	.01
☐ 101T Tom Seaver	.20	.09	.03
☐ 102T Ted Simmons	.10	.05	.01
☐ 103T Sammy Stewart	.05	.02	.01
☐ 104T Kurt Stillwell	.05	.02	.01
☐ 105T Franklin Stubbs	.05	.02	.01
☐ 106T Dale Sveum	.05	.02	.01
☐ 107T Chuck Tanner MG	.10	.05	.01
☐ 108T Danny Tartabull	.10	.05	.01
☐ 109T Tim Teufel	.05	.02	.01
☐ 110T Bob Tewksbury	.10	.05	.01
☐ 111T Andres Thomas	.05	.02	.01
☐ 112T Milt Thompson	.05	.02	.01
☐ 113T Robby Thompson	.10	.05	.01
☐ 114T Jay Tibbs	.05	.02	.01
☐ 115T Wayne Tolleson	.05	.02	.01
☐ 116T Alex Trevino	.05	.02	.01
☐ 117T Manny Trillo	.05	.02	.01
☐ 118T Ed VandeBerg	.05	.02	.01
☐ 119T Ozzie Virgil	.05	.02	.01
☐ 120T Bob Walk	.05	.02	.01
☐ 121T Gene Walter	.05	.02	.01
☐ 122T Claudell Washington	.05	.02	.01
☐ 123T Bill Wegman	.05	.02	.01
☐ 124T Dick Williams MG	.10	.05	.01
☐ 125T Mitch Williams	.10	.05	.01
☐ 126T Bobby Witt	.10	.05	.01
☐ 127T Todd Worrell	.15	.07	.02
☐ 128T George Wright	.05	.02	.01
☐ 129T Ricky Wright	.05	.02	.01
☐ 130T Steve Yeager	.05	.02	.01
☐ 131T Paul Zuvella	.05	.02	.01
☐ 132T Checklist 1T-132T	.05	.02	.01

1986 Topps Traded Tiffany

For the third consecutive season, Topps issued a Tiffany Update issue to go with their regular issue. These 132 cards feature the same players as in the regular set but have a "glossy" front and very clear back. These cards, released through Topps hobby dealers, were sent out only if the dealer ordered the regular Tiffany set. These cards were printed in Topps' Ireland plant.

	MINT	NRMT	EXC
COMPLETE FACT.SET (132)	50.00	22.00	6.25
COMMON CARD (1T-132T)	.20	.09	.03
*STARS: 4X to 8X BASIC CARDS			
*ROOKIES: 2X to 4X BASIC CARDS			

1986 Topps 3-D

This set consists of 30 plastic-sculpted "cards" each measuring 4 3/8" by 6". Each card was individually wrapped in a red paper wrapper. The card back is blank except for two adhesive strips which could used for mounting the card. Cards are numbered on the front in the lower right corner above the name.

	MINT	NRMT	EXC
COMPLETE SET (30)	12.00	5.50	1.50
COMMON CARD (1-30)	.15	.07	.02

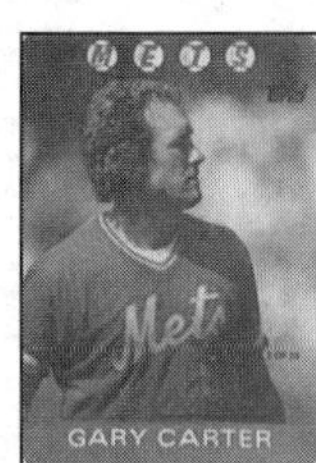

Card	MINT	NRMT	EXC
☐ 1 Bert Blyleven	.15	.07	.02
☐ 2 Gary Carter	.30	.14	.04
☐ 3 Wade Boggs	1.00	.45	.12
☐ 4 Dwight Gooden	.50	.23	.06
☐ 5 George Brett	2.00	.90	.25
☐ 6 Rich Gossage	.30	.14	.04
☐ 7 Darrell Evans	.15	.07	.02
☐ 8 Pedro Guerrero	.15	.07	.02
☐ 9 Ron Guidry	.30	.14	.04
☐ 10 Keith Hernandez	.30	.14	.04
☐ 11 Rickey Henderson	.75	.35	.09
☐ 12 Orel Hershiser	.30	.14	.04
☐ 13 Reggie Jackson	.75	.35	.09
☐ 14 Willie McGee	.30	.14	.04
☐ 15 Don Mattingly	3.00	1.35	.35
☐ 16 Dale Murphy	.50	.23	.06
☐ 17 Jack Morris	.30	.14	.04
☐ 18 Dave Parker	.30	.14	.04
☐ 19 Eddie Murray	1.25	.55	.16
☐ 20 Jeff Reardon	.15	.07	.02
☐ 21 Dan Quisenberry	.15	.07	.02
☐ 22 Pete Rose	1.00	.45	.12
☐ 23 Jim Rice	.30	.14	.04
☐ 24 Mike Schmidt	1.00	.45	.12
☐ 25 Bret Saberhagen	.30	.14	.04
☐ 26 Darryl Strawberry	.30	.14	.04
☐ 27 Dave Stieb	.15	.07	.02
☐ 28 John Tudor	.15	.07	.02
☐ 29 Dave Winfield	.75	.35	.09
☐ 30 Fernando Valenzuela	.30	.14	.04

1986 Topps Gallery of Champions

This 12 card set features various 1985 league leaders or award winners. For the second straight year, these replica cards were issued in either aluminum, bronze or silver. The cards measure approximately 1 1/4" by 1 3/4" and we have sequenced the set in alphabetical order. The bronze cards are valued at 2X to 4X the aluminum cards while the silvers have a value between 5X and 10X of the aluminums.

Card	MINT	NRMT	EXC
COMPLETE SET (12)	75.00	34.00	9.50
COMMON CARD (1-12)	5.00	2.20	.60
☐ 1 Wade Boggs	15.00	6.75	1.85
☐ 2 Vince Coleman	5.00	2.20	.60
☐ 3 Darrell Evans	5.00	2.20	.60
☐ 4 Dwight Gooden	10.00	4.50	1.25
☐ 5 Ozzie Guillen	5.00	2.20	.60
☐ 6 Don Mattingly	25.00	11.00	3.10
☐ 7 Willie McGee	10.00	4.50	1.25
☐ 8 Dale Murphy	15.00	6.75	1.85
☐ 9 Dan Quisenberry	5.00	2.20	.60
☐ 10 Jeff Reardon	5.00	2.20	.60
☐ 11 Pete Rose	20.00	9.00	2.50
☐ 12 Bret Saberhagen	5.00	2.20	.60

1986 Topps Mini Leaders

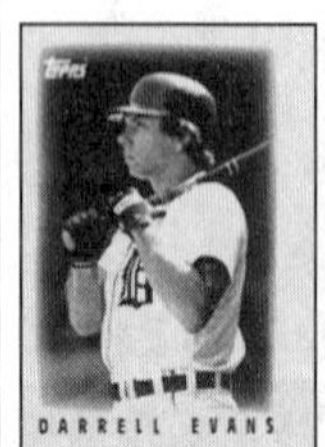

The 1986 Topps Mini set of Major League Leaders features 66 cards of leaders of the various statistical categories for the 1985 season. The cards are numbered on the back and measure approximately 2 1/8" by 2 15/16". They are very similar in design to the Team Leader "Dean" cards in the 1986 Topps regular issue. The order of the set numbering is alphabetical by player's name as well as alphabetical by team city name within league.

Card	MINT	NRMT	EXC
COMPLETE SET (66)	4.00	1.80	.50
COMMON CARD (1-66)	.05	.02	.01
☐ 1 Eddie Murray	.50	.23	.06
☐ 2 Cal Ripken	1.50	.70	.19
☐ 3 Wade Boggs	.40	.18	.05
☐ 4 Dennis Boyd	.05	.02	.01
☐ 5 Dwight Evans	.10	.05	.01
☐ 6 Bruce Hurst	.05	.02	.01
☐ 7 Gary Pettis	.05	.02	.01
☐ 8 Harold Baines	.10	.05	.01
☐ 9 Floyd Bannister	.05	.02	.01
☐ 10 Britt Burns	.05	.02	.01
☐ 11 Carlton Fisk	.30	.14	.04
☐ 12 Brett Butler	.10	.05	.01
☐ 13 Darrell Evans	.10	.05	.01
☐ 14 Jack Morris	.10	.05	.01
☐ 15 Lance Parrish	.05	.02	.01
☐ 16 Walt Terrell	.05	.02	.01
☐ 17 Steve Balboni	.05	.02	.01
☐ 18 George Brett	.75	.35	.09
☐ 19 Charlie Leibrandt	.05	.02	.01
☐ 20 Bret Saberhagen	.15	.07	.02
☐ 21 Lonnie Smith	.05	.02	.01
☐ 22 Willie Wilson	.05	.02	.01
☐ 23 Bert Blyleven	.10	.05	.01
☐ 24 Mike Smithson	.05	.02	.01
☐ 25 Frank Viola	.10	.05	.01
☐ 26 Ron Guidry	.10	.05	.01
☐ 27 Rickey Henderson	.30	.14	.04
☐ 28 Don Mattingly	1.00	.45	.12
☐ 29 Dave Winfield	.25	.11	.03
☐ 30 Mike Moore	.05	.02	.01
☐ 31 Gorman Thomas	.05	.02	.01
☐ 32 Toby Harrah	.05	.02	.01
☐ 33 Charlie Hough	.05	.02	.01
☐ 34 Doyle Alexander	.05	.02	.01
☐ 35 Jimmy Key	.15	.07	.02
☐ 36 Dave Stieb	.05	.02	.01
☐ 37 Dale Murphy	.15	.07	.02
☐ 38 Keith Moreland	.05	.02	.01
☐ 39 Ryne Sandberg	.75	.35	.09
☐ 40 Tom Browning	.05	.02	.01
☐ 41 Dave Parker	.10	.05	.01
☐ 42 Mario Soto	.05	.02	.01
☐ 43 Nolan Ryan	1.50	.70	.19
☐ 44 Pedro Guerrero	.05	.02	.01
☐ 45 Orel Hershiser	.15	.07	.02
☐ 46 Mike Scioscia	.05	.02	.01
☐ 47 Fernando Valenzuela	.10	.05	.01
☐ 48 Bob Welch	.05	.02	.01
☐ 49 Tim Raines	.10	.05	.01
☐ 50 Gary Carter	.15	.07	.02
☐ 51 Sid Fernandez	.05	.02	.01
☐ 52 Dwight Gooden	.15	.07	.02
☐ 53 Keith Hernandez	.10	.05	.01
☐ 54 Juan Samuel	.05	.02	.01
☐ 55 Mike Schmidt	.50	.23	.06
☐ 56 Glenn Wilson	.05	.02	.01
☐ 57 Rick Reuschel	.05	.02	.01
☐ 58 Joaquin Andujar	.05	.02	.01
☐ 59 Jack Clark	.05	.02	.01
☐ 60 Vince Coleman	.10	.05	.01
☐ 61 Danny Cox	.05	.02	.01
☐ 62 Tom Herr	.05	.02	.01
☐ 63 Willie McGee	.10	.05	.01
☐ 64 John Tudor	.05	.02	.01
☐ 65 Tony Gwynn	1.00	.45	.12
☐ 66 Checklist Card	.05	.02	.01

1986 Topps/O-Pee-Chee Stickers

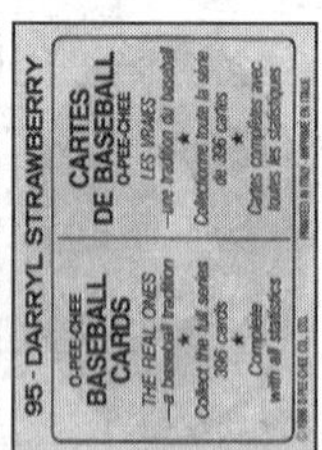

Made in Italy for O-Pee-Chee by Panini, these 315 stickers measure approximately 2 1/8" by 3" and are numbered on both front and back. The fronts feature white-bordered color player photos. The horizontal backs carry a bilingual ad for O-Pee-Chee. An album onto which the stickers could be affixed was available at retail stores. The album and the sticker numbering are organized as follows: 1985 Highlights (1-10), 1985 Championship Series (11-16), 1985 World Series (17-23), Houston Astros (24-33), Atlanta Braves (34-43), St. Louis Cardinals (44-53), Chicago Cubs (54-63), Los Angeles Dodgers (64-73), Montreal Expos (74-83), San Francisco Giants (84-93), New York Mets (94-103), San Diego Padres (104-113), Philadelphia Phillies (114-123), Pittsburgh Pirates (124-133), Cincinnati Reds (134-143), 1985 NL Stat Leaders (144, 145), Foil All-Stars (146-163), 1985 AL Stat Leaders (164, 165), Oakland A's (166-175), California Angels (176-185), Toronto Blue Jays (186-195), Milwaukee Brewers (196-205), Cleveland Indians (206-215), Seattle Mariners (216-225), Baltimore Orioles (226-235), Texas Rangers (236-245), Boston Red Sox (246-255), Kansas City Royals (256-265), Detroit Tigers (266-275), Minnesota Twins (276-285), Chicago White Sox (286-295), New York Yankees (296-305), and Future Stars (306-315). For those stickers featuring more than one player, the other numbers on that sticker are given below in parentheses. The Topps stickers contain offers on the back to obtain either a trip for four to Spring Training of the team of your choice or a complete set of Topps baseball cards directly from Topps.

Card	MINT	NRMT	EXC
COMPLETE SET (315)	15.00	6.75	1.85
COMMON STICKER (1-315)	.05	.02	.01
COMMON FOIL PLAYER	.10	.05	.01
*TOPPS AND OPC: SAME VALUE			
☐ 1 Pete Rose FOIL (Top half)	.60	.25	.07
☐ 2 Pete Rose FOIL (Bottom half)	.60	.25	.07
☐ 3 George Brett (175)	.75	.35	.09
☐ 4 Rod Carew (178)	.40	.18	.05
☐ 5 Vince Coleman (179)	.15	.07	.02
☐ 6 Dwight Gooden (180)	.30	.14	.04
☐ 7 Phil Niekro (181)	.15	.07	.02
☐ 8 Tony Perez (182)	.15	.07	.02
☐ 9 Nolan Ryan (183)	2.00	.90	.25
☐ 10 Tom Seaver (184)	.50	.23	.06
☐ 11 NL Championship (Ozzie Smith batting)	.15	.07	.02
☐ 12 NL Championship (Bill Madlock)	.10	.05	.01
☐ 13 NL Championship (Cardinals celebrate)	.10	.05	.01
☐ 14 AL Championship (Al Oliver swings)	.10	.05	.01
☐ 15 AL Championship (Jim Sundberg)	.05	.02	.01
☐ 16 AL Championship (George Brett swings)	.75	.35	.09
☐ 17 World Series (Bret Saberhagen)	.10	.05	.01
☐ 18 World Series (Dane Iorg swings)	.05	.02	.01
☐ 19 World Series (Tito Landrum)	.05	.02	.01
☐ 20 World Series (John Tudor)	.05	.02	.01
☐ 21 World Series (Buddy Biancalana)	.05	.02	.01
☐ 22 World Series (Darryl Motley)	.05	.02	.01
☐ 23 World Series (George Brett and Frank White)	.30	.14	.04
☐ 24 Nolan Ryan	2.00	.90	.25
☐ 25 Bill Doran	.05	.02	.01
☐ 26 Jose Cruz (185)	.10	.05	.01
☐ 27 Mike Scott (188)	.05	.02	.01
☐ 28 Kevin Bass (189)	.05	.02	.01
☐ 29 Glenn Davis (190)	.10	.05	.01
☐ 30 Mark Bailey (191)	.05	.02	.01
☐ 31 Dave Smith (192)	.05	.02	.01
☐ 32 Phil Garner (193)	.05	.02	.01
☐ 33 Dickie Thon (194)	.05	.02	.01
☐ 34 Bob Horner	.05	.02	.01
☐ 35 Dale Murphy	.15	.07	.02
☐ 36 Glenn Hubbard (195)	.05	.02	.01
☐ 37 Bruce Sutter (198)	.10	.05	.01
☐ 38 Ken Oberkfell (199)	.05	.02	.01
☐ 39 Claudell Washington (200)	.05	.02	.01
☐ 40 Steve Bedrosian (201)	.05	.02	.01
☐ 41 Terry Harper (202)	.05	.02	.01
☐ 42 Rafael Ramirez (203)	.05	.02	.01
☐ 43 Rick Mahler (204)	.05	.02	.01
☐ 44 Joaquin Andujar	.05	.02	.01
☐ 45 Willie McGee	.10	.05	.01
☐ 46 Ozzie Smith (205)	.40	.18	.05
☐ 47 Vince Coleman (208)	.15	.07	.02
☐ 48 Danny Cox (209)	.05	.02	.01
☐ 49 Tom Herr (210)	.05	.02	.01
☐ 50 Jack Clark (211)	.10	.05	.01
☐ 51 Andy Van Slyke (212)	.10	.05	.01
☐ 52 John Tudor (213)	.05	.02	.01
☐ 53 Terry Pendleton (214)	.15	.07	.02
☐ 54 Keith Moreland	.05	.02	.01
☐ 55 Ryne Sandberg	.60	.25	.07
☐ 56 Lee Smith (215)	.15	.07	.02
☐ 57 Steve Trout (218)	.05	.02	.01
☐ 58 Jody Davis (219)	.05	.02	.01
☐ 59 Gary Matthews (220)	.05	.02	.01
☐ 60 Leon Durham (221)	.05	.02	.01
☐ 61 Rick Sutcliffe (222)	.05	.02	.01
☐ 62 Dennis Eckersley (223)	.15	.07	.02
☐ 63 Bob Dernier (224)	.05	.02	.01
☐ 64 Fernando Valenzuela	.10	.05	.01
☐ 65 Pedro Guerrero	.05	.02	.01
☐ 66 Jerry Reuss (225)	.05	.02	.01
☐ 67 Greg Brock (228)	.05	.02	.01
☐ 68 Mike Scioscia (229)	.05	.02	.01
☐ 69 Ken Howell (230)	.05	.02	.01
☐ 70 Bill Madlock (231)	.05	.02	.01
☐ 71 Mike Marshall (232)	.05	.02	.01
☐ 72 Steve Sax (233)	.05	.02	.01
☐ 73 Orel Hershiser (234)	.15	.07	.02
☐ 74 Andre Dawson	.15	.07	.02
☐ 75 Tim Raines	.10	.05	.01
☐ 76 Jeff Reardon (235)	.10	.05	.01
☐ 77 Hubie Brooks (238)	.05	.02	.01
☐ 78 Bill Gullickson (239)	.05	.02	.01
☐ 79 Bryn Smith (240)	.05	.02	.01
☐ 80 Terry Francona (241)	.05	.02	.01
☐ 81 Vance Law (242)	.05	.02	.01
☐ 82 Tim Wallach (243)	.05	.02	.01

☐ 83 He.Winningham (244) .05 .02 .01
☐ 84 Jeff Leonard .05 .02 .01
☐ 85 Chris Brown .05 .02 .01
☐ 86 Scott Garrelts (245) .05 .02 .01
☐ 87 Jose Uribe (248) .05 .02 .01
☐ 88 Manny Trillo (249) .05 .02 .01
☐ 89 Dan Driessen (250) .05 .02 .01
☐ 90 Dan Gladden (251) .05 .02 .01
☐ 91 Mark Davis (252) .05 .02 .01
☐ 92 Bob Brenly (253) .05 .02 .01
☐ 93 Mike Krukow (254) .05 .02 .01
☐ 94 Dwight Gooden .30 .14 .04
☐ 95 Darryl Strawberry .15 .07 .02
☐ 96 Gary Carter (255) .10 .05 .01
☐ 97 Wally Backman (258) .05 .02 .01
☐ 98 Ron Darling (259) .05 .02 .01
☐ 99 Keith Hernandez(260) .10 .05 .01
☐ 100 George Foster (261) .10 .05 .01
☐ 101 Howard Johnson (262) .10 .05 .01
☐ 102 Rafael Santana (263) .05 .02 .01
☐ 103 Roger McDowell (264) .05 .02 .01
☐ 104 Steve Garvey .15 .07 .02
☐ 105 Tony Gwynn 1.00 .45 .12
☐ 106 Graig Nettles (265) .10 .05 .01
☐ 107 Rich Gossage (268) .10 .05 .01
☐ 108 Andy Hawkins (269) .05 .02 .01
☐ 109 Carmelo Martinez (270) .05 .02 .01
☐ 110 Garry Templeton(271) .05 .02 .01
☐ 111 Terry Kennedy (272) .05 .02 .01
☐ 112 Tim Flannery (273) .05 .02 .01
☐ 113 LaMarr Hoyt (274) .05 .02 .01
☐ 114 Mike Schmidt .60 .25 .07
☐ 115 Ozzie Virgil .05 .02 .01
☐ 116 Steve Carlton (275) .40 .18 .05
☐ 117 Garry Maddox (278) .05 .02 .01
☐ 118 Glenn Wilson (279) .05 .02 .01
☐ 119 Kevin Gross (280) .05 .02 .01
☐ 120 Von Hayes (281) .05 .02 .01
☐ 121 Juan Samuel (282) .05 .02 .01
☐ 122 Rick Schu (283) .05 .02 .01
☐ 123 Shane Rawley (284) .05 .02 .01
☐ 124 Johnny Ray .05 .02 .01
☐ 125 Tony Pena .05 .02 .01
☐ 126 Rick Reuschel (285) .05 .02 .01
☐ 127 Sammy Khalifa (288) .05 .02 .01
☐ 128 Marvell Wynne (289) .05 .02 .01
☐ 129 Jason Thompson (290) .05 .02 .01
☐ 130 Rick Rhoden (291) .05 .02 .01
☐ 131 Bill Almon (292) .05 .02 .01
☐ 132 Joe Orsulak (293) .05 .02 .01
☐ 133 Jim Morrison (294) .05 .02 .01
☐ 134 Pete Rose .75 .35 .09
☐ 135 Dave Parker .10 .05 .01
☐ 136 Mario Soto (295) .05 .02 .01
☐ 137 Dave Concepcion(298) .10 .05 .01
☐ 138 Ron Oester (299) .05 .02 .01
☐ 139 Buddy Bell (300) .10 .05 .01
☐ 140 Ted Power (301) .05 .02 .01
☐ 141 Tom Browning (302) .05 .02 .01
☐ 142 John Franco (303) .15 .07 .02
☐ 143 Tony Perez (304) .15 .07 .02
☐ 144 Willie McGee (305) .10 .05 .01
☐ 145 Dale Murphy (306) .15 .07 .02
☐ 146 Tony Gwynn FOIL 1.50 .70 .19
☐ 147 Tom Herr FOIL .10 .05 .01
☐ 148 Steve Garvey FOIL .30 .14 .04
☐ 149 Dale Murphy FOIL .15 .07 .02
☐ 150 Darryl Strawberry FOIL .30 .14 .04
☐ 151 Graig Nettles FOIL .15 .07 .02
☐ 152 Terry Kennedy FOIL .10 .05 .01
☐ 153 Ozzie Smith FOIL .60 .25 .07
☐ 154 LaMarr Hoyt FOIL .10 .05 .01
☐ 155 Rickey Henderson FOIL .40 .18 .05
☐ 156 Lou Whitaker FOIL .10 .05 .01
☐ 157 George Brett FOIL 1.25 .55 .16
☐ 158 Eddie Murray FOIL .50 .23 .06
☐ 159 Cal Ripken FOIL 3.00 1.35 .35
☐ 160 Dave Winfield FOIL .40 .18 .05
☐ 161 Jim Rice FOIL .10 .05 .01
☐ 162 Carlton Fisk FOIL .40 .18 .05
☐ 163 Jack Morris FOIL .10 .05 .01
☐ 164 Wade Boggs (307) .30 .14 .04
☐ 165 Darrell Evans (308) .10 .05 .01
☐ 166 Mike Davis .05 .02 .01
☐ 167 Dave Kingman .10 .05 .01
☐ 168 Alfredo Griffin(309) .05 .02 .01
☐ 169 Carney Lansford(310) .10 .05 .01
☐ 170 Bruce Bochte (311) .05 .02 .01
☐ 171 Dwayne Murphy (312) .05 .02 .01
☐ 172 Dave Collins (313) .05 .02 .01
☐ 173 Chris Codiroli (314) .05 .02 .01
☐ 174 Mike Heath (315) .05 .02 .01
☐ 175 Jay Howell (3) .05 .02 .01
☐ 176 Rod Carew .40 .18 .05
☐ 177 Reggie Jackson .50 .23 .06
☐ 178 Doug DeCinces (4) .05 .02 .01
☐ 179 Bob Boone (5) .10 .05 .01
☐ 180 Ron Romanick (6) .05 .02 .01
☐ 181 Bob Grich (7) .10 .05 .01
☐ 182 Donnie Moore (8) .05 .02 .01
☐ 183 Brian Downing (9) .05 .02 .01
☐ 184 Ruppert Jones (10) .05 .02 .01
☐ 185 Juan Beniquez (26) .05 .02 .01
☐ 186 Dave Stieb .05 .02 .01
☐ 187 George Bell .05 .02 .01
☐ 188 Willie Upshaw (27) .05 .02 .01
☐ 189 Tom Henke (28) .10 .05 .01
☐ 190 Damaso Garcia (29) .05 .02 .01
☐ 191 Jimmy Key (30) .15 .07 .02
☐ 192 Jesse Barfield (31) .05 .02 .01
☐ 193 Dennis Lamp (32) .05 .02 .01
☐ 194 Tony Fernandez (33) .05 .02 .01
☐ 195 Lloyd Moseby (36) .05 .02 .01
☐ 196 Cecil Cooper .10 .05 .01
☐ 197 Robin Yount .15 .07 .02
☐ 198 Rollie Fingers (37) .15 .07 .02
☐ 199 Ted Simmons (38) .10 .05 .01
☐ 200 Ben Oglivie (39) .05 .02 .01
☐ 201 Moose Haas (40) .05 .02 .01
☐ 202 Jim Gantner (41) .05 .02 .01
☐ 203 Paul Molitor (42) .15 .07 .02
☐ 204 Charlie Moore (43) .05 .02 .01
☐ 205 Danny Darwin (46) .05 .02 .01
☐ 206 Brett Butler .10 .05 .01
☐ 207 Brook Jacoby .05 .02 .01
☐ 208 Andre Thornton (47) .05 .02 .01
☐ 209 Tom Waddell (48) .05 .02 .01
☐ 210 Tony Bernazard (49) .05 .02 .01
☐ 211 Julio Franco (50) .10 .05 .01
☐ 212 Pat Tabler (51) .05 .02 .01
☐ 213 Joe Carter (52) .30 .14 .04
☐ 214 George Vukovich (53) .05 .02 .01
☐ 215 Rich Thompson (56) .05 .02 .01
☐ 216 Gorman Thomas .05 .02 .01
☐ 217 Phil Bradley .05 .02 .01
☐ 218 Alvin Davis (57) .05 .02 .01
☐ 219 Jim Presley (58) .05 .02 .01
☐ 220 Matt Young (59) .05 .02 .01
☐ 221 Mike Moore (60) .05 .02 .01
☐ 222 Dave Henderson (61) .05 .02 .01
☐ 223 Ed Nunez (62) .05 .02 .01
☐ 224 Spike Owen (63) .05 .02 .01
☐ 225 Mark Langston (66) .10 .05 .01
☐ 226 Cal Ripken 2.00 .90 .25
☐ 227 Eddie Murray .30 .14 .04
☐ 228 Fred Lynn (67) .10 .05 .01
☐ 229 Lee Lacy (68) .05 .02 .01
☐ 230 Scott McGregor (69) .05 .02 .01
☐ 231 Storm Davis (70) .05 .02 .01
☐ 232 Rick Dempsey (71) .10 .05 .01
☐ 233 Mike Boddicker (72) .05 .02 .01
☐ 234 Mike Young (73) .05 .02 .01
☐ 235 Sammy Stewart (76) .05 .02 .01
☐ 236 Pete O'Brien .05 .02 .01
☐ 237 Oddibe McDowell .05 .02 .01
☐ 238 Toby Harrah (77) .05 .02 .01
☐ 239 Gary Ward (78) .05 .02 .01
☐ 240 Larry Parrish (79) .05 .02 .01
☐ 241 Charlie Hough (80) .10 .05 .01
☐ 242 Burt Hooton (81) .05 .02 .01
☐ 243 Don Slaught (82) .05 .02 .01
☐ 244 Curt Wilkerson (83) .05 .02 .01
☐ 245 Greg Harris (86) .05 .02 .01
☐ 246 Jim Rice .10 .05 .01
☐ 247 Wade Boggs .30 .14 .04
☐ 248 Rich Gedman (87) .05 .02 .01
☐ 249 Dennis Boyd (88) .05 .02 .01
☐ 250 Marty Barrett (89) .05 .02 .01
☐ 251 Dwight Evans (90) .10 .05 .01
☐ 252 Bill Buckner (91) .10 .05 .01
☐ 253 Bob Stanley (92) .05 .02 .01
☐ 254 Tony Armas (93) .05 .02 .01
☐ 255 Mike Easler (96) .05 .02 .01
☐ 256 George Brett .75 .35 .09
☐ 257 Dan Quisenberry .05 .02 .01
☐ 258 Willie Wilson (97) .05 .02 .01
☐ 259 Jim Sundberg (98) .05 .02 .01
☐ 260 Bret Saberhagen (99) .15 .07 .02
☐ 261 Bud Black (100) .05 .02 .01
☐ 262 Charlie Leibrandt (101) .05 .02 .01
☐ 263 Frank White (102) .10 .05 .01
☐ 264 Lonnie Smith (103) .05 .02 .01
☐ 265 Steve Balboni (106) .05 .02 .01
☐ 266 Kirk Gibson .10 .05 .01
☐ 267 Alan Trammell .15 .07 .02
☐ 268 Jack Morris (107) .10 .05 .01
☐ 269 Darrell Evans (108) .10 .05 .01
☐ 270 Dan Petry (109) .05 .02 .01
☐ 271 Larry Herndon (110) .05 .02 .01
☐ 272 Lou Whitaker (111) .10 .05 .01
☐ 273 Lance Parrish (112) .10 .05 .01
☐ 274 Chet Lemon (113) .05 .02 .01
☐ 275 Willie Hernandez (116) .05 .02 .01
☐ 276 Tom Brunansky .05 .02 .01
☐ 277 Kent Hrbek .10 .05 .01
☐ 278 Mark Salas (117) .05 .02 .01
☐ 279 Bert Blyleven (118) .10 .05 .01
☐ 280 Tim Teufel (119) .05 .02 .01
☐ 281 Ron Davis (120) .05 .02 .01
☐ 282 Mike Smithson (121) .05 .02 .01
☐ 283 Gary Gaetti (122) .10 .05 .01
☐ 284 Frank Viola (123) .10 .05 .01
☐ 285 Kirby Puckett (126) 1.50 .70 .19
☐ 286 Carlton Fisk .30 .14 .04
☐ 287 Tom Seaver .50 .23 .06
☐ 288 Harold Baines (127) .10 .05 .01
☐ 289 Ron Kittle (128) .05 .02 .01
☐ 290 Bob James (129) .05 .02 .01
☐ 291 Rudy Law (130) .05 .02 .01
☐ 292 Britt Burns (131) .05 .02 .01
☐ 293 Greg Walker (132) .05 .02 .01
☐ 294 Ozzie Guillen (133) .15 .07 .02
☐ 295 Tim Hulett (136) .05 .02 .01
☐ 296 Don Mattingly 1.50 .70 .19
☐ 297 Rickey Henderson .25 .11 .03
☐ 298 Dave Winfield (137) .15 .07 .02
☐ 299 Butch Wynegar (138) .05 .02 .01
☐ 300 Don Baylor (139) .10 .05 .01
☐ 301 Eddie Whitson (140) .05 .02 .01
☐ 302 Ron Guidry (141) .10 .05 .01
☐ 303 Dave Righetti (142) .05 .02 .01
☐ 304 Bobby Meacham (143) .05 .02 .01
☐ 305 Willie Randolph(144) .10 .05 .01
☐ 306 Vince Coleman (145) .15 .07 .02
☐ 307 Oddibe McDowell(164) .05 .02 .01
☐ 308 Larry Sheets (165) .05 .02 .01
☐ 309 Ozzie Guillen (168) .15 .07 .02
☐ 310 Ernie Riles (169) .05 .02 .01
☐ 311 Chris Brown (170) .05 .02 .01
☐ 312 Brian Fisher and Roger McDowell (171) .05 .02 .01
☐ 313 Tom Browning (172) .05 .02 .01
☐ 314 Glenn Davis (173) .05 .02 .01
☐ 315 Mark Salas (174) .05 .02 .01
☐ xx Album 1.00 .45 .12

1986 Topps Rose

This set of 120 different standard-size cards is dedicated to Pete Rose. The set was sold in a red and white box and distributed by Renata Galasso, Inc. The checklist below gives the distinguishing features of each of the cards. Many of the backs feature a question and answer back. Since many of the pictures are similar, the back question is frequently excerpted below. The first three cards feature traditional statistical backs and the last 30 cards (91-120) feature backs that form a puzzle which, when completely assembled, shows in color all of Pete's Topps baseball cards up through 1985. In the set there are several cards which picture paintings of Pete at various stages of his career by artist Ron Lewis.

	MINT	NRMT	EXC
COMPLETE SET (120)	12.50	5.50	1.55
COMMON CARD (1-120)	.15	.07	.02

☐ 1 Pete Rose .35 .16 .04
Statistics '60s; Lewis painting
☐ 2 Pete Rose .15 .07 .02
Statistics '70s; crew cut photo
☐ 3 Pete Rose .15 .07 .02
Statistics '80s
☐ 4 Pete Rose .15 .07 .02
and kids with Hickok Belt
☐ 5 Pete Rose .15 .07 .02
Pete Rose Jr.
hit number 3631
☐ 6 Pete Rose .15 .07 .02
polishing old roadster
☐ 7 Pete Rose .15 .07 .02
plays softball
☐ 8 Pete Rose .15 .07 .02
4000th hit as Expo
☐ 9 Pete Rose .15 .07 .02
in Army
☐ 10 Pete Rose .15 .07 .02
Did Pete collect
Lewis painting
☐ 11 Pete Rose .15 .07 .02
Hobbies
☐ 12 Pete Rose .15 .07 .02
Sibling relationships
☐ 13 Pete Rose .15 .07 .02
nationality
☐ 14 Pete Rose .15 .07 .02
Think of the Past
☐ 15 Pete Rose .15 .07 .02
Being Drafted
☐ 16 Pete Rose .15 .07 .02
Served in Armed Forces
☐ 17 Pete Rose .15 .07 .02
Association with Dad
☐ 18 Pete Rose .15 .07 .02
No nickname
☐ 19 Pete Rose .15 .07 .02
Typical teenager
☐ 20 Pete Rose .15 .07 .02
All-City Football
Lewis painting
☐ 21 Pete Rose .15 .07 .02
Dad's influence
☐ 22 Pete Rose .15 .07 .02
idol
☐ 23 Pete Rose .15 .07 .02
Misses Dad
☐ 24 Pete Rose .15 .07 .02
Natural Ability
☐ 25 Pete Rose .15 .07 .02
What position
☐ 26 Pete Rose .15 .07 .02
First Tryout
☐ 27 Pete Rose .15 .07 .02
New Drafting System
☐ 28 Pete Rose .15 .07 .02
Natural Switcher
☐ 29 Pete Rose .15 .07 .02
Concentrating on Left
☐ 30 Pete Rose .15 .07 .02
on phone; Lewis painting
☐ 31 Pete Rose .15 .07 .02
Might not make it
☐ 32 Pete Rose .15 .07 .02
First ML game
☐ 33 Pete Rose .15 .07 .02
Nervous in first game
☐ 34 Pete Rose .15 .07 .02
Talked to old timers
☐ 35 Pete Rose .15 .07 .02
Enjoyed talking to the greats
☐ 36 Pete Rose .15 .07 .02
Favorite position
☐ 37 Pete Rose .15 .07 .02
Toughest position
☐ 38 Pete Rose .15 .07 .02
in batting cage
☐ 39 Pete Rose .15 .07 .02
Previous managers
☐ 40 Pete Rose .15 .07 .02
Big adjustment; Lewis painting
☐ 41 Pete Rose .15 .07 .02
30 Triples in 1961
☐ 42 Pete Rose .15 .07 .02
Winter ball
☐ 43 Pete Rose .15 .07 .02
Rookie of the Year
☐ 44 Pete Rose .15 .07 .02
Kennedy assassination
☐ 45 Pete Rose .15 .07 .02
Run to first on walks
☐ 46 Pete Rose .15 .07 .02
Showboating
☐ 47 Pete Rose .15 .07 .02
Remembered for what
☐ 48 Pete Rose .15 .07 .02
Charlie Hustle
☐ 49 Pete Rose .15 .07 .02
Play with enthusiasm
☐ 50 Pete Rose .15 .07 .02
Lose enthusiasm
☐ 51 Pete Rose .15 .07 .02
Enjoy traveling
☐ 52 Pete Rose .15 .07 .02
America
☐ 53 Pete Rose .15 .07 .02
Favorite food
☐ 54 Pete Rose .15 .07 .02
Goal setting
☐ 55 Pete Rose .15 .07 .02
Guess hitter
☐ 56 Pete Rose .15 .07 .02
Tyler Rose
with horse
☐ 57 Pete Rose .15 .07 .02
Artificial turf
☐ 58 Pete Rose .15 .07 .02
Day or Night
☐ 59 Pete Rose .15 .07 .02
Broken Concentration
☐ 60 Pete Rose .15 .07 .02
Favorite park; Lewis painting
☐ 61 Pete Rose .15 .07 .02
Consecutive games
☐ 62 Pete Rose .15 .07 .02
Toughest pitchers
☐ 63 Pete Rose .15 .07 .02
Bear down
☐ 64 Pete Rose .15 .07 .02
Head first slide
☐ 65 Pete Rose .15 .07 .02
Sliding advice
☐ 66 Pete Rose .15 .07 .02
Proudest record
☐ 67 Pete Rose .15 .07 .02
Wanted to be Manager
☐ 68 Pete Rose .15 .07 .02
Ray Fosse
collision
☐ 69 Pete Rose .15 .07 .02
Ray Fosse
Pete got hurt in collision
☐ 70 Pete Rose .15 .07 .02
Bud Harrelson
fight; Lewis painting
☐ 71 Pete Rose .15 .07 .02
Transition to outfield
☐ 72 Pete Rose .15 .07 .02

Asked to outfield
☐ 73 Pete Rose .15 .07 .02
World Champs
☐ 74 Pete Rose .15 .07 .02
Lineup card
☐ 75 Pete Rose .15 .07 .02
On deck before hit 4192
☐ 76 Pete Rose .15 .07 .02
Hit 4192 Swing
☐ 77 Pete Rose .15 .07 .02
Hit 4192 Follow thru
☐ 78 Pete Rose .15 .07 .02
Watching 4192
☐ 79 Pete Rose .15 .07 .02
Keep in shape
☐ 80 Pete Rose .15 .07 .02
Key to Hitting
☐ 81 Pete Rose .15 .07 .02
Batting Practice
☐ 82 Pete Rose .15 .07 .02
How to Pitch to Pete
☐ 83 Pete Rose .15 .07 .02
Pete Rose Jr.
Hugs
☐ 84 Pete Rose .15 .07 .02
Knockdown pitches
☐ 85 Pete Rose .15 .07 .02
Spitball
☐ 86 Pete Rose .15 .07 .02
Illegal pitches
☐ 87 Pete Rose .15 .07 .02
Babe Ruth
☐ 88 Pete Rose .15 .07 .02
Talking to Reagan
☐ 89 Pete Rose .15 .07 .02
Compared to Cobb
☐ 90 Pete Rose .15 .07 .02
Goals Left
☐ 91 Pete Rose .15 .07 .02
Standing in dugout
☐ 92 Pete Rose .15 .07 .02
Expo batting left
☐ 93 Pete Rose .15 .07 .02
Red batting left
☐ 94 Pete Rose .15 .07 .02
Red looking right
☐ 95 Pete Rose .15 .07 .02
Phillies with fence
☐ 96 Pete Rose .15 .07 .02
With goatee
☐ 97 Pete Rose .15 .07 .02
Reds smiling left
☐ 98 Pete Rose .15 .07 .02
Reds batting right
☐ 99 Pete Rose .15 .07 .02
as a boy
☐ 100 Pete Rose .15 .07 .02
Reds holding bat
☐ 101 Pete Rose .15 .07 .02
Reds batting left; Lewis painting
☐ 102 Pete Rose .15 .07 .02
Reds swinging left
☐ 103 Pete Rose .15 .07 .02
Phillies pensive
☐ 104 Pete Rose .15 .07 .02
Reds first base
☐ 105 Pete Rose .15 .07 .02
Reds smiling '60s
☐ 106 Pete Rose .15 .07 .02
Collision at home
☐ 107 Pete Rose .15 .07 .02
Reds looking straight
☐ 108 Pete Rose .15 .07 .02
Reds batting left; looking serious
☐ 109 Pete Rose .15 .07 .02
Head First Slide
☐ 110 Pete Rose .15 .07 .02
Swing follow through
☐ 111 Pete Rose .15 .07 .02
Pre-game warm up
☐ 112 Pete Rose .15 .07 .02
Reds batting; lefty '80s
☐ 113 Pete Rose .15 .07 .02
Diving for pop up
☐ 114 Pete Rose .15 .07 .02
Expo at locker
☐ 115 Pete Rose .15 .07 .02
with son
☐ 116 Pete Rose .15 .07 .02
Collision at plate
☐ 117 Pete Rose .15 .07 .02
In batting cage
☐ 118 Pete Rose .15 .07 .02
Reds batting; lefty '70s
☐ 119 Pete Rose .15 .07 .02
On one knee
☐ 120 Pete Rose .25 .11 .03
Scoreboard

1986 Topps Super

This 60-card set actually consists of giant-sized versions of the Topps regular issue of some of the most popular players. The cards measure 4 7/8" by 6 7/8". Cards are very similar to the Topps regular issue; two exceptions are that on the back they are numbered differently and an

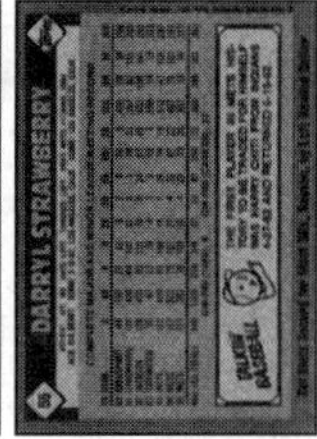

additional line of type is printed at the bottom of the back noting an accomplishment of that player at the end of the 1985 season.

	MINT	NRMT	EXC
COMPLETE SET (60)	14.00	6.25	1.75
COMMON CARD (1-60)	.10	.05	.01
☐ 1 Don Mattingly	2.50	1.10	.30
☐ 2 Willie McGee	.25	.11	.03
☐ 3 Bret Saberhagen	.25	.11	.03
☐ 4 Dwight Gooden	.40	.18	.05
☐ 5 Dan Quisenberry	.10	.05	.01
☐ 6 Jeff Reardon	.10	.05	.01
☐ 7 Ozzie Guillen	.10	.05	.01
☐ 8 Vince Coleman	.25	.11	.03
☐ 9 Harold Baines	.25	.11	.03
☐ 10 Jorge Bell	.10	.05	.01
☐ 11 Bert Blyleven	.25	.11	.03
☐ 12 Wade Boggs	.75	.35	.09
☐ 13 Phil Bradley	.10	.05	.01
☐ 14 George Brett	1.25	.55	.16
☐ 15 Hubie Brooks	.10	.05	.01
☐ 16 Tom Browning	.10	.05	.01
☐ 17 Bill Buckner	.10	.05	.01
☐ 18 Brett Butler	.25	.11	.03
☐ 19 Gary Carter	.40	.18	.05
☐ 20 Cecil Cooper	.10	.05	.01
☐ 21 Darrell Evans	.10	.05	.01
☐ 22 Dwight Evans	.25	.11	.03
☐ 23 Carlton Fisk	.40	.18	.05
☐ 24 Steve Garvey	.40	.18	.05
☐ 25 Kirk Gibson	.25	.11	.03
☐ 26 Rich Gossage	.25	.11	.03
☐ 27 Pedro Guerrero	.10	.05	.01
☐ 28 Ron Guidry	.25	.11	.03
☐ 29 Tony Gwynn	2.00	.90	.25
☐ 30 Rickey Henderson	.60	.25	.07
☐ 31 Keith Hernandez	.25	.11	.03
☐ 32 Tom Herr	.10	.05	.01
☐ 33 Orel Hershiser	.40	.18	.05
☐ 34 Jay Howell	.10	.05	.01
☐ 35 Reggie Jackson	.60	.25	.07
☐ 36 Bob James	.10	.05	.01
☐ 37 Charlie Leibrandt	.10	.05	.01
☐ 38 Jack Morris	.25	.11	.03
☐ 39 Dale Murphy	.40	.18	.05
☐ 40 Eddie Murray	.75	.35	.09
☐ 41 Dave Parker	.25	.11	.03
☐ 42 Tim Raines	.25	.11	.03
☐ 43 Jim Rice	.25	.11	.03
☐ 44 Dave Righetti	.10	.05	.01
☐ 45 Cal Ripken	3.00	1.35	.35
☐ 46 Pete Rose	.75	.35	.09
☐ 47 Nolan Ryan	3.00	1.35	.35
☐ 48 Ryne Sandberg	1.50	.70	.19
☐ 49 Mike Schmidt	.75	.35	.09
☐ 50 Tom Seaver	.50	.23	.06
☐ 51 Bryn Smith	.10	.05	.01
☐ 52 Lee Smith	.40	.18	.05
☐ 53 Ozzie Smith	1.50	.70	.19
☐ 54 Dave Stieb	.10	.05	.01
☐ 55 Darryl Strawberry	.40	.18	.05
☐ 56 Gorman Thomas	.10	.05	.01
☐ 57 John Tudor	.10	.05	.01
☐ 58 Fernando Valenzuela	.25	.11	.03
☐ 59 Willie Wilson	.10	.05	.01
☐ 60 Dave Winfield	.60	.25	.07

1986 Topps Tattoos

This set of 24 different tattoo sheets was distributed one sheet (with gum) per pack as a separate issue by Topps (and also by O-Pee-Chee). Each tattoo sheet measures approximately 3 7/16" by 14 1/4" whereas the individual player tattoos are approximately 1 13/16" by 2 3/8". The wrapper advertises 18 tattoos in the pack, which includes eight small (half-size) generic action shots. The players have their names and team names reverse printed beneath their transfers. The 1986 Topps (or O-Pee-Chee) copyright mark is shown at the bottom right. The checklist below lists only the individual player tattoos; they are listed in order of appearance top to bottom on the sheet. Each tattoo sheet is numbered at the top "X of 24."

MINT NRMT EXC
COMPLETE SET (24) 15.00 6.75 1.85
COMMON SHEET (1-24) .10 .05 .01

☐ 1 Dickie Thon .60 .25 .07
Charlie Leibrandt
Dave Winfield
Lee Smith
Julio Franco
Keith Hernandez
Jack Perconte
Rich Gossage
☐ 2 Dale Murphy .75 .35 .09
Brian Fisher
Bret Saberhagen
Shawon Dunston
Jesse Barfield
Moose Haas
Dennis Eckersley
Mike Moore
☐ 3 Steve Carlton .40 .18 .05
Dan Quisenberry
Bob James
Bob Brenly
George Bell
Jose DeLeon
Andre Thornton
Bob Horner
☐ 4 Johnny Ray 2.50 1.10 .30
Darrell Evans
Mike Davis
Leon Durham
Harold Baines
Cal Ripken
Glenn Hubbard
Ted Simmons
☐ 5 Jesse Orosco .40 .18 .05
Rick Dempsey
John Candelaria
Tony Pena
Brook Jacoby
Gary Matthews
Ozzie Guillen
Steve Garvey
☐ 6 Ron Kittle 1.50 .70 .19
Pete Rose
Sammy Khalifa
Bruce Bochte
Scott McGregor
Mookie Wilson
George Brett
Cecil Cooper
☐ 7 Larry Sheets 2.50 1.10 .30
John Franco
Graig Nettles
Don Mattingly
Carney Lansford
Rick Reuschel
Don Sutton
Mike Schmidt
☐ 8 Phil Niekro 1.00 .45 .12
Ryne Sandberg
Mike Krukow
Fred Lynn
Willie Hernandez
Pat Tabler
Ed Nunez
Cecilio Guante
☐ 9 Chris Codiroli .50 .23 .06
Glenn Wilson
Rick Rhoden
Brett Butler
Robin Yount
Dave Parker
Jim Gantner
Charlie Hough
☐ 10 Chet Lemon .75 .35 .09
Mike Smithson
Ron Darling
Tom Seaver
Von Hayes
Tom Browning
Bruce Sutter
Alan Trammell
☐ 11 Rick Mahler .25 .11 .03
Dave Righetti
Jay Howell
Jose Cruz
Jack Morris
Tony Armas
Mike Young
Rafael Ramirez
☐ 12 Keith Moreland .10 .05 .01
Alvin Davis
Doug DeCinces
John Tudor
Jim Presley
Andy Hawkins
Dennis Lamp
Mario Soto
☐ 13 Charles Hudson 2.00 .90 .25
Dwight Evans
Kirby Puckett
Jody Davis
Eddie Murray
Jose Uribe
Ron Hassey
Hubie Brooks
☐ 14 LaMarr Hoyt .25 .11 .03
Brian Downing
Ron Guidry
Dan Driessen
Tony Bernazard
Garry Maddox
Phil Bradley
Bill Buckner
☐ 15 Tito Landrum .75 .35 .09
Hal McRae
Joe Carter
Jeff Leonard
Tony Fernandez
Juan Samuel
Buddy Bell
Willie Randolph
☐ 16 Scott Garrelts 1.00 .45 .12
Dennis Boyd
Donnie Moore
Tony Perez
Vince Coleman
Alfredo Griffin
Frank White
Ozzie Smith
☐ 17 Claudell Washington 1.00 .45 .12
Rich Gedman
Reggie Jackson
Terry Pendleton
Mark Salas
Mike Marshall
Kent Hrbek
Tim Raines
☐ 18 Ron Davis .25 .11 .03
Glenn Davis
Chris Brown
Burt Hooton
Darryl Strawberry
Tom Brunansky
Tim Wallach
Frank Viola
☐ 19 Jack Clark .25 .11 .03
Toby Harrah
Larry Parrish
Mike Scioscia
Pete O'Brien
Bill Doran
Garry Templeton
Bill Madlock
☐ 20 Dwight Gooden 1.00 .45 .12
Andre Dawson
Roger McDowell
Oddibe McDowell
Gary Carter
Orel Hershiser
Jim Rice
Dwayne Murphy
☐ 21 Steve Balboni .10 .05 .01
Rick Sutcliffe
Charlie Lea
Mike Easler
Steve Sax
Gary Ward
Lloyd Moseby
Willie Wilson
☐ 22 Lance Parrish .75 .35 .09
Tom Herr
Bryn Smith
Kirk Gibson
Jeff Reardon
Gorman Thomas
Wade Boggs
Dave Concepcion
☐ 23 Dave Stieb .75 .35 .09
Willie McGee
Bob Grich
Paul Molitor
Pedro Guerrero
Carlton Fisk
Mike Scott
Lou Whitaker
☐ 24 Tony Gwynn 4.00 1.80 .50
Rickey Henderson
Damaso Garcia
Nolan Ryan
Bert Blyleven
Fernando Valenzuela
Ben Oglivie
Phil Garner

1987 Topps

This set consists of 792 standard-size cards. Cards were primarily issued in 17-card wax packs, 50-card rack packs and factory sets. Card fronts feature wood grain borders encasing a color photo (reminiscent of Topps' classic 1962 baseball set). Subsets include Record Breakers (1-7), Turn Back the Clock (311-315), All-Star selections (595-616) and Team Leaders (scattered throughout the set). The manager cards contain a team checklist on back. The key Rookie Cards in this set are Barry Bonds, Bobby Bonilla, Will Clark, Mike Greenwell, Bo Jackson, Wally Joyner, John Kruk, Barry Larkin, Kevin Mitchell, Rafael Palmiero, Ruben Sierra, and Devon White.

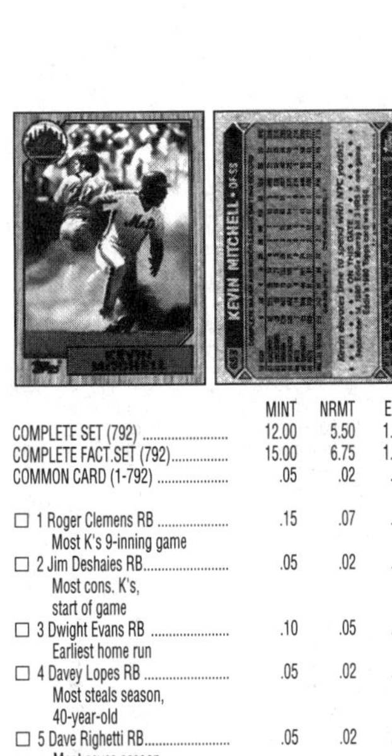

Card	MINT	NRMT	EXC
COMPLETE SET (792)	12.00	5.50	1.50
COMPLETE FACT.SET (792)	15.00	6.75	1.85
COMMON CARD (1-792)	.05	.02	.01
□ 1 Roger Clemens RB Most K's 9-inning game	.15	.07	.02
□ 2 Jim Deshaies RB Most cons. K's, start of game	.05	.02	.01
□ 3 Dwight Evans RB Earliest home run	.10	.05	.01
□ 4 Davey Lopes RB Most steals season, 40-year-old	.05	.02	.01
□ 5 Dave Righetti RB Most saves season	.05	.02	.01
□ 6 Ruben Sierra RB Youngest player to switch hit HR's, game	.15	.07	.02
□ 7 Todd Worrell RB Most saves rookie season	.10	.05	.01
□ 8 Terry Pendleton	.10	.05	.01
□ 9 Jay Tibbs	.05	.02	.01
□ 10 Cecil Cooper	.10	.05	.01
□ 11 Indians Team (Mound conference)	.05	.02	.01
□ 12 Jeff Sellers	.05	.02	.01
□ 13 Nick Esasky	.05	.02	.01
□ 14 Dave Stewart	.10	.05	.01
□ 15 Claudell Washington	.05	.02	.01
□ 16 Pat Clements	.05	.02	.01
□ 17 Pete O'Brien	.05	.02	.01
□ 18 Dick Howser MG (Checklist back)	.10	.05	.01
□ 19 Matt Young	.05	.02	.01
□ 20 Gary Carter	.10	.05	.01
□ 21 Mark Davis	.05	.02	.01
□ 22 Doug DeCinces	.05	.02	.01
□ 23 Lee Smith	.15	.07	.02
□ 24 Tony Walker	.05	.02	.01
□ 25 Bert Blyleven	.10	.05	.01
□ 26 Greg Brock	.05	.02	.01
□ 27 Joe Cowley	.05	.02	.01
□ 28 Rick Dempsey	.10	.05	.01
□ 29 Jimmy Key	.10	.05	.01
□ 30 Tim Raines	.10	.05	.01
□ 31 Braves Team (Glenn Hubbard and Rafael Ramirez)	.05	.02	.01
□ 32 Tim Leary	.05	.02	.01
□ 33 Andy Van Slyke	.10	.05	.01
□ 34 Jose Rijo	.05	.02	.01
□ 35 Sid Bream	.05	.02	.01
□ 36 Eric King	.05	.02	.01
□ 37 Marvell Wynne	.05	.02	.01
□ 38 Dennis Leonard	.05	.02	.01
□ 39 Marty Barrett	.05	.02	.01
□ 40 Dave Righetti	.05	.02	.01
□ 41 Bo Diaz	.05	.02	.01
□ 42 Gary Redus	.05	.02	.01
□ 43 Gene Michael MG (Checklist back)	.05	.02	.01
□ 44 Greg Harris	.05	.02	.01
□ 45 Jim Presley	.05	.02	.01
□ 46 Dan Gladden	.05	.02	.01
□ 47 Dennis Powell	.05	.02	.01
□ 48 Wally Backman	.05	.02	.01
□ 49 Terry Harper	.05	.02	.01
□ 50 Dave Smith	.05	.02	.01
□ 51 Mel Hall	.05	.02	.01
□ 52 Keith Atherton	.05	.02	.01
□ 53 Ruppert Jones	.05	.02	.01
□ 54 Bill Dawley	.05	.02	.01
□ 55 Tim Wallach	.05	.02	.01
□ 56 Brewers Team (Mound conference)	.05	.02	.01
□ 57 Scott Nielsen	.05	.02	.01
□ 58 Thad Bosley	.05	.02	.01
□ 59 Ken Dayley	.05	.02	.01
□ 60 Tony Pena	.05	.02	.01
□ 61 Bobby Thigpen	.10	.05	.01
□ 62 Bobby Meacham	.05	.02	.01
□ 63 Fred Toliver	.05	.02	.01
□ 64 Harry Spilman	.05	.02	.01
□ 65 Tom Browning	.05	.02	.01
□ 66 Marc Sullivan	.05	.02	.01
□ 67 Bill Swift	.05	.02	.01
□ 68 Tony LaRussa MG (Checklist back)	.10	.05	.01
□ 69 Lonnie Smith	.05	.02	.01
□ 70 Charlie Hough	.05	.02	.01
□ 71 Mike Aldrete	.10	.05	.01
□ 72 Walt Terrell	.05	.02	.01
□ 73 Dave Anderson	.05	.02	.01
□ 74 Dan Pasqua	.05	.02	.01
□ 75 Ron Darling	.05	.02	.01
□ 76 Rafael Ramirez	.05	.02	.01
□ 77 Bryan Oelkers	.05	.02	.01
□ 78 Tom Foley	.05	.02	.01
□ 79 Juan Nieves	.05	.02	.01
□ 80 Wally Joyner	.25	.11	.03
□ 81 Padres Team (Andy Hawkins and Terry Kennedy)	.05	.02	.01
□ 82 Rob Murphy	.05	.02	.01
□ 83 Mike Davis	.05	.02	.01
□ 84 Steve Lake	.05	.02	.01
□ 85 Kevin Bass	.05	.02	.01
□ 86 Nate Snell	.05	.02	.01
□ 87 Mark Salas	.05	.02	.01
□ 88 Ed Wojna	.05	.02	.01
□ 89 Ozzie Guillen	.10	.05	.01
□ 90 Dave Stieb	.05	.02	.01
□ 91 Harold Reynolds	.05	.02	.01
□ 92A Urbano Lugo ERR (no trademark)	.15	.07	.02
□ 92B Urbano Lugo COR	.05	.02	.01
□ 93 Jim Leyland MG (Checklist back)	.10	.05	.01
□ 94 Calvin Schiraldi	.05	.02	.01
□ 95 Oddibe McDowell	.05	.02	.01
□ 96 Frank Williams	.05	.02	.01
□ 97 Glenn Wilson	.05	.02	.01
□ 98 Bill Scherrer	.05	.02	.01
□ 99 Darryl Motley (Now with Braves on card front)	.05	.02	.01
□ 100 Steve Garvey	.15	.07	.02
□ 101 Carl Willis	.05	.02	.01
□ 102 Paul Zuvella	.05	.02	.01
□ 103 Rick Aguilera	.10	.05	.01
□ 104 Billy Sample	.05	.02	.01
□ 105 Floyd Youmans	.05	.02	.01
□ 106 Blue Jays Team (George Bell and Jesse Barfield)	.05	.02	.01
□ 107 John Butcher	.05	.02	.01
□ 108 Jim Gantner UER (Brewers logo reversed)	.05	.02	.01
□ 109 R.J. Reynolds	.05	.02	.01
□ 110 John Tudor	.05	.02	.01
□ 111 Alfredo Griffin	.05	.02	.01
□ 112 Alan Ashby	.05	.02	.01
□ 113 Neil Allen	.05	.02	.01
□ 114 Billy Beane	.05	.02	.01
□ 115 Donnie Moore	.05	.02	.01
□ 116 Bill Russell	.05	.02	.01
□ 117 Jim Beattie	.05	.02	.01
□ 118 Bobby Valentine MG (Checklist back)	.05	.02	.01
□ 119 Ron Robinson	.05	.02	.01
□ 120 Eddie Murray	.25	.11	.03
□ 121 Kevin Romine	.05	.02	.01
□ 122 Jim Clancy	.05	.02	.01
□ 123 John Kruk	.15	.07	.02
□ 124 Ray Fontenot	.05	.02	.01
□ 125 Bob Brenly	.05	.02	.01
□ 126 Mike Loynd	.05	.02	.01
□ 127 Vance Law	.05	.02	.01
□ 128 Checklist 1-132	.10	.05	.01
□ 129 Rick Cerone	.05	.02	.01
□ 130 Dwight Gooden	.15	.07	.02
□ 131 Pirates Team (Sid Bream and Tony Pena)	.05	.02	.01
□ 132 Paul Assenmacher	.05	.02	.01
□ 133 Jose Oquendo	.05	.02	.01
□ 134 Rich Yett	.05	.02	.01
□ 135 Mike Easler	.05	.02	.01
□ 136 Ron Romanick	.05	.02	.01
□ 137 Jerry Willard	.05	.02	.01
□ 138 Roy Lee Jackson	.05	.02	.01
□ 139 Devon White	.20	.09	.03
□ 140 Bret Saberhagen	.10	.05	.01
□ 141 Herm Winningham	.05	.02	.01
□ 142 Rick Sutcliffe	.05	.02	.01
□ 143 Steve Boros MG (Checklist back)	.05	.02	.01
□ 144 Mike Scioscia	.05	.02	.01
□ 145 Charlie Kerfeld	.05	.02	.01
□ 146 Tracy Jones	.05	.02	.01
□ 147 Randy Niemann	.05	.02	.01
□ 148 Dave Collins	.05	.02	.01
□ 149 Ray Searage	.05	.02	.01
□ 150 Wade Boggs	.15	.07	.02
□ 151 Mike LaCoss	.05	.02	.01
□ 152 Toby Harrah	.05	.02	.01
□ 153 Duane Ward	.10	.05	.01
□ 154 Tom O'Malley	.05	.02	.01
□ 155 Eddie Whitson	.05	.02	.01
□ 156 Mariners Team (Mound conference)	.05	.02	.01
□ 157 Danny Darwin	.05	.02	.01
□ 158 Tim Teufel	.05	.02	.01
□ 159 Ed Olwine	.05	.02	.01
□ 160 Julio Franco	.10	.05	.01
□ 161 Steve Ontiveros	.05	.02	.01
□ 162 Mike LaValliere	.05	.02	.01
□ 163 Kevin Gross	.05	.02	.01
□ 164 Sammy Khalifa	.05	.02	.01
□ 165 Jeff Reardon	.10	.05	.01
□ 166 Bob Boone	.10	.05	.01
□ 167 Jim Deshaies	.05	.02	.01
□ 168 Lou Piniella MG (Checklist back)	.10	.05	.01
□ 169 Ron Washington	.05	.02	.01
□ 170 Bo Jackson	.50	.23	.06
□ 171 Chuck Cary	.05	.02	.01
□ 172 Ron Oester	.05	.02	.01
□ 173 Alex Trevino	.05	.02	.01
□ 174 Henry Cotto	.05	.02	.01
□ 175 Bob Stanley	.05	.02	.01
□ 176 Steve Buechele	.05	.02	.01
□ 177 Keith Moreland	.05	.02	.01
□ 178 Cecil Fielder	.30	.14	.04
□ 179 Bill Wegman	.05	.02	.01
□ 180 Chris Brown	.05	.02	.01
□ 181 Cardinals Team (Mound conference)	.05	.02	.01
□ 182 Lee Lacy	.05	.02	.01
□ 183 Andy Hawkins	.05	.02	.01
□ 184 Bobby Bonilla	.30	.14	.04
□ 185 Roger McDowell	.05	.02	.01
□ 186 Bruce Benedict	.05	.02	.01
□ 187 Mark Huismann	.05	.02	.01
□ 188 Tony Phillips	.10	.05	.01
□ 189 Joe Hesketh	.05	.02	.01
□ 190 Jim Sundberg	.05	.02	.01
□ 191 Charles Hudson	.05	.02	.01
□ 192 Cory Snyder	.05	.02	.01
□ 193 Roger Craig MG (Checklist back)	.10	.05	.01
□ 194 Kirk McCaskill	.05	.02	.01
□ 195 Mike Pagliarulo	.05	.02	.01
□ 196 Randy O'Neal UER (Wrong ML career W-L totals)	.05	.02	.01
□ 197 Mark Bailey	.05	.02	.01
□ 198 Lee Mazzilli	.05	.02	.01
□ 199 Mariano Duncan	.05	.02	.01
□ 200 Pete Rose	.20	.09	.03
□ 201 John Cangelosi	.05	.02	.01
□ 202 Ricky Wright	.05	.02	.01
□ 203 Mike Kingery	.10	.05	.01
□ 204 Sammy Stewart	.05	.02	.01
□ 205 Graig Nettles	.10	.05	.01
□ 206 Twins Team (Frank Viola and Tim Laudner)	.05	.02	.01
□ 207 George Frazier	.05	.02	.01
□ 208 John Shelby	.05	.02	.01
□ 209 Rick Schu	.05	.02	.01
□ 210 Lloyd Moseby	.05	.02	.01
□ 211 John Morris	.05	.02	.01
□ 212 Mike Fitzgerald	.05	.02	.01
□ 213 Randy Myers	.20	.09	.03
□ 214 Omar Moreno	.05	.02	.01
□ 215 Mark Langston	.10	.05	.01
□ 216 B.J. Surhoff	.15	.07	.02
□ 217 Chris Codiroli	.05	.02	.01
□ 218 Sparky Anderson MG (Checklist back)	.10	.05	.01
□ 219 Cecilio Guante	.05	.02	.01
□ 220 Joe Carter	.20	.09	.03
□ 221 Vern Ruhle	.05	.02	.01
□ 222 Denny Walling	.05	.02	.01
□ 223 Charlie Leibrandt	.05	.02	.01
□ 224 Wayne Tolleson	.05	.02	.01
□ 225 Mike Smithson	.05	.02	.01
□ 226 Max Venable	.05	.02	.01
□ 227 Jamie Moyer	.10	.05	.01
□ 228 Curt Wilkerson	.05	.02	.01
□ 229 Mike Birkbeck	.05	.02	.01
□ 230 Don Baylor	.15	.07	.02
□ 231 Giants Team (Bob Brenly and Jim Gott)	.05	.02	.01
□ 232 Reggie Williams	.05	.02	.01
□ 233 Russ Morman	.05	.02	.01
□ 234 Pat Sheridan	.05	.02	.01
□ 235 Alvin Davis	.05	.02	.01
□ 236 Tommy John	.10	.05	.01
□ 237 Jim Morrison	.05	.02	.01
□ 238 Bill Krueger	.05	.02	.01
□ 239 Juan Espino	.05	.02	.01
□ 240 Steve Balboni	.05	.02	.01
□ 241 Danny Heep	.05	.02	.01
□ 242 Rick Mahler	.05	.02	.01
□ 243 Whitey Herzog MG (Checklist back)	.10	.05	.01
□ 244 Dickie Noles	.05	.02	.01
□ 245 Willie Upshaw	.05	.02	.01
□ 246 Jim Dwyer	.05	.02	.01
□ 247 Jeff Reed	.05	.02	.01
□ 248 Gene Walter	.05	.02	.01
□ 249 Jim Pankovits	.05	.02	.01
□ 250 Teddy Higuera	.05	.02	.01
□ 251 Rob Wilfong	.05	.02	.01
□ 252 Dennis Martinez	.10	.05	.01
□ 253 Eddie Milner	.05	.02	.01
□ 254 Bob Tewksbury	.10	.05	.01
□ 255 Juan Samuel	.05	.02	.01
□ 256 Royals Team (George Brett and Frank White)	.15	.07	.02
□ 257 Bob Forsch	.05	.02	.01
□ 258 Steve Yeager	.05	.02	.01
□ 259 Mike Greenwell	.15	.07	.02
□ 260 Vida Blue	.10	.05	.01
□ 261 Ruben Sierra	.50	.23	.06
□ 262 Jim Winn	.05	.02	.01
□ 263 Stan Javier	.05	.02	.01
□ 264 Checklist 133-264	.10	.05	.01
□ 265 Darrell Evans	.10	.05	.01
□ 266 Jeff Hamilton	.05	.02	.01
□ 267 Howard Johnson	.05	.02	.01
□ 268 Pat Corrales MG (Checklist back)	.10	.05	.01
□ 269 Cliff Speck	.05	.02	.01
□ 270 Jody Davis	.05	.02	.01
□ 271 Mike G. Brown	.05	.02	.01
□ 272 Andres Galarraga	.30	.14	.04
□ 273 Gene Nelson	.05	.02	.01
□ 274 Jeff Hearron UER (Duplicate 1986 stat line on back)	.05	.02	.01
□ 275 LaMarr Hoyt	.05	.02	.01
□ 276 Jackie Gutierrez	.05	.02	.01
□ 277 Juan Agosto	.05	.02	.01
□ 278 Gary Pettis	.05	.02	.01
□ 279 Dan Plesac	.05	.02	.01
□ 280 Jeff Leonard	.05	.02	.01
□ 281 Reds Team (Pete Rose, Bo Diaz, and Bill Gullickson)	.15	.07	.02
□ 282 Jeff Calhoun	.05	.02	.01
□ 283 Doug Drabek	.15	.07	.02
□ 284 John Moses	.05	.02	.01
□ 285 Dennis Boyd	.05	.02	.01
□ 286 Mike Woodard	.05	.02	.01
□ 287 Dave Von Ohlen	.05	.02	.01
□ 288 Tito Landrum	.05	.02	.01
□ 289 Bob Kipper	.05	.02	.01
□ 290 Leon Durham	.05	.02	.01
□ 291 Mitch Williams	.10	.05	.01
□ 292 Franklin Stubbs	.05	.02	.01
□ 293 Bob Rodgers MG (Checklist back, inconsistent design on card back)	.05	.02	.01
□ 294 Steve Jeltz	.05	.02	.01
□ 295 Len Dykstra	.15	.07	.02
□ 296 Andres Thomas	.05	.02	.01
□ 297 Don Schulze	.05	.02	.01
□ 298 Larry Herndon	.05	.02	.01
□ 299 Joel Davis	.05	.02	.01
□ 300 Reggie Jackson	.20	.09	.03
□ 301 Luis Aquino UER (No trademark, never corrected)	.05	.02	.01
□ 302 Bill Schroeder	.05	.02	.01
□ 303 Juan Berenguer	.05	.02	.01
□ 304 Phil Garner	.05	.02	.01
□ 305 John Franco	.10	.05	.01
□ 306 Red Sox Team (Tom Seaver, John McNamara MG, and Rich Gedman)	.15	.07	.02
□ 307 Lee Guetterman	.05	.02	.01
□ 308 Don Slaught	.05	.02	.01
□ 309 Mike Young	.05	.02	.01
□ 310 Frank Viola	.05	.02	.01
□ 311 Rickey Henderson TBC '82	.15	.07	.02
□ 312 Reggie Jackson TBC '77	.15	.07	.02
□ 313 Roberto Clemente TBC '72	.20	.09	.03
□ 314 Carl Yastrzemski UER TBC '67 (Sic, 112 RBI's on back)	.15	.07	.02
□ 315 Maury Wills TBC '62	.10	.05	.01
□ 316 Brian Fisher	.05	.02	.01
□ 317 Clint Hurdle	.05	.02	.01
□ 318 Jim Fregosi MG (Checklist back)	.10	.05	.01
□ 319 Greg Swindell	.15	.07	.02
□ 320 Barry Bonds	1.25	.55	.16
□ 321 Mike Laga	.05	.02	.01
□ 322 Chris Bando	.05	.02	.01
□ 323 Al Newman	.05	.02	.01
□ 324 David Palmer	.05	.02	.01
□ 325 Garry Templeton	.05	.02	.01
□ 326 Mark Gubicza	.05	.02	.01
□ 327 Dale Sveum	.05	.02	.01
□ 328 Bob Welch	.05	.02	.01
□ 329 Ron Roenicke	.05	.02	.01
□ 330 Mike Scott	.05	.02	.01
□ 331 Mets Team (Gary Carter and Darryl Strawberry)	.10	.05	.01
□ 332 Joe Price	.05	.02	.01
□ 333 Ken Phelps	.05	.02	.01
□ 334 Ed Correa	.05	.02	.01
□ 335 Candy Maldonado	.05	.02	.01

☐ 336 Allan Anderson .05 .02 .01
☐ 337 Darrell Miller .05 .02 .01
☐ 338 Tim Conroy .05 .02 .01
☐ 339 Donnie Hill .05 .02 .01
☐ 340 Roger Clemens .40 .18 .05
☐ 341 Mike C. Brown .05 .02 .01
☐ 342 Bob James .05 .02 .01
☐ 343 Hal Lanier MG .10 .05 .01
(Checklist back)
☐ 344A Joe Niekro .05 .02 .01
(Copyright inside
righthand border)
☐ 344B Joe Niekro .05 .02 .01
(Copyright outside
righthand border)
☐ 345 Andre Dawson .15 .07 .02
☐ 346 Shawon Dunston .10 .05 .01
☐ 347 Mickey Brantley .05 .02 .01
☐ 348 Carmelo Martinez .05 .02 .01
☐ 349 Storm Davis .05 .02 .01
☐ 350 Keith Hernandez .10 .05 .01
☐ 351 Gene Garber .05 .02 .01
☐ 352 Mike Felder .05 .02 .01
☐ 353 Ernie Camacho .05 .02 .01
☐ 354 Jamie Quirk .05 .02 .01
☐ 355 Don Carman .05 .02 .01
☐ 356 White Sox Team .05 .02 .01
(Mound conference)
☐ 357 Steve Fireovid .05 .02 .01
☐ 358 Sal Butera .05 .02 .01
☐ 359 Doug Corbett .05 .02 .01
☐ 360 Pedro Guerrero .10 .05 .01
☐ 361 Mark Thurmond .05 .02 .01
☐ 362 Luis Quinones .05 .02 .01
☐ 363 Jose Guzman .05 .02 .01
☐ 364 Randy Bush .05 .02 .01
☐ 365 Rick Rhoden .05 .02 .01
☐ 366 Mark McGwire 1.25 .55 .16
☐ 367 Jeff Lahti .05 .02 .01
☐ 368 John McNamara MG .05 .02 .01
(Checklist back)
☐ 369 Brian Dayett .05 .02 .01
☐ 370 Fred Lynn .10 .05 .01
☐ 371 Mark Eichhorn .05 .02 .01
☐ 372 Jerry Mumphrey .05 .02 .01
☐ 373 Jeff Dedmon .05 .02 .01
☐ 374 Glenn Hoffman .05 .02 .01
☐ 375 Ron Guidry .10 .05 .01
☐ 376 Scott Bradley .05 .02 .01
☐ 377 John Henry Johnson .05 .02 .01
☐ 378 Rafael Santana .05 .02 .01
☐ 379 John Russell .05 .02 .01
☐ 380 Rich Gossage .10 .05 .01
☐ 381 Expos Team .05 .02 .01
(Mound conference)
☐ 382 Rudy Law .05 .02 .01
☐ 383 Ron Davis .05 .02 .01
☐ 384 Johnny Grubb .05 .02 .01
☐ 385 Orel Hershiser .10 .05 .01
☐ 386 Dickie Thon .05 .02 .01
☐ 387 T.R. Bryden .05 .02 .01
☐ 388 Geno Petralli .05 .02 .01
☐ 389 Jeff D. Robinson .05 .02 .01
☐ 390 Gary Matthews .05 .02 .01
☐ 391 Jay Howell .05 .02 .01
☐ 392 Checklist 265-396 .05 .02 .01
☐ 393 Pete Rose MG .25 .11 .03
(Checklist back)
☐ 394 Mike Bielecki .05 .02 .01
☐ 395 Damaso Garcia .05 .02 .01
☐ 396 Tim Lollar .05 .02 .01
☐ 397 Greg Walker .05 .02 .01
☐ 398 Brad Havens .05 .02 .01
☐ 399 Curt Ford .05 .02 .01
☐ 400 George Brett .40 .18 .05
☐ 401 Billy Joe Robidoux .05 .02 .01
☐ 402 Mike Trujillo .05 .02 .01
☐ 403 Jerry Royster .05 .02 .01
☐ 404 Doug Sisk .05 .02 .01
☐ 405 Brook Jacoby .05 .02 .01
☐ 406 Yankees Team .15 .07 .02
(Rickey Henderson and
Don Mattingly)
☐ 407 Jim Acker .05 .02 .01
☐ 408 John Mizerock .05 .02 .01
☐ 409 Milt Thompson .05 .02 .01
☐ 410 Fernando Valenzuela .10 .05 .01
☐ 411 Darnell Coles .05 .02 .01
☐ 412 Eric Davis .15 .07 .02
☐ 413 Moose Haas .05 .02 .01
☐ 414 Joe Orsulak .05 .02 .01
☐ 415 Bobby Witt .10 .05 .01
☐ 416 Tom Nieto .05 .02 .01
☐ 417 Pat Perry .05 .02 .01
☐ 418 Dick Williams MG .10 .05 .01
(Checklist back)
☐ 419 Mark Portugal .10 .05 .01
☐ 420 Will Clark .60 .25 .07
☐ 421 Jose DeLeon .05 .02 .01
☐ 422 Jack Howell .05 .02 .01
☐ 423 Jaime Cocanower .05 .02 .01
☐ 424 Chris Speier .05 .02 .01
☐ 425 Tom Seaver UER .15 .07 .02
Earned Runs amount is wrong
For 86 Red Sox and Career
Also the ERA is wrong for 86 and career
☐ 426 Floyd Rayford .05 .02 .01
☐ 427 Edwin Nunez .05 .02 .01
☐ 428 Bruce Bochy .05 .02 .01
☐ 429 Tim Pyznarski .05 .02 .01
☐ 430 Mike Schmidt .20 .09 .03
☐ 431 Dodgers Team .05 .02 .01
(Mound conference)
☐ 432 Jim Slaton .05 .02 .01
☐ 433 Ed Hearn .05 .02 .01
☐ 434 Mike Fischlin .05 .02 .01
☐ 435 Bruce Sutter .05 .02 .01
☐ 436 Andy Allanson .05 .02 .01
☐ 437 Ted Power .05 .02 .01
☐ 438 Kelly Downs .05 .02 .01
☐ 439 Karl Best .05 .02 .01
☐ 440 Willie McGee .05 .02 .01
☐ 441 Dave Leiper .05 .02 .01
☐ 442 Mitch Webster .05 .02 .01
☐ 443 John Felske MG .05 .02 .01
(Checklist back)
☐ 444 Jeff Russell .05 .02 .01
☐ 445 Dave Lopes .10 .05 .01
☐ 446 Chuck Finley .25 .11 .03
☐ 447 Bill Almon .05 .02 .01
☐ 448 Chris Bosio .10 .05 .01
☐ 449 Pat Dodson .05 .02 .01
☐ 450 Kirby Puckett .75 .35 .09
☐ 451 Joe Sambito .05 .02 .01
☐ 452 Dave Henderson .05 .02 .01
☐ 453 Scott Terry .05 .02 .01
☐ 454 Luis Salazar .05 .02 .01
☐ 455 Mike Boddicker .05 .02 .01
☐ 456 A's Team .05 .02 .01
(Mound conference)
☐ 457 Len Matuszek .05 .02 .01
☐ 458 Kelly Gruber .05 .02 .01
☐ 459 Dennis Eckersley .15 .07 .02
☐ 460 Darryl Strawberry .15 .07 .02
☐ 461 Craig McMurtry .05 .02 .01
☐ 462 Scott Fletcher .05 .02 .01
☐ 463 Tom Candiotti .05 .02 .01
☐ 464 Butch Wynegar .05 .02 .01
☐ 465 Todd Worrell .10 .05 .01
☐ 466 Kal Daniels .05 .02 .01
☐ 467 Randy St.Claire .05 .02 .01
☐ 468 George Bamberger MG .10 .05 .01
(Checklist back)
☐ 469 Mike Diaz .05 .02 .01
☐ 470 Dave Dravecky .10 .05 .01
☐ 471 Ronn Reynolds .05 .02 .01
☐ 472 Bill Doran .05 .02 .01
☐ 473 Steve Farr .05 .02 .01
☐ 474 Jerry Narron .05 .02 .01
☐ 475 Scott Garrelts .05 .02 .01
☐ 476 Danny Tartabull .10 .05 .01
☐ 477 Ken Howell .05 .02 .01
☐ 478 Tim Laudner .05 .02 .01
☐ 479 Bob Sebra .05 .02 .01
☐ 480 Jim Rice .10 .05 .01
☐ 481 Phillies Team .05 .02 .01
(Glenn Wilson,
Juan Samuel and
Von Hayes)
☐ 482 Daryl Boston .05 .02 .01
☐ 483 Dwight Lowry .05 .02 .01
☐ 484 Jim Traber .05 .02 .01
☐ 485 Tony Fernandez .05 .02 .01
☐ 486 Otis Nixon .10 .05 .01
☐ 487 Dave Gumpert .05 .02 .01
☐ 488 Ray Knight .10 .05 .01
☐ 489 Bill Gullickson .05 .02 .01
☐ 490 Dale Murphy .15 .07 .02
☐ 491 Ron Karkovice .10 .05 .01
☐ 492 Mike Heath .05 .02 .01
☐ 493 Tom Lasorda MG .10 .05 .01
(Checklist back)
☐ 494 Barry Jones .05 .02 .01
☐ 495 Gorman Thomas .05 .02 .01
☐ 496 Bruce Bochte .05 .02 .01
☐ 497 Dale Mohorcic .05 .02 .01
☐ 498 Bob Kearney .05 .02 .01
☐ 499 Bruce Ruffin .05 .02 .01
☐ 500 Don Mattingly .50 .23 .06
☐ 501 Craig Lefferts .05 .02 .01
☐ 502 Dick Schofield .05 .02 .01
☐ 503 Larry Andersen .05 .02 .01
☐ 504 Mickey Hatcher .05 .02 .01
☐ 505 Bryn Smith .05 .02 .01
☐ 506 Orioles Team .05 .02 .01
(Mound conference)
☐ 507 Dave L. Stapleton .05 .02 .01
☐ 508 Scott Bankhead .05 .02 .01
☐ 509 Enos Cabell .05 .02 .01
☐ 510 Tom Henke .05 .02 .01
☐ 511 Steve Lyons .05 .02 .01
☐ 512 Dave Magadan .10 .05 .01
☐ 513 Carmen Castillo .05 .02 .01
☐ 514 Orlando Mercado .05 .02 .01
☐ 515 Willie Hernandez .05 .02 .01
☐ 516 Ted Simmons .10 .05 .01
☐ 517 Mario Soto .05 .02 .01
☐ 518 Gene Mauch MG .10 .05 .01
(Checklist back)
☐ 519 Curt Young .05 .02 .01
☐ 520 Jack Clark .10 .05 .01
☐ 521 Rick Reuschel .05 .02 .01
☐ 522 Checklist 397-528 .05 .02 .01
☐ 523 Earnie Riles .05 .02 .01
☐ 524 Bob Shirley .05 .02 .01
☐ 525 Phil Bradley .05 .02 .01
☐ 526 Roger Mason .05 .02 .01
☐ 527 Jim Wohlford .05 .02 .01
☐ 528 Ken Dixon .05 .02 .01
☐ 529 Alvaro Espinoza .05 .02 .01
☐ 530 Tony Gwynn .40 .18 .05
☐ 531 Astros Team .10 .05 .01
(Yogi Berra conference)
☐ 532 Jeff Stone .05 .02 .01
☐ 533 Argenis Salazar .05 .02 .01
☐ 534 Scott Sanderson .05 .02 .01
☐ 535 Tony Armas .05 .02 .01
☐ 536 Terry Mulholland .10 .05 .01
☐ 537 Rance Mulliniks .05 .02 .01
☐ 538 Tom Niedenfuer .05 .02 .01
☐ 539 Reid Nichols .05 .02 .01
☐ 540 Terry Kennedy .05 .02 .01
☐ 541 Rafael Belliard .05 .02 .01
☐ 542 Ricky Horton .05 .02 .01
☐ 543 Dave Johnson MG .10 .05 .01
(Checklist back)
☐ 544 Zane Smith .05 .02 .01
☐ 545 Buddy Bell .10 .05 .01
☐ 546 Mike Morgan .05 .02 .01
☐ 547 Rob Deer .05 .02 .01
☐ 548 Bill Mooneyham .05 .02 .01
☐ 549 Bob Melvin .05 .02 .01
☐ 550 Pete Incaviglia .10 .05 .01
☐ 551 Frank Wills .05 .02 .01
☐ 552 Larry Sheets .05 .02 .01
☐ 553 Mike Maddux .05 .02 .01
☐ 554 Buddy Biancalana .05 .02 .01
☐ 555 Dennis Rasmussen .05 .02 .01
☐ 556 Angels Team .05 .02 .01
(Rene Lachemann CO,
Mike Witt, and
Bob Boone)
☐ 557 John Cerutti .05 .02 .01
☐ 558 Greg Gagne .05 .02 .01
☐ 559 Lance McCullers .05 .02 .01
☐ 560 Glenn Davis .05 .02 .01
☐ 561 Rey Quinones .05 .02 .01
☐ 562 Bryan Clutterbuck .05 .02 .01
☐ 563 John Stefero .05 .02 .01
☐ 564 Larry McWilliams .05 .02 .01
☐ 565 Dusty Baker .10 .05 .01
☐ 566 Tim Hulett .05 .02 .01
☐ 567 Greg Mathews .05 .02 .01
☐ 568 Earl Weaver MG .15 .07 .02
(Checklist back)
☐ 569 Wade Rowdon .05 .02 .01
☐ 570 Sid Fernandez .05 .02 .01
☐ 571 Ozzie Virgil .05 .02 .01
☐ 572 Pete Ladd .05 .02 .01
☐ 573 Hal McRae .10 .05 .01
☐ 574 Manny Lee .05 .02 .01
☐ 575 Pat Tabler .05 .02 .01
☐ 576 Frank Pastore .05 .02 .01
☐ 577 Dann Bilardello .05 .02 .01
☐ 578 Billy Hatcher .05 .02 .01
☐ 579 Rick Burleson .05 .02 .01
☐ 580 Mike Krukow .05 .02 .01
☐ 581 Cubs Team .05 .02 .01
(Ron Cey and
Steve Trout)
☐ 582 Bruce Berenyi .05 .02 .01
☐ 583 Junior Ortiz .05 .02 .01
☐ 584 Ron Kittle .05 .02 .01
☐ 585 Scott Bailes .05 .02 .01
☐ 586 Ben Oglivie .05 .02 .01
☐ 587 Eric Plunk .05 .02 .01
☐ 588 Wallace Johnson .05 .02 .01
☐ 589 Steve Crawford .05 .02 .01
☐ 590 Vince Coleman .05 .02 .01
☐ 591 Spike Owen .05 .02 .01
☐ 592 Chris Welsh .05 .02 .01
☐ 593 Chuck Tanner MG .10 .05 .01
(Checklist back)
☐ 594 Rick Anderson .05 .02 .01
☐ 595 Keith Hernandez AS .10 .05 .01
☐ 596 Steve Sax AS .05 .02 .01
☐ 597 Mike Schmidt AS .15 .07 .02
☐ 598 Ozzie Smith AS .15 .07 .02
☐ 599 Tony Gwynn AS .20 .09 .03
☐ 600 Dave Parker AS .10 .05 .01
☐ 601 Darryl Strawberry AS .15 .07 .02
☐ 602 Gary Carter AS .10 .05 .01
☐ 603A Dwight Gooden AS .10 .05 .01
ERR (no trademark)
☐ 603B Dwight Gooden AS COR .15 .07 .02
☐ 604 Fernando Valenzuela AS .10 .05 .01
☐ 605 Todd Worrell AS .10 .05 .01
☐ 606 Don Mattingly AS COR .25 .11 .03
☐ 606A Don Mattingly AS .75 .35 .09
ERR (no trademark)
☐ 607 Tony Bernazard AS .05 .02 .01
☐ 608 Wade Boggs AS .15 .07 .02
☐ 609 Cal Ripken AS .50 .23 .06
☐ 610 Jim Rice AS .10 .05 .01
☐ 611 Kirby Puckett AS .40 .18 .05
☐ 612 George Bell AS .05 .02 .01
☐ 613 Lance Parrish AS UER .10 .05 .01
(Pitcher heading
on back)
☐ 614 Roger Clemens AS .15 .07 .02
☐ 615 Teddy Higuera AS .05 .02 .01
☐ 616 Dave Righetti AS .05 .02 .01
☐ 617 Al Nipper .05 .02 .01
☐ 618 Tom Kelly MG .10 .05 .01
(Checklist back)
☐ 619 Jerry Reed .05 .02 .01
☐ 620 Jose Canseco .60 .25 .07
☐ 621 Danny Cox .05 .02 .01
☐ 622 Glenn Braggs .05 .02 .01
☐ 623 Kurt Stillwell .05 .02 .01
☐ 624 Tim Burke .05 .02 .01
☐ 625 Mookie Wilson .10 .05 .01
☐ 626 Joel Skinner .05 .02 .01
☐ 627 Ken Oberkfell .05 .02 .01
☐ 628 Bob Walk .05 .02 .01
☐ 629 Larry Parrish .05 .02 .01
☐ 630 John Candelaria .05 .02 .01
☐ 631 Tigers Team .05 .02 .01
(Mound conference)
☐ 632 Rob Woodward .05 .02 .01
☐ 633 Jose Uribe .05 .02 .01
☐ 634 Rafael Palmeiro 1.00 .45 .12
☐ 635 Ken Schrom .05 .02 .01
☐ 636 Darren Daulton .15 .07 .02
☐ 637 Bip Roberts .15 .07 .02
☐ 638 Rich Bordi .05 .02 .01
☐ 639 Gerald Perry .05 .02 .01
☐ 640 Mark Clear .05 .02 .01
☐ 641 Domingo Ramos .05 .02 .01
☐ 642 Al Pulido .05 .02 .01
☐ 643 Ron Shepherd .05 .02 .01
☐ 644 John Denny .05 .02 .01
☐ 645 Dwight Evans .10 .05 .01
☐ 646 Mike Mason .05 .02 .01
☐ 647 Tom Lawless .05 .02 .01
☐ 648 Barry Larkin 1.00 .45 .12
☐ 649 Mickey Tettleton .10 .05 .01
☐ 650 Hubie Brooks .05 .02 .01
☐ 651 Benny Distefano .05 .02 .01
☐ 652 Terry Forster .05 .02 .01
☐ 653 Kevin Mitchell .15 .07 .02
☐ 654 Checklist 529-660 .10 .05 .01
☐ 655 Jesse Barfield .05 .02 .01
☐ 656 Rangers Team .05 .02 .01
(Bobby Valentine MG
and Ricky Wright)
☐ 657 Tom Waddell .05 .02 .01
☐ 658 Robby Thompson .10 .05 .01
☐ 659 Aurelio Lopez .05 .02 .01
☐ 660 Bob Horner .05 .02 .01
☐ 661 Lou Whitaker .10 .05 .01
☐ 662 Frank DiPino .05 .02 .01
☐ 663 Cliff Johnson .05 .02 .01
☐ 664 Mike Marshall .05 .02 .01
☐ 665 Rod Scurry .05 .02 .01
☐ 666 Von Hayes .05 .02 .01
☐ 667 Ron Hassey .05 .02 .01
☐ 668 Juan Bonilla .05 .02 .01
☐ 669 Bud Black .05 .02 .01
☐ 670 Jose Cruz .05 .02 .01
☐ 671A Ray Soff ERR .05 .02 .01
(No D* before
copyright line)
☐ 671B Ray Soff COR .05 .02 .01
(D* before
copyright line)
☐ 672 Chili Davis .10 .05 .01
☐ 673 Don Sutton .15 .07 .02
☐ 674 Bill Campbell .05 .02 .01
☐ 675 Ed Romero .05 .02 .01
☐ 676 Charlie Moore .05 .02 .01
☐ 677 Bob Grich .10 .05 .01
☐ 678 Carney Lansford .10 .05 .01
☐ 679 Kent Hrbek .15 .07 .02
☐ 680 Ryne Sandberg .25 .11 .03
☐ 681 George Bell .05 .02 .01
☐ 682 Jerry Reuss .05 .02 .01
☐ 683 Gary Roenicke .05 .02 .01
☐ 684 Kent Tekulve .05 .02 .01
☐ 685 Jerry Hairston .05 .02 .01
☐ 686 Doyle Alexander .05 .02 .01
☐ 687 Alan Trammell .15 .07 .02
☐ 688 Juan Beniquez .05 .02 .01
☐ 689 Darrell Porter .05 .02 .01
☐ 690 Dane Iorg .05 .02 .01
☐ 691 Dave Parker .10 .05 .01
☐ 692 Frank White .10 .05 .01
☐ 693 Terry Puhl .05 .02 .01
☐ 694 Phil Niekro .15 .07 .02
☐ 695 Chico Walker .05 .02 .01
☐ 696 Gary Lucas .05 .02 .01
☐ 697 Ed Lynch .05 .02 .01
☐ 698 Ernie Whitt .05 .02 .01
☐ 699 Ken Landreaux .05 .02 .01
☐ 700 Dave Bergman .05 .02 .01
☐ 701 Willie Randolph .10 .05 .01
☐ 702 Greg Gross .05 .02 .01
☐ 703 Dave Schmidt .05 .02 .01
☐ 704 Jesse Orosco .05 .02 .01
☐ 705 Bruce Hurst .05 .02 .01
☐ 706 Rick Manning .05 .02 .01

☐ 707 Bob McClure	.05	.02	.01
☐ 708 Scott McGregor	.05	.02	.01
☐ 709 Dave Kingman	.10	.05	.01
☐ 710 Gary Gaetti	.05	.02	.01
☐ 711 Ken Griffey	.10	.05	.01
☐ 712 Don Robinson	.05	.02	.01
☐ 713 Tom Brookens	.05	.02	.01
☐ 714 Dan Quisenberry	.05	.02	.01
☐ 715 Bob Dernier	.05	.02	.01
☐ 716 Rick Leach	.05	.02	.01
☐ 717 Ed VandeBerg	.05	.02	.01
☐ 718 Steve Carlton	.15	.07	.02
☐ 719 Tom Hume	.05	.02	.01
☐ 720 Richard Dotson	.05	.02	.01
☐ 721 Tom Herr	.05	.02	.01
☐ 722 Bob Knepper	.05	.02	.01
☐ 723 Brett Butler	.10	.05	.01
☐ 724 Greg Minton	.05	.02	.01
☐ 725 George Hendrick	.05	.02	.01
☐ 726 Frank Tanana	.05	.02	.01
☐ 727 Mike Moore	.05	.02	.01
☐ 728 Tippy Martinez	.05	.02	.01
☐ 729 Tom Paciorek	.05	.02	.01
☐ 730 Eric Show	.05	.02	.01
☐ 731 Dave Concepcion	.10	.05	.01
☐ 732 Manny Trillo	.05	.02	.01
☐ 733 Bill Caudill	.05	.02	.01
☐ 734 Bill Madlock	.05	.02	.01
☐ 735 Rickey Henderson	.15	.07	.02
☐ 736 Steve Bedrosian	.05	.02	.01
☐ 737 Floyd Bannister	.05	.02	.01
☐ 738 Jorge Orta	.05	.02	.01
☐ 739 Chet Lemon	.05	.02	.01
☐ 740 Rich Gedman	.05	.02	.01
☐ 741 Paul Molitor	.20	.09	.03
☐ 742 Andy McGaffigan	.05	.02	.01
☐ 743 Dwayne Murphy	.05	.02	.01
☐ 744 Roy Smalley	.05	.02	.01
☐ 745 Glenn Hubbard	.05	.02	.01
☐ 746 Bob Ojeda	.05	.02	.01
☐ 747 Johnny Ray	.05	.02	.01
☐ 748 Mike Flanagan	.05	.02	.01
☐ 749 Ozzie Smith	.25	.11	.03
☐ 750 Steve Trout	.05	.02	.01
☐ 751 Garth Iorg	.05	.02	.01
☐ 752 Dan Petry	.05	.02	.01
☐ 753 Rick Honeycutt	.05	.02	.01
☐ 754 Dave LaPoint	.05	.02	.01
☐ 755 Luis Aguayo	.05	.02	.01
☐ 756 Carlton Fisk	.15	.07	.02
☐ 757 Nolan Ryan	.75	.35	.09
☐ 758 Tony Bernazard	.05	.02	.01
☐ 759 Joel Youngblood	.05	.02	.01
☐ 760 Mike Witt	.05	.02	.01
☐ 761 Greg Pryor	.05	.02	.01
☐ 762 Gary Ward	.05	.02	.01
☐ 763 Tim Flannery	.05	.02	.01
☐ 764 Bill Buckner	.10	.05	.01
☐ 765 Kirk Gibson	.10	.05	.01
☐ 766 Don Aase	.05	.02	.01
☐ 767 Ron Cey	.10	.05	.01
☐ 768 Dennis Lamp	.05	.02	.01
☐ 769 Steve Sax	.05	.02	.01
☐ 770 Dave Winfield	.15	.07	.02
☐ 771 Shane Rawley	.05	.02	.01
☐ 772 Harold Baines	.10	.05	.01
☐ 773 Robin Yount	.15	.07	.02
☐ 774 Wayne Krenchicki	.05	.02	.01
☐ 775 Joaquin Andujar	.05	.02	.01
☐ 776 Tom Brunansky	.05	.02	.01
☐ 777 Chris Chambliss	.05	.02	.01
☐ 778 Jack Morris	.10	.05	.01
☐ 779 Craig Reynolds	.05	.02	.01
☐ 780 Andre Thornton	.05	.02	.01
☐ 781 Atlee Hammaker	.05	.02	.01
☐ 782 Brian Downing	.05	.02	.01
☐ 783 Willie Wilson	.05	.02	.01
☐ 784 Cal Ripken	.75	.35	.09
☐ 785 Terry Francona	.05	.02	.01
☐ 786 Jimy Williams MG (Checklist back)	.10	.05	.01
☐ 787 Alejandro Pena	.05	.02	.01
☐ 788 Tim Stoddard	.05	.02	.01
☐ 789 Dan Schatzeder	.05	.02	.01
☐ 790 Julio Cruz	.05	.02	.01
☐ 791 Lance Parrish UER (No trademark, never corrected)	.10	.05	.01
☐ 792 Checklist 661-792	.10	.05	.01

1987 Topps Tiffany

These 792 standard-size cards were a parallel to the regular Topps issue. These cards feature "glossy" fronts and easy to read backs. These cards are in the same style as the regular Topps issue. This set was printed in Ireland and was issued only in factory set form. Unlike previous years, a significantly higher amount of these cards were produced. Therefore, the values of these cards are a much lower mulitplier to the regular cards than previous years.

	MINT	NRMT	EXC
COMPLETE FACT.SET (792)	25.00	11.00	3.10
COMMON CARD (1-792)	.10	.05	.01
*STARS: 2X BASIC CARDS			
*ROOKIES: 2X BASIC CARDS			

1987 Topps Glossy All-Stars

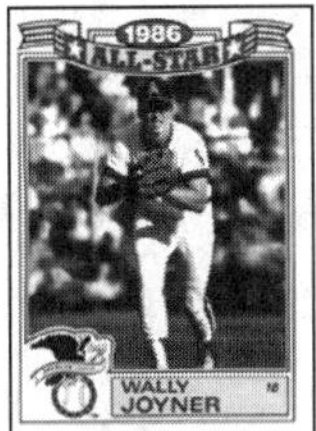

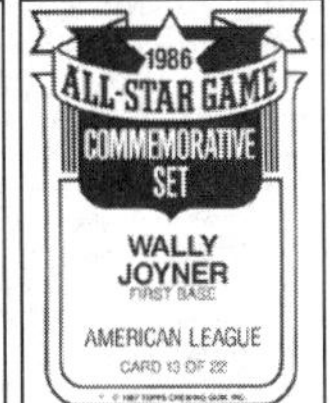

This set of 22 glossy cards was inserted one per rack pack. Players selected for the set are the starting players (plus manager and two pitchers) in the 1986 All-Star Game in Houston. Cards measure the standard size and the backs feature red and blue printing on a white card stock.

	MINT	NRMT	EXC
COMPLETE SET (22)	5.00	2.20	.60
COMMON CARD (1-22)	.05	.02	.01
☐ 1 Whitey Herzog MG	.05	.02	.01
☐ 2 Keith Hernandez	.10	.05	.01
☐ 3 Ryne Sandberg	1.00	.45	.12
☐ 4 Mike Schmidt	.75	.35	.09
☐ 5 Ozzie Smith	1.00	.45	.12
☐ 6 Tony Gwynn	1.25	.55	.16
☐ 7 Dale Murphy	.30	.14	.04
☐ 8 Darryl Strawberry	.10	.05	.01
☐ 9 Gary Carter	.10	.05	.01
☐ 10 Dwight Gooden	.20	.09	.03
☐ 11 Fernando Valenzuela	.10	.05	.01
☐ 12 Dick Howser MG	.05	.02	.01
☐ 13 Wally Joyner	.10	.05	.01
☐ 14 Lou Whitaker	.10	.05	.01
☐ 15 Wade Boggs	.50	.23	.06
☐ 16 Cal Ripken	2.00	.90	.25
☐ 17 Dave Winfield	.40	.18	.05
☐ 18 Rickey Henderson	.40	.18	.05
☐ 19 Kirby Puckett	1.25	.55	.16
☐ 20 Lance Parrish	.05	.02	.01
☐ 21 Roger Clemens	.75	.35	.09
☐ 22 Teddy Higuera	.05	.02	.01

1987 Topps Glossy Send-Ins

Topps issued this set through a mail-in offer explained and advertised on the wax packs. This 60-card set features glossy fronts with each card measuring the standard size. The offer provided your choice of any one of the six 10-card subsets (1-10, 11-20, etc.) for 1.00 plus six of the Special Offer ("Spring Fever Baseball") insert cards, which were found one per wax pack. The last two players (numerically) in each ten-card subset are actually "Hot Prospects."

	MINT	NRMT	EXC
COMPLETE SET (60)	12.50	5.50	1.55
COMMON CARD (1-60)	.10	.05	.01
☐ 1 Don Mattingly	2.00	.90	.25
☐ 2 Tony Gwynn	1.50	.70	.19
☐ 3 Gary Gaetti	.25	.11	.03
☐ 4 Glenn Davis	.10	.05	.01
☐ 5 Roger Clemens	1.00	.45	.12
☐ 6 Dale Murphy	.40	.18	.05
☐ 7 Lou Whitaker	.25	.11	.03
☐ 8 Roger McDowell	.10	.05	.01
☐ 9 Cory Snyder	.10	.05	.01
☐ 10 Todd Worrell	.10	.05	.01
☐ 11 Gary Carter	.25	.11	.03
☐ 12 Eddie Murray	1.00	.45	.12
☐ 13 Bob Knepper	.10	.05	.01
☐ 14 Harold Baines	.25	.11	.03
☐ 15 Jeff Reardon	.25	.11	.03
☐ 16 Joe Carter	.40	.18	.05
☐ 17 Dave Parker	.25	.11	.03
☐ 18 Wade Boggs	.60	.25	.07
☐ 19 Danny Tartabull	.25	.11	.03
☐ 20 Jim Deshaies	.10	.05	.01
☐ 21 Rickey Henderson	.60	.25	.07
☐ 22 Rob Deer	.10	.05	.01
☐ 23 Ozzie Smith	1.25	.55	.16
☐ 24 Dave Righetti	.10	.05	.01
☐ 25 Kent Hrbek	.25	.11	.03
☐ 26 Keith Hernandez	.25	.11	.03
☐ 27 Don Baylor	.25	.11	.03
☐ 28 Mike Schmidt	1.00	.45	.12
☐ 29 Pete Incaviglia	.25	.11	.03
☐ 30 Barry Bonds	2.50	1.10	.30
☐ 31 George Brett	1.50	.70	.19
☐ 32 Darryl Strawberry	.25	.11	.03
☐ 33 Mike Witt	.10	.05	.01
☐ 34 Kevin Bass	.10	.05	.01
☐ 35 Jesse Barfield	.10	.05	.01
☐ 36 Bob Ojeda	.10	.05	.01
☐ 37 Cal Ripken	4.00	1.80	.50
☐ 38 Vince Coleman	.10	.05	.01
☐ 39 Wally Joyner	.25	.11	.03
☐ 40 Robby Thompson	.10	.05	.01
☐ 41 Pete Rose	1.00	.45	.12
☐ 42 Jim Rice	.25	.11	.03
☐ 43 Tony Bernazard	.10	.05	.01
☐ 44 Eric Davis	.25	.11	.03
☐ 45 George Bell	.10	.05	.01
☐ 46 Hubie Brooks	.10	.05	.01
☐ 47 Jack Morris	.25	.11	.03
☐ 48 Tim Raines	.25	.11	.03
☐ 49 Mark Eichhorn	.10	.05	.01
☐ 50 Kevin Mitchell	.25	.11	.03
☐ 51 Dwight Gooden	.40	.18	.05
☐ 52 Doug DeCinces	.10	.05	.01
☐ 53 Fernando Valenzuela	.25	.11	.03
☐ 54 Reggie Jackson	.60	.25	.07
☐ 55 Johnny Ray	.10	.05	.01
☐ 56 Mike Pagliarulo	.10	.05	.01
☐ 57 Kirby Puckett	2.00	.90	.25
☐ 58 Lance Parrish	.25	.11	.03
☐ 59 Jose Canseco	1.00	.45	.12
☐ 60 Greg Mathews	.10	.05	.01

1987 Topps Rookies

Inserted in each supermarket jumbo pack is a card from this series of 22 of 1986's best rookies as determined by Topps. Jumbo packs consisted of 100 (regular issue 1987 Topps baseball) cards with a stick of gum plus the insert "Rookie" card. The card fronts are in full color and measure the standard size. The card backs are printed in red and blue on white card stock and are numbered at the bottom essentially by alphabetical order.

	MINT	NRMT	EXC
COMPLETE SET (22)	10.00	4.50	1.25
COMMON CARD (1-22)	.10	.05	.01
☐ 1 Andy Allanson	.10	.05	.01
☐ 2 John Cangelosi	.10	.05	.01
☐ 3 Jose Canseco	2.50	1.10	.30
☐ 4 Will Clark	2.50	1.10	.30
☐ 5 Mark Eichhorn	.10	.05	.01
☐ 6 Pete Incaviglia	.20	.09	.03
☐ 7 Wally Joyner	.50	.23	.06
☐ 8 Eric King	.10	.05	.01
☐ 9 Dave Magadan	.20	.09	.03
☐ 10 John Morris	.10	.05	.01
☐ 11 Juan Nieves	.10	.05	.01
☐ 12 Rafael Palmeiro	2.00	.90	.25
☐ 13 Billy Joe Robidoux	.10	.05	.01
☐ 14 Bruce Ruffin	.10	.05	.01
☐ 15 Ruben Sierra	.50	.23	.06
☐ 16 Cory Snyder	.10	.05	.01
☐ 17 Kurt Stillwell	.10	.05	.01
☐ 18 Dale Sveum	.10	.05	.01
☐ 19 Danny Tartabull	.50	.23	.06
☐ 20 Andres Thomas	.10	.05	.01
☐ 21 Robby Thompson	.20	.09	.03
☐ 22 Todd Worrell	.20	.09	.03

1987 Topps Wax Box Cards

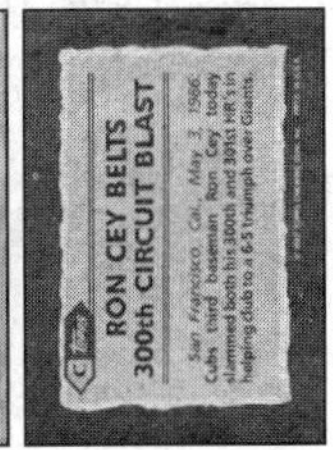

This set of eight cards is really four different sets of two smaller (approximately 2 1/8" by 3") cards which were printed on the side of the wax pack box; these eight cards are lettered A through H and are very similar in design to the Topps regular issue cards. The order of the set is alphabetical by player's name. Complete boxes would be worth an additional 25 percent premium over the prices below. The card backs are done in a newspaper headline style describing something about that player that happened the previous season. The card backs feature blue and yellow ink on gray card stock.

	MINT	NRMT	EXC
COMPLETE SET (8)	3.00	1.35	.35
COMMON CARD (A-H)	.25	.11	.03
☐ A Don Baylor	.35	.16	.04
☐ B Steve Carlton	.75	.35	.09
☐ C Ron Cey	.25	.11	.03
☐ D Cecil Cooper	.25	.11	.03
☐ E Rickey Henderson	1.00	.45	.12
☐ F Jim Rice	.35	.16	.04
☐ G Don Sutton	.50	.23	.06
☐ H Dave Winfield	.60	.25	.07

1987 Topps Traded

This 132-card standard-size Traded set was distributed exclusively in factory set form in a special green and white box through hobby dealers. The card fronts are identical in style to the Topps regular issue except for whiter stock and t-suffixed numbering on back. The cards are ordered alphabetically by player's last name. The key extended Rookie Cards in this set are Ellis Burks, David Cone, Greg Maddux, Fred McGriff and Matt Williams.

	MINT	NRMT	EXC
COMPLETE FACT.SET (132)	8.00	3.60	1.00
COMMON CARD (1T-132T)	.05	.02	.01
☐ 1T Bill Almon	.05	.02	.01
☐ 2T Scott Bankhead	.05	.02	.01
☐ 3T Eric Bell	.05	.02	.01
☐ 4T Juan Beniquez	.05	.02	.01
☐ 5T Juan Berenguer	.05	.02	.01
☐ 6T Greg Booker	.05	.02	.01
☐ 7T Thad Bosley	.05	.02	.01
☐ 8T Larry Bowa MG	.10	.05	.01
☐ 9T Greg Brock	.05	.02	.01
☐ 10T Bob Brower	.05	.02	.01
☐ 11T Jerry Browne	.05	.02	.01
☐ 12T Ralph Bryant	.05	.02	.01
☐ 13T DeWayne Buice	.05	.02	.01
☐ 14T Ellis Burks	.50	.23	.06
☐ 15T Ivan Calderon	.05	.02	.01
☐ 16T Jeff Calhoun	.05	.02	.01
☐ 17T Casey Candaele	.05	.02	.01
☐ 18T John Cangelosi	.05	.02	.01
☐ 19T Steve Carlton	.15	.07	.02
☐ 20T Juan Castillo	.05	.02	.01
☐ 21T Rick Cerone	.05	.02	.01
☐ 22T Ron Cey	.10	.05	.01
☐ 23T John Christensen	.05	.02	.01
☐ 24T David Cone	.50	.23	.06
☐ 25T Chuck Crim	.05	.02	.01
☐ 26T Storm Davis	.05	.02	.01
☐ 27T Andre Dawson	.15	.07	.02
☐ 28T Rick Dempsey	.10	.05	.01
☐ 29T Doug Drabek	.15	.07	.02
☐ 30T Mike Dunne	.05	.02	.01
☐ 31T Dennis Eckersley	.15	.07	.02
☐ 32T Lee Elia MG	.05	.02	.01
☐ 33T Brian Fisher	.05	.02	.01
☐ 34T Terry Francona	.05	.02	.01
☐ 35T Willie Fraser	.05	.02	.01
☐ 36T Billy Gardner MG	.05	.02	.01
☐ 37T Ken Gerhart	.05	.02	.01
☐ 38T Dan Gladden	.05	.02	.01
☐ 39T Jim Gott	.05	.02	.01
☐ 40T Cecilio Guante	.05	.02	.01
☐ 41T Albert Hall	.05	.02	.01
☐ 42T Terry Harper	.05	.02	.01
☐ 43T Mickey Hatcher	.05	.02	.01
☐ 44T Brad Havens	.05	.02	.01
☐ 45T Neal Heaton	.05	.02	.01
☐ 46T Mike Henneman	.15	.07	.02
☐ 47T Donnie Hill	.05	.02	.01
☐ 48T Guy Hoffman	.05	.02	.01
☐ 49T Brian Holton	.05	.02	.01
☐ 50T Charles Hudson	.05	.02	.01
☐ 51T Danny Jackson	.05	.02	.01
☐ 52T Reggie Jackson	.20	.09	.03
☐ 53T Chris James	.05	.02	.01
☐ 54T Dion James	.05	.02	.01
☐ 55T Stan Jefferson	.05	.02	.01
☐ 56T Joe Johnson	.05	.02	.01
☐ 57T Terry Kennedy	.05	.02	.01
☐ 58T Mike Kingery	.10	.05	.01
☐ 59T Ray Knight	.10	.05	.01
☐ 60T Gene Larkin	.05	.02	.01
☐ 61T Mike LaValliere	.05	.02	.01
☐ 62T Jack Lazorko	.05	.02	.01
☐ 63T Terry Leach	.05	.02	.01
☐ 64T Tim Leary	.05	.02	.01
☐ 65T Jim Lindeman	.05	.02	.01

	MINT	NRMT	EXC
☐ 66T Steve Lombardozzi	.05	.02	.01
☐ 67T Bill Long	.05	.02	.01
☐ 68T Barry Lyons	.05	.02	.01
☐ 69T Shane Mack	.10	.05	.01
☐ 70T Greg Maddux	5.00	2.20	.60
☐ 71T Bill Madlock	.05	.02	.01
☐ 72T Joe Magrane	.05	.02	.01
☐ 73T Dave Martinez	.10	.05	.01
☐ 74T Fred McGriff	1.00	.45	.12
☐ 75T Mark McLemore	.05	.02	.01
☐ 76T Kevin McReynolds	.05	.02	.01
☐ 77T Dave Meads	.05	.02	.01
☐ 78T Eddie Milner	.05	.02	.01
☐ 79T Greg Minton	.05	.02	.01
☐ 80T John Mitchell	.05	.02	.01
☐ 81T Kevin Mitchell	.15	.07	.02
☐ 82T Charlie Moore	.05	.02	.01
☐ 83T Jeff Musselman	.05	.02	.01
☐ 84T Gene Nelson	.05	.02	.01
☐ 85T Graig Nettles	.10	.05	.01
☐ 86T Al Newman	.05	.02	.01
☐ 87T Reid Nichols	.05	.02	.01
☐ 88T Tom Niedenfuer	.05	.02	.01
☐ 89T Joe Niekro	.05	.02	.01
☐ 90T Tom Nieto	.05	.02	.01
☐ 91T Matt Nokes	.10	.05	.01
☐ 92T Dickie Noles	.05	.02	.01
☐ 93T Pat Pacillo	.05	.02	.01
☐ 94T Lance Parrish	.10	.05	.01
☐ 95T Tony Pena	.05	.02	.01
☐ 96T Luis Polonia	.15	.07	.02
☐ 97T Randy Ready	.05	.02	.01
☐ 98T Jeff Reardon	.10	.05	.01
☐ 99T Gary Redus	.05	.02	.01
☐ 100T Jeff Reed	.05	.02	.01
☐ 101T Rick Rhoden	.05	.02	.01
☐ 102T Cal Ripken Sr. MG	.10	.05	.01
☐ 103T Wally Ritchie	.05	.02	.01
☐ 104T Jeff M. Robinson	.05	.02	.01
☐ 105T Gary Roenicke	.05	.02	.01
☐ 106T Jerry Royster	.05	.02	.01
☐ 107T Mark Salas	.05	.02	.01
☐ 108T Luis Salazar	.05	.02	.01
☐ 109T Benny Santiago	.10	.05	.01
☐ 110T Dave Schmidt	.05	.02	.01
☐ 111T Kevin Seitzer	.10	.05	.01
☐ 112T John Shelby	.05	.02	.01
☐ 113T Steve Shields	.05	.02	.01
☐ 114T John Smiley	.10	.05	.01
☐ 115T Chris Speier	.05	.02	.01
☐ 116T Mike Stanley	.15	.07	.02
☐ 117T Terry Steinbach	.25	.11	.03
☐ 118T Les Straker	.05	.02	.01
☐ 119T Jim Sundberg	.05	.02	.01
☐ 120T Danny Tartabull	.10	.05	.01
☐ 121T Tom Trebelhorn MG	.05	.02	.01
☐ 122T Dave Valle	.05	.02	.01
☐ 123T Ed VandeBerg	.05	.02	.01
☐ 124T Andy Van Slyke	.10	.05	.01
☐ 125T Gary Ward	.05	.02	.01
☐ 126T Alan Wiggins	.05	.02	.01
☐ 127T Bill Wilkinson	.05	.02	.01
☐ 128T Frank Williams	.05	.02	.01
☐ 129T Matt Williams	2.00	.90	.25
☐ 130T Jim Winn	.05	.02	.01
☐ 131T Matt Young	.05	.02	.01
☐ 132T Checklist 1T-132T	.05	.02	.01

1987 Topps Traded Tiffany

Since the update Tiffany cards were issued in the same quantities as the regular cards, again these cards are not valued as high as a multiplier as the previous years. These 132 standard-size cards parallel the regular cards but have glossy fronts and easy to read backs. These cards were issued in factory set form only.

	MINT	NRMT	EXC
COMPLETE FACT.SET (132)	15.00	6.75	1.85
COMMON CARD (1T-132T)	.10	.05	.01
*STARS: 2X BASIC CARDS			
*ROOKIES: 2X BASIC CARDS			

1987 Topps Coins

This full-color set of 48 coins contains a full-color photo of the player with a scroll at the bottom containing the player's name, position and team. The backs contain the coin number and brief biographical data. Some of the coins have gold rims and some have silver rims. Each coin measures approximately 1 1/2" in diameter. The 1987 set is very similar to the 1988 set of the following year; the 1988 coins have gold stars on the name scroll on the front of the coin.

	MINT	NRMT	EXC
COMPLETE SET (48)	8.00	3.60	1.00
COMMON COIN (1-48)	.05	.02	.01
☐ 1 Harold Baines	.10	.05	.01
☐ 2 Jesse Barfield	.05	.02	.01
☐ 3 George Bell	.05	.02	.01
☐ 4 Wade Boggs	.40	.18	.05
☐ 5 George Brett	.75	.35	.09
☐ 6 Jose Canseco	.75	.35	.09
☐ 7 Joe Carter	.30	.14	.04
☐ 8 Roger Clemens	.50	.23	.06
☐ 9 Alvin Davis	.05	.02	.01
☐ 10 Rob Deer	.05	.02	.01
☐ 11 Kirk Gibson	.10	.05	.01
☐ 12 Rickey Henderson	.30	.14	.04
☐ 13 Kent Hrbek	.10	.05	.01
☐ 14 Pete Incaviglia	.10	.05	.01
☐ 15 Reggie Jackson	.50	.23	.06
☐ 16 Wally Joyner	.30	.14	.04
☐ 17 Don Mattingly	1.00	.45	.12
☐ 18 Jack Morris	.10	.05	.01
☐ 19 Eddie Murray	.50	.23	.06
☐ 20 Kirby Puckett	1.00	.45	.12
☐ 21 Jim Rice	.10	.05	.01
☐ 22 Dave Righetti	.05	.02	.01
☐ 23 Cal Ripken	2.00	.90	.25
☐ 24 Cory Snyder	.05	.02	.01
☐ 25 Danny Tartabull	.05	.02	.01
☐ 26 Dave Winfield	.20	.09	.03
☐ 27 Hubie Brooks	.05	.02	.01
☐ 28 Gary Carter	.10	.05	.01
☐ 29 Vince Coleman	.05	.02	.01
☐ 30 Eric Davis	.10	.05	.01
☐ 31 Glenn Davis	.05	.02	.01
☐ 32 Steve Garvey	.10	.05	.01
☐ 33 Dwight Gooden	.20	.09	.03
☐ 34 Tony Gwynn	1.00	.45	.12
☐ 35 Von Hayes	.05	.02	.01
☐ 36 Keith Hernandez	.10	.05	.01
☐ 37 Dale Murphy	.20	.09	.03
☐ 38 Dave Parker	.10	.05	.01
☐ 39 Tony Pena	.05	.02	.01
☐ 40 Nolan Ryan	2.00	.90	.25
☐ 41 Ryne Sandberg	.75	.35	.09
☐ 42 Steve Sax	.05	.02	.01
☐ 43 Mike Schmidt	.60	.25	.07
☐ 44 Mike Scott	.05	.02	.01
☐ 45 Ozzie Smith	.75	.35	.09
☐ 46 Darryl Strawberry	.20	.09	.03
☐ 47 Fernando Valenzuela	.10	.05	.01
☐ 48 Todd Worrell	.05	.02	.01

1987 Topps Gallery of Champions

These 12 cards, issued in complete set form only, are "metal" versions of regular Topps cards. These 12 players were either 1986 award winners or league leaders. These cards measure approximately 1 14" by 1 3/4" and were issued in aluminum, silver and bronze versions. We have priced the aluminum versions with the bronze valued at 2X to 4X the aluminums and the silvers are 5X to 10X the values listed below. The set is sequenced in alphabetical order.

	MINT	NRMT	EXC
COMPLETE SET (12)	100.00	45.00	12.50
COMMON CARD (1-12)	5.00	2.20	.60
☐ 1 Jesse Barfield	5.00	2.20	.60
☐ 2 Wade Boggs	15.00	6.75	1.85
☐ 3 Jose Canseco	15.00	6.75	1.85
☐ 4 Joe Carter	10.00	4.50	1.25
☐ 5 Roger Clemens	20.00	9.00	2.50
☐ 6 Tony Gwynn	25.00	11.00	3.10
☐ 7 Don Mattingly	20.00	9.00	2.50
☐ 8 Tim Raines	7.50	3.40	.95
☐ 9 Dave Righetti	5.00	2.20	.60
☐ 10 Mike Schmidt	15.00	6.75	1.85
☐ 11 Mike Scott	5.00	2.20	.60
☐ 12 Todd Worrell	7.50	3.40	.95

1987 Topps Mini Leaders

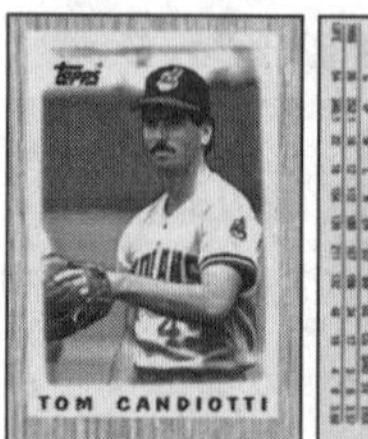

The 1987 Topps Mini set of Major League Leaders features 77 cards of leaders of the various statistical categories for the 1986 season. The cards are numbered on the back and measure approximately 2 5/32" by 3". The card backs are printed in orange and brown on white card stock. They are very similar in design to the Team Leader cards in the 1987 Topps regular issue. The cards were distributed as a separate issue in wax packs of seven for 30 cents. Eleven of the cards were double printed and are hence more plentiful; they are marked DP in the checklist below. The order of the set is alphabetical by player's name within team; the teams themselves are ordered alphabetically by city name within each league.

	MINT	NRMT	EXC
COMPLETE SET (77)	5.00	2.20	.60
COMMON CARD (1-77)	.05	.02	.01
COMMON CARD DP	.03	.01	.01
☐ 1 Bob Horner DP	.03	.01	.01
☐ 2 Dale Murphy	.25	.11	.03
☐ 3 Lee Smith	.25	.11	.03
☐ 4 Eric Davis	.10	.05	.01
☐ 5 John Franco	.10	.05	.01
☐ 6 Dave Parker	.10	.05	.01
☐ 7 Kevin Bass	.05	.02	.01
☐ 8 Glenn Davis DP	.03	.01	.01
☐ 9 Bill Doran DP	.03	.01	.01
☐ 10 Bob Knepper DP	.03	.01	.01
☐ 11 Mike Scott	.05	.02	.01
☐ 12 Dave Smith	.05	.02	.01
☐ 13 Mariano Duncan	.05	.02	.01
☐ 14 Orel Hershiser	.10	.05	.01
☐ 15 Steve Sax DP	.03	.01	.01
☐ 16 Fernando Valenzuela	.10	.05	.01
☐ 17 Tim Raines	.10	.05	.01
☐ 18 Jeff Reardon	.10	.05	.01
☐ 19 Floyd Youmans	.05	.02	.01
☐ 20 Gary Carter DP	.10	.05	.01
☐ 21 Ron Darling	.05	.02	.01
☐ 22 Sid Fernandez	.05	.02	.01
☐ 23 Dwight Gooden	.25	.11	.03
☐ 24 Keith Hernandez	.10	.05	.01
☐ 25 Bob Ojeda	.05	.02	.01
☐ 26 Darryl Strawberry	.10	.05	.01
☐ 27 Steve Bedrosian	.05	.02	.01
☐ 28 Von Hayes DP	.03	.01	.01
☐ 29 Juan Samuel	.05	.02	.01
☐ 30 Mike Schmidt	.50	.23	.06
☐ 31 Rick Rhoden	.05	.02	.01
☐ 32 Vince Coleman	.05	.02	.01
☐ 33 Danny Cox	.05	.02	.01
☐ 34 Todd Worrell	.05	.02	.01
☐ 35 Tony Gwynn	1.00	.45	.12
☐ 36 Mike Krukow	.05	.02	.01
☐ 37 Candy Maldonado	.05	.02	.01
☐ 38 Don Aase	.05	.02	.01
☐ 39 Eddie Murray	.50	.23	.06
☐ 40 Cal Ripken	1.50	.70	.19
☐ 41 Wade Boggs	.30	.14	.04
☐ 42 Roger Clemens	.50	.23	.06
☐ 43 Bruce Hurst	.05	.02	.01
☐ 44 Jim Rice	.10	.05	.01
☐ 45 Wally Joyner	.25	.11	.03
☐ 46 Donnie Moore	.05	.02	.01
☐ 47 Gary Pettis	.05	.02	.01
☐ 48 Mike Witt	.05	.02	.01
☐ 49 John Cangelosi	.05	.02	.01
☐ 50 Tom Candiotti	.05	.02	.01
☐ 51 Joe Carter	.25	.11	.03
☐ 52 Pat Tabler	.05	.02	.01
☐ 53 Kirk Gibson DP	.10	.05	.01
☐ 54 Willie Hernandez	.05	.02	.01
☐ 55 Jack Morris	.10	.05	.01
☐ 56 Alan Trammell DP	.25	.11	.03
☐ 57 George Brett	.75	.35	.09
☐ 58 Willie Wilson	.05	.02	.01
☐ 59 Rob Deer	.05	.02	.01
☐ 60 Teddy Higuera	.05	.02	.01
☐ 61 Bert Blyleven DP	.05	.02	.01
☐ 62 Gary Gaetti DP	.05	.02	.01
☐ 63 Kirby Puckett	1.00	.45	.12
☐ 64 Rickey Henderson	.30	.14	.04
☐ 65 Don Mattingly	1.00	.45	.12
☐ 66 Dennis Rasmussen	.05	.02	.01
☐ 67 Dave Righetti	.05	.02	.01
☐ 68 Jose Canseco	.60	.25	.07
☐ 69 Dave Kingman	.05	.02	.01
☐ 70 Phil Bradley	.05	.02	.01
☐ 71 Mark Langston	.10	.05	.01
☐ 72 Pete O'Brien	.05	.02	.01
☐ 73 Jesse Barfield	.05	.02	.01
☐ 74 George Bell	.05	.02	.01
☐ 75 Tony Fernandez	.05	.02	.01
☐ 76 Tom Henke	.05	.02	.01
☐ 77 Checklist Card	.05	.02	.01

1987 Topps/O-Pee-Chee Stickers

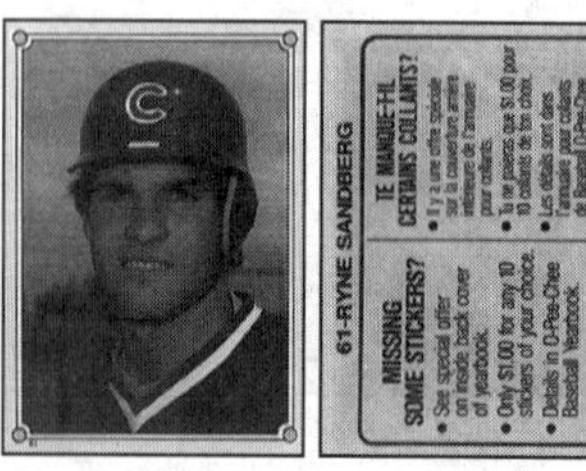

Made in Italy for Topps and O-Pee-Chee by Panini, these 313 stickers measure approximately 2 1/8" by 3" and are numbered on both front and back. The fronts feature white-bordered color player photos. The horizontal backs carry a bilingual ad for O-Pee-Chee. The Topps stickers contain offers on the back to obtain either a trip for four to Spring Training of the team of your choice or a complete set of Topps baseball cards directly from Topps. An album onto which the stickers could be affixed was available at retail stores. The album and the sticker numbering are organized as follows: 1986 Highlights (1-12), 1986 Championship Series (13-18), 1986 World Series (19-25), Houston Astros (26-35), Atlanta Braves (36-45), St. Louis Cardinals (46-55), Chicago Cubs (56-65), Los Angeles Dodgers (66-75), Montreal Expos (76-85), San Francisco Giants (86-95), New York Mets (96-105), San Diego Padres (106-115), Philadelphia Phillies (116-125), Pittsburgh Pirates (126-135), Cincinnati Reds (136-145), Foil All-Stars (146-163), Oakland A's (164-173), California Angels (174-183), Toronto Blue Jays (184-193), Milwaukee Brewers (194-203), Cleveland Indians (204-213), Seattle Mariners (214-223), Baltimore Orioles (224-233), Texas Rangers (234-243), Boston Red Sox (244-253), Kansas City Royals (254-263), Detroit Tigers (264-273), Minnesota Twins (274-283), Chicago White Sox (284-293), New York Yankees (294-303), and Future Stars (304-313). For those stickers featuring more than one player, the other numbers on that sticker are given below in parentheses. There was a variation of this set that was test-marketed by Topps. Its stickers had card backings (precursors of the Super Stars sticker backs) rather than the paper backing Topps had been using in previous years. Apparently the test was successful as both Topps and O-Pee-Chee switched to the home-printed, stiffer-backed stickers the following year.Will Clark and Barry Bonds are featured on stickers during their Rookie Card Year

	MINT	NRMT	EXC
COMPLETE SET (313)	15.00	6.75	1.85
COMMON STICKER (1-145)	.05	.02	.01
COMMON FOIL (146-163)	.10	.05	.01
COMMON STICKER (147-313)	.05	.02	.01
*TOPPS AND OPC: SAME VALUE			
☐ 1 Jim Deshaies (172)	.05	.02	.01
☐ 2 Roger Clemens (175) (Top half)	.15	.07	.02
☐ 3 Roger Clemens (176) (Bottom half)	.15	.07	.02
☐ 4 Dwight Evans (177)	.10	.05	.01
☐ 5 Dwight Gooden (178) (Top half)	.15	.07	.02
☐ 6 Dwight Gooden (180) (Bottom half)	.15	.07	.02
☐ 7 Dave Lopes (181)	.10	.05	.01
☐ 8 Dave Righetti (182) (Top half)	.05	.02	.01
☐ 9 Dave Righetti (183) (Bottom half)	.05	.02	.01
☐ 10 Ruben Sierra (185)	.50	.23	.06
☐ 11 Todd Worrell (186) (Top half)	.05	.02	.01
☐ 12 Todd Worrell (187) (Bottom half)	.05	.02	.01
☐ 13 Len Dykstra LCS	.15	.07	.02
☐ 14 Gary Carter LCS	.10	.05	.01
☐ 15 Mike Scott LCS	.05	.02	.01
☐ 16 Gary Pettis LCS	.05	.02	.01
☐ 17 Jim Rice LCS	.10	.05	.01
☐ 18 Marty Barrett LCS	.05	.02	.01
☐ 19 Bruce Hurst WS	.05	.02	.01
☐ 20 Dwight Evans WS	.10	.05	.01
☐ 21 Len Dykstra WS	.15	.07	.02
☐ 22 Gary Carter WS	.10	.05	.01
☐ 23 Dave Henderson WS	.05	.02	.01
☐ 24 Ray Knight WS	.10	.05	.01
☐ 25 Mets Celebrate WS	.10	.05	.01
☐ 26 Glenn Davis	.05	.02	.01
☐ 27 Nolan Ryan (188)	2.00	.90	.25
☐ 28 Charlie Kerfeld(189)	.05	.02	.01
☐ 29 Jose Cruz (190)	.10	.05	.01
☐ 30 Phil Garner (191)	.10	.05	.01
☐ 31 Bill Doran (192)	.05	.02	.01
☐ 32 Bob Knepper (195)	.05	.02	.01
☐ 33 Denny Walling (196)	.05	.02	.01
☐ 34 Kevin Bass (197)	.05	.02	.01
☐ 35 Mike Scott	.05	.02	.01
☐ 36 Dale Murphy	.15	.07	.02
☐ 37 Paul Assenmacher (198)	.05	.02	.01
☐ 38 Ken Oberkfell (200)	.05	.02	.01
☐ 39 Andres Thomas (201)	.05	.02	.01
☐ 40 Gene Garber (202)	.05	.02	.01
☐ 41 Bob Horner	.05	.02	.01
☐ 42 Rafael Ramirez (203)	.05	.02	.01
☐ 43 Rick Mahler (204)	.05	.02	.01
☐ 44 Omar Moreno (205)	.05	.02	.01
☐ 45 Dave Palmer (206)	.05	.02	.01
☐ 46 Ozzie Smith	.40	.18	.05
☐ 47 Bob Forsch (207)	.05	.02	.01
☐ 48 Willie McGee (209)	.05	.02	.01
☐ 49 Tom Herr (210)	.05	.02	.01
☐ 50 Vince Coleman (211)	.05	.02	.01
☐ 51 Andy Van Slyke (212)	.10	.05	.01
☐ 52 Jack Clark (215)	.10	.05	.01
☐ 53 John Tudor (216)	.05	.02	.01
☐ 54 Terry Pendleton(217)	.10	.05	.01
☐ 55 Todd Worrell	.10	.05	.01
☐ 56 Lee Smith	.15	.07	.02
☐ 57 Leon Durham (218)	.05	.02	.01
☐ 58 Jerry Mumphrey (219)	.05	.02	.01
☐ 59 Shawon Dunston (220)	.10	.05	.01
☐ 60 Scott Sanderson(221)	.05	.02	.01
☐ 61 Ryne Sandberg	.50	.23	.06
☐ 62 Gary Matthews (222)	.05	.02	.01
☐ 63 Dennis Eckersley (225)	.15	.07	.02
☐ 64 Jody Davis (226)	.05	.02	.01

☐ 65 Keith Moreland (227)	.05	.02	.01
☐ 66 Mike Marshall (228)	.05	.02	.01
☐ 67 Bill Madlock (229)	.10	.05	.01
☐ 68 Greg Brock (230)	.05	.02	.01
☐ 69 Pedro Guerrero (231)	.10	.05	.01
☐ 70 Steve Sax	.05	.02	.01
☐ 71 Rick Honeycutt (232)	.05	.02	.01
☐ 72 Franklin Stubbs(235)	.05	.02	.01
☐ 73 Mike Scioscia (236)	.05	.02	.01
☐ 74 Mariano Duncan (237)	.05	.02	.01
☐ 75 Fernando Valenzuela	.10	.05	.01
☐ 76 Hubie Brooks	.05	.02	.01
☐ 77 Andre Dawson (238)	.15	.07	.02
☐ 78 Tim Burke (240)	.05	.02	.01
☐ 79 Floyd Youmans (241)	.05	.02	.01
☐ 80 Tim Wallach (242)	.05	.02	.01
☐ 81 Jeff Reardon (243)	.10	.05	.01
☐ 82 Mitch Webster (244)	.05	.02	.01
☐ 83 Bryn Smith (245)	.05	.02	.01
☐ 84 Andres Galarraga (246)	.50	.23	.06
☐ 85 Tim Raines	.10	.05	.01
☐ 86 Chris Brown	.05	.02	.01
☐ 87 Bob Brenly (247)	.05	.02	.01
☐ 88 Will Clark (249)	1.50	.70	.19
☐ 89 Scott Garrelts (250)	.05	.02	.01
☐ 90 Jeffrey Leonard(251)	.05	.02	.01
☐ 91 Robby Thompson (252)	.10	.05	.01
☐ 92 Mike Krukow (255)	.05	.02	.01
☐ 93 Danny Gladden (256)	.05	.02	.01
☐ 94 Candy Maldonado(257)	.05	.02	.01
☐ 95 Chili Davis	.10	.05	.01
☐ 96 Dwight Gooden	.15	.07	.02
☐ 97 Sid Fernandez (258)	.05	.02	.01
☐ 98 Len Dykstra (259)	.15	.07	.02
☐ 99 Bob Ojeda (260)	.05	.02	.01
☐ 100 Wally Backman (261)	.05	.02	.01
☐ 101 Gary Carter	.10	.05	.01
☐ 102 Keith Hernandez(262)	.10	.05	.01
☐ 103 Darryl Strawberry (265)	.15	.07	.02
☐ 104 Roger McDowell (266)	.05	.02	.01
☐ 105 Ron Darling (267)	.05	.02	.01
☐ 106 Tony Gwynn	.75	.35	.09
☐ 107 Dave Dravecky (268)	.10	.05	.01
☐ 108 Terry Kennedy (269)	.05	.02	.01
☐ 109 Rich Gossage (270)	.10	.05	.01
☐ 110 Garry Templeton(271)	.05	.02	.01
☐ 111 Lance McCullers(272)	.05	.02	.01
☐ 112 Eric Show (275)	.05	.02	.01
☐ 113 John Kruk (276)	.50	.23	.06
☐ 114 Tim Flannery (277)	.05	.02	.01
☐ 115 Steve Garvey	.15	.07	.02
☐ 116 Mike Schmidt	.60	.25	.07
☐ 117 Glenn Wilson (278)	.05	.02	.01
☐ 118 Kent Tekulve (280)	.05	.02	.01
☐ 119 Gary Redus (281)	.05	.02	.01
☐ 120 Shane Rawley (282)	.05	.02	.01
☐ 121 Von Hayes	.05	.02	.01
☐ 122 Don Carman (283)	.05	.02	.01
☐ 123 Bruce Ruffin (285)	.05	.02	.01
☐ 124 Steve Bedrosian(286)	.05	.02	.01
☐ 125 Juan Samuel (287)	.05	.02	.01
☐ 126 Sid Bream (288)	.05	.02	.01
☐ 127 Cecilio Guante (289)	.05	.02	.01
☐ 128 Rick Reuschel (290)	.05	.02	.01
☐ 129 Tony Pena (291)	.05	.02	.01
☐ 130 Rick Rhoden	.05	.02	.01
☐ 131 Barry Bonds (292)	3.00	1.35	.35
☐ 132 Joe Orsulak (295)	.05	.02	.01
☐ 133 Jim Morrison (296)	.05	.02	.01
☐ 134 R.J. Reynolds (297)	.05	.02	.01
☐ 135 Johnny Ray	.05	.02	.01
☐ 136 Eric Davis	.10	.05	.01
☐ 137 Tom Browning (298)	.05	.02	.01
☐ 138 John Franco (300)	.10	.05	.01
☐ 139 Pete Rose (301)	.75	.35	.09
☐ 140 Bill Gullickson(302)	.05	.02	.01
☐ 141 Ron Oester (303)	.05	.02	.01
☐ 142 Bo Diaz (304)	.05	.02	.01
☐ 143 Buddy Bell (305)	.10	.05	.01
☐ 144 Eddie Milner (306)	.05	.02	.01
☐ 145 Dave Parker	.10	.05	.01
☐ 146 Kirby Puckett FOIL	1.25	.55	.16
☐ 147 Rickey Henderson FOIL	.40	.18	.05
☐ 148 Wade Boggs FOIL	.40	.18	.05
☐ 149 Lance Parrish FOIL	.15	.07	.02
☐ 150 Wally Joyner FOIL	.75	.35	.09
☐ 151 Cal Ripken FOIL	3.00	1.35	.35
☐ 152 Dave Winfield FOIL	.40	.18	.05
☐ 153 Lou Whitaker FOIL	.10	.05	.01
☐ 154 Roger Clemens FOIL	.60	.25	.07
☐ 155 Tony Gwynn FOIL	1.25	.55	.16
☐ 156 Ryne Sandberg FOIL	.75	.35	.09
☐ 157 Keith Hernandez FOIL	.10	.05	.01
☐ 158 Gary Carter FOIL	.30	.14	.04
☐ 159 Darryl Strawberry FOIL	.15	.07	.02
☐ 160 Mike Schmidt FOIL	1.00	.45	.12
☐ 161 Dale Murphy FOIL	.30	.14	.04
☐ 162 Ozzie Smith FOIL	.60	.25	.07
☐ 163 Dwight Gooden FOIL	.30	.14	.04
☐ 164 Jose Canseco	.75	.35	.09
☐ 165 Curt Young (307)	.05	.02	.01
☐ 166 Alfredo Griffin(308)	.05	.02	.01
☐ 167 Dave Stewart (309)	.10	.05	.01
☐ 168 Mike Davis (310)	.05	.02	.01
☐ 169 Bruce Bochte (311)	.05	.02	.01
☐ 170 Dwayne Murphy (312)	.05	.02	.01
☐ 171 Carney Lansford(313)	.10	.05	.01
☐ 172 Joaquin Andujar (1)	.05	.02	.01
☐ 173 Dave Kingman	.10	.05	.01
☐ 174 Wally Joyner	.50	.23	.06
☐ 175 Gary Pettis (2)	.05	.02	.01
☐ 176 Dick Schofield (3)	.05	.02	.01
☐ 177 Donnie Moore (4)	.05	.02	.01
☐ 178 Brian Downing (5)	.05	.02	.01
☐ 179 Mike Witt	.05	.02	.01
☐ 180 Bob Boone (6)	.10	.05	.01
☐ 181 Kirk McCaskill (7)	.05	.02	.01
☐ 182 Doug DeCinces (8)	.05	.02	.01
☐ 183 Don Sutton (9)	.15	.07	.02
☐ 184 Jesse Barfield	.05	.02	.01
☐ 185 Tom Henke (10)	.05	.02	.01
☐ 186 Willie Upshaw (11)	.05	.02	.01
☐ 187 Mark Eichhorn (12)	.05	.02	.01
☐ 188 Damaso Garcia (27)	.05	.02	.01
☐ 189 Jim Clancy (28)	.05	.02	.01
☐ 190 Lloyd Moseby (29)	.05	.02	.01
☐ 191 Tony Fernandez (30)	.05	.02	.01
☐ 192 Jimmy Key (31)	.10	.05	.01
☐ 193 George Bell	.05	.02	.01
☐ 194 Rob Deer	.05	.02	.01
☐ 195 Mark Clear (32)	.05	.02	.01
☐ 196 Robin Yount (33)	.25	.11	.03
☐ 197 Jim Gantner (34)	.05	.02	.01
☐ 198 Cecil Cooper (35)	.10	.05	.01
☐ 199 Teddy Higuera	.05	.02	.01
☐ 200 Paul Molitor (38)	.25	.11	.03
☐ 201 Dan Plesac (39)	.05	.02	.01
☐ 202 Billy Joe Robidoux (40)	.05	.02	.01
☐ 203 Earnie Riles (42)	.05	.02	.01
☐ 204 Ken Schrom (43)	.05	.02	.01
☐ 205 Pat Tabler (44)	.05	.02	.01
☐ 206 Mel Hall (45)	.05	.02	.01
☐ 207 Tony Bernazard (47)	.05	.02	.01
☐ 208 Joe Carter	.15	.07	.02
☐ 209 Ernie Camacho (48)	.05	.02	.01
☐ 210 Julio Franco (49)	.10	.05	.01
☐ 211 Tom Candiotti (50)	.05	.02	.01
☐ 212 Brook Jacoby (51)	.05	.02	.01
☐ 213 Cory Snyder	.05	.02	.01
☐ 214 Jim Presley	.05	.02	.01
☐ 215 Mike Moore (52)	.05	.02	.01
☐ 216 Harold Reynolds (53)	.10	.05	.01
☐ 217 Scott Bradley (54)	.05	.02	.01
☐ 218 Matt Young (57)	.05	.02	.01
☐ 219 Mark Langston (58)	.10	.05	.01
☐ 220 Alvin Davis (59)	.05	.02	.01
☐ 221 Phil Bradley (60)	.05	.02	.01
☐ 222 Ken Phelps (62)	.05	.02	.01
☐ 223 Danny Tartabull	.10	.05	.01
☐ 224 Eddie Murray	.30	.14	.04
☐ 225 Rick Dempsey (63)	.05	.02	.01
☐ 226 Fred Lynn (64)	.10	.05	.01
☐ 227 Mike Boddicker (65)	.05	.02	.01
☐ 228 Don Aase (66)	.05	.02	.01
☐ 229 Larry Sheets (67)	.05	.02	.01
☐ 230 Storm Davis (68)	.05	.02	.01
☐ 231 Lee Lacy (69)	.05	.02	.01
☐ 232 Jim Traber (71)	.05	.02	.01
☐ 233 Cal Ripken	2.00	.90	.25
☐ 234 Larry Parrish	.05	.02	.01
☐ 235 Gary Ward (72)	.05	.02	.01
☐ 236 Pete Incaviglia (73)	.10	.05	.01
☐ 237 Scott Fletcher (74)	.05	.02	.01
☐ 238 Greg Harris (77)	.05	.02	.01
☐ 239 Pete O'Brien	.05	.02	.01
☐ 240 Charlie Hough (78)	.05	.02	.01
☐ 241 Don Slaught (79)	.05	.02	.01
☐ 242 Steve Buechele (80)	.05	.02	.01
☐ 243 Oddibe McDowell (81)	.05	.02	.01
☐ 244 Roger Clemens (82)	.40	.18	.05
☐ 245 Bob Stanley (83)	.05	.02	.01
☐ 246 Tom Seaver (84)	.50	.23	.06
☐ 247 Rich Gedman (87)	.05	.02	.01
☐ 248 Jim Rice	.10	.05	.01
☐ 249 Dennis Boyd (88)	.05	.02	.01
☐ 250 Bill Buckner (89)	.10	.05	.01
☐ 251 Dwight Evans (90)	.10	.05	.01
☐ 252 Don Baylor (91)	.10	.05	.01
☐ 253 Wade Boggs	.25	.11	.03
☐ 254 George Brett	.75	.35	.09
☐ 255 Steve Farr (92)	.05	.02	.01
☐ 256 Jim Sundberg (93)	.05	.02	.01
☐ 257 Dan Quisenberry (94)	.05	.02	.01
☐ 258 Charlie Leibrandt(97)	.05	.02	.01
☐ 259 Argenis Salazar (98)	.05	.02	.01
☐ 260 Frank White (99)	.10	.05	.01
☐ 261 Willie Wilson (100)	.05	.02	.01
☐ 262 Lonnie Smith (102)	.05	.02	.01
☐ 263 Steve Balboni	.05	.02	.01
☐ 264 Darrell Evans	.10	.05	.01
☐ 265 Johnny Grubb (103)	.05	.02	.01
☐ 266 Jack Morris (104)	.10	.05	.01
☐ 267 Lou Whitaker (105)	.10	.05	.01
☐ 268 Chet Lemon (107)	.05	.02	.01
☐ 269 Lance Parrish (108)	.10	.05	.01
☐ 270 Alan Trammell (109)	.15	.07	.02
☐ 271 Darnell Coles (110)	.05	.02	.01
☐ 272 Willie Hernandez (111)	.05	.02	.01
☐ 273 Kirk Gibson	.10	.05	.01
☐ 274 Kirby Puckett	.75	.35	.09
☐ 275 Mike Smithson (112)	.05	.02	.01
☐ 276 Mickey Hatcher (113)	.05	.02	.01
☐ 277 Frank Viola (114)	.05	.02	.01
☐ 278 Bert Blyleven (117)	.10	.05	.01
☐ 279 Gary Gaetti	.10	.05	.01
☐ 280 Tom Brunansky (118)	.05	.02	.01
☐ 281 Kent Hrbek (119)	.10	.05	.01
☐ 282 Roy Smalley (120)	.05	.02	.01
☐ 283 Greg Gagne (122)	.05	.02	.01
☐ 284 Harold Baines	.10	.05	.01
☐ 285 Ron Hassey (123)	.05	.02	.01
☐ 286 Floyd Bannister(124)	.05	.02	.01
☐ 287 Ozzie Guillen (125)	.05	.02	.01
☐ 288 Carlton Fisk (126)	.25	.11	.03
☐ 289 Tim Hulett (127)	.05	.02	.01
☐ 290 Joe Cowley (128)	.05	.02	.01
☐ 291 Greg Walker (129)	.05	.02	.01
☐ 292 Neil Allen (131)	.05	.02	.01
☐ 293 John Cangelosi	.05	.02	.01
☐ 294 Don Mattingly	1.00	.45	.12
☐ 295 Mike Easler (132)	.05	.02	.01
☐ 296 Rickey Henderson(133)	.25	.11	.03
☐ 297 Dan Pasqua (134)	.05	.02	.01
☐ 298 Dave Winfield (137)	.25	.11	.03
☐ 299 Dave Righetti	.05	.02	.01
☐ 300 Mike Pagliarulo(138)	.05	.02	.01
☐ 301 Ron Guidry (139)	.10	.05	.01
☐ 302 Willie Randolph(140)	.10	.05	.01
☐ 303 Dennis Rasmussen (141)	.05	.02	.01
☐ 304 Jose Canseco (142)	.75	.35	.09
☐ 305 Andres Thomas (143)	.05	.02	.01
☐ 306 Danny Tartabull(144)	.10	.05	.01
☐ 307 Robby Thompson (165)	.10	.05	.01
☐ 308 Pete Incaviglia(166)	.10	.05	.01
☐ 309 Dale Sveum (167)	.05	.02	.01
☐ 310 Todd Worrell (168)	.10	.05	.01
☐ 311 Andy Allanson (169)	.05	.02	.01
☐ 312 Bruce Ruffin (170)	.05	.02	.01
☐ 313 Wally Joyner (171)	.50	.23	.06
☐ xx Album	1.00	.45	.12

1988 Topps

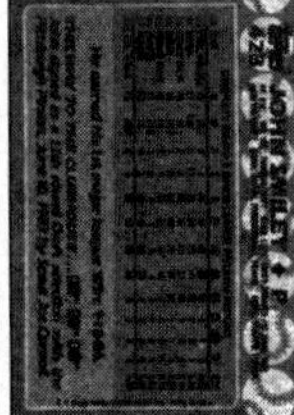

This set consists of 792 standard-size cards. The cards were primarily issued in 15-card wax packs, 42-card rack packs and factory sets. Card fronts feature white borders encasing a color photo with team name running across the top and player name diagonally across the bottom. Subsets include Record Breakers (1-7), All-Stars (386-407), Turn Back the Clock (661-665), and Team Leaders (scattered throughout the set). The manager cards contain a team checklist on back. The key Rookie Cards in this set are Ellis Burks, Ken Caminiti, Tom Glavine, Jeff Montgomery, and Matt Williams.

	MINT	NRMT	EXC
COMPLETE SET (792)	10.00	4.50	1.25
COMPLETE FACT.SET (792)	15.00	6.75	1.85
COMMON CARD (1-792)	.05	.02	.01
☐ 1 Vince Coleman RB 100 Steals for Third Cons. Season	.05	.02	.01
☐ 2 Don Mattingly RB Six Grand Slams	.15	.07	.02
☐ 3 Mark McGwire RB Rookie Homer Record (No white spot)	.30	.14	.04
☐ 3A Mark McGwire RB Rookie Homer Record (White spot behind left foot)	.15	.07	.02
☐ 4 Eddie Murray RB Switch Home Runs, Two Straight Games (No caption on front)	.20	.09	.03
☐ 4A Eddie Murray RB Switch Home Runs, Two Straight Games (Caption in box on card front)	.40	.18	.05
☐ 5 Phil Niekro Joe Niekro RB Brothers Win Record	.10	.05	.01
☐ 6 Nolan Ryan RB 11th 200 K's Season	.40	.18	.05
☐ 7 Benito Santiago RB 34-Game Hitting Streak Rookie Record	.05	.02	.01
☐ 8 Kevin Elster	.15	.07	.02
☐ 9 Andy Hawkins	.05	.02	.01
☐ 10 Ryne Sandberg	.25	.11	.03
☐ 11 Mike Young	.05	.02	.01
☐ 12 Bill Schroeder	.05	.02	.01
☐ 13 Andres Thomas	.05	.02	.01
☐ 14 Sparky Anderson MG (Checklist back)	.10	.05	.01
☐ 15 Chili Davis	.15	.07	.02
☐ 16 Kirk McCaskill	.05	.02	.01
☐ 17 Ron Oester	.05	.02	.01
☐ 18A Al Leiter ERR (Photo actually Steve George, right ear visible)	.15	.07	.02
☐ 18B Al Leiter COR (Left ear visible)	.10	.05	.01
☐ 19 Mark Davidson	.05	.02	.01
☐ 20 Kevin Gross	.05	.02	.01
☐ 21 Red Sox TL Wade Boggs and Spike Owen	.10	.05	.01
☐ 22 Greg Swindell	.05	.02	.01
☐ 23 Ken Landreaux	.05	.02	.01
☐ 24 Jim Deshaies	.05	.02	.01
☐ 25 Andres Galarraga	.15	.07	.02
☐ 26 Mitch Williams	.10	.05	.01
☐ 27 R.J. Reynolds	.05	.02	.01
☐ 28 Jose Nunez	.05	.02	.01
☐ 29 Argenis Salazar	.05	.02	.01
☐ 30 Sid Fernandez	.05	.02	.01
☐ 31 Bruce Bochy	.05	.02	.01
☐ 32 Mike Morgan	.05	.02	.01
☐ 33 Rob Deer	.05	.02	.01
☐ 34 Ricky Horton	.05	.02	.01
☐ 35 Harold Baines	.10	.05	.01
☐ 36 Jamie Moyer	.05	.02	.01
☐ 37 Ed Romero	.05	.02	.01
☐ 38 Jeff Calhoun	.05	.02	.01
☐ 39 Gerald Perry	.05	.02	.01
☐ 40 Orel Hershiser	.10	.05	.01
☐ 41 Bob Melvin	.05	.02	.01
☐ 42 Bill Landrum	.05	.02	.01
☐ 43 Dick Schofield	.05	.02	.01
☐ 44 Lou Piniella MG (Checklist back)	.10	.05	.01
☐ 45 Kent Hrbek	.10	.05	.01
☐ 46 Darnell Coles	.05	.02	.01
☐ 47 Joaquin Andujar	.05	.02	.01
☐ 48 Alan Ashby	.05	.02	.01
☐ 49 Dave Clark	.05	.02	.01
☐ 50 Hubie Brooks	.05	.02	.01
☐ 51 Orioles TL Eddie Murray and Cal Ripken	.40	.18	.05
☐ 52 Don Robinson	.05	.02	.01
☐ 53 Curt Wilkerson	.05	.02	.01
☐ 54 Jim Clancy	.05	.02	.01
☐ 55 Phil Bradley	.05	.02	.01
☐ 56 Ed Hearn	.05	.02	.01
☐ 57 Tim Crews	.10	.05	.01
☐ 58 Dave Magadan	.05	.02	.01
☐ 59 Danny Cox	.05	.02	.01
☐ 60 Rickey Henderson	.15	.07	.02
☐ 61 Mark Knudson	.05	.02	.01
☐ 62 Jeff Hamilton	.05	.02	.01
☐ 63 Jimmy Jones	.05	.02	.01
☐ 64 Ken Caminiti	.75	.35	.09
☐ 65 Leon Durham	.05	.02	.01
☐ 66 Shane Rawley	.05	.02	.01
☐ 67 Ken Oberkfell	.05	.02	.01
☐ 68 Dave Dravecky	.10	.05	.01
☐ 69 Mike Hart	.05	.02	.01
☐ 70 Roger Clemens	.20	.09	.03
☐ 71 Gary Pettis	.05	.02	.01
☐ 72 Dennis Eckersley	.10	.05	.01
☐ 73 Randy Bush	.05	.02	.01
☐ 74 Tom Lasorda MG (Checklist back)	.10	.05	.01
☐ 75 Joe Carter	.15	.07	.02
☐ 76 Dennis Martinez	.10	.05	.01
☐ 77 Tom O'Malley	.05	.02	.01
☐ 78 Dan Petry	.05	.02	.01
☐ 79 Ernie Whitt	.05	.02	.01
☐ 80 Mark Langston	.10	.05	.01
☐ 81 Reds TL Ron Robinson and John Franco	.05	.02	.01
☐ 82 Darrel Akerfelds	.05	.02	.01
☐ 83 Jose Oquendo	.05	.02	.01
☐ 84 Cecilio Guante	.05	.02	.01
☐ 85 Howard Johnson	.05	.02	.01
☐ 86 Ron Karkovice	.05	.02	.01
☐ 87 Mike Mason	.05	.02	.01
☐ 88 Earnie Riles	.05	.02	.01
☐ 89 Gary Thurman	.05	.02	.01
☐ 90 Dale Murphy	.15	.07	.02
☐ 91 Joey Cora	.20	.09	.03
☐ 92 Len Matuszek	.05	.02	.01
☐ 93 Bob Sebra	.05	.02	.01
☐ 94 Chuck Jackson	.05	.02	.01
☐ 95 Lance Parrish	.05	.02	.01
☐ 96 Todd Benzinger	.10	.05	.01
☐ 97 Scott Garrelts	.05	.02	.01
☐ 98 Rene Gonzales	.05	.02	.01

☐ 99 Chuck Finley .10 .05 .01
☐ 100 Jack Clark .10 .05 .01
☐ 101 Allan Anderson .05 .02 .01
☐ 102 Barry Larkin .30 .14 .04
☐ 103 Curt Young .05 .02 .01
☐ 104 Dick Williams MG .10 .05 .01
(Checklist back)
☐ 105 Jesse Orosco .05 .02 .01
☐ 106 Jim Walewander .05 .02 .01
☐ 107 Scott Bailes .05 .02 .01
☐ 108 Steve Lyons .05 .02 .01
☐ 109 Joel Skinner .05 .02 .01
☐ 110 Teddy Higuera .05 .02 .01
☐ 111 Expos TL .05 .02 .01
Hubie Brooks and
Vance Law
☐ 112 Les Lancaster .05 .02 .01
☐ 113 Kelly Gruber .05 .02 .01
☐ 114 Jeff Russell .05 .02 .01
☐ 115 Johnny Ray .05 .02 .01
☐ 116 Jerry Don Gleaton .05 .02 .01
☐ 117 James Steels .05 .02 .01
☐ 118 Bob Welch .05 .02 .01
☐ 119 Robbie Wine .05 .02 .01
☐ 120 Kirby Puckett .40 .18 .05
☐ 121 Checklist 1-132 .10 .05 .01
☐ 122 Tony Bernazard .05 .02 .01
☐ 123 Tom Candiotti .05 .02 .01
☐ 124 Ray Knight .10 .05 .01
☐ 125 Bruce Hurst .05 .02 .01
☐ 126 Steve Jeltz .05 .02 .01
☐ 127 Jim Gott .05 .02 .01
☐ 128 Johnny Grubb .05 .02 .01
☐ 129 Greg Minton .05 .02 .01
☐ 130 Buddy Bell .10 .05 .01
☐ 131 Don Schulze .05 .02 .01
☐ 132 Donnie Hill .05 .02 .01
☐ 133 Greg Mathews .05 .02 .01
☐ 134 Chuck Tanner MG .10 .05 .01
(Checklist back)
☐ 135 Dennis Rasmussen .05 .02 .01
☐ 136 Brian Dayett .05 .02 .01
☐ 137 Chris Bosio .05 .02 .01
☐ 138 Mitch Webster .05 .02 .01
☐ 139 Jerry Browne .05 .02 .01
☐ 140 Jesse Barfield .05 .02 .01
☐ 141 Royals TL .15 .07 .02
George Brett and
Bret Saberhagen
☐ 142 Andy Van Slyke .10 .05 .01
☐ 143 Mickey Tettleton .10 .05 .01
☐ 144 Don Gordon .05 .02 .01
☐ 145 Bill Madlock .05 .02 .01
☐ 146 Donell Nixon .05 .02 .01
☐ 147 Bill Buckner .10 .05 .01
☐ 148 Carmelo Martinez .05 .02 .01
☐ 149 Ken Howell .05 .02 .01
☐ 150 Eric Davis .10 .05 .01
☐ 151 Bob Knepper .05 .02 .01
☐ 152 Jody Reed .10 .05 .01
☐ 153 John Habyan .05 .02 .01
☐ 154 Jeff Stone .05 .02 .01
☐ 155 Bruce Sutter .10 .05 .01
☐ 156 Gary Matthews .05 .02 .01
☐ 157 Atlee Hammaker .05 .02 .01
☐ 158 Tim Hulett .05 .02 .01
☐ 159 Brad Arnsberg .05 .02 .01
☐ 160 Willie McGee .05 .02 .01
☐ 161 Bryn Smith .05 .02 .01
☐ 162 Mark McLemore .05 .02 .01
☐ 163 Dale Mohorcic .05 .02 .01
☐ 164 Dave Johnson MG .10 .05 .01
(Checklist back)
☐ 165 Robin Yount .15 .07 .02
☐ 166 Rick Rodriquez .05 .02 .01
☐ 167 Rance Mulliniks .05 .02 .01
☐ 168 Barry Jones .05 .02 .01
☐ 169 Ross Jones .05 .02 .01
☐ 170 Rich Gossage .15 .07 .02
☐ 171 Cubs TL .05 .02 .01
Shawon Dunston
and Manny Trillo
☐ 172 Lloyd McClendon .05 .02 .01
☐ 173 Eric Plunk .05 .02 .01
☐ 174 Phil Garner .05 .02 .01
☐ 175 Kevin Bass .05 .02 .01
☐ 176 Jeff Reed .05 .02 .01
☐ 177 Frank Tanana .05 .02 .01
☐ 178 Dwayne Henry .05 .02 .01
☐ 179 Charlie Puleo .05 .02 .01
☐ 180 Terry Kennedy .05 .02 .01
☐ 181 David Cone .15 .07 .02
☐ 182 Ken Phelps .05 .02 .01
☐ 183 Tom Lawless .05 .02 .01
☐ 184 Ivan Calderon .05 .02 .01
☐ 185 Rick Rhoden .05 .02 .01
☐ 186 Rafael Palmeiro .25 .11 .03
☐ 187 Steve Kiefer .05 .02 .01
☐ 188 John Russell .05 .02 .01
☐ 189 Wes Gardner .05 .02 .01
☐ 190 Candy Maldonado .05 .02 .01
☐ 191 John Cerutti .05 .02 .01
☐ 192 Devon White .15 .07 .02
☐ 193 Brian Fisher .05 .02 .01
☐ 194 Tom Kelly MG .10 .05 .01
(Checklist back)
☐ 195 Dan Quisenberry .05 .02 .01
☐ 196 Dave Engle .05 .02 .01
☐ 197 Lance McCullers .05 .02 .01
☐ 198 Franklin Stubbs .05 .02 .01
☐ 199 Dave Meads .05 .02 .01
☐ 200 Wade Boggs .15 .07 .02
☐ 201 Rangers TL .05 .02 .01
Bobby Valentine MG
Pete O'Brien,
Pete Incaviglia and
Steve Buechele
☐ 202 Glenn Hoffman .05 .02 .01
☐ 203 Fred Toliver .05 .02 .01
☐ 204 Paul O'Neill .10 .05 .01
☐ 205 Nelson Liriano .05 .02 .01
☐ 206 Domingo Ramos .05 .02 .01
☐ 207 John Mitchell .05 .02 .01
☐ 208 Steve Lake .05 .02 .01
☐ 209 Richard Dotson .05 .02 .01
☐ 210 Willie Randolph .10 .05 .01
☐ 211 Frank DiPino .05 .02 .01
☐ 212 Greg Brock .05 .02 .01
☐ 213 Albert Hall .05 .02 .01
☐ 214 Dave Schmidt .05 .02 .01
☐ 215 Von Hayes .05 .02 .01
☐ 216 Jerry Reuss .05 .02 .01
☐ 217 Harry Spilman .05 .02 .01
☐ 218 Dan Schatzeder .05 .02 .01
☐ 219 Mike Stanley .10 .05 .01
☐ 220 Tom Henke .05 .02 .01
☐ 221 Rafael Belliard .05 .02 .01
☐ 222 Steve Farr .05 .02 .01
☐ 223 Stan Jefferson .05 .02 .01
☐ 224 Tom Trebelhorn MG .05 .02 .01
(Checklist back)
☐ 225 Mike Scioscia .05 .02 .01
☐ 226 Dave Lopes .10 .05 .01
☐ 227 Ed Correa .05 .02 .01
☐ 228 Wallace Johnson .05 .02 .01
☐ 229 Jeff Musselman .05 .02 .01
☐ 230 Pat Tabler .05 .02 .01
☐ 231 Pirates TL .15 .07 .02
Barry Bonds and
Bobby Bonilla
☐ 232 Bob James .05 .02 .01
☐ 233 Rafael Santana .05 .02 .01
☐ 234 Ken Dayley .05 .02 .01
☐ 235 Gary Ward .05 .02 .01
☐ 236 Ted Power .05 .02 .01
☐ 237 Mike Heath .05 .02 .01
☐ 238 Luis Polonia .15 .07 .02
☐ 239 Roy Smalley .05 .02 .01
☐ 240 Lee Smith .10 .05 .01
☐ 241 Damaso Garcia .05 .02 .01
☐ 242 Tom Niedenfuer .05 .02 .01
☐ 243 Mark Ryal .05 .02 .01
☐ 244 Jeff D. Robinson .05 .02 .01
☐ 245 Rich Gedman .05 .02 .01
☐ 246 Mike Campbell .05 .02 .01
☐ 247 Thad Bosley .05 .02 .01
☐ 248 Storm Davis .05 .02 .01
☐ 249 Mike Marshall .05 .02 .01
☐ 250 Nolan Ryan .75 .35 .09
☐ 251 Tom Foley .05 .02 .01
☐ 252 Bob Brower .05 .02 .01
☐ 253 Checklist 133-264 .10 .05 .01
☐ 254 Lee Elia MG .05 .02 .01
(Checklist back)
☐ 255 Mookie Wilson .10 .05 .01
☐ 256 Ken Schrom .05 .02 .01
☐ 257 Jerry Royster .05 .02 .01
☐ 258 Ed Nunez .05 .02 .01
☐ 259 Ron Kittle .05 .02 .01
☐ 260 Vince Coleman .05 .02 .01
☐ 261 Giants TL .05 .02 .01
(Five players)
☐ 262 Drew Hall .05 .02 .01
☐ 263 Glenn Braggs .05 .02 .01
☐ 264 Les Straker .05 .02 .01
☐ 265 Bo Diaz .05 .02 .01
☐ 266 Paul Assenmacher .05 .02 .01
☐ 267 Billy Bean .05 .02 .01
☐ 268 Bruce Ruffin .05 .02 .01
☐ 269 Ellis Burks .40 .18 .05
☐ 270 Mike Witt .05 .02 .01
☐ 271 Ken Gerhart .05 .02 .01
☐ 272 Steve Ontiveros .05 .02 .01
☐ 273 Garth Iorg .05 .02 .01
☐ 274 Junior Ortiz .05 .02 .01
☐ 275 Kevin Seitzer .10 .05 .01
☐ 276 Luis Salazar .05 .02 .01
☐ 277 Alejandro Pena .05 .02 .01
☐ 278 Jose Cruz .05 .02 .01
☐ 279 Randy St.Claire .05 .02 .01
☐ 280 Pete Incaviglia .05 .02 .01
☐ 281 Jerry Hairston .05 .02 .01
☐ 282 Pat Perry .05 .02 .01
☐ 283 Phil Lombardi .05 .02 .01
☐ 284 Larry Bowa MG .10 .05 .01
(Checklist back)
☐ 285 Jim Presley .05 .02 .01
☐ 286 Chuck Crim .05 .02 .01
☐ 287 Manny Trillo .05 .02 .01
☐ 288 Pat Pacillo .05 .02 .01
(Chris Sabo in
background of photo)
☐ 289 Dave Bergman .05 .02 .01
☐ 290 Tony Fernandez .05 .02 .01
☐ 291 Astros TL .05 .02 .01
Billy Hatcher
and Kevin Bass
☐ 292 Carney Lansford .10 .05 .01
☐ 293 Doug Jones .10 .05 .01
☐ 294 Al Pedrique .05 .02 .01
☐ 295 Bert Blyleven .10 .05 .01
☐ 296 Floyd Rayford .05 .02 .01
☐ 297 Zane Smith .05 .02 .01
☐ 298 Milt Thompson .05 .02 .01
☐ 299 Steve Crawford .05 .02 .01
☐ 300 Don Mattingly .50 .23 .06
☐ 301 Bud Black .05 .02 .01
☐ 302 Jose Uribe .05 .02 .01
☐ 303 Eric Show .05 .02 .01
☐ 304 George Hendrick .05 .02 .01
☐ 305 Steve Sax .05 .02 .01
☐ 306 Billy Hatcher .05 .02 .01
☐ 307 Mike Trujillo .05 .02 .01
☐ 308 Lee Mazzilli .05 .02 .01
☐ 309 Bill Long .05 .02 .01
☐ 310 Tom Herr .05 .02 .01
☐ 311 Scott Sanderson .05 .02 .01
☐ 312 Joey Meyer .05 .02 .01
☐ 313 Bob McClure .05 .02 .01
☐ 314 Jimy Williams MG .05 .02 .01
(Checklist back)
☐ 315 Dave Parker .15 .07 .02
☐ 316 Jose Rijo .05 .02 .01
☐ 317 Tom Nieto .05 .02 .01
☐ 318 Mel Hall .05 .02 .01
☐ 319 Mike Loynd .05 .02 .01
☐ 320 Alan Trammell .10 .05 .01
☐ 321 White Sox TL .10 .05 .01
Harold Baines and
Carlton Fisk
☐ 322 Vicente Palacios .05 .02 .01
☐ 323 Rick Leach .05 .02 .01
☐ 324 Danny Jackson .05 .02 .01
☐ 325 Glenn Hubbard .05 .02 .01
☐ 326 Al Nipper .05 .02 .01
☐ 327 Larry Sheets .05 .02 .01
☐ 328 Greg Cadaret .05 .02 .01
☐ 329 Chris Speier .05 .02 .01
☐ 330 Eddie Whitson .05 .02 .01
☐ 331 Brian Downing .05 .02 .01
☐ 332 Jerry Reed .05 .02 .01
☐ 333 Wally Backman .05 .02 .01
☐ 334 Dave LaPoint .05 .02 .01
☐ 335 Claudell Washington .05 .02 .01
☐ 336 Ed Lynch .05 .02 .01
☐ 337 Jim Gantner .05 .02 .01
☐ 338 Brian Holton UER .05 .02 .01
(1987 ERA .389,
should be 3.89)
☐ 339 Kurt Stillwell .05 .02 .01
☐ 340 Jack Morris .15 .07 .02
☐ 341 Carmen Castillo .05 .02 .01
☐ 342 Larry Andersen .05 .02 .01
☐ 343 Greg Gagne .05 .02 .01
☐ 344 Tony LaRussa MG .10 .05 .01
(Checklist back)
☐ 345 Scott Fletcher .05 .02 .01
☐ 346 Vance Law .05 .02 .01
☐ 347 Joe Johnson .05 .02 .01
☐ 348 Jim Eisenreich .10 .05 .01
☐ 349 Bob Walk .05 .02 .01
☐ 350 Will Clark .25 .11 .03
☐ 351 Cardinals TL .10 .05 .01
Red Schoendienst CO
and Tony Pena
☐ 352 Billy Ripken .10 .05 .01
☐ 353 Ed Olwine .05 .02 .01
☐ 354 Marc Sullivan .05 .02 .01
☐ 355 Roger McDowell .05 .02 .01
☐ 356 Luis Aguayo .05 .02 .01
☐ 357 Floyd Bannister .05 .02 .01
☐ 358 Rey Quinones .05 .02 .01
☐ 359 Tim Stoddard .05 .02 .01
☐ 360 Tony Gwynn .40 .18 .05
☐ 361 Greg Maddux 1.25 .55 .16
☐ 362 Juan Castillo .05 .02 .01
☐ 363 Willie Fraser .05 .02 .01
☐ 364 Nick Esasky .05 .02 .01
☐ 365 Floyd Youmans .05 .02 .01
☐ 366 Chet Lemon .05 .02 .01
☐ 367 Tim Leary .05 .02 .01
☐ 368 Gerald Young .05 .02 .01
☐ 369 Greg Harris .05 .02 .01
☐ 370 Jose Canseco .25 .11 .03
☐ 371 Joe Hesketh .05 .02 .01
☐ 372 Matt Williams .75 .35 .09
☐ 373 Checklist 265-396 .10 .05 .01
☐ 374 Doc Edwards MG .05 .02 .01
(Checklist back)
☐ 375 Tom Brunansky .05 .02 .01
☐ 376 Bill Wilkinson .05 .02 .01
☐ 377 Sam Horn .05 .02 .01
☐ 378 Todd Frohwirth .05 .02 .01
☐ 379 Rafael Ramirez .05 .02 .01
☐ 380 Joe Magrane .05 .02 .01
☐ 381 Angels TL .10 .05 .01
Wally Joyner and
Jack Howell
☐ 382 Keith A. Miller .05 .02 .01
☐ 383 Eric Bell .05 .02 .01
☐ 384 Neil Allen .05 .02 .01
☐ 385 Carlton Fisk .15 .07 .02
☐ 386 Don Mattingly AS .20 .09 .03
☐ 387 Willie Randolph AS .05 .02 .01
☐ 388 Wade Boggs AS .15 .07 .02
☐ 389 Alan Trammell AS .10 .05 .01
☐ 390 George Bell AS .05 .02 .01
☐ 391 Kirby Puckett AS .15 .07 .02
☐ 392 Dave Winfield AS .15 .07 .02
☐ 393 Matt Nokes AS .05 .02 .01
☐ 394 Roger Clemens AS .15 .07 .02
☐ 395 Jimmy Key AS .10 .05 .01
☐ 396 Tom Henke AS .05 .02 .01
☐ 397 Jack Clark AS .05 .02 .01
☐ 398 Juan Samuel AS .05 .02 .01
☐ 399 Tim Wallach AS .05 .02 .01
☐ 400 Ozzie Smith AS .15 .07 .02
☐ 401 Andre Dawson AS .10 .05 .01
☐ 402 Tony Gwynn AS .20 .09 .03
☐ 403 Tim Raines AS .10 .05 .01
☐ 404 Benny Santiago AS .05 .02 .01
☐ 405 Dwight Gooden AS .10 .05 .01
☐ 406 Shane Rawley AS .05 .02 .01
☐ 407 Steve Bedrosian AS .05 .02 .01
☐ 408 Dion James .05 .02 .01
☐ 409 Joel McKeon .05 .02 .01
☐ 410 Tony Pena .05 .02 .01
☐ 411 Wayne Tolleson .05 .02 .01
☐ 412 Randy Myers .15 .07 .02
☐ 413 John Christensen .05 .02 .01
☐ 414 John McNamara MG .05 .02 .01
(Checklist back)
☐ 415 Don Carman .05 .02 .01
☐ 416 Keith Moreland .05 .02 .01
☐ 417 Mark Ciardi .05 .02 .01
☐ 418 Joel Youngblood .05 .02 .01
☐ 419 Scott McGregor .05 .02 .01
☐ 420 Wally Joyner .15 .07 .02
☐ 421 Ed VandeBerg .05 .02 .01
☐ 422 Dave Concepcion .10 .05 .01
☐ 423 John Smiley .15 .07 .02
☐ 424 Dwayne Murphy .05 .02 .01
☐ 425 Jeff Reardon .10 .05 .01
☐ 426 Randy Ready .05 .02 .01
☐ 427 Paul Kilgus .05 .02 .01
☐ 428 John Shelby .05 .02 .01
☐ 429 Tigers TL .10 .05 .01
Alan Trammell and
Kirk Gibson
☐ 430 Glenn Davis .05 .02 .01
☐ 431 Casey Candaele .05 .02 .01
☐ 432 Mike Moore .05 .02 .01
☐ 433 Bill Pecota .05 .02 .01
☐ 434 Rick Aguilera .15 .07 .02
☐ 435 Mike Pagliarulo .05 .02 .01
☐ 436 Mike Bielecki .05 .02 .01
☐ 437 Fred Manrique .05 .02 .01
☐ 438 Rob Ducey .05 .02 .01
☐ 439 Dave Martinez .05 .02 .01
☐ 440 Steve Bedrosian .05 .02 .01
☐ 441 Rick Manning .05 .02 .01
☐ 442 Tom Bolton .05 .02 .01
☐ 443 Ken Griffey .05 .02 .01
☐ 444 Cal Ripken, Sr. MG .10 .05 .01
(Checklist back)
UER (two copyrights)
☐ 445 Mike Krukow .05 .02 .01
☐ 446 Doug DeCinces .05 .02 .01
(Now with Cardinals
on card front)
☐ 447 Jeff Montgomery .20 .09 .03
☐ 448 Mike Davis .05 .02 .01
☐ 449 Jeff M. Robinson .05 .02 .01
☐ 450 Barry Bonds .60 .25 .07
☐ 451 Keith Atherton .05 .02 .01
☐ 452 Willie Wilson .05 .02 .01
☐ 453 Dennis Powell .05 .02 .01
☐ 454 Marvell Wynne .05 .02 .01
☐ 455 Shawn Hillegas .05 .02 .01
☐ 456 Dave Anderson .05 .02 .01
☐ 457 Terry Leach .05 .02 .01
☐ 458 Ron Hassey .05 .02 .01
☐ 459 Yankees TL .15 .07 .02
Dave Winfield and
Willie Randolph
☐ 460 Ozzie Smith .25 .11 .03
☐ 461 Danny Darwin .05 .02 .01
☐ 462 Don Slaught .05 .02 .01
☐ 463 Fred McGriff .40 .18 .05
☐ 464 Jay Tibbs .05 .02 .01
☐ 465 Paul Molitor .20 .09 .03
☐ 466 Jerry Mumphrey .05 .02 .01
☐ 467 Don Aase .05 .02 .01
☐ 468 Darren Daulton .10 .05 .01
☐ 469 Jeff Dedmon .05 .02 .01
☐ 470 Dwight Evans .10 .05 .01
☐ 471 Donnie Moore .05 .02 .01
☐ 472 Robby Thompson .05 .02 .01
☐ 473 Joe Niekro .05 .02 .01
☐ 474 Tom Brookens .05 .02 .01
☐ 475 Pete Rose MG .20 .09 .03
(Checklist back)
☐ 476 Dave Stewart .15 .07 .02

☐ 477 Jamie Quirk .05 .02 .01
☐ 478 Sid Bream .05 .02 .01
☐ 479 Brett Butler .10 .05 .01
☐ 480 Dwight Gooden .10 .05 .01
☐ 481 Mariano Duncan .05 .02 .01
☐ 482 Mark Davis .05 .02 .01
☐ 483 Rod Booker .05 .02 .01
☐ 484 Pat Clements .05 .02 .01
☐ 485 Harold Reynolds .05 .02 .01
☐ 486 Pat Keedy .05 .02 .01
☐ 487 Jim Pankovits .05 .02 .01
☐ 488 Andy McGaffigan .05 .02 .01
☐ 489 Dodgers TL .05 .02 .01
Pedro Guerrero and
Fernando Valenzuela
☐ 490 Larry Parrish .05 .02 .01
☐ 491 B.J. Surhoff .10 .05 .01
☐ 492 Doyle Alexander .05 .02 .01
☐ 493 Mike Greenwell .15 .07 .02
☐ 494 Wally Ritchie .05 .02 .01
☐ 495 Eddie Murray .25 .11 .03
☐ 496 Guy Hoffman .05 .02 .01
☐ 497 Kevin Mitchell .10 .05 .01
☐ 498 Bob Boone .10 .05 .01
☐ 499 Eric King .05 .02 .01
☐ 500 Andre Dawson .10 .05 .01
☐ 501 Tim Birtsas .05 .02 .01
☐ 502 Dan Gladden .05 .02 .01
☐ 503 Junior Noboa .05 .02 .01
☐ 504 Bob Rodgers MG .05 .02 .01
(Checklist back)
☐ 505 Willie Upshaw .05 .02 .01
☐ 506 John Cangelosi .05 .02 .01
☐ 507 Mark Gubicza .05 .02 .01
☐ 508 Tim Teufel .05 .02 .01
☐ 509 Bill Dawley .05 .02 .01
☐ 510 Dave Winfield .15 .07 .02
☐ 511 Joel Davis .05 .02 .01
☐ 512 Alex Trevino .05 .02 .01
☐ 513 Tim Flannery .05 .02 .01
☐ 514 Pat Sheridan .05 .02 .01
☐ 515 Juan Nieves .05 .02 .01
☐ 516 Jim Sundberg .05 .02 .01
☐ 517 Ron Robinson .05 .02 .01
☐ 518 Greg Gross .05 .02 .01
☐ 519 Mariners TL .05 .02 .01
Harold Reynolds and
Phil Bradley
☐ 520 Dave Smith .05 .02 .01
☐ 521 Jim Dwyer .05 .02 .01
☐ 522 Bob Patterson .05 .02 .01
☐ 523 Gary Roenicke .05 .02 .01
☐ 524 Gary Lucas .05 .02 .01
☐ 525 Marty Barrett .05 .02 .01
☐ 526 Juan Berenguer .05 .02 .01
☐ 527 Steve Henderson .05 .02 .01
☐ 528A Checklist 397-528 .15 .07 .02
ERR (455 S. Carlton)
☐ 528B Checklist 397-528 .10 .05 .01
COR (455 S. Hillegas)
☐ 529 Tim Burke .05 .02 .01
☐ 530 Gary Carter .10 .05 .01
☐ 531 Rich Yett .05 .02 .01
☐ 532 Mike Kingery .05 .02 .01
☐ 533 John Farrell .05 .02 .01
☐ 534 John Wathan MG .05 .02 .01
(Checklist back)
☐ 535 Ron Guidry .05 .02 .01
☐ 536 John Morris .05 .02 .01
☐ 537 Steve Buechele .05 .02 .01
☐ 538 Bill Wegman .05 .02 .01
☐ 539 Mike LaValliere .05 .02 .01
☐ 540 Bret Saberhagen .10 .05 .01
☐ 541 Juan Beniquez .05 .02 .01
☐ 542 Paul Noce .05 .02 .01
☐ 543 Kent Tekulve .05 .02 .01
☐ 544 Jim Traber .05 .02 .01
☐ 545 Don Baylor .15 .07 .02
☐ 546 John Candelaria .05 .02 .01
☐ 547 Felix Fermin .05 .02 .01
☐ 548 Shane Mack .05 .02 .01
☐ 549 Braves TL .05 .02 .01
Albert Hall,
Dale Murphy,
Ken Griffey
and Dion James
☐ 550 Pedro Guerrero .10 .05 .01
☐ 551 Terry Steinbach .15 .07 .02
☐ 552 Mark Thurmond .05 .02 .01
☐ 553 Tracy Jones .05 .02 .01
☐ 554 Mike Smithson .05 .02 .01
☐ 555 Brook Jacoby .05 .02 .01
☐ 556 Stan Clarke .05 .02 .01
☐ 557 Craig Reynolds .05 .02 .01
☐ 558 Bob Ojeda .05 .02 .01
☐ 559 Ken Williams .05 .02 .01
☐ 560 Tim Wallach .05 .02 .01
☐ 561 Rick Cerone .05 .02 .01
☐ 562 Jim Lindeman .05 .02 .01
☐ 563 Jose Guzman .05 .02 .01
☐ 564 Frank Lucchesi MG .05 .02 .01
(Checklist back)
☐ 565 Lloyd Moseby .05 .02 .01
☐ 566 Charlie O'Brien .05 .02 .01
☐ 567 Mike Diaz .05 .02 .01
☐ 568 Chris Brown .05 .02 .01
☐ 569 Charlie Leibrandt .05 .02 .01
☐ 570 Jeffrey Leonard .05 .02 .01
☐ 571 Mark Williamson .05 .02 .01
☐ 572 Chris James .05 .02 .01
☐ 573 Bob Stanley .05 .02 .01
☐ 574 Graig Nettles .10 .05 .01
☐ 575 Don Sutton .15 .07 .02
☐ 576 Tommy Hinzo .05 .02 .01
☐ 577 Tom Browning .05 .02 .01
☐ 578 Gary Gaetti .05 .02 .01
☐ 579 Mets TL .10 .05 .01
Gary Carter and
Kevin McReynolds
☐ 580 Mark McGwire .60 .25 .07
☐ 581 Tito Landrum .05 .02 .01
☐ 582 Mike Henneman .10 .05 .01
☐ 583 Dave Valle .05 .02 .01
☐ 584 Steve Trout .05 .02 .01
☐ 585 Ozzie Guillen .10 .05 .01
☐ 586 Bob Forsch .05 .02 .01
☐ 587 Terry Puhl .05 .02 .01
☐ 588 Jeff Parrett .05 .02 .01
☐ 589 Geno Petralli .05 .02 .01
☐ 590 George Bell .05 .02 .01
☐ 591 Doug Drabek .10 .05 .01
☐ 592 Dale Sveum .05 .02 .01
☐ 593 Bob Tewksbury .05 .02 .01
☐ 594 Bobby Valentine MG .10 .05 .01
(Checklist back)
☐ 595 Frank White .10 .05 .01
☐ 596 John Kruk .15 .07 .02
☐ 597 Gene Garber .05 .02 .01
☐ 598 Lee Lacy .05 .02 .01
☐ 599 Calvin Schiraldi .05 .02 .01
☐ 600 Mike Schmidt .20 .09 .03
☐ 601 Jack Lazorko .05 .02 .01
☐ 602 Mike Aldrete .05 .02 .01
☐ 603 Rob Murphy .05 .02 .01
☐ 604 Chris Bando .05 .02 .01
☐ 605 Kirk Gibson .10 .05 .01
☐ 606 Moose Haas .05 .02 .01
☐ 607 Mickey Hatcher .05 .02 .01
☐ 608 Charlie Kerfeld .05 .02 .01
☐ 609 Twins TL .10 .05 .01
Gary Gaetti and
Kent Hrbek
☐ 610 Keith Hernandez .10 .05 .01
☐ 611 Tommy John .10 .05 .01
☐ 612 Curt Ford .05 .02 .01
☐ 613 Bobby Thigpen .05 .02 .01
☐ 614 Herm Winningham .05 .02 .01
☐ 615 Jody Davis .05 .02 .01
☐ 616 Jay Aldrich .05 .02 .01
☐ 617 Oddibe McDowell .05 .02 .01
☐ 618 Cecil Fielder .15 .07 .02
☐ 619 Mike Dunne .05 .02 .01
(Inconsistent design,
black name on front)
☐ 620 Cory Snyder .05 .02 .01
☐ 621 Gene Nelson .05 .02 .01
☐ 622 Kal Daniels .05 .02 .01
☐ 623 Mike Flanagan .05 .02 .01
☐ 624 Jim Leyland MG .10 .05 .01
(Checklist back)
☐ 625 Frank Viola .05 .02 .01
☐ 626 Glenn Wilson .05 .02 .01
☐ 627 Joe Boever .05 .02 .01
☐ 628 Dave Henderson .05 .02 .01
☐ 629 Kelly Downs .05 .02 .01
☐ 630 Darrell Evans .10 .05 .01
☐ 631 Jack Howell .05 .02 .01
☐ 632 Steve Shields .05 .02 .01
☐ 633 Barry Lyons .05 .02 .01
☐ 634 Jose DeLeon .05 .02 .01
☐ 635 Terry Pendleton .10 .05 .01
☐ 636 Charles Hudson .05 .02 .01
☐ 637 Jay Bell .20 .09 .03
☐ 638 Steve Balboni .05 .02 .01
☐ 639 Brewers TL .05 .02 .01
Glenn Braggs
and Tony Muser CO
☐ 640 Garry Templeton .05 .02 .01
(Inconsistent design,
green border)
☐ 641 Rick Honeycutt .05 .02 .01
☐ 642 Bob Dernier .05 .02 .01
☐ 643 Rocky Childress .05 .02 .01
☐ 644 Terry McGriff .05 .02 .01
☐ 645 Matt Nokes .05 .02 .01
☐ 646 Checklist 529-660 .10 .05 .01
☐ 647 Pascual Perez .05 .02 .01
☐ 648 Al Newman .05 .02 .01
☐ 649 DeWayne Buice .05 .02 .01
☐ 650 Cal Ripken .75 .35 .09
☐ 651 Mike Jackson .10 .05 .01
☐ 652 Bruce Benedict .05 .02 .01
☐ 653 Jeff Sellers .05 .02 .01
☐ 654 Roger Craig MG .10 .05 .01
(Checklist back)
☐ 655 Len Dykstra .10 .05 .01
☐ 656 Lee Guetterman .05 .02 .01
☐ 657 Gary Redus .05 .02 .01
☐ 658 Tim Conroy .05 .02 .01
(Inconsistent design,
name in white)
☐ 659 Bobby Meacham .05 .02 .01
☐ 660 Rick Reuschel .05 .02 .01
☐ 661 Nolan Ryan TBC '83 .35 .16 .04
☐ 662 Jim Rice TBC '78 .10 .05 .01
☐ 663 Ron Blomberg TBC '73 .05 .02 .01
☐ 664 Bob Gibson TBC '68 .15 .07 .02
☐ 665 Stan Musial TBC '63 .15 .07 .02
☐ 666 Mario Soto .05 .02 .01
☐ 667 Luis Quinones .05 .02 .01
☐ 668 Walt Terrell .05 .02 .01
☐ 669 Phillies TL .05 .02 .01
Lance Parrish
and Mike Ryan CO
☐ 670 Dan Plesac .05 .02 .01
☐ 671 Tim Laudner .05 .02 .01
☐ 672 John Davis .05 .02 .01
☐ 673 Tony Phillips .15 .07 .02
☐ 674 Mike Fitzgerald .05 .02 .01
☐ 675 Jim Rice .15 .07 .02
☐ 676 Ken Dixon .05 .02 .01
☐ 677 Eddie Milner .05 .02 .01
☐ 678 Jim Acker .05 .02 .01
☐ 679 Darrell Miller .05 .02 .01
☐ 680 Charlie Hough .10 .05 .01
☐ 681 Bobby Bonilla .15 .07 .02
☐ 682 Jimmy Key .10 .05 .01
☐ 683 Julio Franco .10 .05 .01
☐ 684 Hal Lanier MG .05 .02 .01
(Checklist back)
☐ 685 Ron Darling .05 .02 .01
☐ 686 Terry Francona .05 .02 .01
☐ 687 Mickey Brantley .05 .02 .01
☐ 688 Jim Winn .05 .02 .01
☐ 689 Tom Pagnozzi .10 .05 .01
☐ 690 Jay Howell .05 .02 .01
☐ 691 Dan Pasqua .05 .02 .01
☐ 692 Mike Birkbeck .05 .02 .01
☐ 693 Benito Santiago .10 .05 .01
☐ 694 Eric Nolte .05 .02 .01
☐ 695 Shawon Dunston .05 .02 .01
☐ 696 Duane Ward .10 .05 .01
☐ 697 Steve Lombardozzi .05 .02 .01
☐ 698 Brad Havens .05 .02 .01
☐ 699 Padres TL .10 .05 .01
Benito Santiago
and Tony Gwynn
☐ 700 George Brett .40 .18 .05
☐ 701 Sammy Stewart .05 .02 .01
☐ 702 Mike Gallego .05 .02 .01
☐ 703 Bob Brenly .05 .02 .01
☐ 704 Dennis Boyd .05 .02 .01
☐ 705 Juan Samuel .05 .02 .01
☐ 706 Rick Mahler .05 .02 .01
☐ 707 Fred Lynn .05 .02 .01
☐ 708 Gus Polidor .05 .02 .01
☐ 709 George Frazier .05 .02 .01
☐ 710 Darryl Strawberry .10 .05 .01
☐ 711 Bill Gullickson .05 .02 .01
☐ 712 John Moses .05 .02 .01
☐ 713 Willie Hernandez .05 .02 .01
☐ 714 Jim Fregosi MG .10 .05 .01
(Checklist back)
☐ 715 Todd Worrell .05 .02 .01
☐ 716 Lenn Sakata .05 .02 .01
☐ 717 Jay Baller .05 .02 .01
☐ 718 Mike Felder .05 .02 .01
☐ 719 Denny Walling .05 .02 .01
☐ 720 Tim Raines .10 .05 .01
☐ 721 Pete O'Brien .05 .02 .01
☐ 722 Manny Lee .05 .02 .01
☐ 723 Bob Kipper .05 .02 .01
☐ 724 Danny Tartabull .05 .02 .01
☐ 725 Mike Boddicker .05 .02 .01
☐ 726 Alfredo Griffin .05 .02 .01
☐ 727 Greg Booker .05 .02 .01
☐ 728 Andy Allanson .05 .02 .01
☐ 729 Blue Jays TL .10 .05 .01
George Bell and
Fred McGriff
☐ 730 John Franco .10 .05 .01
☐ 731 Rick Schu .05 .02 .01
☐ 732 David Palmer .05 .02 .01
☐ 733 Spike Owen .05 .02 .01
☐ 734 Craig Lefferts .05 .02 .01
☐ 735 Kevin McReynolds .05 .02 .01
☐ 736 Matt Young .05 .02 .01
☐ 737 Butch Wynegar .05 .02 .01
☐ 738 Scott Bankhead .05 .02 .01
☐ 739 Daryl Boston .05 .02 .01
☐ 740 Rick Sutcliffe .05 .02 .01
☐ 741 Mike Easler .05 .02 .01
☐ 742 Mark Clear .05 .02 .01
☐ 743 Larry Herndon .05 .02 .01
☐ 744 Whitey Herzog MG .10 .05 .01
(Checklist back)
☐ 745 Bill Doran .05 .02 .01
☐ 746 Gene Larkin .05 .02 .01
☐ 747 Bobby Witt .05 .02 .01
☐ 748 Reid Nichols .05 .02 .01
☐ 749 Mark Eichhorn .05 .02 .01
☐ 750 Bo Jackson .15 .07 .02
☐ 751 Jim Morrison .05 .02 .01
☐ 752 Mark Grant .05 .02 .01
☐ 753 Danny Heep .05 .02 .01
☐ 754 Mike LaCoss .05 .02 .01
☐ 755 Ozzie Virgil .05 .02 .01
☐ 756 Mike Maddux .05 .02 .01
☐ 757 John Marzano .05 .02 .01
☐ 758 Eddie Williams .10 .05 .01
☐ 759 A's TL UER .30 .14 .04
Mark McGwire
and Jose Canseco
(two copyrights)
☐ 760 Mike Scott .05 .02 .01
☐ 761 Tony Armas .05 .02 .01
☐ 762 Scott Bradley .05 .02 .01
☐ 763 Doug Sisk .05 .02 .01
☐ 764 Greg Walker .05 .02 .01
☐ 765 Neal Heaton .05 .02 .01
☐ 766 Henry Cotto .05 .02 .01
☐ 767 Jose Lind .10 .05 .01
☐ 768 Dickie Noles .05 .02 .01
(Now with Tigers
on card front)
☐ 769 Cecil Cooper .10 .05 .01
☐ 770 Lou Whitaker .10 .05 .01
☐ 771 Ruben Sierra .15 .07 .02
☐ 772 Sal Butera .05 .02 .01
☐ 773 Frank Williams .05 .02 .01
☐ 774 Gene Mauch MG .10 .05 .01
(Checklist back)
☐ 775 Dave Stieb .10 .05 .01
☐ 776 Checklist 661-792 .10 .05 .01
☐ 777 Lonnie Smith .05 .02 .01
☐ 778A Keith Comstock ERR 2.00 .90 .25
(White "Padres")
☐ 778B Keith Comstock COR .05 .02 .01
(Blue "Padres")
☐ 779 Tom Glavine .75 .35 .09
☐ 780 Fernando Valenzuela .10 .05 .01
☐ 781 Keith Hughes .05 .02 .01
☐ 782 Jeff Ballard .05 .02 .01
☐ 783 Ron Roenicke .05 .02 .01
☐ 784 Joe Sambito .05 .02 .01
☐ 785 Alvin Davis .05 .02 .01
☐ 786 Joe Price .05 .02 .01
(Inconsistent design,
orange team name)
☐ 787 Bill Almon .05 .02 .01
☐ 788 Ray Searage .05 .02 .01
☐ 789 Indians' TL .15 .07 .02
Joe Carter and
Cory Snyder
☐ 790 Dave Righetti .10 .05 .01
☐ 791 Ted Simmons .10 .05 .01
☐ 792 John Tudor .05 .02 .01

1988 Topps Tiffany

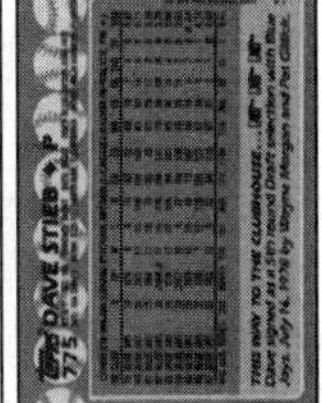

This was the fifth year that Topps issued a "Tiffany" set. These 792 standard-size cards parallel the regular Topps cards. These cards were issued in factory set form only, produced in Topps Irish facility, and only available through Topps hobby dealers. These cards were again produced in relatively large quantities and the mulitplier value is reduced compared to pre-1987 levels.

	MINT	NRMT	EXC
COMPLETE FACT.SET (792)	40.00	18.00	5.00
COMMON CARD (1-792)	.10	.05	.01
*STARS: 3X to 6X BASIC CARDS			
*ROOKIES: 2X to 4X BASIC CARDS			

1988 Topps Glossy All-Stars

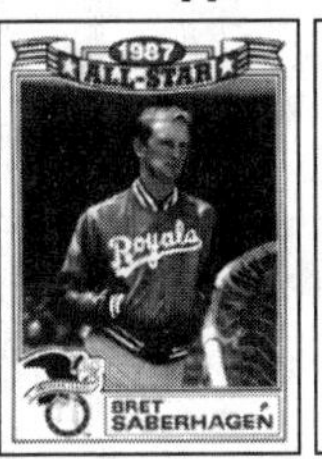

This set of 22 glossy cards was inserted one per rack pack. Players selected for the set are the starting players (plus manager and honorary captain) in the 1987 All-Star Game in Oakland. Cards measure the standard size and the backs feature red and blue printing on a white card stock.

	MINT	NRMT	EXC
COMPLETE SET (22)	4.00	1.80	.50
COMMON CARD (1-22)	.05	.02	.01

Card	MINT	NRMT	EXC
☐ 1 John McNamara MG	.05	.02	.01
☐ 2 Don Mattingly	1.00	.45	.12
☐ 3 Willie Randolph	.05	.02	.01
☐ 4 Wade Boggs	.50	.23	.06
☐ 5 Cal Ripken	2.00	.90	.25
☐ 6 George Bell	.05	.02	.01
☐ 7 Rickey Henderson	.40	.18	.05
☐ 8 Dave Winfield	.40	.18	.05
☐ 9 Terry Kennedy	.05	.02	.01
☐ 10 Bret Saberhagen	.10	.05	.01
☐ 11 Jim Hunter CAPT	.10	.05	.01
☐ 12 Dave Johnson MG	.05	.02	.01
☐ 13 Jack Clark	.10	.05	.01
☐ 14 Ryne Sandberg	1.00	.45	.12
☐ 15 Mike Schmidt	.75	.35	.09
☐ 16 Ozzie Smith	1.00	.45	.12
☐ 17 Eric Davis	.05	.02	.01
☐ 18 Andre Dawson	.20	.09	.03
☐ 19 Darryl Strawberry	.10	.05	.01
☐ 20 Gary Carter	.10	.05	.01
☐ 21 Mike Scott	.05	.02	.01
☐ 22 Billy Williams CAPT	.10	.05	.01

1988 Topps Glossy Send-Ins

Topps issued this set through a mail-in offer explained and advertised on the wax packs. This 60-card set features glossy fronts with each card measuring the standard size. The offer provided your choice of any one of the six 10-card subsets (1-10, 11-20, etc.) for 1.25 plus six of the Special Offer ("Spring Fever Baseball") insert cards, which were found one per wax pack. One complete set was obtainable by sending 7.50 plus 18 special offer cards. The last two players (numerically) in each ten-card subset are actually "Hot Prospects."

	MINT	NRMT	EXC
COMPLETE SET (60)	10.00	4.50	1.25
COMMON CARD (1-60)	.10	.05	.01

Card	MINT	NRMT	EXC
☐ 1 Andre Dawson	.20	.09	.03
☐ 2 Jesse Barfield	.10	.05	.01
☐ 3 Mike Schmidt	1.00	.45	.12
☐ 4 Ruben Sierra	.20	.09	.03
☐ 5 Mike Scott	.10	.05	.01
☐ 6 Cal Ripken	4.00	1.80	.50
☐ 7 Gary Carter	.20	.09	.03
☐ 8 Kent Hrbek	.20	.09	.03
☐ 9 Kevin Seitzer	.20	.09	.03
☐ 10 Mike Henneman	.20	.09	.03
☐ 11 Don Mattingly	2.00	.90	.25
☐ 12 Tim Raines	.20	.09	.03
☐ 13 Roger Clemens	1.25	.55	.16
☐ 14 Ryne Sandberg	1.25	.55	.16
☐ 15 Tony Fernandez	.10	.05	.01
☐ 16 Eric Davis	.20	.09	.03
☐ 17 Jack Morris	.20	.09	.03
☐ 18 Tim Wallach	.10	.05	.01
☐ 19 Mike Dunne	.10	.05	.01
☐ 20 Mike Greenwell	.20	.09	.03
☐ 21 Dwight Evans	.20	.09	.03
☐ 22 Darryl Strawberry	.20	.09	.03
☐ 23 Cory Snyder	.10	.05	.01
☐ 24 Pedro Guerrero	.10	.05	.01
☐ 25 Rickey Henderson	.50	.23	.06
☐ 26 Dale Murphy	.40	.18	.05
☐ 27 Kirby Puckett	1.50	.70	.19
☐ 28 Steve Bedrosian	.10	.05	.01
☐ 29 Devon White	.20	.09	.03
☐ 30 Benito Santiago	.10	.05	.01
☐ 31 George Bell	.10	.05	.01
☐ 32 Keith Hernandez	.20	.09	.03
☐ 33 Dave Stewart	.20	.09	.03
☐ 34 Dave Parker	.20	.09	.03
☐ 35 Tom Henke	.10	.05	.01
☐ 36 Willie McGee	.20	.09	.03
☐ 37 Alan Trammell	.20	.09	.03
☐ 38 Tony Gwynn	2.00	.90	.25
☐ 39 Mark McGwire	2.00	.90	.25
☐ 40 Joe Magrane	.10	.05	.01
☐ 41 Jack Clark	.10	.05	.01
☐ 42 Willie Randolph	.10	.05	.01
☐ 43 Juan Samuel	.10	.05	.01
☐ 44 Joe Carter	.40	.18	.05
☐ 45 Shane Rawley	.10	.05	.01
☐ 46 Dave Winfield	.50	.23	.06
☐ 47 Ozzie Smith	1.25	.55	.16
☐ 48 Wally Joyner	.20	.09	.03
☐ 49 B.J. Surhoff	.20	.09	.03
☐ 50 Ellis Burks	.60	.25	.07
☐ 51 Wade Boggs	.60	.25	.07
☐ 52 Howard Johnson	.10	.05	.01
☐ 53 George Brett	2.00	.90	.25
☐ 54 Dwight Gooden	.20	.09	.03
☐ 55 Jose Canseco	1.00	.45	.12
☐ 56 Lee Smith	.20	.09	.03
☐ 57 Paul Molitor	.75	.35	.09
☐ 58 Andres Galarraga	.50	.23	.06
☐ 59 Matt Nokes	.10	.05	.01
☐ 60 Casey Candaele	.10	.05	.01

1988 Topps Rookies

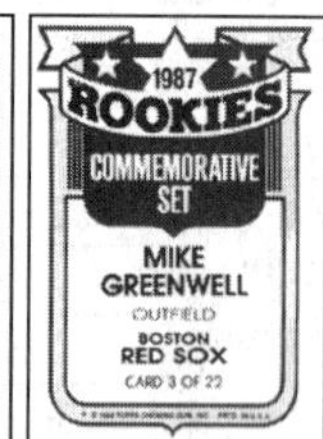

Inserted in each supermarket jumbo pack is a card from this series of 22 of 1987's best rookies as determined by Topps. Jumbo packs consisted of 100 (regular issue 1988 Topps baseball) cards with a stick of gum plus the insert "Rookie" card. The card fronts are in full color and measure the standard size. The card backs are printed in red and blue on white card stock and are numbered at the bottom.

	MINT	NRMT	EXC
COMPLETE SET (22)	4.00	1.80	.50
COMMON CARD (1-22)	.05	.02	.01

Card	MINT	NRMT	EXC
☐ 1 Billy Ripken	.05	.02	.01
☐ 2 Ellis Burks	1.00	.45	.12
☐ 3 Mike Greenwell	.15	.07	.02
☐ 4 DeWayne Buice	.05	.02	.01
☐ 5 Devon White	.40	.18	.05
☐ 6 Fred Manrique	.05	.02	.01
☐ 7 Mike Henneman	.10	.05	.01
☐ 8 Matt Nokes	.05	.02	.01
☐ 9 Kevin Seitzer	.10	.05	.01
☐ 10 B.J. Surhoff	.25	.11	.03
☐ 11 Casey Candaele	.05	.02	.01
☐ 12 Randy Myers	.40	.18	.05
☐ 13 Mark McGwire	2.00	.90	.25
☐ 14 Luis Polonia	.10	.05	.01
☐ 15 Terry Steinbach	.15	.07	.02
☐ 16 Mike Dunne	.05	.02	.01
☐ 17 Al Pedrique	.05	.02	.01
☐ 18 Benito Santiago	.20	.09	.03
☐ 19 Kelly Downs	.05	.02	.01
☐ 20 Joe Magrane	.05	.02	.01
☐ 21 Jerry Browne	.05	.02	.01
☐ 22 Jeff Musselman	.05	.02	.01

1988 Topps Wax Box Cards

The cards in this 16-card set measure the standard size. Cards have essentially the same design as the 1988 Topps regular issue set. The cards were printed on the bottoms of the regular issue wax pack boxes. These 16 cards, "lettered" A through P, are considered a separate set in their own right and are not typically included in a complete set of the regular issue 1988 Topps cards. The value of the panels uncut is slightly greater, perhaps by 25 percent greater, than the value of the individual cards cut up carefully. The card lettering is sequenced alphabetically by player's name.

	MINT	NRMT	EXC
COMPLETE SET (16)	5.00	2.20	.60
COMMON CARD (A-P)	.10	.05	.01

Card	MINT	NRMT	EXC
☐ A Don Baylor	.25	.11	.03
☐ B Steve Bedrosian	.10	.05	.01
☐ C Juan Beniquez	.10	.05	.01
☐ D Bob Boone	.25	.11	.03
☐ E Darrell Evans	.25	.11	.03
☐ F Tony Gwynn	1.25	.55	.16
☐ G John Kruk	.25	.11	.03
☐ H Marvell Wynne	.10	.05	.01
☐ I Joe Carter	.50	.23	.06
☐ J Eric Davis	.30	.14	.04
☐ K Howard Johnson	.10	.05	.01
☐ L Darryl Strawberry	.25	.11	.03
☐ M Rickey Henderson	.60	.25	.07
☐ N Nolan Ryan	2.50	1.10	.30
☐ O Mike Schmidt	1.00	.45	.12
☐ P Kent Tekulve	.10	.05	.01

1988 Topps Traded

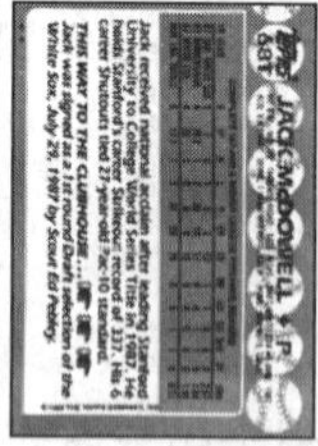

This standard-size 132-card Traded set was distributed exclusively in factory set form in blue and white taped boxes through hobby dealers. The cards are identical in style to the Topps regular issue except for whiter stock and t-suffixed numbering on back. Cards are ordered alphabetically by player's last name. This set generated additional interest upon release due to the inclusion of members of the 1988 U.S. Olympic baseball team. These Olympians are indicated in the checklist below by OLY. The key extended Rookie Cards in this set are Jim Abbott, Roberto Alomar, Brady Anderson, Andy Benes, Jay Buhner, Ron Gant, Mark Grace, Tino Martinez, Jack McDowell, Charles Nagy, Robin Ventura and Walt Weiss.

	MINT	NRMT	EXC
COMPLETE FACT.SET (132)	12.00	5.50	1.50
COMMON CARD (1T-132T)	.05	.02	.01

Card	MINT	NRMT	EXC
☐ 1T Jim Abbott OLY	.30	.14	.04
☐ 2T Juan Agosto	.05	.02	.01
☐ 3T Luis Alicea	.10	.05	.01
☐ 4T Roberto Alomar	4.00	1.80	.50
☐ 5T Brady Anderson	2.00	.90	.25
☐ 6T Jack Armstrong	.05	.02	.01
☐ 7T Don August	.05	.02	.01
☐ 8T Floyd Bannister	.05	.02	.01
☐ 9T Bret Barberie OLY	.10	.05	.01
☐ 10T Jose Bautista	.05	.02	.01
☐ 11T Don Baylor	.15	.07	.02
☐ 12T Tim Belcher	.10	.05	.01
☐ 13T Buddy Bell	.10	.05	.01
☐ 14T Andy Benes OLY	.75	.35	.09
☐ 15T Damon Berryhill	.05	.02	.01
☐ 16T Bud Black	.05	.02	.01
☐ 17T Pat Borders	.10	.05	.01
☐ 18T Phil Bradley	.05	.02	.01
☐ 19T Jeff Branson OLY	.10	.05	.01
☐ 20T Tom Brunansky	.05	.02	.01
☐ 21T Jay Buhner	2.00	.90	.25
☐ 22T Brett Butler	.10	.05	.01
☐ 23T Jim Campanis OLY	.05	.02	.01
☐ 24T Sil Campusano	.05	.02	.01
☐ 25T John Candelaria	.05	.02	.01
☐ 26T Jose Cecena	.05	.02	.01
☐ 27T Rick Cerone	.05	.02	.01
☐ 28T Jack Clark	.10	.05	.01
☐ 29T Kevin Coffman	.05	.02	.01
☐ 30T Pat Combs OLY	.05	.02	.01
☐ 31T Henry Cotto	.05	.02	.01
☐ 32T Chili Davis	.15	.07	.02
☐ 33T Mike Davis	.05	.02	.01
☐ 34T Jose DeLeon	.05	.02	.01
☐ 35T Richard Dotson	.05	.02	.01
☐ 36T Cecil Espy	.05	.02	.01
☐ 37T Tom Filer	.05	.02	.01
☐ 38T Mike Fiore OLY	.05	.02	.01
☐ 39T Ron Gant	.75	.35	.09
☐ 40T Kirk Gibson	.10	.05	.01
☐ 41T Rich Gossage	.15	.07	.02
☐ 42T Mark Grace	1.00	.45	.12
☐ 43T Alfredo Griffin	.05	.02	.01
☐ 44T Ty Griffin OLY	.05	.02	.01
☐ 45T Bryan Harvey	.10	.05	.01
☐ 46T Ron Hassey	.05	.02	.01
☐ 47T Ray Hayward	.05	.02	.01
☐ 48T Dave Henderson	.05	.02	.01
☐ 49T Tom Herr	.05	.02	.01
☐ 50T Bob Horner	.05	.02	.01
☐ 51T Ricky Horton	.05	.02	.01
☐ 52T Jay Howell	.05	.02	.01
☐ 53T Glenn Hubbard	.05	.02	.01
☐ 54T Jeff Innis	.05	.02	.01
☐ 55T Danny Jackson	.05	.02	.01
☐ 56T Darrin Jackson	.10	.05	.01
☐ 57T Roberto Kelly	.15	.07	.02
☐ 58T Ron Kittle	.05	.02	.01
☐ 59T Ray Knight	.10	.05	.01
☐ 60T Vance Law	.05	.02	.01
☐ 61T Jeffrey Leonard	.05	.02	.01
☐ 62T Mike Macfarlane	.15	.07	.02
☐ 63T Scotti Madison	.05	.02	.01
☐ 64T Kirt Manwaring	.10	.05	.01
☐ 65T Mark Marquess OLY CO	.05	.02	.01
☐ 66T Tino Martinez OLY	1.50	.70	.19
☐ 67T Billy Masse OLY	.05	.02	.01
☐ 68T Jack McDowell	.60	.25	.07
☐ 69T Jack McKeon MG	.05	.02	.01
☐ 70T Larry McWilliams	.05	.02	.01
☐ 71T Mickey Morandini OLY	.15	.07	.02
☐ 72T Keith Moreland	.05	.02	.01
☐ 73T Mike Morgan	.05	.02	.01
☐ 74T Charles Nagy OLY	1.50	.70	.19
☐ 75T Al Nipper	.05	.02	.01
☐ 76T Russ Nixon MG	.05	.02	.01
☐ 77T Jesse Orosco	.05	.02	.01
☐ 78T Joe Orsulak	.05	.02	.01
☐ 79T Dave Palmer	.05	.02	.01
☐ 80T Mark Parent	.05	.02	.01
☐ 81T Dave Parker	.15	.07	.02
☐ 82T Dan Pasqua	.05	.02	.01
☐ 83T Melido Perez	.10	.05	.01
☐ 84T Steve Peters	.05	.02	.01
☐ 85T Dan Petry	.05	.02	.01
☐ 86T Gary Pettis	.05	.02	.01
☐ 87T Jeff Pico	.05	.02	.01
☐ 88T Jim Poole OLY	.10	.05	.01
☐ 89T Ted Power	.05	.02	.01
☐ 90T Rafael Ramirez	.05	.02	.01
☐ 91T Dennis Rasmussen	.05	.02	.01
☐ 92T Jose Rijo	.05	.02	.01
☐ 93T Ernie Riles	.05	.02	.01
☐ 94T Luis Rivera	.05	.02	.01
☐ 95T Doug Robbins OLY	.05	.02	.01
☐ 96T Frank Robinson MG	.15	.07	.02
☐ 97T Cookie Rojas MG	.05	.02	.01
☐ 98T Chris Sabo	.10	.05	.01
☐ 99T Mark Salas	.05	.02	.01
☐ 100T Luis Salazar	.05	.02	.01
☐ 101T Rafael Santana	.05	.02	.01
☐ 102T Nelson Santovenia	.05	.02	.01
☐ 103T Mackey Sasser	.05	.02	.01
☐ 104T Calvin Schiraldi	.05	.02	.01
☐ 105T Mike Schooler	.05	.02	.01
☐ 106T Scott Servais OLY	.10	.05	.01
☐ 107T Dave Silvestri OLY	.05	.02	.01
☐ 108T Don Slaught	.05	.02	.01
☐ 109T Joe Slusarski OLY	.05	.02	.01
☐ 110T Lee Smith	.10	.05	.01
☐ 111T Pete Smith	.05	.02	.01
☐ 112T Jim Snyder MG	.05	.02	.01
☐ 113T Ed Sprague OLY	.75	.35	.09
☐ 114T Pete Stanicek	.05	.02	.01
☐ 115T Kurt Stillwell	.05	.02	.01
☐ 116T Todd Stottlemyre	.50	.23	.06
☐ 117T Bill Swift	.05	.02	.01
☐ 118T Pat Tabler	.05	.02	.01
☐ 119T Scott Terry	.05	.02	.01
☐ 120T Mickey Tettleton	.10	.05	.01
☐ 121T Dickie Thon	.05	.02	.01
☐ 122T Jeff Treadway	.05	.02	.01
☐ 123T Willie Upshaw	.05	.02	.01
☐ 124T Robin Ventura OLY	1.50	.70	.19
☐ 125T Ron Washington	.05	.02	.01
☐ 126T Walt Weiss	.10	.05	.01
☐ 127T Bob Welch	.05	.02	.01
☐ 128T David Wells	.15	.07	.02
☐ 129T Glenn Wilson	.05	.02	.01
☐ 130T Ted Wood OLY	.10	.05	.01
☐ 131T Don Zimmer MG	.10	.05	.01
☐ 132T Checklist 1T-132T	.05	.02	.01

1988 Topps Traded Tiffany

As a bonus for those dealers who ordered the regular Tiffany sets, they received an equivalent number of Tiffany update sets. These 132 standard-size cards parallel the regular traded issue. Again issued in the Topps Irish facility, these cards feature glossy fronts and easy to read backs. These sets were only issued in complete factory form.

	MINT	NRMT	EXC
COMPLETE FACT.SET (132)	30.00	13.50	3.70
COMMON CARD (1T-132T)	.10	.05	.01

*STARS: 2.5X to 5X BASIC CARDS
*ROOKIES: 1.25X TO 2.5X BASIC CARDS

1988 Topps Big

This set of 264 cards was issued as three separately distributed series of 88 cards each. Cards were distributed in wax packs with seven cards for a suggested retail of 40 cents. These cards are very reminiscent in style of the 1956 Topps card set. The cards measure approximately 2 5/8" by 3 3/4" and are oriented horizontally.

	MINT	NRMT	EXC
COMPLETE SET (264)	20.00	9.00	2.50
COMMON CARD (1-264)	.05	.02	.01

Card	MINT	NRMT	EXC
☐ 1 Paul Molitor	1.00	.45	.12
☐ 2 Milt Thompson	.05	.02	.01
☐ 3 Billy Hatcher	.05	.02	.01
☐ 4 Mike Witt	.05	.02	.01
☐ 5 Vince Coleman	.05	.02	.01
☐ 6 Dwight Evans	.10	.05	.01
☐ 7 Tim Wallach	.05	.02	.01

☐ 8 Alan Trammell .10 .05 .01
☐ 9 Will Clark 1.00 .45 .12
☐ 10 Jeff Reardon .10 .05 .01
☐ 11 Dwight Gooden .10 .05 .01
☐ 12 Benito Santiago .15 .07 .02
☐ 13 Jose Canseco .75 .35 .09
☐ 14 Dale Murphy .50 .23 .06
☐ 15 George Bell .05 .02 .01
☐ 16 Ryne Sandberg 1.25 .55 .16
☐ 17 Brook Jacoby .05 .02 .01
☐ 18 Fernando Valenzuela .10 .05 .01
☐ 19 Scott Fletcher .05 .02 .01
☐ 20 Eric Davis .25 .11 .03
☐ 21 Willie Wilson .05 .02 .01
☐ 22 B.J. Surhoff .15 .07 .02
☐ 23 Steve Bedrosian .05 .02 .01
☐ 24 Dave Winfield .75 .35 .09
☐ 25 Bobby Bonilla .15 .07 .02
☐ 26 Larry Sheets .05 .02 .01
☐ 27 Ozzie Guillen .10 .05 .01
☐ 28 Checklist 1-88 .05 .02 .01
☐ 29 Nolan Ryan 3.00 1.35 .35
☐ 30 Bob Boone .10 .05 .01
☐ 31 Tom Herr .05 .02 .01
☐ 32 Wade Boggs .60 .25 .07
☐ 33 Neal Heaton .05 .02 .01
☐ 34 Doyle Alexander .05 .02 .01
☐ 35 Candy Maldonado .05 .02 .01
☐ 36 Kirby Puckett 2.00 .90 .25
☐ 37 Gary Carter .10 .05 .01
☐ 38 Lance McCullers .05 .02 .01
☐ 39A Terry Steinbach .15 .07 .02
(Topps logo in black)
☐ 39B Terry Steinbach .15 .07 .02
(Topps logo in white)
☐ 40 Gerald Perry .05 .02 .01
☐ 41 Tom Henke .05 .02 .01
☐ 42 Leon Durham .05 .02 .01
☐ 43 Cory Snyder .05 .02 .01
☐ 44 Dale Sveum .05 .02 .01
☐ 45 Lance Parrish .05 .02 .01
☐ 46 Steve Sax .05 .02 .01
☐ 47 Charlie Hough .05 .02 .01
☐ 48 Kal Daniels .05 .02 .01
☐ 49 Bo Jackson .15 .07 .02
☐ 50 Ron Guidry .05 .02 .01
☐ 51 Bill Doran .05 .02 .01
☐ 52 Wally Joyner .15 .07 .02
☐ 53 Terry Pendleton .10 .05 .01
☐ 54 Marty Barrett .05 .02 .01
☐ 55 Andres Galarraga .60 .25 .07
☐ 56 Larry Herndon .05 .02 .01
☐ 57 Kevin Mitchell .10 .05 .01
☐ 58 Greg Gagne .05 .02 .01
☐ 59 Keith Hernandez .10 .05 .01
☐ 60 John Kruk .15 .07 .02
☐ 61 Mike LaValliere .05 .02 .01
☐ 62 Cal Ripken 3.00 1.35 .35
☐ 63 Ivan Calderon .05 .02 .01
☐ 64 Alvin Davis .05 .02 .01
☐ 65 Luis Polonia .15 .07 .02
☐ 66 Robin Yount .50 .23 .06
☐ 67 Juan Samuel .05 .02 .01
☐ 68 Andres Thomas .05 .02 .01
☐ 69 Jeff Musselman .05 .02 .01
☐ 70 Jerry Mumphrey .05 .02 .01
☐ 71 Joe Carter .50 .23 .06
☐ 72 Mike Scioscia .05 .02 .01
☐ 73 Pete Incaviglia .05 .02 .01
☐ 74 Barry Larkin .75 .35 .09
☐ 75 Frank White .10 .05 .01
☐ 76 Willie Randolph .10 .05 .01
☐ 77 Kevin Bass .05 .02 .01
☐ 78 Brian Downing .05 .02 .01
☐ 79 Willie McGee .10 .05 .01
☐ 80 Ellis Burks .75 .35 .09
☐ 81 Hubie Brooks .05 .02 .01
☐ 82 Darrell Evans .10 .05 .01
☐ 83 Robby Thompson .05 .02 .01
☐ 84 Kent Hrbek .10 .05 .01
☐ 85 Ron Darling .05 .02 .01
☐ 86 Stan Jefferson .05 .02 .01
☐ 87 Teddy Higuera .05 .02 .01
☐ 88 Mike Schmidt .75 .35 .09
☐ 89 Barry Bonds 1.00 .45 .12
☐ 90 Jim Presley .05 .02 .01
☐ 91 Orel Hershiser .10 .05 .01
☐ 92 Jesse Barfield .05 .02 .01
☐ 93 Tom Candiotti .05 .02 .01
☐ 94 Bret Saberhagen .10 .05 .01
☐ 95 Jose Uribe .05 .02 .01
☐ 96 Tom Browning .05 .02 .01
☐ 97 Johnny Ray .05 .02 .01
☐ 98 Mike Morgan .05 .02 .01
☐ 99 Lou Whitaker .10 .05 .01
☐ 100 Jim Sundberg .05 .02 .01
☐ 101 Roger McDowell .05 .02 .01
☐ 102 Randy Ready .05 .02 .01
☐ 103 Mike Gallego .05 .02 .01
☐ 104 Steve Buechele .05 .02 .01
☐ 105 Greg Walker .05 .02 .01
☐ 106 Jose Lind .05 .02 .01
☐ 107 Steve Trout .05 .02 .01
☐ 108 Rick Rhoden .05 .02 .01
☐ 109 Jim Pankovits .05 .02 .01
☐ 110 Ken Griffey Sr. .05 .02 .01
☐ 111 Danny Cox .05 .02 .01
☐ 112 Franklin Stubbs .05 .02 .01
☐ 113 Lloyd Moseby .05 .02 .01
☐ 114 Mel Hall .05 .02 .01
☐ 115 Kevin Seitzer .10 .05 .01
☐ 116 Tim Raines .10 .05 .01
☐ 117 Juan Castillo .05 .02 .01
☐ 118 Roger Clemens .75 .35 .09
☐ 119 Mike Aldrete .05 .02 .01
☐ 120 Mario Soto .05 .02 .01
☐ 121 Jack Howell .05 .02 .01
☐ 122 Rick Schu .05 .02 .01
☐ 123 Jeff D. Robinson .05 .02 .01
☐ 124 Doug Drabek .10 .05 .01
☐ 125 Henry Cotto .05 .02 .01
☐ 126 Checklist 89-176 .05 .02 .01
☐ 127 Gary Gaetti .10 .05 .01
☐ 128 Rick Sutcliffe .05 .02 .01
☐ 129 Howard Johnson .05 .02 .01
☐ 130 Chris Brown .05 .02 .01
☐ 131 Dave Henderson .05 .02 .01
☐ 132 Curt Wilkerson .05 .02 .01
☐ 133 Mike Marshall .05 .02 .01
☐ 134 Kelly Gruber .05 .02 .01
☐ 135 Julio Franco .10 .05 .01
☐ 136 Kurt Stillwell .05 .02 .01
☐ 137 Donnie Hill .05 .02 .01
☐ 138 Mike Pagliarulo .05 .02 .01
☐ 139 Von Hayes .05 .02 .01
☐ 140 Mike Scott .05 .02 .01
☐ 141 Bob Kipper .05 .02 .01
☐ 142 Harold Reynolds .10 .05 .01
☐ 143 Bob Brenly .05 .02 .01
☐ 144 Dave Concepcion .10 .05 .01
☐ 145 Devon White .15 .07 .02
☐ 146 Jeff Stone .05 .02 .01
☐ 147 Chet Lemon .05 .02 .01
☐ 148 Ozzie Virgil .05 .02 .01
☐ 149 Todd Worrell .10 .05 .01
☐ 150 Mitch Webster .05 .02 .01
☐ 151 Rob Deer .05 .02 .01
☐ 152 Rich Gedman .05 .02 .01
☐ 153 Andre Dawson .50 .23 .06
☐ 154 Mike Davis .05 .02 .01
☐ 155 Nelson Liriano .05 .02 .01
☐ 156 Greg Swindell .05 .02 .01
☐ 157 George Brett 1.50 .70 .19
☐ 158 Kevin McReynolds .05 .02 .01
☐ 159 Brian Fisher .05 .02 .01
☐ 160 Mike Kingery .05 .02 .01
☐ 161 Tony Gwynn 1.50 .70 .19
☐ 162 Don Baylor .10 .05 .01
☐ 163 Jerry Browne .05 .02 .01
☐ 164 Dan Pasqua .05 .02 .01
☐ 165 Rickey Henderson .75 .35 .09
☐ 166 Brett Butler .10 .05 .01
☐ 167 Nick Esasky .05 .02 .01
☐ 168 Kirk McCaskill .05 .02 .01
☐ 169 Fred Lynn .05 .02 .01
☐ 170 Jack Morris .15 .07 .02
☐ 171 Pedro Guerrero .05 .02 .01
☐ 172 Dave Stieb .05 .02 .01
☐ 173 Pat Tabler .05 .02 .01
☐ 174 Floyd Bannister .05 .02 .01
☐ 175 Rafael Belliard .05 .02 .01
☐ 176 Mark Langston .10 .05 .01
☐ 177 Greg Mathews .05 .02 .01
☐ 178 Claudell Washington .05 .02 .01
☐ 179 Mark McGwire 2.00 .90 .25
☐ 180 Bert Blyleven .10 .05 .01
☐ 181 Jim Rice .15 .07 .02
☐ 182 Mookie Wilson .05 .02 .01
☐ 183 Willie Fraser .05 .02 .01
☐ 184 Andy Van Slyke .10 .05 .01
☐ 185 Matt Nokes .05 .02 .01
☐ 186 Eddie Whitson .05 .02 .01
☐ 187 Tony Fernandez .05 .02 .01
☐ 188 Rick Reuschel .05 .02 .01
☐ 189 Ken Phelps .05 .02 .01
☐ 190 Juan Nieves .05 .02 .01
☐ 191 Kirk Gibson .10 .05 .01
☐ 192 Glenn Davis .05 .02 .01
☐ 193 Zane Smith .05 .02 .01
☐ 194 Jose DeLeon .05 .02 .01
☐ 195 Gary Ward .05 .02 .01
☐ 196 Pascual Perez .05 .02 .01
☐ 197 Carlton Fisk .60 .25 .07
☐ 198 Oddibe McDowell .05 .02 .01
☐ 199 Mark Gubicza .05 .02 .01
☐ 200 Glenn Hubbard .05 .02 .01
☐ 201 Frank Viola .05 .02 .01
☐ 202 Jody Reed .10 .05 .01
☐ 203 Len Dykstra .10 .05 .01
☐ 204 Dick Schofield .05 .02 .01
☐ 205 Sid Bream .05 .02 .01
☐ 206 Willie Hernandez .05 .02 .01
☐ 207 Keith Moreland .05 .02 .01
☐ 208 Mark Eichhorn .05 .02 .01
☐ 209 Rene Gonzales .05 .02 .01
☐ 210 Dave Valle .05 .02 .01
☐ 211 Tom Brunansky .05 .02 .01
☐ 212 Charles Hudson .05 .02 .01
☐ 213 John Farrell .05 .02 .01
☐ 214 Jeff Treadway .05 .02 .01
☐ 215 Eddie Murray 1.00 .45 .12
☐ 216 Checklist 177-264 .05 .02 .01
☐ 217 Greg Brock .05 .02 .01
☐ 218 John Shelby .05 .02 .01
☐ 219 Craig Reynolds .05 .02 .01
☐ 220 Dion James .05 .02 .01
☐ 221 Carney Lansford .05 .02 .01
☐ 222 Juan Berenguer .05 .02 .01
☐ 223 Luis Rivera .05 .02 .01
☐ 224 Harold Baines .10 .05 .01
☐ 225 Shawon Dunston .05 .02 .01
☐ 226 Luis Aguayo .05 .02 .01
☐ 227 Pete O'Brien .05 .02 .01
☐ 228 Ozzie Smith 1.25 .55 .16
☐ 229 Don Mattingly 2.00 .90 .25
☐ 230 Danny Tartabull .05 .02 .01
☐ 231 Andy Allanson .05 .02 .01
☐ 232 John Franco .10 .05 .01
☐ 233 Mike Greenwell .10 .05 .01
☐ 234 Bob Ojeda .05 .02 .01
☐ 235 Chili Davis .10 .05 .01
☐ 236 Mike Dunne .05 .02 .01
☐ 237 Jim Morrison .05 .02 .01
☐ 238 Carmelo Martinez .05 .02 .01
☐ 239 Ernie Whitt .05 .02 .01
☐ 240 Scott Garrelts .05 .02 .01
☐ 241 Mike Moore .05 .02 .01
☐ 242 Dave Parker .10 .05 .01
☐ 243 Tim Laudner .05 .02 .01
☐ 244 Bill Wegman .05 .02 .01
☐ 245 Bob Horner .05 .02 .01
☐ 246 Rafael Santana .05 .02 .01
☐ 247 Alfredo Griffin .05 .02 .01
☐ 248 Mark Bailey .05 .02 .01
☐ 249 Ron Gant .75 .35 .09
☐ 250 Bryn Smith .05 .02 .01
☐ 251 Lance Johnson .50 .23 .06
☐ 252 Sam Horn .05 .02 .01
☐ 253 Darryl Strawberry .10 .05 .01
☐ 254 Chuck Finley .10 .05 .01
☐ 255 Darnell Coles .05 .02 .01
☐ 256 Mike Henneman .10 .05 .01
☐ 257 Andy Hawkins .05 .02 .01
☐ 258 Jim Clancy .05 .02 .01
☐ 259 Atlee Hammaker .05 .02 .01
☐ 260 Glenn Wilson .05 .02 .01
☐ 261 Larry McWilliams .05 .02 .01
☐ 262 Jack Clark .10 .05 .01
☐ 263 Walt Weiss .15 .07 .02
☐ 264 Gene Larkin .05 .02 .01

1988 Topps Coins

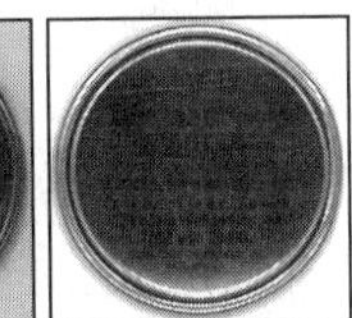

This full-color set of 60 coins contains a full-color photo of the player with a gold-starred scroll at the bottom containing the player's name, position and team. The backs contain the coin number and brief biographical data. Some of the coins have gold rims and some have silver rims. Each coin measures approximately 1 1/2" in diameter. The 1988 set is very similar to the 1987 set of the previous year; the 1988 coins have gold stars on the name scroll on the front of the coin as well as a 1988 copyright at the bottom of the reverse.

	MINT	NRMT	EXC
COMPLETE SET (60)	8.00	3.60	1.00
COMMON COIN (1-60)	.05	.02	.01
☐ 1 George Bell	.05	.02	.01
☐ 2 Roger Clemens	.50	.23	.06
☐ 3 Mark McGwire	1.00	.45	.12
☐ 4 Wade Boggs	.40	.18	.05
☐ 5 Harold Baines	.10	.05	.01
☐ 6 Ivan Calderon	.05	.02	.01
☐ 7 Jose Canseco	.50	.23	.06
☐ 8 Joe Carter	.20	.09	.03
☐ 9 Jack Clark	.05	.02	.01
☐ 10 Alvin Davis	.05	.02	.01
☐ 11 Dwight Evans	.10	.05	.01
☐ 12 Tony Fernandez	.05	.02	.01
☐ 13 Gary Gaetti	.05	.02	.01
☐ 14 Mike Greenwell	.05	.02	.01
☐ 15 Charlie Hough	.05	.02	.01
☐ 16 Wally Joyner	.20	.09	.03
☐ 17 Jimmy Key	.10	.05	.01
☐ 18 Mark Langston	.05	.02	.01
☐ 19 Don Mattingly	1.00	.45	.12
☐ 20 Paul Molitor	.50	.23	.06
☐ 21 Jack Morris	.10	.05	.01
☐ 22 Eddie Murray	.50	.23	.06
☐ 23 Kirby Puckett	1.00	.45	.12
☐ 24 Cal Ripken	2.00	.90	.25
☐ 25 Bret Saberhagen	.10	.05	.01
☐ 26 Ruben Sierra	.20	.09	.03
☐ 27 Cory Snyder	.05	.02	.01
☐ 28 Terry Steinbach	.20	.09	.03
☐ 29 Danny Tartabull	.05	.02	.01
☐ 30 Alan Trammell	.10	.05	.01
☐ 31 Devon White	.20	.09	.03
☐ 32 Robin Yount	.30	.14	.04
☐ 33 Andre Dawson	.10	.05	.01
☐ 34 Steve Bedrosian	.05	.02	.01
☐ 35 Benny Santiago	.05	.02	.01
☐ 36 Tony Gwynn	1.00	.45	.12
☐ 37 Bobby Bonilla	.20	.09	.03
☐ 38 Will Clark	.50	.23	.06
☐ 39 Eric Davis	.05	.02	.01
☐ 40 Mike Dunne	.05	.02	.01
☐ 41 John Franco	.10	.05	.01
☐ 42 Dwight Evans	.10	.05	.01
☐ 43 Pedro Guerrero	.05	.02	.01
☐ 44 Dion James	.05	.02	.01
☐ 45 John Kruk	.20	.09	.03
☐ 46 Jeffrey Leonard	.05	.02	.01
☐ 47 Carmelo Martinez	.05	.02	.01
☐ 48 Dale Murphy	.20	.09	.03
☐ 49 Tim Raines	.10	.05	.01
☐ 50 Nolan Ryan	2.00	.90	.25
☐ 51 Juan Samuel	.05	.02	.01
☐ 52 Ryne Sandberg	.75	.35	.09
☐ 53 Mike Schmidt	.60	.25	.07
☐ 54 Mike Scott	.05	.02	.01
☐ 55 Ozzie Smith	.75	.35	.09
☐ 56 Darryl Strawberry	.10	.05	.01
☐ 57 Rick Sutcliffe	.05	.02	.01
☐ 58 Fernando Valenzuela	.10	.05	.01
☐ 59 Tim Wallach	.05	.02	.01
☐ 60 Todd Worrell	.05	.02	.01

1988 Topps Gallery of Champions

This set marked the fifth consecutive season that Topps issued metal versions of some leading players. The players pictured in this set were either league leaders or award winners. The cards measure approximately 1 1/4" by 1 3/4" and were produced in aluminum, bronze and silver versions. We have priced the aluminum versions and the bronze values are 2X to 4X the aluminum values while the silver cards are valued between 5X and 10X the aluminum cards. We have sequenced this set in alphabetical order.

	MINT	NRMT	EXC
COMPLETE SET (12)	125.00	55.00	15.50
COMMON CARD (1-12)	5.00	2.20	.60
☐ 1 Steve Bedrosian	5.00	2.20	.60
☐ 2 George Bell	5.00	2.20	.60
☐ 3 Wade Boggs	20.00	9.00	2.50
☐ 4 Jack Clark	5.00	2.20	.60
☐ 5 Roger Clemens	20.00	9.00	2.50
☐ 6 Andre Dawson	10.00	4.50	1.25
☐ 7 Tony Gwynn	25.00	11.00	3.10
☐ 8 Mark Langston	5.00	2.20	.60
☐ 9 Mark McGwire	25.00	11.00	3.10
☐ 10 Dave Righetti	5.00	2.20	.60
☐ 11 Nolan Ryan	50.00	22.00	6.25
☐ 12 Benito Santiago	5.00	2.20	.60

1988 Topps Mini Leaders

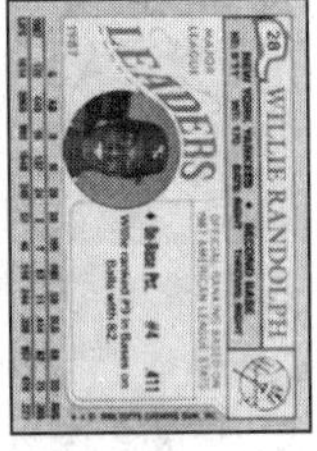

The 1988 Topps Mini set of Major League Leaders features 77 cards of leaders of the various statistical categories for the 1987 season. The cards are numbered on the back and measure approximately 2 1/8" by 3". The set numbering is alphabetical by player within team and the teams themselves are in alphabetical order as well. The card backs are printed in blue, red, and yellow on white card stock. The cards were distributed as a separate issue in wax packs.

	MINT	NRMT	EXC
COMPLETE SET (77)	5.00	2.20	.60
COMMON CARD (1-77)	.05	.02	.01
☐ 1 Wade Boggs	.30	.14	.04
☐ 2 Roger Clemens	.40	.18	.05
☐ 3 Dwight Evans	.10	.05	.01
☐ 4 DeWayne Buice	.05	.02	.01
☐ 5 Brian Downing	.05	.02	.01
☐ 6 Wally Joyner	.10	.05	.01
☐ 7 Ivan Calderon	.05	.02	.01
☐ 8 Carlton Fisk	.30	.14	.04
☐ 9 Gary Redus	.05	.02	.01
☐ 10 Darrell Evans	.10	.05	.01
☐ 11 Jack Morris	.10	.05	.01
☐ 12 Alan Trammell	.10	.05	.01
☐ 13 Lou Whitaker	.10	.05	.01
☐ 14 Bret Saberhagen	.05	.02	.01
☐ 15 Kevin Seitzer	.05	.02	.01
☐ 16 Danny Tartabull	.05	.02	.01
☐ 17 Willie Wilson	.05	.02	.01

□ 18 Teddy Higuera .05 .02 .01
□ 19 Paul Molitor .30 .14 .04
□ 20 Dan Plesac .05 .02 .01
□ 21 Robin Yount .15 .07 .02
□ 22 Kent Hrbek .10 .05 .01
□ 23 Kirby Puckett 1.00 .45 .12
□ 24 Jeff Reardon .10 .05 .01
□ 25 Frank Viola .05 .02 .01
□ 26 Rickey Henderson .30 .14 .04
□ 27 Don Mattingly 1.00 .45 .12
□ 28 Willie Randolph .05 .02 .01
□ 29 Dave Righetti .05 .02 .01
□ 30 Jose Canseco .50 .23 .06
□ 31 Mark McGwire 1.00 .45 .12
□ 32 Dave Stewart .05 .02 .01
□ 33 Phil Bradley .05 .02 .01
□ 34 Mark Langston .05 .02 .01
□ 35 Harold Reynolds .05 .02 .01
□ 36 Charlie Hough .05 .02 .01
□ 37 George Bell .05 .02 .01
□ 38 Tom Henke .05 .02 .01
□ 39 Jimmy Key .10 .05 .01
□ 40 Dion James .05 .02 .01
□ 41 Dale Murphy .15 .07 .02
□ 42 Zane Smith .05 .02 .01
□ 43 Andre Dawson .10 .05 .01
□ 44 Lee Smith .10 .05 .01
□ 45 Rick Sutcliffe .05 .02 .01
□ 46 Eric Davis .10 .05 .01
□ 47 John Franco .10 .05 .01
□ 48 Dave Parker .10 .05 .01
□ 49 Billy Hatcher .05 .02 .01
□ 50 Nolan Ryan 1.50 .70 .19
□ 51 Mike Scott .05 .02 .01
□ 52 Pedro Guerrero .05 .02 .01
□ 53 Orel Hershiser .10 .05 .01
□ 54 Fernando Valenzuela .10 .05 .01
□ 55 Bob Welch .05 .02 .01
□ 56 Andres Galarraga .25 .11 .03
□ 57 Tim Raines .10 .05 .01
□ 58 Tim Wallach .05 .02 .01
□ 59 Len Dykstra .10 .05 .01
□ 60 Dwight Gooden .10 .05 .01
□ 61 Howard Johnson .05 .02 .01
□ 62 Roger McDowell .05 .02 .01
□ 63 Darryl Strawberry .10 .05 .01
□ 64 Steve Bedrosian .05 .02 .01
□ 65 Shane Rawley .05 .02 .01
□ 66 Juan Samuel .05 .02 .01
□ 67 Mike Schmidt .50 .23 .06
□ 68 Mike Dunne .05 .02 .01
□ 69 Jack Clark .05 .02 .01
□ 70 Vince Coleman .05 .02 .01
□ 71 Willie McGee .10 .05 .01
□ 72 Ozzie Smith .75 .35 .09
□ 73 Todd Worrell .05 .02 .01
□ 74 Tony Gwynn 1.00 .45 .12
□ 75 John Kruk .15 .07 .02
□ 76 Rick Reuschel .05 .02 .01
□ 77 Checklist Card .05 .02 .01

1988 Topps/O-Pee-Chee Stickers

Printed in Canada, these 313 stickers measure approximately 2 1/8" by 3" and are numbered on their fronts. The sticker backs are actually cards (1988 O-Pee-Chee Super Stars) and are considered a separate set. The stickers feature yellow- and red-bordered color player photos. An album onto which the stickers could be affixed was available at retail stores. The album and the sticker numbering are organized as follows: 1987 Highlights (1-12), 1987 Championship Series (13-18), 1987 World Series (19-25), Houston Astros (26-35), Atlanta Braves (36-45), St. Louis Cardinals (46-55), Chicago Cubs (56-65), Los Angeles Dodgers (66-75), Montreal Expos (76-85), San Francisco Giants (86-95), New York Mets (96-105), San Diego Padres (106-115), Philadelphia Phillies (116-125), Pittsburgh Pirates (126-135), Cincinnati Reds (136-145), Foil All-Stars (146-163), Oakland A's (164-173), California Angels (174-183), Toronto Blue Jays (184-193), Milwaukee Brewers (194-203), Cleveland Indians (204-213), Seattle Mariners (214-223), Baltimore Orioles (224-233), Texas Rangers (234-243), Boston Red Sox (244-253), Kansas City Royals (254-263), Detroit Tigers (264-273), Minnesota Twins (274-283), Chicago White Sox (284-293), New York Yankees (294-303) and Future Stars (304-313). For those stickers featuring more than one player, the other numbers on that sticker are given below in parentheses. Although the prices listed below are for the stickers only, there are instances where having an especially desirable sticker card back (attached to that sticker) will increase the values listed below.

	MINT	NRMT	EXC
COMPLETE SET (313)	15.00	6.75	1.85
COMMON STICKER (1-145)	.05	.02	.01
COMMON FOIL (146-163)	.10	.05	.01
COMMON STICKER (164-313)	.05	.02	.01

*TOPPS AND OPC: SAME VALUE

□ 1 Mark McGwire (263) .75 .35 .09
□ 2 Benny Santiago (304) .05 .02 .01
□ 3 Don Mattingly (187) 1.00 .45 .12
□ 4 Vince Coleman (223) .05 .02 .01
□ 5 Bob Boone (272) .10 .05 .01
□ 6 Steve Bedrosian(278) .05 .02 .01
□ 7 Nolan Ryan (276) 2.00 .90 .25
□ 8 Darrell Evans (306) .10 .05 .01
□ 9 Mike Schmidt (255) .60 .25 .07
□ 10 Don Baylor (256) .10 .05 .01
□ 11 Eddie Murray (145) .50 .23 .06
□ 12 Juan Beniquez (237) .05 .02 .01
□ 13 John Tudor .05 .02 .01
□ 14 Jeff Reardon .10 .05 .01
□ 15 Tom Brunansky .05 .02 .01
□ 16 Jeffrey Leonard .05 .02 .01
□ 17 Gary Gaetti .10 .05 .01
□ 18 Jose Oquendo .05 .02 .01
□ 19 Dan Gladden .05 .02 .01
□ 20 Bert Blyleven .10 .05 .01
□ 21 John Tudor .05 .02 .01
□ 22 Tom Lawless .05 .02 .01
□ 23 Curt Ford .05 .02 .01
□ 24 Kent Hrbek .10 .05 .01
□ 25 Frank Viola .05 .02 .01
□ 26 Dave Smith (216) .05 .02 .01
□ 27 Jim Deshaies (240) .05 .02 .01
□ 28 Billy Hatcher (171) .05 .02 .01
□ 29 Kevin Bass (196) .05 .02 .01
□ 30 Mike Scott .05 .02 .01
□ 31 Denny Walling (224) .05 .02 .01
□ 32 Alan Ashby (185) .05 .02 .01
□ 33 Ken Caminiti (292) .75 .35 .09
□ 34 Bill Doran (245) .05 .02 .01
□ 35 Glenn Davis .05 .02 .01
□ 36 Ozzie Virgil .05 .02 .01
□ 37 Ken Oberkfell (260) .05 .02 .01
□ 38 Ken Griffey (183) .10 .05 .01
□ 39 Albert Hall (287) .05 .02 .01
□ 40 Zane Smith (310) .05 .02 .01
□ 41 Andres Thomas (207) .05 .02 .01
□ 42 Dion James (178) .05 .02 .01
□ 43 Jim Acker (249) .05 .02 .01
□ 44 Tom Glavine (226) 1.25 .55 .16
□ 45 Dale Murphy .15 .07 .02
□ 46 Jack Clark .10 .05 .01
□ 47 Vince Coleman (269) .05 .02 .01
□ 48 Ricky Horton (221) .05 .02 .01
□ 49 Terry Pendleton(303) .10 .05 .01
□ 50 Tom Herr (271) .05 .02 .01
□ 51 Joe Magrane (265) .05 .02 .01
□ 52 Tony Pena (211) .05 .02 .01
□ 53 Ozzie Smith (298) .40 .18 .05
□ 54 Todd Worrell (169) .05 .02 .01
□ 55 Willie McGee .05 .02 .01
□ 56 Andre Dawson .10 .05 .01
□ 57 Ryne Sandberg (225) .50 .23 .06
□ 58 Keith Moreland (291) .05 .02 .01
□ 59 Greg Maddux (198) 3.00 1.35 .35
□ 60 Jody Davis (290) .05 .02 .01
□ 61 Rick Sutcliffe .05 .02 .01
□ 62 Jamie Moyer (295) .05 .02 .01
□ 63 Leon Durham (172) .05 .02 .01
□ 64 Lee Smith (313) .10 .05 .01
□ 65 Shawon Dunston (250) .05 .02 .01
□ 66 Franklin Stubbs(257) .05 .02 .01
□ 67 Mike Scioscia (235) .05 .02 .01
□ 68 Orel Hershiser (177) .10 .05 .01
□ 69 Mike Marshall (299) .05 .02 .01
□ 70 Fernando Valenzuela .10 .05 .01
□ 71 Mickey Hatcher (281) .05 .02 .01
□ 72 Matt Young (166) .05 .02 .01
□ 73 Bob Welch (236) .05 .02 .01
□ 74 Steve Sax (170) .05 .02 .01
□ 75 Pedro Guerrero .05 .02 .01
□ 76 Tim Raines .10 .05 .01
□ 77 Casey Candaele (252) .05 .02 .01
□ 78 Mike Fitzgerald(248) .05 .02 .01
□ 79 Andres Galarraga (301) .30 .14 .04
□ 80 Neal Heaton (212) .05 .02 .01
□ 81 Hubie Brooks (296) .05 .02 .01
□ 82 Floyd Youmans (258) .05 .02 .01
□ 83 Herm Winningham(201) .05 .02 .01
□ 84 Denny Martinez (307) .10 .05 .01
□ 85 Tim Wallach .05 .02 .01
□ 86 Jeffrey Leonard .05 .02 .01
□ 87 Will Clark (251) .40 .18 .05
□ 88 Kevin Mitchell (288) .10 .05 .01
□ 89 Mike Aldrete (267) .05 .02 .01
□ 90 Scott Garrelts (191) .05 .02 .01
□ 91 Jose Uribe (231) .05 .02 .01
□ 92 Bob Brenly (246) .05 .02 .01
□ 93 Robby Thompson (189) .05 .02 .01
□ 94 Don Robinson (217) .05 .02 .01
□ 95 Candy Maldonado .05 .02 .01
□ 96 Darryl Strawberry .10 .05 .01
□ 97 Keith Hernandez(192) .10 .05 .01
□ 98 Ron Darling (220) .05 .02 .01
□ 99 Howard Johnson (218) .05 .02 .01
□ 100 Roger McDowell (190) .05 .02 .01
□ 101 Dwight Gooden .10 .05 .01
□ 102 Kevin McReynolds (165) .05 .02 .01
□ 103 Sid Fernandez (275) .05 .02 .01
□ 104 Dave Magadan (241) .05 .02 .01
□ 105 Gary Carter (167) .10 .05 .01
□ 106 Carmelo Martinez (302) .05 .02 .01
□ 107 Eddie Whitson (205) .05 .02 .01
□ 108 Tim Flannery (180) .05 .02 .01
□ 109 Stan Jefferson (266) .05 .02 .01
□ 110 John Kruk .15 .07 .02
□ 111 Chris Brown (168) .05 .02 .01
□ 112 Benito Santiago (215) .05 .02 .01
□ 113 Garry Templeton(270) .05 .02 .01
□ 114 Lance McCullers(186) .05 .02 .01
□ 115 Tony Gwynn .75 .35 .09
□ 116 Steve Bedrosian .05 .02 .01
□ 117 Von Hayes (247) .05 .02 .01
□ 118 Kevin Gross (279) .05 .02 .01
□ 119 Bruce Ruffin (238) .05 .02 .01
□ 120 Juan Samuel (184) .05 .02 .01
□ 121 Shane Rawley (182) .05 .02 .01
□ 122 Chris James (222) .05 .02 .01
□ 123 Lance Parrish (199) .05 .02 .01
□ 124 Glenn Wilson (181) .05 .02 .01
□ 125 Mike Schmidt .60 .25 .07
□ 126 Andy Van Slyke .10 .05 .01
□ 127 Jose Lind (297) .10 .05 .01
□ 128 Al Pedrique (176) .05 .02 .01
□ 129 Bobby Bonilla (277) .15 .07 .02
□ 130 Sid Bream (175) .05 .02 .01
□ 131 Mike LaValliere(230) .05 .02 .01
□ 132 Mike Dunne (197) .05 .02 .01
□ 133 Jeff D. Robinson (232) .05 .02 .01
□ 134 Doug Drabek (195) .10 .05 .01
□ 135 Barry Bonds .75 .35 .09
□ 136 Dave Parker .10 .05 .01
□ 137 Nick Esasky (208) .05 .02 .01
□ 138 Buddy Bell (280) .10 .05 .01
□ 139 Kal Daniels (239) .05 .02 .01
□ 140 Barry Larkin (285) .50 .23 .06
□ 141 Eric Davis .05 .02 .01
□ 142 John Franco (227) .10 .05 .01
□ 143 Bo Diaz (229) .05 .02 .01
□ 144 Ron Oester (261) .05 .02 .01
□ 145 Dennis Rasmussen(11) .05 .02 .01
□ 146 Eric Davis FOIL .10 .05 .01
□ 147 Ryne Sandberg FOIL .75 .35 .09
□ 148 Andre Dawson FOIL .30 .14 .04
□ 149 Mike Schmidt FOIL 1.00 .45 .12
□ 150 Jack Clark FOIL .15 .07 .02
□ 151 Darryl Strawberry FOIL .15 .07 .02
□ 152 Gary Carter FOIL .30 .14 .04
□ 153 Ozzie Smith FOIL .60 .25 .07
□ 154 Mike Scott FOIL .10 .05 .01
□ 155 Rickey Henderson FOIL .40 .18 .05
□ 156 Don Mattingly FOIL 1.50 .70 .19
□ 157 Wade Boggs FOIL .40 .18 .05
□ 158 George Bell FOIL .05 .02 .01
□ 159 Dave Winfield FOIL .40 .18 .05
□ 160 Cal Ripken FOIL 3.00 1.35 .35
□ 161 Terry Kennedy FOIL .10 .05 .01
□ 162 Willie Randolph FOIL .15 .07 .02
□ 163 Bret Saberhagen FOIL .10 .05 .01
□ 164 Mark McGwire .75 .35 .09
□ 165 Tony Phillips (102) .10 .05 .01
□ 166 Jay Howell (72) .05 .02 .01
□ 167 Carney Lansford(105) .10 .05 .01
□ 168 Dave Stewart (111) .10 .05 .01
□ 169 Alfredo Griffin (54) .05 .02 .01
□ 170 Dennis Eckersley(74) .10 .05 .01
□ 171 Mike Davis (28) .05 .02 .01
□ 172 Luis Polonia (63) .10 .05 .01
□ 173 Jose Canseco .50 .23 .06
□ 174 Mike Witt .05 .02 .01
□ 175 Jack Howell (130) .05 .02 .01
□ 176 Greg Minton (128) .05 .02 .01
□ 177 Dick Schofield (68) .05 .02 .01
□ 178 Gary Pettis (42) .05 .02 .01
□ 179 Wally Joyner .15 .07 .02
□ 180 DeWayne Buice (108) .05 .02 .01
□ 181 Brian Downing (124) .05 .02 .01
□ 182 Bob Boone (121) .10 .05 .01
□ 183 Devon White (38) .15 .07 .02
□ 184 Jim Clancy (120) .05 .02 .01
□ 185 Willie Upshaw (32) .05 .02 .01
□ 186 Tom Henke (114) .05 .02 .01
□ 187 Ernie Whitt (3) .05 .02 .01
□ 188 George Bell .05 .02 .01
□ 189 Lloyd Moseby (93) .05 .02 .01
□ 190 Jimmy Key (100) .10 .05 .01
□ 191 Dave Stieb (90) .05 .02 .01
□ 192 Jesse Barfield (97) .05 .02 .01
□ 193 Tony Fernandez .05 .02 .01
□ 194 Paul Molitor .25 .11 .03
□ 195 Jim Gantner (134) .05 .02 .01
□ 196 Teddy Higuera (29) .05 .02 .01
□ 197 Glenn Braggs (132) .05 .02 .01
□ 198 Rob Deer (59) .05 .02 .01
□ 199 Dale Sveum (123) .05 .02 .01
□ 200 Bill Wegman (308) .05 .02 .01
□ 201 Robin Yount (83) .25 .11 .03
□ 202 B.J. Surhoff .10 .05 .01
□ 203 Dan Plesac .05 .02 .01
□ 204 Pat Tabler .05 .02 .01
□ 205 Mel Hall (107) .05 .02 .01
□ 206 Scott Bailes (305) .05 .02 .01
□ 207 Julio Franco (41) .10 .05 .01
□ 208 Cory Snyder (137) .05 .02 .01
□ 209 Chris Bando (312) .05 .02 .01
□ 210 Greg Swindell (311) .05 .02 .01
□ 211 Brook Jacoby (52) .05 .02 .01
□ 212 Brett Butler (80) .10 .05 .01
□ 213 Joe Carter .15 .07 .02
□ 214 Mark Langston .10 .05 .01
□ 215 Rey Quinones (112) .05 .02 .01
□ 216 Ed Nunez (16) .05 .02 .01
□ 217 Jim Presley (94) .05 .02 .01
□ 218 Phil Bradley (99) .05 .02 .01
□ 219 Alvin Davis .05 .02 .01
□ 220 Dave Valle (98) .05 .02 .01
□ 221 Harold Reynolds (48) .10 .05 .01
□ 222 Scott Bradley (122) .05 .02 .01
□ 223 Gary Matthews (4) .05 .02 .01
□ 224 Eric Bell (31) .05 .02 .01
□ 225 Terry Kennedy (57) .05 .02 .01
□ 226 Dave Schmidt (44) .05 .02 .01
□ 227 Billy Ripken (142) .05 .02 .01
□ 228 Cal Ripken 2.00 .90 .25
□ 229 Ray Knight (143) .10 .05 .01
□ 230 Larry Sheets (131) .05 .02 .01
□ 231 Mike Boddicker (91) .05 .02 .01
□ 232 Tom Niedenfuer (133) .05 .02 .01
□ 233 Eddie Murray .50 .23 .06
□ 234 Ruben Sierra .15 .07 .02
□ 235 Steve Buechele (67) .05 .02 .01
□ 236 Charlie Hough (73) .10 .05 .01
□ 237 Oddibe McDowell (12) .05 .02 .01
□ 238 Mike Stanley (119) .05 .02 .01
□ 239 Pete Incaviglia(139) .05 .02 .01
□ 240 Pete O'Brien (27) .05 .02 .01
□ 241 Scott Fletcher (104) .05 .02 .01
□ 242 Dale Mohorcic (300) .05 .02 .01
□ 243 Larry Parrish .05 .02 .01
□ 244 Wade Boggs .25 .11 .03
□ 245 Dwight Evans (34) .10 .05 .01
□ 246 Sam Horn (92) .05 .02 .01
□ 247 Jim Rice (117) .10 .05 .01
□ 248 Marty Barrett (78) .05 .02 .01
□ 249 Mike Greenwell (43) .10 .05 .01
□ 250 Ellis Burks (65) .30 .14 .04
□ 251 Roger Clemens (87) .25 .11 .03
□ 252 Rich Gedman (77) .05 .02 .01
□ 253 Bruce Hurst .05 .02 .01
□ 254 Bret Saberhagen .10 .05 .01
□ 255 Frank White (9) .10 .05 .01
□ 256 Dan Quisenberry (10) .05 .02 .01
□ 257 Danny Tartabull (66) .05 .02 .01
□ 258 Bo Jackson (82) .15 .07 .02
□ 259 George Brett .75 .35 .09
□ 260 Charlie Leibrandt(37) .05 .02 .01
□ 261 Kevin Seitzer (144) .10 .05 .01
□ 262 Mark Gubicza (282) .05 .02 .01
□ 263 Willie Wilson (1) .05 .02 .01
□ 264 Frank Tanana (286) .05 .02 .01
□ 265 Darrell Evans (51) .10 .05 .01
□ 266 Bill Madlock (109) .10 .05 .01
□ 267 Kirk Gibson (89) .10 .05 .01
□ 268 Jack Morris .10 .05 .01
□ 269 Matt Nokes (47) .05 .02 .01
□ 270 Lou Whitaker (113) .10 .05 .01
□ 271 Eric King (50) .05 .02 .01
□ 272 Jim Morrison (5) .05 .02 .01
□ 273 Alan Trammell .10 .05 .01
□ 274 Kent Hrbek .10 .05 .01
□ 275 Tom Brunansky (103) .05 .02 .01
□ 276 Bert Blyleven (7) .10 .05 .01
□ 277 Gary Gaetti (129) .10 .05 .01
□ 278 Tim Laudner (6) .05 .02 .01
□ 279 Gene Larkin (118) .10 .05 .01
□ 280 Jeff Reardon (138) .10 .05 .01
□ 281 Danny Gladden (71) .05 .02 .01
□ 282 Frank Viola (262) .05 .02 .01
□ 283 Kirby Puckett .50 .23 .06
□ 284 Ozzie Guillen .10 .05 .01
□ 285 Ivan Calderon (140) .05 .02 .01
□ 286 Donnie Hill (264) .05 .02 .01
□ 287 Ken Williams (39) .05 .02 .01
□ 288 Jim Winn (88) .05 .02 .01
□ 289 Bob James (69) .05 .02 .01
□ 290 Carlton Fisk (60) .25 .11 .03
□ 291 Richard Dotson (58) .05 .02 .01
□ 292 Greg Walker (33) .05 .02 .01
□ 293 Harold Baines .10 .05 .01
□ 294 Willie Randolph .10 .05 .01
□ 295 Mike Pagliarulo (62) .05 .02 .01
□ 296 Ron Guidry (81) .05 .02 .01
□ 297 Rickey Henderson(127) .25 .11 .03
□ 298 Rick Rhoden (53) .05 .02 .01
□ 299 Don Mattingly 1.00 .45 .12
□ 300 Dave Righetti (242) .05 .02 .01
□ 301 Clau.Washington (79) .05 .02 .01
□ 302 Dave Winfield (106) .25 .11 .03
□ 303 Gary Ward (49) .05 .02 .01
□ 304 Al Pedrique (2) .05 .02 .01
□ 305 Casey Candaele (206) .05 .02 .01
□ 306 Kevin Seitzer (8) .10 .05 .01
□ 307 Mike Dunne (84) .05 .02 .01
□ 308 Jeff Musselman (200) .05 .02 .01
□ 309 Mark McGwire .75 .35 .09

☐ 310 Ellis Burks (40)	.30	.14	.04
☐ 311 Matt Nokes (210)	.05	.02	.01
☐ 312 Mike Greenwell (209)	.10	.05	.01
☐ 313 Devon White (64)	.15	.07	.02
☐ xx Album	1.00	.45	.12

1988 Topps/O-Pee-Chee Sticker Backs

These 67 cards were actually the backs of the 1988 O-Pee-Chee Stickers. In previous years O-Pee-Chee had used a disposable peel-off sticker back. The 1988 Super Star sticker back was actually collectible and attractive. In fact, many collectors felt that the sticker backs were more desirable than the stickers. The white-bordered cards measure approximately 2 1/8" by 3" and have either a red (AL, 1-33) or blue (NL, 34-66) background behind the player's photo. The player's 1987 and career statistics were shown at the bottom of each card. The cards are numbered in the statistics box in small print. Three different front (sticker) combinations exist for each of the 66 players and checklist. The cards were retailed in cellophane wax packs at 25 cents for a stick of gum and five sticker cards.

	MINT	NRMT	EXC
COMPLETE SET (67)	6.00	2.70	.75
COMMON CARD (1-67)	.05	.02	.01
☐ 1 Jack Clark	.10	.05	.01
☐ 2 Andres Galarraga	.25	.11	.03
☐ 3 Keith Hernandez	.10	.05	.01
☐ 4 Tom Herr	.05	.02	.01
☐ 5 Juan Samuel	.05	.02	.01
☐ 6 Ryne Sandberg	.50	.23	.06
☐ 7 Terry Pendleton	.10	.05	.01
☐ 8 Mike Schmidt	.50	.23	.06
☐ 9 Tim Wallach	.05	.02	.01
☐ 10 Hubie Brooks	.05	.02	.01
☐ 11 Shawon Dunston	.05	.02	.01
☐ 12 Ozzie Smith	.30	.14	.04
☐ 13 Andre Dawson	.10	.05	.01
☐ 14 Eric Davis	.05	.02	.01
☐ 15 Pedro Guerrero	.05	.02	.01
☐ 16 Tony Gwynn	.60	.25	.07
☐ 17 Jeffrey Leonard	.05	.02	.01
☐ 18 Dale Murphy	.15	.07	.02
☐ 19 Dave Parker	.10	.05	.01
☐ 20 Tim Raines	.10	.05	.01
☐ 21 Darryl Strawberry	.10	.05	.01
☐ 22 Gary Carter	.10	.05	.01
☐ 23 Jody Davis	.05	.02	.01
☐ 24 Ozzie Virgil	.05	.02	.01
☐ 25 Dwight Gooden	.10	.05	.01
☐ 26 Mike Scott	.05	.02	.01
☐ 27 Rick Sutcliffe	.05	.02	.01
☐ 28 Sid Fernandez	.05	.02	.01
☐ 29 Neal Heaton	.05	.02	.01
☐ 30 Fernando Valenzuela	.10	.05	.01
☐ 31 Steve Bedrosian	.05	.02	.01
☐ 32 John Franco	.10	.05	.01
☐ 33 Lee Smith	.10	.05	.01
☐ 34 Wally Joyner	.15	.07	.02
☐ 35 Don Mattingly	.75	.35	.09
☐ 36 Mark McGwire	.40	.18	.05
☐ 37 Willie Randolph	.05	.02	.01
☐ 38 Lou Whitaker	.10	.05	.01
☐ 39 Frank White	.10	.05	.01
☐ 40 Wade Boggs	.20	.09	.03
☐ 41 George Brett	.60	.25	.07
☐ 42 Paul Molitor	.20	.09	.03
☐ 43 Tony Fernandez	.05	.02	.01
☐ 44 Cal Ripken	1.50	.70	.19
☐ 45 Alan Trammell	.10	.05	.01
☐ 46 Jesse Barfield	.05	.02	.01
☐ 47 George Bell	.05	.02	.01
☐ 48 Jose Canseco	.40	.18	.05
☐ 49 Joe Carter	.15	.07	.02
☐ 50 Dwight Evans	.10	.05	.01
☐ 51 Rickey Henderson	.20	.09	.03
☐ 52 Kirby Puckett	.50	.23	.06
☐ 53 Cory Snyder	.05	.02	.01
☐ 54 Dave Winfield	.20	.09	.03
☐ 55 Terry Kennedy	.05	.02	.01
☐ 56 Matt Nokes	.05	.02	.01
☐ 57 B.J. Surhoff	.10	.05	.01
☐ 58 Roger Clemens	.20	.09	.03
☐ 59 Jack Morris	.10	.05	.01
☐ 60 Bret Saberhagen	.10	.05	.01
☐ 61 Ron Guidry	.10	.05	.01
☐ 62 Bruce Hurst	.05	.02	.01
☐ 63 Mark Langston	.10	.05	.01
☐ 64 Tom Henke	.05	.02	.01
☐ 65 Dan Plesac	.05	.02	.01
☐ 66 Dave Righetti	.05	.02	.01
☐ 67 Checklist	.05	.02	.01

1988 Topps Revco League Leaders

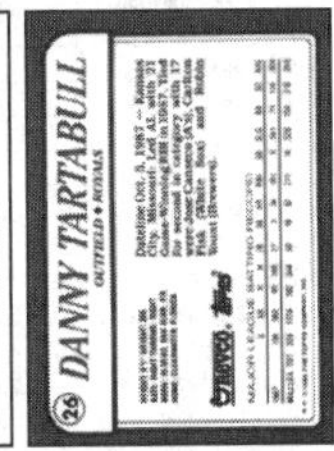

Topps produced this 33-card boxed standard-size set for Revco stores subtitled "League Leaders". The cards feature a high-gloss, full-color photo of the player inside a white border. The card backs are printed in red and black on white card stock. The statistics provided on the card backs cover only two lines, last season and Major League totals.

	MINT	NRMT	EXC
COMPLETE SET (33)	5.00	2.20	.60
COMMON CARD (1-33)	.05	.02	.01
☐ 1 Tony Gwynn	1.00	.45	.12
☐ 2 Andre Dawson	.20	.09	.03
☐ 3 Vince Coleman	.05	.02	.01
☐ 4 Jack Clark	.10	.05	.01
☐ 5 Tim Raines	.10	.05	.01
☐ 6 Tim Wallach	.05	.02	.01
☐ 7 Juan Samuel	.05	.02	.01
☐ 8 Nolan Ryan	2.00	.90	.25
☐ 9 Rick Sutcliffe	.05	.02	.01
☐ 10 Kent Tekulve	.05	.02	.01
☐ 11 Steve Bedrosian	.05	.02	.01
☐ 12 Orel Hershiser	.10	.05	.01
☐ 13 Rick Reuschel	.05	.02	.01
☐ 14 Fernando Valenzuela	.10	.05	.01
☐ 15 Bob Welch	.05	.02	.01
☐ 16 Wade Boggs	.30	.14	.04
☐ 17 Mark McGwire	1.00	.45	.12
☐ 18 George Bell	.05	.02	.01
☐ 19 Harold Reynolds	.05	.02	.01
☐ 20 Paul Molitor	.40	.18	.05
☐ 21 Kirby Puckett	1.00	.45	.12
☐ 22 Kevin Seitzer	.10	.05	.01
☐ 23 Brian Downing	.05	.02	.01
☐ 24 Dwight Evans	.10	.05	.01
☐ 25 Willie Wilson	.05	.02	.01
☐ 26 Danny Tartabull	.05	.02	.01
☐ 27 Jimmy Key	.10	.05	.01
☐ 28 Roger Clemens	.75	.35	.09
☐ 29 Dave Stewart	.10	.05	.01
☐ 30 Mark Eichhorn	.05	.02	.01
☐ 31 Tom Henke	.05	.02	.01
☐ 32 Charlie Hough	.05	.02	.01
☐ 33 Mark Langston	.05	.02	.01

1988 Topps Rite-Aid Team MVP's

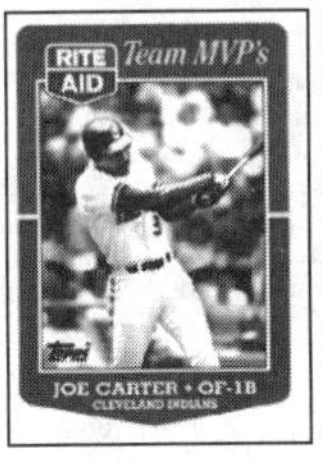

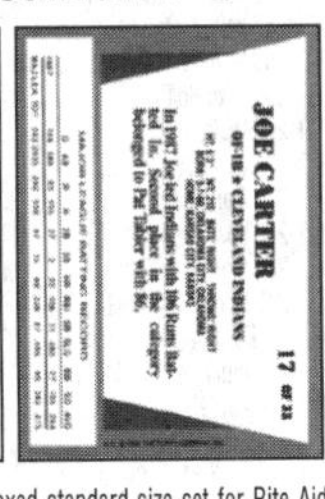

Topps produced this 33-card boxed standard-size set for Rite Aid Drug and Discount Stores subtitled "Team MVP's". The Rite Aid logo is at the top of every obverse. The cards feature a high-gloss, full-color photo of the player inside a red, white, and blue border. The card backs are printed in blue and black on white card stock. The checklist for the set is found on the back panel of the small collector box. The statistics provided on the card backs cover only two lines, last season and Major League totals.

	MINT	NRMT	EXC
COMPLETE SET (33)	4.00	1.80	.50
COMMON CARD (1-33)	.05	.02	.01
☐ 1 Dale Murphy	.20	.09	.03
☐ 2 Andre Dawson	.25	.11	.03
☐ 3 Eric Davis	.10	.05	.01
☐ 4 Mike Scott	.05	.02	.01
☐ 5 Pedro Guerrero	.05	.02	.01
☐ 6 Tim Raines	.10	.05	.01
☐ 7 Darryl Strawberry	.10	.05	.01
☐ 8 Mike Schmidt	.60	.25	.07
☐ 9 Mike Dunne	.05	.02	.01
☐ 10 Jack Clark	.10	.05	.01
☐ 11 Tony Gwynn	1.00	.45	.12
☐ 12 Will Clark	.40	.18	.05
☐ 13 Cal Ripken	2.00	.90	.25
☐ 14 Wade Boggs	.25	.11	.03
☐ 15 Wally Joyner	.20	.09	.03
☐ 16 Harold Baines	.10	.05	.01
☐ 17 Joe Carter	.25	.11	.03
☐ 18 Alan Trammell	.10	.05	.01
☐ 19 Kevin Seitzer	.10	.05	.01
☐ 20 Paul Molitor	.40	.18	.05
☐ 21 Kirby Puckett	1.00	.45	.12
☐ 22 Don Mattingly	1.00	.45	.12
☐ 23 Mark McGwire	1.00	.45	.12
☐ 24 Alvin Davis	.05	.02	.01
☐ 25 Ruben Sierra	.20	.09	.03
☐ 26 George Bell	.05	.02	.01
☐ 27 Jack Morris	.10	.05	.01
☐ 28 Jeff Reardon	.05	.02	.01
☐ 29 John Tudor	.05	.02	.01
☐ 30 Rick Reuschel	.05	.02	.01
☐ 31 Gary Gaetti	.05	.02	.01
☐ 32 Jeffrey Leonard	.05	.02	.01
☐ 33 Frank Viola	.05	.02	.01

1988 Topps UK Minis

The 1988 Topps UK (United Kingdom) Mini set of "American Baseball" features 88 cards. The cards measure approximately 2 1/8" by 3". The card backs are printed in blue, red, and yellow on white card stock. The cards were distributed as a separate issue in packs. A custom black and yellow small set box was also available for holding a complete set; the box has a complete checklist on the back panel. The set player numbering is according to alphabetical order.

	MINT	NRMT	EXC
COMPLETE SET (88)	5.00	2.20	.60
COMMON CARD (1-88)	.05	.02	.01
☐ 1 Harold Baines	.05	.02	.01
☐ 2 Steve Bedrosian	.05	.02	.01
☐ 3 George Bell	.05	.02	.01
☐ 4 Wade Boggs	.30	.14	.04
☐ 5 Barry Bonds	.60	.25	.07
☐ 6 Bob Boone	.10	.05	.01
☐ 7 George Brett	.75	.35	.09
☐ 8 Hubie Brooks	.05	.02	.01
☐ 9 Ivan Calderon	.05	.02	.01
☐ 10 Jose Canseco	.50	.23	.06
☐ 11 Gary Carter	.10	.05	.01
☐ 12 Joe Carter	.15	.07	.02
☐ 13 Jack Clark	.05	.02	.01
☐ 14 Will Clark	.40	.18	.05
☐ 15 Roger Clemens	.50	.23	.06
☐ 16 Vince Coleman	.05	.02	.01
☐ 17 Alvin Davis	.05	.02	.01
☐ 18 Eric Davis	.10	.05	.01
☐ 19 Glenn Davis	.05	.02	.01
☐ 20 Andre Dawson	.15	.07	.02
☐ 21 Mike Dunne	.05	.02	.01
☐ 22 Dwight Evans	.10	.05	.01
☐ 23 Tony Fernandez	.05	.02	.01
☐ 24 John Franco	.10	.05	.01
☐ 25 Gary Gaetti	.10	.05	.01
☐ 26 Kirk Gibson	.10	.05	.01
☐ 27 Dwight Gooden	.10	.05	.01
☐ 28 Pedro Guerrero	.05	.02	.01
☐ 29 Tony Gwynn	1.00	.45	.12
☐ 30 Billy Hatcher	.05	.02	.01
☐ 31 Rickey Henderson	.30	.14	.04
☐ 32 Tom Henke	.05	.02	.01
☐ 33 Keith Hernandez	.10	.05	.01
☐ 34 Orel Hershiser	.10	.05	.01
☐ 35 Teddy Higuera	.05	.02	.01
☐ 36 Charlie Hough	.05	.02	.01
☐ 37 Kent Hrbek	.10	.05	.01
☐ 38 Brook Jacoby	.05	.02	.01
☐ 39 Dion James	.05	.02	.01
☐ 40 Wally Joyner	.10	.05	.01
☐ 41 John Kruk	.10	.05	.01
☐ 42 Mark Langston	.05	.02	.01
☐ 43 Jeffrey Leonard	.05	.02	.01
☐ 44 Candy Maldonado	.05	.02	.01
☐ 45 Don Mattingly	1.00	.45	.12
☐ 46 Willie McGee	.05	.02	.01
☐ 47 Mark McGwire	1.00	.45	.12
☐ 48 Kevin Mitchell	.05	.02	.01
☐ 49 Paul Molitor	.30	.14	.04
☐ 50 Jack Morris	.10	.05	.01
☐ 51 Lloyd Moseby	.05	.02	.01
☐ 52 Dale Murphy	.15	.07	.02
☐ 53 Eddie Murray	.50	.23	.06
☐ 54 Matt Nokes	.05	.02	.01
☐ 55 Dave Parker	.10	.05	.01
☐ 56 Larry Parrish	.05	.02	.01
☐ 57 Kirby Puckett	1.00	.45	.12
☐ 58 Tim Raines	.10	.05	.01
☐ 59 Willie Randolph	.05	.02	.01
☐ 60 Harold Reynolds	.05	.02	.01
☐ 61 Cal Ripken	1.50	.70	.19
☐ 62 Nolan Ryan	1.50	.70	.19
☐ 63 Bret Saberhagen	.10	.05	.01
☐ 64 Juan Samuel	.05	.02	.01
☐ 65 Ryne Sandberg	.75	.35	.09
☐ 66 Benito Santiago	.05	.02	.01
☐ 67 Mike Schmidt	.50	.23	.06
☐ 68 Mike Scott	.05	.02	.01
☐ 69 Kevin Seitzer	.10	.05	.01
☐ 70 Larry Sheets	.05	.02	.01
☐ 71 Ruben Sierra	.10	.05	.01
☐ 72 Ozzie Smith	.75	.35	.09
☐ 73 Zane Smith	.05	.02	.01
☐ 74 Cory Snyder	.05	.02	.01
☐ 75 Dave Stewart	.05	.02	.01
☐ 76 Darryl Strawberry	.10	.05	.01
☐ 77 Rick Sutcliffe	.05	.02	.01
☐ 78 Danny Tartabull	.05	.02	.01
☐ 79 Alan Trammell	.10	.05	.01
☐ 80 Fernando Valenzuela	.10	.05	.01
☐ 81 Andy Van Slyke	.10	.05	.01
☐ 82 Frank Viola	.05	.02	.01
☐ 83 Greg Walker	.05	.02	.01
☐ 84 Tim Wallach	.05	.02	.01
☐ 85 Dave Winfield	.30	.14	.04
☐ 86 Mike Witt	.05	.02	.01
☐ 87 Robin Yount	.15	.07	.02
☐ 88 Checklist Card	.05	.02	.01

1988 Topps UK Minis Tiffany

This set parallels the regular UK mini set. These cards were issued in factory set form only and are valued at a multiple of the regular cards. These cards were issued only in complete factory set form.

	MINT	NRMT	EXC
COMPLETE SET (88)	25.00	11.00	3.10
COMMON CARD (1-88)	.25	.11	.03
*STARS: 3X to 6X BASIC CARDS			

1989 Topps

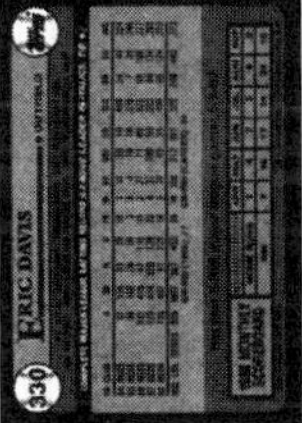

This set consists of 792 standard-size cards. Cards were primarily issued in 15-card wax packs, 42-card rack packs and factory sets. Subsets in the set include Record Breakers (1-7), Turn Back the Clock (661-665), All-Star selections (386-407) and First Draft Picks, Future Stars and Team Leaders (all scattered throughout the set). The manager cards contain a team checklist on back. The key Rookie Cards in this set are Jim Abbott, Sandy Alomar Jr., Brady Anderson, Steve Avery, Andy Benes, Dante Bichette, Craig Biggio, Randy Johnson, Ramon Martinez, Gary Sheffield, John Smoltz, and Robin Ventura.

	MINT	NRMT	EXC
COMPLETE SET (792)	10.00	4.50	1.25
COMPLETE FACT.SET (792)	12.00	5.50	1.50
COMMON CARD (1-792)	.05	.02	.01
☐ 1 George Bell RB Slams 3 Opening Day HR's	.05	.02	.01
☐ 2 Wade Boggs RB 200 Hits 6th Straight Season	.15	.07	.02
☐ 3 Gary Carter RB Career Putouts Record	.10	.05	.01
☐ 4 Andre Dawson RB Logs Double Figures in HR and SB	.10	.05	.01
☐ 5 Orel Hershiser RB 59 Scoreless Innings	.10	.05	.01
☐ 6 Doug Jones RB UER Earns His 15th Straight Save (Photo actually Chris Codiroli)	.05	.02	.01
☐ 7 Kevin McReynolds RB Steals 21 Without Being Caught	.05	.02	.01
☐ 8 Dave Eiland	.05	.02	.01
☐ 9 Tim Teufel	.05	.02	.01
☐ 10 Andre Dawson	.10	.05	.01
☐ 11 Bruce Sutter	.05	.02	.01
☐ 12 Dale Sveum	.05	.02	.01
☐ 13 Doug Sisk	.05	.02	.01
☐ 14 Tom Kelly MG (Team checklist back)	.05	.02	.01
☐ 15 Robby Thompson	.05	.02	.01
☐ 16 Ron Robinson	.05	.02	.01
☐ 17 Brian Downing	.05	.02	.01
☐ 18 Rick Rhoden	.05	.02	.01
☐ 19 Greg Gagne	.05	.02	.01

☐ 20 Steve Bedrosian .05 .02 .01
☐ 21 Chicago White Sox TL .05 .02 .01
Greg Walker
☐ 22 Tim Crews .05 .02 .01
☐ 23 Mike Fitzgerald .05 .02 .01
☐ 24 Larry Andersen .05 .02 .01
☐ 25 Frank White .10 .05 .01
☐ 26 Dale Mohorcic .05 .02 .01
☐ 27A Orestes Destrade .05 .02 .01
(F* next to copyright)
☐ 27B Orestes Destrade .05 .02 .01
(E*F* next to
copyright)
☐ 28 Mike Moore .05 .02 .01
☐ 29 Kelly Gruber .05 .02 .01
☐ 30 Dwight Gooden .10 .05 .01
☐ 31 Terry Francona .05 .02 .01
☐ 32 Dennis Rasmussen .05 .02 .01
☐ 33 B.J. Surhoff .15 .07 .02
☐ 34 Ken Williams .05 .02 .01
☐ 35 John Tudor UER .05 .02 .01
(With Red Sox in '84,should be Pirates)
☐ 36 Mitch Webster .05 .02 .01
☐ 37 Bob Stanley .05 .02 .01
☐ 38 Paul Runge .05 .02 .01
☐ 39 Mike Maddux .05 .02 .01
☐ 40 Steve Sax .05 .02 .01
☐ 41 Terry Mulholland .05 .02 .01
☐ 42 Jim Eppard .05 .02 .01
☐ 43 Guillermo Hernandez .05 .02 .01
☐ 44 Jim Snyder MG .05 .02 .01
(Team checklist back)
☐ 45 Kal Daniels .05 .02 .01
☐ 46 Mark Portugal .05 .02 .01
☐ 47 Carney Lansford .10 .05 .01
☐ 48 Tim Burke .05 .02 .01
☐ 49 Craig Biggio .40 .18 .05
☐ 50 George Bell .05 .02 .01
☐ 51 California Angels TL .05 .02 .01
Mark McLemore
☐ 52 Bob Brenly .05 .02 .01
☐ 53 Ruben Sierra .10 .05 .01
☐ 54 Steve Trout .05 .02 .01
☐ 55 Julio Franco .10 .05 .01
☐ 56 Pat Tabler .05 .02 .01
☐ 57 Alejandro Pena .05 .02 .01
☐ 58 Lee Mazzilli .05 .02 .01
☐ 59 Mark Davis .05 .02 .01
☐ 60 Tom Brunansky .05 .02 .01
☐ 61 Neil Allen .05 .02 .01
☐ 62 Alfredo Griffin .05 .02 .01
☐ 63 Mark Clear .05 .02 .01
☐ 64 Alex Trevino .05 .02 .01
☐ 65 Rick Reuschel .05 .02 .01
☐ 66 Manny Trillo .05 .02 .01
☐ 67 Dave Palmer .05 .02 .01
☐ 68 Darrell Miller .05 .02 .01
☐ 69 Jeff Ballard .05 .02 .01
☐ 70 Mark McGwire .30 .14 .04
☐ 71 Mike Boddicker .05 .02 .01
☐ 72 John Moses .05 .02 .01
☐ 73 Pascual Perez .05 .02 .01
☐ 74 Nick Leyva MG .05 .02 .01
(Team checklist back)
☐ 75 Tom Henke .05 .02 .01
☐ 76 Terry Blocker .05 .02 .01
☐ 77 Doyle Alexander .05 .02 .01
☐ 78 Jim Sundberg .05 .02 .01
☐ 79 Scott Bankhead .05 .02 .01
☐ 80 Cory Snyder .05 .02 .01
☐ 81 Montreal Expos TL .10 .05 .01
Tim Raines
☐ 82 Dave Leiper .05 .02 .01
☐ 83 Jeff Blauser .10 .05 .01
☐ 84 Bill Bene FDP .05 .02 .01
☐ 85 Kevin McReynolds .05 .02 .01
☐ 86 Al Nipper .05 .02 .01
☐ 87 Larry Owen .05 .02 .01
☐ 88 Darryl Hamilton .10 .05 .01
☐ 89 Dave LaPoint .05 .02 .01
☐ 90 Vince Coleman UER .05 .02 .01
(Wrong birth year)
☐ 91 Floyd Youmans .05 .02 .01
☐ 92 Jeff Kunkel .05 .02 .01
☐ 93 Ken Howell .05 .02 .01
☐ 94 Chris Speier .05 .02 .01
☐ 95 Gerald Young .05 .02 .01
☐ 96 Rick Cerone .05 .02 .01
☐ 97 Greg Mathews .05 .02 .01
☐ 98 Larry Sheets .05 .02 .01
☐ 99 Sherman Corbett .05 .02 .01
☐ 100 Mike Schmidt .20 .09 .03
☐ 101 Les Straker .05 .02 .01
☐ 102 Mike Gallego .05 .02 .01
☐ 103 Tim Birtsas .05 .02 .01
☐ 104 Dallas Green MG .05 .02 .01
(Team checklist back)
☐ 105 Ron Darling .05 .02 .01
☐ 106 Willie Upshaw .05 .02 .01
☐ 107 Jose DeLeon .05 .02 .01
☐ 108 Fred Manrique .05 .02 .01
☐ 109 Hipolito Pena .05 .02 .01
☐ 110 Paul Molitor .20 .09 .03
☐ 111 Cincinnati Reds TL .05 .02 .01
Eric Davis
(Swinging bat)
☐ 112 Jim Presley .05 .02 .01
☐ 113 Lloyd Moseby .05 .02 .01
☐ 114 Bob Kipper .05 .02 .01
☐ 115 Jody Davis .05 .02 .01
☐ 116 Jeff Montgomery .10 .05 .01
☐ 117 Dave Anderson .05 .02 .01
☐ 118 Checklist 1-132 .05 .02 .01
☐ 119 Terry Puhl .05 .02 .01
☐ 120 Frank Viola .05 .02 .01
☐ 121 Garry Templeton .05 .02 .01
☐ 122 Lance Johnson .15 .07 .02
☐ 123 Spike Owen .05 .02 .01
☐ 124 Jim Traber .05 .02 .01
☐ 125 Mike Krukow .05 .02 .01
☐ 126 Sid Bream .05 .02 .01
☐ 127 Walt Terrell .05 .02 .01
☐ 128 Milt Thompson .05 .02 .01
☐ 129 Terry Clark .05 .02 .01
☐ 130 Gerald Perry .05 .02 .01
☐ 131 Dave Otto .05 .02 .01
☐ 132 Curt Ford .05 .02 .01
☐ 133 Bill Long .05 .02 .01
☐ 134 Don Zimmer MG .05 .02 .01
(Team checklist back)
☐ 135 Jose Rijo .05 .02 .01
☐ 136 Joey Meyer .05 .02 .01
☐ 137 Geno Petralli .05 .02 .01
☐ 138 Wallace Johnson .05 .02 .01
☐ 139 Mike Flanagan .05 .02 .01
☐ 140 Shawon Dunston .05 .02 .01
☐ 141 Cleveland Indians TL .05 .02 .01
Brook Jacoby
☐ 142 Mike Diaz .05 .02 .01
☐ 143 Mike Campbell .05 .02 .01
☐ 144 Jay Bell .15 .07 .02
☐ 145 Dave Stewart .10 .05 .01
☐ 146 Gary Pettis .05 .02 .01
☐ 147 DeWayne Buice .05 .02 .01
☐ 148 Bill Pecota .05 .02 .01
☐ 149 Doug Dascenzo .05 .02 .01
☐ 150 Fernando Valenzuela .10 .05 .01
☐ 151 Terry McGriff .05 .02 .01
☐ 152 Mark Thurmond .05 .02 .01
☐ 153 Jim Pankovits .05 .02 .01
☐ 154 Don Carman .05 .02 .01
☐ 155 Marty Barrett .05 .02 .01
☐ 156 Dave Gallagher .05 .02 .01
☐ 157 Tom Glavine .25 .11 .03
☐ 158 Mike Aldrete .05 .02 .01
☐ 159 Pat Clements .05 .02 .01
☐ 160 Jeffrey Leonard .05 .02 .01
☐ 161 Gregg Olson FDP UER .15 .07 .02
(Born Scribner, NE,
should be Omaha, NE)
☐ 162 John Davis .05 .02 .01
☐ 163 Bob Forsch .05 .02 .01
☐ 164 Hal Lanier MG .05 .02 .01
(Team checklist back)
☐ 165 Mike Dunne .05 .02 .01
☐ 166 Doug Jennings .05 .02 .01
☐ 167 Steve Searcy FS .05 .02 .01
☐ 168 Willie Wilson .05 .02 .01
☐ 169 Mike Jackson .05 .02 .01
☐ 170 Tony Fernandez .05 .02 .01
☐ 171 Atlanta Braves TL .05 .02 .01
Andres Thomas
☐ 172 Frank Williams .05 .02 .01
☐ 173 Mel Hall .05 .02 .01
☐ 174 Todd Burns .05 .02 .01
☐ 175 John Shelby .05 .02 .01
☐ 176 Jeff Parrett .05 .02 .01
☐ 177 Monty Fariss FDP .05 .02 .01
☐ 178 Mark Grant .05 .02 .01
☐ 179 Ozzie Virgil .05 .02 .01
☐ 180 Mike Scott .05 .02 .01
☐ 181 Craig Worthington .05 .02 .01
☐ 182 Bob McClure .05 .02 .01
☐ 183 Oddibe McDowell .05 .02 .01
☐ 184 John Costello .05 .02 .01
☐ 185 Claudell Washington .05 .02 .01
☐ 186 Pat Perry .05 .02 .01
☐ 187 Darren Daulton .10 .05 .01
☐ 188 Dennis Lamp .05 .02 .01
☐ 189 Kevin Mitchell .10 .05 .01
☐ 190 Mike Witt .05 .02 .01
☐ 191 Sil Campusano .05 .02 .01
☐ 192 Paul Mirabella .05 .02 .01
☐ 193 Sparky Anderson MG .10 .05 .01
(Team checklist back)
UER (553 Salazar)
☐ 194 Greg W. Harris .05 .02 .01
☐ 195 Ozzie Guillen .05 .02 .01
☐ 196 Denny Walling .05 .02 .01
☐ 197 Neal Heaton .05 .02 .01
☐ 198 Danny Heep .05 .02 .01
☐ 199 Mike Schooler .05 .02 .01
☐ 200 George Brett .40 .18 .05
☐ 201 Blue Jays TL .05 .02 .01
Kelly Gruber
☐ 202 Brad Moore .05 .02 .01
☐ 203 Rob Ducey .05 .02 .01
☐ 204 Brad Havens .05 .02 .01
☐ 205 Dwight Evans .10 .05 .01
☐ 206 Roberto Alomar .40 .18 .05
☐ 207 Terry Leach .05 .02 .01
☐ 208 Tom Pagnozzi .05 .02 .01
☐ 209 Jeff Bittiger .05 .02 .01
☐ 210 Dale Murphy .15 .07 .02
☐ 211 Mike Pagliarulo .05 .02 .01
☐ 212 Scott Sanderson .05 .02 .01
☐ 213 Rene Gonzales .05 .02 .01
☐ 214 Charlie O'Brien .05 .02 .01
☐ 215 Kevin Gross .05 .02 .01
☐ 216 Jack Howell .05 .02 .01
☐ 217 Joe Price .05 .02 .01
☐ 218 Mike LaValliere .05 .02 .01
☐ 219 Jim Clancy .05 .02 .01
☐ 220 Gary Gaetti .05 .02 .01
☐ 221 Cecil Espy .05 .02 .01
☐ 222 Mark Lewis FDP .15 .07 .02
☐ 223 Jay Buhner .25 .11 .03
☐ 224 Tony LaRussa MG .10 .05 .01
(Team checklist back)
☐ 225 Ramon Martinez .25 .11 .03
☐ 226 Bill Doran .05 .02 .01
☐ 227 John Farrell .05 .02 .01
☐ 228 Nelson Santovenia .05 .02 .01
☐ 229 Jimmy Key .10 .05 .01
☐ 230 Ozzie Smith .25 .11 .03
☐ 231 San Diego Padres TL .15 .07 .02
Roberto Alomar
(Gary Carter at plate)
☐ 232 Ricky Horton .05 .02 .01
☐ 233 Gregg Jefferies FS .15 .07 .02
☐ 234 Tom Browning .05 .02 .01
☐ 235 John Kruk .10 .05 .01
☐ 236 Charles Hudson .05 .02 .01
☐ 237 Glenn Hubbard .05 .02 .01
☐ 238 Eric King .05 .02 .01
☐ 239 Tim Laudner .05 .02 .01
☐ 240 Greg Maddux .75 .35 .09
☐ 241 Brett Butler .10 .05 .01
☐ 242 Ed VandeBerg .05 .02 .01
☐ 243 Bob Boone .10 .05 .01
☐ 244 Jim Acker .05 .02 .01
☐ 245 Jim Rice .15 .07 .02
☐ 246 Rey Quinones .05 .02 .01
☐ 247 Shawn Hillegas .05 .02 .01
☐ 248 Tony Phillips .15 .07 .02
☐ 249 Tim Leary .05 .02 .01
☐ 250 Cal Ripken .75 .35 .09
☐ 251 John Dopson .05 .02 .01
☐ 252 Billy Hatcher .05 .02 .01
☐ 253 Jose Alvarez .05 .02 .01
☐ 254 Tom Lasorda MG .10 .05 .01
(Team checklist back)
☐ 255 Ron Guidry .05 .02 .01
☐ 256 Benny Santiago .10 .05 .01
☐ 257 Rick Aguilera .10 .05 .01
☐ 258 Checklist 133-264 .05 .02 .01
☐ 259 Larry McWilliams .05 .02 .01
☐ 260 Dave Winfield .15 .07 .02
☐ 261 St.Louis Cardinals TL .05 .02 .01
Tom Brunansky
(With Luis Alicea)
☐ 262 Jeff Pico .05 .02 .01
☐ 263 Mike Felder .05 .02 .01
☐ 264 Rob Dibble .10 .05 .01
☐ 265 Kent Hrbek .10 .05 .01
☐ 266 Luis Aquino .05 .02 .01
☐ 267 Jeff M. Robinson .05 .02 .01
☐ 268 N. Keith Miller .05 .02 .01
☐ 269 Tom Bolton .05 .02 .01
☐ 270 Wally Joyner .10 .05 .01
☐ 271 Jay Tibbs .05 .02 .01
☐ 272 Ron Hassey .05 .02 .01
☐ 273 Jose Lind .05 .02 .01
☐ 274 Mark Eichhorn .05 .02 .01
☐ 275 Danny Tartabull UER .05 .02 .01
(Born San Juan, PR
should be Miami, FL)
☐ 276 Paul Kilgus .05 .02 .01
☐ 277 Mike Davis .05 .02 .01
☐ 278 Andy McGaffigan .05 .02 .01
☐ 279 Scott Bradley .05 .02 .01
☐ 280 Bob Knepper .05 .02 .01
☐ 281 Gary Redus .05 .02 .01
☐ 282 Cris Carpenter .05 .02 .01
☐ 283 Andy Allanson .05 .02 .01
☐ 284 Jim Leyland MG .05 .02 .01
(Team checklist back)
☐ 285 John Candelaria .05 .02 .01
☐ 286 Darrin Jackson .05 .02 .01
☐ 287 Juan Nieves .05 .02 .01
☐ 288 Pat Sheridan .05 .02 .01
☐ 289 Ernie Whitt .05 .02 .01
☐ 290 John Franco .10 .05 .01
☐ 291 New York Mets TL .10 .05 .01
Darryl Strawberry
(With Keith Hernandez
and Kevin McReynolds)
☐ 292 Jim Corsi .05 .02 .01
☐ 293 Glenn Wilson .05 .02 .01
☐ 294 Juan Berenguer .05 .02 .01
☐ 295 Scott Fletcher .05 .02 .01
☐ 296 Ron Gant .15 .07 .02
☐ 297 Oswald Peraza .05 .02 .01
☐ 298 Chris James .05 .02 .01
☐ 299 Steve Ellsworth .05 .02 .01
☐ 300 Darryl Strawberry .10 .05 .01
☐ 301 Charlie Leibrandt .05 .02 .01
☐ 302 Gary Ward .05 .02 .01
☐ 303 Felix Fermin .05 .02 .01
☐ 304 Joel Youngblood .05 .02 .01
☐ 305 Dave Smith .05 .02 .01
☐ 306 Tracy Woodson .05 .02 .01
☐ 307 Lance McCullers .05 .02 .01
☐ 308 Ron Karkovice .05 .02 .01
☐ 309 Mario Diaz .05 .02 .01
☐ 310 Rafael Palmeiro .15 .07 .02
☐ 311 Chris Bosio .05 .02 .01
☐ 312 Tom Lawless .05 .02 .01
☐ 313 Dennis Martinez .10 .05 .01
☐ 314 Bobby Valentine MG .05 .02 .01
(Team checklist back)
☐ 315 Greg Swindell .05 .02 .01
☐ 316 Walt Weiss .05 .02 .01
☐ 317 Jack Armstrong .05 .02 .01
☐ 318 Gene Larkin .05 .02 .01
☐ 319 Greg Booker .05 .02 .01
☐ 320 Lou Whitaker .10 .05 .01
☐ 321 Boston Red Sox TL .05 .02 .01
Jody Reed
☐ 322 John Smiley .05 .02 .01
☐ 323 Gary Thurman .05 .02 .01
☐ 324 Bob Milacki .05 .02 .01
☐ 325 Jesse Barfield .05 .02 .01
☐ 326 Dennis Boyd .05 .02 .01
☐ 327 Mark Lemke .10 .05 .01
☐ 328 Rick Honeycutt .05 .02 .01
☐ 329 Bob Melvin .05 .02 .01
☐ 330 Eric Davis .10 .05 .01
☐ 331 Curt Wilkerson .05 .02 .01
☐ 332 Tony Armas .05 .02 .01
☐ 333 Bob Ojeda .05 .02 .01
☐ 334 Steve Lyons .05 .02 .01
☐ 335 Dave Righetti .05 .02 .01
☐ 336 Steve Balboni .05 .02 .01
☐ 337 Calvin Schiraldi .05 .02 .01
☐ 338 Jim Adduci .05 .02 .01
☐ 339 Scott Bailes .05 .02 .01
☐ 340 Kirk Gibson .15 .07 .02
☐ 341 Jim Deshaies .05 .02 .01
☐ 342 Tom Brookens .05 .02 .01
☐ 343 Gary Sheffield FS .75 .35 .09
☐ 344 Tom Trebelhorn MG .05 .02 .01
(Team checklist back)
☐ 345 Charlie Hough .10 .05 .01
☐ 346 Rex Hudler .05 .02 .01
☐ 347 John Cerutti .05 .02 .01
☐ 348 Ed Hearn .05 .02 .01
☐ 349 Ron Jones .05 .02 .01
☐ 350 Andy Van Slyke .10 .05 .01
☐ 351 San Fran. Giants TL .05 .02 .01
Bob Melvin
(With Bill Fahey CO)
☐ 352 Rick Schu .05 .02 .01
☐ 353 Marvell Wynne .05 .02 .01
☐ 354 Larry Parrish .05 .02 .01
☐ 355 Mark Langston .10 .05 .01
☐ 356 Kevin Elster .10 .05 .01
☐ 357 Jerry Reuss .05 .02 .01
☐ 358 Ricky Jordan .10 .05 .01
☐ 359 Tommy John .10 .05 .01
☐ 360 Ryne Sandberg .25 .11 .03
☐ 361 Kelly Downs .05 .02 .01
☐ 362 Jack Lazorko .05 .02 .01
☐ 363 Rich Yett .05 .02 .01
☐ 364 Rob Deer .05 .02 .01
☐ 365 Mike Henneman .05 .02 .01
☐ 366 Herm Winningham .05 .02 .01
☐ 367 Johnny Paredes .05 .02 .01
☐ 368 Brian Holton .05 .02 .01
☐ 369 Ken Caminiti .25 .11 .03
☐ 370 Dennis Eckersley .10 .05 .01
☐ 371 Manny Lee .05 .02 .01
☐ 372 Craig Lefferts .05 .02 .01
☐ 373 Tracy Jones .05 .02 .01
☐ 374 John Wathan MG .05 .02 .01
(Team checklist back)
☐ 375 Terry Pendleton .10 .05 .01
☐ 376 Steve Lombardozzi .05 .02 .01
☐ 377 Mike Smithson .05 .02 .01
☐ 378 Checklist 265-396 .05 .02 .01
☐ 379 Tim Flannery .05 .02 .01
☐ 380 Rickey Henderson .15 .07 .02
☐ 381 Baltimore Orioles TL .05 .02 .01
Larry Sheets
☐ 382 John Smoltz .75 .35 .09
☐ 383 Howard Johnson .05 .02 .01
☐ 384 Mark Salas .05 .02 .01
☐ 385 Von Hayes .05 .02 .01
☐ 386 Andres Galarraga AS .15 .07 .02
☐ 387 Ryne Sandberg AS .15 .07 .02
☐ 388 Bobby Bonilla AS .15 .07 .02
☐ 389 Ozzie Smith AS .15 .07 .02
☐ 390 Darryl Strawberry AS .10 .05 .01
☐ 391 Andre Dawson AS .10 .05 .01
☐ 392 Andy Van Slyke AS .05 .02 .01
☐ 393 Gary Carter AS .10 .05 .01
☐ 394 Orel Hershiser AS .10 .05 .01
☐ 395 Danny Jackson AS .05 .02 .01
☐ 396 Kirk Gibson AS .15 .07 .02
☐ 397 Don Mattingly AS .25 .11 .03
☐ 398 Julio Franco AS .05 .02 .01

☐ 399 Wade Boggs AS .15 .07 .02
☐ 400 Alan Trammell AS .10 .05 .01
☐ 401 Jose Canseco AS .15 .07 .02
☐ 402 Mike Greenwell AS .05 .02 .01
☐ 403 Kirby Puckett AS .15 .07 .02
☐ 404 Bob Boone AS .05 .02 .01
☐ 405 Roger Clemens AS .15 .07 .02
☐ 406 Frank Viola AS .05 .02 .01
☐ 407 Dave Winfield AS .15 .07 .02
☐ 408 Greg Walker .05 .02 .01
☐ 409 Ken Dayley .05 .02 .01
☐ 410 Jack Clark .10 .05 .01
☐ 411 Mitch Williams .05 .02 .01
☐ 412 Barry Lyons .05 .02 .01
☐ 413 Mike Kingery .05 .02 .01
☐ 414 Jim Fregosi MG .05 .02 .01
(Team checklist back)
☐ 415 Rich Gossage .15 .07 .02
☐ 416 Fred Lynn .05 .02 .01
☐ 417 Mike LaCoss .05 .02 .01
☐ 418 Bob Dernier .05 .02 .01
☐ 419 Tom Filer .05 .02 .01
☐ 420 Joe Carter .15 .07 .02
☐ 421 Kirk McCaskill .05 .02 .01
☐ 422 Bo Diaz .05 .02 .01
☐ 423 Brian Fisher .05 .02 .01
☐ 424 Luis Polonia UER .10 .05 .01
(Wrong birthdate)
☐ 425 Jay Howell .05 .02 .01
☐ 426 Dan Gladden .05 .02 .01
☐ 427 Eric Show .05 .02 .01
☐ 428 Craig Reynolds .05 .02 .01
☐ 429 Minnesota Twins TL .05 .02 .01
Greg Gagne
(Taking throw at 2nd)
☐ 430 Mark Gubicza .05 .02 .01
☐ 431 Luis Rivera .05 .02 .01
☐ 432 Chad Kreuter .05 .02 .01
☐ 433 Albert Hall .05 .02 .01
☐ 434 Ken Patterson .05 .02 .01
☐ 435 Len Dykstra .10 .05 .01
☐ 436 Bobby Meacham .05 .02 .01
☐ 437 Andy Benes FDP .25 .11 .03
☐ 438 Greg Gross .05 .02 .01
☐ 439 Frank DiPino .05 .02 .01
☐ 440 Bobby Bonilla .15 .07 .02
☐ 441 Jerry Reed .05 .02 .01
☐ 442 Jose Oquendo .05 .02 .01
☐ 443 Rod Nichols .05 .02 .01
☐ 444 Moose Stubing MG .05 .02 .01
(Team checklist back)
☐ 445 Matt Nokes .05 .02 .01
☐ 446 Rob Murphy .05 .02 .01
☐ 447 Donell Nixon .05 .02 .01
☐ 448 Eric Plunk .05 .02 .01
☐ 449 Carmelo Martinez .05 .02 .01
☐ 450 Roger Clemens .20 .09 .03
☐ 451 Mark Davidson .05 .02 .01
☐ 452 Israel Sanchez .05 .02 .01
☐ 453 Tom Prince .05 .02 .01
☐ 454 Paul Assenmacher .05 .02 .01
☐ 455 Johnny Ray .05 .02 .01
☐ 456 Tim Belcher .05 .02 .01
☐ 457 Mackey Sasser .05 .02 .01
☐ 458 Donn Pall .05 .02 .01
☐ 459 Seattle Mariners TL .05 .02 .01
Dave Valle
☐ 460 Dave Stieb .05 .02 .01
☐ 461 Buddy Bell .10 .05 .01
☐ 462 Jose Guzman .05 .02 .01
☐ 463 Steve Lake .05 .02 .01
☐ 464 Bryn Smith .05 .02 .01
☐ 465 Mark Grace .20 .09 .03
☐ 466 Chuck Crim .05 .02 .01
☐ 467 Jim Walewander .05 .02 .01
☐ 468 Henry Cotto .05 .02 .01
☐ 469 Jose Bautista .05 .02 .01
☐ 470 Lance Parrish .05 .02 .01
☐ 471 Steve Curry .05 .02 .01
☐ 472 Brian Harper .05 .02 .01
☐ 473 Don Robinson .05 .02 .01
☐ 474 Bob Rodgers MG .05 .02 .01
(Team checklist back)
☐ 475 Dave Parker .10 .05 .01
☐ 476 Jon Perlman .05 .02 .01
☐ 477 Dick Schofield .05 .02 .01
☐ 478 Doug Drabek .10 .05 .01
☐ 479 Mike Macfarlane .10 .05 .01
☐ 480 Keith Hernandez .10 .05 .01
☐ 481 Chris Brown .05 .02 .01
☐ 482 Steve Peters .05 .02 .01
☐ 483 Mickey Hatcher .05 .02 .01
☐ 484 Steve Shields .05 .02 .01
☐ 485 Hubie Brooks .05 .02 .01
☐ 486 Jack McDowell .10 .05 .01
☐ 487 Scott Lusader .05 .02 .01
☐ 488 Kevin Coffman .05 .02 .01
Now with Cubs
☐ 489 Phila. Phillies TL .10 .05 .01
Mike Schmidt
☐ 490 Chris Sabo .05 .02 .01
☐ 491 Mike Birkbeck .05 .02 .01
☐ 492 Alan Ashby .05 .02 .01
☐ 493 Todd Benzinger .05 .02 .01
☐ 494 Shane Rawley .05 .02 .01
☐ 495 Candy Maldonado .05 .02 .01
☐ 496 Dwayne Henry .05 .02 .01
☐ 497 Pete Stanicek .05 .02 .01
☐ 498 Dave Valle .05 .02 .01
☐ 499 Don Heinkel .05 .02 .01
☐ 500 Jose Canseco .15 .07 .02
☐ 501 Vance Law .05 .02 .01
☐ 502 Duane Ward .05 .02 .01
☐ 503 Al Newman .05 .02 .01
☐ 504 Bob Walk .05 .02 .01
☐ 505 Pete Rose MG .20 .09 .03
(Team checklist back)
☐ 506 Kirt Manwaring .05 .02 .01
☐ 507 Steve Farr .05 .02 .01
☐ 508 Wally Backman .05 .02 .01
☐ 509 Bud Black .05 .02 .01
☐ 510 Bob Horner .05 .02 .01
☐ 511 Richard Dotson .05 .02 .01
☐ 512 Donnie Hill .05 .02 .01
☐ 513 Jesse Orosco .05 .02 .01
☐ 514 Chet Lemon .05 .02 .01
☐ 515 Barry Larkin .20 .09 .03
☐ 516 Eddie Whitson .05 .02 .01
☐ 517 Greg Brock .05 .02 .01
☐ 518 Bruce Ruffin .05 .02 .01
☐ 519 New York Yankees TL .05 .02 .01
Willie Randolph
☐ 520 Rick Sutcliffe .05 .02 .01
☐ 521 Mickey Tettleton .10 .05 .01
☐ 522 Randy Kramer .05 .02 .01
☐ 523 Andres Thomas .05 .02 .01
☐ 524 Checklist 397-528 .05 .02 .01
☐ 525 Chili Davis .10 .05 .01
☐ 526 Wes Gardner .05 .02 .01
☐ 527 Dave Henderson .05 .02 .01
☐ 528 Luis Medina .05 .02 .01
(Lower left front
has white triangle)
☐ 529 Tom Foley .05 .02 .01
☐ 530 Nolan Ryan .75 .35 .09
☐ 531 Dave Hengel .05 .02 .01
☐ 532 Jerry Browne .05 .02 .01
☐ 533 Andy Hawkins .05 .02 .01
☐ 534 Doc Edwards MG .05 .02 .01
(Team checklist back)
☐ 535 Todd Worrell UER .05 .02 .01
(4 wins in '88,
should be 5)
☐ 536 Joel Skinner .05 .02 .01
☐ 537 Pete Smith .05 .02 .01
☐ 538 Juan Castillo .05 .02 .01
☐ 539 Barry Jones .05 .02 .01
☐ 540 Bo Jackson .15 .07 .02
☐ 541 Cecil Fielder .10 .05 .01
☐ 542 Todd Frohwirth .05 .02 .01
☐ 543 Damon Berryhill .05 .02 .01
☐ 544 Jeff Sellers .05 .02 .01
☐ 545 Mookie Wilson .10 .05 .01
☐ 546 Mark Williamson .05 .02 .01
☐ 547 Mark McLemore .05 .02 .01
☐ 548 Bobby Witt .05 .02 .01
☐ 549 Chicago Cubs TL .05 .02 .01
Jamie Moyer
(Pitching)
☐ 550 Orel Hershiser .10 .05 .01
☐ 551 Randy Ready .05 .02 .01
☐ 552 Greg Cadaret .05 .02 .01
☐ 553 Luis Salazar .05 .02 .01
☐ 554 Nick Esasky .05 .02 .01
☐ 555 Bert Blyleven .10 .05 .01
☐ 556 Bruce Fields .05 .02 .01
☐ 557 Keith A. Miller .05 .02 .01
☐ 558 Dan Pasqua .05 .02 .01
☐ 559 Juan Agosto .05 .02 .01
☐ 560 Tim Raines .15 .07 .02
☐ 561 Luis Aguayo .05 .02 .01
☐ 562 Danny Cox .05 .02 .01
☐ 563 Bill Schroeder .05 .02 .01
☐ 564 Russ Nixon MG .05 .02 .01
(Team checklist back)
☐ 565 Jeff Russell .05 .02 .01
☐ 566 Al Pedrique .05 .02 .01
☐ 567 David Wells UER .05 .02 .01
(Complete Pitching
Recor)
☐ 568 Mickey Brantley .05 .02 .01
☐ 569 German Jimenez .05 .02 .01
☐ 570 Tony Gwynn UER .40 .18 .05
('88 average should
be italicized as
league leader)
☐ 571 Billy Ripken .05 .02 .01
☐ 572 Atlee Hammaker .05 .02 .01
☐ 573 Jim Abbott FDP .15 .07 .02
☐ 574 Dave Clark .05 .02 .01
☐ 575 Juan Samuel .05 .02 .01
☐ 576 Greg Minton .05 .02 .01
☐ 577 Randy Bush .05 .02 .01
☐ 578 John Morris .05 .02 .01
☐ 579 Houston Astros TL .05 .02 .01
Glenn Davis
(Batting stance)
☐ 580 Harold Reynolds .05 .02 .01
☐ 581 Gene Nelson .05 .02 .01
☐ 582 Mike Marshall .05 .02 .01
☐ 583 Paul Gibson .05 .02 .01
☐ 584 Randy Velarde UER .05 .02 .01
(Signed 1935,
should be 1985)
☐ 585 Harold Baines .10 .05 .01
☐ 586 Joe Boever .05 .02 .01
☐ 587 Mike Stanley .05 .02 .01
☐ 588 Luis Alicea .05 .02 .01
☐ 589 Dave Meads .05 .02 .01
☐ 590 Andres Galarraga .15 .07 .02
☐ 591 Jeff Musselman .05 .02 .01
☐ 592 John Cangelosi .05 .02 .01
☐ 593 Drew Hall .05 .02 .01
☐ 594 Jimy Williams MG .05 .02 .01
(Team checklist back)
☐ 595 Teddy Higuera .05 .02 .01
☐ 596 Kurt Stillwell .05 .02 .01
☐ 597 Terry Taylor .05 .02 .01
☐ 598 Ken Gerhart .05 .02 .01
☐ 599 Tom Candiotti .05 .02 .01
☐ 600 Wade Boggs .15 .07 .02
☐ 601 Dave Dravecky .10 .05 .01
☐ 602 Devon White .10 .05 .01
☐ 603 Frank Tanana .05 .02 .01
☐ 604 Paul O'Neill .10 .05 .01
☐ 605A Bob Welch ERR 2.00 .90 .25
(Missing line on back,
"Complete M.L.
Pitching Record")
☐ 605B Bob Welch COR .05 .02 .01
☐ 606 Rick Dempsey .05 .02 .01
☐ 607 Willie Ansley FDP .05 .02 .01
☐ 608 Phil Bradley .05 .02 .01
☐ 609 Detroit Tigers TL .05 .02 .01
Frank Tanana
(With Alan Trammell
and Mike Heath)
☐ 610 Randy Myers .10 .05 .01
☐ 611 Don Slaught .05 .02 .01
☐ 612 Dan Quisenberry .05 .02 .01
☐ 613 Gary Varsho .05 .02 .01
☐ 614 Joe Hesketh .05 .02 .01
☐ 615 Robin Yount .15 .07 .02
☐ 616 Steve Rosenberg .05 .02 .01
☐ 617 Mark Parent .05 .02 .01
☐ 618 Rance Mulliniks .05 .02 .01
☐ 619 Checklist 529-660 .05 .02 .01
☐ 620 Barry Bonds .40 .18 .05
☐ 621 Rick Mahler .05 .02 .01
☐ 622 Stan Javier .05 .02 .01
☐ 623 Fred Toliver .05 .02 .01
☐ 624 Jack McKeon MG .05 .02 .01
(Team checklist back)
☐ 625 Eddie Murray .25 .11 .03
☐ 626 Jeff Reed .05 .02 .01
☐ 627 Greg A. Harris .05 .02 .01
☐ 628 Matt Williams .25 .11 .03
☐ 629 Pete O'Brien .05 .02 .01
☐ 630 Mike Greenwell .05 .02 .01
☐ 631 Dave Bergman .05 .02 .01
☐ 632 Bryan Harvey .10 .05 .01
☐ 633 Daryl Boston .05 .02 .01
☐ 634 Marvin Freeman .05 .02 .01
☐ 635 Willie Randolph .10 .05 .01
☐ 636 Bill Wilkinson .05 .02 .01
☐ 637 Carmen Castillo .05 .02 .01
☐ 638 Floyd Bannister .05 .02 .01
☐ 639 Oakland A's TL .05 .02 .01
Walt Weiss
☐ 640 Willie McGee .05 .02 .01
☐ 641 Curt Young .05 .02 .01
☐ 642 Argenis Salazar .05 .02 .01
☐ 643 Louie Meadows .05 .02 .01
☐ 644 Lloyd McClendon .05 .02 .01
☐ 645 Jack Morris .10 .05 .01
☐ 646 Kevin Bass .05 .02 .01
☐ 647 Randy Johnson .75 .35 .09
☐ 648 Sandy Alomar FS .20 .09 .03
☐ 649 Stewart Cliburn .05 .02 .01
☐ 650 Kirby Puckett .40 .18 .05
☐ 651 Tom Niedenfuer .05 .02 .01
☐ 652 Rich Gedman .05 .02 .01
☐ 653 Tommy Barrett .05 .02 .01
☐ 654 Whitey Herzog MG .10 .05 .01
(Team checklist back)
☐ 655 Dave Magadan .05 .02 .01
☐ 656 Ivan Calderon .05 .02 .01
☐ 657 Joe Magrane .05 .02 .01
☐ 658 R.J. Reynolds .05 .02 .01
☐ 659 Al Leiter .10 .05 .01
☐ 660 Will Clark .20 .09 .03
☐ 661 Dwight Gooden TBC84 .10 .05 .01
☐ 662 Lou Brock TBC79 .15 .07 .02
☐ 663 Hank Aaron TBC74 .20 .09 .03
☐ 664 Gil Hodges TBC69 .15 .07 .02
☐ 665A Tony Oliva TBC64 2.00 .90 .25
ERR (fabricated card
is enlarged version
of Oliva's 64T card;
Topps copyright
missing)
☐ 665B Tony Oliva TBC64 .10 .05 .01
COR (fabricated
card)
☐ 666 Randy St.Claire .05 .02 .01
☐ 667 Dwayne Murphy .05 .02 .01
☐ 668 Mike Bielecki .05 .02 .01
☐ 669 L.A. Dodgers TL .10 .05 .01
Orel Hershiser
(Mound conference
with Mike Scioscia)
☐ 670 Kevin Seitzer .05 .02 .01
☐ 671 Jim Gantner .05 .02 .01
☐ 672 Allan Anderson .05 .02 .01
☐ 673 Don Baylor .15 .07 .02
☐ 674 Otis Nixon .05 .02 .01
☐ 675 Bruce Hurst .05 .02 .01
☐ 676 Ernie Riles .05 .02 .01
☐ 677 Dave Schmidt .05 .02 .01
☐ 678 Dion James .05 .02 .01
☐ 679 Willie Fraser .05 .02 .01
☐ 680 Gary Carter .10 .05 .01
☐ 681 Jeff D. Robinson .05 .02 .01
☐ 682 Rick Leach .05 .02 .01
☐ 683 Jose Cecena .05 .02 .01
☐ 684 Dave Johnson MG .05 .02 .01
(Team checklist back)
☐ 685 Jeff Treadway .05 .02 .01
☐ 686 Scott Terry .05 .02 .01
☐ 687 Alvin Davis .05 .02 .01
☐ 688 Zane Smith .05 .02 .01
☐ 689A Stan Jefferson .05 .02 .01
(Pink triangle on
front bottom left)
☐ 689B Stan Jefferson .05 .02 .01
(Violet triangle on
front bottom left)
☐ 690 Doug Jones .05 .02 .01
☐ 691 Roberto Kelly UER .10 .05 .01
(83 Oneonita)
☐ 692 Steve Ontiveros .05 .02 .01
☐ 693 Pat Borders .10 .05 .01
☐ 694 Les Lancaster .05 .02 .01
☐ 695 Carlton Fisk .15 .07 .02
☐ 696 Don August .05 .02 .01
☐ 697A Franklin Stubbs .05 .02 .01
(Team name on front
in white)
☐ 697B Franklin Stubbs .05 .02 .01
(Team name on front
in gray)
☐ 698 Keith Atherton .05 .02 .01
☐ 699 Pittsburgh Pirates TL .05 .02 .01
Al Pedrique
(Tony Gwynn sliding)
☐ 700 Don Mattingly .50 .23 .06
☐ 701 Storm Davis .05 .02 .01
☐ 702 Jamie Quirk .05 .02 .01
☐ 703 Scott Garrelts .05 .02 .01
☐ 704 Carlos Quintana .05 .02 .01
☐ 705 Terry Kennedy .05 .02 .01
☐ 706 Pete Incaviglia .10 .05 .01
☐ 707 Steve Jeltz .05 .02 .01
☐ 708 Chuck Finley .10 .05 .01
☐ 709 Tom Herr .05 .02 .01
☐ 710 David Cone .15 .07 .02
☐ 711 Candy Sierra .05 .02 .01
☐ 712 Bill Swift .05 .02 .01
☐ 713 Ty Griffin FDP .05 .02 .01
☐ 714 Joe Morgan MG .05 .02 .01
(Team checklist back)
☐ 715 Tony Pena .05 .02 .01
☐ 716 Wayne Tolleson .05 .02 .01
☐ 717 Jamie Moyer .05 .02 .01
☐ 718 Glenn Braggs .05 .02 .01
☐ 719 Danny Darwin .05 .02 .01
☐ 720 Tim Wallach .05 .02 .01
☐ 721 Ron Tingley .05 .02 .01
☐ 722 Todd Stottlemyre .10 .05 .01
☐ 723 Rafael Belliard .05 .02 .01
☐ 724 Jerry Don Gleaton .05 .02 .01
☐ 725 Terry Steinbach .10 .05 .01
☐ 726 Dickie Thon .05 .02 .01
☐ 727 Joe Orsulak .05 .02 .01
☐ 728 Charlie Puleo .05 .02 .01
☐ 729 Texas Rangers TL .05 .02 .01
Steve Buechele
(Inconsistent design,
team name on front
surrounded by black,
should be white)
☐ 730 Danny Jackson .05 .02 .01
☐ 731 Mike Young .05 .02 .01
☐ 732 Steve Buechele .05 .02 .01
☐ 733 Randy Bockus .05 .02 .01
☐ 734 Jody Reed .05 .02 .01
☐ 735 Roger McDowell .05 .02 .01
☐ 736 Jeff Hamilton .05 .02 .01
☐ 737 Norm Charlton .10 .05 .01
☐ 738 Darnell Coles .05 .02 .01
☐ 739 Brook Jacoby .05 .02 .01
☐ 740 Dan Plesac .05 .02 .01
☐ 741 Ken Phelps .05 .02 .01
☐ 742 Mike Harkey FS .05 .02 .01
☐ 743 Mike Heath .05 .02 .01
☐ 744 Roger Craig MG .05 .02 .01
(Team checklist back)
☐ 745 Fred McGriff .20 .09 .03
☐ 746 German Gonzalez UER .05 .02 .01
(Wrong birthdate)

	MINT	NRMT	EXC
☐ 747 Wil Tejada	.05	.02	.01
☐ 748 Jimmy Jones	.05	.02	.01
☐ 749 Rafael Ramirez	.05	.02	.01
☐ 750 Bret Saberhagen	.10	.05	.01
☐ 751 Ken Oberkfell	.05	.02	.01
☐ 752 Jim Gott	.05	.02	.01
☐ 753 Jose Uribe	.05	.02	.01
☐ 754 Bob Brower	.05	.02	.01
☐ 755 Mike Scioscia	.05	.02	.01
☐ 756 Scott Medvin	.05	.02	.01
☐ 757 Brady Anderson	.60	.25	.07
☐ 758 Gene Walter	.05	.02	.01
☐ 759 Milwaukee Brewers TL Rob Deer	.05	.02	.01
☐ 760 Lee Smith	.10	.05	.01
☐ 761 Dante Bichette	.60	.25	.07
☐ 762 Bobby Thigpen	.05	.02	.01
☐ 763 Dave Martinez	.05	.02	.01
☐ 764 Robin Ventura FDP	.40	.18	.05
☐ 765 Glenn Davis	.05	.02	.01
☐ 766 Cecilio Guante	.05	.02	.01
☐ 767 Mike Capel	.05	.02	.01
☐ 768 Bill Wegman	.05	.02	.01
☐ 769 Junior Ortiz	.05	.02	.01
☐ 770 Alan Trammell	.10	.05	.01
☐ 771 Ron Kittle	.05	.02	.01
☐ 772 Ron Oester	.05	.02	.01
☐ 773 Keith Moreland	.05	.02	.01
☐ 774 Frank Robinson MG (Team checklist back)	.15	.07	.02
☐ 775 Jeff Reardon	.10	.05	.01
☐ 776 Nelson Liriano	.05	.02	.01
☐ 777 Ted Power	.05	.02	.01
☐ 778 Bruce Benedict	.05	.02	.01
☐ 779 Craig McMurtry	.05	.02	.01
☐ 780 Pedro Guerrero	.10	.05	.01
☐ 781 Greg Briley	.05	.02	.01
☐ 782 Checklist 661-792	.05	.02	.01
☐ 783 Trevor Wilson	.05	.02	.01
☐ 784 Steve Avery FDP	.25	.11	.03
☐ 785 Ellis Burks	.15	.07	.02
☐ 786 Melido Perez	.05	.02	.01
☐ 787 Dave West	.05	.02	.01
☐ 788 Mike Morgan	.05	.02	.01
☐ 789 Kansas City Royals TL Bo Jackson (Throwing)	.15	.07	.02
☐ 790 Sid Fernandez	.05	.02	.01
☐ 791 Jim Lindeman	.05	.02	.01
☐ 792 Rafael Santana	.05	.02	.01

1989 Topps Tiffany

Again, Topps issed a standard-size "Glossy" parallel to their regular set. These cards, printed in the Topps Irish facility, have 792 standard-size cards and were issued in complete set form only. These cards have a "shiny" front as well as an easy to read back. These cards were issued only through Topps hobby dealers.

	MINT	NRMT	EXC
COMPLETE FACT.SET (792)	50.00	22.00	6.25
COMMON CARD (1-792)	.10	.05	.01
*STARS: 3X to 6X BASIC CARDS			
*ROOKIES: 2X to 4X BASIC CARDS			

1989 Topps Batting Leaders

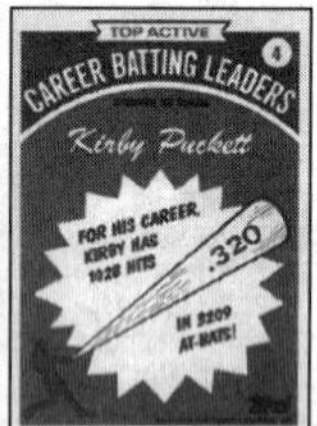

The 1989 Topps Batting Leaders set contains 22 standard-size glossy cards. The fronts are bright red. The set depicts the 22 veterans with the highest lifetime batting averages. The cards were distributed one per Topps blister pack. These blister packs were sold exclusively through K-Mart stores. The cards in the set were numbered by K-Mart essentially in order of highest active career batting average entering the 1989 season.

	MINT	NRMT	EXC
COMPLETE SET (22)	50.00	22.00	6.25
COMMON CARD (1-22)	.50	.23	.06
☐ 1 Wade Boggs	3.00	1.35	.35
☐ 2 Tony Gwynn	10.00	4.50	1.25
☐ 3 Don Mattingly	10.00	4.50	1.25
☐ 4 Kirby Puckett	10.00	4.50	1.25
☐ 5 George Brett	8.00	3.60	1.00
☐ 6 Pedro Guerrero	.50	.23	.06
☐ 7 Tim Raines	1.00	.45	.12
☐ 8 Keith Hernandez	1.00	.45	.12
☐ 9 Jim Rice	1.00	.45	.12
☐ 10 Paul Molitor	5.00	2.20	.60
☐ 11 Eddie Murray	5.00	2.20	.60
☐ 12 Willie McGee	.50	.23	.06
☐ 13 Dave Parker	1.00	.45	.12
☐ 14 Julio Franco	1.00	.45	.12
☐ 15 Rickey Henderson	3.00	1.35	.35
☐ 16 Kent Hrbek	1.00	.45	.12
☐ 17 Willie Wilson	.50	.23	.06
☐ 18 Johnny Ray	.50	.23	.06
☐ 19 Pat Tabler	.50	.23	.06
☐ 20 Carney Lansford	.50	.23	.06
☐ 21 Robin Yount	2.00	.90	.25
☐ 22 Alan Trammell	2.00	.90	.25

1989 Topps Glossy All-Stars

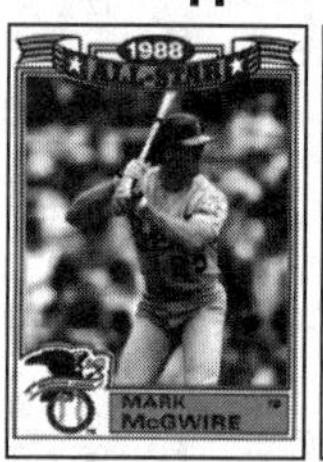

These glossy cards were inserted with Topps rack packs and honor the starting line-ups, managers, and honorary captains of the 1988 National and American League All-Star teams. The standard size cards are very similar in design to what Topps has used since 1984. The backs are printed in red and blue on white card stock.

	MINT	NRMT	EXC
COMPLETE SET (22)	3.00	1.35	.35
COMMON CARD (1-22)	.05	.02	.01
☐ 1 Tom Kelly MG	.05	.02	.01
☐ 2 Mark McGwire	.75	.35	.09
☐ 3 Paul Molitor	.40	.18	.05
☐ 4 Wade Boggs	.25	.11	.03
☐ 5 Cal Ripken	1.50	.70	.19
☐ 6 Jose Canseco	.30	.14	.04
☐ 7 Rickey Henderson	.30	.14	.04
☐ 8 Dave Winfield	.30	.14	.04
☐ 9 Terry Steinbach	.10	.05	.01
☐ 10 Frank Viola	.05	.02	.01
☐ 11 Bobby Doerr CAPT	.10	.05	.01
☐ 12 Whitey Herzog MG	.05	.02	.01
☐ 13 Will Clark	.25	.11	.03
☐ 14 Ryne Sandberg	.50	.23	.06
☐ 15 Bobby Bonilla	.20	.09	.03
☐ 16 Ozzie Smith	.50	.23	.06
☐ 17 Vince Coleman	.05	.02	.01
☐ 18 Andre Dawson	.20	.09	.03
☐ 19 Darryl Strawberry	.10	.05	.01
☐ 20 Gary Carter	.10	.05	.01
☐ 21 Dwight Gooden	.10	.05	.01
☐ 22 Willie Stargell CAPT	.20	.09	.03

1989 Topps Glossy Send-Ins

The 1989 Topps Glossy Send-In set contains 60 standard-size cards. The fronts have color photos with white borders; the backs are light blue. The cards were distributed through the mail by Topps in six groups of ten cards. The last two cards out of each group of ten are young players or prospects.

	MINT	NRMT	EXC
COMPLETE SET (60)	10.00	4.50	1.25
COMMON CARD (1-60)	.10	.05	.01
☐ 1 Kirby Puckett	2.00	.90	.25
☐ 2 Eric Davis	.20	.09	.03
☐ 3 Joe Carter	.40	.18	.05
☐ 4 Andy Van Slyke	.20	.09	.03
☐ 5 Wade Boggs	.50	.23	.06
☐ 6 David Cone	.40	.18	.05
☐ 7 Kent Hrbek	.20	.09	.03
☐ 8 Darryl Strawberry	.20	.09	.03
☐ 9 Jay Buhner	.50	.23	.06
☐ 10 Ron Gant	.50	.23	.06
☐ 11 Will Clark	.50	.23	.06
☐ 12 Jose Canseco	.75	.35	.09
☐ 13 Juan Samuel	.10	.05	.01
☐ 14 George Brett	1.50	.70	.19
☐ 15 Benito Santiago	.10	.05	.01
☐ 16 Dennis Eckersley	.20	.09	.03
☐ 17 Gary Carter	.20	.09	.03
☐ 18 Frank Viola	.10	.05	.01
☐ 19 Roberto Alomar	1.50	.70	.19
☐ 20 Paul Gibson	.10	.05	.01
☐ 21 Dave Winfield	.40	.18	.05
☐ 22 Howard Johnson	.10	.05	.01
☐ 23 Roger Clemens	1.00	.45	.12
☐ 24 Bobby Bonilla	.40	.18	.05
☐ 25 Alan Trammell	.20	.09	.03
☐ 26 Kevin McReynolds	.10	.05	.01
☐ 27 George Bell	.10	.05	.01
☐ 28 Bruce Hurst	.10	.05	.01
☐ 29 Mark Grace	.75	.35	.09
☐ 30 Tim Belcher	.10	.05	.01
☐ 31 Mike Greenwell	.10	.05	.01
☐ 32 Glenn Davis	.10	.05	.01
☐ 33 Gary Gaetti	.10	.05	.01
☐ 34 Ryne Sandberg	1.50	.70	.19
☐ 35 Rickey Henderson	.50	.23	.06
☐ 36 Dwight Evans	.20	.09	.03
☐ 37 Dwight Gooden	.20	.09	.03
☐ 38 Robin Yount	.40	.18	.05
☐ 39 Damon Berryhill	.10	.05	.01
☐ 40 Chris Sabo	.10	.05	.01
☐ 41 Mark McGwire	1.50	.70	.19
☐ 42 Ozzie Smith	1.50	.70	.19
☐ 43 Paul Molitor	.50	.23	.06
☐ 44 Andres Galarraga	.50	.23	.06
☐ 45 Dave Stewart	.20	.09	.03
☐ 46 Tom Browning	.10	.05	.01
☐ 47 Cal Ripken	3.00	1.35	.35
☐ 48 Orel Hershiser	.20	.09	.03
☐ 49 Dave Gallagher	.10	.05	.01
☐ 50 Walt Weiss	.10	.05	.01
☐ 51 Don Mattingly	2.00	.90	.25
☐ 52 Tony Fernandez	.10	.05	.01
☐ 53 Tim Raines	.20	.09	.03
☐ 54 Jeff Reardon	.20	.09	.03
☐ 55 Kirk Gibson	.20	.09	.03
☐ 56 Jack Clark	.10	.05	.01
☐ 57 Danny Jackson	.10	.05	.01
☐ 58 Tony Gwynn	2.00	.90	.25
☐ 59 Cecil Espy	.10	.05	.01
☐ 60 Jody Reed	.10	.05	.01

1989 Topps Rookies

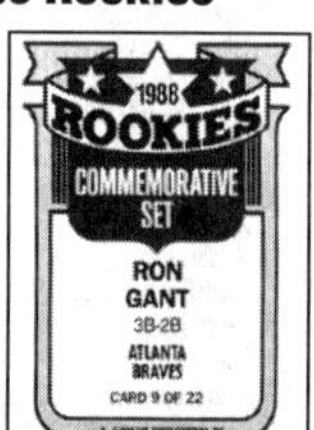

Inserted in each supermarket jumbo pack is a card from this series of 22 of 1988's best rookies as determined by Topps. Jumbo packs consisted of 100 (regular issue 1989 Topps baseball) cards with a stick of gum plus the insert "Rookie" card. The card fronts are in full color and measure the standard size. The card backs are printed in red and blue on white card stock and are numbered at the bottom. The order of the set is alphabetical by player's name.

	MINT	NRMT	EXC
COMPLETE SET (22)	6.00	2.70	.75
COMMON CARD (1-22)	.05	.02	.01
☐ 1 Roberto Alomar	1.50	.70	.19
☐ 2 Brady Anderson	1.25	.55	.16
☐ 3 Tim Belcher	.25	.11	.03
☐ 4 Damon Berryhill	.05	.02	.01
☐ 5 Jay Buhner	1.25	.55	.16
☐ 6 Kevin Elster	.25	.11	.03
☐ 7 Cecil Espy	.05	.02	.01
☐ 8 Dave Gallagher	.05	.02	.01
☐ 9 Ron Gant	.75	.35	.09
☐ 10 Paul Gibson	.05	.02	.01
☐ 11 Mark Grace	1.50	.70	.19
☐ 12 Darrin Jackson	.05	.02	.01
☐ 13 Gregg Jefferies	.25	.11	.03
☐ 14 Ricky Jordan	.05	.02	.01
☐ 15 Al Leiter	.25	.11	.03
☐ 16 Melido Perez	.05	.02	.01
☐ 17 Chris Sabo	.05	.02	.01
☐ 18 Nelson Santovenia	.05	.02	.01
☐ 19 Mackey Sasser	.05	.02	.01
☐ 20 Gary Sheffield	1.50	.70	.19
☐ 21 Walt Weiss	.05	.02	.01
☐ 22 David Wells	.10	.05	.01

1989 Topps Wax Box Cards

The cards in this 16-card set measure the standard size. Cards have essentially the same design as the 1989 Topps regular issue set. The cards were printed on the bottoms of the regular issue wax pack boxes. These 16 cards, "lettered" A through P, are considered a separate set in their own right and are not typically included in a complete set of the regular issue 1989 Topps cards. The order of the set is alphabetical by player's name. The value of the panels uncut is slightly greater, perhaps by 25 percent greater, than the value of the individual cards cut up carefully. The sixteen cards in this set honor players (and one manager) who reached career milestones during the 1988 season.

	MINT	NRMT	EXC
COMPLETE SET (16)	8.00	3.60	1.00
COMMON CARD (A-P)	.10	.05	.01
☐ A George Brett (475th Double)	1.00	.45	.12
☐ B Bill Buckner (2600th Hit)	.25	.11	.03
☐ C Darrell Evans (400th Home Run)	.25	.11	.03
☐ D Rich Gossage (300th Save)	.25	.11	.03
☐ E Greg Gross (125th Pinch Hit)	.10	.05	.01
☐ F Rickey Henderson (775th Stolen Base)	.50	.23	.06
☐ G Keith Hernandez (125th Game-Winning RBI)	.25	.11	.03
☐ H Tom Lasorda MG (1000th Managerial Win)	.40	.18	.05
☐ I Jim Rice (1400th Run Batted In)	.25	.11	.03
☐ J Cal Ripken (1000th Cons. Game)	2.50	1.10	.30
☐ K Nolan Ryan (4700th Strikeout)	2.50	1.10	.30
☐ L Mike Schmidt (1000th Long Hit)	.75	.35	.09
☐ M Bruce Sutter (300th Save)	.25	.11	.03
☐ N Don Sutton (750th Game Started)	.40	.18	.05
☐ O Kent Tekulve (1000th Appearance)	.10	.05	.01
☐ P Dave Winfield (1400th Run Batted In)	.50	.23	.06

1989 Topps Traded

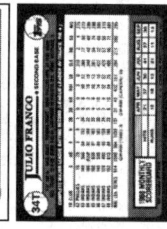

The 1989 Topps Traded set contains 132 standard-size cards. The cards were distributed exclusively in factory set form in red and white taped boxes through hobby dealers. The cards are identical to the 1989 Topps regular issue cards except for whiter stock and t-suffixed numbering on back. Rookie Cards in this set include Ken Griffey Jr., Ken Hill and Deion Sanders.

	MINT	NRMT	EXC
COMPLETE FACT.SET (132)	6.00	2.70	.75
COMMON CARD (1T-132T)	.05	.02	.01
☐ 1T Don Aase	.05	.02	.01
☐ 2T Jim Abbott	.15	.07	.02
☐ 3T Kent Anderson	.05	.02	.01
☐ 4T Keith Atherton	.05	.02	.01
☐ 5T Wally Backman	.05	.02	.01
☐ 6T Steve Balboni	.05	.02	.01
☐ 7T Jesse Barfield	.05	.02	.01
☐ 8T Steve Bedrosian	.05	.02	.01
☐ 9T Todd Benzinger	.05	.02	.01
☐ 10T Geronimo Berroa	.10	.05	.01
☐ 11T Bert Blyleven	.10	.05	.01
☐ 12T Bob Boone	.10	.05	.01
☐ 13T Phil Bradley	.05	.02	.01
☐ 14T Jeff Brantley	.05	.02	.01
☐ 15T Kevin Brown	.15	.07	.02
☐ 16T Jerry Browne	.05	.02	.01
☐ 17T Chuck Cary	.05	.02	.01
☐ 18T Carmen Castillo	.05	.02	.01
☐ 19T Jim Clancy	.05	.02	.01
☐ 20T Jack Clark	.10	.05	.01
☐ 21T Bryan Clutterbuck	.05	.02	.01
☐ 22T Jody Davis	.05	.02	.01
☐ 23T Mike Devereaux	.05	.02	.01
☐ 24T Frank DiPino	.05	.02	.01
☐ 25T Benny Distefano	.05	.02	.01
☐ 26T John Dopson	.05	.02	.01
☐ 27T Len Dykstra	.10	.05	.01
☐ 28T Jim Eisenreich	.10	.05	.01
☐ 29T Nick Esasky	.05	.02	.01
☐ 30T Alvaro Espinoza	.05	.02	.01
☐ 31T Darrell Evans UER (Stat headings on back are for a pitcher)	.10	.05	.01
☐ 32T Junior Felix	.05	.02	.01
☐ 33T Felix Fermin	.05	.02	.01
☐ 34T Julio Franco	.10	.05	.01
☐ 35T Terry Francona	.05	.02	.01
☐ 36T Cito Gaston MG	.10	.05	.01
☐ 37T Bob Geren UER (Photo actually Mike Fennell)	.05	.02	.01
☐ 38T Tom Gordon	.10	.05	.01
☐ 39T Tommy Gregg	.05	.02	.01
☐ 40T Ken Griffey Sr.	.05	.02	.01
☐ 41T Ken Griffey Jr.	5.00	2.20	.60

	MINT	NRMT	EXC
☐ 42T Kevin Gross	.05	.02	.01
☐ 43T Lee Guetterman	.05	.02	.01
☐ 44T Mel Hall	.05	.02	.01
☐ 45T Erik Hanson	.15	.07	.02
☐ 46T Gene Harris	.05	.02	.01
☐ 47T Andy Hawkins	.05	.02	.01
☐ 48T Rickey Henderson	.15	.07	.02
☐ 49T Tom Herr	.05	.02	.01
☐ 50T Ken Hill	.40	.18	.05
☐ 51T Brian Holman	.05	.02	.01
☐ 52T Brian Holton	.05	.02	.01
☐ 53T Art Howe MG	.05	.02	.01
☐ 54T Ken Howell	.05	.02	.01
☐ 55T Bruce Hurst	.05	.02	.01
☐ 56T Chris James	.05	.02	.01
☐ 57T Randy Johnson	.60	.25	.07
☐ 58T Jimmy Jones	.05	.02	.01
☐ 59T Terry Kennedy	.05	.02	.01
☐ 60T Paul Kilgus	.05	.02	.01
☐ 61T Eric King	.05	.02	.01
☐ 62T Ron Kittle	.05	.02	.01
☐ 63T John Kruk	.10	.05	.01
☐ 64T Randy Kutcher	.05	.02	.01
☐ 65T Steve Lake	.05	.02	.01
☐ 66T Mark Langston	.10	.05	.01
☐ 67T Dave LaPoint	.05	.02	.01
☐ 68T Rick Leach	.05	.02	.01
☐ 69T Terry Leach	.05	.02	.01
☐ 70T Jim Lefebvre MG	.05	.02	.01
☐ 71T Al Leiter	.10	.05	.01
☐ 72T Jeffrey Leonard	.05	.02	.01
☐ 73T Derek Lilliquist	.05	.02	.01
☐ 74T Rick Mahler	.05	.02	.01
☐ 75T Tom McCarthy	.05	.02	.01
☐ 76T Lloyd McClendon	.05	.02	.01
☐ 77T Lance McCullers	.05	.02	.01
☐ 78T Oddibe McDowell	.05	.02	.01
☐ 79T Roger McDowell	.05	.02	.01
☐ 80T Larry McWilliams	.05	.02	.01
☐ 81T Randy Milligan	.05	.02	.01
☐ 82T Mike Moore	.05	.02	.01
☐ 83T Keith Moreland	.05	.02	.01
☐ 84T Mike Morgan	.05	.02	.01
☐ 85T Jamie Moyer	.05	.02	.01
☐ 86T Rob Murphy	.05	.02	.01
☐ 87T Eddie Murray	.25	.11	.03
☐ 88T Pete O'Brien	.05	.02	.01
☐ 89T Gregg Olson	.10	.05	.01
☐ 90T Steve Ontiveros	.05	.02	.01
☐ 91T Jesse Orosco	.05	.02	.01
☐ 92T Spike Owen	.05	.02	.01
☐ 93T Rafael Palmeiro	.15	.07	.02
☐ 94T Clay Parker	.05	.02	.01
☐ 95T Jeff Parrett	.05	.02	.01
☐ 96T Lance Parrish	.05	.02	.01
☐ 97T Dennis Powell	.05	.02	.01
☐ 98T Rey Quinones	.05	.02	.01
☐ 99T Doug Rader MG	.05	.02	.01
☐ 100T Willie Randolph	.10	.05	.01
☐ 101T Shane Rawley	.05	.02	.01
☐ 102T Randy Ready	.05	.02	.01
☐ 103T Bip Roberts	.10	.05	.01
☐ 104T Kenny Rogers	.10	.05	.01
☐ 105T Ed Romero	.05	.02	.01
☐ 106T Nolan Ryan	1.25	.55	.16
☐ 107T Luis Salazar	.05	.02	.01
☐ 108T Juan Samuel	.05	.02	.01
☐ 109T Alex Sanchez	.05	.02	.01
☐ 110T Deion Sanders	.75	.35	.09
☐ 111T Steve Sax	.05	.02	.01
☐ 112T Rick Schu	.05	.02	.01
☐ 113T Dwight Smith	.10	.05	.01
☐ 114T Lonnie Smith	.05	.02	.01
☐ 115T Billy Spiers	.05	.02	.01
☐ 116T Kent Tekulve	.05	.02	.01
☐ 117T Walt Terrell	.05	.02	.01
☐ 118T Milt Thompson	.05	.02	.01
☐ 119T Dickie Thon	.05	.02	.01
☐ 120T Jeff Torborg MG	.05	.02	.01
☐ 121T Jeff Treadway	.05	.02	.01
☐ 122T Omar Vizquel	.40	.18	.05
☐ 123T Jerome Walton	.10	.05	.01
☐ 124T Gary Ward	.05	.02	.01
☐ 125T Claudell Washington	.05	.02	.01
☐ 126T Curt Wilkerson	.05	.02	.01
☐ 127T Eddie Williams	.05	.02	.01
☐ 128T Frank Williams	.05	.02	.01
☐ 129T Ken Williams	.05	.02	.01
☐ 130T Mitch Williams	.05	.02	.01
☐ 131T Steve Wilson	.05	.02	.01
☐ 132T Checklist 1T-132T	.05	.02	.01

1989 Topps Traded Tiffany

For each set of regular Tiffany cards ordered, dealers received an update set. These 132 standard-size cards update the regular Topps issue. Again, these cards feature "glossy" fronts as well as easy to read backs. This set was issued only in complete form from the company. Again, the Topps Ireland printing facility produced these cards.

	MINT	NRMT	EXC
COMPLETE FACT.SET (132)	40.00	18.00	5.00
COMMON CARD (1T-132T)	.15	.07	.02
*STARS: 3X to 6X BASIC CARDS			
*ROOKIES: 2X to 4X BASIC CARDS			

1989 Topps Ames 20/20 Club

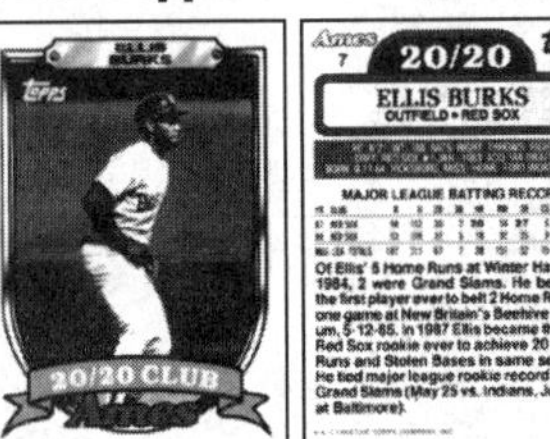

The 1989 (Topps) Ames 20/20 Club set contains 33 standard-size glossy cards. The fronts resemble plaques with gold and silver trim. The vertically oriented backs show career stats. The cards were distributed at Ames department stores as a boxed set. The set was produced by Topps for Ames; the Topps logo is also on the front of each card. The set includes active major leaguers who have had seasons of at least 20 home runs and 20 stolen bases. The backs include lifetime batting records with home run and stolen base totals for their 20/20 years highlighted. The subject list for the set is printed on the back panel of the set's custom box. These numbered cards are ordered alphabetically by player's name.

	MINT	NRMT	EXC
COMPLETE SET (33)	5.00	2.20	.60
COMMON CARD (1-33)	.05	.02	.01
☐ 1 Jesse Barfield	.05	.02	.01
☐ 2 Kevin Bass	.05	.02	.01
☐ 3 Don Baylor	.10	.05	.01
☐ 4 George Bell	.05	.02	.01
☐ 5 Barry Bonds	.60	.25	.07
☐ 6 Phil Bradley	.05	.02	.01
☐ 7 Ellis Burks	.25	.11	.03
☐ 8 Jose Canseco	.40	.18	.05
☐ 9 Joe Carter	.20	.09	.03
☐ 10 Kal Daniels	.05	.02	.01
☐ 11 Eric Davis	.10	.05	.01
☐ 12 Mike Davis	.05	.02	.01
☐ 13 Andre Dawson	.25	.11	.03
☐ 14 Kirk Gibson	.20	.09	.03
☐ 15 Pedro Guerrero	.05	.02	.01
☐ 16 Rickey Henderson	.40	.18	.05
☐ 17 Bo Jackson	.20	.09	.03
☐ 18 Howard Johnson	.05	.02	.01
☐ 19 Jeffrey Leonard	.05	.02	.01
☐ 20 Kevin McReynolds	.05	.02	.01
☐ 21 Dale Murphy	.20	.09	.03
☐ 22 Dwayne Murphy	.05	.02	.01
☐ 23 Dave Parker	.10	.05	.01
☐ 24 Kirby Puckett	.75	.35	.09
☐ 25 Juan Samuel	.05	.02	.01
☐ 26 Ryne Sandberg	.60	.25	.07
☐ 27 Mike Schmidt	.60	.25	.07
☐ 28 Darryl Strawberry	.10	.05	.01
☐ 29 Alan Trammell	.10	.05	.01
☐ 30 Andy Van Slyke	.10	.05	.01
☐ 31 Devon White	.10	.05	.01
☐ 32 Dave Winfield	.30	.14	.04
☐ 33 Robin Yount	.25	.11	.03

1989 Topps Award Winners

This commemorative sheet measures 8 3/4" by 8 1/8" and features the MVP, Cy Young and Rookie of the Year award winners from the AL and the NL. If the cards were cut they would measure the standard size. Fronts feature glossy color player photos with different color inner and outer borders. The player's name and the award he received is listed in a color stripe at the bottom of the card. The backs are blank and unnumbered. The players are checklisted below in alphabetical order. This sheet was included in a blister pack with a complete set of 1990 Topps Stickers.

	MINT	NRMT	EXC
COMPLETE SET (6)	2.00	.90	.25
COMMON CARD (1-6)	.10	.05	.01
☐ 1 Mark Davis	.10	.05	.01
☐ 2 Kevin Mitchell	.10	.05	.01
☐ 3 Gregg Olson	.10	.05	.01
☐ 4 Bret Saberhagen	.50	.23	.06
☐ 5 Jerome Walton	.10	.05	.01
☐ 6 Robin Yount	2.00	.90	.25

1989 Topps Baseball Talk

The BB Talk Soundcards include action photos of players, complete player statistics, exclusive specially recorded baseball programs and player autographs. These cards were produced by Parker Brothers. The fronts of the cards feature oversized replicas of Topps cards.

	MINT	NRMT	EXC
COMPLETE SET (164)	125.00	55.00	15.50
COMMON CARD (1-164)	.25	.11	.03
☐ 1 1975 World Series Game 6	1.50	.70	.19
☐ 2 1986 World Series Game 6	1.00	.45	.12
☐ 3 1986 A.L. Championship Game 5	1.00	.45	.12
☐ 4 1956 World Series Game 5	1.00	.45	.12
☐ 5 1986 N.L. Championship Game 6	1.00	.45	.12
☐ 6 1969 World Series Game 5	1.00	.45	.12
☐ 7 1984 World Series Game 5	1.00	.45	.12
☐ 8 1988 World Series Game 1	1.50	.70	.19
☐ 9 Reggie Jackson	2.50	1.10	.30
☐ 10 Brooks Robinson	2.00	.90	.25
☐ 11 Billy Williams	2.00	.90	.25
☐ 12 Bobby Thomson	1.00	.45	.12
☐ 13 Harmon Killebrew	2.00	.90	.25
☐ 14 Johnny Bench	2.50	1.10	.30
☐ 15 Tom Seaver	2.00	.90	.25
☐ 16 Willie Stargell	2.00	.90	.25
☐ 17 Ernie Banks	3.00	1.35	.35
☐ 18 Gaylord Perry	1.50	.70	.19
☐ 19 Bill Mazeroski	1.00	.45	.12
☐ 20 Babe Ruth	7.50	3.40	.95
☐ 21 Lou Gehrig	6.00	2.70	.75
☐ 22 Ty Cobb	3.00	1.35	.35
☐ 23 Bob Gibson	2.00	.90	.25
☐ 24 Al Kaline	2.00	.90	.25
☐ 25 Rod Carew	2.00	.90	.25
☐ 26 Lou Brock	2.00	.90	.25
☐ 27 Stan Musial	3.00	1.35	.35
☐ 28 Joe L. Morgan	2.00	.90	.25
☐ 29 Willie McCovey	2.00	.90	.25
☐ 30 Duke Snider	2.00	.90	.25
☐ 31 Whitey Ford	2.00	.90	.25
☐ 32 Eddie Mathews	2.00	.90	.25
☐ 33 Carl Yastrzemski	2.00	.90	.25
☐ 34 Pete Rose	4.00	1.80	.50
☐ 35 Hank Aaron	4.00	1.80	.50
☐ 36 Ralph Kiner	1.50	.70	.19
☐ 37 Steve Carlton	2.00	.90	.25
☐ 38 Roberto Clemente	5.00	2.20	.60
☐ 39 Don Drysdale	2.00	.90	.25
☐ 40 Robin Roberts	1.50	.70	.19
☐ 41 Hank Aaron	4.00	1.80	.50
☐ 42 Dave Winfield	2.00	.90	.25
☐ 43 Alan Trammell	1.00	.45	.12
☐ 44 Darryl Strawberry	.50	.23	.06
☐ 45 Ozzie Smith	6.00	2.70	.75
☐ 46 Kirby Puckett	8.00	3.60	1.00
☐ 47 Will Clark	2.50	1.10	.30
☐ 48 Keith Hernandez	.50	.23	.06
☐ 49 Wally Joyner	.25	.11	.03
☐ 50 Mike Scott	.25	.11	.03
☐ 51 Eric Davis	.50	.23	.06
☐ 52 George Brett	6.00	2.70	.75
☐ 53 George Bell	.25	.11	.03
☐ 54 Tommy Lasorda MG	1.50	.70	.19
☐ 55 Rickey Henderson	2.50	1.10	.30
☐ 56 Robin Yount	2.50	1.10	.30
☐ 57 Wade Boggs	2.50	1.10	.30
☐ 58 Roger Clemens	3.00	1.35	.35
☐ 59 Alvin Davis	.25	.11	.03
☐ 60 Jose Canseco	2.50	1.10	.30
☐ 61 Fernando Valenzuela	.50	.23	.06
☐ 62 Tony Gwynn	8.00	3.60	1.00
☐ 63 Dwight Gooden	.50	.23	.06
☐ 64 Mark McGwire	8.00	3.60	1.00
☐ 65 Jack Clark	.25	.11	.03
☐ 66 Dale Murphy	1.50	.70	.19
☐ 67 Kirk Gibson	1.00	.45	.12
☐ 68 Jack Morris	.50	.23	.06
☐ 69 Ryne Sandberg	6.00	2.70	.75
☐ 70 Nolan Ryan	15.00	6.75	1.85
☐ 71 John Tudor	.25	.11	.03
☐ 72 Mike Schmidt	4.00	1.80	.50
☐ 73 Dave Righetti	.25	.11	.03
☐ 74 Pedro Guerrero	.50	.23	.06
☐ 75 Rick Sutcliffe	.25	.11	.03
☐ 76 Gary Carter	.50	.23	.06
☐ 77 Cal Ripken	15.00	6.75	1.85
☐ 78 Andre Dawson	1.00	.45	.12
☐ 79 Andy Van Slyke	.50	.23	.06
☐ 80 Tim Raines	.50	.23	.06
☐ 81 Frank Viola	.25	.11	.03
☐ 82 Orel Hershiser	.50	.23	.06
☐ 83 Rick Reuschel	.25	.11	.03
☐ 84 Willie McGee	.50	.23	.06
☐ 85 Mark Langston	.25	.11	.03
☐ 86 Ron Darling	.25	.11	.03
☐ 87 Gregg Jefferies	1.00	.45	.12
☐ 88 Harold Baines	.50	.23	.06
☐ 89 Eddie Murray	4.00	1.80	.50
☐ 90 Barry Larkin	2.50	1.10	.30
☐ 91 Gary Gaetti	.25	.11	.03
☐ 92 Bret Saberhagen	.50	.23	.06
☐ 93 Roger McDowell	.25	.11	.03
☐ 94 Joe Magrane	.25	.11	.03
☐ 95 Juan Samuel	.25	.11	.03
☐ 96 Bert Blyleven	.25	.11	.03
☐ 97 Kal Daniels	.25	.11	.03
☐ 98 Kevin Bass	.25	.11	.03
☐ 99 Glenn Davis	.25	.11	.03
☐ 100 Steve Sax	.25	.11	.03
☐ 101 Rich Gossage	.50	.23	.06
☐ 102 Roger Craig MG	.25	.11	.03
☐ 103 Carney Lansford	.25	.11	.03
☐ 104 Joe Carter	1.00	.45	.12
☐ 105 Bruce Sutter	.25	.11	.03
☐ 106 Barry Bonds	4.00	1.80	.50
☐ 107 Danny Jackson	.25	.11	.03
☐ 108 Mike Flanagan	.25	.11	.03
☐ 109 Dwight Evans	.50	.23	.06
☐ 110 Ron Guidry	.25	.11	.03
☐ 111 Bruce Hurst	.25	.11	.03
☐ 112 Jim Rice	1.00	.45	.12
☐ 113 Oddibe McDowell	.25	.11	.03
☐ 114 Bobby Bonilla	1.00	.45	.12
☐ 115 Bob Welch	.25	.11	.03
☐ 116 Dave Parker	.50	.23	.06
☐ 117 Tim Wallach	.25	.11	.03
☐ 118 Tom Henke	.25	.11	.03
☐ 119 Mike Greenwell	.25	.11	.03
☐ 120 Kevin Seitzer	.25	.11	.03
☐ 121 Randy Myers	.50	.23	.06
☐ 122 Andres Galarraga	1.00	.45	.12
☐ 123 Don Mattingly	8.00	3.60	1.00
☐ 124 Cory Snyder	.25	.11	.03
☐ 125 Mike Witt	.25	.11	.03
☐ 126 Mike LaValliere	.25	.11	.03
☐ 127 Pete Incaviglia	.25	.11	.03
☐ 128 Dennis Eckersley	1.00	.45	.12
☐ 129 Jimmy Key	.50	.23	.06
☐ 130 John Franco	.50	.23	.06
☐ 131 Dan Plesac	.25	.11	.03
☐ 132 Tony LaRussa MG	.50	.23	.06
☐ 133 Hubie Brooks	.25	.11	.03
☐ 134 Chili Davis	.50	.23	.06
☐ 135 Bob Boone	.50	.23	.06
☐ 136 Jeff Reardon	.50	.23	.06
☐ 137 Candy Maldonado	.25	.11	.03
☐ 138 Mike Marshall	.25	.11	.03
☐ 139 Tommy John	.50	.23	.06
☐ 140 Chris Sabo	.25	.11	.03
☐ 141 Vince Coleman	.25	.11	.03
☐ 142 Frank White	.50	.23	.06
☐ 143 Harold Reynolds	.25	.11	.03
☐ 144 Lee Smith	.50	.23	.06
☐ 145 John Kruk	.50	.23	.06
☐ 146 Tony Fernandez	.25	.11	.03
☐ 147 Steve Bedrosian	.25	.11	.03
☐ 148 Benito Santiago	.50	.23	.06
☐ 149 Ozzie Guillen	.25	.11	.03
☐ 150 Gerald Perry	.25	.11	.03
☐ 151 Carlton Fisk	1.50	.70	.19
☐ 152 Tom Brunansky	.25	.11	.03
☐ 153 Paul Molitor	4.00	1.80	.50
☐ 154 Todd Worrell	.25	.11	.03
☐ 155 Brett Butler	.50	.23	.06
☐ 156 Sparky Anderson MG	.50	.23	.06
☐ 157 Kent Hrbek	.50	.23	.06
☐ 158 Frank Tanana	.25	.11	.03
☐ 159 Kevin Mitchell	.50	.23	.06
☐ 160 Charlie Hough	.25	.11	.03
☐ 161 Doug Jones	.25	.11	.03
☐ 162 Lou Whitaker	.50	.23	.06
☐ 163 Fred Lynn	.25	.11	.03
☐ 164 Checklist	.25	.11	.03

1989 Topps Big

The 1989 Topps Big Baseball set contains 330 glossy cards measuring approximately 2 1/2" by 3 3/4". The fronts feature mug shots superimposed on action photos. The horizontally oriented backs have color cartoons and statistics for the player's previous season and total career. Team members for the United States Olympic team were also included in this set. The set was released in three series of 110 cards. The cards were distributed in seven-card packs marked with the series number.

	MINT	NRMT	EXC
COMPLETE SET (330)	25.00	11.00	3.10
COMMON CARD (1-330)	.05	.02	.01
☐ 1 Orel Hershiser	.10	.05	.01
☐ 2 Harold Reynolds	.10	.05	.01
☐ 3 Jody Davis	.05	.02	.01
☐ 4 Greg Walker	.05	.02	.01
☐ 5 Barry Bonds	1.00	.45	.12
☐ 6 Bret Saberhagen	.10	.05	.01
☐ 7 Johnny Ray	.05	.02	.01
☐ 8 Mike Fiore	.05	.02	.01
☐ 9 Juan Castillo	.05	.02	.01
☐ 10 Todd Burns	.05	.02	.01
☐ 11 Carmelo Martinez	.05	.02	.01
☐ 12 Geno Petralli	.05	.02	.01
☐ 13 Mel Hall	.05	.02	.01
☐ 14 Tom Browning	.05	.02	.01
☐ 15 Fred McGriff	.50	.23	.06
☐ 16 Kevin Elster	.05	.02	.01
☐ 17 Tim Leary	.05	.02	.01
☐ 18 Jim Rice	.15	.07	.02
☐ 19 Bret Barberie	.05	.02	.01
☐ 20 Jay Buhner	.50	.23	.06
☐ 21 Atlee Hammaker	.05	.02	.01
☐ 22 Lou Whitaker	.10	.05	.01
☐ 23 Paul Runge	.05	.02	.01
☐ 24 Carlton Fisk	.50	.23	.06
☐ 25 Jose Lind	.05	.02	.01
☐ 26 Mark Gubicza	.05	.02	.01
☐ 27 Billy Ripken	.05	.02	.01
☐ 28 Mike Pagliarulo	.05	.02	.01
☐ 29 Jim Deshaies	.05	.02	.01
☐ 30 Mark McLemore	.05	.02	.01
☐ 31 Scott Terry	.05	.02	.01
☐ 32 Franklin Stubbs	.05	.02	.01
☐ 33 Don August	.05	.02	.01
☐ 34 Mark McGwire	1.25	.55	.16
☐ 35 Eric Show	.05	.02	.01
☐ 36 Cecil Espy	.05	.02	.01
☐ 37 Ron Tingley	.05	.02	.01
☐ 38 Mickey Brantley	.05	.02	.01
☐ 39 Paul O'Neill	.10	.05	.01
☐ 40 Ed Sprague	.30	.14	.04
☐ 41 Len Dykstra	.10	.05	.01
☐ 42 Roger Clemens	.75	.35	.09
☐ 43 Ron Gant	.40	.18	.05
☐ 44 Dan Pasqua	.05	.02	.01
☐ 45 Jeff D. Robinson	.05	.02	.01
☐ 46 George Brett	1.50	.70	.19
☐ 47 Bryn Smith	.05	.02	.01
☐ 48 Mike Marshall	.05	.02	.01
☐ 49 Doug Robbins	.05	.02	.01
☐ 50 Don Mattingly	2.00	.90	.25
☐ 51 Mike Scott	.05	.02	.01
☐ 52 Steve Jeltz	.05	.02	.01
☐ 53 Dick Schofield	.05	.02	.01
☐ 54 Tom Brunansky	.05	.02	.01
☐ 55 Gary Sheffield	2.00	.90	.25
☐ 56 Dave Valle	.05	.02	.01
☐ 57 Carney Lansford	.05	.02	.01
☐ 58 Tony Gwynn	1.50	.70	.19
☐ 59 Checklist 1-110	.05	.02	.01
☐ 60 Damon Berryhill	.05	.02	.01
☐ 61 Jack Morris	.10	.05	.01
☐ 62 Brett Butler	.10	.05	.01
☐ 63 Mickey Hatcher	.05	.02	.01
☐ 64 Bruce Sutter	.05	.02	.01
☐ 65 Robin Ventura	.75	.35	.09
☐ 66 Junior Ortiz	.05	.02	.01
☐ 67 Pat Tabler	.05	.02	.01
☐ 68 Greg Swindell	.05	.02	.01
☐ 69 Jeff Branson	.05	.02	.01
☐ 70 Manny Lee	.05	.02	.01
☐ 71 Dave Magadan	.05	.02	.01
☐ 72 Rich Gedman	.05	.02	.01
☐ 73 Tim Raines	.15	.07	.02
☐ 74 Mike Maddux	.05	.02	.01
☐ 75 Jim Presley	.05	.02	.01
☐ 76 Chuck Finley	.10	.05	.01
☐ 77 Jose Oquendo	.05	.02	.01
☐ 78 Rob Deer	.05	.02	.01
☐ 79 Jay Howell	.05	.02	.01
☐ 80 Terry Steinbach	.10	.05	.01
☐ 81 Ed Whitson	.05	.02	.01
☐ 82 Ruben Sierra	.10	.05	.01
☐ 83 Bruce Benedict	.05	.02	.01
☐ 84 Fred Manrique	.05	.02	.01
☐ 85 John Smiley	.05	.02	.01
☐ 86 Mike Macfarlane	.10	.05	.01
☐ 87 Rene Gonzales	.05	.02	.01
☐ 88 Charles Hudson	.05	.02	.01
☐ 89 Glenn Davis	.05	.02	.01
☐ 90 Les Straker	.05	.02	.01
☐ 91 Carmen Castillo	.05	.02	.01
☐ 92 Tracy Woodson	.05	.02	.01
☐ 93 Tino Martinez	.60	.25	.07
☐ 94 Herm Winningham	.05	.02	.01
☐ 95 Kelly Gruber	.05	.02	.01
☐ 96 Terry Leach	.05	.02	.01
☐ 97 Jody Reed	.05	.02	.01
☐ 98 Nelson Santovenia	.05	.02	.01
☐ 99 Tony Armas	.05	.02	.01
☐ 100 Greg Brock	.05	.02	.01
☐ 101 Dave Stewart	.10	.05	.01
☐ 102 Roberto Alomar	1.25	.55	.16
☐ 103 Jim Sundberg	.05	.02	.01
☐ 104 Albert Hall	.05	.02	.01
☐ 105 Steve Lyons	.05	.02	.01
☐ 106 Sid Bream	.05	.02	.01
☐ 107 Danny Tartabull	.10	.05	.01
☐ 108 Rick Dempsey	.05	.02	.01
☐ 109 Rich Renteria	.05	.02	.01
☐ 110 Ozzie Smith	1.25	.55	.16
☐ 111 Steve Sax	.05	.02	.01
☐ 112 Kelly Downs	.05	.02	.01
☐ 113 Larry Sheets	.05	.02	.01
☐ 114 Andy Benes	.50	.23	.06
☐ 115 Pete O'Brien	.05	.02	.01
☐ 116 Kevin McReynolds	.05	.02	.01
☐ 117 Juan Berenguer	.05	.02	.01
☐ 118 Billy Hatcher	.05	.02	.01
☐ 119 Rick Cerone	.05	.02	.01
☐ 120 Andre Dawson	.40	.18	.05
☐ 121 Storm Davis	.05	.02	.01
☐ 122 Devon White	.10	.05	.01
☐ 123 Alan Trammell	.10	.05	.01
☐ 124 Vince Coleman	.05	.02	.01
☐ 125 Al Leiter	.15	.07	.02
☐ 126 Dale Sveum	.05	.02	.01
☐ 127 Pete Incaviglia	.05	.02	.01
☐ 128 Dave Stieb	.05	.02	.01
☐ 129 Kevin Mitchell	.10	.05	.01
☐ 130 Dave Schmidt	.05	.02	.01
☐ 131 Gary Redus	.05	.02	.01
☐ 132 Ron Robinson	.05	.02	.01
☐ 133 Darnell Coles	.05	.02	.01
☐ 134 Benito Santiago	.10	.05	.01
☐ 135 John Farrell	.05	.02	.01
☐ 136 Willie Wilson	.05	.02	.01
☐ 137 Steve Bedrosian	.05	.02	.01
☐ 138 Don Slaught	.05	.02	.01
☐ 139 Darryl Strawberry	.10	.05	.01
☐ 140 Frank Viola	.05	.02	.01
☐ 141 Dave Silvestri	.05	.02	.01
☐ 142 Carlos Quintana	.05	.02	.01
☐ 143 Vance Law	.05	.02	.01
☐ 144 Dave Parker	.10	.05	.01
☐ 145 Tim Belcher	.05	.02	.01
☐ 146 Will Clark	.75	.35	.09
☐ 147 Mark Williamson	.05	.02	.01
☐ 148 Ozzie Guillen	.05	.02	.01
☐ 149 Kirk McCaskill	.05	.02	.01
☐ 150 Pat Sheridan	.05	.02	.01
☐ 151 Terry Pendleton	.10	.05	.01
☐ 152 Roberto Kelly	.05	.02	.01
☐ 153 Joey Meyer	.05	.02	.01
☐ 154 Mark Grant	.05	.02	.01
☐ 155 Joe Carter	.30	.14	.04
☐ 156 Steve Buechele	.05	.02	.01
☐ 157 Tony Fernandez	.05	.02	.01
☐ 158 Jeff Reed	.05	.02	.01
☐ 159 Bobby Bonilla	.15	.07	.02
☐ 160 Henry Cotto	.05	.02	.01
☐ 161 Kurt Stillwell	.05	.02	.01
☐ 162 Mickey Morandini	.10	.05	.01
☐ 163 Robby Thompson	.05	.02	.01
☐ 164 Rick Schu	.05	.02	.01
☐ 165 Stan Jefferson	.05	.02	.01
☐ 166 Ron Darling	.05	.02	.01
☐ 167 Kirby Puckett	2.00	.90	.25
☐ 168 Bill Doran	.05	.02	.01
☐ 169 Dennis Lamp	.05	.02	.01
☐ 170 Ty Griffin	.05	.02	.01
☐ 171 Ron Hassey	.05	.02	.01
☐ 172 Dale Murphy	.50	.23	.06
☐ 173 Andres Galarraga	.50	.23	.06
☐ 174 Tim Flannery	.05	.02	.01
☐ 175 Cory Snyder	.05	.02	.01
☐ 176 Checklist 111-220	.05	.02	.01
☐ 177 Tommy Barrett	.05	.02	.01
☐ 178 Dan Petry	.05	.02	.01
☐ 179 Billy Masse	.05	.02	.01
☐ 180 Terry Kennedy	.05	.02	.01
☐ 181 Joe Orsulak	.05	.02	.01
☐ 182 Doyle Alexander	.05	.02	.01
☐ 183 Willie McGee	.10	.05	.01
☐ 184 Jim Gantner	.05	.02	.01
☐ 185 Keith Hernandez	.10	.05	.01
☐ 186 Greg Gagne	.05	.02	.01
☐ 187 Kevin Bass	.05	.02	.01
☐ 188 Mark Eichhorn	.05	.02	.01
☐ 189 Mark Grace	.75	.35	.09
☐ 190 Jose Canseco	.60	.25	.07
☐ 191 Bobby Witt	.05	.02	.01
☐ 192 Rafael Santana	.05	.02	.01
☐ 193 Dwight Evans	.10	.05	.01
☐ 194 Greg Booker	.05	.02	.01
☐ 195 Brook Jacoby	.05	.02	.01
☐ 196 Rafael Belliard	.05	.02	.01
☐ 197 Candy Maldonado	.05	.02	.01
☐ 198 Mickey Tettleton	.10	.05	.01
☐ 199 Barry Larkin	.50	.23	.06
☐ 200 Frank White	.10	.05	.01
☐ 201 Wally Joyner	.10	.05	.01
☐ 202 Chet Lemon	.05	.02	.01
☐ 203 Joe Magrane	.05	.02	.01
☐ 204 Glenn Braggs	.05	.02	.01
☐ 205 Scott Fletcher	.05	.02	.01
☐ 206 Gary Ward	.05	.02	.01
☐ 207 Nelson Liriano	.05	.02	.01
☐ 208 Howard Johnson	.05	.02	.01
☐ 209 Kent Hrbek	.10	.05	.01
☐ 210 Ken Caminiti	.75	.35	.09
☐ 211 Mike Greenwell	.05	.02	.01
☐ 212 Ryne Sandberg	1.25	.55	.16
☐ 213 Joe Slusarski	.05	.02	.01
☐ 214 Donell Nixon	.05	.02	.01
☐ 215 Tim Wallach	.05	.02	.01
☐ 216 John Kruk	.10	.05	.01
☐ 217 Charles Nagy	.50	.23	.06
☐ 218 Alvin Davis	.05	.02	.01
☐ 219 Oswald Peraza	.05	.02	.01
☐ 220 Mike Schmidt	.75	.35	.09
☐ 221 Spike Owen	.05	.02	.01
☐ 222 Mike Smithson	.05	.02	.01
☐ 223 Dion James	.05	.02	.01
☐ 224 Ernie Whitt	.05	.02	.01
☐ 225 Mike Davis	.05	.02	.01
☐ 226 Gene Larkin	.05	.02	.01
☐ 227 Pat Combs	.05	.02	.01
☐ 228 Jack Howell	.05	.02	.01
☐ 229 Ron Oester	.05	.02	.01
☐ 230 Paul Gibson	.05	.02	.01
☐ 231 Mookie Wilson	.10	.05	.01
☐ 232 Glenn Hubbard	.05	.02	.01
☐ 233 Shawon Dunston	.05	.02	.01
☐ 234 Otis Nixon	.10	.05	.01
☐ 235 Melido Perez	.05	.02	.01
☐ 236 Jerry Browne	.05	.02	.01
☐ 237 Rick Rhoden	.05	.02	.01
☐ 238 Bo Jackson	.15	.07	.02
☐ 239 Randy Velarde	.05	.02	.01
☐ 240 Jack Clark	.05	.02	.01
☐ 241 Wade Boggs	.60	.25	.07
☐ 242 Lonnie Smith	.05	.02	.01
☐ 243 Mike Flanagan	.05	.02	.01
☐ 244 Willie Randolph	.10	.05	.01
☐ 245 Oddibe McDowell	.05	.02	.01
☐ 246 Ricky Jordan	.05	.02	.01
☐ 247 Greg Briley	.05	.02	.01
☐ 248 Rex Hudler	.05	.02	.01
☐ 249 Robin Yount	.50	.23	.06
☐ 250 Lance Parrish	.05	.02	.01
☐ 251 Chris Sabo	.05	.02	.01
☐ 252 Mike Henneman	.05	.02	.01
☐ 253 Gregg Jefferies	.30	.14	.04
☐ 254 Curt Young	.05	.02	.01
☐ 255 Andy Van Slyke	.10	.05	.01
☐ 256 Rod Booker	.05	.02	.01
☐ 257 Rafael Palmeiro	.50	.23	.06
☐ 258 Jose Uribe	.05	.02	.01
☐ 259 Ellis Burks	.40	.18	.05
☐ 260 John Smoltz	1.25	.55	.16
☐ 261 Tom Foley	.05	.02	.01
☐ 262 Lloyd Moseby	.05	.02	.01
☐ 263 Jim Poole	.05	.02	.01
☐ 264 Gary Gaetti	.10	.05	.01
☐ 265 Bob Dernier	.05	.02	.01
☐ 266 Harold Baines	.10	.05	.01
☐ 267 Tom Candiotti	.05	.02	.01
☐ 268 Rafael Ramirez	.05	.02	.01
☐ 269 Bob Boone	.10	.05	.01
☐ 270 Buddy Bell	.10	.05	.01
☐ 271 Rickey Henderson	.60	.25	.07
☐ 272 Willie Fraser	.05	.02	.01
☐ 273 Eric Davis	.15	.07	.02
☐ 274 Jeff M. Robinson	.05	.02	.01
☐ 275 Damaso Garcia	.05	.02	.01
☐ 276 Sid Fernandez	.10	.05	.01
☐ 277 Stan Javier	.05	.02	.01
☐ 278 Marty Barrett	.05	.02	.01
☐ 279 Gerald Perry	.05	.02	.01
☐ 280 Rob Ducey	.05	.02	.01
☐ 281 Mike Scioscia	.05	.02	.01
☐ 282 Randy Bush	.05	.02	.01
☐ 283 Tom Herr	.05	.02	.01
☐ 284 Glenn Wilson	.05	.02	.01
☐ 285 Pedro Guerrero	.05	.02	.01
☐ 286 Cal Ripken	3.00	1.35	.35
☐ 287 Randy Johnson	1.25	.55	.16
☐ 288 Julio Franco	.10	.05	.01
☐ 289 Ivan Calderon	.05	.02	.01
☐ 290 Rich Yett	.05	.02	.01
☐ 291 Scott Servais	.05	.02	.01
☐ 292 Bill Pecota	.05	.02	.01
☐ 293 Ken Phelps	.05	.02	.01
☐ 294 Chili Davis	.10	.05	.01
☐ 295 Manny Trillo	.05	.02	.01
☐ 296 Mike Boddicker	.05	.02	.01
☐ 297 Geronimo Berroa	.10	.05	.01
☐ 298 Todd Stottlemyre	.15	.07	.02
☐ 299 Kirk Gibson	.15	.07	.02
☐ 300 Wally Backman	.05	.02	.01
☐ 301 Hubie Brooks	.05	.02	.01
☐ 302 Von Hayes	.05	.02	.01
☐ 303 Matt Nokes	.05	.02	.01
☐ 304 Dwight Gooden	.10	.05	.01
☐ 305 Walt Weiss	.05	.02	.01
☐ 306 Mike LaValliere	.05	.02	.01
☐ 307 Cris Carpenter	.05	.02	.01
☐ 308 Ted Wood	.05	.02	.01
☐ 309 Jeff Russell	.05	.02	.01
☐ 310 Dave Gallagher	.05	.02	.01
☐ 311 Andy Allanson	.05	.02	.01
☐ 312 Craig Reynolds	.05	.02	.01
☐ 313 Kevin Seitzer	.05	.02	.01
☐ 314 Dave Winfield	.60	.25	.07
☐ 315 Andy McGaffigan	.05	.02	.01
☐ 316 Nick Esasky	.05	.02	.01
☐ 317 Jeff Blauser	.10	.05	.01
☐ 318 George Bell	.05	.02	.01
☐ 319 Eddie Murray	1.00	.45	.12
☐ 320 Mark Davidson	.05	.02	.01
☐ 321 Juan Samuel	.05	.02	.01
☐ 322 Jim Abbott	.10	.05	.01
☐ 323 Kal Daniels	.05	.02	.01
☐ 324 Mike Brumley	.05	.02	.01
☐ 325 Gary Carter	.10	.05	.01
☐ 326 Dave Henderson	.05	.02	.01
☐ 327 Checklist 221-330	.05	.02	.01
☐ 328 Garry Templeton	.05	.02	.01
☐ 329 Pat Perry	.05	.02	.01
☐ 330 Paul Molitor	.75	.35	.09

1989 Topps Cap'n Crunch

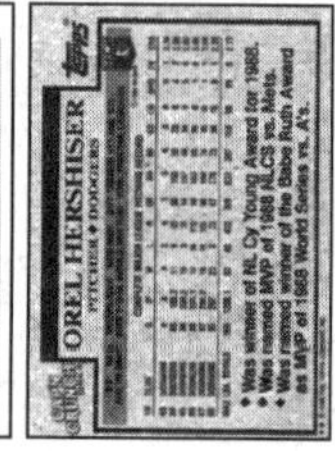

The 1989 Topps Cap'n Crunch set contains 22 standard-size cards. The fronts have red, white and blue borders surrounding "mugshot" photos. The backs are horizontally oriented and show lifetime stats. The team logos have been airbrushed out. Two cards were included (in a cellophane wrapper with a piece of gum) in each specially marked Cap'n Crunch cereal box. The set was not available as a complete set as part of any mail-in offer.

	MINT	NRMT	EXC
COMPLETE SET (22)	12.00	5.50	1.50
COMMON CARD (1-22)	.25	.11	.03
☐ 1 Jose Canseco	.60	.25	.07
☐ 2 Kirk Gibson	.40	.18	.05
☐ 3 Orel Hershiser	.40	.18	.05
☐ 4 Frank Viola	.25	.11	.03
☐ 5 Tony Gwynn	1.50	.70	.19
☐ 6 Cal Ripken	3.00	1.35	.35
☐ 7 Darryl Strawberry	.40	.18	.05
☐ 8 Don Mattingly	1.50	.70	.19
☐ 9 George Brett	1.25	.55	.16
☐ 10 Andre Dawson	.40	.18	.05
☐ 11 Dale Murphy	.60	.25	.07
☐ 12 Alan Trammell	.40	.18	.05
☐ 13 Eric Davis	.25	.11	.03
☐ 14 Jack Clark	.25	.11	.03
☐ 15 Eddie Murray	.75	.35	.09
☐ 16 Mike Schmidt	1.00	.45	.12
☐ 17 Dwight Gooden	.40	.18	.05
☐ 18 Roger Clemens	1.00	.45	.12
☐ 19 Will Clark	.75	.35	.09
☐ 20 Kirby Puckett	1.50	.70	.19
☐ 21 Robin Yount	.60	.25	.07
☐ 22 Mark McGwire	1.25	.55	.16

1989 Topps Coins

The 1989 Topps Coins set contains 60 coins, each measuring approximately 1 1/2" in diameter. The coins were issued in packs of three coins. The set is arranged by league order with the Most Valuable Player, Cy Young Award Winner, Rookie of the Year and Batting Leaders being first, then the rest of the league being arranged alphabetically within the league group. The National League players are 1-28 and the American League players are 29-60.

	MINT	NRMT	EXC
COMPLETE SET (60)	8.00	3.60	1.00
COMMON COIN (1-60)	.05	.02	.01
☐ 1 Kirk Gibson	.20	.09	.03
☐ 2 Orel Hershiser	.10	.05	.01
☐ 3 Chris Sabo	.05	.02	.01
☐ 4 Tony Gwynn	1.00	.45	.12
☐ 5 Bobby Bonilla	.20	.09	.03
☐ 6 Brett Butler	.10	.05	.01

	MINT	NRMT	EXC
☐ 7 Jack Clark	.10	.05	.01
☐ 8 Will Clark	.40	.18	.05
☐ 9 Eric Davis	.10	.05	.01
☐ 10 Glenn Davis	.05	.02	.01
☐ 11 Andre Dawson	.10	.05	.01
☐ 12 John Franco	.10	.05	.01
☐ 13 Andres Galarraga	.30	.14	.04
☐ 14 Dwight Gooden	.10	.05	.01
☐ 15 Mark Grace	.40	.18	.05
☐ 16 Pedro Guerrero	.05	.02	.01
☐ 17 Ricky Jordan	.05	.02	.01
☐ 18 Mike Marshall	.05	.02	.01
☐ 19 Dale Murphy	.20	.09	.03
☐ 20 Eddie Murray	.50	.23	.06
☐ 21 Gerald Perry	.05	.02	.01
☐ 22 Tim Raines	.10	.05	.01
☐ 23 Juan Samuel	.05	.02	.01
☐ 24 Benito Santiago	.05	.02	.01
☐ 25 Ozzie Smith	.75	.35	.09
☐ 26 Darryl Strawberry	.10	.05	.01
☐ 27 Andy Van Slyke	.05	.02	.01
☐ 28 Gerald Young	.05	.02	.01
☐ 29 Jose Canseco	.25	.11	.03
☐ 30 Frank Viola	.05	.02	.01
☐ 31 Walt Weiss	.05	.02	.01
☐ 32 Wade Boggs	.25	.11	.03
☐ 33 Harold Baines	.10	.05	.01
☐ 34 George Brett	1.00	.45	.12
☐ 35 Jay Buhner	.50	.23	.06
☐ 36 Joe Carter	.20	.09	.03
☐ 37 Roger Clemens	.40	.18	.05
☐ 38 Alvin Davis	.05	.02	.01
☐ 39 Tony Fernandez	.05	.02	.01
☐ 40 Carlton Fisk	.30	.14	.04
☐ 41 Mike Greenwell	.05	.02	.01
☐ 42 Kent Hrbek	.10	.05	.01
☐ 43 Don Mattingly	1.00	.45	.12
☐ 44 Fred McGriff	.25	.11	.03
☐ 45 Mark McGwire	1.00	.45	.12
☐ 46 Paul Molitor	.75	.35	.09
☐ 47 Rafael Palmeiro	.30	.14	.04
☐ 48 Kirby Puckett	1.00	.45	.12
☐ 49 Johnny Ray	.05	.02	.01
☐ 50 Cal Ripken	2.00	.90	.25
☐ 51 Ruben Sierra	.10	.05	.01
☐ 52 Pete Stanicek	.05	.02	.01
☐ 53 Dave Stewart	.05	.02	.01
☐ 54 Greg Swindell	.05	.02	.01
☐ 55 Danny Tartabull	.05	.02	.01
☐ 56 Alan Trammell	.10	.05	.01
☐ 57 Lou Whitaker	.10	.05	.01
☐ 58 Dave Winfield	.30	.14	.04
☐ 59 Mike Witt	.05	.02	.01
☐ 60 Robin Yount	.30	.14	.04

1989 Topps Doubleheaders All-Stars

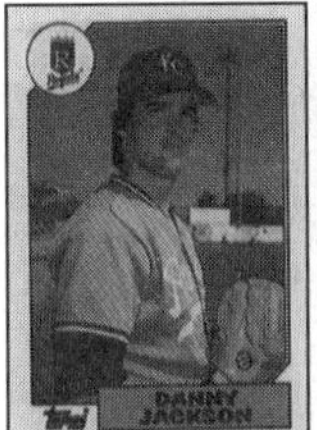

The 1989 Topps Doubleheaders were a novel idea from Topps to capitalize on the interest in rookie cards. The one side of the plastic holder shows a small color photo of the rookie card while the other side shows a photo of the current year Topps card on the other side. The holders measure 2" by 2 1/8". The set contains 24 holders, eight starting players, two starting pitchers, one reliever, and one DH from each league. They are unnumbered. Apparently the twelve from each league are considered by Topps as the "best" at each position.

	MINT	NRMT	EXC
COMPLETE SET (24)	15.00	6.75	1.85
COMMON CARD (1-24)	.25	.11	.03
☐ 1 Don Mattingly	3.00	1.35	.35
☐ 2 Julio Franco	.50	.23	.06
☐ 3 Wade Boggs	1.00	.45	.12
☐ 4 Alan Trammell	.75	.35	.09
☐ 5 Jose Canseco	1.00	.45	.12
☐ 6 Mike Greenwell	.25	.11	.03
☐ 7 Kirby Puckett	3.00	1.35	.35
☐ 8 Carlton Fisk	.75	.35	.09
☐ 9 Roger Clemens	1.50	.70	.19
☐ 10 Frank Viola	.25	.11	.03
☐ 11 Dennis Eckersley	.75	.35	.09
☐ 12 Mark McGwire	2.50	1.10	.30
☐ 13 Will Clark	1.00	.45	.12
☐ 14 Ryne Sandberg	3.00	1.35	.35
☐ 15 Bobby Bonilla	.50	.23	.06
☐ 16 Ozzie Smith	3.00	1.35	.35
☐ 17 Andre Dawson	.75	.35	.09
☐ 18 Darryl Strawberry	.50	.23	.06
☐ 19 Andy Van Slyke	.50	.23	.06
☐ 20 Alan Ashby	.25	.11	.03
☐ 21 Orel Hershiser	.50	.23	.06
☐ 22 Danny Jackson	.25	.11	.03
☐ 23 John Franco	.50	.23	.06
☐ 24 Kirk Gibson	.50	.23	.06

1989 Topps Doubleheaders Mets/Yankees Test

This set of 24 Doubleheaders, which was test marketed by Topps, and is extremely tough to find, features the New York Mets (1-13) and the New York Yankees (14-24). Each item is a clear plastic stand-up holder containing two mini-reproductions of the player's cards. On one side is the 1989 Topps card, and on the reverse is a reproduction of the rookie card.

	MINT	NRMT	EXC
COMPLETE SET (24)	400.00	180.00	50.00
COMMON CARD (1-24)	10.00	4.50	1.25
☐ 1 Darryl Strawberry	15.00	6.75	1.85
☐ 2 Gregg Jefferies	25.00	11.00	3.10
☐ 3 Kevin McReynolds	10.00	4.50	1.25
☐ 4 Gary Carter	15.00	6.75	1.85
☐ 5 Dwight Gooden	15.00	6.75	1.85
☐ 6 David Cone	25.00	11.00	3.10
☐ 7 Ron Darling	15.00	6.75	1.85
☐ 8 Keith Hernandez	15.00	6.75	1.85
☐ 9 Randy Myers	15.00	6.75	1.85
☐ 10 Howard Johnson	15.00	6.75	1.85
☐ 11 Tim Teufel	10.00	4.50	1.25
☐ 12 Len Dykstra	15.00	6.75	1.85
☐ 13 Mookie Wilson	10.00	4.50	1.25
☐ 14 Don Mattingly	100.00	45.00	12.50
☐ 15 Dave Winfield	40.00	18.00	5.00
☐ 16 Rickey Henderson	30.00	13.50	3.70
☐ 17 Claudell Washington	10.00	4.50	1.25
☐ 18 Dave Righetti	15.00	6.75	1.85
☐ 19 Steve Sax	10.00	4.50	1.25
☐ 20 Mike Pagliarulo	10.00	4.50	1.25
☐ 21 Rafael Santana	10.00	4.50	1.25
☐ 22 Richard Dotson	10.00	4.50	1.25
☐ 23 Rick Rhoden	10.00	4.50	1.25
☐ 24 Ken Phelps	10.00	4.50	1.25

1989 Topps Gallery of Champions

These 12 mini "cards" were produced by Topps and sold in complete set form only. The players selected for this set were either award winners or were league leaders. These approximately 1 1/4" by 1 3/4" cards were printed using either aluminum, bronze or silver. We have priced the aluminum versions of these cards. The bronze versions have a value of between 2X to 4X the aluminums while the silvers have a value between 5X to 10X the aluminum cards. We have sequenced this set in alphabetical order.

	MINT	NRMT	EXC
COMPLETE SET (12)	100.00	45.00	12.50
COMMON CARD (1-12)	5.00	2.20	.60
☐ 1 Wade Boggs	20.00	9.00	2.50
☐ 2 Jose Canseco	15.00	6.75	1.85
☐ 3 Will Clark	20.00	9.00	2.50
☐ 4 Dennis Eckersley	10.00	4.50	1.25
☐ 5 John Franco	5.00	2.20	.60
☐ 6 Kirk Gibson	7.50	3.40	.95
☐ 7 Tony Gwynn	25.00	11.00	3.10
☐ 8 Orel Hershiser	7.50	3.40	.95
☐ 9 Chris Sabo	5.00	2.20	.60
☐ 10 Darryl Strawberry	7.50	3.40	.95
☐ 11 Frank Viola	5.00	2.20	.60
☐ 12 Walt Weiss	5.00	2.20	.60

1989 Topps Heads Up Test

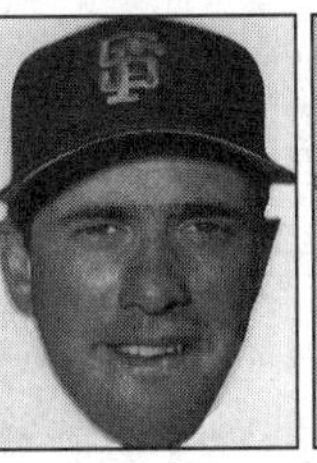

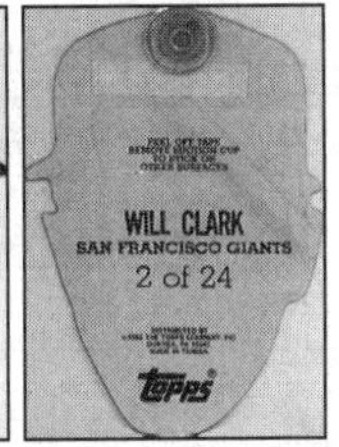

This very limited distribution set features baseball superstars. A large photo of the player's head is featured. These "faces" were released one per pack and the player's name and team are noted on the back.

	MINT	NRMT	EXC
COMPLETE SET (24)	2500.00	1100.00	300.00
COMMON CARD (1-24)	25.00	11.00	3.10
☐ 1 Tony Gwynn	200.00	90.00	25.00
☐ 2 Will Clark	125.00	55.00	15.50
☐ 3 Dwight Gooden	50.00	22.00	6.25
☐ 4 Ricky Jordan	25.00	11.00	3.10
☐ 5 Ken Griffey Jr.	600.00	275.00	75.00
☐ 6 Darryl Strawberry	50.00	22.00	6.25
☐ 7 Frank Viola	25.00	11.00	3.10
☐ 8 Bo Jackson	50.00	22.00	6.25
☐ 9 Ryne Sandberg	200.00	90.00	25.00
☐ 10 Gregg Jefferies	50.00	22.00	6.25
☐ 11 Wade Boggs	100.00	45.00	12.50
☐ 12 Ellis Burks	40.00	18.00	5.00
☐ 13 Gary Sheffield	125.00	55.00	15.50
☐ 14 Mark McGwire	200.00	90.00	25.00
☐ 15 Mark Grace	100.00	45.00	12.50
☐ 16 Jim Abbott	50.00	22.00	6.25
☐ 17 Ozzie Smith	150.00	70.00	19.00
☐ 18 Jose Canseco	100.00	45.00	12.50
☐ 19 Don Mattingly	250.00	110.00	31.00
☐ 20 Kirby Puckett	200.00	90.00	25.00
☐ 21 Eric Davis	50.00	22.00	6.25
☐ 22 Mike Greenwell	25.00	11.00	3.10
☐ 23 Dale Murphy	75.00	34.00	9.50
☐ 24 Mike Schmidt	150.00	70.00	19.00

1989 Topps Hills Team MVP's

The 1989 Topps Hills Team MVP's set contains 33 glossy standard-size cards. The fronts and backs are yellow, red, white and navy. The horizontally oriented backs are green. The cards were distributed through Hills stores as a boxed set. The set was printed in Ireland. These numbered cards are ordered alphabetically by player's name.

	MINT	NRMT	EXC
COMPLETE SET (33)	5.00	2.20	.60
COMMON CARD (1-33)	.05	.02	.01
☐ 1 Harold Baines	.10	.05	.01
☐ 2 Wade Boggs	.30	.14	.04
☐ 3 George Brett	.75	.35	.09
☐ 4 Tom Brunansky	.05	.02	.01
☐ 5 Jose Canseco	.40	.18	.05
☐ 6 Joe Carter	.20	.09	.03
☐ 7 Will Clark	.40	.18	.05
☐ 8 Roger Clemens	.50	.23	.06
☐ 9 David Cone	.20	.09	.03
☐ 10 Glenn Davis	.05	.02	.01
☐ 11 Andre Dawson	.25	.11	.03
☐ 12 Dennis Eckersley	.10	.05	.01
☐ 13 Andres Galarraga	.25	.11	.03
☐ 14 Kirk Gibson	.20	.09	.03
☐ 15 Mike Greenwell	.05	.02	.01
☐ 16 Tony Gwynn	.75	.35	.09
☐ 17 Orel Hershiser	.10	.05	.01
☐ 18 Danny Jackson	.05	.02	.01
☐ 19 Mark Langston	.05	.02	.01
☐ 20 Fred McGriff	.40	.18	.05
☐ 21 Dale Murphy	.20	.09	.03
☐ 22 Eddie Murray	.30	.14	.04
☐ 23 Kirby Puckett	.75	.35	.09
☐ 24 Johnny Ray	.05	.02	.01
☐ 25 Juan Samuel	.05	.02	.01
☐ 26 Ruben Sierra	.10	.05	.01
☐ 27 Dave Stewart	.05	.02	.01
☐ 28 Darryl Strawberry	.10	.05	.01
☐ 29 Alan Trammell	.10	.05	.01
☐ 30 Andy Van Slyke	.05	.02	.01
☐ 31 Frank Viola	.05	.02	.01
☐ 32 Dave Winfield	.40	.18	.05
☐ 33 Robin Yount	.25	.11	.03

1989 Topps Mini Leaders

The 1989 Topps Mini League Leaders set contains 77 cards measuring approximately 2 1/8" by 3". The fronts have color photos with large white borders. The backs are yellow and feature 1988 and career stats. The cards were distributed in seven-card cello packs. These numbered cards are ordered alphabetically by player within team and the teams themselves are ordered alphabetically.

	MINT	NRMT	EXC
COMPLETE SET (77)	5.00	2.20	.60
COMMON CARD (1-77)	.05	.02	.01
☐ 1 Dale Murphy	.20	.09	.03
☐ 2 Gerald Perry	.05	.02	.01
☐ 3 Andre Dawson	.20	.09	.03
☐ 4 Greg Maddux	1.50	.70	.19
☐ 5 Rafael Palmeiro	.25	.11	.03
☐ 6 Tom Browning	.05	.02	.01
☐ 7 Kal Daniels	.05	.02	.01
☐ 8 Eric Davis	.10	.05	.01
☐ 9 John Franco	.10	.05	.01
☐ 10 Danny Jackson	.05	.02	.01
☐ 11 Barry Larkin	.30	.14	.04
☐ 12 Jose Rijo	.05	.02	.01
☐ 13 Chris Sabo	.05	.02	.01
☐ 14 Nolan Ryan	1.50	.70	.19
☐ 15 Mike Scott	.05	.02	.01
☐ 16 Gerald Young	.05	.02	.01
☐ 17 Kirk Gibson	.10	.05	.01
☐ 18 Orel Hershiser	.10	.05	.01
☐ 19 Steve Sax	.05	.02	.01
☐ 20 John Tudor	.05	.02	.01
☐ 21 Hubie Brooks	.05	.02	.01
☐ 22 Andres Galarraga	.20	.09	.03
☐ 23 Otis Nixon	.05	.02	.01
☐ 24 David Cone	.20	.09	.03
☐ 25 Sid Fernandez	.05	.02	.01
☐ 26 Dwight Gooden	.10	.05	.01
☐ 27 Kevin McReynolds	.05	.02	.01
☐ 28 Darryl Strawberry	.10	.05	.01
☐ 29 Juan Samuel	.05	.02	.01
☐ 30 Bobby Bonilla	.20	.09	.03
☐ 31 Sid Bream	.05	.02	.01
☐ 32 Jim Gott	.05	.02	.01
☐ 33 Andy Van Slyke	.05	.02	.01
☐ 34 Vince Coleman	.05	.02	.01
☐ 35 Jose DeLeon	.05	.02	.01
☐ 36 Joe Magrane	.05	.02	.01
☐ 37 Ozzie Smith	.75	.35	.09
☐ 38 Todd Worrell	.05	.02	.01
☐ 39 Tony Gwynn	1.00	.45	.12
☐ 40 Brett Butler	.10	.05	.01
☐ 41 Will Clark	.30	.14	.04
☐ 42 Rick Reuschel	.05	.02	.01
☐ 43 Checklist Card	.05	.02	.01
☐ 44 Eddie Murray	.50	.23	.06
☐ 45 Wade Boggs	.30	.14	.04
☐ 46 Roger Clemens	.50	.23	.06
☐ 47 Dwight Evans	.10	.05	.01
☐ 48 Mike Greenwell	.05	.02	.01
☐ 49 Bruce Hurst	.05	.02	.01
☐ 50 Johnny Ray	.05	.02	.01
☐ 51 Doug Jones	.05	.02	.01
☐ 52 Greg Swindell	.05	.02	.01
☐ 53 Gary Pettis	.05	.02	.01
☐ 54 George Brett	.75	.35	.09
☐ 55 Mark Gubicza	.05	.02	.01
☐ 56 Willie Wilson	.05	.02	.01
☐ 57 Teddy Higuera	.05	.02	.01
☐ 58 Paul Molitor	.30	.14	.04
☐ 59 Robin Yount	.20	.09	.03
☐ 60 Allan Anderson	.05	.02	.01
☐ 61 Gary Gaetti	.10	.05	.01
☐ 62 Kirby Puckett	1.00	.45	.12
☐ 63 Jeff Reardon	.10	.05	.01
☐ 64 Frank Viola	.05	.02	.01
☐ 65 Jack Clark	.05	.02	.01
☐ 66 Rickey Henderson	.30	.14	.04
☐ 67 Dave Winfield	.30	.14	.04
☐ 68 Jose Canseco	.40	.18	.05
☐ 69 Dennis Eckersley	.10	.05	.01
☐ 70 Mark McGwire	.75	.35	.09
☐ 71 Dave Stewart	.05	.02	.01
☐ 72 Alvin Davis	.05	.02	.01
☐ 73 Mark Langston	.05	.02	.01
☐ 74 Harold Reynolds	.05	.02	.01
☐ 75 George Bell	.05	.02	.01
☐ 76 Tony Fernandez	.05	.02	.01
☐ 77 Fred McGriff	.40	.18	.05

1989 Topps/O-Pee-Chee Stickers

Printed in Canada, these 326 stickers measure approximately 2 1/8" by 3" and feature white-bordered color player photos. The borders are highlighted by colored lines and baseball icons. The stickers are numbered at the lower right. The sticker backs are actually cards (1989 O-Pee-Chee Super Stars) and are considered a separate set. An album onto which the stickers could be affixed was available at retail stores. The album and the sticker numbering are organized as follows: 1988 Highlights (1-12), Houston Astros (13-23), Atlanta Braves (24-34), St. Louis Cardinals (35-45), Chicago Cubs (46-56), Los Angeles Dodgers (57-67), Montreal Expos (68-78), San Francisco Giants (79-89), New York Mets (90-100), San Diego Padres (101-111), Philadelphia Phillies (112-122), Pittsburgh Pirates (123-133), Cincinnati Reds (134-144), Foil All-Stars (145-162), Oakland A's (163-173), California Angels (174-184), Toronto Blue Jays (185-195), Milwaukee Brewers (196-206), Cleveland Indians (207-217), Seattle

Mariners (218-228), Baltimore Orioles (229-239), Texas Rangers (240-250), Boston Red Sox (251-261), Kansas City Royals (262-272), Detroit Tigers (273-283), Minnesota Twins (284-294), Chicago White Sox (295-305), New York Yankees (306-316) and Future Stars (317-326). For those stickers featuring more than one player, the other numbers on that sticker are given below in parentheses. Although the prices listed below are for the stickers only, there are instances where having an especially desirable sticker card back (attached to that sticker) will increase the values listed below.

	MINT	NRMT	EXC
COMPLETE SET (326)	15.00	6.75	1.85
COMMON STICKER (1-326)	.05	.02	.01
*TOPPS AND OPC: SAME VALUE			

Sticker	MINT	NRMT	EXC
1 George Bell	.05	.02	.01
2 Gary Carter	.10	.05	.01
3 Doug Jones	.05	.02	.01
4 John Franco	.10	.05	.01
5 Andre Dawson	.10	.05	.01
6 Pat Tabler	.05	.02	.01
7 Tom Browning	.05	.02	.01
8 Jeff Reardon	.10	.05	.01
9 Wade Boggs	.25	.11	.03
10 Kevin McReynolds	.05	.02	.01
11 Jose Canseco	.25	.11	.03
12 Orel Hershiser	.10	.05	.01
13 Dave Smith	.05	.02	.01
14 Kevin Bass	.05	.02	.01
15 Mike Scott	.05	.02	.01
16 Bill Doran	.05	.02	.01
17 Rafael Ramirez	.05	.02	.01
18 Buddy Bell	.10	.05	.01
19 Billy Hatcher	.05	.02	.01
20 Nolan Ryan	2.00	.90	.25
21 Glenn Davis	.05	.02	.01
22 Bob Knepper	.05	.02	.01
23 Gerald Young	.05	.02	.01
24 Dion James	.05	.02	.01
25 Bruce Sutter	.05	.02	.01
26 Andres Thomas	.05	.02	.01
27 Zane Smith	.05	.02	.01
28 Ozzie Virgil	.05	.02	.01
29 Rick Mahler	.05	.02	.01
30 Albert Hall	.05	.02	.01
31 Pete Smith	.05	.02	.01
32 Dale Murphy	.15	.07	.02
33 Gerald Perry	.05	.02	.01
34 Ron Gant	.25	.11	.03
35 Bob Horner	.05	.02	.01
36 Willie McGee	.05	.02	.01
37 Luis Alicea	.05	.02	.01
38 Tony Pena	.05	.02	.01
39 Todd Worrell	.05	.02	.01
40 Pedro Guerrero	.05	.02	.01
41 Tom Brunansky	.05	.02	.01
42 Terry Pendleton	.10	.05	.01
43 Vince Coleman	.05	.02	.01
44 Ozzie Smith	.50	.23	.06
45 Jose Oquendo	.05	.02	.01
46 Vance Law	.05	.02	.01
47 Rafael Palmeiro	.25	.11	.03
48 Greg Maddux	2.50	1.10	.30
49 Shawon Dunston	.05	.02	.01
50 Mark Grace	.40	.18	.05
51 Damon Berryhill	.05	.02	.01
52 Rick Sutcliffe	.05	.02	.01
53 Jamie Moyer	.05	.02	.01
54 Andre Dawson	.10	.05	.01
55 Ryne Sandberg	.50	.23	.06
56 Calvin Schiraldi	.05	.02	.01
57 Steve Sax	.05	.02	.01
58 Mike Scioscia	.05	.02	.01
59 Alfredo Griffin	.05	.02	.01
60 Fernando Valenzuela	.10	.05	.01
61 Jay Howell	.05	.02	.01
62 Tim Leary	.05	.02	.01
63 John Shelby	.05	.02	.01
64 John Tudor	.05	.02	.01
65 Orel Hershiser	.10	.05	.01
66 Kirk Gibson	.15	.07	.02
67 Mike Marshall	.05	.02	.01
68 Luis Rivera	.05	.02	.01
69 Tim Burke	.05	.02	.01
70 Tim Wallach	.05	.02	.01
71 Pascual Perez	.05	.02	.01
72 Hubie Brooks	.05	.02	.01
73 Jeff Parrett	.05	.02	.01
74 Denny Martinez	.10	.05	.01
75 Andy McGaffigan	.05	.02	.01
76 Andres Galarraga	.15	.07	.02
77 Tim Raines	.10	.05	.01
78 Nelson Santovenia	.05	.02	.01
79 Rick Reuschel	.05	.02	.01
80 Mike Aldrete	.05	.02	.01
81 Kelly Downs	.05	.02	.01
82 Jose Uribe	.05	.02	.01
83 Mike Krukow	.05	.02	.01
84 Kevin Mitchell	.05	.02	.01
85 Brett Butler	.10	.05	.01
86 Don Robinson	.05	.02	.01
87 Robby Thompson	.05	.02	.01
88 Will Clark	.30	.14	.04
89 Candy Maldonado	.05	.02	.01
90 Len Dykstra	.10	.05	.01
91 Howard Johnson	.05	.02	.01
92 Roger McDowell	.05	.02	.01
93 Keith Hernandez	.10	.05	.01
94 Gary Carter	.10	.05	.01
95 Kevin McReynolds	.05	.02	.01
96 Dave Cone	.25	.11	.03
97 Randy Myers	.10	.05	.01
98 Darryl Strawberry	.10	.05	.01
99 Dwight Gooden	.10	.05	.01
100 Ron Darling	.05	.02	.01
101 Benito Santiago	.05	.02	.01
102 John Kruk	.10	.05	.01
103 Chris Brown	.05	.02	.01
104 Roberto Alomar	1.00	.45	.12
105 Keith Moreland	.05	.02	.01
106 Randy Ready	.05	.02	.01
107 Marvell Wynne	.05	.02	.01
108 Lance McCullers	.05	.02	.01
109 Tony Gwynn	.75	.35	.09
110 Mark Davis	.05	.02	.01
111 Andy Hawkins	.05	.02	.01
112 Steve Bedrosian	.05	.02	.01
113 Phil Bradley	.05	.02	.01
114 Steve Jeltz	.05	.02	.01
115 Von Hayes	.05	.02	.01
116 Kevin Gross	.05	.02	.01
117 Juan Samuel	.05	.02	.01
118 Shane Rawley	.05	.02	.01
119 Chris James	.05	.02	.01
120 Mike Schmidt	.60	.25	.07
121 Don Carman	.05	.02	.01
122 Bruce Ruffin	.05	.02	.01
123 Bob Walk	.05	.02	.01
124 John Smiley	.05	.02	.01
125 Sid Bream	.05	.02	.01
126 Jose Lind	.05	.02	.01
127 Barry Bonds	.60	.25	.07
128 Mike LaValliere	.05	.02	.01
129 Jeff D. Robinson	.05	.02	.01
130 Mike Dunne	.05	.02	.01
131 Bobby Bonilla	.15	.07	.02
132 Andy Van Slyke	.10	.05	.01
133 Rafael Belliard	.05	.02	.01
134 Nick Esasky	.05	.02	.01
135 Bo Diaz	.05	.02	.01
136 John Franco	.10	.05	.01
137 Barry Larkin	.30	.14	.04
138 Eric Davis	.05	.02	.01
139 Jeff Treadway	.05	.02	.01
140 Jose Rijo	.05	.02	.01
141 Tom Browning	.05	.02	.01
142 Chris Sabo	.05	.02	.01
143 Danny Jackson	.05	.02	.01
144 Kal Daniels	.05	.02	.01
145 Rickey Henderson AS	.15	.07	.02
146 Paul Molitor AS	.15	.07	.02
147 Wade Boggs AS	.15	.07	.02
148 Jose Canseco AS	.15	.07	.02
149 Dave Winfield AS	.15	.07	.02
150 Cal Ripken AS	1.00	.45	.12
151 Mark McGwire AS	.25	.11	.03
152 Terry Steinbach AS	.10	.05	.01
153 Frank Viola AS	.05	.02	.01
154 Vince Coleman AS	.05	.02	.01
155 Ryne Sandberg AS	.25	.11	.03
156 Andre Dawson AS	.10	.05	.01
157 Darryl Strawberry AS	.10	.05	.01
158 Bobby Bonilla AS	.15	.07	.02
159 Will Clark AS	.15	.07	.02
160 Gary Carter AS	.10	.05	.01
161 Ozzie Smith AS	.15	.07	.02
162 Dwight Gooden AS	.10	.05	.01
163 Dave Stewart	.10	.05	.01
164 Dave Henderson	.05	.02	.01
165 Terry Steinbach	.10	.05	.01
166 Bob Welch	.05	.02	.01
167 Dennis Eckersley	.10	.05	.01
168 Walt Weiss	.05	.02	.01
169 Dave Parker	.10	.05	.01
170 Carney Lansford	.10	.05	.01
171 Jose Canseco	.25	.11	.03
172 Mark McGwire	.50	.23	.06
173 Ron Hassey	.05	.02	.01
174 Dick Schofield	.05	.02	.01
175 Bob Boone	.10	.05	.01
176 Mike Witt	.05	.02	.01
177 Chili Davis	.10	.05	.01
178 Brian Downing	.05	.02	.01
179 Devon White	.10	.05	.01
180 Bryan Harvey	.10	.05	.01
181 Jack Howell	.05	.02	.01
182 Johnny Ray	.05	.02	.01
183 Wally Joyner	.10	.05	.01
184 Kirk McCaskill	.05	.02	.01
185 Fred McGriff	.50	.23	.06
186 Jimmy Key	.10	.05	.01
187 Kelly Gruber	.05	.02	.01
188 Lloyd Moseby	.05	.02	.01
189 Tony Fernandez	.05	.02	.01
190 Mike Flanagan	.05	.02	.01
191 Pat Borders	.05	.02	.01
192 Rance Mulliniks	.05	.02	.01
193 George Bell	.05	.02	.01
194 Dave Stieb	.05	.02	.01
195 Tom Henke	.05	.02	.01
196 Glenn Braggs	.05	.02	.01
197 Dan Plesac	.05	.02	.01
198 Teddy Higuera	.05	.02	.01
199 Jeffrey Leonard	.05	.02	.01
200 B.J. Surhoff	.10	.05	.01
201 Greg Brock	.05	.02	.01
202 Rob Deer	.05	.02	.01
203 Jim Gantner	.05	.02	.01
204 Paul Molitor	.25	.11	.03
205 Robin Yount	.25	.11	.03
206 Dale Sveum	.05	.02	.01
207 Andy Allanson	.05	.02	.01
208 Julio Franco	.10	.05	.01
209 Bud Black	.05	.02	.01
210 Cory Snyder	.05	.02	.01
211 Tom Candiotti	.05	.02	.01
212 Brook Jacoby	.05	.02	.01
213 Greg Swindell	.05	.02	.01
214 John Farrell	.05	.02	.01
215 Doug Jones	.05	.02	.01
216 Joe Carter	.15	.07	.02
217 Scott Bailes	.05	.02	.01
218 Henry Cotto	.05	.02	.01
219 Mickey Brantley	.05	.02	.01
220 Mike Moore	.05	.02	.01
221 Mark Langston	.10	.05	.01
222 Steve Balboni	.05	.02	.01
223 Jim Presley	.05	.02	.01
224 Rey Quinones	.05	.02	.01
225 Scott Bradley	.05	.02	.01
226 Harold Reynolds	.10	.05	.01
227 Alvin Davis	.05	.02	.01
228 Bill Swift	.05	.02	.01
229 Jose Bautista	.05	.02	.01
230 Jeff Ballard	.05	.02	.01
231 Mickey Tettleton	.10	.05	.01
232 Pete Stanicek	.05	.02	.01
233 Jim Traber	.05	.02	.01
234 Rene Gonzales	.05	.02	.01
235 Terry Kennedy	.05	.02	.01
236 Tom Niedenfuer	.05	.02	.01
237 Cal Ripken	2.00	.90	.25
238 Eddie Murray	.30	.14	.04
239 Larry Sheets	.05	.02	.01
240 Cecil Espy	.05	.02	.01
241 Jose Guzman	.05	.02	.01
242 Ruben Sierra	.10	.05	.01
243 Jeff Russell	.05	.02	.01
244 Mike Stanley	.05	.02	.01
245 Charlie Hough	.10	.05	.01
246 Scott Fletcher	.05	.02	.01
247 Mitch Williams	.05	.02	.01
248 Pete O'Brien	.05	.02	.01
249 Pete Incaviglia	.05	.02	.01
250 Steve Buechele	.05	.02	.01
251 Lee Smith	.10	.05	.01
252 Dwight Evans	.10	.05	.01
253 Rich Gedman	.05	.02	.01
254 Ellis Burks	.15	.07	.02
255 Mike Greenwell	.05	.02	.01
256 Jim Rice	.10	.05	.01
257 Marty Barrett	.05	.02	.01
258 Bob Stanley	.05	.02	.01
259 Roger Clemens	.25	.11	.03
260 Wade Boggs	.25	.11	.03
261 Mike Boddicker	.05	.02	.01
262 Frank White	.10	.05	.01
263 Bret Saberhagen	.10	.05	.01
264 Kevin Seitzer	.05	.02	.01
265 Bo Jackson	.15	.07	.02
266 Kurt Stillwell	.05	.02	.01
267 Danny Tartabull	.05	.02	.01
268 Willie Wilson	.05	.02	.01
269 Floyd Bannister	.05	.02	.01
270 George Brett	.75	.35	.09
271 Mark Gubicza	.05	.02	.01
272 Steve Farr	.05	.02	.01
273 Mike Henneman	.05	.02	.01
274 Doyle Alexander	.05	.02	.01
275 Frank Tanana	.05	.02	.01
276 Luis Salazar	.05	.02	.01
277 Jack Morris	.10	.05	.01
278 Tom Brookens	.05	.02	.01
279 Gary Pettis	.05	.02	.01
280 Matt Nokes	.05	.02	.01
281 Alan Trammell	.10	.05	.01
282 Lou Whitaker	.10	.05	.01
283 Chet Lemon	.05	.02	.01
284 Jeff Reardon	.10	.05	.01
285 Bert Blyleven	.10	.05	.01
286 Danny Gladden	.05	.02	.01
287 Kent Hrbek	.10	.05	.01
288 Greg Gagne	.05	.02	.01
289 Gary Gaetti	.10	.05	.01
290 Tim Laudner	.05	.02	.01
291 Juan Berenguer	.05	.02	.01
292 Frank Viola	.05	.02	.01
293 Kirby Puckett	.50	.23	.06
294 Gene Larkin	.05	.02	.01
295 Dave Gallagher	.05	.02	.01
296 Melido Perez	.05	.02	.01
297 Ivan Calderon	.05	.02	.01
298 Steve Lyons	.05	.02	.01
299 Carlton Fisk	.25	.11	.03
300 Fred Manrique	.05	.02	.01
301 Dan Pasqua	.05	.02	.01
302 Jack McDowell	.25	.11	.03
303 Ozzie Guillen	.05	.02	.01
304 Harold Baines	.10	.05	.01
305 Bobby Thigpen	.05	.02	.01
306 John Candelaria	.05	.02	.01
307 Dave Righetti	.05	.02	.01
308 Jack Clark	.10	.05	.01
309 Willie Randolph	.10	.05	.01
310 Tommy John	.10	.05	.01
311 Mike Pagliarulo	.05	.02	.01
312 Rickey Henderson	.25	.11	.03
313 Rafael Santana	.05	.02	.01
314 Don Mattingly	1.00	.45	.12
315 Dave Winfield	.25	.11	.03
316 Richard Dotson	.05	.02	.01
317 Tim Belcher	.05	.02	.01
318 Damon Berryhill	.05	.02	.01
319 Jay Buhner	.40	.18	.05
320 Cecil Espy	.05	.02	.01
321 Dave Gallagher	.05	.02	.01
322 Ron Gant	.25	.11	.03
323 Paul Gibson	.05	.02	.01
324 Mark Grace	.40	.18	.05
325 Chris Sabo ROY	.05	.02	.01
326 Walt Weiss ROY	.10	.05	.01
xx Album	1.00	.45	.12

1989 Topps/O-Pee-Chee Sticker Backs

These 67 cards were actually the backs of the 1989 O-Pee-Chee Stickers. The white-bordered cards measure approximately 2 1/8" by 3" and have colorful backgrounds behind the cut-out color player photos. Cards 1-33 feature NL players; cards 34-66 feature AL players. The player's name and position appear in a colored banner near the bottom of the photo. Below are player biography and statistics. The cards are numbered at the lower left.

	MINT	NRMT	EXC
COMPLETE SET (67)	6.00	2.70	.75
COMMON CARD (1-67)	.05	.02	.01

Card	MINT	NRMT	EXC
1 George Brett	.60	.25	.07
2 Don Mattingly	.75	.35	.09
3 Mark McGwire	.25	.11	.03
4 Julio Franco	.10	.05	.01
5 Harold Reynolds	.10	.05	.01
6 Lou Whitaker	.10	.05	.01
7 Wade Boggs	.20	.09	.03
8 Gary Gaetti	.10	.05	.01
9 Paul Molitor	.20	.09	.03
10 Tony Fernandez	.05	.02	.01
11 Cal Ripken	1.50	.70	.19
12 Alan Trammell	.10	.05	.01
13 Jose Canseco	.20	.09	.03
14 Joe Carter	.15	.07	.02
15 Dwight Evans	.10	.05	.01
16 Mike Greenwell	.05	.02	.01
17 Dave Henderson	.05	.02	.01
18 Rickey Henderson	.20	.09	.03
19 Kirby Puckett	.40	.18	.05
20 Dave Winfield	.20	.09	.03
21 Robin Yount	.20	.09	.03
22 Bob Boone	.10	.05	.01
23 Carlton Fisk	.20	.09	.03
24 Geno Petralli	.05	.02	.01
25 Roger Clemens	.20	.09	.03
26 Mark Gubicza	.05	.02	.01
27 Dave Stewart	.10	.05	.01
28 Teddy Higuera	.05	.02	.01
29 Bruce Hurst	.05	.02	.01
30 Frank Viola	.05	.02	.01
31 Dennis Eckersley	.10	.05	.01
32 Doug Jones	.05	.02	.01
33 Jeff Reardon	.10	.05	.01
34 Will Clark	.25	.11	.03
35 Glenn Davis	.05	.02	.01
36 Andres Galarraga	.15	.07	.02
37 Juan Samuel	.05	.02	.01
38 Ryne Sandberg	.40	.18	.05
39 Steve Sax	.05	.02	.01
40 Bobby Bonilla	.15	.07	.02
41 Howard Johnson	.05	.02	.01
42 Vance Law	.05	.02	.01
43 Shawon Dunston	.05	.02	.01
44 Barry Larkin	.25	.11	.03
45 Ozzie Smith	.30	.14	.04
46 Barry Bonds	.50	.23	.06
47 Eric Davis	.05	.02	.01
48 Andre Dawson	.10	.05	.01
49 Kirk Gibson	.15	.07	.02
50 Tony Gwynn	.60	.25	.07

Card	MINT	NRMT	EXC
☐ 51 Kevin McReynolds	.05	.02	.01
☐ 52 Rafael Palmeiro	.20	.09	.03
☐ 53 Darryl Strawberry	.10	.05	.01
☐ 54 Andy Van Slyke	.10	.05	.01
☐ 55 Gary Carter	.10	.05	.01
☐ 56 Mike LaValliere	.05	.02	.01
☐ 57 Benito Santiago	.05	.02	.01
☐ 58 Dave Cone	.20	.09	.03
☐ 59 Dwight Gooden	.10	.05	.01
☐ 60 Orel Hershiser	.10	.05	.01
☐ 61 Tom Browning	.05	.02	.01
☐ 62 Danny Jackson	.05	.02	.01
☐ 63 Bob Knepper	.05	.02	.01
☐ 64 Mark Davis	.05	.02	.01
☐ 65 John Franco	.10	.05	.01
☐ 66 Randy Myers	.10	.05	.01
☐ 67 Checklist	.05	.02	.01

1989 Topps Ritz Mattingly

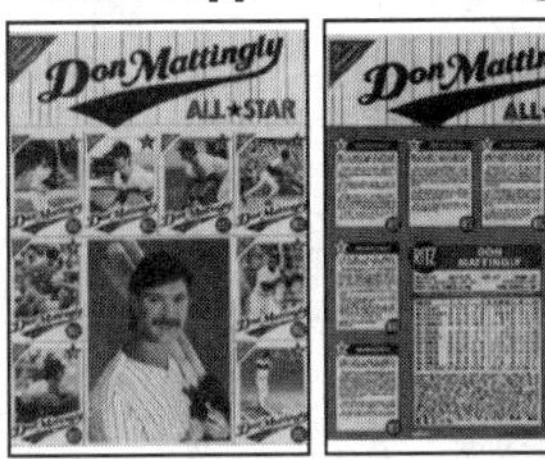

This set is actually a sheet of cards all featuring the career of Don Mattingly. The set was produced by Topps for Nabisco (Ritz Crackers) and was available via a send-in offer involving two proofs of purchase of boxes of Ritz Crackers. The uncut sheet is approximately 14" by 10 5/8". Included on the sheet are eight standard sized cards surrounding one large (5 1/8" by 7") card. In each case the Yankee logo has been airbrushed off the card.

	MINT	NRMT	EXC
COMPLETE SET (9)	7.50	3.40	.95
COMMON CARD (1-9)	1.00	.45	.12
☐ 1 Don Mattingly 1972	1.00	.45	.12
☐ 2 Don Mattingly 1981	1.00	.45	.12
☐ 3 Don Mattingly 1984	1.00	.45	.12
☐ 4 Don Mattingly 1985	1.00	.45	.12
☐ 5 Don Mattingly 1986	1.00	.45	.12
☐ 6 Don Mattingly 1987	1.00	.45	.12
☐ 7 Don Mattingly 1988	1.00	.45	.12
☐ 8 Don Mattingly 1989	1.00	.45	.12
☐ 9 Don Mattingly 5 1/8" by 7"; complete stats	1.00	.45	.12

1989 Topps UK Minis

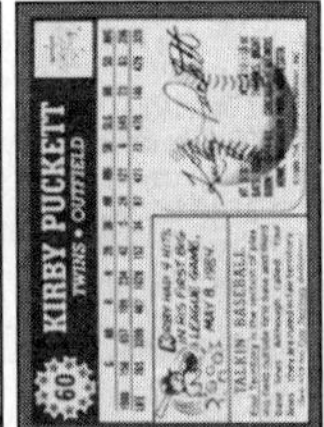

The 1989 Topps UK Minis baseball set contains 88 cards measuring approximately 2 1/8" by 3". The fronts are red, white and blue. The backs are yellow and red, and feature 1988 and career stats. The cards were distributed in five-card poly packs. The card set numbering is in alphabetical order by player's name.

	MINT	NRMT	EXC
COMPLETE SET (88)	12.00	5.50	1.50
COMMON CARD (1-88)	.10	.05	.01
☐ 1 Brady Anderson	1.25	.55	.16
☐ 2 Harold Baines	.20	.09	.03
☐ 3 George Bell	.10	.05	.01
☐ 4 Wade Boggs	.40	.18	.05
☐ 5 Barry Bonds	1.25	.55	.16
☐ 6 Bobby Bonilla	.30	.14	.04
☐ 7 George Brett	1.50	.70	.19
☐ 8 Hubie Brooks	.10	.05	.01
☐ 9 Tom Brunansky	.10	.05	.01
☐ 10 Jay Buhner	.50	.23	.06
☐ 11 Brett Butler	.20	.09	.03
☐ 12 Jose Canseco	.60	.25	.07
☐ 13 Joe Carter	.40	.18	.05
☐ 14 Jack Clark	.10	.05	.01
☐ 15 Will Clark	.50	.23	.06
☐ 16 Roger Clemens	.50	.23	.06
☐ 17 David Cone	.30	.14	.04
☐ 18 Alvin Davis	.10	.05	.01
☐ 19 Eric Davis	.20	.09	.03
☐ 20 Glenn Davis	.10	.05	.01
☐ 21 Andre Dawson	.30	.14	.04
☐ 22 Bill Doran	.10	.05	.01
☐ 23 Dennis Eckersley	.20	.09	.03
☐ 24 Dwight Evans	.20	.09	.03
☐ 25 Tony Fernandez	.10	.05	.01
☐ 26 Carlton Fisk	.60	.25	.07
☐ 27 John Franco	.20	.09	.03
☐ 28 Andres Galarraga	.30	.14	.04
☐ 29 Ron Gant	.40	.18	.05
☐ 30 Kirk Gibson	.20	.09	.03
☐ 31 Dwight Gooden	.20	.09	.03
☐ 32 Mike Greenwell	.10	.05	.01
☐ 33 Mark Gubicza	.10	.05	.01
☐ 34 Pedro Guerrero	.10	.05	.01
☐ 35 Ozzie Guillen	.10	.05	.01
☐ 36 Tony Gwynn	2.00	.90	.25
☐ 37 Rickey Henderson	.50	.23	.06
☐ 38 Orel Hershiser	.20	.09	.03
☐ 39 Teddy Higuera	.10	.05	.01
☐ 40 Charlie Hough	.10	.05	.01
☐ 41 Kent Hrbek	.10	.05	.01
☐ 42 Bruce Hurst	.10	.05	.01
☐ 43 Bo Jackson	.20	.09	.03
☐ 44 Gregg Jefferies	.20	.09	.03
☐ 45 Ricky Jordan	.10	.05	.01
☐ 46 Wally Joyner	.10	.05	.01
☐ 47 Mark Langston	.10	.05	.01
☐ 48 Mike Marshall	.10	.05	.01
☐ 49 Don Mattingly	2.00	.90	.25
☐ 50 Fred McGriff	.50	.23	.06
☐ 51 Mark McGwire	1.50	.70	.19
☐ 52 Kevin McReynolds	.10	.05	.01
☐ 53 Paul Molitor	.40	.18	.05
☐ 54 Jack Morris	.20	.09	.03
☐ 55 Dale Murphy	.30	.14	.04
☐ 56 Eddie Murray	1.00	.45	.12
☐ 57 Pete O'Brien	.10	.05	.01
☐ 58 Rafael Palmeiro	.40	.18	.05
☐ 59 Gerald Perry	.10	.05	.01
☐ 60 Kirby Puckett	2.00	.90	.25
☐ 61 Tim Raines	.20	.09	.03
☐ 62 Johnny Ray	.10	.05	.01
☐ 63 Rick Reuschel	.10	.05	.01
☐ 64 Cal Ripken	4.00	1.80	.50
☐ 65 Chris Sabo	.10	.05	.01
☐ 66 Juan Samuel	.10	.05	.01
☐ 67 Ryne Sandberg	1.50	.70	.19
☐ 68 Benito Santiago	.10	.05	.01
☐ 69 Steve Sax	.10	.05	.01
☐ 70 Mike Schmidt	1.00	.45	.12
☐ 71 Ruben Sierra	.20	.09	.03
☐ 72 Ozzie Smith	1.50	.70	.19
☐ 73 Cory Snyder	.10	.05	.01
☐ 74 Dave Stewart	.10	.05	.01
☐ 75 Darryl Strawberry	.20	.09	.03
☐ 76 Greg Swindell	.10	.05	.01
☐ 77 Alan Trammell	.20	.09	.03
☐ 78 Fernando Valenzuela	.20	.09	.03
☐ 79 Andy Van Slyke	.10	.05	.01
☐ 80 Frank Viola	.10	.05	.01
☐ 81 Claudell Washington	.10	.05	.01
☐ 82 Walt Weiss	.10	.05	.01
☐ 83 Lou Whitaker	.20	.09	.03
☐ 84 Dave Winfield	.50	.23	.06
☐ 85 Mike Witt	.10	.05	.01
☐ 86 Gerald Young	.10	.05	.01
☐ 87 Robin Yount	.30	.14	.04
☐ 88 Checklist Card	.10	.05	.01

1989-90 Topps Senior League

The 1989-90 Topps Senior League baseball set was issued second among the three sets commemorating the first Senior league season. This set was issued in set form in its own box containing all 132 standard-size cards.

	MINT	NRMT	EXC
COMPLETE SET (132)	5.00	2.20	.60
COMMON CARD (1-132)	.05	.02	.01
☐ 1 George Foster	.15	.07	.02
☐ 2 Dwight Lowry	.05	.02	.01
☐ 3 Bob Jones	.05	.02	.01
☐ 4 Clete Boyer MG	.10	.05	.01
☐ 5 Rafael Landestoy	.05	.02	.01
☐ 6 Bob Shirley	.05	.02	.01
☐ 7 Ivan Murrell	.05	.02	.01
☐ 8 Jerry White	.05	.02	.01
☐ 9 Steve Henderson	.05	.02	.01
☐ 10 Marty Castillo	.05	.02	.01
☐ 11 Bruce Kison	.05	.02	.01
☐ 12 George Hendrick	.10	.05	.01
☐ 13 Bernie Carbo	.05	.02	.01
☐ 14 Jerry Martin	.05	.02	.01
☐ 15 Al Hrabosky	.10	.05	.01
☐ 16 Luis Gomez	.05	.02	.01
☐ 17 Dick Drago	.05	.02	.01
☐ 18 Bobby Ramos	.05	.02	.01
☐ 19 Joe Pittman	.05	.02	.01
☐ 20 Ike Blessitt	.05	.02	.01
☐ 21 Bill Travers	.05	.02	.01
☐ 22 Dick Williams MG	.10	.05	.01
☐ 23 Randy Lerch	.05	.02	.01
☐ 24 Tom Spencer	.05	.02	.01
☐ 25 Graig Nettles	.15	.07	.02
☐ 26 Jim Gideon	.05	.02	.01
☐ 27 Al Bumbry	.05	.02	.01
☐ 28 Tom Murphy	.05	.02	.01
☐ 29 Rodney Scott	.05	.02	.01
☐ 30 Alan Bannister	.05	.02	.01
☐ 31 John D'Acquisto	.05	.02	.01
☐ 32 Bert Campaneris	.10	.05	.01
☐ 33 Bill Lee	.10	.05	.01
☐ 34 Jerry Grote	.10	.05	.01
☐ 35 Ken Reitz	.05	.02	.01
☐ 36 Al Oliver	.10	.05	.01
☐ 37 Tim Stoddard	.05	.02	.01
☐ 38 Lenny Randle	.05	.02	.01
☐ 39 Rick Manning	.05	.02	.01
☐ 40 Bobby Bonds	.25	.11	.03
☐ 41 Rick Wise	.05	.02	.01
☐ 42 Sal Butera	.05	.02	.01
☐ 43 Ed Figueroa	.05	.02	.01
☐ 44 Ron Washington	.05	.02	.01
☐ 45 Elias Sosa	.05	.02	.01
☐ 46 Dan Driessen	.05	.02	.01
☐ 47 Wayne Nordhagen	.05	.02	.01
☐ 48 Vida Blue	.10	.05	.01
☐ 49 Butch Hobson	.05	.02	.01
☐ 50 Randy Bass	.05	.02	.01
☐ 51 Paul Mirabella	.05	.02	.01
☐ 52 Steve Kemp	.05	.02	.01
☐ 53 Kim Allen	.05	.02	.01
☐ 54 Stan Cliburn	.05	.02	.01
☐ 55 Derrel Thomas	.05	.02	.01
☐ 56 Pete Falcone	.05	.02	.01
☐ 57 Willie Aikens	.05	.02	.01
☐ 58 Toby Harrah	.10	.05	.01
☐ 59 Bob Tolan	.05	.02	.01
☐ 60 Rick Waits	.05	.02	.01
☐ 61 Jim Morrison	.05	.02	.01
☐ 62 Stan Bahnsen	.05	.02	.01
☐ 63 Gene Richards	.05	.02	.01
☐ 64 Dave Cash	.05	.02	.01
☐ 65 Rollie Fingers	.50	.23	.06
☐ 66 Butch Benton	.05	.02	.01
☐ 67 Tim Ireland	.05	.02	.01
☐ 68 Rick Lysander	.05	.02	.01
☐ 69 Cesar Cedeno	.10	.05	.01
☐ 70 Jim Willoughby	.05	.02	.01
☐ 71 Bill Madlock	.25	.11	.03
☐ 72 Lee Lacy	.05	.02	.01
☐ 73 Milt Wilcox	.05	.02	.01
☐ 74 Ron Pruitt	.05	.02	.01
☐ 75 Wayne Krenchicki	.05	.02	.01
☐ 76 Earl Weaver MG	.50	.23	.06
☐ 77 Pedro Borbon	.05	.02	.01
☐ 78 Jose Cruz	.10	.05	.01
☐ 79 Steve Ontiveros	.05	.02	.01
☐ 80 Mike Easler	.05	.02	.01
☐ 81 Amos Otis	.10	.05	.01
☐ 82 Mickey Mahler	.05	.02	.01
☐ 83 Orlando Gonzalez	.05	.02	.01
☐ 84 Doug Simunic	.05	.02	.01
☐ 85 Felix Millan	.05	.02	.01
☐ 86 Garth Iorg	.05	.02	.01
☐ 87 Pete Broberg	.05	.02	.01
☐ 88 Roy Howell	.05	.02	.01
☐ 89 Dave LaRoche	.05	.02	.01
☐ 90 Jerry Manuel	.05	.02	.01
☐ 91 Tony Scott	.05	.02	.01
☐ 92 Larvell Blanks	.05	.02	.01
☐ 93 Joaquin Andujar	.10	.05	.01
☐ 94 Tito Landrum	.05	.02	.01
☐ 95 Joe Sambito	.05	.02	.01
☐ 96 Pat Dobson	.05	.02	.01
☐ 97 Dan Meyer	.05	.02	.01
☐ 98 Clint Hurdle	.05	.02	.01
☐ 99 Pete LaCock	.05	.02	.01
☐ 100 Bob Galasso	.05	.02	.01
☐ 101 Dave Kingman	.25	.11	.03
☐ 102 Jon Matlack	.05	.02	.01
☐ 103 Larry Harlow	.05	.02	.01
☐ 104 Rick Peterson	.05	.02	.01
☐ 105 Joe Hicks	.05	.02	.01
☐ 106 Bill Campbell	.05	.02	.01
☐ 107 Tom Paciorek	.10	.05	.01
☐ 108 Ray Burris	.05	.02	.01
☐ 109 Ken Landreaux	.05	.02	.01
☐ 110 Steve McCatty	.05	.02	.01
☐ 111 Ron LeFlore	.10	.05	.01
☐ 112 Joe Decker	.05	.02	.01
☐ 113 Leon Roberts	.05	.02	.01
☐ 114 Doug Corbett	.05	.02	.01
☐ 115 Mickey Rivers	.10	.05	.01
☐ 116 Dock Ellis	.05	.02	.01
☐ 117 Ron Jackson	.05	.02	.01
☐ 118 Bob Molinaro	.05	.02	.01
☐ 119 Fergie Jenkins	.50	.23	.06
☐ 120 U.L. Washington	.05	.02	.01
☐ 121 Roy Thomas	.05	.02	.01
☐ 122 Hal McRae	.15	.07	.02
☐ 123 Juan Eichelberger	.05	.02	.01
☐ 124 Gary Rajsich	.05	.02	.01
☐ 125 Dennis Leonard	.05	.02	.01
☐ 126 Walt Williams	.05	.02	.01
☐ 127 Rennie Stennett	.05	.02	.01
☐ 128 Jim Bibby	.05	.02	.01
☐ 129 Dyar Miller	.05	.02	.01
☐ 130 Luis Pujols	.05	.02	.01
☐ 131 Juan Beniquez	.05	.02	.01
☐ 132 Checklist Card	.05	.02	.01

1990 Topps

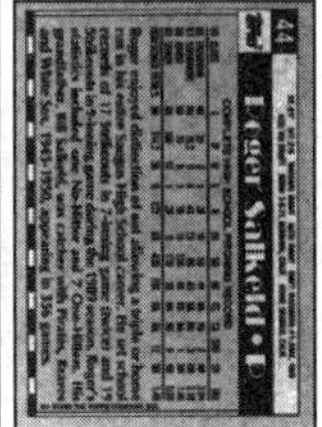

The 1990 Topps set contains 792 standard-size cards. Cards were issued primarily in wax packs, rack packs and hobby and retail factory sets. Card fronts feature various colored borders with the player's name at the bottom and team name at top. Subsets include All-Stars (385-407), Turn Back the Clock (661-665) and Draft Picks (scattered throughout the set). The key Rookie Cards in this set are Juan Gonzalez, Marquis Grissom, Ben McDonald, Sammy Sosa, Frank Thomas, Larry Walker and Bernie Williams. The Thomas card (414A) was printed without his name on front creating a scarce variation. The card is rarely seen and, for a newer issue, has experienced unprecedented growth as far as value. Be careful when purchasing this card as counterfeits have been produced.

	MINT	NRMT	EXC
COMPLETE SET (792)	12.00	5.50	1.50
COMPLETE FACT.SET (792)	15.00	6.75	1.85
COMMON CARD (1-792)	.05	.02	.01
☐ 1 Nolan Ryan	.75	.35	.09
☐ 2 Nolan Ryan Salute New York Mets	.40	.18	.05
☐ 3 Nolan Ryan Salute California Angels	.40	.18	.05
☐ 4 Nolan Ryan Salute Houston Astros	.40	.18	.05
☐ 5 Nolan Ryan Salute Texas Rangers UER (Says Texas Stadium rather than Arlington Stadium)	.40	.18	.05
☐ 6 Vince Coleman RB (50 consecutive SB's	.05	.02	.01
☐ 7 Rickey Henderson RB (40 career leadoff HR's	.15	.07	.02
☐ 8 Cal Ripken RB (20 or more homers for 8 consecutive years, record for shortstops)	.40	.18	.05
☐ 9 Eric Plunk	.05	.02	.01
☐ 10 Barry Larkin	.15	.07	.02
☐ 11 Paul Gibson	.05	.02	.01
☐ 12 Joe Girardi	.10	.05	.01
☐ 13 Mark Williamson	.05	.02	.01
☐ 14 Mike Fetters	.10	.05	.01
☐ 15 Teddy Higuera	.05	.02	.01
☐ 16 Kent Anderson	.05	.02	.01
☐ 17 Kelly Downs	.05	.02	.01
☐ 18 Carlos Quintana	.05	.02	.01
☐ 19 Al Newman	.05	.02	.01
☐ 20 Mark Gubicza	.05	.02	.01
☐ 21 Jeff Torborg MG	.05	.02	.01
☐ 22 Bruce Ruffin	.05	.02	.01
☐ 23 Randy Velarde	.05	.02	.01
☐ 24 Joe Hesketh	.05	.02	.01
☐ 25 Willie Randolph	.10	.05	.01
☐ 26 Don Slaught	.05	.02	.01
☐ 27 Rick Leach	.05	.02	.01
☐ 28 Duane Ward	.05	.02	.01
☐ 29 John Cangelosi	.05	.02	.01
☐ 30 David Cone	.15	.07	.02
☐ 31 Henry Cotto	.05	.02	.01
☐ 32 John Farrell	.05	.02	.01
☐ 33 Greg Walker	.05	.02	.01
☐ 34 Tony Fossas	.05	.02	.01
☐ 35 Benito Santiago	.05	.02	.01
☐ 36 John Costello	.05	.02	.01
☐ 37 Domingo Ramos	.05	.02	.01
☐ 38 Wes Gardner	.05	.02	.01
☐ 39 Curt Ford	.05	.02	.01
☐ 40 Jay Howell	.05	.02	.01

☐ 41 Matt Williams .15 .07 .02
☐ 42 Jeff M. Robinson .05 .02 .01
☐ 43 Dante Bichette .15 .07 .02
☐ 44 Roger Salkeld FDP .05 .02 .01
☐ 45 Dave Parker UER .10 .05 .01
(Born in Jackson, not Calhoun)
☐ 46 Rob Dibble .05 .02 .01
☐ 47 Brian Harper .05 .02 .01
☐ 48 Zane Smith .05 .02 .01
☐ 49 Tom Lawless .05 .02 .01
☐ 50 Glenn Davis .05 .02 .01
☐ 51 Doug Rader MG .05 .02 .01
☐ 52 Jack Daugherty .05 .02 .01
☐ 53 Mike LaCoss .05 .02 .01
☐ 54 Joel Skinner .05 .02 .01
☐ 55 Darrell Evans UER .10 .05 .01
(HR total should be 414, not 424)
☐ 56 Franklin Stubbs .05 .02 .01
☐ 57 Greg Vaughn .15 .07 .02
☐ 58 Keith Miller .05 .02 .01
☐ 59 Ted Power .05 .02 .01
☐ 60 George Brett .40 .18 .05
☐ 61 Deion Sanders .20 .09 .03
☐ 62 Ramon Martinez .15 .07 .02
☐ 63 Mike Pagliarulo .05 .02 .01
☐ 64 Danny Darwin .05 .02 .01
☐ 65 Devon White .10 .05 .01
☐ 66 Greg Litton .05 .02 .01
☐ 67 Scott Sanderson .05 .02 .01
☐ 68 Dave Henderson .05 .02 .01
☐ 69 Todd Frohwirth .05 .02 .01
☐ 70 Mike Greenwell .05 .02 .01
☐ 71 Allan Anderson .05 .02 .01
☐ 72 Jeff Huson .05 .02 .01
☐ 73 Bob Milacki .05 .02 .01
☐ 74 Jeff Jackson FDP .05 .02 .01
☐ 75 Doug Jones .05 .02 .01
☐ 76 Dave Valle .05 .02 .01
☐ 77 Dave Bergman .05 .02 .01
☐ 78 Mike Flanagan .05 .02 .01
☐ 79 Ron Kittle .05 .02 .01
☐ 80 Jeff Russell .05 .02 .01
☐ 81 Bob Rodgers MG .05 .02 .01
☐ 82 Scott Terry .05 .02 .01
☐ 83 Hensley Meulens .05 .02 .01
☐ 84 Ray Searage .05 .02 .01
☐ 85 Juan Samuel .05 .02 .01
☐ 86 Paul Kilgus .05 .02 .01
☐ 87 Rick Luecken .05 .02 .01
☐ 88 Glenn Braggs .05 .02 .01
☐ 89 Clint Zavaras .05 .02 .01
☐ 90 Jack Clark .10 .05 .01
☐ 91 Steve Frey .05 .02 .01
☐ 92 Mike Stanley .05 .02 .01
☐ 93 Shawn Hillegas .05 .02 .01
☐ 94 Herm Winningham .05 .02 .01
☐ 95 Todd Worrell .05 .02 .01
☐ 96 Jody Reed .05 .02 .01
☐ 97 Curt Schilling .05 .02 .01
☐ 98 Jose Gonzalez .05 .02 .01
☐ 99 Rich Monteleone .05 .02 .01
☐ 100 Will Clark .15 .07 .02
☐ 101 Shane Rawley .05 .02 .01
☐ 102 Stan Javier .05 .02 .01
☐ 103 Marvin Freeman .05 .02 .01
☐ 104 Bob Knepper .05 .02 .01
☐ 105 Randy Myers .10 .05 .01
☐ 106 Charlie O'Brien .05 .02 .01
☐ 107 Fred Lynn .05 .02 .01
☐ 108 Rod Nichols .05 .02 .01
☐ 109 Roberto Kelly .05 .02 .01
☐ 110 Tommy Helms MG .05 .02 .01
☐ 111 Ed Whited .05 .02 .01
☐ 112 Glenn Wilson .05 .02 .01
☐ 113 Manny Lee .05 .02 .01
☐ 114 Mike Bielecki .05 .02 .01
☐ 115 Tony Pena .05 .02 .01
☐ 116 Floyd Bannister .05 .02 .01
☐ 117 Mike Sharperson .05 .02 .01
☐ 118 Erik Hanson .10 .05 .01
☐ 119 Billy Hatcher .05 .02 .01
☐ 120 John Franco .05 .02 .01
☐ 121 Robin Ventura .15 .07 .02
☐ 122 Shawn Abner .05 .02 .01
☐ 123 Rich Gedman .05 .02 .01
☐ 124 Dave Dravecky .10 .05 .01
☐ 125 Kent Hrbek .10 .05 .01
☐ 126 Randy Kramer .05 .02 .01
☐ 127 Mike Devereaux .05 .02 .01
☐ 128 Checklist 1 .05 .02 .01
☐ 129 Ron Jones .05 .02 .01
☐ 130 Bert Blyleven .10 .05 .01
☐ 131 Matt Nokes .05 .02 .01
☐ 132 Lance Blankenship .05 .02 .01
☐ 133 Ricky Horton .05 .02 .01
☐ 134 Earl Cunningham FDP .05 .02 .01
☐ 135 Dave Magadan .05 .02 .01
☐ 136 Kevin Brown .15 .07 .02
☐ 137 Marty Pevey .05 .02 .01
☐ 138 Al Leiter .10 .05 .01
☐ 139 Greg Brock .05 .02 .01
☐ 140 Andre Dawson .10 .05 .01
☐ 141 John Hart MG .05 .02 .01
☐ 142 Jeff Wetherby .05 .02 .01
☐ 143 Rafael Belliard .05 .02 .01
☐ 144 Bud Black .05 .02 .01
☐ 145 Terry Steinbach .10 .05 .01
☐ 146 Rob Richie .05 .02 .01
☐ 147 Chuck Finley .10 .05 .01
☐ 148 Edgar Martinez .15 .07 .02
☐ 149 Steve Farr .05 .02 .01
☐ 150 Kirk Gibson .10 .05 .01
☐ 151 Rick Mahler .05 .02 .01
☐ 152 Lonnie Smith .05 .02 .01
☐ 153 Randy Milligan .05 .02 .01
☐ 154 Mike Maddux .05 .02 .01
☐ 155 Ellis Burks .15 .07 .02
☐ 156 Ken Patterson .05 .02 .01
☐ 157 Craig Biggio .15 .07 .02
☐ 158 Craig Lefferts .05 .02 .01
☐ 159 Mike Felder .05 .02 .01
☐ 160 Dave Righetti .05 .02 .01
☐ 161 Harold Reynolds .05 .02 .01
☐ 162 Todd Zeile .10 .05 .01
☐ 163 Phil Bradley .05 .02 .01
☐ 164 Jeff Juden FDP .05 .02 .01
☐ 165 Walt Weiss .05 .02 .01
☐ 166 Bobby Witt .05 .02 .01
☐ 167 Kevin Appier .15 .07 .02
☐ 168 Jose Lind .05 .02 .01
☐ 169 Richard Dotson .05 .02 .01
☐ 170 George Bell .05 .02 .01
☐ 171 Russ Nixon MG .05 .02 .01
☐ 172 Tom Lampkin .05 .02 .01
☐ 173 Tim Belcher .05 .02 .01
☐ 174 Jeff Kunkel .05 .02 .01
☐ 175 Mike Moore .05 .02 .01
☐ 176 Luis Quinones .05 .02 .01
☐ 177 Mike Henneman .05 .02 .01
☐ 178 Chris James .05 .02 .01
☐ 179 Brian Holton .05 .02 .01
☐ 180 Tim Raines .10 .05 .01
☐ 181 Juan Agosto .05 .02 .01
☐ 182 Mookie Wilson .05 .02 .01
☐ 183 Steve Lake .05 .02 .01
☐ 184 Danny Cox .05 .02 .01
☐ 185 Ruben Sierra .10 .05 .01
☐ 186 Dave LaPoint .05 .02 .01
☐ 187 Rick Wrona .05 .02 .01
☐ 188 Mike Smithson .05 .02 .01
☐ 189 Dick Schofield .05 .02 .01
☐ 190 Rick Reuschel .05 .02 .01
☐ 191 Pat Borders .05 .02 .01
☐ 192 Don August .05 .02 .01
☐ 193 Andy Benes .15 .07 .02
☐ 194 Glenallen Hill .10 .05 .01
☐ 195 Tim Burke .05 .02 .01
☐ 196 Gerald Young .05 .02 .01
☐ 197 Doug Drabek .05 .02 .01
☐ 198 Mike Marshall .05 .02 .01
☐ 199 Sergio Valdez .05 .02 .01
☐ 200 Don Mattingly .50 .23 .06
☐ 201 Cito Gaston MG .05 .02 .01
☐ 202 Mike Macfarlane .05 .02 .01
☐ 203 Mike Roesler .05 .02 .01
☐ 204 Bob Dernier .05 .02 .01
☐ 205 Mark Davis .05 .02 .01
☐ 206 Nick Esasky .05 .02 .01
☐ 207 Bob Ojeda .05 .02 .01
☐ 208 Brook Jacoby .05 .02 .01
☐ 209 Greg Mathews .05 .02 .01
☐ 210 Ryne Sandberg .25 .11 .03
☐ 211 John Cerutti .05 .02 .01
☐ 212 Joe Orsulak .05 .02 .01
☐ 213 Scott Bankhead .05 .02 .01
☐ 214 Terry Francona .05 .02 .01
☐ 215 Kirk McCaskill .05 .02 .01
☐ 216 Ricky Jordan .05 .02 .01
☐ 217 Don Robinson .05 .02 .01
☐ 218 Wally Backman .05 .02 .01
☐ 219 Donn Pall .05 .02 .01
☐ 220 Barry Bonds .25 .11 .03
☐ 221 Gary Mielke .05 .02 .01
☐ 222 Kurt Stillwell UER .05 .02 .01
(Graduate misspelled as gradute)
☐ 223 Tommy Gregg .05 .02 .01
☐ 224 Delino DeShields .15 .07 .02
☐ 225 Jim Deshaies .05 .02 .01
☐ 226 Mickey Hatcher .05 .02 .01
☐ 227 Kevin Tapani .10 .05 .01
☐ 228 Dave Martinez .05 .02 .01
☐ 229 David Wells .05 .02 .01
☐ 230 Keith Hernandez .10 .05 .01
☐ 231 Jack McKeon MG .05 .02 .01
☐ 232 Darnell Coles .05 .02 .01
☐ 233 Ken Hill .15 .07 .02
☐ 234 Mariano Duncan .05 .02 .01
☐ 235 Jeff Reardon .10 .05 .01
☐ 236 Hal Morris .10 .05 .01
☐ 237 Kevin Ritz .05 .02 .01
☐ 238 Felix Jose .05 .02 .01
☐ 239 Eric Show .05 .02 .01
☐ 240 Mark Grace .15 .07 .02
☐ 241 Mike Krukow .05 .02 .01
☐ 242 Fred Manrique .05 .02 .01
☐ 243 Barry Jones .05 .02 .01
☐ 244 Bill Schroeder .05 .02 .01
☐ 245 Roger Clemens .20 .09 .03
☐ 246 Jim Eisenreich .05 .02 .01
☐ 247 Jerry Reed .05 .02 .01
☐ 248 Dave Anderson .05 .02 .01
☐ 249 Mike(Texas) Smith .05 .02 .01
☐ 250 Jose Canseco .15 .07 .02
☐ 251 Jeff Blauser .10 .05 .01
☐ 252 Otis Nixon .05 .02 .01
☐ 253 Mark Portugal .05 .02 .01
☐ 254 Francisco Cabrera .05 .02 .01
☐ 255 Bobby Thigpen .05 .02 .01
☐ 256 Marvell Wynne .05 .02 .01
☐ 257 Jose DeLeon .05 .02 .01
☐ 258 Barry Lyons .05 .02 .01
☐ 259 Lance McCullers .05 .02 .01
☐ 260 Eric Davis .10 .05 .01
☐ 261 Whitey Herzog MG .10 .05 .01
☐ 262 Checklist 2 .05 .02 .01
☐ 263 Mel Stottlemyre Jr. .05 .02 .01
☐ 264 Bryan Clutterbuck .05 .02 .01
☐ 265 Pete O'Brien .05 .02 .01
☐ 266 German Gonzalez .05 .02 .01
☐ 267 Mark Davidson .05 .02 .01
☐ 268 Rob Murphy .05 .02 .01
☐ 269 Dickie Thon .05 .02 .01
☐ 270 Dave Stewart .10 .05 .01
☐ 271 Chet Lemon .05 .02 .01
☐ 272 Bryan Harvey .05 .02 .01
☐ 273 Bobby Bonilla .10 .05 .01
☐ 274 Mauro Gozzo .05 .02 .01
☐ 275 Mickey Tettleton .10 .05 .01
☐ 276 Gary Thurman .05 .02 .01
☐ 277 Lenny Harris .05 .02 .01
☐ 278 Pascual Perez .05 .02 .01
☐ 279 Steve Buechele .05 .02 .01
☐ 280 Lou Whitaker .10 .05 .01
☐ 281 Kevin Bass .05 .02 .01
☐ 282 Derek Lilliquist .05 .02 .01
☐ 283 Joey Belle .75 .35 .09
☐ 284 Mark Gardner .05 .02 .01
☐ 285 Willie McGee .05 .02 .01
☐ 286 Lee Guetterman .05 .02 .01
☐ 287 Vance Law .05 .02 .01
☐ 288 Greg Briley .05 .02 .01
☐ 289 Norm Charlton .05 .02 .01
☐ 290 Robin Yount .15 .07 .02
☐ 291 Dave Johnson MG .10 .05 .01
☐ 292 Jim Gott .05 .02 .01
☐ 293 Mike Gallego .05 .02 .01
☐ 294 Craig McMurtry .05 .02 .01
☐ 295 Fred McGriff .15 .07 .02
☐ 296 Jeff Ballard .05 .02 .01
☐ 297 Tommy Herr .05 .02 .01
☐ 298 Dan Gladden .05 .02 .01
☐ 299 Adam Peterson .05 .02 .01
☐ 300 Bo Jackson .10 .05 .01
☐ 301 Don Aase .05 .02 .01
☐ 302 Marcus Lawton .05 .02 .01
☐ 303 Rick Cerone .05 .02 .01
☐ 304 Marty Clary .05 .02 .01
☐ 305 Eddie Murray .25 .11 .03
☐ 306 Tom Niedenfuer .05 .02 .01
☐ 307 Bip Roberts .05 .02 .01
☐ 308 Jose Guzman .05 .02 .01
☐ 309 Eric Yelding .05 .02 .01
☐ 310 Steve Bedrosian .05 .02 .01
☐ 311 Dwight Smith .05 .02 .01
☐ 312 Dan Quisenberry .05 .02 .01
☐ 313 Gus Polidor .05 .02 .01
☐ 314 Donald Harris FDP .05 .02 .01
☐ 315 Bruce Hurst .05 .02 .01
☐ 316 Carney Lansford .10 .05 .01
☐ 317 Mark Guthrie .05 .02 .01
☐ 318 Wallace Johnson .05 .02 .01
☐ 319 Dion James .05 .02 .01
☐ 320 Dave Stieb .05 .02 .01
☐ 321 Joe Morgan MG .05 .02 .01
☐ 322 Junior Ortiz .05 .02 .01
☐ 323 Willie Wilson .05 .02 .01
☐ 324 Pete Harnisch .05 .02 .01
☐ 325 Robby Thompson .05 .02 .01
☐ 326 Tom McCarthy .05 .02 .01
☐ 327 Ken Williams .05 .02 .01
☐ 328 Curt Young .05 .02 .01
☐ 329 Oddibe McDowell .05 .02 .01
☐ 330 Ron Darling .05 .02 .01
☐ 331 Juan Gonzalez 2.00 .90 .25
☐ 332 Paul O'Neill .10 .05 .01
☐ 333 Bill Wegman .05 .02 .01
☐ 334 Johnny Ray .05 .02 .01
☐ 335 Andy Hawkins .05 .02 .01
☐ 336 Ken Griffey Jr. 1.50 .70 .19
☐ 337 Lloyd McClendon .05 .02 .01
☐ 338 Dennis Lamp .05 .02 .01
☐ 339 Dave Clark .05 .02 .01
☐ 340 Fernando Valenzuela .10 .05 .01
☐ 341 Tom Foley .05 .02 .01
☐ 342 Alex Trevino .05 .02 .01
☐ 343 Frank Tanana .05 .02 .01
☐ 344 George Canale .05 .02 .01
☐ 345 Harold Baines .10 .05 .01
☐ 346 Jim Presley .05 .02 .01
☐ 347 Junior Felix .05 .02 .01
☐ 348 Gary Wayne .05 .02 .01
☐ 349 Steve Finley .15 .07 .02
☐ 350 Bret Saberhagen .10 .05 .01
☐ 351 Roger Craig MG .05 .02 .01
☐ 352 Bryn Smith .05 .02 .01
☐ 353 Sandy Alomar Jr. .15 .07 .02
(Not listed as Jr. on card front)
☐ 354 Stan Belinda .05 .02 .01
☐ 355 Marty Barrett .05 .02 .01
☐ 356 Randy Ready .05 .02 .01
☐ 357 Dave West .05 .02 .01
☐ 358 Andres Thomas .05 .02 .01
☐ 359 Jimmy Jones .05 .02 .01
☐ 360 Paul Molitor .20 .09 .03
☐ 361 Randy McCament .05 .02 .01
☐ 362 Damon Berryhill .05 .02 .01
☐ 363 Dan Petry .05 .02 .01
☐ 364 Rolando Roomes .05 .02 .01
☐ 365 Ozzie Guillen .05 .02 .01
☐ 366 Mike Heath .05 .02 .01
☐ 367 Mike Morgan .05 .02 .01
☐ 368 Bill Doran .05 .02 .01
☐ 369 Todd Burns .05 .02 .01
☐ 370 Tim Wallach .05 .02 .01
☐ 371 Jimmy Key .10 .05 .01
☐ 372 Terry Kennedy .05 .02 .01
☐ 373 Alvin Davis .05 .02 .01
☐ 374 Steve Cummings .05 .02 .01
☐ 375 Dwight Evans .10 .05 .01
☐ 376 Checklist 3 UER .05 .02 .01
(Higuera misalphabetized in Brewer list)
☐ 377 Mickey Weston .05 .02 .01
☐ 378 Luis Salazar .05 .02 .01
☐ 379 Steve Rosenberg .05 .02 .01
☐ 380 Dave Winfield .15 .07 .02
☐ 381 Frank Robinson MG .15 .07 .02
☐ 382 Jeff Musselman .05 .02 .01
☐ 383 John Morris .05 .02 .01
☐ 384 Pat Combs .05 .02 .01
☐ 385 Fred McGriff AS .15 .07 .02
☐ 386 Julio Franco AS .05 .02 .01
☐ 387 Wade Boggs AS .15 .07 .02
☐ 388 Cal Ripken AS .40 .18 .05
☐ 389 Robin Yount AS .15 .07 .02
☐ 390 Ruben Sierra AS .10 .05 .01
☐ 391 Kirby Puckett AS .15 .07 .02
☐ 392 Carlton Fisk AS .10 .05 .01
☐ 393 Bret Saberhagen AS .05 .02 .01
☐ 394 Jeff Ballard AS .05 .02 .01
☐ 395 Jeff Russell AS .05 .02 .01
☐ 396 A.Bartlett Giamatti .15 .07 .02
COMM MEM
☐ 397 Will Clark AS .15 .07 .02
☐ 398 Ryne Sandberg AS .15 .07 .02
☐ 399 Howard Johnson AS .05 .02 .01
☐ 400 Ozzie Smith AS .15 .07 .02
☐ 401 Kevin Mitchell AS .05 .02 .01
☐ 402 Eric Davis AS .05 .02 .01
☐ 403 Tony Gwynn AS .20 .09 .03
☐ 404 Craig Biggio AS .15 .07 .02
☐ 405 Mike Scott AS .05 .02 .01
☐ 406 Joe Magrane AS .05 .02 .01
☐ 407 Mark Davis AS .05 .02 .01
☐ 408 Trevor Wilson .05 .02 .01
☐ 409 Tom Brunansky .05 .02 .01
☐ 410 Joe Boever .05 .02 .01
☐ 411 Ken Phelps .05 .02 .01
☐ 412 Jamie Moyer .05 .02 .01
☐ 413 Brian DuBois .05 .02 .01
☐ 414A Frank Thomas FDP 2000.00 900.00 250.00
ERR (Name missing on card front)
☐ 414B Frank Thomas FDP COR 4.00 1.80 .50
☐ 415 Shawon Dunston .05 .02 .01
☐ 416 Dave Johnson (P) .05 .02 .01
☐ 417 Jim Gantner .05 .02 .01
☐ 418 Tom Browning .05 .02 .01
☐ 419 Beau Allred .05 .02 .01
☐ 420 Carlton Fisk .15 .07 .02
☐ 421 Greg Minton .05 .02 .01
☐ 422 Pat Sheridan .05 .02 .01
☐ 423 Fred Toliver .05 .02 .01
☐ 424 Jerry Reuss .05 .02 .01
☐ 425 Bill Landrum .05 .02 .01
☐ 426 Jeff Hamilton UER .05 .02 .01
(Stats say he fanned 197 times in 1987, but he only had 147 at bats)
☐ 427 Carmen Castillo .05 .02 .01
☐ 428 Steve Davis .05 .02 .01
☐ 429 Tom Kelly MG .05 .02 .01
☐ 430 Pete Incaviglia .05 .02 .01
☐ 431 Randy Johnson .25 .11 .03
☐ 432 Damaso Garcia .05 .02 .01
☐ 433 Steve Olin .10 .05 .01
☐ 434 Mark Carreon .05 .02 .01
☐ 435 Kevin Seitzer .05 .02 .01
☐ 436 Mel Hall .05 .02 .01
☐ 437 Les Lancaster .05 .02 .01
☐ 438 Greg Myers .05 .02 .01
☐ 439 Jeff Parrett .05 .02 .01
☐ 440 Alan Trammell .10 .05 .01
☐ 441 Bob Kipper .05 .02 .01
☐ 442 Jerry Browne .05 .02 .01
☐ 443 Cris Carpenter .05 .02 .01

☐ 444 Kyle Abbott FDP .05 .02 .01
☐ 445 Danny Jackson .05 .02 .01
☐ 446 Dan Pasqua .05 .02 .01
☐ 447 Atlee Hammaker .05 .02 .01
☐ 448 Greg Gagne .05 .02 .01
☐ 449 Dennis Rasmussen .05 .02 .01
☐ 450 Rickey Henderson .15 .07 .02
☐ 451 Mark Lemke .10 .05 .01
☐ 452 Luis DeLosSantos .05 .02 .01
☐ 453 Jody Davis .05 .02 .01
☐ 454 Jeff King .10 .05 .01
☐ 455 Jeffrey Leonard .05 .02 .01
☐ 456 Chris Gwynn .05 .02 .01
☐ 457 Gregg Jefferies .10 .05 .01
☐ 458 Bob McClure .05 .02 .01
☐ 459 Jim Lefebvre MG .05 .02 .01
☐ 460 Mike Scott .05 .02 .01
☐ 461 Carlos Martinez .05 .02 .01
☐ 462 Denny Walling .05 .02 .01
☐ 463 Drew Hall .05 .02 .01
☐ 464 Jerome Walton .05 .02 .01
☐ 465 Kevin Gross .05 .02 .01
☐ 466 Rance Mulliniks .05 .02 .01
☐ 467 Juan Nieves .05 .02 .01
☐ 468 Bill Ripken .05 .02 .01
☐ 469 John Kruk .10 .05 .01
☐ 470 Frank Viola .05 .02 .01
☐ 471 Mike Brumley .05 .02 .01
☐ 472 Jose Uribe .05 .02 .01
☐ 473 Joe Price .05 .02 .01
☐ 474 Rich Thompson .05 .02 .01
☐ 475 Bob Welch .05 .02 .01
☐ 476 Brad Komminsk .05 .02 .01
☐ 477 Willie Fraser .05 .02 .01
☐ 478 Mike LaValliere .05 .02 .01
☐ 479 Frank White .10 .05 .01
☐ 480 Sid Fernandez .05 .02 .01
☐ 481 Garry Templeton .05 .02 .01
☐ 482 Steve Carter .05 .02 .01
☐ 483 Alejandro Pena .05 .02 .01
☐ 484 Mike Fitzgerald .05 .02 .01
☐ 485 John Candelaria .05 .02 .01
☐ 486 Jeff Treadway .05 .02 .01
☐ 487 Steve Searcy .05 .02 .01
☐ 488 Ken Oberkfell .05 .02 .01
☐ 489 Nick Leyva MG .05 .02 .01
☐ 490 Dan Plesac .05 .02 .01
☐ 491 Dave Cochrane .05 .02 .01
☐ 492 Ron Oester .05 .02 .01
☐ 493 Jason Grimsley .05 .02 .01
☐ 494 Terry Puhl .05 .02 .01
☐ 495 Lee Smith .10 .05 .01
☐ 496 Cecil Espy UER .05 .02 .01
('88 stats have 3
SB's, should be 33)
☐ 497 Dave Schmidt .05 .02 .01
☐ 498 Rick Schu .05 .02 .01
☐ 499 Bill Long .05 .02 .01
☐ 500 Kevin Mitchell .05 .02 .01
☐ 501 Matt Young .05 .02 .01
☐ 502 Mitch Webster .05 .02 .01
☐ 503 Randy St.Claire .05 .02 .01
☐ 504 Tom O'Malley .05 .02 .01
☐ 505 Kelly Gruber .05 .02 .01
☐ 506 Tom Glavine .15 .07 .02
☐ 507 Gary Redus .05 .02 .01
☐ 508 Terry Leach .05 .02 .01
☐ 509 Tom Pagnozzi .05 .02 .01
☐ 510 Dwight Gooden .10 .05 .01
☐ 511 Clay Parker .05 .02 .01
☐ 512 Gary Pettis .05 .02 .01
☐ 513 Mark Eichhorn .05 .02 .01
☐ 514 Andy Allanson .05 .02 .01
☐ 515 Len Dykstra .10 .05 .01
☐ 516 Tim Leary .05 .02 .01
☐ 517 Roberto Alomar .25 .11 .03
☐ 518 Bill Krueger .05 .02 .01
☐ 519 Bucky Dent MG .05 .02 .01
☐ 520 Mitch Williams .05 .02 .01
☐ 521 Craig Worthington .05 .02 .01
☐ 522 Mike Dunne .05 .02 .01
☐ 523 Jay Bell .10 .05 .01
☐ 524 Daryl Boston .05 .02 .01
☐ 525 Wally Joyner .10 .05 .01
☐ 526 Checklist 4 .05 .02 .01
☐ 527 Ron Hassey .05 .02 .01
☐ 528 Kevin Wickander UER .05 .02 .01
(Monthly scoreboard
strikeout total was 2.2,
that was his innings
pitched total)
☐ 529 Greg A. Harris .05 .02 .01
☐ 530 Mark Langston .10 .05 .01
☐ 531 Ken Caminiti .20 .09 .03
☐ 532 Cecilio Guante .05 .02 .01
☐ 533 Tim Jones .05 .02 .01
☐ 534 Louie Meadows .05 .02 .01
☐ 535 John Smoltz .25 .11 .03
☐ 536 Bob Geren .05 .02 .01
☐ 537 Mark Grant .05 .02 .01
☐ 538 Bill Spiers UER .05 .02 .01
(Photo actually
George Canale)
☐ 539 Neal Heaton .05 .02 .01
☐ 540 Danny Tartabull .05 .02 .01
☐ 541 Pat Perry .05 .02 .01
☐ 542 Darren Daulton .10 .05 .01
☐ 543 Nelson Liriano .05 .02 .01
☐ 544 Dennis Boyd .05 .02 .01
☐ 545 Kevin McReynolds .05 .02 .01
☐ 546 Kevin Hickey .05 .02 .01
☐ 547 Jack Howell .05 .02 .01
☐ 548 Pat Clements .05 .02 .01
☐ 549 Don Zimmer MG .05 .02 .01
☐ 550 Julio Franco .10 .05 .01
☐ 551 Tim Crews .05 .02 .01
☐ 552 Mike(Miss.) Smith .05 .02 .01
☐ 553 Scott Scudder UER .05 .02 .01
(Cedar Rap1ds)
☐ 554 Jay Buhner .15 .07 .02
☐ 555 Jack Morris .10 .05 .01
☐ 556 Gene Larkin .05 .02 .01
☐ 557 Jeff Innis .05 .02 .01
☐ 558 Rafael Ramirez .05 .02 .01
☐ 559 Andy McGaffigan .05 .02 .01
☐ 560 Steve Sax .05 .02 .01
☐ 561 Ken Dayley .05 .02 .01
☐ 562 Chad Kreuter .05 .02 .01
☐ 563 Alex Sanchez .05 .02 .01
☐ 564 Tyler Houston FDP .15 .07 .02
☐ 565 Scott Fletcher .05 .02 .01
☐ 566 Mark Knudson .05 .02 .01
☐ 567 Ron Gant .15 .07 .02
☐ 568 John Smiley .10 .05 .01
☐ 569 Ivan Calderon .05 .02 .01
☐ 570 Cal Ripken .75 .35 .09
☐ 571 Brett Butler .10 .05 .01
☐ 572 Greg W. Harris .05 .02 .01
☐ 573 Danny Heep .05 .02 .01
☐ 574 Bill Swift .05 .02 .01
☐ 575 Lance Parrish .05 .02 .01
☐ 576 Mike Dyer .05 .02 .01
☐ 577 Charlie Hayes .10 .05 .01
☐ 578 Joe Magrane .05 .02 .01
☐ 579 Art Howe MG .05 .02 .01
☐ 580 Joe Carter .10 .05 .01
☐ 581 Ken Griffey Sr. .05 .02 .01
☐ 582 Rick Honeycutt .05 .02 .01
☐ 583 Bruce Benedict .05 .02 .01
☐ 584 Phil Stephenson .05 .02 .01
☐ 585 Kal Daniels .05 .02 .01
☐ 586 Edwin Nunez .05 .02 .01
☐ 587 Lance Johnson .10 .05 .01
☐ 588 Rick Rhoden .05 .02 .01
☐ 589 Mike Aldrete .05 .02 .01
☐ 590 Ozzie Smith .25 .11 .03
☐ 591 Todd Stottlemyre .05 .02 .01
☐ 592 R.J. Reynolds .05 .02 .01
☐ 593 Scott Bradley .05 .02 .01
☐ 594 Luis Sojo .05 .02 .01
☐ 595 Greg Swindell .05 .02 .01
☐ 596 Jose DeJesus .05 .02 .01
☐ 597 Chris Bosio .05 .02 .01
☐ 598 Brady Anderson .15 .07 .02
☐ 599 Frank Williams .05 .02 .01
☐ 600 Darryl Strawberry .10 .05 .01
☐ 601 Luis Rivera .05 .02 .01
☐ 602 Scott Garrelts .05 .02 .01
☐ 603 Tony Armas .05 .02 .01
☐ 604 Ron Robinson .05 .02 .01
☐ 605 Mike Scioscia .05 .02 .01
☐ 606 Storm Davis .05 .02 .01
☐ 607 Steve Jeltz .05 .02 .01
☐ 608 Eric Anthony .10 .05 .01
☐ 609 Sparky Anderson MG .10 .05 .01
☐ 610 Pedro Guerrero .05 .02 .01
☐ 611 Walt Terrell .05 .02 .01
☐ 612 Dave Gallagher .05 .02 .01
☐ 613 Jeff Pico .05 .02 .01
☐ 614 Nelson Santovenia .05 .02 .01
☐ 615 Rob Deer .05 .02 .01
☐ 616 Brian Holman .05 .02 .01
☐ 617 Geronimo Berroa .10 .05 .01
☐ 618 Ed Whitson .05 .02 .01
☐ 619 Rob Ducey .05 .02 .01
☐ 620 Tony Castillo .05 .02 .01
☐ 621 Melido Perez .05 .02 .01
☐ 622 Sid Bream .05 .02 .01
☐ 623 Jim Corsi .05 .02 .01
☐ 624 Darrin Jackson .05 .02 .01
☐ 625 Roger McDowell .05 .02 .01
☐ 626 Bob Melvin .05 .02 .01
☐ 627 Jose Rijo .05 .02 .01
☐ 628 Candy Maldonado .05 .02 .01
☐ 629 Eric Hetzel .05 .02 .01
☐ 630 Gary Gaetti .10 .05 .01
☐ 631 John Wetteland .15 .07 .02
☐ 632 Scott Lusader .05 .02 .01
☐ 633 Dennis Cook .05 .02 .01
☐ 634 Luis Polonia .05 .02 .01
☐ 635 Brian Downing .05 .02 .01
☐ 636 Jesse Orosco .05 .02 .01
☐ 637 Craig Reynolds .05 .02 .01
☐ 638 Jeff Montgomery .10 .05 .01
☐ 639 Tony LaRussa MG .10 .05 .01
☐ 640 Rick Sutcliffe .05 .02 .01
☐ 641 Doug Strange .05 .02 .01
☐ 642 Jack Armstrong .05 .02 .01
☐ 643 Alfredo Griffin .05 .02 .01
☐ 644 Paul Assenmacher .05 .02 .01
☐ 645 Jose Oquendo .05 .02 .01
☐ 646 Checklist 5 .05 .02 .01
☐ 647 Rex Hudler .05 .02 .01
☐ 648 Jim Clancy .05 .02 .01
☐ 649 Dan Murphy .05 .02 .01
☐ 650 Mike Witt .05 .02 .01
☐ 651 Rafael Santana .05 .02 .01
☐ 652 Mike Boddicker .05 .02 .01
☐ 653 John Moses .05 .02 .01
☐ 654 Paul Coleman FDP .05 .02 .01
☐ 655 Gregg Olson .05 .02 .01
☐ 656 Mackey Sasser .05 .02 .01
☐ 657 Terry Mulholland .05 .02 .01
☐ 658 Donell Nixon .05 .02 .01
☐ 659 Greg Cadaret .05 .02 .01
☐ 660 Vince Coleman .05 .02 .01
☐ 661 Dick Howser TBC'85 .05 .02 .01
UER (Seaver's 300th
on 7/11/85, should
be 8/4/85)
☐ 662 Mike Schmidt TBC'80 .15 .07 .02
☐ 663 Fred Lynn TBC'75 .05 .02 .01
☐ 664 Johnny Bench TBC'70 .15 .07 .02
☐ 665 Sandy Koufax TBC'65 .25 .11 .03
☐ 666 Brian Fisher .05 .02 .01
☐ 667 Curt Wilkerson .05 .02 .01
☐ 668 Joe Oliver .05 .02 .01
☐ 669 Tom Lasorda MG .10 .05 .01
☐ 670 Dennis Eckersley .10 .05 .01
☐ 671 Bob Boone .10 .05 .01
☐ 672 Roy Smith .05 .02 .01
☐ 673 Joey Meyer .05 .02 .01
☐ 674 Spike Owen .05 .02 .01
☐ 675 Jim Abbott .10 .05 .01
☐ 676 Randy Kutcher .05 .02 .01
☐ 677 Jay Tibbs .05 .02 .01
☐ 678 Kirt Manwaring UER .05 .02 .01
('88 Phoenix stats
repeated)
☐ 679 Gary Ward .05 .02 .01
☐ 680 Howard Johnson .05 .02 .01
☐ 681 Mike Schooler .05 .02 .01
☐ 682 Dann Bilardello .05 .02 .01
☐ 683 Kenny Rogers .10 .05 .01
☐ 684 Julio Machado .05 .02 .01
☐ 685 Tony Fernandez .05 .02 .01
☐ 686 Carmelo Martinez .05 .02 .01
☐ 687 Tim Birtsas .05 .02 .01
☐ 688 Milt Thompson .05 .02 .01
☐ 689 Rich Yett .05 .02 .01
☐ 690 Mark McGwire .30 .14 .04
☐ 691 Chuck Cary .05 .02 .01
☐ 692 Sammy Sosa .75 .35 .09
☐ 693 Calvin Schiraldi .05 .02 .01
☐ 694 Mike Stanton .10 .05 .01
☐ 695 Tom Henke .05 .02 .01
☐ 696 B.J. Surhoff .10 .05 .01
☐ 697 Mike Davis .05 .02 .01
☐ 698 Omar Vizquel .15 .07 .02
☐ 699 Jim Leyland MG .05 .02 .01
☐ 700 Kirby Puckett .40 .18 .05
☐ 701 Bernie Williams 1.00 .45 .12
☐ 702 Tony Phillips .10 .05 .01
☐ 703 Jeff Brantley .10 .05 .01
☐ 704 Chip Hale .05 .02 .01
☐ 705 Claudell Washington .05 .02 .01
☐ 706 Geno Petralli .05 .02 .01
☐ 707 Luis Aquino .05 .02 .01
☐ 708 Larry Sheets .05 .02 .01
☐ 709 Juan Berenguer .05 .02 .01
☐ 710 Von Hayes .05 .02 .01
☐ 711 Rick Aguilera .10 .05 .01
☐ 712 Todd Benzinger .05 .02 .01
☐ 713 Tim Drummond .05 .02 .01
☐ 714 Marquis Grissom .50 .23 .06
☐ 715 Greg Maddux .60 .25 .07
☐ 716 Steve Balboni .05 .02 .01
☐ 717 Ron Karkovice .05 .02 .01
☐ 718 Gary Sheffield .25 .11 .03
☐ 719 Wally Whitehurst .05 .02 .01
☐ 720 Andres Galarraga .15 .07 .02
☐ 721 Lee Mazzilli .05 .02 .01
☐ 722 Felix Fermin .05 .02 .01
☐ 723 Jeff D. Robinson .05 .02 .01
☐ 724 Juan Bell .05 .02 .01
☐ 725 Terry Pendleton .10 .05 .01
☐ 726 Gene Nelson .05 .02 .01
☐ 727 Pat Tabler .05 .02 .01
☐ 728 Jim Acker .05 .02 .01
☐ 729 Bobby Valentine MG .05 .02 .01
☐ 730 Tony Gwynn .40 .18 .05
☐ 731 Don Carman .05 .02 .01
☐ 732 Ernest Riles .05 .02 .01
☐ 733 John Dopson .05 .02 .01
☐ 734 Kevin Elster .05 .02 .01
☐ 735 Charlie Hough .05 .02 .01
☐ 736 Rick Dempsey .05 .02 .01
☐ 737 Chris Sabo .05 .02 .01
☐ 738 Gene Harris .05 .02 .01
☐ 739 Dale Sveum .05 .02 .01
☐ 740 Jesse Barfield .05 .02 .01
☐ 741 Steve Wilson .05 .02 .01
☐ 742 Ernie Whitt .05 .02 .01
☐ 743 Tom Candiotti .05 .02 .01
☐ 744 Kelly Mann .05 .02 .01
☐ 745 Hubie Brooks .05 .02 .01
☐ 746 Dave Smith .05 .02 .01
☐ 747 Randy Bush .05 .02 .01
☐ 748 Doyle Alexander .05 .02 .01
☐ 749 Mark Parent UER .05 .02 .01
('87 BA .80,
should be .080)
☐ 750 Dale Murphy .15 .07 .02
☐ 751 Steve Lyons .05 .02 .01
☐ 752 Tom Gordon .05 .02 .01
☐ 753 Chris Speier .05 .02 .01
☐ 754 Bob Walk .05 .02 .01
☐ 755 Rafael Palmeiro .15 .07 .02
☐ 756 Ken Howell .05 .02 .01
☐ 757 Larry Walker .60 .25 .07
☐ 758 Mark Thurmond .05 .02 .01
☐ 759 Tom Trebelhorn MG .05 .02 .01
☐ 760 Wade Boggs .15 .07 .02
☐ 761 Mike Jackson .05 .02 .01
☐ 762 Doug Dascenzo .05 .02 .01
☐ 763 Dennis Martinez .10 .05 .01
☐ 764 Tim Teufel .05 .02 .01
☐ 765 Chili Davis .10 .05 .01
☐ 766 Brian Meyer .05 .02 .01
☐ 767 Tracy Jones .05 .02 .01
☐ 768 Chuck Crim .05 .02 .01
☐ 769 Greg Hibbard .05 .02 .01
☐ 770 Cory Snyder .05 .02 .01
☐ 771 Pete Smith .05 .02 .01
☐ 772 Jeff Reed .05 .02 .01
☐ 773 Dave Leiper .05 .02 .01
☐ 774 Ben McDonald .15 .07 .02
☐ 775 Andy Van Slyke .10 .05 .01
☐ 776 Charlie Leibrandt .05 .02 .01
☐ 777 Tim Laudner .05 .02 .01
☐ 778 Mike Jeffcoat .05 .02 .01
☐ 779 Lloyd Moseby .05 .02 .01
☐ 780 Orel Hershiser .10 .05 .01
☐ 781 Mario Diaz .05 .02 .01
☐ 782 Jose Alvarez .05 .02 .01
☐ 783 Checklist 6 .05 .02 .01
☐ 784 Scott Bailes .05 .02 .01
☐ 785 Jim Rice .10 .05 .01
☐ 786 Eric King .05 .02 .01
☐ 787 Rene Gonzales .05 .02 .01
☐ 788 Frank DiPino .05 .02 .01
☐ 789 John Wathan MG .05 .02 .01
☐ 790 Gary Carter .10 .05 .01
☐ 791 Alvaro Espinoza .05 .02 .01
☐ 792 Gerald Perry .05 .02 .01

1990 Topps Tiffany

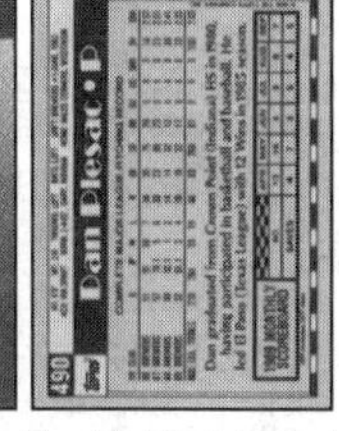

For the seventh year, Topps issued through its hobby dealer network a special "Tiffany" set. These sets which parallel the regular cards consist of 792 standard-size cards. These cards were only issued in complete set form. Since less cards were ordered than in the previous three years, the multiple on these cards are slightly higher than the preceeding sets.

	MINT	NRMT	EXC
COMPLETE FACT.SET (792)	75.00	34.00	9.50
COMMON CARD (1-792)	.10	.05	.01
*STARS: 4X to 8X BASIC CARDS			
* ROOKIES: 3X to 6X BASIC CARDS			

1990 Topps Batting Leaders

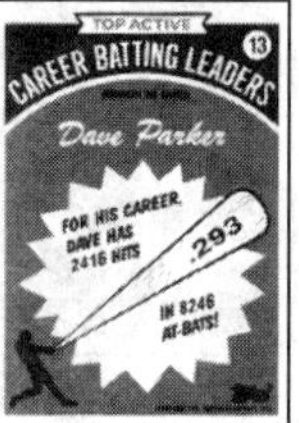

The 1990 Topps Batting Leaders set contains 22 standard-size cards. The front borders are emerald green, and the backs are white, blue and evergreen. This set, like the 1989 set of the same name, depicts the 22 major leaguers with the highest lifetime batting averages (minimum 765 games). The card numbers correspond to the player's rank in terms of career batting average. Many of the photos are the same as those from the 1989 set. The cards were distributed one per special Topps blister pack available only at K-Mart stores and were produced by Topps. The K-Mart logo does not appear anywhere on the cards themselves, although there is a Topps logo on the front and back of each card.

	MINT	NRMT	EXC
COMPLETE SET (22)	50.00	22.00	6.25
COMMON CARD (1-22)	.50	.23	.06
☐ 1 Wade Boggs	3.00	1.35	.35
☐ 2 Tony Gwynn	10.00	4.50	1.25
☐ 3 Kirby Puckett	10.00	4.50	1.25
☐ 4 Don Mattingly	10.00	4.50	1.25
☐ 5 George Brett	8.00	3.60	1.00
☐ 6 Pedro Guerrero	.50	.23	.06
☐ 7 Tim Raines	1.00	.45	.12
☐ 8 Paul Molitor	5.00	2.20	.60
☐ 9 Jim Rice	1.00	.45	.12
☐ 10 Keith Hernandez	1.00	.45	.12
☐ 11 Julio Franco	1.00	.45	.12
☐ 12 Carney Lansford	.50	.23	.06
☐ 13 Dave Parker	1.00	.45	.12
☐ 14 Willie McGee	.50	.23	.06
☐ 15 Robin Yount	2.00	.90	.25
☐ 16 Tony Fernandez	.50	.23	.06
☐ 17 Eddie Murray	4.00	1.80	.50
☐ 18 Johnny Ray	.50	.23	.06
☐ 19 Lonnie Smith	.50	.23	.06
☐ 20 Phil Bradley	.50	.23	.06
☐ 21 Rickey Henderson	3.00	1.35	.35
☐ 22 Kent Hrbek	1.00	.45	.12

1990 Topps Glossy All-Stars

The 1990 Topps Glossy All-Star set contains 22 standard-size glossy cards. The front and back borders are white, and other design elements are red, blue and yellow. This set is almost identical to previous year sets of the same name. One card was included in each 1990 Topps rack pack. The players selected for the set were the starters, managers, and honorary captains in the previous year's All-Star Game.

	MINT	NRMT	EXC
COMPLETE SET (22)	3.00	1.35	.35
COMMON CARD (1-22)	.05	.02	.01
☐ 1 Tom Lasorda MG	.05	.02	.01
☐ 2 Will Clark	.30	.14	.04
☐ 3 Ryne Sandberg	.60	.25	.07
☐ 4 Howard Johnson	.05	.02	.01
☐ 5 Ozzie Smith	.60	.25	.07
☐ 6 Kevin Mitchell	.05	.02	.01
☐ 7 Eric Davis	.05	.02	.01
☐ 8 Tony Gwynn	.75	.35	.09
☐ 9 Benito Santiago	.05	.02	.01
☐ 10 Rick Reuschel	.05	.02	.01
☐ 11 Don Drysdale CAPT	.20	.09	.03
☐ 12 Tony LaRussa MG	.05	.02	.01
☐ 13 Mark McGwire	.50	.23	.06
☐ 14 Julio Franco	.05	.02	.01
☐ 15 Wade Boggs	.25	.11	.03
☐ 16 Cal Ripken	1.50	.70	.19
☐ 17 Bo Jackson	.10	.05	.01
☐ 18 Kirby Puckett	.75	.35	.09
☐ 19 Ruben Sierra	.10	.05	.01
☐ 20 Terry Steinbach	.10	.05	.01
☐ 21 Dave Stewart	.05	.02	.01
☐ 22 Carl Yastrzemski CAPT	.25	.11	.03

1990 Topps Glossy Send-Ins

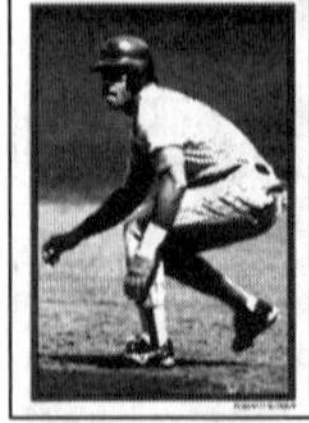

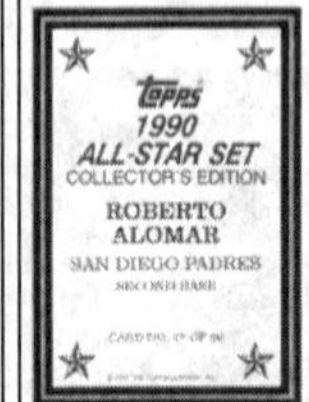

The 1990 Topps Glossy 60 set was issued as a mailaway by Topps for the eighth straight year. This standard-size, 60-card set features two young players among every ten players as Topps again broke down these cards into six series of ten cards each.

	MINT	NRMT	EXC
COMPLETE SET (60)	10.00	4.50	1.25
COMMON CARD (1-60)	.10	.05	.01
☐ 1 Ryne Sandberg	1.25	.55	.16
☐ 2 Nolan Ryan	2.50	1.10	.30
☐ 3 Glenn Davis	.10	.05	.01
☐ 4 Dave Stewart	.25	.11	.03
☐ 5 Barry Larkin	.35	.16	.04
☐ 6 Carney Lansford	.25	.11	.03
☐ 7 Darryl Strawberry	.25	.11	.03
☐ 8 Steve Sax	.10	.05	.01
☐ 9 Carlos Martinez	.10	.05	.01
☐ 10 Gary Sheffield	1.00	.45	.12
☐ 11 Don Mattingly	1.50	.70	.19
☐ 12 Mark Grace	.75	.35	.09
☐ 13 Bret Saberhagen	.10	.05	.01
☐ 14 Mike Scott	.10	.05	.01
☐ 15 Robin Yount	.35	.16	.04
☐ 16 Ozzie Smith	1.25	.55	.16
☐ 17 Jeff Ballard	.10	.05	.01
☐ 18 Rick Reuschel	.10	.05	.01
☐ 19 Greg Briley	.10	.05	.01
☐ 20 Ken Griffey Jr.	4.00	1.80	.50
☐ 21 Kevin Mitchell	.25	.11	.03
☐ 22 Wade Boggs	.50	.23	.06
☐ 23 Dwight Gooden	.25	.11	.03
☐ 24 George Bell	.10	.05	.01
☐ 25 Eric Davis	.25	.11	.03
☐ 26 Ruben Sierra	.10	.05	.01
☐ 27 Roberto Alomar	.75	.35	.09
☐ 28 Gary Gaetti	.25	.11	.03
☐ 29 Gregg Olson	.10	.05	.01
☐ 30 Tom Gordon	.10	.05	.01
☐ 31 Jose Canseco	.60	.25	.07
☐ 32 Pedro Guerrero	.10	.05	.01
☐ 33 Joe Carter	.35	.16	.04
☐ 34 Mike Scioscia	.10	.05	.01
☐ 35 Julio Franco	.25	.11	.03
☐ 36 Joe Magrane	.10	.05	.01
☐ 37 Rickey Henderson	.50	.23	.06
☐ 38 Tim Raines	.25	.11	.03
☐ 39 Jerome Walton	.10	.05	.01
☐ 40 Bob Geren	.10	.05	.01
☐ 41 Andre Dawson	.35	.16	.04
☐ 42 Mark McGwire	1.25	.55	.16
☐ 43 Howard Johnson	.10	.05	.01
☐ 44 Bo Jackson	.25	.11	.03
☐ 45 Shawon Dunston	.10	.05	.01
☐ 46 Carlton Fisk	.35	.16	.04
☐ 47 Mitch Williams	.10	.05	.01
☐ 48 Kirby Puckett	1.50	.70	.19
☐ 49 Craig Worthington	.10	.05	.01
☐ 50 Jim Abbott	.25	.11	.03
☐ 51 Cal Ripken	3.00	1.35	.35
☐ 52 Will Clark	.35	.16	.04
☐ 53 Dennis Eckersley	.25	.11	.03
☐ 54 Craig Biggio	.35	.16	.04
☐ 55 Fred McGriff	.35	.16	.04
☐ 56 Tony Gwynn	2.00	.90	.25
☐ 57 Mickey Tettleton	.10	.05	.01
☐ 58 Mark Davis	.10	.05	.01
☐ 59 Omar Vizquel	.25	.11	.03
☐ 60 Gregg Jefferies	.25	.11	.03

1990 Topps Rookies

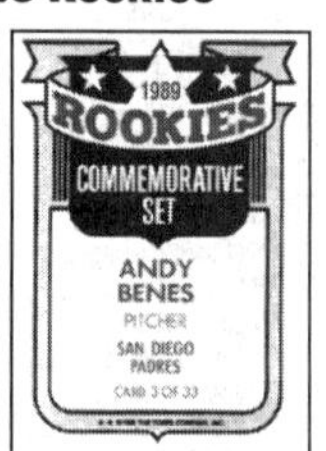

The 1990 Topps Jumbo Rookies set contains 33 standard-size glossy cards. The front and back borders are white, and other design elements are red, blue and yellow. This set is almost identical to previous year sets of the same name except that it contains 33 cards rather than only 22. One card was included in each 1990 Topps "jumbo" pack. The cards are numbered in alphabetical order. Sets of these cards were issued and stamped with various colors so Topps could test for colors of foil stamping.

	MINT	NRMT	EXC
COMPLETE SET (33)	5.00	2.20	.60
COMMON CARD (1-33)	.05	.02	.01
☐ 1 Jim Abbott	.10	.05	.01
☐ 2 Joey Belle	1.25	.55	.16
☐ 3 Andy Benes	.25	.11	.03
☐ 4 Greg Briley	.05	.02	.01
☐ 5 Kevin Brown	.25	.11	.03
☐ 6 Mark Carreon	.05	.02	.01
☐ 7 Mike Devereaux	.05	.02	.01
☐ 8 Junior Felix	.05	.02	.01
☐ 9 Bob Geren	.05	.02	.01
☐ 10 Tom Gordon	.10	.05	.01
☐ 11 Ken Griffey Jr.	2.50	1.10	.30
☐ 12 Pete Harnisch	.05	.02	.01
☐ 13 Greg W. Harris	.05	.02	.01
☐ 14 Greg Hibbard	.05	.02	.01
☐ 15 Ken Hill	.25	.11	.03
☐ 16 Gregg Jefferies	.10	.05	.01
☐ 17 Jeff King	.10	.05	.01
☐ 18 Derek Lilliquist	.05	.02	.01
☐ 19 Carlos Martinez	.05	.02	.01
☐ 20 Ramon Martinez	.25	.11	.03
☐ 21 Bob Milacki	.05	.02	.01
☐ 22 Gregg Olson	.05	.02	.01
☐ 23 Donn Pall	.05	.02	.01
☐ 24 Kenny Rogers	.10	.05	.01
☐ 25 Gary Sheffield	.75	.35	.09
☐ 26 Dwight Smith	.05	.02	.01
☐ 27 Billy Spiers	.05	.02	.01
☐ 28 Omar Vizquel	.25	.11	.03
☐ 29 Jerome Walton	.05	.02	.01
☐ 30 Dave West	.05	.02	.01
☐ 31 John Wetteland	.25	.11	.03
☐ 32 Steve Wilson	.05	.02	.01
☐ 33 Craig Worthington	.05	.02	.01

1990 Topps Wax Box Cards

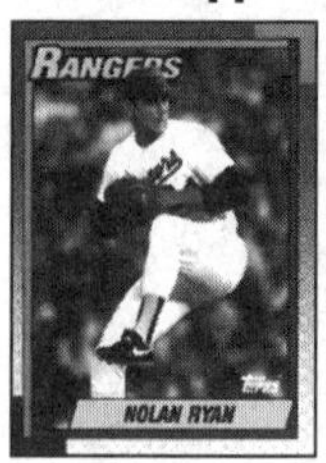

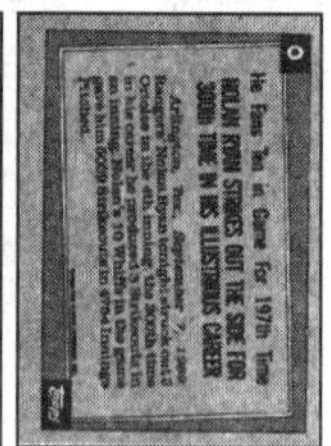

The 1990 Topps wax box cards comprise four different box bottoms with four cards each, for a total of 16 standard-size cards. The front borders are green. The vertically oriented backs are yellowish green. These cards depict various career milestones achieved during the 1989 season. The card numbers are actually the letters A through P. The card ordering is alphabetical by player's name.

	MINT	NRMT	EXC
COMPLETE SET (16)	8.00	3.60	1.00
COMMON CARD (A-P)	.10	.05	.01
☐ A Wade Boggs	.60	.25	.07
☐ B George Brett	1.00	.45	.12
☐ C Andre Dawson	.50	.23	.06
☐ D Darrell Evans	.10	.05	.01
☐ E Dwight Gooden	.25	.11	.03
☐ F Rickey Henderson	.60	.25	.07
☐ G Tom Lasorda MG	.50	.23	.06
☐ H Fred Lynn	.10	.05	.01
☐ I Mark McGwire	1.00	.45	.12
☐ J Dave Parker	.25	.11	.03
☐ K Jeff Reardon	.10	.05	.01
☐ L Rick Reuschel	.10	.05	.01
☐ M Jim Rice	.25	.11	.03
☐ N Cal Ripken	2.50	1.10	.30
☐ O Nolan Ryan	2.50	1.10	.30
☐ P Ryne Sandberg	1.00	.45	.12

1990 Topps Traded

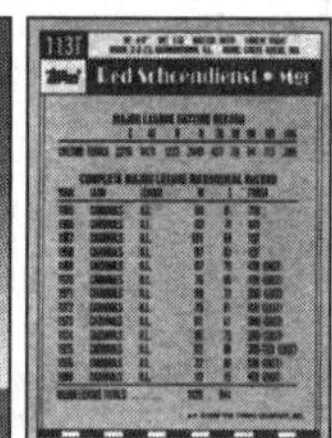

The 1990 Topps Traded Set was the tenth consecutive year Topps issued a 132-card standard-size set at the end of the year. For the first time, Topps not only issued the set in factory set form but also distributed (on a significant basis) the set via 7-card wax packs. Unlike the factory set cards (which feature the whiter paper stock typical of the previous years Traded sets), the wax pack cards feature gray paper stock. Gray and white stock cards are equally valued. This set was arranged alphabetically by player and includes a mix of traded players and rookies for whom Topps did not include a card in the regular set. The key Rookie Cards in this set are Carlos Baerga, Travis Fryman, Todd Hundley and Dave Justice.

	MINT	NRMT	EXC
COMPLETE SET (132)	3.00	1.35	.35
COMPLETE FACT.SET (132)	3.00	1.35	.35
COMMON CARD (1T-132T)	.05	.02	.01
☐ 1T Darrel Akerfelds	.05	.02	.01
☐ 2T Sandy Alomar Jr.	.15	.07	.02
☐ 3T Brad Arnsberg	.05	.02	.01
☐ 4T Steve Avery	.15	.07	.02
☐ 5T Wally Backman	.05	.02	.01
☐ 6T Carlos Baerga	.30	.14	.04
☐ 7T Kevin Bass	.05	.02	.01
☐ 8T Willie Blair	.05	.02	.01
☐ 9T Mike Blowers	.15	.07	.02
☐ 10T Shawn Boskie	.05	.02	.01
☐ 11T Daryl Boston	.05	.02	.01
☐ 12T Dennis Boyd	.05	.02	.01
☐ 13T Glenn Braggs	.05	.02	.01
☐ 14T Hubie Brooks	.05	.02	.01
☐ 15T Tom Brunansky	.05	.02	.01
☐ 16T John Burkett	.10	.05	.01
☐ 17T Casey Candaele	.05	.02	.01
☐ 18T John Candelaria	.05	.02	.01
☐ 19T Gary Carter	.10	.05	.01
☐ 20T Joe Carter	.10	.05	.01
☐ 21T Rick Cerone	.05	.02	.01
☐ 22T Scott Coolbaugh	.05	.02	.01
☐ 23T Bobby Cox MG	.05	.02	.01
☐ 24T Mark Davis	.05	.02	.01
☐ 25T Storm Davis	.05	.02	.01
☐ 26T Edgar Diaz	.05	.02	.01
☐ 27T Wayne Edwards	.05	.02	.01
☐ 28T Mark Eichhorn	.05	.02	.01
☐ 29T Scott Erickson	.15	.07	.02
☐ 30T Nick Esasky	.05	.02	.01
☐ 31T Cecil Fielder	.10	.05	.01
☐ 32T John Franco	.05	.02	.01
☐ 33T Travis Fryman	.40	.18	.05
☐ 34T Bill Gullickson	.05	.02	.01
☐ 35T Darryl Hamilton	.10	.05	.01
☐ 36T Mike Harkey	.05	.02	.01
☐ 37T Bud Harrelson MG	.05	.02	.01
☐ 38T Billy Hatcher	.05	.02	.01
☐ 39T Keith Hernandez	.10	.05	.01
☐ 40T Joe Hesketh	.05	.02	.01
☐ 41T Dave Hollins	.15	.07	.02
☐ 42T Sam Horn	.05	.02	.01
☐ 43T Steve Howard	.05	.02	.01
☐ 44T Todd Hundley	.60	.25	.07
☐ 45T Jeff Huson	.05	.02	.01
☐ 46T Chris James	.05	.02	.01
☐ 47T Stan Javier	.05	.02	.01
☐ 48T Dave Justice	.50	.23	.06
☐ 49T Jeff Kaiser	.05	.02	.01
☐ 50T Dana Kiecker	.05	.02	.01
☐ 51T Joe Klink	.05	.02	.01
☐ 52T Brent Knackert	.05	.02	.01
☐ 53T Brad Komminsk	.05	.02	.01
☐ 54T Mark Langston	.10	.05	.01
☐ 55T Tim Layana	.05	.02	.01
☐ 56T Rick Leach	.05	.02	.01
☐ 57T Terry Leach	.05	.02	.01
☐ 58T Tim Leary	.05	.02	.01
☐ 59T Craig Lefferts	.05	.02	.01
☐ 60T Charlie Leibrandt	.05	.02	.01
☐ 61T Jim Leyritz	.15	.07	.02
☐ 62T Fred Lynn	.05	.02	.01
☐ 63T Kevin Maas	.10	.05	.01
☐ 64T Shane Mack	.05	.02	.01
☐ 65T Candy Maldonado	.05	.02	.01
☐ 66T Fred Manrique	.05	.02	.01
☐ 67T Mike Marshall	.05	.02	.01
☐ 68T Carmelo Martinez	.05	.02	.01
☐ 69T John Marzano	.05	.02	.01
☐ 70T Ben McDonald	.10	.05	.01
☐ 71T Jack McDowell	.15	.07	.02
☐ 72T John McNamara MG	.05	.02	.01
☐ 73T Orlando Mercado	.05	.02	.01
☐ 74T Stump Merrill MG	.05	.02	.01
☐ 75T Alan Mills	.05	.02	.01
☐ 76T Hal Morris	.10	.05	.01
☐ 77T Lloyd Moseby	.05	.02	.01
☐ 78T Randy Myers	.10	.05	.01
☐ 79T Tim Naehring	.15	.07	.02
☐ 80T Junior Noboa	.05	.02	.01
☐ 81T Matt Nokes	.05	.02	.01
☐ 82T Pete O'Brien	.05	.02	.01
☐ 83T John Olerud	.15	.07	.02
☐ 84T Greg Olson	.05	.02	.01
☐ 85T Junior Ortiz	.05	.02	.01
☐ 86T Dave Parker	.10	.05	.01
☐ 87T Rick Parker	.05	.02	.01
☐ 88T Bob Patterson	.05	.02	.01
☐ 89T Alejandro Pena	.05	.02	.01
☐ 90T Tony Pena	.05	.02	.01
☐ 91T Pascual Perez	.05	.02	.01
☐ 92T Gerald Perry	.05	.02	.01
☐ 93T Dan Petry	.05	.02	.01
☐ 94T Gary Pettis	.05	.02	.01
☐ 95T Tony Phillips	.15	.07	.02
☐ 96T Lou Piniella MG	.10	.05	.01
☐ 97T Luis Polonia	.05	.02	.01
☐ 98T Jim Presley	.05	.02	.01
☐ 99T Scott Radinsky	.05	.02	.01
☐ 100T Willie Randolph	.10	.05	.01
☐ 101T Jeff Reardon	.10	.05	.01
☐ 102T Greg Riddoch MG	.05	.02	.01
☐ 103T Jeff Robinson	.05	.02	.01
☐ 104T Ron Robinson	.05	.02	.01
☐ 105T Kevin Romine	.05	.02	.01
☐ 106T Scott Ruskin	.05	.02	.01
☐ 107T John Russell	.05	.02	.01
☐ 108T Bill Sampen	.05	.02	.01
☐ 109T Juan Samuel	.05	.02	.01
☐ 110T Scott Sanderson	.05	.02	.01
☐ 111T Jack Savage	.05	.02	.01
☐ 112T Dave Schmidt	.05	.02	.01
☐ 113T Red Schoendienst MG	.15	.07	.02
☐ 114T Terry Shumpert	.05	.02	.01
☐ 115T Matt Sinatro	.05	.02	.01
☐ 116T Don Slaught	.05	.02	.01
☐ 117T Bryn Smith	.05	.02	.01
☐ 118T Lee Smith	.10	.05	.01
☐ 119T Paul Sorrento	.15	.07	.02
☐ 120T Franklin Stubbs UER ('84 says '99 and has	.05	.02	.01

the same stats as '89,
'83 stats are missing)

☐ 121T Russ Swan	.05	.02	.01
☐ 122T Bob Tewksbury	.05	.02	.01
☐ 123T Wayne Tolleson	.05	.02	.01
☐ 124T John Tudor	.05	.02	.01
☐ 125T Randy Veres	.05	.02	.01
☐ 126T Hector Villanueva	.05	.02	.01
☐ 127T Mitch Webster	.05	.02	.01
☐ 128T Ernie Whitt	.05	.02	.01
☐ 129T Frank Wills	.05	.02	.01
☐ 130T Dave Winfield	.15	.07	.02
☐ 131T Matt Young	.05	.02	.01
☐ 132T Checklist 1T-132T	.05	.02	.01

1990 Topps Traded Tiffany

Again, one of these sets were issued for each regular Tiffany set produced. These 132 standard-size cards parallel the regular Traded issue and feature Glossy fronts and clearer backs. These cards were issued in complete set form only and were distributed through Topps hobby network.

	MINT	NRMT	EXC
COMPLETE FACT.SET (132)	15.00	6.75	1.85
COMMON CARD (1T-132T)	.10	.05	.01
*STARS: 4X to 8X BASIC CARDS			
*ROOKIES: 3X to 6X BASIC CARDS			

1990 Topps Ames All-Stars

The 1990 Topps Ames All-Stars set was issued by Topps for the Ames department stores for the second straight year. This standard-size set featured 33 of the leading hitters active in major league baseball.

	MINT	NRMT	EXC
COMPLETE SET (33)	5.00	2.20	.60
COMMON CARD (1-33)	.05	.02	.01
☐ 1 Dave Winfield	.25	.11	.03
☐ 2 George Brett	.75	.35	.09
☐ 3 Jim Rice	.10	.05	.01
☐ 4 Dwight Evans	.10	.05	.01
☐ 5 Robin Yount	.25	.11	.03
☐ 6 Dave Parker	.10	.05	.01
☐ 7 Eddie Murray	.30	.14	.04
☐ 8 Keith Hernandez	.10	.05	.01
☐ 9 Andre Dawson	.25	.11	.03
☐ 10 Fred Lynn	.05	.02	.01
☐ 11 Dale Murphy	.20	.09	.03
☐ 12 Jack Clark	.10	.05	.01
☐ 13 Rickey Henderson	.50	.23	.06
☐ 14 Paul Molitor	.40	.18	.05
☐ 15 Cal Ripken	2.00	.90	.25
☐ 16 Wade Boggs	.25	.11	.03
☐ 17 Tim Raines	.10	.05	.01
☐ 18 Don Mattingly	1.00	.45	.12
☐ 19 Kent Hrbek	.10	.05	.01
☐ 20 Kirk Gibson	.10	.05	.01
☐ 21 Julio Franco	.10	.05	.01
☐ 22 George Bell	.05	.02	.01
☐ 23 Darryl Strawberry	.10	.05	.01
☐ 24 Kirby Puckett	1.00	.45	.12
☐ 25 Juan Samuel	.05	.02	.01
☐ 26 Alvin Davis	.05	.02	.01
☐ 27 Joe Carter	.10	.05	.01
☐ 28 Eric Davis	.05	.02	.01
☐ 29 Jose Canseco	.40	.18	.05
☐ 30 Wally Joyner	.10	.05	.01
☐ 31 Will Clark	.30	.14	.04
☐ 32 Ruben Sierra	.10	.05	.01
☐ 33 Danny Tartabull	.05	.02	.01

1990 Topps Big

The 1990 Topps Big set contains 330 cards each measuring a slightly over-sized 2 5/8" by 3 3/4". In 1989 Topps had issued two oversize sets (Bigs and Bowmans), but in 1990 only the Topps Big were issued by Topps as an oversize set. The set was issued in three series of 110 cards. Some dealers believe the third series was distributed in far less quantity than the first two series.

	MINT	NRMT	EXC
COMPLETE SET (330)	20.00	9.00	2.50
COMMON CARD (1-330)	.05	.02	.01
☐ 1 Dwight Evans	.10	.05	.01
☐ 2 Kirby Puckett	2.50	1.10	.30
☐ 3 Kevin Gross	.05	.02	.01
☐ 4 Ron Hassey	.05	.02	.01
☐ 5 Lloyd McClendon	.05	.02	.01
☐ 6 Bo Jackson	.10	.05	.01
☐ 7 Lonnie Smith	.05	.02	.01
☐ 8 Alvaro Espinoza	.05	.02	.01
☐ 9 Roberto Alomar	.75	.35	.09
☐ 10 Glenn Braggs	.05	.02	.01
☐ 11 David Cone	.15	.07	.02
☐ 12 Claudell Washington	.05	.02	.01
☐ 13 Pedro Guerrero	.05	.02	.01
☐ 14 Todd Benzinger	.05	.02	.01
☐ 15 Jeff Russell	.05	.02	.01
☐ 16 Terry Kennedy	.05	.02	.01
☐ 17 Kelly Gruber	.05	.02	.01
☐ 18 Alfredo Griffin	.05	.02	.01
☐ 19 Mark Grace	.60	.25	.07
☐ 20 Dave Winfield	.60	.25	.07
☐ 21 Bret Saberhagen	.10	.05	.01
☐ 22 Roger Clemens	1.25	.55	.16
☐ 23 Bob Walk	.05	.02	.01
☐ 24 Dave Magadan	.05	.02	.01
☐ 25 Spike Owen	.05	.02	.01
☐ 26 Jody Davis	.05	.02	.01
☐ 27 Kent Hrbek	.10	.05	.01
☐ 28 Mark McGwire	1.50	.70	.19
☐ 29 Eddie Murray	1.00	.45	.12
☐ 30 Paul O'Neill	.10	.05	.01
☐ 31 Jose DeLeon	.05	.02	.01
☐ 32 Steve Lyons	.05	.02	.01
☐ 33 Dan Plesac	.05	.02	.01
☐ 34 Jack Howell	.05	.02	.01
☐ 35 Greg Briley	.05	.02	.01
☐ 36 Andy Hawkins	.05	.02	.01
☐ 37 Cecil Espy	.05	.02	.01
☐ 38 Rick Sutcliffe	.05	.02	.01
☐ 39 Jack Clark	.05	.02	.01
☐ 40 Dale Murphy	.50	.23	.06
☐ 41 Mike Henneman	.05	.02	.01
☐ 42 Rick Honeycutt	.05	.02	.01
☐ 43 Willie Randolph	.10	.05	.01
☐ 44 Marty Barrett	.05	.02	.01
☐ 45 Willie Wilson	.05	.02	.01
☐ 46 Wallace Johnson	.05	.02	.01
☐ 47 Greg Brock	.05	.02	.01
☐ 48 Tom Browning	.05	.02	.01
☐ 49 Gerald Young	.05	.02	.01
☐ 50 Dennis Eckersley	.10	.05	.01
☐ 51 Scott Garrelts	.05	.02	.01
☐ 52 Gary Redus	.05	.02	.01
☐ 53 Al Newman	.05	.02	.01
☐ 54 Daryl Boston	.05	.02	.01
☐ 55 Ron Oester	.05	.02	.01
☐ 56 Danny Tartabull	.10	.05	.01
☐ 57 Gregg Jefferies	.40	.18	.05
☐ 58 Tom Foley	.05	.02	.01
☐ 59 Robin Yount	.50	.23	.06
☐ 60 Pat Borders	.05	.02	.01
☐ 61 Mike Greenwell	.10	.05	.01
☐ 62 Shawon Dunston	.05	.02	.01
☐ 63 Steve Buechele	.05	.02	.01
☐ 64 Dave Stewart	.10	.05	.01
☐ 65 Jose Oquendo	.05	.02	.01
☐ 66 Ron Gant	.30	.14	.04
☐ 67 Mike Scioscia	.05	.02	.01
☐ 68 Randy Velarde	.05	.02	.01
☐ 69 Von Hayes	.05	.02	.01
☐ 70 Tim Wallach	.05	.02	.01
☐ 71 Eric Show	.05	.02	.01
☐ 72 Eric Davis	.15	.07	.02
☐ 73 Mike Gallego	.05	.02	.01
☐ 74 Rob Deer	.05	.02	.01
☐ 75 Ryne Sandberg	1.50	.70	.19
☐ 76 Kevin Seitzer	.10	.05	.01
☐ 77 Wade Boggs	.60	.25	.07
☐ 78 Greg Gagne	.05	.02	.01
☐ 79 John Smiley	.05	.02	.01
☐ 80 Ivan Calderon	.05	.02	.01
☐ 81 Pete Incaviglia	.05	.02	.01
☐ 82 Orel Hershiser	.10	.05	.01
☐ 83 Carney Lansford	.05	.02	.01
☐ 84 Mike Fitzgerald	.05	.02	.01
☐ 85 Don Mattingly	2.50	1.10	.30
☐ 86 Chet Lemon	.05	.02	.01
☐ 87 Rolando Roomes	.05	.02	.01
☐ 88 Billy Spiers	.05	.02	.01
☐ 89 Pat Tabler	.05	.02	.01
☐ 90 Danny Heep	.05	.02	.01
☐ 91 Andre Dawson	.50	.23	.06
☐ 92 Randy Bush	.05	.02	.01
☐ 93 Tony Gwynn	2.00	.90	.25
☐ 94 Tom Brunansky	.05	.02	.01
☐ 95 Johnny Ray	.05	.02	.01
☐ 96 Matt Williams	.60	.25	.07
☐ 97 Barry Lyons	.05	.02	.01
☐ 98 Jeff Hamilton	.05	.02	.01
☐ 99 Tom Glavine	.50	.23	.06
☐ 100 Ken Griffey Sr.	.10	.05	.01
☐ 101 Tom Henke	.10	.05	.01
☐ 102 Dave Righetti	.05	.02	.01
☐ 103 Paul Molitor	1.00	.45	.12
☐ 104 Mike LaValliere	.05	.02	.01
☐ 105 Frank White	.10	.05	.01
☐ 106 Bob Welch	.05	.02	.01
☐ 107 Ellis Burks	.30	.14	.04
☐ 108 Andres Galarraga	.50	.23	.06
☐ 109 Mitch Williams	.05	.02	.01
☐ 110 Checklist 1-110	.05	.02	.01
☐ 111 Craig Biggio	.40	.18	.05
☐ 112 Dave Stieb	.05	.02	.01
☐ 113 Ron Darling	.05	.02	.01
☐ 114 Bert Blyleven	.10	.05	.01
☐ 115 Dickie Thon	.05	.02	.01
☐ 116 Carlos Martinez	.05	.02	.01
☐ 117 Jeff King	.15	.07	.02
☐ 118 Terry Steinbach	.10	.05	.01
☐ 119 Frank Tanana	.05	.02	.01
☐ 120 Mark Lemke	.05	.02	.01
☐ 121 Chris Sabo	.10	.05	.01
☐ 122 Glenn Davis	.05	.02	.01
☐ 123 Mel Hall	.05	.02	.01
☐ 124 Jim Gantner	.05	.02	.01
☐ 125 Benito Santiago	.10	.05	.01
☐ 126 Milt Thompson	.05	.02	.01
☐ 127 Rafael Palmeiro	.50	.23	.06
☐ 128 Barry Bonds	.75	.35	.09
☐ 129 Mike Bielecki	.05	.02	.01
☐ 130 Lou Whitaker	.10	.05	.01
☐ 131 Bob Ojeda	.05	.02	.01
☐ 132 Dion James	.05	.02	.01
☐ 133 Dennis Martinez	.10	.05	.01
☐ 134 Fred McGriff	.50	.23	.06
☐ 135 Terry Pendleton	.10	.05	.01
☐ 136 Pat Combs	.05	.02	.01
☐ 137 Kevin Mitchell	.10	.05	.01
☐ 138 Marquis Grissom	.75	.35	.09
☐ 139 Chris Bosio	.05	.02	.01
☐ 140 Omar Vizquel	.15	.07	.02
☐ 141 Steve Sax	.05	.02	.01
☐ 142 Nelson Liriano	.05	.02	.01
☐ 143 Kevin Elster	.05	.02	.01
☐ 144 Dan Pasqua	.05	.02	.01
☐ 145 Dave Smith	.05	.02	.01
☐ 146 Craig Worthington	.05	.02	.01
☐ 147 Dan Gladden	.05	.02	.01
☐ 148 Oddibe McDowell	.05	.02	.01
☐ 149 Bip Roberts	.10	.05	.01
☐ 150 Randy Ready	.05	.02	.01
☐ 151 Dwight Smith	.05	.02	.01
☐ 152 Eddie Whitson	.05	.02	.01
☐ 153 George Bell	.05	.02	.01
☐ 154 Tim Raines	.15	.07	.02
☐ 155 Sid Fernandez	.05	.02	.01
☐ 156 Henry Cotto	.05	.02	.01
☐ 157 Harold Baines	.10	.05	.01
☐ 158 Willie McGee	.10	.05	.01
☐ 159 Bill Doran	.05	.02	.01
☐ 160 Steve Balboni	.05	.02	.01
☐ 161 Pete Smith	.05	.02	.01
☐ 162 Frank Viola	.05	.02	.01
☐ 163 Gary Sheffield	.75	.35	.09
☐ 164 Bill Landrum	.05	.02	.01
☐ 165 Tony Fernandez	.05	.02	.01
☐ 166 Mike Heath	.05	.02	.01
☐ 167 Jody Reed	.05	.02	.01
☐ 168 Wally Joyner	.10	.05	.01
☐ 169 Robby Thompson	.05	.02	.01
☐ 170 Ken Caminiti	.50	.23	.06
☐ 171 Nolan Ryan	4.00	1.80	.50
☐ 172 Ricky Jordan	.05	.02	.01
☐ 173 Lance Blankenship	.05	.02	.01
☐ 174 Dwight Gooden	.10	.05	.01
☐ 175 Ruben Sierra	.10	.05	.01
☐ 176 Carlton Fisk	.50	.23	.06
☐ 177 Garry Templeton	.05	.02	.01
☐ 178 Mike Devereaux	.10	.05	.01
☐ 179 Mookie Wilson	.05	.02	.01
☐ 180 Jeff Blauser	.05	.02	.01
☐ 181 Scott Bradley	.05	.02	.01
☐ 182 Luis Salazar	.05	.02	.01
☐ 183 Rafael Ramirez	.05	.02	.01
☐ 184 Vince Coleman	.05	.02	.01
☐ 185 Doug Drabek	.05	.02	.01
☐ 186 Darryl Strawberry	.15	.07	.02
☐ 187 Tim Burke	.05	.02	.01
☐ 188 Jesse Barfield	.05	.02	.01
☐ 189 Barry Larkin	.50	.23	.06
☐ 190 Alan Trammell	.10	.05	.01
☐ 191 Steve Lake	.05	.02	.01
☐ 192 Derek Lilliquist	.05	.02	.01
☐ 193 Don Robinson	.05	.02	.01
☐ 194 Kevin McReynolds	.05	.02	.01
☐ 195 Melido Perez	.05	.02	.01
☐ 196 Jose Lind	.05	.02	.01
☐ 197 Eric Anthony	.05	.02	.01
☐ 198 B.J. Surhoff	.10	.05	.01
☐ 199 John Olerud	.60	.25	.07
☐ 200 Mike Moore	.05	.02	.01
☐ 201 Mark Gubicza	.05	.02	.01
☐ 202 Phil Bradley	.05	.02	.01
☐ 203 Ozzie Smith	1.50	.70	.19
☐ 204 Greg Maddux	2.50	1.10	.30
☐ 205 Julio Franco	.10	.05	.01
☐ 206 Tom Herr	.05	.02	.01
☐ 207 Scott Fletcher	.05	.02	.01
☐ 208 Bobby Bonilla	.10	.05	.01
☐ 209 Bob Geren	.05	.02	.01
☐ 210 Junior Felix	.05	.02	.01
☐ 211 Dick Schofield	.05	.02	.01
☐ 212 Jim Deshaies	.05	.02	.01
☐ 213 Jose Uribe	.05	.02	.01
☐ 214 John Kruk	.10	.05	.01
☐ 215 Ozzie Guillen	.10	.05	.01
☐ 216 Howard Johnson	.05	.02	.01
☐ 217 Andy Van Slyke	.10	.05	.01
☐ 218 Tim Laudner	.05	.02	.01
☐ 219 Manny Lee	.05	.02	.01
☐ 220 Checklist 111-220	.05	.02	.01
☐ 221 Cory Snyder	.05	.02	.01
☐ 222 Billy Hatcher	.05	.02	.01
☐ 223 Bud Black	.05	.02	.01
☐ 224 Will Clark	.60	.25	.07
☐ 225 Kevin Tapani	.25	.11	.03
☐ 226 Mike Pagliarulo	.05	.02	.01
☐ 227 Dave Parker	.10	.05	.01
☐ 228 Ben McDonald	.25	.11	.03
☐ 229 Carlos Baerga	.50	.23	.06
☐ 230 Roger McDowell	.05	.02	.01
☐ 231 Delino DeShields	.15	.07	.02
☐ 232 Mark Langston	.10	.05	.01
☐ 233 Wally Backman	.05	.02	.01
☐ 234 Jim Eisenreich	.10	.05	.01
☐ 235 Mike Schooler	.05	.02	.01
☐ 236 Kevin Bass	.05	.02	.01
☐ 237 John Farrell	.05	.02	.01
☐ 238 Kal Daniels	.05	.02	.01
☐ 239 Tony Phillips	.10	.05	.01
☐ 240 Todd Stottlemyre	.05	.02	.01
☐ 241 Greg Olson	.05	.02	.01
☐ 242 Charlie Hough	.05	.02	.01
☐ 243 Mariano Duncan	.10	.05	.01
☐ 244 Bill Ripken	.05	.02	.01
☐ 245 Joe Carter	.40	.18	.05
☐ 246 Tim Belcher	.05	.02	.01
☐ 247 Roberto Kelly	.05	.02	.01
☐ 248 Candy Maldonado	.05	.02	.01
☐ 249 Mike Scott	.05	.02	.01
☐ 250 Ken Griffey Jr.	5.00	2.20	.60
☐ 251 Nick Esasky	.05	.02	.01
☐ 252 Tom Gordon	.10	.05	.01
☐ 253 John Tudor	.05	.02	.01
☐ 254 Gary Gaetti	.10	.05	.01
☐ 255 Neal Heaton	.05	.02	.01
☐ 256 Jerry Browne	.05	.02	.01
☐ 257 Jose Rijo	.05	.02	.01
☐ 258 Mike Boddicker	.05	.02	.01
☐ 259 Brett Butler	.10	.05	.01
☐ 260 Andy Benes	.15	.07	.02
☐ 261 Kevin Brown	.15	.07	.02
☐ 262 Hubie Brooks	.05	.02	.01
☐ 263 Randy Milligan	.05	.02	.01
☐ 264 John Franco	.10	.05	.01
☐ 265 Sandy Alomar Jr.	.15	.07	.02
☐ 266 Dave Valle	.05	.02	.01
☐ 267 Jerome Walton	.05	.02	.01
☐ 268 Bob Boone	.10	.05	.01
☐ 269 Ken Howell	.05	.02	.01
☐ 270 Jose Canseco	.60	.25	.07
☐ 271 Joe Magrane	.05	.02	.01
☐ 272 Brian DuBois	.05	.02	.01
☐ 273 Carlos Quintana	.05	.02	.01
☐ 274 Lance Johnson	.10	.05	.01
☐ 275 Steve Bedrosian	.05	.02	.01
☐ 276 Brook Jacoby	.05	.02	.01
☐ 277 Fred Lynn UER (Pirates logo on card front)	.10	.05	.01
☐ 278 Jeff Ballard	.05	.02	.01
☐ 279 Otis Nixon	.10	.05	.01
☐ 280 Chili Davis	.10	.05	.01
☐ 281 Joe Oliver	.05	.02	.01
☐ 282 Brian Holman	.05	.02	.01
☐ 283 Juan Samuel	.05	.02	.01
☐ 284 Rick Aguilera	.10	.05	.01
☐ 285 Jeff Reardon	.10	.05	.01
☐ 286 Sammy Sosa	1.50	.70	.19
☐ 287 Carmelo Martinez	.05	.02	.01
☐ 288 Greg Swindell	.05	.02	.01
☐ 289 Erik Hanson	.10	.05	.01
☐ 290 Tony Pena	.05	.02	.01
☐ 291 Pascual Perez	.05	.02	.01
☐ 292 Rickey Henderson	.75	.35	.09

☐ 293 Kurt Stillwell	.05	.02	.01
☐ 294 Todd Zeile	.10	.05	.01
☐ 295 Bobby Thigpen	.05	.02	.01
☐ 296 Larry Walker	1.25	.55	.16
☐ 297 Rob Murphy	.05	.02	.01
☐ 298 Mitch Webster	.05	.02	.01
☐ 299 Devon White	.10	.05	.01
☐ 300 Len Dykstra	.10	.05	.01
☐ 301 Keith Hernandez	.10	.05	.01
☐ 302 Gene Larkin	.05	.02	.01
☐ 303 Jeffrey Leonard	.05	.02	.01
☐ 304 Jim Presley	.05	.02	.01
☐ 305 Lloyd Moseby	.05	.02	.01
☐ 306 John Smoltz	.75	.35	.09
☐ 307 Sam Horn	.05	.02	.01
☐ 308 Greg Litton	.05	.02	.01
☐ 309 Dave Henderson	.05	.02	.01
☐ 310 Mark McLemore	.05	.02	.01
☐ 311 Gary Pettis	.05	.02	.01
☐ 312 Mark Davis	.05	.02	.01
☐ 313 Cecil Fielder	.50	.23	.06
☐ 314 Jack Armstrong	.05	.02	.01
☐ 315 Alvin Davis	.05	.02	.01
☐ 316 Doug Jones	.05	.02	.01
☐ 317 Eric Yelding	.05	.02	.01
☐ 318 Joe Orsulak	.05	.02	.01
☐ 319 Chuck Finley	.10	.05	.01
☐ 320 Glenn Wilson	.05	.02	.01
☐ 321 Harold Reynolds	.10	.05	.01
☐ 322 Teddy Higuera	.05	.02	.01
☐ 323 Lance Parrish	.05	.02	.01
☐ 324 Bruce Hurst	.05	.02	.01
☐ 325 Dave West	.05	.02	.01
☐ 326 Kirk Gibson	.10	.05	.01
☐ 327 Cal Ripken	4.00	1.80	.50
☐ 328 Rick Reuschel	.05	.02	.01
☐ 329 Jim Abbott	.10	.05	.01
☐ 330 Checklist 221-330	.05	.02	.01

1990 Topps Coins

The 1989 Topps Coins set contains 60 coins, each measuring approximately 1 1/2" in diameter. The coins were issued in packs of three coins. The set is arranged by league order with the Most Valuable Player, Cy Young Award Winner, Rookie of the Year and Batting Leaders being first, then the rest of the league being arranged alphabetically within the league group. The American League players are 1-32 and the National League players are 33-60.

	MINT	NRMT	EXC
COMPLETE SET (60)	8.00	3.60	1.00
COMMON COIN (1-60)	.05	.02	.01
☐ 1 Robin Yount	.30	.14	.04
☐ 2 Bret Saberhagen	.10	.05	.01
☐ 3 Gregg Olson	.05	.02	.01
☐ 4 Kirby Puckett	1.50	.70	.19
☐ 5 George Bell	.05	.02	.01
☐ 6 Wade Boggs	.40	.18	.05
☐ 7 Jerry Browne	.05	.02	.01
☐ 8 Ellis Burks	.20	.09	.03
☐ 9 Ivan Calderon	.05	.02	.01
☐ 10 Tom Candiotti	.05	.02	.01
☐ 11 Alvin Davis	.05	.02	.01
☐ 12 Chili Davis	.10	.05	.01
☐ 13 Chuck Finley	.05	.02	.01
☐ 14 Gary Gaetti	.05	.02	.01
☐ 15 Tom Gordon	.05	.02	.01
☐ 16 Ken Griffey Jr.	3.00	1.35	.35
☐ 17 Rickey Henderson	.40	.18	.05
☐ 18 Kent Hrbek	.10	.05	.01
☐ 19 Bo Jackson	.10	.05	.01
☐ 20 Carlos Martinez	.05	.02	.01
☐ 21 Don Mattingly	1.50	.70	.19
☐ 22 Fred McGriff	.50	.23	.06
☐ 23 Paul Molitor	.75	.35	.09
☐ 24 Cal Ripken	2.50	1.10	.30
☐ 25 Nolan Ryan	2.50	1.10	.30
☐ 26 Steve Sax	.05	.02	.01
☐ 27 Gary Sheffield	1.00	.45	.12
☐ 28 Ruben Sierra	.10	.05	.01
☐ 29 Dave Stewart	.05	.02	.01
☐ 30 Mickey Tettleton	.05	.02	.01
☐ 31 Alan Trammell	.10	.05	.01
☐ 32 Lou Whitaker	.10	.05	.01
☐ 33 Kevin Mitchell	.05	.02	.01
☐ 34 Mark Davis	.05	.02	.01
☐ 35 Jerome Walton	.05	.02	.01
☐ 36 Tony Gwynn	1.50	.70	.19
☐ 37 Roberto Alomar	.75	.35	.09
☐ 38 Tim Belcher	.05	.02	.01
☐ 39 Craig Biggio	.30	.14	.04
☐ 40 Barry Bonds	.60	.25	.07
☐ 41 Bobby Bonilla	.10	.05	.01
☐ 42 Joe Carter	.10	.05	.01
☐ 43 Will Clark	.40	.18	.05
☐ 44 Eric Davis	.05	.02	.01
☐ 45 Glenn Davis	.05	.02	.01
☐ 46 Sid Fernandez	.05	.02	.01
☐ 47 Pedro Guerrero	.05	.02	.01
☐ 48 Von Hayes	.05	.02	.01
☐ 49 Tom Herr	.05	.02	.01
☐ 50 Howard Johnson	.05	.02	.01
☐ 51 Barry Larkin	.40	.18	.05
☐ 52 Joe Magrane	.05	.02	.01
☐ 53 Dale Murphy	.20	.09	.03
☐ 54 Tim Raines	.10	.05	.01
☐ 55 Willie Randolph	.10	.05	.01
☐ 56 Ryne Sandberg	1.00	.45	.12
☐ 57 Dwight Smith	.05	.02	.01
☐ 58 Lonnie Smith	.05	.02	.01
☐ 59 Robby Thompson	.05	.02	.01
☐ 60 Tim Wallach	.05	.02	.01

1990 Topps Debut '89

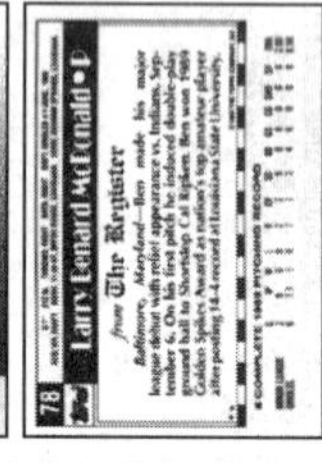

The 1990 Topps Major League Debut Set is a 152-card, standard-size set arranged in alphabetical order by player's name. Each card front features the date of the player's first major league appearance. Strangely enough, even though the set commemorates the 1989 Major League debuts, the set was not issued until the 1990 season had almost begun. Key cards in this set include Joey (Albert) Belle, Juan Gonzalez, Ken Griffey, Jr., David Justice, Deion Sanders and Sammy Sosa

	MINT	NRMT	EXC
COMPLETE SET (152)	12.00	5.50	1.50
COMMON CARD (1-152)	.05	.02	.01
☐ 1 Jim Abbott	.25	.11	.03
☐ 2 Beau Allred	.05	.02	.01
☐ 3 Wilson Alvarez	.40	.18	.05
☐ 4 Kent Anderson	.05	.02	.01
☐ 5 Eric Anthony	.05	.02	.01
☐ 6 Kevin Appier	.40	.18	.05
☐ 7 Larry Arndt	.05	.02	.01
☐ 8 John Barfield	.05	.02	.01
☐ 9 Billy Bates	.05	.02	.01
☐ 10 Kevin Batiste	.05	.02	.01
☐ 11 Blaine Beatty	.05	.02	.01
☐ 12 Stan Belinda	.05	.02	.01
☐ 13 Juan Bell	.05	.02	.01
☐ 14 Joey Belle (Now known as Albert)	3.00	1.35	.35
☐ 15 Andy Benes	.50	.23	.06
☐ 16 Mike Benjamin	.05	.02	.01
☐ 17 Geronimo Berroa	.15	.07	.02
☐ 18 Mike Blowers	.25	.11	.03
☐ 19 Brian Brady	.05	.02	.01
☐ 20 Francisco Cabrera	.15	.07	.02
☐ 21 George Canale	.05	.02	.01
☐ 22 Jose Cano	.05	.02	.01
☐ 23 Steve Carter	.05	.02	.01
☐ 24 Pat Combs	.05	.02	.01
☐ 25 Scott Coolbaugh	.05	.02	.01
☐ 26 Steve Cummings	.05	.02	.01
☐ 27 Pete Dalena	.05	.02	.01
☐ 28 Jeff Datz	.05	.02	.01
☐ 29 Bobby Davidson	.05	.02	.01
☐ 30 Drew Denson	.05	.02	.01
☐ 31 Gary DiSarcina	.15	.07	.02
☐ 32 Brian DuBois	.05	.02	.01
☐ 33 Mike Dyer	.05	.02	.01
☐ 34 Wayne Edwards	.05	.02	.01
☐ 35 Junior Felix	.05	.02	.01
☐ 36 Mike Fetters	.05	.02	.01
☐ 37 Steve Finley	.40	.18	.05
☐ 38 Darrin Fletcher	.15	.07	.02
☐ 39 LaVel Freeman	.05	.02	.01
☐ 40 Steve Frey	.05	.02	.01
☐ 41 Mark Gardner	.05	.02	.01
☐ 42 Joe Girardi	.30	.14	.04
☐ 43 Juan Gonzalez	3.00	1.35	.35
☐ 44 Goose Gozzo	.05	.02	.01
☐ 45 Tommy Greene	.25	.11	.03
☐ 46 Ken Griffey Jr.	5.00	2.20	.60
☐ 47 Jason Grimsley	.05	.02	.01
☐ 48 Marquis Grissom	1.25	.55	.16
☐ 49 Mark Guthrie	.05	.02	.01
☐ 50 Chip Hale	.05	.02	.01
☐ 51 Jack Hardy	.05	.02	.01
☐ 52 Gene Harris	.05	.02	.01
☐ 53 Mike Hartley	.05	.02	.01
☐ 54 Scott Hemond	.05	.02	.01
☐ 55 Xavier Hernandez	.05	.02	.01
☐ 56 Eric Hetzel	.05	.02	.01
☐ 57 Greg Hibbard	.05	.02	.01
☐ 58 Mark Higgins	.05	.02	.01
☐ 59 Glenallen Hill	.15	.07	.02
☐ 60 Chris Hoiles	.35	.16	.04
☐ 61 Shawn Holman	.05	.02	.01
☐ 62 Dann Howitt	.05	.02	.01
☐ 63 Mike Huff	.05	.02	.01
☐ 64 Terry Jorgensen	.05	.02	.01
☐ 65 Dave Justice	1.25	.55	.16
☐ 66 Jeff King	.25	.11	.03
☐ 67 Matt Kinzer	.05	.02	.01
☐ 68 Joe Kraemer	.05	.02	.01
☐ 69 Marcus Lawton	.05	.02	.01
☐ 70 Derek Lilliquist	.05	.02	.01
☐ 71 Scott Little	.05	.02	.01
☐ 72 Greg Litton	.05	.02	.01
☐ 73 Rick Luecken	.05	.02	.01
☐ 74 Julio Machado	.05	.02	.01
☐ 75 Tom Magrann	.05	.02	.01
☐ 76 Kelly Mann	.05	.02	.01
☐ 77 Randy McCament	.05	.02	.01
☐ 78 Ben McDonald	.30	.14	.04
☐ 79 Chuck McElroy	.05	.02	.01
☐ 80 Jeff McKnight	.05	.02	.01
☐ 81 Kent Mercker	.15	.07	.02
☐ 82 Matt Merullo	.05	.02	.01
☐ 83 Hensley Meulens	.05	.02	.01
☐ 84 Kevin Mmahat	.05	.02	.01
☐ 85 Mike Munoz	.05	.02	.01
☐ 86 Dan Murphy	.05	.02	.01
☐ 87 Jaime Navarro	.25	.11	.03
☐ 88 Randy Nosek	.05	.02	.01
☐ 89 John Olerud	.50	.23	.06
☐ 90 Steve Olin	.15	.07	.02
☐ 91 Joe Oliver	.15	.07	.02
☐ 92 Francisco Oliveras	.05	.02	.01
☐ 93 Gregg Olson	.15	.07	.02
☐ 94 John Orton	.05	.02	.01
☐ 95 Dean Palmer	.35	.16	.04
☐ 96 Ramon Pena	.05	.02	.01
☐ 97 Jeff Peterek	.05	.02	.01
☐ 98 Marty Pevey	.05	.02	.01
☐ 99 Rusty Richards	.05	.02	.01
☐ 100 Jeff Richardson	.05	.02	.01
☐ 101 Rob Richie	.05	.02	.01
☐ 102 Kevin Ritz	.05	.02	.01
☐ 103 Rosario Rodriguez	.05	.02	.01
☐ 104 Mike Roesler	.05	.02	.01
☐ 105 Kenny Rogers	.25	.11	.03
☐ 106 Bobby Rose	.05	.02	.01
☐ 107 Alex Sanchez	.05	.02	.01
☐ 108 Deion Sanders	1.25	.55	.16
☐ 109 Jeff Schaefer	.05	.02	.01
☐ 110 Jeff Schulz	.05	.02	.01
☐ 111 Mike Schwabe	.05	.02	.01
☐ 112 Dick Scott	.05	.02	.01
☐ 113 Scott Scudder	.05	.02	.01
☐ 114 Rudy Seanez	.05	.02	.01
☐ 115 Joe Skalski	.05	.02	.01
☐ 116 Dwight Smith	.15	.07	.02
☐ 117 Greg Smith	.05	.02	.01
☐ 118 Mike Smith	.05	.02	.01
☐ 119 Paul Sorrento	.50	.23	.06
☐ 120 Sammy Sosa	1.50	.70	.19
☐ 121 Billy Spiers	.05	.02	.01
☐ 122 Mike Stanton	.05	.02	.01
☐ 123 Phil Stephenson	.05	.02	.01
☐ 124 Doug Strange	.05	.02	.01
☐ 125 Russ Swan	.05	.02	.01
☐ 126 Kevin Tapani	.25	.11	.03
☐ 127 Stu Tate	.05	.02	.01
☐ 128 Greg Vaughn	.40	.18	.05
☐ 129 Robin Ventura	.50	.23	.06
☐ 130 Randy Veres	.05	.02	.01
☐ 131 Jose Vizcaino	.25	.11	.03
☐ 132 Omar Vizquel	.40	.18	.05
☐ 133 Larry Walker	1.50	.70	.19
☐ 134 Jerome Walton	.15	.07	.02
☐ 135 Gary Wayne	.05	.02	.01
☐ 136 Lenny Webster	.05	.02	.01
☐ 137 Mickey Weston	.05	.02	.01
☐ 138 Jeff Wetherby	.05	.02	.01
☐ 139 John Wetteland	.30	.14	.04
☐ 140 Ed Whited	.05	.02	.01
☐ 141 Wally Whitehurst	.05	.02	.01
☐ 142 Kevin Wickander	.05	.02	.01
☐ 143 Dean Wilkins	.05	.02	.01
☐ 144 Dana Williams	.05	.02	.01
☐ 145 Paul Wilmet	.05	.02	.01
☐ 146 Craig Wilson	.05	.02	.01
☐ 147 Matt Winters	.05	.02	.01
☐ 148 Eric Yelding	.05	.02	.01
☐ 149 Clint Zavaras	.05	.02	.01
☐ 150 Todd Zeile	.25	.11	.03
☐ 151 Checklist Card	.05	.02	.01
☐ 152 Checklist Card	.05	.02	.01

1990 Topps Doubleheaders

The 1990 Topps Double Headers set consists of 72 collectibles. Each Double Header consists of a clear plastic holder that contains a mini-reproduction of the player's 1990 card on one side and a mini-reproduction of his rookie card on the other side. The Double Headers were packaged in a paper pouch to conceal the player's identity prior to purchase. Three different checklists (A, B, and C) are printed on the outside of the packs, with the players listed in alphabetical order, and the double headers are checklisted below in alphabetcal order.

	MINT	NRMT	EXC
COMPLETE SET (72)	25.00	11.00	3.10
COMMON CARD (1-72)	.25	.11	.03
☐ 1 Jim Abbott	.50	.23	.06
☐ 2 Jeff Ballard	.25	.11	.03
☐ 3 George Bell	.25	.11	.03
☐ 4 Wade Boggs	1.00	.45	.12
☐ 5 Barry Bonds	2.00	.90	.25
☐ 6 Bobby Bonilla	.50	.23	.06
☐ 7 Ellis Burks	1.00	.45	.12
☐ 8 Jose Canseco	1.50	.70	.19
☐ 9 Joe Carter	.75	.35	.09
☐ 10 Will Clark	1.00	.45	.12
☐ 11 Roger Clemens	1.50	.70	.19
☐ 12 Vince Coleman	.25	.11	.03
☐ 13 Alvin Davis	.25	.11	.03
☐ 14 Eric Davis	.50	.23	.06
☐ 15 Glenn Davis	.25	.11	.03
☐ 16 Mark Davis	.25	.11	.03
☐ 17 Andre Dawson	.75	.35	.09
☐ 18 Shawon Dunston	.25	.11	.03
☐ 19 Dennis Eckersley	.75	.35	.09
☐ 20 Sid Fernandez	.25	.11	.03
☐ 21 Tony Fernandez	.25	.11	.03
☐ 22 Chuck Finley	.25	.11	.03
☐ 23 Carlton Fisk	.75	.35	.09
☐ 24 Julio Franco	.50	.23	.06
☐ 25 Gary Gaetti	.25	.11	.03
☐ 26 Doc Gooden	.50	.23	.06
☐ 27 Mark Grace	1.00	.45	.12
☐ 28 Mike Greenwell	.25	.11	.03
☐ 29 Ken Griffey Jr.	8.00	3.60	1.00
☐ 30 Pedro Guerrero	.25	.11	.03
☐ 31 Tony Gwynn	4.00	1.80	.50
☐ 32 Von Hayes	.25	.11	.03
☐ 33 Rickey Henderson	1.50	.70	.19
☐ 34 Orel Hershiser	.50	.23	.06
☐ 35 Bo Jackson	.50	.23	.06
☐ 36 Gregg Jefferies	.50	.23	.06
☐ 37 Howard Johnson	.25	.11	.03
☐ 38 Ricky Jordan	.25	.11	.03
☐ 39 Carney Lansford	.25	.11	.03
☐ 40 Barry Larkin	1.50	.70	.19
☐ 41 Greg Maddux	5.00	2.20	.60
☐ 42 Joe Magrane	.25	.11	.03
☐ 43 Don Mattingly	4.00	1.80	.50
☐ 44 Fred McGriff	1.00	.45	.12
☐ 45 Mark McGwire	3.00	1.35	.35
☐ 46 Kevin McReynolds	.25	.11	.03
☐ 47 Kevin Mitchell	.25	.11	.03
☐ 48 Gregg Olson	.25	.11	.03
☐ 49 Kirby Puckett	4.00	1.80	.50
☐ 50 Rock Raines	.50	.23	.06
☐ 51 Harold Reynolds	.25	.11	.03
☐ 52 Cal Ripken	6.00	2.70	.75
☐ 53 Nolan Ryan	6.00	2.70	.75
☐ 54 Bret Saberhagen	.25	.11	.03
☐ 55 Ryne Sandberg	3.00	1.35	.35
☐ 56 Benny Santiago	.25	.11	.03
☐ 57 Steve Sax	.25	.11	.03
☐ 58 Mike Scioscia	.25	.11	.03
☐ 59 Mike Scott	.25	.11	.03
☐ 60 Ruben Sierra	.25	.11	.03
☐ 61 Lonnie Smith	.25	.11	.03
☐ 62 Ozzie Smith	3.00	1.35	.35
☐ 63 Dave Stewart	.25	.11	.03
☐ 64 Darryl Strawberry	.50	.23	.06
☐ 65 Greg Swindell	.25	.11	.03
☐ 66 Alan Trammell	.50	.23	.06
☐ 67 Frank Viola	.25	.11	.03
☐ 68 Tim Wallach	.25	.11	.03
☐ 69 Jerome Walton	.25	.11	.03
☐ 70 Lou Whitaker	.50	.23	.06
☐ 71 Mitch Williams	.25	.11	.03
☐ 72 Robin Yount	1.00	.45	.12

1990 Topps Gallery of Champions

This would be the seventh out of eight consecutive seasons that Topps issued small "metal" versions of some leading players from their regular issue set. These 12 cards, issued in complete set form only, feature league leaders and award winners. The cards measure approximately 1 1/4" by 1 3/4" and were produced in aluminum, bronze and silver versions. We have valued the aluminum cards, the bronze cards are valued at 2X to 5X the values of the aluminum versions while the silvers are 7X to 15X the aluminums. We have sequenced this set in alphabetical order.

	MINT	NRMT	EXC
COMPLETE SET (12)	125.00	55.00	15.50
COMMON CARD (1-12)	5.00	2.20	.60

Card	MINT	NRMT	EXC
☐ 1 Mark Davis	5.00	2.20	.60
☐ 2 Jose DeLeon	5.00	2.20	.60
☐ 3 Tony Gwynn	25.00	11.00	3.10
☐ 4 Fred McGriff	20.00	9.00	2.50
☐ 5 Kevin Mitchell	5.00	2.20	.60
☐ 6 Gregg Olson	5.00	2.20	.60
☐ 7 Kirby Puckett	25.00	11.00	3.10
☐ 8 Jeff Russell	5.00	2.20	.60
☐ 9 Nolan Ryan	50.00	22.00	6.25
☐ 10 Bret Saberhagen	5.00	2.20	.60
☐ 11 Jerome Walton	5.00	2.20	.60
☐ 12 Robin Yount	15.00	6.75	1.85

1990 Topps Heads Up

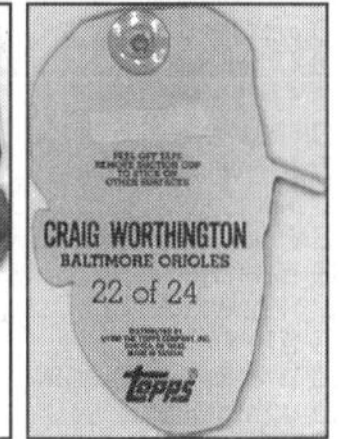

Though this collectible item made a limited appearance in 1989, the 1990 Topps set features 24 different Heads-Up pin-ups. Each item is a die-cut pin-up of a baseball star printed on thick white board, with a suction cup attached to the back. The die-cuts follow the contours of the player's hat and head, and they can be attached to any flat surface. The player's name and number appear on the back. The pin-ups are listed below according to the checklist printed on the back of each wrapper.

	MINT	NRMT	EXC
COMPLETE SET (24)	7.00	3.10	.85
COMMON CARD (1-24)	.15	.07	.02
☐ 1 Tony Gwynn	1.00	.45	.12
☐ 2 Will Clark	.60	.25	.07
☐ 3 Doc Gooden	.30	.14	.04
☐ 4 Dennis Eckersley	.50	.23	.06
☐ 5 Ken Griffey Jr.	2.00	.90	.25
☐ 6 Craig Biggio	.50	.23	.06
☐ 7 Bret Saberhagen	.30	.14	.04
☐ 8 Bo Jackson	.30	.14	.04
☐ 9 Ryne Sandberg	.75	.35	.09
☐ 10 Gregg Olson	.15	.07	.02
☐ 11 John Franco	.15	.07	.02
☐ 12 Rafael Palmeiro	.50	.23	.06
☐ 13 Gary Sheffield	.75	.35	.09
☐ 14 Mark McGwire	1.00	.45	.12
☐ 15 Kevin Mitchell	.15	.07	.02
☐ 16 Jim Abbott	.30	.14	.04
☐ 17 Harold Reynolds	.15	.07	.02
☐ 18 Jose Canseco	.60	.25	.07
☐ 19 Don Mattingly	1.00	.45	.12
☐ 20 Kirby Puckett	1.00	.45	.12
☐ 21 Tom Gordon	.15	.07	.02
☐ 22 Craig Worthington	.15	.07	.02
☐ 23 Dwight Smith	.15	.07	.02
☐ 24 Jerome Walton	.15	.07	.02

1990 Topps Hills Hit Men

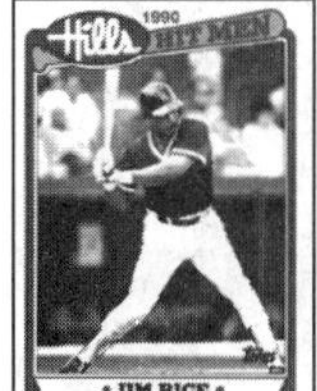

The 1990 Topps Hit Men set is a standard-size 33-card set arranged in order of slugging percentage. The set was produced by Topps for Hills Department stores. Each card in the set has a glossy-coated front.

	MINT	NRMT	EXC
COMPLETE SET (33)	5.00	2.20	.60
COMMON CARD (1-33)	.05	.02	.01
☐ 1 Eric Davis	.05	.02	.01
☐ 2 Will Clark	.40	.18	.05
☐ 3 Don Mattingly	1.00	.45	.12
☐ 4 Darryl Strawberry	.10	.05	.01
☐ 5 Kevin Mitchell	.10	.05	.01
☐ 6 Pedro Guerrero	.10	.05	.01
☐ 7 Jose Canseco	.40	.18	.05
☐ 8 Jim Rice	.10	.05	.01
☐ 9 Danny Tartabull	.05	.02	.01
☐ 10 George Brett	1.00	.45	.12
☐ 11 Kent Hrbek	.10	.05	.01
☐ 12 George Bell	.10	.05	.01
☐ 13 Eddie Murray	.40	.18	.05
☐ 14 Fred Lynn	.05	.02	.01
☐ 15 Andre Dawson	.25	.11	.03
☐ 16 Dale Murphy	.20	.09	.03
☐ 17 Dave Winfield	.40	.18	.05
☐ 18 Jack Clark	.10	.05	.01
☐ 19 Wade Boggs	.30	.14	.04
☐ 20 Ruben Sierra	.10	.05	.01
☐ 21 Dave Parker	.10	.05	.01
☐ 22 Glenn Davis	.05	.02	.01
☐ 23 Dwight Evans	.10	.05	.01
☐ 24 Jesse Barfield	.05	.02	.01
☐ 25 Kirk Gibson	.10	.05	.01
☐ 26 Alvin Davis	.05	.02	.01
☐ 27 Kirby Puckett	1.00	.45	.12
☐ 28 Joe Carter	.10	.05	.01
☐ 29 Carlton Fisk	.40	.18	.05
☐ 30 Harold Baines	.10	.05	.01
☐ 31 Andres Galarraga	.30	.14	.04
☐ 32 Cal Ripken	2.00	.90	.25
☐ 33 Howard Johnson	.05	.02	.01

1990 Topps Mini Leaders

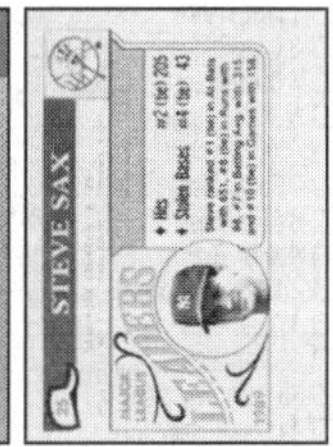

The 1990 Topps League Leader Minis is an 88-card set with cards measuring approximately 2 1/8" by 3". The set features players who finished 1989 in the top five in any major hitting or pitching category. This set marked the fifth year that Topps issued their Mini set. The card numbering is alphabetical by player within team and the teams themselves are ordered alphabetically.

	MINT	NRMT	EXC
COMPLETE SET (88)	5.00	2.20	.60
COMMON CARD (1-88)	.05	.02	.01
☐ 1 Jeff Ballard	.05	.02	.01
☐ 2 Phil Bradley	.05	.02	.01
☐ 3 Wade Boggs	.30	.14	.04
☐ 4 Roger Clemens	.40	.18	.05
☐ 5 Nick Esasky	.05	.02	.01
☐ 6 Jody Reed	.05	.02	.01
☐ 7 Bert Blyleven	.10	.05	.01
☐ 8 Chuck Finley	.10	.05	.01
☐ 9 Kirk McCaskill	.05	.02	.01
☐ 10 Devon White	.10	.05	.01
☐ 11 Ivan Calderon	.05	.02	.01
☐ 12 Bobby Thigpen	.05	.02	.01
☐ 13 Joe Carter	.20	.09	.03
☐ 14 Gary Pettis	.05	.02	.01
☐ 15 Tom Gordon	.05	.02	.01
☐ 16 Bo Jackson	.10	.05	.01
☐ 17 Bret Saberhagen	.10	.05	.01
☐ 18 Kevin Seitzer	.05	.02	.01
☐ 19 Chris Bosio	.05	.02	.01
☐ 20 Paul Molitor	.30	.14	.04
☐ 21 Dan Plesac	.05	.02	.01
☐ 22 Robin Yount	.20	.09	.03
☐ 23 Kirby Puckett	1.00	.45	.12
☐ 24 Don Mattingly	1.00	.45	.12
☐ 25 Steve Sax	.05	.02	.01
☐ 26 Storm Davis	.05	.02	.01
☐ 27 Dennis Eckersley	.10	.05	.01
☐ 28 Rickey Henderson	.30	.14	.04
☐ 29 Carney Lansford	.05	.02	.01
☐ 30 Mark McGwire	.75	.35	.09
☐ 31 Mike Moore	.05	.02	.01
☐ 32 Dave Stewart	.05	.02	.01
☐ 33 Alvin Davis	.05	.02	.01
☐ 34 Harold Reynolds	.05	.02	.01
☐ 35 Mike Schooler	.05	.02	.01
☐ 36 Cecil Espy	.05	.02	.01
☐ 37 Julio Franco	.10	.05	.01
☐ 38 Jeff Russell	.05	.02	.01
☐ 39 Nolan Ryan	1.50	.70	.19
☐ 40 Ruben Sierra	.10	.05	.01
☐ 41 George Bell	.05	.02	.01
☐ 42 Tony Fernandez	.05	.02	.01
☐ 43 Fred McGriff	.30	.14	.04
☐ 44 Dave Stieb	.05	.02	.01
☐ 45 Checklist Card	.05	.02	.01
☐ 46 Lonnie Smith	.05	.02	.01
☐ 47 John Smoltz	.40	.18	.05
☐ 48 Mike Bielecki	.05	.02	.01
☐ 49 Mark Grace	.40	.18	.05
☐ 50 Greg Maddux	1.50	.70	.19
☐ 51 Ryne Sandberg	.75	.35	.09
☐ 52 Mitch Williams	.05	.02	.01
☐ 53 Eric Davis	.10	.05	.01
☐ 54 John Franco	.10	.05	.01
☐ 55 Glenn Davis	.05	.02	.01
☐ 56 Mike Scott	.05	.02	.01
☐ 57 Tim Belcher	.05	.02	.01
☐ 58 Orel Hershiser	.10	.05	.01
☐ 59 Jay Howell	.05	.02	.01
☐ 60 Eddie Murray	.40	.18	.05
☐ 61 Tim Burke	.05	.02	.01
☐ 62 Mark Langston	.05	.02	.01
☐ 63 Tim Raines	.10	.05	.01
☐ 64 Tim Wallach	.05	.02	.01
☐ 65 David Cone	.20	.09	.03
☐ 66 Sid Fernandez	.05	.02	.01
☐ 67 Howard Johnson	.05	.02	.01
☐ 68 Juan Samuel	.05	.02	.01
☐ 69 Von Hayes	.05	.02	.01
☐ 70 Barry Bonds	.50	.23	.06
☐ 71 Bobby Bonilla	.10	.05	.01
☐ 72 Andy Van Slyke	.05	.02	.01
☐ 73 Vince Coleman	.05	.02	.01
☐ 74 Jose DeLeon	.05	.02	.01
☐ 75 Pedro Guerrero	.05	.02	.01
☐ 76 Joe Magrane	.05	.02	.01
☐ 77 Roberto Alomar	.75	.35	.09
☐ 78 Jack Clark	.05	.02	.01
☐ 79 Mark Davis	.05	.02	.01
☐ 80 Tony Gwynn	1.00	.45	.12
☐ 81 Bruce Hurst	.05	.02	.01
☐ 82 Eddie Whitson	.05	.02	.01
☐ 83 Brett Butler	.10	.05	.01
☐ 84 Will Clark	.30	.14	.04
☐ 85 Scott Garrelts	.05	.02	.01
☐ 86 Kevin Mitchell	.05	.02	.01
☐ 87 Rick Reuschel	.05	.02	.01
☐ 88 Robby Thompson	.05	.02	.01

1990 Topps/O-Pee-Chee Stickers

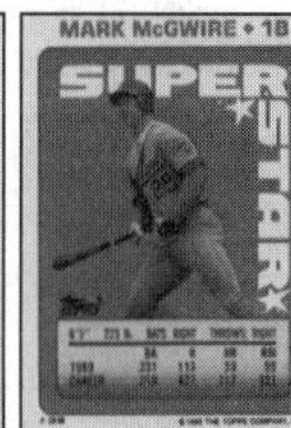

These 328 stickers measure approximately 2 1/8" by 3" and feature color player photos with white borders that have multicolored highlights. The stickers are numbered at the bottom right. The backs are actually cards from the 1990 Topps Super Stars and are considered a separate set. An album onto which the stickers could be affixed was available at retail stores. The album and the sticker numbering are organized as follows: 1989 Highlights (1-12), Houston Astros (13-23), Atlanta Braves (24-34), St. Louis Cardinals (35-45), Chicago Cubs (46-56), Los Angeles Dodgers (57-67), Montreal Expos (68-78), San Francisco Giants (79-89), New York Mets (90-100), San Diego Padres (101-111), Philadelphia Phillies (112-122), Pittsburgh Pirates (123-133), Cincinnati Reds (134-144), Foil All-Stars (145-164), California Angels (165-175), Oakland A's (176-186), Toronto Blue Jays (187-197), Milwaukee Brewers (198-208), Cleveland Indians (209-219), Seattle Mariners (220-230), Baltimore Orioles (231-241), Texas Rangers (242-252), Boston Red Sox (253-263), Kansas City Royals (264-274), Detroit Tigers (275-285), Minnesota Twins (286-296), Chicago White Sox (297-307), New York Yankees (308-318) and Future Stars (319-328). For those stickers featuring more than one player, the other numbers on that sticker are given below in parentheses. Although the prices listed below are for the stickers only, there are instances where having an especially desirable sticker card back (attached to that sticker) will increase the values listed below.

	MINT	NRMT	EXC
COMPLETE SET (328)	15.00	6.75	1.85
COMMON STICKER (1-328)	.05	.02	.01
*TOPPS AND OPC: SAME VALUE			
☐ 1 Rick Cerone HL (321)	.05	.02	.01
☐ 2 Kevin Elster HL (322)	.05	.02	.01
☐ 3 Nolan Ryan HL (323)	1.00	.45	.12
☐ 4 Vince Coleman HL (319)	.05	.02	.01
☐ 5 Cal Ripken HL (240)	1.00	.45	.12
☐ 6 Jeff Reardon HL (328)	.10	.05	.01
☐ 7 Rickey Henderson HL (320)	.15	.07	.02
☐ 8 Wade Boggs HL (324)	.15	.07	.02
☐ 9 Barry Bonds HL (325)	.25	.11	.03
☐ 10 Gregg Olson HL (236)	.05	.02	.01
☐ 11 Tony Fernandez HL (327)	.05	.02	.01
☐ 12 Ryne Sandberg HL (326)	.25	.11	.03
☐ 13 Glenn Davis	.05	.02	.01
☐ 14 Danny Darwin (316)	.05	.02	.01
☐ 15 Bill Doran (298)	.05	.02	.01
☐ 16 Dave Smith (255)	.05	.02	.01
☐ 17 Kevin Bass (278)	.05	.02	.01
☐ 18 Rafael Ramirez (177)	.05	.02	.01
☐ 19 Mike Scott	.05	.02	.01
☐ 20 Ken Caminiti (235)	.15	.07	.02
☐ 21 Jim Deshaies (272)	.05	.02	.01
☐ 22 Gerald Young (314)	.05	.02	.01
☐ 23 Craig Biggio (186)	.30	.14	.04
☐ 24 Lonnie Smith	.05	.02	.01
☐ 25 Dale Murphy (210)	.15	.07	.02
☐ 26 Tom Glavine	.25	.11	.03
☐ 27 Gerald Perry (313)	.05	.02	.01
☐ 28 Jeff Blauser (269)	.05	.02	.01
☐ 29 Jeff Treadway (252)	.05	.02	.01
☐ 30 John Smoltz (299)	.30	.14	.04
☐ 31 Darrell Evans (295)	.10	.05	.01
☐ 32 Oddibe McDowell (265)	.05	.02	.01
☐ 33 Andres Thomas (304)	.05	.02	.01
☐ 34 Joe Boever (191)	.05	.02	.01
☐ 35 Pedro Guerrero	.05	.02	.01
☐ 36 Ken Dayley (226)	.05	.02	.01
☐ 37 Milt Thompson (188)	.05	.02	.01
☐ 38 Jose DeLeon (180)	.05	.02	.01
☐ 39 Vince Coleman (293)	.05	.02	.01
☐ 40 Terry Pendleton (225)	.10	.05	.01
☐ 41 Joe Magrane	.05	.02	.01
☐ 42 Ozzie Smith (179)	.40	.18	.05
☐ 43 Todd Worrell (195)	.05	.02	.01
☐ 44 Jose Oquendo (238)	.05	.02	.01
☐ 45 Tom Brunansky (287)	.05	.02	.01
☐ 46 Ryne Sandberg	.50	.23	.06
☐ 47 Andre Dawson (268)	.10	.05	.01
☐ 48 Mitch Williams	.05	.02	.01
☐ 49 Damon Berryhill (204)	.05	.02	.01
☐ 50 Jerome Walton (274)	.05	.02	.01
☐ 51 Greg Maddux (315)	2.00	.90	.25
☐ 52 Dwight Smith (248)	.05	.02	.01
☐ 53 Shawon Dunston (194)	.05	.02	.01
☐ 54 Mike Bielecki (239)	.05	.02	.01
☐ 55 Rick Sutcliffe (305)	.05	.02	.01
☐ 56 Mark Grace (228)	.25	.11	.03
☐ 57 Eddie Murray	.30	.14	.04
☐ 58 Alfredo Griffin (197)	.05	.02	.01
☐ 59 Fernando Valenzuela (277)	.10	.05	.01
☐ 60 Kirk Gibson (201)	.10	.05	.01
☐ 61 Ramon Martinez (190)	.15	.07	.02
☐ 62 Mike Marshall (309)	.05	.02	.01
☐ 63 Orel Hershiser	.10	.05	.01
☐ 64 Mike Scioscia (271)	.05	.02	.01
☐ 65 Jay Howell (279)	.05	.02	.01
☐ 66 Willie Randolph (283)	.10	.05	.01
☐ 67 Jeff Hamilton (280)	.05	.02	.01
☐ 68 Denny Martinez	.10	.05	.01
☐ 69 Tim Raines (184)	.10	.05	.01
☐ 70 Mark Langston	.10	.05	.01
☐ 71 Dave Martinez (301)	.05	.02	.01
☐ 72 Tim Burke (258)	.05	.02	.01
☐ 73 Spike Owen (232)	.05	.02	.01
☐ 74 Tim Wallach (254)	.05	.02	.01
☐ 75 Andres Galarraga (208)	.15	.07	.02
☐ 76 Kevin Gross (234)	.05	.02	.01
☐ 77 Hubie Brooks (263)	.05	.02	.01
☐ 78 Bryn Smith (207)	.05	.02	.01
☐ 79 Kevin Mitchell	.05	.02	.01
☐ 80 Craig Lefferts (256)	.05	.02	.01
☐ 81 Ernest Riles (247)	.05	.02	.01
☐ 82 Scott Garrelts (185)	.05	.02	.01
☐ 83 Robby Thompson (251)	.05	.02	.01
☐ 84 Don Robinson (282)	.05	.02	.01
☐ 85 Will Clark	.25	.11	.03
☐ 86 Steve Bedrosian (183)	.05	.02	.01
☐ 87 Brett Butler (284)	.10	.05	.01
☐ 88 Matt Williams (227)	.40	.18	.05
☐ 89 Rick Reuschel (291)	.05	.02	.01
☐ 90 Howard Johnson	.05	.02	.01
☐ 91 Darryl Strawberry (246)	.10	.05	.01
☐ 92 Sid Fernandez	.05	.02	.01
☐ 93 David Cone (189)	.15	.07	.02
☐ 94 Kevin McReynolds (311)	.05	.02	.01
☐ 95 Frank Viola (229)	.05	.02	.01
☐ 96 Dwight Gooden (206)	.10	.05	.01
☐ 97 Kevin Elster (267)	.05	.02	.01
☐ 98 Ron Darling (289)	.05	.02	.01
☐ 99 Dave Magadan (257)	.05	.02	.01
☐ 100 Randy Myers (192)	.05	.02	.01
☐ 101 Tony Gwynn	.75	.35	.09
☐ 102 Mark Davis (312)	.05	.02	.01
☐ 103 Bip Roberts (212)	.05	.02	.01
☐ 104 Jack Clark (205)	.10	.05	.01
☐ 105 Chris James (211)	.05	.02	.01
☐ 106 Mike Pagliarulo (199)	.05	.02	.01
☐ 107 Eddie Whitson	.05	.02	.01
☐ 108 Bruce Hurst (245)	.05	.02	.01
☐ 109 Roberto Alomar (202)	.75	.35	.09
☐ 110 Benito Santiago (224)	.05	.02	.01
☐ 111 Eric Show (307)	.05	.02	.01
☐ 112 Ricky Jordan	.05	.02	.01
☐ 113 Steve Jeltz (203)	.05	.02	.01
☐ 114 Von Hayes	.05	.02	.01
☐ 115 Dickie Thon (182)	.05	.02	.01
☐ 116 Ken Howell (213)	.05	.02	.01
☐ 117 John Kruk (306)	.10	.05	.01

☐ 118 Len Dykstra (302)	.10	.05	.01
☐ 119 Jeff Parrett (300)	.05	.02	.01
☐ 120 Randy Ready (230)	.05	.02	.01
☐ 121 Roger McDowell (262)	.05	.02	.01
☐ 122 Tom Herr (250)	.05	.02	.01
☐ 123 Barry Bonds	.50	.23	.06
☐ 124 Andy Van Slyke (219)	.10	.05	.01
☐ 125 Bob Walk (216)	.05	.02	.01
☐ 126 R.J. Reynolds (243)	.05	.02	.01
☐ 127 Gary Redus (249)	.05	.02	.01
☐ 128 Bill Landrum (276)	.05	.02	.01
☐ 129 Bobby Bonilla	.10	.05	.01
☐ 130 Doug Drabek (218)	.05	.02	.01
☐ 131 Jose Lind (221)	.05	.02	.01
☐ 132 John Smiley (241)	.05	.02	.01
☐ 133 Mike LaValliere (214)	.05	.02	.01
☐ 134 Eric Davis	.05	.02	.01
☐ 135 Tom Browning (270)	.05	.02	.01
☐ 136 Barry Larkin	.25	.11	.03
☐ 137 Jose Rijo (318)	.05	.02	.01
☐ 138 Todd Benzinger (292)	.05	.02	.01
☐ 139 Rick Mahler (217)	.05	.02	.01
☐ 140 Chris Sabo (196)	.05	.02	.01
☐ 141 Paul O'Neill (175)	.10	.05	.01
☐ 142 Danny Jackson (273)	.05	.02	.01
☐ 143 Rolando Roomes (261)	.05	.02	.01
☐ 144 John Franco (233)	.05	.02	.01
☐ 145 Ozzie Smith AS	.15	.07	.02
☐ 146 Tony Gwynn AS	.40	.18	.05
☐ 147 Will Clark AS	.15	.07	.02
☐ 148 Kevin Mitchell AS	.05	.02	.01
☐ 149 Eric Davis AS	.05	.02	.01
☐ 150 Howard Johnson AS	.05	.02	.01
☐ 151 Pedro Guerrero AS	.05	.02	.01
☐ 152 Ryne Sandberg AS	.25	.11	.03
☐ 153 Benito Santiago AS	.05	.02	.01
☐ 154 Rick Reuschel AS	.05	.02	.01
☐ 155 Bo Jackson AS	.10	.05	.01
☐ 156 Wade Boggs AS	.15	.07	.02
☐ 157 Kirby Puckett AS	.25	.11	.03
☐ 158 Harold Baines AS	.10	.05	.01
☐ 159 Julio Franco AS	.10	.05	.01
☐ 160 Cal Ripken AS	1.00	.45	.12
☐ 161 Ruben Sierra AS	.10	.05	.01
☐ 162 Mark McGwire AS	.20	.09	.03
☐ 163 Terry Steinbach AS	.10	.05	.01
☐ 164 Dave Stewart AS	.10	.05	.01
☐ 165 Bert Blyleven	.10	.05	.01
☐ 166 Wally Joyner (285)	.10	.05	.01
☐ 167 Kirk McCaskill (290)	.05	.02	.01
☐ 168 Devon White (223)	.10	.05	.01
☐ 169 Brian Downing (294)	.05	.02	.01
☐ 170 Lance Parrish (296)	.10	.05	.01
☐ 171 Chuck Finley	.10	.05	.01
☐ 172 Jim Abbott (317)	.10	.05	.01
☐ 173 Chili Davis (181)	.10	.05	.01
☐ 174 Johnny Ray (260)	.05	.02	.01
☐ 175 Bryan Harvey (141)	.05	.02	.01
☐ 176 Mark McGwire	.50	.23	.06
☐ 177 Jose Canseco (18)	.25	.11	.03
☐ 178 Mike Moore	.05	.02	.01
☐ 179 Dave Parker (42)	.10	.05	.01
☐ 180 Bob Welch (38)	.05	.02	.01
☐ 181 Rickey Henderson (173)	.25	.11	.03
☐ 182 Dennis Eckersley (115)	.10	.05	.01
☐ 183 Carney Lansford (86)	.10	.05	.01
☐ 184 Dave Henderson (69)	.05	.02	.01
☐ 185 Dave Stewart (82)	.10	.05	.01
☐ 186 Terry Steinbach (23)	.10	.05	.01
☐ 187 Fred McGriff	.25	.11	.03
☐ 188 Junior Felix (37)	.05	.02	.01
☐ 189 Ernie Whitt (93)	.05	.02	.01
☐ 190 Dave Smith (61)	.05	.02	.01
☐ 191 Jimmy Key (34)	.05	.02	.01
☐ 192 George Bell (100)	.05	.02	.01
☐ 193 Kelly Gruber	.05	.02	.01
☐ 194 Tony Fernandez (53)	.05	.02	.01
☐ 195 John Cerutti (43)	.05	.02	.01
☐ 196 Tom Henke (140)	.05	.02	.01
☐ 197 Nelson Liriano (58)	.05	.02	.01
☐ 198 Robin Yount	.25	.11	.03
☐ 199 Paul Molitor (106)	.25	.11	.03
☐ 200 Dan Plesac	.05	.02	.01
☐ 201 Teddy Higuera (60)	.05	.02	.01
☐ 202 Gary Sheffield (109)	.30	.14	.04
☐ 203 B.J. Surhoff (113)	.10	.05	.01
☐ 204 Rob Deer (49)	.05	.02	.01
☐ 205 Chris Bosio (104)	.05	.02	.01
☐ 206 Glenn Braggs (96)	.05	.02	.01
☐ 207 Jim Gantner (78)	.05	.02	.01
☐ 208 Greg Brock (75)	.05	.02	.01
☐ 209 Joe Carter	.10	.05	.01
☐ 210 Jerry Browne (25)	.05	.02	.01
☐ 211 Cory Snyder (105)	.05	.02	.01
☐ 212 Joey Belle (103)	2.00	.90	.25
☐ 213 Bud Black (116)	.05	.02	.01
☐ 214 Greg Swindell (133)	.05	.02	.01
☐ 215 Doug Jones	.05	.02	.01
☐ 216 Tom Candiotti (125)	.05	.02	.01
☐ 217 John Farrell (217)	.05	.02	.01
☐ 218 Pete O'Brien (130)	.05	.02	.01
☐ 219 Brook Jacoby (124)	.05	.02	.01
☐ 220 Alvin Davis	.05	.02	.01
☐ 221 Harold Reynolds (131)	.05	.02	.01
☐ 222 Scott Bankhead	.05	.02	.01
☐ 223 Jeffrey Leonard (168)	.05	.02	.01
☐ 224 Jim Presley (110)	.05	.02	.01
☐ 225 Ken Griffey Jr. (40)	3.00	1.35	.35
☐ 226 Greg Briley (36)	.05	.02	.01
☐ 227 Darnell Coles (88)	.05	.02	.01
☐ 228 Mike Schooler (56)	.05	.02	.01
☐ 229 Scott Bradley (95)	.05	.02	.01
☐ 230 Randy Johnson (120)	.50	.23	.06
☐ 231 Cal Ripken	2.00	.90	.25
☐ 232 Jeff Ballard (73)	.05	.02	.01
☐ 233 Randy Milligan (144)	.05	.02	.01
☐ 234 Joe Orsulak (76)	.05	.02	.01
☐ 235 Billy Ripken (20)	.05	.02	.01
☐ 236 Mark Williamson (10)	.05	.02	.01
☐ 237 Mickey Tettleton	.10	.05	.01
☐ 238 Gregg Olson (44)	.05	.02	.01
☐ 239 Craig Worthington (54)	.05	.02	.01
☐ 240 Bob Milacki (5)	.05	.02	.01
☐ 241 Phil Bradley (132)	.05	.02	.01
☐ 242 Nolan Ryan	2.00	.90	.25
☐ 243 Julio Franco (126)	.10	.05	.01
☐ 244 Ruben Sierra	.10	.05	.01
☐ 245 Harold Baines (108)	.10	.05	.01
☐ 246 Jeff Kunkel (91)	.05	.02	.01
☐ 247 Pete Incaviglia (81)	.05	.02	.01
☐ 248 Kevin Brown (52)	.15	.07	.02
☐ 249 Cecil Espy (127)	.05	.02	.01
☐ 250 Rafael Palmeiro (122)	.15	.07	.02
☐ 251 Steve Buechele (83)	.05	.02	.01
☐ 252 Jeff Russell (29)	.05	.02	.01
☐ 253 Wade Boggs	.25	.11	.03
☐ 254 Mike Greenwell (74)	.05	.02	.01
☐ 255 Roger Clemens (16)	.25	.11	.03
☐ 256 Marty Barrett (80)	.05	.02	.01
☐ 257 Dwight Evans (99)	.10	.05	.01
☐ 258 Mike Boddicker (72)	.05	.02	.01
☐ 259 Ellis Burks	.15	.07	.02
☐ 260 John Dopson (174)	.05	.02	.01
☐ 261 Rob Murphy (143)	.05	.02	.01
☐ 262 Lee Smith (121)	.10	.05	.01
☐ 263 Nick Esasky (77)	.05	.02	.01
☐ 264 Bo Jackson	.10	.05	.01
☐ 265 George Brett (32)	.75	.35	.09
☐ 266 Bret Saberhagen	.10	.05	.01
☐ 267 Kevin Seitzer (97)	.05	.02	.01
☐ 268 Tom Gordon (47)	.05	.02	.01
☐ 269 Kurt Stillwell (28)	.05	.02	.01
☐ 270 Steve Farr (135)	.05	.02	.01
☐ 271 Jim Eisenreich (64)	.10	.05	.01
☐ 272 Mark Gubicza (21)	.05	.02	.01
☐ 273 Jeff Montgomery (142)	.05	.02	.01
☐ 274 Danny Tartabull (50)	.05	.02	.01
☐ 275 Lou Whitaker	.10	.05	.01
☐ 276 Jack Morris (128)	.10	.05	.01
☐ 277 Frank Tanana (59)	.05	.02	.01
☐ 278 Chet Lemon (17)	.05	.02	.01
☐ 279 Fred Lynn (65)	.10	.05	.01
☐ 280 Mike Heath (67)	.05	.02	.01
☐ 281 Alan Trammell	.10	.05	.01
☐ 282 Mike Henneman (84)	.05	.02	.01
☐ 283 Gary Pettis (66)	.05	.02	.01
☐ 284 Jeff M. Robinson (87)	.05	.02	.01
☐ 285 Dave Bergman (166)	.05	.02	.01
☐ 286 Kirby Puckett	.50	.23	.06
☐ 287 Kent Hrbek (45)	.10	.05	.01
☐ 288 Gary Gaetti	.05	.02	.01
☐ 289 Jeff Reardon (98)	.10	.05	.01
☐ 290 Brian Harper (167)	.05	.02	.01
☐ 291 Gene Larkin (89)	.05	.02	.01
☐ 292 Dan Gladden (138)	.05	.02	.01
☐ 293 Al Newman (39)	.05	.02	.01
☐ 294 Randy Bush (169)	.05	.02	.01
☐ 295 Greg Gagne (31)	.05	.02	.01
☐ 296 Allan Anderson (170)	.05	.02	.01
☐ 297 Bobby Thigpen	.05	.02	.01
☐ 298 Ozzie Guillen (15)	.05	.02	.01
☐ 299 Ivan Calderon (30)	.05	.02	.01
☐ 300 Carlos Martinez (119)	.05	.02	.01
☐ 301 Steve Lyons (71)	.05	.02	.01
☐ 302 Ron Kittle (118)	.05	.02	.01
☐ 303 Carlton Fisk	.25	.11	.03
☐ 304 Melido Perez (33)	.05	.02	.01
☐ 305 Dave Gallagher (55)	.05	.02	.01
☐ 306 Dan Pasqua (117)	.05	.02	.01
☐ 307 Scott Fletcher (111)	.05	.02	.01
☐ 308 Don Mattingly	1.00	.45	.12
☐ 309 Dan Pasqua (62)	.05	.02	.01
☐ 310 Steve Sax	.05	.02	.01
☐ 311 Alvaro Espinoza (94)	.05	.02	.01
☐ 312 Roberto Kelly (102)	.05	.02	.01
☐ 313 Mel Hall (27)	.05	.02	.01
☐ 314 Jesse Barfield (22)	.05	.02	.01
☐ 315 Chuck Cary (51)	.05	.02	.01
☐ 316 Bob Geren (14)	.05	.02	.01
☐ 317 Andy Hawkins (172)	.05	.02	.01
☐ 318 Don Slaught (137)	.05	.02	.01
☐ 319 Jim Abbott FS (4)	.10	.05	.01
☐ 320 Greg Briley FS (7)	.05	.02	.01
☐ 321 Bob Geren FS (1)	.05	.02	.01
☐ 322 Tom Gordon FS (2)	.05	.02	.01
☐ 323 Ken Griffey Jr. FS (3)	1.50	.70	.19
☐ 324 Gregg Jefferies FS (8)	.10	.05	.01
☐ 325 Carlos Martinez FS (9)	.05	.02	.01
☐ 326 Gary Sheffield FS (12)	.15	.07	.02
☐ 327 Jerome Walton FS (11)	.05	.02	.01
☐ 328 Craig Worthington FS(6)	.05	.02	.01
☐ xx Album	1.00	.45	.12

1990 Topps TV All-Stars

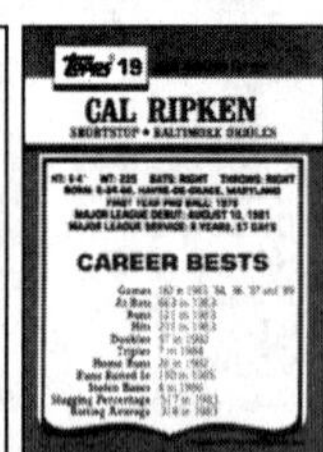

This All-Star team set contains 66 cards measuring the standard size. The fronts feature posed or action color player photos with a high gloss. In block lettering, the words "All-Star" are printed vertically in blue on the left side of the card. The player's name appears in a red plaque below the picture, and white borders round out the card face. The backs are printed in black lettering and have a red and white background. Inside a decal design, biographical information and career bests are superimposed on a blue, pink, and white background. These cards were offered only on television as a complete set for sale through an 800 number.

	MINT	NRMT	EXC
COMPLETE SET (66)	80.00	36.00	10.00
COMMON CARD (1-66)	.60	.25	.07
☐ 1 Mark McGwire	5.00	2.20	.60
☐ 2 Julio Franco	.60	.25	.07
☐ 3 Ozzie Guillen	.60	.25	.07
☐ 4 Carney Lansford	.60	.25	.07
☐ 5 Bo Jackson	1.00	.45	.12
☐ 6 Kirby Puckett	8.00	3.60	1.00
☐ 7 Ruben Sierra	1.00	.45	.12
☐ 8 Carlton Fisk	1.50	.70	.19
☐ 9 Nolan Ryan	15.00	6.75	1.85
☐ 10 Rickey Henderson	1.50	.70	.19
☐ 11 Jose Canseco	2.50	1.10	.30
☐ 12 Mark Davis	.60	.25	.07
☐ 13 Dennis Eckersley	1.00	.45	.12
☐ 14 Chuck Finley	.60	.25	.07
☐ 15 Bret Saberhagen	1.00	.45	.12
☐ 16 Dave Stewart	.60	.25	.07
☐ 17 Don Mattingly	8.00	3.60	1.00
☐ 18 Steve Sax	.60	.25	.07
☐ 19 Cal Ripken	15.00	6.75	1.85
☐ 20 Wade Boggs	2.00	.90	.25
☐ 21 George Bell	.60	.25	.07
☐ 22 Mike Greenwell	.60	.25	.07
☐ 23 Robin Yount	2.50	1.10	.30
☐ 24 Mickey Tettleton	.60	.25	.07
☐ 25 Roger Clemens	3.00	1.35	.35
☐ 26 Fred McGriff	2.50	1.10	.30
☐ 27 Jeff Ballard	.60	.25	.07
☐ 28 Dwight Evans	1.00	.45	.12
☐ 29 Paul Molitor	4.00	1.80	.50
☐ 30 Gregg Olson	.60	.25	.07
☐ 31 Dan Plesac	.60	.25	.07
☐ 32 Greg Swindell	.60	.25	.07
☐ 33 Tony LaRussa MG Cito Gaston MG	.60	.25	.07
☐ 34 Will Clark	2.50	1.10	.30
☐ 35 Roberto Alomar	5.00	2.20	.60
☐ 36 Barry Larkin	2.50	1.10	.30
☐ 37 Ken Caminiti	1.50	.70	.19
☐ 38 Eric Davis	1.00	.45	.12
☐ 39 Tony Gwynn	8.00	3.60	1.00
☐ 40 Kevin Mitchell	.60	.25	.07
☐ 41 Craig Biggio	2.50	1.10	.30
☐ 42 Mike Scott	.60	.25	.07
☐ 43 Joe Carter	2.00	.90	.25
☐ 44 Jack Clark	.60	.25	.07
☐ 45 Glenn Davis	.60	.25	.07
☐ 46 Orel Hershiser	1.00	.45	.12
☐ 47 Jay Howell	.60	.25	.07
☐ 48 Bruce Hurst	.60	.25	.07
☐ 49 Dave Smith	.60	.25	.07
☐ 50 Pedro Guerrero	.60	.25	.07
☐ 51 Ryne Sandberg	6.00	2.70	.75
☐ 52 Ozzie Smith	6.00	2.70	.75
☐ 53 Howard Johnson	.60	.25	.07
☐ 54 Von Hayes	.60	.25	.07
☐ 55 Tim Raines	1.00	.45	.12
☐ 56 Darryl Strawberry	1.00	.45	.12
☐ 57 Mike LaValliere	.60	.25	.07
☐ 58 Dwight Gooden	1.00	.45	.12
☐ 59 Bobby Bonilla	1.00	.45	.12
☐ 60 Tim Burke	.60	.25	.07
☐ 61 Sid Fernandez	.60	.25	.07
☐ 62 Andres Galarraga	2.00	.90	.25
☐ 63 Mark Grace	2.50	1.10	.30
☐ 64 Joe Magrane	.60	.25	.07
☐ 65 Mitch Williams	.60	.25	.07
☐ 66 Roger Craig MG and Don Zimmer MG	.60	.25	.07

1990 Topps TV Cardinals

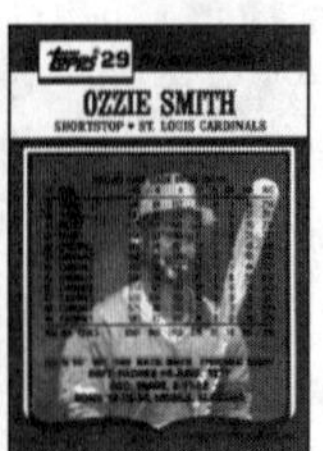

This Cardinals team set contains 66 cards measuring the standard size. The fronts feature posed or action color player photos with a high gloss. In block lettering, the team name is printed vertically in red and pink on the left side of the card. The player's name appears in a blue plaque below the picture, and white borders round out the card face. The backs are printed in black lettering and have a red and white background. Inside a decal design, player information and statistics are superimposed on an indistinct version of the same picture as on the front. Cards numbered 1-36 were with the parent club, while cards 37-66 were in the farm system.

	MINT	NRMT	EXC
COMPLETE SET (66)	35.00	16.00	4.40
COMMON CARD (1-66)	.30	.14	.04
☐ 1 Whitey Herzog MG	.50	.23	.06
☐ 2 Steve Braun CO	.30	.14	.04
☐ 3 Rich Hacker CO	.30	.14	.04
☐ 4 Dave Ricketts CO	.30	.14	.04
☐ 5 Jim Riggleman CO	.30	.14	.04
☐ 6 Mike Roarke CO	.30	.14	.04
☐ 7 Cris Carpenter	.30	.14	.04
☐ 8 John Costello	.30	.14	.04
☐ 9 Danny Cox	.30	.14	.04
☐ 10 Ken Dayley	.30	.14	.04
☐ 11 Jose DeLeon	.30	.14	.04
☐ 12 Frank DiPino	.30	.14	.04
☐ 13 Ken Hill	1.25	.55	.16
☐ 14 Howard Hilton	.30	.14	.04
☐ 15 Ricky Horton	.30	.14	.04
☐ 16 Joe Magrane	.30	.14	.04
☐ 17 Greg Mathews	.30	.14	.04
☐ 18 Bryn Smith	.30	.14	.04
☐ 19 Scott Terry	.30	.14	.04
☐ 20 Bob Tewksbury	.30	.14	.04
☐ 21 John Tudor	.30	.14	.04
☐ 22 Todd Worrell	.50	.23	.06
☐ 23 Tom Pagnozzi	.30	.14	.04
☐ 24 Todd Zeile	.50	.23	.06
☐ 25 Pedro Guerrero	.50	.23	.06
☐ 26 Tim Jones	.30	.14	.04
☐ 27 Jose Oquendo	.30	.14	.04
☐ 28 Terry Pendleton	1.25	.55	.16
☐ 29 Ozzie Smith	20.00	9.00	2.50
☐ 30 Denny Walling	.30	.14	.04
☐ 31 Tom Brunansky	.50	.23	.06
☐ 32 Vince Coleman	.50	.23	.06
☐ 33 Dave Collins	.30	.14	.04
☐ 34 Willie McGee	.50	.23	.06
☐ 35 John Morris	.30	.14	.04
☐ 36 Milt Thompson	.30	.14	.04
☐ 37 Gibson Alba	.30	.14	.04
☐ 38 Scott Arnold	.30	.14	.04
☐ 39 Rod Brewer	.30	.14	.04
☐ 40 Greg Carmona	.30	.14	.04
☐ 41 Mark Clark	.50	.23	.06
☐ 42 Stan Clarke	.30	.14	.04
☐ 43 Paul Coleman	.30	.14	.04
☐ 44 Todd Crosby	.30	.14	.04
☐ 45 Brad DuVall	.30	.14	.04
☐ 46 John Ericks	.30	.14	.04
☐ 47 Bien Figueroa	.30	.14	.04
☐ 48 Terry Francona	.30	.14	.04
☐ 49 Ed Fulton	.30	.14	.04
☐ 50 Bernard Gilkey	4.00	1.80	.50
☐ 51 Ernie Camacho	.30	.14	.04
☐ 52 Mike Hinkle	.30	.14	.04
☐ 53 Ray Lankford	4.00	1.80	.50
☐ 54 Julian Martinez	.30	.14	.04
☐ 55 Jesus Mendez	.30	.14	.04
☐ 56 Mike Milchin	.30	.14	.04
☐ 57 Mauricio Nunez	.30	.14	.04
☐ 58 Omar Olivares	.30	.14	.04
☐ 59 Geronimo Pena	.30	.14	.04
☐ 60 Mike Perez	.30	.14	.04
☐ 61 Gaylen Pitts MG	.30	.14	.04
☐ 62 Mark Riggins CO	.30	.14	.04
☐ 63 Tim Sherrill	.30	.14	.04
☐ 64 Roy Silver	.30	.14	.04
☐ 65 Ray Stephens	.30	.14	.04
☐ 66 Craig Wilson	.30	.14	.04

1990 Topps TV Cubs

This Cubs team set contains 66 standard-size cards. The fronts feature posed or action color player photos with a high gloss. In block lettering, the team name is printed vertically in blue on the left side of the card. The player's name appears in a gold plaque below the picture, and white borders round out the card face. The backs are printed in black and have a red and white background. Inside a decal design, player information and statistics are superimposed on an indistinct version of the same picture as on the front. Cards numbered 1-35 were with the parent club, while cards 36-66 were in the farm system. The key card in this set is Greg Maddux

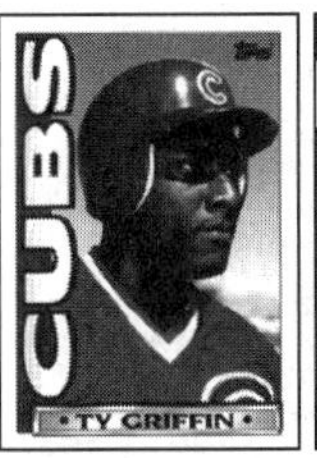

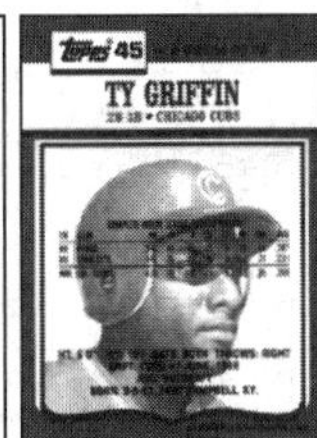

	MINT	NRMT	EXC
COMPLETE SET (66)	65.00	29.00	8.00
COMMON CARD (1-66)	.30	.14	.04
☐ 1 Don Zimmer MG	.50	.23	.06
☐ 2 Joe Altobelli CO	.30	.14	.04
☐ 3 Chuck Cottier CO	.30	.14	.04
☐ 4 Jose Martinez CO	.30	.14	.04
☐ 5 Dick Pole CO	.30	.14	.04
☐ 6 Phil Roof CO	.30	.14	.04
☐ 7 Paul Assenmacher	.30	.14	.04
☐ 8 Mike Bielecki	.30	.14	.04
☐ 9 Mike Harkey	.30	.14	.04
☐ 10 Joe Kraemer	.30	.14	.04
☐ 11 Les Lancaster	.30	.14	.04
☐ 12 Greg Maddux	30.00	13.50	3.70
☐ 13 Jose Nunez	.30	.14	.04
☐ 14 Jeff Pico	.30	.14	.04
☐ 15 Rick Sutcliffe	.50	.23	.06
☐ 16 Dean Wilkins	.30	.14	.04
☐ 17 Mitch Williams	.30	.14	.04
☐ 18 Steve Wilson	.30	.14	.04
☐ 19 Damon Berryhill	.50	.23	.06
☐ 20 Joe Girardi	.50	.23	.06
☐ 21 Rick Wrona	.30	.14	.04
☐ 22 Shawon Dunston	.50	.23	.06
☐ 23 Mark Grace	6.00	2.70	.75
☐ 24 Domingo Ramos	.30	.14	.04
☐ 25 Luis Salazar	.30	.14	.04
☐ 26 Ryne Sandberg	20.00	9.00	2.50
☐ 27 Greg Smith	.30	.14	.04
☐ 28 Curtis Wilkerson	.30	.14	.04
☐ 29 Dave Clark	.30	.14	.04
☐ 30 Doug Dascenzo	.30	.14	.04
☐ 31 Andre Dawson	4.00	1.80	.50
☐ 32 Lloyd McClendon	.30	.14	.04
☐ 33 Dwight Smith	.50	.23	.06
☐ 34 Jerome Walton	.30	.14	.04
☐ 35 Marvell Wynne	.30	.14	.04
☐ 36 Alex Arias	.30	.14	.04
☐ 37 Bob Bafia	.30	.14	.04
☐ 38 Brad Bierley	.30	.14	.04
☐ 39 Shawn Boskie	.30	.14	.04
☐ 40 Danny Clay	.30	.14	.04
☐ 41 Rusty Crockett	.30	.14	.04
☐ 42 Earl Cunningham	.30	.14	.04
☐ 43 Len Damian	.30	.14	.04
☐ 44 Darrin Duffy	.30	.14	.04
☐ 45 Ty Griffin	.30	.14	.04
☐ 46 Brian Guinn	.30	.14	.04
☐ 47 Phil Hannon	.30	.14	.04
☐ 48 Phil Harrison	.30	.14	.04
☐ 49 Jeff Hearron	.30	.14	.04
☐ 50 Greg Kallevig	.30	.14	.04
☐ 51 Ced Landrum	.30	.14	.04
☐ 52 Bill Long	.30	.14	.04
☐ 53 Derrick May	.50	.23	.06
☐ 54 Ray Mullino	.30	.14	.04
☐ 55 Erik Pappas	.30	.14	.04
☐ 56 Steve Parker	.30	.14	.04
☐ 57 Dave Pavlas	.30	.14	.04
☐ 58 Laddie Renfroe	.30	.14	.04
☐ 59 Jeff Small	.30	.14	.04
☐ 60 Doug Strange	.30	.14	.04
☐ 61 Gary Varsho	.30	.14	.04
☐ 62 Hector Villanueva	.30	.14	.04
☐ 63 Rick Wilkins	.50	.23	.06
☐ 64 Dana Williams	.30	.14	.04
☐ 65 Bill Wrona	.30	.14	.04
☐ 66 Fernando Zarranz	.30	.14	.04

1990 Topps TV Mets

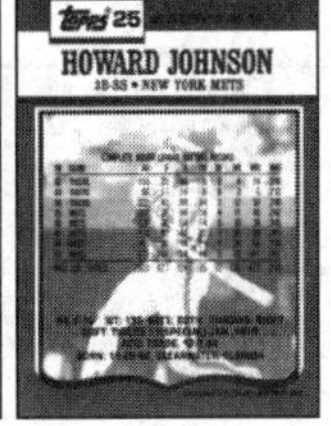

This Mets team set contains 66 cards measuring the standard size. The fronts feature posed or action color player photos with a high gloss. In block lettering, the words 'All Star' are printed vertically in orange and yellow on the left side of the card. The player's name appears in a red plaque below the picture, and white borders round out the card face. The backs are printed in black lettering and have a red and white background. Inside a decal design, player information and statistics are superimposed on an indistinct version of the same picture as on the front. Cards numbered 1-34 were with the parent club, while cards 35-66 were in the farm system.

	MINT	NRMT	EXC
COMPLETE SET (66)	20.00	9.00	2.50
COMMON CARD (1-66)	.30	.14	.04
☐ 1 Dave Johnson MG	.50	.23	.06
☐ 2 Mike Cubbage CO	.30	.14	.04
☐ 3 Doc Edwards CO	.30	.14	.04
☐ 4 Bud Harrelson CO	.30	.14	.04
☐ 5 Greg Pavlick CO	.30	.14	.04
☐ 6 Mel Stottlemyre CO	.30	.14	.04
☐ 7 Blaine Beatty	.30	.14	.04
☐ 8 David Cone	4.00	1.80	.50
☐ 9 Ron Darling	.30	.14	.04
☐ 10 Sid Fernandez	.30	.14	.04
☐ 11 John Franco	.50	.23	.06
☐ 12 Dwight Gooden	3.00	1.35	.35
☐ 13 Jeff Innis	.30	.14	.04
☐ 14 Julio Machado	.30	.14	.04
☐ 15 Jeff Musselman	.30	.14	.04
☐ 16 Bob Ojeda	.30	.14	.04
☐ 17 Alejandro Pena	.30	.14	.04
☐ 18 Frank Viola	.50	.23	.06
☐ 19 Wally Whitehurst	.30	.14	.04
☐ 20 Barry Lyons	.30	.14	.04
☐ 21 Orlando Mercado	.30	.14	.04
☐ 22 Mackey Sasser	.30	.14	.04
☐ 23 Kevin Elster	.30	.14	.04
☐ 24 Gregg Jefferies	2.00	.90	.25
☐ 25 Howard Johnson	.50	.23	.06
☐ 26 Dave Magadan	.30	.14	.04
☐ 27 Mike Marshall	.30	.14	.04
☐ 28 Tom O'Malley	.30	.14	.04
☐ 29 Tim Teufel	.30	.14	.04
☐ 30 Mark Carreon	.30	.14	.04
☐ 31 Kevin McReynolds	.30	.14	.04
☐ 32 Keith Miller	.30	.14	.04
☐ 33 Darryl Strawberry	3.00	1.35	.35
☐ 34 Lou Thornton	.30	.14	.04
☐ 35 Shawn Barton	.30	.14	.04
☐ 36 Tim Bogar	.30	.14	.04
☐ 37 Terry Bross	.30	.14	.04
☐ 38 Kevin Brown	.30	.14	.04
☐ 39 Mike DeButch	.30	.14	.04
☐ 40 Alex Diaz	.30	.14	.04
☐ 41 Chris Donnels	.30	.14	.04
☐ 42 Jeff Gardner	.30	.14	.04
☐ 43 Denny Gonzalez	.30	.14	.04
☐ 44 Kenny Graves	.30	.14	.04
☐ 45 Manny Hernandez	.30	.14	.04
☐ 46 Keith Hughes	.30	.14	.04
☐ 47 Todd Hundley	4.00	1.80	.50
☐ 48 Chris Jelic	.30	.14	.04
☐ 49 Dave Liddell	.30	.14	.04
☐ 50 Terry McDaniel	.30	.14	.04
☐ 51 Cesar Mejia	.30	.14	.04
☐ 52 Scott Nielsen	.30	.14	.04
☐ 53 Dale Plummer	.30	.14	.04
☐ 54 Darren Reed	.30	.14	.04
☐ 55 Gil Roca	.30	.14	.04
☐ 56 Jaime Roseboro	.30	.14	.04
☐ 57 Roger Samuels	.30	.14	.04
☐ 58 Zoilo Sanchez	.30	.14	.04
☐ 59 Pete Schourek	2.00	.90	.25
☐ 60 Craig Shipley	.30	.14	.04
☐ 61 Ray Soff	.30	.14	.04
☐ 62 Steve Swisher MG	.30	.14	.04
☐ 63 Kelvin Torve	.30	.14	.04
☐ 64 Dave Trautwein	.30	.14	.04
☐ 65 Julio Valera	.30	.14	.04
☐ 66 Alan Zinter	.30	.14	.04

1990 Topps TV Red Sox

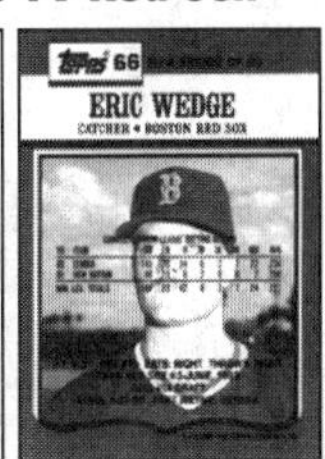

This Red Sox team set contains 66 cards measuring the standard size. The fronts feature posed or action color player photos with a high gloss. In block lettering, the team name is printed vertically in red and yellow on the left side of the card. The player's name appears in a blue plaque below the picture, and white borders round out the card face. The backs are printed in black and have a red and white background. Inside a decal design, player information and statistics are superimposed over an indistinct version of the same picture as on the front. Cards numbered 1-33 were with the parent club, while cards 34-66 were in the farm system. The set features an early card of Mo Vaughn.

	MINT	NRMT	EXC
COMPLETE SET (66)	35.00	16.00	4.40
COMMON CARD (1-66)	.30	.14	.04
☐ 1 Joe Morgan MG	.30	.14	.04
☐ 2 Dick Berardino CO	.30	.14	.04
☐ 3 Al Bumbry CO	.30	.14	.04
☐ 4 Bill Fischer CO	.30	.14	.04
☐ 5 Richie Hebner CO	.30	.14	.04
☐ 6 Rac Slider CO	.30	.14	.04
☐ 7 Mike Boddicker	.30	.14	.04
☐ 8 Roger Clemens	10.00	4.50	1.25
☐ 9 John Dopson	.30	.14	.04
☐ 10 Wes Gardner	.30	.14	.04
☐ 11 Greg A. Harris	.30	.14	.04
☐ 12 Dana Kiecker	.30	.14	.04
☐ 13 Dennis Lamp	.30	.14	.04
☐ 14 Rob Murphy	.30	.14	.04
☐ 15 Jeff Reardon	.50	.23	.06
☐ 16 Mike Rochford	.30	.14	.04
☐ 17 Lee Smith	2.00	.90	.25
☐ 18 Rich Gedman	.30	.14	.04
☐ 19 John Marzano	.30	.14	.04
☐ 20 Tony Pena	.50	.23	.06
☐ 21 Marty Barrett	.30	.14	.04
☐ 22 Wade Boggs	5.00	2.20	.60
☐ 23 Bill Buckner	.50	.23	.06
☐ 24 Danny Heep	.30	.14	.04
☐ 25 Jody Reed	.30	.14	.04
☐ 26 Luis Rivera	.30	.14	.04
☐ 27 Billy Joe Robidoux	.30	.14	.04
☐ 28 Ellis Burks	2.00	.90	.25
☐ 29 Dwight Evans	.50	.23	.06
☐ 30 Mike Greenwell	.50	.23	.06
☐ 31 Randy Kutcher	.30	.14	.04
☐ 32 Carlos Quintana	.30	.14	.04
☐ 33 Kevin Romine	.30	.14	.04
☐ 34 Ed Nottle MG	.30	.14	.04
☐ 35 Mark Meleski CO	.30	.14	.04
☐ 36 Steve Bast	.30	.14	.04
☐ 37 Greg Blosser	.50	.23	.06
☐ 38 Tom Bolton	.30	.14	.04
☐ 39 Scott Cooper	.50	.23	.06
☐ 40 Zach Crouch	.30	.14	.04
☐ 41 Steve Curry	.30	.14	.04
☐ 42 Mike Dalton	.30	.14	.04
☐ 43 John Flaherty	.30	.14	.04
☐ 44 Angel Gonzalez	.30	.14	.04
☐ 45 Eric Hetzel	.30	.14	.04
☐ 46 Daryl Irvine	.30	.14	.04
☐ 47 Joe Johnson	.30	.14	.04
☐ 48 Rick Lancellotti	.30	.14	.04
☐ 49 John Leister	.30	.14	.04
☐ 50 Derek Livernois	.30	.14	.04
☐ 51 Josias Manzanillo	.30	.14	.04
☐ 52 Kevin Morton	.30	.14	.04
☐ 53 Julius McDougal	.30	.14	.04
☐ 54 Tim Naehring	2.00	.90	.25
☐ 55 Jim Pankovits	.30	.14	.04
☐ 56 Mickey Pina	.30	.14	.04
☐ 57 Phil Plantier	.50	.23	.06
☐ 58 Jerry Reed	.30	.14	.04
☐ 59 Larry Shikles	.30	.14	.04
☐ 60 Tito Stewart	.30	.14	.04
☐ 61 Jeff Stone	.30	.14	.04
☐ 62 John Trautwein	.30	.14	.04
☐ 63 Gary Tremblay	.30	.14	.04
☐ 64 Mo Vaughn	12.00	5.50	1.50
☐ 65 Scott Wade	.30	.14	.04
☐ 66 Eric Wedge	.30	.14	.04

1990 Topps TV Yankees

This Yankees team set contains 66 standard-size cards. The fronts feature posed or action color player photos with a high gloss. In block lettering, the team name is printed vertically in light gray on the left side of the card. The player's name appears in a gold plaque below the picture, and white borders round out the card face. The backs are printed in black lettering and have a red and white background. Inside a decal design, player information and statistics are superimposed on an indistinct version of the same picture as on the front. Cards numbered 1-34 were with the parent club, while cards 35-66 were in the farm system. An early card of Deion Sanders is featured in this set.

	MINT	NRMT	EXC
COMPLETE SET (66)	50.00	22.00	6.25
COMMON CARD (1-66)	.30	.14	.04
☐ 1 Bucky Dent MG	.50	.23	.06
☐ 2 Mark Connor CO	.30	.14	.04
☐ 3 Billy Connors CO	.30	.14	.04
☐ 4 Mike Ferraro CO	.30	.14	.04
☐ 5 Joe Sparks CO	.30	.14	.04
☐ 6 Champ Summers CO	.30	.14	.04
☐ 7 Greg Cadaret	.30	.14	.04
☐ 8 Chuck Cary	.30	.14	.04
☐ 9 Lee Guetterman	.30	.14	.04
☐ 10 Andy Hawkins	.30	.14	.04
☐ 11 Dave LaPoint	.30	.14	.04
☐ 12 Tim Leary	.30	.14	.04
☐ 13 Lance McCullers	.30	.14	.04
☐ 14 Alan Mills	.30	.14	.04
☐ 15 Clay Parker	.30	.14	.04
☐ 16 Pascual Perez	.30	.14	.04
☐ 17 Eric Plunk	.30	.14	.04
☐ 18 Dave Righetti	.50	.23	.06
☐ 19 Jeff D. Robinson	.30	.14	.04
☐ 20 Rick Cerone	.30	.14	.04
☐ 21 Bob Geren	.30	.14	.04
☐ 22 Steve Balboni	.30	.14	.04
☐ 23 Mike Blowers	2.00	.90	.25
☐ 24 Alvaro Espinoza	.50	.23	.06
☐ 25 Don Mattingly	30.00	13.50	3.70
☐ 26 Steve Sax	.50	.23	.06
☐ 27 Wayne Tolleson	.30	.14	.04
☐ 28 Randy Velarde	.50	.23	.06
☐ 29 Jesse Barfield	.50	.23	.06
☐ 30 Mel Hall	.30	.14	.04
☐ 31 Roberto Kelly	.50	.23	.06
☐ 32 Luis Polonia	.50	.23	.06
☐ 33 Deion Sanders	6.00	2.70	.75
☐ 34 Dave Winfield	6.00	2.70	.75
☐ 35 Steve Adkins	.30	.14	.04
☐ 36 Oscar Azocar	.30	.14	.04
☐ 37 Bob Brower	.30	.14	.04
☐ 38 Britt Burns	.30	.14	.04
☐ 39 Bob Davidson	.30	.14	.04
☐ 40 Brian Dorsett	.30	.14	.04
☐ 41 Dave Eiland	.30	.14	.04
☐ 42 John Fishel	.30	.14	.04
☐ 43 Andy Fox	.30	.14	.04
☐ 44 John Habyan	.30	.14	.04
☐ 45 Cullen Hartzog	.30	.14	.04
☐ 46 Sterling Hitchcock	.50	.23	.06
☐ 47 Brian Johnson	.30	.14	.04
☐ 48 Jimmy Jones	.30	.14	.04
☐ 49 Scott Kamieniecki	.50	.23	.06
☐ 50 Jim Leyritz	2.00	.90	.25
☐ 51 Mark Leiter	.50	.23	.06
☐ 52 Jason Maas	.30	.14	.04
☐ 53 Kevin Maas	.30	.14	.04
☐ 54 Hensley Meulens	.30	.14	.04
☐ 55 Kevin Mmahat	.30	.14	.04
☐ 56 Rich Monteleone	.30	.14	.04
☐ 57 Vince Phillips	.30	.14	.04
☐ 58 Carlos Rodriguez	.30	.14	.04
☐ 59 Dave Sax	.30	.14	.04
☐ 60 Willie Smith	.30	.14	.04
☐ 61 Van Snider	.30	.14	.04
☐ 62 Andy Stankiewicz	.30	.14	.04
☐ 63 Wade Taylor	.30	.14	.04
☐ 64 Ricky Torres	.30	.14	.04
☐ 65 Jim Walewander	.30	.14	.04
☐ 66 Bernie Williams	10.00	4.50	1.25

1990-93 Topps Magazine

These cards were inserted either four or eight cards per issue of Topps magazine. The cards were all issued in perforated form and when separated measured the standard size. The backs are unnumbered with a TM prefix. Some cards were issued in every Topps magazine from its inagural issue through the magazine's final issue.

	MINT	NRMT	EXC
COMPLETE SET (112)	25.00	11.00	3.10
COMMON CARD (1-112)	.10	.05	.01
☐ 1 Dave Staton	.10	.05	.01
☐ 2 Dan Peltier	.10	.05	.01
☐ 3 Ken Griffey Jr.	2.50	1.10	.30
☐ 4 Ruben Sierra	.10	.05	.01
☐ 5 Bret Saberhagen	.10	.05	.01
☐ 6 Jerome Walton	.10	.05	.01
☐ 7 Kevin Mitchell	.25	.11	.03
☐ 8 Mike Scott	.10	.05	.01
☐ 9 Bo Jackson	.25	.11	.03
☐ 10 Nolan Ryan	1.50	.70	.19
☐ 11 Will Clark	.50	.23	.06
☐ 12 Robin Yount	.40	.18	.05
☐ 13 Joe Morgan	.40	.18	.05
☐ 14 Jim Palmer	.40	.18	.05
☐ 15 Ben McDonald	.10	.05	.01
☐ 16 John Olerud	.25	.11	.03
☐ 17 Don Mattingly	1.00	.45	.12
☐ 18 Eric Davis Barry Larkin Chris Sabo	.40	.18	.05
☐ 19 Jim Abbott	.10	.05	.01
☐ 20 Sandy Alomar	.40	.18	.05
☐ 21 Jose Canseco	.50	.23	.06
☐ 22 Delino DeShields	.10	.05	.01
☐ 23 Wade Boggs	.50	.23	.06
☐ 24 Kirby Puckett	1.00	.45	.12
☐ 25 Ryne Sandberg	.75	.35	.09
☐ 26 Roger Clemens	.60	.25	.07
☐ 27 Ken Griffey Jr. Ken Griffey Sr.	2.00	.90	.25
☐ 28 Cecil Fielder	.25	.11	.03
☐ 29 Steve Avery	.25	.11	.03
☐ 30 Rickey Henderson	.50	.23	.06
☐ 31 Kevin Maas	.10	.05	.01

Card	MINT	NRMT	EXC
☐ 32 Len Dykstra	.25	.11	.03
☐ 33 Darryl Strawberry	.25	.11	.03
☐ 34 Mark McGwire	.60	.25	.07
☐ 35 Matt Williams	.50	.23	.06
☐ 36 David Justice	.50	.23	.06
☐ 37 Cincinnati Reds	.25	.11	.03
☐ 38 Todd Van Poppel	.10	.05	.01
☐ 39 Jose Offerman	.10	.05	.01
☐ 40 Alex Fernandez	.25	.11	.03
☐ 41 Carlton Fisk	.40	.18	.05
☐ 42 Barry Bonds	.60	.25	.07
☐ 43 Bobby Bonilla	.25	.11	.03
☐ 44 Bob Welch	.10	.05	.01
☐ 45 Mo Vaughn	.50	.23	.06
☐ 46 Tino Martinez	.40	.18	.05
☐ 47 D.J. Dozier	.10	.05	.01
☐ 48 Frank Thomas	2.50	1.10	.30
☐ 49 Cal Ripken	2.00	.90	.25
☐ 50 Dave Winfield	.50	.23	.06
☐ 51 Dwight Gooden	.25	.11	.03
☐ 52 Bo Jackson	.25	.11	.03
☐ 53 Kirk Dressendorfer	.10	.05	.01
☐ 54 Gary Scott	.10	.05	.01
☐ 55 Steve Decker	.10	.05	.01
☐ 56 Ray Lankford	.25	.11	.03
☐ 57 Ozzie Smith	.60	.25	.07
☐ 58 Joe Carter	.40	.18	.05
☐ 59 Dave Henderson	.10	.05	.01
☐ 60 Tony Gwynn	1.00	.45	.12
☐ 61 Jeff Bagwell	1.25	.55	.16
☐ 62 Scott Erickson	.10	.05	.01
☐ 63 Pat Kelly	.10	.05	.01
☐ 64 Orlando Merced	.10	.05	.01
☐ 65 Andre Dawson	.40	.18	.05
☐ 66 Reggie Sanders	.25	.11	.03
☐ 67 Phil Plantier	.10	.05	.01
☐ 68 Paul Molitor	.50	.23	.06
☐ 69 Terry Pendleton	.25	.11	.03
☐ 70 Julio Franco	.25	.11	.03
☐ 71 Lee Smith	.40	.18	.05
☐ 72 Minnesota Twins	.25	.11	.03
☐ 73 Royce Clayton	.10	.05	.01
☐ 74 Tom Glavine	.40	.18	.05
☐ 75 Roger Salkeld	.10	.05	.01
☐ 76 Robin Ventura	.25	.11	.03
☐ 77 John Goodman As Babe Ruth	.40	.18	.05
☐ 78 Jack Morris	.25	.11	.03
☐ 79 Brien Taylor	.10	.05	.01
☐ 80 Howard Johnson	.10	.05	.01
☐ 81 Barry Larkin	.40	.18	.05
☐ 82 Deion Sanders	.50	.23	.06
☐ 83 Mike Mussina	.50	.23	.06
☐ 84 Juan Gonzalez	1.25	.55	.16
☐ 85 Roberto Alomar	.60	.25	.07
☐ 86 Fred McGriff	.40	.18	.05
☐ 87 Doug Drabek	.10	.05	.01
☐ 88 George Brett	1.00	.45	.12
☐ 89 Otis Nixon	.10	.05	.01
☐ 90 Brady Anderson	.40	.18	.05
☐ 91 Gary Sheffield	.50	.23	.06
☐ 92 Dave Fleming	.10	.05	.01
☐ 93 Jeff Reardon	.10	.05	.01
☐ 94 Mark McGwire	.75	.35	.09
☐ 95 Larry Walker	.50	.23	.06
☐ 96 John Kruk	.25	.11	.03
☐ 97 Carlos Baerga	.25	.11	.03
☐ 98 Pat Listach	.10	.05	.01
☐ 99 Toronto Blue Jays	.40	.18	.05
☐ 100 Eric Karros	.40	.18	.05
☐ 101 Bret Boone	.10	.05	.01
☐ 102 Al Martin	.10	.05	.01
☐ 103 Wil Cordero	.10	.05	.01
☐ 104 Tim Salmon	.40	.18	.05
☐ 105 Danny Tartabull	.10	.05	.01
☐ 106 J.T. Snow	.25	.11	.03
☐ 107 Mike Piazza	2.00	.90	.25
☐ 108 Frank Viola	.10	.05	.01
☐ 109 Nolan Ryan Mets	1.00	.45	.12
☐ 110 Nolan Ryan Angels	1.00	.45	.12
☐ 111 Nolan Ryan Astros	1.00	.45	.12
☐ 112 Nolan Ryan Rangers	1.00	.45	.12

1991 Topps

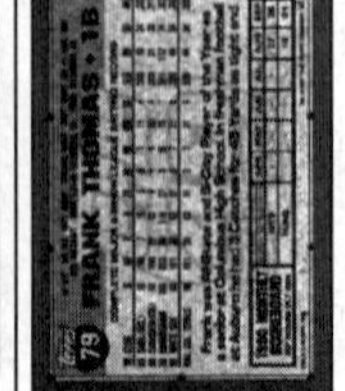

This set marks Topps tenth consecutive year of issuing a 792-card standard-size set. Cards were primarily issued in wax packs, rack packs and factory sets. The fronts feature a full color player photo with a white border. Topps also commemorated their fortieth anniversary by including a "Topps 40" logo on the front and back of each card. Virtually all of the cards have been discovered without the 40th logo on the back. Subsets include Record Breakers (2-8) and All-Stars (386-407). In addition, First Draft Picks and Future Stars subset cards are scattered throughout the set. The key Rookie Cards include Chipper Jones and Brian McRae. As a special promotion Topps inserted (randomly) into their wax packs one of every previous card they ever issued.

	MINT	NRMT	EXC
COMPLETE SET (792)	12.00	5.50	1.50
COMPLETE FACT.SET (792)	15.00	6.75	1.85
COMMON CARD (1-792)	.05	.02	.01

Card	MINT	NRMT	EXC
☐ 1 Nolan Ryan	.75	.35	.09
☐ 2 George Brett RB Batting Title, 3 decades	.20	.09	.03
☐ 3 Carlton Fisk RB Catcher HR Record	.15	.07	.02
☐ 4 Kevin Maas RB Quickest to 10 HR's	.05	.02	.01
☐ 5 Cal Ripken RB Most cons. errorless games	.40	.18	.05
☐ 6 Nolan Ryan RB Oldest pitcher, no-hitter	.40	.18	.05
☐ 7 Ryne Sandberg RB Most cons. errorless games	.15	.07	.02
☐ 8 Bobby Thigpen RB Most saves, season	.05	.02	.01
☐ 9 Darrin Fletcher	.05	.02	.01
☐ 10 Gregg Olson	.05	.02	.01
☐ 11 Roberto Kelly	.05	.02	.01
☐ 12 Paul Assenmacher	.05	.02	.01
☐ 13 Mariano Duncan	.05	.02	.01
☐ 14 Dennis Lamp	.05	.02	.01
☐ 15 Von Hayes	.05	.02	.01
☐ 16 Mike Heath	.05	.02	.01
☐ 17 Jeff Brantley	.05	.02	.01
☐ 18 Nelson Liriano	.05	.02	.01
☐ 19 Jeff D. Robinson	.05	.02	.01
☐ 20 Pedro Guerrero	.05	.02	.01
☐ 21 Joe Morgan MG	.05	.02	.01
☐ 22 Storm Davis	.05	.02	.01
☐ 23 Jim Gantner	.05	.02	.01
☐ 24 Dave Martinez	.05	.02	.01
☐ 25 Tim Belcher	.05	.02	.01
☐ 26 Luis Sojo UER (Born in Barquisimento, not Carquis)	.05	.02	.01
☐ 27 Bobby Witt	.05	.02	.01
☐ 28 Alvaro Espinoza	.05	.02	.01
☐ 29 Bob Walk	.05	.02	.01
☐ 30 Gregg Jefferies	.10	.05	.01
☐ 31 Colby Ward	.05	.02	.01
☐ 32 Mike Simms	.05	.02	.01
☐ 33 Barry Jones	.05	.02	.01
☐ 34 Atlee Hammaker	.05	.02	.01
☐ 35 Greg Maddux	.60	.25	.07
☐ 36 Donnie Hill	.05	.02	.01
☐ 37 Tom Bolton	.05	.02	.01
☐ 38 Scott Bradley	.05	.02	.01
☐ 39 Jim Neidlinger	.05	.02	.01
☐ 40 Kevin Mitchell	.10	.05	.01
☐ 41 Ken Dayley	.05	.02	.01
☐ 42 Chris Hoiles	.05	.02	.01
☐ 43 Roger McDowell	.05	.02	.01
☐ 44 Mike Felder	.05	.02	.01
☐ 45 Chris Sabo	.05	.02	.01
☐ 46 Tim Drummond	.05	.02	.01
☐ 47 Brook Jacoby	.05	.02	.01
☐ 48 Dennis Boyd	.05	.02	.01
☐ 49A Pat Borders ERR (40 steals at Kinston in '86)	.15	.07	.02
☐ 49B Pat Borders COR (0 steals at Kinston in '86)	.05	.02	.01
☐ 50 Bob Welch	.05	.02	.01
☐ 51 Art Howe MG	.05	.02	.01
☐ 52 Francisco Oliveras	.05	.02	.01
☐ 53 Mike Sharperson UER (Born in 1961, not 1960)	.05	.02	.01
☐ 54 Gary Mielke	.05	.02	.01
☐ 55 Jeffrey Leonard	.05	.02	.01
☐ 56 Jeff Parrett	.05	.02	.01
☐ 57 Jack Howell	.05	.02	.01
☐ 58 Mel Stottlemyre Jr.	.05	.02	.01
☐ 59 Eric Yelding	.05	.02	.01
☐ 60 Frank Viola	.05	.02	.01
☐ 61 Stan Javier	.05	.02	.01
☐ 62 Lee Guetterman	.05	.02	.01
☐ 63 Milt Thompson	.05	.02	.01
☐ 64 Tom Herr	.05	.02	.01
☐ 65 Bruce Hurst	.05	.02	.01
☐ 66 Terry Kennedy	.05	.02	.01
☐ 67 Rick Honeycutt	.05	.02	.01
☐ 68 Gary Sheffield	.15	.07	.02
☐ 69 Steve Wilson	.05	.02	.01
☐ 70 Ellis Burks	.10	.05	.01
☐ 71 Jim Acker	.05	.02	.01
☐ 72 Junior Ortiz	.05	.02	.01
☐ 73 Craig Worthington	.05	.02	.01
☐ 74 Shane Andrews	.15	.07	.02
☐ 75 Jack Morris	.10	.05	.01
☐ 76 Jerry Browne	.05	.02	.01
☐ 77 Drew Hall	.05	.02	.01
☐ 78 Geno Petralli	.05	.02	.01
☐ 79 Frank Thomas	2.00	.90	.25
☐ 80A Fernando Valenzuela ERR (104 earned runs in '90 tied for league lead)	.10	.05	.01
☐ 80B Fernando Valenzuela COR (104 earned runs in '90 led league, 20 CG's in 1986 now italicized)	.10	.05	.01
☐ 81 Cito Gaston MG	.05	.02	.01
☐ 82 Tom Glavine	.15	.07	.02
☐ 83 Daryl Boston	.05	.02	.01
☐ 84 Bob McClure	.05	.02	.01
☐ 85 Jesse Barfield	.05	.02	.01
☐ 86 Les Lancaster	.05	.02	.01
☐ 87 Tracy Jones	.05	.02	.01
☐ 88 Bob Tewksbury	.05	.02	.01
☐ 89 Darren Daulton	.10	.05	.01
☐ 90 Danny Tartabull	.05	.02	.01
☐ 91 Greg Colbrunn	.10	.05	.01
☐ 92 Danny Jackson	.05	.02	.01
☐ 93 Ivan Calderon	.05	.02	.01
☐ 94 John Dopson	.05	.02	.01
☐ 95 Paul Molitor	.20	.09	.03
☐ 96 Trevor Wilson	.05	.02	.01
☐ 97A Brady Anderson ERR (September, 2 RBI and 3 hits, should be 3 RBI and 14 hits)	.25	.11	.03
☐ 97B Brady Anderson COR	.15	.07	.02
☐ 98 Sergio Valdez	.05	.02	.01
☐ 99 Chris Gwynn	.05	.02	.01
☐ 100 Don Mattingly COR (101 hits in 1990)	.50	.23	.06
☐ 100A Don Mattingly ERR (10 hits in 1990)	1.00	.45	.12
☐ 101 Rob Ducey	.05	.02	.01
☐ 102 Gene Larkin	.05	.02	.01
☐ 103 Tim Costo	.05	.02	.01
☐ 104 Don Robinson	.05	.02	.01
☐ 105 Kevin McReynolds	.05	.02	.01
☐ 106 Ed Nunez	.05	.02	.01
☐ 107 Luis Polonia	.05	.02	.01
☐ 108 Matt Young	.05	.02	.01
☐ 109 Greg Riddoch MG	.05	.02	.01
☐ 110 Tom Henke	.05	.02	.01
☐ 111 Andres Thomas	.05	.02	.01
☐ 112 Frank DiPino	.05	.02	.01
☐ 113 Carl Everett	.15	.07	.02
☐ 114 Lance Dickson	.05	.02	.01
☐ 115 Hubie Brooks	.05	.02	.01
☐ 116 Mark Davis	.05	.02	.01
☐ 117 Dion James	.05	.02	.01
☐ 118 Tom Edens	.05	.02	.01
☐ 119 Carl Nichols	.05	.02	.01
☐ 120 Joe Carter	.10	.05	.01
☐ 121 Eric King	.05	.02	.01
☐ 122 Paul O'Neill	.10	.05	.01
☐ 123 Greg A. Harris	.05	.02	.01
☐ 124 Randy Bush	.05	.02	.01
☐ 125 Steve Bedrosian	.05	.02	.01
☐ 126 Bernard Gilkey	.10	.05	.01
☐ 127 Joe Price	.05	.02	.01
☐ 128 Travis Fryman (Front has SS back has SS-3B)	.15	.07	.02
☐ 129 Mark Eichhorn	.05	.02	.01
☐ 130 Ozzie Smith	.25	.11	.03
☐ 131A Checklist 1 ERR 727 Phil Bradley	.15	.07	.02
☐ 131B Checklist 1 COR 717 Phil Bradley	.05	.02	.01
☐ 132 Jamie Quirk	.05	.02	.01
☐ 133 Greg Briley	.05	.02	.01
☐ 134 Kevin Elster	.05	.02	.01
☐ 135 Jerome Walton	.05	.02	.01
☐ 136 Dave Schmidt	.05	.02	.01
☐ 137 Randy Ready	.05	.02	.01
☐ 138 Jamie Moyer	.05	.02	.01
☐ 139 Jeff Treadway	.05	.02	.01
☐ 140 Fred McGriff	.15	.07	.02
☐ 141 Nick Leyva MG	.05	.02	.01
☐ 142 Curt Wilkerson	.05	.02	.01
☐ 143 John Smiley	.05	.02	.01
☐ 144 Dave Henderson	.05	.02	.01
☐ 145 Lou Whitaker	.10	.05	.01
☐ 146 Dan Plesac	.05	.02	.01
☐ 147 Carlos Baerga	.15	.07	.02
☐ 148 Rey Palacios	.05	.02	.01
☐ 149 Al Osuna UER (Shown throwing right, but bio says lefty)	.05	.02	.01
☐ 150 Cal Ripken	.75	.35	.09
☐ 151 Tom Browning	.05	.02	.01
☐ 152 Mickey Hatcher	.05	.02	.01
☐ 153 Bryan Harvey	.05	.02	.01
☐ 154 Jay Buhner	.15	.07	.02
☐ 155A Dwight Evans ERR (Led league with 162 games in '82)	.15	.07	.02
☐ 155B Dwight Evans COR (Tied for lead with 162 games in '82)	.10	.05	.01
☐ 156 Carlos Martinez	.05	.02	.01
☐ 157 John Smoltz	.15	.07	.02
☐ 158 Jose Uribe	.05	.02	.01
☐ 159 Joe Boever	.05	.02	.01
☐ 160 Vince Coleman UER (Wrong birth year, born 9/22/60)	.05	.02	.01
☐ 161 Tim Leary	.05	.02	.01
☐ 162 Ozzie Canseco	.05	.02	.01
☐ 163 Dave Johnson	.05	.02	.01
☐ 164 Edgar Diaz	.05	.02	.01
☐ 165 Sandy Alomar Jr.	.10	.05	.01
☐ 166 Harold Baines	.10	.05	.01
☐ 167A Randy Tomlin ERR (Harriburg)	.15	.07	.02
☐ 167B Randy Tomlin COR (Harrisburg)	.05	.02	.01
☐ 168 John Olerud	.10	.05	.01
☐ 169 Luis Aquino	.05	.02	.01
☐ 170 Carlton Fisk	.15	.07	.02
☐ 171 Tony LaRussa MG	.10	.05	.01
☐ 172 Pete Incaviglia	.05	.02	.01
☐ 173 Jason Grimsley	.05	.02	.01
☐ 174 Ken Caminiti	.15	.07	.02
☐ 175 Jack Armstrong	.05	.02	.01
☐ 176 John Orton	.05	.02	.01
☐ 177 Reggie Harris	.05	.02	.01
☐ 178 Dave Valle	.05	.02	.01
☐ 179 Pete Harnisch	.05	.02	.01
☐ 180 Tony Gwynn	.40	.18	.05
☐ 181 Duane Ward	.05	.02	.01
☐ 182 Junior Noboa	.05	.02	.01
☐ 183 Clay Parker	.05	.02	.01
☐ 184 Gary Green	.05	.02	.01
☐ 185 Joe Magrane	.05	.02	.01
☐ 186 Rod Booker	.05	.02	.01
☐ 187 Greg Cadaret	.05	.02	.01
☐ 188 Damon Berryhill	.05	.02	.01
☐ 189 Daryl Irvine	.05	.02	.01
☐ 190 Matt Williams	.15	.07	.02
☐ 191 Willie Blair	.05	.02	.01
☐ 192 Rob Deer	.05	.02	.01
☐ 193 Felix Fermin	.05	.02	.01
☐ 194 Xavier Hernandez	.05	.02	.01
☐ 195 Wally Joyner	.10	.05	.01
☐ 196 Jim Vatcher	.05	.02	.01
☐ 197 Chris Nabholz	.05	.02	.01
☐ 198 R.J. Reynolds	.05	.02	.01
☐ 199 Mike Hartley	.05	.02	.01
☐ 200 Darryl Strawberry	.10	.05	.01
☐ 201 Tom Kelly MG	.05	.02	.01
☐ 202 Jim Leyritz	.10	.05	.01
☐ 203 Gene Harris	.05	.02	.01
☐ 204 Herm Winningham	.05	.02	.01
☐ 205 Mike Perez	.05	.02	.01
☐ 206 Carlos Quintana	.05	.02	.01
☐ 207 Gary Wayne	.05	.02	.01
☐ 208 Willie Wilson	.05	.02	.01
☐ 209 Ken Howell	.05	.02	.01
☐ 210 Lance Parrish	.05	.02	.01
☐ 211 Brian Barnes	.05	.02	.01
☐ 212 Steve Finley	.10	.05	.01
☐ 213 Frank Wills	.05	.02	.01
☐ 214 Joe Girardi	.10	.05	.01
☐ 215 Dave Smith	.05	.02	.01
☐ 216 Greg Gagne	.05	.02	.01
☐ 217 Chris Bosio	.05	.02	.01
☐ 218 Rick Parker	.05	.02	.01
☐ 219 Jack McDowell	.10	.05	.01
☐ 220 Tim Wallach	.05	.02	.01
☐ 221 Don Slaught	.05	.02	.01
☐ 222 Brian McRae	.25	.11	.03
☐ 223 Allan Anderson	.05	.02	.01
☐ 224 Juan Gonzalez	.75	.35	.09
☐ 225 Randy Johnson	.15	.07	.02
☐ 226 Alfredo Griffin	.05	.02	.01
☐ 227 Steve Avery UER (Pitched 13 games for Durham in 1989, not 2)	.15	.07	.02
☐ 228 Rex Hudler	.05	.02	.01
☐ 229 Rance Mulliniks	.05	.02	.01
☐ 230 Sid Fernandez	.05	.02	.01
☐ 231 Doug Rader MG	.05	.02	.01
☐ 232 Jose DeJesus	.05	.02	.01
☐ 233 Al Leiter	.10	.05	.01
☐ 234 Scott Erickson	.10	.05	.01
☐ 235 Dave Parker	.10	.05	.01
☐ 236A Frank Tanana ERR (Tied for lead with 269 K's in '75)	.10	.05	.01
☐ 236B Frank Tanana COR (Led league with 269 K's in '75)	.05	.02	.01
☐ 237 Rick Cerone	.05	.02	.01
☐ 238 Mike Dunne	.05	.02	.01
☐ 239 Darren Lewis	.10	.05	.01
☐ 240 Mike Scott	.05	.02	.01
☐ 241 Dave Clark UER (Career totals 19 HR and 5 3B, should be 22 and 3)	.05	.02	.01
☐ 242 Mike LaCoss	.05	.02	.01
☐ 243 Lance Johnson	.10	.05	.01
☐ 244 Mike Jeffcoat	.05	.02	.01
☐ 245 Kal Daniels	.05	.02	.01

☐ 246 Kevin Wickander	.05	.02	.01
☐ 247 Jody Reed	.05	.02	.01
☐ 248 Tom Gordon	.05	.02	.01
☐ 249 Bob Melvin	.05	.02	.01
☐ 250 Dennis Eckersley	.10	.05	.01
☐ 251 Mark Lemke	.05	.02	.01
☐ 252 Mel Rojas	.10	.05	.01
☐ 253 Garry Templeton	.05	.02	.01
☐ 254 Shawn Boskie	.05	.02	.01
☐ 255 Brian Downing	.05	.02	.01
☐ 256 Greg Hibbard	.05	.02	.01
☐ 257 Tom O'Malley	.05	.02	.01
☐ 258 Chris Hammond	.05	.02	.01
☐ 259 Hensley Meulens	.05	.02	.01
☐ 260 Harold Reynolds	.05	.02	.01
☐ 261 Bud Harrelson MG	.05	.02	.01
☐ 262 Tim Jones	.05	.02	.01
☐ 263 Checklist 2	.05	.02	.01
☐ 264 Dave Hollins	.05	.02	.01
☐ 265 Mark Gubicza	.05	.02	.01
☐ 266 Carmelo Castillo	.05	.02	.01
☐ 267 Mark Knudson	.05	.02	.01
☐ 268 Tom Brookens	.05	.02	.01
☐ 269 Joe Hesketh	.05	.02	.01
☐ 270 Mark McGwire COR (1987 Slugging Pctg. listed as .618)	.30	.14	.04
☐ 270A Mark McGwire ERR (1987 Slugging Pctg. listed as 618)	.50	.23	.06
☐ 271 Omar Olivares	.05	.02	.01
☐ 272 Jeff King	.10	.05	.01
☐ 273 Johnny Ray	.05	.02	.01
☐ 274 Ken Williams	.05	.02	.01
☐ 275 Alan Trammell	.10	.05	.01
☐ 276 Bill Swift	.05	.02	.01
☐ 277 Scott Coolbaugh	.05	.02	.01
☐ 278 Alex Fernandez UER (No '90 White Sox stats)	.15	.07	.02
☐ 279A Jose Gonzalez ERR (Photo actually Billy Bean)	.05	.02	.01
☐ 279B Jose Gonzalez COR	.05	.02	.01
☐ 280 Bret Saberhagen	.10	.05	.01
☐ 281 Larry Sheets	.05	.02	.01
☐ 282 Don Carman	.05	.02	.01
☐ 283 Marquis Grissom	.15	.07	.02
☐ 284 Billy Spiers	.05	.02	.01
☐ 285 Jim Abbott	.10	.05	.01
☐ 286 Ken Oberkfell	.05	.02	.01
☐ 287 Mark Grant	.05	.02	.01
☐ 288 Derrick May	.05	.02	.01
☐ 289 Tim Birtsas	.05	.02	.01
☐ 290 Steve Sax	.05	.02	.01
☐ 291 John Wathan MG	.05	.02	.01
☐ 292 Bud Black	.05	.02	.01
☐ 293 Jay Bell	.10	.05	.01
☐ 294 Mike Moore	.05	.02	.01
☐ 295 Rafael Palmeiro	.15	.07	.02
☐ 296 Mark Williamson	.05	.02	.01
☐ 297 Manny Lee	.05	.02	.01
☐ 298 Omar Vizquel	.15	.07	.02
☐ 299 Scott Radinsky	.05	.02	.01
☐ 300 Kirby Puckett	.40	.18	.05
☐ 301 Steve Farr	.05	.02	.01
☐ 302 Tim Teufel	.05	.02	.01
☐ 303 Mike Boddicker	.05	.02	.01
☐ 304 Kevin Reimer	.05	.02	.01
☐ 305 Mike Scioscia	.05	.02	.01
☐ 306A Lonnie Smith ERR (136 games in '90)	.15	.07	.02
☐ 306B Lonnie Smith COR (135 games in '90)	.05	.02	.01
☐ 307 Andy Benes	.10	.05	.01
☐ 308 Tom Pagnozzi	.05	.02	.01
☐ 309 Norm Charlton	.05	.02	.01
☐ 310 Gary Carter	.10	.05	.01
☐ 311 Jeff Pico	.05	.02	.01
☐ 312 Charlie Hayes	.05	.02	.01
☐ 313 Ron Robinson	.05	.02	.01
☐ 314 Gary Pettis	.05	.02	.01
☐ 315 Roberto Alomar	.20	.09	.03
☐ 316 Gene Nelson	.05	.02	.01
☐ 317 Mike Fitzgerald	.05	.02	.01
☐ 318 Rick Aguilera	.10	.05	.01
☐ 319 Jeff McKnight	.05	.02	.01
☐ 320 Tony Fernandez	.05	.02	.01
☐ 321 Bob Rodgers MG	.05	.02	.01
☐ 322 Terry Shumpert	.05	.02	.01
☐ 323 Cory Snyder	.05	.02	.01
☐ 324A Ron Kittle ERR (Set another standard ...)	.15	.07	.02
☐ 324B Ron Kittle COR (Tied another standard ...)	.05	.02	.01
☐ 325 Brett Butler	.10	.05	.01
☐ 326 Ken Patterson	.05	.02	.01
☐ 327 Ron Hassey	.05	.02	.01
☐ 328 Walt Terrell	.05	.02	.01
☐ 329 Dave Justice UER (Drafted third round on card, should say fourth pick)	.15	.07	.02
☐ 330 Dwight Gooden	.10	.05	.01
☐ 331 Eric Anthony	.05	.02	.01
☐ 332 Kenny Rogers	.05	.02	.01
☐ 333 Chipper Jones FDP	3.00	1.35	.35
☐ 334 Todd Benzinger	.05	.02	.01
☐ 335 Mitch Williams	.05	.02	.01
☐ 336 Matt Nokes	.05	.02	.01
☐ 337A Keith Comstock ERR (Cubs logo on front)	.15	.07	.02
☐ 337B Keith Comstock COR (Mariners logo on front)	.05	.02	.01
☐ 338 Luis Rivera	.05	.02	.01
☐ 339 Larry Walker	.15	.07	.02
☐ 340 Ramon Martinez	.15	.07	.02
☐ 341 John Moses	.05	.02	.01
☐ 342 Mickey Morandini	.05	.02	.01
☐ 343 Jose Oquendo	.05	.02	.01
☐ 344 Jeff Russell	.05	.02	.01
☐ 345 Len Dykstra	.10	.05	.01
☐ 346 Jesse Orosco	.05	.02	.01
☐ 347 Greg Vaughn	.10	.05	.01
☐ 348 Todd Stottlemyre	.05	.02	.01
☐ 349 Dave Gallagher	.05	.02	.01
☐ 350 Glenn Davis	.05	.02	.01
☐ 351 Joe Torre MG	.10	.05	.01
☐ 352 Frank White	.10	.05	.01
☐ 353 Tony Castillo	.05	.02	.01
☐ 354 Sid Bream	.05	.02	.01
☐ 355 Chili Davis	.10	.05	.01
☐ 356 Mike Marshall	.05	.02	.01
☐ 357 Jack Savage	.05	.02	.01
☐ 358 Mark Parent	.05	.02	.01
☐ 359 Chuck Cary	.05	.02	.01
☐ 360 Tim Raines	.10	.05	.01
☐ 361 Scott Garrelts	.05	.02	.01
☐ 362 Hector Villenueva	.05	.02	.01
☐ 363 Rick Mahler	.05	.02	.01
☐ 364 Dan Pasqua	.05	.02	.01
☐ 365 Mike Schooler	.05	.02	.01
☐ 366A Checklist 3 ERR 19 Carl Nichols	.15	.07	.02
☐ 366B Checklist 3 COR 119 Carl Nichols	.05	.02	.01
☐ 367 Dave Walsh	.05	.02	.01
☐ 368 Felix Jose	.05	.02	.01
☐ 369 Steve Searcy	.05	.02	.01
☐ 370 Kelly Gruber	.05	.02	.01
☐ 371 Jeff Montgomery	.10	.05	.01
☐ 372 Spike Owen	.05	.02	.01
☐ 373 Darrin Jackson	.05	.02	.01
☐ 374 Larry Casian	.05	.02	.01
☐ 375 Tony Pena	.05	.02	.01
☐ 376 Mike Harkey	.05	.02	.01
☐ 377 Rene Gonzales	.05	.02	.01
☐ 378A Wilson Alvarez ERR ('89 Port Charlotte and '90 Birmingham stat lines omitted)	.50	.23	.06
☐ 378B Wilson Alvarez COR (Text still says 143 K's in 1988, whereas stats say 134)	.15	.07	.02
☐ 379 Randy Velarde	.05	.02	.01
☐ 380 Willie McGee	.05	.02	.01
☐ 381 Jim Leyland MG	.05	.02	.01
☐ 382 Mackey Sasser	.05	.02	.01
☐ 383 Pete Smith	.05	.02	.01
☐ 384 Gerald Perry	.05	.02	.01
☐ 385 Mickey Tettleton	.10	.05	.01
☐ 386 Cecil Fielder AS	.10	.05	.01
☐ 387 Julio Franco AS	.05	.02	.01
☐ 388 Kelly Gruber AS	.05	.02	.01
☐ 389 Alan Trammell AS	.10	.05	.01
☐ 390 Jose Canseco AS	.15	.07	.02
☐ 391 Rickey Henderson AS	.15	.07	.02
☐ 392 Ken Griffey Jr. AS	.75	.35	.09
☐ 393 Carlton Fisk AS	.15	.07	.02
☐ 394 Bob Welch AS	.05	.02	.01
☐ 395 Chuck Finley AS	.05	.02	.01
☐ 396 Bobby Thigpen AS	.05	.02	.01
☐ 397 Eddie Murray AS	.15	.07	.02
☐ 398 Ryne Sandberg AS	.15	.07	.02
☐ 399 Matt Williams AS	.15	.07	.02
☐ 400 Barry Larkin AS	.15	.07	.02
☐ 401 Barry Bonds AS	.15	.07	.02
☐ 402 Darryl Strawbery AS	.10	.05	.01
☐ 403 Bobby Bonilla AS	.10	.05	.01
☐ 404 Mike Scioscia AS	.05	.02	.01
☐ 405 Doug Drabek AS	.05	.02	.01
☐ 406 Frank Viola AS	.05	.02	.01
☐ 407 John Franco AS	.05	.02	.01
☐ 408 Earnie Riles	.05	.02	.01
☐ 409 Mike Stanley	.05	.02	.01
☐ 410 Dave Righetti	.05	.02	.01
☐ 411 Lance Blankenship	.05	.02	.01
☐ 412 Dave Bergman	.05	.02	.01
☐ 413 Terry Mulholland	.05	.02	.01
☐ 414 Sammy Sosa	.25	.11	.03
☐ 415 Rick Sutcliffe	.05	.02	.01
☐ 416 Randy Milligan	.05	.02	.01
☐ 417 Bill Krueger	.05	.02	.01
☐ 418 Nick Esasky	.05	.02	.01
☐ 419 Jeff Reed	.05	.02	.01
☐ 420 Bobby Thigpen	.05	.02	.01
☐ 421 Alex Cole	.05	.02	.01
☐ 422 Rick Reuschel	.05	.02	.01
☐ 423 Rafael Ramirez UER (Born 1959, not 1958)	.05	.02	.01
☐ 424 Calvin Schiraldi	.05	.02	.01
☐ 425 Andy Van Slyke	.10	.05	.01
☐ 426 Joe Grahe	.05	.02	.01
☐ 427 Rick Dempsey	.05	.02	.01
☐ 428 John Barfield	.05	.02	.01
☐ 429 Stump Merrill MG	.05	.02	.01
☐ 430 Gary Gaetti	.10	.05	.01
☐ 431 Paul Gibson	.05	.02	.01
☐ 432 Delino DeShields	.05	.02	.01
☐ 433 Pat Tabler	.05	.02	.01
☐ 434 Julio Machado	.05	.02	.01
☐ 435 Kevin Maas	.05	.02	.01
☐ 436 Scott Bankhead	.05	.02	.01
☐ 437 Doug Dascenzo	.05	.02	.01
☐ 438 Vicente Palacios	.05	.02	.01
☐ 439 Dickie Thon	.05	.02	.01
☐ 440 George Bell	.05	.02	.01
☐ 441 Zane Smith	.05	.02	.01
☐ 442 Charlie O'Brien	.05	.02	.01
☐ 443 Jeff Innis	.05	.02	.01
☐ 444 Glenn Braggs	.05	.02	.01
☐ 445 Greg Swindell	.05	.02	.01
☐ 446 Craig Grebeck	.05	.02	.01
☐ 447 John Burkett	.10	.05	.01
☐ 448 Craig Lefferts	.05	.02	.01
☐ 449 Juan Berenguer	.05	.02	.01
☐ 450 Wade Boggs	.15	.07	.02
☐ 451 Neal Heaton	.05	.02	.01
☐ 452 Bill Schroeder	.05	.02	.01
☐ 453 Lenny Harris	.05	.02	.01
☐ 454A Kevin Appier ERR ('90 Omaha stat line omitted)	.15	.07	.02
☐ 454B Kevin Appier COR	.15	.07	.02
☐ 455 Walt Weiss	.05	.02	.01
☐ 456 Charlie Leibrandt	.05	.02	.01
☐ 457 Todd Hundley	.15	.07	.02
☐ 458 Brian Holman	.05	.02	.01
☐ 459 Tom Trebelhorn MG UER (Pitching and batting columns switched)	.05	.02	.01
☐ 460 Dave Stieb	.05	.02	.01
☐ 461 Robin Ventura	.15	.07	.02
☐ 462 Steve Frey	.05	.02	.01
☐ 463 Dwight Smith	.05	.02	.01
☐ 464 Steve Buechele	.05	.02	.01
☐ 465 Ken Griffey Sr.	.05	.02	.01
☐ 466 Charles Nagy	.15	.07	.02
☐ 467 Dennis Cook	.05	.02	.01
☐ 468 Tim Hulett	.05	.02	.01
☐ 469 Chet Lemon	.05	.02	.01
☐ 470 Howard Johnson	.05	.02	.01
☐ 471 Mike Lieberthal	.15	.07	.02
☐ 472 Kirt Manwaring	.05	.02	.01
☐ 473 Curt Young	.05	.02	.01
☐ 474 Phil Plantier	.10	.05	.01
☐ 475 Teddy Higuera	.05	.02	.01
☐ 476 Glenn Wilson	.05	.02	.01
☐ 477 Mike Fetters	.05	.02	.01
☐ 478 Kurt Stillwell	.05	.02	.01
☐ 479 Bob Patterson UER (Has a decimal point between 7 and 9)	.05	.02	.01
☐ 480 Dave Magadan	.05	.02	.01
☐ 481 Eddie Whitson	.05	.02	.01
☐ 482 Tino Martinez	.15	.07	.02
☐ 483 Mike Aldrete	.05	.02	.01
☐ 484 Dave LaPoint	.05	.02	.01
☐ 485 Terry Pendleton	.10	.05	.01
☐ 486 Tommy Greene	.05	.02	.01
☐ 487 Rafael Belliard	.05	.02	.01
☐ 488 Jeff Manto	.05	.02	.01
☐ 489 Bobby Valentine MG	.05	.02	.01
☐ 490 Kirk Gibson	.10	.05	.01
☐ 491 Kurt Miller	.05	.02	.01
☐ 492 Ernie Whitt	.05	.02	.01
☐ 493 Jose Rijo	.05	.02	.01
☐ 494 Chris James	.05	.02	.01
☐ 495 Charlie Hough	.05	.02	.01
☐ 496 Marty Barrett	.05	.02	.01
☐ 497 Ben McDonald	.10	.05	.01
☐ 498 Mark Salas	.05	.02	.01
☐ 499 Melido Perez	.05	.02	.01
☐ 500 Will Clark	.15	.07	.02
☐ 501 Mike Bielecki	.05	.02	.01
☐ 502 Carney Lansford	.10	.05	.01
☐ 503 Roy Smith	.05	.02	.01
☐ 504 Julio Valera	.05	.02	.01
☐ 505 Chuck Finley	.10	.05	.01
☐ 506 Darnell Coles	.05	.02	.01
☐ 507 Steve Jeltz	.05	.02	.01
☐ 508 Mike York	.05	.02	.01
☐ 509 Glenallen Hill	.05	.02	.01
☐ 510 John Franco	.05	.02	.01
☐ 511 Steve Balboni	.05	.02	.01
☐ 512 Jose Mesa	.10	.05	.01
☐ 513 Jerald Clark	.05	.02	.01
☐ 514 Mike Stanton	.05	.02	.01
☐ 515 Alvin Davis	.05	.02	.01
☐ 516 Karl Rhodes	.05	.02	.01
☐ 517 Joe Oliver	.05	.02	.01
☐ 518 Cris Carpenter	.05	.02	.01
☐ 519 Sparky Anderson MG	.10	.05	.01
☐ 520 Mark Grace	.15	.07	.02
☐ 521 Joe Orsulak	.05	.02	.01
☐ 522 Stan Belinda	.05	.02	.01
☐ 523 Rodney McCray	.05	.02	.01
☐ 524 Darrel Akerfelds	.05	.02	.01
☐ 525 Willie Randolph	.10	.05	.01
☐ 526A Moises Alou ERR (37 runs in 2 games for '90 Pirates)	.50	.23	.06
☐ 526B Moises Alou COR (0 runs in 2 games for '90 Pirates)	.15	.07	.02
☐ 527A Checklist 4 ERR 105 Keith Miller 719 Kevin McReynolds	.15	.07	.02
☐ 527B Checklist 4 COR 105 Kevin McReynolds 719 Keith Miller	.05	.02	.01
☐ 528 Denny Martinez	.10	.05	.01
☐ 529 Marc Newfield	.15	.07	.02
☐ 530 Roger Clemens	.20	.09	.03
☐ 531 Dave Rohde	.05	.02	.01
☐ 532 Kirk McCaskill	.05	.02	.01
☐ 533 Oddibe McDowell	.05	.02	.01
☐ 534 Mike Jackson	.05	.02	.01
☐ 535 Ruben Sierra UER (Back reads 100 Runs amd 100 RBI's)	.10	.05	.01
☐ 536 Mike Witt	.05	.02	.01
☐ 537 Jose Lind	.05	.02	.01
☐ 538 Bip Roberts	.05	.02	.01
☐ 539 Scott Terry	.05	.02	.01
☐ 540 George Brett	.40	.18	.05
☐ 541 Domingo Ramos	.05	.02	.01
☐ 542 Rob Murphy	.05	.02	.01
☐ 543 Junior Felix	.05	.02	.01
☐ 544 Alejandro Pena	.05	.02	.01
☐ 545 Dale Murphy	.15	.07	.02
☐ 546 Jeff Ballard	.05	.02	.01
☐ 547 Mike Pagliarulo	.05	.02	.01
☐ 548 Jaime Navarro	.05	.02	.01
☐ 549 John McNamara MG	.05	.02	.01
☐ 550 Eric Davis	.10	.05	.01
☐ 551 Bob Kipper	.05	.02	.01
☐ 552 Jeff Hamilton	.05	.02	.01
☐ 553 Joe Klink	.05	.02	.01
☐ 554 Brian Harper	.05	.02	.01
☐ 555 Turner Ward	.05	.02	.01
☐ 556 Gary Ward	.05	.02	.01
☐ 557 Wally Whitehurst	.05	.02	.01
☐ 558 Otis Nixon	.05	.02	.01
☐ 559 Adam Peterson	.05	.02	.01
☐ 560 Greg Smith	.05	.02	.01
☐ 561 Tim McIntosh	.05	.02	.01
☐ 562 Jeff Kunkel	.05	.02	.01
☐ 563 Brent Knackert	.05	.02	.01
☐ 564 Dante Bichette	.15	.07	.02
☐ 565 Craig Biggio	.15	.07	.02
☐ 566 Craig Wilson	.05	.02	.01
☐ 567 Dwayne Henry	.05	.02	.01
☐ 568 Ron Karkovice	.05	.02	.01
☐ 569 Curt Schilling	.05	.02	.01
☐ 570 Barry Bonds	.25	.11	.03
☐ 571 Pat Combs	.05	.02	.01
☐ 572 Dave Anderson	.05	.02	.01
☐ 573 Rich Rodriguez UER (Stats say drafted 4th, but bio says 9th round)	.05	.02	.01
☐ 574 John Marzano	.05	.02	.01
☐ 575 Robin Yount	.15	.07	.02
☐ 576 Jeff Kaiser	.05	.02	.01
☐ 577 Bill Doran	.05	.02	.01
☐ 578 Dave West	.05	.02	.01
☐ 579 Roger Craig MG	.05	.02	.01
☐ 580 Dave Stewart	.10	.05	.01
☐ 581 Luis Quinones	.05	.02	.01
☐ 582 Marty Clary	.05	.02	.01
☐ 583 Tony Phillips	.10	.05	.01
☐ 584 Kevin Brown	.10	.05	.01
☐ 585 Pete O'Brien	.05	.02	.01
☐ 586 Fred Lynn	.05	.02	.01
☐ 587 Jose Offerman UER (Text says he signed 7/24/86, but bio says 1988)	.05	.02	.01
☐ 588 Mark Whiten	.10	.05	.01
☐ 589 Scott Ruskin	.05	.02	.01
☐ 590 Eddie Murray	.25	.11	.03
☐ 591 Ken Hill	.10	.05	.01
☐ 592 B.J. Surhoff	.10	.05	.01
☐ 593A Mike Walker ERR ('90 Canton-Akron stat line omitted)	.15	.07	.02
☐ 593B Mike Walker COR	.05	.02	.01
☐ 594 Rich Garces	.05	.02	.01
☐ 595 Bill Landrum	.05	.02	.01
☐ 596 Ronnie Walden	.05	.02	.01
☐ 597 Jerry Don Gleaton	.05	.02	.01
☐ 598 Sam Horn	.05	.02	.01
☐ 599A Greg Myers ERR ('90 Syracuse stat line omitted)	.15	.07	.02
☐ 599B Greg Myers COR	.05	.02	.01
☐ 600 Bo Jackson	.10	.05	.01
☐ 601 Bob Ojeda	.05	.02	.01

Card	MINT	NRMT	EXC
□ 602 Casey Candaele	.05	.02	.01
□ 603A Wes Chamberlain ERR	.15	.07	.02
(Photo actually Louie Meadows)			
□ 603B Wes Chamberlain COR	.05	.02	.01
□ 604 Billy Hatcher	.05	.02	.01
□ 605 Jeff Reardon	.10	.05	.01
□ 606 Jim Gott	.05	.02	.01
□ 607 Edgar Martinez	.10	.05	.01
□ 608 Todd Burns	.05	.02	.01
□ 609 Jeff Torborg MG	.05	.02	.01
□ 610 Andres Galarraga	.15	.07	.02
□ 611 Dave Eiland	.05	.02	.01
□ 612 Steve Lyons	.05	.02	.01
□ 613 Eric Show	.05	.02	.01
□ 614 Luis Salazar	.05	.02	.01
□ 615 Bert Blyleven	.10	.05	.01
□ 616 Todd Zeile	.10	.05	.01
□ 617 Bill Wegman	.05	.02	.01
□ 618 Sil Campusano	.05	.02	.01
□ 619 David Wells	.05	.02	.01
□ 620 Ozzie Guillen	.05	.02	.01
□ 621 Ted Power	.05	.02	.01
□ 622 Jack Daugherty	.05	.02	.01
□ 623 Jeff Blauser	.05	.02	.01
□ 624 Tom Candiotti	.05	.02	.01
□ 625 Terry Steinbach	.10	.05	.01
□ 626 Gerald Young	.05	.02	.01
□ 627 Tim Layana	.05	.02	.01
□ 628 Greg Litton	.05	.02	.01
□ 629 Wes Gardner	.05	.02	.01
□ 630 Dave Winfield	.15	.07	.02
□ 631 Mike Morgan	.05	.02	.01
□ 632 Lloyd Moseby	.05	.02	.01
□ 633 Kevin Tapani	.05	.02	.01
□ 634 Henry Cotto	.05	.02	.01
□ 635 Andy Hawkins	.05	.02	.01
□ 636 Geronimo Pena	.05	.02	.01
□ 637 Bruce Ruffin	.05	.02	.01
□ 638 Mike Macfarlane	.05	.02	.01
□ 639 Frank Robinson MG	.15	.07	.02
□ 640 Andre Dawson	.10	.05	.01
□ 641 Mike Henneman	.05	.02	.01
□ 642 Hal Morris	.05	.02	.01
□ 643 Jim Presley	.05	.02	.01
□ 644 Chuck Crim	.05	.02	.01
□ 645 Juan Samuel	.05	.02	.01
□ 646 Andujar Cedeno	.05	.02	.01
□ 647 Mark Portugal	.05	.02	.01
□ 648 Lee Stevens	.05	.02	.01
□ 649 Bill Sampen	.05	.02	.01
□ 650 Jack Clark	.10	.05	.01
□ 651 Alan Mills	.05	.02	.01
□ 652 Kevin Romine	.05	.02	.01
□ 653 Anthony Telford	.05	.02	.01
□ 654 Paul Sorrento	.10	.05	.01
□ 655 Erik Hanson	.05	.02	.01
□ 656A Checklist 5 ERR	.15	.07	.02
348 Vicente Palacios			
381 Jose Lind			
537 Mike LaValliere			
665 Jim Leyland			
□ 656B Checklist 5 ERR	.15	.07	.02
433 Vicente Palacios			
(Palacios should be 438)			
537 Jose Lind			
665 Mike LaValliere			
381 Jim Leyland			
□ 656C Checklist 5 COR	.15	.07	.02
438 Vicente Palacios			
537 Jose Lind			
665 Mike LaValliere			
381 Jim Leyland			
□ 657 Mike Kingery	.05	.02	.01
□ 658 Scott Aldred	.05	.02	.01
□ 659 Oscar Azocar	.05	.02	.01
□ 660 Lee Smith	.10	.05	.01
□ 661 Steve Lake	.05	.02	.01
□ 662 Ron Dibble	.05	.02	.01
□ 663 Greg Brock	.05	.02	.01
□ 664 John Farrell	.05	.02	.01
□ 665 Mike LaValliere	.05	.02	.01
□ 666 Danny Darwin	.05	.02	.01
□ 667 Kent Anderson	.05	.02	.01
□ 668 Bill Long	.05	.02	.01
□ 669 Lou Piniella MG	.10	.05	.01
□ 670 Rickey Henderson	.15	.07	.02
□ 671 Andy McGaffigan	.05	.02	.01
□ 672 Shane Mack	.05	.02	.01
□ 673 Greg Olson UER	.05	.02	.01
(6 RBI in '88 at Tidewater and 2 RBI in '87, should be 48 and 15)			
□ 674A Kevin Gross ERR	.15	.07	.02
(89 BB with Phillies in '88 tied for league lead)			
□ 674B Kevin Gross COR	.05	.02	.01
(89 BB with Phillies in '88 led league)			
□ 675 Tom Brunansky	.05	.02	.01
□ 676 Scott Chiamparino	.05	.02	.01
□ 677 Billy Ripken	.05	.02	.01
□ 678 Mark Davidson	.05	.02	.01
□ 679 Bill Bathe	.05	.02	.01
□ 680 David Cone	.10	.05	.01
□ 681 Jeff Schaefer	.05	.02	.01
□ 682 Ray Lankford	.15	.07	.02
□ 683 Derek Lilliquist	.05	.02	.01
□ 684 Milt Cuyler	.05	.02	.01
□ 685 Doug Drabek	.05	.02	.01
□ 686 Mike Gallego	.05	.02	.01
□ 687A John Cerutti ERR	.15	.07	.02
(4.46 ERA in '90)			
□ 687B John Cerutti COR	.05	.02	.01
(4.76 ERA in '90)			
□ 688 Rosario Rodriguez	.05	.02	.01
□ 689 John Kruk	.10	.05	.01
□ 690 Orel Hershiser	.10	.05	.01
□ 691 Mike Blowers	.05	.02	.01
□ 692A Efrain Valdez ERR	.15	.07	.02
(Born 6/11/66)			
□ 692B Efrain Valdez COR	.05	.02	.01
(Born 7/11/66 and two lines of text added)			
□ 693 Francisco Cabrera	.05	.02	.01
□ 694 Randy Veres	.05	.02	.01
□ 695 Kevin Seitzer	.05	.02	.01
□ 696 Steve Olin	.05	.02	.01
□ 697 Shawn Abner	.05	.02	.01
□ 698 Mark Guthrie	.05	.02	.01
□ 699 Jim Lefebvre MG	.05	.02	.01
□ 700 Jose Canseco	.15	.07	.02
□ 701 Pascual Perez	.05	.02	.01
□ 702 Tim Naehring	.10	.05	.01
□ 703 Juan Agosto	.05	.02	.01
□ 704 Devon White	.10	.05	.01
□ 705 Robby Thompson	.05	.02	.01
□ 706A Brad Arnsberg ERR	.15	.07	.02
(68.2 IP in '90)			
□ 706B Brad Arnsberg COR	.05	.02	.01
(62.2 IP in '90)			
□ 707 Jim Eisenreich	.10	.05	.01
□ 708 John Mitchell	.05	.02	.01
□ 709 Matt Sinatro	.05	.02	.01
□ 710 Kent Hrbek	.10	.05	.01
□ 711 Jose DeLeon	.05	.02	.01
□ 712 Ricky Jordan	.05	.02	.01
□ 713 Scott Scudder	.05	.02	.01
□ 714 Marvell Wynne	.05	.02	.01
□ 715 Tim Burke	.05	.02	.01
□ 716 Bob Geren	.05	.02	.01
□ 717 Phil Bradley	.05	.02	.01
□ 718 Steve Crawford	.05	.02	.01
□ 719 Keith Miller	.05	.02	.01
□ 720 Cecil Fielder	.10	.05	.01
□ 721 Mark Lee	.05	.02	.01
□ 722 Wally Backman	.05	.02	.01
□ 723 Candy Maldonado	.05	.02	.01
□ 724 David Segui	.10	.05	.01
□ 725 Ron Gant	.10	.05	.01
□ 726 Phil Stephenson	.05	.02	.01
□ 727 Mookie Wilson	.05	.02	.01
□ 728 Scott Sanderson	.05	.02	.01
□ 729 Don Zimmer MG	.05	.02	.01
□ 730 Barry Larkin	.15	.07	.02
□ 731 Jeff Gray	.05	.02	.01
□ 732 Franklin Stubbs	.05	.02	.01
□ 733 Kelly Downs	.05	.02	.01
□ 734 John Russell	.05	.02	.01
□ 735 Ron Darling	.05	.02	.01
□ 736 Dick Schofield	.05	.02	.01
□ 737 Tim Crews	.05	.02	.01
□ 738 Mel Hall	.05	.02	.01
□ 739 Russ Swan	.05	.02	.01
□ 740 Ryne Sandberg	.25	.11	.03
□ 741 Jimmy Key	.10	.05	.01
□ 742 Tommy Gregg	.05	.02	.01
□ 743 Bryn Smith	.05	.02	.01
□ 744 Nelson Santovenia	.05	.02	.01
□ 745 Doug Jones	.05	.02	.01
□ 746 John Shelby	.05	.02	.01
□ 747 Tony Fossas	.05	.02	.01
□ 748 Al Newman	.05	.02	.01
□ 749 Greg W. Harris	.05	.02	.01
□ 750 Bobby Bonilla	.10	.05	.01
□ 751 Wayne Edwards	.05	.02	.01
□ 752 Kevin Bass	.05	.02	.01
□ 753 Paul Marak UER	.05	.02	.01
(Stats say drafted in Jan. but bio says May)			
□ 754 Bill Pecota	.05	.02	.01
□ 755 Mark Langston	.10	.05	.01
□ 756 Jeff Huson	.05	.02	.01
□ 757 Mark Gardner	.05	.02	.01
□ 758 Mike Devereaux	.05	.02	.01
□ 759 Bobby Cox MG	.10	.05	.01
□ 760 Benny Santiago	.05	.02	.01
□ 761 Larry Andersen	.05	.02	.01
□ 762 Mitch Webster	.05	.02	.01
□ 763 Dana Kiecker	.05	.02	.01
□ 764 Mark Carreon	.05	.02	.01
□ 765 Shawon Dunston	.05	.02	.01
□ 766 Jeff Robinson	.05	.02	.01
□ 767 Dan Wilson	.25	.11	.03
□ 768 Don Pall	.05	.02	.01
□ 769 Tim Sherrill	.05	.02	.01
□ 770 Jay Howell	.05	.02	.01
□ 771 Gary Redus UER	.05	.02	.01
(Born in Tanner, should say Athens)			
□ 772 Kent Mercker UER	.05	.02	.01
(Born in Indianapolis, should say Dublin, Ohio)			
□ 773 Tom Foley	.05	.02	.01
□ 774 Dennis Rasmussen	.05	.02	.01
□ 775 Julio Franco	.10	.05	.01
□ 776 Brent Mayne	.05	.02	.01
□ 777 John Candelaria	.05	.02	.01
□ 778 Dan Gladden	.05	.02	.01
□ 779 Carmelo Martinez	.05	.02	.01
□ 780A Randy Myers ERR	.15	.07	.02
(15 career losses)			
□ 780B Randy Myers COR	.10	.05	.01
(19 career losses)			
□ 781 Darryl Hamilton	.10	.05	.01
□ 782 Jim Deshaies	.05	.02	.01
□ 783 Joel Skinner	.05	.02	.01
□ 784 Willie Fraser	.05	.02	.01
□ 785 Scott Fletcher	.05	.02	.01
□ 786 Eric Plunk	.05	.02	.01
□ 787 Checklist 6	.05	.02	.01
□ 788 Bob Milacki	.05	.02	.01
□ 789 Tom Lasorda MG	.10	.05	.01
□ 790 Ken Griffey Jr.	1.50	.70	.19
□ 791 Mike Benjamin	.05	.02	.01
□ 792 Mike Greenwell	.05	.02	.01

1991 Topps Desert Shield

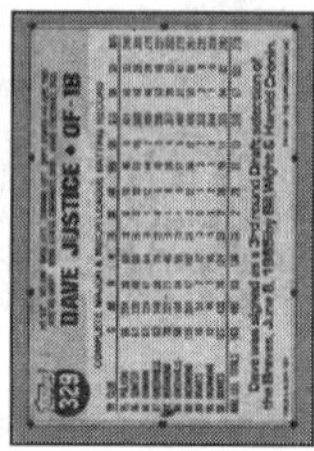

These 792 standard-size cards are parallel to the regular Topps issue. These cards were issued in special packs available only to servicepeople serving in the Desert Shield (later to be Desert Storm) campaign. The cards are differentiated by a "Desert Shield" logo in the upper right corner. There were many different types of forgeries created for these cards so some caution is urged in purchasing any expensive cards from the set.

	MINT	NRMT	EXC
COMPLETE SET (792)	1500.00	700.00	190.00
COMMON CARD (1-792)	1.00	.45	.12
*STARS: 40X to 75X BASIC CARDS			
*ROOKIES: 25X to 50X BASIC CARDS			

1991 Topps Micro

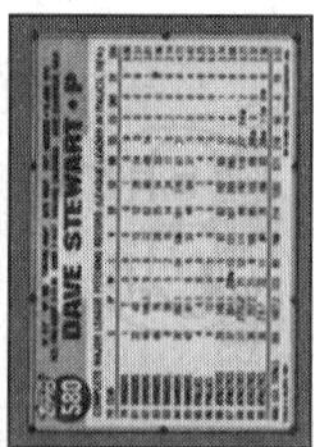

This 792 card set parallels the regular Topps issue. The cards are significantly smaller than the regular Topps cards and are valued at a percentage of the regular 1991 Topps cards.

	MINT	NRMT	EXC
COMPLETE FACT.SET (792)	10.00	4.50	1.25
COMMON CARD (1-792)	.05	.02	.01
*STARS: .5X to 1X BASIC CARDS			

1991 Topps Tiffany

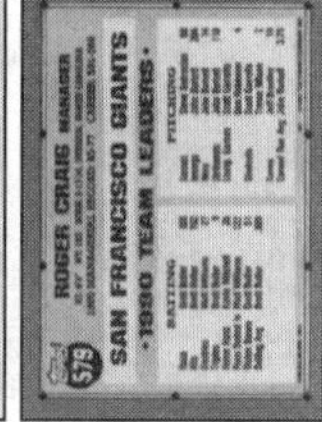

This 792 standard-size set proved to be the final time Topps issued their Tiffany sets. These cards again parallel the regular issue and have "glossy" fronts and easy to read backs. These cards were issued in complete set form only. Since a limited amount of these sets were produced, the multiplier is one of the highest for any of these Topps sets.

	MINT	NRMT	EXC
COMPLETE FACT.SET (792)	200.00	90.00	25.00
COMMON CARD (1-792)	.15	.07	.02
*STARS: 15X to 30X BASIC CARDS			
*ROOKIES: 10X to 20X BASIC CARDS			

1991 Topps Rookies

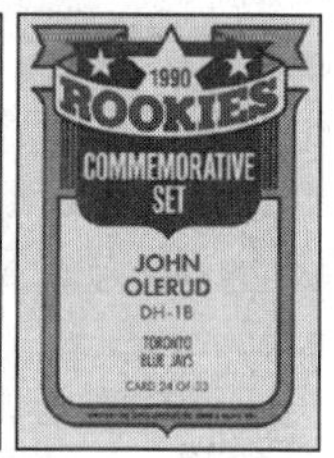

This set contains 33 standard-size cards. The front and back borders are white and other design elements are red, blue, and yellow. This set is identical to the previous year's set. Topps also commemorated its 40th anniversary by including a "Topps 40" logo on the front. The cards are unnumbered and checklisted below in alphabetical order.

	MINT	NRMT	EXC
COMPLETE SET (33)	12.00	5.50	1.50
COMMON CARD (1-33)	.10	.05	.01
□ 1 Sandy Alomar	.20	.09	.03
□ 2 Kevin Appier	.30	.14	.04
□ 3 Steve Avery	.30	.14	.04
□ 4 Carlos Baerga	.30	.14	.04
□ 5 John Burkett	.20	.09	.03
□ 6 Alex Cole	.10	.05	.01
□ 7 Pat Combs	.10	.05	.01
□ 8 Delino DeShields	.20	.09	.03
□ 9 Travis Fryman	.30	.14	.04
□ 10 Marquis Grissom	.30	.14	.04
□ 11 Mike Harkey	.10	.05	.01
□ 12 Glenallen Hill	.20	.09	.03
□ 13 Jeff Huson	.10	.05	.01
□ 14 Felix Jose	.10	.05	.01
□ 15 Dave Justice	.75	.35	.09
□ 16 Jim Leyritz	.20	.09	.03
□ 17 Kevin Maas	.10	.05	.01
□ 18 Ben McDonald	.20	.09	.03
□ 19 Kent Mercker	.10	.05	.01
□ 20 Hal Morris	.10	.05	.01
□ 21 Chris Nabholz	.10	.05	.01
□ 22 Tim Naehring	.30	.14	.04
□ 23 Jose Offerman	.20	.09	.03
□ 24 John Olerud	.50	.23	.06
□ 25 Scott Radinsky	.10	.05	.01
□ 26 Scott Ruskin	.10	.05	.01
□ 27 Kevin Tapani	.20	.09	.03
□ 28 Frank Thomas	6.00	2.70	.75
□ 29 Randy Tomlin	.10	.05	.01
□ 30 Greg Vaughn	.20	.09	.03
□ 31 Robin Ventura	.30	.14	.04
□ 32 Larry Walker	.75	.35	.09
□ 33 Todd Zeile	.30	.14	.04

1991 Topps Wax Box Cards

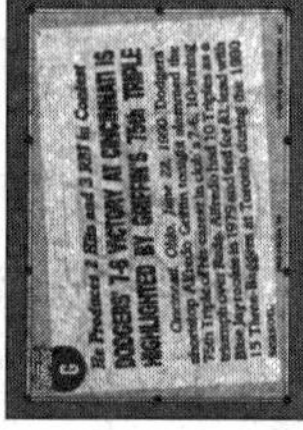

Topps again in 1991 issued cards on the bottom of their wax pack boxes. There are four different boxes, each with four cards and a checklist on the side. These standard-size cards have yellow borders rather than the white borders of the regular issue cards, and they have different photos of the players. The backs are printed in pink and blue on gray cardboard stock and feature outstanding achievements of the players. The cards are numbered by letter on the back. The cards have the typical Topps 1991 design on the front of the card. The set was ordered in alphabetical order and lettered A-P.

	MINT	NRMT	EXC
COMPLETE SET (16)	6.00	2.70	.75
COMMON CARD (A-P)	.10	.05	.01
□ A Bert Blyleven	.25	.11	.03
□ B George Brett	1.00	.45	.12
□ C Brett Butler	.10	.05	.01
□ D Andre Dawson	.40	.18	.05
□ E Dwight Evans	.25	.11	.03
□ F Carlton Fisk	.40	.18	.05
□ G Alfredo Griffin	.10	.05	.01
□ H Rickey Henderson	.50	.23	.06
□ I Willie McGee	.10	.05	.01
□ J Dale Murphy	.40	.18	.05
□ K Eddie Murray	.75	.35	.09

☐ L Dave Parker	.25	.11	.03
☐ M Jeff Reardon	.10	.05	.01
☐ N Nolan Ryan	2.50	1.10	.30
☐ O Juan Samuel	.10	.05	.01
☐ P Robin Yount	.40	.18	.05

1991 Topps Traded

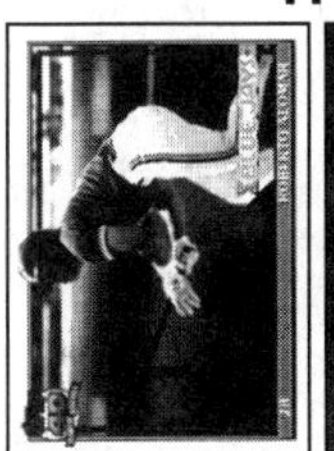

The 1991 Topps Traded set contains 132 standard-size cards. The cards were issued primarily in factory set form through hobby dealers but were also made available on a limited basis in wax packs. The cards in the wax packs (gray backs) and collated factory sets (white backs) are from different card stock. Both versions are valued equally. The card design is identical to the regular issue 1991 Topps cards except for the whiter stock (for factory set cards) and T-suffixed numbering. The set is numbered in alphabetical order. The set includes a Team U.S.A. subset, featuring 25 of America's top collegiate players. The key Rookie Cards in this set are Jeff Bagwell, Jason Giambi, Todd Greene, Charles Johnson and Ivan Rodriguez.

	MINT	NRMT	EXC
COMPLETE SET (132)	5.00	2.20	.60
COMPLETE FACT.SET (132)	5.00	2.20	.60
COMMON CARD (1T-132T)	.05	.02	.01
☐ 1T Juan Agosto	.05	.02	.01
☐ 2T Roberto Alomar	.20	.09	.03
☐ 3T Wally Backman	.05	.02	.01
☐ 4T Jeff Bagwell	2.50	1.10	.30
☐ 5T Skeeter Barnes	.05	.02	.01
☐ 6T Steve Bedrosian	.05	.02	.01
☐ 7T Derek Bell	.15	.07	.02
☐ 8T George Bell	.05	.02	.01
☐ 9T Rafael Belliard	.05	.02	.01
☐ 10T Dante Bichette	.15	.07	.02
☐ 11T Bud Black	.05	.02	.01
☐ 12T Mike Boddicker	.05	.02	.01
☐ 13T Sid Bream	.05	.02	.01
☐ 14T Hubie Brooks	.05	.02	.01
☐ 15T Brett Butler	.10	.05	.01
☐ 16T Ivan Calderon	.05	.02	.01
☐ 17T John Candelaria	.05	.02	.01
☐ 18T Tom Candiotti	.05	.02	.01
☐ 19T Gary Carter	.10	.05	.01
☐ 20T Joe Carter	.10	.05	.01
☐ 21T Rick Cerone	.05	.02	.01
☐ 22T Jack Clark	.10	.05	.01
☐ 23T Vince Coleman	.05	.02	.01
☐ 24T Scott Coolbaugh	.05	.02	.01
☐ 25T Danny Cox	.05	.02	.01
☐ 26T Danny Darwin	.05	.02	.01
☐ 27T Chili Davis	.10	.05	.01
☐ 28T Glenn Davis	.05	.02	.01
☐ 29T Steve Decker	.05	.02	.01
☐ 30T Rob Deer	.05	.02	.01
☐ 31T Rich DeLucia	.05	.02	.01
☐ 32T John Dettmer USA	.10	.05	.01
☐ 33T Brian Downing	.05	.02	.01
☐ 34T Darren Dreifort USA	.15	.07	.02
☐ 35T Kirk Dressendorfer	.05	.02	.01
☐ 36T Jim Essian MG	.05	.02	.01
☐ 37T Dwight Evans	.10	.05	.01
☐ 38T Steve Farr	.05	.02	.01
☐ 39T Jeff Fassero	.15	.07	.02
☐ 40T Junior Felix	.05	.02	.01
☐ 41T Tony Fernandez	.05	.02	.01
☐ 42T Steve Finley	.10	.05	.01
☐ 43T Jim Fregosi MG	.05	.02	.01
☐ 44T Gary Gaetti	.10	.05	.01
☐ 45T Jason Giambi USA	1.00	.45	.12
☐ 46T Kirk Gibson	.10	.05	.01
☐ 47T Leo Gomez	.05	.02	.01
☐ 48T Luis Gonzalez	.15	.07	.02
☐ 49T Jeff Granger USA	.15	.07	.02
☐ 50T Todd Greene USA	.40	.18	.05
☐ 51T Jeffrey Hammonds USA	.25	.11	.03
☐ 52T Mike Hargrove MG	.05	.02	.01
☐ 53T Pete Harnisch	.05	.02	.01
☐ 54T Rick Helling USA UER (Misspelled Hellings on card back)	.10	.05	.01
☐ 55T Glenallen Hill	.05	.02	.01
☐ 56T Charlie Hough	.05	.02	.01
☐ 57T Pete Incaviglia	.05	.02	.01
☐ 58T Bo Jackson	.10	.05	.01
☐ 59T Danny Jackson	.05	.02	.01
☐ 60T Reggie Jefferson	.10	.05	.01
☐ 61T Charles Johnson USA	.75	.35	.09
☐ 62T Jeff Johnson	.05	.02	.01
☐ 63T Todd Johnson USA	.05	.02	.01
☐ 64T Barry Jones	.05	.02	.01
☐ 65T Chris Jones	.05	.02	.01
☐ 66T Scott Kamieniecki	.05	.02	.01
☐ 67T Pat Kelly	.10	.05	.01
☐ 68T Darryl Kile	.05	.02	.01
☐ 69T Chuck Knoblauch	.25	.11	.03
☐ 70T Bill Krueger	.05	.02	.01
☐ 71T Scott Leius	.05	.02	.01
☐ 72T Donnie Leshnock USA	.05	.02	.01
☐ 73T Mark Lewis	.05	.02	.01
☐ 74T Candy Maldonado	.05	.02	.01
☐ 75T Jason McDonald USA	.15	.07	.02
☐ 76T Willie McGee	.05	.02	.01
☐ 77T Fred McGriff	.15	.07	.02
☐ 78T Billy McMillon USA	.15	.07	.02
☐ 79T Hal McRae MG	.05	.02	.01
☐ 80T Dan Melendez USA	.05	.02	.01
☐ 81T Orlando Merced	.15	.07	.02
☐ 82T Jack Morris	.10	.05	.01
☐ 83T Phil Nevin USA	.15	.07	.02
☐ 84T Otis Nixon	.05	.02	.01
☐ 85T Johnny Oates MG	.05	.02	.01
☐ 86T Bob Ojeda	.05	.02	.01
☐ 87T Mike Pagliarulo	.05	.02	.01
☐ 88T Dean Palmer	.15	.07	.02
☐ 89T Dave Parker	.10	.05	.01
☐ 90T Terry Pendleton	.10	.05	.01
☐ 91T Tony Phillips (P) USA	.05	.02	.01
☐ 92T Doug Piatt	.05	.02	.01
☐ 93T Ron Polk USA CO	.10	.05	.01
☐ 94T Tim Raines	.15	.07	.02
☐ 95T Willie Randolph	.10	.05	.01
☐ 96T Dave Righetti	.05	.02	.01
☐ 97T Ernie Riles	.05	.02	.01
☐ 98T Chris Roberts USA	.15	.07	.02
☐ 99T Jeff D. Robinson	.05	.02	.01
☐ 100T Jeff M. Robinson	.05	.02	.01
☐ 101T Ivan Rodriguez	1.50	.70	.19
☐ 102T Steve Rodriguez USA	.05	.02	.01
☐ 103T Tom Runnells MG	.05	.02	.01
☐ 104T Scott Sanderson	.05	.02	.01
☐ 105T Bob Scanlan	.05	.02	.01
☐ 106T Pete Schourek	.15	.07	.02
☐ 107T Gary Scott	.05	.02	.01
☐ 108T Paul Shuey USA	.15	.07	.02
☐ 109T Doug Simons	.05	.02	.01
☐ 110T Dave Smith	.05	.02	.01
☐ 111T Cory Snyder	.05	.02	.01
☐ 112T Luis Sojo	.05	.02	.01
☐ 113T Kennie Steenstra USA	.05	.02	.01
☐ 114T Darryl Strawberry	.10	.05	.01
☐ 115T Franklin Stubbs	.05	.02	.01
☐ 116T Todd Taylor USA	.05	.02	.01
☐ 117T Wade Taylor	.05	.02	.01
☐ 118T Garry Templeton	.05	.02	.01
☐ 119T Mickey Tettleton	.10	.05	.01
☐ 120T Tim Teufel	.05	.02	.01
☐ 121T Mike Timlin	.05	.02	.01
☐ 122T David Tuttle USA	.05	.02	.01
☐ 123T Mo Vaughn	.50	.23	.06
☐ 124T Jeff Ware USA	.10	.05	.01
☐ 125T Devon White	.10	.05	.01
☐ 126T Mark Whiten	.10	.05	.01
☐ 127T Mitch Williams	.05	.02	.01
☐ 128T Craig Wilson USA	.05	.02	.01
☐ 129T Willie Wilson	.05	.02	.01
☐ 130T Chris Wimmer USA	.05	.02	.01
☐ 131T Ivan Zweig USA	.05	.02	.01
☐ 132T Checklist 1T-132T	.05	.02	.01

1991 Topps Traded Tiffany

In the final Tiffany relase, this 132-card standard-size set was released as a parallel issue to the regular Topps Traded issue. These cards were released in very limited quantities and the multiplier for these cards is higher than many previous Tiffany issues. These cards were issued in complete factory set form only.

	MINT	NRMT	EXC
COMPLETE FACT.SET (132)	40.00	18.00	5.00
COMMON CARD (1T-132T)	.15	.07	.02

*STARS: 2X to 4X BASIC CARDS
*YOUNG STARS: 1.5X to 3X BASIC CARDS
*ROOKIES: 1.5X to 3X BASIC CARDS

1991 Topps Cracker Jack I

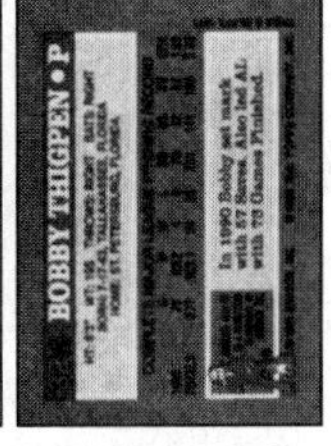

This 36-card set is the first of two 36-card series produced by Topps for Cracker Jack, and the cards were inserted inside specially marked packages of Cracker Jack. These cards were the "toy surprise" inside. The cards measure approximately one-fourth standard-size (1 1/4" by 1 3/4") and are frequently referenced as micro-cards. The micro-cards have color player photos with different color borders but are otherwise identical to the corresponding cards in the Topps regular issue. The horizontally oriented backs are printed in red, blue, and pink, and include biography, complete Major League batting record, career highlights, and the Cracker Jack sailor at the lower left corner. Standard-size cards featuring four micro-cards each were seen at shows but were not inserted inside the product. These were apparently test runs or uncut sheets. Although each mini-card is numbered on the back, the numbering of the four cards on any standard-size card is not consecutive.

	MINT	NRMT	EXC
COMPLETE SET (36)	10.00	4.50	1.25
COMMON CARD (1-36)	.10	.05	.01
☐ 1 Nolan Ryan	2.50	1.10	.30
☐ 2 Paul Molitor	.60	.25	.07
☐ 3 Tim Raines	.20	.09	.03
☐ 4 Frank Viola	.10	.05	.01
☐ 5 Sandy Alomar Jr.	.20	.09	.03
☐ 6 Ryne Sandberg	1.00	.45	.12
☐ 7 Don Mattingly	1.25	.55	.16
☐ 8 Pedro Guerrero	.10	.05	.01
☐ 9 Jose Rijo	.10	.05	.01
☐ 10 Jose Canseco	.50	.23	.06
☐ 11 Dave Parker	.10	.05	.01
☐ 12 Doug Drabek	.10	.05	.01
☐ 13 Cal Ripken	2.50	1.10	.30
☐ 14 Dave Justice	.40	.18	.05
☐ 15 George Brett	1.00	.45	.12
☐ 16 Eric Davis	.10	.05	.01
☐ 17 Mark Langston	.10	.05	.01
☐ 18 Rickey Henderson	.50	.23	.06
☐ 19 Barry Bonds	.60	.25	.07
☐ 20 Kevin Maas	.10	.05	.01
☐ 21 Len Dykstra	.20	.09	.03
☐ 22 Roger Clemens	.60	.25	.07
☐ 23 Robin Yount	.40	.18	.05
☐ 24 Mark Grace	.50	.23	.06
☐ 25 Bo Jackson	.20	.09	.03
☐ 26 Tony Gwynn	1.00	.45	.12
☐ 27 Mark McGwire	1.25	.55	.16
☐ 28 Dwight Gooden	.20	.09	.03
☐ 29 Wade Boggs	.50	.23	.06
☐ 30 Kevin Mitchell	.10	.05	.01
☐ 31 Cecil Fielder	.40	.18	.05
☐ 32 Bobby Thigpen	.10	.05	.01
☐ 33 Benito Santiago	.10	.05	.01
☐ 34 Kirby Puckett	1.25	.55	.16
☐ 35 Will Clark	.50	.23	.06
☐ 36 Ken Griffey Jr.	2.50	1.10	.30

1991 Topps Cracker Jack II

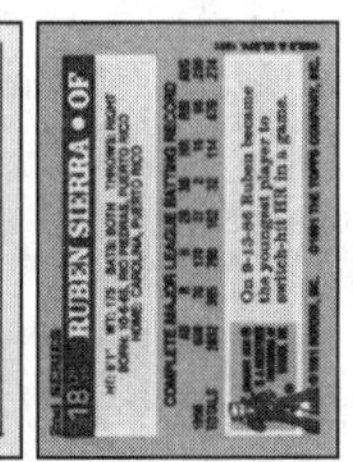

This 36-card set is the second of two different 36-card series produced by Topps for Cracker Jack, and the cards were inserted inside specially marked packages of Cracker Jack. These cards were the "toy surprise" inside. The cards measure approximately one-fourth standard-size (1 1/4" by 1 3/4") and are frequently referenced as micro-cards. The micro-cards have color player photos with different color borders but are otherwise identical to the corresponding cards in the Topps regular issue. The horizontally oriented backs are printed in red, blue, and pink, and include biography, complete Major League batting record, career highlights, and the Cracker Jack sailor at the lower left corner. Standard-size cards featuring four micro-cards each were seen at shows but were not inserted inside the product. These were apparently test runs or uncut sheets. Although each mini-card is numbered on the back, the numbering of the four cards on any standard-size card is not consecutive.

	MINT	NRMT	EXC
COMPLETE SET (36)	6.00	2.70	.75
COMMON CARD (1-36)	.10	.05	.01
☐ 1 Eddie Murray	.60	.25	.07
☐ 2 Carlton Fisk	.40	.18	.05
☐ 3 Eric Anthony	.10	.05	.01
☐ 4 Kelly Gruber	.10	.05	.01
☐ 5 Von Hayes	.10	.05	.01
☐ 6 Ben McDonald	.25	.11	.03
☐ 7 Andre Dawson	.40	.18	.05
☐ 8 Ellis Burks	.40	.18	.05
☐ 9 Matt Williams	.50	.23	.06
☐ 10 Dave Stewart	.10	.05	.01
☐ 11 Barry Larkin	.40	.18	.05
☐ 12 Chuck Finley	.10	.05	.01
☐ 13 Shane Andrews	.25	.11	.03
☐ 14 Bret Saberhagen	.10	.05	.01
☐ 15 Bobby Bonilla	.25	.11	.03
☐ 16 Roberto Kelly	.10	.05	.01
☐ 17 Orel Hershiser	.25	.11	.03
☐ 18 Ruben Sierra	.10	.05	.01
☐ 19 Ron Gant	.40	.18	.05
☐ 20 Frank Thomas	2.50	1.10	.30
☐ 21 Tim Wallach	.10	.05	.01
☐ 22 Gregg Olson	.10	.05	.01
☐ 23 Shawon Dunston	.10	.05	.01
☐ 24 Kent Hrbek	.10	.05	.01
☐ 25 Ramon Martinez	.40	.18	.05
☐ 26 Alan Trammell	.25	.11	.03
☐ 27 Ozzie Smith	1.00	.45	.12
☐ 28 Bob Welch	.10	.05	.01
☐ 29 Chris Sabo	.10	.05	.01
☐ 30 Steve Sax	.10	.05	.01
☐ 31 Bip Roberts	.10	.05	.01
☐ 32 Dave Stieb	.10	.05	.01
☐ 33 Howard Johnson	.10	.05	.01
☐ 34 Mike Greenwell	.10	.05	.01
☐ 35 Delino DeShields	.25	.11	.03
☐ 36 Alex Fernandez	.50	.23	.06

1991 Topps Debut '90

The 1991 Topps Major League Debut Set contains 171 standard-size cards. Although the checklist card is arranged chronologically in order of first major league appearance in 1990, the player cards are arranged alphabetically by the player's last name. The front design features mostly posed color player photos, with two different color stripes on the top and sides of the picture. The card face is white, and the player's name is given in the color stripe below the picture. The horizontally oriented backs have player information and statistics in blue lettering on a pink and white background. Carlos Baerga and Frank Thomas are among the more prominent players featured in this set.

	MINT	NRMT	EXC
COMPLETE SET (171)	20.00	9.00	2.50
COMMON CARD (1-171)	.05	.02	.01
☐ 1 Paul Abbott	.05	.02	.01
☐ 2 Steve Adkins	.05	.02	.01
☐ 3 Scott Aldred	.05	.02	.01
☐ 4 Gerald Alexander	.05	.02	.01
☐ 5 Moises Alou	.60	.25	.07
☐ 6 Steve Avery	.75	.35	.09
☐ 7 Oscar Azocar	.05	.02	.01
☐ 8 Carlos Baerga	1.00	.45	.12
☐ 9 Kevin Baez	.05	.02	.01
☐ 10 Jeff Baldwin	.05	.02	.01
☐ 11 Brian Barnes	.05	.02	.01
☐ 12 Kevin Bearse	.05	.02	.01
☐ 13 Kevin Belcher	.05	.02	.01
☐ 14 Mike Bell	.05	.02	.01
☐ 15 Sean Berry	.25	.11	.03
☐ 16 Joe Bitker	.05	.02	.01
☐ 17 Willie Blair	.05	.02	.01
☐ 18 Brian Bohanon	.05	.02	.01
☐ 19 Mike Bordick	.15	.07	.02
☐ 20 Shawn Boskie	.15	.07	.02
☐ 21 Rod Brewer	.05	.02	.01
☐ 22 Kevin D. Brown	.05	.02	.01
☐ 23 Dave Burba	.25	.11	.03
☐ 24 Jim Campbell	.05	.02	.01
☐ 25 Ozzie Canseco	.05	.02	.01
☐ 26 Chuck Carr	.25	.11	.03
☐ 27 Larry Casian	.05	.02	.01
☐ 28 Andujar Cedeno	.15	.07	.02
☐ 29 Wes Chamberlain	.05	.02	.01
☐ 30 Scott Chiamparino	.05	.02	.01
☐ 31 Steve Chitren	.05	.02	.01
☐ 32 Pete Coachman	.05	.02	.01
☐ 33 Alex Cole	.15	.07	.02
☐ 34 Jeff Conine	2.50	1.10	.30
☐ 35 Scott Cooper	.15	.07	.02
☐ 36 Milt Cuyler	.05	.02	.01
☐ 37 Steve Decker	.05	.02	.01
☐ 38 Rich DeLucia	.05	.02	.01
☐ 39 Delino DeShields	.25	.11	.03
☐ 40 Mark Dewey	.05	.02	.01
☐ 41 Carlos Diaz	.05	.02	.01
☐ 42 Lance Dickson	.05	.02	.01
☐ 43 Narciso Elvira	.05	.02	.01
☐ 44 Luis Encarnacion	.05	.02	.01
☐ 45 Scott Erickson	.30	.14	.04
☐ 46 Paul Faries	.05	.02	.01
☐ 47 Howard Farmer	.05	.02	.01
☐ 48 Alex Fernandez	.75	.35	.09
☐ 49 Travis Fryman	1.25	.55	.16
☐ 50 Rich Garces	.05	.02	.01
☐ 51 Carlos Garcia	.30	.14	.04
☐ 52 Mike Gardiner	.05	.02	.01
☐ 53 Bernard Gilkey	.50	.23	.06
☐ 54 Tom Gilles	.05	.02	.01
☐ 55 Jerry Goff	.05	.02	.01
☐ 56 Leo Gomez	.15	.07	.02
☐ 57 Luis Gonzalez	.25	.11	.03

☐ 58 Joe Grahe	.05	.02	.01
☐ 59 Craig Grebeck	.05	.02	.01
☐ 60 Kip Gross	.05	.02	.01
☐ 61 Eric Gunderson	.05	.02	.01
☐ 62 Chris Hammond	.05	.02	.01
☐ 63 Dave Hansen	.05	.02	.01
☐ 64 Reggie Harris	.05	.02	.01
☐ 65 Bill Haselman	.05	.02	.01
☐ 66 Randy Hennis	.05	.02	.01
☐ 67 Carlos Hernandez	.05	.02	.01
☐ 68 Howard Hilton	.05	.02	.01
☐ 69 Dave Hollins	.25	.11	.03
☐ 70 Darren Holmes	.15	.07	.02
☐ 71 John Hoover	.05	.02	.01
☐ 72 Steve Howard	.05	.02	.01
☐ 73 Thomas Howard	.05	.02	.01
☐ 74 Todd Hundley	1.50	.70	.19
☐ 75 Daryl Irvine	.05	.02	.01
☐ 76 Chris Jelic	.05	.02	.01
☐ 77 Dana Kiecker	.05	.02	.01
☐ 78 Brent Knackert	.05	.02	.01
☐ 79 Jimmy Kremers	.05	.02	.01
☐ 80 Jerry Kutzler	.05	.02	.01
☐ 81 Ray Lankford	2.00	.90	.25
☐ 82 Tim Layana	.05	.02	.01
☐ 83 Terry Lee	.05	.02	.01
☐ 84 Mark Leiter	.25	.11	.03
☐ 85 Scott Leius	.25	.11	.03
☐ 86 Mark Leonard	.05	.02	.01
☐ 87 Darren Lewis	.15	.07	.02
☐ 88 Scott Lewis	.05	.02	.01
☐ 89 Jim Leyritz	.30	.14	.04
☐ 90 Dave Liddell	.05	.02	.01
☐ 91 Luis Lopez	.05	.02	.01
☐ 92 Kevin Maas	.05	.02	.01
☐ 93 Bob MacDonald	.05	.02	.01
☐ 94 Carlos Maldonado	.05	.02	.01
☐ 95 Chuck Malone	.05	.02	.01
☐ 96 Ramon Manon	.05	.02	.01
☐ 97 Jeff Manto	.05	.02	.01
☐ 98 Paul Marak	.05	.02	.01
☐ 99 Tino Martinez	1.25	.55	.16
☐ 100 Derrick May	.15	.07	.02
☐ 101 Brent Mayne	.15	.07	.02
☐ 102 Paul McClellan	.05	.02	.01
☐ 103 Rodney McCray	.05	.02	.01
☐ 104 Tim McIntosh	.05	.02	.01
☐ 105 Brian McRae	.75	.35	.09
☐ 106 Jose Melendez	.05	.02	.01
☐ 107 Orlando Merced	.50	.23	.06
☐ 108 Alan Mills	.05	.02	.01
☐ 109 Gino Minutelli	.05	.02	.01
☐ 110 Mickey Morandini	.15	.07	.02
☐ 111 Pedro Munoz	.25	.11	.03
☐ 112 Chris Nabholz	.05	.02	.01
☐ 113 Tim Naehring	.50	.23	.06
☐ 114 Charles Nagy	.75	.35	.09
☐ 115 Jim Neidlinger	.05	.02	.01
☐ 116 Rafael Novoa	.05	.02	.01
☐ 117 Jose Offerman	.25	.11	.03
☐ 118 Omar Olivares	.05	.02	.01
☐ 119 Javier Ortiz	.05	.02	.01
☐ 120 Al Osuna	.05	.02	.01
☐ 121 Rick Parker	.05	.02	.01
☐ 122 Dave Pavlas	.05	.02	.01
☐ 123 Geronimo Pena	.05	.02	.01
☐ 124 Mike Perez	.05	.02	.01
☐ 125 Phil Plantier	.25	.11	.03
☐ 126 Jim Poole	.15	.07	.02
☐ 127 Tom Quinlan	.05	.02	.01
☐ 128 Scott Radinsky	.05	.02	.01
☐ 129 Darren Reed	.05	.02	.01
☐ 130 Karl Rhodes	.05	.02	.01
☐ 131 Jeff Richardson	.05	.02	.01
☐ 132 Rich Rodriguez	.05	.02	.01
☐ 133 Dave Rohde	.05	.02	.01
☐ 134 Mel Rojas	.30	.14	.04
☐ 135 Vic Rosario	.05	.02	.01
☐ 136 Rich Rowland	.05	.02	.01
☐ 137 Scott Ruskin	.05	.02	.01
☐ 138 Bill Sampen	.05	.02	.01
☐ 139 Andres Santana	.05	.02	.01
☐ 140 David Segui	.40	.18	.05
☐ 141 Jeff Shaw	.05	.02	.01
☐ 142 Tim Sherrill	.05	.02	.01
☐ 143 Terry Shumpert	.05	.02	.01
☐ 144 Mike Simms	.05	.02	.01
☐ 145 Daryl Smith	.05	.02	.01
☐ 146 Luis Sojo	.05	.02	.01
☐ 147 Steve Springer	.05	.02	.01
☐ 148 Ray Stephens	.05	.02	.01
☐ 149 Lee Stevens	.05	.02	.01
☐ 150 Mel Stottlemyre Jr.	.05	.02	.01
☐ 151 Glenn Sutko	.05	.02	.01
☐ 152 Anthony Telford	.05	.02	.01
☐ 153 Frank Thomas	12.00	5.50	1.50
☐ 154 Randy Tomlin	.15	.07	.02
☐ 155 Brian Traxler	.05	.02	.01
☐ 156 Efrain Valdez	.05	.02	.01
☐ 157 Rafael Valdez	.05	.02	.01
☐ 158 Julio Valera	.05	.02	.01
☐ 159 Jim Vatcher	.05	.02	.01
☐ 160 Hector Villanueva	.05	.02	.01
☐ 161 Hector Wagner	.05	.02	.01
☐ 162 Dave Walsh	.05	.02	.01
☐ 163 Steve Wapnick	.05	.02	.01
☐ 164 Colby Ward	.05	.02	.01
☐ 165 Turner Ward	.05	.02	.01
☐ 166 Terry Wells	.05	.02	.01
☐ 167 Mark Whiten	.25	.11	.03
☐ 168 Mike York	.05	.02	.01
☐ 169 Cliff Young	.05	.02	.01
☐ 170 Checklist Card	.05	.02	.01
☐ 171 Checklist Card	.05	.02	.01

1991 Topps East Coast National

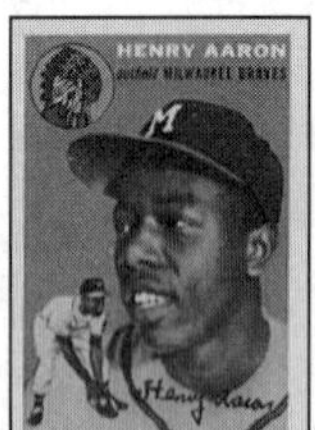

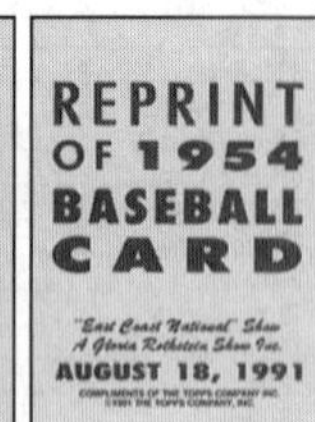

This four-card, standard-size set was included in the paid admission for the 1991 East Coast National Show (August 15-18). Each card is a reproduction of the player's first Topps card: Aaron, ('54 Topps) Mantle, ('52 Topps) Musial, ('58 Topps) and Robinson ('57 Topps). In blue print on white, the backs indicate that these cards are reprints. The cards are unnumbered and checklisted below in alphabetical order.

	MINT	NRMT	EXC
COMPLETE SET (4)	15.00	6.75	1.85
COMMON CARD (1-4)	2.50	1.10	.30
☐ 1 Hank Aaron	5.00	2.20	.60
☐ 2 Mickey Mantle	8.00	3.60	1.00
☐ 3 Stan Musial	4.00	1.80	.50
☐ 4 Frank Robinson	2.50	1.10	.30

1991 Topps Gallery of Champions

In what would be the final season for this issue. Topps issued these 12 cards to honor award winners and league leaders. These "metal" cards measure approximately 1 1/4" by 1 3/4" and were made in aluminum, silver and bronze. We have valued the aluminum versions. The bronze cards are worth 2X to 3X the aluminums while the silvers are worth 4X to 6X the aluminum versions. This set, just as all the other Topps Gallery sets, were issued in complete set form only. We have sequenced this set in alphabetical order.

	MINT	NRMT	EXC
COMPLETE SET (12)	150.00	70.00	19.00
COMMON CARD (1-12)	5.00	2.20	.60
☐ 1 Sandy Alomar	7.50	3.40	.95
☐ 2 Barry Bonds	25.00	11.00	3.10
☐ 3 George Brett	40.00	18.00	5.00
☐ 4 Doug Drabek	5.00	2.20	.60
☐ 5 Cecil Fielder	10.00	4.50	1.25
☐ 6 John Franco	7.50	3.40	.95
☐ 7 Rickey Henderson	25.00	11.00	3.10
☐ 8 Dave Justice	15.00	6.75	1.85
☐ 9 Willie McGee	7.50	3.40	.95
☐ 10 Ryne Sandberg	30.00	13.50	3.70
☐ 11 Bobby Thigpen	5.00	2.20	.60
☐ 12 Bob Welch	5.00	2.20	.60

1991 Topps Glossy All-Stars

These glossy cards were inserted with Topps rack packs and honor the starting lineup, managers and honorary captains of the 1990 National and American League All-Star teams. This would be the final year that this insert set was issued and the design is similar to what Topps produced each year since 1984.

	MINT	NRMT	EXC
COMPLETE SET (22)	8.00	3.60	1.00
COMMON CARD (1-22)	.10	.05	.01
☐ 1 Tony LaRussa MG	.25	.11	.03
☐ 2 Mark McGwire	1.00	.45	.12
☐ 3 Steve Sax	.10	.05	.01
☐ 4 Wade Boggs	.50	.23	.06
☐ 5 Cal Ripken, Jr.	2.00	.90	.25
☐ 6 Rickey Henderson	.50	.23	.06
☐ 7 Ken Griffey, Jr.	2.50	1.10	.30
☐ 8 Jose Canseco	.50	.23	.06
☐ 9 Sandy Alomar, Jr.	.10	.05	.01
☐ 10 Bob Welch	.10	.05	.01
☐ 11 Al Lopez CAPT	.25	.11	.03
☐ 12 Roger Craig MG	.10	.05	.01
☐ 13 Will Clark	.50	.23	.06
☐ 14 Ryne Sandberg	.75	.35	.09
☐ 15 Chris Sabo	.10	.05	.01
☐ 16 Ozzie Smith	1.00	.45	.12
☐ 17 Kevin Mitchell	.10	.05	.01
☐ 18 Len Dykstra	.10	.05	.01
☐ 19 Andre Dawson	.40	.18	.05
☐ 20 Mike Scoscia	.10	.05	.01
☐ 21 Jack Armstrong	.10	.05	.01
☐ 22 Juan Marichal CAPT	.25	.11	.03

1991 Topps Ruth

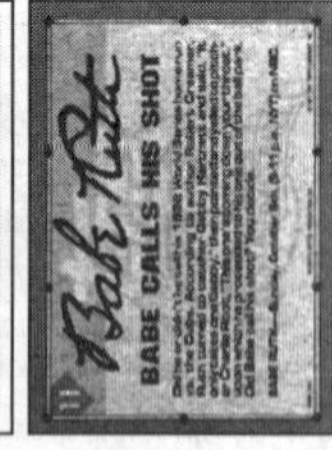

This 11-card set was produced by Topps to commemorate the NBC made-for-television movie about Ruth that aired Sunday, October 6, 1991. The standard-size cards have various color shots from the movie on the fronts, with aqua and red borders on a white card face. The name "Babe Ruth" is written in cursive lettering in the lower right corner of each card, and a caption for each card appears below the picture in the red border. The horizontally oriented backs are printed in dark blue and pink on gray and feature an extended caption to the picture on the front.

	MINT	NRMT	EXC
COMPLETE SET (11)	10.00	4.50	1.25
COMMON CARD (1-11)	1.00	.45	.12
☐ 1 Babe Ruth-Sunday October 6th NBC	1.00	.45	.12
☐ 2 Babe Ruth Stephen Lang as Babe Ruth	1.00	.45	.12
☐ 3 Babe Ruth Bruce Weitz as Miller Huggins	1.00	.45	.12
☐ 4 Babe Ruth Lisa Zane as Claire Ruth	1.00	.45	.12
☐ 5 Babe Ruth Donald Moffat as Jacob Ruppert	1.00	.45	.12
☐ 6 Babe Ruth Neil McDonough as Lou Gehrig	1.00	.45	.12
☐ 7 Babe Ruth Pete Rose as Ty Cobb	2.00	.90	.25
☐ 8 Babe Ruth Rod Carew Baseball Consultant	1.50	.70	.19
☐ 9 Babe Ruth Ruth and Mgr. Huggins	1.00	.45	.12
☐ 10 Babe Ruth Ruth in Action	1.00	.45	.12
☐ 11 Babe Ruth Babe Calls His Shot	1.00	.45	.12

1991 Topps Stand-Ups

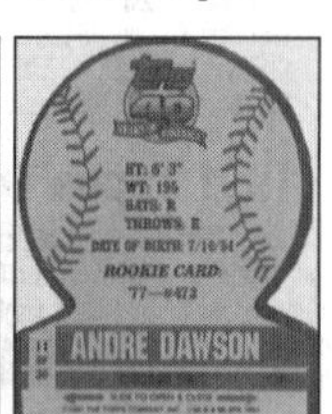

These stand-ups were not widely distributed and therefore appear to be a test issue. The stand-ups are packaged in a wrapper that has a checklist on the back. Each stand-up is actually a 2" by 2 1/2" plastic semi-transparent green container filled with sweet-tart type candy. On the front a color head and shoulders player photo appears, superimposed on a baseball diamond background. The team name appears in a scroll above the player's head, while the player's name is printed in a blue stripe on the base of the stand-up. In a baseball-type design, the back has Topps' 40th anniversary logo, biography, and information on the player's rookie card. The candy is dispensed from the base of the stand-up.

	MINT	NRMT	EXC
COMPLETE SET (36)	125.00	55.00	15.50
COMMON CARD (1-36)	1.00	.45	.12
☐ 1 Jim Abbott	1.00	.45	.12
☐ 2 Sandy Alomar Jr.	2.00	.90	.25
☐ 3 Wade Boggs	4.00	1.80	.50
☐ 4 Barry Bonds	5.00	2.20	.60
☐ 5 Bobby Bonilla	2.00	.90	.25
☐ 6 George Brett	10.00	4.50	1.25
☐ 7 Jose Canseco	4.00	1.80	.50
☐ 8 Will Clark	4.00	1.80	.50
☐ 9 Roger Clemens	5.00	2.20	.60
☐ 10 Eric Davis	1.00	.45	.12
☐ 11 Andre Dawson	2.00	.90	.25
☐ 12 Len Dykstra	2.00	.90	.25
☐ 13 Cecil Fielder	2.00	.90	.25
☐ 14 Carlton Fisk	2.00	.90	.25
☐ 15 Dwight Gooden	2.00	.90	.25
☐ 16 Mark Grace	4.00	1.80	.50
☐ 17 Ken Griffey Jr.	25.00	11.00	3.10
☐ 18 Tony Gwynn	10.00	4.50	1.25
☐ 19 Rickey Henderson	4.00	1.80	.50
☐ 20 Bo Jackson	2.00	.90	.25
☐ 21 Dave Justice	3.00	1.35	.35
☐ 22 Kevin Maas	1.00	.45	.12
☐ 23 Ramon Martinez	3.00	1.35	.35
☐ 24 Don Mattingly	12.50	5.50	1.55
☐ 25 Ben McDonald	2.00	.90	.25
☐ 26 Mark McGwire	7.50	3.40	.95
☐ 27 Kevin Mitchell	1.00	.45	.12
☐ 28 Cal Ripken	20.00	9.00	2.50
☐ 29 Nolan Ryan	20.00	9.00	2.50
☐ 30 Ryne Sandberg	8.00	3.60	1.00
☐ 31 Ozzie Smith	6.00	2.70	.75
☐ 32 Dave Stewart	1.00	.45	.12
☐ 33 Darryl Strawberry	2.00	.90	.25
☐ 34 Frank Viola	1.00	.45	.12
☐ 35 Matt Williams	5.00	2.20	.60
☐ 36 Robin Yount	3.00	1.35	.35

1991 Topps Triple Headers

These balls feature the players' photo and fascimile autographs. Three players per team are featured. A piece of candy was included in each pack. We have sequenced this set in alphabetical order by league. There are reports that the Chicago Cub and St. Louis Cardinal balls were issued less frequently than other teams.

	MINT	NRMT	EXC
COMPLETE SET (26)	90.00	40.00	11.00
COMMON CARD (A1-A14/N1-N12)	2.00	.90	.25
☐ A1 Ben McDonald Cal Ripken Gregg Olson	15.00	6.75	1.85
☐ A2 Wade Boggs Mike Greenwell Roger Clemens	4.00	1.80	.50
☐ A3 Chuck Finley Dave Winfield Wally Joyner	2.00	.90	.25
☐ A4 Carlton Fisk Robin Ventura Frank Thomas	15.00	6.75	1.85
☐ A5 Sandy Alomar Alex Cole Mark Lewis	2.00	.90	.25
☐ A6 Cecil Fielder Tony Phillips Alan Trammell	3.00	1.35	.35
☐ A7 George Brett Danny Tartabull Bret Saberhagen	4.00	1.80	.50
☐ A8 Paul Molitor Robin Yount Greg Vaughn	3.00	1.35	.35
☐ A9 Scott Erickson Kirby Puckett Kent Hrbek	4.00	1.80	.50
☐ A10 Don Mattingly Steve Sax Willie Randolph	10.00	4.50	1.25
☐ A11 Jose Canseco Dave Henderson Rickey Henderson	3.00	1.35	.35
☐ A12 Ken Griffey Jr. Harold Reynolds Ken Griffey Sr.	15.00	6.75	1.85
☐ A13 Julio Franco Nolan Ryan Juan Gonzalez	15.00	6.75	1.85
☐ A14 Roberto Alomar Kelly Gruber Joe Carter	4.00	1.80	.50
☐ N1 Ron Gant Tom Glavine David Justice	3.00	1.35	.35
☐ N2 Ryne Sandberg George Bell Mark Grace	10.00	4.50	1.25
☐ N3 Eric Davis Barry Larkin Chris Sabo	2.00	.90	.25
☐ N4 Jeff Bagwell Craig Biggio Ken Caminiti	5.00	2.20	.60
☐ N5 Ramon Martinez Eddie Murray Darryl Strawberry	3.00	1.35	.35
☐ N6 Delino DeShields Dennis Martinez	2.00	.90	.25

	MINT	NRMT	EXC
Ivan Calderon			
☐ N7 Vince Coleman	2.00	.90	.25
Dwight Gooden			
Howard Johnson			
☐ N8 Len Dykstra	2.00	.90	.25
John Kruk			
Dale Murphy			
☐ N9 Barry Bonds	4.00	1.80	.50
Bobby Bonilla			
Andy Van Slyke			
☐ N10 Fred McGriff	5.00	2.20	.60
Tony Gwynn			
Benito Santiago			
☐ N11 Will Clark	4.00	1.80	.50
Kevin Mitchell			
Matt Williams			
☐ N12 Pedro Guerrero	3.00	1.35	.35
Ozzie Smith			
Todd Zeile			

1991-94 Topps Golden Spikes

From 1991 through 1994, Topps produced a special card for the Golden Spikes award winner that was given away to attendees of the annual United States Baseball Federation luncheon. The USBF sponsors the Golden Spikes award, given to the top amateur baseball player. The unnumbered card backs indicate the player's name, year of award and luncheon date. The card fronts vary -- the 1991 and 1992 cards use slightly altered Topps Major League Debut designs, the 1993 and 1994 cards use slightly altered Topps Traded USA designs.

	MINT	NRMT	EXC
COMPLETE SET (4)	500.00	220.00	60.00
COMMON CARD (1-4)	100.00	45.00	12.50
☐ 1 Alex Fernandez	250.00	110.00	31.00
1991 ML Debut			
☐ 2 Mike Kelly	100.00	45.00	12.50
1992 ML Debut			
☐ 3 Phil Nevin	100.00	45.00	12.50
1993 USA			
☐ 4 Darren Dreifort	100.00	45.00	12.50
1994 USA			

1992 Topps Pre-Production Sheet

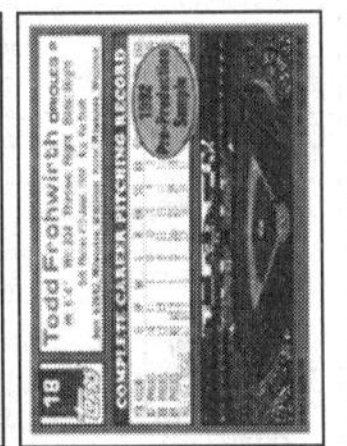

This 1992 Topps pre-production sample sheet measures approximately 7 3/4" by 10 3/4" and features nine player cards. The sheet is unperforated and if cut, the cards would measure the standard size. The fronts have glossy color action photos on a white card face, with different color borders overlaying the picture. In a horizontal format, the backs have biography and complete Major League statistics. Moreover, some of the backs display pictures of baseball stadiums, if the player's career length permits. The cards are numbered on the back with "1992 Pre-Production Sample" prominent. There are two different types of sheets issued. Either sheet has the same value.

	MINT	NRMT	EXC
COMPLETE SET (9)	5.00	2.20	.60
COMMON CARD	.50	.23	.06
☐ 3 Shawon Dunston	1.00	.45	.12
☐ 16 Mike Heath	.50	.23	.06
☐ 18 Todd Frohwirth	.50	.23	.06
☐ 20 Bip Roberts	1.00	.45	.12
☐ 131 Rob Dibble	.50	.23	.06
☐ 174 Otis Nixon	.50	.23	.06
☐ 273 Denny Martinez	1.00	.45	.12
☐ 325 Brett Butler	1.00	.45	.12
☐ 798 Tom Lasorda MG	1.00	.45	.12

1992 Topps Gold Pre-Production Sheet

This 1992 Topps Gold pre-production sample sheet measures approximately 7 3/4" by 10 3/4" and features nine player cards. The sheet is unperforated and if cut, the cards would measure the standard size. The fronts have glossy color action photos on a white card face, with different color borders overlaying the picture. In a horizontal format, the backs have biography and complete Major League statistics. Moreover, some of the backs display pictures of baseball stadiums, if the player's career length permits. The cards are numbered on the back with "1992 Pre-Production Sample" prominent.

	MINT	NRMT	EXC
COMPLETE SET (9)	25.00	11.00	3.10
COMMON CARD	1.00	.45	.12
☐ 1 Nolan Ryan	10.00	4.50	1.25
☐ 15 Denny Martinez	1.50	.70	.19
☐ 20 Bip Roberts	1.50	.70	.19
☐ 40 Cal Ripken	10.00	4.50	1.25
☐ 261 Tom Lasorda MG	1.50	.70	.19
☐ 370 Shawon Dunston	1.50	.70	.19
☐ 512 Mike Heath	1.00	.45	.12
☐ 655 Brett Butler	1.50	.70	.19
☐ 757 Rob Dibble	1.00	.45	.12

1992 Topps

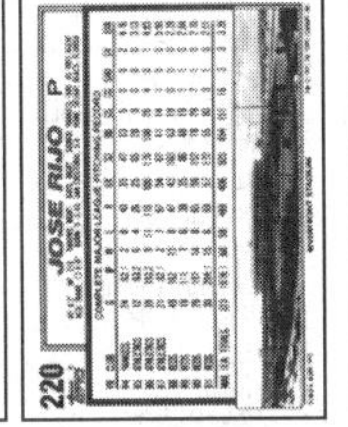

The 1992 Topps set contains 792 standard-size cards. Cards were distributed in plastic wrap packs, jumbo packs, rack packs and factory sets. The fronts have either posed or action color player photos on a white card face. Different color stripes frame the pictures, and the player's name and team name appear in two short color stripes respectively at the bottom. Special subsets included are Record Breakers (2-5), Prospects (58, 126, 179, 473, 551, 591, 618, 656, 676), and All-Stars (386-407). The key Rookie Cards in this set are Shawn Green, John Jaha and Manny Ramirez.

	MINT	NRMT	EXC
COMPLETE SET (792)	25.00	11.00	3.10
COMPLETE FACT.SET (802)	30.00	13.50	3.70
COMP. HOLIDAY SET (811)	35.00	16.00	4.40
COMMON CARD (1-792)	.05	.02	.01
☐ 1 Nolan Ryan	.75	.35	.09
☐ 2 Ricky Henderson RB	.15	.07	.02
Most career SB's			
(Some cards have print			
marks that show 1.991			
on the front)			
☐ 3 Jeff Reardon RB	.05	.02	.01
10 seasons, 20 or more saves			
☐ 4 Nolan Ryan RB	.40	.18	.05
22 cons. 100 K seasons			
☐ 5 Dave Winfield RB	.15	.07	.02
Oldest player, cycle			
☐ 6 Brien Taylor	.10	.05	.01
☐ 7 Jim Olander	.05	.02	.01
☐ 8 Bryan Hickerson	.05	.02	.01
☐ 9 Jon Farrell	.05	.02	.01
☐ 10 Wade Boggs	.15	.07	.02
☐ 11 Jack McDowell	.10	.05	.01
☐ 12 Luis Gonzalez	.05	.02	.01
☐ 13 Mike Scioscia	.05	.02	.01
☐ 14 Wes Chamberlain	.05	.02	.01
☐ 15 Dennis Martinez	.10	.05	.01
☐ 16 Jeff Montgomery	.10	.05	.01
☐ 17 Randy Milligan	.05	.02	.01
☐ 18 Greg Cadaret	.05	.02	.01
☐ 19 Jamie Quirk	.05	.02	.01
☐ 20 Bip Roberts	.05	.02	.01
☐ 21 Buck Rogers MG	.05	.02	.01
☐ 22 Bill Wegman	.05	.02	.01
☐ 23 Chuck Knoblauch	.15	.07	.02
☐ 24 Randy Myers	.10	.05	.01
☐ 25 Ron Gant	.10	.05	.01
☐ 26 Mike Bielecki	.05	.02	.01
☐ 27 Juan Gonzalez	.60	.25	.07
☐ 28 Mike Schooler	.05	.02	.01
☐ 29 Mickey Tettleton	.05	.02	.01
☐ 30 John Kruk	.10	.05	.01
☐ 31 Bryn Smith	.05	.02	.01
☐ 32 Chris Nabholz	.05	.02	.01
☐ 33 Carlos Baerga	.10	.05	.01
☐ 34 Jeff Juden	.05	.02	.01
☐ 35 Dave Righetti	.05	.02	.01
☐ 36 Scott Ruffcorn	.10	.05	.01
☐ 37 Luis Polonia	.05	.02	.01
☐ 38 Tom Candiotti	.05	.02	.01
☐ 39 Greg Olson	.05	.02	.01
☐ 40 Cal Ripken	2.50	1.10	.30
☐ 41 Craig Lefferts	.05	.02	.01
☐ 42 Mike Macfarlane	.05	.02	.01
☐ 43 Jose Lind	.05	.02	.01
☐ 44 Rick Aguilera	.05	.02	.01
☐ 45 Gary Carter	.15	.07	.02
☐ 46 Steve Farr	.05	.02	.01
☐ 47 Rex Hudler	.05	.02	.01
☐ 48 Scott Scudder	.05	.02	.01
☐ 49 Damon Berryhill	.05	.02	.01
☐ 50 Ken Griffey Jr.	1.50	.70	.19
☐ 51 Tom Runnells MG	.05	.02	.01
☐ 52 Juan Bell	.05	.02	.01
☐ 53 Tommy Gregg	.05	.02	.01
☐ 54 David Wells	.05	.02	.01
☐ 55 Rafael Palmeiro	.15	.07	.02
☐ 56 Charlie O'Brien	.05	.02	.01
☐ 57 Donn Pall	.05	.02	.01
☐ 58 1992 Prospects C	.15	.07	.02
Brad Ausmus			
Jim Campanis Jr.			
Dave Nilsson			
Doug Robbins			
☐ 59 Mo Vaughn	.40	.18	.05
☐ 60 Tony Fernandez	.05	.02	.01
☐ 61 Paul O'Neill	.10	.05	.01
☐ 62 Gene Nelson	.05	.02	.01
☐ 63 Randy Ready	.05	.02	.01
☐ 64 Bob Kipper	.05	.02	.01
☐ 65 Willie McGee	.05	.02	.01
☐ 66 Scott Stahoviak	.15	.07	.02
☐ 67 Luis Salazar	.05	.02	.01
☐ 68 Marvin Freeman	.05	.02	.01
☐ 69 Kenny Lofton	1.00	.45	.12
☐ 70 Gary Gaetti	.10	.05	.01
☐ 71 Erik Hanson	.05	.02	.01
☐ 72 Eddie Zosky	.05	.02	.01
☐ 73 Brian Barnes	.05	.02	.01
☐ 74 Scott Leius	.05	.02	.01
☐ 75 Bret Saberhagen	.10	.05	.01
☐ 76 Mike Gallego	.05	.02	.01
☐ 77 Jack Armstrong	.05	.02	.01
☐ 78 Ivan Rodriguez	.40	.18	.05
☐ 79 Jesse Orosco	.05	.02	.01
☐ 80 David Justice	.15	.07	.02
☐ 81 Ced Landrum	.05	.02	.01
☐ 82 Doug Simons	.05	.02	.01
☐ 83 Tommy Greene	.05	.02	.01
☐ 84 Leo Gomez	.05	.02	.01
☐ 85 Jose DeLeon	.05	.02	.01
☐ 86 Steve Finley	.10	.05	.01
☐ 87 Bob MacDonald	.05	.02	.01
☐ 88 Darrin Jackson	.05	.02	.01
☐ 89 Neal Heaton	.05	.02	.01
☐ 90 Robin Yount	.15	.07	.02
☐ 91 Jeff Reed	.05	.02	.01
☐ 92 Lenny Harris	.05	.02	.01
☐ 93 Reggie Jefferson	.10	.05	.01
☐ 94 Sammy Sosa	.25	.11	.03
☐ 95 Scott Bailes	.05	.02	.01
☐ 96 Tom McKinnon	.05	.02	.01
☐ 97 Luis Rivera	.05	.02	.01
☐ 98 Mike Harkey	.05	.02	.01
☐ 99 Jeff Treadway	.05	.02	.01
☐ 100 Jose Canseco	.15	.07	.02
☐ 101 Omar Vizquel	.10	.05	.01
☐ 102 Scott Kamieniecki	.05	.02	.01
☐ 103 Ricky Jordan	.05	.02	.01
☐ 104 Jeff Ballard	.05	.02	.01
☐ 105 Felix Jose	.05	.02	.01
☐ 106 Mike Boddicker	.05	.02	.01
☐ 107 Dan Pasqua	.05	.02	.01
☐ 108 Mike Timlin	.05	.02	.01
☐ 109 Roger Craig MG	.05	.02	.01
☐ 110 Ryne Sandberg	.25	.11	.03
☐ 111 Mark Carreon	.05	.02	.01
☐ 112 Oscar Azocar	.05	.02	.01
☐ 113 Mike Greenwell	.05	.02	.01
☐ 114 Mark Portugal	.05	.02	.01
☐ 115 Terry Pendleton	.10	.05	.01
☐ 116 Willie Randolph	.10	.05	.01
☐ 117 Scott Terry	.05	.02	.01
☐ 118 Chili Davis	.10	.05	.01
☐ 119 Mark Gardner	.05	.02	.01
☐ 120 Alan Trammell	.10	.05	.01
☐ 121 Derek Bell	.15	.07	.02
☐ 122 Gary Varsho	.05	.02	.01
☐ 123 Bob Ojeda	.05	.02	.01
☐ 124 Shawn Livsey	.05	.02	.01
☐ 125 Chris Hoiles	.05	.02	.01
☐ 126 1992 Prospects 1B	.75	.35	.09
Ryan Klesko			
John Jaha			
Rico Brogna			
Dave Staton			
☐ 127 Carlos Quintana	.05	.02	.01
☐ 128 Kurt Stillwell	.05	.02	.01
☐ 129 Melido Perez	.05	.02	.01
☐ 130 Alvin Davis	.05	.02	.01
☐ 131 Checklist 1-132	.05	.02	.01
☐ 132 Eric Show	.05	.02	.01
☐ 133 Rance Mulliniks	.05	.02	.01
☐ 134 Darryl Kile	.05	.02	.01
☐ 135 Von Hayes	.05	.02	.01
☐ 136 Bill Doran	.05	.02	.01
☐ 137 Jeff D. Robinson	.05	.02	.01
☐ 138 Monty Fariss	.05	.02	.01
☐ 139 Jeff Innis	.05	.02	.01
☐ 140 Mark Grace UER	.15	.07	.02
(Home Calie., should			
be Calif.)			
☐ 141 Jim Leyland MG UER	.05	.02	.01
(No closed parenthesis			
after East in 1991)			
☐ 142 Todd Van Poppel	.05	.02	.01
☐ 143 Paul Gibson	.05	.02	.01
☐ 144 Bill Swift	.05	.02	.01
☐ 145 Danny Tartabull	.05	.02	.01
☐ 146 Al Newman	.05	.02	.01
☐ 147 Cris Carpenter	.05	.02	.01
☐ 148 Anthony Young	.05	.02	.01
☐ 149 Brian Bohanon	.05	.02	.01
☐ 150 Roger Clemens UER	.20	.09	.03
(League leading ERA in			
1990 not italicized)			
☐ 151 Jeff Hamilton	.05	.02	.01
☐ 152 Charlie Leibrandt	.05	.02	.01
☐ 153 Ron Karkovice	.05	.02	.01
☐ 154 Hensley Meulens	.05	.02	.01
☐ 155 Scott Bankhead	.05	.02	.01
☐ 156 Manny Ramirez	2.00	.90	.25
☐ 157 Keith Miller	.05	.02	.01
☐ 158 Todd Frohwirth	.05	.02	.01
☐ 159 Darrin Fletcher	.05	.02	.01
☐ 160 Bobby Bonilla	.10	.05	.01
☐ 161 Casey Candaele	.05	.02	.01
☐ 162 Paul Faries	.05	.02	.01
☐ 163 Dana Kiecker	.05	.02	.01
☐ 164 Shane Mack	.05	.02	.01
☐ 165 Mark Langston	.10	.05	.01
☐ 166 Geronimo Pena	.05	.02	.01
☐ 167 Andy Allanson	.05	.02	.01
☐ 168 Dwight Smith	.05	.02	.01
☐ 169 Chuck Crim	.05	.02	.01
☐ 170 Alex Cole	.05	.02	.01
☐ 171 Bill Plummer MG	.05	.02	.01
☐ 172 Juan Berenguer	.05	.02	.01
☐ 173 Brian Downing	.05	.02	.01
☐ 174 Steve Frey	.05	.02	.01
☐ 175 Orel Hershiser	.10	.05	.01
☐ 176 Ramon Garcia	.05	.02	.01
☐ 177 Dan Gladden	.05	.02	.01
☐ 178 Jim Acker	.05	.02	.01
☐ 179 1992 Prospects 2B	.05	.02	.01
Bobby DeJardin			
Cesar Bernhardt			
Armando Moreno			
Andy Stankiewicz			
☐ 180 Kevin Mitchell	.05	.02	.01
☐ 181 Hector Villanueva	.05	.02	.01
☐ 182 Jeff Reardon	.10	.05	.01
☐ 183 Brent Mayne	.05	.02	.01
☐ 184 Jimmy Jones	.05	.02	.01
☐ 185 Benito Santiago	.05	.02	.01
☐ 186 Cliff Floyd	.10	.05	.01
☐ 187 Ernie Riles	.05	.02	.01
☐ 188 Jose Guzman	.05	.02	.01
☐ 189 Junior Felix	.05	.02	.01
☐ 190 Glenn Davis	.05	.02	.01
☐ 191 Charlie Hough	.05	.02	.01
☐ 192 Dave Fleming	.05	.02	.01
☐ 193 Omar Olivares	.05	.02	.01
☐ 194 Eric Karros	.15	.07	.02
☐ 195 David Cone	.10	.05	.01
☐ 196 Frank Castillo	.10	.05	.01
☐ 197 Glenn Braggs	.05	.02	.01
☐ 198 Scott Aldred	.05	.02	.01
☐ 199 Jeff Blauser	.05	.02	.01
☐ 200 Len Dykstra	.10	.05	.01
☐ 201 Buck Showalter MG	.10	.05	.01
☐ 202 Rick Honeycutt	.05	.02	.01
☐ 203 Greg Myers	.05	.02	.01
☐ 204 Trevor Wilson	.05	.02	.01
☐ 205 Jay Howell	.05	.02	.01
☐ 206 Luis Sojo	.05	.02	.01
☐ 207 Jack Clark	.10	.05	.01
☐ 208 Julio Machado	.05	.02	.01
☐ 209 Lloyd McClendon	.05	.02	.01
☐ 210 Ozzie Guillen	.05	.02	.01
☐ 211 Jeremy Hernandez	.05	.02	.01
☐ 212 Randy Velarde	.05	.02	.01
☐ 213 Les Lancaster	.05	.02	.01
☐ 214 Andy Mota	.05	.02	.01
☐ 215 Rich Gossage	.10	.05	.01
☐ 216 Brent Gates	.10	.05	.01
☐ 217 Brian Harper	.05	.02	.01
☐ 218 Mike Flanagan	.05	.02	.01
☐ 219 Jerry Browne	.05	.02	.01
☐ 220 Jose Rijo	.05	.02	.01
☐ 221 Skeeter Barnes	.05	.02	.01
☐ 222 Jaime Navarro	.05	.02	.01
☐ 223 Mel Hall	.05	.02	.01
☐ 224 Bret Barberie	.05	.02	.01
☐ 225 Roberto Alomar	.20	.09	.03
☐ 226 Pete Smith	.05	.02	.01
☐ 227 Daryl Boston	.05	.02	.01
☐ 228 Eddie Whitson	.05	.02	.01
☐ 229 Shawn Boskie	.05	.02	.01
☐ 230 Dick Schofield	.05	.02	.01
☐ 231 Brian Drahman	.05	.02	.01
☐ 232 John Smiley	.05	.02	.01
☐ 233 Mitch Webster	.05	.02	.01
☐ 234 Terry Steinbach	.10	.05	.01
☐ 235 Jack Morris	.10	.05	.01
☐ 236 Bill Pecota	.05	.02	.01
☐ 237 Jose Hernandez	.05	.02	.01

□ 238 Greg Litton .05 .02 .01
□ 239 Brian Holman .05 .02 .01
□ 240 Andres Galarraga .15 .07 .02
□ 241 Gerald Young .05 .02 .01
□ 242 Mike Mussina .30 .14 .04
□ 243 Alvaro Espinoza .05 .02 .01
□ 244 Darren Daulton .10 .05 .01
□ 245 John Smoltz .15 .07 .02
□ 246 Jason Pruitt .05 .02 .01
□ 247 Chuck Finley .10 .05 .01
□ 248 Jim Gantner .05 .02 .01
□ 249 Tony Fossas .05 .02 .01
□ 250 Ken Griffey Sr. .05 .02 .01
□ 251 Kevin Elster .05 .02 .01
□ 252 Dennis Rasmussen .05 .02 .01
□ 253 Terry Kennedy .05 .02 .01
□ 254 Ryan Bowen .05 .02 .01
□ 255 Robin Ventura .10 .05 .01
□ 256 Mike Aldrete .05 .02 .01
□ 257 Jeff Russell .05 .02 .01
□ 258 Jim Lindeman .05 .02 .01
□ 259 Ron Darling .05 .02 .01
□ 260 Devon White .05 .02 .01
□ 261 Tom Lasorda MG .10 .05 .01
□ 262 Terry Lee .05 .02 .01
□ 263 Bob Patterson .05 .02 .01
□ 264 Checklist 133-264 .05 .02 .01
□ 265 Teddy Higuera .05 .02 .01
□ 266 Roberto Kelly .05 .02 .01
□ 267 Steve Bedrosian .05 .02 .01
□ 268 Brady Anderson .15 .07 .02
□ 269 Ruben Amaro Jr. .05 .02 .01
□ 270 Tony Gwynn .40 .18 .05
□ 271 Tracy Jones .05 .02 .01
□ 272 Jerry Don Gleaton .05 .02 .01
□ 273 Craig Grebeck .05 .02 .01
□ 274 Bob Scanlan .05 .02 .01
□ 275 Todd Zeile .05 .02 .01
□ 276 Shawn Green .30 .14 .04
□ 277 Scott Chiamparino .05 .02 .01
□ 278 Darryl Hamilton .05 .02 .01
□ 279 Jim Clancy .05 .02 .01
□ 280 Carlos Martinez .05 .02 .01
□ 281 Kevin Appier .10 .05 .01
□ 282 John Wehner .05 .02 .01
□ 283 Reggie Sanders .15 .07 .02
□ 284 Gene Larkin .05 .02 .01
□ 285 Bob Welch .05 .02 .01
□ 286 Gilberto Reyes .05 .02 .01
□ 287 Pete Schourek .10 .05 .01
□ 288 Andujar Cedeno .05 .02 .01
□ 289 Mike Morgan .05 .02 .01
□ 290 Bo Jackson .10 .05 .01
□ 291 Phil Garner MG .05 .02 .01
□ 292 Ray Lankford .15 .07 .02
□ 293 Mike Henneman .05 .02 .01
□ 294 Dave Valle .05 .02 .01
□ 295 Alonzo Powell .05 .02 .01
□ 296 Tom Brunansky .05 .02 .01
□ 297 Kevin Brown .10 .05 .01
□ 298 Kelly Gruber .05 .02 .01
□ 299 Charles Nagy .10 .05 .01
□ 300 Don Mattingly .50 .23 .06
□ 301 Kirk McCaskill .05 .02 .01
□ 302 Joey Cora .10 .05 .01
□ 303 Dan Plesac .05 .02 .01
□ 304 Joe Oliver .05 .02 .01
□ 305 Tom Glavine .15 .07 .02
□ 306 Al Shirley .10 .05 .01
□ 307 Bruce Ruffin .05 .02 .01
□ 308 Craig Shipley .05 .02 .01
□ 309 Dave Martinez .05 .02 .01
□ 310 Jose Mesa .10 .05 .01
□ 311 Henry Cotto .05 .02 .01
□ 312 Mike LaValliere .05 .02 .01
□ 313 Kevin Tapani .05 .02 .01
□ 314 Jeff Huson .05 .02 .01
(Shows Jose Canseco
sliding into second)
□ 315 Juan Samuel .05 .02 .01
□ 316 Curt Schilling .05 .02 .01
□ 317 Mike Bordick .05 .02 .01
□ 318 Steve Howe .05 .02 .01
□ 319 Tony Phillips .10 .05 .01
□ 320 George Bell .05 .02 .01
□ 321 Lou Piniella MG .10 .05 .01
□ 322 Tim Burke .05 .02 .01
□ 323 Milt Thompson .05 .02 .01
□ 324 Danny Darwin .05 .02 .01
□ 325 Joe Orsulak .05 .02 .01
□ 326 Eric King .05 .02 .01
□ 327 Jay Buhner .15 .07 .02
□ 328 Joel Johnston .05 .02 .01
□ 329 Franklin Stubbs .05 .02 .01
□ 330 Will Clark .15 .07 .02
□ 331 Steve Lake .05 .02 .01
□ 332 Chris Jones .05 .02 .01
□ 333 Pat Tabler .05 .02 .01
□ 334 Kevin Gross .05 .02 .01
□ 335 Dave Henderson .05 .02 .01
□ 336 Greg Anthony .05 .02 .01
□ 337 Alejandro Pena .05 .02 .01
□ 338 Shawn Abner .05 .02 .01
□ 339 Tom Browning .05 .02 .01
□ 340 Otis Nixon .05 .02 .01

□ 341 Bob Geren .05 .02 .01
□ 342 Tim Spehr .05 .02 .01
□ 343 John Vander Wal .05 .02 .01
□ 344 Jack Daugherty .05 .02 .01
□ 345 Zane Smith .05 .02 .01
□ 346 Rheal Cormier .05 .02 .01
□ 347 Kent Hrbek .10 .05 .01
□ 348 Rick Wilkins .05 .02 .01
□ 349 Steve Lyons .05 .02 .01
□ 350 Gregg Olson .05 .02 .01
□ 351 Greg Riddoch MG .05 .02 .01
□ 352 Ed Nunez .05 .02 .01
□ 353 Braulio Castillo .05 .02 .01
□ 354 Dave Bergman .05 .02 .01
□ 355 Warren Newson .05 .02 .01
□ 356 Luis Quinones .05 .02 .01
□ 357 Mike Witt .05 .02 .01
□ 358 Ted Wood .05 .02 .01
□ 359 Mike Moore .05 .02 .01
□ 360 Lance Parrish .05 .02 .01
□ 361 Barry Jones .05 .02 .01
□ 362 Javier Ortiz .05 .02 .01
□ 363 John Candelaria .05 .02 .01
□ 364 Glenallen Hill .05 .02 .01
□ 365 Duane Ward .05 .02 .01
□ 366 Checklist 265-396 .05 .02 .01
□ 367 Rafael Belliard .05 .02 .01
□ 368 Bill Krueger .05 .02 .01
□ 369 Steve Whitaker .05 .02 .01
□ 370 Shawon Dunston .05 .02 .01
□ 371 Dante Bichette .15 .07 .02
□ 372 Kip Gross .05 .02 .01
□ 373 Don Robinson .05 .02 .01
□ 374 Bernie Williams .25 .11 .03
□ 375 Bert Blyleven .10 .05 .01
□ 376 Chris Donnels .05 .02 .01
□ 377 Bob Zupcic .05 .02 .01
□ 378 Joel Skinner .05 .02 .01
□ 379 Steve Chitren .05 .02 .01
□ 380 Barry Bonds .25 .11 .03
□ 381 Sparky Anderson MG .10 .05 .01
□ 382 Sid Fernandez .05 .02 .01
□ 383 Dave Hollins .05 .02 .01
□ 384 Mark Lee .05 .02 .01
□ 385 Tim Wallach .05 .02 .01
□ 386 Will Clark AS .15 .07 .02
□ 387 Ryne Sandberg AS .15 .07 .02
□ 388 Howard Johnson AS .05 .02 .01
□ 389 Barry Larkin AS .15 .07 .02
□ 390 Barry Bonds AS .15 .07 .02
□ 391 Ron Gant AS .10 .05 .01
□ 392 Bobby Bonilla AS .10 .05 .01
□ 393 Craig Biggio AS .10 .05 .01
□ 394 Dennis Martinez AS .05 .02 .01
□ 395 Tom Glavine AS .10 .05 .01
□ 396 Lee Smith AS .10 .05 .01
□ 397 Cecil Fielder AS .10 .05 .01
□ 398 Julio Franco AS .05 .02 .01
□ 399 Wade Boggs AS .15 .07 .02
□ 400 Cal Ripken AS .40 .18 .05
□ 401 Jose Canseco AS .15 .07 .02
□ 402 Joe Carter AS .10 .05 .01
□ 403 Ruben Sierra AS .05 .02 .01
□ 404 Matt Nokes AS .05 .02 .01
□ 405 Roger Clemens AS .15 .07 .02
□ 406 Jim Abbott AS .05 .02 .01
□ 407 Bryan Harvey AS .05 .02 .01
□ 408 Bob Milacki .05 .02 .01
□ 409 Geno Petralli .05 .02 .01
□ 410 Dave Stewart .10 .05 .01
□ 411 Mike Jackson .05 .02 .01
□ 412 Luis Aquino .05 .02 .01
□ 413 Tim Teufel .05 .02 .01
□ 414 Jeff Ware .05 .02 .01
□ 415 Jim Deshaies .05 .02 .01
□ 416 Ellis Burks .10 .05 .01
□ 417 Allan Anderson .05 .02 .01
□ 418 Alfredo Griffin .05 .02 .01
□ 419 Wally Whitehurst .05 .02 .01
□ 420 Sandy Alomar Jr. .10 .05 .01
□ 421 Juan Agosto .05 .02 .01
□ 422 Sam Horn .05 .02 .01
□ 423 Jeff Fassero .10 .05 .01
□ 424 Paul McClellan .05 .02 .01
□ 425 Cecil Fielder .10 .05 .01
□ 426 Tim Raines .10 .05 .01
□ 427 Eddie Taubensee .05 .02 .01
□ 428 Dennis Boyd .05 .02 .01
□ 429 Tony LaRussa MG .10 .05 .01
□ 430 Steve Sax .05 .02 .01
□ 431 Tom Gordon .05 .02 .01
□ 432 Billy Hatcher .05 .02 .01
□ 433 Cal Eldred .05 .02 .01
□ 434 Wally Backman .05 .02 .01
□ 435 Mark Eichhorn .05 .02 .01
□ 436 Mookie Wilson .05 .02 .01
□ 437 Scott Servais .05 .02 .01
□ 438 Mike Maddux .05 .02 .01
□ 439 Chico Walker .05 .02 .01
□ 440 Doug Drabek .05 .02 .01
□ 441 Rob Deer .05 .02 .01
□ 442 Dave West .05 .02 .01
□ 443 Spike Owen .05 .02 .01
□ 444 Tyrone Hill .05 .02 .01
□ 445 Matt Williams .15 .07 .02

□ 446 Mark Lewis .05 .02 .01
□ 447 David Segui .05 .02 .01
□ 448 Tom Pagnozzi .05 .02 .01
□ 449 Jeff Johnson .05 .02 .01
□ 450 Mark McGwire .30 .14 .04
□ 451 Tom Henke .05 .02 .01
□ 452 Wilson Alvarez .15 .07 .02
□ 453 Gary Redus .05 .02 .01
□ 454 Darren Holmes .05 .02 .01
□ 455 Pete O'Brien .05 .02 .01
□ 456 Pat Combs .05 .02 .01
□ 457 Hubie Brooks .05 .02 .01
□ 458 Frank Tanana .05 .02 .01
□ 459 Tom Kelly MG .05 .02 .01
□ 460 Andre Dawson .10 .05 .01
□ 461 Doug Jones .05 .02 .01
□ 462 Rich Rodriguez .05 .02 .01
□ 463 Mike Simms .05 .02 .01
□ 464 Mike Jeffcoat .05 .02 .01
□ 465 Barry Larkin .15 .07 .02
□ 466 Stan Belinda .05 .02 .01
□ 467 Lonnie Smith .05 .02 .01
□ 468 Greg Harris .05 .02 .01
□ 469 Jim Eisenreich .05 .02 .01
□ 470 Pedro Guerrero .05 .02 .01
□ 471 Jose DeJesus .05 .02 .01
□ 472 Rich Rowland .05 .02 .01
□ 473 1992 Prospects 3B UER .15 .07 .02
Frank Bolick
Craig Paquette
Tom Redington
Paul Russo
(Line around top border)
□ 474 Mike Rossiter .05 .02 .01
□ 475 Robby Thompson .05 .02 .01
□ 476 Randy Bush .05 .02 .01
□ 477 Greg Hibbard .05 .02 .01
□ 478 Dale Sveum .05 .02 .01
□ 479 Chito Martinez .05 .02 .01
□ 480 Scott Sanderson .05 .02 .01
□ 481 Tino Martinez .10 .05 .01
□ 482 Jimmy Key .10 .05 .01
□ 483 Terry Shumpert .05 .02 .01
□ 484 Mike Hartley .05 .02 .01
□ 485 Chris Sabo .05 .02 .01
□ 486 Bob Walk .05 .02 .01
□ 487 John Cerutti .05 .02 .01
□ 488 Scott Cooper .05 .02 .01
□ 489 Bobby Cox MG .10 .05 .01
□ 490 Julio Franco .10 .05 .01
□ 491 Jeff Brantley .10 .05 .01
□ 492 Mike Devereaux .05 .02 .01
□ 493 Jose Offerman .05 .02 .01
□ 494 Gary Thurman .05 .02 .01
□ 495 Carney Lansford .10 .05 .01
□ 496 Joe Grahe .05 .02 .01
□ 497 Andy Ashby .10 .05 .01
□ 498 Gerald Perry .05 .02 .01
□ 499 Dave Otto .05 .02 .01
□ 500 Vince Coleman .05 .02 .01
□ 501 Rob Mallicoat .05 .02 .01
□ 502 Greg Briley .05 .02 .01
□ 503 Pascual Perez .05 .02 .01
□ 504 Aaron Sele .15 .07 .02
□ 505 Bobby Thigpen .05 .02 .01
□ 506 Todd Benzinger .05 .02 .01
□ 507 Candy Maldonado .05 .02 .01
□ 508 Bill Gullickson .05 .02 .01
□ 509 Doug Dascenzo .05 .02 .01
□ 510 Frank Viola .05 .02 .01
□ 511 Kenny Rogers .05 .02 .01
□ 512 Mike Heath .05 .02 .01
□ 513 Kevin Bass .05 .02 .01
□ 514 Kim Batiste .05 .02 .01
□ 515 Delino DeShields .05 .02 .01
□ 516 Ed Sprague Jr. .10 .05 .01
□ 517 Jim Gott .05 .02 .01
□ 518 Jose Melendez .05 .02 .01
□ 519 Hal McRae MG .05 .02 .01
□ 520 Jeff Bagwell .60 .25 .07
□ 521 Joe Hesketh .05 .02 .01
□ 522 Milt Cuyler .05 .02 .01
□ 523 Shawn Hillegas .05 .02 .01
□ 524 Don Slaught .05 .02 .01
□ 525 Randy Johnson .15 .07 .02
□ 526 Doug Piatt .05 .02 .01
□ 527 Checklist 397-528 .05 .02 .01
□ 528 Steve Foster .05 .02 .01
□ 529 Joe Girardi .05 .02 .01
□ 530 Jim Abbott .05 .02 .01
□ 531 Larry Walker .15 .07 .02
□ 532 Mike Huff .05 .02 .01
□ 533 Mackey Sasser .05 .02 .01
□ 534 Benji Gil .15 .07 .02
□ 535 Dave Stieb .05 .02 .01
□ 536 Willie Wilson .05 .02 .01
□ 537 Mark Leiter .05 .02 .01
□ 538 Jose Uribe .05 .02 .01
□ 539 Thomas Howard .05 .02 .01
□ 540 Ben McDonald .05 .02 .01
□ 541 Jose Tolentino .05 .02 .01
□ 542 Keith Mitchell .05 .02 .01
□ 543 Jerome Walton .05 .02 .01
□ 544 Cliff Brantley .05 .02 .01
□ 545 Andy Van Slyke .10 .05 .01

□ 546 Paul Sorrento .05 .02 .01
□ 547 Herm Winningham .05 .02 .01
□ 548 Mark Guthrie .05 .02 .01
□ 549 Joe Torre MG .10 .05 .01
□ 550 Darryl Strawberry .10 .05 .01
□ 551 1992 Prospects SS UER 2.00 .90 .25
Wilfredo Cordero
Chipper Jones
Manny Alexander
Alex Arias
(No line around
top border)
□ 552 Dave Gallagher .05 .02 .01
□ 553 Edgar Martinez .10 .05 .01
□ 554 Donald Harris .05 .02 .01
□ 555 Frank Thomas 1.50 .70 .19
□ 556 Storm Davis .05 .02 .01
□ 557 Dickie Thon .05 .02 .01
□ 558 Scott Garrelts .05 .02 .01
□ 559 Steve Olin .05 .02 .01
□ 560 Rickey Henderson .15 .07 .02
□ 561 Jose Vizcaino .05 .02 .01
□ 562 Wade Taylor .05 .02 .01
□ 563 Pat Borders .05 .02 .01
□ 564 Jimmy Gonzalez .05 .02 .01
□ 565 Lee Smith .10 .05 .01
□ 566 Bill Sampen .05 .02 .01
□ 567 Dean Palmer .10 .05 .01
□ 568 Bryan Harvey .05 .02 .01
□ 569 Tony Pena .05 .02 .01
□ 570 Lou Whitaker .10 .05 .01
□ 571 Randy Tomlin .05 .02 .01
□ 572 Greg Vaughn .10 .05 .01
□ 573 Kelly Downs .05 .02 .01
□ 574 Steve Avery UER .10 .05 .01
(Should be 13 games
for Durham in 1989)
□ 575 Kirby Puckett .40 .18 .05
□ 576 Heathcliff Slocumb .05 .02 .01
□ 577 Kevin Seitzer .05 .02 .01
□ 578 Lee Guetterman .05 .02 .01
□ 579 Johnny Oates MG .05 .02 .01
□ 580 Greg Maddux .75 .35 .09
□ 581 Stan Javier .05 .02 .01
□ 582 Vicente Palacios .05 .02 .01
□ 583 Mel Rojas .10 .05 .01
□ 584 Wayne Rosenthal .05 .02 .01
□ 585 Lenny Webster .05 .02 .01
□ 586 Rod Nichols .05 .02 .01
□ 587 Mickey Morandini .05 .02 .01
□ 588 Russ Swan .05 .02 .01
□ 589 Mariano Duncan .05 .02 .01
□ 590 Howard Johnson .05 .02 .01
□ 591 1992 Prospects OF .10 .05 .01
Jeromy Burnitz
Jacob Brumfield
Alan Cockrell
D.J. Dozier
□ 592 Denny Neagle .15 .07 .02
□ 593 Steve Decker .05 .02 .01
□ 594 Brian Barber .10 .05 .01
□ 595 Bruce Hurst .05 .02 .01
□ 596 Kent Mercker .05 .02 .01
□ 597 Mike Magnante .05 .02 .01
□ 598 Jody Reed .05 .02 .01
□ 599 Steve Searcy .05 .02 .01
□ 600 Paul Molitor .20 .09 .03
□ 601 Dave Smith .05 .02 .01
□ 602 Mike Fetters .05 .02 .01
□ 603 Luis Mercedes .05 .02 .01
□ 604 Chris Gwynn .05 .02 .01
□ 605 Scott Erickson .10 .05 .01
□ 606 Brook Jacoby .05 .02 .01
□ 607 Todd Stottlemyre .05 .02 .01
□ 608 Scott Bradley .05 .02 .01
□ 609 Mike Hargrove MG .10 .05 .01
□ 610 Eric Davis .10 .05 .01
□ 611 Brian Hunter .05 .02 .01
□ 612 Pat Kelly .05 .02 .01
□ 613 Pedro Munoz .05 .02 .01
□ 614 Al Osuna .05 .02 .01
□ 615 Matt Merullo .05 .02 .01
□ 616 Larry Andersen .05 .02 .01
□ 617 Junior Ortiz .05 .02 .01
□ 618 1992 Prospects OF .05 .02 .01
Cesar Hernandez
Steve Hosey
Jeff McNeely
Dan Peltier
□ 619 Danny Jackson .05 .02 .01
□ 620 George Brett .40 .18 .05
□ 621 Dan Gakeler .05 .02 .01
□ 622 Steve Buechele .05 .02 .01
□ 623 Bob Tewksbury .05 .02 .01
□ 624 Shawn Estes .15 .07 .02
□ 625 Kevin McReynolds .05 .02 .01
□ 626 Chris Haney .05 .02 .01
□ 627 Mike Sharperson .05 .02 .01
□ 628 Mark Williamson .05 .02 .01
□ 629 Wally Joyner .10 .05 .01
□ 630 Carlton Fisk .15 .07 .02
□ 631 Armando Reynoso .05 .02 .01
□ 632 Felix Fermin .05 .02 .01
□ 633 Mitch Williams .05 .02 .01
□ 634 Manuel Lee .05 .02 .01

Card	MINT	NRMT	EXC
☐ 635 Harold Baines	.10	.05	.01
☐ 636 Greg Harris	.05	.02	.01
☐ 637 Orlando Merced	.05	.02	.01
☐ 638 Chris Bosio	.05	.02	.01
☐ 639 Wayne Housie	.05	.02	.01
☐ 640 Xavier Hernandez	.05	.02	.01
☐ 641 David Howard	.05	.02	.01
☐ 642 Tim Crews	.05	.02	.01
☐ 643 Rick Cerone	.05	.02	.01
☐ 644 Terry Leach	.05	.02	.01
☐ 645 Deion Sanders	.15	.07	.02
☐ 646 Craig Wilson	.05	.02	.01
☐ 647 Marquis Grissom	.10	.05	.01
☐ 648 Scott Fletcher	.05	.02	.01
☐ 649 Norm Charlton	.05	.02	.01
☐ 650 Jesse Barfield	.05	.02	.01
☐ 651 Joe Slusarski	.05	.02	.01
☐ 652 Bobby Rose	.05	.02	.01
☐ 653 Dennis Lamp	.05	.02	.01
☐ 654 Allen Watson	.10	.05	.01
☐ 655 Brett Butler	.10	.05	.01
☐ 656 1992 Prospects OF Rudy Pemberton Henry Rodriguez Lee Tinsley Gerald Williams	.15	.07	.02
☐ 657 Dave Johnson	.05	.02	.01
☐ 658 Checklist 529-660	.05	.02	.01
☐ 659 Brian McRae	.10	.05	.01
☐ 660 Fred McGriff	.15	.07	.02
☐ 661 Bill Landrum	.05	.02	.01
☐ 662 Juan Guzman	.10	.05	.01
☐ 663 Greg Gagne	.05	.02	.01
☐ 664 Ken Hill	.10	.05	.01
☐ 665 Dave Haas	.05	.02	.01
☐ 666 Tom Foley	.05	.02	.01
☐ 667 Roberto Hernandez	.10	.05	.01
☐ 668 Dwayne Henry	.05	.02	.01
☐ 669 Jim Fregosi MG	.05	.02	.01
☐ 670 Harold Reynolds	.05	.02	.01
☐ 671 Mark Whiten	.10	.05	.01
☐ 672 Eric Plunk	.05	.02	.01
☐ 673 Todd Hundley	.10	.05	.01
☐ 674 Mo Sanford	.05	.02	.01
☐ 675 Bobby Witt	.05	.02	.01
☐ 676 1992 Prospects P Sam Militello Pat Mahomes Turk Wendell Roger Salkeld	.05	.02	.01
☐ 677 John Marzano	.05	.02	.01
☐ 678 Joe Klink	.05	.02	.01
☐ 679 Pete Incaviglia	.05	.02	.01
☐ 680 Dale Murphy	.15	.07	.02
☐ 681 Rene Gonzales	.05	.02	.01
☐ 682 Andy Benes	.10	.05	.01
☐ 683 Jim Poole	.05	.02	.01
☐ 684 Trever Miller	.05	.02	.01
☐ 685 Scott Livingstone	.05	.02	.01
☐ 686 Rich DeLucia	.05	.02	.01
☐ 687 Harvey Pulliam	.05	.02	.01
☐ 688 Tim Belcher	.05	.02	.01
☐ 689 Mark Lemke	.05	.02	.01
☐ 690 John Franco	.05	.02	.01
☐ 691 Walt Weiss	.05	.02	.01
☐ 692 Scott Ruskin	.05	.02	.01
☐ 693 Jeff King	.10	.05	.01
☐ 694 Mike Gardiner	.05	.02	.01
☐ 695 Gary Sheffield	.15	.07	.02
☐ 696 Joe Boever	.05	.02	.01
☐ 697 Mike Felder	.05	.02	.01
☐ 698 John Habyan	.05	.02	.01
☐ 699 Cito Gaston MG	.05	.02	.01
☐ 700 Ruben Sierra	.10	.05	.01
☐ 701 Scott Radinsky	.05	.02	.01
☐ 702 Lee Stevens	.05	.02	.01
☐ 703 Mark Wohlers	.15	.07	.02
☐ 704 Curt Young	.05	.02	.01
☐ 705 Dwight Evans	.10	.05	.01
☐ 706 Rob Murphy	.05	.02	.01
☐ 707 Gregg Jefferies	.10	.05	.01
☐ 708 Tom Bolton	.05	.02	.01
☐ 709 Chris James	.05	.02	.01
☐ 710 Kevin Maas	.05	.02	.01
☐ 711 Ricky Bones	.05	.02	.01
☐ 712 Curt Wilkerson	.05	.02	.01
☐ 713 Roger McDowell	.05	.02	.01
☐ 714 Calvin Reese	.15	.07	.02
☐ 715 Craig Biggio	.10	.05	.01
☐ 716 Kirk Dressendorfer	.05	.02	.01
☐ 717 Ken Dayley	.05	.02	.01
☐ 718 B.J. Surhoff	.10	.05	.01
☐ 719 Terry Mulholland	.05	.02	.01
☐ 720 Kirk Gibson	.10	.05	.01
☐ 721 Mike Pagliarulo	.05	.02	.01
☐ 722 Walt Terrell	.05	.02	.01
☐ 723 Jose Oquendo	.05	.02	.01
☐ 724 Kevin Morton	.05	.02	.01
☐ 725 Dwight Gooden	.10	.05	.01
☐ 726 Kirt Manwaring	.05	.02	.01
☐ 727 Chuck McElroy	.05	.02	.01
☐ 728 Dave Burba	.05	.02	.01
☐ 729 Art Howe MG	.05	.02	.01
☐ 730 Ramon Martinez	.10	.05	.01
☐ 731 Donnie Hill	.05	.02	.01
☐ 732 Nelson Santovenia	.05	.02	.01
☐ 733 Bob Melvin	.05	.02	.01
☐ 734 Scott Hatteberg	.05	.02	.01
☐ 735 Greg Swindell	.05	.02	.01
☐ 736 Lance Johnson	.10	.05	.01
☐ 737 Kevin Reimer	.05	.02	.01
☐ 738 Dennis Eckersley	.10	.05	.01
☐ 739 Rob Ducey	.05	.02	.01
☐ 740 Ken Caminiti	.15	.07	.02
☐ 741 Mark Gubicza	.05	.02	.01
☐ 742 Billy Spiers	.05	.02	.01
☐ 743 Darren Lewis	.05	.02	.01
☐ 744 Chris Hammond	.05	.02	.01
☐ 745 Dave Magadan	.05	.02	.01
☐ 746 Bernard Gilkey	.10	.05	.01
☐ 747 Willie Banks	.05	.02	.01
☐ 748 Matt Nokes	.05	.02	.01
☐ 749 Jerald Clark	.05	.02	.01
☐ 750 Travis Fryman	.15	.07	.02
☐ 751 Steve Wilson	.05	.02	.01
☐ 752 Billy Ripken	.05	.02	.01
☐ 753 Paul Assenmacher	.05	.02	.01
☐ 754 Charlie Hayes	.05	.02	.01
☐ 755 Alex Fernandez	.15	.07	.02
☐ 756 Gary Pettis	.05	.02	.01
☐ 757 Rob Dibble	.05	.02	.01
☐ 758 Tim Naehring	.10	.05	.01
☐ 759 Jeff Torborg MG	.05	.02	.01
☐ 760 Ozzie Smith	.25	.11	.03
☐ 761 Mike Fitzgerald	.05	.02	.01
☐ 762 John Burkett	.10	.05	.01
☐ 763 Kyle Abbott	.05	.02	.01
☐ 764 Tyler Green	.10	.05	.01
☐ 765 Pete Harnisch	.05	.02	.01
☐ 766 Mark Davis	.05	.02	.01
☐ 767 Kal Daniels	.05	.02	.01
☐ 768 Jim Thome	.75	.35	.09
☐ 769 Jack Howell	.05	.02	.01
☐ 770 Sid Bream	.05	.02	.01
☐ 771 Arthur Rhodes	.05	.02	.01
☐ 772 Garry Templeton UER (Stat heading in for pitchers)	.05	.02	.01
☐ 773 Hal Morris	.05	.02	.01
☐ 774 Bud Black	.05	.02	.01
☐ 775 Ivan Calderon	.05	.02	.01
☐ 776 Doug Henry	.05	.02	.01
☐ 777 John Olerud	.10	.05	.01
☐ 778 Tim Leary	.05	.02	.01
☐ 779 Jay Bell	.10	.05	.01
☐ 780 Eddie Murray	.25	.11	.03
☐ 781 Paul Abbott	.05	.02	.01
☐ 782 Phil Plantier	.10	.05	.01
☐ 783 Joe Magrane	.05	.02	.01
☐ 784 Ken Patterson	.05	.02	.01
☐ 785 Albert Belle	.50	.23	.06
☐ 786 Royce Clayton	.10	.05	.01
☐ 787 Checklist 661-792	.05	.02	.01
☐ 788 Mike Stanton	.05	.02	.01
☐ 789 Bobby Valentine MG	.05	.02	.01
☐ 790 Joe Carter	.10	.05	.01
☐ 791 Danny Cox	.05	.02	.01
☐ 792 Dave Winfield	.15	.07	.02

1992 Topps Gold

Topps produced a 792-card Topps Gold factory set packaged in a foil display box. Only this set contained an additional card of Brien Taylor, numbered 793 and hand signed by him. The production run was 12,000 sets. The Topps Gold cards were also available in regular series packs. According to Topps, on average collectors would find one Topps Gold card in every 36 wax packs, one in every 18 cello packs, one in every 12 rak packs, five per Vending box, one in every six jumbo packs, and ten per regular factory set. The packs also featured "Match-the-Stats" game cards in which the consumer could save "Runs". For 2.00 and every 100 Runs saved in this game, the consumer could receive through a mail-in offer ten Topps Gold cards. These particular Topps Gold cards carry the word "Winner" in gold foil on the card front. The checklist cards in the regular set were replaced with six individual Rookie player cards (131, 264, 366, 527, 658, 787) in the gold set. There were a number of uncorrected errors in the Gold set. Steve Finley (86) has gold band indicating he is Mark Davidson of the Astros. Andujar Cedeno (288) is listed as a member of the New York Yankees. Mike Huff (532) is listed as a member of the Boston Red Sox. Barry Larkin (465) is listed as a member of the Houston Astros but is correctly listed as a member of the Cincinnati Reds on his Gold Winners cards. Typically the individual cards are sold at a multiple of the player's respective value in the regular set.

	MINT	NRMT	EXC
COMPLETE SET (792)	125.00	55.00	15.50
COMPLETE FACT.SET (793)	130.00	57.50	16.00
COMMON CARD (1-792)	.25	.11	.03

*STARS: 7.5X to 15X BASIC CARDS ..
*YOUNG STARS: 6X to 12X BASIC CARDS

Card	MINT	NRMT	EXC
☐ 131 Terry Mathews (Replaces Checklist 1)	.50	.23	.06
☐ 264 Rod Beck (Replaces Checklist 2)	1.00	.45	.12
☐ 366 Tony Perezchica (Replaces Checklist 3)	.50	.23	.06
☐ 527 Terry McDaniel (Replaces Checklist 4)	.50	.23	.06
☐ 658 John Ramos (Replaces Checklist 5)	.50	.23	.06
☐ 787 Brian Williams (Replaces Checklist 6)	.50	.23	.06
☐ 793 Brien Taylor AU/12000	10.00	4.50	1.25

1992 Topps Gold Winners

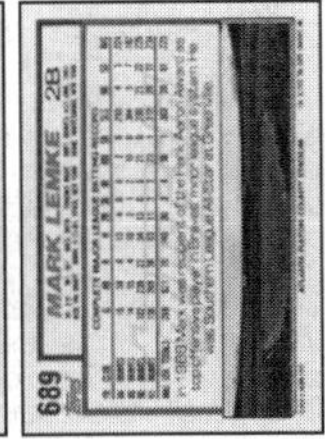

The 1992 Topps baseball card packs featured "Match-the-Stats" game cards in which the consumer could save "Runs". For 2.00 and every 100 Runs saved in this game, the consumer could receive through a mail-in offer ten Topps Gold cards. These particular Topps Gold cards carry the word "Winner" in gold foil on the card front. The checklist cards in the regular set were replaced with six individual Rookie player cards (131, 264, 366, 527, 658, 787) in the gold set. Typically the individual cards are sold at a multiple of the player's respective value in the regular set.

	MINT	NRMT	EXC
COMPLETE SET (792)	60.00	27.00	7.50
COMMON CARD (1-792)	.10	.05	.01

*STARS: 2.5X to 5X BASIC CARDS ....
*YOUNG STARS: 2X to 4X BASIC CARDS

Card	MINT	NRMT	EXC
☐ 131 Terry Mathews (Replaces Checklist 1)	.15	.07	.02
☐ 264 Rod Beck (Replaces Checklist 2)	.30	.14	.04
☐ 366 Tony Perezchica (Replaces Checklist 3)	.15	.07	.02
☐ 527 Terry McDaniel (Replaces Checklist 4)	.15	.07	.02
☐ 658 John Ramos (Replaces Checklist 5)	.15	.07	.02
☐ 787 Brian Williams (Replaces Checklist 6)	.15	.07	.02

1992 Topps Micro

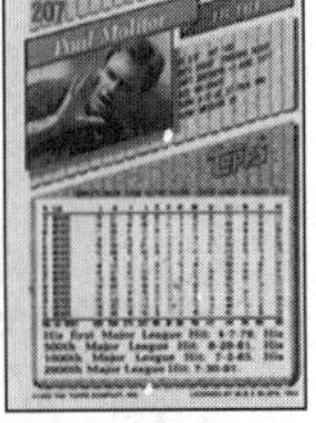

This 804 card parallel set was issued in factory set form only. The set is an exact replica of the regular issue 1992 Topps set (not including the Traded set).The cards, however, measure considerably smaller (1" by 1 3/8") than the regular cards. The set also includes 12 special gold foil parallel mini cards which are listed below. Please refer to the multipliers provided for values on the other singles.

	MINT	NRMT	EXC
COMPLETE FACT.SET (804)	12.50	5.50	1.55
COMMON CARD (1-792)	.05	.02	.01
COMMON GOLD INSERT	.05	.02	.01

*STARS: .5X BASIC CARDS
*YOUNG STARS: .5X BASIC CARDS ..

Card	MINT	NRMT	EXC
☐ G1 Nolan Ryan RB	1.50	.70	.19
☐ G2 Rickey Henderson RB	.25	.11	.03
☐ G10 Wade Boggs Gold	.25	.11	.03
☐ G50 Ken Griffey Jr.	3.00	1.35	.35
☐ G100 Jose Canseco	.25	.11	.03
☐ G270 Tony Gwynn	.75	.35	.09
☐ G300 Don Mattingly	.75	.35	.09
☐ G380 Barry Bonds	.40	.18	.05
☐ G397 Cecil Fielder AS	.10	.05	.01
☐ G403 Ruben Sierra AS	.15	.07	.02
☐ G460 Andre Dawson	.25	.11	.03
☐ G725 Dwight Gooden	.15	.07	.02

1992 Topps Traded

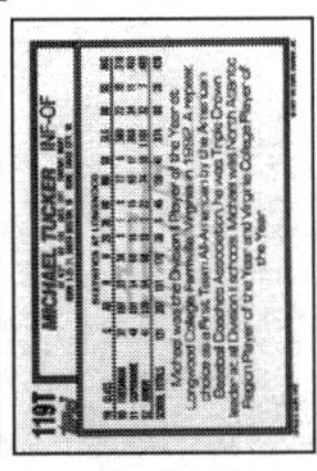

The 1992 Topps Traded set comprises 132 standard-size cards. The set was distributed exclusively in factory set form through hobby dealers. As in past editions, the set focuses on promising rookies, new managers, and players who changed teams. The set also includes a Team U.S.A. subset, featuring 25 of America's top college players and the Team U.S.A. coach. Card design is identical to the regular issue 1992 Topps cards except for the T-suffixed numbering. The cards are arranged in alphabetical order by player's last name. The key Rookie Cards in this set are Nomar Garciaparra, Brian Jordan and Michael Tucker.

	MINT	NRMT	EXC
COMPLETE FACT.SET (132)	15.00	6.75	1.85
COMMON CARD (1T-132T)	.05	.02	.01

Card	MINT	NRMT	EXC
☐ 1T Willie Adams USA	.05	.02	.01
☐ 2T Jeff Alkire USA	.05	.02	.01
☐ 3T Felipe Alou MG	.05	.02	.01
☐ 4T Moises Alou	.30	.14	.04
☐ 5T Ruben Amaro	.05	.02	.01
☐ 6T Jack Armstrong	.05	.02	.01
☐ 7T Scott Bankhead	.05	.02	.01
☐ 8T Tim Belcher	.05	.02	.01
☐ 9T George Bell	.05	.02	.01
☐ 10T Freddie Benavides	.05	.02	.01
☐ 11T Todd Benzinger	.05	.02	.01
☐ 12T Joe Boever	.05	.02	.01
☐ 13T Ricky Bones	.05	.02	.01
☐ 14T Bobby Bonilla	.15	.07	.02
☐ 15T Hubie Brooks	.05	.02	.01
☐ 16T Jerry Browne	.05	.02	.01
☐ 17T Jim Bullinger	.05	.02	.01
☐ 18T Dave Burba	.05	.02	.01
☐ 19T Kevin Campbell	.05	.02	.01
☐ 20T Tom Candiotti	.05	.02	.01
☐ 21T Mark Carreon	.05	.02	.01
☐ 22T Gary Carter	.30	.14	.04
☐ 23T Archi Cianfrocco	.05	.02	.01
☐ 24T Phil Clark	.05	.02	.01
☐ 25T Chad Curtis	.30	.14	.04
☐ 26T Eric Davis	.15	.07	.02
☐ 27T Tim Davis USA	.05	.02	.01
☐ 28T Gary DiSarcina	.05	.02	.01
☐ 29T Darren Dreifort USA	.15	.07	.02
☐ 30T Mariano Duncan	.05	.02	.01
☐ 31T Mike Fitzgerald	.05	.02	.01
☐ 32T John Flaherty	.05	.02	.01
☐ 33T Darrin Fletcher	.05	.02	.01
☐ 34T Scott Fletcher	.05	.02	.01
☐ 35T Ron Fraser CO USA	.15	.07	.02
☐ 36T Andres Galarraga	.30	.14	.04
☐ 37T Dave Gallagher	.05	.02	.01
☐ 38T Mike Gallego	.05	.02	.01
☐ 39T Nomar Garciaparra USA	5.00	2.20	.60
☐ 40T Jason Giambi USA	1.00	.45	.12
☐ 41T Danny Gladden	.05	.02	.01
☐ 42T Rene Gonzales	.05	.02	.01
☐ 43T Jeff Granger USA	.15	.07	.02
☐ 44T Rick Greene USA	.05	.02	.01
☐ 45T Jeffrey Hammonds USA	.30	.14	.04
☐ 46T Charlie Hayes	.05	.02	.01
☐ 47T Von Hayes	.05	.02	.01
☐ 48T Rick Helling USA	.05	.02	.01
☐ 49T Butch Henry	.05	.02	.01
☐ 50T Carlos Hernandez	.05	.02	.01
☐ 51T Ken Hill	.15	.07	.02
☐ 52T Butch Hobson	.05	.02	.01
☐ 53T Vince Horsman	.05	.02	.01
☐ 54T Pete Incaviglia	.05	.02	.01
☐ 55T Gregg Jefferies	.15	.07	.02
☐ 56T Charles Johnson USA	.75	.35	.09
☐ 57T Doug Jones	.05	.02	.01
☐ 58T Brian Jordan	1.00	.45	.12
☐ 59T Wally Joyner	.15	.07	.02
☐ 60T Daron Kirkreit USA	.15	.07	.02
☐ 61T Bill Krueger	.05	.02	.01
☐ 62T Gene Lamont MG	.05	.02	.01
☐ 63T Jim Lefebvre MG	.05	.02	.01
☐ 64T Danny Leon	.05	.02	.01
☐ 65T Pat Listach	.15	.07	.02
☐ 66T Kenny Lofton	2.00	.90	.25
☐ 67T Dave Martinez	.05	.02	.01
☐ 68T Derrick May	.05	.02	.01
☐ 69T Kirk McCaskill	.05	.02	.01
☐ 70T Chad McConnell USA	.15	.07	.02
☐ 71T Kevin McReynolds	.05	.02	.01
☐ 72T Rusty Meacham	.05	.02	.01
☐ 73T Keith Miller	.05	.02	.01
☐ 74T Kevin Mitchell	.15	.07	.02
☐ 75T Jason Moler USA	.05	.02	.01

Card	MINT	NRMT	EXC
□ 76T Mike Morgan	.05	.02	.01
□ 77T Jack Morris	.15	.07	.02
□ 78T Calvin Murray USA	.15	.07	.02
□ 79T Eddie Murray	.40	.18	.05
□ 80T Randy Myers	.15	.07	.02
□ 81T Denny Neagle	.30	.14	.04
□ 82T Phil Nevin USA	.15	.07	.02
□ 83T Dave Nilsson	.30	.14	.04
□ 84T Junior Ortiz	.05	.02	.01
□ 85T Donovan Osborne	.15	.07	.02
□ 86T Bill Pecota	.05	.02	.01
□ 87T Melido Perez	.05	.02	.01
□ 88T Mike Perez	.05	.02	.01
□ 89T Hipolito Pichardo	.05	.02	.01
□ 90T Willie Randolph	.15	.07	.02
□ 91T Darren Reed	.05	.02	.01
□ 92T Bip Roberts	.05	.02	.01
□ 93T Chris Roberts USA	.15	.07	.02
□ 94T Steve Rodriguez USA	.05	.02	.01
□ 95T Bruce Ruffin	.05	.02	.01
□ 96T Scott Ruskin	.05	.02	.01
□ 97T Bret Saberhagen	.15	.07	.02
□ 98T Rey Sanchez	.05	.02	.01
□ 99T Steve Sax	.05	.02	.01
□ 100T Curt Schilling	.05	.02	.01
□ 101T Dick Schofield	.05	.02	.01
□ 102T Gary Scott	.05	.02	.01
□ 103T Kevin Seitzer	.05	.02	.01
□ 104T Frank Seminara	.05	.02	.01
□ 105T Gary Sheffield	.30	.14	.04
□ 106T John Smiley	.05	.02	.01
□ 107T Cory Snyder	.05	.02	.01
□ 108T Paul Sorrento	.05	.02	.01
□ 109T Sammy Sosa	.40	.18	.05
□ 110T Matt Stairs	.05	.02	.01
□ 111T Andy Stankiewicz	.05	.02	.01
□ 112T Kurt Stillwell	.05	.02	.01
□ 113T Rick Sutcliffe	.05	.02	.01
□ 114T Bill Swift	.05	.02	.01
□ 115T Jeff Tackett	.05	.02	.01
□ 116T Danny Tartabull	.05	.02	.01
□ 117T Eddie Taubensee	.05	.02	.01
□ 118T Dickie Thon	.05	.02	.01
□ 119T Michael Tucker USA	.50	.23	.06
□ 120T Scooter Tucker	.05	.02	.01
□ 121T Marc Valdes USA	.05	.02	.01
□ 122T Julio Valera	.05	.02	.01
□ 123T Jason Varitek USA	.50	.23	.06
□ 124T Ron Villone USA	.15	.07	.02
□ 125T Frank Viola	.05	.02	.01
□ 126T B.J. Wallace USA	.15	.07	.02
□ 127T Dan Walters	.05	.02	.01
□ 128T Craig Wilson USA	.05	.02	.01
□ 129T Chris Wimmer USA	.05	.02	.01
□ 130T Dave Winfield	.30	.14	.04
□ 131T Herm Winningham	.05	.02	.01
□ 132T Checklist 1T-132T	.05	.02	.01

1992 Topps Traded Gold

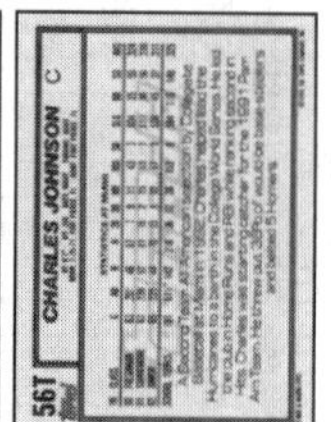

This 132 card standard-size set parallels the regular 1992 Topps Traded set. It was only issued through the Topps dealer network. Six thousand of these sets were produced and the only player difference is that Kerry Woodson replaces the checklist card

	MINT	NRMT	EXC
COMPLETE FACT.SET (132)	25.00	11.00	3.10
COMMON CARDS (1T-132T)	.10	.05	.01
*STARS: 2X BASIC CARDS			
*YOUNG STARS: 2X BASIC CARDS....			
□ 132T Kerry Woodson Replaces Checklist	.40	.18	.05

1992 Topps Cashen

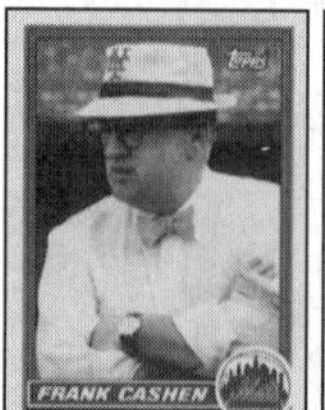

This one-card set was given away at the 1992 New York Sports Commission Luncheon and honors New York Mets General Manager Frank Cashen who was selected as Sportsman of the Year by the Commission.

	MINT	NRMT	EXC
COMPLETE SET (1)	5.00	2.20	.60
COMMON CARD (1)	5.00	2.20	.60
□ 1 Frank Cashen	5.00	2.20	.60

1992 Topps Dairy Queen Team USA

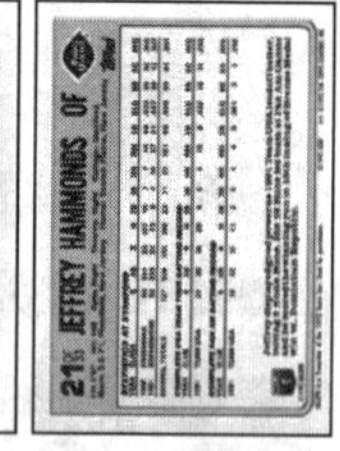

This 33-card standard size set was produced by Topps for Dairy Queen. The set was available in four-card packs with the purchase of a regular-sized sundae in a Team USA helmet during June and July 1992. The set features 16 Team USA players from the 1984 and 1988 teams who are now major league stars as well as 15 1992 Team USA prospects. Completing the set is a 1988 Gold Medal team celebration card and the 1992 Head Coach Ron Fraser. The front design features posed color player photos bordered in blue and red on a white background. The Team USA logo is printed in red and blue at the top. The Dairy Queen logo and the player's name overlay the bottom of the picture. The horizontally oriented backs feature Major League, Team USA tour, and Olympic statistics printed in red and blue on a light blue box.

	MINT	NRMT	EXC
COMPLETE SET (33)	15.00	6.75	1.85
COMMON CARD (1-33)	.25	.11	.03
□ 1 Mark McGwire	3.00	1.35	.35
□ 2 Will Clark	1.50	.70	.19
□ 3 John Marzano	.25	.11	.03
□ 4 Barry Larkin	1.50	.70	.19
□ 5 Bobby Witt	.40	.18	.05
□ 6 Scott Bankhead	.25	.11	.03
□ 7 B.J. Surhoff	.40	.18	.05
□ 8 Shane Mack	.25	.11	.03
□ 9 Jim Abbott	.40	.18	.05
□ 10 Ben McDonald	.40	.18	.05
□ 11 Robin Ventura	.40	.18	.05
□ 12 Charles Nagy	.40	.18	.05
□ 13 Andy Benes	.60	.25	.07
□ 14 Joe Slusarski	.25	.11	.03
□ 15 Ed Sprague	.40	.18	.05
□ 16 Bret Barberie	.25	.11	.03
□ 17 Team USA Strikes Gold	.40	.18	.05
□ 18 Jeff Granger	.40	.18	.05
□ 19 John Dettmer	.25	.11	.03
□ 20 Todd Greene	.60	.25	.07
□ 21 Jeffrey Hammonds	.75	.35	.09
□ 22 Dan Melendez	.25	.11	.03
□ 23 Kennie Steenstra	.40	.18	.05
□ 24 Todd Johnson	.25	.11	.03
□ 25 Chris Roberts	.40	.18	.05
□ 26 Steve Rodriguez	.40	.18	.05
□ 27 Charles Johnson	1.50	.70	.19
□ 28 Chris Wimmer	.25	.11	.03
□ 29 Tony Phillips P	.25	.11	.03
□ 30 Craig Wilson	.25	.11	.03
□ 31 Jason Giambi	2.00	.90	.25
□ 32 Paul Shuey	.40	.18	.05
□ 33 Ron Fraser CO	.25	.11	.03

1992 Topps Debut '91

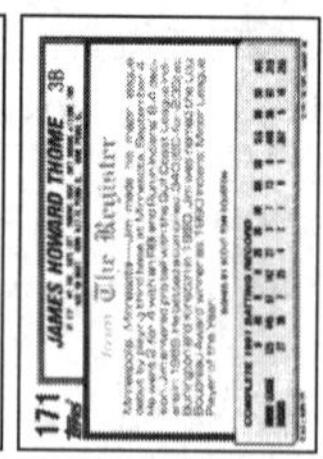

The 1991 Topps Debut '91 set contains 194 standard-size cards. The fronts feature a mix of either posed or action glossy color player photos, framed with two color border stripes on a white card face. The date of the player's first major league appearance is given in a color bar in the lower right corner. In addition to biography and 1991 batting record, the horizontally oriented backs present player profiles in the form of a newspaper article from The Register. Future MVP's Jeff Bagwell and Mo Vaughn are among the featured players in the set.

	MINT	NRMT	EXC
COMPLETE SET (194)	20.00	9.00	2.50
COMMON CARD (1-194)	.05	.02	.01
□ 1 Kyle Abbott	.05	.02	.01
□ 2 Dana Allison	.05	.02	.01
□ 3 Rich Amaral	.15	.07	.02
□ 4 Ruben Amaro Jr.	.05	.02	.01
□ 5 Andy Ashby	.25	.11	.03
□ 6 Jim Austin	.05	.02	.01
□ 7 Jeff Bagwell	4.00	1.80	.50
□ 8 Jeff Banister	.05	.02	.01
□ 9 Willie Banks	.05	.02	.01
□ 10 Bret Barberie	.05	.02	.01
□ 11 Kim Batiste	.05	.02	.01
□ 12 Chris Beasley	.05	.02	.01
□ 13 Rod Beck	.60	.25	.07
□ 14 Derek Bell	.40	.18	.05
□ 15 Esteban Beltre	.05	.02	.01
□ 16 Freddie Benavides	.05	.02	.01
□ 17 Ricky Bones	.15	.07	.02
□ 18 Denis Boucher	.05	.02	.01
□ 19 Ryan Bowen	.05	.02	.01
□ 20 Cliff Brantley	.05	.02	.01
□ 21 John Briscoe	.05	.02	.01
□ 22 Scott Brosius	.25	.11	.03
□ 23 Terry Bross	.05	.02	.01
□ 24 Jarvis Brown	.05	.02	.01
□ 25 Scott Bullett	.05	.02	.01
□ 26 Kevin Campbell	.05	.02	.01
□ 27 Amalio Carreno	.05	.02	.01
□ 28 Matias Carrillo	.05	.02	.01
□ 29 Jeff Carter	.05	.02	.01
□ 30 Vinny Castilla	1.00	.45	.12
□ 31 Braulio Castillo	.05	.02	.01
□ 32 Frank Castillo	.25	.11	.03
□ 33 Darrin Chapin	.05	.02	.01
□ 34 Mike Christopher	.05	.02	.01
□ 35 Mark Clark	.30	.14	.04
□ 36 Royce Clayton	.50	.23	.06
□ 37 Stu Cole	.05	.02	.01
□ 38 Gary Cooper	.05	.02	.01
□ 39 Archie Corbin	.05	.02	.01
□ 40 Rheal Cormier	.15	.07	.02
□ 41 Chris Cron	.05	.02	.01
□ 42 Mike Dalton	.05	.02	.01
□ 43 Mark Davis	.05	.02	.01
□ 44 Francisco DeLaRosa	.05	.02	.01
□ 45 Chris Donnels	.05	.02	.01
□ 46 Brian Drahman	.05	.02	.01
□ 47 Tom Drees	.05	.02	.01
□ 48 Kirk Dressendorfer	.05	.02	.01
□ 49 Bruce Egloff	.05	.02	.01
□ 50 Cal Eldred	.50	.23	.06
□ 51 Jose Escobar	.05	.02	.01
□ 52 Tony Eusebio	.15	.07	.02
□ 53 Hector Fajardo	.05	.02	.01
□ 54 Monty Fariss	.05	.02	.01
□ 55 Jeff Fassero	.25	.11	.03
□ 56 Dave Fleming	.15	.07	.02
□ 57 Kevin Flora	.05	.02	.01
□ 58 Steve Foster	.05	.02	.01
□ 59 Dan Gakeler	.05	.02	.01
□ 60 Ramon Garcia	.05	.02	.01
□ 61 Chris Gardner	.05	.02	.01
□ 62 Jeff Gardner	.05	.02	.01
□ 63 Chris George	.05	.02	.01
□ 64 Ray Giannelli	.05	.02	.01
□ 65 Tom Goodwin	.15	.07	.02
□ 66 Mark Grater	.05	.02	.01
□ 67 Johnny Guzman	.05	.02	.01
□ 68 Juan Guzman	.50	.23	.06
□ 69 Dave Haas	.05	.02	.01
□ 70 Chris Haney	.05	.02	.01
□ 71 Shawn Hare	.05	.02	.01
□ 72 Donald Harris	.05	.02	.01
□ 73 Doug Henry	.05	.02	.01
□ 74 Pat Hentgen	.75	.35	.09
□ 75 Gil Heredia	.05	.02	.01
□ 76 Jeremy Hernandez	.05	.02	.01
□ 77 Jose Hernandez	.05	.02	.01
□ 78 Roberto Hernandez	.50	.23	.06
□ 79 Bryan Hickerson	.05	.02	.01
□ 80 Milt Hill	.05	.02	.01
□ 81 Vince Horsman	.05	.02	.01
□ 82 Wayne Housie	.05	.02	.01
□ 83 Chris Howard	.05	.02	.01
□ 84 David Howard	.05	.02	.01
□ 85 Mike Humphreys	.05	.02	.01
□ 86 Brian Hunter	.05	.02	.01
□ 87 Jim Hunter	.05	.02	.01
□ 88 Mike Ignasiak	.05	.02	.01
□ 89 Reggie Jefferson	.30	.14	.04
□ 90 Jeff Johnson	.05	.02	.01
□ 91 Joel Johnston	.05	.02	.01
□ 92 Calvin Jones	.05	.02	.01
□ 93 Chris Jones	.05	.02	.01
□ 94 Stacy Jones	.05	.02	.01
□ 95 Jeff Juden	.15	.07	.02
□ 96 Scott Kamieniecki	.15	.07	.02
□ 97 Eric Karros	1.50	.70	.19
□ 98 Pat Kelly	.15	.07	.02
□ 99 John Kiely	.05	.02	.01
□ 100 Darryl Kile	.40	.18	.05
□ 101 Wayne Kirby	.15	.07	.02
□ 102 Garland Kiser	.05	.02	.01
□ 103 Chuck Knoblauch	2.00	.90	.25
□ 104 Randy Knorr	.05	.02	.01
□ 105 Tom Kramer	.05	.02	.01
□ 106 Ced Landrum	.05	.02	.01
□ 107 Patrick Lennon	.05	.02	.01
□ 108 Jim Lewis	.05	.02	.01
□ 109 Mark Lewis	.30	.14	.04
□ 110 Doug Lindsey	.05	.02	.01
□ 111 Scott Livingstone	.05	.02	.01
□ 112 Kenny Lofton	4.00	1.80	.50
□ 113 Ever Magallanes	.05	.02	.01
□ 114 Mike Magnante	.05	.02	.01
□ 115 Barry Manuel	.05	.02	.01
□ 116 Josias Manzanillo	.05	.02	.01
□ 117 Chito Martinez	.05	.02	.01
□ 118 Terry Mathews	.05	.02	.01
□ 119 Rob Maurer	.05	.02	.01
□ 120 Tim Mauser	.05	.02	.01
□ 121 Terry McDaniel	.05	.02	.01
□ 122 Rusty Meacham	.05	.02	.01
□ 123 Luis Mercedes	.05	.02	.01
□ 124 Paul Miller	.05	.02	.01
□ 125 Keith Mitchell	.05	.02	.01
□ 126 Bobby Moore	.05	.02	.01
□ 127 Kevin Morton	.05	.02	.01
□ 128 Andy Mota	.05	.02	.01
□ 129 Jose Mota	.05	.02	.01
□ 130 Mike Mussina	2.50	1.10	.30
□ 131 Jeff Mutis	.05	.02	.01
□ 132 Denny Neagle	.50	.23	.06
□ 133 Warren Newson	.05	.02	.01
□ 134 Jim Olander	.05	.02	.01
□ 135 Erik Pappas	.05	.02	.01
□ 136 Jorge Pedre	.05	.02	.01
□ 137 Yorkis Perez	.05	.02	.01
□ 138 Mark Petkovsek	.15	.07	.02
□ 139 Doug Piatt	.05	.02	.01
□ 140 Jeff Plympton	.05	.02	.01
□ 141 Harvey Pulliam	.05	.02	.01
□ 142 John Ramos	.05	.02	.01
□ 143 Mike Remlinger	.05	.02	.01
□ 144 Laddie Renfroe	.05	.02	.01
□ 145 Armando Reynoso	.15	.07	.02
□ 146 Arthur Rhodes	.25	.11	.03
□ 147 Pat Rice	.05	.02	.01
□ 148 Nikco Riesgo	.05	.02	.01
□ 149 Carlos Rodriguez	.05	.02	.01
□ 150 Ivan Rodriguez	3.00	1.35	.35
□ 151 Wayne Rosenthal	.05	.02	.01
□ 152 Rico Rossy	.05	.02	.01
□ 153 Stan Royer	.05	.02	.01
□ 154 Rey Sanchez	.25	.11	.03
□ 155 Reggie Sanders	.50	.23	.06
□ 156 Mo Sanford	.05	.02	.01
□ 157 Bob Scanlan	.05	.02	.01
□ 158 Pete Schourek	.40	.18	.05
□ 159 Gary Scott	.05	.02	.01
□ 160 Tim Scott	.05	.02	.01
□ 161 Tony Scruggs	.05	.02	.01
□ 162 Scott Servais	.05	.02	.01
□ 163 Doug Simons	.05	.02	.01
□ 164 Heathcliff Slocumb	.30	.14	.04
□ 165 Joe Slusarski	.05	.02	.01
□ 166 Tim Spehr	.05	.02	.01
□ 167 Ed Sprague	.30	.14	.04
□ 168 Jeff Tackett	.05	.02	.01
□ 169 Eddie Taubensee	.25	.11	.03
□ 170 Wade Taylor	.05	.02	.01
□ 171 Jim Thome	3.00	1.35	.35
□ 172 Mike Timlin	.25	.11	.03
□ 173 Jose Tolentino	.05	.02	.01
□ 174 John Vander Wal	.15	.07	.02
□ 175 Todd Van Poppel	.05	.02	.01
□ 176 Mo Vaughn	3.00	1.35	.35
□ 177 Dave Wainhouse	.05	.02	.01
□ 178 Don Wakamatsu	.05	.02	.01
□ 179 Bruce Walton	.05	.02	.01
□ 180 Kevin Ward	.05	.02	.01
□ 181 Dave Weathers	.05	.02	.01
□ 182 Eric Wedge	.05	.02	.01
□ 183 John Wehner	.05	.02	.01
□ 184 Rick Wilkins	.25	.11	.03
□ 185 Bernie Williams	2.00	.90	.25
□ 186 Brian Williams	.05	.02	.01
□ 187 Ron Witmeyer	.05	.02	.01
□ 188 Mark Wohlers	.75	.35	.09
□ 189 Ted Wood	.05	.02	.01
□ 190 Anthony Young	.05	.02	.01
□ 191 Eddie Zosky	.05	.02	.01
□ 192 Bob Zupcic	.05	.02	.01
□ 193 Checklist 1	.05	.02	.01
□ 194 Checklist 2	.05	.02	.01

1992 Topps Kids

This 132-card standard size set was packaged in seven-card wax packs with a stick of bubble gum. The front features action and posed player pictures that are part-photo and part-cartoon on a brightly

colored background. The player's name is printed at the bottom in a variety of colors and styles. The backs carry a cartoon with a trivia fact and a "Fun Box" including trivia questions, puzzles, quotable quotes, tips from the pros, or a "Did You Know" feature. Statistical information is shown in a multi-colored grid at the bottom. The set numbering is arranged by teams in alphabetical order within division.

	MINT	NRMT	EXC
COMPLETE SET (132)	12.00	5.50	1.50
COMMON CARD (1-132)	.05	.02	.01
☐ 1 Ryne Sandberg	.75	.35	.09
☐ 2 Andre Dawson	.25	.11	.03
☐ 3 George Bell	.05	.02	.01
☐ 4 Mark Grace	.35	.16	.04
☐ 5 Shawon Dunston	.05	.02	.01
☐ 6 Tim Wallach	.05	.02	.01
☐ 7 Ivan Calderon	.05	.02	.01
☐ 8 Marquis Grissom	.15	.07	.02
☐ 9 Delino DeShields	.05	.02	.01
☐ 10 Dennis Martinez	.15	.07	.02
☐ 11 Dwight Gooden	.15	.07	.02
☐ 12 Howard Johnson	.05	.02	.01
☐ 13 John Franco	.15	.07	.02
☐ 14 Gregg Jefferies	.15	.07	.02
☐ 15 Kevin McReynolds	.05	.02	.01
☐ 16 David Cone	.15	.07	.02
☐ 17 Len Dykstra	.15	.07	.02
☐ 18 John Kruk	.15	.07	.02
☐ 19 Von Hayes	.05	.02	.01
☐ 20 Mitch Williams	.05	.02	.01
☐ 21 Barry Bonds	.40	.18	.05
☐ 22 Bobby Bonilla	.15	.07	.02
☐ 23 Andy Van Slyke	.05	.02	.01
☐ 24 Doug Drabek	.05	.02	.01
☐ 25 Ozzie Smith	.75	.35	.09
☐ 26 Pedro Guerrero	.05	.02	.01
☐ 27 Todd Zeile	.05	.02	.01
☐ 28 Lee Smith	.15	.07	.02
☐ 29 Felix Jose	.05	.02	.01
☐ 30 Jose DeLeon	.05	.02	.01
☐ 31 David Justice	.30	.14	.04
☐ 32 Ron Gant	.15	.07	.02
☐ 33 Terry Pendleton	.15	.07	.02
☐ 34 Tom Glavine	.25	.11	.03
☐ 35 Otis Nixon	.05	.02	.01
☐ 36 Steve Avery	.15	.07	.02
☐ 37 Barry Larkin	.30	.14	.04
☐ 38 Eric Davis	.15	.07	.02
☐ 39 Chris Sabo	.05	.02	.01
☐ 40 Rob Dibble	.05	.02	.01
☐ 41 Paul O'Neill	.15	.07	.02
☐ 42 Jose Rijo	.05	.02	.01
☐ 43 Craig Biggio	.15	.07	.02
☐ 44 Jeff Bagwell	.75	.35	.09
☐ 45 Ken Caminiti	.40	.18	.05
☐ 46 Steve Finley	.25	.11	.03
☐ 47 Darryl Strawberry	.15	.07	.02
☐ 48 Ramon Martinez	.15	.07	.02
☐ 49 Brett Butler	.15	.07	.02
☐ 50 Eddie Murray	.50	.23	.06
☐ 51 Kal Daniels	.05	.02	.01
☐ 52 Orel Hershiser	.15	.07	.02
☐ 53 Tony Gwynn	.75	.35	.09
☐ 54 Benito Santiago	.05	.02	.01
☐ 55 Fred McGriff	.25	.11	.03
☐ 56 Bip Roberts	.05	.02	.01
☐ 57 Tony Fernandez	.05	.02	.01
☐ 58 Will Clark	.25	.11	.03
☐ 59 Kevin Mitchell	.15	.07	.02
☐ 60 Matt Williams	.25	.11	.03
☐ 61 Willie McGee	.15	.07	.02
☐ 62 Dave Righetti	.05	.02	.01
☐ 63 Cal Ripken	1.50	.70	.19
☐ 64 Ben McDonald	.05	.02	.01
☐ 65 Glenn Davis	.05	.02	.01
☐ 66 Gregg Olson	.05	.02	.01
☐ 67 Roger Clemens	.50	.23	.06
☐ 68 Wade Boggs	.35	.16	.04
☐ 69 Mike Greenwell	.05	.02	.01
☐ 70 Ellis Burks	.25	.11	.03
☐ 71 Sandy Alomar Jr.	.15	.07	.02
☐ 72 Greg Swindell	.05	.02	.01
☐ 73 Albert Belle	1.00	.45	.12
☐ 74 Mark Whiten	.05	.02	.01
☐ 75 Alan Trammell	.15	.07	.02
☐ 76 Cecil Fielder	.15	.07	.02
☐ 77 Lou Whitaker	.15	.07	.02
☐ 78 Travis Fryman	.25	.11	.03
☐ 79 Tony Phillips	.05	.02	.01
☐ 80 Robin Yount	.25	.11	.03
☐ 81 Paul Molitor	.40	.18	.05
☐ 82 B.J. Surhoff	.05	.02	.01
☐ 83 Greg Vaughn	.15	.07	.02
☐ 84 Don Mattingly	1.00	.45	.12
☐ 85 Steve Sax	.05	.02	.01
☐ 86 Kevin Maas	.05	.02	.01
☐ 87 Mel Hall	.05	.02	.01
☐ 88 Roberto Kelly	.05	.02	.01
☐ 89 Joe Carter	.25	.11	.03
☐ 90 Roberto Alomar	.40	.18	.05
☐ 91 Dave Stieb	.05	.02	.01
☐ 92 Kelly Gruber	.05	.02	.01
☐ 93 Tom Henke	.05	.02	.01
☐ 94 Chuck Finley	.05	.02	.01
☐ 95 Wally Joyner	.05	.02	.01
☐ 96 Dave Winfield	.25	.11	.03
☐ 97 Jim Abbott	.15	.07	.02
☐ 98 Mark Langston	.05	.02	.01
☐ 99 Frank Thomas	2.00	.90	.25
☐ 100 Ozzie Guillen	.05	.02	.01
☐ 101 Bobby Thigpen	.05	.02	.01
☐ 102 Robin Ventura	.15	.07	.02
☐ 103 Bo Jackson	.15	.07	.02
☐ 104 Tim Raines	.15	.07	.02
☐ 105 George Brett	.75	.35	.09
☐ 106 Danny Tartabull	.05	.02	.01
☐ 107 Bret Saberhagen	.15	.07	.02
☐ 108 Brian McRae	.15	.07	.02
☐ 109 Kirby Puckett	1.00	.45	.12
☐ 110 Scott Erickson	.05	.02	.01
☐ 111 Kent Hrbek	.15	.07	.02
☐ 112 Chuck Knoblauch	.40	.18	.05
☐ 113 Chili Davis	.05	.02	.01
☐ 114 Rick Aguilera	.05	.02	.01
☐ 115 Jose Canseco	.40	.18	.05
☐ 116 Dave Henderson	.05	.02	.01
☐ 117 Dave Stewart	.05	.02	.01
☐ 118 Rickey Henderson	.30	.14	.04
☐ 119 Dennis Eckersley	.15	.07	.02
☐ 120 Harold Baines	.05	.02	.01
☐ 121 Mark McGwire	.75	.35	.09
☐ 122 Ken Griffey Jr.	2.00	.90	.25
☐ 123 Harold Reynolds	.15	.07	.02
☐ 124 Erik Hanson	.05	.02	.01
☐ 125 Edgar Martinez	.15	.07	.02
☐ 126 Randy Johnson	.40	.18	.05
☐ 127 Nolan Ryan	1.50	.70	.19
☐ 128 Ruben Sierra	.05	.02	.01
☐ 129 Julio Franco	.15	.07	.02
☐ 130 Rafael Palmeiro	.25	.11	.03
☐ 131 Juan Gonzalez	1.00	.45	.12
☐ 132 Checklist Card	.05	.02	.01

1992 Topps McDonald's

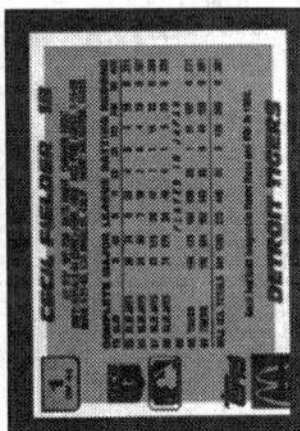

This 44-card standard-size set was produced by Topps for McDonald's and distributed in the New York, New Jersey, and Connecticut areas. The set was subtitled "McDonald's Baseball's Best". For 99 cents with the purchase of an Extra Value Meal or 1.79 with any other food purchase, the collector received a 5-card cello pack. The top card of each pack was always one of eleven different rookies (34-44) randomly packed with four other non-rookie cards. On the fronts, the color player photos are edged with canary yellow and black borders. The player's name and sponsor logo are gold foil stamped at the bottom. The backs are bordered in red and white and display biographical and statistical information on a orange-yellow background. The cards are numbered on the back.

	MINT	NRMT	EXC
COMPLETE SET (44)	30.00	13.50	3.70
COMMON CARD (1-44)	.25	.11	.03
☐ 1 Cecil Fielder	.50	.23	.06
☐ 2 Benny Santiago	.25	.11	.03
☐ 3 Rickey Henderson	.75	.35	.09
☐ 4 Roberto Alomar	1.25	.55	.16
☐ 5 Ryne Sandberg	2.00	.90	.25
☐ 6 George Brett	2.00	.90	.25
☐ 7 Terry Pendleton	.50	.23	.06
☐ 8 Ken Griffey Jr.	5.00	2.20	.60
☐ 9 Bobby Bonilla	.50	.23	.06
☐ 10 Roger Clemens	1.25	.55	.16
☐ 11 Ozzie Smith	2.00	.90	.25
☐ 12 Barry Bonds	1.25	.55	.16
☐ 13 Cal Ripken	4.00	1.80	.50
☐ 14 Ron Gant	.50	.23	.06
☐ 15 Carlton Fisk	.75	.35	.09
☐ 16 Steve Avery	.50	.23	.06
☐ 17 Robin Yount	.75	.35	.09
☐ 18 Will Clark	1.00	.45	.12
☐ 19 Kirby Puckett	2.50	1.10	.30
☐ 20 Jim Abbott	.25	.11	.03
☐ 21 Barry Larkin	.75	.35	.09
☐ 22 Jose Canseco	1.00	.45	.12
☐ 23 Howard Johnson	.25	.11	.03
☐ 24 Nolan Ryan	4.00	1.80	.50
☐ 25 Frank Thomas	5.00	2.20	.60
☐ 26 Danny Tartabull	.25	.11	.03
☐ 27 Julio Franco	.25	.11	.03
☐ 28 David Justice	.75	.35	.09
☐ 29 Joe Carter	.50	.23	.06
☐ 30 Dale Murphy	.75	.35	.09
☐ 31 Andre Dawson	.50	.23	.06
☐ 32 Dwight Gooden	.50	.23	.06
☐ 33 Bo Jackson	.50	.23	.06
☐ 34 Jeff Bagwell	2.50	1.10	.30
☐ 35 Chuck Knoblauch	.75	.35	.09
☐ 36 Derek Bell	.75	.35	.09
☐ 37 Jim Thome	2.50	1.10	.30
☐ 38 Royce Clayton	.50	.23	.06
☐ 39 Ryan Klesko	2.00	.90	.25
☐ 40 Chito Martinez	.25	.11	.03
☐ 41 Ivan Rodriguez	1.50	.70	.19
☐ 42 Todd Hundley	.75	.35	.09
☐ 43 Eric Karros	.75	.35	.09
☐ 44 Todd Van Poppel	.25	.11	.03

1993 Topps Pre-Production

These nine pre-production cards were included in the 1992 Topps Holiday set as a special insert set. The cards are standard size and were done in the style of the 1993 Topps baseball cards. The fronts feature color action player photos bordered in white. A team color-coded horizontal bar and two short diagonal bars accent the pictures at the bottom. The backs carry a color close-up photo, biography, statistics, and (where space allows) a summary of the player's outstanding performance during a game. The cards say "1993 Pre-Production Sample" inside a gray in the middle of the card back.

	MINT	NRMT	EXC
COMPLETE SET (9)	8.00	3.60	1.00
COMMON CARD (1-250)	.30	.14	.04
☐ 1 Robin Yount	.40	.18	.05
☐ 2 Barry Bonds	.75	.35	.09
☐ 11 Eric Karros	.30	.14	.04
☐ 32 Don Mattingly	1.50	.70	.19
☐ 100 Mark McGwire	1.00	.45	.12
☐ 150 Frank Thomas	3.00	1.35	.35
☐ 179 Ken Griffey Jr.	3.00	1.35	.35
☐ 230 Carlton Fisk	.30	.14	.04
☐ 250 Chuck Knoblauch	.50	.23	.06

1993 Topps Pre-Production Sheet

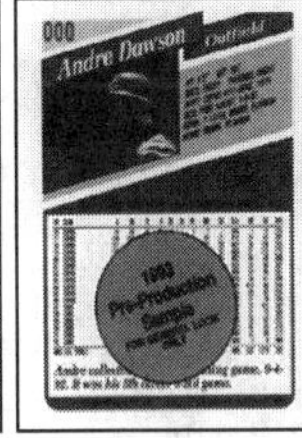

The 1993 Topps Pre-Production sheet was sent out to give collectors a preview of the design of Topps' 1993 regular issue cards. The sheet measures 8" by 11" and features nine standard-size cards. The fronts feature color action player photos with white borders. The player's name appears in a stripe at the bottom of the picture, and this stripe and two short diagonal stripes at the bottom corners of the picture are team color-coded. The backs are colorful and carry a color head shot, biography, complete statistical information, with a career highlight if space permits. A gray circle with the message "1993 Pre-Production Sample: For General Look Only" is superimposed over the statistical section. The cards are all numbered "000" and are therefore checklisted below in alphabetical order.

	MINT	NRMT	EXC
COMPLETE SET (9)	7.00	3.10	.85
COMMON CARD (1-9)	.25	.11	.03
☐ 1 Roberto Alomar	1.25	.55	.16
☐ 2 Bobby Bonilla	.50	.23	.06
☐ 3 Gary Carter	.50	.23	.06
☐ 4 Andre Dawson	.50	.23	.06
☐ 5 Dave Fleming	.25	.11	.03
☐ 6 Ken Griffey Jr.	4.00	1.80	.50
☐ 7 Pete Incaviglia	.25	.11	.03
☐ 8 Spike Owen	.25	.11	.03
☐ 9 Larry Walker	.75	.35	.09

1993 Topps

The 1993 Topps baseball set consists of two series, respectively, of 396 and 429 standard-size cards. A Topps Gold card was inserted in every 15-card pack, and Topps Black Gold cards were randomly inserted throughout the packs. The fronts feature color action player photos with white borders. The player's name appears in a stripe at the bottom of the picture, and this stripe and two short diagonal stripes at the bottom corners of the picture are team color-coded. The backs are colorful and carry a color head shot, biography, complete statistical information, with a career highlight if space permitted. Cards 401-411 comprise an All-Star subset. Rookie Cards in this set include Jim Edmonds, Derek Jeter and Jason Kendall.

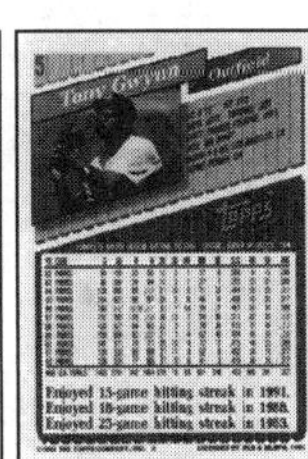

	MINT	NRMT	EXC
COMPLETE SET (825)	30.00	13.50	3.70
COMP.RET.FACT.SET (838)	40.00	18.00	5.00
COMP.HOB.FACT.SET (847)	45.00	20.00	5.50
COMPLETE SERIES 1 (396)	15.00	6.75	1.85
COMPLETE SERIES 2 (429)	15.00	6.75	1.85
COMMON CARD (1-825)	.05	.02	.01
☐ 1 Robin Yount	.15	.07	.02
☐ 2 Barry Bonds	.50	.23	.06
☐ 3 Ryne Sandberg	.50	.23	.06
☐ 4 Roger Clemens	.40	.18	.05
☐ 5 Tony Gwynn	.75	.35	.09
☐ 6 Jeff Tackett	.05	.02	.01
☐ 7 Pete Incaviglia	.05	.02	.01
☐ 8 Mark Wohlers	.10	.05	.01
☐ 9 Kent Hrbek	.10	.05	.01
☐ 10 Will Clark	.15	.07	.02
☐ 11 Eric Karros	.15	.07	.02
☐ 12 Lee Smith	.10	.05	.01
☐ 13 Esteban Beltre	.05	.02	.01
☐ 14 Greg Briley	.05	.02	.01
☐ 15 Marquis Grissom	.10	.05	.01
☐ 16 Dan Plesac	.05	.02	.01
☐ 17 Dave Hollins	.05	.02	.01
☐ 18 Terry Steinbach	.10	.05	.01
☐ 19 Ed Nunez	.05	.02	.01
☐ 20 Tim Salmon	.50	.23	.06
☐ 21 Luis Salazar	.05	.02	.01
☐ 22 Jim Eisenreich	.10	.05	.01
☐ 23 Todd Stottlemyre	.10	.05	.01
☐ 24 Tim Naehring	.05	.02	.01
☐ 25 John Franco	.05	.02	.01
☐ 26 Skeeter Barnes	.05	.02	.01
☐ 27 Carlos Garcia	.05	.02	.01
☐ 28 Joe Orsulak	.05	.02	.01
☐ 29 Dwayne Henry	.05	.02	.01
☐ 30 Fred McGriff	.15	.07	.02
☐ 31 Derek Lilliquist	.05	.02	.01
☐ 32 Don Mattingly	1.00	.45	.12
☐ 33 B.J. Wallace	.05	.02	.01
☐ 34 Juan Gonzalez	1.00	.45	.12
☐ 35 John Smoltz	.15	.07	.02
☐ 36 Scott Servais	.05	.02	.01
☐ 37 Lenny Webster	.05	.02	.01
☐ 38 Chris James	.05	.02	.01
☐ 39 Roger McDowell	.05	.02	.01
☐ 40 Ozzie Smith	.50	.23	.06
☐ 41 Alex Fernandez	.10	.05	.01
☐ 42 Spike Owen	.05	.02	.01
☐ 43 Ruben Amaro	.05	.02	.01
☐ 44 Kevin Seitzer	.05	.02	.01
☐ 45 Dave Fleming	.05	.02	.01
☐ 46 Eric Fox	.05	.02	.01
☐ 47 Bob Scanlan	.05	.02	.01
☐ 48 Bert Blyleven	.10	.05	.01
☐ 49 Brian McRae	.10	.05	.01
☐ 50 Roberto Alomar	.40	.18	.05
☐ 51 Mo Vaughn	.50	.23	.06
☐ 52 Bobby Bonilla	.10	.05	.01
☐ 53 Frank Tanana	.05	.02	.01
☐ 54 Mike LaValliere	.05	.02	.01
☐ 55 Mark McLemore	.05	.02	.01
☐ 56 Chad Mottola	.10	.05	.01
☐ 57 Norm Charlton	.05	.02	.01
☐ 58 Jose Melendez	.05	.02	.01
☐ 59 Carlos Martinez	.05	.02	.01
☐ 60 Roberto Kelly	.05	.02	.01
☐ 61 Gene Larkin	.05	.02	.01
☐ 62 Rafael Belliard	.05	.02	.01
☐ 63 Al Osuna	.05	.02	.01
☐ 64 Scott Chiamparino	.05	.02	.01
☐ 65 Brett Butler	.10	.05	.01
☐ 66 John Burkett	.05	.02	.01
☐ 67 Felix Jose	.05	.02	.01
☐ 68 Omar Vizquel	.10	.05	.01
☐ 69 John Vander Wal	.05	.02	.01
☐ 70 Roberto Hernandez	.10	.05	.01
☐ 71 Ricky Bones	.05	.02	.01
☐ 72 Jeff Grotewold	.05	.02	.01
☐ 73 Mike Moore	.05	.02	.01
☐ 74 Steve Buechele	.05	.02	.01
☐ 75 Juan Guzman	.10	.05	.01
☐ 76 Kevin Appier	.10	.05	.01
☐ 77 Junior Felix	.05	.02	.01
☐ 78 Greg W. Harris	.05	.02	.01
☐ 79 Dick Schofield	.05	.02	.01
☐ 80 Cecil Fielder	.10	.05	.01
☐ 81 Lloyd McClendon	.05	.02	.01
☐ 82 David Segui	.05	.02	.01
☐ 83 Reggie Sanders	.15	.07	.02
☐ 84 Kurt Stillwell	.05	.02	.01

☐ 85 Sandy Alomar .10 .05 .01
☐ 86 John Habyan .05 .02 .01
☐ 87 Kevin Reimer .05 .02 .01
☐ 88 Mike Stanton .05 .02 .01
☐ 89 Eric Anthony .05 .02 .01
☐ 90 Scott Erickson .05 .02 .01
☐ 91 Craig Colbert .05 .02 .01
☐ 92 Tom Pagnozzi .05 .02 .01
☐ 93 Pedro Astacio .05 .02 .01
☐ 94 Lance Johnson .10 .05 .01
☐ 95 Larry Walker .15 .07 .02
☐ 96 Russ Swan .05 .02 .01
☐ 97 Scott Fletcher .05 .02 .01
☐ 98 Derek Jeter 4.00 1.80 .50
☐ 99 Mike Williams .05 .02 .01
☐ 100 Mark McGwire .60 .25 .07
☐ 101 Jim Bullinger .05 .02 .01
☐ 102 Brian Hunter .05 .02 .01
☐ 103 Jody Reed .05 .02 .01
☐ 104 Mike Butcher .05 .02 .01
☐ 105 Gregg Jefferies .10 .05 .01
☐ 106 Howard Johnson .05 .02 .01
☐ 107 John Kiely .05 .02 .01
☐ 108 Jose Lind .05 .02 .01
☐ 109 Sam Horn .05 .02 .01
☐ 110 Barry Larkin .15 .07 .02
☐ 111 Bruce Hurst .05 .02 .01
☐ 112 Brian Barnes .05 .02 .01
☐ 113 Thomas Howard .05 .02 .01
☐ 114 Mel Hall .05 .02 .01
☐ 115 Robby Thompson .05 .02 .01
☐ 116 Mark Lemke .05 .02 .01
☐ 117 Eddie Taubensee .05 .02 .01
☐ 118 David Hulse .05 .02 .01
☐ 119 Pedro Munoz .05 .02 .01
☐ 120 Ramon Martinez .10 .05 .01
☐ 121 Todd Worrell .05 .02 .01
☐ 122 Joey Cora .10 .05 .01
☐ 123 Moises Alou .10 .05 .01
☐ 124 Franklin Stubbs .05 .02 .01
☐ 125 Pete O'Brien .05 .02 .01
☐ 126 Bob Ayrault .05 .02 .01
☐ 127 Carney Lansford .10 .05 .01
☐ 128 Kal Daniels .05 .02 .01
☐ 129 Joe Grahe .05 .02 .01
☐ 130 Jeff Montgomery .10 .05 .01
☐ 131 Dave Winfield .15 .07 .02
☐ 132 Preston Wilson .30 .14 .04
☐ 133 Steve Wilson .05 .02 .01
☐ 134 Lee Guetterman .05 .02 .01
☐ 135 Mickey Tettleton .05 .02 .01
☐ 136 Jeff King .10 .05 .01
☐ 137 Alan Mills .05 .02 .01
☐ 138 Joe Oliver .05 .02 .01
☐ 139 Gary Gaetti .10 .05 .01
☐ 140 Gary Sheffield .15 .07 .02
☐ 141 Dennis Cook .05 .02 .01
☐ 142 Charlie Hayes .05 .02 .01
☐ 143 Jeff Huson .05 .02 .01
☐ 144 Kent Mercker .05 .02 .01
☐ 145 Eric Young .15 .07 .02
☐ 146 Scott Leius .05 .02 .01
☐ 147 Bryan Hickerson .05 .02 .01
☐ 148 Steve Finley .10 .05 .01
☐ 149 Rheal Cormier .05 .02 .01
☐ 150 Frank Thomas UER 2.00 .90 .25
(Categories leading
league are italicized
but not printed in red)
☐ 151 Archi Cianfrocco .05 .02 .01
☐ 152 Rich DeLucia .05 .02 .01
☐ 153 Greg Vaughn .10 .05 .01
☐ 154 Wes Chamberlain .05 .02 .01
☐ 155 Dennis Eckersley .10 .05 .01
☐ 156 Sammy Sosa .15 .07 .02
☐ 157 Gary DiSarcina .05 .02 .01
☐ 158 Kevin Koslofski .05 .02 .01
☐ 159 Doug Linton .05 .02 .01
☐ 160 Lou Whitaker .10 .05 .01
☐ 161 Chad McConnell .05 .02 .01
☐ 162 Joe Hesketh .05 .02 .01
☐ 163 Tim Wakefield .10 .05 .01
☐ 164 Leo Gomez .05 .02 .01
☐ 165 Jose Rijo .05 .02 .01
☐ 166 Tim Scott .05 .02 .01
☐ 167 Steve Olin UER .05 .02 .01
(Born 10/4/65
should say 10/10/65)
☐ 168 Kevin Maas .05 .02 .01
☐ 169 Kenny Rogers .05 .02 .01
☐ 170 David Justice .15 .07 .02
☐ 171 Doug Jones .05 .02 .01
☐ 172 Jeff Reboulet .05 .02 .01
☐ 173 Andres Galarraga .15 .07 .02
☐ 174 Randy Velarde .05 .02 .01
☐ 175 Kirk McCaskill .05 .02 .01
☐ 176 Darren Lewis .05 .02 .01
☐ 177 Lenny Harris .05 .02 .01
☐ 178 Jeff Fassero .10 .05 .01
☐ 179 Ken Griffey Jr. 2.00 .90 .25
☐ 180 Darren Daulton .10 .05 .01
☐ 181 John Jaha .15 .07 .02
☐ 182 Ron Darling .05 .02 .01
☐ 183 Greg Maddux 1.25 .55 .16
☐ 184 Damion Easley .05 .02 .01
☐ 185 Jack Morris .10 .05 .01
☐ 186 Mike Magnante .05 .02 .01
☐ 187 John Dopson .05 .02 .01
☐ 188 Sid Fernandez .05 .02 .01
☐ 189 Tony Phillips .10 .05 .01
☐ 190 Doug Drabek .05 .02 .01
☐ 191 Sean Lowe .10 .05 .01
☐ 192 Bob Milacki .05 .02 .01
☐ 193 Steve Foster .05 .02 .01
☐ 194 Jerald Clark .05 .02 .01
☐ 195 Pete Harnisch .05 .02 .01
☐ 196 Pat Kelly .05 .02 .01
☐ 197 Jeff Frye .05 .02 .01
☐ 198 Alejandro Pena .05 .02 .01
☐ 199 Junior Ortiz .05 .02 .01
☐ 200 Kirby Puckett .75 .35 .09
☐ 201 Jose Uribe .05 .02 .01
☐ 202 Mike Scioscia .05 .02 .01
☐ 203 Bernard Gilkey .10 .05 .01
☐ 204 Dan Pasqua .05 .02 .01
☐ 205 Gary Carter .10 .05 .01
☐ 206 Henry Cotto .05 .02 .01
☐ 207 Paul Molitor .40 .18 .05
☐ 208 Mike Hartley .05 .02 .01
☐ 209 Jeff Parrett .05 .02 .01
☐ 210 Mark Langston .10 .05 .01
☐ 211 Doug Dascenzo .05 .02 .01
☐ 212 Rick Reed .05 .02 .01
☐ 213 Candy Maldonado .05 .02 .01
☐ 214 Danny Darwin .05 .02 .01
☐ 215 Pat Howell .05 .02 .01
☐ 216 Mark Leiter .05 .02 .01
☐ 217 Kevin Mitchell .10 .05 .01
☐ 218 Ben McDonald .05 .02 .01
☐ 219 Bip Roberts .05 .02 .01
☐ 220 Benny Santiago .05 .02 .01
☐ 221 Carlos Baerga .10 .05 .01
☐ 222 Bernie Williams .40 .18 .05
☐ 223 Roger Pavlik .10 .05 .01
☐ 224 Sid Bream .05 .02 .01
☐ 225 Matt Williams .15 .07 .02
☐ 226 Willie Banks .05 .02 .01
☐ 227 Jeff Bagwell .75 .35 .09
☐ 228 Tom Goodwin .05 .02 .01
☐ 229 Mike Perez .05 .02 .01
☐ 230 Carlton Fisk .15 .07 .02
☐ 231 John Wetteland .10 .05 .01
☐ 232 Tino Martinez .10 .05 .01
☐ 233 Rick Greene .05 .02 .01
☐ 234 Tim McIntosh .05 .02 .01
☐ 235 Mitch Williams .05 .02 .01
☐ 236 Kevin Campbell .05 .02 .01
☐ 237 Jose Vizcaino .05 .02 .01
☐ 238 Chris Donnels .05 .02 .01
☐ 239 Mike Boddicker .05 .02 .01
☐ 240 John Olerud .05 .02 .01
☐ 241 Mike Gardiner .05 .02 .01
☐ 242 Charlie O'Brien .05 .02 .01
☐ 243 Rob Deer .05 .02 .01
☐ 244 Denny Neagle .10 .05 .01
☐ 245 Chris Sabo .05 .02 .01
☐ 246 Gregg Olson .05 .02 .01
☐ 247 Frank Seminara UER .05 .02 .01
(Acquired 12/3/98)
☐ 248 Scott Scudder .05 .02 .01
☐ 249 Tim Burke .05 .02 .01
☐ 250 Chuck Knoblauch .15 .07 .02
☐ 251 Mike Bielecki .05 .02 .01
☐ 252 Xavier Hernandez .05 .02 .01
☐ 253 Jose Guzman .05 .02 .01
☐ 254 Cory Snyder .05 .02 .01
☐ 255 Orel Hershiser .10 .05 .01
☐ 256 Wil Cordero .10 .05 .01
☐ 257 Luis Alicea .05 .02 .01
☐ 258 Mike Schooler .05 .02 .01
☐ 259 Craig Grebeck .05 .02 .01
☐ 260 Duane Ward .05 .02 .01
☐ 261 Bill Wegman .05 .02 .01
☐ 262 Mickey Morandini .05 .02 .01
☐ 263 Vince Horsman .05 .02 .01
☐ 264 Paul Sorrento .05 .02 .01
☐ 265 Andre Dawson .10 .05 .01
☐ 266 Rene Gonzales .05 .02 .01
☐ 267 Keith Miller .05 .02 .01
☐ 268 Derek Bell .10 .05 .01
☐ 269 Todd Steverson .05 .02 .01
☐ 270 Frank Viola .05 .02 .01
☐ 271 Wally Whitehurst .05 .02 .01
☐ 272 Kurt Knudsen .05 .02 .01
☐ 273 Dan Walters .05 .02 .01
☐ 274 Rick Sutcliffe .05 .02 .01
☐ 275 Andy Van Slyke .10 .05 .01
☐ 276 Paul O'Neill .10 .05 .01
☐ 277 Mark Whiten .05 .02 .01
☐ 278 Chris Nabholz .05 .02 .01
☐ 279 Todd Burns .05 .02 .01
☐ 280 Tom Glavine .15 .07 .02
☐ 281 Butch Henry .05 .02 .01
☐ 282 Shane Mack .05 .02 .01
☐ 283 Mike Jackson .05 .02 .01
☐ 284 Henry Rodriguez .15 .07 .02
☐ 285 Bob Tewksbury .05 .02 .01
☐ 286 Ron Karkovice .05 .02 .01
☐ 287 Mike Gallego .05 .02 .01
☐ 288 Dave Cochrane .05 .02 .01
☐ 289 Jesse Orosco .05 .02 .01
☐ 290 Dave Stewart .10 .05 .01
☐ 291 Tommy Greene .05 .02 .01
☐ 292 Rey Sanchez .05 .02 .01
☐ 293 Rob Ducey .05 .02 .01
☐ 294 Brent Mayne .05 .02 .01
☐ 295 Dave Stieb .05 .02 .01
☐ 296 Luis Rivera .05 .02 .01
☐ 297 Jeff Innis .05 .02 .01
☐ 298 Scott Livingstone .05 .02 .01
☐ 299 Bob Patterson .05 .02 .01
☐ 300 Cal Ripken 1.50 .70 .19
☐ 301 Cesar Hernandez .05 .02 .01
☐ 302 Randy Myers .10 .05 .01
☐ 303 Brook Jacoby .05 .02 .01
☐ 304 Melido Perez .05 .02 .01
☐ 305 Rafael Palmeiro .15 .07 .02
☐ 306 Damon Berryhill .05 .02 .01
☐ 307 Dan Serafini .30 .14 .04
☐ 308 Darryl Kile .05 .02 .01
☐ 309 J.T. Bruett .05 .02 .01
☐ 310 Dave Righetti .05 .02 .01
☐ 311 Jay Howell .05 .02 .01
☐ 312 Geronimo Pena .05 .02 .01
☐ 313 Greg Hibbard .05 .02 .01
☐ 314 Mark Gardner .05 .02 .01
☐ 315 Edgar Martinez .10 .05 .01
☐ 316 Dave Nilsson .10 .05 .01
☐ 317 Kyle Abbott .05 .02 .01
☐ 318 Willie Wilson .05 .02 .01
☐ 319 Paul Assenmacher .05 .02 .01
☐ 320 Tim Fortugno .05 .02 .01
☐ 321 Rusty Meacham .05 .02 .01
☐ 322 Pat Borders .05 .02 .01
☐ 323 Mike Greenwell .05 .02 .01
☐ 324 Willie Randolph .10 .05 .01
☐ 325 Bill Gullickson .05 .02 .01
☐ 326 Gary Varsho .05 .02 .01
☐ 327 Tim Hulett .05 .02 .01
☐ 328 Scott Ruskin .05 .02 .01
☐ 329 Mike Maddux .05 .02 .01
☐ 330 Danny Tartabull .05 .02 .01
☐ 331 Kenny Lofton .75 .35 .09
☐ 332 Geno Petralli .05 .02 .01
☐ 333 Otis Nixon .05 .02 .01
☐ 334 Jason Kendall 1.00 .45 .12
☐ 335 Mark Portugal .05 .02 .01
☐ 336 Mike Pagliarulo .05 .02 .01
☐ 337 Kirt Manwaring .05 .02 .01
☐ 338 Bob Ojeda .05 .02 .01
☐ 339 Mark Clark .05 .02 .01
☐ 340 John Kruk .10 .05 .01
☐ 341 Mel Rojas .10 .05 .01
☐ 342 Erik Hanson .05 .02 .01
☐ 343 Doug Henry .05 .02 .01
☐ 344 Jack McDowell .10 .05 .01
☐ 345 Harold Baines .10 .05 .01
☐ 346 Chuck McElroy .05 .02 .01
☐ 347 Luis Sojo .05 .02 .01
☐ 348 Andy Stankiewicz .05 .02 .01
☐ 349 Hipolito Pichardo .05 .02 .01
☐ 350 Joe Carter .10 .05 .01
☐ 351 Ellis Burks .10 .05 .01
☐ 352 Pete Schourek .10 .05 .01
☐ 353 Bubby Groom .05 .02 .01
☐ 354 Jay Bell .10 .05 .01
☐ 355 Brady Anderson .15 .07 .02
☐ 356 Freddie Benavides .05 .02 .01
☐ 357 Phil Stephenson .05 .02 .01
☐ 358 Kevin Wickander .05 .02 .01
☐ 359 Mike Stanley .05 .02 .01
☐ 360 Ivan Rodriguez .50 .23 .06
☐ 361 Scott Bankhead .05 .02 .01
☐ 362 Luis Gonzalez .05 .02 .01
☐ 363 John Smiley .05 .02 .01
☐ 364 Trevor Wilson .05 .02 .01
☐ 365 Tom Candiotti .05 .02 .01
☐ 366 Craig Wilson .05 .02 .01
☐ 367 Steve Sax .05 .02 .01
☐ 368 Delino DeShields .05 .02 .01
☐ 369 Jaime Navarro .05 .02 .01
☐ 370 Dave Valle .05 .02 .01
☐ 371 Mariano Duncan .05 .02 .01
☐ 372 Rod Nichols .05 .02 .01
☐ 373 Mike Morgan .05 .02 .01
☐ 374 Julio Valera .05 .02 .01
☐ 375 Wally Joyner .10 .05 .01
☐ 376 Tom Henke .05 .02 .01
☐ 377 Herm Winningham .05 .02 .01
☐ 378 Orlando Merced .10 .05 .01
☐ 379 Mike Munoz .05 .02 .01
☐ 380 Todd Hundley .10 .05 .01
☐ 381 Mike Flanagan .05 .02 .01
☐ 382 Tim Belcher .05 .02 .01
☐ 383 Jerry Browne .05 .02 .01
☐ 384 Mike Benjamin .05 .02 .01
☐ 385 Jim Leyritz .05 .02 .01
☐ 386 Ray Lankford .10 .05 .01
☐ 387 Devon White .05 .02 .01
☐ 388 Jeremy Hernandez .05 .02 .01
☐ 389 Brian Harper .05 .02 .01
☐ 390 Wade Boggs .15 .07 .02
☐ 391 Derrick May .05 .02 .01
☐ 392 Travis Fryman .10 .05 .01
☐ 393 Ron Gant .10 .05 .01
☐ 394 Checklist 1-132 .05 .02 .01
☐ 395 Checklist 133-264 UER .05 .02 .01
(Eckerlsey)
☐ 396 Checklist 265-396 .05 .02 .01
☐ 397 George Brett .75 .35 .09
☐ 398 Bobby Witt .05 .02 .01
☐ 399 Daryl Boston .05 .02 .01
☐ 400 Bo Jackson .10 .05 .01
☐ 401 Fred McGriff .50 .23 .06
Frank Thomas
☐ 402 Ryne Sandberg .10 .05 .01
Carlos Baerga
☐ 403 Gary Sheffield .10 .05 .01
Edgar Martinez
☐ 404 Barry Larkin .10 .05 .01
Travis Fryman
☐ 405 Andy Van Slyke .50 .23 .06
Ken Griffey Jr.
☐ 406 Larry Walker .10 .05 .01
Kirby Puckett
☐ 407 Barry Bonds .10 .05 .01
Joe Carter
☐ 408 Darren Daulton .10 .05 .01
Brian Harper
☐ 409 Greg Maddux .40 .18 .05
Roger Clemens
☐ 410 Tom Glavine .10 .05 .01
Dave Fleming
☐ 411 Lee Smith .10 .05 .01
Dennis Eckersley
☐ 412 Jamie McAndrew .05 .02 .01
☐ 413 Pete Smith .05 .02 .01
☐ 414 Juan Guerrero .05 .02 .01
☐ 415 Todd Frohwirth .05 .02 .01
☐ 416 Randy Tomlin .05 .02 .01
☐ 417 B.J. Surhoff .10 .05 .01
☐ 418 Jim Gott .05 .02 .01
☐ 419 Mark Thompson .05 .02 .01
☐ 420 Kevin Tapani .05 .02 .01
☐ 421 Curt Schilling .05 .02 .01
☐ 422 J.T. Snow .15 .07 .02
☐ 423 1993 Prospects .60 .25 .07
Ryan Klesko
Ivan Cruz
Bubba Smith
Larry Sutton
☐ 424 John Valentin .10 .05 .01
☐ 425 Joe Girardi .05 .02 .01
☐ 426 Nigel Wilson .05 .02 .01
☐ 427 Bob MacDonald .05 .02 .01
☐ 428 Todd Zeile .05 .02 .01
☐ 429 Milt Cuyler .05 .02 .01
☐ 430 Eddie Murray .50 .23 .06
☐ 431 Rich Amaral .05 .02 .01
☐ 432 Pete Young .05 .02 .01
☐ 433 Roger Bailey and .10 .05 .01
Tom Schmidt
☐ 434 Jack Armstrong .05 .02 .01
☐ 435 Willie McGee .05 .02 .01
☐ 436 Greg W. Harris .05 .02 .01
☐ 437 Chris Hammond .05 .02 .01
☐ 438 Ritchie Moody .05 .02 .01
☐ 439 Bryan Harvey .05 .02 .01
☐ 440 Ruben Sierra .10 .05 .01
☐ 441 Don Lemon and .10 .05 .01
Todd Pridy
☐ 442 Kevin McReynolds .05 .02 .01
☐ 443 Terry Leach .05 .02 .01
☐ 444 David Nied .05 .02 .01
☐ 445 Dale Murphy .15 .07 .02
☐ 446 Luis Mercedes .05 .02 .01
☐ 447 Keith Shepherd .05 .02 .01
☐ 448 Ken Caminiti .15 .07 .02
☐ 449 James Austin .05 .02 .01
☐ 450 Darryl Strawberry .10 .05 .01
☐ 451 1993 Prospects .10 .05 .01
Ramon Caraballo
Jon Shave
Brent Gates
Quinton McCracken
☐ 452 Bob Wickman .05 .02 .01
☐ 453 Victor Cole .05 .02 .01
☐ 454 John Johnstone .05 .02 .01
☐ 455 Chili Davis .10 .05 .01
☐ 456 Scott Taylor .05 .02 .01
☐ 457 Tracy Woodson .05 .02 .01
☐ 458 David Wells .05 .02 .01
☐ 459 Derek Wallace .05 .02 .01
☐ 460 Randy Johnson .15 .07 .02
☐ 461 Steve Reed .05 .02 .01
☐ 462 Felix Fermin .05 .02 .01
☐ 463 Scott Aldred .05 .02 .01
☐ 464 Greg Colbrunn .05 .02 .01
☐ 465 Tony Fernandez .05 .02 .01
☐ 466 Mike Felder .05 .02 .01
☐ 467 Lee Stevens .05 .02 .01
☐ 468 Matt Whiteside .05 .02 .01
☐ 469 Dave Hansen .05 .02 .01
☐ 470 Rob Dibble .05 .02 .01
☐ 471 Dave Gallagher .05 .02 .01
☐ 472 Chris Gwynn .05 .02 .01
☐ 473 Dave Henderson .05 .02 .01
☐ 474 Ozzie Guillen .05 .02 .01
☐ 475 Jeff Reardon .10 .05 .01
☐ 476 Mark Voisard and .10 .05 .01

Will Scalzitti
☐ 477 Jimmy Jones .05 .02 .01
☐ 478 Greg Cadaret .05 .02 .01
☐ 479 Todd Pratt .05 .02 .01
☐ 480 Pat Listach .05 .02 .01
☐ 481 Ryan Luzinski .10 .05 .01
☐ 482 Darren Reed .05 .02 .01
☐ 483 Brian Griffiths .05 .02 .01
☐ 484 John Wehner .05 .02 .01
☐ 485 Glenn Davis .05 .02 .01
☐ 486 Eric Wedge .05 .02 .01
☐ 487 Jesse Hollins .05 .02 .01
☐ 488 Manuel Lee .05 .02 .01
☐ 489 Scott Fredrickson .05 .02 .01
☐ 490 Omar Olivares .05 .02 .01
☐ 491 Shawn Hare .05 .02 .01
☐ 492 Tom Lampkin .05 .02 .01
☐ 493 Jeff Nelson .05 .02 .01
☐ 494 1993 Prospects .10 .05 .01
Kevin Young
Adell Davenport
Eduardo Perez
Lou Lucca
☐ 495 Ken Hill .10 .05 .01
☐ 496 Reggie Jefferson .10 .05 .01
☐ 497 Matt Petersen and .10 .05 .01
Willie Brown
☐ 498 Bud Black .05 .02 .01
☐ 499 Chuck Crim .05 .02 .01
☐ 500 Jose Canseco .15 .07 .02
☐ 501 Johnny Oates MG .10 .05 .01
Bobby Cox MG
☐ 502 Butch Hobson MG .05 .02 .01
Jim Lefebvre MG
☐ 503 Buck Rodgers MG .10 .05 .01
Tony Perez MG
☐ 504 Gene Lamont MG .10 .05 .01
Don Baylor MG
☐ 505 Mike Hargrove MG .10 .05 .01
Rene Lachemann MG
☐ 506 Sparky Anderson MG .10 .05 .01
Art Howe MG
☐ 507 Hal McRae MG .10 .05 .01
Tom Lasorda MG
☐ 508 Phil Garner MG .05 .02 .01
Felipe Alou MG
☐ 509 Tom Kelly MG .05 .02 .01
Jeff Torborg MG
☐ 510 Buck Showalter MG .05 .02 .01
Jim Fregosi MG
☐ 511 Tony LaRussa MG .10 .05 .01
Jim Leyland MG
☐ 512 Lou Piniella MG .10 .05 .01
Joe Torre MG
☐ 513 Kevin Kennedy MG .05 .02 .01
Jim Riggleman MG
☐ 514 Cito Gaston MG .10 .05 .01
Dusty Baker MG
☐ 515 Greg Swindell .05 .02 .01
☐ 516 Alex Arias .05 .02 .01
☐ 517 Bill Pecota .05 .02 .01
☐ 518 Benji Grigsby UER .05 .02 .01
(Misspelled Bengi
on card front)
☐ 519 David Howard .05 .02 .01
☐ 520 Charlie Hough .05 .02 .01
☐ 521 Kevin Flora .05 .02 .01
☐ 522 Shane Reynolds .15 .07 .02
☐ 523 Doug Bochtler .05 .02 .01
☐ 524 Chris Hoiles .05 .02 .01
☐ 525 Scott Sanderson .05 .02 .01
☐ 526 Mike Sharperson .05 .02 .01
☐ 527 Mike Fetters .05 .02 .01
☐ 528 Paul Quantrill .05 .02 .01
☐ 529 1993 Prospects 2.50 1.10 .30
Dave Silvestri
Chipper Jones
Benji Gil
Jeff Patzke
☐ 530 Sterling Hitchcock .10 .05 .01
☐ 531 Joe Millette .05 .02 .01
☐ 532 Tom Brunansky .05 .02 .01
☐ 533 Frank Castillo .05 .02 .01
☐ 534 Randy Knorr .05 .02 .01
☐ 535 Jose Oquendo .05 .02 .01
☐ 536 Dave Haas .05 .02 .01
☐ 537 Jason Hutchins and .10 .05 .01
Ryan Turner
☐ 538 Jimmy Baron .05 .02 .01
☐ 539 Kerry Woodson .05 .02 .01
☐ 540 Ivan Calderon .05 .02 .01
☐ 541 Denis Boucher .05 .02 .01
☐ 542 Royce Clayton .10 .05 .01
☐ 543 Reggie Williams .05 .02 .01
☐ 544 Steve Decker .05 .02 .01
☐ 545 Dean Palmer .10 .05 .01
☐ 546 Hal Morris .05 .02 .01
☐ 547 Ryan Thompson .05 .02 .01
☐ 548 Lance Blankenship .05 .02 .01
☐ 549 Hensley Meulens .05 .02 .01
☐ 550 Scott Radinsky .05 .02 .01
☐ 551 Eric Young .15 .07 .02
☐ 552 Jeff Blauser .05 .02 .01
☐ 553 Andujar Cedeno .05 .02 .01
☐ 554 Arthur Rhodes .05 .02 .01
☐ 555 Terry Mulholland .05 .02 .01
☐ 556 Darryl Hamilton .05 .02 .01
☐ 557 Pedro Martinez .15 .07 .02
☐ 558 Ryan Whitman and .10 .05 .01
Mark Skeels
☐ 559 Jamie Arnold .10 .05 .01
☐ 560 Zane Smith .05 .02 .01
☐ 561 Matt Nokes .05 .02 .01
☐ 562 Bob Zupcic .05 .02 .01
☐ 563 Shawn Boskie .05 .02 .01
☐ 564 Mike Timlin .05 .02 .01
☐ 565 Jerald Clark .05 .02 .01
☐ 566 Rod Brewer .05 .02 .01
☐ 567 Mark Carreon .05 .02 .01
☐ 568 Andy Benes .10 .05 .01
☐ 569 Shawn Barton .05 .02 .01
☐ 570 Tim Wallach .05 .02 .01
☐ 571 Dave Mlicki .05 .02 .01
☐ 572 Trevor Hoffman .15 .07 .02
☐ 573 John Patterson .05 .02 .01
☐ 574 De Shawn Warren .10 .05 .01
☐ 575 Monty Fariss .05 .02 .01
☐ 576 1993 Prospects .10 .05 .01
Darrell Sherman
Damon Buford
Cliff Floyd
Michael Moore
☐ 577 Tim Costo .05 .02 .01
☐ 578 Dave Magadan .05 .02 .01
☐ 579 Neil Garret and .10 .05 .01
Jason Bates
☐ 580 Walt Weiss .05 .02 .01
☐ 581 Chris Haney .05 .02 .01
☐ 582 Shawn Abner .05 .02 .01
☐ 583 Marvin Freeman .05 .02 .01
☐ 584 Casey Candaele .05 .02 .01
☐ 585 Ricky Jordan .05 .02 .01
☐ 586 Jeff Tabaka .05 .02 .01
☐ 587 Manny Alexander .05 .02 .01
☐ 588 Mike Trombley .05 .02 .01
☐ 589 Carlos Hernandez .05 .02 .01
☐ 590 Cal Eldred .05 .02 .01
☐ 591 Alex Cole .05 .02 .01
☐ 592 Phil Plantier .05 .02 .01
☐ 593 Brett Merriman .05 .02 .01
☐ 594 Jerry Nielsen .05 .02 .01
☐ 595 Shawon Dunston .05 .02 .01
☐ 596 Jimmy Key .10 .05 .01
☐ 597 Gerald Perry .05 .02 .01
☐ 598 Rico Brogna .10 .05 .01
☐ 599 Clemente Nunez and .10 .05 .01
Daniel Robinson
☐ 600 Bret Saberhagen .10 .05 .01
☐ 601 Craig Shipley .05 .02 .01
☐ 602 Henry Mercedes .05 .02 .01
☐ 603 Jim Thome 1.00 .45 .12
☐ 604 Rod Beck .10 .05 .01
☐ 605 Chuck Finley .05 .02 .01
☐ 606 J. Owens .10 .05 .01
☐ 607 Dan Smith .05 .02 .01
☐ 608 Bill Doran .05 .02 .01
☐ 609 Lance Parrish .05 .02 .01
☐ 610 Denny Martinez .10 .05 .01
☐ 611 Tom Gordon .05 .02 .01
☐ 612 Byron Mathews .05 .02 .01
☐ 613 Joel Adamson .05 .02 .01
☐ 614 Brian Williams .05 .02 .01
☐ 615 Steve Avery .10 .05 .01
☐ 616 1993 Prospects .15 .07 .02
Matt Mieske
Tracy Sanders
Midre Cummings
Ryan Freeburg
☐ 617 Craig Lefferts .05 .02 .01
☐ 618 Tony Pena .05 .02 .01
☐ 619 Billy Spiers .05 .02 .01
☐ 620 Todd Benzinger .05 .02 .01
☐ 621 Mike Kotarski and .10 .05 .01
Greg Boyd
☐ 622 Ben Rivera .05 .02 .01
☐ 623 Al Martin .10 .05 .01
☐ 624 Sam Militello UER .05 .02 .01
(Profile says drafted
in 1988, bio says
drafted in 1990)
☐ 625 Rick Aguilera .05 .02 .01
☐ 626 Dan Gladden .05 .02 .01
☐ 627 Andres Berumen .05 .02 .01
☐ 628 Kelly Gruber .05 .02 .01
☐ 629 Cris Carpenter .05 .02 .01
☐ 630 Mark Grace .15 .07 .02
☐ 631 Jeff Brantley .05 .02 .01
☐ 632 Chris Widger .05 .02 .01
☐ 633 Three Russians UER .10 .05 .01
Rudolf Razjigaev
Eugneyi Puchkov
Ilya Bogatyrev
Bogatyrev is a shortstop,
card has pitching header
☐ 634 Mo Sanford .05 .02 .01
☐ 635 Albert Belle .75 .35 .09
☐ 636 Tim Teufel .05 .02 .01
☐ 637 Greg Myers .05 .02 .01
☐ 638 Brian Bohanon .05 .02 .01
☐ 639 Mike Bordick .05 .02 .01
☐ 640 Dwight Gooden .10 .05 .01
☐ 641 Pat Leahy and .10 .05 .01
Gavin Baugh
☐ 642 Milt Hill .05 .02 .01
☐ 643 Luis Aquino .05 .02 .01
☐ 644 Dante Bichette .15 .07 .02
☐ 645 Bobby Thigpen .05 .02 .01
☐ 646 Rich Scheid .05 .02 .01
☐ 647 Brian Sackinsky .05 .02 .01
☐ 648 Ryan Hawblitzel .05 .02 .01
☐ 649 Tom Marsh .05 .02 .01
☐ 650 Terry Pendleton .10 .05 .01
☐ 651 Rafael Bournigal .05 .02 .01
☐ 652 Dave West .05 .02 .01
☐ 653 Steve Hosey .05 .02 .01
☐ 654 Gerald Williams .05 .02 .01
☐ 655 Scott Cooper .05 .02 .01
☐ 656 Gary Scott .05 .02 .01
☐ 657 Mike Harkey .05 .02 .01
☐ 658 1993 Prospects .10 .05 .01
Jeromy Burnitz
Melvin Nieves
Rich Becker
Shon Walker
☐ 659 Ed Sprague .10 .05 .01
☐ 660 Alan Trammell .15 .07 .02
☐ 661 Garvin Alston and .10 .05 .01
Michael Case
☐ 662 Donovan Osborne .05 .02 .01
☐ 663 Jeff Gardner .05 .02 .01
☐ 664 Calvin Jones .05 .02 .01
☐ 665 Darrin Fletcher .05 .02 .01
☐ 666 Glenallen Hill .05 .02 .01
☐ 667 Jim Rosenbohm .05 .02 .01
☐ 668 Scott Lewis .05 .02 .01
☐ 669 Kip Yaughn .05 .02 .01
☐ 670 Julio Franco .10 .05 .01
☐ 671 Dave Martinez .05 .02 .01
☐ 672 Kevin Bass .05 .02 .01
☐ 673 Todd Van Poppel .05 .02 .01
☐ 674 Mark Gubicza .05 .02 .01
☐ 675 Tim Raines .15 .07 .02
☐ 676 Rudy Seanez .05 .02 .01
☐ 677 Charlie Leibrandt .05 .02 .01
☐ 678 Randy Milligan .05 .02 .01
☐ 679 Kim Batiste .05 .02 .01
☐ 680 Craig Biggio .10 .05 .01
☐ 681 Darren Holmes .05 .02 .01
☐ 682 John Candelaria .05 .02 .01
☐ 683 Jerry Stafford and .10 .05 .01
Eddie Christian
☐ 684 Pat Mahomes .05 .02 .01
☐ 685 Bob Walk .05 .02 .01
☐ 686 Russ Springer .05 .02 .01
☐ 687 Tony Sheffield .05 .02 .01
☐ 688 Dwight Smith .05 .02 .01
☐ 689 Eddie Zosky .05 .02 .01
☐ 690 Bien Figueroa .05 .02 .01
☐ 691 Jim Tatum .05 .02 .01
☐ 692 Chad Kreuter .05 .02 .01
☐ 693 Rich Rodriguez .05 .02 .01
☐ 694 Shane Turner .05 .02 .01
☐ 695 Kent Bottenfield .05 .02 .01
☐ 696 Jose Mesa .10 .05 .01
☐ 697 Darrell Whitmore .05 .02 .01
☐ 698 Ted Wood .05 .02 .01
☐ 699 Chad Curtis .10 .05 .01
☐ 700 Nolan Ryan 1.50 .70 .19
☐ 701 1993 Prospects 2.00 .90 .25
Mike Piazza
Brook Fordyce
Carlos Delgado
Donnie Leshnock
☐ 702 Tim Pugh .05 .02 .01
☐ 703 Jeff Kent .10 .05 .01
☐ 704 Jon Goodrich and .10 .05 .01
Danny Figueroa
☐ 705 Bob Welch .05 .02 .01
☐ 706 Sherard Clinkscales .05 .02 .01
☐ 707 Donn Pall .05 .02 .01
☐ 708 Greg Olson .05 .02 .01
☐ 709 Jeff Juden .05 .02 .01
☐ 710 Mike Mussina .40 .18 .05
☐ 711 Scott Chiamparino .05 .02 .01
☐ 712 Stan Javier .05 .02 .01
☐ 713 John Doherty .05 .02 .01
☐ 714 Kevin Gross .05 .02 .01
☐ 715 Greg Gagne .05 .02 .01
☐ 716 Steve Cooke .05 .02 .01
☐ 717 Steve Farr .05 .02 .01
☐ 718 Jay Buhner .15 .07 .02
☐ 719 Butch Henry .05 .02 .01
☐ 720 David Cone .10 .05 .01
☐ 721 Rick Wilkins .05 .02 .01
☐ 722 Chuck Carr .05 .02 .01
☐ 723 Kenny Felder .05 .02 .01
☐ 724 Guillermo Velasquez .05 .02 .01
☐ 725 Billy Hatcher .05 .02 .01
☐ 726 Mike Veneziale and .10 .05 .01
Ken Kendrena
☐ 727 Jonathan Hurst .05 .02 .01
☐ 728 Steve Frey .05 .02 .01
☐ 729 Mark Leonard .05 .02 .01
☐ 730 Charles Nagy .10 .05 .01
☐ 731 Donald Harris .05 .02 .01
☐ 732 Travis Buckley .05 .02 .01
☐ 733 Tom Browning .05 .02 .01
☐ 734 Anthony Young .05 .02 .01
☐ 735 Steve Shifflett .05 .02 .01
☐ 736 Jeff Russell .05 .02 .01
☐ 737 Wilson Alvarez .10 .05 .01
☐ 738 Lance Painter .05 .02 .01
☐ 739 Dave Weathers .05 .02 .01
☐ 740 Len Dykstra .10 .05 .01
☐ 741 Mike Devereaux .05 .02 .01
☐ 742 1993 Prospects .10 .05 .01
Rene Arocha
Alan Embree
Brien Taylor
Tim Crabtree
☐ 743 Dave Landaker .05 .02 .01
☐ 744 Chris George .05 .02 .01
☐ 745 Eric Davis .10 .05 .01
☐ 746 Mark Strittmatter and .10 .05 .01
Lamarr Rogers
☐ 747 Carl Willis .05 .02 .01
☐ 748 Stan Belinda .05 .02 .01
☐ 749 Scott Kamieniecki .05 .02 .01
☐ 750 Rickey Henderson .15 .07 .02
☐ 751 Eric Hillman .05 .02 .01
☐ 752 Pat Hentgen .15 .07 .02
☐ 753 Jim Corsi .05 .02 .01
☐ 754 Brian Jordan .15 .07 .02
☐ 755 Bill Swift .05 .02 .01
☐ 756 Mike Henneman .05 .02 .01
☐ 757 Harold Reynolds .05 .02 .01
☐ 758 Sean Berry .05 .02 .01
☐ 759 Charlie Hayes .05 .02 .01
☐ 760 Luis Polonia .05 .02 .01
☐ 761 Darrin Jackson .05 .02 .01
☐ 762 Mark Lewis .05 .02 .01
☐ 763 Rob Maurer .05 .02 .01
☐ 764 Willie Greene .10 .05 .01
☐ 765 Vince Coleman .05 .02 .01
☐ 766 Todd Revenig .05 .02 .01
☐ 767 Rich Ireland .05 .02 .01
☐ 768 Mike Macfarlane .05 .02 .01
☐ 769 Francisco Cabrera .05 .02 .01
☐ 770 Robin Ventura .10 .05 .01
☐ 771 Kevin Ritz .05 .02 .01
☐ 772 Chito Martinez .05 .02 .01
☐ 773 Cliff Brantley .05 .02 .01
☐ 774 Curtis Leskanic .05 .02 .01
☐ 775 Chris Bosio .05 .02 .01
☐ 776 Jose Offerman .05 .02 .01
☐ 777 Mark Guthrie .05 .02 .01
☐ 778 Don Slaught .05 .02 .01
☐ 779 Rich Monteleone .05 .02 .01
☐ 780 Jim Abbott .05 .02 .01
☐ 781 Jack Clark .05 .02 .01
☐ 782 Reynol Mendoza and .10 .05 .01
Dan Roman
☐ 783 Heathcliff Slocumb .05 .02 .01
☐ 784 Jeff Branson .05 .02 .01
☐ 785 Kevin Brown .10 .05 .01
☐ 786 1993 Prospects .10 .05 .01
Mike Christopher
Ken Ryan
Aaron Taylor
Gus Gandarillas
☐ 787 Mike Matthews .10 .05 .01
☐ 788 Mackey Sasser .05 .02 .01
☐ 789 Jeff Conine UER .10 .05 .01
(No inclusion of 1990
stats in career total)
☐ 790 George Bell .05 .02 .01
☐ 791 Pat Rapp .10 .05 .01
☐ 792 Joe Boever .05 .02 .01
☐ 793 Jim Poole .05 .02 .01
☐ 794 Andy Ashby .10 .05 .01
☐ 795 Deion Sanders .15 .07 .02
☐ 796 Scott Brosius .05 .02 .01
☐ 797 Brad Pennington .05 .02 .01
☐ 798 Greg Blosser .05 .02 .01
☐ 799 Jim Edmonds 1.50 .70 .19
☐ 800 Shawn Jeter .05 .02 .01
☐ 801 Jesse Levis .05 .02 .01
☐ 802 Phil Clark UER .05 .02 .01
(Word "a" is missing in
sentence beginning
with "In 1992 ...")
☐ 803 Ed Pierce .05 .02 .01
☐ 804 Jose Valentin .30 .14 .04
☐ 805 Terry Jorgensen .05 .02 .01
☐ 806 Mark Hutton .05 .02 .01
☐ 807 Troy Neel .05 .02 .01
☐ 808 Bret Boone .10 .05 .01
☐ 809 Cris Colon .05 .02 .01
☐ 810 Domingo Martinez .05 .02 .01
☐ 811 Javier Lopez .50 .23 .06
☐ 812 Matt Walbeck .05 .02 .01
☐ 813 Dan Wilson .10 .05 .01
☐ 814 Scooter Tucker .05 .02 .01
☐ 815 Billy Ashley .05 .02 .01
☐ 816 Tim Laker .05 .02 .01
☐ 817 Bobby Jones .10 .05 .01
☐ 818 Brad Brink .05 .02 .01
☐ 819 William Pennyfeather .05 .02 .01
☐ 820 Stan Royer .05 .02 .01
☐ 821 Doug Brocail .05 .02 .01
☐ 822 Kevin Rogers .05 .02 .01

☐ 823 Checklist 397-540	.05	.02	.01
☐ 824 Checklist 541-691	.05	.02	.01
☐ 825 Checklist 692-825	.05	.02	.01

1993 Topps Gold

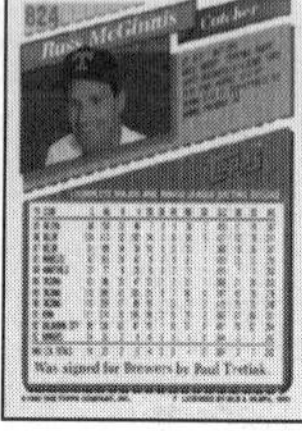

Several insertion schemes were devised for these 825 standard-size cards. Gold cards were inserted one per wax pack, three per rack pack, five per jumbo pack, and ten per factory set. The cards are identical to the regular-issue 1993 Topps baseball cards except that the gold-foil Topps Gold logo appears in an upper corner, and the team color-coded stripe at the bottom of the front, which carried the player's name, has been replaced with an embossed gold-foil stripe. The checklist cards (394-396, 823-825) have been replaced by player cards.

	MINT	NRMT	EXC
COMPLETE GOLD SET (825)	70.00	32.00	8.75
COMPLETE SERIES 1 (396)	40.00	18.00	5.00
COMPLETE SERIES 2 (429)	30.00	13.50	3.70
COMMON CARD (1G-825G)	.10	.05	.01

*STARS: 2X to 4X BASIC CARDS
*YOUNG STARS: 1.5X to 3X BASIC CARDS
*ROOKIES: 1.25X to 2.5X BASIC CARDS

☐ 394 Bernardo Brito Replaces Checklist 1	.25	.11	.03
☐ 395 Jim McNamara Replaces Checklist 2	.25	.11	.03
☐ 396 Rich Sauveur Replaces Checklist 3	.25	.11	.03
☐ 823 Keith Brown Replaces Checklist 4	.25	.11	.03
☐ 824 Russ McGinnis Replaces Checklist 5	.25	.11	.03
☐ 825 Mike Walker UER (Card has 1993 Mariner stats, should be 1992) Replaces Checklist 6	.25	.11	.03

1993 Topps Inaugural Marlins/Rockies

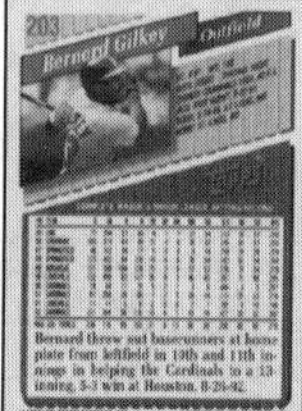

These 825-card standard-size sets were issued by Topps to commemorate the debut seasons of the Colorado Rockies and Florida Marlins. Gold foil Marlins or Rockies logos distinguish these from regular issue cards. These cards were only issued in factory set form. 5,000 Rockies sets and 4,000 Marlins sets were initially printed, but each team had the option of receiving a maximum of 10,000 sets. The Rockies sets were distributed through the four team-owned stores and at Mile High Stadium. The Marlins sets were distributed through FMI and Joe Robbie Stadium.

	MINT	NRMT	EXC
COMPLETE MARLINS FACT.SET (825)	150.00	70.00	19.00
COMPLETE ROCKIES FACT.SET (825)	120.00	55.00	15.00
COMMON CARD (1-825)	.15	.07	.02
COMMON ROCKIES	.30	.14	.04
COMMON MARLINS	.40	.18	.05

*STARS: 3X to 6X BASIC CARDS
*YOUNG STARS: 2X to 4X BASIC CARDS
*ROOKIES: 2X to 4X BASIC CARDS

1993 Topps Micro

This set was only issued in factory set form. It was issued as a 837 card set with the regular 825 card as well as a special 12 card prism insert set. The cards measure 1" by 1 3/8" which is approximately 40 percent of the regular card size. Only the Prism inserts are listed below. Please refer to the multiplier for values on the other other cards. This was the final year Topps issued the Micro factory set.

	MINT	NRMT	EXC
COMPLETE FACT. SET (837)	15.00	6.75	1.85
COMMON CARD (1-825)	.05	.02	.01
COMMON PRISM INSERT	.10	.05	.01

*MICRO: 2X BASIC CARDS

☐ P1 Robin Yount	.40	.18	.05
☐ P20 Tim Salmon	.30	.14	.04
☐ P32 Don Mattingly	.60	.25	.07
☐ P50 Roberto Alomar	.25	.11	.03
☐ P150 Frank Thomas	1.25	.55	.16
☐ P155 Dennis Eckersley	.25	.11	.03
☐ P179 Ken Griffey Jr.	1.25	.55	.16
☐ P200 Kirby Puckett	.60	.25	.07
☐ P397 George Brett	.50	.23	.06
☐ P426 Nigel Wilson	.10	.05	.01
☐ P444 David Nied	.10	.05	.01
☐ P700 Nolan Ryan	1.00	.45	.12

1993 Topps Black Gold

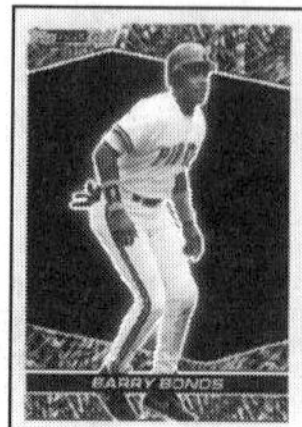

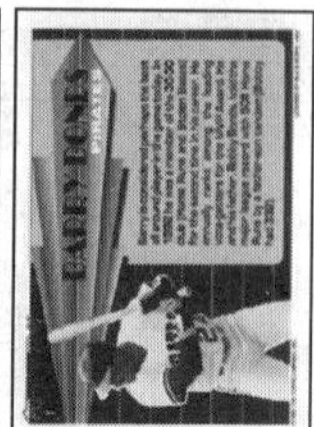

Topps Black Gold cards 1-22 were randomly inserted in series I wax packs while card numbers 23-44 were featured in series II packs. They were also inserted three per factory set. Hobbyists could obtain the set by collecting individual random insert cards or receive 11, 22, or 44 Black Gold cards by mail when they sent in special "You've Just Won" cards, which were randomly inserted in packs. Series I packs featured three different "You've Just Won" cards, entitling the holder to receive Group A (cards 1-11), Group B (cards 12-22), or Groups A and B (Cards 1-22). In a similar fashion, four "You've Just Won" cards were inserted in series II packs and entitled the holder to receive Group C (23-33), Group D (34-44), Groups C and D (23-44), or Groups A-D (1-44). By returning the "You've Just Won" card with 1.50 for postage and handling, the collector received not only the Black Gold cards won but also a special "You've Just Won" card and a congratulatory letter informing the collector that his/her name has been entered into a drawing for one of 500 uncut sheets of all 44 Topps Black Gold cards in a leatherette frame. These standard-size cards feature different color player photos than either the 1993 Topps regular issue or the Topps Gold issue. The player pictures are cut out and superimposed on a black gloss background. Inside white borders, gold refractory foil edges the top and bottom of the card face. On a black-and-gray pinstripe pattern inside white borders, the horizontal backs have a a second cut out player photo and a player profile on a blue panel. The player's name appears in gold foil lettering on a blue-and-gray geometric shape. The first 22 cards are National Leaguers while the second 22 cards are American Leaguers. Winner cards C and D were both originally produced erroneously and later corrected; the error versions show the players from Winner A and B on the respective fronts of Winner cards C and D. There is no value difference in the variations at this time. The winner cards were redeemable until January 31, 1994.

	MINT	NRMT	EXC
COMPLETE SET (44)	10.00	4.50	1.25
COMPLETE SERIES 1 (22)	4.00	1.80	.50
COMPLETE SERIES 2 (22)	6.00	2.70	.75
COMMON CARD (1-44)	.10	.05	.01

☐ 1 Barry Bonds	.75	.35	.09
☐ 2 Will Clark	.50	.23	.06
☐ 3 Darren Daulton	.25	.11	.03
☐ 4 Andre Dawson	.25	.11	.03
☐ 5 Delino DeShields	.25	.11	.03
☐ 6 Tom Glavine	.50	.23	.06
☐ 7 Marquis Grissom	.25	.11	.03
☐ 8 Tony Gwynn	1.25	.55	.16
☐ 9 Eric Karros	.50	.23	.06
☐ 10 Ray Lankford	.25	.11	.03
☐ 11 Barry Larkin	.50	.23	.06
☐ 12 Greg Maddux	2.00	.90	.25
☐ 13 Fred McGriff	.50	.23	.06
☐ 14 Joe Oliver	.10	.05	.01
☐ 15 Terry Pendleton	.25	.11	.03
☐ 16 Bip Roberts	.25	.11	.03
☐ 17 Ryne Sandberg	.75	.35	.09
☐ 18 Gary Sheffield	.50	.23	.06
☐ 19 Lee Smith	.25	.11	.03
☐ 20 Ozzie Smith	.75	.35	.09
☐ 21 Andy Van Slyke	.10	.05	.01
☐ 22 Larry Walker	.50	.23	.06
☐ 23 Roberto Alomar	.60	.25	.07
☐ 24 Brady Anderson	.50	.23	.06
☐ 25 Carlos Baerga	.25	.11	.03
☐ 26 Joe Carter	.25	.11	.03
☐ 27 Roger Clemens	.60	.25	.07
☐ 28 Mike Devereaux	.10	.05	.01
☐ 29 Dennis Eckersley	.25	.11	.03
☐ 30 Cecil Fielder	.25	.11	.03
☐ 31 Travis Fryman	.25	.11	.03
☐ 32 Juan Gonzalez UER (No copyright or licensing on card)	1.50	.70	.19
☐ 33 Ken Griffey Jr.	3.00	1.35	.35
☐ 34 Brian Harper	.10	.05	.01
☐ 35 Pat Listach	.10	.05	.01
☐ 36 Kenny Lofton	1.25	.55	.16
☐ 37 Edgar Martinez	.25	.11	.03
☐ 38 Jack McDowell	.50	.23	.06
☐ 39 Mark McGwire	1.00	.45	.12
☐ 40 Kirby Puckett	1.25	.55	.16
☐ 41 Mickey Tettleton	.25	.11	.03
☐ 42 Frank Thomas UER (No copyright or licensing on card)	3.00	1.35	.35
☐ 43 Robin Ventura	.25	.11	.03
☐ 44 Dave Winfield	.50	.23	.06
☐ A Winner A 1-11	.50	.23	.06
☐ B Winner B 12-22	.50	.23	.06
☐ C Winner C 23-33	.75	.35	.09
☐ D Winner D 34-44	.75	.35	.09
☐ AB Winner AB 1-22 UER (Numbers 10 and 11 have the 1 missing)	1.00	.45	.12
☐ CD Winner C/D 23-44	1.50	.70	.19
☐ ABCD Winner ABCD 1-44	2.50	1.10	.30

1993 Topps Traded

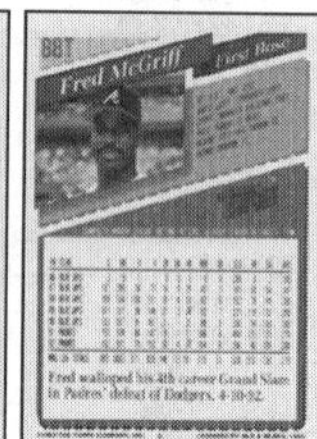

This 132-card standard-size set focuses on promising rookies, new managers, free agents, and players who changed teams. The set also includes 22 members of Team USA. The set has the same design on the front as the regular 1993 Topps issue. The backs are also the same design and carry a head shot, biography, stats, and career highlights. Rookie Cards in this set include Matt Beaumont, Todd Helton, Dante Powell, Todd Walker and Paul Wilson.

	MINT	NRMT	EXC
COMPLETE FACT.SET (132)	15.00	6.75	1.85
COMMON CARD (1T-132T)	.05	.02	.01

☐ 1T Barry Bonds	.50	.23	.06
☐ 2T Rich Renteria	.05	.02	.01
☐ 3T Aaron Sele	.15	.07	.02
☐ 4T Carlton Loewer USA	.15	.07	.02
☐ 5T Erik Pappas	.05	.02	.01
☐ 6T Greg McMichael	.15	.07	.02
☐ 7T Freddie Benavides	.05	.02	.01
☐ 8T Kirk Gibson	.15	.07	.02
☐ 9T Tony Fernandez	.05	.02	.01
☐ 10T Jay Gainer	.05	.02	.01
☐ 11T Orestes Destrade	.05	.02	.01
☐ 12T A.J. Hinch USA	.50	.23	.06
☐ 13T Bobby Munoz	.05	.02	.01
☐ 14T Tom Henke	.05	.02	.01
☐ 15T Rob Butler	.05	.02	.01
☐ 16T Gary Wayne	.05	.02	.01
☐ 17T David McCarty	.05	.02	.01
☐ 18T Walt Weiss	.05	.02	.01
☐ 19T Todd Helton USA	3.00	1.35	.35
☐ 20T Mark Whiten	.05	.02	.01
☐ 21T Ricky Gutierrez	.05	.02	.01
☐ 22T Dustin Hermanson USA	.40	.18	.05
☐ 23T Sherman Obando	.05	.02	.01
☐ 24T Mike Piazza	2.00	.90	.25
☐ 25T Jeff Russell	.05	.02	.01
☐ 26T Jason Bere	.15	.07	.02
☐ 27T Jack Voigt	.05	.02	.01
☐ 28T Chris Bosio	.05	.02	.01
☐ 29T Phil Hiatt	.05	.02	.01
☐ 30T Matt Beaumont USA	.40	.18	.05
☐ 31T Andres Galarraga	.30	.14	.04
☐ 32T Greg Swindell	.05	.02	.01
☐ 33T Vinny Castilla	.30	.14	.04
☐ 34T Pat Clougherty USA	.05	.02	.01
☐ 35T Greg Briley	.05	.02	.01
☐ 36T Dallas Green MG Davey Johnson MG	.05	.02	.01
☐ 37T Tyler Green	.05	.02	.01
☐ 38T Craig Paquette	.05	.02	.01
☐ 39T Danny Sheaffer	.05	.02	.01
☐ 40T Jim Converse	.05	.02	.01
☐ 41T Terry Harvey USA	.05	.02	.01
☐ 42T Phil Plantier	.05	.02	.01
☐ 43T Doug Saunders	.05	.02	.01
☐ 44T Benny Santiago	.05	.02	.01
☐ 45T Dante Powell USA	1.50	.70	.19
☐ 46T Jeff Parrett	.05	.02	.01
☐ 47T Wade Boggs	.30	.14	.04
☐ 48T Paul Molitor	.40	.18	.05
☐ 49T Turk Wendell	.05	.02	.01
☐ 50T David Wells	.05	.02	.01
☐ 51T Gary Sheffield	.30	.14	.04
☐ 52T Kevin Young	.05	.02	.01
☐ 53T Nelson Liriano	.05	.02	.01
☐ 54T Greg Maddux	1.25	.55	.16
☐ 55T Derek Bell	.15	.07	.02
☐ 56T Matt Turner	.05	.02	.01
☐ 57T Charlie Nelson USA	.05	.02	.01
☐ 58T Mike Hampton	.30	.14	.04
☐ 59T Troy O'Leary	.30	.14	.04
☐ 60T Benji Gil	.15	.07	.02
☐ 61T Mitch Lyden	.05	.02	.01
☐ 62T J.T. Snow	.30	.14	.04
☐ 63T Damon Buford	.05	.02	.01
☐ 64T Gene Harris	.05	.02	.01
☐ 65T Randy Myers	.15	.07	.02
☐ 66T Felix Jose	.05	.02	.01
☐ 67T Todd Dunn USA	.15	.07	.02
☐ 68T Jimmy Key	.15	.07	.02
☐ 69T Pedro Castellano	.05	.02	.01
☐ 70T Mark Merila USA	.15	.07	.02
☐ 71T Rich Rodriguez	.05	.02	.01
☐ 72T Matt Mieske	.15	.07	.02
☐ 73T Pete Incaviglia	.05	.02	.01
☐ 74T Carl Everett	.15	.07	.02
☐ 75T Jim Abbott	.05	.02	.01
☐ 76T Luis Aquino	.05	.02	.01
☐ 77T Rene Arocha	.05	.02	.01
☐ 78T Jon Shave	.05	.02	.01
☐ 79T Todd Walker USA	4.00	1.80	.50
☐ 80T Jack Armstrong	.05	.02	.01
☐ 81T Jeff Richardson	.05	.02	.01
☐ 82T Blas Minor	.05	.02	.01
☐ 83T Dave Winfield	.30	.14	.04
☐ 84T Paul O'Neill	.15	.07	.02
☐ 85T Steve Reich USA	.05	.02	.01
☐ 86T Chris Hammond	.05	.02	.01
☐ 87T Hilly Hathaway	.05	.02	.01
☐ 88T Fred McGriff	.30	.14	.04
☐ 89T Dave Telgheder	.05	.02	.01
☐ 90T Richie Lewis	.05	.02	.01
☐ 91T Brent Gates	.15	.07	.02
☐ 92T Andre Dawson	.15	.07	.02
☐ 93T Andy Barkett USA	.15	.07	.02
☐ 94T Doug Drabek	.05	.02	.01
☐ 95T Joe Klink	.05	.02	.01
☐ 96T Willie Blair	.05	.02	.01
☐ 97T Danny Graves USA	.30	.14	.04
☐ 98T Pat Meares	.15	.07	.02
☐ 99T Mike Lansing	.15	.07	.02
☐ 100T Marcos Armas	.05	.02	.01
☐ 101T Darren Grass USA	.05	.02	.01
☐ 102T Chris Jones	.05	.02	.01
☐ 103T Ken Ryan	.05	.02	.01
☐ 104T Ellis Burks	.15	.07	.02
☐ 105T Roberto Kelly	.05	.02	.01
☐ 106T Dave Magadan	.05	.02	.01
☐ 107T Paul Wilson USA	1.00	.45	.12
☐ 108T Rob Natal	.05	.02	.01
☐ 109T Paul Wagner	.05	.02	.01
☐ 110T Jeromy Burnitz	.05	.02	.01
☐ 111T Monty Fariss	.05	.02	.01
☐ 112T Kevin Mitchell	.15	.07	.02
☐ 113T Scott Pose	.05	.02	.01
☐ 114T Dave Stewart	.15	.07	.02
☐ 115T Russ Johnson USA	.75	.35	.09
☐ 116T Armando Reynoso	.05	.02	.01
☐ 117T Geronimo Berroa	.15	.07	.02
☐ 118T Woody Williams	.05	.02	.01
☐ 119T Tim Bogar	.05	.02	.01
☐ 120T Bob Scafa USA	.05	.02	.01
☐ 121T Henry Cotto	.05	.02	.01
☐ 122T Gregg Jefferies	.15	.07	.02
☐ 123T Norm Charlton	.05	.02	.01
☐ 124T Bret Wagner USA	.40	.18	.05
☐ 125T David Cone	.15	.07	.02
☐ 126T Daryl Boston	.05	.02	.01
☐ 127T Tim Wallach	.05	.02	.01
☐ 128T Mike Martin USA	.15	.07	.02
☐ 129T John Cummings	.05	.02	.01
☐ 130T Ryan Bowen	.05	.02	.01
☐ 131T John Powell USA	.15	.07	.02
☐ 132T Checklist 1-132	.05	.02	.01

1993 Topps Commanders of the Hill

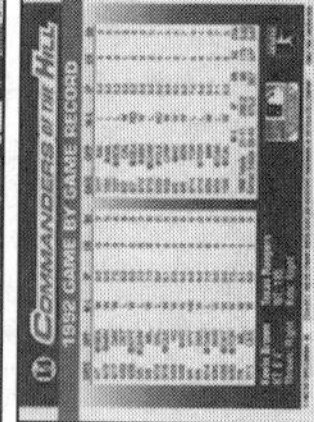

This 30-card set issued by Topps features pitchers of the American and National Leagues. The cards were available individually at commissary on military bases. The standard-size fronts display an action photo with a camouflage design border. The team name is printed vertically along the left edge in brown and outlined in yellow. A banner across the bottom of the picture carries the player's name and his achievement. The horizontal red, white and blue backs carry biography and 1992 game statistics.

	MINT	NRMT	EXC
COMPLETE SET (30)	12.00	5.50	1.50
COMMON CARD (1-30)	.10	.05	.01

☐ 1 Dennis Eckersley	.40	.18	.05
☐ 2 Mike Mussina	1.00	.45	.12
☐ 3 Roger Clemens	1.00	.45	.12
☐ 4 Jim Abbott	.10	.05	.01
☐ 5 Jack McDowell	.25	.11	.03
☐ 6 Charles Nagy	.40	.18	.05
☐ 7 Bill Gullickson	.10	.05	.01
☐ 8 Kevin Appier	.40	.18	.05
☐ 9 Bill Wegman	.10	.05	.01
☐ 10 John Smiley	.10	.05	.01
☐ 11 Melido Perez	.10	.05	.01
☐ 12 Dave Stewart	.10	.05	.01
☐ 13 Dave Fleming	.10	.05	.01
☐ 14 Kevin Brown	.40	.18	.05
☐ 15 Juan Guzman	.25	.11	.03
☐ 16 Randy Johnson	.60	.25	.07
☐ 17 Greg Maddux	4.00	1.80	.50
☐ 18 Tom Glavine	.50	.23	.06
☐ 19 Greg Maddux	4.00	1.80	.50
☐ 20 Jose Rijo	.10	.05	.01
☐ 21 Pete Harnisch	.10	.05	.01
☐ 22 Tom Candiotti	.10	.05	.01
☐ 23 Denny Martinez	.25	.11	.03
☐ 24 Sid Fernandez	.10	.05	.01
☐ 25 Curt Schilling	.10	.05	.01
☐ 26 Doug Drabek	.10	.05	.01
☐ 27 Bob Tewksbury	.10	.05	.01
☐ 28 Andy Benes	.25	.11	.03
☐ 29 Bill Swift	.10	.05	.01
☐ 30 John Smoltz	.60	.25	.07

1993 Topps Full Shots

Issued as one-card inserts in retail re-packs containing a pack each of 1993 Topps Series I and II, and in specially marked jumbo boxes of 1993 Bowman, these 21 cards measure approximately 3 1/2" by 5" and feature on their fronts white-bordered color player action photos. The player's name appears in tan lettering at the top, his team name is printed vertically up one side in ghosted white lettering, and the set's name and logo also appear. The back carries another color player photo, with the player's name and position appearing in white lettering at the top within a brown stripe. The player's team name is shown at the bottom of the picture and below is the player's biography and stats. The set's name and logo round out the back. The cards are numbered on the back. In contrast to many of the oversized cards offered by other baseball card manufacturers, Full Shots were unique cards rather than enlarged versions of existing cards.

	MINT	NRMT	EXC
COMPLETE SET (21)	50.00	22.00	6.25
COMMON CARD (1-21)	.50	.23	.06
☐ 1 Frank Thomas	10.00	4.50	1.25
☐ 2 Ken Griffey Jr.	10.00	4.50	1.25
☐ 3 Barry Bonds	2.50	1.10	.30
☐ 4 Juan Gonzalez	5.00	2.20	.60
☐ 5 Roberto Alomar	2.50	1.10	.30
☐ 6 Mike Piazza	10.00	4.50	1.25
☐ 7 Tony Gwynn	5.00	2.20	.60
☐ 8 Jeff Bagwell	4.00	1.80	.50
☐ 9 Tim Salmon	2.50	1.10	.30
☐ 10 John Olerud	.50	.23	.06
☐ 11 Cal Ripken	8.00	3.60	1.00
☐ 12 David McCarty	.50	.23	.06
☐ 13 Darren Daulton	1.00	.45	.12
☐ 14 Carlos Baerga	1.00	.45	.12
☐ 15 Roger Clemens	2.50	1.10	.30
☐ 16 John Kruk	.50	.23	.06
☐ 17 Barry Larkin	1.50	.70	.19
☐ 18 Gary Sheffield	2.00	.90	.25
☐ 19 Tom Glavine	1.50	.70	.19
☐ 20 Andres Galarraga	1.50	.70	.19
☐ 21 Fred McGriff	1.50	.70	.19

1993 Topps Magazine Jumbo Rookie Cards

This set was inserted in the last four issues of Topps Magazine. When removed from the magazine the cards measure 5" by 7". The players featured autographed 100 of these cards: 50 for subscriber copies and 50 for newstand issues. The cards are all reprinted version of earlier Topps cards. The original Rookie Card year is noted after the player's name

	MINT	NRMT	EXC
COMPLETE SET (4)	5.00	2.20	.60
COMMON CARD (1-4)	.50	.23	.06
☐ 1 Dennis Eckersley 1976	.50	.23	.06
☐ 2 Dave Winfield 1974	1.00	.45	.12
☐ 3 George Brett 1975	1.50	.70	.19
☐ 4 Nolan Ryan 1968	3.00	1.35	.35

1993 Topps Nikon House

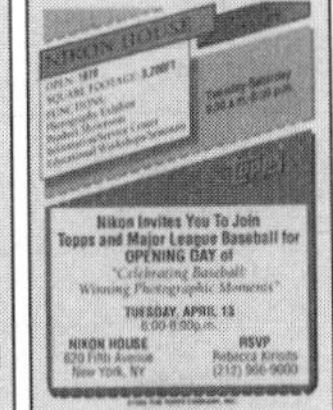

This one-card set commemorates the opening day of the Celebrating Baseball photographic show at Nikon House Photo Gallery on April 13, 1993. The front features a photo of a baseball player batting inside a baseball park. The back displays information about the photo gallery and the Baseball photo show.

	MINT	NRMT	EXC
COMPLETE SET (1)	3.00	1.35	.35
COMMON CARD (1)	3.00	1.35	.35
☐ 1 Batter in Major League Park	3.00	1.35	.35

1993 Topps Postcards

This three-card set is a promotional issue produced by Topps and features a preview of the cards in the 1993 regular Topps set as well as Topps Stadium Club Series II and Series III. Each card displays three different card fronts from the same set. The backs have a postcard format. The cards are unnumbered.

	MINT	NRMT	EXC
COMPLETE SET (3)	10.00	4.50	1.25
COMMON CARD (1-3)	3.00	1.35	.35
☐ 1 Topps Regular Issue Ryne Sandberg Robin Ventura Frank Thomas	4.00	1.80	.50
☐ 2 Topps Stadium Club Walt Weiss Alex Cole Benny Santiago	3.00	1.35	.35
☐ 3 Topps Stadium Club Benny Santiago Walt Weiss Alex Cole	3.00	1.35	.35

1994 Topps Pre-Production

This nine-card standard-size set was issued by Topps for hobby dealers to preview the 1994 Topps regular-issue series. The cards feature glossy color player photos with white borders on the fronts. The player's name is in white cursive lettering at the bottom left, with the team name and player's position printed on a team color-coded bar. There is an inner multi-colored border along the left side that extends obliquely across the bottom. The horizontal backs carry an action shot of the player with biography, statistics, and highlights. The back of each card is identical to the player's regular issue 1994 Topps card back except for a diagonal white box across the statistics stating "PRE-PRODUCTION SAMPLE Design and Photo Selection Subject To Change." These cards were also issued in some of the 1993 Topps factory sets. The factory set versions are worth about the same as the hobby versions. There is both a horizontal and vertical version of Ryan.

	MINT	NRMT	EXC
COMPLETE SET (9)	7.00	3.10	.85
COMMON CARD	.25	.11	.03
☐ 2 Barry Bonds	.75	.35	.09
☐ 6 Jeff Tackett	.25	.11	.03
☐ 34 Juan Gonzalez	1.50	.70	.19
☐ 225 Matt Williams	.50	.23	.06
☐ 294 Carlos Quintana	.25	.11	.03
☐ 331 Kenny Lofton	.75	.35	.09
☐ 390 Wade Boggs	.50	.23	.06
☐ 397 George Brett	1.25	.55	.16
☐ 700 Nolan Ryan	3.00	1.35	.35

1994 Topps

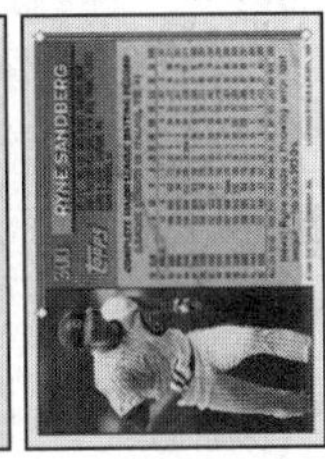

These 792 standard-size cards were issued in two series of 396. Two types of factory sets were also issued. One features the 792 basic cards, ten Topps Gold, three Black Gold and three Finest Pre-Production cards for a total of 808. The other factory set (Bakers Dozen) includes the 792 basic cards, ten Topps Gold, three Black Gold, ten 1995 Topps Pre-Production cards and a sample pack of three special Topps cards for a total of 818. The standard cards feature glossy color player photos with white borders on the fronts. The player's name is in white cursive lettering at the bottom left, with the team name and player's position printed on a team color-coded bar. There is an inner multicolored border along the left side that extends obliquely across the bottom. The horizontal backs carry an action shot of the player with biography, statistics and highlights. Subsets include Draft Picks (201-210/739-762), All-Stars (384-394) and Stat Twins (601-609). Rookie Cards include Alan Benes, Jeff D'Amico, Brooks Kieschnick, Kirk Presley and Pat Watkins.

	MINT	NRMT	EXC
COMPLETE SET (792)	30.00	13.50	3.70
COMP.FACT.SET (808)	50.00	22.00	6.25
COMP.BAKER.FACT.SET (818)	50.00	22.00	6.25
COMPLETE SERIES 1 (396)	15.00	6.75	1.85
COMPLETE SERIES 2 (396)	15.00	6.75	1.85
COMMON CARD (1-792)	.05	.02	.01
☐ 1 Mike Piazza	1.25	.55	.16
☐ 2 Bernie Williams	.40	.18	.05
☐ 3 Kevin Rogers	.05	.02	.01
☐ 4 Paul Carey	.05	.02	.01
☐ 5 Ozzie Guillen	.05	.02	.01
☐ 6 Derrick May	.05	.02	.01
☐ 7 Jose Mesa	.15	.07	.02
☐ 8 Todd Hundley	.15	.07	.02
☐ 9 Chris Haney	.05	.02	.01
☐ 10 John Olerud	.05	.02	.01
☐ 11 Andujar Cedeno	.05	.02	.01
☐ 12 John Smiley	.05	.02	.01
☐ 13 Phil Plantier	.05	.02	.01
☐ 14 Willie Banks	.05	.02	.01
☐ 15 Jay Bell	.15	.07	.02
☐ 16 Doug Henry	.05	.02	.01
☐ 17 Lance Blankenship	.05	.02	.01
☐ 18 Greg W. Harris	.05	.02	.01
☐ 19 Scott Livingstone	.05	.02	.01
☐ 20 Bryan Harvey	.05	.02	.01
☐ 21 Wil Cordero	.15	.07	.02
☐ 22 Roger Pavlik	.05	.02	.01
☐ 23 Mark Lemke	.05	.02	.01
☐ 24 Jeff Nelson	.05	.02	.01
☐ 25 Todd Zeile	.05	.02	.01
☐ 26 Billy Hatcher	.05	.02	.01
☐ 27 Joe Magrane	.05	.02	.01
☐ 28 Tony Longmire	.05	.02	.01
☐ 29 Omar Daal	.05	.02	.01
☐ 30 Kirt Manwaring	.05	.02	.01
☐ 31 Melido Perez	.05	.02	.01
☐ 32 Tim Hulett	.05	.02	.01
☐ 33 Jeff Schwartz	.05	.02	.01
☐ 34 Nolan Ryan	1.50	.70	.19
☐ 35 Jose Guzman	.05	.02	.01
☐ 36 Felix Fermin	.05	.02	.01
☐ 37 Jeff Innis	.05	.02	.01
☐ 38 Brett Mayne	.05	.02	.01
☐ 39 Huck Flener	.05	.02	.01
☐ 40 Jeff Bagwell	.75	.35	.09
☐ 41 Kevin Wickander	.05	.02	.01
☐ 42 Ricky Gutierrez	.05	.02	.01
☐ 43 Pat Mahomes	.05	.02	.01
☐ 44 Jeff King	.15	.07	.02
☐ 45 Cal Eldred	.05	.02	.01
☐ 46 Craig Paquette	.05	.02	.01
☐ 47 Richie Lewis	.05	.02	.01
☐ 48 Tony Phillips	.15	.07	.02
☐ 49 Armando Reynoso	.05	.02	.01
☐ 50 Moises Alou	.15	.07	.02
☐ 51 Manuel Lee	.05	.02	.01
☐ 52 Otis Nixon	.05	.02	.01
☐ 53 Billy Ashley	.05	.02	.01
☐ 54 Mark Whiten	.05	.02	.01
☐ 55 Jeff Russell	.05	.02	.01
☐ 56 Chad Curtis	.05	.02	.01
☐ 57 Kevin Stocker	.05	.02	.01
☐ 58 Mike Jackson	.05	.02	.01
☐ 59 Matt Nokes	.05	.02	.01
☐ 60 Chris Bosio	.05	.02	.01
☐ 61 Damon Buford	.05	.02	.01
☐ 62 Tim Belcher	.05	.02	.01
☐ 63 Glenallen Hill	.05	.02	.01
☐ 64 Bill Wertz	.05	.02	.01
☐ 65 Eddie Murray	.50	.23	.06
☐ 66 Tom Gordon	.05	.02	.01
☐ 67 Alex Gonzalez	.15	.07	.02
☐ 68 Eddie Taubensee	.05	.02	.01
☐ 69 Jacob Brumfield	.05	.02	.01
☐ 70 Andy Benes	.15	.07	.02
☐ 71 Rich Becker	.15	.07	.02
☐ 72 Steve Cooke	.05	.02	.01
☐ 73 Billy Spiers	.05	.02	.01
☐ 74 Scott Brosius	.05	.02	.01
☐ 75 Alan Trammell	.15	.07	.02
☐ 76 Luis Aquino	.05	.02	.01
☐ 77 Jerald Clark	.05	.02	.01
☐ 78 Mel Rojas	.05	.02	.01
☐ 79 Outfield Prospects Billy Masse Stanton Cameron Tim Clark Craig McClure	.30	.14	.04
☐ 80 Jose Canseco	.30	.14	.04
☐ 81 Greg McMichael	.05	.02	.01
☐ 82 Brian Turang	.05	.02	.01
☐ 83 Tom Urbani	.05	.02	.01
☐ 84 Garret Anderson	.30	.14	.04
☐ 85 Tony Pena	.05	.02	.01
☐ 86 Ricky Jordan	.05	.02	.01
☐ 87 Jim Gott	.05	.02	.01
☐ 88 Pat Kelly	.05	.02	.01
☐ 89 Bud Black	.05	.02	.01
☐ 90 Robin Ventura	.15	.07	.02
☐ 91 Rick Sutcliffe	.05	.02	.01
☐ 92 Jose Bautista	.05	.02	.01
☐ 93 Bob Ojeda	.05	.02	.01
☐ 94 Phil Hiatt	.05	.02	.01
☐ 95 Tim Pugh	.05	.02	.01
☐ 96 Randy Knorr	.05	.02	.01
☐ 97 Todd Jones	.05	.02	.01
☐ 98 Ryan Thompson	.05	.02	.01
☐ 99 Tim Mauser	.05	.02	.01
☐ 100 Kirby Puckett	.75	.35	.09
☐ 101 Mark Dewey	.05	.02	.01
☐ 102 B.J. Surhoff	.05	.02	.01
☐ 103 Sterling Hitchcock	.15	.07	.02
☐ 104 Alex Arias	.05	.02	.01
☐ 105 David Wells	.05	.02	.01
☐ 106 Daryl Boston	.05	.02	.01
☐ 107 Mike Stanton	.05	.02	.01
☐ 108 Gary Redus	.05	.02	.01
☐ 109 Delino DeShields	.05	.02	.01
☐ 110 Lee Smith	.15	.07	.02
☐ 111 Greg Litton	.05	.02	.01
☐ 112 Frankie Rodriguez	.15	.07	.02
☐ 113 Russ Springer	.05	.02	.01
☐ 114 Mitch Williams	.05	.02	.01
☐ 115 Eric Karros	.15	.07	.02
☐ 116 Jeff Brantley	.05	.02	.01
☐ 117 Jack Voigt	.05	.02	.01
☐ 118 Jason Bere	.15	.07	.02
☐ 119 Kevin Roberson	.05	.02	.01
☐ 120 Jimmy Key	.15	.07	.02
☐ 121 Reggie Jefferson	.15	.07	.02
☐ 122 Jeromy Burnitz	.05	.02	.01
☐ 123 Billy Brewer	.05	.02	.01
☐ 124 Willie Canate	.05	.02	.01
☐ 125 Greg Swindell	.05	.02	.01
☐ 126 Hal Morris	.05	.02	.01
☐ 127 Brad Ausmus	.05	.02	.01
☐ 128 George Tsamis	.05	.02	.01
☐ 129 Denny Neagle	.15	.07	.02
☐ 130 Pat Listach	.05	.02	.01
☐ 131 Steve Karsay	.05	.02	.01
☐ 132 Bret Barberie	.05	.02	.01
☐ 133 Mark Leiter	.05	.02	.01
☐ 134 Greg Colbrunn	.05	.02	.01
☐ 135 David Nied	.05	.02	.01
☐ 136 Dean Palmer	.15	.07	.02
☐ 137 Steve Avery	.15	.07	.02
☐ 138 Bill Haselman	.05	.02	.01
☐ 139 Tripp Cromer	.05	.02	.01
☐ 140 Frank Viola	.05	.02	.01
☐ 141 Rene Gonzales	.05	.02	.01
☐ 142 Curt Schilling	.05	.02	.01
☐ 143 Tim Wallach	.05	.02	.01
☐ 144 Bobby Munoz	.05	.02	.01
☐ 145 Brady Anderson	.30	.14	.04
☐ 146 Rod Beck	.15	.07	.02
☐ 147 Mike LaValliere	.05	.02	.01
☐ 148 Greg Hibbard	.05	.02	.01
☐ 149 Kenny Lofton	.60	.25	.07
☐ 150 Doc Gooden	.15	.07	.02
☐ 151 Greg Gagne	.05	.02	.01
☐ 152 Ray McDavid	.15	.07	.02
☐ 153 Chris Donnels	.05	.02	.01
☐ 154 Dan Wilson	.15	.07	.02
☐ 155 Todd Stottlemyre	.05	.02	.01
☐ 156 David McCarty	.05	.02	.01
☐ 157 Paul Wagner	.05	.02	.01
☐ 158 Shortstop Prospects Orlando Miller Brandon Wilson Derek Jeter Mike Neal	1.50	.70	.19
☐ 159 Mike Fetters	.05	.02	.01
☐ 160 Scott Lydy	.05	.02	.01
☐ 161 Darrell Whitmore	.05	.02	.01
☐ 162 Bob MacDonald	.05	.02	.01

☐ 163 Vinny Castilla .30 .14 .04
☐ 164 Denis Boucher .05 .02 .01
☐ 165 Ivan Rodriguez .50 .23 .06
☐ 166 Ron Gant .15 .07 .02
☐ 167 Tim Davis .05 .02 .01
☐ 168 Steve Dixon .05 .02 .01
☐ 169 Scott Fletcher .05 .02 .01
☐ 170 Terry Mulholland .05 .02 .01
☐ 171 Greg Myers .05 .02 .01
☐ 172 Brett Butler .15 .07 .02
☐ 173 Bob Wickman .05 .02 .01
☐ 174 Dave Martinez .05 .02 .01
☐ 175 Fernando Valenzuela .15 .07 .02
☐ 176 Craig Grebeck .05 .02 .01
☐ 177 Shawn Boskie .05 .02 .01
☐ 178 Albie Lopez .15 .07 .02
☐ 179 Butch Huskey .15 .07 .02
☐ 180 George Brett .75 .35 .09
☐ 181 Juan Guzman .15 .07 .02
☐ 182 Eric Anthony .05 .02 .01
☐ 183 Rob Dibble .05 .02 .01
☐ 184 Craig Shipley .05 .02 .01
☐ 185 Kevin Tapani .05 .02 .01
☐ 186 Marcus Moore .05 .02 .01
☐ 187 Graeme Lloyd .05 .02 .01
☐ 188 Mike Bordick .05 .02 .01
☐ 189 Chris Hammond .05 .02 .01
☐ 190 Cecil Fielder .15 .07 .02
☐ 191 Curtis Leskanic .15 .07 .02
☐ 192 Lou Frazier .05 .02 .01
☐ 193 Steve Dreyer .05 .02 .01
☐ 194 Javier Lopez .30 .14 .04
☐ 195 Edgar Martinez .15 .07 .02
☐ 196 Allen Watson .05 .02 .01
☐ 197 John Flaherty .05 .02 .01
☐ 198 Kurt Stillwell .05 .02 .01
☐ 199 Danny Jackson .05 .02 .01
☐ 200 Cal Ripken 1.50 .70 .19
☐ 201 Mike Bell FDP .40 .18 .05
☐ 202 Alan Benes FDP .75 .35 .09
☐ 203 Matt Farner FDP .15 .07 .02
☐ 204 Jeff Granger FDP .15 .07 .02
☐ 205 Brooks Kieschnick FDP .40 .18 .05
☐ 206 Jeremy Lee FDP .25 .11 .03
☐ 207 Charles Peterson FDP .30 .14 .04
☐ 208 Alan Rice FDP .15 .07 .02
☐ 209 Billy Wagner FDP .60 .25 .07
☐ 210 Kelly Wunsch FDP .15 .07 .02
☐ 211 Tom Candiotti .05 .02 .01
☐ 212 Domingo Jean .05 .02 .01
☐ 213 John Burkett .05 .02 .01
☐ 214 George Bell .05 .02 .01
☐ 215 Dan Plesac .05 .02 .01
☐ 216 Manny Ramirez .60 .25 .07
☐ 217 Mike Maddux .05 .02 .01
☐ 218 Kevin McReynolds .05 .02 .01
☐ 219 Pat Borders .05 .02 .01
☐ 220 Doug Drabek .05 .02 .01
☐ 221 Larry Luebbers .05 .02 .01
☐ 222 Trevor Hoffman .15 .07 .02
☐ 223 Pat Meares .05 .02 .01
☐ 224 Danny Miceli .05 .02 .01
☐ 225 Greg Vaughn .30 .14 .04
☐ 226 Scott Hemond .05 .02 .01
☐ 227 Pat Rapp .05 .02 .01
☐ 228 Kirk Gibson .15 .07 .02
☐ 229 Lance Painter .05 .02 .01
☐ 230 Larry Walker .30 .14 .04
☐ 231 Benji Gil .05 .02 .01
☐ 232 Mark Wohlers .15 .07 .02
☐ 233 Rich Amaral .05 .02 .01
☐ 234 Eric Pappas .05 .02 .01
☐ 235 Scott Cooper .05 .02 .01
☐ 236 Mike Butcher .05 .02 .01
☐ 237 Outfield Prospects .15 .07 .02
Curtis Pride
Shawn Green
Mark Sweeney
Eddie Davis
☐ 238 Kim Batiste .05 .02 .01
☐ 239 Paul Assenmacher .05 .02 .01
☐ 240 Will Clark .30 .14 .04
☐ 241 Jose Offerman .05 .02 .01
☐ 242 Todd Frohwirth .05 .02 .01
☐ 243 Tim Raines .30 .14 .04
☐ 244 Rick Wilkins .05 .02 .01
☐ 245 Bret Saberhagen .15 .07 .02
☐ 246 Thomas Howard .05 .02 .01
☐ 247 Stan Belinda .05 .02 .01
☐ 248 Rickey Henderson .30 .14 .04
☐ 249 Brian Williams .05 .02 .01
☐ 250 Barry Larkin .30 .14 .04
☐ 251 Jose Valentin .15 .07 .02
☐ 252 Lenny Webster .05 .02 .01
☐ 253 Blas Minor .05 .02 .01
☐ 254 Tim Teufel .05 .02 .01
☐ 255 Bobby Witt .05 .02 .01
☐ 256 Walt Weiss .05 .02 .01
☐ 257 Chad Kreuter .05 .02 .01
☐ 258 Roberto Mejia .05 .02 .01
☐ 259 Cliff Floyd .30 .14 .04
☐ 260 Julio Franco .15 .07 .02
☐ 261 Rafael Belliard .05 .02 .01
☐ 262 Marc Newfield .15 .07 .02
☐ 263 Gerald Perry .05 .02 .01
☐ 264 Ken Ryan .05 .02 .01
☐ 265 Chili Davis .15 .07 .02
☐ 266 Dave West .05 .02 .01
☐ 267 Royce Clayton .15 .07 .02
☐ 268 Pedro Martinez .30 .14 .04
☐ 269 Mark Hutton .05 .02 .01
☐ 270 Frank Thomas 2.00 .90 .25
☐ 271 Brad Pennington .05 .02 .01
☐ 272 Mike Harkey .05 .02 .01
☐ 273 Sandy Alomar .15 .07 .02
☐ 274 Dave Gallagher .05 .02 .01
☐ 275 Wally Joyner .15 .07 .02
☐ 276 Ricky Trlicek .05 .02 .01
☐ 277 Al Osuna .05 .02 .01
☐ 278 Calvin Reese .15 .07 .02
☐ 279 Kevin Higgins .05 .02 .01
☐ 280 Rick Aguilera .05 .02 .01
☐ 281 Orlando Merced .15 .07 .02
☐ 282 Mike Mohler .05 .02 .01
☐ 283 John Jaha .15 .07 .02
☐ 284 Robb Nen .15 .07 .02
☐ 285 Travis Fryman .15 .07 .02
☐ 286 Mark Thompson .15 .07 .02
☐ 287 Mike Lansing .15 .07 .02
☐ 288 Craig Lefferts .05 .02 .01
☐ 289 Damon Berryhill .05 .02 .01
☐ 290 Randy Johnson .30 .14 .04
☐ 291 Jeff Reed .05 .02 .01
☐ 292 Danny Darwin .05 .02 .01
☐ 293 J.T. Snow .15 .07 .02
☐ 294 Tyler Green .05 .02 .01
☐ 295 Chris Hoiles .05 .02 .01
☐ 296 Roger McDowell .05 .02 .01
☐ 297 Spike Owen .05 .02 .01
☐ 298 Salomon Torres .05 .02 .01
☐ 299 Wilson Alvarez .15 .07 .02
☐ 300 Ryne Sandberg .50 .23 .06
☐ 301 Derek Lilliquist .05 .02 .01
☐ 302 Howard Johnson .05 .02 .01
☐ 303 Greg Cadaret .05 .02 .01
☐ 304 Pat Hentgen .15 .07 .02
☐ 305 Craig Biggio .15 .07 .02
☐ 306 Scott Service .05 .02 .01
☐ 307 Melvin Nieves .15 .07 .02
☐ 308 Mike Trombley .05 .02 .01
☐ 309 Carlos Garcia .05 .02 .01
☐ 310 Robin Yount UER .30 .14 .04
(listed with 111 triples in
1988; should be 11)
☐ 311 Marcos Armas .05 .02 .01
☐ 312 Rich Rodriguez .05 .02 .01
☐ 313 Justin Thompson .15 .07 .02
☐ 314 Danny Sheaffer .05 .02 .01
☐ 315 Ken Hill .05 .02 .01
☐ 316 Pitching Prospects .40 .18 .05
Chad Ogea
Duff Brumley
Terrell Wade
Chris Michalak
☐ 317 Cris Carpenter .05 .02 .01
☐ 318 Jeff Blauser .05 .02 .01
☐ 319 Ted Power .05 .02 .01
☐ 320 Ozzie Smith .50 .23 .06
☐ 321 John Dopson .05 .02 .01
☐ 322 Chris Turner .05 .02 .01
☐ 323 Pete Incaviglia .05 .02 .01
☐ 324 Alan Mills .05 .02 .01
☐ 325 Jody Reed .05 .02 .01
☐ 326 Rich Monteleone .05 .02 .01
☐ 327 Mark Carreon .05 .02 .01
☐ 328 Donn Pall .05 .02 .01
☐ 329 Matt Walbeck .05 .02 .01
☐ 330 Charles Nagy .15 .07 .02
☐ 331 Jeff McKnight .05 .02 .01
☐ 332 Jose Lind .05 .02 .01
☐ 333 Mike Timlin .05 .02 .01
☐ 334 Doug Jones .05 .02 .01
☐ 335 Kevin Mitchell .15 .07 .02
☐ 336 Luis Lopez .05 .02 .01
☐ 337 Shane Mack .05 .02 .01
☐ 338 Randy Tomlin .05 .02 .01
☐ 339 Matt Mieske .05 .02 .01
☐ 340 Mark McGwire .60 .25 .07
☐ 341 Nigel Wilson .05 .02 .01
☐ 342 Danny Gladden .05 .02 .01
☐ 343 Mo Sanford .05 .02 .01
☐ 344 Sean Berry .05 .02 .01
☐ 345 Kevin Brown .15 .07 .02
☐ 346 Greg Olson .05 .02 .01
☐ 347 Dave Magadan .05 .02 .01
☐ 348 Rene Arocha .05 .02 .01
☐ 349 Carlos Quintana .05 .02 .01
☐ 350 Jim Abbott .05 .02 .01
☐ 351 Gary DiSarcina .05 .02 .01
☐ 352 Ben Rivera .05 .02 .01
☐ 353 Carlos Hernandez .05 .02 .01
☐ 354 Darren Lewis .05 .02 .01
☐ 355 Harold Reynolds .05 .02 .01
☐ 356 Scott Ruffcorn .05 .02 .01
☐ 357 Mark Gubicza .05 .02 .01
☐ 358 Paul Sorrento .05 .02 .01
☐ 359 Anthony Young .05 .02 .01
☐ 360 Mark Grace .30 .14 .04
☐ 361 Rob Butler .05 .02 .01
☐ 362 Kevin Bass .05 .02 .01
☐ 363 Eric Helfand .05 .02 .01
☐ 364 Derek Bell .15 .07 .02
☐ 365 Scott Erickson .05 .02 .01
☐ 366 Al Martin .05 .02 .01
☐ 367 Ricky Bones .05 .02 .01
☐ 368 Jeff Branson .05 .02 .01
☐ 369 Third Base Prospects .75 .35 .09
Luis Ortiz
David Bell
Jason Giambi
George Arias
☐ 370 Benito Santiago .05 .02 .01
(See also 379)
☐ 371 John Doherty .05 .02 .01
☐ 372 Joe Girardi .05 .02 .01
☐ 373 Tim Scott .05 .02 .01
☐ 374 Marvin Freeman .05 .02 .01
☐ 375 Deion Sanders .30 .14 .04
☐ 376 Roger Salkeld .05 .02 .01
☐ 377 Bernard Gilkey .15 .07 .02
☐ 378 Tony Fossas .05 .02 .01
☐ 379 Mark McLemore UER .05 .02 .01
(Card number is 370)
☐ 380 Darren Daulton .15 .07 .02
☐ 381 Chuck Finley .05 .02 .01
☐ 382 Mitch Webster .05 .02 .01
☐ 383 Gerald Williams .15 .07 .02
☐ 384 Frank Thomas AS .60 .25 .07
Fred McGriff AS
☐ 385 Roberto Alomar AS .15 .07 .02
Robby Thompson AS
☐ 386 Wade Boggs AS .30 .14 .04
Matt Williams AS
☐ 387 Cal Ripken AS .50 .23 .06
Jeff Blauser AS
☐ 388 Ken Griffey Jr. AS .50 .23 .06
Len Dykstra AS
☐ 389 Juan Gonzalez AS .30 .14 .04
David Justice AS
☐ 390 George Belle AS .15 .07 .02
Bobby Bonds AS
☐ 391 Mike Stanley AS .40 .18 .05
Mike Piazza AS
☐ 392 Jack McDowell AS .40 .18 .05
Greg Maddux AS
☐ 393 Jimmy Key AS .15 .07 .02
Tom Glavine AS
☐ 394 Jeff Montgomery AS .05 .02 .01
Randy Myers AS
☐ 395 Checklist 1-198 .05 .02 .01
☐ 396 Checklist 199-396 .05 .02 .01
☐ 397 Tim Salmon .30 .14 .04
☐ 398 Todd Benzinger .05 .02 .01
☐ 399 Frank Castillo .05 .02 .01
☐ 400 Ken Griffey Jr. 2.00 .90 .25
☐ 401 John Kruk .15 .07 .02
☐ 402 Dave Telgheder .05 .02 .01
☐ 403 Gary Gaetti .15 .07 .02
☐ 404 Jim Edmonds .40 .18 .05
☐ 405 Don Slaught .05 .02 .01
☐ 406 Jose Oquendo .05 .02 .01
☐ 407 Bruce Ruffin .05 .02 .01
☐ 408 Phil Clark .05 .02 .01
☐ 409 Joe Klink .05 .02 .01
☐ 410 Lou Whitaker .15 .07 .02
☐ 411 Kevin Seitzer .05 .02 .01
☐ 412 Darrin Fletcher .05 .02 .01
☐ 413 Kenny Rogers .05 .02 .01
☐ 414 Bill Pecota .05 .02 .01
☐ 415 Dave Fleming .05 .02 .01
☐ 416 Luis Alicea .05 .02 .01
☐ 417 Paul Quantrill .05 .02 .01
☐ 418 Damion Easley .05 .02 .01
☐ 419 Wes Chamberlain .05 .02 .01
☐ 420 Harold Baines .15 .07 .02
☐ 421 Scott Radinsky .05 .02 .01
☐ 422 Rey Sanchez .05 .02 .01
☐ 423 Junior Ortiz .05 .02 .01
☐ 424 Jeff Kent .05 .02 .01
☐ 425 Brian McRae .15 .07 .02
☐ 426 Ed Sprague .15 .07 .02
☐ 427 Tom Edens .05 .02 .01
☐ 428 Willie Greene .15 .07 .02
☐ 429 Bryan Hickerson .05 .02 .01
☐ 430 Dave Winfield .30 .14 .04
☐ 431 Pedro Astacio .05 .02 .01
☐ 432 Mike Gallego .05 .02 .01
☐ 433 Dave Burba .05 .02 .01
☐ 434 Bob Walk .05 .02 .01
☐ 435 Darryl Hamilton .05 .02 .01
☐ 436 Vince Horsman .05 .02 .01
☐ 437 Bob Natal .05 .02 .01
☐ 438 Mike Henneman .05 .02 .01
☐ 439 Willie Blair .05 .02 .01
☐ 440 Denny Martinez .15 .07 .02
☐ 441 Dan Peltier .05 .02 .01
☐ 442 Tony Tarasco .05 .02 .01
☐ 443 John Cummings .05 .02 .01
☐ 444 Geronimo Pena .05 .02 .01
☐ 445 Aaron Sele .15 .07 .02
☐ 446 Stan Javier .05 .02 .01
☐ 447 Mike Williams .05 .02 .01
☐ 448 First Base Prospects .30 .14 .04
Greg Pirkl
Roberto Petagine
D.J.Boston
Shawn Wooten
☐ 449 Jim Poole .05 .02 .01
☐ 450 Carlos Baerga .15 .07 .02
☐ 451 Bob Scanlan .05 .02 .01
☐ 452 Lance Johnson .15 .07 .02
☐ 453 Eric Hillman .05 .02 .01
☐ 454 Keith Miller .05 .02 .01
☐ 455 Dave Stewart .15 .07 .02
☐ 456 Pete Harnisch .05 .02 .01
☐ 457 Roberto Kelly .05 .02 .01
☐ 458 Tim Worrell .05 .02 .01
☐ 459 Pedro Munoz .05 .02 .01
☐ 460 Orel Hershiser .15 .07 .02
☐ 461 Randy Velarde .05 .02 .01
☐ 462 Trevor Wilson .05 .02 .01
☐ 463 Jerry Goff .05 .02 .01
☐ 464 Bill Wegman .05 .02 .01
☐ 465 Dennis Eckersley .15 .07 .02
☐ 466 Jeff Conine .15 .07 .02
☐ 467 Joe Boever .05 .02 .01
☐ 468 Dante Bichette .30 .14 .04
☐ 469 Jeff Shaw .05 .02 .01
☐ 470 Rafael Palmeiro .30 .14 .04
☐ 471 Phil Leftwich .05 .02 .01
☐ 472 Jay Buhner .30 .14 .04
☐ 473 Bob Tewksbury .05 .02 .01
☐ 474 Tim Naehring .05 .02 .01
☐ 475 Tom Glavine .30 .14 .04
☐ 476 Dave Hollins .05 .02 .01
☐ 477 Arthur Rhodes .05 .02 .01
☐ 478 Joey Cora .05 .02 .01
☐ 479 Mike Morgan .05 .02 .01
☐ 480 Albert Belle .75 .35 .09
☐ 481 John Franco .05 .02 .01
☐ 482 Hipolito Pichardo .05 .02 .01
☐ 483 Duane Ward .05 .02 .01
☐ 484 Luis Gonzalez .05 .02 .01
☐ 485 Joe Oliver .05 .02 .01
☐ 486 Wally Whitehurst .05 .02 .01
☐ 487 Mike Benjamin .05 .02 .01
☐ 488 Eric Davis .15 .07 .02
☐ 489 Scott Kamieniecki .05 .02 .01
☐ 490 Kent Hrbek .15 .07 .02
☐ 491 John Hope .05 .02 .01
☐ 492 Jesse Orosco .05 .02 .01
☐ 493 Troy Neel .05 .02 .01
☐ 494 Ryan Bowen .05 .02 .01
☐ 495 Mickey Tettleton .05 .02 .01
☐ 496 Chris Jones .05 .02 .01
☐ 497 John Wetteland .15 .07 .02
☐ 498 David Hulse .05 .02 .01
☐ 499 Greg Maddux 1.25 .55 .16
☐ 500 Bo Jackson .15 .07 .02
☐ 501 Donovan Osborne .05 .02 .01
☐ 502 Mike Greenwell .05 .02 .01
☐ 503 Steve Frey .05 .02 .01
☐ 504 Jim Eisenreich .05 .02 .01
☐ 505 Robby Thompson .05 .02 .01
☐ 506 Leo Gomez .05 .02 .01
☐ 507 Dave Staton .05 .02 .01
☐ 508 Wayne Kirby .05 .02 .01
☐ 509 Tim Bogar .05 .02 .01
☐ 510 David Cone .15 .07 .02
☐ 511 Devon White .05 .02 .01
☐ 512 Xavier Hernandez .05 .02 .01
☐ 513 Tim Costo .05 .02 .01
☐ 514 Gene Harris .05 .02 .01
☐ 515 Jack McDowell .15 .07 .02
☐ 516 Kevin Gross .05 .02 .01
☐ 517 Scott Leius .05 .02 .01
☐ 518 Lloyd McClendon .05 .02 .01
☐ 519 Alex Diaz .05 .02 .01
☐ 520 Wade Boggs .30 .14 .04
☐ 521 Bob Welch .05 .02 .01
☐ 522 Henry Cotto .05 .02 .01
☐ 523 Mike Moore .05 .02 .01
☐ 524 Tim Laker .05 .02 .01
☐ 525 Andres Galarraga .30 .14 .04
☐ 526 Jamie Moyer .05 .02 .01
☐ 527 Second Base Prospects .15 .07 .02
Norberto Martin
Ruben Santana
Jason Hardtke
Chris Sexton
☐ 528 Sid Bream .05 .02 .01
☐ 529 Erik Hanson .05 .02 .01
☐ 530 Ray Lankford .15 .07 .02
☐ 531 Rob Deer .05 .02 .01
☐ 532 Rod Correia .05 .02 .01
☐ 533 Roger Mason .05 .02 .01
☐ 534 Mike Devereaux .05 .02 .01
☐ 535 Jeff Montgomery .15 .07 .02
☐ 536 Dwight Smith .05 .02 .01
☐ 537 Jeremy Hernandez .05 .02 .01
☐ 538 Ellis Burks .15 .07 .02
☐ 539 Bobby Jones .15 .07 .02
☐ 540 Paul Molitor .40 .18 .05
☐ 541 Jeff Juden .05 .02 .01
☐ 542 Chris Sabo .05 .02 .01
☐ 543 Larry Casian .05 .02 .01
☐ 544 Jeff Gardner .05 .02 .01
☐ 545 Ramon Martinez .15 .07 .02
☐ 546 Paul O'Neill .15 .07 .02
☐ 547 Steve Hosey .05 .02 .01
☐ 548 Dave Nilsson .15 .07 .02

□ 549 Ron Darling .05 .02 .01
□ 550 Matt Williams .30 .14 .04
□ 551 Jack Armstrong .05 .02 .01
□ 552 Bill Krueger .05 .02 .01
□ 553 Freddie Benavides .05 .02 .01
□ 554 Jeff Fassero .05 .02 .01
□ 555 Chuck Knoblauch .30 .14 .04
□ 556 Guillermo Velasquez .05 .02 .01
□ 557 Joel Johnston .05 .02 .01
□ 558 Tom Lampkin .05 .02 .01
□ 559 Todd Van Poppel .05 .02 .01
□ 560 Gary Sheffield .30 .14 .04
□ 561 Skeeter Barnes .05 .02 .01
□ 562 Darren Holmes .05 .02 .01
□ 563 John Vander Wal .05 .02 .01
□ 564 Mike Ignasiak .05 .02 .01
□ 565 Fred McGriff .30 .14 .04
□ 566 Luis Polonia .05 .02 .01
□ 567 Mike Perez .05 .02 .01
□ 568 John Valentin .15 .07 .02
□ 569 Mike Felder .05 .02 .01
□ 570 Tommy Greene .05 .02 .01
□ 571 David Segui .05 .02 .01
□ 572 Roberto Hernandez .15 .07 .02
□ 573 Steve Wilson .05 .02 .01
□ 574 Willie McGee .05 .02 .01
□ 575 Randy Myers .05 .02 .01
□ 576 Darrin Jackson .05 .02 .01
□ 577 Eric Plunk .05 .02 .01
□ 578 Mike Macfarlane .05 .02 .01
□ 579 Doug Brocail .05 .02 .01
□ 580 Steve Finley .30 .14 .04
□ 581 John Roper .05 .02 .01
□ 582 Danny Cox .05 .02 .01
□ 583 Chip Hale .05 .02 .01
□ 584 Scott Bullett .05 .02 .01
□ 585 Kevin Reimer .05 .02 .01
□ 586 Brent Gates .05 .02 .01
□ 587 Matt Turner .05 .02 .01
□ 588 Rich Rowland .05 .02 .01
□ 589 Kent Bottenfield .05 .02 .01
□ 590 Marquis Grissom .15 .07 .02
□ 591 Doug Strange .05 .02 .01
□ 592 Jay Howell .05 .02 .01
□ 593 Omar Vizquel .15 .07 .02
□ 594 Rheal Cormier .05 .02 .01
□ 595 Andre Dawson .15 .07 .02
□ 596 Hilly Hathaway .05 .02 .01
□ 597 Todd Pratt .05 .02 .01
□ 598 Mike Mussina .40 .18 .05
□ 599 Alex Fernandez .15 .07 .02
□ 600 Don Mattingly 1.00 .45 .12
□ 601 Frank Thomas ST 1.00 .45 .12
□ 602 Ryne Sandberg ST .30 .14 .04
□ 603 Wade Boggs ST .30 .14 .04
□ 604 Cal Ripken ST .75 .35 .09
□ 605 Barry Bonds ST .30 .14 .04
□ 606 Ken Griffey Jr. ST 1.00 .45 .12
□ 607 Kirby Puckett ST .30 .14 .04
□ 608 Darren Daulton ST .15 .07 .02
□ 609 Paul Molitor ST .30 .14 .04
□ 610 Terry Steinbach .15 .07 .02
□ 611 Todd Worrell .05 .02 .01
□ 612 Jim Thome .50 .23 .06
□ 613 Chuck McElroy .05 .02 .01
□ 614 John Habyan .05 .02 .01
□ 615 Sid Fernandez .05 .02 .01
□ 616 Outfield Prospects .50 .23 .06
Eddie Zambrano
Glenn Murray
Chad Mottola
Jermaine Allensworth
□ 617 Steve Bedrosian .05 .02 .01
□ 618 Rob Ducey .05 .02 .01
□ 619 Tom Browning .05 .02 .01
□ 620 Tony Gwynn .75 .35 .09
□ 621 Carl Willis .05 .02 .01
□ 622 Kevin Young .05 .02 .01
□ 623 Rafael Novoa .05 .02 .01
□ 624 Jerry Browne .05 .02 .01
□ 625 Charlie Hough .05 .02 .01
□ 626 Chris Gomez .05 .02 .01
□ 627 Steve Reed .05 .02 .01
□ 628 Kirk Rueter .05 .02 .01
□ 629 Matt Whiteside .05 .02 .01
□ 630 David Justice .30 .14 .04
□ 631 Brad Holman .05 .02 .01
□ 632 Brian Jordan .30 .14 .04
□ 633 Scott Bankhead .05 .02 .01
□ 634 Torey Lovullo .05 .02 .01
□ 635 Len Dykstra .15 .07 .02
□ 636 Ben McDonald .05 .02 .01
□ 637 Steve Howe .05 .02 .01
□ 638 Jose Vizcaino .05 .02 .01
□ 639 Bill Swift .05 .02 .01
□ 640 Darryl Strawberry .15 .07 .02
□ 641 Steve Farr .05 .02 .01
□ 642 Tom Kramer .05 .02 .01
□ 643 Joe Orsulak .05 .02 .01
□ 644 Tom Henke .05 .02 .01
□ 645 Joe Carter .15 .07 .02
□ 646 Ken Caminiti .30 .14 .04
□ 647 Reggie Sanders .15 .07 .02
□ 648 Andy Ashby .15 .07 .02
□ 649 Derek Parks .05 .02 .01
□ 650 Andy Van Slyke .15 .07 .02
□ 651 Juan Bell .05 .02 .01
□ 652 Roger Smithberg .05 .02 .01
□ 653 Chuck Carr .05 .02 .01
□ 654 Bill Gullickson .05 .02 .01
□ 655 Charlie Hayes .05 .02 .01
□ 656 Chris Nabholz .05 .02 .01
□ 657 Karl Rhodes .05 .02 .01
□ 658 Pete Smith .05 .02 .01
□ 659 Bret Boone .15 .07 .02
□ 660 Gregg Jefferies .30 .14 .04
□ 661 Bob Zupcic .05 .02 .01
□ 662 Steve Sax .05 .02 .01
□ 663 Mariano Duncan .05 .02 .01
□ 664 Jeff Tackett .05 .02 .01
□ 665 Mark Langston .15 .07 .02
□ 666 Steve Buechele .05 .02 .01
□ 667 Candy Maldonado .05 .02 .01
□ 668 Woody Williams .05 .02 .01
□ 669 Tim Wakefield .05 .02 .01
□ 670 Danny Tartabull .05 .02 .01
□ 671 Charlie O'Brien .05 .02 .01
□ 672 Felix Jose .05 .02 .01
□ 673 Bobby Ayala .05 .02 .01
□ 674 Scott Servais .05 .02 .01
□ 675 Roberto Alomar .40 .18 .05
□ 676 Pedro Martinez .30 .14 .04
□ 677 Eddie Guardado .05 .02 .01
□ 678 Mark Lewis .05 .02 .01
□ 679 Jaime Navarro .05 .02 .01
□ 680 Ruben Sierra .15 .07 .02
□ 681 Rick Renteria .05 .02 .01
□ 682 Storm Davis .05 .02 .01
□ 683 Cory Snyder .05 .02 .01
□ 684 Ron Karkovice .05 .02 .01
□ 685 Juan Gonzalez 1.00 .45 .12
□ 686 Catchers Prospects .40 .18 .05
Chris Howard
Carlos Delgado
Jason Kendall
Paul Bako
□ 687 John Smoltz .30 .14 .04
□ 688 Brian Dorsett .05 .02 .01
□ 689 Omar Olivares .05 .02 .01
□ 690 Mo Vaughn .50 .23 .06
□ 691 Joe Grahe .05 .02 .01
□ 692 Mickey Morandini .05 .02 .01
□ 693 Tino Martinez .15 .07 .02
□ 694 Brian Barnes .05 .02 .01
□ 695 Mike Stanley .05 .02 .01
□ 696 Mark Clark .05 .02 .01
□ 697 Dave Hansen .05 .02 .01
□ 698 Willie Wilson .05 .02 .01
□ 699 Pete Schourek .15 .07 .02
□ 700 Barry Bonds .50 .23 .06
□ 701 Kevin Appier .15 .07 .02
□ 702 Tony Fernandez .05 .02 .01
□ 703 Darryl Kile .05 .02 .01
□ 704 Archi Cianfrocco .05 .02 .01
□ 705 Jose Rijo .05 .02 .01
□ 706 Brian Harper .05 .02 .01
□ 707 Zane Smith .05 .02 .01
□ 708 Dave Henderson .05 .02 .01
□ 709 Angel Miranda UER .05 .02 .01
(no Topps logo on back)
□ 710 Orestes Destrade .05 .02 .01
□ 711 Greg Gohr .05 .02 .01
□ 712 Eric Young .15 .07 .02
□ 713 Relief Pitchers .15 .07 .02
Prospects
Todd Williams
Ron Watson
Kirk Bullinger
Mike Welch
□ 714 Tim Spehr .05 .02 .01
□ 715 Hank Aaron .50 .23 .06
□ 716 Nate Minchey .05 .02 .01
□ 717 Mike Blowers .05 .02 .01
□ 718 Kent Mercker .05 .02 .01
□ 719 Tom Pagnozzi .05 .02 .01
□ 720 Roger Clemens .40 .18 .05
□ 721 Eduardo Perez .05 .02 .01
□ 722 Milt Thompson .05 .02 .01
□ 723 Gregg Olson .05 .02 .01
□ 724 Kirk McCaskill .05 .02 .01
□ 725 Sammy Sosa .30 .14 .04
□ 726 Alvaro Espinoza .05 .02 .01
□ 727 Henry Rodriguez .15 .07 .02
□ 728 Jim Leyritz .05 .02 .01
□ 729 Steve Scarsone .05 .02 .01
□ 730 Bobby Bonilla .15 .07 .02
□ 731 Chris Gwynn .05 .02 .01
□ 732 Al Leiter .15 .07 .02
□ 733 Bip Roberts .05 .02 .01
□ 734 Mark Portugal .05 .02 .01
□ 735 Terry Pendleton .15 .07 .02
□ 736 Dave Valle .05 .02 .01
□ 737 Paul Kilgus .05 .02 .01
□ 738 Greg A. Harris .05 .02 .01
□ 739 Jon Ratliff DP .15 .07 .02
□ 740 Kirk Presley DP .30 .14 .04
□ 741 Josue Estrada DP .15 .07 .02
□ 742 Wayne Gomes DP .15 .07 .02
□ 743 Pat Watkins DP .30 .14 .04
□ 744 Jamey Wright DP .60 .25 .07
□ 745 Jay Powell DP .15 .07 .02
□ 746 Ryan McGuire DP .15 .07 .02
□ 747 Marc Barcelo DP .15 .07 .02
□ 748 Sloan Smith DP .15 .07 .02
□ 749 John Wasdin DP .40 .18 .05
□ 750 Marc Valdes DP .15 .07 .02
□ 751 Dan Ehler DP .15 .07 .02
□ 752 Andre King DP .15 .07 .02
□ 753 Greg Keagle DP .05 .02 .01
□ 754 Jason Myers DP .15 .07 .02
□ 755 Dax Winslett DP .15 .07 .02
□ 756 Casey Whitten DP .15 .07 .02
□ 757 Tony Fuduric DP .15 .07 .02
□ 758 Greg Norton DP .15 .07 .02
□ 759 Jeff D'Amico DP .50 .23 .06
□ 760 Ryan Hancock DP .15 .07 .02
□ 761 David Cooper DP .15 .07 .02
□ 762 Kevin Orie DP .60 .25 .07
□ 763 John O'Donoghue .05 .02 .01
Mike Oquist
□ 764 Cory Bailey .05 .02 .01
Scott Hatteberg
□ 765 Mark Holzemer .05 .02 .01
Paul Swingle
□ 766 James Baldwin .30 .14 .04
Rod Bolton
□ 767 Jerry Di Poto .15 .07 .02
Julian Tavarez
□ 768 Danny Bautista .15 .07 .02
Sean Bergman
□ 769 Bob Hamelin .05 .02 .01
Joe Vitiello
□ 770 Mark Kiefer .15 .07 .02
Troy O'Leary
□ 771 Denny Hocking .15 .07 .02
Oscar Munoz
□ 772 Russ Davis .15 .07 .02
Brien Taylor
□ 773 Kyle Abbott .15 .07 .02
Miguel Jimenez
□ 774 Kevin King .05 .02 .01
Eric Plantenberg
□ 775 Jon Shave .05 .02 .01
Desi Wilson
□ 776 Domingo Cedeno .05 .02 .01
Paul Spoljaric
□ 777 Chipper Jones 2.50 1.10 .30
Ryan Klesko
□ 778 Steve Trachsel .15 .07 .02
Turk Wendell
□ 779 Johnny Ruffin .05 .02 .01
Jerry Spradlin
□ 780 Jason Bates .15 .07 .02
John Burke
□ 781 Carl Everett .15 .07 .02
Dave Weathers
□ 782 Gary Mota .15 .07 .02
James Mouton
□ 783 Raul Mondesi .30 .14 .04
Ben Van Ryn
□ 784 Gabe White .30 .14 .04
Rondell White
□ 785 Brook Fordyce .15 .07 .02
Bill Pulsipher
□ 786 Kevin Foster .15 .07 .02
Gene Schall
□ 787 Rich Aude .05 .02 .01
Midre Cummings
□ 788 Brian Barber .15 .07 .02
Rich Batchelor
□ 789 Brian Johnson .05 .02 .01
Scott Sanders
□ 790 Ricky Faneyte .05 .02 .01
J.R. Phillips
□ 791 Checklist 3 .05 .02 .01
□ 792 Checklist 4 .05 .02 .01

1994 Topps Gold

The 1994 Topps Gold set is parallel to the basic issue. They were inserted one per wax or mini pack, two per mini jumbo, three per rack pack, four per jumbo, five per jumbo rack and ten per factory set. The only difference between the Gold issue and the basic cards is gold foil on the player's name and the Topps logo. As in previous Gold Sets, player cards replace the Checklist cards.

	MINT	NRMT	EXC
COMPLETE SET (792)	80.00	36.00	10.00
COMPLETE SERIES 1 (396)	40.00	18.00	5.00
COMPLETE SERIES 2 (396)	40.00	18.00	5.00
COMMON CARD (1-792)	.10	.05	.01

*STARS: 2X to 4X BASIC CARDS
*YOUNG STARS: 1.5X to 3X BASIC CARDS

□ 395 Bill Brennan .25 .11 .03
Replaces Checklist 1
□ 396 Jeff Bronkey .25 .11 .03
Replaces Checklist 2
□ 791 Mike Cook .25 .11 .03
Replaces Checklist 3
□ 792 Dan Pasqua .25 .11 .03
Replaces Checklist 4

1994 Topps Spanish

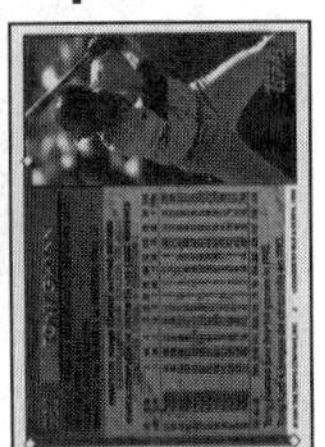

Issued in complete factory set form only, these 792 standard-size cards parallel the regular Topps issue. These cards have the same front photos but are billingual. The factory set also contains the Topps Spanish Legends 10-card set. That set which is entitled 'Topps Legends' features retired Latin players.

	MINT	NRMT	EXC
COMPLETE FACT.SET (802)	125.00	55.00	15.50
COMPLETE SET (792)	120.00	55.00	15.00
SPANISH LEGENDS SET (10)	5.00	2.20	.60
COMMON CARD (1-792)	.20	.09	.03
COMMON LEGENDS (L1-L10)	.25	.11	.03

*STARS: 3X to 6X BASIC CARDS
*YOUNG STARS: 2.5X to 5X BASIC CARDS

□ L1 Felipe Alou .60 .25 .07
□ L2 Ruben Amaro .25 .11 .03
□ L3 Luis Aparicio 1.00 .45 .12
□ L4 Rod Carew 1.00 .45 .12
□ L5 Chico Carrasquel .50 .23 .06
□ L6 Orlando Cepeda .75 .35 .09
□ L7 Juan Marichal 1.00 .45 .12
□ L8 Minnie Minoso .75 .35 .09
□ L9 Cookie Rojas .25 .11 .03
□ L10 Luis Tiant .50 .23 .06

1994 Topps Black Gold

Randomly inserted one in every 72 packs, this 44-card standard-size set was issued in two series of 22. Cards were also issued three per 1994 Topps factory set. Collectors had a chance, through redemption cards to receive all or part of the set. There are seven Winner redemption cards for a total 51 cards associated with this set. The set is considered complete with the 44 player cards. Card fronts feature color player action photos. The player's name at bottom and the team name at top are screened in gold foil. The backs contain a player photo and statistical rankings. The winner cards were redeemable until January 31, 1995

	MINT	NRMT	EXC
COMPLETE SET (44)	25.00	11.00	3.10
COMPLETE SERIES 1 (22)	15.00	6.75	1.85
COMPLETE SERIES 2 (22)	10.00	4.50	1.25
COMMON CARD (1-44)	.25	.11	.03

□ 1 Roberto Alomar .75 .35 .09
□ 2 Carlos Baerga .25 .11 .03
□ 3 Albert Belle 1.50 .70 .19
□ 4 Joe Carter .40 .18 .05
□ 5 Cecil Fielder .40 .18 .05
□ 6 Travis Fryman .40 .18 .05
□ 7 Juan Gonzalez 2.00 .90 .25
□ 8 Ken Griffey Jr. 4.00 1.80 .50
□ 9 Chris Hoiles .25 .11 .03
□ 10 Randy Johnson .60 .25 .07
□ 11 Kenny Lofton 1.25 .55 .16
□ 12 Jack McDowell .40 .18 .05
□ 13 Paul Molitor .60 .25 .07
□ 14 Jeff Montgomery .25 .11 .03
□ 15 John Olerud .25 .11 .03
□ 16 Rafael Palmeiro .60 .25 .07
□ 17 Kirby Puckett 1.50 .70 .19
□ 18 Cal Ripken 3.00 1.35 .35
□ 19 Tim Salmon .60 .25 .07
□ 20 Mike Stanley .25 .11 .03
□ 21 Frank Thomas 4.00 1.80 .50
□ 22 Robin Ventura .40 .18 .05
□ 23 Jeff Bagwell 1.50 .70 .19

☐ 24 Jay Bell	.25	.11	.03
☐ 25 Craig Biggio	.40	.18	.05
☐ 26 Jeff Blauser	.25	.11	.03
☐ 27 Barry Bonds	1.00	.45	.12
☐ 28 Darren Daulton	.40	.18	.05
☐ 29 Len Dykstra	.40	.18	.05
☐ 30 Andres Galarraga	.60	.25	.07
☐ 31 Ron Gant	.40	.18	.05
☐ 32 Tom Glavine	.60	.25	.07
☐ 33 Mark Grace	.60	.25	.07
☐ 34 Marquis Grissom	.40	.18	.05
☐ 35 Gregg Jefferies	.25	.11	.03
☐ 36 David Justice	.40	.18	.05
☐ 37 John Kruk	.25	.11	.03
☐ 38 Greg Maddux	2.50	1.10	.30
☐ 39 Fred McGriff	.60	.25	.07
☐ 40 Randy Myers	.25	.11	.03
☐ 41 Mike Piazza	2.50	1.10	.30
☐ 42 Sammy Sosa	.60	.25	.07
☐ 43 Robby Thompson	.25	.11	.03
☐ 44 Matt Williams	.60	.25	.07
☐ A Winner A 1-11	1.00	.45	.12
☐ B Winner B 12-22	1.00	.45	.12
☐ C Winner C 23-33	1.00	.45	.12
☐ D Winner D 34-44	1.00	.45	.12
☐ AB Winner AB 1-22	2.00	.90	.25
☐ CD Winner CD 23-44	2.00	.90	.25
☐ ABCD Winner ABCD 1-44	4.00	1.80	.50

1994 Topps Traded

This set consists of 132 standard-size cards featuring traded players in their new uniforms, rookies and draft choices. Factory sets consisted of 140 cards including a set of eight Topps Finest cards. Card fronts feature a player photo with the player's name, team and position at the bottom. The horizontal backs have a player photo to the left with complete career statisics and highlights. The cards are numbered with a "T" suffix. Rookie Cards include Brian Anderson, Ben Grieve, Paul Konerko, Terrence Long, Doug Million, Chan Ho Park, Reid Ryan, Mac Suzuki, Terrell Wade and Kevin Witt.

	MINT	NRMT	EXC
COMPLETE FACT.SET (140)	40.00	18.00	5.00
COMPLETE SET (132)	15.00	6.75	1.85
COMMON CARD (1T-132T)	.05	.02	.01
☐ 1T Paul Wilson	.50	.23	.06
☐ 2T Bill Taylor	.05	.02	.01
☐ 3T Dan Wilson	.15	.07	.02
☐ 4T Mark Smith	.05	.02	.01
☐ 5T Toby Borland	.05	.02	.01
☐ 6T Dave Clark	.05	.02	.01
☐ 7T Denny Martinez	.15	.07	.02
☐ 8T Dave Gallagher	.05	.02	.01
☐ 9T Josias Manzanillo	.05	.02	.01
☐ 10T Brian Anderson	.15	.07	.02
☐ 11T Damon Berryhill	.05	.02	.01
☐ 12T Alex Cole	.05	.02	.01
☐ 13T Jacob Shumate	.15	.07	.02
☐ 14T Oddibe McDowell	.05	.02	.01
☐ 15T Willie Banks	.05	.02	.01
☐ 16T Jerry Browne	.05	.02	.01
☐ 17T Donnie Elliott	.05	.02	.01
☐ 18T Ellis Burks	.15	.07	.02
☐ 19T Chuck McElroy	.05	.02	.01
☐ 20T Luis Polonia	.05	.02	.01
☐ 21T Brian Harper	.05	.02	.01
☐ 22T Mark Portugal	.05	.02	.01
☐ 23T Dave Henderson	.05	.02	.01
☐ 24T Mark Acre	.05	.02	.01
☐ 25T Julio Franco	.15	.07	.02
☐ 26T Darren Hall	.05	.02	.01
☐ 27T Eric Anthony	.05	.02	.01
☐ 28T Sid Fernandez	.05	.02	.01
☐ 29T Rusty Greer	1.00	.45	.12
☐ 30T Riccardo Ingram	.05	.02	.01
☐ 31T Gabe White	.05	.02	.01
☐ 32T Tim Belcher	.05	.02	.01
☐ 33T Terrence Long	.75	.35	.09
☐ 34T Mark Dalesandro	.05	.02	.01
☐ 35T Mike Kelly	.05	.02	.01
☐ 36T Jack Morris	.15	.07	.02
☐ 37T Jeff Brantley	.05	.02	.01
☐ 38T Larry Barnes	.15	.07	.02
☐ 39T Brian R. Hunter	.05	.02	.01
☐ 40T Otis Nixon	.05	.02	.01
☐ 41T Bret Wagner	.15	.07	.02
☐ 42T Pedro Martinez TR Delino Deshields	.15	.07	.02
☐ 43T Heathcliff Slocumb	.15	.07	.02
☐ 44T Ben Grieve	3.00	1.35	.35
☐ 45T John Hudek	.05	.02	.01
☐ 46T Shawon Dunston	.05	.02	.01
☐ 47T Greg Colbrunn	.05	.02	.01
☐ 48T Joey Hamilton	.40	.18	.05
☐ 49T Marvin Freeman	.05	.02	.01
☐ 50T Terry Mulholland	.05	.02	.01
☐ 51T Keith Mitchell	.05	.02	.01
☐ 52T Dwight Smith	.05	.02	.01
☐ 53T Shawn Boskie	.05	.02	.01
☐ 54T Kevin Witt	.50	.23	.06
☐ 55T Ron Gant	.15	.07	.02
☐ 56T 1994 Prospects Trenidad Hubbard Jason Schmidt Larry Sutton Stephen Larkin	.50	.23	.06
☐ 57T Jody Reed	.05	.02	.01
☐ 58T Rick Helling	.05	.02	.01
☐ 59T John Powell	.15	.07	.02
☐ 60T Eddie Murray	.50	.23	.06
☐ 61T Joe Hall	.05	.02	.01
☐ 62T Jorge Fabregas	.05	.02	.01
☐ 63T Mike Mordecai	.05	.02	.01
☐ 64T Ed Vosberg	.05	.02	.01
☐ 65T Rickey Henderson	.30	.14	.04
☐ 66T Tim Grieve	.05	.02	.01
☐ 67T Jon Lieber	.05	.02	.01
☐ 68T Chris Howard	.05	.02	.01
☐ 69T Matt Walbeck	.05	.02	.01
☐ 70T Chan Ho Park	.60	.25	.07
☐ 71T Bryan Eversgerd	.05	.02	.01
☐ 72T John Dettmer	.05	.02	.01
☐ 73T Erik Hanson	.05	.02	.01
☐ 74T Mike Thurman	.05	.02	.01
☐ 75T Bobby Ayala	.05	.02	.01
☐ 76T Rafael Palmeiro	.30	.14	.04
☐ 77T Bret Boone	.15	.07	.02
☐ 78T Paul Shuey	.05	.02	.01
☐ 79T Kevin Foster	.05	.02	.01
☐ 80T Dave Magadan	.05	.02	.01
☐ 81T Bip Roberts	.05	.02	.01
☐ 82T Howard Johnson	.05	.02	.01
☐ 83T Xavier Hernandez	.05	.02	.01
☐ 84T Ross Powell	.05	.02	.01
☐ 85T Doug Million	.75	.35	.09
☐ 86T Geronimo Berroa	.15	.07	.02
☐ 87T Mark Farris	.15	.07	.02
☐ 88T Butch Henry	.05	.02	.01
☐ 89T Junior Felix	.05	.02	.01
☐ 90T Bo Jackson	.15	.07	.02
☐ 91T Hector Carrasco	.05	.02	.01
☐ 92T Charlie O'Brien	.05	.02	.01
☐ 93T Omar Vizquel	.15	.07	.02
☐ 94T David Segui	.05	.02	.01
☐ 95T Dustin Hermanson	.15	.07	.02
☐ 96T Gar Finnvold	.05	.02	.01
☐ 97T Dave Stevens	.05	.02	.01
☐ 98T Corey Pointer	.25	.11	.03
☐ 99T Felix Fermin	.05	.02	.01
☐ 100T Lee Smith	.15	.07	.02
☐ 101T Reid Ryan	.15	.07	.02
☐ 102T Bobby Munoz	.05	.02	.01
☐ 103T Deion Sanders TR Roberto Kelly	.30	.14	.04
☐ 104T Turner Ward	.05	.02	.01
☐ 105T W.VanLandingham	.15	.07	.02
☐ 106T Vince Coleman	.05	.02	.01
☐ 107T Stan Javier	.05	.02	.01
☐ 108T Darrin Jackson	.05	.02	.01
☐ 109T C.J. Nitkowski	.15	.07	.02
☐ 110T Anthony Young	.05	.02	.01
☐ 111T Kurt Miller	.05	.02	.01
☐ 112T Paul Konerko	4.00	1.80	.50
☐ 113T Walt Weiss	.05	.02	.01
☐ 114T Daryl Boston	.05	.02	.01
☐ 115T Will Clark	.30	.14	.04
☐ 116T Matt Smith	.15	.07	.02
☐ 117T Mark Leiter	.05	.02	.01
☐ 118T Gregg Olson	.05	.02	.01
☐ 119T Tony Pena	.05	.02	.01
☐ 120T Jose Vizcaino	.05	.02	.01
☐ 121T Rick White	.05	.02	.01
☐ 122T Rich Rowland	.05	.02	.01
☐ 123T Jeff Reboulet	.05	.02	.01
☐ 124T Greg Hibbard	.05	.02	.01
☐ 125T Chris Sabo	.05	.02	.01
☐ 126T Doug Jones	.05	.02	.01
☐ 127T Tony Fernandez	.05	.02	.01
☐ 128T Carlos Reyes	.05	.02	.01
☐ 129T Kevin Brown	.75	.35	.09
☐ 130T Ryne Sandberg Farewell	1.25	.55	.16
☐ 131T Ryne Sandberg Farewell	1.25	.55	.16
☐ 132T Checklist 1-132	.05	.02	.01

1994 Topps Traded Finest Inserts

Each Topps Traded factory set contained a complete 8-card set of Finest Inserts. These cards are numbered separately and designed differently the base cards. Each Finest Insert features a action shot of a player set against purple chrome background. The set highlights the top performers midway through the 1994 season, detailing their performances through July. The cards are numbered on back X of 8.

	MINT	NRMT	EXC
COMPLETE SET (8)	25.00	11.00	3.10
COMMON CARD (1-8)	1.00	.45	.12
☐ 1 Greg Maddux	5.00	2.20	.60
☐ 2 Mike Piazza	5.00	2.20	.60
☐ 3 Matt Williams	1.00	.45	.12
☐ 4 Raul Mondesi	1.00	.45	.12
☐ 5 Ken Griffey Jr.	8.00	3.60	1.00
☐ 6 Kenny Lofton	2.00	.90	.25
☐ 7 Frank Thomas	8.00	3.60	1.00
☐ 8 Manny Ramirez	2.00	.90	.25

1994 Topps Porcelain Promo

Manufactured by R and N China Co. and licensed by Topps, this porcelain promo was issued to herald the March 1994 release of the porcelain version of the 1994 Topps I set. The porcelain promo is actually reproduced from the 1993 Topps set (#700, Nolan Ryan) and the design is identical to that card, aside from having rounded corners and carrying the manufacturer's name and production number at the bottom of the back. The promo was issued in its own box, which also contained a wooden stand for the card and a small certificate of limited issue.

	MINT	NRMT	EXC
COMPLETE SET	30.00	13.50	3.70
COMMON PLAYER	30.00	13.50	3.70
☐ 700 Nolan Ryan	30.00	13.50	3.70

1994 Topps Superstar Samplers

Sold only in retail outlets, each 1994 Topps Baker's Dozen factory set included a cello-wrapped 3-card sampler of a MLB player. Each player is represented by a Bowman, a Finest, and a Stadium Club card. These cards are identical to their regular issue counterparts except for a special "Topps Superstar Sampler" emblem on their backs. The prices listed below are for all three cards; the Finest card represents 50% of the value, while the Bowman or Stadium Club card are worth 25% each of the value.

	MINT	NRMT	EXC
COMPLETE SET (135)	1000.00	450.00	125.00
COMMON BAG (1-45)	4.00	1.80	.50
☐ 1 Roberto Alomar	20.00	9.00	2.50
☐ 2 Carlos Baerga	8.00	3.60	1.00
☐ 3 Jeff Bagwell	40.00	18.00	5.00
☐ 4 Albert Belle	50.00	22.00	6.25
☐ 5 Barry Bonds	20.00	9.00	2.50
☐ 6 Bobby Bonilla	8.00	3.60	1.00
☐ 7 Jose Canseco	15.00	6.75	1.85
☐ 8 Joe Carter	8.00	3.60	1.00
☐ 9 Will Clark	15.00	6.75	1.85
☐ 10 Roger Clemens	25.00	11.00	3.10
☐ 11 Darren Daulton	8.00	3.60	1.00
☐ 12 Len Dykstra	8.00	3.60	1.00
☐ 13 Cecil Fielder	8.00	3.60	1.00
☐ 14 Cliff Floyd	4.00	1.80	.50
☐ 15 Andres Galarraga	12.00	5.50	1.50
☐ 16 Tom Glavine	12.00	5.50	1.50
☐ 17 Juan Gonzalez	50.00	22.00	6.25
☐ 18 Mark Grace	15.00	6.75	1.85
☐ 19 Ken Griffey Jr.	100.00	45.00	12.50
☐ 20 Marquis Grissom	8.00	3.60	1.00
☐ 21 Tony Gwynn	50.00	22.00	6.25
☐ 22 Gregg Jefferies	4.00	1.80	.50
☐ 23 Randy Johnson	15.00	6.75	1.85
☐ 24 David Justice	8.00	3.60	1.00
☐ 25 Barry Larkin	12.00	5.50	1.50
☐ 26 Greg Maddux	60.00	27.00	7.50
☐ 27 Don Mattingly	50.00	22.00	6.25
☐ 28 Jack McDowell	4.00	1.80	.50
☐ 29 Fred McGriff	12.00	5.50	1.50
☐ 30 Paul Molitor	25.00	11.00	3.10
☐ 31 Raul Mondesi	12.00	5.50	1.50
☐ 32 John Olerud	4.00	1.80	.50
☐ 33 Rafael Palmeiro	12.00	5.50	1.50
☐ 34 Mike Piazza	75.00	34.00	9.50
☐ 35 Kirby Puckett	50.00	22.00	6.25
☐ 36 Manny Ramirez	20.00	9.00	2.50
☐ 37 Cal Ripken	80.00	36.00	10.00
☐ 38 Tim Salmon	12.00	5.50	1.50
☐ 39 Ryne Sandberg	40.00	18.00	5.00
☐ 40 Gary Sheffield	15.00	6.75	1.85
☐ 41 Frank Thomas	100.00	45.00	12.50
☐ 42 Andy Van Slyke	4.00	1.80	.50
☐ 43 Mo Vaughn	25.00	11.00	3.10
☐ 44 Larry Walker	15.00	6.75	1.85
☐ 45 Matt Williams	15.00	6.75	1.85

1995 Topps Pre-Production

Each 1994 Topps Baker's Dozen Factory set included a cello bag containing nine pre-production cards as well as one Spectralite version of one of those cards. The standard-size cards feature on their fronts color photos with ragged white borders and the player's name stamped in gold foil. The horizontal backs carry a color closeup photo, biography, major league batting or pitching record, and statistical highlights. The cards are easily distinguished from their regular issue counterparts not only by the "PP" number prefix but also by the words "Pre-Production Sample" printed across the 1994 stat line. The prices below are for the regular pre-production samples; the Spectralite versions are valued at 3X the values below.

	MINT	NRMT	EXC
COMPLETE SET (9)	9.00	4.00	1.10
COMMON CARD (PP1-PP9)	.25	.11	.03
☐ PP1 Larry Walker	.75	.35	.09
☐ PP2 Mike Piazza	4.00	1.80	.50
☐ PP3 Greg Vaughn	.40	.18	.05
☐ PP4 Sandy Alomar	.25	.11	.03
☐ PP5 Travis Fryman	.40	.18	.05
☐ PP6 Ken Griffey Jr.	5.00	2.20	.60
☐ PP7 Mike Devereaux	.25	.11	.03
☐ PP8 Roberto Hernandez	.25	.11	.03
☐ PP9 Alex Fernandez	.75	.35	.09

1995 Topps

These 660 standard-size cards feature color action player photos with white borders on the fronts. This set was released in two series. The first series contained 396 cards while the second series had 264 cards. The player's name in gold-foil appears below the photo, with his position and team name underneath. The horizontal backs carry a color player close-up with a color player cut-out superimposed over it. Player biography, statistics and career highlights complete the backs. One "Own The Game" instant winner card has been inserted in every 120 packs. Rookie cards in this set include Karim Garcia, Jay Payton and Rey Ordonez.

	MINT	NRMT	EXC
COMPLETE SET (660)	45.00	20.00	5.50
COMP.HOB.FACT.SET (677)	50.00	22.00	6.25
COMP.RET.FACT.SET (677)	50.00	22.00	6.25
COMPLETE SERIES 1 (396)	25.00	11.00	3.10
COMPLETE SERIES 2 (264)	20.00	9.00	2.50
COMMON CARD (1-660)	.10	.05	.01
☐ 1 Frank Thomas	3.00	1.35	.35
☐ 2 Mickey Morandini	.10	.05	.01
☐ 3 Babe Ruth 100th B-Day	2.00	.90	.25
☐ 4 Scott Cooper	.10	.05	.01
☐ 5 David Cone	.25	.11	.03
☐ 6 Jacob Shumate	.25	.11	.03
☐ 7 Trevor Hoffman	.25	.11	.03
☐ 8 Shane Mack	.10	.05	.01
☐ 9 Delino DeShields	.10	.05	.01
☐ 10 Matt Williams	.50	.23	.06
☐ 11 Sammy Sosa	.50	.23	.06
☐ 12 Gary DiSarcina	.10	.05	.01
☐ 13 Kenny Rogers	.10	.05	.01
☐ 14 Jose Vizcaino	.10	.05	.01
☐ 15 Lou Whitaker	.25	.11	.03
☐ 16 Ron Darling	.10	.05	.01

Card			
□ 17 Dave Nilsson	.25	.11	.03
□ 18 Chris Hammond	.10	.05	.01
□ 19 Sid Bream	.10	.05	.01
□ 20 Denny Martinez	.25	.11	.03
□ 21 Orlando Merced	.10	.05	.01
□ 22 John Wetteland	.25	.11	.03
□ 23 Mike Devereaux	.10	.05	.01
□ 24 Rene Arocha	.10	.05	.01
□ 25 Jay Buhner	.50	.23	.06
□ 26 Darren Holmes	.10	.05	.01
□ 27 Hal Morris	.10	.05	.01
□ 28 Brian Buchanan	.25	.11	.03
□ 29 Keith Miller	.10	.05	.01
□ 30 Paul Molitor	.60	.25	.07
□ 31 Dave West	.10	.05	.01
□ 32 Tony Tarasco	.10	.05	.01
□ 33 Scott Sanders	.10	.05	.01
□ 34 Eddie Zambrano	.10	.05	.01
□ 35 Ricky Bones	.10	.05	.01
□ 36 John Valentin	.25	.11	.03
□ 37 Kevin Tapani	.10	.05	.01
□ 38 Tim Wallach	.10	.05	.01
□ 39 Darren Lewis	.10	.05	.01
□ 40 Travis Fryman	.25	.11	.03
□ 41 Mark Leiter	.10	.05	.01
□ 42 Jose Bautista	.10	.05	.01
□ 43 Pete Smith	.10	.05	.01
□ 44 Bret Barberie	.10	.05	.01
□ 45 Dennis Eckersley	.25	.11	.03
□ 46 Ken Hill	.10	.05	.01
□ 47 Chad Ogea	.10	.05	.01
□ 48 Pete Harnisch	.10	.05	.01
□ 49 James Baldwin	.25	.11	.03
□ 50 Mike Mussina	.60	.25	.07
□ 51 Al Martin	.25	.11	.03
□ 52 Mark Thompson	.25	.11	.03
□ 53 Matt Smith	.25	.11	.03
□ 54 Joey Hamilton	.50	.23	.06
□ 55 Edgar Martinez	.25	.11	.03
□ 56 John Smiley	.10	.05	.01
□ 57 Rey Sanchez	.10	.05	.01
□ 58 Mike Timlin	.10	.05	.01
□ 59 Ricky Bottalico	.25	.11	.03
□ 60 Jim Abbott	.10	.05	.01
□ 61 Mike Kelly	.10	.05	.01
□ 62 Brian Jordan	.50	.23	.06
□ 63 Ken Ryan	.10	.05	.01
□ 64 Matt Mieske	.25	.11	.03
□ 65 Rick Aguilera	.10	.05	.01
□ 66 Ismael Valdes	.25	.11	.03
□ 67 Royce Clayton	.10	.05	.01
□ 68 Junior Felix	.10	.05	.01
□ 69 Harold Reynolds	.10	.05	.01
□ 70 Juan Gonzalez	1.50	.70	.19
□ 71 Kelly Stinnett	.10	.05	.01
□ 72 Carlos Reyes	.10	.05	.01
□ 73 Dave Weathers	.10	.05	.01
□ 74 Mel Rojas	.10	.05	.01
□ 75 Doug Drabek	.10	.05	.01
□ 76 Charles Nagy	.25	.11	.03
□ 77 Tim Raines	.50	.23	.06
□ 78 Midre Cummings	.10	.05	.01
□ 79 First Base Prospects	.50	.23	.06
Gene Schall			
Scott Talanoa			
Harold Williams			
Ray Brown			
□ 80 Rafael Palmeiro	.50	.23	.06
□ 81 Charlie Hayes	.10	.05	.01
□ 82 Ray Lankford	.25	.11	.03
□ 83 Tim Davis	.10	.05	.01
□ 84 C.J. Nitkowski	.25	.11	.03
□ 85 Andy Ashby	.25	.11	.03
□ 86 Gerald Williams	.10	.05	.01
□ 87 Terry Shumpert	.10	.05	.01
□ 88 Heathcliff Slocumb	.10	.05	.01
□ 89 Domingo Cedeno	.10	.05	.01
□ 90 Mark Grace	.50	.23	.06
□ 91 Brad Woodall	.10	.05	.01
□ 92 Gar Finnvold	.10	.05	.01
□ 93 Jaime Navarro	.10	.05	.01
□ 94 Carlos Hernandez	.10	.05	.01
□ 95 Mark Langston	.10	.05	.01
□ 96 Chuck Carr	.10	.05	.01
□ 97 Mike Gardiner	.10	.05	.01
□ 98 Dave McCarty	.10	.05	.01
□ 99 Cris Carpenter	.10	.05	.01
□ 100 Barry Bonds	.75	.35	.09
□ 101 David Segui	.10	.05	.01
□ 102 Scott Brosius	.10	.05	.01
□ 103 Mariano Duncan	.10	.05	.01
□ 104 Kenny Lofton	.75	.35	.09
□ 105 Ken Caminiti	.50	.23	.06
□ 106 Darrin Jackson	.10	.05	.01
□ 107 Jim Poole	.10	.05	.01
□ 108 Wil Cordero	.10	.05	.01
□ 109 Danny Miceli	.10	.05	.01
□ 110 Walt Weiss	.10	.05	.01
□ 111 Tom Pagnozzi	.10	.05	.01
□ 112 Terrence Long	.50	.23	.06
□ 113 Bret Boone	.25	.11	.03
□ 114 Daryl Boston	.10	.05	.01
□ 115 Wally Joyner	.25	.11	.03
□ 116 Rob Butler	.10	.05	.01
□ 117 Rafael Belliard	.10	.05	.01
□ 118 Luis Lopez	.10	.05	.01
□ 119 Tony Fossas	.10	.05	.01
□ 120 Len Dykstra	.25	.11	.03
□ 121 Mike Morgan	.10	.05	.01
□ 122 Denny Hocking	.10	.05	.01
□ 123 Kevin Gross	.10	.05	.01
□ 124 Todd Benzinger	.10	.05	.01
□ 125 John Doherty	.10	.05	.01
□ 126 Eduardo Perez	.10	.05	.01
□ 127 Dan Smith	.10	.05	.01
□ 128 Joe Orsulak	.10	.05	.01
□ 129 Brent Gates	.10	.05	.01
□ 130 Jeff Conine	.25	.11	.03
□ 131 Doug Henry	.10	.05	.01
□ 132 Paul Sorrento	.10	.05	.01
□ 133 Mike Hampton	.25	.11	.03
□ 134 Tim Spehr	.10	.05	.01
□ 135 Julio Franco	.25	.11	.03
□ 136 Mike Dyer	.10	.05	.01
□ 137 Chris Sabo	.10	.05	.01
□ 138 Rheal Cormier	.10	.05	.01
□ 139 Paul Konerko	2.00	.90	.25
□ 140 Dante Bichette	.50	.23	.06
□ 141 Chuck McElroy	.10	.05	.01
□ 142 Mike Stanley	.10	.05	.01
□ 143 Bob Hamelin	.10	.05	.01
□ 144 Tommy Greene	.10	.05	.01
□ 145 John Smoltz	.50	.23	.06
□ 146 Ed Sprague	.25	.11	.03
□ 147 Ray McDavid	.25	.11	.03
□ 148 Otis Nixon	.10	.05	.01
□ 149 Turk Wendell	.10	.05	.01
□ 150 Chris James	.10	.05	.01
□ 151 Derek Parks	.10	.05	.01
□ 152 Jose Offerman	.10	.05	.01
□ 153 Tony Clark	.75	.35	.09
□ 154 Chad Curtis	.10	.05	.01
□ 155 Mark Portugal	.10	.05	.01
□ 156 Bill Pulsipher	.25	.11	.03
□ 157 Troy Neel	.10	.05	.01
□ 158 Dave Winfield	.50	.23	.06
□ 159 Bill Wegman	.10	.05	.01
□ 160 Benito Santiago	.10	.05	.01
□ 161 Jose Mesa	.10	.05	.01
□ 162 Luis Gonzalez	.10	.05	.01
□ 163 Alex Fernandez	.25	.11	.03
□ 164 Freddie Benavides	.10	.05	.01
□ 165 Ben McDonald	.10	.05	.01
□ 166 Blas Minor	.10	.05	.01
□ 167 Bret Wagner	.25	.11	.03
□ 168 Mac Suzuki	.25	.11	.03
□ 169 Roberto Mejia	.10	.05	.01
□ 170 Wade Boggs	.50	.23	.06
□ 171 Calvin Reese	.10	.05	.01
□ 172 Hipolito Pichardo	.10	.05	.01
□ 173 Kim Batiste	.10	.05	.01
□ 174 Darren Hall	.10	.05	.01
□ 175 Tom Glavine	.50	.23	.06
□ 176 Phil Plantier	.10	.05	.01
□ 177 Chris Howard	.10	.05	.01
□ 178 Karl Rhodes	.10	.05	.01
□ 179 LaTroy Hawkins	.10	.05	.01
□ 180 Raul Mondesi	.50	.23	.06
□ 181 Jeff Reed	.10	.05	.01
□ 182 Milt Cuyler	.10	.05	.01
□ 183 Jim Edmonds	.50	.23	.06
□ 184 Hector Fajardo	.10	.05	.01
□ 185 Jeff Kent	.10	.05	.01
□ 186 Wilson Alvarez	.25	.11	.03
□ 187 Geronimo Berroa	.10	.05	.01
□ 188 Billy Spiers	.10	.05	.01
□ 189 Derek Lilliquist	.10	.05	.01
□ 190 Craig Biggio	.25	.11	.03
□ 191 Roberto Hernandez	.10	.05	.01
□ 192 Bob Natal	.10	.05	.01
□ 193 Bobby Ayala	.10	.05	.01
□ 194 Travis Miller	.25	.11	.03
□ 195 Bob Tewksbury	.10	.05	.01
□ 196 Rondell White	.25	.11	.03
□ 197 Steve Cooke	.10	.05	.01
□ 198 Jeff Branson	.10	.05	.01
□ 199 Derek Jeter	2.00	.90	.25
□ 200 Tim Salmon	.50	.23	.06
□ 201 Steve Frey	.10	.05	.01
□ 202 Kent Mercker	.10	.05	.01
□ 203 Randy Johnson	.50	.23	.06
□ 204 Todd Worrell	.10	.05	.01
□ 205 Mo Vaughn	.75	.35	.09
□ 206 Howard Johnson	.10	.05	.01
□ 207 John Wasdin	.25	.11	.03
□ 208 Eddie Williams	.10	.05	.01
□ 209 Tim Belcher	.25	.11	.03
□ 210 Jeff Montgomery	.25	.11	.03
□ 211 Kirt Manwaring	.10	.05	.01
□ 212 Ben Grieve	1.50	.70	.19
□ 213 Pat Hentgen	.25	.11	.03
□ 214 Shawon Dunston	.10	.05	.01
□ 215 Mike Greenwell	.10	.05	.01
□ 216 Alex Diaz	.10	.05	.01
□ 217 Pat Mahomes	.10	.05	.01
□ 218 Dave Hansen	.10	.05	.01
□ 219 Kevin Rogers	.10	.05	.01
□ 220 Cecil Fielder	.25	.11	.03
□ 221 Andrew Lorraine	.25	.11	.03
□ 222 Jack Armstrong	.10	.05	.01
□ 223 Todd Hundley	.25	.11	.03
□ 224 Mark Acre	.10	.05	.01
□ 225 Darrell Whitmore	.10	.05	.01
□ 226 Randy Milligan	.10	.05	.01
□ 227 Wayne Kirby	.10	.05	.01
□ 228 Darryl Kile	.10	.05	.01
□ 229 Bob Zupcic	.10	.05	.01
□ 230 Jay Bell	.25	.11	.03
□ 231 Dustin Hermanson	.25	.11	.03
□ 232 Harold Baines	.25	.11	.03
□ 233 Alan Benes	.50	.23	.06
□ 234 Felix Fermin	.10	.05	.01
□ 235 Ellis Burks	.25	.11	.03
□ 236 Jeff Brantley	.10	.05	.01
□ 237 Outfield Prospects	3.00	1.35	.35
Brian Hunter			
Jose Malave			
Karim Garcia			
Shane Pullen			
□ 238 Matt Nokes	.10	.05	.01
□ 239 Ben Rivera	.10	.05	.01
□ 240 Joe Carter	.25	.11	.03
□ 241 Jeff Granger	.10	.05	.01
□ 242 Terry Pendelton	.25	.11	.03
□ 243 Melvin Nieves	.25	.11	.03
□ 244 Frankie Rodriguez	.25	.11	.03
□ 245 Darryl Hamilton	.10	.05	.01
□ 246 Brooks Kieschnick	.50	.23	.06
□ 247 Todd Hollandsworth	.50	.23	.06
□ 248 Joe Rosselli	.10	.05	.01
□ 249 Bill Gullickson	.10	.05	.01
□ 250 Chuck Knoblauch	.50	.23	.06
□ 251 Kurt Miller	.10	.05	.01
□ 252 Bobby Jones	.25	.11	.03
□ 253 Lance Blankenship	.10	.05	.01
□ 254 Matt Whiteside	.10	.05	.01
□ 255 Darrin Fletcher	.10	.05	.01
□ 256 Eric Plunk	.10	.05	.01
□ 257 Shane Reynolds	.25	.11	.03
□ 258 Norberto Martin	.10	.05	.01
□ 259 Mike Thurman	.10	.05	.01
□ 260 Andy Van Slyke	.25	.11	.03
□ 261 Dwight Smith	.10	.05	.01
□ 262 Allen Watson	.10	.05	.01
□ 263 Dan Wilson	.25	.11	.03
□ 264 Brent Mayne	.10	.05	.01
□ 265 Bip Roberts	.10	.05	.01
□ 266 Sterling Hitchcock	.25	.11	.03
□ 267 Alex Gonzalez	.25	.11	.03
□ 268 Greg Harris	.10	.05	.01
□ 269 Ricky Jordan	.10	.05	.01
□ 270 Johnny Ruffin	.10	.05	.01
□ 271 Mike Stanton	.10	.05	.01
□ 272 Rich Rowland	.10	.05	.01
□ 273 Steve Trachsel	.10	.05	.01
□ 274 Pedro Munoz	.10	.05	.01
□ 275 Ramon Martinez	.25	.11	.03
□ 276 Dave Henderson	.10	.05	.01
□ 277 Chris Gomez	.10	.05	.01
□ 278 Joe Grahe	.10	.05	.01
□ 279 Rusty Greer	.50	.23	.06
□ 280 John Franco	.10	.05	.01
□ 281 Mike Bordick	.10	.05	.01
□ 282 Jeff D'Amico	.50	.23	.06
□ 283 Dave Magadan	.10	.05	.01
□ 284 Tony Pena	.10	.05	.01
□ 285 Greg Swindell	.10	.05	.01
□ 286 Doug Million	.50	.23	.06
□ 287 Gabe White	.10	.05	.01
□ 288 Trey Beamon	.25	.11	.03
□ 289 Arthur Rhodes	.10	.05	.01
□ 290 Juan Guzman	.25	.11	.03
□ 291 Jose Oquendo	.10	.05	.01
□ 292 Willie Blair	.10	.05	.01
□ 293 Eddie Taubensee	.10	.05	.01
□ 294 Steve Howe	.10	.05	.01
□ 295 Greg Maddux	2.00	.90	.25
□ 296 Mike Macfarlane	.10	.05	.01
□ 297 Curt Schilling	.10	.05	.01
□ 298 Phil Clark	.10	.05	.01
□ 299 Woody Williams	.10	.05	.01
□ 300 Jose Canseco	.50	.23	.06
□ 301 Aaron Sele	.25	.11	.03
□ 302 Carl Willis	.10	.05	.01
□ 303 Steve Buechele	.10	.05	.01
□ 304 Dave Burba	.10	.05	.01
□ 305 Orel Hershiser	.25	.11	.03
□ 306 Damion Easley	.10	.05	.01
□ 307 Mike Henneman	.10	.05	.01
□ 308 Josias Manzanillo	.10	.05	.01
□ 309 Kevin Seitzer	.10	.05	.01
□ 310 Ruben Sierra	.25	.11	.03
□ 311 Bryan Harvey	.10	.05	.01
□ 312 Jim Thome	.60	.25	.07
□ 313 Ramon Castro	.25	.11	.03
□ 314 Lance Johnson	.25	.11	.03
□ 315 Marquis Grissom	.25	.11	.03
□ 316 Starting Pitcher Prospects	.50	.23	.06
Terrell Wade			
Juan Acevedo			
Matt Arrandale			
Eddie Priest			
□ 317 Paul Wagner	.10	.05	.01
□ 318 Jamie Moyer	.10	.05	.01
□ 319 Todd Zeile	.10	.05	.01
□ 320 Chris Bosio	.10	.05	.01
□ 321 Steve Reed	.10	.05	.01
□ 322 Erik Hanson	.10	.05	.01
□ 323 Luis Polonia	.10	.05	.01
□ 324 Ryan Klesko	.50	.23	.06
□ 325 Kevin Appier	.25	.11	.03
□ 326 Jim Eisenreich	.10	.05	.01
□ 327 Randy Knorr	.10	.05	.01
□ 328 Craig Shipley	.10	.05	.01
□ 329 Tim Naehring	.10	.05	.01
□ 330 Randy Myers	.10	.05	.01
□ 331 Alex Cole	.10	.05	.01
□ 332 Jim Gott	.10	.05	.01
□ 333 Mike Jackson	.10	.05	.01
□ 334 John Flaherty	.10	.05	.01
□ 335 Chili Davis	.25	.11	.03
□ 336 Benji Gil	.10	.05	.01
□ 337 Jason Jacome	.10	.05	.01
□ 338 Stan Javier	.10	.05	.01
□ 339 Mike Fetters	.10	.05	.01
□ 340 Rich Renteria	.10	.05	.01
□ 341 Kevin Witt	.25	.11	.03
□ 342 Scott Servais	.10	.05	.01
□ 343 Craig Grebeck	.10	.05	.01
□ 344 Kirk Rueter	.10	.05	.01
□ 345 Don Slaught	.10	.05	.01
□ 346 Armando Benitez	.10	.05	.01
□ 347 Ozzie Smith	.75	.35	.09
□ 348 Mike Blowers	.10	.05	.01
□ 349 Armando Reynoso	.10	.05	.01
□ 350 Barry Larkin	.50	.23	.06
□ 351 Mike Williams	.10	.05	.01
□ 352 Scott Kamieniecki	.10	.05	.01
□ 353 Gary Gaetti	.25	.11	.03
□ 354 Todd Stottlemyre	.10	.05	.01
□ 355 Fred McGriff	.50	.23	.06
□ 356 Tim Mauser	.10	.05	.01
□ 357 Chris Gwynn	.10	.05	.01
□ 358 Frank Castillo	.10	.05	.01
□ 359 Jeff Reboulet	.10	.05	.01
□ 360 Roger Clemens	.60	.25	.07
□ 361 Mark Carreon	.10	.05	.01
□ 362 Chad Kreuter	.10	.05	.01
□ 363 Mark Farris	.25	.11	.03
□ 364 Bob Welch	.10	.05	.01
□ 365 Dean Palmer	.25	.11	.03
□ 366 Jeromy Burnitz	.10	.05	.01
□ 367 B.J. Surhoff	.25	.11	.03
□ 368 Mike Butcher	.10	.05	.01
□ 369 Relief Pitcher Prospects	.25	.11	.03
Brad Clontz			
Steve Phoenix			
Scott Gentile			
Bucky Buckles			
□ 370 Eddie Murray	.75	.35	.09
□ 371 Orlando Miller	.10	.05	.01
□ 372 Ron Karkovice	.10	.05	.01
□ 373 Richie Lewis	.10	.05	.01
□ 374 Lenny Webster	.10	.05	.01
□ 375 Jeff Tackett	.10	.05	.01
□ 376 Tom Urbani	.10	.05	.01
□ 377 Tino Martinez	.25	.11	.03
□ 378 Mark Dewey	.10	.05	.01
□ 379 Charles O'Brien	.10	.05	.01
□ 380 Terry Mulholland	.10	.05	.01
□ 381 Thomas Howard	.10	.05	.01
□ 382 Chris Haney	.10	.05	.01
□ 383 Billy Hatcher	.10	.05	.01
□ 384 Jeff Bagwell AS	.75	.35	.09
Frank Thomas AS			
□ 385 Bret Boone AS	.25	.11	.03
Carlos Baerga AS			
□ 386 Matt Williams AS	.25	.11	.03
Wade Boggs AS			
□ 387 Wil Cordero AS	.50	.23	.06
Cal Ripken AS			
□ 388 Barry Bonds AS	.75	.35	.09
Ken Griffey AS			
□ 389 Tony Gwynn AS	.50	.23	.06
Albert Belle AS			
□ 390 Dante Bichette AS	.25	.11	.03
Kirby Puckett AS			
□ 391 Mike Piazza AS	.50	.23	.06
Mike Stanley AS			
□ 392 Greg Maddux AS	.50	.23	.06
David Cone AS			
□ 393 Danny Jackson AS	.10	.05	.01
Jimmy Key AS			
□ 394 John Franco AS	.10	.05	.01
Lee Smith AS			
□ 395 Checklist 1-198	.10	.05	.01
□ 396 Checklist 199-396	.10	.05	.01
□ 397 Ken Griffey Jr.	3.00	1.35	.35
□ 398 Rick Heiserman	.25	.11	.03
□ 399 Don Mattingly	1.50	.70	.19
□ 400 Henry Rodriguez	.25	.11	.03
□ 401 Lenny Harris	.10	.05	.01
□ 402 Ryan Thompson	.10	.05	.01
□ 403 Darren Oliver	.50	.23	.06
□ 404 Omar Vizquel	.25	.11	.03
□ 405 Jeff Bagwell	1.25	.55	.16
□ 406 Doug Webb	.10	.05	.01
□ 407 Todd Van Poppel	.10	.05	.01

☐ 408 Leo Gomez .10 .05 .01
☐ 409 Mark Whiten .10 .05 .01
☐ 410 Pedro Martinez .25 .11 .03
☐ 411 Reggie Sanders .25 .11 .03
☐ 412 Kevin Foster .10 .05 .01
☐ 413 Danny Tartabull .10 .05 .01
☐ 414 Jeff Blauser .10 .05 .01
☐ 415 Mike Magnante .10 .05 .01
☐ 416 Tom Candiotti .10 .05 .01
☐ 417 Rod Beck .10 .05 .01
☐ 418 Jody Reed .10 .05 .01
☐ 419 Vince Coleman .10 .05 .01
☐ 420 Danny Jackson .10 .05 .01
☐ 421 Ryan Nye .25 .11 .03
☐ 422 Larry Walker .50 .23 .06
☐ 423 Russ Johnson DP .25 .11 .03
☐ 424 Pat Borders .10 .05 .01
☐ 425 Lee Smith .25 .11 .03
☐ 426 Paul O'Neill .25 .11 .03
☐ 427 Devon White .25 .11 .03
☐ 428 Jim Bullinger .10 .05 .01
☐ 429 Starting Pitchers .25 .11 .03
Prospects
Greg Hansell
Brian Sackinsky
Carey Paige
Rob Welch
☐ 430 Steve Avery .25 .11 .03
☐ 431 Tony Gwynn 1.25 .55 .16
☐ 432 Pat Meares .10 .05 .01
☐ 433 Bill Swift .10 .05 .01
☐ 434 David Wells .10 .05 .01
☐ 435 John Briscoe .10 .05 .01
☐ 436 Roger Pavlik .10 .05 .01
☐ 437 Jayson Peterson .25 .11 .03
☐ 438 Roberto Alomar .60 .25 .07
☐ 439 Billy Brewer .10 .05 .01
☐ 440 Gary Sheffield .50 .23 .06
☐ 441 Lou Frazier .10 .05 .01
☐ 442 Terry Steinbach .25 .11 .03
☐ 443 Jay Payton 1.00 .45 .12
☐ 444 Jason Bere .10 .05 .01
☐ 445 Denny Neagle .25 .11 .03
☐ 446 Andres Galarraga .50 .23 .06
☐ 447 Hector Carrasco .10 .05 .01
☐ 448 Bill Risley .10 .05 .01
☐ 449 Andy Benes .10 .05 .01
☐ 450 Jim Leyritz .10 .05 .01
☐ 451 Jose Oliva .10 .05 .01
☐ 452 Greg Vaughn .25 .11 .03
☐ 453 Rich Monteleone .10 .05 .01
☐ 454 Tony Eusebio .10 .05 .01
☐ 455 Chuck Finley .25 .11 .03
☐ 456 Kevin Brown .25 .11 .03
☐ 457 Joe Boever .10 .05 .01
☐ 458 Bobby Munoz .10 .05 .01
☐ 459 Bret Saberhagen .25 .11 .03
☐ 460 Kurt Abbott .10 .05 .01
☐ 461 Bobby Witt .10 .05 .01
☐ 462 Cliff Floyd .25 .11 .03
☐ 463 Mark Clark .10 .05 .01
☐ 464 Andujar Cedeno .10 .05 .01
☐ 465 Marvin Freeman .10 .05 .01
☐ 466 Mike Piazza 2.00 .90 .25
☐ 467 Willie Greene .10 .05 .01
☐ 468 Pat Kelly .10 .05 .01
☐ 469 Carlos Delgado .25 .11 .03
☐ 470 Willie Banks .10 .05 .01
☐ 471 Matt Walbeck .10 .05 .01
☐ 472 Mark McGwire 1.00 .45 .12
☐ 473 McKay Christensen .25 .11 .03
☐ 474 Alan Trammell .25 .11 .03
☐ 475 Tom Gordon .10 .05 .01
☐ 476 Greg Colbrunn .10 .05 .01
☐ 477 Darren Daulton .25 .11 .03
☐ 478 Albie Lopez .10 .05 .01
☐ 479 Robin Ventura .25 .11 .03
☐ 480 Catcher Prospects .25 .11 .03
Eddie Perez
Jason Kendall
Einar Diaz
Bret Hemphill
☐ 481 Bryan Eversgerd .10 .05 .01
☐ 482 Dave Fleming .10 .05 .01
☐ 483 Scott Livingstone .10 .05 .01
☐ 484 Pete Schourek .25 .11 .03
☐ 485 Bernie Williams .60 .25 .07
☐ 486 Mark Lemke .10 .05 .01
☐ 487 Eric Karros .25 .11 .03
☐ 488 Scott Ruffcorn .10 .05 .01
☐ 489 Billy Ashley .10 .05 .01
☐ 490 Rico Brogna .10 .05 .01
☐ 491 John Burkett .25 .11 .03
☐ 492 Cade Gaspar .25 .11 .03
☐ 493 Jorge Fabregas .10 .05 .01
☐ 494 Greg Gagne .10 .05 .01
☐ 495 Doug Jones .10 .05 .01
☐ 496 Troy O'Leary .10 .05 .01
☐ 497 Pat Rapp .10 .05 .01
☐ 498 Butch Henry .10 .05 .01
☐ 499 John Olerud .10 .05 .01
☐ 500 John Hudek .10 .05 .01
☐ 501 Jeff King .25 .11 .03
☐ 502 Bobby Bonilla .25 .11 .03
☐ 503 Albert Belle 1.25 .55 .16
☐ 504 Rick Wilkins .10 .05 .01
☐ 505 John Jaha .25 .11 .03
☐ 506 Nigel Wilson .10 .05 .01
☐ 507 Sid Fernandez .10 .05 .01
☐ 508 Deion Sanders .50 .23 .06
☐ 509 Gil Heredia .10 .05 .01
☐ 510 Scott Elarton .50 .23 .06
☐ 511 Melido Perez .10 .05 .01
☐ 512 Greg McMichael .10 .05 .01
☐ 513 Rusty Meacham .10 .05 .01
☐ 514 Shawn Green .25 .11 .03
☐ 515 Carlos Garcia .10 .05 .01
☐ 516 Dave Stevens .10 .05 .01
☐ 517 Eric Young .25 .11 .03
☐ 518 Omar Daal .10 .05 .01
☐ 519 Kirk Gibson .25 .11 .03
☐ 520 Spike Owen .10 .05 .01
☐ 521 Jacob Cruz .60 .25 .07
☐ 522 Sandy Alomar Jr. .10 .05 .01
☐ 523 Steve Bedrosian .10 .05 .01
☐ 524 Ricky Gutierrez .10 .05 .01
☐ 525 Dave Veres .10 .05 .01
☐ 526 Gregg Jefferies .25 .11 .03
☐ 527 Jose Valentin .25 .11 .03
☐ 528 Robb Nen .10 .05 .01
☐ 529 Jose Rijo .10 .05 .01
☐ 530 Sean Berry .10 .05 .01
☐ 531 Mike Gallego .10 .05 .01
☐ 532 Roberto Kelly .10 .05 .01
☐ 533 Kevin Stocker .10 .05 .01
☐ 534 Kirby Puckett 1.25 .55 .16
☐ 535 Chipper Jones 2.00 .90 .25
☐ 536 Russ Davis .10 .05 .01
☐ 537 Jon Lieber .10 .05 .01
☐ 538 Trey Moore .25 .11 .03
☐ 539 Joe Girardi .10 .05 .01
☐ 540 Second Base Prospects .25 .11 .03
Quilvio Veras
Arquimedez Pozo
Miguel Cairo
Jason Camilli
☐ 541 Tony Phillips .25 .11 .03
☐ 542 Brian Anderson .10 .05 .01
☐ 543 Ivan Rodriguez .75 .35 .09
☐ 544 Jeff Cirillo .25 .11 .03
☐ 545 Joey Cora .10 .05 .01
☐ 546 Chris Hoiles .10 .05 .01
☐ 547 Bernard Gilkey .25 .11 .03
☐ 548 Mike Lansing .10 .05 .01
☐ 549 Jimmy Key .25 .11 .03
☐ 550 Mark Wohlers .25 .11 .03
☐ 551 Chris Clemons .25 .11 .03
☐ 552 Vinny Castilla .25 .11 .03
☐ 553 Mark Guthrie .10 .05 .01
☐ 554 Mike Lieberthal .10 .05 .01
☐ 555 Tommy Davis .25 .11 .03
☐ 556 Robby Thompson .10 .05 .01
☐ 557 Danny Bautista .10 .05 .01
☐ 558 Will Clark .50 .23 .06
☐ 559 Rickey Henderson .50 .23 .06
☐ 560 Todd Jones .10 .05 .01
☐ 561 Jack McDowell .25 .11 .03
☐ 562 Carlos Rodriguez .10 .05 .01
☐ 563 Mark Eichhorn .10 .05 .01
☐ 564 Jeff Nelson .10 .05 .01
☐ 565 Eric Anthony .10 .05 .01
☐ 566 Randy Velarde .10 .05 .01
☐ 567 Javier Lopez .50 .23 .06
☐ 568 Kevin Mitchell .25 .11 .03
☐ 569 Steve Karsay .10 .05 .01
☐ 570 Brian Meadows .30 .14 .04
☐ 571 Rey Ordonez 1.50 .70 .19
Mike Metcalfe
Kevin Orie
Ray Holbert
☐ 572 John Kruk .25 .11 .03
☐ 573 Scott Leius .10 .05 .01
☐ 574 John Patterson .10 .05 .01
☐ 575 Kevin Brown .25 .11 .03
☐ 576 Mike Moore .10 .05 .01
☐ 577 Manny Ramirez .75 .35 .09
☐ 578 Jose Lind .10 .05 .01
☐ 579 Derrick May .10 .05 .01
☐ 580 Cal Eldred .10 .05 .01
☐ 581 Third Base Prospects .30 .14 .04
David Bell
Joel Chelmis
Lino Diaz
Aaron Boone
☐ 582 J.T. Snow .25 .11 .03
☐ 583 Luis Sojo .10 .05 .01
☐ 584 Moises Alou .25 .11 .03
☐ 585 Dave Clark .10 .05 .01
☐ 586 Dave Hollins .10 .05 .01
☐ 587 Nomar Garciaparra 2.00 .90 .25
☐ 588 Cal Ripken 2.50 1.10 .30
☐ 589 Pedro Astacio .10 .05 .01
☐ 590 J.R. Phillips .10 .05 .01
☐ 591 Jeff Frye .10 .05 .01
☐ 592 Bo Jackson .25 .11 .03
☐ 593 Steve Ontiveros .10 .05 .01
☐ 594 David Nied .10 .05 .01
☐ 595 Brad Ausmus .10 .05 .01
☐ 596 Carlos Baerga .25 .11 .03
☐ 597 James Mouton .10 .05 .01
☐ 598 Ozzie Guillen .10 .05 .01
☐ 599 Outfield Prospects 1.00 .45 .12
Ozzie Timmons
Curtis Goodwin
Johnny Damon
Jeff Abbott
☐ 600 Yorkis Perez .10 .05 .01
☐ 601 Rich Rodriguez .10 .05 .01
☐ 602 Mark McLemore .10 .05 .01
☐ 603 Jeff Fassero .10 .05 .01
☐ 604 John Roper .10 .05 .01
☐ 605 Mark Johnson .25 .11 .03
☐ 606 Wes Chamberlain .10 .05 .01
☐ 607 Felix Jose .10 .05 .01
☐ 608 Tony Longmire .10 .05 .01
☐ 609 Duane Ward .10 .05 .01
☐ 610 Brett Butler .25 .11 .03
☐ 611 William VanLandingham .10 .05 .01
☐ 612 Mickey Tettleton .10 .05 .01
☐ 613 Brady Anderson .50 .23 .06
☐ 614 Reggie Jefferson .25 .11 .03
☐ 615 Mike Kingery .10 .05 .01
☐ 616 Derek Bell .25 .11 .03
☐ 617 Scott Erickson .10 .05 .01
☐ 618 Bob Wickman .10 .05 .01
☐ 619 Phil Leftwich .10 .05 .01
☐ 620 David Justice .50 .23 .06
☐ 621 Paul Wilson .50 .23 .06
☐ 622 Pedro Martinez .25 .11 .03
☐ 623 Terry Mathews .10 .05 .01
☐ 624 Brian McRae .25 .11 .03
☐ 625 Bruce Ruffin .10 .05 .01
☐ 626 Steve Finley .25 .11 .03
☐ 627 Ron Gant .25 .11 .03
☐ 628 Rafael Bournigal .10 .05 .01
☐ 629 Darryl Strawberry .25 .11 .03
☐ 630 Luis Alicea .10 .05 .01
☐ 631 Orioles Prospects .25 .11 .03
Mark Smith
Scott Klingenbeck
☐ 632 Red Sox Prospects .25 .11 .03
Cory Bailey
Scott Hatteberg
☐ 633 Angels Prospects .25 .11 .03
Todd Greene
Troy Percival
☐ 634 White Sox Prospects .10 .05 .01
Rod Bolton
Olmedo Saenz
☐ 635 Indians Prospects .25 .11 .03
Steve Kline
Herb Perry
☐ 636 Tigers Prospects .25 .11 .03
Sean Bergman
Shannon Penn
☐ 637 Royals Prospects .25 .11 .03
Joe Randa
Joe Vitiello
☐ 638 Brewers Prospects .25 .11 .03
Jose Mercedes
Duane Singleton
☐ 639 Twins Prospects .50 .23 .06
Marc Barcelo
Marty Cordova
☐ 640 Yankees Prospects 2.00 .90 .25
Andy Pettitte
Ruben Rivera
☐ 641 Athletics Prospects .25 .11 .03
Willie Adams
Scott Spiezio
☐ 642 Mariners Prospects .25 .11 .03
Eddy Diaz
Desi Relaford
☐ 643 Rangers Prospects .10 .05 .01
Terrell Lowery
Jon Shave
☐ 644 Blue Jays Prospects .25 .11 .03
Angel Martinez
Paul Spoljaric
☐ 645 Braves Prospects .50 .23 .06
Tony Graffanino
Damon Hollins
☐ 646 Cubs Prospects .25 .11 .03
Darron Cox
Doug Glanville
☐ 647 Reds Prospects .25 .11 .03
Tim Belk
Pat Watkins
☐ 648 Rockies Prospects .10 .05 .01
Rod Pedraza
Phil Schneider
☐ 649 Marlins Prospects .25 .11 .03
Vic Darensbourg
Marc Valdes
☐ 650 Astros Prospects .25 .11 .03
Rick Huisman
Roberto Petagine
☐ 651 Dodgers Prospects .50 .23 .06
Roger Cedeno
Ron Coomer
☐ 652 Expos Prospects .25 .11 .03
Shane Andrews
Carlos Perez
☐ 653 Mets Prospects .50 .23 .06
Jason Isringhausen
Chris Roberts
☐ 654 Phillies Prospects .25 .11 .03
Wayne Gomes
Kevin Jordan
☐ 655 Pirates Prospects .25 .11 .03
Esteban Loaiza
Steve Pegues
☐ 656 Cardinals Prospects .25 .11 .03
Terry Bradshaw
John Frascatore
☐ 657 Padres Prospects .25 .11 .03
Andres Berumen
Bryce Florie
☐ 658 Giants Prospects .25 .11 .03
Dan Carlson
Keith Williams
☐ 659 Checklist .10 .05 .01
☐ 660 Checklist .10 .05 .01

1995 Topps Cyberstats

The 396-card Cyberstats insert set was issued one per pack and three per jumbo pack. Each 1995 Topps series had 198 Cyberstat cards. The idea was to present prorated statistics for the 1994 strike shortened season. The photos on front are the same as the basic issue. The difference is that the photo is given a glossy or metallic finish. The backs contain yearly and career statistics, including the prorated 1994 numbers.

	MINT	NRMT	EXC
COMPLETE SET (396)	80.00	36.00	10.00
COMPLETE SERIES 1 (198)	40.00	18.00	5.00
COMPLETE SERIES 2 (198)	40.00	18.00	5.00
COMMON CARD (1-396)	.25	.11	.03

☐ 1 Frank Thomas 8.00 3.60 1.00
☐ 2 Mickey Morandini .25 .11 .03
☐ 3 Todd Worrell .25 .11 .03
☐ 4 David Cone .50 .23 .06
☐ 5 Trevor Hoffman .25 .11 .03
☐ 6 Shane Mack .25 .11 .03
☐ 7 Delino DeShields .25 .11 .03
☐ 8 Matt Williams 1.00 .45 .12
☐ 9 Sammy Sosa 1.00 .45 .12
☐ 10 Gary DiSarcina .25 .11 .03
☐ 11 Kenny Rogers .25 .11 .03
☐ 12 Jose Vizcaino .25 .11 .03
☐ 13 Lou Whitaker .50 .23 .06
☐ 14 Ron Darling .25 .11 .03
☐ 15 Dave Nilsson .25 .11 .03
☐ 16 Denny Martinez .25 .11 .03
☐ 17 Orlando Merced .25 .11 .03
☐ 18 John Wetteland .50 .23 .06
☐ 19 Mike Devereaux .25 .11 .03
☐ 20 Rene Arocha .25 .11 .03
☐ 21 Jay Buhner 1.00 .45 .12
☐ 22 Hal Morris .25 .11 .03
☐ 23 Paul Molitor 1.50 .70 .19
☐ 24 Dave West .25 .11 .03
☐ 25 Scott Sanders .25 .11 .03
☐ 26 Eddie Zambrano .25 .11 .03
☐ 27 Ricky Bones .25 .11 .03
☐ 28 John Valentin .25 .11 .03
☐ 29 Kevin Tapani .25 .11 .03
☐ 30 Tim Wallach .25 .11 .03
☐ 31 Darren Lewis .25 .11 .03
☐ 32 Travis Fryman .50 .23 .06
☐ 33 Bret Barberie .25 .11 .03
☐ 34 Dennis Eckersley .50 .23 .06
☐ 35 Ken Hill .25 .11 .03
☐ 36 Pete Harnisch .25 .11 .03
☐ 37 Mike Mussina 1.50 .70 .19
☐ 38 Dave Winfield 1.00 .45 .12
☐ 39 Joey Hamilton 1.00 .45 .12
☐ 40 Edgar Martinez .50 .23 .06
☐ 41 John Smiley .25 .11 .03
☐ 42 Jim Abbott .25 .11 .03
☐ 43 Mike Kelly .25 .11 .03
☐ 44 Brian Jordan 1.00 .45 .12
☐ 45 Ken Ryan .25 .11 .03
☐ 46 Matt Mieske .25 .11 .03
☐ 47 Rick Aguilera .25 .11 .03
☐ 48 Ismael Valdes .50 .23 .06
☐ 49 Royce Clayton .25 .11 .03
☐ 50 Juan Gonzalez 4.00 1.80 .50
☐ 51 Mel Rojas .25 .11 .03
☐ 52 Doug Drabek .25 .11 .03
☐ 53 Charles Nagy .50 .23 .06
☐ 54 Tim Raines .50 .23 .06
☐ 55 Midre Cummings .25 .11 .03
☐ 56 Rafael Palmeiro 1.00 .45 .12
☐ 57 Charlie Hayes .25 .11 .03

☐ 58 Ray Lankford	.50	.23	.06
☐ 59 Tim Davis	.25	.11	.03
☐ 60 Andy Ashby	.25	.11	.03
☐ 61 Mark Grace	1.00	.45	.12
☐ 62 Mark Langston	.25	.11	.03
☐ 63 Chuck Carr	.25	.11	.03
☐ 64 Barry Bonds	2.00	.90	.25
☐ 65 David Segui	.25	.11	.03
☐ 66 Mariano Duncan	.25	.11	.03
☐ 67 Kenny Lofton	2.00	.90	.25
☐ 68 Ken Caminiti	1.00	.45	.12
☐ 69 Darrin Jackson	.25	.11	.03
☐ 70 Wil Cordero	.25	.11	.03
☐ 71 Walt Weiss	.25	.11	.03
☐ 72 Tom Pagnozzi	.25	.11	.03
☐ 73 Bret Boone	.25	.11	.03
☐ 74 Wally Joyner	.25	.11	.03
☐ 75 Luis Lopez	.25	.11	.03
☐ 76 Len Dykstra	.50	.23	.06
☐ 77 Pedro Munoz	.25	.11	.03
☐ 78 Kevin Gross	.25	.11	.03
☐ 79 Eduardo Perez	.25	.11	.03
☐ 80 Brent Gates	.25	.11	.03
☐ 81 Jeff Conine	.50	.23	.06
☐ 82 Paul Sorrento	.25	.11	.03
☐ 83 Julio Franco	.25	.11	.03
☐ 84 Chris Sabo	.25	.11	.03
☐ 85 Dante Bichette	1.00	.45	.12
☐ 86 Mike Stanley	.25	.11	.03
☐ 87 Bob Hamelin	.25	.11	.03
☐ 88 Tommy Greene	.25	.11	.03
☐ 89 Jeff Brantley	.25	.11	.03
☐ 90 Ed Sprague	.25	.11	.03
☐ 91 Otis Nixon	.25	.11	.03
☐ 92 Chad Curtis	.25	.11	.03
☐ 93 Chuck McElroy	.25	.11	.03
☐ 94 Troy Neel	.25	.11	.03
☐ 95 Benny Santiago	.25	.11	.03
☐ 96 Jose Mesa	.25	.11	.03
☐ 97 Luis Gonzalez	.25	.11	.03
☐ 98 Alex Fernandez	.50	.23	.06
☐ 99 Ben McDonald	.25	.11	.03
☐ 100 Wade Boggs	1.00	.45	.12
☐ 101 Tom Glavine	1.00	.45	.12
☐ 102 Phil Plantier	.25	.11	.03
☐ 103 Raul Mondesi	1.00	.45	.12
☐ 104 Jim Edmonds	1.00	.45	.12
☐ 105 Jeff Kent	.25	.11	.03
☐ 106 Wilson Alvarez	.25	.11	.03
☐ 107 Geronimo Berroa	.25	.11	.03
☐ 108 Craig Biggio	.50	.23	.06
☐ 109 Roberto Hernandez	.25	.11	.03
☐ 110 Bobby Ayala	.25	.11	.03
☐ 111 Bob Tewksbury	.25	.11	.03
☐ 112 Rondell White	.50	.23	.06
☐ 113 Steve Cooke	.25	.11	.03
☐ 114 Tim Salmon	1.00	.45	.12
☐ 115 Kent Mercker	.25	.11	.03
☐ 116 Randy Johnson	1.00	.45	.12
☐ 117 Mo Vaughn	2.00	.90	.25
☐ 118 Eddie Williams	.25	.11	.03
☐ 119 Jeff Montgomery	.25	.11	.03
☐ 120 Kirt Manwaring	.25	.11	.03
☐ 121 Pat Hentgen	.50	.23	.06
☐ 122 Shawon Dunston	.25	.11	.03
☐ 123 Tim Belcher	.25	.11	.03
☐ 124 Cecil Fielder	.50	.23	.06
☐ 125 Todd Hundley	.50	.23	.06
☐ 126 Mark Acre	.25	.11	.03
☐ 127 Darrell Whitmore	.25	.11	.03
☐ 128 Darryl Kile	.25	.11	.03
☐ 129 Jay Bell	.25	.11	.03
☐ 130 Harold Baines	.25	.11	.03
☐ 131 Felix Fermin	.25	.11	.03
☐ 132 Ellis Burks	.50	.23	.06
☐ 133 Joe Carter	.50	.23	.06
☐ 134 Terry Pendleton	.25	.11	.03
☐ 135 Junior Felix	.25	.11	.03
☐ 136 Bill Gullickson	.25	.11	.03
☐ 137 Melvin Nieves	.25	.11	.03
☐ 138 Chuck Knoblauch	1.00	.45	.12
☐ 139 Bobby Jones	.25	.11	.03
☐ 140 Darrin Fletcher	.25	.11	.03
☐ 141 Andy Van Slyke	.25	.11	.03
☐ 142 Allen Watson	.25	.11	.03
☐ 143 Dan Wilson	.25	.11	.03
☐ 144 Bip Roberts	.25	.11	.03
☐ 145 Sterling Hitchcock	.25	.11	.03
☐ 146 Johnny Ruffin	.25	.11	.03
☐ 147 Steve Trachsel	.25	.11	.03
☐ 148 Ramon Martinez	.50	.23	.06
☐ 149 Dave Henderson	.25	.11	.03
☐ 150 Chris Gomez	.25	.11	.03
☐ 151 Rusty Greer	1.00	.45	.12
☐ 152 John Franco	.25	.11	.03
☐ 153 Mike Bordick	.25	.11	.03
☐ 154 Dave Magadan	.25	.11	.03
☐ 155 Greg Swindell	.25	.11	.03
☐ 156 Arthur Rhodes	.25	.11	.03
☐ 157 Juan Guzman	.25	.11	.03
☐ 158 Greg Maddux	5.00	2.20	.60
☐ 159 Mike Macfarlane	.25	.11	.03
☐ 160 Curt Schilling	.25	.11	.03
☐ 161 Jose Canseco	1.00	.45	.12
☐ 162 Aaron Sele	.25	.11	.03
☐ 163 Steve Buechele	.25	.11	.03
☐ 164 Orel Hershiser	.50	.23	.06
☐ 165 Mike Henneman	.25	.11	.03
☐ 166 Kevin Seitzer	.25	.11	.03
☐ 167 Ruben Sierra	.25	.11	.03
☐ 168 Alex Cole	.25	.11	.03
☐ 169 Jim Thome	1.50	.70	.19
☐ 170 Lance Johnson	.25	.11	.03
☐ 171 Marquis Grissom	.50	.23	.06
☐ 172 Jamie Moyer	.25	.11	.03
☐ 173 Todd Zeile	.25	.11	.03
☐ 174 Chris Bosio	.25	.11	.03
☐ 175 Steve Howe	.25	.11	.03
☐ 176 Luis Polonia	.25	.11	.03
☐ 177 Ryan Klesko	1.25	.55	.16
☐ 178 Kevin Appier	.50	.23	.06
☐ 179 Tim Naehring	.25	.11	.03
☐ 180 Randy Myers	.25	.11	.03
☐ 181 Mike Jackson	.25	.11	.03
☐ 182 Chili Davis	.25	.11	.03
☐ 183 Jason Jacome	.25	.11	.03
☐ 184 Stan Javier	.25	.11	.03
☐ 185 Scott Servais	.25	.11	.03
☐ 186 Kirk Rueter	.25	.11	.03
☐ 187 Don Slaught	.25	.11	.03
☐ 188 Ozzie Smith	1.50	.70	.19
☐ 189 Barry Larkin	1.00	.45	.12
☐ 190 Gary Gaetti	.25	.11	.03
☐ 191 Fred McGriff	1.00	.45	.12
☐ 192 Roger Clemens	1.00	.45	.12
☐ 193 Dean Palmer	.50	.23	.06
☐ 194 Jeromy Burnitz	.25	.11	.03
☐ 195 Scott Kamieniecki	.25	.11	.03
☐ 196 Eddie Murray	2.00	.90	.25
☐ 197 Ron Karkovice	.25	.11	.03
☐ 198 Tino Martinez	.50	.23	.06
☐ 199 Ken Griffey Jr.	8.00	3.60	1.00
☐ 200 Don Mattingly	4.00	1.80	.50
☐ 201 Henry Rodriguez	.50	.23	.06
☐ 202 Lenny Harris	.25	.11	.03
☐ 203 Ryan Thompson	.25	.11	.03
☐ 204 Darren Oliver	.50	.23	.06
☐ 205 Omar Vizquel	.50	.23	.06
☐ 206 Jeff Bagwell	3.00	1.35	.35
☐ 207 Todd Van Poppel	.25	.11	.03
☐ 208 Leo Gomez	.25	.11	.03
☐ 209 Mark Whiten	.25	.11	.03
☐ 210 Pedro Martinez	.50	.23	.06
☐ 211 Reggie Sanders	.50	.23	.06
☐ 212 Kevin Foster	.25	.11	.03
☐ 213 Danny Tartabull	.25	.11	.03
☐ 214 Jeff Blauser	.25	.11	.03
☐ 215 Mike Magnante	.25	.11	.03
☐ 216 Tom Candiotti	.25	.11	.03
☐ 217 Rod Beck	.25	.11	.03
☐ 218 Jody Reed	.25	.11	.03
☐ 219 Vince Coleman	.25	.11	.03
☐ 220 Danny Jackson	.25	.11	.03
☐ 221 Larry Walker	1.00	.45	.12
☐ 222 Pat Borders	.25	.11	.03
☐ 223 Lee Smith	.50	.23	.06
☐ 224 Paul O'Neill	.50	.23	.06
☐ 225 Devon White	.25	.11	.03
☐ 226 Jim Bullinger	.25	.11	.03
☐ 227 Steve Avery	.25	.11	.03
☐ 228 Tony Gwynn	3.00	1.35	.35
☐ 229 Pat Meares	.25	.11	.03
☐ 230 Bill Swift	.25	.11	.03
☐ 231 David Wells	.25	.11	.03
☐ 232 John Briscoe	.25	.11	.03
☐ 233 Roger Pavlik	.25	.11	.03
☐ 234 Roberto Alomar	1.50	.70	.19
☐ 235 Billy Brewer	.25	.11	.03
☐ 236 Gary Sheffield	1.00	.45	.12
☐ 237 Lou Frazier	.25	.11	.03
☐ 238 Terry Steinbach	.50	.23	.06
☐ 239 Omar Daal	.25	.11	.03
☐ 240 Jason Bere	.25	.11	.03
☐ 241 Denny Neagle	.50	.23	.06
☐ 242 Danny Bautista	.25	.11	.03
☐ 243 Hector Carrasco	.25	.11	.03
☐ 244 Bill Risley	.25	.11	.03
☐ 245 Andy Benes	.50	.23	.06
☐ 246 Jim Leyritz	.25	.11	.03
☐ 247 Jose Oliva	.25	.11	.03
☐ 248 Greg Vaughn	.50	.23	.06
☐ 249 Rich Monteleone	.25	.11	.03
☐ 250 Tony Eusebio	.25	.11	.03
☐ 251 Chuck Finley	.25	.11	.03
☐ 252 Joe Boever	.25	.11	.03
☐ 253 Bobby Munoz	.25	.11	.03
☐ 254 Bret Saberhagen	.25	.11	.03
☐ 255 Kurt Abbott	.25	.11	.03
☐ 256 Bobby Witt	.25	.11	.03
☐ 257 Cliff Floyd	.25	.11	.03
☐ 258 Mark Clark	.25	.11	.03
☐ 259 Andujar Cedeno	.25	.11	.03
☐ 260 Marvin Freeman	.25	.11	.03
☐ 261 Mike Piazza	5.00	2.20	.60
☐ 262 Pat Kelly	.25	.11	.03
☐ 263 Carlos Delgado	.50	.23	.06
☐ 264 Willie Banks	.25	.11	.03
☐ 265 Matt Walbeck	.25	.11	.03
☐ 266 Mark McGwire	2.50	1.10	.30
☐ 267 Alan Trammell	.50	.23	.06
☐ 268 Tom Gordon	.25	.11	.03
☐ 269 Greg Colbrunn	.25	.11	.03
☐ 270 Darren Daulton	.50	.23	.06
☐ 271 Albie Lopez	.25	.11	.03
☐ 272 Robin Ventura	.50	.23	.06
☐ 273 Bryan Eversgerd	.25	.11	.03
☐ 274 Dave Fleming	.25	.11	.03
☐ 275 Scott Livingstone	.25	.11	.03
☐ 276 Pete Schourek	.25	.11	.03
☐ 277 Bernie Williams	1.50	.70	.19
☐ 278 Mark Lemke	.25	.11	.03
☐ 279 Eric Karros	.50	.23	.06
☐ 280 Billy Ashley	.25	.11	.03
☐ 281 Rico Brogna	.25	.11	.03
☐ 282 John Burkett	.25	.11	.03
☐ 283 Jorge Fabregas	.25	.11	.03
☐ 284 Greg Gagne	.25	.11	.03
☐ 285 Doug Jones	.25	.11	.03
☐ 286 Troy O'Leary	.25	.11	.03
☐ 287 Pat Rapp	.25	.11	.03
☐ 288 Butch Henry	.25	.11	.03
☐ 289 John Olerud	.25	.11	.03
☐ 290 John Hudek	.25	.11	.03
☐ 291 Jeff King	.25	.11	.03
☐ 292 Bobby Bonilla	.50	.23	.06
☐ 293 Albert Belle	4.00	1.80	.50
☐ 294 Rick Wilkins	.25	.11	.03
☐ 295 John Jaha	.50	.23	.06
☐ 296 Sid Fernandez	.25	.11	.03
☐ 297 Deion Sanders	1.00	.45	.12
☐ 298 Gil Heredia	.25	.11	.03
☐ 299 Melido Perez	.25	.11	.03
☐ 300 Greg McMichael	.25	.11	.03
☐ 301 Rusty Meacham	.25	.11	.03
☐ 302 Shawn Green	.50	.23	.06
☐ 303 Carlos Garcia	.25	.11	.03
☐ 304 Dave Stevens	.25	.11	.03
☐ 305 Eric Young	.50	.23	.06
☐ 306 Kirk Gibson	.50	.23	.06
☐ 307 Spike Owen	.25	.11	.03
☐ 308 Sandy Alomar Jr.	.25	.11	.03
☐ 309 Ricky Gutierrez	.25	.11	.03
☐ 310 Dave Veres	.25	.11	.03
☐ 311 Gregg Jefferies	.50	.23	.06
☐ 312 Jose Valentin	.25	.11	.03
☐ 313 Robb Nen	.25	.11	.03
☐ 314 Jose Rijo	.25	.11	.03
☐ 315 Sean Berry	.25	.11	.03
☐ 316 Mike Gallego	.25	.11	.03
☐ 317 Roberto Kelly	.25	.11	.03
☐ 318 Kevin Stocker	.25	.11	.03
☐ 319 Kirby Puckett	3.00	1.35	.35
☐ 320 Jon Lieber	.25	.11	.03
☐ 321 Joe Girardi	.25	.11	.03
☐ 322 Tony Phillips	.50	.23	.06
☐ 323 Brian Anderson	.25	.11	.03
☐ 324 Ivan Rodriguez	1.50	.70	.19
☐ 325 Jeff Cirillo	.25	.11	.03
☐ 326 Joey Cora	.25	.11	.03
☐ 327 Chris Hoiles	.25	.11	.03
☐ 328 Bernard Gilkey	.50	.23	.06
☐ 329 Mike Lansing	.25	.11	.03
☐ 330 Jimmy Key	.25	.11	.03
☐ 331 Vinny Castilla	.50	.23	.06
☐ 332 Mark Guthrie	.25	.11	.03
☐ 333 Mike Lieberthal	.25	.11	.03
☐ 334 Will Clark	1.00	.45	.12
☐ 335 Rickey Henderson	1.00	.45	.12
☐ 336 Todd Jones	.25	.11	.03
☐ 337 Jack McDowell	.50	.23	.06
☐ 338 Carlos Rodriguez	.25	.11	.03
☐ 339 Mark Eichhorn	.25	.11	.03
☐ 340 Jeff Nelson	.25	.11	.03
☐ 341 Eric Anthony	.25	.11	.03
☐ 342 Randy Velarde	.25	.11	.03
☐ 343 Javier Lopez	.50	.23	.06
☐ 344 Kevin Mitchell	.25	.11	.03
☐ 345 Steve Bedrosian	.25	.11	.03
☐ 346 John Kruk	.50	.23	.06
☐ 347 Scott Leius	.25	.11	.03
☐ 348 John Patterson	.25	.11	.03
☐ 349 Kevin Brown	.50	.23	.06
☐ 350 Mike Moore	.25	.11	.03
☐ 351 Manny Ramirez	1.50	.70	.19
☐ 352 Jose Lind	.25	.11	.03
☐ 353 Derrick May	.25	.11	.03
☐ 354 Cal Eldred	.25	.11	.03
☐ 355 J.T. Snow	.25	.11	.03
☐ 356 Luis Sojo	.25	.11	.03
☐ 357 Moises Alou	.50	.23	.06
☐ 358 Dave Clark	.25	.11	.03
☐ 359 Dave Hollins	.25	.11	.03
☐ 360 Cal Ripken UER Name spelled Ripkin	6.00	2.70	.75
☐ 361 Pedro Astacio	.25	.11	.03
☐ 362 Tony Longmire	.25	.11	.03
☐ 363 Jeff Frye	.25	.11	.03
☐ 364 Bo Jackson	.50	.23	.06
☐ 365 Steve Ontiveros	.25	.11	.03
☐ 366 David Nied	.25	.11	.03
☐ 367 Brad Ausmus	.25	.11	.03
☐ 368 Carlos Baerga	.50	.23	.06
☐ 369 James Mouton	.25	.11	.03
☐ 370 Ozzie Guillen	.25	.11	.03
☐ 371 Yorkis Perez	.25	.11	.03
☐ 372 Rich Rodriguez	.25	.11	.03
☐ 373 Mark McLemore	.25	.11	.03
☐ 374 Jeff Fassero	.25	.11	.03
☐ 375 John Roper	.25	.11	.03
☐ 376 Wes Chamberlain	.25	.11	.03
☐ 377 Felix Jose	.25	.11	.03
☐ 378 Brett Butler	.50	.23	.06
☐ 379 William VanLandingham	.25	.11	.03
☐ 380 Mickey Tettleton	.25	.11	.03
☐ 381 Brady Anderson	1.00	.45	.12
☐ 382 Reggie Jefferson	.25	.11	.03
☐ 383 Mike Kingery	.25	.11	.03
☐ 384 Derek Bell	.50	.23	.06
☐ 385 Scott Erickson	.25	.11	.03
☐ 386 Bob Wickman	.25	.11	.03
☐ 387 Phil Leftwich	.25	.11	.03
☐ 388 David Justice	.50	.23	.06
☐ 389 Pedro Martinez	.50	.23	.06
☐ 390 Terry Mathews	.25	.11	.03
☐ 391 Brian McRae	.50	.23	.06
☐ 392 Bruce Ruffin	.25	.11	.03
☐ 393 Steve Finley	.50	.23	.06
☐ 394 Rafael Bournigal	.25	.11	.03
☐ 395 Darryl Strawberry	.50	.23	.06
☐ 396 Luis Alicea	.25	.11	.03

1995 Topps Cyber Season in Review

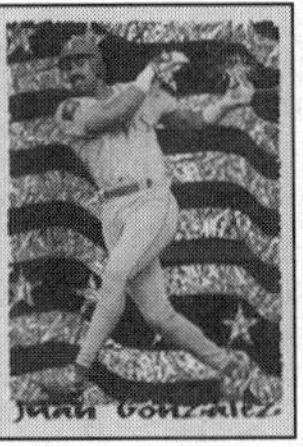

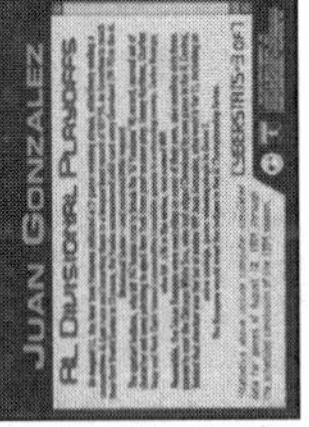

This seven-card set was distributed exclusively in 1995 Topps hobby factory sets. It continues the Cyberstats insert theme used in the regular issue product, which presented "what if" statistics to fill in the strike-shortened 1994 season. The Season in Review cards commemorate projected accomplishments including Barry Bonds' 61 home runs and Kenny Lofton's World Series MVP.

	MINT	NRMT	EXC
COMPLETE SET (7)	5.00	2.20	.60
COMMON CARD (1-7)	.40	.18	.05
☐ 1 Barry Bonds	1.00	.45	.12
☐ 2 Jose Canseco	.75	.35	.09
☐ 3 Juan Gonzalez	2.00	.90	.25
☐ 4 Fred McGriff	.60	.25	.07
☐ 5 Carlos Baerga	.40	.18	.05
☐ 6 Ryan Klesko	.75	.35	.09
☐ 7 Kenny Lofton	1.00	.45	.12

1995 Topps Finest

This 15-card standard-size set was inserted one every 36 Topps series two packs. This set featured the top 15 players in total bases from the 1994 season. The fronts feature a player photo, with his team identification and name on the bottom of the card. The horizontal backs feature another player photo along with a breakdown of how many of each type of hit each player got on the way to their season total. The set is sequenced in order of how they finished in the majors for the 1994 season.

	MINT	NRMT	EXC
COMPLETE SET (15)	70.00	32.00	8.75
COMMON CARD (1-15)	1.50	.70	.19
☐ 1 Jeff Bagwell	8.00	3.60	1.00
☐ 2 Albert Belle	8.00	3.60	1.00
☐ 3 Ken Griffey Jr.	20.00	9.00	2.50
☐ 4 Frank Thomas	20.00	9.00	2.50
☐ 5 Matt Williams	2.50	1.10	.30
☐ 6 Dante Bichette	2.50	1.10	.30
☐ 7 Barry Bonds	5.00	2.20	.60
☐ 8 Moises Alou	1.50	.70	.19
☐ 9 Andres Galarraga	2.50	1.10	.30
☐ 10 Kenny Lofton	5.00	2.20	.60
☐ 11 Rafael Palmeiro	2.50	1.10	.30
☐ 12 Tony Gwynn	8.00	3.60	1.00
☐ 13 Kirby Puckett	8.00	3.60	1.00
☐ 14 Jose Canseco	2.50	1.10	.30
☐ 15 Jeff Conine	1.50	.70	.19

1995 Topps League Leaders

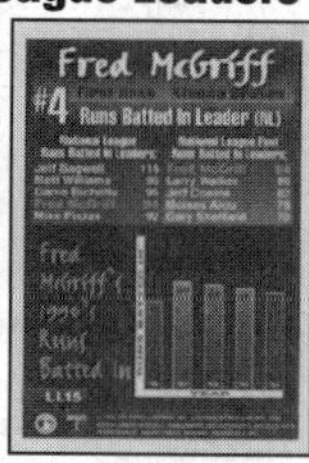

Randomly inserted in jumbo packs at a rate of one in three, this 50-card standard-size set showcases those that were among league leaders in various categories. Card fronts feature a player photo with a black background. The player's name appears in gold foil at the bottom and the category with which he led the league or was among the leaders is in yellow letters up the right side. The backs contain various graphs and where the player placed among the leaders.

	MINT	NRMT	EXC
COMPLETE SET (50)	50.00	22.00	6.25
COMPLETE SERIES 1 (25)	20.00	9.00	2.50
COMPLETE SERIES 2 (25)	30.00	13.50	3.70
COMMON CARD (LL1-LL50)	.50	.23	.06
☐ LL1 Albert Belle	2.50	1.10	.30
☐ LL2 Kevin Mitchell	.50	.23	.06
☐ LL3 Wade Boggs	.75	.35	.09
☐ LL4 Tony Gwynn	2.50	1.10	.30
☐ LL5 Moises Alou	.50	.23	.06
☐ LL6 Andres Galarraga	.75	.35	.09
☐ LL7 Matt Williams	.75	.35	.09
☐ LL8 Barry Bonds	1.50	.70	.19
☐ LL9 Frank Thomas	6.00	2.70	.75
☐ LL10 Jose Canseco	.75	.35	.09
☐ LL11 Jeff Bagwell	2.50	1.10	.30
☐ LL12 Kirby Puckett	2.50	1.10	.30
☐ LL13 Julio Franco	.50	.23	.06
☐ LL14 Albert Belle	2.50	1.10	.30
☐ LL15 Fred McGriff	.75	.35	.09
☐ LL16 Kenny Lofton	1.50	.70	.19
☐ LL17 Otis Nixon	.50	.23	.06
☐ LL18 Brady Anderson	.75	.35	.09
☐ LL19 Deion Sanders	.75	.35	.09
☐ LL20 Chuck Carr	.50	.23	.06
☐ LL21 Pat Hentgen	.50	.23	.06
☐ LL22 Andy Benes	.50	.23	.06
☐ LL23 Roger Clemens	1.25	.55	.16
☐ LL24 Greg Maddux	4.00	1.80	.50
☐ LL25 Pedro Martinez	.50	.23	.06
☐ LL26 Paul O'Neill	.50	.23	.06
☐ LL27 Jeff Bagwell	2.50	1.10	.30
☐ LL28 Frank Thomas	6.00	2.70	.75
☐ LL29 Hal Morris	.50	.23	.06
☐ LL30 Kenny Lofton	1.50	.70	.19
☐ LL31 Ken Griffey Jr.	6.00	2.70	.75
☐ LL32 Jeff Bagwell	2.50	1.10	.30
☐ LL33 Albert Belle	2.50	1.10	.30
☐ LL34 Fred McGriff	.75	.35	.09
☐ LL35 Cecil Fielder	.50	.23	.06
☐ LL36 Matt Williams	.75	.35	.09
☐ LL37 Joe Carter	.50	.23	.06
☐ LL38 Dante Bichette	.75	.35	.09
☐ LL39 Frank Thomas	6.00	2.70	.75
☐ LL40 Mike Piazza	4.00	1.80	.50
☐ LL41 Craig Biggio	.50	.23	.06
☐ LL42 Vince Coleman	.50	.23	.06
☐ LL43 Marquis Grissom	.50	.23	.06
☐ LL44 Chuck Knoblauch	.75	.35	.09
☐ LL45 Darren Lewis	.50	.23	.06
☐ LL46 Randy Johnson	.75	.35	.09
☐ LL47 Jose Rijo	.50	.23	.06
☐ LL48 Chuck Finley	.50	.23	.06
☐ LL49 Bret Saberhagen	.50	.23	.06
☐ LL50 Kevin Appier	.50	.23	.06

1995 Topps Traded

This set contains 165 standard-size cards and was sold in 11-card packs for $1.29. The set features rookies, draft picks and players who had been traded. The fronts contain a photo with a white border. The backs have a player picture in a scoreboard and his statistics and information. All cards are numbered with a "T" prefix. Subsets featured are: At the Break (1T-10T) and All-Stars (156T-164T). Rookie Cards in this set include Ben Davis and Hideo Nomo.

	MINT	NRMT	EXC
COMPLETE SET (165)	20.00	9.00	2.50
COMMON CARD (1T-165T)	.10	.05	.01
☐ 1T Frank Thomas ATB	1.50	.70	.19
☐ 2T Ken Griffey Jr. ATB	1.50	.70	.19
☐ 3T Barry Bonds ATB	.50	.23	.06
☐ 4T Albert Belle ATB	.60	.25	.07
☐ 5T Cal Ripken ATB	1.25	.55	.16
☐ 6T Mike Piazza ATB	1.00	.45	.12
☐ 7T Tony Gwynn ATB	.60	.25	.07
☐ 8T Jeff Bagwell ATB	.60	.25	.07
☐ 9T Mo Vaughn ATB	.50	.23	.06
☐ 10T Matt Williams ATB	.50	.23	.06
☐ 11T Ray Durham	.25	.11	.03
☐ 12T Juan LeBron	.50	.23	.06
☐ 13T Shawn Green	.25	.11	.03
☐ 14T Kevin Gross	.10	.05	.01
☐ 15T Jon Nunnally	.25	.11	.03
☐ 16T Brian Maxcy	.10	.05	.01
☐ 17T Mark Kiefer	.10	.05	.01
☐ 18T Carlos Beltran	.50	.23	.06
☐ 19T Mike Mimbs	.25	.11	.03
☐ 20T Larry Walker	.50	.23	.06
☐ 21T Chad Curtis	.10	.05	.01
☐ 22T Jeff Barry	.10	.05	.01
☐ 23T Joe Oliver	.10	.05	.01
☐ 24T Tomas Perez	.25	.11	.03
☐ 25T Michael Barrett	.25	.11	.03
☐ 26T Brian McRae	.25	.11	.03
☐ 27T Derek Bell	.25	.11	.03
☐ 28T Ray Durham	.25	.11	.03
☐ 29T Todd Williams	.10	.05	.01
☐ 30T Ryan Jaroncyk	.40	.18	.05
☐ 31T Todd Steverson	.10	.05	.01
☐ 32T Mike Devereaux	.10	.05	.01
☐ 33T Rheal Cormier	.10	.05	.01
☐ 34T Benny Santiago	.10	.05	.01
☐ 35T Bobby Higginson	.75	.35	.09
☐ 36T Jack McDowell	.25	.11	.03
☐ 37T Mike Macfarlane	.10	.05	.01
☐ 38T Tony McKnight	.25	.11	.03
☐ 39T Brian Hunter	.25	.11	.03
☐ 40T Hideo Nomo	3.00	1.35	.35
☐ 41T Brett Butler	.25	.11	.03
☐ 42T Donovan Osborne	.10	.05	.01
☐ 43T Scott Karl	.10	.05	.01
☐ 44T Tony Phillips	.25	.11	.03
☐ 45T Marty Cordova	.50	.23	.06
☐ 46T Dave Mlicki	.10	.05	.01
☐ 47T Bronson Arroyo	.40	.18	.05
☐ 48T John Burkett	.25	.11	.03
☐ 49T J.D. Smart	.10	.05	.01
☐ 50T Mickey Tettleton	.10	.05	.01
☐ 51T Todd Stottlemyre	.10	.05	.01
☐ 52T Mike Perez	.10	.05	.01
☐ 53T Terry Mulholland	.10	.05	.01
☐ 54T Edgardo Alfonzo	.25	.11	.03
☐ 55T Zane Smith	.10	.05	.01
☐ 56T Jacob Brumfield	.10	.05	.01
☐ 57T Andujar Cedeno	.10	.05	.01
☐ 58T Jose Parra	.25	.11	.03
☐ 59T Manny Alexander	.10	.05	.01
☐ 60T Tony Tarasco	.10	.05	.01
☐ 61T Orel Hershiser	.25	.11	.03
☐ 62T Tim Scott	.10	.05	.01
☐ 63T Felix Rodriguez	.25	.11	.03
☐ 64T Ken Hill	.10	.05	.01
☐ 65T Marquis Grissom	.25	.11	.03
☐ 66T Lee Smith	.25	.11	.03
☐ 67T Jason Bates	.10	.05	.01
☐ 68T Felipe Lira	.10	.05	.01
☐ 69T Alex Hernandez	.40	.18	.05
☐ 70T Tony Fernandez	.10	.05	.01
☐ 71T Scott Radinsky	.10	.05	.01
☐ 72T Jose Canseco	.50	.23	.06
☐ 73T Mark Grudzielanek	.75	.35	.09
☐ 74T Ben Davis	.75	.35	.09
☐ 75T Jim Abbott	.10	.05	.01
☐ 76T Roger Bailey	.10	.05	.01
☐ 77T Gregg Jefferies	.25	.11	.03
☐ 78T Erik Hanson	.10	.05	.01
☐ 79T Brad Radke	.25	.11	.03
☐ 80T Jaime Navarro	.10	.05	.01
☐ 81T John Wetteland	.25	.11	.03
☐ 82T Chad Fonville	.25	.11	.03
☐ 83T John Mabry	.50	.23	.06
☐ 84T Glenallen Hill	.10	.05	.01
☐ 85T Ken Caminiti	.50	.23	.06
☐ 86T Tom Goodwin	.10	.05	.01
☐ 87T Darren Bragg	.25	.11	.03
☐ 88T Pitching Prospects	.40	.18	.05
Pat Ahearne			
Gary Rath			
Larry Wimberly			
Robbie Bell			
☐ 89T Jeff Russell	.10	.05	.01
☐ 90T Dave Gallagher	.10	.05	.01
☐ 91T Steve Finley	.25	.11	.03
☐ 92T Vaughn Eshelman	.10	.05	.01
☐ 93T Kevin Jarvis	.10	.05	.01
☐ 94T Mark Gubicza	.10	.05	.01
☐ 95T Tim Wakefield	.10	.05	.01
☐ 96T Bob Tewksbury	.10	.05	.01
☐ 97T Sid Roberson	.10	.05	.01
☐ 98T Tom Henke	.10	.05	.01
☐ 99T Michael Tucker	.25	.11	.03
☐ 100T Jason Bates	.10	.05	.01
☐ 101T Otis Nixon	.10	.05	.01
☐ 102T Mark Whiten	.10	.05	.01
☐ 103T Dilson Torres	.10	.05	.01
☐ 104T Melvin Bunch	.10	.05	.01
☐ 105T Terry Pendleton	.25	.11	.03
☐ 106T Corey Jenkins	.50	.23	.06
☐ 107T Glenn Dishman	.25	.11	.03
Rob Grable			
☐ 108T Reggie Taylor	.50	.23	.06
☐ 109T Curtis Goodwin	.25	.11	.03
☐ 110T David Cone	.25	.11	.03
☐ 111T Antonio Osuna	.10	.05	.01
☐ 112T Paul Shuey	.10	.05	.01
☐ 113T Doug Jones	.10	.05	.01
☐ 114T Mark McLemore	.10	.05	.01
☐ 115T Kevin Ritz	.10	.05	.01
☐ 116T John Kruk	.25	.11	.03
☐ 117T Trevor Wilson	.10	.05	.01
☐ 118T Jerald Clark	.10	.05	.01
☐ 119T Julian Tavarez	.10	.05	.01
☐ 120T Tim Pugh	.10	.05	.01
☐ 121T Todd Zeile	.10	.05	.01
☐ 122T Prospects	.75	.35	.09
Mark Sweeney UER			
George Arias			
Richie Sexson			
Brian Schneider			
☐ 123T Bobby Witt	.10	.05	.01
☐ 124T Hideo Nomo	1.25	.55	.16
☐ 125T Joey Cora	.10	.05	.01
☐ 126T Jim Scharrer	.40	.18	.05
☐ 127T Paul Quantrill	.10	.05	.01
☐ 128T Chipper Jones ROY	1.50	.70	.19
☐ 129T Kenny James	.10	.05	.01
☐ 130T Lyle Mouton	.25	.11	.03
Mariano Rivera			
☐ 131T Tyler Green	.10	.05	.01
☐ 132T Brad Clontz	.10	.05	.01
☐ 133T Jon Nunnally	.25	.11	.03
☐ 134T Dave Magadan	.10	.05	.01
☐ 135T Al Leiter	.25	.11	.03
☐ 136T Bret Barberie	.10	.05	.01
☐ 137T Bill Swift	.10	.05	.01
☐ 138T Scott Cooper	.10	.05	.01
☐ 139T Roberto Kelly	.10	.05	.01
☐ 140T Charlie Hayes	.10	.05	.01
☐ 141T Pete Harnisch	.10	.05	.01
☐ 142T Rich Amaral	.10	.05	.01
☐ 143T Rudy Seanez	.10	.05	.01
☐ 144T Pat Listach	.10	.05	.01
☐ 145T Quilvio Veras	.10	.05	.01
☐ 146T Jose Olmeda	.10	.05	.01
☐ 147T Roberto Petagine	.10	.05	.01
☐ 148T Kevin Brown	.25	.11	.03
☐ 149T Phil Plantier	.10	.05	.01
☐ 150T Carlos Perez	.25	.11	.03
☐ 151T Pat Borders	.10	.05	.01
☐ 152T Tyler Green	.10	.05	.01
☐ 153T Stan Belinda	.10	.05	.01
☐ 154T Dave Stewart	.25	.11	.03
☐ 155T Andre Dawson	.10	.05	.01
☐ 156T Frank Thomas AS	.75	.35	.09
Fred McGriff UER			
(McGriff's team shown as Blue Jays)			
☐ 157T Carlos Baerga AS	.25	.11	.03
Craig Biggio			
☐ 158T Wade Boggs AS	.25	.11	.03
Matt Williams			
☐ 159T Cal Ripken AS	.75	.35	.09
Ozzie Smith			
☐ 160T Ken Griffey Jr. AS	.75	.35	.09
Tony Gwynn			
☐ 161T Albert Belle AS	.25	.11	.03
Barry Bonds			
☐ 162T Kirby Puckett	.25	.11	.03
Len Dykstra			
☐ 163T Ivan Rodriguez AS	.25	.11	.03
Mike Piazza			
☐ 164T Randy Johnson AS	.25	.11	.03
Hideo Nomo			
☐ 165T Checklist	.10	.05	.01

1995 Topps Traded Power Boosters

This 10-card standard-size set was inserted in packs at a rate of one in 36. The set is comprised of parallel cards for the first 10 cards of the regular Topps Traded set which was the "At the Break" subset. The cards are done on extra-thick stock. The fronts have an action photo on a "Power Boosted" background, which is similar to diffraction technology, with the words "at the break" on the left side. The backs have a head shot and player information including his mid-season statistics for 1995 and previous years.

	MINT	NRMT	EXC
COMPLETE SET (10)	120.00	55.00	15.00
COMMON CARD (1-10)	4.00	1.80	.50
☐ 1 Frank Thomas	30.00	13.50	3.70
☐ 2 Ken Griffey Jr.	30.00	13.50	3.70
☐ 3 Barry Bonds	8.00	3.60	1.00
☐ 4 Albert Belle	12.00	5.50	1.50
☐ 5 Cal Ripken	25.00	11.00	3.10
☐ 6 Mike Piazza	20.00	9.00	2.50
☐ 7 Tony Gwynn	12.00	5.50	1.50
☐ 8 Jeff Bagwell	12.00	5.50	1.50
☐ 9 Mo Vaughn	8.00	3.60	1.00
☐ 10 Matt Williams	4.00	1.80	.50

1995 Topps Legends of the '60s Medallions

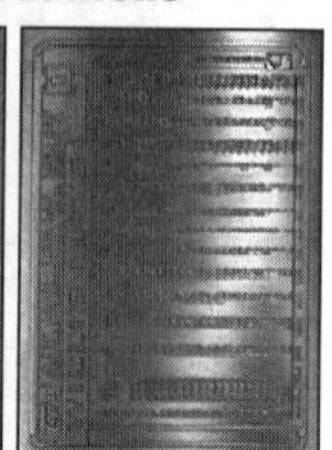

These 12 bronze medallions feature some of the best players of the 60's, duplicating the regular issue Topps cards from various years. This was a special offering for Topps Stadium Club members. One medallion was issued each month; the issue price was $39.95 per card.

	MINT	NRMT	EXC
COMPLETE SET (12)	500.00	220.00	60.00
COMMON CARD (1-12)	40.00	18.00	5.00
☐ 1 Willie Mays 1964	50.00	22.00	6.25
☐ 2 Hank Aaron 1965	50.00	22.00	6.25
☐ 3 Bob Gibson 1964	40.00	18.00	5.00
☐ 4 Don Drysdale 1965	40.00	18.00	5.00
☐ 5 Frank Robinson 1962	40.00	18.00	5.00
☐ 6 Carl Yastrzemski 1966	40.00	18.00	5.00
☐ 7 Willie McCovey 1961	40.00	18.00	5.00
☐ 8 Roberto Clemente 1969	50.00	22.00	6.25
☐ 9 Juan Marichal 1966	40.00	18.00	5.00
☐ 10 Brooks Robinson 1969	40.00	18.00	5.00
☐ 11 Harmon Killebrew 1968	40.00	18.00	5.00
☐ 12 Billy Williams 1967	40.00	18.00	5.00

1996 Topps

This set consists of 440 standard-size cards. These cards were issued in 12-card foil packs with a suggested retail price of $1.29. The fronts feature full-color photos surrounded by a white background. Information on the backs includes a player photo, season and career stats and text. First series subsets include Star Power (1-6, 8-12), Draft Picks (13-26), AAA Stars (101-104), and Future Stars (210-219). A special Mickey Mantle card was issued as card #7 (his uniform number) and became the last card to be issued as card #7 in the Topps brand set. Rookie Cards in this set include Sean Casey and Ron Wright.

	MINT	NRMT	EXC
COMPLETE SET (440)	35.00	16.00	4.40
COMP.HOBBY FACT.SET (449)	50.00	22.00	6.25
COMP.CEREAL FACT.SET (444)	50.00	22.00	6.25
COMPLETE SERIES 1 (220)	20.00	9.00	2.50
COMPLETE SERIES 2 (220)	15.00	6.75	1.85
COMMON CARD (1-220)	.10	.05	.01
COMMON CARD (221-440)	.05	.02	.01
☐ 1 Tony Gwynn STP	.60	.25	.07
☐ 2 Mike Piazza STP	1.00	.45	.12
☐ 3 Greg Maddux STP	1.00	.45	.12
☐ 4 Jeff Bagwell STP	.60	.25	.07

☐ 5 Larry Walker STP .50 .23 .06
☐ 6 Barry Larkin STP .50 .23 .06
☐ 7 Mickey Mantle 4.00 1.80 .50
☐ 8 Tom Glavine STP UER .50 .23 .06
Won 21 games in June 95
☐ 9 Craig Biggio STP .25 .11 .03
☐ 10 Barry Bonds STP .50 .23 .06
☐ 11 Heathcliff Slocumb STP .10 .05 .01
☐ 12 Matt Williams STP .50 .23 .06
☐ 13 Todd Helton 1.25 .55 .16
☐ 14 Mark Redman .25 .11 .03
☐ 15 Michael Barrett .10 .05 .01
☐ 16 Ben Davis .50 .23 .06
☐ 17 Juan LeBron .10 .05 .01
☐ 18 Tony McKnight .10 .05 .01
☐ 19 Ryan Jaroncyk .10 .05 .01
☐ 20 Corey Jenkins .25 .11 .03
☐ 21 Jim Scharrer .10 .05 .01
☐ 22 Mark Bellhorn .30 .14 .04
☐ 23 Jarrod Washburn .25 .11 .03
☐ 24 Geoff Jenkins .40 .18 .05
☐ 25 Sean Casey .75 .35 .09
☐ 26 Brett Tomko .10 .05 .01
☐ 27 Tony Fernandez .10 .05 .01
☐ 28 Rich Becker .25 .11 .03
☐ 29 Andujar Cedeno .10 .05 .01
☐ 30 Paul Molitor .60 .25 .07
☐ 31 Brent Gates .10 .05 .01
☐ 32 Glenallen Hill .25 .11 .03
☐ 33 Mike Macfarlane .10 .05 .01
☐ 34 Manny Alexander .10 .05 .01
☐ 35 Todd Zeile .10 .05 .01
☐ 36 Joe Girardi .10 .05 .01
☐ 37 Tony Tarasco .10 .05 .01
☐ 38 Tim Belcher .10 .05 .01
☐ 39 Tom Goodwin .25 .11 .03
☐ 40 Orel Hershiser .25 .11 .03
☐ 41 Tripp Cromer .10 .05 .01
☐ 42 Sean Bergman .10 .05 .01
☐ 43 Troy Percival .25 .11 .03
☐ 44 Kevin Stocker .10 .05 .01
☐ 45 Albert Belle 1.25 .55 .16
☐ 46 Tony Eusebio .10 .05 .01
☐ 47 Sid Roberson .10 .05 .01
☐ 48 Todd Hollandsworth .25 .11 .03
☐ 49 Mark Wohlers .25 .11 .03
☐ 50 Kirby Puckett 1.25 .55 .16
☐ 51 Darren Holmes .10 .05 .01
☐ 52 Ron Karkovice .10 .05 .01
☐ 53 Al Martin .10 .05 .01
☐ 54 Pat Rapp .10 .05 .01
☐ 55 Mark Grace .50 .23 .06
☐ 56 Greg Gagne .10 .05 .01
☐ 57 Stan Javier .10 .05 .01
☐ 58 Scott Sanders .10 .05 .01
☐ 59 J.T. Snow .50 .23 .06
☐ 60 David Justice .25 .11 .03
☐ 61 Royce Clayton .10 .05 .01
☐ 62 Kevin Foster .10 .05 .01
☐ 63 Tim Naehring .10 .05 .01
☐ 64 Orlando Miller .10 .05 .01
☐ 65 Mike Mussina .60 .25 .07
☐ 66 Jim Eisenreich .10 .05 .01
☐ 67 Felix Fermin .10 .05 .01
☐ 68 Bernie Williams .40 .18 .05
☐ 69 Robb Nen .10 .05 .01
☐ 70 Ron Gant .25 .11 .03
☐ 71 Felipe Lira .10 .05 .01
☐ 72 Jacob Brumfield .10 .05 .01
☐ 73 John Mabry .25 .11 .03
☐ 74 Mark Carreon .10 .05 .01
☐ 75 Carlos Baerga .25 .11 .03
☐ 76 Jim Dougherty .10 .05 .01
☐ 77 Ryan Thompson .10 .05 .01
☐ 78 Scott Leius .10 .05 .01
☐ 79 Roger Pavlik .10 .05 .01
☐ 80 Gary Sheffield .50 .23 .06
☐ 81 Julian Tavarez .10 .05 .01
☐ 82 Andy Ashby .10 .05 .01
☐ 83 Mark Lemke .10 .05 .01
☐ 84 Omar Vizquel .25 .11 .03
☐ 85 Darren Daulton .25 .11 .03
☐ 86 Mike Lansing .10 .05 .01
☐ 87 Rusty Greer .50 .23 .06
☐ 88 Dave Stevens .10 .05 .01
☐ 89 Jose Offerman .10 .05 .01
☐ 90 Tom Henke .25 .11 .03
☐ 91 Troy O'Leary .10 .05 .01
☐ 92 Michael Tucker .25 .11 .03
☐ 93 Marvin Freeman .10 .05 .01
☐ 94 Alex Diaz .10 .05 .01
☐ 95 John Wetteland .25 .11 .03
☐ 96 Cal Ripken 2131 3.00 1.35 .35
☐ 97 Mike Mimbs .10 .05 .01
☐ 98 Bobby Higginson .25 .11 .03
☐ 99 Edgardo Alfonzo .25 .11 .03
☐ 100 Frank Thomas 3.00 1.35 .35
☐ 101 Steve Gibralter .25 .11 .03
Bob Abreu
☐ 102 Brian Givens .10 .05 .01
T.J. Mathews
☐ 103 Chris Pritchett .10 .05 .01
Trenidad Hubbard
☐ 104 Eric Owens .25 .11 .03
Butch Huskey
☐ 105 Doug Drabek .10 .05 .01
☐ 106 Tomas Perez .10 .05 .01
☐ 107 Mark Leiter .10 .05 .01
☐ 108 Joe Oliver .10 .05 .01
☐ 109 Tony Castillo .10 .05 .01
☐ 110 Checklist (1-110) .10 .05 .01
☐ 111 Kevin Seitzer .10 .05 .01
☐ 112 Pete Schourek .25 .11 .03
☐ 113 Sean Berry .10 .05 .01
☐ 114 Todd Stottlemyre .10 .05 .01
☐ 115 Joe Carter .25 .11 .03
☐ 116 Jeff King .25 .11 .03
☐ 117 Dan Wilson .10 .05 .01
☐ 118 Kurt Abbott .10 .05 .01
☐ 119 Lyle Mouton .10 .05 .01
☐ 120 Jose Rijo .10 .05 .01
☐ 121 Curtis Goodwin .10 .05 .01
☐ 122 Jose Valentin .10 .05 .01
☐ 123 Ellis Burks .25 .11 .03
☐ 124 David Cone .25 .11 .03
☐ 125 Eddie Murray .75 .35 .09
☐ 126 Brian Jordan .25 .11 .03
☐ 127 Darrin Fletcher .10 .05 .01
☐ 128 Curt Schilling .10 .05 .01
☐ 129 Ozzie Guillen .10 .05 .01
☐ 130 Kenny Rogers .10 .05 .01
☐ 131 Tom Pagnozzi .10 .05 .01
☐ 132 Garret Anderson .50 .23 .06
☐ 133 Bobby Jones .10 .05 .01
☐ 134 Chris Gomez .10 .05 .01
☐ 135 Mike Stanley .10 .05 .01
☐ 136 Hideo Nomo .75 .35 .09
☐ 137 Jon Nunnally .10 .05 .01
☐ 138 Tim Wakefield .10 .05 .01
☐ 139 Steve Finley .50 .23 .06
☐ 140 Ivan Rodriguez .75 .35 .09
☐ 141 Quilvio Veras .10 .05 .01
☐ 142 Mike Fetters .10 .05 .01
☐ 143 Mike Greenwell .10 .05 .01
☐ 144 Bill Pulsipher .25 .11 .03
☐ 145 Mark McGwire 1.00 .45 .12
☐ 146 Frank Castillo .10 .05 .01
☐ 147 Greg Vaughn .50 .23 .06
☐ 148 Pat Hentgen .25 .11 .03
☐ 149 Walt Weiss .10 .05 .01
☐ 150 Randy Johnson .50 .23 .06
☐ 151 David Segui .10 .05 .01
☐ 152 Benji Gil .10 .05 .01
☐ 153 Tom Candiotti .10 .05 .01
☐ 154 Geronimo Berroa .25 .11 .03
☐ 155 John Franco .10 .05 .01
☐ 156 Jay Bell .25 .11 .03
☐ 157 Mark Gubicza .10 .05 .01
☐ 158 Hal Morris .10 .05 .01
☐ 159 Wilson Alvarez .50 .23 .06
☐ 160 Derek Bell .25 .11 .03
☐ 161 Ricky Bottalico .10 .05 .01
☐ 162 Bret Boone .10 .05 .01
☐ 163 Brad Radke .10 .05 .01
☐ 164 John Valentin .50 .23 .06
☐ 165 Steve Avery .25 .11 .03
☐ 166 Mark McLemore .10 .05 .01
☐ 167 Danny Jackson .10 .05 .01
☐ 168 Tino Martinez .25 .11 .03
☐ 169 Shane Reynolds .10 .05 .01
☐ 170 Terry Pendleton .25 .11 .03
☐ 171 Jim Edmonds .25 .11 .03
☐ 172 Esteban Loaiza .10 .05 .01
☐ 173 Ray Durham .50 .23 .06
☐ 174 Carlos Perez .10 .05 .01
☐ 175 Raul Mondesi .50 .23 .06
☐ 176 Steve Ontiveros .10 .05 .01
☐ 177 Chipper Jones 2.00 .90 .25
☐ 178 Otis Nixon .10 .05 .01
☐ 179 John Burkett .10 .05 .01
☐ 180 Gregg Jefferies .50 .23 .06
☐ 181 Denny Martinez .25 .11 .03
☐ 182 Ken Caminiti .50 .23 .06
☐ 183 Doug Jones .10 .05 .01
☐ 184 Brian McRae .10 .05 .01
☐ 185 Don Mattingly 1.50 .70 .19
☐ 186 Mel Rojas .25 .11 .03
☐ 187 Marty Cordova .25 .11 .03
☐ 188 Vinny Castilla .25 .11 .03
☐ 189 John Smoltz .50 .23 .06
☐ 190 Travis Fryman .25 .11 .03
☐ 191 Chris Hoiles .10 .05 .01
☐ 192 Chuck Finley .10 .05 .01
☐ 193 Ryan Klesko .50 .23 .06
☐ 194 Alex Fernandez .25 .11 .03
☐ 195 Dante Bichette .50 .23 .06
☐ 196 Eric Karros .25 .11 .03
☐ 197 Roger Clemens .60 .25 .07
☐ 198 Randy Myers .10 .05 .01
☐ 199 Tony Phillips .25 .11 .03
☐ 200 Cal Ripken 2.50 1.10 .30
☐ 201 Rod Beck .25 .11 .03
☐ 202 Chad Curtis .10 .05 .01
☐ 203 Jack McDowell .50 .23 .06
☐ 204 Gary Gaetti .25 .11 .03
☐ 205 Ken Griffey Jr. 3.00 1.35 .35
☐ 206 Ramon Martinez .25 .11 .03
☐ 207 Jeff Kent .10 .05 .01
☐ 208 Brad Ausmus .10 .05 .01
☐ 209 Devon White .10 .05 .01
☐ 210 Jason Giambi .50 .23 .06
☐ 211 Nomar Garciaparra 1.25 .55 .16
☐ 212 Billy Wagner .50 .23 .06
☐ 213 Todd Greene .25 .11 .03
☐ 214 Paul Wilson .25 .11 .03
☐ 215 Johnny Damon .25 .11 .03
☐ 216 Alan Benes .50 .23 .06
☐ 217 Karim Garcia .60 .25 .07
☐ 218 Dustin Hermanson .25 .11 .03
☐ 219 Derek Jeter 2.00 .90 .25
☐ 220 Checklist (111-220) .10 .05 .01
☐ 221 Kirby Puckett STP .30 .14 .04
☐ 222 Cal Ripken STP .75 .35 .09
☐ 223 Albert Belle STP .40 .18 .05
☐ 224 Randy Johnson STP .30 .14 .04
☐ 225 Wade Boggs STP .30 .14 .04
☐ 226 Carlos Baerga STP .30 .14 .04
☐ 227 Ivan Rodriguez STP .30 .14 .04
☐ 228 Mike Mussina STP .30 .14 .04
☐ 229 Frank Thomas STP 1.00 .45 .12
☐ 230 Ken Griffey Jr. STP 1.00 .45 .12
☐ 231 Jose Mesa STP .05 .02 .01
☐ 232 Matt Morris RC .40 .18 .05
☐ 233 Craig Wilson RC .30 .14 .04
☐ 234 Alvie Shepherd RC .20 .09 .03
☐ 235 Randy Winn .15 .07 .02
☐ 236 David Yocum .15 .07 .02
☐ 237 Jason Brester .15 .07 .02
☐ 238 Shane Monahan RC .30 .14 .04
☐ 239 Brian McNichol .15 .07 .02
☐ 240 Reggie Taylor .15 .07 .02
☐ 241 Garrett Long .15 .07 .02
☐ 242 Jonathan Johnson RC .30 .14 .04
☐ 243 Jeff Liefer RC .50 .23 .06
☐ 244 Brian Powell .15 .07 .02
☐ 245 Brian Buchanan .15 .07 .02
☐ 246 Mike Piazza 1.25 .55 .16
☐ 247 Edgar Martinez .30 .14 .04
☐ 248 Chuck Knoblauch .30 .14 .04
☐ 249 Andres Galarraga .30 .14 .04
☐ 250 Tony Gwynn .75 .35 .09
☐ 251 Lee Smith .30 .14 .04
☐ 252 Sammy Sosa .30 .14 .04
☐ 253 Jim Thome .40 .18 .05
☐ 254 Frank Rodriguez .15 .07 .02
☐ 255 Charlie Hayes .15 .07 .02
☐ 256 Bernard Gilkey .30 .14 .04
☐ 257 John Smiley .10 .05 .01
☐ 258 Brady Anderson .50 .23 .06
☐ 259 Rico Brogna .15 .07 .02
☐ 260 Kirt Manwaring .05 .02 .01
☐ 261 Len Dykstra .15 .07 .02
☐ 262 Tom Glavine .30 .14 .04
☐ 263 Vince Coleman .15 .07 .02
☐ 264 John Olerud .10 .05 .01
☐ 265 Orlando Merced .15 .07 .02
☐ 266 Kent Mercker .05 .02 .01
☐ 267 Terry Steinbach .15 .07 .02
☐ 268 Brian L. Hunter .15 .07 .02
☐ 269 Jeff Fassero .05 .02 .01
☐ 270 Jay Buhner .30 .14 .04
☐ 271 Jeff Brantley .10 .05 .01
☐ 272 Tim Raines .30 .14 .04
☐ 273 Jimmy Key .15 .07 .02
☐ 274 Mo Vaughn .50 .23 .06
☐ 275 Andre Dawson .30 .14 .04
☐ 276 Jose Mesa .15 .07 .02
☐ 277 Brett Butler .10 .05 .01
☐ 278 Luis Gonzalez .15 .07 .02
☐ 279 Steve Sparks .05 .02 .01
☐ 280 Chili Davis .15 .07 .02
☐ 281 Carl Everett .15 .07 .02
☐ 282 Jeff Cirillo .15 .07 .02
☐ 283 Thomas Howard .05 .02 .01
☐ 284 Paul O'Neill .15 .07 .02
☐ 285 Pat Meares .15 .07 .02
☐ 286 Mickey Tettleton .15 .07 .02
☐ 287 Rey Sanchez .05 .02 .01
☐ 288 Bip Roberts .15 .07 .02
☐ 289 Roberto Alomar .40 .18 .05
☐ 290 Ruben Sierra .15 .07 .02
☐ 291 John Flaherty .05 .02 .01
☐ 292 Bret Saberhagen .15 .07 .02
☐ 293 Barry Larkin .30 .14 .04
☐ 294 Sandy Alomar .15 .07 .02
☐ 295 Ed Sprague .15 .07 .02
☐ 296 Gary DiSarcina .15 .07 .02
☐ 297 Marquis Grissom .30 .14 .04
☐ 298 John Frascatore .10 .05 .01
☐ 299 Will Clark .30 .14 .04
☐ 300 Barry Bonds .50 .23 .06
☐ 301 Ozzie Smith .50 .23 .06
☐ 302 Dave Nilsson .15 .07 .02
☐ 303 Pedro Martinez .15 .07 .02
☐ 304 Joey Cora .05 .02 .01
☐ 305 Rick Aguilera .15 .07 .02
☐ 306 Craig Biggio .30 .14 .04
☐ 307 Jose Vizcaino .15 .07 .02
☐ 308 Jeff Montgomery .10 .05 .01
☐ 309 Moises Alou .15 .07 .02
☐ 310 Robin Ventura .30 .14 .04
☐ 311 David Wells .15 .07 .02
☐ 312 Delino DeShields .15 .07 .02
☐ 313 Trevor Hoffman .15 .07 .02
☐ 314 Andy Benes .15 .07 .02
☐ 315 Deion Sanders .30 .14 .04
☐ 316 Jim Bullinger .05 .02 .01
☐ 317 John Jaha .15 .07 .02
☐ 318 Greg Maddux 1.25 .55 .16
☐ 319 Tim Salmon .30 .14 .04
☐ 320 Ben McDonald .15 .07 .02
☐ 321 Sandy Martinez .05 .02 .01
☐ 322 Dan Miceli .05 .02 .01
☐ 323 Wade Boggs .30 .14 .04
☐ 324 Ismael Valdes .15 .07 .02
☐ 325 Juan Gonzalez 1.00 .45 .12
☐ 326 Charles Nagy .15 .07 .02
☐ 327 Ray Lankford .30 .14 .04
☐ 328 Mark Portugal .05 .02 .01
☐ 329 Bobby Bonilla .30 .14 .04
☐ 330 Reggie Sanders .30 .14 .04
☐ 331 Jamie Brewington .05 .02 .01
☐ 332 Aaron Sele .05 .02 .01
☐ 333 Pete Harnisch .05 .02 .01
☐ 334 Cliff Floyd .15 .07 .02
☐ 335 Cal Eldred .05 .02 .01
☐ 336 Jason Bates .05 .02 .01
☐ 337 Tony Clark .40 .18 .05
☐ 338 Jose Herrera .05 .02 .01
☐ 339 Alex Ochoa .15 .07 .02
☐ 340 Mark Loretta .05 .02 .01
☐ 341 Donne Wall .05 .02 .01
☐ 342 Jason Kendall .30 .14 .04
☐ 343 Shannon Stewart .05 .02 .01
☐ 344 Brooks Kieschnick .05 .02 .01
☐ 345 Chris Snopek .05 .02 .01
☐ 346 Ruben Rivera .40 .18 .05
☐ 347 Jeff Suppan .05 .02 .01
☐ 348 Phil Nevin .15 .07 .02
☐ 349 John Wasdin .05 .02 .01
☐ 350 Jay Payton .30 .14 .04
☐ 351 Tim Crabtree .05 .02 .01
☐ 352 Rick Krivda .05 .02 .01
☐ 353 Bob Wolcott .05 .02 .01
☐ 354 Jimmy Haynes .05 .02 .01
☐ 355 Herb Perry .05 .02 .01
☐ 356 Ryne Sandberg .50 .23 .06
☐ 357 Harold Baines .15 .07 .02
☐ 358 Chad Ogea .05 .02 .01
☐ 359 Lee Tinsley .05 .02 .01
☐ 360 Matt Williams .30 .14 .04
☐ 361 Randy Velarde .05 .02 .01
☐ 362 Jose Canseco .30 .14 .04
☐ 363 Larry Walker .30 .14 .04
☐ 364 Kevin Appier .15 .07 .02
☐ 365 Darryl Hamilton .05 .02 .01
☐ 366 Jose Lima .05 .02 .01
☐ 367 Javy Lopez .30 .14 .04
☐ 368 Dennis Eckersley .30 .14 .04
☐ 369 Jason Isringhausen .15 .07 .02
☐ 370 Mickey Morandini .05 .02 .01
☐ 371 Scott Cooper .05 .02 .01
☐ 372 Jim Abbott .30 .14 .04
☐ 373 Paul Sorrento .15 .07 .02
☐ 374 Chris Hammond .05 .02 .01
☐ 375 Lance Johnson .15 .07 .02
☐ 376 Kevin Brown .15 .07 .02
☐ 377 Luis Alicea .05 .02 .01
☐ 378 Andy Pettitte .60 .25 .07
☐ 379 Dean Palmer .30 .14 .04
☐ 380 Jeff Bagwell .75 .35 .09
☐ 381 Jaime Navarro .05 .02 .01
☐ 382 Rondell White .30 .14 .04
☐ 383 Erik Hanson .05 .02 .01
☐ 384 Pedro Munoz .15 .07 .02
☐ 385 Heathcliff Slocumb .15 .07 .02
☐ 386 Wally Joyner .15 .07 .02
☐ 387 Bob Tewksbury .05 .02 .01
☐ 388 David Bell .05 .02 .01
☐ 389 Fred McGriff .30 .14 .04
☐ 390 Mike Henneman .15 .07 .02
☐ 391 Robby Thompson .05 .02 .01
☐ 392 Norm Charlton .05 .02 .01
☐ 393 Cecil Fielder .30 .14 .04
☐ 394 Benito Santiago .15 .07 .02
☐ 395 Rafael Palmeiro .30 .14 .04
☐ 396 Ricky Bones .05 .02 .01
☐ 397 Rickey Henderson .30 .14 .04
☐ 398 C.J. Nitkowski .05 .02 .01
☐ 399 Shawon Dunston .05 .02 .01
☐ 400 Manny Ramirez .50 .23 .06
☐ 401 Bill Swift .05 .02 .01
☐ 402 Chad Fonville .05 .02 .01
☐ 403 Joey Hamilton .15 .07 .02
☐ 404 Alex Gonzalez .05 .02 .01
☐ 405 Roberto Hernandez .15 .07 .02
☐ 406 Jeff Blauser .05 .02 .01
☐ 407 LaTroy Hawkins .05 .02 .01
☐ 408 Greg Colbrunn .05 .02 .01
☐ 409 Todd Hundley .30 .14 .04
☐ 410 Glenn Dishman .05 .02 .01
☐ 411 Joe Vitiello .05 .02 .01
☐ 412 Todd Worrell .15 .07 .02
☐ 413 Wil Cordero .05 .02 .01
☐ 414 Ken Hill .15 .07 .02
☐ 415 Carlos Garcia .15 .07 .02
☐ 416 Bryan Rekar .05 .02 .01
☐ 417 Shawn Green .05 .02 .01
☐ 418 Tyler Green .05 .02 .01
☐ 419 Mike Blowers .05 .02 .01

Card	MINT	NRMT	EXC
☐ 420 Kenny Lofton	.50	.23	.06
☐ 421 Denny Neagle	.15	.07	.02
☐ 422 Jeff Conine	.15	.07	.02
☐ 423 Mark Langston	.15	.07	.02
☐ 424 Steve Cox	1.50	.70	.19
Jesse Ibarra			
Derrek Lee			
Ron Wright			
☐ 425 Jim Bonnici	.50	.23	.06
Billy Owens			
Richie Sexson			
Daryle Ward			
☐ 426 Kevin Jordan	.15	.07	.02
Bobby Morris			
Desi Relaford			
Adam Riggs			
☐ 427 Tim Harkrider	.15	.07	.02
Rey Ordonez			
Neifi Perez			
Enrique Wilson			
☐ 428 Bartolo Colon	.15	.07	.02
Doug Million			
Rafael Orellano			
Ray Ricken			
☐ 429 Jeff D'Amico	.15	.07	.02
Marty Janzen			
Gary Rath			
Clint Sodowsky			
☐ 430 Matt Drews	.15	.07	.02
Rich Hunter			
Matt Ruebel			
Bret Wagner			
☐ 431 Jaime Bluma	.30	.14	.04
David Coggin			
Steve Montgomery			
Brandon Reed			
☐ 432 Mike Figga	.15	.07	.02
Raul Ibanez			
Paul Konerko			
Julio Mosquera			
☐ 433 Brian Barber	.15	.07	.02
Marc Kroon			
Marc Valdes			
Don Wengert			
☐ 434 George Arias	1.25	.55	.16
Chris Haas			
Scott Rolen			
Scott Spiezio			
☐ 435 Brian Banks	5.00	2.20	.60
Vladimir Guerrero			
Andruw Jones			
Billy McMillon			
☐ 436 Roger Cedeno	1.00	.45	.12
Derrick Gibson			
Ben Grieve			
Shane Spencer			
☐ 437 Anton French	.30	.14	.04
Demond Smith			
Darond Stovall			
Keith Williams			
☐ 438 Michael Coleman	.30	.14	.04
Jacob Cruz			
Richard Hidalgo			
Charles Peterson			
☐ 439 Trey Beamon	.40	.18	.05
Yamil Benitez			
Jermaine Dye			
Angel Echevarria			
☐ 440 Checklist	.05	.02	.01
☐ F7 Mickey Mantle Last Day	8.00	3.60	1.00

1996 Topps Classic Confrontations

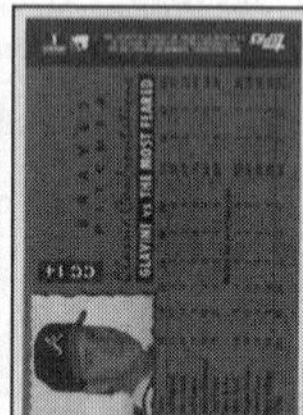

These cards were inserted at a rate of one in every 5-card Series 1 retail pack sold at Walmart. The first ten cards showcase hitters, while the last five cards feature pitchers. Inside white borders, the fronts show player cutouts on a brownish rock background featuring a shadow image of the player. The player's name is gold foil stamped across the bottom. The horizontal backs of the hitters' cards are aqua and present headshots and statistics. The backs of the pitchers cards are purple and present the same information.

	MINT	NRMT	EXC
COMPLETE SET (15)	6.00	2.70	.75
COMMON CARD (CC1-CC15)	.15	.07	.02
☐ CC1 Ken Griffey Jr.	1.50	.70	.19
☐ CC2 Cal Ripken	1.25	.55	.16
☐ CC3 Edgar Martinez	.20	.09	.03
☐ CC4 Kirby Puckett	.60	.25	.07
☐ CC5 Frank Thomas	1.50	.70	.19
☐ CC6 Barry Bonds	.40	.18	.05
☐ CC7 Reggie Sanders	.15	.07	.02
☐ CC8 Andres Galarraga	.25	.11	.03
☐ CC9 Tony Gwynn	.60	.25	.07
☐ CC10 Mike Piazza	1.00	.45	.12
☐ CC11 Randy Johnson	.25	.11	.03
☐ CC12 Mike Mussina	.25	.11	.03
☐ CC13 Roger Clemens	.30	.14	.04
☐ CC14 Tom Glavine	.25	.11	.03
☐ CC15 Greg Maddux	1.00	.45	.12

1996 Topps Mantle

Randomly inserted in Series 1 packs, these cards are reprints of the original Mickey Mantle cards issued from 1951 through 1969. The fronts look the same except for a commemorative stamp, while the backs clearly state that they are "Mickey Mantle Commemorative" cards and have a 1996 copyright date. These cards honor Yankee great Mickey Mantle, who passed away in August 1995 after a gallant battle against cancer. Based on evidence from an uncut sheet auctioned off at the 1996 Kit Young Hawaii Trade Show, some collectors/dealers believe that cards 15 through 19 were slightly shorter printed in relation to the other 14 cards.

	MINT	NRMT	EXC
COMPLETE SET (19)	150.00	70.00	19.00
COMMON MANTLE (1-14)	8.00	3.60	1.00
COMMON MANTLE SP (15-19)	12.00	5.50	1.50
☐ 1 Mickey Mantle 1951 Bowman	15.00	6.75	1.85
☐ 2 Mickey Mantle 1952 Topps	18.00	8.00	2.20
☐ 3 Mickey Mantle 1953 Topps	10.00	4.50	1.25
☐ 4 Mickey Mantle 1954 Bowman	8.00	3.60	1.00
☐ 5 Mickey Mantle 1955 Bowman	8.00	3.60	1.00
☐ 6 Mickey Mantle 1956 Topps	8.00	3.60	1.00
☐ 7 Mickey Mantle 1957 Topps	8.00	3.60	1.00
☐ 8 Mickey Mantle 1958 Topps	8.00	3.60	1.00
☐ 9 Mickey Mantle 1959 Topps	8.00	3.60	1.00
☐ 10 Mickey Mantle 1960 Topps	8.00	3.60	1.00
☐ 11 Mickey Mantle 1961 Topps	8.00	3.60	1.00
☐ 12 Mickey Mantle 1962 Topps	8.00	3.60	1.00
☐ 13 Mickey Mantle 1963 Topps	8.00	3.60	1.00
☐ 14 Mickey Mantle 1964 Topps	8.00	3.60	1.00
☐ 15 Mickey Mantle 1965 Topps	12.00	5.50	1.50
☐ 16 Mickey Mantle 1966 Topps	12.00	5.50	1.50
☐ 17 Mickey Mantle 1967 Topps	12.00	5.50	1.50
☐ 18 Mickey Mantle 1968 Topps	12.00	5.50	1.50
☐ 19 Mickey Mantle 1969 Topps	12.00	5.50	1.50

1996 Topps Mantle Case

These 19 cards were inserted as one per case chiptoppers in second series Hobby, Jumbo or Vending Case. Similar to the regular issue, the last five cards were printed in less quantities than the other 14 cards.

	MINT	NRMT	EXC
COMPLETE SET (19)	1000.00	450.00	125.00
COMMON MANTLE (1-14)	50.00	22.00	6.25
COMMON MANTLE SP (15-19)	60.00	27.00	7.50
☐ 1 Mickey Mantle 1951 Bowman	75.00	34.00	9.50
☐ 2 Mickey Mantle 1952 Topps	125.00	55.00	15.50
☐ 3 Mickey Mantle 1953 Topps	60.00	27.00	7.50
☐ 4 Mickey Mantle 1954 Bowman	50.00	22.00	6.25
☐ 5 Mickey Mantle 1955 Bowman	50.00	22.00	6.25
☐ 6 Mickey Mantle 1956 Topps	50.00	22.00	6.25
☐ 7 Mickey Mantle 1957 Topps	50.00	22.00	6.25
☐ 8 Mickey Mantle 1958 Topps	50.00	22.00	6.25
☐ 9 Mickey Mantle 1959 Topps	50.00	22.00	6.25
☐ 10 Mickey Mantle 1960 Topps	50.00	22.00	6.25
☐ 11 Mickey Mantle 1961 Topps	50.00	22.00	6.25
☐ 12 Mickey Mantle 1962 Topps	50.00	22.00	6.25
☐ 13 Mickey Mantle 1963 Topps	50.00	22.00	6.25
☐ 14 Mickey Mantle 1964 Topps	50.00	22.00	6.25
☐ 15 Mickey Mantle 1965 Topps	60.00	27.00	7.50
☐ 16 Mickey Mantle 1966 Topps	60.00	27.00	7.50
☐ 17 Mickey Mantle 1967 Topps	60.00	27.00	7.50
☐ 18 Mickey Mantle 1968 Topps	60.00	27.00	7.50
☐ 19 Mickey Mantle 1969 Topps	60.00	27.00	7.50

1996 Topps Mantle Finest

Randomly inserted in Series 2 packs at a rate of one in 18, this 19-card set is a reprint of the regular insert set using Finest technology. Each card front is covered with the exclusive Topps Finest Protector to guarantee its brilliant uncirculated condition.

	MINT	NRMT	EXC
COMPLETE SET (19)	150.00	70.00	19.00
COMMON MANTLE (1-14)	8.00	3.60	1.00
COMMON MANTLE SP (15-19)	12.00	5.50	1.50
☐ 1 Mickey Mantle 1951 Bowman	15.00	6.75	1.85
☐ 2 Mickey Mantle 1952 Topps	25.00	11.00	3.10
☐ 3 Mickey Mantle 1953 Topps	10.00	4.50	1.25
☐ 4 Mickey Mantle 1954 Bowman	8.00	3.60	1.00
☐ 5 Mickey Mantle 1955 Bowman	8.00	3.60	1.00
☐ 6 Mickey Mantle 1956 Topps	8.00	3.60	1.00
☐ 7 Mickey Mantle 1957 Topps	8.00	3.60	1.00
☐ 8 Mickey Mantle 1958 Topps	8.00	3.60	1.00
☐ 9 Mickey Mantle 1959 Topps	8.00	3.60	1.00
☐ 10 Mickey Mantle 1960 Topps	8.00	3.60	1.00
☐ 11 Mickey Mantle 1961 Topps	8.00	3.60	1.00
☐ 12 Mickey Mantle 1962 Topps	8.00	3.60	1.00
☐ 13 Mickey Mantle 1963 Topps	8.00	3.60	1.00
☐ 14 Mickey Mantle 1964 Topps	8.00	3.60	1.00
☐ 15 Mickey Mantle 1965 Topps	12.00	5.50	1.50
☐ 16 Mickey Mantle 1966 Topps	12.00	5.50	1.50
☐ 17 Mickey Mantle 1967 Topps	12.00	5.50	1.50
☐ 18 Mickey Mantle 1968 Topps	12.00	5.50	1.50
☐ 19 Mickey Mantle 1969 Topps	12.00	5.50	1.50

1996 Topps Mantle Finest Refractors

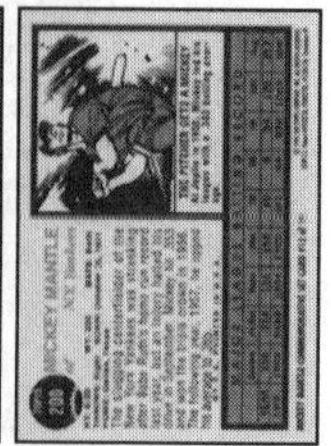

Randomly inserted at the rate of one in 144 Series 2 packs, this 19-card set is parallel to the regular set and is similar in design. It is distinguised from the regular set by the refractive quality of the cards. Just like all the other 96 Mantles, cards 15-19 are printed in 20 percent less quantity than cards 1 through 14.

	MINT	NRMT	EXC
COMPLETE SET (19)	900.00	400.00	110.00
COMMON MANTLE (1-14)	50.00	22.00	6.25
COMMON MANTLE SP (15-19)	60.00	27.00	7.50
☐ 1 Mickey Mantle 1951 Bowman	100.00	45.00	12.50
☐ 2 Mickey Mantle 1952 Topps	200.00	90.00	25.00
☐ 3 Mickey Mantle 1953 Topps	60.00	27.00	7.50
☐ 4 Mickey Mantle 1954 Bowman	50.00	22.00	6.25
☐ 5 Mickey Mantle 1955 Bowman	50.00	22.00	6.25
☐ 6 Mickey Mantle 1956 Topps	50.00	22.00	6.25
☐ 7 Mickey Mantle 1957 Topps	50.00	22.00	6.25
☐ 8 Mickey Mantle 1958 Topps	50.00	22.00	6.25
☐ 9 Mickey Mantle 1959 Topps	50.00	22.00	6.25
☐ 10 Mickey Mantle 1960 Topps	50.00	22.00	6.25
☐ 11 Mickey Mantle 1961 Topps	50.00	22.00	6.25
☐ 12 Mickey Mantle 1962 Topps	50.00	22.00	6.25
☐ 13 Mickey Mantle 1963 Topps	50.00	22.00	6.25
☐ 14 Mickey Mantle 1964 Topps	50.00	22.00	6.25
☐ 15 Mickey Mantle 1965 Topps	60.00	27.00	7.50
☐ 16 Mickey Mantle 1966 Topps	60.00	27.00	7.50
☐ 17 Mickey Mantle 1967 Topps	60.00	27.00	7.50
☐ 18 Mickey Mantle 1968 Topps	60.00	27.00	7.50
☐ 19 Mickey Mantle 1969 Topps	60.00	27.00	7.50

1996 Topps Mantle Redemption

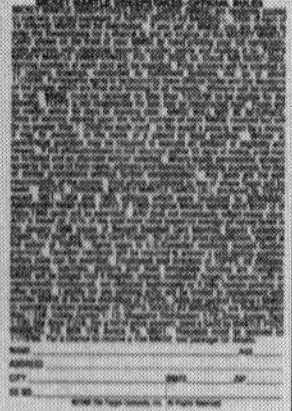

Randomly inserted at the rate of one in 108 Series 2 packs, this 19-card set features redemption cards that made the collector eligible to win the original card whose reprinted design is portrayed on that redemption card front. Only 76 original Mantle cards were to be given away. The redemption deadline for entering the contest was October 15, 1996. The numbers in parentheses next to the player's name indicates how many cards were available through the drawing.

	MINT	NRMT	EXC
COMPLETE SET (19)	350.00	160.00	45.00
COMMON MANTLE (1-19)	20.00	9.00	2.50
☐ 1 Mickey Mantle 1951 Bowman (2)	30.00	13.50	3.70
☐ 2 Mickey Mantle 1952 Topps (1)	50.00	22.00	6.25
☐ 3 Mickey Mantle 1953 Topps (4)	30.00	13.50	3.70
☐ 4 Mickey Mantle 1954 Bowman (2)	20.00	9.00	2.50
☐ 5 Mickey Mantle 1955 Bowman (3)	20.00	9.00	2.50

	MINT	NRMT	EXC
☐ 6 Mickey Mantle 1956 Topps (2)	20.00	9.00	2.50
☐ 7 Mickey Mantle 1957 Topps (2)	20.00	9.00	2.50
☐ 8 Mickey Mantle 1958 Topps (2)	20.00	9.00	2.50
☐ 9 Mickey Mantle 1959 Topps (3)	20.00	9.00	2.50
☐ 10 Mickey Mantle 1960 Topps (3)	20.00	9.00	2.50
☐ 11 Mickey Mantle 1961 Topps (3)	20.00	9.00	2.50
☐ 12 Mickey Mantle 1962 Topps (3)	20.00	9.00	2.50
☐ 13 Mickey Mantle 1963 Topps (3)	20.00	9.00	2.50
☐ 14 Mickey Mantle 1964 Topps (6)	20.00	9.00	2.50
☐ 15 Mickey Mantle 1965 Topps (3)	20.00	9.00	2.50
☐ 16 Mickey Mantle 1966 Topps (10)	20.00	9.00	2.50
☐ 17 Mickey Mantle 1967 Topps (10)	20.00	9.00	2.50
☐ 18 Mickey Mantle 1968 Topps (10)	20.00	9.00	2.50
☐ 19 Mickey Mantle 1969 Topps (4)	20.00	9.00	2.50

1996 Topps Masters of the Game

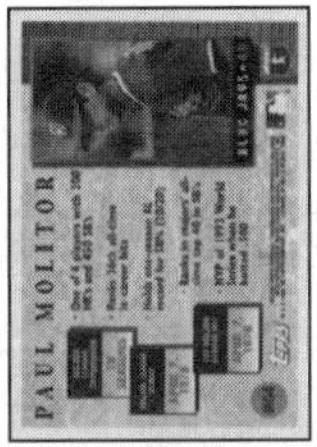

Cards from this 20-card standard-size set were randomly inserted into first-series hobby packs. In addition, every factory set contained two Masters of the Game cards. The horizontal fronts comprise of silver foil set against white borders. The left side of the card has a player photo. The words "Master of the Game" and the playerís name are printed on the right. The horizontal backs have a player photo, a brief write-up and some quick important dates in the playerís career. The cards are numbered with a "MG" prefix in the lower left corner.

	MINT	NRMT	EXC
COMPLETE SET (20)	40.00	18.00	5.00
COMMON CARD (1-20)	.75	.35	.09
☐ 1 Dennis Eckersley	1.00	.45	.12
☐ 2 Denny Martinez	.75	.35	.09
☐ 3 Eddie Murray	2.50	1.10	.30
☐ 4 Paul Molitor	2.00	.90	.25
☐ 5 Ozzie Smith	2.50	1.10	.30
☐ 6 Rickey Henderson	1.25	.55	.16
☐ 7 Tim Raines	.75	.35	.09
☐ 8 Lee Smith	1.00	.45	.12
☐ 9 Cal Ripken	8.00	3.60	1.00
☐ 10 Chili Davis	.75	.35	.09
☐ 11 Wade Boggs	1.25	.55	.16
☐ 12 Tony Gwynn	4.00	1.80	.50
☐ 13 Don Mattingly	5.00	2.20	.60
☐ 14 Bret Saberhagen	.75	.35	.09
☐ 15 Kirby Puckett	4.00	1.80	.50
☐ 16 Joe Carter	1.00	.45	.12
☐ 17 Roger Clemens	2.00	.90	.25
☐ 18 Barry Bonds	2.50	1.10	.30
☐ 19 Greg Maddux	6.00	2.70	.75
☐ 20 Frank Thomas	10.00	4.50	1.25

1996 Topps Mystery Finest

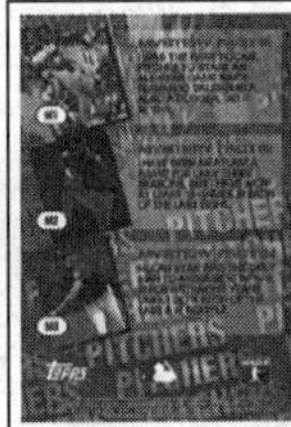

Randomly inserted in first-series packs, this 26-card standard-size set features a bit of a mystery. The fronts have opaque coating that must be removed before the player can be identified. After the opaque coating is removed, the fronts feature a player photo surrounded by silver borders. The backs feature a choice of players along with a corresponding mystery finest trivia fact. Some of these cards were also issued with refractor fronts.

	MINT	NRMT	EXC
COMPLETE SET (26)	150.00	70.00	19.00
COMMON CARD (M1-M26)	1.50	.70	.19
☐ M1 Hideo Nomo	5.00	2.20	.60
☐ M2 Greg Maddux	12.00	5.50	1.50
☐ M3 Randy Johnson	3.00	1.35	.35
☐ M4 Chipper Jones	12.00	5.50	1.50
☐ M5 Marty Cordova	1.50	.70	.19
☐ M6 Garret Anderson	1.50	.70	.19
☐ M7 Cal Ripken	15.00	6.75	1.85
☐ M8 Kirby Puckett	8.00	3.60	1.00
☐ M9 Tony Gwynn	8.00	3.60	1.00
☐ M10 Manny Ramirez	5.00	2.20	.60
☐ M11 Jim Edmonds	1.50	.70	.19
☐ M12 Mike Piazza	12.00	5.50	1.50
☐ M13 Barry Bonds	5.00	2.20	.60
☐ M14 Raul Mondesi	2.50	1.10	.30
☐ M15 Sammy Sosa	3.00	1.35	.35
☐ M16 Ken Griffey Jr.	20.00	9.00	2.50
☐ M17 Albert Belle	8.00	3.60	1.00
☐ M18 Dante Bichette	2.50	1.10	.30
☐ M19 Mo Vaughn	5.00	2.20	.60
☐ M20 Jeff Bagwell	8.00	3.60	1.00
☐ M21 Frank Thomas	20.00	9.00	2.50
☐ M22 Hideo Nomo	5.00	2.20	.60
☐ M23 Cal Ripken	15.00	6.75	1.85
☐ M24 Mike Piazza	12.00	5.50	1.50
☐ M25 Ken Griffey Jr.	20.00	9.00	2.50
☐ M26 Frank Thomas	20.00	9.00	2.50

1996 Topps Mystery Finest Refractors

Parallel to the more common Mystery Finest inserts, these cards differ in their refractive sheen on the card fronts. The cards were randomly inserted into first series packs of 1996 Topps. Please refer to the multiplier for value on singles.

	MINT	NRMT	EXC
COMPLETE SET (26)	450.00	200.00	55.00
COMMON CARD (M1-M26)	5.00	2.20	.60

*STARS: 1.5X TO 3X BASIC CARDS ..

1996 Topps Power Boosters

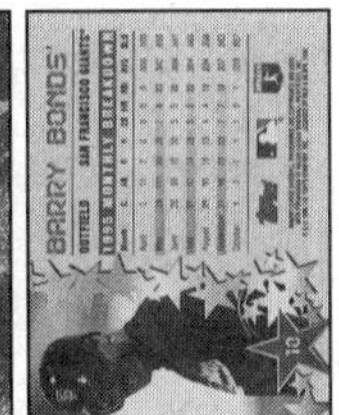

Randomly inserted into packs, these cards are a metallic version of 25 of the first 26 cards from the basic Topps set. Card numbers 1-6 and 8-12 were issued in retail packs, while numbers 13-26 were issued in hobby packs. Inserted in place of two basic cards, they are printed on 28 point stock and the fronts have prismatic foil printing. Card number 7, which is Mickey Mantle in the regular set, was not issued in a Power Booster form.

	MINT	NRMT	EXC
COMPLETE SET (25)	90.00	40.00	11.00
COMP. STAR POWER SET (11)	50.00	22.00	6.25
COMP. DRAFT PICKS SET (14)	40.00	18.00	5.00
COMMON STAR POW. (1-6/8-12)	1.50	.70	.19
COMMON DRAFT PICK (12-26)	2.50	1.10	.30
☐ 1 Tony Gwynn	8.00	3.60	1.00
☐ 2 Mike Piazza	12.00	5.50	1.50
☐ 3 Greg Maddux	12.00	5.50	1.50
☐ 4 Jeff Bagwell	8.00	3.60	1.00
☐ 5 Larry Walker	2.50	1.10	.30
☐ 6 Barry Larkin	2.00	.90	.25
☐ 8 Tom Glavine	2.50	1.10	.30
☐ 9 Craig Biggio	2.00	.90	.25
☐ 10 Barry Bonds	5.00	2.20	.60
☐ 11 Heathcliff Slocumb	1.50	.70	.19
☐ 12 Matt Williams	2.50	1.10	.30
☐ 13 Todd Helton	15.00	6.75	1.85
☐ 14 Mark Redman	2.50	1.10	.30
☐ 15 Michael Barrett	2.50	1.10	.30
☐ 16 Ben Davis	4.00	1.80	.50
☐ 17 Juan LeBron	4.00	1.80	.50
☐ 18 Tony McKnight	2.50	1.10	.30
☐ 19 Ryan Jaroncyk	2.50	1.10	.30
☐ 20 Corey Jenkins	4.00	1.80	.50
☐ 21 Jim Scharrer	2.50	1.10	.30
☐ 22 Mark Bellhorn	2.50	1.10	.30
☐ 23 Jarrod Washburn	2.50	1.10	.30
☐ 24 Geoff Jenkins	4.00	1.80	.50
☐ 25 Sean Casey	4.00	1.80	.50
☐ 26 Brett Tomko	2.50	1.10	.30

1996 Topps Profiles

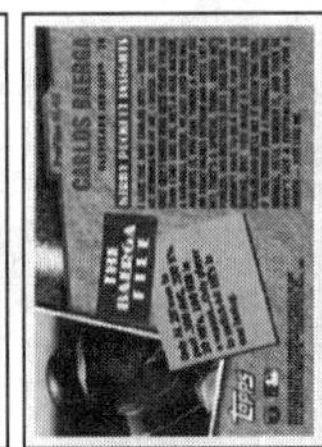

Randomly inserted into Series 1 and 2 packs, this 20-card standard-size set features 10 players from each league. One card from each series was also included in all Topps factory sets. Topps spokesmen Kirby Puckett (AL) and Tony Gwynn (NL) give opinions on players within their league. The fronts feature a player photo set against a silver-foil background. The playerís name is on the bottom. A photo of either Gwynn or Puckett as well as the words "Profiles by ..." is on the right. The backs feature a player photo, some career data as well as Gwynn's or Puckett's opinion about the featured player. The cards are numbered with either an "AL or NL" prefix on the back depending on the playerís league. The cards are sequenced in alphabetical order within league.

	MINT	NRMT	EXC
COMPLETE SET (40)	40.00	18.00	5.00
COMPLETE SERIES 1 (20)	30.00	13.50	3.70
COMPLETE SERIES 2 (20)	10.00	4.50	1.25
COMMON SER.1 (AL1-AL10)	.50	.23	.06
COMMON SER.1 (NL1-NL10)	.50	.23	.06
COMMON SER.2 (AL11-AL20)	.50	.23	.06
COMMON SER.2 (NL11-NL20)	.50	.23	.06
☐ AL1 Roberto Alomar	1.00	.45	.12
☐ AL2 Carlos Baerga	.50	.23	.06
☐ AL3 Albert Belle	2.00	.90	.25
☐ AL4 Cecil Fielder	.75	.35	.09
☐ AL5 Ken Griffey Jr.	5.00	2.20	.60
☐ AL6 Randy Johnson	.75	.35	.09
☐ AL7 Paul O'Neill	.50	.23	.06
☐ AL8 Cal Ripken	4.00	1.80	.50
☐ AL9 Frank Thomas	5.00	2.20	.60
☐ AL10 Mo Vaughn	1.25	.55	.16
☐ AL11 Jay Buhner	.75	.35	.09
☐ AL12 Marty Cordova	.75	.35	.09
☐ AL13 Jim Edmonds	.75	.35	.09
☐ AL14 Juan Gonzalez	2.50	1.10	.30
☐ AL15 Kenny Lofton	1.25	.55	.16
☐ AL16 Edgar Martinez	.75	.35	.09
☐ AL17 Don Mattingly	2.50	1.10	.30
☐ AL18 Mark McGwire	1.50	.70	.19
☐ AL19 Rafael Palmeiro	.75	.35	.09
☐ AL20 Tim Salmon	.75	.35	.09
☐ NL1 Jeff Bagwell	2.00	.90	.25
☐ NL2 Derek Bell	.50	.23	.06
☐ NL3 Barry Bonds	1.25	.55	.16
☐ NL4 Greg Maddux	3.00	1.35	.35
☐ NL5 Fred McGriff	.75	.35	.09
☐ NL6 Raul Mondesi	.75	.35	.09
☐ NL7 Mike Piazza	3.00	1.35	.35
☐ NL8 Reggie Sanders	.50	.23	.06
☐ NL9 Sammy Sosa	.75	.35	.09
☐ NL10 Larry Walker	.75	.35	.09
☐ NL11 Dante Bichette	.75	.35	.09
☐ NL12 Andres Galarraga	.75	.35	.09
☐ NL13 Ron Gant	.75	.35	.09
☐ NL14 Tom Glavine	.75	.35	.09
☐ NL15 Chipper Jones	3.00	1.35	.35
☐ NL16 David Justice	.75	.35	.09
☐ NL17 Barry Larkin	.75	.35	.09
☐ NL18 Hideo Nomo	1.25	.55	.16
☐ NL19 Gary Sheffield	.75	.35	.09
☐ NL20 Matt Williams	.75	.35	.09

1996 Topps Road Warriors

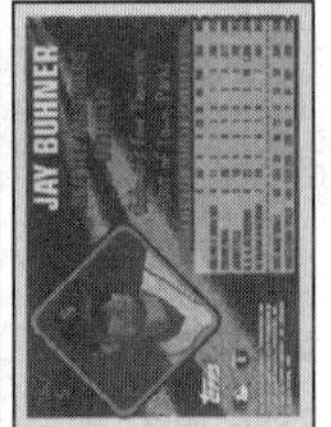

This 20-card set was inserted only into Series 2 WalMart packs and featured leading hitters of the majors. The set is sequenced in alphabetical order.

	MINT	NRMT	EXC
COMPLETE SET (20)	12.00	5.50	1.50
COMMON CARD (RW1-RW20)	.25	.11	.03
☐ RW1 Derek Bell	.25	.11	.03
☐ RW2 Albert Belle	1.50	.70	.19
☐ RW3 Craig Biggio	.35	.16	.04
☐ RW4 Barry Bonds	1.00	.45	.12
☐ RW5 Jay Buhner	.35	.16	.04
☐ RW6 Jim Edmonds	.35	.16	.04
☐ RW7 Gary Gaetti	.25	.11	.03
☐ RW8 Ron Gant	.35	.16	.04
☐ RW9 Edgar Martinez	.35	.16	.04
☐ RW10 Tino Martinez	.50	.23	.06
☐ RW11 Mark McGwire	1.25	.55	.16
☐ RW12 Mike Piazza	2.50	1.10	.30
☐ RW13 Manny Ramirez	1.00	.45	.12
☐ RW14 Tim Salmon	.35	.16	.04
☐ RW15 Reggie Sanders	.25	.11	.03
☐ RW16 Frank Thomas	4.00	1.80	.50
☐ RW17 John Valentin	.25	.11	.03
☐ RW18 Mo Vaughn	1.00	.45	.12
☐ RW19 Robin Ventura	.35	.16	.04
☐ RW20 Matt Williams	.50	.23	.06

1996 Topps Wrecking Crew

Randomly inserted in Series 2 hobby packs, this 15-card set honors some of the hottest home run producers in the League. One card from this set was also inserted into Topps Hobby Factory sets. The cards feature color action player photos with foil stamping.

	MINT	NRMT	EXC
COMPLETE SET (15)	70.00	32.00	8.75
COMMON CARD (1-15)	1.50	.70	.19
☐ WC1 Jeff Bagwell	8.00	3.60	1.00
☐ WC2 Albert Belle	8.00	3.60	1.00
☐ WC3 Barry Bonds	5.00	2.20	.60
☐ WC4 Jose Canseco	2.50	1.10	.30
☐ WC5 Joe Carter	1.50	.70	.19
☐ WC6 Cecil Fielder	1.50	.70	.19
☐ WC7 Ron Gant	1.50	.70	.19
☐ WC8 Juan Gonzalez	10.00	4.50	1.25
☐ WC9 Ken Griffey Jr	20.00	9.00	2.50
☐ WC10 Fred McGriff	2.50	1.10	.30
☐ WC11 Mark McGwire	6.00	2.70	.75
☐ WC12 Mike Piazza	12.00	5.50	1.50
☐ WC13 Frank Thomas	20.00	9.00	2.50
☐ WC14 Mo Vaughn	5.00	2.20	.60
☐ WC15 Matt Williams	2.50	1.10	.30

1996 Topps Big Cards

This nine-card set measures approximately 3 1/2" by 5" and was distributed only by Walmart. One card was packed with the team set of the star player. The fronts feature oversized photos of the Topps cards. The cards are unnumbered and checklisted below in alphabetical order.

	MINT	NRMT	EXC
COMPLETE SET (9)	25.00	11.00	3.10
COMMON CARD (1-9)	2.00	.90	.25
☐ 1 Albert Belle	2.50	1.10	.30
☐ 2 Juan Gonzalez	2.50	1.10	.30
☐ 3 Ken Griffey Jr.	5.00	2.20	.60
☐ 4 Derek Jeter	3.00	1.35	.35
☐ 5 Greg Maddux	3.00	1.35	.35
☐ 6 Hideo Nomo	2.50	1.10	.30
☐ 7 Cal Ripken	4.00	1.80	.50
☐ 8 Ryne Sandberg	2.00	.90	.25
☐ 9 Frank Thomas	5.00	2.20	.60

1996 Topps Bronze League Leaders

This six-card set features color action player images on a background of silver rays, sealed to a bed of solid bronze, and silk-screened with the player's league leading 1995 stats plus career numbers. Only 2,000 of this set was produced.

	MINT	NRMT	EXC
COMPLETE SET (6)	75.00	34.00	9.50
COMMON CARD (1-6)	10.00	4.50	1.25
☐ 1 Barry Larkin	15.00	6.75	1.85
☐ 2 Greg Maddux	25.00	11.00	3.10
☐ 3 Hideo Nomo	20.00	9.00	2.50
☐ 4 Mo Vaughn	15.00	6.75	1.85
☐ 5 Randy Johnson	15.00	6.75	1.85
☐ 6 Marty Cordova			

1997 Topps

This 496-card set was primarily distributed in first and second series 11-card packs with a suggested retail price of $1.29. In addition, 8-card retail packs, 40-card jumbo packs and factory sets were made available. The card fronts feature a color action player photo with a gloss coating and a spot matte finish on the outside border with gold foil stamping. The backs carry another player photo, player information and statistics. The set includes the following subsets: Season Highlights (100-104, 462-466), Prospects (200-207, 487-494), the first ever expansion team cards of the Arizona Diamondbacks (249-251,468-469 and the Tampa Bay Devil Rays (252-253, 470-472) and Draft Picks (269-274, 477-483). Card 42 is a special Jackie Robinson tribute card commemorating the 50th anniversary of his contribution to baseball history and numbered for his Dodgers uniform number. Card #7 does not exist because it was retired in honor of Mickey Mantle. Card #84 does not exist because Mike Fetters' card was incorrectly numbered #61. Card #277 does not exist because Chipper Jones' card was incorrectly numbered #276. 1996 number one draft pick Kris Benson's first card highlights the wide selection of Rookie Cards available in the set.

	MINT	NRMT	EXC
COMPLETE SET (496)	40.00	18.00	5.00
COMPLETE SERIES 1 (276)	20.00	9.00	2.50
COMPLETE SERIES 2 (220)	20.00	9.00	2.50
COMMON CARD (1-496)	.10	.05	.01
☐ 1 Barry Bonds	.75	.35	.09
☐ 2 Tom Pagnozzi	.10	.05	.01
☐ 3 Terrell Wade	.10	.05	.01
☐ 4 Jose Valentin	.10	.05	.01
☐ 5 Mark Clark	.10	.05	.01
☐ 6 Brady Anderson	.25	.11	.03
☐ 8 Wade Boggs	.40	.18	.05
☐ 9 Scott Stahoviak	.10	.05	.01
☐ 10 Andres Galarraga	.40	.18	.05
☐ 11 Steve Avery	.10	.05	.01
☐ 12 Rusty Greer	.25	.11	.03
☐ 13 Derek Jeter	2.00	.90	.25
☐ 14 Ricky Bottalico	.10	.05	.01
☐ 15 Andy Ashby	.10	.05	.01
☐ 16 Paul Shuey	.10	.05	.01
☐ 17 F.P. Santangelo	.10	.05	.01
☐ 18 Royce Clayton	.10	.05	.01
☐ 19 Mike Mohler	.10	.05	.01
☐ 20 Mike Piazza	2.00	.90	.25
☐ 21 Jaime Navarro	.10	.05	.01
☐ 22 Billy Wagner	.25	.11	.03
☐ 23 Mike Timlin	.10	.05	.01
☐ 24 Garret Anderson	.10	.05	.01
☐ 25 Ben McDonald	.10	.05	.01
☐ 26 Mel Rojas	.10	.05	.01
☐ 27 John Burkett	.10	.05	.01
☐ 28 Jeff King	.10	.05	.01
☐ 29 Reggie Jefferson	.10	.05	.01
☐ 30 Kevin Appier	.25	.11	.03
☐ 31 Felipe Lira	.10	.05	.01
☐ 32 Kevin Tapani	.10	.05	.01
☐ 33 Mark Portugal	.10	.05	.01
☐ 34 Carlos Garcia	.10	.05	.01
☐ 35 Joey Cora	.10	.05	.01
☐ 36 David Segui	.10	.05	.01
☐ 37 Mark Grace	.40	.18	.05
☐ 38 Erik Hanson	.10	.05	.01
☐ 39 Jeff D'Amico	.25	.11	.03
☐ 40 Jay Buhner	.40	.18	.05
☐ 41 B.J. Surhoff	.10	.05	.01
☐ 42 Jackie Robinson TRIB	2.50	1.10	.30
☐ 43 Roger Pavlik	.10	.05	.01
☐ 44 Hal Morris	.10	.05	.01
☐ 45 Mariano Duncan	.10	.05	.01
☐ 46 Harold Baines	.10	.05	.01
☐ 47 Jorge Fabregas	.10	.05	.01
☐ 48 Jose Herrera	.10	.05	.01
☐ 49 Jeff Cirillo	.10	.05	.01
☐ 50 Tom Glavine	.40	.18	.05
☐ 51 Pedro Astacio	.10	.05	.01
☐ 52 Mark Gardner	.10	.05	.01
☐ 53 Arthur Rhodes	.10	.05	.01
☐ 54 Troy O'Leary	.10	.05	.01
☐ 55 Bip Roberts	.10	.05	.01
☐ 56 Mike Lieberthal	.10	.05	.01
☐ 57 Shane Andrews	.10	.05	.01
☐ 58 Scott Karl	.10	.05	.01
☐ 59 Gary DiSarcina	.10	.05	.01
☐ 60 Andy Pettitte	.75	.35	.09
☐ 61 Kevin Elster	.10	.05	.01
☐ 62 Mark McGwire	1.00	.45	.12
☐ 63 Dan Wilson	.10	.05	.01
☐ 64 Mickey Morandini	.10	.05	.01
☐ 65 Chuck Knoblauch	.50	.23	.06
☐ 66 Tim Wakefield	.10	.05	.01
☐ 67 Raul Mondesi	.40	.18	.05
☐ 68 Todd Jones	.10	.05	.01
☐ 69 Albert Belle	1.25	.55	.16
☐ 70 Trevor Hoffman	.10	.05	.01
☐ 71 Eric Young	.25	.11	.03
☐ 72 Robert Perez	.10	.05	.01
☐ 73 Butch Huskey	.10	.05	.01
☐ 74 Brian McRae	.10	.05	.01
☐ 75 Jim Edmonds	.25	.11	.03
☐ 76 Mike Henneman	.10	.05	.01
☐ 77 Frank Rodriguez	.10	.05	.01
☐ 78 Danny Tartabull	.10	.05	.01
☐ 79 Robb Nen	.10	.05	.01
☐ 80 Reggie Sanders	.25	.11	.03
☐ 81 Ron Karkovice	.10	.05	.01
☐ 82 Benito Santiago	.10	.05	.01
☐ 83 Mike Lansing	.10	.05	.01
☐ 84 Mike Fetters UER Card numbered 61	.10	.05	.01
☐ 85 Craig Biggio	.25	.11	.03
☐ 86 Mike Bordick	.10	.05	.01
☐ 87 Ray Lankford	.25	.11	.03
☐ 88 Charles Nagy	.25	.11	.03
☐ 89 Paul Wilson	.25	.11	.03
☐ 90 John Wetteland	.25	.11	.03
☐ 91 Tom Candiotti	.10	.05	.01
☐ 92 Carlos Delgado	.25	.11	.03
☐ 93 Derek Bell	.25	.11	.03
☐ 94 Mark Lemke	.10	.05	.01
☐ 95 Edgar Martinez	.25	.11	.03
☐ 96 Rickey Henderson	.40	.18	.05
☐ 97 Greg Myers	.10	.05	.01
☐ 98 Jim Leyritz	.10	.05	.01
☐ 99 Mark Johnson	.10	.05	.01
☐ 100 Dwight Gooden HL	.25	.11	.03
☐ 101 Al Leiter HL	.10	.05	.01
☐ 102 John Mabry HL	.10	.05	.01
☐ 103 Alex Ochoa HL	.10	.05	.01
☐ 104 Mike Piazza HL	1.00	.45	.12
☐ 105 Jim Thome	.10	.05	.01
☐ 106 Ricky Otero	.10	.05	.01
☐ 107 Jamey Wright	.25	.11	.03
☐ 108 Frank Thomas	3.00	1.35	.35
☐ 109 Jody Reed	.10	.05	.01
☐ 110 Orel Hershiser	.25	.11	.03
☐ 111 Terry Steinbach	.10	.05	.01
☐ 112 Mark Loretta	.10	.05	.01
☐ 113 Turk Wendell	.10	.05	.01
☐ 114 Marvin Benard	.10	.05	.01
☐ 115 Kevin Brown	.25	.11	.03
☐ 116 Robert Person	.10	.05	.01
☐ 117 Joey Hamilton	.25	.11	.03
☐ 118 Francisco Cordova	.10	.05	.01
☐ 119 John Smiley	.10	.05	.01
☐ 120 Travis Fryman	.25	.11	.03
☐ 121 Jimmy Key	.10	.05	.01
☐ 122 Tom Goodwin	.10	.05	.01
☐ 123 Mike Greenwell	.10	.05	.01
☐ 124 Juan Gonzalez	1.50	.70	.19
☐ 125 Pete Harnisch	.10	.05	.01
☐ 126 Roger Cedeno	.10	.05	.01
☐ 127 Ron Gant	.25	.11	.03
☐ 128 Mark Langston	.10	.05	.01
☐ 129 Tim Crabtree	.10	.05	.01
☐ 130 Greg Maddux	2.00	.90	.25
☐ 131 William VanLandingham	.10	.05	.01
☐ 132 Wally Joyner	.10	.05	.01
☐ 133 Randy Myers	.10	.05	.01
☐ 134 John Valentin	.10	.05	.01
☐ 135 Bret Boone	.10	.05	.01
☐ 136 Bruce Ruffin	.10	.05	.01
☐ 137 Chris Snopek	.10	.05	.01
☐ 138 Paul Molitor	.60	.25	.07
☐ 139 Mark McLemore	.10	.05	.01
☐ 140 Rafael Palmeiro	.40	.18	.05
☐ 141 Herb Perry	.10	.05	.01
☐ 142 Luis Gonzalez	.10	.05	.01
☐ 143 Doug Drabek	.10	.05	.01
☐ 144 Ken Ryan	.10	.05	.01
☐ 145 Todd Hundley	.25	.11	.03
☐ 146 Ellis Burks	.25	.11	.03
☐ 147 Ozzie Guillen	.10	.05	.01
☐ 148 Rich Becker	.10	.05	.01
☐ 149 Sterling Hitchcock	.10	.05	.01
☐ 150 Bernie Williams	.60	.25	.07
☐ 151 Mike Stanley	.10	.05	.01
☐ 152 Roberto Alomar	.60	.25	.07
☐ 153 Jose Mesa	.10	.05	.01
☐ 154 Steve Trachsel	.10	.05	.01
☐ 155 Alex Gonzalez	.10	.05	.01
☐ 156 Troy Percival	.10	.05	.01
☐ 157 John Smoltz	.50	.23	.06
☐ 158 Pedro Martinez	.25	.11	.03
☐ 159 Jeff Conine	.25	.11	.03
☐ 160 Bernard Gilkey	.10	.05	.01
☐ 161 Jim Eisenreich	.10	.05	.01
☐ 162 Mickey Tettleton	.10	.05	.01
☐ 163 Justin Thompson	.25	.11	.03
☐ 164 Jose Offerman	.10	.05	.01
☐ 165 Tony Phillips	.10	.05	.01
☐ 166 Ismael Valdes	.25	.11	.03
☐ 167 Ryne Sandberg	.75	.35	.09
☐ 168 Matt Mieske	.10	.05	.01
☐ 169 Geronimo Berroa	.10	.05	.01
☐ 170 Otis Nixon	.10	.05	.01
☐ 171 John Mabry	.10	.05	.01
☐ 172 Shawon Dunston	.10	.05	.01
☐ 173 Omar Vizquel	.25	.11	.03
☐ 174 Chris Hoiles	.10	.05	.01
☐ 175 Dwight Gooden	.25	.11	.03
☐ 176 Wilson Alvarez	.10	.05	.01
☐ 177 Todd Hollandsworth	.25	.11	.03
☐ 178 Roger Salkeld	.10	.05	.01
☐ 179 Rey Sanchez	.10	.05	.01
☐ 180 Rey Ordonez	.40	.18	.05
☐ 181 Denny Martinez	.10	.05	.01
☐ 182 Ramon Martinez	.25	.11	.03
☐ 183 Dave Nilsson	.10	.05	.01
☐ 184 Marquis Grissom	.25	.11	.03
☐ 185 Randy Velarde	.10	.05	.01
☐ 186 Ron Coomer	.10	.05	.01
☐ 187 Tino Martinez	.25	.11	.03
☐ 188 Jeff Brantley	.10	.05	.01
☐ 189 Steve Finley	.10	.05	.01
☐ 190 Andy Benes	.10	.05	.01
☐ 191 Terry Adams	.10	.05	.01
☐ 192 Mike Blowers	.10	.05	.01
☐ 193 Russ Davis	.10	.05	.01
☐ 194 Darryl Hamilton	.10	.05	.01
☐ 195 Jason Kendall	.25	.11	.03
☐ 196 Johnny Damon	.10	.05	.01
☐ 197 Dave Martinez	.10	.05	.01
☐ 198 Mike Macfarlane	.10	.05	.01
☐ 199 Norm Charlton	.10	.05	.01
☐ 200 Doug Million Damian Moss Bobby Rodgers	.25	.11	.03
☐ 201 Geoff Jenkins Raul Ibanez Mike Cameron	.25	.11	.03
☐ 202 Sean Casey Jim Bonnici Dmitri Young	.25	.11	.03
☐ 203 Jed Hansen Homer Bush Feilipe Crespo	.25	.11	.03
☐ 204 Kevin Orie Gabe Alvarez Aaron Boone	.25	.11	.03
☐ 205 Ben Davis Kevin Brown Bobby Estalella	.25	.11	.03
☐ 206 Billy McMillon Bubba Trammell Dante Powell	.75	.35	.09
☐ 207 Jarrod Washburn Marc Wilkins Glendon Rusch	.25	.11	.03
☐ 208 Brian Hunter	.10	.05	.01
☐ 209 Jason Giambi	.25	.11	.03
☐ 210 Henry Rodriguez	.25	.11	.03
☐ 211 Edgar Renteria	.40	.18	.05
☐ 212 Edgardo Alfonzo	.10	.05	.01
☐ 213 Fernando Vina	.10	.05	.01
☐ 214 Shawn Green	.10	.05	.01
☐ 215 Ray Durham	.10	.05	.01
☐ 216 Joe Randa	.10	.05	.01
☐ 217 Armando Reynoso	.10	.05	.01
☐ 218 Eric Davis	.10	.05	.01
☐ 219 Bob Tewksbury	.10	.05	.01
☐ 220 Jacob Cruz	.10	.05	.01
☐ 221 Glenallen Hill	.10	.05	.01
☐ 222 Gary Gaetti	.10	.05	.01
☐ 223 Donne Wall	.10	.05	.01
☐ 224 Brad Clontz	.10	.05	.01
☐ 225 Marty Janzen	.10	.05	.01
☐ 226 Todd Worrell	.10	.05	.01
☐ 227 John Franco	.10	.05	.01
☐ 228 David Wells	.10	.05	.01
☐ 229 Gregg Jefferies	.10	.05	.01
☐ 230 Tim Naehring	.10	.05	.01
☐ 231 Thomas Howard	.10	.05	.01
☐ 232 Roberto Hernandez	.10	.05	.01
☐ 233 Kevin Ritz	.10	.05	.01
☐ 234 Julian Tavarez	.10	.05	.01
☐ 235 Ken Hill	.10	.05	.01
☐ 236 Greg Gagne	.10	.05	.01
☐ 237 Bobby Chouinard	.10	.05	.01
☐ 238 Joe Carter	.25	.11	.03
☐ 239 Jermaine Dye	.50	.23	.06
☐ 240 Antonio Osuna	.10	.05	.01
☐ 241 Julio Franco	.10	.05	.01
☐ 242 Mike Grace	.10	.05	.01
☐ 243 Aaron Sele	.10	.05	.01
☐ 244 David Justice	.25	.11	.03
☐ 245 Sandy Alomar Jr.	.10	.05	.01
☐ 246 Jose Canseco	.40	.18	.05
☐ 247 Paul O'Neill	.10	.05	.01
☐ 248 Sean Berry	.10	.05	.01
☐ 249 Nick Bierbrodt Kevin Sweeney	.75	.35	.09
☐ 250 Larry Rodriguez Vladimir Nunez	.50	.23	.06
☐ 251 Ron Hartman David Hayman	.75	.35	.09
☐ 252 Alex Sanchez Matthew Quatraro	.50	.23	.06
☐ 253 Ronni Seberino Pablo Ortego	.50	.23	.06
☐ 254 Rex Hudler	.10	.05	.01
☐ 255 Orlando Miller	.10	.05	.01
☐ 256 Mariano Rivera	.25	.11	.03
☐ 257 Brad Radke	.10	.05	.01
☐ 258 Bobby Higginson	.25	.11	.03
☐ 259 Jay Bell	.10	.05	.01
☐ 260 Mark Grudzielanek	.10	.05	.01
☐ 261 Lance Johnson	.10	.05	.01
☐ 262 Ken Caminiti	.50	.23	.06
☐ 263 J.T. Snow	.10	.05	.01
☐ 264 Gary Sheffield	.50	.23	.06
☐ 265 Darrin Fletcher	.10	.05	.01
☐ 266 Eric Owens	.10	.05	.01
☐ 267 Luis Castillo	.40	.18	.05
☐ 268 Scott Rolen	1.25	.55	.16
☐ 269 Todd Noel John Oliver	.25	.11	.03
☐ 270 Robert Stratton Corey Lee	.25	.11	.03
☐ 271 Gil Meche Matt Halloran	.40	.18	.05
☐ 272 Eric Milton Dermal Brown	.40	.18	.05
☐ 273 Josh Garrett Chris Reitsma	.75	.35	.09
☐ 274 A.J.Zapp Jason Marquis	.50	.23	.06
☐ 275 Checklist	.10	.05	.01
☐ 276 Checklist	.10	.05	.01
☐ 277 Chipper Jones UER incorrectly numbered 276	2.00	.90	.25
☐ 278 Orlando Merced	.10	.05	.01
☐ 279 Ariel Prieto	.10	.05	.01
☐ 280 Al Leiter	.10	.05	.01
☐ 281 Pat Meares	.10	.05	.01
☐ 282 Darryl Strawberry	.25	.11	.03
☐ 283 Jamie Moyer	.10	.05	.01
☐ 284 Scott Servais	.10	.05	.01
☐ 285 Delino DeShields	.10	.05	.01
☐ 286 Danny Graves	.10	.05	.01
☐ 287 Gerald Williams	.10	.05	.01
☐ 288 Todd Greene	.10	.05	.01
☐ 289 Rico Brogna	.10	.05	.01
☐ 290 Derrick Gibson	.50	.23	.06
☐ 291 Joe Girardi	.10	.05	.01
☐ 292 Darren Lewis	.10	.05	.01
☐ 293 Nomar Garciaparra	1.25	.55	.16
☐ 294 Greg Colbrunn	.10	.05	.01
☐ 295 Jeff Bagwell	1.25	.55	.16
☐ 296 Brent Gates	.10	.05	.01
☐ 297 Jose Vizcaino	.10	.05	.01
☐ 298 Alex Ochoa	.10	.05	.01
☐ 299 Sid Fernandez	.10	.05	.01
☐ 300 Ken Griffey Jr.	3.00	1.35	.35
☐ 301 Chris Gomez	.10	.05	.01
☐ 302 Wendell Magee	.25	.11	.03
☐ 303 Darren Oliver	.10	.05	.01
☐ 304 Mel Nieves	.10	.05	.01
☐ 305 Sammy Sosa	.50	.23	.06
☐ 306 George Arias	.10	.05	.01
☐ 307 Jack McDowell	.10	.05	.01
☐ 308 Stan Javier	.10	.05	.01
☐ 309 Kimera Bartee	.10	.05	.01
☐ 310 James Baldwin	.10	.05	.01
☐ 311 Rocky Coppinger	.25	.11	.03
☐ 312 Keith Lockhart	.10	.05	.01
☐ 313 C.J. Nitkowski	.10	.05	.01
☐ 314 Allen Watson	.10	.05	.01
☐ 315 Darryl Kile	.10	.05	.01
☐ 316 Amaury Telemaco	.10	.05	.01
☐ 317 Jason Isringhausen	.25	.11	.03
☐ 318 Manny Ramirez	.75	.35	.09
☐ 319 Terry Pendleton	.10	.05	.01
☐ 320 Tim Salmon	.40	.18	.05
☐ 321 Eric Karros	.25	.11	.03
☐ 322 Mark Whiten	.10	.05	.01
☐ 323 Rick Krivda	.10	.05	.01
☐ 324 Brett Butler	.10	.05	.01
☐ 325 Randy Johnson	.50	.23	.06
☐ 326 Eddie Taubensee	.10	.05	.01
☐ 327 Mark Leiter	.10	.05	.01

☐ 328 Kevin Gross	.10	.05	.01
☐ 329 Ernie Young	.10	.05	.01
☐ 330 Pat Hentgen	.25	.11	.03
☐ 331 Rondell White	.10	.05	.01
☐ 332 Bobby Witt	.10	.05	.01
☐ 333 Eddie Murray	.50	.23	.06
☐ 334 Tim Raines	.10	.05	.01
☐ 335 Jeff Fassero	.10	.05	.01
☐ 336 Chuck Finley	.10	.05	.01
☐ 337 Willie Adams	.10	.05	.01
☐ 338 Chan Ho Park	.40	.18	.05
☐ 339 Jay Powell	.10	.05	.01
☐ 340 Ivan Rodriguez	.75	.35	.09
☐ 341 Jermaine Allensworth	.25	.11	.03
☐ 342 Jay Payton	.40	.18	.05
☐ 343 T.J. Mathews	.10	.05	.01
☐ 344 Tony Batista	.40	.18	.05
☐ 345 Ed Sprague	.10	.05	.01
☐ 346 Jeff Kent	.10	.05	.01
☐ 347 Scott Erickson	.10	.05	.01
☐ 348 Jeff Suppan	.25	.11	.03
☐ 349 Pete Schourek	.10	.05	.01
☐ 350 Kenny Lofton	.75	.35	.09
☐ 351 Alan Benes	.25	.11	.03
☐ 352 Fred McGriff	.40	.18	.05
☐ 353 Charlie O'Brien	.10	.05	.01
☐ 354 Darren Bragg	.10	.05	.01
☐ 355 Alex Fernandez	.25	.11	.03
☐ 356 Al Martin	.10	.05	.01
☐ 357 Bob Wells	.10	.05	.01
☐ 358 Chad Mottola	.10	.05	.01
☐ 359 Devon White	.10	.05	.01
☐ 360 David Cone	.25	.11	.03
☐ 361 Bobby Jones	.10	.05	.01
☐ 362 Scott Sanders	.10	.05	.01
☐ 363 Karim Garcia	.50	.23	.06
☐ 364 Kirt Manwaring	.10	.05	.01
☐ 365 Chili Davis	.10	.05	.01
☐ 366 Mike Hampton	.10	.05	.01
☐ 367 Chad Ogea	.10	.05	.01
☐ 368 Curt Schilling	.10	.05	.01
☐ 369 Phil Nevin	.10	.05	.01
☐ 370 Roger Clemens	.60	.25	.07
☐ 371 Willie Greene	.10	.05	.01
☐ 372 Kenny Rogers	.10	.05	.01
☐ 373 Jose Rijo	.10	.05	.01
☐ 374 Bobby Bonilla	.25	.11	.03
☐ 375 Mike Mussina	.60	.25	.07
☐ 376 Curtis Pride	.10	.05	.01
☐ 377 Todd Walker	1.25	.55	.16
☐ 378 Jason Bere	.10	.05	.01
☐ 379 Heathcliff Slocumb	.10	.05	.01
☐ 380 Dante Bichette	.40	.18	.05
☐ 381 Carlos Baerga	.25	.11	.03
☐ 382 Livan Hernandez	.10	.05	.01
☐ 383 Jason Schmidt	.25	.11	.03
☐ 384 Kevin Stocker	.10	.05	.01
☐ 385 Matt Williams	.40	.18	.05
☐ 386 Bartolo Colon	.40	.18	.05
☐ 387 Will Clark	.40	.18	.05
☐ 388 Dennis Eckersley	.25	.11	.03
☐ 389 Brooks Kieschnick	.25	.11	.03
☐ 390 Ryan Klesko	.50	.23	.06
☐ 391 Mark Carreon	.10	.05	.01
☐ 392 Tim Worrell	.10	.05	.01
☐ 393 Dean Palmer	.10	.05	.01
☐ 394 Wil Cordero	.10	.05	.01
☐ 395 Javy Lopez	.25	.11	.03
☐ 396 Rich Aurilia	.10	.05	.01
☐ 397 Greg Vaughn	.10	.05	.01
☐ 398 Vinny Castilla	.25	.11	.03
☐ 399 Jeff Montgomery	.10	.05	.01
☐ 400 Cal Ripken	2.50	1.10	.30
☐ 401 Walt Weiss	.10	.05	.01
☐ 402 Brad Ausmus	.10	.05	.01
☐ 403 Ruben Rivera	.40	.18	.05
☐ 404 Mark Wohlers	.10	.05	.01
☐ 405 Rick Aguilera	.10	.05	.01
☐ 406 Tony Clark	.50	.23	.06
☐ 407 Lyle Mouton	.10	.05	.01
☐ 408 Bill Pulsipher	.10	.05	.01
☐ 409 Jose Rosado	.40	.18	.05
☐ 410 Tony Gwynn	1.25	.55	.16
☐ 411 Cecil Fielder	.25	.11	.03
☐ 412 John Flaherty	.10	.05	.01
☐ 413 Lenny Dykstra	.25	.11	.03
☐ 414 Ugueth Urbina	.10	.05	.01
☐ 415 Brian Jordan	.25	.11	.03
☐ 416 Bob Abreu	.40	.18	.05
☐ 417 Craig Paquette	.10	.05	.01
☐ 418 Sandy Martinez	.10	.05	.01
☐ 419 Jeff Blauser	.10	.05	.01
☐ 420 Barry Larkin	.40	.18	.05
☐ 421 Kevin Seitzer	.10	.05	.01
☐ 422 Tim Belcher	.10	.05	.01
☐ 423 Paul Sorrento	.10	.05	.01
☐ 424 Cal Eldred	.10	.05	.01
☐ 425 Robin Ventura	.25	.11	.03
☐ 426 John Olerud	.10	.05	.01
☐ 427 Bob Wolcott	.10	.05	.01
☐ 428 Matt Lawton	.10	.05	.01
☐ 429 Rod Beck	.10	.05	.01
☐ 430 Shane Reynolds	.10	.05	.01
☐ 431 Mike James	.10	.05	.01
☐ 432 Steve Wojciechowski	.10	.05	.01
☐ 433 Vladimir Guerrero	2.00	.90	.25
☐ 434 Dustin Hermanson	.10	.05	.01
☐ 435 Marty Cordova	.25	.11	.03
☐ 436 Marc Newfield	.10	.05	.01
☐ 437 Todd Stottlemyre	.10	.05	.01
☐ 438 Jeffrey Hammonds	.10	.05	.01
☐ 439 Dave Stevens	.10	.05	.01
☐ 440 Hideo Nomo	.75	.35	.09
☐ 441 Mark Thompson	.10	.05	.01
☐ 442 Mark Lewis	.10	.05	.01
☐ 443 Quinton McCracken	.10	.05	.01
☐ 444 Cliff Floyd	.10	.05	.01
☐ 445 Denny Neagle	.10	.05	.01
☐ 446 John Jaha	.25	.11	.03
☐ 447 Mike Sweeney	.25	.11	.03
☐ 448 John Wasdin	.10	.05	.01
☐ 449 Chad Curtis	.10	.05	.01
☐ 450 Mo Vaughn	.75	.35	.09
☐ 451 Donovan Osborne	.10	.05	.01
☐ 452 Ruben Sierra	.10	.05	.01
☐ 453 Michael Tucker	.10	.05	.01
☐ 454 Kurt Abbott	.10	.05	.01
☐ 455 Andruw Jones UER	3.00	1.35	.35
Birthdate is incorrectly listed as 1-22-67, should be 1-22-77			
☐ 456 Shannon Stewart	.10	.05	.01
☐ 457 Scott Brosius	.10	.05	.01
☐ 458 Juan Guzman	.10	.05	.01
☐ 459 Ron Villone	.10	.05	.01
☐ 460 Moises Alou	.25	.11	.03
☐ 461 Larry Walker	.25	.11	.03
☐ 462 Eddie Murray SH	.40	.18	.05
☐ 463 Paul Molitor SH	.40	.18	.05
☐ 464 Hideo Nomo SH	.40	.18	.05
☐ 465 Barry Bonds SH	.40	.18	.05
☐ 466 Todd Hundley SH	.25	.11	.03
☐ 467 Rheal Cormier	.10	.05	.01
☐ 468 Jason Conti	.50	.23	.06
Jhensy Sandoval			
☐ 469 Rod Barajas	.50	.23	.06
Jackie Rexrode			
☐ 470 Cedric Bowers	.25	.11	.03
Jared Sandberg			
☐ 471 Chei Gunner	.50	.23	.06
Paul Wilder			
☐ 472 Mike Decelle	.25	.11	.03
Marcus McCain			
☐ 473 Todd Zeile	.10	.05	.01
☐ 474 Neifi Perez	.25	.11	.03
☐ 475 Jeromy Burnitz	.10	.05	.01
☐ 476 Trey Beamon	.10	.05	.01
☐ 477 Braden Looper	.30	.14	.04
John Patterson			
☐ 478 Danny Peoples	.30	.14	.04
Jake Westbrook			
☐ 479 Eric Chavez	.40	.18	.05
Adam Eaton			
☐ 480 Joe Lawrence	.30	.14	.04
Pete Tucci			
☐ 481 Kris Benson	1.50	.70	.19
Billy Koch			
☐ 482 John Nicholson	.25	.11	.03
Andy Prater			
☐ 483 Mark Johnson	1.00	.45	.12
Mark Kotsay			
☐ 484 Armando Benitez	.10	.05	.01
☐ 485 Mike Matheny	.10	.05	.01
☐ 486 Jeff Reed	.10	.05	.01
☐ 487 Mark Bellhorn	.25	.11	.03
Russ Johnson			
Enrique Wilson			
☐ 488 Ben Grieve	.40	.18	.05
Richard Hidalgo			
Scott Morgan			
☐ 489 Paul Konerko	1.00	.45	.12
Derrek Lee UER			
spelled Derek on back			
Ron Wright			
☐ 490 Wes Helms	.75	.35	.09
Bill Mueller			
Brad Seitzer			
☐ 491 Jeff Abbott	.25	.11	.03
Shane Monahan			
Edgard Velazquez			
☐ 492 Jimmy Anderson	.30	.14	.04
Ron Blazier			
Gerald Witasick			
☐ 493 Darin Blood	.40	.18	.05
Heath Murray			
Carl Pavano			
☐ 494 Nelson Figueroa	.25	.11	.03
Mark Redman			
Mike Villano			
☐ 495 Checklist (277-400)	.10	.05	.01
☐ 496 Checklist (401-496)	.10	.05	.01
☐ NNO Derek Jeter AU	125.00	55.00	15.50

1997 Topps All-Stars

Randomly inserted in Series 1 packs at a rate of one in 18, this 22-card set printed on rainbow foilboard features the top 11 players from each league and from each position as voted by the Topps Sports Department. The fronts carry a photo of a "first team" all-star player while the backs carry a different photo of that player alongside the "second team" and "third team" selections. Only the "first team" players are checklisted listed below.

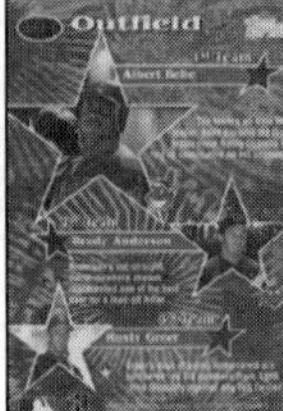

	MINT	NRMT	EXC
COMPLETE SET (22)	60.00	27.00	7.50
COMMON CARD (AS1-AS22)	1.50	.70	.19
☐ AS1 Ivan Rodriguez	4.00	1.80	.50
☐ AS2 Todd Hundley	1.50	.70	.19
☐ AS3 Frank Thomas	15.00	6.75	1.85
☐ AS4 Andres Galarraga	2.00	.90	.25
☐ AS5 Chuck Knoblauch	2.50	1.10	.30
☐ AS6 Eric Young	1.50	.70	.19
☐ AS7 Jim Thome	3.00	1.35	.35
☐ AS8 Chipper Jones	10.00	4.50	1.25
☐ AS9 Cal Ripken	12.00	5.50	1.50
☐ AS10 Barry Larkin	2.00	.90	.25
☐ AS11 Albert Belle	6.00	2.70	.75
☐ AS12 Barry Bonds	4.00	1.80	.50
☐ AS13 Ken Griffey Jr.	15.00	6.75	1.85
☐ AS14 Ellis Burks	1.50	.70	.19
☐ AS15 Juan Gonzalez	8.00	3.60	1.00
☐ AS16 Gary Sheffield	2.50	1.10	.30
☐ AS17 Andy Pettitte	4.00	1.80	.50
☐ AS18 Tom Glavine	2.00	.90	.25
☐ AS19 Pat Hentgen	1.50	.70	.19
☐ AS20 John Smoltz	2.50	1.10	.30
☐ AS21 Roberto Hernandez	1.50	.70	.19
☐ AS22 Mark Wohlers	1.50	.70	.19

1997 Topps Awesome Impact

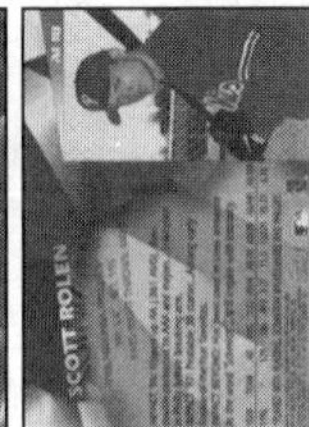

Randomly inserted in second series 11-card retail packs at a rate of 1:18, cards from this 20-card set feature a selection of top young stars and prospects. Each card front features a color player action shot cut out against a silver prismatic background.

	MINT	NRMT	EXC
COMPLETE SET (20)	100.00	45.00	12.50
COMMON CARD (AI1-AI20)	1.50	.70	.19
☐ AI1 Jaime Bluma	1.50	.70	.19
☐ AI2 Tony Clark	4.00	1.80	.50
☐ AI3 Jermaine Dye	4.00	1.80	.50
☐ AI4 Nomar Garciaparra	10.00	4.50	1.25
☐ AI5 Vladimir Guerrero	15.00	6.75	1.85
☐ AI6 Todd Hollandsworth	2.50	1.10	.30
☐ AI7 Derek Jeter	15.00	6.75	1.85
☐ AI8 Andruw Jones	25.00	11.00	3.10
☐ AI9 Chipper Jones	15.00	6.75	1.85
☐ AI10 Jason Kendall	2.50	1.10	.30
☐ AI11 Brooks Kieschnick	2.50	1.10	.30
☐ AI12 Alex Ochoa	1.50	.70	.19
☐ AI13 Rey Ordonez	3.00	1.35	.35
☐ AI14 Neifi Perez	2.50	1.10	.30
☐ AI15 Edgar Renteria	3.00	1.35	.35
☐ AI16 Mariano Rivera	2.50	1.10	.30
☐ AI17 Ruben Rivera	3.00	1.35	.35
☐ AI18 Scott Rolen	10.00	4.50	1.25
☐ AI19 Billy Wagner	2.50	1.10	.30
☐ AI20 Todd Walker	10.00	4.50	1.25

1997 Topps Hobby Masters

Randomly inserted in first and second series hobby packs at a rate of one in 36, cards from this 10-card set honor twenty players picked by hobby dealers from across the country as their all-time favorites. Cards 1-10 were issued in first series packs and 11-20 in second series. Printed on 28-point diffraction foilboard, one card replaces two regular cards when inserted in packs. The fronts feature borderless color player photos on a background of the player's profile. The backs carry player information.

	MINT	NRMT	EXC
COMPLETE SET (20)	110.00	50.00	14.00
COMPLETE SERIES 1 (10)	60.00	27.00	7.50
COMPLETE SERIES 2 (10)	50.00	22.00	6.25
COMMON CARD (HM1-HM20)	2.00	.90	.25
☐ HM1 Ken Griffey Jr.	15.00	6.75	1.85
☐ HM2 Cal Ripken	12.00	5.50	1.50
☐ HM3 Greg Maddux	10.00	4.50	1.25
☐ HM4 Albert Belle	6.00	2.70	.75
☐ HM5 Tony Gwynn	6.00	2.70	.75
☐ HM6 Jeff Bagwell	6.00	2.70	.75
☐ HM7 Randy Johnson	2.50	1.10	.30
☐ HM8 Raul Mondesi	2.00	.90	.25
☐ HM9 Juan Gonzalez	8.00	3.60	1.00
☐ HM10 Kenny Lofton	4.00	1.80	.50
☐ HM11 Frank Thomas	15.00	6.75	1.85
☐ HM12 Mike Piazza	10.00	4.50	1.25
☐ HM13 Chipper Jones	10.00	4.50	1.25
☐ HM14 Brady Anderson	2.00	.90	.25
☐ HM15 Ken Caminiti	2.50	1.10	.30
☐ HM16 Barry Bonds	4.00	1.80	.50
☐ HM17 Mo Vaughn	4.00	1.80	.50
☐ HM18 Derek Jeter	10.00	4.50	1.25
☐ HM19 Sammy Sosa	2.50	1.10	.30
☐ HM20 Andres Galarraga	2.00	.90	.25

1997 Topps Inter-League Finest

Randomly inserted in Series 1 packs at a rate of one in 36, this 14-card set features top individual match-ups from inter-league rivalries. One player from each major league team is represented on each side of this double-sided set with a color photo and is covered with the patented Finest clear protector.

	MINT	NRMT	EXC
COMPLETE SET (14)	60.00	27.00	7.50
COMMON CARD (ILM1-ILM14)	3.00	1.35	.35
☐ ILM1 Mark McGwire	6.00	2.70	.75
Barry Bonds			
☐ ILM2 Tim Salmon	10.00	4.50	1.25
Mike Piazza			
☐ ILM3 Ken Griffey Jr.	15.00	6.75	1.85
Dante Bichette			
☐ ILM4 Juan Gonzalez	10.00	4.50	1.25
Tony Gwynn			
☐ ILM5 Frank Thomas	15.00	6.75	1.85
Sammy Sosa			
☐ ILM6 Albert Belle	6.00	2.70	.75
Barry Larkin			
☐ ILM7 Johnny Damon	3.00	1.35	.35
Brian Jordan			
☐ ILM8 Paul Molitor	4.00	1.80	.50
Jeff King			
☐ ILM9 John Jaha	5.00	2.20	.60
Jeff Bagwell			
☐ ILM10 Bernie Williams	4.00	1.80	.50
Todd Hundley			
☐ ILM11 Joe Carter	3.00	1.35	.35
Henry Rodriguez			
☐ ILM12 Cal Ripken	10.00	4.50	1.25
Gregg Jefferies			
☐ ILM13 Mo Vaughn	10.00	4.50	1.25
Chipper Jones			
☐ ILM14 Travis Fryman	4.00	1.80	.50
Gary Sheffield			

1997 Topps Inter-League Finest Refractors

Randomly inserted into first series packs of 1997 Topps at the rate of one every 216 packs, this 14-card set is distinguished from the more common base Inter-League Finest set by the refractive quality of the cards.

	MINT	NRMT	EXC
COMPLETE SET (14)	300.00	135.00	38.00
COMMON CARD (ILM1-ILM14)	15.00	6.75	1.85

*REFRACTORS: 3X to 6X BASIC INT.LG. FINEST

1997 Topps Mantle

Randomly inserted at the rate of one in 12 Series 1 packs, this 16-card set features authentic reprints of Topps Mickey Mantle cards that were not reprinted last year. Each card is stamped with the commemorative gold foil logo.

	MINT	NRMT	EXC
COMPLETE SET (16)	125.00	55.00	15.50
COMMON MANTLE (21-36)	8.00	3.60	1.00
☐ 21 Mickey Mantle	8.00	3.60	1.00
Hank Bauer			
Yogi Berra			
1953 Bowman			
☐ 22 Mickey Mantle	8.00	3.60	1.00
1953 Bowman			
☐ 23 Mickey Mantle	8.00	3.60	1.00
Yogi Berra			
1957 Topps			
☐ 24 Mickey Mantle	8.00	3.60	1.00
Hank Aaron			
1958 Topps			
☐ 25 Mickey Mantle	8.00	3.60	1.00
1958 Topps AS			
☐ 26 Mickey Mantle	8.00	3.60	1.00
1959 Topps HL			
☐ 27 Mickey Mantle	8.00	3.60	1.00
1959 Topps AS			
☐ 28 Mickey Mantle	8.00	3.60	1.00
Ken Boyer			
1960 Topps			
☐ 29 Mickey Mantle	8.00	3.60	1.00
1960 Topps AS			
☐ 30 Mickey Mantle	8.00	3.60	1.00
1961 Topps HL			
☐ 31 Mickey Mantle	8.00	3.60	1.00
1961 Topps MVP			
☐ 32 Mickey Mantle	8.00	3.60	1.00
1961 Topps AS			
☐ 33 Mickey Mantle	8.00	3.60	1.00
Willie Mays			
1962 Topps			
Hank Aaron and Ernie Banks in background			
☐ 34 Mickey Mantle	8.00	3.60	1.00
1962 Topps IA			
☐ 35 Mickey Mantle	8.00	3.60	1.00
1962 AS			
☐ 36 Mickey Mantle	8.00	3.60	1.00
Roger Maris			
Al Kaline			
Norm Cash			
1964 Topps			

1997 Topps Mantle Finest

Parallel to the first series Mantle inserts, these sixteen Finest style cards were inserted into all second series packs.

	MINT	NRMT	EXC
COMPLETE SET (16)	125.00	55.00	15.50
COMMON CARD (21-36)	8.00	3.60	1.00

1997 Topps Mantle Finest Refractors

Parallel to the first series Mantle inserts and second series Mantle Finest inserts, these sixteen scarce Finest Refractor inserts are randomly seeded into all second series packs. Their refractive sheen differentiates them from the more common Mantle Finest cards.

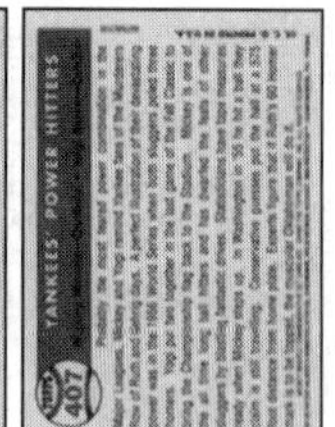

	MINT	NRMT	EXC
COMPLETE SET (16)	600.00	275.00	75.00
COMMON CARD (21-36)	40.00	18.00	5.00

1997 Topps Mays

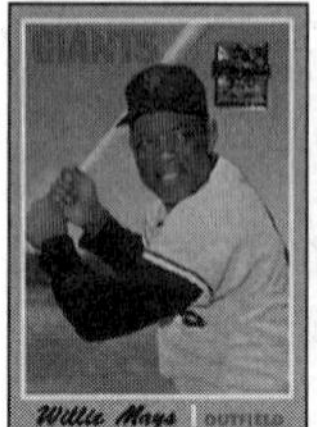

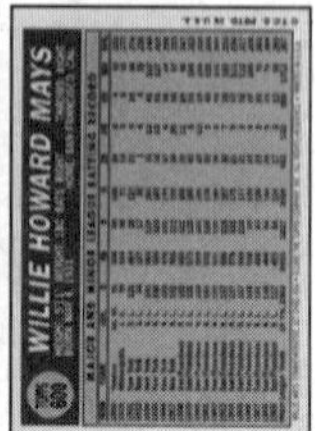

Randomly inserted at the rate of one in eight first series packs, cards from this 27-card set feature reprints of both the Topps and Bowman vintage Mays cards . Each card front is highlighted by a special commemorative gold foil stamp. Randomly inserted in first series hobby packs only (at the rate of one in 2,400) are personally signed cards. According to Topps, Mays signed about 65 each of the following cards: 51B, 52T, 53T, 55T, 57T, 58T, 60T, 60T AS, 61T, 61T AS, 63T, 64T, 65T, 66T, 69T, 70T, 72T, 73T. A special 4 1/4" by 5 3/4" jumbo reprint of the 1952 Topps Willie Mays card was made available exclusively in special series 1 Wal-Mart boxes. Each box (shaped much like a cereal box) contained ten 8-card retail packs and the aforementioned jumbo card and retailed for $10.

	MINT	NRMT	EXC
COMPLETE SET (27)	100.00	45.00	12.50
COMMON MAYS (1-27)	4.00	1.80	.50
☐ 1 Willie Mays	8.00	3.60	1.00
1951 Bowman			
☐ 2 Willie Mays	6.00	2.70	.75
1952 Topps			
☐ 3 Willie Mays	4.00	1.80	.50
1953 Topps			
☐ 4 Willie Mays	4.00	1.80	.50
1954 Bowman			
☐ 5 Willie Mays	4.00	1.80	.50
1954 Topps			
☐ 6 Willie Mays	4.00	1.80	.50
1955 Bowman			
☐ 7 Willie Mays	4.00	1.80	.50
1955 Topps			
☐ 8 Willie Mays	4.00	1.80	.50
1956 Topps			
☐ 9 Willie Mays	4.00	1.80	.50
1957 Topps			
☐ 10 Willie Mays	4.00	1.80	.50
1958 Topps			
☐ 11 Willie Mays	4.00	1.80	.50
1959 Topps			
☐ 12 Willie Mays	4.00	1.80	.50
1960 Topps			
☐ 13 Willie Mays	4.00	1.80	.50
1960 Topps AS			
☐ 14 Willie Mays	4.00	1.80	.50
1961 Topps			
☐ 15 Willie Mays	4.00	1.80	.50
1961 Topps AS			
☐ 16 Willie Mays	4.00	1.80	.50
1962 Topps			
☐ 17 Willie Mays	4.00	1.80	.50
1963 Topps			
☐ 18 Willie Mays	4.00	1.80	.50
1964 Topps			
☐ 19 Willie Mays	4.00	1.80	.50
1965 Topps			
☐ 20 Willie Mays	4.00	1.80	.50
1966 Topps			
☐ 21 Willie Mays	4.00	1.80	.50
1967 Topps			
☐ 22 Willie Mays	4.00	1.80	.50
1968 Topps			
☐ 23 Willie Mays	4.00	1.80	.50
1969 Topps			
☐ 24 Willie Mays	4.00	1.80	.50
1970 Topps			
☐ 25 Willie Mays	4.00	1.80	.50
1971 Topps			
☐ 26 Willie Mays	4.00	1.80	.50
1972 Topps			
☐ 27 Willie Mays	4.00	1.80	.50
1973 Topps			
☐ J261 Willie Mays 1952 Jumbo	10.00	4.50	1.25
☐ NNO Willie Mays AU	100.00	45.00	12.50

1997 Topps Mays Finest

Parallel to the first series Mays inserts, these twenty-seven Finest style cards were inserted into all second series packs.

	MINT	NRMT	EXC
COMPLETE SET (27)	100.00	45.00	12.50
COMMON CARD (1-27)	5.00	2.20	.60

1997 Topps Mays Finest Refractors

Parallel to the first series Mays inserts and second series Mays Finest inserts, these twenty-seven scarce Finest Refractor inserts are randomly seeded into all second series packs. Their refractive sheen differentiates them from the more common Mays Finest cards.

	MINT	NRMT	EXC
COMPLETE SET (27)	500.00	220.00	60.00
COMMON CARD (1-27)	25.00	11.00	3.10

1997 Topps Season's Best

This 25-card set was randomly inserted into Topps Series 2 packs and features five top players from each of the following five statistical categories: Leading Looters (top base stealers), Bleacher Reachers (top home run hitters), Hill Toppers (most wins), Number Crunchers (most RBI's), Kings of Swings (top slugging percentages). The fronts display color player photos printed on prismatic illusion foilboard. The backs carry another player photo and statistics.

	MINT	NRMT	EXC
COMPLETE SET (25)	30.00	13.50	3.70
COMMON CARD (1-25)	.50	.23	.06
☐ SB1 Tony Gwynn	3.00	1.35	.35
☐ SB2 Frank Thomas	8.00	3.60	1.00
☐ SB3 Ellis Burks	.75	.35	.09
☐ SB4 Paul Molitor	1.50	.70	.19
☐ SB5 Chuck Knoblauch	1.25	.55	.16
☐ SB6 Mark McGwire	2.50	1.10	.30
☐ SB7 Brady Anderson	.75	.35	.09
☐ SB8 Ken Griffey Jr.	8.00	3.60	1.00
☐ SB9 Albert Belle	3.00	1.35	.35
☐ SB10 Andres Galarraga			
☐ SB11 Andres Galarraga			
☐ SB12 Albert Belle	3.00	1.35	.35
☐ SB13 Juan Gonzalez	4.00	1.80	.50
☐ SB14 Mo Vaughn	2.00	.90	.25
☐ SB15 Rafael Palmeiro			
☐ SB16 John Smoltz	1.25	.55	.16
☐ SB17 Andy Pettitte	2.00	.90	.25
☐ SB18 Pat Hentgen	.75	.35	.09
☐ SB19 Mike Mussina	1.50	.70	.19
☐ SB20 Andy Benes	.50	.23	.06
☐ SB21 Kenny Lofton	2.00	.90	.25
☐ SB22 Tom Goodwin	.50	.23	.06
☐ SB23 Otis Nixon	.50	.23	.06
☐ SB24 Eric Young	.75	.35	.09
☐ SB25 Lance Johnson	.50	.23	.06

1997 Topps Sweet Strokes

This 15-card retail only set was randomly inserted in series one packs at a rate of one in 12. Printed on Rainbow foilboard, the set features color photos of some of Baseball's top hitters.

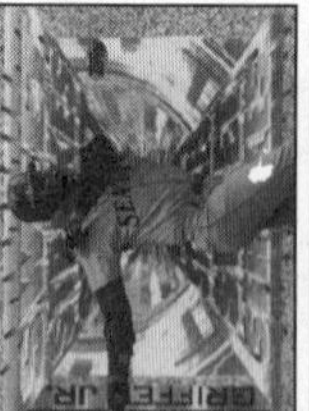

	MINT	NRMT	EXC
COMPLETE SET (15)	40.00	18.00	5.00
COMMON CARD (SS1-SS15)	1.00	.45	.12
☐ SS1 Roberto Alomar	2.00	.90	.25
☐ SS2 Jeff Bagwell	4.00	1.80	.50
☐ SS3 Albert Belle	4.00	1.80	.50
☐ SS4 Barry Bonds	2.50	1.10	.30
☐ SS5 Mark Grace	1.25	.55	.16
☐ SS6 Ken Griffey Jr.	10.00	4.50	1.25
☐ SS7 Tony Gwynn	4.00	1.80	.50
☐ SS8 Chipper Jones	6.00	2.70	.75
☐ SS9 Edgar Martinez	1.00	.45	.12
☐ SS10 Mark McGwire	3.00	1.35	.35
☐ SS11 Rafael Palmeiro	1.25	.55	.16
☐ SS12 Mike Piazza	6.00	2.70	.75
☐ SS13 Gary Sheffield	1.50	.70	.19
☐ SS14 Frank Thomas	10.00	4.50	1.25
☐ SS15 Mo Vaughn	2.50	1.10	.30

1997 Topps Team Timber

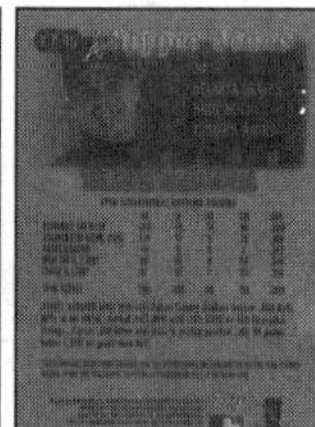

Randomly inserted into all second series packs at a rate of 1:36 and second series Hobby Collector packs at a rate of 1:8, cards from this 16-card set highlight a selection of baseball's top sluggers. Each card features a simulated wood-grain stock, but the fronts are UV-coated, making the cards bow noticeably.

	MINT	NRMT	EXC
COMPLETE SET (16)	80.00	36.00	10.00
COMMON CARD (TT1-TT16)	1.50	.70	.19
☐ TT1 Ken Griffey Jr.	15.00	6.75	1.85
☐ TT2 Ken Caminiti	2.50	1.10	.30
☐ TT3 Bernie Williams	3.00	1.35	.35
☐ TT4 Jeff Bagwell	6.00	2.70	.75
☐ TT5 Frank Thomas	15.00	6.75	1.85
☐ TT6 Andres Galarraga	2.00	.90	.25
☐ TT7 Barry Bonds	4.00	1.80	.50
☐ TT8 Rafael Palmeiro	2.00	.90	.25
☐ TT9 Brady Anderson	1.50	.70	.19
☐ TT10 Juan Gonzalez	8.00	3.60	1.00
☐ TT11 Mo Vaughn	4.00	1.80	.50
☐ TT12 Mark McGwire	5.00	2.20	.60
☐ TT13 Gary Sheffield	2.50	1.10	.30
☐ TT14 Albert Belle	6.00	2.70	.75
☐ TT15 Chipper Jones	10.00	4.50	1.25
☐ TT16 Mike Piazza	10.00	4.50	1.25

1991 Topps Archives 1953

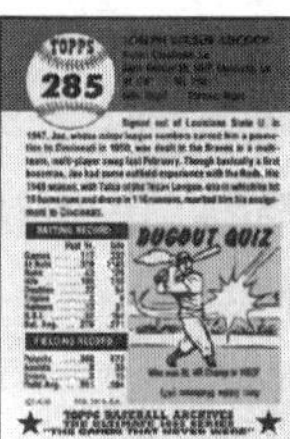

The 1953 Topps Archive set is a reprint of the original 274-card 1953 Topps set. The only card missing from the reprint set is that of Billy Loes (174), who did not give Topps permission to reprint his card. Moreover, the set has been extended by 57 cards, with cards honoring Mrs. Eleanor Engle, Hoyt Wilhelm (who had already been included in the set as card number 151), 1953 HOF inductees Dizzy Dean and Al Simmons, and "prospect" Hank Aaron. Although the original cards measured 2 5/8" by 3 3/4", the reprint cards measure the modern standard size. Production quantities were supposedly limited to not more than 18,000 cases.

	MINT	NRMT	EXC
COMPLETE SET (330)	40.00	18.00	5.00
COMMON CARD (1-220)	.10	.05	.01
COMMON CARD (221-280)	.15	.07	.02
COMMON CARD (281-337)	.20	.09	.03

Card			
☐ 1 Jackie Robinson	6.00	2.70	.75
☐ 2 Luke Easter	.15	.07	.02
☐ 3 George Crowe	.10	.05	.01
☐ 4 Ben Wade	.10	.05	.01
☐ 5 Joe Dobson	.10	.05	.01
☐ 6 Sam Jones	.10	.05	.01
☐ 7 Bob Borkowski	.10	.05	.01
☐ 8 Clem Koshorek	.10	.05	.01
☐ 9 Joe Collins	.15	.07	.02
☐ 10 Smoky Burgess	.15	.07	.02
☐ 11 Sal Yvars	.10	.05	.01
☐ 12 Howie Judson	.10	.05	.01
☐ 13 Conrado Marrero	.10	.05	.01
☐ 14 Clem Labine	.20	.09	.03
☐ 15 Bobo Newsom	.15	.07	.02
☐ 16 Peanuts Lowrey	.10	.05	.01
☐ 17 Billy Hitchcock	.10	.05	.01
☐ 18 Ted Lepcio	.10	.05	.01
☐ 19 Mel Parnell	.10	.05	.01
☐ 20 Hank Thompson	.10	.05	.01
☐ 21 Billy Johnson	.10	.05	.01
☐ 22 Howie Fox	.10	.05	.01
☐ 23 Toby Atwell	.10	.05	.01
☐ 24 Ferris Fain	.10	.05	.01
☐ 25 Ray Boone	.10	.05	.01
☐ 26 Dale Mitchell	.15	.07	.02
☐ 27 Roy Campanella	2.50	1.10	.30
☐ 28 Eddie Pellagrini	.10	.05	.01
☐ 29 Hal Jeffcoat	.10	.05	.01
☐ 30 Willard Nixon	.10	.05	.01
☐ 31 Ewell Blackwell	.15	.07	.02
☐ 32 Clyde Vollmer	.10	.05	.01
☐ 33 Bob Kennedy	.10	.05	.01
☐ 34 George Shuba	.15	.07	.02
☐ 35 Irv Noren	.10	.05	.01
☐ 36 Johnny Groth	.10	.05	.01
☐ 37 Eddie Mathews	1.00	.45	.12
☐ 38 Jim Hearn	.10	.05	.01
☐ 39 Eddie Miksis	.10	.05	.01
☐ 40 John Lipon	.10	.05	.01
☐ 41 Enos Slaughter	.75	.35	.09
☐ 42 Gus Zernial	.15	.07	.02
☐ 43 Gil McDougald	.25	.11	.03
☐ 44 Ellis Kinder	.10	.05	.01
☐ 45 Grady Hatton	.10	.05	.01
☐ 46 Johnny Klippstein	.10	.05	.01
☐ 47 Bubba Church	.10	.05	.01
☐ 48 Bob Del Greco	.10	.05	.01
☐ 49 Faye Throneberry	.10	.05	.01
☐ 50 Chuck Dressen MG	.15	.07	.02
☐ 51 Frank Campos	.10	.05	.01
☐ 52 Ted Gray	.10	.05	.01
☐ 53 Sherm Lollar	.15	.07	.02
☐ 54 Bob Feller	1.50	.70	.19
☐ 55 Maurice McDermott	.10	.05	.01
☐ 56 Gerry Staley	.10	.05	.01
☐ 57 Carl Scheib	.10	.05	.01
☐ 58 George Metkovich	.10	.05	.01
☐ 59 Karl Drews	.10	.05	.01
☐ 60 Cloyd Boyer	.10	.05	.01
☐ 61 Early Wynn	.75	.35	.09
☐ 62 Monte Irvin	.75	.35	.09
☐ 63 Gus Niarhos	.10	.05	.01
☐ 64 Dave Philley	.10	.05	.01
☐ 65 Earl Harrist	.10	.05	.01
☐ 66 Minnie Minoso	.50	.23	.06
☐ 67 Roy Sievers	.15	.07	.02
☐ 68 Del Rice	.10	.05	.01
☐ 69 Dick Brodowski	.10	.05	.01
☐ 70 Ed Yuhas	.10	.05	.01
☐ 71 Tony Bartirome	.10	.05	.01
☐ 72 Fred Hutchinson	.15	.07	.02
☐ 73 Eddie Robinson	.10	.05	.01
☐ 74 Joe Rossi	.10	.05	.01
☐ 75 Mike Garcia	.15	.07	.02
☐ 76 Pee Wee Reese	1.50	.70	.19
☐ 77 Johnny Mize	.75	.35	.09
☐ 78 Red Schoendienst	.75	.35	.09
☐ 79 Johnny Wyrostek	.10	.05	.01
☐ 80 Jim Hegan	.10	.05	.01
☐ 81 Joe Black	.25	.11	.03
☐ 82 Mickey Mantle	20.00	9.00	2.50
☐ 83 Howie Pollet	.10	.05	.01
☐ 84 Bob Hooper	.10	.05	.01
☐ 85 Bobby Morgan	.10	.05	.01
☐ 86 Billy Martin	1.00	.45	.12
☐ 87 Ed Lopat	.25	.11	.03
☐ 88 Willie Jones	.10	.05	.01
☐ 89 Chuck Stobbs	.10	.05	.01
☐ 90 Hank Edwards	.10	.05	.01
☐ 91 Ebba St.Claire	.10	.05	.01
☐ 92 Paul Minner	.10	.05	.01
☐ 93 Hal Rice	.10	.05	.01
☐ 94 Bill Kennedy	.10	.05	.01
☐ 95 Willard Marshall	.10	.05	.01
☐ 96 Virgil Trucks	.10	.05	.01
☐ 97 Don Kolloway	.10	.05	.01
☐ 98 Cal Abrams	.10	.05	.01
☐ 99 Dave Madison	.10	.05	.01
☐ 100 Bill Miller	.10	.05	.01
☐ 101 Ted Wilks	.10	.05	.01
☐ 102 Connie Ryan	.10	.05	.01
☐ 103 Joe Astroth	.10	.05	.01
☐ 104 Yogi Berra	2.50	1.10	.30
☐ 105 Joe Nuxhall	.15	.07	.02
☐ 106 Johnny Antonelli	.15	.07	.02
☐ 107 Danny O'Connell	.10	.05	.01
☐ 108 Bob Porterfield	.10	.05	.01
☐ 109 Alvin Dark	.15	.07	.02
☐ 110 Herman Wehmeier	.10	.05	.01
☐ 111 Hank Sauer	.15	.07	.02
☐ 112 Ned Garver	.10	.05	.01
☐ 113 Jerry Priddy	.10	.05	.01
☐ 114 Phil Rizzuto	1.25	.55	.16
☐ 115 George Spencer	.10	.05	.01
☐ 116 Frank Smith	.10	.05	.01
☐ 117 Sid Gordon	.10	.05	.01
☐ 118 Gus Bell	.15	.07	.02
☐ 119 Johnny Sain	.25	.11	.03
☐ 120 Davey Williams	.10	.05	.01
☐ 121 Walt Dropo	.10	.05	.01
☐ 122 Elmer Valo	.10	.05	.01
☐ 123 Tommy Byrne	.10	.05	.01
☐ 124 Sibby Sisti	.10	.05	.01
☐ 125 Dick Williams	.15	.07	.02
☐ 126 Bill Connelly	.10	.05	.01
☐ 127 Clint Courtney	.10	.05	.01
☐ 128 Wilmer Mizell	.15	.07	.02
☐ 129 Keith Thomas	.10	.05	.01
☐ 130 Turk Lown	.10	.05	.01
☐ 131 Harry Byrd	.10	.05	.01
☐ 132 Tom Morgan	.10	.05	.01
☐ 133 Gil Coan	.10	.05	.01
☐ 134 Rube Walker	.10	.05	.01
☐ 135 Al Rosen	.25	.11	.03
☐ 136 Ken Heintzelman	.10	.05	.01
☐ 137 John Rutherford	.10	.05	.01
☐ 138 George Kell	.75	.35	.09
☐ 139 Sammy White	.10	.05	.01
☐ 140 Tommy Glaviano	.10	.05	.01
☐ 141 Allie Reynolds	.25	.11	.03
☐ 142 Vic Wertz	.15	.07	.02
☐ 143 Billy Pierce	.15	.07	.02
☐ 144 Bob Schultz	.10	.05	.01
☐ 145 Harry Dorish	.10	.05	.01
☐ 146 Granny Hamner	.15	.07	.02
☐ 147 Warren Spahn	1.50	.70	.19
☐ 148 Mickey Grasso	.10	.05	.01
☐ 149 Dom DiMaggio	.50	.23	.06
☐ 150 Harry Simpson	.10	.05	.01
☐ 151 Hoyt Wilhelm	.75	.35	.09
☐ 152 Bob Adams	.10	.05	.01
☐ 153 Andy Seminick	.15	.07	.02
☐ 154 Dick Groat	.25	.11	.03
☐ 155 Dutch Leonard	.10	.05	.01
☐ 156 Jim Rivera	.10	.05	.01
☐ 157 Bob Addis	.10	.05	.01
☐ 158 Johnny Logan	.15	.07	.02
☐ 159 Wayne Terwilliger	.10	.05	.01
☐ 160 Bob Young	.10	.05	.01
☐ 161 Vern Bickford	.10	.05	.01
☐ 162 Ted Kluszewski	.50	.23	.06
☐ 163 Fred Hatfield	.10	.05	.01
☐ 164 Frank Shea	.10	.05	.01
☐ 165 Billy Hoeft	.10	.05	.01
☐ 166 Billy Hunter	.10	.05	.01
☐ 167 Art Schult	.10	.05	.01
☐ 168 Willard Schmidt	.10	.05	.01
☐ 169 Dizzy Trout	.10	.05	.01
☐ 170 Bill Werle	.10	.05	.01
☐ 171 Bill Glynn	.10	.05	.01
☐ 172 Rip Repulski	.10	.05	.01
☐ 173 Preston Ward	.10	.05	.01
☐ 174 Billy Loes (Not printed)			
☐ 175 Ron Kline	.10	.05	.01
☐ 176 Don Hoak	.15	.07	.02
☐ 177 Jim Dyck	.10	.05	.01
☐ 178 Jim Waugh	.10	.05	.01
☐ 179 Gene Hermanski	.10	.05	.01
☐ 180 Virgil Stallcup	.10	.05	.01
☐ 181 Al Zarilla	.10	.05	.01
☐ 182 Bobby Hofman	.10	.05	.01
☐ 183 Stu Miller	.10	.05	.01
☐ 184 Hal Brown	.10	.05	.01
☐ 185 Jim Pendleton	.10	.05	.01
☐ 186 Charlie Bishop	.10	.05	.01
☐ 187 Jim Fridley	.10	.05	.01
☐ 188 Andy Carey	.15	.07	.02
☐ 189 Ray Jablonski	.10	.05	.01
☐ 190 Dixie Walker CO	.15	.07	.02
☐ 191 Ralph Kiner	.75	.35	.09
☐ 192 Wally Westlake	.10	.05	.01
☐ 193 Mike Clark	.10	.05	.01
☐ 194 Eddie Kazak	.10	.05	.01
☐ 195 Ed McGhee	.10	.05	.01
☐ 196 Bob Keegan	.10	.05	.01
☐ 197 Del Crandall	.15	.07	.02
☐ 198 Forrest Main	.10	.05	.01
☐ 199 Marion Fricano	.10	.05	.01
☐ 200 Gordon Goldsberry	.10	.05	.01
☐ 201 Paul LaPalme	.10	.05	.01
☐ 202 Carl Sawatski	.10	.05	.01
☐ 203 Cliff Fannin	.10	.05	.01
☐ 204 Dick Bokelman	.10	.05	.01
☐ 205 Vern Benson	.10	.05	.01
☐ 206 Ed Bailey	.15	.07	.02
☐ 207 Whitey Ford	1.50	.70	.19
☐ 208 Jim Wilson	.10	.05	.01
☐ 209 Jim Greengrass	.10	.05	.01
☐ 210 Bob Cerv	.10	.05	.01
☐ 211 J.W. Porter	.10	.05	.01
☐ 212 Jack Dittmer	.10	.05	.01
☐ 213 Ray Scarborough	.10	.05	.01
☐ 214 Bill Bruton	.10	.05	.01
☐ 215 Gene Conley	.10	.05	.01
☐ 216 Jim Hughes	.10	.05	.01
☐ 217 Murray Wall	.10	.05	.01
☐ 218 Les Fusselman	.10	.05	.01
☐ 219 Pete Runnels UER (Photo actually Don Johnson)	.10	.05	.01
☐ 220 Satchel Paige UER (Misspelled Satchell on card front)	4.00	1.80	.50
☐ 221 Bob Milliken	.15	.07	.02
☐ 222 Vic Janowicz	.20	.09	.03
☐ 223 Johnny O'Brien	.20	.09	.03
☐ 224 Lou Sleater	.15	.07	.02
☐ 225 Bobby Shantz	.20	.09	.03
☐ 226 Ed Erautt	.15	.07	.02
☐ 227 Morrie Martin	.15	.07	.02
☐ 228 Hal Newhouser	1.00	.45	.12
☐ 229 Rocky Krsnich	.15	.07	.02
☐ 230 Johnny Lindell	.15	.07	.02
☐ 231 Solly Hemus	.15	.07	.02
☐ 232 Dick Kokos	.15	.07	.02
☐ 233 Al Aber	.15	.07	.02
☐ 234 Ray Murray	.15	.07	.02
☐ 235 John Hetki	.15	.07	.02
☐ 236 Harry Perkowski	.15	.07	.02
☐ 237 Bud Podbielan	.15	.07	.02
☐ 238 Cal Hogue	.15	.07	.02
☐ 239 Jim Delsing	.15	.07	.02
☐ 240 Fred Marsh	.15	.07	.02
☐ 241 Al Sima	.15	.07	.02
☐ 242 Charlie Silvera	.20	.09	.03
☐ 243 Carlos Bernier	.15	.07	.02
☐ 244 Willie Mays	12.00	5.50	1.50
☐ 245 Bill Norman CO	.15	.07	.02
☐ 246 Roy Face	.30	.14	.04
☐ 247 Mike Sandlock	.15	.07	.02
☐ 248 Gene Stephens	.15	.07	.02
☐ 249 Eddie O'Brien	.20	.09	.03
☐ 250 Bob Wilson	.15	.07	.02
☐ 251 Sid Hudson	.15	.07	.02
☐ 252 Hank Foiles	.15	.07	.02
☐ 253 Does not exist		.07	.02
☐ 254 Preacher Roe	.35	.16	.04
☐ 255 Dixie Howell	.15	.07	.02
☐ 256 Les Peden	.15	.07	.02
☐ 257 Bob Boyd	.15	.07	.02
☐ 258 Jim Gilliam	.50	.23	.06
☐ 259 Roy McMillan	.20	.09	.03
☐ 260 Sam Calderone	.15	.07	.02
☐ 261 Does not exist			
☐ 262 Bob Oldis	.15	.07	.02
☐ 263 Johnny Podres	.35	.16	.04
☐ 264 Gene Woodling	.30	.14	.04
☐ 265 Jackie Jensen	.35	.16	.04
☐ 266 Bob Cain	.15	.07	.02
☐ 267 Does not exist			
☐ 268 Does not exist			
☐ 269 Duane Pillette	.15	.07	.02
☐ 270 Vern Stephens	.20	.09	.03
☐ 271 Does not exist			
☐ 272 Bill Antonello	.15	.07	.02
☐ 273 Harvey Haddix	.20	.09	.03
☐ 274 John Riddle	.15	.07	.02
☐ 275 Does not exist			
☐ 276 Ken Raffensberger	.15	.07	.02
☐ 277 Don Lund	.15	.07	.02
☐ 278 Willie Miranda	.15	.07	.02
☐ 279 Joe Coleman	.15	.07	.02
☐ 280 Milt Bolling	.25	.11	.03
☐ 281 Jimmie Dykes MG	.25	.11	.03
☐ 282 Ralph Houk	.25	.11	.03
☐ 283 Frank Thomas	.25	.11	.03
☐ 284 Bob Lemon	.75	.35	.09
☐ 285 Joe Adcock	.25	.11	.03
☐ 286 Jimmy Piersall	.35	.16	.04
☐ 287 Mickey Vernon	.25	.11	.03
☐ 288 Robin Roberts	1.00	.45	.12
☐ 289 Rogers Hornsby MG	.50	.23	.06
☐ 290 Hank Bauer	.25	.11	.03
☐ 291 Hoot Evers	.20	.09	.03
☐ 292 Whitey Lockman	.25	.11	.03
☐ 293 Ralph Branca	.25	.11	.03
☐ 294 Wally Post	.25	.11	.03
☐ 295 Phil Cavarretta MG	.25	.11	.03
☐ 296 Gil Hodges	1.00	.45	.12
☐ 297 Roy Smalley	.20	.09	.03
☐ 298 Bob Friend	.25	.11	.03
☐ 299 Dusty Rhodes	.20	.09	.03
☐ 300 Eddie Stanky	.20	.09	.03
☐ 301 Harvey Kuenn	.35	.16	.04
☐ 302 Marty Marion	.25	.11	.03
☐ 303 Sal Maglie	.35	.16	.04
☐ 304 Lou Boudreau MG	.50	.23	.06
☐ 305 Carl Furillo	.35	.16	.04
☐ 306 Bobo Holloman	.20	.09	.03
☐ 307 Steve O'Neill MG	.20	.09	.03
☐ 308 Carl Erskine	.35	.16	.04
☐ 309 Leo Durocher MG	.75	.35	.09
☐ 310 Lew Burdette	.25	.11	.03
☐ 311 Richie Ashburn	1.00	.45	.12
☐ 312 Hoyt Wilhelm	.75	.35	.09
☐ 313 Bucky Harris MG	.50	.23	.06
☐ 314 Joe Garagiola	.50	.23	.06
☐ 315 Johnny Pesky	.25	.11	.03
☐ 316 Fred Haney MG	.25	.11	.03
☐ 317 Hank Aaron	10.00	4.50	1.25
☐ 318 Curt Simmons	.25	.11	.03
☐ 319 Ted Williams	10.00	4.50	1.25
☐ 320 Don Newcombe	.50	.23	.06
☐ 321 Charlie Grimm MG	.25	.11	.03
☐ 322 Paul Richards MG	.25	.11	.03
☐ 323 Wes Westrum	.25	.11	.03
☐ 324 Vern Law	.20	.09	.03
☐ 325 Casey Stengel MG	.75	.35	.09
☐ 326 Dizzy Dean and Al Simmons (1953 HOF Inductees)	.50	.23	.06
☐ 327 Duke Snider	2.50	1.10	.30
☐ 328 Bill Rigney	.25	.11	.03
☐ 329 Al Lopez MG	.50	.23	.06
☐ 330 Bobby Thomson	.30	.14	.04
☐ 331 Nellie Fox	1.00	.45	.12
☐ 332 Eleanor Engle	1.00	.45	.12
☐ 333 Larry Doby	.35	.16	.04
☐ 334 Billy Goodman	.25	.11	.03
☐ 335 Checklist 1-140	.20	.09	.03
☐ 336 Checklist 141-280	.20	.09	.03
☐ 337 Checklist 281-337	.20	.09	.03

1994 Topps Archives 1954

The 1954 Archives set includes 248 reprint cards from the original set, plus eight specially created prospect cards (Roberto Clemente, Harmon Killebrew, Bob Grim, Camilo Pascual, Herb Score, Elston Howard, Bill Virdon, and Don Zimmer). No factory sets were sold. Randomly inserted were 1,954 redemption cards good for actual 1954 Topps cards; 1,954 Hank Aaron autographed gold cards; and 1,954 redemption cards for full sets of ToppsGold Archives cards. Each 12-card pack contains 11 Archives cards plus one ToppsGold Archives card. A random insert card replaced the gold card in every 2,210 packs. Ted Williams' cards #1 and #250, as well as a new Mickey Mantle's card #259, were issued as inserts in the 1994 Upper Deck All-Time Heroes series. On a white-bordered color background, the fronts display a color closeup cutout, with the player's name, team name, and team logo across the top. A small black-and-white cutout is superposed next to the color closeup. A facsimile autograph is inscribed across the lower portion of the card. On a white background, the horizontal backs present biography, player profile and, on a green panel, minor league statistics and an "Inside Baseball" feature.

	MINT	NRMT	EXC
COMPLETE SET (256)	30.00	13.50	3.70
COMMON CARD (2-249)	.10	.05	.01
COMMON CARD (251-258)	.15	.07	.02
☐ 1 Not Issued			
☐ 2 Gus Zernial	.15	.07	.02
☐ 3 Monte Irvin	.50	.23	.06
☐ 4 Hank Sauer	.15	.07	.02
☐ 5 Ed Lopat	.15	.07	.02
☐ 6 Pete Runnels	.15	.07	.02
☐ 7 Ted Kluszewski	.20	.09	.03
☐ 8 Bobby Young	.10	.05	.01
☐ 9 Harvey Haddix	.15	.07	.02
☐ 10 Jackie Robinson	4.00	1.80	.50
☐ 11 Paul Smith	.10	.05	.01
☐ 12 Del Crandall	.10	.05	.01
☐ 13 Billy Martin	.50	.23	.06
☐ 14 Preacher Roe	.15	.07	.02
☐ 15 Al Rosen	.20	.09	.03
☐ 16 Vic Janowicz	.20	.09	.03
☐ 17 Phil Rizzuto	.75	.35	.09
☐ 18 Walt Dropo	.10	.05	.01
☐ 19 Johnny Lipon	.10	.05	.01
☐ 20 Warren Spahn	.75	.35	.09
☐ 21 Bobby Shantz	.10	.05	.01
☐ 22 Jim Greengrass	.10	.05	.01
☐ 23 Luke Easter	.15	.07	.02
☐ 24 Granny Hamner	.15	.07	.02
☐ 25 Harvey Kuenn	.15	.07	.02
☐ 26 Ray Jablonski	.10	.05	.01
☐ 27 Ferris Fain	.10	.05	.01
☐ 28 Paul Minner	.10	.05	.01
☐ 29 Jim Hegan	.10	.05	.01
☐ 30 Ed Mathews	.75	.35	.09
☐ 31 Johnny Klippstein	.10	.05	.01
☐ 32 Duke Snider	1.50	.70	.19
☐ 33 Johnny Schmitz	.10	.05	.01
☐ 34 Jim Rivera	.10	.05	.01
☐ 35 Jim Gilliam	.20	.09	.03

☐ 36 Hoyt Wilhelm .50 .23 .06
☐ 37 Whitey Ford .75 .35 .09
☐ 38 Eddie Stanky MG .15 .07 .02
☐ 39 Sherm Lollar .15 .07 .02
☐ 40 Mel Parnell .10 .05 .01
☐ 41 Willie Jones .15 .07 .02
☐ 42 Don Mueller .10 .05 .01
☐ 43 Dick Groat .15 .07 .02
☐ 44 Ned Garver .10 .05 .01
☐ 45 Richie Ashburn .75 .35 .09
☐ 46 Ken Raffensberger .10 .05 .01
☐ 47 Ellis Kinder .10 .05 .01
☐ 48 Billy Hunter .10 .05 .01
☐ 49 Ray Murray .10 .05 .01
☐ 50 Yogi Berra 1.50 .70 .19
☐ 51 Johnny Lindell .10 .05 .01
☐ 52 Vic Power .10 .05 .01
☐ 53 Jack Dittmer .10 .05 .01
☐ 54 Vern Stephens .15 .07 .02
☐ 55 Phil Cavarretta MG .15 .07 .02
☐ 56 Willie Miranda .10 .05 .01
☐ 57 Luis Aloma .10 .05 .01
☐ 58 Bob Wilson .10 .05 .01
☐ 59 Gene Conley .10 .05 .01
☐ 60 Frank Baumholtz .10 .05 .01
☐ 61 Bob Cain .10 .05 .01
☐ 62 Eddie Robinson .10 .05 .01
☐ 63 Johnny Pesky .15 .07 .02
☐ 64 Hank Thompson .10 .05 .01
☐ 65 Bob Swift .10 .05 .01
☐ 66 Ted Lepcio .10 .05 .01
☐ 67 Jim Willis .10 .05 .01
☐ 68 Sammy Calderone .10 .05 .01
☐ 69 Bud Podbielan .10 .05 .01
☐ 70 Larry Doby .20 .09 .03
☐ 71 Frank Smith .10 .05 .01
☐ 72 Preston Ward .10 .05 .01
☐ 73 Wayne Terwilliger .10 .05 .01
☐ 74 Bill Taylor .10 .05 .01
☐ 75 Fred Haney MG .10 .05 .01
☐ 76 Bob Scheffing CO .10 .05 .01
☐ 77 Ray Boone .10 .05 .01
☐ 78 Ted Kazanski .10 .05 .01
☐ 79 Andy Pafko .15 .07 .02
☐ 80 Jackie Jensen .15 .07 .02
☐ 81 Dave Hoskins .10 .05 .01
☐ 82 Milt Bolling .10 .05 .01
☐ 83 Joe Collins .15 .07 .02
☐ 84 Dick Cole .10 .05 .01
☐ 85 Bob Turley .15 .07 .02
☐ 86 Billy Herman CO .20 .09 .03
☐ 87 Roy Face .15 .07 .02
☐ 88 Matt Batts .10 .05 .01
☐ 89 Howie Pollet .10 .05 .01
☐ 90 Willie Mays 6.00 2.70 .75
☐ 91 Bob Oldis .10 .05 .01
☐ 92 Wally Westlake .10 .05 .01
☐ 93 Sid Hudson .10 .05 .01
☐ 94 Ernie Banks 3.00 1.35 .35
☐ 95 Hal Rice .10 .05 .01
☐ 96 Charlie Silvera .15 .07 .02
☐ 97 Jerry Lane .10 .05 .01
☐ 98 Joe Black .20 .09 .03
☐ 99 Bob Hofman .10 .05 .01
☐ 100 Bob Keegan .10 .05 .01
☐ 101 Gene Woodling .15 .07 .02
☐ 102 Gil Hodges .75 .35 .09
☐ 103 Jim Lemon .10 .05 .01
☐ 104 Mike Sandlock .10 .05 .01
☐ 105 Andy Carey .15 .07 .02
☐ 106 Dick Kokos .10 .05 .01
☐ 107 Duane Pillette .10 .05 .01
☐ 108 Thornton Kipper .10 .05 .01
☐ 109 Bill Bruton .15 .07 .02
☐ 110 Harry Dorish .10 .05 .01
☐ 111 Jim Delsing .10 .05 .01
☐ 112 Bill Renna .10 .05 .01
☐ 113 Bob Boyd .10 .05 .01
☐ 114 Dean Stone .10 .05 .01
☐ 115 Rip Repulski .10 .05 .01
☐ 116 Steve Bilko .10 .05 .01
☐ 117 Solly Hemus .10 .05 .01
☐ 118 Carl Scheib .10 .05 .01
☐ 119 Johnny Antonelli .15 .07 .02
☐ 120 Roy McMillan .15 .07 .02
☐ 121 Clem Labine .20 .09 .03
☐ 122 Johnny Logan .15 .07 .02
☐ 123 Bobby Adams .10 .05 .01
☐ 124 Marion Fricano .10 .05 .01
☐ 125 Harry Perkowski .10 .05 .01
☐ 126 Ben Wade .10 .05 .01
☐ 127 Steve O'Neill MG .10 .05 .01
☐ 128 Henry Aaron 6.00 2.70 .75
☐ 129 Forrest Jacobs .10 .05 .01
☐ 130 Hank Bauer .20 .09 .03
☐ 131 Reno Bertoia .10 .05 .01
☐ 132 Tom Lasorda 3.00 1.35 .35
☐ 133 Del Baker CO .10 .05 .01
☐ 134 Cal Hogue .10 .05 .01
☐ 135 Joe Presko .10 .05 .01
☐ 136 Connie Ryan .10 .05 .01
☐ 137 Wally Moon .15 .07 .02
☐ 138 Bob Borkowski .10 .05 .01
☐ 139 Ed O'Brien .15 .07 .02
Johnny O'Brien
☐ 140 Tom Wright .10 .05 .01
☐ 141 Joe Jay .10 .05 .01
☐ 142 Tom Poholsky .10 .05 .01
☐ 143 Rollie Hemsley CO .10 .05 .01
☐ 144 Bill Werle .10 .05 .01
☐ 145 Elmer Valo .10 .05 .01
☐ 146 Don Johnson .10 .05 .01
☐ 147 John Riddle CO .10 .05 .01
☐ 148 Bob Trice .10 .05 .01
☐ 149 Jim Robertson .10 .05 .01
☐ 150 Dick Kryhoski .10 .05 .01
☐ 151 Alex Grammas .10 .05 .01
☐ 152 Mike Blyzka .10 .05 .01
☐ 153 Rube Walker .10 .05 .01
☐ 154 Mike Fornieles .10 .05 .01
☐ 155 Bob Kennedy .10 .05 .01
☐ 156 Joe Coleman .10 .05 .01
☐ 157 Don Lenhardt .10 .05 .01
☐ 158 Peanuts Lowrey .10 .05 .01
☐ 159 Dave Philley .10 .05 .01
☐ 160 Red Kress CO .10 .05 .01
☐ 161 John Hetki .10 .05 .01
☐ 162 Herman Wehmeier .10 .05 .01
☐ 163 Frank House .10 .05 .01
☐ 164 Stu Miller .10 .05 .01
☐ 165 Jim Pendleton .10 .05 .01
☐ 166 Johnny Podres .15 .07 .02
☐ 167 Don Lund .10 .05 .01
☐ 168 Morrie Martin .10 .05 .01
☐ 169 Jim Hughes .10 .05 .01
☐ 170 Jim Rhodes .10 .05 .01
☐ 171 Leo Kiely .10 .05 .01
☐ 172 Hal Brown .10 .05 .01
☐ 173 Jack Harshman .10 .05 .01
☐ 174 Tom Qualters .10 .05 .01
☐ 175 Frank Leja .10 .05 .01
☐ 176 Bob Keely .10 .05 .01
☐ 177 Bob Milliken .10 .05 .01
☐ 178 Bill Glynn .10 .05 .01
☐ 179 Gair Allie .10 .05 .01
☐ 180 Wes Westrum .10 .05 .01
☐ 181 Mel Roach .10 .05 .01
☐ 182 Chuck Harmon .10 .05 .01
☐ 183 Earle Combs CO .20 .09 .03
☐ 184 Ed Bailey .10 .05 .01
☐ 185 Chuck Stobbs .10 .05 .01
☐ 186 Karl Olson .10 .05 .01
☐ 187 Heinie Manush CO .20 .09 .03
☐ 188 Dave Jolly .10 .05 .01
☐ 189 Bob Ross .10 .05 .01
☐ 190 Ray Herbert .10 .05 .01
☐ 191 Dick Schofield .10 .05 .01
☐ 192 Cot Deal CO .10 .05 .01
☐ 193 Johnny Hopp CO .10 .05 .01
☐ 194 Bill Sarni .10 .05 .01
☐ 195 Bill Consolo .10 .05 .01
☐ 196 Stan Jok .10 .05 .01
☐ 197 Schoolboy Rowe CO .15 .07 .02
☐ 198 Carl Sawatski .10 .05 .01
☐ 199 Rocky Nelson .10 .05 .01
☐ 200 Larry Jansen .10 .05 .01
☐ 201 Al Kaline 3.00 1.35 .35
☐ 202 Bob Purkey .10 .05 .01
☐ 203 Harry Brecheen CO .10 .05 .01
☐ 204 Angel Scull .10 .05 .01
☐ 205 Johnny Sain .15 .07 .02
☐ 206 Ray Crone .10 .05 .01
☐ 207 Tom Oliver CO .10 .05 .01
☐ 208 Grady Hatton .10 .05 .01
☐ 209 Charlie Thompson .10 .05 .01
☐ 210 Bob Buhl .10 .05 .01
☐ 211 Don Hoak .10 .05 .01
☐ 212 Mickey Micelotta .10 .05 .01
☐ 213 John Fitzpatrick CO .10 .05 .01
☐ 214 Arnold Portocarrero .10 .05 .01
☐ 215 Ed McGhee .10 .05 .01
☐ 216 Al Sima .10 .05 .01
☐ 217 Paul Schreiber CO .10 .05 .01
☐ 218 Fred Marsh .10 .05 .01
☐ 219 Charlie Kress .10 .05 .01
☐ 220 Ruben Gomez .10 .05 .01
☐ 221 Dick Brodowski .10 .05 .01
☐ 222 Bill Wilson .10 .05 .01
☐ 223 Joe Haynes CO .10 .05 .01
☐ 224 Dick Weik .10 .05 .01
☐ 225 Don Liddle .10 .05 .01
☐ 226 Jehosie Heard .10 .05 .01
☐ 227 Buster Mills CO .10 .05 .01
☐ 228 Gene Hermanski .10 .05 .01
☐ 229 Bob Talbot .10 .05 .01
☐ 230 Bob Kuzava .10 .05 .01
☐ 231 Roy Smalley .10 .05 .01
☐ 232 Lou Limmer .10 .05 .01
☐ 233 Augie Galan .10 .05 .01
☐ 234 Jerry Lynch .10 .05 .01
☐ 235 Vern Law .15 .07 .02
☐ 236 Paul Penson .10 .05 .01
☐ 237 Mike Ryba .10 .05 .01
☐ 238 Al Aber .10 .05 .01
☐ 239 Bill Skowron .20 .09 .03
☐ 240 Sam Mele .10 .05 .01
☐ 241 Bob Miller .10 .05 .01
☐ 242 Curt Roberts .10 .05 .01
☐ 243 Ray Blades CO .10 .05 .01
☐ 244 Leroy Wheat .10 .05 .01
☐ 245 Roy Sievers .15 .07 .02
☐ 246 Howie Fox .10 .05 .01
☐ 247 Eddie Mayo CO .10 .05 .01
☐ 248 Al Smith .10 .05 .01
☐ 249 Wilmer Mizell .15 .07 .02
☐ 250 Not Issued
☐ 251 Roberto Clemente 10.00 4.50 1.25
☐ 252 Bob Grim .15 .07 .02
☐ 253 Elston Howard .25 .11 .03
☐ 254 Harmon Killebrew 2.00 .90 .25
☐ 255 Camilo Pascual .15 .07 .02
☐ 256 Herb Score .20 .09 .03
☐ 257 Bill Virdon .15 .07 .02
☐ 258 Don Zimmer .20 .09 .03
☐ NNO Hank Aaron AU 200.00 90.00 25.00
☐ NNO0 Gold Redemption Card Exp. 3.50 1.55
.45

1994 Topps Archives 1954 Gold

This set parallels the 1994 Topps Archives 1954 reprint series. It has the same design as the regular issue reprint, except that the team logo and the facsimile autograph are gold-foil stamped on the fronts.

	MINT	NRMT	EXC
COMPLETE SET (256)	125.00	55.00	15.50
COMMON CARD (2-258)	.25	.11	.03
*STARS: 2X TO 4X BASIC CARDS			

1995 Topps Archives Brooklyn Dodgers

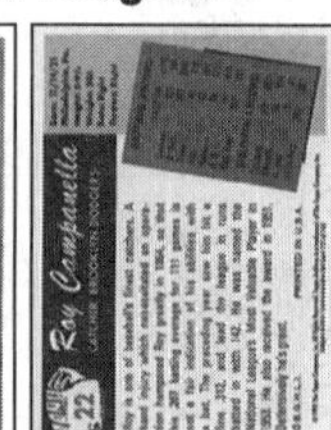

This 165-card set measures the standard size and is a single series release. The set honors the Brooklyn Dodger teams of 1952-1956 and consists of 127 reprints of Topps and Bowman cards produced during that time. The cards "that never were" have been created for the players not featured on Topps and Bowman cards and replicate the design of the card for the year the player would have been pictured. Cards #117-120 commemorate the four games the Dodgers won for the 1955 World Series Championship. Though the cards are numbered as they were originally issued, Topps renumbered them as a complete set and they are checklisted below accordingly. A very limited amount of signed Sandy Koufax cards (#102) were signed and randomly inserted into packs.

	MINT	NRMT	EXC
COMPLETE SET (165)	50.00	22.00	6.25
COMMON CARD (1-165)	.20	.09	.03

☐ 1 Andy Pafko .20 .09 .03
☐ 2 Wayne Terwilliger .20 .09 .03
☐ 3 Billy Loes .30 .14 .04
☐ 4 Gil Hodges 1.00 .45 .12
☐ 5 Duke Snider 1.00 .45 .12
☐ 6 Jim Russell .20 .09 .03
☐ 7 Chris Van Cuyk .20 .09 .03
☐ 8 Preacher Roe .40 .18 .05
☐ 9 Johnny Schmitz .20 .09 .03
☐ 10 Bud Podbielan .20 .09 .03
☐ 11 Phil Haugstad .20 .09 .03
☐ 12 Clyde King .20 .09 .03
☐ 13 Billy Cox .30 .14 .04
☐ 14 Rocky Bridges .20 .09 .03
☐ 15 Carl Erskine .40 .18 .05
☐ 16 Erv Palica .20 .09 .03
☐ 17 Ralph Branca .40 .18 .05
☐ 18 Jackie Robinson 2.00 .90 .25
☐ 19 Roy Campanella 1.00 .45 .12
☐ 20 Rube Walker .20 .09 .03
☐ 21 Johnny Rutherford .20 .09 .03
☐ 22 Joe Black .30 .14 .04
☐ 23 George Shuba .20 .09 .03
☐ 24 Pee Wee Reese 1.00 .45 .12
☐ 25 Clem Labine .40 .18 .05
☐ 26 Bobby Morgan .20 .09 .03
☐ 27 Cookie Lavagetto CO .20 .09 .03
☐ 28 Chuck Dressen MG .20 .09 .03
☐ 29 Ben Wade .20 .09 .03
☐ 30 Rocky Nelson .20 .09 .03
☐ 31 Billy Herman CO .30 .14 .04
☐ 32 Jake Pitler CO .20 .09 .03
☐ 33 Dick Williams .30 .14 .04
☐ 34 Cal Abrams .20 .09 .03
☐ 35 Carl Furillo .40 .18 .05
☐ 36 Don Newcombe .40 .18 .05
☐ 37 Jackie Robinson 2.00 .90 .25
☐ 38 Ben Wade .20 .09 .03
☐ 39 Clem Labine .40 .18 .05
☐ 40 Roy Campanella 1.00 .45 .12
☐ 41 George Shuba .20 .09 .03
☐ 42 Chuck Dressen MG .20 .09 .03
☐ 43 Pee Wee Reese 1.00 .45 .12
☐ 44 Joe Black .30 .14 .04
☐ 45 Bobby Morgan .20 .09 .03
☐ 46 Dick Williams .30 .14 .04
☐ 47 Rube Walker .20 .09 .03
☐ 48 Johnny Rutherford .20 .09 .03
☐ 49 Billy Loes .30 .14 .04
☐ 50 Don Hoak .20 .09 .03
☐ 51 Jim Hughes .20 .09 .03
☐ 52 Bob Milliken .20 .09 .03
☐ 53 Preacher Roe .40 .18 .05
☐ 54 Dixie Howell .20 .09 .03
☐ 55 Junior Gilliam .40 .18 .05
☐ 56 Johnny Podres .40 .18 .05
☐ 57 Bill Antonello .20 .09 .03
☐ 58 Ralph Branca .40 .18 .05
☐ 59 Gil Hodges 1.00 .45 .12
☐ 60 Carl Furillo .40 .18 .05
☐ 61 Carl Erskine .40 .18 .05
☐ 62 Don Newcombe .40 .18 .05
☐ 63 Duke Snider 1.00 .45 .12
☐ 64 Billy Cox .30 .14 .04
☐ 65 Russ Meyer .20 .09 .03
☐ 66 Jackie Robinson 2.00 .90 .25
☐ 67 Preacher Roe .40 .18 .05
☐ 68 Duke Snider 1.00 .45 .12
☐ 69 Junior Gilliam .40 .18 .05
☐ 70 Billy Herman CO .30 .14 .04
☐ 71 Joe Black .30 .14 .04
☐ 72 Gil Hodges 1.00 .45 .12
☐ 73 Clem Labine .40 .18 .05
☐ 74 Ben Wade .20 .09 .03
☐ 75 Tom Lasorda .75 .35 .09
☐ 76 Rube Walker .20 .09 .03
☐ 77 Johnny Podres .40 .18 .05
☐ 78 Jim Hughes .20 .09 .03
☐ 79 Bob Milliken .20 .09 .03
☐ 80 Charlie Thompson .20 .09 .03
☐ 81 Don Hoak .20 .09 .03
☐ 82 Roberto Clemente 3.00 1.35 .35
☐ 83 Don Zimmer .30 .14 .04
☐ 84 Roy Campanella 1.00 .45 .12
☐ 85 Billy Cox .30 .14 .04
☐ 86 Carl Erskine .40 .18 .05
☐ 87 Carl Furillo .40 .18 .05
☐ 88 Don Newcombe .40 .18 .05
☐ 89 Pee Wee Reese 1.00 .45 .12
☐ 90 George Shuba .20 .09 .03
☐ 91 Junior Gilliam .40 .18 .05
☐ 92 Billy Herman CO .30 .14 .04
☐ 93 Johnny Podres .40 .18 .05
☐ 94 Don Hoak .20 .09 .03
☐ 95 Jackie Robinson 2.00 .90 .25
☐ 96 Jim Hughes .20 .09 .03
☐ 97 Sandy Amoros .20 .09 .03
☐ 98 Karl Spooner .20 .09 .03
☐ 99 Don Zimmer .30 .14 .04
☐ 100 Rube Walker .20 .09 .03
☐ 101 Bob Milliken .20 .09 .03
☐ 102 Sandy Koufax 3.00 1.35 .35
☐ 103 Joe Black .30 .14 .04
☐ 104 Clem Labine .40 .18 .05
☐ 105 Gil Hodges 1.00 .45 .12
☐ 106 Ed Roebuck .20 .09 .03
☐ 107 Bert Hamric .20 .09 .03
☐ 108 Duke Snider 1.00 .45 .12
☐ 109 Walter Alston MG .50 .23 .06
☐ 110 Bob Borkowski .20 .09 .03
☐ 111 Roger Craig .40 .18 .05
☐ 112 Don Drysdale 1.50 .70 .19
☐ 113 Dixie Howell .20 .09 .03
☐ 114 Frank Kellert .20 .09 .03
☐ 115 Tom Lasorda .50 .23 .06
☐ 116 Chuck Templeton .20 .09 .03
☐ 117 Jackie Robinson WS 1.00 .45 .12
☐ 118 Gil Hodges WS .50 .23 .06
☐ 119 Duke Snider WS .50 .23 .06
☐ 120 Johnny Podres WS .35 .16 .04
☐ 121 Don Hoak .30 .14 .04
☐ 122 Roy Campanella 1.00 .45 .12
☐ 123 Pee Wee Reese 1.00 .45 .12
☐ 124 Bob Darnell .20 .09 .03
☐ 125 Don Zimmer .40 .18 .05
☐ 126 George Shuba .20 .09 .03
☐ 127 Johnny Podres .50 .23 .06
☐ 128 Junior Gilliam .50 .23 .06
☐ 129 Don Newcombe .50 .23 .06
☐ 130 Jim Hughes .20 .09 .03
☐ 131 Gil Hodges 1.00 .45 .12
☐ 132 Carl Furillo .50 .23 .06
☐ 133 Carl Erskine .50 .23 .06

☐ 134 Erv Palica	.20	.09	.03
☐ 135 Russ Meyer	.20	.09	.03
☐ 136 Billy Loes	.40	.18	.05
☐ 137 Walt Moryn	.20	.09	.03
☐ 138 Chico Fernandez	.20	.09	.03
☐ 139 Charlie Neal	.20	.09	.03
☐ 140 Ken Lehman	.20	.09	.03
☐ 141 Walter Alston MG	.50	.23	.06
☐ 142 Jackie Robinson	2.00	.90	.25
☐ 143 Sandy Amoros	.30	.14	.04
☐ 144 Ed Roebuck	.20	.09	.03
☐ 145 Roger Craig	.40	.18	.05
☐ 146 Sandy Koufax	2.00	.90	.25
☐ 147 Karl Spooner	.20	.09	.03
☐ 148 Don Zimmer	.40	.18	.05
☐ 149 Roy Campanella	1.00	.45	.12
☐ 150 Gil Hodges	1.00	.45	.12
☐ 151 Duke Snider	1.50	.70	.19
☐ 152 Team Card	.40	.18	.05
☐ 153 Johnny Podres	.50	.23	.06
☐ 154 Don Bessent	.20	.09	.03
☐ 155 Carl Furillo	.50	.23	.06
☐ 156 Randy Jackson	.20	.09	.03
☐ 157 Carl Erskine	.50	.23	.06
☐ 158 Don Newcombe	.50	.23	.06
☐ 159 Pee Wee Reese	1.00	.45	.12
☐ 160 Billy Loes	.30	.14	.04
☐ 161 Junior Gilliam	.50	.23	.06
☐ 162 Clem Labine	.50	.23	.06
☐ 163 Charlie Neal	.20	.09	.03
☐ 164 Rube Walker	.20	.09	.03
☐ 165 Checklist	.20	.09	.03
☐ AU Sandy Koufax (Card 102)	500.00	220.00	60.00

1996 Topps Chrome

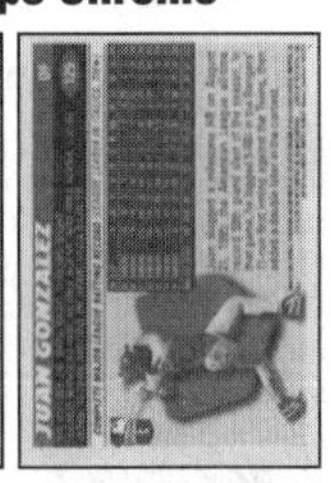

The 1996 Topps Chrome set was issued in one series totalling 165 cards and features the best old and new players from the 1996 Topps regular set. Each chromium card is a replica of its regular version with the exception of the Topps Chrome logo replacing the traditional logo. Included in the set is a Mickey Mantle #7 Commemorative card and a Cal Ripken Tribute card. The four-card packs retail for $3.00 each.

	MINT	NRMT	EXC
COMPLETE SET (165)	80.00	36.00	10.00
COMMON CARD (1-165)	.25	.11	.03
☐ 1 Tony Gwynn STP	1.50	.70	.19
☐ 2 Mike Piazza STP	2.50	1.10	.30
☐ 3 Greg Maddux STP	2.50	1.10	.30
☐ 4 Jeff Bagwell STP	1.50	.70	.19
☐ 5 Larry Walker STP	1.00	.45	.12
☐ 6 Barry Larkin STP	1.00	.45	.12
☐ 7 Mickey Mantle COMM	10.00	4.50	1.25
☐ 8 Tom Glavine STP	1.00	.45	.12
☐ 9 Craig Biggio STP	.50	.23	.06
☐ 10 Barry Bonds STP	1.00	.45	.12
☐ 11 Heathcliff Slocumb STP	.25	.11	.03
☐ 12 Matt Williams STP	1.00	.45	.12
☐ 13 Todd Helton DP	4.00	1.80	.50
☐ 14 Paul Molitor	1.50	.70	.19
☐ 15 Glenallen Hill	.25	.11	.03
☐ 16 Troy Percival	.25	.11	.03
☐ 17 Albert Belle	3.00	1.35	.35
☐ 18 Mark Wohlers	.50	.23	.06
☐ 19 Kirby Puckett	3.00	1.35	.35
☐ 20 Mark Grace	1.00	.45	.12
☐ 21 J.T. Snow	.50	.23	.06
☐ 22 David Justice	.50	.23	.06
☐ 23 Mike Mussina	1.50	.70	.19
☐ 24 Bernie Williams	1.50	.70	.19
☐ 25 Ron Gant	.50	.23	.06
☐ 26 Carlos Baerga	.50	.23	.06
☐ 27 Gary Sheffield	1.25	.55	.16
☐ 28 Cal Ripken 2131	6.00	2.70	.75
☐ 29 Frank Thomas	8.00	3.60	1.00
☐ 30 Kevin Seitzer	.25	.11	.03
☐ 31 Joe Carter	.50	.23	.06
☐ 32 Jeff King	.50	.23	.06
☐ 33 David Cone	.50	.23	.06
☐ 34 Eddie Murray	2.00	.90	.25
☐ 35 Brian Jordan	.50	.23	.06
☐ 36 Garret Anderson	1.00	.45	.12
☐ 37 Hideo Nomo	2.00	.90	.25
☐ 38 Steve Finley	1.00	.45	.12
☐ 39 Ivan Rodriguez	2.00	.90	.25
☐ 40 Quilvio Veras	.25	.11	.03
☐ 41 Mark McGwire	2.50	1.10	.30
☐ 42 Greg Vaughn	1.00	.45	.12
☐ 43 Randy Johnson	1.25	.55	.16
☐ 44 David Segui	.25	.11	.03
☐ 45 Derek Bell	.50	.23	.06
☐ 46 John Valentin	.50	.23	.06
☐ 47 Steve Avery	.50	.23	.06
☐ 48 Tino Martinez	.50	.23	.06
☐ 49 Shane Reynolds	.25	.11	.03
☐ 50 Jim Edmonds	.50	.23	.06
☐ 51 Raul Mondesi	1.00	.45	.12
☐ 52 Chipper Jones	5.00	2.20	.60
☐ 53 Gregg Jefferies	1.00	.45	.12
☐ 54 Ken Caminiti	1.25	.55	.16
☐ 55 Brian McRae	.25	.11	.03
☐ 56 Don Mattingly	4.00	1.80	.50
☐ 57 Marty Cordova	.50	.23	.06
☐ 58 Vinny Castilla	.50	.23	.06
☐ 59 John Smoltz	1.25	.55	.16
☐ 60 Travis Fryman	.50	.23	.06
☐ 61 Ryan Klesko	1.25	.55	.16
☐ 62 Alex Fernandez	.50	.23	.06
☐ 63 Dante Bichette	1.00	.45	.12
☐ 64 Eric Karros	.50	.23	.06
☐ 65 Roger Clemens	1.50	.70	.19
☐ 66 Randy Myers	.25	.11	.03
☐ 67 Cal Ripken	6.00	2.70	.75
☐ 68 Rod Beck	.50	.23	.06
☐ 69 Jack McDowell	1.00	.45	.12
☐ 70 Ken Griffey Jr.	8.00	3.60	1.00
☐ 71 Ramon Martinez	.50	.23	.06
☐ 72 Jason Giambi FS	1.00	.45	.12
☐ 73 Nomar Garciaparra FS	3.00	1.35	.35
☐ 74 Billy Wagner FS	1.00	.45	.12
☐ 75 Todd Greene FS	.50	.23	.06
☐ 76 Paul Wilson FS	.50	.23	.06
☐ 77 Johnny Damon FS	.50	.23	.06
☐ 78 Alan Benes FS	1.00	.45	.12
☐ 79 Karim Garcia FS	1.50	.70	.19
☐ 80 Derek Jeter FS	5.00	2.20	.60
☐ 81 Kirby Puckett STP	1.00	.45	.12
☐ 82 Cal Ripken STP	3.00	1.35	.35
☐ 83 Albert Belle STP	1.50	.70	.19
☐ 84 Randy Johnson STP	1.00	.45	.12
☐ 85 Wade Boggs STP	1.00	.45	.12
☐ 86 Carlos Baerga STP	.50	.23	.06
☐ 87 Ivan Rodriguez STP	1.00	.45	.12
☐ 88 Mike Mussina STP	1.00	.45	.12
☐ 89 Frank Thomas STP	4.00	1.80	.50
☐ 90 Ken Griffey Jr. STP	4.00	1.80	.50
☐ 91 Jose Mesa STP	.25	.11	.03
☐ 92 Matt Morris DP	1.00	.45	.12
☐ 93 Mike Piazza	5.00	2.20	.60
☐ 94 Edgar Martinez	.50	.23	.06
☐ 95 Chuck Knoblauch	1.00	.45	.12
☐ 96 Andres Galarraga	1.00	.45	.12
☐ 97 Tony Gwynn	3.00	1.35	.35
☐ 98 Lee Smith	.50	.23	.06
☐ 99 Sammy Sosa	1.25	.55	.16
☐ 100 Jim Thome	1.50	.70	.19
☐ 101 Bernard Gilkey	.50	.23	.06
☐ 102 Brady Anderson	1.00	.45	.12
☐ 103 Rico Brogna	.25	.11	.03
☐ 104 Len Dykstra	.50	.23	.06
☐ 105 Tom Glavine	1.00	.45	.12
☐ 106 John Olerud	.25	.11	.03
☐ 107 Terry Steinbach	.50	.23	.06
☐ 108 Brian Hunter	.25	.11	.03
☐ 109 Jay Buhner	1.00	.45	.12
☐ 110 Mo Vaughn	2.00	.90	.25
☐ 111 Jose Mesa	.50	.23	.06
☐ 112 Brett Butler	.25	.11	.03
☐ 113 Chili Davis	.25	.11	.03
☐ 114 Paul O'Neill	.25	.11	.03
☐ 115 Roberto Alomar	1.50	.70	.19
☐ 116 Barry Larkin	1.00	.45	.12
☐ 117 Marquis Grissom	.50	.23	.06
☐ 118 Will Clark	1.00	.45	.12
☐ 119 Barry Bonds	2.00	.90	.25
☐ 120 Ozzie Smith	2.00	.90	.25
☐ 121 Pedro Martinez	.50	.23	.06
☐ 122 Craig Biggio	.50	.23	.06
☐ 123 Moises Alou	.50	.23	.06
☐ 124 Robin Ventura	.50	.23	.06
☐ 125 Greg Maddux	5.00	2.20	.60
☐ 126 Tim Salmon	1.00	.45	.12
☐ 127 Wade Boggs	1.00	.45	.12
☐ 128 Ismael Valdes	.50	.23	.06
☐ 129 Juan Gonzalez	4.00	1.80	.50
☐ 130 Ray Lankford	.50	.23	.06
☐ 131 Bobby Bonilla	.50	.23	.06
☐ 132 Reggie Sanders	.50	.23	.06
☐ 133 Alex Ochoa NOW	.50	.23	.06
☐ 134 Mark Loretta NOW	.25	.11	.03
☐ 135 Jason Kendall NOW	1.00	.45	.12
☐ 136 Brooks Kieschnick NOW	1.00	.45	.12
☐ 137 Chris Snopek NOW	.25	.11	.03
☐ 138 Ruben Rivera NOW	1.50	.70	.19
☐ 139 Jeff Suppan NOW	1.00	.45	.12
☐ 140 John Wasdin NOW	.25	.11	.03
☐ 141 Jay Payton NOW	1.00	.45	.12
☐ 142 Rick Krivda NOW	.25	.11	.03
☐ 143 Jimmy Haynes NOW	.25	.11	.03
☐ 144 Ryne Sandberg	2.00	.90	.25
☐ 145 Matt Williams	1.00	.45	.12
☐ 146 Jose Canseco	1.00	.45	.12
☐ 147 Larry Walker	1.00	.45	.12
☐ 148 Kevin Appier	.50	.23	.06
☐ 149 Javy Lopez	.50	.23	.06
☐ 150 Dennis Eckersley	.50	.23	.06
☐ 151 Jason Isringhausen	1.00	.45	.12
☐ 152 Dean Palmer	1.00	.45	.12
☐ 153 Jeff Bagwell	3.00	1.35	.35
☐ 154 Rondell White	.50	.23	.06
☐ 155 Wally Joyner	.25	.11	.03
☐ 156 Fred McGriff	1.00	.45	.12
☐ 157 Cecil Fielder	.50	.23	.06
☐ 158 Rafael Palmeiro	1.00	.45	.12
☐ 159 Rickey Henderson	1.00	.45	.12
☐ 160 Shawon Dunston	.25	.11	.03
☐ 161 Manny Ramirez	2.00	.90	.25
☐ 162 Alex Gonzalez	.25	.11	.03
☐ 163 Shawn Green	.25	.11	.03
☐ 164 Kenny Lofton	2.00	.90	.25
☐ 165 Jeff Conine	.50	.23	.06

1996 Topps Chrome Refractors

Randomly inserted at the rate of one in every 12 packs, this 165-card set is parallel to the regular Chrome set. The difference in design is the refractive quality of the cards.

	MINT	NRMT	EXC
COMPLETE SET (165)	3000.00	1350.00	375.00
COMMON CARD (1-165)	6.00	2.70	.75
*STARS: 10X TO 20X BASIC CARDS			
*YOUNG STARS: 7.5X TO 15X BASIC CARDS			
☐ 1 Tony Gwynn STP	30.00	13.50	3.70
☐ 2 Mike Piazza STP	50.00	22.00	6.25
☐ 3 Greg Maddux STP	40.00	18.00	5.00
☐ 4 Jeff Bagwell STP	30.00	13.50	3.70
☐ 7 Mickey Mantle COMM	175.00	80.00	22.00
☐ 13 Todd Helton	40.00	18.00	5.00
☐ 14 Paul Molitor	30.00	13.50	3.70
☐ 17 Albert Belle	60.00	27.00	7.50
☐ 19 Kirby Puckett	60.00	27.00	7.50
☐ 28 Cal Ripken TRIB	125.00	55.00	15.50
☐ 29 Frank Thomas	150.00	70.00	19.00
☐ 34 Eddie Murray	40.00	18.00	5.00
☐ 37 Hideo Nomo	40.00	18.00	5.00
☐ 39 Ivan Rodriguez	40.00	18.00	5.00
☐ 41 Mark McGwire	50.00	22.00	6.25
☐ 52 Chipper Jones	100.00	45.00	12.50
☐ 56 Don Mattingly	75.00	34.00	9.50
☐ 65 Roger Clemens	30.00	13.50	3.70
☐ 67 Cal Ripken	125.00	55.00	15.50
☐ 70 Ken Griffey Jr.	150.00	70.00	19.00
☐ 73 Nomar Garciaparra	40.00	18.00	5.00
☐ 79 Karim Garcia	30.00	13.50	3.70
☐ 80 Derek Jeter FS	100.00	45.00	12.50
☐ 81 Kirby Puckett STP	30.00	13.50	3.70
☐ 82 Cal Ripken STP	60.00	27.00	7.50
☐ 83 Albert Belle STP	30.00	13.50	3.70
☐ 89 Frank Thomas STP	75.00	34.00	9.50
☐ 90 Ken Griffey Jr. STP	75.00	34.00	9.50
☐ 93 Mike Piazza	100.00	45.00	12.50
☐ 97 Tony Gwynn	60.00	27.00	7.50
☐ 110 Mo Vaughn	40.00	18.00	5.00
☐ 115 Roberto Alomar	30.00	13.50	3.70
☐ 119 Barry Bonds	40.00	18.00	5.00
☐ 120 Ozzie Smith	40.00	18.00	5.00
☐ 125 Greg Maddux	75.00	34.00	9.50
☐ 129 Juan Gonzalez	75.00	34.00	9.50
☐ 144 Ryne Sandberg	40.00	18.00	5.00
☐ 153 Jeff Bagwell	60.00	27.00	7.50
☐ 161 Manny Ramirez	40.00	18.00	5.00
☐ 164 Kenny Lofton	40.00	18.00	5.00

1996 Topps Chrome Masters of the Game

Randomly inserted in packs at a rate of one in 12, this 20-card set honors players who are masters of their playing positions. The fronts feature color action photography with brilliant color metallization.

	MINT	NRMT	EXC
COMPLETE SET (20)	80.00	36.00	10.00
COMMON CARD (1-20)	1.50	.70	.19
☐ 1 Dennis Eckersley	2.00	.90	.25
☐ 2 Denny Martinez	1.50	.70	.19
☐ 3 Eddie Murray	5.00	2.20	.60
☐ 4 Paul Molitor	4.00	1.80	.50
☐ 5 Ozzie Smith	5.00	2.20	.60
☐ 6 Rickey Henderson	3.00	1.35	.35
☐ 7 Tim Raines	1.50	.70	.19
☐ 8 Lee Smith	2.00	.90	.25
☐ 9 Cal Ripken	15.00	6.75	1.85
☐ 10 Chili Davis	1.50	.70	.19
☐ 11 Wade Boggs	3.00	1.35	.35
☐ 12 Tony Gwynn	8.00	3.60	1.00
☐ 13 Don Mattingly	10.00	4.50	1.25
☐ 14 Bret Saberhagen	1.50	.70	.19
☐ 15 Kirby Puckett	8.00	3.60	1.00
☐ 16 Joe Carter	2.00	.90	.25
☐ 17 Roger Clemens	4.00	1.80	.50
☐ 18 Barry Bonds	5.00	2.20	.60
☐ 19 Greg Maddux	12.00	5.50	1.50
☐ 20 Frank Thomas	20.00	9.00	2.50

1996 Topps Chrome Masters of the Game Refractors

Randomly inserted in packs at a rate of one in 36, this 20-card set is parallel to the regular insert set. The difference in design is the refractive quality of the cards.

	MINT	NRMT	EXC
COMPLETE SET (20)	250.00	110.00	31.00
COMMON CARD (1-20)	5.00	2.20	.60
*STARS: 1.5X to 3X BASIC CARDS			

1996 Topps Chrome Wrecking Crew

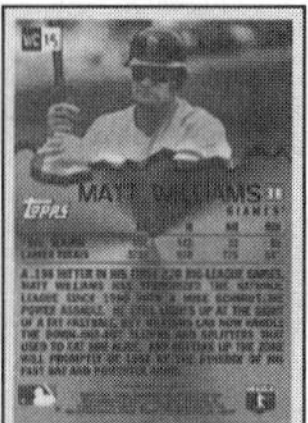

Randomly inserted in packs at a rate of one in 24, this 15-card set features baseball's top hitters and is printed in color action photography with brilliant color metallization.

	MINT	NRMT	EXC
COMPLETE SET (15)	80.00	36.00	10.00
COMMON CARD (WC1-WC15)	2.00	.90	.25
☐ WC1 Jeff Bagwell	10.00	4.50	1.25
☐ WC2 Albert Belle	10.00	4.50	1.25
☐ WC3 Barry Bonds	6.00	2.70	.75
☐ WC4 Jose Canseco	4.00	1.80	.50
☐ WC5 Joe Carter	2.00	.90	.25
☐ WC6 Cecil Fielder	2.00	.90	.25
☐ WC7 Ron Gant	2.00	.90	.25
☐ WC8 Juan Gonzalez	12.00	5.50	1.50
☐ WC9 Ken Griffey Jr.	25.00	11.00	3.10
☐ WC10 Fred McGriff	4.00	1.80	.50
☐ WC11 Mark McGwire	8.00	3.60	1.00
☐ WC12 Mike Piazza	15.00	6.75	1.85
☐ WC13 Frank Thomas	25.00	11.00	3.10
☐ WC14 Mo Vaughn	6.00	2.70	.75
☐ WC15 Matt Williams	4.00	1.80	.50

1996 Topps Chrome Wrecking Crew Refractors

Randomly inserted in packs at a rate of one in 72, this 15-card set is parallel to the regular insert set. The difference in design is the refractive quality of the cards.

	MINT	NRMT	EXC
COMPLETE SET (15)	250.00	110.00	31.00
COMMON CARD (WC1-WC15)	6.00	2.70	.75
*STARS: 1.5X TO 3X BASIC CARDS			

1996 Topps Gallery

The 1996 Topps Gallery set was issued in one series totalling 180 cards. The 8-card packs retail for $3.00 each. The set is divided into 5 themes: Classics (1-90), New Editions (91-108), Modernists (109-126), Futurists (127-144) and Masters (145-180). Each theme features a different design on front, but the bulk of the set has full-bleed, color action shots.

	MINT	NRMT	EXC
COMPLETE SET (180)	40.00	18.00	5.00
COMMON CARD (1-180)	.15	.07	.02
☐ 1 Tom Glavine	.75	.35	.09
☐ 2 Carlos Baerga	.40	.18	.05
☐ 3 Dante Bichette	.75	.35	.09
☐ 4 Mark Langston	.15	.07	.02
☐ 5 Ray Lankford	.40	.18	.05
☐ 6 Moises Alou	.40	.18	.05
☐ 7 Marquis Grissom	.40	.18	.05
☐ 8 Ramon Martinez	.40	.18	.05
☐ 9 Steve Finley	.40	.18	.05
☐ 10 Todd Hundley	.40	.18	.05
☐ 11 Brady Anderson	.75	.35	.09
☐ 12 John Valentin	.40	.18	.05
☐ 13 Heathcliff Slocumb	.15	.07	.02
☐ 14 Ruben Sierra	.15	.07	.02
☐ 15 Jeff Conine	.40	.18	.05
☐ 16 Jay Buhner	.75	.35	.09
☐ 17 Sammy Sosa	.75	.35	.09
☐ 18 Doug Drabek	.15	.07	.02
☐ 19 Jose Mesa	.40	.18	.05
☐ 20 Jeff King	.40	.18	.05
☐ 21 Mickey Tettleton	.40	.18	.05
☐ 22 Jeff Montgomery	.15	.07	.02
☐ 23 Alex Fernandez	.40	.18	.05
☐ 24 Greg Vaughn	.75	.35	.09
☐ 25 Chuck Finley	.15	.07	.02
☐ 26 Terry Steinbach	.40	.18	.05
☐ 27 Rod Beck	.40	.18	.05
☐ 28 Jack McDowell	.75	.35	.09
☐ 29 Mark Wohlers	.75	.35	.09
☐ 30 Len Dykstra	.40	.18	.05
☐ 31 Bernie Williams	1.00	.45	.12
☐ 32 Travis Fryman	.40	.18	.05
☐ 33 Jose Canseco	.75	.35	.09
☐ 34 Ken Caminiti	.75	.35	.09
☐ 35 Devon White	.15	.07	.02
☐ 36 Bobby Bonilla	.40	.18	.05
☐ 37 Paul Sorrento	.15	.07	.02
☐ 38 Ryne Sandberg	1.25	.55	.16
☐ 39 Derek Bell	.40	.18	.05
☐ 40 Bobby Jones	.15	.07	.02
☐ 41 J.T. Snow	.15	.07	.02
☐ 42 Denny Neagle	.40	.18	.05
☐ 43 Tim Wakefield	.15	.07	.02
☐ 44 Andres Galarraga	.75	.35	.09
☐ 45 David Segui	.15	.07	.02
☐ 46 Lee Smith	.40	.18	.05
☐ 47 Mel Rojas	.40	.18	.05
☐ 48 John Franco	.15	.07	.02
☐ 49 Pete Schourek	.15	.07	.02
☐ 50 John Wetteland	.40	.18	.05
☐ 51 Paul Molitor	1.00	.45	.12
☐ 52 Ivan Rodriguez	1.25	.55	.16
☐ 53 Chris Hoiles	.15	.07	.02
☐ 54 Mike Greenwell	.15	.07	.02
☐ 55 Orel Hershiser	.40	.18	.05
☐ 56 Brian McRae	.15	.07	.02
☐ 57 Geronimo Berroa	.40	.18	.05
☐ 58 Craig Biggio	.40	.18	.05
☐ 59 David Justice	.40	.18	.05
☐ 60 Lance Johnson	.40	.18	.05
☐ 61 Andy Ashby	.15	.07	.02
☐ 62 Randy Myers	.15	.07	.02
☐ 63 Gregg Jefferies	.75	.35	.09
☐ 64 Kevin Appier	.40	.18	.05
☐ 65 Rick Aguilera	.15	.07	.02
☐ 66 Shane Reynolds	.15	.07	.02
☐ 67 John Smoltz	.75	.35	.09
☐ 68 Ron Gant	.40	.18	.05
☐ 69 Eric Karros	.40	.18	.05
☐ 70 Jim Thome	1.00	.45	.12
☐ 71 Terry Pendleton	.40	.18	.05
☐ 72 Kenny Rogers	.15	.07	.02
☐ 73 Robin Ventura	.40	.18	.05
☐ 74 Dave Nilsson	.40	.18	.05
☐ 75 Brian Jordan	.40	.18	.05
☐ 76 Glenallen Hill	.15	.07	.02
☐ 77 Greg Colbrunn	.15	.07	.02
☐ 78 Roberto Alomar	1.00	.45	.12
☐ 79 Rickey Henderson	.75	.35	.09
☐ 80 Carlos Garcia	.15	.07	.02
☐ 81 Dean Palmer	.75	.35	.09
☐ 82 Mike Stanley	.15	.07	.02
☐ 83 Hal Morris	.15	.07	.02
☐ 84 Wade Boggs	.75	.35	.09
☐ 85 Chad Curtis	.15	.07	.02
☐ 86 Roberto Hernandez	.40	.18	.05
☐ 87 John Olerud	.15	.07	.02
☐ 88 Frank Castillo	.15	.07	.02
☐ 89 Rafael Palmeiro	.75	.35	.09
☐ 90 Trevor Hoffman	.40	.18	.05
☐ 91 Marty Cordova	.40	.18	.05
☐ 92 Hideo Nomo	1.25	.55	.16
☐ 93 Johnny Damon	.40	.18	.05
☐ 94 Bill Pulsipher	.15	.07	.02
☐ 95 Garret Anderson	.75	.35	.09
☐ 96 Ray Durham	.75	.35	.09
☐ 97 Ricky Bottalico	.15	.07	.02
☐ 98 Carlos Perez	.15	.07	.02
☐ 99 Troy Percival	.15	.07	.02
☐ 100 Chipper Jones	3.00	1.35	.35
☐ 101 Esteban Loaiza	.15	.07	.02
☐ 102 John Mabry	.40	.18	.05
☐ 103 Jon Nunnally	.15	.07	.02
☐ 104 Andy Pettitte	1.50	.70	.19
☐ 105 Lyle Mouton	.15	.07	.02
☐ 106 Jason Isringhausen	.75	.35	.09
☐ 107 Brian L.Hunter	.40	.18	.05
☐ 108 Quilvio Veras	.15	.07	.02
☐ 109 Jim Edmonds	.40	.18	.05
☐ 110 Ryan Klesko	.75	.35	.09
☐ 111 Pedro Martinez	.40	.18	.05
☐ 112 Joey Hamilton	.40	.18	.05
☐ 113 Vinny Castilla	.40	.18	.05
☐ 114 Alex Gonzalez	.15	.07	.02
☐ 115 Raul Mondesi	.75	.35	.09
☐ 116 Rondell White	.40	.18	.05
☐ 117 Dan Miceli	.15	.07	.02
☐ 118 Tom Goodwin	.40	.18	.05
☐ 119 Bret Boone	.15	.07	.02
☐ 120 Shawn Green	.15	.07	.02
☐ 121 Jeff Cirillo	.15	.07	.02
☐ 122 Rico Brogna	.15	.07	.02
☐ 123 Chris Gomez	.15	.07	.02
☐ 124 Ismael Valdes	.40	.18	.05
☐ 125 Javy Lopez	.40	.18	.05
☐ 126 Manny Ramirez	1.25	.55	.16
☐ 127 Paul Wilson	.40	.18	.05
☐ 128 Billy Wagner	.75	.35	.09
☐ 129 Eric Owens	.15	.07	.02
☐ 130 Todd Greene	.40	.18	.05
☐ 131 Karim Garcia	1.00	.45	.12
☐ 132 Jimmy Haynes	.15	.07	.02
☐ 133 Michael Tucker	.40	.18	.05
☐ 134 John Wasdin	.15	.07	.02
☐ 135 Brooks Kieschnick	.75	.35	.09
☐ 136 Alex Ochoa	.40	.18	.05
☐ 137 Ariel Prieto	.15	.07	.02
☐ 138 Tony Clark	1.50	.70	.19
☐ 139 Mark Loretta	.15	.07	.02
☐ 140 Rey Ordonez	.75	.35	.09
☐ 141 Chris Snopek	.15	.07	.02
☐ 142 Roger Cedeno	.15	.07	.02
☐ 143 Derek Jeter	3.00	1.35	.35
☐ 144 Jeff Suppan	.75	.35	.09
☐ 145 Greg Maddux	3.00	1.35	.35
☐ 146 Ken Griffey Jr.	5.00	2.20	.60
☐ 147 Tony Gwynn	2.00	.90	.25
☐ 148 Darren Daulton	.40	.18	.05
☐ 149 Will Clark	.75	.35	.09
☐ 150 Mo Vaughn	1.25	.55	.16
☐ 151 Reggie Sanders	.40	.18	.05
☐ 152 Kirby Puckett	2.00	.90	.25
☐ 153 Paul O'Neill	.15	.07	.02
☐ 154 Tim Salmon	.75	.35	.09
☐ 155 Mark McGwire	1.50	.70	.19
☐ 156 Barry Bonds	1.25	.55	.16
☐ 157 Albert Belle	2.00	.90	.25
☐ 158 Edgar Martinez	.40	.18	.05
☐ 159 Mike Mussina	1.00	.45	.12
☐ 160 Cecil Fielder	.40	.18	.05
☐ 161 Kenny Lofton	1.25	.55	.16
☐ 162 Randy Johnson	.75	.35	.09
☐ 163 Juan Gonzalez	2.50	1.10	.30
☐ 164 Jeff Bagwell	2.00	.90	.25
☐ 165 Joe Carter	.40	.18	.05
☐ 166 Mike Piazza	3.00	1.35	.35
☐ 167 Eddie Murray	1.25	.55	.16
☐ 168 Cal Ripken	4.00	1.80	.50
☐ 169 Barry Larkin	.75	.35	.09
☐ 170 Chuck Knoblauch	.75	.35	.09
☐ 171 Chili Davis	.15	.07	.02
☐ 172 Fred McGriff	.75	.35	.09
☐ 173 Matt Williams	.75	.35	.09
☐ 174 Roger Clemens	1.00	.45	.12
☐ 175 Frank Thomas	5.00	2.20	.60
☐ 176 Dennis Eckersley	.40	.18	.05
☐ 177 Gary Sheffield	.75	.35	.09
☐ 178 David Cone	.40	.18	.05
☐ 179 Larry Walker	.75	.35	.09
☐ 180 Mark Grace	.75	.35	.09
☐ NNO Mantle Masterpiece	20.00	9.00	2.50

1996 Topps Gallery Players Private Issue

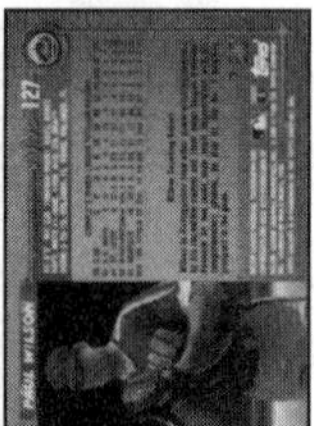

Randomly inserted in packs at a rate of one in 12, this 180-card parallel is foil stamped. The backs are sequentially numbered 0-999, with the first 100 cards (#'s 0-99) sent to the players and the balance inserted in packs.

	MINT	NRMT	EXC
COMPLETE SET (180)	1000.00	450.00	125.00
COMMON CARD (1-180)	2.00	.90	.25
*STARS: 7.5X TO 15X BASIC CARDS			
*YOUNG STARS: 6X TO 12X BASIC CARDS			
☐ 100 Chipper Jones	50.00	22.00	6.25
☐ 143 Derek Jeter	50.00	22.00	6.25
☐ 145 Greg Maddux	50.00	22.00	6.25
☐ 146 Ken Griffey Jr.	80.00	36.00	10.00
☐ 157 Albert Belle	30.00	13.50	3.70
☐ 163 Juan Gonzalez	40.00	18.00	5.00
☐ 166 Mike Piazza	50.00	22.00	6.25
☐ 168 Cal Ripken	60.00	27.00	7.50
☐ 175 Frank Thomas	80.00	36.00	10.00

1996 Topps Gallery Expressionists

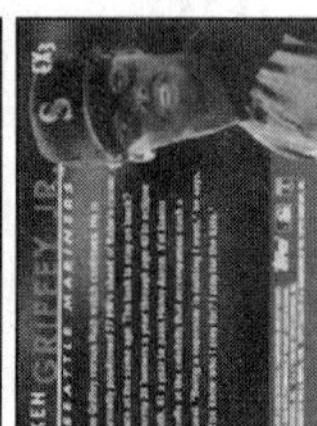

Randomly inserted in packs at a rate of one in 24, this 20-card set features 20 spiritual leaders printed on triple foil stamped and texture embossed cards. Card backs contain a second photo and narrative about the player.

	MINT	NRMT	EXC
COMPLETE SET (20)	120.00	55.00	15.00
COMMON CARD (1-20)	2.00	.90	.25
☐ 1 Mike Piazza	20.00	9.00	2.50
☐ 2 J.T. Snow	2.00	.90	.25
☐ 3 Ken Griffey Jr.	30.00	13.50	3.70
☐ 4 Kirby Puckett	12.00	5.50	1.50
☐ 5 Carlos Baerga	2.00	.90	.25
☐ 6 Chipper Jones	20.00	9.00	2.50
☐ 7 Hideo Nomo	8.00	3.60	1.00
☐ 8 Mark McGwire	10.00	4.50	1.25
☐ 9 Gary Sheffield	5.00	2.20	.60
☐ 10 Randy Johnson	5.00	2.20	.60
☐ 11 Ray Lankford	3.00	1.35	.35
☐ 12 Sammy Sosa	5.00	2.20	.60
☐ 13 Denny Martinez	2.00	.90	.25
☐ 14 Jose Canseco	4.00	1.80	.50
☐ 15 Tony Gwynn	12.00	5.50	1.50
☐ 16 Edgar Martinez	3.00	1.35	.35
☐ 17 Reggie Sanders	2.00	.90	.25
☐ 18 Andres Galarraga	4.00	1.80	.50
☐ 19 Albert Belle	12.00	5.50	1.50
☐ 20 Barry Larkin	3.00	1.35	.35

1996 Topps Gallery Photo Gallery

Randomly inserted in packs at a rate of one in 30, this 15-card set features top photography chronicling baseball's biggest stars and

greatest moments from last year. Each double foil stamped card is printed on 24 pt. stock with customized designs to accentuate the photography.

	MINT	NRMT	EXC
COMPLETE SET (15)	100.00	45.00	12.50
COMMON CARD (PG1-PG15)	1.50	.70	.19
☐ PG1 Eddie Murray	6.00	2.70	.75
☐ PG2 Randy Johnson	4.00	1.80	.50
☐ PG3 Cal Ripken	20.00	9.00	2.50
☐ PG4 Bret Boone	1.50	.70	.19
☐ PG5 Frank Thomas	25.00	11.00	3.10
☐ PG6 Jeff Conine	3.00	1.35	.35
☐ PG7 Johnny Damon	3.00	1.35	.35
☐ PG8 Roger Clemens	5.00	2.20	.60
☐ PG9 Albert Belle	10.00	4.50	1.25
☐ PG10 Ken Griffey Jr.	25.00	11.00	3.10
☐ PG11 Kirby Puckett	10.00	4.50	1.25
☐ PG12 David Justice	1.50	.70	.19
☐ PG13 Bobby Bonilla	3.00	1.35	.35
☐ PG14 Colorado Rockies	4.00	1.80	.50
☐ PG15 Atlanta Braves	4.00	1.80	.50

1996 Topps Laser

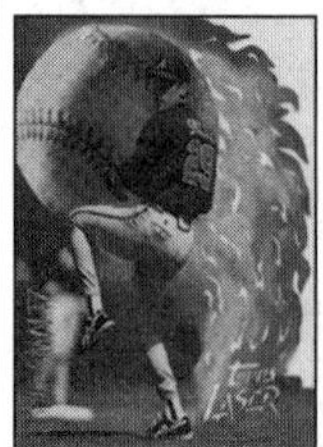

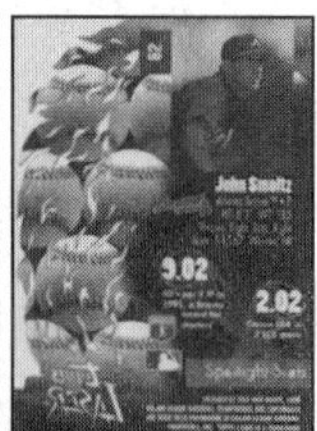

The 1996 Topps Laser contains 128 regular cards that are found on one of four perfected designs. Every card is etch foil-stamped and laser-cut. The four-card packs retail for $5.00 each.

	MINT	NRMT	EXC
COMPLETE SET (128)	120.00	55.00	15.00
COMPLETE SERIES 1 (64)	60.00	27.00	7.50
COMPLETE SERIES 2 (64)	60.00	27.00	7.50
COMMON CARD (1-128)	.50	.23	.06
☐ 1 Moises Alou	.75	.35	.09
☐ 2 Derek Bell	.75	.35	.09
☐ 3 Joe Carter	.75	.35	.09
☐ 4 Jeff Conine	.75	.35	.09
☐ 5 Darren Daulton	.75	.35	.09
☐ 6 Jim Edmonds	.75	.35	.09
☐ 7 Ron Gant	.75	.35	.09
☐ 8 Juan Gonzalez	5.00	2.20	.60
☐ 9 Brian Jordan	.75	.35	.09
☐ 10 Ryan Klesko	1.50	.70	.19
☐ 11 Paul Molitor	2.00	.90	.25
☐ 12 Tony Phillips	.50	.23	.06
☐ 13 Manny Ramirez	2.50	1.10	.30
☐ 14 Sammy Sosa	1.50	.70	.19
☐ 15 Devon White	.50	.23	.06
☐ 16 Bernie Williams	2.00	.90	.25
☐ 17 Garrett Anderson	1.00	.45	.12
☐ 18 Jay Bell	.50	.23	.06
☐ 19 Craig Biggio	.75	.35	.09
☐ 20 Bobby Bonilla	.75	.35	.09
☐ 21 Ken Caminiti	1.50	.70	.19
☐ 22 Shawon Dunston	.50	.23	.06
☐ 23 Mark Grace	1.00	.45	.12
☐ 24 Gregg Jefferies	.75	.35	.09
☐ 25 Jeff King	.75	.35	.09
☐ 26 Javy Lopez	.75	.35	.09
☐ 27 Edgar Martinez	.75	.35	.09
☐ 28 Dean Palmer	1.00	.45	.12
☐ 29 J.T. Snow	.75	.35	.09
☐ 30 Mike Stanley	.50	.23	.06
☐ 31 Terry Steinbach	.75	.35	.09
☐ 32 Robin Ventura	.75	.35	.09
☐ 33 Roberto Alomar	2.00	.90	.25
☐ 34 Jeff Bagwell	4.00	1.80	.50
☐ 35 Dante Bichette	1.00	.45	.12
☐ 36 Wade Boggs	1.00	.45	.12
☐ 37 Barry Bonds	2.50	1.10	.30
☐ 38 Jose Canseco	1.00	.45	.12
☐ 39 Vinny Castilla	.75	.35	.09
☐ 40 Will Clark	1.00	.45	.12
☐ 41 Marty Cordova	.75	.35	.09
☐ 42 Ken Griffey Jr.	10.00	4.50	1.25
☐ 43 Tony Gwynn	4.00	1.80	.50

	MINT	NRMT	EXC
☐ 44 Rickey Henderson	1.00	.45	.12
☐ 45 Chipper Jones	6.00	2.70	.75
☐ 46 Mark McGwire	3.00	1.35	.35
☐ 47 Brian McRae	.50	.23	.06
☐ 48 Ryne Sandberg	2.50	1.10	.30
☐ 49 Andy Ashby	.50	.23	.06
☐ 50 Alan Benes	1.00	.45	.12
☐ 51 Andy Benes	.50	.23	.06
☐ 52 Roger Clemens	2.00	.90	.25
☐ 53 Doug Drabek	.50	.23	.06
☐ 54 Dennis Eckersley	.75	.35	.09
☐ 55 Tom Glavine	1.00	.45	.12
☐ 56 Randy Johnson	1.50	.70	.19
☐ 57 Mark Langston	.50	.23	.06
☐ 58 Denny Martinez	.75	.35	.09
☐ 59 Jack McDowell	1.00	.45	.12
☐ 60 Hideo Nomo	2.50	1.10	.30
☐ 61 Shane Reynolds	.50	.23	.06
☐ 62 John Smoltz	1.50	.70	.19
☐ 63 Paul Wilson	.75	.35	.09
☐ 64 Mark Wohlers	.75	.35	.09
☐ 65 Shawn Green	.50	.23	.06
☐ 66 Marquis Grissom	.75	.35	.09
☐ 67 Dave Hollins	.50	.23	.06
☐ 68 Todd Hundley	.75	.35	.09
☐ 69 David Justice	.75	.35	.09
☐ 70 Eric Karros	.75	.35	.09
☐ 71 Ray Lankford	.75	.35	.09
☐ 72 Fred McGriff	1.00	.45	.12
☐ 73 Hal Morris	.50	.23	.06
☐ 74 Eddie Murray	2.00	.90	.25
☐ 75 Paul O'Neill	.50	.23	.06
☐ 76 Rey Ordonez	1.00	.45	.12
☐ 77 Reggie Sanders	.75	.35	.09
☐ 78 Gary Sheffield	1.50	.70	.19
☐ 79 Jim Thome	1.00	.45	.12
☐ 80 Rondell White	.75	.35	.09
☐ 81 Travis Fryman	.75	.35	.09
☐ 82 Derek Jeter	6.00	2.70	.75
☐ 83 Chuck Knoblauch	1.00	.45	.12
☐ 84 Barry Larkin	1.00	.45	.12
☐ 85 Tino Martinez	.75	.35	.09
☐ 86 Raul Mondesi	1.00	.45	.12
☐ 87 John Olerud	.50	.23	.06
☐ 88 Rafael Palmeiro	1.00	.45	.12
☐ 89 Mike Piazza	6.00	2.70	.75
☐ 90 Cal Ripken	8.00	3.60	1.00
☐ 91 Ivan Rodriguez	2.50	1.10	.30
☐ 92 Frank Thomas	10.00	4.50	1.25
☐ 93 John Valentin	.75	.35	.09
☐ 94 Mo Vaughn	2.50	1.10	.30
☐ 95 Quilvio Veras	.50	.23	.06
☐ 96 Matt Williams	1.00	.45	.12
☐ 97 Brady Anderson	1.00	.45	.12
☐ 98 Carlos Baerga	.75	.35	.09
☐ 99 Albert Belle	4.00	1.80	.50
☐ 100 Jay Buhner	1.00	.45	.12
☐ 101 Johnny Damon	.75	.35	.09
☐ 102 Chili Davis	.50	.23	.06
☐ 103 Ray Durham	1.00	.45	.12
☐ 104 Len Dykstra	.75	.35	.09
☐ 105 Cecil Fielder	.75	.35	.09
☐ 106 Andres Galarraga	1.00	.45	.12
☐ 107 Brian L.Hunter	.75	.35	.09
☐ 108 Kenny Lofton	2.50	1.10	.30
☐ 109 Kirby Puckett	4.00	1.80	.50
☐ 110 Tim Salmon	1.00	.45	.12
☐ 111 Greg Vaughn	1.00	.45	.12
☐ 112 Larry Walker	1.00	.45	.12
☐ 113 Rick Aguilera	.50	.23	.06
☐ 114 Kevin Appier	.75	.35	.09
☐ 115 Kevin Brown	.75	.35	.09
☐ 116 David Cone	.75	.35	.09
☐ 117 Alex Fernandez	.75	.35	.09
☐ 118 Chuck Finley	.50	.23	.06
☐ 119 Joey Hamilton	.75	.35	.09
☐ 120 Jason Isringhausen	1.00	.45	.12
☐ 121 Greg Maddux	6.00	2.70	.75
☐ 122 Pedro Martinez	.75	.35	.09
☐ 123 Jose Mesa	.75	.35	.09
☐ 124 Jeff Montgomery	.50	.23	.06
☐ 125 Mike Mussina	1.00	.45	.12
☐ 126 Randy Myers	.50	.23	.06
☐ 127 Kenny Rogers	.50	.23	.06
☐ 128 Ismael Valdes	.75	.35	.09

1996 Topps Laser Bright Spots

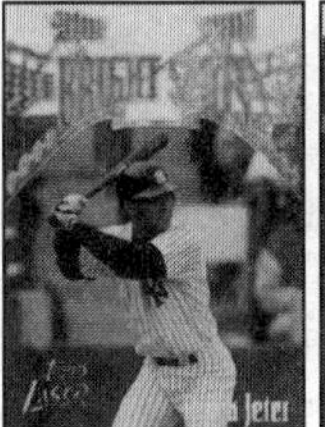

Randomly inserted in packs at a rate of one in 20, this 16-card set highlights top young star players. The cards are printed on etched silver and gold diffraction foil.

	MINT	NRMT	EXC
COMPLETE SET (16)	150.00	70.00	19.00
COMPLETE SERIES 1 (8)	60.00	27.00	7.50
COMPLETE SERIES 2 (8)	100.00	45.00	12.50
COMMON CARD (1-16)	5.00	2.20	.60
☐ 1 Brian L.Hunter	6.00	2.70	.75
☐ 2 Derek Jeter	30.00	13.50	3.70
☐ 3 Jason Kendall	8.00	3.60	1.00
☐ 4 Brooks Kieschnick	6.00	2.70	.75
☐ 5 Rey Ordonez	6.00	2.70	.75
☐ 6 Jason Schmidt	6.00	2.70	.75
☐ 7 Chris Snopek	5.00	2.20	.60
☐ 8 Bob Wolcott	5.00	2.20	.60
☐ 9 Alan Benes	6.00	2.70	.75
☐ 10 Marty Cordova	8.00	3.60	1.00
☐ 11 Jimmy Haynes	5.00	2.20	.60
☐ 12 Todd Hollandsworth	8.00	3.60	1.00
☐ 13 Derek Jeter	30.00	13.50	3.70
☐ 14 Chipper Jones	30.00	13.50	3.70
☐ 15 Hideo Nomo	15.00	6.75	1.85
☐ 16 Paul Wilson	6.00	2.70	.75

1996 Topps Laser Power Cuts

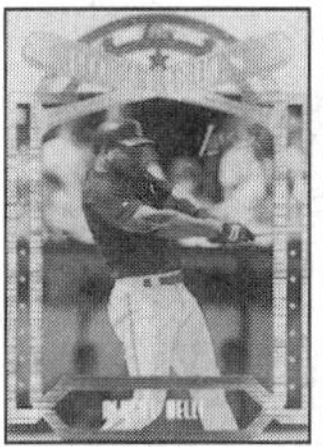

Randomly inserted in packs at a rate of one in 40, this 16-card set features baseball's biggest bats on laser-cut stock polished off with etched silver and gold diffraction foil.

	MINT	NRMT	EXC
COMPLETE SET (16)	250.00	110.00	31.00
COMPLETE SERIES 1 (8)	125.00	55.00	15.50
COMPLETE SERIES 2 (8)	125.00	55.00	15.50
COMMON CARD (1-16)	6.00	2.70	.75
☐ 1 Albert Belle	25.00	11.00	3.10
☐ 2 Jay Buhner	8.00	3.60	1.00
☐ 3 Fred McGriff	8.00	3.60	1.00
☐ 4 Mike Piazza	40.00	18.00	5.00
☐ 5 Tim Salmon	8.00	3.60	1.00
☐ 6 Frank Thomas	60.00	27.00	7.50
☐ 7 Mo Vaughn	15.00	6.75	1.85
☐ 8 Matt Williams	8.00	3.60	1.00
☐ 9 Jeff Bagwell	25.00	11.00	3.10
☐ 10 Barry Bonds	15.00	6.75	1.85
☐ 11 Jose Canseco	8.00	3.60	1.00
☐ 12 Cecil Fielder	6.00	2.70	.75
☐ 13 Juan Gonzalez	30.00	13.50	3.70
☐ 14 Ken Griffey Jr.	60.00	27.00	7.50
☐ 15 Sammy Sosa	10.00	4.50	1.25
☐ 16 Larry Walker	6.00	2.70	.75

1996 Topps Laser Stadium Stars

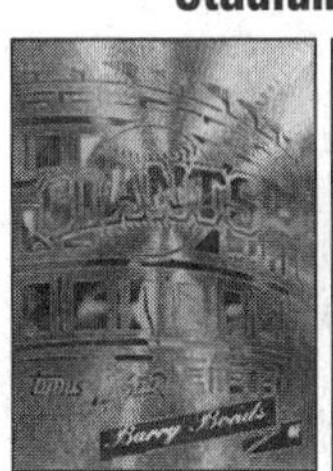

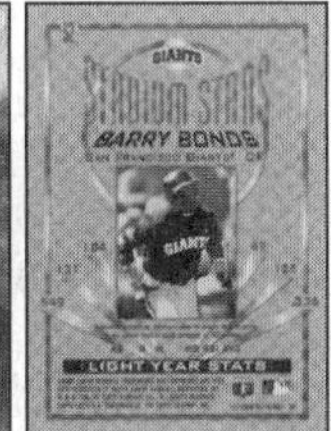

Randomly inserted in packs at a rate of one in 60, this 16-card set features the best and the brightest stars of the baseball diamond. Each highly detailed, laser-sculpted cover folds back to reveal stratied silver and gold etched diffraction foil on every card.

	MINT	NRMT	EXC
COMPLETE SET (16)	300.00	135.00	38.00
COMPLETE SERIES 1 (8)	150.00	70.00	19.00
COMPLETE SERIES 2 (8)	150.00	70.00	19.00
COMMON CARD (1-16)	8.00	3.60	1.00
☐ 1 Carlos Baerga	8.00	3.60	1.00
☐ 2 Barry Bonds	20.00	9.00	2.50
☐ 3 Andres Galarraga	10.00	4.50	1.25
☐ 4 Ken Griffey Jr.	80.00	36.00	10.00
☐ 5 Barry Larkin	10.00	4.50	1.25
☐ 6 Raul Mondesi	10.00	4.50	1.25
☐ 7 Kirby Puckett	30.00	13.50	3.70
☐ 8 Cal Ripken	60.00	27.00	7.50
☐ 9 Will Clark	10.00	4.50	1.25
☐ 10 Roger Clemens	15.00	6.75	1.85
☐ 11 Tony Gwynn	30.00	13.50	3.70
☐ 12 Randy Johnson	12.00	5.50	1.50
☐ 13 Kenny Lofton	20.00	9.00	2.50
☐ 14 Edgar Martinez	8.00	3.60	1.00
☐ 15 Ryne Sandberg	20.00	9.00	2.50
☐ 16 Frank Thomas	80.00	36.00	10.00

1987 Toys'R'Us Rookies

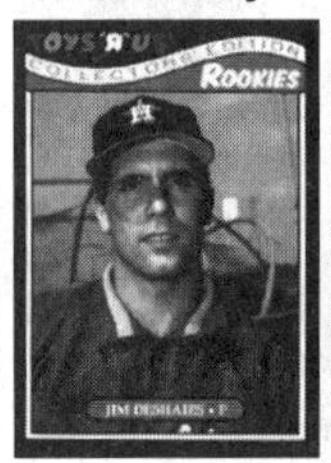

Topps produced this 33-card standard-size boxed set for Toys'R'Us stores. The set is subtitled "Baseball Rookies" and features predominantly younger players. The cards feature a high-gloss, full-color photo of the player inside a black border. The card backs are printed in orange and blue on white card stock. The set numbering is in alphabetical order by player's name.

	MINT	NRMT	EXC
COMPLETE SET (33)	7.50	3.40	.95
COMMON CARD (1-33)	.10	.05	.01
☐ 1 Andy Allanson	.10	.05	.01
☐ 2 Paul Assenmacher	.10	.05	.01
☐ 3 Scott Bailes	.10	.05	.01
☐ 4 Barry Bonds	2.00	.90	.25
☐ 5 Jose Canseco	.75	.35	.09
☐ 6 John Cerutti	.10	.05	.01
☐ 7 Will Clark	.75	.35	.09
☐ 8 Kal Daniels	.10	.05	.01
☐ 9 Jim Deshaies	.10	.05	.01
☐ 10 Mark Eichhorn	.10	.05	.01
☐ 11 Ed Hearn	.10	.05	.01
☐ 12 Pete Incaviglia	.20	.09	.03
☐ 13 Bo Jackson	.50	.23	.06
☐ 14 Wally Joyner	.30	.14	.04
☐ 15 Charlie Kerfeld	.10	.05	.01
☐ 16 Eric King	.10	.05	.01
☐ 17 John Kruk	.50	.23	.06
☐ 18 Barry Larkin	1.00	.45	.12
☐ 19 Mike LaValliere	.10	.05	.01
☐ 20 Greg Mathews	.10	.05	.01
☐ 21 Kevin Mitchell	.20	.09	.03
☐ 22 Dan Plesac	.10	.05	.01
☐ 23 Bruce Ruffin	.10	.05	.01
☐ 24 Ruben Sierra	.50	.23	.06
☐ 25 Cory Snyder	.10	.05	.01
☐ 26 Kurt Stillwell	.10	.05	.01
☐ 27 Dale Sveum	.10	.05	.01
☐ 28 Danny Tartabull	.20	.09	.03
☐ 29 Andres Thomas	.10	.05	.01
☐ 30 Robby Thompson	.20	.09	.03
☐ 31 Jim Traber	.10	.05	.01
☐ 32 Mitch Williams	.20	.09	.03
☐ 33 Todd Worrell	.20	.09	.03

1988 Toys'R'Us Rookies

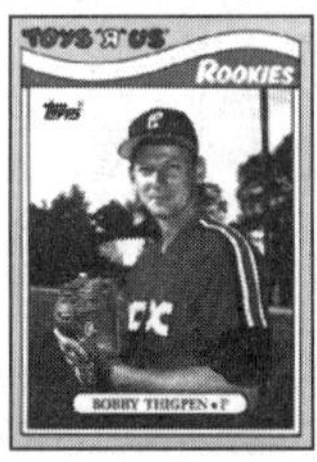

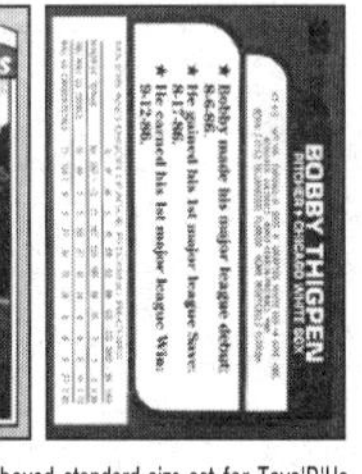

Topps produced this 33-card boxed standard-size set for Toys'R'Us stores. The set is subtitled "Baseball Rookies" and features predominantly younger players. The cards feature a high-gloss, full-color photo of the player inside a blue border. The card backs are printed in pink and blue on white card stock. The checklist for the set is found on the back panel of the small collector box. The statistics provided on the card backs cover only three lines, Minor League totals, last season, and Major League totals. The set numbering is in alphabetical order by player's name.

	MINT	NRMT	EXC
COMPLETE SET (33)	5.00	2.20	.60
COMMON CARD (1-33)	.10	.05	.01
☐ 1 Todd Benzinger	.10	.05	.01
☐ 2 Bob Brower	.10	.05	.01
☐ 3 Jerry Browne	.10	.05	.01
☐ 4 DeWayne Buice	.10	.05	.01
☐ 5 Ellis Burks	.50	.23	.06
☐ 6 Ken Caminiti	1.00	.45	.12
☐ 7 Casey Candaele	.10	.05	.01
☐ 8 Dave Cone	.50	.23	.06
☐ 9 Kelly Downs	.10	.05	.01
☐ 10 Mike Dunne	.10	.05	.01
☐ 11 Ken Gerhart	.10	.05	.01
☐ 12 Mike Greenwell	.20	.09	.03
☐ 13 Mike Henneman	.20	.09	.03
☐ 14 Sam Horn	.10	.05	.01
☐ 15 Joe Magrane	.10	.05	.01
☐ 16 Fred Manrique	.10	.05	.01
☐ 17 John Marzano	.10	.05	.01
☐ 18 Fred McGriff	1.00	.45	.12
☐ 19 Mark McGwire	1.00	.45	.12
☐ 20 Jeff Musselman	.10	.05	.01
☐ 21 Randy Myers	.20	.09	.03
☐ 22 Matt Nokes	.10	.05	.01
☐ 23 Al Pedrique	.10	.05	.01
☐ 24 Luis Polonia	.20	.09	.03
☐ 25 Billy Ripken	.10	.05	.01
☐ 26 Benito Santiago	.20	.09	.03
☐ 27 Kevin Seitzer	.20	.09	.03
☐ 28 John Smiley	.20	.09	.03
☐ 29 Mike Stanley	.20	.09	.03
☐ 30 Terry Steinbach	.30	.14	.04
☐ 31 B.J. Surhoff	.20	.09	.03
☐ 32 Bobby Thigpen	.10	.05	.01
☐ 33 Devon White	.30	.14	.04

1989 Toys'R'Us Rookies

The 1989 Toys'R'Us Rookies set contains 33 standard-size glossy cards. The fronts are yellow and magenta. The horizontally oriented backs are sky blue and red, and feature 1988 and career stats. The cards were distributed through Toys'R'Us stores as a boxed set. The subjects are numbered alphabetically. The set checklist is printed on the back panel of the set's custom box.

	MINT	NRMT	EXC
COMPLETE SET (33)	4.00	1.80	.50
COMMON CARD (1-33)	.10	.05	.01
☐ 1 Roberto Alomar	1.00	.45	.12
☐ 2 Brady Anderson	.60	.25	.07
☐ 3 Tim Belcher	.10	.05	.01
☐ 4 Damon Berryhill	.10	.05	.01
☐ 5 Jay Buhner	.60	.25	.07
☐ 6 Sherman Corbett	.10	.05	.01
☐ 7 Kevin Elster	.20	.09	.03
☐ 8 Cecil Espy	.10	.05	.01
☐ 9 Dave Gallagher	.10	.05	.01
☐ 10 Ron Gant	.40	.18	.05
☐ 11 Paul Gibson	.10	.05	.01
☐ 12 Mark Grace	.60	.25	.07
☐ 13 Bryan Harvey	.20	.09	.03
☐ 14 Darrin Jackson	.10	.05	.01
☐ 15 Gregg Jefferies	.40	.18	.05
☐ 16 Ron Jones	.10	.05	.01
☐ 17 Ricky Jordan	.10	.05	.01
☐ 18 Roberto Kelly	.20	.09	.03
☐ 19 Al Leiter	.20	.09	.03
☐ 20 Jack McDowell	.20	.09	.03
☐ 21 Melido Perez	.10	.05	.01
☐ 22 Jeff Pico	.10	.05	.01
☐ 23 Jody Reed	.10	.05	.01
☐ 24 Chris Sabo	.10	.05	.01
☐ 25 Nelson Santovenia	.10	.05	.01
☐ 26 Mackey Sasser	.10	.05	.01
☐ 27 Mike Schooler	.10	.05	.01
☐ 28 Gary Sheffield	.75	.35	.09
☐ 29 Pete Smith	.10	.05	.01
☐ 30 Pete Stanicek	.10	.05	.01
☐ 31 Jeff Treadway	.10	.05	.01
☐ 32 Walt Weiss	.20	.09	.03
☐ 33 Dave West	.10	.05	.01

1990 Toys'R'Us Rookies

The 1990 Toys'R'Us Rookies set is a 33-card standard-size set of young prospects issued by Topps. For the fourth consecutive year Topps issued a rookie set for Toys'R'Us. There are several players in the set which were on Topps cards for the second time in 1990, i.e., not rookies even for the Topps Company. These players included Gregg Jefferies and Gregg Olson. This set might be more appropriately called the Young Stars set. The cards are numbered, with the numbering being essentially in alphabetical order by player's name. The set checklist is printed on the back panel of the set's custom box.

	MINT	NRMT	EXC
COMPLETE SET (33)	6.00	2.70	.75
COMMON CARD (1-33)	.10	.05	.01
☐ 1 Jim Abbott	.20	.09	.03
☐ 2 Eric Anthony	.10	.05	.01
☐ 3 Joey Belle	1.00	.45	.12
☐ 4 Andy Benes	.30	.14	.04
☐ 5 Greg Briley	.10	.05	.01
☐ 6 Kevin Brown	.30	.14	.04
☐ 7 Mark Carreon	.10	.05	.01
☐ 8 Mike Devereaux	.20	.09	.03
☐ 9 Junior Felix	.10	.05	.01
☐ 10 Mark Gardner	.10	.05	.01
☐ 11 Bob Geren	.10	.05	.01
☐ 12 Tom Gordon	.20	.09	.03
☐ 13 Ken Griffey Jr.	2.00	.90	.25
☐ 14 Pete Harnisch	.20	.09	.03
☐ 15 Ken Hill	.30	.14	.04
☐ 16 Gregg Jefferies	.20	.09	.03
☐ 17 Derek Lilliquist	.10	.05	.01
☐ 18 Carlos Martinez	.10	.05	.01
☐ 19 Ramon Martinez	.30	.14	.04
☐ 20 Bob Milacki	.10	.05	.01
☐ 21 Gregg Olson	.10	.05	.01
☐ 22 Kenny Rogers	.20	.09	.03
☐ 23 Alex Sanchez	.10	.05	.01
☐ 24 Gary Sheffield	.60	.25	.07
☐ 25 Dwight Smith	.20	.09	.03
☐ 26 Billy Spiers	.10	.05	.01
☐ 27 Greg Vaughn	.30	.14	.04
☐ 28 Robin Ventura	.40	.18	.05
☐ 29 Jerome Walton	.10	.05	.01
☐ 30 Dave West	.10	.05	.01
☐ 31 John Wetteland	.30	.14	.04
☐ 32 Craig Worthington	.10	.05	.01
☐ 33 Todd Zeile	.20	.09	.03

1991 Toys'R'Us Rookies

For the fifth year in a row this 33-card standard-size set was produced by Topps for Toys'R'Us, and the sponsor's logo adorns the top of the card front. The front design features glossy color action player photos with yellow borders on a black card face. The words "Topps 1991 Collectors' Edition" appear in a yellow stripe above the picture. The horizontally oriented backs are printed in brown and yellow, and present biographical information, career highlights, and statistics.

	MINT	NRMT	EXC
COMPLETE SET (33)	7.00	3.10	.85
COMMON CARD (1-33)	.10	.05	.01
☐ 1 Sandy Alomar Jr.	.20	.09	.03
☐ 2 Kevin Appier	.30	.14	.04
☐ 3 Steve Avery	.40	.18	.05
☐ 4 Carlos Baerga	.40	.18	.05
☐ 5 Alex Cole	.10	.05	.01
☐ 6 Pat Combs	.10	.05	.01
☐ 7 Delino DeShields	.20	.09	.03
☐ 8 Travis Fryman	.60	.25	.07
☐ 9 Marquis Grissom	.60	.25	.07
☐ 10 Mike Harkey	.10	.05	.01
☐ 11 Glenallen Hill	.20	.09	.03
☐ 12 Jeff Huson	.10	.05	.01
☐ 13 Felix Jose	.10	.05	.01
☐ 14 Dave Justice	.60	.25	.07
☐ 15 Dana Kiecker	.10	.05	.01
☐ 16 Kevin Maas	.10	.05	.01
☐ 17 Ben McDonald	.20	.09	.03
☐ 18 Brian McRae	.20	.09	.03
☐ 19 Kent Mercker	.10	.05	.01
☐ 20 Hal Morris	.20	.09	.03
☐ 21 Chris Nabholz	.10	.05	.01
☐ 22 Tim Naehring	.20	.09	.03
☐ 23 Jose Offerman	.10	.05	.01
☐ 24 John Olerud	.20	.09	.03
☐ 25 Scott Radinsky	.20	.09	.03
☐ 26 Bill Sampen	.10	.05	.01
☐ 27 Frank Thomas	2.00	.90	.25
☐ 28 Randy Tomlin	.10	.05	.01
☐ 29 Greg Vaughn	.20	.09	.03
☐ 30 Robin Ventura	.30	.14	.04
☐ 31 Larry Walker	.30	.14	.04
☐ 32 Wally Whitehurst	.10	.05	.01
☐ 33 Todd Zeile	.20	.09	.03

1993 Toys'R'Us

This 100-card standard-size set produced by Topps Stadium Club for Toys'R'Us features 100 young stars, rookie stars, and future stars. The cards carry glossy, full-bleed color photos with the Toys'R'Us logo in an upper corner. In silver lettering on a blue bar near the bottom of the photo, are the words Future Star, Rookie Star, or Young Star. The player's name is printed on a red bar below. The horizontal backs display a player close-up superimposed on a blue sky with clouds background. Also included are player biography, statistics and some career highlights. The cards were distributed through Toys'R'Us in a molded plastic box designed to resemble a store. 7,500 cases of this product was produced.

	MINT	NRMT	EXC
COMPLETE SET (100)	10.00	4.50	1.25
COMMON CARD (1-100)	.05	.02	.01
☐ 1 Ken Griffey Jr.	2.00	.90	.25
☐ 2 Chad Curtis	.10	.05	.01
☐ 3 Mike Bordick	.05	.02	.01
☐ 4 Ryan Klesko	.40	.18	.05
☐ 5 Pat Listach	.05	.02	.01
☐ 6 Jim Bullinger	.05	.02	.01
☐ 7 Tim Laker	.05	.02	.01
☐ 8 Mike Devereaux	.05	.02	.01
☐ 9 Kevin Young	.05	.02	.01
☐ 10 John Valentin	.10	.05	.01
☐ 11 Pat Mahomes	.05	.02	.01
☐ 12 Todd Hundley	.10	.05	.01
☐ 13 Roberto Alomar	.50	.23	.06
☐ 14 David Justice	.25	.11	.03
☐ 15 Mike Perez	.05	.02	.01
☐ 16 Royce Clayton	.10	.05	.01
☐ 17 Ryan Thompson	.05	.02	.01
☐ 18 Dave Hollins	.05	.02	.01
☐ 19 Brien Taylor	.05	.02	.01
☐ 20 Melvin Nieves	.15	.07	.02
☐ 21 Rheal Cormier	.05	.02	.01
☐ 22 Mike Piazza	2.00	.90	.25
☐ 23 Larry Walker	.40	.18	.05
☐ 24 Tim Wakefield	.05	.02	.01
☐ 25 Tim Costo	.05	.02	.01
☐ 26 Pedro Munoz	.05	.02	.01
☐ 27 Reggie Sanders	.15	.07	.02
☐ 28 Arthur Rhodes	.05	.02	.01
☐ 29 Scott Cooper	.05	.02	.01
☐ 30 Marquis Grissom	.10	.05	.01
☐ 31 Dave Nilsson	.10	.05	.01
☐ 32 John Patterson	.05	.02	.01
☐ 33 Ivan Rodriguez	.50	.23	.06
☐ 34 Andy Stankiewicz	.05	.02	.01
☐ 35 Bret Boone	.10	.05	.01
☐ 36 Gerald Williams	.05	.02	.01
☐ 37 Mike Mussina	.30	.14	.04
☐ 38 Henry Rodriguez	.15	.07	.02
☐ 39 Chuck Knoblauch	.15	.07	.02
☐ 40 Bob Wickman	.05	.02	.01
☐ 41 Donovan Osborne	.05	.02	.01
☐ 42 Mike Timlin	.05	.02	.01
☐ 43 Damion Easley	.05	.02	.01
☐ 44 Pedro Astacio	.05	.02	.01
☐ 45 David Segui	.05	.02	.01
☐ 46 Willie Greene	.10	.05	.01
☐ 47 Mike Trombley	.05	.02	.01
☐ 48 Bernie Williams	.40	.18	.05
☐ 49 Eric Anthony	.05	.02	.01
☐ 50 Tim Naehring	.10	.05	.01
☐ 51 Carlos Baerga	.10	.05	.01
☐ 52 Brady Anderson	.15	.07	.02
☐ 53 Mo Vaughn	.50	.23	.06
☐ 54 Willie Banks	.05	.02	.01
☐ 55 Mark Wohlers	.10	.05	.01
☐ 56 Jeff Bagwell	.75	.35	.09
☐ 57 Frank Seminara	.05	.02	.01
☐ 58 Robin Ventura	.10	.05	.01
☐ 59 Alan Embree	.05	.02	.01
☐ 60 Rey Sanchez	.05	.02	.01
☐ 61 Delino DeShields	.05	.02	.01
☐ 62 Todd Van Poppel	.05	.02	.01
☐ 63 Eric Karros	.15	.07	.02
☐ 64 Gary Sheffield	.30	.14	.04
☐ 65 Dan Wilson	.10	.05	.01
☐ 66 Frank Thomas	2.00	.90	.25
☐ 67 Tim Salmon	.50	.23	.06
☐ 68 Dan Smith	.05	.02	.01
☐ 69 Kenny Lofton	.50	.23	.06
☐ 70 Carlos Garcia	.05	.02	.01
☐ 71 Scott Livingstone	.05	.02	.01
☐ 72 Sam Militello	.05	.02	.01
☐ 73 Juan Guzman	.10	.05	.01
☐ 74 Greg Colbrunn	.10	.05	.01
☐ 75 David Hulse	.05	.02	.01
☐ 76 Rusty Meacham	.05	.02	.01
☐ 77 Dave Fleming	.05	.02	.01
☐ 78 Rene Arocha	.05	.02	.01
☐ 79 Derrick May	.05	.02	.01
☐ 80 Cal Eldred	.05	.02	.01
☐ 81 Bernard Gilkey	.10	.05	.01
☐ 82 Deion Sanders	.15	.07	.02
☐ 83 Reggie Jefferson	.10	.05	.01
☐ 84 Jeff Kent	.10	.05	.01
☐ 85 Juan Gonzalez	1.00	.45	.12
☐ 86 Billy Ashley	.10	.05	.01
☐ 87 Travis Fryman	.10	.05	.01
☐ 88 Roberto Hernandez	.10	.05	.01
☐ 89 Hipolito Pichardo	.05	.02	.01
☐ 90 Wilfredo Cordero	.10	.05	.01
☐ 91 John Jaha	.15	.07	.02
☐ 92 Javier Lopez	.25	.11	.03
☐ 93 Derek Bell	.10	.05	.01
☐ 94 Jeff Juden	.05	.02	.01
☐ 95 Steve Avery	.15	.07	.02
☐ 96 Moises Alou	.10	.05	.01
☐ 97 Brian Jordan	.15	.07	.02
☐ 98 Brian Williams	.05	.02	.01
☐ 99 Bob Zupcic	.05	.02	.01
☐ 100 Ray Lankford	.10	.05	.01

1993 Toys'R'Us Master Photos

This 12-card set of Stadium Club Master Photos was a bonus insert in the 1993 Toys'R'Us 100-card factory set. The photo cards measure approximately 5" by 7" with wide white borders with an inner prismatic gold-foil border. An action photo of the player is below a large colorful Toys 'R' Us logo with the words "Master Photo." The backs are blank, except for copyright symbols, licensing information, and MLBPA logo. The cards are unnumbered and checklisted below in alphabetical order.

	MINT	NRMT	EXC
COMPLETE SET (12)	5.00	2.20	.60
COMMON CARD (1-12)	.10	.05	.01
☐ 1 Moises Alou	.15	.07	.02
☐ 2 Eric Anthony	.10	.05	.01
☐ 3 Carlos Baerga	.10	.05	.01
☐ 4 Willie Greene	.15	.07	.02
☐ 5 Ken Griffey Jr.	2.00	.90	.25
☐ 6 Marquis Grissom	.15	.07	.02
☐ 7 Chuck Knoblauch	.25	.11	.03
☐ 8 Scott Livingstone	.10	.05	.01
☐ 9 Sam Militello	.10	.05	.01
☐ 10 Ivan Rodriguez	.50	.23	.06
☐ 11 Gary Sheffield	.30	.14	.04
☐ 12 Frank Thomas	2.00	.90	.25

1969 Transogram

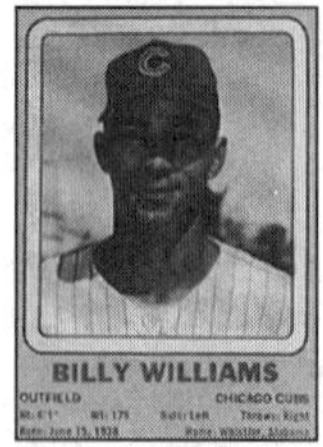

The cards in this 60-card set measure 2 1/2" by 3 1/2". This first Transogram set contains full color, blank backed cards which comprised the backs of boxes containing plastic player statues. The cards are slightly smaller than those of the 1970 set and the Callison photo is reversed. Complete boxes with cards are worth double the price listed below. The cards themselves are not numbered but have been alphabetized and numbered for reference below.

	NRMT	VG-E	GOOD
COMPLETE SET	1500.00	700.00	190.00
COMMON CARD	6.00	2.70	.75
☐ 1 Joe Azcue	6.00	2.70	.75
☐ 2 Willie Horton	7.50	3.40	.95
☐ 3 Luis Tiant	10.00	4.50	1.25
☐ 4 Denny McLain	10.00	4.50	1.25
☐ 5 Jose Cardenal	6.00	2.70	.75
☐ 6 Al Kaline	50.00	22.00	6.25
☐ 7 Tony Oliva	10.00	4.50	1.25
☐ 8 Blue Moon Odom	6.00	2.70	.75
☐ 9 Cesar Tovar	6.00	2.70	.75
☐ 10 Rick Monday	7.50	3.40	.95
☐ 11 Harmon Killebrew	40.00	18.00	5.00
☐ 12 Danny Cater	6.00	2.70	.75
☐ 13 Brooks Robinson	50.00	22.00	6.25
☐ 14 Jim Fregosi	10.00	4.50	1.25
☐ 15 Dave McNally	7.50	3.40	.95
☐ 16 Frank Robinson	50.00	22.00	6.25
☐ 17 Bobby Knoop	6.00	2.70	.75
☐ 18 Rick Reichardt	6.00	2.70	.75
☐ 19 Carl Yastrzemski	50.00	22.00	6.25
☐ 20 Pete Ward	6.00	2.70	.75
☐ 21 Rico Petrocelli	7.50	3.40	.95
☐ 22 Tommy John	10.00	4.50	1.25
☐ 23 Ken Harrelson	10.00	4.50	1.25
☐ 24 Luis Aparicio	30.00	13.50	3.70
☐ 25 Mike Epstein	6.00	2.70	.75
☐ 26 Roy White	7.50	3.40	.95
☐ 27 Camilo Pascual	7.50	3.40	.95
☐ 28 Mel Stottlemyre	7.50	3.40	.95
☐ 29 Frank Howard	10.00	4.50	1.25
☐ 30 Mickey Mantle	275.00	125.00	34.00
☐ 31 Lou Brock	40.00	18.00	5.00
☐ 32 Juan Marichal	40.00	18.00	5.00
☐ 33 Bob Gibson	40.00	18.00	5.00
☐ 34 Willie Mays	150.00	70.00	19.00
☐ 35 Tim McCarver	15.00	6.75	1.85
☐ 36 Willie McCovey	40.00	18.00	5.00
☐ 37 Don Wilson	6.00	2.70	.75
☐ 38 Billy Williams	30.00	13.50	3.70
☐ 39 Rusty Staub	10.00	4.50	1.25
☐ 40 Ernie Banks	50.00	22.00	6.25
☐ 41 Jim Wynn	7.50	3.40	.95
☐ 42 Ron Santo	10.00	4.50	1.25
☐ 43 Tom Haller	6.00	2.70	.75
☐ 44 Ron Swoboda	7.50	3.40	.95
☐ 45 Willie Davis	6.00	2.70	.75
☐ 46 Jerry Koosman	10.00	4.50	1.25
☐ 47 Jim Lefebvre	6.00	2.70	.75
☐ 48 Tom Seaver	75.00	34.00	9.50
☐ 49 Joe Torre	10.00	4.50	1.25
☐ 50 Tony Perez	15.00	6.75	1.85
☐ 51 Felipe Alou	10.00	4.50	1.25
☐ 52 Lee May	7.50	3.40	.95
☐ 53 Hank Aaron	125.00	55.00	15.50
☐ 54 Pete Rose	125.00	55.00	15.50
☐ 55 Cookie Rojas	6.00	2.70	.75
☐ 56 Bob Clemente	175.00	80.00	22.00
☐ 57 Richie Allen	15.00	6.75	1.85
☐ 58 Matty Alou	7.50	3.40	.95
☐ 59 John Callison	7.50	3.40	.95
☐ 60 Bill Mazeroski	15.00	6.75	1.85

1970 Transogram

The cards in this 30-card set measure 2 9/16" by 3 1/2". Blank backed and unnumbered, these 1970 Transogram cards are very similar to those of the preceding year. They were issued in panels of three as the back portion of boxes containing three small plastic statues of ballplayers. The pictures, with the exception of Torre and a corrected Callison, are identical to the 1969 set. They are, however, 1/16" wider than the 1969 cards. The checklist shows the panel combinations and is numbered according to "series" numbers located on each box. Complete panels of three have a value of 50 percent more than the sum of the individual cards on the panel. Complete box prices would be double the sum of the listed prices.

	NRMT	VG-E	GOOD
COMPLETE INDIV. SET	1000.00	450.00	125.00
COMMON CARD	6.00	2.70	.75
☐ 1A Pete Rose	100.00	45.00	12.50
☐ 1B Willie Mays	125.00	55.00	15.50
☐ 1C Cleon Jones	6.00	2.70	.75
☐ 2A Ron Santo	10.00	4.50	1.25
☐ 2B Willie Davis	7.50	3.40	.95
☐ 2C Willie McCovey	30.00	13.50	3.70
☐ 3A Juan Marichal	30.00	13.50	3.70
☐ 3B Joe Torre	10.00	4.50	1.25
☐ 3C Ernie Banks	50.00	22.00	6.25
☐ 4A Hank Aaron	100.00	45.00	12.50
☐ 4B Jim Wynn	7.50	3.40	.95
☐ 4C Tom Seaver	75.00	34.00	9.50
☐ 5A Bob Gibson	30.00	13.50	3.70
☐ 5B Roberto Clemente	175.00	80.00	22.00
☐ 5C Jerry Koosman	10.00	4.50	1.25
☐ 11A Denny McLain	10.00	4.50	1.25
☐ 11B Reggie Jackson	100.00	45.00	12.50
☐ 11C Boog Powell	10.00	4.50	1.25
☐ 12A Frank Robinson	50.00	22.00	6.25
☐ 12B Frank Howard	10.00	4.50	1.25
☐ 12C Rick Reichardt	6.00	2.70	.75

Card			
☐ 13A Carl Yastrzemski	50.00	22.00	6.25
☐ 13B Tony Oliva	10.00	4.50	1.25
☐ 13C Mel Stottlemyre	7.50	3.40	.95
☐ 14A Al Kaline	50.00	22.00	6.25
☐ 14B Jim Fregosi	10.00	4.50	1.25
☐ 14C Sam McDowell	7.50	3.40	.95
☐ 15A Blue Moon Odom	6.00	2.70	.75
☐ 15B Harmon Killebrew	40.00	18.00	5.00
☐ 15C Rico Petrocelli	7.50	3.40	.95

1992 Triple Play Previews

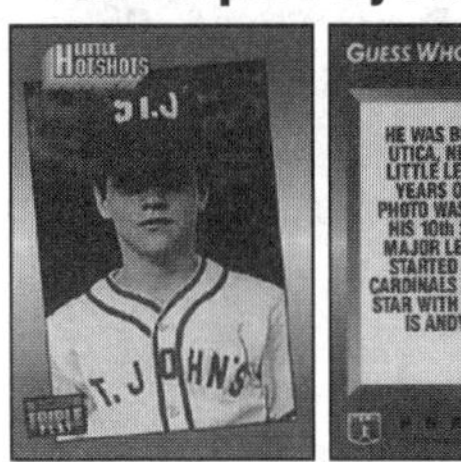

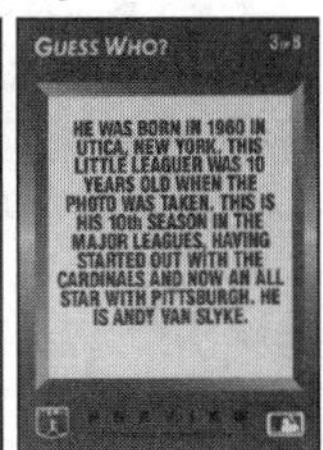

This eight-card standard-size set was issued by Donruss to preview the design of the 264-card 1992 Donruss Triple Play set. The front design and player photos are identical to those in the regular issue set; the only difference is the numbering and the word "preview" appearing across the bottom of the backs.

	MINT	NRMT	EXC
COMPLETE SET (8)	200.00	90.00	25.00
COMMON CARD (1-8)	5.00	2.20	.60
☐ 1 Ken Griffey Jr.	70.00	32.00	8.75
☐ 2 Darryl Strawberry	8.00	3.60	1.00
☐ 3 Andy Van Slyke	8.00	3.60	1.00
☐ 4 Don Mattingly	35.00	16.00	4.40
☐ 5 Gary Carter	5.00	2.20	.60
Steve Finley			
Awesome Action			
☐ 6 Frank Thomas	70.00	32.00	8.75
☐ 7 Kirby Puckett	40.00	18.00	5.00
☐ 8 David Cone	5.00	2.20	.60
John Franco			
Jeff Innis			
Fun at the Ballpark			

1992 Triple Play

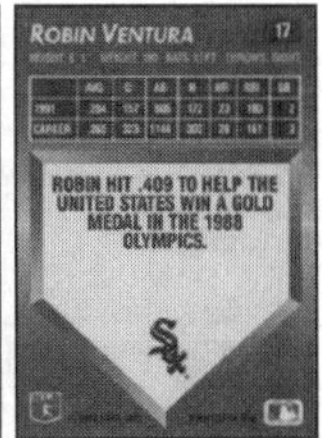

The 1992 Triple Play set contains 264 standard-size cards. Cards were distributed in 15-card foil packs and jumbo packs. Each 15-card foil pack came with one rub off game card. The Triple Play set was created especially for children ages 5-12, featuring bright color borders, player quotes, fun facts.The color action player photos on the fronts are slightly tilted to the left, and the border alternates shades from red to yellow and back to red again as one moves down the card face. Subsets include Little Hotshots (picturing some players when they were kids) and Awesome Action.

	MINT	NRMT	EXC
COMPLETE SET (264)	10.00	4.50	1.25
COMMON CARD (1-264)	.05	.02	.01
☐ 1 SkyDome	.10	.05	.01
☐ 2 Tom Foley	.05	.02	.01
☐ 3 Scott Erickson	.10	.05	.01
☐ 4 Matt Williams	.15	.07	.02
☐ 5 David Valle	.05	.02	.01
☐ 6 Andy Van Slyke LH	.05	.02	.01
☐ 7 Tom Glavine	.15	.07	.02
☐ 8 Kevin Appier	.10	.05	.01
☐ 9 Pedro Guerrero	.05	.02	.01
☐ 10 Terry Steinbach	.10	.05	.01
☐ 11 Terry Mulholland	.05	.02	.01
☐ 12 Mike Boddicker	.05	.02	.01
☐ 13 Gregg Olson	.05	.02	.01
☐ 14 Tim Burke	.05	.02	.01
☐ 15 Candy Maldonado	.05	.02	.01
☐ 16 Orlando Merced	.05	.02	.01
☐ 17 Robin Ventura	.10	.05	.01
☐ 18 Eric Anthony	.05	.02	.01
☐ 19 Greg Maddux	.75	.35	.09
☐ 20 Erik Hanson	.05	.02	.01
☐ 21 Bobby Ojeda	.05	.02	.01
☐ 22 Nolan Ryan	.75	.35	.09
☐ 23 Dave Righetti	.05	.02	.01
☐ 24 Reggie Jefferson	.10	.05	.01
☐ 25 Jody Reed	.05	.02	.01
☐ 26 Steve Finley and	.10	.05	.01
Gary Carter AA			
☐ 27 Chili Davis	.10	.05	.01
☐ 28 Hector Villanueva	.05	.02	.01
☐ 29 Cecil Fielder	.10	.05	.01
☐ 30 Hal Morris	.05	.02	.01
☐ 31 Barry Larkin	.15	.07	.02
☐ 32 Bobby Thigpen	.05	.02	.01
☐ 33 Andy Benes	.10	.05	.01
☐ 34 Harold Baines	.10	.05	.01
☐ 35 David Cone	.10	.05	.01
☐ 36 Mark Langston	.10	.05	.01
☐ 37 Bryan Harvey	.05	.02	.01
☐ 38 John Kruk	.10	.05	.01
☐ 39 Scott Sanderson	.05	.02	.01
☐ 40 Lonnie Smith	.05	.02	.01
☐ 41 Rex Hudler AA	.05	.02	.01
☐ 42 George Bell	.05	.02	.01
☐ 43 Steve Finley	.10	.05	.01
☐ 44 Mickey Tettleton	.05	.02	.01
☐ 45 Robby Thompson	.05	.02	.01
☐ 46 Pat Kelly	.05	.02	.01
☐ 47 Marquis Grissom	.10	.05	.01
☐ 48 Tony Pena	.05	.02	.01
☐ 49 Alex Cole	.05	.02	.01
☐ 50 Steve Buechele	.05	.02	.01
☐ 51 Ivan Rodriguez	.40	.18	.05
☐ 52 John Smiley	.05	.02	.01
☐ 53 Gary Sheffield	.15	.07	.02
☐ 54 Greg Olson	.05	.02	.01
☐ 55 Ramon Martinez	.10	.05	.01
☐ 56 B.J. Surhoff	.10	.05	.01
☐ 57 Bruce Hurst	.05	.02	.01
☐ 58 Todd Stottlemyre	.10	.05	.01
☐ 59 Brett Butler	.10	.05	.01
☐ 60 Glenn Davis	.05	.02	.01
☐ 61 Glenn Braggs and	.05	.02	.01
Kirt Manwaring AA			
☐ 62 Lee Smith	.10	.05	.01
☐ 63 Rickey Henderson	.15	.07	.02
☐ 64 Fun at the Ballpark	.10	.05	.01
Dave Cone			
Jeff Innis			
John Franco			
☐ 65 Rick Aguilera	.05	.02	.01
☐ 66 Kevin Elster	.05	.02	.01
☐ 67 Dwight Evans	.10	.05	.01
☐ 68 Andujar Cedeno	.05	.02	.01
☐ 69 Brian McRae	.10	.05	.01
☐ 70 Benito Santiago	.05	.02	.01
☐ 71 Randy Johnson	.15	.07	.02
☐ 72 Roberto Kelly	.05	.02	.01
☐ 73 Juan Samuel AA	.05	.02	.01
☐ 74 Alex Fernandez	.15	.07	.02
☐ 75 Felix Jose	.05	.02	.01
☐ 76 Brian Harper	.05	.02	.01
☐ 77 Scott Sanderson LH	.05	.02	.01
☐ 78 Ken Caminiti	.15	.07	.02
☐ 79 Mo Vaughn	.40	.18	.05
☐ 80 Roger McDowell	.05	.02	.01
☐ 81 Robin Yount	.15	.07	.02
☐ 82 Dave Magadan	.05	.02	.01
☐ 83 Julio Franco	.10	.05	.01
☐ 84 Roberto Alomar	.20	.09	.03
☐ 85 Steve Avery	.10	.05	.01
☐ 86 Travis Fryman	.15	.07	.02
☐ 87 Fred McGriff	.15	.07	.02
☐ 88 Dave Stewart	.10	.05	.01
☐ 89 Larry Walker	.15	.07	.02
☐ 90 Chris Sabo	.05	.02	.01
☐ 91 Chuck Finley	.05	.02	.01
☐ 92 Dennis Martinez	.10	.05	.01
☐ 93 Jeff Johnson	.05	.02	.01
☐ 94 Len Dykstra	.10	.05	.01
☐ 95 Mark Whiten	.10	.05	.01
☐ 96 Wade Taylor	.05	.02	.01
☐ 97 Lance Dickson	.05	.02	.01
☐ 98 Kevin Tapani	.05	.02	.01
☐ 99 Luis Polonia and	.05	.02	.01
Tony Phillips AA			
☐ 100 Milt Cuyler	.05	.02	.01
☐ 101 Willie McGee	.05	.02	.01
☐ 102 Tony Fernandez AA	.05	.02	.01
☐ 103 Albert Belle	.50	.23	.06
☐ 104 Todd Hundley	.10	.05	.01
☐ 105 Ben McDonald	.05	.02	.01
☐ 106 Doug Drabek	.05	.02	.01
☐ 107 Tim Raines	.15	.07	.02
☐ 108 Joe Carter	.10	.05	.01
☐ 109 Reggie Sanders	.15	.07	.02
☐ 110 John Olerud	.10	.05	.01
☐ 111 Darren Lewis	.05	.02	.01
☐ 112 Juan Gonzalez	.60	.25	.07
☐ 113 Andre Dawson AA	.10	.05	.01
☐ 114 Mark Grace	.15	.07	.02
☐ 115 George Brett	.40	.18	.05
☐ 116 Barry Bonds	.25	.11	.03
☐ 117 Lou Whitaker	.10	.05	.01
☐ 118 Jose Oquendo	.05	.02	.01
☐ 119 Lee Stevens	.05	.02	.01
☐ 120 Phil Plantier	.10	.05	.01
☐ 121 Matt Merullo AA	.05	.02	.01
☐ 122 Greg Vaughn	.10	.05	.01
☐ 123 Royce Clayton	.10	.05	.01
☐ 124 Bob Welch	.05	.02	.01
☐ 125 Juan Samuel	.05	.02	.01
☐ 126 Ron Gant	.10	.05	.01
☐ 127 Edgar Martinez	.10	.05	.01
☐ 128 Andy Ashby	.10	.05	.01
☐ 129 Jack McDowell	.10	.05	.01
☐ 130 Dave Henderson and	.05	.02	.01
Jerry Browne AA			
☐ 131 Leo Gomez	.05	.02	.01
☐ 132 Checklist 1-88	.05	.02	.01
☐ 133 Phillie Phanatic	.15	.07	.02
☐ 134 Bret Barberie	.05	.02	.01
☐ 135 Kent Hrbek	.10	.05	.01
☐ 136 Hall of Fame	.10	.05	.01
☐ 137 Omar Vizquel	.10	.05	.01
☐ 138 The Famous Chicken	.15	.07	.02
☐ 139 Terry Pendleton	.10	.05	.01
☐ 140 Jim Eisenreich	.05	.02	.01
☐ 141 Todd Zeile	.05	.02	.01
☐ 142 Todd Van Poppel	.05	.02	.01
☐ 143 Darren Daulton	.10	.05	.01
☐ 144 Mike Macfarlane	.05	.02	.01
☐ 145 Luis Mercedes	.05	.02	.01
☐ 146 Trevor Wilson	.05	.02	.01
☐ 147 Dave Stieb	.05	.02	.01
☐ 148 Andy Van Slyke	.10	.05	.01
☐ 149 Carlton Fisk	.15	.07	.02
☐ 150 Craig Biggio	.10	.05	.01
☐ 151 Joe Girardi	.05	.02	.01
☐ 152 Ken Griffey Jr.	1.50	.70	.19
☐ 153 Jose Offerman	.05	.02	.01
☐ 154 Bobby Witt	.05	.02	.01
☐ 155 Will Clark	.15	.07	.02
☐ 156 Steve Olin	.05	.02	.01
☐ 157 Greg W. Harris	.05	.02	.01
☐ 158 Dale Murphy LH	.15	.07	.02
☐ 159 Don Mattingly	.50	.23	.06
☐ 160 Shawon Dunston	.05	.02	.01
☐ 161 Bill Gullickson	.05	.02	.01
☐ 162 Paul O'Neill	.10	.05	.01
☐ 163 Norm Charlton	.05	.02	.01
☐ 164 Bo Jackson	.10	.05	.01
☐ 165 Tony Fernandez	.05	.02	.01
☐ 166 Dave Henderson	.05	.02	.01
☐ 167 Dwight Gooden	.10	.05	.01
☐ 168 Junior Felix	.05	.02	.01
☐ 169 Lance Parrish	.05	.02	.01
☐ 170 Pat Combs	.05	.02	.01
☐ 171 Chuck Knoblauch	.15	.07	.02
☐ 172 John Smoltz	.15	.07	.02
☐ 173 Wrigley Field	.10	.05	.01
☐ 174 Andre Dawson	.10	.05	.01
☐ 175 Pete Harnisch	.05	.02	.01
☐ 176 Alan Trammell	.10	.05	.01
☐ 177 Kirk Dressendorfer	.05	.02	.01
☐ 178 Matt Nokes	.05	.02	.01
☐ 179 Wil Cordero	.10	.05	.01
☐ 180 Scott Cooper	.05	.02	.01
☐ 181 Glenallen Hill	.05	.02	.01
☐ 182 John Franco	.05	.02	.01
☐ 183 Rafael Palmeiro	.15	.07	.02
☐ 184 Jay Bell	.10	.05	.01
☐ 185 Bill Wegman	.05	.02	.01
☐ 186 Deion Sanders	.15	.07	.02
☐ 187 Darryl Strawberry	.10	.05	.01
☐ 188 Jaime Navarro	.05	.02	.01
☐ 189 Darrin Jackson	.05	.02	.01
☐ 190 Eddie Zosky	.05	.02	.01
☐ 191 Mike Scioscia	.05	.02	.01
☐ 192 Chito Martinez	.05	.02	.01
☐ 193 Pat Kelly and	.05	.02	.01
Ron Tingley AA			
☐ 194 Ray Lankford	.15	.07	.02
☐ 195 Dennis Eckersley	.10	.05	.01
☐ 196 Ivan Calderon and	.05	.02	.01
Mike Maddux AA			
☐ 197 Shane Mack	.05	.02	.01
☐ 198 Checklist 89-176	.05	.02	.01
☐ 199 Cal Ripken	.75	.35	.09
☐ 200 Jeff Bagwell	.60	.25	.07
☐ 201 Dave Howard	.05	.02	.01
☐ 202 Kirby Puckett	.40	.18	.05
☐ 203 Harold Reynolds	.05	.02	.01
☐ 204 Jim Abbott	.05	.02	.01
☐ 205 Mark Lewis	.05	.02	.01
☐ 206 Frank Thomas	1.50	.70	.19
☐ 207 Rex Hudler	.05	.02	.01
☐ 208 Vince Coleman	.05	.02	.01
☐ 209 Delino DeShields	.05	.02	.01
☐ 210 Luis Gonzalez	.10	.05	.01
☐ 211 Wade Boggs	.15	.07	.02
☐ 212 Orel Hershiser	.10	.05	.01
☐ 213 Cal Eldred	.05	.02	.01
☐ 214 Jose Canseco	.15	.07	.02
☐ 215 Jose Guzman	.05	.02	.01
☐ 216 Roger Clemens	.20	.09	.03
☐ 217 David Justice	.15	.07	.02
☐ 218 Tony Phillips	.10	.05	.01
☐ 219 Tony Gwynn	.40	.18	.05
☐ 220 Mitch Williams	.05	.02	.01
☐ 221 Bill Sampen	.05	.02	.01
☐ 222 Billy Hatcher	.05	.02	.01
☐ 223 Gary Gaetti	.10	.05	.01
☐ 224 Tim Wallach	.05	.02	.01
☐ 225 Kevin Maas	.05	.02	.01
☐ 226 Kevin Brown	.10	.05	.01
☐ 227 Sandy Alomar Jr.	.10	.05	.01
☐ 228 John Habyan	.05	.02	.01
☐ 229 Ryne Sandberg	.25	.11	.03
☐ 230 Greg Gagne	.05	.02	.01
☐ 231 Autographs	.15	.07	.02
(Mark McGwire)			
☐ 232 Mike LaValliere	.05	.02	.01
☐ 233 Mark Gubicza	.05	.02	.01
☐ 234 Lance Parrish LH	.05	.02	.01
☐ 235 Carlos Baerga	.10	.05	.01
☐ 236 Howard Johnson	.05	.02	.01
☐ 237 Mike Mussina	.30	.14	.04
☐ 238 Ruben Sierra	.10	.05	.01
☐ 239 Lance Johnson	.10	.05	.01
☐ 240 Devon White	.10	.05	.01
☐ 241 Dan Wilson	.10	.05	.01
☐ 242 Kelly Gruber	.05	.02	.01
☐ 243 Brett Butler LH	.05	.02	.01
☐ 244 Ozzie Smith	.25	.11	.03
☐ 245 Chuck McElroy	.05	.02	.01
☐ 246 Shawn Boskie	.05	.02	.01
☐ 247 Mark Davis	.05	.02	.01
☐ 248 Bill Landrum	.05	.02	.01
☐ 249 Frank Tanana	.05	.02	.01
☐ 250 Darryl Hamilton	.05	.02	.01
☐ 251 Gary DiSarcina	.05	.02	.01
☐ 252 Mike Greenwell	.05	.02	.01
☐ 253 Cal Ripken LH	.40	.18	.05
☐ 254 Paul Molitor	.20	.09	.03
☐ 255 Tim Teufel	.05	.02	.01
☐ 256 Chris Hoiles	.05	.02	.01
☐ 257 Rob Dibble	.05	.02	.01
☐ 258 Sid Bream	.05	.02	.01
☐ 259 Tino Martinez	.10	.05	.01
☐ 260 Dale Murphy	.15	.07	.02
☐ 261 Greg Hibbard	.05	.02	.01
☐ 262 Mark McGwire	.30	.14	.04
☐ 263 Oriole Park	.10	.05	.01
☐ 264 Checklist 177-264	.05	.02	.01

1992 Triple Play Gallery

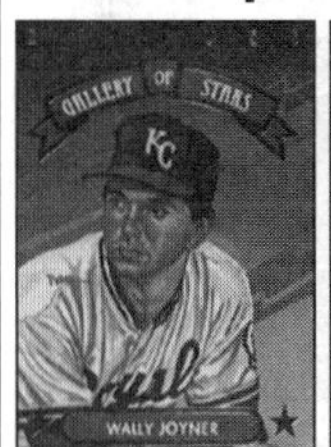

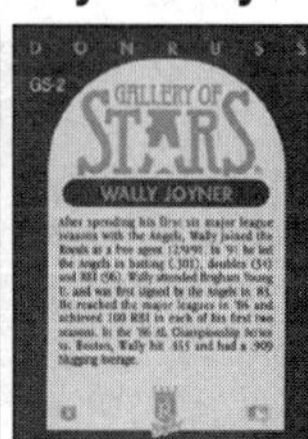

The 1992 Triple Play Gallery of Stars was an insert to the 1992 Triple Play baseball set. Randomly inserted into foil packs, the first six cards feature top players who changed teams in 1992 in their new uniforms. The second six cards were inserted one per jumbo pack. Each group of six cards is sequenced in alphabetical order. On bright-colored backgrounds, the fronts display color player portraits by noted sports artist Dick Perez. The words "Gallery of Stars" appear in a red and silver-foil stamped banner above the portrait, while the player's name appears in a similarly colored bar between two silver foil stars at the card bottom.

	MINT	NRMT	EXC
COMPLETE SET (12)	20.00	9.00	2.50
COMPLETE FOIL SET (6)	2.50	1.10	.30
COMPLETE JUMBO SET (6)	18.00	8.00	2.20
COMMON CARD (GS1-GS6)	.50	.23	.06
COMMON CARD (GS7-GS12)	1.00	.45	.12
☐ GS1 Bobby Bonilla	.50	.23	.06
☐ GS2 Wally Joyner	.50	.23	.06
☐ GS3 Jack Morris	.50	.23	.06
☐ GS4 Steve Sax	.50	.23	.06
☐ GS5 Danny Tartabull	.50	.23	.06
☐ GS6 Frank Viola	.50	.23	.06
☐ GS7 Jeff Bagwell	4.00	1.80	.50
☐ GS8 Ken Griffey Jr.	6.00	2.70	.75
☐ GS9 Dave Justice	1.00	.45	.12
☐ GS10 Ryan Klesko	3.00	1.35	.35
☐ GS11 Cal Ripken	5.00	2.20	.60
☐ GS12 Frank Thomas	6.00	2.70	.75

1993 Triple Play Previews

This 12-card set was issued by Donruss to preview the design of the 264-card 1993 Donruss Triple Play set. The front design and player photos are identical to those in the regular issue with the exception of the word "Preview" printed on the card.

	MINT	NRMT	EXC
COMPLETE SET (12)	100.00	45.00	12.50
COMMON CARD (1-12)	1.00	.45	.12
☐ 1 Ken Griffey Jr.	50.00	22.00	6.25
☐ 2 Roberto Alomar	10.00	4.50	1.25
☐ 3 Cal Ripken	40.00	18.00	5.00
☐ 4 Eric Karros	4.00	1.80	.50
☐ 5 Cecil Fielder	2.00	.90	.25
☐ 6 Gary Sheffield	5.00	2.20	.60
☐ 7 Darren Daulton	2.00	.90	.25
☐ 8 Andy Van Slyke	1.00	.45	.12
☐ 9 Dennis Eckersley	2.00	.90	.25
☐ 10 Ryne Sandberg	12.50	5.50	1.55

	MINT	NRMT	EXC
☐ 11 Mark Grace	5.00	2.20	.60
☐ 12 David Segui Luis Polonia Awesome Action	1.00	.45	.12

1993 Triple Play

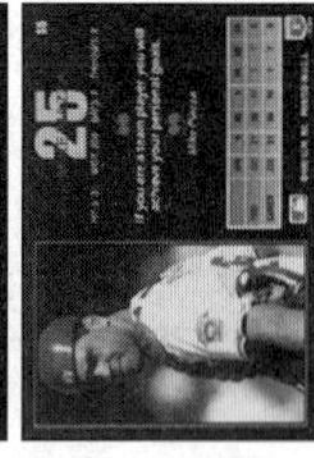

The 1993 Donruss Triple Play baseball set consists of 264 standard-size cards. Approximately eight players from each of the 28 teams is represented in the set. Each pack also included one of thirty Triple Play Action Baseball game cards. The fronts display color action player photos inside a red frame on a black card face. The player's last name appears in silver block lettering across the top of the picture. The team logo is placed at the lower right corner. The horizontal backs feature a color close-up photo, biography, and either trivia questions, fun facts, or player quotes. Scattered throughout the set are seven Little Hotshot (11, 77, 97, 143, 209, 229, 245) and eight Awesome Action (12, 61, 64, 68, 144, 193, 196, 200) cards. There are no key Rookie Cards in this set, however the set does feature the first card of President Bill Clinton.

	MINT	NRMT	EXC
COMPLETE SET (264)	10.00	4.50	1.25
COMMON CARD (1-264)	.05	.02	.01
☐ 1 Ken Griffey Jr.	2.00	.90	.25
☐ 2 Roberto Alomar	.40	.18	.05
☐ 3 Cal Ripken	1.50	.70	.19
☐ 4 Eric Karros	.30	.14	.04
☐ 5 Cecil Fielder	.15	.07	.02
☐ 6 Gary Sheffield	.30	.14	.04
☐ 7 Darren Daulton	.15	.07	.02
☐ 8 Andy Van Slyke	.15	.07	.02
☐ 9 Dennis Eckersley	.15	.07	.02
☐ 10 Ryne Sandberg	.50	.23	.06
☐ 11 Mark Grace LH	.30	.14	.04
☐ 12 David Segui and Luis Polonia AA	.05	.02	.01
☐ 13 Mike Mussina	.40	.18	.05
☐ 14 Vince Coleman	.05	.02	.01
☐ 15 Rafael Belliard	.05	.02	.01
☐ 16 Ivan Rodriguez	.50	.23	.06
☐ 17 Eddie Taubensee	.05	.02	.01
☐ 18 Cal Eldred	.05	.02	.01
☐ 19 Rick Wilkins	.05	.02	.01
☐ 20 Edgar Martinez	.15	.07	.02
☐ 21 Brian McRae	.15	.07	.02
☐ 22 Darren Holmes	.05	.02	.01
☐ 23 Mark Whiten	.05	.02	.01
☐ 24 Todd Zeile	.05	.02	.01
☐ 25 Scott Cooper	.05	.02	.01
☐ 26 Frank Thomas	2.00	.90	.25
☐ 27 Wil Cordero	.15	.07	.02
☐ 28 Juan Guzman	.15	.07	.02
☐ 29 Pedro Astacio	.05	.02	.01
☐ 30 Steve Avery	.15	.07	.02
☐ 31 Barry Larkin	.30	.14	.04
☐ 32 Bill Clinton	1.00	.45	.12
☐ 33 Scott Erickson	.05	.02	.01
☐ 34 Mike Devereaux	.05	.02	.01
☐ 35 Tino Martinez	.15	.07	.02
☐ 36 Brent Mayne	.05	.02	.01
☐ 37 Tim Salmon	.50	.23	.06
☐ 38 Dave Hollins	.05	.02	.01
☐ 39 Royce Clayton	.15	.07	.02
☐ 40 Shawon Dunston	.05	.02	.01
☐ 41 Eddie Murray	.50	.23	.06
☐ 42 Larry Walker	.30	.14	.04
☐ 43 Jeff Bagwell	.75	.35	.09
☐ 44 Milt Cuyler	.05	.02	.01
☐ 45 Mike Bordick	.05	.02	.01
☐ 46 Mike Greenwell	.05	.02	.01
☐ 47 Steve Sax	.05	.02	.01
☐ 48 Chuck Knoblauch	.30	.14	.04
☐ 49 Charles Nagy	.15	.07	.02
☐ 50 Tim Wakefield	.15	.07	.02
☐ 51 Tony Gwynn	.75	.35	.09
☐ 52 Rob Dibble	.05	.02	.01
☐ 53 Mickey Morandini	.05	.02	.01
☐ 54 Steve Hosey	.05	.02	.01
☐ 55 Mike Piazza	2.00	.90	.25
☐ 56 Bill Wegman	.05	.02	.01
☐ 57 Kevin Maas	.05	.02	.01
☐ 58 Gary DiSarcina	.05	.02	.01
☐ 59 Travis Fryman	.15	.07	.02
☐ 60 Ruben Sierra	.15	.07	.02
☐ 61 Ken Caminiti AA	.30	.14	.04
☐ 62 Brian Jordan	.30	.14	.04
☐ 63 Scott Chiamparino	.05	.02	.01
☐ 64 George Brett and Mike Bordick AA	.40	.18	.05
☐ 65 Carlos Garcia	.05	.02	.01
☐ 66 Checklist	.05	.02	.01
☐ 67 John Smoltz	.30	.14	.04
☐ 68 Mark McGwire and Brian Harper AA	.30	.14	.04
☐ 69 Kurt Stillwell	.05	.02	.01
☐ 70 Chad Curtis	.15	.07	.02
☐ 71 Rafael Palmeiro	.30	.14	.04
☐ 72 Kevin Young	.05	.02	.01
☐ 73 Glenn Davis	.05	.02	.01
☐ 74 Dennis Martinez	.15	.07	.02
☐ 75 Sam Militello	.05	.02	.01
☐ 76 Mike Morgan	.05	.02	.01
☐ 77 Frank Thomas LH	1.00	.45	.12
☐ 78 Staying Fit	.05	.02	.01
☐ 79 Steve Buechele	.05	.02	.01
☐ 80 Carlos Baerga	.15	.07	.02
☐ 81 Robby Thompson	.05	.02	.01
☐ 82 Kirk McCaskill	.05	.02	.01
☐ 83 Lee Smith	.15	.07	.02
☐ 84 Gary Scott	.05	.02	.01
☐ 85 Tony Pena	.05	.02	.01
☐ 86 Howard Johnson	.05	.02	.01
☐ 87 Mark McGwire	.60	.25	.07
☐ 88 Bip Roberts	.05	.02	.01
☐ 89 Devon White	.05	.02	.01
☐ 90 John Franco	.05	.02	.01
☐ 91 Tom Browning	.05	.02	.01
☐ 92 Mickey Tettleton	.05	.02	.01
☐ 93 Jeff Conine	.15	.07	.02
☐ 94 Albert Belle	.75	.35	.09
☐ 95 Fred McGriff	.30	.14	.04
☐ 96 Nolan Ryan	1.50	.70	.19
☐ 97 Paul Molitor LH	.15	.07	.02
☐ 98 Juan Bell	.05	.02	.01
☐ 99 Dave Fleming	.05	.02	.01
☐ 100 Craig Biggio	.15	.07	.02
☐ 101A Andy Stankiewicz ERR (Name on front in white)	.15	.07	.02
☐ 101B Andy Stankiewicz ERR (Name on front in red)	.15	.07	.02
☐ 102 Delino DeShields	.05	.02	.01
☐ 103 Damion Easley	.05	.02	.01
☐ 104 Kevin McReynolds	.05	.02	.01
☐ 105 David Nied	.05	.02	.01
☐ 106 Rick Sutcliffe	.05	.02	.01
☐ 107 Will Clark	.30	.14	.04
☐ 108 Tim Raines	.30	.14	.04
☐ 109 Eric Anthony	.05	.02	.01
☐ 110 Mike LaValliere	.05	.02	.01
☐ 111 Dean Palmer	.15	.07	.02
☐ 112 Eric Davis	.15	.07	.02
☐ 113 Damon Berryhill	.05	.02	.01
☐ 114 Felix Jose	.05	.02	.01
☐ 115 Ozzie Guillen	.05	.02	.01
☐ 116 Pat Listach	.05	.02	.01
☐ 117 Tom Glavine	.30	.14	.04
☐ 118 Roger Clemens	.40	.18	.05
☐ 119 Dave Henderson	.05	.02	.01
☐ 120 Don Mattingly	1.00	.45	.12
☐ 121 Orel Hershiser	.15	.07	.02
☐ 122 Ozzie Smith	.50	.23	.06
☐ 123 Joe Carter	.15	.07	.02
☐ 124 Bret Saberhagen	.15	.07	.02
☐ 125 Mitch Williams	.05	.02	.01
☐ 126 Jerald Clark	.05	.02	.01
☐ 127 Mile High Stadium	.15	.07	.02
☐ 128 Kent Hrbek	.15	.07	.02
☐ 129 Equipment Curt Schilling	.05	.02	.01
☐ 130 Gregg Jefferies	.15	.07	.02
☐ 131 John Orton	.05	.02	.01
☐ 132 Checklist	.05	.02	.01
☐ 133 Bret Boone	.15	.07	.02
☐ 134 Pat Borders	.05	.02	.01
☐ 135 Gregg Olson	.05	.02	.01
☐ 136 Brett Butler	.15	.07	.02
☐ 137 Rob Deer	.05	.02	.01
☐ 138 Darrin Jackson	.05	.02	.01
☐ 139 John Kruk	.15	.07	.02
☐ 140 Jay Bell	.15	.07	.02
☐ 141 Bobby Witt	.05	.02	.01
☐ 142 Dan Plesac Randy Myers Jose Guzman New Cubs	.05	.02	.01
☐ 143 Wade Boggs LH	.30	.14	.04
☐ 144 Ken Lofton AA	.40	.18	.05
☐ 145 Ben McDonald	.05	.02	.01
☐ 146 Dwight Gooden	.15	.07	.02
☐ 147 Terry Pendleton	.15	.07	.02
☐ 148 Julio Franco	.15	.07	.02
☐ 149 Ken Caminiti	.30	.14	.04
☐ 150 Greg Vaughn	.15	.07	.02
☐ 151 Sammy Sosa	.30	.14	.04
☐ 152 David Valle	.05	.02	.01
☐ 153 Wally Joyner	.15	.07	.02
☐ 154 Dante Bichette	.30	.14	.04
☐ 155 Mark Lewis	.05	.02	.01
☐ 156 Bob Tewksbury	.05	.02	.01
☐ 157 Billy Hatcher	.05	.02	.01
☐ 158 Jack McDowell	.15	.07	.02
☐ 159 Marquis Grissom	.15	.07	.02
☐ 160 Jack Morris	.15	.07	.02
☐ 161 Ramon Martinez	.15	.07	.02
☐ 162 Deion Sanders	.30	.14	.04
☐ 163 Tim Belcher	.05	.02	.01
☐ 164 Mascots Pirate Parrot	.05	.02	.01
☐ 165 Scott Leius	.05	.02	.01
☐ 166 Brady Anderson	.30	.14	.04
☐ 167 Randy Johnson	.30	.14	.04
☐ 168 Mark Gubicza	.05	.02	.01
☐ 169 Chuck Finley	.05	.02	.01
☐ 170 Terry Mulholland	.05	.02	.01
☐ 171 Matt Williams	.30	.14	.04
☐ 172 Dwight Smith	.05	.02	.01
☐ 173 Bobby Bonilla	.15	.07	.02
☐ 174 Ken Hill	.15	.07	.02
☐ 175 Doug Jones	.05	.02	.01
☐ 176 Tony Phillips	.15	.07	.02
☐ 177 Terry Steinbach	.15	.07	.02
☐ 178 Frank Viola	.05	.02	.01
☐ 179 Robin Ventura	.15	.07	.02
☐ 180 Shane Mack	.05	.02	.01
☐ 181 Kenny Lofton	.75	.35	.09
☐ 182 Jeff King	.15	.07	.02
☐ 183 Tim Teufel	.05	.02	.01
☐ 184 Chris Sabo	.05	.02	.01
☐ 185 Len Dykstra	.15	.07	.02
☐ 186 Trevor Wilson	.05	.02	.01
☐ 187 Darryl Strawberry	.15	.07	.02
☐ 188 Robin Yount	.30	.14	.04
☐ 189 Bob Wickman	.05	.02	.01
☐ 190 Luis Polonia	.05	.02	.01
☐ 191 Alan Trammell	.30	.14	.04
☐ 192 Bob Welch	.05	.02	.01
☐ 193 Omar Vizquel AA	.15	.07	.02
☐ 194 Tom Pagnozzi	.05	.02	.01
☐ 195 Bret Barberie	.05	.02	.01
☐ 196 Mike Scioscia AA	.05	.02	.01
☐ 197 Randy Tomlin	.05	.02	.01
☐ 198 Checklist	.05	.02	.01
☐ 199 Ron Gant	.15	.07	.02
☐ 200 Roberto Alomar AA	.30	.14	.04
☐ 201 Andy Benes	.15	.07	.02
☐ 202 Six Pirates Playing Pepper	.05	.02	.01
☐ 203 Steve Finley	.15	.07	.02
☐ 204 Steve Olin	.05	.02	.01
☐ 205 Chris Hoiles	.05	.02	.01
☐ 206 John Wetteland	.15	.07	.02
☐ 207 Danny Tartabull	.05	.02	.01
☐ 208 Bernard Gilkey	.15	.07	.02
☐ 209 Tom Glavine LH	.30	.14	.04
☐ 210 Benito Santiago	.05	.02	.01
☐ 211 Mark Grace	.30	.14	.04
☐ 212 Glenallen Hill	.05	.02	.01
☐ 213 Jeff Brantley	.05	.02	.01
☐ 214 George Brett	.75	.35	.09
☐ 215 Mark Lemke	.05	.02	.01
☐ 216 Ron Karkovice	.05	.02	.01
☐ 217 Tom Brunansky	.05	.02	.01
☐ 218 Todd Hundley	.15	.07	.02
☐ 219 Rickey Henderson	.30	.14	.04
☐ 220 Joe Oliver	.05	.02	.01
☐ 221 Juan Gonzalez	1.00	.45	.12
☐ 222 John Olerud	.05	.02	.01
☐ 223 Hal Morris	.05	.02	.01
☐ 224 Lou Whitaker	.15	.07	.02
☐ 225 Bryan Harvey	.05	.02	.01
☐ 226 Mike Gallego	.05	.02	.01
☐ 227 Willie McGee	.05	.02	.01
☐ 228 Jose Oquendo	.05	.02	.01
☐ 229 Darren Daulton LH	.15	.07	.02
☐ 230 Curt Schilling	.05	.02	.01
☐ 231 Jay Buhner	.30	.14	.04
☐ 232 Doug Drabek Greg Swindell New Astros	.05	.02	.01
☐ 233 Jaime Navarro	.05	.02	.01
☐ 234 Kevin Appier	.15	.07	.02
☐ 235 Mark Langston	.15	.07	.02
☐ 236 Jeff Montgomery	.15	.07	.02
☐ 237 Joe Girardi	.05	.02	.01
☐ 238 Ed Sprague	.15	.07	.02
☐ 239 Dan Walters	.05	.02	.01
☐ 240 Kevin Tapani	.05	.02	.01
☐ 241 Pete Harnisch	.05	.02	.01
☐ 242 Al Martin	.15	.07	.02
☐ 243 Jose Canseco	.30	.14	.04
☐ 244 Moises Alou	.15	.07	.02
☐ 245 Mark McGwire LH	.30	.14	.04
☐ 246 Luis Rivera	.05	.02	.01
☐ 247 George Bell	.05	.02	.01
☐ 248 B.J. Surhoff	.15	.07	.02
☐ 249 David Justice	.30	.14	.04
☐ 250 Brian Harper	.05	.02	.01
☐ 251 Sandy Alomar Jr.	.15	.07	.02
☐ 252 Kevin Brown	.15	.07	.02
☐ 253 Tim Wallach Todd Worrell Jody Reed New Dodgers	.05	.02	.01
☐ 254 Ray Lankford	.15	.07	.02
☐ 255 Derek Bell	.15	.07	.02
☐ 256 Joe Grahe	.05	.02	.01
☐ 257 Charlie Hayes	.05	.02	.01
☐ 258 Wade Boggs Jim Abbott New Yankees	.30	.14	.04
☐ 259A Joe Robbie Stadium ERR (Misnumbered 129)	.15	.07	.02
☐ 259B Joe Robbie Stadium COR	.15	.07	.02
☐ 260 Kirby Puckett	.75	.35	.09
☐ 261 Jay Bell Fun at the Ballpark	.05	.02	.01
☐ 262 Bill Swift	.05	.02	.01
☐ 263 Roger McDowell Fun at the Ballpark	.05	.02	.01
☐ 264 Checklist	.05	.02	.01

1993 Triple Play Action

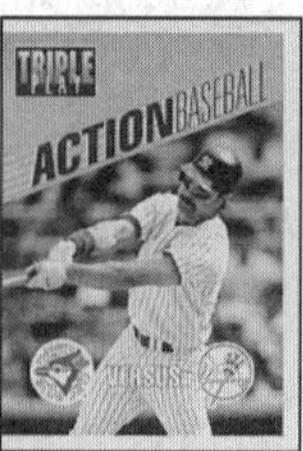

The 1993 Triple Play Action set was inserted one per pack of Triple Play. The cards were designed to serve as a game card with a scratch-off section inside beside a baseball diamond design. The cards are printed on a lighter weight card stock. When unfolded the cards measure approximately 5" by 3 1/2", however when folded they measure the standard size. The front of the folded card features a color action player shot with a wide vertical gray border across the top. Within the upper border are the set title and the words "Action Baseball" printed in black. The player pictured on the card front is not named. Two team logos are superimposed across the photo at the bottom indicating which teams are paired up to play the scratch-off game inside. The inner portion of the card has six game rules printed on the upper left side followed by 32 scratch-off boxes. On the inner right side is a scoreboard printed above a green background baseball diamond. The backs are silver with the Leaf logo printed at the bottom.

	MINT	NRMT	EXC
COMPLETE SET (30)	10.00	4.50	1.25
COMMON CARD (1-30)	.10	.05	.01
☐ 1 Andy Van Slyke	.10	.05	.01
☐ 2 Bobby Bonilla	.20	.09	.03
☐ 3 Ozzie Smith	.50	.23	.06
☐ 4 Ryne Sandberg	.50	.23	.06
☐ 5 Darren Daulton	.20	.09	.03
☐ 6 Larry Walker	.30	.14	.04
☐ 7 Eric Karros	.30	.14	.04
☐ 8 Barry Larkin	.30	.14	.04
☐ 9 Deion Sanders	.30	.14	.04
☐ 10 Gary Sheffield	.30	.14	.04
☐ 11 Will Clark	.30	.14	.04
☐ 12 Jeff Bagwell	.75	.35	.09
☐ 13 Roberto Alomar	.40	.18	.05
☐ 14 Roger Clemens	.40	.18	.05
☐ 15 Cecil Fielder	.20	.09	.03
☐ 16 Robin Yount	.30	.14	.04
☐ 17 Cal Ripken	1.50	.70	.19
☐ 18 Carlos Baerga	.10	.05	.01
☐ 19 Don Mattingly	1.00	.45	.12
☐ 20 Kirby Puckett	.75	.35	.09
☐ 21 Frank Thomas	2.00	.90	.25
☐ 22 Juan Gonzalez	1.00	.45	.12
☐ 23 Mark McGwire	.60	.25	.07
☐ 24 Ken Griffey Jr.	2.00	.90	.25
☐ 25 Wally Joyner	.10	.05	.01
☐ 26 Chad Curtis	.10	.05	.01
☐ 27 Rockies Vs. Marlins	.10	.05	.01
☐ 28 Juan Guzman	.10	.05	.01
☐ 29 David Justice	.20	.09	.03
☐ 30 Joe Carter	.20	.09	.03

1993 Triple Play Gallery

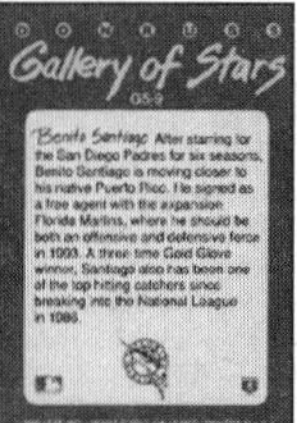

A one per pack insert in 1993 Donruss Triple Play jumbo packs, these ten standard-size cards have fronts that feature color player portraits by noted sports artist Dick Perez. The words "Gallery of Stars" printed in gold foil appear near the top, and the player's name, also in gold foil, rests at the bottom. The backs have a gray-bordered, white rectangle with rounded corners that carries the player's career highlights and team logo. The set name appears above in yellow lettering. The cards are numbered on the back with a "GS" prefix.

	MINT	NRMT	EXC
COMPLETE SET (10)	20.00	9.00	2.50
COMMON CARD (GS1-GS10)	1.50	.70	.19

	MINT	NRMT	EXC
☐ GS1 Barry Bonds	5.00	2.20	.60
☐ GS2 Andre Dawson	2.00	.90	.25
☐ GS3 Wade Boggs	2.50	1.10	.30
☐ GS4 Greg Maddux	12.00	5.50	1.50
☐ GS5 Dave Winfield	2.50	1.10	.30
☐ GS6 Paul Molitor	4.00	1.80	.50
☐ GS7 Jim Abbott	1.50	.70	.19
☐ GS8 J.T. Snow	2.50	1.10	.30
☐ GS9 Benito Santiago	1.50	.70	.19
☐ GS10 David Nied	1.50	.70	.19

1993 Triple Play League Leaders

Randomly inserted in magazine distributor packs only, the six standard-size cards comprising this set feature borderless color action player shots on both sides. A National League leader appears on one side, an American League leader is on the other. The player's league appears in gold-foil lettering across the top. The player's name in white cursive lettering is displayed near the bottom within the set logo, which has a simulated black marble plaque design. The cards are numbered on the American League side with an "L" prefix.

	MINT	NRMT	EXC
COMPLETE SET (6)	35.00	16.00	4.40
COMMON PAIR (L1-L6)	3.00	1.35	.35

	MINT	NRMT	EXC
☐ L1 Barry Bonds Dennis Eckersley	6.00	2.70	.75
☐ L2 Greg Maddux Dennis Eckersley	15.00	6.75	1.85
☐ L3 Eric Karros Pat Listach	3.00	1.35	.35
☐ L4 Fred McGriff Juan Gonzalez	15.00	6.75	1.85
☐ L5 Darren Daulton Cecil Fielder	4.00	1.80	.50
☐ L6 Gary Sheffield Edgar Martinez	5.00	2.20	.60

1993 Triple Play Nicknames

Randomly inserted in foil packs only, this ten-card standard-size set is a new insert set featuring popular player's nicknames. The borderless fronts feature color player action shots. The player's name appears at the bottom, within an irregular red stripe that simulates a stroke of a paintbrush. His nickname appears in large prismatic-foil lettering at the top of the photo. The white back shades to red near the bottom and carries the player's last name in large purplish letters at the top. His first name appears in smaller white cursive lettering superposed upon his last name. The player's biography, set off by thin black lines, is shown below. A color player action shot appears beneath on the left side, and his career highlights are shown alongside on the right. The player's team logo at the bottom rounds out the card.

	MINT	NRMT	EXC
COMPLETE SET (10)	35.00	16.00	4.40
COMMON CARD (1-10)	1.00	.45	.12

	MINT	NRMT	EXC
☐ 1 Frank Thomas Big Hurt	10.00	4.50	1.25
☐ 2 Roger Clemens Rocket	2.00	.90	.25
☐ 3 Ryne Sandberg Ryno	3.00	1.35	.35
☐ 4 Will Clark Thrill	1.25	.55	.16
☐ 5 Ken Griffey Jr. Junior	10.00	4.50	1.25
☐ 6 Dwight Gooden	1.00	.45	.12
☐ 7 Nolan Ryan Express	10.00	4.50	1.25
☐ 8 Deion Sanders Prime Time	1.25	.55	.16
☐ 9 Ozzie Smith Wizard	3.00	1.35	.35
☐ 10 Fred McGriff Crime Dog	1.25	.55	.16

1994 Triple Play Promos

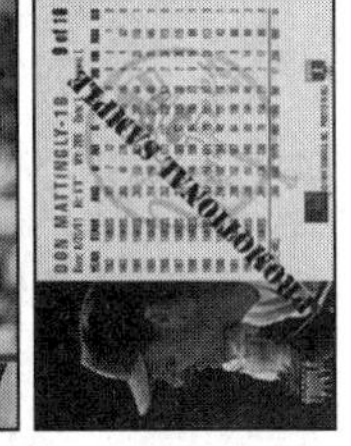

These ten standard-size promos feature on their fronts color player-action shots that are borderless, except at the bottom, where the player's name appears within a colored stripe. The horizontal back carries a posed color player photo on the left side. On the right, beneath the player's name and position, appear biography, statistics, and career highlights on a white background highlighted by his team's ghosted logo. The "Promotional Sample" disclaimer is stenciled obliquely across the front and back.

	MINT	NRMT	EXC
COMPLETE SET (10)	15.00	6.75	1.85
COMMON CARD (1-10)	.50	.23	.06

	MINT	NRMT	EXC
☐ 1 Juan Gonzalez	2.00	.90	.25
☐ 2 Frank Thomas	4.00	1.80	.50
☐ 3 Barry Bonds	1.00	.45	.12
☐ 4 Ken Griffey Jr.	4.00	1.80	.50
☐ 5 Paul Molitor	.75	.35	.09
☐ 6 Mike Piazza	2.50	1.10	.30
☐ 7 Tim Salmon	.50	.23	.06
☐ 8 Lenny Dykstra	.50	.23	.06
☐ 9 Don Mattingly	2.00	.90	.25
☐ 10 Greg Maddux	2.50	1.10	.30

1994 Triple Play

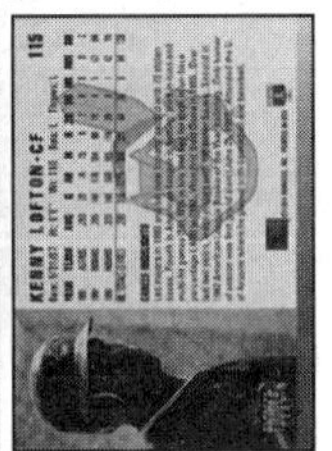

The 1994 Triple Play set consists of 300 standard-size cards, featuring ten players from each team along with a 17-card Rookie Review set. The fronts have color player action shots that are borderless, except at the bottom, where the player's name appears within a colored stripe. The horizontal back carries a posed color player photo on the left side. On the right, beneath the player's name and position, appear biography, statistics, and career highlights on a white background highlighted by his team's ghosted logo. Triple Play game cards, reedemable for various prizes, were inserted one per pack.

	MINT	NRMT	EXC
COMPLETE SET (300)	15.00	6.75	1.85
COMMON CARD (1-300)	.05	.02	.01

	MINT	NRMT	EXC
☐ 1 Mike Bordick	.05	.02	.01
☐ 2 Dennis Eckersley	.15	.07	.02
☐ 3 Brent Gates	.05	.02	.01
☐ 4 Rickey Henderson	.30	.14	.04
☐ 5 Mark McGwire	.60	.25	.07
☐ 6 Troy Neel	.05	.02	.01
☐ 7 Craig Paquette	.05	.02	.01
☐ 8 Ruben Sierra	.15	.07	.02
☐ 9 Terry Steinbach	.15	.07	.02
☐ 10 Bobby Witt	.05	.02	.01
☐ 11 Chad Curtis	.05	.02	.01
☐ 12 Chili Davis	.15	.07	.02
☐ 13 Gary DiSarcina	.05	.02	.01
☐ 14 Damion Easley	.05	.02	.01
☐ 15 Chuck Finley	.05	.02	.01
☐ 16 Joe Grahe	.05	.02	.01
☐ 17 Mark Langston	.15	.07	.02
☐ 18 Eduardo Perez	.05	.02	.01
☐ 19 Tim Salmon	.30	.14	.04
☐ 20 J.T. Snow	.15	.07	.02
☐ 21 Jeff Bagwell	.75	.35	.09
☐ 22 Craig Biggio	.15	.07	.02
☐ 23 Ken Caminiti	.30	.14	.04
☐ 24 Andujar Cedeno	.05	.02	.01
☐ 25 Doug Drabek	.05	.02	.01
☐ 26 Steve Finley	.30	.14	.04
☐ 27 Luis Gonzalez	.05	.02	.01
☐ 28 Pete Harnisch	.05	.02	.01
☐ 29 Darryl Kile	.05	.02	.01
☐ 30 Mitch Williams	.05	.02	.01
☐ 31 Roberto Alomar	.40	.18	.05
☐ 32 Joe Carter	.15	.07	.02
☐ 33 Juan Guzman	.15	.07	.02
☐ 34 Pat Hentgen	.15	.07	.02
☐ 35 Paul Molitor	.40	.18	.05
☐ 36 John Olerud	.05	.02	.01
☐ 37 Ed Sprague	.15	.07	.02
☐ 38 Dave Stewart	.15	.07	.02
☐ 39 Duane Ward	.05	.02	.01
☐ 40 Devon White	.05	.02	.01
☐ 41 Steve Avery	.15	.07	.02
☐ 42 Jeff Blauser	.05	.02	.01
☐ 43 Ron Gant	.15	.07	.02
☐ 44 Tom Glavine	.30	.14	.04
☐ 45 David Justice	.30	.14	.04
☐ 46 Greg Maddux	1.25	.55	.16
☐ 47 Fred McGriff	.30	.14	.04
☐ 48 Terry Pendleton	.15	.07	.02
☐ 49 Deion Sanders	.30	.14	.04
☐ 50 John Smoltz	.30	.14	.04
☐ 51 Ricky Bones	.05	.02	.01
☐ 52 Cal Eldred	.05	.02	.01
☐ 53 Darryl Hamilton	.05	.02	.01
☐ 54 John Jaha	.15	.07	.02
☐ 55 Pat Listach	.05	.02	.01
☐ 56 Jaime Navarro	.05	.02	.01
☐ 57 Dave Nilsson	.15	.07	.02
☐ 58 B.J. Surhoff	.05	.02	.01
☐ 59 Greg Vaughn	.30	.14	.04
☐ 60 Robin Yount	.30	.14	.04
☐ 61 Bernard Gilkey	.15	.07	.02
☐ 62 Gregg Jefferies	.30	.14	.04
☐ 63 Brian Jordan	.30	.14	.04
☐ 64 Ray Lankford	.15	.07	.02
☐ 65 Tom Pagnozzi	.05	.02	.01
☐ 66 Ozzie Smith	.50	.23	.06
☐ 67 Bob Tewksbury	.05	.02	.01
☐ 68 Allen Watson	.05	.02	.01
☐ 69 Mark Whiten	.05	.02	.01
☐ 70 Todd Zeile	.05	.02	.01
☐ 71 Steve Buechele	.05	.02	.01
☐ 72 Mark Grace	.30	.14	.04
☐ 73 Jose Guzman	.05	.02	.01
☐ 74 Derrick May	.05	.02	.01
☐ 75 Mike Morgan	.05	.02	.01
☐ 76 Randy Myers	.05	.02	.01
☐ 77 Ryne Sandberg	.50	.23	.06
☐ 78 Sammy Sosa	.30	.14	.04
☐ 79 Jose Vizcaino	.05	.02	.01
☐ 80 Rick Wilkins	.05	.02	.01
☐ 81 Pedro Astacio	.05	.02	.01
☐ 82 Brett Butler	.15	.07	.02
☐ 83 Delino DeShields	.05	.02	.01
☐ 84 Orel Hershiser	.15	.07	.02
☐ 85 Eric Karros	.15	.07	.02
☐ 86 Ramon Martinez	.15	.07	.02
☐ 87 Jose Offerman	.05	.02	.01
☐ 88 Mike Piazza	1.25	.55	.16
☐ 89 Darryl Strawberry	.15	.07	.02
☐ 90 Tim Wallach	.05	.02	.01
☐ 91 Moises Alou	.15	.07	.02
☐ 92 Wil Cordero	.15	.07	.02
☐ 93 Jeff Fassero	.05	.02	.01
☐ 94 Darrin Fletcher	.05	.02	.01
☐ 95 Marquis Grissom	.15	.07	.02
☐ 96 Ken Hill	.05	.02	.01
☐ 97 Mike Lansing	.15	.07	.02
☐ 98 Kirk Rueter	.05	.02	.01
☐ 99 Larry Walker	.30	.14	.04
☐ 100 John Wetteland	.15	.07	.02
☐ 101 Rod Beck	.15	.07	.02
☐ 102 Barry Bonds	.50	.23	.06
☐ 103 John Burkett	.05	.02	.01
☐ 104 Royce Clayton	.15	.07	.02
☐ 105 Darren Lewis	.05	.02	.01
☐ 106 Kirt Manwaring	.05	.02	.01
☐ 107 Willie McGee	.05	.02	.01
☐ 108 Bill Swift	.05	.02	.01
☐ 109 Robby Thompson	.05	.02	.01
☐ 110 Matt Williams	.30	.14	.04
☐ 111 Sandy Alomar Jr.	.15	.07	.02
☐ 112 Carlos Baerga	.15	.07	.02
☐ 113 Albert Belle	.75	.35	.09
☐ 114 Wayne Kirby	.05	.02	.01
☐ 115 Kenny Lofton	.60	.25	.07
☐ 116 Jose Mesa	.15	.07	.02
☐ 117 Eddie Murray	.50	.23	.06
☐ 118 Charles Nagy	.15	.07	.02
☐ 119 Paul Sorrento	.05	.02	.01
☐ 120 Jim Thome	.50	.23	.06
☐ 121 Rich Amaral	.05	.02	.01
☐ 122 Eric Anthony	.05	.02	.01
☐ 123 Mike Blowers	.05	.02	.01
☐ 124 Chris Bosio	.05	.02	.01
☐ 125 Jay Buhner	.30	.14	.04
☐ 126 Dave Fleming	.05	.02	.01
☐ 127 Ken Griffey Jr.	2.00	.90	.25
☐ 128 Randy Johnson	.30	.14	.04
☐ 129 Edgar Martinez	.15	.07	.02
☐ 130 Tino Martinez	.15	.07	.02
☐ 131 Bret Barberie	.05	.02	.01
☐ 132 Ryan Bowen	.05	.02	.01
☐ 133 Chuck Carr	.05	.02	.01
☐ 134 Jeff Conine	.15	.07	.02
☐ 135 Orestes Destrade	.05	.02	.01
☐ 136 Chris Hammond	.05	.02	.01
☐ 137 Bryan Harvey	.05	.02	.01
☐ 138 Dave Magadan	.05	.02	.01
☐ 139 Benito Santiago	.05	.02	.01
☐ 140 Gary Sheffield	.30	.14	.04
☐ 141 Bobby Bonilla	.15	.07	.02
☐ 142 Jeromy Burnitz	.05	.02	.01
☐ 143 Dwight Gooden	.15	.07	.02
☐ 144 Todd Hundley	.15	.07	.02
☐ 145 Bobby Jones	.15	.07	.02
☐ 146 Jeff Kent	.05	.02	.01
☐ 147 Joe Orsulak	.05	.02	.01
☐ 148 Bret Saberhagen	.15	.07	.02
☐ 149 Pete Schourek	.15	.07	.02
☐ 150 Ryan Thompson	.05	.02	.01
☐ 151 Brady Anderson	.30	.14	.04
☐ 152 Harold Baines	.15	.07	.02
☐ 153 Mike Devereaux	.05	.02	.01
☐ 154 Chris Hoiles	.05	.02	.01
☐ 155 Ben McDonald	.05	.02	.01
☐ 156 Mark McLemore	.05	.02	.01
☐ 157 Mike Mussina	.40	.18	.05
☐ 158 Rafael Palmeiro	.30	.14	.04
☐ 159 Cal Ripken	1.50	.70	.19
☐ 160 Chris Sabo	.05	.02	.01
☐ 161 Brad Ausmus	.05	.02	.01
☐ 162 Derek Bell	.15	.07	.02
☐ 163 Andy Benes	.15	.07	.02
☐ 164 Doug Brocail	.05	.02	.01
☐ 165 Archi Cianfrocco	.05	.02	.01
☐ 166 Ricky Gutierrez	.05	.02	.01
☐ 167 Tony Gwynn	.75	.35	.09
☐ 168 Gene Harris	.05	.02	.01
☐ 169 Pedro Martinez	.15	.07	.02
☐ 170 Phil Plantier	.05	.02	.01
☐ 171 Darren Daulton	.15	.07	.02
☐ 172 Mariano Duncan	.05	.02	.01
☐ 173 Lenny Dykstra	.15	.07	.02
☐ 174 Tommy Greene	.05	.02	.01
☐ 175 Dave Hollins	.05	.02	.01
☐ 176 Danny Jackson	.05	.02	.01
☐ 177 John Kruk	.15	.07	.02
☐ 178 Terry Mulholland	.05	.02	.01
☐ 179 Curt Schilling	.05	.02	.01
☐ 180 Kevin Stocker	.05	.02	.01
☐ 181 Jay Bell	.15	.07	.02
☐ 182 Steve Cooke	.05	.02	.01
☐ 183 Carlos Garcia	.05	.02	.01
☐ 184 Joel Johnston	.05	.02	.01
☐ 185 Jeff King	.15	.07	.02
☐ 186 Al Martin	.05	.02	.01
☐ 187 Orlando Merced	.15	.07	.02
☐ 188 Don Slaught	.05	.02	.01
☐ 189 Andy Van Slyke	.15	.07	.02
☐ 190 Kevin Young	.05	.02	.01
☐ 191 Kevin Brown	.15	.07	.02
☐ 192 Jose Canseco	.30	.14	.04
☐ 193 Will Clark	.30	.14	.04
☐ 194 Juan Gonzalez	1.00	.45	.12
☐ 195 Tom Henke	.05	.02	.01
☐ 196 David Hulse	.05	.02	.01
☐ 197 Dean Palmer	.15	.07	.02
☐ 198 Roger Pavlik	.05	.02	.01
☐ 199 Ivan Rodriguez	.50	.23	.06
☐ 200 Kenny Rogers	.05	.02	.01
☐ 201 Roger Clemens	.40	.18	.05
☐ 202 Scott Cooper	.05	.02	.01
☐ 203 Andre Dawson	.15	.07	.02
☐ 204 Mike Greenwell	.05	.02	.01
☐ 205 Billy Hatcher	.05	.02	.01
☐ 206 Jeff Russell	.05	.02	.01
☐ 207 Aaron Sele	.15	.07	.02
☐ 208 John Valentin	.15	.07	.02
☐ 209 Mo Vaughn	.50	.23	.06
☐ 210 Frank Viola	.05	.02	.01
☐ 211 Rob Dibble	.05	.02	.01
☐ 212 Willie Greene	.15	.07	.02
☐ 213 Roberto Kelly	.05	.02	.01
☐ 214 Barry Larkin	.30	.14	.04
☐ 215 Kevin Mitchell	.15	.07	.02
☐ 216 Hal Morris	.05	.02	.01
☐ 217 Joe Oliver	.05	.02	.01
☐ 218 Jose Rijo	.05	.02	.01
☐ 219 Reggie Sanders	.15	.07	.02
☐ 220 John Smiley	.05	.02	.01
☐ 221 Dante Bichette	.30	.14	.04
☐ 222 Ellis Burks	.15	.07	.02
☐ 223 Andres Galarraga	.30	.14	.04
☐ 224 Joe Girardi	.05	.02	.01
☐ 225 Charlie Hayes	.05	.02	.01
☐ 226 Darren Holmes	.05	.02	.01
☐ 227 Howard Johnson	.05	.02	.01
☐ 228 Roberto Mejia	.05	.02	.01
☐ 229 David Nied	.05	.02	.01
☐ 230 Armando Reynoso	.05	.02	.01
☐ 231 Kevin Appier	.15	.07	.02
☐ 232 David Cone	.15	.07	.02
☐ 233 Greg Gagne	.05	.02	.01
☐ 234 Tom Gordon	.05	.02	.01
☐ 235 Felix Jose	.05	.02	.01
☐ 236 Wally Joyner	.15	.07	.02
☐ 237 Jose Lind	.05	.02	.01
☐ 238 Brian McRae	.15	.07	.02
☐ 239 Mike Macfarliane	.05	.02	.01
☐ 240 Jeff Montgomery	.15	.07	.02
☐ 241 Eric Davis	.15	.07	.02
☐ 242 John Doherty	.05	.02	.01
☐ 243 Cecil Fielder	.15	.07	.02
☐ 244 Travis Fryman	.15	.07	.02
☐ 245 Bill Gullickson	.05	.02	.01
☐ 246 Mike Henneman	.05	.02	.01

☐ 247 Tony Phillips	.15	.07	.02
☐ 248 Mickey Tettleton	.05	.02	.01
☐ 249 Alan Trammell	.15	.07	.02
☐ 250 Lou Whitaker	.15	.07	.02
☐ 251 Rick Aguilera	.05	.02	.01
☐ 252 Scott Erickson	.05	.02	.01
☐ 253 Kent Hrbek	.15	.07	.02
☐ 254 Chuck Knoblauch	.30	.14	.04
☐ 255 Shane Mack	.05	.02	.01
☐ 256 Dave McCarty	.05	.02	.01
☐ 257 Pat Meares	.05	.02	.01
☐ 258 Kirby Puckett	.75	.35	.09
☐ 259 Kevin Tapani	.05	.02	.01
☐ 260 Dave Winfield	.30	.14	.04
☐ 261 Wilson Alvarez	.15	.07	.02
☐ 262 Jason Bere	.15	.07	.02
☐ 263 Alex Fernandez	.15	.07	.02
☐ 264 Ozzie Guillen	.05	.02	.01
☐ 265 Roberto Hernandez	.15	.07	.02
☐ 266 Lance Johnson	.15	.07	.02
☐ 267 Jack McDowell	.15	.07	.02
☐ 268 Tim Raines	.30	.14	.04
☐ 269 Frank Thomas	2.00	.90	.25
☐ 270 Robin Ventura	.15	.07	.02
☐ 271 Jim Abbott	.05	.02	.01
☐ 272 Wade Boggs	.30	.14	.04
☐ 273 Mike Gallego	.05	.02	.01
☐ 274 Pat Kelly	.05	.02	.01
☐ 275 Jimmy Key	.15	.07	.02
☐ 276 Don Mattingly	1.00	.45	.12
☐ 277 Paul O'Neill	.15	.07	.02
☐ 278 Mike Stanley	.05	.02	.01
☐ 279 Danny Tartabull	.05	.02	.01
☐ 280 Bernie Williams	.40	.18	.05
☐ 281 Chipper Jones	1.50	.70	.19
☐ 282 Ryan Klesko	.40	.18	.05
☐ 283 Javier Lopez	.30	.14	.04
☐ 284 Jeffrey Hammonds	.15	.07	.02
☐ 285 Jeff McNeely	.05	.02	.01
☐ 286 Manny Ramirez	.60	.25	.07
☐ 287 Billy Ashley	.05	.02	.01
☐ 288 Raul Mondesi	.30	.14	.04
☐ 289 Cliff Floyd	.30	.14	.04
☐ 290 Rondell White	.30	.14	.04
☐ 291 Steve Karsay	.05	.02	.01
☐ 292 Midre Cummings	.05	.02	.01
☐ 293 Salomon Torres	.05	.02	.01
☐ 294 J.R. Phillips	.05	.02	.01
☐ 295 Marc Newfield	.15	.07	.02
☐ 296 Carlos Delgado	.30	.14	.04
☐ 297 Butch Huskey	.15	.07	.02
☐ 298 Checklist	.05	.02	.01
☐ 299 Checklist	.05	.02	.01
☐ 300 Checklist	.05	.02	.01

1994 Triple Play Bomb Squad

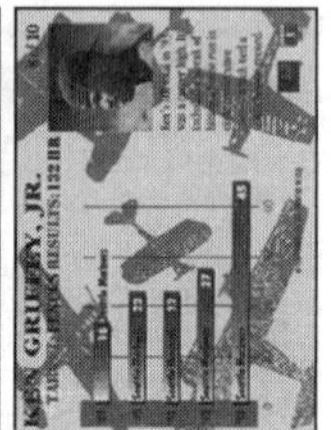

Randomly inserted in regular (one in 18) and jumbo (one in 8) packs, this ten-card standard-size set focuses on the top home run hitters in the majors. Card fronts feature a brown border surrounding a black and white photo. The Bomb Squad logo which includes a pair of wings is at the top. The player's name is at the bottom. Horizontal backs offer more color including a bar graph on yearly home run production with drawings of fighter planes serving as a background.

	MINT	NRMT	EXC
COMPLETE SET (10)	40.00	18.00	5.00
COMMON CARD (1-10)	1.00	.45	.12
☐ 1 Frank Thomas	12.00	5.50	1.50
☐ 2 Cecil Fielder	1.00	.45	.12
☐ 3 Juan Gonzalez	6.00	2.70	.75
☐ 4 Barry Bonds	3.00	1.35	.35
☐ 5 David Justice	1.00	.45	.12
☐ 6 Fred McGriff	1.50	.70	.19
☐ 7 Ron Gant	1.00	.45	.12
☐ 8 Ken Griffey Jr.	12.00	5.50	1.50
☐ 9 Albert Belle	5.00	2.20	.60
☐ 10 Matt Williams	1.50	.70	.19

1994 Triple Play Medalists

Randomly inserted in regular (one in 12) and jumbo packs (one in six), this 15-card standard-size set features the top three players in each league at their position. The players included were determined by statistical rankings over the past two seasons. Each card is horizontally designed with gold, silver and bronze foil on front with three player photos. There are also three player photos and brief highlights on back.

	MINT	NRMT	EXC
COMPLETE SET (15)	35.00	16.00	4.40
COMMON CARD (1-15)	1.00	.45	.12
☐ 1 Chris Hoiles	1.00	.45	.12
Mickey Tettleton			
Brian Harper			
☐ 2 Darren Daulton	1.50	.70	.19
Rick Wilkins			
Kirt Manwaring			
☐ 3 Frank Thomas	8.00	3.60	1.00
Rafael Palmeiro			
John Olerud			
☐ 4 Mark Grace	3.00	1.35	.35
Fred McGriff			
Jeff Bagwell			
☐ 5 Roberto Alomar	2.00	.90	.25
Carlos Baerga			
Lou Whitaker			
☐ 6 Ryne Sandberg	2.50	1.10	.30
Craig Biggio			
Roggie Thompson			
☐ 7 Tony Fernandez	6.00	2.70	.75
Cal Ripken			
Alan Trammell			
☐ 8 Barry Larkin			
Jay Bell			
Jeff Blauser			
☐ 9 Robin Ventura	1.50	.70	.19
Travis Fryman			
Wade Boggs			
☐ 10 Terry Pendleton	1.00	.45	.12
Dave Hollins			
Gary Sheffield			
☐ 11 Ken Griffey Jr.	10.00	4.50	1.25
Kirby Puckett			
Albert Belle			
☐ 12 Barry Bonds	2.00	.90	.25
Andy Van Slyke			
Len Dykstra			
☐ 13 Jack McDowell	1.00	.45	.12
Kevin Brown			
Randy Johnson			
☐ 14 Greg Maddux	5.00	2.20	.60
Jose Rijo			
Bill Swift			
☐ 15 Paul Molitor	1.50	.70	.19
Dave Winfield			
Harold Baines			

1994 Triple Play Nicknames

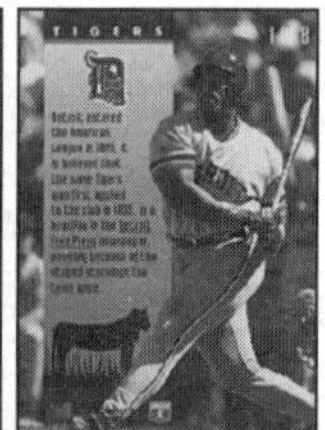

Randomly inserted in regular (one in 36) and jumbo packs (one in 12), this eight-card standard-size set features players with a photo depicting the team name and mascot in the background. The back of each card describes how the team got its nickname as well as a player photo.

	MINT	NRMT	EXC
COMPLETE SET (8)	40.00	18.00	5.00
COMMON CARD (1-8)	2.00	.90	.25
☐ 1 Cecil Fielder	4.00	1.80	.50
☐ 2 Ryne Sandberg	8.00	3.60	1.00
☐ 3 Gary Sheffield	5.00	2.20	.60
☐ 4 Joe Carter	4.00	1.80	.50
☐ 5 John Olerud	2.00	.90	.25
☐ 6 Cal Ripken	25.00	11.00	3.10
☐ 7 Mark McGwire	10.00	4.50	1.25
☐ 8 Gregg Jefferies	4.00	1.80	.50

1986 True Value

The 1986 True Value set consists of 30 cards, each measuring 2 1/2" by 3 1/2", which were printed as panels of four although one of the cards in the panel only pictures a featured product. The complete panel measures approximately 10 3/8" by 3 1/2". The True Value logo is in the upper left corner of the obverse of each card. Supposedly the cards were distributed to customers purchasing 5.00 or more at the store. Cards are frequently found with perforations intact and still in the closed form where only the top card in the folded panel is visible. The card number appears at the bottom of the reverse. Team logos have been surgically removed (airbrushed) from the photos.

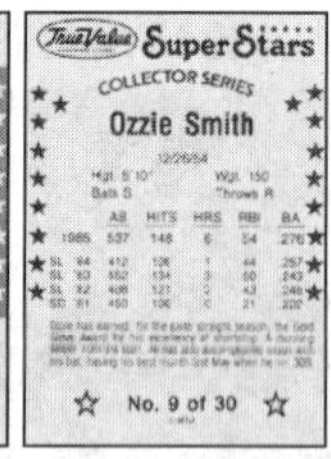

	MINT	NRMT	EXC
COMPLETE SET (30)	15.00	6.75	1.85
COMMON CARD (1-30)	.25	.11	.03
☐ 1 Pedro Guerrero	.25	.11	.03
☐ 2 Steve Garvey	.50	.23	.06
☐ 3 Eddie Murray	1.00	.45	.12
☐ 4 Pete Rose	1.25	.55	.16
☐ 5 Don Mattingly	2.50	1.10	.30
☐ 6 Fernando Valenzuela	.50	.23	.06
☐ 7 Jim Rice	.50	.23	.06
☐ 8 Kirk Gibson	.50	.23	.06
☐ 9 Ozzie Smith	2.00	.90	.25
☐ 10 Dale Murphy	.75	.35	.09
☐ 11 Robin Yount	.75	.35	.09
☐ 12 Tom Seaver	1.00	.45	.12
☐ 13 Reggie Jackson	1.00	.45	.12
☐ 14 Ryne Sandberg	2.00	.90	.25
☐ 15 Bruce Sutter	.25	.11	.03
☐ 16 Gary Carter	.50	.23	.06
☐ 17 George Brett	2.50	1.10	.30
☐ 18 Rick Sutcliffe	.25	.11	.03
☐ 19 Dave Stieb	.25	.11	.03
☐ 20 Buddy Bell	.25	.11	.03
☐ 21 Alvin Davis	.25	.11	.03
☐ 22 Cal Ripken	4.00	1.80	.50
☐ 23 Bill Madlock	.25	.11	.03
☐ 24 Kent Hrbek	.50	.23	.06
☐ 25 Lou Whitaker	.50	.23	.06
☐ 26 Nolan Ryan	4.00	1.80	.50
☐ 27 Dwayne Murphy	.25	.11	.03
☐ 28 Mike Schmidt	1.25	.55	.16
☐ 29 Andre Dawson	.75	.35	.09
☐ 30 Wade Boggs	1.00	.45	.12

1911 Turkey Red T3

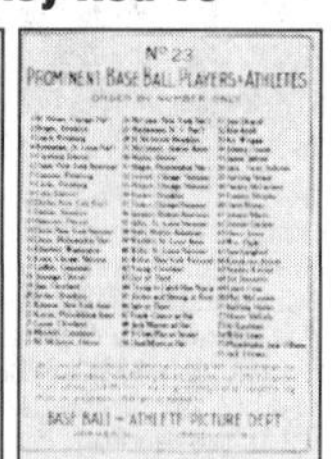

The cards in this 126-card set measure approximately 5 3/4" by 8". The 1911 "Turkey Red" set of color cabinet style cards, designated T3 in the American Card Catalog, is named after the brand of cigarettes with which it was offered as a premium. Cards 1-50 and 77-126 depict baseball players while the middle series (51-76) portrays boxers. The cards themselves are not numbered but were assigned numbers for ordering purposes by the manufacturer. This list appears on the backs of cards in the 77-126 sub-series and has been used in the checklist below. The boxers (51-76) were formerly assigned a separate catalog number (T9) but have now been returned to the classification to which they properly belong and are indicated in the checklist below by BOX. This attractive set has been reprinted recently in 2 1/2" by 3 1/2" form.

	EX-MT	VG-E	GOOD
COMPLETE SET (126)	40000.00	18000.00	5000.00
COMMON BASEBALL (1-50)	225.00	100.00	28.00
COMMON BOXERS (51-76)	200.00	90.00	25.00
COMMON BASEBALL (77-126)	250.00	110.00	31.00
☐ 1 Mordecai Brown: Chicago NL	500.00	220.00	60.00
☐ 2 Bill Bergen: Brooklyn	225.00	100.00	28.00
☐ 3 Fred Leach: Pittsburgh	225.00	100.00	28.00
☐ 4 Roger Bresnahan	450.00	200.00	55.00
☐ 5 Sam Crawford	500.00	220.00	60.00
☐ 6 Hal Chase	275.00	125.00	34.00
☐ 7 Howie Camnitz	225.00	100.00	28.00
☐ 8 Fred Clarke: Pittsburgh	450.00	200.00	55.00
☐ 9 Ty Cobb	5500.00	2500.00	700.00
☐ 10 Art Devlin	225.00	100.00	28.00
☐ 11 Bill Dahlen	275.00	125.00	34.00
☐ 12 Bill Donovan	225.00	100.00	28.00
☐ 13 Larry Doyle	250.00	110.00	31.00
☐ 14 Red Dooin	225.00	100.00	28.00
☐ 15 Kid Elberfeld	225.00	100.00	28.00
☐ 16 Johnny Evers	500.00	220.00	60.00
☐ 17 Clark Griffith	450.00	200.00	55.00
☐ 18 Hughie Jennings	550.00	250.00	70.00
☐ 19 Addie Joss	550.00	250.00	70.00
☐ 20 Tim Jordan	225.00	100.00	28.00
☐ 21 Red Kleinow	225.00	100.00	28.00
☐ 22 Harry Krause	225.00	100.00	28.00
☐ 23 Nap Lajoie	900.00	400.00	110.00
☐ 24 Mike Mitchell	225.00	100.00	28.00
☐ 25 Matty McIntyre	225.00	100.00	28.00
☐ 26 John McGraw	600.00	275.00	75.00
☐ 27 Christy Mathewson	1350.00	600.00	170.00
☐ 28 Harry McIntire	225.00	100.00	28.00
☐ 29 Amby McConnell	225.00	100.00	28.00
☐ 30 George Mullin	225.00	100.00	28.00
☐ 31 Sherry Magee	225.00	100.00	28.00
☐ 32 Orval Overall	225.00	100.00	28.00
☐ 33 Jack Pfeister	225.00	100.00	28.00
☐ 34 Nap Rucker	250.00	110.00	31.00
☐ 35 Joe Tinker	550.00	250.00	70.00
☐ 36 Tris Speaker	900.00	400.00	110.00
☐ 37 Slim Sallee	225.00	100.00	28.00
☐ 38 Jake Stahl	250.00	110.00	31.00
☐ 39 Rube Waddell	500.00	220.00	60.00
☐ 40 Vic Willis	450.00	200.00	55.00
☐ 41 Hooks Wiltse	225.00	100.00	28.00
☐ 42 Cy Young	1200.00	550.00	150.00
☐ 43 Out At Third	225.00	100.00	28.00
☐ 44 Trying to Catch Him Napping	225.00	100.00	28.00
☐ 45 Tim Jordan and Buck Herzog at First	225.00	100.00	28.00
☐ 46 Safe At Third	225.00	100.00	28.00
☐ 47 Frank Chance At Bat	500.00	220.00	60.00
☐ 48 Jack Murray At Bat	225.00	100.00	28.00
☐ 49 Close Play At Second	225.00	100.00	28.00
☐ 50 Chief Myers At Bat (Sic, Meyers)	225.00	100.00	28.00
☐ 51 Jem Driscoll BOX	250.00	110.00	31.00
☐ 52 Abe Attell BOX	400.00	180.00	50.00
☐ 53 Ad. Walgast BOX	200.00	90.00	25.00
☐ 54 Johnny Coulon BOX	200.00	90.00	25.00
☐ 55 James Jeffries BOX	600.00	275.00	75.00
☐ 56 Jack Sullivan BOX Twin	300.00	135.00	38.00
☐ 57 Battling Nelson BOX	250.00	110.00	31.00
☐ 58 Packey McFarland BOX	200.00	90.00	25.00
☐ 59 Tommy Murphy BOX	200.00	90.00	25.00
☐ 60 Owen Moran BOX	250.00	110.00	31.00
☐ 61 Johnny Marto BOX	200.00	90.00	25.00
☐ 62 Jimmie Gardner BOX	200.00	90.00	25.00
☐ 63 Harry Lewis BOX	200.00	90.00	25.00
☐ 64 Wm. Papke BOX	250.00	110.00	31.00
☐ 65 Sam Langford BOX	350.00	160.00	45.00
☐ 66 Knock-out Brown BOX	250.00	110.00	31.00
☐ 67 Stanley Ketchel BOX	600.00	275.00	75.00
☐ 68 Joe Jeannette BOX	300.00	135.00	38.00
☐ 69 Leach Cross BOX	250.00	110.00	31.00
☐ 70 Phil. McGovern BOX	200.00	90.00	25.00
☐ 71 Battling Hurley BOX	200.00	90.00	25.00
☐ 72 Honey Mellody BOX	200.00	90.00	25.00
☐ 73 Al Kaufman BOX	200.00	90.00	25.00
☐ 74 Willie Lewis BOX	200.00	90.00	25.00
☐ 75 Jack O'Brien BOX Philadelphia	300.00	135.00	38.00
☐ 76 Jack Johnson BOX	1000.00	450.00	125.00
☐ 77 Red Ames: New York NL	250.00	110.00	31.00
☐ 78 Frank Baker: Phila. AL Picture probably Jack Barry	450.00	200.00	55.00
☐ 79 George Bell	250.00	110.00	31.00
☐ 80 Chief Bender	500.00	220.00	60.00
☐ 81 Bob Bescher	250.00	110.00	31.00
☐ 82 Kitty Bransfield	250.00	110.00	31.00
☐ 83 Al Bridwell	250.00	110.00	31.00
☐ 84 George Browne	250.00	110.00	31.00
☐ 85 Bill Burns	250.00	110.00	31.00
☐ 86 Bill Carrigan	250.00	110.00	31.00
☐ 87 Eddie Collins	550.00	250.00	70.00
☐ 88 Harry Coveleski	250.00	110.00	31.00
☐ 89 Lou Criger	250.00	110.00	31.00
☐ 90 Mickey Doolan	250.00	110.00	31.00
☐ 91 Tom Downey	250.00	110.00	31.00
☐ 92 Jimmy Dygert	250.00	110.00	31.00
☐ 93 Art Fromme	250.00	110.00	31.00
☐ 94 George Gibson	250.00	110.00	31.00
☐ 95 Peaches Graham	250.00	110.00	31.00
☐ 96 Bob Groom	250.00	110.00	31.00
☐ 97 Bob Hoblitzel	250.00	110.00	31.00
☐ 98 Doc Hofman	250.00	110.00	31.00
☐ 99 Walter Johnson	1600.00	700.00	200.00
☐ 100 Davy Jones	250.00	110.00	31.00
☐ 101 Willie Keeler	750.00	350.00	95.00
☐ 102 Johnny Kling	250.00	110.00	31.00
☐ 103 Ed Konetchy	250.00	110.00	31.00
☐ 104 Ed Lennox	250.00	110.00	31.00
☐ 105 Hans Lobert	250.00	110.00	31.00
☐ 106 Bris Lord	250.00	110.00	31.00
☐ 107 Rube Manning	250.00	110.00	31.00
☐ 108 Fred Merkle	275.00	125.00	34.00
☐ 109 Pat Moran	250.00	110.00	31.00
☐ 110 George McBride	250.00	110.00	31.00
☐ 111 Harry Niles	250.00	110.00	31.00
☐ 112 Dode Paskert	250.00	110.00	31.00
☐ 113 Bugs Raymond	275.00	125.00	34.00
☐ 114 Bob Rhoads	300.00	135.00	38.00
☐ 115 Admiral Schlei	250.00	110.00	31.00
☐ 116 Boss Schmidt	250.00	110.00	31.00

☐ 117 Frank Schulte	250.00	110.00	31.00
☐ 118 Charlie Smith	250.00	110.00	31.00
☐ 119 George Stone	250.00	110.00	31.00
☐ 120 Gabby Street	250.00	110.00	31.00
☐ 121 Billy Sullivan	275.00	125.00	34.00
☐ 122 Fred Tenney	250.00	110.00	31.00
☐ 123 Ira Thomas	250.00	110.00	31.00
☐ 124 Bobby Wallace	550.00	250.00	70.00
☐ 125 Ed Walsh	500.00	220.00	60.00
☐ 126 Chief Wilson	250.00	110.00	31.00

1989 TV Sports Mailbags

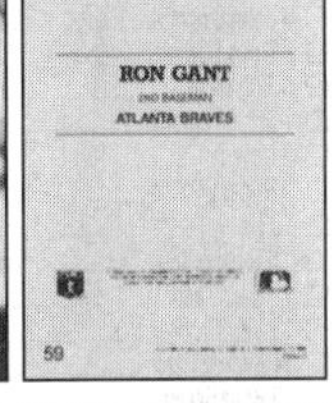

This 140-card set features glossy 8" by 10" color player photos and was distributed in packs with four pictures to a pack at the suggested retail price of $4.95. The backs carry the player's name, playing position, and team name.

	MINT	NRMT	EXC
COMPLETE SET (140)	75.00	34.00	9.50
COMMON CARD (1-140)	.25	.11	.03
☐ 1 Darryl Strawberry	.50	.23	.06
☐ 2 Ron Darling	.25	.11	.03
☐ 3 Dwight Gooden	.50	.23	.06
☐ 4 Keith Hernandez	.50	.23	.06
☐ 5 Kevin McReynolds	.25	.11	.03
☐ 6 David Cone	.75	.35	.09
☐ 7 Randy Myers	.25	.11	.03
☐ 8 Gregg Jefferies	.75	.35	.09
☐ 9 Andy Van Slyke	.25	.11	.03
☐ 10 Bobby Bonilla	.75	.35	.09
☐ 11 Doug Drabek	.25	.11	.03
☐ 12 Barry Bonds	2.00	.90	.25
☐ 13 Tim Raines	.25	.11	.03
☐ 14 Andres Galarraga	.75	.35	.09
☐ 15 Hubie Brooks	.25	.11	.03
☐ 16 Tim Wallach	.25	.11	.03
☐ 17 Mark Grace	1.25	.55	.16
☐ 18 Ryne Sandberg	2.00	.90	.25
☐ 19 Shawon Dunston	.25	.11	.03
☐ 20 Mitch Webster	.25	.11	.03
☐ 21 Andre Dawson	.50	.23	.06
☐ 22 Damon Berryhill	.25	.11	.03
☐ 23 Greg Maddux	4.00	1.80	.50
☐ 24 Vance Law	.25	.11	.03
☐ 25 Ozzie Smith	2.50	1.10	.30
☐ 26 Tom Brunansky	.25	.11	.03
☐ 27 Pedro Guerrero	.25	.11	.03
☐ 28 Vince Coleman	.25	.11	.03
☐ 29 Juan Samuel	.25	.11	.03
☐ 30 Von Hayes	.25	.11	.03
☐ 31 Ricky Jordan	.25	.11	.03
☐ 32 Mike Schmidt	1.00	.45	.12
☐ 33 Kirk Gibson	.75	.35	.09
☐ 34 Orel Hershiser	.50	.23	.06
☐ 35 Mike Marshall	.25	.11	.03
☐ 36 Mike Scioscia	.25	.11	.03
☐ 37 Eric Davis	.25	.11	.03
☐ 38 Chris Sabo	.25	.11	.03
☐ 39 Barry Larkin	1.00	.45	.12
☐ 40 Danny Jackson	.25	.11	.03
☐ 41 Tom Browning	.25	.11	.03
☐ 42 Kal Daniels	.25	.11	.03
☐ 43 John Franco	.50	.23	.06
☐ 44 Paul O'Neill	.50	.23	.06
☐ 45 Tony Gwynn	2.50	1.10	.30
☐ 46 Benito Santiago	.25	.11	.03
☐ 47 Roberto Alomar	2.00	.90	.25
☐ 48 John Kruk	.50	.23	.06
☐ 49 Will Clark	1.00	.45	.12
☐ 50 Rick Reuschel	.25	.11	.03
☐ 51 Kevin Mitchell	.25	.11	.03
☐ 52 Robby Thompson	.25	.11	.03
☐ 53 Mike Scott	.25	.11	.03
☐ 54 Glenn Davis	.25	.11	.03
☐ 55 Billy Hatcher	.25	.11	.03
☐ 56 Gerald Young	.25	.11	.03
☐ 57 Gerald Perry	.25	.11	.03
☐ 58 Dale Murphy	.75	.35	.09
☐ 59 Ron Gant	.75	.35	.09
☐ 60 Jody Davis	.25	.11	.03
☐ 61 Mike Greenwell	.25	.11	.03
☐ 62 Ellis Burks	1.00	.45	.12
☐ 63 Roger Clemens	1.25	.55	.16
☐ 64 Wade Boggs	1.00	.45	.12
☐ 65 Dwight Evans	.50	.23	.06
☐ 66 Marty Barrett	.25	.11	.03
☐ 67 Mike Boddicker	.25	.11	.03
☐ 68 Lee Smith	.50	.23	.06
☐ 69 Alan Trammell	.50	.23	.06
☐ 70 Matt Nokes	.25	.11	.03
☐ 71 Jack Morris	.25	.11	.03
☐ 72 Jeff Robinson	.25	.11	.03
☐ 73 Paul Molitor	1.25	.55	.16
☐ 74 Robin Yount	1.00	.45	.12
☐ 75 Ted Higuera	.25	.11	.03
☐ 76 Jim Gantner	.25	.11	.03
☐ 77 Fred McGriff	1.00	.45	.12
☐ 78 Dave Stieb	.25	.11	.03
☐ 79 George Bell	.25	.11	.03
☐ 80 Tony Fernandez	.25	.11	.03
☐ 81 Dave Winfield	.75	.35	.09
☐ 82 Don Mattingly	2.50	1.10	.30
☐ 83 Rickey Henderson	1.00	.45	.12
☐ 84 Dave Righetti	.25	.11	.03
☐ 85 Joe Carter	.75	.35	.09
☐ 86 Mel Hall	.25	.11	.03
☐ 87 Cory Snyder	.25	.11	.03
☐ 88 Greg Swindell	.25	.11	.03
☐ 89 Cal Ripken	5.00	2.20	.60
☐ 90 Brady Anderson	3.00	1.35	.35
☐ 91 Larry Sheets	.25	.11	.03
☐ 92 Billy Ripken	.25	.11	.03
☐ 93 Jose Canseco	1.00	.45	.12
☐ 94 Walt Weiss	.25	.11	.03
☐ 95 Dave Stewart	.25	.11	.03
☐ 96 Dennis Eckersley	.50	.23	.06
☐ 97 Terry Steinbach	.50	.23	.06
☐ 98 Mark McGwire	3.00	1.35	.35
☐ 99 Carney Lansford	.25	.11	.03
☐ 100 Dave Henderson	.25	.11	.03
☐ 101 Kent Hrbek	.25	.11	.03
☐ 102 Kirby Puckett	2.50	1.10	.30
☐ 103 Frank Viola	.25	.11	.03
☐ 104 Gary Gaetti	.25	.11	.03
☐ 105 George Brett	2.50	1.10	.30
☐ 106 Kevin Seitzer	.25	.11	.03
☐ 107 Danny Tartabull	.25	.11	.03
☐ 108 Bo Jackson	.75	.35	.09
☐ 109 Wally Joyner	.50	.23	.06
☐ 110 Devon White	.50	.23	.06
☐ 111 Johnny Ray	.25	.11	.03
☐ 112 Mike Witt	.25	.11	.03
☐ 113 Harold Baines	.25	.11	.03
☐ 114 Ozzie Guillen	.25	.11	.03
☐ 115 Bobby Thigpen	.25	.11	.03
☐ 116 Dan Pasqua	.25	.11	.03
☐ 117 Ruben Sierra	.50	.23	.06
☐ 118 Pete Incaviglia	.25	.11	.03
☐ 119 Charlie Hough	.25	.11	.03
☐ 120 Scott Fletcher	.25	.11	.03
☐ 121 Mark Langston	.25	.11	.03
☐ 122 Alvin Davis	.25	.11	.03
☐ 123 Harold Reynolds	.25	.11	.03
☐ 124 Jay Buhner	1.25	.55	.16
☐ 125 Jose Canseco	1.00	.45	.12
☐ 126 Wade Boggs	1.00	.45	.12
☐ 127 Rickey Henderson	1.00	.45	.12
☐ 128 Mike Greenwell	.25	.11	.03
☐ 129 Darryl Strawberry	.50	.23	.06
☐ 130 Tony Gwynn	2.50	1.10	.30
☐ 131 Will Clark	1.00	.45	.12
☐ 132 Vince Coleman	.25	.11	.03
☐ 133 Jose Canseco	1.00	.45	.12
☐ 134 Frank Viola	.25	.11	.03
☐ 135 Orel Hershiser	.50	.23	.06
☐ 136 Kirk Gibson	.75	.35	.09
☐ 137 Mark McGwire	3.00	1.35	.35
☐ 138 Benito Santiago	.25	.11	.03
☐ 139 Chris Sabo	.25	.11	.03
☐ 140 Walt Weiss	.25	.11	.03

1992 TV Sports Mailbag/Photo File 500 Home Run Club

This 15-piece set features horizontal, blank-backed, oversized (10" X 8") cards.They are color action shots (except Ruth, Ott, and Foxx, which are black-and-white) on left side. Player's name, biography, teams, and key home run information are printed on the right side. The cards are unnumbered and checklisted below in alphabetical order.

	MINT	NRMT	EXC
COMPLETE SET (15)	30.00	13.50	3.70
COMMON CARD (1-14)	1.00	.45	.12
☐ 1 Hank Aaron	4.00	1.80	.50
☐ 2 Ernie Banks	2.00	.90	.25
☐ 3 Jimmie Foxx	2.00	.90	.25
☐ 4 Reggie Jackson	2.50	1.10	.30
☐ 5 Harmon Killebrew	1.50	.70	.19
☐ 6 Mickey Mantle	5.00	2.20	.60
☐ 7 Eddie Mathews	1.50	.70	.19
☐ 8 Willie Mays	4.00	1.80	.50
☐ 9 Willie McCovey	1.50	.70	.19
☐ 10 Mel Ott	1.50	.70	.19
☐ 11 Frank Robinson	1.50	.70	.19
☐ 12 Babe Ruth	5.00	2.20	.60
☐ 13 Mike Schmidt	2.00	.90	.25
☐ 14 Ted Williams	4.00	1.80	.50
☐ 15 Header card	1.00	.45	.12

1961 Twins Jay Publishing

This 12-card set of the Minnesota Twins measures approximately 5" by 7". The fronts feature black-and-white posed player photos with the

player's and team name printed below in the white border. These cards were packaged 12 to a packet. The backs are blank. The cards are unnumbered and checklisted below in alphabetical order.

	NRMT	VG-E	GOOD
COMPLETE SET (12)	35.00	16.00	4.40
COMMON CARD (1-12)	2.50	1.10	.30
☐ 1 Bob Allison	3.00	1.35	.35
☐ 2 Earl Battey	2.50	1.10	.30
☐ 3 Lenny Green	3.00	1.35	.35
☐ 4 Jim Kaat	4.00	1.80	.50
☐ 5 Harmon Killebrew	10.00	4.50	1.25
☐ 6 John Kralick	2.50	1.10	.30
☐ 7 Don Lee	2.50	1.10	.30
☐ 8 Jim Lemon	2.50	1.10	.30
☐ 9 Sam Mele MG	3.00	1.35	.35
☐ 10 Camilo Pascual	3.00	1.35	.35
☐ 11 Jose Valdivielso	2.50	1.10	.30
☐ 12 Zoilo Versalles	3.00	1.35	.35

1961 Twins Peter's Meats

The cards in this 26 card set measure 3 1/2" by 4 5/8". The 1961 Peter's Meats set of full color numbered cards depicts Minnesota Twins players only. The individual cards served as partial packaging for various meat products and are blank backed and heavily waxed. Complete boxes are sometimes available and are valued approximately 50 percent more than single cards. The catalog designation is F173.

	NRMT	VG-E	GOOD
COMPLETE SET (26)	550.00	250.00	70.00
COMMON CARD (1-26)	15.00	6.75	1.85
☐ 1 Zoilo Versalles	20.00	9.00	2.50
☐ 2 Ed Lopat CO	20.00	9.00	2.50
☐ 3 Pedro Ramos	15.00	6.75	1.85
☐ 4 Chuck Stobbs	15.00	6.75	1.85
☐ 5 Don Mincher	20.00	9.00	2.50
☐ 6 Jack Kralick	15.00	6.75	1.85
☐ 7 Jim Kaat	75.00	34.00	9.50
☐ 8 Hal Naragon	15.00	6.75	1.85
☐ 9 Don Lee	15.00	6.75	1.85
☐ 10 Cookie Lavagetto CO	20.00	9.00	2.50
☐ 11 Pete Whisenant	15.00	6.75	1.85
☐ 12 Elmer Valo	15.00	6.75	1.85
☐ 13 Ray Moore	15.00	6.75	1.85
☐ 14 Billy Gardner	20.00	9.00	2.50
☐ 15 Lenny Green	15.00	6.75	1.85
☐ 16 Sam Mele MG	15.00	6.75	1.85
☐ 17 Jim Lemon	20.00	9.00	2.50
☐ 18 Harmon Killebrew	200.00	90.00	25.00
☐ 19 Paul Giel	20.00	9.00	2.50
☐ 20 Reno Bertoia	15.00	6.75	1.85
☐ 21 Clyde McCullough CO	15.00	6.75	1.85
☐ 22 Earl Battey	20.00	9.00	2.50
☐ 23 Camilo Pascual	20.00	9.00	2.50
☐ 24 Dan Dobbek	15.00	6.75	1.85
☐ 25 Jose Valdivielso	15.00	6.75	1.85
☐ 26 Billy Consolo	15.00	6.75	1.85

1961-62 Twins Cloverleaf Dairy

These large (3 3/4" by 7 3/4") cards are unnumbered; they made up the side of a Cloverleaf Dairy milk carton. Cards still on the carton are valued double the listed price below. The last two digits of the year of issue for each player is given in parentheses. However those players appearing both (BOTH) years are indistinguishable (as to which year they were produced) when cut from the carton. There were 16 cards produced in 1961 and 24 cards produced in 1962. These unnumbered cards are sequenced in alphabetical order. The catalog designation for this set is F103.

	NRMT	VG-E	GOOD
COMPLETE SET (31)	800.00	350.00	100.00
COMMON CARD (1-31)	20.00	9.00	2.50
☐ 1 Bernie Allen 62	25.00	11.00	3.10
☐ 2 George Banks 62	25.00	11.00	3.10
☐ 3 Earl Battey BOTH	20.00	9.00	2.50
☐ 4 Joe Bonikowski 62	25.00	11.00	3.10
☐ 5 Billy Gardner 61	30.00	13.50	3.70
☐ 6 Paul Giel 61	30.00	13.50	3.70
☐ 7 John Goryl 62	25.00	11.00	3.10
☐ 8 Lenny Green BOTH	20.00	9.00	2.50
☐ 9 Jim Kaat BOTH	50.00	22.00	6.25
☐ 10 Harmon Killebrew 61	150.00	70.00	19.00
☐ 11 Jack Kralick BOTH	20.00	9.00	2.50
☐ 12 Don Lee 61	25.00	11.00	3.10
☐ 13 Jim Lemon BOTH	20.00	9.00	2.50
☐ 14 Manager/Coaches 62	25.00	11.00	3.10
☐ 15 Georges Maranda 62	25.00	11.00	3.10
☐ 16 Orlando Martinez 62	25.00	11.00	3.10
☐ 17 Don Mincher BOTH	20.00	9.00	2.50
☐ 18 Ray Moore 62	25.00	11.00	3.10
☐ 19 Hal Naragon 62	25.00	11.00	3.10
☐ 20 Camilo Pascual BOTH	25.00	11.00	3.10
☐ 21 Vic Power 62	25.00	11.00	3.10
☐ 22 Pedro Ramos 61	30.00	13.50	3.70
☐ 23 Rich Rollins 62	30.00	13.50	3.70
☐ 24 Theodore Sadowski 62	25.00	11.00	3.10
☐ 25 Albert Stange 62	25.00	11.00	3.10
☐ 26 Dick Stigman 62	25.00	11.00	3.10
☐ 27 Chuck Stobbs 61	30.00	13.50	3.70
☐ 28 Bill Tuttle BOTH	20.00	9.00	2.50
☐ 29 Jose Valdivielso 61	25.00	11.00	3.10
☐ 30 Zoilo Versalles BOTH	25.00	11.00	3.10
☐ 31 Gerald Zimmerman 62	25.00	11.00	3.10

1963 Twins Jay Publishing

This 12-card set of the Minnesota Twins measures approximately 5" by 7". The fronts feature black-and-white posed player photos with the player's and team name printed below in the white border. These cards were packaged 12 to a packet. The backs are blank. The cards are unnumbered and checklisted below in alphabetical order.

	NRMT	VG-E	GOOD
COMPLETE SET (12)	35.00	16.00	4.40
COMMON CARD (1-12)	2.00	.90	.25
☐ 1 Bernie Allen	2.00	.90	.25
☐ 2 Bob Allison	3.50	1.55	.45
☐ 3 Earl Battey	2.00	.90	.25
☐ 4 Bill Dailey	2.00	.90	.25
☐ 5 Jim Kaat	4.50	2.00	.55
☐ 6 Harmon Killebrew	10.00	4.50	1.25
☐ 7 Sam Mele MG	3.00	1.35	.35
☐ 8 Camilo Pascual	3.50	1.55	.45
☐ 9 Vic Power	2.00	.90	.25
☐ 10 Rich Rollins	2.00	.90	.25
☐ 11 Dick Stigman	2.00	.90	.25
☐ 12 Zoilo Versalles	3.50	1.55	.45

1963 Twins Volpe

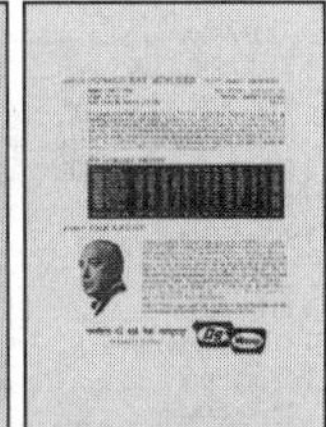

Sponsored by Western Oil and Fuel Company, these eight portraits of the 1963 Minnesota Twins by noted artist Nicholas Volpe measure approximately 8 1/2" by 11". Each white-bordered color reproduction of pastel chalk on a black background features a larger portrait and a smaller action drawing. The player's name appears in black lettering within the white margin at bottom, and also as a white facsimile autograph on the black background. The white back carries the player's name, position, and biography at the top, followed below by career highlights and statistics. Artist information and the sponsor's logo at the bottom round out the backs. The drawings are unnumbered and checklisted below in alphabetical order.

	NRMT	VG-E	GOOD
COMPLETE SET (8)	60.00	27.00	7.50
COMMON CARD (1-8)	8.00	3.60	1.00
☐ 1 Bernie Allen	8.00	3.60	1.00
☐ 2 Bob Allison	10.00	4.50	1.25
☐ 3 Bill Dailey	8.00	3.60	1.00
☐ 4 Lenny Green	8.00	3.60	1.00
☐ 5 Sam Mele MG	8.00	3.60	1.00
☐ 6 Don Mincher	10.00	4.50	1.25
☐ 7 Ray Moore	8.00	3.60	1.00
☐ 8 Lee Stange	8.00	3.60	1.00

1964 Twins Jay Publishing

The 1964 Twins Jay set consists of 12 cards produced by Jay Publishing. The Henry and Oliva cards establish the year of the set, since 1964 was Henry's last year and Oliva's first year with the Twins. The cards measure approximately 5" by 7" and are printed on photographic paper stock. The white fronts feature a black-and-white

player portrait with the player's name and the team name below. The backs are blank. The cards are packaged 12 to a packet. The cards are unnumbered and checklisted below in alphabetical order.

	NRMT	VG-E	GOOD
COMPLETE SET (12)	30.00	13.50	3.70
COMMON CARD (1-12)	2.00	.90	.25
1 Bob Allison	3.00	1.35	.35
2 Earl Battey	2.00	.90	.25
3 Jim Grant	2.00	.90	.25
4 Jimmie Hall	2.00	.90	.25
5 Ron Henry	2.00	.90	.25
6 Jim Kaat	3.50	1.55	.45
7 Harmon Killebrew	5.00	2.20	.60
8 Tony Oliva	3.00	1.35	.35
9 Camilo Pascual	2.50	1.10	.30
10 Rich Rollins	2.50	1.10	.30
11 Dick Stigman	2.00	.90	.25
12 Zorro Versalles	3.00	1.35	.35

1966 Twins Fairway Grocery

This 17-card set features 8" by 10" color player portraits of the Minnesota Twins with player information and statistics on the backs. The cards are unnumbered and checklisted below in alphabetical order.

	NRMT	VG-E	GOOD
COMPLETE SET (17)	100.00	45.00	12.50
COMMON CARD (1-17)	5.00	2.20	.60
1 Bernie Allen	5.00	2.20	.60
2 Bob Allison	10.00	4.50	1.25
3 Earl Battey	5.00	2.20	.60
4 Jim Grant	7.50	3.40	.95
5 Jimmie Hall	5.00	2.20	.60
6 Jim Kaat	5.00	2.20	.60
7 Harmon Killebrew	20.00	9.00	2.50
8 Jim Merritt	5.00	2.20	.60
9 Don Mincher	5.00	2.20	.60
10 Tony Oliva	10.00	4.50	1.25
11 Camilo Pascual	5.00	2.20	.60
12 Jim Perry	5.00	2.20	.60
13 Frank Quilici	5.00	2.20	.60
14 Rich Rollins	5.00	2.20	.60
15 Sandy Valdespino	5.00	2.20	.60
16 Zoilo Versalles	7.50	3.40	.95
17 Al Worthington	5.00	2.20	.60

1969 Twins Team Issue Color

This 10-card set of the Minnesota Twins measures approximately 7" by 8 3/4" with the fronts featuring white-bordered color player photos. The player's name and team is printed in black in the white margin below the picture. The backs are blank. The cards are unnumbered and checklisted below in alphabetical order.

	NRMT	VG-E	GOOD
COMPLETE SET (10)	40.00	18.00	5.00
COMMON CARD (1-10)	3.00	1.35	.35
1 Bob Allison	4.00	1.80	.50
2 Leo Cardenas	4.00	1.80	.50
3 Rod Carew	10.00	4.50	1.25
4 Dean Chance	4.00	1.80	.50
5 Jim Kaat	5.00	2.20	.60
6 Harmon Killebrew	7.50	3.40	.95
7 Billy Martin	7.50	3.40	.95
8 Tony Oliva	6.00	2.70	.75
9 Cesar Tovar	4.00	1.80	.50
10 Ted Uhlaender	3.00	1.35	.35

1978 Twins Frisz

Manufactured by Barry R. Frisz and issued by the Twins in two 25-card series, these cards measure approximately 2 1/2" by 3 3/4" and feature on their fronts white-bordered posed color photos of retired Twins players. The white and gray horizontal back carries the player's name, biography, position, statistics, and career highlights. The cards are numbered on the back.

	NRMT	VG-E	GOOD
COMPLETE SET (50)	25.00	11.00	3.10
COMMON CARD (1-50)	.50	.23	.06
1 Bob Allison	1.50	.70	.19
2 Earl Battey	.50	.23	.06
3 Dave Boswell	.50	.23	.06
4 Dean Chance	1.50	.70	.19
5 Jim Grant	1.00	.45	.12
6 Calvin Griffith PRES	.50	.23	.06
7 Jimmie Hall	.50	.23	.06
8 Harmon Killebrew	2.50	1.10	.30
9 Jim Lemon	.50	.23	.06
10 Billy Martin MG	1.50	.70	.19
11 Gene Mauch MG	.75	.35	.09
12 Sam Mele MG	.50	.23	.06
13 Metropolitan Stadium	1.50	.70	.19
14 Don Mincher	.50	.23	.06
15 Tony Oliva	1.00	.45	.12
16 Camilo Pascual	.75	.35	.09
17 Jim Perry	.50	.23	.06
18 Frank Quilici MG	.50	.23	.06
19 Rich Reese	.50	.23	.06
20 Bill Rigney MG	.50	.23	.06
21 Cesar Tovar	.75	.35	.09
22 Zoilo Versalles	.75	.35	.09
23 Al Worthington	.50	.23	.06
24 Jerry Zimmerman	.50	.23	.06
25 Checklist 1-25	.50	.23	.06
26 Bernie Allen	.50	.23	.06
27 Leo Cardenas	1.00	.45	.12
28 Ray Corbin	.50	.23	.06
29 Joe Decker	.50	.23	.06
30 Johnny Goryl	.50	.23	.06
31 Tom Hall	.50	.23	.06
32 Bill Hands	.50	.23	.06
33 Jim Holt	.50	.23	.06
34 Randy Hundley	1.00	.45	.12
35 Jerry Kindall	.50	.23	.06
36 Johnny Klippstein	.50	.23	.06
37 Jack Kralick	.50	.23	.06
38 Jim Merritt	.50	.23	.06
39 Joe Nossek	.50	.23	.06
40 Ron Perranoski	1.00	.45	.12
41 Bill Pleis	.50	.23	.06
42 Rick Renick	.50	.23	.06
43 Jim Roland	.50	.23	.06
44 Lee Stange	.50	.23	.06
45 Dick Stigman	.50	.23	.06
46 Danny Thompson	.50	.23	.06
47 Ted Uhlaender	.50	.23	.06
48 Sandy Valdespino	1.00	.45	.12
49 Dick Woodson	.50	.23	.06
50 Checklist 25-50	.50	.23	.06

1978 Twins Frisz Postcards

Manufactured by Barry R. Frisz and issued by the Twins, these 25 postcards measure 3 1/2" by 5 1/2" and feature on their fronts borderless color posed-on-field photos of then-current Twins. The back carries the player's name, position, and height and weight at the upper left. Below is a ghosted cartoon logo that carries the words "Win, Twins." The year of the set appears in the vertical lettering bisecting the postcard. The postcards are unnumbered and checklisted below in alphabetical order.

	NRMT	VG-E	GOOD
COMPLETE SET (25)	20.00	9.00	2.50
COMMON CARD (1-25)	.75	.35	.09
1 Glenn Adams	.75	.35	.09
2 Glenn Borgmann	.75	.35	.09
3 Rod Carew	3.50	1.55	.45
4 Rich Chiles	.75	.35	.09
5 Mike Cubbage	.75	.35	.09
6 Roger Erickson	.75	.35	.09
7 Dan Ford	.75	.35	.09
8 Dave Goltz	.75	.35	.09
9 Dave Johnson	.75	.35	.09
10 Tom Johnson	.75	.35	.09
11 Craig Kusick	.75	.35	.09
12 Jose Morales	1.00	.45	.12
13 Willie Norwood	.75	.35	.09
14 Hosken Powell	.75	.35	.09
15 Bob Randall	.75	.35	.09
16 Pete Redfern	.75	.35	.09
17 Bombo Rivera	.75	.35	.09
18 Gary Serum	.75	.35	.09
19 Roy Smalley	1.50	.70	.19
20 Greg Thayer	.75	.35	.09
21 Paul Thormodsgard	.75	.35	.09
22 Rob Wilfong	.75	.35	.09
23 Larry Wolfe	.75	.35	.09
24 Butch Wynegar	1.00	.45	.12
25 Geoff Zahn	.75	.35	.09

1979 Twins Frisz Postcards

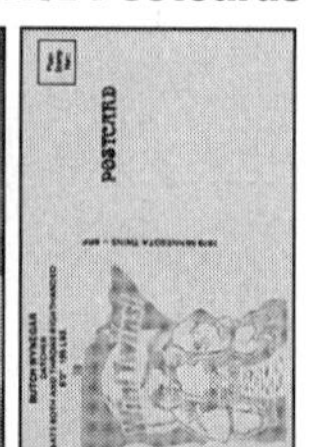

Manufactured by Barry R. Frisz and issued by the Twins, these 30 postcards measure 3 1/2" by 5 1/2" and feature on their fronts borderless color posed-on-field photos of then-current Twins. The back carries the player's name, position, and height and weight at the upper left. Below is a ghosted cartoon logo that carries the words "Win, Twins." The year of the set appears in the vertical lettering bisecting the postcard. The postcards are unnumbered and checklisted below in alphabetical order.

	NRMT	VG-E	GOOD
COMPLETE SET (30)	15.00	6.75	1.85
COMMON CARD (1-30)	.75	.35	.09
1 Glenn Adams	.75	.35	.09
2 Glenn Borgmann	.75	.35	.09
3 John Castino	.75	.35	.09
4 Mike Cubbage	.75	.35	.09
5 Dave Edwards	.75	.35	.09
6 Roger Erickson	.75	.35	.09
7 Dave Goltz	.75	.35	.09
8 John Goryl CO	.75	.35	.09
9 Paul Hartzell	.75	.35	.09
10 Jeff Holly	.75	.35	.09
11 Ron Jackson	.75	.35	.09
12 Jerry Koosman	1.25	.55	.16
13 Karl Kuehl CO	.75	.35	.09
14 Craig Kusick	.75	.35	.09
15 Ken Landreaux	.75	.35	.09
16 Mike Marshall	1.00	.45	.12
17 Gene Mauch MG	1.00	.45	.12
18 Jose Morales	.75	.35	.09
19 Willie Norwood	.75	.35	.09
20 Camilo Pascual CO	1.00	.45	.12
21 Hosken Powell	.75	.35	.09
22 Bobby Randall	.75	.35	.09
23 Pete Redfern	.75	.35	.09
24 Bombo Rivera	.75	.35	.09
25 Gary Serum	.75	.35	.09
26 Roy Smalley	1.00	.45	.12
27 Rob Wilfong	.75	.35	.09
28 Butch Wynegar	.75	.35	.09
29 Geoff Zahn	.75	.35	.09
30 Jerry Zimmerman CO	.75	.35	.09

1982 Twins Postcards

This 34-postcard set features the 1982 Minnesota Twins Baseball Team and features borderless color player photos with a simulated autograph. The backs display a postcard format. The cards are unnumbered and checklisted below in alphabetical order.

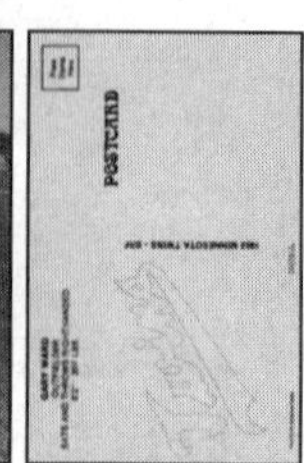

	NRMT	VG-E	GOOD
COMPLETE SET (34)	10.00	4.50	1.25
COMMON CARD (1-34)	.25	.11	.03
1 Fernando Arroyo	.25	.11	.03
2 Sal Butera	.25	.11	.03
3 Bobby Castillo	.25	.11	.03
4 John Castino	.25	.11	.03
5 Doug Corbett	.25	.11	.03
6 Ron Davis	.25	.11	.03
7 Jim Eisenreich	1.25	.55	.16
8 Dave Engle	.25	.11	.03
9 Roger Erickson	.25	.11	.03
10 Lenny Faedo	.25	.11	.03
11 Terry Felton	.25	.11	.03
12 Gary Gaetti	2.50	1.10	.30
13 Billy Gardner MG	.25	.11	.03
14 Mickey Hatcher	.25	.11	.03
15 Brad Havens	.25	.11	.03
16 Kent Hrbek	2.00	.90	.25
17 Darrell Jackson	.25	.11	.03
18 Randy Johnson	.25	.11	.03
19 Karl Kuehl CO	.25	.11	.03
20 Jim Lemon CO	.25	.11	.03
21 Bobby Mitchell	.25	.11	.03
22 Jack O'Connor	.25	.11	.03
23 Johnny Podres CO	.50	.23	.06
24 Pete Redfern	.25	.11	.03
25 Rick Stelmaszek CO	.25	.11	.03
26 Jesus Vega	.25	.11	.03
27 Gary Ward	.25	.11	.03
28 Ron Washington	.25	.11	.03
29 Rob Wilfong	.25	.11	.03
30 Al Williams	.25	.11	.03
31 Butch Wynegar	.25	.11	.03
32 Hubert H. Humphrey Metrodome Outside view	.25	.11	.03
33 Hubert H. Humphrey Metrodome Inside view	.25	.11	.03
34 Team Picture	.25	.11	.03

1983 Twins Team Issue

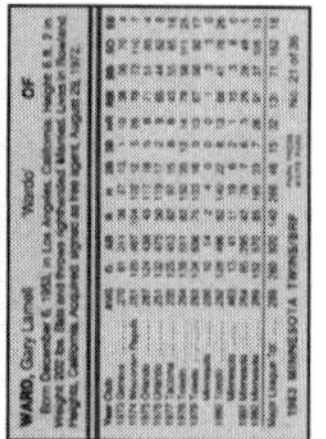

This 36-card set measures the standard size. The fronts feature borderless color player photos with a miniature representation of the player's jersey superimposed on the picture at the bottom. On a white background, biographical information and statistics are printed in red and blue.

	NRMT	VG-E	GOOD
COMPLETE SET (36)	6.00	2.70	.75
COMMON CARD (1-36)	.10	.05	.01
1 John Castino	.10	.05	.01
2 Jim Eisenreich	1.00	.45	.12
3 Ray Smith	.10	.05	.01
4 Scott Ullger	.10	.05	.01
5 Gary Gaetti	1.50	.70	.19
6 Mickey Hatcher	.25	.11	.03
7 Bobby Mitchell	.10	.05	.01
8 Len Faedo	.10	.05	.01
9 Kent Hrbek	.75	.35	.09
10 Tim Laudner	.10	.05	.01
11 Frank Viola	.75	.35	.09
12 Bryan Oelkers	.10	.05	.01
13 Rick Lysander	.10	.05	.01
14 Dave Engle	.10	.05	.01
15 Len Whitehouse	.10	.05	.01
16 Pete Filson	.10	.05	.01
17 Tom Brunansky	.25	.11	.03
18 Randy Bush	.10	.05	.01
19 Brad Havens	.10	.05	.01
20 Al Williams	.10	.05	.01
21 Gary Ward	.10	.05	.01
22 Jack O'Connor	.10	.05	.01
23 Robert Castillo	.10	.05	.01
24 Ron Washington	.10	.05	.01
25 Ron Davis	.10	.05	.01
26 Tom Kelly CO	.25	.11	.03
27 Billy Gardner MG	.10	.05	.01
28 Rich Stelmaszek CO	.10	.05	.01
29 Jim Lemon CO	.10	.05	.01
30 Johnny Podres CO	.25	.11	.03
31 Native Sons Tim Laudner	.50	.23	.06

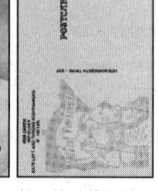

Jim Eisenreich Kent Hrbek			
☐ 32 Twins Catchers Ray Smith Dave Engle Tim Laudner	.10	.05	.01
☐ 33 Lumber Company Tom Brunansky Gary Gaetti Gary Ward Kent Hrbek	.25	.11	.03
☐ 34 Twins Coaches Tom Kelly Rick Stelmaszek Billy Gardner MG Jim Lemon Johnny Podres	.10	.05	.01
☐ 35 Team Photo	.10	.05	.01
☐ 36 Metrodome Checklist	.10	.05	.01

1984 Twins Postcards

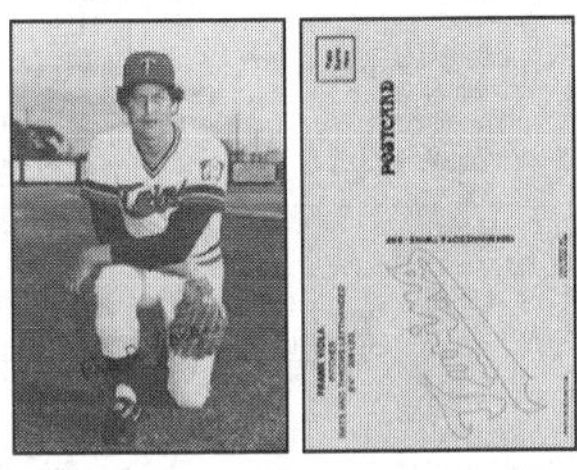

This 34-postcard set features the 1984 Minnesota Twins Baseball Team and features borderless color player photos with a simulated autograph. The backs display a postcard format. The cards are unnumbered and checklisted below in alphabetical order.

	NRMT	VG-E	GOOD
COMPLETE SET (34)	10.00	4.50	1.25
COMMON CARD (1-34)	.25	.11	.03
☐ 1 Darrell Brown	.25	.11	.03
☐ 2 Tom Brunansky	.50	.23	.06
☐ 3 Randy Bush	.25	.11	.03
☐ 4 John Butcher	.25	.11	.03
☐ 5 Bobby Castillo	.25	.11	.03
☐ 6 John Castino	.25	.11	.03
☐ 7 Keith Comstock	.25	.11	.03
☐ 8 Ron Davis	.25	.11	.03
☐ 9 Jim Eisenreich	1.00	.45	.12
☐ 10 Dave Engle	.25	.11	.03
☐ 11 Lenny Faedo	.25	.11	.03
☐ 12 Pete Filson	.25	.11	.03
☐ 13 Gary Gaetti	1.00	.45	.12
☐ 14 Billy Gardner	.25	.11	.03
☐ 15 Mickey Hatcher	.25	.11	.03
☐ 16 Kent Hrbek	.50	.23	.06
☐ 17 Houston Jimenez	.25	.11	.03
☐ 18 Tim Laudner	.25	.11	.03
☐ 19 Tom Kelly CO	.50	.23	.06
☐ 20 Jim Lemon CO	.25	.11	.03
☐ 21 Dave Meier	.25	.11	.03
☐ 22 Larry Pashnick	.25	.11	.03
☐ 23 Johnny Podres CO	.50	.23	.06
☐ 24 Jeff Reed	.25	.11	.03
☐ 25 Ken Schrom	.25	.11	.03
☐ 26 Mike Smithson	.25	.11	.03
☐ 27 Rick Stelmaszek	.25	.11	.03
☐ 28 Tim Teufel	.50	.23	.06
☐ 29 Frank Viola	.75	.35	.09
☐ 30 Mike Walters	.25	.11	.03
☐ 31 Ron Washington	.25	.11	.03
☐ 32 Al Williams	.25	.11	.03
☐ 33 Hubert H. Humphrey Metrodome	.25	.11	.03
☐ 34 Team Picture	.25	.11	.03

1984 Twins Team Issue

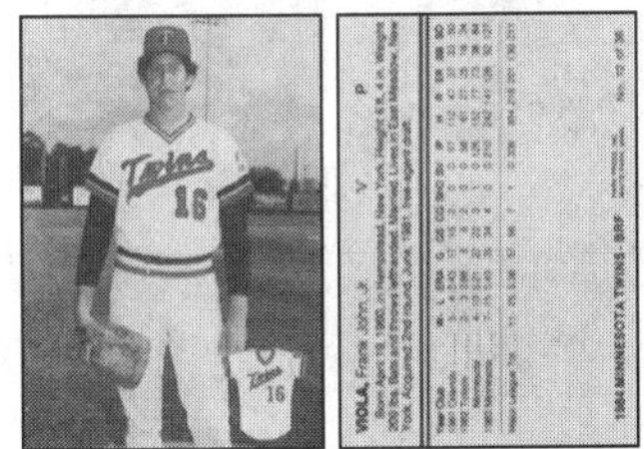

This 36-card set features borderless color player photos of the Minnesota Twins with a small jersey replica in the bottom right displaying the player's jersey number. The backs carry player information and statistics.

	NRMT	VG-E	GOOD
COMPLETE SET (36)	6.00	2.70	.75
COMMON CARD (1-36)	.10	.05	.01
☐ 1 John Castino	.10	.05	.01
☐ 2 Jim Eisenreich	.50	.23	.06
☐ 3 Houston Jimenez	.10	.05	.01
☐ 4 Dave Meier	.10	.05	.01
☐ 5 Gary Gaetti	.75	.35	.09
☐ 6 Mickey Hatcher	.10	.05	.01
☐ 7 Jeff Reed	.10	.05	.01
☐ 8 Tim Teufel	.10	.05	.01
☐ 9 Lenny Faedo	.10	.05	.01
☐ 10 Kent Hrbek	.25	.11	.03
☐ 11 Tim Laudner	.10	.05	.01
☐ 12 Frank Viola	.50	.23	.06
☐ 13 Ken Schrom	.10	.05	.01
☐ 14 Larry Pashnick	.10	.05	.01
☐ 15 Dave Engle	.10	.05	.01
☐ 16 Keith Comstock	.10	.05	.01
☐ 17 Pete Filson	.10	.05	.01
☐ 18 Tom Brunansky	.10	.05	.01
☐ 19 Randy Bush	.10	.05	.01
☐ 20 Darrell Brown	.10	.05	.01
☐ 21 Al Williams	.10	.05	.01
☐ 22 Mike Walters	.10	.05	.01
☐ 23 John Butcher	.10	.05	.01
☐ 24 Bobby Castillo	.10	.05	.01
☐ 25 Ron Washington	.10	.05	.01
☐ 26 Ron Davis	.10	.05	.01
☐ 27 Tom Kelly CO	.25	.11	.03
☐ 28 Billy Gardner MG	.10	.05	.01
☐ 29 Rick Stelmaszek CO	.10	.05	.01
☐ 30 Jim Lemon CO	.10	.05	.01
☐ 31 Johnny Podres CO	.25	.11	.03
☐ 32 Mike Smithson	.10	.05	.01
☐ 33 Harmon Killebrew	1.00	.45	.12
☐ 34 1984 Minnesota Twins Team Picture	.10	.05	.01
☐ 35 Twins Logo Card	.10	.05	.01
☐ 36 Metrodome CL	.10	.05	.01

1985 Twins 7-Eleven

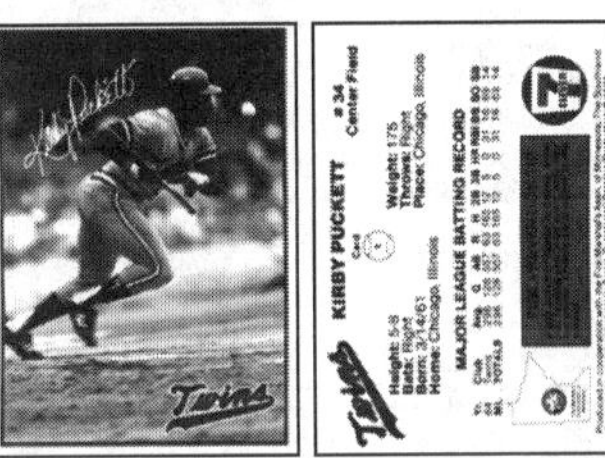

This 13-card set of Minnesota Twins was produced and distributed by the Twins in conjunction with the 7-Eleven stores and the Fire Marshall's Association. The cards measure approximately 2 1/2" by 3 1/2" and are in full color. Supposedly 20,000 sets of cards were distributed during the promotion which began on June 2nd and lasted throughout the month of July. The card backs have some statistics and a fire safety tip. The set features an early Kirby Puckett card.

	NRMT	VG-E	GOOD
COMPLETE SET (13)	15.00	6.75	1.85
COMMON CARD (1-13)	.50	.23	.06
☐ 1 Kirby Puckett	10.00	4.50	1.25
☐ 2 Frank Viola	.75	.35	.09
☐ 3 Mickey Hatcher	.50	.23	.06
☐ 4 Kent Hrbek	1.50	.70	.19
☐ 5 John Butcher	.50	.23	.06
☐ 6 Roy Smalley	.75	.35	.09
☐ 7 Tom Brunansky	.75	.35	.09
☐ 8 Ron Davis	.50	.23	.06
☐ 9 Gary Gaetti	1.50	.70	.19
☐ 10 Tim Teufel	.50	.23	.06
☐ 11 Mike Smithson	.50	.23	.06
☐ 12 Tim Laudner	.50	.23	.06
☐ NNO Checklist Card	.50	.23	.06

1985 Twins Team Issue

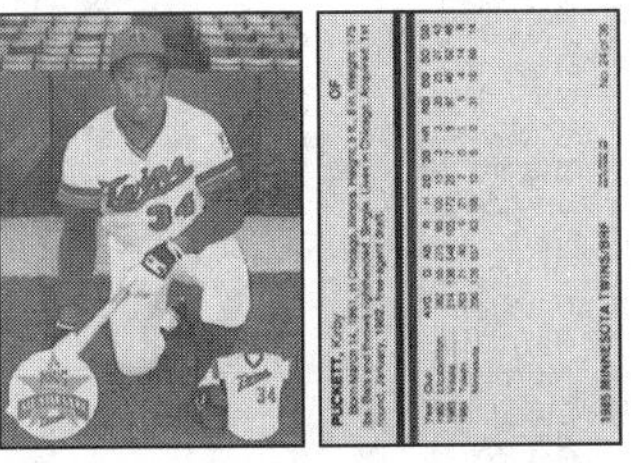

This 36-card set measures the standard size. The fronts feature borderless color player photos with a miniature representation of the player's jersey superimposed on the picture at the lower right corner. The "1985 All-Star Game" logo in the lower left corner rounds out the card face. On a white background, the horizontally oriented backs carry biographical information and statistics printed in red and blue.

	NRMT	VG-E	GOOD
COMPLETE SET (36)	6.00	2.70	.75
COMMON CARD (1-36)	.10	.05	.01
☐ 1 Alvaro Espinoza	.25	.11	.03
☐ 2 Roy Smalley	.25	.11	.03
☐ 3 Tony Oliva CO	.50	.23	.06
☐ 4 Dave Meier	.10	.05	.01
☐ 5 Gary Gaetti	.50	.23	.06
☐ 6 Mickey Hatcher	.25	.11	.03
☐ 7 Jeff Reed	.10	.05	.01
☐ 8 Tim Teufel	.10	.05	.01
☐ 9 Mark Salas	.10	.05	.01
☐ 10 Kent Hrbek	.50	.23	.06
☐ 11 Tim Laudner	.10	.05	.01
☐ 12 Frank Viola	.50	.23	.06
☐ 13 Ken Schrom	.10	.05	.01
☐ 14 Rick Lysander	.10	.05	.01
☐ 15 Dave Engle	.10	.05	.01
☐ 16 Andre David	.10	.05	.01
☐ 17 Len Whitehouse	.10	.05	.01
☐ 18 Pete Filson	.10	.05	.01
☐ 19 Tom Brunansky	.25	.11	.03
☐ 20 Randy Bush	.10	.05	.01
☐ 21 Greg Gagne	.25	.11	.03
☐ 22 John Butcher	.10	.05	.01
☐ 23 Mike Stenhouse	.10	.05	.01
☐ 24 Kirby Puckett	3.00	1.35	.35
☐ 25 Tom Klawitter	.10	.05	.01
☐ 26 Curt Wardle	.10	.05	.01
☐ 27 Rich Yett	.10	.05	.01
☐ 28 Ron Washington	.10	.05	.01
☐ 29 Ron Davis	.10	.05	.01
☐ 30 Tom Kelly CO	.25	.11	.03
☐ 31 Bill Gardner MG	.10	.05	.01
☐ 32 Rick Stelmaszek CO	.10	.05	.01
☐ 33 Johnny Podres CO	.25	.11	.03
☐ 34 Mike Smithson	.10	.05	.01
☐ 35 All-Star Game Logo	.10	.05	.01
☐ 36 Twins Logo/Checklist	.10	.05	.01

1986 Twins Greats TCMA

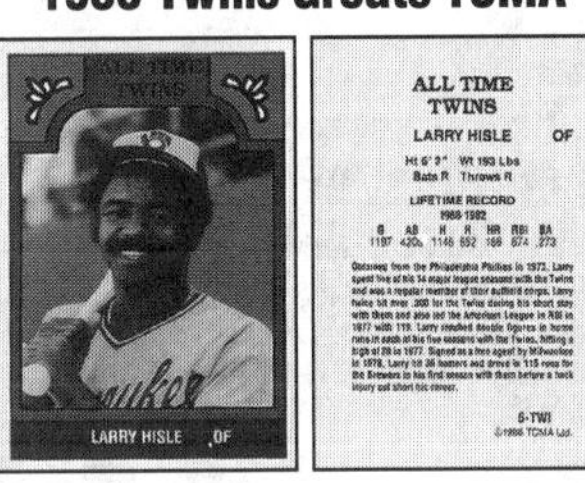

This 12-card standard-size set features some of the best Minnesota Twins from their first 25 seasons. These cards have player photos on the front and player information on the back.

	MINT	NRMT	EXC
COMPLETE SET (12)	5.00	2.20	.60
COMMON CARD (1-12)	.25	.11	.03
☐ 1 Harmon Killebrew	1.00	.45	.12
☐ 2 Rod Carew	1.50	.70	.19
☐ 3 Zoilo Versalles	.25	.11	.03
☐ 4 Cesar Tovar	.25	.11	.03
☐ 5 Bob Allison	.50	.23	.06
☐ 6 Larry Hisle	.25	.11	.03
☐ 7 Tony Oliva	.75	.35	.09
☐ 8 Earl Battey	.25	.11	.03
☐ 9 Jim Perry	.50	.23	.06
☐ 10 Jim Kaat	.75	.35	.09
☐ 11 Al Worthington	.25	.11	.03
☐ 12 Sam Mele MG	.25	.11	.03

1986 Twins Team Issue

These cards feature members of the 1986 Minnesota Twins. Players, coaches and the manager are included in this set.

	MINT	NRMT	EXC
COMPLETE SET (36)	6.00	2.70	.75
COMMON CARD	.10	.05	.01
☐ 1 Chris Pittaro	.10	.05	.01
☐ 2 Steve Lombardozzi	.10	.05	.01
☐ 3 Roy Smalley	.25	.11	.03
☐ 4 Tony Oliva CO	.50	.23	.06
☐ 5 Gary Gaetti	.50	.23	.06
☐ 6 Mickey Hatcher	.25	.11	.03
☐ 7 Jeff Reed	.10	.05	.01
☐ 8 Mark Salas	.10	.05	.01
☐ 9 Kent Hrbek	.50	.23	.06
☐ 10 Tim Laudner	.10	.05	.01
☐ 11 Frank Viola	.35	.16	.04
☐ 12 Dennis Burtt	.10	.05	.01
☐ 13 Alex Sanchez	.10	.05	.01
☐ 14 Roy Smith	.10	.05	.01
☐ 15 Billy Beane	.10	.05	.01
☐ 16 Pete Filson	.10	.05	.01
☐ 17 Tom Brunansky	.25	.11	.03
☐ 18 Randy Bush	.10	.05	.01
☐ 19 Frank Eufemia	.10	.05	.01
☐ 20 Mark Davidson	.10	.05	.01
☐ 21 Bert Blyleven	.50	.23	.06
☐ 22 Greg Gagne	.25	.11	.03
☐ 23 John Butcher	.10	.05	.01
☐ 24 Kirby Puckett	2.50	1.10	.30
☐ 25 Bill Latham	.10	.05	.01
☐ 26 Ron Washington	.10	.05	.01
☐ 27 Ron Davis	.10	.05	.01
☐ 28 Tom Kelly CO	.10	.05	.01
☐ 29 Dick Such CO	.10	.05	.01
☐ 30 Rick Stelmaszek CO	.10	.05	.01
☐ 31 Ray Miller MG	.10	.05	.01
☐ 32 Wayne Terwilliger CO	.10	.05	.01
☐ 33 Mike Smithson	.10	.05	.01
☐ 34 Al Woods	.10	.05	.01
☐ 35 Team Photo	.25	.11	.03
☐ 36 Twins Logo/Checklist	.10	.05	.01

1988 Twins Master Bread Discs

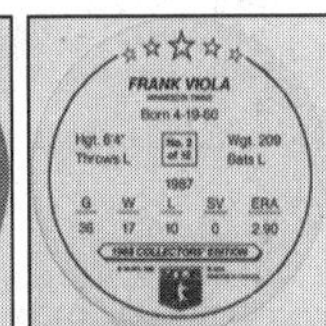

Master Bread introduced a set of 12 discs produced in conjunction with the Major League Baseball Players Association and Mike Schechter Associates. The set commemorates the Minnesota Twins' World Championship the year before and features only Twins players. A single disc was inserted inside each loaf of bread. The discs are numbered on the back and have a medium blue border on the front. Discs are approximately 2 3/4" in diameter. The disc backs contain very sparse personal or statistical information about the player and are printed in blue on white stock.

	MINT	NRMT	EXC
COMPLETE SET (12)	7.50	3.40	.95
COMMON DISC (1-12)	.50	.23	.06
☐ 1 Bert Blyleven	.75	.35	.09
☐ 2 Frank Viola	.75	.35	.09
☐ 3 Juan Berenguer	.50	.23	.06
☐ 4 Jeff Reardon	.75	.35	.09
☐ 5 Tim Laudner	.50	.23	.06
☐ 6 Steve Lombardozzi	.50	.23	.06
☐ 7 Randy Bush	.50	.23	.06
☐ 8 Kirby Puckett	5.00	2.20	.60
☐ 9 Gary Gaetti	.75	.35	.09
☐ 10 Kent Hrbek	.75	.35	.09
☐ 11 Greg Gagne	.50	.23	.06
☐ 12 Tom Brunansky	.50	.23	.06

1988 Twins Smokey Colorgrams

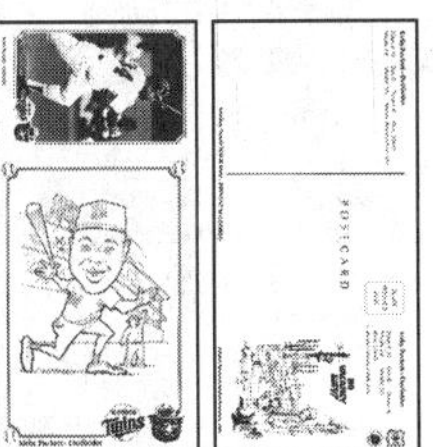

These cards are actually pages of a booklet featuring members of the Minnesota Twins and Smokey's fire safety tips. The booklet has 12 pages each containing a black and white photo card (approximately 2 1/2" by 3 3/4") and a black and white player caricature (oversized head) postcard (approximately 3 3/4" by 5 5/8"). The cards are unnumbered but they have biographical information and a fire-prevention cartoon on the back of the card.

	MINT	NRMT	EXC
COMPLETE SET (12)	20.00	9.00	2.50
COMMON CARD (1-12)	1.00	.45	.12
☐ 1 Frank Viola	1.50	.70	.19
☐ 2 Gary Gaetti	2.00	.90	.25
☐ 3 Kent Hrbek	2.00	.90	.25
☐ 4 Jeff Reardon	1.50	.70	.19
☐ 5 Gene Larkin	1.00	.45	.12
☐ 6 Bert Blyleven	2.00	.90	.25
☐ 7 Tim Laudner	1.00	.45	.12
☐ 8 Greg Gagne	1.25	.55	.16
☐ 9 Randy Bush	1.00	.45	.12
☐ 10 Dan Gladden	1.00	.45	.12
☐ 11 Al Newman	1.00	.45	.12
☐ 12 Kirby Puckett	10.00	4.50	1.25

1988 Twins Team Issue

This 33-card set features borderless color player photos of the 1987 Minnesota Twins World Championship Team. The backs carry player information and season statistics. The cards were pulled from distribution after a dispute with the Commissioner's office.

	MINT	NRMT	EXC
COMPLETE SET (33)	50.00	22.00	6.25
COMMON CARD (1-33)	1.00	.45	.12

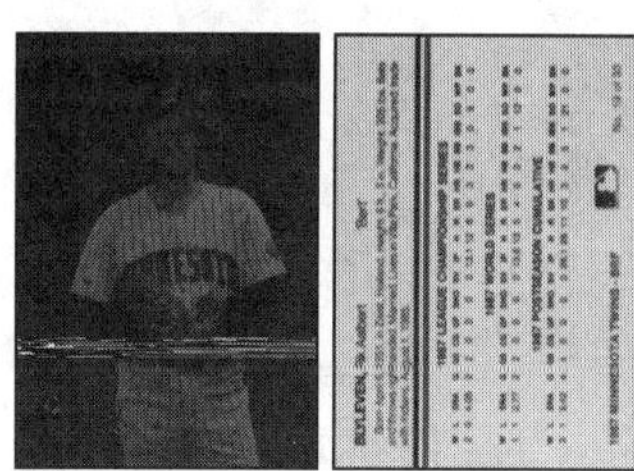

☐ 1 Steve Lombardozzi	1.00	.45	.12
☐ 2 Roy Smalley	1.00	.45	.12
☐ 3 Tony Oliva CO	3.00	1.35	.35
☐ 4 Greg Gagne	1.00	.45	.12
☐ 5 Gary Gaetti	3.00	1.35	.35
☐ 6 Gene Larkin	1.00	.45	.12
☐ 7 Tom Kelly MG	2.00	.90	.25
☐ 8 Kent Hrbek	1.00	.45	.12
☐ 9 Tim Laudner	1.00	.45	.12
☐ 10 Frank Viola	1.50	.70	.19
☐ 11 Les Straker	1.00	.45	.12
☐ 12 Don Baylor	2.00	.90	.25
☐ 13 George Frazier	1.00	.45	.12
☐ 14 Keith Atherton	1.00	.45	.12
☐ 15 Tom Brunansky	1.25	.55	.16
☐ 16 Randy Bush	1.00	.45	.12
☐ 17 Al Newman	1.00	.45	.12
☐ 18 Mark Davidson	1.00	.45	.12
☐ 19 Bert Blyleven	2.00	.90	.25
☐ 20 Dan Schatzeder	1.00	.45	.12
☐ 21 Dan Gladden	1.00	.45	.12
☐ 22 Sal Butera	1.00	.45	.12
☐ 23 Kirby Puckett	25.00	11.00	3.10
☐ 24 Joe Niekro	1.50	.70	.19
☐ 25 Juan Berenguer	1.00	.45	.12
☐ 26 Jeff Reardon	1.50	.70	.19
☐ 27 Dick Such CO	1.00	.45	.12
☐ 28 Rick Stelmaszek CO	1.00	.45	.12
☐ 29 Rick Renick CO	1.00	.45	.12
☐ 30 Wayne Terwilliger CO	1.00	.45	.12
☐ 31 1987 Team Photo	1.00	.45	.12
☐ 32 Twins Championship Logo	1.00	.45	.12
☐ 33 Twins Logo/Checklist	1.00	.45	.12

1932 U.S. Caramel R328

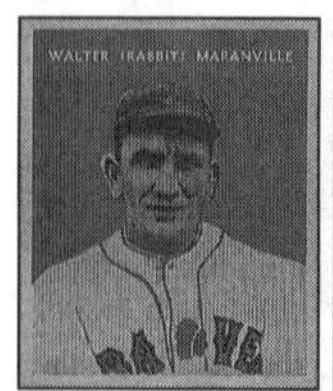

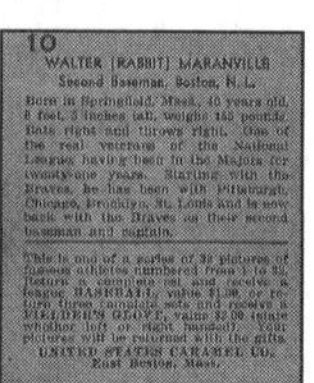

The cards in this 32-card set measure 2 1/2" by 3". The U.S. Caramel set of "Famous Athletes" was issued in 1932. The cards contain black and white bust shots set against an attractive red background. Boxers (BOX) and golfers (GOLF) are included in the set. The existence of card number 16, Fred Lindstrom has only recently been verified. The set price does not include the Lindstrom card.

	EX-MT	VG-E	GOOD
COMPLETE SET (31)	9000.00	4000.00	1100.00
COMMON BASEBALL PLAYER	175.00	80.00	22.00
COMMON BOXER	150.00	70.00	19.00
COMMON GOLFER	150.00	70.00	19.00
☐ 1 Eddie Collins	350.00	160.00	45.00
☐ 2 Paul Waner	350.00	160.00	45.00
☐ 3 Bobby Jones GOLF	200.00	90.00	25.00
☐ 4 Bill Terry	350.00	160.00	45.00
☐ 5 Earl B. Combs	350.00	160.00	45.00
☐ 6 Bill Dickey	350.00	160.00	45.00
☐ 7 Joe Cronin	350.00	160.00	45.00
☐ 8 Charles Hafey	300.00	135.00	38.00
☐ 9 Gene Sarazen GOLF	150.00	70.00	19.00
☐ 10 Rabbit Maranville	300.00	135.00	38.00
☐ 11 Rogers Hornsby	400.00	180.00	50.00
☐ 12 Mickey Cochrane	350.00	160.00	45.00
☐ 13 Lloyd Waner	300.00	135.00	38.00
☐ 14 Ty Cobb	1000.00	450.00	125.00
☐ 15 Gene Tunney BOX	200.00	90.00	25.00
☐ 16 Fred Lindstrom SP	18000.00	8100.00	2200.00
☐ 17 Al Simmons	300.00	135.00	38.00
☐ 18 Anthony Lazzeri	300.00	135.00	38.00
☐ 19 Wally Berger	200.00	90.00	25.00
☐ 20 Charles Ruffing	300.00	135.00	38.00
☐ 21 Chuck Klein	300.00	135.00	38.00
☐ 22 Jack Dempsey BOX	200.00	90.00	25.00
☐ 23 Jimmy Foxx	400.00	180.00	50.00
☐ 24 Lefty O'Doul	175.00	80.00	22.00
☐ 25 Jack Sharkey BOX	150.00	70.00	19.00
☐ 26 Henry Louis Gehrig	1000.00	450.00	125.00
☐ 27 Lefty Grove	400.00	180.00	50.00
☐ 28 Edward Brandt	175.00	80.00	22.00
☐ 29 George Earnshaw	175.00	80.00	22.00
☐ 30 Frank Frisch	300.00	135.00	38.00
☐ 31 Vernon (Lefty) Gomez	300.00	135.00	38.00
☐ 32 Babe Ruth	1200.00	550.00	150.00

1994 U.S. Department of Transportation

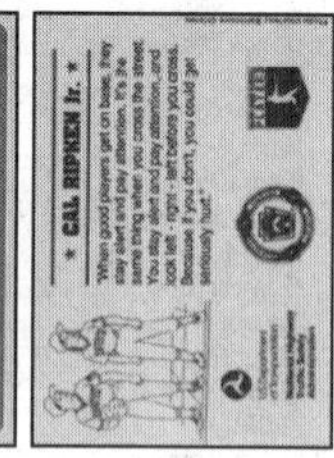

This strip of three cards was co-sponsored by the U.S. Department of Transportation and the National Highway Traffic Safety Administration. The cards were reportedly given out at the Little League World Series. The 8" by 3 1/2" strip is not perforated, but if the cards were cut along the dotted lines, they would measure the standard size. On a white card face, the fronts feature color action player photos that are accented by a pink inner border and a blue outer border. The horizontal backs have a safety message in the form of a player quote and an accompanying illustration. The cards are unnumbered and checklisted below in alphabetical order.

	MINT	NRMT	EXC
COMPLETE SET (3)	10.00	4.50	1.25
COMMON CARD (1-3)	2.00	.90	.25
☐ 1 Mike Piazza	4.00	1.80	.50
☐ 2 Cal Ripken	6.00	2.70	.75
☐ 3 Mo Vaughn	2.00	.90	.25

1991 U.S. Game Systems Baseball Legends

These cards feature leading all time greats. Each player is given one card (Ace, Queen, etc.) in all four suits. This set was issued in its own card box and we have used 1 for Ace, 11 for Jacks, 12 for Queens and 13 for Kings.

	MINT	NRMT	EXC
COMPLETE SET (56)	5.00	2.20	.60
COMMON CARD (1-56)	.10	.05	.01
☐ 1C Ty Cobb	.50	.23	.06
☐ 1D Ty Cobb	.50	.23	.06
☐ 1H Ty Cobb	.50	.23	.06
☐ 1S Ty Cobb	.50	.23	.06
☐ 2C Babe Ruth	.75	.35	.09
☐ 2D Babe Ruth	.75	.35	.09
☐ 2H Babe Ruth	.75	.35	.09
☐ 2S Babe Ruth	.75	.35	.09
☐ 3C Lou Gehrig	.50	.23	.06
☐ 3D Lou Gehrig	.50	.23	.06
☐ 3H Lou Gehrig	.50	.23	.06
☐ 3S Lou Gehrig	.50	.23	.06
☐ 4C Hank Aaron	.50	.23	.06
☐ 4D Hank Aaron	.50	.23	.06
☐ 4H Hank Aaron	.50	.23	.06
☐ 4S Hank Aaron	.50	.23	.06
☐ 5C Satchel Paige	.35	.16	.04
☐ 5D Satchel Paige	.35	.16	.04
☐ 5H Satchel Paige	.35	.16	.04
☐ 5S Satchel Paige	.35	.16	.04
☐ 6C Jimmie Foxx	.20	.09	.03
☐ 6D Jimmie Foxx	.20	.09	.03
☐ 6H Jimmie Foxx	.20	.09	.03
☐ 6S Jimmie Foxx	.20	.09	.03
☐ 7C Rogers Hornsby	.25	.11	.03
☐ 7D Rogers Hornsby	.25	.11	.03
☐ 7H Rogers Hornsby	.25	.11	.03
☐ 7S Rogers Hornsby	.25	.11	.03
☐ 8C Stan Musial	.50	.23	.06
☐ 8D Stan Musial	.50	.23	.06
☐ 8H Stan Musial	.50	.23	.06
☐ 8S Stan Musial	.50	.23	.06
☐ 9C Walter Johnson	.25	.11	.03
☐ 9D Walter Johnson	.25	.11	.03
☐ 9H Walter Johnson	.25	.11	.03
☐ 9S Walter Johnson	.25	.11	.03
☐ 10C Honus Wagner	.25	.11	.03
☐ 10D Honus Wagner	.25	.11	.03
☐ 10H Honus Wagner	.25	.11	.03
☐ 10S Honus Wagner	.25	.11	.03
☐ 11C Roberto Clemente	.50	.23	.06
☐ 11D Roberto Clemente	.50	.23	.06
☐ 11H Roberto Clemente	.50	.23	.06
☐ 11S Roberto Clemente	.50	.23	.06
☐ 12C Christy Mathewson	.25	.11	.03
☐ 12D Christy Mathewson	.25	.11	.03
☐ 12H Christy Mathewson	.25	.11	.03
☐ 12S Christy Mathewson	.25	.11	.03
☐ 13A Cy Young	.20	.09	.03
☐ 13C Cy Young	.20	.09	.03
☐ 13D Cy Young	.20	.09	.03
☐ 13H Cy Young	.20	.09	.03
☐ NNO Title Card	.10	.05	.01

1990 U.S. Playing Card All-Stars

Thse 56 playing standard-size cards have rounded corners and feature color posed and action player photos on white-bordered fronts. The player's name and position appear in a bar at the bottom with the team logo printed in a circle at the top of the bar. The blue and white striped backs carry the set's year and title. The cards are checklisted below in playing card order by suits and assigned numbers to aces (1), jacks (11), queens (12), and kings (13). A limited Silver Series parallel set was produced distinguished from the regular set by the silver foil on the cards' edges.

	MINT	NRMT	EXC
COMPLETE SET (56)	6.00	2.70	.75
COMMON CARD	.05	.02	.01
☐ 1C Bob Welch	.05	.02	.01
☐ 1D Frank Viola	.05	.02	.01
☐ 1H Ramon Martinez	.25	.11	.03
☐ 1S Roger Clemens	.50	.23	.06
☐ 2C Lance Parrish	.05	.02	.01
☐ 2D Greg Olson	.05	.02	.01
☐ 2H Mike Scioscia	.05	.02	.01
☐ 2S Sandy Alomar	.25	.11	.03
☐ 3C Bret Saberhagen	.05	.02	.01
☐ 3D Dennis Martinez	.05	.02	.01
☐ 3H Jeff Brantley	.05	.02	.01
☐ 3S Randy Johnson	.40	.18	.05
☐ 4C Gregg Olson	.05	.02	.01
☐ 4D Roberto Alomar	.40	.18	.05
☐ 4H Ryne Sandberg	.60	.25	.07
☐ 4S Steve Sax	.05	.02	.01
☐ 5C Brook Jacoby	.05	.02	.01
☐ 5D Tim Wallach	.05	.02	.01
☐ 5H Chris Sabo	.05	.02	.01
☐ 5S Kelly Gruber	.05	.02	.01
☐ 6C Ozzie Guillen	.05	.02	.01
☐ 6D Barry Larkin	.25	.11	.03
☐ 6H Ozzie Smith	.75	.35	.09
☐ 6S Cal Ripken	1.50	.70	.19
☐ 7C Ellis Burks	.25	.11	.03
☐ 7D Neal Heaton	.05	.02	.01
☐ 7H John Franco	.15	.07	.02
☐ 7S Doug Jones	.05	.02	.01
☐ 8C Dennis Eckersley	.25	.11	.03
☐ 8D Dave Smith	.05	.02	.01
☐ 8H Matt Williams	.25	.11	.03
☐ 8S Kirby Puckett	.75	.35	.09
☐ 9C Bobby Thigpen	.05	.02	.01
☐ 9D Lenny Dykstra	.05	.02	.01
☐ 9H Andre Dawson	.25	.11	.03
☐ 9S Chuck Finley	.05	.02	.01
☐ 10C Dave Stieb	.05	.02	.01
☐ 10D Shawon Dunston	.05	.02	.01
☐ 10H Benito Santiago	.05	.02	.01
☐ 10S Alan Trammell	.25	.11	.03
☐ 11C Wade Boggs	.40	.18	.05
☐ 11D Tony Gwynn	.75	.35	.09
☐ 11H Bobby Bonilla	.15	.07	.02
☐ 11S Ken Griffey Jr.	2.00	.90	.25
☐ 12C George Bell	.05	.02	.01
☐ 12D Will Clark	.40	.18	.05
☐ 12H Kevin Mitchell	.05	.02	.01
☐ 12S Dave Parker	.05	.02	.01
☐ 13C Rickey Henderson	.40	.18	.05
☐ 13D Barry Bonds	.40	.18	.05
☐ 13H Darryl Strawberry	.15	.07	.02
☐ 13S Cecil Fielder	.15	.07	.02
☐ JKO Jocker Jack Armstrong	.05	.02	.01
☐ JKO Joker Julio Franco	.05	.02	.01
☐ WCO Wild Card Mark McGwire Jose Canseco	.50	.23	.06
☐ WCO Wild Card Rob Dibble Randy Myers	.05	.02	.01

1991 U.S. Playing Card All-Stars

Thse 56 playing standard-size cards have rounded corners and feature color posed and action player photos on white-bordered fronts. The player's name and position appear in a bar at the bottom with the team logo printed in a circle on the top right. The red and white striped backs carry the set's year and title. The cards are checklisted below in playing card order by suits and assigned numbers to aces (1), jacks (11), queens (12), and kings (13). A limited Silver Series parallel set was produced distinguished from the regular set by the silver foil on the cards' edges.

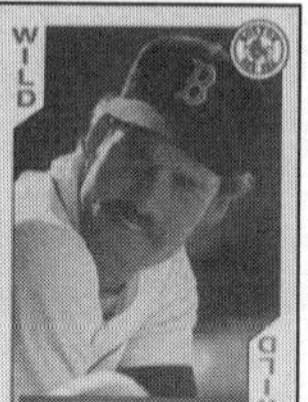

	MINT	NRMT	EXC
COMPLETE SET (56)	6.00	2.70	.75
COMMON CARD	.05	.02	.01
☐ 1C Tony Gwynn	.75	.35	.09
☐ 1D Ken Griffey Jr.	2.00	.90	.25
☐ 1H Jack Morris	.05	.02	.01
☐ 1S Tom Glavine	.40	.18	.05
☐ 2C Paul O'Neill	.05	.02	.01
☐ 2D Carlton Fisk	.25	.11	.03
☐ 2H Ozzie Guillen	.05	.02	.01
☐ 2S Eddie Murray	.50	.23	.06
☐ 3C John Smiley	.05	.02	.01
☐ 3D Scott Sanderson	.05	.02	.01
☐ 3H Jack McDowell	.15	.07	.02
☐ 3S Pete Harnisch	.05	.02	.01
☐ 4C Howard Johnson	.05	.02	.01
☐ 4D Kirby Puckett	.75	.35	.09
☐ 4H Joe Carter	.25	.11	.03
☐ 4S John Kruk	.15	.07	.02
☐ 5C Mike Morgan	.05	.02	.01
☐ 5D Jeff Reardon	.05	.02	.01
☐ 5H Mark Langston	.05	.02	.01
☐ 5S Tom Browning	.05	.02	.01
☐ 6C Barry Larkin	.25	.11	.03
☐ 6D Rafael Palmeiro	.25	.11	.03
☐ 6H Julio Franco	.05	.02	.01
☐ 6S George Bell	.05	.02	.01
☐ 7C Frank Viola	.05	.02	.01
☐ 7D Bryan Harvey	.05	.02	.01
☐ 7H Rick Aguilera	.05	.02	.01
☐ 7S Dennis Martinez	.05	.02	.01
☐ 8C Juan Samuel	.05	.02	.01
☐ 8D Jimmy Key	.05	.02	.01
☐ 8H Paul Molitor	.40	.18	.05
☐ 8S Brett Butler	.05	.02	.01
☐ 9C Craig Biggio	.25	.11	.03
☐ 9D Harold Baines	.05	.02	.01
☐ 9H Ruben Sierra	.05	.02	.01
☐ 9S Felix Jose	.05	.02	.01
☐ 10C Lee Smith	.15	.07	.02
☐ 10D Dennis Eckersley	.25	.11	.03
☐ 10H Roger Clemens	.50	.23	.06
☐ 10S Rob Dibble	.05	.02	.01
☐ 11C Andre Dawson	.25	.11	.03
☐ 11D Sandy Alomar	.05	.02	.01
☐ 11H Rickey Henderson	.25	.11	.03
☐ 11S Benito Santiago	.05	.02	.01
☐ 12C Chris Sabo	.05	.02	.01
☐ 12D Cecil Fielder	.15	.07	.02
☐ 12H Roberto Alomar	.40	.18	.05
☐ 12S Ryne Sandberg	.60	.25	.07
☐ 13C Ivan Calderon	.05	.02	.01
☐ 13D Cal Ripken	1.50	.70	.19
☐ 13H Dave Henderson	.05	.02	.01
☐ 13S Ozzie Smith	.60	.25	.07
☐ JKO Joker Bobby Bonilla	.05	.02	.01
☐ JKO Joker Danny Tartabull	.05	.02	.01
☐ WCO Wild Card Will Clark	.40	.18	.05
☐ WCO Wild Card Wade Boggs	.40	.18	.05

1993 U.S. Playing Cards Aces

This 55-card standard-size set features the top 13 players in four categories according to suits: lowest ERA's, (spades) Most Stolen Bases, (hearts) Most Home Runs, (clubs) and Highest Batting Average (diamonds). The fronts of these rounded-corner cards feature borderless full-color posed and action shots of the players while the backs have the 1993 Major League Baseball Aces design on a red background. The team logo appears in the lower left of each picture. The player's name and position appear in a black stripe that intersects the team logo at the bottom. Since this set is similar to a playing card set, the set is checklisted below as if it were a playing card deck. In the checklist C means Clubs, D means Diamonds, H means Hearts, S means Spades, and JK means Joker. The cards are checklisted in playing order by suits and numbers are assigned to Aces, (1) Jacks, (11) Queens, (12) and Kings (13). The Jokers, Wild Card, and the title card are unnumbered and listed at the end.

	MINT	NRMT	EXC
COMPLETE SET (56)	6.00	2.70	.75
COMMON CARD	.05	.02	.01
☐ 1C Juan Gonzalez	.75	.35	.09
☐ 1D Edgar Martinez	.15	.07	.02
☐ 1H Marquis Grissom	.15	.07	.02
☐ 1S Bill Swift	.05	.02	.01
☐ 2C Dave Hollins	.05	.02	.01
☐ 2D Roberto Alomar	.50	.23	.06
☐ 2H Chad Curtis	.15	.07	.02
☐ 2S Tom Glavine	.25	.11	.03
☐ 3C Darren Daulton	.15	.07	.02
☐ 3D Terry Pendleton	.05	.02	.01
☐ 3H Ozzie Smith	.40	.18	.05
☐ 3S Sid Fernandez	.05	.02	.01
☐ 4C Ken Griffey Jr.	1.50	.70	.19
☐ 4D Carlos Baerga	.15	.07	.02
☐ 4H Bip Roberts	.05	.02	.01
☐ 4S Greg Swindell	.05	.02	.01
☐ 5C Rob Deer	.05	.02	.01
☐ 5D Shane Mack	.05	.02	.01
☐ 5H Steve Finley	.25	.11	.03
☐ 5S Juan Guzman	.05	.02	.01
☐ 6C Mickey Tettleton	.05	.02	.01
☐ 6D Tony Gwynn	.75	.35	.09
☐ 6H Tim Raines	.05	.02	.01
☐ 6S Jose Rijo	.05	.02	.01
☐ 7C Gary Sheffield	.40	.18	.05
☐ 7D Paul Molitor	.30	.14	.04
☐ 7H Delino DeShields	.05	.02	.01
☐ 7S Mike Morgan	.05	.02	.01
☐ 8C Joe Carter	.25	.11	.03
☐ 8D Frank Thomas	1.50	.70	.19
☐ 8H Rickey Henderson	.30	.14	.04
☐ 8S Mike Mussina	.40	.18	.05
☐ 9C Albert Belle	.75	.35	.09
☐ 9D Bip Roberts	.05	.02	.01
☐ 9H Roberto Alomar	.40	.18	.05
☐ 9S Dennis Martinez	.05	.02	.01
☐ 10C Barry Bonds	.40	.18	.05
☐ 10D John Kruk	.05	.02	.01
☐ 10H Luis Polonia	.05	.02	.01
☐ 10S Kevin Appier	.15	.07	.02
☐ 11C Fred McGriff	.25	.11	.03
☐ 11D Andy Van Slyke	.05	.02	.01
☐ 11H Brady Anderson	.30	.14	.04
☐ 11S Roger Clemens	.40	.18	.05
☐ 12C Cecil Fielder	.15	.07	.02
☐ 12D Kirby Puckett	.60	.25	.07
☐ 12H Pat Listach	.05	.02	.01
☐ 12S Curt Schilling	.05	.02	.01
☐ 13C Mark McGwire	.50	.23	.06
☐ 13D Gary Sheffield	.30	.14	.04
☐ 13H Kenny Lofton	.60	.25	.07
☐ 13S Greg Maddux	1.00	.45	.12
☐ JKO American League Logo	.05	.02	.01
☐ WCO Wild Card Cal Ripken	.50	.23	.06
☐ NNO Title Card	.05	.02	.01

1993 U.S. Playing Cards Rookies

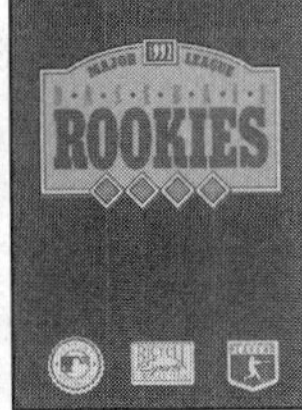

These 56 playing cards from the Bicycle Sports Collection feature outstanding 1992 rookies. The fronts display white bordered color player photos. The player's name appears in white lettering within a green bar at the bottom. His team's logo appears at the upper right. The green back carries the set's title, along with the logos for Major League Baseball, MLBPA, and Bicycle Sports Collection. The set is checklisted below in playing card order by suits and assigned numbers to Aces (1), Jacks (11), Queens (12), Kings (13), and Jokers (JK).

	MINT	NRMT	EXC
COMPLETE SET (56)	5.00	2.20	.60
COMMON CARD (1-56)	.05	.02	.01
☐ 1C Kenny Lofton	1.00	.45	.12
☐ 1D Dave Fleming	.05	.02	.01
☐ 1H Pat Listach	.05	.02	.01
☐ 1S Eric Karros	.40	.18	.05
☐ 2C Eric Fox	.05	.02	.01
☐ 2D Reggie Jefferson	.05	.02	.01
☐ 2H Pat Mahomes	.05	.02	.01
☐ 2S Butch Henry	.05	.02	.01
☐ 3C Mark Wohlers	.15	.07	.02
☐ 3D Anthony Young	.05	.02	.01
☐ 3H Greg Colbrunn	.05	.02	.01
☐ 3S Wilfredo Cordero	.15	.07	.02
☐ 4C John Patterson	.05	.02	.01
☐ 4D Kevin Koslofski	.05	.02	.01
☐ 4H Dan Walters	.05	.02	.01
☐ 4S Pedro Astacio	.05	.02	.01
☐ 5C Eric Young	.25	.11	.03
☐ 5D Brian Williams	.05	.02	.01
☐ 5H John Vanderwal	.05	.02	.01
☐ 5S Derek Bell	.25	.11	.03
☐ 6C Arthur Rhodes	.05	.02	.01
☐ 6D Brian Jordan	.40	.18	.05
☐ 6H Jeff Branson	.05	.02	.01
☐ 6S David Nied	.05	.02	.01
☐ 7C Jeff Frye	.05	.02	.01
☐ 7D John Doherty	.05	.02	.01
☐ 7H Monty Fariss	.05	.02	.01
☐ 7S Jeff Kent	.25	.11	.03
☐ 8C Scott Servais	.05	.02	.01
☐ 8D Lenny Webster	.05	.02	.01
☐ 8H Rey Sanchez	.05	.02	.01
☐ 8S David Haas	.05	.02	.01
☐ 9C Ruben Amaro	.05	.02	.01
☐ 9D Roberto Hernandez	.25	.11	.03
☐ 9H Robert Wickman	.05	.02	.01
☐ 9S Ed Taubensee	.15	.07	.02
☐ 10C Reggie Sanders	.25	.11	.03
☐ 10D Frank Seminara	.05	.02	.01
☐ 10H Derrick May	.05	.02	.01
☐ 10S Royce Clayton	.05	.02	.01
☐ 11C Alan Mills	.05	.02	.01
☐ 11D Scott Cooper	.05	.02	.01
☐ 11H Donovan Osborne	.05	.02	.01
☐ 11S Moises Alou	.25	.11	.03
☐ 12C Bob Zupcic	.05	.02	.01
☐ 12D Andy Stankiewicz	.05	.02	.01
☐ 12H Scott Livingstone	.05	.02	.01
☐ 12S Rusty Meacham	.05	.02	.01
☐ 13C Cal Eldred	.15	.07	.02
☐ 13D Tim Wakefield	.05	.02	.01
☐ 13H Gary DiSarcina	.05	.02	.01
☐ 13S Chad Curtis	.15	.07	.02
☐ JK Pat Listach AL ROY	.05	.02	.01
☐ NNO Alphabetical Checklist	.05	.02	.01

1994 U.S. Playing Cards Aces

These 56 playing standard-size cards have rounded corners, and feature borderless color posed and action player photos on their fronts. The player's name, position, and team logo appear near the bottom. The blue and silver backs carry the set's name, and logos for baseball's 125th Anniversary, MLBPA, and Bicycle Sports Collection. The set is checklisted below in playing card order by suits and assigned numbers to aces (1), jacks (11), queens (12), and kings (13).

	MINT	NRMT	EXC
COMPLETE SET (56)	6.00	2.70	.75
COMMON CARD	.05	.02	.01
☐ 1C Barry Bonds	.50	.23	.06
☐ 1D Andres Galarraga	.25	.11	.03
☐ 1H Kenny Lofton	.50	.23	.06
☐ 1S Greg Maddux	1.00	.45	.12
☐ 2C Phil Plantier	.05	.02	.01
☐ 2D John Kruk	.05	.02	.01
☐ 2H Brett Butler	.05	.02	.01
☐ 2S Tom Candiotti	.05	.02	.01
☐ 3C Bobby Bonilla	.15	.07	.02
☐ 3D Frank Thomas	1.50	.70	.19
☐ 3H Eric Young	.15	.07	.02
☐ 3S Jimmy Key	.05	.02	.01
☐ 4C Mike Piazza	1.00	.45	.12
☐ 4D Mike Piazza	1.00	.45	.12
☐ 4H Delino DeShields	.05	.02	.01
☐ 4S Jack McDowell	.05	.02	.01
☐ 5C Ron Gant	.15	.07	.02
☐ 5D Jeff Bagwell	.60	.25	.07
☐ 5H Darren Lewis	.05	.02	.01
☐ 5S John Burkett	.05	.02	.01
☐ 6C Rafael Palmeiro	.25	.11	.03
☐ 6D Carlos Baerga	.15	.07	.02
☐ 6H Gregg Jefferies	.15	.07	.02
☐ 6S Tom Glavine	.25	.11	.03
☐ 7C Fred McGriff	.25	.11	.03
☐ 7D Mark Grace	.30	.14	.04
☐ 7H Otis Nixon	.05	.02	.01
☐ 7S Pete Harnisch	.05	.02	.01
☐ 8C Matt Williams	.30	.14	.04
☐ 8D Kenny Lofton	.50	.23	.06
☐ 8H Chad Curtis	.15	.07	.02
☐ 8S Wilson Alvarez	.05	.02	.01
☐ 9C Albert Belle	.75	.35	.09
☐ 9D Roberto Alomar	.40	.18	.05
☐ 9H Rickey Henderson	.25	.11	.03
☐ 9S Steve Avery	.15	.07	.02
☐ 10C David Justice	.15	.07	.02
☐ 10D Paul Molitor	.40	.18	.05
☐ 10H Marquis Grissom	.15	.07	.02
☐ 10S Bill Swift	.05	.02	.01
☐ 11C Frank Thomas	1.50	.70	.19
☐ 11D Barry Bonds	.40	.18	.05
☐ 11H Luis Polonia	.05	.02	.01
☐ 11S Mark Portugal	.05	.02	.01
☐ 12C Ken Griffey Jr.	1.50	.70	.19
☐ 12D Gregg Jefferies	.15	.07	.02
☐ 12H Roberto Alomar	.50	.23	.06
☐ 12S Kevin Appier	.15	.07	.02
☐ 13C Juan Gonzalez	.75	.35	.09
☐ 13D John Olerud	.15	.07	.02
☐ 13H Chuck Carr	.05	.02	.01
☐ 13S Jose Rijo	.05	.02	.01
☐ NNO Featured Players	.05	.02	.01

1994 U.S. Playing Cards Rookies

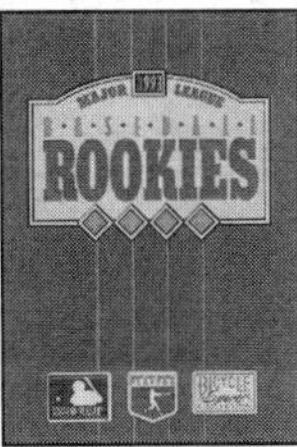

These 56 playing standard-size cards have rounded corners, and feature color posed and action player photos on their white-bordered fronts. The player's name and position appear near the bottom. The purple and gray backs carry the logos for baseball's 125th Anniversary, MLBPA, and Bicycle Sports Collection. The set is checklisted below in playing card order by suits and assigned numbers to aces (1), jacks (11), queens (12), and kings (13).

	MINT	NRMT	EXC
COMPLETE SET (56)	5.00	2.20	.60
COMMON CARD	.05	.02	.01
☐ 1C Mike Piazza	1.00	.45	.12
☐ 1D Chuck Carr	.05	.02	.01
☐ 1H Kevin Stocker	.05	.02	.01
☐ 1S Greg McMichael	.05	.02	.01
☐ 2C Vinny Castilla	.30	.14	.04
☐ 2D Jeff McNeely	.05	.02	.01
☐ 2H Alex Arias	.05	.02	.01
☐ 2S Paul Quantrill	.05	.02	.01
☐ 3C Wil Cordero	.20	.09	.03
☐ 3D Joe Kmak	.05	.02	.01
☐ 3H Carlos Garcia	.05	.02	.01
☐ 3S Steve Reed	.05	.02	.01
☐ 4C Ryan Thompson	.05	.02	.01
☐ 4D Phil Hiatt	.05	.02	.01
☐ 4H Erik Pappas	.05	.02	.01
☐ 4S Trevor Hoffman	.15	.07	.02
☐ 5C Craig Paquette	.05	.02	.01
☐ 5D Brent Gates	.05	.02	.01
☐ 5H Al Martin	.15	.07	.02
☐ 5S Tim Pugh	.05	.02	.01
☐ 6C Carlos Garcia	.05	.02	.01
☐ 6D Wil Cordero	.15	.07	.02
☐ 6H Tim Salmon	.30	.14	.04
☐ 6S Angel Miranda	.05	.02	.01
☐ 7C Jeff Conine	.25	.11	.03
☐ 7D Al Martin	.15	.07	.02
☐ 7H Mike Lansing	.05	.02	.01
☐ 7S Steve Cooke	.05	.02	.01
☐ 8C Bret Boone	.05	.02	.01
☐ 8D Wayne Kirby	.05	.02	.01
☐ 8H Rich Amaral	.05	.02	.01
☐ 8S Aaron Sele	.15	.07	.02
☐ 9C Jeromy Burnitz	.05	.02	.01
☐ 9D Lou Frazier	.05	.02	.01
☐ 9H Brent Gates	.05	.02	.01
☐ 9S Kirk Rueter	.05	.02	.01
☐ 10C J.T. Snow	.15	.07	.02
☐ 10D Carlos Garcia	.05	.02	.01
☐ 10H David Hulse	.05	.02	.01
☐ 10S Rene Arocha	.05	.02	.01
☐ 11C Al Martin	.15	.07	.02
☐ 11D Rich Amaral	.05	.02	.01
☐ 11H Troy Neel	.05	.02	.01
☐ 11S Pedro J. Martinez	.15	.07	.02
☐ 12C Troy Neel	.05	.02	.01
☐ 12D Mike Lansing	.15	.07	.02
☐ 12H Jeff Conine	.25	.11	.03
☐ 12S Armando Reynoso	.05	.02	.01
☐ 13C Tim Salmon	.30	.14	.04
☐ 13D David Hulse	.05	.02	.01
☐ 13H Mike Piazza	1.00	.45	.12
☐ 13S Jason Bere	.15	.07	.02
☐ JK Tim Salmon AL ROY	.30	.14	.04
☐ NNO Rookie Qualification	.05	.02	.01

1995 U.S. Playing Cards Aces

This 52 standard-size card set features leading major league players. The fronts of these rounded-corner cards feature borderless full-color posed and action player shots while the backs have the 1995 Major League Baseball Aces design on a silver and black background. The team logo appears in the lower left of each picture. The player's name and position appear in a reddish-brown stripe to the right of the team logo. Since this set is similar to a playing card set, the set is checklisted below as if it were a playing card deck. In the checklist C means Clubs, D means Diamonds, H means Hearts and S means Spades. The cards are checklisted in playing order by suits and numbers are assigned to Aces (1), Jacks (11), Queens (12) and Kings (13).

	MINT	NRMT	EXC
COMPLETE SET (52)	6.00	2.70	.75
COMMON CARD	.05	.02	.01
☐ 1C Matt Williams	.25	.11	.03
☐ 1D Tony Gwynn	.60	.25	.07
☐ 1H Kenny Lofton	.50	.23	.06
☐ 1S Greg Maddux	1.50	.70	.19
☐ 2C Joe Carter	.25	.11	.03
☐ 2D Gregg Jefferies	.15	.07	.02
☐ 2H Brian McRae	.05	.02	.01
☐ 2S Steve Trachsel	.05	.02	.01
☐ 3C Dante Bichette	.30	.14	.04
☐ 3D Kevin Mitchell	.05	.02	.01
☐ 3H Alex Cole	.05	.02	.01
☐ 3S Randy Johnson	.50	.23	.06
☐ 4C Cecil Fielder	.15	.07	.02
☐ 4D Will Clark	.30	.14	.04
☐ 4H Barry Bonds	.40	.18	.05
☐ 4S Bobby Jones	.05	.02	.01
☐ 5C Kevin Mitchell	.05	.02	.01
☐ 5D Hal Morris	.05	.02	.01
☐ 5H Darren Lewis	.05	.02	.01
☐ 5S Jose Rijo	.05	.02	.01
☐ 6C Andres Galarraga	.25	.11	.03
☐ 6D Moises Alou	.15	.07	.02
☐ 6H Brady Anderson	.40	.18	.05
☐ 6S Mike Mussina	.30	.14	.04
☐ 7C Jose Canseco	.30	.14	.04
☐ 7D Paul Molitor	.30	.14	.04
☐ 7H Chuck Carr	.05	.02	.01
☐ 7S Shane Reynolds	.15	.07	.02
☐ 8C Fred McGriff	.25	.11	.03
☐ 8D Wade Boggs	.30	.14	.04
☐ 8H Chuck Knoblauch	.40	.18	.05
☐ 8S Jeff Fassero	.05	.02	.01
☐ 9C Albert Belle	.75	.35	.09
☐ 9D Kenny Lofton	.50	.23	.06
☐ 9H Marquis Grissom	.15	.07	.02
☐ 9S David Cone	.15	.07	.02
☐ 10C Barry Bonds	.40	.18	.05
☐ 10D Frank Thomas	1.50	.70	.19
☐ 10H Deion Sanders	.40	.18	.05
☐ 10S Roger Clemens	.50	.23	.06
☐ 11C Frank Thomas	1.50	.70	.19
☐ 11D Albert Belle	.75	.35	.09
☐ 11H Craig Biggio	.15	.07	.02
☐ 11S Doug Drabek	.05	.02	.01
☐ 12C Jeff Bagwell	.60	.25	.07
☐ 12D Paul O'Neill	.05	.02	.01
☐ 12H Otis Nixon	.05	.02	.01
☐ 12S Bret Saberhagen	.05	.02	.01
☐ 13C Ken Griffey Jr.	1.50	.70	.19
☐ 13D Jeff Bagwell	.60	.25	.07
☐ 13H Vince Coleman	.05	.02	.01
☐ 13S Steve Ontiveros	.05	.02	.01

1995 UC3

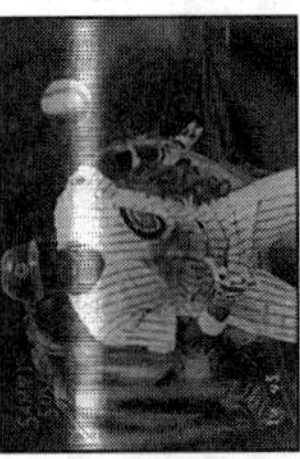

This 147-card standard-size set was issued by Pinnacle Brands. The cards were issued in 16-box cases with 36 packs per box and five cards per pack. The fronts feature a mix of horizontal and vertical designs. The player's photo is shown against a computer generated background. According to Pinnacle, this is the first set issued as an all-3D product. The key Rookie Card in this set is Hideo Nomo.

	MINT	NRMT	EXC
COMPLETE SET (147)	20.00	9.00	2.50
COMMON CARD (1-147)	.10	.05	.01
☐ 1 Frank Thomas	3.00	1.35	.35
☐ 2 Wil Cordero	.10	.05	.01
☐ 3 John Olerud	.10	.05	.01
☐ 4 Deion Sanders	.50	.23	.06
☐ 5 Mike Mussina	.60	.25	.07
☐ 6 Mo Vaughn	.75	.35	.09
☐ 7 Will Clark	.50	.23	.06

☐ 8 Chili Davis	.25	.11	.03
☐ 9 Jimmy Key	.25	.11	.03
☐ 10 John Valentin	.25	.11	.03
☐ 11 Tony Tarasco	.10	.05	.01
☐ 12 Alan Trammell	.25	.11	.03
☐ 13 David Cone	.25	.11	.03
☐ 14 Tim Salmon	.50	.23	.06
☐ 15 Danny Tartabull	.10	.05	.01
☐ 16 Aaron Sele	.25	.11	.03
☐ 17 Alex Fernandez	.25	.11	.03
☐ 18 Barry Bonds	.75	.35	.09
☐ 19 Andres Galarraga	.50	.23	.06
☐ 20 Don Mattingly	1.50	.70	.19
☐ 21 Kevin Appier	.25	.11	.03
☐ 22 Paul Molitor	.60	.25	.07
☐ 23 Omar Vizquel	.25	.11	.03
☐ 24 Andy Benes	.10	.05	.01
☐ 25 Rafael Palmeiro	.50	.23	.06
☐ 26 Barry Larkin	.50	.23	.06
☐ 27 Bernie Williams	.60	.25	.07
☐ 28 Gary Sheffield	.50	.23	.06
☐ 29 Wally Joyner	.25	.11	.03
☐ 30 Wade Boggs	.50	.23	.06
☐ 31 Rico Brogna	.10	.05	.01
☐ 32 Ken Caminiti	.50	.23	.06
☐ 33 Kirby Puckett	1.25	.55	.16
☐ 34 Bobby Bonilla	.25	.11	.03
☐ 35 Hal Morris	.10	.05	.01
☐ 36 Moises Alou	.25	.11	.03
☐ 37 Jim Thome	.60	.25	.07
☐ 38 Chuck Knoblauch	.50	.23	.06
☐ 39 Mike Piazza	2.00	.90	.25
☐ 40 Travis Fryman	.25	.11	.03
☐ 41 Rickey Henderson	.50	.23	.06
☐ 42 Jack McDowell	.25	.11	.03
☐ 43 Carlos Baerga	.25	.11	.03
☐ 44 Gregg Jefferies	.25	.11	.03
☐ 45 Kirk Gibson	.25	.11	.03
☐ 46 Bret Saberhagen	.25	.11	.03
☐ 47 Cecil Fielder	.25	.11	.03
☐ 48 Manny Ramirez	.75	.35	.09
☐ 49 Marquis Grissom	.25	.11	.03
☐ 50 Dave Winfield	.50	.23	.06
☐ 51 Mark McGwire	1.00	.45	.12
☐ 52 Dennis Eckersley	.25	.11	.03
☐ 53 Robin Ventura	.25	.11	.03
☐ 54 Ryan Klesko	.50	.23	.06
☐ 55 Jeff Bagwell	1.25	.55	.16
☐ 56 Ozzie Smith	.75	.35	.09
☐ 57 Brian McRae	.25	.11	.03
☐ 58 Albert Belle	1.25	.55	.16
☐ 59 Darren Daulton	.25	.11	.03
☐ 60 Jose Canseco	.50	.23	.06
☐ 61 Greg Maddux	2.00	.90	.25
☐ 62 Ben McDonald	.10	.05	.01
☐ 63 Lenny Dykstra	.25	.11	.03
☐ 64 Randy Johnson	.50	.23	.06
☐ 65 Fred McGriff	.50	.23	.06
☐ 66 Ray Lankford	.25	.11	.03
☐ 67 Dave Justice	.50	.23	.06
☐ 68 Paul O'Neill	.25	.11	.03
☐ 69 Tony Gwynn	1.25	.55	.16
☐ 70 Matt Williams	.50	.23	.06
☐ 71 Dante Bichette	.50	.23	.06
☐ 72 Craig Biggio	.25	.11	.03
☐ 73 Ken Griffey Jr.	3.00	1.35	.35
☐ 74 Juan Gonzalez	1.50	.70	.19
☐ 75 Cal Ripken	2.50	1.10	.30
☐ 76 Jay Bell	.25	.11	.03
☐ 77 Joe Carter	.25	.11	.03
☐ 78 Roberto Alomar	.60	.25	.07
☐ 79 Mark Langston	.10	.05	.01
☐ 80 Dave Hollins	.10	.05	.01
☐ 81 Tom Glavine	.50	.23	.06
☐ 82 Ivan Rodriguez	.75	.35	.09
☐ 83 Mark Whiten	.10	.05	.01
☐ 84 Raul Mondesi	.50	.23	.06
☐ 85 Kenny Lofton	.75	.35	.09
☐ 86 Ruben Sierra	.25	.11	.03
☐ 87 Mark Grace	.50	.23	.06
☐ 88 Royce Clayton	.10	.05	.01
☐ 89 Billy Ashley	.10	.05	.01
☐ 90 Larry Walker	.50	.23	.06
☐ 91 Sammy Sosa	.50	.23	.06
☐ 92 Jason Bere	.10	.05	.01
☐ 93 Bob Hamelin	.10	.05	.01
☐ 94 Greg Vaughn	.25	.11	.03
☐ 95 Roger Clemens	.60	.25	.07
☐ 96 Scott Ruffcorn	.10	.05	.01
☐ 97 Hideo Nomo	3.00	1.35	.35
☐ 98 Michael Tucker	.25	.11	.03
☐ 99 J.R. Phillips	.10	.05	.01
☐ 100 Roberto Petagine	.10	.05	.01
☐ 101 Chipper Jones	2.00	.90	.25
☐ 102 Armando Benitez	.10	.05	.01
☐ 103 Orlando Miller	.10	.05	.01
☐ 104 Carlos Delgado	.25	.11	.03
☐ 105 Jeff Cirillo	.25	.11	.03
☐ 106 Shawn Green	.25	.11	.03
☐ 107 Joe Randa	.10	.05	.01
☐ 108 Vaughn Eshelman	.10	.05	.01
☐ 109 Frank Rodriguez	.25	.11	.03
☐ 110 Russ Davis	.10	.05	.01
☐ 111 Todd Hollandsworth	.50	.23	.06
☐ 112 Mark Grudzielanek	.75	.35	.09
☐ 113 Jose Oliva	.10	.05	.01
☐ 114 Ray Durham	.25	.11	.03
☐ 115 Alex Rodriguez	4.00	1.80	.50
☐ 116 Alex Gonzalez	.10	.05	.01
☐ 117 Midre Cummings	.10	.05	.01
☐ 118 Marty Cordova	.50	.23	.06
☐ 119 John Mabry	.50	.23	.06
☐ 120 Jason Jacome	.10	.05	.01
☐ 121 Joe Vitiello	.10	.05	.01
☐ 122 Charles Johnson	.25	.11	.03
☐ 123 Cal Ripken ID	1.25	.55	.16
☐ 124 Ken Griffey Jr. ID	1.50	.70	.19
☐ 125 Frank Thomas ID	1.50	.70	.19
☐ 126 Mike Piazza ID	1.00	.45	.12
☐ 127 Matt Williams ID	.50	.23	.06
☐ 128 Barry Bonds ID	.50	.23	.06
☐ 129 Greg Maddux ID	1.00	.45	.12
☐ 130 Randy Johnson ID	.50	.23	.06
☐ 131 Albert Belle ID	.60	.25	.07
☐ 132 Will Clark ID	.50	.23	.06
☐ 133 Tony Gwynn ID	.60	.25	.07
☐ 134 Manny Ramirez ID	.50	.23	.06
☐ 135 Raul Mondesi ID	.50	.23	.06
☐ 136 Mo Vaughn ID	.50	.23	.06
☐ 137 Mark McGwire ID	.50	.23	.06
☐ 138 Kirby Puckett ID	.50	.23	.06
☐ 139 Don Mattingly ID	.75	.35	.09
☐ 140 Carlos Baerga ID	.25	.11	.03
☐ 141 Roger Clemens ID	.50	.23	.06
☐ 142 Fred McGriff ID	.50	.23	.06
☐ 143 Kenny Lofton ID	.50	.23	.06
☐ 144 Jeff Bagwell ID	.60	.25	.07
☐ 145 Larry Walker ID	.50	.23	.06
☐ 146 Joe Carter ID	.25	.11	.03
☐ 147 Rafael Palmeiro ID	.50	.23	.06

1995 UC3 Artist's Proofs

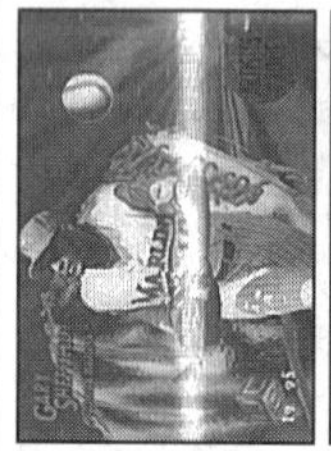
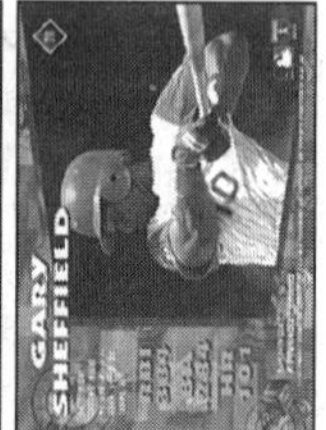

This 147-card standard-size set is a parallel to the regular UC3 set. These cards were inserted one per UC3 box. The only difference between these and the regular UC3 cards is the words "Artist's Proof" in a circle in a bottom corner.

	MINT	NRMT	EXC
COMPLETE SET (147)	800.00	350.00	100.00
COMMON CARD (1-147)	2.50	1.10	.30

*STARS: 10X TO 25X BASIC CARDS ..
*YOUNG STARS: 8X TO 20X BASIC CARDS

1995 UC3 Clear Shots

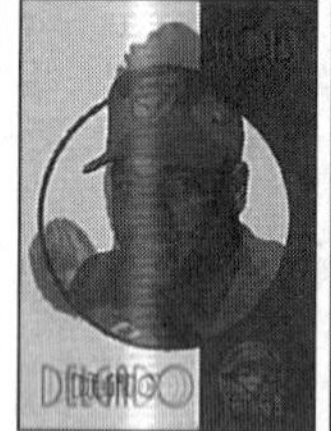

This 12-card standard-size set was inserted approximately one in every 24 packs. The fronts have two photos that alternate when the card is tilted slightly. One photo is a portrait while the other is an action shot. Along with the two photos changing are the words "Clear Shots," and a "UC3 1995" logo which changes with the player's team logo. The backs are opaque, but do have the card number in the upper left corner with a "CS" prefix.

	MINT	NRMT	EXC
COMPLETE SET (12)	70.00	32.00	8.75
COMMON CARD (CS1-CS12)	2.00	.90	.25
☐ CS1 Alex Rodriguez	30.00	13.50	3.70
☐ CS2 Shawn Green	2.00	.90	.25
☐ CS3 Hideo Nomo	15.00	6.75	1.85
☐ CS4 Charles Johnson	2.00	.90	.25
☐ CS5 Orlando Miller	2.00	.90	.25
☐ CS6 Billy Ashley	2.00	.90	.25
☐ CS7 Carlos Delgado	4.00	1.80	.50
☐ CS8 Cliff Floyd	2.00	.90	.25
☐ CS9 Chipper Jones	20.00	9.00	2.50
☐ CS10 Alex Gonzalez	2.00	.90	.25
☐ CS11 J.R. Phillips	2.00	.90	.25
☐ CS12 Michael Tucker	2.00	.90	.25
☐ PCS8 Cliff Floyd Promo	2.00	.90	.25

1995 UC3 Cyclone Squad

This 20-card standard-size set was inserted approximately one in every four packs. The front features a player photo against a background of two circular objects. The "UC3" logo is in the upper left. The bottom has the words "Cyclone Squad" and the player's name and team. The horizontal backs contain a black and white player photo along with some information. The cards are numbered in the upper left with a "CS" prefix.

	MINT	NRMT	EXC
COMPLETE SET (20)	20.00	9.00	2.50
COMMON CARD (CS1-CS20)	.50	.23	.06
☐ CS1 Frank Thomas	4.00	1.80	.50
☐ CS2 Ken Griffey Jr.	4.00	1.80	.50
☐ CS3 Jeff Bagwell	1.50	.70	.19
☐ CS4 Cal Ripken	3.00	1.35	.35
☐ CS5 Barry Bonds	1.00	.45	.12
☐ CS6 Mike Piazza	2.50	1.10	.30
☐ CS7 Matt Williams	.75	.35	.09
☐ CS8 Kirby Puckett	1.50	.70	.19
☐ CS9 Jose Canseco	.75	.35	.09
☐ CS10 Will Clark	.75	.35	.09
☐ CS11 Don Mattingly	2.00	.90	.25
☐ CS12 Albert Belle	1.50	.70	.19
☐ CS13 Tony Gwynn	1.50	.70	.19
☐ CS14 Raul Mondesi	.75	.35	.09
☐ CS15 Bobby Bonilla	.50	.23	.06
☐ CS16 Rafael Palmeiro	.75	.35	.09
☐ CS17 Fred McGriff	.75	.35	.09
☐ CS18 Tim Salmon	.75	.35	.09
☐ CS19 Kenny Lofton	1.00	.45	.12
☐ CS20 Joe Carter	.60	.25	.07

1995 UC3 In Motion

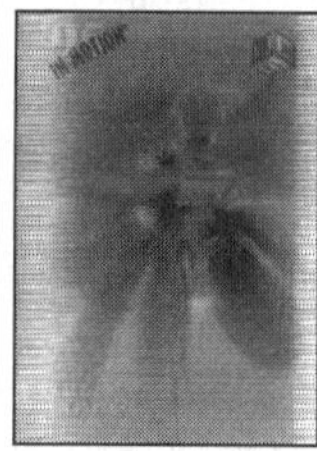

This 10-card standard-size set was inserted approximately one in every 18 packs. The fronts feature a player photo that compresses into many pieces when the card is tilted slightly. The upper left features the words "In Motion 95" with the UC3 logo in the upper right and the player's name in the lower left. The horizontal back features two color photos along with a short informational blurb. The cards are numbered with an "IM" prefix in the upper right corner.

	MINT	NRMT	EXC
COMPLETE SET (10)	40.00	18.00	5.00
COMMON CARD (IM1-IM10)	.75	.35	.09
☐ IM1 Cal Ripken	6.00	2.70	.75
☐ IM2 Ken Griffey Jr.	8.00	3.60	1.00
☐ IM3 Frank Thomas	8.00	3.60	1.00
☐ IM4 Mike Piazza	5.00	2.20	.60
☐ IM5 Barry Bonds	2.00	.90	.25
☐ IM6 Matt Williams	.75	.35	.09
☐ IM7 Kirby Puckett	3.00	1.35	.35
☐ IM8 Greg Maddux	5.00	2.20	.60
☐ IM9 Don Mattingly	4.00	1.80	.50
☐ IM10 Will Clark	.75	.35	.09

1985 Ultimate Baseball Card Set

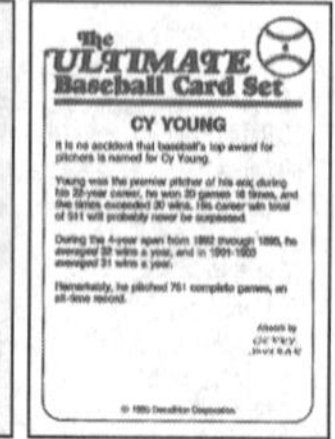

This 15-card set by the Decathlon Corporation measures approximately 4" by 5 5/8". The fronts display color artwork of great players by Gerry Dvorak. The white backs carry the card name, player's name and career information.

	MINT	NRMT	EXC
COMPLETE SET (15)	35.00	16.00	4.40
COMMON CARD (1-15)	1.00	.45	.12
☐ 1 Ty Cobb	7.50	3.40	.95
☐ 2 Honus Wagner	2.50	1.10	.30
☐ 3 Babe Ruth	10.00	4.50	1.25
☐ 4 Lou Gehrig	7.50	3.40	.95
☐ 5 Frank Baker	1.50	.70	.19
☐ 6 Casey Stengel	2.00	.90	.25
☐ 7 Moses Walker	1.00	.45	.12
☐ 8 Cy Young	3.00	1.35	.35
☐ 9 Joe DiMaggio	7.50	3.40	.95
☐ 10 John McGraw	2.00	.90	.25
☐ 11 Josh Gibson	5.00	2.20	.60
☐ 12 Johnny Mize	1.50	.70	.19
☐ 13 Walter Johnson	3.00	1.35	.35
☐ 14 Walter Alston	1.00	.45	.12
☐ 15 Enos Slaughter	1.50	.70	.19

1991 Ultra

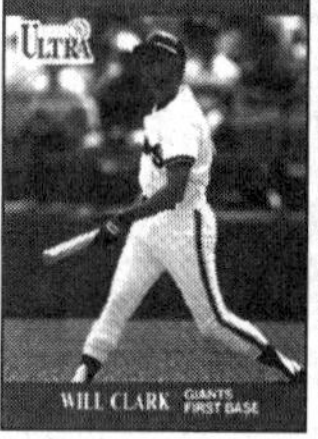

This 400-card standard-size set marked Fleer's first entry into the premium card market. The cards were distributed exclusively in foil-wrapped packs. Fleer claimed in their original press release that there would only be 15 percent the amount of Ultra issued as there was of the regular issue. The cards feature full color action photography on the fronts and three full-color photos on the backs. Fleer also issued the sets in their now traditional alphabetical order as well as the teams in alphabetical order. Subsets include Major League Prospects (373-390), Elite Performance (391-396), and Checklists (397-400). The key Rookie Cards in this set are Jeff Conine, Eric Karros and Brian McRae, Denny Neagle and Henry Rodriguez.

	MINT	NRMT	EXC
COMPLETE SET (400)	20.00	9.00	2.50
COMMON CARD (1-400)	.05	.02	.01
☐ 1 Steve Avery	.30	.14	.04
☐ 2 Jeff Blauser	.05	.02	.01
☐ 3 Francisco Cabrera	.05	.02	.01
☐ 4 Ron Gant	.15	.07	.02
☐ 5 Tom Glavine	.30	.14	.04
☐ 6 Tommy Gregg	.05	.02	.01
☐ 7 Dave Justice	.30	.14	.04
☐ 8 Oddibe McDowell	.05	.02	.01
☐ 9 Greg Olson	.05	.02	.01
☐ 10 Terry Pendleton	.15	.07	.02
☐ 11 Lonnie Smith	.05	.02	.01
☐ 12 John Smoltz	.30	.14	.04
☐ 13 Jeff Treadway	.05	.02	.01
☐ 14 Glenn Davis	.05	.02	.01
☐ 15 Mike Devereaux	.05	.02	.01
☐ 16 Leo Gomez	.05	.02	.01
☐ 17 Chris Hoiles	.05	.02	.01
☐ 18 Dave Johnson	.05	.02	.01
☐ 19 Ben McDonald	.15	.07	.02
☐ 20 Randy Milligan	.05	.02	.01
☐ 21 Gregg Olson	.05	.02	.01
☐ 22 Joe Orsulak	.05	.02	.01
☐ 23 Bill Ripken	.05	.02	.01
☐ 24 Cal Ripken	1.50	.70	.19
☐ 25 David Segui	.15	.07	.02
☐ 26 Craig Worthington	.05	.02	.01
☐ 27 Wade Boggs	.30	.14	.04
☐ 28 Tom Bolton	.05	.02	.01
☐ 29 Tom Brunansky	.05	.02	.01
☐ 30 Ellis Burks	.15	.07	.02
☐ 31 Roger Clemens	.40	.18	.05
☐ 32 Mike Greenwell	.05	.02	.01
☐ 33 Greg A. Harris	.05	.02	.01
☐ 34 Daryl Irvine	.05	.02	.01
☐ 35 Mike Marshall UER (1990 in stats is shown as 990)	.05	.02	.01
☐ 36 Tim Naehring	.15	.07	.02
☐ 37 Tony Pena	.05	.02	.01
☐ 38 Phil Plantier	.15	.07	.02
☐ 39 Carlos Quintana	.05	.02	.01
☐ 40 Jeff Reardon	.15	.07	.02
☐ 41 Jody Reed	.05	.02	.01
☐ 42 Luis Rivera	.05	.02	.01
☐ 43 Jim Abbott	.15	.07	.02
☐ 44 Chuck Finley	.15	.07	.02
☐ 45 Bryan Harvey	.05	.02	.01
☐ 46 Donnie Hill	.05	.02	.01
☐ 47 Jack Howell	.05	.02	.01
☐ 48 Wally Joyner	.15	.07	.02
☐ 49 Mark Langston	.15	.07	.02

☐ 50 Kirk McCaskill	.05	.02	.01
☐ 51 Lance Parrish	.05	.02	.01
☐ 52 Dick Schofield	.05	.02	.01
☐ 53 Lee Stevens	.05	.02	.01
☐ 54 Dave Winfield	.30	.14	.04
☐ 55 George Bell	.05	.02	.01
☐ 56 Damon Berryhill	.05	.02	.01
☐ 57 Mike Bielecki	.05	.02	.01
☐ 58 Andre Dawson	.15	.07	.02
☐ 59 Shawon Dunston	.05	.02	.01
☐ 60 Joe Girardi UER	.15	.07	.02
(Bats right, LH hitter shown is Doug Dascenzo)			
☐ 61 Mark Grace	.30	.14	.04
☐ 62 Mike Harkey	.05	.02	.01
☐ 63 Les Lancaster	.05	.02	.01
☐ 64 Greg Maddux	1.25	.55	.16
☐ 65 Derrick May	.05	.02	.01
☐ 66 Ryne Sandberg	.50	.23	.06
☐ 67 Luis Salazar	.05	.02	.01
☐ 68 Dwight Smith	.05	.02	.01
☐ 69 Hector Villanueva	.05	.02	.01
☐ 70 Jerome Walton	.05	.02	.01
☐ 71 Mitch Williams	.05	.02	.01
☐ 72 Carlton Fisk	.30	.14	.04
☐ 73 Scott Fletcher	.05	.02	.01
☐ 74 Ozzie Guillen	.05	.02	.01
☐ 75 Greg Hibbard	.05	.02	.01
☐ 76 Lance Johnson	.15	.07	.02
☐ 77 Steve Lyons	.05	.02	.01
☐ 78 Jack McDowell	.15	.07	.02
☐ 79 Dan Pasqua	.05	.02	.01
☐ 80 Melido Perez	.05	.02	.01
☐ 81 Tim Raines	.30	.14	.04
☐ 82 Sammy Sosa	.60	.25	.07
☐ 83 Cory Snyder	.05	.02	.01
☐ 84 Bobby Thigpen	.05	.02	.01
☐ 85 Frank Thomas	4.00	1.80	.50
(Card says he is an outfielder)			
☐ 86 Robin Ventura	.30	.14	.04
☐ 87 Todd Benzinger	.05	.02	.01
☐ 88 Glenn Braggs	.05	.02	.01
☐ 89 Tom Browning UER	.05	.02	.01
(Front photo actually Norm Charlton)			
☐ 90 Norm Charlton	.05	.02	.01
☐ 91 Eric Davis	.15	.07	.02
☐ 92 Rob Dibble	.05	.02	.01
☐ 93 Bill Doran	.05	.02	.01
☐ 94 Mariano Duncan UER	.05	.02	.01
(Right back photo is Billy Hatcher)			
☐ 95 Billy Hatcher	.05	.02	.01
☐ 96 Barry Larkin	.30	.14	.04
☐ 97 Randy Myers	.15	.07	.02
☐ 98 Hal Morris	.05	.02	.01
☐ 99 Joe Oliver	.05	.02	.01
☐ 100 Paul O'Neill	.15	.07	.02
☐ 101 Jeff Reed	.05	.02	.01
(See also 104)			
☐ 102 Jose Rijo	.05	.02	.01
☐ 103 Chris Sabo	.05	.02	.01
(See also 106)			
☐ 104 Beau Allred UER	.05	.02	.01
(Card number is 101)			
☐ 105 Sandy Alomar Jr.	.15	.07	.02
☐ 106 Carlos Baerga UER	.30	.14	.04
(Card number is 103)			
☐ 107 Albert Belle	1.00	.45	.12
☐ 108 Jerry Browne	.05	.02	.01
☐ 109 Tom Candiotti	.05	.02	.01
☐ 110 Alex Cole	.05	.02	.01
☐ 111 John Farrell	.05	.02	.01
(See also 114)			
☐ 112 Felix Fermin	.05	.02	.01
☐ 113 Brook Jacoby	.05	.02	.01
☐ 114 Chris James UER	.05	.02	.01
(Card number is 111)			
☐ 115 Doug Jones	.05	.02	.01
☐ 116 Steve Olin	.05	.02	.01
(See also 119)			
☐ 117 Greg Swindell	.05	.02	.01
☐ 118 Turner Ward	.05	.02	.01
☐ 119 Mitch Webster UER	.05	.02	.01
(Card number is 116)			
☐ 120 Dave Bergman	.05	.02	.01
☐ 121 Cecil Fielder	.15	.07	.02
☐ 122 Travis Fryman	.30	.14	.04
☐ 123 Mike Henneman	.05	.02	.01
☐ 124 Lloyd Moseby	.05	.02	.01
☐ 125 Dan Petry	.05	.02	.01
☐ 126 Tony Phillips	.15	.07	.02
☐ 127 Mark Salas	.05	.02	.01
☐ 128 Frank Tanana	.05	.02	.01
☐ 129 Alan Trammell	.30	.14	.04
☐ 130 Lou Whitaker	.15	.07	.02
☐ 131 Eric Anthony	.05	.02	.01
☐ 132 Craig Biggio	.30	.14	.04
☐ 133 Ken Caminiti	.30	.14	.04
☐ 134 Casey Candaele	.05	.02	.01
☐ 135 Andujar Cedeno	.05	.02	.01
☐ 136 Mark Davidson	.05	.02	.01
☐ 137 Jim Deshaies	.05	.02	.01
☐ 138 Mark Portugal	.05	.02	.01
☐ 139 Rafael Ramirez	.05	.02	.01
☐ 140 Mike Scott	.05	.02	.01
☐ 141 Eric Yelding	.05	.02	.01
☐ 142 Gerald Young	.05	.02	.01
☐ 143 Kevin Appier	.30	.14	.04
☐ 144 George Brett	.75	.35	.09
☐ 145 Jeff Conine	.75	.35	.09
☐ 146 Jim Eisenreich	.15	.07	.02
☐ 147 Tom Gordon	.05	.02	.01
☐ 148 Mark Gubicza	.05	.02	.01
☐ 149 Bo Jackson	.15	.07	.02
☐ 150 Brent Mayne	.05	.02	.01
☐ 151 Mike Macfarlane	.05	.02	.01
☐ 152 Brian McRae	.40	.18	.05
☐ 153 Jeff Montgomery	.15	.07	.02
☐ 154 Bret Saberhagen	.15	.07	.02
☐ 155 Kevin Seitzer	.05	.02	.01
☐ 156 Terry Shumpert	.05	.02	.01
☐ 157 Kurt Stillwell	.05	.02	.01
☐ 158 Danny Tartabull	.05	.02	.01
☐ 159 Tim Belcher	.05	.02	.01
☐ 160 Kal Daniels	.05	.02	.01
☐ 161 Alfredo Griffin	.05	.02	.01
☐ 162 Lenny Harris	.05	.02	.01
☐ 163 Jay Howell	.05	.02	.01
☐ 164 Ramon Martinez	.30	.14	.04
☐ 165 Mike Morgan	.05	.02	.01
☐ 166 Eddie Murray	.50	.23	.06
☐ 167 Jose Offerman	.05	.02	.01
☐ 168 Juan Samuel	.05	.02	.01
☐ 169 Mike Scioscia	.05	.02	.01
☐ 170 Mike Sharperson	.05	.02	.01
☐ 171 Darryl Strawberry	.15	.07	.02
☐ 172 Greg Brock	.05	.02	.01
☐ 173 Chuck Crim	.05	.02	.01
☐ 174 Jim Gantner	.05	.02	.01
☐ 175 Ted Higuera	.05	.02	.01
☐ 176 Mark Knudson	.05	.02	.01
☐ 177 Tim McIntosh	.05	.02	.01
☐ 178 Paul Molitor	.40	.18	.05
☐ 179 Dan Plesac	.05	.02	.01
☐ 180 Gary Sheffield	.30	.14	.04
☐ 181 Bill Spiers	.05	.02	.01
☐ 182 B.J. Surhoff	.15	.07	.02
☐ 183 Greg Vaughn	.15	.07	.02
☐ 184 Robin Yount	.30	.14	.04
☐ 185 Rick Aguilera	.15	.07	.02
☐ 186 Greg Gagne	.05	.02	.01
☐ 187 Dan Gladden	.05	.02	.01
☐ 188 Brian Harper	.05	.02	.01
☐ 189 Kent Hrbek	.15	.07	.02
☐ 190 Gene Larkin	.05	.02	.01
☐ 191 Shane Mack	.05	.02	.01
☐ 192 Pedro Munoz	.15	.07	.02
☐ 193 Al Newman	.05	.02	.01
☐ 194 Junior Ortiz	.05	.02	.01
☐ 195 Kirby Puckett	.75	.35	.09
☐ 196 Kevin Tapani	.05	.02	.01
☐ 197 Dennis Boyd	.05	.02	.01
☐ 198 Tim Burke	.05	.02	.01
☐ 199 Ivan Calderon	.05	.02	.01
☐ 200 Delino DeShields	.05	.02	.01
☐ 201 Mike Fitzgerald	.05	.02	.01
☐ 202 Steve Frey	.05	.02	.01
☐ 203 Andres Galarraga	.30	.14	.04
☐ 204 Marquis Grissom	.30	.14	.04
☐ 205 Dave Martinez	.05	.02	.01
☐ 206 Dennis Martinez	.15	.07	.02
☐ 207 Junior Noboa	.05	.02	.01
☐ 208 Spike Owen	.05	.02	.01
☐ 209 Scott Ruskin	.05	.02	.01
☐ 210 Tim Wallach	.05	.02	.01
☐ 211 Daryl Boston	.05	.02	.01
☐ 212 Vince Coleman	.05	.02	.01
☐ 213 David Cone	.15	.07	.02
☐ 214 Ron Darling	.05	.02	.01
☐ 215 Kevin Elster	.05	.02	.01
☐ 216 Sid Fernandez	.05	.02	.01
☐ 217 John Franco	.05	.02	.01
☐ 218 Dwight Gooden	.15	.07	.02
☐ 219 Tom Herr	.05	.02	.01
☐ 220 Todd Hundley	.30	.14	.04
☐ 221 Gregg Jefferies	.15	.07	.02
☐ 222 Howard Johnson	.05	.02	.01
☐ 223 Dave Magadan	.05	.02	.01
☐ 224 Kevin McReynolds	.05	.02	.01
☐ 225 Keith Miller	.05	.02	.01
☐ 226 Mackey Sasser	.05	.02	.01
☐ 227 Frank Viola	.05	.02	.01
☐ 228 Jesse Barfield	.05	.02	.01
☐ 229 Greg Cadaret	.05	.02	.01
☐ 230 Alvaro Espinoza	.05	.02	.01
☐ 231 Bob Geren	.05	.02	.01
☐ 232 Lee Guetterman	.05	.02	.01
☐ 233 Mel Hall	.05	.02	.01
☐ 234 Andy Hawkins UER	.05	.02	.01
(Back center photo is not him)			
☐ 235 Roberto Kelly	.05	.02	.01
☐ 236 Tim Leary	.05	.02	.01
☐ 237 Jim Leyritz	.15	.07	.02
☐ 238 Kevin Maas	.05	.02	.01
☐ 239 Don Mattingly	1.00	.45	.12
☐ 240 Hensley Meulens	.05	.02	.01
☐ 241 Eric Plunk	.05	.02	.01
☐ 242 Steve Sax	.05	.02	.01
☐ 243 Todd Burns	.05	.02	.01
☐ 244 Jose Canseco	.30	.14	.04
☐ 245 Dennis Eckersley	.15	.07	.02
☐ 246 Mike Gallego	.05	.02	.01
☐ 247 Dave Henderson	.05	.02	.01
☐ 248 Rickey Henderson	.30	.14	.04
☐ 249 Rick Honeycutt	.05	.02	.01
☐ 250 Carney Lansford	.15	.07	.02
☐ 251 Mark McGwire	.60	.25	.07
☐ 252 Mike Moore	.05	.02	.01
☐ 253 Terry Steinbach	.15	.07	.02
☐ 254 Dave Stewart	.15	.07	.02
☐ 255 Walt Weiss	.05	.02	.01
☐ 256 Bob Welch	.05	.02	.01
☐ 257 Curt Young	.05	.02	.01
☐ 258 Wes Chamberlain	.05	.02	.01
☐ 259 Pat Combs	.05	.02	.01
☐ 260 Darren Daulton	.15	.07	.02
☐ 261 Jose DeJesus	.05	.02	.01
☐ 262 Len Dykstra	.15	.07	.02
☐ 263 Charlie Hayes	.05	.02	.01
☐ 264 Von Hayes	.05	.02	.01
☐ 265 Ken Howell	.05	.02	.01
☐ 266 John Kruk	.15	.07	.02
☐ 267 Roger McDowell	.05	.02	.01
☐ 268 Mickey Morandini	.05	.02	.01
☐ 269 Terry Mulholland	.05	.02	.01
☐ 270 Dale Murphy	.30	.14	.04
☐ 271 Randy Ready	.05	.02	.01
☐ 272 Dickie Thon	.05	.02	.01
☐ 273 Stan Belinda	.05	.02	.01
☐ 274 Jay Bell	.15	.07	.02
☐ 275 Barry Bonds	.50	.23	.06
☐ 276 Bobby Bonilla	.15	.07	.02
☐ 277 Doug Drabek	.05	.02	.01
☐ 278 Carlos Garcia	.30	.14	.04
☐ 279 Neal Heaton	.05	.02	.01
☐ 280 Jeff King	.15	.07	.02
☐ 281 Bill Landrum	.05	.02	.01
☐ 282 Mike LaValliere	.05	.02	.01
☐ 283 Jose Lind	.05	.02	.01
☐ 284 Orlando Merced	.30	.14	.04
☐ 285 Gary Redus	.05	.02	.01
☐ 286 Don Slaught	.05	.02	.01
☐ 287 Andy Van Slyke	.15	.07	.02
☐ 288 Jose DeLeon	.05	.02	.01
☐ 289 Pedro Guerrero	.05	.02	.01
☐ 290 Ray Lankford	.30	.14	.04
☐ 291 Joe Magrane	.05	.02	.01
☐ 292 Jose Oquendo	.05	.02	.01
☐ 293 Tom Pagnozzi	.05	.02	.01
☐ 294 Bryn Smith	.05	.02	.01
☐ 295 Lee Smith	.15	.07	.02
☐ 296 Ozzie Smith UER	.50	.23	.06
(Born 12-26, 54, should have hyphen)			
☐ 297 Milt Thompson	.05	.02	.01
☐ 298 Craig Wilson	.05	.02	.01
☐ 299 Todd Zeile	.15	.07	.02
☐ 300 Shawn Abner	.05	.02	.01
☐ 301 Andy Benes	.15	.07	.02
☐ 302 Paul Faries	.05	.02	.01
☐ 303 Tony Gwynn	.75	.35	.09
☐ 304 Greg W. Harris	.05	.02	.01
☐ 305 Thomas Howard	.05	.02	.01
☐ 306 Bruce Hurst	.05	.02	.01
☐ 307 Craig Lefferts	.05	.02	.01
☐ 308 Fred McGriff	.30	.14	.04
☐ 309 Dennis Rasmussen	.05	.02	.01
☐ 310 Bip Roberts	.05	.02	.01
☐ 311 Benito Santiago	.05	.02	.01
☐ 312 Garry Templeton	.05	.02	.01
☐ 313 Ed Whitson	.05	.02	.01
☐ 314 Dave Anderson	.05	.02	.01
☐ 315 Kevin Bass	.05	.02	.01
☐ 316 Jeff Brantley	.05	.02	.01
☐ 317 John Burkett	.15	.07	.02
☐ 318 Will Clark	.30	.14	.04
☐ 319 Steve Decker	.05	.02	.01
☐ 320 Scott Garrelts	.05	.02	.01
☐ 321 Terry Kennedy	.05	.02	.01
☐ 322 Mark Leonard	.05	.02	.01
☐ 323 Darren Lewis	.15	.07	.02
☐ 324 Greg Litton	.05	.02	.01
☐ 325 Willie McGee	.05	.02	.01
☐ 326 Kevin Mitchell	.15	.07	.02
☐ 327 Don Robinson	.05	.02	.01
☐ 328 Andres Santana	.05	.02	.01
☐ 329 Robby Thompson	.05	.02	.01
☐ 330 Jose Uribe	.05	.02	.01
☐ 331 Matt Williams	.30	.14	.04
☐ 332 Scott Bradley	.05	.02	.01
☐ 333 Henry Cotto	.05	.02	.01
☐ 334 Alvin Davis	.05	.02	.01
☐ 335 Ken Griffey Sr.	.05	.02	.01
☐ 336 Ken Griffey Jr.	3.00	1.35	.35
☐ 337 Erik Hanson	.05	.02	.01
☐ 338 Brian Holman	.05	.02	.01
☐ 339 Randy Johnson	.30	.14	.04
☐ 340 Edgar Martinez UER	.15	.07	.02
(Listed as playing SS)			
☐ 341 Tino Martinez	.30	.14	.04
☐ 342 Pete O'Brien	.05	.02	.01
☐ 343 Harold Reynolds	.05	.02	.01
☐ 344 Dave Valle	.05	.02	.01
☐ 345 Omar Vizquel	.30	.14	.04
☐ 346 Brad Arnsberg	.05	.02	.01
☐ 347 Kevin Brown	.15	.07	.02
☐ 348 Julio Franco	.15	.07	.02
☐ 349 Jeff Huson	.05	.02	.01
☐ 350 Rafael Palmeiro	.30	.14	.04
☐ 351 Geno Petralli	.05	.02	.01
☐ 352 Gary Pettis	.05	.02	.01
☐ 353 Kenny Rogers	.05	.02	.01
☐ 354 Jeff Russell	.05	.02	.01
☐ 355 Nolan Ryan	1.50	.70	.19
☐ 356 Ruben Sierra	.15	.07	.02
☐ 357 Bobby Witt	.05	.02	.01
☐ 358 Roberto Alomar	.40	.18	.05
☐ 359 Pat Borders	.05	.02	.01
☐ 360 Joe Carter UER	.15	.07	.02
(Reverse negative on back photo)			
☐ 361 Kelly Gruber	.05	.02	.01
☐ 362 Tom Henke	.05	.02	.01
☐ 363 Glenallen Hill	.05	.02	.01
☐ 364 Jimmy Key	.15	.07	.02
☐ 365 Manny Lee	.05	.02	.01
☐ 366 Rance Mulliniks	.05	.02	.01
☐ 367 John Olerud UER	.15	.07	.02
(Throwing left on card; back has throws right; he does throw lefty)			
☐ 368 Dave Stieb	.05	.02	.01
☐ 369 Duane Ward	.05	.02	.01
☐ 370 David Wells	.05	.02	.01
☐ 371 Mark Whiten	.15	.07	.02
☐ 372 Mookie Wilson	.05	.02	.01
☐ 373 Willie Banks MLP	.05	.02	.01
☐ 374 Steve Carter MLP	.05	.02	.01
☐ 375 Scott Chiamparino MLP	.05	.02	.01
☐ 376 Steve Chitren MLP	.05	.02	.01
☐ 377 Darrin Fletcher MLP	.05	.02	.01
☐ 378 Rich Garces MLP	.05	.02	.01
☐ 379 Reggie Jefferson MLP	.15	.07	.02
☐ 380 Eric Karros MLP	1.00	.45	.12
☐ 381 Pat Kelly MLP	.15	.07	.02
☐ 382 Chuck Knoblauch MLP	.50	.23	.06
☐ 383 Denny Neagle MLP	.60	.25	.07
☐ 384 Dan Opperman MLP	.05	.02	.01
☐ 385 John Ramos MLP	.05	.02	.01
☐ 386 Henry Rodriguez MLP	.75	.35	.09
☐ 387 Mo Vaughn MLP	1.00	.45	.12
☐ 388 Gerald Williams MLP	.05	.02	.01
☐ 389 Mike York MLP	.05	.02	.01
☐ 390 Eddie Zosky MLP	.05	.02	.01
☐ 391 Barry Bonds EP	.30	.14	.04
☐ 392 Cecil Fielder EP	.15	.07	.02
☐ 393 Rickey Henderson EP	.30	.14	.04
☐ 394 Dave Justice EP	.30	.14	.04
☐ 395 Nolan Ryan EP	.75	.35	.09
☐ 396 Bobby Thigpen EP	.05	.02	.01
☐ 397 Gregg Jefferies CL	.15	.07	.02
☐ 398 Von Hayes CL	.05	.02	.01
☐ 399 Terry Kennedy CL	.05	.02	.01
☐ 400 Nolan Ryan CL	.30	.14	.04

1991 Ultra Gold

This ten-card standard-size set presents Fleer's 1991 Ultra Team. These cards were randomly inserted into Ultra packs. On a gold background that fades as one moves toward the bottom of the card, the front design has a color head shot, with two cut-out action shots below. Player information is given in a dark blue strip at the bottom of the card face. In blue print on white background with gold borders, the back highlights the player's outstanding achievements. The set is sequenced in alphabetical order.

	MINT	NRMT	EXC
COMPLETE SET (10)	10.00	4.50	1.25
COMMON CARD (1-10)	.25	.11	.03
☐ 1 Barry Bonds	1.00	.45	.12
☐ 2 Will Clark	.50	.23	.06
☐ 3 Doug Drabek	.25	.11	.03
☐ 4 Ken Griffey Jr.	6.00	2.70	.75
☐ 5 Rickey Henderson	.50	.23	.06
☐ 6 Bo Jackson	.35	.16	.04
☐ 7 Ramon Martinez	.50	.23	.06
☐ 8 Kirby Puckett UER	1.50	.70	.19
(Boggs won 1988 batting title, so Puckett didn't win consecutive titles)			
☐ 9 Chris Sabo	.25	.11	.03
☐ 10 Ryne Sandberg UER	1.00	.45	.12

(Johnson and Hornsby didn't hit 40 homers in 1990, Fielder did hit 51 in '90)

1991 Ultra Update

The 120-card set was distributed exclusively in factory set form along with 20 team logo stickers through hobby dealers. The set includes the year's hottest rookies and important veteran players traded after the original Ultra series was produced. Card design is identical to regular issue 1991 cards except for the U-prefixed numbering on back. Cards are ordered alphabetically within and according to teams for each league. Rookie Cards in this set include Jeff Bagwell, Juan Guzman, Mike Mussina, and Ivan Rodriguez.

	MINT	NRMT	EXC
COMPLETE FACT.SET (120)	32.00	14.50	4.00
COMMON CARD (1-120)	.10	.05	.01
☐ 1 Dwight Evans	.25	.11	.03
☐ 2 Chito Martinez	.10	.05	.01
☐ 3 Bob Melvin	.10	.05	.01
☐ 4 Mike Mussina	6.00	2.70	.75
☐ 5 Jack Clark	.25	.11	.03
☐ 6 Dana Kiecker	.10	.05	.01
☐ 7 Steve Lyons	.10	.05	.01
☐ 8 Gary Gaetti	.25	.11	.03
☐ 9 Dave Gallagher	.10	.05	.01
☐ 10 Dave Parker	.25	.11	.03
☐ 11 Luis Polonia	.10	.05	.01
☐ 12 Luis Sojo	.10	.05	.01
☐ 13 Wilson Alvarez	1.00	.45	.12
☐ 14 Alex Fernandez	2.00	.90	.25
☐ 15 Craig Grebeck	.10	.05	.01
☐ 16 Ron Karkovice	.10	.05	.01
☐ 17 Warren Newson	.10	.05	.01
☐ 18 Scott Radinsky	.10	.05	.01
☐ 19 Glenallen Hill	.10	.05	.01
☐ 20 Charles Nagy	1.25	.55	.16
☐ 21 Mark Whiten	.25	.11	.03
☐ 22 Milt Cuyler	.10	.05	.01
☐ 23 Paul Gibson	.10	.05	.01
☐ 24 Mickey Tettleton	.25	.11	.03
☐ 25 Todd Benzinger	.10	.05	.01
☐ 26 Storm Davis	.10	.05	.01
☐ 27 Kirk Gibson	.25	.11	.03
☐ 28 Bill Pecota	.10	.05	.01
☐ 29 Gary Thurman	.10	.05	.01
☐ 30 Darryl Hamilton	.25	.11	.03
☐ 31 Jaime Navarro	.10	.05	.01
☐ 32 Willie Randolph	.25	.11	.03
☐ 33 Bill Wegman	.10	.05	.01
☐ 34 Randy Bush	.10	.05	.01
☐ 35 Chili Davis	.25	.11	.03
☐ 36 Scott Erickson	.25	.11	.03
☐ 37 Chuck Knoblauch	4.00	1.80	.50
☐ 38 Scott Leius	.10	.05	.01
☐ 39 Jack Morris	.25	.11	.03
☐ 40 John Habyan	.10	.05	.01
☐ 41 Pat Kelly	.25	.11	.03
☐ 42 Matt Nokes	.10	.05	.01
☐ 43 Scott Sanderson	.10	.05	.01
☐ 44 Bernie Williams	5.00	2.20	.60
☐ 45 Harold Baines	.25	.11	.03
☐ 46 Brook Jacoby	.10	.05	.01
☐ 47 Earnest Riles	.10	.05	.01
☐ 48 Willie Wilson	.10	.05	.01
☐ 49 Jay Buhner	.75	.35	.09
☐ 50 Rich DeLucia	.10	.05	.01
☐ 51 Mike Jackson	.10	.05	.01
☐ 52 Bill Krueger	.10	.05	.01
☐ 53 Bill Swift	.10	.05	.01
☐ 54 Brian Downing	.10	.05	.01
☐ 55 Juan Gonzalez	15.00	6.75	1.85
☐ 56 Dean Palmer	1.50	.70	.19
☐ 57 Kevin Reimer	.10	.05	.01
☐ 58 Ivan Rodriguez	8.00	3.60	1.00
☐ 59 Tom Candiotti	.10	.05	.01
☐ 60 Juan Guzman	.75	.35	.09
☐ 61 Bob MacDonald	.10	.05	.01
☐ 62 Greg Myers	.10	.05	.01
☐ 63 Ed Sprague	.25	.11	.03
☐ 64 Devon White	.25	.11	.03
☐ 65 Rafael Belliard	.10	.05	.01
☐ 66 Juan Berenguer	.10	.05	.01
☐ 67 Brian R. Hunter	.10	.05	.01
☐ 68 Kent Mercker	.10	.05	.01
☐ 69 Otis Nixon	.10	.05	.01
☐ 70 Danny Jackson	.10	.05	.01
☐ 71 Chuck McElroy	.10	.05	.01
☐ 72 Gary Scott	.10	.05	.01
☐ 73 Heathcliff Slocumb	.50	.23	.06
☐ 74 Chico Walker	.10	.05	.01
☐ 75 Rick Wilkins	.10	.05	.01
☐ 76 Chris Hammond	.10	.05	.01
☐ 77 Luis Quinones	.10	.05	.01
☐ 78 Herm Winningham	.10	.05	.01
☐ 79 Jeff Bagwell	15.00	6.75	1.85
☐ 80 Jim Corsi	.10	.05	.01
☐ 81 Steve Finley	.25	.11	.03
☐ 82 Luis Gonzalez	.50	.23	.06
☐ 83 Pete Harnisch	.10	.05	.01
☐ 84 Darryl Kile	.25	.11	.03
☐ 85 Brett Butler	.25	.11	.03
☐ 86 Gary Carter	.25	.11	.03
☐ 87 Tim Crews	.10	.05	.01
☐ 88 Orel Hershiser	.25	.11	.03
☐ 89 Bob Ojeda	.10	.05	.01
☐ 90 Bret Barberie	.10	.05	.01
☐ 91 Barry Jones	.10	.05	.01
☐ 92 Gilberto Reyes	.10	.05	.01
☐ 93 Larry Walker	1.50	.70	.19
☐ 94 Hubie Brooks	.10	.05	.01
☐ 95 Tim Burke	.10	.05	.01
☐ 96 Rick Cerone	.10	.05	.01
☐ 97 Jeff Innis	.10	.05	.01
☐ 98 Wally Backman	.10	.05	.01
☐ 99 Tommy Greene	.10	.05	.01
☐ 100 Ricky Jordan	.10	.05	.01
☐ 101 Mitch Williams	.10	.05	.01
☐ 102 John Smiley	.10	.05	.01
☐ 103 Randy Tomlin	.10	.05	.01
☐ 104 Gary Varsho	.10	.05	.01
☐ 105 Cris Carpenter	.10	.05	.01
☐ 106 Ken Hill	1.25	.55	.16
☐ 107 Felix Jose	.10	.05	.01
☐ 108 Omar Olivares	.10	.05	.01
☐ 109 Gerald Perry	.10	.05	.01
☐ 110 Jerald Clark	.10	.05	.01
☐ 111 Tony Fernandez	.10	.05	.01
☐ 112 Darrin Jackson	.10	.05	.01
☐ 113 Mike Maddux	.10	.05	.01
☐ 114 Tim Teufel	.10	.05	.01
☐ 115 Bud Black	.10	.05	.01
☐ 116 Kelly Downs	.10	.05	.01
☐ 117 Mike Felder	.10	.05	.01
☐ 118 Willie McGee	.10	.05	.01
☐ 119 Trevor Wilson	.10	.05	.01
☐ 120 Checklist 1-120	.10	.05	.01

1992 Ultra

Consisting of 600 standard-size cards, the 1992 Fleer Ultra set was issued in two series of 300 cards each. Cards were distributed exclusively in foil packs. The glossy color action player photos on the fronts are full-bleed except at the bottom where a diagonal gold-foil stripe edges a green marbleized border. The player's name and team appear on the marble-colored area in bars that are color-coded by team. The cards are numbered on the back and ordered below alphabetically within and according to teams for each league with AL preceding NL. There are no notable Rookie Cards in the set. Some cards have been found without the word Fleer on the front.

	MINT	NRMT	EXC
COMPLETE SET (600)	40.00	18.00	5.00
COMPLETE SERIES 1 (300)	25.00	11.00	3.10
COMPLETE SERIES 2 (300)	15.00	6.75	1.85
COMMON CARD (1-600)	.10	.05	.01
☐ 1 Glenn Davis	.10	.05	.01
☐ 2 Mike Devereaux	.10	.05	.01
☐ 3 Dwight Evans	.15	.07	.02
☐ 4 Leo Gomez	.10	.05	.01
☐ 5 Chris Hoiles	.10	.05	.01
☐ 6 Sam Horn	.10	.05	.01
☐ 7 Chito Martinez	.10	.05	.01
☐ 8 Randy Milligan	.10	.05	.01
☐ 9 Mike Mussina	.60	.25	.07
☐ 10 Billy Ripken	.10	.05	.01
☐ 11 Cal Ripken	1.50	.70	.19
☐ 12 Tom Brunansky	.10	.05	.01
☐ 13 Ellis Burks	.15	.07	.02
☐ 14 Jack Clark	.15	.07	.02
☐ 15 Roger Clemens	.40	.18	.05
☐ 16 Mike Greenwell	.10	.05	.01
☐ 17 Joe Hesketh	.10	.05	.01
☐ 18 Tony Pena	.10	.05	.01
☐ 19 Carlos Quintana	.10	.05	.01
☐ 20 Jeff Reardon	.15	.07	.02
☐ 21 Jody Reed	.10	.05	.01
☐ 22 Luis Rivera	.10	.05	.01
☐ 23 Mo Vaughn	.75	.35	.09
☐ 24 Gary DiSarcina	.10	.05	.01
☐ 25 Chuck Finley	.10	.05	.01
☐ 26 Gary Gaetti	.15	.07	.02
☐ 27 Bryan Harvey	.10	.05	.01
☐ 28 Lance Parrish	.10	.05	.01
☐ 29 Luis Polonia	.10	.05	.01
☐ 30 Dick Schofield	.10	.05	.01
☐ 31 Luis Sojo	.10	.05	.01
☐ 32 Wilson Alvarez	.30	.14	.04
☐ 33 Carlton Fisk	.30	.14	.04
☐ 34 Craig Grebeck	.10	.05	.01
☐ 35 Ozzie Guillen	.10	.05	.01
☐ 36 Greg Hibbard	.10	.05	.01
☐ 37 Charlie Hough	.10	.05	.01
☐ 38 Lance Johnson	.15	.07	.02
☐ 39 Ron Karkovice	.10	.05	.01
☐ 40 Jack McDowell	.15	.07	.02
☐ 41 Donn Pall	.10	.05	.01
☐ 42 Melido Perez	.10	.05	.01
☐ 43 Tim Raines	.30	.14	.04
☐ 44 Frank Thomas	3.00	1.35	.35
☐ 45 Sandy Alomar Jr.	.15	.07	.02
☐ 46 Carlos Baerga	.15	.07	.02
☐ 47 Albert Belle	1.00	.45	.12
☐ 48 Jerry Browne UER (Reversed negative on card back)	.10	.05	.01
☐ 49 Felix Fermin	.10	.05	.01
☐ 50 Reggie Jefferson UER (Born 1968, not 1966)	.15	.07	.02
☐ 51 Mark Lewis	.10	.05	.01
☐ 52 Carlos Martinez	.10	.05	.01
☐ 53 Steve Olin	.10	.05	.01
☐ 54 Jim Thome	1.50	.70	.19
☐ 55 Mark Whiten	.15	.07	.02
☐ 56 Dave Bergman	.10	.05	.01
☐ 57 Milt Cuyler	.10	.05	.01
☐ 58 Rob Deer	.10	.05	.01
☐ 59 Cecil Fielder	.15	.07	.02
☐ 60 Travis Fryman	.30	.14	.04
☐ 61 Scott Livingstone	.10	.05	.01
☐ 62 Tony Phillips	.15	.07	.02
☐ 63 Mickey Tettleton	.10	.05	.01
☐ 64 Alan Trammell	.15	.07	.02
☐ 65 Lou Whitaker	.15	.07	.02
☐ 66 Kevin Appier	.15	.07	.02
☐ 67 Mike Boddicker	.10	.05	.01
☐ 68 George Brett	.75	.35	.09
☐ 69 Jim Eisenreich	.10	.05	.01
☐ 70 Mark Gubicza	.10	.05	.01
☐ 71 David Howard	.10	.05	.01
☐ 72 Joel Johnson	.10	.05	.01
☐ 73 Mike Macfarlane	.10	.05	.01
☐ 74 Brent Mayne	.10	.05	.01
☐ 75 Brian McRae	.15	.07	.02
☐ 76 Jeff Montgomery	.15	.07	.02
☐ 77 Danny Tartabull	.10	.05	.01
☐ 78 Don August	.10	.05	.01
☐ 79 Dante Bichette	.30	.14	.04
☐ 80 Ted Higuera	.10	.05	.01
☐ 81 Paul Molitor	.40	.18	.05
☐ 82 Jaime Navarro	.10	.05	.01
☐ 83 Gary Sheffield	.30	.14	.04
☐ 84 Bill Spiers	.10	.05	.01
☐ 85 B.J. Surhoff	.15	.07	.02
☐ 86 Greg Vaughn	.15	.07	.02
☐ 87 Robin Yount	.30	.14	.04
☐ 88 Rick Aguilera	.10	.05	.01
☐ 89 Chili Davis	.15	.07	.02
☐ 90 Scott Erickson	.15	.07	.02
☐ 91 Brian Harper	.10	.05	.01
☐ 92 Kent Hrbek	.15	.07	.02
☐ 93 Chuck Knoblauch	.30	.14	.04
☐ 94 Scott Leius	.10	.05	.01
☐ 95 Shane Mack	.10	.05	.01
☐ 96 Mike Pagliarulo	.10	.05	.01
☐ 97 Kirby Puckett	.75	.35	.09
☐ 98 Kevin Tapani	.10	.05	.01
☐ 99 Jesse Barfield	.10	.05	.01
☐ 100 Alvaro Espinoza	.10	.05	.01
☐ 101 Mel Hall	.10	.05	.01
☐ 102 Pat Kelly	.10	.05	.01
☐ 103 Roberto Kelly	.10	.05	.01
☐ 104 Kevin Maas	.10	.05	.01
☐ 105 Don Mattingly	1.00	.45	.12
☐ 106 Hensley Meulens	.10	.05	.01
☐ 107 Matt Nokes	.10	.05	.01
☐ 108 Steve Sax	.10	.05	.01
☐ 109 Harold Baines	.15	.07	.02
☐ 110 Jose Canseco	.30	.14	.04
☐ 111 Ron Darling	.10	.05	.01
☐ 112 Mike Gallego	.10	.05	.01
☐ 113 Dave Henderson	.10	.05	.01
☐ 114 Rickey Henderson	.30	.14	.04
☐ 115 Mark McGwire	.60	.25	.07
☐ 116 Terry Steinbach	.15	.07	.02
☐ 117 Dave Stewart	.15	.07	.02
☐ 118 Todd Van Poppel	.10	.05	.01
☐ 119 Bob Welch	.10	.05	.01
☐ 120 Greg Briley	.10	.05	.01
☐ 121 Jay Buhner	.30	.14	.04
☐ 122 Rick DeLucia	.10	.05	.01
☐ 123 Ken Griffey Jr.	3.00	1.35	.35
☐ 124 Erik Hanson	.10	.05	.01
☐ 125 Randy Johnson	.30	.14	.04
☐ 126 Edgar Martinez	.15	.07	.02
☐ 127 Tino Martinez	.15	.07	.02
☐ 128 Pete O'Brien	.10	.05	.01
☐ 129 Harold Reynolds	.10	.05	.01
☐ 130 Dave Valle	.10	.05	.01
☐ 131 Julio Franco	.15	.07	.02
☐ 132 Juan Gonzalez	1.25	.55	.16
☐ 133 Jeff Huson (Shows Jose Canseco sliding into second)	.15	.07	.02
☐ 134 Mike Jeffcoat	.10	.05	.01
☐ 135 Terry Mathews	.10	.05	.01
☐ 136 Rafael Palmeiro	.30	.14	.04
☐ 137 Dean Palmer	.15	.07	.02
☐ 138 Geno Petralli	.10	.05	.01
☐ 139 Ivan Rodriguez	.75	.35	.09
☐ 140 Jeff Russell	.10	.05	.01
☐ 141 Nolan Ryan	1.50	.70	.19
☐ 142 Ruben Sierra	.15	.07	.02
☐ 143 Roberto Alomar	.40	.18	.05
☐ 144 Pat Borders	.10	.05	.01
☐ 145 Joe Carter	.15	.07	.02
☐ 146 Kelly Gruber	.10	.05	.01
☐ 147 Jimmy Key	.15	.07	.02
☐ 148 Manny Lee	.10	.05	.01
☐ 149 Rance Mulliniks	.10	.05	.01
☐ 150 Greg Myers	.10	.05	.01
☐ 151 John Olerud	.15	.07	.02
☐ 152 Dave Stieb	.10	.05	.01
☐ 153 Todd Stottlemyre	.15	.07	.02
☐ 154 Duane Ward	.10	.05	.01
☐ 155 Devon White	.15	.07	.02
☐ 156 Eddie Zosky	.10	.05	.01
☐ 157 Steve Avery	.15	.07	.02
☐ 158 Rafael Belliard	.10	.05	.01
☐ 159 Jeff Blauser	.10	.05	.01
☐ 160 Sid Bream	.10	.05	.01
☐ 161 Ron Gant	.15	.07	.02
☐ 162 Tom Glavine	.30	.14	.04
☐ 163 Brian Hunter	.10	.05	.01
☐ 164 Dave Justice	.30	.14	.04
☐ 165 Mark Lemke	.10	.05	.01
☐ 166 Greg Olson	.10	.05	.01
☐ 167 Terry Pendleton	.15	.07	.02
☐ 168 Lonnie Smith	.10	.05	.01
☐ 169 John Smoltz	.30	.14	.04
☐ 170 Mike Stanton	.10	.05	.01
☐ 171 Jeff Treadway	.10	.05	.01
☐ 172 Paul Assenmacher	.10	.05	.01
☐ 173 George Bell	.10	.05	.01
☐ 174 Shawon Dunston	.10	.05	.01
☐ 175 Mark Grace	.30	.14	.04
☐ 176 Danny Jackson	.10	.05	.01
☐ 177 Les Lancaster	.10	.05	.01
☐ 178 Greg Maddux	1.50	.70	.19
☐ 179 Luis Salazar	.10	.05	.01
☐ 180 Rey Sanchez	.10	.05	.01
☐ 181 Ryne Sandberg	.50	.23	.06
☐ 182 Jose Vizcaino	.10	.05	.01
☐ 183 Chico Walker	.10	.05	.01
☐ 184 Jerome Walton	.10	.05	.01
☐ 185 Glenn Braggs	.10	.05	.01
☐ 186 Tom Browning	.10	.05	.01
☐ 187 Rob Dibble	.10	.05	.01
☐ 188 Bill Doran	.10	.05	.01
☐ 189 Chris Hammond	.10	.05	.01
☐ 190 Billy Hatcher	.10	.05	.01
☐ 191 Barry Larkin	.30	.14	.04
☐ 192 Hal Morris	.10	.05	.01
☐ 193 Joe Oliver	.10	.05	.01
☐ 194 Paul O'Neill	.15	.07	.02
☐ 195 Jeff Reed	.10	.05	.01
☐ 196 Jose Rijo	.10	.05	.01
☐ 197 Chris Sabo	.10	.05	.01
☐ 198 Jeff Bagwell	1.25	.55	.16
☐ 199 Craig Biggio	.15	.07	.02
☐ 200 Ken Caminiti	.30	.14	.04
☐ 201 Andujar Cedeno	.10	.05	.01
☐ 202 Steve Finley	.15	.07	.02
☐ 203 Luis Gonzalez	.15	.07	.02
☐ 204 Pete Harnisch	.10	.05	.01
☐ 205 Xavier Hernandez	.10	.05	.01
☐ 206 Darryl Kile	.10	.05	.01
☐ 207 Al Osuna	.10	.05	.01
☐ 208 Curt Schilling	.10	.05	.01
☐ 209 Brett Butler	.15	.07	.02
☐ 210 Kal Daniels	.10	.05	.01
☐ 211 Lenny Harris	.10	.05	.01
☐ 212 Stan Javier	.10	.05	.01
☐ 213 Ramon Martinez	.15	.07	.02
☐ 214 Roger McDowell	.10	.05	.01
☐ 215 Jose Offerman	.10	.05	.01
☐ 216 Juan Samuel	.10	.05	.01
☐ 217 Mike Scioscia	.10	.05	.01
☐ 218 Mike Sharperson	.10	.05	.01
☐ 219 Darryl Strawberry	.15	.07	.02
☐ 220 Delino DeShields	.10	.05	.01
☐ 221 Tom Foley	.10	.05	.01
☐ 222 Steve Frey	.10	.05	.01
☐ 223 Dennis Martinez	.15	.07	.02

Card			
□ 224 Spike Owen	.10	.05	.01
□ 225 Gilberto Reyes	.10	.05	.01
□ 226 Tim Wallach	.10	.05	.01
□ 227 Daryl Boston	.10	.05	.01
□ 228 Tim Burke	.10	.05	.01
□ 229 Vince Coleman	.10	.05	.01
□ 230 David Cone	.15	.07	.02
□ 231 Kevin Elster	.10	.05	.01
□ 232 Dwight Gooden	.15	.07	.02
□ 233 Todd Hundley	.15	.07	.02
□ 234 Jeff Innis	.10	.05	.01
□ 235 Howard Johnson	.10	.05	.01
□ 236 Dave Magadan	.10	.05	.01
□ 237 Mackey Sasser	.10	.05	.01
□ 238 Anthony Young	.10	.05	.01
□ 239 Wes Chamberlain	.10	.05	.01
□ 240 Darren Daulton	.15	.07	.02
□ 241 Len Dykstra	.15	.07	.02
□ 242 Tommy Greene	.10	.05	.01
□ 243 Charlie Hayes	.10	.05	.01
□ 244 Dave Hollins	.10	.05	.01
□ 245 Ricky Jordan	.10	.05	.01
□ 246 John Kruk	.15	.07	.02
□ 247 Mickey Morandini	.10	.05	.01
□ 248 Terry Mulholland	.10	.05	.01
□ 249 Dale Murphy	.30	.14	.04
□ 250 Jay Bell	.15	.07	.02
□ 251 Barry Bonds	.50	.23	.06
□ 252 Steve Buechele	.10	.05	.01
□ 253 Doug Drabek	.10	.05	.01
□ 254 Mike LaValliere	.10	.05	.01
□ 255 Jose Lind	.10	.05	.01
□ 256 Lloyd McClendon	.10	.05	.01
□ 257 Orlando Merced	.15	.07	.02
□ 258 Don Slaught	.10	.05	.01
□ 259 John Smiley	.10	.05	.01
□ 260 Zane Smith	.10	.05	.01
□ 261 Randy Tomlin	.10	.05	.01
□ 262 Andy Van Slyke	.15	.07	.02
□ 263 Pedro Guerrero	.10	.05	.01
□ 264 Felix Jose	.10	.05	.01
□ 265 Ray Lankford	.30	.14	.04
□ 266 Omar Olivares	.10	.05	.01
□ 267 Jose Oquendo	.10	.05	.01
□ 268 Tom Pagnozzi	.10	.05	.01
□ 269 Bryn Smith	.10	.05	.01
□ 270 Lee Smith UER (1991 record listed as 61-61)	.15	.07	.02
□ 271 Ozzie Smith UER (Comma before year of birth on card back)	.50	.23	.06
□ 272 Milt Thompson	.10	.05	.01
□ 273 Todd Zeile	.10	.05	.01
□ 274 Andy Benes	.15	.07	.02
□ 275 Jerald Clark	.10	.05	.01
□ 276 Tony Fernandez	.10	.05	.01
□ 277 Tony Gwynn	.75	.35	.09
□ 278 Greg W. Harris	.10	.05	.01
□ 279 Thomas Howard	.10	.05	.01
□ 280 Bruce Hurst	.10	.05	.01
□ 281 Mike Maddux	.10	.05	.01
□ 282 Fred McGriff	.30	.14	.04
□ 283 Benito Santiago	.10	.05	.01
□ 284 Kevin Bass	.10	.05	.01
□ 285 Jeff Brantley	.15	.07	.02
□ 286 John Burkett	.15	.07	.02
□ 287 Will Clark	.30	.14	.04
□ 288 Royce Clayton	.15	.07	.02
□ 289 Steve Decker	.10	.05	.01
□ 290 Kelly Downs	.10	.05	.01
□ 291 Mike Felder	.10	.05	.01
□ 292 Darren Lewis	.10	.05	.01
□ 293 Kirt Manwaring	.10	.05	.01
□ 294 Willie McGee	.10	.05	.01
□ 295 Robby Thompson	.10	.05	.01
□ 296 Matt Williams	.30	.14	.04
□ 297 Trevor Wilson	.10	.05	.01
□ 298 Checklist 1-100	.10	.05	.01
□ 299 Checklist 101-200	.10	.05	.01
□ 300 Checklist 201-300	.10	.05	.01
□ 301 Brady Anderson	.30	.14	.04
□ 302 Todd Frohwirth	.10	.05	.01
□ 303 Ben McDonald	.10	.05	.01
□ 304 Mark McLemore	.10	.05	.01
□ 305 Jose Mesa	.15	.07	.02
□ 306 Bob Milacki	.10	.05	.01
□ 307 Gregg Olson	.10	.05	.01
□ 308 David Segui	.10	.05	.01
□ 309 Rick Sutcliffe	.10	.05	.01
□ 310 Jeff Tackett	.10	.05	.01
□ 311 Wade Boggs	.30	.14	.04
□ 312 Scott Cooper	.10	.05	.01
□ 313 John Flaherty	.10	.05	.01
□ 314 Wayne Housie	.10	.05	.01
□ 315 Peter Hoy	.10	.05	.01
□ 316 John Marzano	.10	.05	.01
□ 317 Tim Naehring	.15	.07	.02
□ 318 Phil Plantier	.15	.07	.02
□ 319 Frank Viola	.10	.05	.01
□ 320 Matt Young	.10	.05	.01
□ 321 Jim Abbott	.10	.05	.01
□ 322 Hubie Brooks	.10	.05	.01
□ 323 Chad Curtis	.30	.14	.04
□ 324 Alvin Davis	.10	.05	.01
□ 325 Junior Felix	.10	.05	.01
□ 326 Von Hayes	.10	.05	.01
□ 327 Mark Langston	.15	.07	.02
□ 328 Scott Lewis	.10	.05	.01
□ 329 Don Robinson	.10	.05	.01
□ 330 Bobby Rose	.10	.05	.01
□ 331 Lee Stevens	.10	.05	.01
□ 332 George Bell	.10	.05	.01
□ 333 Esteban Beltre	.10	.05	.01
□ 334 Joey Cora	.15	.07	.02
□ 335 Alex Fernandez	.30	.14	.04
□ 336 Roberto Hernandez	.15	.07	.02
□ 337 Mike Huff	.10	.05	.01
□ 338 Kirk McCaskill	.10	.05	.01
□ 339 Dan Pasqua	.10	.05	.01
□ 340 Scott Radinsky	.10	.05	.01
□ 341 Steve Sax	.10	.05	.01
□ 342 Bobby Thigpen	.10	.05	.01
□ 343 Robin Ventura	.15	.07	.02
□ 344 Jack Armstrong	.10	.05	.01
□ 345 Alex Cole	.10	.05	.01
□ 346 Dennis Cook	.10	.05	.01
□ 347 Glenallen Hill	.10	.05	.01
□ 348 Thomas Howard	.10	.05	.01
□ 349 Brook Jacoby	.10	.05	.01
□ 350 Kenny Lofton	2.50	1.10	.30
□ 351 Charles Nagy	.15	.07	.02
□ 352 Rod Nichols	.10	.05	.01
□ 353 Junior Ortiz	.10	.05	.01
□ 354 Dave Otto	.10	.05	.01
□ 355 Tony Perezchica	.10	.05	.01
□ 356 Scott Scudder	.10	.05	.01
□ 357 Paul Sorrento	.10	.05	.01
□ 358 Skeeter Barnes	.10	.05	.01
□ 359 Mark Carreon	.10	.05	.01
□ 360 John Doherty	.10	.05	.01
□ 361 Dan Gladden	.10	.05	.01
□ 362 Bill Gullickson	.10	.05	.01
□ 363 Shawn Hare	.10	.05	.01
□ 364 Mike Henneman	.10	.05	.01
□ 365 Chad Kreuter	.10	.05	.01
□ 366 Mark Leiter	.10	.05	.01
□ 367 Mike Munoz	.10	.05	.01
□ 368 Kevin Ritz	.10	.05	.01
□ 369 Mark Davis	.10	.05	.01
□ 370 Tom Gordon	.10	.05	.01
□ 371 Chris Gwynn	.10	.05	.01
□ 372 Gregg Jefferies	.15	.07	.02
□ 373 Wally Joyner	.15	.07	.02
□ 374 Kevin McReynolds	.10	.05	.01
□ 375 Keith Miller	.10	.05	.01
□ 376 Rico Rossy	.10	.05	.01
□ 377 Curtis Wilkerson	.10	.05	.01
□ 378 Ricky Bones	.10	.05	.01
□ 379 Chris Bosio	.10	.05	.01
□ 380 Cal Eldred	.10	.05	.01
□ 381 Scott Fletcher	.10	.05	.01
□ 382 Jim Gantner	.10	.05	.01
□ 383 Darryl Hamilton	.10	.05	.01
□ 384 Doug Henry	.10	.05	.01
□ 385 Pat Listach	.15	.07	.02
□ 386 Tim McIntosh	.10	.05	.01
□ 387 Edwin Nunez	.10	.05	.01
□ 388 Dan Plesac	.10	.05	.01
□ 389 Kevin Seitzer	.10	.05	.01
□ 390 Franklin Stubbs	.10	.05	.01
□ 391 William Suero	.10	.05	.01
□ 392 Bill Wegman	.10	.05	.01
□ 393 Willie Banks	.10	.05	.01
□ 394 Jarvis Brown	.10	.05	.01
□ 395 Greg Gagne	.10	.05	.01
□ 396 Mark Guthrie	.10	.05	.01
□ 397 Bill Krueger	.10	.05	.01
□ 398 Pat Mahomes	.10	.05	.01
□ 399 Pedro Munoz	.10	.05	.01
□ 400 John Smiley	.10	.05	.01
□ 401 Gary Wayne	.10	.05	.01
□ 402 Lenny Webster	.10	.05	.01
□ 403 Carl Willis	.10	.05	.01
□ 404 Greg Cadaret	.10	.05	.01
□ 405 Steve Farr	.10	.05	.01
□ 406 Mike Gallego	.10	.05	.01
□ 407 Charlie Hayes	.10	.05	.01
□ 408 Steve Howe	.10	.05	.01
□ 409 Dion James	.10	.05	.01
□ 410 Jeff Johnson	.10	.05	.01
□ 411 Tim Leary	.10	.05	.01
□ 412 Jim Leyritz	.10	.05	.01
□ 413 Melido Perez	.10	.05	.01
□ 414 Scott Sanderson	.10	.05	.01
□ 415 Andy Stankiewicz	.10	.05	.01
□ 416 Mike Stanley	.10	.05	.01
□ 417 Danny Tartabull	.10	.05	.01
□ 418 Lance Blankenship	.10	.05	.01
□ 419 Mike Bordick	.15	.07	.02
□ 420 Scott Brosius	.10	.05	.01
□ 421 Dennis Eckersley	.15	.07	.02
□ 422 Scott Hemond	.10	.05	.01
□ 423 Carney Lansford	.15	.07	.02
□ 424 Henry Mercedes	.10	.05	.01
□ 425 Mike Moore	.10	.05	.01
□ 426 Gene Nelson	.10	.05	.01
□ 427 Randy Ready	.10	.05	.01
□ 428 Bruce Walton	.10	.05	.01
□ 429 Willie Wilson	.10	.05	.01
□ 430 Rich Amaral	.10	.05	.01
□ 431 Dave Cochrane	.10	.05	.01
□ 432 Henry Cotto	.10	.05	.01
□ 433 Calvin Jones	.10	.05	.01
□ 434 Kevin Mitchell	.15	.07	.02
□ 435 Clay Parker	.10	.05	.01
□ 436 Omar Vizquel	.15	.07	.02
□ 437 Floyd Bannister	.10	.05	.01
□ 438 Kevin Brown	.15	.07	.02
□ 439 John Cangelosi	.10	.05	.01
□ 440 Brian Downing	.10	.05	.01
□ 441 Monty Fariss	.10	.05	.01
□ 442 Jose Guzman	.10	.05	.01
□ 443 Donald Harris	.10	.05	.01
□ 444 Kevin Reimer	.10	.05	.01
□ 445 Kenny Rogers	.10	.05	.01
□ 446 Wayne Rosenthal	.10	.05	.01
□ 447 Dickie Thon	.10	.05	.01
□ 448 Derek Bell	.30	.14	.04
□ 449 Juan Guzman	.15	.07	.02
□ 450 Tom Henke	.10	.05	.01
□ 451 Candy Maldonado	.10	.05	.01
□ 452 Jack Morris	.15	.07	.02
□ 453 David Wells	.10	.05	.01
□ 454 Dave Winfield	.30	.14	.04
□ 455 Juan Berenguer	.10	.05	.01
□ 456 Damon Berryhill	.10	.05	.01
□ 457 Mike Bielecki	.10	.05	.01
□ 458 Marvin Freeman	.10	.05	.01
□ 459 Charlie Leibrandt	.10	.05	.01
□ 460 Kent Mercker	.10	.05	.01
□ 461 Otis Nixon	.10	.05	.01
□ 462 Alejandro Pena	.10	.05	.01
□ 463 Ben Rivera	.10	.05	.01
□ 464 Deion Sanders	.30	.14	.04
□ 465 Mark Wohlers	.30	.14	.04
□ 466 Shawn Boskie	.10	.05	.01
□ 467 Frank Castillo	.15	.07	.02
□ 468 Andre Dawson	.15	.07	.02
□ 469 Joe Girardi	.10	.05	.01
□ 470 Chuck McElroy	.10	.05	.01
□ 471 Mike Morgan	.10	.05	.01
□ 472 Ken Patterson	.10	.05	.01
□ 473 Bob Scanlan	.10	.05	.01
□ 474 Gary Scott	.10	.05	.01
□ 475 Dave Smith	.10	.05	.01
□ 476 Sammy Sosa	.50	.23	.06
□ 477 Hector Villanueva	.10	.05	.01
□ 478 Scott Bankhead	.10	.05	.01
□ 479 Tim Belcher	.10	.05	.01
□ 480 Freddie Benavides	.10	.05	.01
□ 481 Jacob Brumfield	.10	.05	.01
□ 482 Norm Charlton	.10	.05	.01
□ 483 Dwayne Henry	.10	.05	.01
□ 484 Dave Martinez	.10	.05	.01
□ 485 Bip Roberts	.10	.05	.01
□ 486 Reggie Sanders	.30	.14	.04
□ 487 Greg Swindell	.10	.05	.01
□ 488 Ryan Bowen	.10	.05	.01
□ 489 Casey Candaele	.10	.05	.01
□ 490 Juan Guerrero UER (photo on front is Andujar Cedeno)	.10	.05	.01
□ 491 Pete Incaviglia	.10	.05	.01
□ 492 Jeff Juden	.10	.05	.01
□ 493 Rob Murphy	.10	.05	.01
□ 494 Mark Portugal	.10	.05	.01
□ 495 Rafael Ramirez	.10	.05	.01
□ 496 Scott Servais	.10	.05	.01
□ 497 Ed Taubensee	.10	.05	.01
□ 498 Brian Williams	.10	.05	.01
□ 499 Todd Benzinger	.10	.05	.01
□ 500 John Candelaria	.10	.05	.01
□ 501 Tom Candiotti	.10	.05	.01
□ 502 Tim Crews	.10	.05	.01
□ 503 Eric Davis	.15	.07	.02
□ 504 Jim Gott	.10	.05	.01
□ 505 Dave Hansen	.10	.05	.01
□ 506 Carlos Hernandez	.10	.05	.01
□ 507 Orel Hershiser	.15	.07	.02
□ 508 Eric Karros	.30	.14	.04
□ 509 Bob Ojeda	.10	.05	.01
□ 510 Steve Wilson	.10	.05	.01
□ 511 Moises Alou	.30	.14	.04
□ 512 Bret Barberie	.10	.05	.01
□ 513 Ivan Calderon	.10	.05	.01
□ 514 Gary Carter	.30	.14	.04
□ 515 Archi Cianfrocco	.10	.05	.01
□ 516 Jeff Fassero	.15	.07	.02
□ 517 Darrin Fletcher	.10	.05	.01
□ 518 Marquis Grissom	.15	.07	.02
□ 519 Chris Haney	.10	.05	.01
□ 520 Ken Hill	.15	.07	.02
□ 521 Chris Nabholz	.10	.05	.01
□ 522 Bill Sampen	.10	.05	.01
□ 523 John Vander Wal	.10	.05	.01
□ 524 Dave Wainhouse	.10	.05	.01
□ 525 Larry Walker	.30	.14	.04
□ 526 John Wetteland	.15	.07	.02
□ 527 Bobby Bonilla	.15	.07	.02
□ 528 Sid Fernandez	.10	.05	.01
□ 529 John Franco	.10	.05	.01
□ 530 Dave Gallagher	.10	.05	.01
□ 531 Paul Gibson	.10	.05	.01
□ 532 Eddie Murray	.50	.23	.06
□ 533 Junior Noboa	.10	.05	.01
□ 534 Charlie O'Brien	.10	.05	.01
□ 535 Bill Pecota	.10	.05	.01
□ 536 Willie Randolph	.15	.07	.02
□ 537 Bret Saberhagen	.15	.07	.02
□ 538 Dick Schofield	.10	.05	.01
□ 539 Pete Schourek	.15	.07	.02
□ 540 Ruben Amaro	.10	.05	.01
□ 541 Andy Ashby	.15	.07	.02
□ 542 Kim Batiste	.10	.05	.01
□ 543 Cliff Brantley	.10	.05	.01
□ 544 Mariano Duncan	.10	.05	.01
□ 545 Jeff Grotewold	.10	.05	.01
□ 546 Barry Jones	.10	.05	.01
□ 547 Julio Peguero	.10	.05	.01
□ 548 Curt Schilling	.10	.05	.01
□ 549 Mitch Williams	.10	.05	.01
□ 550 Stan Belinda	.10	.05	.01
□ 551 Scott Bullett	.10	.05	.01
□ 552 Cecil Espy	.10	.05	.01
□ 553 Jeff King	.15	.07	.02
□ 554 Roger Mason	.10	.05	.01
□ 555 Paul Miller	.10	.05	.01
□ 556 Denny Neagle	.30	.14	.04
□ 557 Vicente Palacios	.10	.05	.01
□ 558 Bob Patterson	.10	.05	.01
□ 559 Tom Prince	.10	.05	.01
□ 560 Gary Redus	.10	.05	.01
□ 561 Gary Varsho	.10	.05	.01
□ 562 Juan Agosto	.10	.05	.01
□ 563 Cris Carpenter	.10	.05	.01
□ 564 Mark Clark	.15	.07	.02
□ 565 Jose DeLeon	.10	.05	.01
□ 566 Rich Gedman	.10	.05	.01
□ 567 Bernard Gilkey	.15	.07	.02
□ 568 Rex Hudler	.10	.05	.01
□ 569 Tim Jones	.10	.05	.01
□ 570 Donovan Osborne	.15	.07	.02
□ 571 Mike Perez	.10	.05	.01
□ 572 Gerald Perry	.10	.05	.01
□ 573 Bob Tewksbury	.10	.05	.01
□ 574 Todd Worrell	.10	.05	.01
□ 575 Dave Eiland	.10	.05	.01
□ 576 Jeremy Hernandez	.10	.05	.01
□ 577 Craig Lefferts	.10	.05	.01
□ 578 Jose Melendez	.10	.05	.01
□ 579 Randy Myers	.15	.07	.02
□ 580 Gary Pettis	.10	.05	.01
□ 581 Rich Rodriguez	.10	.05	.01
□ 582 Gary Sheffield	.30	.14	.04
□ 583 Craig Shipley	.10	.05	.01
□ 584 Kurt Stillwell	.10	.05	.01
□ 585 Tim Teufel	.10	.05	.01
□ 586 Rod Beck	.50	.23	.06
□ 587 Dave Burba	.10	.05	.01
□ 588 Craig Colbert	.10	.05	.01
□ 589 Bryan Hickerson	.10	.05	.01
□ 590 Mike Jackson	.10	.05	.01
□ 591 Mark Leonard	.10	.05	.01
□ 592 Jim McNamara	.10	.05	.01
□ 593 John Patterson	.10	.05	.01
□ 594 Dave Righetti	.10	.05	.01
□ 595 Cory Snyder	.10	.05	.01
□ 596 Bill Swift	.10	.05	.01
□ 597 Ted Wood	.10	.05	.01
□ 598 Checklist 301-400	.10	.05	.01
□ 599 Checklist 401-500	.10	.05	.01
□ 600 Checklist 501-600	.10	.05	.01

1992 Ultra All-Rookies

Cards from this ten-card standard-size set highlighting a selection of top rookies were randomly inserted in 1992 Ultra II foil packs. The fronts feature borderless color action player photos except at the bottom where they are edged by a marbleized black wedge. The words "All-Rookie Team" in gold foil lettering appear in a black marbleized inverted triangle at the lower right corner, with the player's name on a color banner.

	MINT	NRMT	EXC
COMPLETE SET (10)	14.00	6.25	1.75
COMMON CARD (1-10)	.50	.23	.06
□ 1 Eric Karros	2.00	.90	.25
□ 2 Andy Stankiewicz	.50	.23	.06
□ 3 Gary DiSarcina	.50	.23	.06
□ 4 Archi Cianfrocco	.50	.23	.06
□ 5 Jim McNamara	.50	.23	.06
□ 6 Chad Curtis	1.00	.45	.12
□ 7 Kenny Lofton	10.00	4.50	1.25
□ 8 Reggie Sanders	2.00	.90	.25
□ 9 Pat Mahomes	.50	.23	.06
□ 10 Donovan Osborne	1.00	.45	.12

1992 Ultra All-Stars

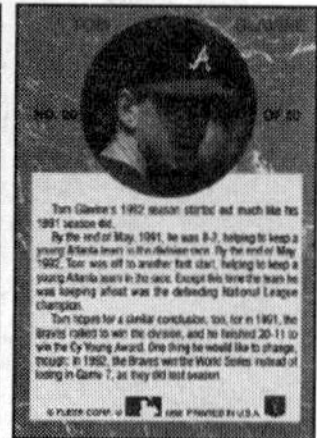

Featuring many of the 1992 season's stars, cards from this 20-card standard-size set were randomly inserted in 1992 Ultra II foil packs. The front design displays color action player photos enclosed by black marbleized borders. The word "All-Star" and the player's name are printed in gold foil lettering in the bottom border.

	MINT	NRMT	EXC
COMPLETE SET (20)	25.00	11.00	3.10
COMMON CARD (1-20)	.50	.23	.06
☐ 1 Mark McGwire	2.00	.90	.25
☐ 2 Roberto Alomar	1.25	.55	.16
☐ 3 Cal Ripken Jr.	6.00	2.70	.75
☐ 4 Wade Boggs	.75	.35	.09
☐ 5 Mickey Tettleton	.50	.23	.06
☐ 6 Ken Griffey Jr.	8.00	3.60	1.00
☐ 7 Roberto Kelly	.50	.23	.06
☐ 8 Kirby Puckett	2.50	1.10	.30
☐ 9 Frank Thomas	8.00	3.60	1.00
☐ 10 Jack McDowell	.60	.25	.07
☐ 11 Will Clark	.75	.35	.09
☐ 12 Ryne Sandberg	1.50	.70	.19
☐ 13 Barry Larkin	.75	.35	.09
☐ 14 Gary Sheffield	1.00	.45	.12
☐ 15 Tom Pagnozzi	.50	.23	.06
☐ 16 Barry Bonds	1.50	.70	.19
☐ 17 Deion Sanders	.75	.35	.09
☐ 18 Darryl Strawberry	.60	.25	.07
☐ 19 David Cone	.60	.25	.07
☐ 20 Tom Glavine	.75	.35	.09

1992 Ultra Award Winners

This 25-card standard-size set features 18 Gold Glove winners, both Cy Young Award winners, both Rookies of the Year, both league MVP's, and the World Series MVP. The cards were randomly inserted in 1992 Fleer Ultra I packs. The fronts carry full-bleed color player photos that have a diagonal blue marbleized border at the bottom. The player's name appears in this bottom border, and a diamond-shaped gold foil seal signifying the award the player won is superimposed at the lower right corner.

	MINT	NRMT	EXC
COMPLETE SET (25)	50.00	22.00	6.25
COMMON CARD (1-25)	.75	.35	.09
☐ 1 Jack Morris	1.00	.45	.12
☐ 2 Chuck Knoblauch	1.50	.70	.19
☐ 3 Jeff Bagwell	8.00	3.60	1.00
☐ 4 Terry Pendleton	1.00	.45	.12
☐ 5 Cal Ripken	10.00	4.50	1.25
☐ 6 Roger Clemens	2.00	.90	.25
☐ 7 Tom Glavine	1.50	.70	.19
☐ 8 Tom Pagnozzi	.75	.35	.09
☐ 9 Ozzie Smith	2.50	1.10	.30
☐ 10 Andy Van Slyke	.75	.35	.09
☐ 11 Barry Bonds	2.50	1.10	.30
☐ 12 Tony Gwynn	4.00	1.80	.50
☐ 13 Matt Williams	1.50	.70	.19
☐ 14 Will Clark	1.50	.70	.19
☐ 15 Robin Ventura	1.00	.45	.12
☐ 16 Mark Langston	.75	.35	.09
☐ 17 Tony Pena	.75	.35	.09
☐ 18 Devon White	.75	.35	.09
☐ 19 Don Mattingly	5.00	2.20	.60
☐ 20 Roberto Alomar	2.00	.90	.25
☐ 21A Cal Ripken ERR (Reversed negative on card back)	15.00	6.75	1.85
☐ 21B Cal Ripken COR	10.00	4.50	1.25
☐ 22 Ken Griffey Jr.	12.00	5.50	1.50
☐ 23 Kirby Puckett	4.00	1.80	.50
☐ 24 Greg Maddux	8.00	3.60	1.00
☐ 25 Ryne Sandberg	2.50	1.10	.30

1992 Ultra Gwynn

Tony Gwynn served as a spokesperson for Ultra during 1992 and was the exclusive subject of this 12-card standard-size set. The first ten cards of this set were randomly inserted in 1992 Ultra I packs. More than 2,000 of these cards were personaly autographed by Gwynn. The fronts display color posed and action shots of Gwynn framed by green marbled borders. The player's name and the words "Commemorative Series" appear in gold-foil lettering in the bottom border. On a green marbled background, the backs features a color head shot, career summary, and highlights. These insert cards are numbered on the back "No. X of 10." An additional special two-card subset was available through a mail-in offer for ten 1992 Ultra baseball wrappers plus 1.00 for shipping and handling. This offer was good through October 31st and, according to Fleer, over 100,000 sets were produced. The standard-size cards display action shots of Gwynn framed by green marbled borders. The player's name and the words "Commemorative Series" appear in gold-foil lettering in the bottom border. On a green marbled background, the backs features a color head shot and either a player profile (Special No. 1 on the card back) or Gwynn's comments about other players or the game itself (Special No. 2 on the card back).

	MINT	NRMT	EXC
COMPLETE SET (10)	10.00	4.50	1.25
COMMON GWYNN (1-10)	1.00	.45	.12
COMMON SEND-OFF (S1/S2)	1.00	.45	.12
☐ 1 Tony Gwynn (Leaping and catching ball at outfield wall)	1.00	.45	.12
☐ 2 Tony Gwynn (Batting stance, brown Padres' uniform)	1.00	.45	.12
☐ 3 Tony Gwynn (Awaiting flyball, glove above head)	1.00	.45	.12
☐ 4 Tony Gwynn (Follow-through on swing)	1.00	.45	.12
☐ 5 Tony Gwynn (Leading off base; crouching at the knees)	1.00	.45	.12
☐ 6 Tony Gwynn (Posed with silver bat and Gold Glove trophy)	1.00	.45	.12
☐ 7 Tony Gwynn (Bunting)	1.00	.45	.12
☐ 8 Tony Gwynn (Full body shot; swinging)	1.00	.45	.12
☐ 9 Tony Gwynn (Taking off for first)	1.00	.45	.12
☐ 10 Tony Gwynn (Batting, following through, sunglasses on)	1.00	.45	.12
☐ S1 Tony Gwynn (Batting)	1.00	.45	.12
☐ S2 Tony Gwynn (Fielding)	1.00	.45	.12
☐ AU0 Tony Gwynn AU (Autographed with certified signature)	175.00	80.00	22.00

1993 Ultra

The 1993 Ultra baseball set was issued in two series and totaled 650 standard-size cards. The full-bleed color-enhanced action photos are edged at the bottom by a gold foil stripe and a fawn-colored border that is streaked with white for a marbleized effect. On a dimensionalized ball park background, the horizontal backs have an action shot, a portrait, last season statistics, and the player's entire professional career totals. The cards are numbered on the back, grouped alphabetically within teams, with NL preceding AL. The first series closes with checklist cards (298-300). The second series features 83 Ultra Rookies, 51 Rockies and Marlins, traded veteran players, and other major league veterans not included in the first series. The Rookie cards show a gold foil stamped Rookie 'flag' as part of the card design. The key Rookie Card in this set is Jim Edmonds.

	MINT	NRMT	EXC
COMPLETE SET (650)	40.00	18.00	5.00
COMPLETE SERIES 1 (300)	20.00	9.00	2.50
COMPLETE SERIES 2 (350)	20.00	9.00	2.50
COMMON CARD (1-650)	.10	.05	.01
☐ 1 Steve Avery	.25	.11	.03
☐ 2 Rafael Belliard	.10	.05	.01
☐ 3 Damon Berryhill	.10	.05	.01
☐ 4 Sid Bream	.10	.05	.01
☐ 5 Ron Gant	.25	.11	.03
☐ 6 Tom Glavine	.40	.18	.05
☐ 7 Ryan Klesko	1.00	.45	.12
☐ 8 Mark Lemke	.10	.05	.01
☐ 9 Javier Lopez	.75	.35	.09
☐ 10 Greg Olson	.10	.05	.01
☐ 11 Terry Pendleton	.25	.11	.03
☐ 12 Deion Sanders	.40	.18	.05
☐ 13 Mike Stanton	.10	.05	.01
☐ 14 Paul Assenmacher	.10	.05	.01
☐ 15 Steve Buechele	.10	.05	.01
☐ 16 Frank Castillo	.10	.05	.01
☐ 17 Shawon Dunston	.10	.05	.01
☐ 18 Mark Grace	.40	.18	.05
☐ 19 Derrick May	.10	.05	.01
☐ 20 Chuck McElroy	.10	.05	.01
☐ 21 Mike Morgan	.10	.05	.01
☐ 22 Bob Scanlan	.10	.05	.01
☐ 23 Dwight Smith	.10	.05	.01
☐ 24 Sammy Sosa	.40	.18	.05
☐ 25 Rick Wilkins	.10	.05	.01
☐ 26 Tim Belcher	.10	.05	.01
☐ 27 Jeff Branson	.10	.05	.01
☐ 28 Bill Doran	.10	.05	.01
☐ 29 Chris Hammond	.10	.05	.01
☐ 30 Barry Larkin	.40	.18	.05
☐ 31 Hal Morris	.10	.05	.01
☐ 32 Joe Oliver	.10	.05	.01
☐ 33 Jose Rijo	.10	.05	.01
☐ 34 Bip Roberts	.10	.05	.01
☐ 35 Chris Sabo	.10	.05	.01
☐ 36 Reggie Sanders	.40	.18	.05
☐ 37 Craig Biggio	.25	.11	.03
☐ 38 Ken Caminiti	.40	.18	.05
☐ 39 Steve Finley	.25	.11	.03
☐ 40 Luis Gonzalez	.10	.05	.01
☐ 41 Juan Guerrero	.10	.05	.01
☐ 42 Pete Harnisch	.10	.05	.01
☐ 43 Xavier Hernandez	.10	.05	.01
☐ 44 Doug Jones	.10	.05	.01
☐ 45 Al Osuna	.10	.05	.01
☐ 46 Eddie Taubensee	.10	.05	.01
☐ 47 Scooter Tucker	.10	.05	.01
☐ 48 Brian Williams	.10	.05	.01
☐ 49 Pedro Astacio	.10	.05	.01
☐ 50 Rafael Bournigal	.10	.05	.01
☐ 51 Brett Butler	.25	.11	.03
☐ 52 Tom Candiotti	.10	.05	.01
☐ 53 Eric Davis	.25	.11	.03
☐ 54 Lenny Harris	.10	.05	.01
☐ 55 Orel Hershiser	.25	.11	.03
☐ 56 Eric Karros	.40	.18	.05
☐ 57 Pedro Martinez	.40	.18	.05
☐ 58 Roger McDowell	.10	.05	.01
☐ 59 Jose Offerman	.10	.05	.01
☐ 60 Mike Piazza	3.00	1.35	.35
☐ 61 Moises Alou	.25	.11	.03
☐ 62 Kent Bottenfield	.10	.05	.01
☐ 63 Archi Cianfrocco	.10	.05	.01
☐ 64 Greg Colbrunn	.10	.05	.01
☐ 65 Wil Cordero	.25	.11	.03
☐ 66 Delino DeShields	.10	.05	.01
☐ 67 Darrin Fletcher	.10	.05	.01
☐ 68 Ken Hill	.25	.11	.03
☐ 69 Chris Nabholz	.10	.05	.01
☐ 70 Mel Rojas	.25	.11	.03
☐ 71 Larry Walker	.40	.18	.05
☐ 72 Sid Fernandez	.10	.05	.01
☐ 73 John Franco	.10	.05	.01
☐ 74 Dave Gallagher	.10	.05	.01
☐ 75 Todd Hundley	.25	.11	.03
☐ 76 Howard Johnson	.10	.05	.01
☐ 77 Jeff Kent	.25	.11	.03
☐ 78 Eddie Murray	.75	.35	.09
☐ 79 Bret Saberhagen	.25	.11	.03
☐ 80 Chico Walker	.10	.05	.01
☐ 81 Anthony Young	.10	.05	.01
☐ 82 Kyle Abbott	.10	.05	.01
☐ 83 Ruben Amaro	.10	.05	.01
☐ 84 Juan Bell	.10	.05	.01
☐ 85 Wes Chamberlain	.10	.05	.01
☐ 86 Darren Daulton	.25	.11	.03
☐ 87 Mariano Duncan	.10	.05	.01
☐ 88 Dave Hollins	.10	.05	.01
☐ 89 Ricky Jordan	.10	.05	.01
☐ 90 John Kruk	.25	.11	.03
☐ 91 Mickey Morandini	.10	.05	.01
☐ 92 Terry Mulholland	.10	.05	.01
☐ 93 Ben Rivera	.10	.05	.01
☐ 94 Mike Williams	.10	.05	.01
☐ 95 Stan Belinda	.10	.05	.01
☐ 96 Jay Bell	.25	.11	.03
☐ 97 Jeff King	.25	.11	.03
☐ 98 Mike LaValliere	.10	.05	.01
☐ 99 Lloyd McClendon	.10	.05	.01
☐ 100 Orlando Merced	.25	.11	.03
☐ 101 Zane Smith	.10	.05	.01
☐ 102 Randy Tomlin	.10	.05	.01
☐ 103 Andy Van Slyke	.25	.11	.03
☐ 104 Tim Wakefield	.25	.11	.03
☐ 105 John Wehner	.10	.05	.01
☐ 106 Bernard Gilkey	.25	.11	.03
☐ 107 Brian Jordan	.40	.18	.05
☐ 108 Ray Lankford	.25	.11	.03
☐ 109 Donovan Osborne	.10	.05	.01
☐ 110 Tom Pagnozzi	.10	.05	.01
☐ 111 Mike Perez	.10	.05	.01
☐ 112 Lee Smith	.25	.11	.03
☐ 113 Ozzie Smith	.75	.35	.09
☐ 114 Bob Tewksbury	.10	.05	.01
☐ 115 Todd Zeile	.10	.05	.01
☐ 116 Andy Benes	.25	.11	.03
☐ 117 Greg W. Harris	.10	.05	.01
☐ 118 Darrin Jackson	.10	.05	.01
☐ 119 Fred McGriff	.40	.18	.05
☐ 120 Rich Rodriguez	.10	.05	.01
☐ 121 Frank Seminara	.10	.05	.01
☐ 122 Gary Sheffield	.40	.18	.05
☐ 123 Craig Shipley	.10	.05	.01
☐ 124 Kurt Stillwell	.10	.05	.01
☐ 125 Dan Walters	.10	.05	.01
☐ 126 Rod Beck	.25	.11	.03
☐ 127 Mike Benjamin	.10	.05	.01
☐ 128 Jeff Brantley	.10	.05	.01
☐ 129 John Burkett	.10	.05	.01
☐ 130 Will Clark	.40	.18	.05
☐ 131 Royce Clayton	.25	.11	.03
☐ 132 Steve Hosey	.10	.05	.01
☐ 133 Mike Jackson	.10	.05	.01
☐ 134 Darren Lewis	.10	.05	.01
☐ 135 Kirt Manwaring	.10	.05	.01
☐ 136 Bill Swift	.10	.05	.01
☐ 137 Robby Thompson	.10	.05	.01
☐ 138 Brady Anderson	.40	.18	.05
☐ 139 Glenn Davis	.10	.05	.01
☐ 140 Leo Gomez	.10	.05	.01
☐ 141 Chito Martinez	.10	.05	.01
☐ 142 Ben McDonald	.10	.05	.01
☐ 143 Alan Mills	.10	.05	.01
☐ 144 Mike Mussina	.60	.25	.07
☐ 145 Gregg Olson	.10	.05	.01
☐ 146 David Segui	.10	.05	.01
☐ 147 Jeff Tackett	.10	.05	.01
☐ 148 Jack Clark	.10	.05	.01
☐ 149 Scott Cooper	.10	.05	.01
☐ 150 Danny Darwin	.10	.05	.01
☐ 151 John Dopson	.10	.05	.01
☐ 152 Mike Greenwell	.10	.05	.01
☐ 153 Tim Naehring	.10	.05	.01
☐ 154 Tony Pena	.10	.05	.01
☐ 155 Paul Quantrill	.10	.05	.01
☐ 156 Mo Vaughn	.75	.35	.09
☐ 157 Frank Viola	.10	.05	.01
☐ 158 Bob Zupcic	.10	.05	.01
☐ 159 Chad Curtis	.25	.11	.03
☐ 160 Gary DiSarcina	.10	.05	.01
☐ 161 Damion Easley	.10	.05	.01
☐ 162 Chuck Finley	.10	.05	.01
☐ 163 Tim Fortugno	.10	.05	.01
☐ 164 Rene Gonzales	.10	.05	.01
☐ 165 Joe Grahe	.10	.05	.01
☐ 166 Mark Langston	.25	.11	.03
☐ 167 John Orton	.10	.05	.01
☐ 168 Luis Polonia	.10	.05	.01
☐ 169 Julio Valera	.10	.05	.01
☐ 170 Wilson Alvarez	.25	.11	.03
☐ 171 George Bell	.10	.05	.01
☐ 172 Joey Cora	.25	.11	.03
☐ 173 Alex Fernandez	.25	.11	.03
☐ 174 Lance Johnson	.25	.11	.03
☐ 175 Ron Karkovice	.10	.05	.01
☐ 176 Jack McDowell	.25	.11	.03
☐ 177 Scott Radinsky	.10	.05	.01
☐ 178 Tim Raines	.40	.18	.05
☐ 179 Steve Sax	.10	.05	.01
☐ 180 Bobby Thigpen	.10	.05	.01
☐ 181 Frank Thomas	3.00	1.35	.35
☐ 182 Sandy Alomar	.25	.11	.03
☐ 183 Carlos Baerga	.25	.11	.03
☐ 184 Felix Fermin	.10	.05	.01
☐ 185 Thomas Howard	.10	.05	.01
☐ 186 Mark Lewis	.10	.05	.01
☐ 187 Derek Lilliquist	.10	.05	.01
☐ 188 Carlos Martinez	.10	.05	.01
☐ 189 Charles Nagy	.25	.11	.03
☐ 190 Scott Scudder	.10	.05	.01
☐ 191 Paul Sorrento	.10	.05	.01
☐ 192 Jim Thome	1.50	.70	.19
☐ 193 Mark Whiten	.10	.05	.01
☐ 194 Milt Cuyler UER (Reversed negative on card front)	.10	.05	.01
☐ 195 Rob Deer	.10	.05	.01
☐ 196 John Doherty	.10	.05	.01
☐ 197 Travis Fryman	.25	.11	.03
☐ 198 Dan Gladden	.10	.05	.01
☐ 199 Mike Henneman	.10	.05	.01
☐ 200 John Kiely	.10	.05	.01
☐ 201 Chad Kreuter	.10	.05	.01
☐ 202 Scott Livingstone	.10	.05	.01
☐ 203 Tony Phillips	.25	.11	.03

Card			
□ 204 Alan Trammell	.40	.18	.05
□ 205 Mike Boddicker	.10	.05	.01
□ 206 George Brett	1.25	.55	.16
□ 207 Tom Gordon	.10	.05	.01
□ 208 Mark Gubicza	.10	.05	.01
□ 209 Gregg Jefferies	.25	.11	.03
□ 210 Wally Joyner	.25	.11	.03
□ 211 Kevin Koslofski	.10	.05	.01
□ 212 Brent Mayne	.10	.05	.01
□ 213 Brian McRae	.25	.11	.03
□ 214 Kevin McReynolds	.10	.05	.01
□ 215 Rusty Meacham	.10	.05	.01
□ 216 Steve Shifflett	.10	.05	.01
□ 217 James Austin	.10	.05	.01
□ 218 Cal Eldred	.10	.05	.01
□ 219 Darryl Hamilton	.10	.05	.01
□ 220 Doug Henry	.10	.05	.01
□ 221 John Jaha	.40	.18	.05
□ 222 Dave Nilsson	.25	.11	.03
□ 223 Jesse Orosco	.10	.05	.01
□ 224 B.J. Surhoff	.25	.11	.03
□ 225 Greg Vaughn	.25	.11	.03
□ 226 Bill Wegman	.10	.05	.01
□ 227 Robin Yount UER (Born in Illinois, not in Virginia)	.40	.18	.05
□ 228 Rick Aguilera	.10	.05	.01
□ 229 J.T. Bruett	.10	.05	.01
□ 230 Scott Erickson	.10	.05	.01
□ 231 Kent Hrbek	.25	.11	.03
□ 232 Terry Jorgensen	.10	.05	.01
□ 233 Scott Leius	.10	.05	.01
□ 234 Pat Mahomes	.10	.05	.01
□ 235 Pedro Munoz	.10	.05	.01
□ 236 Kirby Puckett	1.25	.55	.16
□ 237 Kevin Tapani	.10	.05	.01
□ 238 Lenny Webster	.10	.05	.01
□ 239 Carl Willis	.10	.05	.01
□ 240 Mike Gallego	.10	.05	.01
□ 241 John Habyan	.10	.05	.01
□ 242 Pat Kelly	.10	.05	.01
□ 243 Kevin Maas	.10	.05	.01
□ 244 Don Mattingly	1.50	.70	.19
□ 245 Hensley Meulens	.10	.05	.01
□ 246 Sam Militello	.10	.05	.01
□ 247 Matt Nokes	.10	.05	.01
□ 248 Melido Perez	.10	.05	.01
□ 249 Andy Stankiewicz	.10	.05	.01
□ 250 Randy Velarde	.10	.05	.01
□ 251 Bob Wickman	.10	.05	.01
□ 252 Bernie Williams	.60	.25	.07
□ 253 Lance Blankenship	.10	.05	.01
□ 254 Mike Bordick	.10	.05	.01
□ 255 Jerry Browne	.10	.05	.01
□ 256 Ron Darling	.10	.05	.01
□ 257 Dennis Eckersley	.25	.11	.03
□ 258 Rickey Henderson	.40	.18	.05
□ 259 Vince Horsman	.10	.05	.01
□ 260 Troy Neel	.10	.05	.01
□ 261 Jeff Parrett	.10	.05	.01
□ 262 Terry Steinbach	.25	.11	.03
□ 263 Bob Welch	.10	.05	.01
□ 264 Bobby Witt	.10	.05	.01
□ 265 Rich Amaral	.10	.05	.01
□ 266 Bret Boone	.25	.11	.03
□ 267 Jay Buhner	.40	.18	.05
□ 268 Dave Fleming	.10	.05	.01
□ 269 Randy Johnson	.40	.18	.05
□ 270 Edgar Martinez	.25	.11	.03
□ 271 Mike Schooler	.10	.05	.01
□ 272 Russ Swan	.10	.05	.01
□ 273 Dave Valle	.10	.05	.01
□ 274 Omar Vizquel	.25	.11	.03
□ 275 Kerry Woodson	.10	.05	.01
□ 276 Kevin Brown	.25	.11	.03
□ 277 Julio Franco	.25	.11	.03
□ 278 Jeff Frye	.10	.05	.01
□ 279 Juan Gonzalez	1.50	.70	.19
□ 280 Jeff Huson	.10	.05	.01
□ 281 Rafael Palmeiro	.40	.18	.05
□ 282 Dean Palmer	.25	.11	.03
□ 283 Roger Pavlik	.25	.11	.03
□ 284 Ivan Rodriguez	.75	.35	.09
□ 285 Kenny Rogers	.10	.05	.01
□ 286 Derek Bell	.25	.11	.03
□ 287 Pat Borders	.10	.05	.01
□ 288 Joe Carter	.25	.11	.03
□ 289 Bob MacDonald	.10	.05	.01
□ 290 Jack Morris	.25	.11	.03
□ 291 John Olerud	.10	.05	.01
□ 292 Ed Sprague	.25	.11	.03
□ 293 Todd Stottlemyre	.25	.11	.03
□ 294 Mike Timlin	.10	.05	.01
□ 295 Duane Ward	.10	.05	.01
□ 296 David Wells	.10	.05	.01
□ 297 Devon White	.10	.05	.01
□ 298 Checklist 1-94 Ray Lankford	.25	.11	.03
□ 299 Checklist 95-193 Bobby Witt	.10	.05	.01
□ 300 Checklist 194-300 Mike Piazza	.40	.18	.05
□ 301 Steve Bedrosian	.10	.05	.01
□ 302 Jeff Blauser	.10	.05	.01
□ 303 Francisco Cabrera	.10	.05	.01
□ 304 Marvin Freeman	.10	.05	.01
□ 305 Brian Hunter	.10	.05	.01
□ 306 David Justice	.40	.18	.05
□ 307 Greg Maddux	2.00	.90	.25
□ 308 Greg McMichael	.25	.11	.03
□ 309 Kent Mercker	.10	.05	.01
□ 310 Otis Nixon	.10	.05	.01
□ 311 Pete Smith	.10	.05	.01
□ 312 John Smoltz	.40	.18	.05
□ 313 Jose Guzman	.10	.05	.01
□ 314 Mike Harkey	.10	.05	.01
□ 315 Greg Hibbard	.10	.05	.01
□ 316 Candy Maldonado	.10	.05	.01
□ 317 Randy Myers	.25	.11	.03
□ 318 Dan Plesac	.10	.05	.01
□ 319 Rey Sanchez	.10	.05	.01
□ 320 Ryne Sandberg	.75	.35	.09
□ 321 Tommy Shields	.10	.05	.01
□ 322 Jose Vizcaino	.10	.05	.01
□ 323 Matt Walbeck	.10	.05	.01
□ 324 Willie Wilson	.10	.05	.01
□ 325 Tom Browning	.10	.05	.01
□ 326 Tim Costo	.10	.05	.01
□ 327 Rob Dibble	.10	.05	.01
□ 328 Steve Foster	.10	.05	.01
□ 329 Roberto Kelly	.10	.05	.01
□ 330 Randy Milligan	.10	.05	.01
□ 331 Kevin Mitchell	.25	.11	.03
□ 332 Tim Pugh	.10	.05	.01
□ 333 Jeff Reardon	.25	.11	.03
□ 334 John Roper	.10	.05	.01
□ 335 Juan Samuel	.10	.05	.01
□ 336 John Smiley	.10	.05	.01
□ 337 Dan Wilson	.25	.11	.03
□ 338 Scott Aldred	.10	.05	.01
□ 339 Andy Ashby	.25	.11	.03
□ 340 Freddie Benavides	.10	.05	.01
□ 341 Dante Bichette	.40	.18	.05
□ 342 Willie Blair	.10	.05	.01
□ 343 Daryl Boston	.10	.05	.01
□ 344 Vinny Castilla	.40	.18	.05
□ 345 Jerald Clark	.10	.05	.01
□ 346 Alex Cole	.10	.05	.01
□ 347 Andres Galarraga	.40	.18	.05
□ 348 Joe Girardi	.10	.05	.01
□ 349 Ryan Hawblitzel	.10	.05	.01
□ 350 Charlie Hayes	.10	.05	.01
□ 351 Butch Henry	.10	.05	.01
□ 352 Darren Holmes	.10	.05	.01
□ 353 Dale Murphy	.40	.18	.05
□ 354 David Nied	.10	.05	.01
□ 355 Jeff Parrett	.10	.05	.01
□ 356 Steve Reed	.10	.05	.01
□ 357 Bruce Ruffin	.10	.05	.01
□ 358 Danny Sheaffer	.10	.05	.01
□ 359 Bryn Smith	.10	.05	.01
□ 360 Jim Tatum	.10	.05	.01
□ 361 Eric Young	.40	.18	.05
□ 362 Gerald Young	.10	.05	.01
□ 363 Luis Aquino	.10	.05	.01
□ 364 Alex Arias	.10	.05	.01
□ 365 Jack Armstrong	.10	.05	.01
□ 366 Bret Barberie	.10	.05	.01
□ 367 Ryan Bowen	.10	.05	.01
□ 368 Greg Briley	.10	.05	.01
□ 369 Cris Carpenter	.10	.05	.01
□ 370 Chuck Carr	.10	.05	.01
□ 371 Jeff Conine	.25	.11	.03
□ 372 Steve Decker	.10	.05	.01
□ 373 Orestes Destrade	.10	.05	.01
□ 374 Monty Fariss	.10	.05	.01
□ 375 Junior Felix	.10	.05	.01
□ 376 Chris Hammond	.10	.05	.01
□ 377 Bryan Harvey	.10	.05	.01
□ 378 Trevor Hoffman	.40	.18	.05
□ 379 Charlie Hough	.10	.05	.01
□ 380 Joe Klink	.10	.05	.01
□ 381 Richie Lewis	.10	.05	.01
□ 382 Dave Magadan	.10	.05	.01
□ 383 Bob McClure	.10	.05	.01
□ 384 Scott Pose	.10	.05	.01
□ 385 Rich Renteria	.10	.05	.01
□ 386 Benito Santiago	.10	.05	.01
□ 387 Walt Weiss	.10	.05	.01
□ 388 Nigel Wilson	.10	.05	.01
□ 389 Eric Anthony	.10	.05	.01
□ 390 Jeff Bagwell	1.25	.55	.16
□ 391 Andujar Cedeno	.10	.05	.01
□ 392 Doug Drabek	.10	.05	.01
□ 393 Darryl Kile	.10	.05	.01
□ 394 Mark Portugal	.10	.05	.01
□ 395 Karl Rhodes	.10	.05	.01
□ 396 Scott Servais	.10	.05	.01
□ 397 Greg Swindell	.10	.05	.01
□ 398 Tom Goodwin	.10	.05	.01
□ 399 Kevin Gross	.10	.05	.01
□ 400 Carlos Hernandez	.10	.05	.01
□ 401 Ramon Martinez	.25	.11	.03
□ 402 Raul Mondesi	1.00	.45	.12
□ 403 Jody Reed	.10	.05	.01
□ 404 Mike Sharperson	.10	.05	.01
□ 405 Cory Snyder	.10	.05	.01
□ 406 Darryl Strawberry	.25	.11	.03
□ 407 Rick Trlicek	.10	.05	.01
□ 408 Tim Wallach	.10	.05	.01
□ 409 Todd Worrell	.10	.05	.01
□ 410 Tavo Alvarez	.10	.05	.01
□ 411 Sean Berry	.10	.05	.01
□ 412 Frank Bolick	.10	.05	.01
□ 413 Cliff Floyd	.25	.11	.03
□ 414 Mike Gardiner	.10	.05	.01
□ 415 Marquis Grissom	.25	.11	.03
□ 416 Tim Laker	.10	.05	.01
□ 417 Mike Lansing	.25	.11	.03
□ 418 Dennis Martinez	.25	.11	.03
□ 419 John Vander Wal	.10	.05	.01
□ 420 John Wetteland	.25	.11	.03
□ 421 Rondell White	.40	.18	.05
□ 422 Bobby Bonilla	.25	.11	.03
□ 423 Jeromy Burnitz	.10	.05	.01
□ 424 Vince Coleman	.10	.05	.01
□ 425 Mike Draper	.10	.05	.01
□ 426 Tony Fernandez	.10	.05	.01
□ 427 Dwight Gooden	.25	.11	.03
□ 428 Jeff Innis	.10	.05	.01
□ 429 Bobby Jones	.25	.11	.03
□ 430 Mike Maddux	.10	.05	.01
□ 431 Charlie O'Brien	.10	.05	.01
□ 432 Joe Orsulak	.10	.05	.01
□ 433 Pete Schourek	.25	.11	.03
□ 434 Frank Tanana	.10	.05	.01
□ 435 Ryan Thompson	.10	.05	.01
□ 436 Kim Batiste	.10	.05	.01
□ 437 Mark Davis	.10	.05	.01
□ 438 Jose DeLeon	.10	.05	.01
□ 439 Len Dykstra	.25	.11	.03
□ 440 Jim Eisenreich	.25	.11	.03
□ 441 Tommy Greene	.10	.05	.01
□ 442 Pete Incaviglia	.10	.05	.01
□ 443 Danny Jackson	.10	.05	.01
□ 444 Todd Pratt	.10	.05	.01
□ 445 Curt Schilling	.10	.05	.01
□ 446 Milt Thompson	.10	.05	.01
□ 447 David West	.10	.05	.01
□ 448 Mitch Williams	.10	.05	.01
□ 449 Steve Cooke	.10	.05	.01
□ 450 Carlos Garcia	.10	.05	.01
□ 451 Al Martin	.25	.11	.03
□ 452 Blas Minor	.10	.05	.01
□ 453 Dennis Moeller	.10	.05	.01
□ 454 Denny Neagle	.25	.11	.03
□ 455 Don Slaught	.10	.05	.01
□ 456 Lonnie Smith	.10	.05	.01
□ 457 Paul Wagner	.10	.05	.01
□ 458 Bob Walk	.10	.05	.01
□ 459 Kevin Young	.10	.05	.01
□ 460 Rene Arocha	.10	.05	.01
□ 461 Brian Barber	.10	.05	.01
□ 462 Rheal Cormier	.10	.05	.01
□ 463 Gregg Jefferies	.25	.11	.03
□ 464 Joe Magrane	.10	.05	.01
□ 465 Omar Olivares	.10	.05	.01
□ 466 Geronimo Pena	.10	.05	.01
□ 467 Allen Watson	.10	.05	.01
□ 468 Mark Whiten	.10	.05	.01
□ 469 Derek Bell	.25	.11	.03
□ 470 Phil Clark	.10	.05	.01
□ 471 Pat Gomez	.10	.05	.01
□ 472 Tony Gwynn	1.25	.55	.16
□ 473 Jeremy Hernandez	.10	.05	.01
□ 474 Bruce Hurst	.10	.05	.01
□ 475 Phil Plantier	.10	.05	.01
□ 476 Scott Sanders	.10	.05	.01
□ 477 Tim Scott	.10	.05	.01
□ 478 Darrell Sherman	.10	.05	.01
□ 479 Guillermo Velasquez	.10	.05	.01
□ 480 Tim Worrell	.10	.05	.01
□ 481 Todd Benzinger	.10	.05	.01
□ 482 Bud Black	.10	.05	.01
□ 483 Barry Bonds	.75	.35	.09
□ 484 Dave Burba	.10	.05	.01
□ 485 Bryan Hickerson	.10	.05	.01
□ 486 Dave Martinez	.10	.05	.01
□ 487 Willie McGee	.10	.05	.01
□ 488 Jeff Reed	.10	.05	.01
□ 489 Kevin Rogers	.10	.05	.01
□ 490 Matt Williams	.40	.18	.05
□ 491 Trevor Wilson	.10	.05	.01
□ 492 Harold Baines	.25	.11	.03
□ 493 Mike Devereaux	.10	.05	.01
□ 494 Todd Frohwirth	.10	.05	.01
□ 495 Chris Hoiles	.10	.05	.01
□ 496 Luis Mercedes	.10	.05	.01
□ 497 Sherman Obando	.10	.05	.01
□ 498 Brad Pennington	.10	.05	.01
□ 499 Harold Reynolds	.10	.05	.01
□ 500 Arthur Rhodes	.10	.05	.01
□ 501 Cal Ripken	2.50	1.10	.30
□ 502 Rick Sutcliffe	.10	.05	.01
□ 503 Fernando Valenzuela	.25	.11	.03
□ 504 Mark Williamson	.10	.05	.01
□ 505 Scott Bankhead	.10	.05	.01
□ 506 Greg Blosser	.10	.05	.01
□ 507 Ivan Calderon	.10	.05	.01
□ 508 Roger Clemens	.60	.25	.07
□ 509 Andre Dawson	.25	.11	.03
□ 510 Scott Fletcher	.10	.05	.01
□ 511 Greg A. Harris	.10	.05	.01
□ 512 Billy Hatcher	.10	.05	.01
□ 513 Bob Melvin	.10	.05	.01
□ 514 Carlos Quintana	.10	.05	.01
□ 515 Luis Rivera	.10	.05	.01
□ 516 Jeff Russell	.10	.05	.01
□ 517 Ken Ryan	.10	.05	.01
□ 518 Chili Davis	.25	.11	.03
□ 519 Jim Edmonds	2.50	1.10	.30
□ 520 Gary Gaetti	.25	.11	.03
□ 521 Torey Lovullo	.10	.05	.01
□ 522 Troy Percival	.25	.11	.03
□ 523 Tim Salmon	.75	.35	.09
□ 524 Scott Sanderson	.10	.05	.01
□ 525 J.T. Snow	.40	.18	.05
□ 526 Jerome Walton	.10	.05	.01
□ 527 Jason Bere	.25	.11	.03
□ 528 Rod Bolton	.10	.05	.01
□ 529 Ellis Burks	.25	.11	.03
□ 530 Carlton Fisk	.40	.18	.05
□ 531 Craig Grebeck	.10	.05	.01
□ 532 Ozzie Guillen	.10	.05	.01
□ 533 Roberto Hernandez	.25	.11	.03
□ 534 Bo Jackson	.25	.11	.03
□ 535 Kirk McCaskill	.10	.05	.01
□ 536 Dave Stieb	.10	.05	.01
□ 537 Robin Ventura	.25	.11	.03
□ 538 Albert Belle	1.25	.55	.16
□ 539 Mike Bielecki	.10	.05	.01
□ 540 Glenallen Hill	.10	.05	.01
□ 541 Reggie Jefferson	.25	.11	.03
□ 542 Kenny Lofton	1.25	.55	.16
□ 543 Jeff Mutis	.10	.05	.01
□ 544 Junior Ortiz	.10	.05	.01
□ 545 Manny Ramirez	2.00	.90	.25
□ 546 Jeff Treadway	.10	.05	.01
□ 547 Kevin Wickander	.10	.05	.01
□ 548 Cecil Fielder	.25	.11	.03
□ 549 Kirk Gibson	.25	.11	.03
□ 550 Greg Gohr	.10	.05	.01
□ 551 David Haas	.10	.05	.01
□ 552 Bill Krueger	.10	.05	.01
□ 553 Mike Moore	.10	.05	.01
□ 554 Mickey Tettleton	.10	.05	.01
□ 555 Lou Whitaker	.25	.11	.03
□ 556 Kevin Appier	.25	.11	.03
□ 557 Billy Brewer	.10	.05	.01
□ 558 David Cone	.25	.11	.03
□ 559 Greg Gagne	.10	.05	.01
□ 560 Mark Gardner	.10	.05	.01
□ 561 Phil Hiatt	.10	.05	.01
□ 562 Felix Jose	.10	.05	.01
□ 563 Jose Lind	.10	.05	.01
□ 564 Mike Macfarlane	.10	.05	.01
□ 565 Keith Miller	.10	.05	.01
□ 566 Jeff Montgomery	.25	.11	.03
□ 567 Hipolito Pichardo	.10	.05	.01
□ 568 Ricky Bones	.10	.05	.01
□ 569 Tom Brunansky	.10	.05	.01
□ 570 Joe Kmak	.10	.05	.01
□ 571 Pat Listach	.10	.05	.01
□ 572 Graeme Lloyd	.10	.05	.01
□ 573 Carlos Maldonado	.10	.05	.01
□ 574 Josias Manzanillo	.10	.05	.01
□ 575 Matt Mieske	.25	.11	.03
□ 576 Kevin Reimer	.10	.05	.01
□ 577 Bill Spiers	.10	.05	.01
□ 578 Dickie Thon	.10	.05	.01
□ 579 Willie Banks	.10	.05	.01
□ 580 Jim Deshaies	.10	.05	.01
□ 581 Mark Guthrie	.10	.05	.01
□ 582 Brian Harper	.10	.05	.01
□ 583 Chuck Knoblauch	.40	.18	.05
□ 584 Gene Larkin	.10	.05	.01
□ 585 Shane Mack	.10	.05	.01
□ 586 David McCarty	.10	.05	.01
□ 587 Mike Pagliarulo	.10	.05	.01
□ 588 Mike Trombley	.10	.05	.01
□ 589 Dave Winfield	.40	.18	.05
□ 590 Jim Abbott	.10	.05	.01
□ 591 Wade Boggs	.40	.18	.05
□ 592 Russ Davis	.25	.11	.03
□ 593 Steve Farr	.10	.05	.01
□ 594 Steve Howe	.10	.05	.01
□ 595 Mike Humphreys	.10	.05	.01
□ 596 Jimmy Key	.25	.11	.03
□ 597 Jim Leyritz	.10	.05	.01
□ 598 Bobby Munoz	.10	.05	.01
□ 599 Paul O'Neill	.25	.11	.03
□ 600 Spike Owen	.10	.05	.01
□ 601 Mike Stanley	.10	.05	.01
□ 602 Danny Tartabull	.10	.05	.01
□ 603 Scott Brosius	.10	.05	.01
□ 604 Storm Davis	.10	.05	.01
□ 605 Eric Fox	.10	.05	.01
□ 606 Rich Gossage	.25	.11	.03
□ 607 Scott Hemond	.10	.05	.01
□ 608 Dave Henderson	.10	.05	.01
□ 609 Mark McGwire	1.00	.45	.12
□ 610 Mike Mohler	.10	.05	.01
□ 611 Edwin Nunez	.10	.05	.01
□ 612 Kevin Seitzer	.10	.05	.01
□ 613 Ruben Sierra	.25	.11	.03
□ 614 Chris Bosio	.10	.05	.01
□ 615 Norm Charlton	.10	.05	.01
□ 616 Jim Converse	.10	.05	.01
□ 617 John Cummings	.10	.05	.01
□ 618 Mike Felder	.10	.05	.01

☐ 619 Ken Griffey Jr.	3.00	1.35	.35
☐ 620 Mike Hampton	.40	.18	.05
☐ 621 Erik Hanson	.10	.05	.01
☐ 622 Bill Haselman	.10	.05	.01
☐ 623 Tino Martinez	.25	.11	.03
☐ 624 Lee Tinsley	.25	.11	.03
☐ 625 Fernando Vina	.10	.05	.01
☐ 626 David Wainhouse	.10	.05	.01
☐ 627 Jose Canseco	.40	.18	.05
☐ 628 Benji Gil	.25	.11	.03
☐ 629 Tom Henke	.10	.05	.01
☐ 630 David Hulse	.10	.05	.01
☐ 631 Manuel Lee	.10	.05	.01
☐ 632 Craig Lefferts	.10	.05	.01
☐ 633 Robb Nen	.25	.11	.03
☐ 634 Gary Redus	.10	.05	.01
☐ 635 Bill Ripken	.10	.05	.01
☐ 636 Nolan Ryan	2.50	1.10	.30
☐ 637 Dan Smith	.10	.05	.01
☐ 638 Matt Whiteside	.10	.05	.01
☐ 639 Roberto Alomar	.60	.25	.07
☐ 640 Juan Guzman	.25	.11	.03
☐ 641 Pat Hentgen	.40	.18	.05
☐ 642 Darrin Jackson	.10	.05	.01
☐ 643 Randy Knorr	.10	.05	.01
☐ 644 Domingo Martinez	.10	.05	.01
☐ 645 Paul Molitor	.60	.25	.07
☐ 646 Dick Schofield	.10	.05	.01
☐ 647 Dave Stewart	.25	.11	.03
☐ 648 Checklist 301-421 Rey Sanchez	.10	.05	.01
☐ 649 Checklist 422-537 Jeremy Hernandez	.10	.05	.01
☐ 650 Checklist 538-650 Junior Ortiz	.10	.05	.01

1993 Ultra All-Rookies

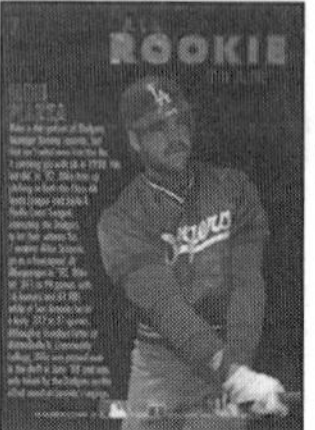

Randomly inserted into series II packs, this ten-card standard-size set features cutout color player action shots that are superposed upon a black background, which carries the player's uniform number, position, team name, and the set's title in multicolored lettering. The player's name appears in gold foil at the bottom. A posed color cutout player shot adorns the back, and is also projected upon a black background. The set's title appears at the top printed in gold foil and red lettering, and the player's name in gold foil precedes his career highlights, printed in white. The set is sequenced in alphabetical order. The key cards in this set are Mike Piazza and Tim Salmon.

	MINT	NRMT	EXC
COMPLETE SET (10)	15.00	6.75	1.85
COMMON CARD (1-10)	.50	.23	.06
☐ 1 Rene Arocha	.50	.23	.06
☐ 2 Jeff Conine	1.50	.70	.19
☐ 3 Phil Hiatt	.50	.23	.06
☐ 4 Mike Lansing	.75	.35	.09
☐ 5 Al Martin	.75	.35	.09
☐ 6 David Nied	.50	.23	.06
☐ 7 Mike Piazza	12.00	5.50	1.50
☐ 8 Tim Salmon	4.00	1.80	.50
☐ 9 J.T. Snow	1.00	.45	.12
☐ 10 Kevin Young	.50	.23	.06

1993 Ultra All-Stars

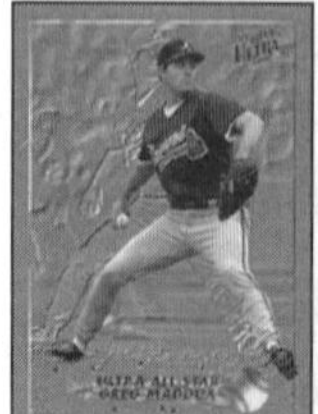
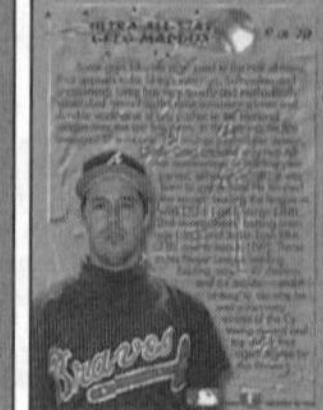

Randomly inserted into series II packs, this 20-card standard-size set features National League (1-10) and American League (11-20) All-Stars. The gray-bordered fronts carry color player action shots that are cutout and superposed upon their original, but faded and shifted, backgrounds. The player's name and the set's title are printed in gold foil upon simulated flames that issue from a baseball icon in the lower right. That same design of the player's name, the set's title, and flaming baseball icon appears again at the top of the gray-bordered back. The player's career highlights follow below.

	MINT	NRMT	EXC
COMPLETE SET (20)	40.00	18.00	5.00
COMMON CARD (1-20)	.75	.35	.09
☐ 1 Darren Daulton	1.00	.45	.12
☐ 2 Will Clark	1.50	.70	.19
☐ 3 Ryne Sandberg	3.00	1.35	.35
☐ 4 Barry Larkin	1.50	.70	.19
☐ 5 Gary Sheffield	2.00	.90	.25
☐ 6 Barry Bonds	3.00	1.35	.35
☐ 7 Ray Lankford	1.00	.45	.12
☐ 8 Larry Walker	1.50	.70	.19
☐ 9 Greg Maddux	8.00	3.60	1.00
☐ 10 Lee Smith	1.00	.45	.12
☐ 11 Ivan Rodriguez	3.00	1.35	.35
☐ 12 Mark McGwire	4.00	1.80	.50
☐ 13 Carlos Baerga	.75	.35	.09
☐ 14 Cal Ripken	10.00	4.50	1.25
☐ 15 Edgar Martinez	1.00	.45	.12
☐ 16 Juan Gonzalez	6.00	2.70	.75
☐ 17 Ken Griffey Jr.	12.00	5.50	1.50
☐ 18 Kirby Puckett	5.00	2.20	.60
☐ 19 Frank Thomas	12.00	5.50	1.50
☐ 20 Mike Mussina	2.50	1.10	.30

1993 Ultra Award Winners

Randomly inserted in first series packs, this first series of 1993 Ultra Award Winners presents the Top Glove for the National (1-9) and American (10-18) Leagues and other major award winners (19-25). The 25 standard-size cards comprising this set feature horizontal black-marbleized card designs and carry two color player photos: an action shot on the left and a posed photo on the right. The player's name appears in gold-foil cursive lettering near the bottom left. The category of award is shown in gold foil below. A gold-foil line highlights the card's lower edge. The horizontal and black-marbleized design continues on the back. A color player head shot appears on the left side. The player's name reappears in gold-foil cursive lettering near the top. Below is the player's award category in gold foil above a gold-foil underline. The player's career highlights are shown in white lettering below.

	MINT	NRMT	EXC
COMPLETE SET (25)	40.00	18.00	5.00
COMMON CARD (1-25)	.75	.35	.09
☐ 1 Greg Maddux	8.00	3.60	1.00
☐ 2 Tom Pagnozzi	.75	.35	.09
☐ 3 Mark Grace	1.50	.70	.19
☐ 4 Jose Lind	.75	.35	.09
☐ 5 Terry Pendleton	1.00	.45	.12
☐ 6 Ozzie Smith	3.00	1.35	.35
☐ 7 Barry Bonds	3.00	1.35	.35
☐ 8 Andy Van Slyke	.75	.35	.09
☐ 9 Larry Walker	1.50	.70	.19
☐ 10 Mark Langston	.75	.35	.09
☐ 11 Ivan Rodriguez	3.00	1.35	.35
☐ 12 Don Mattingly	6.00	2.70	.75
☐ 13 Roberto Alomar	2.50	1.10	.30
☐ 14 Robin Ventura	1.00	.45	.12
☐ 15 Cal Ripken	10.00	4.50	1.25
☐ 16 Ken Griffey	12.00	5.50	1.50
☐ 17 Kirby Puckett	5.00	2.20	.60
☐ 18 Devon White	.75	.35	.09
☐ 19 Pat Listach	.75	.35	.09
☐ 20 Eric Karros	1.50	.70	.19
☐ 21 Pat Borders	.75	.35	.09
☐ 22 Greg Maddux	8.00	3.60	1.00
☐ 23 Dennis Eckersley	1.00	.45	.12
☐ 24 Barry Bonds	3.00	1.35	.35
☐ 25 Gary Sheffield	2.00	.90	.25

1993 Ultra Eckersley

Randomly inserted in first series foil packs, this 10-card (cards 11 and 12 were mail-aways) standard-size set salutes one of baseball's greatest relief pitchers, Dennis Eckersley. The color action player photos on the fronts are full-bleed except at the bottom where a black marbleized border carries the team and years in silver foil lettering. A silver foil "Dennis Eckersley Career Highlights" emblem rounds out the front. On the back, a full-bleed color photo provides the background for a transparent pastel purple panel presenting career highlights in silver foil lettering. The cards are numbered on the back. Two additional cards (11 and 12) were available through a mail-in offer for ten 1993 Fleer Ultra baseball wrappers plus 1.00 for postage and handling. The expiration for this offer was September 30, 1993. Eckersley personally autographed more than 2,000 of these cards. The cards feature silver foil stamping on both sides.

	MINT	NRMT	EXC
COMPLETE SET (10)	5.00	2.20	.60
COMMON ECK (1-10)	.50	.23	.06
COMMON SEND OFF (11-12)	1.00	.45	.12
☐ 1 Dennis Eckersley Perfection	.50	.23	.06
☐ 2 Dennis Eckersley The Kid	.50	.23	.06
☐ 3 Dennis Eckersley The Warrior	.50	.23	.06
☐ 4 Dennis Eckersley Beantown Blazer	.50	.23	.06
☐ 5 Dennis Eckersley Eckspeak	.50	.23	.06
☐ 6 Dennis Eckersley Down to Earth	.50	.23	.06
☐ 7 Dennis Eckersley Wrigley Bound	.50	.23	.06
☐ 8 Dennis Eckersley No Relief	.50	.23	.06
☐ 9 Dennis Eckersley In Control	.50	.23	.06
☐ 10 Dennis Eckersley Simply the Best	.50	.23	.06
☐ 11 Dennis Eckersley Reign of Perfection	1.00	.45	.12
☐ 12 Dennis Eckersley Leaving His Mark	1.00	.45	.12
☐ P1 Dennis Eckersley Promo with Paul Mullan	4.00	1.80	.50
☐ AU0 Dennis Eckersley AU (Certified autograph)	50.00	22.00	6.25

1993 Ultra Home Run Kings

Randomly inserted into all 1993 Ultra packs, this ten-card standard-size set features the best long ball hitters in baseball. The borderless cards carry cutout color action player photos that are superposed upon an outer space scene, which includes a baseball "planet" and background stars. The player's name and team, along with the set's logo, are printed in gold foil and rest at the bottom. The horizontal black-and-stellar back carries a color player close-up on the left side, and the player's name, nickname, and career highlights in white lettering on the right side. The set's logo, printed in gold foil at the upper right, rounds out the card.

	MINT	NRMT	EXC
COMPLETE SET (10)	15.00	6.75	1.85
COMMON CARD (1-10)	1.00	.45	.12
☐ 1 Juan Gonzalez	8.00	3.60	1.00
☐ 2 Mark McGwire	5.00	2.20	.60
☐ 3 Cecil Fielder	1.50	.70	.19
☐ 4 Fred McGriff	2.00	.90	.25
☐ 5 Albert Belle	6.00	2.70	.75
☐ 6 Barry Bonds	4.00	1.80	.50
☐ 7 Joe Carter	1.50	.70	.19
☐ 8 Gary Sheffield	2.50	1.10	.30
☐ 9 Darren Daulton	1.50	.70	.19
☐ 10 Dave Hollins	1.00	.45	.12

1993 Ultra Performers

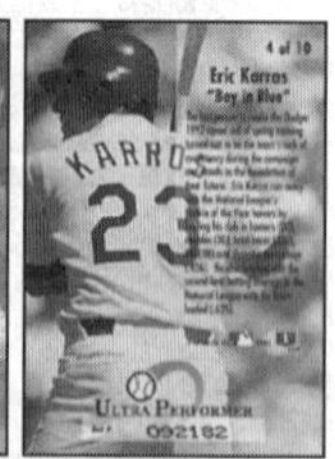

This ten-card standard-size set could only be ordered directly from Fleer by sending in 9.95, five Fleer/Fleer Ultra baseball wrappers, and an order blank found in hobby and sports periodicals. Each borderless front features a color player action shot superposed upon four other player photos, which are ghosted and color-screened. The player's name and the set name, both stamped in gold foil, appear at the bottom. The Ultra Performers set logo, a gold-foil-rimmed baseball icon with a blue trail, lies just above. The gold-foil Fleer Ultra logo appears in an upper corner. The back features a borderless color player action photo that is ghosted and color-screened on one side, where the player's name and career highlights appear. The set logo and gold-foil-stamped name appear below. The set's production number (out of 150,000 produced) rests within a ghosted rectangle at the bottom. The set is sequenced in alphabetical order.

	MINT	NRMT	EXC
COMPLETE SET (10)	25.00	11.00	3.10
COMMON CARD (1-10)	.50	.23	.06
☐ 1 Barry Bonds	2.00	.90	.25
☐ 2 Juan Gonzalez	3.00	1.35	.35
☐ 3 Ken Griffey Jr.	8.00	3.60	1.00
☐ 4 Eric Karros	1.00	.45	.12
☐ 5 Pat Listach	.50	.23	.06
☐ 6 Greg Maddux	5.00	2.20	.60
☐ 7 David Nied	.50	.23	.06
☐ 8 Gary Sheffield	1.25	.55	.16
☐ 9 J.T. Snow	1.00	.45	.12
☐ 10 Frank Thomas	8.00	3.60	1.00

1993 Ultra Strikeout Kings

Randomly inserted into series II packs, this five-card standard-size showcases outstanding pitchers from both leagues. The color cutout action player photo on the front of each card shows a pitcher on the mound superposed upon a background of stars and a metallic baseball. The player's name appears in gold foil at the bottom. The gold foil-stamped set logo also appears on the front. Upon a metallic-baseball-and-stellar background, the horizontal back carries a posed color player photo on the left side, and the player's career highlights in yellow lettering on the right side. The player's name and team, as well as the set's logo, appear in gold foil at the top. The set is sequenced in alphabetical order.

	MINT	NRMT	EXC
COMPLETE SET (5)	20.00	9.00	2.50
COMMON CARD (1-5)	1.00	.45	.12
☐ 1 Roger Clemens	3.00	1.35	.35
☐ 2 Juan Guzman	1.00	.45	.12
☐ 3 Randy Johnson	2.50	1.10	.30
☐ 4 Nolan Ryan	15.00	6.75	1.85
☐ 5 John Smoltz	2.50	1.10	.30

1994 Ultra

The 1994 Ultra baseball set consists of 600 standard-size cards that were issued in two series of 300. Each pack contains at least one insert card, while "Hot Packs" have nothing but insert cards in them. The front features a full-bleed color action player photo except at the bottom, where a gold foil strip edges the picture. The player's name, his position, team name, and company logo are gold foil stamped across the bottom of the front. The horizontal back has a montage of three different player cutouts on a action scene with a team color-coded border. Biography and statistics on a thin panel toward the bottom round out the back. The cards are numbered on the back, grouped alphabetically within teams, and checklisted below alphabetically according to teams for each league with AL preceding NL. Rookie Cards include Ray Durham and Chan Ho Park.

	MINT	NRMT	EXC
COMPLETE SET (600)	50.00	22.00	6.25
COMPLETE SERIES 1 (300)	25.00	11.00	3.10
COMPLETE SERIES 2 (300)	25.00	11.00	3.10
COMMON CARD (1-600)	.10	.05	.01
☐ 1 Jeffrey Hammonds	.25	.11	.03
☐ 2 Chris Hoiles	.10	.05	.01
☐ 3 Ben McDonald	.10	.05	.01
☐ 4 Mark McLemore	.10	.05	.01
☐ 5 Alan Mills	.10	.05	.01
☐ 6 Jamie Moyer	.10	.05	.01
☐ 7 Brad Pennington	.10	.05	.01
☐ 8 Jim Poole	.10	.05	.01
☐ 9 Cal Ripken Jr.	2.50	1.10	.30
☐ 10 Jack Voigt	.10	.05	.01
☐ 11 Roger Clemens	.60	.25	.07
☐ 12 Danny Darwin	.10	.05	.01

☐ 13 Andre Dawson .25 .11 .03
☐ 14 Scott Fletcher .10 .05 .01
☐ 15 Greg A Harris .10 .05 .01
☐ 16 Billy Hatcher .10 .05 .01
☐ 17 Jeff Russell .10 .05 .01
☐ 18 Aaron Sele .25 .11 .03
☐ 19 Mo Vaughn .75 .35 .09
☐ 20 Mike Butcher .10 .05 .01
☐ 21 Rod Correia .10 .05 .01
☐ 22 Steve Frey .10 .05 .01
☐ 23 Phil Leftwich .10 .05 .01
☐ 24 Torey Lovullo .10 .05 .01
☐ 25 Ken Patterson .10 .05 .01
☐ 26 Eduardo Perez UER .10 .05 .01
(listed as a Twin instead of Angel)
☐ 27 Tim Salmon .50 .23 .06
☐ 28 J.T. Snow .25 .11 .03
☐ 29 Chris Turner .10 .05 .01
☐ 30 Wilson Alvarez .25 .11 .03
☐ 31 Jason Bere .25 .11 .03
☐ 32 Joey Cora .10 .05 .01
☐ 33 Alex Fernandez .25 .11 .03
☐ 34 Roberto Hernandez .25 .11 .03
☐ 35 Lance Johnson .25 .11 .03
☐ 36 Ron Karkovice .10 .05 .01
☐ 37 Kirk McCaskill .10 .05 .01
☐ 38 Jeff Schwarz .10 .05 .01
☐ 39 Frank Thomas 3.00 1.35 .35
☐ 40 Sandy Alomar Jr. .25 .11 .03
☐ 41 Albert Belle 1.25 .55 .16
☐ 42 Felix Fermin .10 .05 .01
☐ 43 Wayne Kirby .10 .05 .01
☐ 44 Tom Kramer .10 .05 .01
☐ 45 Kenny Lofton 1.00 .45 .12
☐ 46 Jose Mesa .25 .11 .03
☐ 47 Eric Plunk .10 .05 .01
☐ 48 Paul Sorrento .10 .05 .01
☐ 49 Jim Thome .75 .35 .09
☐ 50 Bill Wertz .10 .05 .01
☐ 51 John Doherty .10 .05 .01
☐ 52 Cecil Fielder .25 .11 .03
☐ 53 Travis Fryman .25 .11 .03
☐ 54 Chris Gomez .10 .05 .01
☐ 55 Mike Henneman .10 .05 .01
☐ 56 Chad Kreuter .10 .05 .01
☐ 57 Bob MacDonald .10 .05 .01
☐ 58 Mike Moore .10 .05 .01
☐ 59 Tony Phillips .25 .11 .03
☐ 60 Lou Whitaker .25 .11 .03
☐ 61 Kevin Appier .25 .11 .03
☐ 62 Greg Gagne .10 .05 .01
☐ 63 Chris Gwynn .10 .05 .01
☐ 64 Bob Hamelin .10 .05 .01
☐ 65 Chris Haney .10 .05 .01
☐ 66 Phil Hiatt .10 .05 .01
☐ 67 Felix Jose .10 .05 .01
☐ 68 Jose Lind .10 .05 .01
☐ 69 Mike Macfarlane .10 .05 .01
☐ 70 Jeff Montgomery .25 .11 .03
☐ 71 Hipolito Pichardo .10 .05 .01
☐ 72 Juan Bell .10 .05 .01
☐ 73 Cal Eldred .10 .05 .01
☐ 74 Darryl Hamilton .10 .05 .01
☐ 75 Doug Henry .10 .05 .01
☐ 76 Mike Ignasiak .10 .05 .01
☐ 77 John Jaha .25 .11 .03
☐ 78 Graeme Lloyd .10 .05 .01
☐ 79 Angel Miranda .10 .05 .01
☐ 80 Dave Nilsson .25 .11 .03
☐ 81 Troy O'Leary .10 .05 .01
☐ 82 Kevin Reimer .10 .05 .01
☐ 83 Willie Banks .10 .05 .01
☐ 84 Larry Casian .10 .05 .01
☐ 85 Scott Erickson .10 .05 .01
☐ 86 Eddie Guardado .10 .05 .01
☐ 87 Kent Hrbek .25 .11 .03
☐ 88 Terry Jorgensen .10 .05 .01
☐ 89 Chuck Knoblauch .50 .23 .06
☐ 90 Pat Meares .10 .05 .01
☐ 91 Mike Trombley .10 .05 .01
☐ 92 Dave Winfield .50 .23 .06
☐ 93 Wade Boggs .50 .23 .06
☐ 94 Scott Kamieniecki .10 .05 .01
☐ 95 Pat Kelly .10 .05 .01
☐ 96 Jimmy Key .25 .11 .03
☐ 97 Jim Leyritz .10 .05 .01
☐ 98 Bobby Munoz .10 .05 .01
☐ 99 Paul O'Neill .25 .11 .03
☐ 100 Melido Perez .10 .05 .01
☐ 101 Mike Stanley .10 .05 .01
☐ 102 Danny Tartabull .10 .05 .01
☐ 103 Bernie Williams .60 .25 .07
☐ 104 Kurt Abbott .25 .11 .03
☐ 105 Mike Bordick .10 .05 .01
☐ 106 Ron Darling .10 .05 .01
☐ 107 Brent Gates .10 .05 .01
☐ 108 Miguel Jimenez .10 .05 .01
☐ 109 Steve Karsay .10 .05 .01
☐ 110 Scott Lydy .10 .05 .01
☐ 111 Mark McGwire 1.00 .45 .12
☐ 112 Troy Neel .10 .05 .01
☐ 113 Craig Paquette .10 .05 .01
☐ 114 Bob Welch .10 .05 .01
☐ 115 Bobby Witt .10 .05 .01
☐ 116 Rich Amaral .10 .05 .01
☐ 117 Mike Blowers .10 .05 .01
☐ 118 Jay Buhner .50 .23 .06
☐ 119 Dave Fleming .10 .05 .01
☐ 120 Ken Griffey Jr. 3.00 1.35 .35
☐ 121 Tino Martinez .25 .11 .03
☐ 122 Marc Newfield .25 .11 .03
☐ 123 Ted Power .10 .05 .01
☐ 124 Mackey Sasser .10 .05 .01
☐ 125 Omar Vizquel .25 .11 .03
☐ 126 Kevin Brown .25 .11 .03
☐ 127 Juan Gonzalez 1.50 .70 .19
☐ 128 Tom Henke .10 .05 .01
☐ 129 David Hulse .10 .05 .01
☐ 130 Dean Palmer .25 .11 .03
☐ 131 Roger Pavlik .10 .05 .01
☐ 132 Ivan Rodriguez .75 .35 .09
☐ 133 Kenny Rogers .10 .05 .01
☐ 134 Doug Strange .10 .05 .01
☐ 135 Pat Borders .10 .05 .01
☐ 136 Joe Carter .25 .11 .03
☐ 137 Darnell Coles .10 .05 .01
☐ 138 Pat Hentgen .25 .11 .03
☐ 139 Al Leiter .25 .11 .03
☐ 140 Paul Molitor .60 .25 .07
☐ 141 John Olerud .10 .05 .01
☐ 142 Ed Sprague .25 .11 .03
☐ 143 Dave Stewart .25 .11 .03
☐ 144 Mike Timlin .10 .05 .01
☐ 145 Duane Ward .10 .05 .01
☐ 146 Devon White .10 .05 .01
☐ 147 Steve Avery .25 .11 .03
☐ 148 Steve Bedrosian .10 .05 .01
☐ 149 Damon Berryhill .10 .05 .01
☐ 150 Jeff Blauser .10 .05 .01
☐ 151 Tom Glavine .50 .23 .06
☐ 152 Chipper Jones 2.50 1.10 .30
☐ 153 Mark Lemke .10 .05 .01
☐ 154 Fred McGriff .50 .23 .06
☐ 155 Greg McMichael .10 .05 .01
☐ 156 Deion Sanders .50 .23 .06
☐ 157 John Smoltz .50 .23 .06
☐ 158 Mark Wohlers .25 .11 .03
☐ 159 Jose Bautista .10 .05 .01
☐ 160 Steve Buechele .10 .05 .01
☐ 161 Mike Harkey .10 .05 .01
☐ 162 Greg Hibbard .10 .05 .01
☐ 163 Chuck McElroy .10 .05 .01
☐ 164 Mike Morgan .10 .05 .01
☐ 165 Kevin Roberson .10 .05 .01
☐ 166 Ryne Sandberg .75 .35 .09
☐ 167 Jose Vizcaino .10 .05 .01
☐ 168 Rick Wilkins .10 .05 .01
☐ 169 Willie Wilson .10 .05 .01
☐ 170 Willie Greene .25 .11 .03
☐ 171 Roberto Kelly .10 .05 .01
☐ 172 Larry Luebbers .10 .05 .01
☐ 173 Kevin Mitchell .25 .11 .03
☐ 174 Joe Oliver .10 .05 .01
☐ 175 John Roper .10 .05 .01
☐ 176 Johnny Ruffin .10 .05 .01
☐ 177 Reggie Sanders .25 .11 .03
☐ 178 John Smiley .10 .05 .01
☐ 179 Jerry Spradlin .10 .05 .01
☐ 180 Freddie Benavides .10 .05 .01
☐ 181 Dante Bichette .50 .23 .06
☐ 182 Willie Blair .10 .05 .01
☐ 183 Kent Bottenfield .10 .05 .01
☐ 184 Jerald Clark .10 .05 .01
☐ 185 Joe Girardi .10 .05 .01
☐ 186 Roberto Mejia .10 .05 .01
☐ 187 Steve Reed .10 .05 .01
☐ 188 Armando Reynoso .10 .05 .01
☐ 189 Bruce Ruffin .10 .05 .01
☐ 190 Eric Young .25 .11 .03
☐ 191 Luis Aquino .10 .05 .01
☐ 192 Bret Barberie .10 .05 .01
☐ 193 Ryan Bowen .10 .05 .01
☐ 194 Chuck Carr .10 .05 .01
☐ 195 Orestes Destrade .10 .05 .01
☐ 196 Richie Lewis .10 .05 .01
☐ 197 Dave Magadan .10 .05 .01
☐ 198 Bob Natal .10 .05 .01
☐ 199 Gary Sheffield .50 .23 .06
☐ 200 Matt Turner .10 .05 .01
☐ 201 Darrell Whitmore .10 .05 .01
☐ 202 Eric Anthony .10 .05 .01
☐ 203 Jeff Bagwell 1.25 .55 .16
☐ 204 Andujar Cedeno .10 .05 .01
☐ 205 Luis Gonzalez .10 .05 .01
☐ 206 Xavier Hernandez .10 .05 .01
☐ 207 Doug Jones .10 .05 .01
☐ 208 Darryl Kile .10 .05 .01
☐ 209 Scott Servais .10 .05 .01
☐ 210 Greg Swindell .10 .05 .01
☐ 211 Brian Williams .10 .05 .01
☐ 212 Pedro Astacio .10 .05 .01
☐ 213 Brett Butler .25 .11 .03
☐ 214 Omar Daal .10 .05 .01
☐ 215 Jim Gott .10 .05 .01
☐ 216 Raul Mondesi .50 .23 .06
☐ 217 Jose Offerman .10 .05 .01
☐ 218 Mike Piazza 2.00 .90 .25
☐ 219 Cory Snyder .10 .05 .01
☐ 220 Tim Wallach .10 .05 .01
☐ 221 Todd Worrell .10 .05 .01
☐ 222 Moises Alou .25 .11 .03
☐ 223 Sean Berry .10 .05 .01
☐ 224 Wil Cordero .25 .11 .03
☐ 225 Jeff Fassero .10 .05 .01
☐ 226 Darrin Fletcher .10 .05 .01
☐ 227 Cliff Floyd .50 .23 .06
☐ 228 Marquis Grissom .25 .11 .03
☐ 229 Ken Hill .10 .05 .01
☐ 230 Mike Lansing .25 .11 .03
☐ 231 Kirk Rueter .10 .05 .01
☐ 232 John Wetteland .25 .11 .03
☐ 233 Rondell White .50 .23 .06
☐ 234 Tim Bogar .10 .05 .01
☐ 235 Jeromy Burnitz .10 .05 .01
☐ 236 Dwight Gooden .25 .11 .03
☐ 237 Todd Hundley .25 .11 .03
☐ 238 Jeff Kent .10 .05 .01
☐ 239 Josias Manzanillo .10 .05 .01
☐ 240 Joe Orsulak .10 .05 .01
☐ 241 Ryan Thompson .10 .05 .01
☐ 242 Kim Batiste .10 .05 .01
☐ 243 Darren Daulton .25 .11 .03
☐ 244 Tommy Greene .10 .05 .01
☐ 245 Dave Hollins .10 .05 .01
☐ 246 Pete Incaviglia .10 .05 .01
☐ 247 Danny Jackson .10 .05 .01
☐ 248 Ricky Jordan .10 .05 .01
☐ 249 John Kruk .25 .11 .03
☐ 250 Mickey Morandini .10 .05 .01
☐ 251 Terry Mulholland .10 .05 .01
☐ 252 Ben Rivera .10 .05 .01
☐ 253 Kevin Stocker .10 .05 .01
☐ 254 Jay Bell .25 .11 .03
☐ 255 Steve Cooke .10 .05 .01
☐ 256 Jeff King .25 .11 .03
☐ 257 Al Martin .10 .05 .01
☐ 258 Danny Miceli .10 .05 .01
☐ 259 Blas Minor .10 .05 .01
☐ 260 Don Slaught .10 .05 .01
☐ 261 Paul Wagner .10 .05 .01
☐ 262 Tim Wakefield .10 .05 .01
☐ 263 Kevin Young .10 .05 .01
☐ 264 Rene Arocha .10 .05 .01
☐ 265 Richard Batchelor .10 .05 .01
☐ 266 Gregg Jefferies .50 .23 .06
☐ 267 Brian Jordan .50 .23 .06
☐ 268 Jose Oquendo .10 .05 .01
☐ 269 Donovan Osborne .10 .05 .01
☐ 270 Erik Pappas .10 .05 .01
☐ 271 Mike Perez .10 .05 .01
☐ 272 Bob Tewksbury .10 .05 .01
☐ 273 Mark Whiten .10 .05 .01
☐ 274 Todd Zeile .10 .05 .01
☐ 275 Andy Ashby .25 .11 .03
☐ 276 Brad Ausmus .10 .05 .01
☐ 277 Phil Clark .10 .05 .01
☐ 278 Jeff Gardner .10 .05 .01
☐ 279 Ricky Gutierrez .10 .05 .01
☐ 280 Tony Gwynn 1.25 .55 .16
☐ 281 Tim Mauser .10 .05 .01
☐ 282 Scott Sanders .10 .05 .01
☐ 283 Frank Seminara .10 .05 .01
☐ 284 Wally Whitehurst .10 .05 .01
☐ 285 Rod Beck .25 .11 .03
☐ 286 Barry Bonds .75 .35 .09
☐ 287 Dave Burba .10 .05 .01
☐ 288 Mark Carreon .10 .05 .01
☐ 289 Royce Clayton .25 .11 .03
☐ 290 Mike Jackson .10 .05 .01
☐ 291 Darren Lewis .10 .05 .01
☐ 292 Kirt Manwaring .10 .05 .01
☐ 293 Dave Martinez .10 .05 .01
☐ 294 Billy Swift .10 .05 .01
☐ 295 Salomon Torres .10 .05 .01
☐ 296 Matt Williams .50 .23 .06
☐ 297 Checklist 1-75 .10 .05 .01
☐ 298 Checklist 76-150 .10 .05 .01
☐ 299 Checklist 151-225 .10 .05 .01
☐ 300 Checklist 226-300 .10 .05 .01
☐ 301 Brady Anderson .50 .23 .06
☐ 302 Harold Baines .25 .11 .03
☐ 303 Damon Buford .10 .05 .01
☐ 304 Mike Devereaux .10 .05 .01
☐ 305 Sid Fernandez .10 .05 .01
☐ 306 Rick Krivda .10 .05 .01
☐ 307 Mike Mussina .60 .25 .07
☐ 308 Rafael Palmeiro .50 .23 .06
☐ 309 Arthur Rhodes .10 .05 .01
☐ 310 Chris Sabo .10 .05 .01
☐ 311 Lee Smith .25 .11 .03
☐ 312 Gregg Zaun .25 .11 .03
☐ 313 Scott Cooper .10 .05 .01
☐ 314 Mike Greenwell .10 .05 .01
☐ 315 Tim Naehring .10 .05 .01
☐ 316 Otis Nixon .10 .05 .01
☐ 317 Paul Quantrill .10 .05 .01
☐ 318 John Valentin .25 .11 .03
☐ 319 Dave Valle .10 .05 .01
☐ 320 Frank Viola .10 .05 .01
☐ 321 Brian Anderson .25 .11 .03
☐ 322 Garret Anderson .50 .23 .06
☐ 323 Chad Curtis .10 .05 .01
☐ 324 Chili Davis .25 .11 .03
☐ 325 Gary DiSarcina .10 .05 .01
☐ 326 Damion Easley .10 .05 .01
☐ 327 Jim Edmonds .60 .25 .07
☐ 328 Chuck Finley .10 .05 .01
☐ 329 Joe Grahe .10 .05 .01
☐ 330 Bo Jackson .25 .11 .03
☐ 331 Mark Langston .25 .11 .03
☐ 332 Harold Reynolds .10 .05 .01
☐ 333 James Baldwin .50 .23 .06
☐ 334 Ray Durham .75 .35 .09
☐ 335 Julio Franco .25 .11 .03
☐ 336 Craig Grebeck .10 .05 .01
☐ 337 Ozzie Guillen .10 .05 .01
☐ 338 Joe Hall .10 .05 .01
☐ 339 Darrin Jackson .10 .05 .01
☐ 340 Jack McDowell .25 .11 .03
☐ 341 Tim Raines .50 .23 .06
☐ 342 Robin Ventura .25 .11 .03
☐ 343 Carlos Baerga .25 .11 .03
☐ 344 Derek Lilliquist .10 .05 .01
☐ 345 Dennis Martinez .25 .11 .03
☐ 346 Jack Morris .25 .11 .03
☐ 347 Eddie Murray .75 .35 .09
☐ 348 Chris Nabholz .10 .05 .01
☐ 349 Charles Nagy .25 .11 .03
☐ 350 Chad Ogea .25 .11 .03
☐ 351 Manny Ramirez 1.00 .45 .12
☐ 352 Omar Vizquel .25 .11 .03
☐ 353 Tim Belcher .10 .05 .01
☐ 354 Eric Davis .25 .11 .03
☐ 355 Kirk Gibson .25 .11 .03
☐ 356 Rick Greene .10 .05 .01
☐ 357 Mickey Tettleton .10 .05 .01
☐ 358 Alan Trammell .25 .11 .03
☐ 359 David Wells .10 .05 .01
☐ 360 Stan Belinda .10 .05 .01
☐ 361 Vince Coleman .10 .05 .01
☐ 362 David Cone .25 .11 .03
☐ 363 Gary Gaetti .25 .11 .03
☐ 364 Tom Gordon .10 .05 .01
☐ 365 Dave Henderson .10 .05 .01
☐ 366 Wally Joyner .25 .11 .03
☐ 367 Brent Mayne .10 .05 .01
☐ 368 Brian McRae .25 .11 .03
☐ 369 Michael Tucker .25 .11 .03
☐ 370 Ricky Bones .10 .05 .01
☐ 371 Brian Harper .10 .05 .01
☐ 372 Tyrone Hill .10 .05 .01
☐ 373 Mark Kiefer .10 .05 .01
☐ 374 Pat Listach .10 .05 .01
☐ 375 Mike Matheny .10 .05 .01
☐ 376 Jose Mercedes .10 .05 .01
☐ 377 Jody Reed .10 .05 .01
☐ 378 Kevin Seitzer .10 .05 .01
☐ 379 B.J. Surhoff .10 .05 .01
☐ 380 Greg Vaughn .50 .23 .06
☐ 381 Turner Ward .10 .05 .01
☐ 382 Wes Weger .10 .05 .01
☐ 383 Bill Wegman .10 .05 .01
☐ 384 Rick Aguilera .10 .05 .01
☐ 385 Rich Becker .25 .11 .03
☐ 386 Alex Cole .10 .05 .01
☐ 387 Steve Dunn .10 .05 .01
☐ 388 Keith Garagozzo .10 .05 .01
☐ 389 LaTroy Hawkins .25 .11 .03
☐ 390 Shane Mack .10 .05 .01
☐ 391 David McCarty .10 .05 .01
☐ 392 Pedro Munoz .10 .05 .01
☐ 393 Derek Parks .10 .05 .01
☐ 394 Kirby Puckett 1.25 .55 .16
☐ 395 Kevin Tapani .10 .05 .01
☐ 396 Matt Walbeck .10 .05 .01
☐ 397 Jim Abbott .10 .05 .01
☐ 398 Mike Gallego .10 .05 .01
☐ 399 Xavier Hernandez .10 .05 .01
☐ 400 Don Mattingly 1.50 .70 .19
☐ 401 Terry Mulholland .10 .05 .01
☐ 402 Matt Nokes .10 .05 .01
☐ 403 Luis Polonia .10 .05 .01
☐ 404 Bob Wickman .10 .05 .01
☐ 405 Mark Acre .10 .05 .01
☐ 406 Fausto Cruz .10 .05 .01
☐ 407 Dennis Eckersley .25 .11 .03
☐ 408 Rickey Henderson .50 .23 .06
☐ 409 Stan Javier .10 .05 .01
☐ 410 Carlos Reyes .10 .05 .01
☐ 411 Ruben Sierra .25 .11 .03
☐ 412 Terry Steinbach .25 .11 .03
☐ 413 Bill Taylor .10 .05 .01
☐ 414 Todd Van Poppel .10 .05 .01
☐ 415 Eric Anthony .10 .05 .01
☐ 416 Bobby Ayala .10 .05 .01
☐ 417 Chris Bosio .10 .05 .01
☐ 418 Tim Davis .10 .05 .01
☐ 419 Randy Johnson .50 .23 .06
☐ 420 Kevin King .10 .05 .01
☐ 421 Anthony Manahan .10 .05 .01
☐ 422 Edgar Martinez .25 .11 .03
☐ 423 Keith Mitchell .10 .05 .01
☐ 424 Roger Salkeld .10 .05 .01
☐ 425 Mac Suzuki .25 .11 .03
☐ 426 Dan Wilson .25 .11 .03
☐ 427 Duff Brumley .10 .05 .01
☐ 428 Jose Canseco .50 .23 .06
☐ 429 Will Clark .50 .23 .06
☐ 430 Steve Dreyer .10 .05 .01

	MINT	NRMT	EXC
☐ 431 Rick Helling	.10	.05	.01
☐ 432 Chris James	.10	.05	.01
☐ 433 Matt Whiteside	.10	.05	.01
☐ 434 Roberto Alomar	.60	.25	.07
☐ 435 Scott Brow	.10	.05	.01
☐ 436 Domingo Cedeno	.10	.05	.01
☐ 437 Carlos Delgado	.50	.23	.06
☐ 438 Juan Guzman	.25	.11	.03
☐ 439 Paul Spoljaric	.10	.05	.01
☐ 440 Todd Stottlemyre	.10	.05	.01
☐ 441 Woody Williams	.10	.05	.01
☐ 442 David Justice	.50	.23	.06
☐ 443 Mike Kelly	.10	.05	.01
☐ 444 Ryan Klesko	.60	.25	.07
☐ 445 Javier Lopez	.50	.23	.06
☐ 446 Greg Maddux	2.00	.90	.25
☐ 447 Kent Mercker	.10	.05	.01
☐ 448 Charlie O'Brien	.10	.05	.01
☐ 449 Terry Pendleton	.25	.11	.03
☐ 450 Mike Stanton	.10	.05	.01
☐ 451 Tony Tarasco	.10	.05	.01
☐ 452 Terrell Wade	.60	.25	.07
☐ 453 Willie Banks	.10	.05	.01
☐ 454 Shawon Dunston	.10	.05	.01
☐ 455 Mark Grace	.50	.23	.06
☐ 456 Jose Guzman	.10	.05	.01
☐ 457 Jose Hernandez	.10	.05	.01
☐ 458 Glenallen Hill	.10	.05	.01
☐ 459 Blaise Ilsley	.10	.05	.01
☐ 460 Brooks Kieschnick	.60	.25	.07
☐ 461 Derrick May	.10	.05	.01
☐ 462 Randy Myers	.10	.05	.01
☐ 463 Karl Rhodes	.10	.05	.01
☐ 464 Sammy Sosa	.50	.23	.06
☐ 465 Steve Trachsel	.25	.11	.03
☐ 466 Anthony Young	.10	.05	.01
☐ 467 Eddie Zambrano	.10	.05	.01
☐ 468 Bret Boone	.25	.11	.03
☐ 469 Tom Browning	.10	.05	.01
☐ 470 Hector Carrasco	.10	.05	.01
☐ 471 Rob Dibble	.10	.05	.01
☐ 472 Erik Hanson	.10	.05	.01
☐ 473 Thomas Howard	.10	.05	.01
☐ 474 Barry Larkin	.50	.23	.06
☐ 475 Hal Morris	.10	.05	.01
☐ 476 Jose Rijo	.10	.05	.01
☐ 477 John Burke	.10	.05	.01
☐ 478 Ellis Burks	.25	.11	.03
☐ 479 Marvin Freeman	.10	.05	.01
☐ 480 Andres Galarraga	.50	.23	.06
☐ 481 Greg W. Harris	.10	.05	.01
☐ 482 Charlie Hayes	.10	.05	.01
☐ 483 Darren Holmes	.10	.05	.01
☐ 484 Howard Johnson	.10	.05	.01
☐ 485 Marcus Moore	.10	.05	.01
☐ 486 David Nied	.10	.05	.01
☐ 487 Mark Thompson	.25	.11	.03
☐ 488 Walt Weiss	.10	.05	.01
☐ 489 Kurt Abbott	.25	.11	.03
☐ 490 Matias Carrillo	.10	.05	.01
☐ 491 Jeff Conine	.25	.11	.03
☐ 492 Chris Hammond	.10	.05	.01
☐ 493 Bryan Harvey	.10	.05	.01
☐ 494 Charlie Hough	.10	.05	.01
☐ 495 Yorkis Perez	.10	.05	.01
☐ 496 Pat Rapp	.10	.05	.01
☐ 497 Benito Santiago	.10	.05	.01
☐ 498 David Weathers	.10	.05	.01
☐ 499 Craig Biggio	.25	.11	.03
☐ 500 Ken Caminiti	.50	.23	.06
☐ 501 Doug Drabek	.10	.05	.01
☐ 502 Tony Eusebio	.10	.05	.01
☐ 503 Steve Finley	.50	.23	.06
☐ 504 Pete Harnisch	.10	.05	.01
☐ 505 Brian Hunter	.50	.23	.06
☐ 506 Domingo Jean	.10	.05	.01
☐ 507 Todd Jones	.10	.05	.01
☐ 508 Orlando Miller	.10	.05	.01
☐ 509 James Mouton	.25	.11	.03
☐ 510 Roberto Petagine	.25	.11	.03
☐ 511 Shane Reynolds	.25	.11	.03
☐ 512 Mitch Williams	.10	.05	.01
☐ 513 Billy Ashley	.10	.05	.01
☐ 514 Tom Candiotti	.10	.05	.01
☐ 515 Delino DeShields	.10	.05	.01
☐ 516 Kevin Gross	.10	.05	.01
☐ 517 Orel Hershiser	.25	.11	.03
☐ 518 Eric Karros	.25	.11	.03
☐ 519 Ramon Martinez	.25	.11	.03
☐ 520 Chan Ho Park	1.00	.45	.12
☐ 521 Henry Rodriguez	.25	.11	.03
☐ 522 Joey Eischen	.10	.05	.01
☐ 523 Rod Henderson	.10	.05	.01
☐ 524 Pedro J. Martinez	.50	.23	.06
☐ 525 Mel Rojas	.10	.05	.01
☐ 526 Larry Walker	.50	.23	.06
☐ 527 Gabe White	.10	.05	.01
☐ 528 Bobby Bonilla	.25	.11	.03
☐ 529 Jonathan Hurst	.10	.05	.01
☐ 530 Bobby Jones	.25	.11	.03
☐ 531 Kevin McReynolds	.10	.05	.01
☐ 532 Bill Pulsipher	.25	.11	.03
☐ 533 Bret Saberhagen	.25	.11	.03
☐ 534 David Segui	.10	.05	.01
☐ 535 Pete Smith	.10	.05	.01
☐ 536 Kelly Stinnett	.10	.05	.01
☐ 537 Dave Telgheder	.10	.05	.01
☐ 538 Quilvio Veras	.25	.11	.03
☐ 539 Jose Vizcaino	.10	.05	.01
☐ 540 Pete Walker	.10	.05	.01
☐ 541 Ricky Bottalico	.50	.23	.06
☐ 542 Wes Chamberlain	.10	.05	.01
☐ 543 Mariano Duncan	.10	.05	.01
☐ 544 Lenny Dykstra	.25	.11	.03
☐ 545 Jim Eisenreich	.10	.05	.01
☐ 546 Phil Geisler	.10	.05	.01
☐ 547 Wayne Gomes	.25	.11	.03
☐ 548 Doug Jones	.10	.05	.01
☐ 549 Jeff Juden	.10	.05	.01
☐ 550 Mike Lieberthal	.10	.05	.01
☐ 551 Tony Longmire	.10	.05	.01
☐ 552 Tom Marsh	.10	.05	.01
☐ 553 Bobby Munoz	.10	.05	.01
☐ 554 Curt Schilling	.10	.05	.01
☐ 555 Carlos Garcia	.10	.05	.01
☐ 556 Ravelo Manzanillo	.10	.05	.01
☐ 557 Orlando Merced	.25	.11	.03
☐ 558 Will Pennyfeather	.10	.05	.01
☐ 559 Zane Smith	.10	.05	.01
☐ 560 Andy Van Slyke	.25	.11	.03
☐ 561 Rick White	.10	.05	.01
☐ 562 Luis Alicea	.10	.05	.01
☐ 563 Brian Barber	.10	.05	.01
☐ 564 Clint Davis	.10	.05	.01
☐ 565 Bernard Gilkey	.25	.11	.03
☐ 566 Ray Lankford	.25	.11	.03
☐ 567 Tom Pagnozzi	.10	.05	.01
☐ 568 Ozzie Smith	.75	.35	.09
☐ 569 Rick Sutcliffe	.10	.05	.01
☐ 570 Allen Watson	.10	.05	.01
☐ 571 Dmitri Young	.60	.25	.07
☐ 572 Derek Bell	.25	.11	.03
☐ 573 Andy Benes	.25	.11	.03
☐ 574 Archi Cianfrocco	.10	.05	.01
☐ 575 Joey Hamilton	.60	.25	.07
☐ 576 Gene Harris	.10	.05	.01
☐ 577 Trevor Hoffman	.25	.11	.03
☐ 578 Tim Hyers	.10	.05	.01
☐ 579 Brian Johnson	.10	.05	.01
☐ 580 Keith Lockhart	.10	.05	.01
☐ 581 Pedro A. Martinez	.10	.05	.01
☐ 582 Ray McDavid	.25	.11	.03
☐ 583 Phil Plantier	.10	.05	.01
☐ 584 Bip Roberts	.10	.05	.01
☐ 585 Dave Staton	.10	.05	.01
☐ 586 Todd Benzinger	.10	.05	.01
☐ 587 John Burkett	.10	.05	.01
☐ 588 Bryan Hickerson	.10	.05	.01
☐ 589 Willie McGee	.10	.05	.01
☐ 590 John Patterson	.10	.05	.01
☐ 591 Mark Portugal	.10	.05	.01
☐ 592 Kevin Rogers	.10	.05	.01
☐ 593 Joe Rosselli	.10	.05	.01
☐ 594 Steve Soderstrom	.25	.11	.03
☐ 595 Robby Thompson	.10	.05	.01
☐ 596 125th Anniversary Card	.10	.05	.01
☐ 597 Checklist	.10	.05	.01
☐ 598 Checklist	.10	.05	.01
☐ 599 Checklist	.10	.05	.01
☐ 600 Checklist	.10	.05	.01
☐ P243 Darren Daulton Promo	.25	.11	.03
☐ P249 John Kruk Promo	2.00	.90	.25

1994 Ultra All-Rookies

This 10-card standard-size set features top rookies of 1994 and were randomly inserted in second series jumbo and foil packs at a rate of one in 10. Card fronts have a color player photo cut-out over a computer generated background that resembles volcanic activity. The player's name and All-Rookie Team logo appear in gold foil at the bottom. On the backs, the player cut-out appears toward the right with text on the left. The background is much the same as the front. The set is sequenced in alphabetical order. Every second series Ultra hobby case included this set in jumbo (3 1/2" by 5") form.

	MINT	NRMT	EXC
COMPLETE SET (10)	10.00	4.50	1.25
COMMON CARD (1-10)	.50	.23	.06
☐ 1 Kurt Abbott	.50	.23	.06
☐ 2 Carlos Delgado	1.50	.70	.19
☐ 3 Cliff Floyd	1.00	.45	.12
☐ 4 Jeffrey Hammonds	1.00	.45	.12
☐ 5 Ryan Klesko	2.50	1.10	.30
☐ 6 Javier Lopez	1.50	.70	.19
☐ 7 Raul Mondesi	2.00	.90	.25
☐ 8 James Mouton	1.00	.45	.12
☐ 9 Chan Ho Park	1.00	.45	.12
☐ 10 Dave Staton	.50	.23	.06

1994 Ultra All-Rookies Jumbo

This 10-card set is a parallel to the regular 1994 Ultra All-Rookie set. It was inserted as a complete set in second series Ultra hobby cases. The cards measure 3 1/2" by 5".

	MINT	NRMT	EXC
COMPLETE SET (10)	20.00	9.00	2.50
COMMON CARD (1-10)	1.00	.45	.12
*JUMBOS: 1X TO 2X BASIC CARDS			

1994 Ultra All-Stars

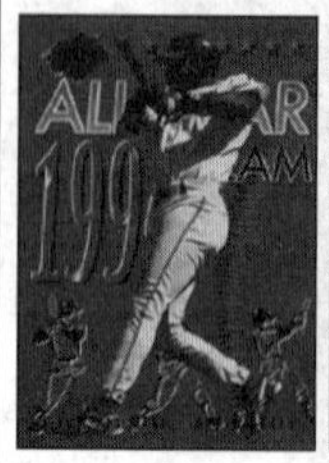
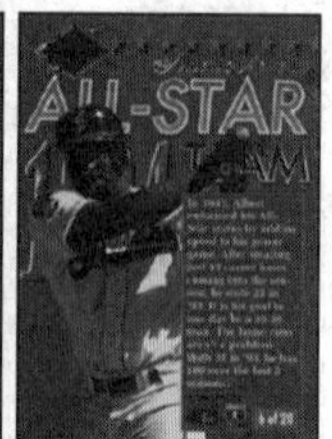

Randomly inserted in second series foil and jumbo packs at a rate of one in three, this 20-card standard-size set contains top major league stars. The fronts have a color player photo superimposed over a bright red (American League players) or dark blue (National League) background. The backs are much the same except they include highlights from 1993.

	MINT	NRMT	EXC
COMPLETE SET (20)	18.00	8.00	2.20
COMMON CARD (1-20)	.25	.11	.03
☐ 1 Chris Hoiles	.25	.11	.03
☐ 2 Frank Thomas	5.00	2.20	.60
☐ 3 Roberto Alomar	1.00	.45	.12
☐ 4 Cal Ripken Jr.	4.00	1.80	.50
☐ 5 Robin Ventura	.40	.18	.05
☐ 6 Albert Belle	2.00	.90	.25
☐ 7 Juan Gonzalez	2.50	1.10	.30
☐ 8 Ken Griffey Jr.	5.00	2.20	.60
☐ 9 John Olerud	.25	.11	.03
☐ 10 Jack McDowell	.40	.18	.05
☐ 11 Mike Piazza	3.00	1.35	.35
☐ 12 Fred McGriff	.60	.25	.07
☐ 13 Ryne Sandberg	1.25	.55	.16
☐ 14 Jay Bell	.25	.11	.03
☐ 15 Matt Williams	.60	.25	.07
☐ 16 Barry Bonds	1.25	.55	.16
☐ 17 Lenny Dykstra	.40	.18	.05
☐ 18 David Justice	.25	.11	.03
☐ 19 Tom Glavine	.60	.25	.07
☐ 20 Greg Maddux	3.00	1.35	.35

1994 Ultra Award Winners

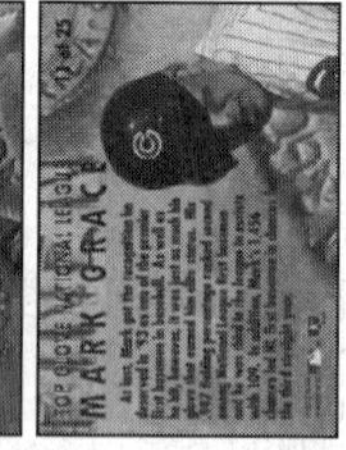

Randomly inserted in all first series packs at a rate of one in three, this 25-card standard-size set features three MVP's, two Rookies of the Year, and 18 Top Glove defensive standouts. The set is divided into American League Top Gloves (1-9), National League Top Gloves (10-18), and Award Winners (19-25). A horizontal design includes a color player cut-out over a gold background on front. Also on front, is a gold foil logo that indicates the honor. The backs have a small photo and text.

	MINT	NRMT	EXC
COMPLETE SET (25)	18.00	8.00	2.20
COMMON CARD (1-25)	.25	.11	.03
☐ 1 Ivan Rodriguez	1.25	.55	.16
☐ 2 Don Mattingly	2.50	1.10	.30
☐ 3 Roberto Alomar	1.00	.45	.12
☐ 4 Robin Ventura	.40	.18	.05
☐ 5 Omar Vizquel	.25	.11	.03
☐ 6 Ken Griffey Jr.	5.00	2.20	.60
☐ 7 Kenny Lofton	1.50	.70	.19
☐ 8 Devon White	.25	.11	.03
☐ 9 Mark Langston	.25	.11	.03
☐ 10 Kirt Manwaring	.25	.11	.03
☐ 11 Mark Grace	.60	.25	.07
☐ 12 Robby Thompson	.25	.11	.03
☐ 13 Matt Williams	.60	.25	.07
☐ 14 Jay Bell	.25	.11	.03
☐ 15 Barry Bonds	1.25	.55	.16
☐ 16 Marquis Grissom	.40	.18	.05
☐ 17 Larry Walker	.60	.25	.07
☐ 18 Greg Maddux	3.00	1.35	.35
☐ 19 Frank Thomas	5.00	2.20	.60
☐ 20 Barry Bonds	1.25	.55	.16
☐ 21 Paul Molitor	1.00	.45	.12
☐ 22 Jack McDowell	.40	.18	.05
☐ 23 Greg Maddux	3.00	1.35	.35
☐ 24 Tim Salmon	.75	.35	.09
☐ 25 Mike Piazza	3.00	1.35	.35

1994 Ultra Career Achievement

Randomly inserted in all second series packs at a rate of one in 21, this five card standard-size set highlights veteran stars and milestones they have reached during their brilliant careers. Horizontally designed cards have fronts that feature a color player photo superimposed over solid color background that contains another player photo. A photo of the player earlier in his career is on back along with text. The cards are sequenced in alphabetical order.

	MINT	NRMT	EXC
COMPLETE SET (5)	12.00	5.50	1.50
COMMON CARD (1-5)	1.00	.45	.12
☐ 1 Joe Carter	1.00	.45	.12
☐ 2 Paul Molitor	2.00	.90	.25
☐ 3 Cal Ripken Jr.	8.00	3.60	1.00
☐ 4 Ryne Sandberg	2.50	1.10	.30
☐ 5 Dave Winfield			

1994 Ultra Firemen

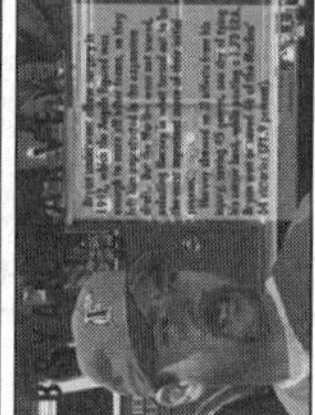

Randomly inserted in all first series packs at a rate of one in 11, this ten-card standard-size set features ten of baseball's top relief pitchers. The fronts feature color player action cutouts superimposed upon borderless backgrounds consisting of pictures of fire-fighting equipment. The player's name appears in gold foil at the bottom. The horizontal back carries a color player head shot on one side, and career highlights inside a ghosted panel on the other, all on a borderless fire-fighting equipment background. The set is arranged according to American League (1-5) and National League (6-10) players.

	MINT	NRMT	EXC
COMPLETE SET (10)	5.00	2.20	.60
COMMON CARD (1-10)	.50	.23	.06
☐ 1 Jeff Montgomery	.50	.23	.06
☐ 2 Duane Ward	.50	.23	.06
☐ 3 Tom Henke	.50	.23	.06
☐ 4 Roberto Hernandez	.50	.23	.06
☐ 5 Dennis Eckersley	1.00	.45	.12
☐ 6 Randy Myers	.50	.23	.06
☐ 7 Rod Beck	.50	.23	.06
☐ 8 Bryan Harvey	.50	.23	.06
☐ 9 John Wetteland	1.00	.45	.12
☐ 10 Mitch Williams	.50	.23	.06

1994 Ultra Hitting Machines

Randomly inserted in all second series packs at a rate of one in five, this 10-card horizontally designed standard-size set features top hitters from 1993. The fronts have a color player cut-out over a "Hitting Machines" background. The back has a smaller player cut-out and text. The set is sequenced in alphabetical order.

	MINT	NRMT	EXC
COMPLETE SET (10)	15.00	6.75	1.85
COMMON CARD (1-10)	.50	.23	.06
☐ 1 Roberto Alomar	1.00	.45	.12
☐ 2 Carlos Baerga	.50	.23	.06
☐ 3 Barry Bonds	1.25	.55	.16
☐ 4 Andres Galarraga	.75	.35	.09
☐ 5 Juan Gonzalez	2.50	1.10	.30
☐ 6 Tony Gwynn	2.00	.90	.25
☐ 7 Paul Molitor	1.00	.45	.12
☐ 8 John Olerud	.50	.23	.06
☐ 9 Mike Piazza	3.00	1.35	.35
☐ 10 Frank Thomas	5.00	2.20	.60

1994 Ultra Home Run Kings

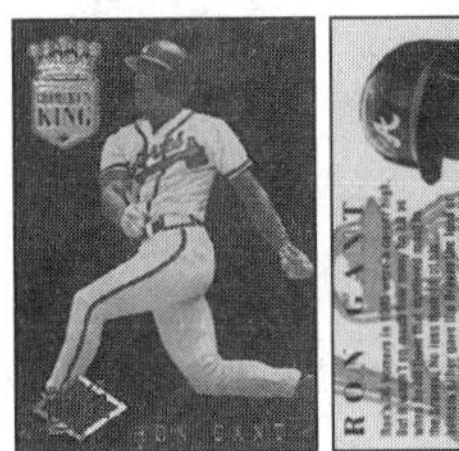

Randomly inserted exclusively in first series foil packs at a rate of one in 36, these 12 standard-size cards highlight home run hitters by an etched metalized look. Cards 1-6 feature American League Home Run Kings while cards 7-12 present National League Home Run Kings.

	MINT	NRMT	EXC
COMPLETE SET (12)	80.00	36.00	10.00
COMMON CARD (1-12)	2.00	.90	.25
☐ 1 Juan Gonzalez	12.00	5.50	1.50
☐ 2 Ken Griffey Jr.	25.00	11.00	3.10
☐ 3 Frank Thomas	25.00	11.00	3.10
☐ 4 Albert Belle	10.00	4.50	1.25
☐ 5 Rafael Palmeiro	3.00	1.35	.35
☐ 6 Joe Carter	2.00	.90	.25
☐ 7 Barry Bonds	6.00	2.70	.75
☐ 8 David Justice	2.00	.90	.25
☐ 9 Matt Williams	3.00	1.35	.35
☐ 10 Fred McGriff	3.00	1.35	.35
☐ 11 Ron Gant	2.00	.90	.25
☐ 12 Mike Piazza	15.00	6.75	1.85

1994 Ultra League Leaders

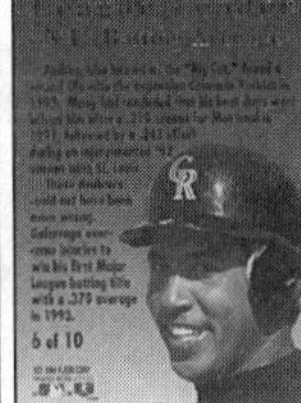

Randomly inserted in all first series packs at a rate of one in 11, this ten-card standard-size set features ten of 1993's leading players. The fronts feature borderless color player action shots, with a color-screening that shades from being imperceptible at the top to washing out the photos' true colors at the bottom. The player's name in gold foil appears across the card face. The borderless back carries a color player head shot in a lower corner with his career highlights appearing above, all on a monochrome background that shades from dark to light, from top to bottom. The set is arranged according to American League (1-5) and National League (6-10) players.

	MINT	NRMT	EXC
COMPLETE SET (10)	5.00	2.20	.60
COMMON CARD (1-10)	.25	.11	.03
☐ 1 John Olerud	.25	.11	.03
☐ 2 Rafael Palmeiro	.50	.23	.06
☐ 3 Kenny Lofton	2.00	.90	.25
☐ 4 Jack McDowell	.35	.16	.04
☐ 5 Randy Johnson	1.00	.45	.12
☐ 6 Andres Galarraga	.50	.23	.06
☐ 7 Lenny Dykstra	.35	.16	.04
☐ 8 Chuck Carr	.25	.11	.03
☐ 9 Tom Glavine	.50	.23	.06
☐ 10 Jose Rijo	.25	.11	.03

1994 Ultra On-Base Leaders

Randomly inserted in second series jumbo packs at a rate of one in 36, this 12-card standard-size set features those that were among the Major League leaders in on-base percentage. Card fronts have the player superimposed over a metallic background that simulates statistics from a sports page. The backs have a player cut-out and text over a statistical background that is not metallic. The set is sequenced in alphabetical order.

	MINT	NRMT	EXC
COMPLETE SET (12)	150.00	70.00	19.00
COMMON CARD (1-12)	4.00	1.80	.50
☐ 1 Roberto Alomar	12.00	5.50	1.50
☐ 2 Barry Bonds	15.00	6.75	1.85
☐ 3 Lenny Dykstra	5.00	2.20	.60
☐ 4 Andres Galarraga	6.00	2.70	.75
☐ 5 Mark Grace	6.00	2.70	.75
☐ 6 Ken Griffey Jr.	60.00	27.00	7.50
☐ 7 Gregg Jefferies	5.00	2.20	.60
☐ 8 Orlando Merced	4.00	1.80	.50
☐ 9 Paul Molitor	12.00	5.50	1.50
☐ 10 John Olerud	5.00	2.20	.60
☐ 11 Tony Phillips	4.00	1.80	.50
☐ 12 Frank Thomas	60.00	27.00	7.50

1994 Ultra Phillies Finest

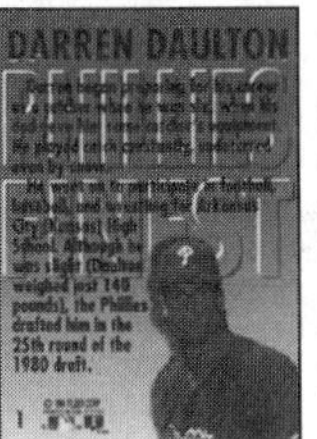

As the "Highlight Series" insert set, this 20-card standard-size set features Darren Daulton and John Kruk of the 1993 National League champion Philadelphia Phillies. The cards were inserted at a rate of one in six first series and one in 10 second series packs. Ten cards spotlight each player's career. Daulton and Kruk each signed more than 1,000 of their cards for random insertion. Moreover, the collector could receive four more cards (two of each player) through a mail-in offer by sending in ten 1994 series I wrappers plus 1.50 for postage and handling. The expiration for this redemption was September 30, 1994. The fronts feature borderless color player action shots. Behind the player, in "transparent" block lettering, the words "Phillies Finest" appear, followed by the player's name. His name also appears in gold foil in a lower corner. The back carries a color player head shot in a lower corner, with career highlights appearing above, all on a borderless red background.

	MINT	NRMT	EXC
COMPLETE SET (20)	10.00	4.50	1.25
COMPLETE SERIES 1 (10)	5.00	2.20	.60
COMPLETE SERIES 2 (10)	5.00	2.20	.60
COMMON DAULTON (1-5/11-15)	.50	.23	.06
COMMON KRUK (6-10/16-20)	.50	.23	.06
COMMON MAIL-IN (M1-M4)	1.00	.45	.12
☐ 1 Darren Daulton (Standing behind home plate)	.50	.23	.06
☐ 2 Darren Daulton (Swinging at a pitch)	.50	.23	.06
☐ 3 Darren Daulton (Blocking home plate)	.50	.23	.06
☐ 4 Darren Daulton (Just completed swing and is headed for fisrt)	.50	.23	.06
☐ 5 Darren Daulton (Looking skyward after connecting with a pitch)	.50	.23	.06
☐ 6 John Kruk (Swinging at a pitch)	.50	.23	.06
☐ 7 John Kruk (Fielding)	.50	.23	.06
☐ 8 John Kruk (Just completed a swing)	.50	.23	.06
☐ 9 John Kruk (On deck)	.50	.23	.06
☐ 10 John Kruk (Breaking out of batters box)	.50	.23	.06
☐ 11 Darren Daulton (Looking skyward after swing)	.50	.23	.06
☐ 12 Darren Daulton	.50	.23	.06
☐ 13 Darren Daulton (Anticipating throw home)	.50	.23	.06
☐ 14 Darren Daulton (Standing at home with ball in hand)	.50	.23	.06
☐ 15 Darren Daulton (Running up first base line with in catching gear)	.50	.23	.06
☐ 16 John Kruk (Follow through of swing)	.50	.23	.06
☐ 17 John Kruk (Waiting on deck)	.50	.23	.06
☐ 18 John Kruk (Follow through from first base dugout angle)	.50	.23	.06
☐ 19 John Kruk (Swinging at pitch) chest high)	.50	.23	.06
☐ 20 John Kruk (Looking out toward left field afer swinging)	.50	.23	.06
☐ M1 Darren Daulton (About to throw down to second base)	1.00	.45	.12
☐ M2 John Kruk (Fielding position)	1.00	.45	.12
☐ M3 Darren Daulton (Awaiting pitch)	1.00	.45	.12
☐ M4 John Kruk (Running)	1.00	.45	.12
☐ AU1 Darren Daulton Certified Autograph	50.00	22.00	6.25
☐ AU2 John Kruk Certified Autograph	50.00	22.00	6.25

1994 Ultra RBI Kings

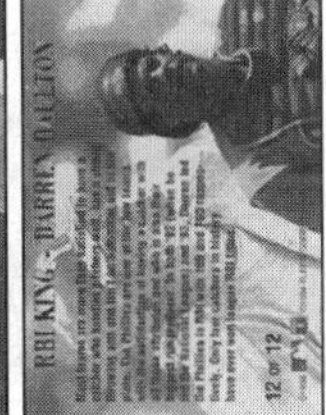

Randomly inserted in first series jumbo packs at a rate of one in 36, this 12-card standard-size set features RBI leaders. These horizontal, metallized cards have a color player photo on front that superimposes a player image.The backs have a write-up and a small color player photo. Cards 1-6 feature American League RBI Kings while cards 7-12 present National League RBI Kings.

	MINT	NRMT	EXC
COMPLETE SET (12)	150.00	70.00	19.00
COMMON CARD (1-12)	6.00	2.70	.75
☐ 1 Albert Belle	25.00	11.00	3.10
☐ 2 Frank Thomas	60.00	27.00	7.50
☐ 3 Joe Carter	6.00	2.70	.75
☐ 4 Juan Gonzalez	30.00	13.50	3.70
☐ 5 Cecil Fielder	6.00	2.70	.75
☐ 6 Carlos Baerga	6.00	2.70	.75
☐ 7 Barry Bonds	15.00	6.75	1.85
☐ 8 David Justice	6.00	2.70	.75
☐ 9 Ron Gant	6.00	2.70	.75
☐ 10 Mike Piazza	40.00	18.00	5.00
☐ 11 Matt Williams	8.00	3.60	1.00
☐ 12 Darren Daulton	6.00	2.70	.75

1994 Ultra Rising Stars

Randomly inserted in second series foil packs and jumbo packs at a rate of one in 36, this 12-card set spotlights top young major league stars. Metallic fronts have the player superimposed over icons resembling outer space. The backs feature the player in the same format along with text. The set is sequenced in alphabetical order.

	MINT	NRMT	EXC
COMPLETE SET (12)	125.00	55.00	15.50
COMMON CARD (1-12)	4.00	1.80	.50
☐ 1 Carlos Baerga	4.00	1.80	.50
☐ 2 Jeff Bagwell	25.00	11.00	3.10
☐ 3 Albert Belle	25.00	11.00	3.10
☐ 4 Cliff Floyd	4.00	1.80	.50
☐ 5 Travis Fryman	6.00	2.70	.75
☐ 6 Marquis Grissom	6.00	2.70	.75
☐ 7 Kenny Lofton	20.00	9.00	2.50
☐ 8 John Olerud	6.00	2.70	.75
☐ 9 Mike Piazza	40.00	18.00	5.00
☐ 10 Kirk Rueter	4.00	1.80	.50
☐ 11 Tim Salmon	10.00	4.50	1.25
☐ 12 Aaron Sele	4.00	1.80	.50

1994 Ultra Second Year Standouts

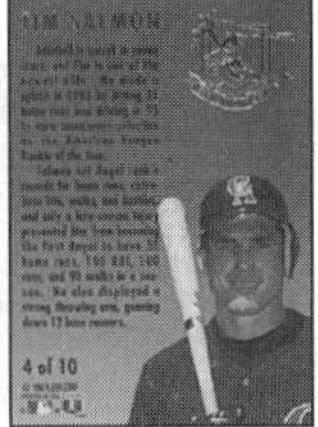

Randomly inserted in all first series packs at a rate of one in 11, this 10-card standard-size set included 10 1993 outstanding rookies who are destined to become future stars. The fronts feature two color playe action cutouts superimposed upon borderless team-colored backgrounds. The player's name appears in gold foil at the bottom. The back carries a color player head shot in a lower corner with his career highlights appearing alongside, all on a borderless team color-coded background. The set is arranged in alphabetical order according to American League (1-5) and National League (6-10) players.

	MINT	NRMT	EXC
COMPLETE SET (10)	15.00	6.75	1.85
COMMON CARD (1-10)	.50	.23	.06
☐ 1 Jason Bere	.50	.23	.06
☐ 2 Brent Gates	.50	.23	.06
☐ 3 Jeffrey Hammonds	.50	.23	.06
☐ 4 Tim Salmon	3.00	1.35	.35
☐ 5 Aaron Sele	1.00	.45	.12
☐ 6 Chuck Carr	.50	.23	.06
☐ 7 Jeff Conine	1.50	.70	.19
☐ 8 Greg McMichael	.50	.23	.06
☐ 9 Mike Piazza	12.00	5.50	1.50
☐ 10 Kevin Stocker	.50	.23	.06

1994 Ultra Strikeout Kings

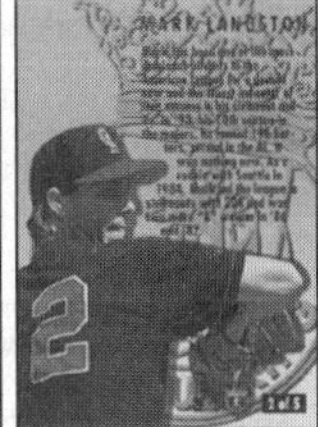

Randomly inserted in all second series packs at a rate of one in seven, this five-card standard-size set features top strikeout artists. Full-bleed fronts offer triple exposure photos and a gold foil Strikeout King logo. The backs contain a photo and write-up with the Strikeout King logo as background. The set is sequenced in alphabetical order.

	MINT	NRMT	EXC
COMPLETE SET (5)	5.00	2.20	.60
COMMON CARD (1-5)	.25	.11	.03
☐ 1 Randy Johnson	.75	.35	.09
☐ 2 Mark Langston	.50	.23	.06
☐ 3 Greg Maddux	3.00	1.35	.35
☐ 4 Jose Rijo	.25	.11	.03
☐ 5 John Smoltz	.75	.35	.09

1995 Ultra

This 450-card standard-size set was issued in two series. The first series contained 250 cards while the second series consisted of 200 cards. They were issued in 12-card packs (either hobby or retail) with a suggested retail price of $1.99. Also, 15-card pre-priced packs with a suggested retail of $2.69. Each pack contained two inserts: one is a Gold Medallion parallel while the other is from one of Ultra's many insert sets. "Hot Packs" contain nothing but insert cards. The full-bleed fronts feature the player's photo with the team name and player's name at the bottom. The '95 Fleer Ultra' logo is in the upper right corner. The backs have a two-photo design; one of which is a full-size duotone shot with the other being a full-color action shot. Personal bio, seasonal and career information are also included on the back. In each series the cards were grouped alphabetically within teams and checklisted alphabetically according to teams for each league with AL preceding NL. There are no key Rookie Cards in this set.

	MINT	NRMT	EXC
COMPLETE SET (450)	30.00	13.50	3.70
COMPLETE SERIES 1 (250)	18.00	8.00	2.20
COMPLETE SERIES 2 (200)	12.00	5.50	1.50
COMMON CARD (1-450)	.10	.05	.01
☐ 1 Brady Anderson	.50	.23	.06
☐ 2 Sid Fernandez	.10	.05	.01
☐ 3 Jeffrey Hammonds	.25	.11	.03
☐ 4 Chris Hoiles	.10	.05	.01
☐ 5 Ben McDonald	.10	.05	.01
☐ 6 Mike Mussina	.60	.25	.07
☐ 7 Rafael Palmeiro	.50	.23	.06
☐ 8 Jack Voigt	.10	.05	.01
☐ 9 Wes Chamberlain	.10	.05	.01
☐ 10 Roger Clemens	.60	.25	.07
☐ 11 Chris Howard	.10	.05	.01
☐ 12 Tim Naehring	.10	.05	.01
☐ 13 Otis Nixon	.10	.05	.01
☐ 14 Rich Rowland	.10	.05	.01
☐ 15 Ken Ryan	.10	.05	.01
☐ 16 John Valentin	.25	.11	.03
☐ 17 Mo Vaughn	.75	.35	.09
☐ 18 Brian Anderson	.10	.05	.01
☐ 19 Chili Davis	.25	.11	.03
☐ 20 Damion Easley	.10	.05	.01
☐ 21 Jim Edmonds	.50	.23	.06
☐ 22 Mark Langston	.10	.05	.01
☐ 23 Tim Salmon	.50	.23	.06
☐ 24 J.T. Snow	.25	.11	.03
☐ 25 Chris Turner	.10	.05	.01
☐ 26 Wilson Alvarez	.25	.11	.03
☐ 27 Joey Cora	.10	.05	.01
☐ 28 Alex Fernandez	.25	.11	.03
☐ 29 Roberto Hernandez	.10	.05	.01
☐ 30 Lance Johnson	.25	.11	.03
☐ 31 Ron Karkovice	.10	.05	.01
☐ 32 Kirk McCaskill	.10	.05	.01
☐ 33 Tim Raines	.50	.23	.06
☐ 34 Frank Thomas	3.00	1.35	.35
☐ 35 Sandy Alomar Jr.	.10	.05	.01
☐ 36 Albert Belle	1.25	.55	.16
☐ 37 Mark Clark	.10	.05	.01
☐ 38 Kenny Lofton	.75	.35	.09
☐ 39 Eddie Murray	.75	.35	.09
☐ 40 Eric Plunk	.10	.05	.01
☐ 41 Manny Ramirez	.75	.35	.09
☐ 42 Jim Thome	.60	.25	.07
☐ 43 Omar Vizquel	.25	.11	.03
☐ 44 Danny Bautista	.10	.05	.01
☐ 45 Junior Felix	.10	.05	.01
☐ 46 Cecil Fielder	.25	.11	.03
☐ 47 Chris Gomez	.10	.05	.01
☐ 48 Chad Kreuter	.10	.05	.01
☐ 49 Mike Moore	.10	.05	.01
☐ 50 Tony Phillips	.25	.11	.03
☐ 51 Alan Trammell	.25	.11	.03
☐ 52 David Wells	.10	.05	.01
☐ 53 Kevin Appier	.25	.11	.03
☐ 54 Billy Brewer	.10	.05	.01
☐ 55 David Cone	.25	.11	.03
☐ 56 Greg Gagne	.10	.05	.01
☐ 57 Bob Hamelin	.10	.05	.01
☐ 58 Jose Lind	.10	.05	.01
☐ 59 Brent Mayne	.10	.05	.01
☐ 60 Brian McRae	.25	.11	.03
☐ 61 Terry Shumpert	.10	.05	.01
☐ 62 Ricky Bones	.10	.05	.01
☐ 63 Mike Fetters	.10	.05	.01
☐ 64 Darryl Hamilton	.10	.05	.01
☐ 65 John Jaha	.25	.11	.03
☐ 66 Graeme Lloyd	.10	.05	.01
☐ 67 Matt Mieske	.25	.11	.03
☐ 68 Kevin Seitzer	.10	.05	.01
☐ 69 Jose Valentin	.25	.11	.03
☐ 70 Turner Ward	.10	.05	.01
☐ 71 Rick Aguilera	.10	.05	.01
☐ 72 Rich Becker	.10	.05	.01
☐ 73 Alex Cole	.10	.05	.01
☐ 74 Scott Leius	.10	.05	.01
☐ 75 Pat Meares	.10	.05	.01
☐ 76 Kirby Puckett	1.25	.55	.16
☐ 77 Dave Stevens	.10	.05	.01
☐ 78 Kevin Tapani	.10	.05	.01
☐ 79 Matt Walbeck	.10	.05	.01
☐ 80 Wade Boggs	.50	.23	.06
☐ 81 Scott Kamieniecki	.10	.05	.01
☐ 82 Pat Kelly	.10	.05	.01
☐ 83 Jimmy Key	.25	.11	.03
☐ 84 Paul O'Neill	.25	.11	.03
☐ 85 Luis Polonia	.10	.05	.01
☐ 86 Mike Stanley	.10	.05	.01
☐ 87 Danny Tartabull	.10	.05	.01
☐ 88 Bob Wickman	.10	.05	.01
☐ 89 Mark Acre	.10	.05	.01
☐ 90 Geronimo Berroa	.10	.05	.01
☐ 91 Mike Bordick	.10	.05	.01
☐ 92 Ron Darling	.10	.05	.01
☐ 93 Stan Javier	.10	.05	.01
☐ 94 Mark McGwire	1.00	.45	.12
☐ 95 Troy Neel	.10	.05	.01
☐ 96 Ruben Sierra	.25	.11	.03
☐ 97 Terry Steinbach	.25	.11	.03
☐ 98 Eric Anthony	.10	.05	.01
☐ 99 Chris Bosio	.10	.05	.01
☐ 100 Dave Fleming	.10	.05	.01
☐ 101 Ken Griffey Jr.	3.00	1.35	.35
☐ 102 Reggie Jefferson	.25	.11	.03
☐ 103 Randy Johnson	.50	.23	.06
☐ 104 Edgar Martinez	.25	.11	.03
☐ 105 Bill Risley	.10	.05	.01
☐ 106 Dan Wilson	.25	.11	.03
☐ 107 Cris Carpenter	.10	.05	.01
☐ 108 Will Clark	.50	.23	.06
☐ 109 Juan Gonzalez	1.50	.70	.19
☐ 110 Rusty Greer	.50	.23	.06
☐ 111 David Hulse	.10	.05	.01
☐ 112 Roger Pavlik	.10	.05	.01
☐ 113 Ivan Rodriguez	.75	.35	.09
☐ 114 Doug Strange	.10	.05	.01
☐ 115 Matt Whiteside	.10	.05	.01
☐ 116 Roberto Alomar	.60	.25	.07
☐ 117 Brad Cornett	.10	.05	.01
☐ 118 Carlos Delgado	.25	.11	.03
☐ 119 Alex Gonzalez	.25	.11	.03
☐ 120 Darren Hall	.10	.05	.01
☐ 121 Pat Hentgen	.25	.11	.03
☐ 122 Paul Molitor	.60	.25	.07
☐ 123 Ed Sprague	.25	.11	.03
☐ 124 Devon White	.25	.11	.03
☐ 125 Tom Glavine	.50	.23	.06
☐ 126 David Justice	.50	.23	.06
☐ 127 Roberto Kelly	.10	.05	.01
☐ 128 Mark Lemke	.10	.05	.01
☐ 129 Greg Maddux	2.00	.90	.25
☐ 130 Greg McMichael	.10	.05	.01
☐ 131 Kent Mercker	.10	.05	.01
☐ 132 Charlie O'Brien	.10	.05	.01
☐ 133 John Smoltz	.50	.23	.06
☐ 134 Willie Banks	.10	.05	.01
☐ 135 Steve Buechele	.10	.05	.01
☐ 136 Kevin Foster	.10	.05	.01
☐ 137 Glenallen Hill	.10	.05	.01
☐ 138 Rey Sanchez	.10	.05	.01
☐ 139 Sammy Sosa	.50	.23	.06
☐ 140 Steve Trachsel	.10	.05	.01
☐ 141 Rick Wilkins	.10	.05	.01
☐ 142 Jeff Brantley	.10	.05	.01
☐ 143 Hector Carrasco	.10	.05	.01
☐ 144 Kevin Jarvis	.10	.05	.01
☐ 145 Barry Larkin	.50	.23	.06
☐ 146 Chuck McElroy	.10	.05	.01
☐ 147 Jose Rijo	.10	.05	.01
☐ 148 Johnny Ruffin	.10	.05	.01
☐ 149 Deion Sanders	.50	.23	.06
☐ 150 Eddie Taubensee	.10	.05	.01
☐ 151 Dante Bichette	.50	.23	.06
☐ 152 Ellis Burks	.25	.11	.03
☐ 153 Joe Girardi	.10	.05	.01
☐ 154 Charlie Hayes	.10	.05	.01
☐ 155 Mike Kingery	.10	.05	.01
☐ 156 Steve Reed	.10	.05	.01
☐ 157 Kevin Ritz	.10	.05	.01
☐ 158 Bruce Ruffin	.10	.05	.01
☐ 159 Eric Young	.25	.11	.03
☐ 160 Kurt Abbott	.10	.05	.01
☐ 161 Chuck Carr	.10	.05	.01
☐ 162 Chris Hammond	.10	.05	.01
☐ 163 Bryan Harvey	.10	.05	.01
☐ 164 Terry Mathews	.10	.05	.01
☐ 165 Yorkis Perez	.10	.05	.01
☐ 166 Pat Rapp	.10	.05	.01
☐ 167 Gary Sheffield	.50	.23	.06
☐ 168 Dave Weathers	.10	.05	.01
☐ 169 Jeff Bagwell	1.25	.55	.16
☐ 170 Ken Caminiti	.50	.23	.06
☐ 171 Doug Drabek	.10	.05	.01
☐ 172 Steve Finley	.25	.11	.03
☐ 173 John Hudek	.10	.05	.01
☐ 174 Todd Jones	.10	.05	.01
☐ 175 James Mouton	.10	.05	.01
☐ 176 Shane Reynolds	.25	.11	.03
☐ 177 Scott Servais	.10	.05	.01
☐ 178 Tom Candiotti	.10	.05	.01
☐ 179 Omar Daal	.10	.05	.01
☐ 180 Darren Dreifort	.10	.05	.01
☐ 181 Eric Karros	.25	.11	.03
☐ 182 Ramon J.Martinez	.25	.11	.03
☐ 183 Raul Mondesi	.50	.23	.06
☐ 184 Henry Rodriguez	.25	.11	.03
☐ 185 Todd Worrell	.10	.05	.01
☐ 186 Moises Alou	.25	.11	.03
☐ 187 Sean Berry	.10	.05	.01
☐ 188 Wil Cordero	.10	.05	.01
☐ 189 Jeff Fassero	.10	.05	.01
☐ 190 Darrin Fletcher	.10	.05	.01
☐ 191 Butch Henry	.10	.05	.01
☐ 192 Ken Hill	.10	.05	.01
☐ 193 Mel Rojas	.10	.05	.01
☐ 194 John Wetteland	.25	.11	.03
☐ 195 Bobby Bonilla	.25	.11	.03
☐ 196 Rico Brogna	.10	.05	.01
☐ 197 Bobby Jones	.25	.11	.03
☐ 198 Jeff Kent	.10	.05	.01
☐ 199 Josias Manzanillo	.10	.05	.01
☐ 200 Kelly Stinnett	.10	.05	.01
☐ 201 Ryan Thompson	.10	.05	.01
☐ 202 Jose Vizcaino	.10	.05	.01
☐ 203 Lenny Dykstra	.25	.11	.03
☐ 204 Jim Eisenreich	.10	.05	.01
☐ 205 Dave Hollins	.10	.05	.01
☐ 206 Mike Lieberthal	.10	.05	.01
☐ 207 Mickey Morandini	.10	.05	.01
☐ 208 Bobby Munoz	.10	.05	.01
☐ 209 Curt Schilling	.10	.05	.01
☐ 210 Heathcliff Slocumb	.10	.05	.01
☐ 211 David West	.10	.05	.01
☐ 212 Dave Clark	.10	.05	.01
☐ 213 Steve Cooke	.10	.05	.01
☐ 214 Midre Cummings	.10	.05	.01
☐ 215 Carlos Garcia	.10	.05	.01
☐ 216 Jeff King	.25	.11	.03
☐ 217 Jon Lieber	.10	.05	.01
☐ 218 Orlando Merced	.10	.05	.01
☐ 219 Don Slaught	.10	.05	.01
☐ 220 Rick White	.10	.05	.01
☐ 221 Rene Arocha	.10	.05	.01
☐ 222 Bernard Gilkey	.25	.11	.03
☐ 223 Brian Jordan	.50	.23	.06
☐ 224 Tom Pagnozzi	.10	.05	.01
☐ 225 Vicente Palacios	.10	.05	.01
☐ 226 Geronimo Pena	.10	.05	.01
☐ 227 Ozzie Smith	.75	.35	.09
☐ 228 Allen Watson	.10	.05	.01
☐ 229 Mark Whiten	.10	.05	.01
☐ 230 Brad Ausmus	.10	.05	.01
☐ 231 Derek Bell	.25	.11	.03
☐ 232 Andy Benes	.10	.05	.01
☐ 233 Tony Gwynn	1.25	.55	.16
☐ 234 Joey Hamilton	.50	.23	.06
☐ 235 Luis Lopez	.10	.05	.01
☐ 236 Pedro A.Martinez	.10	.05	.01
☐ 237 Scott Sanders	.10	.05	.01
☐ 238 Eddie Williams	.10	.05	.01
☐ 239 Rod Beck	.10	.05	.01
☐ 240 Dave Burba	.10	.05	.01
☐ 241 Darren Lewis	.10	.05	.01
☐ 242 Kirt Manwaring	.10	.05	.01
☐ 243 Mark Portugal	.10	.05	.01
☐ 244 Darryl Strawberry	.25	.11	.03
☐ 245 Robby Thompson	.10	.05	.01
☐ 246 Wm.VanLandingham	.10	.05	.01
☐ 247 Matt Williams	.50	.23	.06
☐ 248 Checklist	.10	.05	.01
☐ 249 Checklist	.10	.05	.01
☐ 250 Checklist	.10	.05	.01
☐ 251 Harold Baines	.25	.11	.03
☐ 252 Bret Barberie	.10	.05	.01
☐ 253 Armando Benitez	.10	.05	.01
☐ 254 Mike Devereaux	.10	.05	.01
☐ 255 Leo Gomez	.10	.05	.01
☐ 256 Jamie Moyer	.10	.05	.01
☐ 257 Arthur Rhodes	.10	.05	.01
☐ 258 Cal Ripken	2.50	1.10	.30
☐ 259 Luis Alicea	.10	.05	.01
☐ 260 Jose Canseco	.50	.23	.06
☐ 261 Scott Cooper	.10	.05	.01
☐ 262 Andre Dawson	.25	.11	.03
☐ 263 Mike Greenwell	.10	.05	.01
☐ 264 Aaron Sele	.25	.11	.03
☐ 265 Garret Anderson	.25	.11	.03
☐ 266 Chad Curtis	.10	.05	.01
☐ 267 Gary DiSarcina	.10	.05	.01
☐ 268 Chuck Finley	.25	.11	.03
☐ 269 Rex Hudler	.10	.05	.01
☐ 270 Andrew Lorraine	.25	.11	.03
☐ 271 Spike Owen	.10	.05	.01
☐ 272 Lee Smith	.25	.11	.03
☐ 273 Jason Bere	.10	.05	.01
☐ 274 Ozzie Guillen	.10	.05	.01
☐ 275 Norberto Martin	.10	.05	.01
☐ 276 Scott Ruffcorn	.10	.05	.01
☐ 277 Robin Ventura	.25	.11	.03
☐ 278 Carlos Baerga	.25	.11	.03
☐ 279 Jason Grimsley	.10	.05	.01
☐ 280 Dennis Martinez	.25	.11	.03
☐ 281 Charles Nagy	.25	.11	.03
☐ 282 Paul Sorrento	.10	.05	.01
☐ 283 Dave Winfield	.50	.23	.06
☐ 284 John Doherty	.10	.05	.01
☐ 285 Travis Fryman	.25	.11	.03
☐ 286 Kirk Gibson	.25	.11	.03
☐ 287 Lou Whitaker	.25	.11	.03
☐ 288 Gary Gaetti	.25	.11	.03
☐ 289 Tom Gordon	.10	.05	.01
☐ 290 Mark Gubicza	.10	.05	.01
☐ 291 Wally Joyner	.25	.11	.03
☐ 292 Mike Macfarlane	.10	.05	.01
☐ 293 Jeff Montgomery	.25	.11	.03
☐ 294 Jeff Cirillo	.25	.11	.03
☐ 295 Cal Eldred	.10	.05	.01
☐ 296 Pat Listach	.10	.05	.01
☐ 297 Jose Mercedes	.10	.05	.01
☐ 298 Dave Nilsson	.25	.11	.03
☐ 299 Duane Singleton	.10	.05	.01
☐ 300 Greg Vaughn	.25	.11	.03
☐ 301 Scott Erickson	.10	.05	.01
☐ 302 Denny Hocking	.10	.05	.01
☐ 303 Chuck Knoblauch	.50	.23	.06
☐ 304 Pat Mahomes	.10	.05	.01
☐ 305 Pedro Munoz	.10	.05	.01
☐ 306 Erik Schullstrom	.10	.05	.01
☐ 307 Jim Abbott	.10	.05	.01
☐ 308 Tony Fernandez	.10	.05	.01
☐ 309 Sterling Hitchcock	.25	.11	.03
☐ 310 Jim Leyritz	.10	.05	.01
☐ 311 Don Mattingly	1.50	.70	.19
☐ 312 Jack McDowell	.25	.11	.03
☐ 313 Melido Perez	.10	.05	.01
☐ 314 Bernie Williams	.60	.25	.07
☐ 315 Scott Brosius	.10	.05	.01
☐ 316 Dennis Eckersley	.25	.11	.03
☐ 317 Brent Gates	.10	.05	.01
☐ 318 Rickey Henderson	.50	.23	.06
☐ 319 Steve Karsay	.10	.05	.01
☐ 320 Steve Ontiveros	.10	.05	.01
☐ 321 Bill Taylor	.10	.05	.01
☐ 322 Todd Van Poppel	.10	.05	.01
☐ 323 Bob Welch	.10	.05	.01
☐ 324 Bobby Ayala	.10	.05	.01
☐ 325 Mike Blowers	.10	.05	.01
☐ 326 Jay Buhner	.50	.23	.06
☐ 327 Felix Fermin	.10	.05	.01
☐ 328 Tino Martinez	.25	.11	.03
☐ 329 Marc Newfield	.25	.11	.03
☐ 330 Greg Pirkl	.10	.05	.01
☐ 331 Alex Rodriguez	4.00	1.80	.50
☐ 332 Kevin Brown	.25	.11	.03
☐ 333 John Burkett	.25	.11	.03
☐ 334 Jeff Frye	.10	.05	.01
☐ 335 Kevin Gross	.10	.05	.01
☐ 336 Dean Palmer	.25	.11	.03
☐ 337 Joe Carter	.25	.11	.03
☐ 338 Shawn Green	.25	.11	.03
☐ 339 Juan Guzman	.25	.11	.03
☐ 340 Mike Huff	.10	.05	.01
☐ 341 Al Leiter	.25	.11	.03
☐ 342 John Olerud	.10	.05	.01
☐ 343 Dave Stewart	.25	.11	.03
☐ 344 Todd Stottlemyre	.10	.05	.01
☐ 345 Steve Avery	.25	.11	.03
☐ 346 Jeff Blauser	.10	.05	.01
☐ 347 Chipper Jones	2.00	.90	.25
☐ 348 Mike Kelly	.10	.05	.01
☐ 349 Ryan Klesko	.50	.23	.06
☐ 350 Javier Lopez	.50	.23	.06
☐ 351 Fred McGriff	.50	.23	.06
☐ 352 Jose Oliva	.10	.05	.01
☐ 353 Terry Pendleton	.25	.11	.03
☐ 354 Mike Stanton	.10	.05	.01
☐ 355 Tony Tarasco	.10	.05	.01
☐ 356 Mark Wohlers	.25	.11	.03
☐ 357 Jim Bullinger	.10	.05	.01
☐ 358 Shawon Dunston	.10	.05	.01
☐ 359 Mark Grace	.50	.23	.06
☐ 360 Derrick May	.10	.05	.01
☐ 361 Randy Myers	.10	.05	.01
☐ 362 Karl Rhodes	.10	.05	.01
☐ 363 Bret Boone	.25	.11	.03
☐ 364 Brian Dorsett	.10	.05	.01
☐ 365 Ron Gant	.25	.11	.03
☐ 366 Brian A.Hunter	.10	.05	.01
☐ 367 Hal Morris	.10	.05	.01
☐ 368 Jack Morris	.50	.23	.06
☐ 369 John Roper	.10	.05	.01
☐ 370 Reggie Sanders	.25	.11	.03
☐ 371 Pete Schourek	.25	.11	.03
☐ 372 John Smiley	.10	.05	.01
☐ 373 Marvin Freeman	.10	.05	.01
☐ 374 Andres Galarraga	.50	.23	.06
☐ 375 Mike Munoz	.10	.05	.01
☐ 376 David Nied	.10	.05	.01
☐ 377 Walt Weiss	.10	.05	.01
☐ 378 Greg Colbrunn	.10	.05	.01
☐ 379 Jeff Conine	.25	.11	.03
☐ 380 Charles Johnson	.25	.11	.03
☐ 381 Kurt Miller	.10	.05	.01
☐ 382 Robb Nen	.10	.05	.01
☐ 383 Benito Santiago	.10	.05	.01
☐ 384 Craig Biggio	.25	.11	.03
☐ 385 Tony Eusebio	.10	.05	.01
☐ 386 Luis Gonzalez	.10	.05	.01
☐ 387 Brian L.Hunter	.25	.11	.03
☐ 388 Darryl Kile	.10	.05	.01
☐ 389 Orlando Miller	.10	.05	.01
☐ 390 Phil Plantier	.10	.05	.01
☐ 391 Greg Swindell	.10	.05	.01
☐ 392 Billy Ashley	.10	.05	.01
☐ 393 Pedro Astacio	.10	.05	.01
☐ 394 Brett Butler	.25	.11	.03
☐ 395 Delino DeShields	.10	.05	.01
☐ 396 Orel Hershiser	.25	.11	.03
☐ 397 Garey Ingram	.10	.05	.01
☐ 398 Chan Ho Park	.50	.23	.06
☐ 399 Mike Piazza	2.00	.90	.25
☐ 400 Ismael Valdes	.25	.11	.03
☐ 401 Tim Wallach	.10	.05	.01
☐ 402 Cliff Floyd	.25	.11	.03
☐ 403 Marquis Grissom	.25	.11	.03
☐ 404 Mike Lansing	.10	.05	.01
☐ 405 Pedro J.Martinez	.25	.11	.03
☐ 406 Kirk Rueter	.10	.05	.01
☐ 407 Tim Scott	.10	.05	.01
☐ 408 Jeff Shaw	.10	.05	.01
☐ 409 Larry Walker	.50	.23	.06
☐ 410 Rondell White	.25	.11	.03
☐ 411 John Franco	.10	.05	.01
☐ 412 Todd Hundley	.25	.11	.03
☐ 413 Jason Jacome	.10	.05	.01
☐ 414 Joe Orsulak	.10	.05	.01
☐ 415 Bret Saberhagen	.25	.11	.03

	MINT	NRMT	EXC
☐ 416 David Segui	.10	.05	.01
☐ 417 Darren Daulton	.25	.11	.03
☐ 418 Mariano Duncan	.10	.05	.01
☐ 419 Tommy Greene	.10	.05	.01
☐ 420 Gregg Jefferies	.25	.11	.03
☐ 421 John Kruk	.25	.11	.03
☐ 422 Kevin Stocker	.10	.05	.01
☐ 423 Jay Bell	.25	.11	.03
☐ 424 Al Martin	.25	.11	.03
☐ 425 Denny Neagle	.25	.11	.03
☐ 426 Zane Smith	.10	.05	.01
☐ 427 Andy Van Slyke	.25	.11	.03
☐ 428 Paul Wagner	.10	.05	.01
☐ 429 Tom Henke	.10	.05	.01
☐ 430 Danny Jackson	.10	.05	.01
☐ 431 Ray Lankford	.25	.11	.03
☐ 432 John Mabry	.50	.23	.06
☐ 433 Bob Tewksbury	.10	.05	.01
☐ 434 Todd Zeile	.10	.05	.01
☐ 435 Andy Ashby	.25	.11	.03
☐ 436 Andujar Cedeno	.10	.05	.01
☐ 437 Donnie Elliott	.10	.05	.01
☐ 438 Bryce Florie	.10	.05	.01
☐ 439 Trevor Hoffman	.25	.11	.03
☐ 440 Melvin Nieves	.25	.11	.03
☐ 441 Bip Roberts	.10	.05	.01
☐ 442 Barry Bonds	.75	.35	.09
☐ 443 Royce Clayton	.10	.05	.01
☐ 444 Mike Jackson	.10	.05	.01
☐ 445 John Patterson	.10	.05	.01
☐ 446 J.R. Phillips	.10	.05	.01
☐ 447 Bill Swift	.10	.05	.01
☐ 448 Checklist	.10	.05	.01
☐ 449 Checklist	.10	.05	.01
☐ 450 Checklist	.10	.05	.01

1995 Ultra Gold Medallion

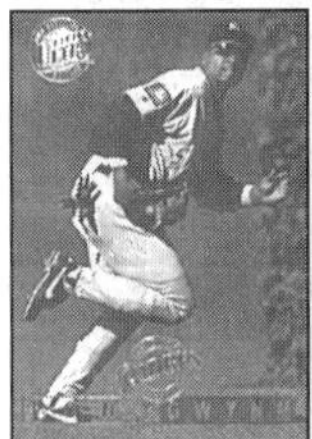

This 450-card parallels the regular Ultra issue. These cards were issued one per pack and are differentiated from the regular cards by the Ultra logo being replaced by the "Ultra Gold Medallion Edition logo."

	MINT	NRMT	EXC
COMPLETE SET (450)	110.00	50.00	14.00
COMPLETE SERIES 1 (250)	60.00	27.00	7.50
COMPLETE SERIES 2 (200)	50.00	22.00	6.25
COMMON CARD (1-450)	.25	.11	.03

*STARS: 2X to 4X BASIC CARDS

*YOUNG STARS: 1.5X to 3X BASIC CARDS

1995 Ultra All-Rookies

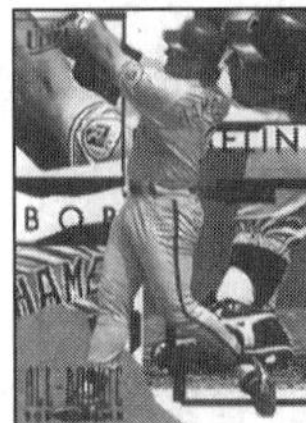

This 10-card standard-size set features rookies who emerged with an impact in 1994. These cards were inserted one in every five second series packs. The fronts feature a player's photo in the middle of the card with each corner devoted to a close-up of part of that action shot. The horizontal backs feature some player information as well as a photo. That same photo is also included in the background as a duotone photo as well. The cards are numbered in the lower left as "X" of 10 and are sequenced in alphabetical order.

	MINT	NRMT	EXC
COMPLETE SET (10)	6.00	2.70	.75
COMMON CARD (1-10)	.25	.11	.03
☐ 1 Cliff Floyd	.35	.16	.04
☐ 2 Chris Gomez	.25	.11	.03
☐ 3 Rusty Greer	.50	.23	.06
☐ 4 Bob Hamelin	.25	.11	.03
☐ 5 Joey Hamilton	1.00	.45	.12
☐ 6 John Hudek	.25	.11	.03
☐ 7 Ryan Klesko	.50	.23	.06
☐ 8 Raul Mondesi	1.00	.45	.12
☐ 9 Manny Ramirez	2.00	.90	.25
☐ 10 Steve Trachsel	.25	.11	.03

1995 Ultra All-Rookies Gold Medallions

This 10 card set parallels the regular All-Rookies insert set. These cards were produced in less quantity than the regular All-Rookie cards and have a Gold Medallion logo on them.

	MINT	NRMT	EXC
COMPLETE SET (10)	18.00	8.00	2.20
COMMON CARD (1-10)	.75	.35	.09

*GOLD MEDALLION: 1.5X TO 3X BASIC CARDS

1995 Ultra All-Stars

This 20-card standard-size set feature players who are considered to be the top players in the game. Cards were inserted one in every four second series packs. The fronts feature two photos. One photo is in full-color while the other is a shaded black and white shot. The player's name, "All-Star" and his team name are at the bottom. The back is split between a player photo and career highlights. The cards are numbered in the bottom left as "X" of 20 and are sequenced in alphabetical order.

	MINT	NRMT	EXC
COMPLETE SET (20)	20.00	9.00	2.50
COMMON CARD (1-20)	.25	.11	.03
☐ 1 Moises Alou	.50	.23	.06
☐ 2 Albert Belle	2.00	.90	.25
☐ 3 Craig Biggio	.50	.23	.06
☐ 4 Wade Boggs	.75	.35	.09
☐ 5 Barry Bonds	1.25	.55	.16
☐ 6 David Cone	.50	.23	.06
☐ 7 Ken Griffey Jr.	5.00	2.20	.60
☐ 8 Tony Gwynn	2.00	.90	.25
☐ 9 Chuck Knoblauch	.75	.35	.09
☐ 10 Barry Larkin	.75	.35	.09
☐ 11 Kenny Lofton	1.25	.55	.16
☐ 12 Greg Maddux	3.00	1.35	.35
☐ 13 Fred McGriff	.75	.35	.09
☐ 14 Paul O'Neill	.25	.11	.03
☐ 15 Mike Piazza	3.00	1.35	.35
☐ 16 Kirby Puckett	2.00	.90	.25
☐ 17 Cal Ripken	4.00	1.80	.50
☐ 18 Ivan Rodriguez	1.25	.55	.16
☐ 19 Frank Thomas	5.00	2.20	.60
☐ 20 Matt Williams	.75	.35	.09

1995 Ultra All-Stars Gold Medallion

This 20 card set parallels the All-Star insert set. The cards are produced in less quantity than the regular All-Star cards and feature a Gold Medallion logo.

	MINT	NRMT	EXC
COMPLETE SET (20)	60.00	27.00	7.50
COMMON CARD (1-20)	.75	.35	.09

*GOLD MEDALLION: 1.5X TO 3X BASIC CARDS

1995 Ultra Award Winners

Featuring players who won major awards in 1994, this 25-card standard-size set was inserted one in every four first series packs. The horizontal fronts feature a full-color photo as well as a "stretched"

duotone photo. The award the player won is indicated at the top while the player's name is on the bottom. The backs feature two more photos as well as reasons for the player winning the given award. The cards are numbered as "X" of 25.

	MINT	NRMT	EXC
COMPLETE SET (25)	20.00	9.00	2.50
COMMON CARD (1-25)	.25	.11	.03
☐ 1 Ivan Rodriguez	1.25	.55	.16
☐ 2 Don Mattingly	2.50	1.10	.30
☐ 3 Roberto Alomar	1.00	.45	.12
☐ 4 Wade Boggs	.60	.25	.07
☐ 5 Omar Vizquel	.40	.18	.05
☐ 6 Ken Griffey Jr.	5.00	2.20	.60
☐ 7 Kenny Lofton	1.25	.55	.16
☐ 8 Devon White	.25	.11	.03
☐ 9 Mark Langston	.25	.11	.03
☐ 10 Tom Pagnozzi	.25	.11	.03
☐ 11 Jeff Bagwell	2.00	.90	.25
☐ 12 Craig Biggio	.40	.18	.05
☐ 13 Matt Williams	.60	.25	.07
☐ 14 Barry Larkin	.60	.25	.07
☐ 15 Barry Bonds	1.25	.55	.16
☐ 16 Marquis Grissom	.40	.18	.05
☐ 17 Darren Lewis	.25	.11	.03
☐ 18 Greg Maddux	3.00	1.35	.35
☐ 19 Frank Thomas	5.00	2.20	.60
☐ 20 Jeff Bagwell	2.00	.90	.25
☐ 21 David Cone	.40	.18	.05
☐ 22 Greg Maddux	3.00	1.35	.35
☐ 23 Bob Hamelin	.25	.11	.03
☐ 24 Raul Mondesi	.60	.25	.07
☐ 25 Moises Alou	.40	.18	.05

1995 Ultra Award Winners Gold Medallion

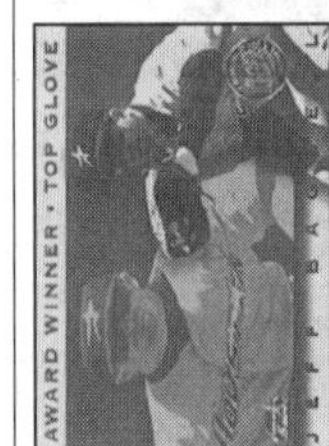

This 25 card set parallels the regular Award Winner insert set. Produced in less quantity than the regular Award Winner set the cards are differentiated by a Gold Medallion logo on the front.

	MINT	NRMT	EXC
COMPLETE SET (25)	60.00	27.00	7.50
COMMON CARD (1-25)	.75	.35	.09

*GOLD MEDALLION: 1.5X TO 3X BASIC CARDS

1995 Ultra Gold Medallion Rookies

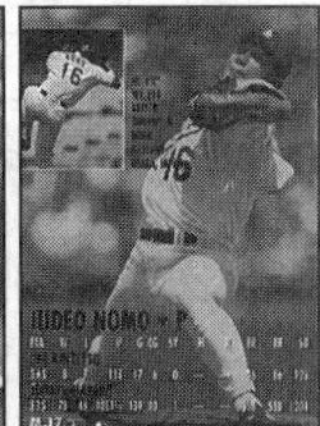

This 20-card standard-size set was available through a mail-in wrapper offer that expired 9/30/95. These players featured were all rookies in 1995 and were not included in the regular Ultra set. The design is essentially the same as the corresponding basic cards save for the medallion in the upper left-hand corner. The cards are numbered with an "M" prefix. The set is sequenced in alphabetical order.

	MINT	NRMT	EXC
COMPLETE SET (20)	15.00	6.75	1.85
COMMON CARD (M1-M20)	.25	.11	.03
UNLISTED STARS	1.00	.45	.12
☐ M1 Manny Alexander	.25	.11	.03
☐ M2 Edgardo Alfonzo	.50	.23	.06
☐ M3 Jason Bates	.25	.11	.03
☐ M4 Andres Berumen	.25	.11	.03
☐ M5 Darren Bragg	.25	.11	.03
☐ M6 Jamie Brewington	.25	.11	.03
☐ M7 Jason Christiansen	.25	.11	.03
☐ M8 Brad Clontz	.25	.11	.03
☐ M9 Marty Cordova	2.00	.90	.25
☐ M10 Johnny Damon	.50	.23	.06
☐ M11 Vaughn Eshelman	.25	.11	.03
☐ M12 Chad Fonville	.25	.11	.03
☐ M13 Curtis Goodwin	.25	.11	.03
☐ M14 Tyler Green	.25	.11	.03
☐ M15 Bob Higginson	1.50	.70	.19
☐ M16 Jason Isringhausen	.25	.11	.03
☐ M17 Hideo Nomo	6.00	2.70	.75
☐ M18 Jon Nunnally	.25	.11	.03
☐ M19 Carlos Perez	.25	.11	.03
☐ M20 Julian Tavarez	.25	.11	.03

1995 Ultra Golden Prospects

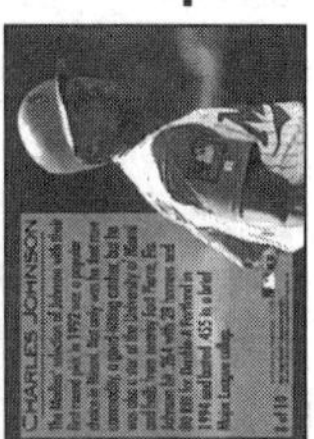

Inserted one every eight first series hobby packs, this 10-card standard-size set features potential impact players. The horizontal fronts feature the same photo with multiple viewpoints giving the impression the photo has been "cut up" into various parts. The words "Golden Prospect" as well as the player's name and team are across the bottom. The horizontal backs have information about his career as well as a normal full-color photo. The cards are numbered as "X" of 10 and are sequenced alphabetically.

	MINT	NRMT	EXC
COMPLETE SET (10)	10.00	4.50	1.25
COMMON CARD (1-10)	.50	.23	.06
☐ 1 James Baldwin	1.25	.55	.16
☐ 2 Alan Benes	.75	.35	.09
☐ 3 Armando Benitez	.50	.23	.06
☐ 4 Ray Durham	.60	.25	.07
☐ 5 LaTroy Hawkins	.50	.23	.06
☐ 6 Brian L.Hunter	1.00	.45	.12
☐ 7 Derek Jeter	5.00	2.20	.60
☐ 8 Charles Johnson	.60	.25	.07
☐ 9 Alex Rodriguez	8.00	3.60	1.00
☐ 10 Michael Tucker	.75	.35	.09

1995 Ultra Golden Prospects Gold Medallion

This 10 card set is a parallel to the regular Golden Prospect set. They are produced in lesser quantity than the regular cards and are differentiated by a Gold Medallion logo on the front.

	MINT	NRMT	EXC
COMPLETE SET (10)	30.00	13.50	3.70
COMMON CARD (1-10)	1.50	.70	.19

*GOLD MEDALLION: 1.5X TO 3X BASIC CARDS

1995 Ultra Hitting Machines

This 10-card standard-size set features some of baseball's leading batters. Inserted one in every eight second-series retail packs, these horizontal cards have the player's photo against a background of the words "Hitting Machine." The player's name and team are identified on the bottom. The horizontal backs feature another player photo and reasons why they are great batters. The cards are numbered as "X" of 10 in the upper right and are sequenced in alphabetical order.

	MINT	NRMT	EXC
COMPLETE SET (10)	15.00	6.75	1.85
COMMON CARD (1-10)	.50	.23	.06

*GOLD MEDALLION: 1.5X TO 3X BASIC CARDS

	MINT	NRMT	EXC
☐ 1 Jeff Bagwell	2.00	.90	.25
☐ 2 Albert Belle	2.00	.90	.25
☐ 3 Dante Bichette	.50	.23	.06
☐ 4 Barry Bonds	1.25	.55	.16
☐ 5 Jose Canseco	.50	.23	.06
☐ 6 Ken Griffey Jr.	5.00	2.20	.60
☐ 7 Tony Gwynn	2.00	.90	.25

	MINT	NRMT	EXC
☐ 8 Fred McGriff	.50	.23	.06
☐ 9 Mike Piazza	3.00	1.35	.35
☐ 10 Frank Thomas	5.00	2.20	.60

1995 Ultra Hitting Machines Gold Medallion

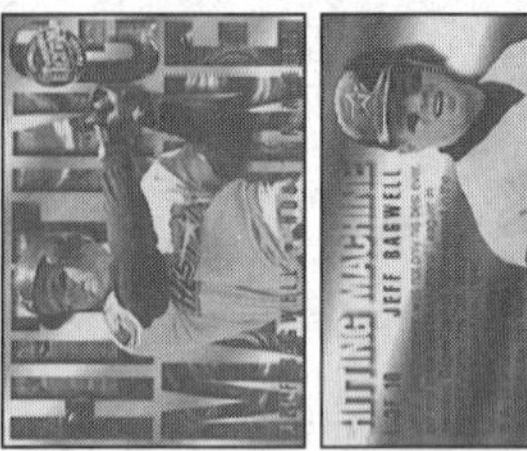

This 10 card set is a parallel to the regular Hitting Machine set. They are printed in less quantity than the regular Hitting Machine set and are differentiated by having a Gold Medallion logo on the front.

	MINT	NRMT	EXC
COMPLETE SET (10)	45.00	20.00	5.50
COMMON CARD (1-10)	1.50	.70	.19

*GOLD MEDALLION: 1.5X TO 3X BASIC CARDS

1995 Ultra Home Run Kings

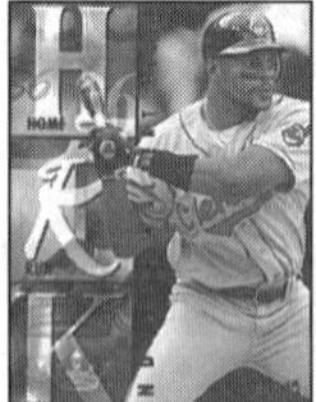

This 10-card standard-size set featured the five leading home run hitters in each league. These cards were issued one every eight first series retail packs. These cards have a player photo on one side with the letters HRK on the other side. The player is identified vertically in the middle. The backs have information about the playeris home run prowess as well as another action photo. The cards are numbered as "X" of 10 and are sequenced by league according to 1994's home rum standings.

	MINT	NRMT	EXC
COMPLETE SET (10)	35.00	16.00	4.40
COMMON CARD (1-10)	1.00	.45	.12
☐ 1 Ken Griffey Jr.	12.00	5.50	1.50
☐ 2 Frank Thomas	12.00	5.50	1.50
☐ 3 Albert Belle	5.00	2.20	.60
☐ 4 Jose Canseco	1.50	.70	.19
☐ 5 Cecil Fielder	1.00	.45	.12
☐ 6 Matt Williams	1.50	.70	.19
☐ 7 Jeff Bagwell	5.00	2.20	.60
☐ 8 Barry Bonds	3.00	1.35	.35
☐ 9 Fred McGriff	1.50	.70	.19
☐ 10 Andres Galarraga	1.50	.70	.19

1995 Ultra Home Run Kings Gold Medallion

This 10 card set parallels the regular Home Run King insert set. These cards, inserted less frequently than the regular Home Run Kings cards, feature a gold medallion logo on the front.

	MINT	NRMT	EXC
COMPLETE SET (10)	100.00	45.00	12.50
COMMON CARD (1-10)	3.00	1.35	.35

*GOLD MEDALLION: 1.5X TO 3X BASIC CARDS

1995 Ultra League Leaders

This 10-card standard-size set was inserted one in three first series packs. The horizontal fronts feature a player photo against a background of his leagueís logo. The player is identified in one corner and the category he led the league in is featured in the other corner. The horizontal backs have a player photo as well as explaining more about the stat with which he paced the field.

	MINT	NRMT	EXC
COMPLETE SET (10)	8.00	3.60	1.00
COMMON CARD (1-10)	.25	.11	.03
☐ 1 Paul O'Neill	.25	.11	.03
☐ 2 Kenny Lofton	1.25	.55	.16
☐ 3 Jimmy Key	.25	.11	.03
☐ 4 Randy Johnson	.75	.35	.09
☐ 5 Lee Smith	.50	.23	.06
☐ 6 Tony Gwynn	2.00	.90	.25
☐ 7 Craig Biggio	.50	.23	.06
☐ 8 Greg Maddux	3.00	1.35	.35
☐ 9 Andy Benes	.25	.11	.03
☐ 10 John Franco	.25	.11	.03

1995 Ultra League Leaders Gold Medallion

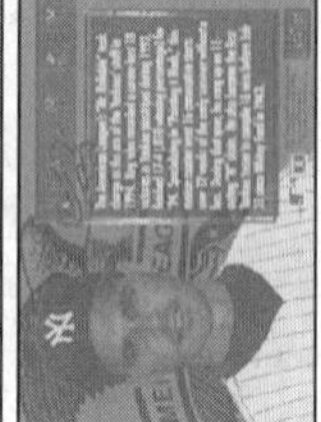

This 10 card set is a parallel to the regular League Leaders set. The cards printed in less quantity than the regular Ultra cards feature a "Gold Medallion" logo on the front.

	MINT	NRMT	EXC
COMPLETE SET (10)	25.00	11.00	3.10
COMMON CARD (1-10)	.75	.35	.09

*GOLD MEDALLION: 1.5X TO 3X BASIC CARDS

1995 Ultra On-Base Leaders

This 10-card standard-size set features ten players who are constantly reaching base safely. These cards were inserted one in every eight pre-priced second series jumbo packs. The fronts have an action photo against a background of several smaller action photos. The words "On-Base Leaders" are featured in the upper right corner along with the player's name. The horizontal backs contain the player's team, some information on how often they get on base and a player photo. The cards are numbered in the upper right corner as "X" of 10 and are sequenced in alphabetical order.

	MINT	NRMT	EXC
COMPLETE SET (10)	40.00	18.00	5.00
COMMON CARD (1-10)	2.50	1.10	.30
☐ 1 Jeff Bagwell	8.00	3.60	1.00
☐ 2 Albert Belle	8.00	3.60	1.00
☐ 3 Craig Biggio	3.00	1.35	.35
☐ 4 Wade Boggs	4.00	1.80	.50
☐ 5 Barry Bonds	5.00	2.20	.60
☐ 6 Will Clark	4.00	1.80	.50
☐ 7 Tony Gwynn	8.00	3.60	1.00
☐ 8 David Justice	2.50	1.10	.30
☐ 9 Paul O'Neill	2.50	1.10	.30
☐ 10 Frank Thomas	20.00	9.00	2.50

1995 Ultra On-Base Leaders Gold Medallion

This 10 card set is a parallel to the On-Base Leaders insert set. Differentiated from the regular cards by a Gold Medallion logo, these cards are printed in shorter supply the regular On-Base leader cards.

	MINT	NRMT	EXC
COMPLETE SET (10)	125.00	55.00	15.50
COMMON CARD (1-10)	7.50	3.40	.95

*GOLD MEDALLION: 1.5X TO 3X BASIC CARDS

1995 Ultra Power Plus

This six-card standard-size set was inserted one in every 37 first series packs. The six players portrayed are not only sluggers, but also excel at another part of the game. Unlike the 1995 Ultra cards and the other insert sets, these cards are 100 percent foil. The fronts have a player photo against a background that has the words "Power Plus" spelled in various size letters. The player and his team are identified on the bottom in gold foil. The backs have a player photo and some player information. The cards are numbered on the bottom right as "X" of 6 and are sequenced in alphabetical order by league.

	MINT	NRMT	EXC
COMPLETE SET (6)	50.00	22.00	6.25
COMMON CARD (1-6)	2.50	1.10	.30
☐ 1 Albert Belle	8.00	3.60	1.00
☐ 2 Ken Griffey Jr.	20.00	9.00	2.50
☐ 3 Frank Thomas	20.00	9.00	2.50
☐ 4 Jeff Bagwell	8.00	3.60	1.00
☐ 5 Barry Bonds	5.00	2.20	.60
☐ 6 Matt Williams	2.50	1.10	.30

1995 Ultra Power Plus Gold Medallion

This six card set parallels the regular Power Plus set. These cards, witha Gold Medallion logo on the front, are printed in lesser quantity than the regular insert cards.

	MINT	NRMT	EXC
COMPLETE SET (6)	150.00	70.00	19.00
COMMON CARD (1-6)	7.50	3.40	.95

*GOLD MEDALLION: 1.5X TO 3X BASIC CARDS

1995 Ultra RBI Kings

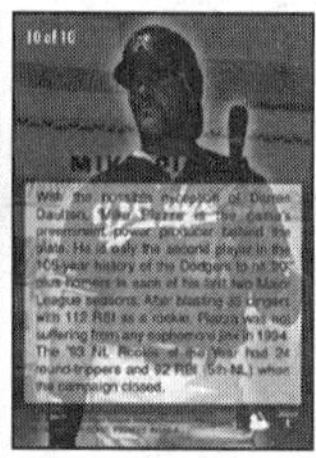

This 10-card standard-size set was inserted into series one jumbo packs at a rate of one every 11. The cards feature a player photo against a multi-colored background. The player's name, the words "RBI King" as well as his team identity are printed in gold foil in the middle. The backs have a player photo as well as some information about the players batting prowess. The cards are numbered in the upper left as "X" of 10 and are sequenced in order by league.

	MINT	NRMT	EXC
COMPLETE SET (10)	50.00	22.00	6.25
COMMON CARD (1-10)	1.50	.70	.19
☐ 1 Kirby Puckett	8.00	3.60	1.00
☐ 2 Joe Carter	2.00	.90	.25
☐ 3 Albert Belle	8.00	3.60	1.00
☐ 4 Frank Thomas	20.00	9.00	2.50
☐ 5 Julio Franco	1.50	.70	.19
☐ 6 Jeff Bagwell	8.00	3.60	1.00
☐ 7 Matt Williams	2.50	1.10	.30
☐ 8 Dante Bichette	2.50	1.10	.30
☐ 9 Fred McGriff	2.50	1.10	.30
☐ 10 Mike Piazza	12.00	5.50	1.50

1995 Ultra RBI Kings Gold Medallion

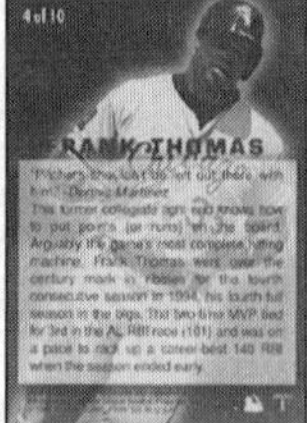

This 10 card set parallels the regular RBI King insert set. These cards are inserted into packs with less frequency than the regular RBI King cards and are valued at a mulitplier of the regular RBI King cards

	MINT	NRMT	EXC
COMPLETE SET (10)	150.00	70.00	19.00
COMMON CARD (1-10)	5.00	2.20	.60

*GOLD MEDALLION: 1.5X TO 3X BASIC CARDS

1995 Ultra Rising Stars

This nine-card standard-size set was inserted one every 37 second series packs. Horizontal fronts feature two photos with the words "Rising Stars" as well as the player's name and team on the bottom left. This front design is set against a shiny background. The backs contain player information as well as a player photo. The cards are numbered "X" of 9 and are sequenced in alphabetical order.

	MINT	NRMT	EXC
COMPLETE SET (9)	80.00	36.00	10.00
COMMON CARD (1-9)	2.00	.90	.25
☐ 1 Moises Alou	2.00	.90	.25
☐ 2 Jeff Bagwell	12.00	5.50	1.50
☐ 3 Albert Belle	12.00	5.50	1.50
☐ 4 Juan Gonzalez	15.00	6.75	1.85
☐ 5 Chuck Knoblauch	4.00	1.80	.50
☐ 6 Kenny Lofton	8.00	3.60	1.00
☐ 7 Raul Mondesi	4.00	1.80	.50
☐ 8 Mike Piazza	20.00	9.00	2.50
☐ 9 Frank Thomas	30.00	13.50	3.70

1995 Ultra Rising Stars Gold Medallion

This nine card set is a parallel to the regular Rising Stars insert set. The cards are differentiated by a Gold Medallion logo on the front and are valued as a multiplier of the regular Rising Cards cards.

	MINT	NRMT	EXC
COMPLETE SET (9)	250.00	110.00	31.00
COMMON CARD (1-9)	6.00	2.70	.75

*GOLD MEDALLION: 1.5X TO 3X BASIC CARDS

	MINT	NRMT	EXC
☐ 1 Moises Alou	4.00	1.80	.50

1995 Ultra Second Year Standouts

This 15-card standard-size set was inserted into first series packs at a rate of not greater than one in six packs. The players in this set were all rookies in 1994 whom big things were expected from in 1995. The horizontal fronts feature the player's photo against a yellowish background. The player, his team's identification as well as the team logo are all printed in gold foil in the middle. The horizontal backs have another player photo as well as information about the player's 1994 season. The cards are numbered in the lower right as "X" of 15 and are sequenced in alphabetical order.

	MINT	NRMT	EXC
COMPLETE SET (15)	10.00	4.50	1.25
COMMON CARD (1-15)	.50	.23	.06
☐ 1 Cliff Floyd	.50	.23	.06
☐ 2 Chris Gomez	.50	.23	.06
☐ 3 Rusty Greer	1.00	.45	.12
☐ 4 Darren Hall	.50	.23	.06
☐ 5 Bob Hamelin	.50	.23	.06
☐ 6 Joey Hamilton	1.50	.70	.19

☐ 7 Jeffrey Hammonds	.50	.23	.06
☐ 8 John Hudek	.50	.23	.06
☐ 9 Ryan Klesko	1.00	.45	.12
☐ 10 Raul Mondesi	1.50	.70	.19
☐ 11 Manny Ramirez	3.00	1.35	.35
☐ 12 Bill Risley	.50	.23	.06
☐ 13 Steve Trachsel	.50	.23	.06
☐ 14 W.VanLandingham	.50	.23	.06
☐ 15 Rondell White	.75	.35	.09

1995 Ultra Second Year Standouts Gold Medallion

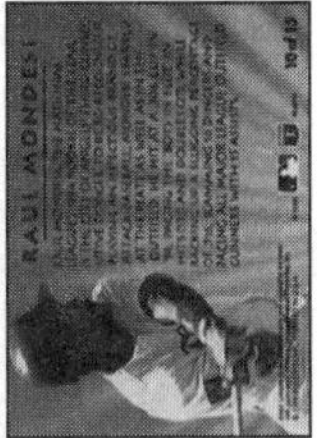

These 15 cards are a parallel to the regular Second Year Standout insert set. The cards are differentiated by a Gold Medallion logo on the front and are printed in lesser quantity than the regular Second Year Standout cards.

	MINT	NRMT	EXC
COMPLETE SET (15)	30.00	13.50	3.70
COMMON CARD (1-15)	1.50	.70	.19

*GOLD MEDALLION: 1.5X TO 3X BASIC CARDS

1995 Ultra Strikeout Kings

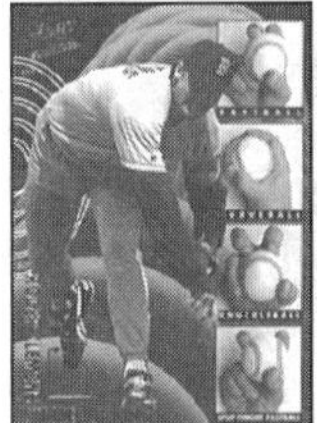
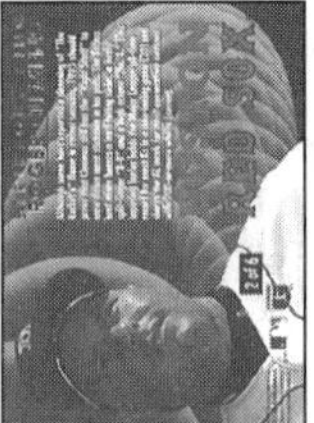

This six-card standard-size set was inserted one every five second series packs. The fronts have a player photo as well as photos of grips for four major pitches. The player's name as well as the words "Strikeout King" is printed in a bottom corner. The horizontal backs feature a player photo, a brief blurb as well as a team logo. The cards are numbered as "X" of 6 and are sequenced in alphabetical order.

	MINT	NRMT	EXC
COMPLETE SET (6)	5.00	2.20	.60
COMMON CARD (1-6)	.25	.11	.03
☐ 1 Andy Benes	.50	.23	.06
☐ 2 Roger Clemens	1.00	.45	.12
☐ 3 Randy Johnson	.75	.35	.09
☐ 4 Greg Maddux	3.00	1.35	.35
☐ 5 Pedro Martinez	.50	.23	.06
☐ 6 Jose Rijo	.25	.11	.03

1995 Ultra Strikeout Kings Gold Medallion

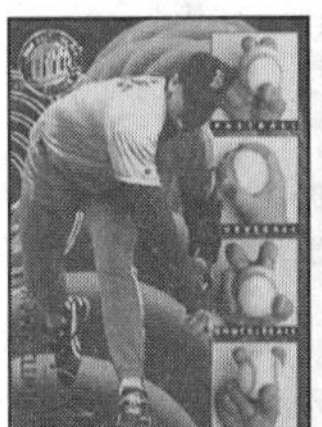

These six cards parallel the regular Strikeout Kings insert cards. These cards, which have a Gold Medallion logo on the front, are printed in lesser quantity than the regular Strikeout King cards and are valued as a multiple of the regular cards.

	MINT	NRMT	EXC
COMPLETE SET (6)	15.00	6.75	1.85
COMMON CARD (1-6)	.75	.35	.09

*GOLD MEDALLION: 1.5X TO 3X BASIC CARDS

1996 Ultra Promos

This 3-card standard-size set previews the 1996 Ultra series. The Griffey card represents the basic set and has the same front and back as its regular issue counterpart. The other two cards are from insert series and carry advertisements on their backs. Each card has the disclaimer "PROMOTIONAL SAMPLE" stamped diagonally across it. Since the cards are unnumbered, they are checklisted below in alphabetical order.

	MINT	NRMT	EXC
COMPLETE SET (3)	5.00	2.20	.60
COMMON CARD (1-3)	1.00	.45	.12
☐ 1 Barry Bonds HR King	1.00	.45	.12
☐ 2 Ken Griffey Jr.	2.00	.90	.25
☐ 3 Cal Ripken Prime Leather	2.00	.90	.25

1996 Ultra

The 1996 Ultra set, produced by Fleer, contains 600 standard-size cards. The cards were distributed in packs that included two inserts. One insert is a Gold Medallion parallel while the other insert comes from one of the many Ultra insert sets. The cards are thicker than their 1995 counterparts and the fronts feature the player in an action shot in full-bleed color. Player's name and team are emblazoned across the bottom in silver foil. Backs show the players in two action shots and one pose. The backs are full-bleed color and include biography and player 1995 statistics in gold print across the bottom. The cards are sequenced in alphabetical order within league and team order.

	MINT	NRMT	EXC
COMPLETE SET (600)	60.00	27.00	7.50
COMPLETE SERIES 1 (300)	30.00	13.50	3.70
COMPLETE SERIES 2 (300)	30.00	13.50	3.70
COMMON CARD (1-600)	.10	.05	.01
☐ 1 Manny Alexander	.10	.05	.01
☐ 2 Brady Anderson	.50	.23	.06
☐ 3 Bobby Bonilla	.25	.11	.03
☐ 4 Scott Erickson	.10	.05	.01
☐ 5 Curtis Goodwin	.10	.05	.01
☐ 6 Chris Hoiles	.10	.05	.01
☐ 7 Doug Jones	.10	.05	.01
☐ 8 Jeff Manto	.10	.05	.01
☐ 9 Mike Mussina	.60	.25	.07
☐ 10 Rafael Palmeiro	.50	.23	.06
☐ 11 Cal Ripken	2.50	1.10	.30
☐ 12 Rick Aguilera	.10	.05	.01
☐ 13 Luis Alicea	.10	.05	.01
☐ 14 Stan Belinda	.10	.05	.01
☐ 15 Jose Canseco	.50	.23	.06
☐ 16 Roger Clemens	.60	.25	.07
☐ 17 Mike Greenwell	.10	.05	.01
☐ 18 Mike Macfarlane	.10	.05	.01
☐ 19 Tim Naehring	.25	.11	.03
☐ 20 Troy O'Leary	.25	.11	.03
☐ 21 John Valentin	.25	.11	.03
☐ 22 Mo Vaughn	.75	.35	.09
☐ 23 Tim Wakefield	.10	.05	.01
☐ 24 Brian Anderson	.10	.05	.01
☐ 25 Garret Anderson	.50	.23	.06
☐ 26 Chili Davis	.10	.05	.01
☐ 27 Gary DiSarcina	.10	.05	.01
☐ 28 Jim Edmonds	.25	.11	.03
☐ 29 Jorge Fabregas	.10	.05	.01
☐ 30 Chuck Finley	.10	.05	.01
☐ 31 Mark Langston	.10	.05	.01
☐ 32 Troy Percival	.25	.11	.03
☐ 33 Tim Salmon	.50	.23	.06
☐ 34 Lee Smith	.25	.11	.03
☐ 35 Wilson Alvarez	.50	.23	.06
☐ 36 Ray Durham	.50	.23	.06
☐ 37 Alex Fernandez	.25	.11	.03
☐ 38 Ozzie Guillen	.10	.05	.01
☐ 39 Roberto Hernandez	.25	.11	.03
☐ 40 Lance Johnson	.25	.11	.03
☐ 41 Ron Karkovice	.10	.05	.01
☐ 42 Lyle Mouton	.10	.05	.01
☐ 43 Tim Raines	.50	.23	.06
☐ 44 Frank Thomas	3.00	1.35	.35
☐ 45 Carlos Baerga	.25	.11	.03
☐ 46 Albert Belle	1.25	.55	.16
☐ 47 Orel Hershiser	.25	.11	.03
☐ 48 Kenny Lofton	.75	.35	.09
☐ 49 Dennis Martinez	.25	.11	.03
☐ 50 Jose Mesa	.25	.11	.03
☐ 51 Eddie Murray	.75	.35	.09
☐ 52 Chad Ogea	.10	.05	.01
☐ 53 Manny Ramirez	.75	.35	.09
☐ 54 Jim Thome	.60	.25	.07
☐ 55 Omar Vizquel	.25	.11	.03
☐ 56 Dave Winfield	.50	.23	.06
☐ 57 Chad Curtis	.10	.05	.01
☐ 58 Cecil Fielder	.25	.11	.03
☐ 59 John Flaherty	.10	.05	.01
☐ 60 Travis Fryman	.25	.11	.03
☐ 61 Chris Gomez	.10	.05	.01
☐ 62 Bob Higginson	.50	.23	.06
☐ 63 Felipe Lira	.10	.05	.01
☐ 64 Brian Maxcy	.10	.05	.01
☐ 65 Alan Trammell	.25	.11	.03
☐ 66 Lou Whitaker	.25	.11	.03
☐ 67 Kevin Appier	.25	.11	.03
☐ 68 Gary Gaetti	.25	.11	.03
☐ 69 Tom Goodwin	.25	.11	.03
☐ 70 Tom Gordon	.10	.05	.01
☐ 71 Jason Jacome	.10	.05	.01
☐ 72 Wally Joyner	.10	.05	.01
☐ 73 Brent Mayne	.10	.05	.01
☐ 74 Jeff Montgomery	.10	.05	.01
☐ 75 Jon Nunnally	.10	.05	.01
☐ 76 Joe Vitiello	.10	.05	.01
☐ 77 Ricky Bones	.10	.05	.01
☐ 78 Jeff Cirillo	.10	.05	.01
☐ 79 Mike Fetters	.10	.05	.01
☐ 80 Darryl Hamilton	.10	.05	.01
☐ 81 David Hulse	.10	.05	.01
☐ 82 Dave Nilsson	.25	.11	.03
☐ 83 Kevin Seitzer	.10	.05	.01
☐ 84 Steve Sparks	.10	.05	.01
☐ 85 B.J. Surhoff	.10	.05	.01
☐ 86 Jose Valentin	.10	.05	.01
☐ 87 Greg Vaughn	.50	.23	.06
☐ 88 Marty Cordova	.25	.11	.03
☐ 89 Chuck Knoblauch	.50	.23	.06
☐ 90 Pat Meares	.10	.05	.01
☐ 91 Pedro Munoz	.10	.05	.01
☐ 92 Kirby Puckett	1.25	.55	.16
☐ 93 Brad Radke	.10	.05	.01
☐ 94 Scott Stahoviak	.10	.05	.01
☐ 95 Dave Stevens	.10	.05	.01
☐ 96 Mike Trombley	.10	.05	.01
☐ 97 Matt Walbeck	.10	.05	.01
☐ 98 Wade Boggs	.50	.23	.06
☐ 99 Russ Davis	.10	.05	.01
☐ 100 Jim Leyritz	.10	.05	.01
☐ 101 Don Mattingly	1.50	.70	.19
☐ 102 Jack McDowell	.50	.23	.06
☐ 103 Paul O'Neill	.10	.05	.01
☐ 104 Andy Pettitte	1.00	.45	.12
☐ 105 Mariano Rivera	.25	.11	.03
☐ 106 Ruben Sierra	.10	.05	.01
☐ 107 Darryl Strawberry	.25	.11	.03
☐ 108 John Wetteland	.25	.11	.03
☐ 109 Bernie Williams	.60	.25	.07
☐ 110 Geronimo Berroa	.25	.11	.03
☐ 111 Scott Brosius	.25	.11	.03
☐ 112 Dennis Eckersley	.25	.11	.03
☐ 113 Brent Gates	.10	.05	.01
☐ 114 Rickey Henderson	.50	.23	.06
☐ 115 Mark McGwire	1.00	.45	.12
☐ 116 Ariel Prieto	.10	.05	.01
☐ 117 Terry Steinbach	.25	.11	.03
☐ 118 Todd Stottlemyre	.10	.05	.01
☐ 119 Todd Van Poppel	.10	.05	.01
☐ 120 Steve Wojciechowski	.10	.05	.01
☐ 121 Rich Amaral	.10	.05	.01
☐ 122 Bobby Ayala	.10	.05	.01
☐ 123 Mike Blowers	.10	.05	.01
☐ 124 Chris Bosio	.10	.05	.01
☐ 125 Joey Cora	.10	.05	.01
☐ 126 Ken Griffey Jr.	3.00	1.35	.35
☐ 127 Randy Johnson	.50	.23	.06
☐ 128 Edgar Martinez	.25	.11	.03
☐ 129 Tino Martinez	.25	.11	.03
☐ 130 Alex Rodriguez	3.00	1.35	.35
☐ 131 Dan Wilson	.10	.05	.01
☐ 132 Will Clark	.50	.23	.06
☐ 133 Jeff Frye	.10	.05	.01
☐ 134 Benji Gil	.10	.05	.01
☐ 135 Juan Gonzalez	1.50	.70	.19
☐ 136 Rusty Greer	.50	.23	.06
☐ 137 Mark McLemore	.10	.05	.01
☐ 138 Roger Pavlik	.10	.05	.01
☐ 139 Ivan Rodriguez	.75	.35	.09
☐ 140 Kenny Rogers	.10	.05	.01
☐ 141 Mickey Tettleton	.25	.11	.03
☐ 142 Roberto Alomar	.60	.25	.07
☐ 143 Joe Carter	.25	.11	.03
☐ 144 Tony Castillo	.10	.05	.01
☐ 145 Alex Gonzalez	.10	.05	.01
☐ 146 Shawn Green	.25	.11	.03
☐ 147 Pat Hentgen	.25	.11	.03
☐ 148 Sandy Martinez	.10	.05	.01
☐ 149 Paul Molitor	.60	.25	.07
☐ 150 John Olerud	.10	.05	.01
☐ 151 Ed Sprague	.25	.11	.03
☐ 152 Jeff Blauser	.10	.05	.01
☐ 153 Brad Clontz	.10	.05	.01
☐ 154 Tom Glavine	.50	.23	.06
☐ 155 Marquis Grissom	.25	.11	.03
☐ 156 Chipper Jones	2.00	.90	.25
☐ 157 David Justice	.25	.11	.03
☐ 158 Ryan Klesko	.50	.23	.06
☐ 159 Javier Lopez	.50	.23	.06
☐ 160 Greg Maddux	2.00	.90	.25
☐ 161 John Smoltz	.50	.23	.06
☐ 162 Mark Wohlers	.25	.11	.03
☐ 163 Jim Bullinger	.10	.05	.01
☐ 164 Frank Castillo	.10	.05	.01
☐ 165 Shawon Dunston	.10	.05	.01
☐ 166 Kevin Foster	.10	.05	.01
☐ 167 Luis Gonzalez	.10	.05	.01
☐ 168 Mark Grace	.50	.23	.06
☐ 169 Rey Sanchez	.10	.05	.01
☐ 170 Scott Servais	.10	.05	.01
☐ 171 Sammy Sosa	.50	.23	.06
☐ 172 Ozzie Timmons	.10	.05	.01
☐ 173 Steve Trachsel	.10	.05	.01
☐ 174 Bret Boone	.10	.05	.01
☐ 175 Jeff Branson	.10	.05	.01
☐ 176 Jeff Brantley	.10	.05	.01
☐ 177 Dave Burba	.10	.05	.01
☐ 178 Ron Gant	.25	.11	.03
☐ 179 Barry Larkin	.50	.23	.06
☐ 180 Darren Lewis	.10	.05	.01
☐ 181 Mark Portugal	.10	.05	.01
☐ 182 Reggie Sanders	.25	.11	.03
☐ 183 Pete Schourek	.25	.11	.03
☐ 184 John Smiley	.10	.05	.01
☐ 185 Jason Bates	.10	.05	.01
☐ 186 Dante Bichette	.50	.23	.06
☐ 187 Ellis Burks	.25	.11	.03
☐ 188 Vinny Castilla	.25	.11	.03
☐ 189 Andres Galarraga	.50	.23	.06
☐ 190 Darren Holmes	.10	.05	.01
☐ 191 Armando Reynoso	.10	.05	.01
☐ 192 Kevin Ritz	.10	.05	.01
☐ 193 Bill Swift	.10	.05	.01
☐ 194 Larry Walker	.50	.23	.06
☐ 195 Kurt Abbott	.10	.05	.01
☐ 196 John Burkett	.10	.05	.01
☐ 197 Greg Colbrunn	.50	.23	.06
☐ 198 Jeff Conine	.25	.11	.03
☐ 199 Andre Dawson	.25	.11	.03
☐ 200 Chris Hammond	.10	.05	.01
☐ 201 Charles Johnson	.25	.11	.03
☐ 202 Robb Nen	.10	.05	.01
☐ 203 Terry Pendleton	.25	.11	.03
☐ 204 Quilvio Veras	.10	.05	.01
☐ 205 Jeff Bagwell	1.25	.55	.16
☐ 206 Derek Bell	.25	.11	.03
☐ 207 Doug Drabek	.10	.05	.01
☐ 208 Tony Eusebio	.10	.05	.01
☐ 209 Mike Hampton	.10	.05	.01
☐ 210 Brian L. Hunter	.25	.11	.03
☐ 211 Todd Jones	.10	.05	.01
☐ 212 Orlando Miller	.10	.05	.01
☐ 213 James Mouton	.10	.05	.01
☐ 214 Shane Reynolds	.25	.11	.03
☐ 215 Dave Veres	.10	.05	.01
☐ 216 Billy Ashley	.10	.05	.01
☐ 217 Brett Butler	.10	.05	.01
☐ 218 Chad Fonville	.10	.05	.01
☐ 219 Todd Hollandsworth	.25	.11	.03
☐ 220 Eric Karros	.25	.11	.03
☐ 221 Ramon Martinez	.25	.11	.03
☐ 222 Raul Mondesi	.50	.23	.06
☐ 223 Hideo Nomo	.75	.35	.09
☐ 224 Mike Piazza	2.00	.90	.25
☐ 225 Kevin Tapani	.10	.05	.01
☐ 226 Ismael Valdes	.25	.11	.03
☐ 227 Todd Worrell	.25	.11	.03
☐ 228 Moises Alou	.25	.11	.03
☐ 229 Wil Cordero	.10	.05	.01
☐ 230 Jeff Fassero	.10	.05	.01
☐ 231 Darrin Fletcher	.10	.05	.01
☐ 232 Mike Lansing	.10	.05	.01
☐ 233 Pedro J.Martinez	.25	.11	.03
☐ 234 Carlos Perez	.10	.05	.01
☐ 235 Mel Rojas	.25	.11	.03
☐ 236 David Segui	.10	.05	.01
☐ 237 Tony Tarasco	.10	.05	.01
☐ 238 Rondell White	.25	.11	.03
☐ 239 Edgardo Alfonzo	.25	.11	.03
☐ 240 Rico Brogna	.10	.05	.01
☐ 241 Carl Everett	.10	.05	.01
☐ 242 Todd Hundley	.25	.11	.03
☐ 243 Butch Huskey	.25	.11	.03
☐ 244 Jason Isringhausen	.50	.23	.06
☐ 245 Bobby Jones	.10	.05	.01
☐ 246 Jeff Kent	.10	.05	.01
☐ 247 Bill Pulsipher	.25	.11	.03
☐ 248 Jose Vizcaino	.10	.05	.01
☐ 249 Ricky Bottalico	.10	.05	.01
☐ 250 Darren Daulton	.25	.11	.03
☐ 251 Jim Eisenreich	.10	.05	.01
☐ 252 Tyler Green	.10	.05	.01
☐ 253 Charlie Hayes	.10	.05	.01
☐ 254 Gregg Jefferies	.50	.23	.06
☐ 255 Tony Longmire	.10	.05	.01
☐ 256 Michael Mimbs	.10	.05	.01
☐ 257 Mickey Morandini	.10	.05	.01
☐ 258 Paul Quantrill	.10	.05	.01
☐ 259 Heathcliff Slocumb	.10	.05	.01
☐ 260 Jay Bell	.25	.11	.03
☐ 261 Jacob Brumfield	.10	.05	.01
☐ 262 Angelo Encarnacion	.10	.05	.01
☐ 263 John Ericks	.10	.05	.01
☐ 264 Mark Johnson	.10	.05	.01
☐ 265 Esteban Loaiza	.10	.05	.01
☐ 266 Al Martin	.10	.05	.01
☐ 267 Orlando Merced	.25	.11	.03
☐ 268 Dan Miceli	.10	.05	.01

☐ 269 Denny Neagle	.25	.11	.03
☐ 270 Brian Barber	.10	.05	.01
☐ 271 Scott Cooper	.10	.05	.01
☐ 272 Tripp Cromer	.10	.05	.01
☐ 273 Bernard Gilkey	.25	.11	.03
☐ 274 Tom Henke	.25	.11	.03
☐ 275 Brian Jordan	.25	.11	.03
☐ 276 John Mabry	.25	.11	.03
☐ 277 Tom Pagnozzi	.10	.05	.01
☐ 278 Mark Petkovsek	.10	.05	.01
☐ 279 Ozzie Smith	.75	.35	.09
☐ 280 Andy Ashby	.10	.05	.01
☐ 281 Brad Ausmus	.10	.05	.01
☐ 282 Ken Caminiti	.50	.23	.06
☐ 283 Glenn Dishman	.10	.05	.01
☐ 284 Tony Gwynn	1.25	.55	.16
☐ 285 Joey Hamilton	.25	.11	.03
☐ 286 Trevor Hoffman	.25	.11	.03
☐ 287 Phil Plantier	.10	.05	.01
☐ 288 Jody Reed	.10	.05	.01
☐ 289 Eddie Williams	.10	.05	.01
☐ 290 Barry Bonds	.75	.35	.09
☐ 291 Jamie Brewington	.10	.05	.01
☐ 292 Mark Carreon	.10	.05	.01
☐ 293 Royce Clayton	.10	.05	.01
☐ 294 Glenallen Hill	.25	.11	.03
☐ 295 Mark Leiter	.10	.05	.01
☐ 296 Kirt Manwaring	.10	.05	.01
☐ 297 J.R. Phillips	.10	.05	.01
☐ 298 Deion Sanders	.50	.23	.06
☐ 299 Wm. VanLandingham	.10	.05	.01
☐ 300 Matt Williams	.50	.23	.06
☐ 301 Roberto Alomar	.60	.25	.07
☐ 302 Armando Benitez	.10	.05	.01
☐ 303 Mike Devereaux	.10	.05	.01
☐ 304 Jeffrey Hammonds	.10	.05	.01
☐ 305 Jimmy Haynes	.10	.05	.01
☐ 306 Scott McClain	.10	.05	.01
☐ 307 Kent Mercker	.10	.05	.01
☐ 308 Randy Myers	.10	.05	.01
☐ 309 B.J. Surhoff	.10	.05	.01
☐ 310 Tony Tarasco	.10	.05	.01
☐ 311 David Wells	.10	.05	.01
☐ 312 Wil Cordero	.10	.05	.01
☐ 313 Alex Delgado	.10	.05	.01
☐ 314 Tom Gordon	.10	.05	.01
☐ 315 Dwayne Hosey	.10	.05	.01
☐ 316 Jose Malave	.10	.05	.01
☐ 317 Kevin Mitchell	.10	.05	.01
☐ 318 Jamie Moyer	.10	.05	.01
☐ 319 Aaron Sele	.10	.05	.01
☐ 320 Heathcliff Slocumb	.10	.05	.01
☐ 321 Mike Stanley	.10	.05	.01
☐ 322 Jeff Suppan	.50	.23	.06
☐ 323 Jim Abbott	.50	.23	.06
☐ 324 George Arias	.10	.05	.01
☐ 325 Todd Greene	.50	.23	.06
☐ 326 Bryan Harvey	.10	.05	.01
☐ 327 J.T. Snow	.25	.11	.03
☐ 328 Randy Velarde	.10	.05	.01
☐ 329 Tim Wallach	.10	.05	.01
☐ 330 Harold Baines	.25	.11	.03
☐ 331 Jason Bere	.10	.05	.01
☐ 332 Darren Lewis	.10	.05	.01
☐ 333 Norberto Martin	.10	.05	.01
☐ 334 Tony Phillips	.25	.11	.03
☐ 335 Bill Simas	.10	.05	.01
☐ 336 Chris Snopek	.10	.05	.01
☐ 337 Kevin Tapani	.10	.05	.01
☐ 338 Danny Tartabull	.10	.05	.01
☐ 339 Robin Ventura	.25	.11	.03
☐ 340 Sandy Alomar Jr.	.10	.05	.01
☐ 341 Julio Franco	.25	.11	.03
☐ 342 Jack McDowell	.50	.23	.06
☐ 343 Charles Nagy	.25	.11	.03
☐ 344 Julian Tavarez	.10	.05	.01
☐ 345 Kimera Bartee	.10	.05	.01
☐ 346 Greg Keagle	.10	.05	.01
☐ 347 Mark Lewis	.10	.05	.01
☐ 348 Jose Lima	.10	.05	.01
☐ 349 Melvin Nieves	.25	.11	.03
☐ 350 Mark Parent	.10	.05	.01
☐ 351 Eddie Williams	.10	.05	.01
☐ 352 Johnny Damon	.25	.11	.03
☐ 353 Sal Fasano	.10	.05	.01
☐ 354 Mark Gubicza	.10	.05	.01
☐ 355 Bob Hamelin	.10	.05	.01
☐ 356 Chris Haney	.10	.05	.01
☐ 357 Keith Lockhart	.10	.05	.01
☐ 358 Mike Macfarlane	.10	.05	.01
☐ 359 Jose Offerman	.10	.05	.01
☐ 360 Bip Roberts	.10	.05	.01
☐ 361 Michael Tucker	.25	.11	.03
☐ 362 Chuck Carr	.10	.05	.01
☐ 363 Bobby Hughes	.10	.05	.01
☐ 364 John Jaha	.25	.11	.03
☐ 365 Mark Loretta	.10	.05	.01
☐ 366 Mike Matheny	.10	.05	.01
☐ 367 Ben McDonald	.10	.05	.01
☐ 368 Matt Mieske	.10	.05	.01
☐ 369 Angel Miranda	.10	.05	.01
☐ 370 Fernando Vina	.10	.05	.01
☐ 371 Rick Aguilera	.10	.05	.01
☐ 372 Rich Becker	.10	.05	.01
☐ 373 LaTroy Hawkins	.10	.05	.01
☐ 374 Dave Hollins	.10	.05	.01
☐ 375 Roberto Kelly	.10	.05	.01
☐ 376 Matt Lawton	.10	.05	.01
☐ 377 Paul Molitor	.60	.25	.07
☐ 378 Dan Naulty	.10	.05	.01
☐ 379 Rich Robertson	.10	.05	.01
☐ 380 Frank Rodriguez	.10	.05	.01
☐ 381 David Cone	.25	.11	.03
☐ 382 Mariano Duncan	.10	.05	.01
☐ 383 Andy Fox	.10	.05	.01
☐ 384 Joe Girardi	.10	.05	.01
☐ 385 Dwight Gooden	.25	.11	.03
☐ 386 Derek Jeter	2.00	.90	.25
☐ 387 Pat Kelly	.10	.05	.01
☐ 388 Jimmy Key	.25	.11	.03
☐ 389 Matt Luke	.10	.05	.01
☐ 390 Tino Martinez	.25	.11	.03
☐ 391 Jeff Nelson	.10	.05	.01
☐ 392 Melido Perez	.10	.05	.01
☐ 393 Tim Raines	.50	.23	.06
☐ 394 Ruben Rivera	.60	.25	.07
☐ 395 Kenny Rogers	.10	.05	.01
☐ 396 Tony Batista	.50	.23	.06
☐ 397 Allen Battle	.10	.05	.01
☐ 398 Mike Bordick	.25	.11	.03
☐ 399 Steve Cox	.10	.05	.01
☐ 400 Jason Giambi	.50	.23	.06
☐ 401 Doug Johns	.10	.05	.01
☐ 402 Pedro Munoz	.10	.05	.01
☐ 403 Phil Plantier	.10	.05	.01
☐ 404 Scott Spiezio	.50	.23	.06
☐ 405 George Williams	.10	.05	.01
☐ 406 Ernie Young	.10	.05	.01
☐ 407 Darren Bragg	.10	.05	.01
☐ 408 Jay Buhner	.50	.23	.06
☐ 409 Norm Charlton	.10	.05	.01
☐ 410 Russ Davis	.10	.05	.01
☐ 411 Sterling Hitchcock	.10	.05	.01
☐ 412 Edwin Hurtado	.10	.05	.01
☐ 413 Raul Ibanez	.10	.05	.01
☐ 414 Mike Jackson	.10	.05	.01
☐ 415 Luis Sojo	.10	.05	.01
☐ 416 Paul Sorrento	.10	.05	.01
☐ 417 Bob Wolcott	.10	.05	.01
☐ 418 Damon Buford	.10	.05	.01
☐ 419 Kevin Gross	.10	.05	.01
☐ 420 Darryl Hamilton UER	.10	.05	.01
☐ 421 Mike Henneman	.10	.05	.01
☐ 422 Ken Hill	.25	.11	.03
☐ 423 Dean Palmer	.50	.23	.06
☐ 424 Bobby Witt	.10	.05	.01
☐ 425 Tilson Brito	.10	.05	.01
☐ 426 Giovanni Carrara	.10	.05	.01
☐ 427 Domingo Cedeno	.10	.05	.01
☐ 428 Felipe Crespo	.10	.05	.01
☐ 429 Carlos Delgado	.25	.11	.03
☐ 430 Juan Guzman	.10	.05	.01
☐ 431 Erik Hanson	.10	.05	.01
☐ 432 Marty Janzen	.10	.05	.01
☐ 433 Otis Nixon	.10	.05	.01
☐ 434 Robert Perez	.10	.05	.01
☐ 435 Paul Quantrill	.10	.05	.01
☐ 436 Bill Risley	.10	.05	.01
☐ 437 Steve Avery	.25	.11	.03
☐ 438 Jermaine Dye	.60	.25	.07
☐ 439 Mark Lemke	.10	.05	.01
☐ 440 Marty Malloy	.10	.05	.01
☐ 441 Fred McGriff	.50	.23	.06
☐ 442 Greg McMichael	.10	.05	.01
☐ 443 Wonderful Monds	.10	.05	.01
☐ 444 Eddie Perez	.10	.05	.01
☐ 445 Jason Schmidt	.50	.23	.06
☐ 446 Terrell Wade	.25	.11	.03
☐ 447 Terry Adams	.10	.05	.01
☐ 448 Scott Bullett	.10	.05	.01
☐ 449 Robin Jennings	.10	.05	.01
☐ 450 Doug Jones	.10	.05	.01
☐ 451 Brooks Kieschnick	.50	.23	.06
☐ 452 Dave Magadan	.10	.05	.01
☐ 453 Jason Maxwell	.10	.05	.01
☐ 454 Brian McRae	.10	.05	.01
☐ 455 Rodney Myers	.10	.05	.01
☐ 456 Jaime Navarro	.10	.05	.01
☐ 457 Ryne Sandberg	.50	.23	.06
☐ 458 Vince Coleman	.10	.05	.01
☐ 459 Eric Davis	.25	.11	.03
☐ 460 Steve Gibralter	.10	.05	.01
☐ 461 Thomas Howard	.10	.05	.01
☐ 462 Mike Kelly	.10	.05	.01
☐ 463 Hal Morris	.10	.05	.01
☐ 464 Eric Owens	.10	.05	.01
☐ 465 Jose Rijo	.10	.05	.01
☐ 466 Chris Sabo	.10	.05	.01
☐ 467 Eddie Taubensee	.10	.05	.01
☐ 468 Trenidad Hubbard	.10	.05	.01
☐ 469 Curt Leskanic	.10	.05	.01
☐ 470 Quinton McCracken	.10	.05	.01
☐ 471 Jayhawk Owens	.10	.05	.01
☐ 472 Steve Reed	.10	.05	.01
☐ 473 Bryan Rekar	.10	.05	.01
☐ 474 Bruce Ruffin	.10	.05	.01
☐ 475 Bret Saberhagen	.10	.05	.01
☐ 476 Walt Weiss	.10	.05	.01
☐ 477 Eric Young	.25	.11	.03
☐ 478 Kevin Brown	.25	.11	.03
☐ 479 Al Leiter	.10	.05	.01
☐ 480 Pat Rapp	.10	.05	.01
☐ 481 Gary Sheffield	.50	.23	.06
☐ 482 Devon White	.10	.05	.01
☐ 483 Bob Abreu	.50	.23	.06
☐ 484 Sean Berry	.10	.05	.01
☐ 485 Craig Biggio	.25	.11	.03
☐ 486 Jim Dougherty	.10	.05	.01
☐ 487 Richard Hidalgo	.50	.23	.06
☐ 488 Darryl Kile	.10	.05	.01
☐ 489 Derrick May	.10	.05	.01
☐ 490 Greg Swindell	.10	.05	.01
☐ 491 Rick Wilkins	.10	.05	.01
☐ 492 Mike Blowers	.10	.05	.01
☐ 493 Tom Candiotti	.10	.05	.01
☐ 494 Roger Cedeno	.25	.11	.03
☐ 495 Delino DeShields	.10	.05	.01
☐ 496 Greg Gagne	.10	.05	.01
☐ 497 Karim Garcia	.60	.25	.07
☐ 498 Wilton Guerrero	1.50	.70	.19
☐ 499 Chan Ho Park	.50	.23	.06
☐ 500 Isreal Alcantara	.10	.05	.01
☐ 501 Shane Andrews	.10	.05	.01
☐ 502 Yamil Benitez	.25	.11	.03
☐ 503 Cliff Floyd	.10	.05	.01
☐ 504 Mark Grudzielanek	.25	.11	.03
☐ 505 Ryan McGuire	.10	.05	.01
☐ 506 Sherman Obando	.10	.05	.01
☐ 507 Jose Paniagua	.10	.05	.01
☐ 508 Henry Rodriguez	.25	.11	.03
☐ 509 Kirk Rueter	.10	.05	.01
☐ 510 Juan Acevedo	.10	.05	.01
☐ 511 John Franco	.10	.05	.01
☐ 512 Bernard Gilkey	.25	.11	.03
☐ 513 Lance Johnson	.25	.11	.03
☐ 514 Rey Ordonez	.50	.23	.06
☐ 515 Robert Person	.10	.05	.01
☐ 516 Paul Wilson	.25	.11	.03
☐ 517 Toby Borland	.10	.05	.01
☐ 518 David Doster	.10	.05	.01
☐ 519 Lenny Dykstra	.25	.11	.03
☐ 520 Sid Fernandez	.10	.05	.01
☐ 521 Mike Grace	.10	.05	.01
☐ 522 Rich Hunter	.10	.05	.01
☐ 523 Benito Santiago	.10	.05	.01
☐ 524 Gene Schall	.10	.05	.01
☐ 525 Curt Schilling	.10	.05	.01
☐ 526 Kevin Sefcik	.10	.05	.01
☐ 527 Lee Tinsley	.10	.05	.01
☐ 528 David West	.10	.05	.01
☐ 529 Mark Whiten	.10	.05	.01
☐ 530 Todd Zeile	.25	.11	.03
☐ 531 Carlos Garcia	.10	.05	.01
☐ 532 Charlie Hayes	.10	.05	.01
☐ 533 Jason Kendall	.50	.23	.06
☐ 534 Jeff King	.25	.11	.03
☐ 535 Mike Kingery	.10	.05	.01
☐ 536 Nelson Liriano	.10	.05	.01
☐ 537 Dan Plesac	.10	.05	.01
☐ 538 Paul Wagner	.10	.05	.01
☐ 539 Luis Alicea	.10	.05	.01
☐ 540 David Bell	.10	.05	.01
☐ 541 Alan Benes	.50	.23	.06
☐ 542 Andy Benes	.10	.05	.01
☐ 543 Mike Busby	.10	.05	.01
☐ 544 Royce Clayton	.10	.05	.01
☐ 545 Dennis Eckersley	.25	.11	.03
☐ 546 Gary Gaetti	.25	.11	.03
☐ 547 Ron Gant	.25	.11	.03
☐ 548 Aaron Holbert	.10	.05	.01
☐ 549 Ray Lankford	.25	.11	.03
☐ 550 T.J. Mathews	.10	.05	.01
☐ 551 Willie McGee	.10	.05	.01
☐ 552 Miguel Mejia	.40	.18	.05
☐ 553 Todd Stottlemyre	.10	.05	.01
☐ 554 Sean Bergman	.10	.05	.01
☐ 555 Willie Blair	.10	.05	.01
☐ 556 Andujar Cedeno	.10	.05	.01
☐ 557 Steve Finley	.50	.23	.06
☐ 558 Rickey Henderson	.50	.23	.06
☐ 559 Wally Joyner	.10	.05	.01
☐ 560 Scott Livingstone	.10	.05	.01
☐ 561 Marc Newfield	.25	.11	.03
☐ 562 Bob Tewksbury	.10	.05	.01
☐ 563 Fernando Valenzuela	.25	.11	.03
☐ 564 Rod Beck	.10	.05	.01
☐ 565 Doug Creek	.10	.05	.01
☐ 566 Shawon Dunston	.10	.05	.01
☐ 567 Osvaldo Fernandez	.25	.11	.03
☐ 568 Stan Javier	.10	.05	.01
☐ 569 Marcus Jensen	.10	.05	.01
☐ 570 Steve Scarsone	.10	.05	.01
☐ 571 Robby Thompson	.10	.05	.01
☐ 572 Allen Watson	.10	.05	.01
☐ 573 Roberto Alomar STA	.50	.23	.06
☐ 574 Jeff Bagwell STA	.60	.25	.07
☐ 575 Albert Belle STA	.60	.25	.07
☐ 576 Wade Boggs STA	.50	.23	.06
☐ 577 Barry Bonds STA	.50	.23	.06
☐ 578 Juan Gonzalez STA	.75	.35	.09
☐ 579 Ken Griffey Jr. STA	1.50	.70	.19
☐ 580 Tony Gwynn STA	.60	.25	.07
☐ 581 Randy Johnson STA	.50	.23	.06
☐ 582 Chipper Jones STA	1.00	.45	.12
☐ 583 Barry Larkin STA	.50	.23	.06
☐ 584 Kenny Lofton STA	.50	.23	.06
☐ 585 Greg Maddux STA	1.00	.45	.12
☐ 586 Raul Mondesi STA	.50	.23	.06
☐ 587 Mike Piazza STA	1.00	.45	.12
☐ 588 Cal Ripken STA	1.25	.55	.16
☐ 589 Tim Salmon STA	.50	.23	.06
☐ 590 Frank Thomas STA	1.50	.70	.19
☐ 591 Mo Vaughn STA	.50	.23	.06
☐ 592 Matt Williams STA	.50	.23	.06
☐ 593 Marty Cordova RAW	.25	.11	.03
☐ 594 Jim Edmonds RAW	.25	.11	.03
☐ 595 Cliff Floyd RAW	.10	.05	.01
☐ 596 Chipper Jones RAW	1.00	.45	.12
☐ 597 Ryan Klesko RAW	.50	.23	.06
☐ 598 Raul Mondesi RAW	.50	.23	.06
☐ 599 Manny Ramirez RAW	.25	.11	.03
☐ 600 Ruben Rivera RAW	.50	.23	.06

1996 Ultra Gold Medallion

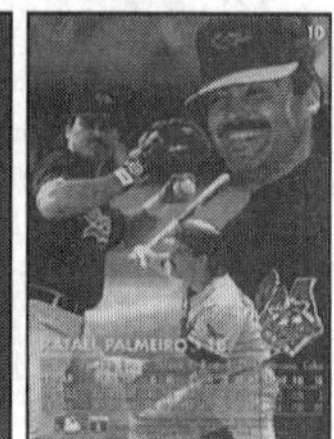

The 1996 Ultra Gold Medallion is a parallel to the regular Ultra issue. The cards were inserted one per pack in both first and second series. The card consists of a full gold foil paper with a full-color player cut out on top. Backs are identical to the regular cards.

	MINT	NRMT	EXC
COMPLETE SET (600)	200.00	90.00	25.00
COMPLETE SERIES 1 (300)	100.00	45.00	12.50
COMPLETE SERIES 2 (300)	100.00	45.00	12.50
COMMON CARD (1-600)	.25	.11	.03

*STARS: 2X to 4X BASIC CARDS
*YOUNG STARS: 1.5X to 3X BASIC CARS

1996 Ultra Call to the Hall

Randomly inserted in packs at a rate of one in 24, this ten-card set features original illustrations of possible future Hall of Famers. The backs state why the player is a possible HOF.

	MINT	NRMT	EXC
COMPLETE SET (10)	80.00	36.00	10.00
COMMON CARD (1-10)	2.00	.90	.25
☐ 1 Barry Bonds	5.00	2.20	.60
☐ 2 Ken Griffey Jr.	20.00	9.00	2.50
☐ 3 Tony Gwynn	8.00	3.60	1.00
☐ 4 Rickey Henderson	2.00	.90	.25
☐ 5 Greg Maddux	12.00	5.50	1.50
☐ 6 Eddie Murray	5.00	2.20	.60
☐ 7 Cal Ripken	15.00	6.75	1.85
☐ 8 Ryne Sandberg	5.00	2.20	.60
☐ 9 Ozzie Smith	5.00	2.20	.60
☐ 10 Frank Thomas	20.00	9.00	2.50

1996 Ultra Call to the Hall Gold Medallion

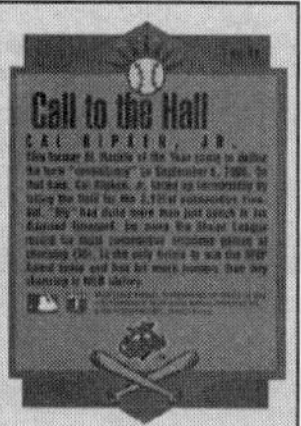

This 10 card set parallels the regular Call to the Hall insert set. These cards are printed less frequently than the regular Call to the Hall set and are valued as a multiplier of the regular cards.

	MINT	NRMT	EXC
COMPLETE SET (10)	250.00	110.00	31.00
COMMON CARD (1-10)	6.00	2.70	.75

*GOLD MEDALLION: 3X BASIC CARDS

1996 Ultra Checklists

Randomly inserted in packs, this set of 10 standard-size cards features superstars of the game. Fronts are full-bleed color action photos of players with "Checklist" written in gold foil across the card. The horizontal backs are numbered and show the different card sets that are included in the Ultra line. The cards are sequenced in alphabetical order. A gold medallion parallel version of each card was issued.

	MINT	NRMT	EXC
COMPLETE SERIES 1 (10)	10.00	4.50	1.25
COMPLETE SERIES 2 (10)	10.00	4.50	1.25
COMMON SERIES 1 (A1-A10)	.50	.23	.06
COMMON SERIES 2 (B1-B10)	.50	.23	.06
☐ A1 Jeff Bagwell	1.50	.70	.19
☐ A2 Barry Bonds	1.00	.45	.12
☐ A3 Juan Gonzalez	2.00	.90	.25
☐ A4 Ken Griffey Jr.	4.00	1.80	.50
☐ A5 Chipper Jones	2.50	1.10	.30
☐ A6 Mike Piazza	2.50	1.10	.30
☐ A7 Manny Ramirez	.75	.35	.09
☐ A8 Cal Ripken	3.00	1.35	.35
☐ A9 Frank Thomas	4.00	1.80	.50
☐ A10 Matt Williams	.50	.23	.06
☐ B1 Albert Belle	1.50	.70	.19
☐ B2 Cecil Fielder	.50	.23	.06
☐ B3 Ken Griffey Jr.	4.00	1.80	.50
☐ B4 Tony Gwynn	1.50	.70	.19
☐ B5 Derek Jeter	2.50	1.10	.30
☐ B6 Jason Kendall	.50	.23	.06
☐ B7 Ryan Klesko	.50	.23	.06
☐ B8 Greg Maddux	2.50	1.10	.30
☐ B9 Cal Ripken	3.00	1.35	.35
☐ B10 Frank Thomas	4.00	1.80	.50

1996 Ultra Checklists Gold Medallion

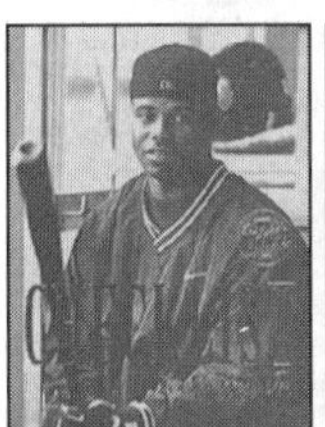
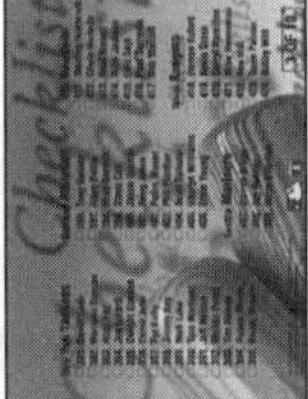

This 20 card set parallels the regular Ultra Checklist insert cards. These cards were randomly seeded at a rate of 1:40 first and second series packs. They can be distinguished from their more common counterparts by the foil "Gold Medallion" logo on the card fronts.

	MINT	NRMT	EXC
COMPLETE SERIES 1 (10)	30.00	13.50	3.70
COMPLETE SERIES 2 (10)	30.00	13.50	3.70
COMMON SERIES 1 (A1-A10)	1.50	.70	.19
COMMON SERIES 2 (B1-B10)	1.50	.70	.19

*GOLD MEDALLION: 3X BASIC CARDS

1996 Ultra Diamond Producers

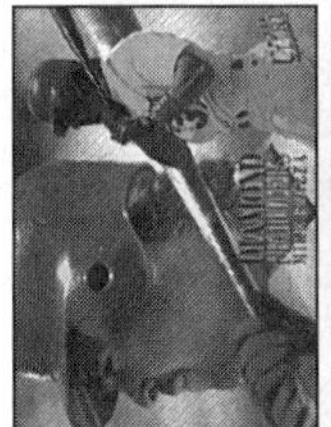

This 12-card standard-size set highlights the achievements of Major League stars. The cards were randomly inserted at a rate of one in 20. The horizontal fronts show the player close-up and an action photo on a metallic-silver paper. "Diamond Producers" and the player's name are printed in silver foil at the bottom of the card. The backs feature the player in an action shot on the left half and a white on black description of the player's career achievements. The cards are sequenced in alphabetical order and there are also gold medallion versions of these cards.

	MINT	NRMT	EXC
COMPLETE SET (12)	60.00	27.00	7.50
COMMON CARD (1-12)	2.00	.90	.25
☐ 1 Albert Belle	6.00	2.70	.75
☐ 2 Barry Bonds	4.00	1.80	.50
☐ 3 Ken Griffey Jr.	15.00	6.75	1.85
☐ 4 Tony Gwynn	6.00	2.70	.75
☐ 5 Greg Maddux	10.00	4.50	1.25
☐ 6 Hideo Nomo	4.00	1.80	.50
☐ 7 Mike Piazza	10.00	4.50	1.25
☐ 8 Kirby Puckett	6.00	2.70	.75
☐ 9 Cal Ripken	12.00	5.50	1.50
☐ 10 Frank Thomas	15.00	6.75	1.85
☐ 11 Mo Vaughn	4.00	1.80	.50
☐ 12 Matt Williams	2.00	.90	.25

1996 Ultra Diamond Producers Gold Medallion

This 12 card set parallels the regular Diamond Producer set. These cards were randomly seeded at a rate of 1:200 first series packs. They can be distinguished from their more common counterparts by the foil "Gold Medallion" logo on the card fronts.

	MINT	NRMT	EXC
COMPLETE SET (12)	180.00	80.00	22.00
COMMON CARD (1-12)	6.00	2.70	.75

*GOLD MEDALLION: 3X BASIC CARDS

1996 Ultra Fresh Foundations

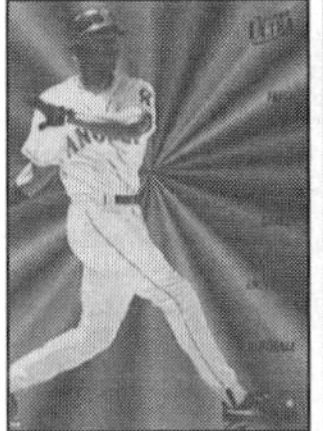
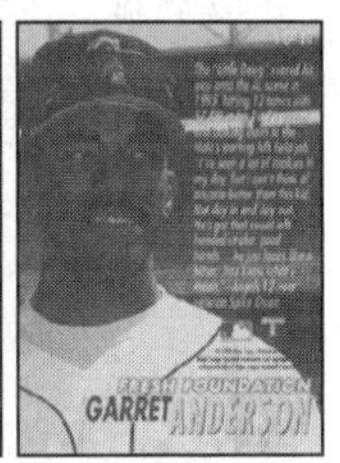

Randomly inserted one every three packs, this 10-card standard-size set highlights the play of hot young players. The fronts feature the player in a full-color action cut-out with a red prismatic background. The Ultra seal, card title, player name and team are printed in silver-foil down the left side of the card. Backs are full-bleed color action shots with player information. The cards are sequenced in alphabetical order and there are also gold medallion versions of these cards.

	MINT	NRMT	EXC
COMPLETE SET (10)	5.00	2.20	.60
COMMON CARD (1-10)	.15	.07	.02
☐ 1 Garret Anderson	.20	.09	.03
☐ 2 Marty Cordova	.20	.09	.03
☐ 3 Jim Edmonds	.20	.09	.03
☐ 4 Brian L.Hunter	.15	.07	.02
☐ 5 Chipper Jones	2.00	.90	.25
☐ 6 Ryan Klesko	.30	.14	.04
☐ 7 Raul Mondesi	.30	.14	.04
☐ 8 Hideo Nomo	.75	.35	.09
☐ 9 Manny Ramirez	.75	.35	.09
☐ 10 Rondell White	.15	.07	.02

1996 Ultra Fresh Foundations Gold Medallions

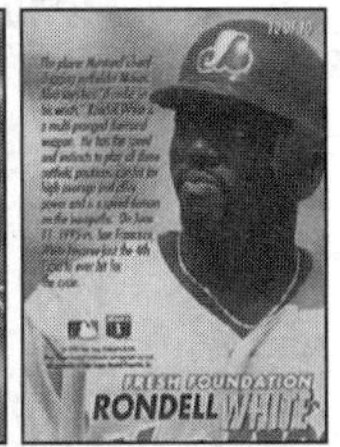

This 10 card set parallels the regular Fresh Foundation insert set. These cards were randomly seeded at a rate of 1:30 first series packs. They can be distinguished from their more common counterparts by the foil "Gold Medallion" logo on the card fronts.

	MINT	NRMT	EXC
COMPLETE SET (10)	15.00	6.75	1.85
COMMON CARD (1-10)	.50	.23	.06

*GOLD MEDALLION: 3X BASIC CARDS

1996 Ultra Golden Prospects

Randomly inserted at a rate of one in five hobby packs, this 10-card standard-size set features players who are likely to make it as major leaguers. The full-bleed fronts have team color-coded tinting over a stadium background. The player is featured in a horizontal action shot with the player's name and team name printed in gold foil. The horizontal backs also feature the minor leaguer in action and player

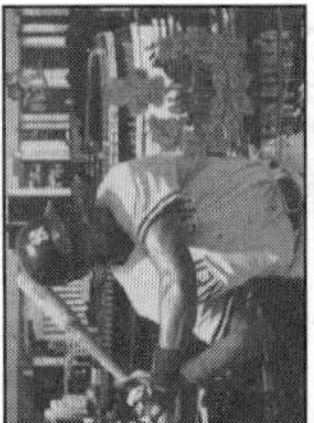

information printed in white type. The cards are sequenced in alphabetical order and there are also gold medallion versions of these cards.

	MINT	NRMT	EXC
COMPLETE SET (10)	5.00	2.20	.60
COMMON CARD (1-10)	.25	.11	.03
☐ 1 Yamil Benitez	.50	.23	.06
☐ 2 Alberto Castillo	.25	.11	.03
☐ 3 Roger Cedeno	.50	.23	.06
☐ 4 Johnny Damon	1.25	.55	.16
☐ 5 Micah Franklin	.25	.11	.03
☐ 6 Jason Giambi	1.50	.70	.19
☐ 7 Jose Herrera	.25	.11	.03
☐ 8 Derek Jeter	5.00	2.20	.60
☐ 9 Kevin Jordan	.25	.11	.03
☐ 10 Ruben Rivera	1.50	.70	.19

1996 Ultra Golden Prospects Gold Medallion

This 10 card set parallels the Golden Prospect insert set. These cards were randomly seeded at a rate of 1:50 first series hobby packs. They can be distinguished from their more common counterparts by the foil "Gold Medallion" logo on the card fronts.

	MINT	NRMT	EXC
COMPLETE SET (10)	15.00	6.75	1.85
COMMON CARD (1-10)	.75	.35	.09

*GOLD MEDALLION: 3X BASIC CARDS

1996 Ultra Golden Prospects Hobby

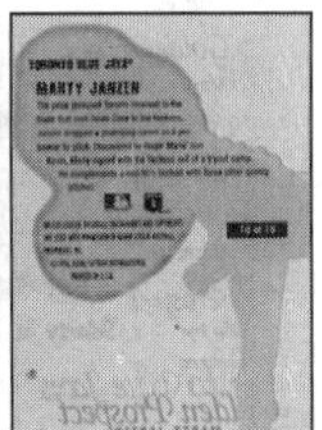

Randomly inserted in hobby packs only at a rate of one in 72, this 15-card set is printed on crystal card stock and showcases players awaiting their Major League debut. The backs carry some of their accomplishments in the Minor League.

	MINT	NRMT	EXC
COMPLETE SET (15)	125.00	55.00	15.50
COMMON CARD (1-15)	6.00	2.70	.75
☐ 1 Bob Abreu	10.00	4.50	1.25
☐ 2 Israel Alcantara	6.00	2.70	.75
☐ 3 Tony Batista	8.00	3.60	1.00
☐ 4 Mike Cameron	15.00	6.75	1.85
☐ 5 Steve Cox	6.00	2.70	.75
☐ 6 Jermaine Dye	15.00	6.75	1.85
☐ 7 Wilton Guerrero	20.00	9.00	2.50
☐ 8 Richard Hidalgo	12.00	5.50	1.50
☐ 9 Raul Ibanez	6.00	2.70	.75
☐ 10 Marty Janzen	6.00	2.70	.75
☐ 11 Robin Jennings	6.00	2.70	.75
☐ 12 Jason Maxwell	6.00	2.70	.75
☐ 13 Scott McClain	6.00	2.70	.75
☐ 14 Wonderful Monds	6.00	2.70	.75
☐ 15 Chris Singleton	6.00	2.70	.75

1996 Ultra Golden Prospects Hobby Gold Medallion

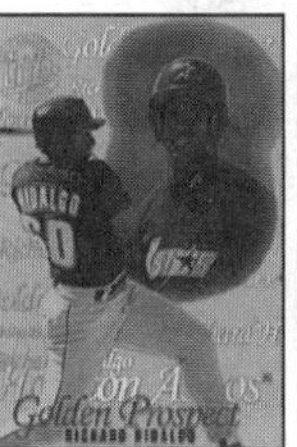

These 15 cards are a parallel to the regular Golden Prospects Hobby insert set. These cards were randomly seeded at a rate of 1:720 second series hobby packs. They can be distinguished from their more common counterparts by the foil "Gold Medallion" logo on the card fronts.

	MINT	NRMT	EXC
COMPLETE SET (15)	375.00	170.00	47.50
COMMON CARD (1-15)	20.00	9.00	2.50

*GOLD MEDALLION: 3X BASIC CARDS

1996 Ultra Hitting Machines

Randomly inserted in second series packs at a rate of one in 288, this 10-card set features players who hit the ball hard and often. The fronts display color action player photos on a die-cut machine gear background. The backs carry a color player portrait and player information.

	MINT	NRMT	EXC
COMPLETE SET (10)	500.00	220.00	60.00
COMMON CARD (1-10)	20.00	9.00	2.50
☐ 1 Albert Belle	60.00	27.00	7.50
☐ 2 Barry Bonds	40.00	18.00	5.00
☐ 3 Juan Gonzalez	75.00	34.00	9.50
☐ 4 Ken Griffey Jr.	150.00	70.00	19.00
☐ 5 Edgar Martinez	20.00	9.00	2.50
☐ 6 Rafael Palmeiro	25.00	11.00	3.10
☐ 7 Mike Piazza	100.00	45.00	12.50
☐ 8 Tim Salmon	25.00	11.00	3.10
☐ 9 Frank Thomas	150.00	70.00	19.00
☐ 10 Matt Williams	25.00	11.00	3.10

1996 Ultra Hitting Machines Gold Medallion

This 10 card set is a parallel to the regular Hitting Machines insert set. These cards were randomly seeded at a rate of 1:2,880 second series packs. They can be distinguished from their more common counterparts by the foil "Gold Medallion" logo on the card fronts.

	MINT	NRMT	EXC
COMPLETE SET (10)	1200.00	550.00	150.00
COMMON CARD (1-10)	50.00	22.00	6.25

*GOLD MEDALLION: 2.5X BASIC CARDS

1996 Ultra Home Run Kings

This 12-card standard-size set features leading power hitters. These cards were randomly inserted at a rate of one in 75 packs. The card fronts are thin wood with a color cut out of the player and HR KING printed diagonally in copper foil down the left side. The Fleer company was not happy with the final look of the card because of the transfer of the copper foil. Therefore all cards were made redemption cards. Backs of the cards have information about how to redeem the cards for replacement. The exchange offer expired on December 1, 1996. The cards are sequenced in alphabetical order.

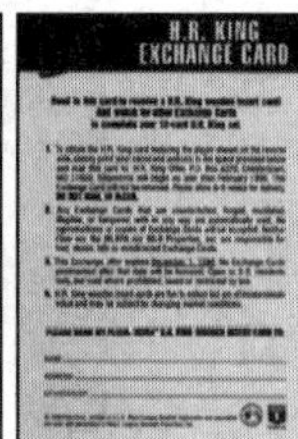

	MINT	NRMT	EXC
COMPLETE SET (12)	60.00	27.00	7.50
COMMON CARD (1-12)	2.50	1.10	.30
☐ 1 Albert Belle	8.00	3.60	1.00
☐ 2 Dante Bichette	2.50	1.10	.30
☐ 3 Barry Bonds	5.00	2.20	.60
☐ 4 Jose Canseco	2.50	1.10	.30
☐ 5 Juan Gonzalez	10.00	4.50	1.25
☐ 6 Ken Griffey Jr.	20.00	9.00	2.50
☐ 7 Mark McGwire	6.00	2.70	.75
☐ 8 Manny Ramirez	5.00	2.20	.60
☐ 9 Tim Salmon	2.50	1.10	.30
☐ 10 Frank Thomas	20.00	9.00	2.50
☐ 11 Mo Vaughn	5.00	2.20	.60
☐ 12 Matt Williams	2.50	1.10	.30

1996 Ultra Home Run Kings Gold Medallion

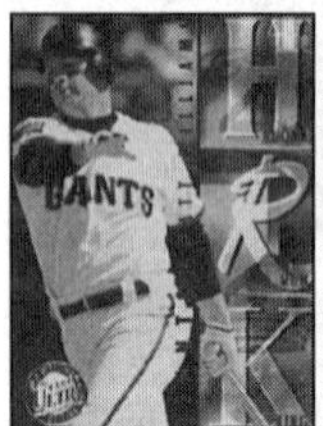
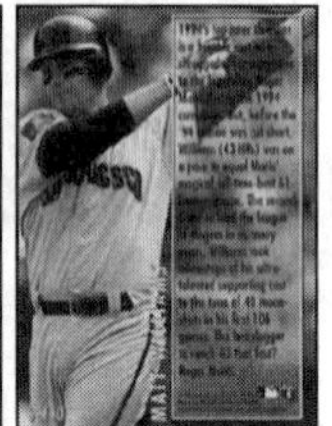

This 12 card insert set parallels the regular Home Run Kings insert set. These cards were randomly seeded at a rate of 1:750 first series packs. They can be distinguished from their more common counterparts by the foil "Gold Medallion" logo on the card fronts.

	MINT	NRMT	EXC
COMPLETE SET (12)	600.00	275.00	75.00
COMMON CARD (1-12)	15.00	6.75	1.85

*GOLD MEDALLION: 6X TO 10X BASIC CARDS

1996 Ultra Home Run Kings Redemption

Collectors could obtain these cards by redeeming the Home Run King cards inserted into first series packs prior to the December 1st, 1996 deadline. Unlike the Home Run Kings cards inserted in packs, these Redemption cards feature simulated wood-grain fronts and carry information about the player on the back.

	MINT	NRMT	EXC
COMPLETE SET (12)	60.00	27.00	7.50
COMMON CARD (1-12)	2.50	1.10	.30

*REDEMPTION CARDS: 1X BASIC CARDS

1996 Ultra On-Base Leaders

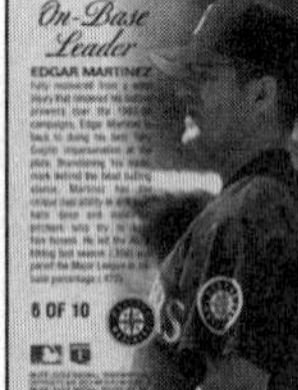

Randomly inserted in second series packs at a rate of one in four, this 10-card set features players with consistently high on-base percentage. The fronts display a color action player image on a black-and-white player background photo with images of bases along the side. The backs carry a color player portrait and player information.

	MINT	NRMT	EXC
COMPLETE SET (10)	6.00	2.70	.75
COMMON CARD (1-10)	.50	.23	.06
☐ 1 Wade Boggs	.50	.23	.06
☐ 2 Barry Bonds	1.00	.45	.12
☐ 3 Tony Gwynn	1.50	.70	.19
☐ 4 Rickey Henderson	.50	.23	.06
☐ 5 Chuck Knoblauch	.50	.23	.06
☐ 6 Edgar Martinez	.50	.23	.06
☐ 7 Mike Piazza	2.50	1.10	.30
☐ 8 Tim Salmon	.50	.23	.06
☐ 9 Frank Thomas	4.00	1.80	.50
☐ 10 Jim Thome	.75	.35	.09

1996 Ultra On-Base Leaders Gold Medallion

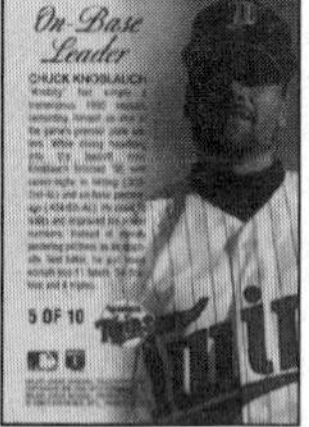

This 10 card set is a parallel to the regular On-Base Leader isnert set. These cards were randomly seeded at a rate of 1:40 second series packs. They can be distinguished from their more common counterparts by the foil "Gold Medallion" logo on the card fronts.

	MINT	NRMT	EXC
COMPLETE SET (10)	18.00	8.00	2.20
COMMON CARD (1-10)	1.50	.70	.19

*GOLD MEDALLION: 3X BASIC CARDS

1996 Ultra Power Plus

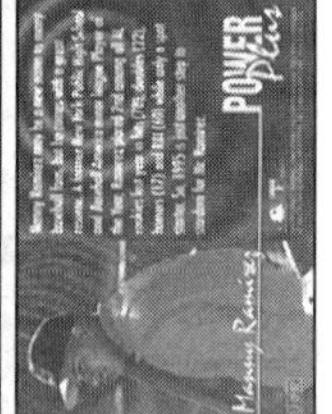

Randomly inserted at a rate of one in ten packs, this 12-card standard-size set features top all-around players. The horizontal fronts feature the player in two cut-out action photos against a multi-colored prismatic wheel background. The player's name and "Power Plus" are stamped in foil across the bottom. The backs are split between a full-color close-up shot of the player and player information printed in white type against a multi-colored circular background. The cards are sequenced in alphabetical order and gold medallion versions of these cards were also issued.

	MINT	NRMT	EXC
COMPLETE SET (12)	25.00	11.00	3.10
COMMON CARD (1-12)	1.00	.45	.12
☐ 1 Jeff Bagwell	4.00	1.80	.50
☐ 2 Barry Bonds	2.50	1.10	.30
☐ 3 Ken Griffey Jr.	10.00	4.50	1.25
☐ 4 Raul Mondesi	1.50	.70	.19
☐ 5 Rafael Palmeiro	1.25	.55	.16
☐ 6 Mike Piazza	6.00	2.70	.75
☐ 7 Manny Ramirez	2.50	1.10	.30
☐ 8 Tim Salmon	1.50	.70	.19
☐ 9 Reggie Sanders	1.00	.45	.12
☐ 10 Frank Thomas	10.00	4.50	1.25
☐ 11 Larry Walker	1.50	.70	.19
☐ 12 Matt Williams	1.50	.70	.19

1996 Ultra Power Plus Gold Medallion

This 12 card set parallels the regular Power Plus insert set. These cards were randomly seeded at a rate of 1:100 first series packs. They can be distinguished from their more common counterparts by the foil "Gold Medallion" logo on the card fronts.

	MINT	NRMT	EXC
COMPLETE SET (12)	75.00	34.00	9.50
COMMON CARD (1-12)	3.00	1.35	.35

*GOLD MEDALLION: 3X BASIC CARDS

1996 Ultra Prime Leather

Eighteen outstanding defensive players are featured in this standard-size set which is inserted approximately one in every eight packs. The horizontal fronts feature a color cut-out shot of the player against an embossed leather-like background. The player's name and team are embossed across the bottom with a black shadow effect. The backs have player's achievements noted in black type with a red outline against a glossy leather background. The other half of the back is a full color shot of the player. The cards are sequenced in alphabetical order and gold medallion versions of these cards were also issued.

	MINT	NRMT	EXC
COMPLETE SET (18)	30.00	13.50	3.70
COMMON CARD (1-18)	1.00	.45	.12
☐ 1 Ivan Rodriguez	2.50	1.10	.30
☐ 2 Will Clark	1.50	.70	.19
☐ 3 Roberto Alomar	2.00	.90	.25
☐ 4 Cal Ripken	8.00	3.60	1.00
☐ 5 Wade Boggs	1.50	.70	.19
☐ 6 Ken Griffey Jr.	10.00	4.50	1.25
☐ 7 Kenny Lofton	2.50	1.10	.30
☐ 8 Kirby Puckett	4.00	1.80	.50
☐ 9 Tim Salmon	1.50	.70	.19
☐ 10 Mike Piazza	6.00	2.70	.75
☐ 11 Mark Grace	1.50	.70	.19
☐ 12 Craig Biggio	1.50	.70	.19
☐ 13 Barry Larkin	1.50	.70	.19
☐ 14 Matt Williams	1.50	.70	.19
☐ 15 Barry Bonds	2.50	1.10	.30
☐ 16 Tony Gwynn	4.00	1.80	.50
☐ 17 Brian McRae	1.00	.45	.12
☐ 18 Raul Mondesi	1.50	.70	.19

1996 Ultra Prime Leather Gold Medallion

This 18 card set parallels the regular Prime Leather insert set. These cards were randomly seeded at a rate of 1:80 first series packs. They can be distinguished from their more common counterparts by the foil "Gold Medallion" logo on the card fronts.

	MINT	NRMT	EXC
COMPLETE SET (18)	90.00	40.00	11.00
COMMON CARD (1-18)	3.00	1.35	.35

*GOLD MEDALLION: 3X BASIC CARDS

1996 Ultra Rawhide

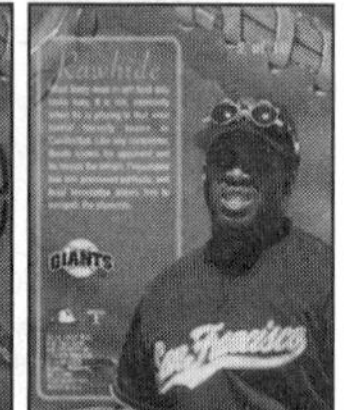

Randomly inserted in second series packs at a rate of one in 8, this 10-card set features leading defensive players. The embossed cards feature the Ultra logo, the word "Rawhide" and the players name against a background of a glove. The back gives a description of the player's defensive abilities.

	MINT	NRMT	EXC
COMPLETE SET (10)	20.00	9.00	2.50
COMMON CARD (1-10)	1.00	.45	.12
☐ 1 Roberto Alomar	1.25	.55	.16
☐ 2 Barry Bonds	1.50	.70	.19
☐ 3 Mark Grace	1.00	.45	.12
☐ 4 Ken Griffey Jr.	6.00	2.70	.75
☐ 5 Kenny Lofton	1.50	.70	.19
☐ 6 Greg Maddux	4.00	1.80	.50
☐ 7 Raul Mondesi	1.00	.45	.12
☐ 8 Mike Piazza	4.00	1.80	.50
☐ 9 Cal Ripken	5.00	2.20	.60
☐ 10 Matt Williams	1.00	.45	.12

1996 Ultra Rawhide Gold Medallion

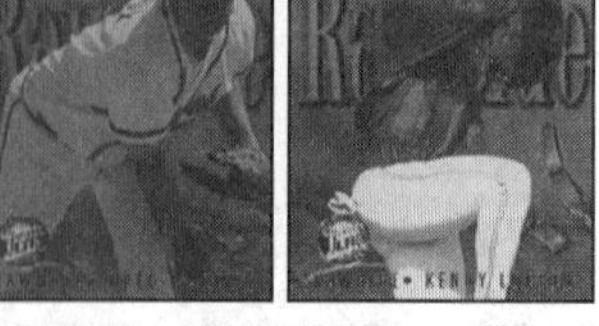

This 10 card set is a parallel to the Rawhide insert set. These cards were randomly seeded at a rate of 1:80 second series packs. They can be distinguished from their more common counterparts by the foil "Gold Medallion" logo on the card fronts.

	MINT	NRMT	EXC
COMPLETE SET (10)	60.00	27.00	7.50
COMMON CARD (1-10)	3.00	1.35	.35

*GOLD MEDALLION: 3X BASIC CARDS

1996 Ultra RBI Kings

This 10-card standard-size set was randomly inserted at a rate of one in five retail packs. This set features top run producers. The full-color, full-bleed fronts feature player cutouts set against a background of baseballs. The player's name and team logo are printed in silver foil across the bottom. The backs show the players on a full-bleed surface with baseballs in the background and player name and accomplishments printed in white with a white box surrounding the type. The cards are sequenced in alphabetical order and gold medallion versions of these cards were also issued.

	MINT	NRMT	EXC
COMPLETE SET (10)	40.00	18.00	5.00
COMMON CARD (1-10)	2.50	1.10	.30
☐ 1 Derek Bell	2.50	1.10	.30
☐ 2 Albert Belle	10.00	4.50	1.25
☐ 3 Dante Bichette	3.00	1.35	.35
☐ 4 Barry Bonds	6.00	2.70	.75
☐ 5 Jim Edmonds	2.50	1.10	.30
☐ 6 Manny Ramirez	6.00	2.70	.75
☐ 7 Reggie Sanders	2.50	1.10	.30
☐ 8 Sammy Sosa	4.00	1.80	.50
☐ 9 Frank Thomas	25.00	11.00	3.10
☐ 10 Mo Vaughn	6.00	2.70	.75

1996 Ultra RBI Kings Gold Medallion

This 10 card set is a parallel to the regular RBI King insert set. These cards were randomly seeded at a rate of 1:50 first series retail packs. They can be distinguished from their more common counterparts by the foil "Gold Medallion" logo on the card fronts.

	MINT	NRMT	EXC
COMPLETE SET (10)	125.00	55.00	15.50
COMMON CARD (1-10)	8.00	3.60	1.00

*GOLD MEDALLION: 3X BASIC CARDS

1996 Ultra Respect

Randomly inserted in second series packs at a rate of one in 18, this 10-card set features players who are well regarded by their peers for both on and off field activies. The fronts consist of a player photo with the word "Respect" as well as his name and the Ultra logo on the right. The back has another player photo as well as reasons why the player has earned his reputation.

	MINT	NRMT	EXC
COMPLETE SET (10)	60.00	27.00	7.50
COMMON CARD (1-10)	1.50	.70	.19
☐ 1 Joe Carter	1.50	.70	.19
☐ 2 Ken Griffey Jr.	15.00	6.75	1.85
☐ 3 Tony Gwynn	6.00	2.70	.75
☐ 4 Greg Maddux	10.00	4.50	1.25
☐ 5 Eddie Murray	4.00	1.80	.50
☐ 6 Kirby Puckett	6.00	2.70	.75
☐ 7 Cal Ripken	12.00	5.50	1.50
☐ 8 Ryne Sandberg	4.00	1.80	.50
☐ 9 Frank Thomas	15.00	6.75	1.85
☐ 10 Mo Vaughn	4.00	1.80	.50

1996 Ultra Respect Gold Medallion

This 10 card set is a parallel to the Ultra Respect insert set. These cards were randomly seeded at a rate of 1:180 second series packs. They can be distinguished from their more common counterparts by the foil "Gold Medallion" logo on the card fronts.

	MINT	NRMT	EXC
COMPLETE SET (10)	180.00	80.00	22.00
COMMON CARD (1-10)	5.00	2.20	.60

*GOLD MEDALLION: 3X BASIC CARDS

1996 Ultra Rising Stars

Randomly inserted in second series packs at a rate of one in 4, this 10-card set features leadgin players of tomorrow. The fronts have a player photo superimposed on a stadium background. The words "Rising Star" as well as the player's name and the Ultra logo are in the middle of the front. The back has another player photo and informaton on the future of these young stars.

	MINT	NRMT	EXC
COMPLETE SET (10)	5.00	2.20	.60
COMMON CARD (1-10)	.25	.11	.03
☐ 1 Garret Anderson	.25	.11	.03
☐ 2 Marty Cordova	.35	.16	.04
☐ 3 Jim Edmonds	.35	.16	.04
☐ 4 Cliff Floyd	.25	.11	.03
☐ 5 Brian L.Hunter	.35	.16	.04
☐ 6 Chipper Jones	2.50	1.10	.30
☐ 7 Ryan Klesko	.50	.23	.06
☐ 8 Hideo Nomo	1.00	.45	.12
☐ 9 Manny Ramirez	1.00	.45	.12
☐ 10 Rondell White	.35	.16	.04

1996 Ultra Rising Stars Gold Medallion

This 10 card set is a parallel to the regular Ultra Rising Stars insert set. These cards were randomly seeded at a rate of 1:40 second series packs. They can be distinguished from their more common counterparts by the foil "Gold Medallion" logo on the card fronts.

	MINT	NRMT	EXC
COMPLETE SET (10)	15.00	6.75	1.85
COMMON CARD (1-10)	.75	.35	.09

*GOLD MEDALLION: 3X BASIC CARDS

1996 Ultra Season Crowns

This set features ten award winners and stat leaders. The cards were randomly inserted at a rate of one in ten. The clear acetate cards feature a full-color player cutout against a background of colored foliage and laurels. Backs include the player's 1995 statistics and other facts on a multi-colored background. The cards are sequenced in alphabetical order and gold medallion versions of these cards were also issued.

	MINT	NRMT	EXC
COMPLETE SET (10)	35.00	16.00	4.40
COMMON CARD (1-10)	.50	.23	.06
☐ 1 Barry Bonds	2.50	1.10	.30
☐ 2 Tony Gwynn	4.00	1.80	.50
☐ 3 Randy Johnson	1.50	.70	.19
☐ 4 Kenny Lofton	2.50	1.10	.30
☐ 5 Greg Maddux	6.00	2.70	.75
☐ 6 Edgar Martinez	.75	.35	.09
☐ 7 Hideo Nomo	2.50	1.10	.30
☐ 8 Cal Ripken	8.00	3.60	1.00
☐ 9 Frank Thomas	10.00	4.50	1.25
☐ 10 Tim Wakefield	.50	.23	.06

1996 Ultra Seasons Crowns Gold Medallion

This 10 card insert set is a parallel to the regular Seasons Crowns insert set. These cards were randomly seeded at a rate of 1:100 first series packs. They can be distinguished from their more common counterparts by the foil "Gold Medallion" logo on the card fronts.

	MINT	NRMT	EXC
COMPLETE SET (10)	100.00	45.00	12.50
COMMON CARD (1-10)	1.50	.70	.19

*GOLD MEDALLION: 3X BASIC CARDS

1996 Ultra Thunderclap

Randomly inserted one in 72 retail packs, these cards feature the leading power hitters. The player's photo is against a background of thunder and lightning and the words "Thunder Clap" and the player's name are on the bottom. The back consists of another player photo as well as a biography as to the player's power skills.

	MINT	NRMT	EXC
COMPLETE SET (20)	400.00	180.00	50.00
COMMON CARD (1-20)	8.00	3.60	1.00
☐ 1 Albert Belle	35.00	16.00	4.40
☐ 2 Barry Bonds	20.00	9.00	2.50
☐ 3 Bobby Bonilla	8.00	3.60	1.00
☐ 4 Jose Canseco	10.00	4.50	1.25
☐ 5 Joe Carter	8.00	3.60	1.00
☐ 6 Will Clark	10.00	4.50	1.25
☐ 7 Andre Dawson	8.00	3.60	1.00
☐ 8 Cecil Fielder	8.00	3.60	1.00
☐ 9 Andres Galarraga	10.00	4.50	1.25
☐ 10 Juan Gonzalez	40.00	18.00	5.00
☐ 11 Ken Griffey Jr.	75.00	34.00	9.50
☐ 12 Fred McGriff	10.00	4.50	1.25
☐ 13 Mark McGwire	25.00	11.00	3.10
☐ 14 Eddie Murray	20.00	9.00	2.50
☐ 15 Rafael Palmeiro	10.00	4.50	1.25
☐ 16 Kirby Puckett	40.00	18.00	5.00
☐ 17 Cal Ripken	60.00	27.00	7.50
☐ 18 Ryne Sandberg	25.00	11.00	3.10
☐ 19 Frank Thomas	75.00	34.00	9.50
☐ 20 Matt Williams	10.00	4.50	1.25

1996 Ultra Thunderclap Gold Medallion

This 20 card set is a parallel to the regular Ultra Thunderclap insert set. These cards were randomly seeded at a rate of 1:720 second series retail packs. They can be distinguished from their more common counterparts by the foil "Gold Medallion" logo on the card fronts.

	MINT	NRMT	EXC
COMPLETE SET (20)	1200.00	550.00	150.00
COMMON CARD (1-20)	25.00	11.00	3.10

*GOLD MEDALLION: 3X BASIC CARDS

1997 Ultra

The 1997 Ultra first series totals 300 cards. The 10-card packs had a suggested retail price of 2.49 each. Each pack had two insert cards, with one insert being a gold medallion parallel and the other insert being from a group of nine different insert sets. As in most Fleer produced sets, the cards are arranged in alphabetical order by league, player and team.

	MINT	NRMT	EXC
COMPLETE SERIES 1 (300)	30.00	13.50	3.70
COMMON CARD (1-300)	.10	.05	.01
☐ 1 Roberto Alomar	.60	.25	.07
☐ 2 Brady Anderson	.25	.11	.03
☐ 3 Rocky Coppinger	.25	.11	.03
☐ 4 Jeffrey Hammonds	.10	.05	.01
☐ 5 Chris Hoiles	.10	.05	.01
☐ 6 Eddie Murray	.75	.35	.09
☐ 7 Mike Mussina	.60	.25	.07
☐ 8 Jimmy Myers	.10	.05	.01
☐ 9 Randy Myers	.10	.05	.01
☐ 10 Arthur Rhodes	.10	.05	.01
☐ 11 Cal Ripken	2.50	1.10	.30
☐ 12 Jose Canseco	.40	.18	.05
☐ 13 Roger Clemens	.60	.25	.07
☐ 14 Tom Gordon	.10	.05	.01
☐ 15 Jose Malave	.10	.05	.01
☐ 16 Tim Naehring	.10	.05	.01
☐ 17 Troy O'Leary	.10	.05	.01
☐ 18 Bill Selby	.10	.05	.01
☐ 19 Heathcliff Slocumb	.10	.05	.01
☐ 20 Mike Stanley	.10	.05	.01
☐ 21 Mo Vaughn	.75	.35	.09
☐ 22 Garret Anderson	.10	.05	.01
☐ 23 George Arias	.10	.05	.01
☐ 24 Chili Davis	.10	.05	.01
☐ 25 Jim Edmonds	.25	.11	.03
☐ 26 Darin Erstad	1.50	.70	.19
☐ 27 Chuck Finley	.10	.05	.01
☐ 28 Todd Greene	.10	.05	.01
☐ 29 Troy Percival	.10	.05	.01
☐ 30 Tim Salmon	.40	.18	.05
☐ 31 Jeff Schmidt	.10	.05	.01
☐ 32 Randy Velarde	.10	.05	.01
☐ 33 Shad Williams	.10	.05	.01
☐ 34 Wilson Alvarez	.10	.05	.01
☐ 35 Harold Baines	.10	.05	.01
☐ 36 James Baldwin	.10	.05	.01
☐ 37 Mike Cameron	.50	.23	.06
☐ 38 Ray Durham	.10	.05	.01
☐ 39 Ozzie Guillen	.10	.05	.01
☐ 40 Roberto Hernandez	.10	.05	.01
☐ 41 Darren Lewis	.10	.05	.01
☐ 42 Jose Munoz	.10	.05	.01
☐ 43 Tony Phillips	.10	.05	.01
☐ 44 Frank Thomas	3.00	1.35	.35
☐ 45 Sandy Alomar Jr.	.10	.05	.01
☐ 46 Albert Belle	1.25	.55	.16
☐ 47 Mark Carreon	.10	.05	.01
☐ 48 Julio Franco	.10	.05	.01
☐ 49 Orel Hershiser	.25	.11	.03
☐ 50 Kenny Lofton	.75	.35	.09
☐ 51 Jack McDowell	.10	.05	.01
☐ 52 Jose Mesa	.10	.05	.01
☐ 53 Charles Nagy	.25	.11	.03
☐ 54 Manny Ramirez	.75	.35	.09
☐ 55 Julian Tavarez	.10	.05	.01
☐ 56 Omar Vizquel	.25	.11	.03
☐ 57 Raul Casanova	.10	.05	.01
☐ 58 Tony Clark	.40	.18	.05
☐ 59 Travis Fryman	.25	.11	.03
☐ 60 Bob Higginson	.25	.11	.03
☐ 61 Melvin Nieves	.10	.05	.01
☐ 62 Curtis Pride	.10	.05	.01
☐ 63 Justin Thompson	.25	.11	.03
☐ 64 Alan Trammell	.25	.11	.03
☐ 65 Kevin Appier	.25	.11	.03
☐ 66 Johnny Damon	.10	.05	.01
☐ 67 Keith Lockhart	.10	.05	.01
☐ 68 Jeff Montgomery	.10	.05	.01
☐ 69 Jose Offerman	.10	.05	.01
☐ 70 Bip Roberts	.10	.05	.01
☐ 71 Jose Rosado	.40	.18	.05
☐ 72 Chris Stynes	.10	.05	.01
☐ 73 Mike Sweeney	.25	.11	.03
☐ 74 Jeff Cirillo	.10	.05	.01
☐ 75 Jeff D'Amico	.25	.11	.03
☐ 76 John Jaha	.25	.11	.03
☐ 77 Scott Karl	.10	.05	.01
☐ 78 Mike Matheny	.10	.05	.01
☐ 79 Ben McDonald	.10	.05	.01
☐ 80 Matt Mieske	.10	.05	.01
☐ 81 Marc Newfield	.10	.05	.01
☐ 82 Dave Nilsson	.10	.05	.01
☐ 83 Jose Valentin	.10	.05	.01
☐ 84 Fernando Vina	.10	.05	.01
☐ 85 Rick Aguilera	.10	.05	.01
☐ 86 Marty Cordova	.25	.11	.03
☐ 87 Chuck Knoblauch	.50	.23	.06
☐ 88 Matt Lawton	.10	.05	.01
☐ 89 Pat Meares	.10	.05	.01
☐ 90 Paul Molitor	.60	.25	.07
☐ 91 Greg Myers	.10	.05	.01
☐ 92 Dan Naulty	.10	.05	.01
☐ 93 Kirby Puckett	1.25	.55	.16
☐ 94 Frank Rodriguez	.10	.05	.01
☐ 95 Wade Boggs	.40	.18	.05
☐ 96 Cecil Fielder	.25	.11	.03
☐ 97 Joe Girardi	.10	.05	.01
☐ 98 Dwight Gooden	.25	.11	.03
☐ 99 Derek Jeter	2.00	.90	.25
☐ 100 Tino Martinez	.25	.11	.03
☐ 101 Ramiro Mendoza	.10	.05	.01
☐ 102 Andy Pettitte	.75	.35	.09
☐ 103 Mariano Rivera	.25	.11	.03
☐ 104 Ruben Rivera	.40	.18	.05
☐ 105 Kenny Rogers	.10	.05	.01
☐ 106 Darryl Strawberry	.25	.11	.03
☐ 107 Bernie Williams	.60	.25	.07
☐ 108 Tony Batista	.40	.18	.05
☐ 109 Geronimo Berroa	.10	.05	.01
☐ 110 Bobby Chouinard	.10	.05	.01
☐ 111 Brent Gates	.10	.05	.01
☐ 112 Jason Giambi	.25	.11	.03
☐ 113 Damon Mashore	.25	.11	.03
☐ 114 Mark McGwire	1.00	.45	.12
☐ 115 Scott Spiezio	.25	.11	.03
☐ 116 John Wasdin	.10	.05	.01
☐ 117 Steve Wojciechowski	.10	.05	.01
☐ 118 Ernie Young	.10	.05	.01
☐ 119 Norm Charlton	.10	.05	.01
☐ 120 Joey Cora	.10	.05	.01
☐ 121 Ken Griffey Jr.	3.00	1.35	.35
☐ 122 Sterling Hitchcock	.10	.05	.01
☐ 123 Raul Ibanez	.10	.05	.01
☐ 124 Randy Johnson	.50	.23	.06
☐ 125 Edgar Martinez	.25	.11	.03
☐ 126 Alex Rodriguez	3.00	1.35	.35
☐ 127 Matt Wagner	.10	.05	.01
☐ 128 Bob Wells	.10	.05	.01
☐ 129 Dan Wilson	.10	.05	.01
☐ 130 Will Clark	.40	.18	.05
☐ 131 Kevin Elster	.10	.05	.01
☐ 132 Juan Gonzalez	1.50	.70	.19
☐ 133 Rusty Greer	.25	.11	.03
☐ 134 Darryl Hamilton	.10	.05	.01
☐ 135 Mike Henneman	.10	.05	.01
☐ 136 Ken Hill	.10	.05	.01
☐ 137 Mark McLemore	.10	.05	.01
☐ 138 Dean Palmer	.10	.05	.01
☐ 139 Roger Pavlik	.10	.05	.01
☐ 140 Ivan Rodriguez	.75	.35	.09
☐ 141 Joe Carter	.25	.11	.03
☐ 142 Carlos Delgado	.25	.11	.03
☐ 143 Alex Gonzalez	.10	.05	.01
☐ 144 Juan Guzman	.10	.05	.01
☐ 145 Pat Hentgen	.25	.11	.03
☐ 146 Marty Janzen	.10	.05	.01
☐ 147 Otis Nixon	.10	.05	.01
☐ 148 Charlie O'Brien	.10	.05	.01
☐ 149 John Olerud	.10	.05	.01
☐ 150 Robert Perez	.10	.05	.01
☐ 151 Jermaine Dye	.50	.23	.06
☐ 152 Tom Glavine	.40	.18	.05
☐ 153 Andruw Jones	3.00	1.35	.35
☐ 154 Chipper Jones	2.00	.90	.25
☐ 155 Ryan Klesko	.50	.23	.06
☐ 156 Javier Lopez	.25	.11	.03
☐ 157 Greg Maddux	2.00	.90	.25
☐ 158 Fred McGriff	.40	.18	.05
☐ 159 Wonderful Monds	.10	.05	.01
☐ 160 John Smoltz	.50	.23	.06
☐ 161 Terrell Wade	.10	.05	.01
☐ 162 Mark Wohlers	.10	.05	.01
☐ 163 Brant Brown	.10	.05	.01
☐ 164 Mark Grace	.40	.18	.05
☐ 165 Tyler Houston	.10	.05	.01
☐ 166 Robin Jennings	.10	.05	.01
☐ 167 Jason Maxwell	.10	.05	.01
☐ 168 Ryne Sandberg	.75	.35	.09
☐ 169 Sammy Sosa	.50	.23	.06
☐ 170 Amaury Telemaco	.10	.05	.01
☐ 171 Steve Trachsel	.10	.05	.01
☐ 172 Pedro Valdes	.10	.05	.01
☐ 173 Tim Belk	.10	.05	.01
☐ 174 Bret Boone	.10	.05	.01
☐ 175 Jeff Brantley	.10	.05	.01
☐ 176 Eric Davis	.10	.05	.01
☐ 177 Barry Larkin	.40	.18	.05
☐ 178 Chad Mottola	.10	.05	.01
☐ 179 Mark Portugal	.10	.05	.01
☐ 180 Reggie Sanders	.25	.11	.03
☐ 181 John Smiley	.10	.05	.01
☐ 182 Eddie Taubensee	.10	.05	.01
☐ 183 Dante Bichette	.40	.18	.05
☐ 184 Ellis Burks	.25	.11	.03
☐ 185 Andres Galarraga	.40	.18	.05
☐ 186 Curt Leskanic	.10	.05	.01
☐ 187 Quinton McCracken	.10	.05	.01
☐ 188 Jeff Reed	.10	.05	.01
☐ 189 Kevin Ritz	.10	.05	.01
☐ 190 Walt Weiss	.10	.05	.01
☐ 191 Jamey Wright	.25	.11	.03
☐ 192 Eric Young	.25	.11	.03
☐ 193 Kevin Brown	.25	.11	.03
☐ 194 Luis Castillo	.40	.18	.05
☐ 195 Jeff Conine	.25	.11	.03
☐ 196 Andre Dawson	.25	.11	.03
☐ 197 Charles Johnson	.10	.05	.01
☐ 198 Al Leiter	.10	.05	.01
☐ 199 Ralph Milliard	.10	.05	.01
☐ 200 Robb Nen	.10	.05	.01
☐ 201 Edgar Renteria	.40	.18	.05
☐ 202 Gary Sheffield	.50	.23	.06

	MINT	NRMT	EXC
☐ 203 Bob Abreu	.40	.18	.05
☐ 204 Jeff Bagwell	1.25	.55	.16
☐ 205 Derek Bell	.25	.11	.03
☐ 206 Sean Berry	.10	.05	.01
☐ 207 Richard Hidalgo	.40	.18	.05
☐ 208 Todd Jones	.10	.05	.01
☐ 209 Darryl Kile	.10	.05	.01
☐ 210 Orlando Miller	.10	.05	.01
☐ 211 Shane Reynolds	.10	.05	.01
☐ 212 Billy Wagner	.25	.11	.03
☐ 213 Donne Wall	.10	.05	.01
☐ 214 Roger Cedeno	.10	.05	.01
☐ 215 Greg Gagne	.10	.05	.01
☐ 216 Karim Garcia	.50	.23	.06
☐ 217 Wilton Guerrero	.50	.23	.06
☐ 218 Todd Hollandsworth	.25	.11	.03
☐ 219 Ramon Martinez	.25	.11	.03
☐ 220 Raul Mondesi	.40	.18	.05
☐ 221 Hideo Nomo	.75	.35	.09
☐ 222 Chan Ho Park	.40	.18	.05
☐ 223 Mike Piazza	2.00	.90	.25
☐ 224 Ismael Valdes	.25	.11	.03
☐ 225 Moises Alou	.25	.11	.03
☐ 226 Derek Aucoin	.10	.05	.01
☐ 227 Yamil Benitez	.10	.05	.01
☐ 228 Jeff Fassero	.10	.05	.01
☐ 229 Darrin Fletcher	.10	.05	.01
☐ 230 Mark Grudzielanek	.10	.05	.01
☐ 231 Barry Manuel	.10	.05	.01
☐ 232 Pedro Martinez	.25	.11	.03
☐ 233 Henry Rodriguez	.25	.11	.03
☐ 234 Ugueth Urbina	.10	.05	.01
☐ 235 Rondell White	.10	.05	.01
☐ 236 Carlos Baerga	.25	.11	.03
☐ 237 John Franco	.10	.05	.01
☐ 238 Bernard Gilkey	.10	.05	.01
☐ 239 Todd Hundley	.25	.11	.03
☐ 240 Butch Huskey	.10	.05	.01
☐ 241 Jason Isringhausen	.25	.11	.03
☐ 242 Lance Johnson	.10	.05	.01
☐ 243 Bobby Jones	.10	.05	.01
☐ 244 Alex Ochoa	.10	.05	.01
☐ 245 Rey Ordonez	.40	.18	.05
☐ 246 Paul Wilson	.25	.11	.03
☐ 247 Ron Blazier	.10	.05	.01
☐ 248 David Doster	.10	.05	.01
☐ 249 Jim Eisenreich	.10	.05	.01
☐ 250 Mike Grace	.10	.05	.01
☐ 251 Mike Lieberthal	.10	.05	.01
☐ 252 Wendell Magee	.25	.11	.03
☐ 253 Mickey Morandini	.10	.05	.01
☐ 254 Ricky Otero	.10	.05	.01
☐ 255 Scott Rolen	1.25	.55	.16
☐ 256 Curt Schilling	.10	.05	.01
☐ 257 Todd Zeile	.10	.05	.01
☐ 258 Jermaine Allensworth	.25	.11	.03
☐ 259 Trey Beamon	.10	.05	.01
☐ 260 Carlos Garcia	.10	.05	.01
☐ 261 Mark Johnson	.10	.05	.01
☐ 262 Jason Kendall	.25	.11	.03
☐ 263 Jeff King	.10	.05	.01
☐ 264 Al Martin	.10	.05	.01
☐ 265 Denny Neagle	.10	.05	.01
☐ 266 Matt Ruebel	.10	.05	.01
☐ 267 Marc Wilkins	.10	.05	.01
☐ 268 Alan Benes	.25	.11	.03
☐ 269 Dennis Eckersley	.25	.11	.03
☐ 270 Ron Gant	.25	.11	.03
☐ 271 Aaron Holbert	.10	.05	.01
☐ 272 Brian Jordan	.25	.11	.03
☐ 273 Ray Lankford	.25	.11	.03
☐ 274 John Mabry	.10	.05	.01
☐ 275 T.J. Mathews	.10	.05	.01
☐ 276 Ozzie Smith	.75	.35	.09
☐ 277 Todd Stottlemyre	.10	.05	.01
☐ 278 Mark Sweeney	.10	.05	.01
☐ 279 Andy Ashby	.10	.05	.01
☐ 280 Steve Finley	.10	.05	.01
☐ 281 John Flaherty	.10	.05	.01
☐ 282 Chris Gomez	.10	.05	.01
☐ 283 Tony Gwynn	1.25	.55	.16
☐ 284 Joey Hamilton	.25	.11	.03
☐ 285 Rickey Henderson	.40	.18	.05
☐ 286 Trevor Hoffman	.10	.05	.01
☐ 287 Jason Thompson	.10	.05	.01
☐ 288 Fernando Valenzuela	.25	.11	.03
☐ 289 Greg Vaughn	.10	.05	.01
☐ 290 Barry Bonds	.75	.35	.09
☐ 291 Jay Canizaro	.10	.05	.01
☐ 292 Jacob Cruz	.10	.05	.01
☐ 293 Shawon Dunston	.10	.05	.01
☐ 294 Shawn Estes	.10	.05	.01
☐ 295 Mark Gardner	.10	.05	.01
☐ 296 Marcus Jensen	.10	.05	.01
☐ 297 Bill Mueller	.10	.05	.01
☐ 298 Chris Singleton	.10	.05	.01
☐ 299 Allen Watson	.10	.05	.01
☐ 300 Matt Williams	.40	.18	.05

1997 Ultra Gold Medallion

This 300 card first series set is a parallel to the regular Ultra set, and were inserted one per pack. Unlike previous Gold Medallion sets, the 1997 edition features different photos than the corresponding regular cards.

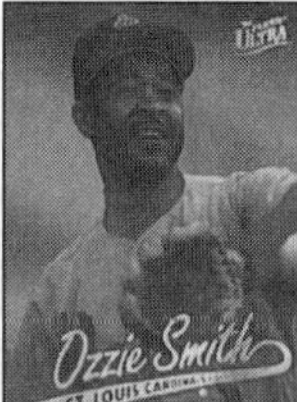

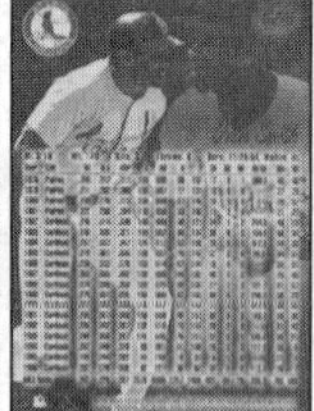

	MINT	NRMT	EXC
COMPLETE SET (300)	150.00	70.00	19.00
COMMON CARD (1-300)	.25	.11	.03

*STARS: 2X to 4X BASIC CARDS........
*YOUNG STARS: 1.5 X to 3X BASIC CARDS

1997 Ultra Platinum Medallion

This 300 card first series set is a parallel to the regular Ultra first series and cards were inserted one per 100 packs. Sparkling platinum lettering on front differentiates these cards from their far more common regular issue brethren. No set price is provided due to scarcity. As with the 1997 Gold Medallion set, the Platinum Medallion set features different photos than the corresponding regular cards.

	MINT	NRMT	EXC
COMMON CARD (1-300)	12.00	5.50	1.50

*STARS: 35X TO 60X BASIC CARDS ..
*YOUNG STARS: 30X TO 50X BASIC CARDS

	MINT	NRMT	EXC
☐ 1 Roberto Alomar	50.00	22.00	6.25
☐ 6 Eddie Murray	60.00	27.00	7.50
☐ 7 Mike Mussina	40.00	18.00	5.00
☐ 11 Cal Ripken	200.00	90.00	25.00
☐ 12 Jose Canseco	30.00	13.50	3.70
☐ 13 Roger Clemens	50.00	22.00	6.25
☐ 21 Mo Vaughn	60.00	27.00	7.50
☐ 26 Darin Erstad	100.00	45.00	12.50
☐ 30 Tim Salmon	30.00	13.50	3.70
☐ 44 Frank Thomas	225.00	100.00	28.00
☐ 46 Albert Belle	100.00	45.00	12.50
☐ 50 Kenny Lofton	60.00	27.00	7.50
☐ 54 Manny Ramirez	50.00	22.00	6.25
☐ 87 Chuck Knoblauch	40.00	18.00	5.00
☐ 90 Paul Molitor	50.00	22.00	6.25
☐ 93 Kirby Puckett	100.00	45.00	12.50
☐ 95 Wade Boggs	30.00	13.50	3.70
☐ 99 Derek Jeter	150.00	70.00	19.00
☐ 102 Andy Pettitte	60.00	27.00	7.50
☐ 104 Ruben Rivera	30.00	13.50	3.70
☐ 107 Bernie Williams	50.00	22.00	6.25
☐ 114 Mark McGwire	75.00	34.00	9.50
☐ 121 Ken Griffey Jr.	250.00	110.00	31.00
☐ 124 Randy Johnson	40.00	18.00	5.00
☐ 126 Alex Rodriguez	250.00	110.00	31.00
☐ 130 Will Clark	30.00	13.50	3.70
☐ 132 Juan Gonzalez	125.00	55.00	15.50
☐ 140 Ivan Rodriguez	60.00	27.00	7.50
☐ 151 Jermaine Dye	30.00	13.50	3.70
☐ 152 Tom Glavine	30.00	13.50	3.70
☐ 153 Andruw Jones	200.00	90.00	25.00
☐ 154 Chipper Jones	150.00	70.00	19.00
☐ 155 Ryan Klesko	30.00	13.50	3.70
☐ 157 Greg Maddux	125.00	55.00	15.50
☐ 158 Fred McGriff	30.00	13.50	3.70
☐ 160 John Smoltz	40.00	18.00	5.00
☐ 168 Ryne Sandberg	60.00	27.00	7.50
☐ 169 Sammy Sosa	40.00	18.00	5.00
☐ 177 Barry Larkin	30.00	13.50	3.70
☐ 183 Dante Bichette	30.00	13.50	3.70
☐ 185 Andres Galarraga	30.00	13.50	3.70
☐ 202 Gary Sheffield	40.00	18.00	5.00
☐ 204 Jeff Bagwell	100.00	45.00	12.50
☐ 216 Karim Garcia	40.00	18.00	5.00
☐ 221 Hideo Nomo	60.00	27.00	7.50
☐ 223 Mike Piazza	150.00	70.00	19.00
☐ 255 Scott Rolen	80.00	36.00	10.00
☐ 276 Ozzie Smith	60.00	27.00	7.50
☐ 283 Tony Gwynn	100.00	45.00	12.50
☐ 290 Barry Bonds	60.00	27.00	7.50
☐ 300 Matt Williams	30.00	13.50	3.70

1997 Ultra Baseball Rules

Randomly inserted into first series retail packs of 1997 Ultra at a rate of 1:36, cards from this 10-card set feature a selection of baseball's

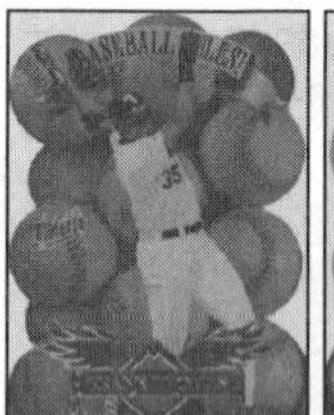

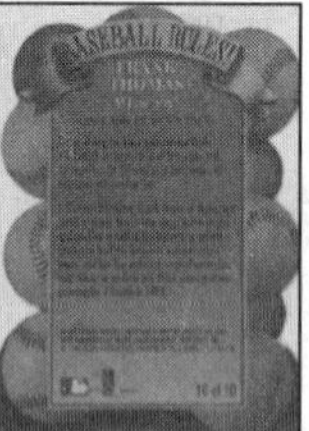

top performers from the 1996 season. The die cut cards feature a player photo surrounded by a group of baseballs. The back explains some of the rules involved in making various awards.

	MINT	NRMT	EXC
COMPLETE SET (10)	120.00	55.00	15.00
COMMON CARD (1-10)	2.00	.90	.25
☐ 1 Barry Bonds	6.00	2.70	.75
☐ 2 Ken Griffey Jr.	25.00	11.00	3.10
☐ 3 Derek Jeter	15.00	6.75	1.85
☐ 4 Chipper Jones	15.00	6.75	1.85
☐ 5 Greg Maddux	15.00	6.75	1.85
☐ 6 Mark McGwire	8.00	3.60	1.00
☐ 7 Troy Percival	2.00	.90	.25
☐ 8 Mike Piazza	15.00	6.75	1.85
☐ 9 Cal Ripken	20.00	9.00	2.50
☐ 10 Frank Thomas	25.00	11.00	3.10

1997 Ultra Checklists

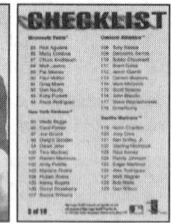

Randomly inserted in all first series packs at a rate of one in four, this 10-card set features player photos on the front along with the word "Checklist", the player's name as well as the "ultra" logo on the bottom. The backs are checklists.

	MINT	NRMT	EXC
COMPLETE SET (10)	8.00	3.60	1.00
COMMON CARD (1-10)	.25	.11	.03
☐ 1 Dante Bichette	.25	.11	.03
☐ 2 Barry Bonds	.50	.23	.06
☐ 3 Ken Griffey Jr.	2.00	.90	.25
☐ 4 Greg Maddux	1.25	.55	.16
☐ 5 Mark McGwire	.60	.25	.07
☐ 6 Mike Piazza	1.25	.55	.16
☐ 7 Cal Ripken	1.50	.70	.19
☐ 8 John Smoltz	.30	.14	.04
☐ 9 Sammy Sosa	.30	.14	.04
☐ 10 Frank Thomas	2.00	.90	.25

1997 Ultra Diamond Producers

Randomly inserted in all first series packs at a rate of one in 288, this 12-card set features "flannel" material mounted on card stock and attempt to look and feel like actual uniforms.

	MINT	NRMT	EXC
COMPLETE SET (12)	650.00	300.00	80.00
COMMON CARD (1-12)	15.00	6.75	1.85
☐ 1 Jeff Bagwell	50.00	22.00	6.25
☐ 2 Barry Bonds	30.00	13.50	3.70
☐ 3 Ken Griffey Jr.	120.00	55.00	15.00
☐ 4 Chipper Jones	80.00	36.00	10.00
☐ 5 Kenny Lofton	30.00	13.50	3.70
☐ 6 Greg Maddux	80.00	36.00	10.00
☐ 7 Mark McGwire	40.00	18.00	5.00
☐ 8 Mike Piazza	80.00	36.00	10.00
☐ 9 Cal Ripken	100.00	45.00	12.50
☐ 10 Alex Rodriguez	120.00	55.00	15.00
☐ 11 Frank Thomas	120.00	55.00	15.00
☐ 12 Matt Williams	15.00	6.75	1.85

1997 Ultra Double Trouble

Randomly inserted in series 1 packs at a rate of one in four, this 20-card set features two players from each team. The horizontal cards feature players photos with their names in silver foil on the bottom and the words "double trouble" on the top. The backs feature information on what the players contributed to their team in 1996

	MINT	NRMT	EXC
COMPLETE SET (20)	20.00	9.00	2.50
COMMON CARD (1-20)	.50	.23	.06
☐ 1 Roberto Alomar Cal Ripken	3.00	1.35	.35
☐ 2 Mo Vaughn Jose Canseco	.75	.35	.09
☐ 3 Jim Edmonds Jim Salmon	.60	.25	.07
☐ 4 Harold Baines Frank Thomas	2.50	1.10	.30
☐ 5 Albert Belle Kenny Lofton	2.00	.90	.25
☐ 6 Marty Cordova Chuck Knoblauch	.60	.25	.07
☐ 7 Derek Jeter Andy Pettitte	2.50	1.10	.30
☐ 8 Jason Giambi Mark McGwire	1.25	.55	.16
☐ 9 Ken Griffey Jr. Alex Rodriguez	6.00	2.70	.75
☐ 10 Juan Gonzalez Will Clark	2.00	.90	.25
☐ 11 Greg Maddux Chipper Jones	4.00	1.80	.50
☐ 12 Mark Grace Sammy Sosa	.60	.25	.07
☐ 13 Dante Bichette Andres Galarraga	.60	.25	.07
☐ 14 Jeff Bagwell Derek Bell	1.50	.70	.19
☐ 15 Hideo Nomo Mike Piazza	2.50	1.10	.30
☐ 16 Henry Rodriguez Moises Alou	.50	.23	.06
☐ 17 Rey Ordonez Alex Ochoa	.50	.23	.06
☐ 18 Ray Lankford Ron Gant	.50	.23	.06
☐ 19 Tony Gwynn Rickey Henderson	1.50	.70	.19
☐ 20 Barry Bonds Matt Williams	.75	.35	.09

1997 Ultra Fielder's Choice

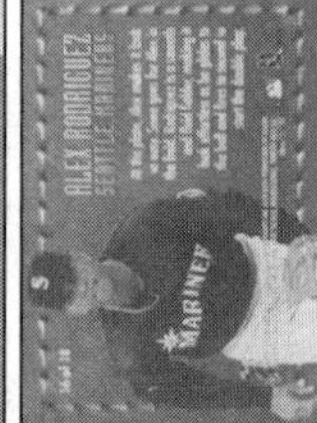

Randomly inserted in series 1 packs at a rate of one in 144, this 18-card set uses leather and gold foil to honor leading defensive players. The horizontal cards also include a player photo on the front as well as the big bold words "97 Fleer Ultra", "Fielder's Choice" and the player's name. The horizontal backs have another player photo as well as information about their defensive prowess.

	MINT	NRMT	EXC
COMPLETE SET (18)	300.00	135.00	38.00
COMMON CARD (1-18)	8.00	3.60	1.00
☐ 1 Roberto Alomar	15.00	6.75	1.85
☐ 2 Jeff Bagwell	30.00	13.50	3.70
☐ 3 Wade Boggs	10.00	4.50	1.25
☐ 4 Barry Bonds	20.00	9.00	2.50
☐ 5 Mark Grace	10.00	4.50	1.25
☐ 6 Ken Griffey Jr.	80.00	36.00	10.00
☐ 7 Marquis Grissom	8.00	3.60	1.00
☐ 8 Charles Johnson	8.00	3.60	1.00
☐ 9 Chuck Knoblauch	12.00	5.50	1.50
☐ 10 Barry Larkin	10.00	4.50	1.25
☐ 11 Kenny Lofton	20.00	9.00	2.50
☐ 12 Greg Maddux	50.00	22.00	6.25
☐ 13 Raul Mondesi	10.00	4.50	1.25

	MINT	NRMT	EXC
☐ 14 Rey Ordonez	10.00	4.50	1.25
☐ 15 Cal Ripken	60.00	27.00	7.50
☐ 16 Alex Rodriguez	80.00	36.00	10.00
☐ 17 Ivan Rodriguez	20.00	9.00	2.50
☐ 18 Matt Williams	10.00	4.50	1.25

1997 Ultra Home Run Kings

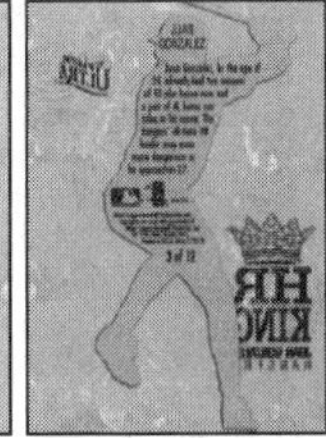

Randomly inserted only in series 1 hobby packs at a rate of one in 36, this 12-card set feaures ultra crystal cards with transparent refractive holo-foil technology. The players pictured are all leading power hitters.

	MINT	NRMT	EXC
COMPLETE SET (12)	100.00	45.00	12.50
COMMON CARD (1-12)	2.50	1.10	.30
☐ 1 Albert Belle	10.00	4.50	1.25
☐ 2 Barry Bonds	6.00	2.70	.75
☐ 3 Juan Gonzalez	12.00	5.50	1.50
☐ 4 Ken Griffey Jr.	25.00	11.00	3.10
☐ 5 Todd Hundley	3.00	1.35	.35
☐ 6 Ryan Klesko	2.50	1.10	.30
☐ 7 Mark McGwire	8.00	3.60	1.00
☐ 8 Mike Piazza	15.00	6.75	1.85
☐ 9 Sammy Sosa	4.00	1.80	.50
☐ 10 Frank Thomas	25.00	11.00	3.10
☐ 11 Mo Vaughn	6.00	2.70	.75
☐ 12 Matt Williams	3.00	1.35	.35

1997 Ultra Power Plus

Randomly inserted in series 1 packs at a rate of one in 24, this 12-card set utilizes silver rainbow holo-foil and features players who not only hit with power but also excel at other parts of the game.

	MINT	NRMT	EXC
COMPLETE SET (12)	80.00	36.00	10.00
COMMON CARD (1-12)	2.50	1.10	.30
☐ 1 Jeff Bagwell	8.00	3.60	1.00
☐ 2 Barry Bonds	5.00	2.20	.60
☐ 3 Juan Gonzalez	10.00	4.50	1.25
☐ 4 Ken Griffey Jr.	20.00	9.00	2.50
☐ 5 Chipper Jones	12.00	5.50	1.50
☐ 6 Mark McGwire	6.00	2.70	.75
☐ 7 Mike Piazza	12.00	5.50	1.50
☐ 8 Cal Ripken	15.00	6.75	1.85
☐ 9 Alex Rodriguez	20.00	9.00	2.50
☐ 10 Sammy Sosa	3.00	1.35	.35
☐ 11 Frank Thomas	20.00	9.00	2.50
☐ 12 Matt Williams	2.50	1.10	.30

1997 Ultra RBI Kings

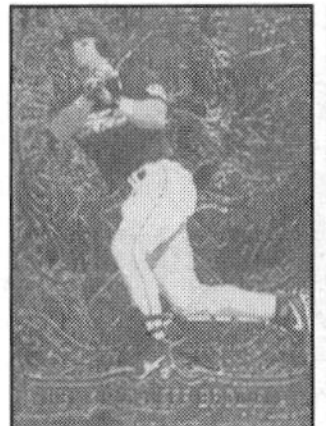
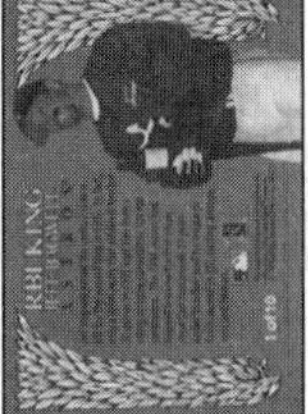

Randomly inserted in series 1 packs at a rate of one in 18, this 10-card set features 100 percent etched-foil cards. The cards feature players who drive in many runs. The horizontal backs contain player information and another player photo.

	MINT	NRMT	EXC
COMPLETE SET (10)	50.00	22.00	6.25
COMMON CARD (1-10)	2.00	.90	.25
☐ 1 Jeff Bagwell	6.00	2.70	.75
☐ 2 Albert Belle	6.00	2.70	.75
☐ 3 Dante Bichette	2.00	.90	.25
☐ 4 Barry Bonds	4.00	1.80	.50
☐ 5 Jay Buhner	2.00	.90	.25
☐ 6 Juan Gonzalez	8.00	3.60	1.00
☐ 7 Ken Griffey Jr.	15.00	6.75	1.85
☐ 8 Sammy Sosa	2.50	1.10	.30
☐ 9 Frank Thomas	15.00	6.75	1.85
☐ 10 Mo Vaughn	4.00	1.80	.50

1997 Ultra Rookie Reflections

Randomly inserted in series 1 packs at a rate of one in 4, this 10-card set uses a silver foil design to feature young players. The horizontal backs contain player information as well as another player photo.

	MINT	NRMT	EXC
COMPLETE SET (10)	8.00	3.60	1.00
COMMON CARD (1-10)	.25	.11	.03
☐ 1 James Baldwin	.25	.11	.03
☐ 2 Jermaine Dye	1.00	.45	.12
☐ 3 Darin Erstad	3.00	1.35	.35
☐ 4 Todd Hollandsworth	.50	.23	.06
☐ 5 Derek Jeter	4.00	1.80	.50
☐ 6 Jason Kendall	.50	.23	.06
☐ 7 Alex Ochoa	.25	.11	.03
☐ 8 Rey Ordonez	.75	.35	.09
☐ 9 Edgar Renteria	.75	.35	.09
☐ 10 Scott Rolen	2.50	1.10	.30

1997 Ultra Season Crowns

Randomly inserted in series 1 packs at a rate of one in 8, this 12-card set features baseball's top stars with etched foil backgrounds.

	MINT	NRMT	EXC
COMPLETE SET (12)	25.00	11.00	3.10
COMMON CARD (1-12)	.75	.35	.09
☐ 1 Albert Belle	3.00	1.35	.35
☐ 2 Dante Bichette	1.00	.45	.12
☐ 3 Barry Bonds	2.00	.90	.25
☐ 4 Kenny Lofton	2.00	.90	.25
☐ 5 Edgar Martinez	.75	.35	.09
☐ 6 Mark McGwire	2.50	1.10	.30
☐ 7 Andy Pettitte	2.00	.90	.25
☐ 8 Mike Piazza	5.00	2.20	.60
☐ 9 Alex Rodriguez	8.00	3.60	1.00
☐ 10 John Smoltz	1.25	.55	.16
☐ 11 Sammy Sosa	1.25	.55	.16
☐ 12 Frank Thomas	8.00	3.60	1.00

1991 United Way Sierra

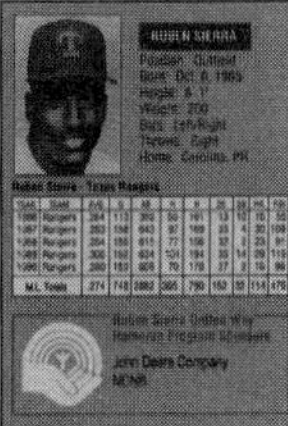

This one-card standard-size set features star outfielder Ruben Sierra. An United Way logo is in the upper left corner. There is also a photo and the player and his team is identified on the bottom. The back has vital statistics and career information about Sierra.

	MINT	NRMT	EXC
COMPLETE SET	1.00	.45	.12
COMMON CARD	1.00	.45	.12
☐ 1 Ruben Sierra	1.00	.45	.12

1988 Upper Deck Promos

The first two cards were test issues given away as samples during the summer of 1988 in anticipation of Upper Deck obtaining licenses from Major League Baseball and the Major League Baseball Players Association. Not many were produced (probably less than 25,000 of each) but few were thrown away as they were distributed basically only to those who would hold on to them. There are three versions based on where the hologram is located. Type A, the most common variety, has a hologram on the bottom that extends as far as the photo. On Type B, the hologram is on the bottom but extends to the edge of the card. Type C, by far the scarcest, has the hologram at the top. Joyner and Buice were supposedly interested in investing in Upper Deck (conflict of interest prohibited them) and apparently were helpful in getting Upper Deck the necessary licenses. Cards were passed out freely to every dealer at the National Sports Collectors Convention in Atlantic City, New Jersey in August 1988.

	MINT	NRMT	EXC
COMPLETE SET (6)	275.00	125.00	34.00
COMPLETE TYPE A SET (2)	35.00	16.00	4.40
COMPLETE TYPE B SET (2)	70.00	32.00	8.75
COMPLETE TYPE C SET (2)	175.00	80.00	22.00
☐ A1 DeWayne Buice	10.00	4.50	1.25
☐ A700 Wally Joyner	30.00	13.50	3.70
☐ B1 DeWayne Buice	20.00	9.00	2.50
☐ B700 Wally Joyner	60.00	27.00	7.50
☐ C1 DeWayne Buice	50.00	22.00	6.25
☐ C700 Wally Joyner	150.00	70.00	19.00

1989 Upper Deck

This attractive 800-card standard-size set was introduced in 1989 as the premier issue by the then-fledgling Upper Deck company. Unlike other 1989 releases, this set was issued in two separate series - a low series numbered 1-700 and a high series numbered 701-800. Cards were primarily issued in fin-wrapped low and high series foil packs, complete 800-card factory sets and 100-card high series factory sets. High series packs contained a mixture of both low and high series cards. Collectors should also note that many dealers consider that Upper Deck's "planned" production of 1,000,000 of each player was increased (perhaps even doubled) later in the year due to the explosion in popularity of the product. The cards feature slick paper stock, full color on both the front and the back and carry a hologram on the reverse to protect against counterfeiting. Subsets include Rookie Stars (1-26) and Collector's Choice art cards (668-693). The more significant variations involving changed photos or changed type are listed below. According to the company, the Murphy and Sheridan cards were corrected very early, after only two percent of the cards had been produced. Similarly, the Sheffield was corrected after 15 percent had been printed; Varsho, Gallego, and Schroeder were corrected after 20 percent; and Holton, Manrique, and Winningham were corrected 30 percent of the way through. Rookie Cards in the set include Jim Abbott, Sandy Alomar Jr., Dante Bichette, Craig Biggio, Steve Finley, Ken Griffey Jr., Erik Hanson, Charlie Hayes, Randy Johnson, Ramon Martinez, Gary Sheffield, John Smoltz and Todd Zeile. Cards with missing or duplicate holograms appear to be relatively common and are generally considered to be flawed copies that sell for substantial discounts.

	MINT	NRMT	EXC
COMPLETE SET (800)	100.00	45.00	12.50
COMPLETE FACT.SET (800)	100.00	45.00	12.50
COMPLETE LO SET (700)	90.00	40.00	11.00
COMPLETE HI SET (100)	10.00	4.50	1.25
COMPLETE HI FACT.SET (100)	8.00	3.60	1.00
COMMON CARD (1-800)	.10	.05	.01
☐ 1 Ken Griffey Jr.	75.00	34.00	9.50
☐ 2 Luis Medina	.10	.05	.01
☐ 3 Tony Chance	.10	.05	.01
☐ 4 Dave Otto	.10	.05	.01
☐ 5 Sandy Alomar Jr. UER (Born 6/16/66, should be 6/18/66)	.75	.35	.09
☐ 6 Rolando Roomes	.10	.05	.01
☐ 7 Dave West	.10	.05	.01
☐ 8 Cris Carpenter	.10	.05	.01
☐ 9 Gregg Jefferies	.50	.23	.06
☐ 10 Doug Dascenzo	.10	.05	.01
☐ 11 Ron Jones	.10	.05	.01
☐ 12 Luis DeLosSantos	.10	.05	.01
☐ 13 Gary Sheffield COR	4.00	1.80	.50
☐ 13A Gary Sheffield ERR (SS upside down on card front)	4.00	1.80	.50
☐ 14 Mike Harkey	.10	.05	.01
☐ 15 Lance Blankenship	.10	.05	.01
☐ 16 William Brennan	.10	.05	.01
☐ 17 John Smoltz	4.00	1.80	.50
☐ 18 Ramon Martinez	1.00	.45	.12
☐ 19 Mark Lemke	.25	.11	.03
☐ 20 Juan Bell	.10	.05	.01
☐ 21 Rey Palacios	.10	.05	.01
☐ 22 Felix Jose	.10	.05	.01
☐ 23 Van Snider	.10	.05	.01
☐ 24 Dante Bichette	3.00	1.35	.35
☐ 25 Randy Johnson	4.00	1.80	.50
☐ 26 Carlos Quintana	.10	.05	.01
☐ 27 Star Rookie CL	.10	.05	.01
☐ 28 Mike Schooler	.10	.05	.01
☐ 29 Randy St.Claire	.10	.05	.01
☐ 30 Jerald Clark	.10	.05	.01
☐ 31 Kevin Gross	.10	.05	.01
☐ 32 Dan Firova	.10	.05	.01
☐ 33 Jeff Calhoun	.10	.05	.01
☐ 34 Tommy Hinzo	.10	.05	.01
☐ 35 Ricky Jordan	.25	.11	.03
☐ 36 Larry Parrish	.10	.05	.01
☐ 37 Bret Saberhagen UER (Hit total 931, should be 1031)	.25	.11	.03
☐ 38 Mike Smithson	.10	.05	.01
☐ 39 Dave Dravecky	.25	.11	.03
☐ 40 Ed Romero	.10	.05	.01
☐ 41 Jeff Musselman	.10	.05	.01
☐ 42 Ed Hearn	.10	.05	.01
☐ 43 Rance Mulliniks	.10	.05	.01
☐ 44 Jim Eisenreich	.25	.11	.03
☐ 45 Sil Campusano	.10	.05	.01
☐ 46 Mike Krukow	.10	.05	.01
☐ 47 Paul Gibson	.10	.05	.01
☐ 48 Mike LaCoss	.10	.05	.01
☐ 49 Larry Herndon	.10	.05	.01
☐ 50 Scott Garrelts	.10	.05	.01
☐ 51 Dwayne Henry	.10	.05	.01
☐ 52 Jim Acker	.10	.05	.01
☐ 53 Steve Sax	.10	.05	.01
☐ 54 Pete O'Brien	.10	.05	.01
☐ 55 Paul Runge	.10	.05	.01
☐ 56 Rick Rhoden	.10	.05	.01
☐ 57 John Dopson	.10	.05	.01
☐ 58 Casey Candaele UER (No stats for Astros for '88 season)	.10	.05	.01
☐ 59 Dave Righetti	.10	.05	.01
☐ 60 Joe Hesketh	.10	.05	.01
☐ 61 Frank DiPino	.10	.05	.01
☐ 62 Tim Laudner	.10	.05	.01
☐ 63 Jamie Moyer	.10	.05	.01
☐ 64 Fred Toliver	.10	.05	.01
☐ 65 Mitch Webster	.10	.05	.01
☐ 66 John Tudor	.10	.05	.01
☐ 67 John Cangelosi	.10	.05	.01
☐ 68 Mike Devereaux	.10	.05	.01
☐ 69 Brian Fisher	.10	.05	.01
☐ 70 Mike Marshall	.10	.05	.01
☐ 71 Zane Smith	.10	.05	.01
☐ 72A Brian Holton ERR (Photo actually Shawn Hillegas)	1.00	.45	.12
☐ 72B Brian Holton COR	.25	.11	.03
☐ 73 Jose Guzman	.10	.05	.01
☐ 74 Rick Mahler	.10	.05	.01
☐ 75 John Shelby	.10	.05	.01
☐ 76 Jim Deshaies	.10	.05	.01
☐ 77 Bobby Meacham	.10	.05	.01
☐ 78 Bryn Smith	.10	.05	.01
☐ 79 Joaquin Andujar	.10	.05	.01
☐ 80 Richard Dotson	.10	.05	.01
☐ 81 Charlie Lea	.10	.05	.01
☐ 82 Calvin Schiraldi	.10	.05	.01
☐ 83 Les Straker	.10	.05	.01
☐ 84 Les Lancaster	.10	.05	.01
☐ 85 Allan Anderson	.10	.05	.01
☐ 86 Junior Ortiz	.10	.05	.01
☐ 87 Jesse Orosco	.10	.05	.01
☐ 88 Felix Fermin	.10	.05	.01
☐ 89 Dave Anderson	.10	.05	.01
☐ 90 Rafael Belliard UER (Born '61, not '51)	.10	.05	.01
☐ 91 Franklin Stubbs	.10	.05	.01
☐ 92 Cecil Espy	.10	.05	.01
☐ 93 Albert Hall	.10	.05	.01
☐ 94 Tim Leary	.10	.05	.01
☐ 95 Mitch Williams	.10	.05	.01
☐ 96 Tracy Jones	.10	.05	.01
☐ 97 Danny Darwin	.10	.05	.01
☐ 98 Gary Ward	.10	.05	.01
☐ 99 Neal Heaton	.10	.05	.01
☐ 100 Jim Pankovits	.10	.05	.01
☐ 101 Bill Doran	.10	.05	.01
☐ 102 Tim Wallach	.10	.05	.01

☐ 103 Joe Magrane .10 .05 .01
☐ 104 Ozzie Virgil .10 .05 .01
☐ 105 Alvin Davis .10 .05 .01
☐ 106 Tom Brookens .10 .05 .01
☐ 107 Shawon Dunston .10 .05 .01
☐ 108 Tracy Woodson .10 .05 .01
☐ 109 Nelson Liriano .10 .05 .01
☐ 110 Devon White UER .25 .11 .03
(Doubles total 46,
should be 56)
☐ 111 Steve Balboni .10 .05 .01
☐ 112 Buddy Bell .25 .11 .03
☐ 113 German Jimenez .10 .05 .01
☐ 114 Ken Dayley .10 .05 .01
☐ 115 Andres Galarraga .50 .23 .06
☐ 116 Mike Scioscia .10 .05 .01
☐ 117 Gary Pettis .10 .05 .01
☐ 118 Ernie Whitt .10 .05 .01
☐ 119 Bob Boone .25 .11 .03
☐ 120 Ryne Sandberg 1.00 .45 .12
☐ 121 Bruce Benedict .10 .05 .01
☐ 122 Hubie Brooks .10 .05 .01
☐ 123 Mike Moore .10 .05 .01
☐ 124 Wallace Johnson .10 .05 .01
☐ 125 Bob Horner .10 .05 .01
☐ 126 Chili Davis .25 .11 .03
☐ 127 Manny Trillo .10 .05 .01
☐ 128 Chet Lemon .10 .05 .01
☐ 129 John Cerutti .10 .05 .01
☐ 130 Orel Hershiser .25 .11 .03
☐ 131 Terry Pendleton .25 .11 .03
☐ 132 Jeff Blauser .25 .11 .03
☐ 133 Mike Fitzgerald .10 .05 .01
☐ 134 Henry Cotto .10 .05 .01
☐ 135 Gerald Young .10 .05 .01
☐ 136 Luis Salazar .10 .05 .01
☐ 137 Alejandro Pena .10 .05 .01
☐ 138 Jack Howell .10 .05 .01
☐ 139 Tony Fernandez .10 .05 .01
☐ 140 Mark Grace .75 .35 .09
☐ 141 Ken Caminiti 1.00 .45 .12
☐ 142 Mike Jackson .10 .05 .01
☐ 143 Larry McWilliams .10 .05 .01
☐ 144 Andres Thomas .10 .05 .01
☐ 145 Nolan Ryan 3X 3.00 1.35 .35
☐ 146 Mike Davis .10 .05 .01
☐ 147 DeWayne Buice .10 .05 .01
☐ 148 Jody Davis .10 .05 .01
☐ 149 Jesse Barfield .10 .05 .01
☐ 150 Matt Nokes .10 .05 .01
☐ 151 Jerry Reuss .10 .05 .01
☐ 152 Rick Cerone .10 .05 .01
☐ 153 Storm Davis .10 .05 .01
☐ 154 Marvell Wynne .10 .05 .01
☐ 155 Will Clark .75 .35 .09
☐ 156 Luis Aguayo .10 .05 .01
☐ 157 Willie Upshaw .10 .05 .01
☐ 158 Randy Bush .10 .05 .01
☐ 159 Ron Darling .10 .05 .01
☐ 160 Kal Daniels .10 .05 .01
☐ 161 Spike Owen .10 .05 .01
☐ 162 Luis Polonia .25 .11 .03
☐ 163 Kevin Mitchell UER .25 .11 .03
('88/total HR's 18/52,
should be 19/53)
☐ 164 Dave Gallagher .10 .05 .01
☐ 165 Benito Santiago .25 .11 .03
☐ 166 Greg Gagne .10 .05 .01
☐ 167 Ken Phelps .10 .05 .01
☐ 168 Sid Fernandez .10 .05 .01
☐ 169 Bo Diaz .10 .05 .01
☐ 170 Cory Snyder .10 .05 .01
☐ 171 Eric Show .10 .05 .01
☐ 172 Robby Thompson .10 .05 .01
☐ 173 Marty Barrett .10 .05 .01
☐ 174 Dave Henderson .10 .05 .01
☐ 175 Ozzie Guillen .10 .05 .01
☐ 176 Barry Lyons .10 .05 .01
☐ 177 Kelvin Torve .10 .05 .01
☐ 178 Don Slaught .10 .05 .01
☐ 179 Steve Lombardozzi .10 .05 .01
☐ 180 Chris Sabo .10 .05 .01
☐ 181 Jose Uribe .10 .05 .01
☐ 182 Shane Mack .10 .05 .01
☐ 183 Ron Karkovice .10 .05 .01
☐ 184 Todd Benzinger .10 .05 .01
☐ 185 Dave Stewart .25 .11 .03
☐ 186 Julio Franco .25 .11 .03
☐ 187 Ron Robinson .10 .05 .01
☐ 188 Wally Backman .10 .05 .01
☐ 189 Randy Velarde .10 .05 .01
☐ 190 Joe Carter .50 .23 .06
☐ 191 Bob Welch .10 .05 .01
☐ 192 Kelly Paris .10 .05 .01
☐ 193 Chris Brown .10 .05 .01
☐ 194 Rick Reuschel .10 .05 .01
☐ 195 Roger Clemens .75 .35 .09
☐ 196 Dave Concepcion .25 .11 .03
☐ 197 Al Newman .10 .05 .01
☐ 198 Brook Jacoby .10 .05 .01
☐ 199 Mookie Wilson .25 .11 .03
☐ 200 Don Mattingly 2.00 .90 .25
☐ 201 Dick Schofield .10 .05 .01
☐ 202 Mark Gubicza .10 .05 .01
☐ 203 Gary Gaetti .10 .05 .01
☐ 204 Dan Pasqua .10 .05 .01
☐ 205 Andre Dawson .25 .11 .03
☐ 206 Chris Speier .10 .05 .01
☐ 207 Kent Tekulve .10 .05 .01
☐ 208 Rod Scurry .10 .05 .01
☐ 209 Scott Bailes .10 .05 .01
☐ 210 Rickey Henderson UER .50 .23 .06
(Throws Right)
☐ 211 Harold Baines .25 .11 .03
☐ 212 Tony Armas .10 .05 .01
☐ 213 Kent Hrbek .25 .11 .03
☐ 214 Darrin Jackson .10 .05 .01
☐ 215 George Brett 1.50 .70 .19
☐ 216 Rafael Santana .10 .05 .01
☐ 217 Andy Allanson .10 .05 .01
☐ 218 Brett Butler .25 .11 .03
☐ 219 Steve Jeltz .10 .05 .01
☐ 220 Jay Buhner 1.00 .45 .12
☐ 221 Bo Jackson .50 .23 .06
☐ 222 Angel Salazar .10 .05 .01
☐ 223 Kirk McCaskill .10 .05 .01
☐ 224 Steve Lyons .10 .05 .01
☐ 225 Bert Blyleven .25 .11 .03
☐ 226 Scott Bradley .10 .05 .01
☐ 227 Bob Melvin .10 .05 .01
☐ 228 Ron Kittle .10 .05 .01
☐ 229 Phil Bradley .10 .05 .01
☐ 230 Tommy John .25 .11 .03
☐ 231 Greg Walker .10 .05 .01
☐ 232 Juan Berenguer .10 .05 .01
☐ 233 Pat Tabler .10 .05 .01
☐ 234 Terry Clark .10 .05 .01
☐ 235 Rafael Palmeiro 1.00 .45 .12
☐ 236 Paul Zuvella .10 .05 .01
☐ 237 Willie Randolph .25 .11 .03
☐ 238 Bruce Fields .10 .05 .01
☐ 239 Mike Aldrete .10 .05 .01
☐ 240 Lance Parrish .10 .05 .01
☐ 241 Greg Maddux 4.00 1.80 .50
☐ 242 John Moses .10 .05 .01
☐ 243 Melido Perez .10 .05 .01
☐ 244 Willie Wilson .10 .05 .01
☐ 245 Mark McLemore .10 .05 .01
☐ 246 Von Hayes .10 .05 .01
☐ 247 Matt Williams 1.00 .45 .12
☐ 248 John Candelaria UER .10 .05 .01
(Listed as Yankee for
part of '87,
should be Mets)
☐ 249 Harold Reynolds .10 .05 .01
☐ 250 Greg Swindell .10 .05 .01
☐ 251 Juan Agosto .10 .05 .01
☐ 252 Mike Felder .10 .05 .01
☐ 253 Vince Coleman .10 .05 .01
☐ 254 Larry Sheets .10 .05 .01
☐ 255 George Bell .10 .05 .01
☐ 256 Terry Steinbach .25 .11 .03
☐ 257 Jack Armstrong .10 .05 .01
☐ 258 Dickie Thon .10 .05 .01
☐ 259 Ray Knight .10 .05 .01
☐ 260 Darryl Strawberry .25 .11 .03
☐ 261 Doug Sisk .10 .05 .01
☐ 262 Alex Trevino .10 .05 .01
☐ 263 Jeffrey Leonard .10 .05 .01
☐ 264 Tom Henke .10 .05 .01
☐ 265 Ozzie Smith 1.00 .45 .12
☐ 266 Dave Bergman .10 .05 .01
☐ 267 Tony Phillips .50 .23 .06
☐ 268 Mark Davis .10 .05 .01
☐ 269 Kevin Elster .25 .11 .03
☐ 270 Barry Larkin .75 .35 .09
☐ 271 Manny Lee .10 .05 .01
☐ 272 Tom Brunansky .10 .05 .01
☐ 273 Craig Biggio 2.00 .90 .25
☐ 274 Jim Gantner .10 .05 .01
☐ 275 Eddie Murray 1.00 .45 .12
☐ 276 Jeff Reed .10 .05 .01
☐ 277 Tim Teufel .10 .05 .01
☐ 278 Rick Honeycutt .10 .05 .01
☐ 279 Guillermo Hernandez .10 .05 .01
☐ 280 John Kruk .25 .11 .03
☐ 281 Luis Alicea .10 .05 .01
☐ 282 Jim Clancy .10 .05 .01
☐ 283 Billy Ripken .10 .05 .01
☐ 284 Craig Reynolds .10 .05 .01
☐ 285 Robin Yount .50 .23 .06
☐ 286 Jimmy Jones .10 .05 .01
☐ 287 Ron Oester .10 .05 .01
☐ 288 Terry Leach .10 .05 .01
☐ 289 Dennis Eckersley .25 .11 .03
☐ 290 Alan Trammell .25 .11 .03
☐ 291 Jimmy Key .25 .11 .03
☐ 292 Chris Bosio .10 .05 .01
☐ 293 Jose DeLeon .10 .05 .01
☐ 294 Jim Traber .10 .05 .01
☐ 295 Mike Scott .10 .05 .01
☐ 296 Roger McDowell .10 .05 .01
☐ 297 Garry Templeton .10 .05 .01
☐ 298 Doyle Alexander .10 .05 .01
☐ 299 Nick Esasky .10 .05 .01
☐ 300 Mark McGwire UER 1.25 .55 .16
(Doubles total 52,
should be 51)
☐ 301 Darryl Hamilton .25 .11 .03
☐ 302 Dave Smith .10 .05 .01
☐ 303 Rick Sutcliffe .10 .05 .01
☐ 304 Dave Stapleton .10 .05 .01
☐ 305 Alan Ashby .10 .05 .01
☐ 306 Pedro Guerrero .25 .11 .03
☐ 307 Ron Guidry .10 .05 .01
☐ 308 Steve Farr .10 .05 .01
☐ 309 Curt Ford .10 .05 .01
☐ 310 Claudell Washington .10 .05 .01
☐ 311 Tom Prince .10 .05 .01
☐ 312 Chad Kreuter .10 .05 .01
☐ 313 Ken Oberkfell .10 .05 .01
☐ 314 Jerry Browne .10 .05 .01
☐ 315 R.J. Reynolds .10 .05 .01
☐ 316 Scott Bankhead .10 .05 .01
☐ 317 Milt Thompson .10 .05 .01
☐ 318 Mario Diaz .10 .05 .01
☐ 319 Bruce Ruffin .10 .05 .01
☐ 320 Dave Valle .10 .05 .01
☐ 321A Gary Varsho ERR 2.00 .90 .25
(Back photo actually
Mike Bielecki bunting)
☐ 321B Gary Varsho COR .10 .05 .01
(In road uniform)
☐ 322 Paul Mirabella .10 .05 .01
☐ 323 Chuck Jackson .10 .05 .01
☐ 324 Drew Hall .10 .05 .01
☐ 325 Don August .10 .05 .01
☐ 326 Israel Sanchez .10 .05 .01
☐ 327 Denny Walling .10 .05 .01
☐ 328 Joel Skinner .10 .05 .01
☐ 329 Danny Tartabull .10 .05 .01
☐ 330 Tony Pena .10 .05 .01
☐ 331 Jim Sundberg .10 .05 .01
☐ 332 Jeff D. Robinson .10 .05 .01
☐ 333 Oddibe McDowell .10 .05 .01
☐ 334 Jose Lind .10 .05 .01
☐ 335 Paul Kilgus .10 .05 .01
☐ 336 Juan Samuel .10 .05 .01
☐ 337 Mike Campbell .10 .05 .01
☐ 338 Mike Maddux .10 .05 .01
☐ 339 Darnell Coles .10 .05 .01
☐ 340 Bob Dernier .10 .05 .01
☐ 341 Rafael Ramirez .10 .05 .01
☐ 342 Scott Sanderson .10 .05 .01
☐ 343 B.J. Surhoff .50 .23 .06
☐ 344 Billy Hatcher .10 .05 .01
☐ 345 Pat Perry .10 .05 .01
☐ 346 Jack Clark .25 .11 .03
☐ 347 Gary Thurman .10 .05 .01
☐ 348 Tim Jones .10 .05 .01
☐ 349 Dave Winfield .50 .23 .06
☐ 350 Frank White .25 .11 .03
☐ 351 Dave Collins .10 .05 .01
☐ 352 Jack Morris .25 .11 .03
☐ 353 Eric Plunk .10 .05 .01
☐ 354 Leon Durham .10 .05 .01
☐ 355 Ivan DeJesus .10 .05 .01
☐ 356 Brian Holman .10 .05 .01
☐ 357A Dale Murphy ERR 15.00 6.75 1.85
(Front has
reverse negative)
☐ 357B Dale Murphy COR .50 .23 .06
☐ 358 Mark Portugal .10 .05 .01
☐ 359 Andy McGaffigan .10 .05 .01
☐ 360 Tom Glavine 1.00 .45 .12
☐ 361 Keith Moreland .10 .05 .01
☐ 362 Todd Stottlemyre .25 .11 .03
☐ 363 Dave Leiper .10 .05 .01
☐ 364 Cecil Fielder .25 .11 .03
☐ 365 Carmelo Martinez .10 .05 .01
☐ 366 Dwight Evans .25 .11 .03
☐ 367 Kevin McReynolds .10 .05 .01
☐ 368 Rich Gedman .10 .05 .01
☐ 369 Len Dykstra .25 .11 .03
☐ 370 Jody Reed .10 .05 .01
☐ 371 Jose Canseco UER .50 .23 .06
(Strikeout total 391,
should be 491)
☐ 372 Rob Murphy .10 .05 .01
☐ 373 Mike Henneman .10 .05 .01
☐ 374 Walt Weiss .10 .05 .01
☐ 375 Rob Dibble .25 .11 .03
☐ 376 Kirby Puckett 1.50 .70 .19
(Mark McGwire
in background)
☐ 377 Dennis Martinez .25 .11 .03
☐ 378 Ron Gant .50 .23 .06
☐ 379 Brian Harper .10 .05 .01
☐ 380 Nelson Santovenia .10 .05 .01
☐ 381 Lloyd Moseby .10 .05 .01
☐ 382 Lance McCullers .10 .05 .01
☐ 383 Dave Stieb .10 .05 .01
☐ 384 Tony Gwynn 1.50 .70 .19
☐ 385 Mike Flanagan .10 .05 .01
☐ 386 Bob Ojeda .10 .05 .01
☐ 387 Bruce Hurst .10 .05 .01
☐ 388 Dave Magadan .10 .05 .01
☐ 389 Wade Boggs .50 .23 .06
☐ 390 Gary Carter .25 .11 .03
☐ 391 Frank Tanana .10 .05 .01
☐ 392 Curt Young .10 .05 .01
☐ 393 Jeff Treadway .10 .05 .01
☐ 394 Darrell Evans .25 .11 .03
☐ 395 Glenn Hubbard .10 .05 .01
☐ 396 Chuck Cary .10 .05 .01
☐ 397 Frank Viola .10 .05 .01
☐ 398 Jeff Parrett .10 .05 .01
☐ 399 Terry Blocker .10 .05 .01
☐ 400 Dan Gladden .10 .05 .01
☐ 401 Louie Meadows .10 .05 .01
☐ 402 Tim Raines .50 .23 .06
☐ 403 Joey Meyer .10 .05 .01
☐ 404 Larry Andersen .10 .05 .01
☐ 405 Rex Hudler .10 .05 .01
☐ 406 Mike Schmidt .75 .35 .09
☐ 407 John Franco .25 .11 .03
☐ 408 Brady Anderson 3.00 1.35 .35
☐ 409 Don Carman .10 .05 .01
☐ 410 Eric Davis .25 .11 .03
☐ 411 Bob Stanley .10 .05 .01
☐ 412 Pete Smith .10 .05 .01
☐ 413 Jim Rice .50 .23 .06
☐ 414 Bruce Sutter .10 .05 .01
☐ 415 Oil Can Boyd .10 .05 .01
☐ 416 Ruben Sierra .25 .11 .03
☐ 417 Mike LaValliere .10 .05 .01
☐ 418 Steve Buechele .10 .05 .01
☐ 419 Gary Redus .10 .05 .01
☐ 420 Scott Fletcher .10 .05 .01
☐ 421 Dale Sveum .10 .05 .01
☐ 422 Bob Knepper .10 .05 .01
☐ 423 Luis Rivera .10 .05 .01
☐ 424 Ted Higuera .10 .05 .01
☐ 425 Kevin Bass .10 .05 .01
☐ 426 Ken Gerhart .10 .05 .01
☐ 427 Shane Rawley .10 .05 .01
☐ 428 Paul O'Neill .25 .11 .03
☐ 429 Joe Orsulak .10 .05 .01
☐ 430 Jackie Gutierrez .10 .05 .01
☐ 431 Gerald Perry .10 .05 .01
☐ 432 Mike Greenwell .10 .05 .01
☐ 433 Jerry Royster .10 .05 .01
☐ 434 Ellis Burks .50 .23 .06
☐ 435 Ed Olwine .10 .05 .01
☐ 436 Dave Rucker .10 .05 .01
☐ 437 Charlie Hough .25 .11 .03
☐ 438 Bob Walk .10 .05 .01
☐ 439 Bob Brower .10 .05 .01
☐ 440 Barry Bonds 1.50 .70 .19
☐ 441 Tom Foley .10 .05 .01
☐ 442 Rob Deer .10 .05 .01
☐ 443 Glenn Davis .10 .05 .01
☐ 444 Dave Martinez .10 .05 .01
☐ 445 Bill Wegman .10 .05 .01
☐ 446 Lloyd McClendon .10 .05 .01
☐ 447 Dave Schmidt .10 .05 .01
☐ 448 Darren Daulton .25 .11 .03
☐ 449 Frank Williams .10 .05 .01
☐ 450 Don Aase .10 .05 .01
☐ 451 Lou Whitaker .25 .11 .03
☐ 452 Goose Gossage .50 .23 .06
☐ 453 Ed Whitson .10 .05 .01
☐ 454 Jim Walewander .10 .05 .01
☐ 455 Damon Berryhill .10 .05 .01
☐ 456 Tim Burke .10 .05 .01
☐ 457 Barry Jones .10 .05 .01
☐ 458 Joel Youngblood .10 .05 .01
☐ 459 Floyd Youmans .10 .05 .01
☐ 460 Mark Salas .10 .05 .01
☐ 461 Jeff Russell .10 .05 .01
☐ 462 Darrell Miller .10 .05 .01
☐ 463 Jeff Kunkel .10 .05 .01
☐ 464 Sherman Corbett .10 .05 .01
☐ 465 Curtis Wilkerson .10 .05 .01
☐ 466 Bud Black .10 .05 .01
☐ 467 Cal Ripken 3.00 1.35 .35
☐ 468 John Farrell .10 .05 .01
☐ 469 Terry Kennedy .10 .05 .01
☐ 470 Tom Candiotti .10 .05 .01
☐ 471 Roberto Alomar 1.50 .70 .19
☐ 472 Jeff M. Robinson .10 .05 .01
☐ 473 Vance Law .10 .05 .01
☐ 474 Randy Ready UER .10 .05 .01
(Strikeout total 136,
should be 115)
☐ 475 Walt Terrell .10 .05 .01
☐ 476 Kelly Downs .10 .05 .01
☐ 477 Johnny Paredes .10 .05 .01
☐ 478 Shawn Hillegas .10 .05 .01
☐ 479 Bob Brenly .10 .05 .01
☐ 480 Otis Nixon .10 .05 .01
☐ 481 Johnny Ray .10 .05 .01
☐ 482 Geno Petralli .10 .05 .01
☐ 483 Stu Cliburn .10 .05 .01
☐ 484 Pete Incaviglia .25 .11 .03
☐ 485 Brian Downing .10 .05 .01
☐ 486 Jeff Stone .10 .05 .01
☐ 487 Carmen Castillo .10 .05 .01
☐ 488 Tom Niedenfuer .10 .05 .01
☐ 489 Jay Bell .50 .23 .06
☐ 490 Rick Schu .10 .05 .01
☐ 491 Jeff Pico .10 .05 .01
☐ 492 Mark Parent .10 .05 .01
☐ 493 Eric King .10 .05 .01
☐ 494 Al Nipper .10 .05 .01
☐ 495 Andy Hawkins .10 .05 .01
☐ 496 Daryl Boston .10 .05 .01
☐ 497 Ernie Riles .10 .05 .01
☐ 498 Pascual Perez .10 .05 .01
☐ 499 Bill Long UER .10 .05 .01

(Games started total
70, should be 44)
☐ 500 Kirt Manwaring .10 .05 .01
☐ 501 Chuck Crim .10 .05 .01
☐ 502 Candy Maldonado .10 .05 .01
☐ 503 Dennis Lamp .10 .05 .01
☐ 504 Glenn Braggs .10 .05 .01
☐ 505 Joe Price .10 .05 .01
☐ 506 Ken Williams .10 .05 .01
☐ 507 Bill Pecota .10 .05 .01
☐ 508 Rey Quinones .10 .05 .01
☐ 509 Jeff Bittiger .10 .05 .01
☐ 510 Kevin Seitzer .10 .05 .01
☐ 511 Steve Bedrosian .10 .05 .01
☐ 512 Todd Worrell .10 .05 .01
☐ 513 Chris James .10 .05 .01
☐ 514 Jose Oquendo .10 .05 .01
☐ 515 David Palmer .10 .05 .01
☐ 516 John Smiley .10 .05 .01
☐ 517 Dave Clark .10 .05 .01
☐ 518 Mike Dunne .10 .05 .01
☐ 519 Ron Washington .10 .05 .01
☐ 520 Bob Kipper .10 .05 .01
☐ 521 Lee Smith .25 .11 .03
☐ 522 Juan Castillo .10 .05 .01
☐ 523 Don Robinson .10 .05 .01
☐ 524 Kevin Romine .10 .05 .01
☐ 525 Paul Molitor .75 .35 .09
☐ 526 Mark Langston .25 .11 .03
☐ 527 Donnie Hill .10 .05 .01
☐ 528 Larry Owen .10 .05 .01
☐ 529 Jerry Reed .10 .05 .01
☐ 530 Jack McDowell .25 .11 .03
☐ 531 Greg Mathews .10 .05 .01
☐ 532 John Russell .10 .05 .01
☐ 533 Dan Quisenberry .10 .05 .01
☐ 534 Greg Gross .10 .05 .01
☐ 535 Danny Cox .10 .05 .01
☐ 536 Terry Francona .10 .05 .01
☐ 537 Andy Van Slyke .25 .11 .03
☐ 538 Mel Hall .10 .05 .01
☐ 539 Jim Gott .10 .05 .01
☐ 540 Doug Jones .10 .05 .01
☐ 541 Craig Lefferts .10 .05 .01
☐ 542 Mike Boddicker .10 .05 .01
☐ 543 Greg Brock .10 .05 .01
☐ 544 Atlee Hammaker .10 .05 .01
☐ 545 Tom Bolton .10 .05 .01
☐ 546 Mike Macfarlane .25 .11 .03
☐ 547 Rich Renteria .10 .05 .01
☐ 548 John Davis .10 .05 .01
☐ 549 Floyd Bannister .10 .05 .01
☐ 550 Mickey Brantley .10 .05 .01
☐ 551 Duane Ward .10 .05 .01
☐ 552 Dan Petry .10 .05 .01
☐ 553 Mickey Tettleton UER .25 .11 .03
(Walks total 175,
should be 136)
☐ 554 Rick Leach .10 .05 .01
☐ 555 Mike Witt .10 .05 .01
☐ 556 Sid Bream .10 .05 .01
☐ 557 Bobby Witt .10 .05 .01
☐ 558 Tommy Herr .10 .05 .01
☐ 559 Randy Milligan .10 .05 .01
☐ 560 Jose Cecena .10 .05 .01
☐ 561 Mackey Sasser .10 .05 .01
☐ 562 Carney Lansford .25 .11 .03
☐ 563 Rick Aguilera .25 .11 .03
☐ 564 Ron Hassey .10 .05 .01
☐ 565 Dwight Gooden .25 .11 .03
☐ 566 Paul Assenmacher .10 .05 .01
☐ 567 Neil Allen .10 .05 .01
☐ 568 Jim Morrison .10 .05 .01
☐ 569 Mike Pagliarulo .10 .05 .01
☐ 570 Ted Simmons .25 .11 .03
☐ 571 Mark Thurmond .10 .05 .01
☐ 572 Fred McGriff .75 .35 .09
☐ 573 Wally Joyner .25 .11 .03
☐ 574 Jose Bautista .10 .05 .01
☐ 575 Kelly Gruber .10 .05 .01
☐ 576 Cecilio Guante .10 .05 .01
☐ 577 Mark Davidson .10 .05 .01
☐ 578 Bobby Bonilla UER .50 .23 .06
(Total steals 2 in '87,
should be 3)
☐ 579 Mike Stanley .10 .05 .01
☐ 580 Gene Larkin .10 .05 .01
☐ 581 Stan Javier .10 .05 .01
☐ 582 Howard Johnson .10 .05 .01
☐ 583A Mike Gallego ERR 1.00 .45 .12
(Front reversed
negative)
☐ 583B Mike Gallego COR .50 .23 .06
☐ 584 David Cone .75 .35 .09
☐ 585 Doug Jennings .10 .05 .01
☐ 586 Charles Hudson .10 .05 .01
☐ 587 Dion James .10 .05 .01
☐ 588 Al Leiter .25 .11 .03
☐ 589 Charlie Puleo .10 .05 .01
☐ 590 Roberto Kelly .25 .11 .03
☐ 591 Thad Bosley .10 .05 .01
☐ 592 Pete Stanicek .10 .05 .01
☐ 593 Pat Borders .25 .11 .03
☐ 594 Bryan Harvey .25 .11 .03
☐ 595 Jeff Ballard .10 .05 .01
☐ 596 Jeff Reardon .25 .11 .03
☐ 597 Doug Drabek .25 .11 .03
☐ 598 Edwin Correa .10 .05 .01
☐ 599 Keith Atherton .10 .05 .01
☐ 600 Dave LaPoint .10 .05 .01
☐ 601 Don Baylor .50 .23 .06
☐ 602 Tom Pagnozzi .10 .05 .01
☐ 603 Tim Flannery .10 .05 .01
☐ 604 Gene Walter .10 .05 .01
☐ 605 Dave Parker .25 .11 .03
☐ 606 Mike Diaz .10 .05 .01
☐ 607 Chris Gwynn .10 .05 .01
☐ 608 Odell Jones .10 .05 .01
☐ 609 Carlton Fisk .50 .23 .06
☐ 610 Jay Howell .10 .05 .01
☐ 611 Tim Crews .10 .05 .01
☐ 612 Keith Hernandez .25 .11 .03
☐ 613 Willie Fraser .10 .05 .01
☐ 614 Jim Eppard .10 .05 .01
☐ 615 Jeff Hamilton .10 .05 .01
☐ 616 Kurt Stillwell .10 .05 .01
☐ 617 Tom Browning .10 .05 .01
☐ 618 Jeff Montgomery .25 .11 .03
☐ 619 Jose Rijo .10 .05 .01
☐ 620 Jamie Quirk .10 .05 .01
☐ 621 Willie McGee .10 .05 .01
☐ 622 Mark Grant UER .10 .05 .01
(Glove on wrong hand)
☐ 623 Bill Swift .10 .05 .01
☐ 624 Orlando Mercado .10 .05 .01
☐ 625 John Costello .10 .05 .01
☐ 626 Jose Gonzalez .10 .05 .01
☐ 627A Bill Schroeder ERR 1.00 .45 .12
(Back photo actually
Ronn Reynolds buckling
shin guards)
☐ 627B Bill Schroeder COR .50 .23 .06
☐ 628A Fred Manrique ERR .50 .23 .06
(Back photo actually
Ozzie Guillen throwing)
☐ 628B Fred Manrique COR .10 .05 .01
(Swinging bat on back)
☐ 629 Ricky Horton .10 .05 .01
☐ 630 Dan Plesac .10 .05 .01
☐ 631 Alfredo Griffin .10 .05 .01
☐ 632 Chuck Finley .25 .11 .03
☐ 633 Kirk Gibson .50 .23 .06
☐ 634 Randy Myers .25 .11 .03
☐ 635 Greg Minton .10 .05 .01
☐ 636A Herm Winningham .50 .23 .06
ERR (W1nningham
on back)
☐ 636B Herm Winningham COR .10 .05 .01
☐ 637 Charlie Leibrandt .10 .05 .01
☐ 638 Tim Birtsas .10 .05 .01
☐ 639 Bill Buckner .25 .11 .03
☐ 640 Danny Jackson .10 .05 .01
☐ 641 Greg Booker .10 .05 .01
☐ 642 Jim Presley .10 .05 .01
☐ 643 Gene Nelson .10 .05 .01
☐ 644 Rod Booker .10 .05 .01
☐ 645 Dennis Rasmussen .10 .05 .01
☐ 646 Juan Nieves .10 .05 .01
☐ 647 Bobby Thigpen .10 .05 .01
☐ 648 Tim Belcher .10 .05 .01
☐ 649 Mike Young .10 .05 .01
☐ 650 Ivan Calderon .10 .05 .01
☐ 651 Oswaldo Peraza .10 .05 .01
☐ 652A Pat Sheridan ERR 8.00 3.60 1.00
(No position on front)
☐ 652B Pat Sheridan COR .10 .05 .01
☐ 653 Mike Morgan .10 .05 .01
☐ 654 Mike Heath .10 .05 .01
☐ 655 Jay Tibbs .10 .05 .01
☐ 656 Fernando Valenzuela .25 .11 .03
☐ 657 Lee Mazzilli .10 .05 .01
☐ 658 Frank Viola AL CY .10 .05 .01
☐ 659A Jose Canseco AL MVP .50 .23 .06
(Eagle logo in black)
☐ 659B Jose Canseco AL MVP .50 .23 .06
(Eagle logo in blue)
☐ 660 Walt Weiss AL ROY .10 .05 .01
☐ 661 Orel Hershiser NL CY .25 .11 .03
☐ 662 Kirk Gibson NL MVP .50 .23 .06
☐ 663 Chris Sabo NL ROY .10 .05 .01
☐ 664 Dennis Eckersley .25 .11 .03
ALCS MVP
☐ 665 Orel Hershiser .25 .11 .03
NLCS MVP
☐ 666 Kirk Gibson WS .50 .23 .06
☐ 667 Orel Hershiser WS MVP .25 .11 .03
☐ 668 Wally Joyner TC .25 .11 .03
☐ 669 Nolan Ryan TC .75 .35 .09
☐ 670 Jose Canseco TC .50 .23 .06
☐ 671 Fred McGriff TC .50 .23 .06
☐ 672 Dale Murphy TC .50 .23 .06
☐ 673 Paul Molitor TC .50 .23 .06
☐ 674 Ozzie Smith TC .50 .23 .06
☐ 675 Ryne Sandberg TC .50 .23 .06
☐ 676 Kirk Gibson TC .50 .23 .06
☐ 677 Andres Galarraga TC .50 .23 .06
☐ 678 Will Clark TC .50 .23 .06
☐ 679 Cory Snyder TC .10 .05 .01
☐ 680 Alvin Davis TC .10 .05 .01
☐ 681 Darryl Strawberry TC .25 .11 .03
☐ 682 Cal Ripken TC .75 .35 .09
☐ 683 Tony Gwynn TC .50 .23 .06
☐ 684 Mike Schmidt TC .50 .23 .06
☐ 685 Andy Van Slyke TC UER .10 .05 .01
(96 Junior Ortiz)
☐ 686 Ruben Sierra TC .25 .11 .03
☐ 687 Wade Boggs TC .50 .23 .06
☐ 688 Eric Davis TC .25 .11 .03
☐ 689 George Brett TC .50 .23 .06
☐ 690 Alan Trammell TC .25 .11 .03
☐ 691 Frank Viola TC .10 .05 .01
☐ 692 Harold Baines TC .25 .11 .03
☐ 693 Don Mattingly TC .50 .23 .06
☐ 694 Checklist 1-100 .10 .05 .01
☐ 695 Checklist 101-200 .10 .05 .01
☐ 696 Checklist 201-300 .10 .05 .01
☐ 697 Checklist 301-400 .10 .05 .01
☐ 698 Checklist 401-500 UER .10 .05 .01
(467 Cal Ripkin Jr.)
☐ 699 Checklist 501-600 UER .10 .05 .01
(543 Greg Booker)
☐ 700 Checklist 601-700 .10 .05 .01
☐ 701 Checklist 701-800 .10 .05 .01
☐ 702 Jesse Barfield .10 .05 .01
☐ 703 Walt Terrell .10 .05 .01
☐ 704 Dickie Thon .10 .05 .01
☐ 705 Al Leiter .25 .11 .03
☐ 706 Dave LaPoint .10 .05 .01
☐ 707 Charlie Hayes .50 .23 .06
☐ 708 Andy Hawkins .10 .05 .01
☐ 709 Mickey Hatcher .10 .05 .01
☐ 710 Lance McCullers .10 .05 .01
☐ 711 Ron Kittle .10 .05 .01
☐ 712 Bert Blyleven .25 .11 .03
☐ 713 Rick Dempsey .10 .05 .01
☐ 714 Ken Williams .10 .05 .01
☐ 715 Steve Rosenberg .10 .05 .01
☐ 716 Joe Skalski .10 .05 .01
☐ 717 Spike Owen .10 .05 .01
☐ 718 Todd Burns .10 .05 .01
☐ 719 Kevin Gross .10 .05 .01
☐ 720 Tommy Herr .10 .05 .01
☐ 721 Rob Ducey .10 .05 .01
☐ 722 Gary Green .10 .05 .01
☐ 723 Gregg Olson .25 .11 .03
☐ 724 Greg W. Harris .10 .05 .01
☐ 725 Craig Worthington .10 .05 .01
☐ 726 Tom Howard .10 .05 .01
☐ 727 Dale Mohorcic .10 .05 .01
☐ 728 Rich Yett .10 .05 .01
☐ 729 Mel Hall .10 .05 .01
☐ 730 Floyd Youmans .10 .05 .01
☐ 731 Lonnie Smith .10 .05 .01
☐ 732 Wally Backman .10 .05 .01
☐ 733 Trevor Wilson .10 .05 .01
☐ 734 Jose Alvarez .10 .05 .01
☐ 735 Bob Milacki .10 .05 .01
☐ 736 Tom Gordon .25 .11 .03
☐ 737 Wally Whitehurst .10 .05 .01
☐ 738 Mike Aldrete .10 .05 .01
☐ 739 Keith Miller .10 .05 .01
☐ 740 Randy Milligan .10 .05 .01
☐ 741 Jeff Parrett .10 .05 .01
☐ 742 Steve Finley 1.00 .45 .12
☐ 743 Junior Felix .10 .05 .01
☐ 744 Pete Harnisch .25 .11 .03
☐ 745 Bill Spiers .10 .05 .01
☐ 746 Hensley Meulens .10 .05 .01
☐ 747 Juan Bell .10 .05 .01
☐ 748 Steve Sax .10 .05 .01
☐ 749 Phil Bradley .10 .05 .01
☐ 750 Rey Quinones .10 .05 .01
☐ 751 Tommy Gregg .10 .05 .01
☐ 752 Kevin Brown .50 .23 .06
☐ 753 Derek Lilliquist .10 .05 .01
☐ 754 Todd Zeile .50 .23 .06
☐ 755 Jim Abbott .50 .23 .06
(Triple exposure)
☐ 756 Ozzie Canseco .10 .05 .01
☐ 757 Nick Esasky .10 .05 .01
☐ 758 Mike Moore .10 .05 .01
☐ 759 Rob Murphy .10 .05 .01
☐ 760 Rick Mahler .10 .05 .01
☐ 761 Fred Lynn .10 .05 .01
☐ 762 Kevin Blankenship .10 .05 .01
☐ 763 Eddie Murray 1.00 .45 .12
☐ 764 Steve Searcy .10 .05 .01
☐ 765 Jerome Walton .25 .11 .03
☐ 766 Erik Hanson .50 .23 .06
☐ 767 Bob Boone .25 .11 .03
☐ 768 Edgar Martinez .75 .35 .09
☐ 769 Jose DeJesus .10 .05 .01
☐ 770 Greg Briley .10 .05 .01
☐ 771 Steve Peters .10 .05 .01
☐ 772 Rafael Palmeiro 1.00 .45 .12
☐ 773 Jack Clark .25 .11 .03
☐ 774 Nolan Ryan 3.00 1.35 .35
(Throwing football)
☐ 775 Lance Parrish .10 .05 .01
☐ 776 Joe Girardi .50 .23 .06
☐ 777 Willie Randolph .25 .11 .03
☐ 778 Mitch Williams .10 .05 .01
☐ 779 Dennis Cook .10 .05 .01
☐ 780 Dwight Smith .25 .11 .03
☐ 781 Lenny Harris .10 .05 .01
☐ 782 Torey Lovullo .10 .05 .01
☐ 783 Norm Charlton .25 .11 .03
☐ 784 Chris Brown .10 .05 .01
☐ 785 Todd Benzinger .10 .05 .01
☐ 786 Shane Rawley .10 .05 .01
☐ 787 Omar Vizquel 2.00 .90 .25
☐ 788 LaVel Freeman .10 .05 .01
☐ 789 Jeffrey Leonard .10 .05 .01
☐ 790 Eddie Williams .10 .05 .01
☐ 791 Jamie Moyer .10 .05 .01
☐ 792 Bruce Hurst UER .10 .05 .01
(Workd Series)
☐ 793 Julio Franco .25 .11 .03
☐ 794 Claudell Washington .10 .05 .01
☐ 795 Jody Davis .10 .05 .01
☐ 796 Oddibe McDowell .10 .05 .01
☐ 797 Paul Kilgus .10 .05 .01
☐ 798 Tracy Jones .10 .05 .01
☐ 799 Steve Wilson .10 .05 .01
☐ 800 Pete O'Brien .10 .05 .01

1989 Upper Deck Sheets

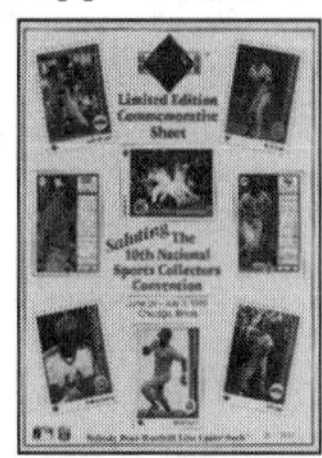

These blank-backed, 8 1/2" by 11" sheets feature pictures of Upper Deck baseball cards and were distributed at conventions in Chicago and Washington, D.C. The sheets carried a production run number but not the total number produced. The sheets are listed below in chronological order.

	MINT	NRMT	EXC
COMPLETE SET (3)	35.00	16.00	4.40
COMMON SHEET (1-3)	10.00	4.50	1.25

☐ 1 10th National Sports 10.00 4.50 1.25
Collectors Convention
Chicago, Illinois
June 29-July 2, 1989
Kevin Mitchell
Mickey Tettleton
Dwight Gooden
Harold Baines
Mark Grace
Jim Abbott
Wade Boggs
Will Clark
☐ 2 National Candy 20.00 9.00 2.50
Wholesalers Expo
Washington, D.C.
July 27-29, 1989
Ken Griffey Jr.
Mark McGwire
Junior Felix
Cal Ripken
Barry Larkin
Todd Zeile
Tim Raines
Todd Benzinger
☐ 3 Sun-Times Card Show 10.00 4.50 1.25
Chicago, Illinois
Dec. 16-17, 1989
Ken Griffey Jr.
Gary Gaetti
Don Mattingly
Andre Dawson
Kevin Seitzer
Tom Browning
Andres Galarraga
Kevin Mitchell

1990 Upper Deck

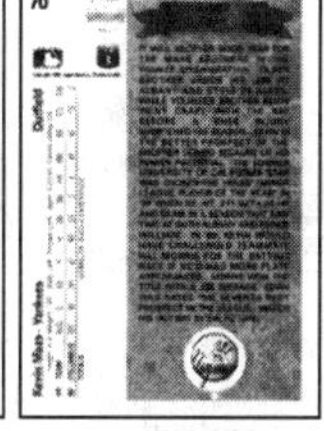

The 1990 Upper Deck set contains 800 standard-size cards issued in two series, low numbers (1-700) and high numbers (701-800). Cards were distributed in fin-wrapped low and high series foil packs, complete 800-card factory sets and 100-card high series factory sets. High series foil packs contained a mixture of low and high series cards. The front and back borders are white, and both sides feature full-color photos. The horizontally oriented backs have recent stats and anti-counterfeiting holograms. Team checklist cards are mixed in with the first 100 cards of the set. Rookie Cards in the set include

Wilson Alvarez, Carlos Baerga, Juan Gonzalez, Marquis Grissom, Todd Hundley, David Justice, Ray Lankford, Ben McDonald, Dean Palmer, Sammy Sosa and Larry Walker. The high series contains a Nolan Ryan variation; all cards produced before August 12th only discuss Ryan's sixth no-hitter while the later-issue cards include a stripe honoring Ryan's 300th victory. Card 702 (Rookie Threats) was originally scheduled to be Mike Witt. A few Witt cards with 702 on back and checklist cards showing Witt as 702 escaped into early packs; they are characterized by a black rectangle covering much of the card's back.

	MINT	NRMT	EXC
COMPLETE SET (800)	20.00	9.00	2.50
COMPLETE FACT.SET (800)	20.00	9.00	2.50
COMPLETE LO SET (700)	16.00	7.25	2.00
COMPLETE HI SET (100)	4.00	1.80	.50
COMPLETE HI FACT.SET (100)	4.00	1.80	.50
COMMON CARD (1-800)	.05	.02	.01

Card	MINT	NRMT	EXC
☐ 1 Star Rookie Checklist	.05	.02	.01
☐ 2 Randy Nosek	.05	.02	.01
☐ 3 Tom Drees UER (11th line, hulred, should be hurled)	.05	.02	.01
☐ 4 Curt Young	.05	.02	.01
☐ 5 Devon White TC	.15	.07	.02
☐ 6 Luis Salazar	.05	.02	.01
☐ 7 Von Hayes TC	.05	.02	.01
☐ 8 Jose Bautista	.05	.02	.01
☐ 9 Marquis Grissom	1.00	.45	.12
☐ 10 Orel Hershiser TC	.15	.07	.02
☐ 11 Rick Aguilera	.15	.07	.02
☐ 12 Benito Santiago TC	.05	.02	.01
☐ 13 Deion Sanders	.40	.18	.05
☐ 14 Marvell Wynne	.05	.02	.01
☐ 15 Dave West	.05	.02	.01
☐ 16 Bobby Bonilla TC	.15	.07	.02
☐ 17 Sammy Sosa	1.50	.70	.19
☐ 18 Steve Sax TC	.05	.02	.01
☐ 19 Jack Howell	.05	.02	.01
☐ 20 Mike Schmidt Special UER (Suprising, should be surprising)	.50	.23	.06
☐ 21 Robin Ventura UER (Samta Maria)	.30	.14	.04
☐ 22 Brian Meyer	.05	.02	.01
☐ 23 Blaine Beatty	.05	.02	.01
☐ 24 Ken Griffey Jr. TC	.75	.35	.09
☐ 25 Greg Vaughn UER (Association misspelled as assiocation)	.30	.14	.04
☐ 26 Xavier Hernandez	.05	.02	.01
☐ 27 Jason Grimsley	.05	.02	.01
☐ 28 Eric Anthony UER (Ashville, should be Asheville)	.15	.07	.02
☐ 29 Tim Raines TC UER (Wallach listed before Walker)	.15	.07	.02
☐ 30 David Wells	.05	.02	.01
☐ 31 Hal Morris	.15	.07	.02
☐ 32 Bo Jackson TC	.15	.07	.02
☐ 33 Kelly Mann	.05	.02	.01
☐ 34 Nolan Ryan Special	.75	.35	.09
☐ 35 Scott Service UER (Born Cincinatti on 7/27/67, should be Cincinnati 2/27)	.05	.02	.01
☐ 36 Mark McGwire TC	.30	.14	.04
☐ 37 Tino Martinez	.30	.14	.04
☐ 38 Chili Davis	.15	.07	.02
☐ 39 Scott Sanderson	.05	.02	.01
☐ 40 Kevin Mitchell TC	.05	.02	.01
☐ 41 Lou Whitaker TC	.15	.07	.02
☐ 42 Scott Coolbaugh UER (Definately)	.05	.02	.01
☐ 43 Jose Cano UER (Born 9/7/62, should be 3/7/62)	.05	.02	.01
☐ 44 Jose Vizcaino	.30	.14	.04
☐ 45 Bob Hamelin	.15	.07	.02
☐ 46 Jose Offerman UER (Posesses)	.15	.07	.02
☐ 47 Kevin Blankenship	.05	.02	.01
☐ 48 Kirby Puckett TC	.30	.14	.04
☐ 49 Tommy Greene UER (Livest, should be liveliest)	.05	.02	.01
☐ 50 Will Clark Special UER (Perenial, should be perennial)	.30	.14	.04
☐ 51 Rob Nelson	.05	.02	.01
☐ 52 Chris Hammond UER (Chatanooga)	.05	.02	.01
☐ 53 Joe Carter TC	.15	.07	.02
☐ 54A Ben McDonald ERR (No Rookie designation on card front)	8.00	3.60	1.00
☐ 54B Ben McDonald COR	.30	.14	.04
☐ 55 Andy Benes UER (Whichita)	.30	.14	.04
☐ 56 John Olerud	.30	.14	.04
☐ 57 Roger Clemens TC	.30	.14	.04
☐ 58 Tony Armas	.05	.02	.01
☐ 59 George Canale	.05	.02	.01
☐ 60A Mickey Tettleton TC ERR (683 Jamie Weston)	2.00	.90	.25
☐ 60B Mickey Tettleton TC COR (683 Mickey Weston)	.05	.02	.01
☐ 61 Mike Stanton	.15	.07	.02
☐ 62 Dwight Gooden TC	.15	.07	.02
☐ 63 Kent Mercker UER (Albuguerque)	.15	.07	.02
☐ 64 Francisco Cabrera	.05	.02	.01
☐ 65 Steve Avery UER (Born NJ, should be MI, Merker should be Mercker)	.30	.14	.04
☐ 66 Jose Canseco	.30	.14	.04
☐ 67 Matt Merullo	.05	.02	.01
☐ 68 Vince Coleman TC UER (Guerrero)	.05	.02	.01
☐ 69 Ron Karkovice	.05	.02	.01
☐ 70 Kevin Maas	.15	.07	.02
☐ 71 Dennis Cook UER (Shown with righty glove on card back)	.05	.02	.01
☐ 72 Juan Gonzalez UER (135 games for Tulsa in '89, should be 133)	4.00	1.80	.50
☐ 73 Andre Dawson TC	.15	.07	.02
☐ 74 Dean Palmer UER (Permanent misspelled as perminant)	.75	.35	.09
☐ 75 Bo Jackson Special UER (Monsterous, should be monstrous)	.15	.07	.02
☐ 76 Rob Richie	.05	.02	.01
☐ 77 Bobby Rose UER (Pickin, should be pick in)	.05	.02	.01
☐ 78 Brian DuBois UER (Commiting)	.05	.02	.01
☐ 79 Ozzie Guillen TC	.05	.02	.01
☐ 80 Gene Nelson	.05	.02	.01
☐ 81 Bob McClure	.05	.02	.01
☐ 82 Julio Franco TC	.05	.02	.01
☐ 83 Greg Minton	.05	.02	.01
☐ 84 John Smoltz TC UER (Oddibe not Odibbe)	.30	.14	.04
☐ 85 Willie Fraser	.05	.02	.01
☐ 86 Neal Heaton	.05	.02	.01
☐ 87 Kevin Tapani UER (24th line has excpet, should be except)	.15	.07	.02
☐ 88 Mike Scott TC	.05	.02	.01
☐ 89A Jim Gott ERR (Photo actually Rick Reed)	2.50	1.10	.30
☐ 89B Jim Gott COR	.05	.02	.01
☐ 90 Lance Johnson	.15	.07	.02
☐ 91 Robin Yount TC UER (Checklist on back has 178 Rob Deer and 176 Mike Felder)	.30	.14	.04
☐ 92 Jeff Parrett	.05	.02	.01
☐ 93 Julio Machado UER (Valenzuelan, should be Venezuelan)	.05	.02	.01
☐ 94 Ron Jones	.05	.02	.01
☐ 95 George Bell TC	.05	.02	.01
☐ 96 Jerry Reuss	.05	.02	.01
☐ 97 Brian Fisher	.05	.02	.01
☐ 98 Kevin Ritz UER (Amercian)	.05	.02	.01
☐ 99 Barry Larkin TC	.30	.14	.04
☐ 100 Checklist 1-100	.05	.02	.01
☐ 101 Gerald Perry	.05	.02	.01
☐ 102 Kevin Appier	.30	.14	.04
☐ 103 Julio Franco	.15	.07	.02
☐ 104 Craig Biggio	.30	.14	.04
☐ 105 Bo Jackson UER ('89 BA wrong, should be .256)	.15	.07	.02
☐ 106 Junior Felix	.05	.02	.01
☐ 107 Mike Harkey	.05	.02	.01
☐ 108 Fred McGriff	.30	.14	.04
☐ 109 Rick Sutcliffe	.05	.02	.01
☐ 110 Pete O'Brien	.05	.02	.01
☐ 111 Kelly Gruber	.05	.02	.01
☐ 112 Dwight Evans	.15	.07	.02
☐ 113 Pat Borders	.05	.02	.01
☐ 114 Dwight Gooden	.15	.07	.02
☐ 115 Kevin Batiste	.05	.02	.01
☐ 116 Eric Davis	.15	.07	.02
☐ 117 Kevin Mitchell UER (Career HR total 99, should be 100)	.15	.07	.02
☐ 118 Ron Oester	.05	.02	.01
☐ 119 Brett Butler	.15	.07	.02
☐ 120 Danny Jackson	.05	.02	.01
☐ 121 Tommy Gregg	.05	.02	.01
☐ 122 Ken Caminiti	.40	.18	.05
☐ 123 Kevin Brown	.30	.14	.04
☐ 124 George Brett UER (133 runs, should be 1300)	.75	.35	.09
☐ 125 Mike Scott	.05	.02	.01
☐ 126 Cory Snyder	.05	.02	.01
☐ 127 George Bell	.05	.02	.01
☐ 128 Mark Grace	.30	.14	.04
☐ 129 Devon White	.15	.07	.02
☐ 130 Tony Fernandez	.05	.02	.01
☐ 131 Don Aase	.05	.02	.01
☐ 132 Rance Mulliniks	.05	.02	.01
☐ 133 Marty Barrett	.05	.02	.01
☐ 134 Nelson Liriano	.05	.02	.01
☐ 135 Mark Carreon	.05	.02	.01
☐ 136 Candy Maldonado	.05	.02	.01
☐ 137 Tim Birtsas	.05	.02	.01
☐ 138 Tom Brookens	.05	.02	.01
☐ 139 John Franco	.05	.02	.01
☐ 140 Mike LaCoss	.05	.02	.01
☐ 141 Jeff Treadway	.05	.02	.01
☐ 142 Pat Tabler	.05	.02	.01
☐ 143 Darrell Evans	.15	.07	.02
☐ 144 Rafael Ramirez	.05	.02	.01
☐ 145 Oddibe McDowell UER (Misspelled Odibbe)	.05	.02	.01
☐ 146 Brian Downing	.05	.02	.01
☐ 147 Curt Wilkerson	.05	.02	.01
☐ 148 Ernie Whitt	.05	.02	.01
☐ 149 Bill Schroeder	.05	.02	.01
☐ 150 Domingo Ramos UER (Says throws right, but shows him throwing lefty)	.05	.02	.01
☐ 151 Rick Honeycutt	.05	.02	.01
☐ 152 Don Slaught	.05	.02	.01
☐ 153 Mitch Webster	.05	.02	.01
☐ 154 Tony Phillips	.30	.14	.04
☐ 155 Paul Kilgus	.05	.02	.01
☐ 156 Ken Griffey Jr. UER (Simultaniously)	3.00	1.35	.35
☐ 157 Gary Sheffield	.50	.23	.06
☐ 158 Wally Backman	.05	.02	.01
☐ 159 B.J. Surhoff	.15	.07	.02
☐ 160 Louie Meadows	.05	.02	.01
☐ 161 Paul O'Neill	.15	.07	.02
☐ 162 Jeff McKnight	.05	.02	.01
☐ 163 Alvaro Espinoza	.05	.02	.01
☐ 164 Scott Scudder	.05	.02	.01
☐ 165 Jeff Reed	.05	.02	.01
☐ 166 Gregg Jefferies	.15	.07	.02
☐ 167 Barry Larkin	.30	.14	.04
☐ 168 Gary Carter	.15	.07	.02
☐ 169 Robby Thompson	.05	.02	.01
☐ 170 Rolando Roomes	.05	.02	.01
☐ 171 Mark McGwire UER (Total games 427 and hits 479, should be 467 and 427)	.60	.25	.07
☐ 172 Steve Sax	.05	.02	.01
☐ 173 Mark Williamson	.05	.02	.01
☐ 174 Mitch Williams	.05	.02	.01
☐ 175 Brian Holton	.05	.02	.01
☐ 176 Rob Deer	.05	.02	.01
☐ 177 Tim Raines	.30	.14	.04
☐ 178 Mike Felder	.05	.02	.01
☐ 179 Harold Reynolds	.05	.02	.01
☐ 180 Terry Francona	.05	.02	.01
☐ 181 Chris Sabo	.05	.02	.01
☐ 182 Darryl Strawberry	.15	.07	.02
☐ 183 Willie Randolph	.15	.07	.02
☐ 184 Bill Ripken	.05	.02	.01
☐ 185 Mackey Sasser	.05	.02	.01
☐ 186 Todd Benzinger	.05	.02	.01
☐ 187 Kevin Elster UER (16 homers in 1989, should be 10)	.05	.02	.01
☐ 188 Jose Uribe	.05	.02	.01
☐ 189 Tom Browning	.05	.02	.01
☐ 190 Keith Miller	.05	.02	.01
☐ 191 Don Mattingly	1.00	.45	.12
☐ 192 Dave Parker	.15	.07	.02
☐ 193 Roberto Kelly UER (96 RBI, should be 62)	.15	.07	.02
☐ 194 Phil Bradley	.05	.02	.01
☐ 195 Ron Hassey	.05	.02	.01
☐ 196 Gerald Young	.05	.02	.01
☐ 197 Hubie Brooks	.05	.02	.01
☐ 198 Bill Doran	.05	.02	.01
☐ 199 Al Newman	.05	.02	.01
☐ 200 Checklist 101-200	.05	.02	.01
☐ 201 Terry Puhl	.05	.02	.01
☐ 202 Frank DiPino	.05	.02	.01
☐ 203 Jim Clancy	.05	.02	.01
☐ 204 Bob Ojeda	.05	.02	.01
☐ 205 Alex Trevino	.05	.02	.01
☐ 206 Dave Henderson	.05	.02	.01
☐ 207 Henry Cotto	.05	.02	.01
☐ 208 Rafael Belliard UER (Born 1961, not 1951)	.05	.02	.01
☐ 209 Stan Javier	.05	.02	.01
☐ 210 Jerry Reed	.05	.02	.01
☐ 211 Doug Dascenzo	.05	.02	.01
☐ 212 Andres Thomas	.05	.02	.01
☐ 213 Greg Maddux	1.25	.55	.16
☐ 214 Mike Schooler	.05	.02	.01
☐ 215 Lonnie Smith	.05	.02	.01
☐ 216 Jose Rijo	.05	.02	.01
☐ 217 Greg Gagne	.05	.02	.01
☐ 218 Jim Gantner	.05	.02	.01
☐ 219 Allan Anderson	.05	.02	.01
☐ 220 Rick Mahler	.05	.02	.01
☐ 221 Jim Deshaies	.05	.02	.01
☐ 222 Keith Hernandez	.15	.07	.02
☐ 223 Vince Coleman	.05	.02	.01
☐ 224 David Cone	.30	.14	.04
☐ 225 Ozzie Smith	.50	.23	.06
☐ 226 Matt Nokes	.05	.02	.01
☐ 227 Barry Bonds	.50	.23	.06
☐ 228 Felix Jose	.05	.02	.01
☐ 229 Dennis Powell	.05	.02	.01
☐ 230 Mike Gallego	.05	.02	.01
☐ 231 Shawon Dunston UER ('89 stats are Andre Dawson's)	.05	.02	.01
☐ 232 Ron Gant	.30	.14	.04
☐ 233 Omar Vizquel	.30	.14	.04
☐ 234 Derek Lilliquist	.05	.02	.01
☐ 235 Erik Hanson	.15	.07	.02
☐ 236 Kirby Puckett UER (824 games, should be 924)	.75	.35	.09
☐ 237 Bill Spiers	.05	.02	.01
☐ 238 Dan Gladden	.05	.02	.01
☐ 239 Bryan Clutterbuck	.05	.02	.01
☐ 240 John Moses	.05	.02	.01
☐ 241 Ron Darling	.05	.02	.01
☐ 242 Joe Magrane	.05	.02	.01
☐ 243 Dave Magadan	.05	.02	.01
☐ 244 Pedro Guerrero UER (Misspelled Guererro)	.05	.02	.01
☐ 245 Glenn Davis	.05	.02	.01
☐ 246 Terry Steinbach	.15	.07	.02
☐ 247 Fred Lynn	.05	.02	.01
☐ 248 Gary Redus	.05	.02	.01
☐ 249 Ken Williams	.05	.02	.01
☐ 250 Sid Bream	.05	.02	.01
☐ 251 Bob Welch UER (2587 career strike-outs, should be 1587)	.05	.02	.01
☐ 252 Bill Buckner	.05	.02	.01
☐ 253 Carney Lansford	.15	.07	.02
☐ 254 Paul Molitor	.40	.18	.05
☐ 255 Jose DeJesus	.05	.02	.01
☐ 256 Orel Hershiser	.15	.07	.02
☐ 257 Tom Brunansky	.05	.02	.01
☐ 258 Mike Davis	.05	.02	.01
☐ 259 Jeff Ballard	.05	.02	.01
☐ 260 Scott Terry	.05	.02	.01
☐ 261 Sid Fernandez	.05	.02	.01
☐ 262 Mike Marshall	.05	.02	.01
☐ 263 Howard Johnson UER (192 SO, should be 592)	.05	.02	.01
☐ 264 Kirk Gibson UER (659 runs, should be 669)	.15	.07	.02
☐ 265 Kevin McReynolds	.05	.02	.01
☐ 266 Cal Ripken	1.50	.70	.19
☐ 267 Ozzie Guillen UER (Career triples 27, should be 29)	.05	.02	.01
☐ 268 Jim Traber	.05	.02	.01
☐ 269 Bobby Thigpen UER (31 saves in 1989, should be 34)	.05	.02	.01
☐ 270 Joe Orsulak	.05	.02	.01
☐ 271 Bob Boone	.15	.07	.02
☐ 272 Dave Stewart UER (Totals wrong due to omission of '86 stats)	.15	.07	.02
☐ 273 Tim Wallach	.05	.02	.01
☐ 274 Luis Aquino UER (Says throws lefty, but shows him throwing righty)	.05	.02	.01
☐ 275 Mike Moore	.05	.02	.01
☐ 276 Tony Pena	.05	.02	.01
☐ 277 Eddie Murray UER (Several typos in career total stats)	.50	.23	.06
☐ 278 Milt Thompson	.05	.02	.01
☐ 279 Alejandro Pena	.05	.02	.01
☐ 280 Ken Dayley	.05	.02	.01
☐ 281 Carmen Castillo	.05	.02	.01
☐ 282 Tom Henke	.05	.02	.01
☐ 283 Mickey Hatcher	.05	.02	.01
☐ 284 Roy Smith	.05	.02	.01
☐ 285 Manny Lee	.05	.02	.01
☐ 286 Dan Pasqua	.05	.02	.01
☐ 287 Larry Sheets	.05	.02	.01
☐ 288 Garry Templeton	.05	.02	.01
☐ 289 Eddie Williams	.05	.02	.01
☐ 290 Brady Anderson UER (Home: Silver Springs, not Siver Springs)	.30	.14	.04
☐ 291 Spike Owen	.05	.02	.01
☐ 292 Storm Davis	.05	.02	.01
☐ 293 Chris Bosio	.05	.02	.01
☐ 294 Jim Eisenreich	.05	.02	.01
☐ 295 Don August	.05	.02	.01
☐ 296 Jeff Hamilton	.05	.02	.01
☐ 297 Mickey Tettleton	.15	.07	.02
☐ 298 Mike Scioscia	.05	.02	.01
☐ 299 Kevin Hickey	.05	.02	.01
☐ 300 Checklist 201-300	.05	.02	.01
☐ 301 Shawn Abner	.05	.02	.01
☐ 302 Kevin Bass	.05	.02	.01
☐ 303 Bip Roberts	.05	.02	.01
☐ 304 Joe Girardi	.15	.07	.02
☐ 305 Danny Darwin	.05	.02	.01

☐ 306 Mike Heath .05 .02 .01
☐ 307 Mike Macfarlane .05 .02 .01
☐ 308 Ed Whitson .05 .02 .01
☐ 309 Tracy Jones .05 .02 .01
☐ 310 Scott Fletcher .05 .02 .01
☐ 311 Darnell Coles .05 .02 .01
☐ 312 Mike Brumley .05 .02 .01
☐ 313 Bill Swift .05 .02 .01
☐ 314 Charlie Hough .05 .02 .01
☐ 315 Jim Presley .05 .02 .01
☐ 316 Luis Polonia .05 .02 .01
☐ 317 Mike Morgan .05 .02 .01
☐ 318 Lee Guetterman .05 .02 .01
☐ 319 Jose Oquendo .05 .02 .01
☐ 320 Wayne Tolleson .05 .02 .01
☐ 321 Jody Reed .05 .02 .01
☐ 322 Damon Berryhill .05 .02 .01
☐ 323 Roger Clemens .40 .18 .05
☐ 324 Ryne Sandberg .50 .23 .06
☐ 325 Benito Santiago UER .05 .02 .01
(Misspelled Santago
on card back)
☐ 326 Bret Saberhagen UER .15 .07 .02
(1140 hits, should be
1240; 56 CG, should
be 52)
☐ 327 Lou Whitaker .15 .07 .02
☐ 328 Dave Gallagher .05 .02 .01
☐ 329 Mike Pagliarulo .05 .02 .01
☐ 330 Doyle Alexander .05 .02 .01
☐ 331 Jeffrey Leonard .05 .02 .01
☐ 332 Torey Lovullo .05 .02 .01
☐ 333 Pete Incaviglia .05 .02 .01
☐ 334 Rickey Henderson .30 .14 .04
☐ 335 Rafael Palmeiro .30 .14 .04
☐ 336 Ken Hill .30 .14 .04
☐ 337 Dave Winfield UER .30 .14 .04
(1418 RBI, should
be 1438)
☐ 338 Alfredo Griffin .05 .02 .01
☐ 339 Andy Hawkins .05 .02 .01
☐ 340 Ted Power .05 .02 .01
☐ 341 Steve Wilson .05 .02 .01
☐ 342 Jack Clark UER .15 .07 .02
(916 BB, should be
1006; 1142 SO,
should be 1130)
☐ 343 Ellis Burks .30 .14 .04
☐ 344 Tony Gwynn UER .75 .35 .09
(Doubles stats on
card back are wrong)
☐ 345 Jerome Walton UER .05 .02 .01
(Total At Bats 476,
should be 475)
☐ 346 Roberto Alomar UER .50 .23 .06
(61 doubles, should
be 51)
☐ 347 Carlos Martinez UER .05 .02 .01
(Born 8/11/64, should
be 8/11/65)
☐ 348 Chet Lemon .05 .02 .01
☐ 349 Willie Wilson .05 .02 .01
☐ 350 Greg Walker .05 .02 .01
☐ 351 Tom Bolton .05 .02 .01
☐ 352 German Gonzalez .05 .02 .01
☐ 353 Harold Baines .15 .07 .02
☐ 354 Mike Greenwell .05 .02 .01
☐ 355 Ruben Sierra .15 .07 .02
☐ 356 Andres Galarraga .30 .14 .04
☐ 357 Andre Dawson .15 .07 .02
☐ 358 Jeff Brantley .15 .07 .02
☐ 359 Mike Bielecki .05 .02 .01
☐ 360 Ken Oberkfell .05 .02 .01
☐ 361 Kurt Stillwell .05 .02 .01
☐ 362 Brian Holman .05 .02 .01
☐ 363 Kevin Seitzer UER .05 .02 .01
(Career triples total
does not add up)
☐ 364 Alvin Davis .05 .02 .01
☐ 365 Tom Gordon .05 .02 .01
☐ 366 Bobby Bonilla UER .15 .07 .02
(Two steals in 1987,
should be 3)
☐ 367 Carlton Fisk .30 .14 .04
☐ 368 Steve Carter UER .05 .02 .01
(Charlotesville)
☐ 369 Joel Skinner .05 .02 .01
☐ 370 John Cangelosi .05 .02 .01
☐ 371 Cecil Espy .05 .02 .01
☐ 372 Gary Wayne .05 .02 .01
☐ 373 Jim Rice .30 .14 .04
☐ 374 Mike Dyer .05 .02 .01
☐ 375 Joe Carter .15 .07 .02
☐ 376 Dwight Smith .05 .02 .01
☐ 377 John Wetteland .30 .14 .04
☐ 378 Earnie Riles .05 .02 .01
☐ 379 Otis Nixon .05 .02 .01
☐ 380 Vance Law .05 .02 .01
☐ 381 Dave Bergman .05 .02 .01
☐ 382 Frank White .15 .07 .02
☐ 383 Scott Bradley .05 .02 .01
☐ 384 Israel Sanchez UER .05 .02 .01
(Totals don't in-
clude '89 stats)
☐ 385 Gary Pettis .05 .02 .01
☐ 386 Donn Pall .05 .02 .01
☐ 387 John Smiley .15 .07 .02
☐ 388 Tom Candiotti .05 .02 .01
☐ 389 Junior Ortiz .05 .02 .01
☐ 390 Steve Lyons .05 .02 .01
☐ 391 Brian Harper .05 .02 .01
☐ 392 Fred Manrique .05 .02 .01
☐ 393 Lee Smith .15 .07 .02
☐ 394 Jeff Kunkel .05 .02 .01
☐ 395 Claudell Washington .05 .02 .01
☐ 396 John Tudor .05 .02 .01
☐ 397 Terry Kennedy UER .05 .02 .01
(Career totals all
wrong)
☐ 398 Lloyd McClendon .05 .02 .01
☐ 399 Craig Lefferts .05 .02 .01
☐ 400 Checklist 301-400 .05 .02 .01
☐ 401 Keith Moreland .05 .02 .01
☐ 402 Rich Gedman .05 .02 .01
☐ 403 Jeff D. Robinson .05 .02 .01
☐ 404 Randy Ready .05 .02 .01
☐ 405 Rick Cerone .05 .02 .01
☐ 406 Jeff Blauser .15 .07 .02
☐ 407 Larry Andersen .05 .02 .01
☐ 408 Joe Boever .05 .02 .01
☐ 409 Felix Fermin .05 .02 .01
☐ 410 Glenn Wilson .05 .02 .01
☐ 411 Rex Hudler .05 .02 .01
☐ 412 Mark Grant .05 .02 .01
☐ 413 Dennis Martinez .15 .07 .02
☐ 414 Darrin Jackson .05 .02 .01
☐ 415 Mike Aldrete .05 .02 .01
☐ 416 Roger McDowell .05 .02 .01
☐ 417 Jeff Reardon .15 .07 .02
☐ 418 Darren Daulton .15 .07 .02
☐ 419 Tim Laudner .05 .02 .01
☐ 420 Don Carman .05 .02 .01
☐ 421 Lloyd Moseby .05 .02 .01
☐ 422 Doug Drabek .05 .02 .01
☐ 423 Lenny Harris UER .05 .02 .01
(Walks 2 in '89,
should be 20)
☐ 424 Jose Lind .05 .02 .01
☐ 425 Dave Johnson (P) .05 .02 .01
☐ 426 Jerry Browne .05 .02 .01
☐ 427 Eric Yelding .05 .02 .01
☐ 428 Brad Komminsk .05 .02 .01
☐ 429 Jody Davis .05 .02 .01
☐ 430 Mariano Duncan .05 .02 .01
☐ 431 Mark Davis .05 .02 .01
☐ 432 Nelson Santovenia .05 .02 .01
☐ 433 Bruce Hurst .05 .02 .01
☐ 434 Jeff Huson .05 .02 .01
☐ 435 Chris James .05 .02 .01
☐ 436 Mark Guthrie .05 .02 .01
☐ 437 Charlie Hayes .15 .07 .02
☐ 438 Shane Rawley .05 .02 .01
☐ 439 Dickie Thon .05 .02 .01
☐ 440 Juan Berenguer .05 .02 .01
☐ 441 Kevin Romine .05 .02 .01
☐ 442 Bill Landrum .05 .02 .01
☐ 443 Todd Frohwirth .05 .02 .01
☐ 444 Craig Worthington .05 .02 .01
☐ 445 Fernando Valenzuela .15 .07 .02
☐ 446 Joey Belle 1.50 .70 .19
☐ 447 Ed Whited UER .05 .02 .01
(Ashville, should
be Asheville)
☐ 448 Dave Smith .05 .02 .01
☐ 449 Dave Clark .05 .02 .01
☐ 450 Juan Agosto .05 .02 .01
☐ 451 Dave Valle .05 .02 .01
☐ 452 Kent Hrbek .15 .07 .02
☐ 453 Von Hayes .05 .02 .01
☐ 454 Gary Gaetti .15 .07 .02
☐ 455 Greg Briley .05 .02 .01
☐ 456 Glenn Braggs .05 .02 .01
☐ 457 Kirt Manwaring .05 .02 .01
☐ 458 Mel Hall .05 .02 .01
☐ 459 Brook Jacoby .05 .02 .01
☐ 460 Pat Sheridan .05 .02 .01
☐ 461 Rob Murphy .05 .02 .01
☐ 462 Jimmy Key .15 .07 .02
☐ 463 Nick Esasky .05 .02 .01
☐ 464 Rob Ducey .05 .02 .01
☐ 465 Carlos Quintana UER .05 .02 .01
(Internatinoal)
☐ 466 Larry Walker 1.25 .55 .16
☐ 467 Todd Worrell .05 .02 .01
☐ 468 Kevin Gross .05 .02 .01
☐ 469 Terry Pendleton .15 .07 .02
☐ 470 Dave Martinez .05 .02 .01
☐ 471 Gene Larkin .05 .02 .01
☐ 472 Len Dykstra UER .15 .07 .02
('89 and total runs
understated by 10)
☐ 473 Barry Lyons .05 .02 .01
☐ 474 Terry Mulholland .05 .02 .01
☐ 475 Chip Hale .05 .02 .01
☐ 476 Jesse Barfield .05 .02 .01
☐ 477 Dan Plesac .05 .02 .01
☐ 478A Scott Garrelts ERR 2.00 .90 .25
(Photo actually
Bill Bathe)
☐ 478B Scott Garrelts COR .05 .02 .01
☐ 479 Dave Righetti .05 .02 .01
☐ 480 Gus Polidor UER .05 .02 .01
(Wearing 14 on front,
but 10 on back)
☐ 481 Mookie Wilson .05 .02 .01
☐ 482 Luis Rivera .05 .02 .01
☐ 483 Mike Flanagan .05 .02 .01
☐ 484 Dennis Boyd .05 .02 .01
☐ 485 John Cerutti .05 .02 .01
☐ 486 John Costello .05 .02 .01
☐ 487 Pascual Perez .05 .02 .01
☐ 488 Tommy Herr .05 .02 .01
☐ 489 Tom Foley .05 .02 .01
☐ 490 Curt Ford .05 .02 .01
☐ 491 Steve Lake .05 .02 .01
☐ 492 Tim Teufel .05 .02 .01
☐ 493 Randy Bush .05 .02 .01
☐ 494 Mike Jackson .05 .02 .01
☐ 495 Steve Jeltz .05 .02 .01
☐ 496 Paul Gibson .05 .02 .01
☐ 497 Steve Balboni .05 .02 .01
☐ 498 Bud Black .05 .02 .01
☐ 499 Dale Sveum .05 .02 .01
☐ 500 Checklist 401-500 .05 .02 .01
☐ 501 Tim Jones .05 .02 .01
☐ 502 Mark Portugal .05 .02 .01
☐ 503 Ivan Calderon .05 .02 .01
☐ 504 Rick Rhoden .05 .02 .01
☐ 505 Willie McGee .05 .02 .01
☐ 506 Kirk McCaskill .05 .02 .01
☐ 507 Dave LaPoint .05 .02 .01
☐ 508 Jay Howell .05 .02 .01
☐ 509 Johnny Ray .05 .02 .01
☐ 510 Dave Anderson .05 .02 .01
☐ 511 Chuck Crim .05 .02 .01
☐ 512 Joe Hesketh .05 .02 .01
☐ 513 Dennis Eckersley .15 .07 .02
☐ 514 Greg Brock .05 .02 .01
☐ 515 Tim Burke .05 .02 .01
☐ 516 Frank Tanana .05 .02 .01
☐ 517 Jay Bell .15 .07 .02
☐ 518 Guillermo Hernandez .05 .02 .01
☐ 519 Randy Kramer UER .05 .02 .01
(Codiroli misspelled
as Codoroli)
☐ 520 Charles Hudson .05 .02 .01
☐ 521 Jim Corsi .05 .02 .01
(Word "originally" is
misspelled on back)
☐ 522 Steve Rosenberg .05 .02 .01
☐ 523 Cris Carpenter .05 .02 .01
☐ 524 Matt Winters .05 .02 .01
☐ 525 Melido Perez .05 .02 .01
☐ 526 Chris Gwynn UER .05 .02 .01
(Albeguergue)
☐ 527 Bert Blyleven UER .15 .07 .02
(Games career total is
wrong, should be 644)
☐ 528 Chuck Cary .05 .02 .01
☐ 529 Daryl Boston .05 .02 .01
☐ 530 Dale Mohorcic .05 .02 .01
☐ 531 Geronimo Berroa .15 .07 .02
☐ 532 Edgar Martinez .30 .14 .04
☐ 533 Dale Murphy .30 .14 .04
☐ 534 Jay Buhner .30 .14 .04
☐ 535 John Smoltz UER .50 .23 .06
(HEA Stadium)
☐ 536 Andy Van Slyke .15 .07 .02
☐ 537 Mike Henneman .05 .02 .01
☐ 538 Miguel Garcia .05 .02 .01
☐ 539 Frank Williams .05 .02 .01
☐ 540 R.J. Reynolds .05 .02 .01
☐ 541 Shawn Hillegas .05 .02 .01
☐ 542 Walt Weiss .05 .02 .01
☐ 543 Greg Hibbard .05 .02 .01
☐ 544 Nolan Ryan 1.50 .70 .19
☐ 545 Todd Zeile .15 .07 .02
☐ 546 Hensley Meulens .05 .02 .01
☐ 547 Tim Belcher .05 .02 .01
☐ 548 Mike Witt .05 .02 .01
☐ 549 Greg Cadaret UER .05 .02 .01
(Aquiring, should
be Acquiring)
☐ 550 Franklin Stubbs .05 .02 .01
☐ 551 Tony Castillo .05 .02 .01
☐ 552 Jeff M. Robinson .05 .02 .01
☐ 553 Steve Olin .15 .07 .02
☐ 554 Alan Trammell .15 .07 .02
☐ 555 Wade Boggs 4X .30 .14 .04
(Bo Jackson
in background)
☐ 556 Will Clark .30 .14 .04
☐ 557 Jeff King .15 .07 .02
☐ 558 Mike Fitzgerald .05 .02 .01
☐ 559 Ken Howell .05 .02 .01
☐ 560 Bob Kipper .05 .02 .01
☐ 561 Scott Bankhead .05 .02 .01
☐ 562A Jeff Innis ERR 2.00 .90 .25
(Photo actually
David West)
☐ 562B Jeff Innis COR .05 .02 .01
☐ 563 Randy Johnson .50 .23 .06
☐ 564 Wally Whitehurst .05 .02 .01
☐ 565 Gene Harris .05 .02 .01
☐ 566 Norm Charlton .05 .02 .01
☐ 567 Robin Yount UER .30 .14 .04
(7602 career hits,
should be 2606)
☐ 568 Joe Oliver UER .05 .02 .01
(Fl.orida)
☐ 569 Mark Parent .05 .02 .01
☐ 570 John Farrell UER .05 .02 .01
(Loss total added wrong)
☐ 571 Tom Glavine .30 .14 .04
☐ 572 Rod Nichols .05 .02 .01
☐ 573 Jack Morris .15 .07 .02
☐ 574 Greg Swindell .05 .02 .01
☐ 575 Steve Searcy .05 .02 .01
☐ 576 Ricky Jordan .05 .02 .01
☐ 577 Matt Williams .30 .14 .04
☐ 578 Mike LaValliere .05 .02 .01
☐ 579 Bryn Smith .05 .02 .01
☐ 580 Bruce Ruffin .05 .02 .01
☐ 581 Randy Myers .15 .07 .02
☐ 582 Rick Wrona .05 .02 .01
☐ 583 Juan Samuel .05 .02 .01
☐ 584 Les Lancaster .05 .02 .01
☐ 585 Jeff Musselman .05 .02 .01
☐ 586 Rob Dibble .05 .02 .01
☐ 587 Eric Show .05 .02 .01
☐ 588 Jesse Orosco .05 .02 .01
☐ 589 Herm Winningham .05 .02 .01
☐ 590 Andy Allanson .05 .02 .01
☐ 591 Dion James .05 .02 .01
☐ 592 Carmelo Martinez .05 .02 .01
☐ 593 Luis Quinones .05 .02 .01
☐ 594 Dennis Rasmussen .05 .02 .01
☐ 595 Rich Yett .05 .02 .01
☐ 596 Bob Walk .05 .02 .01
☐ 597A Andy McGaffigan ERR .15 .07 .02
(Photo actually
Rich Thompson)
☐ 597B Andy McGaffigan COR .05 .02 .01
☐ 598 Billy Hatcher .05 .02 .01
☐ 599 Bob Knepper .05 .02 .01
☐ 600 Checklist 501-600 UER .05 .02 .01
(599 Bob Kneppers)
☐ 601 Joey Cora .15 .07 .02
☐ 602 Steve Finley .30 .14 .04
☐ 603 Kal Daniels UER .05 .02 .01
(12 hits in '87, should
be 123; 335 runs,
should be 235)
☐ 604 Gregg Olson .05 .02 .01
☐ 605 Dave Stieb .05 .02 .01
☐ 606 Kenny Rogers .15 .07 .02
(Shown catching
football)
☐ 607 Zane Smith .05 .02 .01
☐ 608 Bob Geren UER .05 .02 .01
(Origionally)
☐ 609 Chad Kreuter .05 .02 .01
☐ 610 Mike Smithson .05 .02 .01
☐ 611 Jeff Wetherby .05 .02 .01
☐ 612 Gary Mielke .05 .02 .01
☐ 613 Pete Smith .05 .02 .01
☐ 614 Jack Daugherty UER .05 .02 .01
(Born 7/30/60, should
be 7/3/60)
☐ 615 Lance McCullers .05 .02 .01
☐ 616 Don Robinson .05 .02 .01
☐ 617 Jose Guzman .05 .02 .01
☐ 618 Steve Bedrosian .05 .02 .01
☐ 619 Jamie Moyer .05 .02 .01
☐ 620 Atlee Hammaker .05 .02 .01
☐ 621 Rick Luecken UER .05 .02 .01
(Innings pitched wrong)
☐ 622 Greg W. Harris .05 .02 .01
☐ 623 Pete Harnisch .05 .02 .01
☐ 624 Jerald Clark .05 .02 .01
☐ 625 Jack McDowell UER .30 .14 .04
(Career totals for Games
and GS don't include
1987 season)
☐ 626 Frank Viola .05 .02 .01
☐ 627 Teddy Higuera .05 .02 .01
☐ 628 Marty Pevey .05 .02 .01
☐ 629 Bill Wegman .05 .02 .01
☐ 630 Eric Plunk .05 .02 .01
☐ 631 Drew Hall .05 .02 .01
☐ 632 Doug Jones .05 .02 .01
☐ 633 Geno Petralli UER .05 .02 .01
(Sacremento)
☐ 634 Jose Alvarez .05 .02 .01
☐ 635 Bob Milacki .05 .02 .01
☐ 636 Bobby Witt .05 .02 .01
☐ 637 Trevor Wilson .05 .02 .01
☐ 638 Jeff Russell UER .05 .02 .01
(Shutout stats wrong)
☐ 639 Mike Krukow .05 .02 .01
☐ 640 Rick Leach .05 .02 .01
☐ 641 Dave Schmidt .05 .02 .01
☐ 642 Terry Leach .05 .02 .01
☐ 643 Calvin Schiraldi .05 .02 .01
☐ 644 Bob Melvin .05 .02 .01
☐ 645 Jim Abbott .15 .07 .02
☐ 646 Jaime Navarro .05 .02 .01
☐ 647 Mark Langston UER .15 .07 .02
(Several errors in
stats totals)

☐ 648 Juan Nieves	.05	.02	.01
☐ 649 Damaso Garcia	.05	.02	.01
☐ 650 Charlie O'Brien	.05	.02	.01
☐ 651 Eric King	.05	.02	.01
☐ 652 Mike Boddicker	.05	.02	.01
☐ 653 Duane Ward	.05	.02	.01
☐ 654 Bob Stanley	.05	.02	.01
☐ 655 Sandy Alomar Jr.	.30	.14	.04
☐ 656 Danny Tartabull UER	.05	.02	.01
(395 BB, should be 295)			
☐ 657 Randy McCament	.05	.02	.01
☐ 658 Charlie Leibrandt	.05	.02	.01
☐ 659 Dan Quisenberry	.05	.02	.01
☐ 660 Paul Assenmacher	.05	.02	.01
☐ 661 Walt Terrell	.05	.02	.01
☐ 662 Tim Leary	.05	.02	.01
☐ 663 Randy Milligan	.05	.02	.01
☐ 664 Bo Diaz	.05	.02	.01
☐ 665 Mark Lemke UER	.15	.07	.02
(Richmond misspelled as Richomond)			
☐ 666 Jose Gonzalez	.05	.02	.01
☐ 667 Chuck Finley UER	.15	.07	.02
(Born 11/16/62, should be 11/26/62)			
☐ 668 John Kruk	.15	.07	.02
☐ 669 Dick Schofield	.05	.02	.01
☐ 670 Tim Crews	.05	.02	.01
☐ 671 John Dopson	.05	.02	.01
☐ 672 John Orton	.05	.02	.01
☐ 673 Eric Hetzel	.05	.02	.01
☐ 674 Lance Parrish	.05	.02	.01
☐ 675 Ramon Martinez	.30	.14	.04
☐ 676 Mark Gubicza	.05	.02	.01
☐ 677 Greg Litton	.05	.02	.01
☐ 678 Greg Mathews	.05	.02	.01
☐ 679 Dave Dravecky	.15	.07	.02
☐ 680 Steve Farr	.05	.02	.01
☐ 681 Mike Devereaux	.05	.02	.01
☐ 682 Ken Griffey Sr.	.05	.02	.01
☐ 683A Mickey Weston ERR	2.00	.90	.25
(Listed as Jamie on card)			
☐ 683B Mickey Weston COR	.05	.02	.01
(Technically still an error as birthdate is listed as 3/26/81)			
☐ 684 Jack Armstrong	.05	.02	.01
☐ 685 Steve Buechele	.05	.02	.01
☐ 686 Bryan Harvey	.05	.02	.01
☐ 687 Lance Blankenship	.05	.02	.01
☐ 688 Dante Bichette	.30	.14	.04
☐ 689 Todd Burns	.05	.02	.01
☐ 690 Dan Petry	.05	.02	.01
☐ 691 Kent Anderson	.05	.02	.01
☐ 692 Todd Stottlemyre	.15	.07	.02
☐ 693 Wally Joyner UER	.15	.07	.02
(Several stats errors)			
☐ 694 Mike Rochford	.05	.02	.01
☐ 695 Floyd Bannister	.05	.02	.01
☐ 696 Rick Reuschel	.05	.02	.01
☐ 697 Jose DeLeon	.05	.02	.01
☐ 698 Jeff Montgomery	.15	.07	.02
☐ 699 Kelly Downs	.05	.02	.01
☐ 700A Checklist 601-700	2.00	.90	.25
(683 Jamie Weston)			
☐ 700B Checklist 601-700	.05	.02	.01
(683 Mickey Weston)			
☐ 701 Jim Gott	.05	.02	.01
☐ 702 Rookie Threats	.50	.23	.06
Delino DeShields			
Marquis Grissom			
Larry Walker			
☐ 703 Alejandro Pena	.05	.02	.01
☐ 704 Willie Randolph	.15	.07	.02
☐ 705 Tim Leary	.05	.02	.01
☐ 706 Chuck McElroy	.05	.02	.01
☐ 707 Gerald Perry	.05	.02	.01
☐ 708 Tom Brunansky	.05	.02	.01
☐ 709 John Franco	.05	.02	.01
☐ 710 Mark Davis	.05	.02	.01
☐ 711 David Justice	1.00	.45	.12
☐ 712 Storm Davis	.05	.02	.01
☐ 713 Scott Ruskin	.05	.02	.01
☐ 714 Glenn Braggs	.05	.02	.01
☐ 715 Kevin Bearse	.05	.02	.01
☐ 716 Jose Nunez	.05	.02	.01
☐ 717 Tim Layana	.05	.02	.01
☐ 718 Greg Myers	.05	.02	.01
☐ 719 Pete O'Brien	.05	.02	.01
☐ 720 John Candelaria	.05	.02	.01
☐ 721 Craig Grebeck	.05	.02	.01
☐ 722 Shawn Boskie	.05	.02	.01
☐ 723 Jim Leyritz	.30	.14	.04
☐ 724 Bill Sampen	.05	.02	.01
☐ 725 Scott Radinsky	.05	.02	.01
☐ 726 Todd Hundley	1.25	.55	.16
☐ 727 Scott Hemond	.05	.02	.01
☐ 728 Lenny Webster	.05	.02	.01
☐ 729 Jeff Reardon	.15	.07	.02
☐ 730 Mitch Webster	.05	.02	.01
☐ 731 Brian Bohanon	.05	.02	.01
☐ 732 Rick Parker	.05	.02	.01
☐ 733 Terry Shumpert	.05	.02	.01
☐ 734A Ryan's 6th No-Hitter	3.00	1.35	.35
(No stripe on front)			
☐ 734B Ryan's 6th No-Hitter	.75	.35	.09
(stripe added on card front for 300th win)			
☐ 735 John Burkett	.15	.07	.02
☐ 736 Derrick May	.30	.14	.04
☐ 737 Carlos Baerga	.60	.25	.07
☐ 738 Greg Smith	.05	.02	.01
☐ 739 Scott Sanderson	.05	.02	.01
☐ 740 Joe Kraemer	.05	.02	.01
☐ 741 Hector Villanueva	.05	.02	.01
☐ 742 Mike Fetters	.15	.07	.02
☐ 743 Mark Gardner	.05	.02	.01
☐ 744 Matt Nokes	.05	.02	.01
☐ 745 Dave Winfield	.30	.14	.04
☐ 746 Delino DeShields	.15	.07	.02
☐ 747 Dann Howitt	.05	.02	.01
☐ 748 Tony Pena	.05	.02	.01
☐ 749 Oil Can Boyd	.05	.02	.01
☐ 750 Mike Benjamin	.05	.02	.01
☐ 751 Alex Cole	.15	.07	.02
☐ 752 Eric Gunderson	.05	.02	.01
☐ 753 Howard Farmer	.05	.02	.01
☐ 754 Joe Carter	.15	.07	.02
☐ 755 Ray Lankford	1.00	.45	.12
☐ 756 Sandy Alomar Jr.	.30	.14	.04
☐ 757 Alex Sanchez	.05	.02	.01
☐ 758 Nick Esasky	.05	.02	.01
☐ 759 Stan Belinda	.05	.02	.01
☐ 760 Jim Presley	.05	.02	.01
☐ 761 Gary DiSarcina	.30	.14	.04
☐ 762 Wayne Edwards	.05	.02	.01
☐ 763 Pat Combs	.05	.02	.01
☐ 764 Mickey Pina	.05	.02	.01
☐ 765 Wilson Alvarez	.50	.23	.06
☐ 766 Dave Parker	.15	.07	.02
☐ 767 Mike Blowers	.30	.14	.04
☐ 768 Tony Phillips	.30	.14	.04
☐ 769 Pascual Perez	.05	.02	.01
☐ 770 Gary Pettis	.05	.02	.01
☐ 771 Fred Lynn	.05	.02	.01
☐ 772 Mel Rojas	.30	.14	.04
☐ 773 David Segui	.30	.14	.04
☐ 774 Gary Carter	.15	.07	.02
☐ 775 Rafael Valdez	.05	.02	.01
☐ 776 Glenallen Hill	.15	.07	.02
☐ 777 Keith Hernandez	.15	.07	.02
☐ 778 Billy Hatcher	.05	.02	.01
☐ 779 Marty Clary	.05	.02	.01
☐ 780 Candy Maldonado	.05	.02	.01
☐ 781 Mike Marshall	.05	.02	.01
☐ 782 Billy Joe Robidoux	.05	.02	.01
☐ 783 Mark Langston	.15	.07	.02
☐ 784 Paul Sorrento	.30	.14	.04
☐ 785 Dave Hollins	.30	.14	.04
☐ 786 Cecil Fielder	.15	.07	.02
☐ 787 Matt Young	.05	.02	.01
☐ 788 Jeff Huson	.05	.02	.01
☐ 789 Lloyd Moseby	.05	.02	.01
☐ 790 Ron Kittle	.05	.02	.01
☐ 791 Hubie Brooks	.05	.02	.01
☐ 792 Craig Lefferts	.05	.02	.01
☐ 793 Kevin Bass	.05	.02	.01
☐ 794 Bryn Smith	.05	.02	.01
☐ 795 Juan Samuel	.05	.02	.01
☐ 796 Sam Horn	.05	.02	.01
☐ 797 Randy Myers	.15	.07	.02
☐ 798 Chris James	.05	.02	.01
☐ 799 Bill Gullickson	.05	.02	.01
☐ 800 Checklist 701-800	.05	.02	.01

1990 Upper Deck Jackson Heroes

This ten-card standard-size set was issued as an insert in 1990 Upper Deck High Number packs as part of the Upper Deck promotional giveaway of 2,500 officially signed and personally numbered Reggie Jackson cards. Signed cards ending with 00 have the words "Mr. October" added to the autograph. These cards cover Jackson's major league career. The complete set price refers only to the unautographed card set of ten. One-card packs of over-sized (3 1/2" by 5") versions of these cards were later inserted into retail blister repacks containing one foil pack each of 1993 Upper Deck Series I and II. These cards were later inserted into various forms of repackaging. The larger cards are also distinguishable by the Upper Deck Fifth Anniversary logo and "1993 Hall of Fame Inductee" logo on the front of the card. These over-sized cards were a limited edition of 10,000 numbered cards and have no extra value than the basic cards.

	MINT	NRMT	EXC
COMPLETE SET (10)	20.00	9.00	2.50
COMMON REGGIE (1-9)	2.00	.90	.25

☐ 1 Reggie Jackson	2.00	.90	.25
1969 Emerging Superstar			
☐ 2 Reggie Jackson	2.00	.90	.25
1973 An MVP Year			
☐ 3 Reggie Jackson	2.00	.90	.25
1977 Mr. October			
☐ 4 Reggie Jackson	2.00	.90	.25
1978 vs. Bob Welch			
☐ 5 Reggie Jackson	2.00	.90	.25
1982 Under the Halo			
☐ 6 Reggie Jackson	2.00	.90	.25
1984 500 Homers			
☐ 7 Reggie Jackson	2.00	.90	.25
1986 Moving Up the List			
☐ 8 Reggie Jackson	2.00	.90	.25
1987 A Great Career Ends			
☐ 9 Jackson Heroes art/CL	2.00	.90	.25
☐ AU1 Reggie Jackson AU	300.00	135.00	38.00
(Signed and Numbered out of 2500)			
☐ NNO0 Reggie Jackson	4.00	1.80	.50
Header Card			

1990 Upper Deck Sheets

These blank-backed, 8 1/2" by 11" sheets feature pictures of Upper Deck baseball cards and were distributed at various specific events and times around the country. The sheets carried a production run number but not necessarily a total number produced. There were four regionally-issued sheets bound inside Street and Smith's 1990 Baseball Annual magazines to celebrate its 50th anniversary. The top five 1990 Upper Deck cards featured on all four sheets were the same: Carlton Fisk, Tim Raines, Jose Canseco and Will Clark. The Street and Smith sheets are listed below by their regions and regional players. The sheets are listed below in chronological order.

	MINT	NRMT	EXC
COMPLETE SET (5)	40.00	18.00	5.00
COMMON SHEET (1-5)	8.00	3.60	1.00

☐ 1 11th Annual National	10.00	4.50	1.25
Sports Collectors Convention			
Arlington, Texas			
July 5-8, 1990			
(26,000)			
Pat Combs			
Bill Doran			
Ruben Sierra			
Mark McGwire			
Howard Johnson			
Nolan Ryan			
Bugs Bunny			
Daffy Duck			
(Comic Ball)			
☐ 2 San Francisco	8.00	3.60	1.00
Conv. Center Show			
Aug. 31-Sept. 3, 1990			
(45,000 est.)			
Marquis Grissom			
Delino DeShields			
Larry Walker			
Matt Williams			
Kevin Maas			
Nolan Ryan			
Bob Welch			
Cecil Fielder			
Reggie Jackson			
☐ 3 Street/Smith: West	15.00	6.75	1.85
Ken Griffey Jr.			
Roberto Alomar			
Bert Blyleven			
☐ 4 Street/Smith: East	8.00	3.60	1.00
Gregg Olson			
Wade Boggs			
Gregg Jefferies			
☐ 5 Street/Smith: Midwest	10.00	4.50	1.25
Tom Gordon			
Pedro Guerrero			
Ryne Sandberg			

1991 Upper Deck

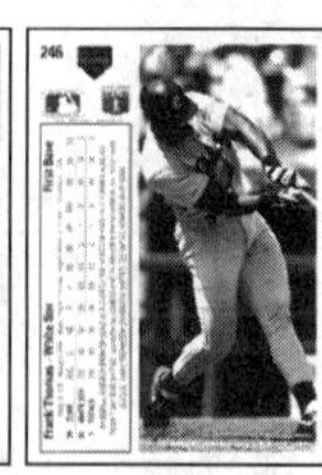

This set marked the third year Upper Deck issued a 800-card standard-size set in two separate series of 700 and 100 cards respectively. Cards were distributed in low and high series foil packs and factory sets. The 100-card extended or high-number series was issued by Upper Deck several months after the release of their first series. For the first time in Upper Deck's three-year history, they did not issue a factory Extended set. The basic cards are made on the typical Upper Deck slick, white card stock and features full-color photos on both the front and the back. Subsets include Star Rookies (1-26), Team Cards (28-34, 43-49, 77-82, 95-99) and Top Prospects (50-76). Several other special achievement cards are seeded throughout the set. The team checklist (TC) cards in the set feature an attractive Vernon Wells drawing of a featured player for that particular team. Rookie Cards in this set include Jeff Bagwell, Jeff Conine, Chipper Jones, Eric Karros, Brian McRae, Mike Mussina and Reggie Sanders. A special Michael Jordan card (numbered SP1) was randomly included in packs on a somewhat limited basis. The Hank Aaron hologram card was randomly inserted in the 1991 Upper Deck high number foil packs. Neither card is included in the price of the regular issue set.

	MINT	NRMT	EXC
COMPLETE SET (800)	20.00	9.00	2.50
COMPLETE FACT.SET (800)	20.00	9.00	2.50
COMPLETE LO SET (700)	16.00	7.25	2.00
COMPLETE HI SET (100)	4.00	1.80	.50
COMMON CARD (1-800)	.05	.02	.01

☐ 1 Star Rookie Checklist	.05	.02	.01
☐ 2 Phil Plantier	.10	.05	.01
☐ 3 D.J. Dozier	.05	.02	.01
☐ 4 Dave Hansen	.05	.02	.01
☐ 5 Maurice Vaughn	.50	.23	.06
☐ 6 Leo Gomez	.05	.02	.01
☐ 7 Scott Aldred	.05	.02	.01
☐ 8 Scott Chiamparino	.05	.02	.01
☐ 9 Lance Dickson	.05	.02	.01
☐ 10 Sean Berry	.10	.05	.01
☐ 11 Bernie Williams	.30	.14	.04
☐ 12 Brian Barnes UER	.05	.02	.01
(Photo either not him or in wrong jersey)			
☐ 13 Narciso Elvira	.05	.02	.01
☐ 14 Mike Gardiner	.05	.02	.01
☐ 15 Greg Colbrunn	.10	.05	.01
☐ 16 Bernard Gilkey	.10	.05	.01
☐ 17 Mark Lewis	.05	.02	.01
☐ 18 Mickey Morandini	.05	.02	.01
☐ 19 Charles Nagy	.15	.07	.02
☐ 20 Geronimo Pena	.05	.02	.01
☐ 21 Henry Rodriguez	.50	.23	.06
☐ 22 Scott Cooper	.05	.02	.01
☐ 23 Andujar Cedeno UER	.05	.02	.01
(Shown batting left, back says right)			
☐ 24 Eric Karros	.60	.25	.07
☐ 25 Steve Decker UER	.05	.02	.01
(Lewis-Clark State College, not Lewis and Clark)			
☐ 26 Kevin Belcher	.05	.02	.01
☐ 27 Jeff Conine	.50	.23	.06
☐ 28 Dave Stewart TC	.10	.05	.01
☐ 29 Carlton Fisk TC	.15	.07	.02
☐ 30 Rafael Palmeiro TC	.15	.07	.02
☐ 31 Chuck Finley TC	.05	.02	.01
☐ 32 Harold Reynolds TC	.05	.02	.01
☐ 33 Bret Saberhagen TC	.10	.05	.01
☐ 34 Gary Gaetti TC	.05	.02	.01
☐ 35 Scott Leius	.05	.02	.01
☐ 36 Neal Heaton	.05	.02	.01
☐ 37 Terry Lee	.05	.02	.01
☐ 38 Gary Redus	.05	.02	.01
☐ 39 Barry Jones	.05	.02	.01
☐ 40 Chuck Knoblauch	.25	.11	.03
☐ 41 Larry Andersen	.05	.02	.01
☐ 42 Darryl Hamilton	.10	.05	.01
☐ 43 Mike Greenwell TC	.05	.02	.01
☐ 44 Kelly Gruber TC	.05	.02	.01
☐ 45 Jack Morris TC	.10	.05	.01
☐ 46 Sandy Alomar Jr. TC	.10	.05	.01
☐ 47 Gregg Olson TC	.05	.02	.01
☐ 48 Dave Parker TC	.10	.05	.01
☐ 49 Roberto Kelly TC	.05	.02	.01
☐ 50 Top Prospect Checklist	.05	.02	.01
☐ 51 Kyle Abbott	.05	.02	.01
☐ 52 Jeff Juden	.05	.02	.01
☐ 53 Todd Van Poppel UER	.10	.05	.01
(Born Arlington and attended John Martin HS, should say Hinsdale and James Martin HS)			
☐ 54 Steve Karsay	.15	.07	.02
☐ 55 Chipper Jones	4.00	1.80	.50
☐ 56 Chris Johnson UER	.05	.02	.01
(Called Tim on back)			
☐ 57 John Ericks	.05	.02	.01
☐ 58 Gary Scott	.05	.02	.01
☐ 59 Kiki Jones	.05	.02	.01
☐ 60 Wil Cordero	.15	.07	.02
☐ 61 Royce Clayton	.15	.07	.02

Card			
☐ 62 Tim Costo	.05	.02	.01
☐ 63 Roger Salkeld	.05	.02	.01
☐ 64 Brook Fordyce	.05	.02	.01
☐ 65 Mike Mussina	1.25	.55	.16
☐ 66 Dave Staton	.05	.02	.01
☐ 67 Mike Lieberthal	.15	.07	.02
☐ 68 Kurt Miller	.05	.02	.01
☐ 69 Dan Peltier	.05	.02	.01
☐ 70 Greg Blosser	.05	.02	.01
☐ 71 Reggie Sanders	.50	.23	.06
☐ 72 Brent Mayne	.05	.02	.01
☐ 73 Rico Brogna	.10	.05	.01
☐ 74 Willie Banks	.05	.02	.01
☐ 75 Len Brutcher	.05	.02	.01
☐ 76 Pat Kelly	.10	.05	.01
☐ 77 Chris Sabo TC	.05	.02	.01
☐ 78 Ramon Martinez TC	.15	.07	.02
☐ 79 Matt Williams TC	.15	.07	.02
☐ 80 Roberto Alomar TC	.15	.07	.02
☐ 81 Glenn Davis TC	.05	.02	.01
☐ 82 Ron Gant TC	.10	.05	.01
☐ 83 Cecil Fielder FEAT	.10	.05	.01
☐ 84 Orlando Merced	.15	.07	.02
☐ 85 Domingo Ramos	.05	.02	.01
☐ 86 Tom Bolton	.05	.02	.01
☐ 87 Andres Santana	.05	.02	.01
☐ 88 John Dopson	.05	.02	.01
☐ 89 Kenny Williams	.05	.02	.01
☐ 90 Marty Barrett	.05	.02	.01
☐ 91 Tom Pagnozzi	.05	.02	.01
☐ 92 Carmelo Martinez	.05	.02	.01
☐ 93 Bobby Thigpen SAVE	.05	.02	.01
☐ 94 Barry Bonds TC	.15	.07	.02
☐ 95 Gregg Jefferies TC	.10	.05	.01
☐ 96 Tim Wallach TC	.05	.02	.01
☐ 97 Len Dykstra TC	.10	.05	.01
☐ 98 Pedro Guerrero TC	.05	.02	.01
☐ 99 Mark Grace TC	.15	.07	.02
☐ 100 Checklist 1-100	.05	.02	.01
☐ 101 Kevin Elster	.05	.02	.01
☐ 102 Tom Brookens	.05	.02	.01
☐ 103 Mackey Sasser	.05	.02	.01
☐ 104 Felix Fermin	.05	.02	.01
☐ 105 Kevin McReynolds	.05	.02	.01
☐ 106 Dave Stieb	.05	.02	.01
☐ 107 Jeffrey Leonard	.05	.02	.01
☐ 108 Dave Henderson	.05	.02	.01
☐ 109 Sid Bream	.05	.02	.01
☐ 110 Henry Cotto	.05	.02	.01
☐ 111 Shawon Dunston	.05	.02	.01
☐ 112 Mariano Duncan	.05	.02	.01
☐ 113 Joe Girardi	.10	.05	.01
☐ 114 Billy Hatcher	.05	.02	.01
☐ 115 Greg Maddux	.60	.25	.07
☐ 116 Jerry Browne	.05	.02	.01
☐ 117 Juan Samuel	.05	.02	.01
☐ 118 Steve Olin	.05	.02	.01
☐ 119 Alfredo Griffin	.05	.02	.01
☐ 120 Mitch Webster	.05	.02	.01
☐ 121 Joel Skinner	.05	.02	.01
☐ 122 Frank Viola	.05	.02	.01
☐ 123 Cory Snyder	.05	.02	.01
☐ 124 Howard Johnson	.05	.02	.01
☐ 125 Carlos Baerga	.15	.07	.02
☐ 126 Tony Fernandez	.05	.02	.01
☐ 127 Dave Stewart	.10	.05	.01
☐ 128 Jay Buhner	.15	.07	.02
☐ 129 Mike LaValliere	.05	.02	.01
☐ 130 Scott Bradley	.05	.02	.01
☐ 131 Tony Phillips	.10	.05	.01
☐ 132 Ryne Sandberg	.25	.11	.03
☐ 133 Paul O'Neill	.10	.05	.01
☐ 134 Mark Grace	.15	.07	.02
☐ 135 Chris Sabo	.05	.02	.01
☐ 136 Ramon Martinez	.15	.07	.02
☐ 137 Brook Jacoby	.05	.02	.01
☐ 138 Candy Maldonado	.05	.02	.01
☐ 139 Mike Scioscia	.05	.02	.01
☐ 140 Chris James	.05	.02	.01
☐ 141 Craig Worthington	.05	.02	.01
☐ 142 Manny Lee	.05	.02	.01
☐ 143 Tim Raines	.15	.07	.02
☐ 144 Sandy Alomar Jr.	.10	.05	.01
☐ 145 John Olerud	.10	.05	.01
☐ 146 Ozzie Canseco (With Jose)	.10	.05	.01
☐ 147 Pat Borders	.05	.02	.01
☐ 148 Harold Reynolds	.05	.02	.01
☐ 149 Tom Henke	.05	.02	.01
☐ 150 R.J. Reynolds	.05	.02	.01
☐ 151 Mike Gallego	.05	.02	.01
☐ 152 Bobby Bonilla	.10	.05	.01
☐ 153 Terry Steinbach	.10	.05	.01
☐ 154 Barry Bonds	.25	.11	.03
☐ 155 Jose Canseco	.15	.07	.02
☐ 156 Gregg Jefferies	.10	.05	.01
☐ 157 Matt Williams	.15	.07	.02
☐ 158 Craig Biggio	.15	.07	.02
☐ 159 Daryl Boston	.05	.02	.01
☐ 160 Ricky Jordan	.05	.02	.01
☐ 161 Stan Belinda	.05	.02	.01
☐ 162 Ozzie Smith	.25	.11	.03
☐ 163 Tom Brunansky	.05	.02	.01
☐ 164 Todd Zeile	.10	.05	.01
☐ 165 Mike Greenwell	.05	.02	.01
☐ 166 Kal Daniels	.05	.02	.01
☐ 167 Kent Hrbek	.10	.05	.01
☐ 168 Franklin Stubbs	.05	.02	.01
☐ 169 Dick Schofield	.05	.02	.01
☐ 170 Junior Ortiz	.05	.02	.01
☐ 171 Hector Villanueva	.05	.02	.01
☐ 172 Dennis Eckersley	.10	.05	.01
☐ 173 Mitch Williams	.05	.02	.01
☐ 174 Mark McGwire	.30	.14	.04
☐ 175 Fernando Valenzuela 3X	.10	.05	.01
☐ 176 Gary Carter	.10	.05	.01
☐ 177 Dave Magadan	.05	.02	.01
☐ 178 Robby Thompson	.05	.02	.01
☐ 179 Bob Ojeda	.05	.02	.01
☐ 180 Ken Caminiti	.15	.07	.02
☐ 181 Don Slaught	.05	.02	.01
☐ 182 Luis Rivera	.05	.02	.01
☐ 183 Jay Bell	.10	.05	.01
☐ 184 Jody Reed	.05	.02	.01
☐ 185 Wally Backman	.05	.02	.01
☐ 186 Dave Martinez	.05	.02	.01
☐ 187 Luis Polonia	.05	.02	.01
☐ 188 Shane Mack	.05	.02	.01
☐ 189 Spike Owen	.05	.02	.01
☐ 190 Scott Bailes	.05	.02	.01
☐ 191 John Russell	.05	.02	.01
☐ 192 Walt Weiss	.05	.02	.01
☐ 193 Jose Oquendo	.05	.02	.01
☐ 194 Carney Lansford	.10	.05	.01
☐ 195 Jeff Huson	.05	.02	.01
☐ 196 Keith Miller	.05	.02	.01
☐ 197 Eric Yelding	.05	.02	.01
☐ 198 Ron Darling	.05	.02	.01
☐ 199 John Kruk	.10	.05	.01
☐ 200 Checklist 101-200	.05	.02	.01
☐ 201 John Shelby	.05	.02	.01
☐ 202 Bob Geren	.05	.02	.01
☐ 203 Lance McCullers	.05	.02	.01
☐ 204 Alvaro Espinoza	.05	.02	.01
☐ 205 Mark Salas	.05	.02	.01
☐ 206 Mike Pagliarulo	.05	.02	.01
☐ 207 Jose Uribe	.05	.02	.01
☐ 208 Jim Deshaies	.05	.02	.01
☐ 209 Ron Karkovice	.05	.02	.01
☐ 210 Rafael Ramirez	.05	.02	.01
☐ 211 Donnie Hill	.05	.02	.01
☐ 212 Brian Harper	.05	.02	.01
☐ 213 Jack Howell	.05	.02	.01
☐ 214 Wes Gardner	.05	.02	.01
☐ 215 Tim Burke	.05	.02	.01
☐ 216 Doug Jones	.05	.02	.01
☐ 217 Hubie Brooks	.05	.02	.01
☐ 218 Tom Candiotti	.05	.02	.01
☐ 219 Gerald Perry	.05	.02	.01
☐ 220 Jose DeLeon	.05	.02	.01
☐ 221 Wally Whitehurst	.05	.02	.01
☐ 222 Alan Mills	.05	.02	.01
☐ 223 Alan Trammell	.10	.05	.01
☐ 224 Dwight Gooden	.10	.05	.01
☐ 225 Travis Fryman	.15	.07	.02
☐ 226 Joe Carter	.10	.05	.01
☐ 227 Julio Franco	.10	.05	.01
☐ 228 Craig Lefferts	.05	.02	.01
☐ 229 Gary Pettis	.05	.02	.01
☐ 230 Dennis Rasmussen	.05	.02	.01
☐ 231A Brian Downing ERR (No position on front)	.05	.02	.01
☐ 231B Brian Downing COR (DH on front)	.10	.05	.01
☐ 232 Carlos Quintana	.05	.02	.01
☐ 233 Gary Gaetti	.10	.05	.01
☐ 234 Mark Langston	.10	.05	.01
☐ 235 Tim Wallach	.05	.02	.01
☐ 236 Greg Swindell	.05	.02	.01
☐ 237 Eddie Murray	.25	.11	.03
☐ 238 Jeff Manto	.05	.02	.01
☐ 239 Lenny Harris	.05	.02	.01
☐ 240 Jesse Orosco	.05	.02	.01
☐ 241 Scott Lusader	.05	.02	.01
☐ 242 Sid Fernandez	.05	.02	.01
☐ 243 Jim Leyritz	.10	.05	.01
☐ 244 Cecil Fielder	.10	.05	.01
☐ 245 Darryl Strawberry	.10	.05	.01
☐ 246 Frank Thomas UER (Comiskey Park misspelled Comisky)	2.00	.90	.25
☐ 247 Kevin Mitchell	.10	.05	.01
☐ 248 Lance Johnson	.10	.05	.01
☐ 249 Rick Reuschel	.05	.02	.01
☐ 250 Mark Portugal	.05	.02	.01
☐ 251 Derek Lilliquist	.05	.02	.01
☐ 252 Brian Holman	.05	.02	.01
☐ 253 Rafael Valdez UER (Born 4/17/68, should be 12/17/67)	.05	.02	.01
☐ 254 B.J. Surhoff	.10	.05	.01
☐ 255 Tony Gwynn	.40	.18	.05
☐ 256 Andy Van Slyke	.10	.05	.01
☐ 257 Todd Stottlemyre	.05	.02	.01
☐ 258 Jose Lind	.05	.02	.01
☐ 259 Greg Myers	.05	.02	.01
☐ 260 Jeff Ballard	.05	.02	.01
☐ 261 Bobby Thigpen	.05	.02	.01
☐ 262 Jimmy Kremers	.05	.02	.01
☐ 263 Robin Ventura	.15	.07	.02
☐ 264 John Smoltz	.15	.07	.02
☐ 265 Sammy Sosa	.25	.11	.03
☐ 266 Gary Sheffield	.15	.07	.02
☐ 267 Len Dykstra	.10	.05	.01
☐ 268 Bill Spiers	.05	.02	.01
☐ 269 Charlie Hayes	.05	.02	.01
☐ 270 Brett Butler	.10	.05	.01
☐ 271 Bip Roberts	.05	.02	.01
☐ 272 Rob Deer	.05	.02	.01
☐ 273 Fred Lynn	.05	.02	.01
☐ 274 Dave Parker	.10	.05	.01
☐ 275 Andy Benes	.10	.05	.01
☐ 276 Glenallen Hill	.05	.02	.01
☐ 277 Steve Howard	.05	.02	.01
☐ 278 Doug Drabek	.05	.02	.01
☐ 279 Joe Oliver	.05	.02	.01
☐ 280 Todd Benzinger	.05	.02	.01
☐ 281 Eric King	.05	.02	.01
☐ 282 Jim Presley	.05	.02	.01
☐ 283 Ken Patterson	.05	.02	.01
☐ 284 Jack Daugherty	.05	.02	.01
☐ 285 Ivan Calderon	.05	.02	.01
☐ 286 Edgar Diaz	.05	.02	.01
☐ 287 Kevin Bass	.05	.02	.01
☐ 288 Don Carman	.05	.02	.01
☐ 289 Greg Brock	.05	.02	.01
☐ 290 John Franco	.05	.02	.01
☐ 291 Joey Cora	.10	.05	.01
☐ 292 Bill Wegman	.05	.02	.01
☐ 293 Eric Show	.05	.02	.01
☐ 294 Scott Bankhead	.05	.02	.01
☐ 295 Garry Templeton	.05	.02	.01
☐ 296 Mickey Tettleton	.10	.05	.01
☐ 297 Luis Sojo	.05	.02	.01
☐ 298 Jose Rijo	.05	.02	.01
☐ 299 Dave Johnson	.05	.02	.01
☐ 300 Checklist 201-300	.05	.02	.01
☐ 301 Mark Grant	.05	.02	.01
☐ 302 Pete Harnisch	.05	.02	.01
☐ 303 Greg Olson	.05	.02	.01
☐ 304 Anthony Telford	.05	.02	.01
☐ 305 Lonnie Smith	.05	.02	.01
☐ 306 Chris Hoiles	.05	.02	.01
☐ 307 Bryn Smith	.05	.02	.01
☐ 308 Mike Devereaux	.05	.02	.01
☐ 309A Milt Thompson ERR (Under yr information has print dot)	.15	.07	.02
☐ 309B Milt Thompson COR (Under yr information says 86)	.05	.02	.01
☐ 310 Bob Melvin	.05	.02	.01
☐ 311 Luis Salazar	.05	.02	.01
☐ 312 Ed Whitson	.05	.02	.01
☐ 313 Charlie Hough	.05	.02	.01
☐ 314 Dave Clark	.05	.02	.01
☐ 315 Eric Gunderson	.05	.02	.01
☐ 316 Dan Petry	.05	.02	.01
☐ 317 Dante Bichette UER (Assists misspelled as assissts)	.15	.07	.02
☐ 318 Mike Heath	.05	.02	.01
☐ 319 Damon Berryhill	.05	.02	.01
☐ 320 Walt Terrell	.05	.02	.01
☐ 321 Scott Fletcher	.05	.02	.01
☐ 322 Dan Plesac	.05	.02	.01
☐ 323 Jack McDowell	.10	.05	.01
☐ 324 Paul Molitor	.20	.09	.03
☐ 325 Ozzie Guillen	.05	.02	.01
☐ 326 Gregg Olson	.05	.02	.01
☐ 327 Pedro Guerrero	.05	.02	.01
☐ 328 Bob Milacki	.05	.02	.01
☐ 329 John Tudor UER ('90 Cardinals, should be '90 Dodgers)	.05	.02	.01
☐ 330 Steve Finley UER (Born 3/12/65, should be 5/12)	.10	.05	.01
☐ 331 Jack Clark	.10	.05	.01
☐ 332 Jerome Walton	.05	.02	.01
☐ 333 Andy Hawkins	.05	.02	.01
☐ 334 Derrick May	.05	.02	.01
☐ 335 Roberto Alomar	.20	.09	.03
☐ 336 Jack Morris	.10	.05	.01
☐ 337 Dave Winfield	.15	.07	.02
☐ 338 Steve Searcy	.05	.02	.01
☐ 339 Chili Davis	.10	.05	.01
☐ 340 Larry Sheets	.05	.02	.01
☐ 341 Ted Higuera	.05	.02	.01
☐ 342 David Segui	.10	.05	.01
☐ 343 Greg Cadaret	.05	.02	.01
☐ 344 Robin Yount	.15	.07	.02
☐ 345 Nolan Ryan	.75	.35	.09
☐ 346 Ray Lankford	.15	.07	.02
☐ 347 Cal Ripken	.75	.35	.09
☐ 348 Lee Smith	.10	.05	.01
☐ 349 Brady Anderson	.15	.07	.02
☐ 350 Frank DiPino	.05	.02	.01
☐ 351 Hal Morris	.05	.02	.01
☐ 352 Deion Sanders	.15	.07	.02
☐ 353 Barry Larkin	.15	.07	.02
☐ 354 Don Mattingly	.50	.23	.06
☐ 355 Eric Davis	.10	.05	.01
☐ 356 Jose Offerman	.05	.02	.01
☐ 357 Mel Rojas	.10	.05	.01
☐ 358 Rudy Seanez	.05	.02	.01
☐ 359 Oil Can Boyd	.05	.02	.01
☐ 360 Nelson Liriano	.05	.02	.01
☐ 361 Ron Gant	.10	.05	.01
☐ 362 Howard Farmer	.05	.02	.01
☐ 363 David Justice	.15	.07	.02
☐ 364 Delino DeShields	.05	.02	.01
☐ 365 Steve Avery	.15	.07	.02
☐ 366 David Cone	.10	.05	.01
☐ 367 Lou Whitaker	.10	.05	.01
☐ 368 Von Hayes	.05	.02	.01
☐ 369 Frank Tanana	.05	.02	.01
☐ 370 Tim Teufel	.05	.02	.01
☐ 371 Randy Myers	.10	.05	.01
☐ 372 Roberto Kelly	.05	.02	.01
☐ 373 Jack Armstrong	.05	.02	.01
☐ 374 Kelly Gruber	.05	.02	.01
☐ 375 Kevin Maas	.05	.02	.01
☐ 376 Randy Johnson	.15	.07	.02
☐ 377 David West	.05	.02	.01
☐ 378 Brent Knackert	.05	.02	.01
☐ 379 Rick Honeycutt	.05	.02	.01
☐ 380 Kevin Gross	.05	.02	.01
☐ 381 Tom Foley	.05	.02	.01
☐ 382 Jeff Blauser	.05	.02	.01
☐ 383 Scott Ruskin	.05	.02	.01
☐ 384 Andres Thomas	.05	.02	.01
☐ 385 Dennis Martinez	.10	.05	.01
☐ 386 Mike Henneman	.05	.02	.01
☐ 387 Felix Jose	.05	.02	.01
☐ 388 Alejandro Pena	.05	.02	.01
☐ 389 Chet Lemon	.05	.02	.01
☐ 390 Craig Wilson	.05	.02	.01
☐ 391 Chuck Crim	.05	.02	.01
☐ 392 Mel Hall	.05	.02	.01
☐ 393 Mark Knudson	.05	.02	.01
☐ 394 Norm Charlton	.05	.02	.01
☐ 395 Mike Felder	.05	.02	.01
☐ 396 Tim Layana	.05	.02	.01
☐ 397 Steve Frey	.05	.02	.01
☐ 398 Bill Doran	.05	.02	.01
☐ 399 Dion James	.05	.02	.01
☐ 400 Checklist 301-400	.05	.02	.01
☐ 401 Ron Hassey	.05	.02	.01
☐ 402 Don Robinson	.05	.02	.01
☐ 403 Gene Nelson	.05	.02	.01
☐ 404 Terry Kennedy	.05	.02	.01
☐ 405 Todd Burns	.05	.02	.01
☐ 406 Roger McDowell	.05	.02	.01
☐ 407 Bob Kipper	.05	.02	.01
☐ 408 Darren Daulton	.10	.05	.01
☐ 409 Chuck Cary	.05	.02	.01
☐ 410 Bruce Ruffin	.05	.02	.01
☐ 411 Juan Berenguer	.05	.02	.01
☐ 412 Gary Ward	.05	.02	.01
☐ 413 Al Newman	.05	.02	.01
☐ 414 Danny Jackson	.05	.02	.01
☐ 415 Greg Gagne	.05	.02	.01
☐ 416 Tom Herr	.05	.02	.01
☐ 417 Jeff Parrett	.05	.02	.01
☐ 418 Jeff Reardon	.10	.05	.01
☐ 419 Mark Lemke	.05	.02	.01
☐ 420 Charlie O'Brien	.05	.02	.01
☐ 421 Willie Randolph	.10	.05	.01
☐ 422 Steve Bedrosian	.05	.02	.01
☐ 423 Mike Moore	.05	.02	.01
☐ 424 Jeff Brantley	.05	.02	.01
☐ 425 Bob Welch	.05	.02	.01
☐ 426 Terry Mulholland	.05	.02	.01
☐ 427 Willie Blair	.05	.02	.01
☐ 428 Darrin Fletcher	.05	.02	.01
☐ 429 Mike Witt	.05	.02	.01
☐ 430 Joe Boever	.05	.02	.01
☐ 431 Tom Gordon	.05	.02	.01
☐ 432 Pedro Munoz	.10	.05	.01
☐ 433 Kevin Seitzer	.05	.02	.01
☐ 434 Kevin Tapani	.05	.02	.01
☐ 435 Bret Saberhagen	.10	.05	.01
☐ 436 Ellis Burks	.10	.05	.01
☐ 437 Chuck Finley	.10	.05	.01
☐ 438 Mike Boddicker	.05	.02	.01
☐ 439 Francisco Cabrera	.05	.02	.01
☐ 440 Todd Hundley	.15	.07	.02
☐ 441 Kelly Downs	.05	.02	.01
☐ 442 Dann Howitt	.05	.02	.01
☐ 443 Scott Garrelts	.05	.02	.01
☐ 444 Rickey Henderson 3X	.15	.07	.02
☐ 445 Will Clark	.15	.07	.02
☐ 446 Ben McDonald	.10	.05	.01
☐ 447 Dale Murphy	.15	.07	.02
☐ 448 Dave Righetti	.05	.02	.01
☐ 449 Dickie Thon	.05	.02	.01
☐ 450 Ted Power	.05	.02	.01
☐ 451 Scott Coolbaugh	.05	.02	.01
☐ 452 Dwight Smith	.05	.02	.01
☐ 453 Pete Incaviglia	.05	.02	.01
☐ 454 Andre Dawson	.10	.05	.01
☐ 455 Ruben Sierra	.10	.05	.01
☐ 456 Andres Galarraga	.15	.07	.02
☐ 457 Alvin Davis	.05	.02	.01
☐ 458 Tony Castillo	.05	.02	.01
☐ 459 Pete O'Brien	.05	.02	.01
☐ 460 Charlie Leibrandt	.05	.02	.01
☐ 461 Vince Coleman	.05	.02	.01
☐ 462 Steve Sax	.05	.02	.01

☐ 463 Omar Olivares .05 .02 .01
☐ 464 Oscar Azocar .05 .02 .01
☐ 465 Joe Magrane .05 .02 .01
☐ 466 Karl Rhodes .05 .02 .01
☐ 467 Benito Santiago .05 .02 .01
☐ 468 Joe Klink .05 .02 .01
☐ 469 Sil Campusano .05 .02 .01
☐ 470 Mark Parent .05 .02 .01
☐ 471 Shawn Boskie UER .05 .02 .01
(Depleted misspelled
as depleated)
☐ 472 Kevin Brown .10 .05 .01
☐ 473 Rick Sutcliffe .05 .02 .01
☐ 474 Rafael Palmeiro .15 .07 .02
☐ 475 Mike Harkey .05 .02 .01
☐ 476 Jaime Navarro .05 .02 .01
☐ 477 Marquis Grissom UER .15 .07 .02
(DeShields misspelled
as DeSheilds)
☐ 478 Marty Clary .05 .02 .01
☐ 479 Greg Briley .05 .02 .01
☐ 480 Tom Glavine .15 .07 .02
☐ 481 Lee Guetterman .05 .02 .01
☐ 482 Rex Hudler .05 .02 .01
☐ 483 Dave LaPoint .05 .02 .01
☐ 484 Terry Pendleton .10 .05 .01
☐ 485 Jesse Barfield .05 .02 .01
☐ 486 Jose DeJesus .05 .02 .01
☐ 487 Paul Abbott .05 .02 .01
☐ 488 Ken Howell .05 .02 .01
☐ 489 Greg W. Harris .05 .02 .01
☐ 490 Roy Smith .05 .02 .01
☐ 491 Paul Assenmacher .05 .02 .01
☐ 492 Geno Petralli .05 .02 .01
☐ 493 Steve Wilson .05 .02 .01
☐ 494 Kevin Reimer .05 .02 .01
☐ 495 Bill Long .05 .02 .01
☐ 496 Mike Jackson .05 .02 .01
☐ 497 Oddibe McDowell .05 .02 .01
☐ 498 Bill Swift .05 .02 .01
☐ 499 Jeff Treadway .05 .02 .01
☐ 500 Checklist 401-500 .05 .02 .01
☐ 501 Gene Larkin .05 .02 .01
☐ 502 Bob Boone .10 .05 .01
☐ 503 Allan Anderson .05 .02 .01
☐ 504 Luis Aquino .05 .02 .01
☐ 505 Mark Guthrie .05 .02 .01
☐ 506 Joe Orsulak .05 .02 .01
☐ 507 Dana Kiecker .05 .02 .01
☐ 508 Dave Gallagher .05 .02 .01
☐ 509 Greg A. Harris .05 .02 .01
☐ 510 Mark Williamson .05 .02 .01
☐ 511 Casey Candaele .05 .02 .01
☐ 512 Mookie Wilson .05 .02 .01
☐ 513 Dave Smith .05 .02 .01
☐ 514 Chuck Carr .05 .02 .01
☐ 515 Glenn Wilson .05 .02 .01
☐ 516 Mike Fitzgerald .05 .02 .01
☐ 517 Devon White .10 .05 .01
☐ 518 Dave Hollins .05 .02 .01
☐ 519 Mark Eichhorn .05 .02 .01
☐ 520 Otis Nixon .05 .02 .01
☐ 521 Terry Shumpert .05 .02 .01
☐ 522 Scott Erickson .10 .05 .01
☐ 523 Danny Tartabull .05 .02 .01
☐ 524 Orel Hershiser .10 .05 .01
☐ 525 George Brett .40 .18 .05
☐ 526 Greg Vaughn .10 .05 .01
☐ 527 Tim Naehring .10 .05 .01
☐ 528 Curt Schilling .05 .02 .01
☐ 529 Chris Bosio .05 .02 .01
☐ 530 Sam Horn .05 .02 .01
☐ 531 Mike Scott .05 .02 .01
☐ 532 George Bell .05 .02 .01
☐ 533 Eric Anthony .05 .02 .01
☐ 534 Julio Valera .05 .02 .01
☐ 535 Glenn Davis .05 .02 .01
☐ 536 Larry Walker UER .15 .07 .02
(Should have comma
after Expos in text)
☐ 537 Pat Combs .05 .02 .01
☐ 538 Chris Nabholz .05 .02 .01
☐ 539 Kirk McCaskill .05 .02 .01
☐ 540 Randy Ready .05 .02 .01
☐ 541 Mark Gubicza .05 .02 .01
☐ 542 Rick Aguilera .10 .05 .01
☐ 543 Brian McRae .25 .11 .03
☐ 544 Kirby Puckett .40 .18 .05
☐ 545 Bo Jackson .10 .05 .01
☐ 546 Wade Boggs .15 .07 .02
☐ 547 Tim McIntosh .05 .02 .01
☐ 548 Randy Milligan .05 .02 .01
☐ 549 Dwight Evans .10 .05 .01
☐ 550 Billy Ripken .05 .02 .01
☐ 551 Erik Hanson .05 .02 .01
☐ 552 Lance Parrish .05 .02 .01
☐ 553 Tino Martinez .15 .07 .02
☐ 554 Jim Abbott .10 .05 .01
☐ 555 Ken Griffey Jr. UER 1.50 .70 .19
(Second most votes for
1991 All-Star Game)
☐ 556 Milt Cuyler .05 .02 .01
☐ 557 Mark Leonard .05 .02 .01
☐ 558 Jay Howell .05 .02 .01
☐ 559 Lloyd Moseby .05 .02 .01

☐ 560 Chris Gwynn .05 .02 .01
☐ 561 Mark Whiten .10 .05 .01
☐ 562 Harold Baines .10 .05 .01
☐ 563 Junior Felix .05 .02 .01
☐ 564 Darren Lewis .10 .05 .01
☐ 565 Fred McGriff .15 .07 .02
☐ 566 Kevin Appier .15 .07 .02
☐ 567 Luis Gonzalez .15 .07 .02
☐ 568 Frank White .10 .05 .01
☐ 569 Juan Agosto .05 .02 .01
☐ 570 Mike Macfarlane .05 .02 .01
☐ 571 Bert Blyleven .10 .05 .01
☐ 572 Ken Griffey Sr. .50 .23 .06
Ken Griffey Jr.
☐ 573 Lee Stevens .05 .02 .01
☐ 574 Edgar Martinez .10 .05 .01
☐ 575 Wally Joyner .10 .05 .01
☐ 576 Tim Belcher .05 .02 .01
☐ 577 John Burkett .10 .05 .01
☐ 578 Mike Morgan .05 .02 .01
☐ 579 Paul Gibson .05 .02 .01
☐ 580 Jose Vizcaino .05 .02 .01
☐ 581 Duane Ward .05 .02 .01
☐ 582 Scott Sanderson .05 .02 .01
☐ 583 David Wells .05 .02 .01
☐ 584 Willie McGee .05 .02 .01
☐ 585 John Cerutti .05 .02 .01
☐ 586 Danny Darwin .05 .02 .01
☐ 587 Kurt Stillwell .05 .02 .01
☐ 588 Rich Gedman .05 .02 .01
☐ 589 Mark Davis .05 .02 .01
☐ 590 Bill Gullickson .05 .02 .01
☐ 591 Matt Young .05 .02 .01
☐ 592 Bryan Harvey .05 .02 .01
☐ 593 Omar Vizquel .15 .07 .02
☐ 594 Scott Lewis .05 .02 .01
☐ 595 Dave Valle .05 .02 .01
☐ 596 Tim Crews .05 .02 .01
☐ 597 Mike Bielecki .05 .02 .01
☐ 598 Mike Sharperson .05 .02 .01
☐ 599 Dave Bergman .05 .02 .01
☐ 600 Checklist 501-600 .05 .02 .01
☐ 601 Steve Lyons .05 .02 .01
☐ 602 Bruce Hurst .05 .02 .01
☐ 603 Donn Pall .05 .02 .01
☐ 604 Jim Vatcher .05 .02 .01
☐ 605 Dan Pasqua .05 .02 .01
☐ 606 Kenny Rogers .05 .02 .01
☐ 607 Jeff Schulz .05 .02 .01
☐ 608 Brad Arnsberg .05 .02 .01
☐ 609 Willie Wilson .05 .02 .01
☐ 610 Jamie Moyer .05 .02 .01
☐ 611 Ron Oester .05 .02 .01
☐ 612 Dennis Cook .05 .02 .01
☐ 613 Rick Mahler .05 .02 .01
☐ 614 Bill Landrum .05 .02 .01
☐ 615 Scott Scudder .05 .02 .01
☐ 616 Tom Edens .05 .02 .01
☐ 617 1917 Revisited .10 .05 .01
(White Sox in vin-
tage uniforms)
☐ 618 Jim Gantner .05 .02 .01
☐ 619 Darrel Akerfelds .05 .02 .01
☐ 620 Ron Robinson .05 .02 .01
☐ 621 Scott Radinsky .05 .02 .01
☐ 622 Pete Smith .05 .02 .01
☐ 623 Melido Perez .05 .02 .01
☐ 624 Jerald Clark .05 .02 .01
☐ 625 Carlos Martinez .05 .02 .01
☐ 626 Wes Chamberlain .05 .02 .01
☐ 627 Bobby Witt .05 .02 .01
☐ 628 Ken Dayley .05 .02 .01
☐ 629 John Barfield .05 .02 .01
☐ 630 Bob Tewksbury .05 .02 .01
☐ 631 Glenn Braggs .05 .02 .01
☐ 632 Jim Neidlinger .05 .02 .01
☐ 633 Tom Browning .05 .02 .01
☐ 634 Kirk Gibson .10 .05 .01
☐ 635 Rob Dibble .05 .02 .01
☐ 636 Rickey Henderson SB .30 .14 .04
Lou Brock
May 1, 1991 on front)
☐ 636A Rickey Henderson SB .15 .07 .02
Lou Brock
no date on card)
☐ 637 Jeff Montgomery .10 .05 .01
☐ 638 Mike Schooler .05 .02 .01
☐ 639 Storm Davis .05 .02 .01
☐ 640 Rich Rodriguez .05 .02 .01
☐ 641 Phil Bradley .05 .02 .01
☐ 642 Kent Mercker .05 .02 .01
☐ 643 Carlton Fisk .15 .07 .02
☐ 644 Mike Bell .05 .02 .01
☐ 645 Alex Fernandez .15 .07 .02
☐ 646 Juan Gonzalez .75 .35 .09
☐ 647 Ken Hill .10 .05 .01
☐ 648 Jeff Russell .05 .02 .01
☐ 649 Chuck Malone .05 .02 .01
☐ 650 Steve Buechele .05 .02 .01
☐ 651 Mike Benjamin .05 .02 .01
☐ 652 Tony Pena .05 .02 .01
☐ 653 Trevor Wilson .05 .02 .01
☐ 654 Alex Cole .05 .02 .01
☐ 655 Roger Clemens .20 .09 .03
☐ 656 Mark McGwire BASH .15 .07 .02

☐ 657 Joe Grahe .05 .02 .01
☐ 658 Jim Eisenreich .10 .05 .01
☐ 659 Dan Gladden .05 .02 .01
☐ 660 Steve Farr .05 .02 .01
☐ 661 Bill Sampen .05 .02 .01
☐ 662 Dave Rohde .05 .02 .01
☐ 663 Mark Gardner .05 .02 .01
☐ 664 Mike Simms .05 .02 .01
☐ 665 Moises Alou .15 .07 .02
☐ 666 Mickey Hatcher .05 .02 .01
☐ 667 Jimmy Key .10 .05 .01
☐ 668 John Wetteland .15 .07 .02
☐ 669 John Smiley .05 .02 .01
☐ 670 Jim Acker .05 .02 .01
☐ 671 Pascual Perez .05 .02 .01
☐ 672 Reggie Harris UER .05 .02 .01
(Opportunity misspelled
as oppurtinty)
☐ 673 Matt Nokes .05 .02 .01
☐ 674 Rafael Novoa .05 .02 .01
☐ 675 Hensley Meulens .05 .02 .01
☐ 676 Jeff M. Robinson .05 .02 .01
☐ 677 Ground Breaking .10 .05 .01
(New Comiskey Park;
Carlton Fisk and
Robin Ventura)
☐ 678 Johnny Ray .05 .02 .01
☐ 679 Greg Hibbard .05 .02 .01
☐ 680 Paul Sorrento .10 .05 .01
☐ 681 Mike Marshall .05 .02 .01
☐ 682 Jim Clancy .05 .02 .01
☐ 683 Rob Murphy .05 .02 .01
☐ 684 Dave Schmidt .05 .02 .01
☐ 685 Jeff Gray .05 .02 .01
☐ 686 Mike Hartley .05 .02 .01
☐ 687 Jeff King .10 .05 .01
☐ 688 Stan Javier .05 .02 .01
☐ 689 Bob Walk .05 .02 .01
☐ 690 Jim Gott .05 .02 .01
☐ 691 Mike LaCoss .05 .02 .01
☐ 692 John Farrell .05 .02 .01
☐ 693 Tim Leary .05 .02 .01
☐ 694 Mike Walker .05 .02 .01
☐ 695 Eric Plunk .05 .02 .01
☐ 696 Mike Fetters .05 .02 .01
☐ 697 Wayne Edwards .05 .02 .01
☐ 698 Tim Drummond .05 .02 .01
☐ 699 Willie Fraser .05 .02 .01
☐ 700 Checklist 601-700 .05 .02 .01
☐ 701 Mike Heath .05 .02 .01
☐ 702 Rookie Threats .75 .35 .09
Luis Gonzalez
Karl Rhodes
Jeff Bagwell
☐ 703 Jose Mesa .10 .05 .01
☐ 704 Dave Smith .05 .02 .01
☐ 705 Danny Darwin .05 .02 .01
☐ 706 Rafael Belliard .05 .02 .01
☐ 707 Rob Murphy .05 .02 .01
☐ 708 Terry Pendleton .10 .05 .01
☐ 709 Mike Pagliarulo .05 .02 .01
☐ 710 Sid Bream .05 .02 .01
☐ 711 Junior Felix .05 .02 .01
☐ 712 Dante Bichette .15 .07 .02
☐ 713 Kevin Gross .05 .02 .01
☐ 714 Luis Sojo .05 .02 .01
☐ 715 Bob Ojeda .05 .02 .01
☐ 716 Julio Machado .05 .02 .01
☐ 717 Steve Farr .05 .02 .01
☐ 718 Franklin Stubbs .05 .02 .01
☐ 719 Mike Boddicker .05 .02 .01
☐ 720 Willie Randolph .10 .05 .01
☐ 721 Willie McGee .05 .02 .01
☐ 722 Chili Davis .10 .05 .01
☐ 723 Danny Jackson .05 .02 .01
☐ 724 Cory Snyder .05 .02 .01
☐ 725 MVP Lineup .15 .07 .02
Andre Dawson
George Bell
Ryne Sandberg
☐ 726 Rob Deer .05 .02 .01
☐ 727 Rich DeLucia .05 .02 .01
☐ 728 Mike Perez .05 .02 .01
☐ 729 Mickey Tettleton .10 .05 .01
☐ 730 Mike Blowers .05 .02 .01
☐ 731 Gary Gaetti .10 .05 .01
☐ 732 Brett Butler .10 .05 .01
☐ 733 Dave Parker .10 .05 .01
☐ 734 Eddie Zosky .05 .02 .01
☐ 735 Jack Clark .10 .05 .01
☐ 736 Jack Morris .10 .05 .01
☐ 737 Kirk Gibson .10 .05 .01
☐ 738 Steve Bedrosian .05 .02 .01
☐ 739 Candy Maldonado .05 .02 .01
☐ 740 Matt Young .05 .02 .01
☐ 741 Rich Garces .05 .02 .01
☐ 742 George Bell .05 .02 .01
☐ 743 Deion Sanders .15 .07 .02
☐ 744 Bo Jackson .10 .05 .01
☐ 745 Luis Mercedes .05 .02 .01
☐ 746 Reggie Jefferson UER .10 .05 .01
(Throwing left on card;
back has throws right)
☐ 747 Pete Incaviglia .05 .02 .01
☐ 748 Chris Hammond .05 .02 .01

☐ 749 Mike Stanton .05 .02 .01
☐ 750 Scott Sanderson .05 .02 .01
☐ 751 Paul Faries .05 .02 .01
☐ 752 Al Osuna .05 .02 .01
☐ 753 Steve Chitren .05 .02 .01
☐ 754 Tony Fernandez .05 .02 .01
☐ 755 Jeff Bagwell UER 2.50 1.10 .30
(Strikeout and walk
totals reversed)
☐ 756 Kirk Dressendorfer .05 .02 .01
☐ 757 Glenn Davis .05 .02 .01
☐ 758 Gary Carter .10 .05 .01
☐ 759 Zane Smith .05 .02 .01
☐ 760 Vance Law .05 .02 .01
☐ 761 Denis Boucher .05 .02 .01
☐ 762 Turner Ward .05 .02 .01
☐ 763 Roberto Alomar .20 .09 .03
☐ 764 Albert Belle .50 .23 .06
☐ 765 Joe Carter .10 .05 .01
☐ 766 Pete Schourek .15 .07 .02
☐ 767 Heathcliff Slocumb .15 .07 .02
☐ 768 Vince Coleman .05 .02 .01
☐ 769 Mitch Williams .05 .02 .01
☐ 770 Brian Downing .05 .02 .01
☐ 771 Dana Allison .05 .02 .01
☐ 772 Pete Harnisch .05 .02 .01
☐ 773 Tim Raines .15 .07 .02
☐ 774 Darryl Kile .05 .02 .01
☐ 775 Fred McGriff .15 .07 .02
☐ 776 Dwight Evans .10 .05 .01
☐ 777 Joe Slusarski .05 .02 .01
☐ 778 Dave Righetti .05 .02 .01
☐ 779 Jeff Hamilton .05 .02 .01
☐ 780 Ernest Riles .05 .02 .01
☐ 781 Ken Dayley .05 .02 .01
☐ 782 Eric King .05 .02 .01
☐ 783 Devon White .10 .05 .01
☐ 784 Beau Allred .05 .02 .01
☐ 785 Mike Timlin .05 .02 .01
☐ 786 Ivan Calderon .05 .02 .01
☐ 787 Hubie Brooks .05 .02 .01
☐ 788 Juan Agosto .05 .02 .01
☐ 789 Barry Jones .05 .02 .01
☐ 790 Wally Backman .05 .02 .01
☐ 791 Jim Presley .05 .02 .01
☐ 792 Charlie Hough .05 .02 .01
☐ 793 Larry Andersen .05 .02 .01
☐ 794 Steve Finley .10 .05 .01
☐ 795 Shawn Abner .05 .02 .01
☐ 796 Jeff M. Robinson .05 .02 .01
☐ 797 Joe Bitker .05 .02 .01
☐ 798 Eric Show .05 .02 .01
☐ 799 Bud Black .05 .02 .01
☐ 800 Checklist 701-800 .05 .02 .01
☐ HH1 Hank Aaron Hologram 2.00 .90 .25
☐ SP1 Michael Jordan SP 15.00 6.75 1.85
(Shown batting in
White Sox uniform)
☐ SP2 Rickey Henderson 2.50 1.10 .30
Nolan Ryan
May 1, 1991 Records

1991 Upper Deck Aaron Heroes

These standard-size cards were issued in honor of Hall of Famer Hank Aaron and inserted in Upper Deck high number wax packs. The fronts have color player photos superimposed over a circular shot. Inside a red border stripe, a tan background fills in the rest of the card face. The Baseball Heroes logo adorns the card face. The backs have a similar design, except with an extended caption presented on a light gray background. Aaron autographed 2,500 of card number 27, which featured his portrait by noted sports artist Vernon Wells. The cards are numbered on the back in continuation of the Baseball Heroes set.

	MINT	NRMT	EXC
COMPLETE SET (10)	5.00	2.20	.60
COMMON AARON (19-27)	.50	.23	.06

☐ 19 Hank Aaron .50 .23 .06
1954 Rookie Year
☐ 20 Hank Aaron .50 .23 .06
1957 MVP
☐ 21 Hank Aaron .50 .23 .06
1966 Move to Atlanta
☐ 22 Hank Aaron .50 .23 .06
1970 3,000 Hits
☐ 23 Hank Aaron .50 .23 .06
1974 715 Homers
☐ 24 Hank Aaron .50 .23 .06
1975 Return to Milwaukee
☐ 25 Hank Aaron .50 .23 .06

	MINT	NRMT	EXC
1976 755 Homers			
☐ 26 Hank Aaron	.50	.23	.06
1982 Hall of Fame			
☐ 27 Checklist 19-27	.50	.23	.06
☐ AU3 Hank Aaron AU (Signed and Numbered out of 2500)	300.00	135.00	38.00
☐ NNO0 Title/Header card SP	2.00	.90	.25

1991 Upper Deck Heroes of Baseball

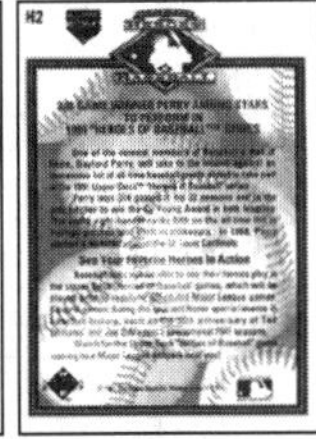

These standard-size cards were randomly inserted in Upper Deck Baseball Heroes wax packs. On a white card face, the fronts of the first three cards have sepia-toned player photos, with red, gold, and blue border stripes. The player's name appears in a gold border stripe beneath the picture, with the Upper Deck "Heroes of Baseball" logo in the lower right corner. The backs have a similar design to the fronts, except with a career summary and an advertisement for Upper Deck "Heroes of Baseball" games that will be played prior to regularly scheduled Major League games. The fourth card features a color portrait of the three players by noted sports artist Vernon Wells.

	MINT	NRMT	EXC
COMPLETE SET (4)	30.00	13.50	3.70
COMMON CARD (H1-H4)	8.00	3.60	1.00
☐ H1 Harmon Killebrew	8.00	3.60	1.00
☐ H2 Gaylord Perry	8.00	3.60	1.00
☐ H3 Ferguson Jenkins	8.00	3.60	1.00
☐ H4 Harmon Killebrew DRAW Ferguson Jenkins Gaylord Perry	8.00	3.60	1.00
☐ AU1 Harmon Killebrew AU/3000	75.00	34.00	9.50
☐ AU2 Gaylord Perry AU/3000	60.00	27.00	7.50
☐ AU3 Ferguson Jenkins AU/3000	75.00	34.00	9.50

1991 Upper Deck Ryan Heroes

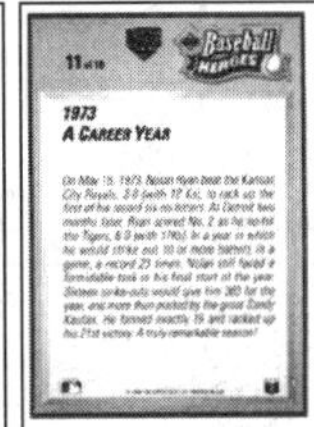

This nine-card standard-size set was included in first series 1991 Upper Deck packs. The set which honors Nolan Ryan and is numbered as a continuation of the Baseball Heroes set which began with Reggie Jackson in 1990. This set honors Ryan's long career and his place in Baseball History. Card number 18 features the artwork of Vernon Wells while the other cards are photos. The complete set price below does not include the signed Ryan card of which only 2500 were made. Signed cards ending with 00 have the expression "Strikeout King" added. These Ryan cards were apparently issued on 100-card sheets with the following configuration: ten each of the nine Ryan Baseball Heroes cards, five Michael Jordan cards and five Baseball Heroes header cards. The Baseball Heroes header card is a standard size card which explains the continuation of the Baseball Heroes series on the back while the front just says Baseball Heroes.

	MINT	NRMT	EXC
COMPLETE SET (10)	5.00	2.20	.60
COMMON RYAN (10-18)	.50	.23	.06
☐ 10 Nolan Ryan Tom Seaver Jerry Koosman 1968 Victory 1	.50	.23	.06
☐ 11 Nolan Ryan 1973 A Career Year	.50	.23	.06
☐ 12 Nolan Ryan 1975 Double Milestone	.50	.23	.06
☐ 13 Nolan Ryan 1979 Back Home	.50	.23	.06
☐ 14 Nolan Ryan 1981 All Time Leader	.50	.23	.06
☐ 15 Nolan Ryan 1989 5,000 K's	.50	.23	.06
☐ 16 Nolan Ryan 1990 6th No-Hitter	.50	.23	.06
☐ 17 Nolan Ryan 1990 And Still Counting	.50	.23	.06
☐ 18 NBlan Ryan Checklist Card Vernon Wells drawing with 5 poses of Ryan including each team he played for	.50	.23	.06
☐ AU2 Nolan Ryan AU (Signed and Numbered out of 2500)	600.00	275.00	75.00
☐ NNO0 Baseball Heroes SP (Header card)	2.00	.90	.25

1991 Upper Deck Silver Sluggers

The Upper Deck Silver Slugger set features nine players from each league, representing the nine batting positions on the team. The cards were issued one per 1991 Upper Deck jumbo pack. The cards measure the standard size. The fronts have glossy color action player photos, with white borders on three sides and a "Silver Slugger" bat serving as the border on the left side. The player's name appears in a tan stripe below the picture, with the team logo superimposed at the lower right corner. The card back is dominated by another color action photo with career highlights in a horizontally oriented rectangle to the left of the picture. The cards are numbered on the back with an SS prefix.

	MINT	NRMT	EXC
COMPLETE SET (18)	15.00	6.75	1.85
COMMON CARD (SS1-SS18)	.50	.23	.06
☐ SS1 Julio Franco	.75	.35	.09
☐ SS2 Alan Trammell	.75	.35	.09
☐ SS3 Rickey Henderson	1.25	.55	.16
☐ SS4 Jose Canseco	1.25	.55	.16
☐ SS5 Barry Bonds	2.00	.90	.25
☐ SS6 Eddie Murray	1.25	.55	.16
☐ SS7 Kelly Gruber	.50	.23	.06
☐ SS8 Ryne Sandberg	2.00	.90	.25
☐ SS9 Darryl Strawberry	.75	.35	.09
☐ SS10 Ellis Burks	.75	.35	.09
☐ SS11 Lance Parrish	.50	.23	.06
☐ SS12 Cecil Fielder	.75	.35	.09
☐ SS13 Matt Williams	1.25	.55	.16
☐ SS14 Dave Parker	.75	.35	.09
☐ SS15 Bobby Bonilla	.75	.35	.09
☐ SS16 Don Robinson	.50	.23	.06
☐ SS17 Benito Santiago	.50	.23	.06
☐ SS18 Barry Larkin	1.25	.55	.16

1991 Upper Deck Final Edition

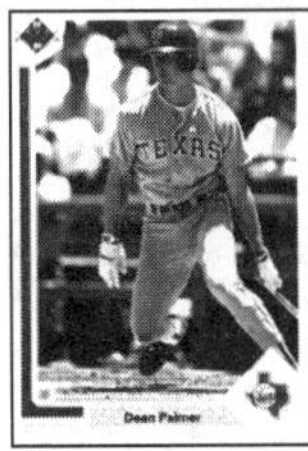

The 1991 Upper Deck Final Edition boxed set contains 100 standard-size cards and showcases players who made major contributions during their team's late-season pennant drive. In addition to the late season traded and impact rookie cards (22-78), the set includes two special subsets: Diamond Skills cards (1-21), depicting the best Minor League prospects, and All-Star cards (80-99). Six assorted team logo hologram cards were issued with each set. The basic card fronts feature posed or action color player photos on a white card face, with the upper left corner of the picture cut out to provide space for the Upper Deck logo. The pictures are bordered in green on the left, with the player's name in a tan border below the picture. The cards are numbered on the back with an F suffix. Among the outstanding Rookie Cards in this set are Ryan Klesko, Kenny Lofton, Pedro Martinez, Ivan Rodriguez, Jim Thome, Rondell White, and Dmitri Young.

	MINT	NRMT	EXC
COMPLETE FACT.SET (100)	5.00	2.20	.60
COMMON CARD (1F-100F)	.05	.02	.01
☐ 1F Ryan Klesko CL Reggie Sanders	.25	.11	.03
☐ 2F Pedro Martinez	.40	.18	.05
☐ 3F Lance Dickson	.05	.02	.01
☐ 4F Royce Clayton	.10	.05	.01
☐ 5F Scott Bryant	.05	.02	.01
☐ 6F Dan Wilson	.25	.11	.03
☐ 7F Dmitri Young	.50	.23	.06
☐ 8F Ryan Klesko	1.00	.45	.12
☐ 9F Tom Goodwin	.10	.05	.01
☐ 10F Rondell White	.40	.18	.05
☐ 11F Reggie Sanders	.25	.11	.03
☐ 12F Todd Van Poppel	.10	.05	.01
☐ 13F Arthur Rhodes	.10	.05	.01
☐ 14F Eddie Zosky	.05	.02	.01
☐ 15F Gerald Williams	.05	.02	.01
☐ 16F Robert Eenhoorn	.05	.02	.01
☐ 17F Jim Thome	1.25	.55	.16
☐ 18F Marc Newfield	.15	.07	.02
☐ 19F Kerwin Moore	.05	.02	.01
☐ 20F Jeff McNeely	.05	.02	.01
☐ 21F Frankie Rodriguez	.15	.07	.02
☐ 22F Andy Mota	.05	.02	.01
☐ 23F Chris Haney	.05	.02	.01
☐ 24F Kenny Lofton	2.00	.90	.25
☐ 25F Dave Nilsson	.15	.07	.02
☐ 26F Derek Bell	.15	.07	.02
☐ 27F Frank Castillo	.10	.05	.01
☐ 28F Candy Maldonado	.05	.02	.01
☐ 29F Chuck McElroy	.05	.02	.01
☐ 30F Chito Martinez	.05	.02	.01
☐ 31F Steve Howe	.05	.02	.01
☐ 32F Freddie Benavides	.05	.02	.01
☐ 33F Scott Kamieniecki	.05	.02	.01
☐ 34F Denny Neagle	.40	.18	.05
☐ 35F Mike Humphreys	.05	.02	.01
☐ 36F Mike Remlinger	.05	.02	.01
☐ 37F Scott Coolbaugh	.05	.02	.01
☐ 38F Darren Lewis	.10	.05	.01
☐ 39F Thomas Howard	.05	.02	.01
☐ 40F John Candelaria	.05	.02	.01
☐ 41F Todd Benzinger	.05	.02	.01
☐ 42F Wilson Alvarez	.15	.07	.02
☐ 43F Patrick Lennon	.05	.02	.01
☐ 44F Rusty Meacham	.05	.02	.01
☐ 45F Ryan Bowen	.05	.02	.01
☐ 46F Rick Wilkins	.05	.02	.01
☐ 47F Ed Sprague	.10	.05	.01
☐ 48F Bob Scanlan	.05	.02	.01
☐ 49F Tom Candiotti	.05	.02	.01
☐ 50F Dennis Martinez (Perfecto)	.10	.05	.01
☐ 51F Oil Can Boyd	.05	.02	.01
☐ 52F Glenallen Hill	.05	.02	.01
☐ 53F Scott Livingstone	.05	.02	.01
☐ 54F Brian R. Hunter	.05	.02	.01
☐ 55F Ivan Rodriguez	1.25	.55	.16
☐ 56F Keith Mitchell	.05	.02	.01
☐ 57F Roger McDowell	.05	.02	.01
☐ 58F Otis Nixon	.05	.02	.01
☐ 59F Juan Bell	.05	.02	.01
☐ 60F Bill Krueger	.05	.02	.01
☐ 61F Chris Donnels	.05	.02	.01
☐ 62F Tommy Greene	.05	.02	.01
☐ 63F Doug Simons	.05	.02	.01
☐ 64F Andy Ashby	.15	.07	.02
☐ 65F Anthony Young	.05	.02	.01
☐ 66F Kevin Morton	.05	.02	.01
☐ 67F Bret Barberie	.05	.02	.01
☐ 68F Scott Servais	.05	.02	.01
☐ 69F Ron Darling	.05	.02	.01
☐ 70F Tim Burke	.05	.02	.01
☐ 71F Vicente Palacios	.05	.02	.01
☐ 72F Gerald Alexander	.05	.02	.01
☐ 73F Reggie Jefferson	.10	.05	.01
☐ 74F Dean Palmer	.15	.07	.02
☐ 75F Mark Whiten	.10	.05	.01
☐ 76F Randy Tomlin	.05	.02	.01
☐ 77F Mark Wohlers	.40	.18	.05
☐ 78F Brook Jacoby	.05	.02	.01
☐ 79F Ken Griffey Jr. CL Ryne Sandberg	.40	.18	.05
☐ 80F Jack Morris AS	.10	.05	.01
☐ 81F Sandy Alomar Jr. AS	.10	.05	.01
☐ 82F Cecil Fielder AS	.10	.05	.01
☐ 83F Roberto Alomar AS	.15	.07	.02
☐ 84F Wade Boggs AS	.15	.07	.02
☐ 85F Cal Ripken AS	.40	.18	.05
☐ 86F Rickey Henderson AS	.15	.07	.02
☐ 87F Ken Griffey Jr. AS	.75	.35	.09
☐ 88F Dave Henderson AS	.05	.02	.01
☐ 89F Danny Tartabull AS	.05	.02	.01
☐ 90F Tom Glavine AS	.15	.07	.02
☐ 91F Benito Santiago AS	.05	.02	.01
☐ 92F Will Clark AS	.15	.07	.02
☐ 93F Ryne Sandberg AS	.15	.07	.02
☐ 94F Chris Sabo AS	.05	.02	.01
☐ 95F Ozzie Smith AS	.10	.05	.01
☐ 96F Ivan Calderon AS	.05	.02	.01
☐ 97F Tony Gwynn AS	.20	.09	.03
☐ 98F Andre Dawson AS	.10	.05	.01
☐ 99F Bobby Bonilla AS	.10	.05	.01
☐ 100F Checklist 1-100	.05	.02	.01

1991 Upper Deck Comic Ball Promos

These promo cards measure the standard size and are horizontally oriented. The fronts feature color photos of the players with Looney Tunes characters superimposed on the pictures. An orange banner on the top of each picture has the Looney Tunes and Upper Deck logos.

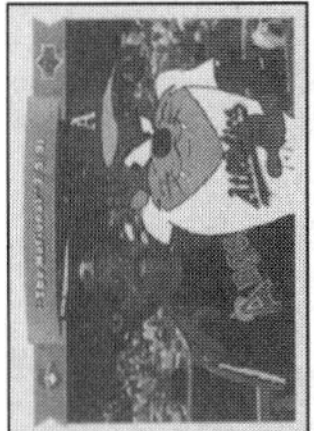

The backs of all four cards form a composite cartoon in which Tweety is standing on the pitcher's mound as Sylvester drags it from the field. The cards are unnumbered and checklisted below by the date of distribution at the 1991 National Sports Collectors Convention in Anaheim.

	MINT	NRMT	EXC
COMPLETE SET (4)	12.00	5.50	1.50
COMMON CARD (1-4)	2.50	1.10	.30
☐ 1 The National 7/4/91 Nolan Ryan with Daffy Duck and Bugs Bunny	5.00	2.20	.60
☐ 2 The National 7/5/91 Reggie Jackson and the Tasmanian Devil	2.50	1.10	.30
☐ 3 The National 7/6/91 Nolan Ryan and Speedy Gonzales	5.00	2.20	.60
☐ 4 The National 7/7/91 Reggie Jackson, Elmer Fudd, and Sylvester	2.50	1.10	.30

1991 Upper Deck Comic Ball 2

This 198-card set of Upper Deck's animation-style trading cards contains special cards featuring Reggie Jackson and Nolan Ryan with their Looney Toons teammates.

	MINT	NRMT	EXC
COMPLETE SET (198)	10.00	4.50	1.25
COMMON CARD (1-198)	.05	.02	.01
COMMON CARD W/REGGIE	.10	.05	.01
COMMON CARD W/RYAN	.20	.09	.03
COMMON REGGIE HOLOGRAM	1.00	.45	.12
COMMON RYAN HOLOGRAM	3.00	1.35	.35

1991 Upper Deck Heroes of Baseball 5x7

This unnumbered sheet measures 5" by 7" and was distributed to herald the 1991 Heroes of Baseball sheets, listing on its back the dates and sites of the old-timers games where they were to be distributed. The front features artist renderings of the players listed below.

	MINT	NRMT	EXC
COMPLETE SET (1)	20.00	9.00	2.50
COMMON SHEET	20.00	9.00	2.50
☐ 1 Date sheet 5x7 Reggie Jackson Lou Brock Harmon Killebrew Boog Powell Gaylord Perry Ferguson Jenkins	20.00	9.00	2.50

1991 Upper Deck Sheets

These 23 commemorative sheets were issued in 1991 to fans attending old-timers games preceding major league games. The sheets measure 8 1/2" by 11" and feature artist renderings of players from the teams recreated for the old-timers game. The front carries the individual production number out of the total number produced, but otherwise the sheets are unnumbered and so listed below in chronological order. The cover sheet was produced in two different versions, one numbered to 10,000, the other to 20,000. After the original 10,000 were produced, another 10,000 were needed for promotions.

	MINT	NRMT	EXC
COMPLETE SET (22)	175.00	80.00	22.00
COMMON SHEET (1-22)	5.00	2.20	.60
☐ 1 Cover sheet Reggie Jackson	5.00	2.20	.60

(20,000)
Dates and sites of
Old-Timers Games

☐ 1 Philadelphia Scholars Fund Sports Show Oct. 17, 1991 (21,500) Mike Schmidt Charles Barkley Rick Tocchet Reggie White	15.00	6.75	1.85
☐ 2 Tribute to Baltimore Orioles Heroes April 21, 1991 (17,000) Memorial Stadium Frank Robinson Earl Weaver Brooks Robinson Robin Roberts Boog Powell	12.00	5.50	1.50
☐ 3 Tribute to Joe DiMaggio and Ted Williams in celebration of their Summer of '41 May 11, 1991 (17,000) Fenway Park Ken Keltner Dom DiMaggio Johnny Pesky Bobby Doerr Mickey Owen	12.00	5.50	1.50
☐ 4 Heroes of the '70s May 18, 1991 (22,000) Cleveland Municipal Stadium Ray Fosse Reggie Jackson Gaylord Perry Boog Powell Mark Fidrych	10.00	4.50	1.25
☐ 5 Atlanta Braves Heroes vs. National League Heroes June 8, 1991 (22,000) Fulton County Stadium Rico Carty Chris Chambliss Jeff Burroughs Darrell Evans Lou Brock	10.00	4.50	1.25
☐ 6 Oakland A's June 9, 1991 (22,000) Oakland Coliseum Jim(Catfish) Hunter	10.00	4.50	1.25
☐ 7 World Series Heroes June 15, 1991 (47,000) Shea Stadium Ron Swoboda Yogi Berra MG Ray Knight Donn Clendenon Tug McGraw	7.00	3.10	.85
☐ 8 Cincinnati Reds Heroes vs. World Series Heroes June 22, 1991 (22,000) Riverfront Stadium Leo Cardenas Ed Bailey Joe Nuxhall John Edwards Tony Perez	15.00	6.75	1.85
☐ 9 1981 American League Divisional Playoff Heroes June 29, 1991 (27,000) County Stadium Ben Oglivie Charlie Moore Cecil Cooper Rollie Fingers Gorman Thomas	7.00	3.10	.85
☐ 10 A Tribute to All-Star Heroes Toronto July 8, 1991 (95,000) SkyDome Reggie Jackson Ferguson Jenkins Brooks Robinson Lou Brock Bob Gibson	5.00	2.20	.60
☐ 11 Tribute to Home Run Heroes July 14, 1991 (44,000) Anaheim Stadium George Foster Bobby Grich Bobby Bonds Reggie Jackson Billy Williams	7.00	3.10	.85
☐ 12 Pittsburgh Pirates July 20, 1991 (18,000) Three Rivers Stadium Steve Blass Bruce Kison Willie Stargell Al Oliver Richie Hebner	10.00	4.50	1.25
☐ 13 Battle of Missouri July 21, 1991 (17,000) Busch Stadium Mike Shannon Al Hrabosky Bob Gibson Red Schoendeinst Lou Brock	12.00	5.50	1.50
☐ 14 David vs. Goliath July 27, 1991 (17,000) Astrodome Lou Brock Eddie Mathews Cesar Cedeno Gaylord Perry Billy Williams	12.00	5.50	1.50
☐ 15 45th Annual Old-Timer's Day Classic July 27, 1991 (47,000) Yankee Stadium Joe Pepitone Bobby Murcer Catfish Hunter Ron Guidry Bobby Richardson	7.00	3.10	.85
☐ 16 1971 Phillies vs. Upper Deck Heroes Aug. 10, 1991 (42,000) Veterans Stadium Larry Bowa Willie Montanez Don Money Jim Bunning	7.00	3.10	.85
☐ 17 Tribute to Hall of Famers Aug. 10, 1991 (17,000) Arlington Stadium Ferguson Jenkins Gaylord Perry	10.00	4.50	1.25
☐ 18 All-Star Joes vs. All-Star Bobs Aug. 16, 1991 (27,000) Jack Murphy Stadium Bobby Bonds Bobby Doerr Bob Gibson Joe Pepitone Joe Rudi	8.00	3.60	1.00
☐ 19 Giants Reunion with Newest Hall of Famer Aug. 18, 1991 (42,000) Candlestick Park Gaylord Perry	7.00	3.10	.85
☐ 20 American League vs. National League Aug. 24, 1991 (22,000) Wrigley Field Ron Santo Don Kessinger Billy Williams Dave Kingman Ferguson Jenkins	10.00	4.50	1.25
☐ 21 Tribute to 1971 Heroes Aug. 25, 1991 (32,000) Tiger Stadium Bill Freehan Mickey Lolich Al Kaline Willie Horton	9.00	4.00	1.10
☐ 22 10th Anniversary of Expos' Divisional Championship Sept. 1, 1991 (22,000) Olympic Stadium Larry Parrish Chris Speier Jerry White Steve Rogers Charlie Lea	7.00	3.10	.85

1992 Upper Deck

The 1992 Upper Deck set contains 800 standard-size cards issued in two separate series of 700 and 100 cards respectively. The cards were distributed in low and high series foil packs in addition to factory sets. Factory sets feature a unique gold-foil hologram on the card backs (in contrast to the silver hologram on foil pack cards). The basic issue card fronts features shadow-bordered action color player photos on a white card face. The player's name appears above the photo, with the team name superimposed at the lower right corner. Special subsets included in the set are Star Rookies (1-27), Team Checklists (29-40/86-99), with player portraits by Vernon Wells; Top Prospects (52-77); Bloodlines (79-85), Diamond Skills (640-650/711-721) and Diamond Debuts (771-780). Rookie Cards in the set include Shawn Green, Joey Hamilton, Brian Jordan and Manny Ramirez. A special card picturing Tom Selleck and Frank Thomas, commemorating the forgettable movie "Mr. Baseball", was randomly inserted into high series packs. A standard-size Ted Williams hologram card was randomly inserted into low series packs. By mailing in 15 low series foil wrappers, a completed order form, and a handling fee, the collector could receive an 8 1/2" by 11" numbered, black and white lithograph picturing Ted Williams in his batting swing.

	MINT	NRMT	EXC
COMPLETE SET (800)	15.00	6.75	1.85
COMPLETE FACT.SET (800)	20.00	9.00	2.50
COMPLETE LO SET (700)	12.00	5.50	1.50
COMPLETE HI SET (100)	3.00	1.35	.35
COMMON CARD (1-800)	.05	.02	.01
☐ 1 Ryan Klesko CL Jim Thome	.50	.23	.06
☐ 2 Royce Clayton SR	.10	.05	.01
☐ 3 Brian Jordan SR	.50	.23	.06
☐ 4 Dave Fleming SR	.05	.02	.01
☐ 5 Jim Thome SR	.75	.35	.09
☐ 6 Jeff Juden SR	.05	.02	.01
☐ 7 Roberto Hernandez SR	.10	.05	.01
☐ 8 Kyle Abbott SR	.05	.02	.01
☐ 9 Chris George SR	.05	.02	.01
☐ 10 Rob Maurer SR	.05	.02	.01
☐ 11 Donald Harris SR	.05	.02	.01
☐ 12 Ted Wood SR	.05	.02	.01
☐ 13 Patrick Lennon SR	.05	.02	.01
☐ 14 Willie Banks SR	.05	.02	.01
☐ 15 Roger Salkeld SR UER (Bill was his grand- father, not his father)	.05	.02	.01
☐ 16 Wil Cordero SR	.10	.05	.01
☐ 17 Arthur Rhodes SR	.05	.02	.01
☐ 18 Pedro Martinez SR	.25	.11	.03
☐ 19 Andy Ashby SR	.10	.05	.01
☐ 20 Tom Goodwin SR	.10	.05	.01
☐ 21 Braulio Castillo SR	.05	.02	.01
☐ 22 Todd Van Poppel SR	.05	.02	.01
☐ 23 Brian Williams SR	.05	.02	.01
☐ 24 Ryan Klesko SR	.50	.23	.06
☐ 25 Kenny Lofton SR	1.00	.45	.12
☐ 26 Derek Bell SR	.15	.07	.02
☐ 27 Reggie Sanders SR	.15	.07	.02
☐ 28 Dave Winfield's 400th	.15	.07	.02
☐ 29 David Justice TC	.10	.05	.01
☐ 30 Rob Dibble TC	.05	.02	.01
☐ 31 Craig Biggio TC	.10	.05	.01
☐ 32 Eddie Murray TC	.15	.07	.02
☐ 33 Fred McGriff TC	.15	.07	.02
☐ 34 Willie McGee TC	.05	.02	.01
☐ 35 Shawon Dunston TC	.05	.02	.01
☐ 36 Delino DeShields TC	.05	.02	.01
☐ 37 Howard Johnson TC	.05	.02	.01
☐ 38 John Kruk TC	.05	.02	.01
☐ 39 Doug Drabek TC	.05	.02	.01
☐ 40 Todd Zeile TC	.05	.02	.01
☐ 41 Steve Avery Playoff Perfection	.10	.05	.01
☐ 42 Jeremy Hernandez	.05	.02	.01
☐ 43 Doug Henry	.05	.02	.01
☐ 44 Chris Donnels	.05	.02	.01
☐ 45 Mo Sanford	.05	.02	.01
☐ 46 Scott Kamieniecki	.05	.02	.01
☐ 47 Mark Lemke	.05	.02	.01
☐ 48 Steve Farr	.05	.02	.01
☐ 49 Francisco Oliveras	.05	.02	.01
☐ 50 Ced Landrum	.05	.02	.01
☐ 51 Rondell White CL Mark Newfield	.15	.07	.02
☐ 52 Eduardo Perez TP	.10	.05	.01
☐ 53 Tom Nevers TP	.05	.02	.01
☐ 54 David Zancanaro TP	.05	.02	.01
☐ 55 Shawn Green TP	.30	.14	.04
☐ 56 Mark Wohlers TP	.15	.07	.02
☐ 57 Dave Nilsson TP	.15	.07	.02
☐ 58 Dmitri Young TP	.25	.11	.03
☐ 59 Ryan Hawblitzel TP	.05	.02	.01
☐ 60 Raul Mondesi TP	.60	.25	.07
☐ 61 Rondell White TP	.30	.14	.04
☐ 62 Steve Hosey TP	.05	.02	.01
☐ 63 Manny Ramirez TP	2.00	.90	.25
☐ 64 Marc Newfield TP	.15	.07	.02
☐ 65 Jeromy Burnitz TP	.10	.05	.01
☐ 66 Mark Smith TP	.10	.05	.01
☐ 67 Joey Hamilton TP	.75	.35	.09
☐ 68 Tyler Green TP	.10	.05	.01
☐ 69 Jon Farrell TP	.05	.02	.01
☐ 70 Kurt Miller TP	.05	.02	.01
☐ 71 Jeff Plympton TP	.05	.02	.01
☐ 72 Dan Wilson TP	.10	.05	.01
☐ 73 Joe Vitiello TP	.10	.05	.01
☐ 74 Rico Brogna TP	.10	.05	.01
☐ 75 David McCarty TP	.05	.02	.01
☐ 76 Bob Wickman TP	.05	.02	.01
☐ 77 Carlos Rodriguez TP	.05	.02	.01
☐ 78 Jim Abbott Stay In School	.05	.02	.01
☐ 79 Ramon Martinez Pedro Martinez	.15	.07	.02
☐ 80 Kevin Mitchell Keith Mitchell	.05	.02	.01
☐ 81 Sandy Alomar Jr. Roberto Alomar	.15	.07	.02
☐ 82 Cal Ripken Billy Ripken	.50	.23	.06
☐ 83 Tony Gwynn Chris Gwynn	.15	.07	.02
☐ 84 Dwight Gooden Gary Sheffield	.10	.05	.01
☐ 85 Ken Griffey Sr. Ken Griffey Jr. Craig Griffey	.75	.35	.09
☐ 86 Jim Abbott TC	.05	.02	.01
☐ 87 Frank Thomas TC	.75	.35	.09
☐ 88 Danny Tartabull TC	.05	.02	.01
☐ 89 Scott Erickson TC	.05	.02	.01
☐ 90 Rickey Henderson TC	.15	.07	.02
☐ 91 Edgar Martinez TC	.10	.05	.01
☐ 92 Nolan Ryan TC	.40	.18	.05
☐ 93 Ben McDonald TC	.05	.02	.01
☐ 94 Ellis Burks TC	.10	.05	.01
☐ 95 Greg Swindell TC	.05	.02	.01
☐ 96 Cecil Fielder TC	.10	.05	.01
☐ 97 Greg Vaughn TC	.10	.05	.01
☐ 98 Kevin Maas TC	.05	.02	.01
☐ 99 Dave Stieb TC	.05	.02	.01
☐ 100 Checklist 1-100	.05	.02	.01
☐ 101 Joe Oliver	.05	.02	.01
☐ 102 Hector Villanueva	.05	.02	.01
☐ 103 Ed Whitson	.05	.02	.01
☐ 104 Danny Jackson	.05	.02	.01
☐ 105 Chris Hammond	.05	.02	.01
☐ 106 Ricky Jordan	.05	.02	.01
☐ 107 Kevin Bass	.05	.02	.01
☐ 108 Darrin Fletcher	.05	.02	.01
☐ 109 Junior Ortiz	.05	.02	.01
☐ 110 Tom Bolton	.05	.02	.01
☐ 111 Jeff King	.10	.05	.01
☐ 112 Dave Magadan	.05	.02	.01
☐ 113 Mike LaValliere	.05	.02	.01
☐ 114 Hubie Brooks	.05	.02	.01
☐ 115 Jay Bell	.10	.05	.01
☐ 116 David Wells	.05	.02	.01
☐ 117 Jim Leyritz	.05	.02	.01
☐ 118 Manuel Lee	.05	.02	.01
☐ 119 Alvaro Espinoza	.05	.02	.01
☐ 120 B.J. Surhoff	.10	.05	.01
☐ 121 Hal Morris	.05	.02	.01
☐ 122 Shawon Dawson	.05	.02	.01
☐ 123 Chris Sabo	.05	.02	.01
☐ 124 Andre Dawson	.10	.05	.01
☐ 125 Eric Davis	.10	.05	.01
☐ 126 Chili Davis	.10	.05	.01
☐ 127 Dale Murphy	.15	.07	.02
☐ 128 Kirk McCaskill	.05	.02	.01
☐ 129 Terry Mulholland	.05	.02	.01
☐ 130 Rick Aguilera	.05	.02	.01
☐ 131 Vince Coleman	.05	.02	.01
☐ 132 Andy Van Slyke	.10	.05	.01
☐ 133 Gregg Jefferies	.10	.05	.01
☐ 134 Barry Bonds	.25	.11	.03
☐ 135 Dwight Gooden	.10	.05	.01
☐ 136 Dave Stieb	.05	.02	.01
☐ 137 Albert Belle	.50	.23	.06
☐ 138 Teddy Higuera	.05	.02	.01
☐ 139 Jesse Barfield	.05	.02	.01
☐ 140 Pat Borders	.05	.02	.01
☐ 141 Bip Roberts	.05	.02	.01
☐ 142 Rob Dibble	.05	.02	.01
☐ 143 Mark Grace	.15	.07	.02
☐ 144 Barry Larkin	.15	.07	.02
☐ 145 Ryne Sandberg	.25	.11	.03
☐ 146 Scott Erickson	.10	.05	.01
☐ 147 Luis Polonia	.05	.02	.01
☐ 148 John Burkett	.10	.05	.01
☐ 149 Luis Sojo	.05	.02	.01
☐ 150 Dickie Thon	.05	.02	.01
☐ 151 Walt Weiss	.05	.02	.01
☐ 152 Mike Scioscia	.05	.02	.01
☐ 153 Mark McGwire	.30	.14	.04
☐ 154 Matt Williams	.15	.07	.02
☐ 155 Rickey Henderson	.15	.07	.02
☐ 156 Sandy Alomar Jr.	.10	.05	.01
☐ 157 Brian McRae	.10	.05	.01
☐ 158 Harold Baines	.10	.05	.01
☐ 159 Kevin Appier	.10	.05	.01
☐ 160 Felix Fermin	.05	.02	.01
☐ 161 Leo Gomez	.05	.02	.01
☐ 162 Craig Biggio	.10	.05	.01
☐ 163 Ben McDonald	.05	.02	.01
☐ 164 Randy Johnson	.15	.07	.02
☐ 165 Cal Ripken	.75	.35	.09
☐ 166 Frank Thomas	1.50	.70	.19
☐ 167 Delino DeShields	.05	.02	.01
☐ 168 Greg Gagne	.05	.02	.01
☐ 169 Ron Karkovice	.05	.02	.01
☐ 170 Charlie Leibrandt	.05	.02	.01
☐ 171 Dave Righetti	.05	.02	.01
☐ 172 Dave Henderson	.05	.02	.01
☐ 173 Steve Decker	.05	.02	.01
☐ 174 Darryl Strawberry	.10	.05	.01
☐ 175 Will Clark	.15	.07	.02
☐ 176 Ruben Sierra	.10	.05	.01
☐ 177 Ozzie Smith	.25	.11	.03

☐ 178 Charles Nagy	.10	.05	.01
☐ 179 Gary Pettis	.05	.02	.01
☐ 180 Kirk Gibson	.10	.05	.01
☐ 181 Randy Milligan	.05	.02	.01
☐ 182 Dave Valle	.05	.02	.01
☐ 183 Chris Hoiles	.05	.02	.01
☐ 184 Tony Phillips	.10	.05	.01
☐ 185 Brady Anderson	.15	.07	.02
☐ 186 Scott Fletcher	.05	.02	.01
☐ 187 Gene Larkin	.05	.02	.01
☐ 188 Lance Johnson	.10	.05	.01
☐ 189 Greg Olson	.05	.02	.01
☐ 190 Melido Perez	.05	.02	.01
☐ 191 Lenny Harris	.05	.02	.01
☐ 192 Terry Kennedy	.05	.02	.01
☐ 193 Mike Gallego	.05	.02	.01
☐ 194 Willie McGee	.05	.02	.01
☐ 195 Juan Samuel	.05	.02	.01
☐ 196 Jeff Huson (Shows Jose Canseco sliding into second)	.10	.05	.01
☐ 197 Alex Cole	.05	.02	.01
☐ 198 Ron Robinson	.05	.02	.01
☐ 199 Joel Skinner	.05	.02	.01
☐ 200 Checklist 101-200	.05	.02	.01
☐ 201 Kevin Reimer	.05	.02	.01
☐ 202 Stan Belinda	.05	.02	.01
☐ 203 Pat Tabler	.05	.02	.01
☐ 204 Jose Guzman	.05	.02	.01
☐ 205 Jose Lind	.05	.02	.01
☐ 206 Spike Owen	.05	.02	.01
☐ 207 Joe Orsulak	.05	.02	.01
☐ 208 Charlie Hayes	.05	.02	.01
☐ 209 Mike Devereaux	.05	.02	.01
☐ 210 Mike Fitzgerald	.05	.02	.01
☐ 211 Willie Randolph	.10	.05	.01
☐ 212 Rod Nichols	.05	.02	.01
☐ 213 Mike Boddicker	.05	.02	.01
☐ 214 Bill Spiers	.05	.02	.01
☐ 215 Steve Olin	.05	.02	.01
☐ 216 David Howard	.05	.02	.01
☐ 217 Gary Varsho	.05	.02	.01
☐ 218 Mike Harkey	.05	.02	.01
☐ 219 Luis Aquino	.05	.02	.01
☐ 220 Chuck McElroy	.05	.02	.01
☐ 221 Doug Drabek	.05	.02	.01
☐ 222 Dave Winfield	.15	.07	.02
☐ 223 Rafael Palmeiro	.15	.07	.02
☐ 224 Joe Carter	.10	.05	.01
☐ 225 Bobby Bonilla	.10	.05	.01
☐ 226 Ivan Calderon	.05	.02	.01
☐ 227 Gregg Olson	.05	.02	.01
☐ 228 Tim Wallach	.05	.02	.01
☐ 229 Terry Pendleton	.10	.05	.01
☐ 230 Gilberto Reyes	.05	.02	.01
☐ 231 Carlos Baerga	.10	.05	.01
☐ 232 Greg Vaughn	.10	.05	.01
☐ 233 Bret Saberhagen	.10	.05	.01
☐ 234 Gary Sheffield	.15	.07	.02
☐ 235 Mark Lewis	.05	.02	.01
☐ 236 George Bell	.05	.02	.01
☐ 237 Danny Tartabull	.05	.02	.01
☐ 238 Willie Wilson	.05	.02	.01
☐ 239 Doug Dascenzo	.05	.02	.01
☐ 240 Bill Pecota	.05	.02	.01
☐ 241 Julio Franco	.10	.05	.01
☐ 242 Ed Sprague	.10	.05	.01
☐ 243 Juan Gonzalez	.60	.25	.07
☐ 244 Chuck Finley	.05	.02	.01
☐ 245 Ivan Rodriguez	.40	.18	.05
☐ 246 Len Dykstra	.10	.05	.01
☐ 247 Deion Sanders	.15	.07	.02
☐ 248 Dwight Evans	.10	.05	.01
☐ 249 Larry Walker	.15	.07	.02
☐ 250 Billy Ripken	.05	.02	.01
☐ 251 Mickey Tettleton	.05	.02	.01
☐ 252 Tony Pena	.05	.02	.01
☐ 253 Benito Santiago	.05	.02	.01
☐ 254 Kirby Puckett	.40	.18	.05
☐ 255 Cecil Fielder	.10	.05	.01
☐ 256 Howard Johnson	.05	.02	.01
☐ 257 Andujar Cedeno	.05	.02	.01
☐ 258 Jose Rijo	.05	.02	.01
☐ 259 Al Osuna	.05	.02	.01
☐ 260 Todd Hundley	.10	.05	.01
☐ 261 Orel Hershiser	.10	.05	.01
☐ 262 Ray Lankford	.15	.07	.02
☐ 263 Robin Ventura	.10	.05	.01
☐ 264 Felix Jose	.05	.02	.01
☐ 265 Eddie Murray	.25	.11	.03
☐ 266 Kevin Mitchell	.10	.05	.01
☐ 267 Gary Carter	.15	.07	.02
☐ 268 Mike Benjamin	.05	.02	.01
☐ 269 Dick Schofield	.05	.02	.01
☐ 270 Jose Uribe	.05	.02	.01
☐ 271 Pete Incaviglia	.05	.02	.01
☐ 272 Tony Fernandez	.05	.02	.01
☐ 273 Alan Trammell	.10	.05	.01
☐ 274 Tony Gwynn	.40	.18	.05
☐ 275 Mike Greenwell	.05	.02	.01
☐ 276 Jeff Bagwell	.60	.25	.07
☐ 277 Frank Viola	.05	.02	.01
☐ 278 Randy Myers	.10	.05	.01
☐ 279 Ken Caminiti	.15	.07	.02
☐ 280 Bill Doran	.05	.02	.01
☐ 281 Dan Pasqua	.05	.02	.01
☐ 282 Alfredo Griffin	.05	.02	.01
☐ 283 Jose Oquendo	.05	.02	.01
☐ 284 Kal Daniels	.05	.02	.01
☐ 285 Bobby Thigpen	.05	.02	.01
☐ 286 Robby Thompson	.05	.02	.01
☐ 287 Mark Eichhorn	.05	.02	.01
☐ 288 Mike Felder	.05	.02	.01
☐ 289 Dave Gallagher	.05	.02	.01
☐ 290 Dave Anderson	.05	.02	.01
☐ 291 Mel Hall	.05	.02	.01
☐ 292 Jerald Clark	.05	.02	.01
☐ 293 Al Newman	.05	.02	.01
☐ 294 Rob Deer	.05	.02	.01
☐ 295 Matt Nokes	.05	.02	.01
☐ 296 Jack Armstrong	.05	.02	.01
☐ 297 Jim Deshaies	.05	.02	.01
☐ 298 Jeff Innis	.05	.02	.01
☐ 299 Jeff Reed	.05	.02	.01
☐ 300 Checklist 201-300	.05	.02	.01
☐ 301 Lonnie Smith	.05	.02	.01
☐ 302 Jimmy Key	.10	.05	.01
☐ 303 Junior Felix	.05	.02	.01
☐ 304 Mike Heath	.05	.02	.01
☐ 305 Mark Langston	.10	.05	.01
☐ 306 Greg W. Harris	.05	.02	.01
☐ 307 Brett Butler	.10	.05	.01
☐ 308 Luis Rivera	.05	.02	.01
☐ 309 Bruce Ruffin	.05	.02	.01
☐ 310 Paul Faries	.05	.02	.01
☐ 311 Terry Leach	.05	.02	.01
☐ 312 Scott Brosius	.05	.02	.01
☐ 313 Scott Leius	.05	.02	.01
☐ 314 Harold Reynolds	.05	.02	.01
☐ 315 Jack Morris	.10	.05	.01
☐ 316 David Segui	.05	.02	.01
☐ 317 Bill Gullickson	.05	.02	.01
☐ 318 Todd Frohwirth	.05	.02	.01
☐ 319 Mark Leiter	.05	.02	.01
☐ 320 Jeff M. Robinson	.05	.02	.01
☐ 321 Gary Gaetti	.10	.05	.01
☐ 322 John Smoltz	.15	.07	.02
☐ 323 Andy Benes	.10	.05	.01
☐ 324 Kelly Gruber	.05	.02	.01
☐ 325 Jim Abbott	.05	.02	.01
☐ 326 John Kruk	.10	.05	.01
☐ 327 Kevin Seitzer	.05	.02	.01
☐ 328 Darrin Jackson	.05	.02	.01
☐ 329 Kurt Stillwell	.05	.02	.01
☐ 330 Mike Maddux	.05	.02	.01
☐ 331 Dennis Eckersley	.10	.05	.01
☐ 332 Dan Gladden	.05	.02	.01
☐ 333 Jose Canseco	.15	.07	.02
☐ 334 Kent Hrbek	.10	.05	.01
☐ 335 Ken Griffey Sr.	.05	.02	.01
☐ 336 Greg Swindell	.05	.02	.01
☐ 337 Trevor Wilson	.05	.02	.01
☐ 338 Sam Horn	.05	.02	.01
☐ 339 Mike Henneman	.05	.02	.01
☐ 340 Jerry Browne	.05	.02	.01
☐ 341 Glenn Braggs	.05	.02	.01
☐ 342 Tom Glavine	.15	.07	.02
☐ 343 Wally Joyner	.10	.05	.01
☐ 344 Fred McGriff	.15	.07	.02
☐ 345 Ron Gant	.10	.05	.01
☐ 346 Ramon Martinez	.10	.05	.01
☐ 347 Wes Chamberlain	.05	.02	.01
☐ 348 Terry Shumpert	.05	.02	.01
☐ 349 Tim Teufel	.05	.02	.01
☐ 350 Wally Backman	.05	.02	.01
☐ 351 Joe Girardi	.05	.02	.01
☐ 352 Devon White	.10	.05	.01
☐ 353 Greg Maddux	.75	.35	.09
☐ 354 Ryan Bowen	.05	.02	.01
☐ 355 Roberto Alomar	.20	.09	.03
☐ 356 Don Mattingly	.50	.23	.06
☐ 357 Pedro Guerrero	.05	.02	.01
☐ 358 Steve Sax	.05	.02	.01
☐ 359 Joey Cora	.10	.05	.01
☐ 360 Jim Gantner	.05	.02	.01
☐ 361 Brian Barnes	.05	.02	.01
☐ 362 Kevin McReynolds	.05	.02	.01
☐ 363 Bret Barberie	.05	.02	.01
☐ 364 David Cone	.10	.05	.01
☐ 365 Dennis Martinez	.10	.05	.01
☐ 366 Brian Hunter	.05	.02	.01
☐ 367 Edgar Martinez	.10	.05	.01
☐ 368 Steve Finley	.10	.05	.01
☐ 369 Greg Briley	.05	.02	.01
☐ 370 Jeff Blauser	.05	.02	.01
☐ 371 Todd Stottlemyre	.10	.05	.01
☐ 372 Luis Gonzalez	.10	.05	.01
☐ 373 Rick Wilkins	.05	.02	.01
☐ 374 Darryl Kile	.05	.02	.01
☐ 375 John Olerud	.10	.05	.01
☐ 376 Lee Smith	.10	.05	.01
☐ 377 Kevin Maas	.05	.02	.01
☐ 378 Dante Bichette	.15	.07	.02
☐ 379 Tom Pagnozzi	.05	.02	.01
☐ 380 Mike Flanagan	.05	.02	.01
☐ 381 Charlie O'Brien	.05	.02	.01
☐ 382 Dave Martinez	.05	.02	.01
☐ 383 Keith Miller	.05	.02	.01
☐ 384 Scott Ruskin	.05	.02	.01
☐ 385 Kevin Elster	.05	.02	.01
☐ 386 Alvin Davis	.05	.02	.01
☐ 387 Casey Candaele	.05	.02	.01
☐ 388 Pete O'Brien	.05	.02	.01
☐ 389 Jeff Treadway	.05	.02	.01
☐ 390 Scott Bradley	.05	.02	.01
☐ 391 Mookie Wilson	.05	.02	.01
☐ 392 Jimmy Jones	.05	.02	.01
☐ 393 Candy Maldonado	.05	.02	.01
☐ 394 Eric Yelding	.05	.02	.01
☐ 395 Tom Henke	.05	.02	.01
☐ 396 Franklin Stubbs	.05	.02	.01
☐ 397 Milt Thompson	.05	.02	.01
☐ 398 Mark Carreon	.05	.02	.01
☐ 399 Randy Velarde	.05	.02	.01
☐ 400 Checklist 301-400	.05	.02	.01
☐ 401 Omar Vizquel	.10	.05	.01
☐ 402 Joe Boever	.05	.02	.01
☐ 403 Bill Krueger	.05	.02	.01
☐ 404 Jody Reed	.05	.02	.01
☐ 405 Mike Schooler	.05	.02	.01
☐ 406 Jason Grimsley	.05	.02	.01
☐ 407 Greg Myers	.05	.02	.01
☐ 408 Randy Ready	.05	.02	.01
☐ 409 Mike Timlin	.05	.02	.01
☐ 410 Mitch Williams	.05	.02	.01
☐ 411 Garry Templeton	.05	.02	.01
☐ 412 Greg Cadaret	.05	.02	.01
☐ 413 Donnie Hill	.05	.02	.01
☐ 414 Wally Whitehurst	.05	.02	.01
☐ 415 Scott Sanderson	.05	.02	.01
☐ 416 Thomas Howard	.05	.02	.01
☐ 417 Neal Heaton	.05	.02	.01
☐ 418 Charlie Hough	.05	.02	.01
☐ 419 Jack Howell	.05	.02	.01
☐ 420 Greg Hibbard	.05	.02	.01
☐ 421 Carlos Quintana	.05	.02	.01
☐ 422 Kim Batiste	.05	.02	.01
☐ 423 Paul Molitor	.20	.09	.03
☐ 424 Ken Griffey Jr.	1.50	.70	.19
☐ 425 Phil Plantier	.10	.05	.01
☐ 426 Denny Neagle	.15	.07	.02
☐ 427 Von Hayes	.05	.02	.01
☐ 428 Shane Mack	.05	.02	.01
☐ 429 Darren Daulton	.10	.05	.01
☐ 430 Dwayne Henry	.05	.02	.01
☐ 431 Lance Parrish	.05	.02	.01
☐ 432 Mike Humphreys	.05	.02	.01
☐ 433 Tim Burke	.05	.02	.01
☐ 434 Bryan Harvey	.05	.02	.01
☐ 435 Pat Kelly	.05	.02	.01
☐ 436 Ozzie Guillen	.05	.02	.01
☐ 437 Bruce Hurst	.05	.02	.01
☐ 438 Sammy Sosa	.25	.11	.03
☐ 439 Dennis Rasmussen	.05	.02	.01
☐ 440 Ken Patterson	.05	.02	.01
☐ 441 Jay Buhner	.15	.07	.02
☐ 442 Pat Combs	.05	.02	.01
☐ 443 Wade Boggs	.15	.07	.02
☐ 444 George Brett	.40	.18	.05
☐ 445 Mo Vaughn	.40	.18	.05
☐ 446 Chuck Knoblauch	.15	.07	.02
☐ 447 Tom Candiotti	.05	.02	.01
☐ 448 Mark Portugal	.05	.02	.01
☐ 449 Mickey Morandini	.05	.02	.01
☐ 450 Duane Ward	.05	.02	.01
☐ 451 Otis Nixon	.05	.02	.01
☐ 452 Bob Welch	.05	.02	.01
☐ 453 Rusty Meacham	.05	.02	.01
☐ 454 Keith Mitchell	.05	.02	.01
☐ 455 Marquis Grissom	.10	.05	.01
☐ 456 Robin Yount	.15	.07	.02
☐ 457 Harvey Pulliam	.05	.02	.01
☐ 458 Jose DeLeon	.05	.02	.01
☐ 459 Mark Gubicza	.05	.02	.01
☐ 460 Darryl Hamilton	.05	.02	.01
☐ 461 Tom Browning	.05	.02	.01
☐ 462 Monty Fariss	.05	.02	.01
☐ 463 Jerome Walton	.05	.02	.01
☐ 464 Paul O'Neill	.10	.05	.01
☐ 465 Dean Palmer	.10	.05	.01
☐ 466 Travis Fryman	.15	.07	.02
☐ 467 John Smiley	.05	.02	.01
☐ 468 Lloyd Moseby	.05	.02	.01
☐ 469 John Wehner	.05	.02	.01
☐ 470 Skeeter Barnes	.05	.02	.01
☐ 471 Steve Chitren	.05	.02	.01
☐ 472 Kent Mercker	.05	.02	.01
☐ 473 Terry Steinbach	.10	.05	.01
☐ 474 Andres Galarraga	.15	.07	.02
☐ 475 Steve Avery	.10	.05	.01
☐ 476 Tom Gordon	.05	.02	.01
☐ 477 Cal Eldred	.05	.02	.01
☐ 478 Omar Olivares	.05	.02	.01
☐ 479 Julio Machado	.05	.02	.01
☐ 480 Bob Milacki	.05	.02	.01
☐ 481 Les Lancaster	.05	.02	.01
☐ 482 John Candelaria	.05	.02	.01
☐ 483 Brian Downing	.05	.02	.01
☐ 484 Roger McDowell	.05	.02	.01
☐ 485 Scott Scudder	.05	.02	.01
☐ 486 Zane Smith	.05	.02	.01
☐ 487 John Cerutti	.05	.02	.01
☐ 488 Steve Buechele	.05	.02	.01
☐ 489 Paul Gibson	.05	.02	.01
☐ 490 Curtis Wilkerson	.05	.02	.01
☐ 491 Marvin Freeman	.05	.02	.01
☐ 492 Tom Foley	.05	.02	.01
☐ 493 Juan Berenguer	.05	.02	.01
☐ 494 Ernest Riles	.05	.02	.01
☐ 495 Sid Bream	.05	.02	.01
☐ 496 Chuck Crim	.05	.02	.01
☐ 497 Mike Macfarlane	.05	.02	.01
☐ 498 Dale Sveum	.05	.02	.01
☐ 499 Storm Davis	.05	.02	.01
☐ 500 Checklist 401-500	.05	.02	.01
☐ 501 Jeff Reardon	.10	.05	.01
☐ 502 Shawn Abner	.05	.02	.01
☐ 503 Tony Fossas	.05	.02	.01
☐ 504 Cory Snyder	.05	.02	.01
☐ 505 Matt Young	.05	.02	.01
☐ 506 Allan Anderson	.05	.02	.01
☐ 507 Mark Lee	.05	.02	.01
☐ 508 Gene Nelson	.05	.02	.01
☐ 509 Mike Pagliarulo	.05	.02	.01
☐ 510 Rafael Belliard	.05	.02	.01
☐ 511 Jay Howell	.05	.02	.01
☐ 512 Bob Tewksbury	.05	.02	.01
☐ 513 Mike Morgan	.05	.02	.01
☐ 514 John Franco	.05	.02	.01
☐ 515 Kevin Gross	.05	.02	.01
☐ 516 Lou Whitaker	.10	.05	.01
☐ 517 Orlando Merced	.05	.02	.01
☐ 518 Todd Benzinger	.05	.02	.01
☐ 519 Gary Redus	.05	.02	.01
☐ 520 Walt Terrell	.05	.02	.01
☐ 521 Jack Clark	.10	.05	.01
☐ 522 Dave Parker	.10	.05	.01
☐ 523 Tim Naehring	.10	.05	.01
☐ 524 Mark Whiten	.10	.05	.01
☐ 525 Ellis Burks	.10	.05	.01
☐ 526 Frank Castillo	.10	.05	.01
☐ 527 Brian Harper	.05	.02	.01
☐ 528 Brook Jacoby	.05	.02	.01
☐ 529 Rick Sutcliffe	.05	.02	.01
☐ 530 Joe Klink	.05	.02	.01
☐ 531 Terry Bross	.05	.02	.01
☐ 532 Jose Offerman	.05	.02	.01
☐ 533 Todd Zeile	.05	.02	.01
☐ 534 Eric Karros	.15	.07	.02
☐ 535 Anthony Young	.05	.02	.01
☐ 536 Milt Cuyler	.05	.02	.01
☐ 537 Randy Tomlin	.05	.02	.01
☐ 538 Scott Livingstone	.05	.02	.01
☐ 539 Jim Eisenreich	.05	.02	.01
☐ 540 Don Slaught	.05	.02	.01
☐ 541 Scott Cooper	.05	.02	.01
☐ 542 Joe Grahe	.05	.02	.01
☐ 543 Tom Brunansky	.05	.02	.01
☐ 544 Eddie Zosky	.05	.02	.01
☐ 545 Roger Clemens	.20	.09	.03
☐ 546 David Justice	.15	.07	.02
☐ 547 Dave Stewart	.10	.05	.01
☐ 548 David West	.05	.02	.01
☐ 549 Dave Smith	.05	.02	.01
☐ 550 Dan Plesac	.05	.02	.01
☐ 551 Alex Fernandez	.15	.07	.02
☐ 552 Bernard Gilkey	.10	.05	.01
☐ 553 Jack McDowell	.10	.05	.01
☐ 554 Tino Martinez	.10	.05	.01
☐ 555 Bo Jackson	.10	.05	.01
☐ 556 Bernie Williams	.25	.11	.03
☐ 557 Mark Gardner	.05	.02	.01
☐ 558 Glenallen Hill	.05	.02	.01
☐ 559 Oil Can Boyd	.05	.02	.01
☐ 560 Chris James	.05	.02	.01
☐ 561 Scott Servais	.05	.02	.01
☐ 562 Rey Sanchez	.05	.02	.01
☐ 563 Paul McClellan	.05	.02	.01
☐ 564 Andy Mota	.05	.02	.01
☐ 565 Darren Lewis	.05	.02	.01
☐ 566 Jose Melendez	.05	.02	.01
☐ 567 Tommy Greene	.05	.02	.01
☐ 568 Rich Rodriguez	.05	.02	.01
☐ 569 Heathcliff Slocumb	.05	.02	.01
☐ 570 Joe Hesketh	.05	.02	.01
☐ 571 Carlton Fisk	.15	.07	.02
☐ 572 Erik Hanson	.05	.02	.01
☐ 573 Wilson Alvarez	.15	.07	.02
☐ 574 Rheal Cormier	.05	.02	.01
☐ 575 Tim Raines	.15	.07	.02
☐ 576 Bobby Witt	.05	.02	.01
☐ 577 Roberto Kelly	.05	.02	.01
☐ 578 Kevin Brown	.10	.05	.01
☐ 579 Chris Nabholz	.05	.02	.01
☐ 580 Jesse Orosco	.05	.02	.01
☐ 581 Jeff Brantley	.10	.05	.01
☐ 582 Rafael Ramirez	.05	.02	.01
☐ 583 Kelly Downs	.05	.02	.01
☐ 584 Mike Simms	.05	.02	.01
☐ 585 Mike Remlinger	.05	.02	.01
☐ 586 Dave Hollins	.05	.02	.01
☐ 587 Larry Andersen	.05	.02	.01
☐ 588 Mike Gardiner	.05	.02	.01
☐ 589 Craig Lefferts	.05	.02	.01
☐ 590 Paul Assenmacher	.05	.02	.01
☐ 591 Bryn Smith	.05	.02	.01
☐ 592 Donn Pall	.05	.02	.01
☐ 593 Mike Jackson	.05	.02	.01
☐ 594 Scott Radinsky	.05	.02	.01
☐ 595 Brian Holman	.05	.02	.01

☐ 596 Geronimo Pena	.05	.02	.01
☐ 597 Mike Jeffcoat	.05	.02	.01
☐ 598 Carlos Martinez	.05	.02	.01
☐ 599 Geno Petralli	.05	.02	.01
☐ 600 Checklist 501-600	.05	.02	.01
☐ 601 Jerry Don Gleaton	.05	.02	.01
☐ 602 Adam Peterson	.05	.02	.01
☐ 603 Craig Grebeck	.05	.02	.01
☐ 604 Mark Guthrie	.05	.02	.01
☐ 605 Frank Tanana	.05	.02	.01
☐ 606 Hensley Meulens	.05	.02	.01
☐ 607 Mark Davis	.05	.02	.01
☐ 608 Eric Plunk	.05	.02	.01
☐ 609 Mark Williamson	.05	.02	.01
☐ 610 Lee Guetterman	.05	.02	.01
☐ 611 Bobby Rose	.05	.02	.01
☐ 612 Bill Wegman	.05	.02	.01
☐ 613 Mike Hartley	.05	.02	.01
☐ 614 Chris Beasley	.05	.02	.01
☐ 615 Chris Bosio	.05	.02	.01
☐ 616 Henry Cotto	.05	.02	.01
☐ 617 Chico Walker	.05	.02	.01
☐ 618 Russ Swan	.05	.02	.01
☐ 619 Bob Walk	.05	.02	.01
☐ 620 Billy Swift	.05	.02	.01
☐ 621 Warren Newson	.05	.02	.01
☐ 622 Steve Bedrosian	.05	.02	.01
☐ 623 Ricky Bones	.05	.02	.01
☐ 624 Kevin Tapani	.05	.02	.01
☐ 625 Juan Guzman	.10	.05	.01
☐ 626 Jeff Johnson	.05	.02	.01
☐ 627 Jeff Montgomery	.10	.05	.01
☐ 628 Ken Hill	.10	.05	.01
☐ 629 Gary Thurman	.05	.02	.01
☐ 630 Steve Howe	.05	.02	.01
☐ 631 Jose DeJesus	.05	.02	.01
☐ 632 Kirk Dressendorfer	.05	.02	.01
☐ 633 Jaime Navarro	.05	.02	.01
☐ 634 Lee Stevens	.05	.02	.01
☐ 635 Pete Harnisch	.05	.02	.01
☐ 636 Bill Landrum	.05	.02	.01
☐ 637 Rich DeLucia	.05	.02	.01
☐ 638 Luis Salazar	.05	.02	.01
☐ 639 Rob Murphy	.05	.02	.01
☐ 640 Jose Canseco CL Rickey Henderson	.15	.07	.02
☐ 641 Roger Clemens DS	.15	.07	.02
☐ 642 Jim Abbott DS	.05	.02	.01
☐ 643 Travis Fryman DS	.15	.07	.02
☐ 644 Jesse Barfield DS	.05	.02	.01
☐ 645 Cal Ripken DS	.40	.18	.05
☐ 646 Wade Boggs DS	.15	.07	.02
☐ 647 Cecil Fielder DS	.10	.05	.01
☐ 648 Rickey Henderson DS	.15	.07	.02
☐ 649 Jose Canseco DS	.15	.07	.02
☐ 650 Ken Griffey Jr. DS	.75	.35	.09
☐ 651 Kenny Rogers	.05	.02	.01
☐ 652 Luis Mercedes	.05	.02	.01
☐ 653 Mike Stanton	.05	.02	.01
☐ 654 Glenn Davis	.05	.02	.01
☐ 655 Nolan Ryan	.75	.35	.09
☐ 656 Reggie Jefferson	.10	.05	.01
☐ 657 Javier Ortiz	.05	.02	.01
☐ 658 Greg A. Harris	.05	.02	.01
☐ 659 Mariano Duncan	.05	.02	.01
☐ 660 Jeff Shaw	.05	.02	.01
☐ 661 Mike Moore	.05	.02	.01
☐ 662 Chris Haney	.05	.02	.01
☐ 663 Joe Slusarski	.05	.02	.01
☐ 664 Wayne Housie	.05	.02	.01
☐ 665 Carlos Garcia	.10	.05	.01
☐ 666 Bob Ojeda	.05	.02	.01
☐ 667 Bryan Hickerson	.05	.02	.01
☐ 668 Tim Belcher	.05	.02	.01
☐ 669 Ron Darling	.05	.02	.01
☐ 670 Rex Hudler	.05	.02	.01
☐ 671 Sid Fernandez	.05	.02	.01
☐ 672 Chito Martinez	.05	.02	.01
☐ 673 Pete Schourek	.10	.05	.01
☐ 674 Armando Reynoso	.05	.02	.01
☐ 675 Mike Mussina	.30	.14	.04
☐ 676 Kevin Morton	.05	.02	.01
☐ 677 Norm Charlton	.05	.02	.01
☐ 678 Danny Darwin	.05	.02	.01
☐ 679 Eric King	.05	.02	.01
☐ 680 Ted Power	.05	.02	.01
☐ 681 Barry Jones	.05	.02	.01
☐ 682 Carney Lansford	.10	.05	.01
☐ 683 Mel Rojas	.10	.05	.01
☐ 684 Rick Honeycutt	.05	.02	.01
☐ 685 Jeff Fassero	.10	.05	.01
☐ 686 Cris Carpenter	.05	.02	.01
☐ 687 Tim Crews	.05	.02	.01
☐ 688 Scott Terry	.05	.02	.01
☐ 689 Chris Gwynn	.05	.02	.01
☐ 690 Gerald Perry	.05	.02	.01
☐ 691 John Barfield	.05	.02	.01
☐ 692 Bob Melvin	.05	.02	.01
☐ 693 Juan Agosto	.05	.02	.01
☐ 694 Alejandro Pena	.05	.02	.01
☐ 695 Jeff Russell	.05	.02	.01
☐ 696 Carmelo Martinez	.05	.02	.01
☐ 697 Bud Black	.05	.02	.01
☐ 698 Dave Otto	.05	.02	.01
☐ 699 Billy Hatcher	.05	.02	.01
☐ 700 Checklist 601-700	.05	.02	.01
☐ 701 Clemente Nunez	.15	.07	.02
☐ 702 Rookie Threats Mark Clark Donovan Osborne Brian Jordan	.15	.07	.02
☐ 703 Mike Morgan	.05	.02	.01
☐ 704 Keith Miller	.05	.02	.01
☐ 705 Kurt Stillwell	.05	.02	.01
☐ 706 Damon Berryhill	.05	.02	.01
☐ 707 Von Hayes	.05	.02	.01
☐ 708 Rick Sutcliffe	.05	.02	.01
☐ 709 Hubie Brooks	.05	.02	.01
☐ 710 Ryan Turner	.05	.02	.01
☐ 711 Barry Bonds CL Andy Van Slyke	.10	.05	.01
☐ 712 Jose Rijo DS	.05	.02	.01
☐ 713 Tom Glavine DS	.10	.05	.01
☐ 714 Shawon Dunston DS	.05	.02	.01
☐ 715 Andy Van Slyke DS	.05	.02	.01
☐ 716 Ozzie Smith DS	.15	.07	.02
☐ 717 Tony Gwynn DS	.20	.09	.03
☐ 718 Will Clark DS	.15	.07	.02
☐ 719 Marquis Grissom DS	.10	.05	.01
☐ 720 Howard Johnson DS	.05	.02	.01
☐ 721 Barry Bonds DS	.15	.07	.02
☐ 722 Kirk McCaskill	.05	.02	.01
☐ 723 Sammy Sosa	.25	.11	.03
☐ 724 George Bell	.05	.02	.01
☐ 725 Gregg Jefferies	.10	.05	.01
☐ 726 Gary DiSarcina	.05	.02	.01
☐ 727 Mike Bordick	.10	.05	.01
☐ 728 Eddie Murray 400 Home Run Club	.15	.07	.02
☐ 729 Rene Gonzales	.05	.02	.01
☐ 730 Mike Bielecki	.05	.02	.01
☐ 731 Calvin Jones	.05	.02	.01
☐ 732 Jack Morris	.10	.05	.01
☐ 733 Frank Viola	.05	.02	.01
☐ 734 Dave Winfield	.15	.07	.02
☐ 735 Kevin Mitchell	.10	.05	.01
☐ 736 Bill Swift	.05	.02	.01
☐ 737 Dan Gladden	.05	.02	.01
☐ 738 Mike Jackson	.05	.02	.01
☐ 739 Mark Carreon	.05	.02	.01
☐ 740 Kirt Manwaring	.05	.02	.01
☐ 741 Randy Myers	.10	.05	.01
☐ 742 Kevin McReynolds	.05	.02	.01
☐ 743 Steve Sax	.05	.02	.01
☐ 744 Wally Joyner	.10	.05	.01
☐ 745 Gary Sheffield	.15	.07	.02
☐ 746 Danny Tartabull	.05	.02	.01
☐ 747 Julio Valera	.05	.02	.01
☐ 748 Denny Neagle	.15	.07	.02
☐ 749 Lance Blankenship	.05	.02	.01
☐ 750 Mike Gallego	.05	.02	.01
☐ 751 Bret Saberhagen	.10	.05	.01
☐ 752 Ruben Amaro	.05	.02	.01
☐ 753 Eddie Murray	.25	.11	.03
☐ 754 Kyle Abbott	.05	.02	.01
☐ 755 Bobby Bonilla	.10	.05	.01
☐ 756 Eric Davis	.10	.05	.01
☐ 757 Eddie Taubensee	.05	.02	.01
☐ 758 Andres Galarraga	.15	.07	.02
☐ 759 Pete Incaviglia	.05	.02	.01
☐ 760 Tom Candiotti	.05	.02	.01
☐ 761 Tim Belcher	.05	.02	.01
☐ 762 Ricky Bones	.05	.02	.01
☐ 763 Bip Roberts	.05	.02	.01
☐ 764 Pedro Munoz	.05	.02	.01
☐ 765 Greg Swindell	.05	.02	.01
☐ 766 Kenny Lofton	1.00	.45	.12
☐ 767 Gary Carter	.15	.07	.02
☐ 768 Charlie Hayes	.05	.02	.01
☐ 769 Dickie Thon	.05	.02	.01
☐ 770 Donovan Osborne DD CL	.05	.02	.01
☐ 771 Bret Boone DD	.15	.07	.02
☐ 772 Archi Cianfrocco DD	.05	.02	.01
☐ 773 Mark Clark DD	.10	.05	.01
☐ 774 Chad Curtis DD	.10	.05	.01
☐ 775 Pat Listach DD	.10	.05	.01
☐ 776 Pat Mahomes DD	.05	.02	.01
☐ 777 Donovan Osborne DD	.10	.05	.01
☐ 778 John Patterson DD	.05	.02	.01
☐ 779 Andy Stankiewicz DD	.05	.02	.01
☐ 780 Turk Wendell DD	.10	.05	.01
☐ 781 Bill Krueger	.05	.02	.01
☐ 782 Rickey Henderson Grand Theft	.15	.07	.02
☐ 783 Kevin Seitzer	.05	.02	.01
☐ 784 Dave Martinez	.05	.02	.01
☐ 785 John Smiley	.05	.02	.01
☐ 786 Matt Stairs	.05	.02	.01
☐ 787 Scott Scudder	.05	.02	.01
☐ 788 John Wetteland	.10	.05	.01
☐ 789 Jack Armstrong	.05	.02	.01
☐ 790 Ken Hill	.10	.05	.01
☐ 791 Dick Schofield	.05	.02	.01
☐ 792 Mariano Duncan	.05	.02	.01
☐ 793 Bill Pecota	.05	.02	.01
☐ 794 Mike Kelly	.05	.02	.01
☐ 795 Willie Randolph	.10	.05	.01
☐ 796 Butch Henry	.05	.02	.01
☐ 797 Carlos Hernandez	.05	.02	.01
☐ 798 Doug Jones	.05	.02	.01
☐ 799 Melido Perez	.05	.02	.01
☐ 800 Checklist 701-800	.05	.02	.01
☐ HH2 Ted Williams Hologram (Top left corner says 91 Upper Deck 92)	2.00	.90	.25
☐ SP3 Deion Sanders FB/BB	3.00	1.35	.35
☐ SP4 Tom Selleck Frank Thomas SP (Mr. Baseball)	5.00	2.20	.60

1992 Upper Deck Bench/Morgan Heroes

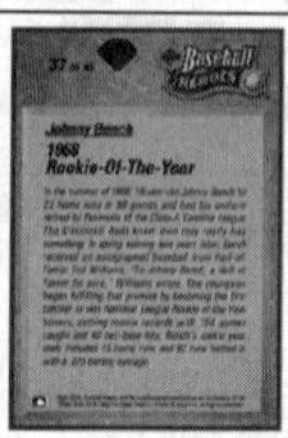

This standard size 10-card set was randomly inserted in 1992 Upper Deck high number packs. Both Bench and Morgan autographed 2,500 of card number 45, which displays a portrait by sports artist Vernon Wells. The fronts feature color photos of Bench (37-39), Morgan (40-42), or both (43-44) at various stages of their baseball careers. These pictures are partially contained within a blue and white bordered circle. The photos rest on a parchment card face trimmed with a brick red and white border. The Upper Deck Baseball Heroes logo appears in the lower right corner. The back design displays career highlights on a gray plaque resting on the same parchment background as on the front.

	MINT	NRMT	EXC
COMPLETE SET (10)	12.00	5.50	1.50
COMMON BENCH/MORG (37-45)	1.00	.45	.12
☐ 37 Johnny Bench 1968 Rookie-of-the-Year	1.00	.45	.12
☐ 38 Johnny Bench 1968-77 Ten Straight Gold Gloves	1.00	.45	.12
☐ 39 Johnny Bench 1970 and 1972 MVP	1.00	.45	.12
☐ 40 Joe Morgan 1965 Rookie Year	1.00	.45	.12
☐ 41 Joe Morgan 1975-76 Back-to-Back MVP	1.00	.45	.12
☐ 42 Johnny Bench 1980-83 The Golden Years	1.00	.45	.12
☐ 43 Johnny Bench Joe Morgan 1972-79 Big Red Machine	1.00	.45	.12
☐ 44 Johnny Bench Joe Morgan 1989 and 1990 Hall of Fame	1.00	.45	.12
☐ 45 Checklist-Heroes 37-45	1.00	.45	.12
☐ AU5 Johnny Bench and Joe Morgan AU (Signed and Numbered of 2500)	200.00	90.00	25.00
☐ NNO0 Baseball Heroes SP (Header card)	5.00	2.20	.60

1992 Upper Deck College POY Holograms

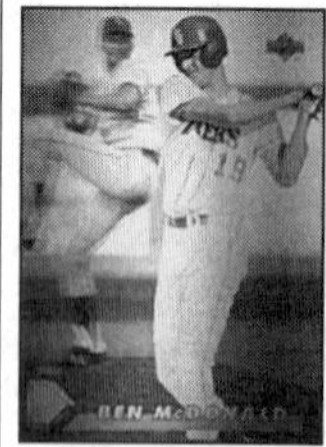

This three-card standard-size set was randomly inserted in 1992 Upper Deck high series foil packs. This set features College Player of the Year winners for 1989 through 1991. The full-bleed fronts display two action player holographic photos. The player's name is superimposed at the bottom edge over a team color-coded bar. The backs carry a second action player shot on the right side with the player's name and the year he made POY printed on a color-coded bar along the left side. In a vertical format, the player's career summary is printed on the left. The cards are numbered on the back with the prefix "CP".

	MINT	NRMT	EXC
COMPLETE SET (3)	2.00	.90	.25
COMMON CARD (CP1-CP3)	.75	.35	.09
☐ CP1 David McCarty	.75	.35	.09
☐ CP2 Mike Kelly	.75	.35	.09
☐ CP3 Ben McDonald	.75	.35	.09

1992 Upper Deck Heroes of Baseball

Continuing a popular insert set introduced the previous year, Upper Deck produced four new commemorative cards, including three player cards and one portrait card by sports artist Vernon Wells. These cards were randomly inserted in 1992 Upper Deck baseball low number foil packs. Three thousand of each card were personally numbered and autographed by each player. On a white card face, the fronts carry sepia-tone player photos with red, gold, and blue border stripes. The player's name appears in a gold border stripe beneath the picture, with the Upper Deck "Heroes of Baseball" logo in the lower right corner.

	MINT	NRMT	EXC
COMPLETE SET (4)	15.00	6.75	1.85
COMMON CARD (H5-H8)	3.00	1.35	.35
☐ H5 Vida Blue	3.00	1.35	.35
☐ H6 Lou Brock	5.00	2.20	.60
☐ H7 Rollie Fingers	4.00	1.80	.50
☐ H8 Vida Blue ART Lou Brock Rollie Fingers	4.00	1.80	.50
☐ AU5 Vida Blue AU/3000	40.00	18.00	5.00
☐ AU6 Lou Brock AU/3000	70.00	32.00	8.75
☐ AU7 R.Fingers AU/3000	60.00	27.00	7.50

1992 Upper Deck Heroes Highlights

To dealers participating in Heroes of Baseball Collectors shows, Upper Deck made available this ten-card insert standard-size set, which commemorates one of the greatest moments in the careers of ten of baseball's all-time players. The cards were primarily randomly inserted in high number packs sold at these shows. However at the first Heroes show in Anaheim, the cards were inserted into low number packs. The fronts feature color player photos with a shadowed strip for a three-dimensional effect. The player's name and the date of the great moment in the hero's career appear with a "Heroes Highlights" logo in a bottom border of varying shades of brown and blue-green. The backs have white borders and display a blue-green and brown bordered monument design accented with baseballs. The major portion of the design is parchment-textured and contains text highlighting a special moment in the player's career. The cards are numbered on the back with an "HI" prefix. The card numbering follows alphabetical order by player's name.

	MINT	NRMT	EXC
COMPLETE SET (10)	20.00	9.00	2.50
COMMON CARD (HI1-HI10)	1.00	.45	.12
☐ HI1 Bobby Bonds	1.00	.45	.12
☐ HI2 Lou Brock	4.00	1.80	.50
☐ HI3 Rollie Fingers	2.50	1.10	.30
☐ HI4 Bob Gibson	4.00	1.80	.50
☐ HI5 Reggie Jackson	6.00	2.70	.75
☐ HI6 Gaylord Perry	2.50	1.10	.30
☐ HI7 Robin Roberts	2.50	1.10	.30
☐ HI8 Brooks Robinson	5.00	2.20	.60
☐ HI9 Billy Williams	2.50	1.10	.30
☐ HI10 Ted Williams	8.00	3.60	1.00

1992 Upper Deck Home Run Heroes

This 26-card standard-size set was inserted one per pack into 1992 Upper Deck low series jumbo packs. The set spotlights the 1991 home run leaders from each of the 26 Major League teams. The fronts display color action player photos with a shadow strip around the picture for a three-dimensional effect. A gold bat icon runs vertically down the left side and contains the words "Homerun Heroes" printed in white.

	MINT	NRMT	EXC
COMPLETE SET (26)	15.00	6.75	1.85
COMMON CARD (HR1-HR26)	.25	.11	.03

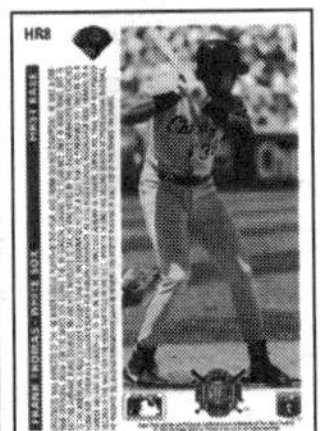

	MINT	NRMT	EXC
☐ HR1 Jose Canseco	.60	.25	.07
☐ HR2 Cecil Fielder	.40	.18	.05
☐ HR3 Howard Johnson	.25	.11	.03
☐ HR4 Cal Ripken	4.00	1.80	.50
☐ HR5 Matt Williams	.60	.25	.07
☐ HR6 Joe Carter	.40	.18	.05
☐ HR7 Ron Gant	.40	.18	.05
☐ HR8 Frank Thomas	4.00	1.80	.50
☐ HR9 Andre Dawson	.40	.18	.05
☐ HR10 Fred McGriff	.60	.25	.07
☐ HR11 Danny Tartabull	.25	.11	.03
☐ HR12 Chili Davis	.40	.18	.05
☐ HR13 Albert Belle	1.25	.55	.16
☐ HR14 Jack Clark	.25	.11	.03
☐ HR15 Paul O'Neill	.40	.18	.05
☐ HR16 Darryl Strawberry	.40	.18	.05
☐ HR17 Dave Winfield	.60	.25	.07
☐ HR18 Jay Buhner	.60	.25	.07
☐ HR19 Juan Gonzalez	1.50	.70	.19
☐ HR20 Greg Vaughn	.40	.18	.05
☐ HR21 Barry Bonds	.75	.35	.09
☐ HR22 Matt Nokes	.25	.11	.03
☐ HR23 John Kruk	.40	.18	.05
☐ HR24 Ivan Calderon	.25	.11	.03
☐ HR25 Jeff Bagwell	2.00	.90	.25
☐ HR26 Todd Zeile	.25	.11	.03

1992 Upper Deck Scouting Report

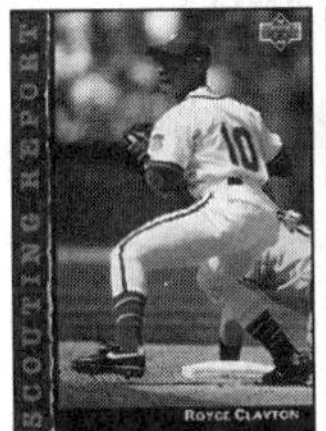

Inserted one per high series jumbo pack, cards from this 25-card standard-size set feature outstanding prospects in baseball. The fronts carry color action player photos that are full-bleed on the top and right, bordered below by a black stripe with the player's name, and by a black jagged left border that resembles torn paper. The words "Scouting Report" are printed vertically in silver lettering in the left border.

	MINT	NRMT	EXC
COMPLETE SET (25)	15.00	6.75	1.85
COMMON CARD (SR1-SR25)	.25	.11	.03
☐ SR1 Andy Ashby	.35	.16	.04
☐ SR2 Willie Banks	.25	.11	.03
☐ SR3 Kim Batiste	.25	.11	.03
☐ SR4 Derek Bell	1.00	.45	.12
☐ SR5 Archi Cianfrocco	.25	.11	.03
☐ SR6 Royce Clayton	.35	.16	.04
☐ SR7 Gary DiSarcina	.25	.11	.03
☐ SR8 Dave Fleming	.25	.11	.03
☐ SR9 Butch Henry	.25	.11	.03
☐ SR10 Todd Hundley	1.25	.55	.16
☐ SR11 Brian Jordan	2.50	1.10	.30
☐ SR12 Eric Karros	1.50	.70	.19
☐ SR13 Pat Listach	.35	.16	.04
☐ SR14 Scott Livingstone	.25	.11	.03
☐ SR15 Kenny Lofton	8.00	3.60	1.00
☐ SR16 Pat Mahomes	.25	.11	.03
☐ SR17 Denny Neagle	1.00	.45	.12
☐ SR18 Dave Nilsson	.50	.23	.06
☐ SR19 Donovan Osborne	.25	.11	.03
☐ SR20 Reggie Sanders	1.50	.70	.19
☐ SR21 Andy Stankiewicz	.25	.11	.03
☐ SR22 Jim Thome	6.00	2.70	.75
☐ SR23 Julio Valera	.25	.11	.03
☐ SR24 Mark Wohlers	.75	.35	.09
☐ SR25 Anthony Young	.25	.11	.03

1992 Upper Deck Williams Best

This 20-card standard-size set contains Ted Williams' choices of best current and future hitters in the game. The cards were randomly inserted in Upper Deck high number foil packs. The fronts feature full-

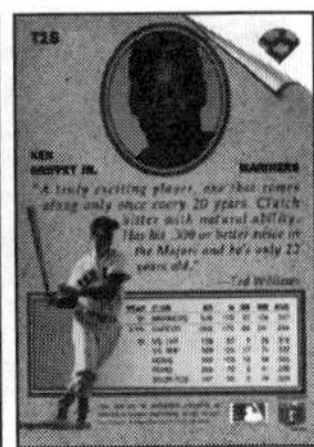

bleed color action photos with the player's name in a black field separated from the picture by Ted Williams' gold-stamped signature.

	MINT	NRMT	EXC
COMPLETE SET (20)	30.00	13.50	3.70
COMMON CARD (T1-T20)	.50	.23	.06
☐ T1 Wade Boggs	.75	.35	.09
☐ T2 Barry Bonds	1.25	.55	.16
☐ T3 Jose Canseco	.75	.35	.09
☐ T4 Will Clark	.75	.35	.09
☐ T5 Cecil Fielder	.60	.25	.07
☐ T6 Tony Gwynn	1.50	.70	.19
☐ T7 Rickey Henderson	.75	.35	.09
☐ T8 Fred McGriff	.75	.35	.09
☐ T9 Kirby Puckett	1.50	.70	.19
☐ T10 Ruben Sierra	.50	.23	.06
☐ T11 Roberto Alomar	1.00	.45	.12
☐ T12 Jeff Bagwell	3.00	1.35	.35
☐ T13 Albert Belle	2.50	1.10	.30
☐ T14 Juan Gonzalez	3.00	1.35	.35
☐ T15 Ken Griffey Jr.	8.00	3.60	1.00
☐ T16 Chris Hoiles	.50	.23	.06
☐ T17 David Justice	.60	.25	.07
☐ T18 Phil Plantier	.50	.23	.06
☐ T19 Frank Thomas	8.00	3.60	1.00
☐ T20 Robin Ventura	.60	.25	.07

1992 Upper Deck Williams Heroes

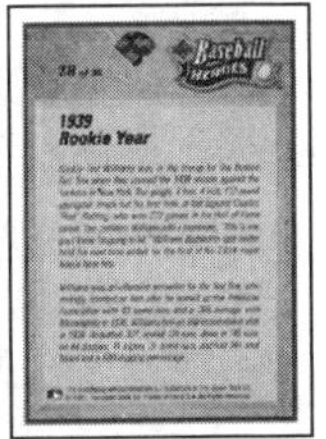

This standard-size ten-card set was randomly inserted in 1992 Upper Deck low number foil packs. Williams autographed 2,500 of card 36, which displays his portrait by sports artist Vernon Wells. The fronts features sepia-tone photos of Williams in various stages of his career that are partially contained within a blue and white bordered circle. The photos rest on a parchment card face trimmed with a brick red and white border. The Upper Deck Baseball Heroes logo appears in the lower right corner. The back design displays career highlights on a gray plaque resting on the same parchment background as on the front. The cards are numbered on the back in continuation of the Upper Deck heroes series.

	MINT	NRMT	EXC
COMPLETE SET (10)	7.00	3.10	.85
COMMON WILLIAMS (28-36)	.50	.23	.06
☐ 28 Ted Williams 1939 Rookie Year	.50	.23	.06
☐ 29 Ted Williams 1941 .406 BA	.50	.23	.06
☐ 30 Ted Williams 1942 Triple Crown Year	.50	.23	.06
☐ 31 Ted Williams 1946 and 1949 MVP	.50	.23	.06
☐ 32 Ted Williams 1947 2nd Triple Crown	.50	.23	.06
☐ 33 Ted Williams 1950s Player of the Decade	.50	.23	.06
☐ 34 Ted Williams 1960 500 Home Run Club	.50	.23	.06
☐ 35 Ted Williams 1966 Hall of Fame	.50	.23	.06
☐ 36 Baseball Heroes CL	.50	.23	.06
☐ AU4 Ted Williams (Signed and Numbered of 2500)	500.00	220.00	60.00
☐ NNO0 Baseball Heroes SP (Header card)	4.00	1.80	.50

1992 Upper Deck Williams Wax Boxes

These eight oversized "cards," measuring approximately 5 1/4" by 7 1/4", were featured on the bottom panels of 1992 Upper Deck low series wax boxes. They are identical in design to the Williams Heroes insert cards, displaying color player photos in an oval frame. The backs are blank and they are unnumbered. We have checklisted them below according to the numbering of the Heroes cards.

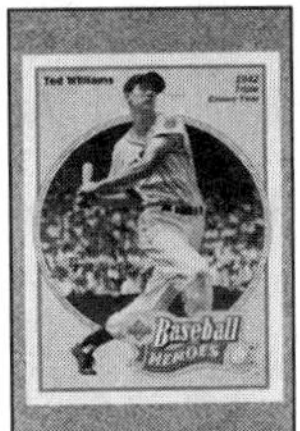

	MINT	NRMT	EXC
COMPLETE SET (8)	3.00	1.35	.35
COMMON CARD (28-35)	.50	.23	.06
☐ 28 1939 Rookie Year	.50	.23	.06
☐ 29 1941 .406	.50	.23	.06
☐ 30 1942 Triple Crown Year	.50	.23	.06
☐ 31 1946 and 1949 MVP	.50	.23	.06
☐ 32 1947 Second Triple Crown	.50	.23	.06
☐ 33 1950s Player of the Decade	.50	.23	.06
☐ 34 1960 500 Home Run Club	.50	.23	.06
☐ 35 1966 Hall of Fame	.50	.23	.06

1992 Upper Deck Comic Ball 3

This 198-card set of Upper Deck's animation-style trading cards contains ten 18-card stories; 16 special cards featuring Ken Griffey, Sr., Ken Griffey, Jr. and Jim Abbott with their Looney Toons teammates; and two checklist cards.

	MINT	NRMT	EXC
COMPLETE SET (198)	10.00	4.50	1.25
COMMON CARD (1-198)	.05	.02	.01
COMMON CARD W/GRIFFEY JR	.20	.09	.03
COMMON HOLOGRAM	1.00	.45	.12
COMMON HOLOGRAM W/GRIFFEY JR	5.00	2.20	.60

1992 Upper Deck FanFest

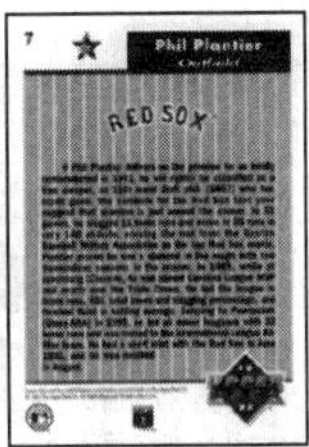

As a title sponsor of the 1992 All-Star FanFest in San Diego, Upper Deck produced this 54-card standard size set to commemorate past, present, and future All-Stars Heroes of Major League Baseball. Sixty sets were packaged in a case, and each case had at least one gold foil set. Cards 1-10 feature ten Future Heroes that are, in Upper Deck's opinion, sure bets to make an upcoming team; cards 11-44 present active All-Star alumni; and cards 45-54 salute All-Star Heroes of the past with ten fan favorites. The glossy action color photos on the front are borderless except for a pinstripe-patterned bottom border and an All-Star FanFest insignia superimposed at the lower left corner. The bottom border on the ten Future Heroes cards is navy blue and silver while the bottom border on the All-Star Heroes is silver and white. The player's name is superimposed on the photo in silver and runs vertically down the left edge of the card. The backs display the team name and career and personal information on a gray and white pinstripe panel. The player's name and position appear in a navy bar in the upper right corner.

	MINT	NRMT	EXC
COMPLETE SET (54)	6.00	2.70	.75
COMMON CARD (1-54)	.05	.02	.01
*GOLD CARDS: 15X VALUE	.05	.02	.01
☐ 1 Steve Avery	.10	.05	.01
☐ 2 Ivan Rodriguez	.30	.14	.04
☐ 3 Jeff Bagwell	.50	.23	.06
☐ 4 Delino DeShields	.05	.02	.01
☐ 5 Royce Clayton	.05	.02	.01
☐ 6 Robin Ventura	.10	.05	.01
☐ 7 Phil Plantier	.05	.02	.01
☐ 8 Ray Lankford	.15	.07	.02
☐ 9 Juan Gonzalez	.60	.25	.07
☐ 10 Frank Thomas	1.25	.55	.16
☐ 11 Roberto Alomar	.30	.14	.04
☐ 12 Sandy Alomar Jr.	.10	.05	.01
☐ 13 Wade Boggs	.20	.09	.03
☐ 14 Barry Bonds	.30	.14	.04
☐ 15 Bobby Bonilla	.10	.05	.01
☐ 16 George Brett	.50	.23	.06
☐ 17 Jose Canseco	.20	.09	.03
☐ 18 Will Clark	.20	.09	.03
☐ 19 Roger Clemens	.20	.09	.03
☐ 20 Eric Davis	.05	.02	.01
☐ 21 Rob Dibble	.05	.02	.01
☐ 22 Cecil Fielder	.10	.05	.01
☐ 23 Dwight Gooden	.10	.05	.01
☐ 24 Ken Griffey Jr.	1.25	.55	.16
☐ 25 Tony Gwynn	.60	.25	.07
☐ 26 Bryan Harvey	.05	.02	.01
☐ 27 Rickey Henderson	.20	.09	.03
☐ 28 Howard Johnson	.05	.02	.01
☐ 29 Wally Joyner	.05	.02	.01
☐ 30 Barry Larkin	.20	.09	.03
☐ 31 Don Mattingly	.60	.25	.07
☐ 32 Mark McGwire	.40	.18	.05
☐ 33 Dale Murphy	.15	.07	.02
☐ 34 Rafael Palmeiro	.15	.07	.02
☐ 35 Kirby Puckett	.50	.23	.06
☐ 36 Cal Ripken	1.25	.55	.16
☐ 37 Nolan Ryan	1.00	.45	.12
☐ 38 Chris Sabo	.05	.02	.01
☐ 39 Ryne Sandberg	.40	.18	.05
☐ 40 Benito Santiago	.05	.02	.01
☐ 41 Ruben Sierra	.05	.02	.01
☐ 42 Ozzie Smith	.40	.18	.05
☐ 43 Darryl Strawberry	.10	.05	.01
☐ 44 Robin Yount	.20	.09	.03
☐ 45 Rollie Fingers	.10	.05	.01
☐ 46 Reggie Jackson	.20	.09	.03
☐ 47 Billy Williams	.10	.05	.01
☐ 48 Lou Brock	.20	.09	.03
☐ 49 Gaylord Perry	.10	.05	.01
☐ 50 Ted Williams	.50	.23	.06
☐ 51 Brooks Robinson	.20	.09	.03
☐ 52 Bob Gibson	.20	.09	.03
☐ 53 Bobby Bonds	.05	.02	.01
☐ 54 Robin Roberts	.10	.05	.01

1992 Upper Deck Heroes of Baseball 5x7

This sheet measures approximately 5" by 7" and was distributed to herald the 1992 Heroes of Baseball sheets. Superimposed upon a black-and-white photo of Ted Williams, the back carries the dates and sites of the old-timers games at which the sheets were to be distributed. The front carries a story about the Baseball Assistance Team, (BAT) an organization that offers help to members of the baseball family who may have fallen on hard times. A total of 5,000 were produced.

	MINT	NRMT	EXC
COMPLETE SET (1)	50.00	22.00	6.25
COMMON SHEET	50.00	22.00	6.25
☐ 1 Date sheet 5x7#Ted Williams	50.00	22.00	6.25

1992 Upper Deck Sheets

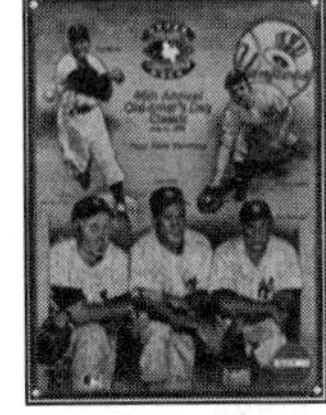

The 34 commemorative sheets listed below in chronological order were issued by Upper Deck in 1992. The Upper Deck Heroes of Baseball made stops in all 26 MLB ballparks, as well as Mile High Stadium in Denver. They sponsored old-timer baseball games and donated $10,000 to the Baseball Assistance Team, a group dedicated to helping members of the baseball family that have fallen upon hard times. At each game a limited edition commemorative sheet was distributed. Four other commemorative sheets were produced in honor of other events. When the Orioles moved to Oriole Park at Camden Yards on April 6, Upper Deck distributed 17,000 individually numbered sheets free to fans. These sheets feature four artistic views of the new stadium. The first 1992 sheet listed below was issued at the Yankee Fan Festival held at the Jacob Javits Convention Center in New York Jan. 31-Feb. 2. Sheets 17 and 18 were issued at the All-Star Game in San Diego. Sheets 31 and 32 were inserted into retail repacks of eight 1992 Upper Deck foil packs. Displaying different player cards, sheets 33-34 are two different versions of the same sheet and list dates and locations of collectors shows. All the sheets measure 8 1/2" by 11" and most feature artist renderings of players from the teams recreated for the old-timers games. The front carries the individual production number out of the total number produced, but otherwise the sheets are unnumbered.

	MINT	NRMT	EXC
COMPLETE SET (34)	250.00	110.00	31.00
COMMON SHEET (1-34)	5.00	2.20	.60

	MINT	NRMT	EXC
☐ 1 Yankee Fan Festival Jan. 31-Feb. 2, 1992 (12,500) Pictures regular-issue 1992 Upper Deck cards Don Mattingly Mel Hall Pat Kelly Matt Nokes Alvaro Espinoza Bernie Williams	15.00	6.75	1.85
☐ 2 Opening of Oriole Park at Camden Yards April 6, 1992 (17,000) Features four artist renderings of the Park	30.00	13.50	3.70
☐ 3 Toronto Blue Jays April 25, 1992 (52,000) SkyDome Bob Bailor John Mayberry Rick Bosetti Balor Moore Garth Iorg	5.00	2.20	.60
☐ 4 '72 Upper Deck Heroes vs. Atlanta Braves Heroes May 1, 1992 (22,000) Fulton County Coliseum Bruce Benedict Darrell Evans Glenn Hubbard Dave Johnson Reggie Jackson	8.00	3.60	1.00
☐ 5 Rangers Heroes vs. White Sox Heroes May 3, 1992 (22,000) Comiskey Park Bill Melton Dick Allen Wilbur Wood Carlos May Chuck Tanner MG	7.00	3.10	.85
☐ 6 Silver Anniversary of the Impossible Dream May 16, 1992 (38,000) Fenway Park Jim Lonborg George Scott Carl Yastrzemski Tony Conigliaro Dick Williams MG	7.00	3.10	.85
☐ 7 Nickname Heroes at the 'Stick May 17, 1992 (37,000) Candlestick Park Orlando Cepeda Jim Davenport Juan Marichal Dave Kingman John Montefusco	7.00	3.10	.85
☐ 8 American League Heroes vs. National League Heroes May 30, 1992 (17,000) Astrodome Tony Oliva Joe Niekro Jose Cruz Mark Fidrych Jim Wynn	9.00	4.00	1.10
☐ 9 Harvey's Wallbangers May 30, 1992 (32,000) County Stadium Ben Oglivie Harvey Kuenn Cecil Cooper Gorman Thomas	7.00	3.10	.85
☐ 10 30 Years of Mets Baseball June 13, 1992 (47,000) Shea Stadium Cleon Jones Bud Harrelson Rusty Staub Jerry Koosman Ed Kranepool	5.00	2.20	.60
☐ 11 Cardinals' 100th Anniversary June 14, 1992 (22,000) Busch Stadium Red Schoendeinst Bob Gibson Enos Slaughter Lou Brock	10.00	4.50	1.25
☐ 12 National League Heroes vs. American League Heroes June 20, 1992 (47,000) Arlington Stadium former Texas Rangers Jim Sundberg Toby Harrah Jim Kern Al Oliver Jim Spencer	5.00	2.20	.60
☐ 13 Record Setters June 21, 1992 (52,000) Anaheim Stadium Nolan Ryan Jim Abbott Jimmie Reese CO	15.00	6.75	1.85
☐ 14 Cubs Heroes vs. Reds Heroes June 28, 1992 (27,000) Riverfront Stadium George Foster Gary Nolan Pedro Borbon Cesar Cedeno Bernie Carbo	8.00	3.60	1.00
☐ 15 The Record-Setting Infield July 5, 1992 (62,000) Dodger Stadium Bill Russell Davey Lopes Steve Garvey Ron Cey	7.00	3.10	.85
☐ 16 46th Annual Old-Timers Day Classic July 11, 1992 (50,000) Yankee Stadium Phil Rizzuto Bobby Brown Allie Reynolds Hank Bauer Tom Henrich	7.00	3.10	.85
☐ 17 Heroes of Baseball All-Star Game July 13, 1992 (67,000) Jack Murphy Stadium Reggie Jackson Rollie Fingers Steve Garvey Brooks Robinson Bob Feller	8.00	3.60	1.00
☐ 18 All-Star Fanfest July 13, 1992 (12,000) Jack Murphy Stadium Larry Doby Steve Garvey Rollie Fingers	15.00	6.75	1.85
☐ 19 All-Star Game Heroes July 18, 1992 (27,000) Three Rivers Stadium Kent Tekulve Frank Thomas Elroy Face Bob Veale Chuck Tanner	8.00	3.60	1.00
☐ 20 Royals Hall of Fame Inductees July 18-19, 1992 (42,000) Royal Stadium Fred Patek Joe Burke GM Larry Gura	5.00	2.20	.60
☐ 21 More Than 100 Years of Baseball in Montreal July 26, 1992 (22,000) Olympic Stadium Claude Raymond Duke Snider Jean-Pierre Roy ANN Rusty Staub Steve Rogers	9.00	4.00	1.10
☐ 22 Seattle Mariners Heroes of Baseball July 26, 1992 Kingdome Gorman Thomas	7.00	3.10	.85
☐ 23 A Tribute to Rocky Colavito Aug. 1, 1992 (22,000) Municipal Stadium	9.00	4.00	1.10
☐ 24 '70s A's vs. '76 Phillies Aug. 8, 1992 (44,000) Veterans Stadium Tug McGraw Steve Carlton Greg Luzinski Larry Bowa Dick Allen	8.00	3.60	1.00
☐ 25 Rollie Fingers Hall of Fame Day Aug. 9, 1992 (32,000) County Stadium Rollie Fingers	7.00	3.10	.85
☐ 26 200 Club Aug. 9, 1992 (50,000) Camden Yards Luis Aparicio J.R. Richard Brooks Robinson Milt Pappas Bill Buckner	8.00	3.60	1.00
☐ 27 25th Anniversary of the Oakland Athletics Aug. 15, 1992 (22,000) Oakland-Alameda County Stadium Jim(Catfish) Hunter Reggie Jackson Rollie Fingers Vida Blue Bert Campaneris	10.00	4.50	1.25
☐ 28 Minnesota Twins World Series Heroes Aug. 23, 1992 (22,000) Metrodome Maury Wills Bob Gibson Zoilo Versalles Jim(Mudcat) Grant Tony Oliva	9.00	4.00	1.10
☐ 29 1972 Division Winners Detroit Tigers Aug. 30, 1992 (32,000) Bert Campaneris Aurelio Rodriguez Sparky Anderson MG Al Oliver	8.00	3.60	1.00
☐ 30 Upper Deck Authenticated Salutes The Legends: Past, Present and Future Nov. 13-15, 1992 (18,000) Midwest Sports Collectors Show List of Tri-Star Sports, Inc., shows	5.00	2.20	.60
☐ 31 50 Year Anniversary of the 1942 Triple Crown Season by Ted Williams (Numbered, but without total production number) Ted Williams	12.00	5.50	1.50
☐ 32 Upper Deck Honors Lou Brock Vida Blue Rollie Fingers (50,000)	8.00	3.60	1.00
☐ 33 Upper Deck Heroes of Baseball Shows Rollie Fingers Reggie Jackson Gaylord Perry Brooks Robinson Ted Williams (76,400)	5.00	2.20	.60
☐ 34 Upper Deck Heroes of Baseball Shows Bobby Bonds Lou Brock Bob Gibson Robin Roberts Billy Williams (76,400)	5.00	2.20	.60

1992 Upper Deck Team MVP Holograms

The 54 hologram cards in this standard size set feature the top offensive player and pitcher from each Major League team plus two checklist cards. Only 216,000 number sets were produced, and each set was packaged in a custom-designed box with protective sleeve and included a numbered certificate. To display the set, Upper Deck also made available a custom album through a mail-in offer for 10.00. The horizontally oriented fronts display the players in action and close-up in three-dimensional form. The player's name appears at the bottom in a striped border. In the lower right corner, a baseball image on a black home plate design radiates streaks of light up into the picture. The backs are also horizontally oriented and show the player in action in a full-color picture. A green-bordered pale yellow panel contains a career summary. Cards 1-2 feature the AL and NL MVPs (with checklists) while cards 3-54 are arranged in alphabetical order.

	MINT	NRMT	EXC
COMPLETE SET (54)	20.00	9.00	2.50
COMMON CARD (1-54)	.15	.07	.02
☐ 1 Cal Ripken MVP CL	1.50	.70	.19
☐ 2 Terry Pendleton MVP CL	.25	.11	.03
☐ 3 Jim Abbott	.15	.07	.02
☐ 4 Roberto Alomar	.75	.35	.09
☐ 5 Kevin Appier	.25	.11	.03
☐ 6 Steve Avery	.25	.11	.03
☐ 7 Jeff Bagwell	1.25	.55	.16
☐ 8 Albert Belle	1.50	.70	.19
☐ 9 Andy Benes	.25	.11	.03
☐ 10 Wade Boggs	.50	.23	.06
☐ 11 Barry Bonds	.75	.35	.09
☐ 12 George Brett	1.25	.55	.16
☐ 13 Ivan Calderon	.15	.07	.02
☐ 14 Jose Canseco	.50	.23	.06
☐ 15 Will Clark	.50	.23	.06
☐ 16 Roger Clemens	.60	.25	.07
☐ 17 David Cone	.25	.11	.03
☐ 18 Doug Drabek	.15	.07	.02
☐ 19 Dennis Eckersley	.25	.11	.03
☐ 20 Scott Erickson	.15	.07	.02
☐ 21 Cecil Fielder	.25	.11	.03
☐ 22 Ken Griffey Jr.	3.00	1.35	.35
☐ 23 Bill Gullickson	.15	.07	.02
☐ 24 Juan Guzman	.25	.11	.03
☐ 25 Pete Harnisch	.15	.07	.02
☐ 26 Howard Johnson	.15	.07	.02
☐ 27 Randy Johnson	.60	.25	.07
☐ 28 John Kruk	.15	.07	.02
☐ 29 Barry Larkin	.40	.18	.05
☐ 30 Greg Maddux	2.50	1.10	.30
☐ 31 Dennis Martinez	.25	.11	.03
☐ 32 Ramon Martinez	.25	.11	.03
☐ 33 Don Mattingly	1.50	.70	.19
☐ 34 Jack McDowell	.15	.07	.02
☐ 35 Fred McGriff	.40	.18	.05
☐ 36 Paul Molitor	.75	.35	.09
☐ 37 Charles Nagy	.25	.11	.03
☐ 38 Gregg Olson	.15	.07	.02
☐ 39 Terry Pendleton	.25	.11	.03
☐ 40 Luis Polonia	.15	.07	.02
☐ 41 Kirby Puckett	1.50	.70	.19
☐ 42 Dave Righetti	.15	.07	.02
☐ 43 Jose Rijo	.15	.07	.02
☐ 44 Cal Ripken	3.00	1.35	.35
☐ 45 Nolan Ryan	3.00	1.35	.35
☐ 46 Ryne Sandberg	1.25	.55	.16
☐ 47 Scott Sanderson	.15	.07	.02
☐ 48 Ruben Sierra	.15	.07	.02
☐ 49 Lee Smith	.25	.11	.03
☐ 50 Ozzie Smith	1.25	.55	.16
☐ 51 Darryl Strawberry	.25	.11	.03
☐ 52 Frank Thomas	3.00	1.35	.35
☐ 53 Bill Wegman	.15	.07	.02
☐ 54 Mitch Williams	.15	.07	.02

1993 Upper Deck

The 1993 Upper Deck set consists of two series of 420 standard-size cards. A special card (SP5) was randomly inserted in first series packs to commemorate the 3,000th hit of George Brett and Robin Yount. A special card (SP6) commemorating Nolan Ryan's last season was randomly inserted into second series packs. The front designs features color action player photos bordered in white. The company name is printed along the photo surface of the card top. The player's name appears in script in a color stripe cutting across the bottom of the picture while the team name and his position appear in another color stripe immediately below. The backs have a color close-up photo on the upper portion and biography, statistics, and career higlights on the lower portion. Special subsets featured include Star Rookies (1-29), Community Heroes (30-40), and American League Teammates (41-55), Top Prospects (421-449), Inside the Numbers (450-470), Team Stars (471-485), Award Winners (486-499), and Diamond Debuts (500-510). Derek Jeter is the only notable Rookie Card in this set.

	MINT	NRMT	EXC
COMPLETE SET (840)	40.00	18.00	5.00
COMPLETE FACT.SET (840)	40.00	18.00	5.00
COMPLETE SERIES 1 (420)	20.00	9.00	2.50
COMPLETE SERIES 2 (420)	20.00	9.00	2.50
COMMON CARD (1-840)	.05	.02	.01
☐ 1 Tim Salmon CL	.30	.14	.04
☐ 2 Mike Piazza SR	2.00	.90	.25
☐ 3 Rene Arocha SR	.05	.02	.01
☐ 4 Willie Greene SR	.15	.07	.02
☐ 5 Manny Alexander SR	.05	.02	.01
☐ 6 Dan Wilson SR	.15	.07	.02
☐ 7 Dan Smith SR	.05	.02	.01
☐ 8 Kevin Rogers SR	.05	.02	.01
☐ 9 Kurt Miller SR	.05	.02	.01
☐ 10 Joe Vitko SR	.05	.02	.01
☐ 11 Tim Costo SR	.05	.02	.01
☐ 12 Alan Embree SR	.05	.02	.01
☐ 13 Jim Tatum SR	.05	.02	.01
☐ 14 Cris Colon SR	.05	.02	.01
☐ 15 Steve Hosey SR	.05	.02	.01
☐ 16 Sterling Hitchcock SR	.15	.07	.02
☐ 17 Dave Mlicki SR	.05	.02	.01
☐ 18 Jessie Hollins SR	.05	.02	.01
☐ 19 Bobby Jones SR	.15	.07	.02
☐ 20 Kurt Miller SR	.05	.02	.01

☐ 21 Melvin Nieves SR .30 .14 .04
☐ 22 Billy Ashley SR .05 .02 .01
☐ 23 J.T. Snow SR .30 .14 .04
☐ 24 Chipper Jones SR 2.50 1.10 .30
☐ 25 Tim Salmon SR .50 .23 .06
☐ 26 Tim Pugh SR .05 .02 .01
☐ 27 David Nied SR .05 .02 .01
☐ 28 Mike Trombley SR .05 .02 .01
☐ 29 Javier Lopez SR .50 .23 .06
☐ 30 Jim Abbott CL .05 .02 .01
☐ 31 Jim Abbott CH .05 .02 .01
☐ 32 Dale Murphy CH .30 .14 .04
☐ 33 Tony Pena CH .05 .02 .01
☐ 34 Kirby Puckett CH .30 .14 .04
☐ 35 Harold Reynolds CH .05 .02 .01
☐ 36 Cal Ripken CH .75 .35 .09
☐ 37 Nolan Ryan CH .75 .35 .09
☐ 38 Ryne Sandberg CH .30 .14 .04
☐ 39 Dave Stewart CH .05 .02 .01
☐ 40 Dave Winfield CH .30 .14 .04
☐ 41 Joe Carter CL .30 .14 .04
Mark McGwire
☐ 42 Blockbuster Trade .30 .14 .04
Joe Carter
Roberto Alomar
☐ 43 Brew Crew .30 .14 .04
Paul Molitor
Pat Listach
Robin Yount
☐ 44 Iron and Steel .50 .23 .06
Cal Ripken
Brady Anderson
☐ 45 Youthful Tribe .50 .23 .06
Albert Belle
Sandy Alomar Jr.
Jim Thome
Carlos Baerga
Kenny Lofton
☐ 46 Motown Mashers .15 .07 .02
Cecil Fielder
Mickey Tettleton
☐ 47 Yankee Pride .30 .14 .04
Roberto Kelly
Don Mattingly
☐ 48 Boston Cy Sox .15 .07 .02
Frank Viola
Roger Clemens
☐ 49 Bash Brothers .15 .07 .02
Ruben Sierra
Mark McGwire
☐ 50 Twin Titles .30 .14 .04
Kent Hrbek
Kirby Puckett
☐ 51 Southside Sluggers .50 .23 .06
Robin Ventura
Frank Thomas
☐ 52 Latin Stars .50 .23 .06
Juan Gonzalez
Jose Canseco
Ivan Rodriguez
Rafael Palmeiro
☐ 53 Lethal Lefties .15 .07 .02
Mark Langston
Jim Abbott
Chuck Finley
☐ 54 Royal Family .15 .07 .02
Wally Joyner
Gregg Jefferies
George Brett
☐ 55 Pacific Sock Exchange .50 .23 .06
Kevin Mitchell
Ken Griffey Jr.
Jay Buhner
☐ 56 George Brett .75 .35 .09
☐ 57 Scott Cooper .05 .02 .01
☐ 58 Mike Maddux .05 .02 .01
☐ 59 Rusty Meacham .05 .02 .01
☐ 60 Wil Cordero .15 .07 .02
☐ 61 Tim Teufel .05 .02 .01
☐ 62 Jeff Montgomery .15 .07 .02
☐ 63 Scott Livingstone .05 .02 .01
☐ 64 Doug Dascenzo .05 .02 .01
☐ 65 Bret Boone .15 .07 .02
☐ 66 Tim Wakefield .15 .07 .02
☐ 67 Curt Schilling .05 .02 .01
☐ 68 Frank Tanana .05 .02 .01
☐ 69 Len Dykstra .15 .07 .02
☐ 70 Derek Lilliquist .05 .02 .01
☐ 71 Anthony Young .05 .02 .01
☐ 72 Hipolito Pichardo .05 .02 .01
☐ 73 Rod Beck .15 .07 .02
☐ 74 Kent Hrbek .15 .07 .02
☐ 75 Tom Glavine .30 .14 .04
☐ 76 Kevin Brown .15 .07 .02
☐ 77 Chuck Finley .05 .02 .01
☐ 78 Bob Walk .05 .02 .01
☐ 79 Rheal Cormier UER .05 .02 .01
(Born in New Brunswick,
not British Columbia)
☐ 80 Rick Sutcliffe .05 .02 .01
☐ 81 Harold Baines .15 .07 .02
☐ 82 Lee Smith .15 .07 .02
☐ 83 Geno Petralli .05 .02 .01
☐ 84 Jose Oquendo .05 .02 .01
☐ 85 Mark Gubicza .05 .02 .01

☐ 86 Mickey Tettleton .05 .02 .01
☐ 87 Bobby Witt .05 .02 .01
☐ 88 Mark Lewis .05 .02 .01
☐ 89 Kevin Appier .15 .07 .02
☐ 90 Mike Stanton .05 .02 .01
☐ 91 Rafael Belliard .05 .02 .01
☐ 92 Kenny Rogers .05 .02 .01
☐ 93 Randy Velarde .05 .02 .01
☐ 94 Luis Sojo .05 .02 .01
☐ 95 Mark Leiter .05 .02 .01
☐ 96 Jody Reed .05 .02 .01
☐ 97 Pete Harnisch .05 .02 .01
☐ 98 Tom Candiotti .05 .02 .01
☐ 99 Mark Portugal .05 .02 .01
☐ 100 Dave Valle .05 .02 .01
☐ 101 Shawon Dunston .05 .02 .01
☐ 102 B.J. Surhoff .15 .07 .02
☐ 103 Jay Bell .15 .07 .02
☐ 104 Sid Bream .05 .02 .01
☐ 105 Frank Thomas CL .30 .14 .04
☐ 106 Mike Morgan .05 .02 .01
☐ 107 Bill Doran .05 .02 .01
☐ 108 Lance Blankenship .05 .02 .01
☐ 109 Mark Lemke .05 .02 .01
☐ 110 Brian Harper .05 .02 .01
☐ 111 Brady Anderson .30 .14 .04
☐ 112 Bip Roberts .05 .02 .01
☐ 113 Mitch Williams .05 .02 .01
☐ 114 Craig Biggio .15 .07 .02
☐ 115 Eddie Murray .50 .23 .06
☐ 116 Matt Nokes .05 .02 .01
☐ 117 Lance Parrish .05 .02 .01
☐ 118 Bill Swift .05 .02 .01
☐ 119 Jeff Innis .05 .02 .01
☐ 120 Mike LaValliere .05 .02 .01
☐ 121 Hal Morris .05 .02 .01
☐ 122 Walt Weiss .05 .02 .01
☐ 123 Ivan Rodriguez .50 .23 .06
☐ 124 Andy Van Slyke .15 .07 .02
☐ 125 Roberto Alomar .40 .18 .05
☐ 126 Robby Thompson .05 .02 .01
☐ 127 Sammy Sosa .30 .14 .04
☐ 128 Mark Langston .15 .07 .02
☐ 129 Jerry Browne .05 .02 .01
☐ 130 Chuck McElroy .05 .02 .01
☐ 131 Frank Viola .05 .02 .01
☐ 132 Leo Gomez .05 .02 .01
☐ 133 Ramon Martinez .15 .07 .02
☐ 134 Don Mattingly 1.00 .45 .12
☐ 135 Roger Clemens .40 .18 .05
☐ 136 Rickey Henderson .30 .14 .04
☐ 137 Darren Daulton .15 .07 .02
☐ 138 Ken Hill .15 .07 .02
☐ 139 Ozzie Guillen .05 .02 .01
☐ 140 Jerald Clark .05 .02 .01
☐ 141 Dave Fleming .05 .02 .01
☐ 142 Delino DeShields .05 .02 .01
☐ 143 Matt Williams .30 .14 .04
☐ 144 Larry Walker .30 .14 .04
☐ 145 Ruben Sierra .15 .07 .02
☐ 146 Ozzie Smith .50 .23 .06
☐ 147 Chris Sabo .05 .02 .01
☐ 148 Carlos Hernandez .05 .02 .01
☐ 149 Pat Borders .05 .02 .01
☐ 150 Orlando Merced .15 .07 .02
☐ 151 Royce Clayton .15 .07 .02
☐ 152 Kurt Stillwell .05 .02 .01
☐ 153 Dave Hollins .05 .02 .01
☐ 154 Mike Greenwell .05 .02 .01
☐ 155 Nolan Ryan 1.50 .70 .19
☐ 156 Felix Jose .05 .02 .01
☐ 157 Junior Felix .05 .02 .01
☐ 158 Derek Bell .15 .07 .02
☐ 159 Steve Buechele .05 .02 .01
☐ 160 John Burkett .05 .02 .01
☐ 161 Pat Howell .05 .02 .01
☐ 162 Milt Cuyler .05 .02 .01
☐ 163 Terry Pendleton .15 .07 .02
☐ 164 Jack Morris .15 .07 .02
☐ 165 Tony Gwynn .75 .35 .09
☐ 166 Deion Sanders .30 .14 .04
☐ 167 Mike Devereaux .05 .02 .01
☐ 168 Ron Darling .05 .02 .01
☐ 169 Orel Hershiser .15 .07 .02
☐ 170 Mike Jackson .05 .02 .01
☐ 171 Doug Jones .05 .02 .01
☐ 172 Dan Walters .05 .02 .01
☐ 173 Darren Lewis .05 .02 .01
☐ 174 Carlos Baerga .15 .07 .02
☐ 175 Ryne Sandberg .50 .23 .06
☐ 176 Gregg Jefferies .15 .07 .02
☐ 177 John Jaha .30 .14 .04
☐ 178 Luis Polonia .05 .02 .01
☐ 179 Kirt Manwaring .05 .02 .01
☐ 180 Mike Magnante .05 .02 .01
☐ 181 Billy Ripken .05 .02 .01
☐ 182 Mike Moore .05 .02 .01
☐ 183 Eric Anthony .05 .02 .01
☐ 184 Lenny Harris .05 .02 .01
☐ 185 Tony Pena .05 .02 .01
☐ 186 Mike Felder .05 .02 .01
☐ 187 Greg Olson .05 .02 .01
☐ 188 Rene Gonzales .05 .02 .01
☐ 189 Mike Bordick .05 .02 .01
☐ 190 Mel Rojas .15 .07 .02

☐ 191 Todd Frohwirth .05 .02 .01
☐ 192 Darryl Hamilton .05 .02 .01
☐ 193 Mike Fetters .05 .02 .01
☐ 194 Omar Olivares .05 .02 .01
☐ 195 Tony Phillips .15 .07 .02
☐ 196 Paul Sorrento .05 .02 .01
☐ 197 Trevor Wilson .05 .02 .01
☐ 198 Kevin Gross .05 .02 .01
☐ 199 Ron Karkovice .05 .02 .01
☐ 200 Brook Jacoby .05 .02 .01
☐ 201 Mariano Duncan .05 .02 .01
☐ 202 Dennis Cook .05 .02 .01
☐ 203 Daryl Boston .05 .02 .01
☐ 204 Mike Perez .05 .02 .01
☐ 205 Manuel Lee .05 .02 .01
☐ 206 Steve Olin .05 .02 .01
☐ 207 Charlie Hough .05 .02 .01
☐ 208 Scott Scudder .05 .02 .01
☐ 209 Charlie O'Brien .05 .02 .01
☐ 210 Barry Bonds CL .30 .14 .04
☐ 211 Jose Vizcaino .05 .02 .01
☐ 212 Scott Leius .05 .02 .01
☐ 213 Kevin Mitchell .15 .07 .02
☐ 214 Brian Barnes .05 .02 .01
☐ 215 Pat Kelly .05 .02 .01
☐ 216 Chris Hammond .05 .02 .01
☐ 217 Rob Deer .05 .02 .01
☐ 218 Cory Snyder .05 .02 .01
☐ 219 Gary Carter .15 .07 .02
☐ 220 Danny Darwin .05 .02 .01
☐ 221 Tom Gordon .05 .02 .01
☐ 222 Gary Sheffield .30 .14 .04
☐ 223 Joe Carter .15 .07 .02
☐ 224 Jay Buhner .30 .14 .04
☐ 225 Jose Offerman .05 .02 .01
☐ 226 Jose Rijo .05 .02 .01
☐ 227 Mark Whiten .05 .02 .01
☐ 228 Randy Milligan .05 .02 .01
☐ 229 Bud Black .05 .02 .01
☐ 230 Gary DiSarcina .05 .02 .01
☐ 231 Steve Finley .15 .07 .02
☐ 232 Dennis Martinez .15 .07 .02
☐ 233 Mike Mussina .30 .14 .04
☐ 234 Joe Oliver .05 .02 .01
☐ 235 Chad Curtis .15 .07 .02
☐ 236 Shane Mack .05 .02 .01
☐ 237 Jaime Navarro .05 .02 .01
☐ 238 Brian McRae .15 .07 .02
☐ 239 Chili Davis .15 .07 .02
☐ 240 Jeff King .15 .07 .02
☐ 241 Dean Palmer .15 .07 .02
☐ 242 Danny Tartabull .05 .02 .01
☐ 243 Charles Nagy .15 .07 .02
☐ 244 Ray Lankford .15 .07 .02
☐ 245 Barry Larkin .30 .14 .04
☐ 246 Steve Avery .15 .07 .02
☐ 247 John Kruk .15 .07 .02
☐ 248 Derrick May .05 .02 .01
☐ 249 Stan Javier .05 .02 .01
☐ 250 Roger McDowell .05 .02 .01
☐ 251 Dan Gladden .05 .02 .01
☐ 252 Wally Joyner .15 .07 .02
☐ 253 Pat Listach .05 .02 .01
☐ 254 Chuck Knoblauch .30 .14 .04
☐ 255 Sandy Alomar Jr. .15 .07 .02
☐ 256 Jeff Bagwell .75 .35 .09
☐ 257 Andy Stankiewicz .05 .02 .01
☐ 258 Darrin Jackson .05 .02 .01
☐ 259 Brett Butler .15 .07 .02
☐ 260 Joe Orsulak .05 .02 .01
☐ 261 Andy Benes .15 .07 .02
☐ 262 Kenny Lofton .75 .35 .09
☐ 263 Robin Ventura .15 .07 .02
☐ 264 Ron Gant .15 .07 .02
☐ 265 Ellis Burks .15 .07 .02
☐ 266 Juan Guzman .15 .07 .02
☐ 267 Wes Chamberlain .05 .02 .01
☐ 268 John Smiley .05 .02 .01
☐ 269 Franklin Stubbs .05 .02 .01
☐ 270 Tom Browning .05 .02 .01
☐ 271 Dennis Eckersley .15 .07 .02
☐ 272 Carlton Fisk .30 .14 .04
☐ 273 Lou Whitaker .15 .07 .02
☐ 274 Phil Plantier .05 .02 .01
☐ 275 Bobby Bonilla .15 .07 .02
☐ 276 Ben McDonald .05 .02 .01
☐ 277 Bob Zupcic .05 .02 .01
☐ 278 Terry Steinbach .15 .07 .02
☐ 279 Terry Mulholland .05 .02 .01
☐ 280 Lance Johnson .15 .07 .02
☐ 281 Willie McGee .05 .02 .01
☐ 282 Bret Saberhagen .15 .07 .02
☐ 283 Randy Myers .15 .07 .02
☐ 284 Randy Tomlin .05 .02 .01
☐ 285 Mickey Morandini .05 .02 .01
☐ 286 Brian Williams .05 .02 .01
☐ 287 Tino Martinez .15 .07 .02
☐ 288 Jose Melendez .05 .02 .01
☐ 289 Jeff Huson .05 .02 .01
☐ 290 Joe Grahe .05 .02 .01
☐ 291 Mel Hall .05 .02 .01
☐ 292 Otis Nixon .05 .02 .01
☐ 293 Todd Hundley .15 .07 .02
☐ 294 Casey Candaele .05 .02 .01
☐ 295 Kevin Seitzer .05 .02 .01

☐ 296 Eddie Taubensee .05 .02 .01
☐ 297 Moises Alou .15 .07 .02
☐ 298 Scott Radinsky .05 .02 .01
☐ 299 Thomas Howard .05 .02 .01
☐ 300 Kyle Abbott .05 .02 .01
☐ 301 Omar Vizquel .15 .07 .02
☐ 302 Keith Miller .05 .02 .01
☐ 303 Rick Aguilera .05 .02 .01
☐ 304 Bruce Hurst .05 .02 .01
☐ 305 Ken Caminiti .30 .14 .04
☐ 306 Mike Pagliarulo .05 .02 .01
☐ 307 Frank Seminara .05 .02 .01
☐ 308 Andre Dawson .15 .07 .02
☐ 309 Jose Lind .05 .02 .01
☐ 310 Joe Boever .05 .02 .01
☐ 311 Jeff Parrett .05 .02 .01
☐ 312 Alan Mills .05 .02 .01
☐ 313 Kevin Tapani .05 .02 .01
☐ 314 Darryl Kile .05 .02 .01
☐ 315 Will Clark CL .15 .07 .02
☐ 316 Mike Sharperson .05 .02 .01
☐ 317 John Orton .05 .02 .01
☐ 318 Bob Tewksbury .05 .02 .01
☐ 319 Xavier Hernandez .05 .02 .01
☐ 320 Paul Assenmacher .05 .02 .01
☐ 321 John Franco .05 .02 .01
☐ 322 Mike Timlin .05 .02 .01
☐ 323 Jose Guzman .05 .02 .01
☐ 324 Pedro Martinez .30 .14 .04
☐ 325 Bill Spiers .05 .02 .01
☐ 326 Melido Perez .05 .02 .01
☐ 327 Mike Macfarlane .05 .02 .01
☐ 328 Ricky Bones .05 .02 .01
☐ 329 Scott Bankhead .05 .02 .01
☐ 330 Rich Rodriguez .05 .02 .01
☐ 331 Geronimo Pena .05 .02 .01
☐ 332 Bernie Williams .40 .18 .05
☐ 333 Paul Molitor .40 .18 .05
☐ 334 Carlos Garcia .05 .02 .01
☐ 335 David Cone .15 .07 .02
☐ 336 Randy Johnson .30 .14 .04
☐ 337 Pat Mahomes .05 .02 .01
☐ 338 Erik Hanson .05 .02 .01
☐ 339 Duane Ward .05 .02 .01
☐ 340 Al Martin .15 .07 .02
☐ 341 Pedro Munoz .05 .02 .01
☐ 342 Greg Colbrunn .05 .02 .01
☐ 343 Julio Valera .05 .02 .01
☐ 344 John Olerud .05 .02 .01
☐ 345 George Bell .05 .02 .01
☐ 346 Devon White .05 .02 .01
☐ 347 Donovan Osborne .05 .02 .01
☐ 348 Mark Gardner .05 .02 .01
☐ 349 Zane Smith .05 .02 .01
☐ 350 Wilson Alvarez .15 .07 .02
☐ 351 Kevin Koslofski .05 .02 .01
☐ 352 Roberto Hernandez .15 .07 .02
☐ 353 Glenn Davis .05 .02 .01
☐ 354 Reggie Sanders .30 .14 .04
☐ 355 Ken Griffey Jr. 2.00 .90 .25
☐ 356 Marquis Grissom .15 .07 .02
☐ 357 Jack McDowell .15 .07 .02
☐ 358 Jimmy Key .15 .07 .02
☐ 359 Stan Belinda .05 .02 .01
☐ 360 Gerald Williams .05 .02 .01
☐ 361 Sid Fernandez .05 .02 .01
☐ 362 Alex Fernandez .15 .07 .02
☐ 363 John Smoltz .30 .14 .04
☐ 364 Travis Fryman .15 .07 .02
☐ 365 Jose Canseco .30 .14 .04
☐ 366 David Justice .30 .14 .04
☐ 367 Pedro Astacio .05 .02 .01
☐ 368 Tim Belcher .05 .02 .01
☐ 369 Steve Sax .05 .02 .01
☐ 370 Gary Gaetti .15 .07 .02
☐ 371 Jeff Frye .05 .02 .01
☐ 372 Bob Wickman .05 .02 .01
☐ 373 Ryan Thompson .05 .02 .01
☐ 374 David Hulse .05 .02 .01
☐ 375 Cal Eldred .05 .02 .01
☐ 376 Ryan Klesko .60 .25 .07
☐ 377 Damion Easley .05 .02 .01
☐ 378 John Kiely .05 .02 .01
☐ 379 Jim Bullinger .05 .02 .01
☐ 380 Brian Bohanon .05 .02 .01
☐ 381 Rod Brewer .05 .02 .01
☐ 382 Fernando Ramsey .05 .02 .01
☐ 383 Sam Militello .05 .02 .01
☐ 384 Arthur Rhodes .05 .02 .01
☐ 385 Eric Karros .30 .14 .04
☐ 386 Rico Brogna .15 .07 .02
☐ 387 John Valentin .15 .07 .02
☐ 388 Kerry Woodson .05 .02 .01
☐ 389 Ben Rivera .05 .02 .01
☐ 390 Matt Whiteside .05 .02 .01
☐ 391 Henry Rodriguez .30 .14 .04
☐ 392 John Wetteland .15 .07 .02
☐ 393 Kent Mercker .05 .02 .01
☐ 394 Bernard Gilkey .15 .07 .02
☐ 395 Doug Henry .05 .02 .01
☐ 396 Mo Vaughn .50 .23 .06
☐ 397 Scott Erickson .05 .02 .01
☐ 398 Bill Gullickson .05 .02 .01
☐ 399 Mark Guthrie .05 .02 .01
☐ 400 Dave Martinez .05 .02 .01

□ 401 Jeff Kent .15 .07 .02
□ 402 Chris Hoiles .05 .02 .01
□ 403 Mike Henneman .05 .02 .01
□ 404 Chris Nabholz .05 .02 .01
□ 405 Tom Pagnozzi .05 .02 .01
□ 406 Kelly Gruber .05 .02 .01
□ 407 Bob Welch .05 .02 .01
□ 408 Frank Castillo .05 .02 .01
□ 409 John Dopson .05 .02 .01
□ 410 Steve Farr .05 .02 .01
□ 411 Henry Cotto .05 .02 .01
□ 412 Bob Patterson .05 .02 .01
□ 413 Todd Stottlemyre .15 .07 .02
□ 414 Greg A. Harris .05 .02 .01
□ 415 Denny Neagle .15 .07 .02
□ 416 Bill Wegman .05 .02 .01
□ 417 Willie Wilson .05 .02 .01
□ 418 Terry Leach .05 .02 .01
□ 419 Willie Randolph .15 .07 .02
□ 420 Mark McGwire CL .30 .14 .04
□ 421 Calvin Murray CL .05 .02 .01
□ 422 Pete Janicki TP .05 .02 .01
□ 423 Todd Jones TP .15 .07 .02
□ 424 Mike Neill TP .05 .02 .01
□ 425 Carlos Delgado TP .50 .23 .06
□ 426 Jose Oliva TP .05 .02 .01
□ 427 Tyrone Hill TP .05 .02 .01
□ 428 Dmitri Young TP .50 .23 .06
□ 429 Derek Wallace TP .05 .02 .01
□ 430 Michael Moore TP .05 .02 .01
□ 431 Cliff Floyd TP .15 .07 .02
□ 432 Calvin Murray TP .05 .02 .01
□ 433 Manny Ramirez TP 1.25 .55 .16
□ 434 Marc Newfield TP .15 .07 .02
□ 435 Charles Johnson TP .40 .18 .05
□ 436 Butch Huskey TP .30 .14 .04
□ 437 Brad Pennington TP .05 .02 .01
□ 438 Ray McDavid TP .15 .07 .02
□ 439 Chad McConnell TP .05 .02 .01
□ 440 Midre Cummings TP .15 .07 .02
□ 441 Benji Gil TP .15 .07 .02
□ 442 Frankie Rodriguez TP .15 .07 .02
□ 443 Chad Mottola TP .15 .07 .02
□ 444 John Burke TP .05 .02 .01
□ 445 Michael Tucker TP .30 .14 .04
□ 446 Rick Greene TP .05 .02 .01
□ 447 Rich Becker TP .15 .07 .02
□ 448 Mike Robertson TP .05 .02 .01
□ 449 Derek Jeter TP 4.00 1.80 .50
□ 450 Ivan Rodriguez CL .15 .07 .02
David McCarty
□ 451 Jim Abbott IN .05 .02 .01
□ 452 Jeff Bagwell IN .40 .18 .05
□ 453 Jason Bere IN .15 .07 .02
□ 454 Delino DeShields IN .05 .02 .01
□ 455 Travis Fryman IN .15 .07 .02
□ 456 Alex Gonzalez IN .30 .14 .04
□ 457 Phil Hiatt IN .05 .02 .01
□ 458 Dave Hollins IN .05 .02 .01
□ 459 Chipper Jones IN 1.25 .55 .16
□ 460 David Justice IN .15 .07 .02
□ 461 Ray Lankford IN .15 .07 .02
□ 462 David McCarty IN .05 .02 .01
□ 463 Mike Mussina IN .30 .14 .04
□ 464 Jose Offerman IN .05 .02 .01
□ 465 Dean Palmer IN .15 .07 .02
□ 466 Geronimo Pena IN .05 .02 .01
□ 467 Eduardo Perez IN .05 .02 .01
□ 468 Ivan Rodriguez IN .30 .14 .04
□ 469 Reggie Sanders IN .30 .14 .04
□ 470 Bernie Williams IN .30 .14 .04
□ 471 Barry Bonds CL .30 .14 .04
Matt Williams
Will Clark
□ 472 Strike Force .50 .23 .06
Greg Maddux
Steve Avery
John Smoltz
Tom Glavine
□ 473 Red October .05 .02 .01
Jose Rijo
Rob Dibble
Roberto Kelly
Reggie Sanders
Barry Larkin
□ 474 Four Corners .30 .14 .04
Gary Sheffield
Phil Plantier
Tony Gwynn
Fred McGriff
□ 475 Shooting Stars .15 .07 .02
Doug Drabek
Craig Biggio
Jeff Bagwell
□ 476 Giant Sticks .30 .14 .04
Will Clark
Barry Bonds
Matt Williams
□ 477 Boyhood Friends .15 .07 .02
Eric Davis
Darryl Strawberry
□ 478 Rock Solid Foundation .30 .14 .04
Dante Bichette
David Nied
Andres Galarraga

□ 479 Inaugural Catch .05 .02 .01
Dave Magadan
Orestes Destrade
Bret Barberie
Jeff Conine
□ 480 Steel City Champions .05 .02 .01
Tim Wakefield
Andy Van Slyke
Jay Bell
□ 481 Les Grandes Etoiles .15 .07 .02
Marquis Grissom
Delino DeShields
Dennis Martinez
Larry Walker
□ 482 Runnin' Redbirds .15 .07 .02
Geronimo Pena
Ray Lankford
Ozzie Smith
Bernard Gilkey
□ 483 Ivy Leaguers .15 .07 .02
Randy Myers
Ryne Sandberg
Mark Grace
□ 484 Big Apple Power Switch .15 .07 .02
Eddie Murray
Howard Johnson
Bobby Bonilla
□ 485 Hammers and Nails .05 .02 .01
John Kruk
Dave Hollins
Darren Daulton
Len Dykstra
□ 486 Barry Bonds AW .30 .14 .04
□ 487 Dennis Eckersley AW .15 .07 .02
□ 488 Greg Maddux AW .60 .25 .07
□ 489 Dennis Eckersley AW .15 .07 .02
□ 490 Eric Karros AW .30 .14 .04
□ 491 Pat Listach AW .05 .02 .01
□ 492 Gary Sheffield AW .30 .14 .04
□ 493 Mark McGwire AW .30 .14 .04
□ 494 Gary Sheffield AW .30 .14 .04
□ 495 Edgar Martinez AW .15 .07 .02
□ 496 Fred McGriff AW .30 .14 .04
□ 497 Juan Gonzalez AW .50 .23 .06
□ 498 Darren Daulton AW .15 .07 .02
□ 499 Cecil Fielder AW .15 .07 .02
□ 500 Brent Gates CL .05 .02 .01
□ 501 Tavo Alvarez DD .05 .02 .01
□ 502 Rod Bolton DD .05 .02 .01
□ 503 John Cummings DD .05 .02 .01
□ 504 Brent Gates DD .15 .07 .02
□ 505 Tyler Green DD .05 .02 .01
□ 506 Jose Martinez DD .05 .02 .01
□ 507 Troy Percival DD .15 .07 .02
□ 508 Kevin Stocker DD .15 .07 .02
□ 509 Matt Walbeck DD .05 .02 .01
□ 510 Rondell White DD .30 .14 .04
□ 511 Billy Ripken .05 .02 .01
□ 512 Mike Moore .05 .02 .01
□ 513 Jose Lind .05 .02 .01
□ 514 Chito Martinez .05 .02 .01
□ 515 Jose Guzman .05 .02 .01
□ 516 Kim Batiste .05 .02 .01
□ 517 Jeff Tackett .05 .02 .01
□ 518 Charlie Hough .05 .02 .01
□ 519 Marvin Freeman .05 .02 .01
□ 520 Carlos Martinez .05 .02 .01
□ 521 Eric Young .30 .14 .04
□ 522 Pete Incaviglia .05 .02 .01
□ 523 Scott Fletcher .05 .02 .01
□ 524 Orestes Destrade .05 .02 .01
□ 525 Ken Griffey Jr. CL .30 .14 .04
□ 526 Ellis Burks .15 .07 .02
□ 527 Juan Samuel .05 .02 .01
□ 528 Dave Magadan .05 .02 .01
□ 529 Jeff Parrett .05 .02 .01
□ 530 Bill Krueger .05 .02 .01
□ 531 Frank Bolick .05 .02 .01
□ 532 Alan Trammell .30 .14 .04
□ 533 Walt Weiss .05 .02 .01
□ 534 David Cone .15 .07 .02
□ 535 Greg Maddux 1.25 .55 .16
□ 536 Kevin Young .05 .02 .01
□ 537 Dave Hansen .05 .02 .01
□ 538 Alex Cole .05 .02 .01
□ 539 Greg Hibbard .05 .02 .01
□ 540 Gene Larkin .05 .02 .01
□ 541 Jeff Reardon .15 .07 .02
□ 542 Felix Jose .05 .02 .01
□ 543 Jimmy Key .15 .07 .02
□ 544 Reggie Jefferson .15 .07 .02
□ 545 Gregg Jefferies .15 .07 .02
□ 546 Dave Stewart .15 .07 .02
□ 547 Tim Wallach .05 .02 .01
□ 548 Spike Owen .05 .02 .01
□ 549 Tommy Greene .05 .02 .01
□ 550 Fernando Valenzuela .15 .07 .02
□ 551 Rich Amaral .05 .02 .01
□ 552 Bret Barberie .05 .02 .01
□ 553 Edgar Martinez .15 .07 .02
□ 554 Jim Abbott .05 .02 .01
□ 555 Frank Thomas 2.00 .90 .25
□ 556 Wade Boggs .30 .14 .04
□ 557 Tom Henke .05 .02 .01
□ 558 Milt Thompson .05 .02 .01

□ 559 Lloyd McClendon .05 .02 .01
□ 560 Vinny Castilla .30 .14 .04
□ 561 Ricky Jordan .05 .02 .01
□ 562 Andujar Cedeno .05 .02 .01
□ 563 Greg Vaughn .15 .07 .02
□ 564 Cecil Fielder .15 .07 .02
□ 565 Kirby Puckett .75 .35 .09
□ 566 Mark McGwire 1.00 .45 .12
□ 567 Barry Bonds .50 .23 .06
□ 568 Jody Reed .05 .02 .01
□ 569 Todd Zeile .05 .02 .01
□ 570 Mark Carreon .05 .02 .01
□ 571 Joe Girardi .05 .02 .01
□ 572 Luis Gonzalez .05 .02 .01
□ 573 Mark Grace .30 .14 .04
□ 574 Rafael Palmeiro .30 .14 .04
□ 575 Darryl Strawberry .15 .07 .02
□ 576 Will Clark .30 .14 .04
□ 577 Fred McGriff .30 .14 .04
□ 578 Kevin Reimer .05 .02 .01
□ 579 Dave Righetti .05 .02 .01
□ 580 Juan Bell .05 .02 .01
□ 581 Jeff Brantley .05 .02 .01
□ 582 Brian Hunter .05 .02 .01
□ 583 Tim Naehring .05 .02 .01
□ 584 Glenallen Hill .05 .02 .01
□ 585 Cal Ripken 1.50 .70 .19
□ 586 Albert Belle .75 .35 .09
□ 587 Robin Yount .30 .14 .04
□ 588 Chris Bosio .05 .02 .01
□ 589 Pete Smith .05 .02 .01
□ 590 Chuck Carr .05 .02 .01
□ 591 Jeff Blauser .05 .02 .01
□ 592 Kevin McReynolds .05 .02 .01
□ 593 Andres Galarraga .30 .14 .04
□ 594 Kevin Maas .05 .02 .01
□ 595 Eric Davis .15 .07 .02
□ 596 Brian Jordan .30 .14 .04
□ 597 Tim Raines .30 .14 .04
□ 598 Rick Wilkins .05 .02 .01
□ 599 Steve Cooke .05 .02 .01
□ 600 Mike Gallego .05 .02 .01
□ 601 Mike Munoz .05 .02 .01
□ 602 Luis Rivera .05 .02 .01
□ 603 Junior Ortiz .05 .02 .01
□ 604 Brent Mayne .05 .02 .01
□ 605 Luis Alicea .05 .02 .01
□ 606 Damon Berryhill .05 .02 .01
□ 607 Dave Henderson .05 .02 .01
□ 608 Kirk McCaskill .05 .02 .01
□ 609 Jeff Fassero .15 .07 .02
□ 610 Mike Harkey .05 .02 .01
□ 611 Francisco Cabrera .05 .02 .01
□ 612 Rey Sanchez .05 .02 .01
□ 613 Scott Servais .05 .02 .01
□ 614 Darrin Fletcher .05 .02 .01
□ 615 Felix Fermin .05 .02 .01
□ 616 Kevin Seitzer .05 .02 .01
□ 617 Bob Scanlan .05 .02 .01
□ 618 Billy Hatcher .05 .02 .01
□ 619 John Vander Wal .05 .02 .01
□ 620 Joe Hesketh .05 .02 .01
□ 621 Hector Villanueva .05 .02 .01
□ 622 Randy Milligan .05 .02 .01
□ 623 Tony Tarasco .15 .07 .02
□ 624 Russ Swan .05 .02 .01
□ 625 Willie Wilson .05 .02 .01
□ 626 Frank Tanana .05 .02 .01
□ 627 Pete O'Brien .05 .02 .01
□ 628 Lenny Webster .05 .02 .01
□ 629 Mark Clark .05 .02 .01
□ 630 Roger Clemens CL .30 .14 .04
□ 631 Alex Arias .05 .02 .01
□ 632 Chris Gwynn .05 .02 .01
□ 633 Tom Bolton .05 .02 .01
□ 634 Greg Briley .05 .02 .01
□ 635 Kent Bottenfield .05 .02 .01
□ 636 Kelly Downs .05 .02 .01
□ 637 Manuel Lee .05 .02 .01
□ 638 Al Leiter .15 .07 .02
□ 639 Jeff Gardner .05 .02 .01
□ 640 Mike Gardiner .05 .02 .01
□ 641 Mark Gardner .05 .02 .01
□ 642 Jeff Branson .05 .02 .01
□ 643 Paul Wagner .05 .02 .01
□ 644 Sean Berry .05 .02 .01
□ 645 Phil Hiatt .05 .02 .01
□ 646 Kevin Mitchell .15 .07 .02
□ 647 Charlie Hayes .05 .02 .01
□ 648 Jim Deshaies .05 .02 .01
□ 649 Dan Pasqua .05 .02 .01
□ 650 Mike Maddux .05 .02 .01
□ 651 Domingo Martinez .05 .02 .01
□ 652 Greg McMichael .15 .07 .02
□ 653 Eric Wedge .05 .02 .01
□ 654 Mark Whiten .05 .02 .01
□ 655 Roberto Kelly .05 .02 .01
□ 656 Julio Franco .15 .07 .02
□ 657 Gene Harris .05 .02 .01
□ 658 Pete Schourek .15 .07 .02
□ 659 Mike Bielecki .05 .02 .01
□ 660 Ricky Gutierrez .05 .02 .01
□ 661 Chris Hammond .05 .02 .01
□ 662 Tim Scott .05 .02 .01
□ 663 Norm Charlton .05 .02 .01

□ 664 Doug Drabek .05 .02 .01
□ 665 Dwight Gooden .15 .07 .02
□ 666 Jim Gott .05 .02 .01
□ 667 Randy Myers .15 .07 .02
□ 668 Darren Holmes .05 .02 .01
□ 669 Tim Spehr .05 .02 .01
□ 670 Bruce Ruffin .05 .02 .01
□ 671 Bobby Thigpen .05 .02 .01
□ 672 Tony Fernandez .05 .02 .01
□ 673 Darrin Jackson .05 .02 .01
□ 674 Gregg Olson .05 .02 .01
□ 675 Rob Dibble .05 .02 .01
□ 676 Howard Johnson .05 .02 .01
□ 677 Mike Lansing .15 .07 .02
□ 678 Charlie Leibrandt .05 .02 .01
□ 679 Kevin Bass .05 .02 .01
□ 680 Hubie Brooks .05 .02 .01
□ 681 Scott Brosius .05 .02 .01
□ 682 Randy Knorr .05 .02 .01
□ 683 Dante Bichette .30 .14 .04
□ 684 Bryan Harvey .05 .02 .01
□ 685 Greg Gohr .05 .02 .01
□ 686 Willie Banks .05 .02 .01
□ 687 Robb Nen .15 .07 .02
□ 688 Mike Sciosia .05 .02 .01
□ 689 John Farrell .05 .02 .01
□ 690 John Candelaria .05 .02 .01
□ 691 Damon Buford .05 .02 .01
□ 692 Todd Worrell .05 .02 .01
□ 693 Pat Hentgen .30 .14 .04
□ 694 John Smiley .05 .02 .01
□ 695 Greg Swindell .05 .02 .01
□ 696 Derek Bell .15 .07 .02
□ 697 Terry Jorgensen .05 .02 .01
□ 698 Jimmy Jones .05 .02 .01
□ 699 David Wells .05 .02 .01
□ 700 Dave Martinez .05 .02 .01
□ 701 Steve Bedrosian .05 .02 .01
□ 702 Jeff Russell .05 .02 .01
□ 703 Joe Magrane .05 .02 .01
□ 704 Matt Mieske .15 .07 .02
□ 705 Paul Molitor .40 .18 .05
□ 706 Dale Murphy .30 .14 .04
□ 707 Steve Howe .05 .02 .01
□ 708 Greg Gagne .05 .02 .01
□ 709 Dave Eiland .05 .02 .01
□ 710 David West .05 .02 .01
□ 711 Luis Aquino .05 .02 .01
□ 712 Joe Orsulak .05 .02 .01
□ 713 Eric Plunk .05 .02 .01
□ 714 Mike Felder .05 .02 .01
□ 715 Joe Klink .05 .02 .01
□ 716 Lonnie Smith .05 .02 .01
□ 717 Monty Fariss .05 .02 .01
□ 718 Craig Lefferts .05 .02 .01
□ 719 John Habyan .05 .02 .01
□ 720 Willie Blair .05 .02 .01
□ 721 Darnell Coles .05 .02 .01
□ 722 Mark Williamson .05 .02 .01
□ 723 Bryn Smith .05 .02 .01
□ 724 Greg W. Harris .05 .02 .01
□ 725 Graeme Lloyd .05 .02 .01
□ 726 Cris Carpenter .05 .02 .01
□ 727 Chico Walker .05 .02 .01
□ 728 Tracy Woodson .05 .02 .01
□ 729 Jose Uribe .05 .02 .01
□ 730 Stan Javier .05 .02 .01
□ 731 Jay Howell .05 .02 .01
□ 732 Freddie Benavides .05 .02 .01
□ 733 Jeff Reboulet .05 .02 .01
□ 734 Scott Sanderson .05 .02 .01
□ 735 Ryne Sandberg CL .30 .14 .04
□ 736 Archi Cianfrocco .05 .02 .01
□ 737 Daryl Boston .05 .02 .01
□ 738 Craig Grebeck .05 .02 .01
□ 739 Doug Dascenzo .05 .02 .01
□ 740 Gerald Young .05 .02 .01
□ 741 Candy Maldonado .05 .02 .01
□ 742 Joey Cora .15 .07 .02
□ 743 Don Slaught .05 .02 .01
□ 744 Steve Decker .05 .02 .01
□ 745 Blas Minor .05 .02 .01
□ 746 Storm Davis .05 .02 .01
□ 747 Carlos Quintana .05 .02 .01
□ 748 Vince Coleman .05 .02 .01
□ 749 Todd Burns .05 .02 .01
□ 750 Steve Frey .05 .02 .01
□ 751 Ivan Calderon .05 .02 .01
□ 752 Steve Reed .05 .02 .01
□ 753 Danny Jackson .05 .02 .01
□ 754 Jeff Conine .15 .07 .02
□ 755 Juan Gonzalez 1.00 .45 .12
□ 756 Mike Kelly .05 .02 .01
□ 757 John Doherty .05 .02 .01
□ 758 Jack Armstrong .05 .02 .01
□ 759 John Wehner .05 .02 .01
□ 760 Scott Bankhead .05 .02 .01
□ 761 Jim Tatum .05 .02 .01
□ 762 Scott Pose .05 .02 .01
□ 763 Andy Ashby .15 .07 .02
□ 764 Ed Sprague .15 .07 .02
□ 765 Harold Baines .15 .07 .02
□ 766 Kirk Gibson .15 .07 .02
□ 767 Troy Neel .05 .02 .01
□ 768 Dick Schofield .05 .02 .01

☐ 769 Dickie Thon	.05	.02	.01
☐ 770 Butch Henry	.05	.02	.01
☐ 771 Junior Felix	.05	.02	.01
☐ 772 Ken Ryan	.05	.02	.01
☐ 773 Trevor Hoffman	.30	.14	.04
☐ 774 Phil Plantier	.05	.02	.01
☐ 775 Bo Jackson	.15	.07	.02
☐ 776 Benito Santiago	.05	.02	.01
☐ 777 Andre Dawson	.15	.07	.02
☐ 778 Bryan Hickerson	.05	.02	.01
☐ 779 Dennis Moeller	.05	.02	.01
☐ 780 Ryan Bowen	.05	.02	.01
☐ 781 Eric Fox	.05	.02	.01
☐ 782 Joe Kmak	.05	.02	.01
☐ 783 Mike Hampton	.30	.14	.04
☐ 784 Darrell Sherman	.05	.02	.01
☐ 785 J.T. Snow	.30	.14	.04
☐ 786 Dave Winfield	.30	.14	.04
☐ 787 Jim Austin	.05	.02	.01
☐ 788 Craig Shipley	.05	.02	.01
☐ 789 Greg Myers	.05	.02	.01
☐ 790 Todd Benzinger	.05	.02	.01
☐ 791 Cory Snyder	.05	.02	.01
☐ 792 David Segui	.05	.02	.01
☐ 793 Armando Reynoso	.05	.02	.01
☐ 794 Chili Davis	.15	.07	.02
☐ 795 Dave Nilsson	.15	.07	.02
☐ 796 Paul O'Neill	.15	.07	.02
☐ 797 Jerald Clark	.05	.02	.01
☐ 798 Jose Mesa	.15	.07	.02
☐ 799 Brain Holman	.05	.02	.01
☐ 800 Jim Eisenreich	.15	.07	.02
☐ 801 Mark McLemore	.05	.02	.01
☐ 802 Luis Sojo	.05	.02	.01
☐ 803 Harold Reynolds	.05	.02	.01
☐ 804 Dan Plesac	.05	.02	.01
☐ 805 Dave Stieb	.05	.02	.01
☐ 806 Tom Brunansky	.05	.02	.01
☐ 807 Kelly Gruber	.05	.02	.01
☐ 808 Bob Ojeda	.05	.02	.01
☐ 809 Dave Burba	.05	.02	.01
☐ 810 Joe Boever	.05	.02	.01
☐ 811 Jeremy Hernandez	.05	.02	.01
☐ 812 Tim Salmon TC	.30	.14	.04
☐ 813 Jeff Bagwell TC	.40	.18	.05
☐ 814 Dennis Eckersley TC	.15	.07	.02
☐ 815 Roberto Alomar TC	.30	.14	.04
☐ 816 Steve Avery TC	.05	.02	.01
☐ 817 Pat Listach TC	.05	.02	.01
☐ 818 Gregg Jefferies TC	.15	.07	.02
☐ 819 Sammy Sosa TC	.30	.14	.04
☐ 820 Darryl Strawberry TC	.15	.07	.02
☐ 821 Dennis Martinez TC	.05	.02	.01
☐ 822 Robby Thompson TC	.05	.02	.01
☐ 823 Albert Belle TC	.40	.18	.05
☐ 824 Randy Johnson TC	.30	.14	.04
☐ 825 Nigel Wilson TC	.05	.02	.01
☐ 826 Bobby Bonilla TC	.15	.07	.02
☐ 827 Glenn Davis TC	.05	.02	.01
☐ 828 Gary Sheffield TC	.30	.14	.04
☐ 829 Darren Daulton TC	.15	.07	.02
☐ 830 Jay Bell TC	.05	.02	.01
☐ 831 Juan Gonzalez TC	.50	.23	.06
☐ 832 Andre Dawson TC	.15	.07	.02
☐ 833 Hal Morris TC	.05	.02	.01
☐ 834 David Nied TC	.05	.02	.01
☐ 835 Felix Jose TC	.05	.02	.01
☐ 836 Travis Fryman TC	.15	.07	.02
☐ 837 Shane Mack TC	.05	.02	.01
☐ 838 Robin Ventura TC	.15	.07	.02
☐ 839 Danny Tartabull TC	.05	.02	.01
☐ 840 Roberto Alomar CL	.30	.14	.04
☐ SP5 George Brett Robin Yount 3,000th Hit	1.50	.70	.19
☐ SP6 Nolan Ryan	4.00	1.80	.50

1993 Upper Deck Gold

These gold parallel cards were made available exclusively in factory set form. One set in every 20 ct. case of factory sets featured cards with gold foil holograms on the card backs, rather than the traditional silver foil holograms. Please refer to the multipliers provided below for values on single cards.

	MINT	NRMT	EXC
COMPLETE FACT.SET (840)	80.00	36.00	10.00
COMMON CARD (1-840)	.10	.05	.01
*GOLD STARS: 1X TO 2X BASIC CARDS			

1993 Upper Deck Clutch Performers

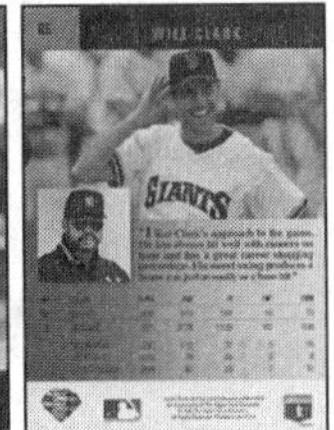

These 20 standard-size cards were randomly inserted into series II retail foil packs, as well as inserted one per series II retail jumbo packs. The fronts feature color player action shots that are borderless, except at the bottom, where a black stripe is set off by a gold-foil line and carries the set's title and Reggie Jackson's gold-foil signature. The player's name printed in white lettering rests at the bottom of the photo. The back carries a color player action shot below a black bar at the top that carries the player's name in gold-colored lettering. Below the picture appears a small black-and-white head shot of Reggie Jackson alongside his comments on the player. A player stat table appears below. The cards are numbered on the back with an "R" prefix and appear in alphabetical order. These 20 cards represent Reggie Jackson's selection of players who have come through under pressure.

	MINT	NRMT	EXC
COMPLETE SET (20)	20.00	9.00	2.50
COMMON CARD (R1-R20)	.25	.11	.03
☐ R1 Roberto Alomar	1.00	.45	.12
☐ R2 Wade Boggs	.60	.25	.07
☐ R3 Barry Bonds	1.25	.55	.16
☐ R4 Jose Canseco	.60	.25	.07
☐ R5 Joe Carter	.40	.18	.05
☐ R6 Will Clark	.60	.25	.07
☐ R7 Roger Clemens	1.00	.45	.12
☐ R8 Dennis Eckersley	.40	.18	.05
☐ R9 Cecil Fielder	.40	.18	.05
☐ R10 Juan Gonzalez	2.50	1.10	.30
☐ R11 Ken Griffey Jr.	5.00	2.20	.60
☐ R12 Rickey Henderson	.60	.25	.07
☐ R13 Barry Larkin	.60	.25	.07
☐ R14 Don Mattingly	2.50	1.10	.30
☐ R15 Fred McGriff	.60	.25	.07
☐ R16 Terry Pendleton	.25	.11	.03
☐ R17 Kirby Puckett	2.00	.90	.25
☐ R18 Ryne Sandberg	1.25	.55	.16
☐ R19 John Smoltz	.75	.35	.09
☐ R20 Frank Thomas	5.00	2.20	.60

1993 Upper Deck Fifth Anniversary

This 15-card standard-size set celebrates Upper Deck's five years in the sports card business.The cards are essentially reprinted versions of some of Upper Deck's most popular cards in the last five years. These cards were randomly inserted in second series hobby packs. The black-bordered fronts feature player photos that previously appeared on an Upper Deck card. The Five-Year Anniversary logo is located in one of the corners and the player's name is printed in gold-foil along the lower black border. The black backs carry a picture of the original card on the left side with narrative historical information on Upper Deck and a brief career summary of the player. The gold-colored year of issue of the original card is prominently displayed in the middle of the text. The cards are numbered on the back with an A prefix. One over-sized (3 1/2" by 5") version of each of these cards was initially inserted into retail blister repacks, which contained one foil pack each of 1993 Upper Deck Series I and II. These cards are individually numbered out of 10,000 and were later inserted into various forms of repackaging.

	MINT	NRMT	EXC
COMPLETE SET (15)	20.00	9.00	2.50
COMMON CARD (A1-A15)	.25	.11	.03
*JUMBO CARDS: 2X VALUE			
☐ A1 Ken Griffey Jr.	8.00	3.60	1.00
☐ A2 Gary Sheffield	.60	.25	.07
☐ A3 Roberto Alomar	1.00	.45	.12
☐ A4 Jim Abbott	.40	.18	.05
☐ A5 Nolan Ryan	5.00	2.20	.60
☐ A6 Juan Gonzalez	2.50	1.10	.30
☐ A7 David Justice	.40	.18	.05
☐ A8 Carlos Baerga	.40	.18	.05
☐ A9 Reggie Jackson	.75	.35	.09
☐ A10 Eric Karros	.60	.25	.07
☐ A11 Chipper Jones	4.00	1.80	.50
☐ A12 Ivan Rodriguez	1.25	.55	.16
☐ A13 Pat Listach	.25	.11	.03
☐ A14 Frank Thomas	5.00	2.20	.60
☐ A15 Tim Salmon	1.00	.45	.12

1993 Upper Deck Future Heroes

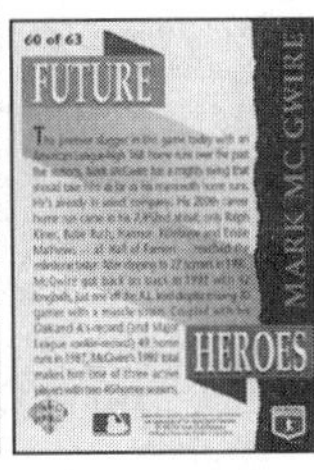

Randomly inserted in second series foil packs and continuing the Heroes insert set begun in the 1990 Upper Deck high-number set, this ten-card standard-size set features eight different "Future Heroes" along with a checklist and header card. The fronts feature borderless color player action shots that bear the player's simulated autograph in gold foil in an upper corner. The player's name appears within a black stripe formed by the simulated tearing away of a piece of the photo. The player's name appears below. The back carries the player's name vertically within a black "tear-away" stripe along the right edge. Career highlights are displayed within a white, gray, and tan panel on the left.

	MINT	NRMT	EXC
COMPLETE SET (10)	12.00	5.50	1.50
COMMON CARD (55-63)	.50	.23	.06
☐ 55 Roberto Alomar	1.00	.45	.12
☐ 56 Barry Bonds	1.25	.55	.16
☐ 57 Roger Clemens	1.00	.45	.12
☐ 58 Juan Gonzalez	2.50	1.10	.30
☐ 59 Ken Griffey Jr.	5.00	2.20	.60
☐ 60 Mark McGwire	1.50	.70	.19
☐ 61 Kirby Puckett	2.00	.90	.25
☐ 62 Frank Thomas	5.00	2.20	.60
☐ 63 Checklist	.50	.23	.06
☐ NNO Header Card SP	.75	.35	.09

1993 Upper Deck Home Run Heroes

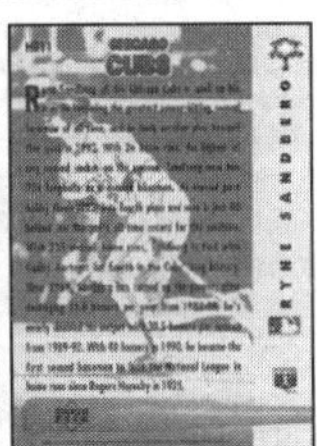

This 28-card standard-size set features the home run leader from each Major League team. Each 1993 first series 27-card jumbo pack contained one of these cards. The cards feature action color player photos with a three-dimensional baseball bat design at the bottom. Featuring embossed printing, the bat looks and feels as if it stands off the card, and a shadow design below it adds to the effect. The words "Homerun Heroes" are printed vertically down the left. The backs show a team color-coded photo as the background for player information. The player's name appears in a white border on the right. The baseball bat design is repeated at the bottom. The cards are numbered on the back with an "HR" prefix and the set is arranged in descending order according to the number of home runs.

	MINT	NRMT	EXC
COMPLETE SET (28)	15.00	6.75	1.85
COMMON CARD (HR1-HR28)	.25	.11	.03
☐ HR1 Juan Gonzalez	2.50	1.10	.30
☐ HR2 Mark McGwire	1.50	.70	.19
☐ HR3 Cecil Fielder	.40	.18	.05
☐ HR4 Fred McGriff	.60	.25	.07
☐ HR5 Albert Belle	2.00	.90	.25
☐ HR6 Barry Bonds	1.25	.55	.16
☐ HR7 Joe Carter	.40	.18	.05
☐ HR8 Darren Daulton	.40	.18	.05
☐ HR9 Ken Griffey Jr.	5.00	2.20	.60
☐ HR10 Dave Hollins	.25	.11	.03
☐ HR11 Ryne Sandberg	1.25	.55	.16
☐ HR12 George Bell	.25	.11	.03
☐ HR13 Danny Tartabull	.40	.18	.05
☐ HR14 Mike Devereaux	.25	.11	.03
☐ HR15 Greg Vaughn	.40	.18	.05
☐ HR16 Larry Walker	.60	.25	.07
☐ HR17 David Justice	.40	.18	.05
☐ HR18 Terry Pendleton	.25	.11	.03
☐ HR19 Eric Karros	.60	.25	.07
☐ HR20 Ray Lankford	.40	.18	.05
☐ HR21 Matt Williams	.60	.25	.07
☐ HR22 Eric Anthony	.25	.11	.03
☐ HR23 Bobby Bonilla	.40	.18	.05
☐ HR24 Kirby Puckett	2.00	.90	.25
☐ HR25 Mike Macfarlane	.25	.11	.03
☐ HR26 Tom Brunansky	.25	.11	.03
☐ HR27 Paul O'Neill	.40	.18	.05
☐ HR28 Gary Gaetti	.40	.18	.05

1993 Upper Deck looss Collection

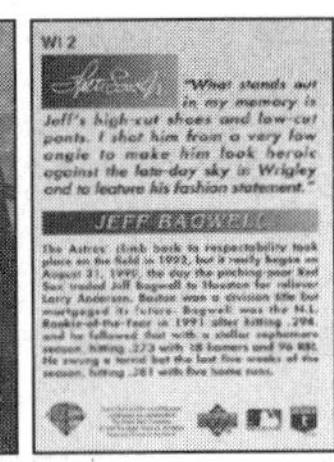

This 27-card standard-size set spotlights the work of famous sports photographer Walter looss Jr. by presenting 26 of the game's current greats in a candid photo set. The cards were randomly inserted in series I foil packs purchased from major retail outlets only. The posed color player photos on the fronts are full-bleed and either horizontally or vertically oriented. The words "The Upper Deck looss Collection" are printed in gold foil. The back carries a quote from looss about the shoot and the player's career highlights. The text blocks on the card backs are separated by a gradated bars of varying colors. The cards are numbered on the back with a "WI" prefix. One over-sized version of each of these cards were initially inserted into retail blister repacks containing one foil pack each of 1993 Upper Deck Series I and II. These over-sized (3 1/2" by 5") cards are individually numbered out of 10,000 and were later inserted in various forms of repackaging.

	MINT	NRMT	EXC
COMPLETE SET (27)	25.00	11.00	3.10
COMMON CARD (WI1-WI26)	.30	.14	.04
*JUMBO CARDS: 2X VALUE			
☐ WI1 Tim Salmon	1.25	.55	.16
☐ WI2 Jeff Bagwell	2.50	1.10	.30
☐ WI3 Mark McGwire	2.00	.90	.25
☐ WI4 Roberto Alomar	1.25	.55	.16
☐ WI5 Steve Avery	.30	.14	.04
☐ WI6 Paul Molitor	1.25	.55	.16
☐ WI7 Ozzie Smith	1.50	.70	.19
☐ WI8 Mark Grace	.75	.35	.09
☐ WI9 Eric Karros	.75	.35	.09
☐ WI10 Delino DeShields	.50	.23	.06
☐ WI11 Will Clark	.75	.35	.09
☐ WI12 Albert Belle	2.50	1.10	.30
☐ WI13 Ken Griffey Jr.	6.00	2.70	.75
☐ WI14 Howard Johnson	.30	.14	.04
☐ WI15 Cal Ripken Jr.	5.00	2.20	.60
☐ WI16 Fred McGriff	.75	.35	.09
☐ WI17 Darren Daulton	.50	.23	.06
☐ WI18 Andy Van Slyke	.30	.14	.04
☐ WI19 Nolan Ryan	5.00	2.20	.60
☐ WI20 Wade Boggs	.75	.35	.09
☐ WI21 Barry Larkin	.75	.35	.09
☐ WI22 George Brett	2.50	1.10	.30
☐ WI23 Cecil Fielder	.50	.23	.06
☐ WI24 Kirby Puckett	2.50	1.10	.30
☐ WI25 Frank Thomas	6.00	2.70	.75
☐ WI26 Don Mattingly	3.00	1.35	.35
☐ NNO Title Card looss Header	.50	.23	.06

1993 Upper Deck Mays Heroes

This standard-size ten-card set was randomly inserted in 1993 Upper Deck first series foil packs. The fronts feature color photos of Mays at various stages of his career that are partially contained within a black bordered circle. The photos rest on a rough-edged sports page from a newspaper. The Upper Deck Baseball Heroes logo appears in the lower right corner. The back design displays career highlights on a blank newspaper page. The cards are numbered in continuation of Upper Deck's Heroes series.

	MINT	NRMT	EXC
COMPLETE SET (10)	3.00	1.35	.35
COMMON MAYS (46-54)	.50	.23	.06
☐ 46 Willie Mays 1951 Rookie-of-the-Year	.50	.23	.06
☐ 47 Willie Mays 1954 The Catch	.50	.23	.06
☐ 48 Willie Mays 1956-57 30-30 Club	.50	.23	.06
☐ 49 Willie Mays 1961 Four-Homer Game	.50	.23	.06
☐ 50 Willie Mays 1965 Most Valuable Player	.50	.23	.06
☐ 51 Willie Mays 1969 600-Home Run Club	.50	.23	.06
☐ 52 Willie Mays 1972 New York Homecoming	.50	.23	.06
☐ 53 Willie Mays 1979 Hall of Fame	.50	.23	.06
☐ 54 Baseball Heroes CL	.50	.23	.06

	MINT	NRMT	EXC
Vernon Wells Portrait			
☐ NNO0 Baseball Heroes SP	.50	.23	.06
(Header card)			

1993 Upper Deck On Deck

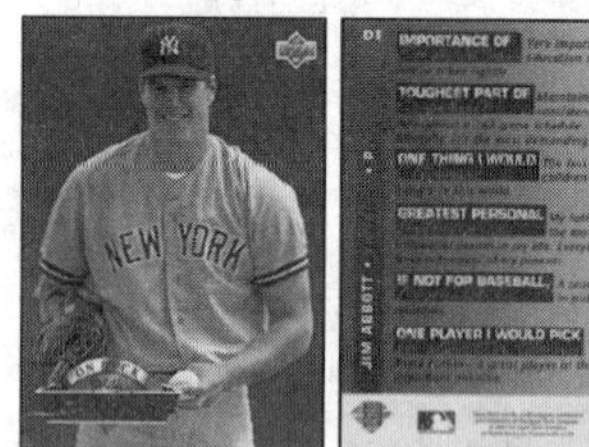

Inserted one per series II jumbo packs, these 25 standard-size cards profile baseball's top players. The fronts feature borderless color player photos, some action, others posed, and carry the player's simulated gold-foil signature within a team color-coded stripe that appears as part of the set's logo. The gradated-tan-colored back carries the player's name, position, and team vertically within a team color-coded stripe near the left edge. The player's answers to personal questions rounds out the back. The cards are numbered on the back with a "D" prefix in alphabetical order by name.

	MINT	NRMT	EXC
COMPLETE SET (25)	20.00	9.00	2.50
COMMON CARD (D1-D25)	.25	.11	.03
☐ D1 Jim Abbott	.25	.11	.03
☐ D2 Roberto Alomar	1.00	.45	.12
☐ D3 Carlos Baerga	.25	.11	.03
☐ D4 Albert Belle	2.00	.90	.25
☐ D5 Wade Boggs	.60	.25	.07
☐ D6 George Brett	2.00	.90	.25
☐ D7 Jose Canseco	.60	.25	.07
☐ D8 Will Clark	.60	.25	.07
☐ D9 Roger Clemens	1.00	.45	.12
☐ D10 Dennis Eckersley	.40	.18	.05
☐ D11 Cecil Fielder	.40	.18	.05
☐ D12 Juan Gonzalez	2.50	1.10	.30
☐ D13 Ken Griffey Jr.	5.00	2.20	.60
☐ D14 Tony Gwynn	2.00	.90	.25
☐ D15 Bo Jackson	.40	.18	.05
☐ D16 Chipper Jones	4.00	1.80	.50
☐ D17 Eric Karros	.60	.25	.07
☐ D18 Mark McGwire	1.50	.70	.19
☐ D19 Kirby Puckett	2.00	.90	.25
☐ D20 Nolan Ryan	5.00	2.20	.60
☐ D21 Tim Salmon	1.00	.45	.12
☐ D22 Ryne Sandberg	1.25	.55	.16
☐ D23 Darryl Strawberry	.40	.18	.05
☐ D24 Frank Thomas	5.00	2.20	.60
☐ D25 Andy Van Slyke	.25	.11	.03

1993 Upper Deck Season Highlights

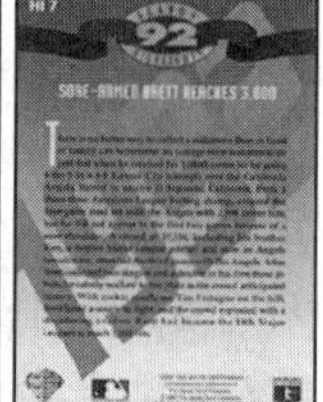

This 20-card standard-size insert set captures great moments of the 1992 Major League Baseball season. The set was randomly packed into specially marked cases that were available only at Upper Deck Heroes of Baseball Card Shows and through the purchase of a specified quantity of second series cases. The fronts display a full-bleed color action photo with a special "92 Season Highlights" logo running across the bottom. The ribbon intersecting the logo is blue on the American League cards and red on the National League. The date of the player's outstanding achievement is gold-foil stamped at the lower right. On backs that fade from the league color to white, a description of the achievement is presented. The year 1992 is printed diagonally across the backs. The cards are numbered on the back with an "HI" prefix in alphabetical order by player's name.

	MINT	NRMT	EXC
COMPLETE SET (20)	160.00	70.00	20.00
COMMON CARD (HI1-HI20)	2.50	1.10	.30
☐ HI1 Roberto Alomar	10.00	4.50	1.25
☐ HI2 Steve Avery	2.50	1.10	.30
☐ HI3 Harold Baines	3.00	1.35	.35
☐ HI4 Damon Berryhill	2.50	1.10	.30
☐ HI5 Barry Bonds	12.00	5.50	1.50
☐ HI6 Bret Boone	2.50	1.10	.30
☐ HI7 George Brett	20.00	9.00	2.50
☐ HI8 Francisco Cabrera	2.50	1.10	.30
☐ HI9 Ken Griffey Jr.	50.00	22.00	6.25
☐ HI10 Rickey Henderson	5.00	2.20	.60
☐ HI11 Kenny Lofton	15.00	6.75	1.85
☐ HI12 Mickey Morandini	2.50	1.10	.30
☐ HI13 Eddie Murray	12.00	5.50	1.50
☐ HI14 David Nied	2.50	1.10	.30
☐ HI15 Jeff Reardon	3.00	1.35	.35
☐ HI16 Bip Roberts	2.50	1.10	.30
☐ HI17 Nolan Ryan	50.00	22.00	6.25
☐ HI18 Ed Sprague	3.00	1.35	.35
☐ HI19 Dave Winfield	5.00	2.20	.60
☐ HI20 Robin Yount	5.00	2.20	.60

1993 Upper Deck Then And Now

This 18-card, standard-size hologram set highlights veteran stars in their rookie year and today, reflecting on how they and the game have changed. Cards 1-9 were randomly inserted in series I foil packs; cards 10-18 were randomly inserted in series II foil packs. The nine lithogram cards in the second series feature one card each of Hall of Famers Reggie Jackson, Mickey Mantle, and Willie Mays, as well as six active players. The horizontal fronts have a color close-up photo cutout and superimposed at the left corner of a full-bleed hologram portraying the player in an action scene. The skyline of the player's city serves as the background for the holograms. The player's name and the manufacturer's name form a right angle at the upper right corner. At the upper left corner, a "Then And Now" logo which includes the length of the player's career in years rounds out the front. On a sand-colored panel that resembles a postage stamp, the backs present career summary. The cards are numbered on the back with a "TN" prefix and arranged alphabetically within subgroup according to player's last name.

	MINT	NRMT	EXC
COMPLETE SET (18)	50.00	22.00	6.25
COMPLETE SERIES 1 (9)	20.00	9.00	2.50
COMPLETE SERIES 2 (9)	30.00	13.50	3.70
COMMON CARD (TN1-TN18)	.50	.23	.06
☐ TN1 Wade Boggs	1.00	.45	.12
☐ TN2 George Brett	4.00	1.80	.50
☐ TN3 Rickey Henderson	1.00	.45	.12
☐ TN4 Cal Ripken	8.00	3.60	1.00
☐ TN5 Nolan Ryan	8.00	3.60	1.00
☐ TN6 Ryne Sandberg	2.50	1.10	.30
☐ TN7 Ozzie Smith	2.50	1.10	.30
☐ TN8 Darryl Strawberry	.75	.35	.09
☐ TN9 Dave Winfield	1.00	.45	.12
☐ TN10 Dennis Eckersley	.75	.35	.09
☐ TN11 Tony Gwynn	4.00	1.80	.50
☐ TN12 Howard Johnson	.50	.23	.06
☐ TN13 Don Mattingly	5.00	2.20	.60
☐ TN14 Eddie Murray	2.50	1.10	.30
☐ TN15 Robin Yount	1.00	.45	.12
☐ TN16 Reggie Jackson	2.50	1.10	.30
☐ TN17 Mickey Mantle	15.00	6.75	1.85
☐ TN18 Willie Mays	8.00	3.60	1.00

1993 Upper Deck Triple Crown

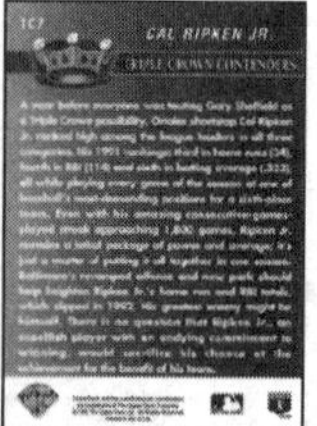

This ten-card, standard-size insert set highlights ten players who were selected by Upper Deck as having the best shot at winning Major League Baseball's Triple Crown. The cards were randomly inserted in series I foil packs sold by hobby dealers only. The fronts display glossy full-bleed color player photos. At the bottom, a purple ribbon edged in gold foil carries the words "Triple Crown Contenders," while the player's name appears in gold foil lettering immediately below on a gradated black background. A crown overlays the ribbon at the lower left corner and rounds out the front. On a gradated black background, the backs summarize the player's performance in home runs, RBIs, and batting average. The cards are numbered on the back with a "TC" prefix and arranged alphabetically by player's last name.

	MINT	NRMT	EXC
COMPLETE SET (10)	30.00	13.50	3.70
COMMON CARD (TC1-TC10)	1.00	.45	.12
☐ TC1 Barry Bonds	2.50	1.10	.30
☐ TC2 Jose Canseco	1.00	.45	.12
☐ TC3 Will Clark	1.00	.45	.12
☐ TC4 Ken Griffey Jr.	10.00	4.50	1.25
☐ TC5 Fred McGriff	1.00	.45	.12
☐ TC6 Kirby Puckett	4.00	1.80	.50
☐ TC7 Cal Ripken Jr.	8.00	3.60	1.00
☐ TC8 Gary Sheffield	1.50	.70	.19
☐ TC9 Frank Thomas	10.00	4.50	1.25
☐ TC10 Larry Walker	1.00	.45	.12

1993 Upper Deck All-Time Heroes Preview

This four-card boxed preview set was distributed to herald the release of the 165-card main set. The cards are patterned after the T-202 Hassan Triple Folders cards, which first appeared in 1912. The cards measure approximately 2 1/4" by 5 1/4" and feature two side panels and a larger middle panel. The fronts feature two-player color drawings by Todd Reigle in their middle panels. The side panels feature photos of the two players. The white backs include player biographies and career highlights printed in red lettering. The cards are numbered on the back with an "HOB" prefix.

	MINT	NRMT	EXC
COMPLETE SET (4)	5.00	2.20	.60
COMMON CARD (1-4)	1.50	.70	.19
☐ 1 Ted Williams Mickey Mantle	1.50	.70	.19
☐ 2 Reggie Jackson Mickey Mantle	1.50	.70	.19
☐ 3 Ted Williams Reggie Jackson	1.50	.70	.19
☐ 4 Reggie Jackson Mickey Mantle Ted Williams	1.50	.70	.19

1993 Upper Deck All-Time Heroes

This 165-card set of All-Time Heroes of Baseball is patterned after the T-202 Hassan Triple Folders cards, which first appeared in 1912. The cards measure approximately 2 1/4" by 5 1/4" and feature two side panels and a larger middle panel. The set consists of 130 regular cards and the Classic Combinations subset (131-165). The fronts feature candid or action photos of the featured player on the center panel, along with a portrait on one of the side panels and the B.A.T. (Baseball Assistance Team) logo on the other. The backs include player biographies and career highlights, as well as an explanation of the B.A.T. cause. The Classic Combinations subset have center panels that feature either artwork by Todd Reigle or a photograph of multiple greats. The side panels feature photos of two players. The backs include player biographies on the side panels, with the center panel detailing the association between the players. Cards from the ten-card T202 Reprints set were randomly inserted in 1993 Upper Deck All-Time Heroes of Baseball foil packs. The foil packs contained 12 cards per pack. Each card is holographically enhanced. The stated odds (on the box) of finding a T202 Reprint insert card were one in five packs. Reggie Jackson and Mickey Mantle were the spokespersons for this set and they are featured prominently on the front of the box. The grand prize for the set's mail-in contest was an actual, original set of T202 Hassan Triplefolders, which Upper Deck had purchased in the open hobby market expressly for the promotion.

	MINT	NRMT	EXC
COMPLETE SET (165)	20.00	9.00	2.50
COMMON CARD (1-165)	.10	.05	.01
☐ 1 Hank Aaron	1.50	.70	.19
☐ 2 Tommie Agee	.10	.05	.01
☐ 3 Bob Allison	.10	.05	.01
☐ 4 Matty Alou	.10	.05	.01
☐ 5 Sal Bando	.10	.05	.01
☐ 6 Hank Bauer	.10	.05	.01
☐ 7 Don Baylor	.15	.07	.02
☐ 8 Glenn Beckert	.10	.05	.01
☐ 9 Yogi Berra	.75	.35	.09
☐ 10 Buddy Biancalana	.10	.05	.01
☐ 11 Jack Billingham	.10	.05	.01
☐ 12 Joe Black	.15	.07	.02
☐ 13 Paul Blair	.10	.05	.01
☐ 14 Steve Blass	.10	.05	.01
☐ 15 Ray Boone	.10	.05	.01
☐ 16 Lou Boudreau	.20	.09	.03
☐ 17 Ken Brett	.10	.05	.01
☐ 18 Nellie Briles	.10	.05	.01
☐ 19 Bobby Brown	.15	.07	.02
☐ 20 Bill Buckner	.15	.07	.02
☐ 21 Don Buford	.10	.05	.01
☐ 22 Al Bumbry	.10	.05	.01
☐ 23 Lew Burdette	.15	.07	.02
☐ 24 Jeff Burroughs	.10	.05	.01
☐ 25 Johnny Callison	.10	.05	.01
☐ 26 Bert Campaneris	.10	.05	.01
☐ 27 Rico Carty	.10	.05	.01
☐ 28 Dave Cash	.10	.05	.01
☐ 29 Cesar Cedeno	.15	.07	.02
☐ 30 Frank Chance	.20	.09	.03
☐ 31 Joe Charboneau	.15	.07	.02
☐ 32 Ty Cobb	1.50	.70	.19
☐ 33 Jerry Coleman	.10	.05	.01
☐ 34 Cecil Cooper	.10	.05	.01
☐ 35 Frankie Crosetti	.10	.05	.01
☐ 36 Alvin Dark	.10	.05	.01
☐ 37 Tommy Davis	.10	.05	.01
☐ 38 Dizzy Dean	.30	.14	.04
☐ 39 Doug DeCinces	.10	.05	.01
☐ 40 Bucky Dent	.10	.05	.01
☐ 41 Larry Dierker	.10	.05	.01
☐ 42 Larry Doby	.15	.07	.02
☐ 43 Moe Drabowsky	.10	.05	.01
☐ 44 Dave Dravecky	.10	.05	.01
☐ 45 Del Ennis	.10	.05	.01
☐ 46 Carl Erskine	.15	.07	.02
☐ 47 Johnny Evers	.20	.09	.03
☐ 48 Elroy Face	.10	.05	.01
☐ 49 Rick Ferrell	.20	.09	.03
☐ 50 Mark Fidrych	.15	.07	.02
☐ 51 Curt Flood	.15	.07	.02
☐ 52 Whitey Ford	.60	.25	.07
☐ 53 George Foster	.15	.07	.02
☐ 54 Jimmie Foxx	.40	.18	.05
☐ 55 Jim Fregosi	.15	.07	.02
☐ 56 Phil Garner	.10	.05	.01
☐ 57 Ralph Garr	.10	.05	.01
☐ 58 Lou Gehrig	2.00	.90	.25
☐ 59 Bobby Grich	.15	.07	.02
☐ 60 Jerry Grote	.10	.05	.01
☐ 61 Harvey Haddix	.10	.05	.01
☐ 62 Toby Harrah	.10	.05	.01
☐ 63 Bud Harrelson	.15	.07	.02
☐ 64 Jim Hegan	.10	.05	.01
☐ 65 Gil Hodges	.25	.11	.03
☐ 66 Ken Holtzman	.10	.05	.01
☐ 67 Bob Horner	.10	.05	.01
☐ 68 Rogers Hornsby	.40	.18	.05
☐ 69 Carl Hubbell	.20	.09	.03
☐ 70 Ron Hunt	.10	.05	.01
☐ 71 Monte Irvin	.20	.09	.03
☐ 72 Reggie Jackson	.75	.35	.09
☐ 73 Larry Jansen	.10	.05	.01
☐ 74 Ferguson Jenkins	.20	.09	.03
☐ 75 Tommy John	.15	.07	.02
☐ 76 Cliff Johnson	.10	.05	.01
☐ 77 Davey Johnson	.15	.07	.02
☐ 78 Walter Johnson	.40	.18	.05
☐ 79 George Kell	.20	.09	.03
☐ 80 Don Kessinger	.10	.05	.01
☐ 81 Vern Law	.10	.05	.01
☐ 82 Dennis Leonard	.10	.05	.01
☐ 83 Johnny Logan	.10	.05	.01
☐ 84 Mickey Lolich	.15	.07	.02
☐ 85 Jim Lonborg	.10	.05	.01
☐ 86 Bill Madlock	.10	.05	.01
☐ 87 Mickey Mantle	3.00	1.35	.35
☐ 88 Billy Martin	.20	.09	.03
☐ 89 Christy Mathewson	.40	.18	.05
☐ 90 Lee May	.10	.05	.01
☐ 91 Willie Mays	1.50	.70	.19
☐ 92 Bill Mazeroski	.15	.07	.02
☐ 93 Gil McDougald	.15	.07	.02
☐ 94 Sam McDowell	.10	.05	.01
☐ 95 Minnie Minoso	.15	.07	.02
☐ 96 Johnny Mize	.20	.09	.03
☐ 97 Rick Monday	.10	.05	.01
☐ 98 Wally Moon	.10	.05	.01
☐ 99 Manny Mota	.10	.05	.01
☐ 100 Bobby Murcer	.10	.05	.01
☐ 101 Ron Necciai	.10	.05	.01
☐ 102 Al Oliver	.15	.07	.02
☐ 103 Mel Ott	.20	.09	.03
☐ 104 Mel Parnell	.10	.05	.01
☐ 105 Jimmy Piersall	.15	.07	.02
☐ 106 Johnny Podres	.10	.05	.01
☐ 107 Bobby Richardson	.15	.07	.02
☐ 108 Robin Roberts	.20	.09	.03
☐ 109 Al Rosen	.15	.07	.02
☐ 110 Babe Ruth	3.00	1.35	.35
☐ 111 Joe Sambito	.10	.05	.01
☐ 112 Manny Sanguillen	.10	.05	.01
☐ 113 Ron Santo	.15	.07	.02
☐ 114 Bill Skowron	.10	.05	.01
☐ 115 Enos Slaughter	.20	.09	.03
☐ 116 Warren Spahn	.20	.09	.03
☐ 117 Tris Speaker	.20	.09	.03

☐ 118 Frank Thomas	.10	.05	.01
☐ 119 Bobby Thomson	.15	.07	.02
☐ 120 Andre Thornton	.10	.05	.01
☐ 121 Marv Throneberry	.10	.05	.01
☐ 122 Luis Tiant	.15	.07	.02
☐ 123 Joe Tinker	.20	.09	.03
☐ 124 Honus Wagner	.40	.18	.05
☐ 125 Bill White	.15	.07	.02
☐ 126 Ted Williams	2.00	.90	.25
☐ 127 Earl Wilson	.10	.05	.01
☐ 128 Joe Wood	.15	.07	.02
☐ 129 Cy Young	.20	.09	.03
☐ 130 Richie Zisk	.10	.05	.01
☐ 131 Babe Ruth Lou Gehrig	1.50	.70	.19
☐ 132 Ted Williams Rogers Hornsby	.75	.35	.09
☐ 133 Lou Gehrig Babe Ruth	1.50	.70	.19
☐ 134 Babe Ruth Mickey Mantle	1.50	.70	.19
☐ 135 Mickey Mantle Reggie Jackson	1.00	.45	.12
☐ 136 Mel Ott Carl Hubbell	.15	.07	.02
☐ 137 Mickey Mantle Willie Mays	1.25	.55	.16
☐ 138 Cy Young Walter Johnson	.20	.09	.03
☐ 139 Honus Wagner Rogers Hornsby	.20	.09	.03
☐ 140 Mickey Mantle Whitey Ford	1.00	.45	.12
☐ 141 Mickey Mantle Billy Martin	1.00	.45	.12
☐ 142 Cy Young Walter Johnson	.20	.09	.03
☐ 143 Christy Mathewson Walter Johnson	.20	.09	.03
☐ 144 Warren Spahn Christy Mathewson	.20	.09	.03
☐ 145 Honus Wagner Ty Cobb	.75	.35	.09
☐ 146 Babe Ruth Ty Cobb	1.50	.70	.19
☐ 147 Joe Tinker Johnny Evers	.20	.09	.03
☐ 148 Johnny Evers Frank Chance	.20	.09	.03
☐ 149 Hank Aaron Babe Ruth	1.50	.70	.19
☐ 150 Willie Mays Hank Aaron	1.00	.45	.12
☐ 151 Babe Ruth Willie Mays	1.50	.70	.19
☐ 152 Babe Ruth Whitey Ford	1.00	.45	.12
☐ 153 Larry Doby Minnie Minoso	.10	.05	.01
☐ 154 Joe Black Monte Irvin	.15	.07	.02
☐ 155 Joe Wood Christy Mathewson	.15	.07	.02
☐ 156 Christy Mathewson Cy Young	.20	.09	.03
☐ 157 Cy Young Joe Wood	.15	.07	.02
☐ 158 Cy Young Whitey Ford	.15	.07	.02
☐ 159 Cy Young Ferguson Jenkins	.15	.07	.02
☐ 160 Ty Cobb Rogers Hornsby	.75	.35	.09
☐ 161 Tris Speaker Ted Williams	.75	.35	.09
☐ 162 Rogers Hornsby Ted Williams	.75	.35	.09
☐ 163 Willie Mays Monte Irvin	.60	.25	.07
☐ 164 Willie Mays Bobby Thomson	.60	.25	.07
☐ 165 Reggie Jackson Mickey Mantle	1.25	.55	.16

1993 Upper Deck T202 Reprints

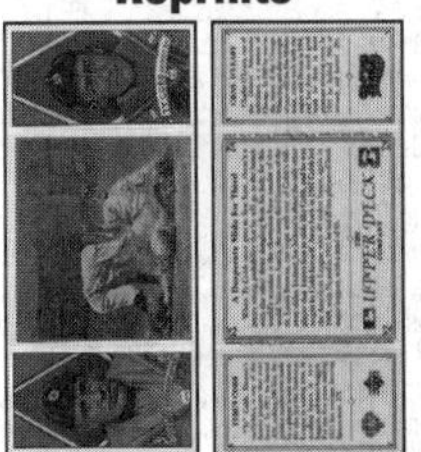

Randomly inserted in 1993 Upper Deck All-Time Heroes of Baseball foil packs, this ten-card set of reprints feature players from the 1912 Hassan "Triplefolders. The Hassan cigarette ads were replaced by the Upper Deck hologram and their designation of "T202" comes from their assignment in the American Card Catalog. The reprints are unnumbered and appear alphabetically

	MINT	NRMT	EXC
COMPLETE SET (10)	15.00	6.75	1.85
COMMON CARD (1-10)	1.00	.45	.12
☐ 1 Art Devlin Christy Mathewson	1.00	.45	.12
☐ 2 Hugh Jennings Ty Cobb	2.50	1.10	.30
☐ 3 John Kling Cy Young	1.00	.45	.12
☐ 4 Jack Knight Walter Johnson	1.00	.45	.12
☐ 5 John McGraw Hugh Jennings	1.50	.70	.19
☐ 6 George Moriarty Ty Cobb	2.00	.90	.25
☐ 7 Charles O'Leary Ty Cobb	2.00	.90	.25
☐ 8 Charles O'Leary Ty Cobb	2.00	.90	.25
☐ 9 Joe Tinker Frank Chance	2.50	1.10	.30
☐ 10 Joe Wood Tris Speaker	1.00	.45	.12

1993 Upper Deck Clark Reggie Jackson

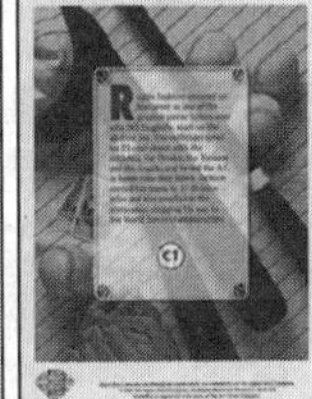

Issued to promote the reintroduction of the Reggie bar by the Clark Candy Co., these three standard-size cards highlight Jackson's career and feature on their fronts white-bordered color photos of Jackson as an Athletic and as a Yankee, with all team logos airbrushed out. Jackson's name and achievement appear in a bar at the bottom that shades from blue to black left to right. The Clark logo appears in the upper left and the Upper Deck logo rests in the lower right. Within a white rectangle superposed upon a photo of pintstripes, baseballs, bats, and a cap and glove, the white-bordered back recounts Jackson's achievement cited on the front. The Upper Deck hologram in the lower left rounds out the back. The cards are numbered on the back with a "C" prefix. One card was inserted in each Reggie bar and Jackson autographed 200 cards that were randomly inserted into the candy bar packages.

	MINT	NRMT	EXC
COMPLETE SET (3)	5.00	2.20	.60
COMMON CARD (C1-C3)	2.00	.90	.25
☐ C1 Reggie Jackson Inducted into HOF, 1993	2.00	.90	.25
☐ C2 Reggie Jackson Mr. October, 1977	2.00	.90	.25
☐ C3 Reggie Jackson AL MVP, 1973	2.00	.90	.25

1993 Upper Deck Diamond Gallery

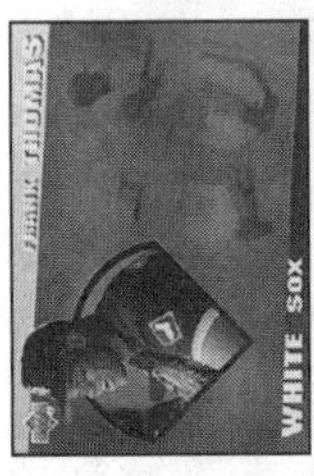

This 38-card standard-size boxed set features two player action photos on its horizontal fronts. One is a hologram, the other is a color action shot of the player, which is displayed on the left side projecting from a baseball diamond design. In the hologram, the player's uniform number appears behind him. The front is borderless on the sides and has oblique team-colored borders on the top and bottom, which contain the player's name and team, respectively. The back features another player action photo. This photo is borderless at the top, and ghosted in the oblique side borders and at the bottom of the photo, where the player's biography, stats and highlights appear. The cards are numbered on the back, with cards 29-31 belonging to the Gallery Heroes subset, and cards 32-36 belonging to the Diamonds in the Rough subset. Also included in the set are the checklist bearing the production number out of 123,600 sets produced, and a mail-away card for the Diamond Gallery card album.

	MINT	NRMT	EXC
COMPLETE SET (38)	18.00	8.00	2.20
COMMON CARD (1-36)	.15	.07	.02
☐ 1 Tim Salmon	.75	.35	.09
☐ 2 Jeff Bagwell	1.25	.55	.16
☐ 3 Mark McGwire	1.00	.45	.12
☐ 4 Roberto Alomar	.75	.35	.09
☐ 5 Terry Pendleton	.15	.07	.02
☐ 6 Robin Yount	.50	.23	.06
☐ 7 Ray Lankford	.30	.14	.04
☐ 8 Ryne Sandberg	1.00	.45	.12
☐ 9 Darryl Strawberry	.30	.14	.04
☐ 10 Marquis Grissom	.30	.14	.04
☐ 11 Barry Bonds	.75	.35	.09
☐ 12 Carlos Baerga	.15	.07	.02
☐ 13 Ken Griffey Jr.	3.00	1.35	.35
☐ 14 Benito Santiago	.15	.07	.02
☐ 15 Dwight Gooden	.30	.14	.04
☐ 16 Cal Ripken	3.00	1.35	.35
☐ 17 Tony Gwynn	1.50	.70	.19
☐ 18 Dave Hollins	.15	.07	.02
☐ 19 Andy Van Slyke	.15	.07	.02
☐ 20 Juan Gonzalez	1.50	.70	.19
☐ 21 Roger Clemens	.60	.25	.07
☐ 22 Barry Larkin	.50	.23	.06
☐ 23 David Nied	.15	.07	.02
☐ 24 George Brett	1.25	.55	.16
☐ 25 Travis Fryman	.30	.14	.04
☐ 26 Kirby Puckett	1.50	.70	.19
☐ 27 Frank Thomas	3.00	1.35	.35
☐ 28 Don Mattingly	1.50	.70	.19
☐ 29 Rickey Henderson	.50	.23	.06
☐ 30 Nolan Ryan	2.50	1.10	.30
☐ 31 Ozzie Smith	1.00	.45	.12
☐ 32 Wil Cordero	.15	.07	.02
☐ 33 Phil Hiatt	.15	.07	.02
☐ 34 Mike Piazza	3.00	1.35	.35
☐ 35 J.T. Snow	.40	.18	.05
☐ 36 Kevin Young	.15	.07	.02
☐ NNO Checklist Card	.15	.07	.02
☐ NNO Album Offer Card	.15	.07	.02

1993 Upper Deck Jackson Heroes Jumbo

This jumbo set (3 1/2" by 5") utilizes the same design as the 1990 standard-size high series inserts. It is currently uncertain whether the unnumbered header card was reproduced in jumbo form. The jumbos were issued in 1993 as a retail blister pack insert in a pack which included one pack of each 1993 Upper Deck series. These cards also include a 5th Anniversary Upper Deck logo and "1993 Hall of Fame inductee" on the front. Ten thousand of each card were issued.

	MINT	NRMT	EXC
COMPLETE SET (9)	20.00	9.00	2.50
COMMON REGGIE (1-9)	3.00	1.35	.35
☐ 1 Reggie Jackson 1969 Emerging Superstar	3.00	1.35	.35
☐ 2 Reggie Jackson 1973 An MVP Year	3.00	1.35	.35
☐ 3 Reggie Jackson 1977 Mr. October	3.00	1.35	.35
☐ 4 Reggie Jackson 1978 vs. Bob Welch	3.00	1.35	.35
☐ 5 Reggie Jackson 1982 Under the Halo	3.00	1.35	.35
☐ 6 Reggie Jackson 1984 500 Homers	3.00	1.35	.35
☐ 7 Reggie Jackson 1986 Moving Up the List	3.00	1.35	.35
☐ 8 Reggie Jackson 1987 A Great Career Ends	3.00	1.35	.35
☐ 9 Jackson Heroes art/CL	3.00	1.35	.35

1993 Upper Deck Sheets

The 29 commemorative sheets listed below in chronological order were issued by Upper Deck in 1993. The Upper Deck Heroes of Baseball made stops in MLB ballparks and sponsored old-timer baseball games preceding major league games. At each game a limited edition commemorative sheet was distributed. Commemorative sheets were produced in honor of other events. Days prior to the All-Star Game, sheets 16 and 17 were issued to fans who were at Camden Yards to watch the All-Star Workout. Sheet 19 was issued at the National in Chicago. Sheet 21 commemorates the World Children's Baseball Fair. And sheet 29 was handed out at by Upper Deck to collectors at various shows during the year. All the sheets measure 8 1/2" by 11" and most feature artist renderings of players from the teams recreated for the old-timers games. The front of each sheet carries the individual production number out of the total number produced, but otherwise the sheets are unnumbered.

	MINT	NRMT	EXC
COMPLETE SET (29)	175.00	80.00	22.00
COMMON SHEET (1-29)	2.00	.90	.25
☐ 1 Blue Jays Heroes vs. Upper Deck Heroes April 25, 1993 (53,600) SkyDome Bob Bailor Reggie Jackson Ferguson Jenkins Alan Ashby	7.00	3.10	.85
☐ 2 Atlanta Braves Heroes vs. Upper Deck Award Winners May 14, 1993 (44,100) Fulton County Coliseum Jeff Burroughs George Kell Gary Matthews Earl Williams Ralph Garr	7.00	3.10	.85
☐ 3 Upper Deck Heroes of Baseball vs. St. Louis Cardinals May 15, 1993 (51,600) Busch Stadium Art Shamsky Reggie Jackson Dick Williams Earl Weaver MG Ken Holtzman Bob Feller	7.00	3.10	.85
☐ 4 '69 Royals vs. '69 Twins May 22, 1993 (42,600) Royal Stadium Bob Oliver Ellie Rodriguez Moe Drabowsky Dick Drago Joe Keough	6.00	2.70	.75
☐ 5 Ewing M. Kauffman Induction into Royals Hall of Fame May 23, 1993 (42,600) Royal Stadium Ewing M. Kauffman	5.00	2.20	.60
☐ 6 Upper Deck Heroes vs. Red Sox Heroes May 29, 1993 (36,600) Fenway Park Minnie Minoso Ernie Banks Earl Wilson Carl Yastrzemski	8.00	3.60	1.00
☐ 7 Heroes of the '60s June 6, 1993 (31,600) Candlestick Park Jim Ray Hart Jim Davenport Tom Haller Juan Marichal Orlando Cepeda	7.00	3.10	.85
☐ 8 125 Years of Cincinnati Baseball June 6, 1993 (51,600) Riverfront Stadium Tommy Helms Bobby Tolan Brooks Lawrence Gordy Coleman	5.00	2.20	.60
☐ 9 Nickname Heroes Milwaukee County Stad. June 12, 1993 (31,600) County Stadium Bill Madlock Mark Fidrych Jerry Augustine John Montefusco Cecil Cooper	7.00	3.10	.85
☐ 10 20th Anniversary of the 1973 World Series June 12, 1993 (46,600) Shea Stadium Felix Millan Dick Williams MG Vida Blue Jerry Grote Wayne Garrett	7.00	3.10	.85
☐ 11 Colorado Rockies Inaugural Season June 19, 1993 (21,600) Mile High Stadium Roger Freed Johnny Blanchard Graig Nettles J.R. Richard	10.00	4.50	1.25
☐ 12 '83 Phillies vs. '83 Heroes June 19, 1993 (56,600) Veterans Stadium Mike Schmidt Gary Matthews John Denny Joe Morgan Al Holland	9.00	4.00	1.10
☐ 13 25 Years of Padres	7.00	3.10	.85

Baseball
June 25, 1993 (41,600)
Jack Murphy Stadium
Randy Jones
Dick Williams MG
Graig Nettles
Steve Garvey
Nate Colbert

	MINT	EXC	G-VG
□ 14 White Sox 1983	6.00	2.70	.75

Winning Ugly vs.
1983 Baltimore Orioles
July 4, 1993 (21,600)
Comiskey Park
Dick Tidrow
Floyd Bannister
Tom Paciorek
Richard Dotson
Julio Cruz

□ 15 All-Time Home Run	8.00	3.60	1.00

Hitters
July 4, 1993 (21,600)
Metrodome
Dick Allen
George Foster
Harmon Killebrew
Tony Oliva
Willie Horton

□ 16 1993 Upper Deck	2.00	.90	.25

All-Star FanFest
Autograph Sheet
July 8-13, 1993
(unnumbered)

□ 17 A Celebration of	8.00	3.60	1.00

Early Black Baseball
July 10, 1993 (50,000)
Camden Yards
Roy Campanella
Bill Wright
Andy Porter
Leon Day
Henry Kimbro
Luis Villodas
Buck Leonard
Verdell Mathis
Buck O'Neil
Ray Dandridge
Piper Davis
Ted Radcliffe

□ 18 Upper Deck	6.00	2.70	.75

Heroes of Baseball
All-Star Game
July 12, 1993 (unnumbered)
Camden Yards
Reggie Jackson
Brooks Robinson
Frank Robinson
Jim Palmer
Al Kaline

□ 19 The 1993 National	7.00	3.10	.85

Chicago
Upper Deck Five Year
Anniversary
July 20-25, 1993
(unnumbered)
Tim Salmon
Gary Sheffield
Nolan Ryan
Juan Gonzalez
Dave Justice
Ivan Rodriguez
Ken Griffey Jr.
Frank Thomas
Ken Griffey Jr.

□ 20 1978 Yankees	7.00	3.10	.85

22nd World Championship
July 24, 1993 (51,600)
Yankee Stadium
Thurman Munson
Mike Torrez
Reggie Jackson
Steve Garvey
Dennis Leonard

□ 21 World Children's	8.00	3.60	1.00

Baseball Fair
July 31, 1993 (61,000)
Jack Murphy Stadium
Randy Jones
Sachio Kinugasa
George Foster
Orlando Cepeda
Minnie Minoso
Bill Madlock
Sadaharu Oh

□ 22 Reggie Jackson	7.00	3.10	.85

Hall of Fame
Induction
Aug. 1, 1993 (51,600)
Anaheim Stadium
Reggie Jackson

□ 23 A Tribute to	6.00	2.70	.75

Billy Ball
Billy Martin
Aug. 15, 1993 (46,600)
Oakland-Alameda
County Stadium
Billy Martin

□ 24 25th Anniversary	10.00	4.50	1.25

of the 1968 World Series
August 22, 1993 (31,600)
Tiger Stadium
Curt Flood
Lou Brock
Mickey Lolich
Jim Northrup
Willie Horton

□ 25 The Expos' 25th	6.00	2.70	.75

Anniversary
August 28, 1993 (41,600)
Olympic Stadium
Warren Cromartie
Rusty Staub
Gene Mauch MG
Steve Rogers
Gary Carter

□ 26 Florida Marlins	8.00	3.60	1.00

Inaugural Season
September 25, 1993 (47,600)
Tony Perez
Minnie Minoso
Luis Tiant
Orlando Cepeda
Cookie Rojas

□ 27 Upper Deck Company	5.00	2.20	.60

Salutes the Heroes of
Arlington Stadium
October 2, 1993 (46,600)
Arlington Stadium

□ 28 Tribute to Cleveland	5.00	2.20	.60

Stadium
October 2, 1993 (76,600)
Cleveland Stadium
Andre Thornton
Mel Harder
Bob Feller
Lou Boudreau

□ 29 Upper Deck Heroes of	2.00	.90	.25

Baseball
Autograph Sheet
No date (21,600)

1994 Upper Deck

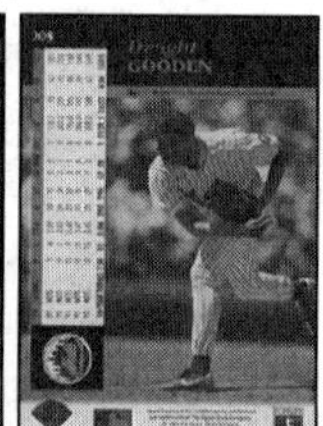

The 1994 Upper Deck set was issued in two series of 280 and 270 standard-size cards for a total of 550. Card fronts feature a color photo of the player with a smaller version of the same photo along the left-hand border. The player's name appears in a black box in the upper left-hand corner. There are number of topical subsets including Star Rookies (1-30), Fantasy Team (31-40), The Future is Now (41-55), Home Field Advantage (267-294), Upper Deck Classic Alumni (295-299), Diamond Debuts (511-522) and Top Prospects (523-550). Three autograph cards were randomly inserted into first series retail packs. They are Ken Griffey Jr. (KG), Mickey Mantle (MM) and a combo card with Griffey and Mantle (GM). An Alex Rodriguez (298A) autograph card was randomly inserted into second series retail packs. Rookie Cards include Alan Benes, Michael Jordan, Derrek Lee, Chan Ho Park, Alex Rodriguez and Billy Wagner. Many cards have been found with a significant variation on the back. The player's name, the horizontal bar containing the biographical information and the vertical bar containing the stats header are normally printed in copper-gold color. On the variation cards, these areas are printed in silver. It is not known exactly how many of the 550 cards have silver versions, nor has any premium been established for them. Also, all of the American League Home Field Advantage subset cards (#281-294) are minor uncorrected errors because the Upper Deck logos on the front are missing the year "1994".

	MINT	EXC	G-VG
COMPLETE SET (550)	50.00	22.00	6.25
COMPLETE SERIES 1 (280)	30.00	13.50	3.70
COMPLETE SERIES 2 (270)	20.00	9.00	2.50
COMMON CARD (1-550)	.10	.05	.01

□ 1 Brian Anderson	.25	.11	.03
□ 2 Shane Andrews	.25	.11	.03
□ 3 James Baldwin	.50	.23	.06
□ 4 Rich Becker	.25	.11	.03
□ 5 Greg Blosser	.10	.05	.01
□ 6 Ricky Bottalico	.50	.23	.06
□ 7 Midre Cummings	.10	.05	.01
□ 8 Carlos Delgado	.50	.23	.06
□ 9 Steve Dreyer	.10	.05	.01
□ 10 Joey Eischen	.10	.05	.01
□ 11 Carl Everett	.10	.05	.01
□ 12 Cliff Floyd UER (text indicates he throws left; should be right)	.50	.23	.06
□ 13 Alex Gonzalez	.25	.11	.03
□ 14 Jeff Granger	.25	.11	.03
□ 14 Jorge Fabregas	.10	.05	.01
□ 15 Shawn Green	.25	.11	.03
□ 16 Brian Hunter	.50	.23	.06
□ 17 Butch Huskey	.25	.11	.03
□ 18 Mark Hutton	.10	.05	.01
□ 19 Michael Jordan	10.00	4.50	1.25
□ 20 Steve Karsay	.10	.05	.01
□ 21 Jeff McNeely	.10	.05	.01
□ 22 Marc Newfield	.25	.11	.03
□ 23 Manny Ramirez	1.00	.45	.12
□ 24 Alex Rodriguez	10.00	4.50	1.25
□ 25 Scott Ruffcorn UER (photo on back is Robert Ellis)	.10	.05	.01
□ 26 Paul Spoljaric UER (Expos logo on back)	.10	.05	.01
□ 27 Salomon Torres	.10	.05	.01
□ 28 Steve Trachsel	.25	.11	.03
□ 29 Chris Turner	.10	.05	.01
□ 30 Gabe White	.10	.05	.01
□ 31 Randy Johnson FT	.50	.23	.06
□ 32 John Wetteland FT	.25	.11	.03
□ 33 Mike Piazza FT	1.00	.45	.12
□ 34 Rafael Palmeiro FT	.50	.23	.06
□ 35 Roberto Alomar FT	.50	.23	.06
□ 36 Matt Williams FT	.50	.23	.06
□ 37 Travis Fryman FT	.25	.11	.03
□ 38 Barry Bonds FT	.50	.23	.06
□ 39 Marquis Grissom FT	.25	.11	.03
□ 40 Albert Belle FT	.60	.25	.07
□ 41 Steve Avery FUT	.10	.05	.01
□ 42 Jason Bere FUT	.10	.05	.01
□ 43 Alex Fernandez FUT	.25	.11	.03
□ 44 Mike Mussina FUT	.50	.23	.06
□ 45 Aaron Sele FUT	.10	.05	.01
□ 46 Rod Beck FUT	.10	.05	.01
□ 47 Mike Piazza FUT	1.00	.45	.12
□ 48 John Olerud FUT	.10	.05	.01
□ 49 Carlos Baerga FUT	.25	.11	.03
□ 50 Gary Sheffield FUT	.50	.23	.06
□ 51 Travis Fryman FUT	.25	.11	.03
□ 52 Juan Gonzalez FUT	.75	.35	.09
□ 53 Ken Griffey Jr. FUT	1.50	.70	.19
□ 54 Tim Salmon FUT	.50	.23	.06
□ 55 Frank Thomas FUT	1.50	.70	.19
□ 56 Tony Phillips	.25	.11	.03
□ 57 Julio Franco	.25	.11	.03
□ 58 Kevin Mitchell	.25	.11	.03
□ 59 Raul Mondesi	.50	.23	.06
□ 60 Rickey Henderson	.50	.23	.06
□ 61 Jay Buhner	.50	.23	.06
□ 62 Bill Swift	.10	.05	.01
□ 63 Brady Anderson	.50	.23	.06
□ 64 Ryan Klesko	.60	.25	.07
□ 65 Darren Daulton	.25	.11	.03
□ 66 Damion Easley	.10	.05	.01
□ 67 Mark McGwire	1.00	.45	.12
□ 68 John Roper	.10	.05	.01
□ 69 Dave Telgheder	.10	.05	.01
□ 70 Dave Nied	.10	.05	.01
□ 71 Mo Vaughn	.75	.35	.09
□ 72 Tyler Green	.10	.05	.01
□ 73 Dave Magadan	.10	.05	.01
□ 74 Chili Davis	.25	.11	.03
□ 75 Archi Cianfrocco	.10	.05	.01
□ 76 Joe Girardi	.10	.05	.01
□ 77 Chris Hoiles	.10	.05	.01
□ 78 Ryan Bowen	.10	.05	.01
□ 79 Greg Gagne	.10	.05	.01
□ 80 Aaron Sele	.25	.11	.03
□ 81 Dave Winfield	.50	.23	.06
□ 82 Chad Curtis	.10	.05	.01
□ 83 Andy Van Slyke	.25	.11	.03
□ 84 Kevin Stocker	.10	.05	.01
□ 85 Deion Sanders	.50	.23	.06
□ 86 Bernie Williams	.60	.25	.07
□ 87 John Smoltz	.50	.23	.06
□ 88 Ruben Santana	.10	.05	.01
□ 89 Dave Stewart	.25	.11	.03
□ 90 Don Mattingly	1.50	.70	.19
□ 91 Joe Carter	.25	.11	.03
□ 92 Ryne Sandberg	.75	.35	.09
□ 93 Chris Gomez	.10	.05	.01
□ 94 Tino Martinez	.25	.11	.03
□ 95 Terry Pendleton	.25	.11	.03
□ 96 Andre Dawson	.25	.11	.03
□ 97 Wil Cordero	.25	.11	.03
□ 98 Kent Hrbek	.25	.11	.03
□ 99 John Olerud	.10	.05	.01
□ 100 Kirt Manwaring	.10	.05	.01
□ 101 Tim Bogar	.10	.05	.01
□ 102 Mike Mussina	.60	.25	.07
□ 103 Nigel Wilson	.10	.05	.01
□ 104 Ricky Gutierrez	.10	.05	.01
□ 105 Roberto Mejia	.10	.05	.01
□ 106 Tom Pagnozzi	.10	.05	.01
□ 107 Mike Macfarlane	.10	.05	.01
□ 108 Jose Bautista	.10	.05	.01
□ 109 Luis Ortiz	.10	.05	.01
□ 110 Brent Gates	.10	.05	.01
□ 111 Tim Salmon	.50	.23	.06
□ 112 Wade Boggs	.50	.23	.06
□ 113 Tripp Cromer	.10	.05	.01
□ 114 Denny Hocking	.10	.05	.01
□ 115 Carlos Baerga	.25	.11	.03
□ 116 J.R. Phillips	.10	.05	.01
□ 117 Bo Jackson	.25	.11	.03
□ 118 Lance Johnson	.25	.11	.03
□ 119 Bobby Jones	.25	.11	.03
□ 120 Bobby Witt	.10	.05	.01
□ 121 Ron Karkovice	.10	.05	.01
□ 122 Jose Vizcaino	.10	.05	.01
□ 123 Danny Darwin	.10	.05	.01
□ 124 Eduardo Perez	.10	.05	.01
□ 125 Brian Looney	.10	.05	.01
□ 125 Johnny Damon	.50	.23	.06
□ 126 Pat Hentgen	.25	.11	.03
□ 127 Frank Viola	.10	.05	.01
□ 128 Darren Holmes	.10	.05	.01
□ 129 Wally Whitehurst	.10	.05	.01
□ 130 Matt Walbeck	.10	.05	.01
□ 131 Albert Belle	1.25	.55	.16
□ 132 Steve Cooke	.10	.05	.01
□ 133 Kevin Appier	.25	.11	.03
□ 134 Joe Oliver	.10	.05	.01
□ 135 Benji Gil	.10	.05	.01
□ 136 Steve Buechele	.10	.05	.01
□ 137 Devon White	.10	.05	.01
□ 138 Sterling Hitchcock UER (two losses for career; should be four)	.25	.11	.03
□ 139 Phil Leftwich	.10	.05	.01
□ 140 Jose Canseco	.50	.23	.06
□ 141 Rick Aguilera	.10	.05	.01
□ 142 Rod Beck	.25	.11	.03
□ 143 Jose Rijo	.10	.05	.01
□ 144 Tom Glavine	.50	.23	.06
□ 145 Phil Plantier	.10	.05	.01
□ 146 Jason Bere	.25	.11	.03
□ 147 Jamie Moyer	.10	.05	.01
□ 148 Wes Chamberlain	.10	.05	.01
□ 149 Glenallen Hill	.10	.05	.01
□ 150 Mark Whiten	.10	.05	.01
□ 151 Bret Barberie	.10	.05	.01
□ 152 Chuck Knoblauch	.50	.23	.06
□ 153 Trevor Hoffman	.25	.11	.03
□ 154 Rick Wilkins	.10	.05	.01
□ 155 Juan Gonzalez	1.50	.70	.19
□ 156 Ozzie Guillen	.10	.05	.01
□ 157 Jim Eisenreich	.10	.05	.01
□ 158 Pedro Astacio	.10	.05	.01
□ 159 Joe Magrane	.10	.05	.01
□ 160 Ryan Thompson	.10	.05	.01
□ 161 Jose Lind	.10	.05	.01
□ 162 Jeff Conine	.25	.11	.03
□ 163 Todd Benzinger	.10	.05	.01
□ 164 Roger Salkeld	.10	.05	.01
□ 165 Gary DiSarcina	.10	.05	.01
□ 166 Kevin Gross	.10	.05	.01
□ 167 Charlie Hayes	.10	.05	.01
□ 168 Tim Costo	.10	.05	.01
□ 169 Wally Joyner	.25	.11	.03
□ 170 Johnny Ruffin	.10	.05	.01
□ 171 Kirk Rueter	.10	.05	.01
□ 172 Lenny Dykstra	.25	.11	.03
□ 173 Ken Hill	.10	.05	.01
□ 174 Mike Bordick	.10	.05	.01
□ 175 Billy Hall	.10	.05	.01
□ 176 Rob Butler	.10	.05	.01
□ 177 Jay Bell	.25	.11	.03
□ 178 Jeff Kent	.10	.05	.01
□ 179 David Wells	.10	.05	.01
□ 180 Dean Palmer	.25	.11	.03
□ 181 Mariano Duncan	.10	.05	.01
□ 182 Orlando Merced	.25	.11	.03
□ 183 Brett Butler	.25	.11	.03
□ 184 Milt Thompson	.10	.05	.01
□ 185 Chipper Jones	2.50	1.10	.30
□ 186 Paul O'Neill	.25	.11	.03
□ 187 Mike Greenwell	.10	.05	.01
□ 188 Harold Baines	.25	.11	.03
□ 189 Todd Stottlemyre	.10	.05	.01
□ 190 Jeromy Burnitz	.10	.05	.01
□ 191 Rene Arocha	.10	.05	.01
□ 192 Jeff Fassero	.10	.05	.01
□ 193 Robby Thompson	.10	.05	.01
□ 194 Greg W. Harris	.10	.05	.01
□ 195 Todd Van Poppel	.10	.05	.01
□ 196 Jose Guzman	.10	.05	.01
□ 197 Shane Mack	.10	.05	.01
□ 198 Carlos Garcia	.10	.05	.01
□ 199 Kevin Roberson	.10	.05	.01
□ 200 David McCarty	.10	.05	.01
□ 201 Alan Trammell	.25	.11	.03
□ 202 Chuck Carr	.10	.05	.01
□ 203 Tommy Greene	.10	.05	.01
□ 204 Wilson Alvarez	.25	.11	.03
□ 205 Dwight Gooden	.25	.11	.03
□ 206 Tony Tarasco	.10	.05	.01
□ 207 Darren Lewis	.10	.05	.01
□ 208 Eric Karros	.25	.11	.03
□ 209 Chris Hammond	.10	.05	.01
□ 210 Jeffrey Hammonds	.25	.11	.03
□ 211 Rich Amaral	.10	.05	.01
□ 212 Danny Tartabull	.10	.05	.01
□ 213 Jeff Russell	.10	.05	.01
□ 214 Dave Staton	.10	.05	.01
□ 215 Kenny Lofton	1.00	.45	.12
□ 216 Manuel Lee	.10	.05	.01
□ 217 Brian Koelling	.10	.05	.01
□ 218 Scott Lydy	.10	.05	.01

☐ 219 Tony Gwynn	1.25	.55	.16
☐ 220 Cecil Fielder	.25	.11	.03
☐ 221 Royce Clayton	.25	.11	.03
☐ 222 Reggie Sanders	.25	.11	.03
☐ 223 Brian Jordan	.50	.23	.06
☐ 224 Ken Griffey Jr.	3.00	1.35	.35
☐ 225 Fred McGriff	.50	.23	.06
☐ 226 Felix Jose	.10	.05	.01
☐ 227 Brad Pennington	.10	.05	.01
☐ 228 Chris Bosio	.10	.05	.01
☐ 229 Mike Stanley	.10	.05	.01
☐ 230 Willie Greene	.25	.11	.03
☐ 231 Alex Fernandez	.25	.11	.03
☐ 232 Brad Ausmus	.10	.05	.01
☐ 233 Darrell Whitmore	.10	.05	.01
☐ 234 Marcus Moore	.10	.05	.01
☐ 235 Allen Watson	.10	.05	.01
☐ 236 Jose Offerman	.10	.05	.01
☐ 237 Rondell White	.50	.23	.06
☐ 238 Jeff King	.25	.11	.03
☐ 239 Luis Alicea	.10	.05	.01
☐ 240 Dan Wilson	.25	.11	.03
☐ 241 Ed Sprague	.25	.11	.03
☐ 242 Todd Hundley	.25	.11	.03
☐ 243 Al Martin	.10	.05	.01
☐ 244 Mike Lansing	.25	.11	.03
☐ 245 Ivan Rodriguez	.75	.35	.09
☐ 246 Dave Fleming	.10	.05	.01
☐ 247 John Doherty	.10	.05	.01
☐ 248 Mark McLemore	.10	.05	.01
☐ 249 Bob Hamelin	.10	.05	.01
☐ 250 Curtis Pride	.25	.11	.03
☐ 251 Zane Smith	.10	.05	.01
☐ 252 Eric Young	.25	.11	.03
☐ 253 Brian McRae	.25	.11	.03
☐ 254 Tim Raines	.50	.23	.06
☐ 255 Javier Lopez	.50	.23	.06
☐ 256 Melvin Nieves	.25	.11	.03
☐ 257 Randy Myers	.10	.05	.01
☐ 258 Willie McGee	.10	.05	.01
☐ 259 Jimmy Key UER (birthdate missing on back)	.25	.11	.03
☐ 260 Tom Candiotti	.10	.05	.01
☐ 261 Eric Davis	.25	.11	.03
☐ 262 Craig Paquette	.10	.05	.01
☐ 263 Robin Ventura	.25	.11	.03
☐ 264 Pat Kelly	.10	.05	.01
☐ 265 Gregg Jefferies	.50	.23	.06
☐ 266 Cory Snyder	.10	.05	.01
☐ 267 David Justice HFA	.25	.11	.03
☐ 268 Sammy Sosa HFA	.50	.23	.06
☐ 269 Barry Larkin HFA	.50	.23	.06
☐ 270 Andres Galarraga HFA	.50	.23	.06
☐ 271 Gary Sheffield HFA	.50	.23	.06
☐ 272 Jeff Bagwell HFA	.60	.25	.07
☐ 273 Mike Piazza HFA	1.00	.45	.12
☐ 274 Larry Walker HFA	.50	.23	.06
☐ 275 Bobby Bonilla HFA	.25	.11	.03
☐ 276 John Kruk HFA	.10	.05	.01
☐ 277 Jay Bell HFA	.10	.05	.01
☐ 278 Ozzie Smith HFA	.50	.23	.06
☐ 279 Tony Gwynn HFA	.60	.25	.07
☐ 280 Barry Bonds HFA	.50	.23	.06
☐ 281 Cal Ripken Jr. HFA	1.25	.55	.16
☐ 282 Mo Vaughn HFA	.50	.23	.06
☐ 283 Tim Salmon HFA	.50	.23	.06
☐ 284 Frank Thomas HFA	1.50	.70	.19
☐ 285 Albert Belle HFA	.60	.25	.07
☐ 286 Cecil Fielder HFA	.25	.11	.03
☐ 287 Wally Joyner HFA	.10	.05	.01
☐ 288 Greg Vaughn HFA	.25	.11	.03
☐ 289 Kirby Puckett HFA	.50	.23	.06
☐ 290 Don Mattingly HFA	.75	.35	.09
☐ 291 Terry Steinbach HFA	.10	.05	.01
☐ 292 Ken Griffey Jr. HFA	1.50	.70	.19
☐ 293 Juan Gonzalez HFA	.75	.35	.09
☐ 294 Paul Molitor HFA	.50	.23	.06
☐ 295 Tavo Alvarez UDC	.10	.05	.01
☐ 296 Matt Brunson UDC	.25	.11	.03
☐ 297 Shawn Green UDC	.25	.11	.03
☐ 298 Alex Rodriguez UDC	4.00	1.80	.50
☐ 299 Shannon Stewart UDC	.25	.11	.03
☐ 300 Frank Thomas	3.00	1.35	.35
☐ 301 Mickey Tettleton	.10	.05	.01
☐ 302 Pedro Munoz	.10	.05	.01
☐ 303 Jose Valentin	.25	.11	.03
☐ 304 Orestes Destrade	.10	.05	.01
☐ 305 Pat Listach	.10	.05	.01
☐ 306 Scott Brosius	.10	.05	.01
☐ 307 Kurt Miller	.10	.05	.01
☐ 308 Rob Dibble	.10	.05	.01
☐ 309 Mike Blowers	.10	.05	.01
☐ 310 Jim Abbott	.10	.05	.01
☐ 311 Mike Jackson	.10	.05	.01
☐ 312 Craig Biggio	.25	.11	.03
☐ 313 Kurt Abbott	.25	.11	.03
☐ 314 Chuck Finley	.10	.05	.01
☐ 315 Andres Galarraga	.50	.23	.06
☐ 316 Mike Moore	.10	.05	.01
☐ 317 Doug Strange	.10	.05	.01
☐ 318 Pedro J. Martinez	.50	.23	.06
☐ 319 Kevin McReynolds	.10	.05	.01
☐ 320 Greg Maddux	2.00	.90	.25
☐ 321 Mike Henneman	.10	.05	.01
☐ 322 Scott Leius	.10	.05	.01
☐ 323 John Franco	.10	.05	.01
☐ 324 Jeff Blauser	.10	.05	.01
☐ 325 Kirby Puckett	1.25	.55	.16
☐ 326 Darryl Hamilton	.10	.05	.01
☐ 327 John Smiley	.10	.05	.01
☐ 328 Derrick May	.10	.05	.01
☐ 329 Jose Vizcaino	.10	.05	.01
☐ 330 Randy Johnson	.50	.23	.06
☐ 331 Jack Morris	.25	.11	.03
☐ 332 Graeme Lloyd	.10	.05	.01
☐ 333 Dave Valle	.10	.05	.01
☐ 334 Greg Myers	.10	.05	.01
☐ 335 John Wetteland	.25	.11	.03
☐ 336 Jim Gott	.10	.05	.01
☐ 337 Tim Naehring	.10	.05	.01
☐ 338 Mike Kelly	.10	.05	.01
☐ 339 Jeff Montgomery	.25	.11	.03
☐ 340 Rafael Palmeiro	.50	.23	.06
☐ 341 Eddie Murray	.50	.23	.06
☐ 342 Xavier Hernandez	.10	.05	.01
☐ 343 Bobby Munoz	.10	.05	.01
☐ 344 Bobby Bonilla	.25	.11	.03
☐ 345 Travis Fryman	.25	.11	.03
☐ 346 Steve Finley	.50	.23	.06
☐ 347 Chris Sabo	.10	.05	.01
☐ 348 Armando Reynoso	.10	.05	.01
☐ 349 Ramon Martinez	.25	.11	.03
☐ 350 Will Clark	.50	.23	.06
☐ 351 Moises Alou	.25	.11	.03
☐ 352 Jim Thome	.75	.35	.09
☐ 353 Bob Tewksbury	.10	.05	.01
☐ 354 Andujar Cedeno	.10	.05	.01
☐ 355 Orel Hershiser	.25	.11	.03
☐ 356 Mike Devereaux	.10	.05	.01
☐ 357 Mike Perez	.10	.05	.01
☐ 358 Dennis Martinez	.25	.11	.03
☐ 359 Dave Nilsson	.25	.11	.03
☐ 360 Ozzie Smith	.75	.35	.09
☐ 361 Eric Anthony	.10	.05	.01
☐ 362 Scott Sanders	.10	.05	.01
☐ 363 Paul Sorrento	.10	.05	.01
☐ 364 Tim Belcher	.10	.05	.01
☐ 365 Dennis Eckersley	.25	.11	.03
☐ 366 Mel Rojas	.10	.05	.01
☐ 367 Tom Henke	.10	.05	.01
☐ 368 Randy Tomlin	.10	.05	.01
☐ 369 B.J. Surhoff	.10	.05	.01

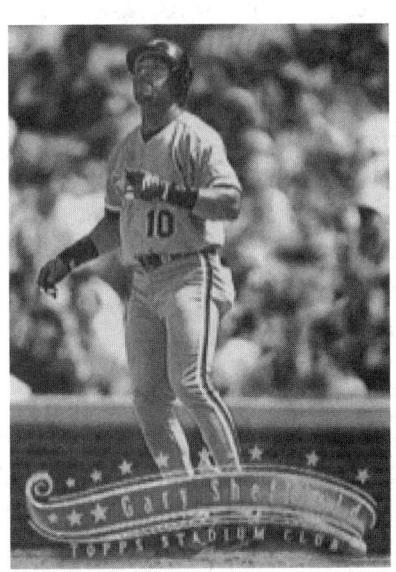

□ 370 Larry Walker	.50	.23	.06
□ 371 Joey Cora	.10	.05	.01
□ 372 Mike Harkey	.10	.05	.01
□ 373 John Valentin	.25	.11	.03
□ 374 Doug Jones	.10	.05	.01
□ 375 David Justice	.50	.23	.06
□ 376 Vince Coleman	.10	.05	.01
□ 377 David Hulse	.10	.05	.01
□ 378 Kevin Seitzer	.10	.05	.01
□ 379 Pete Harnisch	.10	.05	.01
□ 380 Ruben Sierra	.25	.11	.03
□ 381 Mark Lewis	.10	.05	.01
□ 382 Bip Roberts	.10	.05	.01
□ 383 Paul Wagner	.10	.05	.01
□ 384 Stan Javier	.10	.05	.01
□ 385 Barry Larkin	.50	.23	.06
□ 386 Mark Portugal	.10	.05	.01
□ 387 Roberto Kelly	.10	.05	.01
□ 388 Andy Benes	.25	.11	.03
□ 389 Felix Fermin	.10	.05	.01
□ 390 Marquis Grissom	.25	.11	.03
□ 391 Troy Neel	.10	.05	.01
□ 392 Chad Kreuter	.10	.05	.01
□ 393 Gregg Olson	.10	.05	.01
□ 394 Charles Nagy	.25	.11	.03
□ 395 Jack McDowell	.25	.11	.03
□ 396 Luis Gonzalez	.10	.05	.01
□ 397 Benito Santiago	.10	.05	.01
□ 398 Chris James	.10	.05	.01
□ 399 Terry Mulholland	.10	.05	.01
□ 400 Barry Bonds	.75	.35	.09
□ 401 Joe Grahe	.10	.05	.01
□ 402 Duane Ward	.10	.05	.01
□ 403 John Burkett	.10	.05	.01
□ 404 Scott Servais	.10	.05	.01
□ 405 Bryan Harvey	.10	.05	.01
□ 406 Bernard Gilkey	.25	.11	.03
□ 407 Greg McMichael	.10	.05	.01
□ 408 Tim Wallach	.10	.05	.01
□ 409 Ken Caminiti	.50	.23	.06
□ 410 John Kruk	.25	.11	.03
□ 411 Darrin Jackson	.10	.05	.01
□ 412 Mike Gallego	.10	.05	.01
□ 413 David Cone	.25	.11	.03
□ 414 Lou Whitaker	.25	.11	.03
□ 415 Sandy Alomar Jr.	.25	.11	.03
□ 416 Bill Wegman	.10	.05	.01
□ 417 Pat Borders	.10	.05	.01
□ 418 Roger Pavlik	.10	.05	.01
□ 419 Pete Smith	.10	.05	.01
□ 420 Steve Avery	.25	.11	.03
□ 421 David Segui	.10	.05	.01
□ 422 Rheal Cormier	.10	.05	.01
□ 423 Harold Reynolds	.10	.05	.01
□ 424 Edgar Martinez	.25	.11	.03
□ 425 Cal Ripken Jr.	2.50	1.10	.30
□ 426 Jaime Navarro	.10	.05	.01
□ 427 Sean Berry	.10	.05	.01
□ 428 Bret Saberhagen	.25	.11	.03
□ 429 Bob Welch	.10	.05	.01
□ 430 Juan Guzman	.25	.11	.03
□ 431 Cal Eldred	.10	.05	.01
□ 432 Dave Hollins	.10	.05	.01
□ 433 Sid Fernandez	.10	.05	.01
□ 434 Willie Banks	.10	.05	.01
□ 435 Darryl Kile	.10	.05	.01
□ 436 Henry Rodriguez	.25	.11	.03
□ 437 Tony Fernandez	.10	.05	.01
□ 438 Walt Weiss	.10	.05	.01
□ 439 Kevin Tapani	.10	.05	.01
□ 440 Mark Grace	.50	.23	.06
□ 441 Brian Harper	.10	.05	.01
□ 442 Kent Mercker	.10	.05	.01
□ 443 Anthony Young	.10	.05	.01
□ 444 Todd Zeile	.10	.05	.01
□ 445 Greg Vaughn	.50	.23	.06
□ 446 Ray Lankford	.25	.11	.03
□ 447 Dave Weathers	.10	.05	.01
□ 448 Bret Boone	.25	.11	.03
□ 449 Charlie Hough	.10	.05	.01
□ 450 Roger Clemens	.60	.25	.07
□ 451 Mike Morgan	.10	.05	.01
□ 452 Doug Drabek	.10	.05	.01
□ 453 Danny Jackson	.10	.05	.01
□ 454 Dante Bichette	.50	.23	.06
□ 455 Roberto Alomar	.60	.25	.07
□ 456 Ben McDonald	.10	.05	.01
□ 457 Kenny Rogers	.10	.05	.01
□ 458 Bill Gullickson	.10	.05	.01
□ 459 Darrin Fletcher	.10	.05	.01
□ 460 Curt Schilling	.10	.05	.01
□ 461 Billy Hatcher	.10	.05	.01
□ 462 Howard Johnson	.10	.05	.01
□ 463 Mickey Morandini	.10	.05	.01
□ 464 Frank Castillo	.10	.05	.01
□ 465 Delino DeShields	.10	.05	.01
□ 466 Gary Gaetti	.25	.11	.03
□ 467 Steve Farr	.10	.05	.01
□ 468 Roberto Hernandez	.25	.11	.03
□ 469 Jack Armstrong	.10	.05	.01
□ 470 Paul Molitor	.60	.25	.07
□ 471 Melido Perez	.10	.05	.01
□ 472 Greg Hibbard	.10	.05	.01
□ 473 Jody Reed	.10	.05	.01
□ 474 Tom Gordon	.10	.05	.01
□ 475 Gary Sheffield	.50	.23	.06
□ 476 John Jaha	.25	.11	.03
□ 477 Shawon Dunston	.10	.05	.01
□ 478 Reggie Jefferson	.25	.11	.03
□ 479 Don Slaught	.10	.05	.01
□ 480 Jeff Bagwell	1.25	.55	.16
□ 481 Tim Pugh	.10	.05	.01
□ 482 Kevin Young	.10	.05	.01
□ 483 Ellis Burks	.25	.11	.03
□ 484 Greg Swindell	.10	.05	.01
□ 485 Mark Langston	.25	.11	.03
□ 486 Omar Vizquel	.25	.11	.03
□ 487 Kevin Brown	.25	.11	.03
□ 488 Terry Steinbach	.25	.11	.03
□ 489 Mark Lemke	.10	.05	.01
□ 490 Matt Williams	.50	.23	.06
□ 491 Pete Incaviglia	.10	.05	.01
□ 492 Karl Rhodes	.10	.05	.01
□ 493 Shawn Green	.25	.11	.03
□ 494 Hal Morris	.10	.05	.01
□ 495 Derek Bell	.25	.11	.03
□ 496 Luis Polonia	.10	.05	.01
□ 497 Otis Nixon	.10	.05	.01
□ 498 Ron Darling	.10	.05	.01
□ 499 Mitch Williams	.10	.05	.01
□ 500 Mike Piazza	2.00	.90	.25
□ 501 Pat Meares	.10	.05	.01
□ 502 Scott Cooper	.10	.05	.01
□ 503 Scott Erickson	.10	.05	.01
□ 504 Jeff Juden	.10	.05	.01
□ 505 Lee Smith	.25	.11	.03
□ 506 Bobby Ayala	.10	.05	.01
□ 507 Dave Henderson	.10	.05	.01
□ 508 Erik Hanson	.10	.05	.01
□ 509 Bob Wickman	.10	.05	.01
□ 510 Sammy Sosa	.50	.23	.06
□ 511 Hector Carrasco DD	.10	.05	.01
□ 512 Tim Davis DD	.10	.05	.01
□ 513 Joey Hamilton DD	.60	.25	.07
□ 514 Robert Eenhoorn DD	.10	.05	.01
□ 515 Jorge Fabregas DD	.10	.05	.01
□ 516 Tim Hyers DD	.10	.05	.01
□ 517 John Hudek DD	.10	.05	.01
□ 518 James Mouton DD	.25	.11	.03
□ 519 Herbert Perry DD	.25	.11	.03
□ 520 Chan Ho Park DD	1.00	.45	.12
□ 521 W.Van Landingham DD	.25	.11	.03
□ 522 Paul Shuey DD	.10	.05	.01
□ 523 Ryan Hancock TP	.25	.11	.03
□ 524 Billy Wagner TP	1.00	.45	.12
□ 525 Jason Giambi	.75	.35	.09
□ 526 Jose Silva TP	.25	.11	.03
□ 527 Terrell Wade TP	.60	.25	.07
□ 528 Todd Dunn TP	.10	.05	.01
□ 529 Alan Benes TP	1.25	.55	.16
□ 530 Brooks Kieschnick TP	.60	.25	.07
□ 531 Todd Hollandsworth TP	.75	.35	.09
□ 532 Brad Fullmer TP	.75	.35	.09
□ 533 Steve Soderstrom TP	.25	.11	.03
□ 534 Daron Kirkreit TP	.25	.11	.03
□ 535 Arquimedez Pozo TP	.40	.18	.05
□ 536 Charles Johnson TP	.50	.23	.06
□ 537 Preston Wilson TP	.25	.11	.03
□ 538 Alex Ochoa TP	.25	.11	.03
□ 539 Derrek Lee TP	2.00	.90	.25
□ 540 Wayne Gomes TP	.25	.11	.03
□ 541 Jermaine Allensworth TP	.75	.35	.09
□ 542 Mike Bell TP	.60	.25	.07
□ 543 Trot Nixon TP	.50	.23	.06
□ 544 Pokey Reese TP	.25	.11	.03
□ 545 Neifi Perez TP	.75	.35	.09
□ 546 Johnny Damon TP	.50	.23	.06
□ 547 Matt Brunson TP	.25	.11	.03
□ 548 LaTroy Hawkins TP	.25	.11	.03
□ 549 Eddie Pearson TP	.50	.23	.06
□ 550 Derek Jeter TP	2.50	1.10	.30
□ A298 Alex Rodriguez AU	200.00	90.00	25.00
□ GM1 Ken Griffey Jr. AU Mickey Mantle AU/1000	1200.00	550.00	150.00
□ KG1 Ken Griffey Jr. AU1000	250.00	110.00	31.00
□ MM1 Mickey Mantle AU1000	600.00	275.00	75.00

1994 Upper Deck Electric Diamond

This 550-card set is a parallel issue to the basic 1994 Upper Deck cards. The cards were issued one per foil pack and two per mini jumbo. The only differences between these and the basic cards is the "Electric Diamond" in silver foil toward the bottom and the player's name is also in silver foil.

	MINT	NRMT	EXC
COMPLETE SET (550)	125.00	55.00	15.50
COMPLETE SERIES 1 (280)	80.00	36.00	10.00
COMPLETE SERIES 2 (270)	50.00	22.00	6.25
COMMON CARD (1-550)	.15	.07	.02

*STARS: 2X to 4X BASIC CARDS
*YOUNG STARS: 1.5X to 3X BASIC CARDS

1994 Upper Deck Diamond Collection

This 30-card standard-size set was inserted regionally in first series hobby packs at a rate of one in 18. The three regions are Central (C1-C10), East (E1-E10) and West (W1-W10). While each card has the same horizontal format, the color scheme differs by region. The Central cards have a blue background, the East green and the West a deep shade of red. Color player photos are superimposed over the backgrounds. Each card has, "The Upper Deck Diamond Collection" as part of the background. The backs have a small photo and career highlights.

	MINT	NRMT	EXC
COMPLETE SET (30)	325.00	145.00	40.00
COMPLETE CENTRAL (10)	150.00	70.00	19.00
COMPLETE EAST (10)	75.00	34.00	9.50
COMPLETE WEST (10)	100.00	45.00	12.50
COMMON CARD	2.50	1.10	.30
□ C1 Jeff Bagwell	15.00	6.75	1.85
□ C2 Michael Jordan	50.00	22.00	6.25
□ C3 Barry Larkin	5.00	2.20	.60
□ C4 Kirby Puckett	15.00	6.75	1.85
□ C5 Manny Ramirez	12.00	5.50	1.50
□ C6 Ryne Sandberg	10.00	4.50	1.25
□ C7 Ozzie Smith	10.00	4.50	1.25
□ C8 Frank Thomas	40.00	18.00	5.00
□ C9 Andy Van Slyke	2.50	1.10	.30
□ C10 Robin Yount	5.00	2.20	.60
□ E1 Roberto Alomar	6.00	2.70	.75
□ E2 Roger Clemens	6.00	2.70	.75
□ E3 Lenny Dykstra	3.00	1.35	.35
□ E4 Cecil Fielder	3.00	1.35	.35
□ E5 Cliff Floyd	2.50	1.10	.30
□ E6 Dwight Gooden	3.00	1.35	.35
□ E7 David Justice	3.00	1.35	.35
□ E8 Don Mattingly	15.00	6.75	1.85
□ E9 Cal Ripken Jr.	30.00	13.50	3.70
□ E10 Gary Sheffield	6.00	2.70	.75
□ W1 Barry Bonds	10.00	4.50	1.25
□ W2 Andres Galarraga	5.00	2.20	.60
□ W3 Juan Gonzalez	20.00	9.00	2.50
□ W4 Ken Griffey Jr.	40.00	18.00	5.00
□ W5 Tony Gwynn	15.00	6.75	1.85
□ W6 Rickey Henderson	5.00	2.20	.60
□ W7 Bo Jackson	2.50	1.10	.30
□ W8 Mark McGwire	12.00	5.50	1.50
□ W9 Mike Piazza	20.00	9.00	2.50
□ W10 Tim Salmon	6.00	2.70	.75

1994 Upper Deck Griffey Jumbos

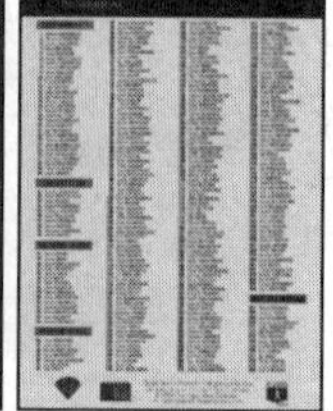

Measuring 4 7/8" by 6 13/16", these four Griffey cards serve as checklists for first series Upper Deck issues. They were issued one per first series hobby foil box. Card fronts have a full color photo with a small Griffey hologram. The first three cards provide a numerical, alphabetical and team organized checklist for the basic set. The fourth card is a checklist of inserts. Each card was printed in different quantities with CL1 the most plentiful and CL4 the more scarce. The backs are numbered with a CL prefix.

	MINT	NRMT	EXC
COMPLETE SET (4)	20.00	9.00	2.50
COMMON GRIFFEY (CL1-CL4)	4.00	1.80	.50
□ CL1 Numerical CL TP	4.00	1.80	.50
□ CL2 Alphabetical CL DP	5.00	2.20	.60
□ CL3 Team CL	6.00	2.70	.75
□ CL4 Insert CL SP	8.00	3.60	1.00

1994 Upper Deck Mantle Heroes

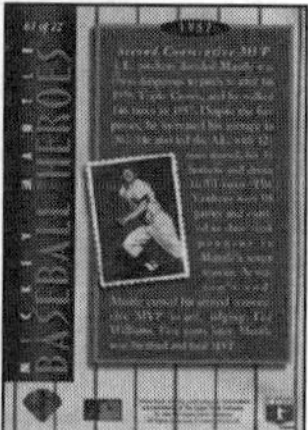

Randomly inserted in second series packs at a rate of one in 20, this 10-card standard-size set looks at various moments from The Mick's career. Metallic fronts feature a vintage photo with the card title at the bottom. The backs contain career highlights with a small scrapbook like photo. The numbering (64-72) is a continuation from previous Heroes sets.

	MINT	NRMT	EXC
COMPLETE SET (10)	100.00	45.00	12.50
COMMON MANTLE (64-72)	12.00	5.50	1.50
□ 64 Mickey Mantle 1951 The Early Years	12.00	5.50	1.50
□ 65 Mickey Mantle 1953 Tape-Measure Home Runs	12.00	5.50	1.50
□ 66 Mickey Mantle 1956 Triple Crown Season	12.00	5.50	1.50
□ 67 Mickey Mantle 1957 Second Consecutive MVP	12.00	5.50	1.50
□ 68 Mickey Mantle 1961 Chasing the Babe	12.00	5.50	1.50
□ 69 Mickey Mantle 1964 Series Home Run Record	12.00	5.50	1.50
□ 70 Mickey Mantle 1967 500th Home Run	12.00	5.50	1.50
□ 71 Mickey Mantle 1974 Hall of Fame	12.00	5.50	1.50
□ 72 Mickey Mantle Checklist	12.00	5.50	1.50
□ NNO0 Mickey Mantle Header Card	12.00	5.50	1.50

1994 Upper Deck Mantle's Long Shots

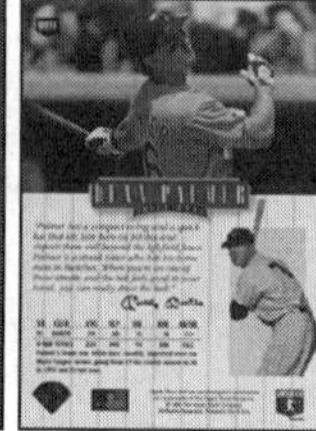

Randomly inserted in first series retail packs at a rate of one in 18, this 21-card silver foil standard-size set features top longball hitters as selected by Mickey Mantle. Card fronts are horizontal with a color player photo standing out from a dulled holographic image. The backs have a vertical format with a player photo at the top, a small photo of Mickey Mantle, a quote from The Mick and career power numbers. The cards are numbered on the back with a "MM" prefix and sequenced in alphabetical order. Two trade cards, were also random inserts and were redeemable (expiration: December 31, 1994) for either the basic silver foil set version (Silver Trade card) or the Electric Diamond version (blue Trade card).

	MINT	NRMT	EXC
COMPLETE SET (21)	50.00	22.00	6.25
COMMON CARD (MM1-MM21)	.50	.23	.06
□ MM1 Jeff Bagwell	4.00	1.80	.50
□ MM2 Albert Belle	4.00	1.80	.50
□ MM3 Barry Bonds	2.50	1.10	.30
□ MM4 Jose Canseco	1.25	.55	.16
□ MM5 Joe Carter	.75	.35	.09
□ MM6 Carlos Delgado	1.25	.55	.16
□ MM7 Cecil Fielder	.75	.35	.09
□ MM8 Cliff Floyd	.50	.23	.06
□ MM9 Juan Gonzalez	5.00	2.20	.60
□ MM10 Ken Griffey Jr.	10.00	4.50	1.25
□ MM11 David Justice	.75	.35	.09
□ MM12 Fred McGriff	1.25	.55	.16
□ MM13 Mark McGwire	3.00	1.35	.35
□ MM14 Dean Palmer	.75	.35	.09
□ MM15 Mike Piazza	6.00	2.70	.75
□ MM16 Manny Ramirez	3.00	1.35	.35
□ MM17 Tim Salmon	1.50	.70	.19
□ MM18 Frank Thomas	10.00	4.50	1.25
□ MM19 Mo Vaughn	2.50	1.10	.30
□ MM20 Matt Williams	1.25	.55	.16

	MINT	NRMT	EXC
☐ MM21 Mickey Mantle	15.00	6.75	1.85
☐ NNO M.Mantle Silver Trade	6.00	2.70	.75
☐ NNO M.Mantle Blue ED Trade	12.00	5.50	1.50

1994 Upper Deck Mantle's Long Shots Electric Diamond

This 21 card set was a parallel to the regular Mantle's Long Shots insert set. The only difference in these cards is that they have an "Electric Diamond" logo on the bottom.

	MINT	NRMT	EXC
COMPLETE SET (21)	60.00	27.00	7.50
COMMON CARD (MM1-MM21)	.60	.25	.07
*ELEC.DIAMOND: 6X TO 1.2X BASIC CARDS			

1994 Upper Deck Next Generation

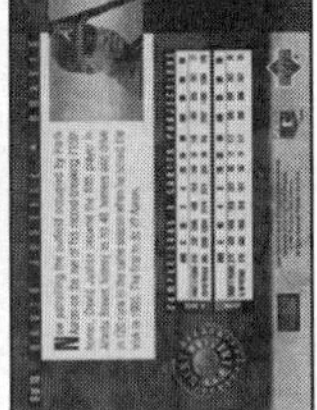

Randomly inserted in second series retail packs at a rate of one in 35, this 18-card standard-size set spotlights young established stars and promising prospects. The set is sequenced in alphabetical order. Metallic fronts feature a color player photo on solid background. A small player hologram is halfway up the card on the right and comes between the player's first and last name. The Next Generation logo is at bottom left. Horizontal backs contain statistical comparisons, where applicable, to Hall of Famers and brief write-up noting the comparisons. A Next Generation Electric Diamond Trade Card and a Next Generation Trade Card were randomly in second series hobby packs. Each card could be redeemed for that set. Expiration date for redemption was October 31, 1994.

	MINT	NRMT	EXC
COMPLETE SET (18)	140.00	65.00	17.50
COMMON CARD (1-18)	2.00	.90	.25
☐ 1 Roberto Alomar	6.00	2.70	.75
☐ 2 Carlos Delgado	4.00	1.80	.50
☐ 3 Cliff Floyd	2.00	.90	.25
☐ 4 Alex Gonzalez	2.00	.90	.25
☐ 5 Juan Gonzalez	12.00	5.50	1.50
☐ 6 Ken Griffey Jr.	30.00	13.50	3.70
☐ 7 Jeffrey Hammonds	2.00	.90	.25
☐ 8 Michael Jordan	40.00	18.00	5.00
☐ 9 David Justice	2.50	1.10	.30
☐ 10 Ryan Klesko	6.00	2.70	.75
☐ 11 Javier Lopez	4.00	1.80	.50
☐ 12 Raul Mondesi	5.00	2.20	.60
☐ 13 Mike Piazza	20.00	9.00	2.50
☐ 14 Kirby Puckett	12.00	5.50	1.50
☐ 15 Manny Ramirez	10.00	4.50	1.25
☐ 16 Alex Rodriguez	40.00	18.00	5.00
☐ 17 Tim Salmon	5.00	2.20	.60
☐ 18 Gary Sheffield	5.00	2.20	.60
☐ NNO Expired NG Trade Card	4.00	1.80	.50
☐ NNO Expired NG Trade Card	4.00	1.80	.50

1994 Upper Deck Next Generation Electric Diamond

This 18 card set parallels the regular Next Generation insert set. The cards are differentiated by an "Electric Diamond" logo on the bottom.

	MINT	NRMT	EXC
COMPLETE SET (18)	175.00	80.00	22.00
COMMON CARD (1-18)	2.50	1.10	.30
*ELEC.DIAMOND: .6X TO 1.2X BASIC CARDS			

1994 Upper Deck All-Star Jumbos

This 48-card boxed set captures the photography of Walter Iooss Jr. Iooss shot 42 of the 49 cards in the set. The set included an order form for an album. The cards are oversized, measuring 3 1/2" by 5 1/4". The full-bleed color player photos are edged on one side by a green stripe carrying the player's name. A special green foil All-Star logo appears in one of the lower corners. One set per 40-box case uses gold foil in place of green. The horizontal back has a thick black stripe carrying a small color photo and Iooss' comments on the left, with a career summary and another closeup photo on the remainder of the back. The set closes with six cards commemorating historic events during the 125-year history of baseball (43-48). Some dealers believe that gold production was limited to 1,200 sets.

	MINT	NRMT	EXC
COMPLETE SET (48)	18.00	8.00	2.20
COMMON CARD (1-48)	.10	.05	.01
*GOLD CARDS: 10X VALUE			
☐ 1 Ken Griffey Jr.	2.50	1.10	.30
☐ 2 Ruben Sierra	.10	.05	.01
Todd Van Poppel			
☐ 3 Bryan Harvey	.20	.09	.03
Gary Sheffield			
☐ 4 Gregg Jefferies	.20	.09	.03
Brian Jordan			
☐ 5 Ryne Sandberg	1.00	.45	.12
☐ 6 Matt Williams	.30	.14	.04
John Burkett			
☐ 7 Darren Daulton	.20	.09	.03
John Kruk			
☐ 8 Don Mattingly	1.25	.55	.16
Wade Boggs			
☐ 9 Pat Listach	.10	.05	.01
Greg Vaughn			
☐ 10 Tim Salmon	.40	.18	.05
Eduardo Perez			
☐ 11 Fred McGriff	.50	.23	.06
Tom Glavine			
☐ 12 Mo Vaughn	.60	.25	.07
Andre Dawson			
☐ 13 Brian McRae	.10	.05	.01
Kevin Appier			
☐ 14 Kirby Puckett	1.25	.55	.16
Kent Hrbek			
☐ 15 Cal Ripken	2.50	1.10	.30
☐ 16 Roberto Alomar	1.00	.45	.12
Paul Molitor			
☐ 17 Tony Gwynn	1.00	.45	.12
Phil Plantier			
☐ 18 Greg Maddux	2.00	.90	.25
Steve Avery			
☐ 19 Mike Mussina	.40	.18	.05
Chris Hoiles			
☐ 20 Randy Johnson	.60	.25	.07
☐ 21 Roger Clemens	.50	.23	.06
Aaron Sele			
☐ 22 Will Clark	.30	.14	.04
Dean Palmer			
☐ 23 Cecil Fielder	.20	.09	.03
Travis Fryman			
☐ 24 John Olerud	.20	.09	.03
Joe Carter			
☐ 25 Juan Gonzalez	1.25	.55	.16
☐ 26 Jose Rijo	.30	.14	.04
Barry Larkin			
☐ 27 Andy Van Slyke	.10	.05	.01
Jeff King			
☐ 28 Larry Walker	.50	.23	.06
Marquis Grissom			
☐ 29 Kenny Lofton	1.25	.55	.16
Albert Belle			
☐ 30 Mark Grace	.60	.25	.07
Sammy Sosa			
☐ 31 Mike Piazza	2.00	.90	.25
☐ 32 Ramon Martinez	.20	.09	.03
Pedro Martinez			
Orel Hershiser			
☐ 33 David Justice	.30	.14	.04
Terry Pendleton			
☐ 34 Ivan Rodriguez	.60	.25	.07
Jose Canseco			
☐ 35 Barry Bonds	.60	.25	.07
☐ 36 Jeff Bagwell	1.00	.45	.12
Craig Biggio			
☐ 37 Jay Bell	.10	.05	.01
Orlando Merced			
☐ 38 Jeff Kent	.10	.05	.01
Dwight Gooden			
☐ 39 Andres Galarraga	.30	.14	.04
Charlie Hayes			
☐ 40 Frank Thomas	2.50	1.10	.30
☐ 41 Bobby Bonilla	.20	.09	.03
☐ 42 Jack McDowell	.10	.05	.01
Tim Raines			
☐ 43 1869 Red Stockings	.10	.05	.01
☐ 44 Ty Cobb 25th Ann.	.60	.25	.07
☐ 45 Babe Ruth 50th Ann.	1.25	.55	.16
☐ 46 Mickey Mantle 75th Ann.	2.50	1.10	.30
☐ 47 Hank Aaron 100th Ann.	.60	.25	.07
☐ 48 Ken Griffey Jr. 125th Ann.	2.50	1.10	.30

1994 Upper Deck All-Time Heroes

This set consists of 225 standard-size cards. According to Upper Deck, production was limited to 4,015 numbered cases. Mantle and three other superstars (Reggie Jackson, Tom Seaver, and George Brett) each autographed 1,000 cards that were randomly inserted into

but did not. Instead, Brett signed an additional 1,000 cards). According to Upper Deck, a signed card would be found in one of every 385 packs. Also cards from the parallel and gold foil-highlighted version of the All-Time Heroes set were inserted at a rate on one card per pack. The fronts feature black-and-white player photos with black borders above and below. The player's name, team name, and position appear at the lower left. A second photo "pops out" of a baseball diamond icon at the lower right. The backs include a small player photo, biography, and statistics. Special subsets featured are Off The Wire (1-18), All-Time Heroes (101-125), Diamond Legends (151-177), and Heroes of Baseball (208-224).

	MINT	NRMT	EXC
COMPLETE SET (225)	12.00	5.50	1.50
COMMON CARD (1-225)	.05	.02	.01
☐ 1 Ted Williams	.50	.23	.06
☐ 2 Johnny Vander Meer	.05	.02	.01
☐ 3 Lou Brock	.10	.05	.01
☐ 4 Lou Gehrig	1.00	.45	.12
☐ 5 Hank Aaron	.25	.11	.03
☐ 6 Tommie Agee	.05	.02	.01
☐ 7 Mickey Mantle	.50	.23	.06
☐ 8 Bill Mazeroski	.10	.05	.01
☐ 9 Reggie Jackson	.20	.09	.03
☐ 10 Willie Mays	1.00	.45	.12
Mickey Mantle			
☐ 11 Roy Campanella	.12	.05	.01
☐ 12 Harvey Haddix	.05	.02	.01
☐ 13 Jimmy Piersall	.05	.02	.01
☐ 14 Enos Slaughter	.10	.05	.01
☐ 15 Nolan Ryan	.50	.23	.06
☐ 16 Bobby Thomson	.05	.02	.01
☐ 17 Willie Mays	.25	.11	.03
☐ 18 Bucky Dent	.05	.02	.01
☐ 19 Joe Garagiola	.10	.05	.01
☐ 20 George Brett	.50	.23	.06
☐ 21 Cecil Cooper	.05	.02	.01
☐ 22 Ray Boone	.05	.02	.01
☐ 23 King Kelly	.10	.05	.01
☐ 24 Willie Mays	.50	.23	.06
☐ 25 Napoleon Lajoie	.15	.07	.02
☐ 26 Gil McDougald	.05	.02	.01
☐ 27 Nelson Briles	.05	.02	.01
☐ 28 Bucky Dent	.05	.02	.01
☐ 29 Manny Sanguillen	.05	.02	.01
☐ 30 Ty Cobb	.50	.23	.06
☐ 31 Jim Grant	.05	.02	.01
☐ 32 Del Ennis	.05	.02	.01
☐ 33 Ron Hunt	.05	.02	.01
☐ 34 Nolan Ryan	1.00	.45	.12
☐ 35 Christy Mathewson	.15	.07	.02
☐ 36 Robin Roberts	.15	.07	.02
☐ 37 Frank Crosetti	.05	.02	.01
☐ 38 Johnny Vander Meer	.05	.02	.01
☐ 39 Virgil Trucks	.05	.02	.01
☐ 40 Lou Gehrig	1.00	.45	.12
☐ 41 Luke Appling	.10	.05	.01
☐ 42 Rico Petrocelli	.05	.02	.01
☐ 43 Harry Walker	.05	.02	.01
☐ 44 Reggie Jackson	.40	.18	.05
☐ 45 Mel Ott	.15	.07	.02
☐ 46 Phil Cavarretta	.05	.02	.01
☐ 47 Larry Doby	.10	.05	.01
☐ 48 Johnny Mize	.10	.05	.01
☐ 49 Ralph Kiner	.15	.07	.02
☐ 50 Ted Williams	1.00	.45	.12
☐ 51 Bobby Thomson	.10	.05	.01
☐ 52 Joe Black	.05	.02	.01
☐ 53 Monte Irvin	.10	.05	.01
☐ 54 Bill Virdon	.05	.02	.01
☐ 55 Honus Wagner	.15	.07	.02
☐ 56 Herb Score	.05	.02	.01
☐ 57 Jerry Coleman	.05	.02	.01
☐ 58 Jimmie Foxx	.10	.05	.01
☐ 59 Elroy Face	.05	.02	.01
☐ 60 Babe Ruth	1.00	.45	.12
☐ 61 Jimmy Piersall	.05	.02	.01
☐ 62 Ed Charles	.05	.02	.01
☐ 63 Johnny Podres	.05	.02	.01
☐ 64 Charlie Neal	.05	.02	.01
☐ 65 Bill White	.10	.05	.01
☐ 66 Bill Skowron	.05	.02	.01
☐ 67 Al Rosen	.05	.02	.01
☐ 68 Eddie Lopat	.05	.02	.01
☐ 69 Bud Harrelson	.05	.02	.01
☐ 70 Steve Carlton	.25	.11	.03
☐ 71 Vida Blue	.05	.02	.01
☐ 72 Don Newcombe	.05	.02	.01
☐ 73 Al Bumbry	.05	.02	.01
☐ 74 Bill Madlock	.05	.02	.01
☐ 75 Hank Aaron CL	.10	.05	.01
☐ 76 Bill Mazeroski	.10	.05	.01
☐ 77 Ron Cey	.05	.02	.01
☐ 78 Tommy John	.10	.05	.01
☐ 79 Lou Brock	.15	.07	.02
☐ 80 Walter Johnson	.15	.07	.02
☐ 81 Harvey Haddix	.05	.02	.01
☐ 82 Al Oliver	.05	.02	.01
☐ 83 Johnny Logan	.05	.02	.01
☐ 84 Dave Dravecky	.05	.02	.01
☐ 85 Tony Oliva	.10	.05	.01
☐ 86 Dave Kingman	.05	.02	.01
☐ 87 Luis Tiant	.05	.02	.01
☐ 88 Sal Bando	.05	.02	.01
☐ 89 Cesar Cedeno	.05	.02	.01
☐ 90 Warren Spahn	.15	.07	.02
☐ 91 Mickey Lolich	.05	.02	.01
☐ 92 Lew Burdette	.05	.02	.01
☐ 93 Hank Bauer	.05	.02	.01
☐ 94 Marv Throneberry	.05	.02	.01
☐ 95 Willie Stargell	.15	.07	.02
☐ 96 George Kell	.10	.05	.01
☐ 97 Ferguson Jenkins	.10	.05	.01
☐ 98 Al Kaline	.15	.07	.02
☐ 99 Billy Martin	.10	.05	.01
☐ 100 Mickey Mantle	1.00	.45	.12
☐ 101 1869 Red Stockings	.05	.02	.01
☐ 102 King Kelly	.10	.05	.01
☐ 103 Nap Lajoie	.10	.05	.01
☐ 104 Christy Mathewson	.10	.05	.01
☐ 105 Cy Young	.10	.05	.01
☐ 106 Ty Cobb	.25	.11	.03
☐ 107 Reggie Jackson CL	.10	.05	.01
☐ 108 Rogers Hornsby	.10	.05	.01
☐ 109 Walter Johnson	.10	.05	.01
☐ 110 Babe Ruth	.50	.23	.06
☐ 111 Hack Wilson	.10	.05	.01
☐ 112 Lou Gehrig	.50	.23	.06
☐ 113 Ted Williams	.50	.23	.06
☐ 114 Yogi Berra	.10	.05	.01
☐ 115 Bobby Thomson	.10	.05	.01
☐ 116 Mickey Mantle	.50	.23	.06
☐ 117 Willie Mays	.25	.11	.03
☐ 118 Bill Mazeroski	.10	.05	.01
☐ 119 Bob Gibson	.10	.05	.01
☐ 120 1969 Miracle Mets	.40	.18	.05
Nolan Ryan			
Tom Seaver			
Tommie Agee			
☐ 121 Hank Aaron	.25	.11	.03
☐ 122 Reggie Jackson	.20	.09	.03
☐ 123 George Brett	.25	.11	.03
☐ 124 Steve Carlton	.12	.05	.01
☐ 125 Nolan Ryan	.50	.23	.06
☐ 126 Frank Thomas	.05	.02	.01
☐ 127 Sam McDowell	.05	.02	.01
☐ 128 Jim Lonborg	.05	.02	.01
☐ 129 Bert Campaneris	.05	.02	.01
☐ 130 Bob Gibson	.15	.07	.02
☐ 131 Bobby Richardson	.10	.05	.01
☐ 132 Bobby Grich	.05	.02	.01
☐ 133 Billy Pierce	.05	.02	.01
☐ 134 Enos Slaughter	.10	.05	.01
☐ 135 Mickey Mantle CL	.25	.11	.03
☐ 136 Orlando Cepeda	.10	.05	.01
☐ 137 Rennie Stennett	.05	.02	.01
☐ 138 Gene Alley	.05	.02	.01
☐ 139 Manny Mota	.05	.02	.01
☐ 140 Rogers Hornsby	.20	.09	.03
☐ 141 Joe Charboneau	.05	.02	.01
☐ 142 Rick Ferrell	.10	.05	.01
☐ 143 Toby Harrah	.05	.02	.01
☐ 144 Hank Aaron	.50	.23	.06
☐ 145 Yogi Berra	.20	.09	.03
☐ 146 Whitey Ford	.20	.09	.03
☐ 147 Roy Campanella	.25	.11	.03
☐ 148 Graig Nettles	.10	.05	.01
☐ 149 Bobby Brown	.05	.02	.01
☐ 150 Willie Mays CL	.10	.05	.01
☐ 151 Cy Young	.10	.05	.01
☐ 152 Walter Johnson	.10	.05	.01
☐ 153 Christy Mathewson	.10	.05	.01
☐ 154 Warren Spahn	.10	.05	.01
☐ 155 Steve Carlton	.12	.05	.01
☐ 156 Bob Gibson	.10	.05	.01
☐ 157 Whitey Ford	.10	.05	.01
☐ 158 Yogi Berra	.10	.05	.01
☐ 159 Roy Campanella	.10	.05	.01
☐ 160 Lou Gehrig	.50	.23	.06
☐ 161 Johnny Mize	.10	.05	.01
☐ 162 Rogers Hornsby	.10	.05	.01
☐ 163 Honus Wagner	.10	.05	.01
☐ 164 Hank Aaron	.25	.11	.03
☐ 165 Babe Ruth	.50	.23	.06
☐ 166 Willie Mays	.25	.11	.03
☐ 167 Reggie Jackson	.20	.09	.03
☐ 168 Mickey Mantle	.50	.23	.06
☐ 169 Jimmie Foxx	.10	.05	.01
☐ 170 Ted Williams	.50	.23	.06
☐ 171 Mel Ott	.10	.05	.01
☐ 172 Willie Stargell	.10	.05	.01
☐ 173 Al Kaline	.10	.05	.01
☐ 174 Ty Cobb	.25	.11	.03
☐ 175 Napoleon Lajoie	.10	.05	.01
☐ 176 Lou Brock	.10	.05	.01
☐ 177 Tom Seaver	.12	.05	.01

☐ 178 Mark Fidrych	.10	.05	.01
☐ 179 Don Baylor	.05	.02	.01
☐ 180 Tom Seaver	.25	.11	.03
☐ 181 Jerry Grote	.05	.02	.01
☐ 182 George Foster	.05	.02	.01
☐ 183 Buddy Bell	.05	.02	.01
☐ 184 Ralph Garr	.05	.02	.01
☐ 185 Steve Garvey	.10	.05	.01
☐ 186 Joe Torre	.05	.02	.01
☐ 187 Carl Erskine	.05	.02	.01
☐ 188 Tommy Davis	.05	.02	.01
☐ 189 Bill Buckner	.05	.02	.01
☐ 190 Hack Wilson	.10	.05	.01
☐ 191 Steve Blass	.05	.02	.01
☐ 192 Ken Brett	.05	.02	.01
☐ 193 Lee May	.05	.02	.01
☐ 194 Bob Horner	.05	.02	.01
☐ 195 Boog Powell	.10	.05	.01
☐ 196 Darrell Evans	.05	.02	.01
☐ 197 Paul Blair	.05	.02	.01
☐ 198 Johnny Callison	.05	.02	.01
☐ 199 Jimmie Reese	.05	.02	.01
☐ 200 Cy Young	.15	.07	.02
☐ 201 Ron Santo	.10	.05	.01
☐ 202 Rico Carty	.05	.02	.01
☐ 203 Ron Necciai	.05	.02	.01
☐ 204 Lou Boudreau	.10	.05	.01
☐ 205 Minnie Minoso	.10	.05	.01
☐ 206 Eddie Yost	.05	.02	.01
☐ 207 Tommie Agee	.05	.02	.01
☐ 208 Dave Kingman	.05	.02	.01
☐ 209 Tony Oliva	.10	.05	.01
☐ 210 Reggie Jackson	.20	.09	.03
☐ 211 Paul Blair	.05	.02	.01
☐ 212 Ferguson Jenkins	.10	.05	.01
☐ 213 Steve Garvey	.10	.05	.01
☐ 214 Bert Campaneris	.05	.02	.01
☐ 215 Orlando Cepeda	.10	.05	.01
☐ 216 Bill Madlock	.05	.02	.01
☐ 217 Rennie Stennett	.05	.02	.01
☐ 218 Frank Thomas	.05	.02	.01
☐ 219 Bob Gibson	.10	.05	.01
☐ 220 Lou Brock	.10	.05	.01
☐ 221 Rico Carty	.05	.02	.01
☐ 222 Mickey Mantle	.50	.23	.06
☐ 223 Robin Roberts	.10	.05	.01
☐ 224 Manny Sanguillen	.05	.02	.01
☐ 225 Mickey Mantle CL	.50	.23	.06
☐ P44 Reggie Jackson Promo	3.00	1.35	.35
☐ AU1 George Brett (2,000)	125.00	55.00	15.50
☐ AU2 Reggie Jackson (1,000)	100.00	45.00	12.50
☐ AU3 Mickey Mantle (1,000)	325.00	145.00	40.00
☐ AU4 Tom Seaver (1,000)	75.00	34.00	9.50

1994 Upper Deck All-Time Heroes 125th

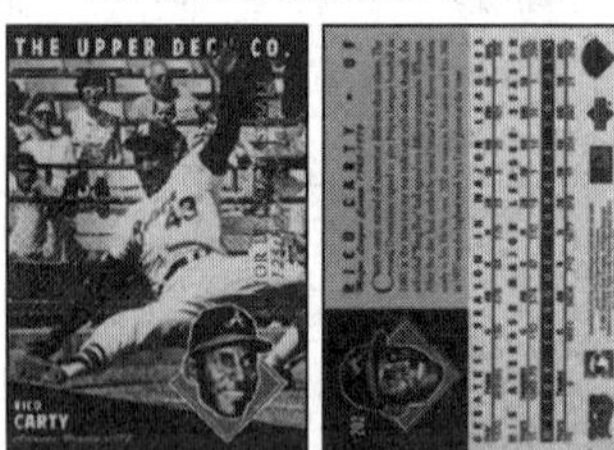

This 225-card standard-size set is identical to the regular issue 1994 Upper Deck All-Time Heroes of Baseball series, except that each card has on its front "Major League Baseball" and "125th Anniversary" stamped in bronze foil along the right edge. Every pack contained one 125th Anniversary gold card.

	MINT	NRMT	EXC
COMPLETE SET (225)	40.00	18.00	5.00
COMMON CARD (1-225)	.20	.09	.03
*STARS: 2X to 4X BASIC CARDS			

1994 Upper Deck All-Time Heroes 1954 Archives

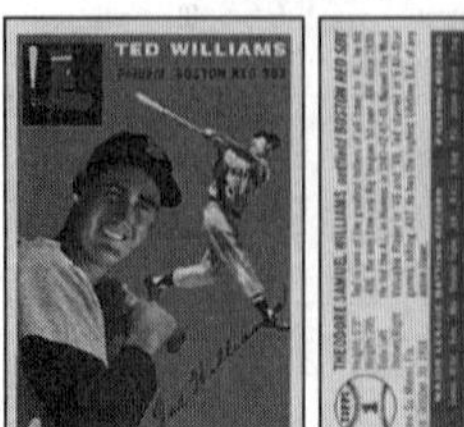

Measuring the standard-size, these three chase cards were randomly inserted in the foil packs at a ratio of one card per 30 ten-card foil packs. Cards #1 and #250 of Ted Williams, which are similar in design to the two that were originally issued by Topps in 1954, were not included in that company's 1954 Archives edition due to the terms of his contract with Upper Deck. Like Williams, Mickey Mantle had an exclusive agreement with Upper Deck that precluded his appearance in the 1954 Topps Archives set. Mantle didn't even appear in the original 1954 Topps set due to his then exclusive contract with Bowman. This "card that never was" is similar to the original 1954 set design.

	MINT	NRMT	EXC
COMPLETE SET (3)	70.00	32.00	8.75
COMMON CARD	20.00	9.00	2.50
☐ 1 Ted Williams	20.00	9.00	2.50
☐ 250 Ted Williams	20.00	9.00	2.50
☐ 259 Mickey Mantle	40.00	18.00	5.00

1994 Upper Deck All-Time Heroes Next In Line

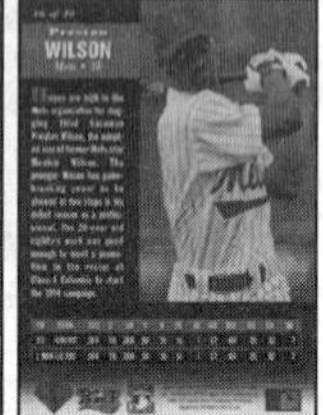

Capturing up and coming Minor League stars, this 20-card standard-size set was randomly inserted at a ratio of one in every 39 packs. Production was limited to 2,500 of each card. The fronts have a metallic finish with a color player cutout on the left, silhouetted by a blue-foil line. A black border on the right features the words "Next In Line," a color player headshot, and the player's name. The backs carry another color player photo, player information, and 1993 statistics. The cards are numbered on the back as "X of 20".

	MINT	NRMT	EXC
COMPLETE SET (20)	125.00	55.00	15.50
COMMON CARD (1-20)	3.00	1.35	.35
☐ 1 Mike Bell	7.00	3.10	.85
☐ 2 Alan Benes	10.00	4.50	1.25
☐ 3 D.J. Boston	3.00	1.35	.35
☐ 4 Johnny Damon	15.00	6.75	1.85
☐ 5 Brad Fullmer	3.00	1.35	.35
☐ 6 LaTroy Hawkins	3.00	1.35	.35
☐ 7 Derek Jeter	30.00	13.50	3.70
☐ 8 Daron Kirkreit	3.00	1.35	.35
☐ 9 Trot Nixon	5.00	2.20	.60
☐ 10 Alex Ochoa	10.00	4.50	1.25
☐ 11 Kirk Presley	3.00	1.35	.35
☐ 12 Jose Silva	3.00	1.35	.35
☐ 13 Terrell Wade	4.00	1.80	.50
☐ 14 Billy Wagner	5.00	2.20	.60
☐ 15 Glenn Williams	6.00	2.70	.75
☐ 16 Preston Wilson	4.00	1.80	.50
☐ 17 Wayne Gomes	3.00	1.35	.35
☐ 18 Ben Grieve	15.00	6.75	1.85
☐ 19 Dustin Hermanson	4.00	1.80	.50
☐ 20 Paul Wilson	8.00	3.60	1.00

1994 Upper Deck: The American Epic

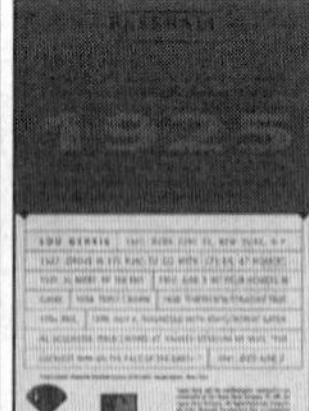

This 80-card boxed standard-size set recounts the story behind the PBS documentary "Baseball: The American Epic," produced by Ken Burns and sponsored by GM. The suggested retail price for the set, including the storage container, was 19.95. It was available from leading retail stores, the QVC television network, direct mail solicitation, and the Upper Deck Authenticated catalog. The fronts display full-bleed, color-tinted black-and-white player photos. The year celebrated and the player's name are printed in white lettering along the edges. The upper panel of the backs is either brown, purple, or green; the lower panel on all cards is white. The upper presents player profile while the lower records biography and career highlights. Like the documentary, the set is divided into "nine innings" and arranged chronologically as follows: 1st Inning (the 19th century [1-10]), 2nd Inning (the 1900s [11-20]), 3rd Inning (the 1910s [21-29]), 4th Inning (the 1920s [30-39]), 5th Inning (the 1930s [40-49]), 6th Inning (the 1940s [50-56]), 7th Inning (the 1950s [57-64]), 8th Inning (the 1960s [65-71]), and 9th Inning (1970-present [72-80]). Three insert cards were included with the set. A Michael Jordan card was available for direct mail customers, a Babe Ruth card for retail customers and a Mickey Mantle card for QVC customers. These cards are horizontal, full-bleed cards with black and white player photos. The backs are black and white with player information. The set price applies to either of the three versions and includes either of the three inserts.

	MINT	NRMT	EXC
COMPLETE SET (81)	15.00	6.75	1.85
COMMON CARD (1-80)	.05	.02	.01
☐ 1 Our Game 1800s	.05	.02	.01
☐ 2 Alexander Cartwright 1845	.10	.05	.01
☐ 3 Henry Chadwick 1857	.05	.02	.01
☐ 4 The Fair Sex 1866	.05	.02	.01
☐ 5 Harry Wright 1869	.05	.02	.01
☐ 6 Albert Goodwill Spalding 1876	.10	.05	.01
☐ 7 Cap Anson 1883	.15	.07	.02
☐ 8 Moses Fleetwood Walker 1884	.10	.05	.01
☐ 9 King Kelly 1886	.10	.05	.01
☐ 10 John Montgomery Ward 1890	.10	.05	.01
☐ 11 Ty Cobb 1909	1.00	.45	.12
☐ 12 John McGraw 1904	.15	.07	.02
☐ 13 Rube Waddell 1904	.10	.05	.01
☐ 14 Christy Mathewson 1905	.25	.11	.03
☐ 15 Walter Johnson 1907	.30	.14	.04
☐ 16 Alta Weiss 1908	.05	.02	.01
☐ 17 Fred Merkle 1908	.05	.02	.01
☐ 18 Take Me Out To The Ballgame	.05	.02	.01
☐ 19 John Henry(Pop) Lloyd 1909	.10	.05	.01
☐ 20 Honus Wagner 1909	.60	.25	.07
☐ 21 Woodrow Wilson 1915	.10	.05	.01
☐ 22 Nap Lajoie 1910	.10	.05	.01
☐ 23 Addie Joss 1911	.10	.05	.01
☐ 24 Joe Wood 1912	.05	.02	.01
☐ 25 Royal Rooters 1912	.05	.02	.01
☐ 26 Ebbets Field 1913	.05	.02	.01
☐ 27 Johnny Evers 1914	.10	.05	.01
☐ 28 World War I 1918	.05	.02	.01
☐ 29 Joe Jackson 1919	.75	.35	.09
☐ 30 Babe Ruth 1927	2.00	.90	.25
☐ 31 George(Rube) Foster 1920	.05	.02	.01
☐ 32 Ray Chapman 1920	.05	.02	.01
☐ 33 Kenesaw M. Landis 1921	.10	.05	.01
☐ 34 Yankee Stadium 1923	.05	.02	.01
☐ 35 Rogers Hornsby 1923	.30	.14	.04
☐ 36 Warren G. Harding 1924	.05	.02	.01
☐ 37 Lou Gehrig 1925	2.00	.90	.25
☐ 38 Grover C. Alexander 1926	.10	.05	.01
☐ 39 House of David 1929	.05	.02	.01
☐ 40 Satchel Paige 1933	.60	.25	.07
☐ 41 Lefty Grove 1931	.10	.05	.01
☐ 42 Jimmie Foxx 1932	.15	.07	.02
☐ 43 Connie Mack 1932	.15	.07	.02
☐ 44 Josh Gibson 1937	.25	.11	.03
☐ 45 Dizzy Dean 1934	.10	.05	.01
☐ 46 Carl Hubbell 1934	.10	.05	.01
☐ 47 Franklin D. Roosevelt 1937	.15	.07	.02
☐ 48 Bob Feller 1938	.10	.05	.01
☐ 49 Cool Papa Bell 1939	.10	.05	.01
☐ 50 Jackie Robinson 1947	1.50	.70	.19
☐ 51 Ted Williams 1941	2.00	.90	.25
☐ 52 Sym-phony Band 1941	.05	.02	.01
☐ 53 Annabel Lee 1944	.05	.02	.01
☐ 54 Hank Greenberg 1945	.10	.05	.01
☐ 55 Branch Rickey 1947	.10	.05	.01
☐ 56 Harry S. Truman 1948	.15	.07	.02
☐ 57 Casey Stengel 1953	.25	.11	.03
☐ 58 Bobby Thomson 1951	.10	.05	.01
☐ 59 Dwight D. Eisenhower 1952	.10	.05	.01
☐ 60 Mario Cuomo 1952	.10	.05	.01
☐ 61 Buck O'Neil 1945	.10	.05	.01
☐ 62 Yogi Berra 1955	.40	.18	.05
☐ 63 Mickey Mantle 1956	2.50	1.10	.30
☐ 64 Don Larsen 1956	.10	.05	.01
☐ 65 John F. Kennedy 1960	.75	.35	.09
☐ 66 Bill Mazeroski 1960	.10	.05	.01
☐ 67 Roger Maris 1961	.25	.11	.03
☐ 68 Frank Robinson 1966	.10	.05	.01
☐ 69 Bob Gibson 1968	.10	.05	.01
☐ 70 Tom Seaver 1969	.30	.14	.04
☐ 71 Curt Flood 1969	.05	.02	.01
☐ 72 Roberto Clemente 1972	1.50	.70	.19
☐ 73 Luis Tiant 1975	.05	.02	.01
☐ 74 Marvin Miller 1975	.05	.02	.01
☐ 75 Reggie Jackson 1977	.40	.18	.05
☐ 76 Willie(Pops) Stargell 1979	.10	.05	.01
☐ 77 Pete Rose 1985	.50	.23	.06
☐ 78 Bill Clinton 1988	.75	.35	.09
☐ 79 Nolan Ryan 1991	2.00	.90	.25
☐ 80 George Brett 1993	1.00	.45	.12
☐ BC1 Babe Ruth (Retail insert)	5.00	2.20	.60
☐ BC2 Michael Jordan (Direct mail insert)	5.00	2.20	.60
☐ BC3 Mickey Mantle (Home shopping insert)	5.00	2.20	.60

1994 Upper Deck: The American Epic GM

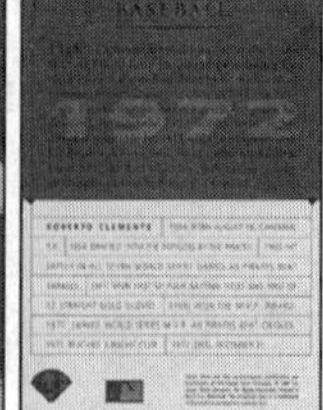

This 9-card set recounts part of the story behind the PBS documentary "Baseball: The American Epic," produced by Ken Burns and sponsored by GM. A GM Merchandise and Memorabilia Catalog was based on the American Epic series and available at GM dealers. The catalog included an offer for this 9-card set for 1.00. The fronts display full-bleed, color-tinted black-and-white player photos. The year celebrated and the player's name are printed in white lettering along the edges. The GM logo appears in the lower right corner. The upper panel of the backs is either brown, purple, or green; the lower panel on all cards is white. The upper presents player profile while the lower records biography and career highlights.

	MINT	NRMT	EXC
COMPLETE SET (9)	4.00	1.80	.50
COMMON CARD (1-9)	.10	.05	.01
☐ 1 Hank Aaron 1974	.50	.23	.06
☐ 2 Roberto Clemente	1.00	.45	.12

1972			
☐ 3 Ty Cobb	.50	.23	.06
1909			
☐ 4 Hank Greenberg	.10	.05	.01
1945			
☐ 5 Mickey Mantle	1.25	.55	.16
1956			
☐ 6 Satchel Paige	.25	.11	.03
1941			
☐ 7 Jackie Robinson	.75	.35	.09
1947			
☐ 8 Babe Ruth	1.25	.55	.16
1927			
☐ 9 Ted Williams	1.00	.45	.12
1941			

1994 Upper Deck: The American Epic Little Debbies

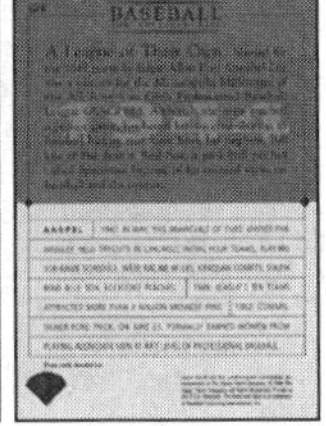

This 15-card set recounts part of the story behind the PBS documentary "Baseball: The American Epic," produced by Ken Burns. The cards could be ordered through an on-pack offer on Little Debbies cakes for 3.99. The fronts display full-bleed, color-tinted black-and-white player photos. The year celebrated and the player's name are printed in white lettering along the edges. The upper panel of the backs is either brown, purple, or green; the lower panel on all cards is white. The upper presents player profile while the lower records biography and career highlights. The Little Debbies logo appears on the bottom of the checklist card.

	MINT	NRMT	EXC
COMPLETE SET (15)	5.00	2.20	.60
COMMON CARD (LD1-LD15)	.10	.05	.01
☐ LD1 Our Game CL	.10	.05	.01
☐ LD2 Alexander Cartwright	.10	.05	.01
1845			
☐ LD3 King Kelly	.10	.05	.01
1886			
☐ LD4 John McGraw	.20	.09	.03
1904			
☐ LD5 Christy Mathewson	.20	.09	.03
1905			
☐ LD6 Walter Johnson	.40	.18	.05
1907			
☐ LD7 Ted Williams	1.50	.70	.19
1941			
☐ LD8 Annabel Lee	.10	.05	.01
1944			
☐ LD9 Jackie Robinson	1.00	.45	.12
1947			
☐ LD10 Bobby Thomson	.20	.09	.03
1951			
☐ LD11 Buck O'Neil	.20	.09	.03
1954			
☐ LD12 Mickey Mantle	1.50	.70	.19
1956			
☐ LD13 Bob Gibson	.40	.18	.05
1968			
☐ LD14 Curt Flood	.10	.05	.01
1969			
☐ LD15 Reggie Jackson	.60	.25	.07
1977			

1994 Upper Deck Mantle Phone Cards

Upper Deck in conjunction with Global Telecommunication Solutions produced this set of 10 phone cards to honor Mickey Mantle, the greatest switch-hitter in baseball history. The set was issued in two five-card sets: series 1 in early October, and series 2 later that year. Each five-card set retailed for $59.95. Chronicling his career from 1951 until his 1974 Hall of Fame Induction, the set is a replica of the "Baseball Heroes" insert cards featured in the 1994 Upper Deck baseball series 2. Just 5,000 sets of series 1 were produced, with each card including a bonus one-minute Mantle highlight replay moment. As an added bonus, 500 1869 Cincinnati Red Stockings phone cards were randomly inserted in series 1 sets, while Upper Deck distributed its allotment to the first 450 orders received from hobby dealers. Only 2,000 Red Stocking cards were produced. The fronts feature either black-and-white or color photos set on a pinstripe background. The white backs present instructions for the use of the phone card. The phone cards are unnumbered and checklisted below in chronological order.

	MINT	NRMT	EXC
COMPLETE SET (11)	70.00	32.00	8.75
COMMON CARD (1-10)	8.00	3.60	1.00
☐ 1 Mickey Mantle	8.00	3.60	1.00
Portrait Card			
☐ 2 Mickey Mantle	8.00	3.60	1.00
1951: The Early Years			
☐ 3 Mickey Mantle	8.00	3.60	1.00
1953: Tape-Measure Home Runs			
☐ 4 Mickey Mantle	8.00	3.60	1.00
1956: Triple Crown Season			
☐ 5 Mickey Mantle	8.00	3.60	1.00
1957: Second Consecutive MVP			
☐ 6 Mickey Mantle	8.00	3.60	1.00
1961: Chasing the Babe			
☐ 7 Mickey Mantle	8.00	3.60	1.00
1964: Series Home Run Record			
☐ 8 Mickey Mantle	8.00	3.60	1.00
1967: 500th Home Run			
☐ 9 Mickey Mantle	8.00	3.60	1.00
1974: Hall of Fame			
☐ 10 Mickey Mantle	8.00	3.60	1.00
(Color Portrait)			
☐ NNO 1869 Cincinnati Red Stockings	10.00	4.50	1.25

1994 Upper Deck Sheets

These six 8 1/2" by 11" sheets were produced by Upper Deck. They were issued to commemorate various special events sponsored by Upper Deck. We have listed the production quantities when known.

	MINT	NRMT	EXC
COMPLETE SET (6)	35.00	16.00	4.40
COMMON SHEET (1-6)	2.00	.90	.25
☐ 1 Tribute to the 1964 Season	8.00	3.60	1.00
June 4, 1994 (50,000)			
Lou Brock			
Dick Groat			
Bobby Richardson			
Bob Gibson			
☐ 2 Hollywood Softball Game	7.00	3.10	.85
June 26			
☐ 3 Heroes of Baseball	7.00	3.10	.85
All-Star Game			
July 11, 1994 (60,000)			
Bill Mazeroski			
Reggie Jackson			
Chuck Tanner			
Steve Garvey			
Willie Stargell			
☐ 4 25th Anniversary of the 1969 Season and the Miracle Mets	8.00	3.60	1.00
July 17			
☐ 5 All-Time Homerun Kings	8.00	3.60	1.00
July 23			
☐ 6 All Star Fanfest	2.00	.90	.25
Autograph Sheet			
Drawing of baseball field			

1994-96 Upper Deck Griffey Promos

Each year Upper Deck produces promo issues to preview various product lines. The featured player, Ken Griffey Jr., is a spokesman for Upper Deck. These cards are easily distinguished form their regular issue counterparts by the disclaimer "For Promotional Use Only" printed diagonally across them.

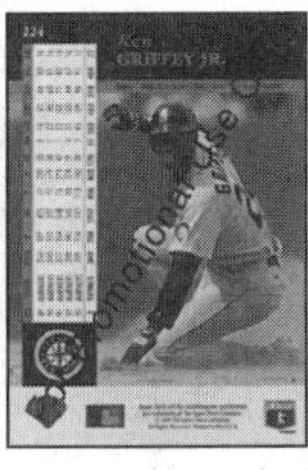

	MINT	NRMT	EXC
COMPLETE SET (10)	25.00	11.00	3.10
COMMON CARD	1.00	.45	.12
☐ 172 Ken Griffey Jr.	3.00	1.35	.35
1995 Collector's Choice			
☐ 50 Ken Griffey Jr.	1.00	.45	.12
1994 Collector's Choice			
☐ 24 Ken Griffey Jr.	3.00	1.35	.35
1994 Fun Pack			
☐ 224 Ken Griffey Jr.	3.00	1.35	.35
1994 Upper Deck			
☐ 48 Ken Griffey Jr.	5.00	2.20	.60
1994 UD All-Star Jumbo			
☐ 24 Ken Griffey Jr.	3.00	1.35	.35
1994 UD SP			
☐ 6 Ken Griffey Jr.	5.00	2.20	.60
1994 UD Top Ten			
☐ 125 Ken Griffey Jr.	3.00	1.35	.35
1995 Collector's Choice SE			
☐ 100 Ken Griffey Jr.	3.00	1.35	.35
1995 Upper Deck			
☐ 100 Ken Griffey Jr.	3.00	1.35	.35
1996 Collector's Choice			

1995 Upper Deck

The 1995 Upper Deck baseball set was issued in two series of 225 cards for a total of 450. The cards were distributed in 12-card packs (36 per box) with a suggested retail price of $1.99. The fronts display full-bleed color action photos, with the player's name in copper foil across the bottom. The backs carry another photo, biography, and season and career statistics. Subsets include Top Prospect (1-15, 251-265), 90's Midpoint (101-110), Star Rookie (211-240), and Diamond Debuts (241-250). Rookie Cards in this set include Karim Garcia and Hideo Nomo. Five randomly inserted Trade Cards were each redeemable for nine updated cards of new rookies or players who changed teams, comprising a 45-card Trade Redemption set. The Trade cards expired Feb 1, 1996. Autographed jumbo cards (Roger Clemens for series one, Alex Rodriguez for either series) were available through a wrapper redemption offer.

	MINT	NRMT	EXC
COMPLETE SET (450)	60.00	27.00	7.50
COMPLETE SERIES 1 (225)	30.00	13.50	3.70
COMPLETE SERIES 2 (225)	30.00	13.50	3.70
COMMON CARD (1-450)	.10	.05	.01
COMP.TRADE SET (45)	12.00	5.50	1.50
COMMON TRADE (451T-495T)	.25	.11	.03
☐ 1 Ruben Rivera	1.00	.45	.12
☐ 2 Bill Pulsipher	.25	.11	.03
☐ 3 Ben Grieve	1.50	.70	.19
☐ 4 Curtis Goodwin	.25	.11	.03
☐ 5 Damon Hollins	.25	.11	.03
☐ 6 Todd Greene	.25	.11	.03
☐ 7 Glenn Williams	.25	.11	.03
☐ 8 Bret Wagner	.25	.11	.03
☐ 9 Karim Garcia	3.00	1.35	.35
☐ 10 Nomar Garciaparra	2.00	.90	.25
☐ 11 Raul Casanova	.75	.35	.09
☐ 12 Matt Smith	.25	.11	.03
☐ 13 Paul Wilson	.50	.23	.06
☐ 14 Jason Isringhausen	.50	.23	.06
☐ 15 Reid Ryan	.50	.23	.06
☐ 16 Lee Smith	.25	.11	.03
☐ 17 Chili Davis	.25	.11	.03
☐ 18 Brian Anderson	.10	.05	.01
☐ 19 Gary DiSarcina	.10	.05	.01
☐ 20 Bo Jackson	.25	.11	.03
☐ 21 Chuck Finley	.25	.11	.03
☐ 22 Darryl Kile	.10	.05	.01
☐ 23 Shane Reynolds	.25	.11	.03
☐ 24 Tony Eusebio	.10	.05	.01
☐ 25 Craig Biggio	.25	.11	.03
☐ 26 Doug Drabek	.10	.05	.01
☐ 27 Brian L. Hunter	.25	.11	.03
☐ 28 James Mouton	.10	.05	.01
☐ 29 Geronimo Berroa	.10	.05	.01
☐ 30 Rickey Henderson	.50	.23	.06
☐ 31 Steve Karsay	.10	.05	.01
☐ 32 Steve Ontiveros	.10	.05	.01
☐ 33 Ernie Young	.25	.11	.03
☐ 34 Dennis Eckersley	.25	.11	.03
☐ 35 Mark McGwire	1.00	.45	.12
☐ 36 Dave Stewart	.25	.11	.03
☐ 37 Pat Hentgen	.25	.11	.03
☐ 38 Carlos Delgado	.25	.11	.03
☐ 39 Joe Carter	.25	.11	.03
☐ 40 Roberto Alomar	.60	.25	.07
☐ 41 John Olerud	.10	.05	.01
☐ 42 Devon White	.25	.11	.03
☐ 43 Roberto Kelly	.10	.05	.01
☐ 44 Jeff Blauser	.10	.05	.01
☐ 45 Fred McGriff	.50	.23	.06
☐ 46 Tom Glavine	.50	.23	.06
☐ 47 Mike Kelly	.10	.05	.01
☐ 48 Javier Lopez	.50	.23	.06
☐ 49 Greg Maddux	2.00	.90	.25
☐ 50 Matt Mieske	.25	.11	.03
☐ 51 Troy O'Leary	.10	.05	.01
☐ 52 Jeff Cirillo	.25	.11	.03
☐ 53 Cal Eldred	.10	.05	.01
☐ 54 Pat Listach	.10	.05	.01
☐ 55 Jose Valentin	.25	.11	.03
☐ 56 John Mabry	.50	.23	.06
☐ 57 Bob Tewksbury	.10	.05	.01
☐ 58 Brian Jordan	.50	.23	.06
☐ 59 Gregg Jefferies	.25	.11	.03
☐ 60 Ozzie Smith	.75	.35	.09
☐ 61 Geronimo Pena	.10	.05	.01
☐ 62 Mark Whiten	.10	.05	.01
☐ 63 Rey Sanchez	.10	.05	.01
☐ 64 Willie Banks	.10	.05	.01
☐ 65 Mark Grace	.50	.23	.06
☐ 66 Randy Myers	.10	.05	.01
☐ 67 Steve Trachsel	.10	.05	.01
☐ 68 Derrick May	.10	.05	.01
☐ 69 Brett Butler	.25	.11	.03
☐ 70 Eric Karros	.25	.11	.03
☐ 71 Tim Wallach	.10	.05	.01
☐ 72 Delino DeShields	.10	.05	.01
☐ 73 Darren Dreifort	.10	.05	.01
☐ 74 Orel Hershiser	.25	.11	.03
☐ 75 Billy Ashley	.10	.05	.01
☐ 76 Sean Berry	.10	.05	.01
☐ 77 Ken Hill	.10	.05	.01
☐ 78 John Wetteland	.25	.11	.03
☐ 79 Moises Alou	.25	.11	.03
☐ 80 Cliff Floyd	.25	.11	.03
☐ 81 Marquis Grissom	.25	.11	.03
☐ 82 Larry Walker	.50	.23	.06
☐ 83 Rondell White	.25	.11	.03
☐ 84 William VanLandingham	.10	.05	.01
☐ 85 Matt Williams	.50	.23	.06
☐ 86 Rod Beck	.10	.05	.01
☐ 87 Darren Lewis	.10	.05	.01
☐ 88 Robby Thompson	.10	.05	.01
☐ 89 Darryl Strawberry	.25	.11	.03
☐ 90 Kenny Lofton	.75	.35	.09
☐ 91 Charles Nagy	.25	.11	.03
☐ 92 Sandy Alomar Jr.	.10	.05	.01
☐ 93 Mark Clark	.10	.05	.01
☐ 94 Dennis Martinez	.25	.11	.03
☐ 95 Dave Winfield	.50	.23	.06
☐ 96 Jim Thome	.60	.25	.07
☐ 97 Manny Ramirez	.75	.35	.09
☐ 98 Goose Gossage	.25	.11	.03
☐ 99 Tino Martinez	.25	.11	.03
☐ 100 Ken Griffey Jr.	3.00	1.35	.35
☐ 101 Greg Maddux ANA	1.00	.45	.12
☐ 102 Randy Johnson ANA	.50	.23	.06
☐ 103 Barry Bonds ANA	.50	.23	.06
☐ 104 Juan Gonzalez ANA	.30	.14	.04
☐ 105 Frank Thomas ANA	1.50	.70	.19
☐ 106 Matt Williams ANA	.50	.23	.06
☐ 107 Paul Molitor ANA	.50	.23	.06
☐ 108 Fred McGriff ANA	.50	.23	.06
☐ 109 Carlos Baerga ANA	.25	.11	.03
☐ 110 Ken Griffey Jr. ANA	1.50	.70	.19
☐ 111 Reggie Jefferson	.25	.11	.03
☐ 112 Randy Johnson	.50	.23	.06
☐ 113 Marc Newfield	.25	.11	.03
☐ 114 Robb Nen	.10	.05	.01
☐ 115 Jeff Conine	.25	.11	.03
☐ 116 Kurt Abbott	.10	.05	.01
☐ 117 Charlie Hough	.10	.05	.01
☐ 118 Dave Weathers	.10	.05	.01
☐ 119 Juan Castillo	.10	.05	.01
☐ 120 Bret Saberhagen	.25	.11	.03
☐ 121 Rico Brogna	.10	.05	.01
☐ 122 John Franco	.10	.05	.01
☐ 123 Todd Hundley	.25	.11	.03
☐ 124 Jason Jacome	.10	.05	.01
☐ 125 Bobby Jones	.25	.11	.03
☐ 126 Bret Barberie	.10	.05	.01
☐ 127 Ben McDonald	.10	.05	.01
☐ 128 Harold Baines	.25	.11	.03
☐ 129 Jeffrey Hammonds	.25	.11	.03
☐ 130 Mike Mussina	.60	.25	.07
☐ 131 Chris Hoiles	.10	.05	.01
☐ 132 Brady Anderson	.50	.23	.06
☐ 133 Eddie Williams	.10	.05	.01
☐ 134 Andy Benes	.10	.05	.01
☐ 135 Tony Gwynn	1.25	.55	.16
☐ 136 Bip Roberts	.10	.05	.01
☐ 137 Joey Hamilton	.50	.23	.06
☐ 138 Luis Lopez	.10	.05	.01
☐ 139 Ray McDavid	.25	.11	.03
☐ 140 Lenny Dykstra	.25	.11	.03

□ 141 Mariano Duncan	.10	.05	.01
□ 142 Fernando Valenzuela	.25	.11	.03
□ 143 Bobby Munoz	.10	.05	.01
□ 144 Kevin Stocker	.10	.05	.01
□ 145 John Kruk	.25	.11	.03
□ 146 Jon Lieber	.10	.05	.01
□ 147 Zane Smith	.10	.05	.01
□ 148 Steve Cooke	.10	.05	.01
□ 149 Andy Van Slyke	.25	.11	.03
□ 150 Jay Bell	.25	.11	.03
□ 151 Carlos Garcia	.10	.05	.01
□ 152 John Dettmer	.10	.05	.01
□ 153 Darren Oliver	.50	.23	.06
□ 154 Dean Palmer	.25	.11	.03
□ 155 Otis Nixon	.10	.05	.01
□ 156 Rusty Greer	.50	.23	.06
□ 157 Rick Helling	.10	.05	.01
□ 158 Jose Canseco	.50	.23	.06
□ 159 Roger Clemens	.60	.25	.07
□ 160 Andre Dawson	.25	.11	.03
□ 161 Mo Vaughn	.75	.35	.09
□ 162 Aaron Sele	.25	.11	.03
□ 163 John Valentin	.25	.11	.03
□ 164 Brian R. Hunter	.10	.05	.01
□ 165 Bret Boone	.25	.11	.03
□ 166 Hector Carrasco	.10	.05	.01
□ 167 Pete Schourek	.25	.11	.03
□ 168 Willie Greene	.10	.05	.01
□ 169 Kevin Mitchell	.25	.11	.03
□ 170 Deion Sanders	.50	.23	.06
□ 171 John Roper	.10	.05	.01
□ 172 Charlie Hayes	.10	.05	.01
□ 173 David Nied	.10	.05	.01
□ 174 Ellis Burks	.25	.11	.03
□ 175 Dante Bichette	.50	.23	.06
□ 176 Marvin Freeman	.10	.05	.01
□ 177 Eric Young	.25	.11	.03
□ 178 David Cone	.25	.11	.03
□ 179 Greg Gagne	.10	.05	.01
□ 180 Bob Hamelin	.10	.05	.01
□ 181 Wally Joyner	.25	.11	.03
□ 182 Jeff Montgomery	.25	.11	.03
□ 183 Jose Lind	.10	.05	.01
□ 184 Chris Gomez	.10	.05	.01
□ 185 Travis Fryman	.25	.11	.03
□ 186 Kirk Gibson	.25	.11	.03
□ 187 Mike Moore	.10	.05	.01
□ 188 Lou Whitaker	.25	.11	.03
□ 189 Sean Bergman	.10	.05	.01
□ 190 Shane Mack	.10	.05	.01
□ 191 Rick Aguilera	.10	.05	.01
□ 192 Denny Hocking	.10	.05	.01
□ 193 Chuck Knoblauch	.50	.23	.06
□ 194 Kevin Tapani	.10	.05	.01
□ 195 Kent Hrbek	.25	.11	.03
□ 196 Ozzie Guillen	.10	.05	.01
□ 197 Wilson Alvarez	.25	.11	.03
□ 198 Tim Raines	.50	.23	.06
□ 199 Scott Ruffcorn	.10	.05	.01
□ 200 Michael Jordan	4.00	1.80	.50
□ 201 Robin Ventura	.25	.11	.03
□ 202 Jason Bere	.10	.05	.01
□ 203 Darrin Jackson	.10	.05	.01
□ 204 Russ Davis	.10	.05	.01
□ 205 Jimmy Key	.25	.11	.03
□ 206 Jack McDowell	.25	.11	.03
□ 207 Jim Abbott	.10	.05	.01
□ 208 Paul O'Neill	.25	.11	.03
□ 209 Bernie Williams	.60	.25	.07
□ 210 Don Mattingly	1.50	.70	.19
□ 211 Orlando Miller	.10	.05	.01
□ 212 Alex Gonzalez	.25	.11	.03
□ 213 Terrell Wade	.50	.23	.06
□ 214 Jose Oliva	.10	.05	.01
□ 215 Alex Rodriguez	4.00	1.80	.50
□ 216 Garret Anderson	.25	.11	.03
□ 217 Alan Benes	.50	.23	.06
□ 218 Armando Benitez	.10	.05	.01
□ 219 Dustin Hermanson	.25	.11	.03
□ 220 Charles Johnson	.25	.11	.03
□ 221 Julian Tavarez	.10	.05	.01
□ 222 Jason Giambi	.60	.25	.07
□ 223 LaTroy Hawkins	.10	.05	.01
□ 224 Todd Hollandsworth	.50	.23	.06
□ 225 Derek Jeter	2.00	.90	.25
□ 226 Hideo Nomo	3.00	1.35	.35
□ 227 Tony Clark	.75	.35	.09
□ 228 Roger Cedeno	.25	.11	.03
□ 229 Scott Stahoviak	.10	.05	.01
□ 230 Michael Tucker	.25	.11	.03
□ 231 Joe Rosselli	.10	.05	.01
□ 232 Antonio Osuna	.10	.05	.01
□ 233 Bobby Higginson	.75	.35	.09
□ 234 Mark Grudzielanek	.75	.35	.09
□ 235 Ray Durham	.25	.11	.03
□ 236 Frank Rodriguez	.25	.11	.03
□ 237 Quilvio Veras	.10	.05	.01
□ 238 Darren Bragg	.25	.11	.03
□ 239 Ugueth Urbina	.10	.05	.01
□ 240 Jason Bates	.10	.05	.01
□ 241 David Bell	.10	.05	.01
□ 242 Ron Villone	.10	.05	.01
□ 243 Joe Randa	.10	.05	.01
□ 244 Carlos Perez	.25	.11	.03
□ 245 Brad Clontz	.10	.05	.01
□ 246 Steve Rodriguez	.10	.05	.01
□ 247 Joe Vitiello	.10	.05	.01
□ 248 Ozzie Timmons	.10	.05	.01
□ 249 Rudy Pemberton	.10	.05	.01
□ 250 Marty Cordova	.50	.23	.06
□ 251 Tony Graffanino	.10	.05	.01
□ 252 Mark Johnson	.25	.11	.03
□ 253 Tomas Perez	.25	.11	.03
□ 254 Jimmy Hurst	.25	.11	.03
□ 255 Edgardo Alfonzo	.25	.11	.03
□ 256 Jose Malave	.10	.05	.01
□ 257 Brad Radke	.25	.11	.03
□ 258 Jon Nunnally	.25	.11	.03
□ 259 Dilson Torres	.10	.05	.01
□ 260 Esteban Loaiza	.10	.05	.01
□ 261 Freddy Garcia	.25	.11	.03
□ 262 Don Wengert	.10	.05	.01
□ 263 Robert Person	.10	.05	.01
□ 264 Tim Unroe	.25	.11	.03
□ 265 Juan Acevedo	.10	.05	.01
□ 266 Eduardo Perez	.10	.05	.01
□ 267 Tony Phillips	.25	.11	.03
□ 268 Jim Edmonds	.50	.23	.06
□ 269 Jorge Fabregas	.10	.05	.01
□ 270 Tim Salmon	.50	.23	.06
□ 271 Mark Langston	.10	.05	.01
□ 272 J.T. Snow	.25	.11	.03
□ 273 Phil Plantier	.10	.05	.01
□ 274 Derek Bell	.25	.11	.03
□ 275 Jeff Bagwell	1.25	.55	.16
□ 276 Luis Gonzalez	.10	.05	.01
□ 277 John Hudek	.10	.05	.01
□ 278 Todd Stottlemyre	.10	.05	.01
□ 279 Mark Acre	.10	.05	.01
□ 280 Ruben Sierra	.25	.11	.03
□ 281 Mike Bordick	.10	.05	.01
□ 282 Ron Darling	.10	.05	.01
□ 283 Brent Gates	.10	.05	.01
□ 284 Todd Van Poppel	.10	.05	.01
□ 285 Paul Molitor	.60	.25	.07
□ 286 Ed Sprague	.25	.11	.03
□ 287 Juan Guzman	.25	.11	.03
□ 288 David Cone	.25	.11	.03
□ 289 Shawn Green	.25	.11	.03
□ 290 Marquis Grissom	.25	.11	.03
□ 291 Kent Mercker	.10	.05	.01
□ 292 Steve Avery	.25	.11	.03
□ 293 Chipper Jones	2.00	.90	.25
□ 294 John Smoltz	.50	.23	.06
□ 295 David Justice	.50	.23	.06
□ 296 Ryan Klesko	.50	.23	.06
□ 297 Joe Oliver	.10	.05	.01
□ 298 Ricky Bones	.10	.05	.01
□ 299 John Jaha	.25	.11	.03
□ 300 Greg Vaughn	.25	.11	.03
□ 301 Dave Nilsson	.25	.11	.03
□ 302 Kevin Seitzer	.10	.05	.01
□ 303 Bernard Gilkey	.25	.11	.03
□ 304 Allen Battle	.10	.05	.01
□ 305 Ray Lankford	.25	.11	.03
□ 306 Tom Pagnozzi	.10	.05	.01
□ 307 Allen Watson	.10	.05	.01
□ 308 Danny Jackson	.10	.05	.01
□ 309 Ken Hill	.10	.05	.01
□ 310 Todd Zeile	.10	.05	.01
□ 311 Kevin Roberson	.10	.05	.01
□ 312 Steve Buechele	.10	.05	.01
□ 313 Rick Wilkins	.10	.05	.01
□ 314 Kevin Foster	.10	.05	.01
□ 315 Sammy Sosa	.50	.23	.06
□ 316 Howard Johnson	.10	.05	.01
□ 317 Greg Hansell	.10	.05	.01
□ 318 Pedro Astacio	.10	.05	.01
□ 319 Rafael Bournigal	.10	.05	.01
□ 320 Mike Piazza	2.00	.90	.25
□ 321 Ramon Martinez	.25	.11	.03
□ 322 Raul Mondesi	.50	.23	.06
□ 323 Ismael Valdes	.25	.11	.03
□ 324 Wil Cordero	.10	.05	.01
□ 325 Tony Tarasco	.10	.05	.01
□ 326 Roberto Kelly	.10	.05	.01
□ 327 Jeff Fassero	.10	.05	.01
□ 328 Mike Lansing	.10	.05	.01
□ 329 Pedro J. Martinez	.25	.11	.03
□ 330 Kirk Rueter	.10	.05	.01
□ 331 Glenallen Hill	.10	.05	.01
□ 332 Kirt Manwaring	.10	.05	.01
□ 333 Royce Clayton	.10	.05	.01
□ 334 J.R. Phillips	.10	.05	.01
□ 335 Barry Bonds	.75	.35	.09
□ 336 Mark Portugal	.10	.05	.01
□ 337 Terry Mulholland	.10	.05	.01
□ 338 Omar Vizquel	.25	.11	.03
□ 339 Carlos Baerga	.25	.11	.03
□ 340 Albert Belle	1.25	.55	.16
□ 341 Eddie Murray	.75	.35	.09
□ 342 Wayne Kirby	.10	.05	.01
□ 343 Chad Ogea	.10	.05	.01
□ 344 Tim Davis	.10	.05	.01
□ 345 Jay Buhner	.50	.23	.06
□ 346 Bobby Ayala	.10	.05	.01
□ 347 Mike Blowers	.10	.05	.01
□ 348 Dave Fleming	.10	.05	.01
□ 349 Edgar Martinez	.25	.11	.03
□ 350 Andre Dawson	.25	.11	.03
□ 351 Darrell Whitmore	.10	.05	.01
□ 352 Chuck Carr	.10	.05	.01
□ 353 John Burkett	.25	.11	.03
□ 354 Chris Hammond	.10	.05	.01
□ 355 Gary Sheffield	.50	.23	.06
□ 356 Pat Rapp	.10	.05	.01
□ 357 Greg Colbrunn	.10	.05	.01
□ 358 David Segui	.10	.05	.01
□ 359 Jeff Kent	.10	.05	.01
□ 360 Bobby Bonilla	.25	.11	.03
□ 361 Pete Harnisch	.10	.05	.01
□ 362 Ryan Thompson	.10	.05	.01
□ 363 Jose Vizcaino	.10	.05	.01
□ 364 Brett Butler	.25	.11	.03
□ 365 Cal Ripken Jr.	2.50	1.10	.30
□ 366 Rafael Palmeiro	.50	.23	.06
□ 367 Leo Gomez	.10	.05	.01
□ 368 Andy Van Slyke	.25	.11	.03
□ 369 Arthur Rhodes	.10	.05	.01
□ 370 Ken Caminiti	.50	.23	.06
□ 371 Steve Finley	.25	.11	.03
□ 372 Melvin Nieves	.25	.11	.03
□ 373 Andujar Cedeno	.10	.05	.01
□ 374 Trevor Hoffman	.25	.11	.03
□ 375 Fernando Valenzuela	.25	.11	.03
□ 376 Ricky Bottalico	.25	.11	.03
□ 377 Dave Hollins	.10	.05	.01
□ 378 Charlie Hayes	.10	.05	.01
□ 379 Tommy Greene	.10	.05	.01
□ 380 Darren Daulton	.25	.11	.03
□ 381 Curt Schilling	.10	.05	.01
□ 382 Midre Cummings	.10	.05	.01
□ 383 Al Martin	.25	.11	.03
□ 384 Jeff King	.25	.11	.03
□ 385 Orlando Merced	.10	.05	.01
□ 386 Denny Neagle	.25	.11	.03
□ 387 Don Slaught	.10	.05	.01
□ 388 Dave Clark	.10	.05	.01
□ 389 Kevin Gross	.10	.05	.01
□ 390 Will Clark	.50	.23	.06
□ 391 Ivan Rodriguez	.75	.35	.09
□ 392 Benji Gil	.10	.05	.01
□ 393 Jeff Frye	.10	.05	.01
□ 394 Kenny Rogers	.10	.05	.01
□ 395 Juan Gonzalez	1.50	.70	.19
□ 396 Mike Macfarlane	.10	.05	.01
□ 397 Lee Tinsley	.10	.05	.01
□ 398 Tim Naehring	.10	.05	.01
□ 399 Tim Vanegmond	.10	.05	.01
□ 400 Mike Greenwell	.10	.05	.01
□ 401 Ken Ryan	.10	.05	.01
□ 402 John Smiley	.10	.05	.01
□ 403 Tim Pugh	.10	.05	.01
□ 404 Reggie Sanders	.25	.11	.03
□ 405 Barry Larkin	.50	.23	.06
□ 406 Hal Morris	.10	.05	.01
□ 407 Jose Rijo	.10	.05	.01
□ 408 Lance Painter	.10	.05	.01
□ 409 Joe Girardi	.10	.05	.01
□ 410 Andres Galarraga	.50	.23	.06
□ 411 Mike Kingery	.10	.05	.01
□ 412 Roberto Mejia	.10	.05	.01
□ 413 Walt Weiss	.10	.05	.01
□ 414 Bill Swift	.10	.05	.01
□ 415 Larry Walker	.50	.23	.06
□ 416 Billy Brewer	.10	.05	.01
□ 417 Pat Borders	.10	.05	.01
□ 418 Tom Gordon	.10	.05	.01
□ 419 Kevin Appier	.25	.11	.03
□ 420 Gary Gaetti	.25	.11	.03
□ 421 Greg Gohr	.10	.05	.01
□ 422 Felipe Lira	.10	.05	.01
□ 423 John Doherty	.10	.05	.01
□ 424 Chad Curtis	.10	.05	.01
□ 425 Cecil Fielder	.25	.11	.03
□ 426 Alan Trammell	.25	.11	.03
□ 427 David McCarty	.10	.05	.01
□ 428 Scott Erickson	.10	.05	.01
□ 429 Pat Mahomes	.10	.05	.01
□ 430 Kirby Puckett	1.25	.55	.16
□ 431 Dave Stevens	.10	.05	.01
□ 432 Pedro Munoz	.10	.05	.01
□ 433 Chris Sabo	.10	.05	.01
□ 434 Alex Fernandez	.25	.11	.03
□ 435 Frank Thomas	3.00	1.35	.35
□ 436 Roberto Hernandez	.10	.05	.01
□ 437 Lance Johnson	.25	.11	.03
□ 438 Jim Abbott	.10	.05	.01
□ 439 John Wetteland	.25	.11	.03
□ 440 Melido Perez	.10	.05	.01
□ 441 Tony Fernandez	.10	.05	.01
□ 442 Pat Kelly	.10	.05	.01
□ 443 Mike Stanley	.10	.05	.01
□ 444 Danny Tartabull	.10	.05	.01
□ 445 Wade Boggs	.50	.23	.06
□ 446 Robin Yount	.50	.23	.06
□ 447 Ryne Sandberg	.60	.25	.07
□ 448 Nolan Ryan	2.50	1.10	.30
□ 449 George Brett	1.00	.45	.12
□ 450 Mike Schmidt	.60	.25	.07
□ 451T Jim Abbott TRADE	.50	.23	.06
□ 452T Danny Tartabull TRADE	.50	.23	.06
□ 453T Ariel Prieto TRADE	.25	.11	.03
□ 454T Scott Cooper TRADE	.10	.05	.01
□ 455T Tom Henke TRADE	.25	.11	.03
□ 456T Todd Zeile TRADE	.25	.11	.03
□ 457T Brian McRae TRADE	.25	.11	.03
□ 458T Luis Gonzalez TRADE	.25	.11	.03
□ 459T Julio Navarro TRADE	.10	.05	.01
□ 460T Todd Worrell TRADE	.25	.11	.03
□ 461T Roberto Kelly TRADE	.10	.05	.01
□ 462T Chad Fonville TRADE	.25	.11	.03
□ 463T Shane Andrews TRADE	.25	.11	.03
□ 464T David Segui TRADE	.25	.11	.03
□ 465T Deion Sanders TRADE	.50	.23	.06
□ 466T Orel Hershiser TRADE	.25	.11	.03
□ 467T Ken Hill TRADE	.25	.11	.03
□ 468T Andy Benes TRADE	.10	.05	.01
□ 469T Terry Pendleton TRADE	.25	.11	.03
□ 470T Bobby Bonilla TRADE	.25	.11	.03
□ 471T Scott Erickson TRADE	.10	.05	.01
□ 472T Kevin Brown TRADE	.25	.11	.03
□ 473T Glenn Dishman TRADE	.25	.11	.03
□ 474T Phil Plantier TRADE	.10	.05	.01
□ 475T Gregg Jefferies TRADE	.50	.23	.06
□ 476T Tyler Green TRADE	.10	.05	.01
□ 477T Heathcliff Slocumb TRADE	.25	.11	.03
□ 478T Mark Whiten TRADE	.25	.11	.03
□ 479T Mickey Tettleton TRADE	.25	.11	.03
□ 480T Tim Wakefield TRADE	.25	.11	.03
□ 481T Vaughn Eshelman TRADE	.10	.05	.01
□ 482T Rick Aguilera TRADE	.25	.11	.03
□ 483T Erik Hanson TRADE	.10	.05	.01
□ 484T Willie McGee TRADE	.25	.11	.03
□ 485T Troy O'Leary TRADE	.25	.11	.03
□ 486T Benito Santiago TRADE	.25	.11	.03
□ 487T Darren Lewis TRADE	.10	.05	.01
□ 488T Dave Burba TRADE	.10	.05	.01
□ 489T Ron Gant TRADE	.25	.11	.03
□ 490T Bret Saberhagen TRADE	.25	.11	.03
□ 491T Vinny Castilla TRADE	.25	.11	.03
□ 492T Frank Rodriguez TRADE	.25	.11	.03
□ 493T Andy Pettitte TRADE	6.00	2.70	.75
□ 494T Ruben Sierra TRADE	.25	.11	.03
□ 495T David Cone TRADE	.25	.11	.03
□ J159 R. Clemens Jumbo AU	25.00	11.00	3.10
□ J215 A. Rodriguez Jumbo AU	80.00	36.00	10.00
□ TC1 Orel Hershiser	1.00	.45	.12
□ TC2 Terry Pendleton	1.00	.45	.12
□ TC3 Benito Santiago	1.00	.45	.12
□ TC4 Kevin Brown	1.00	.45	.12
□ TC5 Gregg Jefferies	1.00	.45	.12

1995 Upper Deck Electric Diamond

This 450-card parallel set was inserted one per retail pack or two per mini-jumbo pack. These cards are distinguished from their regular issue counterparts in that they are printed on a heavier cardstock and use a special foil treatment.

	MINT	NRMT	EXC
COMPLETE SET (450)	110.00	50.00	14.00
COMPLETE SERIES 1 (225)	50.00	22.00	6.25
COMPLETE SERIES 2 (225)	60.00	27.00	7.50
COMMON CARD (1-450)	.15	.07	.02

*STARS: 2X to 4X BASIC CARDS
*YOUNG STARS: 1.5X to 3X BASIC CARDS

1995 Upper Deck Electric Diamond Gold

This 450-card parallel standard-size set was randomly inserted in retail and mini-jumbo packs. These cards are identical to the Electric Diamond series except for the special gold foil treatment.

	MINT	NRMT	EXC
COMPLETE SET (450)	1500.00	700.00	190.00
COMPLETE SERIES 1 (225)	700.00	325.00	90.00
COMPLETE SERIES 2 (225)	800.00	350.00	100.00
COMMON CARD (1-450)	4.00	1.80	.50

*STARS: 20X TO 40X BASIC CARDS
*YOUNG STARS: 12.5X TO 25X BASIC CARDS

1995 Upper Deck Autographs

Trade cards to redeem these autographed issues were randomly seeded into second series packs. The actual signed cards share the same front design as the basic issue 1995 Upper Deck cards. The cards are unnumbered on back and therefore we have sequenced them in alphabetical order.

	MINT	NRMT	EXC
COMPLETE SET (5)	200.00	90.00	25.00
COMMON CARD	30.00	13.50	3.70

☐ 1 Roger Clemens	30.00	13.50	3.70
☐ 2 Reggie Jackson	30.00	13.50	3.70
☐ 3 Willie Mays	80.00	36.00	10.00
☐ 4 Raul Mondesi	40.00	18.00	5.00
☐ 5 Frank Robinson	40.00	18.00	5.00

1995 Upper Deck Checklists

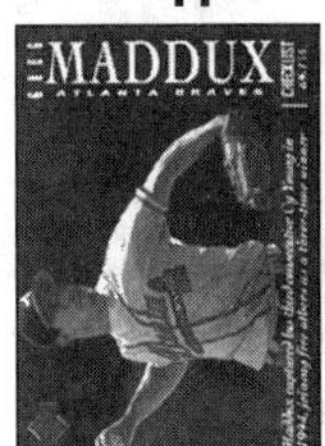
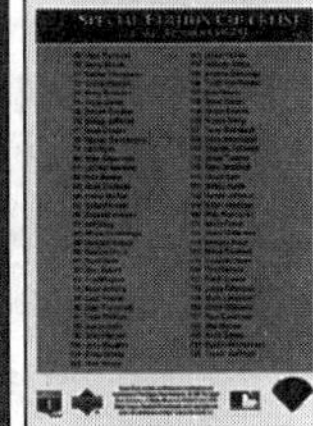

Each of these 10 cards features a star player(s) on the front and a checklist on the back. The cards were randomly inserted in hobby and retail packs at a rate of one in 17. The horizontal fronts feature a player photo along with a sentence about the 1994 highlight. The cards are numbered as "X" of 5 in the upper left.

	MINT	NRMT	EXC
COMPLETE SET (5)	25.00	11.00	3.10
COMPLETE SERIES 1 (5)	10.00	4.50	1.25
COMPLETE SERIES 2 (5)	15.00	6.75	1.85
COMMON CARD (1A-5A)	.75	.35	.09
COMMON CARD (1B-5B)	.75	.35	.09
☐ 1A Montreal Expos	.75	.35	.09
☐ 2A Fred McGriff	1.25	.55	.16
☐ 3A John Valentin	.75	.35	.09
☐ 4A Kenny Rogers	.75	.35	.09
☐ 5A Greg Maddux	6.00	2.70	.75
☐ 1B Cecil Fielder	1.00	.45	.12
☐ 2B Tony Gwynn	4.00	1.80	.50
☐ 3B Greg Maddux	6.00	2.70	.75
☐ 4B Randy Johnson	1.25	.55	.16
☐ 5B Mike Schmidt	2.50	1.10	.30

1995 Upper Deck Predictor Award Winners

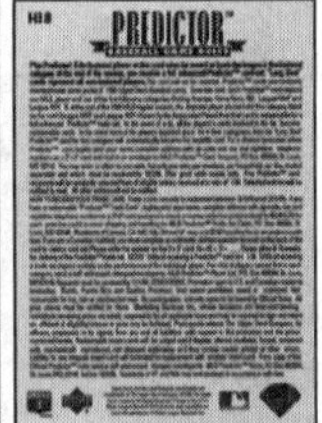

This set was inserted in hobby packs at a rate of approximately one in 30. This 40-card standard-size set features nine players and a Long Shot in each league for each of two categories -- MVP and Rookie of the Year. If the player pictured on the card won his category, the card was redeemable for a special foil version of all 20 Hobby Predictor cards. Fronts are full-color player action photos. Backs include the rules of the contest. These cards were redeemable until December 31, 1995. The cards are numbered in the upper left with an "H" prefix.

	MINT	NRMT	EXC
COMPLETE SET (40)	100.00	45.00	12.50
COMPLETE SERIES 1 (20)	60.00	27.00	7.50
COMPLETE SERIES 2 (20)	40.00	18.00	5.00
COMMON CARD (H1-H40)	1.00	.45	.12
*AW EXCHANGE CARDS: .25X PREDICTORS			
☐ H1 Albert Belle MVP	4.00	1.80	.50
☐ H2 Juan Gonzalez MVP	5.00	2.20	.60
☐ H3 Ken Griffey Jr. MVP	10.00	4.50	1.25
☐ H4 Kirby Puckett MVP	4.00	1.80	.50
☐ H5 Frank Thomas MVP	10.00	4.50	1.25
☐ H6 Jeff Bagwell MVP	4.00	1.80	.50
☐ H7 Barry Bonds MVP	2.50	1.10	.30
☐ H8 Mike Piazza MVP	6.00	2.70	.75
☐ H9 Matt Williams MVP	1.50	.70	.19
☐ H10 MVP Wild Card	1.00	.45	.12
☐ H11 Armando Benitez ROY	1.00	.45	.12
☐ H12 Alex Gonzalez ROY	1.25	.55	.16
☐ H13 Shawn Green ROY	1.25	.55	.16
☐ H14 Derek Jeter ROY	6.00	2.70	.75
☐ H15 Alex Rodriguez ROY	10.00	4.50	1.25
☐ H16 Alan Benes ROY	1.50	.70	.19
☐ H17 Brian L.Hunter ROY	1.25	.55	.16
☐ H18 Charles Johnson ROY	1.25	.55	.16
☐ H19 Jose Oliva ROY	1.00	.45	.12
☐ H20 ROY Wild Card	1.00	.45	.12
☐ H21 Cal Ripken MVP	8.00	3.60	1.00
☐ H22 Don Mattingly MVP	5.00	2.20	.60
☐ H23 Roberto Alomar MVP	2.00	.90	.25
☐ H24 Kenny Lofton MVP	2.50	1.10	.30
☐ H25 Will Clark MVP	1.50	.70	.19
☐ H26 Mark McGwire MVP	3.00	1.35	.35
☐ H27 Greg Maddux MVP	6.00	2.70	.75
☐ H28 Fred McGriff MVP	1.50	.70	.19
☐ H29 Andres Galarraga MVP	1.50	.70	.19
☐ H30 Jose Canseco MVP	1.50	.70	.19
☐ H31 Ray Durham ROY	1.25	.55	.16
☐ H32 Mark Grudzielanek ROY	1.25	.55	.16
☐ H33 Scott Ruffcorn ROY	1.00	.45	.12
☐ H34 Michael Tucker ROY	1.25	.55	.16
☐ H35 Garret Anderson ROY	1.25	.55	.16
☐ H36 Darren Bragg ROY	1.00	.45	.12
☐ H37 Quilvio Veras ROY	1.00	.45	.12
☐ H38 Hideo Nomo ROY W	5.00	2.20	.60
☐ H39 Chipper Jones ROY	6.00	2.70	.75
☐ H40 Marty Cordova ROY W	1.50	.70	.19

1995 Upper Deck Predictor League Leaders

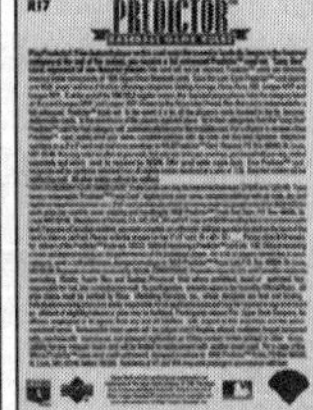

This 60-card standard-size insert set was available only in retail packs. The set included nine players and a Long Shot in each league for each of three categories -- Batting Average Leader, Home Run Leader and Runs Batted In Leader. If the player pictured on the card won his category, the card was redeemable for a special foil version of all 60 Retail Predictor cards. These cards were redeemable until December 31, 1995. Card fronts are full-color action photos of the player emerging from a marble diamond. Backs list the rules of the game. The cards are numbered in the upper left with an "R" prefix.

	MINT	NRMT	EXC
COMPLETE SET (60)	130.00	57.50	16.00
COMPLETE SERIES 1 (30)	80.00	36.00	10.00
COMPLETE SERIES 2 (30)	50.00	22.00	6.25
COMMON CARD (R1-R60)	1.00	.45	.12
*AW EXCHANGE CARDS: .25X PREDICTORS			
☐ R1 Albert Belle HR W	4.00	1.80	.50
☐ R2 Jose Canseco HR	1.50	.70	.19
☐ R3 Juan Gonzalez HR	5.00	2.20	.60
☐ R4 Ken Griffey Jr. HR	10.00	4.50	1.25
☐ R5 Frank Thomas HR	10.00	4.50	1.25
☐ R6 Jeff Bagwell HR	4.00	1.80	.50
☐ R7 Barry Bonds HR	2.50	1.10	.30
☐ R8 Fred McGriff HR	1.50	.70	.19
☐ R9 Matt Williams HR	1.50	.70	.19
☐ R10 HR Wild Card W	1.00	.45	.12
☐ R11 Albert Belle RBI W	4.00	1.80	.50
☐ R12 Joe Carter RBI	1.25	.55	.16
☐ R13 Cecil Fielder RBI	1.25	.55	.16
☐ R14 Kirby Puckett RBI	4.00	1.80	.50
☐ R15 Frank Thomas RBI	10.00	4.50	1.25
☐ R16 Jeff Bagwell RBI	4.00	1.80	.50
☐ R17 Barry Bonds RBI	2.50	1.10	.30
☐ R18 Mike Piazza RBI	6.00	2.70	.75
☐ R19 Matt Williams RBI	1.50	.70	.19
☐ R20 RBI Wild Card W	1.00	.45	.12
☐ R21 Wade Boggs BAT	1.50	.70	.19
☐ R22 Kenny Lofton BAT	2.50	1.10	.30
☐ R23 Paul Molitor BAT	1.25	.55	.16
☐ R24 Paul O'Neill BAT	1.25	.55	.16
☐ R25 Frank Thomas BAT	10.00	4.50	1.25
☐ R26 Jeff Bagwell BAT	4.00	1.80	.50
☐ R27 Tony Gwynn BAT W	4.00	1.80	.50
☐ R28 Gregg Jefferies BAT	1.00	.45	.12
☐ R29 Hal Morris BAT	1.00	.45	.12
☐ R30 Batting Wild Card W	1.00	.45	.12
☐ R31 Joe Carter HR	1.25	.55	.16
☐ R32 Cecil Fielder HR	1.25	.55	.16
☐ R33 Rafael Palmeiro HR	1.50	.70	.19
☐ R34 Larry Walker HR	1.50	.70	.19
☐ R35 Manny Ramirez HR	2.50	1.10	.30
☐ R36 Tim Salmon HR	1.50	.70	.19
☐ R37 Mike Piazza HR	6.00	2.70	.75
☐ R38 Andres Galarraga HR	1.50	.70	.19
☐ R39 David Justice HR	1.25	.55	.16
☐ R40 Gary Sheffield HR	1.50	.70	.19
☐ R41 Juan Gonzalez RBI	5.00	2.20	.60
☐ R42 Jose Canseco RBI	1.50	.70	.19
☐ R43 Will Clark RBI	1.50	.70	.19
☐ R44 Rafael Palmeiro RBI	1.50	.70	.19
☐ R45 Ken Griffey Jr. RBI	10.00	4.50	1.25
☐ R46 Ruben Sierra RBI	1.00	.45	.12
☐ R47 Larry Walker RBI	1.50	.70	.19
☐ R48 Fred McGriff RBI	1.50	.70	.19
☐ R49 Dante Bichette RBI W	1.50	.70	.19
☐ R50 Darren Daulton RBI	1.25	.55	.16
☐ R51 Will Clark BAT	1.50	.70	.19
☐ R52 Ken Griffey Jr. BAT	10.00	4.50	1.25
☐ R53 Don Mattingly BAT	5.00	2.20	.60
☐ R54 John Olerud BAT	1.25	.55	.16
☐ R55 Kirby Puckett BAT	4.00	1.80	.50
☐ R56 Raul Mondesi BAT	1.50	.70	.19
☐ R57 Moises Alou BAT	1.25	.55	.16
☐ R58 Bret Boone BAT	1.00	.45	.12
☐ R59 Albert Belle BAT	4.00	1.80	.50
☐ R60 Mike Piazza BAT	6.00	2.70	.75

1995 Upper Deck Ruth Heroes

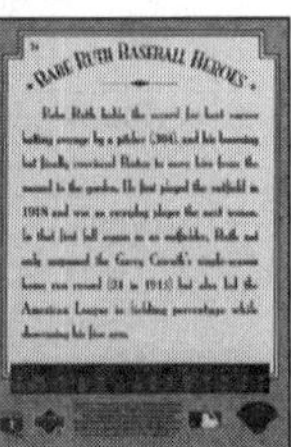

Randomly inserted in second series packs, this set of 10 standard-size cards celebrates the achievements of one of baseball's all-time greats. The set was issued on the Centennial of Ruth's birth. The fronts have silver foil paper and feature the Bambino in colorized action photos on a sepia-tone background. Backs highlight interesting moments from Ruth's career and statistics from separate years are featured at the bottom. The numbering (73-81) is a continuation from previous Heroes sets.

	MINT	NRMT	EXC
COMPLETE SET (10)	120.00	55.00	15.00
COMMON RUTH (73-81)	15.00	6.75	1.85
☐ 73 Babe Ruth 1914-18 Pitching Career	15.00	6.75	1.85
☐ 74 Babe Ruth 1919 Move to Outfield	15.00	6.75	1.85
☐ 75 Babe Ruth 1920 Renaissance Man	15.00	6.75	1.85
☐ 76 Babe Ruth 1923 House that Ruth Built	15.00	6.75	1.85
☐ 77 Babe Ruth 1927 60-home run Season	15.00	6.75	1.85
☐ 78 Babe Ruth 1928 Three Homers in Game 4	15.00	6.75	1.85
☐ 79 Babe Ruth 1932 The Called Shot	15.00	6.75	1.85
☐ 80 Babe Ruth 1930-35 Milestones	15.00	6.75	1.85
☐ 81 Babe Ruth 1935 The Last Hurrah	15.00	6.75	1.85
☐ NNO Babe Ruth Header Card An American Hero	15.00	6.75	1.85

1995 Upper Deck Special Edition

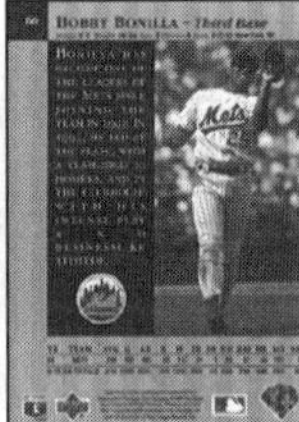

Inserted at a rate of one per pack, this 270 standard-size card set features full color action shots of players on a silver foil background. The back highlights the player's previous performance, including 1994 and career statistics. Another player photo is also featured on the back.

	MINT	NRMT	EXC
COMPLETE SET (270)	200.00	90.00	25.00
COMPLETE SERIES 1 (135)	80.00	36.00	10.00
COMPLETE SERIES 2 (135)	120.00	55.00	15.00
COMMON CARD (1-270)	.25	.11	.03
☐ 1 Cliff Floyd	1.25	.55	.16
☐ 2 Wil Cordero	.50	.23	.06
☐ 3 Pedro J. Martinez	1.25	.55	.16
☐ 4 Larry Walker	1.25	.55	.16
☐ 5 Derek Jeter	6.00	2.70	.75
☐ 6 Mike Stanley	.50	.23	.06
☐ 7 Melido Perez	.25	.11	.03
☐ 8 Jim Leyritz	.25	.11	.03
☐ 9 Danny Tartabull	.50	.23	.06
☐ 10 Wade Boggs	1.25	.55	.16
☐ 11 Ryan Klesko	1.25	.55	.16
☐ 12 Steve Avery	.50	.23	.06
☐ 13 Damon Hollins	1.25	.55	.16
☐ 14 Chipper Jones	6.00	2.70	.75
☐ 15 David Justice	1.25	.55	.16
☐ 16 Glenn Williams	.50	.23	.06
☐ 17 Jose Oliva	.25	.11	.03
☐ 18 Terrell Wade	1.25	.55	.16
☐ 19 Alex Fernandez	.50	.23	.06
☐ 20 Frank Thomas	10.00	4.50	1.25
☐ 21 Ozzie Guillen	.50	.23	.06
☐ 22 Roberto Hernandez	.50	.23	.06
☐ 23 Albie Lopez	.25	.11	.03
☐ 24 Eddie Murray	2.50	1.10	.30
☐ 25 Albert Belle	4.00	1.80	.50
☐ 26 Omar Vizquel	.50	.23	.06
☐ 27 Carlos Baerga	.50	.23	.06
☐ 28 Jose Rijo	.25	.11	.03
☐ 29 Hal Morris	.25	.11	.03
☐ 30 Reggie Sanders	.50	.23	.06
☐ 31 Jack Morris	1.25	.55	.16
☐ 32 Raul Mondesi	1.25	.55	.16
☐ 33 Karim Garcia	8.00	3.60	1.00
☐ 34 Todd Hollandsworth	1.25	.55	.16
☐ 35 Mike Piazza	6.00	2.70	.75
☐ 36 Chan Ho Park	1.25	.55	.16
☐ 37 Ramon Martinez	.50	.23	.06
☐ 38 Kenny Rogers	.25	.11	.03
☐ 39 Will Clark	1.25	.55	.16
☐ 40 Juan Gonzalez	5.00	2.20	.60
☐ 41 Ivan Rodriguez	2.50	1.10	.30
☐ 42 Orlando Miller	.50	.23	.06
☐ 43 John Hudek	.25	.11	.03
☐ 44 Luis Gonzalez	.50	.23	.06
☐ 45 Jeff Bagwell	4.00	1.80	.50
☐ 46 Cal Ripken	8.00	3.60	1.00
☐ 47 Mike Oquist	.25	.11	.03
☐ 48 Armando Benitez	.25	.11	.03
☐ 49 Ben McDonald	.50	.23	.06
☐ 50 Rafael Palmeiro	1.25	.55	.16
☐ 51 Curtis Goodwin	.25	.11	.03
☐ 52 Vince Coleman	.50	.23	.06
☐ 53 Tom Gordon	.25	.11	.03
☐ 54 Mike Macfarlane	.25	.11	.03
☐ 55 Brian McRae	.50	.23	.06
☐ 56 Matt Smith	.25	.11	.03
☐ 57 David Segui	.50	.23	.06
☐ 58 Paul Wilson	1.25	.55	.16
☐ 59 Bill Pulsipher	.50	.23	.06
☐ 60 Bobby Bonilla	.50	.23	.06
☐ 61 Jeff Kent	.50	.23	.06
☐ 62 Ryan Thompson	.25	.11	.03
☐ 63 Jason Isringhausen	1.25	.55	.16
☐ 64 Ed Sprague	.50	.23	.06
☐ 65 Paul Molitor	2.00	.90	.25
☐ 66 Juan Guzman	.50	.23	.06
☐ 67 Alex Gonzalez	.50	.23	.06
☐ 68 Shawn Green	.50	.23	.06
☐ 69 Mark Portugal	.25	.11	.03
☐ 70 Barry Bonds	2.50	1.10	.30
☐ 71 Robby Thompson	.25	.11	.03
☐ 72 Royce Clayton	.50	.23	.06
☐ 73 Ricky Bottalico	.50	.23	.06
☐ 74 Doug Jones	.25	.11	.03
☐ 75 Darren Daulton	.50	.23	.06
☐ 76 Gregg Jefferies	1.25	.55	.16
☐ 77 Scott Cooper	.25	.11	.03
☐ 78 Nomar Garciaparra	5.00	2.20	.60
☐ 79 Ken Ryan	.25	.11	.03
☐ 80 Mike Greenwell	.50	.23	.06
☐ 81 LaTroy Hawkins	.25	.11	.03
☐ 82 Rich Becker	.50	.23	.06
☐ 83 Scott Erickson	.50	.23	.06
☐ 84 Pedro Munoz	.50	.23	.06
☐ 85 Kirby Puckett	4.00	1.80	.50
☐ 86 Orlando Merced	.50	.23	.06
☐ 87 Jeff King	.50	.23	.06
☐ 88 Midre Cummings	.25	.11	.03
☐ 89 Bernard Gilkey	1.25	.55	.16
☐ 90 Ray Lankford	.50	.23	.06
☐ 91 Todd Zeile	.50	.23	.06
☐ 92 Alan Benes	1.25	.55	.16
☐ 93 Bret Wagner	.25	.11	.03
☐ 94 Rene Arocha	.25	.11	.03
☐ 95 Cecil Fielder	.50	.23	.06
☐ 96 Alan Trammell	.50	.23	.06
☐ 97 Tony Phillips	.50	.23	.06
☐ 98 Junior Felix	.25	.11	.03
☐ 99 Brian Harper	.25	.11	.03
☐ 100 Greg Vaughn	1.25	.55	.16
☐ 101 Ricky Bones	.25	.11	.03
☐ 102 Walt Weiss	.25	.11	.03
☐ 103 Lance Painter	.25	.11	.03
☐ 104 Roberto Mejia	.25	.11	.03
☐ 105 Andres Galarraga	1.25	.55	.16
☐ 106 Todd Van Poppel	.25	.11	.03
☐ 107 Ben Grieve	4.00	1.80	.50
☐ 108 Brent Gates	.25	.11	.03
☐ 109 Jason Giambi	2.00	.90	.25
☐ 110 Ruben Sierra	.50	.23	.06
☐ 111 Terry Steinbach	.50	.23	.06
☐ 112 Chris Hammond	.25	.11	.03
☐ 113 Charles Johnson	.50	.23	.06
☐ 114 Jesus Tavarez	.25	.11	.03
☐ 115 Gary Sheffield	1.25	.55	.16
☐ 116 Chuck Carr	.25	.11	.03
☐ 117 Bobby Ayala	.25	.11	.03
☐ 118 Randy Johnson	1.25	.55	.16
☐ 119 Edgar Martinez	.50	.23	.06
☐ 120 Alex Rodriguez	10.00	4.50	1.25
☐ 121 Kevin Foster	.25	.11	.03
☐ 122 Kevin Roberson	.25	.11	.03
☐ 123 Sammy Sosa	1.25	.55	.16
☐ 124 Steve Trachsel	.25	.11	.03
☐ 125 Eduardo Perez	.25	.11	.03
☐ 126 Tim Salmon	1.25	.55	.16
☐ 127 Todd Greene	.50	.23	.06
☐ 128 Jorge Fabregas	.25	.11	.03

Card	MINT	NRMT	EXC
☐ 129 Mark Langston	.50	.23	.06
☐ 130 Mitch Williams	.50	.23	.06
☐ 131 Raul Casanova	2.00	.90	.25
☐ 132 Mel Nieves	.50	.23	.06
☐ 133 Andy Benes	.50	.23	.06
☐ 134 Dustin Hermanson	.25	.11	.03
☐ 135 Trevor Hoffman	.50	.23	.06
☐ 136 Mark Grudzielanek	2.00	.90	.25
☐ 137 Ugueth Urbina	.50	.23	.06
☐ 138 Moises Alou	.50	.23	.06
☐ 139 Roberto Kelly	.25	.11	.03
☐ 140 Rondell White	.50	.23	.06
☐ 141 Paul O'Neill	.50	.23	.06
☐ 142 Jimmy Key	.50	.23	.06
☐ 143 Jack McDowell	1.25	.55	.16
☐ 144 Ruben Rivera	2.50	1.10	.30
☐ 145 Don Mattingly	5.00	2.20	.60
☐ 146 John Wetteland	.50	.23	.06
☐ 147 Tom Glavine	1.25	.55	.16
☐ 148 Marquis Grissom	.50	.23	.06
☐ 149 Javier Lopez	1.25	.55	.16
☐ 150 Fred McGriff	1.25	.55	.16
☐ 151 Greg Maddux	6.00	2.70	.75
☐ 152 Chris Sabo	.25	.11	.03
☐ 153 Ray Durham	1.25	.55	.16
☐ 154 Robin Ventura	.50	.23	.06
☐ 155 Jim Abbott	1.25	.55	.16
☐ 156 Jimmy Hurst	.25	.11	.03
☐ 157 Tim Raines	1.25	.55	.16
☐ 158 Dennis Martinez	.50	.23	.06
☐ 159 Kenny Lofton	2.50	1.10	.30
☐ 160 Dave Winfield	1.25	.55	.16
☐ 161 Manny Ramirez	2.50	1.10	.30
☐ 162 Jim Thome	2.00	.90	.25
☐ 163 Barry Larkin	1.25	.55	.16
☐ 164 Bret Boone	.50	.23	.06
☐ 165 Deion Sanders	1.25	.55	.16
☐ 166 Ron Gant	.50	.23	.06
☐ 167 Benito Santiago	.50	.23	.06
☐ 168 Hideo Nomo	8.00	3.60	1.00
☐ 169 Billy Ashley	.25	.11	.03
☐ 170 Roger Cedeno	.50	.23	.06
☐ 171 Ismael Valdes	.50	.23	.06
☐ 172 Eric Karros	.50	.23	.06
☐ 173 Rusty Greer	1.25	.55	.16
☐ 174 Rick Helling	.25	.11	.03
☐ 175 Nolan Ryan	8.00	3.60	1.00
☐ 176 Dean Palmer	1.25	.55	.16
☐ 177 Phil Plantier	.25	.11	.03
☐ 178 Darryl Kile	.25	.11	.03
☐ 179 Derek Bell	1.25	.55	.16
☐ 180 Doug Drabek	.50	.23	.06
☐ 181 Craig Biggio	.50	.23	.06
☐ 182 Kevin Brown	.50	.23	.06
☐ 183 Harold Baines	.50	.23	.06
☐ 184 Jeffrey Hammonds	.50	.23	.06
☐ 185 Chris Hoiles	.50	.23	.06
☐ 186 Mike Mussina	2.00	.90	.25
☐ 187 Bob Hamelin	.25	.11	.03
☐ 188 Jeff Montgomery	.50	.23	.06
☐ 189 Michael Tucker	1.25	.55	.16
☐ 190 George Brett	4.00	1.80	.50
☐ 191 Edgardo Alfonzo	.50	.23	.06
☐ 192 Brett Butler	.50	.23	.06
☐ 193 Bobby Jones	.50	.23	.06
☐ 194 Todd Hundley	1.25	.55	.16
☐ 195 Bret Saberhagen	.50	.23	.06
☐ 196 Pat Hentgen	1.25	.55	.16
☐ 197 Roberto Alomar	2.00	.90	.25
☐ 198 David Cone	.50	.23	.06
☐ 199 Carlos Delgado	1.25	.55	.16
☐ 200 Joe Carter	.50	.23	.06
☐ 201 Wm. VanLandingham	.25	.11	.03
☐ 202 Rod Beck	.50	.23	.06
☐ 203 J.R. Phillips	.25	.11	.03
☐ 204 Darren Lewis	.25	.11	.03
☐ 205 Matt Williams	1.25	.55	.16
☐ 206 Lenny Dykstra	.50	.23	.06
☐ 207 Dave Hollins	.25	.11	.03
☐ 208 Mike Schmidt	2.50	1.10	.30
☐ 209 Charlie Hayes	.50	.23	.06
☐ 210 Mo Vaughn	2.50	1.10	.30
☐ 211 Jose Malave	.25	.11	.03
☐ 212 Roger Clemens	2.00	.90	.25
☐ 213 Jose Canseco	1.25	.55	.16
☐ 214 Mark Whiten	.50	.23	.06
☐ 215 Marty Cordova	1.25	.55	.16
☐ 216 Rick Aguilera	.50	.23	.06
☐ 217 Kevin Tapani	.50	.23	.06
☐ 218 Chuck Knoblauch	1.25	.55	.16
☐ 219 Al Martin	.50	.23	.06
☐ 220 Jay Bell	.50	.23	.06
☐ 221 Carlos Garcia	.50	.23	.06
☐ 222 Freddy Garcia	.50	.23	.06
☐ 223 Jon Lieber	.25	.11	.03
☐ 224 Danny Jackson	.25	.11	.03
☐ 225 Ozzie Smith	2.50	1.10	.30
☐ 226 Brian Jordan	1.25	.55	.16
☐ 227 Ken Hill	.25	.11	.03
☐ 228 Scott Cooper	.25	.11	.03
☐ 229 Chad Curtis	.50	.23	.06
☐ 230 Lou Whitaker	.50	.23	.06
☐ 231 Kirk Gibson	.50	.23	.06
☐ 232 Travis Fryman	.50	.23	.06
☐ 233 Jose Valentin	.50	.23	.06
☐ 234 Dave Nilsson	.50	.23	.06
☐ 235 Cal Eldred	.25	.11	.03
☐ 236 Matt Mieske	.50	.23	.06
☐ 237 Bill Swift	.25	.11	.03
☐ 238 Marvin Freeman	.25	.11	.03
☐ 239 Jason Bates	.25	.11	.03
☐ 240 Larry Walker	1.25	.55	.16
☐ 241 Dave Nied	.25	.11	.03
☐ 242 Dante Bichette	1.25	.55	.16
☐ 243 Dennis Eckersley	.50	.23	.06
☐ 244 Todd Stottlemyre	.50	.23	.06
☐ 245 Rickey Henderson	1.25	.55	.16
☐ 246 Geronimo Berroa	.50	.23	.06
☐ 247 Mark McGwire	3.00	1.35	.35
☐ 248 Quilvio Veras	.25	.11	.03
☐ 249 Terry Pendleton	.50	.23	.06
☐ 250 Andre Dawson	.50	.23	.06
☐ 251 Jeff Conine	.50	.23	.06
☐ 252 Kurt Abbott	.25	.11	.03
☐ 253 Jay Buhner	1.25	.55	.16
☐ 254 Darren Bragg	.25	.11	.03
☐ 255 Ken Griffey Jr.	10.00	4.50	1.25
☐ 256 Tino Martinez	.50	.23	.06
☐ 257 Mark Grace	1.25	.55	.16
☐ 258 Ryne Sandberg	2.50	1.10	.30
☐ 259 Randy Myers	.50	.23	.06
☐ 260 Howard Johnson	.50	.23	.06
☐ 261 Lee Smith	.50	.23	.06
☐ 262 J.T. Snow	.25	.11	.03
☐ 263 Chili Davis	.50	.23	.06
☐ 264 Chuck Finley	.50	.23	.06
☐ 265 Eddie Williams	.25	.11	.03
☐ 266 Joey Hamilton	1.25	.55	.16
☐ 267 Ken Caminiti	1.25	.55	.16
☐ 268 Andujar Cedeno	.25	.11	.03
☐ 269 Steve Finley	1.25	.55	.16
☐ 270 Tony Gwynn	4.00	1.80	.50

1995 Upper Deck Special Edition Gold

The Gold set parallels the basic Special Edition set and features the player in a full color photo on gold foil paper. Backs include the player's close-up photo and outstanding achievements. Season and career statistics are featured at the bottom of the cards.

	MINT	NRMT	EXC
COMPLETE SET (270)	2600.00	1150.00	325.00
COMPLETE SERIES 1 (135)	1200.00	550.00	150.00
COMPLETE SERIES 2 (135)	1400.00	650.00	180.00
COMMON CARD (1-270)	4.00	1.80	.50

*STARS: 6X TO 12X BASIC CARDS ....
*YOUNG STARS: 4X TO 8X BASIC CARDS

1995 Upper Deck Steal of a Deal

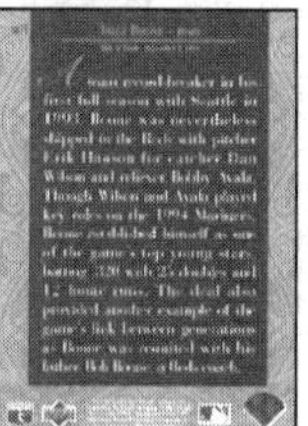

This set was inserted in hobby and retail packs at a rate of approximately one in 34. This 15-card standard-size set focuses on players who were acquired through, according to Upper Deck, "astute trades" or low round draft picks. The horizontal fronts feature a player cutout on a green background with a bronze seal. Backs feature information of how the player was acquired and past performance. The cards are numbered in the upper left with an "SD" prefix.

	MINT	NRMT	EXC
COMPLETE SET (15)	100.00	45.00	12.50
COMMON CARD (SD1-SD15)	2.00	.90	.25
☐ SD1 Mike Piazza	20.00	9.00	2.50
☐ SD2 Fred McGriff	4.00	1.80	.50
☐ SD3 Kenny Lofton	8.00	3.60	1.00
☐ SD4 Jose Oliva	2.00	.90	.25
☐ SD5 Jeff Bagwell	12.00	5.50	1.50
☐ SD6 Roberto Alomar Joe Carter	6.00	2.70	.75
☐ SD7 Steve Karsay	2.00	.90	.25
☐ SD8 Ozzie Smith	8.00	3.60	1.00
☐ SD9 Dennis Eckersley	3.00	1.35	.35
☐ SD10 Jose Canseco	4.00	1.80	.50
☐ SD11 Carlos Baerga	2.00	.90	.25
☐ SD12 Cecil Fielder	3.00	1.35	.35
☐ SD13 Don Mattingly	15.00	6.75	1.85
☐ SD14 Bret Boone	2.00	.90	.25
☐ SD15 Michael Jordan	30.00	13.50	3.70

1995 Upper Deck/GTS Phone Cards

Upper Deck joined with GTS (Global Telecommunication Solutions Inc.) to produce a series of MLB player phone cards. Each card contained 15 minutes of long distance phone time and was priced at $12.00. Card numbers 1-5 were released March 1, April 15, and May 15, for a total of fifteen cards. Moreover, other cards were to be released later in the year. The cards are unnumbered and checklisted below in alphabetical order in two sections--the first five that were released (MLB1-MLB5) and then the other ten cards (MLB6-MLB15).

	MINT	NRMT	EXC
COMPLETE SET (15)	125.00	55.00	15.50
COMMON CARD (MLB1-MLB15)	4.00	1.80	.50
☐ MLB1 Tony Gwynn	12.00	5.50	1.50
☐ MLB2 Fred McGriff	4.00	1.80	.50
☐ MLB3 Frank Thomas	25.00	11.00	3.10
☐ MLB4 Ken Griffey Jr.	25.00	11.00	3.10
☐ MLB5 Cecil Fielder	4.00	1.80	.50
☐ MLB6 Roberto Alomar	8.00	3.60	1.00
☐ MLB7 Jeff Bagwell	10.00	4.50	1.25
☐ MLB8 Barry Bonds	6.00	2.70	.75
☐ MLB9 Roger Clemens	8.00	3.60	1.00
☐ MLB10 David Justice	4.00	1.80	.50
☐ MLB11 Don Mattingly	12.00	5.50	1.50
☐ MLB12 Kirby Puckett	10.00	4.50	1.25
☐ MLB13 Cal Ripken	25.00	11.00	3.10
☐ MLB14 Gary Sheffield	4.00	1.80	.50
☐ MLB15 Ozzie Smith	8.00	3.60	1.00

1995 Upper Deck Sheets

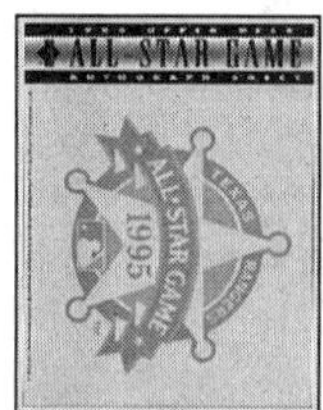

This one 8 1/2" by 11" sheet was issued so fans at Fan Fest could have an item for players to sign at the show. The sheet has very little on the front so more signatures can be signed and the back is blank.

	MINT	NRMT	EXC
COMPLETE SET	2.00	.90	.25
COMMON CARD	2.00	.90	.25
☐ 1 1995 All-Star Game Autograph Sheet	2.00	.90	.25

1995 Upper Deck Sonic Heroes of Baseball

These standard-size cards were given out in three-card cello packs to customers who purchased a combo meal at participating Sonic Restaurants. The fronts feature black-and-white player photos with white borders. The words "Exclusive Edition" are printed in a blue bar at the top, with the player's name in a red bar directly below. The team name and the player's position appear on the bottom. The backs carry stats, career highlights, and sponsor and producer logos.

	MINT	NRMT	EXC
COMPLETE SET (20)	8.00	3.60	1.00
COMMON CARD (1-20)	.20	.09	.03
☐ 1 Whitey Ford	.40	.18	.05
☐ 2 Cy Young	.50	.23	.06
☐ 3 Babe Ruth	1.25	.55	.16
☐ 4 Lou Gehrig	.75	.35	.09
☐ 5 Mike Schmidt	.75	.35	.09
☐ 6 Nolan Ryan	1.00	.45	.12
☐ 7 Robin Yount	.30	.14	.04
☐ 8 Gary Carter	.30	.14	.04
☐ 9 Tom Seaver	.40	.18	.05
☐ 10 Reggie Jackson	.40	.18	.05
☐ 11 Bob Gibson	.30	.14	.04
☐ 12 Gil Hodges	.40	.18	.05
☐ 13 Monte Irvin	.20	.09	.03
☐ 14 Minnie Minoso	.20	.09	.03
☐ 15 Willie Stargell	.30	.14	.04
☐ 16 Al Kaline	.30	.14	.04
☐ 17 Joe Jackson	.75	.35	.09
☐ 18 Walter Johnson	.50	.23	.06
☐ 19 Ty Cobb	.75	.35	.09
☐ 20 Satchel Paige	.50	.23	.06

1995 Upper Deck Sports Drink Jackson

Upper Deck and Energy Foods have joined together to produce the Upper Deck Authentic Sports Drink. The drink was available in four flavors (lemon lime, madarin orange, fruit cooler and tropical berry), and each package included one of three Reggie Jackson Heroes cards. Six-bottle packages retail for $2.00. The cards are similar to those that were included with Reggie Candy Bars in 1993, and come with and without a gold facsimile autograph. The cards are numbered on the back "X of 3."

	MINT	NRMT	EXC
COMPLETE SET (3)	5.00	2.20	.60
COMMON CARD (1-3)	2.00	.90	.25
☐ 1 Reggie Jackson	2.00	.90	.25
☐ 2 Reggie Jackson	2.00	.90	.25
☐ 3 Reggie Jackson	2.00	.90	.25

1996 Upper Deck

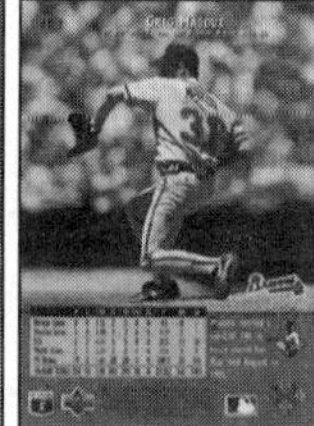

The 1996 Upper Deck set was issued in two series of 240 cards, and a 30 card update set, for a total of 510 cards. The cards were distributed in 10-card packs with a suggested retail price of $1.99, and 28 packs were contained in each box. The attractive fronts feature a full-bleed photo above a bronze foil bar that includes the player's name, team and position in a white oval. Subsets include Young at Heart (100-117), Beat the Odds (145-153), Postseason Checklist (218-222), Best of a Generation (370-387), Strange But True (415-423) and Managerial Salute Checklists (476-480).

	MINT	NRMT	EXC
COMPLETE SET (480)	65.00	29.00	8.00
COMP.FACT.SET (510)	80.00	36.00	10.00
COMPLETE SERIES 1 (240)	35.00	16.00	4.40
COMPLETE SERIES 2 (240)	30.00	13.50	3.70
COMMON CARD (1-480)	.10	.05	.01
COMP.UPDATE SET (30)	8.00	3.60	1.00
COMMON UPDATE (481U-510U)	.25	.11	.03
☐ 1 Cal Ripken 2131	4.00	1.80	.50
☐ 2 Eddie Murray 3000 Hits	.75	.35	.09
☐ 3 Mark Wohlers	.25	.11	.03
☐ 4 David Justice	.25	.11	.03
☐ 5 Chipper Jones	2.00	.90	.25
☐ 6 Javier Lopez	.50	.23	.06
☐ 7 Mark Lemke	.10	.05	.01
☐ 8 Marquis Grissom	.25	.11	.03
☐ 9 Tom Glavine	.50	.23	.06
☐ 10 Greg Maddux	2.00	.90	.25
☐ 11 Manny Alexander	.10	.05	.01
☐ 12 Curtis Goodwin	.10	.05	.01
☐ 13 Scott Erickson	.10	.05	.01
☐ 14 Chris Hoiles	.10	.05	.01
☐ 15 Rafael Palmeiro	.50	.23	.06
☐ 16 Rick Krivda	.10	.05	.01
☐ 17 Jeff Manto	.10	.05	.01
☐ 18 Mo Vaughn	.75	.35	.09
☐ 19 Tim Wakefield	.10	.05	.01
☐ 20 Roger Clemens	.60	.25	.07
☐ 21 Tim Naehring	.10	.05	.01
☐ 22 Troy O'Leary	.10	.05	.01
☐ 23 Mike Greenwell	.10	.05	.01
☐ 24 Stan Belinda	.10	.05	.01
☐ 25 John Valentin	.25	.11	.03
☐ 26 J.T. Snow	.25	.11	.03
☐ 27 Gary DiSarcina	.10	.05	.01
☐ 28 Mark Langston	.10	.05	.01
☐ 29 Brian Anderson	.10	.05	.01
☐ 30 Jim Edmonds	.25	.11	.03
☐ 31 Garret Anderson	.50	.23	.06
☐ 32 Orlando Palmeiro	.10	.05	.01
☐ 33 Brian McRae	.10	.05	.01
☐ 34 Kevin Foster	.10	.05	.01
☐ 35 Sammy Sosa	.50	.23	.06
☐ 36 Todd Zeile	.25	.11	.03
☐ 37 Jim Bullinger	.10	.05	.01
☐ 38 Luis Gonzalez	.10	.05	.01
☐ 39 Lyle Mouton	.10	.05	.01
☐ 40 Ray Durham	.50	.23	.06
☐ 41 Ozzie Guillen	.10	.05	.01

□ 42 Alex Fernandez .25 .11 .03
□ 43 Brian Keyser .10 .05 .01
□ 44 Robin Ventura .25 .11 .03
□ 45 Reggie Sanders .25 .11 .03
□ 46 Pete Schourek .25 .11 .03
□ 47 John Smiley .10 .05 .01
□ 48 Jeff Brantley .10 .05 .01
□ 49 Thomas Howard .10 .05 .01
□ 50 Bret Boone .10 .05 .01
□ 51 Kevin Jarvis .10 .05 .01
□ 52 Jeff Branson .10 .05 .01
□ 53 Carlos Baerga .25 .11 .03
□ 54 Jim Thome .60 .25 .07
□ 55 Manny Ramirez .75 .35 .09
□ 56 Omar Vizquel .25 .11 .03
□ 57 Jose Mesa .25 .11 .03
□ 58 Julian Tavarez UER .10 .05 .01
□ 59 Orel Hershiser .25 .11 .03
□ 60 Larry Walker .50 .23 .06
□ 61 Bret Saberhagen .10 .05 .01
□ 62 Vinny Castilla .25 .11 .03
□ 63 Eric Young .25 .11 .03
□ 64 Bryan Rekar .10 .05 .01
□ 65 Andres Galarraga .50 .23 .06
□ 66 Steve Reed .10 .05 .01
□ 67 Chad Curtis .10 .05 .01
□ 68 Bobby Higginson .25 .11 .03
□ 69 Phil Nevin .10 .05 .01
□ 70 Cecil Fielder .25 .11 .03
□ 71 Felipe Lira .10 .05 .01
□ 72 Chris Gomez .10 .05 .01
□ 73 Charles Johnson .25 .11 .03
□ 74 Quilvio Veras .10 .05 .01
□ 75 Jeff Conine .25 .11 .03
□ 76 John Burkett .10 .05 .01
□ 77 Greg Colbrunn .10 .05 .01
□ 78 Terry Pendleton .10 .05 .01
□ 79 Shane Reynolds .10 .05 .01
□ 80 Jeff Bagwell 1.25 .55 .16
□ 81 Orlando Miller .10 .05 .01
□ 82 Mike Hampton .10 .05 .01
□ 83 James Mouton .10 .05 .01
□ 84 Brian L. Hunter .25 .11 .03
□ 85 Derek Bell .25 .11 .03
□ 86 Kevin Appier .25 .11 .03
□ 87 Joe Vitiello .10 .05 .01
□ 88 Wally Joyner .10 .05 .01
□ 89 Michael Tucker .25 .11 .03
□ 90 Johnny Damon .25 .11 .03
□ 91 Jon Nunnally .10 .05 .01
□ 92 Jason Jacome .10 .05 .01
□ 93 Chad Fonville .10 .05 .01
□ 94 Chan Ho Park .50 .23 .06
□ 95 Hideo Nomo .75 .35 .09
□ 96 Ismael Valdes .25 .11 .03
□ 97 Greg Gagne .10 .05 .01
□ 98 Diamondbacks-Devil Rays .10 .05 .01
□ 99 Raul Mondesi .50 .23 .06
□ 100 Dave Winfield YH .50 .23 .06
□ 101 Dennis Eckersley YH .25 .11 .03
□ 102 Andre Dawson YH .25 .11 .03
□ 103 Dennis Martinez YH .25 .11 .03
□ 104 Lance Parrish YH .25 .11 .03
□ 105 Eddie Murray YH .50 .23 .06
□ 106 Alan Trammell YH .25 .11 .03
□ 107 Lou Whitaker YH .25 .11 .03
□ 108 Ozzie Smith YH .50 .23 .06
□ 109 Paul Molitor YH .60 .25 .07
□ 110 Rickey Henderson YH .50 .23 .06
□ 111 Tim Raines YH .25 .11 .03
□ 112 Harold Baines YH .25 .11 .03
□ 113 Lee Smith YH .25 .11 .03
□ 114 Fernando Valenzuela YH .25 .11 .03
□ 115 Cal Ripken YH 1.25 .55 .16
□ 116 Tony Gwynn YH .60 .25 .07
□ 117 Wade Boggs .50 .23 .06
□ 118 Todd Hollandsworth .25 .11 .03
□ 119 Dave Nilsson .25 .11 .03
□ 120 Jose Valentin .10 .05 .01
□ 121 Steve Sparks .10 .05 .01
□ 122 Chuck Carr .10 .05 .01
□ 123 John Jaha .25 .11 .03
□ 124 Scott Karl .10 .05 .01
□ 125 Chuck Knoblauch .50 .23 .06
□ 126 Brad Radke .10 .05 .01
□ 127 Pat Meares .10 .05 .01
□ 128 Ron Coomer .10 .05 .01
□ 129 Pedro Munoz .10 .05 .01
□ 130 Kirby Puckett 1.25 .55 .16
□ 131 David Segui .10 .05 .01
□ 132 Mark Grudzielanek .25 .11 .03
□ 133 Mike Lansing .10 .05 .01
□ 134 Sean Berry .10 .05 .01
□ 135 Rondell White .25 .11 .03
□ 136 Pedro J. Martinez .25 .11 .03
□ 137 Carl Everett .10 .05 .01
□ 138 Dave Mlicki .10 .05 .01
□ 139 Bill Pulsipher .10 .05 .01
□ 140 Jason Isringhausen .50 .23 .06
□ 141 Rico Brogna .10 .05 .01
□ 142 Edgardo Alfonzo .25 .11 .03
□ 143 Jeff Kent .10 .05 .01
□ 144 Andy Pettitte 1.00 .45 .12
□ 145 Mike Piazza BO 1.00 .45 .12
□ 146 Cliff Floyd BO .10 .05 .01

□ 147 Jason Isringhausen BO .50 .23 .06
□ 148 Tim Wakefield BO .10 .05 .01
□ 149 Chipper Jones BO 1.00 .45 .12
□ 150 Hideo Nomo BO .50 .23 .06
□ 151 Mark McGwire BO 1.00 .45 .12
□ 152 Ron Gant BO .25 .11 .03
□ 153 Gary Gaetti BO .25 .11 .03
□ 154 Don Mattingly 1.50 .70 .19
□ 155 Paul O'Neill .10 .05 .01
□ 156 Derek Jeter 2.00 .90 .25
□ 157 Joe Girardi .10 .05 .01
□ 158 Ruben Sierra .10 .05 .01
□ 159 Jorge Posada .10 .05 .01
□ 160 Geronimo Berroa .25 .11 .03
□ 161 Steve Ontiveros .10 .05 .01
□ 162 George Williams .10 .05 .01
□ 163 Doug Johns .10 .05 .01
□ 164 Ariel Prieto .10 .05 .01
□ 165 Scott Brosius .10 .05 .01
□ 166 Mike Bordick .10 .05 .01
□ 167 Tyler Green .10 .05 .01
□ 168 Mickey Morandini .10 .05 .01
□ 169 Darren Daulton .25 .11 .03
□ 170 Gregg Jefferies .25 .11 .03
□ 171 Jim Eisenreich .10 .05 .01
□ 172 Heathcliff Slocumb .10 .05 .01
□ 173 Kevin Stocker .10 .05 .01
□ 174 Esteban Loaiza .10 .05 .01
□ 175 Jeff King .25 .11 .03
□ 176 Mark Johnson .10 .05 .01
□ 177 Denny Neagle .25 .11 .03
□ 178 Orlando Merced .25 .11 .03
□ 179 Carlos Garcia .10 .05 .01
□ 180 Brian Jordan .25 .11 .03
□ 181 Mike Morgan .10 .05 .01
□ 182 Mark Petkovsek .10 .05 .01
□ 183 Bernard Gilkey .25 .11 .03
□ 184 John Mabry .25 .11 .03
□ 185 Tom Henke .25 .11 .03
□ 186 Glenn Dishman .10 .05 .01
□ 187 Andy Ashby .10 .05 .01
□ 188 Bip Roberts .10 .05 .01
□ 189 Melvin Nieves .10 .05 .01
□ 190 Ken Caminiti .50 .23 .06
□ 191 Brad Ausmus .10 .05 .01
□ 192 Deion Sanders .50 .23 .06
□ 193 Jamie Brewington .10 .05 .01
□ 194 Glenallen Hill .10 .05 .01
□ 195 Barry Bonds .75 .35 .09
□ 196 Wm. Van Landingham .10 .05 .01
□ 197 Mark Carreon .10 .05 .01
□ 198 Royce Clayton .10 .05 .01
□ 199 Joey Cora .10 .05 .01
□ 200 Ken Griffey Jr. 3.00 1.35 .35
□ 201 Jay Buhner .50 .23 .06
□ 202 Alex Rodriguez 3.00 1.35 .35
□ 203 Norm Charlton .10 .05 .01
□ 204 Andy Benes .10 .05 .01
□ 205 Edgar Martinez .25 .11 .03
□ 206 Juan Gonzalez 1.50 .70 .19
□ 207 Will Clark .50 .23 .06
□ 208 Kevin Gross .10 .05 .01
□ 209 Roger Pavlik .10 .05 .01
□ 210 Ivan Rodriguez .75 .35 .09
□ 211 Rusty Greer .50 .23 .06
□ 212 Angel Martinez .10 .05 .01
□ 213 Tomas Perez .10 .05 .01
□ 214 Alex Gonzalez .10 .05 .01
□ 215 Joe Carter .25 .11 .03
□ 216 Shawn Green .10 .05 .01
□ 217 Edwin Hurtado .10 .05 .01
□ 218 Edgar Martinez .25 .11 .03
Tony Pena CL
□ 219 Chipper Jones .75 .35 .09
Barry Larkin CL
□ 220 Orel Hershiser CL .25 .11 .03
□ 221 Mike Devereaux CL .10 .05 .01
□ 222 Tom Glavine CL .50 .23 .06
□ 223 Karim Garcia .60 .25 .07
□ 224 Arquimedez Pozo .10 .05 .01
□ 225 Billy Wagner .50 .23 .06
□ 226 John Wasdin .10 .05 .01
□ 227 Jeff Suppan .50 .23 .06
□ 228 Steve Gibralter .10 .05 .01
□ 229 Jimmy Haynes .10 .05 .01
□ 230 Ruben Rivera .60 .25 .07
□ 231 Chris Snopek .10 .05 .01
□ 232 Alex Ochoa .25 .11 .03
□ 233 Shannon Stewart .10 .05 .01
□ 234 Quinton McCracken .10 .05 .01
□ 235 Trey Beamon .10 .05 .01
□ 236 Billy McMillon .10 .05 .01
□ 237 Steve Cox .10 .05 .01
□ 238 George Arias .10 .05 .01
□ 239 Jose Herrera .10 .05 .01
□ 240 Todd Greene .50 .23 .06
□ 241 Jason Kendall .50 .23 .06
□ 242 Brooks Kieschnick .50 .23 .06
□ 243 Osvaldo Fernandez .10 .05 .01
□ 244 Livan Hernandez .10 .05 .01
□ 245 Rey Ordonez .50 .23 .06
□ 246 Mike Grace .10 .05 .01
□ 247 Jay Canizaro .10 .05 .01
□ 248 Bob Wolcott .10 .05 .01
□ 249 Jermaine Dye .60 .25 .07

□ 250 Jason Schmidt .50 .23 .06
□ 251 Mike Sweeney .60 .25 .07
□ 252 Marcus Jensen .10 .05 .01
□ 253 Mendy Lopez .25 .11 .03
□ 254 Wilton Guerrero 1.50 .70 .19
□ 255 Paul Wilson .25 .11 .03
□ 256 Edgar Renteria .50 .23 .06
□ 257 Richard Hidalgo .50 .23 .06
□ 258 Bob Abreu .50 .23 .06
□ 259 Robert Smith .50 .23 .06
□ 260 Sal Fasano .10 .05 .01
□ 261 Enrique Wilson .50 .23 .06
□ 262 Rich Hunter .10 .05 .01
□ 263 Sergio Nunez .25 .11 .03
□ 264 Dan Serafini .10 .05 .01
□ 265 David Doster .10 .05 .01
□ 266 Ryan McGuire .10 .05 .01
□ 267 Scott Spiezio .50 .23 .06
□ 268 Rafael Orellano .10 .05 .01
□ 269 Steve Avery .25 .11 .03
□ 270 Fred McGriff .50 .23 .06
□ 271 John Smoltz .50 .23 .06
□ 272 Ryan Klesko .50 .23 .06
□ 273 Jeff Blauser .10 .05 .01
□ 274 Brad Clontz .10 .05 .01
□ 275 Roberto Alomar .60 .25 .07
□ 276 B.J. Surhoff .10 .05 .01
□ 277 Jeffrey Hammonds .10 .05 .01
□ 278 Brady Anderson .50 .23 .06
□ 279 Bobby Bonilla .25 .11 .03
□ 280 Cal Ripken 2.50 1.10 .30
□ 281 Mike Mussina .60 .25 .07
□ 282 Wil Cordero .10 .05 .01
□ 283 Mike Stanley .10 .05 .01
□ 284 Aaron Sele .10 .05 .01
□ 285 Jose Canseco .50 .23 .06
□ 286 Tom Gordon .10 .05 .01
□ 287 Heathcliff Slocumb .10 .05 .01
□ 288 Lee Smith .25 .11 .03
□ 289 Troy Percival .25 .11 .03
□ 290 Tim Salmon .50 .23 .06
□ 291 Chuck Finley .10 .05 .01
□ 292 Jim Abbott .50 .23 .06
□ 293 Chili Davis .10 .05 .01
□ 294 Steve Trachsel .10 .05 .01
□ 295 Mark Grace .50 .23 .06
□ 296 Rey Sanchez .10 .05 .01
□ 297 Scott Servais .10 .05 .01
□ 298 Jaime Navarro .10 .05 .01
□ 299 Frank Castillo .10 .05 .01
□ 300 Frank Thomas 3.00 1.35 .35
□ 301 Jason Bere .10 .05 .01
□ 302 Danny Tartabull .10 .05 .01
□ 303 Darren Lewis .10 .05 .01
□ 304 Roberto Hernandez .25 .11 .03
□ 305 Tony Phillips .25 .11 .03
□ 306 Wilson Alvarez .50 .23 .06
□ 307 Jose Rijo .10 .05 .01
□ 308 Hal Morris .10 .05 .01
□ 309 Mark Portugal .10 .05 .01
□ 310 Barry Larkin .50 .23 .06
□ 311 Dave Burba .10 .05 .01
□ 312 Ed Taubensee .10 .05 .01
□ 313 Sandy Alomar Jr. .10 .05 .01
□ 314 Dennis Martinez .25 .11 .03
□ 315 Albert Belle 1.25 .55 .16
□ 316 Eddie Murray .75 .35 .09
□ 317 Charles Nagy .25 .11 .03
□ 318 Chad Ogea .10 .05 .01
□ 319 Kenny Lofton .75 .35 .09
□ 320 Dante Bichette .50 .23 .06
□ 321 Armando Reynoso .10 .05 .01
□ 322 Walt Weiss .10 .05 .01
□ 323 Ellis Burks .25 .11 .03
□ 324 Kevin Ritz .10 .05 .01
□ 325 Bill Swift .10 .05 .01
□ 326 Jason Bates .10 .05 .01
□ 327 Tony Clark .60 .25 .07
□ 328 Travis Fryman .25 .11 .03
□ 329 Mark Parent .10 .05 .01
□ 330 Alan Trammell .25 .11 .03
□ 331 C.J. Nitkowski .10 .05 .01
□ 332 Jose Lima .10 .05 .01
□ 333 Phil Plantier .10 .05 .01
□ 334 Kurt Abbott .10 .05 .01
□ 335 Andre Dawson .25 .11 .03
□ 336 Chris Hammond .10 .05 .01
□ 337 Robb Nen .10 .05 .01
□ 338 Pat Rapp .10 .05 .01
□ 339 Al Leiter .10 .05 .01
□ 340 Gary Sheffield UER .50 .23 .06
(HR total says 17
□ 341 Todd Jones .10 .05 .01
□ 342 Doug Drabek .10 .05 .01
□ 343 Greg Swindell .10 .05 .01
□ 344 Tony Eusebio .10 .05 .01
□ 345 Craig Biggio .25 .11 .03
□ 346 Darryl Kile .10 .05 .01
□ 347 Mike Macfarlane .10 .05 .01
□ 348 Jeff Montgomery .10 .05 .01
□ 349 Chris Haney .10 .05 .01
□ 350 Bip Roberts .10 .05 .01
□ 351 Tom Goodwin .25 .11 .03
□ 352 Mark Gubicza .10 .05 .01
□ 353 Joe Randa .10 .05 .01

□ 354 Ramon Martinez .25 .11 .03
□ 355 Eric Karros .25 .11 .03
□ 356 Delino DeShields .10 .05 .01
□ 357 Brett Butler .10 .05 .01
□ 358 Todd Worrell .50 .23 .06
□ 359 Mike Blowers .10 .05 .01
□ 360 Mike Piazza 2.00 .90 .25
□ 361 Ben McDonald .10 .05 .01
□ 362 Ricky Bones .10 .05 .01
□ 363 Greg Vaughn .50 .23 .06
□ 364 Matt Mieske .10 .05 .01
□ 365 Kevin Seitzer .10 .05 .01
□ 366 Jeff Cirillo .10 .05 .01
□ 367 LaTroy Hawkins .10 .05 .01
□ 368 Frank Rodriguez .10 .05 .01
□ 369 Rick Aguilera .10 .05 .01
□ 370 Roberto Alomar BG .50 .23 .06
□ 371 Albert Belle BG .60 .25 .07
□ 372 Wade Boggs BG .50 .23 .06
□ 373 Barry Bonds BG .50 .23 .06
□ 374 Roger Clemens BG .50 .23 .06
□ 375 Dennis Eckersley BG .25 .11 .03
□ 376 Ken Griffey Jr. BG 1.50 .70 .19
□ 377 Tony Gwynn BG .60 .25 .07
□ 378 Rickey Henderson BG .50 .23 .06
□ 379 Greg Maddux BG 1.00 .45 .12
□ 380 Fred McGriff BG .50 .23 .06
□ 381 Paul Molitor BG .50 .23 .06
□ 382 Eddie Murray BG .50 .23 .06
□ 383 Mike Piazza BG 1.00 .45 .12
□ 384 Kirby Puckett BG .50 .23 .06
□ 385 Cal Ripken BG 1.25 .55 .16
□ 386 Ozzie Smith BG .50 .23 .06
□ 387 Frank Thomas BG 1.50 .70 .19
□ 388 Matt Walbeck .10 .05 .01
□ 389 Dave Stevens .10 .05 .01
□ 390 Marty Cordova .25 .11 .03
□ 391 Darrin Fletcher .10 .05 .01
□ 392 Cliff Floyd .10 .05 .01
□ 393 Mel Rojas .10 .05 .01
□ 394 Shane Andrews .10 .05 .01
□ 395 Moises Alou .25 .11 .03
□ 396 Carlos Perez .10 .05 .01
□ 397 Jeff Fassero .10 .05 .01
□ 398 Bobby Jones .10 .05 .01
□ 399 Todd Hundley .25 .11 .03
□ 400 John Franco .10 .05 .01
□ 401 Jose Vizcaino .10 .05 .01
□ 402 Bernard Gilkey .25 .11 .03
□ 403 Pete Harnisch .10 .05 .01
□ 404 Pat Kelly .10 .05 .01
□ 405 David Cone .25 .11 .03
□ 406 Bernie Williams .60 .25 .07
□ 407 John Wetteland .25 .11 .03
□ 408 Scott Kamieniecki .10 .05 .01
□ 409 Tim Raines .50 .23 .06
□ 410 Wade Boggs .50 .23 .06
□ 411 Terry Steinbach .25 .11 .03
□ 412 Jason Giambi .50 .23 .06
□ 413 Todd Van Poppel .10 .05 .01
□ 414 Pedro Munoz .10 .05 .01
□ 415 Eddie Murray SBT .50 .23 .06
□ 416 Dennis Eckersley SBT .25 .11 .03
□ 417 Bip Roberts SBT .10 .05 .01
□ 418 Glenallen Hill SBT .10 .05 .01
□ 419 John Hudek SBT .10 .05 .01
□ 420 Derek Bell SBT .25 .11 .03
□ 421 Larry Walker SBT .50 .23 .06
□ 422 Greg Maddux SBT 1.00 .45 .12
□ 423 Ken Caminiti SBT .50 .23 .06
□ 424 Brent Gates .10 .05 .01
□ 425 Mark McGwire 1.00 .45 .12
□ 426 Mark Whiten .10 .05 .01
□ 427 Sid Fernandez .10 .05 .01
□ 428 Ricky Bottalico .10 .05 .01
□ 429 Mike Mimbs .10 .05 .01
□ 430 Lenny Dykstra .25 .11 .03
□ 431 Todd Zeile .25 .11 .03
□ 432 Benito Santiago .10 .05 .01
□ 433 Danny Miceli .10 .05 .01
□ 434 Al Martin .10 .05 .01
□ 435 Jay Bell .25 .11 .03
□ 436 Charlie Hayes .10 .05 .01
□ 437 Mike Kingery .10 .05 .01
□ 438 Paul Wagner .10 .05 .01
□ 439 Tom Pagnozzi .10 .05 .01
□ 440 Ozzie Smith .75 .35 .09
□ 441 Ray Lankford .25 .11 .03
□ 442 Dennis Eckersley .25 .11 .03
□ 443 Ron Gant .25 .11 .03
□ 444 Alan Benes .50 .23 .06
□ 445 Rickey Henderson .50 .23 .06
□ 446 Jody Reed .10 .05 .01
□ 447 Trevor Hoffman .25 .11 .03
□ 448 Andujar Cedeno .10 .05 .01
□ 449 Steve Finley .50 .23 .06
□ 450 Tony Gwynn 1.25 .55 .16
□ 451 Joey Hamilton .25 .11 .03
□ 452 Mark Leiter .10 .05 .01
□ 453 Rod Beck .10 .05 .01
□ 454 Kirt Manwaring .10 .05 .01
□ 455 Matt Williams .50 .23 .06
□ 456 Robby Thompson .10 .05 .01
□ 457 Shawon Dunston .10 .05 .01
□ 458 Russ Davis .10 .05 .01

☐ 459 Paul Sorrento	.10	.05	.01
☐ 460 Randy Johnson	.50	.23	.06
☐ 461 Chris Bosio	.10	.05	.01
☐ 462 Luis Sojo	.10	.05	.01
☐ 463 Sterling Hitchcock	.10	.05	.01
☐ 464 Benji Gil	.10	.05	.01
☐ 465 Mickey Tettleton	.25	.11	.03
☐ 466 Mark McLemore	.10	.05	.01
☐ 467 Darryl Hamilton	.10	.05	.01
☐ 468 Ken Hill	.25	.11	.03
☐ 469 Dean Palmer	.50	.23	.06
☐ 470 Carlos Delgado	.25	.11	.03
☐ 471 Ed Sprague	.25	.11	.03
☐ 472 Otis Nixon	.10	.05	.01
☐ 473 Pat Hentgen	.25	.11	.03
☐ 474 Juan Guzman	.10	.05	.01
☐ 475 John Olerud	.10	.05	.01
☐ 476 Buck Showalter CL	.10	.05	.01
☐ 477 Bobby Cox CL	.10	.05	.01
☐ 478 Tommy Lasorda CL	.50	.23	.06
☐ 479 Buck Showalter CL	.10	.05	.01
☐ 480 Sparky Anderson CL	.25	.11	.03
☐ 481U Randy Myers	.25	.11	.03
☐ 482U Kent Mercker	.25	.11	.03
☐ 483U David Wells	.25	.11	.03
☐ 484U Kevin Mitchell	.25	.11	.03
☐ 485U Randy Velarde	.25	.11	.03
☐ 486U Ryne Sandberg	1.50	.70	.19
☐ 487U Doug Jones	.25	.11	.03
☐ 488U Terry Adams	.25	.11	.03
☐ 489U Kevin Tapani	.25	.11	.03
☐ 490U Harold Baines	.50	.23	.06
☐ 491U Eric Davis	.25	.11	.03
☐ 492U Julio Franco	.25	.11	.03
☐ 493U Jack McDowell	.50	.23	.06
☐ 494U Devon White	.25	.11	.03
☐ 495U Kevin Brown	.25	.11	.03
☐ 496U Rick Wilkins	.25	.11	.03
☐ 497U Sean Berry	.25	.11	.03
☐ 498U Keith Lockhart	.25	.11	.03
☐ 499U Mark Loretta	.25	.11	.03
☐ 500U Paul Molitor	1.25	.55	.16
☐ 501U Roberto Kelly	.25	.11	.03
☐ 502U Lance Johnson	.50	.23	.06
☐ 503U Tino Martinez	.50	.23	.06
☐ 504U Kenny Rogers	.25	.11	.03
☐ 505U Todd Stottlemyre	.25	.11	.03
☐ 506U Gary Gaetti	.25	.11	.03
☐ 507U Royce Clayton	.25	.11	.03
☐ 508U Andy Benes	.25	.11	.03
☐ 509U Wally Joyner	.25	.11	.03
☐ 510U Erik Hanson	.25	.11	.03

1996 Upper Deck Blue Chip Prospects

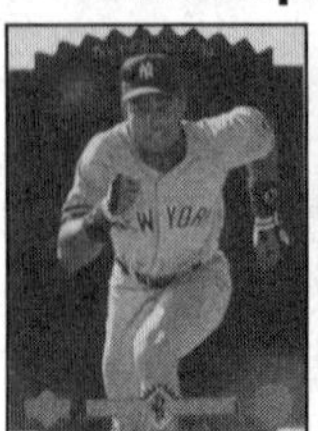
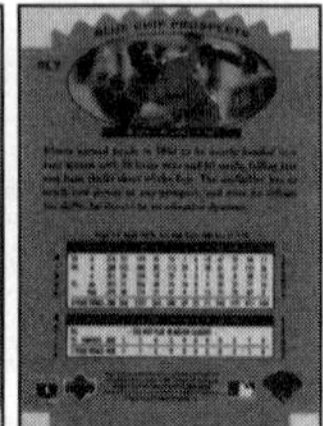

Randomly inserted in retail packs at a rate of one in 72, this 20-card set, diecut on the top and bottom, features some of the best young stars in the majors against a bluish background.

	MINT	NRMT	EXC
COMPLETE SET (20)	200.00	90.00	25.00
COMMON CARD (BC1-BC20)	6.00	2.70	.75
☐ BC1 Hideo Nomo	20.00	9.00	2.50
☐ BC2 Johnny Damon	7.00	3.10	.85
☐ BC3 Jason Isringhausen	6.00	2.70	.75
☐ BC4 Bill Pulsipher	6.00	2.70	.75
☐ BC5 Marty Cordova	7.00	3.10	.85
☐ BC6 Michael Tucker	7.00	3.10	.85
☐ BC7 John Wasdin	6.00	2.70	.75
☐ BC8 Karim Garcia	12.00	5.50	1.50
☐ BC9 Ruben Rivera	10.00	4.50	1.25
☐ BC10 Chipper Jones	40.00	18.00	5.00
☐ BC11 Billy Wagner	8.00	3.60	1.00
☐ BC12 Brooks Kieschnick	7.00	3.10	.85
☐ BC13 Alan Benes	8.00	3.60	1.00
☐ BC14 Roger Cedeno	6.00	2.70	.75
☐ BC15 Alex Rodriguez	60.00	27.00	7.50
☐ BC16 Jason Schmidt	7.00	3.10	.85
☐ BC17 Derek Jeter	40.00	18.00	5.00
☐ BC18 Brian L.Hunter	7.00	3.10	.85
☐ BC19 Garret Anderson	7.00	3.10	.85
☐ BC20 Manny Ramirez	15.00	6.75	1.85

1996 Upper Deck Diamond Destiny

Issued one per WalMark pack, these 40 cards feature leading players of baseball. The cards have two photos on the front with the player's name listed on the bottom. The backs have another photo along with biographical information. The cards are numbered with a "DD" prefix.

	MINT	NRMT	EXC
COMPLETE SET (40)	150.00	70.00	19.00
COMMON CARD (DD1-DD40)	1.50	.70	.19
☐ DD1 Chipper Jones	10.00	4.50	1.25
☐ DD2 Fred McGriff	2.50	1.10	.30
☐ DD3 John Smoltz	2.50	1.10	.30
☐ DD4 Ryan Klesko	2.50	1.10	.30
☐ DD5 Greg Maddux	10.00	4.50	1.25
☐ DD6 Cal Ripken	12.00	5.50	1.50
☐ DD7 Roberto Alomar	3.00	1.35	.35
☐ DD8 Eddie Murray	4.00	1.80	.50
☐ DD9 Brady Anderson	2.50	1.10	.30
☐ DD10 Mo Vaughn	4.00	1.80	.50
☐ DD11 Roger Clemens	3.00	1.35	.35
☐ DD12 Darin Erstad	8.00	3.60	1.00
☐ DD13 Sammy Sosa	2.50	1.10	.30
☐ DD14 Frank Thomas	15.00	6.75	1.85
☐ DD15 Barry Larkin	1.50	.70	.19
☐ DD16 Albert Belle	6.00	2.70	.75
☐ DD17 Manny Ramirez	4.00	1.80	.50
☐ DD18 Kenny Lofton	4.00	1.80	.50
☐ DD19 Dante Bichette	2.50	1.10	.30
☐ DD20 Gary Sheffield	2.50	1.10	.30
☐ DD21 Jeff Bagwell	6.00	2.70	.75
☐ DD22 Hideo Nomo	4.00	1.80	.50
☐ DD23 Mike Piazza	10.00	4.50	1.25
☐ DD24 Kirby Puckett	6.00	2.70	.75
☐ DD25 Paul Molitor	3.00	1.35	.35
☐ DD26 Chuck Knoblauch	2.50	1.10	.30
☐ DD27 Wade Boggs	2.50	1.10	.30
☐ DD28 Derek Jeter	10.00	4.50	1.25
☐ DD29 Rey Ordonez	2.50	1.10	.30
☐ DD30 Mark McGwire	5.00	2.20	.60
☐ DD31 Ozzie Smith	4.00	1.80	.50
☐ DD32 Tony Gwynn	6.00	2.70	.75
☐ DD33 Barry Bonds	4.00	1.80	.50
☐ DD34 Matt Williams	2.50	1.10	.30
☐ DD35 Ken Griffey Jr.	15.00	6.75	1.85
☐ DD36 Jay Buhner	2.50	1.10	.30
☐ DD37 Randy Johnson	2.50	1.10	.30
☐ DD38 Alex Rodriguez	15.00	6.75	1.85
☐ DD39 Juan Gonzalez	8.00	3.60	1.00
☐ DD40 Joe Carter	1.50	.70	.19

1996 Upper Deck Diamond Destiny Gold

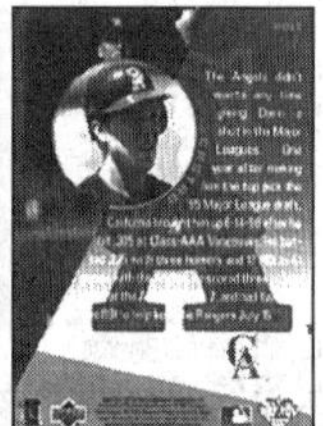

Randomly inserted in Wal-Mart packs at a rate of one in 143, these cards are parallel to the regular Diamond Destiny cards.

	MINT	NRMT	EXC
COMPLETE SET (40)	2500.00	1100.00	300.00
COMMON CARD (DD1-DD40)	30.00	13.50	3.70

*STARS: 12X TO 20X BASIC CARDS ..

1996 Upper Deck Diamond Destiny Silver

Randomly inserted in packs in Walmart packs at a rate of one in 35, these cards are parallel to the regular Diamond Destiny cards.

	MINT	NRMT	EXC
COMPLETE SET (40)	600.00	275.00	75.00
COMMON CARD (DD1-DD40)	8.00	3.60	1.00

*STARS: 2.5X to 5X BASIC CARDS ....

1996 Upper Deck Future Stock Prospects

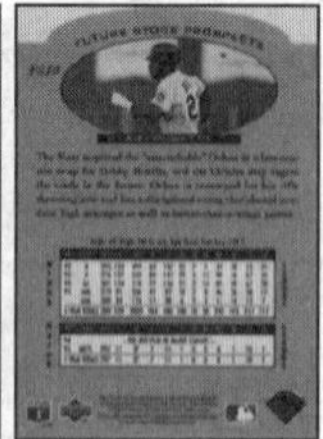

Randomly inserted in packs at a rate of one in 6, this 20-card set highlights the top prospects who made their major league debuts in 1995. The cards are diecut at the top and feature a purple border surrounding the player's picture.

	MINT	NRMT	EXC
COMPLETE SET (20)	12.00	5.50	1.50
COMMON CARD (FS1-FS20)	1.00	.45	.12
☐ FS1 George Arias	1.00	.45	.12
☐ FS2 Brian Barber	1.00	.45	.12
☐ FS3 Trey Beamon	1.00	.45	.12
☐ FS4 Yamil Benitez	1.50	.70	.19
☐ FS5 Jamie Brewington	1.00	.45	.12
☐ FS6 Tony Clark	4.00	1.80	.50
☐ FS7 Steve Cox	1.00	.45	.12
☐ FS8 Carlos Delgado	1.50	.70	.19
☐ FS9 Chad Fonville	1.00	.45	.12
☐ FS10 Alex Ochoa	1.50	.70	.19
☐ FS11 Curtis Goodwin	1.00	.45	.12
☐ FS12 Todd Greene	1.00	.45	.12
☐ FS13 Jimmy Haynes	1.00	.45	.12
☐ FS14 Quinton McCracken	1.00	.45	.12
☐ FS15 Billy McMillon	1.00	.45	.12
☐ FS16 Chan Ho Park	2.00	.90	.25
☐ FS17 Arquimedez Pozo	1.00	.45	.12
☐ FS18 Chris Snopek	1.00	.45	.12
☐ FS19 Shannon Stewart	1.00	.45	.12
☐ FS20 Jeff Suppan	2.00	.90	.25

1996 Upper Deck Gameface

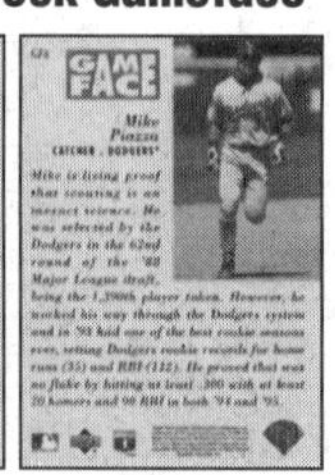

These Gameface cards were seeded at a rate of one per Upper Deck and Collector's Choice Wal Mart retail pack. The Upper Deck packs contained eight cards and the Collector's Choice packs contained sixteen cards. Both packs carried a suggested retail price of $1.50. The card fronts feature the player's photo surrounded by a "cloudy" white border along with a Gameface logo at the bottom.

	MINT	NRMT	EXC
COMPLETE SET (10)	12.00	5.50	1.50
COMMON CARD (GF1-GF10)	.30	.14	.04
☐ GF1 Ken Griffey Jr.	2.50	1.10	.30
☐ GF2 Frank Thomas	2.50	1.10	.30
☐ GF3 Barry Bonds	.60	.25	.07
☐ GF4 Albert Belle	1.00	.45	.12
☐ GF5 Cal Ripken	2.00	.90	.25
☐ GF6 Mike Piazza	1.50	.70	.19
☐ GF7 Chipper Jones	1.50	.70	.19
☐ GF8 Matt Williams	.30	.14	.04
☐ GF9 Hideo Nomo	.60	.25	.07
☐ GF10 Greg Maddux	1.50	.70	.19

1996 Upper Deck Hot Commodities

This 20 card set double die-cut set was randomly inserted into series two Upper Deck packs at a rate of one in 37. The set features some of baseball's most popular players.

	MINT	NRMT	EXC
COMPLETE SET (20)	200.00	90.00	25.00
COMMON CARD (HC1-HC20)	4.00	1.80	.50
☐ HC1 Ken Griffey Jr.	30.00	13.50	3.70
☐ HC2 Hideo Nomo	8.00	3.60	1.00
☐ HC3 Roberto Alomar	6.00	2.70	.75
☐ HC4 Paul Wilson	4.00	1.80	.50
☐ HC5 Albert Belle	12.00	5.50	1.50
☐ HC6 Manny Ramirez	8.00	3.60	1.00
☐ HC7 Kirby Puckett	12.00	5.50	1.50
☐ HC8 Johnny Damon	4.00	1.80	.50
☐ HC9 Randy Johnson	5.00	2.20	.60
☐ HC10 Greg Maddux	20.00	9.00	2.50
☐ HC11 Chipper Jones	20.00	9.00	2.50
☐ HC12 Barry Bonds	8.00	3.60	1.00
☐ HC13 Mo Vaughn	8.00	3.60	1.00
☐ HC14 Mike Piazza	20.00	9.00	2.50
☐ HC15 Cal Ripken	25.00	11.00	3.10
☐ HC16 Tim Salmon	4.00	1.80	.50
☐ HC17 Sammy Sosa	5.00	2.20	.60
☐ HC18 Kenny Lofton	8.00	3.60	1.00
☐ HC19 Tony Gwynn	12.00	5.50	1.50
☐ HC20 Frank Thomas	30.00	13.50	3.70

1996 Upper Deck V.J. Lovero Showcase

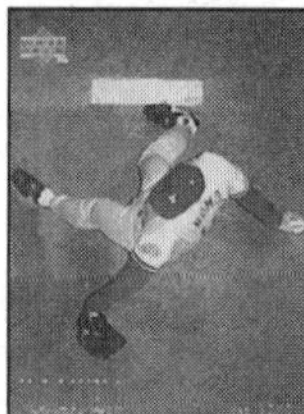

Upper Deck utilized photos from the files of V.J. Lovero to produce this set. The cards feature the photos along with a story of how Lovero took the photos. The cards are numbered with a "VJ" prefix.

	MINT	NRMT	EXC
COMPLETE SET (19)	25.00	11.00	3.10
COMMON CARD (VJ1-VJ19)	.50	.23	.06
☐ VJ1 Jim Abbott	.50	.23	.06
☐ VJ2 Hideo Nomo	2.00	.90	.25
☐ VJ3 Derek Jeter	4.00	1.80	.50
☐ VJ4 Barry Bonds	2.00	.90	.25
☐ VJ5 Greg Maddux	5.00	2.20	.60
☐ VJ6 Mark McGwire	2.50	1.10	.30
☐ VJ7 Jose Canseco	1.00	.45	.12
☐ VJ8 Ken Caminiti	1.00	.45	.12
☐ VJ9 Raul Mondesi	1.00	.45	.12
☐ VJ10 Ken Griffey Jr.	8.00	3.60	1.00
☐ VJ11 Jay Buhner	1.00	.45	.12
☐ VJ12 Randy Johnson	1.25	.55	.16
☐ VJ13 Roger Clemens	1.50	.70	.19
☐ VJ14 Brady Anderson	1.00	.45	.12
☐ VJ15 Frank Thomas	8.00	3.60	1.00
☐ VJ16 Garret Anderson Jim Edmonds Tim Salmon	.50	.23	.06
☐ VJ17 Mike Piazza	5.00	2.20	.60
☐ VJ18 Dante Bichette	1.00	.45	.12
☐ VJ19 Tony Gwynn	3.00	1.35	.35

1996 Upper Deck Nomo Highlights

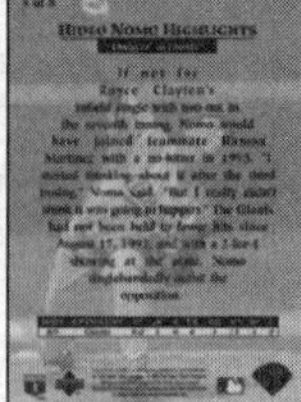

Los Angeles Dodgers star pitcher and Upper Deck spokesperson Hideo Nomo was featured in this special five card set. The cards were randomly seeded into second series packs and feature game action as well as descriptions of some of Nomo's key 1995 games.

	MINT	NRMT	EXC
COMPLETE SET (5)	20.00	9.00	2.50
COMMON CARD (1-5)	5.00	2.20	.60
☐ 1 Hideo Nomo Dodgers at Giants First Career Start	5.00	2.20	.60
☐ 2 Hideo Nomo	5.00	2.20	.60
☐ 3 Hideo Nomo 1995 All-Star Game	5.00	2.20	.60
☐ 4 Hideo Nomo Dodgers at Giants	5.00	2.20	.60

One-Hitter			
□ 5 Hideo Nomo	5.00	2.20	.60
Dodgers at Padres			
Season-Ending Performance			

1996 Upper Deck Power Driven

Randomly inserted in packs at a rate of one in 36, this 20-card set consists of embossed rainbow foil inserts of baseball's top power hitters.

	MINT	NRMT	EXC
COMPLETE SET (20)	125.00	55.00	15.50
COMMON CARD (PD1-PD20)	2.50	1.10	.30
□ PD1 Albert Belle	12.00	5.50	1.50
□ PD2 Barry Bonds	8.00	3.60	1.00
□ PD3 Jay Buhner	4.00	1.80	.50
□ PD4 Jose Canseco	4.00	1.80	.50
□ PD5 Cecil Fielder	2.50	1.10	.30
□ PD6 Juan Gonzalez	15.00	6.75	1.85
□ PD7 Ken Griffey Jr.	30.00	13.50	3.70
□ PD8 Eric Karros	2.50	1.10	.30
□ PD9 Fred McGriff	4.00	1.80	.50
□ PD10 Mark McGwire	10.00	4.50	1.25
□ PD11 Rafael Palmeiro	4.00	1.80	.50
□ PD12 Mike Piazza	20.00	9.00	2.50
□ PD13 Manny Ramirez	8.00	3.60	1.00
□ PD14 Tim Salmon	4.00	1.80	.50
□ PD15 Reggie Sanders	2.50	1.10	.30
□ PD16 Sammy Sosa	5.00	2.20	.60
□ PD17 Frank Thomas	30.00	13.50	3.70
□ PD18 Mo Vaughn	8.00	3.60	1.00
□ PD19 Larry Walker	4.00	1.80	.50
□ PD20 Matt Williams	4.00	1.80	.50

1996 Upper Deck Predictor Hobby

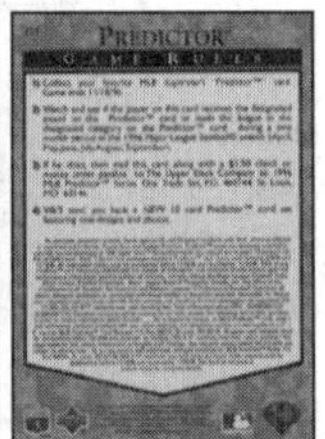

Randomly inserted in hobby packs at a rate of one in 12, this 60-card predictor set offers unique prizes as Major League Baseball players compete for monthly milestones and awards. The fronts feature a cutout player photo against a pinstriped background surrounded by a gray marble border.

	MINT	NRMT	EXC
COMPLETE SET (60)	110.00	50.00	14.00
COMPLETE SERIES 1 (30)	60.00	27.00	7.50
COMPLETE SERIES 2 (30)	50.00	22.00	6.25
COMMON CARD (H1-H60)	1.00	.45	.12
*EXCHANGE CARDS: .25X to .5X BASIC CARDS			
□ H1 Albert Belle	4.00	1.80	.50
□ H2 Kenny Lofton	2.50	1.10	.30
□ H3 Rafael Palmeiro	1.50	.70	.16
□ H4 Ken Griffey Jr.	10.00	4.50	1.25
□ H5 Tim Salmon	1.50	.70	.16
□ H6 Cal Ripken	8.00	3.60	1.00
□ H7 Mark McGwire W	3.00	1.35	.35
□ H8 Frank Thomas W	10.00	4.50	1.25
□ H9 Mo Vaughn W	2.50	1.10	.30
□ H10 Player of Month Longshot	1.00	.45	.12
□ H11 Roger Clemens	2.00	.90	.25
□ H12 David Cone	1.25	.55	.16
□ H13 Jose Mesa	1.00	.45	.12
□ H14 Randy Johnson	1.50	.70	.16
□ H15 Chuck Finley	1.00	.45	.12
□ H16 Mike Mussina	2.00	.90	.25
□ H17 Kevin Appier	1.25	.55	.16
□ H18 Kenny Rogers	1.00	.45	.12
□ H19 Lee Smith	1.00	.45	.12
□ H20 Pitcher of Month Longshot W	1.00	.45	.12
□ H21 George Arias	1.00	.45	.12
□ H22 Jose Herrera	1.00	.45	.12
□ H23 Tony Clark	2.00	.90	.25
□ H24 Todd Greene	1.00	.45	.12
□ H25 Derek Jeter W	6.00	2.70	.75
□ H26 Arquimedez Pozo	1.00	.45	.12
□ H27 Matt Lawton	1.00	.45	.12
□ H28 Shannon Stewart	1.00	.45	.12
□ H29 Chris Snopek	1.00	.45	.12
□ H30 Most Rookie Hits Longshot	1.00	.45	.12
□ H31 Jeff Bagwell W	4.00	1.80	.50
□ H32 Dante Bichette	1.50	.70	.16
□ H33 Barry Bonds W	2.50	1.10	.30
□ H34 Tony Gwynn	4.00	1.80	.50
□ H35 Chipper Jones	6.00	2.70	.75
□ H36 Eric Karros	1.25	.55	.16
□ H37 Barry Larkin	1.25	.55	.16
□ H38 Mike Piazza	6.00	2.70	.75
□ H39 Matt Williams	1.50	.70	.16
□ H40 Long Shot Card	5.00	2.20	.60
□ H41 Osvaldo Fernandez	1.00	.45	.12
□ H42 Tom Glavine	1.50	.70	.16
□ H43 Jason Isringhausen	1.00	.45	.12
□ H44 Greg Maddux	6.00	2.70	.75
□ H45 Pedro Martinez	1.50	.70	.16
□ H46 Hideo Nomo	2.50	1.10	.30
□ H47 Pete Schourek	1.00	.45	.12
□ H48 Paul Wilson	1.00	.45	.12
□ H49 Mark Wohlers	1.00	.45	.12
□ H50 Long Shot Card	1.00	.45	.12
□ H51 Bob Abreu	1.50	.70	.16
□ H52 Trey Beamon	1.00	.45	.12
□ H53 Yamil Benitez	1.25	.55	.16
□ H54 Roger Cedeno	1.50	.70	.16
□ H55 Todd Hollandsworth	1.25	.55	.16
□ H56 Marvin Benard	1.00	.45	.12
□ H57 Jason Kendall	1.50	.70	.16
□ H58 Brooks Kieschnick	1.50	.70	.16
□ H59 Rey Ordonez W	1.50	.70	.16
□ H60 Long Shot Card	1.00	.45	.12

1996 Upper Deck Predictor Retail

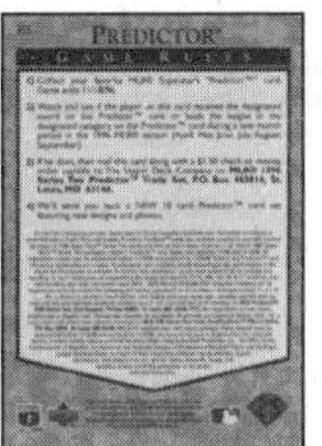

Randomly inserted in retail packs at a rate of one in 12, this 60-card predictor set offers unique prizes as Major League Baseball players compete for "monthly milestones and awards." The fronts feature a "cutout" player photo against a pinstriped background surrounded by a gray marble border.

	MINT	NRMT	EXC
COMPLETE SET (60)	150.00	70.00	19.00
COMPLETE SERIES 1 (30)	100.00	45.00	12.50
COMPLETE SERIES 2 (30)	50.00	22.00	6.25
COMMON CARD (R1-R60)	1.00	.45	.12
*EXCHANGE CARDS: .25X to .5X BASIC CARDS			
□ R1 Albert Belle W	4.00	1.80	.50
□ R2 Jay Buhner W	1.50	.70	.19
□ R3 Juan Gonzalez	5.00	2.20	.60
□ R4 Ken Griffey Jr.	10.00	4.50	1.25
□ R5 Mark McGwire W	3.00	1.35	.35
□ R6 Rafael Palmeiro	1.50	.70	.19
□ R7 Tim Salmon	1.50	.70	.19
□ R8 Frank Thomas	10.00	4.50	1.25
□ R9 Mo Vaughn W	2.50	1.10	.30
□ R10 Monthly HR Ldr Longshot W	1.00	.45	.12
□ R11 Albert Belle W	4.00	1.80	.50
□ R12 Jay Buhner	1.50	.70	.19
□ R13 Jim Edmonds	1.25	.55	.16
□ R14 Cecil Fielder	1.25	.55	.16
□ R15 Ken Griffey Jr.	10.00	4.50	1.25
□ R16 Edgar Martinez	1.25	.55	.16
□ R17 Manny Ramirez	2.50	1.10	.30
□ R18 Frank Thomas	10.00	4.50	1.25
□ R19 Mo Vaughn W	2.50	1.10	.30
□ R20 Monthly RBI Ldr Longshot	1.00	.45	.12
□ R21 Roberto Alomar W	2.00	.90	.25
□ R22 Carlos Baerga	1.25	.55	.16
□ R23 Wade Boggs	1.50	.70	.19
□ R24 Ken Griffey Jr.	10.00	4.50	1.25
□ R25 Chuck Knoblauch	1.50	.70	.19
□ R26 Kenny Lofton	2.50	1.10	.30
□ R27 Edgar Martinez	1.25	.55	.16
□ R28 Tim Salmon	1.50	.70	.19
□ R29 Frank Thomas	10.00	4.50	1.25
□ R30 Monthly Hits Ldr Longshot W	1.00	.45	.12
□ R31 Dante Bichette	1.50	.70	.19
□ R32 Barry Bonds W	2.50	1.10	.30
□ R33 Ron Gant	1.25	.55	.16
□ R34 Chipper Jones	6.00	2.70	.75
□ R35 Fred McGriff	1.50	.70	.19
□ R36 Mike Piazza	6.00	2.70	.75
□ R37 Sammy Sosa	1.50	.70	.19
□ R38 Larry Walker	1.50	.70	.19
□ R39 Matt Williams	1.50	.70	.19
□ R40 Long Shot Card	1.00	.45	.12
□ R41 Jeff Bagwell W	4.00	1.80	.50
□ R42 Dante Bichette	1.50	.70	.19
□ R43 Barry Bonds W	2.50	1.10	.30
□ R44 Jeff Conine	1.25	.55	.16
□ R45 Andres Galarraga	1.50	.70	.19
□ R46 Mike Piazza	6.00	2.70	.75
□ R47 Reggie Sanders	1.00	.45	.12
□ R48 Sammy Sosa	1.50	.70	.19
□ R49 Matt Williams	1.50	.70	.19
□ R50 Long Shot Card	1.00	.45	.12
□ R51 Jeff Bagwell	4.00	1.80	.50
□ R52 Derek Bell	1.25	.55	.16
□ R53 Dante Bichette	1.50	.70	.19
□ R54 Craig Biggio	1.25	.55	.16
□ R55 Barry Bonds	2.50	1.10	.30
□ R56 Bret Boone	1.00	.45	.12
□ R57 Tony Gwynn	4.00	1.80	.50
□ R58 Barry Larkin	1.25	.55	.16
□ R59 Mike Piazza W	6.00	2.70	.75
□ R60 Long Shot Card	1.00	.45	.12

1996 Upper Deck Ripken Collection

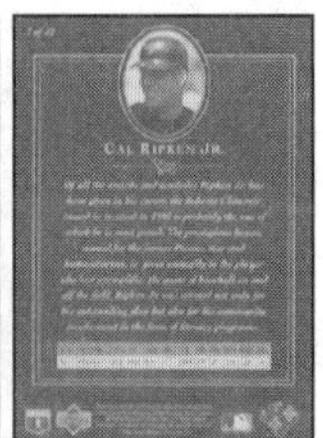

This 23 card set was issued across all the various Upper Deck brands. The cards were issued to commemorate Cal Ripken's career, which had been capped the previous season by the breaking of the consecutive game streak long held by Lou Gehrig.

	MINT	NRMT	EXC
COMPLETE SET (23)	125.00	55.00	15.50
COMP.COLC SER.1 (5)	15.00	6.75	1.85
COMP.UD SER.1 (4)	25.00	11.00	3.10
COMP.COLC SER.2 (4)	12.00	5.50	1.50
COMP.UD SER.2 (5)	25.00	11.00	3.10
COMPLETE SP SET (5)	50.00	22.00	6.25
COMMON COLC (1-4/9-12)	4.00	1.80	.50
COMMON UD (5-8/13-17)	6.00	2.70	.75
COMMON SP (18-22)	12.00	5.50	1.50
□ 1 Cal Ripken COLC	4.00	1.80	.50
After playing in 2,131 consecutive games			
□ 2 Cal Ripken COLC	4.00	1.80	.50
Barry Bonds#(1995 All-Star Game			
□ 3 Cal Ripken COLC	4.00	1.80	.50
300th home run			
□ 4 Cal Ripken COLC	4.00	1.80	.50
Chasing Pop-up#(1994			
□ 5 Cal Ripken UD	6.00	2.70	.75
Running to first#(1995			
□ 6 Cal Ripken UD	6.00	2.70	.75
Brian McRae sliding into second#(1992			
□ 7 Cal Ripken UD	6.00	2.70	.75
1992 Roberto Clemente Award			
□ 8 Cal Ripken UD	6.00	2.70	.75
Batting pose#(1991			
□ 9 Cal Ripken COLC	4.00	1.80	.50
Batting follow-through#(1991			
□ 10 Cal Ripken COLC	4.00	1.80	.50
1991 1st Gold Glove			
□ 11 Cal Ripken COLC	4.00	1.80	.50
Midway through swing#(1991			
□ 12 Cal Ripken COLC	4.00	1.80	.50
Fielding and throwing Ball#(1990			
□ 13 Cal Ripken UD	6.00	2.70	.75
Black uniform top in field#(1990			
□ 14 Cal Ripken UD	6.00	2.70	.75
Batting follow-through#(1987			
□ 15 Cal Ripken UD	6.00	2.70	.75
In Backswing#(1986			
□ 16 Cal Ripken UD	6.00	2.70	.75
Midway through swing#(1984			
□ 17 Cal Ripken UD	6.00	2.70	.75
Ball about to enter glove#(1983			
□ 18 Cal Ripken SP	12.00	5.50	1.50
Throwing#(1983			
□ 19 Cal Ripken SP	12.00	5.50	1.50
Batting, Orange Uniform#(1983			
□ 20 Cal Ripken SP	12.00	5.50	1.50
Batting follow-through#(1982			
□ 21 Cal Ripken SP	12.00	5.50	1.50
Fielding at third#(Mark Belanger in background#(1981			
□ 22 Cal Ripken SP	12.00	5.50	1.50
Eddie Murray#(1981			
□ NNO Cal Ripken Header COLC	4.00	1.80	.50

1996 Upper Deck Run Producers

This 20 card set was randomly inserted into series two packs at a rate of one every 71 packs. The cards are thermographically printed, which gives the card a rubber surface texture. The cards are double die-cut and are foil stamped. These cards are designed to show off the technology of the Upper Deck cards.

	MINT	NRMT	EXC
COMPLETE SET (20)	225.00	100.00	28.00
COMMON CARD (RP1-RP20)	4.00	1.80	.50
□ RP1 Albert Belle	15.00	6.75	1.85
□ RP2 Dante Bichette	5.00	2.20	.60
□ RP3 Barry Bonds	10.00	4.50	1.25
□ RP4 Jay Buhner	5.00	2.20	.60
□ RP5 Jose Canseco	5.00	2.20	.60
□ RP6 Juan Gonzalez	20.00	9.00	2.50
□ RP7 Ken Griffey Jr.	40.00	18.00	5.00
□ RP8 Tony Gwynn	15.00	6.75	1.85
□ RP9 Kenny Lofton	10.00	4.50	1.25
□ RP10 Edgar Martinez	4.00	1.80	.50
□ RP11 Fred McGriff	5.00	2.20	.60
□ RP12 Mark McGwire	12.00	5.50	1.50
□ RP13 Rafael Palmeiro	5.00	2.20	.60
□ RP14 Mike Piazza	25.00	11.00	3.10
□ RP15 Manny Ramirez	10.00	4.50	1.25
□ RP16 Tim Salmon	5.00	2.20	.60
□ RP17 Sammy Sosa	6.00	2.70	.75
□ RP18 Frank Thomas	40.00	18.00	5.00
□ RP19 Mo Vaughn	10.00	4.50	1.25
□ RP20 Matt Williams	5.00	2.20	.60

1996 Upper Deck All-Stars

This 18-card set measures approximately 3 1/2" by 5" with a suggested retail price of $19.95 a set. The fronts feature borderless color player photos and are foil stamped with the official 1996 Major League Baseball All-Star game logo. The backs carry another player photo with player information and statistics. The cards are checklisted below in alphabetical order.

	MINT	NRMT	EXC
COMPLETE SET (18)	20.00	9.00	2.50
COMMON CARD (1-18)	.30	.14	.04
□ 1 Roberto Alomar	1.00	.45	.12
□ 2 Sandy Alomar Jr.	.30	.14	.04
□ 3 Jeff Bagwell	1.50	.70	.19
□ 4 Albert Belle	2.00	.90	.25
□ 5 Dante Bichette	.75	.35	.09
□ 6 Craig Biggio	.50	.23	.06
□ 7 Wade Boggs	.75	.35	.09
□ 8 Barry Bonds	1.00	.45	.12
□ 9 Ken Griffey Jr.	4.00	1.80	.50
□ 10 Tony Gwynn	2.00	.90	.25
□ 11 Barry Larkin	.50	.23	.06
□ 12 Kenny Lofton	1.00	.45	.12
□ 13 Charles Nagy	.50	.23	.06
□ 14 Mike Piazza	3.00	1.35	.35
□ 15 Cal Ripken Jr.	4.00	1.80	.50
□ 16 John Smoltz	.75	.35	.09
□ 17 Frank Thomas	4.00	1.80	.50
□ 18 Matt Williams	.75	.35	.09

1996 Upper Deck Meet the Stars Griffey Redemption

This one-card set features a postcard-size action photo of Ken Grifey Jr. with a "Magic Moment" from a 1995 Post-Season game printed on one side of the three-sided black-and-aqua border. The back is blank.

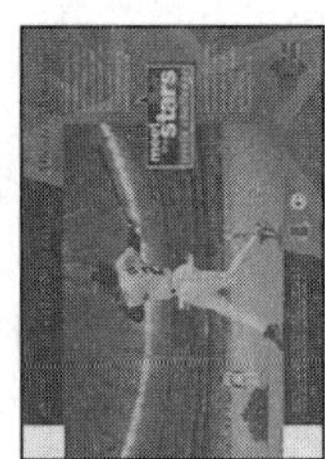

	MINT	NRMT	EXC
COMPLETE SET (1)	3.00	1.35	.35
COMMON CARD	3.00	1.35	.35
☐ 1 Ken Griffey Jr - 1995 Post-Season	3.00	1.35	.35

1996 Upper Deck Ripken Collection Jumbos

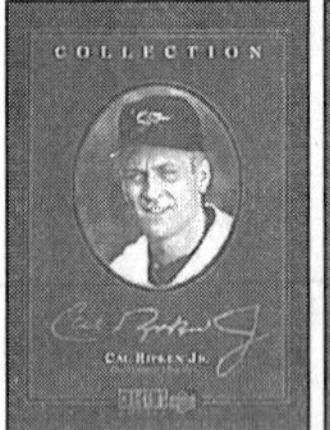

With a suggested retail price of $19.95, cards from this 22-card boxed set measures approximately 3 1/2" by 5" and features color borderless photos of Cal Ripken Jr. with a gold foil facsimile autograph. The cards parallel the standard Ripken Collection inserted into various 1996 Upper Deck Baseball products. The backs carry information about the player.

	MINT	NRMT	EXC
COMPLETE SET	20.00	9.00	2.50
COMMON CARD	1.00	.45	.12
☐ 1 Cal Ripken COLC	2.00	.90	.25
after playing in 2131 consecutive games			
☐ 2 Cal Ripken COLC	1.00	.45	.12
Barry Bonds			
1995 All-Star Game			
☐ 3 Cal Ripken COLC	1.00	.45	.12
300th home run			
☐ 4 Cal Ripken COLC	1.00	.45	.12
Chasing Pop-up			
1994			
☐ 5 Cal Ripken UD	1.00	.45	.12
Running to first			
1995			
☐ 6 Cal Ripken UD	1.00	.45	.12
Brian McRae sliding into second			
1992			
☐ 7 Cal Ripken UD	1.00	.45	.12
1992 Roberto Clemente Award			
☐ 8 Cal Ripken UD	1.00	.45	.12
Batting pose			
1991			
☐ 9 Cal Ripken COLC	1.00	.45	.12
Batting follow through			
1991			
☐ 10 Cal Ripken COLC	1.00	.45	.12
1991 1st Gold Glove			
☐ 11 Cal Ripken COLC	1.00	.45	.12
Midway through swing			
1991			
☐ 12 Cal Ripken COLC	1.00	.45	.12
Fielding and throwing ball			
1990			
☐ 13 Cal Ripken UD	1.00	.45	.12
Black uniform top in field			
1990			
☐ 14 Cal Ripken UD	1.00	.45	.12
Batting follow through			
1987			
☐ 15 Cal Ripken UD	1.00	.45	.12
in Backswing			
1986			
☐ 16 Cal Ripken UD	1.00	.45	.12
Midway through swing			
1984			
☐ 17 Cal Ripken UD	1.00	.45	.12
Ball about to enter glove			
1983			
☐ 18 Cal Ripken SP	1.00	.45	.12
Throwing			
1983			
☐ 19 Cal Ripken SP	1.00	.45	.12
Batting. Orange uniform			
1983			
☐ 20 Cal Ripken SP	1.00	.45	.12
Batting follow-through			
1982			
☐ 21 Cal Ripken SP	1.00	.45	.12
Fielding at third			
Mark Belanger in background			
1981			
☐ 22 Cal Ripken SP	1.00	.45	.12
Eddie Murray			
1981			

1996 Upper Deck Nomo ROY Japanese

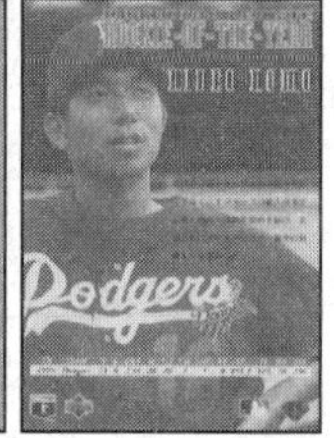

Produced by Upper Deck, this 3 1/2" by 5" card commemorates Hideo Nomo being named the Rookie-of-the-Year of the National League for 1995. The front features a color action player photo while the back displays a blue-tinted player portrait with player information in Japanese.

	MINT	NRMT	EXC
COMPLETE SET (1)	5.00	2.20	.60
COMMON CARD (1)	5.00	2.20	.60
☐ 1 Hideo Nomo	5.00	2.20	.60

1997 Upper Deck

The 1997 Upper Deck first series totals 240 cards. The 12-card packs retail for $2.49 each. Among the susbets in the first series are Star Rookies, Global Impact, Defensive Gems, Strike Force, Season Highlights and a nine card Jackie Robinson 50th anniversary set to lead off the 97 issue. Many cards have dates on the front to identify when, and when possible, what significant event is pictured. The backs include a player photo, stats and a brief blurb to go with vital statistics. A 30-card update set (numbered 241-270) was available to collectors that mailed in 10 series one wrappers along with $3 for postage and handling. The Update set is composed primarily of 1996 post-season highlights.

	MINT	NRMT	EXC
COMPLETE SERIES 1 (260)	30.00	13.50	3.70
COMMON CARD (1-240)	.10	.05	.01
COMP.UPDATE SET (30)	6.00	2.70	.75
COMMON UPDATE (241-270)	.10	.05	.01
☐ 1 Jackie Robinson	.50	.23	.06
The Beginnings			
☐ 2 Jackie Robinson	.50	.23	.06
Breaking the Barrier			
☐ 3 Jackie Robinson	.50	.23	.06
The MVP Season, 1949			
☐ 4 Jackie Robinson	.50	.23	.06
1951 season			
☐ 5 Jackie Robinson	.50	.23	.06
1952 and 1953 seasons			
☐ 6 Jackie Robinson	.50	.23	.06
1954 season			
☐ 7 Jackie Robinson	.50	.23	.06
1955 season			
☐ 8 Jackie Robinson	.50	.23	.06
1956 season			
☐ 9 Jackie Robinson	.50	.23	.06
Hall of Fame			
☐ 10 Chipper Jones	2.00	.90	.25
☐ 11 Marquis Grissom	.25	.11	.03
☐ 12 Jermaine Dye	.50	.23	.06
☐ 13 Mark Lemke	.10	.05	.01
☐ 14 Terrell Wade	.10	.05	.01
☐ 15 Fred McGriff	.40	.18	.05
☐ 16 Tom Glavine	.40	.18	.05
☐ 17 Mark Wohlers	.10	.05	.01
☐ 18 Randy Myers	.10	.05	.01
☐ 19 Roberto Alomar	.60	.25	.07
☐ 20 Cal Ripken	2.50	1.10	.30
☐ 21 Rafael Palmeiro	.40	.18	.05
☐ 22 Mike Mussina	.60	.25	.07
☐ 23 Brady Anderson	.25	.11	.03
☐ 24 Jose Canseco	.40	.18	.05
☐ 25 Mo Vaughn	.75	.35	.09
☐ 26 Roger Clemens	.60	.25	.07
☐ 27 Tim Naehring	.10	.05	.01
☐ 28 Jeff Suppan	.25	.11	.03
☐ 29 Troy Percival	.10	.05	.01
☐ 30 Sammy Sosa	.50	.23	.06
☐ 31 Amaury Telemaco	.10	.05	.01
☐ 32 Rey Sanchez	.10	.05	.01
☐ 33 Scott Servais	.10	.05	.01
☐ 34 Steve Trachsel	.10	.05	.01
☐ 35 Mark Grace	.40	.18	.05
☐ 36 Wilson Alvarez	.10	.05	.01
☐ 37 Harold Baines	.10	.05	.01
☐ 38 Tony Phillips	.10	.05	.01
☐ 39 James Baldwin	.10	.05	.01
☐ 40 Frank Thomas	3.00	1.35	.35
☐ 41 Lyle Mouton	.10	.05	.01
☐ 42 Chris Snopek	.10	.05	.01
☐ 43 Hal Morris	.10	.05	.01
☐ 44 Eric Davis	.10	.05	.01
☐ 45 Barry Larkin	.40	.18	.05
☐ 46 Reggie Sanders	.25	.11	.03
☐ 47 Pete Schourek	.10	.05	.01
☐ 48 Lee Smith	.25	.11	.03
☐ 49 Charles Nagy	.25	.11	.03
☐ 50 Albert Belle	1.25	.55	.16
☐ 51 Julio Franco	.10	.05	.01
☐ 52 Kenny Lofton	.75	.35	.09
☐ 53 Orel Hershiser	.25	.11	.03
☐ 54 Omar Vizquel	.25	.11	.03
☐ 55 Eric Young	.25	.11	.03
☐ 56 Curtis Leskanic	.10	.05	.01
☐ 57 Quinton McCracken	.10	.05	.01
☐ 58 Kevin Ritz	.10	.05	.01
☐ 59 Walt Weiss	.10	.05	.01
☐ 60 Dante Bichette	.40	.18	.05
☐ 61 Mark Lewis	.10	.05	.01
☐ 62 Tony Clark	.40	.18	.05
☐ 63 Travis Fryman	.25	.11	.03
☐ 64 John Smoltz SF	.25	.11	.03
☐ 65 Greg Maddux SF	1.00	.45	.12
☐ 66 Tom Glavine SF	.25	.11	.03
☐ 67 Mike Mussina SF	.25	.11	.03
☐ 68 Andy Pettitte SF	.40	.18	.05
☐ 69 Mariano Rivera SF	.25	.11	.03
☐ 70 Hideo Nomo SF	.40	.18	.05
☐ 71 Kevin Brown SF	.25	.11	.03
☐ 72 Randy Johnson SF	.25	.11	.03
☐ 73 Felipe Lira	.10	.05	.01
☐ 74 Kimera Bartee	.10	.05	.01
☐ 75 Alan Trammell	.25	.11	.03
☐ 76 Kevin Brown	.25	.11	.03
☐ 77 Edgar Renteria	.40	.18	.05
☐ 78 Al Leiter	.10	.05	.01
☐ 79 Charles Johnson	.10	.05	.01
☐ 80 Andre Dawson	.25	.11	.03
☐ 81 Billy Wagner	.25	.11	.03
☐ 82 Donne Wall	.10	.05	.01
☐ 83 Jeff Bagwell	1.25	.55	.16
☐ 84 Keith Lockhart	.10	.05	.01
☐ 85 Jeff Montgomery	.10	.05	.01
☐ 86 Tom Goodwin	.10	.05	.01
☐ 87 Tim Belcher	.10	.05	.01
☐ 88 Mike Macfarlane	.10	.05	.01
☐ 89 Joe Randa	.10	.05	.01
☐ 90 Brett Butler	.10	.05	.01
☐ 91 Todd Worrell	.10	.05	.01
☐ 92 Todd Hollandsworth	.25	.11	.03
☐ 93 Ismael Valdes	.25	.11	.03
☐ 94 Hideo Nomo	.75	.35	.09
☐ 95 Mike Piazza	2.00	.90	.25
☐ 96 Jeff Cirillo	.10	.05	.01
☐ 97 Ricky Bones	.10	.05	.01
☐ 98 Fernando Vina	.10	.05	.01
☐ 99 Ben McDonald	.10	.05	.01
☐ 100 John Jaha	.25	.11	.03
☐ 101 Mark Loretta	.10	.05	.01
☐ 102 Paul Molitor	.60	.25	.07
☐ 103 Rick Aguilera	.10	.05	.01
☐ 104 Marty Cordova	.25	.11	.03
☐ 105 Kirby Puckett	1.25	.55	.16
☐ 106 Dan Naulty	.10	.05	.01
☐ 107 Frank Rodriguez	.10	.05	.01
☐ 108 Shane Andrews	.10	.05	.01
☐ 109 Henry Rodriguez	.25	.11	.03
☐ 110 Mark Grudzielanek	.10	.05	.01
☐ 111 Pedro Martinez	.25	.11	.03
☐ 112 Ugueth Urbina	.10	.05	.01
☐ 113 David Segui	.10	.05	.01
☐ 114 Rey Ordonez	.40	.18	.05
☐ 115 Bernard Gilkey	.10	.05	.01
☐ 116 Butch Huskey	.10	.05	.01
☐ 117 Paul Wilson	.25	.11	.03
☐ 118 Alex Ochoa	.10	.05	.01
☐ 119 John Franco	.10	.05	.01
☐ 120 Dwight Gooden	.25	.11	.03
☐ 121 Ruben Rivera	.40	.18	.05
☐ 122 Andy Pettitte	.75	.35	.09
☐ 123 Tino Martinez	.25	.11	.03
☐ 124 Bernie Williams	.60	.25	.07
☐ 125 Wade Boggs	.40	.18	.05
☐ 126 Paul O'Neill	.10	.05	.01
☐ 127 Scott Brosius	.10	.05	.01
☐ 128 Ernie Young	.10	.05	.01
☐ 129 Doug Johns	.10	.05	.01
☐ 130 Geronimo Berroa	.10	.05	.01
☐ 131 Jason Giambi	.25	.11	.03
☐ 132 John Wasdin	.10	.05	.01
☐ 133 Jim Eisenreich	.10	.05	.01
☐ 134 Ricky Otero	.10	.05	.01
☐ 135 Ricky Bottalico	.10	.05	.01
☐ 136 Mark Langston DG	.10	.05	.01
☐ 137 Greg Maddux DG	1.00	.45	.12
☐ 138 Ivan Rodriguez DG	.40	.18	.05
☐ 139 Charles Johnson DG	.10	.05	.01
☐ 140 J.T. Snow DG	.10	.05	.01
☐ 141 Mark Grace DG	.25	.11	.03
☐ 142 Roberto Alomar DG	.25	.11	.03
☐ 143 Craig Biggio DG	.25	.11	.03
☐ 144 Ken Caminiti DG	.25	.11	.03
☐ 145 Matt Williams DG	.25	.11	.03
☐ 146 Omar Vizquel DG	.25	.11	.03
☐ 147 Cal Ripken DG	1.25	.55	.16
☐ 148 Ozzie Smith DG	.40	.18	.05
☐ 149 Rey Ordonez DG	.25	.11	.03
☐ 150 Ken Griffey Jr. DG	1.50	.70	.19
☐ 151 Devon White DG	.10	.05	.01
☐ 152 Barry Bonds DG	.40	.18	.05
☐ 153 Kenny Lofton DG	.40	.18	.05
☐ 154 Mickey Morandini	.10	.05	.01
☐ 155 Gregg Jefferies	.10	.05	.01
☐ 156 Curt Schilling	.10	.05	.01
☐ 157 Jason Kendall	.25	.11	.03
☐ 158 Francisco Cordova	.10	.05	.01
☐ 159 Dennis Eckersley	.25	.11	.03
☐ 160 Ron Gant	.25	.11	.03
☐ 161 Ozzie Smith	.75	.35	.09
☐ 162 Brian Jordan	.25	.11	.03
☐ 163 John Mabry	.10	.05	.01
☐ 164 Andy Ashby	.10	.05	.01
☐ 165 Steve Finley	.10	.05	.01
☐ 166 Fernando Valenzuela	.25	.11	.03
☐ 167 Archi Cianfrocco	.10	.05	.01
☐ 168 Wally Joyner	.10	.05	.01
☐ 169 Greg Vaughn	.10	.05	.01
☐ 170 Barry Bonds	.75	.35	.09
☐ 171 William VanLandingham	.10	.05	.01
☐ 172 Marvin Benard	.10	.05	.01
☐ 173 Rich Aurilia	.10	.05	.01
☐ 174 Jay Canizaro	.10	.05	.01
☐ 175 Ken Griffey Jr.	3.00	1.35	.35
☐ 176 Bob Wells	.10	.05	.01
☐ 177 Jay Buhner	.40	.18	.05
☐ 178 Sterling Hitchcock	.10	.05	.01
☐ 179 Edgar Martinez	.25	.11	.03
☐ 180 Rusty Greer	.25	.11	.03
☐ 181 Dave Nilsson GI	.10	.05	.01
☐ 182 Larry Walker GI	.25	.11	.03
☐ 183 Edgar Renteria GI	.25	.11	.03
☐ 184 Rey Ordonez GI	.25	.11	.03
☐ 185 Rafael Palmeiro GI	.25	.11	.03
☐ 186 Osvaldo Fernandez GI	.10	.05	.01
☐ 187 Raul Mondesi GI	.25	.11	.03
☐ 188 Manny Ramirez GI	.40	.18	.05
☐ 189 Sammy Sosa GI	.25	.11	.03
☐ 190 Robert Eenhoorn GI	.10	.05	.01
☐ 191 Devon White GI	.10	.05	.01
☐ 192 Hideo Nomo GI	.40	.18	.05
☐ 193 Mac Suzuki GI	.10	.05	.01
☐ 194 Chan Ho Park GI	.25	.11	.03
☐ 195 Fernando Valenzuela GI	.25	.11	.03
☐ 196 Andruw Jones GI	1.50	.70	.19
☐ 197 Vinny Castilla GI	.25	.11	.03
☐ 198 Dennis Martinez GI	.10	.05	.01
☐ 199 Ruben Rivera GI	.25	.11	.03
☐ 200 Juan Gonzalez GI	.75	.35	.09
☐ 201 Roberto Alomar GI	.25	.11	.03
☐ 202 Edgar Martinez GI	.25	.11	.03
☐ 203 Ivan Rodriguez GI	.40	.18	.05
☐ 204 Carlos Delgado GI	.25	.11	.03
☐ 205 Andres Galarraga GI	.25	.11	.03
☐ 206 Ozzie Guillen GI	.10	.05	.01
☐ 207 Midre Cummings GI	.10	.05	.01
☐ 208 Roger Pavlik	.10	.05	.01
☐ 209 Darren Oliver	.10	.05	.01
☐ 210 Dean Palmer	.10	.05	.01
☐ 211 Ivan Rodriguez	.75	.35	.09
☐ 212 Otis Nixon	.10	.05	.01
☐ 213 Pat Hentgen	.25	.11	.03
☐ 214 Ozzie Smith	.25	.11	.03
Andre Dawson			
Kirby Puckett HL/CL			
☐ 215 Barry Bonds	.25	.11	.03
Gary Sheffield			
Brady Anderson HL/CL			
☐ 216 Ken Caminiti HL/CL	.25	.11	.03
☐ 217 John Smoltz HL/CL	.25	.11	.03
☐ 218 Eric Young HL/CL	.25	.11	.03
☐ 219 Juan Gonzalez HL/CL	.50	.23	.06
☐ 220 Eddie Murray HL/CL	.40	.18	.05
☐ 221 Tommy Lasorda HL/CL	.25	.11	.03
☐ 222 Paul Molitor HL/CL	.25	.11	.03
☐ 223 Luis Castillo	.40	.18	.05
☐ 224 Justin Thompson	.25	.11	.03
☐ 225 Rocky Coppinger	.25	.11	.03
☐ 226 Jermaine Allensworth	.25	.11	.03
☐ 227 Jeff D'Amico	.25	.11	.03
☐ 228 Jamey Wright	.25	.11	.03
☐ 229 Scott Rolen	1.25	.55	.16
☐ 230 Darin Erstad	1.50	.70	.19
☐ 231 Marty Janzen	.10	.05	.01
☐ 232 Jacob Cruz	.10	.05	.01
☐ 233 Raul Ibanez	.10	.05	.01
☐ 234 Nomar Garciaparra	1.25	.55	.16
☐ 235 Todd Walker	1.50	.70	.19
☐ 236 Brian Giles	.10	.05	.01
☐ 237 Matt Beech	.10	.05	.01
☐ 238 Mike Cameron	.50	.23	.06

☐ 239 Jose Paniagua	.10	.05	.01
☐ 240 Andruw Jones	3.00	1.35	.35
☐ 241 Brant Brown	.10	.05	.01
☐ 242 Robin Jennings	.10	.05	.01
☐ 243 Willie Adams	.10	.05	.01
☐ 244 Ken Caminiti UPD	.50	.23	.06
☐ 245 Brian Jordan UPD	.25	.11	.03
☐ 246 Chipper Jones UPD	1.00	.45	.12
☐ 247 Juan Gonzalez UPD	.75	.35	.09
☐ 248 Bernie Williams UPD	.30	.14	.04
☐ 249 Roberto Alomar UPD	.30	.14	.04
☐ 250 Bernie Williams UPD	.30	.14	.04
☐ 251 David Wells UPD	.10	.05	.01
☐ 252 Cecil Fielder UPD	.20	.09	.03
☐ 253 Darryl Strawberry UPD	.20	.09	.03
☐ 254 Andy Pettitte UPD	.40	.18	.05
☐ 255 Javier Lopez UPD	.25	.11	.03
☐ 256 Gary Gaetti UPD	.10	.05	.01
☐ 257 Ron Gant UPD	.20	.09	.03
☐ 258 Brian Jordan UPD	.25	.11	.03
☐ 259 John Smoltz UPD	.50	.23	.06
☐ 260 Greg Maddux UPD	1.00	.45	.12
☐ 261 Tom Glavine UPD	.25	.11	.03
☐ 262 Andruw Jones UPD	1.50	.70	.19
☐ 263 Greg Maddux UPD	1.00	.45	.12
☐ 264 David Cone UPD	.25	.11	.03
☐ 265 Jim Leyritz UPD	.10	.05	.01
☐ 266 Andy Pettitte UPD	.40	.18	.05
☐ 267 John Wetteland UPD	.25	.11	.03
☐ 268 Dario Veras UPD	.10	.05	.01
☐ 269 Neifi Perez UPD	.10	.05	.01
☐ 270 Bill Mueller UPD	.10	.05	.01

1997 Upper Deck Amazing Greats

Randomly inserted in all first series packs at a rate of one in 138, this 20-card set features a horizontal design along with two player photos on the front. The cards feature translucent player images against a real wood grain stock.

	MINT	NRMT	EXC
COMPLETE SET (20)	600.00	275.00	75.00
COMMON CARD (AG1-AG20)	10.00	4.50	1.25
☐ AG1 Ken Griffey Jr.	80.00	36.00	10.00
☐ AG2 Roberto Alomar	20.00	9.00	2.50
☐ AG3 Alex Rodriguez	80.00	36.00	10.00
☐ AG4 Paul Molitor	15.00	6.75	1.85
☐ AG5 Chipper Jones	50.00	22.00	6.25
☐ AG6 Tony Gwynn	30.00	13.50	3.70
☐ AG7 Kenny Lofton	20.00	9.00	2.50
☐ AG8 Albert Belle	30.00	13.50	3.70
☐ AG9 Matt Williams	10.00	4.50	1.25
☐ AG10 Frank Thomas	80.00	36.00	10.00
☐ AG11 Greg Maddux	50.00	22.00	6.25
☐ AG12 Sammy Sosa	12.00	5.50	1.50
☐ AG13 Kirby Puckett	30.00	13.50	3.70
☐ AG14 Jeff Bagwell	30.00	13.50	3.70
☐ AG15 Cal Ripken	60.00	27.00	7.50
☐ AG16 Manny Ramirez	20.00	9.00	2.50
☐ AG17 Barry Bonds	20.00	9.00	2.50
☐ AG18 Mo Vaughn	20.00	9.00	2.50
☐ AG19 Eddie Murray	20.00	9.00	2.50
☐ AG20 Mike Piazza	50.00	22.00	6.25

1997 Upper Deck Game Jersey

Randomly inserted in all first series packs at a rate of one in 660, this 3-card set feaures swatches of real game-worn jerseys cut up and placed on the cards.

	MINT	NRMT	EXC
COMPLETE SET (3)	750.00	350.00	95.00
COMMON CARD (GJ1-GJ3)	110.00	50.00	14.00
☐ GJ1 Ken Griffey Jr.	450.00	200.00	55.00
☐ GJ2 Tony Gwynn	250.00	110.00	31.00
☐ GJ3 Rey Ordonez	110.00	50.00	14.00

1997 Upper Deck Power Package

Randomly inserted in all first series packs at a rate of one in 23, this 20-card set feaures some of the best longball hitters. The die cut cards feature some of baseball's leading power hitters. Non-die cut jumbo (5 x 7) versions were distributed one per 1997 Series 1 Upper Deck retail Sam's box on the bottom of the box under the packs.

	MINT	NRMT	EXC
COMPLETE SET (20)	125.00	55.00	15.50
COMMON CARD (PP1-PP20)	3.00	1.35	.35
☐ PP1 Ken Griffey Jr.	30.00	13.50	3.70
☐ PP2 Joe Carter	3.00	1.35	.35
☐ PP3 Rafael Palmeiro	4.00	1.80	.50
☐ PP4 Jay Buhner	4.00	1.80	.50
☐ PP5 Sammy Sosa	5.00	2.20	.60
☐ PP6 Fred McGriff	4.00	1.80	.50
☐ PP7 Jeff Bagwell	12.00	5.50	1.50
☐ PP8 Albert Belle	12.00	5.50	1.50
☐ PP9 Matt Williams	4.00	1.80	.50
☐ PP10 Mark McGwire	10.00	4.50	1.25
☐ PP11 Gary Sheffield	5.00	2.20	.60
☐ PP12 Tim Salmon	4.00	1.80	.50
☐ PP13 Ryan Klesko	5.00	2.20	.60
☐ PP14 Manny Ramirez	8.00	3.60	1.00
☐ PP15 Mike Piazza	20.00	9.00	2.50
☐ PP16 Barry Bonds	8.00	3.60	1.00
☐ PP17 Mo Vaughn	8.00	3.60	1.00
☐ PP18 Jose Canseco	4.00	1.80	.50
☐ PP19 Juan Gonzalez	15.00	6.75	1.85
☐ PP20 Frank Thomas	30.00	13.50	3.70

1997 Upper Deck Power Package Jumbo

These cards measure 5" by 7" and parallel the regular power package cards

	MINT	NRMT	EXC
COMPLETE SET (20)	65.00	29.00	8.00
COMMON CARD (PP1-PP20)	2.00	.90	.25

*JUMBOS .25X to .5X BASIC CARDS

1997 Upper Deck Rock Solid Foundation

Randomly inserted in all first series packs at a rate of one in seven, this 20-card set features players 25 and under who have made an impact in the majors. The fronts feature a player photo against a "silver" type background. The backs give player information as well as another player photo and are numbered with a "RS" prefix.

	MINT	NRMT	EXC
COMPLETE SET (20)	50.00	22.00	6.25
COMMON CARD (RS1-RS20)	1.00	.45	.12
☐ RS1 Alex Rodriguez	15.00	6.75	1.85
☐ RS2 Rey Ordonez	2.00	.90	.25
☐ RS3 Derek Jeter	10.00	4.50	1.25
☐ RS4 Darin Erstad	8.00	3.60	1.00
☐ RS5 Chipper Jones	10.00	4.50	1.25
☐ RS6 Johnny Damon	1.00	.45	.12
☐ RS7 Ryan Klesko	2.50	1.10	.30
☐ RS8 Charles Johnson	1.00	.45	.12
☐ RS9 Andy Pettitte	4.00	1.80	.50
☐ RS10 Manny Ramirez	4.00	1.80	.50
☐ RS11 Ivan Rodriguez	4.00	1.80	.50
☐ RS12 Jason Kendall	1.50	.70	.19
☐ RS13 Rondell White	1.00	.45	.12
☐ RS14 Alex Ochoa	1.00	.45	.12
☐ RS15 Javier Lopez	1.50	.70	.19
☐ RS16 Pedro Martinez	1.50	.70	.19
☐ RS17 Carlos Delgado	1.50	.70	.19
☐ RS18 Paul Wilson	1.50	.70	.19
☐ RS19 Alan Benes	1.50	.70	.19
☐ RS20 Raul Mondesi	2.00	.90	.25

1997 Upper Deck Ticket To Stardom

Randomly inserted in all first series packs at a rate of one in 34, this 20-card set is designed in the form of a ticket and are designed to be matched. The horizontal fronts feature two player photos as well as using "light f/x technology and embossed player images.

	MINT	NRMT	EXC
COMPLETE SET (20)	150.00	70.00	19.00
COMMON CARD (TS1-TS20)	3.00	1.35	.35
☐ TS1 Chipper Jones	25.00	11.00	3.10
☐ TS2 Jermaine Dye	6.00	2.70	.75
☐ TS3 Rey Ordonez	5.00	2.20	.60
☐ TS4 Alex Ochoa	3.00	1.35	.35
☐ TS5 Derek Jeter	25.00	11.00	3.10
☐ TS6 Ruben Rivera	5.00	2.20	.60
☐ TS7 Billy Wagner	4.00	1.80	.50
☐ TS8 Jason Kendall	4.00	1.80	.50
☐ TS9 Darin Erstad	20.00	9.00	2.50
☐ TS10 Alex Rodriguez	40.00	18.00	5.00
☐ TS11 Bob Abreu	5.00	2.20	.60
☐ TS12 Richard Hidalgo	5.00	2.20	.60
☐ TS13 Karim Garcia	6.00	2.70	.75
☐ TS14 Andruw Jones	40.00	18.00	5.00
☐ TS15 Carlos Delgado	4.00	1.80	.50
☐ TS16 Rocky Coppinger	4.00	1.80	.50
☐ TS17 Jeff D'Amico	4.00	1.80	.50
☐ TS18 Johnny Damon	3.00	1.35	.35
☐ TS19 John Wasdin	3.00	1.35	.35
☐ TS20 Manny Ramirez	10.00	4.50	1.25

1997 Upper Deck Award Winner Jumbos

This 23-card set measures approximately 3 1/2" by 5" and features borderless color player photos with gold and silver foil highlights of both American and National League award winners. The backs carry another player photo and statistics with a sentence about winning his award. The set was issued through retail outlets and television promotions with a suggested retail set price of $19.95.

	MINT	NRMT	EXC
COMPLETE SET (23)	2.00	.90	.25
COMMON CARD (1-23)	.50	.23	.06
☐ 1 Alex Rodriguez American League Batting Leader	5.00	2.20	.60
☐ 2 Tony Gwynn National League Batting Leader	2.00	.90	.25
☐ 3 Mark McGwire American League HR Leader	1.50	.70	.19
☐ 4 Andres Galarraga National League HR Leader	.75	.35	.09
☐ 5 Albert Belle American League RBI Leader	2.00	.90	.25
☐ 6 Andres Galarraga Nation League RBI Leader	.75	.35	.09
☐ 7 Kenny Lofton American League SB Leader	1.50	.70	.19
☐ 8 Eric Young National League SB Leader	.50	.23	.06
☐ 9 Andy Pettitte American League WIN Leader	.75	.35	.09
☐ 10 John Smoltz National League WIN Leader	1.00	.45	.12
☐ 11 Roger Clemens American League K Leader	1.50	.70	.19
☐ 12 John Smoltz National League K Leader	1.00	.45	.12
☐ 13 Juan Guzman American League ERA Leader	.50	.23	.06
☐ 14 Kevin Brown National League ERA Leader	.50	.23	.06
☐ 15 John Wetteland American League SAVE Leader	.50	.23	.06
☐ 16 Jeff Brantley National League SAVE Co-Leader	.50	.23	.06
☐ 17 Todd Worrell National League SAVE Co-Leader	.50	.23	.06
☐ 18 Derek Jeter American League ROY Leader	3.00	1.35	.35
☐ 19 Todd Hollandsworth National League ROY Leader	.50	.23	.06
☐ 20 Juan Gonzalez American League MVP Leader	2.50	1.10	.30
☐ 21 Ken Caminiti National League MVP Leader	1.50	.70	.19
☐ 22 Pat Hentgen American League CY Young Leader	1.00	.45	.12
☐ 23 John Smoltz National League CY Young Leader	1.00	.45	.12

1997 Upper Deck UD3

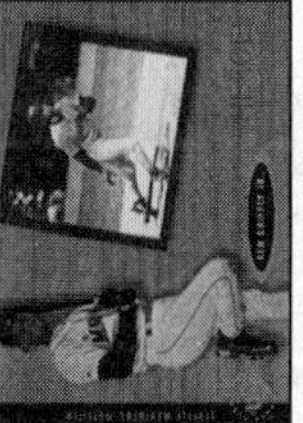

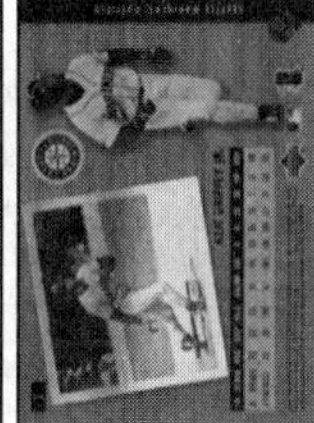

This 60-card standard-size super premium set was released by Upper Deck exclusively to retail outlets in mid-April,1997. The set is broken up into three distinct 20-card subsets: Homerun Heroes (1-20) featuring Electric Wood technology, Pro-Motion (21-40) featuring Light F/X technology and Future Impact (41-60) featuring Cel Chrome technology. Packs carried a suggested retail price of $3.99. Each pack contained three cards, one from each of the subsets. Boxes contained 24 packs.

	MINT	NRMT	EXC
COMPLETE SET (60)	60.00	27.00	7.50
COMMON CARD (1-60)	.50	.23	.06
☐ 1 Mark McGwire	2.00	.90	.25
☐ 2 Brady Anderson	1.00	.45	.12
☐ 3 Ken Griffey Jr.	6.00	2.70	.75
☐ 4 Albert Belle	2.50	1.10	.30
☐ 5 Andres Galarraga	.75	.35	.09
☐ 6 Juan Gonzalez	3.00	1.35	.35
☐ 7 Jay Buhner	1.00	.45	.12
☐ 8 Mo Vaughn	1.50	.70	.19
☐ 9 Barry Bonds	1.50	.70	.19
☐ 10 Gary Sheffield	1.00	.45	.12
☐ 11 Todd Hundley	1.00	.45	.12
☐ 12 Ellis Burks	.75	.35	.09
☐ 13 Ken Caminiti	1.00	.45	.12
☐ 14 Vinny Castilla	.75	.35	.09
☐ 15 Sammy Sosa	1.00	.45	.12
☐ 16 Frank Thomas	6.00	2.70	.75
☐ 17 Rafael Palmeiro	.75	.35	.09
☐ 18 Mike Piazza	4.00	1.80	.50
☐ 19 Matt Williams	1.00	.45	.12
☐ 20 Eddie Murray	1.50	.70	.19
☐ 21 Roger Clemens	1.25	.55	.16
☐ 22 Tim Salmon	1.00	.45	.12
☐ 23 Robin Ventura	.50	.23	.06
☐ 24 Ron Gant	.75	.35	.09
☐ 25 Cal Ripken	5.00	2.20	.60
☐ 26 Bernie Williams	1.25	.55	.16
☐ 27 Hideo Nomo	1.50	.70	.19
☐ 28 Ivan Rodriguez	1.50	.70	.19
☐ 29 John Smoltz	1.00	.45	.12
☐ 30 Paul Molitor	1.25	.55	.16
☐ 31 Greg Maddux	4.00	1.80	.50
☐ 32 Raul Mondesi	1.00	.45	.12
☐ 33 Roberto Alomar	1.25	.55	.16
☐ 34 Barry Larkin	1.00	.45	.12
☐ 35 Tony Gwynn	2.50	1.10	.30
☐ 36 Jim Thome	1.25	.55	.16
☐ 37 Kenny Lofton	1.50	.70	.19
☐ 38 Jeff Bagwell	2.50	1.10	.30
☐ 39 Ozzie Smith	1.50	.70	.19
☐ 40 Kirby Puckett	2.50	1.10	.30
☐ 41 Andruw Jones	6.00	2.70	.75
☐ 42 Vladimir Guerrero	4.00	1.80	.50
☐ 43 Edgar Renteria	.50	.23	.06
☐ 44 Luis Castillo	.50	.23	.06
☐ 45 Darin Erstad	3.00	1.35	.35
☐ 46 Nomar Garciaparra	2.50	1.10	.30
☐ 47 Todd Greene	.50	.23	.06

☐ 48 Jason Kendall	.75	.35	.09
☐ 49 Rey Ordonez	.50	.23	.06
☐ 50 Alex Rodriguez	6.00	2.70	.75
☐ 51 Manny Ramirez	1.50	.70	.19
☐ 52 Todd Walker	2.50	1.10	.30
☐ 53 Ruben Rivera	.75	.35	.09
☐ 54 Andy Pettitte	1.50	.70	.19
☐ 55 Derek Jeter	4.00	1.80	.50
☐ 56 Todd Hollandsworth	.75	.35	.09
☐ 57 Rocky Coppinger	.50	.23	.06
☐ 58 Scott Rolen	2.50	1.10	.30
☐ 59 Jermaine Dye	.50	.23	.06
☐ 60 Chipper Jones	4.00	1.80	.50

1997 Upper Deck UD3 Generation Next

Randomly seeded into one in every 11 packs, cards from this 20-card set feature a selection of the game's top prospects. The horizontal card fronts feature a full-color cut-out player photo set against a metallized background with another picture of the player in action. Card backs include 1996 season statistics, a rarity for insert issues.

	MINT	NRMT	EXC
COMPLETE SET (20)	150.00	70.00	19.00
COMMON CARD (1-20)	2.00	.90	.25
☐ GN1 Alex Rodriguez	25.00	11.00	3.10
☐ GN2 Vladimir Guerrero	15.00	6.75	1.85
☐ GN3 Luis Castillo	2.00	.90	.25
☐ GN4 Rey Ordonez	3.00	1.35	.35
☐ GN5 Andruw Jones	25.00	11.00	3.10
☐ GN6 Darin Erstad	12.00	5.50	1.50
☐ GN7 Edgar Renteria	3.00	1.35	.35
☐ GN8 Jason Kendall	3.00	1.35	.35
☐ GN9 Jermaine Dye	3.00	1.35	.35
☐ GN10 Chipper Jones	15.00	6.75	1.85
☐ GN11 Rocky Coppinger	2.00	.90	.25
☐ GN12 Andy Pettitte	6.00	2.70	.75
☐ GN13 Todd Greene	2.00	.90	.25
☐ GN14 Todd Hollandsworth	3.00	1.35	.35
☐ GN15 Derek Jeter	15.00	6.75	1.85
☐ GN16 Ruben Rivera	3.00	1.35	.35
☐ GN17 Todd Walker	10.00	4.50	1.25
☐ GN18 Nomar Garciaparra	10.00	4.50	1.25
☐ GN19 Scott Rolen	10.00	4.50	1.25
☐ GN20 Manny Ramirez	6.00	2.70	.75

1997 Upper Deck UD3 Marquee Attraction

Randomly seed into one in every 144 packs, cards from this 10-card set feature a selection of the game's top veteran stars. Horizontal card fronts feature a small color action player photo set against a bold diamond-shaped holographic image of the player. Card backs feature silver foil, statistics, another photo and text.

	MINT	NRMT	EXC
COMPLETE SET (10)	500.00	220.00	60.00
COMMON CARD (MA1-MA10)	25.00	11.00	3.10
☐ MA1 Ken Griffey Jr.	100.00	45.00	12.50
☐ MA2 Mark McGwire	30.00	13.50	3.70
☐ MA3 Juan Gonzalez	50.00	22.00	6.25
☐ MA4 Barry Bonds	25.00	11.00	3.10
☐ MA5 Frank Thomas	100.00	45.00	12.50
☐ MA6 Albert Belle	40.00	18.00	5.00
☐ MA7 Mike Piazza	60.00	27.00	7.50
☐ MA8 Cal Ripken	80.00	36.00	10.00
☐ MA9 Mo Vaughn	25.00	11.00	3.10
☐ MA10 Alex Rodriguez	100.00	45.00	12.50

1997 Upper Deck UD3 Superb Signatures

Randomly seeded into one in every 1,500 packs, cards from this 4-card set feature actual autographs from some of baseball's top stars.

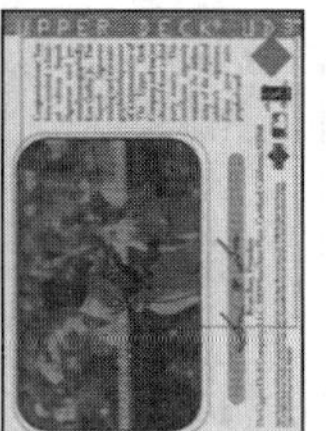

Horizontal wood-cel card fronts feature a rectangular clear plastic player photo, statistics on height, weight, date of birth and hometown, plus of course a real autograph at the base of the card. Card backs feature text congratulating the bearer of the card plus the signature of Upper Deck's president Brian Burr.

	MINT	NRMT	EXC
COMPLETE SET (4)	1150.00	525.00	145.00
COMMON CARD	125.00	55.00	15.50
☐ 1 Ken Caminiti	125.00	55.00	15.50
☐ 2 Ken Griffey Jr.	600.00	275.00	75.00
☐ 3 Vladimir Guerrero	200.00	90.00	25.00
☐ 4 Derek Jeter	250.00	110.00	31.00

1989 USPS Legends Stamp Cards

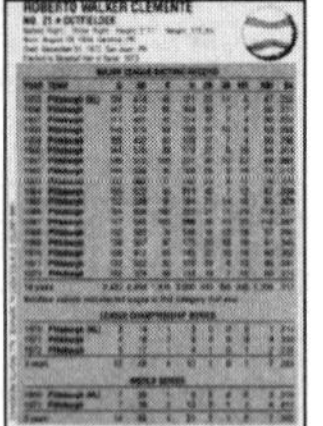

The 1989 USPS Legends Stamp Cards set includes four cards each measuring 2 1/2" by 3 9/16". On the fronts, the cards depict the four baseball-related stamp designs which featured actual players. The outer front borders are white; the inner front borders are orange and purple. The vertically oriented backs are beige and pink. These cards were sold by the U.S. Postal Service as a set (kit) for $7.95 along with the actual stamps, an attractive booklet, and other materials. The first printing of the set was sold out and so a second printing was made. The first printing cards did not have the USPS copyright logo. All the stamps in the set are drawings; for example, the Gehrig stamp was painted by noted sports artist, Bart Forbes. All of the stamps except Gehrig (25 cents) are 20-cent stamps.

	MINT	NRMT	EXC
COMPLETE SET (4)	25.00	11.00	3.10
COMMON CARD (1-4)	6.00	2.70	.75
☐ 1 Roberto Clemente Issued August 17, 1984	6.00	2.70	.75
☐ 2 Lou Gehrig Issued June 10, 1989	6.00	2.70	.75
☐ 3 Jackie Robinson Issued August 2, 1982	6.00	2.70	.75
☐ 4 Babe Ruth Issued July 6, 1983	7.50	3.40	.95

1915 Victory T214

The cards in this 30-card set measure 1 1/2" by 2 5/8". The set is easily distinguished by the presence of the reference to Victory Tobacco on the card backs. The players in this unnumbered set have been alphabetized and numbered for reference in the checklist below. The set can be dated to 1915 with Chief Bender's appearence as a Baltimore Federal.

	EX-MT	VG-E	GOOD
COMPLETE SET (30)	11000.00	5000.00	1400.00
COMMON CARD (1-30)	350.00	160.00	45.00
☐ 1 Chief Bender	550.00	250.00	70.00
☐ 2 Roger Bresnahan	550.00	250.00	70.00
☐ 3 Howie Camnitz	350.00	160.00	45.00
☐ 4 Ty Cobb	2000.00	900.00	250.00
☐ 5 Birdie Cree	350.00	160.00	45.00
☐ 6 Ray Demmitt	350.00	160.00	45.00
☐ 7 Mickey Doolan	350.00	160.00	45.00
☐ 8 Tom Downey	350.00	160.00	45.00
☐ 9 Kid Elberfeld	450.00	200.00	55.00
☐ 10 Russ Ford	350.00	160.00	45.00
☐ 11 Art Fromme	350.00	160.00	45.00
☐ 12 Rube Geyer	350.00	160.00	45.00
☐ 13 Clark Griffith MG	550.00	250.00	70.00
☐ 14 Bob Groom	350.00	160.00	45.00
☐ 15 Walter Johnson	1000.00	450.00	125.00
☐ 16 Ed Konetchy	350.00	160.00	45.00
☐ 17 Nap Lajoie	600.00	275.00	75.00
☐ 18 Ed Lennox	350.00	160.00	45.00
☐ 19 Sherry Magee	350.00	160.00	45.00
☐ 20 Chief Meyers	450.00	200.00	55.00
☐ 21 George Mullin	350.00	160.00	45.00
☐ 22 Tom Needham	350.00	160.00	45.00
☐ 23 Rebel Oakes	350.00	160.00	45.00
☐ 24 Jack Quinn	350.00	160.00	45.00
☐ 25 Frank Schulte	350.00	160.00	45.00
☐ 26 Ed Sweeney	350.00	160.00	45.00
☐ 27 Joe Tinker	550.00	250.00	70.00
☐ 28 Heinie Wagner	350.00	160.00	45.00
☐ 29 Zack Wheat	550.00	250.00	70.00
☐ 30 Hooks Wiltse	350.00	160.00	45.00

1990 W/R Mark Grace

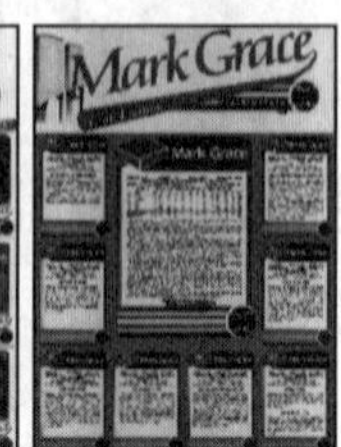

Produced and distributed by W/R Associates in care of Baseball Cards-N-More (Louisville, KY), the sheet has an 5 1/8" by 7" oversized color portrait of Grace in its center, surrounded on three sides by standard-size cards that trace Grace's career. The color photos on the fronts have blue and green inner borders and a white outer border, while the year is printed on a base icon at the upper left corner. On a white panel with a light blue outer border, the backs have biography and summarize chapters from his career. The cards are unnumbered and checklisted below in chronological order.

	MINT	NRMT	EXC
COMPLETE SET (9)	4.00	1.80	.50
COMMON CARD (1-9)	.50	.23	.06
☐ 1 Mark Grace '73 Una Recreational League	.50	.23	.06
☐ 2 Mark Grace '83 San Diego State Aztecs	.50	.23	.06
☐ 3 Mark Grace '86 Peoria Chiefs	.50	.23	.06
☐ 4 Mark Grace '87 Pittsfield Cubs	.50	.23	.06
☐ 5 Mark Grace '88 To Have and To Hold	.50	.23	.06
☐ 6 Mark Grace '88 Iowa Cubs Chicago Cubs	.50	.23	.06
☐ 7 Mark Grace '89 Chicago Cubs	.50	.23	.06
☐ 8 Mark Grace '89 Chicago Cubs	.50	.23	.06
☐ 9 Mark Grace (Oversized card 5 1/8" by 7")	.50	.23	.06

1909 W.W. Smith Postcards

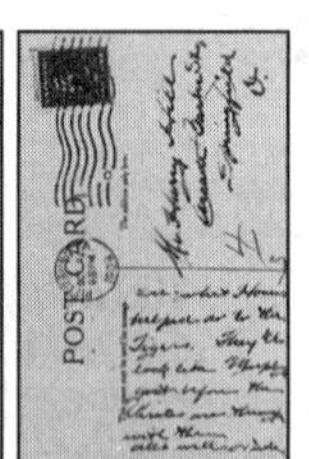

In 1909 W.W. Smith of Pittsburgh produced a set of Postcards for the 1909 World Series between the Pittsburgh Pirates and Detroit Tigers. One card is titled "World's Series Souvenir" titled two of a kind featuring the stars of each team, Ty Cobb of the Tigers and Honus Wagner of the Pirates featuring caracitures of the two stars. The other known card titled "The Mighty Honus" shows a caraciture of Wagner. It is possible that a caraciture of Cobb exists as well as some of the other prominent players from both teams but they have yet to be identified.

	MINT	NRMT	EXC
COMPLETE SET (2)	700.00	325.00	90.00
COMMON CARD (1-2)	250.00	110.00	31.00
☐ 1 Ty Cobb Honus Wagner World Series Souvenir	500.00	220.00	60.00
☐ 2 Honus Wagner The Mighty Honus	250.00	110.00	31.00

1923 W501

This 120-card set, referenced by the catalog designation W501, measures approximately 1 15/16" by 3 1/2". The cards have white borders which frame a posed black and white photo. The cards are blank backed and have the number in the upper right hand corner. The cards are thought to have been issued about 1923.

	EX-MT	VG-E	GOOD
COMPLETE SET (120)	4000.00	1800.00	500.00
COMMON CARD (1-120)	20.00	9.00	2.50
☐ 1 Ed Rommel	20.00	9.00	2.50
☐ 2 Urban Shocker	35.00	16.00	4.40
☐ 3 Frank Davis	20.00	9.00	2.50
☐ 4 George Sisler	100.00	45.00	12.50
☐ 5 Bobby Veach	20.00	9.00	2.50
☐ 6 Harry Heilmann	75.00	34.00	9.50
☐ 7 Ira Flagstead	20.00	9.00	2.50
☐ 8 Ty Cobb	300.00	135.00	38.00
☐ 9 Oscar Vitt	35.00	16.00	4.40
☐ 10 Muddy Ruel	20.00	9.00	2.50
☐ 11 Del Pratt	20.00	9.00	2.50
☐ 12 Joe Gharrity	20.00	9.00	2.50
☐ 13 Joe Judge	20.00	9.00	2.50
☐ 14 Sam Rice	50.00	22.00	6.25
☐ 15 Clyde Milan	20.00	9.00	2.50
☐ 16 Joe Sewell	50.00	22.00	6.25
☐ 17 Walter Johnson	200.00	90.00	25.00
☐ 18 Stuffy McInnis	35.00	16.00	4.40
☐ 19 Tris Speaker	125.00	55.00	15.50
☐ 20 Jim Bagby	20.00	9.00	2.50
☐ 21 Stan Coveleski	50.00	22.00	6.25
☐ 22 Bill Wambsganss	35.00	16.00	4.40
☐ 23 John Mails	20.00	9.00	2.50
☐ 24 Larry Gardner	20.00	9.00	2.50
☐ 25 Aaron Ward	20.00	9.00	2.50
☐ 26 Miller Huggins MG	20.00	9.00	2.50
☐ 27 Wally Schang	35.00	16.00	4.40
☐ 28 Thomas Rogers	20.00	9.00	2.50
☐ 29 Carl Mays	35.00	16.00	4.40
☐ 30 Everett Scott	20.00	9.00	2.50
☐ 31 Bob Shawkey	20.00	9.00	2.50
☐ 32 Waite Hoyt	75.00	34.00	9.50
☐ 33 Mike McNally	20.00	9.00	2.50
☐ 34 Joe Bush	20.00	9.00	2.50
☐ 35 Bob Meusel	35.00	16.00	4.40
☐ 36 Irish Meusel	35.00	16.00	4.40
☐ 37 Dickie Kerr	20.00	9.00	2.50
☐ 38 Eddie Collins	75.00	34.00	9.50
☐ 39 Kid Gleason MG	35.00	16.00	4.40
☐ 40 Johnny Mostil	20.00	9.00	2.50
☐ 41 Bibb Falk	20.00	9.00	2.50
☐ 42 Clarence Hodge	20.00	9.00	2.50
☐ 43 Ray Schalk	50.00	22.00	6.25
☐ 44 Amos Strunk	20.00	9.00	2.50
☐ 45 Edward Mulligan	20.00	9.00	2.50
☐ 46 Earl Sheely	20.00	9.00	2.50
☐ 47 Harry Hooper	75.00	34.00	9.50
☐ 48 Red Faber	50.00	22.00	6.25
☐ 49 Babe Ruth	500.00	220.00	60.00
☐ 50 Ivy Wingo	35.00	16.00	4.40
☐ 51 Greasy Neale	20.00	9.00	2.50
☐ 52 Jake Daubert	35.00	16.00	4.40
☐ 53 Edd Roush	75.00	34.00	9.50
☐ 54 Eppa Rixey	50.00	22.00	6.25
☐ 55 Speed Martin	20.00	9.00	2.50
☐ 56 Bill Killifer	20.00	9.00	2.50
☐ 57 Charlie Hollocher	20.00	9.00	2.50
☐ 58 Zeb Terry	100.00	45.00	12.50
☐ 59 Grover Alexander	100.00	45.00	12.50
☐ 60 Turner Barber	20.00	9.00	2.50
☐ 61 Johnny Rawlings	20.00	9.00	2.50
☐ 62 Frankie Frisch	125.00	55.00	15.50
☐ 63 Red Shea	20.00	9.00	2.50
☐ 64 Dave Bancroft	50.00	22.00	6.25
☐ 65 Red Causey	20.00	9.00	2.50
☐ 66 Pancho Snyder	20.00	9.00	2.50
☐ 67 Heinie Groh	35.00	16.00	4.40
☐ 68 Ross Youngs	50.00	22.00	6.25
☐ 69 Fred Toney	20.00	9.00	2.50
☐ 70 Art Nehf	20.00	9.00	2.50
☐ 71 Earl Smith	20.00	9.00	2.50
☐ 72 George Kelly	50.00	22.00	6.25
☐ 73 John McGraw MG	75.00	34.00	9.50
☐ 74 Phil Douglas	20.00	9.00	2.50
☐ 75 Rosy Ryan	20.00	9.00	2.50
☐ 76 Jesse Haines	50.00	22.00	6.25
☐ 77 Milt Stock	20.00	9.00	2.50
☐ 78 Bill Doak	20.00	9.00	2.50
☐ 79 Specs Toporcer	20.00	9.00	2.50
☐ 80 Wilbur Cooper	20.00	9.00	2.50
☐ 81 Possum Whitted	20.00	9.00	2.50
☐ 82 Charlie Grimm	50.00	22.00	6.25
☐ 83 Rabbit Maranville	50.00	22.00	6.25
☐ 84 Babe Adams	20.00	9.00	2.50
☐ 85 Carson Bigbee	20.00	9.00	2.50
☐ 86 Max Carey	75.00	34.00	9.50
☐ 87 Whitey Glazner	20.00	9.00	2.50
☐ 89 George Gibson	20.00	9.00	2.50
☐ 90 Billy Southworth	35.00	16.00	4.40
☐ 91 Hank Gowdy	20.00	9.00	2.50
☐ 92 Walter Holke	20.00	9.00	2.50
☐ 93 Joe Oeschger	20.00	9.00	2.50
☐ 94 Pete Kilduff	20.00	9.00	2.50
☐ 95 Chief Meyers	35.00	16.00	4.40
☐ 96 Otto Miller	20.00	9.00	2.50
☐ 97 Wilbert Robinson MG	20.00	9.00	2.50
☐ 98 Zack Wheat	50.00	22.00	6.25
☐ 99 Dutch Ruether	20.00	9.00	2.50
☐ 100 Tilly Walker	20.00	9.00	2.50
☐ 101 Cy Williams	20.00	9.00	2.50
☐ 102 Dave Danforth	20.00	9.00	2.50
☐ 103 Ed Rommell	20.00	9.00	2.50

	EX-MT	VG-E	GOOD
☐ 104 John McGraw MG	75.00	34.00	9.50
☐ 105 Frank Frisch	75.00	34.00	9.50
☐ 106 Al DeVormer	20.00	9.00	2.50
☐ 107 Tommy Griffith	20.00	9.00	2.50
☐ 108 George Harper	20.00	9.00	2.50
☐ 109 Doc Lavan	20.00	9.00	2.50
☐ 110 Elmer Smith	20.00	9.00	2.50
☐ 111 Hooks Dauss	20.00	9.00	2.50
☐ 112 Alex Gaston	20.00	9.00	2.50
☐ 113 Jack Graney	20.00	9.00	2.50
☐ 114 Irish Meusel	35.00	16.00	4.40
☐ 115 Rogers Hornsby	125.00	55.00	15.50
☐ 116 Les Nunamaker	20.00	9.00	2.50
☐ 117 Steve O'Neill	35.00	16.00	4.40
☐ 118 Max Flack	20.00	9.00	2.50
☐ 119 Art Nehf	20.00	9.00	2.50
☐ 120 Chick Fewster	20.00	9.00	2.50

1928 W502

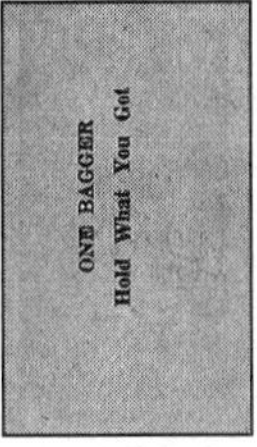

This 60-card set, referenced by the catalog designation W502, measures approximately 1 5/16" by 2 1/2". The photo is a black and white action-posed photo, while the back reads "One Bagger. Hold what you've got." The cards are thought to have been issued about 1928.

	EX-MT	VG-E	GOOD
COMPLETE SET (60)	1500.00	700.00	190.00
COMMON CARD (1-60)	12.00	5.50	1.50
☐ 1 Burleigh Grimes	25.00	11.00	3.10
☐ 2 Walter Reuther	12.00	5.50	1.50
☐ 3 Joe Dugan	15.00	6.75	1.85
☐ 4 Red Faber	25.00	11.00	3.10
☐ 5 Gabby Hartnett	25.00	11.00	3.10
☐ 6 Babe Ruth	200.00	90.00	25.00
☐ 7 Bob Meusel	15.00	6.75	1.85
☐ 8 Herb Pennock	25.00	11.00	3.10
☐ 9 George Burns	12.00	5.50	1.50
☐ 10 Joe Sewell	25.00	11.00	3.10
☐ 11 George Uhle	12.00	5.50	1.50
☐ 12 Bob O'Farrell	12.00	5.50	1.50
☐ 13 Rogers Hornsby	50.00	22.00	6.25
☐ 14 Pie Traynor	30.00	13.50	3.70
☐ 15 Clarence Mitchell	12.00	5.50	1.50
☐ 16 Eppa Rixey	25.00	11.00	3.10
☐ 17 Carl Mays	15.00	6.75	1.85
☐ 18 Adolfo Luque	12.00	5.50	1.50
☐ 19 Dave Bancroft	25.00	11.00	3.10
☐ 20 George Kelly	25.00	11.00	3.10
☐ 21 Earl Combs	25.00	11.00	3.10
☐ 22 Harry Heilmann	30.00	13.50	3.70
☐ 23 Ray W. Schalk	25.00	11.00	3.10
☐ 24 Johnny Mostil	12.00	5.50	1.50
☐ 25 Hack Wilson	30.00	13.50	3.70
☐ 26 Lou Gehrig	125.00	55.00	15.50
☐ 27 Ty Cobb	125.00	55.00	15.50
☐ 28 Tris Speaker	50.00	22.00	6.25
☐ 29 Tony Lazzeri	25.00	11.00	3.10
☐ 30 Waite Hoyt	25.00	11.00	3.10
☐ 31 Sherwood Smith	12.00	5.50	1.50
☐ 32 Max Carey	25.00	11.00	3.10
☐ 33 Eugene Hargrave	12.00	5.50	1.50
☐ 34 Miguel J. Gonzalez	12.00	5.50	1.50
☐ 35 Joe Judge	12.00	5.50	1.50
☐ 36 E.C. (Sam) Rice	25.00	11.00	3.10
☐ 37 Earl Sheely	12.00	5.50	1.50
☐ 38 Sam Jones	12.00	5.50	1.50
☐ 39 Bob A. Falk	12.00	5.50	1.50
☐ 40 Willie Kamm	15.00	6.75	1.85
☐ 41 Stanley Harris	25.00	11.00	3.10
☐ 42 John J. McGraw	30.00	13.50	3.70
☐ 43 Artie Nehf	12.00	5.50	1.50
☐ 44 Grover Alexander	50.00	22.00	6.25
☐ 45 Paul Waner	25.00	11.00	3.10
☐ 46 William H. Terry	30.00	13.50	3.70
☐ 47 Glenn Wright	12.00	5.50	1.50
☐ 48 Earl Smith	12.00	5.50	1.50
☐ 49 Leon (Goose) Goslin	25.00	11.00	3.10
☐ 50 Frank Frisch	30.00	13.50	3.70
☐ 51 Joe Harris	12.00	5.50	1.50
☐ 52 Fred (Cy) Wiliams	25.00	11.00	3.10
☐ 53 Ed Roush	25.00	11.00	3.10
☐ 54 George Sisler	30.00	13.50	3.70
☐ 55 Ed Rommel	12.00	5.50	1.50
☐ 56 Roger Peckinpaugh	12.00	5.50	1.50
☐ 57 Stanley Coveleski	25.00	11.00	3.10
☐ 58 Lester Bell	12.00	5.50	1.50
☐ 59 Lloyd Waner	25.00	11.00	3.10
☐ 60 John P. McInnis	25.00	11.00	3.10

1923 W503

This 64-card set, referenced by the catalog designation W503, measures approximately 1 3/4" by 2 3/4". The cards have white borders which frame a black-and-white player portrait or action photo and the card number. The backs are blank, and there is no evidence of a manufacturer. The set is thought to have been issued in early 1923.

	EX-MT	VG-E	GOOD
COMPLETE SET (64)	2500.00	1100.00	300.00
COMMON CARD (1-64)	25.00	11.00	3.10
☐ 1 Joe Bush	35.00	16.00	4.40
☐ 2 Wally Schang	35.00	16.00	4.40
☐ 3 Dave Robertson	25.00	11.00	3.10
☐ 4 Wally Pipp	25.00	11.00	3.10
☐ 5 Bill Ryan	25.00	11.00	3.10
☐ 6 George Kelly	50.00	22.00	6.25
☐ 7 Frank Snyder	25.00	11.00	3.10
☐ 8 Jimmy O'Connell	25.00	11.00	3.10
☐ 9 Bill Cunningham	25.00	11.00	3.10
☐ 10 Norman McMillan	25.00	11.00	3.10
☐ 11 Waite Hoyt	75.00	34.00	9.50
☐ 12 Art Nehf	25.00	11.00	3.10
☐ 13 George Sisler	100.00	45.00	12.50
☐ 14 Al Devormer	25.00	11.00	3.10
☐ 15 Casey Stengel	125.00	55.00	15.50
☐ 16 Ken Williams	35.00	16.00	4.40
☐ 17 Joe Dugan	25.00	11.00	3.10
☐ 18 Irish Muesel	25.00	11.00	3.10
☐ 19 Bob Meusel	35.00	16.00	4.40
☐ 20 Carl Mays	35.00	16.00	4.40
☐ 21 Frank Frisch	75.00	34.00	9.50
☐ 22 Jess Barnes	25.00	11.00	3.10
☐ 23 Walter Johnson	150.00	70.00	19.00
☐ 24 Claude Jonnard	25.00	11.00	3.10
☐ 25 Dave Bancroft	50.00	22.00	6.25
☐ 26 Johnny Rawlings	25.00	11.00	3.10
☐ 27 Pep Young	25.00	11.00	3.10
☐ 28 Earl Smith	25.00	11.00	3.10
☐ 29 Willie Kamm	25.00	11.00	3.10
☐ 30 Art Fletcher	25.00	11.00	3.10
☐ 31 Kid Gleason MG	25.00	11.00	3.10
☐ 32 Babe Ruth	500.00	220.00	60.00
☐ 33 Guy Morton	25.00	11.00	3.10
☐ 34 Heinie Groh	25.00	11.00	3.10
☐ 35 Leon Cadore	25.00	11.00	3.10
☐ 36 Joe Tobin	25.00	11.00	3.10
☐ 37 Rube Marquard	75.00	34.00	9.50
☐ 38 Grover Alexander	125.00	55.00	15.50
☐ 39 George Burns	25.00	11.00	3.10
☐ 40 Joe Oeschger	25.00	11.00	3.10
☐ 41 Chick Shorten	25.00	11.00	3.10
☐ 42 Roger Hornsby UER misspelled Rogers	150.00	70.00	19.00
☐ 43 Adolfo Luque	50.00	22.00	6.25
☐ 44 Zack Wheat	75.00	34.00	9.50
☐ 45 Hub Pruett UER misspelled Herb	25.00	11.00	3.10
☐ 46 Rabbit Maranville	75.00	34.00	9.50
☐ 47 Jimmy Ring	25.00	11.00	3.10
☐ 48 Sherrod Smith	25.00	11.00	3.10
☐ 49 Lea Meadows UER misspelled Lee	25.00	11.00	3.10
☐ 50 Aaron Ward	25.00	11.00	3.10
☐ 51 Herb Pennock	75.00	34.00	9.50
☐ 52 Carlson Bigbee UER misspelled Carson	25.00	11.00	3.10
☐ 53 Max Carey	75.00	34.00	9.50
☐ 54 Charles Robertson	25.00	11.00	3.10
☐ 55 Urban Shocker	35.00	16.00	4.40
☐ 56 Dutch Ruether	25.00	11.00	3.10
☐ 57 Jake Daubert	35.00	16.00	4.40
☐ 58 Louis Guisto	25.00	11.00	3.10
☐ 59 Ivy Wingo	25.00	11.00	3.10
☐ 60 Bill Pertica	25.00	11.00	3.10
☐ 61 Luke Sewell	25.00	11.00	3.10
☐ 62 Hank Gowdy	25.00	11.00	3.10
☐ 63 Jack Scott	25.00	11.00	3.10
☐ 64 Stan Coveleskie UER misspelled Coveleski	75.00	34.00	9.50

1928 W512 *

This set, referenced by the catalog designation W512, measures approximately 1 3/16" by 2 3/16". The cards are blank backed and the set includes most of the athletes that made the 1920s "The Golden Age of Sports," Babe Ruth, Bill Tilden, Johnny Weismuller, Walter Hagen, and Jack Dempsey. The cards are thought to have been issued about 1928. The set is sometimes titled as "Athletes, Aviators, Movie Stars and Boxers."

	EX-MT	VG-E	GOOD
COMPLETE SET (50)	375.00	170.00	47.50
COMMON BASEBALL (1-10)	8.00	3.60	1.00
COMMON NON-BB (31-50)	6.00	2.70	.75
☐ 1 Dave Bancroft	15.00	6.75	1.85
☐ 2 Grover Alexander	30.00	13.50	3.70
☐ 3 Ty Cobb	60.00	27.00	7.50
☐ 4 Tris Speaker	30.00	13.50	3.70
☐ 5 Glenn Wright	10.00	4.50	1.25
☐ 6 Babe Ruth	125.00	55.00	15.50
☐ 7 Everett Scott	10.00	4.50	1.25
☐ 8 Frank Frisch	20.00	9.00	2.50
☐ 9 Rogers Hornsby	30.00	13.50	3.70
☐ 10 Dazzy Vance	15.00	6.75	1.85
☐ 31 Gladys Robinson	6.00	2.70	.75
☐ 32 Lt. R.L. Maugham	6.00	2.70	.75
☐ 33 Helen Wills	8.00	3.60	1.00
☐ 34 Jack Wardle	6.00	2.70	.75
☐ 35 Clarence DeMar	6.00	2.70	.75
☐ 36 Bill Tilden	10.00	4.50	1.25
☐ 37 Helen Wainright	6.00	2.70	.75
☐ 38 Johnny Weismuller	15.00	6.75	1.85
☐ 39 Walter Hagen	8.00	3.60	1.00
☐ 40 Aileen Riggin	6.00	2.70	.75
☐ 41 Jack Dempsey	15.00	6.75	1.85
☐ 42 Pancho Villa	15.00	6.75	1.85
☐ 43 Johnny Dundee	6.00	2.70	.75
☐ 44 Gene Tunney	15.00	6.75	1.85
☐ 45 Mickey Walker	8.00	3.60	1.00
☐ 46 Luis Firpo	8.00	3.60	1.00
☐ 47 Geo. Carpentier	8.00	3.60	1.00
☐ 48 Benny Leonard	8.00	3.60	1.00
☐ 49 Abe Goldstein	8.00	3.60	1.00
☐ 50 Charley Ledoux	8.00	3.60	1.00

1928 W513 *

This set, referenced by the catalog designation W513, continues the numbering sequence started with W512. This set contains drawings and the cards which measure approximately 1 3/16" by 2 3/16" are blank backed. The most famous athletes outside the baseball players are Jack Sharkey, the heavyweight champion and Rene LaCoste, the famed tennis player and entrepeneur. The cards are thought to have been issued about 1928. The set is sometimes titled as "Athletes, Aviators, Movie Stars and Boxers."

	EX-MT	VG-E	GOOD
COMPLETE SET (42)	4500.00	2000.00	550.00
COMMON BASEBALL	10.00	4.50	1.25
COMMON OTHERS	8.00	3.60	1.00
☐ 61 Eddie Roush	20.00	9.00	2.50
☐ 62 Waite Hoyt	20.00	9.00	2.50
☐ 63 Gink Hundrick	10.00	4.50	1.25
☐ 64 Jumbo Elliott	10.00	4.50	1.25
☐ 65 John Miljus	10.00	4.50	1.25
☐ 66 Jumping Joe Dugan	10.00	4.50	1.25
☐ 67 Smiling Bill Terry	25.00	11.00	3.10
☐ 68 Herb Pennock	20.00	9.00	2.50
☐ 69 Rube Benton	10.00	4.50	1.25
☐ 70 Paul Waner	20.00	9.00	2.50
☐ 71 Adolfo Luque	10.00	4.50	1.25
☐ 72 Burleigh Grimes	20.00	9.00	2.50
☐ 73 Lloyd Waner	20.00	9.00	2.50
☐ 74 Hack Wilson	20.00	9.00	2.50
☐ 75 Hal Carlson	10.00	4.50	1.25
☐ 76 L. Grantham	10.00	4.50	1.25
☐ 77 Wilcey Moore	10.00	4.50	1.25
☐ 78 Jess Haines	20.00	9.00	2.50
☐ 79 Tony Lazzeri	20.00	9.00	2.50
☐ 80 Al De Vormer	10.00	4.50	1.25
☐ 81 Joe Harris	10.00	4.50	1.25
☐ 82 Pie Traynor	20.00	9.00	2.50
☐ 83 Mark Koenig	10.00	4.50	1.25
☐ 84 Babe Herman	12.50	5.50	1.55
☐ 85 George Harper	10.00	4.50	1.25
☐ 86 Earl Combs	20.00	9.00	2.50
☐ 87 Jack Sharkey	10.00	4.50	1.25
☐ 88 Paolino Uzcudun	8.00	3.60	1.00
☐ 89 Tom Heeney	8.00	3.60	1.00
☐ 90 Jack Delaney	8.00	3.60	1.00
☐ 91 Billy 'Young' Stribling	8.00	3.60	1.00
☐ 92 Babe Herman	8.00	3.60	1.00
☐ 93 Phil Scott	8.00	3.60	1.00
☐ 94 Benny Touchstone	8.00	3.60	1.00
☐ 95 Sammy Mandell	8.00	3.60	1.00
☐ 96 Fedel La Barbra	8.00	3.60	1.00
☐ 97 Tony Canzoneri	8.00	3.60	1.00
☐ 98 Louis Kid Kaplan	8.00	3.60	1.00
☐ 99 Charlie Phil Rosenberg	8.00	3.60	1.00
☐ 100 Rene LaCoste	10.00	4.50	1.25

1919 W514

This 120-card set measures approximately 1 7/16" by 2 1/2" and are numbered in the lower right The cards portray drawings of the athletes portrayed. The cards are thought to have been issued about 1919.

	EX-MT	VG-E	GOOD
COMPLETE SET (120)	1500.00	700.00	190.00
COMMON CARD (1-120)	10.00	4.50	1.25
☐ 1 Ira Flagstead	10.00	4.50	1.25
☐ 2 Babe Ruth	200.00	90.00	25.00
☐ 3 Happy Felsch	20.00	9.00	2.50
☐ 4 Doc Lavan	10.00	4.50	1.25
☐ 5 Phil Douglas	10.00	4.50	1.25
☐ 6 Earl Neale	12.50	5.50	1.55
☐ 7 Leslie Nunamaker	10.00	4.50	1.25
☐ 8 Sam Jones	10.00	4.50	1.25
☐ 9 Claude Hendrix	10.00	4.50	1.25
☐ 10 Frank Schulte	10.00	4.50	1.25
☐ 11 Cactus Cravath	10.00	4.50	1.25
☐ 12 Pat Moran	10.00	4.50	1.25
☐ 13 Dick Rudolph	10.00	4.50	1.25
☐ 14 Arthur Fletcher	10.00	4.50	1.25
☐ 15 Joe Jackson	150.00	70.00	19.00
☐ 16 Bill Southworth	10.00	4.50	1.25
☐ 17 Ad Luque	10.00	4.50	1.25
☐ 18 Charlie Deal	10.00	4.50	1.25
☐ 19 Al Mamaux	10.00	4.50	1.25
☐ 20 Stuffy McInnis	12.50	5.50	1.55
☐ 21 Rabbit Maranville	15.00	6.75	1.85
☐ 22 Max Carey	20.00	9.00	2.50
☐ 23 Dick Kerr	10.00	4.50	1.25
☐ 24 George Burns	10.00	4.50	1.25
☐ 25 Eddie Collins	20.00	9.00	2.50
☐ 26 Steve O'Neil	10.00	4.50	1.25
☐ 27 Bill Fisher	10.00	4.50	1.25
☐ 28 Rube Bressler	10.00	4.50	1.25
☐ 29 Bob Shawkey	10.00	4.50	1.25
☐ 30 Donie Bush	10.00	4.50	1.25
☐ 31 Chick Gandil	20.00	9.00	2.50
☐ 32 Ollie Zeider	10.00	4.50	1.25
☐ 33 Vean Gregg	10.00	4.50	1.25
☐ 34 Miller Huggins	20.00	9.00	2.50
☐ 35 Lefty Williams	10.00	4.50	1.25
☐ 36 Tub Spencer	10.00	4.50	1.25
☐ 37 Lew McCarthy	10.00	4.50	1.25
☐ 38 Hod Eller	10.00	4.50	1.25
☐ 39 Joe Gedeon	10.00	4.50	1.25
☐ 40 Dave Bancroft	15.00	6.75	1.85
☐ 41 Clark Griffith	20.00	9.00	2.50
☐ 42 Wilbur Cooper	10.00	4.50	1.25
☐ 43 Ty Cobb	75.00	34.00	9.50
☐ 44 Roger Peckinpaugh	12.50	5.50	1.55
☐ 45 Nic Carter	10.00	4.50	1.25
☐ 46 Heinie Groh	10.00	4.50	1.25
☐ 47 Bob Roth	10.00	4.50	1.25
☐ 48 Frank Davis	10.00	4.50	1.25
☐ 49 Leslie Mann	10.00	4.50	1.25
☐ 50 Fielder Jones	10.00	4.50	1.25
☐ 51 Bill Doak	10.00	4.50	1.25
☐ 52 John J. McGraw MG	25.00	11.00	3.10
☐ 53 Charles Hollocher	10.00	4.50	1.25
☐ 54 Babe Adams	10.00	4.50	1.25
☐ 55 Dode Paskert	10.00	4.50	1.25
☐ 56 Rogers Hornsby	30.00	13.50	3.70
☐ 57 Max Rath	10.00	4.50	1.25
☐ 58 Jeff Pfeffer	10.00	4.50	1.25
☐ 59 Nick Cullop	10.00	4.50	1.25
☐ 60 Ray Schalk	15.00	6.75	1.85
☐ 61 Bill Jacobson	10.00	4.50	1.25
☐ 62 Nap Lajoie	25.00	11.00	3.10
☐ 63 George Gibson	10.00	4.50	1.25
☐ 64 Harry Hooper	20.00	9.00	2.50
☐ 65 Grover Alexander	25.00	11.00	3.10
☐ 66 Ping Bodie	10.00	4.50	1.25
☐ 67 Hank Gowdy	12.50	5.50	1.55
☐ 68 Jake Daubert	12.50	5.50	1.55
☐ 69 Red Faber	15.00	6.75	1.85
☐ 70 Ivan Olson	10.00	4.50	1.25
☐ 71 Pickles Dilhoefer	10.00	4.50	1.25
☐ 72 Christy Mathewson	30.00	13.50	3.70
☐ 73 Ira Wingo	10.00	4.50	1.25
☐ 74 Fred Merkle	12.50	5.50	1.55
☐ 75 Frank Baker	20.00	9.00	2.50
☐ 76 Bert Gallia	10.00	4.50	1.25
☐ 77 Milton Watson	10.00	4.50	1.25
☐ 78 Bert Shotten	10.00	4.50	1.25
☐ 79 Sam Rice	15.00	6.75	1.85
☐ 80 Dan Greiner	10.00	4.50	1.25
☐ 81 Larry Doyle	12.50	5.50	1.55
☐ 82 Eddie Cicotte	25.00	11.00	3.10
☐ 83 Hugo Bezdek	10.00	4.50	1.25
☐ 84 Wally Pipp	12.50	5.50	1.55
☐ 85 Eddie Roush	15.00	6.75	1.85
☐ 86 Slim Sallee	10.00	4.50	1.25
☐ 87 Bill Killifer	10.00	4.50	1.25
☐ 88 Bob Veach	10.00	4.50	1.25
☐ 89 Jim Burke	10.00	4.50	1.25
☐ 90 Everett Scott	10.00	4.50	1.25
☐ 91 Buck Weaver	20.00	9.00	2.50
☐ 92 George Whitted	10.00	4.50	1.25
☐ 93 Ed Konetchy	10.00	4.50	1.25
☐ 94 Walter Johnson	30.00	13.50	3.70
☐ 95 Sam Crawford	15.00	6.75	1.85

	EX-MT	VG-E	GOOD
☐ 96 Fred Mitchell	10.00	4.50	1.25
☐ 97 Ira Thomas	10.00	4.50	1.25
☐ 98 Jimmy Ring	10.00	4.50	1.25
☐ 99 Wally Schang	10.00	4.50	1.25
☐ 100 Benny Kauff	10.00	4.50	1.25
☐ 101 George Sisler	25.00	11.00	3.10
☐ 102 Tris Speaker	25.00	11.00	3.10
☐ 103 Carl Mays	10.00	4.50	1.25
☐ 104 Buck Herzog	10.00	4.50	1.25
☐ 105 Swede Risberg	15.00	6.75	1.85
☐ 106 Hugh Jennings MG	20.00	9.00	2.50
☐ 107 Pep Young	20.00	9.00	2.50
☐ 108 Walter Reuther	10.00	4.50	1.25
☐ 109 Joe Gharrity	10.00	4.50	1.25
☐ 110 Zack Wheat	15.00	6.75	1.85
☐ 111 Jim Vaughn	10.00	4.50	1.25
☐ 112 Kid Gleason MG	10.00	4.50	1.25
☐ 113 Casey Stengel	30.00	13.50	3.70
☐ 114 Hal Chase	12.50	5.50	1.55
☐ 115 Oscar Stanage	10.00	4.50	1.25
☐ 116 Larry Shean	10.00	4.50	1.25
☐ 117 Steve Pendergast	10.00	4.50	1.25
☐ 118 Larry Kopf	10.00	4.50	1.25
☐ 119 Charles Whiteman	10.00	4.50	1.25
☐ 120 Jesse Barnes	10.00	4.50	1.25
☐ 53 Wilbert Robinson MG	20.00	9.00	2.50
☐ 54 George Burns	8.00	3.60	1.00
☐ 55 Rogers Hornsby	35.00	16.00	4.40
☐ 56 Zack Wheat	15.00	6.75	1.85
☐ 57 Eddie Roush	20.00	9.00	2.50
☐ 58 Eddie Collins	20.00	9.00	2.50
☐ 59 Charlie Hollocher	8.00	3.60	1.00
☐ 60 Red Faber	15.00	6.75	1.85

1923 W515

This 60-card set, referenced by the catalog designation W515, measures approximately 1 5/16" by 2 3/16". The cards are blank backed and feature drawings on the front with the name of the player, his position, and his team on the bottom of the card.

	EX-MT	VG-E	GOOD
COMPLETE SET (60)	1000.00	450.00	125.00
COMMON CARD (1-60)	8.00	3.60	1.00
☐ 1 Bill Cunningham	8.00	3.60	1.00
☐ 2 Al Mamaux	8.00	3.60	1.00
☐ 3 Babe Ruth	150.00	70.00	19.00
☐ 4 Dave Bancroft	15.00	6.75	1.85
☐ 5 Ed Rommell	8.00	3.60	1.00
☐ 6 Babe Adams	8.00	3.60	1.00
☐ 7 Clarence Walker	8.00	3.60	1.00
☐ 8 Waite Hoyt	15.00	6.75	1.85
☐ 9 Bob Shawkey	8.00	3.60	1.00
☐ 10 Ty Cobb	75.00	34.00	9.50
☐ 11 George Sisler	25.00	11.00	3.10
☐ 12 Jack Bentley	8.00	3.60	1.00
☐ 13 Jim O'Connell	8.00	3.60	1.00
☐ 14 Frank Frisch	25.00	11.00	3.10
☐ 15 Frank Baker	20.00	9.00	2.50
☐ 16 Burleigh Grimes	15.00	6.75	1.85
☐ 17 Wally Schang	8.00	3.60	1.00
☐ 18 Harry Heilman	20.00	9.00	2.50
☐ 19 Aaron Ward	8.00	3.60	1.00
☐ 20 Carl Mays	10.00	4.50	1.25
☐ 21 The Meusel Bros.	10.00	4.50	1.25
☐ 22 Arthur Nehf	8.00	3.60	1.00
☐ 23 Lee Meadows	8.00	3.60	1.00
☐ 24 Casey Stengel	35.00	16.00	4.40
☐ 25 Jack Scott	8.00	3.60	1.00
☐ 26 Kenneth Williams	8.00	3.60	1.00
☐ 27 Joe Bush	8.00	3.60	1.00
☐ 28 Tris Speaker	25.00	11.00	3.10
☐ 29 Ross Youngs	15.00	6.75	1.85
☐ 30 Joe Dugan	10.00	4.50	1.25
☐ 31 The Barnes Bros.	10.00	4.50	1.25
☐ 32 George Kelly	15.00	6.75	1.85
☐ 33 Hugh McQuillen	8.00	3.60	1.00
☐ 34 Hugh Jennings MG	15.00	6.75	1.85
☐ 35 Tom Griffith	8.00	3.60	1.00
☐ 36 Miller Huggins MG	20.00	9.00	2.50
☐ 37 Whitey Witt	8.00	3.60	1.00
☐ 38 Walter Johnson	35.00	16.00	4.40
☐ 39 Wally Pipp	10.00	4.50	1.25
☐ 40 Dutch Reuther	8.00	3.60	1.00
☐ 41 Jim Johnston	8.00	3.60	1.00
☐ 42 Willie Kamm	10.00	4.50	1.25
☐ 43 Sam Jones	8.00	3.60	1.00
☐ 44 Frank Snyder	8.00	3.60	1.00
☐ 45 John McGraw MG	20.00	9.00	2.50
☐ 46 Everett Scott	8.00	3.60	1.00
☐ 47 Babe Ruth	150.00	70.00	19.00
☐ 48 Urban Shocker	10.00	4.50	1.25
☐ 49 Grover Alexander	25.00	11.00	3.10
☐ 50 Rabbit Maranville	15.00	6.75	1.85
☐ 51 Ray Schalk	15.00	6.75	1.85
☐ 52 Heinie Groh	10.00	4.50	1.25

1920 W516-1

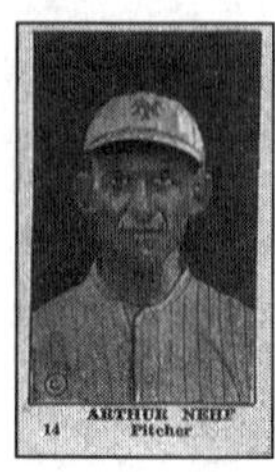

This 30-card set, referenced by the catalog designation W516, measures approximately 1 7/16" by 2 5/16". The cards have colorful photos with a blank back. The copyright is reversed on the front of the card. There is also the name of the player and position on the bottom of the card.

	EX-MT	VG-E	GOOD
COMPLETE SET (30)	600.00	275.00	75.00
COMMON CARD (1-30)	8.00	3.60	1.00
☐ 1 Babe Ruth	175.00	80.00	22.00
☐ 2 Heine Groh	10.00	4.50	1.25
☐ 3 Ping Bodie	8.00	3.60	1.00
☐ 4 Ray Shalk (sic)	20.00	9.00	2.50
☐ 5 Tris Speaker	40.00	18.00	5.00
☐ 6 Ty Cobb	75.00	34.00	9.50
☐ 7 Roger Hornsby (sic)	60.00	27.00	7.50
☐ 8 Walter Johnson	60.00	27.00	7.50
☐ 9 Grover Alexander	40.00	18.00	5.00
☐ 10 George Burns	8.00	3.60	1.00
☐ 11 Jimmy Ring	8.00	3.60	1.00
☐ 12 Jess Barnes	8.00	3.60	1.00
☐ 13 Larry Doyle	12.50	5.50	1.55
☐ 14 Arty Fletcher	8.00	3.60	1.00
☐ 15 Dick Rudolph	8.00	3.60	1.00
☐ 16 Benny Dauff	8.00	3.60	1.00
☐ 17 Art Nehf	8.00	3.60	1.00
☐ 18 Babe Adams	8.00	3.60	1.00
☐ 19 Will Cooper	8.00	3.60	1.00
☐ 20 R.Peckingpaugh (sic)	12.50	5.50	1.55
☐ 21 Eddie Cicotte	25.00	11.00	3.10
☐ 22 Hank Gowdy	12.50	5.50	1.55
☐ 23 Eddie Collins	25.00	11.00	3.10
☐ 24 Christy Mathewson	60.00	27.00	7.50
☐ 25 Clyde Milan	8.00	3.60	1.00
☐ 26 M. Kelley	8.00	3.60	1.00
☐ 27 Ed Hooper	8.00	3.60	1.00
☐ 28 Pep Young	20.00	9.00	2.50
☐ 29 Eddie Rousch (sic)	20.00	9.00	2.50
☐ 30 George Bancroft	8.00	3.60	1.00

1931 W517

The cards in this 54-card set measure approximately 3" by 4". This 1931 set of numbered, blank-backed cards was placed in the "W" category in the original American Card Catalog because (1) its producer was unknown and (2) it was issued in strips of three. The photo is black and white but the entire obverse of each card is generally found tinted in tones of sepia, blue, green, yellow, rose, black or gray. The cards are numbered in a small circle on the front. A solid dark line at one end of a card entitled the purchaser to another piece of candy as a prize. There are two different cards of both Babe Ruth and Mickey Cochrane. There may be other variations in this set: such as cards without numbers (e.g., Paul Waner and Dazzy Vance) as well as Chalmer Cissell with both Chicago and Cleveland, Chick Hafey with both the Cardinals and Cincinnati, and George Kelly and Lefty O'Doul with Brooklyn.

	EX-MT	VG-E	GOOD
COMPLETE SET (54)	7500.00	3400.00	950.00
COMMON CARD (1-54)	40.00	18.00	5.00
☐ 1 Earle Combs	80.00	36.00	10.00
☐ 2 Pie Traynor	100.00	45.00	12.50
☐ 3 Eddie Roush (Wearing Cincinnati uniform, but listed as a New York Giant)	100.00	45.00	12.50
☐ 4 Babe Ruth (Throwing)	1500.00	700.00	190.00
☐ 5 Chalmer Cissell	40.00	18.00	5.00
☐ 6 Bill Sherdel	40.00	18.00	5.00
☐ 7 Bill Shore	40.00	18.00	5.00
☐ 8 George Earnshaw	40.00	18.00	5.00
☐ 9 Bucky Harris	80.00	36.00	10.00
☐ 10 Chuck Klein	100.00	45.00	12.50
☐ 11 George Kelly	80.00	36.00	10.00
☐ 12 Travis Jackson	80.00	36.00	10.00
☐ 13 Willie Kamm	40.00	18.00	5.00
☐ 14 Harry Heilmann	100.00	45.00	12.50
☐ 15 Grover Alexander	150.00	70.00	19.00
☐ 16 Frank Frisch	100.00	45.00	12.50
☐ 17 Jack Quinn	40.00	18.00	5.00
☐ 18 Cy Williams	50.00	22.00	6.25
☐ 19 Kiki Cuyler	80.00	36.00	10.00
☐ 20 Babe Ruth (Portrait)	1800.00	800.00	220.00
☐ 21 Jimmy Foxx	250.00	110.00	31.00
☐ 22 Jimmy Dykes	50.00	22.00	6.25
☐ 23 Bill Terry	125.00	55.00	15.50
☐ 24 Freddy Lindstrom	80.00	36.00	10.00
☐ 25 Hugh Critz	40.00	18.00	5.00
☐ 26 Pete Donahue	40.00	18.00	5.00
☐ 27 Tony Lazzeri	100.00	45.00	12.50
☐ 28 Heinie Manush	80.00	36.00	10.00
☐ 29 Chick Hafey	80.00	36.00	10.00
☐ 30 Melvin Ott	175.00	80.00	22.00
☐ 31 Bing Miller	40.00	18.00	5.00
☐ 32 Mule Haas	40.00	18.00	5.00
☐ 33 Lefty O'Doul	50.00	22.00	6.25
☐ 34 Paul Waner	80.00	36.00	10.00
☐ 35 Lou Gehrig	900.00	400.00	110.00
☐ 36 Dazzy Vance	80.00	36.00	10.00
☐ 37 Mickey Cochrane (Catching pose)	125.00	55.00	15.50
☐ 38 Rogers Hornsby	250.00	110.00	31.00
☐ 39 Lefty Grove	175.00	80.00	22.00
☐ 40 Al Simmons	100.00	45.00	12.50
☐ 41 Rube Walberg	40.00	18.00	5.00
☐ 42 Hack Wilson	125.00	55.00	15.50
☐ 43 Art Shires	40.00	18.00	5.00
☐ 44 Sammy Hale	40.00	18.00	5.00
☐ 45 Ted Lyons	80.00	36.00	10.00
☐ 46 Joe Sewell	80.00	36.00	10.00
☐ 47 Goose Goslin	80.00	36.00	10.00
☐ 48 Lou Fonseca	40.00	18.00	5.00
☐ 49 Bob Meusel	50.00	22.00	6.25
☐ 50 Lu Blue	40.00	18.00	5.00
☐ 51 Earl Averill	80.00	36.00	10.00
☐ 52 Eddie Collins	100.00	45.00	12.50
☐ 53 Joe Judge	40.00	18.00	5.00
☐ 54 Mickey Cochrane (Portrait)	125.00	55.00	15.50

1930 W554

This set corresponds to the poses in R316 and R306. The cards measure 5" by 7" and are reasonably available within the Hobby.

	EX-MT	VG-E	GOOD
COMPLETE SET (18)	1500.00	700.00	190.00
COMMON CARD (1-18)	25.00	11.00	3.10
☐ 1 Gordon S. (Mickey) Cochrane	75.00	33.00	9.30
☐ 2 Lewis A. Fonseca	25.00	11.00	3.10
☐ 3 Jimmy Foxx	100.00	45.00	12.00
☐ 4 Lou Gehrig	250.00	110.00	31.00
☐ 5 Burleigh Grimes	75.00	33.00	9.30
☐ 6 Robert M. Grove	75.00	33.00	9.30
☐ 7 Waite Hoyt	75.00	33.00	9.30
☐ 8 Joe Judge	25.00	11.00	3.10
☐ 9 Charles(Chuck)Klein	75.00	33.00	9.30
☐ 10 Douglas McWeeny	25.00	11.00	3.10
☐ 11 Frank O'Doul	50.00	22.00	6.20
☐ 12 Melvin Ott	75.00	33.00	9.30
☐ 13 Herbert Pennock	75.00	33.00	9.30
☐ 14 Eddie Rommel	50.00	22.00	6.20
☐ 15 Babe Ruth	350.00	160.00	44.00
☐ 16 Al Simmons	75.00	33.00	9.30
☐ 17 Lloyd Waner	75.00	33.00	9.30
☐ 18 Hack Wilson	75.00	33.00	9.30

1910 W555

This 66 card set measures 1 1/8" by 1 3/16" and have sepia pictures surrounded by a black border, which is framed by a white line. Little is known about how these cards were released and it is speculated they they are part of the strip card family which explains why they have the "W" designation. Eight cards: Bates, Bescher, Byrne, Collins, Crawford, Devlin, Lake and Mowery are frequently found on want lists. The Eddie Cicotte card was the most recent discovery and is also assumed to be one of the tougher cards. The set is also considered to be related to the E93, E94, E97 and E98 sets.

	EX-MT	VG-E	GOOD
COMPLETE SET (66)	5000.00	2200.00	600.00
COMMON CARD (1-66)	35.00	16.00	4.40
☐ 1 Red Ames	35.00	16.00	4.40
☐ 2 Jimmy Austin	35.00	16.00	4.40
☐ 3 Johnny Bates	75.00	34.00	9.50
☐ 4 Chief Bender	100.00	45.00	12.50
☐ 5 Bob Bescher	75.00	34.00	9.50
☐ 6 Joe Birmingham	35.00	16.00	4.40
☐ 7 Bill Bradley	35.00	16.00	4.40
☐ 8 Kitty Bransfield	35.00	16.00	4.40
☐ 9 Mordecai Brown	100.00	45.00	12.50
☐ 10 Bobby Byrne	75.00	34.00	9.50
☐ 11 Frank Chance	100.00	45.00	12.50
☐ 12 Hal Chase	75.00	34.00	9.50
☐ 13 Eddie Cicotte	100.00	45.00	12.50
☐ 14 Fred Clarke	100.00	45.00	12.50
☐ 15 Ty Cobb	500.00	220.00	60.00
☐ 16 Eddie Collins dark uniform	300.00	135.00	38.00
☐ 17 Eddie Collins light uniform	300.00	135.00	38.00
☐ 18 Harry Covelskie	35.00	16.00	4.40
☐ 19 Sam Crawford	150.00	70.00	19.00
☐ 20 Harry Davis	35.00	16.00	4.40
☐ 21 Jim Delahanty	35.00	16.00	4.40
☐ 22 Art Devlin	75.00	34.00	9.50
☐ 23 Josh Devore	35.00	16.00	4.40
☐ 24 Bill Donovan	50.00	22.00	6.25
☐ 25 Red Dooin	35.00	16.00	4.40
☐ 26 Mickey Doolan	35.00	16.00	4.40
☐ 27 Bull Durham	35.00	16.00	4.40
☐ 28 Jimmy Dygert	35.00	16.00	4.40
☐ 29 Johnny Evers	125.00	55.00	15.50
☐ 30 Russ Ford	35.00	16.00	4.40
☐ 31 George Gibson	35.00	16.00	4.40
☐ 32 Clark Griffith	100.00	45.00	12.50
☐ 33 Topsy Hartsell	35.00	16.00	4.40
☐ 34 Bill Hinchman Sic, Heinchman	35.00	16.00	4.40
☐ 35 Charlie Hemphill	35.00	16.00	4.40
☐ 36 Hugh Jennings MG	100.00	45.00	12.50
☐ 37 Davy Jones	35.00	16.00	4.40
☐ 38 Addie Joss	100.00	45.00	12.50
☐ 39 Willie Keeler	100.00	45.00	12.50
☐ 40 Red Kleinow	35.00	16.00	4.40
☐ 41 Nap Lajoie	150.00	70.00	19.00
☐ 42 Joe Lake	35.00	16.00	4.40
☐ 43 Fred Leach	35.00	16.00	4.40
☐ 44 Sherry Magee	35.00	16.00	4.40
☐ 45 Christy Mathewson	200.00	90.00	25.00
☐ 46 Ambrose McConnell	35.00	16.00	4.40
☐ 47 John McGraw MG	150.00	70.00	19.00
☐ 48 Chief Meyers	50.00	22.00	6.25
☐ 49 Earl Moore	35.00	16.00	4.40
☐ 50 Mike Mowrey	35.00	16.00	4.40
☐ 51 George Mullin	35.00	16.00	4.40
☐ 52 Red Murray	35.00	16.00	4.40
☐ 53 Simon Nicholls	35.00	16.00	4.40
☐ 54 Jim Pastorius	35.00	16.00	4.40
☐ 55 Deacon Phillipe	50.00	22.00	6.25
☐ 56 Eddie Plank	100.00	45.00	12.50
☐ 57 Fred Snodgrass	35.00	16.00	4.40
☐ 58 Harry Steinfeldt	50.00	22.00	6.25
☐ 59 Joe Tinker	125.00	55.00	15.50
☐ 60 Hippo Vaughn	35.00	16.00	4.40
☐ 61 Honus Wagner	250.00	110.00	31.00
☐ 62 Rube Waddell	100.00	45.00	12.50
☐ 63 Hoooks Wiltse	35.00	16.00	4.40
☐ 64 Cy Young Cleveland Amer.	200.00	90.00	25.00
☐ 65 Cy Young Same pose as E93	200.00	90.00	25.00
☐ 66 Cy Young Same pose as E97-8	200.00	90.00	25.00

1922 W572

This 119-card set was issued in 1922 in ten-card strips along with strips of boxer cards. The cards measure approximately 1 5/16" by 2 1/2" and are blank backed. Most of the player photos on the fronts are black and white, although a few photos are sepia-toned. The pictures are the same ones used in the E120 set, but they have been cropped to fit on the smaller format. The player's signature and team appear at the bottom of the pictures, along with an IFS (International Feature Service) copyright notice. The cards are unnumbered and checklisted below in alphabetical order.

	EX-MT	VG-E	GOOD
COMPLETE SET (119)	4000.00	1800.00	500.00
COMMON CARD (1-119)	15.00	6.75	1.85
☐ 1 Eddie Ainsmith	15.00	6.75	1.85
☐ 2 Vic Aldridge	15.00	6.75	1.85
☐ 3 Grover C. Alexander	100.00	45.00	12.50
☐ 4 Dave Bancroft	30.00	13.50	3.70
☐ 5 Jesse Barnes	15.00	6.75	1.85
☐ 6 John Bassler	15.00	6.75	1.85
☐ 7 Lu Blue	15.00	6.75	1.85
☐ 8 Norm Boeckel	15.00	6.75	1.85
☐ 9 George Burns	15.00	6.75	1.85
☐ 10 Joe Bush	18.00	8.00	2.20
☐ 11 Leon Cadore	15.00	6.75	1.85
☐ 12 Virgil Cheevers	15.00	6.75	1.85
☐ 13 Ty Cobb	500.00	220.00	60.00
☐ 14 Eddie Collins	40.00	18.00	5.00
☐ 15 John Collins	15.00	6.75	1.85
☐ 16 Wilbur Cooper	15.00	6.75	1.85
☐ 17 Stanley Coveleski	30.00	13.50	3.70
☐ 18 Walton Cruise	15.00	6.75	1.85
☐ 19 Dave Danforth	15.00	6.75	1.85
☐ 20 Jake Daubert	18.00	8.00	2.20
☐ 21 Hank DeBerry	15.00	6.75	1.85
☐ 22 Lou DeVormer	15.00	6.75	1.85
☐ 23 Bill Doak	15.00	6.75	1.85
☐ 24 Pete Donohue	15.00	6.75	1.85
☐ 25 Pat Duncan	15.00	6.75	1.85
☐ 26 Jimmy Dykes	18.00	8.00	2.20
☐ 27 Urban Faber	30.00	13.50	3.70
☐ 28 Bibb Falk	15.00	6.75	1.85
☐ 29 Frank Frisch	45.00	20.00	5.50
☐ 30 Chick Galloway	15.00	6.75	1.85
☐ 31 Ed Gharrity	15.00	6.75	1.85
☐ 32 Charles Glazner	15.00	6.75	1.85
☐ 33 Hank Gowdy	18.00	8.00	2.20
☐ 34 Tom Griffith	15.00	6.75	1.85
☐ 35 Burleigh Grimes	30.00	13.50	3.70
☐ 36 Ray Grimes	15.00	6.75	1.85
☐ 37 Heinie Groh	18.00	8.00	2.20
☐ 38 Joe Harris	15.00	6.75	1.85
☐ 39 Bucky Harris	30.00	13.50	3.70
☐ 40 Joe Hauser	15.00	6.75	1.85
☐ 41 Harry Heilmann	40.00	18.00	5.00
☐ 42 Walter Henline	15.00	6.75	1.85
☐ 43 Charles Hollocher	15.00	6.75	1.85
☐ 44 Harry Hooper	40.00	18.00	5.00
☐ 45 Rogers Hornsby	125.00	55.00	15.50
☐ 46 Waite Hoyt	30.00	13.50	3.70
☐ 47 Wilbur Hubbell	15.00	6.75	1.85
☐ 48 William Jacobson	15.00	6.75	1.85
☐ 49 Charles Jamieson	15.00	6.75	1.85
☐ 50 Syl Johnson	15.00	6.75	1.85
☐ 51 Walter Johnson	175.00	80.00	22.00
☐ 52 Jimmy Johnston	15.00	6.75	1.85
☐ 53 Joe Judge	18.00	8.00	2.20
☐ 54 George Kelly	30.00	13.50	3.70
☐ 55 Lee King	15.00	6.75	1.85
☐ 56 Larry Kopf	15.00	6.75	1.85
☐ 57 George Leverette	15.00	6.75	1.85
☐ 58 Al Mamaux	15.00	6.75	1.85
☐ 59 Rabbit Maranville	30.00	13.50	3.70
☐ 60 Rube Marquard	30.00	13.50	3.70
☐ 61 Martin McManus	15.00	6.75	1.85
☐ 62 Lee Meadows	15.00	6.75	1.85
☐ 63 Mike Menosky	15.00	6.75	1.85
☐ 64 Bob Meusel	20.00	9.00	2.50
☐ 65 Emil Meusel	18.00	8.00	2.20
☐ 66 George Mogridge	15.00	6.75	1.85
☐ 67 John Morrison	15.00	6.75	1.85
☐ 68 Johnny Mostil	15.00	6.75	1.85
☐ 69 Roleine Naylor	15.00	6.75	1.85
☐ 70 Art Nehf	15.00	6.75	1.85
☐ 71 Joe Oeschger	15.00	6.75	1.85
☐ 72 Bob O'Farrell	15.00	6.75	1.85
☐ 73 Steve O'Neill	18.00	8.00	2.20
☐ 74 Frank Parkinson	15.00	6.75	1.85
☐ 75 Ralph Perkins	15.00	6.75	1.85
☐ 76 Herman Pillette	15.00	6.75	1.85
☐ 77 Babe Pinelli	15.00	6.75	1.85
☐ 78 Wallie Pipp	20.00	9.00	2.50
☐ 79 Ray Powell	15.00	6.75	1.85
☐ 80 Jack Quinn	15.00	6.75	1.85
☐ 81 Goldie Rapp	15.00	6.75	1.85
☐ 82 Walt Reuther	18.00	8.00	2.20
☐ 83 Sam Rice	30.00	13.50	3.70
☐ 84 Emory Rigney	15.00	6.75	1.85
☐ 85 Eppa Rixey	30.00	13.50	3.70
☐ 86 Ed Rommel	18.00	8.00	2.20
☐ 87 Eddie Roush	45.00	20.00	5.50
☐ 88 Babe Ruth	1000.00	450.00	125.00
☐ 89 Ray Schalk	30.00	13.50	3.70
☐ 90 Wally Schang	18.00	8.00	2.20
☐ 91 Walter Schmidt	15.00	6.75	1.85
☐ 92 Joe Schultz	15.00	6.75	1.85
☐ 93 Hank Severeid	15.00	6.75	1.85
☐ 94 Joe Sewell	30.00	13.50	3.70
☐ 95 Bob Shawkey	15.00	6.75	1.85
☐ 96 Earl Sheely	15.00	6.75	1.85
☐ 97 Will Sherdel	15.00	6.75	1.85
☐ 98 Urban Shocker	18.00	8.00	2.20
☐ 99 George Sisler	75.00	34.00	9.50
☐ 100 Earl Smith	15.00	6.75	1.85
☐ 101 Elmer Smith	15.00	6.75	1.85
☐ 102 Jack Smith	15.00	6.75	1.85
☐ 103 Bill Southworth	18.00	8.00	2.20
☐ 104 Tris Speaker	100.00	45.00	12.50
☐ 105 Milton Stock	15.00	6.75	1.85
☐ 106 Jim Tierney	15.00	6.75	1.85
☐ 107 Harold Traynor	40.00	18.00	5.00
☐ 108 George Uhle	15.00	6.75	1.85
☐ 109 Bob Veach	15.00	6.75	1.85
☐ 110 Clarence Walker	15.00	6.75	1.85
☐ 111 Curtis Walker	15.00	6.75	1.85
☐ 112 Bill Wambsganss	18.00	8.00	2.20
☐ 113 Aaron Ward	15.00	6.75	1.85
☐ 114 Zach Wheat	30.00	13.50	3.70
☐ 115 Fred Williams	15.00	6.75	1.85
☐ 116 Ken Williams	20.00	9.00	2.50
☐ 117 Ivy Wingo	15.00	6.75	1.85
☐ 118 Joe Wood	30.00	13.50	3.70
☐ 119 Tom Zachary	15.00	6.75	1.85

1922 W573

This set's design is similiar to the E120 American Caramel set. The backs are blank. These cards have been described as a "small strip card type of E120.

	EX-MT	VG-E	GOOD
COMPLETE SET (142)	2000.00	900.00	250.00
COMMON CARD (1-142)	10.00	4.50	1.25
☐ 1 Babe Adams	10.00	4.50	1.25
☐ 2 Eddie Ainsmith	10.00	4.50	1.25
☐ 3 Vic Aldridge	10.00	4.50	1.25
☐ 4 Grover C. Alexander	60.00	27.00	7.50
☐ 5 Frank Baker	25.00	11.00	3.10
☐ 6 Dave Bancroft	20.00	9.00	2.50
☐ 7 Turner Barber	10.00	4.50	1.25
☐ 8 Jesse Barnes	10.00	4.50	1.25
☐ 9 Johnny Bassler	10.00	4.50	1.25
☐ 10 Carson Bigbee	10.00	4.50	1.25
☐ 11 Lu Blue	10.00	4.50	1.25
☐ 12 Tony Boeckel	10.00	4.50	1.25
☐ 13 George H. Burns	10.00	4.50	1.25
☐ 14 George J. Burns	10.00	4.50	1.25
☐ 15 Marty Callaghan	10.00	4.50	1.25
☐ 16 Max Carey	20.00	9.00	2.50
☐ 17 Ike Caveney	10.00	4.50	1.25
☐ 18 Verne Clemons	10.00	4.50	1.25
☐ 19 Ty Cobb	150.00	70.00	19.00
☐ 20 Al Cole	10.00	4.50	1.25
☐ 21 Eddie Collins	25.00	11.00	3.10
☐ 22 Pat Collins	10.00	4.50	1.25
☐ 23 Wilbur Cooper	10.00	4.50	1.25
☐ 24 Dick Cox	10.00	4.50	1.25
☐ 25 Bill Cunningham	10.00	4.50	1.25
☐ 26 George Cutshaw	10.00	4.50	1.25
☐ 27 Dave Danforth	10.00	4.50	1.25
☐ 28 Hooks Dauss	10.00	4.50	1.25
☐ 29 Dixie Davis	10.00	4.50	1.25
☐ 30 Hank DeBerry	10.00	4.50	1.25
☐ 31 Al DeVormer	10.00	4.50	1.25
☐ 32 Bill Doak	10.00	4.50	1.25
☐ 33 Joe Dugan	12.50	5.50	1.55
☐ 34 Howard Ehmke	12.50	5.50	1.55
☐ 35 Frank Ellerbe	10.00	4.50	1.25
☐ 36 Red Faber	20.00	9.00	2.50
☐ 37 Bibb Falk	10.00	4.50	1.25
☐ 38 Max Flack	10.00	4.50	1.25
☐ 39 Ira Flagstead	10.00	4.50	1.25
☐ 40 Art Fletcher	10.00	4.50	1.25
☐ 41 Hod Ford	10.00	4.50	1.25
☐ 42 Jacques Fournier	10.00	4.50	1.25
☐ 43 Frank Frisch	40.00	18.00	5.00
☐ 44 Ollie Fuhrman	10.00	4.50	1.25
☐ 45 Chick Galloway	10.00	4.50	1.25
☐ 46 Wally Gerber	10.00	4.50	1.25
☐ 47 Patsy Gharrity	10.00	4.50	1.25
☐ 48 Whitey Glazner	10.00	4.50	1.25
☐ 49 Goose Goslin	20.00	9.00	2.50
☐ 50 Hank Gowdy	12.50	5.50	1.55
☐ 51 Jack Graney	10.00	4.50	1.25
☐ 52 Burleigh Grimes	20.00	9.00	2.50
☐ 53 Heinie Groh	12.50	5.50	1.55
☐ 54 Jesse Haines	20.00	9.00	2.50
☐ 55 Bubbles Hargrave	10.00	4.50	1.25
☐ 56 Joe Harris	10.00	4.50	1.25
☐ 57 Earl Hamilton	10.00	4.50	1.25
☐ 58 Cliff Heathcote	10.00	4.50	1.25
☐ 59 Harry Heilmann	25.00	11.00	3.10
☐ 60 Clarence Hodge	10.00	4.50	1.25
☐ 61 Charlie Hollocher	10.00	4.50	1.25
☐ 62 Harry Hooper	20.00	9.00	2.50
☐ 63 Rogers Hornsby	75.00	34.00	9.50
☐ 64 Waite Hoyt	20.00	9.00	2.50
☐ 65 Ernie Johnson	10.00	4.50	1.25
☐ 66 Syl Johnson	10.00	4.50	1.25
☐ 67 Walter Johnson	75.00	34.00	9.50
☐ 68 Paul Johnson	10.00	4.50	1.25
☐ 69 Sam Jones	10.00	4.50	1.25
☐ 70 Benjamin Karr	10.00	4.50	1.25
☐ 71 Doc Lavan	10.00	4.50	1.25
☐ 72 Dixie Levrette	10.00	4.50	1.25
☐ 73 Rabbit Maranville	20.00	9.00	2.50
☐ 74 Cliff Markle	10.00	4.50	1.25
☐ 75 Carl Mays	12.50	5.50	1.55
☐ 76 Harvey McClellan	10.00	4.50	1.25
☐ 77 Marty McManus	10.00	4.50	1.25
☐ 78 Lee Meadows	10.00	4.50	1.25
☐ 79 Mike Menosky	10.00	4.50	1.25
☐ 80 Irish Meusel	12.50	5.50	1.55
☐ 81 Clyde Milan	10.00	4.50	1.25
☐ 82 Bing Miller	10.00	4.50	1.25
☐ 83 Elmer Miller	10.00	4.50	1.25
☐ 84 Ralph Miller	10.00	4.50	1.25
☐ 85 Hack Miller	10.00	4.50	1.25
☐ 86 Clarence Mitchell	10.00	4.50	1.25
☐ 87 George Mogridge	10.00	4.50	1.25
☐ 88 John Morrison	10.00	4.50	1.25
☐ 89 Johnny Mostil	10.00	4.50	1.25
☐ 90 Elmer Myers	10.00	4.50	1.25
☐ 91 Roleine Naylor	10.00	4.50	1.25
☐ 92 Les Nunamaker	10.00	4.50	1.25
☐ 93 Bob O'Farrell	10.00	4.50	1.25
☐ 94 Steve O'Neill	12.50	5.50	1.55
☐ 95 Herb Pennock	20.00	9.00	2.50
☐ 96 Cy Perkins	10.00	4.50	1.25
☐ 97 Thomas Phillips	10.00	4.50	1.25
☐ 98 Val Picinich	10.00	4.50	1.25
☐ 99 Herman Pillette	12.50	5.50	1.55
☐ 100 Babe Pinelli	10.00	4.50	1.25
☐ 101 Wally Pipp	12.50	5.50	1.55
☐ 102 Clark Pittenger	10.00	4.50	1.25
☐ 103 Del Pratt	10.00	4.50	1.25
☐ 104 Goldie Rapp	10.00	4.50	1.25
☐ 105 Johnny Rawlings	10.00	4.50	1.25
☐ 106 Topper Rigney	10.00	4.50	1.25
☐ 107 Charlie Robertson	10.00	4.50	1.25
☐ 108 Ed Rommel	10.00	4.50	1.25
☐ 109 Muddy Ruel	10.00	4.50	1.25
☐ 110 Dutch Ruether	10.00	4.50	1.25
☐ 111 Babe Ruth	250.00	110.00	31.00
☐ 112 Ray Schalk	20.00	9.00	2.50
☐ 113 Wally Schang	12.50	5.50	1.55
☐ 114 Ray Schmandt	10.00	4.50	1.25
☐ 115 Walter Schmidt	10.00	4.50	1.25
☐ 116 Germany Schultz	10.00	4.50	1.25
☐ 117 Henry Severeid	10.00	4.50	1.25
☐ 118 Joe Sewell	20.00	9.00	2.50
☐ 119 Bob Shawkey	10.00	4.50	1.25
☐ 120 Earl Sheely	10.00	4.50	1.25
☐ 121 Ralph Shinners	10.00	4.50	1.25
☐ 122 Urban Shocker	10.00	4.50	1.25
☐ 123 George Sisler	40.00	18.00	5.00
☐ 124 Earl L. Smith	10.00	4.50	1.25
☐ 125 Earl S. Smith	10.00	4.50	1.25
☐ 126 Jack Smith	10.00	4.50	1.25
☐ 127 Allen Sothoron	10.00	4.50	1.25
☐ 128 Tris Speaker	60.00	27.00	7.50
☐ 129 Amos Strunk	10.00	4.50	1.25
☐ 130 Cotton Tierney	10.00	4.50	1.25
☐ 131 Jack Tobin	10.00	4.50	1.25
☐ 132 Specs Toporcer	10.00	4.50	1.25
☐ 133 George Uhle	10.00	4.50	1.25
☐ 134 Bobby Veach	10.00	4.50	1.25
☐ 135 John Watson	10.00	4.50	1.25
☐ 136 Zack Wheat	20.00	9.00	2.50
☐ 137 Ken Williams	12.50	5.50	1.55
☐ 138 Cy Williams	10.00	4.50	1.25
☐ 139 Charles Woodall	10.00	4.50	1.25
☐ 140 Russell Wrightstone	10.00	4.50	1.25
☐ 141 Ross Youngs	20.00	9.00	2.50
☐ 142 Tom Zachary	10.00	4.50	1.25

1922 W575

This 154-card set, referenced by the catalog designation W575, measures approximately 1 15/16" by 3 3/16". The cards have a black and white action posed photo are are blank backed. The players name and position are under the photo on the front. Cards that are part of the "autograph on shoulder" series are marked with an asterisk in the checklist below and are worth a little more.

	EX-MT	VG-E	GOOD
COMPLETE SET (154)	2750.00	1250.00	350.00
COMMON CARD (1-154)	10.00	4.50	1.25
☐ 1 Babe Adams	10.00	4.50	1.25
☐ 2 Grover C. Alexander (2)	50.00	22.00	6.25
☐ 3 Jim Bagby	10.00	4.50	1.25
☐ 4 Frank Baker	30.00	13.50	3.70
☐ 5 Dave Bancroft (2)	50.00	22.00	6.25
☐ 6 Jesse Barnes	10.00	4.50	1.25
☐ 7 Johnny Bassler	20.00	9.00	2.50
☐ 8 Joe Berry	10.00	4.50	1.25
☐ 9 Carson Bigbee	10.00	4.50	1.25
☐ 10 Ping Bodie	10.00	4.50	1.25
☐ 11 Eddie Brown	10.00	4.50	1.25
☐ 12 Jesse Burkett CO	10.00	4.50	1.25
☐ 13 George H. Burns	10.00	4.50	1.25
☐ 14 Donie Bush	20.00	9.00	2.50
☐ 15 Joe Bush	10.00	4.50	1.25
☐ 16 Max Carey (2)	25.00	11.00	3.10
☐ 17 Ty Cobb	150.00	70.00	19.00
☐ 18 Eddie Collins*	30.00	13.50	3.70
☐ 19 Rip Collins	10.00	4.50	1.25
☐ 20 Stan Coveleski*	25.00	11.00	3.10
☐ 21 Bill Cunningham	10.00	4.50	1.25
☐ 22 Jake Daubert	20.00	9.00	2.50
☐ 23 Hooks Dauss (2)	10.00	4.50	1.25
☐ 24 Dixie Davis	10.00	4.50	1.25
☐ 25 Charlie Deal (2)	10.00	4.50	1.25
☐ 26 Al Devormer	10.00	4.50	1.25
☐ 27 Bill Doak	10.00	4.50	1.25
☐ 28 Bill Donovan MG	10.00	4.50	1.25
☐ 29 Phil Douglas	10.00	4.50	1.25
☐ 30 Joe Dugan	20.00	9.00	2.50
☐ 31 Johnny Evers MG (2)	30.00	13.50	3.70
☐ 32 Red Faber	25.00	11.00	3.10
☐ 33 Bibb Falk	10.00	4.50	1.25
☐ 34 Alex Ferguson	10.00	4.50	1.25
☐ 35 Chick Fewster	10.00	4.50	1.25
☐ 36 Eddie Foster	10.00	4.50	1.25
☐ 37 Frank Frisch	50.00	22.00	6.25
☐ 38 Larry Gardner	10.00	4.50	1.25
☐ 39 Alex Gaston	10.00	4.50	1.25
☐ 40 Wally Gerber	20.00	9.00	2.50
☐ 41 Patsy Gharrity	10.00	4.50	1.25
☐ 42 Whitey Glazner	10.00	4.50	1.25
☐ 43 Kid Gleason MG	15.00	6.75	1.85
☐ 44 Mike Gonzales	10.00	4.50	1.25
☐ 45 Hank Gowdy	15.00	6.75	1.85
☐ 46 Jack Graney (2)	10.00	4.50	1.25
☐ 47 Tommy Griffith	10.00	4.50	1.25
☐ 48 Charlie Grimm	15.00	6.75	1.85
☐ 49 Heinie Groh	15.00	6.75	1.85
New York NL			
☐ 50 Henie Groh	15.00	6.75	1.85
Cincinnati NL			
☐ 51 Jesse Haines	20.00	9.00	2.50
☐ 52 Harry Harper	10.00	4.50	1.25
☐ 53 Chicken Hawks	10.00	4.50	1.25
☐ 54 Harry Heilmann	25.00	11.00	3.10
☐ 55 Fred Hoffman	10.00	4.50	1.25
☐ 56 Walter Holke (3)	10.00	4.50	1.25
☐ 57 Charlie Hollocher (2)	10.00	4.50	1.25
☐ 58 Harry Hooper	25.00	11.00	3.10
☐ 59 Rogers Hornsby	60.00	27.00	7.50
☐ 60 Waite Hoyt	25.00	11.00	3.10
☐ 61 Miller Huggins MG	30.00	13.50	3.70
☐ 62 Baby Doll Jacobson	10.00	4.50	1.25
☐ 63 Hugh Jennings CO	30.00	13.50	3.70
☐ 64 Walter Johnson (2)	100.00	45.00	12.50
☐ 65 Jimmy Johnston	10.00	4.50	1.25
☐ 66 Joe Judge	20.00	9.00	2.50
☐ 67 George Kelly (2)	30.00	13.50	3.70
☐ 68 Dickie Kerr	10.00	4.50	1.25
☐ 69 Pete Kilduff	10.00	4.50	1.25
☐ 70 Doc Lavan	10.00	4.50	1.25
☐ 71 Nemo Leibold	10.00	4.50	1.25
☐ 72 Duffy Lewis	10.00	4.50	1.25
☐ 73 Al Mamaux	10.00	4.50	1.25
☐ 74 Rabbit Maranville*	25.00	11.00	3.10
☐ 75 Rube Marquard	30.00	13.50	3.70
☐ 76 Carl Mays (2)	15.00	6.75	1.85
☐ 77 John McGraw MG	50.00	22.00	6.25
☐ 78 Stuffy McInnis	15.00	6.75	1.85
☐ 79 Mike McNally	10.00	4.50	1.25
☐ 80 Bob Meusel	15.00	6.75	1.85
☐ 81 Irish Meusel	15.00	6.75	1.85
☐ 82 Clyde Milan	10.00	4.50	1.25
☐ 83 Elmer Miller	10.00	4.50	1.25
☐ 84 Otto Miller	10.00	4.50	1.25
☐ 85 Johnny Mitchell	10.00	4.50	1.25
☐ 86 Guy Morton	20.00	9.00	2.50
☐ 87 Eddie Mulligan	10.00	4.50	1.25
☐ 88 Eddie Murphy	10.00	4.50	1.25
☐ 89 Hy Myers (3)	10.00	4.50	1.25
☐ 90 Greasy Neale	15.00	6.75	1.85
☐ 91 Art Nehf	20.00	9.00	2.50
☐ 92 Joe Oeschger	10.00	4.50	1.25
☐ 93 Charley O'Leary CO	10.00	4.50	1.25
☐ 94 Steve O'Neill	15.00	6.75	1.85
☐ 95 Roger Peckinpaugh (2)	15.00	6.75	1.85
☐ 96 Percy	10.00	4.50	1.25
New York AL			
☐ 97 Jeff Pfeffer	10.00	4.50	1.25
Brook. NL			
☐ 98 Jeff Pfeffer	10.00	4.50	1.25
St. L. NL			
☐ 99 Wally Pipp	15.00	6.75	1.85
☐ 100 Jack Quinn	10.00	4.50	1.25
☐ 101 Johnny Rawlings (2)	10.00	4.50	1.25
☐ 102 Sam Rice (2)	20.00	9.00	2.50
☐ 103 Jimmy Ring	20.00	9.00	2.50
☐ 104 Eppa Rixey	25.00	11.00	3.10
☐ 105 Charlie Robertson*	20.00	9.00	2.50
☐ 106 Wilbert Robinson MG	20.00	9.00	2.50
☐ 107 Tom Rogers	10.00	4.50	1.25
☐ 108 Ed Rommel	20.00	9.00	2.50
☐ 109 Braggo Roth	10.00	4.50	1.25
☐ 110 Edd Roush (2)	25.00	11.00	3.10
☐ 111 Muddy Ruel	10.00	4.50	1.25
☐ 112 Babe Ruth (2)	250.00	110.00	31.00
☐ 113 Rosy Ryan (2)	10.00	4.50	1.25
☐ 114 Slim Sallee (2)	10.00	4.50	1.25
☐ 115 Ray Schalk (2)	20.00	9.00	2.50
☐ 116 Wally Schang* (2)	20.00	9.00	2.50
☐ 117 Ferd Schupp (2)	10.00	4.50	1.25
☐ 118 Everett Scott	20.00	9.00	2.50
Boston AL			
☐ 119 Everett Scott	10.00	4.50	1.25
New York AL			
☐ 120 Hank Severeid	20.00	9.00	2.50
☐ 121 Joe Sewell*	25.00	11.00	3.10
☐ 122 Bob Shawkey	10.00	4.50	1.25
☐ 123 Red Shea	10.00	4.50	1.25
☐ 124 Earl Sheely	10.00	4.50	1.25
☐ 125 Urban Shocker	10.00	4.50	1.25
☐ 126 George Sisler* (2)	50.00	22.00	6.25

☐ 127 Elmer Smith	10.00	4.50	1.25
☐ 128 Earl Smith	10.00	4.50	1.25
☐ 129 Pancho Snyder	10.00	4.50	1.25
☐ 130 Tris Speaker* (2)	50.00	22.00	6.25
☐ 131 Casey Stengel New York NL	50.00	22.00	6.25
☐ 132 Casey Stengel Phila. NL	50.00	22.00	6.25
☐ 133 Riggs Stephenson	20.00	9.00	2.50
☐ 134 Milt Stock	10.00	4.50	1.25
☐ 135 Amos Strunk (2)	10.00	4.50	1.25
☐ 136 Zeb Terry	50.00	22.00	6.25
☐ 137 Pinch Thomas	10.00	4.50	1.25
☐ 138 Fred Toney (2)	10.00	4.50	1.25
☐ 139 Specs Torporcer	10.00	4.50	1.25
☐ 140 Lefty Tyler	10.00	4.50	1.25
☐ 141 Hippo Vaughn (2)	15.00	6.75	1.85
☐ 142 Bobby Veach (3)	20.00	9.00	2.50
☐ 143 Ossie Vitt	10.00	4.50	1.25
☐ 144 Frank Walker	20.00	9.00	2.50
☐ 145 Curt Walker	20.00	9.00	2.50
☐ 146 Bill Wambsganss (2)	15.00	6.75	1.85
☐ 147 Zack Wheat	30.00	13.50	3.70
☐ 148 Possum Whitted	10.00	4.50	1.25
☐ 149 Williams Chicago AL *	20.00	9.00	2.50
☐ 150 Cy Williams	10.00	4.50	1.25
☐ 151 Ivy Wingo	10.00	4.50	1.25
☐ 152 Joe Wood	15.00	6.75	1.85
☐ 153 Ralph Young	50.00	22.00	6.25
☐ 154 Ross Youngs	10.00	4.50	1.25

1920 Walter Mails WG7

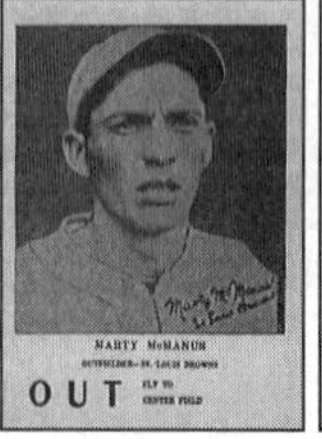

These cards were distributed as part of a baseball game produced in 1920. The cards each measure approximately 2 5/16" by 3 1/4" and have rounded corners. The card fronts show a black and white photo of the player, his name, position, his team, and the game outcome associated with that particular card. The card backs are all the same, each showing an ornate red and white design with "Walter Mails" inside a red circle in the middle all surrounded by a thin white outer border. Since the cards are unnumbered, they are listed below in alphabetical order.

	EX-MT	VG-E	GOOD
COMPLETE SET	3600.00	1600.00	450.00
COMMON CARD (1-56)	50.00	22.00	6.25
☐ 1 Buzz Arlett	50.00	22.00	6.25
☐ 2 Jim Bagby	50.00	22.00	6.25
☐ 3 Dave Bancroft	125.00	55.00	15.50
☐ 4 Johnny Bassler Sic, Basseler	50.00	22.00	6.25
☐ 5 Jack Bentley	50.00	22.00	6.25
☐ 6 Rube Benton	50.00	22.00	6.25
☐ 7 George Burns	50.00	22.00	6.25
☐ 8 Joe Bush	50.00	22.00	6.25
☐ 9 Harold P. Chavez	50.00	22.00	6.25
☐ 10 Hugh Critz	50.00	22.00	6.25
☐ 11 Jake Daubert	75.00	34.00	9.50
☐ 12 Wheezer Dell	50.00	22.00	6.25
☐ 13 Joe Dugan	60.00	27.00	7.50
☐ 14 Pat Duncan	50.00	22.00	6.25
☐ 15 Howard Ehmke	50.00	22.00	6.25
☐ 16 Lew Fonseca	50.00	22.00	6.25
☐ 17 Ray French	50.00	22.00	6.25
☐ 18 Ed Gharity Sic, Gharitty	50.00	22.00	6.25
☐ 19 Heinie Groh	75.00	34.00	9.50
☐ 20 George Grove	50.00	22.00	6.25
☐ 21 Bubbles Hargrave	50.00	22.00	6.25
☐ 22 Elmer Jacobs	50.00	22.00	6.25
☐ 23 Walter Johnson	500.00	220.00	60.00
☐ 24 Duke Kenworthy	50.00	22.00	6.25
☐ 25 Harry Krause	50.00	22.00	6.25
☐ 26 Ray Kremer	50.00	22.00	6.25
☐ 27 Walter Mails	50.00	22.00	6.25
☐ 28 Rabbit Maranville	125.00	55.00	15.50
☐ 29 Stuffy McInnis	75.00	34.00	9.50
☐ 30 Marty McManus	50.00	22.00	6.25
☐ 31 Bob Meusel	75.00	34.00	9.50
☐ 32 Hack Miller	50.00	22.00	6.25
☐ 33 Pat J. Moran	60.00	27.00	7.50
☐ 34 Guy Morton	50.00	22.00	6.25
☐ 35 Johnny Mostil	50.00	22.00	6.25
☐ 36 Red Murphy	50.00	22.00	6.25
☐ 37 Jimmy O'Connell	50.00	22.00	6.25
☐ 38 Joe Oeschger	50.00	22.00	6.25
☐ 39 Steve O'Neil	60.00	27.00	7.50
☐ 40 Roger Peckinpaugh	75.00	34.00	9.50
☐ 41 Babe Pinelli	50.00	22.00	6.25
☐ 42 Wally Pipp	100.00	45.00	12.50
☐ 43 Elmer Ponder	50.00	22.00	6.25
☐ 44 Sam Rice	125.00	55.00	15.50
☐ 45 Ed Rommell	50.00	22.00	6.25
☐ 46 Walter Schmidt	50.00	22.00	6.25
☐ 47 Joe Sewell	125.00	55.00	15.50
☐ 48 Pat Shea	50.00	22.00	6.25
☐ 49 Wilford Shupe	50.00	22.00	6.25
☐ 50 Paddy Siglin	50.00	22.00	6.25
☐ 51 George Sisler	150.00	70.00	19.00
☐ 52 Bill Skiff	50.00	22.00	6.25
☐ 53 Jack Smith	50.00	22.00	6.25
☐ 54 Suds Sutherland	50.00	22.00	6.25
☐ 55 Cotton Tierney	50.00	22.00	6.25
☐ 56 George Uhle	50.00	22.00	6.25

1934 Ward Baking Sporties Pins PB6

This 8-pin set was put out by Ward Baking Co. around 1934. Each pin measures approximately 1 1/4" in diameter. The color scheme is red, white and blue. Since the pins are not numbered, they are ordered below alphabetically.

	EX-MT	VG-E	GOOD
COMPLETE SET (8)	750.00	350.00	95.00
COMMON PIN (1-8)	50.00	22.00	6.25
☐ 1 Dizzy Dean	250.00	110.00	31.00
☐ 2 Jimmie Dykes	50.00	22.00	6.25
☐ 3 Jimmy Foxx	250.00	110.00	31.00
☐ 4 Frankie Frisch	100.00	45.00	12.50
☐ 5 Charlie Gehringer	100.00	45.00	12.50
☐ 6 Charlie Grimm	50.00	22.00	6.25
☐ 7 Schoolboy Rowe	50.00	22.00	6.25
☐ 8 Jimmie Wilson	50.00	22.00	6.25

1994 Wendy's Clemente

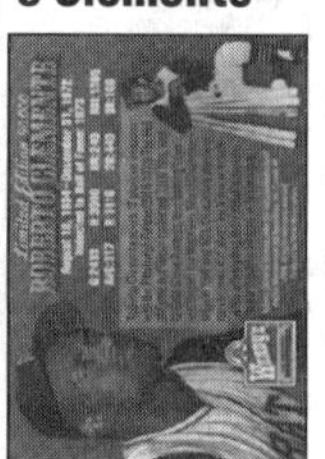

Sponsored by Wendy's restaurants, this standard-size hologram card commemorates Hall of Famer Roberto Clemente. Reportedly only 90,000 of these hologram cards were produced. Framed by black borders, the horizontal front pictures Clemente in batting posture awaiting the pitch. When the holograph is rotated slightly, he is pictured hitting the ball. His name, the team name, and "3000" are printed in the holograph. The horizontal backs presents two color photos of Clemente and career summary. The card is unnumbered.

	MINT	NRMT	EXC
COMPLETE SET (1)	5.00	2.20	.60
COMMON CARD	5.00	2.20	.60
☐ 1 Roberto Clemente	5.00	2.20	.60

1888 WG1 Card Game

These cards were distributed as part of a baseball game. The cards each measure approximately 2 1/2" by 3 1/2" and have rounded corners. The card fronts show a color drawing of the player, his name, his position, and the game outcome associated with that particular card. The card backs are all the same, each showing a geometric graphic design in blue. Since the cards are unnumbered, they are listed below in alphabetical order within each of the eight teams.

	EX-MT	VG-E	GOOD
COMPLETE SET (72)	30000.00	13500.00	3800.00
COMMON CARD (1-72)	350.00	160.00	45.00
☐ 1 Tom Brown	350.00	160.00	45.00
☐ 2 John Clarkson	1000.00	450.00	125.00
☐ 3 Joe Hornung	350.00	160.00	45.00
☐ 4 Dick Johnston	350.00	160.00	45.00
☐ 5 King Kelly	1500.00	700.00	190.00
☐ 6 John Morrill	350.00	160.00	45.00
☐ 7 Billy Nash	350.00	160.00	45.00
☐ 8 Ezra Sutton	350.00	160.00	45.00
☐ 9 Sam Wise	350.00	160.00	45.00
☐ 10 Cap Anson	2500.00	1100.00	300.00
☐ 11 Tom Burns	350.00	160.00	45.00
☐ 12 Silver Flint	350.00	160.00	45.00
☐ 13 Bob Pettit	350.00	160.00	45.00
☐ 14 Fred Pfeffer	350.00	160.00	45.00
☐ 15 Jimmy Ryan	350.00	160.00	45.00
☐ 16 Marty Sullivan	750.00	350.00	95.00
☐ 17 George Van Haltren	350.00	160.00	45.00
☐ 18 Ned Williamson	350.00	160.00	45.00
☐ 19 Charlie Bennett	350.00	160.00	45.00
☐ 20 Dan Brouthers	1250.00	550.00	160.00
☐ 21 Charlie Getzein	350.00	160.00	45.00
☐ 22 Ned Hanlon	350.00	160.00	45.00
☐ 23 Hardy Richardson	350.00	160.00	45.00
☐ 24 Jack Rowet	350.00	160.00	45.00
☐ 25 Sam Thompson	1000.00	450.00	125.00
☐ 26 Larry Twitchell	350.00	160.00	45.00
☐ 27 Deacon White	350.00	160.00	45.00
☐ 28 Charley Bassett	350.00	160.00	45.00
☐ 29 Henry Boyle	350.00	160.00	45.00
☐ 30 Jerry Denny	350.00	160.00	45.00
☐ 31 Dude Esterbrook	350.00	160.00	45.00
☐ 32 Jack Glasscock	750.00	350.00	95.00
☐ 33 Paul Hines	350.00	160.00	45.00
☐ 34 George Meyers	350.00	160.00	45.00
☐ 35 Emmett Seery	350.00	160.00	45.00
☐ 36 Jumbo Shoeneck	350.00	160.00	45.00
☐ 37 Roger Connor	1000.00	450.00	125.00
☐ 38 Buck Ewing	1250.00	550.00	160.00
☐ 39 Elmer Foster	350.00	160.00	45.00
☐ 40 George Gore	350.00	160.00	45.00
☐ 41 Tim Keefe	1000.00	450.00	125.00
☐ 42 Jim O'Rourke	1000.00	450.00	125.00
☐ 43 Danny Richardson	350.00	160.00	45.00
☐ 44 Mike Tiernan	350.00	160.00	45.00
☐ 45 John Ward	1250.00	550.00	160.00
☐ 46 Ed Andrews	350.00	160.00	45.00
☐ 47 Charlie Bastian	350.00	160.00	45.00
☐ 48 Don Casey	350.00	160.00	45.00
☐ 49 Jack Clements	350.00	160.00	45.00
☐ 50 Sid Farrar	350.00	160.00	45.00
☐ 51 Jim Fogarty	350.00	160.00	45.00
☐ 52 Arthur Irwin	350.00	160.00	45.00
☐ 53 Joe Mulvey	350.00	160.00	45.00
☐ 54 George Wood	350.00	160.00	45.00
☐ 55 Fred Carroll	350.00	160.00	45.00
☐ 56 John Coleman	350.00	160.00	45.00
☐ 57 Abner Dalrymple	350.00	160.00	45.00
☐ 58 Fred Dunlap	350.00	160.00	45.00
☐ 59 Pud Galvin	1000.00	450.00	125.00
☐ 60 Willie Kuehne	350.00	160.00	45.00
☐ 61 Al Maul	350.00	160.00	45.00
☐ 62 Pop Smith	350.00	160.00	45.00
☐ 63 Billy Sunday	1000.00	450.00	125.00
☐ 64 Jim Donelly	350.00	160.00	45.00
☐ 65 Dummy Hoy	750.00	350.00	95.00
☐ 66 John Irwin	350.00	160.00	45.00
☐ 67 Connie Mack	1500.00	700.00	190.00
☐ 68 Al Myers	350.00	160.00	45.00
☐ 69 Billy O'Brien	350.00	160.00	45.00
☐ 70 George Shoch	350.00	160.00	45.00
☐ 71 Jim Whitney	350.00	160.00	45.00
☐ 72 Walt Wilmot	350.00	160.00	45.00

1993 Whataburger Ryan

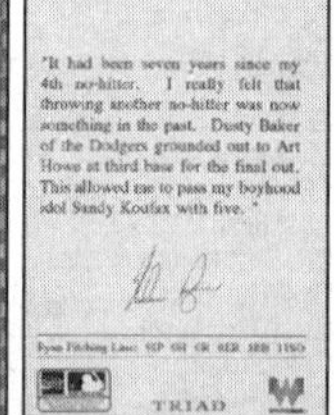

Subtitled "Recollections," these ten plastic-coated cards were produced by Triad and distributed by Whataburger. The standard-size fronts have a prismatic border and color action shots of Ryan, which lay under the diffraction grating plastic coating that gives a 3-D appearance. The borderless white backs carry a brief comment by Ryan and a facsimile autograph. The cards are unnumbered.

	MINT	NRMT	EXC
COMPLETE SET (10)	5.00	2.20	.60
COMMON CARD (1-10)	.50	.23	.06
☐ 1 Nolan Ryan On horse	.50	.23	.06
☐ 2 Nolan Ryan 1st No-hitter	.50	.23	.06
☐ 3 Nolan Ryan 2nd No-hitter	.50	.23	.06
☐ 4 Nolan Ryan 3rd No-hitter	.50	.23	.06
☐ 5 Nolan Ryan 4th No-hitter	.50	.23	.06
☐ 6 Nolan Ryan 5th No-hitter	.50	.23	.06
☐ 7 Nolan Ryan 6th No-hitter	.50	.23	.06
☐ 8 Nolan Ryan 7th No-hitter	.50	.23	.06
☐ 9 Nolan Ryan 300th Win	.50	.23	.06
☐ 10 Nolan Ryan 5,000th Strikeout	.50	.23	.06

1935 Wheaties BB1

This set is referred to as "Fancy Frame with Script Signature". These cards (which made up the back of the Wheaties cereal box) measure 6" by 6 1/4" with the frame and about 5" by 5 1/2" if the frame is trimmed off. The player photo appears in blue on a blue-tinted field with a solid orange background behind the player. The player's facsimile autograph is displayed at the bottom of the card.

	EX-MT	VG-E	GOOD
COMPLETE SET (27)	2000.00	900.00	250.00
COMMON CARD (1-25)	35.00	16.00	4.40
☐ 1 Jack Armstrong (batting pose) (fictional character)	35.00	16.00	4.40
☐ 2 Jack Armstrong (throwing) (your friend) (fictional character)	35.00	16.00	4.40
☐ 3 Wally Berger (batting follow through) Sincerely Yours	35.00	16.00	4.40
☐ 4 Tommy Bridges (pitching)	35.00	16.00	4.40
☐ 5A Mickey Cochrane (squatting, wearing black hat and uniform with stripes)	75.00	34.00	9.50
☐ 5B Mickey Cochrane (squatting, wearing white hat and uniform with no stripes)	250.00	110.00	31.00
☐ 6 James "Rip" Collins (jumping)	35.00	16.00	4.40
☐ 7 Dizzy Dean (pitching follow through)	150.00	70.00	19.00
☐ 8 Dizzy Dean and Paul Dean (squatting)	100.00	45.00	12.50
☐ 9 Paul Dean (pitching)	50.00	22.00	6.25
☐ 10 William Delancey (catching)	35.00	16.00	4.40
☐ 11 Jimmie Foxx (facing camera knee up)	125.00	55.00	15.50
☐ 12 Frank Frisch (stooping to field)	75.00	34.00	9.50
☐ 13 Lou Gehrig (batting follow through)	450.00	200.00	55.00
☐ 14 Goose Goslin (batting)	75.00	34.00	9.50
☐ 15 Lefty Grove (holding trophy)	125.00	55.00	15.50
☐ 16 Carl Hubbell (pitching)	75.00	34.00	9.50
☐ 17 Travis C. Jackson (stooping to field)	50.00	22.00	6.25
☐ 18 Chuck Klein (with four bats)	75.00	34.00	9.50
☐ 19 Gus Mancuso (catching)	35.00	16.00	4.40
☐ 20A Pepper Martin (batting)	35.00	16.00	4.40
☐ 20B Pepper Martin (portrait) Sincerely Yours	35.00	16.00	4.40
☐ 21 Joe Medwick (batting follow through)	75.00	34.00	9.50
☐ 22 Mel Ott (batting follow through)	125.00	55.00	15.50
☐ 23 Harold Schumacher (pitching)	35.00	16.00	4.40
☐ 24 Al Simmons (batting follow through) Sincerely Yours	75.00	34.00	9.50
☐ 25 Jo Jo White (batting follow through)	35.00	16.00	4.40

1936 Wheaties BB3

This set is referred to as "Fancy Frame with Printed Name and Data." These cards (which made up the back of the Wheaties cereal box) measure 6" by 6 1/4" with the frame and about 5" by 5 1/2" if the frame is trimmed off. This set is distinguished from BB1 (above) in that this set also shows the player's name and some fact about him. The

player's facsimile autograph is displayed at the bottom of the card. In the checklist below, the first few words of the printed data found on the card is also provided.

	EX-MT	VG-E	GOOD
COMPLETE SET (12)	850.00	375.00	105.00
COMMON CARD	35.00	16.00	4.40
☐ 1 Earl Averill (batting) Star Outfielder	50.00	22.00	6.25
☐ 2 Mickey Cochrane (catching) Manager, World Champion Detroit	100.00	45.00	12.50
☐ 3 Jimmie Foxx (batting) All Around Star	125.00	55.00	15.50
☐ 4 Lou Gehrig (stooping to field) Iron Man	400.00	180.00	50.00
☐ 5 Hank Greenberg (jumping) Home Run Champion	100.00	45.00	12.50
☐ 6 Gabby Hartnett (squatting) Catcher Voted Most Valuable	75.00	34.00	9.50
☐ 7 Carl Hubbell (ready to throw) Star Pitcher	75.00	34.00	9.50
☐ 8 Pepper Martin (jumping) Heavy Hitter	35.00	16.00	4.40
☐ 9 Van L. Mungo (pitching) Star Pitcher	35.00	16.00	4.40
☐ 10 Buck Newsom (pitching) Star Pitcher	35.00	16.00	4.40
☐ 11 Arky Vaughan (batting) Batting Champion	50.00	22.00	6.25
☐ 12 Jimmy Wilson (squatting) Manager and Star Catcher	35.00	16.00	4.40

1936 Wheaties BB4

This set is refered to as the "Thin Orange Border / Figures in Border." These unnumbered cards (which made up the back of the Wheaties cereal box) mwasure 6" by 8 1/2". The set is the first in this larger size. The figures in the border include drawings of men and women competing baseball, football, hockey, track, golf, tennis, skiing and swimming. A train and an airplane also appear. The rectangular photo of the player appears in a box above an endorsment for Wheaties. The player's name is in script below the endorsment, A printed name, team and other information is near the top in the solid orange background.

	EX-MT	VG-E	GOOD
COMPLETE SET (12)	750.00	350.00	95.00
COMMON CARD (1-12)	35.00	16.00	4.40
☐ 1 Curt Davis Philadelphia Phillies	35.00	16.00	4.40
☐ 2 Lou Gehrig New York Yankees	350.00	160.00	45.00
☐ 3 Charlie Gehringer Detroit Tigers	75.00	34.00	9.50
☐ 4 Lefty Grove Boston Red Sox	100.00	45.00	12.50
☐ 5 Rollie Hemsley St. Louis Browns	35.00	16.00	4.40
☐ 6 Billy Herman Chicago Cubs	50.00	22.00	6.25
☐ 7 Joe Medwick St. Louis Cardinals	75.00	34.00	9.50
☐ 8 Mel Ott New York Giants	100.00	45.00	12.50
☐ 9 Schoolboy Rowe Detroit Tigers	35.00	16.00	4.40
☐ 10 Arky Vaughan Detroit Tigers	50.00	22.00	6.25
☐ 11 Joe Vosmik Cleveland Indians	35.00	16.00	4.40
☐ 12 Lon Warneke Chicago Cubs	35.00	16.00	4.40

1936 Wheaties BB5

This set is referred to as "How to Play Winning Baseball." These cards, which made up the back of the Wheaties box. measure 6" X 8 1/2" These panels combine a photo of the player with a series of blue and white drawings illustrating playing instrutions. All of the players are shown in full length poses, except Earl Averill, who is pictured to the thighs. The players appear aganist a solid orange background. In addition to the numbers 1 thru 12, these panels are also found with a small number 28 combined with captial letters "A" thru "L." However, panels are know without these letter-number combinations. This set is sometimes refered to as the "28 Series."

	EX-MT	VG-E	GOOD
COMPLETE SET (13)	650.00	300.00	80.00
COMMON CARD (1-12)	35.00	16.00	4.40
☐ 1 Lefty Gomez (28E) Pitching, How to Throw the Fast Ball	50.00	22.00	6.25
☐ 2 Billy Herman	40.00	18.00	5.00
☐ 3 Luke Appling (28C) Shortstop, Putting 'Em Out at Second	40.00	18.00	5.00
☐ 4 Jimmie Foxx (28A) Tells How to Play First Base...	75.00	34.00	9.50
☐ 5 Joe Medwick (28K) Tells How to Play Outfield...	50.00	22.00	6.25
☐ 6 Charlie Gehringer(28G) Tells How to Play Second Base...	60.00	27.00	7.50
☐ 7A Mel Ott Bunting, Put 'Em Where They Count (large figure, tips in vertical sequence)	75.00	34.00	9.50
☐ 7B Mel Ott (28H) Bunting, Put 'Em Where They Count" (small figure, tips in two horiz. rows)	75.00	34.00	9.50
☐ 8 Odell Hale (28B) Third Base -- Fine Play at Hot Corner	35.00	16.00	4.40
☐ 9 Bill Dickey (28I) Catching Pointers Behind the Plate	75.00	34.00	9.50
☐ 10 Lefty Grove (28J) Tells You About Pitching...	60.00	27.00	7.50
☐ 11 Carl Hubbell	50.00	22.00	6.25
☐ 12 Earl Averill (28L) Batting -- Get Those Extra Bases	40.00	18.00	5.00

1937 Wheaties BB6

This set is referred to as "How to Star in Baseball." These numbered cards, which made up the back of the cereal box, measure 6" X 8 1/4". This series is very similar to BB5. Both are instructional series' and the text and drawings used to illuatrate the tips are similar and in some cases identical. Each panel is a full length photo, The players name, team and script signature also appears on the card.

	EX-MT	VG-E	GOOD
COMPLETE SET (12)	800.00	350.00	100.00
COMMON CARD (1-12)	35.00	16.00	4.40
☐ 1 Bill Dickey How to Catch	100.00	45.00	12.50
☐ 2 Red Ruffing Pitching the Fast Ball	60.00	27.00	7.50
☐ 3 Zeke Bonura First Base - Make More Outs	35.00	16.00	4.40
☐ 4 Charlie Gehringer Second Base as the Stars Play It	100.00	45.00	12.50
☐ 5 Arky Vaughan Shortstop, Play It Right	60.00	27.00	7.50
☐ 6 Carl Hubbell Pitching the Slow Ball	75.00	34.00	9.50
☐ 7 John Lewis Third Base, Field Those Hot Ones	35.00	16.00	4.40
☐ 8 Heinie Manush Fielding for Extra Outs	60.00	27.00	7.50
☐ 9 Lefty Grove Pitching the Outdrop Ball	100.00	45.00	12.50
☐ 10 Billy Herman How to Score (baserunning)	60.00	27.00	7.50
☐ 11 Joe DiMaggio Bat Like a Home Run King	350.00	160.00	45.00
☐ 12 Joe Medwick Batting for Extra Bases	60.00	27.00	7.50

1937 Wheaties BB7

This set is refered to as the "29 Series" These numbered cards which make up the back of the box measure 6" X 8 1/4". The players name, position, team and some information about him are printed near the top. His signature appears on the lower part of the panel near a printed endorsment for the cereal. This set contains several different card designs. One design shows the player outlined aganist an orange (nearly red) background. A two or three line endorsment is at the bottom. DiMaggio, Bonura and Bridges appear in this form. Another design shows a player against a solid white background , but the panel is rimmed by a red, white and blue border. Players shown in this fashion are Moore, Radcliff and Martin. A third style offers a panel with an orange border and a large orange circle behind the player. The rest of the background is white. Lombardi, Travis and Mungo appear in this design. The final style is a titled, orange background picture of the player with white and blue framing the photo. Trosky, Demaree and Vaughan show up in this design. The set also has three known Pacific Coast League players. One number, 29N, which could be a PCL player, is unknown.

	EX-MT	VG-E	GOOD
COMPLETE SET (15)	900.00	400.00	110.00
COMMON CARD	35.00	16.00	4.40
☐ 29A Zeke Bonura (batting)	35.00	16.00	4.40
☐ 29B Cecil Travis (reaching left)	35.00	16.00	4.40
☐ 29C Frank Demaree (batting)	35.00	16.00	4.40
☐ 29D Joe Moore (batting)	35.00	16.00	4.40
☐ 29E Ernie Lombardi (crouch)	50.00	22.00	6.25
☐ 29F John L. "Pepper" Martin (reaching)	35.00	16.00	4.40
☐ 29G Harold Trosky (batting)	35.00	16.00	4.40
☐ 29H Ray Radcliff (batting)	35.00	16.00	4.40
☐ 29I Joe DiMaggio (batting)	400.00	180.00	50.00
☐ 29J Tommy Bridges (hands over head)	35.00	16.00	4.40
☐ 29K Van L. Mungo (pitching)	35.00	16.00	4.40
☐ 29L Arky Vaughan (batting)	50.00	22.00	6.25
☐ 29M Arnold Statz (PCL)	150.00	70.00	19.00
☐ 29N Uuknown	35.00	16.00	4.40
☐ 29O Fred Muller (PCL)	150.00	70.00	19.00
☐ 29P Gene Lillard (PCL)	150.00	70.00	19.00

1937 Wheaties BB8

This set is refered to as the "Speckled Orange, White and Blue Series." These unnumbered cards which made up the back of the Wheaties box measure 6" X 8 1/2". The set contains several different card designs. One design (DiMaggio and Feller) shows the player surrounded by orange sprecklės on a white backgroung with a group of four blue and white drawings of players in action along the panel's right side. Another design shows the panel divided into four rectangles -- white at upper right and lower left and orange on the other two. -- with the players (Appling and Averill) leaping to catch the ball. Blue circles surrounded by orange and white speckles appear on the pictures of Hubbel and Grove. Medwick and Gehringer appear on white panels with a cloud of orange speckles behind them. The player's name in script style appears along with printed data about his 1936 season and a brief endorsement for the cereal.

	EX-MT	VG-E	GOOD
COMPLETE SET (8)	750.00	350.00	95.00
COMMON CARD (1-8)	50.00	22.00	6.25
☐ 1 Luke Appling (reaching)	50.00	22.00	6.25
☐ 2 Earl Averill (reaching)	50.00	22.00	6.25
☐ 3 Joe DiMaggio (batting)	400.00	180.00	50.00
☐ 4 Bob Feller (throwing)	125.00	55.00	15.50
☐ 5 Charlie Gehringer (batting)	75.00	34.00	9.50
☐ 6 Lefty Grove (throwing)	75.00	34.00	9.50
☐ 7 Carl Hubbell (throwing)	75.00	34.00	9.50
☐ 8 Joe Medwick (fielding)	50.00	22.00	6.25

1937 Wheaties BB9

This set is refered to as the "Color Series." These unnumbered cards measure 6" X 8 1/2" Photos of the players appear in circles. "V" shapes and rectangles, and stars among others. A player from every major League team is included. The player's name is in script with the team name below. The name , endorsment and player's 1936 highlights are printed near the bottom. John Moore and Harland Cliff have been reported on paper stock. Whether they were part of a store display is unknown.

	EX-MT	VG-E	GOOD
COMPLETE SET (16)	1000.00	450.00	125.00
COMMON CARD	35.00	16.00	4.40
☐ 1 Zeke Bonura Chicago White Sox (fielding, crossed bats, glove, ball at upper left)	35.00	16.00	4.40
☐ 2 Tom Bridges Detroit Tigers (pitching, figure in large orange circle)	35.00	16.00	4.40
☐ 3 Harland Clift St. Louis Browns (batting, large baseball behind him)	35.00	16.00	4.40
☐ 4 Kiki Cuyler Cincinnati Reds (batting on green background)	50.00	22.00	6.25
☐ 5 Joe DiMaggio New York Yankees (leaping, green and white circle behind)	400.00	180.00	50.00
☐ 6 Bob Feller Cleveland Indians (pitching, blue circle on left knee)	125.00	55.00	15.50
☐ 7 Lefty Grove	100.00	45.00	12.50

	EX-MT	VG-E	GOOD
Boston Red Sox (pitching, red orange home plate)			
☐ 8 Billy Herman Chicago Cubs (throwing, yellow star behind him)	50.00	22.00	6.25
☐ 9 Carl Hubbell New York Giants (pitching, orange, yellow V's behind)	75.00	34.00	9.50
☐ 10 Buck Jordan Boston Bees (batting, dark orange rectangle, blue sides)	35.00	16.00	4.40
☐ 11 Pepper Martin St. Louis Cardinals (reaching, orange rectangle)	40.00	18.00	5.00
☐ 12 John Moore Philadelphia Phillies (batting, blue background, stands on green)	35.00	16.00	4.40
☐ 13 Wally Moses Philadelphia A's (leaping, dark orange background, yellow and blue)	35.00	16.00	4.40
☐ 14 Van L. Mungo Brooklyn Dodgers (pitching, green background, orange and blue)	40.00	18.00	5.00
☐ 15 Cecil Travis Washington Senators (batting, orange lightning)	35.00	16.00	4.40
☐ 16 Arky Vaughan Pittsburgh Pirates (batting, blue diamond, green frame)	50.00	22.00	6.25

1937 Wheaties BB14

This set is referred to as the "Small Panels with Orange Background Series." These numbered (and unnumbered) cards, which made up the back of the Wheaties individual serving cereal box, measure about 2 5/8" by 3 7/8". These small panels have orange backgrounds and some, but not all, use poses that appear in some of the regular sized panels. Joe DiMaggio, for example, is the same pose as in the large Wheaties BB7 set and the Mel Ott is similar to the BB5 pose, but cropped a little differently. Some panels have been seen with and without the number 29 in combination with a letter, so apparently there were several printings. The player's name is in all capitals with his position and team in smaller caps. A printed block of data about him is on the main part of the card with a Wheaties endorsement in a white strip at the bottom.

	EX-MT	VG-E	GOOD
COMPLETE SET (17)	1600.00	700.00	200.00
COMMON CARD	60.00	27.00	7.50
☐ 1 Zeke Bonura (29A) Led all A.L. First Basemen (BB7 pose)	60.00	27.00	7.50
☐ 2 Tommy Bridges (29J) Struck Out Most Batters, 173 ..." (not BB7 pose)	60.00	27.00	7.50
☐ 3 Dolph Camilli Most Put Outs, 1446 ..." (unnumbered)	75.00	34.00	9.50
☐ 4 Frank Demaree	60.00	27.00	7.50
☐ 5 Joe DiMaggio (29I) Outstanding Rookie, 1936 ..." (BB7 pose)	500.00	220.00	60.00
☐ 6 Billy Herman Lifetime .300 Hitter ... (unnumbered)	100.00	45.00	12.50
☐ 7 Carl Hubbell Won Most Games, 26 ... (unnumbered)	150.00	70.00	19.00
☐ 8 Ernie Lombardi	100.00	45.00	12.50
☐ 9 Pepper Martin	75.00	34.00	9.50
☐ 10 Joe Moore	60.00	27.00	7.50
☐ 11 Van L. Mungo	75.00	34.00	9.50
☐ 12 Mel Ott	150.00	70.00	19.00
☐ 13 Raymond Radcliff (29H) (most one-base hits) (BB7 pose)	60.00	27.00	7.50
☐ 14 Cecil Travis (29B) One of the Leading Bats in ... (BB7 pose)	60.00	27.00	7.50
☐ 15 Harold Trosky	60.00	27.00	7.50
☐ 16A Arky Vaughan (unnumbered)	125.00	55.00	15.50
☐ 16B Arky Vaughan (29L) Lifetime .300 Hitter who ..." (BB7 pose)	125.00	55.00	15.50

1938 Wheaties BB10

This set is refered to as the "Biggest Thrills in Baseball." These numbered cards which make up the back of the cereal box measure 6" X 8 1/2." A player from every Major League team is included. Each panel describes the player's greatest thrill playing the game. The thrill is announced in large banner headline type and described in a block of copy over the players script signature, His team name and position are printed below the name. All sixteen are known to exist on both paper stock as well as heavy cardboard.

	EX-MT	VG-E	GOOD
COMPLETE SET (16)	1000.00	450.00	125.00
COMMON CARD	35.00	16.00	4.40
☐ 1 Bob Feller Cleveland Indians (Two Hits in One Inning for Feller)	125.00	55.00	15.50
☐ 2 Cecil Travis Washington Nationals (Clicks in First Big League Games)	35.00	16.00	4.40
☐ 3 Joe Medwick St. Louis Cardinals (Goes on Batting Spree Twice)	60.00	27.00	7.50
☐ 4 Gerald Walker Chicago White Sox (World Series Game, 1934, Gives ...)	35.00	16.00	4.40
☐ 5 Carl Hubbell New York Giants (Strikes Out Murderer's Row)	75.00	34.00	9.50
☐ 6 Bob Johnson Philadelphia A's (Setting New A.L. Record)	35.00	16.00	4.40
☐ 7 Beau Bell St. Louis Browns (Smacks First Major League Homer)	35.00	16.00	4.40
☐ 8 Ernie Lombardi Cincinnati Reds (Sold to Majors)	50.00	22.00	6.25
☐ 9 Lefty Grove Boston Red Sox (Fans Babe Ruth)	100.00	45.00	12.50
☐ 10 Lou Fette Boston Bees (Wins 20 Games)	35.00	16.00	4.40
☐ 11 Joe DiMaggio New York Yankees (Home Run King Gets Biggest Thrill ...)	400.00	180.00	50.00
☐ 12 Pinky Whitney Philadelphia Phillies (Hits Three in a Row)	35.00	16.00	4.40
☐ 13 Dizzy Dean Chicago Cubs (11-0 Victory Clinches World Series)	100.00	45.00	12.50
☐ 14 Charlie Gehringer Detroit Tigers (Homers Off Dizzy Dean)	75.00	34.00	9.50
☐ 15 Paul Waner Pittsburgh Pirates (Four Perfect Sixes)	50.00	22.00	6.25
☐ 16 Dolph Camilli Brooklyn Dodgers (First Hit a Homer)	40.00	18.00	5.00

1938 Wheaties BB11

This set is refered to as the "Dress Clothes or Civies Series." The cards are unnumbered and measure 6" 8 1/4" The panels feature the players and their friends in blue photos. The remainder of the panel uses the traditional orange, blue and white Wheaties colors.

	EX-MT	VG-E	GOOD
COMPLETE SET (8)	300.00	135.00	38.00
COMMON CARD	35.00	16.00	4.40
☐ 1 Lou Fette (pouring milk over his Wheaties)	35.00	16.00	4.40
☐ 2 Jimmie Foxx (slices banana for his son's Wheaties)	60.00	27.00	7.50
☐ 3 Charlie Gehringer (and his young fan)	50.00	22.00	6.25
☐ 4 Lefty Grove (watches waitress pour Wheaties)	50.00	22.00	6.25
☐ 5 Hank Greenberg and Roxie Lawson (eat breakfast)	60.00	27.00	7.50
☐ 6 Ernie Lombardi and Lee Grissom (prepare to eat)	35.00	16.00	4.40
☐ 7 Joe Medwick (pours milk over cereal)	40.00	18.00	5.00
☐ 8 Lon Warneke (smiles in anticip- ation of Wheaties)	35.00	16.00	4.40

1938 Wheaties BB15

This set is referred to as the "Small Panels with Orange, Blue and White Background Series." These numbered (and unnumbered) cards, which made up the back of the Wheaties individual serving cereal box, measure about 2 5/8" by 3 7/8". These small panels have orange, blue and white backgrounds and some, but not all, use poses that appear in some of the regular, larger-sized panels. Greenberg and Lewis are featured with a horizontal (HOR) pose.

	EX-MT	VG-E	GOOD
COMPLETE SET (11)	1000.00	450.00	125.00
COMMON CARD	50.00	22.00	6.25
☐ 1 Zeke Bonura (batted .345)	50.00	22.00	6.25
☐ 2 Joe DiMaggio (46 home runs)	400.00	180.00	50.00
☐ 3A Charlie Gehringer (leaping, MVP, American League)	100.00	45.00	12.50
☐ 3B Charlie Gehringer (batting, 1937 batting king)	100.00	45.00	12.50
☐ 4 Hank Greenberg HOR (second in home runs)	125.00	55.00	15.50
☐ 5 Lefty Grove (17-9 won-lost record)	125.00	55.00	15.50
☐ 6 Carl Hubbell (star pitcher, 1937 Giants)	100.00	45.00	12.50
☐ 7 John (Buddy) Lewis (batted .314) HOR	50.00	22.00	6.25
☐ 8 Heinie Manush (batted .332)	75.00	34.00	9.50
☐ 9 Joe Medwick	75.00	34.00	9.50
☐ 10 Arky Vaughan	75.00	34.00	9.50

1939 Wheaties BB12

This set is refered to as the "Personal Pointers Series." These numbered cards measure 6" X 8 1/4'. The panels feature an

instructional format similar to both the BB5 and BB6 Wheaties sets. Drawings again illustrate the tips on batting and pitching. The colors are orange, blue and white and the players appear in photographs.

	EX-MT	VG-E	GOOD
COMPLETE SET (9)	500.00	220.00	60.00
COMMON CARD	35.00	16.00	4.40
☐ 1 Ernie Lombardi How to Place Hits For Scores	60.00	27.00	7.50
☐ 2 Johnny Allen It's Windup That Counts	35.00	16.00	4.40
☐ 3 Lefty Gomez Delivery That Keeps 'Em Guessing	75.00	34.00	9.50
☐ 4 Bill Lee Follow Through For Stops	35.00	16.00	4.40
☐ 5 Jimmie Foxx Stance Helps Sluggers	100.00	45.00	12.50
☐ 6 Joe Medwick Power-Drive Grip	60.00	27.00	7.50
☐ 7 Hank Greenberg Smooth Swing	100.00	45.00	12.50
☐ 8 Mel Ott Study That Pitcher	75.00	34.00	9.50
☐ 9 Arky Vaughan Beat 'Em With Bunts	60.00	27.00	7.50

1939 Wheaties BB13

This set is referred to as the "100 Years of Baseball or Baseball Centennial Series." These numbered cards which make up the back of the Wheaties box measure 6" X 6 3/4". Each panel has a drawing that depicts various aspects and events in baseball in the traditional orange, blue and white Wheaties colors.

	EX-MT	VG-E	GOOD
COMPLETE SET (8)	200.00	90.00	25.00
COMMON CARD	25.00	11.00	3.10
☐ 1 Design of First Diamond with Picture of Abner Doubleday - 1938	35.00	16.00	4.40
☐ 2 Lincoln Gets News of Nomination on Base- ball Field - 1860	35.00	16.00	4.40
☐ 3 Crowd Boos First Baseball Glove (pictures of gloves) - 1869	25.00	11.00	3.10
☐ 4 Curve Ball Just an Illusion Say Scientists - 1877	25.00	11.00	3.10
☐ 5 Fencer's Mask is Pattern for First Catcher's Cage - 1877	25.00	11.00	3.10
☐ 6 Baseball Gets "All Dressed Up" pictures of uniforms) - 1890	25.00	11.00	3.10
☐ 7 Modern Bludgeon Enters Game (pictures of bats) - 1895	25.00	11.00	3.10
☐ 8 Casey at the Bat (eight verses of the famous Mudville poem)	35.00	16.00	4.40

1940 Wheaties M4

This set is refered to as the "Champs in the USA" The cards measure about 6" 8 1'4" and are numbered. The drawing portion (inside the dotted lines) measure approximately 6" X 6". Baseball players are on each card joined by football players and coaches, race car drivers, airline pilots, a circus clown, ice skater, hockey star and golfers. Eaxh athelete appears in what looks like a stamp with a serrated edge. The stamps appear one above the other with a brief block of copy describing his or her achievements. There appears to have been three printings, resulting in some variation panels. The full panels tell the cereal buyer to look for either 27, 39, or 63 champ stamps. The first nine panels apparently were printed more than once, since all the unknown variations occur with those numbers.

	EX-MT	VG-E	GOOD
COMPLETE SET (20)	800.00	350.00	100.00
COMMON CARD	25.00	11.00	3.10
☐ 1A Charles "Red" Ruffing Lynn Patrick Bob Feller (27 stamp series)	75.00	34.00	9.50
☐ 1B Charles "Red" Ruffing Lynn Patrick Leo Durocher (39 stamp series)	50.00	22.00	6.25
☐ 2A Joe DiMaggio Hank Greenberg Don Duge (27 stamp series)	200.00	90.00	25.00
☐ 2B Joe DiMaggio Mel Ott Ellsworth Vines (39 stamp series)	200.00	90.00	25.00
☐ 3 Jimmie Foxx Bernie Bierman Bill Dickey	60.00	27.00	7.50
☐ 4 Morris Arnovich Earl "Dutch" Clark Capt R.L. Baker	25.00	11.00	3.10
☐ 5 Joe Medwick Madison(Matty) Bell Ab Jenkins	25.00	11.00	3.10
☐ 6A John Mize Davey O'Brien Ralph Guldahl (27 stamp series)	25.00	11.00	3.10
☐ 6B John Mize Bob Feller Rudy York (39 stamp series)	75.00	34.00	9.50
☐ 6C Gabby Hartnett Davey O'Brien Ralph Guldahl (unknown series)	25.00	11.00	3.10
☐ 7A Joe Cronin Cecil Isbell Byron Nelson (27 stamp series)	25.00	11.00	3.10
☐ 7B Joe Cronin Hank Greenberg Byron Nelson (unknown series)	50.00	22.00	6.25
☐ 7C Paul Derringer Cecil Isbell Byron Nelson (unknown series)	25.00	11.00	3.10
☐ 8A Jack Manders Ernie Lombardi George I. Myers (27 stamp series)	25.00	11.00	3.10
☐ 8B Paul Derringer Ernie Lombardi George I. Myers (39 stamp series)	25.00	11.00	3.10
☐ 9 Bob Bartlett Terrell Jacobs Captain R.C.Hanson	25.00	11.00	3.10
☐ 10 Adele Inge Lowell "Red" Dawson Billy Herman	25.00	11.00	3.10
☐ 11 Dolph Camilli Antoinette Concello Wallace Wade	25.00	11.00	3.10
☐ 12 Hugh McManus Luke Appling Stanley Hack	25.00	11.00	3.10
☐ 13 Felix Adler Hal Trosky Mabel Vinson	25.00	11.00	3.10

1941 Wheaties M5

This set is also referred to as "Champs of the U.S.A." These numbered cards made up the back of the Wheaties box; the whole panel measures 6" X 8 1/4" but the drawing portion (inside the dotted lines) is apparently 6" X 6". Each athlete appears in what looks like a stamp with a serrated edge. The stamps appear one above the other with a brief block of copy describing his or her achievements. The format is the same as the previous M4 set -- even the numbering system continues where the M4 set stops.

	EX-MT	VG-E	GOOD
COMPLETE SET (8)	350.00	160.00	45.00
COMMON CARD	25.00	11.00	3.10
☐ 14 Jimmie Foxx Felix Adler Capt. R.G. Hanson	50.00	22.00	6.25
☐ 15 Bernie Bierman Bob Feller Jessie McLeod	40.00	18.00	5.00
☐ 16 Hank Greenberg Lowell "Red" Dawson J.W. Stoker	40.00	18.00	5.00
☐ 17 Joe DiMaggio Byron Nelson Antoinette Concello	200.00	90.00	25.00
☐ 18 Pee Wee" Reese Capt. R.L. Baker Frank "Buck" McCormick	50.00	22.00	6.25
☐ 19 W. Robbins/G. Sarazen	25.00	11.00	3.10
☐ 20 B. Walters/Barney McCosky	25.00	11.00	3.10
☐ 21 Joe "Flash" Gordon George I. Myers Stan Hack	25.00	11.00	3.10

1951 Wheaties *

The cards in this 6-card set measure 2 1/2" by 3 1/4". Cards of the 1951 Wheaties set are actually the backs of small individual boxes of Wheaties. The cards are waxed and depict three baseball players, one football player, one basketball player and one golfer. They are occasionally found as complete boxes, which are worth 50 percent more than the prices listed below. The catalog designation for this set is F272-3. The cards are blank-backed and unnumbered; they are numbered below in alphabetical order for convenience.

	NRMT	VG-E	GOOD
COMPLETE SET (6)	500.00	220.00	60.00
COMMON CARD (1-6)	60.00	27.00	7.50
☐ 1 Bob Feller (baseball)	75.00	34.00	9.50
☐ 2 Johnny Lujack (football)	60.00	27.00	7.50
☐ 3 George Mikan (basketball)	175.00	80.00	22.00
☐ 4 Stan Musial (baseball)	125.00	55.00	15.50
☐ 5 Sam Snead (golfer)	60.00	27.00	7.50
☐ 6 Ted Williams (baseball)	150.00	70.00	19.00

1952 Wheaties *

The cards in this 60-card set measure 2" by 2 3/4". The 1952 Wheaties set of orange, blue and white, unnumbered cards was issued in panels of eight or ten cards on the backs of Wheaties cereal boxes. Each player appears in an action pose designated in the checklist with an "A" and as a portrait listed in the checklist with a "B". The catalog designation is F272-4. The cards are blank-backed and unnumbered; they are numbered below in alphabetical order for convenience.

	NRMT	VG-E	GOOD
COMPLETE SET (60)	1200.00	550.00	150.00
COMMON BASEBALL	15.00	6.75	1.85
COMMON FOOTBALL	15.00	6.75	1.85
COMMON NON-BASEBALL	5.00	2.20	.60
☐ 1A Alice Bauer	5.00	2.20	.60
☐ 1B Alice Bauer	5.00	2.20	.60
☐ 2A Marlene Bauer	5.00	2.20	.60
☐ 2B Marlene Bauer	5.00	2.20	.60
☐ 3A Patty Berg	5.00	2.20	.60
☐ 3B Patty Berg	5.00	2.20	.60
☐ 4A Yogi Berra	40.00	18.00	5.00
☐ 4B Yogi Berra	40.00	18.00	5.00
☐ 5A Roy Campanella	50.00	22.00	6.25
☐ 5B Roy Campanella	50.00	22.00	6.25
☐ 6A Bob Davies	30.00	13.50	3.70
☐ 6B Bob Davies	30.00	13.50	3.70
☐ 7A Glenn Davis	15.00	6.75	1.85
☐ 7B Glenn Davis	15.00	6.75	1.85
☐ 8A Ned Day	5.00	2.20	.60
☐ 8B Ned Day	5.00	2.20	.60
☐ 9A Charles Diehl	5.00	2.20	.60
☐ 9B Charles Diehl	5.00	2.20	.60
☐ 10A Tom Fears	15.00	6.75	1.85
☐ 10B Tom Fears	15.00	6.75	1.85
☐ 11A Bob Feller	40.00	18.00	5.00
☐ 11B Bob Feller	40.00	18.00	5.00
☐ 12A Gretchen Fraser	5.00	2.20	.60
☐ 12B Gretchen Fraser	5.00	2.20	.60
☐ 13A Otto Graham	35.00	16.00	4.40
☐ 13B Otto Graham	35.00	16.00	4.40
☐ 14A Ben Hogan	20.00	9.00	2.50
☐ 14B Ben Hogan	20.00	9.00	2.50
☐ 15A George Kell	25.00	11.00	3.10
☐ 15B George Kell	25.00	11.00	3.10
☐ 16A Ralph Kiner	25.00	11.00	3.10
☐ 16B Ralph Kiner	25.00	11.00	3.10
☐ 17A Jack Kramer	7.50	3.40	.95
☐ 17B Jack Kramer	7.50	3.40	.95
☐ 18A Bob Lemon	25.00	11.00	3.10
☐ 18B Bob Lemon	25.00	11.00	3.10
☐ 19A Johnny Lujack	15.00	6.75	1.85
☐ 19B Johnny Lujack	15.00	6.75	1.85
☐ 20A Lloyd Mangrum	5.00	2.20	.60
☐ 20B Lloyd Mangrum	5.00	2.20	.60
☐ 21A George Mikan	125.00	55.00	15.50
☐ 21B George Mikan	125.00	55.00	15.50
☐ 22A Stan Musial	75.00	34.00	9.50
☐ 22B Stan Musial	75.00	34.00	9.50
☐ 23A Jimmy Patterson	5.00	2.20	.60
☐ 23B Jimmy Patterson	5.00	2.20	.60
☐ 24A Jim Pollard	35.00	16.00	4.40
☐ 24B Jim Pollard	35.00	16.00	4.40
☐ 25A Phil Rizzuto	30.00	13.50	3.70
☐ 25B Phil Rizzuto	30.00	13.50	3.70
☐ 26A Preacher Roe	12.50	5.50	1.55
☐ 26B Preacher Roe	12.50	5.50	1.55
☐ 27A Sam Snead	15.00	6.75	1.85
☐ 27B Sam Snead	15.00	6.75	1.85
☐ 28A Doak Walker	25.00	11.00	3.10
☐ 28B Doak Walker	25.00	11.00	3.10
☐ 29A Bob Waterfield	25.00	11.00	3.10
☐ 29B Bob Waterfield	25.00	11.00	3.10
☐ 30A Ted Williams	100.00	45.00	12.50
☐ 30B Ted Williams	100.00	45.00	12.50

1964 Wheaties Stamps

In 1964 General Mills issued the Wheaties Major League All-Star Baseball Player Stamp Album. The album is orange, blue and white and measures approximately 8 3/8" by 11"; it contains 48 pages with places for one or two stamps per page. The individual stamps are in full color with a thick white border and measure approximately 2 9/16" by 2 3/4". The stamps are unnumbered so they listed below in alphabetical order.

	NRMT	VG-E	GOOD
COMPLETE SET (50)	140.00	65.00	17.50
COMMON STAMP (1-50)	1.00	.45	.12
☐ 1 Hank Aaron	15.00	6.75	1.85
☐ 2 Bob Allison	1.25	.55	.16
☐ 3 Luis Aparicio	4.00	1.80	.50
☐ 4 Ed Bailey	1.00	.45	.12
☐ 5 Steve Barber	1.00	.45	.12
☐ 6 Earl Battey	1.00	.45	.12
☐ 7 Jim Bouton	1.25	.55	.16
☐ 8 Ken Boyer	1.50	.70	.19
☐ 9 Jim Bunning	4.00	1.80	.50
☐ 10 Orlando Cepeda	2.50	1.10	.30
☐ 11 Roberto Clemente	20.00	9.00	2.50
☐ 12 Ray Culp	1.00	.45	.12
☐ 13 Tommy Davis	1.25	.55	.16
☐ 14 John Edwards	1.00	.45	.12
☐ 15 Whitey Ford	6.00	2.70	.75
☐ 16 Nelson Fox	2.00	.90	.25
☐ 18 Jim Gilliam	1.50	.70	.19
☐ 19 Jim Grant	1.00	.45	.12
☐ 20 Dick Groat	1.25	.55	.16
☐ 21 Elston Howard	1.50	.70	.19
☐ 22 Larry Jackson	1.00	.45	.12
☐ 23 Julian Javier	1.00	.45	.12
☐ 24 Al Kaline	8.00	3.60	1.00
☐ 25 Harmon Killebrew	6.00	2.70	.75
☐ 26 Don Leppert	1.00	.45	.12
☐ 27 Frank Malzone	1.25	.55	.16
☐ 28 Juan Marichal	5.00	2.20	.60
☐ 29 Willie Mays	15.00	6.75	1.85
☐ 30 Ken McBride	1.00	.45	.12
☐ 31 Willie McCovey	5.00	2.20	.60
☐ 32 Jim O'Toole	1.00	.45	.12
☐ 33 Albie Pearson	1.00	.45	.12
☐ 34 Joe Pepitone	1.25	.55	.16
☐ 35 Ron Perranoski	1.25	.55	.16
☐ 36 Juan Pizarro	1.00	.45	.12
☐ 37 Dick Radatz	1.00	.45	.12
☐ 38 Bobby Richardson	2.00	.90	.25
☐ 39 Brooks Robinson	8.00	3.60	1.00
☐ 40 Ron Santo	2.00	.90	.25
☐ 41 Norm Siebern	1.00	.45	.12
☐ 42 Duke Snider	8.00	3.60	1.00
☐ 43 Warren Spahn	8.00	3.60	1.00
☐ 44 Joe Torre	2.00	.90	.25
☐ 45 Tom Tresh	1.25	.55	.16
☐ 46 Zoilo Versalles	1.25	.55	.16
☐ 47 Leon Wagner	1.00	.45	.12
☐ 48 Bill White	1.25	.55	.16
☐ 49 Hal Woodeshick	1.00	.45	.12
☐ 50 Carl Yastrzemski	1.00	.45	.12

1907 White Sox George W. Hull

This 12 card set measures 3 1/2" by 5 1/2" and contains World Champion White Sox players only. Each postcard contains club president Charles Comiskey's picture in a circle on the lower left on the front; assorted White Sox players pictures in ovals on socks in a clothesline; and the subject player's picture on the right side of the card. The George W. Hall identification is also pictured on the front.

	EX-MT	VG-E	GOOD
COMPLETE SET (12)	1200.00	550.00	150.00
COMMON CARD (1-12)	100.00	45.00	12.50
☐ 1 Nick Altrock	125.00	55.00	15.50
☐ 2 George Davis	100.00	45.00	12.50
☐ 3 Jiggs Donohue	100.00	45.00	12.50
☐ 4 Pat Dougherty	100.00	45.00	12.50
☐ 5 Frank Isbell	100.00	45.00	12.50
☐ 6 Fielder Jones	100.00	45.00	12.50
☐ 7 Ed McFarland	100.00	45.00	12.50
☐ 8 Frank Owens	100.00	45.00	12.50
☐ 9 Ray Patterson	100.00	45.00	12.50
☐ 10 Frank Smith	100.00	45.00	12.50
☐ 11 Ed Walsh	250.00	110.00	31.00
☐ 12 Doc White	100.00	45.00	12.50

1939 White Sox Team Issue

These 23 photos measure approximately 5 1/4" by 6 3/4". They feature player photos and a fascimile autograph. The backs are blank and we have sequenced them in alphabetical order.

	EX-MT	VG-E	GOOD
COMPLETE SET (23)	80.00	36.00	10.00
COMMON CARD (1-23)	3.00	1.35	.35
☐ 1 Pete Appleton	3.00	1.35	.35
☐ 2 Luke Appling	10.00	4.50	1.25
☐ 3 Clint Brown	3.00	1.35	.35
☐ 4 Bill Dietrich	3.00	1.35	.35
☐ 5 Mule Haas	3.00	1.35	.35
☐ 6 Jack Hayes	3.00	1.35	.35
☐ 7 Bob Kennedy	3.00	1.35	.35
☐ 8 Jack Knott	3.00	1.35	.35
☐ 9 Mike Kreevich	3.00	1.35	.35
☐ 10 Joe Kuhel	3.00	1.35	.35
☐ 11 Thornton Lee	5.00	2.20	.60
☐ 12 Ted Lyons	10.00	4.50	1.25
☐ 13 Eric McNair	3.00	1.35	.35
☐ 14 John Rigney	3.00	1.35	.35
☐ 15 Larry Rosenthal	3.00	1.35	.35
☐ 16 Ken Silvestri	3.00	1.35	.35
☐ 17 Eddie Smith	3.00	1.35	.35
☐ 18 Moose Solters	3.00	1.35	.35

	NRMT	VG-E	GOOD
☐ 19 Monty Stratton	7.50	3.40	.95
☐ 20 Mike Tresh	3.00	1.35	.35
☐ 21 Skeeter Webb	3.00	1.35	.35
☐ 22 Ed Weiland	3.00	1.35	.35
☐ 23 Taft Wright	3.00	1.35	.35

1948 White Sox Team Issue

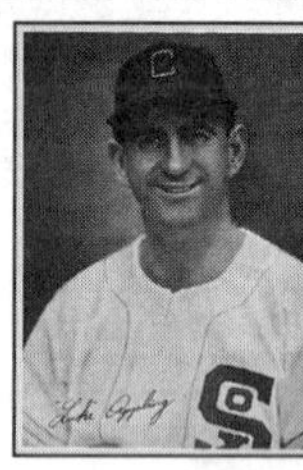

These 30 photos represent members of the 1948 Chicago White Sox. They measure approximately 6 1/2" by 9" are black and white and have blank backs. We have sequenced this set in alphabetical order.

	NRMT	VG-E	GOOD
COMPLETE SET (30)	150.00	70.00	19.00
COMMON CARD (1-30)	3.50	1.55	.45
☐ 1 Luke Appling	20.00	9.00	2.50
☐ 2 Floyd Baker	3.50	1.55	.45
☐ 3 Fred Bradley	3.50	1.55	.45
☐ 4 Earl Caldwell	3.50	1.55	.45
☐ 5 Red Faber CO	15.00	6.75	1.85
☐ 6 Bob Gillespie	3.50	1.55	.45
☐ 7 Jim Goodwin	3.50	1.55	.45
☐ 8 Orval Grove	3.50	1.55	.45
☐ 9 Earl Harrist	3.50	1.55	.45
☐ 10 Joe Haynes	3.50	1.55	.45
☐ 11 Ralph Hodgin	3.50	1.55	.45
☐ 12 Howie Judson	3.50	1.55	.45
☐ 13 Bob Kennedy	5.00	2.20	.60
☐ 14 Don Kolloway	3.50	1.55	.45
☐ 15 Tony Lupien	3.50	1.55	.45
☐ 16 Ted Lyons MG	15.00	6.75	1.85
☐ 17 Cass Michaels	3.50	1.55	.45
☐ 18 Bing Miller CO	3.50	1.55	.45
☐ 19 Buster Mills CO	3.50	1.55	.45
☐ 20 Glen Moulder	3.50	1.55	.45
☐ 21 Frank Papish	3.50	1.55	.45
☐ 22 Ike Pearson	3.50	1.55	.45
☐ 23 Dave Philley	3.50	1.55	.45
☐ 24 Aaron Robinson	3.50	1.55	.45
☐ 25 Mike Tresh	3.50	1.55	.45
☐ 26 Jack Wallaesa	3.50	1.55	.45
☐ 27 Ralph Weigel	3.50	1.55	.45
☐ 28 Bill Wight	3.50	1.55	.45
☐ 29 Taft Wright	3.50	1.55	.45
☐ 30 Team Photo	25.00	11.00	3.10

1952 White Sox Hawthorn-Mellody

This set of 11 pins is described on each pin as "Club of Champs." The set was issued about 1952 by Hawthorn-Mellody Dairy in Chicago featuring members of the Chicago White Sox. The coloring of each pin is brownish sepia and white. Since the pins are unnumbered, they are ordered below in alphabetical order. The player's name only (no position) is given on the front of the pin. Each pin measures approximately 1 3/8" in diameter. The set also technically includes an eleventh pin, the "Club of Champs Member" pin; since this pin has no player pictured or even any baseball reference on the pin, it is not checklisted or priced below with the players in the set.

	NRMT	VG-E	GOOD
COMPLETE SET (10)	350.00	160.00	45.00
COMMON PLAYER (1-10)	30.00	13.50	3.70
☐ 1 Ray Coleman	30.00	13.50	3.70
☐ 2 Sam Dente	30.00	13.50	3.70
☐ 3 Joe Dobson	30.00	13.50	3.70
☐ 4 Nellie Fox	75.00	34.00	9.50
☐ 5 Sherman Lollar	40.00	18.00	5.00
☐ 6 Billy Pierce	50.00	22.00	6.25
☐ 7 Eddie Robinson	30.00	13.50	3.70
☐ 8 Hector Rodriguez	30.00	13.50	3.70
☐ 9 Eddie Stewart	30.00	13.50	3.70
☐ 10 Al Zarilla	30.00	13.50	3.70

1958 White Sox Jay Publishing

This 12-card set of the Chicago White Sox measures approximately 5" by 7" and features black-and-white player photos in a white border. These cards were packaged 12 to a packet. The backs are blank. The cards are unnumbered and checklisted below in alphabetical order.

	NRMT	VG-E	GOOD
COMPLETE SET (12)	35.00	16.00	4.40
COMMON CARD (1-12)	2.50	1.10	.30
☐ 1 Luis Aparicio	5.00	2.20	.60
☐ 2 Dick Donovan	2.50	1.10	.30
☐ 3 Nelson Fox	5.00	2.20	.60
☐ 4 Tito Francona	2.50	1.10	.30
☐ 5 Bill Goodman	2.50	1.10	.30
☐ 6 Sherman Lollar	2.50	1.10	.30
☐ 7 Ray Moore	2.50	1.10	.30
☐ 8 Billy Pierce	2.50	1.10	.30
☐ 9 Jim Rivera	2.50	1.10	.30
☐ 10 Al Smith	2.50	1.10	.30
☐ 11 Jim Wilson	2.50	1.10	.30
☐ 12 Early Wynn	5.00	2.20	.60

1960 White Sox Jay Publishing

This 12-card set of the Chicago White Sox measures approximately 5" by 7" and features black-and-white player photos in a white border. These cards were packaged 12 to a packet. The backs are blank. The cards are unnumbered and checklisted below in alphabetical order.

	NRMT	VG-E	GOOD
COMPLETE SET (12)	30.00	13.50	3.70
COMMON CARD (1-12)	2.00	.90	.25
☐ 1 Luis Aparicio	5.00	2.20	.60
☐ 2 Nelson Fox	5.00	2.20	.60
☐ 3 Gene Freese	2.00	.90	.25
☐ 4 Ted Kluszewski	4.00	1.80	.50
☐ 5 Jim Landis	2.00	.90	.25
☐ 6 Sherman Lollar	2.00	.90	.25
☐ 7 Al Lopez MG	3.00	1.35	.35
☐ 8 Orestes Minoso	4.00	1.80	.50
☐ 9 Bob Shaw	2.00	.90	.25
☐ 10 Roy Sievers	2.50	1.10	.30
☐ 11 Al Smith	2.00	.90	.25
☐ 12 Early Wynn	6.00	2.70	.75

1960 White Sox Ticket Stubs

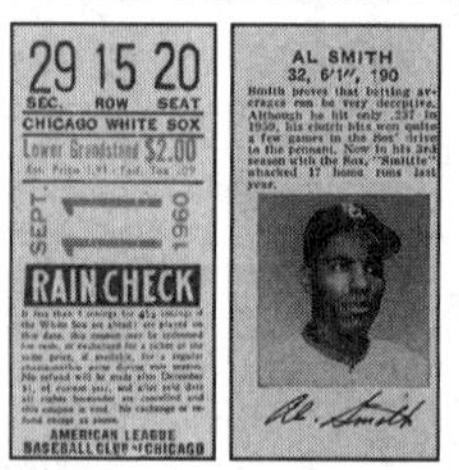

This set was the brainchild of famed owner Bill Veeck. Player's photos were put on a ticket stub so they could be collected. The players marked UNC below in the checklist are unconfirmed at this time and may not exist.

	NRMT	VG-E	GOOD
COMPLETE SET	90.00	40.00	11.00
COMMON PLAYER	3.00	1.35	.35
☐ 1 Luis Aparicio	7.50	3.40	.95
☐ 2 Earl Battey UNC	3.00	1.35	.35
☐ 3 Frank Baumann	3.00	1.35	.35
☐ 4 Dick Donovan	3.00	1.35	.35
☐ 5 Nelson Fox	10.00	4.50	1.25
☐ 6 Gene Freese	3.00	1.35	.35
☐ 7 Billy Goodman UNC	3.00	1.35	.35
☐ 8 Ted Kluzewski	7.50	3.40	.95
☐ 9 Jim Landis	3.00	1.35	.35
☐ 10 Barry Latman	3.00	1.35	.35
☐ 11 Sherman Lollar	3.00	1.35	.35
☐ 12 Al Lopez MG	5.00	2.20	.60
☐ 13 Turk Lown	3.00	1.35	.35
☐ 14 Orestes Minoso	7.50	3.40	.95
☐ 15 Billy Pierce	5.00	2.20	.60
☐ 16 Jim Rivera	3.00	1.35	.35
☐ 17 Bob Shaw	3.00	1.35	.35
☐ 18 Roy Sievers	3.00	1.35	.35
☐ 19 Al Smith	3.00	1.35	.35
☐ 20 Gerry Staley	3.00	1.35	.35
☐ 21 Earl Torgeson UNC	3.00	1.35	.35
☐ 22 Early Wynn	7.50	3.40	.95

1961 White Sox Ticket Stubs

For the second year, the White Sox placed player photos on ticket stubs to promote interest in their players.

	NRMT	VG-E	GOOD
COMPLETE SET	75.00	34.00	9.50
COMMON PLAYER	3.00	1.35	.35
☐ 1 Luis Aparicio	6.00	2.70	.75
☐ 2 Frank Baumann	3.00	1.35	.35
☐ 3 Cam Carreon	3.00	1.35	.35
☐ 4 Sam Esposito	3.00	1.35	.35

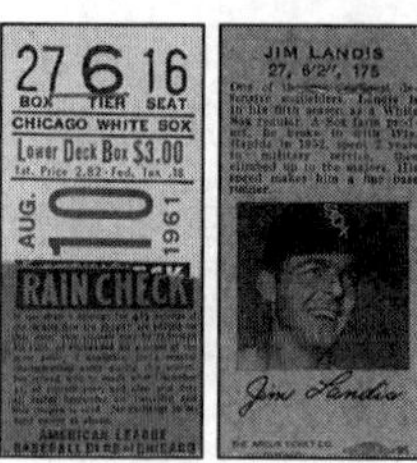

	NRMT	VG-E	GOOD
☐ 5 Nelson Fox	7.50	3.40	.95
☐ 6 Jim Landis	3.00	1.35	.35
☐ 7 Sherm Lollar	3.00	1.35	.35
☐ 8 Al Lopez MG	5.00	2.20	.60
☐ 9 Cal McLish	3.00	1.35	.35
☐ 10 J.C. Martin	3.00	1.35	.35
☐ 11 Orestes Minoso	7.50	3.40	.95
☐ 12 Billy Pierce	5.00	2.20	.60
☐ 13 Juan Pizarro	4.00	1.80	.50
☐ 14 Bob Roselli	3.00	1.35	.35
☐ 15 Herb Score	5.00	2.20	.60
☐ 16 Bob Shaw	3.00	1.35	.35
☐ 17 Roy Sievers	4.00	1.80	.50
☐ 18 Al Smith	3.00	1.35	.35
☐ 19 Gerry Staley	3.00	1.35	.35
☐ 20 Early Wynn	7.50	3.40	.95

1962 White Sox Jay Publishing

This 12-card set of the Chicago White Sox measures approximately 5" by 7". The fronts feature black-and-white posed player photos with the player's and team name printed below in the white border. These cards were packaged 12 to a packet. The backs are blank. The cards are unnumbered and checklisted below in alphabetical order.

	NRMT	VG-E	GOOD
COMPLETE SET (12)	30.00	13.50	3.70
COMMON CARD (1-12)	2.50	1.10	.30
☐ 1 Luis Aparicio	5.00	2.20	.60
☐ 2 Frank Baumann	2.50	1.10	.30
☐ 3 Nellie Fox	5.00	2.20	.60
☐ 4 Russ Kemmerer	2.50	1.10	.30
☐ 5 Jim Landis	2.50	1.10	.30
☐ 6 Sherm Lollar	2.50	1.10	.30
☐ 7 Al Lopez MG	3.50	1.55	.45
☐ 8 Joe Martin	2.50	1.10	.30
☐ 9 Juan Pizzaro	3.00	1.35	.35
☐ 10 Floyd Robinson	2.50	1.10	.30
☐ 11 Al Smith	2.50	1.10	.30
☐ 12 Early Wynn	5.00	2.20	.60

1962 White Sox Ticket Stubs

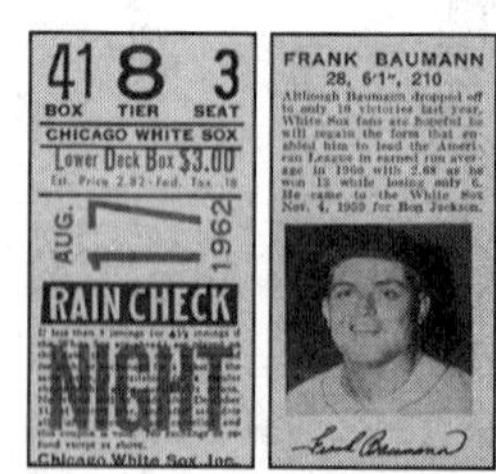

This stubs featured White Sox players. The stubs had the player photo imprinted so fans could have more keepsakes of their favorite players.

	NRMT	VG-E	GOOD
COMPLETE SET	85.00	38.00	10.50
COMMON TICKET STUB	3.00	1.35	.35
☐ 1 Luis Aparicio	7.50	3.40	.95
☐ 2 Frank Baumann	3.00	1.35	.35
☐ 3 John Buzhardt	3.00	1.35	.35
☐ 4 Camilo Carreon	3.00	1.35	.35
☐ 5 Joe Cunningham	3.00	1.35	.35
☐ 6 Bob Farley	3.00	1.35	.35
☐ 7 Eddie Fisher	3.00	1.35	.35
☐ 8 Nelson Fox	7.50	3.40	.95
☐ 9 Jim Landis	3.00	1.35	.35
☐ 10 Sherm Lollar	4.00	1.80	.50
☐ 11 Al Lopez MG	5.00	2.20	.60
☐ 12 Turk Lown	3.00	1.35	.35
☐ 13 J.C. Martin	3.00	1.35	.35
☐ 14 Cal McLish	3.00	1.35	.35
☐ 15 Gary Peters	4.00	1.80	.50
☐ 16 Juan Pizarro	4.00	1.80	.50
☐ 17 Floyd Robinson	3.00	1.35	.35
☐ 18 Bob Roselli	3.00	1.35	.35
☐ 19 Herb Score	5.00	2.20	.60
☐ 20 Al Smith	3.00	1.35	.35
☐ 21 Charles Smith	3.00	1.35	.35
☐ 22 Early Wynn	10.00	4.50	1.25

1963 White Sox Jay Publishing

This 12-card set of the Chicago White Sox measures approximately 5" by 7". The fronts feature black-and-white posed player photos with the player's and team name printed below in the white border. These cards were packaged 12 to a packet. The backs are blank. The cards are unnumbered and checklisted below in alphabetical order.

	NRMT	VG-E	GOOD
COMPLETE SET (12)	25.00	11.00	3.10
COMMON CARD (1-12)	2.00	.90	.25
☐ 1 Camilio Carreon	2.00	.90	.25
☐ 2 Joe Cunningham	2.00	.90	.25
☐ 3 Ron Hansen	2.00	.90	.25
☐ 4 Ray Herbert	2.00	.90	.25
☐ 5 Mike Hershberger	2.00	.90	.25
☐ 6 Joel Horlen	2.00	.90	.25
☐ 7 Jim Landis	2.00	.90	.25
☐ 8 Al Lopez MG	4.00	1.80	.50
☐ 9 Dave Nicholson	2.00	.90	.25
☐ 10 Gary Peters	3.00	1.35	.35
☐ 11 Juan Pizarro	3.00	1.35	.35
☐ 12 Pete Ward	2.00	.90	.25

1963 White Sox Ticket Stubs

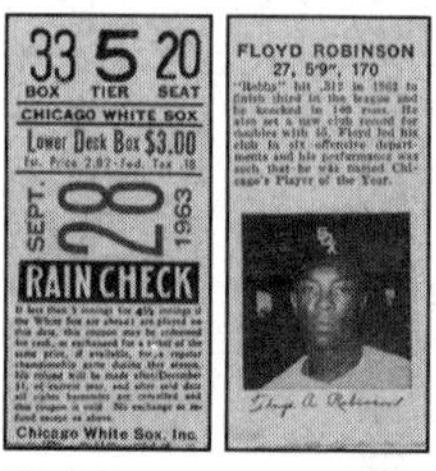

Again, the White Sox featured player photos on their ticket stubs. These photos were originally the idea of Hall of Famer Bill Vecck, but the promotion continued even after he had sold all his interest in the White Sox.

	NRMT	VG-E	GOOD
COMPLETE SET	85.00	38.00	10.50
COMMON PLAYER	3.00	1.35	.35
☐ 1 Frank Baumann	3.00	1.35	.35
☐ 2 John Buzhardt	3.00	1.35	.35
☐ 3 Camilo Carreon	3.00	1.35	.35
☐ 4 Joe Cunningham	3.00	1.35	.35
☐ 5 Dave DeBusschere	5.00	2.20	.60
☐ 6 Eddie Fisher	3.00	1.35	.35
☐ 7 Nelson Fox	7.50	3.40	.95
☐ 8 Ron Hansen	4.00	1.80	.50
☐ 9 Ray Herbert	3.00	1.35	.35
☐ 10 Mike Hershberger	3.00	1.35	.35
☐ 11 Grover Jones	3.00	1.35	.35
☐ 12 Mike Joyce	3.00	1.35	.35
☐ 13 Frank Kreutzer	3.00	1.35	.35
☐ 14 Jim Landis	3.00	1.35	.35
☐ 15 Al Lopez MG	5.00	2.20	.60
☐ 16 J.C. Martin	3.00	1.35	.35
☐ 17 Charlie Maxwell	3.00	1.35	.35
☐ 18 Dave Nicholson	3.00	1.35	.35
☐ 19 Juan Pizarro	4.00	1.80	.50
☐ 20 Floyd Robinson	3.00	1.35	.35
☐ 21 Charlie Smith	3.00	1.35	.35
☐ 22 Pete Ward	3.00	1.35	.35
☐ 23 Al Weis	3.00	1.35	.35
☐ 24 Hoyt Wilhelm	7.50	3.40	.95

1964 White Sox Ticket Stubs

For the fifth consecutive year, White Sox players were featured on these collector strips. These stubs were collected so fans could have another way of collecting memorabilia of their favorite players.

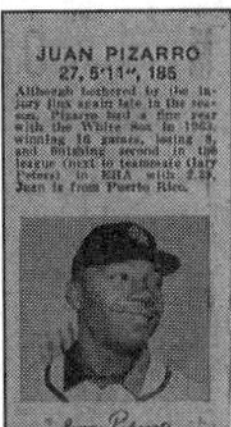

	NRMT	VG-E	GOOD
COMPLETE SET	75.00	34.00	9.50
COMMON PLAYER	3.50	1.55	.45
☐ 1 Fritz Ackley	3.50	1.55	.45
☐ 2 Frank Baumann	3.50	1.55	.45
☐ 3 Don Buford	3.50	1.55	.45
☐ 4 John Buzhardt	3.50	1.55	.45
☐ 5 Camilo Carreon	3.50	1.55	.45
☐ 6 Joe Cunningham	3.50	1.55	.45
☐ 7 Dave DeBusschere	5.00	2.20	.60
☐ 8 Eddie Fisher	3.50	1.55	.45
☐ 9 Jim Golden	3.50	1.55	.45
☐ 10 Ron Hansen	3.50	1.55	.45
☐ 11 Ray Herbert	3.50	1.55	.45
☐ 12 Mike Hershberger	3.50	1.55	.45
☐ 13 Joe Horlen	3.50	1.55	.45
☐ 14 Jim Landis	3.50	1.55	.45
☐ 15 Al Lopez MG	5.00	2.20	.60
☐ 16 J.C. Martin	3.50	1.55	.45
☐ 17 Dave Nicholson	3.50	1.55	.45
☐ 18 Gary Peters	4.00	1.80	.50
☐ 20 Floyd Robinson	3.50	1.55	.45
☐ 21 Gene Stephens	3.50	1.55	.45
☐ 22 Pete Ward	4.00	1.80	.50
☐ 23 Hoyt Wilhelm	5.00	2.20	.60

1965 White Sox Jay Publishing

This 12-card set of the Chicago White Sox measures approximately 5" by 7". The fronts feature black-and-white posed player photos with the player's and team name printed below in the white border. These cards were packaged 12 to a packet. The backs are blank. The cards are unnumbered and checklisted below in alphabetical order.

	NRMT	VG-E	GOOD
COMPLETE SET (12)	25.00	11.00	3.10
COMMON CARD (1-12)	2.00	.90	.25
☐ 1 Ron Hansen	2.00	.90	.25
☐ 2 Al Lopez MG	3.50	1.55	.45
☐ 3 J.C. Martin	2.00	.90	.25
☐ 4 Tom McCraw	2.00	.90	.25
☐ 5 Dave Nicholson	2.00	.90	.25
☐ 6 Gary Peters	2.50	1.10	.30
☐ 7 Juan Pizzaro	2.50	1.10	.30
☐ 8 Floyd Robinson	2.00	.90	.25
☐ 9 John Romano	2.00	.90	.25
☐ 10 Bill Skowron	2.00	.90	.25
☐ 11 Pete Ward	2.00	.90	.25
☐ 12 Hoyt Wilhelm	3.50	1.55	.45

1966 White Sox Team Issue

This 12-card set of the Chicago White Sox measures 4 7/8" by 7" and features black-and-white player photos in a white border with blank backs. These cards were originally packaged 12 to a packet. The cards are unnumbered and checklisted below in alphabetical order.

	NRMT	VG-E	GOOD
COMPLETE SET (12)	25.00	11.00	3.10
COMMON CARD (1-12)	2.00	.90	.25
☐ 1 Jerry Adair	2.00	.90	.25
☐ 2 Tom Agee	2.00	.90	.25
☐ 3 Ken Berry	2.00	.90	.25
☐ 4 Don Buford	2.00	.90	.25
☐ 5 Ron Hansen	2.00	.90	.25
☐ 6 Joe Horlen	2.00	.90	.25
☐ 7 Tommy John	5.00	2.20	.60
☐ 8 Duane Josephson	2.00	.90	.25
☐ 9 Tom McCraw	2.00	.90	.25
☐ 10 Gary Peters	2.00	.90	.25
☐ 11 Ed Stanky MG	2.00	.90	.25
☐ 12 Pete Ward	2.00	.90	.25

1969 White Sox Team Issue

This 12-card set of the Chicago White Sox measures approximately 4 1/4" by 7". The fronts display black-and-white player portraits bordered in white. The player's name and team are printed in the top margin. The backs are blank. The cards are unnumbered and checklisted below in alphabetical order.

	NRMT	VG-E	GOOD
COMPLETE SET (12)	20.00	9.00	2.50
COMMON CARD (1-12)	1.50	.70	.19
☐ 1 Sandy Alomar	2.00	.90	.25
☐ 2 Luis Aparicio	3.00	1.35	.35
☐ 3 Ken Berry	1.50	.70	.19
☐ 4 Charles Bradford	1.50	.70	.19
☐ 5 Joe Horlen	1.50	.70	.19
☐ 6 Tommy John	2.50	1.10	.30
☐ 7 Duane Josephson	1.50	.70	.19
☐ 8 Al Lopez	2.50	1.10	.30
☐ 9 Carlos May	1.50	.70	.19
☐ 10 Bill Melton	2.00	.90	.25
☐ 11 Gary Peters	2.00	.90	.25
☐ 12 Pete Ward	1.50	.70	.19

1970 White Sox Team Issue

This 12-card set of the Chicago White Sox measures approximately 4 1/4" by 7" and features black-and-white player photos in a white border. Packaged 12 to a packet with blank backs, the cards are unnumbered and checklisted below in alphabetical order.

	NRMT	VG-E	GOOD
COMPLETE CARD (12)	30.00	13.50	3.70
COMMON CARD (1-12)	2.00	.90	.25
☐ 1 Luis Aparicio	7.50	3.40	.95
☐ 2 Ken Berry	2.00	.90	.25
☐ 3 Charles Bradford	2.00	.90	.25
☐ 4 Don Gutteridge MG	2.00	.90	.25
☐ 5 Gail Hopkins	2.00	.90	.25
☐ 6 Joe Horlen	2.00	.90	.25
☐ 7 Tommy John	5.00	2.20	.60
☐ 8 Duane Josephson	2.00	.90	.25
☐ 9 Bobby Knoop	2.00	.90	.25
☐ 10 Carlos May	3.00	1.35	.35
☐ 11 Bill Melton	3.00	1.35	.35
☐ 12 Walter Williams	2.00	.90	.25

1972 White Sox

The 1972 Chicago White Sox are featured in this set of 12 approximately 7 1/2" by 9 3/8" glossy color player photos. The photos are bordered in white, and the player's name is given below the picture. The backs are blank and the photos are checklisted below in alphabetical order.

	NRMT	VG-E	GOOD
COMPLETE SET (12)	28.00	12.50	3.50
COMMON CARD (1-12)	2.50	1.10	.30
☐ 1 Dick Allen	3.50	1.55	.45
☐ 2 Stan Bahnsen	3.00	1.35	.35
☐ 3 Terry Forster	3.00	1.35	.35
☐ 4 Ken Henderson	2.50	1.10	.30
☐ 5 Ed Herrmann	2.50	1.10	.30
☐ 6 Pat Kelly	3.00	1.35	.35
☐ 7 Eddie Leon	2.50	1.10	.30
☐ 8 Carlos May	2.50	1.10	.30
☐ 9 Bill Melton	3.00	1.35	.35
☐ 10 Jorge Orta	3.00	1.35	.35
☐ 11 Steve Stone	3.50	1.55	.45
☐ 12 Wilbur Wood	3.00	1.35	.35

1972 White Sox Chi-Foursome

These drawings feature members of the Chicago White Sox. These drawings measure 11" by 14" and also have the player's fascimile signature. The backs are blank and we have sequenced this set in alphabetical order.

	NRMT	VG-E	GOOD
COMPLETE SET (7)	40.00	18.00	5.00
COMMON CARD (1-7)	5.00	2.20	.60
☐ 1 Mike Andrews	5.00	2.20	.60
☐ 2 Ed Herrmann	5.00	2.20	.60
☐ 3 Pat Kelly	5.00	2.20	.60
☐ 4 Carlos May	6.50	2.90	.80
☐ 5 Bill Melton	6.50	2.90	.80
☐ 6 Chuck Tanner MG	6.50	2.90	.80
☐ 7 Wilbur Wood	7.50	3.40	.95

1972 White Sox Durochrome Stickers

These stickers measure 3 1/2" by 4 1/2". They are unnumbered and we have sequenced them in alphabetical order.

	NRMT	VG-E	GOOD
COMPLETE SET (6)	12.00	5.50	1.50
COMMON PLAYER (1-6)	1.50	.70	.19
☐ 1 Dick Allen	3.50	1.55	.45
☐ 2 Ed Herrmann	1.50	.70	.19
☐ 3 Bart Johnson	1.50	.70	.19
☐ 4 Carlos May	1.50	.70	.19
☐ 5 Bill Melton	2.00	.90	.25
☐ 6 Wilbur Wood	3.00	1.35	.35

1975 White Sox 1919 TCMA

This 28-card set features the 1919 Chicago White Sox Team. The fronts display black-and-white player photos while the backs carry player statistics. The set includes one team picture jumbo card which measures approximately 3 1/2" by 4 3/4". The cards are unnumbered and checklisted below in alphabetical order.

	NRMT	VG-E	GOOD
COMPLETE SET (28)	25.00	11.00	3.10
COMMON CARD (1-28)	.50	.23	.06
☐ 1 Joe Benz	.50	.23	.06
☐ 2 Eddie Cicotte	2.00	.90	.25
☐ 3 Eddie Collins	3.00	1.35	.35
☐ 4 Shano Collins	.50	.23	.06
☐ 5 Dave Danforth	.50	.23	.06
☐ 6 Red Faber	2.00	.90	.25
☐ 7 Happy Felsch	1.50	.70	.19
☐ 8 Charles "Chick" Gandil	1.50	.70	.19
☐ 9 Kid Gleason MG	1.00	.45	.12
☐ 10 Joe Jackson	5.00	2.20	.60
☐ 11 Bill James	.50	.23	.06
☐ 12 Dickie Kerr	1.00	.45	.12
☐ 13 Nemo Leibold	.50	.23	.06
☐ 14 Byrd Lynn	.50	.23	.06
☐ 15 Erskine Mayer	.50	.23	.06
☐ 16 Harvey McClellan	.50	.23	.06
☐ 17 Fred McMullin	.50	.23	.06
☐ 18 Eddie Murphy	.50	.23	.06
☐ 19 Pat Ragan	.50	.23	.06
☐ 20 Swede Risberg	1.00	.45	.12
☐ 21 Charlie Robertson	.50	.23	.06
☐ 22 Red Russell	.50	.23	.06
☐ 23 Ray Schalk	2.00	.90	.25
☐ 24 Frank Shellenback	.50	.23	.06
Grover Lowdermilk			
Joe Jenkins			
Dickie Kerr			
Ray Schalk			
☐ 25 Buck Weaver	2.00	.90	.25
☐ 26 Roy Wilkinson	.50	.23	.06
☐ 27 Lefty Williams	.50	.23	.06
☐ 28 Team Picture	1.00	.45	.12

1976 White Sox TCMA All-Time Greats

All-Time Chicago White Sox

Eddie Robinson	1B
Eddie Collins	2B
Willie Kamm	3B
Luke Appling	SS
Ray Schalk	C
Al Simmons	LF
Johnny Mostil	CF
Harry Hooper	RF
Ted Lyons	RHP
Billy Pierce	LHP
Gerry Staley	RP
Al Lopez	Mgr

This 12-card set of the All-Time Chicago White Sox Team features black-and-white player photos bordered in white with the player's name and position printed in red in the bottom margin. The white backs carry the roster of the team. The cards are unnumbered and checklisted below in alphabetical order.

	NRMT	VG-E	GOOD
COMPLETE SET (12)	10.00	4.50	1.25
COMMON CARD (1-12)	.50	.23	.06
☐ 1 Luke Appling	1.00	.45	.12
☐ 2 Eddie Collins	1.50	.70	.19
☐ 3 Harry Hooper	1.00	.45	.12
☐ 4 Willie Kamm	.50	.23	.06
☐ 5 Al Lopez MG	.75	.35	.09
☐ 6 Ted Lyons	1.00	.45	.12
☐ 7 Johnny Mostil	.50	.23	.06
☐ 8 Billy Pierce	.75	.35	.09
☐ 9 Eddie Robinson	.50	.23	.06
☐ 10 Ray Schalk	.75	.35	.09
☐ 11 Al Simmons	1.50	.70	.19
☐ 12 Gerry Staley	.50	.23	.06

1977 White Sox Jewel Tea

This 16-card set of the Chicago White Sox measures approximately 5 7/8" by 9". The white-bordered fronts feature color player head photos with a facsimile autograph below. The backs are blank. The cards are unnumbered and checklisted below in alphabetical order.

	NRMT	VG-E	GOOD
COMPLETE SET (16)	15.00	6.75	1.85
COMMON CARD (1-16)	1.00	.45	.12
☐ 1 Alan Bannister	1.00	.45	.12
☐ 2 Francisco Barrios	1.00	.45	.12
☐ 3 Jim Essian	1.00	.45	.12
☐ 4 Oscar Gamble	1.50	.70	.19
☐ 5 Ralph Garr	1.50	.70	.19
☐ 6 Lamar Johnson	1.00	.45	.12
☐ 7 Chris Knapp	1.00	.45	.12
☐ 8 Ken Kravec	1.00	.45	.12

☐ 9 Lerrin LaGrow	1.00	.45	.12
☐ 10 Chet Lemon	1.50	.70	.19
☐ 11 Jorge Orta	1.00	.45	.12
☐ 12 Eric Soderholm	1.00	.45	.12
☐ 13 Jim Spencer	1.00	.45	.12
☐ 14 Steve Stone	1.50	.70	.19
☐ 15 Wilbur Wood	1.00	.45	.12
☐ 16 Richie Zisk	1.50	.70	.19

1980 White Sox Greats TCMA

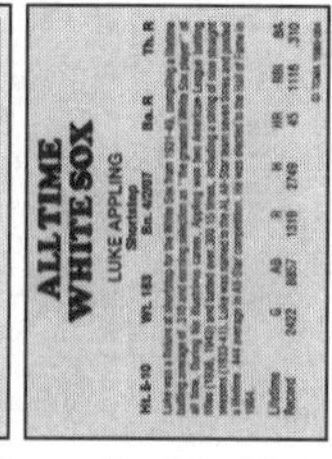

This 12-card standard-size set features various all-time White Sox greats. The fronts display a player photo, while the backs carry information about the player.

	MINT	NRMT	EXC
COMPLETE SET (12)	5.00	2.20	.60
COMMON CARD (1-12)	.25	.11	.03
☐ 1 Ted Lyons	.75	.35	.09
☐ 2 Eddie Collins	1.00	.45	.12
☐ 3 Al Lopez MG	.50	.23	.06
☐ 4 Luke Appling	1.00	.45	.12
☐ 5 Billy Pierce	.50	.23	.06
☐ 6 Willie Kamm	.25	.11	.03
☐ 7 Johnny Mostil	.25	.11	.03
☐ 8 Al Simmons	.75	.35	.09
☐ 9 Ray Schalk	.75	.35	.09
☐ 10 Gerry Staley	.25	.11	.03
☐ 11 Harry Hooper	.75	.35	.09
☐ 12 Eddie Robinson	.25	.11	.03

1983 White Sox True Value

This 23-card set was sponsored by True Value Hardware Stores and features full-color (approximately 2 5/8" by 4 1/4") cards of the Chicago White Sox. Most of the set was intended for distribution two cards per game at selected White Sox Tuesday night home games. The cards are unnumbered except for uniform number given in the lower right corner of the obverse. The card backs contain statistical information in basic black and white. The cards of Harold Baines, Salome Barojas, and Marc Hill were not issued at the park; hence they are more difficult to obtain than the other 20 cards and are marked SP in the checklist below.

	NRMT	VG-E	GOOD
COMPLETE SET (23)	35.00	16.00	4.40
COMMON CARD	.50	.23	.06
☐ 1 Scott Fletcher	.50	.23	.06
☐ 3 Harold Baines SP	.75	.35	.09
☐ 5 Vance Law	.50	.23	.06
☐ 7 Marc Hill SP	5.00	2.20	.60
☐ 10 Tony LaRussa MG	1.50	.70	.19
☐ 11 Rudy Law	.50	.23	.06
☐ 14 Tony Bernazard	.50	.23	.06
☐ 17 Jerry Hairston	.50	.23	.06
☐ 19 Greg Luzinski	1.25	.55	.16
☐ 24 Floyd Bannister	.50	.23	.06
☐ 25 Mike Squires	.50	.23	.06
☐ 30 Salome Barojas SP	5.00	2.20	.60
☐ 31 LaMarr Hoyt	.75	.35	.09
☐ 34 Richard Dotson	.50	.23	.06
☐ 36 Jerry Koosman	1.00	.45	.12
☐ 40 Britt Burns	.50	.23	.06
☐ 41 Dick Tidrow	.50	.23	.06
☐ 42 Ron Kittle	1.25	.55	.16
☐ 44 Tom Paciorek	1.00	.45	.12
☐ 45 Kevin Hickey	.50	.23	.06
☐ 53 Dennis Lamp	.50	.23	.06
☐ 67 Jim Kern	.50	.23	.06
☐ 72 Carlton Fisk	7.50	3.40	.95

1984 White Sox True Value

This 30-card set features full color (approximately 2 1/2" by 4") cards of the Chicago White Sox. Most of the set was distributed two cards per game at selected White Sox Tuesday home games. Faust and Minoso were not given out although their cards were available

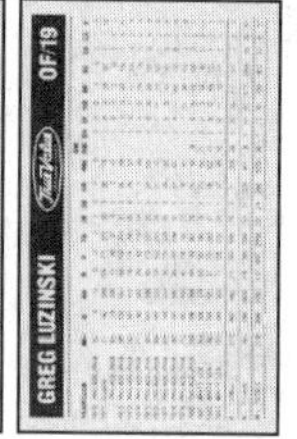

through direct (promotional) contact with them. Brennan and Hulett were not released directly since they were sent down to the minors. The cards are unnumbered except for uniform number given in the lower right corner of the obverse; they are arbitrarily listed below in alphabetical order. The card backs contain statistical information in basic black and white.

	NRMT	VG-E	GOOD
COMPLETE SET (30)	25.00	11.00	3.10
COMMON CARD (1-30)	.50	.23	.06
☐ 1 Juan Agosto	.50	.23	.06
☐ 2 Luis Aparicio	3.00	1.35	.35
☐ 3 Harold Baines	2.00	.90	.25
☐ 4 Floyd Bannister	.50	.23	.06
☐ 5 Salome Barojas	.50	.23	.06
☐ 6 Tom Brennan SP	3.00	1.35	.35
☐ 7 Britt Burns	.50	.23	.06
☐ 8 Coaching Staff (Blank back)	.75	.35	.09
☐ 9 Julio Cruz	.50	.23	.06
☐ 10 Richard Dotson	.50	.23	.06
☐ 11 Jerry Dybzinski	.50	.23	.06
☐ 12 Nancy Faust ORG (Blank back)	2.00	.90	.25
☐ 13 Carlton Fisk	6.00	2.70	.75
☐ 14 Scott Fletcher	.50	.23	.06
☐ 15 Jerry Hairston	.50	.23	.06
☐ 16 Marc Hill	.50	.23	.06
☐ 17 LaMarr Hoyt	.50	.23	.06
☐ 18 Tim Hulett SP	3.00	1.35	.35
☐ 19 Ron Kittle	.75	.35	.09
☐ 20 Tony LaRussa MG	1.25	.55	.16
☐ 21 Rudy Law	.50	.23	.06
☐ 22 Vance Law	.50	.23	.06
☐ 23 Greg Luzinski	1.25	.55	.16
☐ 24 Minnie Minoso	3.00	1.35	.35
☐ 25 Tom Paciorek	1.00	.45	.12
☐ 26 Ron Reed	.50	.23	.06
☐ 27 Tom Seaver	6.00	2.70	.75
☐ 28 Dave Stegman	.50	.23	.06
☐ 29 Mike Squires	.50	.23	.06
☐ 30 Greg Walker	.75	.35	.09

1985 White Sox Coke

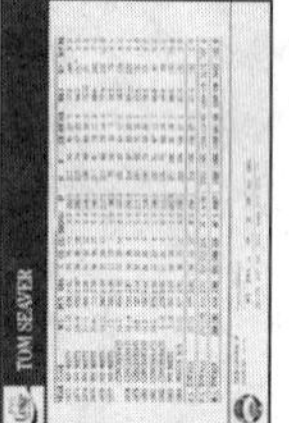

This 30-card set features present and past Chicago White Sox players and personnel. Cards measure approximately 2 5/8" by 4 1/8" and feature a red band at the bottom of the card. Within the red band are the White Sox logo, the player's name, position, uniform number, and a small oval portrait of an all-time White Sox Great at a similar position. The cards were available two at a time at Tuesday night White Sox home games or as a complete set through membership in the Coca-Cola White Sox Fan Club. The cards below are numbered by uniform number; the last three cards are unnumbered.

	NRMT	VG-E	GOOD
COMPLETE SET (30)	12.00	5.50	1.50
COMMON PAIR	.25	.11	.03
☐ 0 Oscar Gamble Zeke Bonura	.25	.11	.03
☐ 1 Scott Fletcher Luke Appling	1.00	.45	.12
☐ 3 Harold Baines Bill Melton	.75	.35	.09
☐ 5 Luis Salazar Chico Carrasquel	.25	.11	.03
☐ 7 Marc Hill Sherm Lollar	.25	.11	.03
☐ 8 Daryl Boston Jim Landis	.25	.11	.03
☐ 10 Tony LaRussa MG Al Lopez MG	1.00	.45	.12
☐ 12 Julio Cruz Nellie Fox	1.00	.45	.12
☐ 13 Ozzie Guillen Luis Aparicio	2.50	1.10	.30
☐ 17 Jerry Hairston Smoky Burgess	.25	.11	.03
☐ 20 Joe DeSa Carlos May	.25	.11	.03
☐ 22 Joel Skinner J.C. Martin	.25	.11	.03
☐ 23 Rudy Law Bill Skowron	.25	.11	.03
☐ 24 Floyd Bannister Red Faber	.50	.23	.06
☐ 29 Greg Walker Dick Allen	.75	.35	.09
☐ 30 Gene Nelson Early Wynn	1.00	.45	.12
☐ 32 Tim Hulett Pete Ward	.25	.11	.03
☐ 34 Richard Dotson Ed Walsh	.50	.23	.06
☐ 37 Dan Spillner Thornton Lee	.25	.11	.03
☐ 40 Britt Burns Gary Peters	.25	.11	.03
☐ 41 Tom Seaver Ted Lyons	2.50	1.10	.30
☐ 42 Ron Kittle Minnie Minoso	1.00	.45	.12
☐ 43 Bob James Hoyt Wilhelm	.25	.11	.03
☐ 44 Tom Paciorek Eddie Collins	1.00	.45	.12
☐ 46 Tim Lollar Billy Pierce	.50	.23	.06
☐ 50 Juan Agosto Wilbur Wood	.25	.11	.03
☐ 72 Carlton Fisk Ray Schalk	2.50	1.10	.30
☐ NNO Comiskey Park	.25	.11	.03
☐ NNO Nancy Faust ORG	.25	.11	.03
☐ NNO Ribbie and Roobarb	.25	.11	.03

1986 White Sox Coke

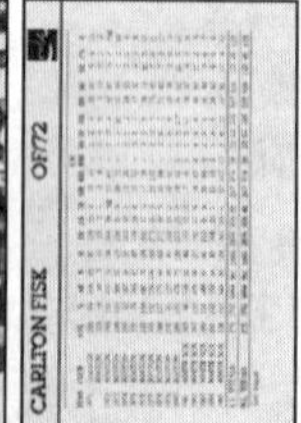

This colorful 30-card set features a borderless photo on top of a blue-on-white name, position, and uniform number. Card backs provide complete major and minor season-by-season career statistical information. Since the cards are unnumbered, they are numbered below according to uniform number. The cards measure approximately 2 5/8" by 4". The five unnumbered non-player cards are listed at the end of the checklist below.

	MINT	NRMT	EXC
COMPLETE SET (30)	12.00	5.50	1.50
COMMON CARD	.25	.11	.03
☐ 1 Wayne Tolleson	.25	.11	.03
☐ 3 Harold Baines	1.25	.55	.16
☐ 7 Marc Hill	.25	.11	.03
☐ 8 Daryl Boston	.25	.11	.03
☐ 12 Julio Cruz	.25	.11	.03
☐ 13 Ozzie Guillen	1.25	.55	.16
☐ 17 Jerry Hairston	.25	.11	.03
☐ 19 Floyd Bannister	.25	.11	.03
☐ 20 Reid Nichols	.25	.11	.03
☐ 22 Joel Skinner	.25	.11	.03
☐ 24 Dave Schmidt	.25	.11	.03
☐ 26 Bobby Bonilla	3.00	1.35	.35
☐ 29 Greg Walker	.25	.11	.03
☐ 30 Gene Nelson	.25	.11	.03
☐ 32 Tim Hulett	.25	.11	.03
☐ 33 Neil Allen	.25	.11	.03
☐ 34 Richard Dotson	.25	.11	.03
☐ 40 Joe Cowley	.25	.11	.03
☐ 41 Tom Seaver	3.00	1.35	.35
☐ 42 Ron Kittle	.50	.23	.06
☐ 43 Bob James	.25	.11	.03
☐ 44 John Cangelosi	.25	.11	.03
☐ 50 Juan Agosto	.25	.11	.03
☐ 52 Joel Davis	.25	.11	.03
☐ 72 Carlton Fisk	3.00	1.35	.35
☐ NNO Nancy Faust ORG	.25	.11	.03
☐ NNO Ken(Hawk) Harrelson GM	.50	.23	.06
☐ NNO Tony LaRussa MG	.75	.35	.09
☐ NNO Minnie Minoso CO	.75	.35	.09
☐ NNO Ribbie and Roobarb	.25	.11	.03

1987 White Sox Coke

This colorful 30-card set features a card front with a blue-bordered photo and name, position, and uniform number. Card backs provide complete major and minor season-by-season career statistical information. Since the cards are unnumbered, they are numbered below in alphabetical order. The cards measure approximately 2 5/8" by 4". The card set, sponsored by Coca-Cola, is an exclusive for fan club members who join (for 10.00) in 1987.

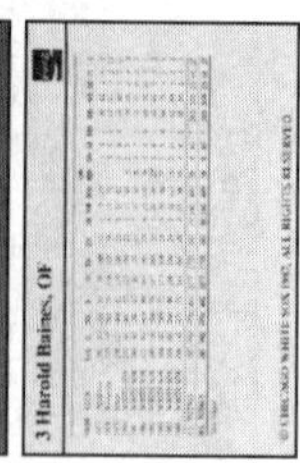

	MINT	NRMT	EXC
COMPLETE SET (30)	12.00	5.50	1.50
COMMON CARD (1-30)	.25	.11	.03
☐ 1 Neil Allen	.25	.11	.03
☐ 2 Harold Baines	1.50	.70	.19
☐ 3 Floyd Bannister	.25	.11	.03
☐ 4 Daryl Boston	.25	.11	.03
☐ 5 Ivan Calderon	.50	.23	.06
☐ 6 Joel Davis	.25	.11	.03
☐ 7 Jose DeLeon	.25	.11	.03
☐ 8 Richard Dotson	.25	.11	.03
☐ 9 Nancy Faust ORG	.25	.11	.03
☐ 10 Carlton Fisk	3.00	1.35	.35
☐ 11 Jim Fregosi MG	.25	.11	.03
☐ 12 Ozzie Guillen	.75	.35	.09
☐ 13 Jerry Hairston	.25	.11	.03
☐ 14 Ron Hassey	.25	.11	.03
☐ 15 Donnie Hill	.25	.11	.03
☐ 16 Tim Hulett	.25	.11	.03
☐ 17 Bob James	.25	.11	.03
☐ 18 Ron Karkovice	.50	.23	.06
☐ 19 Steve Lyons	.25	.11	.03
☐ 20 Fred Manrique	.25	.11	.03
☐ 21 Joel McKeon	.25	.11	.03
☐ 22 Minnie Minoso	1.00	.45	.12
☐ 23 Russ Morman	.25	.11	.03
☐ 24 Gary Redus	.25	.11	.03
☐ 25 Ribbie and Roobarb	.25	.11	.03
☐ 26 Jerry Royster	.25	.11	.03
☐ 27 Ray Searage	.25	.11	.03
☐ 28 Bobby Thigpen	.50	.23	.06
☐ 29 Greg Walker	.25	.11	.03
☐ 30 Jim Winn	.25	.11	.03

1988 White Sox Coke

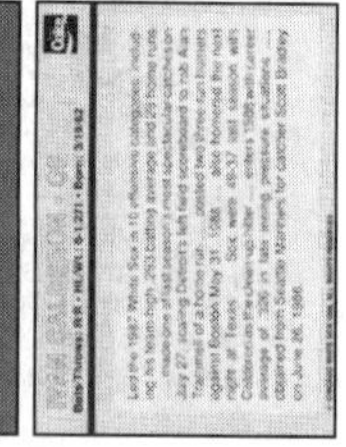

This colorful 30-card set features a card front with a red-bordered photo and name and position. Card backs provide a narrative without any statistical tables. Since the cards are unnumbered, they are numbered below in alphabetical order according to the subject's name or card's title. The cards measure approximately 2 5/8" by 3 1/2". The card set, sponsored by Coca-Cola, was for fan club members who join (for 10.00) in 1988. The cards were also given out at the May 22nd game at Comiskey Park. These cards do not even list the player's uniform number anywhere on the card. Card backs are printed in black and gray on thin white card stock.

	MINT	NRMT	EXC
COMPLETE SET (30)	8.00	3.60	1.00
COMMON CARD (1-30)	.25	.11	.03
☐ 1 Harold Baines	1.00	.45	.12
☐ 2 Daryl Boston	.25	.11	.03
☐ 3 Ivan Calderon	.25	.11	.03
☐ 4 Comiskey Park	.25	.11	.03
☐ 5 John Davis	.25	.11	.03
☐ 6 Nancy Faust ORG	.25	.11	.03
☐ 7 Jim Fregosi MG	.25	.11	.03
☐ 8 Carlton Fisk	2.00	.90	.25
☐ 9 Ozzie Guillen	.75	.35	.09
☐ 10 Donnie Hill	.25	.11	.03
☐ 11 Ricky Horton	.25	.11	.03
☐ 12 Lance Johnson	2.00	.90	.25
☐ 13 Dave LaPoint	.25	.11	.03
☐ 14 Bill Long	.25	.11	.03
☐ 15 Steve Lyons	.25	.11	.03
☐ 16 Jack McDowell	2.50	1.10	.30
☐ 17 Fred Manrique	.25	.11	.03
☐ 18 Minnie Minoso CO	1.00	.45	.12
☐ 19 Dan Pasqua	.25	.11	.03
☐ 20 John Pawlowski	.25	.11	.03
☐ 21 Melido Perez	.25	.11	.03
☐ 22 Billy Pierce	.50	.23	.06
☐ 23 Jerry Reuss	.50	.23	.06
☐ 24 Gary Redus	.25	.11	.03
☐ 25 Ribbie and Roobarb	.25	.11	.03
☐ 26 Mark Salas	.25	.11	.03
☐ 27 Jose Segura	.25	.11	.03

☐ 28 Bobby Thigpen	.50	.23	.06
☐ 29 Greg Walker	.25	.11	.03
☐ 30 Kenny Williams	.25	.11	.03

1988 White Sox Kodak

This five-card, approximately 8" by 11 1/2" set was issued by Kodak including members of the 1988 Chicago White Sox. The cards are borderless and say "1988 Kodak Collectible Series" on top with the player's photo dominating the middle of the photo. Underneath the photo is a facsimile autograph and on the bottom left of the photo is an advertisment for Kodak and the bottom right of the card the White Sox logo is featured.

	MINT	NRMT	EXC
COMPLETE SET (5)	8.00	3.60	1.00
COMMON CARD (1-5)	1.50	.70	.19
☐ 1 Ozzie Guillen	2.50	1.10	.30
☐ 2 Carlton Fisk	4.00	1.80	.50
☐ 3 Rick Horton	1.50	.70	.19
☐ 4 Ivan Calderon	1.50	.70	.19
☐ 5 Harold Baines	3.00	1.35	.35

1989 White Sox Coke

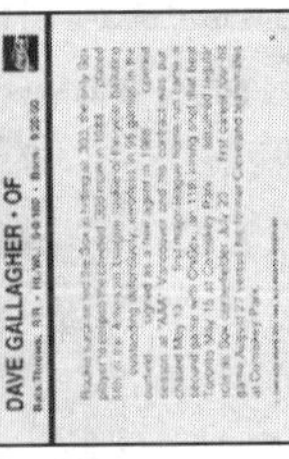

The 1989 Coke Chicago White Sox set contains 30 cards measuring approximately 2 5/8" by 3 1/2". The players in the set represent the White Sox opening day roster. The fronts are blue. The horizontally oriented backs are gray and white, and feature biographical information. The set was a promotional give-away August 10, 1989 at the Baseball Card Night game against the Oakland A's to the first 15,000 fans. The set includes a special "New Comiskey Park, 1991" card. The complete set was also available with (10.00) membership in the Chi-Sox Fan Club. The cards in the set are numbered on the backs in the lower right corner in very small print.

	MINT	NRMT	EXC
COMPLETE SET (30)	8.00	3.60	1.00
COMMON CARD (1-30)	.25	.11	.03
☐ 1 New Comiskey Park 1991	.25	.11	.03
☐ 2 Comiskey Park	.25	.11	.03
☐ 3 Jeff Torborg MG	.25	.11	.03
☐ 4 Coaching Staff	.25	.11	.03
☐ 5 Harold Baines	.75	.35	.09
☐ 6 Daryl Boston	.25	.11	.03
☐ 7 Ivan Calderon	.50	.23	.06
☐ 8 Carlton Fisk	1.50	.70	.19
☐ 9 Dave Gallagher	.25	.11	.03
☐ 10 Ozzie Guillen	.75	.35	.09
☐ 11 Shawn Hillegas	.25	.11	.03
☐ 12 Barry Jones	.25	.11	.03
☐ 13 Ron Karkovice	.25	.11	.03
☐ 14 Eric King	.25	.11	.03
☐ 15 Ron Kittle	.25	.11	.03
☐ 16 Bill Long	.25	.11	.03
☐ 17 Steve Lyons	.25	.11	.03
☐ 18 Donn Pall	.25	.11	.03
☐ 19 Dan Pasqua	.25	.11	.03
☐ 20 Ken Patterson	.25	.11	.03
☐ 21 Melido Perez	.25	.11	.03
☐ 22 Jerry Reuss	.50	.23	.06
☐ 23 Billy Joe Robidoux	.25	.11	.03
☐ 24 Steve Rosenberg	.25	.11	.03
☐ 25 Jeff Schaefer	.25	.11	.03
☐ 26 Bobby Thigpen	.25	.11	.03
☐ 27 Greg Walker	.25	.11	.03
☐ 28 Eddie Williams	.25	.11	.03
☐ 29 Nancy Faust ORG	.25	.11	.03
☐ 30 Minnie Minoso	.75	.35	.09

1989 White Sox Kodak

For the second consecutive year Kodak in conjunction with the Chicago White Sox issued a set about the White Sox. The 1989 set was marked by a color photo of the active star dominating the upper right half of the card with the bottom half of the card depicting two other famous White Sox players at the same position that the current

star played. This six-card, approximately 8" by 11 1/2", set was given away at various games at Comiskey Park.

	MINT	NRMT	EXC
COMPLETE SET (6)	8.00	3.60	1.00
COMMON CARD (1-6)	1.50	.70	.19
☐ 1 Greg Walker Dick Allen Ted Kluszewski	1.50	.70	.19
☐ 2 Steve Lyons Eddie Collins Nellie Fox	2.00	.90	.25
☐ 3 Carlton Fisk Sherm Lollar Ray Schalk	3.00	1.35	.35
☐ 4 Harold Baines Minnie Minoso Jim Landis	1.50	.70	.19
☐ 5 Bobby Thigpen Gerry Staley Hoyt Wilhelm	1.50	.70	.19
☐ 6 Ozzie Guillen Luke Appling Luis Aparicio	3.00	1.35	.35

1990 White Sox Coke

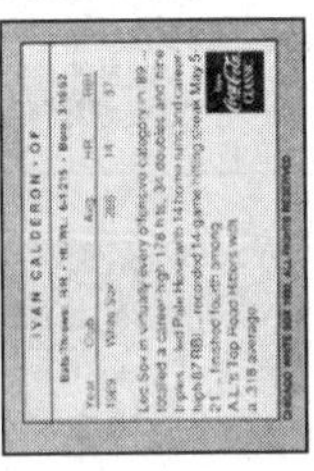

The 1990 Coca Cola White Sox set contains 30 cards. The set is a beautiful full-color set commemorating the 1990 White Sox who were celebrating the eightieth and last season played in old Comiskey Park. This (approximately) 2 5/8" by 3 1/2" set has a Comiskey Park logo on the front with 1989 statistics and a brief biography on the back. The set is checklisted alphabetically. The set features cards of Sammy Sosa and Frank Thomas appearing in their Rookie Card year.

	MINT	NRMT	EXC
COMPLETE SET (30)	30.00	13.50	3.70
COMMON CARD (1-30)	.25	.11	.03
☐ 1 Ivan Calderon	.25	.11	.03
☐ 2 Wayne Edwards	.25	.11	.03
☐ 3 Carlton Fisk	2.00	.90	.25
☐ 4 Scott Fletcher	.25	.11	.03
☐ 5 Dave Gallagher	.25	.11	.03
☐ 6 Craig Grebeck	.25	.11	.03
☐ 7 Ozzie Guillen	.75	.35	.09
☐ 8 Greg Hibbard	.25	.11	.03
☐ 9 Lance Johnson	1.00	.45	.12
☐ 10 Barry Jones	.25	.11	.03
☐ 11 Ron Karkovice	.25	.11	.03
☐ 12 Eric King	.25	.11	.03
☐ 13 Ron Kittle	.25	.11	.03
☐ 14 Jerry Kutzler	.25	.11	.03
☐ 15 Steve Lyons	.25	.11	.03
☐ 16 Carlos Martinez	.25	.11	.03
☐ 17 Jack McDowell	1.50	.70	.19
☐ 18 Donn Pall	.25	.11	.03
☐ 19 Dan Pasqua	.25	.11	.03
☐ 20 Ken Patterson	.25	.11	.03
☐ 21 Melido Perez	.25	.11	.03
☐ 22 Scott Radinsky	.25	.11	.03
☐ 23 Sammy Sosa	4.00	1.80	.50
☐ 24 Bobby Thigpen	.50	.23	.06
☐ 25 Frank Thomas	20.00	9.00	2.50
☐ 26 Jeff Torborg MG	.50	.23	.06
☐ 27 Robin Ventura	2.00	.90	.25
☐ 28 Rookies: Jerry Kutzler Wayne Edwards Craig Grebeck Scott Radinsky Robin Ventura	.75	.35	.09
☐ 29 Captains Ozzie Guillen Carlton Fisk	.50	.23	.06
☐ 30 Coaches: Barry Foote Sammy Ellis Walt Hriniak Terry Bevington Dave LaRoche Joe Nossek Ron Clark	.25	.11	.03

1990 White Sox Kodak

In 1990 Kodak again in conjunction with the Chicago White Sox issued a beautiful six-card set about some key members of the 1990 White Sox. This was slightly reduced in size (from the previous two years) to be approximately 7" by 11" and featured a full-color picture with an advertisement for Kodak on the lower left corner of the front of the card and the White Sox logo in the lower right hand corner. The cards were again borderless and blank-backed.

	MINT	NRMT	EXC
COMPLETE SET (6)	8.00	3.60	1.00
COMMON CARD (1-6)	1.25	.55	.16
☐ 1 Carlton Fisk	4.00	1.80	.50
☐ 2 Melido Perez	1.25	.55	.16
☐ 3 Ozzie Guillen	1.50	.70	.19
☐ 4 Ron Kittle	1.25	.55	.16
☐ 5 Scott Fletcher	1.25	.55	.16
☐ 6 Comiskey Park	1.25	.55	.16

1991 White Sox Kodak

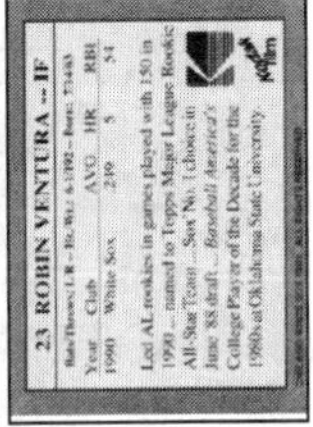

This 28-card set was sponsored by Kodak and measures approximately 2 5/8" by 3 1/2". The front design depicts borderless glossy color action player photos. A Comiskey Park insignia is superimposed at the upper left corner of the picture. The player's name appears in black lettering in a silver stripe toward the card bottom, with a black oversized (uniform) number in the lower left corner. In a horizontal format, the backs are printed in black on white with gray borders, and provide 1990 statistics and highlights. The cards are skip-numbered by uniform number and checklisted below accordingly, with the unnumbered cards listed at the end.

	MINT	NRMT	EXC
COMPLETE SET (28)	15.00	6.75	1.85
COMMON CARD	.25	.11	.03
☐ 1 Lance Johnson	1.25	.55	.16
☐ 5 Matt Merullo	.25	.11	.03
☐ 7 Scott Fletcher	.25	.11	.03
☐ 8 Bo Jackson	1.50	.70	.19
☐ 10 Jeff Torborg MG	.25	.11	.03
☐ 13 Ozzie Guillen	.75	.35	.09
☐ 14 Craig Grebeck	.25	.11	.03
☐ 20 Ron Karkovice	.25	.11	.03
☐ 21 Joey Cora	.50	.23	.06
☐ 22 Donn Pall	.25	.11	.03
☐ 23 Robin Ventura	1.50	.70	.19
☐ 25 Sammy Sosa	3.00	1.35	.35
☐ 27 Greg Hibbard	.25	.11	.03
☐ 28 Cory Snyder	.25	.11	.03
☐ 29 Jack McDowell	1.25	.55	.16
☐ 30 Tim Raines	.75	.35	.09
☐ 31 Scott Radinsky	.25	.11	.03
☐ 32 Alex Fernandez	3.00	1.35	.35
☐ 33 Melido Perez	.25	.11	.03
☐ 34 Ken Patterson	.25	.11	.03
☐ 35 Frank Thomas	7.50	3.40	.95
☐ 37 Bobby Thigpen	.25	.11	.03
☐ 44 Dan Pasqua	.25	.11	.03
☐ 45 Wayne Edwards	.25	.11	.03
☐ 49 Charlie Hough	.50	.23	.06
☐ 50 Brian Drahman	.25	.11	.03
☐ 72 Carlton Fisk	2.50	1.10	.30
☐ NNO First Draft Choices Jack McDowell Robin Ventura Alex Fernandez Frank Thomas	5.00	2.20	.60
☐ NNO0 1991 Co-Captains Carlton Fisk Ozzie Guillen	.75	.35	.09
☐ NNO 1991 Coaching Staff Walt Hriniak Sammy Ellis Terry Bevington Barry Foote Joe Nossek John Stephenson Dave LaRoche	.25	.11	.03

1992 White Sox Kodak

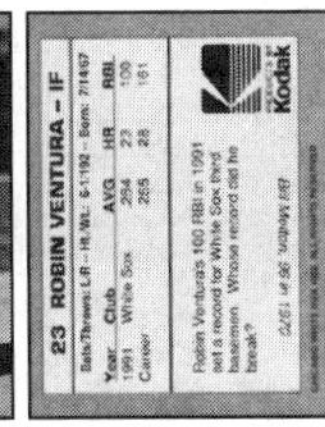

This 30-card set was sponsored by Kodak and measures slightly larger (2 5/8" by 3 1/2") than standard size. The set was distributed at a White Sox vs. Milwaukee four-game series at Comiskey Park. The fronts display glossy borderless color player photos. All the players are pictured in black attire, in keeping with the "Good Guys Wear Black" team slogan, which is tilted slightly to the left and superimposed at the upper left corner. The player's name appears in a black diagonal stripe that cuts across the bottom of the picture; at the lower right corner, it intersects a diamond bearing his jersey number. The horizontally oriented backs have gray borders and feature biography, statistics (1991 and career), and a White Sox trivia question and answer. The cards are skip-numbered on the front by uniform number and checklisted below accordingly.

	MINT	NRMT	EXC
COMPLETE SET (30)	15.00	6.75	1.85
COMMON CARD	.25	.11	.03
☐ 0 Waldo the Wolf	.25	.11	.03
☐ 1 Lance Johnson	1.00	.45	.12
☐ 5 Matt Merullo	.25	.11	.03
☐ 7 Steve Sax	.25	.11	.03
☐ 12 Mike Huff	.25	.11	.03
☐ 13 Ozzie Guillen	.75	.35	.09
☐ 14 Craig Grebeck	.25	.11	.03
☐ 20 Ron Karkovice	.25	.11	.03
☐ 21 George Bell	.50	.23	.06
☐ 22 Donn Pall	.25	.11	.03
☐ 23 Robin Ventura	2.00	.90	.25
☐ 24 Warren Newson	.25	.11	.03
☐ 25 Kirk McCaskill	.25	.11	.03
☐ 27 Greg Hibbard	.25	.11	.03
☐ 28 Joey Cora	.50	.23	.06
☐ 29 Jack McDowell	1.50	.70	.19
☐ 30 Tim Raines	.75	.35	.09
☐ 31 Scott Radinsky	.25	.11	.03
☐ 32 Alex Fernandez	2.50	1.10	.30
☐ 33 Gene Lamont MG	.25	.11	.03
☐ 34 Terry Leach	.25	.11	.03
☐ 35 Frank Thomas	7.50	3.40	.95
☐ 37 Bobby Thigpen	.25	.11	.03
☐ 39 Roberto Hernandez	2.00	.90	.25
☐ 40 Wilson Alvarez	2.00	.90	.25
☐ 44 Dan Pasqua	.25	.11	.03
☐ 45 Shawn Abner	.25	.11	.03
☐ 49 Charlie Hough	.50	.23	.06
☐ 72 Carlton Fisk	2.00	.90	.25
☐ NNO Coaching Staff Walt Hriniak Doug Mansolino Dave Huppert Mike Squires Terry Bevington Gene Lamont MG Joe Nossek Jackie Brown	.25	.11	.03

1993 White Sox Kodak

This 30-card set measures approximately 2 5/8" by 3 1/2" and features color player action photos on the fronts. The White Sox logo appears in an upper corner and the player's team number, name, and position appear on a light blue stripe at the lower edge, the only bordered side. The horizontal backs are printed in black and white with a gray border. The player's name, team number and position, biography, 1992 statistics, and career average appear in the top half of the card. The lower half contains a brief career summary with the Kodak logo located in the lower right. The cards are unnumbered and checklisted below in alphabetical order.

	MINT	NRMT	EXC
COMPLETE SET (30)	15.00	6.75	1.85
COMMON CARD (1-30)	.25	.11	.03
☐ 1 Wilson Alvarez	1.25	.55	.16
☐ 2 George Bell	.50	.23	.06
☐ 3 Jason Bere	.50	.23	.06
☐ 4 Rod Bolton	.25	.11	.03
☐ 5 Ellis Burks	1.00	.45	.12
☐ 6 Chuck Cary	.25	.11	.03
☐ 7 Joey Cora	.50	.23	.06
☐ 8 Alex Fernandez	1.50	.70	.19
☐ 9 Craig Grebeck	.25	.11	.03
☐ 10 Ozzie Guillen	.75	.35	.09
☐ 11 Roberto Hernandez	.75	.35	.09
☐ 12 Mike Huff	.25	.11	.03
☐ 13 Bo Jackson	.50	.23	.06
☐ 14 Lance Johnson	1.00	.45	.12
☐ 15 Ron Karkovice	.25	.11	.03
☐ 16 Gene Lamont MG	.25	.11	.03
☐ 17 Mike LaValliere	.25	.11	.03
☐ 18 Terry Leach	.25	.11	.03
☐ 19 Kirk McCaskill	.25	.11	.03
☐ 20 Jack McDowell	1.25	.55	.16
☐ 21 Donn Pall	.25	.11	.03
☐ 22 Dan Pasqua	.25	.11	.03
☐ 23 Scott Radinsky	.25	.11	.03
☐ 24 Tim Raines	.75	.35	.09
☐ 25 Steve Sax	.25	.11	.03
☐ 26 Jeff Schwarz	.25	.11	.03
☐ 27 Bobby Thigpen	.25	.11	.03
☐ 28 Frank Thomas	6.00	2.70	.75
☐ 29 Robin Ventura	1.25	.55	.16
☐ 30 Coaching Staff	.25	.11	.03

Jose Antigua
Terry Bevington
Jackie Brown
Walt Hriniak
Gene Lamont MG
Doug Mansolino
Joe Nossek
Dewey Robinson

1994 White Sox Kodak

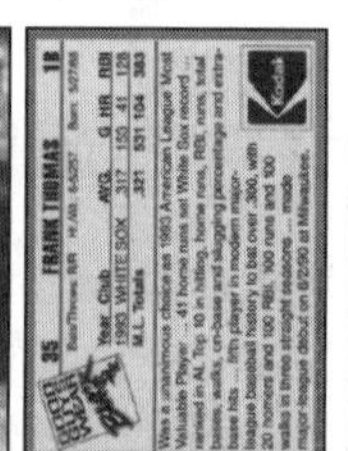

These 30 cards measure 2 5/8" by 3 1/2" and feature borderless color player action shots on their fronts. The player's facsimile autograph appears in silver-colored ink near the bottom. The silver-bordered horizontal back carries the player's name, uniform number, and position at the top, followed below by biography, statistics, and career highlights. The cards are unnumbered and checklisted below in alphabetical order.

	MINT	NRMT	EXC
COMPLETE SET (30)	15.00	6.75	1.85
COMMON CARD (1-30)	.25	.11	.03
☐ 1 Wilson Alvarez	1.25	.55	.16
☐ 2 Paul Assenmacher	.25	.11	.03
☐ 3 Jason Bere	.25	.11	.03
☐ 4 Dennis Cook	.25	.11	.03
☐ 5 Joey Cora	.25	.11	.03
☐ 6 Jose DeLeon	.25	.11	.03
☐ 7 Alex Fernandez	2.00	.90	.25
☐ 8 Julio Franco	.75	.35	.09
☐ 9 Craig Grebeck	.25	.11	.03
☐ 10 Ozzie Guillen	.75	.35	.09
☐ 11 Joe Hall	.25	.11	.03
☐ 12 Roberto Hernandez	.25	.11	.03
☐ 13 Dann Howitt	.25	.11	.03
☐ 14 Darrin Jackson	.25	.11	.03
☐ 15 Dane Johnson	.25	.11	.03
☐ 16 Lance Johnson	1.00	.45	.12
☐ 17 Ron Karkovice	.25	.11	.03
☐ 18 Gene Lamont MG	.25	.11	.03
☐ 19 Mike LaValliere	.25	.11	.03
☐ 20 Norberto Martin	.25	.11	.03
☐ 21 Kirk McCaskill	.25	.11	.03
☐ 22 Jack McDowell	1.25	.55	.16
☐ 23 Warren Newson	.25	.11	.03
☐ 24 Dan Pasqua	.25	.11	.03
☐ 25 Tim Raines	.75	.35	.09
☐ 26 Scott Sanderson	.25	.11	.03
☐ 27 Frank Thomas	7.50	3.40	.95
☐ 28 Robin Ventura	1.50	.70	.19
☐ 29 Bob Zupcic	.25	.11	.03
☐ 30 Coaches Card	.25	.11	.03

Doug Mansolino
Rick Peterson
Roly de Armas
Jackie Brown
Gene Lamont MG
Terry Bevington
Joe Nossek
Walt Hriniak

1995 White Sox Kodak

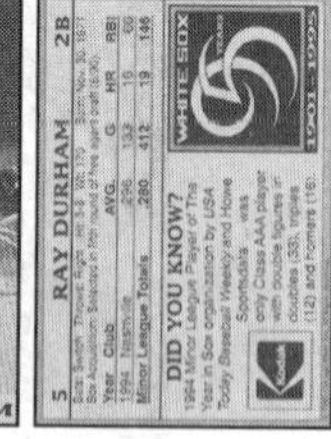

Sponsored by Kodak, this 31-card set commemorates the 95th anniversary of the Chicago White Sox. The cards measure 2 5/8" by 3 1/2". The fronts feature full-bleed color action photos except at the bottom, where the player's name is reversed out on a black-and-white bar. The horizontal backs carry biography, statistics, a "Did You Know?" trivia feature, the sponsor logo, and a special logo celebrating 95 years of White Sox baseball. The cards are unnumbered and checklisted below in alphabetical order.

	MINT	NRMT	EXC
COMPLETE SET (31)	12.50	5.50	1.55
COMMON CARD (1-31)	.25	.11	.03
☐ 1 Jim Abbott	.50	.23	.06
☐ 2 Wilson Alvarez	1.25	.55	.16
☐ 3 Jason Bere	.25	.11	.03
☐ 4 Terry Bevington MG	.25	.11	.03
☐ 5 Jose DeLeon	.25	.11	.03
☐ 6 Mike Devereaux	.25	.11	.03
☐ 7 Rob Dibble	.25	.11	.03
☐ 8 Ray Durham	1.25	.55	.16
☐ 9 Alex Fernandez	1.50	.70	.19
☐ 10 Tim Fortugno	.25	.11	.03
☐ 11 Craig Grebeck	.25	.11	.03
☐ 12 Ozzie Guillen	.75	.35	.09
☐ 13 Roberto Hernandez	.75	.35	.09
☐ 14 Lance Johnson	1.00	.45	.12
☐ 15 Ron Karkovice	.25	.11	.03
☐ 16 Brian Keyser	.25	.11	.03
☐ 17 John Kruk	.50	.23	.06
☐ 18 Mike LaValliere	.25	.11	.03
☐ 19 Norberto Martin	.25	.11	.03
☐ 20 Dave Martinez	.25	.11	.03
☐ 21 Kirk McCaskill	.25	.11	.03
☐ 22 Warren Newson	.25	.11	.03
☐ 24 Steve Odgers Dir. of Conditioning	.25	.11	.03
☐ 25 Scott Radinsky	.25	.11	.03
☐ 26 Tim Raines	.75	.35	.09
☐ 27 Herm Schneider TR Mark Anderson TR	.25	.11	.03
☐ 28 Frank Thomas	6.00	2.70	.75
☐ 29 Frank Thomas AS	3.00	1.35	.35
☐ 30 Robin Ventura	1.50	.70	.19
☐ 31 Coaching Staff	.25	.11	.03

Terry Bevington MG
Don Cooper
Walt Hriniak
Joe Nossek
Doug Mansolino
Ron Jackson
Mark Salas
Roly de Armas

1992 Whitehall Prototypes

This five-card standard-size set features color close-up photos inside a tan inner border and a white outer border. By a process known as Photonix, old photographs from the National Baseball Library underwent extensive pixel value recomputation to restore contrast, resolution, and light balance. The backs feature a miniature reproduction of the original black-and-white vintage photo and a discussion of the Photonix process. The cards are stamped "Prototype" across the text. The cards are unnumbered and checklisted below in alphabetical order.

	MINT	NRMT	EXC
COMPLETE SET (5)	12.00	5.50	1.50
COMMON CARD (1-5)	2.00	.90	.25
☐ 1 Ty Cobb	4.00	1.80	.50
☐ 2 Lou Gehrig	4.00	1.80	.50
☐ 3 Babe Ruth	6.00	2.70	.75
☐ 4 Honus Wagner	3.00	1.35	.35
☐ 5 Cy Young	2.00	.90	.25

1992 Whitehall Legends to Life

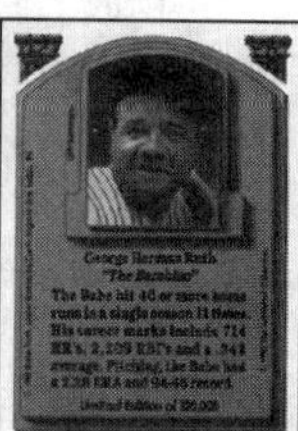

This five-card hologram set from the Whitehall Collection, which measures the standard size, features hologram images created from actual photographs on the card fronts. The players are shown in action in front of the scene in the original photo. The pictures are bordered and have striped banners at the corners. The player's name appears in an arch at the top. The words "Whitehall Collection" and "Limited Edition" are printed at the top and bottom respectively. The back design shows a "color" close-up photo colorized with a special process called Photonix. The picture is displayed on a tan monument-shaped graphic design with antiquated roman pillars partially visible at the top corners. Below the photo are the player's name and a career summary. The cards are unnumbered and checklisted below in alphabetical order.

	MINT	NRMT	EXC
COMPLETE SET (5)	12.00	5.50	1.50
COMMON CARD (1-5)	2.00	.90	.25
☐ 1 Ty Cobb	4.00	1.80	.50
☐ 2 Lou Gehrig	4.00	1.80	.50
☐ 3 Babe Ruth	6.00	2.70	.75
☐ 4 Honus Wagner	3.00	1.35	.35
☐ 5 Cy Young	2.00	.90	.25

1978 Wiffle Ball Discs

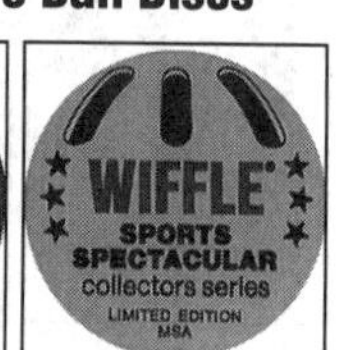

These discs were on the side of Wiffle Ball boxes. Even though the copyright date on the discs are 1976, the player selection implies that this set was issued early in 1978. For some reason, Thurman Munson discs seem to be available in significantly higher quantities and we have labeled Munson as a DP. These discs are ununmbered and we have sequenced this set in alphabetical order.

	NRMT	VG-E	GOOD
COMPLETE SET (79)	125.00	55.00	15.50
COMMON DISC	.25	.11	.03
☐ 1 Sal Bando	.50	.23	.06
☐ 2 Buddy Bell	1.00	.45	.12
☐ 3 Johnny Bench	7.50	3.40	.95
☐ 4 Vida Blue	1.00	.45	.12
☐ 5 Bert Blyleven	1.00	.45	.12
☐ 6 Bobby Bonds	1.00	.45	.12
☐ 7 George Brett	25.00	11.00	3.10
☐ 8 Lou Brock	5.00	2.20	.60
☐ 9 Ray Burris	.25	.11	.03
☐ 10 Bill Buckner	.25	.11	.03
☐ 11 Jeff Burroughs	.25	.11	.03
☐ 12 Campy Campaneris	.50	.23	.06
☐ 13 Rod Carew	5.00	2.20	.60
☐ 14 Steve Carlton	5.00	2.20	.60
☐ 15 Dave Cash	.25	.11	.03
☐ 16 Cesar Cedeno	.50	.23	.06
☐ 17 Ron Cey	1.00	.45	.12
☐ 18 Chris Chambliss	.25	.11	.03
☐ 19 Dave Concepcion	1.00	.45	.12
☐ 20 Dennis Eckersley	5.00	2.20	.60
☐ 21 Mark Fidrych	4.00	1.80	.50
☐ 22 Rollie Fingers	5.00	2.20	.60
☐ 23 Carlton Fisk	7.50	3.40	.95
☐ 24 George Foster	1.00	.45	.12
☐ 25 Wayne Garland	.25	.11	.03
☐ 26 Ralph Garr	.25	.11	.03
☐ 27 Steve Garvey	4.00	1.80	.50
☐ 28 Don Gullett	.25	.11	.03
☐ 29 Larry Hisle	.25	.11	.03
☐ 30 Al Hrabosky	.25	.11	.03
☐ 31 Catfish Hunter	5.00	2.20	.60
☐ 32 Reggie Jackson	10.00	4.50	1.25
☐ 33 Randy Jones	.25	.11	.03
☐ 34 Dave Kingman	2.00	.90	.25
☐ 35 Jerry Koosman	1.00	.45	.12
☐ 36 Ed Kranepool	.25	.11	.03
☐ 37 Ron LeFlore	.50	.23	.06
☐ 38 Sixto Lezcano	.25	.11	.03
☐ 39 Davey Lopes	.50	.23	.06
☐ 40 Greg Luzinski	1.00	.45	.12
☐ 41 Fred Lynn	.50	.23	.06
☐ 42 Garry Maddox	.25	.11	.03
☐ 43 Jon Matlack	.25	.11	.03
☐ 44 Gary Matthews	.50	.23	.06
☐ 45 Lee May	.50	.23	.06
☐ 46 John Mayberry	.25	.11	.03
☐ 47 Bake McBride	.25	.11	.03
☐ 48 Tug McGraw	1.00	.45	.12
☐ 49 Hal McRae	1.00	.45	.12
☐ 50 Andy Messersmith	.25	.11	.03
☐ 51 Randy Moffitt	.25	.11	.03
☐ 52 Joe Morgan	5.00	2.20	.60
☐ 53 Thurman Munson DP	2.50	1.10	.30
☐ 54 Graig Nettles	.50	.23	.06
☐ 55 Al Oliver	1.00	.45	.12
☐ 56 Jorge Orta	.25	.11	.03
☐ 57 Jim Palmer	5.00	2.20	.60
☐ 58 Dave Parker	1.00	.45	.12
☐ 59 Tony Perez	4.00	1.80	.50
☐ 60 Gaylord Perry	5.00	2.20	.60
☐ 61 Jim Rice	2.00	.90	.25
☐ 62 Steve Rogers	.25	.11	.03
☐ 63 Pete Rose	10.00	4.50	1.25
☐ 64 Joe Rudi	.25	.11	.03
☐ 65 Nolan Ryan	30.00	13.50	3.70
☐ 66 Manny Sanguillen	.25	.11	.03
☐ 67 Mike Schmidt	10.00	4.50	1.25
☐ 68 Tom Seaver	10.00	4.50	1.25
☐ 69 Ted Simmons	1.00	.45	.12
☐ 70 Reggie Smith	.50	.23	.06
☐ 71 Willie Stargell	5.00	2.20	.60
☐ 72 Rusty Staub	1.00	.45	.12
☐ 73 Frank Tanana	.50	.23	.06
☐ 74 Gene Tenace	.25	.11	.03
☐ 75 Luis Tiant	1.00	.45	.12
☐ 76 Manny Trillo	.25	.11	.03
☐ 77 Bob Watson	1.00	.45	.12
☐ 78 Carl Yastrzemski	5.00	2.20	.60
☐ 79 Richie Zisk	.25	.11	.03

1923 Willards Chocolates V100

Issued in Canada by Willards Chocolates, these 180 blank-backed cards measure approximately 2" by 3 1/4". The catalog designation for this set is V100. The white-bordered fronts feature sepia-tone player photos. The player's facsimile autograph appears on the card face. The cards are unnumbered and checklisted below in alphabetical order.

	EX-MT	VG-E	GOOD
COMPLETE SET (180)	10500.00	4700.00	1300.00
COMMON CARD (1-180)	40.00	18.00	5.00
☐ 1 Babe Adams	50.00	22.00	6.25
☐ 2 Grover C. Alexander	150.00	70.00	19.00
☐ 3 James Austin MG	40.00	18.00	5.00
☐ 4 Jim Bagby	40.00	18.00	5.00
☐ 5 Frank Baker	80.00	36.00	10.00
☐ 6 Dave Bancroft	80.00	36.00	10.00
☐ 7 Turner Barber	40.00	18.00	5.00
☐ 8 Jesse L. Barnes	40.00	18.00	5.00
☐ 9 John Bassler	40.00	18.00	5.00
☐ 10 Lu Blue	40.00	18.00	5.00
☐ 11 Norman Boekel	40.00	18.00	5.00
☐ 12 Frank Brazill	40.00	18.00	5.00
☐ 13 George H. Burns	40.00	18.00	5.00
☐ 14 George J. Burns	40.00	18.00	5.00
☐ 15 Leon Cadore	50.00	22.00	6.25
☐ 16 Max Carey	80.00	36.00	10.00
☐ 17 Harold G. Carlson	40.00	18.00	5.00
☐ 18 Lloyd Christenberry	40.00	18.00	5.00
☐ 19 Vernon J. Clemons	40.00	18.00	5.00
☐ 20 Ty Cobb	750.00	350.00	95.00
☐ 21 Bert Cole	40.00	18.00	5.00
☐ 22 John F. Collins	40.00	18.00	5.00
☐ 23 Stan Coveleski	80.00	36.00	10.00
☐ 24 Walton E. Cruise	40.00	18.00	5.00
☐ 25 George W. Cutshaw	40.00	18.00	5.00
☐ 26 Jake Daubert	50.00	22.00	6.25
☐ 27 George Dauss	40.00	18.00	5.00
☐ 28 Frank Davis	40.00	18.00	5.00
☐ 29 Charles A. Deal	40.00	18.00	5.00
☐ 30 William L. Doak	40.00	18.00	5.00
☐ 31 Wild Bill Donovan MG	40.00	18.00	5.00
☐ 32 Hugh Duffy MG	80.00	36.00	10.00
☐ 33 Joe Dugan	50.00	22.00	6.25
☐ 34 Louis B. Duncan	40.00	18.00	5.00
☐ 35 Jimmy Dykes	50.00	22.00	6.25
☐ 36 Howard Ehmke	50.00	22.00	6.25
☐ 37 Francis R. Ellerbe	40.00	18.00	5.00

☐ 38 Eric G. Erickson	40.00	18.00	5.00
☐ 39 Johnny Evers MG	80.00	36.00	10.00
☐ 40 Urban Faber	80.00	36.00	10.00
☐ 41 Bibb Falk	40.00	18.00	5.00
☐ 42 Max Flack	40.00	18.00	5.00
☐ 43 Lee Fohl MG	40.00	18.00	5.00
☐ 44 Jack Fournier	40.00	18.00	5.00
☐ 45 Frank Frisch	100.00	45.00	12.50
☐ 46 C.E. Galloway	40.00	18.00	5.00
☐ 47 Billy Gardner	40.00	18.00	5.00
☐ 48 Edward Gharrity	40.00	18.00	5.00
☐ 49 George Gibson	40.00	18.00	5.00
☐ 50 Kid Gleason MG	60.00	27.00	7.50
☐ 51 William Gleason	40.00	18.00	5.00
☐ 52 Hank Gowdy	50.00	22.00	6.25
☐ 53 I.M. Griffin	40.00	18.00	5.00
☐ 54 Thomas Griffith	40.00	18.00	5.00
☐ 55 Burleigh Grimes	80.00	36.00	10.00
☐ 56 Charlie Grimm	50.00	22.00	6.25
☐ 57 Jesse Haines	80.00	36.00	10.00
☐ 58 Bill Harris	40.00	18.00	5.00
☐ 59 Bucky Harris	80.00	36.00	10.00
☐ 60 Robert Hasty	40.00	18.00	5.00
☐ 61 Harry Heilmann	100.00	45.00	12.50
☐ 62 Walter Henline	40.00	18.00	5.00
☐ 63 Walter Holke	40.00	18.00	5.00
☐ 64 Charles Hollocher	40.00	18.00	5.00
☐ 65 Harry Hooper	80.00	36.00	10.00
☐ 66 Rogers Hornsby	250.00	110.00	31.00
☐ 67 Waite Hoyt	80.00	36.00	10.00
☐ 68 Miller Huggins MG	100.00	45.00	12.50
☐ 69 W.C. Jacobson	40.00	18.00	5.00
☐ 70 Charlie Jamieson	40.00	18.00	5.00
☐ 71 E. Johnson	40.00	18.00	5.00
☐ 72 Walter Johnson	350.00	160.00	45.00
☐ 73 James H. Johnston	40.00	18.00	5.00
☐ 74 Bob Jones	40.00	18.00	5.00
☐ 75 Sam Jones	50.00	22.00	6.25
☐ 76 Joe Judge	50.00	22.00	6.25
☐ 77 James W. Keenan	40.00	18.00	5.00
☐ 78 Geo. L. Kelly	80.00	36.00	10.00
☐ 79 Peter J. Kilduff	40.00	18.00	5.00
☐ 80 William Killefer	40.00	18.00	5.00
☐ 81 Lee King	40.00	18.00	5.00
☐ 82 Ray Kolp	40.00	18.00	5.00
☐ 83 John Lavan	40.00	18.00	5.00
☐ 84 Harry Leibold	40.00	18.00	5.00
☐ 85 Connie Mack MG	150.00	70.00	19.00
☐ 86 Duster Mails	40.00	18.00	5.00
☐ 87 Walter Maranville	80.00	36.00	10.00
☐ 88 Richard W. Marquard	80.00	36.00	10.00
☐ 89 Carl W. Mays	50.00	22.00	6.25
☐ 90 Geo. F. McBride	40.00	18.00	5.00
☐ 91 Harvey McClellan	40.00	18.00	5.00
☐ 92 John J. McGraw MG	125.00	55.00	15.50
☐ 93 Austin B. McHenry	40.00	18.00	5.00
☐ 94 Snuffy McInnis	50.00	22.00	6.25
☐ 95 Douglas McWeeny	40.00	18.00	5.00
☐ 96 Mike Menosky	40.00	18.00	5.00
☐ 97 Emil F. Meusel	40.00	18.00	5.00
☐ 98 Bob Meusel	50.00	22.00	6.25
☐ 99 Henry W. Meyers	40.00	18.00	5.00
☐ 100 Clyde Milan MG	50.00	22.00	6.25
☐ 101 John K. Miljus	40.00	18.00	5.00
☐ 102 Edmund J. Miller	50.00	22.00	6.25
☐ 103 Elmer Miller	40.00	18.00	5.00
☐ 104 Otto L. Miller	40.00	18.00	5.00
☐ 105 Fred Mitchell MG	40.00	18.00	5.00
☐ 106 Geo. Mogridge	40.00	18.00	5.00
☐ 107 Patrick J. Moran MG	40.00	18.00	5.00
☐ 108 John D. Morrison	40.00	18.00	5.00
☐ 109 Johnny Mostil	40.00	18.00	5.00
☐ 110 Clarence F. Mueller	40.00	18.00	5.00
☐ 111 Greasy Neale	60.00	27.00	7.50
☐ 112 Joseph Oeschger	40.00	18.00	5.00
☐ 113 Robert J. O'Farrell	40.00	18.00	5.00
☐ 114 John Oldham	40.00	18.00	5.00
☐ 115 Ivy Olson	40.00	18.00	5.00
☐ 116 Geo. M. O'Neil	40.00	18.00	5.00
☐ 117 Steve O'Neill	50.00	22.00	6.25
☐ 118 Frank J. Parkinson	40.00	18.00	5.00
☐ 119 Dode Paskert	40.00	18.00	5.00
☐ 120 Roger Peckinpaugh	50.00	22.00	6.25
☐ 121 Herb Pennock	80.00	36.00	10.00
☐ 122 Ralph Perkins	40.00	18.00	5.00
☐ 123 Jeff Pfeffer	40.00	18.00	5.00
☐ 124 Wally Pipp	50.00	22.00	6.25
☐ 125 Charles Ponder	40.00	18.00	5.00
☐ 126 Raymond R. Powell	40.00	18.00	5.00
☐ 127 Del Pratt	40.00	18.00	5.00
☐ 128 Joseph Rapp	40.00	18.00	5.00
☐ 129 John H. Rawlings	40.00	18.00	5.00
☐ 130 Edgar Rice	80.00	36.00	10.00
☐ 131 Branch Rickey MG	125.00	55.00	15.50
☐ 132 James J. Ring	40.00	18.00	5.00
☐ 133 Eppa J. Rixey	80.00	36.00	10.00
☐ 134 Davis A. Robertson	40.00	18.00	5.00
☐ 135 Edwin Rommel	50.00	22.00	6.25
☐ 136 Edd J. Roush	80.00	36.00	10.00
☐ 137 Harold Ruel	40.00	18.00	5.00
☐ 138 Allen Russell	40.00	18.00	5.00
☐ 139 Babe Ruth	1200.00	550.00	150.00
☐ 140 Wilfred D. Ryan	40.00	18.00	5.00
☐ 141 Henry F. Sallee	40.00	18.00	5.00
☐ 142 Wally Schang	50.00	22.00	6.25
☐ 143 Raymond H. Schmandt	40.00	18.00	5.00
☐ 144 Everett Scott	50.00	22.00	6.25
☐ 145 Henry Severeid	40.00	18.00	5.00
☐ 146 Joseph W. Sewell	80.00	36.00	10.00
☐ 147 Howard S. Shanks	40.00	18.00	5.00
☐ 148 Earl Sheely	40.00	18.00	5.00
☐ 149 Ralph Shinners	40.00	18.00	5.00
☐ 150 Urban J. Shocker	50.00	22.00	6.25
☐ 151 George H. Sisler	125.00	55.00	15.50
☐ 152 Earl L. Smith	40.00	18.00	5.00
☐ 153 Earl S. Smith	40.00	18.00	5.00
☐ 154 George A. Smith	40.00	18.00	5.00
☐ 155 John Smith	40.00	18.00	5.00
☐ 156 Tris Speaker MG	150.00	70.00	19.00
☐ 157 Arnold Staatz	40.00	18.00	5.00
☐ 158 Riggs Stephenson	60.00	27.00	7.50
☐ 159 Milton J. Stock	40.00	18.00	5.00
☐ 160 John L. Sullivan	40.00	18.00	5.00
☐ 161 Herb Thormahlen	40.00	18.00	5.00
☐ 162 James A. Tierney	40.00	18.00	5.00
☐ 163 John Tobin	40.00	18.00	5.00
☐ 164 James L. Vaughn	40.00	18.00	5.00
☐ 165 Bobby Veach	40.00	18.00	5.00
☐ 166 Tilly Walker	40.00	18.00	5.00
☐ 167 Aaron Ward	40.00	18.00	5.00
☐ 168 Zack D. Wheat	80.00	36.00	10.00
☐ 169 George B. Whitted	40.00	18.00	5.00
☐ 170 Irvin K. Wilhelm	40.00	18.00	5.00
☐ 171 Roy H. Wilkinson	40.00	18.00	5.00
☐ 172 Fred C. Williams	50.00	22.00	6.25
☐ 173 Ken Williams	50.00	22.00	6.25
☐ 174 Samuel W. Wilson	40.00	18.00	5.00
☐ 175 Ivy B. Wingo	40.00	18.00	5.00
☐ 176 Whitey Witt	50.00	22.00	6.25
☐ 177 Joseph Wood	60.00	27.00	7.50
☐ 178 Clarence Yaryan	40.00	18.00	5.00
☐ 179 Ralph Young	40.00	18.00	5.00
☐ 180 Ross Youngs	80.00	36.00	10.00

1922 William Paterson V89

This 50-card set was inserted in packages of caramel candy. The cards measure approximately 2" by 3 1/4". the fronts feature sepia-toned player photos framed by white borders. The following information appears in the bottom border beneath the picture: card number, player's name, team name and imprint information (Wm. Paterson, Limited; Brantford, Canada). The backs are blank.

	EX-MT	VG-E	GOOD
COMPLETE SET (50)	5500.00	2500.00	700.00
COMMON CARD (1-50)	50.00	22.00	6.25
☐ 1 Ed Roush	100.00	45.00	12.50
☐ 2 Unknown	50.00	22.00	6.25
☐ 3 Del Gainer	50.00	22.00	6.25
☐ 4 George Sisler	125.00	55.00	15.50
☐ 5 Joe Bush	60.00	27.00	7.50
☐ 6 Joe Oeschger	50.00	22.00	6.25
☐ 7 Willie Kamm	50.00	22.00	6.25
☐ 8 John Watson	50.00	22.00	6.25
☐ 9 Adolfo Luque	60.00	27.00	7.50
☐ 10 Miller Huggins MG	100.00	45.00	12.50
☐ 11 Wally Schang	60.00	27.00	7.50
☐ 12 Unknown	50.00	22.00	6.25
☐ 13 Tris Speaker MG	125.00	55.00	15.50
☐ 14 Hugh McQuillen	50.00	22.00	6.25
☐ 15 George Kelly	100.00	45.00	12.50
☐ 16 Ray Schalk	100.00	45.00	12.50
☐ 17 Sam Jones	60.00	27.00	7.50
☐ 18 Grover Alexander	150.00	70.00	19.00
☐ 19 Bob Meusel	60.00	27.00	7.50
☐ 20 Emil Meusel	50.00	22.00	6.25
☐ 21 Rogers Hornsby	200.00	90.00	25.00
☐ 22 Harry Heilmann	100.00	45.00	12.50
☐ 23 Heinie Groh	60.00	27.00	7.50
☐ 24 Frankie Frisch	100.00	45.00	12.50
☐ 25 Babe Ruth	1250.00	550.00	160.00
☐ 26 Jack Bentley	50.00	22.00	6.25
☐ 27 Unknown	50.00	22.00	6.25
☐ 28 Max Carey	100.00	45.00	12.50
☐ 29 Chick Fewster	50.00	22.00	6.25
☐ 30 Cy Williams	60.00	27.00	7.50
☐ 31 Burleigh Grimes	100.00	45.00	12.50
☐ 32 Waite Hoyt	100.00	45.00	12.50
☐ 33 Frank Snyder	50.00	22.00	6.25
☐ 34 Clyde Milan MG	50.00	22.00	6.25
☐ 35 Eddie Collins	125.00	55.00	15.50
☐ 36 Travis Jackson	100.00	45.00	12.50
☐ 37 Ken Williams	60.00	27.00	7.50
☐ 38 Dave Bancroft	100.00	45.00	12.50
☐ 39 Mike McNally	50.00	22.00	6.25
☐ 40 John McGraw MG	150.00	70.00	19.00
☐ 41 Art Nehf	60.00	27.00	7.50
☐ 42 Rabbit Maranville	100.00	45.00	12.50
☐ 43 Charlie Grimm	60.00	27.00	7.50
☐ 44 Joe Judge	60.00	27.00	7.50
☐ 45 Wally Pipp	60.00	27.00	7.50
☐ 46 Ty Cobb	600.00	275.00	75.00
☐ 47 Walter Johnson	250.00	110.00	31.00
☐ 48 Jake Daubert	50.00	22.00	6.25
☐ 49 Zach Wheat	100.00	45.00	12.50
☐ 50 Herb Pennock	100.00	45.00	12.50

1910 Williams Caramels E103

The cards in this 30-card set measure 1 1/2" by 2 3/4". E103 is distinctive for its black and white player portraits set onto a solid red background. Player names and teams are listed below each photo, with "Williams", the manufacturer's name, in the line below. Printed on thin cardboard, the blank back Williams set was released to the public about 1910. Since the cards are unnumbered, they are ordered below alphabetically

	EX-MT	VG-E	GOOD
COMPLETE SET (30)	7500.00	3400.00	950.00
COMMON CARD (1-30)	125.00	55.00	15.50
☐ 1 Chief Bender	250.00	110.00	31.00
☐ 2 Roger Bresnahan	250.00	110.00	31.00
☐ 3 Mordecai Brown	300.00	135.00	38.00
☐ 4 Frank Chance	300.00	135.00	38.00
☐ 5 Hal Chase	200.00	90.00	25.00
☐ 6 Ty Cobb	2000.00	900.00	250.00
☐ 7 Eddie Collins	250.00	110.00	31.00
☐ 8 Sam Crawford	250.00	110.00	31.00
☐ 9 Harry Davis	125.00	55.00	15.50
☐ 10 Art Devlin	125.00	55.00	15.50
☐ 11 Bill Donovan	125.00	55.00	15.50
☐ 12 Red Dooin	125.00	55.00	15.50
☐ 13 Larry Doyle	125.00	55.00	15.50
☐ 14 John Ewing	125.00	55.00	15.50
☐ 15 George Gibson	125.00	55.00	15.50
☐ 16 Hugh Jennings	250.00	110.00	31.00
☐ 17 Davy Jones	125.00	55.00	15.50
☐ 18 Tim Jordan	125.00	55.00	15.50
☐ 19 Napoleon Lajoie	450.00	200.00	55.00
☐ 20 Tommy Leach	125.00	55.00	15.50
☐ 21 Harry Lord	125.00	55.00	15.50
☐ 22 Christy Mathewson	650.00	300.00	80.00
☐ 23 Larry McLean	125.00	55.00	15.50
☐ 24 George McQuillan	125.00	55.00	15.50
☐ 25 Jim Pastorious	125.00	55.00	15.50
☐ 26 Nap Rucker	125.00	55.00	15.50
☐ 27 Fred Tenney	125.00	55.00	15.50
☐ 28 Ira Thomas	125.00	55.00	15.50
☐ 29 Honus Wagner	750.00	350.00	95.00
☐ 30 Joe Wood	200.00	90.00	25.00

1988 Willard Mullin Postcards

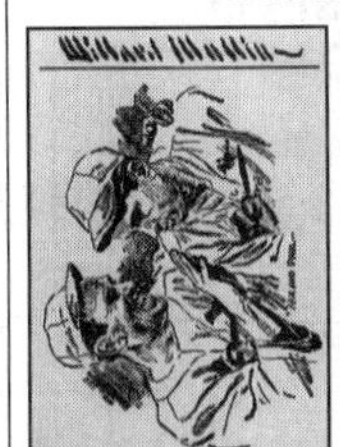

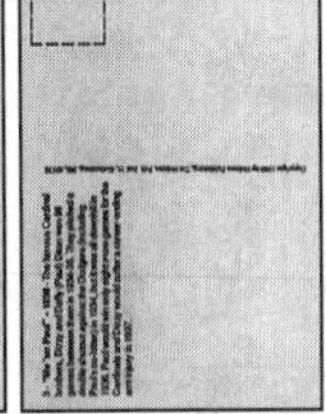

These 24 postcards feature the drawings of Willard Mullin, among the most known sports cartoonists. These cards were issued by Holmes Publishing in 1988. The cards measure 3 1/2" by 5" and feature reprints of Mullin's best works.

	MINT	NRMT	EXC
COMPLETE SET (24)	12.50	5.50	1.55
COMMON CARD (1-24)	.10	.05	.01
☐ 1 Williard Mullin	.10	.05	.01
☐ 2 Casey Stengel	1.00	.45	.12
☐ 3 Dizzy Dean Paul Dean	.50	.23	.06
☐ 4 Joe DiMaggio	2.00	.90	.25
☐ 5 Babe Ruth Hank Greenberg	2.00	.90	.25
☐ 6 Brooklyn Bum #1	.10	.05	.01
☐ 7 Pete Reiser	.25	.11	.03
☐ 8 Dixie Walker	.25	.11	.03
☐ 9 Branch Rickey Bum #2 Flatbush Willie	.25	.11	.03
☐ 10 Jackie Robinson Abraham Lincoln	3.00	1.35	.35
☐ 11 George Weiss Casey Stengel	.50	.23	.06
☐ 12 Flatbush Willie	.10	.05	.01
☐ 13 Flatbush Willie	.10	.05	.01
☐ 14 Jim Gilliam	.25	.11	.03
☐ 15 Duke Snider	1.00	.45	.12
☐ 16 Flatbush Willie Walt Alston	.25	.11	.03
☐ 17 Flatbush Willie	.10	.05	.01
☐ 18 Stan Musial	1.50	.70	.19
☐ 19 Giants leave NY	.10	.05	.01
☐ 20 Flatbush Willie	.10	.05	.01
☐ 21 Unknown	.10	.05	.01
☐ 22 Willie Mays	2.00	.90	.25
☐ 23 Mickey Mantle	3.00	1.35	.35
☐ 24 Amazing Mets	.25	.11	.03

1984 Willie Mays

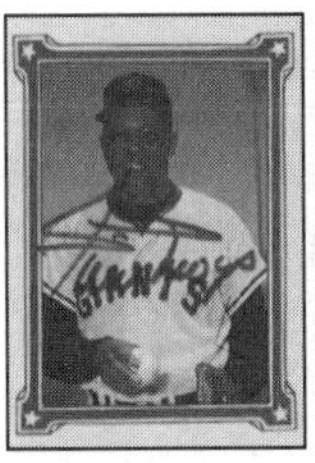

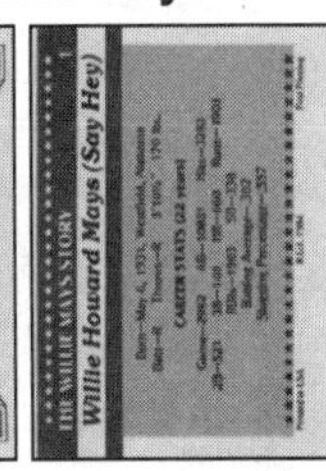

This ninety-card standard-size set was issued by ASA and printed by Renata Gallaso Inc. to honor the life and career of Willie Mays. These cards were issued in set form only. Sets were issued with and without the number one card being signed by Mays. The complete set does not include the autograph card which is valued seperately. Cards 1-45 contain biographical information about Mays while cards 46-90 have a puzzle back. The puzzle when put together features a collage of all Willie Mays baseball cards.

	MINT	NRMT	EXC
COMPLETE SET (90)	15.00	6.75	1.85
COMMON CARD (1-90)	.15	.07	.02
☐ 1A Willie Mays Say Hey, autographed	75.00	34.00	9.50
☐ 1B Willie Mays Say Hey unautographed	.15	.07	.02
☐ 2 Willie Mays Tearing up the Minor Leagues	.15	.07	.02
☐ 3 Willie Mays Called up to the Majors	.15	.07	.02
☐ 4 Willie Mays Leo Durocher Hank Thompson Monte Irvin 1951 Rookie Season	.25	.11	.03
☐ 5 Willie Mays Joins the Army	.15	.07	.02
☐ 6 Willie Mays MVP Season	.15	.07	.02
☐ 7 Willie Mays THE Catch	.50	.23	.06
☐ 8 Willie Mays Winter Ball	.15	.07	.02
☐ 9 Willie Mays Billiards for Willie	.15	.07	.02
☐ 10 Willie Mays Endorsements	.15	.07	.02
☐ 11 Willie Mays Honors for Willie	.15	.07	.02
☐ 12 Willie Mays Horace Stoneham OWN A Sportsman and A Gentleman	.25	.11	.03
☐ 13 Willie Mays Duke Snider The Toast of New York	.35	.16	.04
☐ 14 Willie Mays A Superb Fielder	.15	.07	.02
☐ 15 Willie Mays Giants Move to San Francisco	.15	.07	.02
☐ 16 Willie Mays A Favorite with Fans	.15	.07	.02
☐ 17 Willie Mays Making Adjustments	.15	.07	.02
☐ 18 Willie Mays Coming Home	.15	.07	.02
☐ 19 Willie Mays Roberto Clemente 3,000 Hitters	.35	.16	.04
☐ 20 Willie Mays 4 Homers in One Game	.15	.07	.02
☐ 21 Willie Mays Always Hustling	.15	.07	.02
☐ 22 Willie Mays Concentration	.15	.07	.02
☐ 23 Willie Mays San Francisco Wins 1st Pennant	.15	.07	.02

☐ 24 Willie Mays / Whitey Ford / Tom Tresh / Friendly Foes UER / Tresh is spelled Thresh	.35	.16	.04
☐ 25 Willie Mays / The One That Didn't / Get Away	.15	.07	.02
☐ 26 Willie Mays / Dick Stuart / Earl Wilson / Spring Training	.25	.11	.03
☐ 27 Willie Mays / Warren Giles PRES / Another MVP Season	.25	.11	.03
☐ 28 Willie Mays / N.L. Home Run King	.15	.07	.02
☐ 29 Willie Mays / Mickey Mantle	.75	.35	.09
☐ 30 Willie Mays / Stan Musial / Pride of the N.L.	.50	.23	.06
☐ 31 Willie Mays / Roy Hofheinz OWN / The Birthday Boy	.25	.11	.03
☐ 32 Willie Mays / Ernie Banks / 500 Home Run Hitters	.25	.11	.03
☐ 33 Willie Mays / #600	.35	.16	.04
☐ 34 Willie Mays / Returns to New York	.15	.07	.02
☐ 35 Willie Mays / Don Drysdale / All-Stars	.35	.16	.04
☐ 36 Willie Mays / Retirement	.15	.07	.02
☐ 37 Willie Mays / Cover Boy	.15	.07	.02
☐ 38 Willie Mays / John Lindsay MAYOR / Willie Mays Day	.25	.11	.03
☐ 39 Willie Mays / Queen Elizabeth / Ronald Reagan / Holding Court	.75	.35	.09
☐ 40 Willie Mays / Hank Aaron / Home Run Kings	.50	.23	.06
☐ 41 Willie Mays / Hall of Fame	.15	.07	.02
☐ 42 Willie Mays / Santa	.15	.07	.02
☐ 43 Willie Mays / Mae Mays / The Exhibit	.25	.11	.03
☐ 44 Willie Mays / Joe DiMaggio / Baseball Immortals	.75	.35	.09
☐ 45 Willie Mays / Greatest of Them All	.15	.07	.02
☐ 46 Willie Mays / Mrs. Willie Mays / Bill Cosby	.50	.23	.06
☐ 47 Willie Mays / Head shot	.15	.07	.02
☐ 48 Willie Mays / Batting stance / stadium background	.15	.07	.02
☐ 49 Willie Mays / Follow-through	.15	.07	.02
☐ 50 Willie Mays / Crouching, two bats on ground	.15	.07	.02
☐ 51 Willie Mays / Posed, bat on right shoulder	.15	.07	.02
☐ 52 Willie Mays / Hank Aaron	.50	.23	.06
☐ 53 Willie Mays / On one knee / resting knee on bat	.15	.07	.02
☐ 54 Willie Mays / Looking over left shoulder	.15	.07	.02
☐ 55 Willie Mays / Head shot, no hat	.15	.07	.02
☐ 56 Willie Mays / Head shot, hat on	.15	.07	.02
☐ 57 Willie Mays / Head shot, looking right	.15	.07	.02
☐ 58 Willie Mays / Posed batting stance	.15	.07	.02
☐ 59 Willie Mays / On one knee, frowning	.15	.07	.02
☐ 60 Willie Mays / Bat in air over / left shoulder	.15	.07	.02
☐ 61 Willie Mays / Posed, bat over left shoulder	.15	.07	.02
☐ 62 Willie Mays / Posed, looking left / bat held straight up	.15	.07	.02
☐ 63 Willie Mays / Side view / bat on right shoulder	.15	.07	.02
☐ 64 Willie Mays / Smiling, no hat	.15	.07	.02
☐ 65 Willie Mays / Two bats / resting on right shoulder	.15	.07	.02
☐ 66 Willie Mays / Mets uniform / bat in air	.15	.07	.02
☐ 67 Willie Mays / Posed / bat on right shoulder / smiling	.15	.07	.02
☐ 68 Willie Mays / Portrait, frown on face	.15	.07	.02
☐ 69 Willie Mays / Right shoulder to camera / looking serious	.15	.07	.02
☐ 70 Willie Mays / Posed, bat on right shoulder / Giants' player / 30 in background	.15	.07	.02
☐ 71 Willie Mays / Running with / sunglasses flipped up	.15	.07	.02
☐ 72 Willie Mays / Holding right hand / in glove with a / stadium background	.15	.07	.02
☐ 73 Willie Mays / Swinging	.15	.07	.02
☐ 74 Willie Mays / Portrait / wearing black turtleneck / under uniform	.15	.07	.02
☐ 75 Willie Mays / Head shot / hands gripping bat on left	.15	.07	.02
☐ 76 Willie Mays / Portrait, Mets uniform / batting cage	.15	.07	.02
☐ 77 Willie Mays / Head shot, faded color	.15	.07	.02
☐ 78 Willie Mays / Posed, swinging	.15	.07	.02
☐ 79 Willie Mays / Head shot, no bat	.15	.07	.02
☐ 80 Willie Mays / Preparing to field	.15	.07	.02
☐ 81 Willie Mays / Side view / bat in air / over right shoulder	.15	.07	.02
☐ 82 Willie Mays / Head shot, serious look	.15	.07	.02
☐ 83 Willie Mays / Posed, batting stance	.15	.07	.02
☐ 84 Willie Mays / Autographing fan's baseball	.15	.07	.02
☐ 85 Willie Mays / Holding bat across chest	.15	.07	.02
☐ 86 Willie Mays / Smiling, head shot	.15	.07	.02
☐ 87 Willie Mays / Faded color / posed batting stance	.15	.07	.02
☐ 88 Willie Mays / Side portrait	.15	.07	.02
☐ 89 Willie Mays / In batting cage / wearing Mets uniform	.15	.07	.02
☐ 90 Willie Mays / Horizontal view / holding bat extended / straight out	.15	.07	.02

1954 Wilson

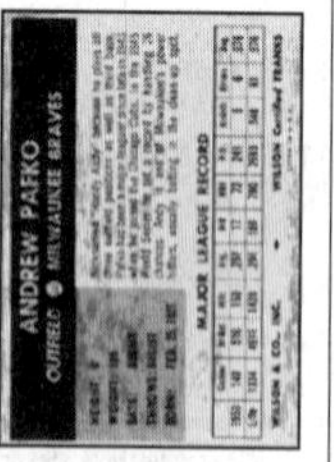

The cards in this 20-card set measure approximately 2 5/8" by 3 3/4". The 1954 "Wilson Wieners" set contains 20 full color, unnumbered cards. The obverse design of a package of hot dogs appearing to fly through the air is a distinctive feature of this set. Uncut sheets have been seen. Cards are numbered below alphabetically by player's name.

	NRMT	VG-E	GOOD
COMPLETE SET (20)	7500.00	3400.00	950.00
COMMON CARD (1-20)	150.00	70.00	19.00
☐ 1 Roy Campanella	750.00	350.00	95.00
☐ 2 Del Ennis	175.00	80.00	22.00
☐ 3 Carl Erskine	175.00	80.00	22.00
☐ 4 Ferris Fain	150.00	70.00	19.00
☐ 5 Bob Feller	500.00	220.00	60.00
☐ 6 Nellie Fox	350.00	160.00	45.00
☐ 7 Johnny Groth	150.00	70.00	19.00
☐ 8 Stan Hack MG	150.00	70.00	19.00
☐ 9 Gil Hodges	400.00	180.00	50.00
☐ 10 Ray Jablonski	150.00	70.00	19.00
☐ 11 Harvey Kuenn	175.00	80.00	22.00
☐ 12 Roy McMillan	150.00	70.00	19.00
☐ 13 Andy Pafko	150.00	70.00	19.00
☐ 14 Paul Richards MG	150.00	70.00	19.00
☐ 15 Hank Sauer	150.00	70.00	19.00
☐ 16 Red Schoendienst	350.00	160.00	45.00
☐ 17 Enos Slaughter	350.00	160.00	45.00
☐ 18 Vern Stephens	150.00	70.00	19.00
☐ 19 Sammy White	150.00	70.00	19.00
☐ 20 Ted Williams	3000.00	1350.00	375.00

1959-61 Wilson Sporting Goods

This seven-card set measures approximately 8" by 10" and features white-bordered black-and-white player photos with a facsimile autograph. The player's and sponsor's names are printed in the bottom margin. The backs are blank. The cards are unnumbered and checklisted below in alphabetical order.

	NRMT	VG-E	GOOD
COMPLETE SET	125.00	55.00	15.50
COMMON CARD	10.00	4.50	1.25
☐ 1 Luis Aparicio	25.00	11.00	3.10
☐ 2 Ernie Banks	30.00	13.50	3.70
☐ 3 Nellie Fox	25.00	11.00	3.10
☐ 4 Harmon Killebrew	30.00	13.50	3.70
☐ 5 Billy Pierce	15.00	6.75	1.85
☐ 6 Pete Runnels	10.00	4.50	1.25
☐ 7 Larry Sherry	10.00	4.50	1.25

1961 Wilson Sporting Goods H828

This three-card set features black-and-white player images on a gray background with a black border and looks as if the cards were cut from boxes. A player facsimile autograph is printed at the bottom. The cards measure approximately 1 7/8" by 5 1/4" and the catalog number is H828. The cards are unnumbered and checklisted below in alphabetical order.

	NRMT	VG-E	GOOD
COMPLETE SET (3)	250.00	110.00	31.00
COMMON CARD (1-3)	100.00	45.00	12.50
☐ 1 Don Hoak	100.00	45.00	12.50
☐ 2 Harvey Kuenn	100.00	45.00	12.50
☐ 3 Jim Piersall	100.00	45.00	12.50

1961 Wilson Sporting Goods H828-1

This six card set measures approximately 2 1/4" by 4" and features black and white blank backed photos containing a blue facsimile autograph and "Member - Advisory Staff Wilson Sporting Goods Co." across the bottom of the card. According to old hobby experts, this set may very well have more than six players. All additions to this checklist are appreciated. The catalog designation for this set is H828-1.

	NRMT	VG-E	GOOD
COMPLETE SET (6)	60.00	27.00	7.50
COMMON CARD (1-6)	10.00	4.50	1.25
☐ 1 Dick Ellsworth	10.00	4.50	1.25
☐ 2 Don Hoak	10.00	4.50	1.25
☐ 3 Harvey Kuenn	10.00	4.50	1.25
☐ 4 Roy McMillan	10.00	4.50	1.25
☐ 5 Jim Piersall	15.00	6.75	1.85
☐ 6 Ron Santo	20.00	9.00	2.50

1990 Windwalker Discs

This nine-disc set features 1990 American League All-Stars. The discs measure approximately 3 13/16" in diameter. Inside a pale yellow outer border with red baseball stitching, the fronts have a color action player photo. A facsimile autograph is inscribed across the picture. The player's name and the words "1990 All-Star" appear below the picture. The reverse of each disc features a different player. The discs are unnumbered; they are listed below in alphabetical order according to the player on one of the sides.

	MINT	NRMT	EXC
COMPLETE SET (9)	25.00	11.00	3.10
COMMON DISC (1-9)	1.00	.45	.12
☐ 1 Sandy Alomar Jr. / Dave Parker	1.50	.70	.19
☐ 2 Wade Boggs / Kirby Puckett	5.00	2.20	.60
☐ 3 Roger Clemens / Bob Welch	2.50	1.10	.30
☐ 4 Cecil Fielder / Bret Saberhagen	2.00	.90	.25
☐ 5 Chuck Finley / Kelly Gruber	1.00	.45	.12
☐ 6 Julio Franco / George Bell	1.50	.70	.19
☐ 7 Ken Griffey Jr. / Steve Sax	7.50	3.40	.95
☐ 8 Rickey Henderson / Jose Canseco	4.00	1.80	.50
☐ 9 Cal Ripken Jr. / Ozzie Guillen	6.00	2.70	.75

1990 Wonder Bread Stars

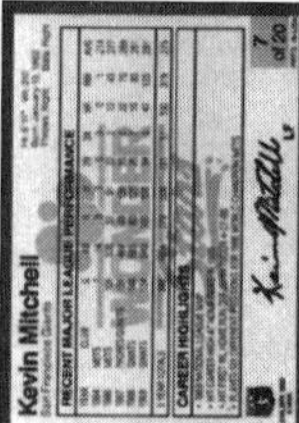

The 1990 Wonder Bread set was issued in 1990 by MSA (Michael Schechter Associates) in conjunction with Wonder Bread. One card was issued inside each specially marked package of Wonder Bread. Cards were available in grocery stores through June 15, 1990. The card was sealed in a pouch in the bread wrapper. This standard-size card set was issued without logos like many of the sets produced by MSA. Cards were printed on thin stock and hence were easily creased during bread handling making the set more difficult to put together one card at a time for condition-conscious collectors. Cards are numbered on the back in the lower right corner. Wonder Bread also offered sets in uncut sheet form to collectors mailing in with 3.00 and five proofs of purchase.

	MINT	NRMT	EXC
COMPLETE SET (20)	20.00	9.00	2.50
COMMON CARD (1-20)	.25	.11	.03
☐ 1 Bo Jackson	.50	.23	.06
☐ 2 Roger Clemens	1.25	.55	.16
☐ 3 Jim Abbott	.25	.11	.03
☐ 4 Orel Hershiser	.50	.23	.06
☐ 5 Ozzie Smith	2.00	.90	.25
☐ 6 Don Mattingly	2.50	1.10	.30
☐ 7 Kevin Mitchell	.25	.11	.03
☐ 8 Jerome Walton	.25	.11	.03
☐ 9 Kirby Puckett	2.50	1.10	.30
☐ 10 Darryl Strawberry	.50	.23	.06
☐ 11 Robin Yount	.75	.35	.09
☐ 12 Tony Gwynn	2.50	1.10	.30
☐ 13 Alan Trammell	.50	.23	.06
☐ 14 Jose Canseco	1.00	.45	.12
☐ 15 Greg Swindell	.25	.11	.03
☐ 16 Nolan Ryan	4.00	1.80	.50
☐ 17 Howard Johnson	.25	.11	.03
☐ 18 Ken Griffey Jr.	5.00	2.20	.60
☐ 19 Will Clark	1.25	.55	.16
☐ 20 Ryne Sandberg	2.00	.90	.25

1985 Woolworth's

This 44-card standard-size set features color as well as black and white cards of All Time Record Holders. The cards are printed with blue ink on an orange and white back. The set was produced for Woolworth's by Topps and was packaged in a colorful box which contained a checklist of the cards in the set on the back panel. The numerical order of the cards coincides alphabetically with the player's name.

	NRMT	VG-E	GOOD
COMPLETE SET (44)	4.00	1.80	.50
COMMON CARD (1-44)	.05	.02	.01
☐ 1 Hank Aaron	.75	.35	.09
☐ 2 Grover C. Alexander	.25	.11	.03
☐ 3 Ernie Banks	.25	.11	.03
☐ 4 Yogi Berra	.25	.11	.03
☐ 5 Lou Brock	.15	.07	.02
☐ 6 Steve Carlton	.25	.11	.03
☐ 7 Jack Chesbro	.05	.02	.01
☐ 8 Ty Cobb	.75	.35	.09
☐ 9 Sam Crawford	.15	.07	.02
☐ 10 Rollie Fingers	.15	.07	.02
☐ 11 Whitey Ford	.25	.11	.03
☐ 12 John Frederick	.05	.02	.01
☐ 13 Frankie Frisch	.15	.07	.02
☐ 14 Lou Gehrig	.75	.35	.09
☐ 15 Jim Gentile	.05	.02	.01
☐ 16 Dwight Gooden	.50	.23	.06
☐ 17 Rickey Henderson	.35	.16	.04
☐ 18 Rogers Hornsby	.25	.11	.03
☐ 19 Frank Howard	.10	.05	.01
☐ 20 Cliff Johnson	.05	.02	.01
☐ 21 Walter Johnson	.25	.11	.03
☐ 22 Hub Leonard	.05	.02	.01
☐ 23 Mickey Mantle	1.00	.45	.12
☐ 24 Roger Maris	.50	.23	.06
☐ 25 Christy Mathewson	.25	.11	.03
☐ 26 Willie Mays	.75	.35	.09
☐ 27 Stan Musial	.50	.23	.06
☐ 28 Dan Quisenberry	.05	.02	.01
☐ 29 Frank Robinson	.25	.11	.03
☐ 30 Pete Rose	.50	.23	.06
☐ 31 Babe Ruth	1.00	.45	.12
☐ 32 Nolan Ryan	1.00	.45	.12
☐ 33 George Sisler	.25	.11	.03
☐ 34 Tris Speaker	.25	.11	.03
☐ 35 Ed Walsh	.15	.07	.02
☐ 36 Lloyd Waner	.15	.07	.02
☐ 37 Earl Webb	.05	.02	.01
☐ 38 Ted Williams	.75	.35	.09
☐ 39 Maury Wills	.10	.05	.01
☐ 40 Hack Wilson	.15	.07	.02
☐ 41 Owen Wilson	.05	.02	.01
☐ 42 Willie Wilson	.05	.02	.01
☐ 43 Rudy York	.05	.02	.01
☐ 44 Cy Young	.25	.11	.03

1986 Woolworth's

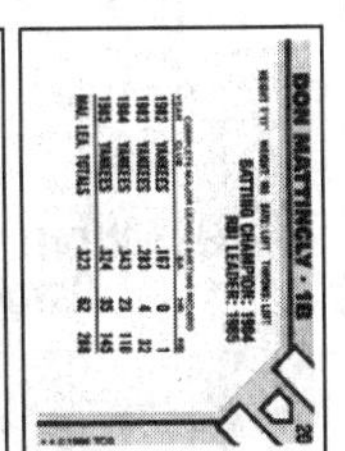

This boxed set of 33 standard-size cards was produced by Topps for Woolworth's variety stores. The set features players who hold or have held hitting, home run or RBI titles. The cards have a glossy finish. The card fronts are bordered in yellow with the subtitle "Topps Collectors' Series" across the top. The card backs are printed in green and blue ink on white card stock. The custom box gives the set checklist on the back.

	MINT	NRMT	EXC
COMPLETE SET (33)	4.00	1.80	.50
COMMON CARD (1-33)	.05	.02	.01
☐ 1 Tony Armas	.05	.02	.01
☐ 2 Don Baylor	.10	.05	.01
☐ 3 Wade Boggs	.30	.14	.04
☐ 4 George Brett	1.00	.45	.12
☐ 5 Bill Buckner	.05	.02	.01
☐ 6 Rod Carew	.30	.14	.04
☐ 7 Gary Carter	.10	.05	.01
☐ 8 Cecil Cooper	.10	.05	.01
☐ 9 Darrell Evans	.05	.02	.01
☐ 10 Dwight Evans	.10	.05	.01
☐ 11 George Foster	.10	.05	.01
☐ 12 Bob Grich	.05	.02	.01
☐ 13 Tony Gwynn	1.00	.45	.12
☐ 14 Keith Hernandez	.10	.05	.01
☐ 15 Reggie Jackson	.40	.18	.05
☐ 16 Dave Kingman	.05	.02	.01
☐ 17 Carney Lansford	.05	.02	.01
☐ 18 Fred Lynn	.10	.05	.01
☐ 19 Bill Madlock	.05	.02	.01
☐ 20 Don Mattingly	1.50	.70	.19
☐ 21 Willie McGee	.10	.05	.01
☐ 22 Hal McRae	.05	.02	.01
☐ 23 Dale Murphy	.20	.09	.03
☐ 24 Eddie Murray	.50	.23	.06
☐ 25 Ben Oglivie	.05	.02	.01
☐ 26 Al Oliver	.05	.02	.01
☐ 27 Dave Parker	.10	.05	.01
☐ 28 Jim Rice	.10	.05	.01
☐ 29 Pete Rose	.75	.35	.09
☐ 30 Mike Schmidt	.75	.35	.09
☐ 31 Gorman Thomas	.05	.02	.01
☐ 32 Willie Wilson	.05	.02	.01
☐ 33 Dave Winfield	.40	.18	.05

1987 Woolworth's

Topps produced this 33-card standard-size set for Woolworth's stores. The set is subtitled "Topps Collectors Series Baseball Highlights" and consists of high gloss card fronts with full-color photos. The cards show and describe highlights of the previous season. The card backs are printed in gold and purple and are numbered. The set was sold nationally in Woolworth's for a 1.99 suggested retail price.

	MINT	NRMT	EXC
COMPLETE SET (33)	4.00	1.80	.50
COMMON CARD (1-33)	.05	.02	.01
☐ 1 Steve Carlton	.25	.11	.03
☐ 2 Cecil Cooper	.10	.05	.01
☐ 3 Rickey Henderson	.30	.14	.04
☐ 4 Reggie Jackson	.40	.18	.05
☐ 5 Jim Rice	.10	.05	.01
☐ 6 Don Sutton	.25	.11	.03
☐ 7 Roger Clemens	.75	.35	.09
☐ 8 Mike Schmidt	.60	.25	.07
☐ 9 Jesse Barfield	.05	.02	.01
☐ 10 Wade Boggs	.30	.14	.04
☐ 11 Tim Raines	.10	.05	.01
☐ 12 Jose Canseco	.75	.35	.09
☐ 13 Todd Worrell	.05	.02	.01
☐ 14 Dave Righetti	.05	.02	.01
☐ 15 Don Mattingly	1.00	.45	.12
☐ 16 Tony Gwynn	1.00	.45	.12
☐ 17 Marty Barrett	.05	.02	.01
☐ 18 Mike Scott	.05	.02	.01
☐ 19 Bruce Hurst	.05	.02	.01
☐ 20 Calvin Schiraldi	.05	.02	.01
☐ 21 Dwight Evans	.10	.05	.01
☐ 22 Dave Henderson	.05	.02	.01
☐ 23 Len Dykstra	.20	.09	.03
☐ 24 Bob Ojeda	.05	.02	.01
☐ 25 Gary Carter	.10	.05	.01
☐ 26 Ron Darling	.05	.02	.01
☐ 27 Jim Rice	.10	.05	.01
☐ 28 Bruce Hurst	.05	.02	.01
☐ 29 Darryl Strawberry	.20	.09	.03
☐ 30 Ray Knight	.05	.02	.01
☐ 31 Keith Hernandez	.10	.05	.01
☐ 32 Mets Celebration	.10	.05	.01
☐ 33 Ray Knight	.10	.05	.01

1988 Woolworth's

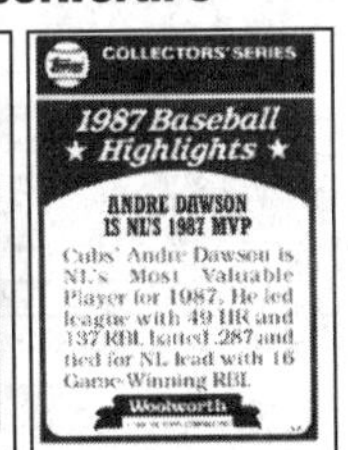

COLLECTORS' SERIES
1987 Baseball
★ Highlights ★
ANDRE DAWSON
IS NL'S 1987 MVP

Topps produced this 33-card standard-size set for Woolworth's stores. The set is subtitled "Topps Collectors' Series Baseball Highlights" and consists of high gloss card fronts with full-color photos. The cards show and describe highlights of the previous season. Cards 19-33 commemorate the World Series with highlights and key players of each game in the series. The card backs are printed in red and blue on white card stock and are numbered. The set was sold nationally in Woolworth's for a 1.99 suggested retail price.

	MINT	NRMT	EXC
COMPLETE SET (33)	4.00	1.80	.50
COMMON CARD (1-33)	.05	.02	.01
☐ 1 Don Baylor	.10	.05	.01
☐ 2 Vince Coleman	.05	.02	.01
☐ 3 Darrell Evans	.05	.02	.01
☐ 4 Don Mattingly	1.00	.45	.12
☐ 5 Eddie Murray	.50	.23	.06
☐ 6 Nolan Ryan	2.00	.90	.25
☐ 7 Mike Schmidt	.60	.25	.07
☐ 8 Andre Dawson	.20	.09	.03
☐ 9 George Bell	.05	.02	.01
☐ 10 Steve Bedrosian	.05	.02	.01
☐ 11 Roger Clemens	.75	.35	.09
☐ 12 Tony Gwynn	1.00	.45	.12
☐ 13 Wade Boggs	.25	.11	.03
☐ 14 Benito Santiago	.05	.02	.01
☐ 15 Mark McGwire UER (Referenced on card back as NL ROY, sic)	1.00	.45	.12
☐ 16 Dave Righetti	.05	.02	.01
☐ 17 Jeffrey Leonard	.05	.02	.01
☐ 18 Gary Gaetti	.05	.02	.01
☐ 19 Frank Viola WS1	.05	.02	.01
☐ 20 Dan Gladden WS1	.05	.02	.01
☐ 21 Bert Blyleven WS2	.10	.05	.01
☐ 22 Gary Gaetti WS2	.05	.02	.01
☐ 23 John Tudor WS3	.05	.02	.01
☐ 24 Todd Worrell WS3	.05	.02	.01
☐ 25 Tom Lawless WS4	.05	.02	.01
☐ 26 Willie McGee WS4	.05	.02	.01
☐ 27 Danny Cox WS5	.05	.02	.01
☐ 28 Curt Ford WS5	.05	.02	.01
☐ 29 Don Baylor WS6	.10	.05	.01
☐ 30 Kent Hrbek WS6	.10	.05	.01
☐ 31 Kirby Puckett WS7	1.00	.45	.12
☐ 32 Greg Gagne WS7	.05	.02	.01
☐ 33 Frank Viola WS-MVP	.05	.02	.01

1989 Woolworth's

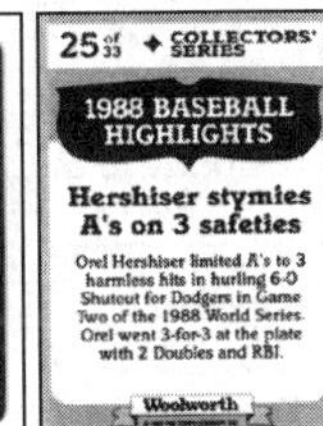

1988 BASEBALL HIGHLIGHTS
Hershiser stymies A's on 3 safeties

The 1989 Woolworth's Highlights set contains 33 standard-size glossy cards. The fronts have red and white borders. The vertically oriented backs are yellow and red, and describe highlights from the 1988 season including the World Series. The cards were distributed through Woolworth stores as a boxed set.

	MINT	NRMT	EXC
COMPLETE SET (33)	3.00	1.35	.35
COMMON CARD (1-33)	.05	.02	.01
☐ 1 Jose Canseco MVP	.50	.23	.06
☐ 2 Kirk Gibson MVP	.20	.09	.03
☐ 3 Frank Viola CY	.05	.02	.01
☐ 4 Orel Hershiser CY	.10	.05	.01
☐ 5 Walt Weiss ROY	.05	.02	.01
☐ 6 Chris Sabo ROY	.05	.02	.01
☐ 7 George Bell	.05	.02	.01
☐ 8 Wade Boggs	.30	.14	.04
☐ 9 Tom Browning	.05	.02	.01
☐ 10 Gary Carter	.10	.05	.01
☐ 11 Andre Dawson	.10	.05	.01
☐ 12 John Franco	.10	.05	.01
☐ 13 Randy Johnson	1.00	.45	.12
☐ 14 Doug Jones	.05	.02	.01
☐ 15 Kevin McReynolds	.05	.02	.01
☐ 16 Gene Nelson	.05	.02	.01
☐ 17 Jeff Reardon	.05	.02	.01
☐ 18 Pat Tabler	.05	.02	.01
☐ 19 Tim Belcher	.05	.02	.01
☐ 20 Dennis Eckersley	.10	.05	.01
☐ 21 Orel Hershiser	.10	.05	.01
☐ 22 Gregg Jefferies	.20	.09	.03
☐ 23 Jose Canseco	.50	.23	.06
☐ 24 Kirk Gibson	.20	.09	.03
☐ 25 Orel Hershiser	.10	.05	.01
☐ 26 Mike Marshall	.05	.02	.01
☐ 27 Mark McGwire	1.00	.45	.12
☐ 28 Rick Honeycutt	.05	.02	.01
☐ 29 Tim Belcher	.05	.02	.01
☐ 30 Jay Howell	.05	.02	.01
☐ 31 Mickey Hatcher	.05	.02	.01
☐ 32 Mike Davis	.05	.02	.01
☐ 33 Orel Hershiser	.10	.05	.01

1990 Woolworth's

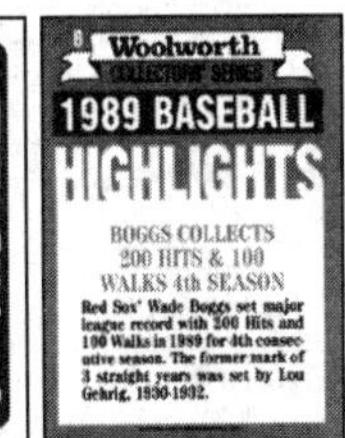

Woolworth
1989 BASEBALL HIGHLIGHTS
BOGGS COLLECTS 200 HITS & 100 WALKS 4th SEASON

The 1990 Woolworth set is a 33-card standard-size set highlighting some of the more important events of the 1989 season. This set is broken down between major award winners, career highlights, and post-season heroes. The first six cards of the set feature the award winners while the last 11 cards of the set feature post-season heroes.

	MINT	NRMT	EXC
COMPLETE SET (33)	5.00	2.20	.60
COMMON CARD (1-33)	.05	.02	.01
☐ 1 Robin Yount MVP	.25	.11	.03
☐ 2 Kevin Mitchell MVP	.05	.02	.01
☐ 3 Bret Saberhagen CY	.10	.05	.01
☐ 4 Mark Davis CY	.05	.02	.01
☐ 5 Gregg Olson ROY	.05	.02	.01
☐ 6 Jerome Walton ROY	.05	.02	.01
☐ 7 Bert Blyleven	.10	.05	.01
☐ 8 Wade Boggs	.30	.14	.04
☐ 9 George Brett	1.00	.45	.12
☐ 10 Vince Coleman	.05	.02	.01
☐ 11 Andre Dawson	.10	.05	.01
☐ 12 Dwight Evans	.05	.02	.01
☐ 13 Carlton Fisk	.30	.14	.04
☐ 14 Rickey Henderson	.40	.18	.05
☐ 15 Dale Murphy	.20	.09	.03
☐ 16 Eddie Murray	.50	.23	.06
☐ 17 Jeff Reardon	.05	.02	.01
☐ 18 Rick Reuschel	.05	.02	.01
☐ 19 Cal Ripken	2.00	.90	.25
☐ 20 Nolan Ryan	2.00	.90	.25
☐ 21 Ryne Sandberg	.75	.35	.09
☐ 22 Robin Yount	.40	.18	.05
☐ 23 Rickey Henderson	.40	.18	.05
☐ 24 Will Clark	.50	.23	.06
☐ 25 Dave Stewart	.05	.02	.01
☐ 26 Walt Weiss	.05	.02	.01
☐ 27 Mike Moore	.05	.02	.01
☐ 28 Terry Steinbach	.10	.05	.01
☐ 29 Dave Henderson	.05	.02	.01
☐ 30 Matt Williams	.50	.23	.06
☐ 31 Rickey Henderson	.40	.18	.05
☐ 32 Kevin Mitchell	.05	.02	.01
☐ 33 Dave Stewart	.05	.02	.01

1991 Woolworth's

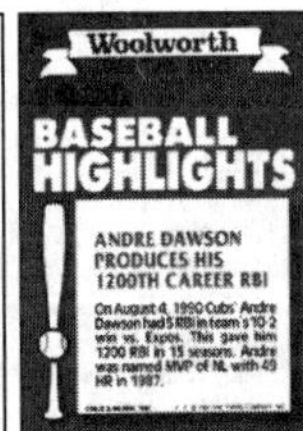

Woolworth
BASEBALL HIGHLIGHTS
ANDRE DAWSON PRODUCES HIS 1200TH CAREER RBI

Topps produced this 33-card boxed standard-size set for Woolworth stores. The cards feature glossy color player photos on the fronts, with yellow borders on a white card face. The backs are printed in red, black, and white, and commemorate outstanding achievements of the players featured on the cards. The set can be subdivided as follows: MVPs (1-2), Cy Young winners (3-4), ROYs (5-6), '90 highlights in alphabetical order (7-22), playoff MVPs (23-24), and World Series action in chronological order (25-33).

	MINT	NRMT	EXC
COMPLETE SET (33)	5.00	2.20	.60
COMMON CARD (1-33)	.05	.02	.01
☐ 1 Barry Bonds	.50	.23	.06
☐ 2 Rickey Henderson (Bat on shoulder)	.30	.14	.04
☐ 3 Doug Drabek	.05	.02	.01
☐ 4 Bob Welch	.05	.02	.01
☐ 5 David Justice	.20	.09	.03
☐ 6 Sandy Alomar Jr.	.10	.05	.01
☐ 7 Bert Blyleven	.10	.05	.01
☐ 8 George Brett	1.00	.45	.12
☐ 9 Andre Dawson	.25	.11	.03
☐ 10 Dwight Evans	.05	.02	.01
☐ 11 Alex Fernandez	.40	.18	.05
☐ 12 Carlton Fisk	.30	.14	.04
☐ 13 Kevin Maas	.05	.02	.01
☐ 14 Dale Murphy	.20	.09	.03
☐ 15 Eddie Murray	.50	.23	.06
☐ 16 Dave Parker	.10	.05	.01
☐ 17 Jeff Reardon	.05	.02	.01
☐ 18 Cal Ripken	2.00	.90	.25
☐ 19 Nolan Ryan	2.00	.90	.25
☐ 20 Ryne Sandberg	.75	.35	.09
☐ 21 Bobby Thigpen	.05	.02	.01
☐ 22 Robin Yount	.30	.14	.04
☐ 23 Rob Dibble and Randy Myers	.05	.02	.01
☐ 24 Dave Stewart	.05	.02	.01
☐ 25 Eric Davis	.05	.02	.01
☐ 26 Rickey Henderson (Running bases)	.30	.14	.04
☐ 27 Billy Hatcher	.05	.02	.01
☐ 28 Joe Oliver	.05	.02	.01
☐ 29 Chris Sabo	.05	.02	.01
☐ 30 Barry Larkin	.30	.14	.04
☐ 31 Jose Rijo (Pitching Game 4)	.05	.02	.01
☐ 32 Reds Celebrate (1990 World Champions)	.05	.02	.01
☐ 33 Jose Rijo World Series MVP	.05	.02	.01

1936 World Wide Gum V355

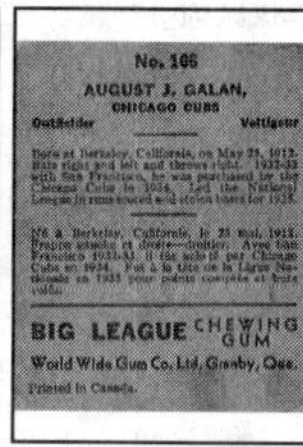

The cards in this 135-card set measure approximately 2 1/2" by 3". The 1936 Canadian Goudey set was issued by World Wide Gum Company and contains black and white cards. This issue is the most difficult to obtain of the Canadian Goudeys. The fronts feature player photos with white borders. The bilingual (French and English) backs carry player biography and career highlights. The World Wide Gum Company has its location listed as Granby, Quebec on these cards (as opposed to Montreal on earlier issues). The cards are numbered on both sides.

	EX-MT	VG-E	GOOD
COMPLETE SET (135)	16000.00	7200.00	2000.00
COMMON CARD (1-135)	60.00	27.00	7.50
☐ 1 Jimmy Dykes	75.00	34.00	9.50
☐ 2 Paul Waner	125.00	55.00	15.50
☐ 3 Cy Blanton	60.00	27.00	7.50
☐ 4 Sam Leslie	60.00	27.00	7.50
☐ 5 Johnny Vergez	60.00	27.00	7.50
☐ 6 Arky Vaughan	125.00	55.00	15.50
☐ 7 Bill Terry	150.00	70.00	19.00
☐ 8 Joe Moore	60.00	27.00	7.50
☐ 9 Gus Mancuso	60.00	27.00	7.50
☐ 10 Fred Marberry	60.00	27.00	7.50
☐ 11 George Selkirk	75.00	34.00	9.50
☐ 12 Spud Davis	60.00	27.00	7.50
☐ 13 Chuck Klein	75.00	34.00	9.50
☐ 14 Fred Fitzsimmons	75.00	34.00	9.50
☐ 15 Bill DeLancey	60.00	27.00	7.50
☐ 16 Billy Herman	125.00	55.00	15.50
☐ 17 George Davis	60.00	27.00	7.50
☐ 18 Rip Collins	60.00	27.00	7.50
☐ 19 Dizzy Dean	350.00	160.00	45.00
☐ 20 Roy Parmelee	60.00	27.00	7.50
☐ 21 Vic Sorrell	60.00	27.00	7.50
☐ 22 Harry Danning	60.00	27.00	7.50
☐ 23 Hal Schumacher	75.00	34.00	9.50
☐ 24 Cy Perkins	60.00	27.00	7.50
☐ 25 Leo Durocher	200.00	90.00	25.00
☐ 26 Glenn Myatt	60.00	27.00	7.50
☐ 27 Bob Seeds	60.00	27.00	7.50
☐ 28 Jimmy Ripple	60.00	27.00	7.50
☐ 29 Al Schacht	75.00	34.00	9.50
☐ 30 Pete Fox	60.00	27.00	7.50
☐ 31 Del Baker	60.00	27.00	7.50
☐ 32 Herman(Flea) Clifton	60.00	27.00	7.50
☐ 33 Tommy Bridges	75.00	34.00	9.50
☐ 34 Bill Dickey	200.00	90.00	25.00
☐ 35 Wally Berger	75.00	34.00	9.50
☐ 36 Slick Castleman	60.00	27.00	7.50
☐ 37 Dick Bartell	75.00	34.00	9.50
☐ 38 Red Rolfe	75.00	34.00	9.50
☐ 39 Waite Hoyt	125.00	55.00	15.50
☐ 40 Wes Ferrell	75.00	34.00	9.50
☐ 41 Hank Greenberg	200.00	90.00	25.00
☐ 42 Charlie Gehringer	150.00	70.00	19.00
☐ 43 Goose Goslin	125.00	55.00	15.50
☐ 44 Schoolboy Rowe	75.00	34.00	9.50
☐ 45 Mickey Cochrane MG	150.00	70.00	19.00
☐ 46 Joe Cronin	150.00	70.00	19.00
☐ 47 Jimmie Foxx	300.00	135.00	38.00
☐ 48 Jerry Walker	60.00	27.00	7.50
☐ 49 Charlie Gelbert	60.00	27.00	7.50
☐ 50 Ray Hayworth	60.00	27.00	7.50
☐ 51 Joe DiMaggio	3500.00	1600.00	450.00
☐ 52 Billy Rogell	60.00	27.00	7.50
☐ 53 John McCarthy	60.00	27.00	7.50
☐ 54 Phil Cavarretta	75.00	34.00	9.50
☐ 55 KiKi Cuyler	125.00	55.00	15.50
☐ 56 Lefty Gomez	150.00	70.00	19.00
☐ 57 Gabby Hartnett	125.00	55.00	15.50
☐ 58 John Marcum	60.00	27.00	7.50
☐ 59 Burgess Whitehead	60.00	27.00	7.50
☐ 60 Whitey Whitehill	60.00	27.00	7.50
☐ 61 Bucky Walters	75.00	34.00	9.50
☐ 62 Luke Sewell	75.00	34.00	9.50
☐ 63 Joe Kuhel	60.00	27.00	7.50
☐ 64 Lou Finney	60.00	27.00	7.50
☐ 65 Fred Lindstrom	125.00	55.00	15.50
☐ 66 Paul Derringer	75.00	34.00	9.50
☐ 67 Steve O'Neill MG	75.00	34.00	9.50
☐ 68 Mule Haas	60.00	27.00	7.50
☐ 69 Marv Owen	60.00	27.00	7.50
☐ 70 Bill Hallahan	60.00	27.00	7.50
☐ 71 Billy Urbanski	60.00	27.00	7.50
☐ 72 Dan Taylor	60.00	27.00	7.50
☐ 73 Heinie Manush	125.00	55.00	15.50
☐ 74 Jo Jo White	60.00	27.00	7.50
☐ 75 Joe Medwick	150.00	70.00	19.00
☐ 76 Joe Vosmik	60.00	27.00	7.50
☐ 77 Al Simmons	150.00	70.00	19.00
☐ 78 Shaug Shaughnessy	60.00	27.00	7.50
☐ 79 Harry Smythe	60.00	27.00	7.50
☐ 80 Bennie Tate	60.00	27.00	7.50
☐ 81 Billy Rheil	60.00	27.00	7.50
☐ 82 Lauri Myllykangas	60.00	27.00	7.50
☐ 83 Ben Sankey	60.00	27.00	7.50
☐ 84 Crip Polli	60.00	27.00	7.50
☐ 85 Jim Bottomley	125.00	55.00	15.50
☐ 86 Watson Clark	60.00	27.00	7.50
☐ 87 Ossie Bluege	75.00	34.00	9.50
☐ 88 Lefty Grove	200.00	90.00	25.00
☐ 89 Charlie Grimm MG	75.00	34.00	9.50
☐ 90 Ben Chapman	75.00	34.00	9.50
☐ 91 Frank Crosetti	100.00	45.00	12.50
☐ 92 John Pomorski	60.00	27.00	7.50
☐ 93 Jess Haines	125.00	55.00	15.50
☐ 94 Chick Hafey	125.00	55.00	15.50
☐ 95 Tony Piet	60.00	27.00	7.50
☐ 96 Lou Gehrig	2500.00	1100.00	300.00
☐ 97 Billy Jurges	75.00	34.00	9.50
☐ 98 Smead Jolley	75.00	34.00	9.50
☐ 99 Jimmy Wilson	75.00	34.00	9.50
☐ 100 Lon Warneke	75.00	34.00	9.50
☐ 101 Vito Tamulis	60.00	27.00	7.50
☐ 102 Red Ruffing	125.00	55.00	15.50
☐ 103 Earl Grace	60.00	27.00	7.50
☐ 104 Rox Lawson	60.00	27.00	7.50
☐ 105 Stan Hack	75.00	34.00	9.50
☐ 106 Augie Galan	60.00	27.00	7.50
☐ 107 Frank Frisch MG	125.00	55.00	15.50
☐ 108 Bill McKechnie MG	125.00	55.00	15.50
☐ 109 Bill Lee	75.00	34.00	9.50
☐ 110 Connie Mack MG	150.00	70.00	19.00
☐ 111 Frank Reiber	60.00	27.00	7.50
☐ 112 Zeke Bonura	75.00	34.00	9.50
☐ 113 Luke Appling	125.00	55.00	15.50
☐ 114 Monte Pearson	60.00	27.00	7.50
☐ 115 Bob O'Farrell	60.00	27.00	7.50
☐ 116 Marvin Duke	60.00	27.00	7.50
☐ 117 Paul Florence	60.00	27.00	7.50
☐ 118 John Berley	60.00	27.00	7.50
☐ 119 Tom Oliver	60.00	27.00	7.50
☐ 120 Norman Kies	60.00	27.00	7.50
☐ 121 Hal King	60.00	27.00	7.50
☐ 122 Tom Abernathy	60.00	27.00	7.50
☐ 123 Phil Hensich	60.00	27.00	7.50
☐ 124 Ray Schalk	125.00	55.00	15.50
☐ 125 Paul Dunlap	60.00	27.00	7.50
☐ 126 Benny Bates	60.00	27.00	7.50
☐ 127 George Puccinelli	60.00	27.00	7.50
☐ 128 Stevie Stevenson	60.00	27.00	7.50
☐ 129 Rabbit Maranville MG	125.00	55.00	15.50
☐ 130 Bucky Harris MG	125.00	55.00	15.50
☐ 131 Al Lopez	125.00	55.00	15.50
☐ 132 Buddy Myer	75.00	34.00	9.50
☐ 133 Cliff Bolton	60.00	27.00	7.50
☐ 134 Estel Crabtree	60.00	27.00	7.50
☐ 135 Phil Weintraub	60.00	27.00	7.50

1939 World Wide Gum V351A

These 25 photos measure approximately 4" by 5 3/4" and feature on their fronts white-bordered sepia-toned posed player photos. The player's facsimile autograph appears across the picture. The backs carry tips printed in brown ink on how to play baseball. The photos are unnumbered and checklisted below in alphabetical order.

	EX-MT	VG-E	GOOD
COMPLETE SET (25)	2000.00	900.00	250.00
COMMON CARD (1-25)	30.00	13.50	3.70
☐ 1 Morris Arnovich	30.00	13.50	3.70
☐ 2 Sam Bell	30.00	13.50	3.70
☐ 3 Zeke Bonura	40.00	18.00	5.00
☐ 4 Earl Caldwell	30.00	13.50	3.70
☐ 5 Flea Clifton	30.00	13.50	3.70
☐ 6 Frank Crosetti	50.00	22.00	6.25
☐ 7 Harry Danning	30.00	13.50	3.70
☐ 8 Dizzy Dean	150.00	70.00	19.00
☐ 9 Emile De Jonghe	30.00	13.50	3.70
☐ 10 Paul Derringer	30.00	13.50	3.70
☐ 11 Joe DiMaggio	600.00	275.00	75.00
☐ 12 Vince DiMaggio	75.00	34.00	9.50
☐ 13 Charles Gehringer	125.00	55.00	15.50
☐ 14 Gene Hasson	30.00	13.50	3.70
☐ 15 Tom Henrich	60.00	27.00	7.50
☐ 16 Fred Hutchinson	50.00	22.00	6.25
☐ 17 Phil Marchildon	40.00	18.00	5.00
☐ 18 Mike Meola	30.00	13.50	3.70
☐ 19 Arnold Moser	30.00	13.50	3.70
☐ 20 Frank Pytlak	30.00	13.50	3.70
☐ 21 Frank Reiber	30.00	13.50	3.70
☐ 22 Lee Rogers	30.00	13.50	3.70
☐ 23 Cecil Travis	40.00	18.00	5.00
☐ 24 Hal Trosky	40.00	18.00	5.00
☐ 25 Ted Williams	600.00	275.00	75.00

1939 World Wide Gum Trimmed Premiums V351B

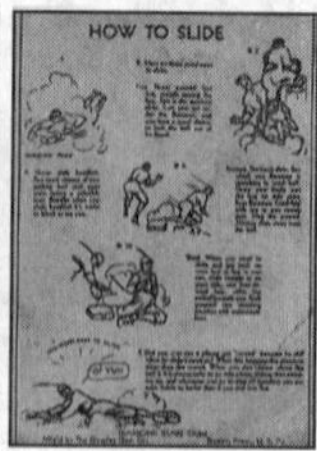

These 48 photos measure approximately 4" by 5 3/4" and feature on their fronts white-bordered sepia-toned posed player photos. The set is essentially a re-issue of the R303A set. The white borders at the top and bottom were trimmed (during the manufacturing process) to the same size as the Series A photos. The player's facsimile autograph appears across the photo. The backs carry tips printed in brown ink on how to play baseball. The photos are unnumbered and checklisted below in alphabetical order.

	EX-MT	VG-E	GOOD
COMPLETE SET (48)	1600.00	700.00	200.00
COMMON CARD (1-48)	20.00	9.00	2.50
☐ 1 Luke Appling	40.00	18.00	5.00
☐ 2 Earl Averill	40.00	18.00	5.00
☐ 3 Wally Berger	30.00	13.50	3.70
☐ 4 Darrell Blanton	20.00	9.00	2.50
☐ 5 Zeke Bonura	30.00	13.50	3.70
☐ 6 Mace Brown	20.00	9.00	2.50
☐ 7 George Case	20.00	9.00	2.50
☐ 8 Ben Chapman	20.00	9.00	2.50
☐ 9 Joe Cronin	40.00	18.00	5.00
☐ 10 Frank Crosetti	25.00	11.00	3.10
☐ 11 Paul Derringer	25.00	11.00	3.10
☐ 12 Bill Dickey	50.00	22.00	6.25
☐ 13 Joe DiMaggio	250.00	110.00	31.00
☐ 14 Bob Feller	75.00	34.00	9.50
☐ 15 Jimmy Foxx	60.00	27.00	7.50
☐ 16 Charlie Gehringer	40.00	18.00	5.00
☐ 17 Lefty Gomez	40.00	18.00	5.00
☐ 18 Ival Goodman	20.00	9.00	2.50
☐ 19 Joe Gordon	25.00	11.00	3.10
☐ 20 Hank Greenberg	50.00	22.00	6.25
☐ 21 Buddy Hassett	20.00	9.00	2.50
☐ 22 Jeff Heath	20.00	9.00	2.50
☐ 23 Tom Henrich	30.00	13.50	3.70
☐ 24 Billy Herman	40.00	18.00	5.00
☐ 25 Frank Higgins	20.00	9.00	2.50
☐ 26 Fred Hutchinson	25.00	11.00	3.10
☐ 27 Bob Johnson	25.00	11.00	3.10
☐ 28 Ken Keltner	25.00	11.00	3.10
☐ 29 Mike Kreevich	20.00	9.00	2.50
☐ 30 Ernie Lombardi	40.00	18.00	5.00
☐ 31 Gus Mancuso	20.00	9.00	2.50
☐ 32 Eric McNair	20.00	9.00	2.50
☐ 33 Van Mungo	25.00	11.00	3.10
☐ 34 Buck Newsom	25.00	11.00	3.10
☐ 35 Mel Ott	40.00	18.00	5.00
☐ 36 Marvin Owen	20.00	9.00	2.50
☐ 37 Frankie Pytlak	20.00	9.00	2.50
☐ 38 Woody Rich	20.00	9.00	2.50
☐ 39 Charlie Root	25.00	11.00	3.10
☐ 40 Al Simmons	40.00	18.00	5.00
☐ 41 Jim Tabor	20.00	9.00	2.50
☐ 42 Cecil Travis	20.00	9.00	2.50
☐ 43 Hal Trosky	20.00	9.00	2.50
☐ 44 Arky Vaughan	40.00	18.00	5.00
☐ 45 Joe Vosmik	20.00	9.00	2.50
☐ 46 Lon Warneke	20.00	9.00	2.50
☐ 47 Ted Williams	250.00	110.00	31.00
☐ 48 Rudy York	25.00	11.00	3.10

1950 World Wide Gum V362

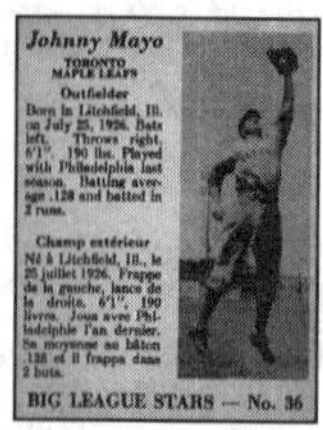

The cards in this 48-card set measure approximately 2 1/2" by 3 1/4". In 1950, long after its former parent company had disappeared from the card market, the World Wide Gum Company issued a set of blue printed cards depicting players from the International League. The fronts feature player photos with bilingual (French and English) biographies. The backs are blank. The series was entitled "Big League Stars". The catalog designation for this set is V362. The cards are numbered on the front.

	NRMT	VG-E	GOOD
COMPLETE SET (48)	4000.00	1800.00	500.00
COMMON CARD (1-48)	75.00	34.00	9.50
☐ 1 Rocky Bridges	100.00	45.00	12.50
☐ 2 Chuck Connors	350.00	160.00	45.00
☐ 3 Jake Wade	75.00	34.00	9.50
☐ 4 Al Cihocki	75.00	34.00	9.50
☐ 5 John Simmons	75.00	34.00	9.50
☐ 6 Frank Trechock	75.00	34.00	9.50
☐ 7 Steve Lembo	75.00	34.00	9.50
☐ 8 Johnny Welaj	75.00	34.00	9.50
☐ 9 Seymour Block	75.00	34.00	9.50
☐ 10 Pat McGlothlin	75.00	34.00	9.50
☐ 11 Bryan Stephens	75.00	34.00	9.50
☐ 12 Clarence Podbielan	100.00	45.00	12.50
☐ 13 Clem Hausmann	75.00	34.00	9.50
☐ 14 Turk Lown	100.00	45.00	12.50
☐ 15 Joe Payne	75.00	34.00	9.50
☐ 16 Coaker Triplett	100.00	45.00	12.50
☐ 17 Nick Strincevich	75.00	34.00	9.50
☐ 18 Charlie Thompson	75.00	34.00	9.50
☐ 19 Eric Silverman	75.00	34.00	9.50
☐ 20 George Schmees	75.00	34.00	9.50
☐ 21 George Binks	75.00	34.00	9.50
☐ 22 Gino Cimoli	100.00	45.00	12.50
☐ 23 Marty Tabacheck	75.00	34.00	9.50
☐ 24 Al Gionfriddo	100.00	45.00	12.50
☐ 25 Ronnie Lee	75.00	34.00	9.50
☐ 26 Clyde King	100.00	45.00	12.50
☐ 27 Harry Heslet	75.00	34.00	9.50
☐ 28 Jerry Scala	75.00	34.00	9.50
☐ 29 Boris Woyt	75.00	34.00	9.50
☐ 30 Jack Collum	75.00	34.00	9.50
☐ 31 Chet Laabs	100.00	45.00	12.50
☐ 32 Carden Gillenwater	75.00	34.00	9.50
☐ 33 Irving Medlinger	75.00	34.00	9.50
☐ 34 Toby Atwell	75.00	34.00	9.50
☐ 35 Charlie Marshall	75.00	34.00	9.50
☐ 36 Johnny Mayo	75.00	34.00	9.50
☐ 37 Gene Markland	75.00	34.00	9.50
☐ 38 Russ Kerns	75.00	34.00	9.50
☐ 39 Jim Prendergast	75.00	34.00	9.50
☐ 40 Lou Welaj	75.00	34.00	9.50
☐ 41 Clyde Kluttz	100.00	45.00	12.50
☐ 42 Bill Glynn	75.00	34.00	9.50
☐ 43 Don Richmond	75.00	34.00	9.50
☐ 44 Hank Biasatti	75.00	34.00	9.50
☐ 45 Tom Lasorda	400.00	180.00	50.00
☐ 46 Al Roberge	75.00	34.00	9.50
☐ 47 George Byam	75.00	34.00	9.50
☐ 48 Dutch Mele	100.00	45.00	12.50

1993 World University Games*

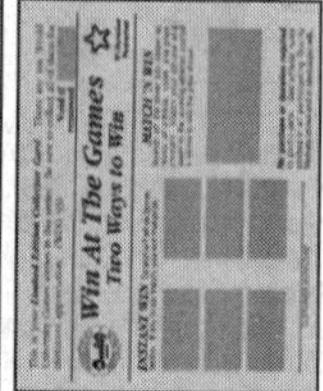

This 10-card set features borderless photos of various sporting events at the World University Games in Buffalo in 1993. The backs display two different ways the collector could win prizes in two different scratch-off games. The cards are unnumbered and checklisted below alphabetically according to the sport pictured on the card front.

	MINT	NRMT	EXC
COMPLETE SET (10)	3.00	1.35	.35
COMMON CARD (1-10)	.25	.11	.03
☐ 1 Baseball Charles Johnson batting	1.00	.45	.12
☐ 2 Basketball	.25	.11	.03
☐ 3 Gymnastics	.25	.11	.03
☐ 4 Pilot Field	.25	.11	.03
☐ 5 Rich Stadium	.25	.11	.03
☐ 6 Rowing	.25	.11	.03
☐ 7 Soccer	.25	.11	.03
☐ 8 Swimming	.25	.11	.03
☐ 9 Tennis	.25	.11	.03
☐ 10 Track and Field	.25	.11	.03

1943 Yankees Stamps

This stamp set commemorates the New York Yankees and their World Series victory in 1943. The stamps were perforated together in a sheet with five rows of six stamps across. The stamps are ordered alphabetically on the stamp sheet left to right. Each stamp measures approximately 1 3/4" by 2 3/8" and is in full color. The player's name is printed in white on a red background at the bottom of each stamp. An album for the set was issued but it is more difficult to find than the stamps. The catalog designation for this set is ST101.

	EX-MT	VG-E	GOOD
COMPLETE SET (30)	50.00	22.00	6.25
COMMON CARD (1-30)	1.50	.70	.19
☐ 1 Ernie Bonham	3.00	1.35	.35
☐ 2 Hank Borowy	3.00	1.35	.35
☐ 3 Marvin Breuer	1.50	.70	.19
☐ 4 Tommy Byrne	2.50	1.10	.30
☐ 5 Spud Chandler	3.00	1.35	.35
☐ 6 Earl Combs CO	5.00	2.20	.60
☐ 7 Frank Crosetti	3.00	1.35	.35
☐ 8 Bill Dickey	8.00	3.60	1.00
☐ 9 Atley Donald	1.50	.70	.19
☐ 10 Nick Etten	1.50	.70	.19
☐ 11 Art Fletcher CO	1.50	.70	.19
☐ 12 Joe Gordon	3.00	1.35	.35
☐ 13 Oscar Grimes	1.50	.70	.19
☐ 14 Rollie Hemsley	1.50	.70	.19
☐ 15 Bill Johnson	1.50	.70	.19
☐ 16 Charlie Keller	3.00	1.35	.35
☐ 17 John Lindell	2.00	.90	.25
☐ 18 Joe McCarthy MG	5.00	2.20	.60
☐ 19 Bud Metheny	1.50	.70	.19
☐ 20 Johnny Murphy	2.00	.90	.25
☐ 21 Pat O'Dougherty	1.50	.70	.19
☐ 22 Marius Russo	1.50	.70	.19
☐ 23 John Schulte	1.50	.70	.19
☐ 24 Ken Sears	1.50	.70	.19
☐ 25 Tuck Stainback	1.50	.70	.19
☐ 26 George Stirnweiss	2.50	1.10	.30
☐ 27 Jim Turner	2.50	1.10	.30
☐ 28 Roy Weatherly	1.50	.70	.19
☐ 29 Charley Wensloff	1.50	.70	.19
☐ 30 Bill Zuber	1.50	.70	.19
☐ XX Album	20.00	9.00	2.50

1948 Yankees Team Issue

These 26 photos measure approximately 6 1/2" by 9". They feature members of the 1948 New York Yankees. These black and white photos also feature a facsimile signature and are framed by white borders. The photos are unnumbered and we have sequenced them in alphabetical order.

	NRMT	VG-E	GOOD
COMPLETE SET (26)	275.00	125.00	34.00
COMMON CARD (1-26)	3.50	1.55	.45
☐ 1 Mel Allen ANN	15.00	6.75	1.85
☐ 2 Yogi Berra	30.00	13.50	3.70
☐ 3 Bobby Brown	5.00	2.20	.60
☐ 4 Red Corriden CO	3.50	1.55	.45
☐ 5 Frank Crosetti	15.00	6.75	1.85
☐ 6 Joe DiMaggio	75.00	34.00	9.50
☐ 7 Chuck Dressen CO	7.50	3.40	.95
☐ 8 Karl Drews	3.50	1.55	.45
☐ 9 Red Embree	3.50	1.55	.45
☐ 10 Randy Gumpert	3.50	1.55	.45
☐ 11 Bucky Harris MG	10.00	4.50	1.25
☐ 12 Tom Henrich	15.00	6.75	1.85
☐ 13 Frank Hiller	3.50	1.55	.45
☐ 14 Bill Johnson	3.50	1.55	.45
☐ 15 Charlie Keller	5.00	2.20	.60
☐ 16 Ed Lopat	10.00	4.50	1.25
☐ 17 John Lindell	5.00	2.20	.60
☐ 18 Cliff Mapes	3.50	1.55	.45
☐ 19 Gus Niarhos	3.50	1.55	.45
☐ 20 George McQuinn	3.50	1.55	.45
☐ 21 Joe Page	10.00	4.50	1.25
☐ 22 Vic Raschi	5.00	2.20	.60
☐ 23 Allie Reynolds	10.00	4.50	1.25
☐ 24 Phil Rizzuto	25.00	11.00	3.10
☐ 25 Frank Shea	3.50	1.55	.45
☐ 26 Snuffy Stirnweiss	5.00	2.20	.60

1952-3 Yankees A.J. Begyn-Silvercraft

This 1952-3 set measures 3 1/2' by 5 1/2" and features three New York Yankee players. The reverse contains the A.J. Begyn identification at the left and the Silvercraft-Dexter Press identification vertically at the center. The player's name and the New York Yankees team identification are also contained on the reverse.

	NRMT	VG-E	GOOD
COMPLETE SET (3)	50.00	22.00	6.25
COMMON CARD (1-3)	15.00	6.75	1.85
☐ 1 Jerry Coleman	15.00	6.75	1.85
☐ 2 Irv Noren	15.00	6.75	1.85
☐ 3 Gene Woodling	20.00	9.00	2.50

1957 Yankees Jay Publishing

This 12-card set of the New York Yankees measures approximately 5" X 7". The fronts feature black-and-white posed player photos with the player's and team name printed below in the white border. These cards were packaged 12 to a packet and originally sold for 25 cents. The backs are blank. The cards are unnumbered and checklisted below in alphabetical order.

	NRMT	VG-E	GOOD
COMPLETE SET (12)	175.00	80.00	22.00
COMMON CARD (1-12)	3.50	1.55	.45
☐ 1 Hank Bauer	10.00	4.50	1.25
☐ 2 Larry Berra	25.00	11.00	3.10
☐ 3 Ed (Whitey) Ford	20.00	9.00	2.50
☐ 4 Elston Howard	7.50	3.40	.95
☐ 5 Johnny Kucks	3.50	1.55	.45
☐ 6 Don Larsen	7.50	3.40	.95
☐ 7 Mickey Mantle	60.00	27.00	7.50
☐ 8 Billy Martin	15.00	6.75	1.85
☐ 9 Gil McDougald	7.50	3.40	.95
☐ 10 Bill Skowron	7.50	3.40	.95
☐ 11 Casey Stengel MG	15.00	6.75	1.85
☐ 12 Tom Sturdivant	3.50	1.55	.45

1958 Yankees Jay Publishing

This 12-card set of the New York Yankees measures approximately 5" by 7" and features black-and-white player photos in a white border. These cards were packaged 12 to a packet. The backs are blank. The cards are unnumbered and checklisted below in alphabetical order.

	NRMT	VG-E	GOOD
COMPLETE SET (12)	50.00	22.00	6.25
COMMON CARD (1-12)	3.00	1.35	.35
☐ 1 Hank Bauer	3.50	1.55	.45
☐ 2 Larry Berra	5.00	2.20	.60
☐ 3 Whitey Ford	5.00	2.20	.60
☐ 4 Tony Kubek	3.50	1.55	.45
☐ 5 Don Larsen	3.00	1.35	.35
☐ 6 Jerry Lumpe	3.00	1.35	.35
☐ 7 Mickey Mantle	15.00	6.75	1.85
☐ 8 Gil McDougald	3.00	1.35	.35
☐ 9 Bobby Shantz	3.00	1.35	.35
☐ 10 Bill Skowron	3.50	1.55	.45
☐ 11 Tom Sturdivant	3.00	1.35	.35
☐ 12 Bob Turley	3.00	1.35	.35

1960 Yankees Jay Publishing

This 12-card set of the New York Yankees measures approximately 5" by 7" and features black-and-white player photos in a white border. These cards were packaged 12 to a packet. The backs are blank. The cards are unnumbered and checklisted below in alphabetical order.

	NRMT	VG-E	GOOD
COMPLETE SET (12)	75.00	34.00	9.50
COMMON CARD (1-12)	2.50	1.10	.30
☐ 1 Yogi Berra	15.00	6.75	1.85
☐ 2 Andy Carey	2.50	1.10	.30
☐ 3 Whitey Ford	10.00	4.50	1.25
☐ 4 Elston Howard	3.00	1.35	.35
☐ 5 Tony Kubek	3.00	1.35	.35
☐ 6 Hector Lopez	2.50	1.10	.30
☐ 7 Mickey Mantle	25.00	11.00	3.10
☐ 8 Roger Maris	10.00	4.50	1.25
☐ 9 Gil McDougald	2.50	1.10	.30
☐ 10 Bill Skowron	3.00	1.35	.35
☐ 11 Casey Stengel MG	10.00	4.50	1.25
☐ 12 Bob Turley	2.50	1.10	.30

1961 Yankees Jay Publishing

This 12-card set of the New York Yankees measures approximately 5" by 7". The fronts feature black-and-white posed player photos with the player's and team name printed below in the white border. These cards were packaged 12 to a packet. The backs are blank. The cards are unnumbered and checklisted below in alphabetical order.

	NRMT	VG-E	GOOD
COMPLETE SET (12)	100.00	45.00	12.50
COMMON CARD (1-12)	2.50	1.10	.30
☐ 1 Yogi Berra	20.00	9.00	2.50
☐ 2 Clete Boyer	3.50	1.55	.45
☐ 3 Art Ditmar	2.50	1.10	.30
☐ 4 Whitey Ford	20.00	9.00	2.50
☐ 5 Ralph Houk MG	3.50	1.55	.45
☐ 6 Elston Howard	5.00	2.20	.60
☐ 7 Tony Kubek	5.00	2.20	.60
☐ 8 Mickey Mantle	35.00	16.00	4.40
☐ 9 Roger Maris	20.00	9.00	2.50
☐ 10 Bobby Richardson	5.00	2.20	.60
☐ 11 Bill Skowron	5.00	2.20	.60
☐ 12 Bob Turley	2.50	1.10	.30

1962 Yankees Jay Publishing

This 12-card set of the New York Yankees measures approximately 5" by 7". The fronts feature black-and-white posed player photos with the player's and team name printed below in the white border. These cards were packaged 12 to a packet. The backs are blank. The cards are unnumbered and checklisted below in alphabetical order.

	NRMT	VG-E	GOOD
COMPLETE SET (12)	75.00	34.00	9.50
COMMON CARD (1-12)	2.50	1.10	.30
☐ 1 Luis Arroyo	2.50	1.10	.30
☐ 2 Yogi Berra	15.00	6.75	1.85
☐ 3 John Blanchard	2.50	1.10	.30
☐ 4 Cletis Boyer	2.50	1.10	.30
☐ 5 Bud Daley	2.50	1.10	.30
☐ 6 Whitey Ford	15.00	6.75	1.85
☐ 7 Ralph Houk MG	3.50	1.55	.45
☐ 8 Elston Howard	5.00	2.20	.60
☐ 9 Mickey Mantle	35.00	16.00	4.40
☐ 10 Roger Maris	15.00	6.75	1.85
☐ 11 Bobby Richardson	5.00	2.20	.60
☐ 12 Bill Skowron	5.00	2.20	.60

1963 Yankees Jay Publishing

This 12-card set of the New York Yankees measures approximately 5" by 7". The fronts feature black-and-white posed player photos with the player's and team name printed below in the white border. These cards were packaged 12 to a packet. The backs are blank. The cards are unnumbered and checklisted below in alphabetical order.

	NRMT	VG-E	GOOD
COMPLETE SET (12)	80.00	36.00	10.00
COMMON CARD (1-12)	2.50	1.10	.30
☐ 1 Yogi Berra	12.50	5.50	1.55
☐ 2 Clete Boyer	3.00	1.35	.35
☐ 3 Whitey Ford	10.00	4.50	1.25
☐ 4 Ralph Houk MG	3.50	1.55	.45
☐ 5 Elston Howard	5.00	2.20	.60
☐ 6 Tony Kubek	5.00	2.20	.60
☐ 7 Mickey Mantle	35.00	16.00	4.40
☐ 8 Roger Maris	15.00	6.75	1.85
☐ 9 Joe Pepitone	7.50	3.40	.95
☐ 10 Bobby Richardson	5.00	2.20	.60
☐ 11 Ralph Terry	2.50	1.10	.30
☐ 12 Tom Tresh	4.00	1.80	.50

1963-67 Yankee Requena K Postcards

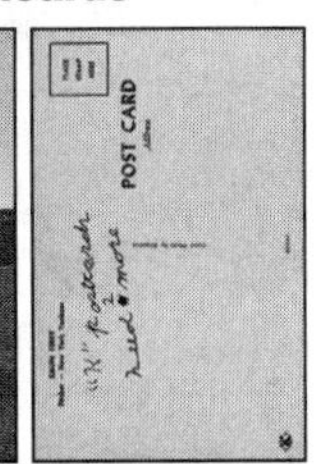

Issued over a period of several years this set features New York Yankee players only, except for a single card of Ron Swoboda of the Mets. The set features two types -- one in color, the other in black and white. Bridges only appears in black and white. We have sequenced this set in alphabetical order. Similar to the Dormand and Bill and Bob postcard, Requena postcards feature a K in the lower left of the reverse.

	NRMT	VG-E	GOOD
COMPLETE SET	350.00	160.00	45.00
COMMON CARD	15.00	6.75	1.85
☐ 1 Steve Barber	15.00	6.75	1.85
☐ 2 Yogi Berra	50.00	22.00	6.25
☐ 3 Johnny Blanchard	15.00	6.75	1.85
☐ 4 Jim Bouton	25.00	11.00	3.10
☐ 5 Clete Boyer	20.00	9.00	2.50
☐ 6 Marshall Bridges	15.00	6.75	1.85
☐ 7 Whitey Ford (2)	50.00	22.00	6.25
☐ 8 Elston Howard	25.00	11.00	3.10
☐ 9 Tony Kubek	25.00	11.00	3.10
☐ 10 Phil Linz	15.00	6.75	1.85
☐ 11 Fritz Peterson	15.00	6.75	1.85
☐ 12 Joe Pepitone	20.00	9.00	2.50
☐ 13 Pedro Ramos	15.00	6.75	1.85
☐ 14 Bobby Richardson	15.00	6.75	1.85
☐ 15 Bill Stafford	15.00	6.75	1.85
☐ 16 Mel Stottlemyre	20.00	9.00	2.50
☐ 17 Ron Swoboda	15.00	6.75	1.85
☐ 18 Ralph Terry	15.00	6.75	1.85
☐ 19 Tom Tresh (2)	20.00	9.00	2.50

1964 Yankees Jay Publishing

This 12-card set of the New York Yankees measures approximately 5" by 7". The fronts feature black-and-white posed player photos with the player's and team name printed below in the white border. These cards were packaged 12 to a packet. The backs are blank. The cards are unnumbered and checklisted below in alphabetical order.

	NRMT	VG-E	GOOD
COMPLETE SET (12)	80.00	36.00	10.00
COMMON CARD (1-12)	2.50	1.10	.30
☐ 1 Yogi Berra MG	10.00	4.50	1.25
☐ 2 Clete Boyer	3.00	1.35	.35
☐ 3 Al Downing	2.50	1.10	.30
☐ 4 Whitey Ford	7.50	3.40	.95
☐ 5 Elston Howard	5.00	2.20	.60
☐ 6 Tony Kubek	5.00	2.20	.60
☐ 7 Mickey Mantle	35.00	16.00	4.40
☐ 8 Roger Maris	15.00	6.75	1.85
☐ 9 Joe Pepitone	5.00	2.20	.60
☐ 10 Bobby Richardson	5.00	2.20	.60
☐ 11 Ralph Terry	2.50	1.10	.30
☐ 12 Tom Tresh	3.00	1.35	.35

1966 Yankees Team Issue

This 12-card set of the New York Yankees measures 4 7/8" by 7" and features black-and-white player photos in a white border with blank backs. These cards were originally packaged 12 to a packet with a price of 25 cents. The cards are unnumbered and checklisted below in alphabetical order.

	NRMT	VG-E	GOOD
COMPLETE SET (12)	60.00	27.00	7.50
COMMON CARD (1-12)	2.00	.90	.25

Card	NRMT	VG-E	GOOD
☐ 1 Clete Boyer	2.00	.90	.25
☐ 2 Al Downing	2.00	.90	.25
☐ 3 Whitey Ford	15.00	6.75	1.85
☐ 4 Elston Howard	3.00	1.35	.35
☐ 5 Johnny Keane MG	2.00	.90	.25
☐ 6 Hector Lopez	2.00	.90	.25
☐ 7 Mickey Mantle	25.00	11.00	3.10
☐ 8 Roger Maris	15.00	6.75	1.85
☐ 9 Joe Pepitone	2.00	.90	.25
☐ 10 Bobby Richardson	5.00	2.20	.60
☐ 11 Mel Stottlemyre	3.00	1.35	.35
☐ 12 Tom Tresh	2.00	.90	.25

1970 Yankee Clinic Day Postcards

During the 1970 season, The New York Yankees had a promotion where fans could meet their favorite players before a game. These postcards were issued so the fans could have something to sign. These cards are sequenced in order of the player's appearance. Some cards are known to be in much shorter supply. The card of Roy White is extremely difficult since the game was rained out. The Murcer card was issued early in the season is difficult as well. Both cards are noted with a SP in the listings.

	NRMT	VG-E	GOOD
COMPLETE SET	50.00	22.00	6.25
COMMON CARD	1.00	.45	.12

Card	NRMT	VG-E	GOOD
☐ 1 Bobby Murcer SP	5.00	2.20	.60
☐ 2 Roy White SP	25.00	11.00	3.10
☐ 3 Curt Blefary	1.00	.45	.12
☐ 4 Fritz Peterson	1.00	.45	.12
☐ 5 Danny Cater	1.00	.45	.12
☐ 6 Horace Clarke	1.00	.45	.12
☐ 7 Gene Michael	1.00	.45	.12
☐ 8 Stan Bahnsen	1.00	.45	.12
☐ 9 Thurman Munson	10.00	4.50	1.25
☐ 10 John Ellis	1.00	.45	.12
☐ 11 Jerry Kenney	1.00	.45	.12
☐ 12 Mel Stottlemyre	2.00	.90	.25
☐ 13 Joe DiMaggio and Mickey Mantle	10.00	4.50	1.25

1971 Yankees Arco Oil

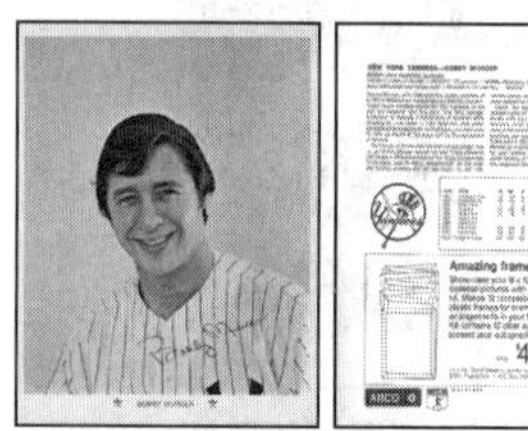

Sponsored by Arco Oil, these 12 pictures of the 1971 New York Yankees measure approximately 8" by 10" and feature on their fronts white-bordered posed color player photos. The player's name is shown in black lettering within the white margin below the photo. His facsimile autograph appears across the picture. The white back carries the team's and player's names at the top, followed below by position, biography, career highlights, and statistics. An ad at the bottom for picture frames rounds out the back. The cards are unnumbered and checklisted below in alphabetical order.

	NRMT	VG-E	GOOD
COMPLETE SET (12)	40.00	18.00	5.00
COMMON CARD (1-12)	3.00	1.35	.35

Card	NRMT	VG-E	GOOD
☐ 1 Jack Aker	3.00	1.35	.35
☐ 2 Stan Bahnsen	3.00	1.35	.35
☐ 3 Frank Baker	3.00	1.35	.35
☐ 4 Danny Cater	3.00	1.35	.35
☐ 5 Horace Clarke	4.00	1.80	.50
☐ 6 John Ellis	3.00	1.35	.35
☐ 7 Gene Michael	4.00	1.80	.50
☐ 8 Thurman Munson	10.00	4.50	1.25
☐ 9 Bobby Murcer	5.00	2.20	.60
☐ 10 Fritz Peterson	3.00	1.35	.35
☐ 11 Mel Stottlemyre	5.00	2.20	.60
☐ 12 Roy White	4.00	1.80	.50

1971 Yankee Clinic Day Postcards

Similar to the 1970 promotion, the New York Yankees again had days where the fans could meet their favorite players before selected home

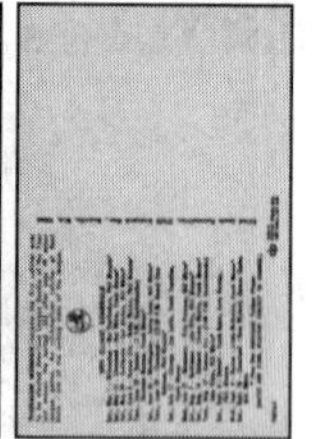

games. These cards were issued so fans could have an item for the player to sign. We have sequenced this set in alphabetical order.

	NRMT	VG-E	GOOD
COMPLETE SET (16)	50.00	22.00	6.25
COMMON CARD (1-16)	1.00	.45	.12

Card	NRMT	VG-E	GOOD
☐ 1 Stan Bahnsen	1.00	.45	.12
☐ 2 Curt Blefary	1.00	.45	.12
☐ 3 Danny Cater	1.00	.45	.12
☐ 4 Horace Clarke Gene Michael	1.00	.45	.12
☐ 5 John Ellis	1.00	.45	.12
☐ 6 Jake Gibbs	1.00	.45	.12
☐ 7 Ralph Houk MG	1.00	.45	.12
☐ 8 Jerry Kenney Frank Baker	1.00	.45	.12
☐ 9 Jim Lyttle Felipe Alou	1.00	.45	.12
☐ 10 Mickey Mantle	25.00	11.00	3.10
☐ 11 Lindy McDaniel	1.00	.45	.12
☐ 12 Thurman Munson	10.00	4.50	1.25
☐ 13 Bobby Murcer	3.00	1.35	.35
☐ 14 Fritz Peterson	1.00	.45	.12
☐ 15 Mel Stottlemyre	2.00	.90	.25
☐ 16 Roy White	3.00	1.35	.35

1973 Yankees

This six-card set of the New York Yankees measures approximately 7" by 8 3/4" and features color player photos in a white border. The player's name and team are printed in the wide bottom margin. The backs are blank. The cards are unnumbered and checklisted in alphabetical order.

	NRMT	VG-E	GOOD
COMPLETE SET (6)	25.00	11.00	3.10
COMMON CARD (1-6)	3.00	1.35	.35

Card	NRMT	VG-E	GOOD
☐ 1 Ron Blomberg	3.00	1.35	.35
☐ 2 Sparky Lyle	5.00	2.20	.60
☐ 3 Bobby Murcer	5.00	2.20	.60
☐ 4 Graig Nettles	5.00	2.20	.60
☐ 5 Fritz Peterson	3.00	1.35	.35
☐ 6 Roy White	5.00	2.20	.60

1975 Yankee Dynasty 1936-39 TCMA

The first 49 cards in this set measure 2 3/4" by 4" and feature black-and-white player photos with white borders. The last five cards are 4" by 5 1/2" and feature photos of Yankees from 1936-39. The player's name and position are printed in blue below the picture. The phrase "1936-1939 Yankee Dynasty" is at the top except for card numbers 50-53, which have "World Champions -- 19XX" printed at the top. The backs carry statistics printed in blue. The cards are unnumbered and checklisted below in alphabetical order.

	NRMT	VG-E	GOOD
COMPLETE SET (55)	40.00	18.00	5.00
COMMON CARD (1-55)	.50	.23	.06

Card	NRMT	VG-E	GOOD
☐ 1 Ivy Paul Andrews	.50	.23	.06
☐ 2 Joe Beggs	.50	.23	.06
☐ 3 Marv Breuer	.50	.23	.06
☐ 4 Johnny Broaca	.50	.23	.06
☐ 5 Jumbo Brown	.50	.23	.06
☐ 6 Spud Chandler	.75	.35	.09
☐ 7 Ben Chapman	.50	.23	.06
☐ 8 Earl Combs CO	1.00	.45	.12
☐ 9 Frankie Crosetti	1.00	.45	.12
☐ 10 Babe Dahlgren	.50	.23	.06
☐ 11 Joe DiMaggio	6.00	2.70	.75
☐ 12 Bill Dickey	1.50	.70	.19
☐ 13 Atley Donald	.50	.23	.06
☐ 14 Wes Farrell	.50	.23	.06
☐ 15 Artie Fletcher CO	.50	.23	.06
☐ 16 Lou Gehrig	6.00	2.70	.75
☐ 17 Joe Glenn	.50	.23	.06
☐ 18 Lefty Gomez	1.00	.45	.12
☐ 19 Joe Gordon	1.00	.45	.12
☐ 20 Bump Hadley	.50	.23	.06
☐ 21 Don Heffner	.50	.23	.06
☐ 22 Tommy Henrich	1.00	.45	.12
☐ 23 Oral Hildebrand	.50	.23	.06
☐ 24 Myril Hoag	.50	.23	.06
☐ 25 Roy Johnson	.50	.23	.06
☐ 26 Art Jorgens	.50	.23	.06
☐ 27 Charlie Keller	.75	.35	.09
☐ 28 Ted Kleinhans	.50	.23	.06
☐ 29 Billy Knickerbocker	.50	.23	.06
☐ 30 Tony Lazzeri	1.00	.45	.12
☐ 31 Frank Makosky	.50	.23	.06
☐ 32 Pat Malone	.50	.23	.06
☐ 33 Joe McCarthy MG Jacob Ruppert OWN	1.00	.45	.12
☐ 34 Johnny Murphy	.50	.23	.06
☐ 35 Monty Pearson	.50	.23	.06
☐ 36 Jake Powell	.50	.23	.06
☐ 37 Red Rolfe	.75	.35	.09
☐ 38 Buddy Rosar	.50	.23	.06
☐ 39 Red Ruffing	1.00	.45	.12
☐ 40 Marius Russo	.50	.23	.06
☐ 41 Jack Saltzgaver	.50	.23	.06
☐ 42 Paul Schreiber	.50	.23	.06
☐ 43 Johnny Schulte	.50	.23	.06
☐ 44 Bob Seeds	.50	.23	.06
☐ 45 Twinkletoes Selkirk	.75	.35	.09
☐ 46 Steve Sundra	.50	.23	.06
☐ 47 Sandy Vance	.50	.23	.06
☐ 48 Dixie Walker	.75	.35	.09
☐ 49 Kemp Wicker	.50	.23	.06
☐ 50 World Champions 1936 (Team celebrating)	4.00	1.80	.50
☐ 51 World Champions 1937 Joe DiMaggio Frankie Crosetti Tony Lazzeri Bill Dickey Lou Gehrig Jake Powell Twinkletoes Selkirk	4.00	1.80	.50
☐ 52 World Champions 1938 Red Rolfe Tony Lazzeri Lou Gehrig Frankie Crosetti	1.50	.70	.19
☐ 53 World Champions 1939 Lou Gehrig Joe DiMaggio	4.00	1.80	.50
☐ 54 Lou Gehrig Hits Another	4.00	1.80	.50

1975 Yankees SSPC

This 23-card standard-size set of New York Yankees features white-bordered posed color player photos on their fronts, which are free of any other markings. The white back carries the player's name in red lettering above his blue-lettered biography and career highlights. The cards are numbered on the back within a circle formed by the player's team name. A similar set of New York Mets was produced at the same time. This set is dated 1975 because that was Ed Brinkman's only season with the Yankees.

	NRMT	VG-E	GOOD
COMPLETE SET (23)	18.00	8.00	2.20
COMMON CARD (1-23)	.50	.23	.06

Card	NRMT	VG-E	GOOD
☐ 1 Jim Hunter	4.00	1.80	.50
☐ 2 Bobby Bonds	1.25	.55	.16
☐ 3 Ed Brinkman	.50	.23	.06
☐ 4 Ron Blomberg	.60	.25	.07
☐ 5 Thurman Munson	5.00	2.20	.60
☐ 6 Roy White	.75	.35	.09
☐ 7 Larry Gura	.50	.23	.06
☐ 8 Ed Herrmann	.50	.23	.06
☐ 9 Bill Virdon MG	.60	.25	.07
☐ 10 Elliott Maddox	.60	.25	.07
☐ 11 Lou Piniella	1.25	.55	.16
☐ 12 Rick Dempsey	.75	.35	.09
☐ 13 Fred Stanley	.50	.23	.06
☐ 14 Chris Chambliss	1.00	.45	.12
☐ 15 George Medich	.50	.23	.06
☐ 16 Pat Dobson	.60	.25	.07
☐ 17 Alex Johnson	.60	.25	.07
☐ 18 Jim Mason	.50	.23	.06
☐ 19 Sandy Alomar	.60	.25	.07
☐ 20 Graig Nettles	1.25	.55	.16
☐ 21 Walt Williams	.50	.23	.06
☐ 22 Sparky Lyle	.75	.35	.09
☐ 23 Dick Tidrow	.50	.23	.06

1977 Yankees Burger King

The cards in this 24-card set measure 2 1/2" by 3 1/2". The cards in this set marked with an asterisk have different poses than the cards in the regular 1977 Topps set. The checklist card is unnumbered and the Piniella card was issued subsequent to the original printing. The complete set price below refers to all 24 cards listed, including Piniella.

	NRMT	VG-E	GOOD
COMPLETE SET (24)	40.00	18.00	5.00
COMMON CARD (1-23)	.25	.11	.03

Card	NRMT	VG-E	GOOD
☐ 1 Yankees Team Billy Martin MG	1.50	.70	.19
☐ 2 Thurman Munson * UER (Facsimile autograph misspelled)	8.00	3.60	1.00
☐ 3 Fran Healy	.25	.11	.03
☐ 4 Jim Hunter	2.50	1.10	.30
☐ 5 Ed Figueroa	.25	.11	.03
☐ 6 Don Gullett * (Mouth closed)	.50	.23	.06
☐ 7 Mike Torrez * (Shown as A's in 1977 Topps)	.50	.23	.06
☐ 8 Ken Holtzman	.50	.23	.06
☐ 9 Dick Tidrow	.25	.11	.03
☐ 10 Sparky Lyle	.50	.23	.06
☐ 11 Ron Guidry	.75	.35	.09
☐ 12 Chris Chambliss	.50	.23	.06
☐ 13 Willie Randolph * (No rookie trophy)	.75	.35	.09
☐ 14 Bucky Dent * (Shown as White Sox in 1977 Topps)	.50	.23	.06
☐ 15 Graig Nettles * (Closer photo than in 1977 Topps)	1.50	.70	.19
☐ 16 Fred Stanley	.25	.11	.03
☐ 17 Reggie Jackson * (Looking up with bat)	12.50	5.50	1.55
☐ 18 Mickey Rivers	.50	.23	.06
☐ 19 Roy White	.50	.23	.06
☐ 20 Jim Wynn * (Shown as Brave in 1977 Topps)	.75	.35	.09
☐ 21 Paul Blair * (Shown as Oriole in 1977 Topps)	.75	.35	.09
☐ 22 Carlos May * (Shown as White Sox in 1977 Topps)	.50	.23	.06
☐ 23 Lou Piniella SP	20.00	9.00	2.50
☐ NNO Checklist Card TP	.25	.11	.03

1978 Yankees Burger King

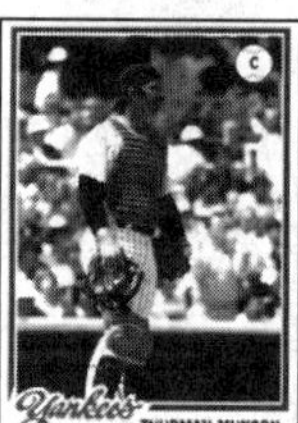

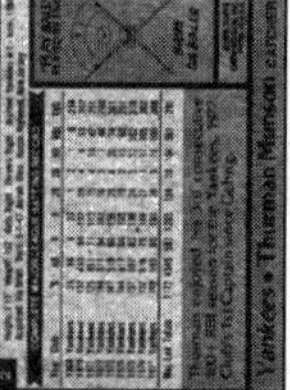

The cards in this 23-card set measure 2 1/2" by 3 1/2". These cards were distributed in packs of three players plus a checklist at Burger King's New York area outlets. Cards with an asterisk have different poses than those in the Topps regular issue.

	NRMT	VG-E	GOOD
COMPLETE SET (23)	12.00	5.50	1.50
COMMON CARD (1-22)	.25	.11	.03

	NRMT	VG-E	GOOD
☐ 1 Billy Martin MG	.75	.35	.09
☐ 2 Thurman Munson	4.00	1.80	.50
☐ 3 Cliff Johnson	.25	.11	.03
☐ 4 Ron Guidry	1.25	.55	.16
☐ 5 Ed Figueroa	.25	.11	.03
☐ 6 Dick Tidrow	.25	.11	.03
☐ 7 Jim Hunter	2.50	1.10	.30
☐ 8 Don Gullett	.25	.11	.03
☐ 9 Sparky Lyle	.50	.23	.06
☐ 10 Rich Gossage *	1.25	.55	.16
☐ 11 Rawly Eastwick *	.25	.11	.03
☐ 12 Chris Chambliss	.50	.23	.06
☐ 13 Willie Randolph	.50	.23	.06
☐ 14 Graig Nettles	.75	.35	.09
☐ 15 Bucky Dent	.60	.25	.07
☐ 16 Jim Spencer *	.25	.11	.03
☐ 17 Fred Stanley	.25	.11	.03
☐ 18 Lou Piniella	1.00	.45	.12
☐ 19 Roy White	.50	.23	.06
☐ 20 Mickey Rivers	.50	.23	.06
☐ 21 Reggie Jackson	4.00	1.80	.50
☐ 22 Paul Blair	.25	.11	.03
☐ NNO Checklist Card TP	.15	.07	.02

1978 Yankees SSPC Diary

This 27 card standard-size set was inserted into the 1978 Yankees Yearbook and Diary of a Champion Yankee. These cards are full bleed and the backs have 1977 seasonal highlights.

	NRMT	VG-E	GOOD
COMPLETE SET (27)	10.00	4.50	1.25
COMMON CARD (1-27)	.10	.05	.01
☐ 1 Thurman Munson	3.00	1.35	.35
☐ 2 Cliff Johnson	.10	.05	.01
☐ 3 Lou Piniella	.75	.35	.09
☐ 4 Dell Alston	.10	.05	.01
☐ 5 Yankee Stadium	.10	.05	.01
☐ 6 Ken Holtzman	.10	.05	.01
☐ 7 Chris Chambliss	.25	.11	.03
☐ 8 Roy White	.10	.05	.01
☐ 9 Ed Figueroa	.10	.05	.01
☐ 10 Dick Tidrow	.10	.05	.01
☐ 11 Sparky Lyle	.25	.11	.03
☐ 12 Fred Stanley	.10	.05	.01
☐ 13 Mickey Rivers	.10	.05	.01
☐ 14 Billy Martin MG	.25	.11	.03
☐ 15 George Zeber	.10	.05	.01
☐ 16 Ken Clay	.10	.05	.01
☐ 17 Ron Guidry	1.00	.45	.12
☐ 18 Don Gullett	.10	.05	.01
☐ 19 Fran Healy	.10	.05	.01
☐ 20 Paul Blair	.10	.05	.01
☐ 21 Mickey Klutts	.10	.05	.01
☐ 22 Yankee Team	.10	.05	.01
☐ 23 Catfish Hunter	2.00	.90	.25
☐ 24 Bucky Dent	.25	.11	.03
☐ 25 Graig Nettles	.75	.35	.09
☐ 26 Reggie Jackson	3.00	1.35	.35
☐ 27 Willie Randolph	1.00	.45	.12

1979 Yankees Burger King

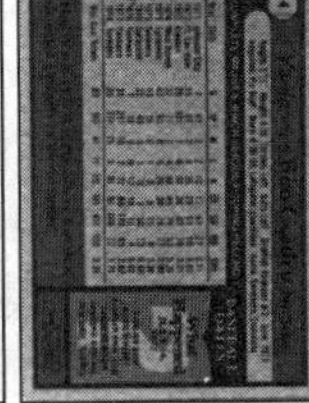

The cards in this 23-card set measure 2 1/2" by 3 1/2". There are 22 numbered cards and one unnumbered checklist in the 1979 Burger King Yankee set. The poses of Guidry, Tiant, John and Beniquez, each marked with an asterisk below, are different from their poses appearing in the regular Topps issue. The team card has a picture of Lemon rather than Martin.

	NRMT	VG-E	GOOD
COMPLETE SET (23)	10.00	4.50	1.25
COMMON CARD (1-22)	.25	.11	.03
☐ 1 Yankees Team: Bob Lemon MG *	.75	.35	.09
☐ 2 Thurman Munson	4.00	1.80	.50
☐ 3 Cliff Johnson	.25	.11	.03
☐ 4 Ron Guidry *	.35	.16	.04
☐ 5 Jay Johnstone	.35	.16	.04
☐ 6 Jim Hunter	2.50	1.10	.30
☐ 7 Jim Beattie	.25	.11	.03
☐ 8 Luis Tiant * (Shown as Red Sox in 1979 Topps)	.75	.35	.09
☐ 9 Tommy John * (Shown as Dodgers in 1979 Topps)	1.25	.55	.16
☐ 10 Rich Gossage	.75	.35	.09
☐ 11 Ed Figueroa	.25	.11	.03
☐ 12 Chris Chambliss	.50	.23	.06
☐ 13 Willie Randolph	.75	.35	.09
☐ 14 Bucky Dent	.50	.23	.06
☐ 15 Graig Nettles	.75	.35	.09
☐ 16 Fred Stanley	.25	.11	.03
☐ 17 Jim Spencer	.25	.11	.03
☐ 18 Lou Piniella	1.00	.45	.12
☐ 19 Roy White	.50	.23	.06
☐ 20 Mickey Rivers	.50	.23	.06
☐ 21 Reggie Jackson	4.00	1.80	.50
☐ 22 Juan Beniquez *	.35	.16	.04
☐ NNO Checklist Card TP	.15	.07	.02

1979 Yankees Picture Album

This 32-page Picture Album of the 1979 New York Yankees measures approximately 8" by 8" and features posed color player photos in white borders with a facsimile autograph across the bottom. The backs are blank. The cards are unnumbered and checklisted below in alphabetical order.

	NRMT	VG-E	GOOD
COMPLETE SET (34)	20.00	9.00	2.50
COMMON CARD (1-34)	.25	.11	.03
☐ 1 Jim Beattie	.25	.11	.03
☐ 2 Juan Beniquez	.25	.11	.03
☐ 3 Yogi Berra CO	2.00	.90	.25
☐ 4 Bobby Brown	.25	.11	.03
☐ 5 Ray Burris	.25	.11	.03
☐ 6 Chris Chambliss	.50	.23	.06
☐ 7 Ken Clay	.25	.11	.03
☐ 8 Ron Davis	.25	.11	.03
☐ 9 Bucky Dent	.50	.23	.06
☐ 10 Brian Doyle	.25	.11	.03
☐ 11 Mike Ferraro	.25	.11	.03
☐ 12 Ed Figueroa	.25	.11	.03
☐ 13 Art Fowler CO	.25	.11	.03
☐ 14 Rich Gossage	1.00	.45	.12
☐ 15 Ron Guidry	1.00	.45	.12
☐ 16 Don Gullett	.25	.11	.03
☐ 17 Jim Hegan CO	.25	.11	.03
☐ 18 Don Hood	.25	.11	.03
☐ 19 Jim Hunter	1.50	.70	.19
☐ 20 Reggie Jackson	2.50	1.10	.30
☐ 21 Tommy John	1.00	.45	.12
☐ 22 Jim Kaat	1.00	.45	.12
☐ 23 Charley Lau CO	.25	.11	.03
☐ 24 Billy Martin MG	1.00	.45	.12
☐ 25 Thurman Munson	2.00	.90	.25
☐ 26 Bobby Murcer	1.00	.45	.12
☐ 27 Jerry Narron	.25	.11	.03
☐ 28 Graig Nettles	1.00	.45	.12
☐ 29 Lou Piniella	1.00	.45	.12
☐ 30 Willie Randolph	1.00	.45	.12
☐ 31 Jim Spencer	.25	.11	.03
☐ 32 Fred Stanley	.25	.11	.03
☐ 33 Luis Tiant	.50	.23	.06
☐ 34 Roy White	.50	.23	.06

1980 Yankees Greats TCMA

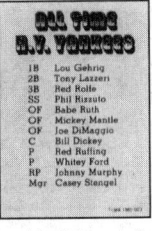

These 12 standard-size cards feature all-time Yankee greats. The fronts have a player photo and the backs display a checklist of who is in the set.

	NRMT	VG-E	GOOD
COMPLETE SET (12)	10.00	4.50	1.25
COMMON CARD (1-12)	.25	.11	.03
☐ 1 Lou Gehrig	2.50	1.10	.30
☐ 2 Tony Lazzeri	.50	.23	.06
☐ 3 Red Rolfe	.25	.11	.03
☐ 4 Phil Rizzuto	1.00	.45	.12
☐ 5 Babe Ruth	3.00	1.35	.35
☐ 6 Mickey Mantle	3.00	1.35	.35
☐ 7 Joe DiMaggio	2.50	1.10	.30
☐ 8 Bill Dickey	.75	.35	.09
☐ 9 Red Ruffing	.75	.35	.09
☐ 10 Whitey Ford	1.25	.55	.16
☐ 11 Johnny Murphy	.25	.11	.03
☐ 12 Casey Stengel MG	.75	.35	.09

1983 Yankee A-S Fifty Years

With the great New York Yankee tradition, this set commemorates the first 50 years of Yankee All-Stars. Other than the Mickey Mantle checklist card, this set is sequenced in alphabetical order.

	NRMT	VG-E	GOOD
COMPLETE SET (50)	12.50	5.50	1.55
COMMON CARD (1-50)	.10	.05	.01
☐ 1 Mickey Mantle CL	1.00	.45	.12
☐ 2 Luis Arroyo	.10	.05	.01
☐ 3 Hank Bauer	.25	.11	.03
☐ 4 Yogi Berra	1.00	.45	.12
☐ 5 Tommy Byrne	.10	.05	.01
☐ 6 Spud Chandler	.10	.05	.01
☐ 7 Ben Chapman	.10	.05	.01
☐ 8 Jim Coates	.10	.05	.01
☐ 9 Bill Dickey	.75	.35	.09
☐ 10 Joe DiMaggio	1.50	.70	.19
☐ 11 Al Downing	.10	.05	.01
☐ 12 Ryne Duren	.10	.05	.01
☐ 13 Whitey Ford PORT	1.00	.45	.12
☐ 14 Whitey Ford PIT	1.00	.45	.12
☐ 15 Lou Gehrig	1.50	.70	.19
☐ 16 Lefty Gomez	.75	.35	.09
☐ 17 Bob Grim	.10	.05	.01
☐ 18 Tommy Henrich	.50	.23	.06
☐ 20 Catfish Hunter	.75	.35	.09
☐ 21 Billy Johnson	.10	.05	.01
☐ 22 Charlie Keller	.25	.11	.03
☐ 23 Johnny Kucks	.10	.05	.01
☐ 24 Eddie Lopat	.25	.11	.03
☐ 25 Sparky Lyle	.25	.11	.03
☐ 26 Mickey Mantle	2.00	.90	.25
☐ 27 Roger Maris	1.25	.55	.16
☐ 28 Billy Martin	1.00	.45	.12
☐ 29 Johnny Mize	.75	.35	.09
☐ 30 Bobby Murcer	.50	.23	.06
☐ 31 Irv Noren	.10	.05	.01
☐ 32 Joe Pepitone	.50	.23	.06
☐ 33 Fritz Peterson	.10	.05	.01
☐ 34 Vic Raschi	.10	.05	.01
☐ 35 Allie Reynolds	.25	.11	.03
☐ 36 Bobby Richardson	.50	.23	.06
☐ 37 Phil Rizzuto	1.00	.45	.12
☐ 38 Marius Russo	.10	.05	.01
☐ 40 Johnny Sain	.50	.23	.06
☐ 41 George Selkirk	.10	.05	.01
☐ 42 Bobby Shantz	.10	.05	.01
☐ 43 Spec Shea	.10	.05	.01
☐ 44 Moose Skowron	.50	.23	.06
☐ 45 Casey Stengel	1.00	.45	.12
☐ 46 Mel Stottlemyre	.25	.11	.03
☐ 47 Ralph Terry	.10	.05	.01
☐ 48 Tom Tresh	.10	.05	.01
☐ 49 Bob Turley	.10	.05	.01
☐ 50 Roy White	.10	.05	.01

1983 Yankees Roy Rogers Discs

This disc set features members of the 1983 New York Yankees team. The set was licensed by the Major League Baseball Players Association in conjunction with Mike Schechter Associates and was distributed at Roy Rogers Restaurants in the New York and New Jersey area. These round cards measure approximately 3 1/2" in diameter and were actually a round card with a red plastic rim. Cards were blank backed and the the player photo used is black and white. The discs are unnumbered and so they are ordered below in alphabetical order. These discs are also sometimes found with the printing of Roy Rogers missing at the top of the disc.

	NRMT	VG-E	GOOD
COMPLETE SET (12)	30.00	13.50	3.70
COMMON DISC (1-12)	2.00	.90	.25
☐ 1 Rick Cerone	2.00	.90	.25
☐ 2 Rich Gossage	4.00	1.80	.50
☐ 3 Ken Griffey	4.00	1.80	.50
☐ 4 Ron Guidry	4.00	1.80	.50
☐ 5 Steve Kemp	2.00	.90	.25
☐ 6 Jerry Mumphrey	2.00	.90	.25
☐ 7 Graig Nettles	4.00	1.80	.50
☐ 8 Lou Piniella	4.00	1.80	.50
☐ 9 Willie Randolph	4.00	1.80	.50
☐ 10 Andre Robertson	2.00	.90	.25
☐ 11 Roy Smalley	2.00	.90	.25
☐ 12 Dave Winfield	6.00	2.70	.75

1983 Yankee Yearbook Insert TCMA

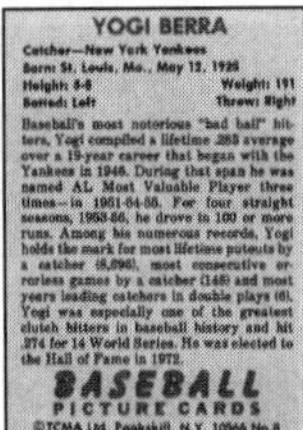

Subtitled Baseball Picture Cards, this uncut sheet produced by TCMA features 18 American League players of the past (nine Yankees and nine from other AL teams) and measures approximately 16 1/2" by 10 7/8". If cut into singles, each card would measure the standard size. The fronts feature white-bordered color drawings of the players. The player's name appears in white lettering within a black rectangle near the bottom. The back carries the player's name in red lettering at the top, followed below by biography and career highlights.

	NRMT	VG-E	GOOD
COMPLETE SET (18)	10.00	4.50	1.25
COMMON CARD (1-18)	.25	.11	.03
☐ 1 Joe DiMaggio	2.50	1.10	.30
☐ 2 Billy Pierce	.50	.23	.06
☐ 3 Phil Rizzuto	1.25	.55	.16
☐ 4 Ted Williams	2.50	1.10	.30
☐ 5 Billy Martin	.75	.35	.09
☐ 6 Mel Parnell	.25	.11	.03
☐ 7 Harmon Killebrew	1.00	.45	.12
☐ 8 Yogi Berra	1.00	.45	.12
☐ 9 Roy Sievers	.25	.11	.03
☐ 10 Bill Dickey	.75	.35	.09
☐ 11 Hank Greenberg	.75	.35	.09
☐ 12 Allie Reynolds	.50	.23	.06
☐ 13 Joe Sewell	.75	.35	.09
☐ 14 Virgil Trucks	.25	.11	.03
☐ 15 Mickey Mantle	3.00	1.35	.35
☐ 16 Boog Powell	.50	.23	.06
☐ 17 Whitey Ford	1.50	.70	.19
☐ 18 Lou Boudreau	.75	.35	.09

1986 Yankees TCMA

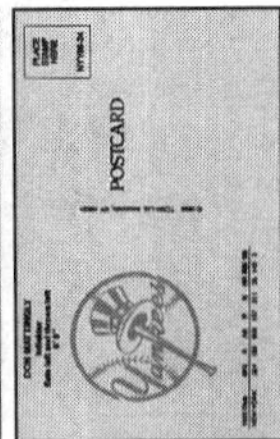

This 3 1/2" by 5 1/2" postcard set features members of the 1986 Yankees. The set has full-bleed color photographs. The backs have the players name and usually 1995 stats. The cards are numbered in the upper right corner with a "NYY86" prefix.

	MINT	NRMT	EXC
COMPLETE SET (40)	12.00	5.50	1.50
COMMON CARD (1-40)	.25	.11	.03
☐ 1 Tommy John	.75	.35	.09
☐ 2 Brad Arnsberg UER (Name spelled Arnsburg)	.25	.11	.03
☐ 3 Al Holland UER (Name spelled All)	.25	.11	.03
☐ 4 Mike Armstrong	.25	.11	.03
☐ 5 Marty Bystrom	.25	.11	.03
☐ 6 Doug Drabek	.75	.35	.09
☐ 7 Brian Fisher	.25	.11	.03
☐ 8 Stump Merrill CO	.25	.11	.03
☐ 9 Ron Guidry	.50	.23	.06
☐ 10 Joe Niekro	.50	.23	.06
☐ 12 Dennis Rasmussen	.25	.11	.03
☐ 13 Dave Righetti	.50	.23	.06
☐ 14 Rod Scurry	.25	.11	.03
☐ 15 Bob Shirley	.25	.11	.03
☐ 16 Bob Tewksbury	.25	.11	.03
☐ 17 Ed Whitson	.25	.11	.03
☐ 18 Gene Michael CO	.25	.11	.03
☐ 18 Britt Burns	.25	.11	.03
☐ 19 Butch Wynegar	.25	.11	.03
☐ 20 Ron Hassey	.25	.11	.03
☐ 21 Dale Berra	.25	.11	.03
☐ 22 Jeff Torborg CO	.25	.11	.03

Card	MINT	NRMT	EXC
☐ 23 Mike Fischlin	.25	.11	.03
☐ 24 Don Mattingly	4.00	1.80	.50
☐ 25 Bobby Meacham	.25	.11	.03
☐ 26 Mike Pagliarulo	.25	.11	.03
☐ 27 Willie Randolph	.50	.23	.06
☐ 28 Andre Robertson	.25	.11	.03
☐ 29 Roy White CO	.50	.23	.06
☐ 31 Henry Cotto	.25	.11	.03
☐ 32 Ken Griffey	.50	.23	.06
☐ 33 Rickey Henderson	2.00	.90	.25
☐ 34 Vic Mata	.25	.11	.03
☐ 35 Dan Pasqua	.25	.11	.03
☐ 36 Dave Winfield	1.50	.70	.19
☐ 37 Gary Roenicke	.25	.11	.03
☐ 38 Lou Piniella MG	.75	.35	.09
☐ 39 Joe Altobelli CO	.25	.11	.03
☐ 40 Sammy Ellis CO	.25	.11	.03
☐ 45 Mike Easler	.25	.11	.03

1987 Yankees 1927 TCMA

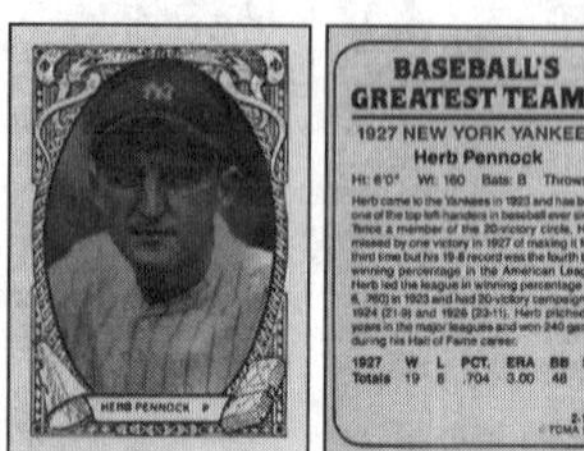

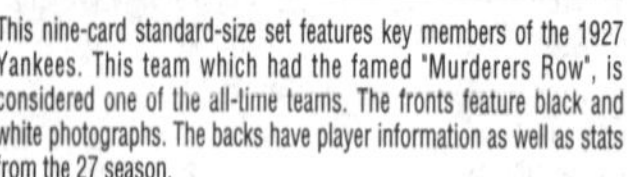

This nine-card standard-size set features key members of the 1927 Yankees. This team which had the famed "Murderers Row", is considered one of the all-time teams. The fronts feature black and white photographs. The backs have player information as well as stats from the 27 season.

	MINT	NRMT	EXC
COMPLETE SET (9)	6.00	2.70	.75
COMMON CARD (1-9)	.25	.11	.03
☐ 1 Miller Huggins MG	.50	.23	.06
☐ 2 Herb Pennock	.75	.35	.09
☐ 3 Tony Lazzeri	.75	.35	.09
☐ 4 Waite Hoyt	.75	.35	.09
☐ 5 Wilcy Moore	.25	.11	.03
☐ 6 Earle Combs	.75	.35	.09
☐ 7 Bob Meusel	.50	.23	.06
☐ 8 Lou Gehrig	2.00	.90	.25
☐ 9 Babe Ruth	2.50	1.10	.30

1987 Yankees 1961 TCMA

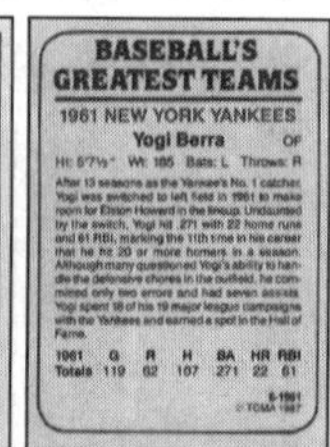

This nine-card standard-size set features members of the 1961 Yankees. This team set a major league record with 240 homers in a season and was led by Roger Maris and Mickey Mantle who combined for 115 of those blasts. The fronts display color photos, the player's name and position. The backs carry player information as well as more details about the 1961 season.

	MINT	NRMT	EXC
COMPLETE SET (9)	6.00	2.70	.75
COMMON CARD (1-9)	.25	.11	.03
☐ 1 Bill Skowron	.50	.23	.06
☐ 2 Mickey Mantle	2.50	1.10	.30
☐ 3 Bobby Richardson	.75	.35	.09
☐ 4 Tony Kubek	.50	.23	.06
☐ 5 Elston Howard	.75	.35	.09
☐ 6 Yogi Berra	1.25	.55	.16
☐ 7 Whitey Ford	1.25	.55	.16
☐ 8 Roger Maris	1.25	.55	.16
☐ 9 Ralph Houk MG	.25	.11	.03

1989 Yankee Citgo All-Time Greats

These six cards feature great New York Yankees. Since the cards are unnumbered we have checklisted them below in alphabetical order.

	MINT	NRMT	EXC
COMPLETE SET (6)	17.50	8.00	2.20
COMMON CARD (1-6)	1.50	.70	.19
☐ 1 Whitey Ford	3.00	1.35	.35
☐ 2 Lou Gehrig	5.00	2.20	.60

Card	MINT	NRMT	EXC
☐ 3 Lefty Gomez	2.50	1.10	.30
☐ 4 Phil Rizzuto	2.50	1.10	.30
☐ 5 Babe Ruth	7.50	3.40	.95
☐ 6 Casey Stengel	1.50	.70	.19

1989 Yankees Score Nat West

The 1989 Score National Westminster Bank New York Yankees set features 33 standard-size cards. The fronts and backs are navy; the backs have color mug shots, 1988 and career stats. The set was given away at a 1989 Yankees' home game.

	MINT	NRMT	EXC
COMPLETE SET (33)	20.00	9.00	2.50
COMMON CARD (1-33)	.25	.11	.03
☐ 1 Don Mattingly	8.00	3.60	1.00
☐ 2 Steve Sax	.75	.35	.09
☐ 3 Alvaro Espinoza	.25	.11	.03
☐ 4 Luis Polonia	1.00	.45	.12
☐ 5 Jesse Barfield	.25	.11	.03
☐ 6 Dave Righetti	.50	.23	.06
☐ 7 Dave Winfield	4.00	1.80	.50
☐ 8 John Candelaria	.25	.11	.03
☐ 9 Wayne Tolleson	.25	.11	.03
☐ 10 Ken Phelps	.25	.11	.03
☐ 11 Rafael Santana	.25	.11	.03
☐ 12 Don Slaught	.25	.11	.03
☐ 13 Mike Pagliarulo	.25	.11	.03
☐ 14 Lance McCullers	.25	.11	.03
☐ 15 Dave LaPoint	.25	.11	.03
☐ 16 Dale Mohorcic	.25	.11	.03
☐ 17 Steve Balboni	.25	.11	.03
☐ 18 Roberto Kelly	.50	.23	.06
☐ 19 Andy Hawkins	.25	.11	.03
☐ 20 Mel Hall	.25	.11	.03
☐ 21 Tom Brookens	.25	.11	.03
☐ 22 Deion Sanders	5.00	2.20	.60
☐ 23 Richard Dotson	.25	.11	.03
☐ 24 Lee Guetterman	.25	.11	.03
☐ 25 Bob Geren	.25	.11	.03
☐ 26 Jimmy Jones	.25	.11	.03
☐ 27 Chuck Cary	.25	.11	.03
☐ 28 Ron Guidry	1.00	.45	.12
☐ 29 Hal Morris	1.00	.45	.12
☐ 30 Clay Parker	.25	.11	.03
☐ 31 Dallas Green MG	.50	.23	.06
☐ 32 Thurman Munson MEM	5.00	2.20	.60
☐ 33 Yankees Team Card	.50	.23	.06

1990 Yankees 61 Ron Lewis

These 42 oversized cards feature members of the 1961 New York Yankees. The fronts feature artwork by noted sports artist Ron Lewis.

	MINT	NRMT	EXC
COMPLETE SET (42)	25.00	11.00	3.10
COMMON CARD (1-42)	.50	.23	.06
☐ 1 Team Photo	1.00	.45	.12
☐ 2 Bobby Richardson	1.50	.70	.19
☐ 3 Roger Maris	2.50	1.10	.30
☐ 4 Elston Howard	1.50	.70	.19
☐ 5 Bill Skowron	1.50	.70	.19
☐ 6 Clete Boyer	1.00	.45	.12
☐ 7 Mickey Mantle	5.00	2.20	.60
☐ 8 Yogi Berra	2.50	1.10	.30
☐ 9 Johnny Blanchard	.50	.23	.06
☐ 10 Hector Lopez	.50	.23	.06
☐ 11 Whitey Ford	2.50	1.10	.30
☐ 12 Ralph Terry	.50	.23	.06
☐ 13 Bill Stafford	.50	.23	.06
☐ 14 Bud Daley	.50	.23	.06
☐ 15 Billy Gardner	.50	.23	.06
☐ 16 Jim Coates	.50	.23	.06
☐ 17 Luis Arroyo	.50	.23	.06
☐ 18 Tex Clevenger	.50	.23	.06
☐ 19 Bob Cerv	.50	.23	.06
☐ 20 Art Ditmar	.50	.23	.06
☐ 21 Bob Turley	.50	.23	.06
☐ 22 Joe DeMaestri	.50	.23	.06
☐ 23 Rollie Sheldon	.50	.23	.06
☐ 24 Earl Torgeson	.50	.23	.06
☐ 25 Hal Reniff	.50	.23	.06
☐ 26 Ralph Houk MG	1.00	.45	.12
☐ 27 Johnny James	.50	.23	.06
☐ 28 Bob Hale	.50	.23	.06
☐ 29 Danny McDevitt	.50	.23	.06
☐ 30 Duke Maas	.50	.23	.06
☐ 31 Jim Hegan CO	.50	.23	.06
☐ 32 Wally Moses CO	.50	.23	.06
☐ 33 Frank Crosetti CO	1.00	.45	.12
☐ 34 Lee Thomas	.50	.23	.06
☐ 35 Al Downing	.50	.23	.06
☐ 36 Jack Reed	.50	.23	.06
☐ 37 Ryne Duren	.50	.23	.06
☐ 38 Tom Tresh	1.00	.45	.12
☐ 39 Johnny Sain CO	1.00	.45	.12
☐ 40 Jesse Gonder	.50	.23	.06
☐ 41 Deron Johnson	.50	.23	.06
☐ 42 Tony Kubek	1.50	.70	.19

1990 Yankees Score Nat West

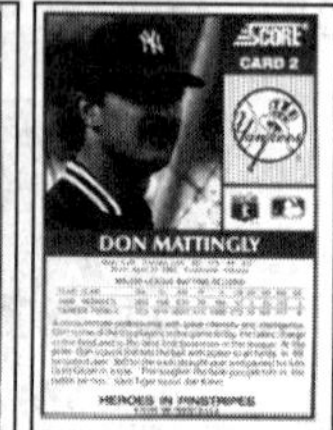

1990 Score National Westminster Bank Yankees is a 32-card, standard-size set featuring members of the 1990 New York Yankees. This set also has a special Billy Martin memorial card which honored the late Yankee manager who died in a truck accident on 12/25/89.

	MINT	NRMT	EXC
COMPLETE SET (32)	15.00	6.75	1.85
COMMON CARD (1-32)	.25	.11	.03
☐ 1 Stump Merrill MG	.25	.11	.03
☐ 2 Don Mattingly	7.50	3.40	.95
☐ 3 Steve Sax	.50	.23	.06
☐ 4 Alvaro Espinoza	.25	.11	.03
☐ 5 Jesse Barfield	.50	.23	.06
☐ 6 Roberto Kelly	.50	.23	.06
☐ 7 Mel Hall	.25	.11	.03
☐ 8 Claudell Washington	.50	.23	.06
☐ 9 Bob Geren	.25	.11	.03
☐ 10 Jim Leyritz	1.50	.70	.19
☐ 11 Pascual Perez	.25	.11	.03
☐ 12 Dave LaPoint	.25	.11	.03
☐ 13 Tim Leary	.25	.11	.03
☐ 14 Mike Witt	.25	.11	.03
☐ 15 Chuck Cary	.25	.11	.03
☐ 16 Dave Righetti	.50	.23	.06
☐ 17 Lee Guetterman	.25	.11	.03
☐ 18 Andy Hawkins	.25	.11	.03
☐ 19 Greg Cadaret	.25	.11	.03
☐ 20 Eric Plunk	.25	.11	.03
☐ 21 Jimmy Jones	.25	.11	.03
☐ 22 Deion Sanders	2.50	1.10	.30
☐ 23 Jeff D. Robinson	.25	.11	.03
☐ 24 Matt Nokes	.25	.11	.03
☐ 25 Steve Balboni	.25	.11	.03
☐ 26 Wayne Tolleson	.25	.11	.03
☐ 27 Randy Velarde	.25	.11	.03
☐ 28 Rick Cerone	.25	.11	.03
☐ 29 Alan Mills	.50	.23	.06
☐ 30 Billy Martin MEM	2.50	1.10	.30
☐ 31 Stadium Card	.50	.23	.06
☐ 32 All-Time Yankee Record	.50	.23	.06

1992 Yankees WIZ 60s

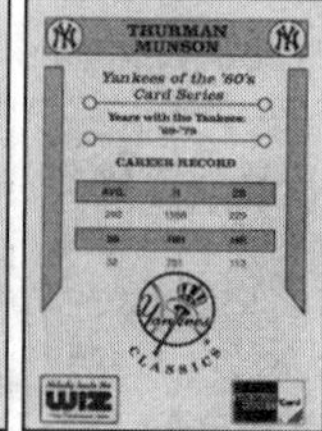

This 140-card set was sponsored by WIZ Home Entertainment Centers and American Express. The set was issued on 10" by 9" perforated sheets yielding cards measuring approximately 2" by 3". The fronts have black-and-white action and posed shots of the players on a white background enhanced with a blue bridge design. The player's name appears in a blue bordered box at the bottom. The backs have blue lettering and include the player's name, career record, and number of years with the Yankees. The team and sponsor logos are also on the back. The cards are unnumbered and checklisted below in alphabetical order.

	MINT	NRMT	EXC
COMPLETE SET (140)	30.00	13.50	3.70
COMMON CARD (1-140)	.10	.05	.01
☐ 1 Jack Aker	.10	.05	.01
☐ 2 Ruben Amaro	.10	.05	.01
☐ 3 Luis Arroyo	.10	.05	.01
☐ 4 Stan Bahnsen	.10	.05	.01
☐ 5 Steve Barber	.10	.05	.01
☐ 6 Ray Barker	.10	.05	.01
☐ 7 Rich Beck	.10	.05	.01
☐ 8 Yogi Berra	4.00	1.80	.50
☐ 9 Johnny Blanchard	.25	.11	.03
☐ 10 Gil Blanco	.10	.05	.01
☐ 11 Ron Blomberg	.10	.05	.01
☐ 12 Len Boehmer	.10	.05	.01
☐ 13 Jim Bouton	.50	.23	.06
☐ 14 Clete Boyer	.25	.11	.03
☐ 15 Jim Brenneman	.10	.05	.01
☐ 16 Marshall Bridges	.10	.05	.01
☐ 17 Harry Bright	.10	.05	.01
☐ 18 Hal Brown	.10	.05	.01
☐ 19 Billy Bryan	.10	.05	.01
☐ 20 Bill Burbach	.10	.05	.01
☐ 21 Andy Carey	.25	.11	.03
☐ 22 Duke Carmel	.10	.05	.01
☐ 23 Bob Cerv	.25	.11	.03
☐ 24 Horace Clarke	.10	.05	.01
☐ 25 Tex Clevenger	.10	.05	.01
☐ 26 Lu Clinton	.10	.05	.01
☐ 27 Jim Coates	.10	.05	.01
☐ 28 Rocky Colavito	2.00	.90	.25
☐ 29 Billy Cowan	.10	.05	.01
☐ 30 Bobby Cox	.50	.23	.06
☐ 31 Jack Cullen	.10	.05	.01
☐ 32 John Cumberland	.10	.05	.01
☐ 33 Bud Daley	.10	.05	.01
☐ 34 Joe DeMaestri	.10	.05	.01
☐ 35 Art Ditmar	.10	.05	.01
☐ 36 Al Downing	.25	.11	.03
☐ 37 Ryne Duren	.25	.11	.03
☐ 38 Doc Edwards	.10	.05	.01
☐ 39 John Ellis	.10	.05	.01
☐ 40 Frank Fernandez	.10	.05	.01
☐ 41 Mike Ferraro	.10	.05	.01
☐ 42 Whitey Ford	4.00	1.80	.50
☐ 43 Bob Friend	.25	.11	.03
☐ 44 John Gabler	.10	.05	.01
☐ 45 Billy Gardner	.10	.05	.01
☐ 46 Jake Gibbs	.25	.11	.03
☐ 47 Jesse Gonder	.10	.05	.01
☐ 48 Pedro Gonzalez	.10	.05	.01
☐ 49 Eli Grba	.10	.05	.01
☐ 50 Kent Hadley	.10	.05	.01
☐ 51 Bob Hale	.10	.05	.01
☐ 52 Jimmie Hall	.10	.05	.01
☐ 53 Steve Hamilton	.10	.05	.01
☐ 54 Mike Hegan	.10	.05	.01
☐ 55 Bill Henry	.10	.05	.01
☐ 56 Elston Howard	1.00	.45	.12
☐ 57 Dick Howser	.25	.11	.03
☐ 58 Ken Hunt	.10	.05	.01
☐ 59 Johnny James	.10	.05	.01
☐ 60 Deron Johnson	.25	.11	.03
☐ 61 Ken Johnson	.10	.05	.01
☐ 62 Elvio Jimenez	.10	.05	.01
☐ 63 Mike Jurewicz	.10	.05	.01
☐ 64 Mike Kekich	.10	.05	.01
☐ 65 John Kennedy	.10	.05	.01
☐ 66 Jerry Kenney	.10	.05	.01
☐ 67 Fred Kipp	.10	.05	.01
☐ 68 Ron Klimkowski	.10	.05	.01
☐ 69 Andy Kosco	.10	.05	.01
☐ 70 Tony Kubek	1.00	.45	.12
☐ 71 Bill Kunkel	.10	.05	.01
☐ 72 Phil Linz	.25	.11	.03
☐ 73 Dale Long	.25	.11	.03
☐ 74 Art Lopez	.10	.05	.01
☐ 75 Hector Lopez	.25	.11	.03
☐ 76 Jim Lyttle	.10	.05	.01
☐ 77 Duke Maas	.10	.05	.01
☐ 78 Mickey Mantle	10.00	4.50	1.25
☐ 79 Roger Maris	4.00	1.80	.50
☐ 80 Lindy McDaniel	.25	.11	.03
☐ 81 Danny McDevitt	.10	.05	.01
☐ 82 Dave McDonald	.10	.05	.01
☐ 83 Gil McDougald	.50	.23	.06
☐ 84 Tom Metcalf	.10	.05	.01
☐ 85 Bob Meyer	.10	.05	.01
☐ 86 Gene Michael	.25	.11	.03
☐ 87 Pete Mikkelsen	.10	.05	.01
☐ 88 John Miller	.10	.05	.01
☐ 89 Bill Monbouquette	.10	.05	.01
☐ 90 Archie Moore	.10	.05	.01
☐ 91 Ross Moschitto	.10	.05	.01
☐ 92 Thurman Munson	2.00	.90	.25
☐ 93 Bobby Murcer	.50	.23	.06
☐ 94 Don Nottebart	.10	.05	.01
☐ 95 Nate Oliver	.10	.05	.01
☐ 96 Joe Pepitone	.25	.11	.03
☐ 97 Cecil Perkins	.10	.05	.01
☐ 98 Fritz Peterson	.10	.05	.01
☐ 99 Jim Pisoni	.10	.05	.01
☐ 100 Pedro Ramos	.10	.05	.01
☐ 101 Jack Reed	.10	.05	.01
☐ 102 Hal Reniff	.10	.05	.01

☐ 103 Roger Repoz	.10	.05	.01
☐ 104 Bobby Richardson	1.00	.45	.12
☐ 105 Dale Roberts	.10	.05	.01
☐ 106 Bill Robinson	.25	.11	.03
☐ 107 Ellie Rodriguez	.10	.05	.01
☐ 108 Charlie Sands	.10	.05	.01
☐ 109 Bob Schmidt	.10	.05	.01
☐ 110 Dick Schofield	.10	.05	.01
☐ 111 Billy Shantz	.10	.05	.01
☐ 112 Bobby Shantz	.25	.11	.03
☐ 113 Rollie Sheldon	.10	.05	.01
☐ 114 Tom Shopay	.10	.05	.01
☐ 115 Bill Short	.10	.05	.01
☐ 116 Dick Simpson	.10	.05	.01
☐ 117 Bill Skowron	.50	.23	.06
☐ 118 Charley Smith	.10	.05	.01
☐ 119 Tony Solaita	.10	.05	.01
☐ 120 Bill Stafford	.10	.05	.01
☐ 121 Mel Stottlemyre	.25	.11	.03
☐ 122 Hal Stowe	.10	.05	.01
☐ 123 Fred Talbot	.10	.05	.01
☐ 124 Frank Tepedino	.10	.05	.01
☐ 125 Ralph Terry	.25	.11	.03
☐ 126 Lee Thomas	.25	.11	.03
☐ 127 Bobby Tiefenauer	.10	.05	.01
☐ 128 Bob Tillman	.10	.05	.01
☐ 129 Thad Tillotson	.10	.05	.01
☐ 130 Earl Torgeson	.10	.05	.01
☐ 131 Tom Tresh	.25	.11	.03
☐ 132 Bob Turley	.25	.11	.03
☐ 133 Elmer Valo	.10	.05	.01
☐ 134 Joe Verbanic	.10	.05	.01
☐ 135 Steve Whitaker	.10	.05	.01
☐ 136 Roy White	.25	.11	.03
☐ 137 Stan Williams	.25	.11	.03
☐ 138 Dooley Womack	.10	.05	.01
☐ 139 Ron Woods	.10	.05	.01
☐ 140 John Wyatt	.10	.05	.01

1992 Yankees WIZ 70s

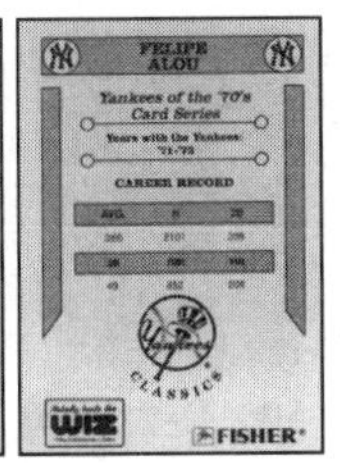

This 172-card set was sponsored by WIZ Home Entertainment Centers and Fisher. The set was issued on 10" by 9" perforated sheets yielding cards measuring approximately 2" by 3". The fronts have black-and-white action and posed shots of the players on a white background enhanced with a blue bridge design. The player's name appears in a blue bordered box at the bottom. The backs have blue lettering and include the player's name, career record, and number of years with the Yankees. The team and sponsor logos are also on the back. The cards are unnumbered and checklisted below in alphabetical order.

	MINT	NRMT	EXC
COMPLETE SET (172)	30.00	13.50	3.70
COMMON CARD (1-172)	.10	.05	.01
☐ 1 Jack Aker	.10	.05	.01
☐ 2 Doyle Alexander	.25	.11	.03
☐ 3 Bernie Allen	.10	.05	.01
☐ 4 Sandy Alomar	.25	.11	.03
☐ 5 Felipe Alou	.50	.23	.06
☐ 6 Matty Alou	.25	.11	.03
☐ 7 Dell Alston	.10	.05	.01
☐ 8 Rick Anderson	.10	.05	.01
☐ 9 Stan Bahnsen	.10	.05	.01
☐ 10 Frank Baker	.10	.05	.01
☐ 11 Jim Beattie	.10	.05	.01
☐ 12 Fred Beene	.10	.05	.01
☐ 13 Juan Beniquez	.10	.05	.01
☐ 14 Dave Bergman	.10	.05	.01
☐ 15 Juan Bernhardt	.10	.05	.01
☐ 16 Rick Bladt	.10	.05	.01
☐ 17 Paul Blair	.25	.11	.03
☐ 18 Wade Blasingame	.10	.05	.01
☐ 19 Steve Blateric	.10	.05	.01
☐ 20 Curt Blefary	.10	.05	.01
☐ 21 Ron Blomberg	.25	.11	.03
☐ 22 Len Boehmer	.10	.05	.01
☐ 23 Bobby Bonds	1.00	.45	.12
☐ 24 Ken Brett	.10	.05	.01
☐ 25 Ed Brinkman	.10	.05	.01
☐ 26 Bobby Brown	.10	.05	.01
☐ 27 Bill Burbach	.10	.05	.01
☐ 28 Ray Burris	.10	.05	.01
☐ 29 Tom Buskey	.10	.05	.01
☐ 30 Johnny Callison	.25	.11	.03
☐ 31 Danny Cater	.10	.05	.01
☐ 32 Chris Chambliss	.25	.11	.03
☐ 33 Horace Clarke	.10	.05	.01
☐ 34 Ken Clay	.10	.05	.01
☐ 35 Al Closter	.10	.05	.01
☐ 36 Rich Coggins	.10	.05	.01
☐ 37 Loyd Colson	.10	.05	.01
☐ 38 Casey Cox	.10	.05	.01
☐ 39 John Cumberland	.10	.05	.01
☐ 40 Ron Davis	.10	.05	.01
☐ 41 Jim Deidel	.10	.05	.01
☐ 42 Rick Dempsey	.25	.11	.03
☐ 43 Bucky Dent	.50	.23	.06
☐ 44 Kerry Dineen	.10	.05	.01
☐ 45 Pat Dobson	.25	.11	.03
☐ 46 Brian Doyle	.10	.05	.01
☐ 47 Rawly Eastwick	.10	.05	.01
☐ 48 Dock Ellis	.10	.05	.01
☐ 49 John Ellis	.10	.05	.01
☐ 50 Ed Figueroa	.10	.05	.01
☐ 51 Oscar Gamble	.25	.11	.03
☐ 52 Damaso Garcia	.10	.05	.01
☐ 53 Rob Gardner	.10	.05	.01
☐ 54 Jake Gibbs	.25	.11	.03
☐ 55 Fernando Gonzalez	.10	.05	.01
☐ 56 Rich Gossage	1.00	.45	.12
☐ 57 Larry Gowell	.10	.05	.01
☐ 58 Wayne Granger	.10	.05	.01
☐ 59 Mike Griffin	.10	.05	.01
☐ 60 Ron Guidry	.50	.23	.06
☐ 61 Brad Gulden	.10	.05	.01
☐ 62 Don Gullett	.25	.11	.03
☐ 63 Larry Gura	.10	.05	.01
☐ 64 Roger Hambright	.10	.05	.01
☐ 65 Steve Hamilton	.10	.05	.01
☐ 66 Ron Hansen	.10	.05	.01
☐ 67 Jim Hardin	.10	.05	.01
☐ 68 Jim Ray Hart	.25	.11	.03
☐ 69 Fran Healy	.10	.05	.01
☐ 70 Mike Heath	.10	.05	.01
☐ 71 Mike Hegan	.10	.05	.01
☐ 72 Elrod Hendricks	.10	.05	.01
☐ 73 Ed Herrmann	.10	.05	.01
☐ 74 Rich Hinton	.10	.05	.01
☐ 75 Ken Holtzman	.25	.11	.03
☐ 76 Don Hood	.10	.05	.01
☐ 77 Catfish Hunter	1.00	.45	.12
☐ 78 Grant Jackson	.10	.05	.01
☐ 79 Reggie Jackson	5.00	2.20	.60
☐ 80 Tommy John	.50	.23	.06
☐ 81 Alex Johnson	.25	.11	.03
☐ 82 Cliff Johnson	.25	.11	.03
☐ 83 Jay Johnstone	.50	.23	.06
☐ 84 Darryl Jones	.10	.05	.01
☐ 85 Gary Jones	.10	.05	.01
☐ 86 Jim Kaat	.50	.23	.06
☐ 87 Bob Kammeyer	.10	.05	.01
☐ 88 Mike Kekich	.10	.05	.01
☐ 89 Jerry Kenney	.10	.05	.01
☐ 90 Dave Kingman	.50	.23	.06
☐ 91 Ron Klimkowski	.10	.05	.01
☐ 92 Steve Kline	.10	.05	.01
☐ 93 Mickey Klutts	.10	.05	.01
☐ 94 Hal Lanier	.10	.05	.01
☐ 95 Eddie Leon	.10	.05	.01
☐ 96 Terry Ley	.10	.05	.01
☐ 97 Paul Lindblad	.10	.05	.01
☐ 98 Gene Locklear	.10	.05	.01
☐ 99 Sparky Lyle	.50	.23	.06
☐ 100 Jim Lyttle	.10	.05	.01
☐ 101 Elliott Maddox	.10	.05	.01
☐ 102 Jim Magnuson	.10	.05	.01
☐ 103 Tippy Martinez	.25	.11	.03
☐ 104 Jim Mason	.10	.05	.01
☐ 105 Carlos May	.10	.05	.01
☐ 106 Rudy May	.10	.05	.01
☐ 107 Larry McCall	.10	.05	.01
☐ 108 Mike McCormick	.25	.11	.03
☐ 109 Lindy McDaniel	.25	.11	.03
☐ 110 Sam McDowell	.25	.11	.03
☐ 111 Rich McKinney	.10	.05	.01
☐ 112 George Medich	.10	.05	.01
☐ 113 Andy Messersmith	.25	.11	.03
☐ 114 Gene Michael	.25	.11	.03
☐ 115 Paul Mirabella	.10	.05	.01
☐ 116 Bobby Mitchell	.10	.05	.01
☐ 117 Gerry Moses	.10	.05	.01
☐ 118 Thurman Munson	2.50	1.10	.30
☐ 119 Bobby Murcer	.50	.23	.06
☐ 120 Larry Murray	.10	.05	.01
☐ 121 Jerry Narron	.10	.05	.01
☐ 122 Graig Nettles	1.00	.45	.12
☐ 123 Bob Oliver	.10	.05	.01
☐ 124 Dave Pagan	.10	.05	.01
☐ 125 Gil Patterson	.10	.05	.01
☐ 126 Marty Perez	.10	.05	.01
☐ 127 Fritz Peterson	.25	.11	.03
☐ 128 Lou Piniella	.50	.23	.06
☐ 129 Dave Rajsich	.10	.05	.01
☐ 130 Domingo Ramos	.10	.05	.01
☐ 131 Lenny Randle	.10	.05	.01
☐ 132 Willie Randolph	.50	.23	.06
☐ 133 Dave Righetti	.25	.11	.03
☐ 134 Mickey Rivers	.25	.11	.03
☐ 135 Bruce Robinson	.10	.05	.01
☐ 136 Jim Roland	.10	.05	.01
☐ 137 Celerino Sanchez	.10	.05	.01
☐ 138 Rick Sawyer	.10	.05	.01
☐ 139 George Scott	.25	.11	.03
☐ 140 Duke Sims	.10	.05	.01
☐ 141 Roger Slagle	.10	.05	.01
☐ 142 Jim Spencer	.10	.05	.01
☐ 143 Charlie Spikes	.10	.05	.01
☐ 144 Roy Staiger	.10	.05	.01
☐ 145 Fred Stanley	.10	.05	.01
☐ 146 Bill Sudakis	.10	.05	.01
☐ 147 Ron Swoboda	.25	.11	.03
☐ 148 Frank Tepedino	.10	.05	.01
☐ 149 Stan Thomas	.10	.05	.01
☐ 150 Gary Thomasson	.10	.05	.01
☐ 151 Luis Tiant	.50	.23	.06
☐ 152 Dick Tidrow	.10	.05	.01
☐ 153 Rusty Torres	.10	.05	.01
☐ 154 Mike Torrez	.25	.11	.03
☐ 155 Cesar Tovar	.10	.05	.01
☐ 156 Cecil Upshaw	.10	.05	.01
☐ 157 Otto Velez	.10	.05	.01
☐ 158 Joe Verbanic	.10	.05	.01
☐ 159 Mike Wallace	.10	.05	.01
☐ 160 Danny Walton	.10	.05	.01
☐ 161 Pete Ward	.10	.05	.01
☐ 162 Gary Waslewski	.10	.05	.01
☐ 163 Dennis Werth	.10	.05	.01
☐ 164 Roy White	.25	.11	.03
☐ 165 Terry Whitfield	.10	.05	.01
☐ 166 Walt Williams	.10	.05	.01
☐ 167 Ron Woods	.10	.05	.01
☐ 168 Dick Woodson	.10	.05	.01
☐ 169 Ken Wright	.10	.05	.01
☐ 170 Jimmy Wynn	.25	.11	.03
☐ 171 Jim York	.10	.05	.01
☐ 172 George Zeber	.10	.05	.01

1992 Yankees WIZ 80s

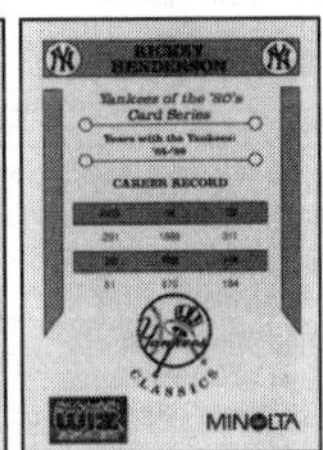

This 206-card set was sponsored by WIZ Home Entertainment Centers and Minolta. The set was issued on 10" by 9" perforated sheets yielding cards measuring approximately 2" by 3". The fronts have black-and-white action and posed shots of the players on a white background enhanced with a blue bridge design. The player's name appears in a blue bordered box at the bottom. The backs have blue lettering and include the player's name, career record, and number of years with the Yankees. The team and sponsor logos are also on the back. The cards are unnumbered and checklisted below in alphabetical order.

	MINT	NRMT	EXC
COMPLETE SET (206)	30.00	13.50	3.70
COMMON CARD (1-206)	.10	.05	.01
☐ 1 Luis Aguayo	.10	.05	.01
☐ 2 Doyle Alexander	.25	.11	.03
☐ 3 Neil Allen	.10	.05	.01
☐ 4 Mike Armstrong	.10	.05	.01
☐ 5 Brad Arnsberg	.10	.05	.01
☐ 6 Tucker Ashford	.10	.05	.01
☐ 7 Steve Balboni	.10	.05	.01
☐ 8 Jesse Barfield	.25	.11	.03
☐ 9 Don Baylor	.50	.23	.06
☐ 10 Dale Berra	.10	.05	.01
☐ 11 Doug Bird	.10	.05	.01
☐ 12 Paul Blair	.25	.11	.03
☐ 13 Mike Blowers	.25	.11	.03
☐ 14 Juan Bonilla	.10	.05	.01
☐ 15 Rick Bordi	.10	.05	.01
☐ 16 Scott Bradley	.10	.05	.01
☐ 17 Marshall Brant	.10	.05	.01
☐ 18 Tom Brookens	.10	.05	.01
☐ 19 Bob Brower	.10	.05	.01
☐ 20 Bobby Brown	.10	.05	.01
☐ 21 Curt Brown	.10	.05	.01
☐ 22 Jay Buhner	2.00	.90	.25
☐ 23 Marty Bystrom	.10	.05	.01
☐ 24 Greg Cadaret	.10	.05	.01
☐ 25 Bert Campaneris	.25	.11	.03
☐ 26 John Candelaria	.25	.11	.03
☐ 27 Chuck Cary	.10	.05	.01
☐ 28 Bill Castro	.10	.05	.01
☐ 29 Rick Cerone	.10	.05	.01
☐ 30 Chris Chambliss	.25	.11	.03
☐ 31 Clay Christiansen	.10	.05	.01
☐ 32 Jack Clark	.25	.11	.03
☐ 33 Pat Clements	.10	.05	.01
☐ 34 Dave Collins	.10	.05	.01
☐ 35 Don Cooper	.10	.05	.01
☐ 36 Henry Cotto	.10	.05	.01
☐ 37 Joe Cowley	.10	.05	.01
☐ 38 Jose Cruz	.25	.11	.03
☐ 39 Bobby Davidson	.10	.05	.01
☐ 40 Ron Davis	.10	.05	.01
☐ 41 Brian Dayett	.10	.05	.01
☐ 42 Ivan DeJesus	.10	.05	.01
☐ 43 Bucky Dent	.25	.11	.03
☐ 44 Jim Deshaies	.10	.05	.01
☐ 45 Orestes Destrade	.10	.05	.01
☐ 46 Brian Dorsett	.10	.05	.01
☐ 47 Richard Dotson	.10	.05	.01
☐ 48 Brian Doyle	.10	.05	.01
☐ 49 Doug Drabek	.50	.23	.06
☐ 50 Mike Easler	.25	.11	.03
☐ 51 Dave Eiland	.10	.05	.01
☐ 52 Roger Erickson	.10	.05	.01
☐ 53 Juan Espino	.10	.05	.01
☐ 54 Alvaro Espinoza	.10	.05	.01
☐ 55 Barry Evans	.10	.05	.01
☐ 56 Ed Figueroa	.10	.05	.01
☐ 57 Pete Filson	.10	.05	.01
☐ 58 Mike Fischlin	.10	.05	.01
☐ 59 Brian Fisher	.10	.05	.01
☐ 60 Tim Foli	.10	.05	.01
☐ 61 Ray Fontenot	.10	.05	.01
☐ 62 Barry Foote	.10	.05	.01
☐ 63 George Frazier	.10	.05	.01
☐ 64 Bill Fulton	.10	.05	.01
☐ 65 Oscar Gamble	.25	.11	.03
☐ 66 Bob Geren	.10	.05	.01
☐ 67 Rich Gossage	.75	.35	.09
☐ 68 Mike Griffin	.10	.05	.01
☐ 69 Ken Griffey	.50	.23	.06
☐ 70 Cecilio Guante	.10	.05	.01
☐ 71 Lee Guetterman	.10	.05	.01
☐ 72 Ron Guidry	.50	.23	.06
☐ 73 Brad Gulden	.10	.05	.01
☐ 74 Don Gullett	.25	.11	.03
☐ 75 Bill Gullickson	.25	.11	.03
☐ 76 Mel Hall	.10	.05	.01
☐ 77 Toby Harrah	.25	.11	.03
☐ 78 Ron Hassey	.10	.05	.01
☐ 79 Andy Hawkins	.10	.05	.01
☐ 80 Rickey Henderson	3.00	1.35	.35
☐ 81 Leo Hernandez	.10	.05	.01
☐ 82 Butch Hobson	.10	.05	.01
☐ 83 Al Holland	.10	.05	.01
☐ 84 Roger Holt	.10	.05	.01
☐ 85 Jay Howell	.10	.05	.01
☐ 86 Rex Hudler	.10	.05	.01
☐ 87 Charles Hudson	.10	.05	.01
☐ 88 Keith Hughes	.10	.05	.01
☐ 89 Reggie Jackson	3.00	1.35	.35
☐ 90 Stan Javier	.10	.05	.01
☐ 91 Stan Jefferson	.10	.05	.01
☐ 92 Tommy John	.50	.23	.06
☐ 93 Jimmy Jones	.10	.05	.01
☐ 94 Ruppert Jones	.10	.05	.01
☐ 95 Jim Kaat	.75	.35	.09
☐ 96 Curt Kaufman	.10	.05	.01
☐ 97 Roberto Kelly	.25	.11	.03
☐ 98 Steve Kemp	.25	.11	.03
☐ 99 Matt Keough	.10	.05	.01
☐ 100 Steve Kiefer	.10	.05	.01
☐ 101 Ron Kittle	.10	.05	.01
☐ 102 Dave LaPoint	.10	.05	.01
☐ 103 Marcus Lawton	.10	.05	.01
☐ 104 Joe Lefebvre	.10	.05	.01
☐ 105 Al Leiter	1.00	.45	.12
☐ 106 Jim Lewis	.10	.05	.01
☐ 107 Bryan Little	.10	.05	.01
☐ 108 Tim Lollar	.10	.05	.01
☐ 109 Phil Lombardi	.10	.05	.01
☐ 110 Vic Mata	.10	.05	.01
☐ 111 Don Mattingly	7.50	3.40	.95
☐ 112 Rudy May	.10	.05	.01
☐ 113 John Mayberry	.25	.11	.03
☐ 114 Lee Mazzilli	.10	.05	.01
☐ 115 Lance McCullers	.10	.05	.01
☐ 116 Andy McGaffigan	.10	.05	.01
☐ 117 Lynn McGlothen	.10	.05	.01
☐ 118 Bobby Meacham	.10	.05	.01
☐ 119 Hensley Meulens	.10	.05	.01
☐ 120 Larry Milbourne	.10	.05	.01
☐ 121 Kevin Mmahat	.10	.05	.01
☐ 122 Dale Mohorcic	.10	.05	.01
☐ 123 John Montefusco	.10	.05	.01
☐ 124 Omar Moreno	.10	.05	.01
☐ 125 Mike Morgan	.10	.05	.01
☐ 126 Jeff Moronko	.10	.05	.01
☐ 127 Hal Morris	.50	.23	.06
☐ 128 Jerry Mumphrey	.10	.05	.01
☐ 129 Bobby Murcer	.50	.23	.06
☐ 130 Dale Murray	.10	.05	.01
☐ 131 Gene Nelson	.10	.05	.01
☐ 132 Joe Niekro	.25	.11	.03
☐ 133 Phil Niekro	1.00	.45	.12
☐ 134 Scott Nielsen	.10	.05	.01
☐ 135 Otis Nixon	.50	.23	.06
☐ 136 Johnny Oates	.25	.11	.03
☐ 137 Mike O'Berry	.10	.05	.01
☐ 138 Rowland Office	.10	.05	.01
☐ 139 John Pacella	.10	.05	.01
☐ 140 Mike Pagliarulo	.25	.11	.03
☐ 141 Clay Parker	.10	.05	.01
☐ 142 Dan Pasqua	.10	.05	.01
☐ 143 Mike Patterson	.10	.05	.01
☐ 144 Hipolito Pena	.10	.05	.01
☐ 145 Gaylord Perry	1.00	.45	.12
☐ 146 Ken Phelps	.10	.05	.01
☐ 147 Lou Piniella	.75	.35	.09
☐ 148 Eric Plunk	.10	.05	.01

☐ 149 Luis Polonia	.50	.23	.06
☐ 150 Alfonso Pulido	.10	.05	.01
☐ 151 Jamie Quirk	.10	.05	.01
☐ 152 Bobby Ramos	.10	.05	.01
☐ 153 Willie Randolph	.50	.23	.06
☐ 154 Dennis Rasmussen	.10	.05	.01
☐ 155 Shane Rawley	.10	.05	.01
☐ 156 Rick Reuschel	.25	.11	.03
☐ 157 Dave Revering	.10	.05	.01
☐ 158 Rick Rhoden	.10	.05	.01
☐ 159 Dave Righetti	.25	.11	.03
☐ 160 Jose Rijo	.10	.05	.01
☐ 161 Andre Robertson	.10	.05	.01
☐ 162 Bruce Robinson	.10	.05	.01
☐ 163 Aurelio Rodriguez	.10	.05	.01
☐ 164 Edwin Rodriguez	.10	.05	.01
☐ 165 Gary Roenicke	.10	.05	.01
☐ 166 Jerry Royster	.10	.05	.01
☐ 167 Lenn Sakata	.10	.05	.01
☐ 168 Mark Salas	.10	.05	.01
☐ 169 Billy Sample	.10	.05	.01
☐ 170 Deion Sanders	3.00	1.35	.35
☐ 171 Rafael Santana	.10	.05	.01
☐ 172 Steve Sax	.25	.11	.03
☐ 173 Don Schulze	.10	.05	.01
☐ 174 Rodney Scott	.10	.05	.01
☐ 175 Rod Scurry	.10	.05	.01
☐ 176 Dennis Sherrill	.10	.05	.01
☐ 177 Steve Shields	.10	.05	.01
☐ 179 Bob Shirley	.10	.05	.01
☐ 180 Joel Skinner	.10	.05	.01
☐ 181 Don Slaught	.25	.11	.03
☐ 182 Roy Smalley	.25	.11	.03
☐ 183 Keith Smith	.10	.05	.01
☐ 184 Eric Soderholm	.10	.05	.01
☐ 185 Jim Spencer	.10	.05	.01
☐ 186 Fred Stanley	.10	.05	.01
☐ 187 Dave Stegman	.10	.05	.01
☐ 188 Tim Stoddard	.10	.05	.01
☐ 189 Walt Terrell	.10	.05	.01
☐ 190 Bob Tewksbury	.50	.23	.06
☐ 191 Luis Tiant	.50	.23	.06
☐ 192 Wayne Tolleson	.10	.05	.01
☐ 193 Steve Trout	.10	.05	.01
☐ 194 Tom Underwood	.10	.05	.01
☐ 195 Randy Velarde	.10	.05	.01
☐ 196 Gary Ward	.10	.05	.01
☐ 197 Claudell Washington	.25	.11	.03
☐ 198 Bob Watson	.50	.23	.06
☐ 199 Dave Wehrmeister	.10	.05	.01
☐ 200 Dennis Werth	.10	.05	.01
☐ 201 Stefan Wever	.10	.05	.01
☐ 202 Ed Whitson	.10	.05	.01
☐ 203 Ted Wilborn	.10	.05	.01
☐ 204 Dave Winfield	3.00	1.35	.35
☐ 205 Butch Wynegar	.25	.11	.03
☐ 206 Paul Zuvella	.10	.05	.01

1992 Yankees WIZ All-Stars

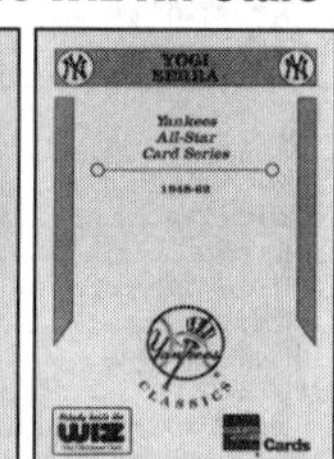

This 86-card set was sponsored by WIZ Home Entertainment Centers and American Express. The set was issued on five 15-card sheets and one 11-card title sheet, all measuring approximately 10" by 9". The perforated sheets yielded cards measuring approximately 2" by 3". The fronts have black-and-white action and posed shots of the players on a white background enhanced with a blue bridge design. The player's name appears in a blue bordered box at the bottom. The team logo in the upper left corner completes the card face. The backs have blue lettering and include the player's name and years with the team. The team and sponsor logos are also on the back. The cards are unnumbered and checklisted below in alphabetical order.

	MINT	NRMT	EXC
COMPLETE SET (86)	30.00	13.50	3.70
COMMON CARD (1-86)	.10	.05	.01
☐ 1 Luis Arroyo	.10	.05	.01
☐ 2 Hank Bauer	.25	.11	.03
☐ 3 Yogi Berra	2.00	.90	.25
☐ 4 Bobby Bonds	.50	.23	.06
☐ 5 Ernie Bonham	.10	.05	.01
☐ 6 Hank Borowy	.10	.05	.01
☐ 7 Jim Bouton	.50	.23	.06
☐ 8 Tommy Byrne	.10	.05	.01
☐ 9 Chris Chambliss	.25	.11	.03
☐ 10 Spud Chandler	.25	.11	.03
☐ 11 Ben Chapman	.10	.05	.01
☐ 12 Jim Coates	.10	.05	.01
☐ 13 Jerry Coleman	.10	.05	.01
☐ 14 Frank Crosetti	.25	.11	.03
☐ 15 Ron Davis	.10	.05	.01
☐ 16 Bucky Dent	.25	.11	.03
☐ 17 Bill Dickey	1.00	.45	.12
☐ 18 Joe DiMaggio	5.00	2.20	.60
☐ 19 Al Downing	.10	.05	.01
☐ 20 Ryne Duren	.25	.11	.03
☐ 21 Whitey Ford	2.00	.90	.25
☐ 22 Lou Gehrig	5.00	2.20	.60
☐ 23 Lefty Gomez	1.00	.45	.12
☐ 24 Joe Gordon	.25	.11	.03
☐ 25 Rich Gossage	.50	.23	.06
☐ 26 Bob Grim	.10	.05	.01
☐ 27 Ron Guidry	.50	.23	.06
☐ 28 Rollie Hemsley	.10	.05	.01
☐ 29 Rickey Henderson	1.50	.70	.19
☐ 30 Tommy Henrich	.50	.23	.06
☐ 31 Elston Howard	.50	.23	.06
☐ 32 Catfish Hunter	1.00	.45	.12
☐ 33 Reggie Jackson	2.00	.90	.25
☐ 34 Tommy John	.50	.23	.06
☐ 35 Billy Johnson	.10	.05	.01
☐ 36 Charlie Keller	.25	.11	.03
☐ 37 Tony Kubek	.25	.11	.03
☐ 38 Johnny Kucks	.10	.05	.01
☐ 39 Tony Lazzeri	1.00	.45	.12
☐ 40 Johnny Lindell	.10	.05	.01
☐ 41 Ed Lopat	.50	.23	.06
☐ 42 Sparky Lyle	.25	.11	.03
☐ 43 Mickey Mantle	7.50	3.40	.95
☐ 44 Roger Maris	2.00	.90	.25
☐ 45 Billy Martin	.75	.35	.09
☐ 46 Don Mattingly	3.00	1.35	.35
☐ 47 Gil McDougald	.25	.11	.03
☐ 48 George McQuinn	.10	.05	.01
☐ 49 Johnny Mize	1.00	.45	.12
☐ 50 Thurman Munson	1.50	.70	.19
☐ 51 Bobby Murcer	.25	.11	.03
☐ 52 Johnny Murphy	.10	.05	.01
☐ 53 Graig Nettles	.50	.23	.06
☐ 54 Phil Niekro	1.00	.45	.12
☐ 55 Irv Noren	.10	.05	.01
☐ 56 Joe Page	.10	.05	.01
☐ 57 Monte Pearson	.10	.05	.01
☐ 58 Joe Pepitone	.25	.11	.03
☐ 59 Fritz Peterson	.10	.05	.01
☐ 60 Willie Randolph	.25	.11	.03
☐ 61 Vic Raschi	.25	.11	.03
☐ 62 Allie Reynolds	.50	.23	.06
☐ 63 Bobby Richardson	.50	.23	.06
☐ 64 Dave Righetti	.25	.11	.03
☐ 65 Mickey Rivers	.25	.11	.03
☐ 66 Phil Rizzuto	1.50	.70	.19
☐ 67 Aaron Robinson	.10	.05	.01
☐ 68 Red Rolfe	.10	.05	.01
☐ 69 Buddy Rosar	.10	.05	.01
☐ 70 Red Ruffing	1.00	.45	.12
☐ 71 Marius Russo	.10	.05	.01
☐ 72 Babe Ruth	7.50	3.40	.95
☐ 73 Johnny Sain	.50	.23	.06
☐ 74 Scott Sanderson	.10	.05	.01
☐ 75 Steve Sax	.25	.11	.03
☐ 76 George Selkirk	.10	.05	.01
☐ 77 Bobby Shantz	.25	.11	.03
☐ 78 Spec Shea	.10	.05	.01
☐ 79 Bill Skowron	.25	.11	.03
☐ 80 Snuffy Stirnweiss	.10	.05	.01
☐ 81 Mel Stottlemyre	.25	.11	.03
☐ 82 Ralph Terry	.10	.05	.01
☐ 83 Tom Tresh	.25	.11	.03
☐ 84 Bob Turley	.25	.11	.03
☐ 85 Roy White	.25	.11	.03
☐ 86 Dave Winfield	2.00	.90	.25

1992 Yankees WIZ HOF

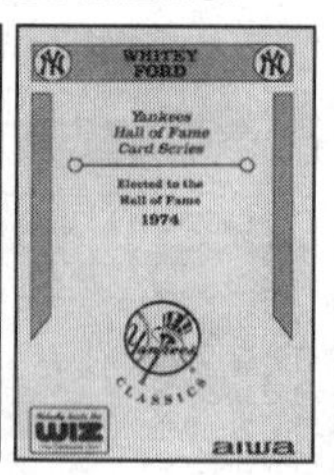

This 35-card set was sponsored by WIZ Home Entertainment Centers and Aiwa. The set was issued on two 15-card sheets and one five-card title sheet, all measuring approximately 10" by 9". The perforated sheets yielded cards measuring approximately 2" by 3". The fronts have black-and-white action and posed shots of the players on a white background enhanced with a blue bridge design. A white banner with the words "Hall of Fame" in the upper left corner completes the card face. The player's name appears in a blue bordered box at the bottom. The backs have blue lettering and include the player's name and the year he was inducted into the Hall of Fame. The team and sponsor logos are also on the back. The cards are unnumbered and checklisted below in alphabetical order.

	MINT	NRMT	EXC
COMPLETE SET (35)	20.00	9.00	2.50
COMMON CARD (1-35)	.25	.11	.03
☐ 1 Home Run Baker	.25	.11	.03
☐ 2 Edward G. Barrow	.25	.11	.03
☐ 3 Yogi Berra	2.00	.90	.25
☐ 4 Frank Chance	.25	.11	.03
☐ 5 Jack Chesbro	.25	.11	.03
☐ 6 Earle Combs	.25	.11	.03
☐ 7 Stan Coveleski	.25	.11	.03
☐ 8 Bill Dickey	.75	.35	.09
☐ 9 Joe DiMaggio	5.00	2.20	.60
☐ 10 Whitey Ford	2.00	.90	.25
☐ 11 Lou Gehrig	4.00	1.80	.50
☐ 12 Lefty Gomez	.50	.23	.06
☐ 13 Clark C. Griffith	.25	.11	.03
☐ 14 Burleigh Grimes	.25	.11	.03
☐ 15 Bucky Harris	.25	.11	.03
☐ 16 Waite Hoyt	.25	.11	.03
☐ 17 Miller Huggins	.25	.11	.03
☐ 18 Catfish Hunter	.50	.23	.06
☐ 19 Willie Keeler	.25	.11	.03
☐ 20 Tony Lazzeri	.25	.11	.03
☐ 21 Larry MacPhail	.25	.11	.03
☐ 22 Mickey Mantle	5.00	2.20	.60
☐ 23 Joe McCarthy MG	.25	.11	.03
☐ 24 Johnny Mize	.50	.23	.06
☐ 25 Herb Pennock	.25	.11	.03
☐ 26 Gaylord Perry	.50	.23	.06
☐ 27 Branch Rickey	.25	.11	.03
☐ 28 Red Ruffing	.25	.11	.03
☐ 29 Babe Ruth	5.00	2.20	.60
☐ 30 Joe Sewell	.25	.11	.03
☐ 31 Enos Slaughter	.50	.23	.06
☐ 32 Casey Stengel	.75	.35	.09
☐ 33 Dazzy Vance	.25	.11	.03
☐ 34 Paul Waner	.25	.11	.03
☐ 35 George M. Weiss GM	.25	.11	.03

1956 Yellow Basepath Pins

This relatively scarce set was probably issued around 1956 judging by the players included. If this set were produced in 1956, it would provide a possible explanation for the apparent scarcity of the Dale Long pin. Long was a relative unknown until going on his record-setting consecutive game homer-hitting spree in May 1956; perhaps he was a late addition to the set. These pins were supposedly issued as premiums or prizes in one-cent bubblegum machines. Each pin measures approximately 7/8" in diameter. The front of the pin also contains a green "infield" background with a black and white photo of the player in the center.

	NRMT	VG-E	GOOD
COMPLETE SET (32)	5000.00	2200.00	600.00
COMMON PIN (1-32)	75.00	34.00	9.50
☐ 1 Hank Aaron	350.00	160.00	45.00
☐ 2 Joe Adcock	100.00	45.00	12.50
☐ 3 Luis Aparicio	150.00	70.00	19.00
☐ 4 Richie Ashburn	150.00	70.00	19.00
☐ 5 Gene Baker	75.00	34.00	9.50
☐ 6 Ernie Banks	250.00	110.00	31.00
☐ 7 Yogi Berra	300.00	135.00	38.00
☐ 8 Bill Bruton	75.00	34.00	9.50
☐ 9 Larry Doby	100.00	45.00	12.50
☐ 10 Bob Friend	75.00	34.00	9.50
☐ 11 Nellie Fox	150.00	70.00	19.00
☐ 12 Jim Greengrass	75.00	34.00	9.50
☐ 13 Steve Gromek	75.00	34.00	9.50
☐ 14 Johnny Groth	75.00	34.00	9.50
☐ 15 Gil Hodges	150.00	70.00	19.00
☐ 16 Al Kaline	250.00	110.00	31.00
☐ 17 Ted Kluzewski (sic, Kluszewski)	125.00	55.00	15.50
☐ 18 Johnny Logan	75.00	34.00	9.50
☐ 19 Dale Long	175.00	80.00	22.00
☐ 20 Mickey Mantle	900.00	400.00	110.00
☐ 21 Eddie Matthews (sic, Mathews)	200.00	90.00	25.00
☐ 22 Minnie Minoso	125.00	55.00	15.50
☐ 23 Stan Musial	350.00	160.00	45.00
☐ 24 Don Newcombe	100.00	45.00	12.50
☐ 25 Bob Porterfield	75.00	34.00	9.50
☐ 26 Pee Wee Reese	250.00	110.00	31.00
☐ 27 Robin Roberts	150.00	70.00	19.00
☐ 28 Red Schoendienst	125.00	55.00	15.50
☐ 29 Duke Snider	300.00	135.00	38.00
☐ 30 Vern Stephens	75.00	34.00	9.50
☐ 31 Gene Woodling	100.00	45.00	12.50
☐ 32 Gus Zernial	75.00	34.00	9.50

1958 Yoo-Hoo Match Book Cover

This yellow match book cover was issued by the Yoo-Hoo chocolate drink company and featured a photo of Yogi Berra on the back. The sepia, head shot photo is encircled with a bottle cap design and above and below the cap are the words "Me for Yoo-Hoo". Yogi Berra's name is printed on the lower portion of the picture. The inner portion of the match book cover carries an offer to mail in the empty cover with $2.50 and receive a book entitled "The Story of Yogi Berra".

	NRMT	VG-E	GOOD
COMPLETE SET	25.00	11.00	3.10
COMMON PLAYER	25.00	11.00	3.10

1959 Yoo-Hoo

These cards are black and white, with no printing on the back. They feature New York Yankee ballplayers, and were distributed as a premium in the New York area with a six-pack of Yoo-Hoo. There were six cards issued in the set. A facsimile signature of the player, along with the phrase "Me for Yoo-Hoo" appears on the front. The cards have a 15/16" tab at the bottom. The cards measure approximately 2 7/16" by 3 9/16" without the tab and 2 7/16" by 4 1/2" with the tab. The cards are valued below as being with tabs intact.

	NRMT	VG-E	GOOD
COMPLETE SET (6)	2250.00	1000.00	275.00
COMMON CARD (1-6)	100.00	45.00	12.50
☐ 1 Yogi Berra	500.00	220.00	60.00
☐ 2 Whitey Ford	250.00	110.00	31.00
☐ 3 Tony Kubek	125.00	55.00	15.50
☐ 4 Mickey Mantle SP	1750.00	800.00	220.00
☐ 5 Gil McDougald	100.00	45.00	12.50
☐ 6 Moose Skowron	125.00	55.00	15.50

1993 Yoo-Hoo

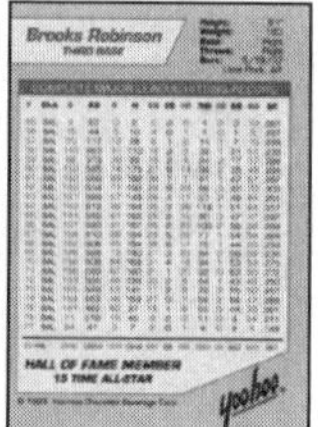

This standard-size 20-card set was issued by Yoo-Hoo Chocolate Beverage Corporation and celebrates some of baseball's legends. The fronts and backs are bright yellow and carry a posed or action color photo that is edged in red. The Yoo-Hoo logo is in the upper left and the player's name is printed in red on a white bar in the lower left. The Baseball Legends Limited Edition logo is in the lower right. The backs contain biography, player position, and career statistics. The cards are unnumbered and checklisted below in alphabetical order.

	MINT	NRMT	EXC
COMPLETE SET (20)	10.00	4.50	1.25
COMMON CARD (1-20)	.40	.18	.05
☐ 1 Johnny Bench	.75	.35	.09
☐ 2 Yogi Berra	1.00	.45	.12
☐ 3 Lou Brock	.75	.35	.09
☐ 4 Rod Carew	.75	.35	.09
☐ 5 Bob Feller	1.00	.45	.12
☐ 6 Whitey Ford	.75	.35	.09
☐ 7 Steve Garvey	.40	.18	.05
☐ 8 Al Kaline	1.00	.45	.12
☐ 9 Willie McCovey	.50	.23	.06
☐ 10 Joe Morgan	.60	.25	.07
☐ 11 Stan Musial	1.25	.55	.16
☐ 12 Gaylord Perry	.50	.23	.06
☐ 13 Graig Nettles	.40	.18	.05
☐ 14 Jim Rice	.40	.18	.05
☐ 15 Phil Rizzuto	.75	.35	.09
☐ 16 Brooks Robinson	1.00	.45	.12
☐ 17 Pete Rose	1.25	.55	.16
☐ 18 Tom Seaver	1.00	.45	.12
☐ 19 Duke Snider	1.00	.45	.12
☐ 20 Willie Stargell	.60	.25	.07

1994 Yoo-Hoo

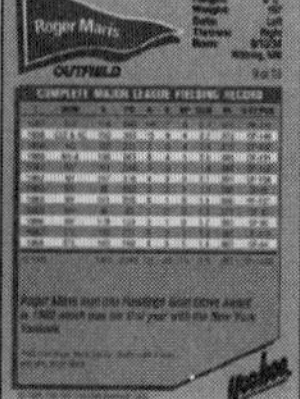

Issued in conjunction with Rawlings in two ten-card sets, each set consisting of eight player cards and two fact cards, this 20-card set features past winners of Rawlings Gold Glove Award. The first series was introduced in May, while the second series was released in August. The entire set could be received for proofs-of-purchase as well as postage and handling; a toll free number on Yoo-Hoo products could be called to obtain the details of the offer. The standard-size cards feature color player photos on their yellow-bordered fronts. Team logo have been airbrushed out. The player's name appears in white lettering within a red banner at the lower left. The yellow-bordered back carries the player's name in white lettering in a red banner at the top left, with biography appearing alongside on the right and statistics below. The Fact Cards are numbered 1-4 on their fronts and backs, and have been arbitrarily assigned an "F" prefix below to distinguish them from the player cards.

	MINT	NRMT	EXC
COMPLETE SET (20)	10.00	4.50	1.25
COMMON CARD (1-16)	.50	.23	.06
☐ 1 Luis Aparicio	.75	.35	.09
☐ 2 Bobby Bonds	.40	.18	.05
☐ 3 Bob Boone	.75	.35	.09
☐ 4 Steve Carlton	1.00	.45	.12
☐ 5 Roberto Clemente	2.50	1.10	.30
☐ 6 Bob Gibson	1.00	.45	.12
☐ 7 Keith Hernandez	.75	.35	.09
☐ 8 Jim Kaat	.75	.35	.09
☐ 9 Roger Maris	1.50	.70	.19
☐ 10 Don Mattingly	1.50	.70	.19
☐ 11 Thurman Munson	.50	.23	.06
☐ 12 Phil Rizzuto	1.00	.45	.12
☐ 13 Brooks Robinson	1.00	.45	.12
☐ 14 Ryne Sandberg	1.50	.70	.19
☐ 15 Mike Schmidt	1.00	.45	.12
☐ 16 Carl Yastrzemski	1.00	.45	.12
☐ F1 Fact Card 1	.25	.11	.03
☐ F2 Fact Card 2	.25	.11	.03
☐ F3 Fact Card 3	.25	.11	.03
☐ F4 Fact Card 4	.25	.11	.03

1927 York Caramel E210

The cards in this 60-card set measure 1 3/8" by 2 1/2". This set contains numbered cards with black and white photos of baseball players in the series of "most prominent baseball stars" issued by the York Caramel Company. They were released to the public in 1927. Number 12 has been found with two spellings; number 58 appears with either Bell or Galloway; and numbers 9, 25, 31 and 46 have incorrect photos of players with the same last names. An interesting feature is the caption which appears under the players's name on back, e.g., Burleigh Grimes is dubbed "A Sterling National League Pitcher." The complete set price includes all variation cards listed in the checklist below.

	EX-MT	VG-E	GOOD
COMPLETE SET (64)	6000.00	2700.00	750.00
COMMON CARD (1-60)	60.00	27.00	7.50
☐ 1 Burleigh Grimes	100.00	45.00	12.50
☐ 2 Walter Reuther (sic, Ruether)	60.00	27.00	7.50
☐ 3A Joe Duggan ERR (sic, Dugan)	75.00	34.00	9.50
☐ 3B Joe Dugan COR	75.00	34.00	9.50
☐ 4 Red Faber	100.00	45.00	12.50
☐ 5 Gabby Hartnett	125.00	55.00	15.50
☐ 6 Babe Ruth	1200.00	550.00	150.00
☐ 7 Bob Meusel	75.00	34.00	9.50
☐ 8 Herb Pennock	100.00	45.00	12.50
☐ 9 George (H.) Burns (photo actually George J. Burns)	60.00	27.00	7.50
☐ 10 Joe Sewell	100.00	45.00	12.50
☐ 11 George Uhle	60.00	27.00	7.50
☐ 12A Bob O'Farrel ERR	75.00	34.00	9.50
☐ 12B Bob O'Farrell COR	75.00	34.00	9.50
☐ 13 Rogers Hornsby	250.00	110.00	31.00
☐ 14 Pie Traynor	150.00	70.00	19.00
☐ 15 Clarence Mitchell	60.00	27.00	7.50
☐ 16 Eppa Rixey	100.00	45.00	12.50
☐ 17 Carl Mays	75.00	34.00	9.50
☐ 18 Dolf Luque	60.00	27.00	7.50
☐ 19 Dave Bancroft	100.00	45.00	12.50
☐ 20 George Kelly	100.00	45.00	12.50
☐ 21 Ira Flagstead	60.00	27.00	7.50
☐ 22 Harry Heilmann	125.00	55.00	15.50
☐ 23 Ray Schalk	100.00	45.00	12.50
☐ 24 Johnny Mostil	60.00	27.00	7.50
☐ 25 Hack Wilson (photo actually Art Wilson)	200.00	90.00	25.00
☐ 26 Tom Zachary	60.00	27.00	7.50
☐ 27 Ty Cobb	900.00	400.00	110.00
☐ 28 Tris Speaker	250.00	110.00	31.00
☐ 29 Ralph Perkins	60.00	27.00	7.50
☐ 30 Jess Haines (sic, Jesse)	100.00	45.00	12.50
☐ 31 Sherwood Smith (photo actually Jack Coombs)	60.00	27.00	7.50
☐ 32 Max Carey	100.00	45.00	12.50
☐ 33 Eugene Hargraves	60.00	27.00	7.50
☐ 34 Miguel L. Gonzales	60.00	27.00	7.50
☐ 35A Clifton Heathcot ERR	75.00	34.00	9.50
☐ 35B Clifton Heathcote COR	75.00	34.00	9.50
☐ 36 Sam Rice	100.00	45.00	12.50
☐ 37 Earl Sheely	60.00	27.00	7.50
☐ 38 Emory E. Rigney	60.00	27.00	7.50
☐ 39 Bib Falk	60.00	27.00	7.50
☐ 40 Nick Altrock	60.00	27.00	7.50
☐ 41 Stanley Harris	100.00	45.00	12.50
☐ 42 John J. McGraw MG	200.00	90.00	25.00
☐ 43 Wilbert Robinson MG	150.00	70.00	19.00
☐ 44 Grover Cleveland Alexander	250.00	110.00	31.00
☐ 45 Walter Johnson	300.00	135.00	38.00
☐ 46 William H. Terry (photo actually Zeb Terry)	150.00	70.00	19.00
☐ 47 Eddie Collins	125.00	55.00	15.50
☐ 48 Marty McManus	60.00	27.00	7.50
☐ 49 Goose Goslin	125.00	55.00	15.50
☐ 50 Frankie Frisch	200.00	90.00	25.00
☐ 51 Jimmy Dykes	75.00	34.00	9.50
☐ 52 Cy Williams	75.00	34.00	9.50
☐ 53 Ed Roush	125.00	55.00	15.50
☐ 54 George Sisler	200.00	90.00	25.00
☐ 55 Ed Rommel	75.00	34.00	9.50
☐ 56 Rogers Peckinpaugh (sic, Roger)	75.00	34.00	9.50
☐ 57 Stan Coveleskie	100.00	45.00	12.50
☐ 58A Clarence Galloway	75.00	34.00	9.50
☐ 58B Lester Bell	75.00	34.00	9.50
☐ 59 Bob Shawkey	75.00	34.00	9.50
☐ 60 John P. McInnis	75.00	34.00	9.50

1928 Yuenglings

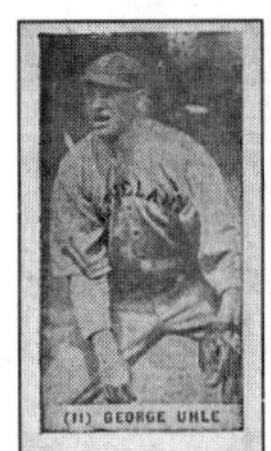

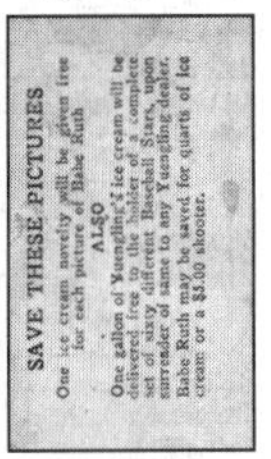

The cards in this 60-card set measure approximately 1 3/8" by 2 9/16". This black and white, numbered set contains many Hall of Famers. The card backs are the same as those found in sets of E210 and W502. The Paul Waner card, number 45, actually contains a picture of Clyde Barnhardt. Each back contains an offer to redeem pictures of Babe Ruth for ice cream. The catalog designation for this set is F50.

	EX-MT	VG-E	GOOD
COMPLETE SET (60)	3000.00	1350.00	375.00
COMMON CARD (1-60)	15.00	6.75	1.85
☐ 1 Burleigh Grimes	30.00	13.50	3.70
☐ 2 Walter Reuther	15.00	6.75	1.85
☐ 3 Joe Dugan	18.00	8.00	2.20
☐ 4 Red Faber	30.00	13.50	3.70
☐ 5 Gabby Hartnett	35.00	16.00	4.40
☐ 6 Babe Ruth	800.00	350.00	100.00
☐ 7 Bob Meusel	18.00	8.00	2.20
☐ 8 Herb Pennock	30.00	13.50	3.70
☐ 9 George Burns	15.00	6.75	1.85
☐ 10 Joe Sewell	30.00	13.50	3.70
☐ 11 George Uhle	15.00	6.75	1.85
☐ 12 Bob O'Farrell	15.00	6.75	1.85
☐ 13 Rogers Hornsby	100.00	45.00	12.50
☐ 14 Pie Traynor	35.00	16.00	4.40
☐ 15 Clarence Mitchell	15.00	6.75	1.85
☐ 16 Eppa Rixey	30.00	13.50	3.70
☐ 17 Carl Mays	20.00	9.00	2.50
☐ 18 Adolfo Luque	25.00	11.00	3.10
☐ 19 Dave Bancroft	30.00	13.50	3.70
☐ 20 George Kelly	30.00	13.50	3.70
☐ 21 Earle Combs	30.00	13.50	3.70
☐ 22 Harry Heilmann	35.00	16.00	4.40
☐ 23 Ray Schalk	30.00	13.50	3.70
☐ 24 John Mostil	15.00	6.75	1.85
☐ 25 Hack Wilson	45.00	20.00	5.50
☐ 26 Lou Gehrig	450.00	200.00	55.00
☐ 27 Ty Cobb	450.00	200.00	55.00
☐ 28 Tris Speaker	75.00	34.00	9.50
☐ 29 Tony Lazzeri	45.00	20.00	5.50
☐ 30 Waite Hoyt	30.00	13.50	3.70
☐ 31 Sherwood Smith	15.00	6.75	1.85
☐ 32 Max Carey	30.00	13.50	3.70
☐ 33 Gene Hargrave	15.00	6.75	1.85
☐ 34 Miguel Gonzalez	18.00	8.00	2.20
☐ 35 Joe Judge	18.00	8.00	2.20
☐ 36 Sam Rice	30.00	13.50	3.70
☐ 37 Earl Sheely	15.00	6.75	1.85
☐ 38 Sam Jones	18.00	8.00	2.20
☐ 39 Bibb Falk	15.00	6.75	1.85
☐ 40 Willie Kamm	15.00	6.75	1.85
☐ 41 Bucky Harris	25.00	11.00	3.10
☐ 42 John McGraw MG	50.00	22.00	6.25
☐ 43 Art Nehf	18.00	8.00	2.20
☐ 44 Grover C. Alexander	90.00	40.00	11.00
☐ 45 Paul Waner	35.00	16.00	4.40
☐ 46 Bill Terry	60.00	27.00	7.50
☐ 47 Glenn Wright	15.00	6.75	1.85
☐ 48 Earl Smith	15.00	6.75	1.85
☐ 49 Goose Goslin	30.00	13.50	3.70
☐ 50 Frank Frisch	40.00	18.00	5.00
☐ 51 Joe Harris	15.00	6.75	1.85
☐ 52 Cy Williams	18.00	8.00	2.20
☐ 53 Eddie Roush	40.00	18.00	5.00
☐ 54 George Sisler	60.00	27.00	7.50
☐ 55 Ed Rommel	18.00	8.00	2.20
☐ 56 Roger Peckinpaugh	18.00	8.00	2.20
☐ 57 Stanley Coveleskie	30.00	13.50	3.70
☐ 58 Lester Bell	15.00	6.75	1.85
☐ 59 Lloyd Waner	30.00	13.50	3.70
☐ 60 John McInnis	18.00	8.00	2.20

1993 Z-Silk Clemente

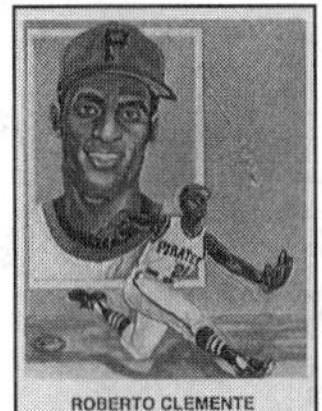

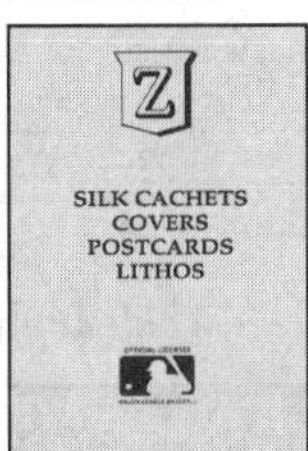

This ten-card set of silk cachets features artist's paintings of Roberto Clemente. The cards measure the standard-size and have white borders. Roberto Clemente's name is printed along the bottom edge. Each card displays a portrait head view with an overlaid action picture that is printed on silk. The white backs carry the 'Z' company logo and a list of products they produce. The cards are unnumbered. The cards may be most easily distinguished by the differing overlaid action pictures described below.

	MINT	NRMT	EXC
COMPLETE SET (10)	7.50	3.40	.95
COMMON CARD (1-10)	.75	.35	.09
☐ 1 Roberto Clemente (Bat behind after hit)	.75	.35	.09
☐ 2 Roberto Clemente (Batting stance)	.75	.35	.09
☐ 3 Roberto Clemente (Climbing outfield fence to catch fly ball)	.75	.35	.09
☐ 4 Roberto Clemente (Running to first)	.75	.35	.09
☐ 5 Roberto Clemente (On deck kneeling with two bats)	.75	.35	.09
☐ 6 Roberto Clemente (Sprinting to catch fly ball in outfield)	.75	.35	.09
☐ 7 Roberto Clemente (Saluting with hat raised over head)	.75	.35	.09
☐ 8 Roberto Clemente (Bat extended straight out)	.75	.35	.09
☐ 9 Roberto Clemente (In major, minor and winter league uniforms)	.75	.35	.09
☐ 10 Roberto Clemente	.75	.35	.09

1995 Zenith

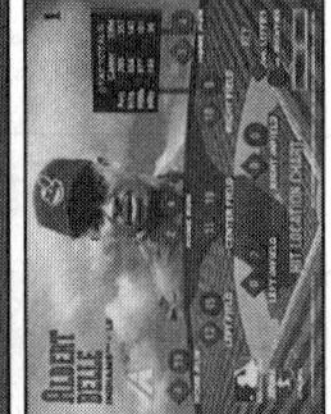

The complete 1995 Zenith set consists of 150 standard-size cards. The cards are made of thick stock and are borderless. The fronts have an action photo with a pyramid design serving as background. The player's name appears vertically up the left side with the Pinnacle logo in the upper right corner. The backs have a head shot and statistical information such as pitcheris strike frequency and what part of the field batters have the tendency to go to most. Included is a subset of 50 Rookies (111-150). The regular issued cards are in alphabetical order by first name. Rookie Cards in this set include Bobby Higginson and Hideo Nomo.

	MINT	NRMT	EXC
COMPLETE SET (150)	40.00	18.00	5.00
COMMON CARD (1-150)	.15	.07	.02
☐ 1 Albert Belle	2.00	.90	.25
☐ 2 Alex Fernandez	.30	.14	.04
☐ 3 Andy Benes	.15	.07	.02
☐ 4 Barry Larkin	.75	.35	.09
☐ 5 Barry Bonds	1.25	.55	.16
☐ 6 Ben McDonald	.15	.07	.02
☐ 7 Bernard Gilkey	.30	.14	.04
☐ 8 Billy Ashley	.15	.07	.02
☐ 9 Bobby Bonilla	.30	.14	.04
☐ 10 Bret Saberhagen	.30	.14	.04
☐ 11 Brian Jordan	.75	.35	.09
☐ 12 Cal Ripken	4.00	1.80	.50
☐ 13 Carlos Baerga	.30	.14	.04
☐ 14 Carlos Delgado	.30	.14	.04
☐ 15 Cecil Fielder	.30	.14	.04
☐ 16 Chili Davis	.30	.14	.04
☐ 17 Chuck Knoblauch	.75	.35	.09
☐ 18 Craig Biggio	.30	.14	.04
☐ 19 Danny Tartabull	.15	.07	.02
☐ 20 Dante Bichette	.75	.35	.09
☐ 21 Darren Daulton	.30	.14	.04
☐ 22 David Justice	.75	.35	.09
☐ 23 Dave Winfield	.75	.35	.09
☐ 24 David Cone	.30	.14	.04
☐ 25 Dean Palmer	.30	.14	.04
☐ 26 Deion Sanders	.75	.35	.09
☐ 27 Dennis Eckersley	.30	.14	.04
☐ 28 Derek Bell	.30	.14	.04
☐ 29 Don Mattingly	2.50	1.10	.30
☐ 30 Edgar Martinez	.30	.14	.04
☐ 31 Eric Karros	.30	.14	.04
☐ 32 James Mouton	.15	.07	.02
☐ 33 Frank Thomas	5.00	2.20	.60
☐ 34 Fred McGriff	.75	.35	.09
☐ 35 Gary Sheffield	.75	.35	.09
☐ 36 Gary Gaetti	.30	.14	.04
☐ 37 Greg Maddux	3.00	1.35	.35
☐ 38 Gregg Jefferies	.30	.14	.04
☐ 39 Ivan Rodriguez	1.25	.55	.16
☐ 40 Kenny Rogers	.15	.07	.02
☐ 41 J.T. Snow	.30	.14	.04
☐ 42 Hal Morris	.15	.07	.02
☐ 43 Eddie Murray 3000th Hit	1.25	.55	.16
☐ 44 Javier Lopez	.75	.35	.09
☐ 45 Jay Bell	.30	.14	.04
☐ 46 Jeff Conine	.30	.14	.04
☐ 47 Jeff Bagwell	2.00	.90	.25
☐ 48 Hideo Nomo Japanese	5.00	2.20	.60
☐ 49 Jeff Kent	.15	.07	.02
☐ 50 Jeff King	.30	.14	.04
☐ 51 Jim Thome	1.00	.45	.12
☐ 52 Jimmy Key	.30	.14	.04
☐ 53 Joe Carter	.30	.14	.04
☐ 54 John Valentin	.30	.14	.04
☐ 55 John Olerud	.15	.07	.02
☐ 56 Jose Canseco	.75	.35	.09
☐ 57 Jose Rijo	.15	.07	.02
☐ 58 Jose Offerman	.15	.07	.02
☐ 59 Juan Gonzalez	2.50	1.10	.30
☐ 60 Ken Caminiti	.75	.35	.09
☐ 61 Ken Griffey Jr.	5.00	2.20	.60
☐ 62 Kenny Lofton	1.25	.55	.16
☐ 63 Kevin Appier	.30	.14	.04
☐ 64 Kevin Seitzer	.15	.07	.02
☐ 65 Kirby Puckett	2.00	.90	.25
☐ 66 Kirk Gibson	.30	.14	.04
☐ 67 Larry Walker	.75	.35	.09
☐ 68 Lenny Dykstra	.30	.14	.04
☐ 69 Manny Ramirez	1.25	.55	.16
☐ 70 Mark Grace	.75	.35	.09
☐ 71 Mark McGwire	1.50	.70	.19
☐ 72 Marquis Grissom	.30	.14	.04
☐ 73 Jim Edmonds	.75	.35	.09
☐ 74 Matt Williams	.75	.35	.09
☐ 75 Mike Mussina	1.00	.45	.12
☐ 76 Mike Piazza	3.00	1.35	.35
☐ 77 Mo Vaughn	1.25	.55	.16
☐ 78 Moises Alou	.30	.14	.04
☐ 79 Ozzie Smith	1.25	.55	.16
☐ 80 Paul O'Neill	.30	.14	.04
☐ 81 Paul Molitor	1.00	.45	.12
☐ 82 Rafael Palmeiro	.75	.35	.09
☐ 83 Randy Johnson	.75	.35	.09
☐ 84 Raul Mondesi	.75	.35	.09
☐ 85 Ray Lankford	.30	.14	.04
☐ 86 Reggie Sanders	.30	.14	.04
☐ 87 Rickey Henderson	.75	.35	.09
☐ 88 Rico Brogna	.15	.07	.02
☐ 89 Roberto Alomar	1.00	.45	.12
☐ 90 Robin Ventura	.30	.14	.04
☐ 91 Roger Clemens	1.00	.45	.12
☐ 92 Ron Gant	.30	.14	.04
☐ 93 Rondell White	.30	.14	.04
☐ 94 Royce Clayton	.15	.07	.02
☐ 95 Ruben Sierra	.30	.14	.04
☐ 96 Rusty Greer	.75	.35	.09
☐ 97 Ryan Klesko	.75	.35	.09
☐ 98 Sammy Sosa	.75	.35	.09
☐ 99 Shawon Dunston	.15	.07	.02
☐ 100 Steve Ontiveros	.15	.07	.02
☐ 101 Tim Naehring	.15	.07	.02
☐ 102 Tim Salmon	.75	.35	.09
☐ 103 Tino Martinez	.30	.14	.04
☐ 104 Tony Gwynn	2.00	.90	.25
☐ 105 Travis Fryman	.30	.14	.04

Card	MINT	NRMT	EXC
□ 106 Vinny Castilla	.30	.14	.04
□ 107 Wade Boggs	.75	.35	.09
□ 108 Wally Joyner	.30	.14	.04
□ 109 Wil Cordero	.15	.07	.02
□ 110 Will Clark	.75	.35	.09
□ 111 Chipper Jones	3.00	1.35	.35
□ 112 Armando Benitez	.15	.07	.02
□ 113 Curtis Goodwin	.30	.14	.04
□ 114 Gabe White	.15	.07	.02
□ 115 Vaughn Eshelman	.15	.07	.02
□ 116 Marty Cordova	.75	.35	.09
□ 117 Dustin Hermanson	.30	.14	.04
□ 118 Rich Becker	.15	.07	.02
□ 119 Ray Durham	.30	.14	.04
□ 120 Shane Andrews	.15	.07	.02
□ 121 Scott Ruffcorn	.15	.07	.02
□ 122 Mark Grudzielanek	1.25	.55	.16
□ 123 James Baldwin	.30	.14	.04
□ 124 Carlos Perez	.30	.14	.04
□ 125 Julian Tavarez	.15	.07	.02
□ 126 Joe Vitiello	.15	.07	.02
□ 127 Jason Bates	.15	.07	.02
□ 128 Edgardo Alfonzo	.30	.14	.04
□ 129 Juan Acevedo	.15	.07	.02
□ 130 Bill Pulsipher	.30	.14	.04
□ 131 Bob Higginson	1.25	.55	.16
□ 132 Russ Davis	.15	.07	.02
□ 133 Charles Johnson	.30	.14	.04
□ 134 Derek Jeter	3.00	1.35	.35
□ 135 Orlando Miller	.15	.07	.02
□ 136 LaTroy Hawkins	.15	.07	.02
□ 137 Brian L.Hunter	.30	.14	.04
□ 138 Roberto Petagine	.15	.07	.02
□ 139 Midre Cummings	.15	.07	.02
□ 140 Garret Anderson	.30	.14	.04
□ 141 Ugueth Urbina	.15	.07	.02
□ 142 Antonio Osuna	.15	.07	.02
□ 143 Michael Tucker	.30	.14	.04
□ 144 Benji Gil	.15	.07	.02
□ 145 Jon Nunnally	.30	.14	.04
□ 146 Alex Rodriguez	6.00	2.70	.75
□ 147 Todd Hollandsworth	.75	.35	.09
□ 148 Alex Gonzalez	.15	.07	.02
□ 149 Hideo Nomo	5.00	2.20	.60
□ 150 Shawn Green	.30	.14	.04

1995 Zenith All-Star Salute

This 18-card set was randomly inserted in packs at a rate of one in six. The set commemorates many of the memorable plays of the 1995 All-Star Game played in Arlington, TX. The fronts have an action photo set out against the background of the game giving it a 3D look. The words "All-Star Salute" are in gold on the left with the player's name at the bottom. The backs have a color photo with personal All-Star Game tidbits. The cards are numbered "X of 18."

	MINT	NRMT	EXC
COMPLETE SET (18)	60.00	27.00	7.50
COMMON CARD (1-18)	1.00	.45	.12
□ 1 Cal Ripken	8.00	3.60	1.00
□ 2 Frank Thomas	10.00	4.50	1.25
□ 3 Mike Piazza	6.00	2.70	.75
□ 4 Kirby Puckett	4.00	1.80	.50
□ 5 Manny Ramirez	2.50	1.10	.30
□ 6 Tony Gwynn	4.00	1.80	.50
□ 7 Hideo Nomo	6.00	2.70	.75
□ 8 Matt Williams	1.25	.55	.16
□ 9 Randy Johnson	1.50	.70	.19
□ 10 Raul Mondesi	1.25	.55	.16
□ 11 Albert Belle	4.00	1.80	.50
□ 12 Ivan Rodriguez	2.50	1.10	.30
□ 13 Barry Bonds	2.50	1.10	.30
□ 14 Carlos Baerga	1.00	.45	.12
□ 15 Ken Griffey Jr.	10.00	4.50	1.25
□ 16 Jeff Conine	1.00	.45	.12
□ 17 Frank Thomas	10.00	4.50	1.25
□ 18 Cal Ripken Barry Bonds	6.00	2.70	.75

1995 Zenith Rookie Roll Call

This 18-card, Dufex-designed standard-size set was randomly inserted in packs at a rate of one in 24. The set is comprised of 18 top rookies from 1995. The fronts have two photos and a colorful star in the background with which rays of color emanate. The backs are laid out horizontally with a color photo on a multi-color foil background. Player information of previous accomplishments is also on the back and the cards are numbered "X of 18."

	MINT	NRMT	EXC
COMPLETE SET (18)	225.00	100.00	28.00
COMMON CARD (1-18)	8.00	3.60	1.00
□ 1 Alex Rodriguez	80.00	36.00	10.00
□ 2 Derek Jeter	50.00	22.00	6.25
□ 3 Chipper Jones	50.00	22.00	6.25
□ 4 Shawn Green	10.00	4.50	1.25
□ 5 Todd Hollandsworth	12.00	5.50	1.50
□ 6 Bill Pulsipher	8.00	3.60	1.00
□ 7 Hideo Nomo	40.00	18.00	5.00
□ 8 Ray Durham	8.00	3.60	1.00
□ 9 Curtis Goodwin	8.00	3.60	1.00
□ 10 Brian L.Hunter	10.00	4.50	1.25
□ 11 Julian Tavarez	8.00	3.60	1.00
□ 12 Marty Cordova UER Kevin Maas pictured	12.00	5.50	1.50
□ 13 Michael Tucker	10.00	4.50	1.25
□ 14 Edgardo Alfonzo	8.00	3.60	1.00
□ 15 LaTroy Hawkins	8.00	3.60	1.00
□ 16 Carlos Perez	8.00	3.60	1.00
□ 17 Charles Johnson	10.00	4.50	1.25
□ 18 Benji Gil	8.00	3.60	1.00

1995 Zenith Z-Team

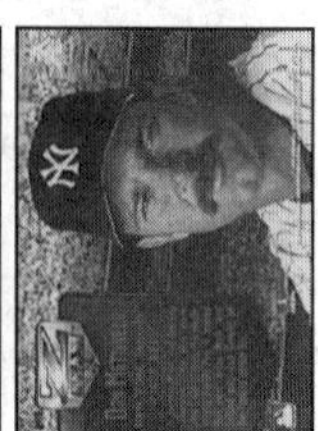

This 18-card standard-size set was randomly inserted in packs at a rate of one in 72. The set is comprised of the best players in baseball and is done in 3-D Dufex. The fronts have a player action photo positioned on home plate which has the words "Z Team". There are multi-colored rays coming out of the card background. The back is laid out horizontally with a color head shot and a stadium crowd background. The back also has player information and a "Z Team" emblem.

	MINT	NRMT	EXC
COMPLETE SET (18)	400.00	180.00	50.00
COMMON CARD (1-18)	8.00	3.60	1.00
□ 1 Cal Ripken	50.00	22.00	6.25
□ 2 Ken Griffey Jr.	60.00	27.00	7.50
□ 3 Frank Thomas	60.00	27.00	7.50
□ 4 Matt Williams	10.00	4.50	1.25
□ 5 Mike Piazza UER (Card says started at first base Piazza is a catcher)	40.00	18.00	5.00
□ 6 Barry Bonds	15.00	6.75	1.85
□ 7 Raul Mondesi	10.00	4.50	1.25
□ 8 Greg Maddux	40.00	18.00	5.00
□ 9 Jeff Bagwell	25.00	11.00	3.10
□ 10 Manny Ramirez	15.00	6.75	1.85
□ 11 Larry Walker	10.00	4.50	1.25
□ 12 Tony Gwynn	25.00	11.00	3.10
□ 13 Will Clark	10.00	4.50	1.25
□ 14 Albert Belle	25.00	11.00	3.10
□ 15 Kenny Lofton	15.00	6.75	1.85
□ 16 Rafael Palmeiro	10.00	4.50	1.25
□ 17 Don Mattingly	30.00	13.50	3.70
□ 18 Carlos Baerga	8.00	3.60	1.00

1996 Zenith

This 1996 Zenith set was issued in one series totalling 150 cards. The six-card packs retail for $3.99 each. The set contains the subset: Honor Roll (131-150). The fronts feature a color player cutout over an arrangement of baseball bats on a black background. The backs carry a hit location chart and player statistics. The only notable Rookie Card is of Darin Erstad.

	MINT	NRMT	EXC
COMPLETE SET (150)	40.00	18.00	5.00
COMMON CARD (1-150)	.15	.07	.02
□ 1 Ken Griffey Jr.	4.00	1.80	.50
□ 2 Ozzie Smith	1.00	.45	.12
□ 3 Greg Maddux	2.50	1.10	.30
□ 4 Rondell White	.30	.14	.04
□ 5 Mark McGwire	1.25	.55	.16
□ 6 Jim Thome	.75	.35	.09
□ 7 Ivan Rodriguez	1.00	.45	.12
□ 8 Marc Newfield	.30	.14	.04
□ 9 Travis Fryman	.30	.14	.04
□ 10 Fred McGriff	.60	.25	.07
□ 11 Shawn Green	.15	.07	.02
□ 12 Mike Piazza	2.50	1.10	.30
□ 13 Dante Bichette	.60	.25	.07
□ 14 Tino Martinez	.30	.14	.04
□ 15 Sterling Hitchcock	.15	.07	.02
□ 16 Ryne Sandberg	1.00	.45	.12
□ 17 Rico Brogna	.15	.07	.02
□ 18 Roberto Alomar	.75	.35	.09
□ 19 Barry Larkin	.60	.25	.07
□ 20 Bernie Williams	.75	.35	.09
□ 21 Gary Sheffield	.60	.25	.07
□ 22 Frank Thomas	4.00	1.80	.50
□ 23 Gregg Jefferies	.60	.25	.07
□ 24 Jeff Bagwell	1.50	.70	.19
□ 25 Marty Cordova	.30	.14	.04
□ 26 Jim Edmonds	.30	.14	.04
□ 27 Jay Bell	.30	.14	.04
□ 28 Ben McDonald	.15	.07	.02
□ 29 Barry Bonds	1.00	.45	.12
□ 30 Mo Vaughn	1.00	.45	.12
□ 31 Johnny Damon	.30	.14	.04
□ 32 Dean Palmer	.60	.25	.07
□ 33 Ismael Valdes	.30	.14	.04
□ 34 Manny Ramirez	1.00	.45	.12
□ 35 Edgar Martinez	.30	.14	.04
□ 36 Cecil Fielder	.30	.14	.04
□ 37 Ryan Klesko	.60	.25	.07
□ 38 Ray Lankford	.30	.14	.04
□ 39 Tim Salmon	.60	.25	.07
□ 40 Joe Carter	.30	.14	.04
□ 41 Jason Isringhausen	.60	.25	.07
□ 42 Rickey Henderson	.60	.25	.07
□ 43 Lenny Dykstra	.30	.14	.04
□ 44 Andre Dawson	.30	.14	.04
□ 45 Paul O'Neill	.15	.07	.02
□ 46 Ray Durham	.60	.25	.07
□ 47 Raul Mondesi	.60	.25	.07
□ 48 Jay Buhner	.60	.25	.07
□ 49 Eddie Murray	1.00	.45	.12
□ 50 Henry Rodriguez	.30	.14	.04
□ 51 Hal Morris	.15	.07	.02
□ 52 Mike Mussina	.75	.35	.09
□ 53 Wally Joyner	.15	.07	.02
□ 54 Will Clark	.60	.25	.07
□ 55 Chipper Jones	2.50	1.10	.30
□ 56 Brian Jordan	.30	.14	.04
□ 57 Larry Walker	.60	.25	.07
□ 58 Wade Boggs	.60	.25	.07
□ 59 Melvin Nieves	.30	.14	.04
□ 60 Charles Johnson	.30	.14	.04
□ 61 Juan Gonzalez	2.00	.90	.25
□ 62 Carlos Delgado	.30	.14	.04
□ 63 Reggie Sanders	.30	.14	.04
□ 64 Brian L.Hunter	.30	.14	.04
□ 65 Edgardo Alfonzo	.15	.07	.02
□ 66 Kenny Lofton	1.00	.45	.12
□ 67 Paul Molitor	.75	.35	.09
□ 68 Mike Bordick	.15	.07	.02
□ 69 Garret Anderson	.60	.25	.07
□ 70 Orlando Merced	.15	.07	.02
□ 71 Craig Biggio	.30	.14	.04
□ 72 Chuck Knoblauch	.60	.25	.07
□ 73 Mark Grace	.60	.25	.07
□ 74 Jack McDowell	.60	.25	.07
□ 75 Randy Johnson	.60	.25	.07
□ 76 Cal Ripken	3.00	1.35	.35
□ 77 Matt Williams	.60	.25	.07
□ 78 Benji Gil	.15	.07	.02
□ 79 Moises Alou	.30	.14	.04
□ 80 Robin Ventura	.30	.14	.04
□ 81 Greg Vaughn	.60	.25	.07
□ 82 Carlos Baerga	.30	.14	.04
□ 83 Roger Clemens	.75	.35	.09
□ 84 Hideo Nomo	1.00	.45	.12
□ 85 Pedro Martinez	.30	.14	.04
□ 86 John Valentin	.30	.14	.04
□ 87 Andres Galarraga	.60	.25	.07
□ 88 Andy Pettitte	1.25	.55	.16
□ 89 Derek Bell	.30	.14	.04
□ 90 Kirby Puckett	1.50	.70	.19
□ 91 Tony Gwynn	1.50	.70	.19
□ 92 Brady Anderson	.60	.25	.07
□ 93 Derek Jeter	2.50	1.10	.30
□ 94 Michael Tucker	.30	.14	.04
□ 95 Albert Belle	1.50	.70	.19
□ 96 David Cone	.30	.14	.04
□ 97 J.T. Snow	.30	.14	.04
□ 98 Tom Glavine	.60	.25	.07
□ 99 Alex Rodriguez	4.00	1.80	.50
□ 100 Sammy Sosa	.60	.25	.07
□ 101 Karim Garcia	.75	.35	.09
□ 102 Alan Benes	.60	.25	.07
□ 103 Chad Mottola	.15	.07	.02
□ 104 Robin Jennings	.15	.07	.02
□ 105 Bob Abreu	.60	.25	.07
□ 106 Tony Clark	.75	.35	.09
□ 107 George Arias	.15	.07	.02
□ 108 Jermaine Dye	.75	.35	.09
□ 109 Jeff Suppan	.60	.25	.07
□ 110 Ralph Milliard	.15	.07	.02
□ 111 Ruben Rivera	.75	.35	.09
□ 112 Billy Wagner	.60	.25	.07
□ 113 Jason Kendall	.60	.25	.07
□ 114 Mike Grace	.15	.07	.02
□ 115 Edgar Renteria	.60	.25	.07
□ 116 Jason Schmidt	.60	.25	.07
□ 117 Paul Wilson	.30	.14	.04
□ 118 Rey Ordonez	.60	.25	.07
□ 119 Rocky Coppinger	.75	.35	.09
□ 120 Wilton Guerrero	2.00	.90	.25
□ 121 Brooks Kieschnick	.60	.25	.07
□ 122 Raul Casanova	.30	.14	.04
□ 123 Alex Ochoa	.30	.14	.04
□ 124 Chan Ho Park	.60	.25	.07
□ 125 John Wasdin	.15	.07	.02
□ 126 Eric Owens	.15	.07	.02
□ 127 Justin Thompson	.30	.14	.04
□ 128 Chris Snopek	.15	.07	.02
□ 129 Terrell Wade	.30	.14	.04
□ 130 Darin Erstad	4.00	1.80	.50
□ 131 Albert Belle HON	.75	.35	.09
□ 132 Cal Ripken HON	1.50	.70	.19
□ 133 Frank Thomas HON	2.00	.90	.25
□ 134 Greg Maddux HON	1.25	.55	.16
□ 135 Ken Griffey Jr. HON	2.00	.90	.25
□ 136 Mo Vaughn HON	.60	.25	.07
□ 137 Chipper Jones HON	1.25	.55	.16
□ 138 Mike Piazza HON	1.25	.55	.16
□ 139 Ryan Klesko HON	.60	.25	.07
□ 140 Hideo Nomo HON	.60	.25	.07
□ 141 Roberto Alomar HON	.60	.25	.07
□ 142 Manny Ramirez HON	.30	.14	.04
□ 143 Gary Sheffield HON	.60	.25	.07
□ 144 Barry Bonds HON	.60	.25	.07
□ 145 Matt Williams HON	.60	.25	.07
□ 146 Jim Edmonds HON	.30	.14	.04
□ 147 Derek Jeter HON	1.25	.55	.16
□ 148 Sammy Sosa HON	.60	.25	.07
□ 149 Kirby Puckett HON	.60	.25	.07
□ 150 Tony Gwynn HON	.75	.35	.09

1996 Zenith Artist's Proofs

Randomly inserted in packs at a rate of one in 35, this 150-card set is parallel to the regular Zenith set. The cards are distinguished from the regular set by the "Artist's Proof" all-gold, rainbow holographic foil stamp on the front.

	MINT	NRMT	EXC
COMPLETE SET (150)	2000.00	900.00	250.00
COMMON CARD (1-150)	3.00	1.35	.35

*STARS: 10X TO 25X BASIC CARDS ..
*YOUNG STARS: 8X TO 20X BASIC CARDS

1996 Zenith Diamond Club

Randomly inserted in packs at a rate of one in 24, cards from this 20-card set honor top performers on a Spectroetch card design printed on thick foil stock with etched highlights. The fronts feature an above-the-waist color action player cutout over a diamond-shaped opening on a grass-green background. The backs carry player information.

	MINT	NRMT	EXC
COMPLETE SET (20)	250.00	110.00	31.00
COMMON CARD (1-20)	4.00	1.80	.50
□ 1 Albert Belle	12.00	5.50	1.50
□ 2 Mo Vaughn	8.00	3.60	1.00
□ 3 Ken Griffey Jr.	30.00	13.50	3.70
□ 4 Mike Piazza	20.00	9.00	2.50

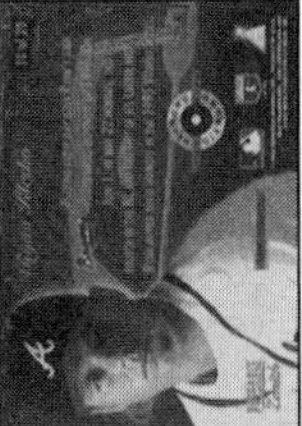

☐ 5 Cal Ripken	25.00	11.00	3.10
☐ 6 Jermaine Dye	5.00	2.20	.60
☐ 7 Jeff Bagwell	12.00	5.50	1.50
☐ 8 Frank Thomas	30.00	13.50	3.70
☐ 9 Alex Rodriguez	30.00	13.50	3.70
☐ 10 Ryan Klesko	5.00	2.20	.60
☐ 11 Roberto Alomar	6.00	2.70	.75
☐ 12 Sammy Sosa	5.00	2.20	.60
☐ 13 Matt Williams	4.00	1.80	.50
☐ 14 Gary Sheffield	5.00	2.20	.60
☐ 15 Ruben Rivera	5.00	2.20	.60
☐ 16 Darin Erstad	25.00	11.00	3.10
☐ 17 Randy Johnson	5.00	2.20	.60
☐ 18 Greg Maddux	20.00	9.00	2.50
☐ 19 Karim Garcia	6.00	2.70	.75
☐ 20 Chipper Jones	20.00	9.00	2.50

1996 Zenith Diamond Club Parallel

Randomly inserted in packs at the rate of one in 350, cards from this 20-card insert set parallel the regular Diamond Club cards. The difference lies in the fact that this insert set actually contains a diamond chip incorporated into the card design. Please refer to the multipliers provided below to ascertain value for singles.

	MINT	NRMT	EXC
COMPLETE SET (20)	1500.00	700.00	190.00
COMMON CARD (1-20)	25.00	11.00	3.10
*STARS: 3X to 6X BASIC CARDS			

1996 Zenith Mozaics

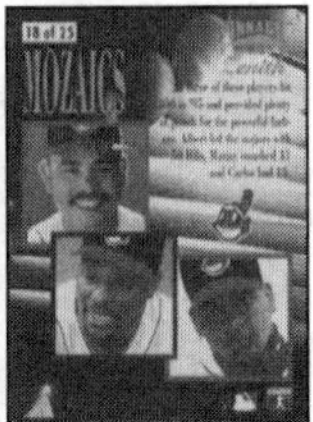

Randomly inserted in packs at a rate of one in 10, this 25-card set features three-player image cards of the hottest superstars. The fronts display multiple player images representing the core of each of the 28 teams and are printed on rainbow holographic foil.

	MINT	NRMT	EXC
COMPLETE SET (25)	200.00	90.00	25.00
COMMON CARD (1-25)	4.00	1.80	.50
☐ 1 Greg Maddux	25.00	11.00	3.10
Chipper Jones			
Ryan Klesko			
☐ 2 Juan Gonzalez	15.00	6.75	1.85
Will Clark			
Ivan Rodriguez			
☐ 3 Frank Thomas	25.00	11.00	3.10
Robin Ventura			
Ray Durham			
☐ 4 Matt Williams	6.00	2.70	.75
Barry Bonds			
Osvaldo Fernandez			
☐ 5 Ken Griffey Jr.	35.00	16.00	4.40
Randy Johnson			
Alex Rodriguez			
☐ 6 Sammy Sosa	8.00	3.60	1.00
Ryne Sandberg			
Mark Grace			
☐ 7 Jim Edmonds	4.00	1.80	.50
Tim Salmon			
Garret Anderson			
☐ 8 Cal Ripken	25.00	11.00	3.10
Roberto Alomar			
Mike Mussina			
☐ 9 Mo Vaughn	10.00	4.50	1.25
Roger Clemens			
John Valentin			
☐ 10 Barry Larkin	4.00	1.80	.50
Reggie Sanders			
Hal Morris			
☐ 11 Ray Lankford	8.00	3.60	1.00
Brian Jordan			
Ozzie Smith			
☐ 12 Dante Bichette	6.00	2.70	.75
Larry Walker			
Andres Galarraga			
☐ 13 Mike Piazza	20.00	9.00	2.50
Hideo Nomo			
Raul Mondesi			
☐ 14 Ben McDonald	4.00	1.80	.50
Greg Vaughn			
Kevin Seitzer			
☐ 15 Joe Carter	4.00	1.80	.50
Carlos Delgado			
Alex Gonzalez			
☐ 16 Gary Sheffield	4.00	1.80	.50
Charles Johnson			
Jeff Conine			
☐ 17 Rondell White	4.00	1.80	.50
Moises Alou			
Henry Rodriguez			
☐ 18 Albert Belle	12.00	5.50	1.50
Manny Ramirez			
Carlos Baerga			
☐ 19 Kirby Puckett	12.00	5.50	1.50
Paul Molitor			
Chuck Knoblauch			
☐ 20 Tony Gwynn	10.00	4.50	1.25
Rickey Henderson			
Wally Joyner			
☐ 21 Mark McGwire	8.00	3.60	1.00
Mike Bordick			
Scott Brosius			
☐ 22 Paul O'Neill	8.00	3.60	1.00
Bernie Williams			
Wade Boggs			
☐ 23 Jay Bell	4.00	1.80	.50
Orlando Merced			
Jason Kendall			
☐ 24 Rico Brogna	4.00	1.80	.50
Paul Wilson			
Jason Isringhausen			
☐ 25 Jeff Bagwell	10.00	4.50	1.25
Craig Biggio			
Derek Bell			

1996 Zenith Z-Team

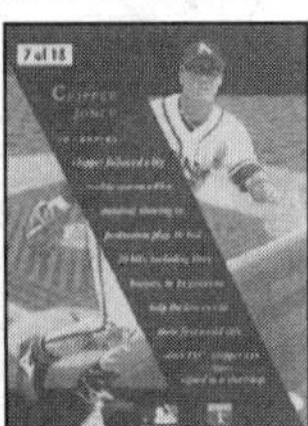

Randomly inserted in packs at a rate of one in 72, this 18-card set features a color action player cutout on a clear micro-etched design with a gold foil Z-Team logo and a see-through green baseball field background. The backs carry player information printed on the back of the Z.

	MINT	NRMT	EXC
COMPLETE SET (18)	500.00	220.00	60.00
COMMON CARD (1-18)	10.00	4.50	1.25
☐ 1 Ken Griffey Jr.	80.00	36.00	10.00
☐ 2 Albert Belle	30.00	13.50	3.70
☐ 3 Cal Ripken	60.00	27.00	7.50
☐ 4 Frank Thomas	80.00	36.00	10.00
☐ 5 Greg Maddux	50.00	22.00	6.25
☐ 6 Mo Vaughn	20.00	9.00	2.50
☐ 7 Chipper Jones	50.00	22.00	6.25
☐ 8 Mike Piazza	50.00	22.00	6.25
☐ 9 Ryan Klesko	12.00	5.50	1.50
☐ 10 Hideo Nomo	20.00	9.00	2.50
☐ 11 Roberto Alomar	15.00	6.75	1.85
☐ 12 Manny Ramirez	20.00	9.00	2.50
☐ 13 Gary Sheffield	12.00	5.50	1.50
☐ 14 Barry Bonds	20.00	9.00	2.50
☐ 15 Matt Williams	10.00	4.50	1.25
☐ 16 Jim Edmonds	10.00	4.50	1.25
☐ 17 Kirby Puckett	30.00	13.50	3.70
☐ 18 Sammy Sosa	12.00	5.50	1.50

1992 Ziploc

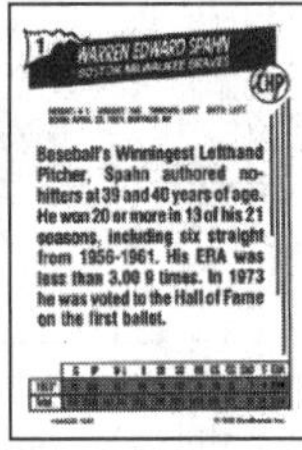

This 11-card standard-size set features posed player photos of many of the game's all-time greats. The Ziploc logo appears diagonally in the upper left corner, while the player's name is printed in black in a bright-yellow stripe accented with red and blue stars at the bottom. The team logo is superimposed over the photo at the upper right. The back design displays the player's full name and team in a slightly diagonal red stripe at the top. A biography, career summary, and statistics are printed in medium blue on a white background. The set was available via a mail-in offer for 50 cents and two UPC's from Ziploc sandwich bags. Individual cards were found one per specially marked package.

	MINT	NRMT	EXC
COMPLETE SET (11)	10.00	4.50	1.25
COMMON CARD (1-11)	.75	.35	.09
☐ 1 Warren Spahn	1.00	.45	.12
☐ 2 Bob Gibson	1.00	.45	.12
☐ 3 Rollie Fingers	.75	.35	.09
☐ 4 Carl Yastrzemski	1.25	.55	.16
☐ 5 Brooks Robinson	1.50	.70	.19
☐ 6 Pee Wee Reese	1.00	.45	.12
☐ 7 Willie McCovey	1.00	.45	.12
☐ 8 Willie Mays	2.00	.90	.25
☐ 9 Nellie Fox	.75	.35	.09
☐ 10 Yogi Berra	1.50	.70	.19
☐ 11 Hank Aaron	2.00	.90	.25

1888 S.F. Hess and Co. Creole N321

It is not known why S.F. Hess based in Rochester, N.Y., produced this set of regional ballplayers from the California League. Each card has a color drawing of a ballplayer and is copyrighted 1888. The teams represented are G and M's, Haverlys, Pioneers and Stocktons; in the checklist below these teams are coded GM, HAV, PIO and STOCK, respectively. There are 41 cards known (36 players and five variations) and all carry advertising for Creole cigarettes.

	EX-MT	VG-E	GOOD
COMPLETE SET	27500.00	12400.00	3400.00
COMMON CARD	750.00	350.00	95.00
☐ 1 Bennett HAV	750.00	350.00	95.00
☐ 2 Borchers: GM	750.00	350.00	95.00
☐ 3 Buckley HAV	750.00	350.00	95.00
☐ 4A Burke STOCK (pitching)	750.00	350.00	95.00
☐ 4B Burke STOCK (batting)	750.00	350.00	95.00
☐ 5 Burnett: GM	750.00	350.00	95.00
☐ 6 Carroll PIO	750.00	350.00	95.00
☐ 7 Donahue PIO	750.00	350.00	95.00
☐ 8 Donovan: GM	750.00	350.00	95.00
☐ 9 Finn PIO	750.00	350.00	95.00
☐ 10 Gagus HAV	750.00	350.00	95.00
☐ 11 Hanley HAV	750.00	350.00	95.00
☐ 12A Hardie: GM (Catcher)	750.00	350.00	95.00
☐ 12B Hardie: GM (Center Field)	750.00	350.00	95.00
☐ 13 Hayes STOCK	750.00	350.00	95.00
☐ 14 Lawton HAV	750.00	350.00	95.00
☐ 15 Levy HAV	750.00	350.00	95.00
☐ 16 Long: GM	750.00	350.00	95.00
☐ 17 McCord: GM	750.00	350.00	95.00
☐ 18 Meegan HAV	750.00	350.00	95.00
☐ 19 Moore STOCK	750.00	350.00	95.00
☐ 20 Mullane PIO	750.00	350.00	95.00
☐ 21 Newhart: GM	750.00	350.00	95.00
☐ 22 Noonan PIO	750.00	350.00	95.00
☐ 23 O'Day STOCK	750.00	350.00	95.00
☐ 24 Perrier PIO	750.00	350.00	95.00
☐ 25A Powers HAV (first base)	750.00	350.00	95.00
☐ 25B Powers HAV (first base and Capt.)	750.00	350.00	95.00
☐ 26 Ryan: GM	750.00	350.00	95.00
☐ 27 Selna STOCK	750.00	350.00	95.00
☐ 28 Shea: GM	750.00	350.00	95.00
☐ 29 J. Sheridan (Umpire)	750.00	350.00	95.00
☐ 30 Big Smith PIO	750.00	350.00	95.00
☐ 31 H. Smith PIO	750.00	350.00	95.00
☐ 32 J. Smith PIO	750.00	350.00	95.00
☐ 33A Stockwell STOCK (catching)	750.00	350.00	95.00
☐ 33B Stockwell STOCK (batting)	750.00	350.00	95.00
☐ 34 Sweeney HAV	750.00	350.00	95.00
☐ 35 Swett HAV	750.00	350.00	95.00
☐ 36 Whitehead STOCK	750.00	350.00	95.00

1909-11 Obak T212

The catalog designation T212 actually encompasses three separate minor league sets (listed in sequence in the checklist below). Each card measures 1 7/16" by 2 5/8". Set 1 (1-76) features 76 colored player cards representing six PCL teams and was issued in 1909. The obverse captions are stylized (slanted), and the word "Obak" on the reverse is inscribed in "Old English" letters. Set 2 contains 175 colored cards (77-251) of players from six PCL and four NWL teams. The captions are not slanted, and "Obak" appears in large block letters on the back. Reverses advertise either "150" or "175" subjects, and some 35 different slogans exist. The backs of sets 1 and 2 are printed in blue. In contrast, the 1911 set of 175 colored cards has red-printed backs which contain a short biography and some statistics (252-426). The PCL and NWL are each represented by six teams in this set. Note that there is a Portland club in each league. The Obak brand was produced and distributed in California by a branch of the American Tobacco Company. Cards are ordered below alphabetically within team. Type 1 consists of Los Angeles (1-8), Oakland (9-20), Portland (23-33), Sacramento (34-46), San Francisco (47-62) and Vernon (63-76). Type 2 consists of Los Angeles (77-96), Oakland (97-113), Portland (114-132), Sacramento (133-151), San Francisco (152-172), Vernon (173-188), Seattle NWL (189-204), Spokane NWL (205-219), Tacoma NWL (220-235) and Vancouver NWL (236-251). Type 3 consists of Los Angeles (252-268), Oakland (269-287), Portland PCL (288-303), Sacramento (304-320), San Francisco (321-339), Vernon (340-358), Portland NWL (359-368), Seattle NWL (369-380), Spokane NWL (381-392), Tacoma NWL (393-403), Vancouver NWL (404-415), and Victoria NWL (416-426).

	EX-MT	VG-E	GOOD
COMPLETE SET	10000.00	4500.00	1250.00
COMMON CARD (1-76)	60.00	27.00	7.50
COMMON CARD (77-251)	20.00	9.00	2.50
COMMON CARD (252-426)	20.00	9.00	2.50
☐ 1 Beall	60.00	27.00	7.50
☐ 2 Delmas	60.00	27.00	7.50
☐ 3 Dillon	60.00	27.00	7.50
☐ 4 Howard	60.00	27.00	7.50
☐ 5 Nagle	60.00	27.00	7.50
☐ 6 Ornsdorff	60.00	27.00	7.50
☐ 7 Smith	60.00	27.00	7.50
☐ 8 Wheeler	60.00	27.00	7.50
☐ 9 Boyce	60.00	27.00	7.50
☐ 10 Cameron	60.00	27.00	7.50
☐ 11 Carrol	60.00	27.00	7.50
☐ 12 Christian	60.00	27.00	7.50
☐ 13 Hogan	60.00	27.00	7.50
☐ 14 La Longe	60.00	27.00	7.50
☐ 15 Lewis	60.00	27.00	7.50
☐ 16 D. Lewis	60.00	27.00	7.50
☐ 17 McKune	60.00	27.00	7.50
☐ 18 Murphy	60.00	27.00	7.50
☐ 19 Nelson	60.00	27.00	7.50
☐ 20 Ragan	60.00	27.00	7.50
☐ 20 Wiggs	60.00	27.00	7.50
☐ 21 Reidy	60.00	27.00	7.50
☐ 23 Breen	60.00	27.00	7.50
☐ 24 Carson	60.00	27.00	7.50
☐ 25 Fisher	60.00	27.00	7.50
☐ 26 Garrett	60.00	27.00	7.50
☐ 27 Graney	60.00	27.00	7.50
☐ 28 Guyn	60.00	27.00	7.50
☐ 29 McCredie	60.00	27.00	7.50
☐ 30 Olson	60.00	27.00	7.50
☐ 31 Ort	60.00	27.00	7.50
☐ 32 Ryan	60.00	27.00	7.50
☐ 33 Speas	60.00	27.00	7.50
☐ 34 Baum	60.00	27.00	7.50
☐ 35 Brown	60.00	27.00	7.50
☐ 36 Byrnes	60.00	27.00	7.50
☐ 37 Ehman	60.00	27.00	7.50
☐ 38 Fitzgerald	60.00	27.00	7.50
☐ 39 Flannagan	60.00	27.00	7.50
☐ 40 Gandil	200.00	90.00	25.00
☐ 41 Graham	60.00	27.00	7.50
☐ 42 Howse	60.00	27.00	7.50
☐ 43 Jansing	60.00	27.00	7.50
☐ 44 Raymer	60.00	27.00	7.50
☐ 45 Shinn	60.00	27.00	7.50
☐ 46 Whalen	60.00	27.00	7.50
☐ 47 Berry	60.00	27.00	7.50
☐ 48 Bodie	60.00	27.00	7.50
☐ 49 Browning	60.00	27.00	7.50
☐ 50 Easterly	60.00	27.00	7.50
☐ 51 Griffen	60.00	27.00	7.50
☐ 52 Henley	60.00	27.00	7.50
☐ 53 F. Lewis	60.00	27.00	7.50
☐ 54 McArdle	60.00	27.00	7.50
☐ 55 Melchior	60.00	27.00	7.50
☐ 56 Mohler	60.00	27.00	7.50
☐ 57 Mundorff	60.00	27.00	7.50
☐ 58 Tennant	60.00	27.00	7.50
☐ 59 F. Williams	60.00	27.00	7.50
☐ 60 R. Williams	60.00	27.00	7.50
☐ 61 Willis	60.00	27.00	7.50
☐ 62 Zeider	60.00	27.00	7.50
☐ 63 Bernard	60.00	27.00	7.50
☐ 64 Brockenridge	60.00	27.00	7.50
☐ 65 Brashear	60.00	27.00	7.50
☐ 66 D. Brown	60.00	27.00	7.50
☐ 67 Coy	60.00	27.00	7.50
☐ 68 Eagan	60.00	27.00	7.50
☐ 69 Haley	60.00	27.00	7.50
☐ 70 Harkins	60.00	27.00	7.50
☐ 71 Hitt	60.00	27.00	7.50
☐ 72 W. Hogan	60.00	27.00	7.50
☐ 73 Martinke	60.00	27.00	7.50
☐ 74 Mott	60.00	27.00	7.50
☐ 75 Stoval	60.00	27.00	7.50
☐ 76 Willett	60.00	27.00	7.50
☐ 77 Agnew	20.00	9.00	2.50
☐ 78 Bernard	20.00	9.00	2.50
☐ 79 Briswalter	20.00	9.00	2.50

☐ 80 Casellton 20.00 9.00 2.50
☐ 81 Criger 20.00 9.00 2.50
☐ 82 Daley 20.00 9.00 2.50
☐ 83 Delhi 20.00 9.00 2.50
☐ 84 Delmas 20.00 9.00 2.50
☐ 85 Dillon 20.00 9.00 2.50
☐ 86 Howard 20.00 9.00 2.50
☐ 87 Klein 20.00 9.00 2.50
☐ 88 Murphy 20.00 9.00 2.50
☐ 89 Nagle 20.00 9.00 2.50
☐ 90 Orendorff 20.00 9.00 2.50
☐ 91 Roth 20.00 9.00 2.50
☐ 92 H. Smith 20.00 9.00 2.50
☐ 93 J. Smith 20.00 9.00 2.50
☐ 94 Thorsen 20.00 9.00 2.50
☐ 95 Tozer 20.00 9.00 2.50
☐ 96 Waring 20.00 9.00 2.50
☐ 97 Cameron 20.00 9.00 2.50
☐ 98 Carroll 20.00 9.00 2.50
☐ 99 Christian 20.00 9.00 2.50
☐ 100 Cutshaw 25.00 11.00 3.10
☐ 101 Harkins 20.00 9.00 2.50
☐ 102 Logan 20.00 9.00 2.50
☐ 103 Lively 20.00 9.00 2.50
☐ 104 Manush 25.00 11.00 3.10
☐ 105 Mitze 20.00 9.00 2.50
☐ 106 Moser 20.00 9.00 2.50
☐ 107 Nelson 20.00 9.00 2.50
☐ 108 Spiesman 20.00 9.00 2.50
☐ 109 Swander 20.00 9.00 2.50
☐ 110 Thomas 20.00 9.00 2.50
☐ 111 Tonnesen 20.00 9.00 2.50
☐ 112 Wares 20.00 9.00 2.50
☐ 113 Wolverton 20.00 9.00 2.50
☐ 114 Armbruster 20.00 9.00 2.50
☐ 115 Casey 20.00 9.00 2.50
☐ 116 Fisher 20.00 9.00 2.50
☐ 117 Garrett 20.00 9.00 2.50
☐ 118 Greggs 20.00 9.00 2.50
☐ 119 Hetling 20.00 9.00 2.50
☐ 120 Krapp 20.00 9.00 2.50
☐ 121 McCredie 20.00 9.00 2.50
☐ 122 Netzel 20.00 9.00 2.50
☐ 123 Olson 20.00 9.00 2.50
☐ 124 Ort 20.00 9.00 2.50
☐ 125 Perrine 20.00 9.00 2.50
☐ 126 Rapps 20.00 9.00 2.50
☐ 127 D. Roan 20.00 9.00 2.50
☐ 128 J. Ryan 20.00 9.00 2.50
☐ 129 Seaton 20.00 9.00 2.50
☐ 130 Smith 20.00 9.00 2.50
☐ 131 Speas 20.00 9.00 2.50
☐ 132 Steen 20.00 9.00 2.50
☐ 133 Baum 20.00 9.00 2.50
☐ 134 Boardman 20.00 9.00 2.50
☐ 135 Briggs 20.00 9.00 2.50
☐ 136 Brown 20.00 9.00 2.50
☐ 137 Danzig 20.00 9.00 2.50
☐ 138 Daringer 20.00 9.00 2.50
☐ 139 Fitzgerald 20.00 9.00 2.50
☐ 140 Fournier 20.00 9.00 2.50
☐ 141 Hiester 20.00 9.00 2.50
☐ 142 Hollis 20.00 9.00 2.50
☐ 143 Hunt 20.00 9.00 2.50
☐ 144 LaLonge 20.00 9.00 2.50
☐ 145 Nourse 20.00 9.00 2.50
☐ 146 Perry 20.00 9.00 2.50
☐ 147 Persons 20.00 9.00 2.50
☐ 148 Raymer 20.00 9.00 2.50
☐ 149 Shinn 20.00 9.00 2.50
☐ 150 Van Buren 20.00 9.00 2.50
☐ 151 Whalen 20.00 9.00 2.50
☐ 152 Ames 20.00 9.00 2.50
☐ 153 Berry 20.00 9.00 2.50
☐ 154 Bodie 20.00 9.00 2.50
☐ 155 Browning 20.00 9.00 2.50
☐ 156 Byrd 20.00 9.00 2.50
☐ 157 Eastley 20.00 9.00 2.50
☐ 158A Griffin (175) 20.00 9.00 2.50
☐ 158B Griffin (150) 20.00 9.00 2.50
☐ 159 Henley 20.00 9.00 2.50
☐ 160 Lewis 20.00 9.00 2.50
☐ 161 McArdle 20.00 9.00 2.50
☐ 162 Melchoir 20.00 9.00 2.50
☐ 163 Miller 20.00 9.00 2.50
☐ 164 Mohler 20.00 9.00 2.50
☐ 165 Mundorff 100.00 45.00 12.50
☐ 166 Shaw 20.00 9.00 2.50
☐ 167 Stewart 20.00 9.00 2.50
☐ 168 Sutor 20.00 9.00 2.50
☐ 169 Tennant 20.00 9.00 2.50
☐ 170 Vitt 25.00 11.00 3.10
☐ 171 Williams 20.00 9.00 2.50
☐ 172 Willis 20.00 9.00 2.50
☐ 173 Brackenridge 20.00 9.00 2.50
☐ 174 N. Brashear 20.00 9.00 2.50
☐ 175 R. Brashear 20.00 9.00 2.50
☐ 176 Brown 20.00 9.00 2.50
☐ 177 Burrell 20.00 9.00 2.50
☐ 178 Carlisle 20.00 9.00 2.50
☐ 179 Coy 20.00 9.00 2.50
☐ 180 Fisher 20.00 9.00 2.50
☐ 181 Hensling 20.00 9.00 2.50
☐ 182 Hitt 20.00 9.00 2.50
☐ 183 Hogan 20.00 9.00 2.50
☐ 184 Lindsay 20.00 9.00 2.50
☐ 185 Martinke 20.00 9.00 2.50
☐ 186 Shafer 20.00 9.00 2.50
☐ 187 Stovell 20.00 9.00 2.50
☐ 188 Willett 20.00 9.00 2.50
☐ 189 Akin 20.00 9.00 2.50
☐ 190 Bennett 20.00 9.00 2.50
☐ 191 Custer 20.00 9.00 2.50
☐ 192 Dretchko 20.00 9.00 2.50
☐ 193 Frisk 20.00 9.00 2.50
☐ 194 Hall 20.00 9.00 2.50
☐ 195 Hendrix 20.00 9.00 2.50
☐ 196 Johnston 20.00 9.00 2.50
☐ 197 Lynch 20.00 9.00 2.50
☐ 198 Miller 20.00 9.00 2.50
☐ 199 Pennington 20.00 9.00 2.50
☐ 200 Raymond 20.00 9.00 2.50
☐ 201 Seaton 20.00 9.00 2.50
☐ 202 Shea 20.00 9.00 2.50
☐ 203 Thompson 20.00 9.00 2.50
☐ 204 Zackert 20.00 9.00 2.50
☐ 205 Baker 20.00 9.00 2.50
☐ 206 Bonner 20.00 9.00 2.50
☐ 207 Brooks 20.00 9.00 2.50
☐ 208 Cartwright 20.00 9.00 2.50
☐ 209 Cooney 20.00 9.00 2.50
☐ 210 Davis 20.00 9.00 2.50
☐ 211 Flood 20.00 9.00 2.50
☐ 212 Hickey 20.00 9.00 2.50
☐ 213 Holm 20.00 9.00 2.50
☐ 214 Keener 20.00 9.00 2.50
☐ 215 Killilay 20.00 9.00 2.50
☐ 216 Kippert 20.00 9.00 2.50
☐ 217 Nordyke 20.00 9.00 2.50
☐ 218 Ostdiek 20.00 9.00 2.50
☐ 219 Weed 20.00 9.00 2.50
☐ 220 Annis 20.00 9.00 2.50
☐ 221 Bassey 20.00 9.00 2.50
☐ 222 Blankenship 20.00 9.00 2.50
☐ 223 Byrnes 20.00 9.00 2.50
☐ 224 Coleman 20.00 9.00 2.50
☐ 225 Gaddy 20.00 9.00 2.50
☐ 226 Gurney 20.00 9.00 2.50
☐ 227 Hall 20.00 9.00 2.50
☐ 228 Hartman 20.00 9.00 2.50
☐ 229 Jansing 20.00 9.00 2.50
☐ 230 Mott 20.00 9.00 2.50
☐ 231 Rockenfield 20.00 9.00 2.50
☐ 232 Schmutz 20.00 9.00 2.50
☐ 233 Starkell 20.00 9.00 2.50
☐ 234 Stevens 20.00 9.00 2.50
☐ 235 Warren 20.00 9.00 2.50
☐ 236 Breen 20.00 9.00 2.50
☐ 237 Brinker 20.00 9.00 2.50
☐ 238 Brown 20.00 9.00 2.50
☐ 239 Capron 20.00 9.00 2.50
☐ 240 Chenault 20.00 9.00 2.50
☐ 241 Erickson 20.00 9.00 2.50
☐ 242 Flannagan 20.00 9.00 2.50
☐ 243 Gardner 20.00 9.00 2.50
☐ 244 James 20.00 9.00 2.50
☐ 245 Jensen 20.00 9.00 2.50
☐ 246 Kusel 20.00 9.00 2.50
☐ 247 Lewis 20.00 9.00 2.50
☐ 248 Scharnweber 20.00 9.00 2.50
☐ 249 Streib 20.00 9.00 2.50
☐ 250 Sugden 20.00 9.00 2.50
☐ 251 Swain 20.00 9.00 2.50
☐ 252 Abbott 20.00 9.00 2.50
☐ 253 Agnew 20.00 9.00 2.50
☐ 254 Akin 20.00 9.00 2.50
☐ 255 Bernard 20.00 9.00 2.50
☐ 256 Criger 20.00 9.00 2.50
☐ 257 Daley 20.00 9.00 2.50
☐ 258 Delhi 20.00 9.00 2.50
☐ 259 Delmas 20.00 9.00 2.50
☐ 260 Dillon 20.00 9.00 2.50
☐ 261 Grindle 20.00 9.00 2.50
☐ 262 Howard 20.00 9.00 2.50
☐ 263 Metzger 20.00 9.00 2.50
☐ 264 Moore 20.00 9.00 2.50
☐ 265 H. Smith 20.00 9.00 2.50
☐ 266 Thorsen 20.00 9.00 2.50
☐ 267 Tozer 20.00 9.00 2.50
☐ 268 Wheeler 20.00 9.00 2.50
☐ 269 Ables 20.00 9.00 2.50
☐ 270 Christian 20.00 9.00 2.50
☐ 271 Coy 20.00 9.00 2.50
☐ 272 Cutshaw 25.00 11.00 3.10
☐ 273 Flater 20.00 9.00 2.50
☐ 274 Hetling 20.00 9.00 2.50
☐ 275 Hoffman 20.00 9.00 2.50
☐ 276 Knight 20.00 9.00 2.50
☐ 277 Maggert 20.00 9.00 2.50
☐ 278 Miller 20.00 9.00 2.50
☐ 279 Mitze 20.00 9.00 2.50
☐ 280 Pearce 20.00 9.00 2.50
☐ 281 Pernoll 20.00 9.00 2.50
☐ 282 Pfyl 20.00 9.00 2.50
☐ 283 Tiedeman 20.00 9.00 2.50
☐ 284 Wares 20.00 9.00 2.50
☐ 285 Wiggs 20.00 9.00 2.50
☐ 286 Wolverton 20.00 9.00 2.50
☐ 287 Zacher 20.00 9.00 2.50
☐ 288 Barry 20.00 9.00 2.50
☐ 289 Chadbourne 20.00 9.00 2.50
☐ 290 Fullerton 20.00 9.00 2.50
☐ 291 J. Henderson 20.00 9.00 2.50
☐ 292 Koestner 20.00 9.00 2.50
☐ 293 Krueger 20.00 9.00 2.50
☐ 294 Kuhn 20.00 9.00 2.50
☐ 295 McCredie 20.00 9.00 2.50
☐ 296 Murray 20.00 9.00 2.50
☐ 297 Peckinpaugh 20.00 9.00 2.50
☐ 298 Rapps 20.00 9.00 2.50
☐ 299 Rodgers 20.00 9.00 2.50
☐ 300 J. Ryan 20.00 9.00 2.50
☐ 301 Seaton 20.00 9.00 2.50
☐ 302 Sheehan 20.00 9.00 2.50
☐ 303 Steen 20.00 9.00 2.50
☐ 304 Arrelanes 20.00 9.00 2.50
☐ 305 Baum 20.00 9.00 2.50
☐ 306 Byram 20.00 9.00 2.50
☐ 307 Danzig 20.00 9.00 2.50
☐ 308 Fitzgerald 20.00 9.00 2.50
☐ 309 Hiester 20.00 9.00 2.50
☐ 310 Hunt 20.00 9.00 2.50
☐ 311 LaLonge 20.00 9.00 2.50
☐ 312 Lerchen 20.00 9.00 2.50
☐ 313 Mahoney 20.00 9.00 2.50
☐ 314 Nourse 20.00 9.00 2.50
☐ 315 O'Rourke 20.00 9.00 2.50
☐ 316 Shinn 20.00 9.00 2.50
☐ 317 Thomas 20.00 9.00 2.50
☐ 318 Thompson 20.00 9.00 2.50
☐ 319 Thornton 20.00 9.00 2.50
☐ 320 Van Buren 20.00 9.00 2.50
☐ 321 Berry 20.00 9.00 2.50
☐ 322 Browning 20.00 9.00 2.50
☐ 323 Henley 20.00 9.00 2.50
☐ 324 Madden 20.00 9.00 2.50
☐ 325 McArdle 20.00 9.00 2.50
☐ 326 Meikle 20.00 9.00 2.50
☐ 327 Melchoir 20.00 9.00 2.50
☐ 328 Miller 20.00 9.00 2.50
☐ 329 Mohler 20.00 9.00 2.50
☐ 330 Moskiman 20.00 9.00 2.50
☐ 331 Powell 20.00 9.00 2.50
☐ 332 Ryan 20.00 9.00 2.50
☐ 333 Schmidt 20.00 9.00 2.50
☐ 334 Shaw 20.00 9.00 2.50
☐ 335 Sutor 20.00 9.00 2.50
☐ 336 Tennant 20.00 9.00 2.50
☐ 337 Vitt 25.00 11.00 3.10
☐ 338 Weaver 150.00 70.00 19.00
☐ 339 Zamlock 20.00 9.00 2.50
☐ 340 Brackenridge 20.00 9.00 2.50
☐ 341 R. Brashear 20.00 9.00 2.50
☐ 342 Brown 20.00 9.00 2.50
☐ 343 Burrell 20.00 9.00 2.50
☐ 344 Carlisle 20.00 9.00 2.50
☐ 345 Carson 20.00 9.00 2.50
☐ 346 Castleton 20.00 9.00 2.50
☐ 347 Hitt 20.00 9.00 2.50
☐ 348 Hogan 20.00 9.00 2.50
☐ 349 Hosp 20.00 9.00 2.50
☐ 350 Kane 20.00 9.00 2.50
☐ 351 McDonnell 20.00 9.00 2.50
☐ 352 Patterson 20.00 9.00 2.50
☐ 353 Raleigh 20.00 9.00 2.50
☐ 354 Ross 20.00 9.00 2.50
☐ 355 Sheehan 20.00 9.00 2.50
☐ 356 Stewart 20.00 9.00 2.50
☐ 357 Stinson 20.00 9.00 2.50
☐ 358 Willett 20.00 9.00 2.50
☐ 359 Bloomfield 20.00 9.00 2.50
☐ 360 Casey 20.00 9.00 2.50
☐ 361 Garrett 20.00 9.00 2.50
☐ 362 Harris 20.00 9.00 2.50
☐ 363 Lamline 20.00 9.00 2.50
☐ 364 Mensor 20.00 9.00 2.50
☐ 365 Mundorff 20.00 9.00 2.50
☐ 366 Speas 20.00 9.00 2.50
☐ 367 Stovall 25.00 11.00 3.10
☐ 368 Williams 20.00 9.00 2.50
☐ 369 Bues 20.00 9.00 2.50
☐ 370 Butler 20.00 9.00 2.50
☐ 371 Cruikshank 20.00 9.00 2.50
☐ 372 Kading 20.00 9.00 2.50
☐ 373 Leard 20.00 9.00 2.50
☐ 374 Raymond 20.00 9.00 2.50
☐ 375 Seaton 20.00 9.00 2.50
☐ 376 Shea 20.00 9.00 2.50
☐ 377 Skeels 20.00 9.00 2.50
☐ 378 Spencer 20.00 9.00 2.50
☐ 379 Weed 20.00 9.00 2.50
☐ 380 Zackert 20.00 9.00 2.50
☐ 381 Bonner 20.00 9.00 2.50
☐ 382 Cartwright 20.00 9.00 2.50
☐ 383 Cooney 20.00 9.00 2.50
☐ 384 Frisk 20.00 9.00 2.50
☐ 385 Hasty 20.00 9.00 2.50
☐ 386 Holm 20.00 9.00 2.50
☐ 387 Kippert 20.00 9.00 2.50
☐ 388 Netzel 20.00 9.00 2.50
☐ 389 Nordyke 20.00 9.00 2.50
☐ 390 Ostdiek 20.00 9.00 2.50
☐ 391 Strand 20.00 9.00 2.50
☐ 392 Zimmerman 20.00 9.00 2.50
☐ 393 Annis 20.00 9.00 2.50
☐ 394 Bassey 20.00 9.00 2.50
☐ 395 Burns 20.00 9.00 2.50
☐ 396 Coleman 20.00 9.00 2.50
☐ 397 Gordon 20.00 9.00 2.50
☐ 398 Hall 20.00 9.00 2.50
☐ 399 Higgins 20.00 9.00 2.50
☐ 400 Morse 20.00 9.00 2.50
☐ 401 Rockenfield 20.00 9.00 2.50
☐ 402 Schmutz 20.00 9.00 2.50
☐ 403 Warren 20.00 9.00 2.50
☐ 404 Adams 20.00 9.00 2.50
☐ 405 Bennett 20.00 9.00 2.50
☐ 406 Brasher 20.00 9.00 2.50
☐ 407 Brinker 20.00 9.00 2.50
☐ 408 Engel 20.00 9.00 2.50
☐ 409 Erickson 20.00 9.00 2.50
☐ 410 James 20.00 9.00 2.50
☐ 411 Jensen 20.00 9.00 2.50
☐ 412 Lewis 20.00 9.00 2.50
☐ 413 Scharnweber 20.00 9.00 2.50
☐ 414 Spiesman 20.00 9.00 2.50
☐ 415 Swain 20.00 9.00 2.50
☐ 416 Dashwood 20.00 9.00 2.50
☐ 417 Davis 20.00 9.00 2.50
☐ 418 Goodman 20.00 9.00 2.50
☐ 419 Householder 20.00 9.00 2.50
☐ 420 Raymer 20.00 9.00 2.50
☐ 421 Reddick 20.00 9.00 2.50
☐ 422 Roche 20.00 9.00 2.50
☐ 423 Starkel 20.00 9.00 2.50
☐ 424 Ten Million 20.00 9.00 2.50
☐ 425 Thomas 20.00 9.00 2.50
☐ 426 Ward 20.00 9.00 2.50

1910 Bishop Coast League E99

The cards in this 30-card set measure 1 1/2" by 2 3/4". Although there is no manufacturer's name to be found on the cards of this series, the similarities to set E100 almost certainly mark it as a product of Bishop and Co. The subjects are Coast League players, portrayed in black and white photos on solid color backgrounds. The cards are unnumbered but are back listed (starting with "Knapp"). The set was issued about 1910, and some players are found with more than one background color. The cards have been alphabetized and assigned numbers in the checklist below.

	EX-MT	VG-E	GOOD
COMPLETE SET (30)	4200.00	1900.00	525.00
COMMON CARD (1-30)	150.00	70.00	19.00

☐ 1 Ping Bodie 200.00 90.00 25.00
☐ 2 N. Brashear 150.00 70.00 19.00
☐ 3 Briggs 150.00 70.00 19.00
☐ 4 Byones 150.00 70.00 19.00
sic, Byrnes
☐ 5 Cameron 150.00 70.00 19.00
☐ 6 Casey 150.00 70.00 19.00
☐ 7 Cutshaw 150.00 70.00 19.00
☐ 8 Delmas 150.00 70.00 19.00
☐ 9 Dillon 150.00 70.00 19.00
☐ 10 Hasty 150.00 70.00 19.00
☐ 11 Hitt 150.00 70.00 19.00
☐ 12 Hap. Hogan 150.00 70.00 19.00
☐ 13 Hunt 150.00 70.00 19.00
☐ 14 Krapp 150.00 70.00 19.00
☐ 15 Lindsay 150.00 70.00 19.00
☐ 16 Maggert 150.00 70.00 19.00
☐ 17 McArdle 150.00 70.00 19.00
☐ 18 McCredie 150.00 70.00 19.00
sic, McCreedie
☐ 19 Melchoir 150.00 70.00 19.00
☐ 20 Mohler 150.00 70.00 19.00
☐ 21 Nagle 150.00 70.00 19.00
☐ 22 Nelson 150.00 70.00 19.00
☐ 23 Nourse 150.00 70.00 19.00
☐ 24 Olsen 150.00 70.00 19.00
☐ 25 Raymer 150.00 70.00 19.00
☐ 26 Smith 150.00 70.00 19.00
☐ 27 Tennent 150.00 70.00 19.00
sic, Tennant
☐ 28 Thorsen 150.00 70.00 19.00
☐ 29 Van Buren 150.00 70.00 19.00
☐ 30 Wolverton 150.00 70.00 19.00

1910 Contentnea T209

These baseball cards (each measuring 1 1/2" by 2 5/8") found as inserts in packs of Contentnea Cigarettes were released to the public in 1909 and 1910. Although both sets depict players from the Virginia, Carolina Association and Eastern Carolina leagues, they are otherwise dissimilar. The 16-card color series, known as Type I, is much

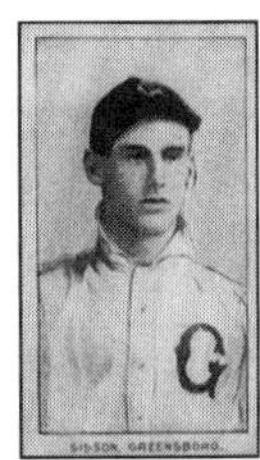

tougher and more valuable. The obverse captions are printed in blue and are located in the white border at the bottom. The reverse is marked "First Series", but no subsequent printings are known. There are also 219 of the Type II black and white "Photo Series" listed below, although more are believed to exist. The captions on this type are printed in black and are found within a white panel inside the picture area. Both types are unnumbered. Type I cards are alphabetized below. while Type II cards are arranged in alphabetical order within team. Teams in Type II are Anderson (17-27), Charlotte (28-40), Danville (41-50), Fayetteville (51-58), Goldsboro (59-72), Greensboro (73-85), Greenville (86-98), Lynchburg (99-110), Norfolk (111-123), Portsmouth (124-134), Raleigh (135-153), Richmond (154-167), Roanoke (168-180), Rocky Mount (181-187), Spartanburg (188-199), Wilmington (200-210), Wilson (211-222), and Winston-Salem (223-235).

	EX-MT	VG-E	GOOD
COMPLETE SET (235)	8000.00	3600.00	1000.00
COMMON TYPE I (1-16)	175.00	80.00	22.00
COMMON TYPE II (17-235)	25.00	11.00	3.10
☐ 1 Armstrong (Wilson)	175.00	80.00	22.00
☐ 2 Booles (Raleigh)	175.00	80.00	22.00
☐ 3 Bourquise (Rocky Mount)	175.00	80.00	22.00
☐ 4 Cooper (Wilson)	175.00	80.00	22.00
☐ 5 Cowell (Wilson)	175.00	80.00	22.00
☐ 6 Crockett (Goldsboro)	175.00	80.00	22.00
☐ 7 Fullenwider (Raleigh)	175.00	80.00	22.00
☐ 8 Gilmore (Winston-Salem)	175.00	80.00	22.00
☐ 9 Hoffman (Raleigh)	175.00	80.00	22.00
☐ 10 Lane (Wilson)	175.00	80.00	22.00
☐ 12 McGeehan (Wilson)	175.00	80.00	22.00
☐ 13 Pope (Raleigh)	175.00	80.00	22.00
☐ 14 Sisson (Greensboro)	175.00	80.00	22.00
☐ 15 Stubbe (Goldsboro)	175.00	80.00	22.00
☐ 16 Walsh (Goldsboro)	175.00	80.00	22.00
☐ 17 Byrd	25.00	11.00	3.10
☐ 18 Corbett	25.00	11.00	3.10
☐ 19 Farmer	25.00	11.00	3.10
☐ 20 Gorham	25.00	11.00	3.10
☐ 21 Harley	25.00	11.00	3.10
☐ 22 Kelly	25.00	11.00	3.10
☐ 23 A. McCarthy	25.00	11.00	3.10
☐ 24 J. McCarthy	25.00	11.00	3.10
☐ 25 Peloguin	25.00	11.00	3.10
☐ 26 Roth	25.00	11.00	3.10
☐ 27 Wehrell	25.00	11.00	3.10
☐ 28 Bausewein	25.00	11.00	3.10
☐ 29 Brazelle	25.00	11.00	3.10
☐ 30 Coutts	25.00	11.00	3.10
☐ 31 Cross	25.00	11.00	3.10
☐ 32 Dobard	25.00	11.00	3.10
☐ 33 Duvie	25.00	11.00	3.10
☐ 34 Francisco	25.00	11.00	3.10
☐ 35 Garman	25.00	11.00	3.10
☐ 36 Hargrave	25.00	11.00	3.10
☐ 37 Hemphrey	25.00	11.00	3.10
☐ 38 McHugh	25.00	11.00	3.10
☐ 39 Taxis	25.00	11.00	3.10
☐ 40 Williams	25.00	11.00	3.10
☐ 41 Bussey	25.00	11.00	3.10
☐ 42 Callahan	25.00	11.00	3.10
☐ 43 Griffin	25.00	11.00	3.10
☐ 44 Hooker	25.00	11.00	3.10
☐ 45 Mayberry	25.00	11.00	3.10
☐ 46 Mullinix	25.00	11.00	3.10
☐ 47 Priest	25.00	11.00	3.10
☐ 48 Rickert	25.00	11.00	3.10
☐ 49 Schrader	25.00	11.00	3.10
☐ 50 Sullivan	25.00	11.00	3.10
☐ 51 Boyle	25.00	11.00	3.10
☐ 52 Dobson	25.00	11.00	3.10
☐ 53 Galvin	25.00	11.00	3.10
☐ 54 Lavoia	25.00	11.00	3.10
☐ 55 Luyster	25.00	11.00	3.10
☐ 56 Schumaker	25.00	11.00	3.10
☐ 57 Waters	25.00	11.00	3.10
☐ 58 Wamack	25.00	11.00	3.10
☐ 59 Dailey	25.00	11.00	3.10
☐ 60 Evans	25.00	11.00	3.10
☐ 61 Fulton	25.00	11.00	3.10
☐ 62 Gates	25.00	11.00	3.10
☐ 63 Gunderson	25.00	11.00	3.10
☐ 64 Handiboe	25.00	11.00	3.10
☐ 65 Kelly	25.00	11.00	3.10
☐ 66 Malcolm	25.00	11.00	3.10
☐ 67 Merchant	25.00	11.00	3.10
☐ 68 Morgan	25.00	11.00	3.10
☐ 69 Sharp	25.00	11.00	3.10
☐ 70 Stoehr	25.00	11.00	3.10
☐ 71 Webb	25.00	11.00	3.10
☐ 72 Wolf	25.00	11.00	3.10
☐ 73 Bentley	25.00	11.00	3.10
☐ 74 Beusse	25.00	11.00	3.10
☐ 75 Doak	25.00	11.00	3.10
☐ 76 Eldridge	25.00	11.00	3.10
☐ 77 Hammersley	25.00	11.00	3.10
☐ 78 Hicks	25.00	11.00	3.10
☐ 79 Jackson	25.00	11.00	3.10
☐ 80 Martin	25.00	11.00	3.10
☐ 81 Pickard	25.00	11.00	3.10
☐ 82 Ridgeway	25.00	11.00	3.10
☐ 83 Springs	25.00	11.00	3.10
☐ 84 Walters	25.00	11.00	3.10
☐ 85 Weldon	25.00	11.00	3.10
☐ 86 Blackstone	25.00	11.00	3.10
☐ 87 F. Derrck (sic, Derrick)	25.00	11.00	3.10
☐ 88 C. Derrick	25.00	11.00	3.10
☐ 89 Drumm	25.00	11.00	3.10
☐ 90 Flowers	25.00	11.00	3.10
☐ 91 Jenkins	25.00	11.00	3.10
☐ 92 McFarlin	25.00	11.00	3.10
☐ 93 Noojin	25.00	11.00	3.10
☐ 94 Ochs	25.00	11.00	3.10
☐ 95 Redfern	25.00	11.00	3.10
☐ 96 Stouch	25.00	11.00	3.10
☐ 97 Wingo	25.00	11.00	3.10
☐ 98 Workman	25.00	11.00	3.10
☐ 99 Brandon	25.00	11.00	3.10
☐ 100 Griffin	25.00	11.00	3.10
☐ 101 Hoffman	25.00	11.00	3.10
☐ 102 Howedel	25.00	11.00	3.10
☐ 103 Levy	25.00	11.00	3.10
☐ 104 Lloyd	25.00	11.00	3.10
☐ 105 Lucia	25.00	11.00	3.10
☐ 106 Rawe	25.00	11.00	3.10
☐ 107 Sexton	25.00	11.00	3.10
☐ 108 A. Smith	25.00	11.00	3.10
☐ 109 D. Smith	25.00	11.00	3.10
☐ 110 Woolums	25.00	11.00	3.10
☐ 111 Armstrong	25.00	11.00	3.10
☐ 112 Banner	25.00	11.00	3.10
☐ 113 Busch	25.00	11.00	3.10
☐ 114 Chandler	25.00	11.00	3.10
☐ 115 Clark	25.00	11.00	3.10
☐ 116 Johnson	25.00	11.00	3.10
☐ 117 Mullany	25.00	11.00	3.10
☐ 118 Munsen	25.00	11.00	3.10
☐ 119 Murdock	25.00	11.00	3.10
☐ 120 Reggy	25.00	11.00	3.10
☐ 121 Tiedmann	25.00	11.00	3.10
☐ 122 Walker	25.00	11.00	3.10
☐ 123 Walsh	25.00	11.00	3.10
☐ 124 Bowen	25.00	11.00	3.10
☐ 125 Clunk	25.00	11.00	3.10
☐ 126 Guiheen	25.00	11.00	3.10
☐ 127 Hamilton	25.00	11.00	3.10
☐ 128 Hannifen	25.00	11.00	3.10
☐ 129 Kunkle	25.00	11.00	3.10
☐ 130 McFarland	25.00	11.00	3.10
☐ 131 Smith	25.00	11.00	3.10
☐ 132 Toner	25.00	11.00	3.10
☐ 133 Vail	25.00	11.00	3.10
☐ 134 Welsher	25.00	11.00	3.10
☐ 135 Beatty	25.00	11.00	3.10
☐ 136 Biel	25.00	11.00	3.10
☐ 137 Bigbie	25.00	11.00	3.10
☐ 138 Clemens	25.00	11.00	3.10
☐ 139 Hart	25.00	11.00	3.10
☐ 140 Hawkins	25.00	11.00	3.10
☐ 141 Hobbs	25.00	11.00	3.10
☐ 142 Jobson	25.00	11.00	3.10
☐ 143 Keating	25.00	11.00	3.10
☐ 144 King Kelly	25.00	11.00	3.10
☐ 145 Lathrop	25.00	11.00	3.10
☐ 146 McCormick	25.00	11.00	3.10
☐ 147 Mundell	25.00	11.00	3.10
☐ 148 Phoenix	25.00	11.00	3.10
☐ 149 Prim	25.00	11.00	3.10
☐ 150 Richardson	25.00	11.00	3.10
☐ 151 Simmons	25.00	11.00	3.10
☐ 152 Turner	25.00	11.00	3.10
☐ 153 Wright	25.00	11.00	3.10
☐ 154 Baker	25.00	11.00	3.10
☐ 155 Bigbie	25.00	11.00	3.10
☐ 156 Brown	25.00	11.00	3.10
☐ 157 Cowan	25.00	11.00	3.10
☐ 158 Hale	25.00	11.00	3.10
☐ 159 Irvine	25.00	11.00	3.10
☐ 160 Landgraff	25.00	11.00	3.10
☐ 161 Missitt	25.00	11.00	3.10
☐ 162 Morrissey	25.00	11.00	3.10
☐ 163 Salve	25.00	11.00	3.10
☐ 164 Shaw	25.00	11.00	3.10
☐ 165 Titman	25.00	11.00	3.10
☐ 166 Verbout	25.00	11.00	3.10
☐ 167 Wallace	25.00	11.00	3.10
☐ 168 Andrada	25.00	11.00	3.10
☐ 169 Cafalu	25.00	11.00	3.10
☐ 170 Doyle	25.00	11.00	3.10
☐ 171 Fisher	25.00	11.00	3.10
☐ 172 Halland	25.00	11.00	3.10
☐ 173 Jenkins	25.00	11.00	3.10
☐ 174 Newton	25.00	11.00	3.10
☐ 175 Powell	25.00	11.00	3.10
☐ 176 Presley and Pritchard (sic, Pressley)	25.00	11.00	3.10
☐ 177 Pritchard	25.00	11.00	3.10
☐ 178 Schmidt	25.00	11.00	3.10
☐ 179 Shanghnessy	25.00	11.00	3.10
☐ 180 Spratt	25.00	11.00	3.10
☐ 181 Bonner	25.00	11.00	3.10
☐ 182 Creagan	25.00	11.00	3.10
☐ 183 Forque	25.00	11.00	3.10
☐ 184 Gatmeyer	25.00	11.00	3.10
☐ 185 Gillespie	25.00	11.00	3.10
☐ 186 Novak	25.00	11.00	3.10
☐ 187 Phealean	25.00	11.00	3.10
☐ 188 Abercrombie	25.00	11.00	3.10
☐ 189 Averett	25.00	11.00	3.10
☐ 190 Fairbanks	25.00	11.00	3.10
☐ 191 Gardin	25.00	11.00	3.10
☐ 192 Harrington	25.00	11.00	3.10
☐ 193 Harris	25.00	11.00	3.10
☐ 194 Jackson	25.00	11.00	3.10
☐ 195 Thompson	25.00	11.00	3.10
☐ 196 Vickery	25.00	11.00	3.10
☐ 197 Walker	25.00	11.00	3.10
☐ 198 Wood	25.00	11.00	3.10
☐ 199 Wynne	25.00	11.00	3.10
☐ 200 Bourquin	25.00	11.00	3.10
☐ 201 Cooper	25.00	11.00	3.10
☐ 202 Doak	25.00	11.00	3.10
☐ 203 Ebinger	25.00	11.00	3.10
☐ 204 Foltz	25.00	11.00	3.10
☐ 205 Gehring	25.00	11.00	3.10
☐ 206 Howard	25.00	11.00	3.10
☐ 207 Hyames	25.00	11.00	3.10
☐ 208 Kelley	25.00	11.00	3.10
☐ 209 Kite	25.00	11.00	3.10
☐ 210 Tydeman	25.00	11.00	3.10
☐ 211 Clapp	25.00	11.00	3.10
☐ 212 Cowells	25.00	11.00	3.10
☐ 213 Foreman	25.00	11.00	3.10
☐ 214 Hearne	25.00	11.00	3.10
☐ 215 Hudson	25.00	11.00	3.10
☐ 216 Lane	25.00	11.00	3.10
☐ 217 C. McGeehan	25.00	11.00	3.10
☐ 218 Dan McGeehan	25.00	11.00	3.10
☐ 219 Miller	25.00	11.00	3.10
☐ 220 Stewart	25.00	11.00	3.10
☐ 221 B.E. Thompson	25.00	11.00	3.10
☐ 222 Westlake	25.00	11.00	3.10
☐ 223 Brent	25.00	11.00	3.10
☐ 224 Cote	25.00	11.00	3.10
☐ 225 Ferrell	25.00	11.00	3.10
☐ 226 Fogarty	25.00	11.00	3.10
☐ 227 King	25.00	11.00	3.10
☐ 228 Loval	25.00	11.00	3.10
☐ 229 MacConachie	25.00	11.00	3.10
☐ 230 McKeavitt	25.00	11.00	3.10
☐ 231 Midkiff	25.00	11.00	3.10
☐ 232 Painter	25.00	11.00	3.10
☐ 233 Swindell	25.00	11.00	3.10
☐ 234 Templin	25.00	11.00	3.10
☐ 235 Willis	25.00	11.00	3.10

1910 Old Mill T210

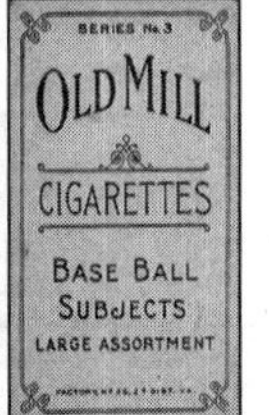

At 640 cards, this is the largest 20th Century tobacco-issued baseball series, and it presents a formidable challenge to the collector. Each card measures 1 1/2" by 2 5/8". Eight minor leagues are each represented by a specific numbered series indicated on the reverse of each card. Each player's name and team are printed in black within the bottom white picture area. The list below is ordered alphabetically by player's name within team within series. Series 1 (South Atlantic League) teams are Augusta (1-13), Columbia (14-26), Columbus (27-39), Jacksonville (40-51), Macon (52-63) and Savannah (64-75). Series 2 (Virginia League) teams are Danville (76-88), Lynchburg (89-105), Norfolk (106-117), Portsmouth (118-132), Richmond (133-151), and Roanoke (152-162). Series 3 (Texas League) teams are Dallas (163-181), Ft. Worth (182-197), Galveston (198-204), Houston (205-216), Oklahoma City (217-221), San Antonio (222-230), Shreveport (231-243) and Waco (244-257). Series 4 (Virginia Valley League) teams are Charleston (258-272), Huntington (273-285), Montgomery (286-296) and Mt. Pleasant (297-306). Series 5 (Carolina Association) teams are Anderson (307-320), Charlotte (321-335), Greensboro (336-348), Greenville (349-364), Spartanburg (365-379) and Winston-Salem (380-393). Series 6 (Blue Grass League) teams are Frankfort (394-401), Lexington (402-414), Maysville (415-422), Paris (423-433), Richmond (434-443), Shelbyville (444-446) and Winchester (447-459). Series 7 (Eastern Carolina League) teams are Fayetteville (460-468), Goldsboro (469-490), Raleigh (491-504), Rocky Mount (505-519), Wilmington (520) and Wilson (521-526). Series 8 (Southern Association) teams are Atlanta (527-539), Birmingham (540-556), Chattanooga (557-566), Memphis (567-580), Mobile (581-592), Montgomery (593-608), Nashville (609-625) and New Orleans (626-640). The two key cards in the set are Casey Stengel and Joe Jackson.

	EX-MT	VG-E	GOOD
COMPLETE SET (640)	15000.00	6800.00	1900.00
COMMON SERIES 1 (1-75)	20.00	9.00	2.50
COMMON SERIES 2 (76-162)	15.00	6.75	1.85
COMMON SERIES 3 (163-257)	20.00	9.00	2.50
COMMON SERIES 4 (258-306)	20.00	9.00	2.50
COMMON SERIES 5 (307-393)	20.00	9.00	2.50
COMMON SERIES 6 (394-459)	18.00	8.00	2.20
COMMON SERIES 7 (460-526)	25.00	11.00	3.10
COMMON SERIES 8 (527-640)	20.00	9.00	2.50
☐ 1 Bagwell	15.00	6.75	1.85
☐ 2 Bierkorttle	20.00	9.00	2.50
☐ 3 Dudley	20.00	9.00	2.50
☐ 4 Edwards	20.00	9.00	2.50
☐ 5 Hannifan	20.00	9.00	2.50
☐ 6 Hauser	20.00	9.00	2.50
☐ 7 McMahon	20.00	9.00	2.50
☐ 8 Norcum	20.00	9.00	2.50
☐ 9 Pierce	20.00	9.00	2.50
☐ 10 Shields	20.00	9.00	2.50
☐ 11 Smith	20.00	9.00	2.50
☐ 12 Viola	20.00	9.00	2.50
☐ 13 Wagner	20.00	9.00	2.50
☐ 14 Breitenstein	20.00	9.00	2.50
☐ 15 Cavender	20.00	9.00	2.50
☐ 16 Collins	20.00	9.00	2.50
☐ 17 Dwyer	20.00	9.00	2.50
☐ 18 Jones	20.00	9.00	2.50
☐ 19 Lewis	20.00	9.00	2.50
☐ 20 Marshall	20.00	9.00	2.50
☐ 21 Martin	20.00	9.00	2.50
☐ 22 Massing	20.00	9.00	2.50
☐ 23 Mulldowney	20.00	9.00	2.50
☐ 24 Redfern	20.00	9.00	2.50
☐ 25 Schwietzka	20.00	9.00	2.50
☐ 26 Wohlleben	20.00	9.00	2.50
☐ 27 Becker	20.00	9.00	2.50
☐ 28 Bensen	20.00	9.00	2.50
☐ 29 Fox	20.00	9.00	2.50
☐ 30 Harley	20.00	9.00	2.50
☐ 31 Hille	20.00	9.00	2.50
☐ 32 Krebs	20.00	9.00	2.50
☐ 33 Lewis	20.00	9.00	2.50
☐ 34 Long	20.00	9.00	2.50
☐ 35 McLeod	20.00	9.00	2.50
☐ 36 Radebaugh	20.00	9.00	2.50
☐ 37 Reynolds	20.00	9.00	2.50
☐ 38 Sisson	20.00	9.00	2.50
☐ 39 Toren	20.00	9.00	2.50
☐ 40 Bierman	20.00	9.00	2.50
☐ 41 Bremmerhoff	20.00	9.00	2.50
☐ 42 Carter	20.00	9.00	2.50
☐ 43 DeFraites	20.00	9.00	2.50
☐ 44 Hoyt	20.00	9.00	2.50
☐ 45 Hubner	20.00	9.00	2.50
☐ 46 Lee	20.00	9.00	2.50
☐ 47 Manion	20.00	9.00	2.50
☐ 48 Mullaney	20.00	9.00	2.50
☐ 49 Pope	20.00	9.00	2.50
☐ 50 Taffee	20.00	9.00	2.50
☐ 51 Sahl	20.00	9.00	2.50
☐ 52 Benton	20.00	9.00	2.50
☐ 53 Enbanks	20.00	9.00	2.50
☐ 54 Eubank	20.00	9.00	2.50
☐ 55 Ison	20.00	9.00	2.50
☐ 56 Kalkhoff	20.00	9.00	2.50
☐ 57 Lawrence	20.00	9.00	2.50
☐ 58 Lee	20.00	9.00	2.50
☐ 59 Lipe (portrait)	20.00	9.00	2.50
☐ 60 Lipe (batting)	20.00	9.00	2.50
☐ 61 Morse	20.00	9.00	2.50
☐ 62 Schulze	20.00	9.00	2.50
☐ 63 Weems	20.00	9.00	2.50
☐ 64 Balenti	20.00	9.00	2.50
☐ 65 Howard	20.00	9.00	2.50
☐ 66 Magoon	20.00	9.00	2.50
☐ 67 Martina	20.00	9.00	2.50
☐ 68 Murch	20.00	9.00	2.50
☐ 69 Pelkey	20.00	9.00	2.50
☐ 70 Petit	20.00	9.00	2.50
☐ 71 Regan	20.00	9.00	2.50
☐ 72 Reynolds	20.00	9.00	2.50
☐ 73 Schulz	20.00	9.00	2.50
☐ 74 Sweeney	20.00	9.00	2.50
☐ 75 Wells	20.00	9.00	2.50
☐ 76 Bussey	15.00	6.75	1.85
☐ 77 Gaston	15.00	6.75	1.85

Card			
☐ 78 Griffin	15.00	6.75	1.85
☐ 79 Hanks	15.00	6.75	1.85
☐ 80 Hooker	15.00	6.75	1.85
☐ 81 Kinkel	15.00	6.75	1.85
☐ 82 Larkins	15.00	6.75	1.85
☐ 83 Laughlin	15.00	6.75	1.85
☐ 84 Lloyd	15.00	6.75	1.85
☐ 85 Loos	15.00	6.75	1.85
☐ 86 Mayberry	15.00	6.75	1.85
☐ 87 Schrader	15.00	6.75	1.85
☐ 88 Tydeman	15.00	6.75	1.85
☐ 89 Beham	15.00	6.75	1.85
☐ 90 Brandon	15.00	6.75	1.85
☐ 91 Breivogel	15.00	6.75	1.85
☐ 92 Eddowes	15.00	6.75	1.85
☐ 93 Gehring	15.00	6.75	1.85
☐ 94 Griffen	15.00	6.75	1.85
☐ 95 Hoffman	15.00	6.75	1.85
☐ 96 Jackson	15.00	6.75	1.85
☐ 97 Levy	15.00	6.75	1.85
☐ 98 Lucia	15.00	6.75	1.85
☐ 99 Michel	15.00	6.75	1.85
☐ 100 Rowe	15.00	6.75	1.85
☐ 101 Sharp	15.00	6.75	1.85
☐ 102 Smith (at bat)	15.00	6.75	1.85
☐ 103 Smith (catching)	15.00	6.75	1.85
☐ 104 Woolums	15.00	6.75	1.85
☐ 105 Zimmerman	15.00	6.75	1.85
☐ 106 Bonner	15.00	6.75	1.85
☐ 107 Busch	15.00	6.75	1.85
☐ 108 Chandler	15.00	6.75	1.85
☐ 109 Clarke	15.00	6.75	1.85
☐ 110 Fox	15.00	6.75	1.85
☐ 111 Jackson	15.00	6.75	1.85
☐ 112 Lovell	15.00	6.75	1.85
☐ 113 MacConachie	15.00	6.75	1.85
☐ 114 Mullaney	15.00	6.75	1.85
☐ 115 Munson	15.00	6.75	1.85
☐ 116 Nimmo	15.00	6.75	1.85
☐ 117 Walker	15.00	6.75	1.85
☐ 118 Bowen	15.00	6.75	1.85
☐ 119 Clunk	15.00	6.75	1.85
☐ 120 Cote	15.00	6.75	1.85
☐ 121 Cowan	15.00	6.75	1.85
☐ 122 Foxen	15.00	6.75	1.85
☐ 123 Hamilton	15.00	6.75	1.85
☐ 124 Hannifan	15.00	6.75	1.85
☐ 125 Jackson	15.00	6.75	1.85
☐ 126 Kirkpatrick	15.00	6.75	1.85
☐ 127 McFarland	15.00	6.75	1.85
☐ 128 Norris	15.00	6.75	1.85
☐ 129 Smith	15.00	6.75	1.85
☐ 130 Spicer	15.00	6.75	1.85
☐ 131 Toner	15.00	6.75	1.85
☐ 132 Vail	15.00	6.75	1.85
☐ 133 Archer	15.00	6.75	1.85
☐ 134 Baker	15.00	6.75	1.85
☐ 135 Brooks	15.00	6.75	1.85
☐ 136 Brown	15.00	6.75	1.85
☐ 137 Decker	15.00	6.75	1.85
☐ 138 Hale	15.00	6.75	1.85
☐ 139 Irvine	15.00	6.75	1.85
☐ 140 Jackson	15.00	6.75	1.85
☐ 141 Keifel	15.00	6.75	1.85
☐ 142 Landgradd	15.00	6.75	1.85
☐ 143 Lawlor	15.00	6.75	1.85
☐ 144 Messitt	15.00	6.75	1.85
☐ 145 Peterson	15.00	6.75	1.85
☐ 146 Revelle	15.00	6.75	1.85
☐ 147 Shaw	15.00	6.75	1.85
☐ 148 Titman	15.00	6.75	1.85
☐ 149 Verbout	15.00	6.75	1.85
☐ 150 Wallace	15.00	6.75	1.85
☐ 151 Waymack	15.00	6.75	1.85
☐ 152 Anrada	15.00	6.75	1.85
☐ 153 Cefalu	15.00	6.75	1.85
☐ 154 Doyle	15.00	6.75	1.85
☐ 155 Fisher	15.00	6.75	1.85
☐ 156 Holland	15.00	6.75	1.85
☐ 157 Jenkins	15.00	6.75	1.85
☐ 158 Newton	15.00	6.75	1.85
☐ 159 Powell	15.00	6.75	1.85
☐ 160 Presley	15.00	6.75	1.85
☐ 161 Pritchard	15.00	6.75	1.85
☐ 162 Schmidt	15.00	6.75	1.85
☐ 163 Berlick	20.00	9.00	2.50
☐ 164 Dale	20.00	9.00	2.50
☐ 165 Doyle	20.00	9.00	2.50
☐ 166 Enos	20.00	9.00	2.50
☐ 167 Evans	20.00	9.00	2.50
☐ 168 Glawe	20.00	9.00	2.50
☐ 169 Gowdy	20.00	9.00	2.50
☐ 170 Hicks	20.00	9.00	2.50
☐ 171 Hirsch	20.00	9.00	2.50
☐ 172 Maloney	20.00	9.00	2.50
☐ 173 Meagher	20.00	9.00	2.50
☐ 174 Mullen	20.00	9.00	2.50
☐ 175 Ogle	20.00	9.00	2.50
☐ 176 Onslow	20.00	9.00	2.50
☐ 177 Robertson	20.00	9.00	2.50
☐ 178 Shindel	20.00	9.00	2.50
☐ 179 Shontz	20.00	9.00	2.50
☐ 180 Storch	20.00	9.00	2.50
☐ 181 Woodburn	20.00	9.00	2.50
☐ 182 Ash	20.00	9.00	2.50
☐ 183 Belew	20.00	9.00	2.50
☐ 184 Burk	20.00	9.00	2.50
☐ 185 Coyle	20.00	9.00	2.50
☐ 186 Deardoff	20.00	9.00	2.50
☐ 187 Fillman	20.00	9.00	2.50
☐ 188 Francis	20.00	9.00	2.50
☐ 189 Jolley	20.00	9.00	2.50
☐ 190 McKay	20.00	9.00	2.50
☐ 191 Morris	20.00	9.00	2.50
☐ 192 Pendelton	20.00	9.00	2.50
☐ 193 Powell	20.00	9.00	2.50
☐ 194 Salazor	20.00	9.00	2.50
☐ 195 Weber	20.00	9.00	2.50
☐ 196 Weeks	20.00	9.00	2.50
☐ 197 Wertherford	20.00	9.00	2.50
☐ 198 Cable	20.00	9.00	2.50
☐ 199 Donnelley	20.00	9.00	2.50
☐ 200 Hise	20.00	9.00	2.50
☐ 201 Kaphan	20.00	9.00	2.50
☐ 202 Riley	20.00	9.00	2.50
☐ 203 Spangler	20.00	9.00	2.50
☐ 204 Stringer	20.00	9.00	2.50
☐ 205 Bell	20.00	9.00	2.50
☐ 206 Burch	20.00	9.00	2.50
☐ 207 Carlin	20.00	9.00	2.50
☐ 208 Corkhill	20.00	9.00	2.50
☐ 209 Hill	20.00	9.00	2.50
☐ 210 Hornsby	20.00	9.00	2.50
☐ 211 Malloy	20.00	9.00	2.50
☐ 212 Merritt	20.00	9.00	2.50
☐ 213 Norten	20.00	9.00	2.50
☐ 214 Rose	20.00	9.00	2.50
☐ 215 Watson	20.00	9.00	2.50
☐ 216 Wickenhorf	20.00	9.00	2.50
☐ 217 Bandy	20.00	9.00	2.50
☐ 218 Davis	20.00	9.00	2.50
☐ 219 Jones	20.00	9.00	2.50
☐ 220 Nagel	20.00	9.00	2.50
☐ 221 Walsh	20.00	9.00	2.50
☐ 222 Alexander	20.00	9.00	2.50
☐ 223 Billiard	20.00	9.00	2.50
☐ 224 Blanding	20.00	9.00	2.50
☐ 225 Firestone	20.00	9.00	2.50
☐ 226 Kipp	20.00	9.00	2.50
☐ 227 Leidy	20.00	9.00	2.50
☐ 228 Slaven	20.00	9.00	2.50
☐ 229 Stinson	20.00	9.00	2.50
☐ 230 Yantz	20.00	9.00	2.50
☐ 231 Barenkamp	20.00	9.00	2.50
☐ 232 Cowans	20.00	9.00	2.50
☐ 233 Galloway	20.00	9.00	2.50
☐ 234 Gardner	20.00	9.00	2.50
☐ 235 Gear	20.00	9.00	2.50
☐ 236 Harper	20.00	9.00	2.50
☐ 237 Hinninger	20.00	9.00	2.50
☐ 238 Howell	20.00	9.00	2.50
☐ 239 Mills	20.00	9.00	2.50
☐ 240 Smith (Bat over right shoulder)	20.00	9.00	2.50
☐ 241 Smith (Bat at right hip)	20.00	9.00	2.50
☐ 242 Stadeli	20.00	9.00	2.50
☐ 243 Tesreau	20.00	9.00	2.50
☐ 244 Bennett	20.00	9.00	2.50
☐ 245 Blue	20.00	9.00	2.50
☐ 246 Conoway	20.00	9.00	2.50
☐ 247 Curry	20.00	9.00	2.50
☐ 248 Drucke	20.00	9.00	2.50
☐ 249 Dugey	20.00	9.00	2.50
☐ 250 Gordon	20.00	9.00	2.50
☐ 251 Harbison	20.00	9.00	2.50
☐ 252 Hooks	20.00	9.00	2.50
☐ 253 Johnston	20.00	9.00	2.50
☐ 254 Munsell	20.00	9.00	2.50
☐ 255 Thebo	20.00	9.00	2.50
☐ 256 Tullas	20.00	9.00	2.50
☐ 257 Williams	20.00	9.00	2.50
☐ 258 Benny	20.00	9.00	2.50
☐ 259 Carney	20.00	9.00	2.50
☐ 260 Conolly	20.00	9.00	2.50
☐ 261 Donnel	20.00	9.00	2.50
☐ 262 Erlewein	20.00	9.00	2.50
☐ 263 Ferrell	20.00	9.00	2.50
☐ 264 Heady	20.00	9.00	2.50
☐ 265 Hollis	20.00	9.00	2.50
☐ 266 Johnson	20.00	9.00	2.50
☐ 267 Moore	20.00	9.00	2.50
☐ 268 Pick	20.00	9.00	2.50
☐ 269 Stanley	20.00	9.00	2.50
☐ 270 Stockum	20.00	9.00	2.50
☐ 271 Willis	20.00	9.00	2.50
☐ 272 Zurlage	20.00	9.00	2.50
☐ 273 Bonno	20.00	9.00	2.50
☐ 274 Brumfield	20.00	9.00	2.50
☐ 275 Campbell	20.00	9.00	2.50
☐ 276 Canepa	20.00	9.00	2.50
☐ 277 Carter	20.00	9.00	2.50
☐ 278 Collier	20.00	9.00	2.50
☐ 279 Halterman	20.00	9.00	2.50
☐ 280 Kane	20.00	9.00	2.50
☐ 281 Leonard	20.00	9.00	2.50
☐ 282 McClain	20.00	9.00	2.50
☐ 283 Seaman	20.00	9.00	2.50
☐ 284 Titlow	20.00	9.00	2.50
☐ 285 Young	20.00	9.00	2.50
☐ 286 Aylor	20.00	9.00	2.50
☐ 287 Cochrane	20.00	9.00	2.50
☐ 288 Davis	20.00	9.00	2.50
☐ 289 Geary	20.00	9.00	2.50
☐ 290 Lux	20.00	9.00	2.50
☐ 291 Moye	20.00	9.00	2.50
☐ 292 O'Connor	20.00	9.00	2.50
☐ 293 Orcutt	20.00	9.00	2.50
☐ 294 Spicer	20.00	9.00	2.50
☐ 295 Waldron	20.00	9.00	2.50
☐ 296 Womach	20.00	9.00	2.50
☐ 297 Best	20.00	9.00	2.50
☐ 298 Boshmer	20.00	9.00	2.50
☐ 299 Brown	20.00	9.00	2.50
☐ 300 Dougherty	20.00	9.00	2.50
☐ 301 Hunter	20.00	9.00	2.50
☐ 302 Kuehn	20.00	9.00	2.50
☐ 303 Mollenkamp	20.00	9.00	2.50
☐ 304 Pickels	20.00	9.00	2.50
☐ 305 Schafer	20.00	9.00	2.50
☐ 306 Witter	20.00	9.00	2.50
☐ 307 Brannon	20.00	9.00	2.50
☐ 308 Corbett (3/4 pose)	20.00	9.00	2.50
☐ 309 Corbett (full pose)	20.00	9.00	2.50
☐ 310 Farmer	20.00	9.00	2.50
☐ 311 Finn	20.00	9.00	2.50
☐ 312 Gorham	20.00	9.00	2.50
☐ 313 Harley	20.00	9.00	2.50
☐ 314 Kelly	20.00	9.00	2.50
☐ 315 Lothrop	20.00	9.00	2.50
☐ 316 A. McCarthy	20.00	9.00	2.50
☐ 317 J. McCarthy	20.00	9.00	2.50
☐ 318 McEnvoe	20.00	9.00	2.50
☐ 319 Mangum	20.00	9.00	2.50
☐ 320 Wehrell	20.00	9.00	2.50
☐ 321 Bausewein	20.00	9.00	2.50
☐ 322 Brazell	20.00	9.00	2.50
☐ 323 L. Cross	20.00	9.00	2.50
☐ 324 Coutts	20.00	9.00	2.50
☐ 325 Dobard	20.00	9.00	2.50
☐ 326 Duvie	20.00	9.00	2.50
☐ 327 Francisco	20.00	9.00	2.50
☐ 328 Gorman	20.00	9.00	2.50
☐ 329 Hargrave	20.00	9.00	2.50
☐ 330 Hayes	20.00	9.00	2.50
☐ 331 Humphrey	20.00	9.00	2.50
☐ 332 Johnson	20.00	9.00	2.50
☐ 333 McHugh	20.00	9.00	2.50
☐ 334 Taxis	20.00	9.00	2.50
☐ 335 Williams	20.00	9.00	2.50
☐ 336 Bentley	20.00	9.00	2.50
☐ 337 C. Beusse	20.00	9.00	2.50
☐ 338 E. Beusse	20.00	9.00	2.50
☐ 339 Eldridge	20.00	9.00	2.50
☐ 340 Hammersley	20.00	9.00	2.50
☐ 341 Hicks	20.00	9.00	2.50
☐ 342 Jackson	20.00	9.00	2.50
☐ 343 James	20.00	9.00	2.50
☐ 344 Rickard	20.00	9.00	2.50
☐ 345 Smith	20.00	9.00	2.50
☐ 346 Thrasher	20.00	9.00	2.50
☐ 347 Walters	20.00	9.00	2.50
☐ 348 Weldon	20.00	9.00	2.50
☐ 349 Blackstone	20.00	9.00	2.50
☐ 350 Cashion	20.00	9.00	2.50
☐ 351 C. Derrick	20.00	9.00	2.50
☐ 352 F. Derrick	20.00	9.00	2.50
☐ 353 Drumm	20.00	9.00	2.50
☐ 354 Flowers	20.00	9.00	2.50
☐ 355 Jenkins	20.00	9.00	2.50
☐ 356 McFarlin	20.00	9.00	2.50
☐ 357 Noojin	20.00	9.00	2.50
☐ 358 Ochs	20.00	9.00	2.50
☐ 359 Redfern	20.00	9.00	2.50
☐ 360 Stouch	20.00	9.00	2.50
☐ 361 Trammel	20.00	9.00	2.50
☐ 362 Wingo	20.00	9.00	2.50
☐ 363 Workman	20.00	9.00	2.50
☐ 364 Wysong	20.00	9.00	2.50
☐ 365 Abercrombie	20.00	9.00	2.50
☐ 366 Avarett	20.00	9.00	2.50
☐ 367 Bigbee	20.00	9.00	2.50
☐ 368 Bullock	20.00	9.00	2.50
☐ 369 Crouch	20.00	9.00	2.50
☐ 370 Ehrhardt	20.00	9.00	2.50
☐ 371 Fairbanks	20.00	9.00	2.50
☐ 372 Gardin	20.00	9.00	2.50
☐ 373 Harrington	20.00	9.00	2.50
☐ 374 Harris	20.00	9.00	2.50
☐ 375 Roth (at bat)	20.00	9.00	2.50
☐ 376 Roth (fielding)	20.00	9.00	2.50
☐ 377 Springs	20.00	9.00	2.50
☐ 378 Walker	20.00	9.00	2.50
☐ 379 Wynne	20.00	9.00	2.50
☐ 380 Bievens	20.00	9.00	2.50
☐ 381 Brent	20.00	9.00	2.50
☐ 382 Ferrell	20.00	9.00	2.50
☐ 383 Fogarty	20.00	9.00	2.50
☐ 384 Gilmore	20.00	9.00	2.50
☐ 385 Guss	20.00	9.00	2.50
☐ 386 Laval	20.00	9.00	2.50
☐ 387 MacConachie	20.00	9.00	2.50
☐ 388 McKevitt	20.00	9.00	2.50
☐ 389 Midkiff	20.00	9.00	2.50
☐ 390 Moore	20.00	9.00	2.50
☐ 391 Painter	20.00	9.00	2.50
☐ 392 Reis	20.00	9.00	2.50
☐ 393 Templin	20.00	9.00	2.50
☐ 394 Angermeier (sic, Angermeir)	18.00	8.00	2.20
☐ 395 Angermeir	18.00	8.00	2.20
☐ 396 Beard	18.00	8.00	2.20
☐ 397 Bohannon	18.00	8.00	2.20
☐ 398 Cornell	18.00	8.00	2.20
☐ 399 Hicks	18.00	8.00	2.20
☐ 400 Hoffman	18.00	8.00	2.20
☐ 401 McIlvain	18.00	8.00	2.20
☐ 402 Badger	18.00	8.00	2.20
☐ 403 Ellis	18.00	8.00	2.20
☐ 404 Endington	18.00	8.00	2.20
☐ 405 Haines	18.00	8.00	2.20
☐ 406 Hevevon	18.00	8.00	2.20
☐ 407 Keifel	18.00	8.00	2.20
☐ 408 Kinbrough	18.00	8.00	2.20
☐ 409 L'Heuveux	18.00	8.00	2.20
☐ 410 Meyers	18.00	8.00	2.20
☐ 411 Sinex	18.00	8.00	2.20
☐ 412 Fan Landingham	18.00	8.00	2.20
☐ 413 Viox	18.00	8.00	2.20
☐ 414 Yancy	18.00	8.00	2.20
☐ 415 Chase	18.00	8.00	2.20
☐ 416 Dailey	18.00	8.00	2.20
☐ 417 Everden	18.00	8.00	2.20
☐ 418 Gisler	18.00	8.00	2.20
☐ 419 Oyler	18.00	8.00	2.20
☐ 420 Ross	18.00	8.00	2.20
☐ 421 Schultz	18.00	8.00	2.20
☐ 422 Casey Stengel	750.00	350.00	95.00
☐ 423 Barnett	18.00	8.00	2.20
☐ 424 Chapman	18.00	8.00	2.20
☐ 425 Goodman	18.00	8.00	2.20
☐ 426 Harold	18.00	8.00	2.20
☐ 427 Kaiser	18.00	8.00	2.20
☐ 428 Kuhlman	18.00	8.00	2.20
☐ 429 Kuhlmann	18.00	8.00	2.20
☐ 430 McKernon	18.00	8.00	2.20
☐ 431 Scheneberg (head and shoulders)	18.00	8.00	2.20
☐ 432 Scheneberg (fielding)	18.00	8.00	2.20
☐ 433 Scott	18.00	8.00	2.20
☐ 434 Creager	18.00	8.00	2.20
☐ 435 Elgin	18.00	8.00	2.20
☐ 436 Moloney	18.00	8.00	2.20
☐ 437 Olson	18.00	8.00	2.20
☐ 438 Thoss	18.00	8.00	2.20
☐ 439 Tilford	18.00	8.00	2.20
☐ 440 Walden	18.00	8.00	2.20
☐ 441 Whitaker	18.00	8.00	2.20
☐ 442 Willis	18.00	8.00	2.20
☐ 443 Wright	18.00	8.00	2.20
☐ 444 Kircher	18.00	8.00	2.20
☐ 445 Van Landingham	18.00	8.00	2.20
☐ 446 Womble	18.00	8.00	2.20
☐ 447 Atwell	18.00	8.00	2.20
☐ 448 Barney	18.00	8.00	2.20
☐ 449 Callahan	18.00	8.00	2.20
☐ 450 Coleman	18.00	8.00	2.20
☐ 451 Cornell	18.00	8.00	2.20
☐ 452 Goostree (leaning on bat)	18.00	8.00	2.20
☐ 453 Goostree (hands behind back)	18.00	8.00	2.20
☐ 454 Horn	18.00	8.00	2.20
☐ 455 Kircher	18.00	8.00	2.20
☐ 456 Mullin	18.00	8.00	2.20
☐ 457 Reed	18.00	8.00	2.20
☐ 458 Toney	18.00	8.00	2.20
☐ 459 Yeager	18.00	8.00	2.20
☐ 460 Brandt	25.00	11.00	3.10
☐ 461 Cantwell	25.00	11.00	3.10
☐ 462 Dwyer	25.00	11.00	3.10
☐ 463 Galvin	25.00	11.00	3.10
☐ 464 Hartley	25.00	11.00	3.10
☐ 465 Luyster	25.00	11.00	3.10
☐ 466 Mayer	25.00	11.00	3.10
☐ 467 O'Halloran	25.00	11.00	3.10
☐ 468 Schumaker	25.00	11.00	3.10
☐ 469 Brown	25.00	11.00	3.10
☐ 470 Crockett	25.00	11.00	3.10
☐ 471 Dailey	25.00	11.00	3.10
☐ 472 Evans	25.00	11.00	3.10
☐ 473 Fulton	25.00	11.00	3.10
☐ 474 Gates	25.00	11.00	3.10
☐ 475 Gunderson	25.00	11.00	3.10
☐ 476 Handibe	25.00	11.00	3.10
☐ 477 Irving	25.00	11.00	3.10
☐ 478 Kaiser	25.00	11.00	3.10
☐ 479 Kelly	25.00	11.00	3.10
☐ 480 Kelly (Mascot)	25.00	11.00	3.10
☐ 481 MacDonald	25.00	11.00	3.10
☐ 482 Malcolm	25.00	11.00	3.10
☐ 483 Merchant	25.00	11.00	3.10
☐ 484 Morgan	25.00	11.00	3.10
☐ 485 Sharp	25.00	11.00	3.10
☐ 486 Steinback	25.00	11.00	3.10
☐ 487 Stoehr	25.00	11.00	3.10
☐ 488 Taylor	25.00	11.00	3.10
☐ 489 Webb	25.00	11.00	3.10
☐ 490 Wolf	25.00	11.00	3.10
☐ 491 Beatty	25.00	11.00	3.10

☐ 492 Biel 25.00 11.00 3.10
☐ 493 Carrol 25.00 11.00 3.10
☐ 494 Ham 25.00 11.00 3.10
☐ 495 Hart 25.00 11.00 3.10
☐ 496 Hobbs 25.00 11.00 3.10
☐ 497 Kelley 25.00 11.00 3.10
☐ 498 McCormac 25.00 11.00 3.10
☐ 499 Newman 25.00 11.00 3.10
☐ 500 Prim 25.00 11.00 3.10
☐ 501 Richardson 25.00 11.00 3.10
☐ 502 Sherrill 25.00 11.00 3.10
☐ 503 Simmons 25.00 11.00 3.10
☐ 504 Wright 25.00 11.00 3.10
☐ 505 Bonner 25.00 11.00 3.10
☐ 506 Creagan 25.00 11.00 3.10
☐ 507 Cooney 25.00 11.00 3.10
☐ 508 Dobbs 25.00 11.00 3.10
☐ 509 Dussault 25.00 11.00 3.10
☐ 510 Forgue 25.00 11.00 3.10
☐ 511 Gastmeyer (batting) 25.00 11.00 3.10
☐ 512 Gastmeyer (fielding) 25.00 11.00 3.10
☐ 513 Gillespie 25.00 11.00 3.10
☐ 514 Griffin 25.00 11.00 3.10
☐ 515 Morris 25.00 11.00 3.10
☐ 516 Munson 25.00 11.00 3.10
☐ 517 Noval 25.00 11.00 3.10
☐ 518 Phelan 25.00 11.00 3.10
☐ 519 Reeves 25.00 11.00 3.10
☐ 520 Hyames 25.00 11.00 3.10
☐ 521 Armstrong 25.00 11.00 3.10
☐ 522 Cooper 25.00 11.00 3.10
☐ 523 Cowell 25.00 11.00 3.10
☐ 524 McGeehan 25.00 11.00 3.10
☐ 525 Mills 25.00 11.00 3.10
☐ 526 Whelan 25.00 11.00 3.10
☐ 527 Bartley 20.00 9.00 2.50
☐ 528 Bayless 20.00 9.00 2.50
☐ 529 Fisher 20.00 9.00 2.50
☐ 530 Griffin 20.00 9.00 2.50
☐ 531 Hanks 20.00 9.00 2.50
☐ 532 Hohnhorst 20.00 9.00 2.50
☐ 533 Jordan 20.00 9.00 2.50
☐ 534 Moran 20.00 9.00 2.50
☐ 535 Rogers 20.00 9.00 2.50
☐ 536 Seitz 20.00 9.00 2.50
☐ 537 Sid. Smith 20.00 9.00 2.50
☐ 538 Sweeney 20.00 9.00 2.50
☐ 539 Walker 20.00 9.00 2.50
☐ 540 Bauer 20.00 9.00 2.50
☐ 541 Elliott 20.00 9.00 2.50
☐ 542 Emery 20.00 9.00 2.50
☐ 543 Fleharty 20.00 9.00 2.50
☐ 544 Gygli 20.00 9.00 2.50
☐ 545 Kane 20.00 9.00 2.50
☐ 546 Larsen 20.00 9.00 2.50
☐ 547 Manuel 20.00 9.00 2.50
☐ 548 Marcan 20.00 9.00 2.50
☐ 549 McBride 20.00 9.00 2.50
☐ 550 McGilvray 20.00 9.00 2.50
☐ 551 McTigue 20.00 9.00 2.50
☐ 552 Molesworth 20.00 9.00 2.50
☐ 553 Newton 20.00 9.00 2.50
☐ 554 Owen 20.00 9.00 2.50
☐ 555 Schopp 20.00 9.00 2.50
☐ 556 Wagner 20.00 9.00 2.50
☐ 557 Carson 20.00 9.00 2.50
☐ 558 Collins 20.00 9.00 2.50
☐ 559 Demaree 20.00 9.00 2.50
☐ 560 Dobbs 20.00 9.00 2.50
☐ 561 McLaurin 20.00 9.00 2.50
☐ 562 Miller 20.00 9.00 2.50
☐ 563 Patterson 20.00 9.00 2.50
☐ 564 Rhodes 20.00 9.00 2.50
☐ 565 Schlitzer 20.00 9.00 2.50
☐ 566 Yerkes 20.00 9.00 2.50
☐ 567 Allen 20.00 9.00 2.50
☐ 568 Babb 20.00 9.00 2.50
☐ 569 Crandall 20.00 9.00 2.50
☐ 570 Cross 20.00 9.00 2.50
☐ 571 Davis 20.00 9.00 2.50
☐ 572 Dick 20.00 9.00 2.50
☐ 573 Dudley 20.00 9.00 2.50
☐ 574 Farrell 20.00 9.00 2.50
☐ 575 Fritz 20.00 9.00 2.50
☐ 576 Peters 20.00 9.00 2.50
☐ 577 Rementer 20.00 9.00 2.50
☐ 578 Steele 20.00 9.00 2.50
☐ 579 Wanner 20.00 9.00 2.50
☐ 580 Whitney 20.00 9.00 2.50
☐ 581 Allen 20.00 9.00 2.50
☐ 582 Berger 20.00 9.00 2.50
☐ 583 Bittroff 20.00 9.00 2.50
☐ 584 Chappelle 20.00 9.00 2.50
☐ 585 Dunn 20.00 9.00 2.50
☐ 586 Hickman 20.00 9.00 2.50
☐ 587 Huelsman 20.00 9.00 2.50
☐ 588 Kerwin 20.00 9.00 2.50
☐ 589 Rhoton 20.00 9.00 2.50
☐ 590 Swacina 20.00 9.00 2.50
☐ 591 Wagner 20.00 9.00 2.50
☐ 592 Wilder 20.00 9.00 2.50
☐ 593 Burnett 20.00 9.00 2.50
☐ 594 Daly 20.00 9.00 2.50
☐ 595 Graninger 20.00 9.00 2.50
☐ 596 Gribbin 20.00 9.00 2.50
☐ 597 Hart 20.00 9.00 2.50
☐ 598 McCreery 20.00 9.00 2.50
☐ 599 Miller 20.00 9.00 2.50
☐ 600 Nolley 20.00 9.00 2.50
☐ 601 Osteen 20.00 9.00 2.50
☐ 602 Pepe 20.00 9.00 2.50
☐ 603 Phillips 20.00 9.00 2.50
☐ 604 Pratt 20.00 9.00 2.50
☐ 605 Smith 20.00 9.00 2.50
☐ 606 Thomas (portrait) 20.00 9.00 2.50
☐ 607 Thomas (fielding) 20.00 9.00 2.50
☐ 608 Whiteman 20.00 9.00 2.50
☐ 609 Anderson 20.00 9.00 2.50
☐ 610 Bay 20.00 9.00 2.50
☐ 611 Bernard 20.00 9.00 2.50
☐ 612 Bronkie 20.00 9.00 2.50
☐ 613 Case 20.00 9.00 2.50
☐ 614 Cohen 20.00 9.00 2.50
☐ 615 Erloff 20.00 9.00 2.50
☐ 616 Flood 20.00 9.00 2.50
☐ 617 Kelly 20.00 9.00 2.50
☐ 618 Keupper 20.00 9.00 2.50
☐ 619 Lynch 20.00 9.00 2.50
☐ 620 Perdue 20.00 9.00 2.50
☐ 621 Seabough 20.00 9.00 2.50
☐ 622 Siegle 20.00 9.00 2.50
☐ 623 Vinson 20.00 9.00 2.50
☐ 624 Weif 20.00 9.00 2.50
☐ 625 Wiseman 20.00 9.00 2.50
☐ 626 Breitenstein 20.00 9.00 2.50
☐ 627 Brooks 20.00 9.00 2.50
☐ 628 Cafalu 20.00 9.00 2.50
☐ 629 DeMontreville 20.00 9.00 2.50
☐ 630 E. DeMontreville 20.00 9.00 2.50
☐ 631 Doster 20.00 9.00 2.50
☐ 632 Hess 20.00 9.00 2.50
☐ 633 Joe Jackson 4000.00 1800.00 500.00
☐ 634 LaFitte 20.00 9.00 2.50
☐ 635 Lindsay 20.00 9.00 2.50
☐ 636 Manush 20.00 9.00 2.50
☐ 637 Maxwell 20.00 9.00 2.50
☐ 638 Paige 20.00 9.00 2.50
☐ 639 Robertson 20.00 9.00 2.50
☐ 640 Rohe 20.00 9.00 2.50

1910 Red Sun T211

The green-bordered cards in this 75-card set measure approximately 1 1/2" by 2 5/8". The obverse design of this 1910 issue resembles that of the the T210 set except for the green borders surrounding the black and white picture area. All players in the set are from the Southern Association and all also appear in the T210 Series 8. The players have been alphabetized within team and numbered for reference in the checklist below. The teams are also ordered alphabetically: Atlanta (1-13), Birmingham (14-16), Memphis (17-22), Mobile (23-34), Montgomery (35-45), Nashville (46-62) and New Orleans (63-75).

	EX-MT	VG-E	GOOD
COMPLETE SET (75)	3200.00	1450.00	400.00
COMMON CARD (1-75)	50.00	22.00	6.25

☐ 1 Bartley 50.00 22.00 6.25
☐ 2 Bayless 50.00 22.00 6.25
☐ 3 Fisher 50.00 22.00 6.25
☐ 4 Griffin 50.00 22.00 6.25
☐ 5 Gornhorst 50.00 22.00 6.25
☐ 6 Hanks 50.00 22.00 6.25
☐ 7 Jordan 50.00 22.00 6.25
☐ 8 Moran 50.00 22.00 6.25
☐ 9 Rogers 50.00 22.00 6.25
☐ 10 Seitz 50.00 22.00 6.25
☐ 11 Sid Smith 50.00 22.00 6.25
☐ 12 Sweeney 50.00 22.00 6.25
☐ 13 Walker 50.00 22.00 6.25
☐ 14 Gygli 50.00 22.00 6.25
☐ 15 Kane 50.00 22.00 6.25
☐ 16 Molesworth 50.00 22.00 6.25
☐ 17 Babb 50.00 22.00 6.25
☐ 18 Cross 50.00 22.00 6.25
☐ 19 Davis 50.00 22.00 6.25
☐ 20 Dick 50.00 22.00 6.25
☐ 21 Fritz 50.00 22.00 6.25
☐ 22 Steele 50.00 22.00 6.25
☐ 23 Allen 50.00 22.00 6.25
☐ 24 Berger 50.00 22.00 6.25
☐ 25 Bittroff 50.00 22.00 6.25
☐ 26 Chappelle 50.00 22.00 6.25
☐ 27 Dunn 50.00 22.00 6.25
☐ 28 Hickman 50.00 22.00 6.25
☐ 29 Huelsman 50.00 22.00 6.25
☐ 30 Kerwin 50.00 22.00 6.25
☐ 31 Rhoton 50.00 22.00 6.25
☐ 32 Swacina 50.00 22.00 6.25
☐ 33 Wagner 50.00 22.00 6.25
☐ 34 Wilder 50.00 22.00 6.25
☐ 35 Jud Daly 50.00 22.00 6.25
☐ 36 Greminger 50.00 22.00 6.25
☐ 37 Gribbin 50.00 22.00 6.25
☐ 38 Hart 50.00 22.00 6.25
☐ 39 McCreary 50.00 22.00 6.25
☐ 40 Miller 50.00 22.00 6.25
☐ 41 Nolley 50.00 22.00 6.25
☐ 42 Pepe 50.00 22.00 6.25
☐ 43 Pratt 50.00 22.00 6.25
☐ 44 Smith 50.00 22.00 6.25
☐ 45 Thomas 50.00 22.00 6.25
☐ 46 Anderson 50.00 22.00 6.25
☐ 47 Bay 50.00 22.00 6.25
☐ 48 Bernard 50.00 22.00 6.25
☐ 49 Bronkie 50.00 22.00 6.25
☐ 50 Case 50.00 22.00 6.25
☐ 51 Cohen 50.00 22.00 6.25
☐ 52 Erloff 50.00 22.00 6.25
☐ 53 Flood 50.00 22.00 6.25
☐ 54 Kelly 50.00 22.00 6.25
☐ 55 Keupper 50.00 22.00 6.25
☐ 56 Lynch 50.00 22.00 6.25
☐ 57 Perdue 50.00 22.00 6.25
☐ 58 Seabrough 50.00 22.00 6.25
☐ 59 Siegel 50.00 22.00 6.25
☐ 60 Vinson 50.00 22.00 6.25
☐ 61 Wiseman 50.00 22.00 6.25
☐ 62 Welf 50.00 22.00 6.25
☐ 63 Breitenstein 50.00 22.00 6.25
☐ 64 Brooks 50.00 22.00 6.25
☐ 65 Cafalu 50.00 22.00 6.25
☐ 66 DeMontreville 50.00 22.00 6.25
☐ 67 E. DeMontreville 50.00 22.00 6.25
☐ 68 Foster 50.00 22.00 6.25
☐ 69 Hess 50.00 22.00 6.25
☐ 70 LaFitte 50.00 22.00 6.25
☐ 71 Lindsay 50.00 22.00 6.25
☐ 72 Manush 50.00 22.00 6.25
☐ 73 Paige 50.00 22.00 6.25
☐ 74 Robertson 50.00 22.00 6.25
☐ 75 Rohe 50.00 22.00 6.25

1911 Bishop Coast League E100

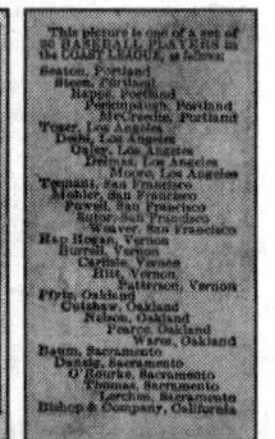

The cards in this 30-card set measure 1 1/2" by 2 3/4". Each of the cards of this Coast League set have the inscription "Bishop and Co." printed on the reverse at the bottom. Otherwise, the style of the cards is similar to set E99. They have black and white photos set on solid color backgrounds, they are backlisted (starts with "Seaton"), and they are unnumbered. There are color variations for many players. Subjects marked by an asterisk are found also in a blank-backed, slightly larger (photo on) card with a green or orange backgound. These blank-backed (Type II) cards are valued double the prices below. According to some hobbyists, there has never been a type two found in better than vg/ex condition. The cards in the set have been alphabetized and numbered in the checklist below. The set was produced around 1910.

	EX-MT	VG-E	GOOD
COMPLETE SET (30)	3800.00	1700.00	475.00
COMMON CARD (1-30)	125.00	55.00	15.50

☐ 1 Baum 125.00 55.00 15.50
☐ 2 Burrell 125.00 55.00 15.50
☐ 3 Carlisle 125.00 55.00 15.50
☐ 4 Cutshaw 125.00 55.00 15.50
☐ 5 Daley 125.00 55.00 15.50
☐ 6 Danzig 125.00 55.00 15.50
☐ 7 Delhi 125.00 55.00 15.50
☐ 8 Delmas 125.00 55.00 15.50
☐ 9 Hitt 125.00 55.00 15.50
☐ 10 Hogan 125.00 55.00 15.50
☐ 11 Lerchen 125.00 55.00 15.50
☐ 12 McCreedie 125.00 55.00 15.50
☐ 13 Mohler 125.00 55.00 15.50
☐ 14 Moore 125.00 55.00 15.50
☐ 15 Nelson 125.00 55.00 15.50
☐ 16 O'Rourke 125.00 55.00 15.50
☐ 17 Patterson 125.00 55.00 15.50
☐ 18 Pearce 125.00 55.00 15.50
☐ 19 Peckinpaugh 150.00 70.00 19.00
☐ 20 Pfyle 125.00 55.00 15.50
sic, Pfyl
☐ 21 Powell 125.00 55.00 15.50
☐ 22 Rapps 125.00 55.00 15.50
☐ 23 Seaton 125.00 55.00 15.50
☐ 24 Steen 125.00 55.00 15.50
☐ 25 Suter 125.00 55.00 15.50
☐ 26 Tennant 125.00 55.00 15.50
☐ 27 Thomas 125.00 55.00 15.50
☐ 28 Tozer 125.00 55.00 15.50
☐ 29 Wares 125.00 55.00 15.50
☐ 30 Buck Weaver 600.00 275.00 75.00

1911 Big Eater E-Unc.

This 20-card set of the Pacific Coast League's team, the Sacramento Senators, features black-and-white player photos which measure approximately 2 1/8" by 4". Each card has a three line capiton giving the name of the player, the team as "SAC'TO" and the words, "HE EATS 'BIG EATER' " which is presumed to be the name of a candy. These cards are rarely found in a better condition than g-vg. There is speculation that these were issued by a candy company -- therefore the cards are listed with the "E" designation.

	EX-MT	VG-E	GOOD
COMPLETE SET (20)	5000.00	2200.00	600.00
COMMON CARD (1-20)	250.00	110.00	31.00

☐ 1 Arellanes 250.00 110.00 31.00
☐ 2 Baum 250.00 110.00 31.00
☐ 3 Byram 250.00 110.00 31.00
☐ 4 Hal Danzig 250.00 110.00 31.00
☐ 5 John Fitzgerald 250.00 110.00 31.00
☐ 6 Gaddy 250.00 110.00 31.00
(unidentified player)
☐ 7 Heister 250.00 110.00 31.00
☐ 8 Hunt 250.00 110.00 31.00
☐ 9 Kerns 250.00 110.00 31.00
☐ 10 LaLonge 250.00 110.00 31.00
☐ 11 Lerchen 250.00 110.00 31.00
☐ 12 Jim Lewis 250.00 110.00 31.00
☐ 13 Mahoney 250.00 110.00 31.00
☐ 14 Nebinger 250.00 110.00 31.00
☐ 15 O'Rourke 250.00 110.00 31.00
☐ 16 Shinn 250.00 110.00 31.00
☐ 17 Thomas 250.00 110.00 31.00
☐ 18 Thompson 250.00 110.00 31.00
☐ 19 Thornton 250.00 110.00 31.00
☐ 20 Van Buren 250.00 110.00 31.00

1912 Imperial Tobacco C46

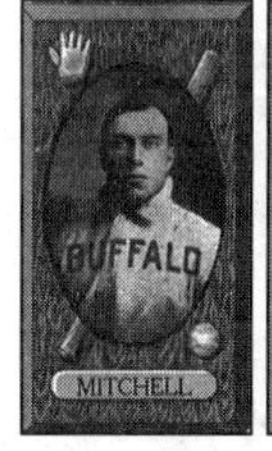

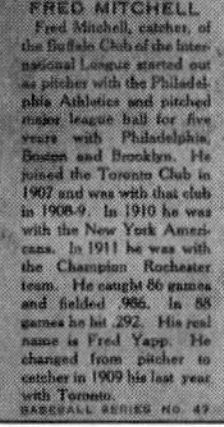

FRED MITCHELL
Fred Mitchell, catcher, of the Buffalo Club of the International League started out as pitcher with the Philadelphia Athletics and pitched major league ball for five years with Philadelphia, Boston and Brooklyn. He joined the Toronto Club in 1907 and was with that club in 1908-9. In 1910 he was with the New York Americans. In 1911 he was with the Champion Rochester team. He caught 86 games and fielded .986. In 88 games he hit .292. His real name is Fred Yapp. He changed from pitcher to catcher in 1909 his last year with Toronto.
BASEBALL SERIES NO. 49

The cards in this 90-card set measure approximately 1 1/2" by 2 3/4". The 1912 C46 set features numbered cards which were issued with unidentified brands of cigarettes although there is speculation that Imperial Tobacco was the sponsor of the set. The set features International League players and is styled with a brown wood-grain look. Card backs feature brief biographical information.

	EX-MT	VG-E	GOOD
COMPLETE SET (90)	4500.00	2000.00	550.00
COMMON CARD (1-90)	50.00	22.00	6.25

☐ 1 William O'Hara 150.00 70.00 19.00
☐ 2 James McGinley 50.00 22.00 6.25
☐ 3 Geo.Frenchy LeClaire 50.00 22.00 6.25
☐ 4 John White 50.00 22.00 6.25
☐ 5 James Murray 50.00 22.00 6.25
☐ 6 Joe Ward 50.00 22.00 6.25
☐ 7 Whitey Alperman 50.00 22.00 6.25
☐ 8 Natty Nattress 50.00 22.00 6.25
☐ 9 Fred Sline 50.00 22.00 6.25
☐ 10 Royal Rock 50.00 22.00 6.25
☐ 11 Ray Demmitt 60.00 27.00 7.50
☐ 12 Butcher Boy Schmidt 50.00 22.00 6.25
☐ 13 Samuel Frock 50.00 22.00 6.25
☐ 14 Fred Burchell 50.00 22.00 6.25
☐ 15 Jack Kelley 50.00 22.00 6.25
☐ 16 Frank Barberich 50.00 22.00 6.25
☐ 17 Frank Corridon 50.00 22.00 6.25
☐ 18 Doc Adkins 50.00 22.00 6.25
☐ 19 Jack Dunn MG 60.00 27.00 7.50
☐ 20 James Walsh 50.00 22.00 6.25
☐ 21 Charles Handford 50.00 22.00 6.25
☐ 22 Dick Rudolph 60.00 27.00 7.50
☐ 23 Curt Elston 50.00 22.00 6.25
☐ 24 Silton 50.00 22.00 6.25
☐ 25 Charlie French 50.00 22.00 6.25
☐ 26 John Ganzel 50.00 22.00 6.25
☐ 27 Joe Kelley 200.00 90.00 25.00
☐ 28 Benny Meyers 50.00 22.00 6.25
☐ 29 George Schirm 50.00 22.00 6.25
☐ 30 William Purtell 50.00 22.00 6.25
☐ 31 Bayard Sharpe 50.00 22.00 6.25
☐ 32 Tony Smith 50.00 22.00 6.25
☐ 33 John Lush 50.00 22.00 6.25
☐ 34 William Collins 50.00 22.00 6.25
☐ 35 Art Phelan 50.00 22.00 6.25
☐ 36 Edward Phelps 50.00 22.00 6.25

	EX-MT	VG-E	GOOD
☐ 37 Rube Vickers	60.00	27.00	7.50
☐ 38 Cy Seymour	75.00	34.00	9.50
☐ 39 Shadow Carroll	50.00	22.00	6.25
☐ 40 Jake Gettman	50.00	22.00	6.25
☐ 41 Luther Taylor	60.00	27.00	7.50
☐ 42 Walter Justis	50.00	22.00	6.25
☐ 43 Robert Fisher	50.00	22.00	6.25
☐ 44 Fred Parent	60.00	27.00	7.50
☐ 45 James Dygert	50.00	22.00	6.25
☐ 46 Johnnie Butler	50.00	22.00	6.25
☐ 47 Fred Mitchell	50.00	22.00	6.25
☐ 48 Heine Batch	50.00	22.00	6.25
☐ 49 Michael Corcoran	50.00	22.00	6.25
☐ 50 Edward Doescher	50.00	22.00	6.25
☐ 51 Wheeler	50.00	22.00	6.25
☐ 52 Elijah Jones	50.00	22.00	6.25
☐ 53 Fred Truesdale	50.00	22.00	6.25
☐ 54 Fred Beebe	50.00	22.00	6.25
☐ 55 Louis Brockett	50.00	22.00	6.25
☐ 56 Wells	50.00	22.00	6.25
☐ 57 Lew McAllister	50.00	22.00	6.25
☐ 58 Ralph Stroud	50.00	22.00	6.25
☐ 59 Manser	50.00	22.00	6.25
☐ 60 Ducky Holmes	50.00	22.00	6.25
☐ 61 Rube Dessau	50.00	22.00	6.25
☐ 62 Fred Jacklitsch	50.00	22.00	6.25
☐ 63 Graham	50.00	22.00	6.25
☐ 64 Noah Henline	50.00	22.00	6.25
☐ 65 Chick Gandil	250.00	110.00	31.00
☐ 66 Tom Hughes	75.00	34.00	9.50
☐ 67 Joseph Delehanty	60.00	27.00	7.50
☐ 68 Pierce	50.00	22.00	6.25
☐ 69 Gaunt	50.00	22.00	6.25
☐ 70 Edward Fitzpatrick	50.00	22.00	6.25
☐ 71 Wyatt Lee	50.00	22.00	6.25
☐ 72 John Kissinger	50.00	22.00	6.25
☐ 73 William Malarkey	50.00	22.00	6.25
☐ 74 William Byers	50.00	22.00	6.25
☐ 75 George Simmons	50.00	22.00	6.25
☐ 76 Daniel Moeller	50.00	22.00	6.25
☐ 77 Joseph McGinnity	200.00	90.00	25.00
☐ 78 Alex Hardy	50.00	22.00	6.25
☐ 79 Bob Holmes	50.00	22.00	6.25
☐ 80 William Baxter	50.00	22.00	6.25
☐ 81 Edward Spencer	50.00	22.00	6.25
☐ 82 Bradley Kocher	50.00	22.00	6.25
☐ 83 Robert Shaw	50.00	22.00	6.25
☐ 84 Joseph Yeager	50.00	22.00	6.25
☐ 85 Carlo	50.00	22.00	6.25
☐ 86 William Abstein	60.00	27.00	7.50
☐ 87 Tim Jordan	50.00	22.00	6.25
☐ 88 Dick Breen	50.00	22.00	6.25
☐ 89 Tom McCarty	50.00	22.00	6.25
☐ 90 Ed Curtis	50.00	22.00	6.25

1912 Home Run Kisses E136-1

The cards in this 90-card set measure 2" by 4". This is perhaps the most distinctive of all the baseball series issued by the Collins-McCarthy company because of the clever product name and the distinctive ornate frame surrounding the picture area of the card. The players are from six different Pacific Coast League teams in the set. The name "Home Run Kisses" and the player's name and team are printed within the picture area; the picture itself is sepia. Some cards are found with premium advertising on the reverse but the great majority have only a simple easel design on the back. They were issued in 1912. The cards have been alphabetized and numbered in the checklist below.

	EX-MT	VG-E	GOOD
COMPLETE SET (90)	10000.00	4500.00	1250.00
COMMON CARD (1-90)	125.00	55.00	15.50
☐ 1 Boles	125.00	55.00	15.50
☐ 2 Brooks	125.00	55.00	15.50
☐ 3 Check	125.00	55.00	15.50
☐ 4 Core	125.00	55.00	15.50
☐ 5 Daley	125.00	55.00	15.50
☐ 6 Dillon	125.00	55.00	15.50
☐ 7 Driscoll	175.00	80.00	22.00
☐ 8 Flater	125.00	55.00	15.50
☐ 9 Heitmuller	125.00	55.00	15.50
☐ 10 Leverenz	175.00	80.00	22.00
☐ 11 Lober	125.00	55.00	15.50
☐ 12 Metzler	175.00	80.00	22.00
☐ 13 Nagle	125.00	55.00	15.50
☐ 14 Page	125.00	55.00	15.50
☐ 15 Slagle	125.00	55.00	15.50
☐ 16 Smith	125.00	55.00	15.50
☐ 17 Tozer	125.00	55.00	15.50
☐ 18 Ables	125.00	55.00	15.50
☐ 19 Brooks	125.00	55.00	15.50
☐ 20 Coy	125.00	55.00	15.50
☐ 21 Gregory	125.00	55.00	15.50
☐ 22 Hoffman	125.00	55.00	15.50
☐ 23 Leard	125.00	55.00	15.50
☐ 24 Malarkey	125.00	55.00	15.50
☐ 25 Martinoni	125.00	55.00	15.50
☐ 26 Olmstead	125.00	55.00	15.50
☐ 27 Parkins	125.00	55.00	15.50
☐ 28 Patterson	125.00	55.00	15.50
☐ 29 Pernoll	125.00	55.00	15.50
☐ 30 Tiedman	125.00	55.00	15.50
☐ 31 Zacher	125.00	55.00	15.50
☐ 32 Dave Bancroft	300.00	135.00	38.00
☐ 33 Butler	125.00	55.00	15.50
☐ 34 Chadbourne	125.00	55.00	15.50
☐ 35 Doane	125.00	55.00	15.50
☐ 36 Fisher	125.00	55.00	15.50
☐ 37 Gregg	125.00	55.00	15.50
☐ 38 Harkness	125.00	55.00	15.50
☐ 39 Howley	125.00	55.00	15.50
☐ 40 Klawitter	125.00	55.00	15.50
☐ 41 Kreuger	125.00	55.00	15.50
☐ 42 Lindsay	125.00	55.00	15.50
☐ 43 McDowell	125.00	55.00	15.50
☐ 44 Rogers	125.00	55.00	15.50
☐ 45 Stone	125.00	55.00	15.50
☐ 46 Arrelanes	125.00	55.00	15.50
☐ 47 Gaddy	125.00	55.00	15.50
☐ 48 Hiester	125.00	55.00	15.50
☐ 49 Ireland	125.00	55.00	15.50
☐ 50 Kreitz	125.00	55.00	15.50
☐ 51 Lewis	125.00	55.00	15.50
☐ 52 O'Rourke	125.00	55.00	15.50
☐ 53 Price	125.00	55.00	15.50
☐ 54 Schwenk	125.00	55.00	15.50
☐ 55 Sheehan	125.00	55.00	15.50
☐ 56 Shinn	125.00	55.00	15.50
☐ 57 Swain	125.00	55.00	15.50
☐ 58 Van Buren	125.00	55.00	15.50
☐ 59 Williams	125.00	55.00	15.50
☐ 60 Altman	125.00	55.00	15.50
☐ 61 Auer	125.00	55.00	15.50
☐ 62 Berry	125.00	55.00	15.50
☐ 63 Corhan	125.00	55.00	15.50
☐ 64 Henley	125.00	55.00	15.50
☐ 65 Johnson	125.00	55.00	15.50
☐ 66 McArdle	125.00	55.00	15.50
☐ 67 McCorry	125.00	55.00	15.50
☐ 68 McIver	125.00	55.00	15.50
☐ 69 Miller	125.00	55.00	15.50
☐ 70 Mundorf	125.00	55.00	15.50
☐ 71 Noyes	125.00	55.00	15.50
☐ 72 Powell	125.00	55.00	15.50
☐ 73 Raferty	125.00	55.00	15.50
☐ 74 Schmidt	125.00	55.00	15.50
☐ 75 Taylor	125.00	55.00	15.50
☐ 76 Toner	125.00	55.00	15.50
☐ 77 Agnew	125.00	55.00	15.50
☐ 78 Bayless	125.00	55.00	15.50
☐ 79 Brashear	125.00	55.00	15.50
☐ 80 Brown	125.00	55.00	15.50
☐ 81 Burrell	125.00	55.00	15.50
☐ 82 Carlisle	175.00	80.00	22.00
☐ 83 Carson	125.00	55.00	15.50
☐ 84 Castleton	125.00	55.00	15.50
☐ 85 Hogan	125.00	55.00	15.50
☐ 86 Hosp	125.00	55.00	15.50
☐ 87 Kane	125.00	55.00	15.50
☐ 88 Litschi	125.00	55.00	15.50
☐ 89 Patterson	125.00	55.00	15.50
☐ 90 Raleigh	125.00	55.00	15.50

1920 Mrs. Sherlock's Pins PB5-1

This set of pins is subtitled "Mrs. Sherlocks Home Made Bread" at the top of each pin. Players pictured in the set are members of the Toledo Mud Hens. The pins measure approximately 7/8" in diameter and are done totally in black and white. Since the pins are unnumbered, they are listed below in alphabetical order.

	EX-MT	VG-E	GOOD
COMPLETE SET (19)	700.00	325.00	90.00
COMMON PIN (1-19)	40.00	18.00	5.00
☐ 1 Brady P	40.00	18.00	5.00
☐ 2 Roger Bresnahan MG	150.00	70.00	19.00
☐ 3 Dubuc P	40.00	18.00	5.00
☐ 4 Dyer 2B	40.00	18.00	5.00
☐ 5 Fox Utility	40.00	18.00	5.00
☐ 6 Hyatt 1B	40.00	18.00	5.00
☐ 7 Jones SS	40.00	18.00	5.00
☐ 8 J. Kelly CF	40.00	18.00	5.00
☐ 9 M. Kelly C	40.00	18.00	5.00
☐ 10 Kores 3B	40.00	18.00	5.00
☐ 11 McColl P	40.00	18.00	5.00
☐ 12 McNeill C	40.00	18.00	5.00
☐ 13 Middleton P	40.00	18.00	5.00
☐ 14 Murphy C	40.00	18.00	5.00
☐ 15 Nelson P	40.00	18.00	5.00
☐ 16 Stryker P	40.00	18.00	5.00
☐ 17 Thompson Utility	40.00	18.00	5.00
☐ 18 Wickland RF	40.00	18.00	5.00
☐ 19 Wilhoit LF	40.00	18.00	5.00

1922 Mrs. Sherlock's Pins PB5-2

This set of pins is subtitled "Eat Mrs. Sherlocks Bread" at the top of each pin. Players pictured in the set are members of the Toledo Mud Hens. The pins measure approximately 5/8" in diameter and are done totally in brownish sepia (or green) and white. The catalog are numbered.

	EX-MT	VG-E	GOOD
COMPLETE SET	1000.00	450.00	125.00
COMMON PIN (1-21)	50.00	22.00	6.25
☐ 1 Roger Bresnahan MG	150.00	70.00	19.00
☐ 2 Kocher	50.00	22.00	6.25
☐ 3 Hill	50.00	22.00	6.25
☐ 4 Huber	50.00	22.00	6.25
☐ 5 Doc Ayers	50.00	22.00	6.25
☐ 6 Parks	50.00	22.00	6.25
☐ 7 Giard	50.00	22.00	6.25
☐ 8 Grimes	50.00	22.00	6.25
☐ 9 McCullough	50.00	22.00	6.25
☐ 10 Shoup	50.00	22.00	6.25
☐ 11 Wickland	50.00	22.00	6.25
☐ 12 Baker	50.00	22.00	6.25
☐ 13 Schauffle	50.00	22.00	6.25
☐ 14 Wright	50.00	22.00	6.25
☐ 15 Lamar	50.00	22.00	6.25
☐ 16 Sallee	50.00	22.00	6.25
☐ 17 Luderus	50.00	22.00	6.25
☐ 18 Walgomat	50.00	22.00	6.25
☐ 19 Konetchy	50.00	22.00	6.25
☐ 20 O'Neill	50.00	22.00	6.25
☐ 21 Bedient	50.00	22.00	6.25

1922-23 Kolbs Mothers' Bread Pins PB4

These pins may have been issued over a two year period. The pins however are essentially indistinguishable as to which year they may have been produced. Pins measure approximately 7/8" in diameter. Players pictured in the set are from the Reading Baseball Club of the International League. The pins are styled in black and white with red trim.

	EX-MT	VG-E	GOOD
COMPLETE SET (32)	1250.00	550.00	160.00
COMMON PIN (1-32)	40.00	18.00	5.00
☐ 1 Spencer Abbott MG	40.00	18.00	5.00
☐ 2 Babington F	40.00	18.00	5.00
☐ 3 Barrett INF	40.00	18.00	5.00
☐ 4 R. Bates 1B	40.00	18.00	5.00
☐ 5 Chief Bender MG	150.00	70.00	19.00
☐ 6 M. Brown P	40.00	18.00	5.00
☐ 7 Carts P	40.00	18.00	5.00
☐ 8 Clarke C	40.00	18.00	5.00
☐ 9 T. Connelly F	40.00	18.00	5.00
☐ 10 Getz 2B	40.00	18.00	5.00
☐ 11 Gilhooley F	40.00	18.00	5.00
☐ 12 Gordonier P	40.00	18.00	5.00
☐ 13 Haines F	40.00	18.00	5.00
☐ 14 Karpp P	40.00	18.00	5.00
☐ 15 J. Kelley F	40.00	18.00	5.00
☐ 16 Kotch F	40.00	18.00	5.00
☐ 17 Lightner RF	40.00	18.00	5.00
☐ 18 Lynn C	40.00	18.00	5.00
☐ 19 Al Mamaux	40.00	18.00	5.00
☐ 20 Martin P	40.00	18.00	5.00
☐ 21 R. Miller 3B	40.00	18.00	5.00
☐ 22 Pahlman 1B	40.00	18.00	5.00
☐ 23 Sam Post	40.00	18.00	5.00
☐ 24 Al Schacht	75.00	34.00	9.50
☐ 25 Scott INF	40.00	18.00	5.00
☐ 26 Smallwood P	40.00	18.00	5.00
☐ 27 Swartz P	40.00	18.00	5.00
☐ 28 F. Thomas 3B	40.00	18.00	5.00
☐ 29 M. Thomas P	40.00	18.00	5.00
☐ 30 Tragesser C	40.00	18.00	5.00
☐ 31 Washburn 2B	40.00	18.00	5.00
☐ 32 Wolfe SS	40.00	18.00	5.00

1928 Exhibits PCL

Exhibit card collectors speculate that this 32-card set, produced in 1928, was distributed regionally, in California only, in conjunction with the Exhibit Company's regular series of major league players. The cards are blue in color (as are the major league cards) and contain pictures of ball players from the six California teams of the PCL. There are no cards known for Portland and Seattle (and given that 32 cards is the exact length of a one-half sheet printing, none can be expected to appear). The cards have plain backs and carry a divided legend (two lines on each side) on the front. Several names are misspelled, several more are wrongly assigned ("Carl" instead of "Walter" Berger), and the Hollywood team name should read "Sheiks". Several of the cards are oriented horizontally (HOR). Each card measures 3 3/8" by 5 3/8". The catalog designation for this set is W465.

	EX-MT	VG-E	GOOD
COMPLETE SET (32)	5000.00	2200.00	600.00
COMMON CARD (1-32)	150.00	70.00	19.00
☐ 1 Buzz Arlett	200.00	90.00	25.00
☐ 2 Earl Averill	300.00	135.00	38.00
☐ 3 Carl Berger Walter, sic	200.00	90.00	25.00
☐ 4 Ping Bodie	200.00	90.00	25.00
☐ 5 Carl Dittmar HOR	150.00	70.00	19.00
☐ 6 Jack Penton	150.00	70.00	19.00
☐ 7 Neal "Mickey" Finn Cornelius, sic	200.00	90.00	25.00
☐ 8 Tony Governor	150.00	70.00	19.00
☐ 9 Truck Hannah HOR	200.00	90.00	25.00
☐ 10 Mickey Heath HOR	150.00	70.00	19.00
☐ 11 Wally Hood	150.00	70.00	19.00
☐ 12 Fuzzy Hufft	150.00	70.00	19.00
☐ 13 Snead Jolly (Smead Jolley, sic)	200.00	90.00	25.00
☐ 14 Bobby "Ducky" Jones	150.00	70.00	19.00
☐ 15 Rudy Kallio	150.00	70.00	19.00
☐ 16 Johnny Kerr HOR	150.00	70.00	19.00
☐ 17 Harry Krause	150.00	70.00	19.00
☐ 18 Lynford H. Larry (sic, Lary)	200.00	90.00	25.00
☐ 19 Dudley Lee	150.00	70.00	19.00
☐ 20 Walter "Duster" Mails	200.00	90.00	25.00
☐ 21 Jimmy Reese	250.00	110.00	31.00
☐ 22 Dusty Rhodes	150.00	70.00	19.00
☐ 23 Hal Rhyne	150.00	70.00	19.00
☐ 24 Hank Severied Severeid, sic	150.00	70.00	19.00
☐ 25 Earl Sheely	200.00	90.00	25.00
☐ 26 Frank Shellenback	200.00	90.00	25.00
☐ 27 Gordon Slade	150.00	70.00	19.00
☐ 28 Hollis Thurston	200.00	90.00	25.00
☐ 29 Babe Twombly	150.00	70.00	19.00
☐ 30 Earl "Tex" Weathersby	150.00	70.00	19.00
☐ 31 Ray French	150.00	70.00	19.00
☐ 32 Ray Keating	150.00	70.00	19.00

1928-32 La Presse

These color retouched photos of Canadian ballplayers of the late '20s and early '30s were published in La Presse, a French-language newspaper of Montreal. The pictures measure approximately 10" by 16"; the player's name, followed by career highlights, appear within a rectangle below. The drawings are unnumbered and checklisted below in chronological order of publication.

	EX-MT	VG-E	GOOD
COMPLETE SET (28)	650.00	300.00	80.00
COMMON CARD (1-28)	25.00	11.00	3.10
☐ 1 Bob Shawkey (June 2, 1928)	50.00	22.00	6.25
☐ 2 Lachine Club (June 9, 1928)	25.00	11.00	3.10
☐ 3 Buckalew Dunagan Smith Radwan Fowler Gulley (June 16, 1928)	25.00	11.00	3.10
☐ 4 Seymour Bailey (June 23, 1928)	25.00	11.00	3.10
☐ 5 Wilson Fewster (June 30, 1928)	25.00	11.00	3.10
☐ 6 Tom Daly (July 14, 1928)	25.00	11.00	3.10
☐ 7 Red Holt (August 11, 1928)	25.00	11.00	3.10
☐ 8 Johnny Prud'homme (November 3, 1928)	25.00	11.00	3.10
☐ 9 Walter Gautreau (April 13, 1929)	25.00	11.00	3.10
☐ 10 Herb Thormahlen (April 27, 1929)	25.00	11.00	3.10
☐ 11 Elon Hogsett (July 13, 1929)	25.00	11.00	3.10
☐ 12 Del Bissonette (June 28, 1930)	25.00	11.00	3.10
☐ 13 Smith Thormalen Griffin Pomorski (May 31, 1930)	25.00	11.00	3.10
☐ 14 Head Jimmy Ripple Conley Celeran (June 7, 1930)	25.00	11.00	3.10
☐ 15 Joe Hauser (July 12, 1930)	50.00	22.00	6.25
☐ 16 Gowell Classet (September 13, 1930)	25.00	11.00	3.10
☐ 17 Jimmy Ripple (July 4, 1930)	25.00	11.00	3.10
☐ 18 Sol Mishkin (July 18, 1930)	25.00	11.00	3.10
☐ 19 Walter Brown (August 15, 1931)	25.00	11.00	3.10
☐ 20 Johnny Grabowski (May 28, 1932)	25.00	11.00	3.10
☐ 21 John Clancy (June 25, 1932)	25.00	11.00	3.10
☐ 22 Buck Walters (July 2, 1932)	50.00	22.00	6.25
☐ 23 Bill McAfee (July 9, 1932)	25.00	11.00	3.10
☐ 24 George Puccinelli (July 16, 1932)	25.00	11.00	3.10
☐ 25 Buck Crouse (August 6, 1932)	25.00	11.00	3.10
☐ 26 Olie Carnegie (August 13, 1932)	25.00	11.00	3.10
☐ 27 Leo Mangum (August 20, 1932)	25.00	11.00	3.10
☐ 28 Roy Parmalee (October 19, 1932)	25.00	11.00	3.10

1933 Mrs. Sherlock's Pins PB5-3

This set of pins is subtitled "Mrs. Sherlocks Home Made Bread" at the top of each pin. Players pictured in the set are members of the Toledo Mud Hens. The pins measure approximately 7/8" in diameter and are done in black and white with red subtitle at top. Since the pins are unnumbered, they are listed below in alphabetical order. In the set the position of each player is spelled out next to the player's last name at the bottom of the pin.

	EX-MT	VG-E	GOOD
COMPLETE SET (18)	600.00	275.00	75.00
COMMON PIN (1-18)	35.00	16.00	4.40
☐ 1 Bachman	35.00	16.00	4.40
☐ 2 Detore	35.00	16.00	4.40
☐ 3 Doljack	35.00	16.00	4.40
☐ 4 Galatzer	35.00	16.00	4.40
☐ 5 Henline	35.00	16.00	4.40
☐ 6 Lawson	35.00	16.00	4.40
☐ 7 Lee	35.00	16.00	4.40
☐ 8 Montague	35.00	16.00	4.40
☐ 9 O'Neill	35.00	16.00	4.40
☐ 10 Pearson	35.00	16.00	4.40
☐ 11 Reis	35.00	16.00	4.40
☐ 12 Scott	35.00	16.00	4.40
☐ 13 Sweeney	35.00	16.00	4.40
☐ 14 Twogood	35.00	16.00	4.40
☐ 15 Trosky	50.00	22.00	6.25
☐ 16 Turgeon	35.00	16.00	4.40
☐ 17 West	40.00	18.00	5.00
☐ 18 Winegarner	35.00	16.00	4.40

1940 Solons Hughes

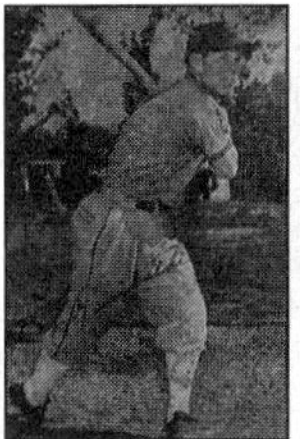
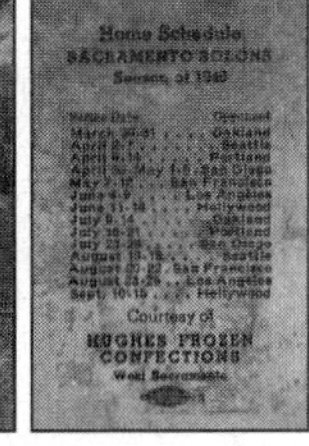

This unnumbered set features 20 members of the Sacramento Solons of the Pacific Coast League. The cards measure approximately 2" by 3" and are printed in black and white on rather thick card stock. Each card has a facsimile autograph on the front and a 1940 season home game schedule for the Sacramento Solons. The bottom of the reverse shows "Courtesy of Hughes Frozen Confections" and a tiny union label.

	EX-MT	VG-E	GOOD
COMPLETE SET (20)	1800.00	800.00	220.00
COMMON CARD (1-20)	100.00	45.00	12.50
☐ 1 Mel Almada	100.00	45.00	12.50
☐ 2 Frank Asbell	100.00	45.00	12.50
☐ 3 Larry Barton	100.00	45.00	12.50
☐ 4 Robert Blattner	100.00	45.00	12.50
☐ 5 Bennie Borgmann	100.00	45.00	12.50
☐ 6 Tony Freitas	100.00	45.00	12.50
☐ 7 Art Garibaldi	100.00	45.00	12.50
☐ 8 Jim Grilk	100.00	45.00	12.50
☐ 9 Gene Handley	100.00	45.00	12.50
☐ 10 Oscar Judd	100.00	45.00	12.50
☐ 11 Lynn King	100.00	45.00	12.50
☐ 12 Norbert Kleinke	100.00	45.00	12.50
☐ 13 Max Marshall	100.00	45.00	12.50
☐ 14 Wm. McLaughlin	100.00	45.00	12.50
☐ 15 Bruce Ogrodowski	100.00	45.00	12.50
☐ 16 Franich Riel	100.00	45.00	12.50
☐ 17 Bill Schmidt	100.00	45.00	12.50
☐ 18 Melvin Wasley	100.00	45.00	12.50
☐ 19 Chet Wieczorek	100.00	45.00	12.50
☐ 20 Deb Williams	100.00	45.00	12.50

1943 Centennial Flour

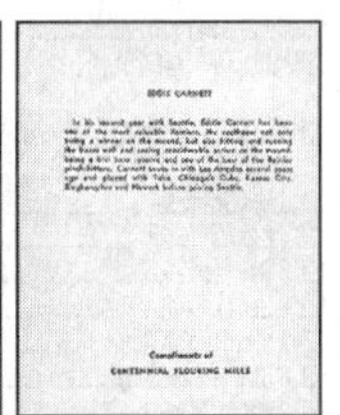

This set of 25 black and white cards features members of the Seattle Rainiers of the Pacific Coast League. The cards measure approximately 4" by 5" and contain a brief biographical sketch on the back. The cards are unnumbered and hence they are listed below alphabetically. This set can be distinguished from the other Centennial sets by looking at the obverse; Compliments of Centennial Flouring Mills is printed at the bottom.

	EX-MT	VG-E	GOOD
COMPLETE SET (25)	950.00	425.00	120.00
COMMON CARD (1-25)	50.00	22.00	6.25
☐ 1 John Babich	50.00	22.00	6.25
☐ 2 Nick Bonarigo	50.00	22.00	6.25
☐ 3 Eddie Carnett	50.00	22.00	6.25
☐ 4 Loyd Christopher	50.00	22.00	6.25
☐ 5 Joe Demoran	50.00	22.00	6.25
☐ 6 Joe Dobbins	50.00	22.00	6.25
☐ 7 Glenn Elliott	50.00	22.00	6.25
☐ 8 Carl Fischer	50.00	22.00	6.25
☐ 9 Leonard Gabrielson	50.00	22.00	6.25
☐ 10 Stanley Gray	50.00	22.00	6.25
☐ 11 Dick Gyselman	50.00	22.00	6.25
☐ 12 Jim Jewell	50.00	22.00	6.25
☐ 13 Sylvester Johnson	75.00	34.00	9.50
☐ 14 Pete Jonas	50.00	22.00	6.25
☐ 15 Bill Kats	50.00	22.00	6.25
☐ 16 Lynn King	50.00	22.00	6.25
☐ 17 Bill Lawrence	50.00	22.00	6.25
☐ 18 Clarence Marshall	50.00	22.00	6.25
☐ 19 Bill Matheson	50.00	22.00	6.25
☐ 20 Ford Mullen	50.00	22.00	6.25
☐ 21 Bill Skiff	50.00	22.00	6.25
☐ 22 Byron Speece	50.00	22.00	6.25
☐ 23 Hal Sueme	50.00	22.00	6.25
☐ 24 Hal Turpin	50.00	22.00	6.25
☐ 25 John Yelovic	50.00	22.00	6.25

1944 Centennial Flour

This set of 25 black and white cards features members of the Seattle Rainiers of the Pacific Coast League. The cards measure approximately 4" by 5" and contain a brief biographical sketch on the

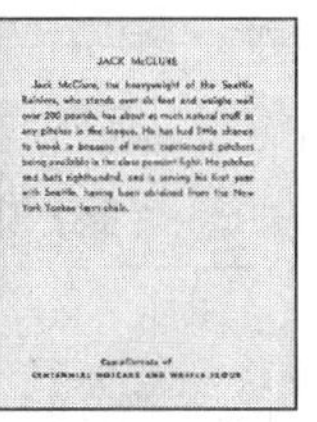

back. The cards are unnumbered and hence they are listed below alphabetically. This set can be distinguished from the other Centennial sets by looking at the obverse; Compliments of Centennial Hotcake and Waffle Flour is printed at the bottom.

	EX-MT	VG-E	GOOD
COMPLETE SET (25)	950.00	425.00	120.00
COMMON CARD (1-25)	50.00	22.00	6.25
☐ 1 John Babich	50.00	22.00	6.25
☐ 2 Paul Carpenter	50.00	22.00	6.25
☐ 3 Loyd Christopher	50.00	22.00	6.25
☐ 4 Joe Demoran	50.00	22.00	6.25
☐ 5 Joe Dobbins	50.00	22.00	6.25
☐ 6 Glenn Elliott	50.00	22.00	6.25
☐ 7 Carl Fischer	50.00	22.00	6.25
☐ 8 Bob Garbould	50.00	22.00	6.25
☐ 9 Stanley Gray	50.00	22.00	6.25
☐ 10 Dick Gyselman	50.00	22.00	6.25
☐ 11 Gene Holt	50.00	22.00	6.25
☐ 12 Roy Johnson	50.00	22.00	6.25
☐ 13 Sylvester Johnson	75.00	34.00	9.50
☐ 14 Al Libke	50.00	22.00	6.25
☐ 15 Billy Lyman	50.00	22.00	6.25
☐ 16 Bill Matheson	50.00	22.00	6.25
☐ 17 Jack McClure	50.00	22.00	6.25
☐ 18 Jimmy Ripple	75.00	34.00	9.50
☐ 19 Sicks Stadium	50.00	22.00	6.25
☐ 20 Bill Skiff MG	50.00	22.00	6.25
☐ 21 Byron Speece	50.00	22.00	6.25
☐ 22 Hal Sueme	50.00	22.00	6.25
☐ 23 Frank Tincup	50.00	22.00	6.25
☐ 24 Jack Treece	50.00	22.00	6.25
☐ 25 Hal Turpin	50.00	22.00	6.25

1945 Centennial Flour

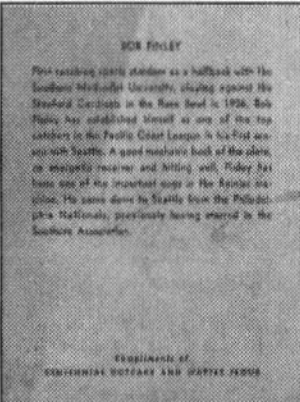

This set of 27 black and white cards features members of the Seattle Rainiers of the Pacific Coast League. The cards measure approximately 3 7/8" by 5 1/16" and contain a brief biographical sketch on the back. The picture of the player on the front is borderless and contains the player's name and team in a black strip at the bottom. The cards are unnumbered and hence they are listed below alphabetically.

	EX-MT	VG-E	GOOD
COMPLETE SET (27)	900.00	400.00	110.00
COMMON CARD (1-27)	40.00	18.00	5.00
☐ 1 Charley Aleno	40.00	18.00	5.00
☐ 2 Dick Briskey	40.00	18.00	5.00
☐ 3 John Carpenter	40.00	18.00	5.00
☐ 4 Joe Demoran	40.00	18.00	5.00
☐ 5 Joe Dobbins	40.00	18.00	5.00
☐ 6 Glenn Elliott	40.00	18.00	5.00
☐ 7 Bob Finley	40.00	18.00	5.00
☐ 8 Carl Fischer	40.00	18.00	5.00
☐ 9 Keith Frazier	40.00	18.00	5.00
☐ 10 Johnny Gill	40.00	18.00	5.00
☐ 11 Bob Gorbould	40.00	18.00	5.00
☐ 12 Chet Johnson	40.00	18.00	5.00
☐ 13 Sylvester Johnson	60.00	27.00	7.50
☐ 14 Bill Kats	40.00	18.00	5.00
☐ 15 Billy Lyman	40.00	18.00	5.00
☐ 16 Bill Matheson	40.00	18.00	5.00
☐ 17 George McDonald	40.00	18.00	5.00
☐ 18 Ted Norbert	40.00	18.00	5.00
☐ 19 Alex Palica	40.00	18.00	5.00
☐ 20 Joe Passero	40.00	18.00	5.00
☐ 21 Hal Patchett	40.00	18.00	5.00
☐ 22 Bill Skiff MG	40.00	18.00	5.00
☐ 23 Byron Speece	40.00	18.00	5.00
☐ 24 Hal Sueme	40.00	18.00	5.00
☐ 25 Eddie Taylor	40.00	18.00	5.00
☐ 26 Hal Turpin	40.00	18.00	5.00
☐ 27 Jack Whipple	40.00	18.00	5.00

1946 Remar Bread

The 1946 Remar Bread set of 23 black and white cards was issued one player per week in stores carrying Remar Bread. The cards are

easily identified by the "red loaf" of Remar bread on the back. The first cards issued were not numbered, but the rest were, beginning with No. 5. Raimondi was the first card issued and is scarce. The set depicts Oakland Oaks players only. Even though we have numbered the last five cards, they are actually unnumbered. The catalog designation is D317-1. Cards in this set measure approximately 2" by 3".

	EX-MT	VG-E	GOOD
COMPLETE SET (23)	400.00	180.00	50.00
COMMON CARD (5-27)	15.00	6.75	1.85
☐ 5 Herschel Martin	15.00	6.75	1.85
☐ 6 Bill Hart	15.00	6.75	1.85
☐ 7 Chuck Gassaway	15.00	6.75	1.85
☐ 8 Wally Westlake	20.00	9.00	2.50
☐ 9 Ora Burnett	15.00	6.75	1.85
☐ 10 Casey Stengel MG	100.00	45.00	12.50
☐ 11 Charles Metro	20.00	9.00	2.50
☐ 12 Tom Hafey	15.00	6.75	1.85
☐ 13 Tony Sabol	15.00	6.75	1.85
☐ 14 Ed Kearse	20.00	9.00	2.50
☐ 15 Bud Foster ANN	15.00	6.75	1.85
☐ 16 Johnny Price	15.00	6.75	1.85
☐ 17 Gene Bearden	20.00	9.00	2.50
☐ 18 Floyd Speer	15.00	6.75	1.85
☐ 19 Bryan Stephens	15.00	6.75	1.85
☐ 20 Rinaldo Ardizola	15.00	6.75	1.85
☐ 21 Ralph Buxton	15.00	6.75	1.85
☐ 22 Ambrose Palica	15.00	6.75	1.85
☐ 23 Brooks Holder	20.00	9.00	2.50
☐ 24 Henry Pippen	20.00	9.00	2.50
☐ 25 Bill Raimondi	60.00	27.00	7.50
☐ 26 Les Scarsella	20.00	9.00	2.50
☐ 27 Glen Stewart	20.00	9.00	2.50

1946 Sunbeam Bread

The 1946 Sunbeam Bread set of 21 black and white, unnumbered cards features the Sacramento Solons only. There is a reference to the "1946 Solons" on the fronts of the cards and small yellow and red bread loafs on the backs of the cards. The backs are in blue print and give a brief biography and a Sunbeam Bread ad. The catalog designation is D315-1. Cards in this set measure approximately 2" by 3".

	EX-MT	VG-E	GOOD
COMPLETE SET (21)	800.00	350.00	100.00
COMMON CARD (1-21)	35.00	16.00	4.40
☐ 1 Bud Beasley	35.00	16.00	4.40
☐ 2 Jack Calvey	35.00	16.00	4.40
☐ 3 Gene Corbett	35.00	16.00	4.40
☐ 4 Bill Conroy	35.00	16.00	4.40
☐ 5 Guy Fletcher	35.00	16.00	4.40
☐ 6 Tony Freitas	35.00	16.00	4.40
☐ 7 Ted Greenhalgh	35.00	16.00	4.40
☐ 8 Al Jarlett	35.00	16.00	4.40
☐ 9 Landrum	35.00	16.00	4.40
☐ 10 Gene Lillard	40.00	18.00	5.00
☐ 11 Garth Mann	35.00	16.00	4.40
☐ 12 Lilo Marcucci	40.00	18.00	5.00
☐ 13 Joe Marty	200.00	90.00	25.00
☐ 14 Steve Mesner	35.00	16.00	4.40
☐ 15 Herm Pillette	35.00	16.00	4.40
☐ 16 Earl Sheely	35.00	16.00	4.40
☐ 17 Al Smith	40.00	18.00	5.00
☐ 18 Gerald Staley	50.00	22.00	6.25
☐ 19 Averett Thompson	35.00	16.00	4.40
☐ 20 Jo Jo White	40.00	18.00	5.00
☐ 21 Bud Zipay	35.00	16.00	4.40

1947 Centennial Flour

This set of 32 black and white cards features members of the Seattle Rainiers of the Pacific Coast League. The cards measure approximately 3 7/8" by 5 1/8" and contain a brief biographical sketch on the back. The picture of the player on the front is borderless and contains the player's name and team in a black strip at the bottom.

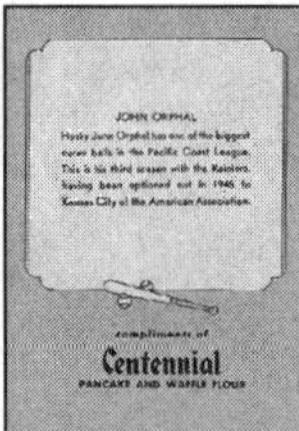

The cards are unnumbered and hence they are listed below alphabetically. This set can be distinguished from the other Centennial sets by looking at the obverse; Compliments of Centennial Pancake and Waffle Flour is printed at the bottom.

	EX-MT	VG-E	GOOD
COMPLETE SET (32)	750.00	350.00	95.00
COMMON CARD (1-32)	25.00	11.00	3.10
☐ 1 Dick Barrett	35.00	16.00	4.40
☐ 2 Joe Buzas	25.00	11.00	3.10
☐ 3 Paul Carpenter	25.00	11.00	3.10
☐ 4 Rex Cecil	25.00	11.00	3.10
☐ 5 Tony Criscola	25.00	11.00	3.10
☐ 6 Walter Dubiel	25.00	11.00	3.10
☐ 7 Doug Ford	25.00	11.00	3.10
☐ 8 Rollie Hemsley	35.00	16.00	4.40
☐ 9 Jim Hill	25.00	11.00	3.10
☐ 10 Jim Hopper	25.00	11.00	3.10
☐ 11 Sigmund Jakucki	35.00	16.00	4.40
☐ 12 Bob Johnson	35.00	16.00	4.40
☐ 13 Pete Jonas	25.00	11.00	3.10
☐ 14 Joe Kaney	25.00	11.00	3.10
☐ 15 Hillis Layne	25.00	11.00	3.10
☐ 16 Lou Novikoff	35.00	16.00	4.40
☐ 17 Johnny O'Neil	25.00	11.00	3.10
☐ 18 John Orphal	25.00	11.00	3.10
☐ 19 Ike Pearson	25.00	11.00	3.10
☐ 20 Bill Posedel	35.00	16.00	4.40
☐ 21 Don Pulford	25.00	11.00	3.10
☐ 22 Tom Reis	25.00	11.00	3.10
☐ 23 Charley Ripple	25.00	11.00	3.10
☐ 24 Mickey Rocco	25.00	11.00	3.10
☐ 25 Johnny Rucker	25.00	11.00	3.10
☐ 26 Earl Sheely	25.00	11.00	3.10
☐ 27 Bob Stagg	25.00	11.00	3.10
☐ 28 Hal Sueme	25.00	11.00	3.10
☐ 29 Eddie Taylor	25.00	11.00	3.10
☐ 30 Edo Vanni	25.00	11.00	3.10
☐ 31 Jo Jo White	35.00	16.00	4.40
☐ 32 Tony York	25.00	11.00	3.10

1947 Remar Bread

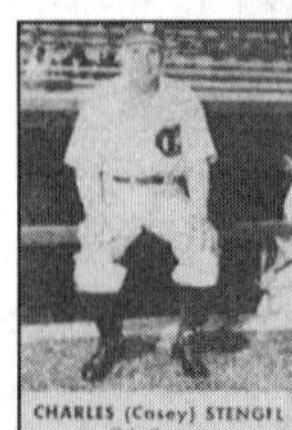

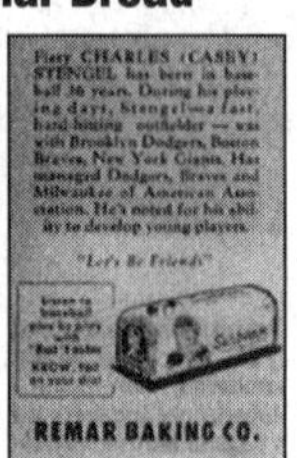

The 1947 Remar Bread set of 25 black and white, numbered cards features Oakland Oaks players only. Many cards are identical to the 1946 issue on the front except for the numbering. These cards are listed with an asterisk in the checklist. The backs are distinguishable from the 1946 issue by a "blue loaf" of Remar Bread. The backs are printed in blue and include player biographies and an ad for the Oakland Oaks radio station. The cards are on very thin stock. The catalog designation is D317-2. Cards in this set measure approximately 2" by 3".

	EX-MT	VG-E	GOOD
COMPLETE SET	300.00	135.00	38.00
COMMON CARD (1-25)	10.00	4.50	1.25
☐ 1 Bill Raimondi	10.00	4.50	1.25
☐ 2 Les Scarsella	10.00	4.50	1.25
☐ 3 Brooks Holder	10.00	4.50	1.25
☐ 4 Chuck Gassaway	10.00	4.50	1.25
☐ 5 Ora Burnett	10.00	4.50	1.25
☐ 6 Ralph Buxton	10.00	4.50	1.25
☐ 7 Ed Kearse	10.00	4.50	1.25
☐ 8 Casey Stengel MG	100.00	45.00	12.50
☐ 9 Bud Foster ANN	10.00	4.50	1.25
☐ 10 Ambrose Palica	10.00	4.50	1.25
☐ 11 Tom Hafey	10.00	4.50	1.25
☐ 12 Herschel Martin	10.00	4.50	1.25
☐ 13 Henry Pippen	10.00	4.50	1.25
☐ 14 Floyd Speer	10.00	4.50	1.25
☐ 15 Tony Sabol	10.00	4.50	1.25
☐ 16 Will Hafey	10.00	4.50	1.25
☐ 17 Ray Hamrick	10.00	4.50	1.25
☐ 18 Maurice Van Robays	10.00	4.50	1.25
☐ 19 Dario Lodigiani	10.00	4.50	1.25
☐ 20 Mel Duezabou	10.00	4.50	1.25
☐ 21 Damon Hayes	10.00	4.50	1.25
☐ 22 Gene Lillard	10.00	4.50	1.25
☐ 23 Al Wilkie	10.00	4.50	1.25
☐ 24 Tony Soriano	10.00	4.50	1.25
☐ 25 Glenn Crawford	10.00	4.50	1.25

1947 Signal Oil

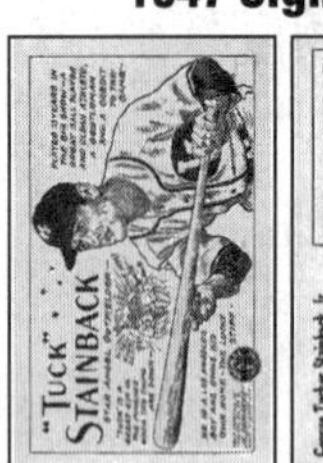

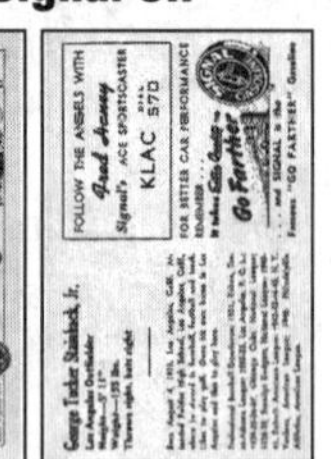

The 1947 Signal Oil set of 89 black and white, unnumbered drawings, by Al DeMaree, features Pacific Coast League players from five teams -- Hollywood Stars (1-20), Los Angeles Angels (21-38), Oakland Oaks (39-57), Sacramento Solons (58-73) and Seattle Rainiers (74-89). Numbers are assigned alphabetically within teams. The Sacramento player cards and to a greater extent the Seattle player cards are more difficult to obtain. The highlights of the careers of the players appear on the backgrounds of the cards as cartoons. Four players appear with two teams -- Frank Dasso, Guy Fletcher, Red Mann and Bill Ramsey. Woody Williams is considered quite scarce and Charles Ripple is somewhat less scarce. The catalog designation is U011. Cards in this set measure approximately 5 1/2" by 3 1/2".

	EX-MT	VG-E	GOOD
COMPLETE SET (89)	5000.00	2200.00	600.00
COMMON CARD (1-38)	30.00	13.50	3.70
COMMON CARD (39-57)	20.00	9.00	2.50
COMMON CARD (58-73)	50.00	22.00	6.25
COMMON CARD (74-89)	100.00	45.00	12.50
☐ 1 Ed Albosta	30.00	13.50	3.70
☐ 2 Carl Cox	30.00	13.50	3.70
☐ 3 Frank Dasso	30.00	13.50	3.70
☐ 4 Tod Davis	30.00	13.50	3.70
☐ 5 Jimmy Delsing	35.00	16.00	4.40
☐ 6 Jimmy Dykes MG	50.00	22.00	6.25
☐ 7 Paul Gregory	30.00	13.50	3.70
☐ 8 Fred Haney GM	35.00	16.00	4.40
☐ 9 Francis Kelleher	30.00	13.50	3.70
☐ 10 Joe Krakauskas	30.00	13.50	3.70
☐ 11 Al Libke	30.00	13.50	3.70
☐ 12 Tony Lupien	35.00	16.00	4.40
☐ 13 Xavier Rescigno	30.00	13.50	3.70
☐ 14 Jack Sherman	30.00	13.50	3.70
☐ 15 Andy Skurski	30.00	13.50	3.70
☐ 16 Glen Stewart	30.00	13.50	3.70
☐ 17 Al Unser	35.00	16.00	4.40
☐ 18 Fred Vaughn	30.00	13.50	3.70
☐ 19 Woody Williams	800.00	350.00	100.00
☐ 20 Dutch Zernial	50.00	22.00	6.25
☐ 21 Red Adams	30.00	13.50	3.70
☐ 22 Larry Barton	30.00	13.50	3.70
☐ 23 Cliff Chambers	35.00	16.00	4.40
☐ 24 Loyd Christopher	30.00	13.50	3.70
☐ 25 Cece Garriott	30.00	13.50	3.70
☐ 26 Al Glossops	30.00	13.50	3.70
☐ 27 Bill Kelly	30.00	13.50	3.70
☐ 28 Red Lynn	30.00	13.50	3.70
☐ 29 Eddie Malone	30.00	13.50	3.70
☐ 30 Dutch McCall	30.00	13.50	3.70
☐ 31 Don Osborn	30.00	13.50	3.70
☐ 32 John Ostrowski	30.00	13.50	3.70
☐ 33 Reggie Otero	30.00	13.50	3.70
☐ 34 Ray Prim	30.00	13.50	3.70
☐ 35 Ed Sauer	30.00	13.50	3.70
☐ 36 Bill Schuster	30.00	13.50	3.70
☐ 37 Tuck Stainback	35.00	16.00	4.40
☐ 38 Lou Stringer	30.00	13.50	3.70
☐ 39 Vic Buccola	20.00	9.00	2.50
☐ 40 Mickey Burnett	20.00	9.00	2.50
☐ 41 Ralph Buxton	20.00	9.00	2.50
☐ 42 Vince DiMaggio	100.00	45.00	12.50
☐ 43 Dizz Duezabou	20.00	9.00	2.50
☐ 44 Bud Foster ANN	20.00	9.00	2.50
☐ 45 Sherriff Gassaway	20.00	9.00	2.50
☐ 46 Tom Hafey	20.00	9.00	2.50
☐ 47 Brooks Holder	20.00	9.00	2.50
☐ 48 Gene Lillard	20.00	9.00	2.50
☐ 49 Dario Lodigiani	20.00	9.00	2.50
☐ 50 Hershel Martin	20.00	9.00	2.50
☐ 51 Cotton Pippen	20.00	9.00	2.50
☐ 52 Bill Raimondi	20.00	9.00	2.50
☐ 53 Tony Sabol	20.00	9.00	2.50
☐ 54 Les Scarsella	20.00	9.00	2.50
☐ 55 Floyd Speer	20.00	9.00	2.50
☐ 56 Casey Stengel MG	200.00	90.00	25.00
☐ 57 Maurice Van Robays	30.00	13.50	3.70
☐ 58 Bud Beasley	50.00	22.00	6.25
☐ 59 Frank Dasso	50.00	22.00	6.25
☐ 60 Ed Fitzgerald	50.00	22.00	6.25
☐ 61 Guy Fletcher	50.00	22.00	6.25
☐ 62 Tony Freitas	50.00	22.00	6.25
☐ 63 Red Mann	50.00	22.00	6.25
☐ 64 Joe Marty	50.00	22.00	6.25
☐ 65 Steve Mesner	50.00	22.00	6.25
☐ 66 Bill Ramsey	50.00	22.00	6.25
☐ 67 Chas. Ripple	350.00	160.00	45.00
☐ 68 John Rizzo	50.00	22.00	6.25
☐ 69 Al Smith	60.00	27.00	7.50
☐ 70 Ronnie Smith	50.00	22.00	6.25
☐ 71 Tommy Thompson	50.00	22.00	6.25
☐ 72 Jim Warner	60.00	27.00	7.50
☐ 73 Ed Zipay	50.00	22.00	6.25
☐ 74 Kewpie Barrett	125.00	55.00	15.50
☐ 75 Herman Besse	100.00	45.00	12.50
☐ 76 Guy Fletcher	100.00	45.00	12.50
☐ 77 Jack Jakucki	125.00	55.00	15.50
☐ 78 Bob Johnson	125.00	55.00	15.50
☐ 79 Pete Jonas	100.00	45.00	12.50
☐ 80 Hillis Layne	100.00	45.00	12.50
☐ 81 Red Mann	100.00	45.00	12.50
☐ 82 Lou Novikoff	125.00	55.00	15.50
☐ 83 John O'Neill	100.00	45.00	12.50
☐ 84 Bill Ramsey	100.00	45.00	12.50
☐ 85 Mickey Rocco	100.00	45.00	12.50
☐ 86 Geo. Scharein	100.00	45.00	12.50
☐ 87 Hal Sueme	100.00	45.00	12.50
☐ 88 Jo Jo White	125.00	55.00	15.50
☐ 89 Tony York	100.00	45.00	12.50

1947 Smith's Clothing

The 1947 Smith's Clothing set of 25 black and white, numbered cards features players from the Oakland Oaks only and is similar to the Remar Bread set. The backs give brief player biographies and a Smith's ad. The set is on very thin stock paper. The Max Marshall card is quite scarce, while the Gillespie, Hayes and Faria cards are tougher to find. The catalog designation is H801-3A. Cards in this set measure approximately 2" by 3".

	EX-MT	VG-E	GOOD
COMPLETE SET (25)	800.00	350.00	100.00
COMMON CARD (1-25)	25.00	11.00	3.10
☐ 1 Casey Stengel MG	150.00	70.00	19.00
☐ 2 Billy Raimondi	25.00	11.00	3.10
☐ 3 Les Scarsella	25.00	11.00	3.10
☐ 4 Brooks Holder	25.00	11.00	3.10
☐ 5 Ray Hamrick	25.00	11.00	3.10
☐ 6 Gene Lillard	25.00	11.00	3.10
☐ 7 Maurice Van Robays	25.00	11.00	3.10
☐ 8 Charlie Gassaway	25.00	11.00	3.10
☐ 9 Henry Pippen	25.00	11.00	3.10
☐ 10 James Arnold	25.00	11.00	3.10
☐ 11 Ralph Buxton	25.00	11.00	3.10
☐ 12 Ambrose Palica	25.00	11.00	3.10
☐ 13 Tony Sabol	25.00	11.00	3.10
☐ 14 Ed Kearse	25.00	11.00	3.10
☐ 15 Bill Hart	25.00	11.00	3.10
☐ 16 Snuffy Smith	25.00	11.00	3.10
☐ 17 Mickey Burnett	25.00	11.00	3.10
☐ 18 Tom Hafey	25.00	11.00	3.10
☐ 19 Will Hafey	25.00	11.00	3.10
☐ 20 Paul Gillespie	50.00	22.00	6.25
☐ 21 Damon Hayes	50.00	22.00	6.25
☐ 22 Max Marshall	125.00	55.00	15.50
☐ 23 Mel Duezabou	25.00	11.00	3.10
☐ 24 Mel Reeves	25.00	11.00	3.10
☐ 25 Joe Faria	50.00	22.00	6.25

1947 Sunbeam Bread

The 1947 Sunbeam Bread set of 26 black and white, unnumbered cards features the Sacramento Solons only. This set is distinguishable from the 1946 set by a reference to the "1947 Solons" on the fronts of the cards and a colored Sunbeam Bread loaf filling the entire back of the card. This issue is printed on very thin paper stock. The catalog designation is D315-2. Cards in this set measure approximately 2" by 3".

	EX-MT	VG-E	GOOD
COMPLETE SET (26)	800.00	350.00	100.00
COMMON CARD (1-26)	30.00	13.50	3.70
☐ 1 Gene Babbit	30.00	13.50	3.70
☐ 2 Bob Barthelson	30.00	13.50	3.70
☐ 3 Bud Beasley	30.00	13.50	3.70
☐ 4 Chuck Cronin	30.00	13.50	3.70
☐ 5 Eddie Fernandes	30.00	13.50	3.70
☐ 6 Ed Fitzgerald	30.00	13.50	3.70
☐ 7 Van Fletcher	30.00	13.50	3.70
☐ 8 Tony Freitas	30.00	13.50	3.70
☐ 9 Garth Mann	30.00	13.50	3.70
☐ 10 Joe Marty	75.00	34.00	9.50
☐ 11 Lou McCollum	30.00	13.50	3.70
☐ 12 Steve Mesner	30.00	13.50	3.70
☐ 13 Frank Nelson	30.00	13.50	3.70
☐ 14 Tommy Nelson	30.00	13.50	3.70
☐ 15 Joe Orengo	30.00	13.50	3.70
☐ 16 Hugh Orhan	30.00	13.50	3.70
☐ 17 Nick Pesut	30.00	13.50	3.70
☐ 18 Bill Ramsey	30.00	13.50	3.70
☐ 19 Johnny Rizzo	40.00	18.00	5.00
☐ 20 Mike Schemer	30.00	13.50	3.70
☐ 21 Al Smith	50.00	22.00	6.25
☐ 22 Tommy Thompson	30.00	13.50	3.70
☐ 23 Jim Warner	50.00	22.00	6.25
☐ 24 Mel Wasley	50.00	22.00	6.25
☐ 25 Leo Wells	30.00	13.50	3.70
☐ 26 Eddie Zipay	30.00	13.50	3.70

1948 Signal Oil

This set of 24 color photos of Oakland Oaks (Pacific Coast League) was given away at local gas stations. The cards are not numbered and are found with either blue or black printing on the back. Nicholas Etten and Brooks Holder are considered to be harder to find than the other cards in this set; they are notated with SP below. The catalog designation is U010. The cards are listed below in alphabetical order. The cards in this set measure approximately 2 3/8" by 3 1/2".

	NRMT	VG-E	GOOD
COMPLETE SET (24)	700.00	325.00	90.00
COMMON CARD (1-24)	20.00	9.00	2.50
☐ 1 John Babich	20.00	9.00	2.50
☐ 2 Ralph Buxton	20.00	9.00	2.50
☐ 3 Loyd Christopher	20.00	9.00	2.50
☐ 4 Merrill Combs	20.00	9.00	2.50
☐ 5 Melvin Duezabou	20.00	9.00	2.50
☐ 6 Nicholas Etten SP	35.00	16.00	4.40
☐ 7 Bud Foster ANN	20.00	9.00	2.50
☐ 8 Charles Gassaway	20.00	9.00	2.50
☐ 9 Will Hafey	20.00	9.00	2.50
☐ 10 Ray Hamrick	20.00	9.00	2.50
☐ 11 Brooks Holder SP	50.00	22.00	6.25
☐ 12 Earl Jones	20.00	9.00	2.50
☐ 13 Cookie Lavagetto	30.00	13.50	3.70
☐ 14 Robert Lillard	20.00	9.00	2.50
☐ 15 Dario Lodigiani	20.00	9.00	2.50
☐ 16 Ernie Lombardi	75.00	34.00	9.50
☐ 17 Alfred Martin	100.00	45.00	12.50
☐ 18 George Metkovich	25.00	11.00	3.10
☐ 19 William Raimondi	20.00	9.00	2.50
☐ 20 Les Scarsella	20.00	9.00	2.50
☐ 21 Floyd Speer	20.00	9.00	2.50
☐ 22 Casey Stengel MG	125.00	55.00	15.50
☐ 23 Maurice Van Robays	20.00	9.00	2.50
☐ 24 Aldon Wilkie	20.00	9.00	2.50

1948 Smith's Clothing

The 1948 Smith's Clothing set of 25 black and white numbered cards features Oakland Oaks players only and is printed on a much heavier stock than the 1947 Smith's set. The cards have a glossy finish. All cards feature full body shots showing players in either fielding, batting or pitching positions. The catalog designation is H801-3B. Cards in this set measure approximately 2" by 3".

	NRMT	VG-E	GOOD
COMPLETE SET (25)	650.00	300.00	80.00
COMMON CARD (1-25)	20.00	9.00	2.50
☐ 1 Billy Raimondi	20.00	9.00	2.50
☐ 2 Brooks Holder	20.00	9.00	2.50
☐ 3 Will Hafey	30.00	13.50	3.70
☐ 4 Nick Etten	30.00	13.50	3.70
☐ 5 Loyd Christopher	20.00	9.00	2.50
☐ 6 Les Scarsella	20.00	9.00	2.50
☐ 7 Ray Hamrick	20.00	9.00	2.50
☐ 8 Gene Lillard	20.00	9.00	2.50
☐ 9 Maurice Van Robays	20.00	9.00	2.50
☐ 10 Charlie Gassaway	20.00	9.00	2.50
☐ 11 Ralph Buxton	20.00	9.00	2.50
☐ 12 Tom Hafey	20.00	9.00	2.50
☐ 13 Damon Hayes	20.00	9.00	2.50

	NRMT	VG-E	GOOD
☐ 14 Mel "Dizz" Duezabou	20.00	9.00	2.50
☐ 15 Dario Lodigiani	20.00	9.00	2.50
☐ 16 Vic Buccola	20.00	9.00	2.50
☐ 17 Billy Martin	100.00	45.00	12.50
☐ 18 Floyd Speer	20.00	9.00	2.50
☐ 19 Eddie Samcoff	20.00	9.00	2.50
☐ 20 Casey Stengel MG	125.00	55.00	15.50
☐ 21 Floyd Hittle	20.00	9.00	2.50
☐ 22 John Babich	20.00	9.00	2.50
☐ 23 Merrill Combs	20.00	9.00	2.50
☐ 24 Eddie Murphy	30.00	13.50	3.70
☐ 25 Bob Klinger	30.00	13.50	3.70

1948 Sommer and Kaufman

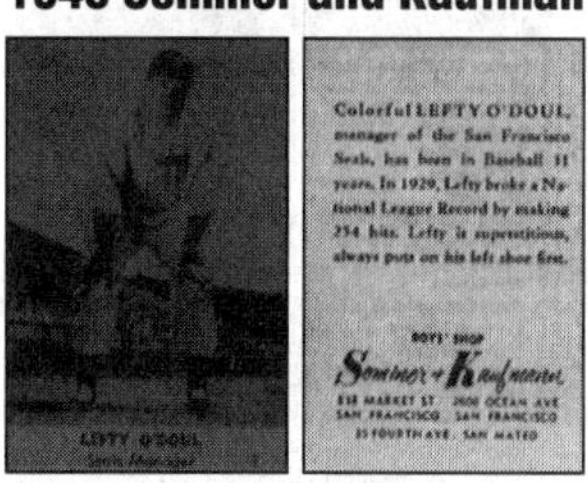

The 1948 Sommer and Kaufman set of 30 numbered, black and white cards features players from the San Francisco Seals of the Pacific Coast League. The catalog designation is H801-4A. The backs give brief player biographies and a Sommer and Kaufman ad. The 1948 set can be distinguished from the 1949 set by the script writing of "Sommer and Kaufman". The 1949 set has "Sommer and Kaufman" in fancy print. Cards in this set measure approximately 2" by 3".

	NRMT	VG-E	GOOD
COMPLETE SET (30)	1400.00	650.00	180.00
COMMON CARD (1-30)	40.00	18.00	5.00
☐ 1 Lefty O'Doul	60.00	27.00	7.50
☐ 2 Jack Brewer	40.00	18.00	5.00
☐ 3 Cornelius Dempsey	50.00	22.00	6.25
☐ 4 Tommy Fine	40.00	18.00	5.00
☐ 5 Kenneth Gables	40.00	18.00	5.00
☐ 6 Robert Joyce	40.00	18.00	5.00
☐ 7 Alfred Lien	40.00	18.00	5.00
☐ 8 Cliff Melton	50.00	22.00	6.25
☐ 9 Frank S. Shofner	40.00	18.00	5.00
☐ 10 Don Trower	40.00	18.00	5.00
☐ 11 Joe Brovia	40.00	18.00	5.00
☐ 12 Dino Paul Restelli	50.00	22.00	6.25
☐ 13 Gene Woodling	60.00	27.00	7.50
☐ 14 Benjamin Guintini	40.00	18.00	5.00
☐ 15 Felix Mackiewicz	40.00	18.00	5.00
☐ 16 John Patrick Tobin	40.00	18.00	5.00
☐ 17 Manuel Perez Jr.	40.00	18.00	5.00
☐ 18 William Werle	40.00	18.00	5.00
☐ 19 Homer E. Howell Jr.	40.00	18.00	5.00
☐ 20 Wilfred Leonard	40.00	18.00	5.00
☐ 21 Bruce Ogrodowski	40.00	18.00	5.00
☐ 22 R. Dick Lajeskie	40.00	18.00	5.00
☐ 23 Hugh Luby	40.00	18.00	5.00
☐ 24 Roy Melvin Nicely	40.00	18.00	5.00
☐ 25 Raymond Orteig	40.00	18.00	5.00
☐ 26 Michael D. Rocco	40.00	18.00	5.00
☐ 27 Del Edward Young	40.00	18.00	5.00
☐ 28 Joe Sprinz	40.00	18.00	5.00
☐ 29 Leo Doc Hughes	40.00	18.00	5.00
☐ 30 Don Rode Albert Bero Charlie Barnes Bat Boys	40.00	18.00	5.00

1949 Bowman PCL

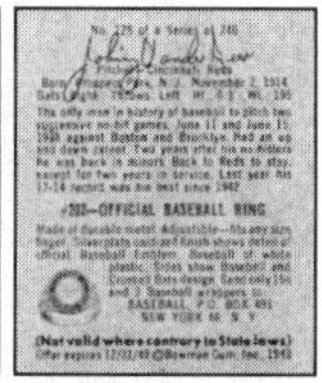

The 1949 Bowman Pacific Coast League set is recognized as one of the scarcest sets of the post-war period. Each card measures 2 1/16" by 2 1/2". Marketed regionally on the West Coast, it is thought that it may have been sold in sheets in candy and variety stores rather than in gum packs. The format of tinted photographs on colored backgrounds is identical to the regular 1949 Bowman issue.

	NRMT	VG-E	GOOD
COMPLETE SET (36)	7000.00	3200.00	900.00
COMMON CARD (1-36)	200.00	90.00	25.00
☐ 1 Lee Anthony	200.00	90.00	25.00
☐ 2 George Metkovich	200.00	90.00	25.00
☐ 3 Ralph Hodgin	200.00	90.00	25.00
☐ 4 George Woods	200.00	90.00	25.00
☐ 5 Xavier Rescigno	200.00	90.00	25.00
☐ 6 Mickey Grasso	200.00	90.00	25.00
☐ 7 Johnny Rucker	200.00	90.00	25.00
☐ 8 Jack Brewer	200.00	90.00	25.00
☐ 9 Dom D'Allessandro	200.00	90.00	25.00
☐ 10 Charlie Gassaway	200.00	90.00	25.00
☐ 11 Tony Freitas	200.00	90.00	25.00
☐ 12 Gordon Maltzberger	200.00	90.00	25.00
☐ 13 John Jensen	200.00	90.00	25.00
☐ 14 Joyner White	200.00	90.00	25.00
☐ 15 Harvey Storey	200.00	90.00	25.00
☐ 16 Dick Lajeski	200.00	90.00	25.00
☐ 17 Albie Glossup	200.00	90.00	25.00
☐ 18 Bill Raimondi	200.00	90.00	25.00
☐ 19 Ken Holcombe	200.00	90.00	25.00
☐ 20 Don Ross	200.00	90.00	25.00
☐ 21 Pete Coscarart	200.00	90.00	25.00
☐ 22 Tony York	200.00	90.00	25.00
☐ 23 Jake Mooty	200.00	90.00	25.00
☐ 24 Charles Adams	200.00	90.00	25.00
☐ 25 Les Scarsella	200.00	90.00	25.00
☐ 26 Joe Marty	200.00	90.00	25.00
☐ 27 Frank Kelleher	200.00	90.00	25.00
☐ 28 Lee Handley	200.00	90.00	25.00
☐ 29 Herman Besse	200.00	90.00	25.00
☐ 30 John Lazor	200.00	90.00	25.00
☐ 31 Eddie Malone	200.00	90.00	25.00
☐ 32 Maurice Van Robays	200.00	90.00	25.00
☐ 33 Jim Tabor	200.00	90.00	25.00
☐ 34 Gene Handley	200.00	90.00	25.00
☐ 35 Tom Seats	200.00	90.00	25.00
☐ 36 Ora Burnett	200.00	90.00	25.00

1949 Remar Bread

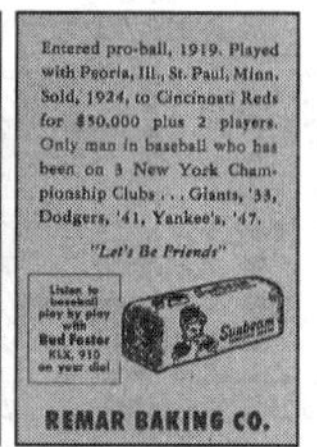

The 1949 Remar Bread set of 32 black and white picture cards depicts Oakland Oaks players only. The backs, in blue print on white stock, give vital statistics, 1948 records and show a Sunbeam bread loaf. Some cards were printed in limited quantities (marked with an asterisk) and the players have been placed in alphabetical order and numbered in the checklist, although the cards themselves are not numbered. The catalog designation is D317-4. Cards in this set measure approximately 2" by 3".

	NRMT	VG-E	GOOD
COMPLETE SET (32)	450.00	200.00	55.00
COMMON CARD (1-32)	8.00	3.60	1.00
☐ 1 Ralph Buxton	8.00	3.60	1.00
☐ 2 Mario Candini	25.00	11.00	3.10
☐ 3 Rex Cecil	25.00	11.00	3.10
☐ 4 Loyd Christopher	8.00	3.60	1.00
☐ 5 Mel Duezabou	8.00	3.60	1.00
☐ 6 Chuck Dressen MG	25.00	11.00	3.10
☐ 7 Bud Foster ANN	8.00	3.60	1.00
☐ 8 Clarence Gassaway	8.00	3.60	1.00
☐ 9 Ray Hamrick	8.00	3.60	1.00
☐ 10 Jackie Jensen	40.00	18.00	5.00
☐ 11 Earl Jones	8.00	3.60	1.00
☐ 12 George Kelly	25.00	11.00	3.10
☐ 13 Frank Kerr	25.00	11.00	3.10
☐ 14 Dick Kryhoski	25.00	11.00	3.10
☐ 15 Cookie Lavagetto	30.00	13.50	3.70
☐ 16 Dario Lodigiani	8.00	3.60	1.00
☐ 17 Billy Martin	75.00	34.00	9.50
☐ 18 George Metkovich	8.00	3.60	1.00
☐ 19 Frank Nelson	8.00	3.60	1.00
☐ 20 Don Padgett	8.00	3.60	1.00
☐ 21 Alonzo Perry	25.00	11.00	3.10
☐ 22 Bill Raimondi	8.00	3.60	1.00
☐ 23 Earl Rapp	8.00	3.60	1.00
☐ 24 Ed Samcoff	8.00	3.60	1.00
☐ 25 Les Scarsella	8.00	3.60	1.00
☐ 26 Forest Thompson	25.00	11.00	3.10
☐ 27 Earl Toolson	25.00	11.00	3.10
☐ 28 Louis Tost	25.00	11.00	3.10
☐ 29 Maurice Van Robays	10.00	4.50	1.25
☐ 30 Jim Wallace	8.00	3.60	1.00
☐ 31 Artie Wilson	10.00	4.50	1.25
☐ 32 Parnell Woods	30.00	13.50	3.70

1949 Solon Sunbeam/Pureta PC759

This set was co-issued by Sunbeam Bread and Pureta Sausage and features Sacramento Solons. The fronts feature the player and an microphone insert with station call letters printed on it. The backs feature ads for both Sunbeam Bread and Pureta Sausage.

	NRMT	VG-E	GOOD
COMPLETE SET (12)	550.00	250.00	70.00
COMMON CARD (1-12)	50.00	22.00	6.25
☐ 1 Del Baker	50.00	22.00	6.25
☐ 2 Frankie Dasso	50.00	22.00	6.25
☐ 3 Walt Dropo	75.00	34.00	9.50
☐ 4 Joe Grace	50.00	22.00	6.25
☐ 5 Bob Gillespie	50.00	22.00	6.25
☐ 6 Ralph Hodgin	50.00	22.00	6.25
☐ 7 Freddie Marsh	50.00	22.00	6.25
☐ 8 Joe Marty	50.00	22.00	6.25
☐ 9 Len Ratto	50.00	22.00	6.25
☐ 10 Jim Tabor	50.00	22.00	6.25
☐ 11 Al White	50.00	22.00	6.25
☐ 12 Bill Wilson	50.00	22.00	6.25

1949 Sommer and Kaufman

The 1949 Sommer and Kaufman set of 28 numbered, black and white cards features players of the San Francisco Seals of the Pacific Coast League. Card No. 24 is not known to exist. The catalog designation is H801-4B. Cards in this set measure approximately 2" by 3".

	NRMT	VG-E	GOOD
COMPLETE SET (28)	1200.00	550.00	150.00
COMMON CARD (1-29)	40.00	18.00	5.00
☐ 1 Lefty O'Doul	60.00	27.00	7.50
☐ 2 Jack Brewer	40.00	18.00	5.00
☐ 3 Kenneth H. Gables	40.00	18.00	5.00
☐ 4 Con Dempsey	50.00	22.00	6.25
☐ 5 Alfred Lien	40.00	18.00	5.00
☐ 6 Cliff Melton	50.00	22.00	6.25
☐ 7 Steve Nagy	40.00	18.00	5.00
☐ 8 Manny Perez	40.00	18.00	5.00
☐ 9 Roy Jarvis	40.00	18.00	5.00
☐ 10 Roy Partee	40.00	18.00	5.00
☐ 11 Reno Cheso	40.00	18.00	5.00
☐ 12 Dick Lajeskie	40.00	18.00	5.00
☐ 13 Roy M. Nicely	40.00	18.00	5.00
☐ 14 Mickey Rocco	40.00	18.00	5.00
☐ 15 Frank Shofner	40.00	18.00	5.00
☐ 16 Richard Holder	40.00	18.00	5.00
☐ 17 Dino Restelli	50.00	22.00	6.25
☐ 18 Arky Vaughan	60.00	27.00	7.50
☐ 19 Jackie Baccioccu	40.00	18.00	5.00
☐ 20 Robert F. Drilling	40.00	18.00	5.00
☐ 21 Del E. Young	40.00	18.00	5.00
☐ 22 Joseph D. Sprinz	40.00	18.00	5.00
☐ 23 Leo E.Doc Hughes	40.00	18.00	5.00
☐ 25 Bert Singleton	40.00	18.00	5.00
☐ 26 John Gene Brocker	40.00	18.00	5.00
☐ 27 Jack Tobin	40.00	18.00	5.00
☐ 28 Walter Judnich	50.00	22.00	6.25
☐ 29 Harry (Hal) Foldman	40.00	18.00	5.00

1950 Remar Bread

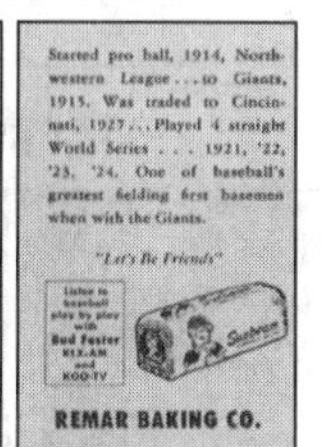

The 1950 Remar Bread set of 27 black and white, unnumbered cards features Oakland Oaks players only. The format is identical to the 1949 set except that the backs include 1949 records. The catalog designation is D317-5. The cards are listed below in alphabetical order. Cards in this set measure approximately 2" by 3".

	NRMT	VG-E	GOOD
COMPLETE SET (27)	250.00	110.00	31.00
COMMON CARD (1-27)	7.50	3.40	.95
☐ 1 George Bamberger	20.00	9.00	2.50
☐ 2 Hank Behrman	7.50	3.40	.95
☐ 3 Loyd Christopher	7.50	3.40	.95
☐ 4 Chuck Dressen	15.00	6.75	1.85
☐ 5 Mel Duezabou	7.50	3.40	.95
☐ 6 Augie Galan	10.00	4.50	1.25
☐ 7 Clarence Gassaway	7.50	3.40	.95
☐ 8 Allen Gettel	7.50	3.40	.95
☐ 9 Ernie Groth	10.00	4.50	1.25
☐ 10 Ray Hamrick	7.50	3.40	.95
☐ 11 Earl Harrist	7.50	3.40	.95
☐ 12 Billy Herman	30.00	13.50	3.70
☐ 13 Bob Hofman	7.50	3.40	.95
☐ 14 George Kelly	30.00	13.50	3.70
☐ 15 Cookie Lavagetto	15.00	6.75	1.85
☐ 16 Eddie Malone	7.50	3.40	.95
☐ 17 George Metkovich	7.50	3.40	.95
☐ 18 Frank Nelson	7.50	3.40	.95
☐ 19 Ray Noble	7.50	3.40	.95
☐ 20 Don Padgett	7.50	3.40	.95
☐ 21 Earl Rapp	7.50	3.40	.95
☐ 22 Clyde Shoun	7.50	3.40	.95
☐ 23 Forest Thompson	7.50	3.40	.95
☐ 24 Louis Tost	7.50	3.40	.95
☐ 25 Dick Wakefield	15.00	6.75	1.85
☐ 26 Artie Wilson	10.00	4.50	1.25
☐ 27 Roy Zimmerman	7.50	3.40	.95

1952 La Patrie

These posed color photos of Canadian baseball players of 1952 comprised an "Album Sportif" in La Patrie, a French-language Montreal newspaper. They are bordered in red, white and blue and measure approximately 11" by 15 1/4". The player's name appears at the upper right. The photos are unnumbered and checklisted below in alphabetical order.

	NRMT	VG-E	GOOD
COMPLETE SET (17)	175.00	80.00	22.00
COMMON CARD (1-17)	10.00	4.50	1.25
☐ 1 Bob Alexander	10.00	4.50	1.25
☐ 2 Georges Carpentier	10.00	4.50	1.25
☐ 3 Hampton Coleman	10.00	4.50	1.25
☐ 4 Walter Fiala	10.00	4.50	1.25
☐ 5 Jim Gilliam UER (Gilliams printed on front)	40.00	18.00	5.00
☐ 6 Tom Hackett	10.00	4.50	1.25
☐ 7 Don Hoak	20.00	9.00	2.50
☐ 8 Herbie Lash	10.00	4.50	1.25
☐ 9 Mal Mallatte	10.00	4.50	1.25
☐ 10 Georges Maranda	10.00	4.50	1.25
☐ 11 Carmen Mauro	10.00	4.50	1.25
☐ 12 Solly Mohn	10.00	4.50	1.25
☐ 13 Jacques Monette	10.00	4.50	1.25
☐ 14 Ed Roebuck	15.00	6.75	1.85
☐ 15 Charlie Thompson	10.00	4.50	1.25
☐ 16 Don Thompson	10.00	4.50	1.25
☐ 17 John Wingo	10.00	4.50	1.25

1952 Laval Provinciale

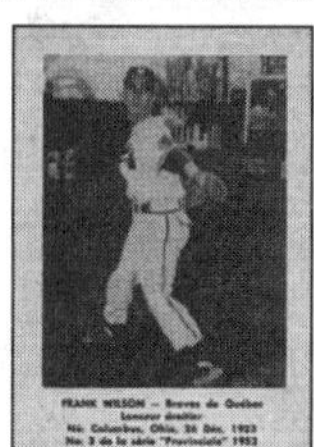

Issued by Laval Dairies of Quebec, these 114 blank-backed cards measure approximately 1 1/4" by 2 1/2" and feature white-bordered black-and-white posed player photos. The player's name, team, position, birthplace and birthdate appear in the white margin below the photo. All text is in French. The cards are numbered on the front.

	NRMT	VG-E	GOOD
COMPLETE SET (114)	1000.00	450.00	125.00
COMMON CARD (1-114)	10.00	4.50	1.25
☐ 1 Georges McQuinn	20.00	9.00	2.50
☐ 2 Cliff Statham	10.00	4.50	1.25
☐ 3 Frank Wilson	10.00	4.50	1.25
☐ 4 Frank Neri	10.00	4.50	1.25
☐ 5 Georges Maranda	15.00	6.75	1.85
☐ 6 Richard Cordeiro	10.00	4.50	1.25
☐ 7 Roger McCardell	10.00	4.50	1.25
☐ 8 Joseph Janiak	10.00	4.50	1.25
☐ 9 Herbert Shankman	10.00	4.50	1.25
☐ 10 Joe Subbiondo	10.00	4.50	1.25
☐ 11 Jack Brenner	10.00	4.50	1.25
☐ 12 Donald Buchanan	10.00	4.50	1.25
☐ 13 Bob Smith	15.00	6.75	1.85
☐ 14 Raymond Lague	10.00	4.50	1.25
☐ 15 Mike Fandozzi	10.00	4.50	1.25
☐ 16 Dick Moler	10.00	4.50	1.25
☐ 17 Edward Bazydlo	10.00	4.50	1.25
☐ 18 Danny Mazurek	10.00	4.50	1.25
☐ 19 Edwin Charles	15.00	6.75	1.85
☐ 20 Jack Mullaney	10.00	4.50	1.25
☐ 21 Bob Bolan	10.00	4.50	1.25
☐ 22 Bob Long	10.00	4.50	1.25

☐ 23 Cleo Lewright	10.00	4.50	1.25
☐ 24 Herb Taylor	10.00	4.50	1.25
☐ 25 Frank Gaeta	10.00	4.50	1.25
☐ 26 Bill Truitt	10.00	4.50	1.25
☐ 27 Jean Prats	10.00	4.50	1.25
☐ 28 Tex Taylor	10.00	4.50	1.25
☐ 29 Ronnie Delbianco	10.00	4.50	1.25
☐ 30 Joe Dilorenzo	10.00	4.50	1.25
☐ 31 John Paszek	10.00	4.50	1.25
☐ 32 Ken Suess	10.00	4.50	1.25
☐ 33 Harry Sims	10.00	4.50	1.25
☐ 34 William Jackson	10.00	4.50	1.25
☐ 35 Jerry Mayers	10.00	4.50	1.25
☐ 36 Gordon Maltzberger	15.00	6.75	1.85
☐ 37 Gerry Cabana	10.00	4.50	1.25
☐ 38 Gary Rutkay	10.00	4.50	1.25
☐ 39 Ken Hatcher	10.00	4.50	1.25
☐ 40 Vincent Cosenza	10.00	4.50	1.25
☐ 41 Edward Yaeger	10.00	4.50	1.25
☐ 42 Jimmy Orr	10.00	4.50	1.25
☐ 43 John Dimartino	10.00	4.50	1.25
☐ 44 Len Wisnaski	10.00	4.50	1.25
☐ 45 Pete Caniglia	10.00	4.50	1.25
☐ 46 Guy Coleman	10.00	4.50	1.25
☐ 47 Herb Fleischer	10.00	4.50	1.25
☐ 48 Charles Yahrling	10.00	4.50	1.25
☐ 49 Roger Bedard	10.00	4.50	1.25
☐ 50 Al Barillari	10.00	4.50	1.25
☐ 51 Hugh Mulcahy	15.00	6.75	1.85
☐ 52 Vincent Canepa	10.00	4.50	1.25
☐ 53 Bob Loranger	10.00	4.50	1.25
☐ 54 Georges Carpentier	10.00	4.50	1.25
☐ 55 Bill Hamilton	10.00	4.50	1.25
☐ 56 Hector Lopez	25.00	11.00	3.10
☐ 57 Joe Taylor	10.00	4.50	1.25
☐ 58 Alonso Brathwaite	10.00	4.50	1.25
☐ 59 Carl McQuillen	10.00	4.50	1.25
☐ 60 Robert Trice	15.00	6.75	1.85
☐ 61 John Dworak	10.00	4.50	1.25
☐ 62 Lal Pinkston	10.00	4.50	1.25
☐ 63 William Shannon	10.00	4.50	1.25
☐ 64 Stanley Watychowics	10.00	4.50	1.25
☐ 65 Roger Hebert	10.00	4.50	1.25
☐ 66 Troy Spencer	10.00	4.50	1.25
☐ 67 Johnny Rahan	10.00	4.50	1.25
☐ 68 John Sosh	10.00	4.50	1.25
☐ 69 Raymond Mason	10.00	4.50	1.25
☐ 70 Tom Smith	10.00	4.50	1.25
☐ 71 Douglas McBean	10.00	4.50	1.25
☐ 72 Bill Babik	10.00	4.50	1.25
☐ 73 Dante Cozzi	10.00	4.50	1.25
☐ 74 Melvil Doxtator	10.00	4.50	1.25
☐ 75 William(Bill) Gilday	10.00	4.50	1.25
☐ 76 Armando Diaz	10.00	4.50	1.25
☐ 77 Ackroyd Smith	10.00	4.50	1.25
☐ 78 Germain Pizarro	10.00	4.50	1.25
☐ 79 James Heap	10.00	4.50	1.25
☐ 80 Herbert B. Crompton	10.00	4.50	1.25
☐ 81 Howard J. Bodell	10.00	4.50	1.25
☐ 82 Andre Schreiser	10.00	4.50	1.25
☐ 83 John Wingo	10.00	4.50	1.25
☐ 84 Salvatore Arduini	10.00	4.50	1.25
☐ 85 Fred Paccito	10.00	4.50	1.25
☐ 86 Aaron Osofsky	10.00	4.50	1.25
☐ 87 Jack Digrace	10.00	4.50	1.25
☐ 88 Alfonzo Gerard	10.00	4.50	1.25
☐ 89 Manuel Trabous	10.00	4.50	1.25
☐ 90 Tom Barnes	10.00	4.50	1.25
☐ 91 Humberto Robinson	15.00	6.75	1.85
☐ 92 Jack Buxowatz	10.00	4.50	1.25
☐ 93 Marco Mainini	10.00	4.50	1.25
☐ 94 Claude St-Vincent	10.00	4.50	1.25
☐ 95 Fernand Brousseau	10.00	4.50	1.25
☐ 96 John Malangone	10.00	4.50	1.25
☐ 97 Pierre Nantel	10.00	4.50	1.25
☐ 98 Donald Stevens	10.00	4.50	1.25
☐ 99 Jim Prappas	10.00	4.50	1.25
☐ 100 Richard Fitzgerald	10.00	4.50	1.25
☐ 101 Yves Aubin	10.00	4.50	1.25
☐ 102 Frank Novosel	10.00	4.50	1.25
☐ 103 Tony Campos	10.00	4.50	1.25
☐ 104 Gelso Oviedo	10.00	4.50	1.25
☐ 105 July Becker	10.00	4.50	1.25
☐ 106 Aurelio Ala	10.00	4.50	1.25
☐ 107 Orlando Andux	10.00	4.50	1.25
☐ 108 Tom Hackett	10.00	4.50	1.25
☐ 109 Guillaume Vargas	10.00	4.50	1.25
☐ 110 Francisco Salfran	10.00	4.50	1.25
☐ 111 Jean-Marc Blais	10.00	4.50	1.25
☐ 112 Vince Pizzitola	10.00	4.50	1.25
☐ 113 John Olsen	10.00	4.50	1.25
☐ 114 Jacques Monette	10.00	4.50	1.25

1952 Mothers Cookies

The cards in this 64-card set measure 2 3/16" by 3 1/2". The 1952 Mother's Cookies set contains numbered, full-color cards. They feature PCL players only and were distributed on the West Coast in bags of Mothers Cookies. Reported scarcities are 29 Peterson, 43 Erautt, 37 Welmaker, 11 MacCawley and 16 Talbot. Chuck Connors (4), the "Rifleman," is not scarce but is widely sought after. The catalog designation is D357-1. Johnny Lindell (#1) and Fred Haney (#13) are also known to exist with schedule backs. These backs are very scarce and are worth approximately 10 times the value of the regular cards.

	NRMT	VG-E	GOOD
COMPLETE SET (64)	2000.00	900.00	250.00
COMMON CARD (1-64)	25.00	11.00	3.10
☐ 1 Johnny Lindell	30.00	13.50	3.70
☐ 2 Jim Davis	25.00	11.00	3.10
☐ 3 Al Gettel	25.00	11.00	3.10
☐ 4 Chuck Connors	250.00	110.00	31.00
☐ 5 Joe Grace	25.00	11.00	3.10
☐ 6 Eddie Basinski	25.00	11.00	3.10
☐ 7 Gene Handley	25.00	11.00	3.10
☐ 8 Walt Judnich	25.00	11.00	3.10
☐ 9 Jim Marshall	25.00	11.00	3.10
☐ 10 Max West	25.00	11.00	3.10
☐ 11 Bill MacCawley SP	60.00	27.00	7.50
☐ 12 Moreno Pieretti	25.00	11.00	3.10
☐ 13 Fred Haney MG	30.00	13.50	3.70
☐ 14 Earl Johnson	25.00	11.00	3.10
☐ 15 Dave Dahle	25.00	11.00	3.10
☐ 16 Bob Talbot SP	60.00	27.00	7.50
☐ 17 Smokey Singleton	25.00	11.00	3.10
☐ 18 Frank Austin	25.00	11.00	3.10
☐ 19 Joe Gordon MG	40.00	18.00	5.00
☐ 20 Joe Marty	25.00	11.00	3.10
☐ 21 Bob Gillespie	25.00	11.00	3.10
☐ 22 Red Embree	25.00	11.00	3.10
☐ 23 Lefty Olsen	25.00	11.00	3.10
☐ 24 Whitey Wietelmann	25.00	11.00	3.10
☐ 25 Lefty O'Doul MG	40.00	18.00	5.00
☐ 26 Memo Luna	25.00	11.00	3.10
☐ 27 John Davis	25.00	11.00	3.10
☐ 28 Dick Faber	25.00	11.00	3.10
☐ 29 Buddy Peterson SP	150.00	70.00	19.00
☐ 30 Hank Schenz	25.00	11.00	3.10
☐ 31 Tookie Gilbert	25.00	11.00	3.10
☐ 32 Mel Ott MG	100.00	45.00	12.50
☐ 33 Sam Chapman	30.00	13.50	3.70
☐ 34 John Ragni	25.00	11.00	3.10
☐ 35 Dick Cole	25.00	11.00	3.10
☐ 36 Tom Saffel	25.00	11.00	3.10
☐ 37 Roy Welmaker SP	100.00	45.00	12.50
☐ 38 Lou Stringer	25.00	11.00	3.10
☐ 39 Chuck Stevens	25.00	11.00	3.10
☐ 40 Artie Wilson	25.00	11.00	3.10
☐ 41 Charlie Schanz	25.00	11.00	3.10
☐ 42 Al Lyons	25.00	11.00	3.10
☐ 43 Joe Erautt SP	150.00	70.00	19.00
☐ 44 Clarence Maddern	25.00	11.00	3.10
☐ 45 Gene Baker	30.00	13.50	3.70
☐ 46 Tom Heath	25.00	11.00	3.10
☐ 47 Al Lien	25.00	11.00	3.10
☐ 48 Bill Reeder	25.00	11.00	3.10
☐ 49 Bob Thurman	30.00	13.50	3.70
☐ 50 Ray Orteig	25.00	11.00	3.10
☐ 51 Joe Brovia	25.00	11.00	3.10
☐ 52 Jim Russell	25.00	11.00	3.10
☐ 53 Fred Sanford	25.00	11.00	3.10
☐ 54 Jim Gladd	25.00	11.00	3.10
☐ 55 Clay Hopper MG	25.00	11.00	3.10
☐ 56 Bill Glynn	25.00	11.00	3.10
☐ 57 Mike McCormick	25.00	11.00	3.10
☐ 58 Richie Myers	25.00	11.00	3.10
☐ 59 Vinnie Smith	25.00	11.00	3.10
☐ 60 Stan Hack MG	30.00	13.50	3.70
☐ 61 Bob Spicer	25.00	11.00	3.10
☐ 62 Jack Hollis	25.00	11.00	3.10
☐ 63 Ed Chandler	25.00	11.00	3.10
☐ 64 Bill Moisan	25.00	11.00	3.10

1952 Parkhurst

The 100 cards comprising the 1952 Parkhurst/Frostade set measure approximately 2" by 2 1/2" and depict players from three Canadian International League teams: Montreal Royals (49-76), Ottawa Athletics (77-100) and Toronto Maple Leafs (1-26). The fronts feature white-bordered black-and-white player photos. The plain backs have red print and carry the player's name, team, position and biography at the top; an ad for Frostade follows below. The set also includes a number of playing tip and play diagram cards (27-48). The catalog designation for this set is V338-1. Cards oriented horizontally are indicated below by HOR.

	NRMT	VG-E	GOOD
COMPLETE SET (100)	1650.00	750.00	210.00
COMMON CARD (1-25)	15.00	6.75	1.85
COMMON CARD (26-48)	10.00	4.50	1.25
COMMON CARD (49-100)	15.00	6.75	1.85
☐ 1 Joe Becker MG	20.00	9.00	2.50
☐ 2 Bobby Rhawn HOR	15.00	6.75	1.85
☐ 3 Aaron Silverman	15.00	6.75	1.85
☐ 4 Russ Bauers HOR	15.00	6.75	1.85
☐ 5 William Jennings HOR	15.00	6.75	1.85
☐ 6 Grover Bowers	15.00	6.75	1.85
☐ 7 Vic Lombardi	20.00	9.00	2.50
☐ 8 Billy DeMars	20.00	9.00	2.50
☐ 9 Frank Colman	15.00	6.75	1.85
☐ 10 Charles Grant	15.00	6.75	1.85
☐ 11 Irving Medlinger	15.00	6.75	1.85
☐ 12 Burke McLaughlin	15.00	6.75	1.85
☐ 13 Lew Morton	15.00	6.75	1.85
☐ 14 Red Barrett	20.00	9.00	2.50
☐ 15 Leon Foulk	15.00	6.75	1.85
☐ 16 Neil Sheridan	15.00	6.75	1.85
☐ 17 Ferrell(Andy) Anderson	15.00	6.75	1.85
☐ 18 Ray Shore	15.00	6.75	1.85
☐ 19 Duke Markell	15.00	6.75	1.85
☐ 20 Robert Balcena	15.00	6.75	1.85
☐ 21 Wilmer Fields	15.00	6.75	1.85
☐ 22 Charles White HOR	15.00	6.75	1.85
☐ 23 Gerald Fahr	15.00	6.75	1.85
☐ 24 Jose Bracho HOR	15.00	6.75	1.85
☐ 25 Edward Stevens HOR	20.00	9.00	2.50
☐ 26 Maple Leaf Stadium HOR	20.00	9.00	2.50
☐ 27 Throwing Home HOR	10.00	4.50	1.25
☐ 28 Regulation Baseball Diamond HOR	10.00	4.50	1.25
☐ 29 Gripping The Bat	10.00	4.50	1.25
☐ 30 Hiding Kind of Pitch	10.00	4.50	1.25
☐ 31 Catcher's Stance	10.00	4.50	1.25
☐ 32 Quiz Question How long does a batter have to see, swing at, and hit a fast ball	10.00	4.50	1.25
☐ 33 Finger and Arm Exercises HOR	10.00	4.50	1.25
☐ 34 First Baseman	10.00	4.50	1.25
☐ 35 Pitcher's Stance	10.00	4.50	1.25
☐ 36 Swinging Bats	10.00	4.50	1.25
☐ 37 Quiz Question HOR Can a player advance a base when a foul is caught	10.00	4.50	1.25
☐ 38 Watch the Ball HOR	10.00	4.50	1.25
☐ 39 Quiz Question HOR Can a team ever win a game with less runs than their opponents	10.00	4.50	1.25
☐ 40 Quiz Question Can a player put his own teammate out	10.00	4.50	1.25
☐ 41 How to Bunt	10.00	4.50	1.25
☐ 42 Wrist Snap	10.00	4.50	1.25
☐ 43 Pitching Practice	10.00	4.50	1.25
☐ 44 Stealing Bases	10.00	4.50	1.25
☐ 45 Pitching I	10.00	4.50	1.25
☐ 46 Pitching II	10.00	4.50	1.25
☐ 47 Signals	10.00	4.50	1.25
☐ 48 Regulation Baseballs	10.00	4.50	1.25
☐ 49 Albert Ronning	15.00	6.75	1.85
☐ 50 William C. Lane	15.00	6.75	1.85
☐ 51 William Samson	15.00	6.75	1.85
☐ 52 Charles Thompson	15.00	6.75	1.85
☐ 53 Ezra McGlothin	15.00	6.75	1.85
☐ 54 Forrest Jacobs	20.00	9.00	2.50
☐ 55 Arthur Fabbro	15.00	6.75	1.85
☐ 56 James Hughes	20.00	9.00	2.50
☐ 57 Don Hoak	25.00	11.00	3.10
☐ 58 Tommy Lasorda	200.00	90.00	25.00
☐ 59 Gilbert Mills	15.00	6.75	1.85
☐ 60 Malcolm Mallette	15.00	6.75	1.85
☐ 61 Glenn Nelson	20.00	9.00	2.50
☐ 62 John Simmons	15.00	6.75	1.85
☐ 63 R.S. Alex Alexander	15.00	6.75	1.85
☐ 64 Dan Bankhead	20.00	9.00	2.50
☐ 65 Solomon Coleman	15.00	6.75	1.85
☐ 66 Walter Alston MG	100.00	45.00	12.50
☐ 67 Walter Fiala	15.00	6.75	1.85
☐ 68 Jim Gilliam	60.00	27.00	7.50
☐ 69 Jim Pendleton	20.00	9.00	2.50
☐ 70 Gino Cimoli	20.00	9.00	2.50
☐ 71 Carmen Mauro	15.00	6.75	1.85
☐ 72 Walt Moryn	20.00	9.00	2.50
☐ 73 James Romano	15.00	6.75	1.85
☐ 74 Rollin Lutz	15.00	6.75	1.85
☐ 75 Ed Roebuck	20.00	9.00	2.50
☐ 76 John Podres	50.00	22.00	6.25
☐ 77 Walter Novick	15.00	6.75	1.85
☐ 78 Lefty Gohl	15.00	6.75	1.85
☐ 79 Thomas Kirk	15.00	6.75	1.85
☐ 80 Robert Betz	15.00	6.75	1.85
☐ 81 Bill Hockenbury	15.00	6.75	1.85
☐ 82 Albert Rubeling HOR	15.00	6.75	1.85
☐ 83 Julius Watlington	15.00	6.75	1.85
☐ 84 Frank Fanovich	15.00	6.75	1.85
☐ 85 Hank Foiles	20.00	9.00	2.50
☐ 86 Lou Limmer HOR	20.00	9.00	2.50
☐ 87 Edward Hrabcsak	15.00	6.75	1.85
☐ 88 Bob Gardner	15.00	6.75	1.85
☐ 89 John Metkovich	15.00	6.75	1.85
☐ 90 Jean-Pierre Roy	15.00	6.75	1.85
☐ 91 Frank Skaff MG	15.00	6.75	1.85
☐ 92 Harry Desert	15.00	6.75	1.85
☐ 93 Stan Jok	20.00	9.00	2.50
☐ 94 Russ Swingle	15.00	6.75	1.85
☐ 95 Bob Wellman	15.00	6.75	1.85
☐ 96 John Conway HOR	15.00	6.75	1.85
☐ 97 George Maskovich HOR	15.00	6.75	1.85
☐ 98 Charles Bishop	15.00	6.75	1.85
☐ 99 Joseph Murray	15.00	6.75	1.85
☐ 100 Mike Kume	20.00	9.00	2.50

1953 Mothers Cookies

The cards in this 63-card set measure 2 3/16" by 3 1/2". The 1953 Mother's Cookies set features PCL players only. The cards are numbered and the corners are rounded in "playing-card" style. The set has different numbers than the 1952 series and carries a "trading card album" offer on the back. Eleven cards are marked with DP in the checklist below as they essentially were double printed and are much more plentiful than the other numbers in the set. The catalog designation of the set is D357-2.

	NRMT	VG-E	GOOD
COMPLETE SET (63)	850.00	375.00	105.00
COMMON CARD (1-63)	15.00	6.75	1.85
COMMON CARD DP	7.50	3.40	.95
☐ 1 Lee Winters	25.00	11.00	3.10
☐ 2 Joe Ostrowski	15.00	6.75	1.85
☐ 3 Willie Ramsdell	15.00	6.75	1.85
☐ 4 Bobby Bragan	20.00	9.00	2.50
☐ 5 Fletcher Robbe	15.00	6.75	1.85
☐ 6 Aaron Robinson	17.50	8.00	2.20
☐ 7 Augie Galan	20.00	9.00	2.50
☐ 8 Buddy Peterson	15.00	6.75	1.85
☐ 9 Lefty O'Doul	40.00	18.00	5.00
☐ 10 Walt Poceday	15.00	6.75	1.85
☐ 11 Nini Tornay	15.00	6.75	1.85
☐ 12 Jim Moran	15.00	6.75	1.85
☐ 13 George Schmees	15.00	6.75	1.85
☐ 14 Al Widmar	15.00	6.75	1.85
☐ 15 Richie Myers	15.00	6.75	1.85
☐ 16 Bill Howerton	15.00	6.75	1.85
☐ 17 Chuck Stevens	15.00	6.75	1.85
☐ 18 Joe Brovia	15.00	6.75	1.85
☐ 19 Max West	17.50	8.00	2.20
☐ 20 Eddie Malone	15.00	6.75	1.85
☐ 21 Gene Handley	15.00	6.75	1.85
☐ 22 William D. McCawley	15.00	6.75	1.85
☐ 23 Bill Sweeney	15.00	6.75	1.85
☐ 24 Tom Alston	15.00	6.75	1.85
☐ 25 George Vico	15.00	6.75	1.85
☐ 26 Hank Arft	15.00	6.75	1.85
☐ 27 Al Benton	17.50	8.00	2.20
☐ 28 Pete Milne	15.00	6.75	1.85
☐ 29 Jim Gladd	15.00	6.75	1.85
☐ 30 Earl Rapp	15.00	6.75	1.85
☐ 31 Ray Orteig	15.00	6.75	1.85
☐ 32 Eddie Basinski	15.00	6.75	1.85
☐ 33 Reno Cheso	15.00	6.75	1.85
☐ 34 Clarence Maddern	15.00	6.75	1.85
☐ 35 Marino Pieretti	15.00	6.75	1.85
☐ 36 Bill Raimondi	15.00	6.75	1.85
☐ 37 Frank Kelleher	15.00	6.75	1.85
☐ 38 George Bamberger	30.00	13.50	3.70
☐ 39 Dick Smith	15.00	6.75	1.85
☐ 40 Charley Schanz	15.00	6.75	1.85
☐ 41 John Van Cuyk	15.00	6.75	1.85
☐ 42 Lloyd Hittle	15.00	6.75	1.85
☐ 43 Tommy Heath	15.00	6.75	1.85
☐ 44 Frank Kalin	15.00	6.75	1.85
☐ 45 Jack Tobin DP	7.50	3.40	.95
☐ 46 Jim Davis	15.00	6.75	1.85
☐ 47 Claude Christy	15.00	6.75	1.85
☐ 48 Elvin Tappe	15.00	6.75	1.85
☐ 49 Stan Hack	20.00	9.00	2.50
☐ 50 Fred Richards DP	7.50	3.40	.95
☐ 51 Clay Hopper DP	7.50	3.40	.95
☐ 52 Roy Welmaker	15.00	6.75	1.85
☐ 53 Red Adams DP	7.50	3.40	.95
☐ 54 Piper Davis DP	7.50	3.40	.95
☐ 55 Spider Jorgensen	17.50	8.00	2.20
☐ 56 Lee Walls	17.50	8.00	2.20
☐ 57 Jack Phillips DP	7.50	3.40	.95
☐ 58 Red Lynn DP	7.50	3.40	.95
☐ 59 Eddie Robinson DP	15.00	6.75	1.85
☐ 60 Gene Desautels DP	7.50	3.40	.95
☐ 61 Bob Dillinger DP	15.00	6.75	1.85
☐ 62 Al Federoff	15.00	6.75	1.85
☐ 63 Bill Boemler DP	7.50	3.40	.95

1957 Hygrade Meats

This 12-card set features Seattle Rainiers of the Pacific Coast League (PCL) only. The cards measure 3 3/4" by 4 1/2" and they are unnumbered. The catalog designation for this scarce set is F178. These cards, along with Milwaukee Sausage and the Henry House issues were in direct contact with hot dog meats. Therefore, these cards are usually found in vg or less condition in these sets and a significant premium is attached for nm/mt cards or better.

	NRMT	VG-E	GOOD
COMPLETE SET (12)	2500.00	1100.00	300.00
COMMON CARD (1-12)	200.00	90.00	25.00
☐ 1 Dick Aylward	200.00	90.00	25.00
☐ 2 Bob Balcena	200.00	90.00	25.00
☐ 3 Jim Dyck	200.00	90.00	25.00
☐ 4 Marion Fricano	200.00	90.00	25.00
☐ 5 Billy Glynn	200.00	90.00	25.00
☐ 6 Larry Jansen	250.00	110.00	31.00
☐ 7 Bill Kennedy	200.00	90.00	25.00
☐ 8 Jack Wayne (Lucky) Lohrke	200.00	90.00	25.00
☐ 9 Lefty O'Doul	250.00	110.00	31.00
☐ 10 Ray Orteig	200.00	90.00	25.00
☐ 11 Joe Taylor	200.00	90.00	25.00
☐ 12 Morrie Wills (sic, Maury)	500.00	220.00	60.00

1958 Union Oil

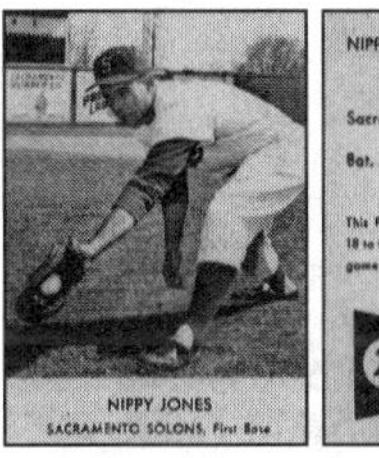

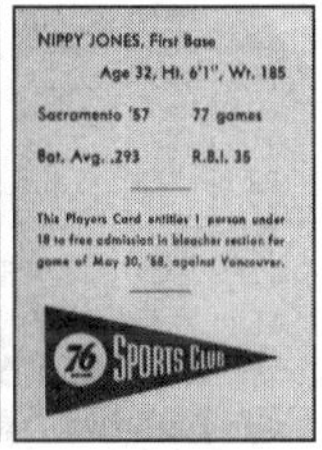

The 1958 Union Olil set of ten black and white, unnumbered cards depicts members of the Sacramento Solons. Each card has a white strip containing the player's name, team and position below the picture. The back has a pennant design advertising the '76 Sports Club' and states that the card is redeemable for free admission to a specific Solons game. The cards measure approximately 2 1/2" by 3 1/2".

	NRMT	VG-E	GOOD
COMPLETE SET (10)	200.00	90.00	25.00
COMMON CARD (1-10)	15.00	6.75	1.85
☐ 1 Marshall Bridges	50.00	22.00	6.25
☐ 2 Dick Cole	15.00	6.75	1.85
☐ 3 Jim Greengrass	20.00	9.00	2.50
☐ 4 Al Heist	20.00	9.00	2.50
☐ 5 Nippy Jones	20.00	9.00	2.50
☐ 6 Carlos Paula	20.00	9.00	2.50
☐ 7 Kal Segrist	15.00	6.75	1.85
☐ 8 Sibbi Sisti	20.00	9.00	2.50
☐ 9 Joe Stanka	15.00	6.75	1.85
☐ 10 Bud Watkins	30.00	13.50	3.70

1959 Darigold Farms

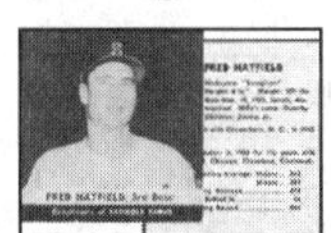

The cards in this 22-card set measure 2 1/2" by 2 3/8". Darigold Farms produced this 1959 set to spotlight the Spokane Indians baseball team. The cards are unnumbered and contain black and white photos set against colored backgrounds (1-8 have yellow, 9-16 have red and 17-22 have blue). The cards were attached to milk cartons by tabs and carry the catalog number F115-1. The cards have been alphabetized and assigned numbers in the checklist below.

	NRMT	VG-E	GOOD
COMPLETE SET (22)	600.00	275.00	75.00
COMMON CARD (1-22)	35.00	16.00	4.40
☐ 1 Facundo Barragan	35.00	16.00	4.40
☐ 2 Steve Bilko	40.00	18.00	5.00
☐ 3 Bobby Bragan MG	40.00	18.00	5.00
☐ 4 Chuck Churn	35.00	16.00	4.40
☐ 5 Tommy Davis	60.00	27.00	7.50
☐ 6 Dom Domenichelli	35.00	16.00	4.40
☐ 7 Bob Giallombardo	35.00	16.00	4.40
☐ 8 Connie Grob	35.00	16.00	4.40
☐ 9 Fred Hatfield	35.00	16.00	4.40
☐ 10 Bob Lillis	40.00	18.00	5.00
☐ 11 Lloyd Merritt	35.00	16.00	4.40
☐ 12 Larry Miller	35.00	16.00	4.40
☐ 13 Chris Nicolosi	35.00	16.00	4.40
☐ 14 Allen Norris	35.00	16.00	4.40
☐ 15 Phil Ortega	35.00	16.00	4.40
☐ 16 Phillips Paine	35.00	16.00	4.40
☐ 17 Bill Parsons	35.00	16.00	4.40
☐ 18 Hisel Patrick	35.00	16.00	4.40
☐ 19 Tony Roig	35.00	16.00	4.40
☐ 20 Tom Saffell	35.00	16.00	4.40
☐ 21 Norm Sherry	40.00	18.00	5.00
☐ 22 Ben Wade	35.00	16.00	4.40

1960 Darigold Farms

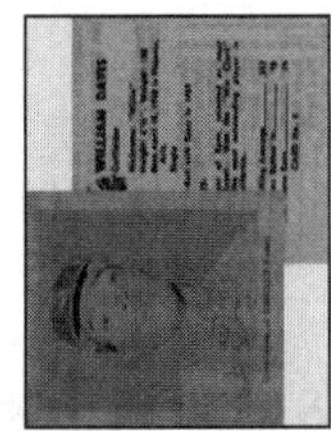

The cards in this 24-card set measure 2 3/8" by 2 9/16". The 1960 Darigold edition of the Spokane Indians has several distinguishing features which allow it to be separated from the similar set produced the year before. Most importantly, the cards are numbered and there are 24 in the set. The sequential use of color background was retained, but cards 9-16 have green and 17-24 have red. A facsimile autograph was added to the front of each card. The catalog designation is F115-2.

	NRMT	VG-E	GOOD
COMPLETE SET (24)	900.00	400.00	110.00
COMMON CARD (1-24)	35.00	16.00	4.40
☐ 1 Chris Nicolosi	35.00	16.00	4.40
☐ 2 Jim Pagliaroni	50.00	22.00	6.25
☐ 3 Roy Smalley	50.00	22.00	6.25
☐ 4 Bill Bethee	35.00	16.00	4.40
☐ 5 Joe Liscio	35.00	16.00	4.40
☐ 6 Curt Roberts	35.00	16.00	4.40
☐ 7 Ed Palmquist	35.00	16.00	4.40
☐ 8 Willie Davis	60.00	27.00	7.50
☐ 9 Bob Giallombardo	35.00	16.00	4.40
☐ 10 Pedro Gomez	50.00	22.00	6.25
☐ 11 Mel Nelson	35.00	16.00	4.40
☐ 12 Charlie Smith	40.00	18.00	5.00
☐ 13 Clarence Churn	35.00	16.00	4.40
☐ 14 Ramon Conde	35.00	16.00	4.40
☐ 15 George O'Donnell	35.00	16.00	4.40
☐ 16 Tony Roig	35.00	16.00	4.40
☐ 17 Frank Howard	75.00	34.00	9.50
☐ 18 Billy Harris	35.00	16.00	4.40
☐ 19 Mike Brumley	35.00	16.00	4.40
☐ 20 Earl Robinson	35.00	16.00	4.40
☐ 21 Ron Fairly	60.00	27.00	7.50
☐ 22 Joe Frazier	35.00	16.00	4.40
☐ 23 Allen Norris	35.00	16.00	4.40
☐ 24 Ford Young	35.00	16.00	4.40

1960 Henry House Wieners

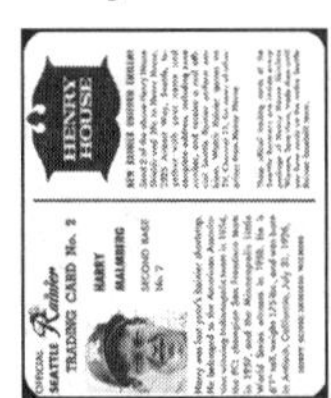

This 18-card set features Seattle Rainiers of the Pacific Coast League (PCL) only. The cards measure 3 3/4" by 4 1/2" and they are skip-numbered by uniform number. Cards are printed on stiff cardboard with red ink. The catalog designation for this scarce set is F171.

	NRMT	VG-E	GOOD
COMPLETE SET (18)	4000.00	1800.00	500.00
COMMON CARD (1-18)	250.00	110.00	31.00
☐ 2 Harry Malmberg	250.00	110.00	31.00
☐ 3 Francisco Obregon	250.00	110.00	31.00
☐ 4 Johnny O'Brien	300.00	135.00	38.00
☐ 5 Gordon Coleman	300.00	135.00	38.00
☐ 6 Bill Hain	250.00	110.00	31.00
☐ 8 Dick Sisler	300.00	135.00	38.00
☐ 9 Jerry Zimmerman	250.00	110.00	31.00
☐ 10 Hal Bevan	250.00	110.00	31.00
☐ 14 Rudy Regalado	250.00	110.00	31.00
☐ 15 Paul Pettit	250.00	110.00	31.00
☐ 16 Buddy Gilbert	250.00	110.00	31.00
☐ 21 Erv Palica	250.00	110.00	31.00
☐ 22 Joe Taylor	250.00	110.00	31.00
☐ 25 Bill Kennedy	250.00	110.00	31.00
☐ 26 Dave Stenhouse	250.00	110.00	31.00
☐ 28 Ray Ripplemeyer	250.00	110.00	31.00
☐ 30 Charlie Beamon	250.00	110.00	31.00
☐ 33 Don Rudolph	250.00	110.00	31.00

1960 Maple Leafs Shopsy's Frankfurters

These 23 blank-backed cards measure approximately 2 3/16" by 3 1/4" and feature players from the Toronto Maple Leafs of the International League. The white-bordered cards carry posed black-and-white player photos. The player's name and position appear in black lettering within the bottom white margin; the words "Shopsy's Player Photo" appear in black lettering within the top white margin. The catalog designation for this set is FC35. The cards are unnumbered and checklisted below in alphabetical order.

	NRMT	VG-E	GOOD
COMPLETE SET (23)	900.00	400.00	110.00
COMMON CARD (1-23)	40.00	18.00	5.00
☐ 1 George Anderson	125.00	55.00	15.50
☐ 2 Bob Chakales	40.00	18.00	5.00
☐ 3 Al Cicotte	40.00	18.00	5.00
☐ 4 Rip Coleman	40.00	18.00	5.00
☐ 5 Steve Demeter	40.00	18.00	5.00
☐ 6 Don Dillard	40.00	18.00	5.00
☐ 7 Frank Funk	40.00	18.00	5.00
☐ 8 Russ Heman	40.00	18.00	5.00
☐ 9 Earl Hersh	40.00	18.00	5.00
☐ 10 Allen Jones	40.00	18.00	5.00
☐ 11 Jim King	40.00	18.00	5.00
☐ 12 Jack Kubiszyn	40.00	18.00	5.00
☐ 13 Mel McGaha CO	40.00	18.00	5.00
☐ 14 Bill Moran	40.00	18.00	5.00
☐ 15 Ron Negray	40.00	18.00	5.00
☐ 16 Herb Plews	40.00	18.00	5.00
☐ 17 Steve Ridzik	40.00	18.00	5.00
☐ 18 Pat Scantlebury	40.00	18.00	5.00
☐ 19 Bill Smith	40.00	18.00	5.00
☐ 20 Bob Smith	40.00	18.00	5.00
☐ 21 Tim Thompson	40.00	18.00	5.00
☐ 22 Jack Waters	40.00	18.00	5.00
☐ 23 Archie Wilson	40.00	18.00	5.00

1960 Tacoma Bank

The Tacoma National Bank of Washington set features 21 large cards each measuring 3" by 5". The set exclusively features players from the Tacoma Giants of the Pacific Coast League (PCL). Several of the players went on to later play for the big league Giants. The catalog designation is H801-14.

	NRMT	VG-E	GOOD
COMPLETE SET (21)	450.00	200.00	55.00
COMMON CARD (1-21)	20.00	9.00	2.50
☐ 1 Matty Alou	30.00	13.50	3.70
☐ 2 Ossie Alvarez	20.00	9.00	2.50
☐ 3 Don Choate	20.00	9.00	2.50
☐ 4 Red Davis	20.00	9.00	2.50
☐ 5 Bob Farley	20.00	9.00	2.50
☐ 6 Eddie Fisher	25.00	11.00	3.10
☐ 7 Tom Haller	25.00	11.00	3.10
☐ 8 Sherman Jones	20.00	9.00	2.50
☐ 9 Juan Marichal	75.00	34.00	9.50
☐ 10 Ramon Monzant	20.00	9.00	2.50
☐ 11 Danny O'Connell	30.00	13.50	3.70
☐ 12 Jose Pagan	25.00	11.00	3.10
☐ 13 Bob Perry	20.00	9.00	2.50
☐ 14 Dick Phillips	20.00	9.00	2.50
☐ 15 Bobby Prescott	20.00	9.00	2.50
☐ 16 Marshall Renfroe	20.00	9.00	2.50
☐ 17 Frank Reveira	20.00	9.00	2.50
☐ 18 Dusty Rhodes	30.00	13.50	3.70
☐ 19 Sal Taormina	20.00	9.00	2.50
☐ 20 Verle Tiefenthaler	20.00	9.00	2.50
☐ 21 Dom Zanni	20.00	9.00	2.50

1960 Union Oil

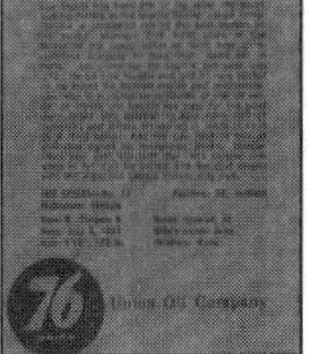

The 1960 Union Oil set consists of nine full-color, skip-numbered cards spotlighting the Seattle Rainers. These cards were given away by Union Oil stations in the Seattle area. The fronts contain full-length action photos taken at Sicks Stadium. Ripplemeyer and Obregon are considered the "scarcities" of the set. The biographical material on the back is entitled "Thumb Nail Sketches". Cards in this set measure approximately 3 1/8" by 4".

	NRMT	VG-E	GOOD
COMPLETE SET (9)	225.00	100.00	28.00
COMMON CARD (1-22)	12.00	5.50	1.50
☐ 4 Francisco Obregon	30.00	13.50	3.70
☐ 6 Drew Gilbert	12.00	5.50	1.50
☐ 7 Bill Hain	12.00	5.50	1.50
☐ 10 Ray Ripplemeyer	125.00	55.00	15.50
☐ 13 Joe Taylor	12.00	5.50	1.50
☐ 15 Lou Skizas	12.00	5.50	1.50
☐ 17 Don Rudolph	15.00	6.75	1.85
☐ 19 Gordy Coleman	20.00	9.00	2.50
☐ 22 Hal Bevan	12.00	5.50	1.50

1961 Maple Leafs Bee Hive

BEE HIVE PLAYER PHOTO
CHUCK TANNER, outfielder - 1961

These 24 blank-backed cards measure approximately 2 3/16" by 3 3/16" and are printed on thin stock. The set features white-bordered black-and-white photos of the 1961 Toronto Maple Leafs of the International League. The player's name and position appear in black lettering within the lower white margin. The catalog designation for this set is FC36. The cards are unnumbered and checklisted below in alphabetical order.

	NRMT	VG-E	GOOD
COMPLETE SET (24)	1000.00	450.00	125.00
COMMON CARD (1-24)	40.00	18.00	5.00
☐ 1 Sparky Anderson	150.00	70.00	19.00
☐ 2 Fritzie Brickell	40.00	18.00	5.00
☐ 3 Ellis Burton	40.00	18.00	5.00
☐ 4 Bob Chakales	40.00	18.00	5.00
☐ 5 Rip Coleman	40.00	18.00	5.00
☐ 6 Steve Demeter	40.00	18.00	5.00
☐ 7 Joe Hannah	40.00	18.00	5.00
☐ 8 Earl Hersh	40.00	18.00	5.00
☐ 9 Lou Jackson	40.00	18.00	5.00
☐ 10 Ken Johnson	50.00	22.00	6.25
☐ 11 Lou Johnson	50.00	22.00	6.25
☐ 12 John Lipon	40.00	18.00	5.00
☐ 13 Carl Mathias	40.00	18.00	5.00
☐ 14 Bill Moran	40.00	18.00	5.00
☐ 15 Ron Negray	40.00	18.00	5.00
☐ 16 Herb Plews	40.00	18.00	5.00
☐ 17 Dave Pope	40.00	18.00	5.00
☐ 18 Steve Ridzik	40.00	18.00	5.00
☐ 19 Raul Sanchez	40.00	18.00	5.00
☐ 20 Pat Scantlebury	40.00	18.00	5.00
☐ 21 Bill Smith	40.00	18.00	5.00
☐ 22 Bob Smith	40.00	18.00	5.00
☐ 23 Chuck Tanner	60.00	27.00	7.50
☐ 24 Tim Thompson	40.00	18.00	5.00

1961 Tacoma Bank

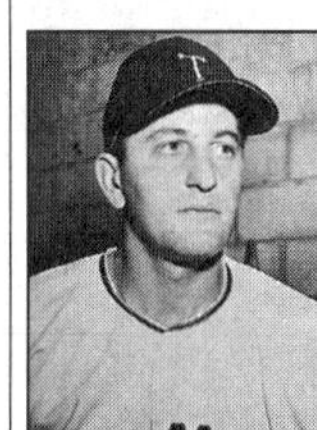

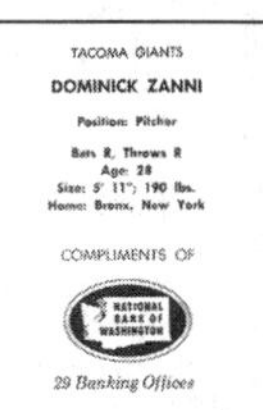

TACOMA GIANTS
DOMINICK ZANNI
Position: Pitcher
Bats R, Throws R
Age: 28
Size: 5' 11"; 190 lbs.
Home: Bronx, New York
COMPLIMENTS OF
NATIONAL BANK OF WASHINGTON
29 Banking Offices

The Tacoma National Bank of Washington set again consists of 21 large (3" by 5") cards. The asterisked cards use the same photo as the 1961 Union Oil issue. The set exclusively features players from the Tacoma Giants of the Pacific Coast League (PCL). Several of the players went on to later play for the big league Giants. The catalog designation is H801-15.

	NRMT	VG-E	GOOD
COMMON CARD	300.00	135.00	38.00
COMMON CARD	15.00	6.75	1.85
☐ 1 Rafael Alomar	15.00	6.75	1.85
☐ 2 Ernie Bowman	15.00	6.75	1.85
☐ 3 Bud Byerly	15.00	6.75	1.85
☐ 4 Ray Daviault	15.00	6.75	1.85
☐ 5 Red Davis	15.00	6.75	1.85
☐ 6 Bob Farley	15.00	6.75	1.85
☐ 7 Gil Garrido	15.00	6.75	1.85
☐ 8 John Goetz	15.00	6.75	1.85

	NRMT	VG-E	GOOD
☐ 9 Bill Hain	15.00	6.75	1.85
☐ 10 Ronald Herbel	15.00	6.75	1.85
☐ 11 Lynn Lovenguth	15.00	6.75	1.85
☐ 12 Georges H. Maranda	15.00	6.75	1.85
☐ 13 Manny Mota	20.00	9.00	2.50
☐ 14 John Orsino	15.00	6.75	1.85
☐ 15 Gaylord Perry	50.00	22.00	6.25
☐ 16 Bob Perry	15.00	6.75	1.85
☐ 17 Dick Phillips	15.00	6.75	1.85
☐ 18 Frank Reveira	15.00	6.75	1.85
☐ 19 Dusty Rhodes	20.00	9.00	2.50
☐ 20 Verle Tiefenthaler	15.00	6.75	1.85
☐ 21 Dom Zanni	15.00	6.75	1.85

1961 Union Oil

DIEGO SEGUI

Union Oil Company

The cards in the 67-card set measure 3" by 4". The 1961 Union Oil set of sepia, unnumbered cards contains players from six Pacific Coast League teams. Individual player cards were available only in their respective cities at Union 76 stations. The backs are in blue print and give player biographies and depict the Union 76 logo. Spokane players are more difficult to obtain than players from other teams. The Gomez and Prescott cards are scarce. The Mike Hershberger card actually depicts Bobby Knoop. Cards are numbered alphabetically with team (except Tacoma's uniform numbering) and have a prefix before the number indicating the team, i.e. Hawaii (H), Portland (P), San Diego (SD), Sacramento (S), Spokane (SP) and Tacoma (T)

	NRMT	VG-E	GOOD
COMPLETE SET (67)	1250.00	550.00	160.00
COMMON CARD (P/S)	12.00	5.50	1.50
COMMON CARD (SD/T)	12.00	5.50	1.50
COMMON CARD (H/SP)	25.00	11.00	3.10

	NRMT	VG-E	GOOD
☐ H1 Ray Jablonski	30.00	13.50	3.70
☐ H2 Jim McManus	25.00	11.00	3.10
☐ H3 George Prescott	100.00	45.00	12.50
☐ H4 Diego Segui	30.00	13.50	3.70
☐ H5 Rachel Slider	25.00	11.00	3.10
☐ H6 Jim Small	25.00	11.00	3.10
☐ H7 Milt Smith	25.00	11.00	3.10
☐ H8 Dave Thies	25.00	11.00	3.10
☐ H9 Jay Ward	25.00	11.00	3.10
☐ H10 Bill Werle	25.00	11.00	3.10
☐ P1 Ed Bauta	12.00	5.50	1.50
☐ P2 Vern Benson	12.00	5.50	1.50
☐ P3 Jerry Buchek	12.00	5.50	1.50
☐ P4 Bob Burda	12.00	5.50	1.50
☐ P5 Duke Carmel	12.00	5.50	1.50
☐ P6 Don Choate	12.00	5.50	1.50
☐ P7 Phil Gagliano	12.00	5.50	1.50
☐ P8 Jim Hickman	15.00	6.75	1.85
☐ P9 Ray Katt	12.00	5.50	1.50
☐ P10 Mel Nelson	12.00	5.50	1.50
☐ P11 Jim Schaffer	12.00	5.50	1.50
☐ P12 Mike Shannon	25.00	11.00	3.10
☐ P13 Clint Stark	12.00	5.50	1.50
☐ S1 Galen Cisco	12.00	5.50	1.50
☐ S2 Lou Clinton	12.00	5.50	1.50
☐ S3 Marlan Coughtry	12.00	5.50	1.50
☐ S4 Harry Malmberg	12.00	5.50	1.50
☐ S5 Dave Mann	12.00	5.50	1.50
☐ S6 Derrell Martin	12.00	5.50	1.50
☐ S7 Erv Palica	12.00	5.50	1.50
☐ S8 John Pesky	20.00	9.00	2.50
☐ S9 Bob Tillman	12.00	5.50	1.50
☐ S10 Marv Toft	12.00	5.50	1.50
☐ S11 Tom Umphlett	12.00	5.50	1.50
☐ T10 Red Davis	12.00	5.50	1.50
☐ T12 Dick Phillips	12.00	5.50	1.50
☐ T17 Gil Garrido	12.00	5.50	1.50
☐ T20 Georges Maranda	12.00	5.50	1.50
☐ T25 John Orsino	12.00	5.50	1.50
☐ T26 Dusty Rhodes	25.00	11.00	3.10
☐ T28 Ron Herbel	12.00	5.50	1.50
☐ T29 Gaylord Perry	125.00	55.00	15.50
☐ T30 Rafael Alomar	12.00	5.50	1.50
☐ T34 Bob Farley	12.00	5.50	1.50
☐ SD1 Dick Barone	12.00	5.50	1.50
☐ SD2 Jim Bolger	12.00	5.50	1.50
☐ SD3 Kent Hadley	12.00	5.50	1.50
☐ SD4 Norman Hershberger	12.00	5.50	1.50
☐ SD5 Stan Johnson	12.00	5.50	1.50
☐ SD6 Dick Lines	12.00	5.50	1.50
☐ SD7 Jim Napier	12.00	5.50	1.50
☐ SD8 Tony Roig	12.00	5.50	1.50
☐ SD9 Herb Score	50.00	22.00	6.25
☐ SD10 Harry Simpson	15.00	6.75	1.85
☐ SD11 Joe Taylor	12.00	5.50	1.50
☐ SD12 Ben Wade	12.00	5.50	1.50
☐ SP1 Doug Camilli	25.00	11.00	3.10
☐ SP2 Ramon Conde	25.00	11.00	3.10
☐ SP3 Bob Giallombardo	25.00	11.00	3.10
☐ SP4 Mike Goliat	25.00	11.00	3.10
☐ SP5 Preston Gomez	100.00	45.00	12.50
☐ SP6 Rod Graber	25.00	11.00	3.10
☐ SP7 Tim Harkness	25.00	11.00	3.10
☐ SP8 Jim Harwell	25.00	11.00	3.10
☐ SP9 Howie Reed	25.00	11.00	3.10
☐ SP10 Curt Roberts	25.00	11.00	3.10
☐ SP11 Rene Valdes	25.00	11.00	3.10

1962 Kahn's Atlanta

The cards in this 24-card set measure 3 1/4" X 4". The 1962 Kahn's Wieners Atlanta set features unnumbered, black and white cards of the Atlanta Crackers of the International League. The backs contain player statistical information as well as instructions on how to obtain free tickets. The catalog designation is F155-9. The cards are listed and numbered below in alphabetical order by the subject's name.

	NRMT	VG-E	GOOD
COMPLETE SET (24)	375.00	170.00	47.50
COMMON CARD (1-24)	12.50	5.50	1.55

	NRMT	VG-E	GOOD
☐ 1 Jim Beauchamp	15.00	6.75	1.85
☐ 2 Gerry Buchek	12.50	5.50	1.55
☐ 3 Bob Burda	12.50	5.50	1.55
☐ 4 Dick Dietz	15.00	6.75	1.85
☐ 5 Bob Duliba	12.50	5.50	1.55
☐ 6 Harry Fanok	12.50	5.50	1.55
☐ 7 Phil Gagliano	15.00	6.75	1.85
☐ 8 John Glenn	12.50	5.50	1.55
☐ 9 Leroy Gregory	12.50	5.50	1.55
☐ 10 Dick Hughes	12.50	5.50	1.55
☐ 11 Johnny Kucks	15.00	6.75	1.85
☐ 12 Johnny Lewis	15.00	6.75	1.85
☐ 13 Tim McCarver	75.00	34.00	9.50
☐ 14 Bob Milliken	12.50	5.50	1.55
☐ 15 Joe M. Morgan	15.00	6.75	1.85
☐ 16 Ron Plaza	12.50	5.50	1.55
☐ 17 Bob Sadowski	12.50	5.50	1.55
☐ 18 Jim Saul	12.50	5.50	1.55
☐ 19 Willard Schmidt	12.50	5.50	1.55
☐ 20 Joe Schultz MG	15.00	6.75	1.85
☐ 21 Mike Shannon	35.00	16.00	4.40
☐ 22 Paul Toth	12.50	5.50	1.55
☐ 23 Lou Vickery	12.50	5.50	1.55
☐ 24 Fred Whitfield	15.00	6.75	1.85

1963 Milwaukee Sausage

This 11-card set features Seattle Rainiers of the Pacific Coast League (PCL) only. The cards measure approximately 4 1/2" by 4 9/16" and they are unnumbered. Cards are printed on stiff cardboard with blue ink. The Milwaukee brand logo is featured in the upper right corner in red and yellow. The catalog designation for this scarce set is F180.

	NRMT	VG-E	GOOD
COMPLETE SET (11)	2200.00	1000.00	275.00
COMMON CARD (1-11)	200.00	90.00	25.00

	NRMT	VG-E	GOOD
☐ 1 Dave Hall	200.00	90.00	25.00
☐ 2 Bill Harrell	200.00	90.00	25.00
☐ 3 Pete Jernigan	200.00	90.00	25.00
☐ 4 Bill McLeod	200.00	90.00	25.00
☐ 5 Mel Parnell	250.00	110.00	31.00
☐ 6 Elmer Singleton	200.00	90.00	25.00
☐ 7 Archie Skeen	200.00	90.00	25.00
☐ 8 Paul Smith	250.00	110.00	31.00
☐ 9 Pete Smith	200.00	90.00	25.00
☐ 10 Bill Spanswick	200.00	90.00	25.00
☐ 11 George Spencer	200.00	90.00	25.00

1972 Cedar Rapids Cardinals TCMA

This set is considered complete at 29 cards. The team photo card #30 was a late issue and is very scarce. The regular cards in the set measure 2-1/8" X 3-1/4" and are black and white. The team photo card measures 4-15/16" X 3-7/16" and is also black and white. We have priced the set with and without the team card.

	NRMT	VG-E	GOOD
COMPLETE SET (30)	300.00	135.00	38.00

☐ 1 Bill Pinkham
☐ 2 Mark Hale
☐ 3 Tom Zimmer
☐ 4 Don Buchheister
☐ 5 Jethro Mills
☐ 6 John Sawatski
☐ 7 Jim Gregory
☐ 8 Duke Wheeler
☐ 9 Victor Diaz
☐ 10 Jim Dunham
☐ 11 Mike Carmuso
☐ 12 Bruce Henderson
☐ 13 Manny Abreu
☐ 14 Luis Gonzales
☐ 15 Gary Trumbauer
☐ 16 Randy Reucor
☐ 17 Gary Geiger
☐ 18 Burt Nordstrom
☐ 19 Mike Proffitt
☐ 20 Milo Voskovitch
☐ 21 Jim Silvey
☐ 22 Joe Mazzella
☐ 23 Craig Burns
☐ 24 Leon Lee
☐ 25 Larry Aubel
☐ 26 Mark Mueller
☐ 27 Tony Velasquez
☐ 28 Bill Poe
☐ 29 Monte Bolinger
☐ 30 Team Photo

1973 Cedar Rapids Astros TCMA

The cards measure 2-3/16" X 3-5/8" and are black and white.

	NRMT	VG-E	GOOD
COMPLETE SET (28)	75.00	34.00	9.50

☐ 1 Arturo Gonzales
☐ 2 Ramon Perez
☐ 3 Al Williams
☐ 4 Guillermo Forster
☐ 5 Bob Dean
☐ 6 Fred Mims
☐ 7 Art Gardner
☐ 8 Jesus Reyes
☐ 9 Don Buchheister
☐ 10 Neil Rasmussen
☐ 11 Luis Pujols
☐ 12 George Vasquez
☐ 13 Paulo Deleon
☐ 14 Mike Stanton
☐ 15 Luis Sanchez
☐ 16 Jose Sosa
☐ 17 Luis Melendez
☐ 18 Steve Englishby
☐ 19 Rafael Tatis
☐ 20 Richard Williams
☐ 21 Alfredo Javier
☐ 22 Romauldo Blanco
☐ 23 Bob Youse
☐ 24 Heleno Cuen
☐ 25 Leo Posada MGR
☐ 26 Team Picture
☐ 27 Pancho Lopez
☐ 28 Jorge Moreno

1973 Syracuse Chiefs Team Issue

This 1973 Syracuse Chiefs team issued set features major league players as well as minor league players from the Yankee organization. The cards are black and white and measure 4" X 5". The cards were inserted one at a time inside the Syracuse Chiefs minor league programs. Card #22 was a late addition to the set.

	NRMT	VG-E	GOOD
COMPLETE SET (29)	150.00	70.00	19.00
COMPLETE SET W/PAZIK (30)	225.00	100.00	28.00

☐ 1 Felipe Alou
☐ 2 Marty Alou
☐ 3 Ron Blumberg
☐ 4 John Callison
☐ 5 Horace Clark
☐ 6 Alan Closter
☐ 7 Joe DiMaggio
☐ 8 Lou Gehrig
☐ 9 Larry Gowell
☐ 10 Ralph Houk
☐ 11 Mike Kekich
☐ 12 Ron Klimkowski
☐ 13 Steve Kline
☐ 14 Sparky Lyle
☐ 15 Mickey Mantle
☐ 16 Lindy McDaniel
☐ 17 George Medich
☐ 18 Gene Michael
☐ 19 Thurman Munson
☐ 20 Bobby Murcer
☐ 21 Graig Nettles
☐ 22 Mike Pazik (Late Issue)
☐ 23 Fritz Peterson
☐ 24 Babe Ruth
☐ 25 Cellie Sanchez
☐ 26 Mel Stottlemyre
☐ 27 Frank Tepedino
☐ 28 Otto Velez
☐ 29 Roy White
☐ 30 Geroge Zeber

1973 Tacoma Twins Caruso

These cards measure 2-3/8" X 3-1/8" and have blank backs.

	NRMT	VG-E	GOOD
COMPLETE SET (21)	15.00	6.75	1.85

☐ 1 Vic Albury
☐ 2 Glenn Borgmann
☐ 3 Mike Brooks
☐ 4 Bill Campbell
☐ 5 Glenn Ezell
☐ 6 Kerby Farrell
☐ 7 Dan Fife
☐ 8 Bob Gebhard
☐ 9 Ken Gill
☐ 10 Bucky Guth
☐ 11 Jim Hoppe
☐ 12 Tom Kelly
☐ 13 Craig Kusick
☐ 14 John Matias
☐ 15 Mike McCormick
☐ 16 Jim Nettles
☐ 17 Tom Norton
☐ 18 Rick Renick
☐ 19 Eric Soderholm
☐ 20 Bob Storm
☐ 21 Jim Strickland

1973 Wichita Aeros Kansas State Bank

These cards measure 3-3/4"X 5" and are black and white. Variation cards of Jim Hibbs #4 and Ron Tompkins #17 exist with their names printed with both small and large lettering.

	NRMT	VG-E	GOOD
COMPLETE SET (19)	100.00	45.00	12.50
COMPLETE SET W/VAR (21)	125.00	55.00	15.50

☐ 1 Matt Alexander
☐ 2 Tom Badcock
☐ 3 Clint Compton
☐ 4A Jim Hibbs (Large)
☐ 4B Jim Hibbs (Small)
☐ 5 Pete La Cock
☐ 6 Tony La Russa
☐ 7 Tom Lundstedt
☐ 8 J.C. Martin
☐ 9 Jim Marshall
☐ 10 Al Montreuil
☐ 11 Jose Ortiz
☐ 12 Griggy Porter
☐ 13 Paul Reulschel
☐ 14 Ralph Rickey
☐ 15 Dave Rosello
☐ 16 Jim Todd
☐ 17A Ron Tompkins (Large)
☐ 17B Ron Tompkins (Small)
☐ 18 Chris Ward
☐ 19 Floyd Weaver

1974 Albuquerque Dukes Caruso

	NRMT	VG-E	GOOD
COMPLETE SET (16)	15.00	6.75	1.85

☐ 64 Hnery Cruz
☐ 65 Tom Tischinski
☐ 66 Orlando Alvarez
☐ 67 Terry McDermott
☐ 68 Ivan De Jesus
☐ 69 Kevin Pasley
☐ 70 Phil Keller
☐ 71 Eddie Solomon
☐ 72 Charlie Manuel
☐ 73 Greg Shanahan
☐ 74 Lee Robinson
☐ 75 P.R. Powell
☐ 76 Jerry Royster
☐ 77 Stan Wasiak
☐ 78 Bobby Randall
☐ 79 Jim Allen

1974 Albuquerque Dukes Team Issue

	NRMT	VG-E	GOOD
COMPLETE SET (23)	400.00	180.00	50.00

☐ 1 Orlando Alvarez
☐ 2 Bernie Beckman
☐ 3 Wayne Burney
☐ 4 Henry Cruz
☐ 5 Ivan De Jesus
☐ 6 Greg Heydeman

☐ 7 Rex Hudson
☐ 8 Phil Keller
☐ 9 Charlie Manuel
☐ 10 Terry McDermott
☐ 11 Rick Nitz
☐ 12 Kevin Pasley
☐ 13 P.R. Powell
☐ 14 Bobby Randall
☐ 15 Rick Rhoden
☐ 16 Lee Robinson
☐ 17 Jerry Royster
☐ 18 Greg Shanahan
☐ 19 Eddie Solomon
☐ 20 Mike Strahler
☐ 21 Tom Tischinski
☐ 22 Stan Wall
☐ 23 Stan Wasiak

1974 Cedar Rapids Astros TCMA

	NRMT	VG-E	GOOD
COMPLETE SET (28)	100.00	45.00	12.50

☐ 1 Bob Renninger
☐ 2 Bob Youse
☐ 3 Jesus Reyes
☐ 4 Arturo Gonzalez
☐ 5 Tom Rima
☐ 6 Joe Sambito
☐ 7 Dave Aloi
☐ 8 Mike Jones
☐ 9 Calvin Partley
☐ 10 Alejandro Taveras
☐ 11 Luis Pujols
☐ 12 Eric Brown
☐ 13 Luis Sanchez
☐ 14 Jose Alfaro
☐ 15 Jorge Moreno
☐ 16 Fred Mims
☐ 17 Fernado Tatis
☐ 18 Tom Twellman
☐ 19 Kevin Drake
☐ 20 Guillermo Forster
☐ 21 Pastor Perez
☐ 22 Bob Cluck
☐ 23 Larry Elenes
☐ 24 Jose Sosa
☐ 25 Leo Posada
☐ 26 Mike Holland
☐ 27 Pablo Deleon
☐ 28 Don Buchheister

1974 Gastonia Rangers TCMA

Approximately 1,100 sets were produced. Black and White

	NRMT	VG-E	GOOD
COMPLETE SET (24)	125.00	55.00	15.50

☐ 1 Curt Arnett
☐ 2 Jon Astroth
☐ 3 Mike Bacsik
☐ 4 Len Barker
☐ 5 Don Bodenhamer
☐ 6 Don Bright
☐ 7 Gary Cooper
☐ 8 Rich Donnelly
☐ 9 Dan Duran
☐ 10 Dave Fendrick
☐ 11 Lindsey Graham
☐ 12 Tim Murphy
☐ 13 Fred Nichols
☐ 14 Drew Nickerson
☐ 15 Ed Nottle
☐ 16 Wally Pontiff
☐ 17 Ray Rainbolt
☐ 18 Rich Shubert
☐ 19 Rick Simon
☐ 20 Keith Smith
☐ 21 John Sutton
☐ 22 Mark Tanner
☐ 23 Don Thomas
☐ 24 Bobby Thompson

1974 Hawaii Islanders Caruso

	NRMT	VG-E	GOOD
COMPLETE SET (8)	15.00	6.75	1.85

☐ 101 Gene Locklear
☐ 102 Gary Jestadt
☐ 103 Hector Torres
☐ 104 Ed Acosta
☐ 105 Pat Corrales
☐ 106 Bill Almon
☐ 107 Bill Chiles
☐ 108 Roy Hartsfield

1974 Phoenix Giants Caruso

	NRMT	VG-E	GOOD
COMPLETE SET (11)	15.00	6.75	1.85

☐ 80 Skip James
☐ 81 Mike Sadek
☐ 82 Leon Brown
☐ 83 Glenn Redmon
☐ 84 Ed Sukla
☐ 85 Glenn Adams
☐ 86 Bruce Christensen
☐ 87 Jimmy Rosario
☐ 88 Frank Johnson
☐ 89 Glenn Ezell
☐ 90 Rocky Bridges

1974 Sacramento Solons Caruso

	NRMT	VG-E	GOOD
COMPLETE SET (18)	20.00	9.00	2.50

☐ 46 Tom Reynolds
☐ 47 Art Kusnyer
☐ 48 Gorman Thomas
☐ 49 Bill McNulty
☐ 50 Tom Bianco
☐ 51 Gary Cavallo
☐ 52 Tom Hausman
☐ 53 Roger Miller
☐ 54 Tom King
☐ 55 Craig Glassco
☐ 56 Jose Salado
☐ 57 Sixto Lezcano
☐ 58 Steve McCartney
☐ 59 Juan Lopez
☐ 60 Jack Lind
☐ 61 Rob Ellis
☐ 62 Bob Lemon
☐ 63 Bob Sheldon

1974 Salt Lake City Angels Caruso

	NRMT	VG-E	GOOD
COMPLETE SET (10)	15.00	6.75	1.85

☐ 91 Rudy Meoli
☐ 92 Bob Marcano
☐ 93 Frankie George
☐ 94 Dave Chorley
☐ 95 Morris Nettles
☐ 96 Bruce Bochte
☐ 97 Norm Sherry
☐ 98 Jerry Bell
☐ 99 Paul Dade
☐ 100 Danny Briggs

1974 Spokane Indians Caruso

	NRMT	VG-E	GOOD
COMPLETE SET (18)	15.00	6.75	1.85

☐ 28 Steve Dunning
☐ 29 Bob Johnson
☐ 30 Rick Henninger
☐ 31 Jim Shellenback
☐ 32 Rick Waits
☐ 33 Dave Criscione
☐ 34 Bill Fahey
☐ 35 Don Castle
☐ 36 Bob Jones
☐ 37 Dave Moates
☐ 38 Tom Robson
☐ 39 Mike Cubbage
☐ 40 Steve Greenberg
☐ 41 Roy Howell
☐ 42 Pete Mackanin
☐ 43 Vern Wilkins
☐ 44 Marty Martinez
☐ 45 Del Wilber

1974 Syracuse Chiefs Team Issue

This 1974 Syracuse Chiefs team issued set features major league players as well as minor league players from the Yankee organization. The cards are black and white and measure 4" X 5". The cards were inserted one at a time inside the Syracuse Chiefs minor league programs. Card #7 was a late addition to the set.

	NRMT	VG-E	GOOD
COMPLETE SET (29)	150.00	70.00	19.00
COMPLETE SET W/FRAZIER (30)	200.00	90.00	25.00

☐ 1 Ron Blomberg
☐ 2 Rick Bladt
☐ 3 Tom Buskey
☐ 4 Rick Dempsey
☐ 5 Joe DiMaggio
☐ 6 Pat Dobson
☐ 7 Fred Frazier (Late Issue)
☐ 8 Lou Gehrig
☐ 9 Roger Hambright
☐ 10 Mike Hegan
☐ 11 Elston Howard
☐ 12 Steve Kline
☐ 13 Sparky Lyle
☐ 14 Mickey Mantle
☐ 15 Sam McDowell
☐ 16 George Medich
☐ 17 Gene Michael
☐ 18 Thurman Munson
☐ 19 Bobby Murcer
☐ 20 Graig Nettles
☐ 21 Dave Pagan
☐ 22 Fritz Peterson
☐ 23 Babe Ruth
☐ 24 Celerino Sanchez
☐ 25 Fred Stanley
☐ 26 Mel Stottlemeyre
☐ 27 Otto Velez
☐ 28 Bill Virdon
☐ 29 Roy White
☐ 30 Whitey Ford

1974 Tacoma Twins Caruso

	NRMT	VG-E	GOOD
COMPLETE SET (27)	15.00	6.75	1.85

☐ 1 Jim Obardovich
☐ 2 Dale Soderholm
☐ 3 Craig Kusick
☐ 4 Cal Ermer MG
☐ 5 Eddie Bane
☐ 6 Dan Fife
☐ 7 Jim Hughes
☐ 8 Mike Pazik
☐ 9 Frank Schuster
☐ 10 Coley Smith
☐ 11 Earl Stephenson
☐ 12 Juan Veintidos
☐ 13 Dan Vossler
☐ 14 Mark Wiley
☐ 15 Sam Ceci
☐ 16 George Pena
☐ 17 Sergio Ferrer
☐ 18 Doug Howard
☐ 19 Bill Ralston
☐ 20 Rick Renick
☐ 21 Jim Van Wyck
☐ 22 Mike Adams
☐ 23 Lyman Bostock
☐ 24 Jim Fairey
☐ 25 Tom Kelly
☐ 26 Ed Palat
☐ 27 Danny Walton

1974 Wichita Aeros One Day Film

	NRMT	VG-E	GOOD
COMPLETE SET (28)	100.00	45.00	12.50
COMPLETE SET (29)	125.00	55.00	15.50

☐ 101 Francisco Lopez
☐ 102 Paul Zahn
☐ 103A Walter Babcock Jr.
☐ 103B Tom Babcock (Late Issue)
☐ 104 Roberto M. Rodriguez
☐ 105 George Manz
☐ 106 Tom Dettore Jr.
☐ 107 David La Roche
☐ 108 Daniel Corder
☐ 109 Mike Roarke
☐ 110 James Todd Jr.
☐ 111 Wilford Prall
☐ 112 Paul Reuschel
☐ 113 Cleo James
☐ 114 Al Montreuil
☐ 115 Ron Matney
☐ 116 Robert Sperring
☐ 117 Jack Hiatt P/CO
☐ 118 Griggy Porter Jr.
☐ 119 Ron Dunn
☐ 120 Gene Hiser
☐ 121 Alfredo Zavala
☐ 122 Dave Arrington
☐ 123 Steven Swisher
☐ 124 Pete LaCock
☐ 125 Scipio R. Spinks
☐ 126 Bob Drew MG
☐ 127 John Wallenstein MG
☐ 128 Paul St. Onge TR

1975 Albuquerque Dukes Caruso

	NRMT	VG-E	GOOD
COMPLETE SET (21)	25.00	11.00	3.10

☐ 1 Orlando Alvarez
☐ 2 Joe Simpson
☐ 3 Jerry Royster
☐ 4 Lee Robinson
☐ 5 John Hale
☐ 6 Bobby Randall
☐ 7 Terry McDermott
☐ 8 Terry Collins
☐ 9 Cleo Smith
☐ 10 Wayne Burney
☐ 11 Dick Selma
☐ 12 Greg Shanahan
☐ 13 Rex Hudson
☐ 14 Stan Hudson
☐ 15 Pablo Peguero
☐ 16 Rick Nitz
☐ 17 Stan Wall
☐ 18 Jim Allen
☐ 19 Jim Haller
☐ 20 Dennis Lewallyn
☐ 21 Wayne Miller

1975 Anderson Rangers TCMA

	NRMT	VG-E	GOOD
COMPLETE SET (25)	50.00	22.00	6.25

☐ 1 Tommy Smith
☐ 2 Rick Lisi
☐ 3 Mark Miller
☐ 8 Tim Brookens
☐ 9 Keath Chauncey
☐ 10 Glenn Purvis
☐ 15 Gary Gray
☐ 16 Curt Runyon
☐ 17 Terry Olson
☐ 18 Jim Crall
☐ 20 Dave McCarthy
☐ 23 Kerry Getter
☐ 25 Danny Tidwell
☐ 28 Wes Goodale
☐ 29 Jeff Byrd
☐ 32 Jim Clancy
☐ 37 Bob Carroll
☐ 39 Bill Patten
☐ 42 Freeman Evans
☐ 43 Don Bright
☐ 46 Joe Russell
☐ 47 Ward Smith
☐ 57 Drew Nickerson
☐ 67 Darrel Frolin
☐ NNO Ed Nottle

1975 Appleton Foxes TCMA

	NRMT	VG-E	GOOD
COMPLETE SET (29)	50.00	22.00	6.25

☐ 1 Fred Anyzeski
☐ 2 Kevin Bell
☐ 3 Robert Bianco
☐ 4 Paul Bock
☐ 5 Bobby Combs
☐ 6 Roy Coulter
☐ 7 Bob Flynn
☐ 8 Bill Kautzer
☐ 9 Tom King
☐ 10 Bob Klein
☐ 11 Odie Koehnke
☐ 12 Tony Komadina
☐ 13 Juan Leonardo
☐ 14 Ted Loehr
☐ 15 Gordon Lund
☐ 16 Bobby McClellan
☐ 17 Candy Mercado
☐ 18 Larry Monroe
☐ 19 Johnny Narron
☐ 20 Phil Nerone
☐ 21 Ed Olszta
☐ 22 Bob Palmer
☐ 23 Harris Price
☐ 24 Scott Richartz
☐ 25 Silvano Robles
☐ 26 Eric Thomas
☐ 27 Tom Toman
☐ 28 Ed Wheeler
☐ 29 Batboys

1975 Burlington Bees TCMA

	NRMT	VG-E	GOOD
COMPLETE SET (29)	70.00	32.00	8.75

☐ 1 John Buffamoyer
☐ 2 Gary Conn
☐ 3 Barry Cort
☐ 4 Marty DeMerritt
☐ 5 Butch Edge
☐ 6 Terry Erwin
☐ 7 Matt Galante
☐ 8 Miguel Garcia
☐ 9 Frank Gaton
☐ 10 Moose Haas
Sic, Hass
☐ 11 Dennis Holmberg
☐ 12 Sam Jones
☐ 13 Sam Killingsworth
☐ 14 Esteban Maria
☐ 15 Victor Marichal
☐ 16 Marcos Mejias
☐ 17 Sam Monteau
☐ 18 Willie Mueller
☐ 19 Abelino Pena
☐ 20 Neil Rasmussen
☐ 21 Alex Rodriquez

- ☐ 22 Sal Rosario
- ☐ 23 Pedro Sanchez
- ☐ 24 Carey Scarborough
- ☐ 25 Joe Slaymaker
- ☐ 26 Ron Smith
- ☐ 27 Gil Stafford
- ☐ 28 Dave Sylvia
- ☐ 29 John Whiting

1975 Cedar Rapids Giants TCMA

	NRMT	VG-E	GOOD
COMPLETE SET (32)	50.00	22.00	6.25

- ☐ 1 Tom Hughes
- ☐ 2 Mike Wilbins
- ☐ 3 Steve Cline
- ☐ 4 Joe Heinen
- ☐ 5 German De Los Santos
- ☐ 6 John Riddle
- ☐ 7 Bob Thompson
- ☐ 8 Jeff Yurak
- ☐ 9 Terry Lee
- ☐ 10 Dan Beitey
- ☐ 11 John Nix
- ☐ 12 Don Sasser
- ☐ 13 Brian Felda
- ☐ 14 John Johnson
- ☐ 15 Mike Cash
- ☐ 16 Jim Ray
- ☐ 17 Dan Smith
- ☐ 18 Bob Hartsfield and Don Buchheister
- ☐ 19 Bob Hartsfield
- ☐ 20 Barney Wilson
- ☐ 21 Frank Ferrell
- ☐ 22 Mike Dodd
- ☐ 23 Jim Ayers
- ☐ 24 Jerry Stamps
- ☐ 25 Mark Woodbrey
- ☐ 26 Don Benedetti
- ☐ 27 Ron Hodges
- ☐ 28 Wayne Bradley
- ☐ 29 Calvin Moore
- ☐ 30 Garet Strong
- ☐ 31 Terry Kenny
- ☐ 32 Ernie Young

1975 Clinton Pilots TCMA

	NRMT	VG-E	GOOD
COMPLETE SET (30)	125.00	55.00	15.50

- ☐ 1 Jim Leyland
- ☐ 2 Dave Rozema
- ☐ 3 Dwight Carter
- ☐ 4 Brian Kelly
- ☐ 5 Greg Kline
- ☐ 6 Steve Gamby
- ☐ 7 Bill Michael
- ☐ 8 Randy Haas
- ☐ 9 Isaac Giminez
- ☐ 10 Ray Giminez
- ☐ 11 Jim Murray
- ☐ 12 John Dinkelmeyer
- ☐ 13 Larry Feola
- ☐ 14 Tom Lantz
- ☐ 15 Dave Holm
- ☐ 16 Mike Uremovich
- ☐ 17 Kevin Slattery
- ☐ 18 Mark Wagner
- ☐ 19 Ben Hunt
- ☐ 20 Greg Shippy
- ☐ 21 Luis Atilano
- ☐ 22 Tom Perkins
- ☐ 23 Al Baker
- ☐ 24 Steve Trella
- ☐ 24 Jose Centeno
- ☐ 25 Harry Schulz
- ☐ 26 Mike Bartell
- ☐ 27 Al Callis
- ☐ 29 Venoy Garrison
- ☐ 30 Jeff Reinke

1975 Dubuque Packers TCMA

	NRMT	VG-E	GOOD
COMPLETE SET (32)	60.00	27.00	7.50

- ☐ 1 Clancy (Mascot)
- ☐ 2 Terry Puhl
- ☐ 3 Jeff Smith
- ☐ 4 Tom Rima
- ☐ 5 Arnaldo Alvarado
- ☐ 6 Fay Thompson
- ☐ 7 Bob Dean
- ☐ 8 Mike Mendoza
- ☐ 9 John McLaren
- ☐ 10 Bob Cluck
- ☐ 11 Romo Blanco
- ☐ 12 Roger Polanco
- ☐ 13 Eleno Cuen
- ☐ 14 Rick Haynes
- ☐ 15 J.J. Cannon
- ☐ 16 Fernando Tatis
- ☐ 17 Mike Weeber
- ☐ 18 Alan Knicely
- ☐ 19 Tom Dixon
- ☐ 20 Paulo DeLeon
- ☐ 21 Luis Pujols
- ☐ 22 Jose Alfaro
- ☐ 23 Gordon Pladson
- ☐ 24 Dave Aloi
- ☐ 25 Jorge Moreno
- ☐ 26 Tom Twellman
- ☐ 27 George Lazarique
- ☐ 28 Arnie Costell
- ☐ 29 Kevin Drake
- ☐ 30 Mike Hasley
- ☐ 31 Jack Goetz
- ☐ 32 Alvin Osofsky

1975 Fort Lauderdale Yanks Sussman

	NRMT	VG-E	GOOD
COMPLETE SET (29)	120.00	55.00	15.00
COMPLETE SET W/FIGUEROA (30)	70.00	32.00	8.75

- ☐ 1 Scott Norris
- ☐ 2 Mike Ferraro
- ☐ 3 Benny Perez
- ☐ 4 Neil Liebovitz
- ☐ 5 Dave Wright
- ☐ 6 Rich Meltz
- ☐ 7 Dave Rajsick
- ☐ 8 Greg Diehl
- ☐ 9 Tony DeRosa
- ☐ 10 Rick Fleshman
- ☐ 11 Pat Peterson
- ☐ 12 Jim Sullivan
- ☐ 13 Marv Thompson
- ☐ 14 Joe Alvarez
- ☐ 15 Ken Kruppa
- ☐ 16 Jim Beirman
- ☐ 17 Doug Melvin
- ☐ 18 Joe Kwasny
- ☐ 19 Mike Heath
- ☐ 20 Sheldon Gill
- ☐ 21 Dennis Werth
- ☐ 22 Jesus Figueroa
- ☐ 23 Wilson Plunkett
- ☐ 24 Jose Alcantara
- ☐ 25 Leo Posada
- ☐ 26 Garth Iorg
- ☐ 27 Scott Delgatti
- ☐ 28 Mike Rusk
- ☐ 29 Team Photo
- ☐ 30 Jerry Narron

1975 Hawaii Islanders Caruso

	NRMT	VG-E	GOOD
COMPLETE SET (21)	20.00	9.00	2.50

- ☐ 1 Gus Gil
- ☐ 2 Steve Huntz
- ☐ 3 Bob Davis
- ☐ 4 Randy Elliott
- ☐ 5 Dave Roberts
- ☐ 6 Rod Gasper
- ☐ 7 Jim Fairey
- ☐ 8 Jerry Turner
- ☐ 9 Marve Galliher
- ☐ 10 Sonny Jackson
- ☐ 11 Bill Almon
- ☐ 12 Brent Strom
- ☐ 13 Frank Linzy
- ☐ 14 Jim Shellenback
- ☐ 15 Larry Hardy
- ☐ 16 Gary Ross
- ☐ 17 Bob Strampe
- ☐ 18 Jerry Johnson
- ☐ 19 Butch Metzger
- ☐ 20 Dave Wehrmeister
- ☐ 21 Bob Miller

1975 International League All-Stars TCMA

	NRMT	VG-E	GOOD
COMPLETE SET (31)	40.00	18.00	5.00

- ☐ 1 Jerry White
- ☐ 2 Dyar Miller
- ☐ 3 Mike Krizmanich
- ☐ 4 Earl Stephenson
- ☐ 5 Mike Reinbach
- ☐ 6 Jerry White
- ☐ 7 John Stearns
- ☐ 8 Lee Elia
- ☐ 9 Dave Pagan
- ☐ 10 Rob Andrews
- ☐ 11 Jim Hutto
- ☐ 12 Chris Coletta
- ☐ 13 Ron Clark
- ☐ 14 Bill Kirkpatrick

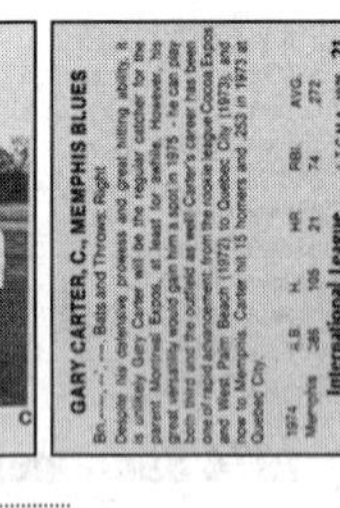

- ☐ 15 Fred Frazier
- ☐ 16 Joe Altobelli
- ☐ 17 Jim Hutto
- ☐ 18 Mike Willis
- ☐ 19 Glenn Stitzel
- ☐ 20 Fred Frazier
- ☐ 21 Gary Carter
- ☐ 22 Steve Dillard
- ☐ 23 Mike Krizmanich
- ☐ 24 Hank Webb
- ☐ 25 Karl Kuehl
- ☐ 26 Lee Elia
- ☐ 27 Chris Coletta
- ☐ 28 Mike Willis
- ☐ 29 Bob Gebhard
- ☐ 30 Dick Wissel
- ☐ 31 Dick Wissel

1975 International League All-Stars Broder

	NRMT	VG-E	GOOD
COMPLETE SET (36)	50.00	22.00	6.25

- ☐ 1 Orlando Alvarez
- ☐ 2 Ed Bane
- ☐ 3 Charlie Chant
- ☐ 4 Tommy Cruz
- ☐ 5 Bob Davis
- ☐ 6 Rob Dressler
- ☐ 7 Bob Hansen
- ☐ 8 Chuck Hartenstein
- ☐ 9 Roy Hartsfield
- ☐ 10 Leon Hooten
- ☐ 11 Steve Huntz
- ☐ 12 Ron Jackson
- ☐ 13 Jerry Johnson
- ☐ 14 Bob Jones
- ☐ 15 Art Kusnyer
- ☐ 16 John LeMaster
- ☐ 17 Dave McKay
- ☐ 18 Sid Monge
- ☐ 19 Buzz Nitschke
- ☐ 20 Rick Nitz
- ☐ 21 Kevin Pasley
- ☐ 22 Tony Pepper
- ☐ 23 Stan Perzanowski
- ☐ 24 Bobby Randall
- ☐ 25 Barry Raziano
- ☐ 26 Tommy Reynolds
- ☐ 27 Dave Roberts
- ☐ 28 Tom Robson
- ☐ 29 Gary Ross
- ☐ 30 Jerry Royster
- ☐ 31 Norm Sherry
- ☐ 32 Joe Simpson
- ☐ 33 Horace Speed
- ☐ 34 Rocky Stone
- ☐ 35 Jerry Turner
- ☐ 36 Stan Wall

1975 Iowa Oaks TCMA

	NRMT	VG-E	GOOD
COMPLETE SET (21)	150.00	70.00	19.00

- ☐ 1 Carlos Alfonso
- ☐ 2 Ron Boone
- ☐ 3 Ray Busse
- ☐ 4 Mike Cosgrove
- ☐ 5 Jerry Davanon
- ☐ 6 Bob Didier
- ☐ 7 Mike Easler
- ☐ 8 Art Gardner
- ☐ 9 Alfredo Javier
- ☐ 10 Jesus DeLaRosa
- ☐ 11 Ramon De Los Santos
- ☐ 12 Joe Niekro
- ☐ 13 George Pena
- ☐ 14 Ramon Perez
- ☐ 15 Russ Rothermal
- ☐ 16 Ron Roznovsky
- ☐ 17 Paul Siebert
- ☐ 18 Joe Sparks
- ☐ 19 Scipio Spinks
- ☐ 20 Mike Stanton
- ☐ 21 Alejandro Taveras

1975 Lafayette Drillers TCMA

	NRMT	VG-E	GOOD
COMPLETE SET (32)	150.00	70.00	19.00

- ☐ 1 Chico Del Orbe
- ☐ 2 Wendell Kim
- ☐ 3 Joey Martin
- ☐ 4 Scott Wolfe
- ☐ 5 Tommy Smith
- ☐ 6 Jake Brown
- ☐ 7 Gary Atwell
- ☐ 8 Ernie Young
- ☐ 9 Craig Barnes
- ☐ 10 John Yeglinski
- ☐ 11 Tom Stedman
- ☐ 12 Gary Alexander
- ☐ 13 Jack Clark
- ☐ 14 Reggie Walton
- ☐ 15 Frank Riccelli
- ☐ 16 Rob Dressler
- ☐ 17 Kyle Hypes
- ☐ 18 Jay Dillard
- ☐ 19 Jeff Little
- ☐ 20 Julio Divison
- ☐ 21 Silvano Quezada
- ☐ 22 David Fuqua
- ☐ 23 Terry Cornutt
- ☐ 24 John Steigerwald
- ☐ 25 Bob Drew
- ☐ 26 Don Steele
- ☐ 27 Al Stuckeman
- ☐ 28 Dan Adams
- ☐ 29 Ducky Crandall
- ☐ 30 Denny Sommers
- ☐ 31 Clark Field
- ☐ 32 Drillers Batboys

1975 Lynchburg Rangers TCMA

	NRMT	VG-E	GOOD
COMPLETE SET (26)	50.00	22.00	6.25

- ☐ 1 Rich Albert
- ☐ 2 Curt Arnett
- ☐ 3 George Ban
- ☐ 4 Mel Barrow
- ☐ 5 Larry Bradford
- ☐ 6 Bobby Buford
- ☐ 7 Bobby Cuellar
- ☐ 8 Amado Dinzey
- ☐ 9 Brian Doyle
- ☐ 10 Dan Duran
- ☐ 11 Chuck Hammond
- ☐ 12 Eddie Holman
- ☐ 13 William Johnson
- ☐ 14 Jerome Johnson
- ☐ 15 Robert Long
- ☐ 16 Ken Miller
- ☐ 17 Brian Nakamoto
- ☐ 18 Wayne Terwilliger
- ☐ 19 Don Thomas
- ☐ 20 Bobby Thompson
- ☐ 21 Pat Putnam
- ☐ 22 Ray Rainbolt
- ☐ 23 Ron Rockhill
- ☐ 24 Jeff Scott
- ☐ 25 Glenn Smith
- ☐ 26 Mark Tanner

1975 Oklahoma City 89ers Team Issue

	NRMT	VG-E	GOOD
COMPLETE SET (24)	10.00	4.50	1.25

- ☐ 1 Robert Grossman
- ☐ 2 Barry Lersch
- ☐ 3 Thomas McGough
- ☐ 4 Richard Henninger
- ☐ 5 Thomas Brennan
- ☐ 6 Bruce Ellingsen
- ☐ 7 Larry Anderson
- ☐ 8 James Kern
- ☐ 9 James Strickland
- ☐ 10 Rick Waits
- ☐ 11 John Siracusa
- ☐ 12 Benjamin Heise
- ☐ 13 Orlando Gonzalez
- ☐ 14 Brian Ostrosser
- ☐ 15 Tommy Smith
- ☐ 16 Thomas McMillan
- ☐ 17 James Norris
- ☐ 18 Mike Hannah
- ☐ 19 Nelson Garcia
- ☐ 20 Joseph Lis
- ☐ 21 Gene Dusan
- ☐ 22 Michael Brooks
- ☐ 23 John Davis
- ☐ 24 Rex Rosser

1975 Omaha Royals Team Issue

	NRMT	VG-E	GOOD
COMPLETE SET (18)	100.00	45.00	12.50

☐ 1 Norm Angelini
☐ 2 Al Autry
☐ 3 Hal Baird
☐ 4 Greg Chlan
☐ 5 Mickey Cobb
☐ 6 Bobby Floyd
☐ 7 Ruppert Jones
☐ 8 Gary Lance
☐ 9 Mark Littell
☐ 10 Keith Marshall
☐ 11 Gary Martz
☐ 12 Frank Ortenzio
☐ 13 Craig Perkins
☐ 14 Jamie Quirk
☐ 15 Steve Staggs
☐ 16 George Throop
☐ 17 U.L. Washington
☐ 18 John(Duke) Wathan

1975 Pacific Coast League All-Stars Broder

	NRMT	VG-E	GOOD
COMPLETE SET (36)	100.00	45.00	12.50
COMPLETE SET (37)	125.00	55.00	15.50

☐ 1 Orlando Alvarez
☐ 2 Ed Bane
☐ 3 Charlie Chant
☐ 4 Tommy Cruz
☐ 5 Bob Davis
☐ 6 Rob Dressler
☐ 7 Bob Hansen
☐ 8 Chuck Hartenstein
☐ 9 Roy Hartsfield
☐ 10 Leon Hooten
☐ 11 Steve Huntz
☐ 12 Ron Jackson
☐ 13 Jerry Johnson
☐ 14 Bob Jones
☐ 15 Art Kusnyer
☐ 16 John LeMaster
☐ 17 Dave McKay
☐ 18 Sid Monge
☐ 19 Buzz Nitschke
☐ 20 Rick Nitz
☐ 21 Kevin Pasley
☐ 22 Tony Pepper
☐ 23 Stan Perzanowski
☐ 24 Bobby Randall
☐ 25 Barry Raziano
☐ 26 Tommy Reynolds
☐ 27 Dave Roberts
☐ 28 Tom Robson
☐ 29 Gary Ross
☐ 30 Jerry Royster
☐ 31 Norm Sherry
☐ 32 Joe Simpson
☐ 33A Horace Speed
Portrait
☐ 33B Horace Speed
Action Shot
☐ 34 Rocky Stone
☐ 35 Jerry Turner
☐ 36 Stan Wall

1975 Phoenix Giants Caruso

	NRMT	VG-E	GOOD
COMPLETE SET (21)	25.00	11.00	3.10

☐ 1 Leon Brown
☐ 2 Jim Williams
☐ 3 Horace Speed
☐ 4 Tony Pepper
☐ 5 Skip James
☐ 6 Jack Mull
☐ 7 Rick Bradley
☐ 8 Glenn Redmon
☐ 9 Larry Herndon
☐ 10 Bruce Christensen
☐ 11 Mike Edan
☐ 12 John LeMaster
☐ 13 Tom Heintzelman
☐ 14 Rob Dressler
☐ 15 Greg Minton
☐ 16 Bob Knepper
☐ 17 Tommy Toms
☐ 18 Ed Sulka
☐ 19 Tony Gonzalez
☐ 20 Kyle Hydes
☐ 21 Don Rose

1975 Phoenix Giants Circle K

	NRMT	VG-E	GOOD
COMPLETE SET (26)	7.00	3.10	.85

☐ 1 Rocky Bridges
☐ 2 Jack Mull
☐ 3 Mike Sadek
☐ 4 Bob Nolan
☐ 5 Tony Gonzalez
☐ 6 Ed Sulka
☐ 7 Don Rose
☐ 8 Greg Minton
☐ 9 Tom Bradley
☐ 10 Bob Knepper
☐ 11 Rob Dressler
☐ 12 John LeMaster
☐ 13 Glenn Redmon
☐ 14 Skip James
☐ 15 Bruce Christiansen
☐ 16 Mike Eden
☐ 17 Tom Heintzelman
☐ 18 Tony Pepper
☐ 19 Jim Williams
☐ 20 Larry Herndon
☐ 21 Leon Brown
☐ 22 Horace Speed
☐ 23 Frank Johnson
☐ 24 Harry K. Jordan
☐ 25 Ethan Blackaby
☐ 26 Michael J. Cramer

1975 Quad City Angels TCMA

	NRMT	VG-E	GOOD
COMPLETE SET (34)	70.00	32.00	8.75

☐ 1 Rick Young
☐ 2 Ralph Botting
☐ 3 Willie Aikens
☐ 4 Bryant Fahrow
☐ 5 Stan Cliburn
☐ 6 Bobby Knoop
☐ 7 Jim Dorsey
☐ 8 Julio Cruz
☐ 9 Carl Person
☐ 10 Steve Mulliniks
☐ 11 Alex Guerrero
☐ 12 Manuel Jiminez
☐ 13 Rafael Kelly
☐ 14 Mike Howard
☐ 15 Carl Meche
☐ 16 Carlos Perez
☐ 17 Pat Kelly
☐ 18 John Hund
☐ 19 Mark Wulfemeyer
☐ 20 Steve Powers
☐ 21 John Roslund
☐ 22 Doug Slettvet
☐ 23 Billy Taylor
☐ 24 Mal Washington
☐ 25 Paul Hartzell
☐ 26 Steve Kelley
☐ 27 Andy Castillo
☐ 28 Danny Miller
☐ 29 Thad Bosley
☐ 30 Steve Brisbin
☐ 31 Kim Allen
☐ 32 Mark Stipetich
☐ 33 Mike Martinson
☐ 34 John Caneira

1975 Sacramento Solons Caruso

	NRMT	VG-E	GOOD
COMPLETE SET (22)	25.00	11.00	3.10

☐ 1 Bob Hansen
☐ 2 Dave Lindsey
☐ 3 Tommie Reynolds
☐ 4 Jack Lind
☐ 5 Toby Bianco
☐ 6 Bill McNulty
☐ 7 Duane Espy
☐ 8 Bob Sheldon
☐ 9 George Vasquez
☐ 10 Art Kusnyer
☐ 11 Rob Ellis
☐ 12 Jimmy Rosario
☐ 13 Steve Bowling
☐ 14 Rick Austin
☐ 15 Tom Widmar
☐ 16 Carl Austerman
☐ 17 Carlos Velasquez
☐ 18 Gordy Crane
☐ 19 Roger Miller
☐ 20 Bill Travers
☐ 21 Pat Osborn
☐ 22 Juan Lopez

1975 Salt Lake City Caruso

	NRMT	VG-E	GOOD
COMPLETE SET (20)	25.00	11.00	3.10

☐ 1 Rusty Torres
☐ 2 Dave Collins
☐ 3 John Balaz
☐ 4 Ron Jackson
☐ 5 Dan Briggs
☐ 6 John Doherty
☐ 7 Frankie George
☐ 8 Bob Miley
☐ 9 Darrell Darrow
☐ 10 Rocky Jordan
☐ 11 Ike Hampton
☐ 12 Gary Wheelock
☐ 13 Charlie Hockenberry
☐ 14 Gary Ryerson
☐ 15 Barry Raziano
☐ 16 Louis Quintana
☐ 17 Sid Monge
☐ 18 Charlie Hudson
☐ 19 Steve Blateric
☐ 20 Norm Sherry

1975 San Antonio Brewers TCMA

	NRMT	VG-E	GOOD
COMPLETE SET (22)	40.00	18.00	5.00

☐ 1 Wil Aaron
☐ 2 Ed Arsenault
☐ 3 Jerry Bell
☐ 4 Mike Brooks
☐ 5 Gary Cleverly
☐ 6 Joe Garcia
☐ 7 Bob Grossman
☐ 8 Rich Guerra
☐ 9 Mike Hannah
☐ 10 Bob Hickey
☐ 11 Bill Hiss
☐ 12 Dennis Kinney
☐ 13 Manny Lantigua
☐ 14 Tom Linnert
☐ 15 Tony Manning
☐ 16 Steve Rametta
☐ 17 Andy Rodriguez
☐ 18 Ron Salyer
☐ 19 Woody Smith
☐ 20 Paul Starkovich
☐ 21 Gary Weese
☐ 22 Norm Werd

1975 Shreveport Captains TCMA

	NRMT	VG-E	GOOD
COMPLETE SET (23)	50.00	22.00	6.25

☐ 1 Paul Djakonow
☐ 2 Mike Edwards
☐ 3 Mike Gonzalez
☐ 4 Frank Grundler
☐ 5 Randy Hopkins
☐ 6 Tim Jones
☐ 7 Mike Kavanagh
☐ 8 Rick Langford
☐ 9 Don Leshnock
☐ 10 Ken Melvin
☐ 11 Ron Mitchell
☐ 12 Tim Murtaugh
☐ 13 Dave Nelson
☐ 14 Doug Nelson
☐ 15 Steve Nicosia
☐ 16 Max Oliveras
☐ 17 Mitch Page
☐ 18 Harry Saferight
☐ 19 Randy Sealy
☐ 20 Jim Sexton
☐ 21 Rich Standart
☐ 22 Tom Thomas
☐ 23 Steve Williams

1975 Spokane Indians Caruso

	NRMT	VG-E	GOOD
COMPLETE SET (21)	20.00	9.00	2.50

☐ 1 Tom Robson
☐ 2 Dave Moates
☐ 3 Rudy Kinard
☐ 4 Charlie Borders
☐ 5 Rick Guarnera
☐ 6 Roy Smalley
☐ 7 Ken Pape
☐ 8 Tommy Cruz
☐ 9 Bob Jones
☐ 10 Doug Ault
☐ 11 Ron Pruitt
☐ 12 Dave Criscione
☐ 13 John Astroth
☐ 14 Mike Cubbage
☐ 15 Rick Kemp
☐ 16 Rick Waits
☐ 17 Jerry Bostic
☐ 18 Mike Bacsik
☐ 19 Dave Moharter
☐ 20 Art DeFillipis
☐ 21 Ron Norman

1975 Syracuse Chiefs Team Issue

This 1975 Syracuse Chiefs team issued set features major league players as well as minor league players from the Yankee organization. The cards are black and white and measure 2'1/2" X 3'1/2". The cards were inserted one at a time inside the Syracuse Chiefs minor league programs. Rich Bladt was a late addition to the set.

	NRMT	VG-E	GOOD
COMPLETE SET (24)	140.00	65.00	17.50
COMPLETE SET W/BLADT (25)	200.00	90.00	25.00

☐ 1 Ron Blomberg
☐ 2 Bobby Cox MG
☐ 3 Rick Dempsey
☐ 4 Pat Dobson
☐ 5 Whitey Ford CO
☐ 6 Elston Howard CO
☐ 7 Jerry Kenney
☐ 8 Sparky Lyle
☐ 9 Mickey Mantle
☐ 10 Tippy Martinez
☐ 11 Scott McGregor
☐ 12 George Medich
☐ 13 Thurman Munson
☐ 14 Graig Nettles
☐ 15 Dave Pagan
☐ 16 Billy Parker
☐ 17 Babe Ruth
☐ 18 Rick Sawyer
☐ 19 Fred Stanley
☐ 20 Mel Stottlemyre
☐ 21 Otto Velez
☐ 22 Bill Virdon
☐ 23 Roy White
☐ 24 Terry Whitfield
☐ NNO Rick Bladt (Late Issue)

1975 Tacoma Twins KMMO

	NRMT	VG-E	GOOD
COMPLETE SET (21)	10.00	4.50	1.25

☐ 1 Mark Wiley
☐ 2 Dave McKay
☐ 3 Jerry Terrell
☐ 4 Tom Lundstedt
☐ 5 Bill Ralston
☐ 6 Randy Beach
☐ 7 Randy Bass
☐ 8 Rick Renick
☐ 9 Bob Gorinski
☐ 10 Cal Ermer MG
☐ 11 Tom Johnson
☐ 12 Rocky Stone
☐ 13 Eddie Bane
☐ 14 Mike Pazik
☐ 15 Greg Thayer
☐ 16 Brad Cutler
☐ 17 Coley Smith
☐ 18 Juan Veintidos
☐ 19 Tom Kelly
☐ 20 Ed Palat
☐ 21 Mike Poepping

1975 Tidewater Tides Team Issue

	NRMT	VG-E	GOOD
COMPLETE SET (24)	150.00	70.00	19.00

☐ 1 Benny Ayala
☐ 2 Bob Bartlett
☐ 3 Dwight Bernard
☐ 4 Kent Biggerstaff
☐ 5 Bruce Boisclair
☐ 6 Nardi Contreras Jr.
☐ 7 Jerry Cram
☐ 8 Mark DeJohn
☐ 9 Ron Diggle
☐ 10 Nino Espinosa
☐ 11 Leo Foster
☐ 12 Joe Frazier
☐ 13 Ron Hodges
☐ 14 Jay Kleven
☐ 15 Bill Laxton
☐ 16 Gary Manderbach
☐ 17 Brock Pemberton
☐ 18 Terry Senn
☐ 19 Ray Staiger
☐ 20 Randy Sterling
☐ 21 Craig Swan
☐ 22 George Theodore
☐ 23 Mike Vail
☐ 24 Mike Wegener

1975 Tucson Toros Caruso

	NRMT	VG-E	GOOD
COMPLETE SET (21)	15.00	6.75	1.85

☐ 1 Bill Grabarkewitz
☐ 2 Tom Sandt
☐ 3 Ramon Webster
☐ 4 Gaylen Pitts
☐ 5 Buzz Nitschke
☐ 6 Mike Weathers
☐ 7 Dale Sanner
☐ 8 Charlie Chant
☐ 9 Ike Blessitt
☐ 10 Keith Lieppman
☐ 11 Rich McKinney
☐ 12 Juan Gomez
☐ 13 Lew Krausse
☐ 14 Craig Mitchell
☐ 15 Leo Mazzone
☐ 16 Skip Lockwood
☐ 17 Leon Hooten
☐ 18 Alan Griffin
☐ 19 Skip Pitlock
☐ 20 Roger Nelson
☐ 21 Hank Aquirre

1975 Tucson Toros Team Issue

	NRMT	VG-E	GOOD
COMPLETE SET (24)	40.00	18.00	5.00

☐ 1 Hank Aquirre
☐ 2 Charlie Chant
☐ 3 Juan Gomez
☐ 4 Bill Grabarkewitz
☐ 5 Alan Griffin
☐ 6 Leon Hooten
☐ 7 Lew Krausse
☐ 8 Chester Lemon
☐ 9 Skip Lockwood
☐ 10 Leo Mazzone
☐ 11 Rich McKinney
☐ 12 Craig Mitchell
☐ 13 Roger Nelson
☐ 14 Buzz Nitschke
☐ 15 Orlando Pena
☐ 16 Galyen Pitts
☐ 17 Charlie Sands
☐ 18 Tom Sandt
☐ 19 Dale Sanner
☐ 20 Mike Weathers
☐ 21 Ramon Webster
☐ 22 Larry Davis
☐ 23 Freddie The Toro
☐ NNO Autograph Card

1975 Tulsa Oilers 7-11

	NRMT	VG-E	GOOD
COMPLETE SET (24)	100.00	45.00	12.50

☐ 1 Hector Cruz
☐ 2 Leon Lee
☐ 3 Ken Boyer
☐ 4 Kenneth Reynolds
☐ 5 Richard Leon
☐ 6 Kenneth Crosby
☐ 7 Michael Kelleher
☐ 8 Harold Lanier
☐ 9 James Willoughby
☐ 10 William Parsons
☐ 11 Harold Rasmussen
☐ 12 Larry Herndon
☐ 13 Douglas Howard
☐ 14 Michael Proly
☐ 15 Gregory Terlecky
☐ 16 Jerry Mumphrey
☐ 17 Randall Wiles
☐ 18 Joseph Lindsey
☐ 19 John Johnson
☐ 20 James Foor
☐ 21 Sergio Robles
☐ 22 Thomas Harmon
☐ 23 Mario Guerreo
☐ 24 Richard Billings

1975 Waterbury Dodgers TCMA

Approximately 1,100 sets were produced. Black and White

	NRMT	VG-E	GOOD
COMPLETE SET (22)	50.00	22.00	6.25

☐ 1 Tom Badcock
☐ 2 Jose Baez
☐ 3 Glenn Burke
☐ 4 Larry Corrigan
☐ 5 Bob Detherage
☐ 6 Mike Dimmel
☐ 7 Art Fischetti
☐ 8 Dewey Forry
☐ 9 Rafael Landestoy
☐ 10 Dave Lanfair
☐ 11 Don LeJohn
☐ 12 Bob Lesslie
☐ 13 Rich Magner
☐ 14 Barney Mestek
☐ 15 Steve Patchin
☐ 16 Thad Philyaw
☐ 17 Lance Rautzham
☐ 18 Jim Riggleman
☐ 19 Don Standley
☐ 20 Tim Steele
☐ 21 Jim Van Der Beck
☐ 22 Marvin Webb

1975 Waterloo Royals TCMA

	NRMT	VG-E	GOOD
COMPLETE SET (34)	90.00	40.00	11.00
COMPLETE SET W/LATE ISSUE (35)	120.00	55.00	15.00

☐ 1A German Barranca (Waterloo Logo)
☐ 1B German Barranca (Dubuque Logo--Late Issue)
☐ 2 Al Bartlinski
☐ 3 John Bass
☐ 4 Charlie Beamon
☐ 5 Roy Branch
☐ 6 Dave/Brenda Brunk
☐ 7 Willie Clark
☐ 8 Pat Curran
☐ 9 Karel Deleeuw
☐ 10 Bobby Edmondson
☐ 11 Bobby Flacon
☐ 12 Craig Flanders
☐ 13 Joe Gates
☐ 14 Luis Gonzalez
☐ 15 John Hart
☐ 16 Dave Hrovat
☐ 17 Steve Lacy
☐ 18 Kevin Lahey
☐ 19 Tom Laseter
☐ 20 Manuel Moreta
☐ 21 Lou Olsen
☐ 22 Darrell Parker
☐ 23 Jerry Peterson
☐ 24 Dan Quisenberry
☐ 25 Ed Sempsprott
☐ 26 Luis Silverio
☐ 27 Dick Smotherman
☐ 28 Mark Souza
☐ 29 John Sullivan
☐ 30 Roy Tanner
☐ 31 Hal Thomasson
☐ 32 Gary Williams
☐ 33 Mike Williams
☐ 34 Willie Wilson

1975 West Palm Beach Expos Sussman

This 32-card standard-size set of the 1975 West Palm Beach Expos, a Class A Florida State League affiliate of the Montreal Expos, features white-bordered posed black-and-white player photos on its fronts. The team name appears above the photo, while the player's name and position are printed on the bottom. The backs are blank. The cards are numbered on the front in the upper left corner.

	NRMT	VG-E	GOOD
COMPLETE SET (29)	30.00	13.50	3.70
COMPLETE SET W/LATE ISSUES (32)	50.00	22.00	6.25

☐ 1 Julio Perez
☐ 2 Gary Gingrich
☐ 3 Jim Baby
☐ 4A Team Photo
☐ 4B Fred Whitacre (Late Issue)
☐ 5 Mark Ewell
☐ 6 Jose Bastian
☐ 7 Roberto Ramos
☐ 8 Carlos Ledezma
☐ 9 Joe Kerrigan
☐ 10 Hal Dues
☐ 11 Marcel Lachemann
☐ 12 Godfrey Evans
☐ 13 Jerry Fry
☐ 14 Ron Staggs
☐ 15 Mike Curran
☐ 16 William Welsh
☐ 17 Gordon MacKenzie
☐ 18 Chris Wood
☐ 19 Mike Grabowski
☐ 20 Bob Woodland
☐ 21 Shane Rawley
☐ 22 Gary Horstmann
☐ 23 Mike Finlayson
☐ 24 Dave MacQuarrie
☐ 25 Larry Horn
☐ 26 Mark Knose
☐ 27 Ron Sorey
☐ 28 Guy Krause
☐ 29A Antonio Bernazand
☐ 29B Guy Krause (Late Issue)
☐ 30 Antonio Bernazand (Late Issue)

1976 Appleton Foxes TCMA

	NRMT	VG-E	GOOD
COMPLETE SET (29)	50.00	22.00	6.25

☐ 1 Jay Attardi
☐ 2 Roy Coulter
☐ 3 Curt Etchandy
☐ 4 Rick Evans
☐ 5 Mike Farrell
☐ 6 Bob Flynn
☐ 7 Jim Handley
☐ 8 Marshal Harper
☐ 9 Tom Joyce
☐ 10 Bill Kautzer
☐ 11 Bill Lehman
☐ 12 Mitch Lukevics
☐ 13 Bob Madden
☐ 14 Pete Maropis
☐ 15 Candy Mercado
☐ 16 Phil Nerone
☐ 17 Mike Nored
☐ 18 Ed Olszta
☐ 19 Harris Price
☐ 20 Curt Ramstack
☐ 21 Scott Richartz
☐ 22 Silvano Robles
☐ 23 Ted Schultz
☐ 24 Randy Seltzer
☐ 25 Mike Smith
☐ 26 Tommy Toman
☐ 27 Ed Yesenchak
☐ 28 Ed Holtz and Jim Napier
☐ 29 Batboys

1976 Arkansas Travelers TCMA

Approximately 1,100 sets were produced. Black and White.

	NRMT	VG-E	GOOD
COMPLETE SET (12)	175.00	80.00	22.00

☐ 1 Cardell Camper
☐ 2 Manny Castillo
☐ 3 Bill Caudill
☐ 4 Jack Krol
☐ 5 Ryan Kurosaki
☐ 6 Terry Landrum
☐ 7 Ken Oberkfell
☐ 8 Mike Ramsey
☐ 9 John Urrea
☐ 10 Bill Valentine
☐ 11 Randy Wiles
☐ 12 John Young

1976 Asheville Tourists TCMA

	NRMT	VG-E	GOOD
COMPLETE SET (25)	50.00	22.00	6.25

☐ 1 Joe Russell
☐ 2 Randy Reynolds
☐ 3 Paul Mirabella
☐ 4 David Rivera
☐ 5 Bob Carroll
☐ 6 Bill Stone
☐ 7 Riccardo Lisi
☐ 8 Ward Smith
☐ 9 Wayne Pinkerton
☐ 10 David McCarthy
☐ 11 Wayne Pinkerton
☐ 12 Richard Couch
☐ 13 Mike Arrington
☐ 14 Jerry Gaines
☐ 15 Patrick Putnam
☐ 16 Patrick Moock
☐ 17 Mark Miller
☐ 18 LaRue Washington
☐ 19 Danny Tidwell
☐ 20 Wayne Terwilliger
☐ 21 Glen Purvis
☐ 22 Len Glowzenski
☐ 23 Mark Soroko
☐ 24 Edward Miller
☐ 25 Joseph Stewart

1976 Batavia Trojans Team Issue

	NRMT	VG-E	GOOD
COMPLETE SET (29	150.00	70.00	19.00

☐ 1 Ron Arp
☐ 2 John Brown
☐ 3 Rocky Bullard
☐ 4 John Buszka
☐ 5 Al Cajide
☐ 6 Jack Cassini
☐ 7 Denny Doss
☐ 8 Dave Fowlkes
☐ 9 Ray Gault
☐ 10 Tim Glass
☐ 11 Larry Harmon
☐ 12 Craig Harvey
☐ 13 Kevin Jeansonne
☐ 14 Bill Mitchell
☐ 15 Steve Narleski
☐ 16 Ken Preseren
☐ 17 Nate Puryear
☐ 18 Julian Rodriguez
☐ 19 Mike Rowe
☐ 20 Reggie Smith
☐ 21 John Spence
☐ 22 Sam Spence
☐ 23 Paul Tasker
☐ 24 John Teising
☐ 25 Jeff Tomski
☐ 26 Tony Toups
☐ 27 Terry Tyson
☐ 28 Troy Wilder
☐ 29 Bubba Wilson

1976 Baton Rouge Cougars TCMA

	NRMT	VG-E	GOOD
COMPLETE SET (21)	50.00	22.00	6.25

☐ 1 Sterling Allen
☐ 2 Nick Baltz
☐ 3 Matt Batts
☐ 4 Randy Benson
☐ 5 Mike Brooks
☐ 6 Tom Brown
☐ 7 Jim Carruth
☐ 8 Winston Cole
☐ 9 Robbie Cox
☐ 10 Kevin Fogg
☐ 11 Gary Grunsky
☐ 12 Larry Keenum
☐ 13 Paul Kennemur
☐ 14 Terry Leach
☐ 15 Mickey Miller
☐ 16 Dave Obal
☐ 17 Ken Palmer
☐ 18 Gerry Poche
☐ 19 Ed Stephenson
☐ 20 Bob Taylor
☐ 21 Curtis Wallace

1976 Burlington Bees TCMA

	NRMT	VG-E	GOOD
COMPLETE SET (33)	50.00	22.00	6.25

☐ 1 Greg Anderson
☐ 2 Gary Conn
☐ 3 Roger Danson
☐ 4 John Dempsey
☐ 5 Bill Dick
☐ 6 Alvin Edge
☐ 7 Butch Edge
☐ 8 Miguel Encarcion
☐ 9 Adalberto Flores
☐ 10 Rich Ford
☐ 11 Elliott Franklin
☐ 12 George Frazier
☐ 13 Matt Galante
☐ 14 Frank Gaton
☐ 15 Gary Gingrich
☐ 16 Dave Globig
☐ 17 John Hannon
☐ 18 Dennis Holmberg
☐ 19 Sam Jones
☐ 20 Gary Larocque
☐ 21 Shawn McCarthy
☐ 22 Sam Monteau
☐ 23 Willie Mueller
☐ 24 Rick O'Keeffe
☐ 25 Jay Passmore
☐ 26 Abelino Pena
☐ 27 Eric Restin
☐ 28 Edgardo Romero
☐ 29 Chuck Ross
☐ 30 Dave Smith
☐ 31 Ron Smith
☐ 32 Talmage Tanks
☐ 33 Ron Wrona

1976 Cedar Rapids Giants TCMA

	NRMT	VG-E	GOOD
COMPLETE SET (37)	40.00	18.00	5.00
COMPLETE SET (39)	80.00	36.00	10.00

☐ 1 Terry Adams
☐ 2 Dave Anderson
☐ 3 Ted Barnicle
☐ 4 Jose Barrios
☐ 5 Ken Barton
☐ 6 Bryan Boyne
☐ 7 Don Buchheister
☐ 8 Ken Burton
☐ 9 Wayne Cato
☐ 10 Mike Clinatsis
☐ 11A Steve Grimes (Incorrect name on back)
☐ 11B Steve Grimes (Correct name on back)
☐ 12 Ron Hodges

☐ 13 John Johnson
☐ 14 Steven McKown
☐ 15 Dave Mendoza
☐ 16 Stan Moline
☐ 17 Dick Murray
☐ 18 Billy Ray Parker
☐ 19 Francis Parker
☐ 20 Wayne Pechek
☐ 21 Tim Peterson
☐ 22 Jim Pryor
☐ 23 Mike Rex
☐ 24 Pat Roy
☐ 25 German De Los Santos
☐ 26 Don Sasser
☐ 27 Ted Schoenhaus
☐ 28 Steve Sherman
☐ 29 Bill Tullish
☐ 30 Lozando Washington
☐ 31 Steve Watson
☐ 32 Steve Wilkins
☐ 33 Barney Wilson
☐ 34A Mark Woodbrey
(Incorrect name on back)
☐ 34B Mark Woodbrey
(Correct name on back)
☐ 35 Ernie Young
☐ 36 Jeff Yurak
☐ 37 Cedar Rapids Team

1976 Clinton Pilots TCMA

	NRMT	VG-E	GOOD
COMPLETE SET (35)	125.00	55.00	15.50
COMPLETE SET W/LATE ISSUES (37)	175.00	80.00	22.00

☐ 1 Phil Bauer
☐ 2 Mike Bigusiak
☐ 3 Ken Bokek
☐ 4 Bobby Buford
☐ 5 Davy Burress
☐ 6 Felan Byrd
☐ 7 Tom Carlson
☐ 8 George Davis
☐ 9 Fred Dipietro
☐ 10 Julian Ditto
☐ 11 Tim Doerr
☐ 12 Mike Elders
☐ 13 Freeman Evans
☐ 14 Popilio Fermin
☐ 15 Don Fletcher
☐ 16 Miguel Garcia
☐ 17 Kerry Getter
☐ 18 Juan Gonzalez
☐ 19 Bob Hartsfield
☐ 20 Kent Hunziker
☐ 21 Joe Jackson
☐ 22 Tom King
☐ 23 Greg Kline (Late Issue)
☐ 24 Willie Mueller
☐ 25 Denzil Palmer
☐ 26 Jack Parish
☐ 27 Gene Quick
☐ 28 Silvano Robles (Late Issue)
☐ 29 Phil Trucks
☐ 30 Jackie Uhey
☐ 31 Mike Vaughn
☐ 32 Paul Vavruska
☐ 33 Larry Walbring
☐ 34 Mal Washington
☐ 35 Ward Wilson
☐ 36 Dave Wood
☐ 37 Donna Colschen
Fritz Colschen

1976 Dubuque Packers TCMA

	NRMT	VG-E	GOOD
COMPLETE SET (40)	50.00	22.00	6.25

☐ 1 Jose Alvarez
☐ 2 Edward Anderson
☐ 3 Reno Aragon
☐ 4 Bruce Bochy
☐ 5 Leroy Clark
☐ 6 John Clothery
☐ 7 Robert Cluck MGR
☐ 8 Neal Cooper
☐ 9 Martin DeMerritt
☐ 10 Jeff Ellison
☐ 11 Larry Eubanks
☐ 12 Barry Glabman
☐ 13 Larry Green
☐ 14 Robert Hallgren
☐ 15 Michael Hasley
☐ 16 Ray Hutchinson
☐ 17 Alan Knicely
☐ 18 Kenneth LaHonta
☐ 19 George Lauzerique CO
☐ 20 John Lee
☐ 21 William Melendez
☐ 22 Michael Mendoza
☐ 23 Richard Miller
☐ 24 Raul Nieves
☐ 25 Martin Perez
☐ 26 Donald Pisker
☐ 27 Joseph Pittman

☐ 28 Gordon Pladson
☐ 29 Pedro Prieto TR
☐ 30 Bill Roberts
☐ 31 Alberto Rondon
☐ 32 Simon Rosario
☐ 33 Randy Rouse
☐ 34 Jeffrey Smith
☐ 35 Ray Thompson
☐ 36 Tom Twellman
☐ 37 Michael Tyler
☐ 38 Jerry Willeford
☐ 39 Gary Wilson
☐ 40 George Lauzerique
Bob Cluck
Steve Greenberg

1976 Fort Lauderdale Yanks Sussman

	NRMT	VG-E	GOOD
COMPLETE SET (30)	80.00	36.00	10.00

☐ 1 Jesus Figueroa
☐ 2 Duke Drawdy
☐ 3 Jerry Narron
☐ 4 Joe Alcantara
☐ 5 Jim McDonald
☐ 6 Tom Davis
☐ 7 Bernardo Estevez
☐ 8 Jim Lysgaard
☐ 9 Domingo Ramos
☐ 10 Ken Kruppa
☐ 11 Nate Chapman
☐ 12 Antonio Bautista
☐ 13 Darnell Waters
☐ 14 Mike Heath
☐ 15 Damaso Garcia
☐ 16 Marty Caffrey
☐ 17 Mike Ferraro
☐ 18 Orlando Pena
☐ 19 Dave Wright
☐ 20 Greg Diehl
☐ 21 Willie Upshaw
☐ 22 Roger Slagle
☐ 23 Rick Stenholm
☐ 24 Benny Perez
☐ 25 Tim Lewis
☐ 26 Bevan Luis
☐ 27 Doug Melvin
☐ 28 Randy Niemann
☐ 29 Juan Espino
☐ 30 Sandy Valdespino

1976 Hawaii Islanders Caruso

	NRMT	VG-E	GOOD
COMPLETE SET (21)	30.00	13.50	3.70

☐ 1 Chuck Hartenstein
☐ 2 Jim Shellenback
☐ 3 Eddie Watt
☐ 4 Roy Hartsfield
☐ 5 Dave Roberts
☐ 6 Bobby Valentine
☐ 7 John Scott
☐ 8 Jerry Stone
☐ 9 Dave Hilton
☐ 10 Bill Almon
☐ 11 Joe Pepitone
☐ 12 Gaylen McSpadden
☐ 13 Gene Richards
☐ 14 Ken Reynolds
☐ 15 Jim Fairey
☐ 16 Dave Freisleben
☐ 17 Kala Kaaihue
☐ 18 Rod Gaspar
☐ 19 Jerry Johnson
☐ 20 Steve Huntz
☐ 21 Mike Champion

1976 Indianapolis Indians Team Issue

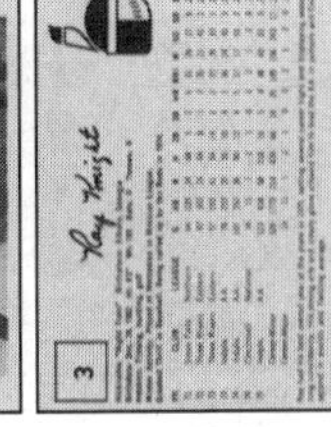

	NRMT	VG-E	GOOD
COMPLETE SET (26)	40.00	18.00	5.00

☐ 1 Jim Snyder MG
☐ 2 Larry Payne
☐ 3 Ray Knight
☐ 4 Arturo DeFreites

☐ 5 Joe Henderson
☐ 6 Tom Spencer
☐ 7 Dave Revering
☐ 8 Jeff Sovern
☐ 9 Tom Hume
☐ 10 Rudy Meoli
☐ 11 Sonny Ruberto
☐ 12 Tom Carroll
☐ 13 Junior Kennedy
☐ 14 Lorin Grow
☐ 15 Dave Schneck
☐ 16 Manny Sarmiento
☐ 17 Don Werner
☐ 18 Mike Thompson
☐ 19 Keith Marshall
☐ 20 Rick Hinton
☐ 21 John Knox
☐ 22 Mac Scarce
☐ 23 Tony Franklin
☐ 24 Carlos Alfonso
☐ 25 Ron McClain TR
☐ 26 Checklist

1976 Oklahoma City 89ers Team Issue

	NRMT	VG-E	GOOD
COMPLETE SET (24)	90.00	40.00	11.00

☐ 1 Terry Jones
☐ 2 Sergio Ferrer
☐ 3 Ronald Clark CO
☐ 4 Lonnie Smith
☐ 6 James Morrison
☐ 7 Michael Buskey
☐ 8 Dane Iorg
☐ 10 Richard Bosetti
☐ 11 Jesus Hernaiz
☐ 12 Fred Andrews Jr.
☐ 14 James Bunning MG
☐ 15 Randy Lerch
☐ 16 Danny Boitano
☐ 18 Willie Hernandez
☐ 19 William Nahorodny
☐ 20 Ruben Amaro CO
☐ 21 David Wallace
☐ 22 Wayne Nordhagen
☐ 23 Quency Hill
☐ 24 John Bastable
☐ 25 John Montague Jr.
☐ 26 Manuel Seoane
☐ 28 Larry Kiser
☐ 30 Robert Oliver

1976 Omaha Royals Top Trophies

	NRMT	VG-E	GOOD
COMPLETE SET (27)	100.00	45.00	12.50

☐ 1 Hall of Fame Members
☐ 2 Hal Baird
☐ 3 Mark Ballinger
☐ 4 Tom Bruno
☐ 5 Jerry Cram
☐ 6 Dave Cripe
☐ 7 Dave Hasbach
☐ 8 Bob Johnson
☐ 9 Ruppert Jones
☐ 10 Gary Lance
☐ 11 Sheldon Mallory
☐ 12 Gary Martz
☐ 13 Bob McClure
☐ 14 Lynn McKinney
☐ 15 Brian Murphy
☐ 16 Roger Nelson
☐ 17 Lew Olsen
☐ 18 Frank Ortenzio
☐ 19 Steve Patchin
☐ 20 Max Patkin
☐ 21 Craig Perkins
☐ 22 Steve Staggs
☐ 23 Bill Sudakis
☐ 24 George Throop
☐ 25 U.L. Washington
☐ 26 Duke Wathan
☐ 27 Joe Zbed

1976 Phoenix Giants Caruso

	NRMT	VG-E	GOOD
COMPLETE SET (20)	30.00	13.50	3.70

☐ 1 John LeMaster
☐ 2 Bruce Christensen
☐ 3 Kyle Hypes
☐ 4 Silvano Quezada
☐ 5 Skip James
☐ 6 Rocky Bridges
☐ 7 Frank Riccelli
☐ 8 Horace Speed
☐ 9 Terry Cornutt
☐ 10 Mike Wegener
☐ 11 Gary Alexander
☐ 12 Tommy Toms

☐ 13 Bob Gallagher
☐ 14 Mike Eden
☐ 15 Bob Knepper
☐ 16 Tom Heintzelman
☐ 17 Joey Martin
☐ 18 Ed Plank
☐ 19 Jack Clark
☐ 20 Bruce Miller

1976 Phoenix Giants Coca Cola

	NRMT	VG-E	GOOD
COMPLETE SET (24)	15.00	6.75	1.85

☐ 1 Gary Alexander
☐ 2 Ethan Blackaby
General Manager
☐ 3 Rocky Bridges MG
☐ 4 Terry Cornutt
☐ 5 Bruce Christensen
☐ 6 Jack Clark
☐ 7 Rob Dressler
☐ 8 Mike Eden
☐ 9 Bob Gallagher
☐ 10 Tom Heintzelman
☐ 11 Larry Herndon
☐ 12 Kyle Hypes
☐ 13 Skip James
☐ 14 Bob Knepper
☐ 15 Johnnie Le Master
☐ 16 Jack Mull
☐ 17 Bruce Miller
☐ 18 Ed Plank
☐ 19 Silvano Quezada
☐ 20 Frank Riccelli
☐ 21 Horace Speed
☐ 22 Tommy Toms
☐ 23 Mike Wegener
☐ 24 Harry Jordan TR
Tommy Gonzales
Stadium Supervisor
(Checklist)

1976 Phoenix Giants Cramer

	NRMT	VG-E	GOOD
COMPLETE SET (24)	30.00	13.50	3.70

☐ 2 Johnnie LeMaster
☐ 10 Jack Mull
☐ 11 Larry Herndon
☐ 14 Bruce Miller
☐ 15 Skip James
☐ 17 Bruce Christensen
☐ 18 Bob Gallagher
☐ 19 Mike Eden
☐ 20 Horace Speed
☐ 22 Jack Clark
☐ 23 Tom Heintzelman
☐ 25 Gary Alexander
☐ 26 Rocky Bridges
☐ 28 Ed Plank
☐ 30 Frank Ricelli
☐ 32 Silvano Quezada
☐ 33 Tommy Toms
☐ 34 Bob Knepper
☐ 35 Mike Wegener
☐ 36 Kyle Hypes
☐ 37 Rob Dressler
☐ 38 Terry Cornutt
☐ NNO Harry Jordan
Tommy Gonzalez CL
☐ NNO Ethan Blackaby

1976 Phoenix Giants Valley National Bank

	NRMT	VG-E	GOOD
COMPLETE SET (24)	20.00	9.00	2.50

☐ 1 Gary Alexander
☐ 2 Rocky Bridges
☐ 3 Bruce Christensen
☐ 4 Jack Clark
☐ 5 Terry Cornutt
☐ 6 Jay Dillard
☐ 7 Bob Gallagher
☐ 8 Don Hahn
☐ 9 Tom Heintzelman
☐ 10 Kyle Hypes
☐ 11 Skip James
☐ 12 Harry Jordan
☐ 13 Bob Knepper
☐ 14 Johnny LeMaster
☐ 15 Joey Martin
☐ 16 Bruce Miller
☐ 17 Greg Minton
☐ 18 Jack Mull
☐ 19 Ed Plank
☐ 20 Silvano Quezada
☐ 21 Frank Ricelli
☐ 22 Horace Speed
☐ 23 Tommy Toms
☐ 24 Mike Wegener

1976 Quad City Angels TCMA

Card #21 Manuel Mercedes is a scarce late issue.

	NRMT	VG-E	GOOD
COMPLETE SET (39)	150.00	70.00	19.00
COMPLETE SET W/LATE ISSUE (40)	200.00	90.00	25.00

☐ 1 Dan Beerbrower
☐ 2 Ned Bergert TR
☐ 3 Ralph Botting
☐ 4 Bob Boyd
☐ 5 Gary Boyle
☐ 6 Rich Brewster
☐ 7 Jim Brown
☐ 8 Jerry Brust
☐ 9 Bob Clark
☐ 10 Mark Clear
☐ 11 Stan Cliburn
☐ 12 Steve Eddy
☐ 13 Bill Ewing
☐ 14 Bob Ferris
☐ 15 John Flannery
☐ 16 David Hollifield
☐ 17 Rafael Kelly
☐ 18 Carney Lansford
☐ 19 Joe Maddon
☐ 20 Mike Martinson
☐ 21 Manuel Mercedes (Late Issue)
☐ 22 Scott Moffit
☐ 23 Don Mraz
☐ 24 Mystery Infielder
Harry Pells
☐ 25 Jim Officer
☐ 26 Harry Pells GM
☐ 27 Charles Porter
☐ 28 Jerry Quigley
☐ 29 John Ricanelli
☐ 30 Bob Slater
☐ 31 Doug Slettvet
☐ 32 Randy Smith
☐ 33 Bob Starks
☐ 34 Dave Steck
☐ 35 Larry "Moose" Stubing MGR
☐ 36 Billy Taylor
☐ 37 Steve Tebbetts
☐ 38 Richard Thon
☐ 39 Steve Whitehead
☐ 40 Ken Wright

1976 Sacramento Solons Caruso

	NRMT	VG-E	GOOD
COMPLETE SET (23)	25.00	11.00	3.10

☐ 1 Dave Criscione
☐ 2 Keith Smith
☐ 3 Dave Moharter
☐ 4 Craig Skok
☐ 5 Bob Jones
☐ 6 Mike Bacsik
☐ 7 Tommy Cruz
☐ 8 Tommy Boggs
☐ 9 Doug Ault
☐ 10 Greg Pryor
☐ 11 Charlie Bordes
☐ 12 Art DeFillippis
☐ 13 John Sutton
☐ 14 Ed Nottle
☐ 15 Jim Gideon
☐ 16 Don Thomas
☐ 17 Bump Wills
☐ 18 Lew Beasley
☐ 19 Jerry Bostic
☐ 20 Len Barker
☐ 21 David Clyde
☐ 22 Rick Donnelly
☐ 23 Greg Mahlberg

1976 Salt Lake City Gulls Caruso

	NRMT	VG-E	GOOD
COMPLETE SET (22)	20.00	9.00	2.50

☐ 1 Darrell Darrow
☐ 2 Gary Wheelock
☐ 3 Mike Overy
☐ 4 Frankie George
☐ 5 Carlos Lopez
☐ 6 Mike Miley
☐ 7 Mike Martinson
☐ 8 Ed Kurpiel
☐ 9 Billy Smith
☐ 10 Pat Cristelli
☐ 11 Orlando Alvarez
☐ 12 Ike Hampton
☐ 13 Chuck Hockenberry
☐ 14 Wayne Simpson
☐ 15 Dick Lange
☐ 16 Skip Pitlock
☐ 17 Luis Quintana
☐ 18 Paul Dade
☐ 19 Dave Collins
☐ 20 Dan Briggs
☐ 21 Charlie Hudson
☐ 22 Gil Flores

1976 San Antonio Brewers Team Issue

	NRMT	VG-E	GOOD
COMPLETE SET (26)	90.00	40.00	11.00

☐ 1 Mel Barrow
☐ 2 Frank Bolick
☐ 3 Don Bright
☐ 4 Mike Bucci
☐ 5 Jeffrey Byrd
☐ 6 Keith Chauncey
☐ 7 Jim Clancy
☐ 8 Bobby Cuellar
☐ 9 Doug Duncan
☐ 10 Dan Duran
☐ 11 Gary Gray
☐ 12 Ed Holman
☐ 13 Rudy Jaramillo
☐ 14 Marty Martinez
☐ 15 Brian Nakamoto
☐ 16 Ron Norman
☐ 17 Wayne Pinkerton
☐ 18 John Poloni
☐ 19 Ray Rainbolt
☐ 20 Rich Shubert
☐ 21 Mike Steen
☐ 22 Blair Stouffer
☐ 23 Don G. Thomas
☐ 24 Jim Thomas
☐ 25 Bobby Thompson
☐ 26 Dan Wheat

1976 Seattle Rainiers Cramer

B/W cards; measure 2" by 3", blank backs.

	NRMT	VG-E	GOOD
COMPLETE SET (20)	10.00	4.50	1.25

☐ 1 Russ Attebery
☐ 2 Vince Barbisan
☐ 3 George Benson
☐ 4 Xavier Dixon
☐ 5 Kevin Gilmartin
☐ 6 Paul Gilmartin
☐ 7 Ken Kanikeberg
☐ 8 Bob Kraft
☐ 9 Ken May
☐ 10 Danny Miller
☐ 11 Ken Peters
☐ 12 Art Peterson
☐ 13 Dennis Peterson
☐ 14 Doug Peterson
☐ 15 Terry Sheehan
☐ 16 Dave Sloan
☐ 17 Dave Stewart
☐ 18 Steve Stillwell
☐ 19 Steve Watson
☐ 20 Jimmy Williams

1976 Shreveport Captains TCMA

Card #23 Barry Weinberg was a late issue. The oversized team photo card (5 3/8" by 3 1/2") is considered very scarce.

	NRMT	VG-E	GOOD
COMPLETE SET (23)	50.00	22.00	6.25
COMPLETE SET W/WEINBERG (24)	125.00	55.00	15.50
COMPLETE SET W/TEAM PHOTO (25)	225.00	100.00	28.00

☐ 1 Gary Hargis
☐ 2 Rich Standart
☐ 3 Rich Anderson
☐ 4 Doug Nelson
☐ 5 Luke Wrenn
☐ 6 Mike Gonzalez
☐ 7 Rod Scurry
☐ 8 Jim Sexton
☐ 9 Paul Djakonow
☐ 10 Dave Nelson
☐ 11 Mike Edwards
☐ 12 Randy Sealy
☐ 13 John Lipon
☐ 14 Albert Louis
☐ 15 Silvio Martinez
☐ 16 Steve Blomberg
☐ 17 Frank Grundler
☐ 18 Harry Saferight
☐ 19 Chet Gunter
☐ 20 Rafael Cariel
☐ 21 Ron Mitchell
☐ 22 Randy Hopkins
☐ 23 Barry Weinberg (Late Issue)
☐ NNO Tim Murtaugh MGR
☐ NNO Team Photo

1976 Spokane Indians Caruso

	NRMT	VG-E	GOOD
COMPLETE SET (21)	25.00	11.00	3.10

☐ 1 Bobby Sheldon
☐ 2 Jimmy Rosario
☐ 3 Sam Ceci
☐ 4 Tom Widmar
☐ 5 Ron Jacobs
☐ 6 Bob Ellis
☐ 7 Juan Lopez
☐ 8 Kevin Kobel
☐ 9 Bob Strampe
☐ 10 Moose Haas
☐ 11 Perry Danforth
☐ 12 Art Kusnyer
☐ 13 Frank Howard
☐ 14 Gary Beare
☐ 15 Kurt Bevacqua
☐ 16 Tommie Reynolds
☐ 17 Bob Hansen
☐ 18 Steve Bowling
☐ 19 Len Sakata
☐ 20 Toby Bianco
☐ 21 Rick Austin

1976 Tacoma Twins Dairy Queen

	NRMT	VG-E	GOOD
COMPLETE SET (24)	30.00	13.50	3.70

☐ 1 Paul Ausman
☐ 2 Randy Bass
☐ 3 Bill Butler
☐ 4 Larry Cox
☐ 5 Tom Epperly
☐ 6 Cal Ermer
☐ 7 Jim Gideon
☐ 8 Bob Gorinski
☐ 9 Tom Johnson
☐ 10 Jack Maloof
☐ 11 Bob Maneely
☐ 12 Davis May
☐ 13 Dave McKay
☐ 14 Willie Norwood
☐ 15 Mike Pazik
☐ 16 Mike Pepping
☐ 17 Rick Renick
☐ 18 Tommy Sain
☐ 19 Dale Soderholm
☐ 20 Jim Van Wyck
☐ 21 Juan Veintidos
☐ 22 Mark Wiley
☐ 23 Rob Wilfong
☐ 24 Al Woods

1976 Tucson Toros Caruso

	NRMT	VG-E	GOOD
COMPLETE SET (20)	15.00	6.75	1.85

☐ 1 Bob Picciolo
☐ 2 Don Hopkins
☐ 3 Keith Lieppman
☐ 4 Gary Woods
☐ 5 Mike Weathers
☐ 6 Angel Manguel
☐ 7 Bob Lacey
☐ 8 Rich McKinney
☐ 9 Harry Bright
☐ 10 Wayne Gross
☐ 11 JIm Holt
☐ 12 Leon Hooten
☐ 13 Alan Griffin
☐ 14 Gaylen Pitts
☐ 15 Craig Mitchell
☐ 16 Tom Bradley
☐ 17 Rick Lysander
☐ 18 Charlie Hudson
☐ 19 Jeff Newman
☐ 20 Charlie Sands

1976 Tucson Toros Cramer

	NRMT	VG-E	GOOD
COMPLETE SET (24)	10.00	4.50	1.25

☐ 2 Mike Weathers
☐ 3 Gary Woods
☐ 6 Keith Lieppman
☐ 8 Angel Manguel
☐ 9 Rob Picciolo
☐ 10 Chris Batton
☐ 11 Don Hopkins
☐ 12 Jeff Newman
☐ 14 Dale Sanner
☐ 15 Wayne Kirby
☐ 16 Leon Hooten
☐ 19 Bob Lacey
☐ 22 Rich McKinney
☐ 23 Harry Bright
☐ 25 Wayne Gross
☐ 28 Rick Lysander
☐ 32 Craig Mitchell
☐ 33 Juan Gomez
☐ 34 Alan Griffin
☐ 35 Tom Bradley
☐ 37 Jim Holt
☐ 39 Charlie Sands
☐ 42 Gaylen Pitts
☐ 44 Skip Pitlock

1976 Tulsa Oilers Goof's Pants

	NRMT	VG-E	GOOD
COMPLETE SET (26)	250.00	110.00	31.00

☐ 1 Ken Boyer
☐ 2 Lloyd Allen
☐ 3 Tom Harmon
☐ 4 Stan Butkus
☐ 5 Doug Clary
☐ 6 Mike Easler
☐ 7 Doug Capilla
☐ 8 Stan Mejias
☐ 9 Ed Crosby
☐ 10 Jimmy Freeman
☐ 11 John Tamargo
☐ 12 Leon Lee
☐ 13 Lerrin LaGrow
☐ 14 Luis Alvarado
☐ 15 Mike Potter
☐ 16 Mike Proly
☐ 17 Bill Rothan
☐ 18 Garry Templeton
☐ 19 Tom Walker
☐ 20 Charlie Chant
☐ 21 Steve Waterbury
☐ 22 Randy Wiles
☐ 23 Satchel Paige (Autographed)
☐ 24 Paul Dean (Autographed)
☐ 25 Earl Bass
☐ 26 Lee Landers

1976 Waterloo Royals TCMA

	NRMT	VG-E	GOOD
COMPLETE SET (33)	75.00	34.00	9.50

☐ 1 Bob Barr
☐ 2 German Barranca
☐ 3 Steve Beene
☐ 4 Kent Cvejdlik
☐ 5 Karel DeLeeuw
☐ 6 Rich Dubee
☐ 7 Craig Eaton
☐ 8 Richard Gale
☐ 9 Danny Garcia
☐ 10 Kevin Gillen
☐ 11 Dale Hrovat
☐ 12 Jack Hudson
☐ 13 Clint Hurdle
☐ 14 Bryan Jones
☐ 15 Ron Kainer
☐ 16 Steve Lacy
☐ 17 Tom Laseter
☐ 18 Fernando Llodrat
☐ 19 Manuel Moreta
☐ 20 Darrell Parker
☐ 21 Ricky Passalacqua
☐ 22 Jerry Peterson
☐ 23 Ken Phelps
☐ 24 Dan Quisenberry
☐ 25 Ed Sempsrott
☐ 26 Luis Silverio
☐ 27 Ron Smith
☐ 28 Mark Souza
☐ 29 John Sullivan
☐ 30 Roy Tanner
☐ 31 Hal Thomasson
☐ 32 Alan Viebrock
☐ 33 Mike Williams

1976 Wausau Mets TCMA

	NRMT	VG-E	GOOD
COMPLETE SET (25)	50.00	22.00	6.25

☐ 1 Gene Bardot
☐ 2 Bob Barger
☐ 3 Dave Bedrosian
☐ 4 Butch Benton
☐ 5 Keith Bodie
☐ 6 Randy Brown
☐ 7 Paul Cacciatore
☐ 8 Larry Calufetti
☐ 9 Ed Cipot
☐ 10 Russell Clark
☐ 11 Steve Darnell
☐ 12 Tony Echols
☐ 13 Ed Hicks
☐ 14 Steve Kessels
☐ 15 Steve Love
☐ 16 Luis Lunar
☐ 17 Jim Miles
☐ 18 Jeryl McIver
☐ 19 Juan Monasterio

☐ 20 Bill Monbouquette
☐ 21 Ted O'Neill
☐ 22 Mario Ramirez
☐ 23 Willie Simon
☐ 24 Fred Westfall
☐ 25 Mike Feder and Jim Brown

1976 Williamsport Tomahawks TCMA

	NRMT	VG-E	GOOD
COMPLETE SET (23)	50.00	22.00	6.25

☐ 1 Wil Aaron
☐ 2 Ed Arsenault
☐ 3 Stan Bockewitz
☐ 4 Wayne Cage
☐ 5 Red Davis
☐ 6 Bob Grossman
☐ 7 Rich Guerra
☐ 8 Mike Hannah
☐ 9 Tom Linnert
☐ 10 Tom McGough
☐ 11 Mike Dolf
☐ 12 Lou Isaac
☐ 13 Pete Ithier
☐ 14 Dennis Kinney
☐ 15 George Mahan
☐ 16 Tim Norrid
☐ 17 Rick Oliver
☐ 18 Bob Servoss
☐ 19 Glenn Redmon
☐ 20 Pat Washko
☐ 21 Gary Weese
☐ 22 Kris Yoder
☐ 23 Checklist Card

1977 Appleton Foxes TCMA

This 30-card standard-size set of the 1977 Appleton Foxes, a Class A Midwest League affiliate of the Chicago White Sox, features white-bordered posed black-and-white player photos on its fronts. The player's name, position and Foxes logo appear in the orange section near the bottom. The league affiliation appears across an upper corner. The plain white back carries the McDonalds logo and the words "Appleton Foxes" in bold letters. The cards are unnumbered and checklisted below in alphabetical order. Card #16B Orestes Minoso Jr. is a late issue.

	NRMT	VG-E	GOOD
COMPLETE SET (29)	60.00	27.00	7.50
COMP. SET W/LATE ISSUE (30)	90.00	40.00	11.00

☐ 1 Appleton Foxes Staff
☐ 2 Tom Bright
☐ 3 Brad Calhoun
☐ 4 Bobby Combs
☐ 5 Marvis Foley
☐ 6 Lorenzo Gray
☐ 7 Marshall Harper
☐ 8 Greg Herman
☐ 9 Clay Hicks
☐ 10 A.J. Hill
☐ 11 Fred Howard
☐ 12 Kent Hunziker
☐ 13 Bob Madden
☐ 14 John Martin
☐ 15 Candy Mercado
☐ 16A Orestes Minosi Jr. ERR
☐ 16B Orestes Minoso Jr. COR (Late Issue)
☐ 17 Ed Olszta
☐ 18 Andy Pasillas
☐ 19 Joel Perez
☐ 20 Carlos Rios
☐ 21 Keith Rokosz
☐ 22 Randy Seltzer
☐ 23 Michael Sivik
☐ 24 Paul Soth
☐ 25 Leo Sutherland
☐ 26 Rick Thoren
☐ 27 Steve Trout
☐ 28 Mike Tulacz
☐ 29 Ed Yesenchak

1977 Arkansas Travelers TCMA

This 21-card standard-size set of the 1977 Arkansas Travelers, a Class AA Texas League affiliate of the St. Louis Cardinals, features white-bordered posed black-and-white player photos on its fronts. The player's name, position and Travelers logo appear in the orange section near the bottom. The league affiliation appears across an upper corner. The plain white back carries the player's name, position and biography. The cards are unnumbered and checklisted below in alphabetical order. Several of the players below have variations.

	NRMT	VG-E	GOOD
COMPLETE SET (12)	75.00	34.00	9.50
COMPLETE SET (21)	200.00	90.00	25.00

☐ 1 Ray Winder Field
☐ 2A Buzzy Keller MGR
☐ 2B Carlton Roy (Buzz) Keller MGR
☐ 3A Ryan Kurosaki (Logo on right)
☐ 3B Ryan Kurosaki (Logo on left)
☐ 4A Terry Landrum
☐ 4B Teto Landrum
☐ 5A Nick Leyva
☐ 5B Nick Leyva (Hand only slightly showing)
☐ 6 Mike Murphy
☐ 7A Mike Ramsey (Logo on right)
☐ 7B Mike Ramsey (Logo on left)
☐ 8A Andy Replogle (Logo on right)
☐ 8B Andy Replogle (Logo on left)
☐ 9A Jim Riggleman (Logo on right)
☐ 9B Jim Riggleman (Logo on left)
☐ 10 Steve Stanland
☐ 11A John R. Yeglinski
☐ 11B John Yeglinski
☐ 12A John Young
☐ 12B John Young (A on cap clear)

1977 Asheville Tourists TCMA

This 29-card standard-size set of the 1977 Asheville Tourists, a Class A Western Carolinas League affiliate of the Texas Rangers, features white-bordered posed black-and-white player photos on its fronts. The player's name, position and Tourists logo appear in the orange section near the bottom. The league affiliation appears across an upper corner. The plain white back carries the player's name, position and biography. The cards are unnumbered and checklisted below in alphabetical order.

	NRMT	VG-E	GOOD
COMPLETE SET (29)	30.00	13.50	3.70

☐ 1 Bryan Allard
☐ 2 Steve Bianchi
☐ 3 Richard Couch
☐ 4 Dennis Doyle
☐ 5 Steve Finch
☐ 6 Jerry Gaines
☐ 7 Mike Griffin
☐ 8 Mike Hicks
☐ 9 Mike Jaccar
☐ 10 Stan Jakubowski
☐ 11 Greg Jemison
☐ 12 Kerry Keenan
☐ 13 Vic Mabee
☐ 14 Dave McCarthy
☐ 15 Arnold McCrary
☐ 16 Ron Patrick
☐ 17 Scott Peterson
☐ 18 Dave Rivera
☐ 19 Phil Roddy
☐ 20 Jeff Scott CO
☐ 21 Bill Simpson
☐ 22 John Takacs
☐ 23 Wayne Terwilliger MGR
☐ 24 Al Thompson
☐ 25 Phil Watson
☐ 26 Len Whitehouse
☐ 27 Wayne Wilkerson
☐ 28 Glenn Williams
☐ 29 Mike Williamson

1977 Bristol Red Sox TCMA

This 20-card standard-size set of the 1977 Bristol Red Sox, a Class AA Eastern League affiliate of the Boston Red Sox, features white-bordered posed black-and-white player photos on its fronts. The player's name, position and Red Sox logo appear in the orange section near the bottom. The league affiliation appears across an upper corner. The plain white back carries the words "Bristol Red Sox" in large letters along with the player's name, position and biography. The cards are unnumbered and checklisted below in alphabetical order.

	NRMT	VG-E	GOOD
COMPLETE SET (20)	175.00	80.00	22.00

☐ 1 Erwin Bryant
☐ 2 Mark Buba
☐ 3 Jose Caldera
☐ 4 Tom Farias
☐ 5 Glenn Fisher
☐ 6 Joel Finch
☐ 7 Otis Foster
☐ 8 Ken Huizenga
☐ 9 Ed Jurak
☐ 10 Dave Koza
☐ 11 Joe Krsnich
☐ 12 Dave Labossiere TR
☐ 13 Breen Newcomer
☐ 14 Mike O'Berry
☐ 15 Gary Purcell
☐ 16 Win Remmerswaal Sic, Remmerswael
☐ 17 Burke Suter
☐ 18 Steve Tarbell
☐ 19 John Tudor
☐ 20 Rich Waller

1977 Burlington Bees TCMA

This 27-card standard-size set of the 1977 Burlington Bees, a Class A Midwest League affiliate of the Milwaukee Brewers, features white-bordered posed black-and-white player photos on its fronts. The player's name, position and Bees logo appear in the orange section near the bottom. The league affiliation appears across an upper corner. The plain white back carries the player's name, position and biography. The cards are unnumbered and checklisted below in alphabetical order. Card #12 Gary Halls and #17 Candy Mercado are late issues.

	NRMT	VG-E	GOOD
COMPLETE SET (25)	50.00	22.00	6.25
COMP. SET W/LATE ISSUE (27)	125.00	55.00	15.50

☐ 1 Daryl Bailey
☐ 2 Tim Bannister
☐ 3 Jesus Vega
☐ 4 Mike Dempsey
☐ 5 Bill Dick
☐ 6 Gary Donovan
☐ 7 Larry Edwards
☐ 8 Bert Flores
☐ 9 Richard Ford
☐ 10 Gary Gingerich
☐ 11 Steve Greene
☐ 12 Gary Halls (Late Issue)
☐ 13 Dave Hersh GM
☐ 14 Al Manning
☐ 15 Brad Meagher
☐ 16 Dennis Menke MGR
☐ 17 Candy Mercado (Late Issue)
☐ 18 Larry Montgomery
☐ 19 Willie Mueller
☐ 20 Jose Oppenheimer
☐ 21 Glenn Partridge
☐ 22 Jay Passmore
☐ 23 Rene Quinones
☐ 24 Eric Restin
☐ 25 Chuck Ross
☐ 26 Terry Shoebridge
☐ 27 Steve Splitt

1977 Cedar Rapids Giants TCMA

This 25-card standard-size set of the 1977 Cedar Rapids Giants, a Class A Midwest League affiliate of the San Francisco Giants, features white-bordered posed black-and-white player photos on its fronts. The player's name, position and Giants logo appear in the orange section near the bottom. The league affiliation appears across an upper corner. The plain white back carries the player's name, position and biography. The cards are unnumbered and checklisted below in alphabetical order. John Laubhan was a late addition to the set.

	NRMT	VG-E	GOOD
COMPLETE SET (24)	75.00	34.00	9.50
COMP. SET W/LATE ISSUE (25)	125.00	55.00	15.50

☐ 1 Rich Murray
☐ 2 Bob Brenly
☐ 3 Dave Anderson
☐ 4 John Sylvester
☐ 5 Ken Feinburg
☐ 6 Brian Moulton
☐ 7 Phil Nastu
☐ 8 Henry Macias
☐ 9 Gary Ledbetter
☐ 10 Ken Barton
☐ 11 Jack Mull MGR
☐ 12 Drew Nickerson
☐ 13 Jim Pryor
☐ 14 Mike Wardlow
☐ 15 Dave Myers
☐ 16 Bart Bass
☐ 17 Steve Sherman
☐ 18 Jon Harper
☐ 19 Don "Bucky" Buchhiester GM
☐ 20 Mark Kuecker
☐ 21 Dan Hartwig
☐ 22 Chris Bourjos
☐ 23 Jeff Shourds
☐ 24 Steve Pearce
☐ NNO John Laubhan (Late Issue)

1977 Charleston Patriots TCMA

This 25-card standard-size set of the 1977 Charleston Patriots, a Class A Western Carolinas League affiliate of the Pittsburgh Pirates, features white-bordered posed black-and-white player photos on its fronts. The player's name, position and Patriots logo appear in the orange section near the bottom. The league affiliation appears across an upper corner. The plain white back carries the words "Charleston Patriots" in large letters followed by the player's name, position and biography. The cards are unnumbered and checklisted below in alphabetical order.

	NRMT	VG-E	GOOD
COMPLETE SET (25)	30.00	13.50	3.70

☐ 1 Tom Burke III
☐ 2 Jorge Carty
☐ 3 Arcadio Cruz
☐ 4 Bienvenido De La Rosa
☐ 5 Rick "Bubba" Evans
☐ 6 Stan Floyd
☐ 7 Skip Leech
☐ 8 Jim Mahoney MGR
☐ 9 Jim Miller
☐ 10 Adalberto Ortiz
☐ 11 Jim Parke
☐ 12 Pascual Perez
☐ 13 Eric "Ricky" Peterson
☐ 14 Fred Rein
☐ 15 Martin Rivas
☐ 16 Bob Rock
☐ 17 Richard Rodriquez
☐ 18 Chuck Rouse
☐ 19 Simon Santana
☐ 20 Brian Schwerman
☐ 21 Bob Semerano
☐ 22 Jim Smith
☐ 23 Alfredo Torres
☐ 24 Candido Ventura
☐ 25 Jerry Yandrick

1977 Clinton Dodgers TCMA

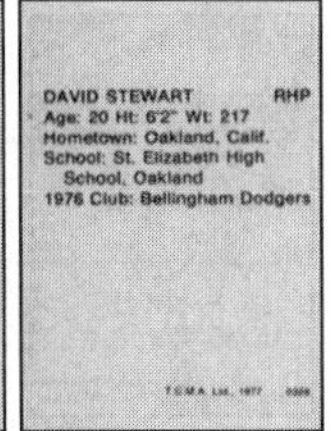

This 29-card standard-size set of the 1977 Clinton Dodgers, a Class A Midwest League affiliate of the Los Angeles Dodgers, features white-bordered posed black-and-white player photos on its fronts. The player's name, position and Dodgers logo appear in the orange section near the bottom. The league affiliation appears across an upper corner. The plain white back carries the player's name, position and biography. The cards are unnumbered and checklisted below in alphabetical order. Approximately 1,100 sets were produced.

	NRMT	VG-E	GOOD
COMPLETE SET (29)	120.00	55.00	15.00

☐ 1 Paul Bain
☐ 2 Paul Bock
☐ 3 Dave Cohea TR
☐ 4 Gerry De La Cruz
☐ 5 Jim Del Vecchio
☐ 6 Charles Dorgan
☐ 7 Jim Evans
☐ 8 Chuck Gardner
☐ 9 Rich Goulding
☐ 10 Dan Henry
☐ 11 Tim Jones
☐ 12 George Kaage
☐ 13 Ron Kittle
☐ 14 Mark Kryka
☐ 15 Mickey Lashley
☐ 16 Don LeJohn Jr.
☐ 17 Dick "Mac" McLaughlin MGR
☐ 18 Damon Middleton
☐ 19 Jim Peterson
☐ 20 Jose Reyes
☐ 21 Tim Roche
☐ 22 Eric Schimdt
☐ 23 Mike Scioscia
☐ 24 Hilario Soriano
☐ 25 Dave Stewart
☐ 26 Bill Swoope
☐ 27 Ken Townsend
☐ 28 Max Venable
☐ 29 Mike Wilson

1977 Cocoa Astros TCMA

This 25-card standard-size set of the 1977 Cocoa Astros, a Class A Florida State League affiliate of the Houston Astros, features white-bordered posed black-and-white player photos on its fronts. The player's name, position and Astros logo appear in the orange section near the bottom. The league affiliation appears across an upper corner. The cards are unnumbered and checklisted below in alphabetical order.

	NRMT	VG-E	GOOD
COMPLETE SET (25)	40.00	18.00	5.00

☐ 1 Ed Anderson
☐ 2 Reno Aragon
☐ 3 Bruce Bochy
☐ 4 Cocoa Astros Staff
☐ 5 Jeff Ellison
☐ 6 Larry Eubanks
☐ 7 Bob Hallgren
☐ 8 Don Harkness
☐ 9 Phil Klimas
☐ 10 Randy Lamb
☐ 11 Ramon Leader
☐ 12 Diago Melendez
☐ 13 Mark Miggins
☐ 14 Dennis Miscik
☐ 15 Jose Mota
☐ 16 Jim Pankovits

☐ 17 Gordy Pladson
☐ 18 George Ploucher
☐ 19 Pete Prieto TR
☐ 20 Gary Rajsich
☐ 21 Bert Roberge
☐ 22 Simon Rosario
☐ 23 Randy Rouse
☐ 24 Dave Smith
☐ 25 Tom Wiedenbauer

1977 Columbus Clippers TCMA

This 24-card standard-size set of the 1977 Columbus Clippers, a Class AAA International League affiliate of the New York Yankees, features white-bordered posed black-and-white player photos on its fronts. The player's name and Clippers logo appear in the orange section near the bottom. The league affiliation appears across an upper corner. The plain white back carries the 1977 Clippers home schedule. The cards are unnumbered and checklisted below in alphabetical order. Approximately 1,100 sets were produced.

	NRMT	VG-E	GOOD
COMPLETE SET (22)	250.00	110.00	31.00
COMPLETE SET W/COR (24)	350.00	160.00	45.00

☐ 1 Dave Augustine
☐ 2 Chris Batton
☐ 3 Dale Berra
☐ 4 Mike Easler
☐ 5 Mike Edwards
☐ 6 Gary Hargis
☐ 7 Red Hartman
☐ 8 Randy Hopkins
☐ 9 Tim Jones
☐ 10A Alberto Lois
(Wrong photo: Lowell Palmer)
☐ 10B Alberto Lois (Correct photo)
☐ 11 Ken Macha
☐ 12 Ron Mitchell
☐ 13 Tim Murtaugh
☐ 14 Doug Nelson
☐ 15 Jim Nettles
☐ 16 Steve Nicosia
☐ 17 Bob Oliver
☐ 18A Lowell Palmer
(Wrong photo: Alberto Lois)
☐ 18B Lowell Palmer (Correct photo)
☐ 19 Ray Price
☐ 20 Fred Scherman
☐ 21 Rich Standart
☐ 22 Ed Whitson

1977 Daytona Beach Islanders TCMA

This 27-card standard-size set of the 1977 Daytona Beach Islanders, a Class A Florida State League affiliate of the Kansas City Royals, features white-bordered posed black-and-white player photos on its fronts. The player's name, position and Islanders logo appear in the orange section near the bottom. The league affiliation appears across an upper corner. The plain white back carries the words "Daytona Beach Islanders" in large letters followed by the player's name, position and biography. The cards are unnumbered and checklisted below in alphabetical order.

	NRMT	VG-E	GOOD
COMPLETE SET (27)	30.00	13.50	3.70

☐ 1 Steve Beene
☐ 2 Ed Cowan
☐ 3 Rich Dubee
☐ 4 Craig Eaton
☐ 5 Bob Engelmeyer
☐ 6 Jack Fleming
☐ 7 Henry Greene
☐ 8 Ben Grzybeck
☐ 9 John Hoscheidt
☐ 10 Sam Jones
☐ 11 Tom Krattli
☐ 12 Steve Lacey
☐ 13 Mel Lowman
☐ 14 Jose Martinez MGR
☐ 15 Ken Phelps
☐ 16 Ray Prince
☐ 17 Phil Pulido
☐ 18 Tim Riley
☐ 19 Cliff Roberts
☐ 20 Juan Rodrigues
☐ 21 Ed Sempsrott
☐ 22 Marty Serrano
☐ 23 Brad Simmons
☐ 24 Paul Stevens
☐ 25 Roy Tanner CO
☐ 26 Hal Thomasson
☐ 27 Buddy Yarbrough

1977 Evansville Triplets TCMA

This 25-card standard-size set of the 1977 Evansville Triplets, a Class AAA American Association affiliate of the Detroit Tigers, features white-bordered posed black-and-white player photos on its fronts. The player's name, position and Triplets logo appear in the orange section near the bottom. The league affiliation appears across an upper corner. The plain white back carries the player's name, position and biography along with the words "Evansville Triplets" across the top of the card. The cards are unnumbered and checklisted below in alphabetical order.

	NRMT	VG-E	GOOD
COMPLETE SET (25)	400.00	180.00	50.00

☐ 1 Bob Adams
☐ 2 Julio Alonso
☐ 3 Tom Bianco
☐ 4 Tom Brookens
☐ 5 George Cappuzzello
☐ 6 Tim Corcoran
☐ 7 Charles "Boots" Day
☐ 8 Pio DiSalvo TR
☐ 9 Jim Eschen
☐ 10 Gary Geiger CO
☐ 11 Eddie Glynn
☐ 12 Dan Gonzales
☐ 13 Glenn Gulliver
☐ 14 Frank Harris
☐ 15 Roric Harrison
☐ 16 Artie James
☐ 17 Marvin Lane
☐ 18 Jerry Manuel
☐ 19 Bob Molinaro
☐ 20 Jack Morris
☐ 21 Les Moss MG
☐ 22 Lance Parrish
☐ 23 Bruce Taylor
☐ 24 John Valle
☐ 25 Milt Wilcox

1977 Fort Lauderdale Yankees Sussman

	NRMT	VG-E	GOOD
COMPLETE SET (31)	80.00	36.00	10.00

☐ 1 Pat Callahan
☐ 2 Woody Keys
☐ 3 Johnny Crawford
☐ 4 Jose Alcantara
☐ 5 Mark Theil
☐ 6 Joe LeFebvre
☐ 7 Beban Luis
☐ 8 Ted Wilborn
☐ 9 Gerry Gaube
☐ 10 Nat Showalter
☐ 11 Mark Softy
☐ 12 Jose Paulino
☐ 13 Roger Holt
☐ 14 Jim McDonald
☐ 15 Jim Kibbee
☐ 16 Tom Guess
☐ 17 Sam Ellis
☐ 18 Pat Tabler
☐ 19 Dave Wright
☐ 20 Steve Peters
☐ 21 Don Hogestyn
☐ 22 Scott Delgatti
☐ 23 Don Fisk
☐ 24 Stan Saleski
☐ 25 Jimmy DePaola
☐ 26 Mark Burlingame
☐ 27 Gus Gil
☐ 28 Butch Riggar
☐ 29 Juan Espino
☐ 30 Tony Cameron
☐ 31 Eddie Napoleon

1977 Holyoke Millers TCMA

This 26-card standard-size set of the 1977 Holyoke Millers, a Class AA Eastern League affiliate of the Milwaukee Brewers, features white-bordered posed black-and-white player photos on its fronts. The player's name, position and Millers logo appear in the orange section near the bottom. The league affiliation appears across an upper corner. The cards are unnumbered and checklisted below in alphabetical order.

	NRMT	VG-E	GOOD
COMPLETE SET (26)	25.00	11.00	3.10

☐ 1 Ike Blessitt
☐ 2 Mark Bomback
☐ 3 John Buffamoyer
☐ 4 Doug Clarey
☐ 5 Garry Conn
☐ 6 Gene Delyon
☐ 7 Bill Dick
☐ 8 Greg Erardi
☐ 9 Rick Ford
☐ 10 George Frazier
☐ 11 Matt Galante MGR
☐ 12 John Hannon
☐ 13 Lynn B. Herzig PRES
☐ 14 Gary Holle
☐ 15 Dale Hrovat
☐ 16 Ron Jacobs
☐ 17 Tom Kayser GM
☐ 18 Gary LaRocque
☐ 19 Lanny Phillips
☐ 20 Neil Rasmussen
☐ 21 Ed Romero
☐ 22 Bill Severns
☐ 23 Rich Shubert
☐ 24 Dave Smith
☐ 25 Ron Wrona
☐ 26 Jeff Yurak

1977 Indianapolis Indians Team Issue

	NRMT	VG-E	GOOD
COMPLETE SET (27)	15.00	6.75	1.85

☐ 1 Team Card
☐ 2 Roy Majtyka MG
☐ 3 Joe Henderson
☐ 4 Dave Revering
☐ 5 Tom Hume
☐ 6 Ron Oester
☐ 7 Larry Payne
☐ 8 Don Werner
☐ 9 Paul Moskau
☐ 10 Dan Norman
☐ 11 Mike LaCoss
☐ 12 Mike Grace
☐ 13 Dan Dumoulin
☐ 14 Steve Henderson
☐ 15 Mac Scarce
☐ 16 Tommy Mutz
☐ 17 Larry Rothschild
☐ 18 Rudy Meoli
☐ 19 Raul Ferreyra
☐ 20 Arturo DeFreites
☐ 21 Mario Soto
☐ 22 Hugh Yancy
☐ 23 Barry Moss
☐ 24 Jack Maloof
☐ 25 Manny Sarmiento
☐ 26 Ron McClain TR
☐ 27 Checklist Card
(unnumbered)

1977 Jacksonville Suns TCMA

This 22-card standard-size set of the 1977 Jacksonville Suns, a Class AA Southern League affiliate of the Kansas City Royals, features white-bordered posed black-and-white player photos on its fronts. The player's name, position and Suns logo appear in the orange section near the bottom. The league affiliation appears across an upper corner. The plain white back carries the words "Jacksonville Suns" logo in bold letters. The cards are unnumbered and checklisted below in alphabetical order.

	NRMT	VG-E	GOOD
COMPLETE SET (22)	75.00	34.00	9.50

☐ 1 Mark Ballanger
☐ 2 German Barranca
☐ 3 Steve Burke
☐ 4 Mike Denevi
☐ 5 Rich Gale
☐ 6 Joe Gates
☐ 7 Jim Gaudet
☐ 8 Kevin Gillen
☐ 9 Bobby Glass
☐ 10 Tim Ireland
☐ 11 Dennis Kaspryzak TR
☐ 12 Pete Koegel
☐ 13 Gordon MacKenzie MGR
☐ 14 Frank McCann
☐ 15 Randy McGilberry
☐ 16 Lew Olsen
☐ 17 Darrell Parker
☐ 18 Bill Paschall
☐ 19 Ken Phelps
☐ 20 Dan Quisenberry
☐ 21 Luis Silverio
☐ 22 Gary Williams

1977 Lodi Dodgers TCMA

This 25-card standard-size set of the 1977 Lodi Dodgers, a Class A Carolina League affiliate of the Los Angeles Dodgers, features white-bordered posed black-and-white player photos on its fronts. The player's name, position and Dodgers logo appear in the orange section near the bottom. The league affiliation appears across an upper corner. The plain white back carries the player's name, position and biography along with the "Lodi Dodgers" logo in bold letters. The cards are unnumbered and checklisted below in alphabetical order.

	NRMT	VG-E	GOOD
COMPLETE SET (25)	50.00	22.00	6.25

☐ 1 Charles Barrett
☐ 2 Mark Bradley
☐ 3 Marv Garrison
☐ 4 Brad Gulden
☐ 5 Dan Henry
☐ 6 Ubaldo Heredia
☐ 7 Hank Jones
☐ 8 Mike Lake
☐ 9 Rudy Law
☐ 10 Tony Martin
☐ 11 Dave Patterson
☐ 12 Pablo Peguero
☐ 13 Jack Perconte
☐ 14 Charlie Phillips
☐ 15 Don Ruzek
☐ 16 Rick Sander
☐ 17 Ed Santos
☐ 18 Rod Scheller
☐ 19 Steve Shirley
☐ 20 Kelly Snider
☐ 21 Mike Tennant
☐ 22 Miguel Vallaran
☐ 23 Stan Wasiak MGR
☐ 24 Myron White
☐ 25 Mike Williams

1977 Lynchburg Mets TCMA

This 34-card standard-size set of the 1977 Lynchburg Mets, a Class A Carolina League affiliate of the New York Mets, features white-bordered posed black-and-white player photos on its fronts. The player's name, position and Mets logo appear in the orange section near the bottom. The league affiliation appears across an upper corner. The cards are unnumbered and checklisted below in alphabetical order. This set contains a few of variations which are listed below.

	NRMT	VG-E	GOOD
COMPLETE SET (30)	100.00	45.00	12.50
COMPLETE SET W/2B/4B (32)	225.00	100.00	28.00
COMPLETE SET W/REARDON (33)	325.00	145.00	40.00
COMPLETE SET W/16B (34)	450.00	200.00	55.00

☐ 1 Jack Aker
☐ 2A Neil Allen
(Pirates logo)
☐ 2B Neil Allen
(Mets logo)
☐ 3 Gene Bardot
☐ 4A Butch Benton (Knee)
☐ 4B Butch Benton (Ankle)
☐ 5 George Bradbury
☐ 6 Mike Brown
☐ 7 Randy Brown
☐ 8 Robert Bryant
☐ 9 Russell Clark
☐ 10 Carmen Coppol
☐ 11 Dave Covert
☐ 12 Curt Fisher
☐ 13 Ron Gill
☐ 14 Scott Goodfarm
☐ 15 Bob Grant
☐ 16A Stu Greenstein
Knee showing
☐ 16B Stu Greenstein
☐ 17 Bob Healy
☐ 18 Steve Keesses
☐ 19 Jerry McIver
☐ 20 Juan Monasterio
☐ 21 Ted O'Neill
☐ 22 Pacho Perez
☐ 23 Mario Ramirez
☐ 24 Jeff Reardon
☐ 25 Bob Rossen
☐ 26 Cliff Speck
☐ 27 Randy Tate
☐ 28 David Van Ohlen
☐ 29 Fred Westfall
☐ 30 Ward Wilson
☐ 31 Steve Yost

1977 Modesto A's Chong

This 22-card set of the 1977 Modesto A's, a Class A California League affiliate of the Oakland Athletics, features white-bordered posed black-and-white player photos on its fronts. This issue includes the minor league card debut of Rickey Henderson. Approximately 400 sets were produced.

	MINT	NRMT	EXC
COMPLETE SET (22)			

☐ 1 Ted Smith
☐ 2 Barry Wright
☐ 3 Craig Minetto
☐ 4 Dominic Scala
☐ 5 Rickey Henderson
Sic, Ricky
☐ 6 Jesse Wright
☐ 7 Mike Rodriguez
☐ 8 Ernie Camacho
☐ 9 Pat Dempsey

- ☐ 10 Randy Green
- ☐ 11 Mike Patterson
- ☐ 12 Mace Harrison
- ☐ 13 Rod Patterson
- ☐ 14 Monte Bothwell
- ☐ 15 Bart Braun
- ☐ 16 Rich Oziomiela
- ☐ 17 Tom Trebelhorn
- ☐ 18 Rod McNeely
- ☐ 19 Ron Beaurivage
- ☐ 20 Brian Meyl
- ☐ 21 John Eisinger
- ☐ 22 Juan Gomez
  Tom Trebelhorn

1977 Newark Co-Pilots TCMA

This 29-card standard-size set of the 1977 Newark Co-Pilots, a Class A New York-Penn League affiliate of the Milwaukee Brewers, features white-bordered posed black-and-white player photos on its fronts. The player's name, position and Pilots logo appear in the orange section near the bottom. The league affiliation appears across an upper corner. The plain white back carries the words "Newark Co-Pilots" in large letters followed by the player's name, position and biography. The cards are unnumbered and checklisted below in alphabetical order. Approximately 1,100 sets were produced.

	NRMT	VG-E	GOOD
COMPLETE SET (29)	40.00	18.00	5.00

- ☐ 1 Kevin Bass
- ☐ 2 Manuel Betemit
- ☐ 3 Rick Broas
- ☐ 4 Ronald Buggs TR
- ☐ 5 Chris Carstensen
- ☐ 6 Pablo Caualło
- ☐ 7 Stan Davis
- ☐ 8 Steve Day
- ☐ 9 Tom DeRosa
- ☐ 10 Ron Driver
- ☐ 11 Gerry Erb
- ☐ 12 Brian Fisher
- ☐ 13 Adelberto Flores
- ☐ 14 Bill Foley
- ☐ 15 Eric Frey
- ☐ 16 Jeff Harryman
- ☐ 17 Dennis Holmberg MGR
- ☐ 18 Gary House
- ☐ 19 Jerry Jenkins
- ☐ 20 Tim Jordan
- ☐ 21 David LaPoint
- ☐ 22 Joe Mitchell
- ☐ 23 Steve Manderfield
- ☐ 24 Chester Nelson
- ☐ 25 Rick Nicholson
- ☐ 26 Joe Polese
- ☐ 27 James Quinn
- ☐ 28 John Roesch
- ☐ 29 John Skorochocki

1977 Orlando Twins TCMA

This 24-card standard-size set of the 1977 Orlando Twins, a Class AA Southern League affiliate of the Minnesota Twins, features white-bordered posed black-and-white player photos on its fronts. The player's name, position and Twins logo appear in the orange section near the bottom. The league affiliation appears across an upper corner. The plain white back carries the words "Orlando Twins" in large letters followed by the player's name, position and biography. The cards are unnumbered and checklisted below in alphabetical order. Both Terry Felton variation cards #9A and #9B are late issues.

	NRMT	VG-E	GOOD
COMPLETE SET (22)	50.00	22.00	6.25
COMPLETE SET (23)	90.00	40.00	11.00
COMP. SET W/BOTH FELTONS (24)	110.00	50.00	14.00

- ☐ 1 Archie Amerson
- ☐ 2 Paul Ausman
- ☐ 3 Terry "Bud" Bulling
- ☐ 4 John Castino
- ☐ 5 Wayne Caughey
- ☐ 6 Julian Dito
- ☐ 7 Tom Epperly CO
- ☐ 8 Frank "Doc" J. Estes
- ☐ 9A Terry Felton
  (logo on right--Late Issue)
- ☐ 9B Terry Felton
  (logo on left--Late Issue)
- ☐ 10 Greg Field
- ☐ 11 Mike Gatlin
- ☐ 12 John Goryl MGR
- ☐ 13 Bill Harris
- ☐ 14 Bruce MacPherson
- ☐ 15 Dennis Mantick
- ☐ 16 Johnny Pittman
- ☐ 17 Brian Rothrock
- ☐ 18 Gary Serum
- ☐ 19 Dale Soderholm
- ☐ 20 Mark Souza
- ☐ 21 Greg Thayer
- ☐ 22 Steve Wagner
- ☐ 23 Jeff Youngbauer

1977 Phoenix Giants Coke Premium

	NRMT	VG-E	GOOD
COMPLETE SET (24)	25.00	11.00	3.10

- ☐ 1 Gary Alexander
- ☐ 2 Chris Arnold
- ☐ 3 Rick Bradley
- ☐ 4 Rocky Bridges
- ☐ 5 Rob Dressler
- ☐ 6 Don Hahn
- ☐ 7 Vic Harris
- ☐ 8 Dave Heaverlo
- ☐ 9 Kyles Hypes
- ☐ 10 Skip James
- ☐ 11 Skip James
- ☐ 12 Garry Jestadt
- ☐ 13 Harry Jordan
- ☐ 14 Junior Kennedy
- ☐ 15 Wendell Kim
- ☐ 16 Bob Knepper
- ☐ 17 Joey Martin
- ☐ 18 Greg Minton
- ☐ 19 Ed Plank
- ☐ 20 Frank Ricelli
- ☐ 21 Rick Sanderlin
- ☐ 22 Horace Speed
- ☐ 23 Tommy Toms
- ☐ 24 Mike Wegener

1977 Phoenix Giants Cramer Coke

	NRMT	VG-E	GOOD
COMPLETE SET (24)	5.00	2.20	.60

- ☐ 1 Gary Alexander
- ☐ 2 Chris Arnold
- ☐ 3 Ethan Blackaby
- ☐ 4 Rick Bradley
- ☐ 5 Rocky Bridges
- ☐ 6 Rob Dressler
- ☐ 7 Don Hahn
- ☐ 8 Vic Harris
- ☐ 9 Dave Heaverlo
- ☐ 10 Kyle Hypes
- ☐ 11 Skip James
- ☐ 12 Garry Jestadt
- ☐ 13 Harry Jordan
- ☐ 14 Junior Kennedy
- ☐ 15 Wendell Kim
- ☐ 16 Bob Knepper
- ☐ 17 Joey Martin
- ☐ 18 Greg Minton
- ☐ 19 Ed Plank
- ☐ 20 Frank Riccelli
- ☐ 21 Rick Sanderlin
- ☐ 22 Horace Speed
- ☐ 23 Tommy Toms
- ☐ 24 Michael Wegener

1977 Quad City Angels TCMA

This 29-card standard-size set of the 1977 Quad City Angels, a Class A Midwest League affiliate of the California Angels, features white-bordered posed black-and-white player photos on its fronts. The player's name, position and Angels logo appear in the orange section near the bottom. The league affiliation appears across an upper corner. The plain white back carries the player's name, position, biography and the words "Quad City Angels" in bold letters. The cards are unnumbered and checklisted below in alphabetical order.

	NRMT	VG-E	GOOD
COMPLETE SET (29)	50.00	22.00	6.25

- ☐ 1 Jim Ball
- ☐ 2 Gary Balla
- ☐ 3 Ned Bergert TR
- ☐ 4 Mike Bishop
- ☐ 5 Arturo Bonitio
- ☐ 6 Bob Boyd
- ☐ 7 Rich Brewster
- ☐ 8 Scott Carnes
- ☐ 9 Mark Clear
- ☐ 10 Keith Comstock
- ☐ 11 Frank Coppenbarger
- ☐ 12 Chuck Cottier MGR
- ☐ 13 Joel Crisler
- ☐ 14 John Harris
- ☐ 15 Bob Healy
- ☐ 16 John Henderson
- ☐ 17 Craig Hendrickson
- ☐ 18 Dave Hollifield
- ☐ 19 Greg Johnson
- ☐ 20 Donny Jones
- ☐ 21 Scott Moffitt
- ☐ 22 Steve Oliva
- ☐ 23 Harry Pells GM
- ☐ 24 Ken Schrom
- ☐ 25 Rick Sentlinger
- ☐ 26 Doug Slettvet
- ☐ 27 Fernando Tarin
- ☐ 28 Steve Tebbetts
- ☐ 29 Ken Wright

1977 Reading Phillies TCMA

This 23-card standard-size set of the 1977 Reading Phillies, a Class AA Eastern League affiliate of the Philadelphia Phillies, features white-bordered posed black-and-white player photos on its fronts. The player's name, position and Phillies logo appear in the orange section near the bottom. The league affiliation appears across an upper corner. The plain white back carries the words "Reading Phillies" in large letters followed by the player's name, position and biography. The cards are unnumbered and checklisted below in alphabetical order.

	NRMT	VG-E	GOOD
COMPLETE SET (23)	250.00	110.00	31.00

- ☐ 1 Garv Begnaud
- ☐ 2 George Benson
- ☐ 3 Todd Brenizer
- ☐ 4 Franco Ciammachilli
- ☐ 5 Narda Contreras
- ☐ 6 Rafael Contreras
- ☐ 7 Phil Convertino
- ☐ 8 Todd Cruz
- ☐ 9 Bobby Demeo
- ☐ 10 Lee Elia
- ☐ 11 Dan Greenhalgh
- ☐ 12 Glenn Gregson
- ☐ 13 John Guarnaccia
- ☐ 14 Jesus Hernaiz
- ☐ 15 Mark Klein
- ☐ 16 Pete Manos
- ☐ 17 Jose Moreno
- ☐ 18 Ed Olivaros
- ☐ 19 Mell Roberts
- ☐ 20 Kevin Saucier
- ☐ 21 Tom Silicato
- ☐ 22 Rocky Skalisky
- ☐ 23 Tom White

1977 Rochester Red Wings McCurdy's

	NRMT	VG-E	GOOD
COMPLETE SET (24)	150.00	70.00	19.00

- ☐ 1 David Criscione
- ☐ 3 Pedro Liranzo
- ☐ 4 Michael Parrott
- ☐ 5 Taylor Duncan
- ☐ 6 David Ford
- ☐ 7 Earl Stephenson
- ☐ 8 Blake Doyle
- ☐ 9 Richard Bladt
- ☐ 10 Terry Crowley
- ☐ 11 Tony Chavez
- ☐ 12 John Flinn
- ☐ 13 Larry Harlow
- ☐ 14 John O'Rear
- ☐ 15 Randy Miller
- ☐ 16 Mike Fiore
- ☐ 17 Creighton Tevlin
- ☐ 18 Ed Farmer
- ☐ 19 John McCall
- ☐ 20 Myrl Smith
- ☐ 21 Gershan Jarquin
- ☐ 22 Dave Harper
- ☐ 23 Dennis Blair
- ☐ 24 Kevin Kennedy
- ☐ 25 Ken Boyer

1977 Salem Pirates TCMA

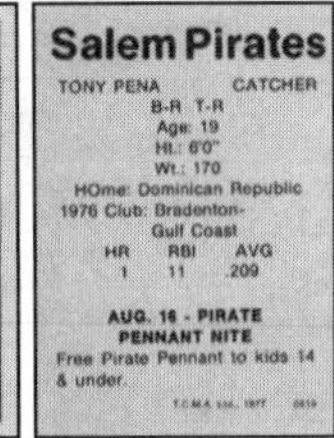

This 35-card standard-size set of the 1977 Salem Pirates, a Class A Carolina League affiliate of the Pittsburgh Pirates, features white-bordered posed black-and-white player photos on its fronts. The player's name, position and Pirates logo appear in the orange section near the bottom. The league affiliation appears across an upper corner. The plain white back carries the words "Salem Pirates" in large letters followed by the player's name, position and biography. The cards are unnumbered and checklisted below in alphabetical order. This set contains numerous variations which are listed below.

	NRMT	VG-E	GOOD
COMPLETE SET (24)	90.00	40.00	11.00
COMPLETE SET W/LATE ISSUES (35)	225.00	100.00	28.00

- ☐ 1 Paul Anthony
- ☐ 2 Jim Brady
- ☐ 3 Randy Brandt
- ☐ 4 Bryan Clark
- ☐ 5 Casey Clark
- ☐ 6 Stewart Cliburn
- ☐ 7 Wink Cole
- ☐ 8 Eugenio Cotes
- ☐ 9A Pablo Cruz
  (no shadow on face)
- ☐ 9B Pablo Cruz
  (shadow on face--Late Issue)
- ☐ 10 Dennis "Doc" Davis
- ☐ 11A John Dean
  (uniform #4 visible)
- ☐ 11B John Dean
  (uniform #4 not visible--Late Issue)
- ☐ 12 Dan DeBattista
- ☐ 13 Steve Demeter MGR
- ☐ 14 Bob Mazur
- ☐ 15A Jerry McDonald
  (uniform #14 visible)
- ☐ 15B Jerry McDonald
  (uniform #14 not visible--Late Issue)
- ☐ 16A Ossie Oliveras
- ☐ 16B Ossie Oliveras (batting--Late Issue)
- ☐ 17 Tony Pena
- ☐ 18 Alphie Perdue
- ☐ 19 Jeff Pinkus
- ☐ 20A Steve Powers
  (logo on left)
- ☐ 20B Steve Powers
  (logo on right--Late Issue)
- ☐ 21 Fred Rein (Late Issue)
- ☐ 22 Dave Rogers (Late Issue)
- ☐ 23 Luis Salazar
- ☐ 24 Chick Valley
- ☐ 25 Rafael Vasquez
- ☐ 26A Dick Walterhouse
- ☐ 26B Dick Walterhouse (batting--Late Issue)
- ☐ 27A Bob Wiesmiller
  (logo on left)
- ☐ 27B Bob Weismiller
  (logo on right--Late Issue)
- ☐ 28 Ernie Young

1977 Salt Lake City Gulls Cramer

	NRMT	VG-E	GOOD
COMPLETE SET (24)	5.00	2.20	.60

- ☐ 1 Jimy Williams
- ☐ 2 Fred Frazier
- ☐ 4 Rance Mulliniks
- ☐ 5 Gilberto Flores
- ☐ 6 Chuck Dobson
- ☐ 7 Danny Goodwin
- ☐ 8 Tom Donohue
- ☐ 9 Thad Bosley
- ☐ 10 Pat Cristelli
- ☐ 11 Dave Machemer
- ☐ 12 Fred Kuhaulua
- ☐ 13 Orlando Alvarez
- ☐ 14 Frankie George
- ☐ 15 Bob Nolan
- ☐ 16 Luis Quintana
- ☐ 17 Stan Perzanowski
- ☐ 18 John Caneira
- ☐ 19 Frank Panick
- ☐ 20 Dick Lange
- ☐ 21 Mike Barlow
- ☐ 22 Willie Aikens
- ☐ 24 Mike Overy
- ☐ 25 Butch Alberts
- ☐ NNO Leonard Garcia

1977 San Jose Missions Mr. Chef's

	NRMT	VG-E	GOOD
COMPLETE SET (25)	15.00	6.75	1.85

- ☐ 1 Team Photo CL
- ☐ 2 Rene Lachemann
- ☐ 3 Blue Moon Odom
- ☐ 4 Derek Bryant
- ☐ 5 Milt Ramirez
- ☐ 6 Mark Williams
- ☐ 7 Jim Tyrone
- ☐ 8 Greg Sinatro
- ☐ 9 Charlie Beamon
- ☐ 10 Tim Hosley
- ☐ 11 Denny Haines
- ☐ 12 Mike Weathers
- ☐ 13 Don Hopkins
- ☐ 14 Bob Lacey
- ☐ 15 Craig Mitchell
- ☐ 16 Randy Boyd
- ☐ 17 Denny Walling
- ☐ 18 Randy Scarberry
- ☐ 19 Brian Kingman
- ☐ 20 Ron Bell
- ☐ 21 Randy Taylor
- ☐ 22 Jimmy Sexton
- ☐ 23 Brian Abraham
- ☐ 24 Dave Johnson
- ☐ 25 Paul Mitchell

1977 Shreveport Captains TCMA

This 23-card standard-size set of the 1977 Shreveport Captains, a Class AA Texas League affiliate of the Pittsburgh Pirates, features white-bordered posed black-and-white player photos on its fronts. The player's name, position and Captains logo appear in the orange section near the bottom. The league affiliation appears across an upper corner. The cards are unnumbered and checklisted below in alphabetical order.

	NRMT	VG-E	GOOD
COMPLETE SET (23)	100.00	45.00	12.50

- ☐ 1 Doe Boyland
- ☐ 2 Fred Breining
- ☐ 3 Jim Busby
- ☐ 4 Juan Deliza
- ☐ 5 Paul Djakonow
- ☐ 6 Chet Gunter
- ☐ 7 Al Holland
- ☐ 8 Rick Honeycutt
- ☐ 9 Rusty Johnston
- ☐ 10 Mike Kavanagh
- ☐ 11 Jim Kidder
- ☐ 12 John Lipon
- ☐ 13 Larry Littleton
- ☐ 14 Tim Murtaugh
- ☐ 15 Doug Nelson
- ☐ 16 Nelson Norman
- ☐ 17 Leo Ortiz
- ☐ 18 Don Robinson
- ☐ 19 Felix Rodriguez
- ☐ 20 Harry Saferight
- ☐ 21 Rod Scurry
- ☐ 22 Tommy Thomas
- ☐ 23 Luke Wrenn

1977 Spartanburg Phillies TCMA

This 24-card standard-size set of the 1977 Spartanburg Phillies, a Class A Western Carolinas League affiliate of the Philadelphia Phillies, features white-bordered posed black-and-white player photos on its fronts. The player's name, position and Phillies logo appear in the orange section near the bottom. The league affiliation appears across an upper corner. The plain white back carries the Spartanburg Phillies 1977 schedule.

	NRMT	VG-E	GOOD
COMPLETE SET (24)	125.00	55.00	15.50

- ☐ 1 Pablo Minier
- ☐ 2 Tom Brunswick
- ☐ 3 Marty Bystrom
- ☐ 4 Jim Nickerson
- ☐ 5 Jarrell Whalley
- ☐ 6 Wally Nunn
- ☐ 7 Henry Mack
- ☐ 8 Jim Lasek
- ☐ 9 Joe Jones
- ☐ 10 Nick Popovich
- ☐ 11 Ricky Burdette
- ☐ 12 Armand Abreu
- ☐ 13 Ronnie Mattson
- ☐ 14 Glenn Ballard
- ☐ 15 Tony Gonzalez CO
- ☐ 16 Brian Watts
- ☐ 17 Elijah Bonaparte
- ☐ 18 Jeff Kraus
- ☐ 19 Mike Compton MGR
- ☐ 20 Bob Roman
- ☐ 21 Ozzie Virgil
- ☐ 22 Barry Janney
- ☐ 23 Sam Welborn
- ☐ 24 Ken Berger

1977 Spokane Indians Cramer

	NRMT	VG-E	GOOD
COMPLETE SET (24)	15.00	6.75	1.85

- ☐ 1 Duane Espy
- ☐ 2 Bill McLaurine
- ☐ 4 Jim Gantner
- ☐ 6 Bill Sharp
- ☐ 7 Perry Danforth
- ☐ 8 Stev Ruling
- ☐ 10 Art Kusnyer
- ☐ 11 Lenn Sakata
- ☐ 12 Bob Sheldon
- ☐ 13 Gorman Thomas
- ☐ 14 Juan Lopez
- ☐ 15 Tommie Reynolds
- ☐ 16 Ron Diggle
- ☐ 17 Sam Hinds
- ☐ 18 Tom Hausman
- ☐ 19 Lary Sorensen
- ☐ 20 Ken Sanders
- ☐ 21 Dick Davis
- ☐ 22 Kevin Kobel
- ☐ 24 Bob Ellis
- ☐ 25 Roger Miller
- ☐ 26 John Felske
- ☐ 28 Rich Folkers
- ☐ NNO Mark Voorhees

1977 St. Petersburg Cardinals TCMA

This 26-card standard-size set of the 1977 St. Petersburg Cardinals, a Class A Florida State League affiliate of the St. Louis Cardinals, features white-bordered posed black-and-white player photos on its fronts. The player's name, position and Cardinals logo appear in the orange section near the bottom. The league affiliation appears across an upper corner. The plain white back carries the St. Petersburg Cardinals 1977 home games schedule. NNO Mike Nagle was a late issue to the set.

	NRMT	VG-E	GOOD
COMPLETE SET (25)	75.00	34.00	9.50
COMPLETE SET (26)	150.00	70.00	19.00

- ☐ 1 Kelly Paris
- ☐ 2 William Bowman
- ☐ 3 Felipe Zayas
- ☐ 4 John Littlefield
- ☐ 5 Denzel Martindale
- ☐ 6 John Fulgham
- ☐ 7 Raymond Searge
- ☐ 8 Frank Hunsacker
- ☐ 9 Michael Stone
- ☐ 10 Terry Gray
- ☐ 11 Daniel O'Brien
- ☐ 12 Jorge Arazamendi
- ☐ 13 Hub Kittle MGR
- ☐ 14 Thomas Herr
- ☐ 15 Raymond Donaghue
- ☐ 16 Henry Mays
- ☐ 17 Scott Boras
- ☐ 18 Claude Crockett
- ☐ 19 Michael Pisarkiewicz
- ☐ 20 Robert Harrison
- ☐ 21 Hector Eduardo
- ☐ 22 Alfred Meyer
- ☐ 23 David Pennial
- ☐ 24 Benny Joe Edelen
- ☐ 25 Ralph Miller Jr. GM
- ☐ NNO Mike Nagle

1977 Tacoma Twins Dairy Queen

The cards measure 2 3/4" by 3 9/16" and have blank backs. Card #8 Tim Loiberg, #16B Rob Wilfong and #24B Jeff Holly were not issued with the original set and thus not considered part of the regular set.

	NRMT	VG-E	GOOD
COMPLETE SET (27)	25.00	11.00	3.10
COMPLETE SET (30)	40.00	18.00	5.00

- ☐ 1 Jim Van Wyck
- ☐ 2A Wayne Caughey
- ☐ 2B Luis Gomez
- ☐ 3 Dave Edwards
- ☐ 4 Sam Perlozzo
- ☐ 5 Sal Butera
- ☐ 6 Hosken Powell
- ☐ 7 Tommy Sain
- ☐ 8A Tim Loberg (Unissued)
- ☐ 8B Willie Norwood
- ☐ 9 John Lonchar
- ☐ 10 Tom Kelly CO
- ☐ 11 Eddie Bane
- ☐ 12 Davis May
- ☐ 13 Tom Hall
- ☐ 14 Gregg Bemis
- ☐ 15 Gary Ward
- ☐ 16A Gary Serum
- ☐ 16B Rob Wilfong (Unissued)
- ☐ 17 Mike Proly
- ☐ 18 Steve Luebber
- ☐ 19 Art DeFillippis
- ☐ 20 Jim Gideon
- ☐ 21 Jim Hughes
- ☐ 22 Juan Veintidos
- ☐ 23 Randy Bass
- ☐ 24A Bill Butler
- ☐ 24B Jeff Holly (Unissued)
- ☐ 25 Dan Graham
- ☐ 26 Del Wilber MGR

1977 Tucson Toros Cramer

	NRMT	VG-E	GOOD
COMPLETE SET (24)	5.00	2.20	.60

- ☐ 2 Dave Moates
- ☐ 4 Lew Beasley
- ☐ 5 Ken Pape
- ☐ 6 Wayne Pinkerton
- ☐ 7 Larue Washington
- ☐ 8 Greg Mahlberg
- ☐ 11 Keith Smith
- ☐ 12 Keathel Chauncey
- ☐ 13 David Moharter
- ☐ 14 Rich Donnelly
- ☐ 17 Rick Stelmaszek
- ☐ 19 Gary Gray
- ☐ 20 Bob Babcock
- ☐ 27 Ed Nottle
- ☐ 32 David Clyde
- ☐ 33 Kurt Bevacqua
- ☐ 35 John Poloni
- ☐ 40 Len Barker
- ☐ 45 Mark Soroko
- ☐ 51 Pat Putnam
- ☐ 52 Mike Bacsik
- ☐ 53 Bobby Cuellar
- ☐ 59 David Harper
- ☐ NNO Chip Steger

1977 Phoenix Giants Valley National Bank

	NRMT	VG-E	GOOD
COMPLETE SET (24)	25.00	11.00	3.10

- ☐ 1 Chris Arnold
- ☐ 2 Rick Bradley
- ☐ 3 Rocky Bridges
- ☐ 4 Terry Cornutt
- ☐ 5 Rob Dressler
- ☐ 6 Monroe Greenfield
- ☐ 7 Don Hahn
- ☐ 8 Randy Hammon
- ☐ 9 Tom Heintzelman
- ☐ 10 Kyle Hypes
- ☐ 11 Skip James
- ☐ 12 Garry Jestadt
- ☐ 13 Harry Jordan
- ☐ 14 Junior Kennedy
- ☐ 15 Wendell Kim
- ☐ 16 Bob Knepper
- ☐ 17 Joey Martin
- ☐ 18 Greg Minton
- ☐ 19 Ed Plank
- ☐ 20 Frank Riccelli
- ☐ 21 Rick Sanderlin
- ☐ 22 Horace Speed
- ☐ 23 Tommy Toms
- ☐ 24 Michael Wegener

1977 Visalia Oaks TCMA

This 17-card standard-size set of the 1977 Visalia Oaks, a Class A California League affiliate of the Minnesota Twins, features white-bordered posed black-and-white player photos on its fronts. The player's name, position and Oaks logo appear in the orange section near the bottom. The league affiliation appears across an upper corner. The plain white back carries the words "Visalia Oaks" in large letters followed by the player's name, position and biography. The cards are unnumbered and checklisted below in alphabetical order.

	NRMT	VG-E	GOOD
COMPLETE SET (17)	30.00	13.50	3.70

- ☐ 1 John Altman
- ☐ 2 Leland Byrd
- ☐ 3 Bob Carroll
- ☐ 4 Tim Costello
- ☐ 5 Doug Duncan
- ☐ 6 Rick Green
- ☐ 7 James LaFountain
- ☐ 8 Roy McMillian MGR
- ☐ 9 Dean Olson
- ☐ 10 Glenn Purvis
- ☐ 11 Frank Quintero
- ☐ 12 Charlie Renneau
- ☐ 13 Ray Smith
- ☐ 14 Rick Sofield
- ☐ 15 Kevin Stanfield
- ☐ 16 Joe Stewart
- ☐ 17 Bill Stone

1977 Waterloo Indians TCMA

This 32-card standard-size set of the 1977 Waterloo Indians, a Class A Midwest League affiliate of the Cleveland Indians, features white-bordered posed black-and-white player photos on its fronts. The player's name, position and Indians logo appear in the orange section near the bottom. The league affiliation appears across an upper corner. The plain white back carries the player's name and position followed by a biography. The cards are unnumbered and checklisted below in alphabetical order. Card #2 John Arnold and #23 Dave Strickfaden are late issues. Card #3B Thomas Brennan with the corrected Midwest League affiliation on front is considered scarce.

	NRMT	VG-E	GOOD
COMPLETE SET (29)	75.00	34.00	9.50
COMPLETE SET W/LATE ISSUES (31)	125.00	55.00	15.50
COMP. SET W/BRENNAN COR (32)	175.00	80.00	22.00

- ☐ 1 Craig Adams
- ☐ 2 John Arnold (Late Issue)
- ☐ 3A Thomas Brennan (Texas League Affiliation)
- ☐ 3B Thomas Brennan (Midwest League Affiliation)
- ☐ 4 John Buszka
- ☐ 5 Norman Churchhill
- ☐ 6 Dennis Doss
- ☐ 7 Gene Dusan CO
- ☐ 8 David Fowlkes
- ☐ 9 Pedro Garcia
- ☐ 10 Raymond Gault
- ☐ 11 Craig Harvey
- ☐ 12 William Hiss
- ☐ 13 Rick Howerton
- ☐ 14 Kevin Jeansonne
- ☐ 15 Steven Narleski
- ☐ 16 Thomas Pulchinski GM
- ☐ 17 Nathaniel Puryear
- ☐ 18 Junior Roman
- ☐ 19 David Schuler
- ☐ 20 Daniel Skiba
- ☐ 21 Forest "Woody" Smith MGR
- ☐ 22 Samuel Spence
- ☐ 23 Dave Strickfaden (Late Issue)
- ☐ 24 Jeffery Tomski
- ☐ 25 Tony Toups
- ☐ 26 Terry Tyson
- ☐ 27 Michael Vaughn
- ☐ 28 Patrick Washko
- ☐ 29 Steven Widner
- ☐ 30 Al Wihtol
- ☐ 31 Dwain "Bubba" Wilson

1977 Wausau Mets TCMA

This 24-card standard-size set of the 1977 Wausau Mets, a Class A Midwest League Independent, features white-bordered posed black-and-white player photos on its fronts. The player's name, position and Mets logo appear in the orange section near the bottom. The league affiliation appears across an upper corner. The plain white back carries the words "Wausau Mets" in large letters followed by the player's name, position and biography. The cards are unnumbered and checklisted below in alphabetical order.

	NRMT	VG-E	GOOD
COMPLETE SET (24)	50.00	22.00	6.25

- ☐ 1 Kevan Aman
- ☐ 2 Rick Armer
- ☐ 3 Paul Cacciatore
- ☐ 4 Buddy Cardwell
- ☐ 5 Kelvin Chapman
- ☐ 6 Alexander Coghen
- ☐ 7 Gary Corrado
- ☐ 8 Bob Grant
- ☐ 9 James "Pete" Hammer
- ☐ 10 Randy Holman
- ☐ 11 Luis Lunar
- ☐ 12 Bill Muth
- ☐ 13 Bob Pappageorgas
- ☐ 14 Rick Patterson
- ☐ 15 Don Pearson
- ☐ 16 Dennis Sandoval
- ☐ 17 Kim Seaman
- ☐ 18 Keith Shermeyer
- ☐ 19 Tony Thomas
- ☐ 20 Tom Thurberg
- ☐ 21 Alex Trevino
- ☐ 22 Charlie Warren
- ☐ 23 Rick Wolf
- ☐ 24 Tom Egan MGR

1977 West Haven Yankees TCMA

This 25-card standard-size set of the 1977 West Haven Yankees, a Class AA Eastern League affiliate of the Oakland Athletics, features white-bordered posed black-and-white player photos on its fronts. The player's name, position and Yankees logo appear in the orange section near the bottom. The league affiliation appears across an upper corner. The plain white back carries the words "West Haven Yankees" in big letters across the top. The cards are unnumbered and checklisted below in alphabetical order.

	NRMT	VG-E	GOOD
COMPLETE SET (25)	150.00	70.00	19.00

- ☐ 1 Richard Anderson
- ☐ 2 Antonio Bautista
- ☐ 3 Jim Beattie
- ☐ 4 Donald Castle
- ☐ 5 Steven Coulson
- ☐ 6 Duke Drawdy
- ☐ 7 Michael D. Ferraro MGR
- ☐ 8 Jesus Figueroa
- ☐ 9 Richard Fleshman
- ☐ 10 Damaso Garcia
- ☐ 11 Michael Heath
- ☐ 12 Lloyd Kern
- ☐ 13 Timothy Lewis
- ☐ 14 Jim Lysgaard
- ☐ 15 Douglas Melvin
- ☐ 16 Carl Merrill
- ☐ 17 Jerry Narron
- ☐ 18 Nelson Pichardo
- ☐ 19 Domingo Ramos
- ☐ 20 Roger Slagle
- ☐ 21 Garry J. Smith
- ☐ 22 Richard Stenholm
- ☐ 23 Sandy Valdespino
- ☐ 24 Will Verhoeff
- ☐ 25 Bob Zeig GM

1978 Appleton Foxes TCMA

This 25-card standard-size set of the 1978 Appleton Foxes, a Class A Midwest League affiliate of the Chicago White Sox, features white-bordered posed black-and-white player photos on its fronts. The player's name and Foxes logo appear in the green section near the bottom. The league affiliation appears across an upper corner. The plain white horizontal back carries the words "The Minors - 1978 Appleton Foxes" at the top. The cards are unnumbered and checklisted below in alphabetical order.

	NRMT	VG-E	GOOD
COMPLETE SET (25)	50.00	22.00	6.25

☐ 1 Rod Allen
☐ 2 Edward Bahne
☐ 3 Phil Bauer
☐ 4 Ross Baumgarten
☐ 5 Harry Chappas
☐ 6 Roy Coulter
☐ 7 David Daniels
☐ 8 Mark Esser
☐ 9 Curt Etohandy
☐ 10 Lorenzo Gray
☐ 11 John Hanely
☐ 12 Dave Hersh
☐ 13 Clay Hicks
☐ 14 Lamar Hoyt
☐ 15 Dewey Robinson
☐ 16 Mike Sivik
☐ 17 Jackie Smith
☐ 18 Paul Soth
☐ 19 Leo Sutherland
☐ 20 Richard Thoren
☐ 21 Tom Toman
☐ 22 Phil Trucks
☐ 23 Michael Tulacz
☐ 24 Jeffery Vuksan
☐ 25 Victor Walters

1978 Arkansas Travelers TCMA

This 23-card standard-size set of the 1978 Arkansas Travelers, a Class AA Texas League affiliate of the St. Louis Cardinals, features white-bordered posed black-and-white player photos on its fronts. The player's name and Cardinals logo appear in the green section near the bottom. The league affiliation appears across an upper corner. The plain white horizontal back carries the words "The Minors - 1978 Arkansas Travelers" at the top. The cards are unnumbered and checklisted below in alphabetical order. Approximately 1,100 sets were produced.

	NRMT	VG-E	GOOD
COMPLETE SET (23)	225.00	100.00	28.00

☐ 1 Jose Aranzamendi
☐ 2 Earl Bass
☐ 3 Dave Boyer
☐ 4 Glenn Brummer
☐ 5 Mike Calise
☐ 6 Roy Donaghue
☐ 7 Gene Dotson
☐ 8 Leon Durham
☐ 9 Joe Edelen
☐ 10 John Fulgham
☐ 11 Nelson Garcia
☐ 12 R.J. Harrison
☐ 13 Tommy Herr
☐ 14 Terry Kennedy
☐ 15 Ryan Kurosaki
☐ 16 Jim Lentine
☐ 17 John Littlefield
☐ 18 Dan O'Brien
☐ 19 Dave Penniall
☐ 20 Len Strelitz
☐ 21 Randy Thomas
☐ 22 Tommy Thompson
☐ 23 Fred Tisdale

1978 Asheville Tourists TCMA

This 29-card standard-size set of the 1978 Asheville Tourists, a Class A Western Carolinas League affiliate of the Texas Rangers, features white-bordered posed black-and-white player photos on its fronts. The player's name and Tourists logo appear in the green section near the bottom. The league affiliation appears across an upper corner. The plain white horizontal back carries the words "The Minors - 1978 Asheville Tourists" at the top. The cards are unnumbered and checklisted below in alphabetical order.

	NRMT	VG-E	GOOD
COMPLETE SET (29)	40.00	18.00	5.00

☐ 1 Jim Barbe
☐ 2 John Butcher
☐ 3 Jim Capowski
☐ 4 Ron Carney
☐ 5 Joe Carrol
☐ 6 Ted Davis
☐ 7 Luis Gonzalez
☐ 8 Issie Gutierrez
☐ 9 Bob Hallgren
☐ 10 Dave Hibner
☐ 11 Mike Jirschele
☐ 12 Bobby Johnson
☐ 13 Bill LaRosa
☐ 14 Check Lamson
☐ 15 Ed Lynch
☐ 16 Jim Mathews
☐ 17 Arnold McCrary
☐ 18 Mark Mercer
☐ 19 Linvel Mosby
☐ 20 Pat Nelson
☐ 21 Steve Nielsen
☐ 22 Scott Peterson
☐ 23 Miguel Pizarro
☐ 24 Steve Righetti
☐ 25 Bill Simpson
☐ 26 Mike Vickers
☐ 27 Len Whitehouse
☐ 28 Arnold Wilhoite
☐ 29 George Wright

1978 Burlington Bees TCMA

This 28-card standard-size set of the 1978 Burlington Bees, a Class A Midwest League affiliate of the Milwaukee Brewers, features white-bordered posed black-and-white player photos on its fronts. The player's name and Bees logo appear in the green section near the bottom. The league affiliation appears across an upper corner. The plain white horizontal back carries the words "The Minors - 1978 Burlington Bees" at the top. The cards are unnumbered and checklisted below in alphabetical order.

	NRMT	VG-E	GOOD
COMPLETE SET (28)	50.00	22.00	6.25

☐ 1 John Adams
☐ 2 Daryl Bailey
☐ 3 Tim Bannister
☐ 4 Devin Bass
☐ 5 Manuel Betemit
☐ 6 Terry Bevington
☐ 7 Chris Carstensen
☐ 8 Tom DeRosa
☐ 9 Bill Dick
☐ 10 Frank DiPino
☐ 11 Alvin Edge
☐ 12 Larry Edwards
☐ 13 Bill Foley
☐ 14 Ed Gilliam
☐ 15 Jeff Harryman
☐ 16 Jerry Jenkins
☐ 17 Jim Jordan
☐ 18 David LaPoint
☐ 19 Doug Loman
☐ 20 Melvin Manning
☐ 21 Larry Montgomery
☐ 22 Steve Reed
☐ 23 Ivan Rodriquez
☐ 24 Terry Shoebridge
☐ 25 Lee Sigman
☐ 26 John Skorochocki
☐ 27 Bob Smith
☐ 28 Weldon Swift

1978 Cedar Rapids Giants TCMA

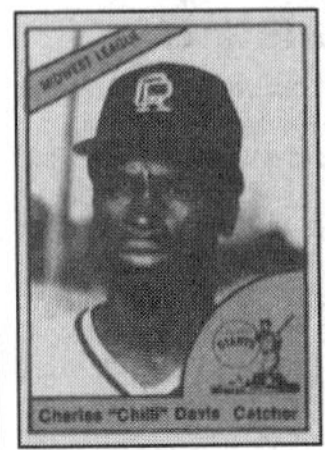

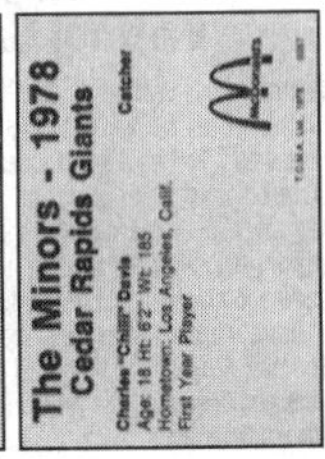

This 29-card standard-size set of the 1978 Cedar Rapids Giants, a Class A Midwest League affiliate of the San Francisco Giants, features white-bordered posed black-and-white player photos on its fronts. The player's name and Giants logo appear in the green section near the bottom. The league affiliation appears across an upper corner. The plain white horizontal back carries the words "The Minors - 1978 Wisconsin Rapids Twins" at the top. The cards are unnumbered and checklisted below in alphabetical order.

	NRMT	VG-E	GOOD
COMPLETE SET (29)	125.00	55.00	15.50

☐ 1 Pat Alexander
☐ 2 Darnell Baker
☐ 3 Jeff Borruel
☐ 4 DeWayne Buice
☐ 5 Don Buchheister
☐ 6 Raymondo Coslo
☐ 7 Charles "Chili" Davis
☐ 8 Ken Feinberg
☐ 9 Rob Henderson
☐ 10 Craig Hendrick
☐ 11 Steve Holman
☐ 12 Bob Kearney
☐ 13 Craig Landis
☐ 14 Doug Landuyt
☐ 15 Javier Lopes
☐ 16 Henry Macias
☐ 17 Louis Marietta
☐ 18 Jack Mull
☐ 19 Venice Murray
☐ 20 Bob Omo
☐ 21 Juan Oppenheimer
☐ 22 Ron Pisel
☐ 23 Francisco Rojas
☐ 24 Alfonso Rosario
☐ 25 John Smith
☐ 26 Jeff Stadler
☐ 27 Jeff Stember
☐ 28 Frankie Thon
☐ 29 Veterans Mem. Stadium

1978 Charleston Charlies TCMA

This 20-card standard-size set of the 1978 Charleston Charlies, a Class AAA International League affiliate of the Houston Astros, features white-bordered posed color player photos on its fronts. The white back carries the year, league, team name, the player's name, position, biography and statistics. The cards are unnumbered and checklisted below in alphabetical order.

	NRMT	VG-E	GOOD
COMPLETE SET (20)	15.00	6.75	1.85

☐ 1 Dave Augustine
☐ 2 Jim Beauchamp
☐ 3 Craig Cacek
☐ 4 Joe Cannon
☐ 5 Bob Coluccio
☐ 6 Keith Drumright
☐ 7 Mike Fischlin
☐ 8 Larry Hardy
☐ 9 Bo McLaughlin
Sic, McLaughton
☐ 10 Jim O'Bradovich
☐ 11 Ramon Perez
☐ 12 Don Pisker
☐ 13 Luis Pujols
☐ 14 Vern Ruhle
Sic, Ruhl
☐ 15 Jose Sosa
☐ 16 Rob Sperring
☐ 17 Roy Thomas
☐ 18 Mike Tyler
☐ 19 Randy Wiles
☐ 20 Rick Williams

1978 Charleston Pirates TCMA

This 24-card standard-size set of the 1978 Charleston Pirates, a Class A Western Carolinas League affiliate of the Pittsburgh Pirates, features white-bordered posed black-and-white player photos on its fronts. The player's name and Pirates logo appear in the green section near the bottom. The league affiliation appears across an upper corner. The plain white horizontal back carries the words "The Minors - 1978 Charleston Pirates" at the top. The cards are unnumbered and checklisted below in alphabetical order.

	NRMT	VG-E	GOOD
COMPLETE SET (24)	25.00	11.00	3.10

☐ 1 Doug Britt
☐ 2 Bryan Clark
☐ 3 Casey Clark
☐ 4 Steve Farr
☐ 5 Rick Federici
☐ 6 Doug Frobel
☐ 7 Tim Ganch
☐ 8 Gene Gentile
☐ 9 Wendell Hibbett
☐ 10 Woody Huyke
☐ 11 Luis Jimenez
☐ 12 Jean Leduc
☐ 13 Brian Lucas
☐ 14 Ed Lynch
☐ 15 Vic Marte
☐ 16 Tony Nicely
☐ 17 Adalberto Ortiz
☐ 18 Mike Pill
☐ 19 Charlie Powell
☐ 20 Wascar Reyes
☐ 21 Carlos Rios
☐ 22 Brian Schwerman
☐ 23 Billy Scripture
☐ 24 Ed Vargas

1978 Clinton Dodgers TCMA

This 33-card standard-size set of the 1978 Clinton Dodgers, a Class A Midwest League affiliate of the Los Angeles Dodgers, features white-bordered posed black-and-white player photos on its fronts. The player's name and Dodgers logo appear in the green section near the bottom. The league affiliation appears across an upper corner. The plain white horizontal back carries the words "The Minors - 1978 Clinton Dodgers" at the top. The cards are unnumbered and checklisted below in alphabetical order. Approximately 1,100 sets were produced.

	NRMT	VG-E	GOOD
COMPLETE SET (33)	50.00	22.00	6.25

☐ 1 Rick Bach
Jan Bach
☐ 2 Jerry Bass
☐ 3 Clinton Batboys
☐ 4 Riverview Stadium
☐ 5 Rocky Cordova
☐ 6 Dean Craig
☐ 7 Mark Elliott
☐ 8 Larry Ferst
☐ 9 Rick Ford
☐ 10 Doug Foster
☐ 11 Miguel Franjul
☐ 12 Diug Harrison
☐ 13 Leonardo Hernandez
☐ 14 Mike Holt
☐ 15 Mike Howard
☐ 16 Tim Jones
☐ 17 Kevin Joyce
☐ 18 Mark Kryka
☐ 19 Don LeJohn
☐ 20 Jack Littrell
☐ 21 Evon Martinson
☐ 22 Rusty McDonald
☐ 23 Dick McLaughlin
☐ 24 Chris Mulden
☐ 25 Rick Ollar
☐ 26 Joe Purpura
☐ 27 German Rivera
☐ 28 Mike Stone
☐ 29 Steve Sunker
☐ 30 Bill Swoope
☐ 31 Mark Van Bever
☐ 32 Mitch Webster
☐ 33 Larry Wright

1978 Columbus Clippers TCMA

This 27-card standard-size set of the 1978 Columbus Clippers, a Class AAA International League affiliate of the Pittsburgh Pirates, features white-bordered posed color player photos on its fronts. The white back carries the year, league, team name, the player's name, position, biography and statistics. The cards are unnumbered and checklisted below in alphabetical order.

	NRMT	VG-E	GOOD
COMPLETE SET (27)	25.00	11.00	3.10

☐ 1 Dale Berra
☐ 2 Dorian Boyland
☐ 3 Fred Briening
☐ 4 Cot Deal
☐ 5 Mike Easler
☐ 6 Mike Fiore
☐ 7 Jim Fuller
☐ 8 Fernando Gonzales
☐ 9 Gary Hargis
☐ 10 Al Holland
☐ 11 Randy Hopkins
☐ 12 Odell Jones
☐ 13 John Lipon
☐ 14 Alberto Lois
☐ 15 Ken Macha
☐ 16 Ron Mitchell
☐ 17 Roger Nelson
☐ 18 Steve Nicosia
☐ 19 Cosie Olivares
☐ 20 Dave Pagan
☐ 21 Harry Saferight
☐ 22 Mickey Scott
☐ 23 Rod Scurry
☐ 24 Tom Shopay
☐ 25 Randy Tate
☐ 26 Tom Walker
☐ 27 Ed Whitson

1978 Daytona Beach Astros TCMA

This 26-card standard-size set of the 1978 Daytona Beach Astros, a Class A Florida State League affiliate of the Houston Astros, features white-bordered posed black-and-white player photos on its fronts. The player's name and Astros logo appear in the green section near the bottom. The league affiliation appears across an upper corner. The plain white horizontal back carries the words "The Minors - 1978 Daytona Beach Astros" at the top. The cards are unnumbered and checklisted below in alphabetical order.

	NRMT	VG-E	GOOD
COMPLETE SET (26)	25.00	11.00	3.10

☐ 1 Ricky Adams
☐ 2 Rick Aponte
☐ 3 Julio Beltran
☐ 4 Al Cajide
☐ 5 John Cloherty
☐ 6 Paul Cooper
☐ 7 Steve Englishbey
☐ 8 George Gross
☐ 9 Don Harkness
☐ 10 Pete Hernandez
☐ 11 Kevin Houston

☐ 12 Doug Jackson
☐ 13 Ramon Leader
☐ 14 Del Leatherwood
☐ 15 Stan Leland
☐ 16 Scott Loucks
☐ 17 Jim MacDonald
☐ 18 Diego Melendez
☐ 19 Fred Morris
☐ 20 Jose Mota
☐ 21 Leo Posado
☐ 22 Simon Rosario
☐ 23 Randy Rouse
☐ 24 Billy Smith
☐ 25 Jose Turner
☐ 26 Randy Walraven

1978 Dunedin Blue Jays TCMA

This 27-card standard-size set of the 1978 Dunedin Blue Jays, a Class A Florida State League affiliate of the Toronto Blue Jays, features white-bordered posed black-and-white player photos on its fronts. The player's name and Blue Jays logo appear in the green section near the bottom. The league affiliation appears across an upper corner. The plain white horizontal back carries the words "The Minors - 1978 Dunedin Blue Jays" at the top. This issue includes the first minor league appearance of Jesse Barfield. The cards are unnumbered and checklisted below in alphabetical order.

	NRMT	VG-E	GOOD
COMPLETE SET (27)	50.00	22.00	6.25

☐ 1 Jesse Barfield
☐ 2 Larry Bullard
☐ 3 Jeff Carsley
☐ 4 Rick Counts GM
☐ 5 Tom Dejak
☐ 6 Eduardo Dennis
☐ 7 Wayne DeWright
☐ 8 Roberto Galvez
☐ 9 Miguel Gomez
☐ 10 Scott Gregory
☐ 11 Rick Hertel
☐ 12 Darryl Hill
☐ 13 Jack Hollis
☐ 14 Dennis Holmberg CO UER (Misspelled Homberg on front)
☐ 15 Mike Lebo
☐ 16 Denis Menke MG
☐ 17 Benny Perez
☐ 18 Jay Robertson
☐ 19 Dave Rohm
☐ 20 Jose Rosario
☐ 21 Pete Rowe
☐ 22 Ron Sorey
☐ 23 Fay Thompson
☐ 24 Greg Wells
☐ 25 Ralph Wheeler
☐ 26 Randy Wiens
☐ 27 Andre Wood

1978 Greenwood Braves TCMA

This 29-card standard-size set of the 1978 Greenwood Braves, a Class A Western Carolinas League affiliate of the Atlanta Braves, features white-bordered posed black-and-white player photos on its fronts. The player's name and Braves logo appear in the green section near the bottom. The league affiliation appears across an upper corner. The plain white horizontal back carries the words "The Minors - 1978 Greenwood Braves" at the top. The cards are unnumbered and checklisted below in alphabetical order.

	NRMT	VG-E	GOOD
COMPLETE SET (29)	25.00	11.00	3.10

☐ 1 Terry Abbott
☐ 2 Tom Ballard
☐ 3 Tim Barr
☐ 4 Clete Boyer
☐ 5 Smokey Burgess
☐ 6 Tim Cole
☐ 7 Joe Cowley
☐ 8 John Dyer
☐ 9 Andre Forbes
☐ 10 Alan Gallagher
☐ 11 Bill Haley
☐ 12 Steve Hammond
☐ 13 Bill Haslerig
☐ 14 Danny Lucia
☐ 15 Jeff Matthews
☐ 16 Tommy Mee
☐ 17 Alvin Moore
☐ 18 Felix Pettaway
☐ 19 Bob Porter
☐ 20 Rafael Ramirez
☐ 21 George Ramos
☐ 22 Andre Sams
☐ 23 Brian Snitker
☐ 24 Scott Thayer
☐ 25 Bruce Tonascia
☐ 26 Wyatt Tonkin
☐ 27 William Tucker
☐ 28 Bob Veale
☐ 29 Richard Wieters

1978 Holyoke Millers TCMA

This 24-card standard-size set of the 1978 Holyoke Millers, a Class AA Eastern League affiliate of the Milwaukee Brewers, features white-bordered posed color player photos on its fronts. The white back carries the year, league, team name, the player's name, position, biography and statistics. The cards are unnumbered and checklisted below in alphabetical order. Approximately 5,000 sets were produced.

	NRMT	VG-E	GOOD
COMPLETE SET (24)	15.00	6.75	1.85

☐ 1 Jeff Barker
☐ 2 Ken Biggerstaff
☐ 3 Ed Carroll
☐ 4 Mike Dempsey
☐ 5 Bill Dick
☐ 6 Ronnie Driver
☐ 7 Marshall Edwards
☐ 8 George Farson
☐ 9 Steve Green
☐ 10 Steve Grimes
☐ 11 Mike Henderson
☐ 12 Lynn B. Herzig
☐ 13 Gary Holle
☐ 14 Ron Jacobs
☐ 15 Bernado Leonard
☐ 16 Willie Mueller
☐ 17 Rick Nicholson
☐ 18 Neil Rasmussen
☐ 19 Chuck Ross
☐ 20 Dave Smith
☐ 21 Steve Splitt
☐ 22 Esteban Texidor
☐ 23 Don Whiting
☐ 24 Jeff Yurak

1978 Indianapolis Indians Team Issue

	NRMT	VG-E	GOOD
COMPLETE SET (27)	25.00	11.00	3.10

☐ 1 Team Picture
☐ 2 Roy Majtyka MG
☐ 3 Paul Moskau
☐ 4 Mike LaCoss
☐ 5 Harry Spilman
☐ 6 Ron Oester
☐ 7 Dan Dumoulin
☐ 8 Ed Armbrister
☐ 9 Mario Soto
☐ 10 Tommy Mutz
☐ 11 Dave Moore
☐ 12 John Summers
☐ 13 Larry Payne
☐ 14 John Valle
☐ 15 George Cappuzzello
☐ 16 Mike Grace
☐ 17 Rafael Santo Domingo
☐ 18 Angel Torres
☐ 19 Vic Correll
☐ 20 Lynn Jones
☐ 21 Raul Ferreyra
☐ 22 Arturo DeFreites
☐ 23 Frank Pastore
☐ 24 Randy Davidson
☐ 25 Jeff Sovern
☐ 26 Ron McClain TR
☐ 27 Checklist

1978 Knoxville Knox Sox TCMA

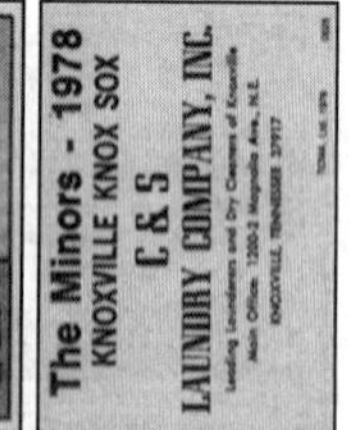

This 25-card standard-size set of the 1978 Knoxville Knox Sox, a Class A Southern League affiliate of the Chicago White Sox, features white-bordered posed black-and-white player photos on its fronts. The player's name and Knox Sox logo appear in the green section near the bottom. The league affiliation appears across an upper corner. The plain white horizontal back carries the words "The Minors - 1978 Knoxville Knox Sox" at the top. The cards are unnumbered and checklisted below in alphabetical order. Approximately 1,100 sets were produced.

	NRMT	VG-E	GOOD
COMPLETE SET (25)	250.00	110.00	31.00

☐ 1 Harold Baines
☐ 2 Richard Barnes
☐ 3 Richard Dotson
☐ 4 Marvis Foley
☐ 5 Ken Frailing
☐ 6 Fred Frazier
☐ 7 Joe Gates
☐ 8 Quincy Hill
☐ 9 Fred Howard
☐ 10 Rusty Kuntz
☐ 11 Tony LaRussa
☐ 12 Mitch Lukevics
☐ 13 Larry Monroe
☐ 14 Bill Moran
☐ 15 Mark Naehring
☐ 16 Chris Nyman
☐ 17 Andy Pasillas
☐ 18 Donn Seidholz
☐ 19 Duane Shaffer
☐ 20 Ken Silvestri
☐ 21 Tom Spencer
☐ 22 Willie Thompson
☐ 23 Tommy Toman
☐ 24 Steve Trout
☐ 25 Mike Wolf

1978 Lodi Dodgers TCMA

This 26-card standard-size set of the 1978 Lodi Dodgers, a Class A California League affiliate of the Los Angeles Dodgers, features white-bordered posed black-and-white player photos on its fronts. The player's name and Dodgers logo appear in the green section near the bottom. The league affiliation appears across an upper corner. The plain white horizontal back carries the words "The Minors - 1978 Lodi Dodgers" at the top. The cards are unnumbered and checklisted below in alphabetical order.

	NRMT	VG-E	GOOD
COMPLETE SET (25)	30.00	13.50	3.70
COMPLETE SET (26)	50.00	22.00	6.25

☐ 1 Paul Bain
☐ 2 Bobby Brown
☐ 3 H.P. Drake
☐ 4 Larry Fobbs
☐ 5 Marv Garrison
☐ 6 Rick Goulding
☐ 7 Brian Hayes
☐ 8 Ubaldo Heredia
☐ 9 Hank Jones
☐ 10 George Kaage
☐ 11 Mike Lake
☐ 12 Mickey Lashley
☐ 13 Dave Richards
☐ 14 Tim Roche
☐ 15 Ron Roenicke
☐ 16 Don Ruzek
☐ 17A Rod Scheller ERR (wrong name on back)
☐ 17B Rod Scheller COR (correct name on back)
☐ 18 Eric Schmidt
☐ 19 Steve Shirley
☐ 20 John Shoemaker
☐ 21 Mike Stone
☐ 22 Ken Townsend
☐ 23 Max Venable
☐ 24 John Walker
☐ 25 Stan Wasiak

1978 Memphis Chicks Britling Cafeterias

Printed on thin card stock, this 10-card set of the 1978 Memphis Chicks, a Class AA Southern League affiliate of the Montreal Expos, measures 2 3/4" by 3 7/8" and features white-bordered and blue-screened posed player photos on its fronts. The player's name and logos for the Chicks and Britling appear within the wide white bottom margin. The red, white, and blue horizontal back carries the player's name and biography at the top, followed by career highlights and statistics. Although some cards are numbered on the back (e.g., #1 Perez; #2 Hemm; #3 McMullen; #4 Goldetsky), the rest carry no card numbers. Therefore, the cards are listed below alphabetically by player's last name.

	NRMT	VG-E	GOOD
COMPLETE SET (10)	25.00	11.00	3.10

☐ 1 Felipe Alou MG
☐ 2 Ray Crowley
☐ 3 Godfrey Evans
☐ 4 Larry Goldetsky
☐ 5 Warren Hemm
☐ 6 Dale McMullen
☐ 7 Julio Perez
☐ 8 Joe Pettini
☐ 9 John Scoras
☐ 10 Rick Williams

1978 Newark Wayne Co-Pilots TCMA

This 45-card standard-size set of the 1978 Newark Wayne Co-Pilots, a Class A New York-Penn League affiliate of the Milwaukee Brewers, features white-bordered posed black-and-white player photos on its fronts. The player's name and Co-Pilots logo appear in the green section near the bottom. The league affiliation appears across an upper corner. The plain white horizontal back carries the words "The Minors - 1978 Newark Wayne Co-Pilots" at the top. The cards are unnumbered and checklisted below in alphabetical order.

	NRMT	VG-E	GOOD
COMPLETE SET (45)	30.00	13.50	3.70

☐ 1 Bert Acosta
☐ 2 Sally Beal
☐ 3 Randy Boyce
☐ 4 Eddie Brunson
☐ 5 Ron Buggs
☐ 6 Pablo Cavallo
☐ 7 Rafael Cuevas
☐ 8 Stan Davis
☐ 9 Greg DeHart
☐ 10 Jorge DeJuses
☐ 11 Roberto Diaz
☐ 12 Duke Duncan
☐ 13 Lance Ediger
☐ 14 Willie Flowers
☐ 15 Steve Gibson
☐ 16 Sam Giergan
☐ 17 Dan Gilmartin
☐ 18 Dean Hall
☐ 19 Rocky Hall
☐ 20 Nick Hernandez
☐ 21 Doug Jones
☐ 22 Tim Jordan
☐ 23 Eligio Kelly
☐ 24 Harvey Kuenn
☐ 25 David Lebron
☐ 26 Jerry Lewis
☐ 27 Steve Maderfield
☐ 28 Ray Manship
☐ 29 Dan Maxaon
☐ 30 Tom McLish
☐ 31 Steve Norwood
☐ 32 Rick Olsen
☐ 33 Jim Padula
☐ 34 Vince Pone
☐ 35 Luis Ramirez
☐ 36 Russell Ramirez
☐ 37 Kenny Richardson
☐ 38 Jim Robinson
☐ 39 John Roesch
☐ 40 Pat Seegers
☐ 41 Tom Soto
☐ 42 John Stevenson
☐ 43 Al Wesolowski
☐ 44 Nick Willhite
☐ 45 Porter Wyatt

1978 Orlando Twins TCMA

This 23-card standard-size set of the 1978 Orlando Twins, a Class AA Southern League affiliate of the Minnesota Twins, features white-bordered posed black-and-white player photos on its fronts. The player's name and Twins logo appear in the green section near the bottom. The league affiliation appears across an upper corner. The plain white horizontal back carries the words "The Minors - 1978 Orlando Twins" at the top. The cards are unnumbered and checklisted below in alphabetical order.

	NRMT	VG-E	GOOD
COMPLETE SET (23)	20.00	9.00	2.50

☐ 1 Terry Bulling
☐ 2 John Castino
☐ 3 Mark Clapham
☐ 4 Rich Dalton
☐ 5 Rick Duncan
☐ 6 Frank Estes
☐ 7 John Goryl
☐ 8 Jeff Holly
☐ 9 Darrell Jackson
☐ 10 Curt Lewis
☐ 11 Bruce MacPherson
☐ 12 Dennis Mantick
☐ 13 Marty Maxwell
☐ 14 Kevin McWhirter
☐ 15 Warren Mertens
☐ 16 Frank Quintero
☐ 17 Tom Sain
☐ 18 Terry Sheehan
☐ 19 Ray Smith
☐ 20 Dan Spain
☐ 21 Jesus Vega
☐ 22 Steve Wagner
☐ 23 Kurt Whitmayer

1978 Phoenix Giants Cramer

	NRMT	VG-E	GOOD
COMPLETE SET (25)	5.00	2.20	.60

☐ 1 Ethan Blackaby
☐ 2 Rick Bradley
☐ 3 Rocky Bridges
☐ 4 Don Carrithers
☐ 5 Mike Cash
☐ 6 Terry Cornutt
☐ 7 Rob Dressler
☐ 8 Art Gardner
☐ 9 Randy Hammon
☐ 10 Kyle Hypes
☐ 11 Greg Johnston
☐ 12 Harry Jordan
☐ 13 Wendell Kim
☐ 14 Jeff Little

☐ 15 Dennis Littlejohn
☐ 16 Greg Minton
☐ 17 Howie Mitchell
☐ 18 Rich Murray
☐ 19 Phil Nastu
☐ 20 Casey Parsons
☐ 21 Ed Plank
☐ 22 Mike Rowland
☐ 23 Rick Sanderlin
☐ 24 Joe Strain
☐ 25 Guy Sularz

1978 Quad City Angels TCMA

This 30-card standard-size set of the 1978 Quad City Angels, a Class A Midwest League affiliate of the California Angels, features white-bordered posed black-and-white player photos on its fronts. The player's name and Angels logo appear in the green section near the bottom. The league affiliation appears across an upper corner. The plain white horizontal back carries the words "The Minors - 1978 Quad City Angels" at the top. The cards are unnumbered and checklisted below in alphabetical order.

	NRMT	VG-E	GOOD
COMPLETE SET (30)	100.00	45.00	12.50

☐ 1 Gary Balla
☐ 2 Ned Bergert
☐ 3 Jeff Bertoni
☐ 4 Joe Blyleven
☐ 5 Arturo Bonitto
☐ 6 Bob Border
☐ 7 Jeff Connor
☐ 8 Brian Harper
☐ 9 Brad Havens
☐ 10 Mike Heaton
☐ 11 Don Jones
☐ 12 Guy Jones
☐ 13 Monte Mendenhall
☐ 14 Mark Miller
☐ 15 Charles Nash MGR
☐ 16 Steve Oliva
☐ 17 Harry Pells GM
☐ 18 John Pound
☐ 19 Melvin Quarles
☐ 20 Bran Riffle UER
(Name misspelled Riffel on card front)
☐ 21 Greg Ris
☐ 22 Andy Rodriguez
☐ 23 Wade Schexnayder
☐ 24 Darryl Sconiers
☐ 25 Mike Stover
☐ 26 Doug Thomson
☐ 27 Jim Vallone
☐ 28 Steve Van Deren
☐ 29 Alan Wiggins
☐ 30 Waterloo Municipal Stadium

1978 Richmond Braves TCMA

This 20-card standard-size set of the 1978 Richmond Braves, a Class AAA International League affiliate of the Atlanta Braves, features white-bordered posed color player photos on its fronts. The white back carries the year, league, team name, the player's name, position, biography and statistics. The cards are unnumbered and checklisted below in alphabetical order.

	NRMT	VG-E	GOOD
COMPLETE SET (20)	20.00	9.00	2.50

☐ 1 Tommie Aaron
☐ 2 James Arline
☐ 3 Bruce Benedict
☐ 4 Larry Bradford
☐ 5 Glenn Hubbard
☐ 6 Frank LaCorte
☐ 7 Michael Macha
☐ 8 Jerry Maddox
☐ 9 Richard Mahler
☐ 10 Joey McLaughlin
☐ 11 Edward Miller
☐ 12 Jon Richardson
☐ 13 Chico Ruiz
☐ 14 John Sain
☐ 15 Hank Small
☐ 16 Duane Theiss
☐ 17 Larry Whisenton
☐ 18 Kris Yoder
☐ 19 Front Office
☐ 20 Seymore Baseball and Chief Powa Hitta

1978 Rochester Red Wings TCMA

This 17-card standard-size set of the 1978 Rochester Red Wings, a Class AAA International League affiliate of the Baltimore Orioles, features white-bordered posed color player photos on its fronts. The white back carries the year, league, team name, the player's name, position, biography and statistics. The cards are unnumbered and checklisted below in alphabetical order.

	NRMT	VG-E	GOOD
COMPLETE SET (17)	30.00	13.50	3.70

☐ 1 Ray Bare
☐ 2 Tom Bianco
☐ 3 Don Cardoza
☐ 4 Tony Chevez
☐ 5 Tom Chism
☐ 6 Dave Criscione
☐ 7 Mike Dimmel
☐ 8 Blake Doyle
☐ 9 Skeeter Jarquin
☐ 10 Kevin Kennedy
☐ 11 Wayne Krenchicki
☐ 12 Rafael Liranzo
☐ 13 Marty Parrill
☐ 14 Jeff Rineer
☐ 15 Frank Robinson
☐ 16 Earl Stephenson
☐ 17 Tim Stoddard

1978 Salem Pirates TCMA

This 18-card standard-size set of the 1978 Salem Pirates, a Class A Carolina League affiliate of the Pittsburgh Pirates, features white-bordered posed black-and-white player photos on its fronts. The player's name and Pirates logo appear in the green section near the bottom. The league affiliation appears across an upper corner. The plain white horizontal back carries the words "The Minors - 1978 Salem Pirates" at the top. The cards are unnumbered and checklisted below in alphabetical order.

	NRMT	VG-E	GOOD
COMPLETE SET (18)	25.00	11.00	3.10

☐ 1 Juan Arias
☐ 2 Pablo Cruz
☐ 3 Phil Cyburt
☐ 4 Rickey Evans
☐ 5 Marc Gelinas
☐ 6 Sandy Hill
☐ 7 Rick Lancelotti
☐ 8 Robert Long
☐ 9 Jim Mahoney
☐ 10 Frank Miloszewski
☐ 11 Bob Parsons
☐ 12 Rick Peterson
☐ 13 Dean Rick
☐ 14 Bob Rock
☐ 15 Luis Salazar
☐ 16 Alfredo Torres
☐ 17 Chich Valley
☐ 18 Ben Wiltbank

1978 Salt Lake City Gulls Cramer

	NRMT	VG-E	GOOD
COMPLETE SET (24)	10.00	4.50	1.25

☐ 1 Tommy Smith
☐ 2 Jim Anderson
☐ 3 Dave Machemer
☐ 4 Dickie Thon
☐ 5 Kim Allen
☐ 6 Gil Flores
☐ 7 Deron Johnson
☐ 8 Tom Donohue
☐ 9 Steve Stroughter
☐ 10 Pat Cristelli
☐ 11 John Racanelli
☐ 14 Stan Cliburn
☐ 15 Bobby Jones
☐ 16 Gil Kubski
☐ 17 Chuck Porter
☐ 18 John Caneira
☐ 19 Bob Ferris
☐ 20 Dave Schuler
☐ 21 Mike Barlow
☐ 22 Willie Aikens
☐ 24 Mike Overy
☐ 25 Dave Frost
☐ 26 Carlos Perez
☐ NNO Leonard Garcia

1978 San Jose Missions Mr. Chef's

	NRMT	VG-E	GOOD
COMPLETE SET (24)	40.00	18.00	5.00

☐ 1 Checklist Card
☐ 2 Rene Lachemann MG
☐ 3 Greg Biercevicz
☐ 4 Frank MacCormack
☐ 5 Ed Crosby
☐ 6 Joe Decker
☐ 7 Jose Elguezabal
☐ 8 Gary Wheelock
☐ 9 Alan Griffin
☐ 10 Pete Ithier
☐ 11 Rick Baldwin
☐ 12 Charlie Beamon
☐ 13 Juan Bernhardt
☐ 14 Luis Delgado
☐ 15 Steve Hamrick
☐ 16 Tom Brown
☐ 17 Byron McLaughlin
☐ 18 Tommy McMillan
☐ 19 Bill Plummer
☐ 20 George Mitterwald
☐ 21 Archie Amerson
☐ 22 Manny Estrada
☐ 23 Jack Pierce
☐ 24 Mike Kekich

1978 Spokane Indians Cramer

	NRMT	VG-E	GOOD
COMPLETE SET (24)	5.00	2.20	.60

☐ 1 Duane Espy
☐ 2 William McLaurine
☐ 3 Ronnie Diggle
☐ 4 Dale Hrovat
☐ 5 James Quirk
☐ 6 Lanny Phillips
☐ 7 Billy Severns
☐ 8 Tony Muser
☐ 9 Jack Heidemann
☐ 10 Edgardo Romero
☐ 11 Stephen Ruling
☐ 12 Craighton Tevlin
☐ 13 Juan Lopez
☐ 15 Tommie Reynolds
☐ 17 Ron Wrona
☐ 18 Barry Cort
☐ 19 Samuel Hinds
☐ 20 John Buffamoyer
☐ 21 Robert Galasso
☐ 22 Edward Farmer
☐ 24 Lynn McKinney
☐ 26 John Felske
☐ 27 Gary Beare
☐ 28 Edgar Yost

1978 Springfield Redbirds Wiener King

	NRMT	VG-E	GOOD
COMPLETE SET (24)	100.00	45.00	12.50

☐ 1 Ken Oberkfell
☐ 2 Ron Farkas
☐ 3 Mike Potter
☐ 4 John Scott
☐ 5 Mike Ramsey
☐ 6 Nyls Nyman
☐ 7 David Bialas
☐ 8 Benny Ayala
☐ 9 Manny Castillo
☐ 10 John Tamargo
☐ 11 Eddie Daves
☐ 12 Lee Landers TR
☐ 13 Jimy Williams MG
☐ 14 Tommy Toms
☐ 15 Al Autry
☐ 16 Tom Bruno
☐ 17 Frank Riccelli
☐ 18 Silvio Martinez
☐ 19 Bill Rothan
☐ 20 Gregory Terlecky
☐ 21 Ron Selak
☐ 22 Aurelio Lopez
☐ 23 George Frazier
☐ 24 Ken Rudolph CO

1978 St. Petersburg Cardinals TCMA

This 29-card standard-size set of the 1978 St. Petersburg Cardinals, a Class A Florida State League affiliate of the St. Louis Cardinals, features white-bordered posed black-and-white player photos on its fronts. The player's name and Cardinals logo appear in the green section near the bottom. The league affiliation appears across an upper corner. The plain white horizontal back carries the words "The Minors - 1978 St. Petersburg Cardinals" at the top. The cards are unnumbered and checklisted below in alphabetical order.

	NRMT	VG-E	GOOD
COMPLETE SET (29)	25.00	11.00	3.10

☐ 1 Fulvio Bertolotti
☐ 2 Jack Boag
☐ 3 Mark Bumstead
☐ 4 Tom Chamberlain
☐ 5 Donnie Chesire
☐ 6 Dennis Cirbo
☐ 7 Glenn Comoletti
☐ 8 Chris Davis
☐ 9 Hector Eduardo
☐ 10 Niel Fiala
☐ 11 Julian Gutierrez
☐ 12 Brett Houser
☐ 13 Dave Johnson
☐ 14 Dave Jorn
☐ 15 Arno Kirchenwitz
☐ 16 Terry Landrum
☐ 17 Chris Lombardo
☐ 18 Ralph Miller Jr.
☐ 19 Kelly Paris
☐ 20 Mike Pisarkiewicz
☐ 21 Mike Pope
☐ 22 Jim Reeves
☐ 23 Gene Roof
☐ 24 Larry Silver
☐ 25 Elliot Waller
☐ 26 Ray Williams
☐ 27 Hal Witt
☐ 28 Felipe Zayas
☐ 29 Hal Lanier

1978 Syracuse Chiefs TCMA

This 22-card standard-size set of the 1978 Syracuse Chiefs, a Class AAA International League affiliate of the Toronto Blue Jays, features white-bordered posed color player photos on its fronts. The white back carries the year, league, team name, the player's name, position, biography and statistics. This issue includes Danny Ainge's first appearance on a minor league card. The cards are unnumbered and checklisted below in alphabetical order.

	NRMT	VG-E	GOOD
COMPLETE SET (22)	50.00	22.00	6.25

☐ 1 Danny Ainge
☐ 2 Butch Alberts
☐ 3 Vern Benson MG
☐ 4 Jeff Byrd
☐ 5 Victor Cruz
☐ 6 Mike Darr
☐ 7 Andy Dyes
☐ 8 Butch Edge
☐ 9 Sam Ewing
☐ 10 Chuck Fore
☐ 11 Steve Grilli
☐ 12 Pat Kelly
☐ 13 Sheldon Mallory
☐ 14 Luis Melendez
☐ 15 Ken Pape
☐ 16 Ken Reynolds
☐ 17 Tom Sandt
☐ 18 Mike Stanton
☐ 19 Hector Torres
☐ 20 Ernie Whitt
☐ 21 Alvis Woods
☐ 22 Garry Woods

1978 Tacoma Yankees Cramer

	NRMT	VG-E	GOOD
COMPLETE SET (25)	8.00	3.60	1.00

☐ 1 Mike Ferraro
☐ 8 Ed Napoleon
☐ 9 Dennis Werth
☐ 10 Roger Slagle
☐ 14 Dennis Irwin
☐ 15 Darryl Jones
☐ 17 Domingo Ramos
☐ 18 Jim Lysgaard
☐ 19 Jim Curnal
☐ 20 George Zeber
☐ 21 Bob Kammeyer
☐ 22 Marv Thompson
☐ 23 Roy Staiger
☐ 25 Steve Taylor
☐ 27 Dell Alston
☐ 28 Dave Rajsich
☐ 29 Larry McCall
☐ 38 Jerry Narron
☐ 39A Brian Doyle
☐ 39B Garry Smith
☐ 42 Damaso Garcia
☐ 43 Bob Polinsky
☐ 44 Tommy Cruz
☐ 47 Hoyt Wilhelm
☐ 54 Neal Mersch

1978 Tidewater Tides TCMA

This 27-card standard-size set of the 1978 Tidewater Tides, a Class AAA International League affiliate of the New York Mets, features white-bordered posed color player photos on its fronts. The white back carries the year, league, team name, the player's name, position, biography and statistics. The cards are unnumbered and checklisted below in alphabetical order.

	NRMT	VG-E	GOOD
COMPLETE SET (27)	25.00	11.00	3.10

☐ 1 Neil Allen
☐ 2 Fred Andrews
☐ 3 Juan Berenguer
☐ 4 Dwight Bernard
☐ 5 Marshall Brant
☐ 6 Mike Bruhart
☐ 7 Ed Cipot
☐ 8 Mardie Cornejo
☐ 9 Sergio Ferrer
☐ 10 Tom Hausman
☐ 11 Roy Lee Jackson
☐ 12 Ed Kurpiel
☐ 13 Pepe Mangual
☐ 14 Rich Miller

☐ 15 Bob Myrick
☐ 16 Dan Norman
☐ 17 John Pacella
☐ 18 Greg Pavlick
☐ 19 Marty Perez
☐ 20 Mario Ramirez
☐ 21 Randy Rogers
☐ 22 Luis Rosado
☐ 23 Mike Scott
☐ 24 Dan Smith
☐ 25 Alex Trevino
☐ 26 Mike Van DeCasteele
☐ 27 Frank Verdi

1978 Tucson Toros Cramer

	NRMT	VG-E	GOOD
COMPLETE SET (25)	5.00	2.20	.60

☐ 2 LaRue Washington
☐ 4 Nelson Norman
☐ 9 Wayne Pinkerton
☐ 10 Paul Mirabella
☐ 12 Keith Chauncey
☐ 13 David Moharter
☐ 14 Bill Fahey
☐ 15A Mike Bucci
☐ 15B Keith Smith
☐ 19 Bill Sample
☐ 20 Bob Babcock
☐ 21 Don Bright
☐ 22 Stan Thomas
☐ 24 Greg Mahlberg
☐ 27 Gary Gray
☐ 28 Danny Darwin
☐ 32 Pat Putnam
☐ 35 Rusty Torres
☐ 39 Jackie Brown
☐ 42 Rich Donnelly
☐ 45 Mike Bacsik
☐ 46 Bobby Cuellar
☐ 48 Jerry Ready
☐ 59A David Harper
☐ 59B Jim Hughes

1978 Waterloo Indians TCMA

This 26-card standard-size set of the 1978 Waterloo Indians, a Class A Midwest League affiliate of the Cleveland Indians, features white-bordered posed black-and-white player photos on its fronts. The player's name and Indians logo appear in the green section near the bottom. The league affiliation appears across an upper corner. The plain white horizontal back carries the words "The Minors - 1978 Waterloo Indians" at the top. The cards are unnumbered and checklisted below in alphabetical order.

	NRMT	VG-E	GOOD
COMPLETE SET (26)	15.00	6.75	1.85

☐ 1 Tom Anderson
☐ 2 Ken Bolek
☐ 3 Juan Bonilla
☐ 4 Tim Brill
☐ 5 John Buszka
☐ 6 Bob Conley
☐ 7 Sammy Davis
☐ 8 Jack Dubeau
☐ 9 Jerry Dybzinski
☐ 10 Robin Fuson
☐ 11 Tim Glass
☐ 12 Vic Homstedt
☐ 13 Don Hubbard
☐ 14 Angelo LoGrande
☐ 15 Carl Nicholson
☐ 16 Thomas Pulchinski
☐ 17 Al Rauch
☐ 18 Kevin Rhomberg
☐ 19 Ramon Romero
☐ 20 Ed Saavedra
☐ 21 Forest Smith
☐ 22 Sam Spence
☐ 23 John Teising
☐ 24 Lloyd Turner
☐ 25 Glenn Wendt
☐ 26 Troy Wilder

1978 Wausau Mets TCMA

This 25-card standard-size set of the 1978 Wausau Mets, a Class A Midwest League affiliate of the New York Mets, features white-bordered posed black-and-white player photos on its fronts. The player's name and Mets logo appear in the green section near the bottom. The league affiliation appears across an upper corner. The plain white horizontal back carries the words "The Minors - 1978 Wausau Mets" at the top. The cards are unnumbered and checklisted below in alphabetical order.

	NRMT	VG-E	GOOD
COMPLETE SET (25)	40.00	18.00	5.00

☐ 1 Curt Baker
☐ 2 Don Brazell
☐ 3 Stewart Bringhurst
☐ 4 Greg Brown
☐ 5 Bill Chamberlain
☐ 6 Al Coghen
☐ 7 Ed Cuervo
☐ 8 Bruce Ferguson
☐ 9 Jeff Franklin
☐ 10 Brent Gaff
☐ 11 John Hinkel
☐ 12 Chris Jones
☐ 13 Ken Jones
☐ 14 Chris Kirby
☐ 15 Randy Lamb
☐ 16 Steve Lowe
☐ 17 Mike Lowry
☐ 18 John McDonald Stadium
☐ 19 Dan Monzon
☐ 20 Jim Noonan
☐ 21 Darryl Paquette
☐ 22 Don Pearson
☐ 23 Junior Roman
☐ 24 Frank Sanchez
☐ 25 Keith Shermeyer

1978 Wisconsin Rapids Twins TCMA

This 18-card standard-size set of the 1978 Wisconsin Rapids Twins, a Class A Midwest League affiliate of the Minnesota Twins, features white-bordered posed black-and-white player photos on its fronts. The player's name and Twins logo appear in the green section near the bottom. The league affiliation appears across an upper corner. The plain white horizontal back carries the words "The Minors - 1978 Wisconsin Rapids Twins" at the top. The cards are unnumbered and checklisted below in alphabetical order.

	NRMT	VG-E	GOOD
COMPLETE SET (18)	15.00	6.75	1.85

☐ 1 Greg Allen
☐ 2 Paul Croft
☐ 3 George Dierburger
☐ 4 Gary Dobbs
☐ 5 Mark Funderburk
☐ 6 Michael Gustave
☐ 7 Lance Hallberg
☐ 8 Elmore Hill
☐ 9 Joe Keith Isaac
☐ 10 Abner Johnson
☐ 11 Elmer Lingerman
☐ 12 Ronnie Mears
☐ 13 John Minarcin
☐ 14 Dean Moranda
☐ 15 Eric Prevost
☐ 16 Clyde Reichard
☐ 17 Harold Rowe
☐ 18 Richard Stelmaszek

1979 Albuquerque Dukes TCMA

This 23-card standard-size set of the 1979 Albuquerque Dukes, a Class AAA Pacific Coast League affiliate of the Los Angeles Dodgers, features white-bordered posed color player photos on its fronts. The player's name and position appear in the lower yellow portion of the front. The horizontal back carries the player's name, position, team, and league at the top, followed by biography and statistics.

	NRMT	VG-E	GOOD
COMPLETE SET (23)	60.00	27.00	7.50

☐ 1 Pablo Peguero
☐ 2 Mike Tennent
☐ 3 Mike Williams
☐ 4 Bill Swiacki
☐ 5 Dave Stewart
☐ 6 Dave Patterson
☐ 7 Dennis Lewallyn
☐ 8 Kevin Keefe
☐ 9 Gerry Hannahs
☐ 10 Mike Scioscia
☐ 11 Mickey Hatcher
☐ 12 John O'Rear
☐ 13 Jack Perconte
☐ 14 Kelly Snider
☐ 15 Alex Taveras
☐ 16 Pedro Guerrero
☐ 17 Rich Magner
☐ 18 Bobby Mitchell
☐ 19 Rudy Law
☐ 20 Joe Beckwith
☐ 21 Claude Westmoreland
☐ 22 Bobby Castillo
☐ 23 Bobby Padilla

1979 Appleton Foxes TCMA

This 25-card standard-size set of the 1979 Appleton Foxes, a Class A Midwest League affiliate of the Chicago White Sox, features white-bordered posed black-and-white player photos on its fronts. The player's name and position appear in the lower orange portion of the front. The horizontal back carries the player's name, position, team, and league at the top, followed by biography and statistics.

	NRMT	VG-E	GOOD
COMPLETE SET (25)	50.00	22.00	6.25

☐ 1 Paul Soth
☐ 2 Dennis Keating
☐ 3 Vito Lucarelli
☐ 4 Ed Bahns
☐ 5 Dave White
☐ 6 Kevin Hickey
☐ 7 Clancy Woods
☐ 8 Jeff Vuksan
☐ 9 Lorenzo Gray
☐ 10 Mike Johnson
☐ 11 Dave Daniels
☐ 12 Ivan Mesa
☐ 13 Mike Sivik
☐ 14 Phil Bauer
☐ 15 Mark Teutsch
☐ 16 Luis Estrada
☐ 17 Jim Breazeale
☐ 18 Vince Bienek
☐ 19 Bob Umdenstock
☐ 20 Mike Mattland
☐ 21 Duane Shaffer
☐ 22 Mark Platel
☐ 23 Don Kraeger
☐ 24 Vic Walters
☐ 25 Paul Gbur

1979 Arkansas Travelers TCMA

This 23-card standard-size set of the 1979 Arkansas Travelers, a Class AA Texas League affiliate of the St. Louis Cardinals, features white-bordered posed color player photos on its fronts. The player's name and position appear in the lower yellow portion of the front. The horizontal back carries the player's name, position, team, and league at the top, followed by biography and statistics.

	NRMT	VG-E	GOOD
COMPLETE SET (23)	15.00	6.75	1.85

☐ 1 Arno Kirchenwitz
☐ 2 Len Strelitz
☐ 3 Raymond Williams
☐ 4 Terry Landrum
☐ 5 Jim Riggleman
☐ 6 John Littlefield
☐ 7 Thomas N. Thompson
☐ 8 Joseph Dotson
☐ 9 Elliott Waller
☐ 10 Joseph DeSa
☐ 11 Fred Tisdale
☐ 12 Jorge Aranzamendi
☐ 13 Neil Fiala
☐ 14 Mike McCormick
☐ 15 Fulvio Bertolotti
☐ 16 Dennis Delaney
☐ 17 Chris Davis
☐ 18 Randy Thomas
☐ 19A Tom Chamberlain
☐ 19B Hector Eduardo
☐ 20 Ray Searage
☐ 21 David Johnson
☐ 22 Gene Roof

1979 Asheville Tourists TCMA

This 28-card standard-size set of the 1979 Asheville Tourists, a Class A Western Carolinas League affiliate of the Texas Rangers, features white-bordered posed black-and-white player photos on its fronts. The player's name and position appear in the lower orange portion of the front. The horizontal back carries the player's name, position, team, and league at the top, followed by biography and statistics.

	NRMT	VG-E	GOOD
COMPLETE SET (28)	100.00	45.00	12.50

☐ 1 Luis Gonzalez
☐ 2 Tracy Cowger
☐ 3 Tom McGivney
☐ 4 Linvel Mosby
☐ 5 Wayne Terwilliger
☐ 6 Jim Farr
☐ 7 Dave Chapman
☐ 8 Andy Tam
☐ 9 Jeff Zitek
☐ 10 George Wright
☐ 11 Dave Miller
☐ 12 Wes Williams
☐ 13 Jim McWilliams
☐ 14 Al Ortiz
☐ 15 Steve Righetti
☐ 16 Bobby Tanzi
☐ 17 Amos Lewis
☐ 18 Arnold Wilhoit
☐ 19 Pat Nelson
☐ 20 Mike Childs
☐ 21 Mike Vickers
☐ 22 Jeff Scott
☐ 23 Dan Dixon
☐ 24 Chuck Kwolek
☐ 25 Dave Hibner
☐ 26 Mike Richardt
☐ 27 Stan Reese
☐ 28 Gene Nelson

1979 Buffalo Bisons TCMA

This 21-card standard-size set of the 1979 Buffalo Bisons, a Class AA Eastern League affiliate of the Pittsburgh Pirates, features white-bordered posed color player photos on its fronts. The player's name and position appear in the lower orange portion of the front. The horizontal back carries the player's name, position, team, and league at the top, followed by biography and statistics.

	NRMT	VG-E	GOOD
COMPLETE SET (21)	75.00	34.00	9.50

☐ 1 Dave Dravecky
☐ 2 Stu Cliburn
☐ 3 Rick Lancellotti
☐ 4 Joe Galante
☐ 5 Tony Pena
☐ 6 Jerry McDonald
☐ 7 Steve Demeter
☐ 8 Ernie Young
☐ 9 Bubba Evans
☐ 10 Marck Galinas
☐ 11 Juan Arias
☐ 12 Harry Dorish
and Bob Weismiller
☐ 13 Fred Breining
☐ 14 Chuck Valley
☐ 15 Tom McMillan
☐ 16 Luis Salazar
☐ 17 Jim Smith
☐ 18 Al Torres
☐ 19 Dick Walterhouse
☐ 20 Robert Long
☐ 21 Paul Djakonow

1979 Burlington Bees TCMA

This 25-card standard-size set of the 1979 Burlington Bees, a Class A Midwest League affiliate of the Milwaukee Brewers, features white-bordered posed black-and-white player photos on its fronts. The player's name and position appear in the lower orange portion of the front. The horizontal back carries the player's name, position, team, and league at the top, followed by biography and statistics.

	NRMT	VG-E	GOOD
COMPLETE SET (25)	25.00	11.00	3.10

☐ 1 Larry Edwards
☐ 2 Russell Ramirez
☐ 3 Pat Seegers
☐ 4 Jim Robinson
☐ 5 Sam Gierham
☐ 6 Rocky Hall
☐ 7 Willie Lozado
☐ 8 Nick Hernandez
☐ 9 Ron Buggs
☐ 10 Dan Gilmartin
☐ 11 Mark Lepson
☐ 12 Doug Jones
☐ 13 Steve Gibson
☐ 14 Bob Gibson
☐ 15 Johnny Evans
☐ 16 Roberto Diaz
☐ 17 Duane Espy
☐ 18 Vince Bailey
☐ 19 Randy Boyce
☐ 20 Greg De Hart
☐ 21 Stan Davis
☐ 22 Vince Pone
☐ 23 Jim Padula
☐ 24 Steve Norwood
☐ 25 Steve Manderfield

1979 Cedar Rapids Giants TCMA

This 32-card standard-size set of the 1979 Cedar Rapids Giants, a Class A Midwest League affiliate of the San Francisco Giants, features white-bordered posed black-and-white player photos on its fronts. The player's name and position appear in the lower orange portion of the front. The horizontal back carries the player's name, position, team, and league at the top, followed by biography and statistics.

	NRMT	VG-E	GOOD
COMPLETE SET (32)	100.00	45.00	12.50

☐ 1 Steve Duckhorn
☐ 2 Jesus Cruz
☐ 3 Mark Benson
☐ 4 Jorge Mundroig
☐ 5 John Rabb
☐ 6 Robbie Henderson
☐ 7 Jeff Stadler
☐ 8 Matt Sutherland
☐ 9 Francisco Fojas
☐ 10 Rick Doss
☐ 11 Bruce Oliver
☐ 12 Bill Bellomo
☐ 13 Glen Fisher
☐ 14 Bud Curran
☐ 15 Wayne Cato
☐ 16 Jeff Stember
☐ 17 Paul Plinski
☐ 18 Jose Chue
☐ 19 Rick Mean

☐ 20 George Torassa
☐ 21 Ned Raines
☐ 22 Lou Merietta
☐ 23 Craig Hedrick
☐ 24 Kelly Anderson
☐ 25 Harry Wing
☐ 26 Juan Oppenheimer
☐ 27 Ray Cosio
☐ 28 Rob Deer
☐ 29 Don Buchheister
☐ 30 Phil Sutton
☐ 31 Doug Linduyt
☐ 32 Bob Cummins

1979 Charleston Charlies TCMA

This 21-card standard-size set of the 1979 Charleston Charlies, a Class AAA International League affiliate of the Houston Astros, features white-bordered posed color player photos on its fronts. The player's name and position appear in the lower yellow portion of the front. The horizontal back carries the player's name, position, team, and league at the top, followed by biography and statistics.

	NRMT	VG-E	GOOD
COMPLETE SET (19)	15.00	6.75	1.85
COMPLETE SET (21)	30.00	13.50	3.70

☐ 1 Keith Drumright
☐ 2 Jim Beauchamp
☐ 3 Russ Rothermel
☐ 4 Reggie Baldwin
☐ 5 Gary Woods
☐ 6 Mike Fischlin
☐ 7 Mike Tyler
☐ 8 Dave Bergman
☐ 9 Ramon Perez
☐ 10A Mark Miggins
(Dave Smith photo)
☐ 10B Mark Miggins (Correct photo)
☐ 11A David Smith
(Mark Miggins photo)
☐ 11B Dave Smith (Correct photo) ..
☐ 12 Dave Augustine
☐ 13 Gordy Pladson
☐ 14 Luis Pujols
☐ 15 Larry Hardy
☐ 16 Rob Sperring
☐ 17 Wilbur Howard
☐ 18 Gary Wilson
☐ 19 Mike Mendoza

1979 Clinton Dodgers TCMA

This 28-card standard-size set of the 1979 Clinton Dodgers, a Class A Midwest League affiliate of the Los Angeles Dodgers, features white-bordered posed black-and-white player photos on its fronts. The player's name and position appear in the lower orange portion of the front. The horizontal back carries the player's name, position, team, and league at the top, followed by biography and statistics.

	NRMT	VG-E	GOOD
COMPLETE SET (28)	50.00	22.00	6.25

☐ 1 Mark Elliott
☐ 2 Clay Smith
☐ 3 Johnny Lee Robbins
☐ 4 Roberto Alexander
☐ 5 Matt Reeves
☐ 6 Alan Wiggins
☐ 7 Otis Bradley
☐ 8 Paul Popovich
☐ 9 Alejandro Pena
☐ 10 Steve Sax
☐ 11 Mitch Webster
☐ 12 Eric Schmidt
☐ 13 Chris Gandy
☐ 14 Kent Johnson
☐ 15 Marcos Rodriguez
☐ 16 Leonardo Hernandez
☐ 17 Dick McLaughlin
☐ 18 Dave Sax
☐ 19 Dave LaPoint
☐ 20 Rod Nelson
☐ 21 Bob Giesecke
☐ 22 Larry Wright
☐ 23 Steve Maples
☐ 24 Kevin Joyce
☐ 25 Bob White
☐ 26 Candido Maldonado
☐ 27 Frank Wilczewski
☐ 28 Larry Ferst

1979 Columbus Clippers TCMA

This 29-card standard-size set of the 1979 Columbus Clippers, a Class AAA International League affiliate of the New York Yankees, features white-bordered posed color player photos on its fronts. The player's name and position appear in the lower yellow portion of the front. The horizontal back carries the player's name, position, team, and league at the top, followed by biography and statistics.

	NRMT	VG-E	GOOD
COMPLETE SET (29)	15.00	6.75	1.85

☐ 1 Brad Gulden
☐ 2 Roy Staiger
☐ 3 Paul Semall
☐ 4 Damaso Garcia
☐ 5 Garry Smith
☐ 6 Stan Williams
☐ 7 Gene Michael
☐ 8 Jim Beattie
☐ 9 Gerry McNertney
☐ 10 Dennis Werth
☐ 11 Mark Letendre
☐ 12 Marvin Thompson
☐ 13 Tommy Cruz
☐ 14 Ron Davis
☐ 15 Bob Polinsky
☐ 16 Bruce Robinson
☐ 17 Greg Cochran
☐ 18 Rodger Holt
☐ 19 Dennis Sherrill
☐ 20 Steve Taylor
☐ 21 Rich Anderson
☐ 22 Nathan Chapman
☐ 23 Bob Kammeyer
☐ 24 Chris Welsh
☐ 25 Howard Cassidy
☐ 26 Paul Mirabella
☐ 27 Bobby Brown
☐ 28 Daryl Jones
☐ 29 Mickey Vernon

1979 Elmira Pioneer Red Sox TCMA

This 28-card standard-size set of the 1979 Elmira Pioneer Red Sox, a Class A New York-Penn League affiliate of the Boston Red Sox, features white-bordered posed black-and-white player photos on its fronts. The player's name and position appear in the lower orange portion of the front. The horizontal back carries the player's name, position, team, and league at the top, followed by biography and statistics.

	NRMT	VG-E	GOOD
COMPLETE SET (28)	75.00	34.00	9.50

☐ 1 Lloyd Bessard
☐ 2 Jay Fredlund
☐ 3 Ken Hagemann
☐ 4 Danny Huffstickler
☐ 5 Arturo Samaniego
☐ 6 Glenn Eddins Jr.
☐ 7 Joaquin Gutierrez
☐ 8 Tom McCarthy
☐ 9 Steve Fortune
☐ 10 Don Hayford
☐ 11 Eddie Lee
☐ 12 Russell Lee Pruitt
☐ 13 Scott Gering
☐ 14 Dave Holt
☐ 15 Steve Schaefer
☐ 16 Tony Cleary
☐ 17 Andy Serrano
☐ 18 Francisco Vasquez
☐ 19 Gus Malespin
☐ 20 Hal Natupsky
☐ 21 Dick Berardino
☐ 22 Ed Berroa
☐ 23 Bill Limoncelli
☐ 24 Bob Birrell
☐ 25 Wayne Tremblay
☐ 26 Tom Brunner
☐ 27 Tom DeSanto
☐ 28 Mark Saunders

1979 Hawaii Islanders Cramer

	NRMT	VG-E	GOOD
COMPLETE SET (24)	5.00	2.20	.60

☐ 1 Cover Card
☐ 3 Al Zarilla
☐ 5 Sam Perlozzo
☐ 8 Tucker Ashford
☐ 9 Steve Brye
☐ 10 Vic Bernal
☐ 11 Chuck Baker
☐ 12 Bob Mitchell
☐ 13 Juan Eichelberger
☐ 14 Craig Stimac
☐ 16 Tom Tellmann
☐ 17 Dennis Kinney
☐ 18 Rick Sweet
☐ 19 Al Fitzmorris
☐ 20 Lynn McKinney
☐ 21 Jim Beswick
☐ 22 Randy Fierbaugh
☐ 23 Fred Kuhaulua
☐ 24 Dick Phillips
☐ 25 Jim Wilhelm
☐ 26 Gary Lucas
☐ 27 Tony Castillo
☐ 28 Andy Dyes
☐ 29 Dave Wehrmeister

1979 Hawaii Islanders TCMA

This 24-card standard-size set of the 1979 Hawaii Islanders, a Class AAA Pacific Coast affiliate of the San Diego Padres, features white-bordered posed color player photos on its fronts. The player's name and position appear in the lower yellow portion of the front. The horizontal back carries the player's name, position, team, and league at the top, followed by biography and statistics.

	NRMT	VG-E	GOOD
COMPLETE SET (24)	10.00	4.50	1.25

☐ 1 Bob Mitchell
☐ 2 Lynn McKinney
☐ 3 Rick Sweet
☐ 4 Craig Stimac
☐ 5 Andy Dyes
☐ 6 Dick Phillips
☐ 7 Jim Wilhelm
☐ 8 Vic Bernal
☐ 9 Gary Lucas
☐ 10 Jim Beswick
☐ 11 Sam Perlozzo
☐ 12 Steve Brye
☐ 13 Don Reynolds
☐ 14 Steve Smith
☐ 15 Al Zarilla
☐ 16 Chuck Baker
☐ 17 Alan Fitzmorris
☐ 18 Dennis Kinney
☐ 19 Mike Dupree
☐ 20 Fred Kahaulua
☐ 21 Juan Eichelberger
☐ 22 Dennis Blair
☐ 23 Tom Tellmann
☐ 24 Tony Castillo

1979 Holyoke Millers TCMA

This 30-card standard-size set of the 1979 Holyoke Millers, a Class AA Eastern League affiliate of the Milwaukee Brewers, features white-bordered posed color player photos on its fronts. The player's name and position appear in the lower yellow portion of the front. The horizontal back carries the player's name, position, team, and league at the top, followed by biography and statistics.

	NRMT	VG-E	GOOD
COMPLETE SET (30)	10.00	4.50	1.25

☐ 1 Rene Quinones
☐ 2 Terry Bevington
☐ 3 Bill Foley
☐ 4 Ed Carroll
☐ 5 Kevin Bass
☐ 6 Bobby Smith
☐ 7 Mark Schuster
☐ 8 George Farson
☐ 9 Rick Olsen
☐ 10 Tom Soto
☐ 11 Ron Driver
☐ 12 Tom Cook
☐ 13 Gersan Jarquin
☐ 14 Rick Duran
☐ 15 Don Whiting
☐ 16 Brian Thorson
☐ 17 Mike Henderson
☐ 18 Butch Riggar
☐ 19 Steve Splitt
☐ 20 Larry Rush
☐ 21 Steve Reed
☐ 22 Darryl Bailey
☐ 23 Weldon Swift
☐ 24 Rocky Hall
☐ 25 Lance Rautzhan
☐ 26 Barry Cort
☐ 27 Duke Duncan
☐ 28 Jeff Yurak
☐ 29 Sam Hinds
☐ 30 Tom Kayser

1979 Indianapolis Indians Team Issue

	NRMT	VG-E	GOOD
COMPLETE SET (32)	25.00	11.00	3.10

☐ 1 Team Picture
☐ 2 Roy Majtyka MG
☐ 3 Ron Oester
☐ 4 Dave Moore
☐ 5 Harry Spilman
☐ 6 The Outfielders
☐ 7 Charlie Leibrandt
☐ 8 Tommy Mutz
☐ 9 Lary Rothschild
☐ 10 Eddie Milner
☐ 11 The Infielders
☐ 12 Doug Corbett
☐ 13 Randy Davidson
☐ 14 Bruce Berenyi
☐ 15 Don Lyle
☐ 16 George Cappuzzello
☐ 17 The Catchers
☐ 18 Mike Grace
☐ 19 Geoff Combe
☐ 20 Steve Bowling
☐ 21 Manny Sarmiento
☐ 22 Don Werner
☐ 23 The Relievers
☐ 24 Jay Howell
☐ 25 John Valle
☐ 26 Dan Dumoulin
☐ 27 Mickey Duval
☐ 28 Mario Soto
☐ 29 The Starters
☐ 30 Ron McClain TR
☐ 31 Bush Stadium
☐ 32 Checklist

1979 Iowa Oaks Police

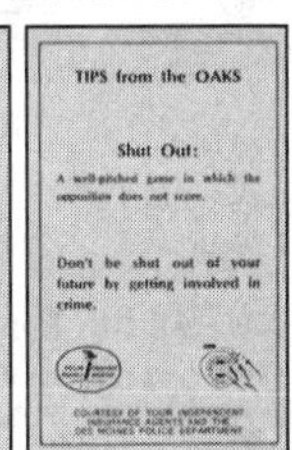

Black and White.

	NRMT	VG-E	GOOD
COMPLETE SET (14)	200.00	90.00	25.00

☐ 1 Tony LaRussa MG
☐ 2 Lloyd Allen
☐ 3 Harold Baines
☐ 4 Kevin Bell
☐ 5 Harry Chappas
☐ 6 Mike Colbern
☐ 7 Fred Frazier
☐ 8 Guy Hoffman
☐ 9 Dewey Hoyt
☐ 10 Art Kusnyer
☐ 11 Bob Molinaro
☐ 12 Chris Nyman
☐ 13 Dewey Robinson
☐ 14 John Sutton

1979 Jackson Mets TCMA

This 25-card standard-size set of the 1979 Jackson Mets, a Class AA Texas League affiliate of the New York Mets, features white-bordered posed color player photos on its fronts. The player's name and position appear in the lower yellow portion of the front. The horizontal back carries the player's name, position, team, and league at the top, followed by biography and statistics. Approximately 2,500 sets were produced.

	NRMT	VG-E	GOOD
COMPLETE SET (25)	20.00	9.00	2.50

☐ 1 Paco Perez
☐ 2 Wally Backman
☐ 3 Hubie Brooks
☐ 4 Wayne Sexton
☐ 5 Paul Wiener
☐ 6 Bob Wellman
☐ 7 Jody Davis
Sic, Jodie
☐ 8 Bob Grote
☐ 9 Sergio Beltre
☐ 10 Paul Cacciatore
☐ 11 Keith Bodie
☐ 12 Pete Hamner
☐ 13 Luis Lunar
☐ 14 Mike Howard
☐ 15 Dave Von Ohlen
☐ 16 Rick Anderson
☐ 17 Dan Smith
☐ 18 Rich Miller Jr.
☐ 19 Bobby Bryant
☐ 20 Russell Clark
☐ 21 Greg Harris
☐ 22A Stan Hough
☐ 22B Front Office Staff
☐ 23 Ronald Macdonald
☐ 24 Fred Martinez

1979 Knoxville Knox Sox TCMA

This 26-card standard-size set of the 1979 Knoxville Knox Sox, a Class AA Southern League affiliate of the Chicago White Sox, features white-bordered posed black-and-white player photos on its fronts. The player's name and position appear in the lower orange portion of the front. The horizontal back carries the player's name, position, team, and league at the top, followed by biography and statistics.

	NRMT	VG-E	GOOD
COMPLETE SET (26)	60.00	27.00	7.50

☐ 1 Mark Naihing
☐ 2 Phil Trucks
☐ 3 Luis Guzman

☐ 4 Gordy Lund
☐ 5 Richard Barnes
☐ 6 Britt Burns
☐ 7 Leo Sutherland
☐ 8 Richard Dotson
☐ 9 Don Seidholz
☐ 10 John Flannery
☐ 11 Mitch Lukevics
☐ 12 Ron Kittle
☐ 13 Willie Gutierrez
☐ 14 Larry Monroe
☐ 15 John Hanley
☐ 16 Joel Perez
☐ 17 Jackie Smith
☐ 18 Bruce Dal Canton
☐ 19 Ray Murillo
☐ 20 Andy Pasillas
☐ 21 Ted Barnicle
☐ 22 H.A. Hill
☐ 23 Ray Torres
☐ 24 Rod Allen
☐ 25 Tom Spencer
☐ 26 Willie Thompson

1979 Lodi Dodgers TCMA

This 21-card standard-size set of the 1979 Lodi Dodgers, a Class A California League affiliate of the Los Angeles Dodgers, features white-bordered posed black-and-white player photos on its fronts. The player's name and position appear in the lower orange portion of the front. The horizontal back carries the player's name, position, team, and league at the top, followed by biography and statistics.

	NRMT	VG-E	GOOD
COMPLETE SET (21)	125.00	55.00	15.50

☐ 1 Rod Kemp
☐ 2 Augie Ruiz
☐ 3 Paul Bain
☐ 4 Alfredo Mejia
☐ 5 Skip Mann
☐ 6 Mike Marshall
☐ 7 Rocky Cordova
☐ 8 Steve Perry
☐ 9 Jesse Baez
☐ 10 Jim Nobles
☐ 11 Larry Powers
☐ 12 Johnny Walker
☐ 13 Bill Swoope
☐ 14 Stan Wasiak
☐ 15 Miguel Franjul
☐ 16 Jerry Bass
☐ 17 Bob Foster
☐ 18 Chris Malden
☐ 19 Brian Hayes
☐ 20 Hank Jones
☐ 21 Evon Martinson

1979 Memphis Chicks TCMA

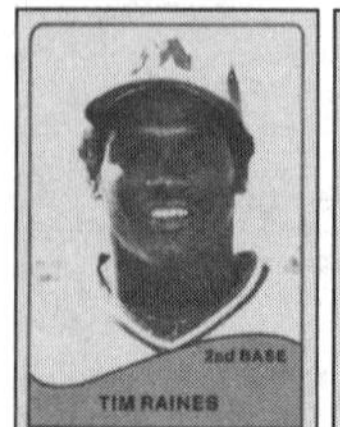

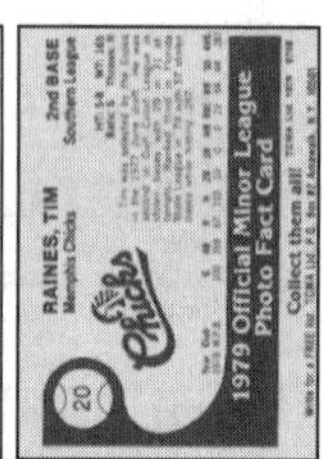

This 24-card standard-size set of the 1979 Memphis Chicks, a Class AA Southern League affiliate of the Montreal Expos, features white-bordered posed black-and-white player photos on its fronts. The player's name and position appear within an orange area near the bottom. The white and black horizontal back carries the player's name and position at the top, followed by biography, career highlights, and statistics. This issue includes the only minor league card appearance of Tim Raines. Approximately 1,500 sets were produced.

	NRMT	VG-E	GOOD
COMPLETE SET (24)	300.00	135.00	38.00

☐ 1 Steve Lovins
☐ 2 Steve Michael
☐ 3 Bill Armstrong TR
☐ 4 Julio Perez
☐ 5 Bryn Smith
☐ 6 Larry Goldetsky
☐ 7 Doug Simunic
☐ 8 Charlie Lea
☐ 9 Dave Hostetler
☐ 10 Anthony Johnson
☐ 11 Randy Schafer
☐ 12 Mike Finlayson
☐ 13 Rick Williams
☐ 14 Rick Engle
☐ 15 Bob Tenenini
☐ 16 Ray Crowley
☐ 17 John Scoras
☐ 18 Jeff Gingrich
☐ 19 Dennis Sherow
☐ 20 Tim Raines
☐ 21 Billy Gardner MG
☐ 22 Pat Rooney
☐ 23 Warren Hemm
☐ 24 Godfrey Evans

1979 Nashville Sounds Team Issue

	NRMT	VG-E	GOOD
COMPLETE SET (25)	30.00	13.50	3.70

☐ 1 Team Photo
☐ 2 Soundettes
☐ 3 Mike Armstrong
☐ 4 Skeeter Barnes
☐ 5 Scott Brown
☐ 6 Geoff W. Combe
☐ 7 Bill Dawley
☐ 8 Rick Duncan
☐ 9 Raul Ferreyra
☐ 10 Bob Hamilton
☐ 11 Paul Householder
☐ 12 Greg Hughes
☐ 13 Bill Kelly
☐ 14 Bob Mayer
☐ 15 Gene Menees
☐ 16 Mark Miller
☐ 17 Eddie Milner
☐ 18 Farrell Owens
☐ 19 Joe Price
☐ 20 R. Santo Domingo
☐ 21 George R. Scherger
☐ 22 Larry Schmittou
☐ 23 Tom Sohns
☐ 24 Dave Van Gorder
☐ 25 Duane Walker

1979 Newark Co-Pilots TCMA

This 24-card standard-size set of the 1979 Newark Co-Pilots, a Class A New York-Penn League Independent, features white-bordered posed black-and-white player photos on its fronts. The player's name and position appear in the lower orange portion of the front. The horizontal back carries the player's name, position, team, and league at the top, followed by biography and statistics.

	NRMT	VG-E	GOOD
COMPLETE SET (24)	25.00	11.00	3.10

☐ 1 Tom Dann
☐ 2 Steve Nicastro
☐ 3 Joe Rigoli
☐ 4 Bob Bill
☐ 5 Mike Overton
☐ 6 Mike Fichman
☐ 7 Steve Dembowski
☐ 8 Mike Oleksak
☐ 9 Don Clatterbuck
☐ 10 Michael Lacasse
☐ 11 Kevin MacDonald
☐ 12 Joe McCann
☐ 13 Harry White
☐ 14 Mark Grier
☐ 15 Carl Adams
☐ 16 Bob Cross
☐ 17 Billy Clay
☐ 18 Keith Gainer
☐ 19 Richard Block
☐ 20 Kevin Rose
☐ 21 Mitch Wright
☐ 22 Len Spicer
☐ 23 Lance Viola
☐ 24 Andy Pascarella

1979 Ogden A's TCMA

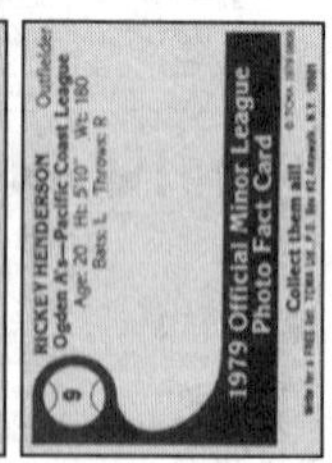

This 26-card standard-size set of the 1979 Ogden A's, a Class AAA Pacific Coast League affiliate of the Oakland Athletics, features white-bordered posed color player photos on its fronts. The player's name and position appear in the lower yellow portion of the front. The horizontal back carries the player's name, position, team, and league at the top, followed by biography and statistics. Approximately 3,000 sets were produced.

	NRMT	VG-E	GOOD
COMPLETE SET (26)	200.00	90.00	25.00

☐ 1 Terry Enyart
☐ 2 Tim Hosley
☐ 3 Mike Morgan
☐ 4 Mike Rodriguez
☐ 5 Craig Mitchell
☐ 6 Jose Pagan
☐ 7 Mack Harrison
☐ 8 Dennis Haines
☐ 9 Rickey Henderson
☐ 10 Brian Abraham
☐ 11 Richard Lysander
☐ 12 Jeff Cox
☐ 13 Brian Kingman
☐ 14 Royle Stillman
☐ 15 Danny Goodwin
☐ 16 Ray Cosey
☐ 17 Mark Souza
☐ 18 Mark Budaska
☐ 19 Frank Kolarek
☐ 20 Pat Dempsey
☐ 21 Craig Mitchell
☐ 22 Allen Wirth
☐ 23 Jeff Jones
☐ 24 Mike Patterson
☐ 25 Bob Grandas
☐ 26 Keith Lieppman

1979 Phoenix Giants Valley National Bank

	NRMT	VG-E	GOOD
COMPLETE SET (24)	5.00	2.20	.60

☐ 1 Doug Schaefer
☐ 2 Kyle Hypes
☐ 3 Mike Rowland
☐ 4 Jeff Little
☐ 5 Rocky Bridges
☐ 6 Phil Nastu
☐ 7 Bill Bordley
☐ 8 Ed Plank
☐ 9 Joe Strain
☐ 10 Greg Johnston
☐ 11 Don Carrithers
☐ 12 Tom Heintzelman
☐ 13 Randy Hammon
☐ 14 Rick Bradley
☐ 15 Terry Cornutt
☐ 16 Chris Bourjos
☐ 17 Casey Parsons
☐ 18 Rich Murray
☐ 19 Dennis Littlejohn
☐ 20 Mark Kuecker
☐ 21 Rick Sanderlin
☐ 22 Guy Sularz
☐ 23 Mike Rex
☐ 24 Harry Jordan
Tommy Gonzales
Ethan Blackaby

1979 Portland Beavers TCMA

This 24-card standard-size set of the 1979 Portland Beavers, a Class AAA Pacific Coast League affiliate of the Pittsburgh Pirates, features white-bordered posed color player photos on its fronts. The player's name and position appear in the lower yellow portion of the front. The horizontal back carries the player's name, position, team, and league at the top, followed by biography and statistics.

	NRMT	VG-E	GOOD
COMPLETE SET (24)	15.00	6.75	1.85

☐ 1 Al Holland
☐ 2 Ossie Olivares
☐ 3 Greg Field
☐ 4 Ben Wiltbank
☐ 5 Vance Law
☐ 6 Tom Sandt
☐ 7 Dorian Boyland
☐ 8 Ron Mitchell
☐ 9 John Lipon
☐ 10 Gene Cotes
☐ 11 Joe Coleman
☐ 12 Gene Pentz
☐ 13 Gary Hargis
☐ 14 Alberto Lois
☐ 15 Mike Garman
☐ 16 Manny Lantigua
☐ 17 Dan Warthen
☐ 18 Craig Cacek
☐ 19 Larry Littleton
☐ 20 Pascual Perez
☐ 21 Harry Saferight
☐ 22 Rod Scurry
☐ 23 Rick Jones
☐ 24 Rod Gilbreath

1979 Quad City Cubs TCMA

This 27-card standard-size set of the 1979 Quad City Cubs, a Class A Midwest League affiliate of the Chicago Cubs, features white-bordered posed black-and-white player photos on its fronts. The player's name and position appear in the lower orange portion of the front. The horizontal back carries the player's name, position, team, and league at the top, followed by biography and statistics.

	NRMT	VG-E	GOOD
COMPLETE SET (27)	50.00	22.00	6.25

☐ 1 Mike Wright
☐ 2 Ed Mohr
☐ 3 Ed Moore
☐ 4 Roger Crow
☐ 5 Bill Morgan
☐ 6 Wayne Rohlfing
☐ 7 Ted May
☐ 8 Joe McClain
☐ 9 Rich McClure
☐ 10 J.W. Mitchell
☐ 11 Joe Hicks
☐ 12 Mark Gilbert
☐ 13 Joey Cole
☐ 14 Randy Clark
☐ 15 Hal Kizer
☐ 16 Craig Kornfeld
☐ 17 Bob Maddon
☐ 18 Gordon Hodgson
☐ 19 John Bargfeldt
☐ 20 Andy Walker
☐ 21 Freddy Forgeur
☐ 22 Jim Napier
☐ 23 Tom Spino
☐ 24 Mike Shepston
☐ 25 Steve Viskas
☐ 26 Bob Oliver
☐ 27 Norm Churchill

1979 Richmond Braves TCMA

This 25-card standard-size set of the 1979 Richmond Braves, a Class AAA International League affiliate of the Atlanta Braves, features white-bordered posed color player photos on its fronts. The player's name and position appear in the lower yellow portion of the front. The horizontal back carries the player's name, position, team, and league at the top, followed by biography and statistics.

	NRMT	VG-E	GOOD
COMPLETE SET (25)	10.00	4.50	1.25

☐ 1 Joey McLaughlin
☐ 2 Mike Reynolds
☐ 3 John Sain
☐ 4 Larry Whisenton
☐ 5 Larry Owen
☐ 6 Jerry Maddox
☐ 7 Jon Richardson
☐ 8 Seymour B-ball
and Chief Powa-Hitta
☐ 9 Radio Voices
☐ 10 Front Office
☐ 11 Jamie Easterly
☐ 12 Roger Alexander
☐ 13 Chico Ruiz
☐ 14 Terry Harper
☐ 15 Tom Burgess
☐ 16 Duane Thesis
☐ 17 Larry Bradford
☐ 18 Dan Morogiello
☐ 19 Jerry Keller
☐ 20 Pat Rockett
☐ 21 Rick Camp
☐ 22 Tommy Boggs
☐ 23 Jim Arline
☐ 24 Ed Miller
☐ 25 Tony Brizzolara

1979 Rochester Red Wings TCMA

This 20-card standard-size set of the 1979 Rochester Red Wings, a Class AAA International League affiliate of the Baltimore Orioles, features white-bordered posed color player photos on its fronts. The player's name and position appear in the lower yellow portion of the front. The horizontal back carries the player's name, position, team, and league at the top, followed by biography and statistics.

	NRMT	VG-E	GOOD
COMPLETE SET (20)	10.00	4.50	1.25

☐ 1 Jeff Youngbauer
☐ 2 Joe Kerrigan
☐ 3 Kevin Kennedy
☐ 4 Blake Doyle
☐ 5 Willie Royster
☐ 6 Art James
☐ 7 Tony Franklin
☐ 8 Carlos Lopez
☐ 9 Mike Eden
☐ 10 Howard Edwards
☐ 11 Tom Bianco
☐ 12 Gerry Pirtle
☐ 13 Jim Smith
☐ 14 Ron Diggle
☐ 15 Mark Corey
☐ 16 Jeff Rineer
☐ 17 Jose Bastian
☐ 18 Tom Chism
☐ 19 Tony Chevez
☐ 20 Dave Ford

1979 Salt Lake City Gulls TCMA

This 23-card standard-size set of the 1979 Salt Lake City Gulls, a Class AAA Pacific Coast League affiliate of the California Angels, features white-bordered posed color player photos on its fronts. The player's name and position appear in the lower yellow portion of the front. The horizontal back carries the player's name, position, team, and league at the top, followed by biography and statistics.

	NRMT	VG-E	GOOD
COMPLETE SET (23)	10.00	4.50	1.25

☐ 9 Mike Overy
☐ 10 Bob Ferris
☐ 11 Rance Mulliniks
☐ 12 Bob Clark
☐ 13 Bill Ewing
☐ 14 Jim Dorsey
☐ 15 Joel Crisler
☐ 16A John Harris
☐ 16B Gil Kubski
☐ 17A Dave Schuler
☐ 17B Darrell Darrow
☐ 18A Carlos Perez
☐ 18B Rick Foley
☐ 19A Chuck Porter
☐ 19B Dan Whitmer
☐ 20A Jay Peters
☐ 20B Floyd Rayford
☐ 21A Bob Slater
☐ 21B Bobby Ramos
☐ 22A Pepe Manguel
☐ 22B Jimmy Williams
☐ 23A Leonard Garcia
☐ 23B Daniel Boone

1979 Savannah Braves TCMA

This 26-card standard-size set of the 1979 Savannah Braves, a Class AA Southern League affiliate of the Atlanta Braves, features white-bordered posed color player photos on its fronts. The player's name and position appear in the lower yellow portion of the front. The horizontal back carries the player's name, position, team, and league at the top, followed by biography and statistics.

	NRMT	VG-E	GOOD
COMPLETE SET (26)	20.00	9.00	2.50

☐ 1 Dom Chiti
☐ 2 Gary Cooper
☐ 3 Rufino Linares
(no number)
☐ 4 Bill Haslerig
☐ 5 Brian Snitker
☐ 6 Tim Brill
☐ 7 Tim Graven
☐ 8 Sonny Jackson
☐ 9 Mike Shields
☐ 10 Greg Johnson
☐ 11 Clay Elliott
☐ 12 Jose Alvarez
☐ 13 Kris Yoder
☐ 14 Steve Bedrosian
☐ 15 Joe Cowley
☐ 16 Richard Wieters
Eddie Haas back
☐ 17 Leo Mazzone
☐ 18 Eddie Haas
Richard Wieters back
☐ 19 Terry Leach
☐ 20 Tim Cole
☐ 21 Louis Pratt
☐ 22 Bob Porter
☐ 23 Rafael Ramirez
☐ 24 Kenny Smith
☐ 25 Mike Miller
☐ 26 Jim Wessinger

1979 Spokane Indians TCMA

This 25-card standard-size set of the 1979 Spokane Indians, a Class AAA Pacific Coast League affiliate of the Seattle Mariners, features white-bordered posed color player photos on its fronts. The player's name and position appear in the lower yellow portion of the front. The horizontal back carries the player's name, position, team, and league at the top, followed by biography and statistics.

	NRMT	VG-E	GOOD
COMPLETE SET (25)	10.00	4.50	1.25

☐ 1 Ed Crosby
☐ 2 Royle Stillman
☐ 3 Mike Porter
☐ 4 Danny Walton
☐ 5 Rod Craig
☐ 6 Charlie Beamon
☐ 7 Jack L. Pierce
☐ 8 Ken Pape
☐ 9 Reggie Walton
☐ 10 Bill Plummer
☐ 11 Gary Lance
☐ 12 George Decker
☐ 13 Jim Lewis
☐ 14 Mike Davey
☐ 15 Jack Heidemann
☐ 16 Rene Lachemann
☐ 17 Gary Wheelock
☐ 18 Rob Pietroburgo
☐ 19 Rob Dressler
☐ 20 Karl Anderson
☐ 21 Greg Biercevicz
☐ 22 Steve Burke
☐ 23 Terry Bulling
☐ 24 Moncho Berhardt
☐ 25 Manny Estrada

1979 Syracuse Chiefs TCMA

This 20-card standard-size set of the 1979 Syracuse Chiefs, a Class AAA International League affiliate of the Toronto Blue Jays, features white-bordered posed color player photos on its fronts. The player's name and position appear in the lower yellow portion of the front. The horizontal back carries the player's name, position, team, and league at the top, followed by biography and statistics.

	NRMT	VG-E	GOOD
COMPLETE SET (20)	15.00	6.75	1.85

☐ 1 Greg Wells
☐ 2 Vern Benson MG
☐ 3 Ernie Whitt
☐ 4 Willie Upshaw
☐ 5 Mark Wiley
☐ 6 Domingo Ramos
☐ 7 Joe Cannon
☐ 8 Don Pisker
☐ 9 Butch Edge
☐ 10 Mike Sember
☐ 11 Dave Baker
☐ 12 Garth Iorg
☐ 13 Jackson Todd
☐ 14 Chuck Fore
☐ 15 Doug Ault
☐ 16 Davis May
☐ 17 Steve Grilli
☐ 18 Luis Rosado
☐ 19 Ken Reynolds
☐ 20 Steve Luebber

1979 Syracuse Chiefs Team Issue

	NRMT	VG-E	GOOD
COMPLETE SET (24)	90.00	40.00	11.00

☐ 1 Domingo Ramos
☐ 2 Papo Rosado
☐ 3 Chuck Scrivener
☐ 4 Dan Ainge
☐ 5 Dave Baker
☐ 6 Pat Kelly
☐ 7 Don Pisker
☐ 8 Vern Benson MG
☐ 9 Garth Iorg
☐ 10 Mike Sember
☐ 12 Ernie Whitt
☐ 14 Butch Alberts
☐ 15 Ken Reynolds
☐ 16 Jackson Todd
☐ 17 Doug Ault
☐ 19 Butch Edge
☐ 21 Steve Grilli
☐ 22 Davis May
☐ 23 Joe Cannon
☐ 25 Jerry Garvin
☐ 26 Willie Upshaw
☐ 27 Mark Wiley
☐ 29 Tom Buskey
☐ 31 Steve Luebber

1979 Tacoma Tugs TCMA

This 26-card standard-size set of the 1979 Tacoma Tugs, a Class AAA Pacific Coast League affiliate of the Cleveland Indians, features white-bordered posed color player photos on its fronts. The player's name and position appear in the lower yellow portion of the front. The horizontal back carries the player's name, position, team, and league at the top, followed by biography and statistics.

	NRMT	VG-E	GOOD
COMPLETE SET (26)	15.00	6.75	1.85

☐ 1 Ron Hassey
☐ 2 Tom Brown
☐ 3 Rick Borchers
☐ 4 Larry Andersen
☐ 5 Tom Brennan
☐ 6 Juan Berenguer
☐ 7 Bobby Cuellar
☐ 8 Todd Heimer
☐ 9 Gary Melson
☐ 10 Hugh Yancy
☐ 11 Sal Rende
☐ 12 Dave Oliver
☐ 13 Jerry Dybzinski
☐ 14 Mike Champion
☐ 15 Bob Allietta
☐ 16 Sandy Wihtol
☐ 17 Nate Puryear
☐ 18 Carl Nicholson
☐ 19 Del Alston
☐ 20 Rich Chiles
☐ 21 Sheldon Mallory
☐ 22 Tim Norrid
☐ 23 Rob Ellis
☐ 24 Gene Dusan
☐ 25 Fred Gladding
☐ 26 Wayne Cage

1979 Tidewater Tides TCMA

This 25-card standard-size set of the 1979 Tidewater Tides, a Class AAA International League affiliate of the New York Mets, features white-bordered posed color player photos on its fronts. The player's name and position appear in the lower yellow portion of the front. The horizontal back carries the player's name, position, team, and league at the top, followed by biography and statistics. Approximately 4,000 sets were produced.

	NRMT	VG-E	GOOD
COMPLETE SET (25)	70.00	32.00	8.75

☐ 1 Roy Lee Jackson
☐ 2 John Pacella
☐ 3 Jose Moreno
☐ 4 Frank Verdi
☐ 5 Jeff Reardon
☐ 6 Dwight Bernard
☐ 7 Mookie Wilson
☐ 8 Butch Benton
☐ 9 Ron Washington
☐ 10 Jim Buckner
☐ 11 Dan Norman
☐ 12 Mario Ramirez
☐ 13 Marshall Brant
☐ 14 Ed Cipot
☐ 15 Mike Scott
☐ 16 Stan Hough
☐ 17 Scott Holman
☐ 18 Kelvin Chapman
☐ 19 Mike Van De Casteele
☐ 20 Greg Pavlick
☐ 21 Bobby Bryant
☐ 22 Russell Clark
☐ 23 Jesse Orosco
☐ 24 Bob Gorinski
☐ 25 Earl Stephenson

1979 Toledo Mud Hens TCMA

This 22-card standard-size set of the 1979 Toledo Mud Hens, a Class AAA International League affiliate of the Minnesota Twins, features white-bordered posed color player photos on its fronts. The player's name and position appear in the lower yellow portion of the front. The horizontal back carries the player's name, position, team, and league at the top, followed by biography and statistics.

	NRMT	VG-E	GOOD
COMPLETE SET (22)	10.00	4.50	1.25

☐ 1 Gary Ward
☐ 2 Paul Thormodsgard
☐ 3 Cal Ermer
☐ 4 Archie Amerson
☐ 5 Kevin Stanfield
☐ 6 Dan Graham
☐ 7 Dave Engle
☐ 8 Sal Butera
☐ 9 Terry Felton
☐ 10 Terry Sheehan
☐ 11 Wayne Caughey
☐ 12 John Verhoeven
☐ 13 Buck Chamberlin
☐ 14 Jim Buckner
☐ 15 Tom Sain
☐ 16 Greg Thayer
☐ 17 Dave Coleman
☐ 18 Darrell Jackson
☐ 19 Frank Viloria
☐ 20 Jesus Vega
☐ 21 Dennis Mantick
☐ 22 Ray Smith

1979 Tucson Toros TCMA

This 24-card standard-size set of the 1979 Tucson Toros, a Class AAA Pacific Coast League affiliate of the Texas Rangers, features white-bordered posed color player photos on its fronts. The player's name and position appear in the lower yellow portion of the front. The horizontal back carries the player's name, position, team, and league at the top, followed by biography and statistics.

	NRMT	VG-E	GOOD
COMPLETE SET (24)	10.00	4.50	1.25

☐ 1 Gary Gray
☐ 2 Myrl Smith
☐ 3 Mike Bruhardt
☐ 4 Brian Allard
☐ 5 Mike Bucci
☐ 6 Stan Jakubowski
☐ 7 Ron Gooch
☐ 8 Rich Donnelly
☐ 9 Steve Bianchi
☐ 10 Marty Scott
☐ 11 Don Kainer
☐ 12 Wayne Pinkerton
☐ 13 Fla Strawn
☐ 14 Tom Grieve
☐ 15 Greg Mahlberg
☐ 16 Dave Moharter
☐ 17 Mike Hart
☐ 18 Odie Davis
☐ 19 Deathel Chauncey
☐ 20 Ed Lynch
☐ 21 Bob Myrick
☐ 22 Mel Barrow
☐ 23 Larry McCall
☐ 24 Jim Umbarger

1979 Tulsa Drillers TCMA

This 24-card standard-size set of the 1979 Tulsa Drillers, a Class AA Texas League affiliate of the Texas Rangers, features white-bordered posed color player photos on its fronts. The player's name and position appear in the lower yellow portion of the front. The horizontal back carries the player's name, position, team, and league at the top, followed by biography and statistics.

	NRMT	VG-E	GOOD
COMPLETE SET (24)	18.00	8.00	2.20

☐ 1 Wayne Tolleson
☐ 2 Joe Russell
☐ 3 Len Whitehouse
☐ 4 Jim Capowski
☐ 5 Fla Strawn
☐ 6 Steve Finch
☐ 7 Dan Dixon
☐ 8 Ray Rainbolt
☐ 9 Steve Nielsen
☐ 10 Mark Mercer
☐ 11 Ron Gooch
☐ 12 Jack Ramirez
☐ 13 Jim Schaffer
☐ 14 Rick Lisi
☐ 15 Terry Bogener
☐ 16 John Butcher
☐ 17 Jim Barbe
☐ 18 Ron Carney
☐ 19 Dave Crutcher
☐ 20 Nick Capra
☐ 21 Mel Barrow
☐ 22 Hal Kelly
☐ 23 Bill Rollings
☐ 24 Roy Clark

1979 Vancouver Canadians TCMA

This 25-card standard-size set of the 1979 Vancouver Canadians, a Class AAA Pacific Coast League affiliate of the Milwaukee Brewers, features white-bordered posed color player photos on its fronts. The player's name and position appear in the lower yellow portion of the front. The horizontal back carries the player's name, position, team, and league at the top, followed by biography and statistics.

	NRMT	VG-E	GOOD
COMPLETE SET (25)	10.00	4.50	1.25

☐ 1 Skip James
☐ 2 Vic Harris
☐ 3 Ron Jacobs
☐ 4 Marshall Edwards
☐ 5 Craig Ryan
☐ 6 Tim Nordbrook
☐ 7 Mark Bomback
☐ 8 Andy Replogle
☐ 9 Danny Boitano
☐ 10 Rickey Keeton
☐ 11 Gus Quiros
☐ 12 Juan Lopez
☐ 13 Ned Yost
☐ 14 Clay Carroll
☐ 15 Kuni Ogawa
☐ 16 Randy Stein
☐ 17 Ed Romero
☐ 18 Jeff Yurak
☐ 19 Sam Hinds
☐ 20 John Felske
☐ 21 Billy Severns
☐ 22A Kent Biggerstaff
☐ 22B Lenn Sakata
☐ 23A Creighton Tevlin
☐ 23B Willie Mueller

1979 Waterbury A's TCMA

This 25-card standard-size set of the 1979 Waterbury A's, a Class AA Eastern League affiliate of the Oakland Athletics, features white-bordered posed black-and-white player photos on its fronts. The player's name and position appear in the lower orange portion of the front. The horizontal back carries the player's name, position, team, and league at the top, followed by biography and statistics.

	NRMT	VG-E	GOOD
COMPLETE SET (25)	80.00	36.00	10.00

☐ 1 Dennis De Barr
☐ 2 Rick Tronerud
☐ 3 Walt Horn
☐ 4 Bart Braun
☐ 5 Dennis Wysznaski
☐ 6 Keith Atherton
☐ 7 Leroy Robbins
☐ 8 Frank Kolarek
☐ 9 Ed Nottle

- ☐ 10 Al Armstead
- ☐ 11 Shotty Babitt
- ☐ 12 Randy Green
- ☐ 13 Rob Klebba
- ☐ 14 Mike Patterson
- ☐ 15 Mike Davis
- ☐ 16 Al Minker
- ☐ 17 Larry Groover
- ☐ 18 Paul Mize
- ☐ 19 Bruce Fournier
- ☐ 20 Bob Grandas
- ☐ 21 Ron McNeely
- ☐ 22 Tim Conroy
- ☐ 23 Scott Meyer
- ☐ 24 Dave Beard
- ☐ 25 Robert Moore

1979 Waterloo Indians TCMA

This 36-card standard-size set of the 1979 Waterloo Indians, a Class A Midwest League affiliate of the Cleveland Indians, features white-bordered posed black-and-white player photos on its fronts. The player's name and position appear in the lower orange portion of the front. The horizontal back carries the player's name, position, team, and league at the top, followed by biography and statistics.

	NRMT	VG-E	GOOD
COMPLETE SET (36)	80.00	36.00	10.00

- ☐ 1A Lynn Garrett
- ☐ 1B Matt Bullinger
- ☐ 2A Tim Glass
- ☐ 2B Lou Ganci
- ☐ 3A Bill Hallstrom
- ☐ 3B Ron Linfonte
- ☐ 4A Jeff Klein
- ☐ 4B Keith Hendry
- ☐ 5 Troy Wilder
- ☐ 6 Jerry Stutzrien
- ☐ 7 Frank Regan
- ☐ 8 Gary Hinson
- ☐ 9 Steve McMurray
- ☐ 10 Sammy Davis
- ☐ 11 Rick Barnhart
- ☐ 12 John Asbell
- ☐ 13 Tom Anderson
- ☐ 14 Dane Anthony
- ☐ 15 Reid Cassidy
- ☐ 16 Scott Dwyer
- ☐ 17 Randy Rambis
- ☐ 18 Marcus Clark
- ☐ 19 Carmelo Castillo
- ☐ 20 Rick Colzie
- ☐ 21 Ed Saaverdra
- ☐ 22 Bob Diering
- ☐ 23 Mel Queen
- ☐ 24 Cal Emory
- ☐ 25 Pete Peltz
- ☐ 26 Tommy Martinez
- ☐ 27 Robbie Alvarez
- ☐ 28 John Walters
- ☐ 29 Dave Hudgins
- ☐ 30 Greg Johnson
- ☐ 31 Rod Hudson
- ☐ 32 Ray Richard

1979 Wausau Timbers TCMA

This 25-card standard-size set of the 1979 Wausau Timbers, a Class A Midwest League Independent, features white-bordered posed black-and-white player photos on its fronts. The player's name and position appear in the lower orange portion of the front. The horizontal back carries the player's name, position, team, and league at the top, followed by biography and statistics. Approximately 1,100 sets were produced.

	NRMT	VG-E	GOOD
COMPLETE SET (25)	25.00	11.00	3.10

- ☐ 1 Brent Gaff
- ☐ 2 Jerry Stutzriem
- ☐ 3 Todd Winterfeldt
- ☐ 4 Kerry Keenan
- ☐ 5 Dave Stockstill
- ☐ 6 Vic Mabee
- ☐ 7 Israel Gutierrez
- ☐ 8 Wally Goff
- ☐ 9 Joe Nemeth
- ☐ 10 Lloyd Turner
- ☐ 11 John Zisk
- ☐ 12 Bob Johnson
- ☐ 13 Rick Barnhart
- ☐ 14 Ramon Romero
- ☐ 15 Jack Littrell
- ☐ 16 Tom Robson
- ☐ 17 Donald Lowe
- ☐ 18 Dean Craig
- ☐ 19 Alex Christianson
- ☐ 20 Ted Davis
- ☐ 21 Mike Jirschele
- ☐ 22 Cameron Killebrew
- ☐ 23 Arnold McCrary
- ☐ 24 Jim Payne
- ☐ 25 Tom Owens

1979 West Haven Yankees TCMA

This 30-card standard-size set of the 1979 West Haven Yankees, a Class AA Eastern League affiliate of the New York Yankees, features white-bordered posed color player photos on its fronts. The player's name and position appear in the lower yellow portion of the front. The horizontal back carries the player's name, position, team, and league at the top, followed by biography and statistics. Approximately 2,000 sets were produced.

	NRMT	VG-E	GOOD
COMPLETE SET (30)	50.00	22.00	6.25

- ☐ 1 Mark Johnston
- ☐ 2 Ed Napoleon
- ☐ 3 Don Cooper
- ☐ 4 Brian Dayett
- ☐ 5 Dan Schmitz
- ☐ 6 Pat Callahan
- ☐ 7 Nat Showalter
- ☐ 8 Carl Merrill
- ☐ 9 Dan Ledduke
- ☐ 10 Jim McDonald
- ☐ 11 Tom Filer
- ☐ 12 Kenny Baker
- ☐ 13 Willie McGee
- ☐ 14 Andy McGaffigan
- ☐ 15 Greg Jemison
- ☐ 16 Mark Softy
- ☐ 17 Mike Griffin
- ☐ 18 Tim Lewis
- ☐ 19 Steve Donohue
- ☐ 20 Tim Lollar
- ☐ 21 Dave Righetti
- ☐ 22 Batboys
- ☐ 23 Robert Zeig
- ☐ 24 Juan Espino
- ☐ 25 Joe Lefebvre
- ☐ 26 Mark Harris
- ☐ 27 Hoyt Wilhelm
- ☐ 28 Lloyd Kern
- ☐ 29 Front Office Staff
- ☐ 30 Neal Mersch

1979 Wisconsin Rapids Twins TCMA

This 23-card standard-size set of the 1979 Wisconsin Rapids Twins, a Class A Midwest League affiliate of the Minnesota Twins, features white-bordered posed black-and-white player photos on its fronts. The player's name and position appear in the lower orange portion of the front. The horizontal back carries the player's name, position, team, and league at the top, followed by biography and statistics.

	NRMT	VG-E	GOOD
COMPLETE SET (23)	30.00	13.50	3.70

- ☐ 1 Antonio Lopez
- ☐ 2 Mike Ungs
- ☐ 3 Mike Riley
- ☐ 4 George Dierberger
- ☐ 5 Bob Blake
- ☐ 6 Alex Dovalis
- ☐ 7 Ron Grout
- ☐ 8 Matt Henderson
- ☐ 9 Steve Mapel
- ☐ 10 John Minarcin
- ☐ 11 Kim Nelson
- ☐ 12 Scott Stoltenberg
- ☐ 13 Bob Bohnet
- ☐ 14 Tarry Boelter
- ☐ 15 Gary Dobbs
- ☐ 16 Stan Cannon
- ☐ 17 Luis Bravo
- ☐ 18 Rubio Malone
- ☐ 19 Ted Kromy
- ☐ 20 Chuck Belk
- ☐ 21 Jose Rodriguez
- ☐ 22 Jack Schumate
- ☐ 23 Rich Stelmaszek

1980 Albuquerque Dukes TCMA

This 27-card standard-size set of the 1980 Albuquerque Dukes, a Class AAA Pacific Coast League affiliate of the Los Angeles Dodgers, features red-bordered posed color player photos with rounded corners on its fronts. The player's name and position appear in a white bar under the photo, and the team name is printed under this bar. The horizontal back carries the player's name, position, team, league, and biography.

	MINT	NRMT	EXC
COMPLETE SET (27)	40.00	18.00	5.00

- ☐ 1 Dave Stewart
- ☐ 2 Joe Beckwith
- ☐ 3 Pablo Peguero
- ☐ 4 Kelly Snider
- ☐ 5 Bill Swiacki
- ☐ 6 Ron Roenicke
- ☐ 7 John O'Rear
- ☐ 8 Dennis Lewallyn
- ☐ 9 Doug Harrison
- ☐ 10 Dave Patterson
- ☐ 11 Claude Westmoreland
- ☐ 12 Myron White
- ☐ 13 Gary Weiss
- ☐ 14 Teddy Martinez
- ☐ 15 Mike Wilson
- ☐ 16 Jack Perconte
- ☐ 17 Kevin Keefe
- ☐ 18 Wayne Caughey
- ☐ 19 Terry Collins
- ☐ 20 Bobby Mitchell
- ☐ 21 Mark Nipp
- ☐ 22 Ted Power
- ☐ 23 Del Crandall
- ☐ 24 Paul Padilla
- ☐ 25 Gerald Hannahs
- ☐ 26 Mike Scioscia
- ☐ 27 Don Crow

1980 Anderson Braves TCMA

This 29-card standard-size set of the 1980 Anderson Braves, a Class A South Atlantic League affiliate of the Atlanta Braves, features red-bordered posed color player photos with rounded corners on its fronts. The player's name and position appear in a white bar under the photo, and the team name is printed under this bar. The horizontal back carries the player's name, position, team, league, and biography.

	MINT	NRMT	EXC
COMPLETE SET (29)	30.00	13.50	3.70

- ☐ 1 Dan Church
- ☐ 2 Arcilio Castaigne
- ☐ 3 Duane Theiss
- ☐ 4 Tim Fuller
- ☐ 5 Larry Edwards
- ☐ 6 Tim Alexander
- ☐ 7 Dave Coghill
- ☐ 8 Sonny Jackson
- ☐ 9 Scott Patterson
- ☐ 10 Ken Ames
- ☐ 11 Felipe Arroyo
- ☐ 12 Dave Chase
- ☐ 13 Mark Moses
- ☐ 14 Bill Nice
- ☐ 15 Mike Payne
- ☐ 16 Carlos Rymer
- ☐ 17 Buddy Bailey
- ☐ 18 Roy North
- ☐ 19 Randy Whistler
- ☐ 20 Eric Ayala
- ☐ 21 Mike Koperda
- ☐ 22 Mike Garcia
- ☐ 23 Ken Scanlon
- ☐ 24 Miguel Sosa
- ☐ 25 Harold Williams
- ☐ 26 Brett Butler
- ☐ 27 Brook Jacoby
- ☐ 28 Brad Komminsk
- ☐ 29 Rafael Quezada

1980 Appleton Foxes TCMA

This 30-card standard-size set of the 1980 Appleton Foxes, a Class A Midwest League affiliate of the Chicago White Sox, features red-bordered posed black-and-white player photos with rounded corners on its fronts. The player's name and position appear in a white bar under the photo, and the team name is printed under this bar. The horizontal back carries the player's name, position, team, league, and biography.

	MINT	NRMT	EXC
COMPLETE SET (30)	100.00	45.00	12.50

- ☐ 1 Luis Estrada
- ☐ 2 Bob Fallon
- ☐ 3 Diego Helendez
- ☐ 4 William Mills
- ☐ 5 Rick Naumann
- ☐ 6 J.B. Brown
- ☐ 7 Jeff Vuksan
- ☐ 8 Vito Lucarelli
- ☐ 9 Ron Kittle
- ☐ 10 Larry Wright
- ☐ 11 Dennis Vasguez
- ☐ 12 Nelson Rodreguez
- ☐ 13 Steve Pastrovich
- ☐ 14 Daniel Ortega
- ☐ 15 Keith Brown
- ☐ 16 Jim English
- ☐ 17 A.J. Hill
- ☐ 18 Mitch Olson
- ☐ 19 Greg Stewart
- ☐ 20 Greg Walker
- ☐ 21 David White
- ☐ 22 Tim Carroll
- ☐ 23 Dave Daniels
- ☐ 24 Dennis Keatting
- ☐ 25 Bill Luzinski
- ☐ 26 Larry Doby
- ☐ 27 Larry Hall
- ☐ 28 Mike Maitland
- ☐ 29 Gordy Lund
- ☐ 30 Ron Wollenhaupt

1980 Arkansas Travelers TCMA

This 25-card standard-size set of the 1980 Arkansas Travelers, a Class AA Texas League affiliate of the St. Louis Cardinals, features red-bordered posed color player photos with rounded corners on its fronts. The player's name and position appear in a white bar under the photo, and the team name is printed under this bar. The horizontal back carries the player's name, position, team, league, and biography.

	MINT	NRMT	EXC
COMPLETE SET (25)	10.00	4.50	1.25

- ☐ 1 Benny (Joe) Edelen
- ☐ 2 George Bjorkman
- ☐ 3 Jorge Aranzamendi
- ☐ 4 James Riggleman
- ☐ 5 Sonny Ruberto MGR
- ☐ 6 Mike Calise
- ☐ 7 Luis DeLeon
- ☐ 8 Mike Dimmel
- ☐ 9 Andrew Rincon
- ☐ 10 Dave Penniall
- ☐ 11 Alan Olmsted
- ☐ 12 James McIntyre
- ☐ 13 Ryan Kurosaki
- ☐ 14 David Johnson
- ☐ 15 Frank Hunsaker
- ☐ 16 Julian Gutierrez
- ☐ 17 Nelson Garcia
- ☐ 18 Freddie Tisdale
- ☐ 19 Felipe Zayas
- ☐ 20 Ray Williams
- ☐ 21 John Murphy
- ☐ 22 Kelly Paris
- ☐ 23 Bill Valentine
- ☐ 24 Mike McCormick
- ☐ 25 David Jorn

1980 Asheville Tourists TCMA

This 28-card standard-size set of the 1980 Asheville Tourists, a Class A South Atlantic League affiliate of the Texas Rangers, features red-bordered posed color player photos with rounded corners on its fronts. The player's name and position appear in a white bar under the photo, and the team name is printed under this bar. The horizontal back carries the player's name, position, team, league, and biography. Approximately 2,500 sets were produced.

	MINT	NRMT	EXC
COMPLETE SET (28)	25.00	11.00	3.10

- ☐ 1 Billy Goodman
- ☐ 2 Tom Robson
- ☐ 3 George Gomez
- ☐ 4 Melvin Gilliam
- ☐ 5 Andy Hancock
- ☐ 6 Jim Schaefer
- ☐ 7 Tony Fossas
  Sic, Toni
- ☐ 8 Dave Hibner
- ☐ 9 Ron McKee
- ☐ 10 Bobby Ball
- ☐ 11 Jimmy Tjader
- ☐ 12 Joe Nemeth
- ☐ 13 Pete O'Brien
- ☐ 14 Ron Carney
- ☐ 15 Kerry Kenan
- ☐ 16 Jim Maxwell
- ☐ 17 Jay Pettibone
- ☐ 18 Bill Taylor
- ☐ 19 Daryl Smith
- ☐ 20 Linvel Mosby
- ☐ 21 Donnie Scott
- ☐ 22 Larry Donofrio
- ☐ 23 Frank Garcia
- ☐ 24 Rick Burdette
- ☐ 25 Dave Schmidt
- ☐ 26 George Eason
- ☐ 27 Shelton McMath
- ☐ 28 Mike Jirschele

1980 Batavia Trojans TCMA

This 30-card standard-size set of the 1980 Batavia Trojans, a Class A New York-Penn League affiliate of the Cleveland Indians, features red-bordered posed black-and-white player photos with rounded corners on its fronts. The player's name and position appear in a white bar under the photo, and the team name is printed under this bar. The horizontal back carries the player's name, position, team, league, and biography.

	MINT	NRMT	EXC
COMPLETE SET (30)	125.00	55.00	15.50

- ☐ 1 Angelo Gilbert
- ☐ 2 Terry Norman
- ☐ 3 Mark Bajus
- ☐ 4 Todd Richards
- ☐ 5 Mike Kolodny
- ☐ 6 Kirk Jones
- ☐ 7 Tom Blackmon
- ☐ 8 Tom Burns
- ☐ 9 Monty Holland

☐ 10 Mike Schwarber
☐ 11 Orestes Moldes
☐ 12 Chuck Hollowell
☐ 13 Tom Stiboro
☐ 14 Brian Meier
☐ 15 Rick Elkin
☐ 16 Luis Duarte
☐ 17 Chuck Melito
☐ 18 Darold Ellison
☐ 19 Kevin Malone
☐ 20 Andy Alvis
☐ 21 Kelly Gruber
☐ 22 Rick Colzie
☐ 23 Justo Saavedra
☐ 24 Matt Minium
☐ 25 Dave Gallagher
☐ 26 Pat Grady
☐ 27 Chris Rehbaum
☐ 28 Jeff Moronko
☐ 29 Nelson Ruiz
☐ 30 Mark Wright

1980 Buffalo Bisons TCMA

This 16-card standard-size set of the 1980 Buffalo Bisons, a Class AA Eastern League affiliate of the Pittsburgh Pirates, features red-bordered posed color player photos with rounded corners on its fronts. The player's name and position appear in a white bar under the photo, and the team name is printed under this bar. The horizontal back carries the player's name, position, team, league, and biography.

	MINT	NRMT	EXC
COMPLETE SET (16)	30.00	13.50	3.70

☐ 1 Mike Barnes
☐ 2 Ron Mitchell
☐ 3 Rick Federici
☐ 4 Dave Dravecky
☐ 5 Jim Buckner
☐ 6 Drew Macaluey
☐ 7 Steve Farr
☐ 8 Rick "Bubba" Evans
☐ 9 Al Ortiz Jr.
(no number on back)
☐ 10 Paul Djakonow
☐ 11 Mike Allen
☐ 12 Bob Rock
☐ 13 Al Torres
☐ 14 Larry Nicholson
☐ 15 Ed Vargas
☐ 16 Steve Demeter

1980 Burlington Bees TCMA

This 29-card standard-size set of the 1980 Burlington Bees, a Class A Midwest League affiliate of the Milwaukee Brewers, features red-bordered posed black-and-white player photos with rounded corners on its fronts. The player's name and position appear in a white bar under the photo, and the team name is printed under this bar. The horizontal back carries the player's name, position, team, league, and biography.

	MINT	NRMT	EXC
COMPLETE SET (29)	40.00	18.00	5.00

☐ 1 Steve Gibson
☐ 2 Kevin McCoy
☐ 3 Mike Donovan
☐ 4 Mark Lepson
☐ 5 Dave Grier
☐ 6 Greg Dehart
☐ 7 Orlando Gonzalez
☐ 8 Steve Manderfield
☐ 9 Brian Thorson
☐ 10 Duane Espy
☐ 11 Vince Pone
☐ 12 Jesse Vasquez
☐ 13 Al Walker
☐ 14 Ty Coleman
☐ 15 Steve Norwood
☐ 16 Rich Bach
☐ 17 Greg Cicotte
☐ 18 Mike Anderson
☐ 19 Kurt Kingsolver
☐ 20 Walt Steele
☐ 21 Jorge DeJesus
☐ 22 Juan Castillo
☐ 23 Mark Higgins
☐ 24 Kirk Downs
☐ 25 John Evans
☐ 26 Curt Watanabe
☐ 27 Stan Levi
☐ 28 Karl McKay
☐ 29 Bengie Biggus

1980 Cedar Rapids Reds TCMA

This 26-card standard-size set of the 1980 Cedar Rapids Reds, a Class A Midwest League affiliate of the Cincinnati Reds, features red-bordered posed color player photos with rounded corners on its fronts. The player's name and position appear in a white bar under the photo, and the team name is printed under this bar. The horizontal back carries the player's name, position, team, league, and biography.

	MINT	NRMT	EXC
COMPLETE SET (26)	10.00	4.50	1.25

☐ 1 Mark Moore
☐ 2 Newt Box
☐ 3 Dave Hoenstine
☐ 4 Emil Drzayich
☐ 5 Larry Buckle
☐ 6 Carlos Porte
☐ 7 Eski Viltz
☐ 8 Steve Hughes
☐ 9 Tony Masone
☐ 10 Bob Lapple
☐ 11 Rick Jendra
☐ 12 Charlie McKinney
☐ 13 Jose Mota
☐ 14 Steve Skaggs
☐ 15 Frank DeJulio
☐ 16 Mark Miller
☐ 17 Les Straker
☐ 18 Paul Gibson
☐ 19 Jeff Jones
☐ 20 Mike Messaros
☐ 21 Don Buchheister
☐ 22 Jim Lett
☐ 23 Mike Kripner
☐ 24 Steve Daniels
☐ 25 Kevin Waller
☐ 26 Wayne Guinn

1980 Charleston Charlies TCMA

This 17-card standard-size set of the 1980 Charleston Charlies, a Class AAA International League affiliate of the Texas Rangers, features red-bordered posed color player photos with rounded corners on its fronts. The player's name and position appear in a white bar under the photo, and the team name is printed under this bar. The horizontal back carries the player's name, position, team, league, and biography.

	MINT	NRMT	EXC
COMPLETE SET (17)	10.00	4.50	1.25

☐ 1 Tom Burgess
☐ 2 Mark Scott
☐ 3 Wayne Pinkerton
☐ 4 Nelson Norman
☐ 5 Brian Allard
☐ 6 Greg Mahlberg
☐ 7 Dave Moharter
☐ 8 Mike Richardt
☐ 9 Richard Lisi
☐ 10 Mike Hart
☐ 11 Mark Mercer
☐ 12 Dan Duran
☐ 13 John Butcher
☐ 14 Fla Strawn
☐ 15 Odie David
☐ 16 Tucker Ashford
☐ 17 Bob Babcock

1980 Charlotte O's Police

This 28-card standard-size set of the 1980 Charlotte O's, a Class AA Southern League affiliate of the Baltimore Orioles, features orange-bordered posed color player photos. The player's name and position appear in white letters across the bottom of the card with the team's logo printed on the right. The back carries player tips and crime prevention tips. Single cards from the set were given out one or two at a time to local school children. Less than a dozen complete sets are known to exist. This issue features the minor league card debut of Cal Ripken Jr.

	MINT	NRMT	EXC
COMPLETE SET (25)	2500.00	1100.00	300.00

☐ 1 Larry Anderson
☐ 2 John Buffamoyer
☐ 3 Brooks Carey
☐ 4 Doc Cole TR
☐ 5 John Denman
☐ 6 Tommy Eaton
☐ 7 Kurt Fabrizio
☐ 8 Will George
☐ 9 Jose Gonzales
☐ 10 Drungo Hazewood
☐ 11 Dave Huppert
☐ 12 Minnie Mendoza CO
☐ 13 Edwin Neal
☐ 14 Russ Pensiero
☐ 15 Billy Presley
☐ 16 Luis Quintana
☐ 17 Dan Ramirez
☐ 18 Cal Ripken Jr.
☐ 19 Willie Royster
☐ 20 John Shelby
☐ 21 Tommy Smith
☐ 22 Don Welchel
☐ 23 Cat Whitfield
☐ 24 Jimmy Williams MGR
☐ 25 The Pepper Girls

1980 Charlotte O's W3TV

This 28-card standard-size set of the 1980 Charlotte O's, a Class AA Southern League affiliate of the Baltimore Orioles, features blue-bordered posed color player photos. The player's name and position appear in white letters across the bottom of the card with the team's logo printed on the right and the sponsor's logo printed on the left. The back carries the player's name, position, team, league, and biography. This issue features the minor league card debut of Cal Ripken Jr.

	MINT	NRMT	EXC
COMPLETE SET (28)	1500.00	700.00	190.00

☐ 1 Larry Anderson
☐ 2 John Buffamoyer
☐ 3 Brooks Carey
☐ 4 Doc Cole TR
☐ 5 John Denman
☐ 6 Tommy Eaton
☐ 7 Kurt Fabrizio
☐ 8 Will George
☐ 9 Jose Gonzales
☐ 10 Drungo Hazewood
☐ 11 Marshall Hester
☐ 12 Dave Huppert
☐ 13 Minnie Mendoza CO
☐ 14 Edwin Neal
☐ 15 Russ Pensiero
☐ 16 Billy Presley
☐ 17 Luis Quintana
☐ 18 Dan Ramirez
☐ 19 Cal Ripken Jr.
☐ 20 Willie Royster
☐ 21 John Shelby
☐ 22 Tommy Smith
☐ 23 Don Welchel
☐ 24 Cat Whitfield
☐ 25 Jimmy Williams MGR
☐ 26 Cover Card
☐ 27 O's Team Photo
☐ 28 'The Pepper Girls'

1980 Clinton Giants TCMA

This 27-card standard-size set of the 1980 Clinton Giants, a Class A Midwest League affiliate of the San Francisco Giants, features red-bordered posed black-and-white player photos with rounded corners on its fronts. The player's name and position appear in a white bar under the photo, and the team name is printed under this bar. The horizontal back carries the player's name, position, team, league, and biography.

	MINT	NRMT	EXC
COMPLETE SET (27)	100.00	45.00	12.50

☐ 1 Dave Wilhelmi
☐ 2 Dennis Rathjen
☐ 3 Jose Chue
☐ 4 Ramon Bautista
☐ 5 Jerry Stoval
☐ 6 Chris Goodchild
☐ 7 Ron Matrisciano
☐ 8 Ken Schwab
☐ 9 Tim Hagemann
☐ 10 Scott Garrelts
☐ 11 Art Maese
☐ 12 Kevin Johnson
☐ 13 David Fonseca
☐ 14 Randy Kutcher
☐ 15 Tim Painton
☐ 16 Chris Brown
☐ 17 Frank Thon
☐ 18 Rafael Estepan
☐ 19 Glen Moon
☐ 20 Rob Deer
☐ 21 Ron Perodin
☐ 22 Stan Morton
☐ 23 Richard Figueroa
☐ 24 Bob Cummings
☐ 25 Gilbert Albright
☐ 26 Wayne Cato
☐ 27 Yommy Jones

1980 Columbus Astros TCMA

This 22-card standard-size set of the 1980 Columbus Astros, a Class AA Southern League affiliate of the Houston Astros, features red-bordered posed black-and-white player photos with rounded corners on its fronts. The player's name and position appear in a white bar under the photo, and the team name is printed under this bar. The horizontal back carries the player's name, position, team, league, and biography.

	MINT	NRMT	EXC
COMPLETE SET (22)	30.00	13.50	3.70

☐ 1 Greg Cypret
☐ 2 Val Primmante
☐ 3 Tim Tolman
☐ 4 Stan Leland
☐ 5 Del Letherwood
☐ 6 Chick Valley
☐ 7 Johnny Ray
☐ 8 Bert Pena
☐ 9 Doug Stokke
☐ 10 Matt Galante
☐ 11 Greg Dahl
☐ 12 Rod Boxberger
☐ 13 John Hessler
☐ 14 Simone Rosario
☐ 15 Reggie Waller
☐ 16 Riccardo Aponte
☐ 17 Scott Loucks
☐ 18 Keith Bodie
☐ 19 Ron Meridith
☐ 20 Jim MacDonald
☐ 21 Mark Miggins
☐ 22 Rex Jones

1980 Columbus Clippers Police

	MINT	NRMT	EXC
COMPLETE SET (25)	15.00	6.75	1.85

☐ 2 Brian Doyle
☐ 11 Roger Holt
☐ 12 Dennis Sherrill
☐ 14 Joe Lefebvre
☐ 15 Garry Smith
☐ 16 Joe Altobelli MG
☐ 17 Dave Coleman
☐ 18 Roger Slagle
☐ 20 Brad Gulden
☐ 21 Jim Lewis
☐ 22 Marv Thompson
☐ 23 Tim Lollar
☐ 24 Dave Righetti
☐ 25 Roy Staiger
☐ 26 Bruce Robinson
☐ 27 Greg Cochran
☐ 28 Jim Nettles
☐ 29 Bob Kammeyer
☐ 30 Dave Wehrmeister
☐ 31 Jim McDonald
☐ 33 Marshall Brant
☐ 34 Chris Welsh
☐ 36 Ken Clay
☐ NNO Coaches/Trainer
Sammy Ellis CO
Mark Letendre TR
Jerry McNertney CO
☐ NNO George Sisler Jr. GM

1980 Columbus Clippers TCMA

This 28-card standard-size set of the 1980 Columbus Clippers, a Class AAA International League affiliate of the New York Yankees, features red-bordered posed color player photos with rounded corners on its fronts. The player's name and position appear in a white bar under the photo, and the team name is printed under this bar. The horizontal back carries the player's name, position, team, league, and biography.

	MINT	NRMT	EXC
COMPLETE SET (28)	30.00	13.50	3.70

☐ 1 Tim Lollar
☐ 2 Roger Slagle
☐ 3 Chris Welsh
☐ 4 Wayne Harer
☐ 5 Garry Smith
☐ 6 Brad Gullen
☐ 7 Roger Holt
☐ 8 Joe Altobelli
☐ 9 Roy Staiger
☐ 10 Bob Kammeyer
☐ 11 Jim McDonald
☐ 12 Jim Nettles
☐ 13 Brian Doyle
☐ 14 Sammy Ellis
☐ 15 Bruce Robinson
☐ 16 Jim Lewis
☐ 17 Dave Righetti
☐ 18 Mark Letendre
☐ 19 Dave Coleman
☐ 20 Marshall Brant
☐ 21 Greg Cochran
☐ 22 Jerry McNertney
☐ 23 Dennis Sherrill
☐ 24 Marv Thompson
☐ 25 Dave Wehrmeister
☐ 26 Joe Lefebvre
☐ 27 George Sisler Jr.
☐ 28 Juan Espino

1980 El Paso Diablos TCMA

This 24-card standard-size set of the 1980 El Paso Diablos, a Class AA Texas League affiliate of the Milwaukee Brewers, features red-bordered posed color player photos with rounded corners on its fronts. The player's name and position appear in a white bar under the photo, and the team name is printed under this bar. The horizontal back carries the player's name, position, team, league, and biography.

	MINT	NRMT	EXC
COMPLETE SET (24)	18.00	8.00	2.20

☐ 1 Brandt Humphrey
☐ 2 Dennis Gilbert
☐ 3 Scott Carnes
☐ 4 Rick Steirer
☐ 5 Tom Chevolek
☐ 6 Rich Rommel

☐ 7 Jim Saul
☐ 8 Mark Miller
☐ 9 Brian Harper
☐ 10 Bob Border
☐ 11 Joel Crisler
☐ 12 Mike Bishop
☐ 13 Tom Bhagwat
☐ 14 Daryl Sconiers
☐ 15 Don Smelser
☐ 16 Steve Brown
☐ 17 Tom Brunansky
☐ 18 Donny Jones
☐ 19 Perry Morrison
☐ 20 Rich Brewster
☐ 21 Rick Adams
☐ 22 Mike Walters
☐ 23 Jamie Hamilton
☐ 24 Charlie Phillips

1980 Elmira Pioneer Red Sox TCMA

This 44-card standard-size set of the 1980 Elmira Pioneer, a Class A New York-Penn League affiliate of the Boston Red Sox, features red-bordered posed black-and-white player photos with rounded corners on its fronts. The player's name and position appear in a white bar under the photo, and the team name is printed under this bar. The horizontal back carries the player's name, position, team, league, and biography. Approximately 1,100 sets were produced.

	MINT	NRMT	EXC
COMPLETE SET (44)	100.00	45.00	12.50

☐ 1 Alan Barnes
☐ 2 Tom Bolton
☐ 3 Allan Bowlin
☐ 4 Dennis Boyd
☐ 5 Brice Cote
☐ 6 Steve Garrett
☐ 7 George Greco
☐ 8 Ty Herman
☐ 9 Ron Hill
☐ 10 Kevin Keenan
☐ 11 Jeff Hall
☐ 12 John Ackley
☐ 13 Mark Weinbrecht
☐ 14 Bob Sandling
☐ 15 Brandon Plainte
☐ 16 George Mecerod
☐ 17 Tom McCarthy
☐ 18 Mitch Johnson
☐ 19 Don Leach
☐ 20 Tim Duncan
☐ 21 Jeff Hunter
☐ 22 Tony Stevens
☐ 23 Ron Oddo
☐ 24 Wolf Ramos
☐ 25 Mike Bryant
☐ 26 Gus Burgess
☐ 27 Mike Ciampa
☐ 28 Simon Glenn
☐ 29 Dick Berardino
☐ 30 Parker Wilson
☐ 31 Brian Zell
☐ 32 Gilberto Gonzalez
☐ 33 Bob Crandall
☐ 34 Marve Handler
☐ 35 Bill Limoncelli
☐ 36 Bruce Butera
☐ 37 Sam Mele
☐ 38 Frank Malzone
☐ 39 Charlie Wagner
☐ 40 Jay La Bare
☐ 41 Charlie Lynch
☐ 42 Alan Mintz
☐ 43 Rodolfo Santana
☐ 44 Miguel Valdez

1980 Evansville Tripletts TCMA

This 24-card standard-size set of the 1980 Evansville Triplets, a Class AAA American Association affiliate of the Detroit Tigers, features red-bordered posed color player photos with rounded corners on its fronts. The player's name and position appear in a white bar under the photo, and the team name is printed under this bar. The horizontal back carries the player's name, position, team, league, and biography.

	MINT	NRMT	EXC
COMPLETE SET (24)	15.00	6.75	1.85

☐ 1 Roger Weaver
☐ 2 Mark DeJohn
☐ 3 James Gaudet
☐ 4 David Steffen
☐ 5 Michael Chris
☐ 6 Mark Fidrych
☐ 7 Ed Putnam
☐ 8 Altar Greene
☐ 9 David Rucker
☐ 10 Gerald Ujdur
☐ 11 Darrell Brown
☐ 12 Steve Baker
☐ 13 Go Giannotta
☐ 14 John Martin
☐ 15 Ralph Treuel
☐ 16 David Machemer
☐ 17 Jim Leyland
☐ 18 Bruce Robbins
☐ 19 Martin Castillo
☐ 20 Dan Gonzales
☐ 21 Glenn Gulliver
☐ 22 Steve Patchin
☐ 23 Juan Lopez
☐ 24 Richard Leach

1980 Glen Falls White Sox Color TCMA

This 30-card standard-size set of the 1980 Glens Falls White Sox, a Class AA Eastern League affiliate of the Chicago White Sox, features red-bordered posed color player photos with rounded corners on its fronts. The player's name and position appear in a white bar under the photo, and the team name is printed under this bar. The horizontal back carries the player's name, position, team, league, and biography.

	MINT	NRMT	EXC
COMPLETE SET (30)	25.00	11.00	3.10

☐ 1 Ron Perry
☐ 2 Len Bradley
☐ 3 Mark Teutsch
☐ 4 Randy Johnson
☐ 5 Mark Esser
☐ 6 Andy Pasillas
☐ 7 Kevin Hickey
☐ 8 Rick Seilheimer
☐ 9 Mark Platel
☐ 10 Julio Perez
☐ 11 Vince Bienek
☐ 12 Fran Mullins
☐ 13 Rick Wieters
☐ 14 Dom Fucci
☐ 15 Randy Evans
☐ 16 Steve Pastrovich
☐ 17 Luis Rois
☐ 18 Reggie Patterson
☐ 19 Ted Barnicle
☐ 20 Sox Infield
☐ 21 Mike Pazik
☐ 22 Abner Haines
☐ 23 Bob Bolster
☐ 24 Duane Shaffer
☐ 25 Orlando Cepeda
☐ 26 Lorenzo Gray
☐ 27 Ray Torres
☐ 28 Tom Johnson
☐ 29 Batboys
☐ 30 A.J. Hill

1980 Glens Falls White Sox B/W TCMA

This 29-card standard-size set of the 1980 Glens Falls White Sox, a Class AA Eastern League affiliate of the Chicago White Sox, features red-bordered posed black-and-white player photos with rounded corners on its fronts. The player's name and position appear in a white bar under the photo, and the team name is printed under this bar. The horizontal back carries the player's name, position, team, league, and biography.

	MINT	NRMT	EXC
COMPLETE SET (29)	175.00	80.00	22.00

☐ 1 Steve Pastrovich
☐ 2 Len Bradley
☐ 3 Tom Johnson
☐ 4 Randy Evans
☐ 5 Mark Platel
☐ 6 Luis Rois
☐ 7 Rick Seilheimer
☐ 8 Ray Torres
☐ 9 Reggie Patterson
☐ 10 Kevin Hickey
☐ 11 Ted Barnicle
☐ 12 Rick Wieters
☐ 13 Mark Teutsch
☐ 14 Mark Esser
☐ 15 Andy Pasillas
☐ 16 Julio Perez
☐ 17 Ron Perry
☐ 18 Randy Johnson
☐ 19 Dom Fucci
☐ 20 Vince Bienek
☐ 21 A.J. Hill
☐ 22 Lorenzo Gray
☐ 23 Fran Mullins
☐ 24 Mike Pazik
☐ 25 Duane Shaffer
☐ 26 Orlando Cepeda
☐ 27 Allan Haines
☐ 28 Batboys
☐ 29 Bob Bolster

1980 Hawaii Islanders TCMA

This 25-card standard-size set of the 1980 Hawaii Islanders, a Class AAA Pacific Coast League affiliate of the San Diego Padres, features red-bordered posed color player photos with rounded corners on its fronts. The player's name and position appear in a white bar under the photo, and the team name is printed under this bar. The horizontal back carries the player's name, position, team, league, and biography.

	MINT	NRMT	EXC
COMPLETE SET (25)	10.00	4.50	1.25

☐ 1 Chuck Baker
☐ 2 Doug Rader
☐ 3 Bob Duensing
☐ 4 Juan Eichelberger
☐ 5 Eric Mustad
☐ 6 Craig Stimac
☐ 7 Craig Kusick
☐ 8 Jim Beswick
☐ 9 Dennis Blair
☐ 10 Bobby Mitchell
☐ 11 Chuck Hartenstein
☐ 12 John Yandle
☐ 13 Greg Wilkes
☐ 14 Tom Tellmann
☐ 15 George Stablein
☐ 16 Mike Armstrong
☐ 17 Mark Lee
☐ 18 Steve Smith
☐ 19 Bill Flannery
☐ 20 Rick Sweet
☐ 21 Tony Castillo
☐ 22 Broderick Perkins
☐ 23 Don Reynolds
☐ 24 Andy Dyes
☐ 25 Fred Kuhaulua

1980 Holyoke Millers TCMA

This 25-card standard-size set of the 1980 Holyoke Millers, a Class AA Eastern League affiliate of the Milwaukee Brewers, features red-bordered posed color player photos with rounded corners on its fronts. The player's name and position appear in a white bar under the photo, and the team name is printed under this bar. The horizontal back carries the player's name, position, team, league, and biography.

	MINT	NRMT	EXC
COMPLETE SET (25)	10.00	4.50	1.25

☐ 1 Rick Kranitz
☐ 2 John Skorochocki
☐ 3 Mark Schuster
☐ 4 Barry Cort
☐ 5 Frank Thomas
☐ 6 Ivan Rodriguez
☐ 7 Eddie Brunson
☐ 8 Kuni Ogawa
☐ 9 Terry Shoebridge
☐ 10 Tom Kayser
☐ 11 Weldon Swift
☐ 12 Frank DiPino
☐ 13 Kevin Bass
☐ 14 David Green
☐ 15 Doug Loman
☐ 16 John Adams
☐ 17 Steve Lake
☐ 18 Steve Reed
☐ 19 Ed Carroll
☐ 20 Larry Montgomery
☐ 21 Terry Lee
☐ 22 Dave Curran
☐ 23 Gerald Ako
☐ 24 Tony Torres
☐ 25 Lee Sigman

1980 Indianapolis Indians Team Issue

	MINT	NRMT	EXC
COMPLETE SET (32)	30.00	13.50	3.70

☐ 1 Team Picture
☐ 2 Jim Beauchamp MG
☐ 3 Sheldon Burnside
☐ 4 Mike Grace
☐ 5 Joe Price
☐ 6 John Hale
☐ 7 Geoff Combe
☐ 8 Dave Van Gorder
☐ 9 Bruce Berenyi
☐ 10 Eddie Milner
☐ 11 Jay Howell
☐ 12 Paul O'Neill
☐ 13 The Braintrust
☐ 14 Larry Rothschild
☐ 15 Paul Householder
☐ 16 The Relievers
☐ 17 Scott Brown
☐ 18 Mark Miller
☐ 19 The Starters
☐ 20 Blake Doyle
☐ 21 Gene Menees
☐ 22 Rafael Santo Domingo
☐ 23 Bill Kelly
☐ 24 Don Lyle
☐ 25 Bill Dawley
☐ 26 Duane Walker
☐ 27 Angel Torres
☐ 28 The Catchers
☐ 29 The Infielders
☐ 30 The Outfielders
☐ 31 John Young TR
☐ 32 Checklist

1980 Iowa Oaks Police

(White Sox) [#2B and #12B are scarce cards]

	MINT	NRMT	EXC
COMPLETE SET (14)	200.00	90.00	25.00
COMPLETE SET (16)	400.00	180.00	50.00

☐ 1 Richard Barnes
☐ 2A Mike Colbern
(has the word
"Rhubarb" on back)
☐ 2B Mike Colbern
(has the word
"The Walk" on back)
☐ 3 Nardi Contreras
☐ 4 Henry Cruz
☐ 5 Fred Frazier
☐ 6 Joe Gates
☐ 7 Guy Hoffman
☐ 8 Lamarr Hoyt
☐ 9 Chris Nyman
☐ 10 Dewey Robinson
☐ 11 Leo Sutherland
☐ 12A Raymundo Torres
(has the word
"A Walk on back)
☐ 12B Raymundo Torres
(has the word
"Rhubarb" on back)
☐ 13 Pete Ward
☐ 14 Mike Wolf

1980 Knoxville Blue Jays TCMA

This 28-card standard-size set of the 1980 Knoxville Blue Jays, a Class AA Southern League affiliate of the Toronto Blue Jays, features red-bordered posed black-and-white player photos with rounded corners on its fronts. The player's name and position appear in a white bar under the photo, and the team name is printed under this bar. The horizontal back carries the player's name, position, team, league, and biography.

	MINT	NRMT	EXC
COMPLETE SET (28)	75.00	34.00	9.50

☐ 1 Chuck Fore
☐ 2 Gene Petralli
☐ 3 John Poloni
☐ 4 Pete Rowe
☐ 5 Paul Hodgson
☐ 6 Mark Stober
☐ 7 Davis May
☐ 8 Jesse Flores
☐ 9 Bob Silverman
☐ 10 Shaun McCarthy
☐ 11 Ralph Santana
☐ 12 Mike Cuellar Jr.
☐ 13 Jesse Barfield
☐ 14 Ed Dennis
☐ 15 Tim Thompson
☐ 16 Tom Dejak
☐ 17 Pedro Hernandez
☐ 18 Larry Hardy
☐ 19 Dave Gibson
☐ 20 Jesus DeLaRosa
☐ 21 Charlie Puleo
☐ 22 Andre Wood
☐ 23 Keith Walker
☐ 24 Rocket Wheeler
☐ 25 Bob Humphreys
☐ 26 Rick Morgan
☐ 27 Duane Larson
☐ 28 Ed Holtz

1980 Lynn Sailors TCMA

This 23-card standard-size set of the 1980 Lynn Sailors, a Class AAA Eastern League affiliate of the Seattle Mariners, features red-bordered posed color player photos with rounded corners on its fronts. The player's name and position appear in a white bar under the photo, and the team name is printed under this bar. The horizontal back carries the player's name, position, team, league, and biography.

	MINT	NRMT	EXC
COMPLETE SET (23)	10.00	4.50	1.25

☐ 1 Mike Moore
☐ 2 Larry Patterson
☐ 3 Rodney Hobbs
☐ 4 Bobby Floyd
☐ 5 Chuck Lindsay
☐ 6 Rob Simond
☐ 7 Mike Hart
☐ 8 Don Minnick
☐ 9 Orlando Mercado
☐ 10 Miguel Negron
☐ 11 Karl Best
☐ 12 Jeff Cary
☐ 13 Manny Estrada

☐ 14 Gary Pellant
☐ 15 Mickey Bowers
☐ 16 Tom Hunt
☐ 17 Joe Georger
☐ 18 Jamie Allen
☐ 19 R.J. Harrison
☐ 20 Roy Clark
☐ 21 Sam Welborn
☐ 22 Lloyd Kern
☐ 23 Ron Musselman

1980 Memphis Chicks TCMA

This 30-card standard-size set of the 1980 Memphis Chicks, a Class AA Southern League affiliate of the Montreal Expos, features red-bordered posed black-and-white player photos on its fronts. The player's name and position appear near the bottom. The white and blue horizontal back carries the player's name and position at the top, followed by biography, career highlights, and statistics. This set includes the first minor league card of Tony Phillips.

	MINT	NRMT	EXC
COMPLETE SET (30)	60.00	27.00	7.50

☐ 1 Steve Lovins
☐ 2 Charlie Lea
☐ 3 Anthony Johnson
☐ 4 Tom Gorman
☐ 5 Greg Bargar
☐ 6 Joe Abone
☐ 7 Larry Goldetsky CO
☐ 8 Larry Bearnarth MG
☐ 9 Mike Gates
☐ 10 Glen Franklin
☐ 11 Ray Crowley
☐ 12 Leonel Carrion
☐ 13 Terry Francona
☐ 14 Kevin Mendon
☐ 15 Brad Mills
☐ 16 Tony Phillips
☐ 17 Pat Rooney
☐ 18 Dennis Sherow
☐ 19 Tommy Joe Shimp
☐ 20 Bryn Smith
☐ 21 Chris Smith
☐ 22 Doug Simunic
☐ 23 Bob Tenenini
☐ 24 Grayling Tobias
☐ 25 Tom Wieghaus
☐ 26 Rick Williams
☐ 27 Steve Winfield
☐ 28 Frank Wren
☐ 29 Bud Yanus
☐ 30 Audie Thor TR

1980 Nashville Sounds Team Issue

	MINT	NRMT	EXC
COMPLETE SET (25)	25.00	11.00	3.10

☐ 1 Ken Baker
☐ 2 Steve Balboni
☐ 3 Paul Boris
☐ 4 Pat Callahan
☐ 5 Nate Chapman
☐ 6 Don Cooper
☐ 7 Brian Dayett
☐ 8 Pat Dobson
☐ 9 Tom Filer
☐ 10 Brad Guilden
☐ 11 Greg Jemison
☐ 12 Dan Ledduke
☐ 13 Andy McGaffigan
☐ 14 Willie McGee
☐ 15 Carl "Stump" Merrill
☐ 16 Eddie Napoleon
☐ 17 Brian Ryder
☐ 18 Rafel Santana
☐ 19 Danny Schmitz
☐ 20 Buck Showalter
☐ 21 Roger Slagle
☐ 22 Pat Tabler
☐ 23 Steve Taylor
☐ 24 James Werly
☐ 25 Ted Wilborn

1980 Ogden A's TCMA

This 23-card standard-size set of the 1980 Ogden A's, a Class AAA Pacific Coast League affiliate of the Oakland Athletics, features red-bordered posed color player photos with rounded corners on its fronts. The player's name and position appear in a white bar under the photo, and the team name is printed under this bar. The horizontal back carries the player's name, position, team, league, and biography.

	MINT	NRMT	EXC
COMPLETE SET (23)	10.00	4.50	1.25

☐ 1 Tim Hosley
☐ 2 Ray Cosey
☐ 3 Craig Minetto
☐ 4 Derek Bryant
☐ 5 Randy Green
☐ 6 Rich Lysander
☐ 7 Mark Budska
☐ 8 Terry Enyart
☐ 9 Brian Abraham
☐ 10 Mark Souza
☐ 11 Bob Grandas
☐ 12 Frank Harris
☐ 13 John Sutton
☐ 14 Milt Ramirez
☐ 15 David Beard
☐ 16 Bruce Fournier
☐ 17 Allen Wirth
☐ 18 Royle Stillman
☐ 19 Jeff Cox
☐ 20 Kelvin Moore
☐ 21 Shooty Babbitt
☐ 22 Pat Dempsey
☐ 23 Jose Pagan

1980 Omaha Royals Police

	MINT	NRMT	EXC
COMPLETE SET (24)	70.00	32.00	8.75

☐ 1 Dave Augustine
☐ 2 German Barranca
☐ 3 Leon Brown
☐ 4 Steve Busby
☐ 5 Manny Castillo
☐ 6 Craig Chamberlain
☐ 7 Jerry Cram
☐ 8 Ken Cvejdlik
☐ 9 Bob Detherage
☐ 10 Keith Drumright
☐ 11 Dan Fischer
☐ 12 Danny Garcia
☐ 13 Jim Gaudet
☐ 14 Kelly Heath
☐ 15 Tim Ireland
☐ 16 Bill Laskey
☐ 17 Randy McGilberry
☐ 18 Mike Morley
☐ 19 Tom Mutz
☐ 20 Bill Paschall
☐ 21 Ken Phelps
☐ 22 Jeff Schattinger
☐ 23 Joe Sparks
☐ 24 Jeff Twitty

1980 Orlando Twins TCMA

This 22-card standard-size set of the 1980 Orlando Twins, a Class AA Southern League affiliate of the Minnesota Twins, features red-bordered posed black-and-white player photos with rounded corners on its fronts. The player's name and position appear in a white bar under the photo, and the team name is printed under this bar. The horizontal back carries the player's name, position, team, league, and biography.

	MINT	NRMT	EXC
COMPLETE SET (22)	100.00	45.00	12.50

☐ 1 Wade Adamson
☐ 2 Tim Barr
☐ 3 Tom Biko
☐ 4 Steve Green
☐ 5 Eddie Hodge
☐ 6 Steve Mapel
☐ 7 Jose Reyes
☐ 8 Lance Hallberg
☐ 9 Doc Estes
☐ 10 Lenny Faedo
☐ 11 Steve Benson
☐ 12 Tim Laudner
☐ 13 Chino Cadahia
☐ 14 Butch Ballard
☐ 15 Mike Ungs
☐ 16 Terry Sheehan
☐ 17 Steve McManaman
☐ 18 Alex Ramirez
☐ 19 Mark Funderburk
☐ 20 Kevin McWhirter
☐ 21 Scott Ullger
☐ 22 Roy McMillan

1980 Peninsula Pilots B/W TCMA

This 27-card standard-size set of the 1980 Peninsula Pilots, a Class A Carolina League affiliate of the Philadelphia Phillies, features red-bordered posed black-and-white player photos with rounded corners on its fronts. The player's name and position appear in a white bar under the photo, and the team name is printed under this bar. The horizontal back carries the player's name, position, team, league, and biography. Approximately 1,100 sets were produced.

	MINT	NRMT	EXC
COMPLETE SET (27)	75.00	34.00	9.50

☐ 1 Phil Teston
☐ 2 Daryl Adams
☐ 3 Carlos Cabassa
☐ 4 Miguel Alicea
☐ 5 Fred Warner
☐ 6 Kelly Faulk
☐ 7 Wally Goff
☐ 8 Wil Culmer
☐ 9 Keith Washington
☐ 10 Bob Tiefenauer
☐ 11 Don Carman
☐ 12 Roy Smith
☐ 13 Jim Wright
☐ 14 Randy Greer
☐ 15 Joe Bruno
☐ 16 Al White
☐ 17 Paul Kiess
☐ 18 Russ Hamric
☐ 19 Ray Borucki
☐ 20 Ron Smith
☐ 21 Julio Franco
☐ 22 Jeff Ulrich
☐ 23 Herb Orensky
☐ 24 John Fierro
☐ 25 Bob Neal
☐ 26 Frank Funk
☐ 27 Bill Dancy

1980 Peninsula Pilots Color TCMA

This 27-card standard-size set of the 1980 Peninsula Pilots, a Class A Carolina League affiliate of the Philadelphia Phillies, features red-bordered posed color player photos with rounded corners on its fronts. The player's name and position appear in a white bar under the photo, and the team name is printed under this bar. The horizontal back carries the player's name, position, team, league, and biography. Approximately 2,500 sets were produced.

	MINT	NRMT	EXC
COMPLETE SET (27)	60.00	27.00	7.50

☐ 1 Phil Teston
☐ 2 Daryl Adams
☐ 3 Carlos Cabassa
☐ 4 Roy Smith
☐ 5 Don Carman
☐ 6 Miguel Alicea
☐ 7 Jim Wright
☐ 8 Fred Warner
☐ 9 Bob Neal
☐ 10 John Fierro
☐ 11 George Farson
☐ 12 Bill Dancy
☐ 13 Kelly Faulk
☐ 14 Wally Goff
☐ 15 Herb Grensky
☐ 16 Jeff Ulrihe
☐ 17 Julio Franco
☐ 18 Keith Washington
☐ 19 Wil Culmer
☐ 20 Randy Greer
☐ 21 Joe Bruno
☐ 22 Al White
☐ 23 Paul Kiess
☐ 24 Russ Hamric
☐ 25 Ray Borucki
☐ 26 Ron Smith
☐ 27 Bob Tiefenauer

1980 Phoenix Giants Valley National Bank

	MINT	NRMT	EXC
COMPLETE SET (26)	5.00	2.20	.60

☐ 1 Mike Williams
☐ 2 Bob Tufts
☐ 3 Doug Schaefer
☐ 4 Mike Rowland
☐ 5 Larry Prewitt
☐ 6 Ed Plank
☐ 7 Phil Nastu
☐ 8 Terry Cornutt
☐ 9 Fred Breining
☐ 10 Bill Bordley
☐ 11 Chris Bourjos
☐ 12 Max Venable
☐ 13 Casey Parsons
☐ 14 Craig Landis
☐ 15 Bob Kearney
☐ 16 Dennis Littlejohn
☐ 17 Jose Barrios
☐ 18 Mike Rex
☐ 19 Rich Murray
☐ 20 Joe Pettini
☐ 21 Guy Sularz
☐ 22 Rocky Bridges MG
☐ 23 Jim Duffalo CO
☐ 24 Ethan Blackaby GM
☐ 25 Tommy Gonzales SVR
☐ 26 Harry Jordan TR

1980 Portland Beavers TCMA

This 26-card standard-size set of the 1980 Portland Beavers, a Class AAA Pacific Coast League affiliate of the Pittsburgh Pirates, features red-bordered posed color player photos with rounded corners on its fronts. The player's name and position appear in a white bar under the photo, and the team name is printed under this bar. The horizontal back carries the player's name, position, team, league, and biography.

	MINT	NRMT	EXC
COMPLETE SET (26)	15.00	6.75	1.85

☐ 1 Mike Tyler
☐ 2 Dorian Boyland
☐ 3 Craig Cacek
☐ 4 Jerry McDonald
☐ 5 Rob Ellis
☐ 6 Jim Mahoney
☐ 7 Pascual Perez
☐ 8 Tommy Sandt
☐ 9 Vance Law
☐ 9 Luis Salazar
☐ 10 Mickey Mahler
☐ 11 Dick Pole
☐ 12 Bill Fortinberry
☐ 13 Stewart Cliburn
☐ 14 Harry Dorish
☐ 15 Gary Hargis
☐ 17 Odell Jones
☐ 18 Tom Trebelhorn
☐ 19 Mike Davey
☐ 20 Rick Lancellotti
☐ 21 Robert Long
☐ 22 Rod Gilbreath
☐ 23 Larry Anderson
☐ 24 Tony Pena
☐ 25 Gene Pentz
☐ 26 Dan Warthen
☐ 27 Rick Rhoden

1980 Quad City Cubs TCMA

This 32-card standard-size set of the 1980 Quad City Cubs, a Class A Midwest League affiliate of the Chicago Cubs, features red-bordered posed black-and-white player photos with rounded corners on its fronts. The player's name and position appear in a white bar under the photo, and the team name is printed under this bar. The horizontal back carries the player's name, position, team, league, and biography.

	MINT	NRMT	EXC
COMPLETE SET (32)	75.00	34.00	9.50

☐ 1 Mike Thompson
☐ 2 Gerry Mims
☐ 3 Tim Millner
☐ 4 Ed Moore
☐ 5 Tom Morris
☐ 6 Glenn Swaggerty
☐ 7 Ray Soff
☐ 8 Carlos Gil
☐ 9 Richard Renwick
☐ 10 Mark Wilkins
☐ 11 Bob Maddon
☐ 12 Norm Churchill
☐ 13 Mike Diaz
☐ 14 Pete Bazan
☐ 15 Ted Trevino
☐ 16 Jack Upton
☐ 17 Craig Kornfield
☐ 18 Jim Payne
☐ 19 Glenn Millhauser
☐ 20 Bruce Compton
☐ 21 Mike Kelley
☐ 22 Dennis Mork
☐ 23 Gordy Hodgson
☐ 24 Wayne Rohlfing
☐ 25 Phil Belmonte
☐ 26 Mike Wilson
☐ 27 Rich DeLoach
☐ 28 John Stockstill
☐ 29 Carmelo Martinez
☐ 30 Jim Napier
☐ 31 Davey Nesmoe
☐ 32 Roger Crow

1980 Reading Phillies TCMA

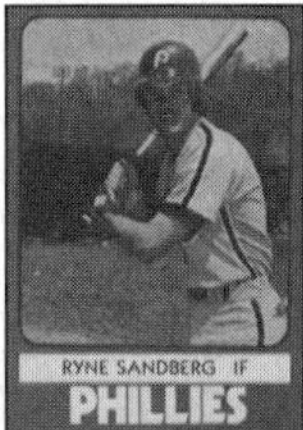

This 24-card standard-size set of the 1980 Reading Phillies, a Class AA Eastern League affiliate of the Philadelphia Phillies, features red-bordered posed black-and-white player photos with rounded corners on its fronts. The player's name and position appear in a white bar under the photo, and the team name is printed under this bar. The horizontal back carries the player's name, position, team, league, and biography. This issue inlcudes the minor league card debuts of Ryne Sandberg and George Bell. Approximately 1,100 sets were produced.

	MINT	NRMT	EXC
COMPLETE SET (24)	1100.00	500.00	140.00

☐ 1 Wayne Williams
☐ 2 Jose Castro
☐ 3 Ozzie Virgil

- ☐ 4 Mark Davis
- ☐ 5 Don Fowler
- ☐ 6 Miguel Ibarra
- ☐ 7 Joe Jones
- ☐ 8 Jeff Kraus
- ☐ 9 Tommy Hart
- ☐ 10 Ernie Gause
- ☐ 11 Darren Burroughs
- ☐ 12 Tom Lombarski
- ☐ 13 Jorge Bell
- ☐ 14 John Devincenzo
- ☐ 15 Bob Dernier
- ☐ 16 Manny Abreu
- ☐ 17 Ron Clark
- ☐ 18 Roly DeArmas
- ☐ 19 Cliff Speck
- ☐ 20 Dan Prior
- ☐ 21 Tony McDonald
- ☐ 22 Ryne Sandberg
- ☐ 23 Jesus Hernaiz
- ☐ 24 Steve Curry

1980 Richmond Braves TCMA

This 23-card standard-size set of the 1980 Richmond Braves, a Class AAA International League affiliate of the Atlanta Braves, features red-bordered posed color player photos with rounded corners on its fronts. The player's name and position appear in a white bar under the photo, and the team name is printed under this bar. The horizontal back carries the player's name, position, team, league, and biography.

	MINT	NRMT	EXC
COMPLETE SET (23)	10.00	4.50	1.25

- ☐ 1 Danny Morogiello
- ☐ 2 Rafael Ramirez
- ☐ 3 Butch Edge
- ☐ 4 Larry Whisenton
- ☐ 5 Fred Hatfield
- ☐ 6 Steve Hammond
- ☐ 7 Tony Brizzolara
- ☐ 8 Gary Melson
- ☐ 9 John Sain
- ☐ 10 Danny O'Brien
- ☐ 11 Rick Mahler
- ☐ 12 Charlie Keller
- ☐ 13 Butch Metzger
- ☐ 14 Horace Speed
- ☐ 15 Glenn Hubbard
- ☐ 16 Harry Saferight
- ☐ 17 Terry Harper
- ☐ 18 Ken Smith
- ☐ 19 Bob Beall
- ☐ 20 Craig Skok
- ☐ 21 Jim Wessinger
- ☐ 22 Eddie Miller
- ☐ 23 Bo McLaughlin

1980 Rochester Red Wings TCMA

This 21-card standard-size set of the 1980 Rochester Red Wings, a Class AAA International League affiliate of the Baltimore Orioles, features red-bordered posed color player photos with rounded corners on its fronts. The player's name and position appear in a white bar under the photo, and the team name is printed under this bar. The horizontal back carries the player's name, position, team, league, and biography.

	MINT	NRMT	EXC
COMPLETE SET (21)	10.00	4.50	1.25

- ☐ 1 Bob Bonner
- ☐ 2 Dallas Williams
- ☐ 3 Vern Thomas
- ☐ 4 Dan Logan
- ☐ 5 Mark Corey
- ☐ 6 Mike Boddicker
- ☐ 7 Larry Jones
- ☐ 8 Jeff Rineer
- ☐ 9 Tom Rowe
- ☐ 10 Jeff Schneider
- ☐ 11 Kevin Kennedy
- ☐ 12 Mike Eden
- ☐ 13 Doc Edwards
- ☐ 14 John Valle
- ☐ 15 Steve Luebber
- ☐ 16 Wayne Krenchicki
- ☐ 17 Jim Smith
- ☐ 18 Floyd Rayford
- ☐ 19 Tom Smith
- ☐ 20 Larry Johnson
- ☐ 21 Pete Torrez

1980 Salt Lake City Gulls TCMA

This 26-card standard-size set of the 1980 Salt Lake City Gulls, a Class AAA Pacific Coast League affiliate of the California Angels, features red-bordered posed color player photos with rounded corners on its fronts. The player's name and position appear in a white bar under the photo, and the team name is printed under this bar. The horizontal back carries the player's name, position, team, league, and biography.

	MINT	NRMT	EXC
COMPLETE SET (26)	10.00	4.50	1.25

- ☐ 1 Ralph Botting
- ☐ 2 Dan Whitmer
- ☐ 3 Craig Eaton
- ☐ 4 Scott Moffitt
- ☐ 5 Mark Nocciolo
- ☐ 6 Dave Schuler
- ☐ 7 Ken Schrom
- ☐ 8 Charlie Phillips
- ☐ 9 Jeff Bertoni
- ☐ 10 Rick Oliver
- ☐ 11 Jay Peters
- ☐ 12 John Harris
- ☐ 13 Carlos Perez
- ☐ 14 Steve Lubratich
- ☐ 15 Rick Foley
- ☐ 16 Jim Dorsey
- ☐ 17 Steve Eddy
- ☐ 18 Moose Stubing
- ☐ 19 Leonard Garcia
- ☐ 20 Sterling Gull
- ☐ 21 Gil Kubski
- ☐ 22 Pete Mangual
- ☐ 23 Bob Clark
- ☐ 24 Bob Ferris
- ☐ 25 Fernando Gonzalez
- ☐ 26 Mike Overy

1980 San Jose Missions Jack in the Box

	MINT	NRMT	EXC
COMPLETE SET (21)	50.00	22.00	6.25

- ☐ 1 Bill Plummer
- ☐ 2 Ed Aponte
- ☐ 3 Mark Batten
- ☐ 4 Bud Black
- ☐ 5 Mark Chelette
- ☐ 6 Ramon Estepa
- ☐ 7 Chris Flammang
- ☐ 8 Bill Gaffney
- ☐ 9 Rick Graser
- ☐ 10 Tracy Harris
- ☐ 11 Tim Hallgren
- ☐ 12 Steve Knight
- ☐ 13 Chris Krajewski
- ☐ 14 Jed Murray
- ☐ 15 Tito Nanni
- ☐ 16 Brian Snyder
- ☐ 17 Kevin Steger
- ☐ 18 Jeff Stottlemyre
- ☐ 19 Scott Stranski
- ☐ 20 Dave Valle
- ☐ 21 Checklist

1980 Spokane Indians TCMA

This 24-card standard-size set of the 1980 Spokane Indians, a Class AAA Pacific Coast League affiliate of the Seattle Mariners, features red-bordered posed color player photos with rounded corners on its fronts. The player's name and position appear in a white bar under the photo, and the team name is printed under this bar. The horizontal back carries the player's name, position, team, league, and biography.

	MINT	NRMT	EXC
COMPLETE SET (24)	25.00	11.00	3.10

- ☐ 1 Bob Stoddard
- ☐ 2 Dave Smith
- ☐ 3 Greg Biercevicz
- ☐ 4 Carlos Diaz
- ☐ 5 Joe Coleman
- ☐ 6 Ron McGee
- ☐ 7 Roy Branch
- ☐ 8 Bryan Clark
- ☐ 9 Vance McHenry
- ☐ 10 Terry Bulling
- ☐ 11 Kip Young
- ☐ 12 Manny Sarmiento
- ☐ 13 Randy Stein
- ☐ 14 Jim Maler
- ☐ 15 Dave Edler
- ☐ 16 Dave Henderson
- ☐ 17 Gary Wheelock
- ☐ 18 Rene Lachemann
- ☐ 19 Kim Allen
- ☐ 20 Rich Anderson
- ☐ 21 Reggie Walton
- ☐ 22 Dan Firova
- ☐ 23 Steve Stroughter
- ☐ 24 Charlie Beamon

1980 Syracuse Chiefs TCMA

This 23-card standard-size set of the 1980 Syracuse Chiefs, a Class AAA International League affiliate of the Toronto Blue Jays, features red-bordered posed color player photos on its fronts. The player's name and position appear in a white bar under the photo, and the team name is printed under this bar. The horizontal back carries the player's name, position, team, and league at the top, followed by biography and statistics.

	MINT	NRMT	EXC
COMPLETE SET (23)	30.00	13.50	3.70

- ☐ 1 Garth Iorg
- ☐ 2 Doug Ault
- ☐ 3 Kevin Pasley
- ☐ 4 Jackson Todd
- ☐ 5 Pat Rockett
- ☐ 6 Jay Robertson
- ☐ 7 Mike Willis
- ☐ 8 Tom Brown
- ☐ 9 Phil Huffman
- ☐ 10 Butch Alberts
- ☐ 11 Jack Kucek
- ☐ 12 Mitch Webster
- ☐ 13 Mike Barlow
- ☐ 14 Greg Wells
- ☐ 15 Pat Kelly
- ☐ 16 Lloyd Moseby
- ☐ 17 Dave Baker
- ☐ 18 Randy Benson
- ☐ 19 Harry Warner MG
- ☐ 20 Danny Ainge
- ☐ 21 Willie Upshaw
- ☐ 22 Domingo Ramos
- ☐ 23 Don Pisker

1980 Syracuse Chiefs Team Issue

This 24-card set of the 1980 Syracuse Chiefs, a Class AAA International League affiliate of the Toronto Blue Jays, measures about 3 1/4" by 5" and features white-bordered posed black-and-white photos on its fronts. The player's uniform number and name appear in the bottom wider border. The backs are blank. The cards are unnumbered and checklisted below in alphabetical order.

	MINT	NRMT	EXC
COMPLETE SET (24)	90.00	40.00	11.00

- ☐ 1 Butch Alberts
- ☐ 2 Doug Ault
- ☐ 3 Dave Baker
- ☐ 4 Mike Barlow
- ☐ 5 Randy Benson
- ☐ 6 Tom Brown
- ☐ 7 Steve Davis
- ☐ 8 Tony DeRosa TR
- ☐ 9 Steve Grilli
- ☐ 10 Phil Huffman
- ☐ 11 Garth Iorg
- ☐ 12 Pat Kelly
- ☐ 13 Jack Kucek
- ☐ 14 Luis Leal
- ☐ 15 Lloyd Moseby
- ☐ 16 Kevin Pasley
- ☐ 17 Don Pisker
- ☐ 18 Jay Robertson
- ☐ 19 Pat Rockett
- ☐ 20 Jackson Todd
- ☐ 21 Harry Warner MG
- ☐ 22 Mitchell Webster
- ☐ 23 Greg Wells
- ☐ 24 Mike Willis

1980 Tacoma Tigers TCMA

This 28-card standard-size set of the 1980 Tacoma Tigers, a Class AAA Pacific Coast League affiliate of the Cleveland Indians, features red-bordered posed color player photos with rounded corners on its fronts. The player's name and position appear in a white bar under the photo, and the team name is printed under this bar. The horizontal back carries the player's name, position, team, league, and biography.

	MINT	NRMT	EXC
COMPLETE SET (28)	10.00	4.50	1.25

- ☐ 1 Rob Pietroburgo (no number on back)
- ☐ 2 Tim Norrid
- ☐ 3 Larry Littleton
- ☐ 4 Wayne Cage
- ☐ 5 Don Collins
- ☐ 6 Bobbi Cuellar
- ☐ 7 Mel Queen
- ☐ 8 Larry McCall
- ☐ 9 Raphael Vasquez
- ☐ 10 Sandy Wihtol
- ☐ 11 Bob Allietta
- ☐ 12 Tom Brennan
- ☐ 13 Mike Bucci
- ☐ 14 Sal Rende
- ☐ 15 Dave Oliver
- ☐ 16 Mike Champion
- ☐ 17 Gary Gray
- ☐ 18 Todd Heimer
- ☐ 19 John Bonilla
- ☐ 20 Kevin Rhomberg
- ☐ 21 Rick Borchers
- ☐ 22 Art Popham
- ☐ 23 Gene Dusan
- ☐ 24 Del Alston
- ☐ 25 Eric Wilkins
- ☐ 26 Steve Ciszczon
- ☐ 27 Luis DeLeon
- ☐ 27 Mike Paxton

1980 Tidewater Tides TCMA

This 24-card standard-size set of the 1980 Tidewater Tides, a Class AAA International League affiliate of the New York Mets, features red-bordered posed color player photos with rounded corners on its fronts. The player's name and position appear in a white bar under the photo, and the team name is printed under this bar. The horizontal back carries the player's name, position, team, league, and biography.

	MINT	NRMT	EXC
COMPLETE SET (24)	30.00	13.50	3.70

- ☐ 1 Dave Von Ohlen
- ☐ 2 Jose Moreno
- ☐ 3 Juan Berenguer
- ☐ 4 Wally Backman
- ☐ 5 Sergio Ferrer
- ☐ 6 Gil Flores
- ☐ 7 Ed Cipot
- ☐ 8 Butch Benton
- ☐ 9 Ron MacDonald
- ☐ 10 Dyar Miller
- ☐ 11 Greg Harris
- ☐ 12 Tom Dixon
- ☐ 13 Reggie Baldwin
- ☐ 14 Fred Beene
- ☐ 15 Hubie Brooks
- ☐ 17 Mookie Wilson
- ☐ 18 Kelvin Chapman
- ☐ 19 Roy Lee Jackson
- ☐ 20 Jimmy Smith
- ☐ 21 Ed Lynch
- ☐ 22 Papo Rosado
- ☐ 23 Mike Scott
- ☐ 24 Frank Verdi
- ☐ 25 Randi McGilberry

1980 Toledo Mud Hens TCMA

This 20-card standard-size set of the 1980 Toledo Mud Hens, a Class AAA International League affiliate of the Minnesota Twins, features red-bordered posed color player photos with rounded corners on its fronts. The player's name and position appear in a white bar under the photo, and the team name is printed under this bar. The horizontal back carries the player's name, position, team, league, and biography.

	MINT	NRMT	EXC
COMPLETE SET (20)	10.00	4.50	1.25

- ☐ 1 Steve Mapel
- ☐ 2 Bob Randall
- ☐ 3 Cal Ermer MGR
- ☐ 4 Bruce MacPherson
- ☐ 5 Gary Serum
- ☐ 6 Ron Washington
- ☐ 7 Terry Felton
- ☐ 8 Randy Bush
- ☐ 9 John Walker
- ☐ 10 Willie Norwood
- ☐ 11 Jesus Vega
- ☐ 12 Walfredo Sarmiento
- ☐ 13 Steve Herz
- ☐ 14 Buck Chamberlin TR
- ☐ 15 Dave Engle
- ☐ 16 Ray Smith
- ☐ 17 Al Williams
- ☐ 18 Jeff Brueggemann
- ☐ 19 Bob Veselic
- ☐ 20 Kurt Seibert

1980 Tucson Toros TCMA

This 24-card standard-size set of the 1980 Tucson Toros, a Class AAA Pacific Coast League affiliate of the Houston Astros, features red-bordered posed color player photos with rounded corners on its fronts. The player's name and position appear in a white bar under the photo, and the team name is printed under this bar. The horizontal back carries the player's name, position, team, league, and biography.

	MINT	NRMT	EXC
COMPLETE SET (24)	10.00	4.50	1.25

- ☐ 1 Danny Heep
- ☐ 2 Jimmy Sexton
- ☐ 3 Joe Pittman
- ☐ 4 Rick Williams
- ☐ 5 Gary Wilson
- ☐ 6 Bob Sprowl
- ☐ 7 Jack Fleming
- ☐ 8 Tom Wiedenbauer
- ☐ 9 Jimmy Johnson MGR
- ☐ 10 George Gross
- ☐ 11 Billy Smith
- ☐ 12 Dave LaBossiere TR
- ☐ 13 Dennis Miscik
- ☐ 14 Alan Knicely
- ☐ 15 Tom Spencer
- ☐ 16 Gary Rajsich
- ☐ 17 Mike Fischlin
- ☐ 18 Gordy Pladson
- ☐ 19 Jim Plankovits
- ☐ 20 Brent Strom
- ☐ 21 Mike Mendoza
- ☐ 22 Gary Woods

☐ 23 Bert Roberge
☐ 24 Doug Stokke

1980 Tulsa Drillers TCMA

This 26-card standard-size set of the 1980 Tulsa Drillers, a Class AA Texas League affiliate of the Texas Rangers, features red-bordered posed color player photos with rounded corners on its fronts. The player's name and position appear in a white bar under the photo, and the team name is printed under this bar. The horizontal back carries the player's name, position, team, league, and biography.

	MINT	NRMT	EXC
COMPLETE SET (26)	10.00	4.50	1.25

☐ 1 Jerry Gleaton
☐ 2 Dave Crutcher
☐ 3 Tony Hudson
☐ 4 Ted Davis
☐ 5 Mike Roberts
☐ 6 Jack Lazorko
☐ 7 Jim Farr
☐ 8 Nick Capra
☐ 9 Larry Reynolds
☐ 10 George Wright
☐ 11 Mel Barrow
☐ 12 Frank Garcia
☐ 13 Phil Klimas
☐ 14 Luis Gonzalez
☐ 15 Mike Jirschele
☐ 16 Wayne Tolleson
☐ 17 Ronnie Gooch
☐ 18 Tracy Cowger
☐ 19 Steve Nielsen
☐ 20 Chuck Lamson
☐ 21 Bobby Johnson
☐ 22 Dave Schmidt
☐ 23 Darrell Ortiz TR
☐ 24 Wayne Terwilliger MGR
☐ 25 Mike Vickers
☐ 26 Mitch Fletcher CO

1980 Utica Blue Jays TCMA

This 33-card standard-size set of the 1980 Utica Blue Jays, a Class A New York-Penn League affiliate of the Toronto Blue Jays, features red-bordered posed black-and-white player photos with rounded corners on its fronts. The player's name and position appear in a white bar under the photo, and the team name is printed under this bar. The horizontal back carries the player's name, position, team, league, and biography.

	MINT	NRMT	EXC
COMPLETE SET (33)	40.00	18.00	5.00

☐ 1 Larry Hardy MGR
☐ 2 Rich White
☐ 3 Carlos Cabrera
☐ 4 Jim Baker
☐ 5 Felix Feliciano
☐ 6 Rafael Harris
☐ 7 Tom Norko
☐ 8 Siverio Valdez
☐ 9 Jon Woodworth TR
☐ 10 Bob Wilbur CO
☐ 11 Hector Torres CO
☐ 12 Tomas Castillo
☐ 13 Juan Castillo
☐ 14 Roberto Cerrud
☐ 15 Jose Escobar
☐ 16 Tony Gilmore
☐ 17 Luis Guzman
☐ 18 Toby Hernandez
☐ 19 Mark Holton
☐ 20 Dennis Howard
☐ 21 Miguel Ortiz
☐ 22 Tom O'Dowd
☐ 23 Al Montgomery
☐ 24 Bob McNair
☐ 25 Tom Lukish
☐ 26 Herman Lewis
☐ 27 Carlos Leal
☐ 28 Paul Langfield
☐ 29 Mike Hurdle
☐ 30 Bill Reade
☐ 31 Rafael Rivas
☐ 32 Miguel Rodriguez
☐ 33 Rico Sutton

1980 Vancouver Canadians TCMA

This 22-card standard-size set of the 1980 Vancouver Canadians, a Class AAA Pacific Coast League affiliate of the Milwaukee Brewers, features red-bordered posed color player photos with rounded corners on its fronts. The player's name and position appear in a white bar under the photo, and the team name is printed under this bar. The horizontal back carries the player's name, position, team, league, and biography.

	MINT	NRMT	EXC
COMPLETE SET (22)	10.00	4.50	1.25

☐ 1 Lawrence Rush
☐ 2 Willie Mueller
☐ 3 Ned Yost
☐ 4 Gus Quiros
☐ 5 Bobby Glen Smith
☐ 6 Terry Bevington
☐ 7 Dave LaPoint
☐ 8 Billy Severns
☐ 9 Lance Rautzhan
☐ 10 Tim Nordbrook
☐ 11 Bob Didier MGR
☐ 12 Kent Biggerstaff TR
☐ 13 Ed Romero
☐ 14 Dan Boitano
☐ 15 Craig Ryan
☐ 16 Rene Quinones
☐ 17 Mike Henderson
☐ 18 Fred Holdsworth
☐ 19 Marshall Edwards
☐ 20 Bob Galasso
☐ 21 Vic Harris
☐ 22 Rick Olsen

1980 Waterbury Reds TCMA

This 22-card standard-size set of the 1980 Waterbury Reds, a Class AA Eastern League affiliate of the Cincinnati Reds, features red-bordered posed black-and-white player photos with rounded corners on its fronts. The player's name and position appear in a white bar under the photo, and the team name is printed under this bar. The horizontal back carries the player's name, position, team, league, and biography.

	MINT	NRMT	EXC
COMPLETE SET (22)	125.00	55.00	15.50

☐ 1 Nick Fiorillo
☐ 2 Jeff Lahti
☐ 3 Steve Christmas
☐ 4 Doug Neuenschwander
☐ 5 Paul Herring
☐ 6 Randy Town
☐ 7 Bill Scherrer
☐ 8 Scott Dye
☐ 9 Lee Garrett TR
☐ 10 Mike Compton MGR
☐ 11 Rick O'Keeffe
☐ 12 Jose Brito
☐ 13 Bob Hamilton
☐ 14 Mark Gilbert
☐ 15 Skeeter Barnes
☐ 16 Tom Sohns
☐ 17 Dan Sarrett
☐ 18 Tom Lawless
☐ 19 Tom Foley
☐ 20 Russ Aldrich
☐ 21 Nick Esasky
☐ 22 Greg Hughes

1980 Waterloo Indians TCMA

This 35-card standard-size set of the 1980 Waterloo Indians, a Class A Midwest League affiliate of the Cleveland Indians, features red-bordered posed black-and-white player photos with rounded corners on its fronts. The player's name and position appear in a white bar under the photo, and the team name is printed under this bar. The horizontal back carries the player's name, position, team, league, and biography.

	MINT	NRMT	EXC
COMPLETE SET (35)	50.00	22.00	6.25

☐ 1 John Hoban
☐ 2 Dane Anthony
☐ 3 Ron Leach
☐ 4 Larry White
☐ 5 Tim Glass
☐ 6 Ramon Romero
☐ 7 Alan Willis
☐ 8 Jack Nuismer
☐ 9 John Bohnet
☐ 10 John Asbell
☐ 11 Larry Hrynko
☐ 12 Kirk Jones
☐ 13 Rick Barnhart
☐ 14 Daryl Fazzio
☐ 15 Bryan Meier
☐ 16 Chris Rehbaum
☐ 17 Sammy Torres
☐ 18 Bruce Chaney
☐ 19 Erik Peterson
☐ 20 George Cechetti
☐ 21 Robert Bohnet
☐ 22 Don Nicolet
☐ 23 Gary Hinson
☐ 24 Frank Regan
☐ 25 Everett Rey
☐ 26 Rick Baker
☐ 27 Carmelo Castillo
☐ 28 Tommy Martinez
☐ 29 Mike Taylor
☐ 30 Cal Emery MGR
☐ 31 Chuck Stobbs CO
☐ 32 Bob Gariglio TR
☐ 33 Rich Blumeyer GM
☐ 34 Wes Mitchell
☐ 35 Von Hayes

1980 Wausau Timbers TCMA

This 23-card standard-size set of the 1980 Wausau Timbers, a Class A Midwest League Independent, features red-bordered posed black-and-white player photos with rounded corners on its fronts. The player's name and position appear in a white bar under the photo, and the team name is printed under this bar. The horizontal back carries the player's name, position, team, league, and biography.

	MINT	NRMT	EXC
COMPLETE SET (23)	30.00	13.50	3.70

☐ 1 Tom Brennan
☐ 2 John Burden
☐ 3 Mark Cahill
☐ 4 Tony Jordan
☐ 5 Martin Little
☐ 6 Edwin Nunez
☐ 7 Steve Roche
☐ 8 Elias Salva
☐ 9 Mark Softy
☐ 10 John Zisk
☐ 11 Takashi Upshur
☐ 12 Bobby Tanzi
☐ 13 Jimmy Presley
☐ 14 Mario Diaz
☐ 15 Enrique Diaz
☐ 16 Mike Hood
☐ 17 Chris Henry
☐ 18 Rick Graser
☐ 19 Mike Frierson
☐ 20 Kevin King
☐ 21 Werner Lajszky
☐ 22 Arnie McCrary
☐ 23 Orlando Martinez

1980 West Haven White Caps TCMA

This 31-card standard-size set of the 1980 West Haven White Caps, a Class AA Eastern League affiliate of the Oakland Athletics, features red-bordered posed color player photos with rounded corners on its fronts. The player's name and position appear in a white bar under the photo, and the team name is printed under this bar. The horizontal back carries the player's name, position, team, league, and biography.

	MINT	NRMT	EXC
COMPLETE SET (31)	10.00	4.50	1.25

☐ 1 Al Minker
☐ 2 Dennis Wyszynski
☐ 3 LeRoy Robbins
☐ 4 Don Morris
☐ 5 Bruce Fournier
☐ 6 Rob Klebba
☐ 7 Paul Stevens
☐ 8 Paul Mize
☐ 9 Scott Meyer
☐ 10 Bert Bradley
☐ 11 Craig Harris
☐ 12 Bobby Markham
☐ 13 Fred Devito
☐ 14 Darryl Ciaz
☐ 15 Mike Patterson
☐ 16 Keith Atherton
☐ 17 Shooty Babbitt
☐ 18A Nick Beamon
☐ 18B Staff
☐ 19A John Gosse
☐ 19B Keith Comstock
☐ 20A Ed Nottle MGR
☐ 20B David Goldstein PRES
☐ 21A Keathel Chauncey
☐ 21B Rich Lynch
☐ 21C Bob Moore
☐ 22A Aggie Maggio
☐ 22B Tim Conroy
☐ 23A Coach Benson
☐ 23B Randy Sealy
☐ 24 Rick Tronerud

1980 Wichita Aeros TCMA

This 22-card standard-size set of the 1980 Wichita Aeros, a Class AAA American Association affiliate of the Chicago Cubs, features red-bordered posed color player photos with rounded corners on its fronts. The player's name and position appear in a white bar under the photo, and the team name is printed under this bar. The horizontal back carries the player's name, position, team, league, and biography. Approximately 2,500 sets were produced.

	MINT	NRMT	EXC
COMPLETE SET (22)	90.00	40.00	11.00

☐ 1 Karl Pagel
☐ 2 Jim Tracy
☐ 3 Kim Buettemeyer
☐ 4 Mark Parker
☐ 5 Bill Hayes
☐ 6 Danny Rohn
☐ 7 Randy Martz
☐ 8 Jack Hiatt
☐ 9 Jesus Figeroa
☐ 10 Ignacio Javier
☐ 11 Mike Turgeon
☐ 12 Lee Smith
☐ 13 Mike Allen
☐ 14 Jesus Alfaro
☐ 15 Paul Semall
☐ 16 Jared Martin
☐ 17 Brian Rosinski
☐ 18 Steve Macko
☐ 19 Vince Valentini
☐ 20 George Riley
☐ 21 Manny Seoane
☐ 22 Mark Lemongello

1980 Wisconsin Rapids Twins TCMA

This 27-card standard-size set of the 1980 Wisconsin Rapids Twins, a Class A Midwest League affiliate of the Minnesota Twins, features red-bordered posed black-and-white player photos with rounded corners on its fronts. The player's name and position appear in a white bar under the photo, and the team name is printed under this bar. The horizontal back carries the player's name, position, team, league, and biography.

	MINT	NRMT	EXC
COMPLETE SET (27)	150.00	70.00	19.00

☐ 1 Sam Arrington
☐ 2 Luis Santos
☐ 3 Robert Mulligan
☐ 4 Larry May
☐ 5 Manuel Lunar
☐ 6 William Lamkey
☐ 7 Bob Konopa
☐ 8 Hal Jackson
☐ 9 Ken Francingues
☐ 10 Conrad Everett
☐ 11 Chris Thomas
☐ 12 Paul Voight
☐ 13 Richard Ray Austin
☐ 14 Glenn Ballard
☐ 15 James Christensen
☐ 16 Manuel Colletti
☐ 17 Gary Gaetti
☐ 18 Kent Hrbek
☐ 19 Kevin Miller
☐ 20 Norberto Molina
☐ 21 Brad Carlson
☐ 22 Matt Henderson
☐ 23 Joe Kubit
☐ 24 Bruce Stocker
☐ 25 Ray Stein
☐ 26 Rich Stelmaszek
☐ 27 Tony Oliva

1981 Albuquerque Dukes TCMA

This 26-card standard-size set of the 1981 Albuquerque Dukes, a Class AAA Pacific Coast League affiliate of the Los Angeles Dodgers, features white-bordered posed color player photos on its fronts. The player's name and position appear in red letters below the photo. The horizontal back carries the player's name, position, team, and league at the top, followed by biography and statistics.

	MINT	NRMT	EXC
COMPLETE SET (26)	70.00	32.00	8.75

☐ 1 Dave Moore
☐ 2 Dave Patterson
☐ 3 Steve Shirley
☐ 4 Alejandro Pena
☐ 5 Ted Power
☐ 6 Bill Swiacki
☐ 7 Ricky Wright
☐ 8 Dave Richards
☐ 9 Ron Roenicke
☐ 10 Brian Holton
☐ 11 Kevin Keefe
☐ 12 Brent Strom
☐ 13 Don Crow
☐ 14 Wayne Caughey
☐ 15 Larry Fobbs
☐ 16 Mike Marshall
☐ 17 Jack Perconte
☐ 18 Alex Taveras
☐ 19 Gary Weiss
☐ 20 Rudy Law
☐ 21 Candy Maldonado
☐ 22 Bobby Mitchell
☐ 23A Tack Wilson
☐ 23B Sandy Koufax
☐ 25 Del Crandall
☐ 26 Dick McLauchlin

1981 Appleton Foxes TCMA

This 29-card standard-size set of the 1981 Appleton Foxes, a Class A Midwest League affiliate of the Chicago White Sox, features white-bordered posed color player photos on its fronts. The player's name and position appear in red letters below the photo. The horizontal back carries the player's name, position, team, and league at the top, followed by biography and statistics.

	MINT	NRMT	EXC
COMPLETE SET (29)	15.00	6.75	1.85

☐ 1 Jesse Anderson
☐ 2 Jeff Barnard
☐ 3 Keith Desjarlais
☐ 4 Kevin Flannery
☐ 5 Tom Mullen
☐ 6 Rick Naumann
☐ 7 Dan Ortega
☐ 8 Steve Pastrovich
☐ 9 Mark Platel
☐ 10 Jim Siwy
☐ 11 Roy Schumacher
☐ 12 Wayne Schukert
☐ 13 Larry Donofrio
☐ 14 Cecil Espy
☐ 15 Leo Garcia
☐ 16 Ike Golden
☐ 17 John Hanley
☐ 18 A.J. Hill
☐ 19 Scott Meier
☐ 20 Mike Morse
☐ 21 Dave Nix
☐ 22 Gary Robinette
☐ 23 Ramon Romero
☐ 24 Mark Seeger
☐ 25 Ray Torres
☐ 26 Wes Kent
☐ 27 Dave Wall
☐ 28 Sam Ewing
☐ 29 Doug Wiesner

1981 Arkansas Travelers TCMA

This 23-card standard-size set of the 1981 Arkansas Travelers, a Class AA Texas League affiliate of the St. Louis Cardinals, features white-bordered posed black-and-white player photos on its fronts. The player's name and position appear in black letters below the photo. The horizontal back carries the player's name, position, team, and league at the top, followed by biography and statistics.

	MINT	NRMT	EXC
COMPLETE SET (23)	25.00	11.00	3.10

☐ 1 Felipe Zayas
☐ 2 Steve Turco
☐ 3 Donald Moore
☐ 4 Dennis Delany
☐ 5 Fred Tisdale
☐ 6 Rhadames Mills
☐ 7 Jeffrey Doyle
☐ 8 Jorge Aranzamendi
☐ 9 David Kable
☐ 10 Kerry Burchett
☐ 11 Jerry Johnson
☐ 12 David Jorn
☐ 13 Rafael Pimentel
☐ 14 Mark Riggins
☐ 15 Daniel Winslow
☐ 16 Kevin Hagen
☐ 17 James Gott
☐ 18 Ralph Citarella
☐ 19 James Riggleman
☐ 20 Louis Pratt
☐ 21 Gaylen Pitts
☐ 22 Jerry McKune
☐ 23 Arkansas Travelerettes

1981 Batavia Trojans TCMA

This 30-card standard-size set of the 1981 Batavia Trojans, a Class A New York-Penn League affiliate of the Cleveland Indians, features white-bordered posed black-and-white player photos on its fronts. The player's name and position appear in black letters below the photo. The horizontal back carries the player's name, position, team, and league at the top, followed by biography and statistics. Approximately 1,100 sets were produced.

	MINT	NRMT	EXC
COMPLETE SET (30)	15.00	6.75	1.85

☐ 1 Mark Bajus
☐ 2 Tom Burns
☐ 3 Jose Roman
☐ 4 Steve Cushing
☐ 5 Mike Piondexter
☐ 6 Todd Richard
☐ 7 Brian Silvas
☐ 8 Phil Deriso
☐ 9 Bart Mackie
☐ 10 Adelberto Nieves
☐ 11 Rick Elkin
☐ 12 Arnold Cochran
☐ 13 Ray Martinez
☐ 14 Jerry Nalley
☐ 15 Junior Noboa
☐ 16 Ed Tanner
☐ 17 Sam Martin
☐ 18 John Merchant
☐ 19 Scott Collins
☐ 20 Bernardo Brito
☐ 21 Gary Holden
☐ 22 Eric Jones
☐ 23 Chris Rehbaum
☐ 24 Randy Washington
☐ 25 George Alpert
☐ 26 Miguel Roman
☐ 27 Dave Oliver
☐ 28 Luis Isaac
☐ 29 Paul Seymour
☐ 30 John Jakubowski

1981 Birmingham Barons TCMA

This 25-card standard-size set of the 1981 Birmingham Barons, a Class AA Southern League affiliate of the Detroit Tigers, features white-bordered posed black-and-white color player photos on its fronts. The player's name and position appear in black letters below the photo. The horizontal back carries the player's name, position, team, and league at the top, followed by biography and statistics.

	MINT	NRMT	EXC
COMPLETE SET (25)	75.00	34.00	9.50

☐ 1 John Lackey
☐ 2 Roy Majtyka
☐ 3 Dwight Lowry
☐ 4 Manny Seoane
☐ 5 Ron Mathis
☐ 6 Bruce Robbins
☐ 7 Mark Dacko
☐ 8 Mike Laga
☐ 9 Frank Hunsaker
☐ 10 Glenn Wilson
☐ 11 Gary Bozich
☐ 12 Howard Johnson
☐ 13 Jeff Kenaga
☐ 14 Bob Nandin
☐ 15 Jack Smith
☐ 16 Bruce Chaney
☐ 17 Stan Younger
☐ 18 Nick O'Connor
☐ 19 Dick Pole
☐ 20 Stine Poole
☐ 21 Darrell Woodard
☐ 22 Barbaro Garbey
☐ 23 Augie Ruiz
☐ 24 Paul Josephson
☐ 25 Mike Beecroft

1981 Bristol Red Sox TCMA

This 22-card standard-size set of the 1981 Bristol Red Sox, a Class AA Eastern League affiliate of the Boston Red Sox, features white-bordered posed color player photos on its fronts. The player's name and position appear in red letters below the photo. The horizontal back carries the player's name, position, team, and league at the top, followed by biography and statistics.

	MINT	NRMT	EXC
COMPLETE SET (22)	15.00	6.75	1.85

☐ 1 Craig Brooks
☐ 2 Bill Molony
☐ 3 Kevin Kane
☐ 4 Gene Gentile
☐ 5 Reggie Whittemore
☐ 6 Jim Wilson
☐ 7 Brian Denman
☐ 8 Tony Torchia
☐ 9 Dave Schoppee
☐ 10 Rick Colbert
☐ 11 Chuck Sandberg
☐ 12 Ed Jurak
☐ 13 Jerry King
☐ 14 Kenny Young
☐ 15 Jay Fredlund
☐ 16 Erwin Bryant
☐ 17 Steve Shields
☐ 18 Glenn Eddins
☐ 19 Dave Tyler
☐ 20 Clint Johnson
☐ 21 Dennis Burtt
☐ 22 Jim Watkins

1981 Buffalo Bisons TCMA

This 25-card standard-size set of the 1981 Buffalo Bisons, a Class AA Eastern League affiliate of the Pittsburgh Pirates, features white-bordered posed color player photos on its fronts. The player's name and position appear in red letters below the photo. The horizontal back carries the player's name, position, team, and league at the top, followed by biography and statistics.

	MINT	NRMT	EXC
COMPLETE SET (25)	10.00	4.50	1.25

☐ 1 John Lipon
☐ 2 John Holland
☐ 3 Doug Britt
☐ 4 Jose DeLeon
☐ 5 Ben Wiltbank
☐ 6 Benny DeLarosa
☐ 7 Drew Macauley
☐ 8 Carlos Ledezema
☐ 9 Stew Cliburn
☐ 10 Bob Rock
☐ 11 Rafael Vasquez
☐ 12 Dan Warthen
☐ 13 Jose Rodriquez
☐ 14 Billy Waag
☐ 15 Gary Hargis
☐ 16 Jose Calderon
☐ 17 Angel Barez
☐ 18 Steve Farr
☐ 19 Carlos Rios
☐ 20 Tony Incaviglia
☐ 21 Terry Salazar
☐ 22 Doug Frobel
☐ 23 Eddie Vargas
☐ 24 Frank Riccelli
☐ 25 Reggie Buchanan

1981 Burlington Bees TCMA

This 29-card standard-size set of the 1981 Burlington Bees, a Class A Midwest League affiliate of the Milwaukee Brewers, features white-bordered posed black-and-white player photos on its fronts. The player's name and position appear in black letters below the photo. The horizontal back carries the player's name, position, team, and league at the top, followed by biography and statistics.

	MINT	NRMT	EXC
COMPLETE SET (29)	35.00	16.00	4.40

☐ 1 Dave Morris
☐ 2 Vince Pone
☐ 3 Kevin McCoy
☐ 4 Steve Noewood
☐ 5 Gene Smith
☐ 6 Raymond Gallo
☐ 7 Craig Herberholz
☐ 9 Mark Lepson
☐ 10 Tim Crews
☐ 11 Steve Gibson
☐ 12 Johnson Wood
☐ 13 Murphy Su'a
☐ 14 Angel Morris
☐ 15 Henry Contreras
☐ 16 Steve Jordan
☐ 17 Randy Ready
☐ 18 Butch Kirby
☐ 19 Mike Samuel
☐ 20 Juan Castillo
☐ 21 Brad Dekraai
☐ 22 Carlos Ponce
☐ 23 Mark Higgins
☐ 24 Gerry Miller
☐ 25 Ronnie Jones
☐ 26 Karl McKay
☐ 27 Joel Parker
☐ 28 Bill Nowlan
☐ 29 Lawrence Avery
☐ 30 Terry Bevington

1981 Cedar Rapids Reds TCMA

This 26-card standard-size set of the 1981 Cedar Rapids Reds, a Class A Midwest League affiliate of the Cincinnati Reds, features white-bordered posed color player photos on its fronts. The player's name and position appear in red letters below the photo. The horizontal back carries the player's name, position, team, and league at the top, followed by biography and statistics.

	MINT	NRMT	EXC
COMPLETE SET (26)	35.00	16.00	4.40

☐ 1 Larry Jackson
☐ 2 Kurt Kepshire
☐ 3 Brad Lesley
☐ 4 Rick Myles
☐ 5 Mike Raines
☐ 6 Don Robinson
☐ 7 Mark Rothey
☐ 8 Ray Corbet
☐ 9 Dave Miley
☐ 10 Emil Drzavich
☐ 11 Kevin Hinds
☐ 12 Dave Hoenstine
☐ 13 Dean Seats
☐ 14 Mike Sorel
☐ 15 Tom Wesley
☐ 16 Jeff Jones
☐ 17 Ken Scarpace
☐ 18 Scott Terry
☐ 19 Randy Davidson
☐ 20 Don Buchheister
☐ 21 Jeff Clay
☐ 22 Mark Bowden
☐ 23 Bob Buchanan
☐ 24 Scott Ender
☐ 25 Greg McKinney
☐ 26 Dave Hall

1981 Charleston Charlies TCMA

This 24-card standard-size set of the 1981 Charleston Charlies, a Class AAA International League affiliate of the Cleveland Indians, features white-bordered posed color player photos on its fronts. The player's name and position appear in red letters below the photo. The horizontal back carries the player's name, position, team, and league at the top, followed by biography and statistics.

	MINT	NRMT	EXC
COMPLETE SET (24)	15.00	6.75	1.85

☐ 1 Tom Brennan
☐ 2 Bobby Cuellar
☐ 3 Gordy Glaser
☐ 4 Ed Glynn
☐ 5 Mike Paxton
☐ 6 Eric Wilkins
☐ 7 Sandy Wihtol
☐ 8 Chris Bando
☐ 9 Tim Norrid
☐ 10 Kenny Barton
☐ 11 Mike Bucci
☐ 12 Len Faedo
☐ 13 Mike Fischlin
☐ 14 Anglelo Logrande
☐ 15 Von Hayes
☐ 16 Odie Davis
☐ 17 Jim Lentine
☐ 18 Karl Pagel
☐ 19 Rodney Craig
☐ 20 Vassie Gardner
☐ 21 Mel Queen
☐ 22 Nate Puryear
☐ 23 Rob Pietroburgo
☐ 24 Cal Emery

1981 Charleston Royals TCMA

This 26-card standard-size set of the 1981 Charleston Royals, a Class A South Atlantic League affiliate of the Kansas City Royals, features white-bordered posed black-and-white player photos on its fronts. The player's name and position appear in black letters below the photo. The horizontal back carries the player's name, position, team, and league at the top, followed by biography and statistics.

	MINT	NRMT	EXC
COMPLETE SET (26)	15.00	6.75	1.85

☐ 1 Greg Johnson
☐ 2 Hector Arroyo
☐ 3 David Wong
☐ 4 Mike Olson
☐ 5 Hal Hatcher
☐ 6 Roger Hanson
☐ 7 Glenn Ray
☐ 8 Theo Shaw
☐ 9 Dave Albright
☐ 10 Bob Hegman
☐ 11 Fran Cutty
☐ 12 Doug Cook
☐ 13 Russell Stephans
☐ 14 Chuck McMichael
☐ 15 Ben Cadahia
☐ 16 Cliff Pastornicky
☐ 17 Jeff Gladden
☐ 18 Mark Huismann
☐ 19 Abner Johnson
☐ 20 Randy Meier
☐ 21 Bill Best
☐ 22 Larry Grahek
☐ 23 Rick Rizzo
☐ 24 Tad Venger
☐ 25 Willie Neal
☐ 26 Rick Mathews

1981 Chattanooga Lookouts TCMA

This 25-card standard-size set of the 1981 Chattanooga Lookouts, a Class AA Southern League affiliate of the Cleveland Indians, features white-bordered posed black-and-white player photos on its fronts. The player's name and position appear in black letters below the photo. The horizontal back carries the player's name, position, team, and league at the top, followed by biography and statistics. Approximately 1,100 sets were produced.

	MINT	NRMT	EXC
COMPLETE SET (25)	15.00	6.75	1.85

☐ 1 Robert Gariglio
☐ 2 John Burden
☐ 3 Robbie Alvarez
☐ 4 Luis Deleon
☐ 5 Steve Narleski
☐ 6 Matt Bullinger
☐ 7 Jack Nuismer
☐ 8 Steve Roche
☐ 9 Everett Rey
☐ 10 Todd Heimer
☐ 11 Tim Glass
☐ 12 Jeff Moronko
☐ 13 John Bohnet
☐ 14 George Cecchetti
☐ 15 Ricky Baker
☐ 16 Carmelo Castillo
☐ 17 Sal Rende
☐ 18 Rick Burchers
☐ 19 Chuck Stobbs
☐ 20 Craig Adams
☐ 21 Larry White
☐ 22 Jeff Tomski
☐ 23 Kevin Rhomberg

☐ 24 Woody Smith
☐ 25 Bud Anderson

1981 Clinton Giants TCMA

This 29-card standard-size set of the 1981 Clinton Giants, a Class A Midwest League affiliate of the San Francisco Giants, features white-bordered posed black-and-white player photos on its fronts. The player's name and position appear in black letters below the photo. The horizontal back carries the player's name, position, team, and league at the top, followed by biography and statistics.

	MINT	NRMT	EXC
COMPLETE SET (29)	10.00	4.50	1.25

☐ 1 Joe Banach
☐ 2 Wendell Kim
☐ 3 Steve Cline
☐ 4 Dave Wilhelmi
☐ 5 Bruce Oliver
☐ 6 Ben Gallo
☐ 7 Jose Chue
☐ 8 Art Gomez
☐ 9 Kevin May
☐ 10 Greg Bangert
☐ 11 Mark O'Connell
☐ 12 Matt Young
☐ 13 Dennis Schafer
☐ 14 Louis D'Amore
☐ 15 Gus Stokes
☐ 16 Kirk Ortega
☐ 17 John Taylor
☐ 18 Ken Frazier
☐ 19 James Johnson
☐ 20 Sean Toerner
☐ 21 Dave Wilson
☐ 22 Joe Henderson
☐ 23 Mike Lenti
☐ 24 Tom McLaughlin
☐ 25 Greg McSparron
☐ 26 Rollo Adams
☐ 27 Lance Junker
☐ 28 Rich Figueroa
☐ 29 Mark Tudor

1981 Columbus Clippers Police

	MINT	NRMT	EXC
COMPLETE SET (25)	10.00	4.50	1.25

☐ 2 Andre Robertson
☐ 6 Dan Schmitz
☐ 11 Buck Showalter
☐ 12 Tucker Ashford
☐ 13 Garry Smith
☐ 15 Rick Stenholm
☐ 17 Dave Coleman
☐ 21 Jim Lewis
☐ 22 Wayne Harer
☐ 23 Pat Callahan
☐ 24 Dave Righetti
☐ 25 Pat Tabler
☐ 26 Frank Verdi MG
☐ 27 Greg Cochran
☐ 28 Dave Wehrmeister
☐ 29 Juan Espino
☐ 30 John Pacella
☐ 31 Paul Boris
☐ 33 Marshall Brant
☐ 35 Brian Ryder
☐ 36 Mike Griffin
☐ 37 Steve Balboni
☐ NNO Coaches/Trainer
Sammy Ellis CO
Mark Letendre TR
Jerry McNertney CO
☐ NNO Sgt. Dick Hoover (Policeman)
☐ NNO George Sisler Jr. GM

1981 Columbus Clippers TCMA

This 28-card standard-size set of the 1981 Columbus Clippers, a Class AAA International League affiliate of the New York Yankees, features white-bordered posed color player photos on its fronts. The player's name and position appear in red letters below the photo. The horizontal back carries the player's name, position, team, and league at the top, followed by biography and statistics.

	MINT	NRMT	EXC
COMPLETE SET (28)	40.00	18.00	5.00

☐ 1 Dick Stenholm
☐ 2 Tucker Ashford
☐ 3 Andre Robertson
☐ 4 Pat Callahan
☐ 5 Danny Schmitz
☐ 6 Jim Lewis
☐ 7 Paul Boris
☐ 8 Andy McGaffigan
☐ 9 Dave Righetti
☐ 10 Mike Griffin
☐ 11 Steve Balboni
☐ 12 Greg Cochran
☐ 13 Marshall Brant
☐ 14 Brian Ryder
☐ 15 Juan Espino
☐ 16 Pat Tabler
☐ 17 Frank Verdi
☐ 18 Dave Coleman
☐ 19 Wayne Harer
☐ 20 Bill Showalter
☐ 21 Gary Smith
☐ 22 John Pacella
☐ 23 Dave Wehrmeister
☐ 24 Tom Filer
☐ 25 Mark Letenore
☐ 26 Sam Ellis
☐ 27 George H. Sisler
☐ 28 Jerry McNertney

1981 Durham Bulls TCMA

This 24-card standard-size set of the 1981 Durham Bulls, a Class A Carolina League affiliate of the Atlanta Braves, features white-bordered posed black-and-white player photos on its fronts. The player's name and position appear in black letters below the photo. The horizontal back carries the player's name, position, team, and league at the top, followed by biography and statistics.

	MINT	NRMT	EXC
COMPLETE SET (24)	20.00	9.00	2.50

☐ 1 Miguel Sosa
☐ 2 Mike Garcia
☐ 3 Kevin Rigby
☐ 4 Ken Scanlon
☐ 5 Tommy Thompson
☐ 6 Gary Cooper
☐ 7 Tom Hayes
☐ 8 Harold Williams
☐ 9 Keith Hagman
☐ 10 Brad Komminsk
☐ 11 Glen Buckhorn
☐ 12 Jeff Vuksan
☐ 13 Alvin Moore
☐ 14 Alan Gallagher
☐ 15 Rick Behenna
☐ 16 Rick Coatney
☐ 17 Jeff Dedmon
☐ 18 Glen Germer
☐ 19 Hoot Gibson
☐ 20 Danny Lucia
☐ 21 Roy North
☐ 22 Scott Patterson
☐ 23 Mike Payne
☐ 24 Gary Reiter

1981 Edmonton Trappers Red Rooster

	MINT	NRMT	EXC
COMPLETE SET (24)	10.00	4.50	1.25

☐ 1 Gary Holle
☐ 2 John Poff
☐ 3 Dan Williams
☐ 4 Nardi Contreras
☐ 5 Juan Agosto
☐ 6 Guy Hoffman
☐ 7 Chris Nyman
☐ 8 Gord Lund
☐ 9 Vern Thomas
☐ 10 Rich Barnes
☐ 11 John Flannery
☐ 12 Bill Atkinson
☐ 13 Hector Eduardo
☐ 14 Leo Sutherland
☐ 15 Ray Murillo
☐ 16 Joe Gates
☐ 17 Julio Perez
☐ 18 Marv Foley
☐ 19 Mike Colbern
☐ 20 Fran Mullins
☐ 21 Rod Allen
☐ 22 Reggie Patterson
☐ 23 Jay Loviglio
☐ 24 Mark Teutsch

1981 El Paso Diablos TCMA

This 24-card standard-size set of the 1981 El Paso Diablos, a Class AA Texas League affiliate of the Milwaukee Brewers, features white-bordered posed color player photos on its fronts. The player's name and position appear in red letters below the photo. The horizontal back carries the player's name, position, team, and league at the top, followed by biography and statistics.

	MINT	NRMT	EXC
COMPLETE SET (24)	15.00	6.75	1.85

☐ 1 Ed Irvine
☐ 2 Willie Lozado
☐ 3 Al Manning
☐ 4 John Skorochocki
☐ 5 Terry Shoebridge
☐ 6 Stan Davis
☐ 7 Jerry Lane
☐ 8 Doug Loman
☐ 9 Gerry Ako
☐ 10 Jim Koontz
☐ 11 Doug Jones
☐ 12 Larry Montgomery
☐ 13 Bill Schroeder
☐ 14 Mike Madden
☐ 15 Bob Skube
☐ 16 Chick Valley
☐ 17 Rick Kranitz
☐ 18 Tony Torres
☐ 19 Weldon Swift
☐ 20 Tim Cook
☐ 21 Johnny Evans
☐ 22 Tom Candiotti
☐ 23 Tony Muser
☐ 24 Al Price

1981 Evansville Triplets TCMA

This 22-card standard-size set of the 1981 Evansville Triplets, a Class AAA American Association affiliate of the Detroit Tigers, features white-bordered posed color player photos on its fronts. The player's name and position appear in red letters below the photo. The horizontal back carries the player's name, position, team, and league at the top, followed by biography and statistics.

	MINT	NRMT	EXC
COMPLETE SET (22)	15.00	6.75	1.85

☐ 1 Jim Leyland
☐ 2 George Cappuzzello
☐ 3 Mike Chris
☐ 4 Mark Fidrych
☐ 5 Larry Pashnick
☐ 6 Larry Rothschild
☐ 7 Manny Seoane
☐ 8 Jerry Ujdur
☐ 9 Pat Underwood
☐ 10 Roger Weaver
☐ 11 Marty Castillo
☐ 12 Larry Johnson
☐ 13 Mark DeJohn
☐ 14 Vern Followell
☐ 15 Glenn Gulliver
☐ 16 Craig Kusick
☐ 17 Juan Lopez
☐ 18 Tim Corcoran
☐ 19 Les Filkins
☐ 20 Eddie Gates
☐ 21 Ken Houston
☐ 22 Dennis Kinney

1981 Glens Falls White Sox TCMA

This 24-card standard-size set of the 1981 Glens Falls White Sox, a Class AA Eastern League affiliate of the Chicago White Sox, features white-bordered posed color player photos on its fronts. The player's name and position appear in red letters below the photo. The horizontal back carries the player's name, position, team, and league at the top, followed by biography and statistics.

	MINT	NRMT	EXC
COMPLETE SET(24)	30.00	13.50	3.70

☐ 1 Luis Estrada
☐ 2 Randy Evans
☐ 3 Robert Fallon
☐ 4 Chuck Johnson
☐ 5 Mickey Maitland
☐ 6 Tom Mullen
☐ 7 Dennis Vasquez
☐ 8 Richard Wieters
☐ 9 Ricky Seilheimer
☐ 10 Andy Pasillas
☐ 11 Dom Fucci
☐ 12 Tim Hulett
☐ 13 Ivan Mesa
☐ 14 Peter Peltz
☐ 15 Ron Perry
☐ 16 Greg Walker
☐ 17 Vince Bienex
☐ 18 Randy Johnson
☐ 19 Ron Kittle
☐ 20 Luis Rois
☐ 21 Raymundo Torres
☐ 22 Jim Mahoney
☐ 23 Len Bradley
☐ 24 Larry Edwards

1981 Hawaii Islanders TCMA

This 23-card standard-size set of the 1981 Hawaii Islanders, a Class AAA Pacific Coast League affiliate of the San Diego Padres, features white-bordered posed color player photos on its fronts. The player's name and position appear in red letters below the photo. The horizontal back carries the player's name, position, team, and league at the top, followed by biography and statistics.

	MINT	NRMT	EXC
COMPLETE SET (23)	10.00	4.50	1.25

☐ 1 Tim Flannery
☐ 2 Jose Moreno
☐ 3 Gary Ashby
☐ 4 Steve Smith
☐ 5 Doug Gwosdz
☐ 6 Tony Castillo
☐ 7 Jim Beswick
☐ 8 Alan Wiggins
☐ 9 Rick Lancellotti
☐ 10 Curtis Reed
☐ 11 Mike Armstrong
☐ 12 Steve Fireovid
☐ 13 Alan Olmsted
☐ 14 George Stablein
☐ 15 Tom Tellman
☐ 16 Kim Seaman
☐ 17 Fred Kuhualua
☐ 18 Floyd Chiffer
☐ 19 Eric Show
☐ 20 Larry Duensing
☐ 21 Doug Rader
☐ 22 Chuck Hartenstein
☐ 23 Mario Ramirez

1981 Holyoke Millers TCMA

This 26-card standard-size set of the 1981 Holyoke Millers, a Class AA Eastern League affiliate of the California Angels, features white-bordered posed color player photos on its fronts. The player's name and position appear in red letters below the photo. The horizontal back carries the player's name, position, team, and league at the top, followed by biography and statistics.

	MINT	NRMT	EXC
COMPLETE SET (26)	15.00	6.75	1.85

☐ 1 Ed Rodriguez
☐ 2 Jim Saul
☐ 3 Tom Kayser
☐ 4 T.J. Byrne
☐ 5 Dave Thomas
Dave Comforti
☐ 6 John Yandle
☐ 7 Ricky Adams
☐ 8 Mike Brown
☐ 9 Chris Clark
☐ 10 Dennis Gilbert
☐ 11 Curt Brown
☐ 12 Jeff Connor
☐ 13 Lonnie Dugger
☐ 14 Dave Durna
☐ 15 Rick Foley
☐ 16 Pat Keedy
☐ 17 Darrell Miller
☐ 18 Mark Nocciolo
☐ 19 Les Pearsey
☐ 20 Gary Pettis
☐ 21 Gustavo Polidor
☐ 22 Brandt Humphry
☐ 23 Bill Moonyham
☐ 24 Perry Morrison
☐ 25 Dennis Rasmussen
☐ 26 Rick Rommell

1981 Indianapolis Indians Team Issue

	MINT	NRMT	EXC
COMPLETE SET (32)	25.00	11.00	3.10

☐ 1 Team Picture
☐ 2 Jim Beauchamp MG
☐ 3 Geoff Combe
☐ 4 Paul Householder
☐ 5 Charlie Leibrandt
☐ 6 Dave Van Gorder
☐ 7 Tom Foley
☐ 8 Kip Young
☐ 9 Eddie Milner
☐ 10 The Relievers
☐ 11 Jose Brito
☐ 12 Greg Mahlberg
☐ 13 Bill Bonham
☐ 14 The Teachers
☐ 15 Nick Esasky
☐ 16 Jeff Lahti
☐ 17 The Lightning Squad
☐ 18 Gene Menees
☐ 19 Scott Brown
☐ 20 The Outfielders
☐ 21 Duane Walker
☐ 22 Bill Kelly
☐ 23 The Infielders
☐ 24 Joe Kerrigan
☐ 25 German Barranca
☐ 26 The Starters
☐ 27 Paul Herring
☐ 28 Bill Dawley
☐ 29 Skeeter Barnes
☐ 30 The Catchers
☐ 31 Sergio Ferrer
☐ 32 John Young TR

1981 Lynn Sailors TCMA

This 29-card standard-size set of the 1981 Lynn Sailors, a Class AA Eastern League affiliate of the Seattle Mariners, features white-bordered posed color player photos on its fronts. The player's name and position appear in red letters below the photo. The horizontal back carries the player's name, position, team, and league at the top, followed by biography and statistics.

	MINT	NRMT	EXC
COMPLETE SET (29)	25.00	11.00	3.10

□ 1 Karl Best
□ 2 Bud Black
□ 3 Mark Cahill
□ 4 Joe Georger
□ 5 Tracy Harris
□ 6 R.J. Harrison
□ 7 Steve Krueger
□ 8 Jed Murray
□ 9 Dave Sheriff
□ 10 Rob Simond
□ 11 Dave Smith
□ 12 Matt Young
□ 13 Jim Nelson
□ 14 Dave Valle
□ 15 Edwin Aponte
□ 16 Billy Crone
□ 17 Mario Diaz
□ 18 Paul Serna
□ 19 Mike White
□ 20 Al Chambers
□ 21 Ramon Estepa
□ 22 Rodney Hobbs
□ 23 Tito Nanni
□ 24 Bobby Floyd MGR
□ 25 Mickey Bowers CO
□ 26 Lloyd D. Kern PRES
□ 26 Bob Randolph
□ 27 Jeff Stottlemyre
□ 28 Clark Crist

1981 Miami Orioles TCMA

This 23-card standard-size set of the 1981 Miami Orioles, a Class A Florida State League affiliate of the Baltimore Orioles, features white-bordered posed black-and-white player photos on its fronts. The player's name and position appear in black letters below the photo. The horizontal back carries the player's name, position, team, and league at the top, followed by biography and statistics.

	MINT	NRMT	EXC
COMPLETE SET (21)	10.00	4.50	1.25
COMPLETE SET W/22/23 (23)	125.00	55.00	15.50

□ 1 Ron Dillard
□ 2 Al Pardo
□ 3 Freddie Smith
□ 4 Mark Brown
□ 5 Don Murelli
□ 6 Minnie Mendoza
□ 7 John Deleon
□ 8 Pat Dumouchelle
□ 9 Satch Sanders
□ 10 Francisco Oliveras
□ 11 Mike Alvarez
□ 12 Skip Clark
□ 13 Andy Timko
□ 14 Frank Ferroni
□ 15 Lonnie Ivie
□ 16 Neal Herrick
□ 17 Leon Hoke
□ 18 Tim Maples
□ 19 Jeff Williams
□ 20 Bret Gold
□ 21 Scott Johnson
□ 22 Chris Willsher
□ 23 Mike Young

1981 Nashville Sounds Team Issue

	MINT	NRMT	EXC
COMPLETE SET (25)	25.00	11.00	3.10

□ 1 Rod Boxberger
□ 2 Pat Callahan
□ 3 Nate Chapman
□ 4 Brian Dayett
□ 5 Dan Hanggie
□ 6 Curt Kaufman
□ 7 Dan Led Duke
□ 8 Don Mattingly
□ 9 Willie McGee
□ 10 Mike Morgan
□ 11 Otis Nixon
□ 12 Erik Peterson
□ 13 Brian Poldberg
□ 14 Bob Jamison
□ 15 Frank Ricci
□ 16 Wes Robbins
□ 17 Buck Showalter
□ 18 Roger Slagle
□ 19 Jeff Taylor
□ 20 Steve Taylor
□ 21 Rafael Villaman
□ 22 Jamie Werly
□ 23 Ted Wilborn
□ 24 Manager,Trainer and Coaches
□ 25 Team Photo

1981 Oklahoma City 89ers TCMA

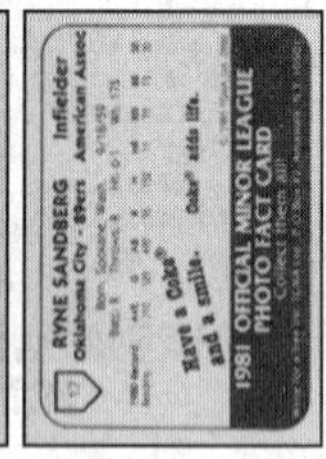

This 26-card standard-size set of the 1981 Oklahoma City 89ers, a Class AAA American Association affiliate of the Philadelphia Phillies, features white-bordered posed color player photos on its fronts. The player's name and position appear in red letters below the photo. The horizontal back carries the player's name, position, team, and league at the top, followed by biography and statistics. This issue includes a second year card of Ryne Sandberg. Approximately 3,500 sets were produced.

	MINT	NRMT	EXC
COMPLETE SET (26)	150.00	70.00	19.00

□ 1 Porfirio Altamirano
□ 2 Carlos Arroyo
□ 3 Eli Bonaparte
□ 4 Warren Brusstar
□ 5 Bob Dernier
□ 6 Mark Davis
□ 7 Dan Larson
□ 8 Orlando Isales
□ 9 Don McCormack
□ 10 Lenny Matuszek
□ 11 Dennis Miscik
□ 12 Manny McDonald
□ 13 Scott Munninghoff
□ 14 Dickie Noles
□ 15 John Reelhorn
□ 16 Luis Rodriguez
□ 17 Ryne Sandberg
□ 18 Bill Suter
□ 19 Osvaldo Virgil
□ 20 George Vukovich
□ 21 Bob Demeo
□ 22 Ellis Deal
□ 23 Jim Snyder
□ 24 Jose Castro
□ 25 Jim Rasmussen
□ 26 Jeff Ulrich

1981 Omaha Royals TCMA

This 24-card standard-size set of the 1981 Omaha Royals, a Class AAA American Association affiliate of the Kansas City Royals, features white-bordered posed color player photos on its fronts. The player's name and position appear in red letters below the photo. The horizontal back carries the player's name, position, team, and league at the top, followed by biography and statistics.

	MINT	NRMT	EXC
COMPLETE SET (24)	15.00	6.75	1.85

□ 1 Joe Sparks
□ 2 Jerry Cram
□ 3 Paul McGannon
□ 4 Craig Chamberlain
□ 5 Gary Christenson
□ 6 Atlee Hammaker
□ 7 Dan Fischer
□ 8 Don Hood
□ 9 Mike Jones
□ 10 Bill Laskey
□ 11 Bill Paschall
□ 12 Jeff Schattinger
□ 13 Jim Gaudet
□ 14 Greg Keatly
□ 15 Manny Castillo
□ 16 Onix Concepcion
□ 17 Kelly Heath
□ 18 Tim Ireland
□ 19 Ron Johnson
□ 20 Jim Buckner
□ 21 Bob Detherage
□ 22 Darryl Motley
□ 23 Bombo Rivera
□ 24 Pat Sheridan

1981 Pawtucket Red Sox TCMA

This 24-card standard-size set of the 1981 Pawtucket Red Sox, a Class AAA International League affiliate of the Boston Red Sox, features white-bordered posed color player photos on its fronts. The

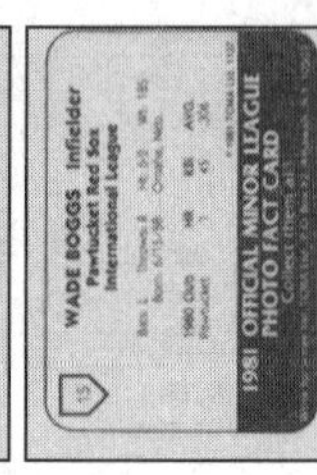

player's name and position appear in red letters below the photo. The horizontal back carries the player's name, position, team, and league at the top, followed by biography and statistics. This issue includes the only minor league card of Wade Boggs. Approximately 3,500 sets were produced.

	MINT	NRMT	EXC
COMPLETE SET (24)	150.00	70.00	19.00

□ 1 Joel Finch
□ 2 Mike Howard
□ 3 Bruce Hurst
□ 4 Keith MacWhorter
□ 5 Bob Ojeda
□ 6 Danny Parks
□ 7 Win Remmerswaal
□ 8 Luis Aponte
□ 9 Jim Dorsey
□ 10 Manny Sarmiento
□ 11 Mike Smithson
□ 12 Joe Morgan
□ 13 Dale Robertson
□ 14 Marty Barrett
□ 15 Wade Boggs
□ 16 Dave Koza
□ 17 Julio Valdez
□ 18 Sam Bowen
□ 19 Lee Graham
□ 20 Russ Laribee
□ 21 Mike Ongarato
□ 22 Chico Walker
□ 23 Roger LaFrancois
□ 24 Rich Gedman

1981 Phoenix Giants Valley National Bank

	MINT	NRMT	EXC
COMPLETE SET (27)	10.00	4.50	1.25

□ 1 Phoenix Booster Rooster CL
□ 2 Harry Jordan
□ 3 Bob Tufts
□ 4 Bob Brenly
□ 5 Jeff Stember
□ 6 Max Venable
□ 7 Doug Schaefer
□ 8 Mike Williams
□ 9 Mark Calvert
□ 10 Mike Rowland
□ 11 Mike Rex
□ 12 Jose Barrios
□ 13 Al Hargesheimer
□ 14 Dave Wiggins
□ 15 Guy Sularz
□ 16 Tommy Jones
□ 17 Phil Hinrichs
□ 18 Dennis Littlejohn
□ 19 Wayne Pechek
□ 20 Gene Pentz
□ 21 Joe Pettini
□ 22 Jeff Ranson
□ 23 Tom Runnells
□ 24 Rich Murray
□ 25 Rocky Bridges
□ 26 Tommy Gonzales
□ 27 Ethan Blackaby

1981 Portland Beavers TCMA

This 27-card standard-size set of the 1981 Portland Beavers, a Class AAA Pacific Coast League affiliate of the Pittsburgh Pirates, features white-bordered posed color player photos on its fronts. The player's name and position appear in red letters below the photo. The horizontal back carries the player's name, position, team, and league at the top, followed by biography and statistics.

	MINT	NRMT	EXC
COMPLETE SET (27)	10.00	4.50	1.25

□ 1 Pete Ward
□ 2 Tom Trebelhorn
□ 3 Santo Alcala
□ 4 Matt Alexander
□ 5 Mike Anderson
□ 6 Dave Augustine
□ 7 Bob Beall
□ 8 Doe Boyland
□ 9 Craig Cacek
□ 10 Cecilio Guante
□ 11 Dave Hilton
□ 12 Willie Horton
□ 13 Odell Jones
□ 14 Vance Law
□ 15 Mark Lee
□ 16 Robert Long
□ 17 Dale Mohorcic
□ 18 Bobby Mitchell
□ 19 Junior Ortiz
□ 20 Pascual Perez
□ 21 Tommy Sandt
□ 22 Jimmy Smith
□ 23 Luis Tiant
□ 24 Alfredo Torres
□ 25 Rusty Torres
□ 26 Eleno Cuen
□ 27 Kent Biggerstaff

1981 Quad City Cubs TCMA

This 33-card standard-size set of the 1981 Quad City Cubs, a Class A Midwest League affiliate of the Chicago Cubs, features white-bordered posed black-and-white player photos on its fronts. The player's name and position appear in black letters below the photo. The horizontal back carries the player's name, position, team, and league at the top, followed by biography and statistics.

	MINT	NRMT	EXC
COMPLETE SET (33)	10.00	4.50	1.25

□ 1 Dave Pagel
□ 2 Don Hyman
□ 3 Greg Tarnow
□ 4 Rusty Piggot
□ 5 Fritz Connally
□ 6 Mike Buckley
□ 7 Shane Allen
□ 8 Mickey Tenney
□ 9 Dennis Webb
□ 10 Kevin Schoendienst
□ 11 Jim Walsh
□ 12 Terry Austin
□ 13 Tom Johnson
□ 14 Gary Monroe
□ 15 Henry Cotto
□ 16 Dan Cataline
□ 17 Mike King
□ 18 Tom Smith
□ 19 Stan Kyles
□ 20 Joe Housey
□ 21 John Miglio
□ 22 Ken Pryce
□ 23 Ray Soff
□ 24 Mark Vaji
□ 25 Glenn Swaggerty
□ 26 Craig Weissman
□ 27 Jim Gerlach
□ 28 Mark Wilkins
□ 29 Don Schultze
□ 30 Rich Morales
□ 31 Gene Oliver
□ 32 Roger Crow
□ 33 Mike Palmer

1981 Reading Phillies TCMA

This 24-card standard-size set of the 1981 Reading Phillies, a Class AA Eastern League affiliate of the Philadelphia Phillies, features white-bordered posed black-and-white player photos on its fronts. The player's name and position appear in black letters below the photo. The horizontal back carries the player's name, position, team, and league at the top, followed by biography and statistics.

	MINT	NRMT	EXC
COMPLETE SET (24)	120.00	55.00	15.00

□ 1 Jerry Reed
□ 2 Kelly Faulk
□ 3 Tom Hart
□ 4 Darren Burroughs
□ 5 Dan Prior
□ 6 Miguel Alicea
□ 7 Leroy Smith
□ 8 Don Carman
□ 9 Carlos Cabassa
□ 10 Wally Goff
□ 11 Herb Orensky
□ 12 Miguel Ibarra
□ 13 Jim Wright
□ 14 Russ Hamric
□ 15 Ron Smith
□ 16 Tom Lombarski
□ 17 Julio Franco
□ 18 Ray Borucki
□ 19 Keith Washington
□ 20 Joe Bruno
□ 21 Wil Culmer
□ 22 Al Sanchez
□ 23 Ron Clark
□ 24 George Culver

1981 Redwood Pioneers TCMA

This 30-card standard-size set of the 1981 Redwood Pioneers, a Class A California League affiliate of the California Angels, features white-bordered posed black-and-white photos on its fronts. The player's name and position appear in black letters below the photo. The horizontal back carries the player's name, position, team, and league at the top, followed by biography and statistics.

	MINT	NRMT	EXC
COMPLETE SET (30)	15.00	6.75	1.85

- ☐ 1 Robert Bastian
- ☐ 2 Brian Buckley
- ☐ 3 Tom Crisler
- ☐ 4 Jay Kibbe
- ☐ 5 Ron Romanick
- ☐ 6 Jeff Smith
- ☐ 7 Ron Sylvia
- ☐ 8 Mike Venezia
- ☐ 9 Doug Rau
- ☐ 10 Aldo Bagiotti
- ☐ 11 Duffy Ryan
- ☐ 12 Wade Schexnayder
- ☐ 13 Harry Francis
- ☐ 14 Matt Gundelfinger
- ☐ 15 Ron Hunt
- ☐ 16 Marion Hunter
- ☐ 17 Tim Krauss
- ☐ 18 Mark Sproesser
- ☐ 19 Leo Lemon
- ☐ 20 Ken Tillman
- ☐ 21 Luis Zambrana
- ☐ 22 Warren Spahn
- ☐ 23 Tom Leonard
- ☐ 24 Kathy Leonard
- ☐ 25 David Levinson
- ☐ 26 Ralph Hartman
- ☐ 27 Chris Bankowski
- ☐ 28 Chris Cannizzaro
- ☐ 29 Barton Braun
- ☐ 30 Steve Levinson

1981 Richmond Braves TCMA

This 25-card standard-size set of the 1981 Richmond Braves, a Class AAA International League affiliate of the Atlanta Braves, features white-bordered posed color player photos on its fronts. The player's name and position appear in red letters below the photo. The horizontal back carries the player's name, position, team, and league at the top, followed by biography and statistics.

	MINT	NRMT	EXC
COMPLETE SET (25)	30.00	13.50	3.70

- ☐ 1 John Sain
- ☐ 2 Tony Brizzolara
- ☐ 3 Jerry Keller
- ☐ 4 Ken Smith
- ☐ 5 Craig Landis
- ☐ 6 Larry Whisenton
- ☐ 7 Bob Porter
- ☐ 8 Brett Butler
- ☐ 9 Chico Ruiz
- ☐ 10 Paul Runge
- ☐ 11 Butch Edge
- ☐ 12 Steve Bedrosian
- ☐ 13 Carlos Diaz
- ☐ 14 Larry McWilliams
- ☐ 15 Jose Alvarez
- ☐ 16 Steve Hammond
- ☐ 17 Steve Curry
- ☐ 18 Dan O'Brien
- ☐ 19 Ken Dayley
- ☐ 20 Matt Sinatro
- ☐ 21 Eddie Haas
- ☐ 22 Randy Johnson
- ☐ 23 Craig Robinson
- ☐ 24 Harry Saferight
- ☐ 25 Sam Ayoub

1981 Rochester Red Wings TCMA

This 23-card standard-size set of the 1981 Rochester Red Wings, a Class AAA International League affiliate of the Baltimore Orioles, features white-bordered posed color player photos on its fronts. The player's name and position appear in red letters below the photo. The horizontal back carries the player's name, position, team, and league at the top, followed by biography and statistics. This issue includes a second year card of Cal Ripken Jr. Approximately 3,500 sets were produced.

	MINT	NRMT	EXC
COMPLETE SET (25)	400.00	180.00	50.00

- ☐ 1 Mike Boddicker
- ☐ 2 Bill Bonner
- ☐ 3 Brooks Carey
- ☐ 4 Tom Chism
- ☐ 5 Tom Eaton
- ☐ 6 Johnny Hale
- ☐ 7 Mike Hart
- ☐ 8 Drungo Hazewood
- ☐ 9 Dave Huppert
- ☐ 10 Kevin Kennedy
- ☐ 11 Dan Logan
- ☐ 12 Steve Luebber
- ☐ 13 Ed Putnam
- ☐ 14 Floyd Rayford
- ☐ 15 Cal Ripken Jr.
- ☐ 16 Tom Rowe
- ☐ 17 John Valle
- ☐ 18 Don Welchel
- ☐ 19 Larry Jones
- ☐ 20 Richie Bancells TR
- ☐ 21 Chris Bourjos
- ☐ 22 Doc Edwards MGR
- ☐ 23 Dallas Williams

1981 Rochester Red Wings WTF

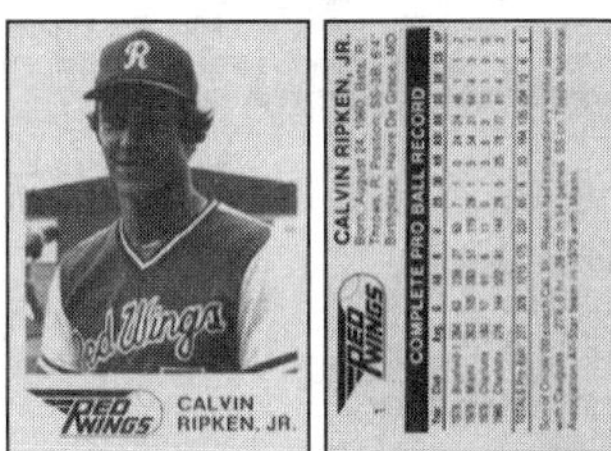

This 25-card standard-size set of the 1981 Rochester Red Wings, a Class AAA International League affiliate of the Baltimore Orioles, features white-bordered posed black-and-white player photos on its fronts. This issue includes a second year card of Cal Ripken Jr.

	MINT	NRMT	EXC
COMPLETE SET (25)	500.00	220.00	60.00

- ☐ 1 Cal Ripken Jr.
- ☐ 2 Dallas Williams
- ☐ 3 Chris Bourjos
- ☐ 4 Mark Corey
- ☐ 5 Doc Edwards
- ☐ 6 Tom Rowe
- ☐ 7 Jeff Schneider
- ☐ 8 Jim Umbarger
- ☐ 9 Don Welchel
- ☐ 10 Larry Jones
- ☐ 11 Dan Logan
- ☐ 12 Steve Luebber
- ☐ 13 Ed Putman
- ☐ 14 Floyd Rayford
- ☐ 15 Dave Huppert
- ☐ 16 Drungo Hazewood
- ☐ 17 James Hart
- ☐ 18 John Hale
- ☐ 19 Tom Eaton
- ☐ 20 Team Photo
- ☐ 21 Bob Bonner
- ☐ 22 Brooks Carey
- ☐ 23 Mike Boddicker
- ☐ 24 Thomas Chism
- ☐ 25 Silver Stadium

1981 Salt Lake City Gulls TCMA

This 26-card standard-size set of the 1981 Salt Lake City Gulls, a Class AAA Pacific Coast League affiliate of the Seattle Mariners, features white-bordered posed color player photos on its fronts. The player's name and position appear in red letters below the photo. The horizontal back carries the player's name, position, team, and league at the top, followed by biography and statistics.

	MINT	NRMT	EXC
COMPLETE SET (26)	15.00	6.75	1.85

- ☐ 1 Leonard Garcia
- ☐ 2 Ralph Botting
- ☐ 3 Steve Brown
- ☐ 4 Craig Eaton
- ☐ 5 Bob Ferris
- ☐ 6 Dave Frost
- ☐ 7 Christian Knapp
- ☐ 8 Mike Mahler
- ☐ 9 Alfredo Martinez
- ☐ 10 Carlos Perez
- ☐ 11 Dave Schuler
- ☐ 12 Ricky Steirer
- ☐ 13 Mike Walters
- ☐ 14 Mike Bishop
- ☐ 15 Brian Harper
- ☐ 16 Jeff Bertoni
- ☐ 17 Scott Carnes
- ☐ 18 Fernando Gonzales
- ☐ 19 Steve Lubratich
- ☐ 20 Daryl Sconiers
- ☐ 21 Tom Brunansky
- ☐ 22 Pepe Mangual
- ☐ 23 Scott Moffitt
- ☐ 24 Don Pisker
- ☐ 25 Moose Stubing
- ☐ 26 Bob Davis

1981 Shreveport Captains TCMA

This 23-card standard-size set of the 1981 Shreveport Captains, a Class AA Texas League affiliate of the San Francisco Giants, features white-bordered posed black-and-white player photos on its fronts. The player's name and position appear in black letters below the photo. The horizontal back carries the player's name, position, team, and league at the top, followed by biography and statistics.

	MINT	NRMT	EXC
COMPLETE SET (23)	20.00	9.00	2.50

- ☐ 1 Jack Mull
- ☐ 2 John Rabb
- ☐ 3 Jim Dunn
- ☐ 4 Tom O'Malley
- ☐ 5 Jim Wojcik
- ☐ 6 Glenn Fisher
- ☐ 7 Alan Fowlkes
- ☐ 8 Mike Tucker
- ☐ 9 Dan Gladden
- ☐ 10 Brad Bauman
- ☐ 11 Mark Dempsey
- ☐ 12 Paul Szymarek
- ☐ 13 Jim Duffalo
- ☐ 14 Doug Landuyt
- ☐ 15 Doran Perdue
- ☐ 16 Greg Baker
- ☐ 17 Ron Quick
- ☐ 18 Doug Wabeke
- ☐ 19 Jim Rothford
- ☐ 20 Scott Garrelts
- ☐ 21 Mark Lohuis
- ☐ 22 Greg Moyer
- ☐ 23 Pat Alexander

1981 Spokane Indians TCMA

This 32-card standard-size set of the 1981 Spokane Indians, a Class AAA Pacific Coast League affiliate of the Seattle Mariners, features white-bordered posed color player photos on its fronts. The player's name and position appear in red letters below the photo. The horizontal back carries the player's name, position, team, and league at the top, followed by biography and statistics.

	MINT	NRMT	EXC
COMPLETE SET (32)	10.00	4.50	1.25

- ☐ 1 Chris Flammang
- ☐ 2 Manny Estrada
- ☐ 3 Scott Stranski
- ☐ 4 Sam Welborn
- ☐ 5 Orlando Mercado
- ☐ 6 Roy Clark
- ☐ 7 Mike Hart
- ☐ 8 Greg Biercevicz
- ☐ 9 Bob Galasso
- ☐ 10 Brain Allard
- ☐ 11 Steve Finch
- ☐ 12 Doug Merrifield
- ☐ 13 Rene Lachemann
- ☐ 14 Reggie Walton
- ☐ 15 Ed Vande Berg
- ☐ 16 Ted Cox
- ☐ 17 Ron Musselman
- ☐ 18 Bob Stoddard
- ☐ 19 Joe Coleman
- ☐ 20 Vance McHenry
- ☐ 21 Ken Page
- ☐ 22 Jim Mahler
- ☐ 23 Larry Patterson
- ☐ 24 Randy Stein
- ☐ 25 Allen Wirth
- ☐ 26 Casey Parsons
- ☐ 27 Kim Allen
- ☐ 28 Rich Anderson
- ☐ 29 Jim Beattie
- ☐ 30 Brad Gulden
- ☐ 31 Jamie Allen
- ☐ 32 Marty Martinez

1981 Syracuse Chiefs TCMA

This 24-card standard-size set of the 1981 Syracuse Chiefs, a Class AAA International League affiliate of the Toronto Blue Jays, features white-bordered posed color player photos on its fronts. The player's name and position appear in red letters below the photo. The horizontal back carries the player's name, position, team, and league at the top, followed by biography and statistics.

	MINT	NRMT	EXC
COMPLETE SET (24)	10.00	4.50	1.25

- ☐ 1 Steve Baker
- ☐ 2 Tom Brown
- ☐ 3 Chuck Fore
- ☐ 4 Steve Grilli
- ☐ 5 Phil Huffman
- ☐ 6 Jack Kucek
- ☐ 7 Dale Murray
- ☐ 8 Kevin Pasley
- ☐ 9 Geno Petralli
- ☐ 10 Ramon Lora
- ☐ 11 Dave Baker
- ☐ 12 Charlie Beamon
- ☐ 13 Keith Chapman
- ☐ 14 Mike Davis
- ☐ 15 Pedro Hernandez
- ☐ 16 Greg Wells
- ☐ 17 Joe Cannon
- ☐ 18 Gil Kubski
- ☐ 19 Crieghton Telvin
- ☐ 20 Marv Thompson
- ☐ 21 Ken Schrom
- ☐ 22 Dave Tomlin
- ☐ 23 Bob Humphreys MG
- ☐ 24 Tony DeRosa TR

1981 Syracuse Chiefs Team Issue

Cards measure 3 1/2" by 5" and the backs are blank.

	MINT	NRMT	EXC
COMPLETE SET (24)	75.00	34.00	9.50

- ☐ 1 Dave Baker
- ☐ 2 Steve Baker
- ☐ 3 Charlie Beamon
- ☐ 4 Tom Brown
- ☐ 5 J.J. Cannon
- ☐ 6 Kelvin Chapman
- ☐ 7 Steve Davis
- ☐ 8 Chuck Fore
- ☐ 9 Pedro Hernandez
- ☐ 10 Phil Huffman
- ☐ 11 Bob Humphreys
- ☐ 12 Jack Kucek
- ☐ 13 Ramon Lora
- ☐ 14 Paul Mirabella
- ☐ 15 Dale Murray
- ☐ 16 Geno Petralli
- ☐ 17 Domingo Ramos
- ☐ 18 Ken Schrom
- ☐ 19 Creighton Tevlin
- ☐ 20 Marv Thompson
- ☐ 21 Dave Tomlin
- ☐ 22 Greg Wells
- ☐ 23 Dan Whitmer
- ☐ 24 Jim Wright

1981 Tacoma Tigers TCMA

This 32-card standard-size set of the 1981 Tacoma Tigers, a Class AAA Pacific Coast League affiliate of the Oakland Athletics, features white-bordered posed color player photos on its fronts. The player's name and position appear in red letters below the photo. The horizontal back carries the player's name, position, team, and league at the top, followed by biography and statistics.

	MINT	NRMT	EXC
COMPLETE SET (32)	10.00	4.50	1.25

- ☐ 1 Larry Davis
- ☐ 2 Rick Randahl
- ☐ 3 Art Popham
- ☐ 4 Eric Mustad
- ☐ 5 Bob Kearney
- ☐ 6 Ed Nottle
- ☐ 7 Pat Dempsey
- ☐ 8 Dave Hamilton
- ☐ 9 Derek Bryant
- ☐ 10 Rich Bordi
- ☐ 11 Mike Davis
- ☐ 12 Jim Nettles
- ☐ 13 Mark Budaska
- ☐ 14 Don Fowler
- ☐ 15 Jim Sexton
- ☐ 16 Paul Mize
- ☐ 17 Keith Drumright
- ☐ 18 Kelvin Moore
- ☐ 19 Jeff Cox
- ☐ 20 Roy Thomas
- ☐ 21 Fred Holdsworth
- ☐ 22 Mark Souza
- ☐ 23 Rick Lysander
- ☐ 24 Dave Beard
- ☐ 25 Kevin Bell
- ☐ 26 Dave Heaverlo
- ☐ 27 Bob Grandas
- ☐ 28 Tiger Mascot
- ☐ 29 Charlie Harigen
  Ted Henderson
  Shawn Holland
- ☐ 30 Stan Naccarato
- ☐ 31 Jim Perry
- ☐ 32 Ed Figueroa

1981 Tidewater Tides TCMA

This 29-card standard-size set of the 1981 Tidewater Tides, a Class AAA International League affiliate of the New York Mets, features white-bordered posed color player photos on its fronts. The player's name and position appear in red letters below the photo. The horizontal back carries the player's name, position, team, and league at the top, followed by biography and statistics. Approximately 3,000 sets were produced.

	MINT	NRMT	EXC
COMPLETE SET (29)	15.00	6.75	1.85

- ☐ 1 Rick Sweet
- ☐ 2 Bruce Bochy
- ☐ 3 Ronald McDonald
- ☐ 4 Brian Giles

- ☐ 5 Ron Gardenhire
- ☐ 6 Phil Mankowski
- ☐ 7 Todd Einterfeldt
- ☐ 8 Wally Backman
- ☐ 9 Gary Rajsich
- ☐ 10 Sergio Beltre
- ☐ 11 Gil Flores
- ☐ 12 Mike Howard
- ☐ 13 Charlie Puleo
- ☐ 14 Tom Dixon
- ☐ 15 Scott Dye
- ☐ 16 Ed Lynch
- ☐ 17 Brent Gaff
- ☐ 18 Dave Von Ohlen
- ☐ 19 Mike Mendoza
- ☐ 20 Jesse Orosco
- ☐ 21 Jack Aker
- ☐ 22 Sam Perlozzo
- ☐ 23 Greg Harris
- ☐ 24 Ray Searage
- ☐ 25 Mark Daly
- ☐ 26 Rick Anderson
- ☐ 27 Danny Boitano
- ☐ 28 Dan Norman
- ☐ 29 Terry Leach

1981 Toledo Mud Hens TCMA

This 22-card standard-size set of the 1981 Toledo Mud Hens, a Class AAA International League affiliate of the Minnesota Twins, features white-bordered posed color player photos on its fronts. The player's name and position appear in red letters below the photo. The horizontal back carries the player's name, position, team, and league at the top, followed by biography and statistics.

	MINT	NRMT	EXC
COMPLETE SET (22)	10.00	4.50	1.25

- ☐ 1 Cal Ermer
- ☐ 2 Buck Chamberlin
- ☐ 3 Jose Bastian
- ☐ 4 Terry Felton
- ☐ 5 Gerry Hannahs
- ☐ 6 Mike Kinnunen
- ☐ 7 Bruce MacPherson
- ☐ 8 Wally Sarmieto
- ☐ 9 Bob Veselic
- ☐ 10 Ric Williams
- ☐ 11 Aurelio Cadahia
- ☐ 12 Steve Hero
- ☐ 13 Dave Machemer
- ☐ 14 Kurt Seibert
- ☐ 15 Kelly Snider
- ☐ 16 Jesus Vega
- ☐ 17 John Walker
- ☐ 18 Ron Washington
- ☐ 19 Keathel Chauncey
- ☐ 20 Ed Cipot
- ☐ 21 Frank Estes
- ☐ 22 Steve Stroughter

1981 Tucson Toros TCMA

This 26-card standard-size set of the 1981 Tucson Toros, a Class AAA Pacific Coast League affiliate of the Houston Astros, features white-bordered posed color player photos on its fronts. The player's name and position appear in red letters below the photo. The horizontal back contains safety tips.

	MINT	NRMT	EXC
COMPLETE SET (26)	15.00	6.75	1.85

- ☐ 1 Greg Cypret
- ☐ 2 Dell Leayherwood
- ☐ 3 Joe Pittman
- ☐ 4 Alan Knicely
- ☐ 5 Bob Cluck
- ☐ 6 Tom Vessey
- ☐ 7 Bert Pena
- ☐ 8 Simon Rosario
- ☐ 9 Mark Miggins
- ☐ 10 Johnny Ray
- ☐ 11 Scott Loucks
- ☐ 12 Jimmy Johnson
- ☐ 13 Tom Spencer
- ☐ 14 Dave Labossiere
- ☐ 15 Stan Leland
- ☐ 16 Ron Meredith
- ☐ 17 Jim Planouits
- ☐ 18 Gordon Pladson
- ☐ 19 Pete Ladd
- ☐ 20 Tim Tolman
- ☐ 21 Bert Roberge
- ☐ 22 George Gross
- ☐ 23 Jim Macdonald
- ☐ 24 Billy Smith
- ☐ 25 Jack Donovan
- ☐ 26 Tom Wiedenbauer

1981 Tulsa Drillers TCMA

This 30-card standard-size set of the 1981 Tulsa Drillers, a Class AA Texas League affiliate of the Texas Rangers, features white-bordered posed color player photos on its fronts. The player's name and position appear in red letters below the photo. The horizontal back carries the player's name, position, team, and league at the top, followed by biography and statistics.

	MINT	NRMT	EXC
COMPLETE SET (30)	18.00	8.00	2.20

- ☐ 1 George Wright
- ☐ 2 Tracy Cowger
- ☐ 3 Phil Klimas
- ☐ 4 Marty Scott
- ☐ 5 Dave Stockstill
- ☐ 6 Mel Barrow
- ☐ 7 Larry Reynolds
- ☐ 8 Ted Davis
- ☐ 9 Steve Nielsen
- ☐ 10 Ron Carney
- ☐ 11 Joe Nemeth
- ☐ 12 Walt Terrell
- ☐ 13 Don Scott
- ☐ 14 Dennis Long
- ☐ 15 Dave Crutcher
- ☐ 16A Tony Fossas
- ☐ 16B Pete O'Brien
- ☐ 17 Mike Roberts
- ☐ 18 Ron Darling
- ☐ 19 Jack Lazorko
- ☐ 20 Tom Burgess
- ☐ 21 Tony Hudson
- ☐ 22 Kevin Richards
- ☐ 23 Greg Hughes
- ☐ 24 Brooks Wallace
- ☐ 25 Lindy Duncan
- ☐ 26 Bobby Ball
- ☐ 27 Joe Russell
- ☐ 28 Ron Gooch
- ☐ 29 Mike Jirschele

1981 Vancouver Canadians TCMA

This 25-card standard-size set of the 1981 Vancouver Canadians, a Class AAA Pacific Coast League affiliate of the Milwaukee Brewers, features white-bordered posed color player photos on its fronts. The player's name and position appear in red letters below the photo. The horizontal back carries the player's name, position, team, and league.

	MINT	NRMT	EXC
COMPLETE SET (25)	10.00	4.50	1.25

- ☐ 1 Jamie Cocanower
- ☐ 2 Chuck Porter
- ☐ 3 Doug Wanz
- ☐ 4 Dwight Bernard
- ☐ 5 Mark Schuster
- ☐ 6 Frank Thomas
- ☐ 7 Brian Thorson TR
- ☐ 8 Ivan Rodriguez
- ☐ 9 Gil Kubski
- ☐ 10 Baylor Moore
- ☐ 11 Gus Quiros
- ☐ 12 Larry Rush
- ☐ 13 Rich Olsen
- ☐ 14 Terry Lee
- ☐ 15 Willie Mueller
- ☐ 16 Andy Replogle
- ☐ 17 Frank DiPino
- ☐ 18 Rene Quinones
- ☐ 19 Bobby Smith
- ☐ 20 Lee Stigman MG
- ☐ 21 John Flinn
- ☐ 22 Gerry Ako
- ☐ 23 Tom Soto
- ☐ 24 Kevin Bass
- ☐ 25 Steve Lake

1981 Vero Beach Dodgers TCMA

This 27-card standard-size set of the 1981 Vero Beach Dodgers, a Class A Florida State League affiliate of the Los Angeles Dodgers, features white-bordered posed black-and-white player photos on its fronts. The player's name and position appear in black letters below the photo. The horizontal back carries the player's name, position, team, and league at the top, followed by biography and statistics.

	MINT	NRMT	EXC
COMPLETE SET (27)	15.00	6.75	1.85

- ☐ 1 Ed Amelung
- ☐ 2 Paul Bard
- ☐ 3 Frank Bryant
- ☐ 4 John Debus
- ☐ 5 Dan Forer
- ☐ 6 Art Hammond
- ☐ 7 Bobby Kenyon
- ☐ 8 Tony Lachowetz
- ☐ 9 Dave Lanning
- ☐ 10 Skip Mann
- ☐ 11 Holly Martin
- ☐ 12 Mike Martin
- ☐ 13 Mike O'Malley
- ☐ 14 Steve Perry
- ☐ 15 Pat Raimondo
- ☐ 16 Curtis Reade
- ☐ 17 R.J. Reynolds
- ☐ 18 Greg Smith
- ☐ 19 Bill Sobbe
- ☐ 20 Terry Sutcliffe
- ☐ 21 Ricky Thomas
- ☐ 22 Brad Thorp
- ☐ 23 Juan Villascusa
- ☐ 24 Brett Wise
- ☐ 25 David Wallace
- ☐ 26 John Shoemaker
- ☐ 27 Stan Wasiak

1981 Waterbury Reds TCMA

This 23-card standard-size set of the 1981 Waterbury Reds, a Class AA Eastern League affiliate of the Cincinnati Reds, features white-bordered posed black-and-white player photos on its fronts. The player's name and position appear in black letters below the photo. The horizontal back carries the player's name, position, team, and league at the top, followed by biography and statistics.

	MINT	NRMT	EXC
COMPLETE SET (23)	30.00	13.50	3.70

- ☐ 1 Rich Carlucci
- ☐ 2 Keefe Cato
- ☐ 3 Mike Dowless
- ☐ 4 Ken Jones
- ☐ 5 Doug Neuenschwander
- ☐ 6 Rick O'Keeffe
- ☐ 7 Bill Scherrer
- ☐ 8 Lester Straker
- ☐ 9 Mike Sullivan
- ☐ 10 Randy Town
- ☐ 11 Anthony Walker
- ☐ 12 Steve Christmas
- ☐ 13 Adokfo Feliz
- ☐ 14 Tom Lawless
- ☐ 15 Gary Redus
- ☐ 16 Hector Rincones
- ☐ 17 Eski Viltz
- ☐ 18 Russ Aldrich
- ☐ 19 Mark Gilbert
- ☐ 20 Dave Bisceglia
- ☐ 21 Tony Walker
- ☐ 22 George Scherger
- ☐ 23 Lee Garrett

1981 Waterloo Indians TCMA

This 34-card standard-size set of the 1981 Waterloo Indians, a Class A Midwest League affiliate of the Cleveland Indians, features white-bordered posed black-and-white player photos on its fronts. The player's name and position appear in black letters below the photo. The horizontal back carries the player's name, position, team, and league at the top, followed by biography and statistics.

	MINT	NRMT	EXC
COMPLETE SET (34)	35.00	16.00	4.40

- ☐ 1 Gomer Hodge
- ☐ 2 Rick Colzie
- ☐ 3 Dennis Brogna
- ☐ 4 Larry Hrynko
- ☐ 5 John Asbell
- ☐ 6 Mark Bajus
- ☐ 7 Tom Burns
- ☐ 8 Mike Dixon
- ☐ 9 John Hoban
- ☐ 10 Mike Jeffcoat
- ☐ 11 Ricky Lintz
- ☐ 12 Tom Owens
- ☐ 13 Greg Pope
- ☐ 14 Ramon Romero
- ☐ 15 Mike Schwarber
- ☐ 16 Rich Thompson
- ☐ 17 Louis Duarte (no number on back)
- ☐ 18 Jack Fimple
- ☐ 19 John Malkin
- ☐ 20 Arnold Cochran
- ☐ 21 Shanie Dugas
- ☐ 22 Kelly Gruber
- ☐ 23 Marlin Methven
- ☐ 24 Juan Pacho
- ☐ 25 Larry Dotson
- ☐ 26 Dave Gallagher
- ☐ 27 Ed Saavedra
- ☐ 28 Mike Taylor
- ☐ 29 Winston Ficklin
- ☐ 30 Adalberto Nieves
- ☐ 31 Bernardo Brito
- ☐ 32 Steve Cushing
- ☐ 33 Ralph Elpin
- ☐ 34 Bob Feller

1981 Wausau Timbers TCMA

This 29-card standard-size set of the 1981 Wausau Timbers, a Class A Midwest League affiliate of the Seattle Mariners, features white-bordered posed black-and-white player photos on its fronts. The player's name and position appear in black letters below the photo. The horizontal back carries the player's name, position, team, and league at the top, followed by biography and statistics.

	MINT	NRMT	EXC
COMPLETE SET (29)	35.00	16.00	4.40

- ☐ 1 Kevin Steger
- ☐ 2 Jeff Stottlemyre
- ☐ 3 Bob Hudson
- ☐ 4 Edwin Nunez
- ☐ 5 Tom Brennan
- ☐ 6 Mark Pedersen
- ☐ 7 Brian Snyder
- ☐ 8 Mark Batten
- ☐ 9 Chris Hunger
- ☐ 10 Don McKenzie
- ☐ 11 David Blume
- ☐ 12 Eddie Yampierre
- ☐ 13 Jesse Baez
- ☐ 14 Rick Adair
- ☐ 15 Jeff Cary
- ☐ 16 Enrique Diaz
- ☐ 17 Donell Nixon
- ☐ 18 Harold Reynolds
- ☐ 19 Darnell Coles
- ☐ 20 Jimmy Presley
- ☐ 21 Clark Crist
- ☐ 22 Omar Minaya
- ☐ 23 Mark Chelette
- ☐ 24 Glenn Walker
- ☐ 25 John Moses
- ☐ 26 Ivan Calderon
- ☐ 27 Kevin King
- ☐ 28 Tom Hunt
- ☐ 29 Bill Plummer

1981 West Haven A's TCMA

This 23-card standard-size set of the 1981 West Haven A's, a Class AA Eastern League affiliate of the Oakland Athletics, features white-bordered posed color player photos on its fronts. The player's name and position appear in red letters below the photo. The horizontal back carries the player's name, position, team, and league at the top, followed by biography and statistics.

	MINT	NRMT	EXC
COMPLETE SET (23)	30.00	13.50	3.70

- ☐ 1 Robert Didler
- ☐ 2 Keith Atherton
- ☐ 3 Bert Bradley
- ☐ 4 Dewayne Buice
- ☐ 5 Darryl Cias
- ☐ 6 Keith Comstock
- ☐ 7 Tim Conroy
- ☐ 8 Jim Durrman
- ☐ 9 Bobby Garrett
- ☐ 10 Bruce Fournier
- ☐ 11 Lynn Garrett
- ☐ 12 Steve Gelfarb
- ☐ 13 Rick Holloway
- ☐ 14 Tony Phillips
- ☐ 15 Ricky Tronerud
- ☐ 16 Don Morris
- ☐ 17 Mike Woodard
- ☐ 18 Alan Abraham
- ☐ 19 Dennis Sherow
- ☐ 20 Gorman Heimueller
- ☐ 21 Scott Meyer
- ☐ 22 Dick Lynch
- ☐ 23 Scott Pyle

1981 Wisconsin Rapids Twins TCMA

This 23-card standard-size set of the 1981 Wisconsin Rapids Twins, a Class A Midwest League affiliate of the Minnesota Twins, features white-bordered posed black-and-white player photos on its fronts. The player's name and position appear in black letters below the photo. The horizontal back carries the player's name, position, team, and league at the top, followed by biography and statistics.

	MINT	NRMT	EXC
COMPLETE SET (23)	30.00	13.50	3.70

- ☐ 1 Ken Staples
- ☐ 2 Tom Leix
- ☐ 3 Smokey Everett
- ☐ 4 Tony Guerrero
- ☐ 5 Larry Harris
- ☐ 6 Kirby Krueger
- ☐ 7 Jeorge Ortiz
- ☐ 8 Adriano Pena
- ☐ 9 Luis Suarez
- ☐ 10 Mike Ungs
- ☐ 11 Mark Wright
- ☐ 12 Richard Yett
- ☐ 13 Ken Chandler
- ☐ 14 Jeff Reed
- ☐ 15 Michael Cole
- ☐ 16 Ken Foster
- ☐ 17 Jim Payne
- ☐ 18 Bill Price
- ☐ 19 Mandy Smith
- ☐ 20 Talbot Aiello
- ☐ 21 Jim Eisenreich
- ☐ 22 John Palica
- ☐ 23 Nelson Suarez

1982 Albuquerque Dukes TCMA

This 27-card standard-size set of the 1982 Albuquerque Dukes, a Class AAA Pacific Coast League affiliate of the Los Angeles Dodgers, features white-bordered posed color player photos on its fronts. Most are horizontally oriented. The player's name and position appear at the (vertical) bottom. The white and black back carries the team name at the top, followed below by the league affiliation, and then the player's name, biography and statistics. This issue includes the minor league card debut of Orel Hershiser.

	MINT	NRMT	EXC
COMPLETE SET (27)	60.00	27.00	7.50

☐ 1 Joe Beckwith
☐ 2 John Franco
☐ 3 Burt Gieger
☐ 4 Orel Hershiser
☐ 5 Brian Holton
☐ 6 Dave Moore
☐ 7 Tom Niedenfuer
☐ 8 Tom Shirley
☐ 9 Rick Rodas
☐ 10 Larry White
☐ 11 Rick Wright
☐ 12 Don Crow
☐ 13 Dave Sax
☐ 14 Dave Anderson
☐ 15 Greg Brock
☐ 16 Larry Fobbs
☐ 17 Ross Jones
☐ 18 Alex Taveras
☐ 19 Mark Bradley
☐ 20 Dave Holman
☐ 21 Candy Maldonado
☐ 22 Mike Marshall
☐ 23 Tack Wilson
☐ 24 Del Crandall
☐ 25 Dave Cohea
☐ 26 Dick McLaughlin
☐ 27 Brent Strom

1982 Alexandria Dukes TCMA

This 27-card standard-size set of the 1982 Alexandria Dukes, a Class A Carolina League affiliate of the Pittsburgh Pirates, features white-bordered posed black-and-white player photos on its fronts. The player's name and position appear at the bottom. The white and black back carries the team name at the top, followed below by the league affiliation, and then the player's name, biography and statistics.

	MINT	NRMT	EXC
COMPLETE SET (27)	30.00	13.50	3.70

☐ 1 Johnny Taylor
☐ 2 Lee Marcheskie
☐ 3 Larry Lamonde
☐ 4 Ray Krawczyk
☐ 5 Jeffrey Horne
☐ 6 Christopher Green
☐ 7 Fernando Gonzales
☐ 8 Lance Dodd
☐ 9 Wilfrido Cordoba
☐ 10 Mike Quade
☐ 11 Brad Garnett
☐ 12 Marvin Clack
☐ 13 Nick Castaneda
☐ 14 Pete Rowe
☐ 15 Burk Goldthorn
☐ 16 James Churchill
☐ 17 Jeffrey Zaske
☐ 18 Timothy Wheeler
☐ 19 Brian McCann
☐ 20 Dan Warthen
☐ 21 John Lipon
☐ 22 Joe Orsulak
☐ 23 Ken Ford
☐ 24 Jim Felt
☐ 25 Nelson Delarosa
☐ 26 Andy Snaith
☐ 27 Rick Renteria

1982 Amarillo Gold Sox TCMA

This 25-card standard-size set of the 1982 Amarillo Gold Sox, a Class AA Texas League affiliate of the San Diego Padres, features white-bordered posed black-and-white player photos on its fronts. The player's name and position appear at the bottom. The white and black back carries the team name at the top, followed below by the league affiliation, and then the player's name, biography and statistics.

	MINT	NRMT	EXC
COMPLETE SET (25)	25.00	11.00	3.10

☐ 1 George Hinshaw
☐ 2 Brian Greer
☐ 3 John Stevenson
☐ 4 Joe Scherger
☐ 5 Gerry Davis
☐ 6 Bob Macias
☐ 7 Jeff Ronk
☐ 8 Dan Purpura
☐ 9 Mike Martin
☐ 10 Mark Parent
☐ 11 James Steels
☐ 12 Jim Coffman
☐ 13 John White
☐ 14 Tom Biko
☐ 15 Neil Bryant
☐ 16 Mike Couchee
☐ 17 Steve Stone
☐ 18 Bill Long
☐ 19 Willie Hardwick
☐ 20 Marty Kain
☐ 21 Randy Kaczmarski
☐ 22 Rick Shaw
☐ 23 Glen Ezell
☐ 24 Mike Hebrard
☐ 25 Tom House

1982 Appleton Foxes Fritsch

	MINT	NRMT	EXC
COMPLETE SET (31)	5.00	2.20	.60

☐ 1 Checklist
☐ 2 Jeff Overton
☐ 3 Leo Garcia
☐ 4 Jim Sutton
☐ 5 Wade L. Rowdon
☐ 6 Ramon Romero
☐ 7 Al Jones
☐ 8 John Taylor
☐ 9 Scott Meier
☐ 10 Jesse Anderson
☐ 11 Steve Pastrovich
☐ 12 Curt Reed
☐ 13 Wes Kent
☐ 14 John Skinner
☐ 15 Dave Nix
☐ 16 Joseph J. Paglino
☐ 17 Donn Koch
☐ 18 Wayne Schuckert
☐ 19 Bill Babcock
☐ 20 Eddie Miles
☐ 21 Kevin Flannery
☐ 22 Scott Gibson
☐ 23 Art Niemann
☐ 24 Daryl Boston
☐ 25 Michael J. Tanzi
☐ 26 Michael J. Buggs
☐ 27 Pat Adams
☐ 28 Al Heath
☐ 29 Doug Wiesner TR
☐ 30 Mike Pazik CO
☐ 31 Adrian Garrett MGR

1982 Arkansas Travelers TCMA

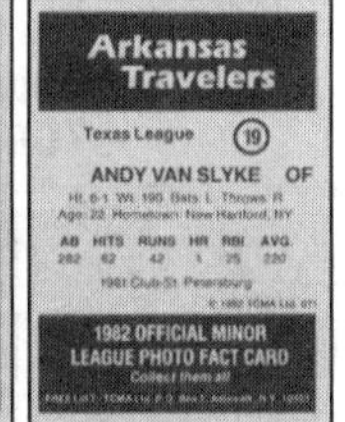

This 24-card standard-size set of the 1982 Arkansas Travelers, a Class AA Texas League affiliate of the St. Louis Cardinals, features white-bordered posed black-and-white player photos on its fronts. The player's name and position appear at the bottom. The white and black back carries the team name at the top, followed below by the league affiliation, and then the player's name, biography and statistics.

	MINT	NRMT	EXC
COMPLETE SET (24)	120.00	55.00	15.00

☐ 1 Scott Arigoni
☐ 2 Kevin Hagen
☐ 3 Ricky Horton
☐ 4 Jeff Keener
☐ 5 Rafael Pimentel
☐ 6 Gerry Perry
☐ 7 Mark Riggins
☐ 8 Ed Sanford
☐ 9 Buddy Schultz
☐ 10 Tom Thurberg
☐ 11 Mark Salas
☐ 12 Tom Nieto
☐ 13 Jose Gonzales
☐ 14 Greg Guin
☐ 15 Peachy Guiterrez
☐ 16 Luis Ojeda
☐ 17 Don Moore
☐ 18 Jim Adduci
☐ 19 Andy Van Slyke
☐ 20 Jack Ayer
☐ 21 Larry Reynolds
☐ 22 Gaylen Pitts
☐ 23 Dave England
☐ 24 Jorge Aranzamendi

1982 Auburn Astros TCMA

This 19-card standard-size set of the 1982 Auburn Astros, a Class A New York-Penn League affiliate of the Houston Astros, features white-bordered posed black-and-white player photos on its fronts. The player's name and position appear at the bottom. The white and black back carries the team name at the top, followed below by the league affiliation, and then the player's name, biography and statistics.

	MINT	NRMT	EXC
COMPLETE SET (19)	10.00	4.50	1.25

☐ 1 Tom Roarke
☐ 2 Bob Hartsfield
☐ 3 Jeff Jacobson
☐ 4 Mike Stellern
☐ 5 Ray Perkins
☐ 6 Eric Anderson
☐ 7 Jeff Meadows
☐ 8 Mike Hogan
☐ 9 Larry McIver
☐ 10 Bob Hinson
☐ 11 Jeff Datz
☐ 12 Tracy Dophied
☐ 13 Rich Bombard
☐ 14 Craig Kizer
☐ 15 Tom Riewerts
☐ 16 Steve Swain
☐ 17 Ricardo Rivera
☐ 18 Carlos Alfonso
☐ 19 Rick Thompson

1982 Beloit Brewers Fritsch

	MINT	NRMT	EXC
COMPLETE SET (27)	10.00	4.50	1.25

☐ 1 Checklist
☐ 2 Joe Henderson
☐ 3 Gerry Miller
☐ 4 Bill Wegman
☐ 5 Johnson C. Wood
☐ 6 Ty Van Burkleo
☐ 7 John Hoban
☐ 8 John Gibbons
☐ 9 Fritz Fedor
☐ 10 Marcos Gomez
☐ 11 Dewey James
☐ 12 Mike Myerchin
☐ 13 Collin Tanabe
☐ 14 Kenny Clayton
☐ 15 Butch Kirby
☐ 16 Joe Edwin Morales
☐ 17 Gary Evans
☐ 18 Danny Gilmartin
☐ 19 Mike Samuel
☐ 20 Bryan Clutterbuck
☐ 21 Bill Max
☐ 22 Brad DeKraai
☐ 23 Martin Antunez
☐ 24 Terry Bevington MG
☐ 25 Bill Nowlan TR
☐ 26 Angel Morris Jr.
☐ 27 Ted Pallas

1982 Birmingham Barons TCMA

This 24-card standard-size set of the 1982 Birmingham Barons, a Class AA Southern League affiliate of the Detroit Tigers, features white-bordered posed color player photos on its fronts. Most are horizontally oriented. The player's name and position appear at the (vertical) bottom. The white and black back carries the team name at the top, followed below by the league affiliation, and then the player's name, biography and statistics.

	MINT	NRMT	EXC
COMPLETE SET (24)	10.00	4.50	1.25

☐ 1 Stan Younger
☐ 2 Barbaro Garbey
☐ 3 Darrell Woodard
☐ 4 Homer Moncrief
☐ 5 Dave Gumpert
☐ 6 Mike Beecroft
☐ 7 Bob Melvin
☐ 8 Randy O'Neal
☐ 9 Chuck Cary
☐ 10 Kenny Baker
☐ 11 Bruce Fields
☐ 12 Randy Harvey
☐ 13 Rondal Rollins
☐ 14 Gary Hinson
☐ 15 John Flannery
☐ 16 Dave Hawarney
☐ 17 Kevin Pasley
☐ 18 Jerry Bass
☐ 19 Frank McCann
☐ 20 Steve Quealey
☐ 21 Charlie Nail
☐ 22 Emilio Carrasquel
☐ 23 Paul Gibson
☐ 24 Ed Brinkman

1982 Buffalo Bisons TCMA

This 18-card standard-size set of the 1982 Buffalo Bisons, a Class AA Eastern League affiliate of the Pittsburgh Pirates, features white-bordered posed color player photos on its fronts. Most are horizontally oriented. The player's name and position appear at the (vertical) bottom. The white and black back carries the team name at the top, followed below by the league affiliation, and then the player's name, biography and statistics.

	MINT	NRMT	EXC
COMPLETE SET (18)	15.00	6.75	1.85

☐ 1 Rich Leggat
☐ 2 Bob Misak
☐ 3 Connor McGeehee
☐ 4 Drew McCauley
☐ 5 Greg Pastors
☐ 6 John Schaive
☐ 7 Al Torres
☐ 8 Keith Thibodeaux
☐ 9 Tim Wheeler
☐ 10 Kevin Houston
☐ 11 Ron Wotus
☐ 12 John Holland
☐ 13 Steve Farr
☐ 14 Eleno Cuen
☐ 15 Tim Burke
☐ 16 Mike Bielecki
☐ 17 Rick Peterson
☐ 18 Tom Sandt

1982 Burlington Rangers Fritsch

	MINT	NRMT	EXC
COMPLETE SET (30)	5.00	2.20	.60

☐ 1 Checklist
☐ 2 Lawrence Avery GM
☐ 3 Kevin Buckley
☐ 4 Dwayne Henry
☐ 5 Al Hartman
☐ 6 Tony Triplett
☐ 7 Ray Warren
☐ 8 Frank Brosious
☐ 9 Garry Venner
☐ 10 Keith Jones
☐ 11 Rod Hodde
☐ 12 Jorge Gomez
☐ 13 Curtis Wilkerson
☐ 14 Tim Henry
☐ 15 Greg Tabor
☐ 16 Chuckie Canady
☐ 17 Mark Gammage
☐ 18 Mike Schmid
☐ 19 Gary Sharp
☐ 20 Larry McLane
☐ 21 Tony Hudson
☐ 22 Doug Davis
☐ 23 Glen Cook
☐ 24 Whitney Harry
☐ 25 Jim Jeffries
☐ 26 Greg Campbell TR
☐ 27 Otto Gonzalez
☐ 28 Marty Scott MG
☐ 29 Tim Maki
☐ 30 Steve Nielsen CO

1982 Burlington Rangers TCMA

This 27-card standard-size set of the 1982 Burlington Rangers, a Class A Midwest League affiliate of the Texas Rangers, features white-bordered posed black-and-white player photos on its fronts. The player's name and position appear at the bottom. The white and black back carries the team name at the top, followed below by the league affiliation, and then the player's name, biography and statistics.

	MINT	NRMT	EXC
COMPLETE SET (26)	20.00	9.00	2.50
COMPLETE SET W/LATE ISSUE (27)	50.00	22.00	6.25

☐ 1 Timothy Henry
☐ 2 Rodney Hodde
☐ 3 Anthony Hudson
☐ 4 James Jeffries
☐ 5 Keith Jones
☐ 6 Timothy Maki
☐ 7 Larry McLane
☐ 8 Michael Schmid
☐ 9 Gary Sharp
☐ 10 Gregory Tabor
☐ 11 Antonio Triplett
☐ 12 Raymond Warren
☐ 13 Curtis Wilkerson
☐ 14 Frank Brosious
☐ 15 Kevin Buckley
☐ 16 Chuckie Canady
☐ 17 Glen Cook
☐ 18 Douglas Davis
☐ 19 Mike Gammage
☐ 20 Jorge Gomez
☐ 21 Otto Gonzalez
☐ 22 Whitney Harry
☐ 23 Albert Hartman
☐ 24 Dwayne Henry
☐ 25 Martin Scott
☐ 26 Steven Nielsen
☐ 27 Larry Avery (Late Issue)

1982 Cedar Rapids Reds TCMA

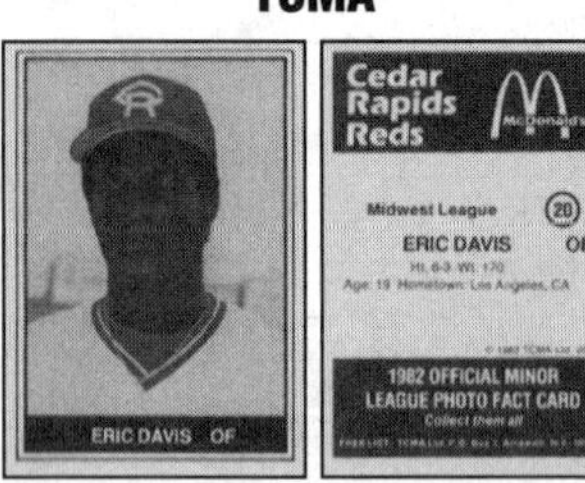

This 27-card standard-size set of the 1982 Cedar Rapids Reds, a Class A Midwest League affiliate of the Cincinnati Reds, features white-bordered posed color player photos on its fronts. Most are horizontally oriented. The player's name and position appear at the (vertical) bottom. The white and black back carries the team name at the top, followed below by the league affiliation, and then the player's name, biography and statistics. This issue includes the minor league card debut of Eric Davis. Approximately 3,000 sets were produced.

	MINT	NRMT	EXC
COMPLETE SET (27)	75.00	34.00	9.50

☐ 1 Mark Rothey
☐ 2 Rob Murphy
☐ 3 Curt Heidenreich
☐ 4 Steve Lowrey
☐ 5 Kurt Kepshire
☐ 6 Mike Riley
☐ 7 Freddie Toliver
☐ 8 Mike Ferguson
☐ 9 Mike Hennessy
☐ 10 Jim Pettibone
☐ 11 Larry Freeburg
☐ 12 Danny Lamar
☐ 13 Mark Matzen
☐ 14 Paul Kirsch
☐ 15 Adolfo Feliz
☐ 16 Tony Burley
☐ 17 Byron Peyton
☐ 18 Bill Metil
☐ 19 Dave Hall
☐ 20 Eric Davis
☐ 21 Paul O'Neill
☐ 22 Tim Stout
☐ 23 Scott Terry
☐ 24 Jeff Jones
☐ 25 Randy Davidson
☐ 26 David Clay
☐ 27 Don Buchheister

1982 Charleston Charlies TCMA

This 24-card standard-size set of the 1982 Charleston Charlies, a Class AAA International League affiliate of the Cleveland Indians, features white-bordered posed color player photos on its fronts. Most are horizontally oriented. The player's name and position appear at the (vertical) bottom. The white and black back carries the team name at the top, followed below by the league affiliation, and then the player's name, biography and statistics.

	MINT	NRMT	EXC
COMPLETE SET (24)	10.00	4.50	1.25

☐ 1 Bud Anderson
☐ 2 John Bohnet
☐ 3 Gordy Glaser
☐ 4 Ed Glynn
☐ 5 Neal Heaton
☐ 6 Harry Hrynko
☐ 7 Silvio Martinez
☐ 8 Jack Nulsmer
☐ 9 Rob Pietroburgo
☐ 10 Ray Searage
☐ 11 Bill Nahorodny
☐ 12 Tim Norrid
☐ 13 Craig Stimac
☐ 14 Luis Deleon
☐ 15 Angelo LoGrande
☐ 16 Rich Murray
☐ 17 Kevin Rhomberg
☐ 18 Dave Rosello
☐ 19 Carmelo Castillo
☐ 20 Larry Littleton
☐ 21 Karl Pagel
☐ 22 Dave Rivera
☐ 23 Doc Edwards
☐ 24 Chuck Estrada

1982 Charleston Royals TCMA

This 24-card standard-size set of the 1982 Charleston Royals, a Class A South Atlantic League affiliate of the Kansas City Royals, features white-bordered posed black-and-white player photos on its fronts. The player's name and position appear at the bottom. The white and black back carries the team name at the top, followed below by the league affiliation, and then the player's name, biography and statistics. This issue includes the minor league card debut of David Cone.

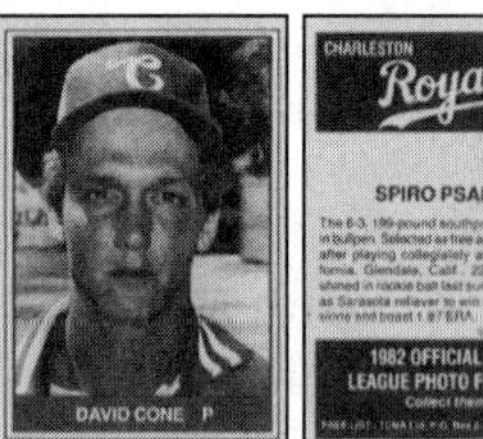

	MINT	NRMT	EXC
COMPLETE SET (24)	75.00	34.00	9.50

☐ 1 Jim Miner
☐ 2 Roger Hansen
☐ 3 Mike Sorrel
☐ 4 Tom McHugh
☐ 5 John Bryant
☐ 6 Danny Jackson
☐ 7 Mitch Ashmore
☐ 8 Perry Swanson
☐ 9 Bert Johnson
☐ 10 Chris Bryeans
☐ 11 Bob Umdenstock
☐ 12 Mike Kingery
☐ 13 Tim Ballard
☐ 14 Dick Vitato
☐ 15 Ron Krauss
☐ 16 Ken Patterson
☐ 17 Roland Druna
☐ 18 Den Swank
☐ 19 Spiro Psaltis
☐ 20 Dave Cone
☐ 21 Cliff Pastornicky
☐ 22 Wille Neal
☐ 23 Mark Farnsworth
☐ 24 Roy Tanner

1982 Chattanooga Lookouts TCMA

This 25-card standard-size set of the 1982 Chattanooga Lookouts, a Class AA Southern League affiliate of the Cleveland Indians, features white-bordered posed black-and-white player photos on its fronts. The player's name and position appear at the bottom. The white and black back carries the team name at the top, followed below by the league affiliation, and then the player's name, biography and statistics.

	MINT	NRMT	EXC
COMPLETE SET (25)	40.00	18.00	5.00

☐ 1 Nate Puryear
☐ 2 Scott Munninghoff
☐ 3 Everett Rey
☐ 4 Ed Saavedra
☐ 5 Richard Thompson
☐ 6 Tim Glass
☐ 7 Ricky Baker
☐ 8 Dane Anthony
☐ 9 Tom Owens
☐ 10 Mike Schwarber
☐ 11 Sal Rende
☐ 12 Marlin Methvin
☐ 13 Shanie Dugas
☐ 14 George Ceechetti
☐ 15 Steve Roche
☐ 16 Kelly Gruber
☐ 17 Dave Gallagher
☐ 18 Robin Fuson
☐ 19 Steve Narleski
☐ 20 Rick Borchers
☐ 21 Jeff Moronko
☐ 22 Craig Adams
☐ 23 Al Gallagher
☐ 24 Chuck Stobbs
☐ 25 Hank Gaughan

1982 Clinton Giants Fritsch

	MINT	NRMT	EXC
COMPLETE SET (32)	15.00	6.75	1.85

☐ 1 Checklist
☐ 2 Wendell Kim MG
☐ 3 Steve Cline CO
☐ 4 Matt Nokes
☐ 5 Phil Ouellette
☐ 6 Glenn Barling
☐ 7 Michael Jones
☐ 8 Todd Zacher
☐ 9 David Nenad
☐ 10 Everett Graham
☐ 11 Steve Wilcox
☐ 12 Randy Saunier
☐ 13 Ramon Bautista
☐ 14 Mike Dunner
☐ 15 Marty Baiern
☐ 16 Kerman Ronan
☐ 17 Gene Lambert
☐ 18 Allen Smoot
☐ 19 Larry Crews
☐ 20 Brian Murtha
☐ 21 Glenn Jones
☐ 22 Eric Erickson
☐ 23 Mark Grant
☐ 24 Randy Ebersberger
☐ 25 Bob O'Connor
☐ 26 Mark Tudor TR
☐ 27 Gus Stokes GM
☐ 28 John Marks AGM
☐ 29 Jim Weir
☐ 30 Mickey Swenson
☐ 31 Mark Swenson
☐ 32 Mickey Swenson
Mark Swenson
Clinton Giants

1982 Columbus Clippers Police

	MINT	NRMT	EXC
COMPLETE SET (25)	50.00	22.00	6.25

☐ 2 Andre Robertson
☐ 6 Dan Schmitz
☐ 11 Scott Patterson
☐ 12 Tucker Ashford
☐ 13 Garry Smith
☐ 14 Mike Patterson
☐ 15 Jamie Werly
☐ 17 John Pacella
☐ 19 Don Mattingly
☐ 21 Jim Lewis
☐ 22 Wayne Harer
☐ 23 Dave Stegman
☐ 24 Curt Kaufman
☐ 25 Mike Bruhert
☐ 26 Frank Verdi
☐ 27 Greg Cochran
☐ 28 Dave Wehrmeister
☐ 29 Juan Espino
☐ 30 Pete Filson
☐ 31 Bobby Ramos
☐ 33 Marshall Brant
☐ 35 Steve Balboni
☐ 38 Bob Sykes
☐ NNO Clippers' Staff
Sammy Ellis 32 CO
Jerry McNertney 34 CO
Steve Donohue TR
☐ NNO George H. Sisler Jr.
General Manager

1982 Columbus Clippers TCMA

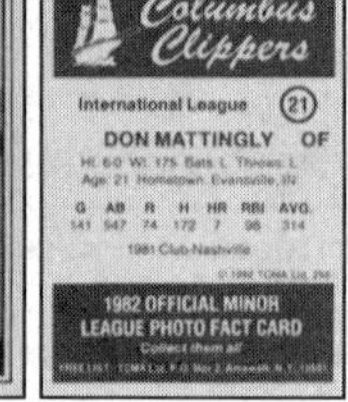

This 26-card standard-size set of the 1982 Columbus Clippers, a Class AAA International League affiliate of the New York Yankees, features white-bordered posed color player photos on its fronts. Most are horizontally oriented. The player's name and position appear at the (vertical) bottom. The white and black back carries the team name at the top, followed below by the league affiliation, and then the player's name, biography and statistics. This issue includes a second year minor league card of Don Mattingly. Approximately 3,500 sets were produced.

	MINT	NRMT	EXC
COMPLETE SET (26)	300.00	135.00	38.00

☐ 1 John Pacella
☐ 2 Tucker Ashford
☐ 3 Wayne Harer
☐ 4 Steve Balboni
☐ 5 Curt Kaufman
☐ 6 Marshall Brant
☐ 7 Mike Bruhert
☐ 8 Greg Cochran
☐ 9 Pete Filson
☐ 10 Jamie Werley
☐ 11 Dave Wehrmeister
☐ 12 Bob Sykes
☐ 13 David Stegman
☐ 14 Garry Smith
☐ 15 Dick Scott
☐ 16 Dan Schmitz
☐ 17 Andre Robertson
☐ 18 Bobby Ramos
☐ 19 Scott Patterson
☐ 20 Mike Patterson
☐ 21 Don Mattingly
☐ 22 Jim Lewis
☐ 23 Juan Espino
☐ 24 Sammy Ellis
Jerry McNertney
Steve Donohue
☐ 25 Frank Verdi
☐ 26 George H. Sisler Jr.

1982 Danville Suns Fritsch

	MINT	NRMT	EXC
COMPLETE SET (28)	25.00	11.00	3.10

☐ 1 Checklist
☐ 2 Gus Gil MG
☐ 3 Jeff Ahern
☐ 4 T.R. Bryden
☐ 5 Mark Bingham
☐ 6 Bill White
☐ 7 Rick Turner
☐ 8 Jack Crawford
☐ 9 Kevin Price
☐ 10 Butch Dowies
☐ 11 Carlos Matos
☐ 12 Doug Lindsey
☐ 13 Tony Gonzalez CO
☐ 14 Marcel Lachemann CO
☐ 15 Richard Zaleski TR
☐ 16 Scott Oliver
☐ 17 Ellie Barros
☐ 18 Willie D. Williams
☐ 19 Freddy Machuca
☐ 20 Bill Worden
☐ 21 Devon White
☐ 22 Joe King
☐ 23 Mike Saverino
☐ 24 Brian Hartsock
☐ 25 Mark Bonner
☐ 26 Rafael Lugo
☐ 27 Dick Schofield
☐ 28 Norman Carrasco

1982 Daytona Beach Astros TCMA

This 25-card standard-size set of the 1982 Daytona Beach Astros, a Class A Florida State League affiliate of the Houston Astros, features white-bordered posed black-and-white player photos on its fronts. The player's name and position appear at the bottom. The white and black back carries the team name at the top, followed below by the league affiliation, and then the player's name, biography and statistics. Approximately 1,100 sets were produced.

	MINT	NRMT	EXC
COMPLETE SET (25)	30.00	13.50	3.70

☐ 1 Guillermo Castro
☐ 2 Mitch Coplon
☐ 3 Joe Ferrante
☐ 4 Scott Gardner
☐ 5 Manny Hernandez
☐ 6 Uvaldo Regalado
☐ 7 Rex Schimpf
☐ 8 Ben Snyder
☐ 9 Roberto Yan
☐ 10 Doug Britt
☐ 11 Steve Dunnegan
☐ 12 Eric Bullock
☐ 13 Ty Gainey
☐ 14 Ira Lane
☐ 15 Neil Simons
☐ 16 Eric Swanson
☐ 17 Mark Campbell
☐ 18 Robbie McGorkle
☐ 19 Jamie Williams
☐ 20 Glenn Davis
☐ 21 Jim McKnight
☐ 22 Val Medina
☐ 23 Larry Simcox
☐ 24 Phil Smith
☐ 25 Mark Strucher

1982 Durham Bulls TCMA

This 25-card standard-size set of the 1982 Durham Bulls, a Class A Carolina League affiliate of the Atlanta Braves, features white-bordered posed black-and-white player photos on its fronts. The player's name and position appear at the bottom. The white and black back carries the team name at the top, followed below by the league affiliation, and then the player's name, biography and statistics.

	MINT	NRMT	EXC
COMPLETE SET (25)	50.00	22.00	6.25

☐ 1 Mike Garcia
☐ 2 Keith Hagman
☐ 3 Scott Hood
☐ 4 Joe Lorenz
☐ 5 Bob Luzon
☐ 6 Bryan Neal
☐ 7 Ken Scanlon
☐ 8 Rick Siriano
☐ 9 Miguel Sosa
☐ 10 Jim Stefanski
☐ 11 Tommy Thompson
☐ 12 Freddy Tiburcio
☐ 13 Bob Tumpane
☐ 14 Dave Clay

☐ 15 Rick Coatney
☐ 16 Jeff Dedmon
☐ 17 Brian Fisher
☐ 18 Rick Hatcher
☐ 19 Mike Payne
☐ 20 Gary Rieter
☐ 21 Andre Treadway
☐ 22 Bruce Dal Canton
☐ 23 Buddy Bailey
☐ 24 Gene Lane
☐ 25 Bob Dews

1982 Edmonton Trappers TCMA

This 25-card standard-size set of the 1982 Edmonton Trappers, a Class AAA Pacific Coast League affiliate of the Chicago White Sox, features white-bordered posed color player photos on its fronts. Most are horizontally oriented. The player's name and position appear at the (vertical) bottom. The white and black back carries the team name at the top, followed below by the league affiliation, and then the player's name, biography and statistics.

	MINT	NRMT	EXC
COMPLETE SET (25)	20.00	9.00	2.50

☐ 1 Carlos Ibarra
☐ 2 Jose Castro
☐ 3 Jim Siwy
☐ 4 Steve Dillard
☐ 5 Chris Nyman
☐ 6 Guy Hoffman
☐ 7 Keith Disjarlais
☐ 8 Jay Loviglio
☐ 9 Fran Mullins
☐ 10 Lorenzo Gray
☐ 11 Leo Sutherland
☐ 12 Woody Agosto
☐ 13 Ron Kittle
☐ 14 Nardi Contreras CO
☐ 15 Reggie Patterson
☐ 16 David Hogg
☐ 17 Len Bradley
☐ 18 Dom Fucci
☐ 19 Rich Barnes
☐ 20 Rusty Kuntz
☐ 21 Rick Seilheimer
☐ 22 Gordy Lund MG
☐ 23 Geoff Combe
☐ 24 Dave Grossman TR
☐ 25 Jeff Schattinger

1982 El Paso Diablos TCMA

This 24-card standard-size set of the 1982 El Paso Diablos, a Class AA Texas League affiliate of the Milwaukee Brewers, features white-bordered posed color player photos on its fronts. The player's name and position appear at the bottom. The white and black back carries the team name at the top, followed below by the league affiliation, and then the player's name, biography and statistics.

	MINT	NRMT	EXC
COMPLETE SET (24)	20.00	9.00	2.50

☐ 1 Eric Peyton
☐ 2 Dion James
☐ 3 Ron Koenigsfeld
☐ 4 Kurt Kingsolver
☐ 5 Dan Davidsmeier
☐ 6 Bill Foley
☐ 7 Randy Ready
☐ 8 Mark Schuster
☐ 9 Don Whiting
☐ 10 Mark Johnston
☐ 11 Joe Hansen
☐ 12 Steve Michael
☐ 13 Jerry Jenkins
☐ 14 Andy Beene
☐ 15 Steve Manderfield
☐ 16 Bob Schroeck
☐ 17 Dave Grier
☐ 18 Jack Uhey
☐ 19 Steve Parrott
☐ 20 Jim Koontz
☐ 21 Bob Gibson
☐ 22 Derek Tatsuno
☐ 23 Tony Muser
☐ 24 Al Price

1982 Evansville Triplets TCMA

This 25-card standard-size set of the 1982 Evansville Triplets, a Class AAA American Association affiliate of the Detroit Tigers, features white-bordered posed color player photos on its fronts. The player's name and position appear at the bottom. The white and black back carries the team name at the top, followed below by the league affiliation, and then the player's name, biography and statistics.

	MINT	NRMT	EXC
COMPLETE SET (25)	10.00	4.50	1.25

☐ 1 Howard Bailey
☐ 2 Juan Berenguer
☐ 3 Mark Dacko
☐ 4 Mark Lee
☐ 5 Rick Matula
☐ 6 Bruce Robbins
☐ 7 Larry Rothschild
☐ 8 Dave Rucker
☐ 9 Augie Ruiz
☐ 10 Gerald Ujdur
☐ 11 Marty Castillo
☐ 12 Don McCormack
☐ 13 Stine Poole
☐ 14 Jeff Cox
☐ 15 Paul Djakonow
☐ 16 Mike Laga
☐ 17 Juan Lopez
☐ 18 Vern Followell
☐ 19 Les Filkins
☐ 20 Eddie Gates
☐ 21 Ray Hampton
☐ 22 Jeff Kenaga
☐ 23 Mark Corey
☐ 24 Ken Houston
☐ 25 Roy Majtyka

1982 Fort Myers Royals TCMA

This 23-card standard-size set of the 1982 Fort Myers Royals, a Class A Florida State League affiliate of the Kansas City Royals, features white-bordered posed black-and-white player photos on its fronts. The player's name and position appear at the bottom. The white and black back carries the team name at the top, followed below by the league affiliation, and then the player's name, biography and statistics.

	MINT	NRMT	EXC
COMPLETE SET (23)	15.00	6.75	1.85

☐ 1 Rick Rizzo
☐ 2 Hal Hatcher
☐ 3 Tommy Thompson
☐ 4 Benny Cadahia
☐ 5 Warren Oliver
☐ 6 Greg Jonson
☐ 7 Nick Harsh
☐ 8 Mickey Palmer
☐ 9 Rick Plautz
☐ 10 Duane Gustavson
☐ 11 Tony Ferreira
☐ 12 Mike Alvarez
☐ 13 Jeff Gladden
☐ 14 Dave Wong
☐ 15 Fran Cutty
☐ 16 Mark Huismann
☐ 17 James Gleissner
☐ 18 Bill Best
☐ 19 Lester Strode
☐ 20 Mark Newman
☐ 21 Bill Pecota
☐ 22 Rick Mathews
☐ 23 Steve Morrow

1982 Glens Falls White Sox TCMA

This 23-card standard-size set of the 1982 Glens Falls White Sox, a Class AA Eastern League affiliate of the Chicago White Sox, features white-faced fronts bordered by two thin red lines framing posed black-and-white player portraits. A red stripe below the photo carries the player's name and position. The white back carries the team name at the top, followed by the player's name, position, biography and statistics.

	MINT	NRMT	EXC
COMPLETE SET (23)	150.00	70.00	19.00

☐ 1 Vince Bienek
☐ 2 J.B. Brown
☐ 3 Ed Cipot
☐ 4 Larry Donofrio
☐ 5 Dom Fucci
☐ 6 Tim Hulett
☐ 7 Phil Klimas
☐ 8 Mike Morse
☐ 9 Pete Peltz
☐ 10 Joel Skinner
☐ 11 Vern Thomas
☐ 12 Dan Williams
☐ 13 Dave Yobs
☐ 16 Larry Edwards
☐ 17 Bob Fallon
☐ 18 Jack Hardy
☐ 19 Chuck Johnson
☐ 20 John Lackey
☐ 21 Mike Maitland
☐ 22 Tom Mullen
☐ 23 Mark Teutsch
☐ 24 Mike Withrow
☐ 25 Jim Mahoney

1982 Hawaii Islanders TCMA

This 25-card standard-size set of the 1982 Hawaii Islanders, a Class AAA Pacific Coast League affiliate of the San Diego Padres, features white-bordered posed color player photos on its fronts. The player's name and position appear at the bottom. The white and black back carries the team name at the top, followed below by the league affiliation, and then the player's name, biography and statistics. This issue includes the only minor league card of Tony Gwynn.

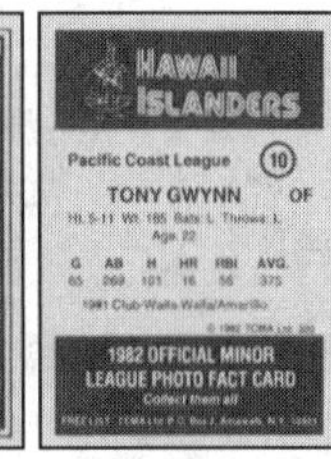

	MINT	NRMT	EXC
COMPLETE SET (25)	325.00	145.00	40.00

☐ 1 Ron Tingley
☐ 2 Dave Richards
☐ 3 Steve Smith
☐ 4 Jim Pankovits
☐ 5 Jerry Johnson
☐ 6 Joe Lansford
☐ 7 Jerry De Simone
☐ 8 Dan Gausepohl
☐ 9 Aaron Cain
☐ 10 Tony Gwynn
☐ 11 Rick Lancellotti
☐ 12 Jeff Pyburn
☐ 13 Steve Fireovid
☐ 14 Andy Hawkins
☐ 15 George Stablein
☐ 16 Ron Meredith
☐ 17 Fred Kuhaulua
☐ 18 Tim Hamm
☐ 19 Tom Tellmann
☐ 20 Dave Dravecky
☐ 21 Mark Thurmond
☐ 22 Kim Seaman
☐ 23 Doug Rader
☐ 24 Chuck Hartenstein
☐ 25 Larry Duensing

1982 Holyoke Millers TCMA

This 26-card standard-size set of the 1982 Holyoke Millers, a Class AA Eastern League affiliate of the California Angels, features white-bordered posed color player photos on its fronts. The player's name and position appear at the bottom. The white and black back carries the team name at the top, followed below by the league affiliation, and then the player's name, biography and statistics.

	MINT	NRMT	EXC
COMPLETE SET (26)	10.00	4.50	1.25

☐ 1 Michael Barba
☐ 2 Brian Buckley
☐ 3 Jeff Conner
☐ 4 Lonnie Dugger
☐ 5 Dave Duran
☐ 6 Bill Mooneyham
☐ 7 Perry Morrison
☐ 8 Ron Romanick
☐ 9 David A. Smith
☐ 10 David W. Smith
☐ 11 Bob Palmer
☐ 12 Larry Patterson
☐ 13 Rick Adams
☐ 14 Bob Bohnet
☐ 15 Ron Hunt
☐ 16 Pat Keedy
☐ 17 Tim Krauss
☐ 18 Gus Polidor
☐ 19 Chris Clark
☐ 20 Harry Francis
☐ 21 Dennis Gilbert
☐ 22 Darrell Miller
☐ 23 Jack Hiatt
☐ 24 Marc Terrazas
☐ 25 George Como
☐ 26 Ben Surner

1982 Idaho Falls Athletics TCMA

This 33-card standard-size set of the 1982 Idaho Falls Athletics, a Rookie Class Pioneer League affiliate of the Oakland Athletics, features white-faced fronts bordered by two thin red lines framing posed black-and-white player portraits. A red stripe below the photo carries the player's name and position. The white back carries the team name at the top, followed by the player's name, position, biography and statistics.

	MINT	NRMT	EXC
COMPLETE SET (33)	15.00	6.75	1.85

☐ 1 Dav Baehr
☐ 2 Jim Bailey
☐ 3 Mark Border
☐ 4 Eric Brown
☐ 5 Tom Conquest
☐ 6 Doug Farrow
☐ 7 Todd Fischer
☐ 8 Angelo Gilbert
☐ 9 Mark Kochanski
☐ 10 Tim Lambert
☐ 11 Dave Leiper
☐ 12 Tenoa Stevenson
☐ 13 Steve Travers
☐ 14 Shawn Gill
☐ 15 Russ Wortmann
☐ 16 Leon Baham
☐ 17 Bill Davis
☐ 18 Mark Dye
☐ 19 John Michel
☐ 20 Clemente Oropeza
☐ 21 Greg Robles
☐ 22 Kenny Clayton
☐ 23 Steve Campbell
☐ 24 Rob Loscalzo
☐ 25 Eddie Malone
☐ 26 Gary McGraw
☐ 27 Jorge Oquendo
☐ 28 Ricky Thomas
☐ 29 Dave Wilder
☐ 30 Keith Lieppman
☐ 31 Grady Fuson
☐ 32 Mark Doberenz
☐ 33 Dave Sheriff

1982 Indianapolis Indians Team Issue

1,200 sets were produced.

	MINT	NRMT	EXC
COMPLETE SET (32)	15.00	6.75	1.85

☐ 1 Team Picture
☐ 2 George Scherger MG
☐ 3 Kip Young
☐ 4 Nick Esasky
☐ 5 Brad Lesley
☐ 6 Duane Walker
☐ 7 Bill Dawley
☐ 8 The Instructors
☐ 9 Brooks Carey
☐ 10 Orlando Isales
☐ 11 Brian Ryder
☐ 12 Dave Van Gorder
☐ 13 Greg Harris
☐ 14 The Bullpen
☐ 15 Tom Lawless
☐ 16 Mike Dowless
☐ 17 Gary Redus
☐ 18 The Catchers
☐ 19 Rich Carlucci
☐ 20 Tom Foley
☐ 21 Ben Hayes
☐ 22 Steve Christmas
☐ 23 The Outfielders
☐ 24 Ron Farkas
☐ 25 Dave Tomlin
☐ 26 Dallas Williams
☐ 27 The Infielders
☐ 28 Gil Kubski
☐ 29 Neil Fiala
☐ 30 Starting Pitchers
☐ 31 Lee Garrett TR
☐ 32 Behind The Scenes

1982 Iowa Cubs TCMA

This 32-card standard-size set of the 1982 Iowa Cubs, a Class AAA American Association affiliate of the Chicago Cubs, features white-bordered posed color player photos on its fronts. The player's name and position appear at the bottom. The white and black back carries the team name at the top, followed below by the league affiliation, and then the player's name, biography and statistics.

	MINT	NRMT	EXC
COMPLETE SET (32)	35.00	16.00	4.40

☐ 1 Alfred Benton
☐ 2 Scott Fletcher
☐ 3 Tom Grant
☐ 4 Mel Hall
☐ 5 Bill Hayes
☐ 6 Randy Lavigne
☐ 7 Jared Martin
☐ 8 Danny Rohn
☐ 9 Joe Strain
☐ 10 Pat Tabler
☐ 11 Scot Thompson
☐ 12 Jack Upton
☐ 13 Elliott Waller
☐ 14 Robert Blyth
☐ 15 Tom Filer
☐ 16 Jay Howell
☐ 17 Larry Jones
☐ 18 Chris Knapp
☐ 19 Ken Kravec
☐ 20 Craig Lefferts
☐ 21 Mark Parker
☐ 22 Mike Proly
☐ 23 Herman Sagelke
☐ 24 Randy Stein
☐ 25 Jim Napier

☐ 26 Scott Breeden
☐ 27 Ken Grandquist
☐ 28 Bob Reynolds
☐ 29 Tom Butts
☐ 30 Frank Macy
☐ 31 Kim Hart
☐ 32 Dr. Richard Evans

1982 Jackson Mets TCMA

This 25-card standard-size set of the 1982 Jackson Mets, a Class AA Texas League affiliate of the New York Mets, features white-bordered posed color player photos on its fronts. The player's name and position appear at the bottom. The white and black back carries the team name at the top, followed below by the league affiliation, and then the player's name, biography and statistics. This issue includes the minor league card debut of Darryl Strawberry. Approximately 2,500 sets were produced.

	MINT	NRMT	EXC
COMPLETE SET (25)	70.00	32.00	8.75

☐ 1 Jeff Bittiger
☐ 2 Matt Bullinger
☐ 3 Ted Davis
☐ 4 Scott Dye
☐ 5 Steve Ibarguen
☐ 6 Jody Johnston
☐ 7 Brian Kolbe
☐ 8 Jose Rodriguez
☐ 9 John Semprini
☐ 10 Doug Sisk
☐ 11 Ronn Reynolds
☐ 12 Dave Duff
☐ 13 Rick Poe
☐ 14 Mike Anicich
☐ 15 Rick McMullen
☐ 16 Al Pedrique
☐ 17 Jim Woodward
☐ 18 Bill Rittweger
☐ 19 Billy Beane
☐ 20 Terry Blocker
☐ 21 Darryl Strawberry
☐ 22 Gene Dusan
☐ 23 Bob Apodaca
☐ 24 Bob Sikes
☐ 25 Bill Walberg

1982 Knoxville Blue Jays TCMA

This 23-card standard-size set of the 1982 Knoxville Blue Jays, a Class AA Southern League affiliate of the Toronto Blue Jays, features white-faced fronts bordered by two thin red lines framing posed black-and-white player portraits. A red stripe below the photo carries the player's name and position. The white back carries the team name at the top, followed by the player's name, position, biography and statistics.

	MINT	NRMT	EXC
COMPLETE SET (23)	10.00	4.50	1.25

☐ 1 Team Photo
☐ 2 Scott Elam
☐ 3 Randy Ford
☐ 4 Dennis Howard
☐ 5 Tom Lukish
☐ 6 Colin McLaughlin
☐ 7 Keith Walker
☐ 8 Matt Williams
☐ 9 Brian Stemberger
☐ 10 Brian Milner
☐ 11 Dan Whitmer
☐ 12 Tim Thompson
☐ 13 Paul Hodgson
☐ 14 Andre Wood
☐ 15 Carlos Rios
☐ 16 Ed Dennis
☐ 17 Vern Ramie
☐ 18 J.J. Cannon
☐ 19 Vassie Gardner
☐ 20 Ron Shepherd
☐ 21 Larry Hardy MG
☐ 22 Hector Torres CO
☐ 23 John Woodworth TR

1982 Louisville Redbirds Ehrlers

	MINT	NRMT	EXC
COMPLETE SET (30)	25.00	11.00	3.10

☐ 1 George A. Bjorkman
☐ 2 Glenn E. Brummer
☐ 3 Jose Oscar Brito
☐ 4 Michael S. Calise
☐ 5 Ralph A. Citarella
☐ 6 Joseph De Sa
☐ 7 Jeffrey D. Doyle
☐ 8 Joseph F. Frazier
☐ 9 John T. Fulgham
☐ 10 David A. Green
☐ 11 Ricky N. Horton
☐ 12 David B. Kable
☐ 13 Jeffrey Allen Lahti
☐ 14 William Allen Lyons
☐ 15 John R. Martin
☐ 16 Willie D. McGee
☐ 17 Jerry McKune
☐ 18 Dyar K. Miller
☐ 19 Gotay Mills
☐ 20 Daniel J. Morogiello
☐ 21 Alan R. Olmsted
☐ 22 Kelly J. Paris
☐ 23 Gaylen R. Pitts
☐ 24 Andrew J. Rincon
☐ 25 Eugene L. (Gene) Roof
☐ 26 Orlando Sanchez
☐ 27 Rafael Santana
☐ 28 Jed Smith
☐ 29 John A. Stuper
☐ 30 Steven W. Winfield

1982 Lynchburg Mets TCMA

This 23-card standard-size set of the 1982 Lynchburg Mets, a Class A Carolina League affiliate of the New York Mets, features white-bordered posed black-and-white player photos on its fronts. The player's name and position appear at the bottom. The white and black back carries the team name at the top, followed below by the league affiliation, and then the player's name, biography and statistics.

	MINT	NRMT	EXC
COMPLETE SET (23)	50.00	22.00	6.25

☐ 1 Danny Monzon
☐ 2 Laschelle Tarver
☐ 3 Herman Winningham
☐ 4 John De Imonte
☐ 5 Bruce Kastelic
☐ 6 Kevin Mitchell
☐ 7 Dewayne Vaughn
☐ 8 Ed Rech
☐ 9 Jeff Sunderlage
☐ 10 Paul Wilmet
☐ 11 Tom Miller
☐ 12 Roger Frash
☐ 13 Duane Evans
☐ 14 Chuck Schnoor
☐ 15 Randy Milligan
☐ 16 Lloyd McClendon
☐ 17 Rick Myles
☐ 18 Roger Begue
☐ 19 Jay Tibbs
☐ 20 Bill Fultz
☐ 21 Rich Webster
☐ 22 Jody Johnston
☐ 23 John Raeside

1982 Lynn Sailors TCMA

This 18-card standard-size set of the 1982 Lynn Sailors, a Class AA Eastern League affiliate of the Seattle Mariners, features white-bordered posed black-and-white player photos on its fronts. The player's name and position appear at the bottom. The white and black back carries the team name at the top, followed below by the league affiliation, and then the player's name, biography and statistics.

	MINT	NRMT	EXC
COMPLETE SET (18)	25.00	11.00	3.10

☐ 1 Rick Adair
☐ 2 Carl Best
☐ 3 Kevin Dukes
☐ 4 Joe Georger
☐ 5 Steve Krueger
☐ 6 Jed Murray
☐ 7 Jeff Stottlemyre
☐ 8 Scott Stranski (photo actually Jeff Stottlemyre)
☐ 9 Jim Nelson
☐ 10 Clark Crist
☐ 11 Bill Crone (photo actually John Moses)
☐ 12 Mario Diaz
☐ 13 Jim Presley
☐ 14 Ramon Estepa (photo actually Tito Nanni)
☐ 15 Tito Nanni
☐ 16 Glenn Walker
☐ 17 Harold Reynolds
☐ 18 Mickey Bowers

1982 Madison Muskies Fritsch

	MINT	NRMT	EXC
COMPLETE SET (34)	5.00	2.20	.60

☐ 1 Checklist
☐ 2 Joel Boni
☐ 3 Steve Kiefer
☐ 4 Mike Flinn
☐ 5 John(Duke) Smith
☐ 6 Chuck Kolotka
☐ 7 Kevin Coughlon
☐ 8 Tom Heckman
☐ 9 Gene Ransom
☐ 10 Scott Anderson
☐ 11 Scot Mitchell
☐ 12 Mark Jarrett
☐ 13 Jeff Tipton
☐ 14 Mark Fellows
☐ 15 Monte R. McAbee
☐ 16 Ron Wilkinson
☐ 17 Allen Edwards
☐ 18 Frank Harris CO
☐ 19 Brad Fischer
☐ 20 James Feeley
☐ 21 Ron Harrison
☐ 22 Kevin D. Waller
☐ 23 Mike Ashman
☐ 24 Rob Vavrock
☐ 25 Jeff Kobernus
☐ 26 Keith Call
☐ 27 Pat O'Hara
☐ 28 Thomas Romano
☐ 29 Mark(Mac) McDonald
☐ 30 Bruce Amador
☐ 31 Jeff Cary
☐ 32 Hector Perez TR
☐ 33 Ed Janus MG
☐ 34 Michael Duval GM
Bob Drew VP

1982 Miami Marlins TCMA

This 22-card standard-size set of the 1982 Miami Marlins, a Class A Florida State League affiliate of the San Diego Padres, features white-bordered posed black-and-white player photos on its fronts. The player's name and position appear at the bottom. The white and black back carries the team name at the top, followed below by the league affiliation, and then the player's name, biography and statistics.

	MINT	NRMT	EXC
COMPLETE SET (22)	10.00	4.50	1.25

☐ 1 Will George
☐ 2 Mike Glinatsis
☐ 3 Marcos Gonzalez
☐ 4 Brian McDonough
☐ 5 Carlos Moreno
☐ 6 Joel Pyfrom
☐ 7 Tony Wadley
☐ 8 Jose Caballero
☐ 9 Ron Cardieri
☐ 10 Jorge Curbelo
☐ 11 Jorge Llano
☐ 12 Robbie Alvarez
☐ 13 Julio Beltran
☐ 14 Bob Boyce
☐ 15 Edgar Castro
☐ 16 Rick Rembielak
☐ 17 Angel Valdez
☐ 18 Raul Tovar
☐ 19 Lee Granger
☐ 20 Mike Kutner
☐ 21 Frank Contreras
☐ 22 John Tamargo

1982 Nashville Sounds Team Issue

	MINT	NRMT	EXC
COMPLETE SET (28)	5.00	2.20	.60

☐ 1 Dave Banes
☐ 2 Mike Browning
☐ 3 Brian Butterfield
☐ 4 Ben Callahan
☐ 5 Pat Callahan
☐ 6 Nate Chapman
☐ 7 Clay Christiansen
☐ 8 Dean Craig
☐ 9 Brian Dayett
☐ 10 Tommie Dodd
☐ 11 Guy Elston
☐ 12 Ray Fontenot
☐ 13 Paul Grayner
☐ 14 Rex Hudler
☐ 15 Tim Knight
☐ 16 Chris Lein
☐ 17 Erik Peterson
☐ 18 Brian Poldberg
☐ 19 Frank Ricci
☐ 20 Mark Salas
☐ 21 Dan Schmitz
☐ 22 Buck Showalter
☐ 23 Roger Slagle
☐ 24 Garry Smith
☐ 25 Bob Sykes
☐ 26 Rafael Villaman
☐ 27 Stefan Wever
☐ 28 Managers And Coaches
Hoyt Wilhelm CO
John Oates MG
Eddie Napoleon CO

1982 Oklahoma City 89ers TCMA

This 25-card standard-size set of the 1982 Oklahoma City 89ers, a Class AAA American Association affiliate of the Texas Rangers, features white-bordered posed color player photos on its fronts. The player's name and position appear at the bottom. The white and black back carries the team name at the top, followed below by the league affiliation, and then the player's name, biography and statistics.

	MINT	NRMT	EXC
COMPLETE SET (25)	40.00	18.00	5.00

☐ 1 Mike Willis
☐ 2 Rowland Office
☐ 3 Tim Corcoran
☐ 4 Ramon Aviles
☐ 5 Ellis Deal
☐ 6 Ron Clark
☐ 7 Al Sanchez
☐ 8 Len Matuszek
☐ 9 Jerry Reed
☐ 10 Rusty Hamric
☐ 11 Julio Franco
☐ 12 Mark Davis
☐ 13 Joe Kerrigan
☐ 14 Tom Lombarski
☐ 15 Tony McDonald
☐ 16 Luis Rasmussen
☐ 17 Jeff Ulrich
☐ 18 Jim Rasmussen
☐ 19 Jon Reelhorn
☐ 20 Herb Orensky
☐ 21 Kelly Downs
☐ 22 Marty Decker
☐ 23 Darren Burroughs
☐ 24 Don Carman
☐ 25 Will Culmer

1982 Omaha Royals TCMA

This 29-card standard-size set of the 1982 Omaha Royals, a Class AAA American Association affiliate of the Kansas City Royals, features white-bordered posed color player photos on its fronts. The player's name and position appear at the bottom. The white and black back carries the team name at the top, followed below by the league affiliation, and then the player's name, biography and statistics.

	MINT	NRMT	EXC
COMPLETE SET (27)	15.00	6.75	1.85
COMPLETE SET (29)	60.00	27.00	7.50

☐ 1 Mike Armstrong
☐ 2 Ralph Botting
☐ 3 Keith Creel
☐ 4 Dan Fischer
☐ 5 Don Hood
☐ 6 Phil Huffman
☐ 7 Bill Kelly
☐ 8 Dave Schuler
☐ 9 Bob Tufts
☐ 10 Frank Wills
☐ 11 Greg Keatley
☐ 12 Don Slaught
☐ 13 Mitch Ashmore
☐ 14 Buddy Biancalana
☐ 15 Manuel Colletti
☐ 16 Dave Edler
☐ 17A Ron Johnson (Photo of Dan Wieser)
☐ 17B Ron Johnson (White uniform)
☐ 18A Dan Wieser (Photo of Ron Johnson)
☐ 18B Dan Weiser (Blue uniform)
☐ 19 Darryl Motley
☐ 20 Bombo Rivera
☐ 21 Mark Ryal
☐ 22 Pat Sheridan
☐ 23 Luis Silverio
☐ 24 Bill Gorman GM
☐ 25 Joe Sparks MGR
☐ 26 Jerry Cram CO
☐ 27 Paul McGannon TR

1982 Oneonta Yankees TCMA

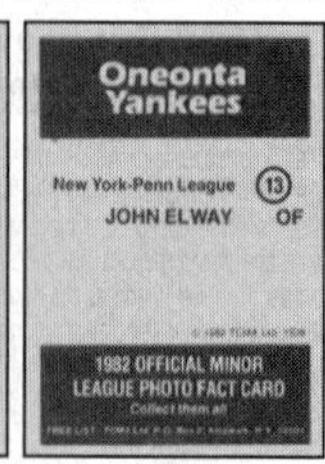

This 17-card standard-size set of the 1982 Oneonta Yankees, a Class A New York-Penn League affiliate of the New York Yankees, features white-bordered posed black-and-white player photos on its fronts.

The player's name and position appear at the bottom. The white and black back carries the team name at the top, followed below by the league affiliation, and then the player's name, biography and statistics. This issue includes the only minor league card of Denver Broncos' quarterback John Elway. Approximately 1,100 sets were produced.

	MINT	NRMT	EXC
COMPLETE SET (17)	350.00	160.00	45.00

☐ 1 Orestes Destrade
☐ 2 Jim Riggs
☐ 3 Brent Giesdal
☐ 4 Ken Berry
☐ 5 Dan O'Regan
☐ 6 Q.V. Lowe
☐ 7 Stan Sanders
☐ 8 Tim Birtsas
☐ 9 Steve Campagno
☐ 10 Pate Bone
☐ 11 Tim Byron
☐ 12 Jesus Alcala
☐ 13 John Elway
☐ 14 Mike Fennell
☐ 15 Jim Ferguson
☐ 16 Mike Gatlin
☐ 17 Pedro Medina

1982 Orlando Twins 81 SL Champs TCMA

This 24-card standard-size set of the 1982 Orlando Twins, a Class AA Southern League affiliate of the Minnesota Twins, features white-bordered posed black-and-white player photos on its fronts. The player's name and position appear at the bottom. The white and black back carries the team name at the top, followed below by the league affiliation, and then the player's name, biography and statistics. The words Southern League Champs is printed on the front of each card.

	MINT	NRMT	EXC
COMPLETE SET (24)	50.00	22.00	6.25

☐ 1 Rod Booker
☐ 2 Randy Bush
☐ 3 Chino Cadahia
☐ 4 Manny Colletti
☐ 5 Andre David
☐ 6 Steve Douglas
☐ 7 Gary Gaetti
☐ 8 Tim Laudner
☐ 9 Tim Teufel
☐ 10 Scott Ullger
☐ 11 Lance Hallberg
☐ 12 Tom Kelly
☐ 13 Eric Broersma
☐ 14 Scott Gleckel
☐ 15 Steve Green
☐ 16 Brad Havens
☐ 17 Jacks Hobbs
☐ 18 Bob Konopa
☐ 19 Ted Kromy
☐ 20 Steve Mapel
☐ 21 Bob Mulligan
☐ 22 Jose Reyes
☐ 23 Gary Serum
☐ 24 Frank Viola

1982 Orlando Twins TCMA

This 24-card standard-size set of the 1982 Orlando Twins, a Class AA Southern League affiliate of the Minnesota Twins, features white-bordered posed black-and-white player photos on its fronts. The player's name and position appear at the bottom. The white and black back carries the team name at the top, followed below by the league affiliation, and then the player's name, biography and statistics.

	MINT	NRMT	EXC
COMPLETE SET (24)	40.00	18.00	5.00

☐ 1 Kevin Williams
☐ 2 Lee Belanger
☐ 3 Eric Broersma
☐ 4 Smokey Everett
☐ 5 Jack Hobbs
☐ 6 Bob Konopa
☐ 7 Mark Funderburk
☐ 8 Greg Gagne
☐ 9 Dave Meier
☐ 10 Mike McClain
☐ 11 Tony Pilla
☐ 12 Tim Teufel
☐ 13 Tom Kelly
☐ 14 Rick Austin
☐ 15 Chino Cadahia
☐ 16 Andre David
☐ 17 Steve Douglas
☐ 18 Ken Foster
☐ 19 Ted Kromy
☐ 20 Larry May
☐ 21 Bob Mulligan
☐ 22 Jay Pettibone
☐ 23 Sam Arrington
☐ 24 Eddie Hodge

1982 Phoenix Giants Valley National Bank

	MINT	NRMT	EXC
COMPLETE SET (27)	10.00	4.50	1.25

☐ 1 Team Photo
☐ 2 Mike Chris
☐ 3 Ted Wilborn
☐ 4 Mike Rowland
☐ 5 John Rabb
☐ 6 Paul Szymarek
☐ 7 Rocky Bridges
☐ 8 Dave Roberts
☐ 9 Harry Jordan
Tommy Gonzales
☐ 10 Mike Tucker
☐ 11 Ethan Blackaby
☐ 12 Craig Chamberlain
☐ 13 Ron Pruitt
☐ 14 Mark Dempsey
☐ 15 Dorian Boyland
☐ 16 Jeff Stember
☐ 17 Mike Turgeon
☐ 18 Giantettes
☐ 19 Andy McGaffigan
☐ 20 Kelly Smith
☐ 21 Tom Runnells
☐ 22 Dan Gladden
☐ 23 Tom O'Malley
☐ 24 Jose Barrios
☐ 25 Booster Rooster
☐ 26 Mike Rex
☐ 27 Al Hargesheimer

1982 Portland Beavers TCMA

This 25-card standard-size set of the 1982 Portland Beavers, a Class AAA Pacific Coast League affiliate of the Pittsburgh Pirates, features white-bordered posed color player photos on its fronts. The player's name and position appear at the bottom. The white and black back carries the team name at the top, followed below by the league affiliation, and then the player's name, biography and statistics.

	MINT	NRMT	EXC
COMPLETE SET (25)	15.00	6.75	1.85

☐ 1 Jose DeLeon
☐ 2 Butch Edge
☐ 3 Cecilio Guante
☐ 4 Odell Jones
☐ 5 Robert Long
☐ 6 Randy Niemann
Sic, Nieman
☐ 7 Pascual Perez
Sic, Pasqual
☐ 8 Manny Sarmiento
☐ 9 Lee Tunnell
☐ 10 Stan Cliburn
☐ 11 Junior Ortiz
☐ 12 Wayne Caughey
☐ 13 Denny Gonzalez
☐ 14 Willie Horton
☐ 15 Bobby Mitchell
☐ 16 Nelson Norman
☐ 17 Eddie Vargas
☐ 18 Dave Augustine
☐ 19 Trench Davis
☐ 20 Doug Frobel
☐ 21 Jose Rodriguez
☐ 22 Reggie Walton
☐ 23 Jim Saul MGR
☐ 24 Vern Law CO/Jim Saul MGR
☐ 26 Carlos Lezedma TR

1982 Quad City Cubs TCMA

This 28-card standard-size set of the 1982 Quad City Cubs, a Class A Midwest League affiliate of the Chicago Cubs, features white-bordered posed black-and-white player photos on its fronts. The player's name and position appear at the bottom. The white and black back carries the team name at the top, followed below by the league affiliation, and then the player's name, biography and statistics.

	MINT	NRMT	EXC
COMPLETE SET (28)	15.00	6.75	1.85

☐ 1 Darryl Banks
☐ 2 Allen Black
☐ 3 Russ Brahms
☐ 4 Rich Buonantony
☐ 5 Jorge Carpio
☐ 6 Tim Clarke
☐ 7 Mitch Cooke
☐ 8 Jeff Fruge
☐ 9 Ron Kaufman
☐ 10 Vance Lovelace
☐ 11 Mike Shulleetta
☐ 12 Roger Crow
☐ 13 Craig Weissman
☐ 14 Lee George
☐ 15 Wendell Henderson
☐ 16 Jeff Remo
☐ 17 James Allen
☐ 18 Ken Arnerich
☐ 19 Jeff Rutledge
☐ 20 Otis Tramble
☐ 21 Antonion Cordova
☐ 22 Darrin Jackson
☐ 23 Scott Miller
☐ 24 Rolando Roomes
☐ 25 Jim Walsh
☐ 26 George Enright
☐ 27 Quency Hill
☐ 28 Randy Roetter

1982 Reading Phillies TCMA

This 22-card standard-size set of the 1982 Reading Phillies, a Class AA Eastern League affiliate of the Philadelphia Phillies, features white-bordered posed black-and-white player photos on its fronts. The player's name and position appear at the bottom. The white and black back carries the team name at the top, followed below by the league affiliation, and then the player's name, biography and statistics.

	MINT	NRMT	EXC
COMPLETE SET (22)	25.00	11.00	3.10

☐ 1 Jay Baller
☐ 2 Kelly Faulk
☐ 3 Butch Hughes
☐ 4 Kyle Money
☐ 5 John Palmieri
☐ 6 Dan Prior
☐ 7 Jim Rasmussen
☐ 8 Leroy Smith
☐ 9 Dennis Thomas
☐ 10 Richard Wortham
☐ 11 Gerry Willard
☐ 12 Al Velasquez
☐ 13 Dave Enos
☐ 14 Paul Fryer
☐ 15 Steve Jeltz
☐ 16 Jon Lindsey
☐ 17 Joe Nemeth
☐ 18 Randy Salava
☐ 19 Keith Washington
☐ 20 Steve Harvey
☐ 21 Tony McDonald
☐ 22 John Felske

1982 Redwood Pioneers TCMA

This 27-card standard-size set of the 1982 Redwood Pioneers, a Class A California League affiliate of the California Angels, features white-bordered posed black-and-white player photos on its fronts. The player's name and position appear at the bottom. The white and black back carries the team name at the top, followed below by the league affiliation, and then the player's name, biography and statistics.

	MINT	NRMT	EXC
COMPLETE SET (27)	15.00	6.75	1.85

☐ 1 Michael Brooks
☐ 2 Steven Eakes
☐ 3 Craig Gerber
☐ 4 Kevin Halicki
☐ 5 Gordon Jones
☐ 6 Tim Kammeyer
☐ 7 Steve Liddle
☐ 8 James Randall
☐ 9 Esmyel Romero
☐ 10 Michael Saatzer
☐ 11 Mark Smelko
☐ 12 Jeff Smith
☐ 13 Mark Sproesser
☐ 14 Darryl Stephens
☐ 15 Richard Sundberg
☐ 16 Ronald Sylvia
☐ 17 Paul Wright
☐ 18 Luis Zambrana
☐ 19 Harry Oliver
☐ 20 Glen Fisher
☐ 21 Ronald Hunt
☐ 22 Terry Harper
☐ 23 Kevin Jacobson
☐ 24 Barton Barun
☐ 25 Chris Cannizzaro
☐ 26 Brian Parfrey
☐ 27 Ralph Hartman

1982 Richmond Braves TCMA

This 32-card standard-size set of the 1982 Richmond Braves, a Class AAA International League affiliate of the Atlanta Braves, features white-bordered posed color player photos on its fronts. The player's name and position appear at the bottom. The white and black back carries the team name at the top, followed below by the league affiliation, and then the player's name, biography and statistics.

	MINT	NRMT	EXC
COMPLETE SET (31)	25.00	11.00	3.10
COMPLETE SET (32)	75.00	34.00	9.50

☐ 1 Jose Alvarez
☐ 2A Tony Brizzolara
☐ 2B Tony Brizzolara (Catching)
☐ 3 Tim Cole
☐ 4 John D'Acquisto
☐ 5 Carlos Diaz
☐ 6 Craig McMurtry
☐ 7 Donnie Moore
☐ 8 Jeff Twitty
☐ 9 Roger Weaver
☐ 10 Jerry Keller
☐ 11 Larry Owen
☐ 12 Matt Sinatro
☐ 13 Brook Jacoby
☐ 14 Gerald Perry
☐ 15 Chico Ruiz
☐ 16 Paul Runge
☐ 17 Paul Zuvella
☐ 18 Mike Reynolds
☐ 19 Albert Hall
☐ 20 Leonel Vargas
☐ 21 Bob Porter
☐ 22 Mike Colbern
☐ 23 Ken Smith
☐ 24 Terry Harper
☐ 25 Ken Dayley
☐ 26 Mike Smith
☐ 27 Eddie Haas MGR
☐ 28 Johnny Sain CO
☐ 29 Craig Robinson CO
☐ 30 Sam Ayoub TR
☐ 31 Albert Hall
Brook Jacoby
Gerald Perry
Terry Harper
and Roger Weaver

1982 Rochester Red Wings TCMA

This 22-card standard-size set of the 1982 Rochester Red Wings, a Class AAA International League affiliate of the Baltimore Orioles, features white-bordered posed color player photos on its fronts. The player's name and position appear at the bottom. The white and black back carries the team name at the top, followed below by the league affiliation, and then the player's name, biography and statistics.

	MINT	NRMT	EXC
COMPLETE SET (22)	15.00	6.75	1.85

☐ 1 Mike Boddicker
☐ 2 John Flinn
☐ 3 Bruce MacPherson
☐ 4 Craig Minetto
☐ 5 Allan Ramirez
☐ 6 Cliff Speck
☐ 7 Bill Swaggerty
☐ 8 Don Welchel
☐ 9 Tim Derryberry
☐ 10 Dan Graham
☐ 11 Willie Royster
☐ 12 Glenn Gulliver
☐ 13 Rick Jones
☐ 14 Rick Lisi
☐ 15 Dan Logan
☐ 16 Vic Rodriguez
☐ 17 John Shelby
☐ 18 John Valle
☐ 19 Mike Young
☐ 20 Lance Nichols
☐ 21 Tom Chism
☐ 22 Ken Rowe

1982 Salt Lake City Gulls TCMA

This 25-card standard-size set of the 1982 Salt Lake City Gulls, a Class AAA Pacific Coast League affiliate of the Seattle Mariners, features white-bordered posed color player photos on its fronts. The player's name and position appear at the bottom. The white and black back carries the team name at the top, followed below by the league affiliation, and then the player's name, biography and statistics.

	MINT	NRMT	EXC
COMPLETE SET (25)	10.00	4.50	1.25

☐ 1 Doug Merrifield
☐ 2 Jamie Allen
☐ 3 Rod Allen
☐ 4 Rich Bordi
☐ 5 Al Chambers
☐ 6 Bryan Clark
☐ 7 Roy Clark
☐ 8 Steve Finch
☐ 9 Gary Gray
☐ 10 Tracy Harris
☐ 11 Mike Hart
☐ 12 Vance McHenry
☐ 13 Orlando Mercado
☐ 14 Ron Musselman
☐ 15 Casey Parsons
☐ 16 Domingo Ramos
☐ 17 Brian Snyder
☐ 18 Bob Stoddard
☐ 19 Roy Thomas
☐ 20 Dave Valle
☐ 21 Sammye Welborn
☐ 22 Matt Young
☐ 23 Manny Estrada
☐ 24 Bobby Floyd
☐ 25 Joe Decker

1982 Spokane Indians TCMA

This 26-card standard-size set of the 1982 Spokane Indians, a Class AAA Pacific Coast League affiliate of the California Angels, features white-bordered posed color player photos on its fronts. The player's name and position appear at the bottom. The white and black back carries the team name at the top, followed below by the league affiliation, and then the player's name, biography and statistics.

	MINT	NRMT	EXC
COMPLETE SET (26)	10.00	4.50	1.25

- ☐ 1 Steve Brown
- ☐ 2 Craig Eaton
- ☐ 3 Rick Foley
- ☐ 4 Mickey Mahler
- ☐ 5 Fred Martinez
- ☐ 6 Paul Olden
- ☐ 7 Jeff Schneider
- ☐ 8 Rick Steirer
- ☐ 9 Mike Walters
- ☐ 10 Mike Bishop
- ☐ 11 Steve Herz
- ☐ 12 Jerry Narron
- ☐ 13 Jeff Bertoni
- ☐ 14 Craig Cacer
- ☐ 15 Scott Carnes
- ☐ 16 John Harris
- ☐ 17 Steve Lubratich
- ☐ 18 Les Pearsey
- ☐ 19 Mike Brown
- ☐ 20 Tom Brunansky
- ☐ 21 Ron Jackson
- ☐ 22 Pepe Mangual
- ☐ 23 Gary Pettis
- ☐ 24 Moose Stubing
- ☐ 25 Joe Coleman
- ☐ 26 Leonard Garcia

1982 Springfield Cardinals Fritsch

	MINT	NRMT	EXC
COMPLETE SET (24)	5.00	2.20	.60

- ☐ 1 Checklist
- ☐ 2 Dave Bialas MG
- ☐ 3 Bruce(Pic) Miller TR
- ☐ 4 Bill Lyons
- ☐ 5 Mike Pittman
- ☐ 6 Freddie Silva
- ☐ 7 Robert Hicks
- ☐ 8 Tom Epple
- ☐ 9 Dan Stryffeler
- ☐ 10 Gus Malespin
- ☐ 11 Steve Winfield
- ☐ 12 Danny Cox
- ☐ 13 Greg Dunn
- ☐ 14 Bobby Kish
- ☐ 15 Tom Dozier
- ☐ 16 Marty Mason
- ☐ 17 Alan Hunsinger
- ☐ 18 Don Collins
- ☐ 19 Mike Harris
- ☐ 20 Randy Hunt
- ☐ 21 Deron Thomas
- ☐ 22 Harry McCulla
- ☐ 23 Brad Bennett
- ☐ 24 Francisco Batista

1982 Syracuse Chiefs TCMA

This 29-card standard-size set of the 1982 Syracuse Chiefs, a Class AAA International League affiliate of the Toronto Blue Jays, features white-bordered posed color player photos on its fronts. The player's name and position appear at the bottom. The white and black back carries the team name at the top, followed below by the league affiliation, and then the player's name, biography and statistics. This issue includes Tony Fernandez' minor league debut. Two cards were issued bearing number 27; those and number 28 were late issues.

	MINT	NRMT	EXC
COMPLETE SET (26)	40.00	18.00	5.00
COMPLETE SET W/LATE ISSUES (29)	70.00	32.00	8.75

- ☐ 1 Mike Barlow
- ☐ 2 Tom Dixon
- ☐ 3 Mark Eichhorn
- ☐ 4 Mark Geisel
- ☐ 5 John Littlefield
- ☐ 6 Frank Ricelli
- ☐ 7 Ken Schrom
- ☐ 8 Steve Senteney
- ☐ 9 Jackson Todd
- ☐ 10 Jim Wright
- ☐ 11 Jim Gaudet
- ☐ 12 Ramon Lora
- ☐ 13 Gene Petralli
- ☐ 14 Dave Baker
- ☐ 15 Charlie Beamon
- ☐ 16 Brian Doyle
- ☐ 17 Tony Fernandez
- ☐ 18 Fred Manrique
- ☐ 19 Glenn Adams
- ☐ 20 George Bell
- ☐ 21 Pedro Hernandez
- ☐ 22 Creighton Tevlin
- ☐ 23 Mitch Webster
- ☐ 24 Doug Ault
- ☐ 25 Tom Craig TR
- ☐ 26 Jim Beauchamp MG
- ☐ 27A Duane Larson CO (Late Issue)
- ☐ 27B Rick O'Keeffe (Late Issue
- ☐ 28 Dan Whitmer (Late Issue)

1982 Syracuse Chiefs Team Issue

This issue includes Tony Fernandez' minor league card debut.

	MINT	NRMT	EXC
COMPLETE SET (24)	100.00	45.00	12.50

- ☐ 1 Glenn Adams
- ☐ 2 Doug Ault
- ☐ 3 Dave Baker
- ☐ 4 Mike Barlow
- ☐ 5 Charlie Beamon
- ☐ 6 Jim Beauchamp
- ☐ 7 George Bell
- ☐ 8 Pete Dempsey
- ☐ 9 Tom Dixon
- ☐ 10 Brian Doyle
- ☐ 11 Mark Eichhorn
- ☐ 12 Tony Fernandez
- ☐ 13 Dave Geisel
- ☐ 14 Pedro Hernandez
- ☐ 15 John Littlefield
- ☐ 16 Fred Manrique
- ☐ 17 Rick O'Keefe
- ☐ 18 Geno Petralli
- ☐ 19 Ken Schrom
- ☐ 20 Steve Senteney
- ☐ 21 Creighton Tevlin
- ☐ 22 Jackson Todd
- ☐ 23 Mitch Webster
- ☐ 24 Dan Whitmer

1982 Tacoma Tigers TCMA

This 39-card standard-size set of the 1982 Tacoma Tigers, a Class AAA Pacific Coast League affiliate of the Oakland Athletics, features white-bordered posed color player photos on its fronts. The player's name and position appear at the bottom. The white and black back carries the team name at the top, followed below by the league affiliation, and then the player's name, biography and statistics.

	MINT	NRMT	EXC
COMPLETE SET (39)	10.00	4.50	1.25

- ☐ 1 DeWayne Buice
- ☐ 2 Don Fowler
- ☐ 3 Dave Heaverlo
- ☐ 4 Bill Castro
- ☐ 5 Gorman Heimueller
- ☐ 6 Dennis Kinney
- ☐ 7 Eric Mustad
- ☐ 8 Dave Patterson
- ☐ 9 Bill Swiacki
- ☐ 10 Ed Figueroa
- ☐ 11 Darryl Cias
- ☐ 12 Tim Hosley
- ☐ 13 Kevin Bell
- ☐ 14 Danny Goodwin
- ☐ 15 Paul Mize
- ☐ 16 Johnny Evans
- ☐ 17 Jim Nettles
- ☐ 18 Dennis Sherow
- ☐ 19 Ed Nottle
- ☐ 20 Larry Davis
- ☐ 21 Art Popham
- ☐ 22 Stan Naccarato
- ☐ 23 Keith Atherton
- ☐ 24 Jeff Jones
- ☐ 25 Brian Kingman
- ☐ 26 Pat Dempsey
- ☐ 27 Robert Kearney
- ☐ 28 Mack Babitt
- ☐ 29 Keith Drumright
- ☐ 30 Mike Gallego
- ☐ 31 Kelvin Moore
- ☐ 32 Tony Phillips
- ☐ 33 Rick Bosetti
- ☐ 34 Michael Davis
- ☐ 35 Bob Grandas
- ☐ 36 Mitchell Page
- ☐ 37 Tiger Mascott
- ☐ 38 Jommy Sexton
- ☐ 39 Keith Comstock

1982 Tidewater Tides TCMA

This 26-card standard-size set of the 1982 Tidewater Tides, a Class AAA International League affiliate of the New York Mets, features white-bordered posed color player photos on its fronts. The player's name and position appear at the bottom. The white and black back carries the team name at the top, followed below by the league affiliation, and then the player's name, biography and statistics.

	MINT	NRMT	EXC
COMPLETE SET (26)	25.00	11.00	3.10

- ☐ 1 Rick Ownbey
- ☐ 2 Kelvin Chapman
- ☐ 3 Mike Davis
- ☐ 4 Mike Fitzgerald
- ☐ 5 Mike Howard
- ☐ 6 Bruce Bochy
- ☐ 7 Gil Flores
- ☐ 8 Brian Giles
- ☐ 9 Phil Mankowski
- ☐ 10 Ronald MacDonald
- ☐ 11 Rusty Tillman
- ☐ 12 Rick Anderson
- ☐ 13 Ron Darling
- ☐ 14 Terry Leach
- ☐ 15 Jose Oquendo
- ☐ 16 Marvell Wynne
- ☐ 17 Greg Biercevicz
- ☐ 18 Scott Holman
- ☐ 19 Jack Aker
- ☐ 20 Brent Gaff
- ☐ 21 Steve Ratzer
- ☐ 22 Bob Schaefer
- ☐ 23 Dave Von Ohlen
- ☐ 24 Walt Terrell
- ☐ 25 Mike Anicich
- ☐ 26 Mike Cubbage

1982 Toledo Mud Hens TCMA

This 27-card standard-size set of the 1982 Toledo Mud Hens, a Class AAA International League affiliate of the Minnesota Twins, features white-bordered posed color player photos on its fronts. The player's name and position appear at the bottom. The white and black back carries the team name at the top, followed below by the league affiliation, and then the player's name, biography and statistics.

	MINT	NRMT	EXC
COMPLETE SET (24)	30.00	13.50	3.70
COMPLETE SET W/LATE ISSUES (27)	60.00	27.00	7.50

- ☐ 1 Don Cooper
- ☐ 2 Glenn Dooner
- ☐ 3 Steve Korczyk
- ☐ 4 Jeff Little
- ☐ 5 Jack O'Connor
- ☐ 6 Bob Veselic
- ☐ 7 Frank Viola
- ☐ 8 Mike Walters
- ☐ 9 Rick Williams
- ☐ 10 Harry Saferight
- ☐ 11 Ray Smith
- ☐ 12 Rod Booker
- ☐ 13 Jim Christensen
- ☐ 14 Dave Machemer
- ☐ 15 Ivan Mesa
- ☐ 16 Kelly Snider
- ☐ 17 Greg Wells
- ☐ 18 Mike Sodders
- ☐ 19 Elijah Bonaparte
- ☐ 20 Randy Bush
- ☐ 21 Rick Sofield
- ☐ 22 Scott Ullger
- ☐ 23 Cal Ermer
- ☐ 24 Buck Chamberlin
- ☐ 26 Pete Filson (Late Issue)
- ☐ 27 Doug Fregin (Late Issue)
- ☐ 28 Bob Mitchell (Late Issue)

1982 Tucson Toros TCMA

This 28-card standard-size set of the 1982 Tucson Toros, a Class AAA Pacific Coast League affiliate of the Houston Astros, features white-bordered posed color player photos on its fronts. The player's name and position appear at the bottom. The white and black back carries safety tips.

	MINT	NRMT	EXC
COMPLETE SET (28)	20.00	9.00	2.50

- ☐ 1 Bert Pena
- ☐ 2 Chris Jones
- ☐ 3 Mark Ross
- ☐ 4 Tom Vessey
- ☐ 5 Steve Lake
- ☐ 6 Greg Cypret
- ☐ 7 Billy Doran
- ☐ 8 Tim Tolman
- ☐ 9 Jim Tracy
- ☐ 10 Larry Ray
- ☐ 11 Harry Spillman
- ☐ 12 Jim McDonald
- ☐ 13 Rickey Keeton
- ☐ 14 Zacarias Paris
- ☐ 15 Bert Roberge
- ☐ 16 Rick Lysander
- ☐ 17 Mark Miggins
- ☐ 18 Billy Smith
- ☐ 19 Bobby Sprowl
- ☐ 20 George Cappuzzello
- ☐ 21 Gordy Pladson
- ☐ 22 Bill Wood
- ☐ 23 James Hand
- ☐ 24 Jim Johnson
- ☐ 25 Gary Tuck
- ☐ 26 Denis Menke
  Sic, Dennis
- ☐ 27 Dave Labossiere
- ☐ 28 Bat Boys

1982 Tulsa Drillers TCMA

This 28-card standard-size set of the 1982 Tulsa Drillers, a Class AA Texas League affiliate of the Texas Rangers, features white-bordered posed color player photos on its fronts. The player's name and position appear at the bottom. The white and black back carries the team name at the top, followed below by the league affiliation, and then the player's name, biography and statistics.

	MINT	NRMT	EXC
COMPLETE SET (28)	30.00	13.50	3.70

- ☐ 1 Tom Henke
- ☐ 2 Brad Mengwasser
- ☐ 3 Martin Leach
- ☐ 4 Dennis Long
- ☐ 5 Mike Mason
- ☐ 6 Tim Henry
- ☐ 7 Al Lachowicz
- ☐ 8 Kevin Richards
- ☐ 9 Jim Gideon
- ☐ 10 Tom Dunbar
- ☐ 11 Don Scott
- ☐ 12 Tracy Cowger
- ☐ 13 Steve Moore
- ☐ 14 Carmelo Aguayo
- ☐ 15 Dave Stockstill
- ☐ 16 Oscar Mejia
- ☐ 17 Dan Murphy
- ☐ 18 Ron Dillard
- ☐ 19 Mike Jirschele
- ☐ 20 Gerry Neufang
- ☐ 21 Robert Ball
- ☐ 22 Tom Burgess
- ☐ 23 Orlando Gomez
- ☐ 24 Joe Nemeth
- ☐ 25 Curtis Wilkerson
- ☐ 26 Brett Benza
- ☐ 27 Steve Buechele
- ☐ 28 Mike Rubel

1982 Vancouver Canadians TCMA

This 24-card standard-size set of the 1982 Vancouver Canadians, a Class AAA Pacific Coast League affiliate of the Milwaukee Brewers, features white-bordered posed color player photos on its fronts. The player's name and position appear at the bottom. The white and black back carries the team name at the top, followed below by the league affiliation, and then the player's name, biography and statistics.

	MINT	NRMT	EXC
COMPLETE SET (24)	10.00	4.50	1.25

- ☐ 1 Bob Skube
- ☐ 2 Frank Thomas
- ☐ 3 Bill Schroder
- ☐ 4 Kevin Bass
- ☐ 5 Willie Lozada
- ☐ 6 John Skorochocki
- ☐ 7 Lawrence Rush
- ☐ 8 Ed Irvine
- ☐ 9 Stan Davis
- ☐ 10 Doug Loman
- ☐ 11 Steve Herz
- ☐ 12 Tim Cook
- ☐ 13 Doug Jones
- ☐ 14 Mike Madden
- ☐ 15 Rich Olsen
- ☐ 16 Frank DiPino
- ☐ 17 Pete Ladd
- ☐ 18 Chuck Valley
- ☐ 19 Rick Kranitz
- ☐ 20 Jamie Cocanower
- ☐ 21 Chuck Porter
- ☐ 22 Mike Anderson
- ☐ 23 Eli Grba CO
- ☐ 24 Brian Thorson TR

1982 Vero Beach Dodgers TCMA

This 29-card standard-size set of the 1982 Vero Beach Dodgers, a Class A Florida State League affiliate of the Los Angeles Dodgers, features white-bordered posed black-and-white player photos on its fronts. The player's name and position appear at the bottom. The white and black back carries the team name at the top, followed below by the league affiliation, and then the player's name, biography and statistics.

	MINT	NRMT	EXC
COMPLETE SET (29)	40.00	18.00	5.00

- ☐ 1 Roberto Alexander
- ☐ 2 Ernie Borbon
- ☐ 3 Paul Cozzolino
- ☐ 4 Dave Daniel
- ☐ 5 Rich Felt
- ☐ 6 Sid Fernandez

☐ 7 Robert Kenyon
☐ 8 Steve Martin
☐ 9 Peyton Mosher
☐ 10 Matt Reeves
☐ 11 Robert Slezak
☐ 12 Paul Bard
☐ 13 Steve Boncore
☐ 14 Jack Fimple
☐ 15 Robert Allen
☐ 16 Carmelo Alvarez
☐ 17 Jerry Bendorf
☐ 18 Sid Bream
☐ 19 Harold Perkins
☐ 20 Larry See
☐ 21 Ralph Bryant
☐ 22 Cecil Espy
☐ 23 Tony Lachowetz
☐ 24 Stu Pederson
☐ 25 Bob Seymour
☐ 26 Terry Collins
☐ 27 Rob Giesecke
☐ 28 Dave Wallace
☐ 29 John Shoemaker

1982 Waterbury Reds TCMA

This 23-card standard-size set of the 1982 Waterbury Reds, a Class AA Eastern League affiliate of the Cincinnati Reds, features white-bordered posed color photos on its fronts. The player's name and position appear at the bottom. The white and black back carries the team name at the top, followed below by the league affiliation, and then the player's name, biography and statistics. This issue includes the minor league card debut of Danny Tartabull. Approximately 1,600 sets were produced.

	MINT	NRMT	EXC
COMPLETE SET (23)	40.00	18.00	5.00

☐ 1 Bill Landrum
☐ 2 Larry Buckle
☐ 3 Keefe Cato
☐ 4 Kenneth Jones
☐ 5 Gene Menees
☐ 6 Clem Freeman
☐ 7 Bob Buchanan
☐ 8 Jeff Russell
☐ 9 Ronald Robinson
☐ 10 Nicholas Fiorillo
☐ 11 Raymond Corbett
☐ 12 Michael Kripner
☐ 13 Skeeter Barnes
☐ 14 Danny Tartabull
☐ 15 Eski Viltz
☐ 16 Paul Herring
☐ 17 Glen Franklin
☐ 18 Mark Gilbert
☐ 19 Kenneth Scarpace
☐ 20 Tony Walker
☐ 21 Ronald Little
☐ 22 Crestwell Pratt
☐ 23 Jim Lett

1982 Waterloo Indians Fritsch

	MINT	NRMT	EXC
COMPLETE SET (28)	5.00	2.20	.60

☐ 1 Checklist
☐ 2 Gomer Hodge MG
☐ 3 Vic Albury CO
☐ 4 Ron Wollenhaupt TR
☐ 5 Ricky Lintz
☐ 6 Jerry Nalley
☐ 7 Phil Wilson
☐ 8 Rod McDonald
☐ 9 Rod Carraway
☐ 10 Steve Roche
☐ 11 Dave Gallagher
☐ 12 Ralph Elpin
☐ 13 Dave Wick
☐ 14 Mike Gertz
☐ 15 Steve Cushing
☐ 16 John Miglio
☐ 17 Chris Rehbaum
☐ 18 Marlin Methven
☐ 19 Winston Ficklin
☐ 20 John Malkin
☐ 21 Sammy Martin
☐ 22 Ed Tanner
☐ 23 Rich Doyle
☐ 24 Jose Roman
☐ 25 Wayne Johnson
☐ 26 Randy Washington
☐ 27 George Alpert
☐ 28 Junior Noboa

1982 Waterloo Indians TCMA

This 28-card standard-size set of the 1982 Waterloo Indians, a Class A Midwest League affiliate of the Cleveland Indians, features white-bordered posed black-and-white player photos on its fronts. The player's name and position appear at the bottom. The white and black back carries the team name at the top, followed below by the league affiliation, and then the player's name, biography and statistics.

	MINT	NRMT	EXC
COMPLETE SET (25)	10.00	4.50	1.25
COMPLETE SET W/LATE ISSUES (28)	80.00	36.00	10.00

☐ 1 Steve Cushing
☐ 2 Rich Doyle
☐ 3 Ralph Elpin
☐ 4 Mike Jeffcoat
☐ 5 Wayne Johnson
☐ 6 Ricky Lintz
☐ 7 Rodney McDonald
☐ 8 John Miglio
☐ 9 Ramon Romero
☐ 10 David Wick
☐ 11 Alan Willis
☐ 12 John Malkin
☐ 13 Phillip Wilson
☐ 14 Rod Carraway
☐ 15 Winston Ficklin
☐ 16 Mike Gertz
☐ 17 Sam Martin
☐ 18 Junior Noboa
☐ 19 Ed Tanner
☐ 20 George Albert
☐ 21 Jerry Nalley
☐ 22 Chris Rehbaum
☐ 23 Dwight Taylor
☐ 24 Mike Taylor
☐ 25 Randy Washington
☐ 26 Gomer Hodge (Late Issue)
☐ 27 Vic Albury (Late Issue)
☐ 28 Ron Wollenhaupt (Late Issue)

1982 Wausau Timbers Fritsch

	MINT	NRMT	EXC
COMPLETE SET (31)	10.00	4.50	1.25

☐ 1 Checklist
☐ 2 Team Photo
1981 Midwest League
Champs
☐ 3 Jack Roeder GM
☐ 4 Stan Edmonds
☐ 5 Curtis Kouba
☐ 6 Bart Mackie
☐ 7 Joe Benes
☐ 8 Randy Meier
☐ 9 Donell Nixon
☐ 10 Ivan Calderon
☐ 11 Eric Parent
☐ 12 Mike Bucci CO
☐ 13 Bret McAfee
☐ 14 Ronn Dixon
☐ 15 Martin O. Enriquez
☐ 16 Luis T. Castillo
☐ 17 R.J. Harrison MG
☐ 18 Mike Johnson
☐ 19 Mitch Zwolensky
☐ 20 Donny Holland
☐ 21 Jay Michael Erdahl
☐ 22 Mike Evans
☐ 23 Gary Pellant CO
☐ 24 Don Diego Pierce
☐ 25 Angel Fonseca
☐ 26 Bill Taylor
☐ 27 Ric Wilson
☐ 28 Chip Conklin
☐ 29 Terry Hayes
☐ 30 Tom Hunt TR
☐ 31 Bob Gisselman EQMG

1982 West Haven A's TCMA

This 29-card standard-size set of the 1982 West Haven A's, a Class AA Eastern League affiliate of the Oakland Athletics, features white-bordered posed black-and-white player photos on its fronts. The player's name and position appear at the bottom. The white and black back carries the team name at the top, followed below by the league affiliation, and then the player's name, biography and statistics.

	MINT	NRMT	EXC
COMPLETE SET (29)	15.00	6.75	1.85

☐ 1 Brian Abraham
☐ 2 Bert Bradley
☐ 3 Jeff Carey
☐ 4 Chris Codiroli
☐ 5 Keith Comstock
☐ 6 Chuck Hensley
☐ 7 Bill Krueger
☐ 8 Lou Marietta
☐ 9 Jack Smith
☐ 10 Bill Bathe
☐ 11 Chuck Fick
☐ 12 Mike Gallego
☐ 13 Steve Gelfarb
☐ 14 Donnie Hill
☐ 15 Monte McAbee
☐ 16 Paul Mize
☐ 17 Tim Pyznarski
☐ 18 Ron Wilkerson
☐ 19 Mike Woodard
☐ 20 Jim Bemmett
☐ 21 Lynn Garrett
☐ 22 Rodney Hobbs
☐ 23 Rusty McNealy
☐ 24 Luis Rojas
☐ 25 Dennis Sherow
☐ 26 Bob Didier
☐ 27 Keith Lieppman
☐ 28 Scott Pyle
☐ 29 Walt Horn
(photo actually
Dick Lynch)

1982 Wichita Aeros Team Issue

This 20-card standard-size set of the 1982 Wichita Aeros, a Class AAA American Association affiliate of the Montreal Expos, features white-bordered posed color player photos on its fronts. The player's name, team, and position appear at the bottom. The white back carries the Aeros All Time Single Season Batting Records. The cards are unnumbered and checklisted below in alphabetical order.

	MINT	NRMT	EXC
COMPLETE SET (20)	20.00	9.00	2.50

☐ 1 Joseph Abone
☐ 2 Felipe Alou MG
☐ 3 Douglas Capilla
☐ 4 Mike Gates
☐ 5 Tom Gorman
☐ 6 Roy Johnson
☐ 7 Roy Johnson
Ken Phelps
Batting Leaders
☐ 8 Wally Johnson
☐ 9 Rich Little
☐ 10 Willard Mueller
☐ 11 Richard Murray
☐ 12 Ken Phelps
☐ 13 Luis Quintana
☐ 14 Richard Ramos
☐ 15 Pat Rooney
☐ 16 William Sattler
☐ 17 Kim Seaman
☐ 18 Christopher Smith
☐ 19 Mike Stenhouse
☐ 20 Thomas Weighaus

1982 Wisconsin Rapids Twins Fritsch

	MINT	NRMT	EXC
COMPLETE SET (27)	10.00	4.50	1.25

☐ 1 Checklist
☐ 2 Greg Kipfer GM
☐ 3 Ken Staples MG
☐ 4 Mike Weiermiller
☐ 5 Dave Hoyt
☐ 6 Mark Wright
☐ 7 Alvaro(Espi) Espinoza
☐ 8 Paul Fleming
☐ 9 Johnny Salery
☐ 10 Herbert Carter
☐ 11 Rick Scheetz
☐ 12 Larry James Mikesell
☐ 13 Sebby Borriello
☐ 14 Mark Portugal
☐ 15 Jose Gil
☐ 16 Barry(B.C.) Houston
☐ 17 Dick Henkemeyer
☐ 18 Phil Franko
☐ 19 John Foster
☐ 20 Eric Porter
☐ 21 Willi Flores
☐ 22 Mark Larcom
☐ 23 Steve Aragon
☐ 24 Marc J. Page
☐ 25 Jeff Arney
☐ 26 Craig Henderson
☐ 27 Rhett Whisman

1983 Albany-Colonie A's TCMA

This 20-card standard-size set of the 1983 Albany A's, a Class AA Eastern League affiliate of the Oakland Athletics, features white-bordered posed color player photos on its fronts. The player's name and position appear within a blue stripe at the bottom. The plain back carries the team name at the top, followed below by the league affiliation, and then the player's name, biography and statistics.

	MINT	NRMT	EXC
COMPLETE SET (20)	50.00	22.00	6.25

☐ 1 Jesse Anderson
☐ 2 Allen Edwards
☐ 3 Mark Fellows
☐ 4 Mark Ferguson
☐ 5 Paul Josephson
☐ 6 Mike Lynes
☐ 7 Steve Ontiveros
☐ 8 Gary Wex
☐ 9 Jim Durrman
☐ 10 Charlie O'Brien
☐ 11 Mike Ashman
☐ 12 Steve Kiefer
☐ 13 Tim Pyznarski
☐ 14 Luis Quinones
☐ 15 Phil Stephenson
☐ 16 Sly Young
☐ 17 Luis Bravo
☐ 18 Ron Harrison
☐ 19 Tom Romano
☐ 20 Pete Whisenant

1983 Albuquerque Dukes TCMA

This 25-card standard-size set of the 1983 Albuquerque Dukes, a Class AAA Pacific Coast League affiliate of the Los Angeles Dodgers, features white-bordered posed color player photos on its fronts. The player's name and position appear within a blue stripe at the bottom. The plain back carries the team name at the top, followed below by the league affiliation, and then the player's name, biography and statistics. This issue includes a second year card of Orel Hershiser.

	MINT	NRMT	EXC
COMPLETE SET (25)	50.00	22.00	6.25

☐ 1 Franklin Stubbs
☐ 2 Bert Geiger
☐ 3 Orel Hershiser
☐ 4 Brian Holton
☐ 5 Dean Rennicke
☐ 6 Rich Rodas
☐ 7 Paul Voigt
☐ 8 Larry White
☐ 9 Steve Perry
☐ 10 Alex Taveras
☐ 11 Jack Fimple
☐ 12 Scotti Madison
☐ 13 Brent Strom
☐ 14 Candy Maldonado
☐ 15 Sid Bream
☐ 16 Ross Jones
☐ 17 German Rivera
☐ 18 Greg Schultz
☐ 19 Ed Amelung
☐ 20 Tony Brewer
☐ 21 Ernesto Borbon
☐ 22 Lemmie Miller
☐ 23 Del Crandall
☐ 24 Dave Cohea
☐ 25 Dick McLaughlin

1983 Alexandria Dukes TCMA

This 31-card standard-size set of the 1983 Alexandria Dukes, a Class A Carolina League affiliate of the Pittsburgh Pirates, features white-bordered posed color player photos on its fronts. The player's name and position appear within a blue stripe at the bottom. The plain back carries the team name at the top, followed below by the league affiliation, and then the player's name, biography and statistics. This issue includes the minor league card debut of Bobby Bonilla. Approximately 1,100 sets were produced.

	MINT	NRMT	EXC
COMPLETE SET (31)	100.00	45.00	12.50

☐ 1 Bobby Lyons
☐ 2 Sam Khalifa
☐ 3 Chuck Meadows
☐ 4 Scott Borland
☐ 5 Nick Castaneda
☐ 6 Jim Opie
☐ 7 Marvin Clack
☐ 8 Pete Rice
☐ 9 Art Ray
☐ 10 Scott Bailes
☐ 11 John Lipon
☐ 12 Johnny Taylor
☐ 13 Jim Aulenback
☐ 14 Chris Lein
☐ 15 David Tumbas
☐ 16 Roberto Bonilla
☐ 17 Thomas Martinez
☐ 18 Sean Faherty
☐ 19 Craig Brown
☐ 20 David Johnson
☐ 21 Steve Susce
☐ 22 Jim Felt
☐ 23 Nelson De LaRussa
☐ 24 Eric Zimmerman
☐ 25 Steve Lewis
☐ 26 Rubin Rodriguez
☐ 27 Ravelo Manzanillo
☐ 28 Mike Quade
☐ 29 Jim Buckmier
☐ 30 Dorn Taylor
☐ 31 Lorenzo Bundy

1983 Anderson Braves TCMA

This 33-card standard-size set of the 1983 Anderson Braves, a Class A South Atlantic League affiliate of the Atlanta Braves, features white-bordered posed color player photos on its fronts. The player's name and position appear within a blue stripe at the bottom. The plain back carries the team name at the top, followed below by the league affiliation, and then the player's name, biography and statistics.

	MINT	NRMT	EXC
COMPLETE SET (33)	20.00	9.00	2.50

- ☐ 1 Bill MacKay
- ☐ 2 Rick Albert
- ☐ 3 Skip Weisman
- ☐ 4 Randy Ingle
- ☐ 5 Dave May
- ☐ 6 Buzz Capra
- ☐ 7 John Baker
- ☐ 8 Jose Cano
- ☐ 9 Al Candelaria
- ☐ 10 Chip Reese
- ☐ 11 Ken Lynn
- ☐ 12 Charlie Morelock
- ☐ 13 John Mortillaro
- ☐ 14 Jim Rivera
- ☐ 15 Randy Rogers
- ☐ 16 Maximo Rosario
- ☐ 17 Rudy Torres
- ☐ 18 Sylverio Valdez
- ☐ 19 Ramon Vargas
- ☐ 20 Dave Griffin
- ☐ 21 Ralph Giansanti
- ☐ 22 Jay Palma
- ☐ 23 Andres Thomas
- ☐ 24 Dave Van Horn
- ☐ 25 Russ Anglin
- ☐ 26 Clint Brill
- ☐ 27 Jerry Ragsdale
- ☐ 28 Paul Llewellyn
- ☐ 29 Dave Morris
- ☐ 30 Larry Moser
- ☐ 31 Jay Roberts
- ☐ 32 Rich Thompson
- ☐ 33 Jeff Wagner

1983 Appleton Foxes Fritsch

	MINT	NRMT	EXC
COMPLETE SET (30)	15.00	6.75	1.85

- ☐ 1 Bill Smith GM
- ☐ 2 Mike Trujillo
- ☐ 3 Dave McLaughlin
- ☐ 4 Kim Christensen
- ☐ 5 Joel McKeon
- ☐ 6 Jim Best TR
- ☐ 7 Rich DeVincenzo
- ☐ 8 Pat Adams
- ☐ 9 Steve Noworyta
- ☐ 10 Craig Smajstrla
- ☐ 11 Mike Henley
- ☐ 12 Rolando Pino
- ☐ 13 John Cangelosi
- ☐ 14 Ken Williams
- ☐ 15 Team Card (Right Half)
- ☐ 16 Team Card (Left Half)
- ☐ 17 Edwin Correa
- ☐ 18 Ed Sedar
- ☐ 19 Bill Atkinson CO
- ☐ 20 Al Jones
- ☐ 21 Greg Tarnow
- ☐ 22 Ron Karkovice
- ☐ 23 David Kinsel
- ☐ 24 Johnny Moses
- ☐ 25 John Boles MG
- ☐ 26 Garry Keeton
- ☐ 27 Don Ruzek
- ☐ 28 Bill Sandry
- ☐ 29 Al Heath
- ☐ 30 Team Logo

1983 Arkansas Travelers TCMA

This 25-card standard-size set of the 1983 Arkansas Travelers, a Class AA Texas League affiliate of the St. Louis Cardinals, features white-bordered posed color player photos on its fronts. The player's name and position appear within a blue stripe at the bottom. The plain back carries the team name at the top, followed below by the league affiliation, and then the player's name, biography and statistics.

	MINT	NRMT	EXC
COMPLETE SET (25)	70.00	32.00	8.75

- ☐ 1 Mike Rhodes
- ☐ 2 Ruben Gotay
- ☐ 3 Terry Clark
- ☐ 4 Kurt Kepshire
- ☐ 5 Walter Pierce
- ☐ 6 Mike Barba
- ☐ 7 Bill Thomas
- ☐ 8 Steve Winfield
- ☐ 9 Jerry Johnson
- ☐ 10 John Adams
- ☐ 11 Randy Hunt
- ☐ 12 Mark Salas
- ☐ 13 Mike Harris
- ☐ 14 Mike Wolters
- ☐ 15 Terry Pendelton
- ☐ 16 Luis Ojeda
- ☐ 17 Greg Guin
- ☐ 18 Alan Hunsinger
- ☐ 19 Rod Booker
- ☐ 20 Fran Batista
- ☐ 21 Gotay Mills
- ☐ 22 Larry Reynolds
- ☐ 23 Nick Leyva
- ☐ 24 Jorge Aranzamendi
- ☐ 25 Dave England

1983 Beaumont Golden Gators TCMA

This 23-card standard-size set of the 1983 Beaumont Golden Gators, a Class AA Texas League affiliate of the San Diego Padres, features white-bordered posed color player photos on its fronts. The player's name and position appear within a blue stripe at the bottom. The plain back carries the team name at the top, followed below by the league affiliation, and then the player's name, biography and statistics.

	MINT	NRMT	EXC
COMPLETE SET (23)	70.00	32.00	8.75

- ☐ 1 Mike Martin
- ☐ 2 Ozzie Guillen
- ☐ 3 Steve Johnson
- ☐ 4 Randy Kaczmarski
- ☐ 5 Walt Vanderbush
- ☐ 6 Jim Leopold
- ☐ 7 Bob Patterson
- ☐ 8 Mark Williamson
- ☐ 9 Marty Lain
- ☐ 10 Dan Purpura
- ☐ 11 John Kruk
- ☐ 12 Steve Garcia
- ☐ 13 Mark Parent
- ☐ 14 Jeff Ronk
- ☐ 15 Mark Gillaspie
- ☐ 16 Pat Casey
- ☐ 17 Frank Ricci
- ☐ 18 Willie Hardwick
- ☐ 19 Ray Haywood Jr.
- ☐ 20 James Steels
- ☐ 21 Jack Maloof
- ☐ 22 Allen Gerhardt
- ☐ 23 Gene Confreda

1983 Beloit Brewers Fritsch

	MINT	NRMT	EXC
COMPLETE SET (30)	18.00	8.00	2.20

- ☐ 1 Butch Kirby
- ☐ 2 Woolsey Rice
- ☐ 3 Dewey James
- ☐ 4 Jeff Gyarmati
- ☐ 5 John Mitchell
- ☐ 6 John Antonelli
- ☐ 7 Hank Landers
- ☐ 8 Jay Aldrich
- ☐ 9 Bruce Williams
- ☐ 10 Mark Johnston
- ☐ 11 Doug Norton
- ☐ 12 Steve Anderson
- ☐ 13 Bill Nowlan TR
- ☐ 14 Don Whiting
- ☐ 15A Team Logo (right half)
- ☐ 15B Team Logo (left half)
- ☐ 16 Tim Nordbrook MG
- ☐ 17 Dave Tarrolly GM
- ☐ 18 Brian Finley
- ☐ 19 Jim Teahan
- ☐ 20 Tim Utecht
- ☐ 21 Billy Joe Robidoux
- ☐ 22 Chuck Crim
- ☐ 23 Edgar Diaz
- ☐ 24 Fritz Fedor
- ☐ 25 Dan Scarpetta
- ☐ 26 Hector Quinones
- ☐ 27 Chris Bosio
- ☐ 28 Stan Boroski
- ☐ 29 Joel Weatherford

1983 Birmingham Barons TCMA

This 25-card standard-size set of the 1983 Birmingham Barons, a Class AA Southern League affiliate of the DetroitTigers, features white-bordered posed color player photos on its fronts. The player's name and position appear within a blue stripe at the bottom. The plain back carries the team name at the top, followed below by the league affiliation, and then the player's name, biography and statistics.

	MINT	NRMT	EXC
COMPLETE SET (25)	10.00	4.50	1.25

- ☐ 1 Raul Tovar
- ☐ 2 Don Gordon
- ☐ 3 Dan Williams
- ☐ 4 Dwight Lowry
- ☐ 5 Stan Younger
- ☐ 6 Dave Hawarny
- ☐ 7 Mark Smith
- ☐ 8 Doug Baker
- ☐ 9 Don Heinker
- ☐ 10 Bruce Robbins
- ☐ 11 George Foussianes
- ☐ 12 Bob Melvin
- ☐ 13 Greg Norman
- ☐ 14 Chuck Cary
- ☐ 15 Scott Tabor
- ☐ 16 Nelson Simmons
- ☐ 17 Scottie Earl
- ☐ 18 Ted Davis
- ☐ 19 Colin Ward
- ☐ 20 Jon Furman
- ☐ 21 Pedro Chavez
- ☐ 22 Keith Comstock
- ☐ 23 Troy Dixon
- ☐ 24 Roger Mason
- ☐ 25 Roy Majtyka

1983 Buffalo Bisons TCMA

This 25-card standard-size set of the 1983 Buffalo Bisons, a Class AA Eastern League affiliate of the Cleveland Indians, features white-bordered posed color player photos on its fronts. The player's name and position appear within a blue stripe at the bottom. The plain back carries the team name at the top, followed below by the league affiliation, and then the player's name, biography and statistics.

	MINT	NRMT	EXC
COMPLETE SET (25)	25.00	11.00	3.10

- ☐ 1 Robin Fuson
- ☐ 2 Wayne Johnson
- ☐ 3 Rich Doyle
- ☐ 4 Gordie Glaser
- ☐ 5 Rod McDonald
- ☐ 6 Tom Owens
- ☐ 7 Rich Thompson
- ☐ 8 Jeff Green
- ☐ 9 Ramon Romero
- ☐ 10 John Malkin
- ☐ 11 Tim Glass
- ☐ 12 Everett Rey
- ☐ 13 Sal Rende
- ☐ 14 Jim Wilson
- ☐ 15 Shanie Dugas
- ☐ 16 Kelly Gruber
- ☐ 17 Jeff Moronko
- ☐ 18 Rene Quinones
- ☐ 19 Dave Gallagher
- ☐ 20 Ed Saavedra
- ☐ 21 Dwight Taylor
- ☐ 22 George Cecchetti
- ☐ 23 Joe Charboneau
- ☐ 24 Al Gallagher
- ☐ 25 Jack Aker

1983 Burlington Rangers Fritsch

	MINT	NRMT	EXC
COMPLETE SET (30)	5.00	2.20	.60

- ☐ 1 Bob Hausladen
- ☐ 2 Todd Schulte
- ☐ 3 Sam Sorce
- ☐ 4 George Crum
- ☐ 5 Randy Kramer
- ☐ 6 Antonio Triplett
- ☐ 7 Jose Guzman
- ☐ 8 Elijah Ben
- ☐ 9 Barry Bass
- ☐ 10 Terry Johnson
- ☐ 11 Bobby Brower
- ☐ 12 Glen Cook
- ☐ 13 Bob Gergen
- ☐ 14 Ron Dillard
- ☐ 15 Whitney J. Harry
- ☐ 16 Chris Joslin
- ☐ 17 Otto Gonzalez
- ☐ 18 Brendan Hennessy
- ☐ 19 Tim Maki
- ☐ 20 John Buckley
- ☐ 21 Mark Sutton
- ☐ 22 Kevin Stock
- ☐ 23 David Hopkins
- ☐ 24 Jeff Mace
- ☐ 25 Greg Campbell TR
- ☐ 26 Greg Jemison CO
- ☐ 27 Orlando Gomez MG
- ☐ 28 Team Logo (right half)
- ☐ 29 Team Logo (left half)
- ☐ 30 Special Offers

1983 Burlington Rangers TCMA

This 28-card standard-size set of the 1983 Burlington Rangers, a Class A Midwest League affiliate of the Texas Rangers, features white-bordered posed color player photos on its fronts. The player's name and position appear within a blue stripe at the bottom. The plain back carries the team name at the top, followed below by the league affiliation, and then the player's name, biography and statistics.

	MINT	NRMT	EXC
COMPLETE SET (28)	25.00	11.00	3.10

- ☐ 1 Barry Bass
- ☐ 2 John Buckley
- ☐ 3 Glenn Cook
- ☐ 4 Jose Guzman
- ☐ 5 Dave Hopkins
- ☐ 6 Terry Johnson
- ☐ 7 Chris Joslin
- ☐ 8 Randy Kramer
- ☐ 9 Tim Maki
- ☐ 10 Todd Schulte
- ☐ 11 Mike Soper
- ☐ 12 Elijah Ben
- ☐ 13 Bob Brower
- ☐ 14 George Crum
- ☐ 15 Ron Dillard
- ☐ 16 Bob Gergen
- ☐ 17 Otto Gonzales
- ☐ 18 Whitney Harry
- ☐ 19 Bob Hausladen
- ☐ 20 Brendan Hennessey
- ☐ 21 Jeff Mace
- ☐ 22 Sam Sorce
- ☐ 23 Kevin Stock
- ☐ 24 Mark Sutton
- ☐ 25 Tony Triplett
- ☐ 26 Orlando Gomez
- ☐ 27 Greg Jemison
- ☐ 28 Greg Campbell

1983 Butte Copper Kings TCMA

This 33-card standard-size set of the 1983 Butte Copper Kings, a Rookie Class Pioneer League affiliate of the Kansas City Royals, features white-bordered posed color player photos on its fronts. The player's name and position appear within a blue stripe at the bottom. The plain back carries the team name at the top, followed below by the league affiliation, and then the player's name, biography and statistics. Approximately 1,100 sets were produced.

	MINT	NRMT	EXC
COMPLETE SET (33)	35.00	16.00	4.40

- ☐ 1 Dennis Boatright
- ☐ 2 Dan Chelini
- ☐ 3 Dave Digirolama
- ☐ 4 Tom Edens
- ☐ 5 Phil George
- ☐ 6 Gary Klein
- ☐ 7 Stefan Lipson
- ☐ 8 Charley Luman
- ☐ 9 Randy Robinson
- ☐ 10 John Serritella
- ☐ 11 Jose Torres
- ☐ 12 Rob Vodvarka
- ☐ 13 Dave Landrith
- ☐ 14 Tom Niemann
- ☐ 15 Stan Oxner
- ☐ 16 Jim Bagnall
- ☐ 17 Vic Davila
- ☐ 18 Jere Longenecker
- ☐ 19 Mike Miller
- ☐ 20 Kevin Seitzer
- ☐ 21 Kevin Stanley
- ☐ 22 Mark Van Blaricom
- ☐ 23 Edward Allen
- ☐ 24 John Devich
- ☐ 25 Tommy Mohr
- ☐ 26 Dave Rooker
- ☐ 27 John Rubel
- ☐ 28 Jeff Schulz
- ☐ 29 Joe Kasunick
- ☐ 30 Tommy Jones
- ☐ 31 Guy Hansen
- ☐ 32 Bruce Piatt
- ☐ 33 Tom Osowski

1983 Cedar Rapids Reds Fritsch

	MINT	NRMT	EXC
COMPLETE SET (26)	10.00	4.50	1.25

- ☐ 1 Tim Reynolds
- ☐ 2 Buddy Pryor
- ☐ 3 Tim Scott
- ☐ 4 Joe Stalp
- ☐ 5 Tom Riley
- ☐ 6 Wayne Harmon TR
- ☐ 7 Jay Munson
- ☐ 8 Dave Lochner
- ☐ 9 Mike Knox
- ☐ 10 Billy Hawley
- ☐ 11 Dave Haberle
- ☐ 12 Louie Trujillo
- ☐ 13 Terry Lee
- ☐ 14 Mike Konderla
- ☐ 15 Jeff Rhodes
- ☐ 16 Glenn Spagnola
- ☐ 17 Kal Daniels
- ☐ 18 Scott Jones
- ☐ 19 Vin Rover

☐ 20 Mike Manfre
☐ 21 Scott Radloff
☐ 22 Bruce Kimm MG
☐ 23 Orsino Hill
☐ 24 Rob Murphy
☐ 25 Steve Padia
☐ 26 Team Logo

1983 Cedar Rapids Reds TCMA

This 28-card standard-size set of the 1983 Cedar Rapids Reds, a Class A Midwest League affiliate of the Cincinnati Reds, features white-bordered posed color player photos on its fronts. The player's name and position appear within a blue stripe at the bottom. The plain back carries the team name at the top, followed below by the league affiliation, and then the player's name, biography and statistics.

	MINT	NRMT	EXC
COMPLETE SET (28)	25.00	11.00	3.10

☐ 1 Bruce Kimm
☐ 2 Scott Jones
☐ 3 Dave Lochner
☐ 4 Mike Knox
☐ 5 Glen Spagnola
☐ 6 Billy Rawley
☐ 7 Mike Konderla
☐ 8 Tim Scott
☐ 9 Tim Reynolds
☐ 10 Joe Stalp
☐ 11 Louie Trujillo
☐ 12 Steve Padia
☐ 13 Rob Murphy
☐ 14 Buddy Pryor
☐ 15 Scott Radloff
☐ 16 Tom Riley
☐ 17 Delwyn Young
☐ 18 Dave Haberle
☐ 19 Terry Lee
☐ 20 Mike Manfre
☐ 21 Vince Rover
☐ 22 Kal Daniels
☐ 23 Orsino Hill
☐ 24 Jeff Rhodes
☐ 25 Jay Munson
☐ 26 Don Buchheister
☐ 27 Batboys
☐ 28 Wayne Harmon

1983 Charleston Charlies TCMA

This 22-card standard-size set of the 1983 Charleston Royals, a Class AAA International League affiliate of the Cleveland Indians, features white-bordered posed color player photos on its fronts. The player's name and position appear within a blue stripe at the bottom. The plain back carries the team name at the top, followed below by the league affiliation, and then the player's name, biography and statistics.

	MINT	NRMT	EXC
COMPLETE SET (22)	10.00	4.50	1.25

☐ 1 Jay Baller
☐ 2 Mike Jeffcoat
☐ 3 Larry Hrynko
☐ 4 Jerry Reed
☐ 5 Roy Smith
☐ 6 Sandy Whitol
☐ 7 Doug Simunic
☐ 8 Jerry Willard
☐ 9 Luis Deleon
☐ 10 Angelo Logrande
☐ 11 Juan Pacho
☐ 12 Karl Pagel
☐ 13 Jack Perconte
☐ 14 Tim Norrid
☐ 15 Rodney Craig
☐ 16 Wil Culmer
☐ 17 Kevin Rhomberg
☐ 18 Otto Velez
☐ 19 Ed Glynn
☐ 20 Vic Albury
☐ 21 Steve Cisczon
☐ 22 Doc Edwards

1983 Charleston Royals TCMA

This 26-card standard-size set of the 1983 Charleston Royals, a Class A South Atlantic League affiliate of the Kansas City Royals, features white-bordered posed color player photos on its fronts. The player's name and position appear within a blue stripe at the bottom. The plain back carries the team name at the top, followed below by the league affiliation, and then the player's name, biography and statistics.

	MINT	NRMT	EXC
COMPLETE SET (26)	15.00	6.75	1.85

☐ 1 Mark Pirruccello
☐ 2 Nicky Richards
☐ 3 Joe Szekely
☐ 4 Jim Bagnall
☐ 5 Chris Bryeans
☐ 6 Craig Goodin
☐ 7 Keith Hempfield
☐ 8 Bill Phillips
☐ 9 Rich Vitato
☐ 10 Edward Allen
☐ 11 Roland Oruna
☐ 12 Jack Shuffield
☐ 13 Van Snider
☐ 14 Richard Aube
☐ 15 John Bryant
☐ 16 Doug Cook
☐ 17 John Davis
☐ 18 Bob De Bord
☐ 19 Tom Drizmala
☐ 20 Rich Goodin
☐ 21 Ron McCormack
☐ 22 Israel Sanchez
☐ 23 John Serritella
☐ 24 Roy Tanner
☐ 25 Duane Gustavson
☐ 26 Mark Farnsworth

1983 Chattanooga Lookouts TCMA

This 28-card standard-size set of the 1983 Chattanooga Lookouts, a Class AA Southern League affiliate of the Seattle Mariners, features white-bordered posed color player photos on its fronts. The player's name and position appear within a blue stripe at the bottom. The plain back carries the team name at the top, followed below by the league affiliation, and then the player's name, biography and statistics. This issue includes the minor league card debut of Mark Langston.

	MINT	NRMT	EXC
COMPLETE SET (28)	130.00	57.50	16.00

☐ 1 Darnell Coles
☐ 2 Paul Serna
☐ 3 Chris Hunger
☐ 4 Joe Whitmer
☐ 5 Ramon Estepa
☐ 6 Danny Tartabull
☐ 7 Vic Martin
☐ 8 Alvin Davis
☐ 9 Mike Bucci
☐ 10 Miguel Negron
☐ 11 Mark Langston
☐ 12 Mickey Bowers
☐ 13 Bob Randolph
☐ 14 Robert Hudson
☐ 15 Don (Clay) Hill
☐ 16 Jeff Stottlemyre
☐ 17 Tracy Harris
☐ 18 Kevin King
☐ 19 Kevin Dukes
☐ 20 John Burden
☐ 21 Mark Cahill
☐ 22 Kevin Steger
☐ 23 Tom Hunt
☐ 24 Cheif Lookout
☐ 25 Harry Landreth
☐ 26 Dave Valle
☐ 27 Ivan Caldron
☐ 28 1983 Chatt. Lookouts

1983 Clinton Giants Fritsch

	MINT	NRMT	EXC
COMPLETE SET (30)	5.00	2.20	.60

☐ 1 Gus Stokes GM
Bill Kuehn AGM
☐ 2 Eric Halberg
☐ 3 Scott Norman
☐ 4 Billy Cabell
☐ 5 Jim Weir
☐ 6 Greg Lynn TR
☐ 7 Marty Baier
☐ 8 Ramon Bautista
☐ 9 Scott Rainey
☐ 10 Gene Lambert
☐ 11 Orlando Blackwell
☐ 12 Davis Tavarez
☐ 13 Bob Naber
☐ 14 Alonzo Powell
☐ 15 Mike Empting
☐ 16 John Hughes
☐ 17 Brian Bargerhuff
☐ 18 Alan Marr
☐ 19 Ken Mills
☐ 20 Kelvin Smith
☐ 21 Van Sowards
☐ 22 Kurt Mattson
☐ 23 Ed Stewart
☐ 24 Dennie Taft
☐ 25 Marty DeMerritt
☐ 26 Scott Blanke
☐ 27 Randy Weibel
☐ 28 Jeff Gladden
☐ 29 Bill Lachemann MG
☐ 30 Team Logo

1983 Columbus Astros TCMA

This 24-card standard-size set of the 1983 Columbus Astros, a Class AA Southern League affiliate of the Houston Astros, features white-bordered posed color player photos on its fronts. The player's name and position appear within a blue stripe at the bottom. The plain back carries the team name at the top, followed below by the league affiliation, and then the player's name, biography and statistics.

	MINT	NRMT	EXC
COMPLETE SET (24)	40.00	18.00	5.00

☐ 1 George Bjorkman
☐ 2 Ed Cuervo
☐ 3 John Csefalvay
☐ 4 Mike Grace
☐ 5 Jim Sherman
☐ 6 Mark Strucher
☐ 7 Larry Simcox
☐ 8 Steve Benson
☐ 9 Eric Bullock
☐ 10 Ty Gainey
☐ 11 Glenn Davis
☐ 12 Fransisco Jabalera
☐ 13 Jeff Calhoun
☐ 14 Jeff Heathcock
☐ 15 Jim McDonald
☐ 16 Tim Meckes
☐ 17 Zac Paris
☐ 18 Pat Perry
☐ 19 Ben Snyder
☐ 20 Jack Smith
☐ 21 Bob Sprowl
☐ 22 Jack Hiatt
☐ 23 Ken Bolek
☐ 24 Rex Jones

1983 Columbus Clippers TCMA

This 27-card standard-size set of the 1983 Columbus Clippers, a Class AAA International League affiliate of the New York Yankees, features white-bordered posed color player photos on its fronts. The player's name and position appear within a blue stripe at the bottom. The plain back carries the team name at the top, followed below by the league affiliation, and then the player's name, biography and statistics.

	MINT	NRMT	EXC
COMPLETE SET (27)	30.00	13.50	3.70

☐ 1 Johnny Oates
☐ 2 Coaching Staff
☐ 3 Juan Espino
☐ 4 Bradley Culden
☐ 5 Silton Fontenot
☐ 6 David Wehrmeister
☐ 7 Timothy Burke
☐ 8 Dennis Rasmussen
☐ 9 Clay Christiansen
☐ 10 Stefan Wever
☐ 11 Curt Kaufman
☐ 12 Jesus Hernaiz
☐ 13 Guy Elston
☐ 14 Benjamin Callahan III
☐ 15 Stephen Balboni
☐ 16 Marshall Brant
☐ 17 Bert Campaneris
☐ 18 Edwin Rodriguez
☐ 19 Barry Evans
☐ 20 Robert Meacham
☐ 21 Clell Hobson , Jr.
☐ 22 Michael Patterson
☐ 23 Matthew Winters
☐ 24 James Hart
☐ 25 Otis Nixon
☐ 26 Brian Dayett
☐ 27 Rowland Office

1983 Daytona Beach Astros TCMA

This 27-card standard-size set of the 1983 Daytona Beach Astros, a Class A Florida State League affiliate of the Houston Astros, features white-bordered posed color player photos on its fronts. The player's name and position appear within a blue stripe at the bottom. The plain back carries the team name at the top, followed below by the league affiliation, and then the player's name, biography and statistics.

	MINT	NRMT	EXC
COMPLETE SET (27)	10.00	4.50	1.25

☐ 1 Dave Cripe
☐ 2 Stan Hough
☐ 3 Rich Bombard
☐ 4 Mike Callahan
☐ 5 Guillermo Castro
☐ 6 Manny Hernandez
☐ 7 Mark Knudson
☐ 8 Mike Hogan
☐ 9 Uvaldo Regaldo
☐ 10 Ed Reilly
☐ 11 Rex Schimpf
☐ 12 Jamey Shouppe
☐ 13 Tom Wiedenbauer
☐ 14 Don Berti
☐ 15 Jeff Datz
☐ 16 Jamie Williams
☐ 17 Randy Braun
☐ 18 Glenn Carpenter
☐ 19 Juan Delgado
☐ 20 Gary D'Onofrio
☐ 21 Steve McAllister
☐ 22 Ricardo Rivera
☐ 23 Jim Thomas
☐ 24 Mike Botkin
☐ 25 Curtis Burke
☐ 26 Louie Meadows
☐ 27 Tony Walker

1983 Durham Bulls TCMA

This 29-card standard-size set of the 1983 Durham Bulls, a Class A Carolina League affiliate of the Atlanta Braves, features white-bordered posed color player photos on its fronts. The player's name and position appear within a blue stripe at the bottom. The plain back carries the team name at the top, followed below by the league affiliation, and then the player's name, biography and statistics.

	MINT	NRMT	EXC
COMPLETE SET (29)	25.00	11.00	3.10

☐ 1 Chip Childress
☐ 2 Steve Chmil
☐ 3 Terry Cormack
☐ 4 Inocencio Guerrero
☐ 5 Johnny Hatcher
☐ 6 Pat Hodge
☐ 7 Scott Hood
☐ 8 Mike Knox
☐ 9 Bob Luzon
☐ 10 Bryan Neal
☐ 11 Tony Neuendorff
☐ 12 Ken Scanlon
☐ 13 Rick Siriano
☐ 14 Freddy Tiburcio
☐ 15 Bob Tumpane
☐ 16 Mike Bormann
☐ 17 Dave Clay
☐ 18 Tim Cole
☐ 19 Mark Lance
☐ 20 Rich Leggatt
☐ 21 Dennis Lubert
☐ 22 Ike Pettaway
☐ 23 Allen Sears
☐ 24 Zane Smith
☐ 25 Duane Ward
☐ 26 Matt West
☐ 27 Tim Alexander
☐ 28 Brian Snitker
☐ 29 Leo Mazzone

1983 El Paso Diablos TCMA

This 25-card standard-size set of the 1983 El Paso Diablos, a Class AA Texas League affiliate of the Milwaukee Brewers, features white-bordered posed color player photos on its fronts. The player's name and position appear within a blue stripe at the bottom. The plain back carries the team name at the top, followed below by the league affiliation, and then the player's name, biography and statistics.

	MINT	NRMT	EXC
COMPLETE SET (25)	10.00	4.50	1.25

☐ 1 Dan Burns
☐ 2 Eric Peyton
☐ 3 Joe Henderson
☐ 4 Jim Paciorek
☐ 5 Bryan Duquette
☐ 6 Stan Davis
☐ 7 Mark Effrig
☐ 8 Rene Quinones
☐ 9 Mike Felder
☐ 10 Juan Castillo
☐ 11 Stan Levi
☐ 12 Garrett Nago
☐ 13 Bill Max
☐ 14 Ray Gallo
☐ 15 Bryan Clutterbuck
☐ 16 Steve Parrott
☐ 17 Tim Crews
☐ 18 Al Price
☐ 19 Carlos Ponce
☐ 20 Kevin McCoy
☐ 21 Ernest Riles
☐ 22 Frank Thomas
☐ 23 Jack Lazorko
☐ 24 Bob Schroeck
☐ 25 Lee Sigman

1983 Erie Cardinals TCMA

This 25-card standard-size set of the 1983 Erie Cardinals, a Class A New York-Penn League affiliate of the St. Louis Cardinals, features white-bordered posed color player photos on its fronts. The player's name and position appear within a blue stripe at the bottom. The plain back carries the team name at the top, followed below by the league affiliation, and then the player's name, biography and statistics.

	MINT	NRMT	EXC
COMPLETE SET (25)	25.00	11.00	3.10

☐ 1 Paul Mangiardi
☐ 2 Joe Rigoli
☐ 3 John Rigos
☐ 4 Jim ReBoulet

☐ 5 Wilfredo Martinez
☐ 6 Bill Packer
☐ 7 Mark Dougherty
☐ 8 Keith Turnbull
☐ 9 Jamie Brisco
☐ 10 Brian Farley
☐ 11 Mike Behrend
☐ 12 Mark Angelo
☐ 13 Jeff Pasquali
☐ 14 Scott Pleis
☐ 15 Chuck McGrath
☐ 16 Jeff Gass
☐ 17 Phil Burwell
☐ 18 John Costello
☐ 19 Tim Kavanaugh
☐ 20 Tom Pagnozzi
☐ 21 Tom Rossi
☐ 22 Ernie Carrasco
☐ 23 Tom Caulfield
☐ 24 Mike Robinson
☐ 25 Kurt Kaull

1983 Evansville Triplets TCMA

This 25-card standard-size set of the 1983 Evansville Triplets, a Class AAA American Association affiliate of the Detroit Tigers, features white-bordered posed color player photos on its fronts. The player's name and position appear within a blue stripe at the bottom. The plain back carries the team name at the top, followed below by the league affiliation, and then the player's name, biography and statistics.

	MINT	NRMT	EXC
COMPLETE SET (25)	10.00	4.50	1.25

☐ 1 Mark Dacko
☐ 2 Craig Eaton
☐ 3 David Grumpert
☐ 4 Bryan Kelly
☐ 5 Steven Luebber
☐ 6 Charles Nail
☐ 7 Randall O'Neill
☐ 8 Larry Pashnick
☐ 9 Davis Rucker
☐ 10 Patrick Underwood
☐ 11 Martin Castillo
☐ 12 Willie Royster
☐ 13 Jeffery Bertoni
☐ 14 Julio Gonzales
☐ 15 Mike Laga
☐ 16 Juan Lopez
☐ 17 Kenneth Baker
☐ 18 Barbaro Garbey
☐ 19 Bob Grandas
☐ 20 Jeffrey Kenaga
☐ 21 Darryl Motley
☐ 22 Gordon MacKenzie
☐ 23 William Armstrong
☐ 24 Mark De John
☐ 25 German Barranca

1983 Glen Falls White Sox TCMA

This 24-card standard-size set of the 1983 Glen Falls White Sox, a Class AA Eastern League affiliate of the Chicago White Sox, features white-bordered posed color player photos on its fronts. The player's name and position appear within a blue stripe at the bottom. The plain back carries the team name at the top, followed below by the league affiliation, and then the player's name, biography and statistics.

	MINT	NRMT	EXC
COMPLETE SET (24)	70.00	32.00	8.75

☐ 1 Darryl Boston
☐ 2 J.B. Brown
☐ 3 Wes Kent
☐ 4 Monte McAbee
☐ 5 Scott Meier
☐ 6 Ed Miles
☐ 7 Mike Morse
☐ 8 Dave Nix
☐ 9 Curt Reed
☐ 10 Ramon Romero
☐ 11 Pat Kelly
☐ 12 Tom Brennan
☐ 13 Keith Desjarlais
☐ 14 Mike Maitland
☐ 15 Homer Moncrief
☐ 16 Robert Moore
☐ 17 Tom Mullen
☐ 18 Steve Pastrovich
☐ 19 Wayne Schuckert
☐ 20 Mike Tanzi
☐ 21 Mike Withrow
☐ 22 Adrian Garrett
☐ 23 Lori Corcoran
☐ 24 Dick Manning

1983 Greensboro Hornets TCMA

This 30-card standard-size set of the 1983 Greensboro Hornets, a Class A South Atlantic League affiliate of the New York Yankees, features white-bordered posed color player photos on its fronts. The player's name and position appear within a blue stripe at the bottom. The plain back carries the team name at the top, followed below by the league affiliation, and then the player's name, biography and statistics.

	MINT	NRMT	EXC
COMPLETE SET (30)	50.00	22.00	6.25

☐ 1 Johnny Baldwin
☐ 2 Scott Beahan
☐ 3 Ozzie Canseco
☐ 4 Jim Corsi
☐ 5 Logan Easley
☐ 6 John Gaston
☐ 7 Steve George
☐ 8 Randy Graham
☐ 9 Rich Gumbert
☐ 10 Daryl Humphrey
☐ 11 Steve Ray
☐ 12 Dick Seidel
☐ 13 Randy White
☐ 14 Fredi Gonzales
☐ 15 Phil Lombardi
☐ 16 Mark Blaser
☐ 17 Maurice Ching
☐ 18 Mike Fennell
☐ 19 Roberto Kelly
☐ 20 Pedro Medina
☐ 21 Felix Perdomo
☐ 22 Jim Riggs
☐ 23 Jose Rivera
☐ 24 Stan Javier
☐ 25 Joe MacKay
☐ 26 Tony Russell
☐ 27 Carlos Tosca
☐ 28 Bill Evers
☐ 29 Q.V. Lowe
☐ 30 Don McGann

1983 Idaho Falls Athletics TCMA

This 34-card standard-size set of the 1983 Idaho Falls Athletics, a Rookie Class A Pioneer League affiliate of the Oakland Athletics, features white-bordered posed color player photos on its fronts. The player's name and position appear within a blue stripe at the bottom. The plain back carries the team name at the top, followed below by the league affiliation, and then the player's name, biography and statistics.

	MINT	NRMT	EXC
COMPLETE SET (34)	15.00	6.75	1.85

☐ 1 Steve Bowens
☐ 2 Steve Chasteen
☐ 3 Oscar DeChavez
☐ 4 Wayne Giddings
☐ 5 Dave Hanna
☐ 6 Darel Hansen
☐ 7 Perry Johnson
☐ 8 Mark Leonette
☐ 9 Wade Mangum
☐ 10 Camilo Pascual
☐ 11 Larry Smith
☐ 12 Bob Vantrease
☐ 13 Tony Wadley
☐ 14 Joe Law
☐ 15 Eric Garrett
☐ 16 Matt Held
☐ 17 Mike Rojas
☐ 18 Steve Chumas
☐ 19 Darrell Dull
☐ 20 Rich Borowski
☐ 21 Twayne Harris
☐ 22 Rob Nelson
☐ 23 Felix Pagan
☐ 24 Mike Rantz
☐ 25 Mike Wilder
☐ 26 Maurice Castain
☐ 27 Steve Howard
☐ 28 Sly Humphrey
☐ 29 Tony Moncrief
☐ 30 Jim Nettles
☐ 31 Grady Fuson
☐ 32 Gary Lance
☐ 33 Mark Doberenz
☐ 34 Dave Sheriff

1983 Indianapolis Indians Team Issue

1,200 sets were produced.

	MINT	NRMT	EXC
COMPLETE SET (32)	15.00	6.75	1.85

☐ 1 Team Picture
☐ 2 1982 Pennant
☐ 3 Roy Hartsfield MG
☐ 4 Charlie Leibrandt
☐ 5 Nick Esasky
☐ 6 Greg Harris
☐ 7 Dallas Williams
☐ 8 Joe Edelen
☐ 9 The Starters
☐ 10 Willie Lozado
☐ 11 Brian Ryder
☐ 12 Tom Lawless
☐ 13 The Bullpen
☐ 14 Jeff Russell
☐ 15 Ray Corbett
☐ 16 Rich Carlucci
☐ 17 The Infielders
☐ 18 Orlando Isales
☐ 19 Freddie Toliver
☐ 20 Ron Little
☐ 21 The Catchers
☐ 22 Mark Gilbert
☐ 23 Mike Dowless
☐ 24 Glen Franklin
☐ 25 The Outfielders
☐ 26 Brad Lesley
☐ 27 Dave Van Gorder
☐ 28 Bob Buchanan
☐ 29 John Harris
☐ 30 The Instructors
☐ 31 Skeeter Barnes
☐ 32 Lee Garrett TR

1983 Iowa Cubs TCMA

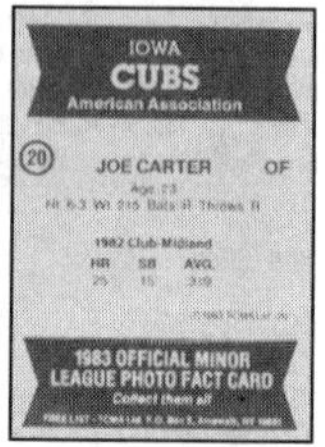

This 31-card standard-size set of the 1983 Iowa Cubs, a Class AAA American Association affiliate of the Chicago Cubs, features white-bordered posed color player photos on its fronts. The player's name and position appear within a blue stripe at the bottom. The plain back carries the team name at the top, followed below by the league affiliation, and then the player's name, biography and statistics. This issue includes the minor league card debut of Joe Carter.

	MINT	NRMT	EXC
COMPLETE SET (30)	150.00	70.00	19.00
COMPLETE SET W/LATE ISSUE (31)	160.00	70.00	20.00

☐ 1 Rich Bordi
☐ 2 Bill Earley
☐ 3 Tom Filer
☐ 4 Alan Hargesheimer
☐ 5 Larry Jones
☐ 6 Dan Larson
☐ 7 Reggie Patterson
☐ 8 John Perlman
☐ 9 Dan Schulze
☐ 10 Randy Stein
☐ 11 Mike Diaz
☐ 12 Bill Hayes
☐ 13 Fritz Connally
☐ 14 Joe Hicks
☐ 15 Jay Loviglio
☐ 16 Carmelo Martinez
☐ 17 Jerry Manuel
☐ 18 Dave Owen
☐ 19 Dan Rohn
☐ 20 Joe Carter
☐ 21 Henry Cotto
☐ 22 Tom Grant
☐ 23 Carlos Lezcano
☐ 24 Steve Carroll
☐ 25 Front Office Team
☐ 26 Jim Narier
☐ 27 Scott Breeden
☐ 28 Kim Hart
☐ 29 Ken Grandquist
☐ 30 Cubby (Mascot)
☐ NNO Cubby (Late Issue)

1983 Kinston Blue Jays Team Issue

This 28-card standard size unnumbered set of the 1983 Kinston Blue Jays was issued by Tony Kelly's Studio. This set includes a card of former Washington Redskins' quarterback Jay Schroeder.

	MINT	NRMT	EXC
COMPLETE SET (28)	125.00	55.00	15.50

☐ 1 Jim Bishop
☐ 2 J.J. Cannon
☐ 3 Ron Clark
☐ 4 Scot Elam
☐ 5 Jose Escobar
☐ 6 Keith Gilliam
☐ 7 Devallon Harper
☐ 8 Moe Hazelette
☐ 9 Ken Kinnard
☐ 10 Chris Knapp
☐ 11 Tom Layton
☐ 12 Perry Lychak
☐ 13 Perry Mader
☐ 14 Alex Marte
☐ 15 Mark Poole
☐ 16 Joe Pursell
☐ 17 Steve Reish
☐ 18 Derrick Reutter
☐ 19 Ralph Rivas
☐ 20 Tim Rodgers
☐ 21 Randy Romagna
☐ 22 Eddie Santos
☐ 23 Jay Schroeder
☐ 24 Mike Sharperson
☐ 25 Rico Sutton
☐ 26 Bernie Tatis
☐ 27 Guillermo Valenzuela
☐ 28 David Wells

1983 Knoxville Blue Jays TCMA

This 22-card standard-size set of the 1983 Knoxville Blue Jays, a Class AA Southern League affiliate of the Toronto Blue Jays, features white-bordered posed color player photos on its fronts. The player's name and position appear within a blue stripe at the bottom. The plain back carries the team name at the top, followed below by the league affiliation, and then the player's name, biography and statistics.

	MINT	NRMT	EXC
COMPLETE SET (22)	20.00	9.00	2.50

☐ 1 Tom Blackmon
☐ 2 Stan Clarke
☐ 3 John Cerutti
☐ 4 Mercedes Esquer
☐ 5 Jack McKnight
☐ 6 Chris Phillips
☐ 7 Dave Shipanoff
☐ 8 Bill Pinkham
☐ 9 Dan Whitmer
☐ 10 Carry Harris
☐ 11 Chris Johnston
☐ 12 Augie Schmidt
☐ 13 Andre Wood
☐ 14 Chris Shaddy
☐ 15 Kevin Aitcheson
☐ 16 Eddie Dennis
☐ 17 Greg Griffin
☐ 18 Paul Hodgson
☐ 19 John McLaren
☐ 20 Doug Ault
☐ 21 John Woodworth
☐ 22 Gary McCune

1983 Las Vegas Stars Baseball Hobby News

	MINT	NRMT	EXC
COMPLETE SET (22)	20.00	9.00	2.50

☐ 1 Greg Booker
☐ 2 Bobby Brown
☐ 3 Larry Brown
☐ 4 Tim Cook
☐ 5 Gerry Davis
☐ 6 Gerry DeSimone
☐ 7 Harry Dunlop
☐ 8 Steve Fireovid
☐ 9 Larry Harlow
☐ 10 George Hinshaw
☐ 11 Tom House
☐ 12 Jerry Johnson
☐ 13 Joe Lansford
☐ 14 Bill Long
☐ 15 Kevin McReynolds
☐ 16 Felix Oroz
☐ 17 Joe Pittman
☐ 18 Larry Rothschild
☐ 19 Cecilio Ruiz
☐ 20 James Steels
☐ 21 Mark Thurmond
☐ 22 Ron Tingley

1983 Louisville Redbirds Riley's

	MINT	NRMT	EXC
COMPLETE SET (30)	25.00	11.00	3.10

☐ 1 Jim Fregosi
☐ 2 Gaylen Pitts
☐ 3 Jerry McKune
☐ 4 Dyar Miller
☐ 5 Gene Roof
☐ 6 Kevin Hagen
☐ 7 Joe De Sa
☐ 8 David Von Ohlen
☐ 9 Tom Nieto
☐ 10 Jeff Keener
☐ 11 Jeff Doyle
☐ 12 Tito Landrum
☐ 13 Jose Gonzalez
☐ 14 Jose Brito
☐ 15 Gene Dotson

☐ 16 Ralph Citarella
☐ 17 Andy Rincon
☐ 18 Andy Van Slyke
☐ 19 Jim Adduci
☐ 20 John Fulgham
☐ 21 Mike Calise
☐ 22 Dennis Werth
☐ 23 Ricky Horton
☐ 24 Orlando Sanchez
☐ 25 Tom Thurberg
☐ 26 Todd Worrell
☐ 27 Bill Lyons
☐ 28 Dave Kable
☐ 29 Doyle Harris
☐ 30 Jed Smith

1983 Lynchburg Mets TCMA

This 23-card standard-size set of the 1983 Lynchburg Mets, a Class A Carolina League affiliate of the New York Mets, features white-bordered posed color player photos on its fronts. The player's name and position appear within a blue stripe at the bottom. The plain back carries the team name at the top, followed below by the league affiliation, and then the player's name, biography and statistics. This issue includes the minor league card debuts of Lenny Dykstra and Dwight Gooden. Approximately 4,000 sets were produced.

	MINT	NRMT	EXC
COMPLETE SET (23)	75.00	34.00	9.50

☐ 1 Reggie Jackson
☐ 2 Larry McNutt
☐ 3 Bill Latham
☐ 4 Jeff Bettendorf
☐ 5 Bill Fultz
☐ 6 Darryl Denby
☐ 7 Randy Milligan
☐ 8 Greg Olson
☐ 9 Bruce Morrison
☐ 10 Dwight Gooden
☐ 11 Sam Perlozzo
☐ 13 John Cumberland
☐ 14A Mark Carreon
☐ 14B Dave Cochrane
☐ 15 Lenny Dykstra
☐ 16 Jay Tibbs
☐ 17 John Heller
☐ 18 Jeff Sunderlage
☐ 19 Dave Wyatt
☐ 20 Joe Graves
☐ 21 Rich Pickett
☐ 22 Ed Hearn
☐ 23 Wes Gardner

1983 Lynn Pirates TCMA

This 27-card standard-size set of the 1983 Lynn Pirates, a Class AA Eastern League affiliate of the Pittsburgh Pirates, features white-bordered posed color player photos on its fronts. The player's name and position appear within a blue stripe at the bottom. The plain back carries the team name at the top, followed below by the league affiliation, and then the player's name, biography and statistics.

	MINT	NRMT	EXC
COMPLETE SET (27)	50.00	22.00	6.25

☐ 1 Mike Bielecki
☐ 2 Wilfredo Cordoba
☐ 3 Fernando Gonzales
☐ 4 John Lackey
☐ 5 Lee Marcheskie
☐ 6 Dale Mahorcic
☐ 7 Craig Pippin
☐ 8 Keith Thibodeaux
☐ 9 Tim Wheeler
☐ 11 Stan Cliburn
☐ 12 Burke Goldthorn
☐ 13 Peter Rowe
☐ 14 Rafael Belliard
☐ 15 Nelson Norman
☐ 16 Greg Pastors
☐ 17 Rich Renteria
☐ 18 John Schaive
☐ 19 Benny Distefano
☐ 20 Ken Ford
☐ 21 Connor McGehee
☐ 22 Jose Rodriguez
☐ 23 Tommy Sandt
☐ 24 Frank Leger
☐ 25 Brian McCann
☐ 26 Thomas Lynn
☐ 27 Gary Fitzpatrick
☐ 28 Jay Walsh

1983 Madison Muskies Fritsch

This issue include the minor league card debut of Jose Canseco.

	MINT	NRMT	EXC
COMPLETE SET (32)	35.00	16.00	4.40

☐ 1 Ed Janus GM
Bob Drew PRES
☐ 2 Stephen Charry TD
Mike DuVal AGM
☐ 3 Dave Collins DB
☐ 4 Todd Fischer
☐ 5 Dave Wilder
☐ 6 Ray Alonzo
☐ 7 Dennis Gonsalves
☐ 8 Jorge Diaz
☐ 9 Thad Reece
☐ 10 Ed Retzer
☐ 11 Shawn Gill
☐ 12 Tom Conquest
☐ 13 Jose Canseco
☐ 14 Keith Call
☐ 15 Bob Loscalzo
☐ 16 Bob Hallas
☐ 17 Eddie Escribano
☐ 18 Gene Ransom
☐ 19 John Michel
☐ 20 Mikki Jackson
☐ 21 Juan Cruz
☐ 22 Greg Robles
☐ 23 Pete Kendrick
☐ 24 Gary Dawson
☐ 25 Glenn Godwin
☐ 26 John Huey
☐ 27 Dave Leiper
☐ 28 Brian Graham
☐ 29 Hector Perez TR
☐ 30 Frank Trucchio CO
☐ 31 Brad Fischer MG
☐ 32 Team Logo

1983 Memphis Chicks TCMA

This 24-card standard-size set of the 1983 Memphis Chicks, a Class AA Southern League affiliate of the Montreal Expos, features white-bordered posed color player photos on its fronts. The player's name and position appear within a blue stripe at the bottom. The plain back carries the team name at the top, followed below by the league affiliation, and then the player's name, biography and statistics.

	MINT	NRMT	EXC
COMPLETE SET (24)	25.00	11.00	3.10

☐ 1 Shooty Babitt
☐ 2 Georgie Cruz
☐ 3 Rene Gonzales
☐ 4 John Damon
☐ 5 Jeff Carl
☐ 6 Larry Goldetsky CO
☐ 7 Don Carter
☐ 8 Nelson Santovenia
☐ 9 Dave Hoeksema
☐ 10 Tommy Joe Shimp
☐ 11 Tim Cates
☐ 12 Bud Yanus
☐ 13 Rod Nealeigh
☐ 14 Jeff Taylor
☐ 15 Leonel Carrion
☐ 16 Jim Auten
☐ 17 Bob Tenenini
☐ 18 Larry Glasscock
☐ 19 Joe Hesketh
☐ 20 Greg Bargar
☐ 21 Razor Shines
☐ 22 Jeff Porter
☐ 23 Rick Renick
☐ 24 Mike Kinnunen

1983 Miami Marlins TCMA

This 28-card standard-size set of the 1983 Miami Marlins, a Class A Florida State League affiliate of the San Diego Padres, features white-bordered posed color player photos on its fronts. The player's name and position appear within a blue stripe at the bottom. The plain back carries the team name at the top, followed below by the league affiliation, and then the player's name, biography and statistics. This issue includes the minor league card debut of Benito Santiago.

	MINT	NRMT	EXC
COMPLETE SET (28)	75.00	34.00	9.50

☐ 1 Will George
☐ 2 Mike McClain
☐ 3 Scott Gardner
☐ 4 Francisco Cota
☐ 5 Gene Walter
☐ 6 Sergio Del Rosario
☐ 7 Bill Gerhardt
☐ 8 Chuck Kolotka
☐ 9 Greg Raymer
☐ 10 Kevin Rhodas
☐ 11 Jeff Dean
☐ 12 Ray Nodell
☐ 13 Billy Ireland
☐ 14 Jose Gomez
☐ 15 Dan Jones
☐ 16 Al Simmons
☐ 17 Paul Noce
☐ 18 Manny Del Rosario
☐ 19 John Frierson
☐ 20 Benito Santiago
☐ 21 Bob Allinger
☐ 22 Tim Cannon
☐ 23 Tommy Francis
☐ 24 Steve Sayles
☐ 25 Jim Breazeale
☐ 26 Mark Miggins
☐ 27 Dennis Maley
☐ 28 Todd Hutcheson

1983 Midland Cubs TCMA

This 26-card standard-size set of the 1983 Midland Angels, a Class AA Texas League affiliate of the Chicago Cubs, features white-bordered posed color player photos on its fronts. The player's name and position appear within a blue stripe at the bottom. The plain back carries the team name at the top, followed below by the league affiliation, and then the player's name, biography and statistics.

	MINT	NRMT	EXC
COMPLETE SET (26)	25.00	11.00	3.10

☐ 1 Bill Schammel
☐ 2 Tommy Harmon
☐ 3 Glen Gregson
☐ 4 Jim Walsh
☐ 5 Neil Bryant
☐ 6 Dennis Brogna
☐ 7 Carlos Gil
☐ 8 Doug Weleno
☐ 9 Tim Millner
☐ 10 Bruce Chanye
☐ 11 Ken Pryce
☐ 12 Darrel Banks
☐ 13 Bill Hatcher
☐ 14 Tom Lombarski
☐ 15 George Borges
☐ 16 Trey Brooks
☐ 17 Don Hyman
☐ 18 Ron Richardson
☐ 19 Stan Kyles
☐ 20 Mike Anicich
☐ 21 Jim Gerlach
☐ 22 Ray Soff
☐ 23 Tom Johnson
☐ 24 Randy LaVigne
☐ 25 Rick Baker
☐ 26 A.J. Hill

1983 Nashua Angels TCMA

This 27-card standard-size set of the 1983 Nashua Angels, a Class AA Eastern League affiliate of the California Angels, features white-bordered posed color player photos on its fronts. The player's name and position appear within a blue stripe at the bottom. The plain back carries the team name at the top, followed below by the league affiliation, and then the player's name, biography and statistics.

	MINT	NRMT	EXC
COMPLETE SET (27)	10.00	4.50	1.25

☐ 1 Bob Bastian
☐ 2 Rod Boxberger
☐ 3 Stewart Cliburn
☐ 4 Jeff Connor
☐ 5 Bill Mooneyham
☐ 6 Ron Romanick
☐ 7 Mickey Saatzer
☐ 8 D.W. Smith
☐ 9 Ron Sylvia
☐ 10 Steve Liddle
☐ 11 Larry Patterson
☐ 12 Harry Francis
☐ 13 Craig Gerber
☐ 14 Gustavo Polidor
☐ 15 Darryl Stephens
☐ 16 Frank Vilorio
☐ 17 Jim Beswick
☐ 18 Sap Randall
☐ 19 Al Romero
☐ 20 Winston Llenas
☐ 21 Frank Reberger
☐ 22 Richard Zaleski
☐ 23 Mark McCormack
☐ 24 Ben Surner
☐ 25 Jerry Mileur
☐ 26 George Como
☐ 27 Nashua Angel Chicken

1983 Nashville Sounds Team Issue

	MINT	NRMT	EXC
COMPLETE SET (25)	10.00	4.50	1.25

☐ 1 Scott Bradley
☐ 2 Mike Browning
☐ 3 Tim Burke
☐ 4 Ben Callahan
☐ 5 Pete Dalena
☐ 6 Matt Gallegos
☐ 7 Paul Grayner TR
☐ 8 Doug Holmquist MG
☐ 9 Frank Kneuer
☐ 10 Tim Knight
☐ 11 Vic Mata
☐ 12 Derwin McNealy
☐ 13 Ed Olwine
☐ 14 Mike Pagliarulo
☐ 15 Scott Patterson
☐ 16 Erik Peterson
☐ 17 Mike Reddish
☐ 18 Jim Saul CO
☐ 19 Kelly Scott
☐ 20 Mark Shifflett
☐ 21 Buck Showalter
☐ 22 Mark Silva
☐ 23 Keith Smith
☐ 24 Dave Szymczak
☐ 25 Hoyt Wilhelm CO

1983 Oklahoma City 89ers TCMA

This 24-card standard-size set of the 1983 Oklahoma City 89ers, a Class AAA American Association affiliate of the Texas Rangers, features white-bordered posed color player photos on its fronts. The player's name and position appear within a blue stripe at the bottom. The plain back carries the team name at the top, followed below by the league affiliation, and then the player's name, biography and statistics.

	MINT	NRMT	EXC
COMPLETE SET (24)	25.00	11.00	3.10

☐ 1 Bill Stearns
☐ 2 Tommy Burgess
☐ 3 Terry Bogener
☐ 4 Nick Capra
☐ 5 Tracy Cowger
☐ 6 Victor Cruz
☐ 7 Tommy Dunbar
☐ 8 Mike Griffin
☐ 9 Thomas Henke
☐ 10 Michael Jirschele
☐ 11 Robert Jones
☐ 12 Peter MacKanin
☐ 13 Mark Mercer
☐ 14 Ron Musselman
☐ 15 David Rajsich
☐ 16 Paul Semall
☐ 17 David Stockstill
☐ 18 Don Werner
☐ 19 Curt Wilkerson
☐ 20 Mike Mason
☐ 21 Joe Strain
☐ 22 Jim Farr
☐ 23 Don Scott
☐ 24 Danny Wheat

1983 Omaha Royals TCMA

This 26-card standard-size set of the 1983 Omaha Royals, a Class AAA American Association affiliate of the Kansas City Royals, features white-bordered posed color player photos on its fronts. The player's name and position appear within a blue stripe at the bottom. The plain back carries the team name at the top, followed below by the league affiliation, and then the player's name, biography and statistics.

	MINT	NRMT	EXC
COMPLETE SET (26)	25.00	11.00	3.10

☐ 1 Mike Alverez
☐ 2 Bud Black
☐ 3 Derek Botelho
☐ 4 Scott Brown
☐ 5 Keith Creel
☐ 6 Danny Jackson
☐ 7 Mike Parrott
☐ 8 Dan St. Clair
☐ 9 Dave Schuler
☐ 10 Vince Yuhas
☐ 11 Brian Poldberg
☐ 12 Russ Stephans
☐ 13 Buddy Biancalana
☐ 14 Jeff Cox
☐ 15 Mark Funderburk
☐ 16 Kelly Heath
☐ 17 Cliff Pastornicky
☐ 18 Steve Hammond
☐ 19 Bombo Rivera
☐ 20 Mark Ryal
☐ 21 Pat Sheridan
☐ 22 Dave Leeper
☐ 23 Bill Gorman
☐ 24 Joe Sparks
☐ 25 Jerry Cram
☐ 26 Paul McGannon

1983 Orlando Twins TCMA

This 23-card standard-size set of the 1983 Orlando Twins, a Class AA Southern League affiliate of the Minnesota Twins, features white-bordered posed color player photos on its fronts. The player's name and position appear within a blue stripe at the bottom. The plain back carries the team name at the top, followed below by the league affiliation, and then the player's name, biography and statistics.

	MINT	NRMT	EXC
COMPLETE SET (22)	10.00	4.50	1.25
COMPLETE SET W/LATE ISSUE (23)	50.00	22.00	6.25

☐ 1 Phil Roof
☐ 2 Tony Pilla
☐ 3 Jim Weaver

- ☐ 4 Kevin Williams
- ☐ 5 Jeff Reed
- ☐ 6 Steve Lombardozzi
- ☐ 7 Mike McCain
- ☐ 8 John Palica
- ☐ 9 Mike Sodders
- ☐ 10 Chris Cadahia
- ☐ 11 Ken Foster
- ☐ 12 Jerry Lomastro
- ☐ 13 Manny Pena
- ☐ 14 Jay Pettibone
- ☐ 15 Rich Yett
- ☐ 16 Jack Hobbs
- ☐ 17 Ted Kromy
- ☐ 18 Kirby Krueger
- ☐ 19 Eric Broersma
- ☐ 20 Paul Gibson
- ☐ 21 Mike Giordano
- ☐ 22 Tony Guerrero
- ☐ 25 Carson Carroll (Late Issue)

1983 Pawtucket Red Sox TCMA

This 26-card standard-size set of the 1983 Pawtucket Red Sox, a Class AAA International League affiliate of the Boston Red Sox, features white-bordered posed color player photos on its fronts. The player's name and position appear within a blue stripe at the bottom. The plain back carries the team name at the top, followed below by the league affiliation, and then the player's name, biography and statistics.

	MINT	NRMT	EXC
COMPLETE SET (26)	30.00	13.50	3.70

- ☐ 1 Bob Birrell
- ☐ 2 Dennis Boyd
- ☐ 3 Dennis Burtt
- ☐ 4 Steve Crawford
- ☐ 5 Brian Denman
- ☐ 6 Jim Dorsey
- ☐ 7 Mark Fidrych
- ☐ 8 Keith MacWhorter
- ☐ 9 Bill Moloney
- ☐ 10 Dave Schoppee
- ☐ 11 Steve Shields
- ☐ 12 Roger LaFrancois
- ☐ 13 John Lickert
- ☐ 14 Marty Barrett
- ☐ 15 Juan Bustabad
- ☐ 16 Mike Davis
- ☐ 17 Dava Koza
- ☐ 18 Jim Wilson
- ☐ 19 Reggie Whittemore
- ☐ 20 Gus Burgess
- ☐ 21 Geno Gentile
- ☐ 22 Lee Graham
- ☐ 23 Juan Pautt
- ☐ 24 Chico Walker
- ☐ 25 Tony Torchia
- ☐ 26 Mike Roarke

1983 Peoria Suns Fritsch

	MINT	NRMT	EXC
COMPLETE SET (30)	18.00	8.00	2.20

- ☐ 1 Ray Jimenez
- ☐ 2 Joe King
- ☐ 3 Kevin Davis
- ☐ 4 Scott Glanz
- ☐ 5 Donald Groh
- ☐ 6 Dave Heath
- ☐ 7 Kris Kline
- ☐ 8 Dougl McKenzie
- ☐ 9 Mark McLemore
- ☐ 10 Tom Smith
- ☐ 11 Rick Stromer
- ☐ 12 Jose Valdez
- ☐ 13 Don Timberlake
- ☐ 14 Mike Rizzo
- ☐ 15 Jack Crawford
- ☐ 16 Tom Rentschler
- ☐ 17 Jeff Salazar
- ☐ 18 Jay Lewis
- ☐ 19 Al Christy
- ☐ 20 Rafael Lugo
- ☐ 21 Scott Suehr
- ☐ 22 Devon White
- ☐ 23 Julian Gonzalez
- ☐ 24 Brian Hartsock
- ☐ 25 Bob Kipper
- ☐ 26 Ron Phipps TR
- ☐ 27 Mike Saverino CO
- ☐ 28 Eddie Rodriguez CO
- ☐ 29 Joe Coleman MG
- ☐ 30 Team Logo

1983 Phoenix Giants Baseball Hobby News

	MINT	NRMT	EXC
COMPLETE SET (28)	20.00	9.00	2.50

- ☐ 1 John Rabb
- ☐ 2 Mark Calvert
- ☐ 3 Scott Garrelts
- ☐ 4 Brian Asselstine
- ☐ 5 Jeff Ransom
- ☐ 6 Rich Murray
- ☐ 7 Jeff Cornell
- ☐ 8 Dan Gladden
- ☐ 9 Tom Runnells
- ☐ 10 Kernan Ronan
- ☐ 11 Phil Hinrichs
- ☐ 12 Kelvin Torve
- ☐ 13 Herman Segelke
- ☐ 14 Guy Sularz
- ☐ 15 Randy Kutcher
- ☐ 16 Ted Wilborn
- ☐ 17 Mike Brecht
- ☐ 18 Butch Hughes
- ☐ 19 Ron Pisel
- ☐ 20 Mark Davis
- ☐ 21 Mark Dempsey
- ☐ 22 Chris Smith
- ☐ 23 Craig Chamberlain
- ☐ 24 Jack Mull MG
- ☐ 25 Doug Landuyt TR
- ☐ 26 Ethan Blackaby GM
- ☐ 27 Phoenix Giants Rooster
- ☐ 28 Tommy Gonzalez Stadium Supervisor

1983 Portland Beavers TCMA

This 25-card standard-size set of the 1983 Portland Beavers, a Class AAA Pacific Coast League affiliate of the Philadelphia Phillies, features white-bordered posed color player photos on its fronts. The player's name and position appear within a blue stripe at the bottom. The plain back carries the team name at the top, followed below by the league affiliation, and then the player's name, biography and statistics.

	MINT	NRMT	EXC
COMPLETE SET (22)	75.00	34.00	9.50
COMPLETE SET (25)	125.00	55.00	15.50

- ☐ 1 Luis Aguayo
- ☐ 2 Juan Samuel
- ☐ 3 Larry Andersen
- ☐ 4 Kyle Money
- ☐ 5 Kevin Gross
- ☐ 6 Steve Jeltz
- ☐ 7 Jerry Keller
- ☐ 8 Len Matuszek
- ☐ 9 Kelly Downs
- ☐ 10 Ramon Aviles
- ☐ 11 Tim Corcoran
- ☐ 12 George Culver
- ☐ 13 John Felske
- ☐ 14 Chris Bourjos
- ☐ 15 Porfi Altamirano
- ☐ 16 Dick Davis
- ☐ 17 John Russell
- ☐ 18 Marty Decker
- ☐ 19 Charlie Hudson
- ☐ 20 Ed Miller
- ☐ 21 Ron Pruitt
- ☐ 22 Alejandro Sanchez
- ☐ 23 Stan Bahnsen
- ☐ 24 Larry Bradford
- ☐ 25 Kiko Garcia

1983 Quad City Cubs TCMA

This 27-card standard-size set of the 1983 Quad City Cubs, a Class A Midwest League affiliate of the Chicago Cubs, features white-bordered posed color player photos on its fronts. The player's name and position appear within a blue stripe at the bottom. The plain back carries the team name at the top, followed below by the league affiliation, and then the player's name, biography and statistics. This issue includes the minor league card debut of Shawon Dunston.

	MINT	NRMT	EXC
COMPLETE SET (27)	35.00	16.00	4.40

- ☐ 1 Roger Crow
- ☐ 2 Larry Cox
- ☐ 3 Dick Pole
- ☐ 4 Mario Panetta
- ☐ 5 David Barber Kyle Benjamin
- ☐ 6 Mark Baker
- ☐ 7 Steve Balmer
- ☐ 8 Brad Blevins
- ☐ 9 Mitch Cook
- ☐ 10 Jeff Fruge
- ☐ 11 Rene German
- ☐ 12 Tim Grachen
- ☐ 13 Randy Lockie
- ☐ 14 Rudy Serafini
- ☐ 15 Brian Tuller
- ☐ 16 Steve Roadcap
- ☐ 17 Juan Velazquez
- ☐ 18 Jim Allen
- ☐ 19 Steve Cordner
- ☐ 20 Shawon Dunston
- ☐ 21 Gary Jones
- ☐ 22 Tony Woods
- ☐ 23 Jose Rivera
- ☐ 24 Stan Broderick
- ☐ 25 Damon Farmar
- ☐ 26 Dave Martinez
- ☐ 27 Rolando Roomes

1983 Reading Phillies TCMA

This 24-card standard-size set of the 1983 Reading Phillies, a Class AA Eastern League affiliate of the Philadelphia Phillies, features white-bordered posed color player photos on its fronts. The player's name and position appear within a blue stripe at the bottom. The plain back carries the team name at the top, followed below by the league affiliation, and then the player's name, biography and statistics. This issue includes the minor league card debut of Darren Daulton.

	MINT	NRMT	EXC
COMPLETE SET (24)	150.00	70.00	19.00

- ☐ 1 Bud Bartholow
- ☐ 2 Darren Burroughs
- ☐ 3 Don Carman
- ☐ 4 Jay Davisson
- ☐ 5 Rich Gaynor
- ☐ 6 Frankie Griffin
- ☐ 7 Bill Johnson
- ☐ 8 George Riley
- ☐ 9 Denny Thomas
- ☐ 10 Ed Wojna
- ☐ 11 Darren Daulton
- ☐ 12 Mike LaValliere
- ☐ 13 Den Dowell
- ☐ 14 Greg Legg
- ☐ 15 Francisco Melendez
- ☐ 16 Julio Perez
- ☐ 17 Juan Samuel
- ☐ 18 Willie Darkis
- ☐ 19 Randy Salava
- ☐ 20 Jeff Stone
- ☐ 21 Keith Washington
- ☐ 22 Mel Williams
- ☐ 23 Bill Dancy
- ☐ 24 Bob Tiefenauer

1983 Redwood Pioneers TCMA

This 32-card standard-size set of the 1983 Redwood Pioneers, a Class A California League affiliate of the California Angels, features white-bordered posed color player photos on its fronts. The player's name and position appear within a blue stripe at the bottom. The plain back carries the team name at the top, followed below by the league affiliation, and then the player's name, biography and statistics.

	MINT	NRMT	EXC
COMPLETE SET (32)	15.00	6.75	1.85

- ☐ 1 Jeff Ahern
- ☐ 2 Ken Angulo
- ☐ 3 Kris Bankowski
- ☐ 4 Mark Bonner
- ☐ 5 Norman Carrasco
- ☐ 6 Dave Brady
- ☐ 7 T.R. Bryden
- ☐ 8 Kevin Davis
- ☐ 9 Steve Eakes
- ☐ 10 Lonnie Garza
- ☐ 11 Dennis Gilbert
- ☐ 12 Terry Harper
- ☐ 13 Lee Jones
- ☐ 14 Lance Junker
- ☐ 15 Tim Kammeyer
- ☐ 16 Greg Key
- ☐ 17 Tony Mack
- ☐ 18 Mike Madril
- ☐ 19 Kirk McCaskill
- ☐ 20 Scott Oliver
- ☐ 21 Kevin Price
- ☐ 22 Tom Rentschuler
- ☐ 23 Mark Smelko
- ☐ 24 Rick Turner
- ☐ 25 Bill Worden
- ☐ 26 Goldie Wright
- ☐ 27 Luis Zambrana
- ☐ 28 Don Rowe
- ☐ 29 Bernie Smith
- ☐ 30 Jack Lind
- ☐ 31 Mark Terrazas
- ☐ 32 Pioneer Pete

1983 Richmond Braves TCMA

This 25-card standard-size set of the 1983 Richmond Braves, a Class AAA International League affiliate of the Atlanta Braves, features white-bordered posed color player photos on its fronts. The player's name and position appear within a blue stripe at the bottom. The plain back carries the team name at the top, followed below by the league affiliation, and then the player's name, biography and statistics.

	MINT	NRMT	EXC
COMPLETE SET (25)	20.00	9.00	2.50

- ☐ 1 Jose Alvarez
- ☐ 2 Tony Brizzolaria
- ☐ 3 Joe Cowley
- ☐ 4 Ken Daley
- ☐ 5 Greg Field
- ☐ 6 Chuck Fore
- ☐ 7 Sam Ayoub
- ☐ 8 Gary Reiter
- ☐ 9 Angie Ruiz
- ☐ 10 Bob Walk
- ☐ 11 Matt Sinatro
- ☐ 12 Steve Swisher
- ☐ 13 Brook Jacoby
- ☐ 14 Gerald Perry
- ☐ 15 Chico Ruiz
- ☐ 16 Paul Runge
- ☐ 17 Paul Zuvella
- ☐ 18 Albert Hall
- ☐ 19 Brad Komminsk
- ☐ 20 Bob Porter
- ☐ 21 Leonel Vargas
- ☐ 22 Larry Whisenton
- ☐ 23 Eddie Haas
- ☐ 24 Craig Robinson
- ☐ 25 Johnny Sain

1983 Rochester Red Wings TCMA

This 25-card standard-size set of the 1983 Rochester Red Wings, a Class AAA International League affiliate of the Baltimore Orioles, features white-bordered posed color player photos on its fronts. The player's name and position appear within a blue stripe at the bottom. The plain back carries the team name at the top, followed below by the league affiliation, and then the player's name, biography and statistics.

	MINT	NRMT	EXC
COMPLETE SET (25)	20.00	9.00	2.50

- ☐ 1 Lance Nichols
- ☐ 2 Mark Brown
- ☐ 3 John Flinn
- ☐ 4 Dave Ford
- ☐ 5 Craig Minetto
- ☐ 6 Dan Morogiello
- ☐ 7 Allan Ramirez
- ☐ 8 Mark Smith
- ☐ 9 Cliff Speck
- ☐ 10 Bill Swaggerty
- ☐ 11 Dave Huppert
- ☐ 12 Al Pardo
- ☐ 13 Floyd Rayford
- ☐ 14 Bob Bonner
- ☐ 15 Glenn Gulliver
- ☐ 16 Rick Jones
- ☐ 17 Dan Logan
- ☐ 18 Jone Valle
- ☐ 19 Elijah Bonaparte
- ☐ 20 Drungo Hazewood
- ☐ 21 Ric Lisi
- ☐ 22 Mike Young
- ☐ 23 Tom Chism
- ☐ 24 Richie Bancells
- ☐ 25 Mark Wiley

1983 Salt Lake City Gulls TCMA

This 26-card standard-size set of the 1983 Salt Lake City Gulls, a Class AAA Pacific Coast League affiliate of the Seattle Mariners, features white-bordered posed color player photos on its fronts. The player's name and position appear within a blue stripe at the bottom. The plain back carries the team name at the top, followed below by the league affiliation, and then the player's name, biography and statistics.

	MINT	NRMT	EXC
COMPLETE SET (26)	20.00	9.00	2.50

- ☐ 1 Edwin Nunez
- ☐ 2 Jerry Gleaton
- ☐ 3 Robert Babcock
- ☐ 4 Brian Snyder
- ☐ 5 Karl Best
- ☐ 6 Brian Allard
- ☐ 7 Mike Moore
- ☐ 8 Rick Adair
- ☐ 9 Jed Murray
- ☐ 10 Joe Decker
- ☐ 11 Phil Bradley
- ☐ 12 Mark Woodmansee
- ☐ 13 Tito Nanni

☐ 14 Rod Allen
☐ 15 Bud Bulling
☐ 16 Jamie Nelson
☐ 17 Jim Maler
☐ 18 Bill Crone
☐ 19 John Moses
☐ 20 Glen Walker
☐ 21 Al Chambers
☐ 22 Harold Reynolds
☐ 23 Spike Owen
☐ 24 Bobby Floyd
☐ 25 Manny Estrada
☐ 26 Doug Merrifield

1983 San Jose Bees Colla

This standard size set of the San Jose Bees, a Class A California League Co-op team of the Baltimore Orioles and Seibu Lions was produced by collector Barry Colla.

	MINT	NRMT	EXC
COMPLETE SET (26)	10.00	4.50	1.25

☐ 1 Frank Verdi MG
☐ 2 Hiromi Wada CO
☐ 3 Charlie Bertucio
☐ 4 Lee Granger
☐ 5 Brian McDonough
☐ 6 Gary Springer
☐ 7 Dan McInerny
☐ 8 Osamu Abe
☐ 9 Yukiichi Komazaki
☐ 10 Hiro Shirahata
☐ 11 Mark Butler
☐ 12 Mark Jacob
☐ 13 Kerry Cook
☐ 14 Bruce Fields
☐ 15 Gary Legumina
☐ 16 Sadahito Ueda
☐ 17 Kraig Priessman
☐ 18 Katsuya Soma
☐ 19 Mike Daughterty
☐ 20 Carl Nichols
☐ 21 Jeff Gilbert
☐ 22 Jeff Summers
☐ 23 Leon Hoke
☐ 24 Kurt Leiter
☐ 25 Greg Dehart
☐ 26 Harry Steve GM

1983 Springfield Cardinals Fritsch

	MINT	NRMT	EXC
COMPLETE SET (26)	10.00	4.50	1.25

☐ 1 Pete Stoll TR
☐ 2 David Clements
☐ 3 Paul Cherry
☐ 4 Sammy Martin
☐ 5 Dave Droschak
☐ 6 Curtis Ford
☐ 7 Marty Mason
☐ 8 Ed Tanner
☐ 9 Scott Arigoni
☐ 10 Brett Benza
☐ 11 Mick Shade
☐ 12 Joe Silkwood
☐ 13 Bob Geren
☐ 14 Greg Dunn
☐ 15 John Young
☐ 16 Dave Hoyt
☐ 17 Harry McCulla
☐ 18 Matt Gundelfinger
☐ 19 Randy Martinez
☐ 20 Mike Pittman
☐ 21 Dan Stryffeler
☐ 22 Dave Bialas MG
☐ 23 Mike Gambeski
☐ 24 Allen Morlock
☐ 25 Gus Malespin
☐ 26 Team Logo

1983 St. Petersburg Cardinals TCMA

This 30-card standard-size set of the 1983 St. Petersburg Cardinals, a Class A Florida State League affiliate of the St. Louis Cardinals, features white-bordered posed color player photos on its fronts. The player's name and position appear within a blue stripe at the bottom. The plain back carries the team name at the top, followed below by the league affiliation, and then the player's name, biography and statistics.

	MINT	NRMT	EXC
COMPLETE SET (30)	30.00	13.50	3.70

☐ 1 Joseph Boever
☐ 2 Javier Carranza
☐ 3 Henry Carson
☐ 4 Danny Cox
☐ 5 Thomas Dozier
☐ 6 Thomas Epple
☐ 7 Michael Hartley
☐ 8 Robert Kish
☐ 9 John Martin
☐ 10 Christian Martinez
☐ 11 Mark Riggins
☐ 12 Freddie Silva
☐ 13 Scott Young
☐ 14 Randall Champion
☐ 15 Timothy Wallace
☐ 16 James Burns
☐ 17 Frank Garcia
☐ 18 Brad Luther
☐ 19 Deron Thomas
☐ 20 Francisco Batista
☐ 21 Robert Helsom
☐ 22 Richard James
☐ 23 Jose Rodreguez
☐ 24 Barry Sayler
☐ 25 Steve F. Turco
☐ 26 Stephen Turgion
☐ 27 Ralph Miller, Jr.
☐ 28 Karl Rogozenski
☐ 29 James Riggleman
☐ 30 Dave Link

1983 Syracuse Chiefs TCMA

This 26-card standard-size set of the 1983 Syracuse Chiefs, a Class AAA International League affiliate of the Toronto Blue Jays, features white-bordered posed color player photos on its fronts. The player's name and position appear within a blue stripe at the bottom. The plain back carries the team name at the top, followed below by the league affiliation, and then the player's name, biography and statistics.

	MINT	NRMT	EXC
COMPLETE SET (26)	50.00	22.00	6.25

☐ 1 Jim Beauchamp MG
☐ 2 Bernie Beckman CO
☐ 3 Tommy Craig TR
☐ 4 Jim Baker
☐ 5 Mark Bomback
☐ 6 Don Cooper
☐ 7 Mark Eichhorn
☐ 8 Dennis Howard
☐ 9 Tom Lukish
☐ 10 Colin McLaughlin
☐ 11 Jeff Schneider
☐ 12 Keith Walker
☐ 13 Matt Williams
☐ 14 Toby Hernandez
☐ 15 Geno Petralli
☐ 16 Tony Fernandez
☐ 17 Fred Manrique
☐ 18 Bob Nandin
☐ 19 Jeff Reynolds
☐ 20 Tim Thompson
☐ 21 George Bell
☐ 22 Anthony Johnson
☐ 23 Vern Ramie
☐ 24 Ron Shepherd
☐ 25 Mitch Webster
☐ 26 Bob Humphreys CO

1983 Tacoma Tigers TCMA

This 36-card standard-size set of the 1983 Tacoma Tigers, a Class AAA Pacific Coast League affiliate of the Oakland Athletics, features white-bordered posed color player photos on its fronts. The player's name and position appear within a blue stripe at the bottom. The plain back carries the team name at the top, followed below by the league affiliation, and then the player's name, biography and statistics.

	MINT	NRMT	EXC
COMPLETE SET (31)	10.00	4.50	1.25
COMPLETE SET (36)	80.00	36.00	10.00

☐ 1 Keith Atherton
☐ 2 Bert Bradley
☐ 3 DeWayne Buice
☐ 4 Gorman Heimueller
☐ 5 Chuck Hensley
☐ 6 Jerome King
☐ 7 Russ McDonald
☐ 8 Curt Young
☐ 9 Daryl Cias
☐ 10 Bill Bathe
☐ 11 Donnie Hill
☐ 12 John Hotchkiss
☐ 13 Mike Woodard
☐ 14 Jim Bennett
☐ 15 Lynn Garrett
☐ 16 Dave Hudgens
☐ 17 Rusty McNealy
☐ 18 Bob Didier
☐ 19 Stan Naccarato
☐ 20 Jim Nettles
☐ 21 Dave Heaverlo
☐ 22 Larry Davis
☐ 23 Art Popham
☐ 24 Tiger Mascot
☐ 25A Danny Goodwin
☐ 25B Bob Christofferson
☐ 26 Scott Pyle
☐ 27 Dennis Sherow
☐ 28 Jeff Jones
☐ 29A Rickey Peters
☐ 29B Dave McKay
☐ 30A Jim Christiansen
☐ 30B Dave Rodriguez
☐ 31 Ed Retzer
☐ 32 Kelvin Moore
☐ 33 Shawn Perry

1983 Tampa Tarpons TCMA

This 29-card standard-size set of the 1983 Tampa Tarpons, a Class A Florida State League affiliate of the Cincinnati Reds, features white-bordered posed color player photos on its fronts. The player's name and position appear within a blue stripe at the bottom. The plain back carries the team name at the top, followed below by the league affiliation, and then the player's name, biography and statistics.

	MINT	NRMT	EXC
COMPLETE SET (29)	70.00	32.00	8.75

☐ 1 Tony Burley
☐ 2 Virg Conley
☐ 3 L.C. Culver
☐ 4 Tony Evans
☐ 5 Tom Browning
☐ 7 Tim Dodd
☐ 8 Jason Felice
☐ 9 Adolfo Feliz
☐ 10 Fergy Ferguson
☐ 11 Jack Foley
☐ 12 Clem Freeman Jr.
☐ 13 Orlando Gonzales
☐ 14 Dave Hall
☐ 15 Ty Hubbard III
☐ 16 Danny LaMar
☐ 17 Ted Langdon
☐ 18 Terrence McGriff
☐ 19 Paul O'Neill
☐ 20 Cressy Pratt
☐ 21 Kevin Steinmetz
☐ 22 Allen Swindle
☐ 23 Scott Terry
☐ 24 Tony Threatt
☐ 25 Steve Watson
☐ 26 Tracy Jones
☐ 27 Nick Fiorillo
☐ 28 Jim Hoff
☐ 29 Mike Sims
☐ 30 Bull Norman

1983 Tidewater Tides TCMA

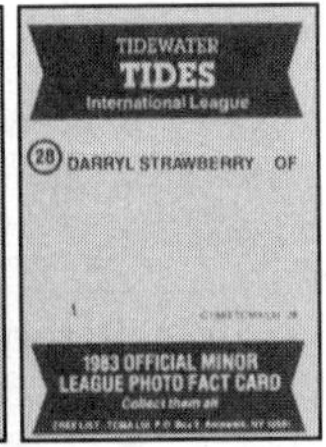

This 29-card standard-size set of the 1983 Tidewater Tides, a Class AAA International League affiliate of the New York Mets, features white-bordered posed color player photos on its fronts. The player's name and position appear within a blue stripe at the bottom. The plain back carries the team name at the top, followed below by the league affiliation, and then the player's name, biography and statistics. Approximately 4,000 sets were produced.

	MINT	NRMT	EXC
COMPLETE SET (29)	40.00	18.00	5.00

☐ 1 Ron Darling
☐ 2 Mike Fitzgerald
☐ 3 Wally Backman
☐ 4 Clint Hurdle
☐ 5 Terry Leach
☐ 6 Mike Bishop
☐ 7 Kelvin Chapman
☐ 8 Gary Rajsich
☐ 9 Tim Leary
☐ 10 Steve Senteney
☐ 11 Tom Gorman
☐ 12 Walt Terrell
☐ 13 Jeff Bittiger
☐ 14 Scott Dye
☐ 15 Greg Biercevicz
☐ 16 Brent Gaff
☐ 17 Dan Schmitz
☐ 18 Mike Howard
☐ 19 Rusty Tillman
☐ 20 Ron Gardenhire
☐ 21 Marvell Wynne
☐ 22 Gil Flores
☐ 23 Davey Johnson
☐ 24 Al Jackson
☐ 25 Josh Wakana
☐ 26 Tucker Ashford
☐ 27 Bob Sikes
☐ 28 Darryl Strawberry
☐ 29 Jose Oquendo

1983 Toledo Mud Hens TCMA

This 29-card standard-size set of the 1983 Toledo Mud Hens, a Class AAA International League affiliate of the Minnesota Twins, features white-bordered posed color player photos on its fronts. The player's name and position appear within a blue stripe at the bottom. The plain back carries the team name at the top, followed below by the league affiliation, and then the player's name, biography and statistics.

	MINT	NRMT	EXC
COMPLETE SET (25)	20.00	9.00	2.50
COMPLETE SET (29)	100.00	45.00	12.50

☐ 1 Paul Boris
☐ 2 Terry Felton
☐ 3 Kevin Flannery
☐ 4 Ed Hodge
☐ 5 Steve Korczyk
☐ 6 Jim Lewis
☐ 7 Jeff Little
☐ 8 Bob Mulligan
☐ 9 Ken Schrom
☐ 10 Mike Walters
☐ 11 Rick Austin
☐ 12 Stine Poole
☐ 13 Dave Baker
☐ 14 Greg Gagne
☐ 15 Houston Jimenez
☐ 16 Tim Teufel
☐ 17 Jesus Vega
☐ 18 Michael Wilson
☐ 19 Andre David
☐ 20 Mike Hart
☐ 21 Randy Johnson
☐ 22 Dave Meier
☐ 23 Cal Ermer
☐ 24 Tim Agan
Kevin Flannery
☐ 25 Scott Tellgren
☐ 26 Eric Broersma
☐ 27 Mike McCain
☐ 28 Bryan Oelkers
☐ 29 Jack O'Conner

1983 Tri-Cities Triplets TCMA

This 28-card standard-size set of the 1983 Tri-Cities Triplets, a Class A Northwest League affiliate of the Texas Rangers, features white-bordered posed color player photos on its fronts. The player's name and position appear within a blue stripe at the bottom. The plain back carries the team name at the top, followed below by the league affiliation, and then the player's name, biography and statistics.

	MINT	NRMT	EXC
COMPLETE SET (28)	10.00	4.50	1.25

☐ 1 Bob Sebra
☐ 2 Steve Kordish
☐ 3 Bruce Kipper
☐ 4 Kerry Burns
☐ 5 Dennis Knight
☐ 6 Mark Cipres
☐ 7 John Munley
☐ 8 Robin Keathley
☐ 9 Nick Esposito
☐ 10 John Fryhoff
☐ 11 Dan Lindquist
☐ 12 Jim Allison
☐ 13 Bill Hance
☐ 14 Tony Carlucci
☐ 15 Reggie Mosley
☐ 16 Mark Gile
☐ 17 Ron Hansen
☐ 18 Mike Keehn
☐ 19 Vince Sakowski
☐ 20 Bert Martinez
☐ 21 Greg Bailey
☐ 22 Danny Simpson
☐ 23 Jim Cesarlo
☐ 24 Brendan Hennessy
☐ 25 Clint Curry
☐ 26 Dave Oliver
☐ 27 Gary Venner
☐ 28 Bob Bill

1983 Tucson Toros TCMA

This 26-card standard-size set of the 1983 Tucson Toros, a Class AAA Pacific Coast League affiliate of the Houston Astros, features white-bordered posed color player photos on its fronts. The player's name and position appear within a blue stripe at the bottom. The back contains safety tips.

	MINT	NRMT	EXC
COMPLETE SET (25)	10.00	4.50	1.25
COMPLETE SET W/LATE ISSUE (26)	50.00	22.00	6.25

☐ 1 Ed Bonine
☐ 2 Dan Boone
☐ 3 Buster Keeton
☐ 4 Ron Mathis
☐ 5 Ron Meredith
☐ 6 Jeff Morris
☐ 7 Gordie Pladson

- ☐ 8 Bert Roberge
- ☐ 9 Bob Vesclic
- ☐ 10 Sam Welborn
- ☐ 11 Julio Solano
- ☐ 12 Steve Christmas
- ☐ 13 Luis Pujols
- ☐ 14 Wes Clements
- ☐ 15 Greg Cypret
- ☐ 16 Jim Pankovits
- ☐ 17 Bert Pena
- ☐ 18 Cliff Wherry
- ☐ 19 Chris Jones
- ☐ 20 Larry Ray
- ☐ 21 Bob Pate
- ☐ 22 Scott Loucks
- ☐ 23 Matt Galante
- ☐ 24 Gary Tuck
- ☐ 25 Dave Labossiere
- ☐ 26 Ruben Robles (Late Issue)

1983 Tulsa Drillers TCMA

This 25-card standard-size set of the 1983 Tulsa Drillers, a Class AA Texas League affiliate of the Texas Rangers, features white-bordered posed color player photos on its fronts. The player's name and position appear within a blue stripe at the bottom. The plain back carries the team name at the top, followed below by the league affiliation, and then the player's name, biography and statistics.

	MINT	NRMT	EXC
COMPLETE SET (25)	15.00	6.75	1.85

- ☐ 1 Jorge Gomez
- ☐ 2 Glen Cook
- ☐ 3 Tony Fossas
- ☐ 4 Rob Clark
- ☐ 5 Billy Taylor
- ☐ 6 Larry McLane
- ☐ 7 Daryl Smith
- ☐ 8 Dennis Long
- ☐ 9 Mitch Zwolensky
- ☐ 10 Tim Henry
- ☐ 11 Dwayne Henry
- ☐ 12 Kirk Killingsworth
- ☐ 13 Bob Brower
- ☐ 14 Chuckie Canady
- ☐ 15 Mike Rubel
- ☐ 16 John Buckley
- ☐ 17 Tracy Cowger
- ☐ 18 Steve Nielsen
- ☐ 19 Joe Nemeth
- ☐ 20 Jim Foit
- ☐ 21 Dan Murphy
- ☐ 22 Steve Buechele
- ☐ 23 Jerry Neufang
- ☐ 24 Terry Johnson
- ☐ 25 Marty Scott

1983 Vero Beach Dodgers TCMA

This 29-card standard-size set of the 1983 Vero Beach Dodgers, a Class A Florida State League affiliate of the Los Angeles Dodgers, features white-bordered posed color player photos on its fronts. The player's name and position appear within a blue stripe at the bottom. The plain back carries the team name at the top, followed below by the league affiliation, and then the player's name, biography and statistics.

	MINT	NRMT	EXC
COMPLETE SET (29)	30.00	13.50	3.70

- ☐ 1 Mike Beuder
- ☐ 2 Tom Duffy
- ☐ 3 Rick Felt
- ☐ 4 Mike Gentle
- ☐ 5 Brian Innis
- ☐ 6 Charlie Jones
- ☐ 7 Vance Lovelace
- ☐ 8 Morris Madden
- ☐ 9 Rafael Montalvo
- ☐ 10 Bill Scudder
- ☐ 11 Chris Thomas
- ☐ 12 Rob Slezak
- ☐ 13 Luis Rivera
- ☐ 14 Steve Boncore
- ☐ 15 Bob Gilles
- ☐ 16 Mariano Duncan
- ☐ 17 John Gregory
- ☐ 18 Hector Guzman
- ☐ 19 Gary Newsom
- ☐ 20 Harold Perkins
- ☐ 21 Billy White
- ☐ 22 Ralph Bryant
- ☐ 23 Jerald Cain
- ☐ 24 Dan Cataline
- ☐ 25 Reggie Williams
- ☐ 26 John Shoemaker
- ☐ 27 Rob Giesecke
- ☐ 28 Stan Wesiak
- ☐ 29 Dennis Lewallyn

1983 Visalia Oaks Fritsch

This 25-card set of the 1983 Visalia Oaks, a Class A California League affiliate of the Minnesota Twins, features the only minor league card of Kirby Puckett.

	MINT	NRMT	EXC
COMPLETE SET (25)	325.00	145.00	40.00

- ☐ 1 Lee Belanger
- ☐ 2 Jeff Arney
- ☐ 3 Steve Aragon
- ☐ 4 Sam Arrington
- ☐ 5 Phil Franko
- ☐ 6 Kirby Puckett
- ☐ 7 Frank Rampen
- ☐ 8 Bob DeCosta
- ☐ 9 Jack McMahon
- ☐ 10 Stan Holmes
- ☐ 11 Frank Eufemia
- ☐ 12 Ron McKelvie TR
- ☐ 13 Harry Warner MG
- ☐ 14 Jeff Brueggeman GM
- ☐ 15 Erez Borowsky
- ☐ 16 Mark Cartwright
- ☐ 17 Joe Kubit
- ☐ 18 Curt Wardle
- ☐ 19 Bennie Richie
- ☐ 20 Craig Henderson
- ☐ 21 Greg Howe
- ☐ 22 Curt Kindred
- ☐ 23 Alvaro Espinoza
- ☐ 24 Mark Portugal
- ☐ 25 Brian Rupe

1983 Waterbury Reds TCMA

This 19-card standard-size set of the 1983 Waterbury Reds, a Class AA Eastern League affiliate of the Cincinnati Reds, features white-bordered posed color player photos on its fronts. The player's name and position appear within a blue stripe at the bottom. The plain back carries the team name at the top, followed below by the league affiliation, and then the player's name, biography and statistics. This issue includes a second year card of Eric Davis. Approximately 1,600 sets were produced.

	MINT	NRMT	EXC
COMPLETE SET (19)	40.00	18.00	5.00

- ☐ 1 Keefe Cato
- ☐ 2 Bryan Funk
- ☐ 3 Curt Heidenreich
- ☐ 4 Ken Jones
- ☐ 5 Bill Landrum
- ☐ 6 Jim Pettibone
- ☐ 7 Mark Rothey
- ☐ 8 Lester Straker
- ☐ 9 Lloyd McClendon
- ☐ 10 Dave Miley
- ☐ 11 Adolfo Feliz
- ☐ 12 Carlos Porte
- ☐ 13 Hector Rincones
- ☐ 14 Wade Rowdon
- ☐ 15 Eric Davis
- ☐ 16 Dexter Day
- ☐ 17 Leo Garcia
- ☐ 18 Ruben Guzman
- ☐ 19 Jim Lett

1983 Waterloo Indians Fritsch

	MINT	NRMT	EXC
COMPLETE SET (29)	5.00	2.20	.60

- ☐ 1 Randy Washington
- ☐ 2 Edwin Aponte
- ☐ 3 Ben Piphus
- ☐ 4 Eddie Diaz
- ☐ 5 Andy Ortiz
- ☐ 6 Juan Lopez
- ☐ 7 Nelson Pedraza
- ☐ 8 Junior Noboa
- ☐ 9 Jay"Devo' Keeler
- ☐ 10 Wilson Valera
- ☐ 11 John Miglio
- ☐ 12 Jose Roman
- ☐ 13 Miguel Roman
- ☐ 14 Phil Wilson
- ☐ 15 Reggie Ritter
- ☐ 16 Pookie Bernstine
- ☐ 17 Bernardo Brito
- ☐ 18 Winston Ficklin
- ☐ 19 Ray Martinez
- ☐ 20 Jeff Barkley
- ☐ 21 Dane Anthony
- ☐ 22 Mike Gertz
- ☐ 23 West Pierorazio
- ☐ 24 Mike Poindexter
- ☐ 25 Rich Diaz
- ☐ 26 Rick Henkie TR
- ☐ 27 Vic Albury CO
- ☐ 28 Gomer Hodge MG
- ☐ 29 Team Logo

1983 Wausau Timbers Fritsch

	MINT	NRMT	EXC
COMPLETE SET (31)	5.00	2.20	.60

- ☐ 1 K.R. Houston TR
- ☐ 2 John Poloni CO
- ☐ 3 Gary Pellant CO
- ☐ 4 Tom Burns
- ☐ 5 Martin Enriquez
- ☐ 6 Brian David
- ☐ 7 Ronn Dixon
- ☐ 8 Tim Slavin
- ☐ 9 Terry Taylor
- ☐ 10 Eric Parent
- ☐ 11 Chip Conklin
- ☐ 12 David Myers
- ☐ 13 Kevin Roy
- ☐ 14 Todd Francis
- ☐ 15 Randy Meier
- ☐ 16 Robby Vollmer
- ☐ 17 Jesse Baez
- ☐ 18 Scott Barnhouse
- ☐ 19 Paul Schneider
- ☐ 20 Scott Roebuck
- ☐ 21 Tom Duggan
- ☐ 22 Bob Baldrick
- ☐ 23 Sam Haley
- ☐ 24 Ron Sismondo
- ☐ 25 Randy Newman
- ☐ 26 John Duncan
- ☐ 27 Dave Smith
- ☐ 28 Wray Bergendahl
- ☐ 29 Kenny Briggs
- ☐ 30 R.J. Harrison MG
- ☐ 31 Team Logo

1983 Wichita Aeros Dog'n Shake

Sponsored by Dog'n'Shake and produced by Rock's Dugout, this 24-card standard-size set of the 1983 Wichita Aeros, a Class AAA American Association affiliate of the Montreal Expos, features white-bordered posed color player photos on its fronts. The player's name and position, and team and sponsor's logos, appear at the bottom. The white horizontal back carries the player's name, biography and statistics.

	MINT	NRMT	EXC
COMPLETE SET (24)	20.00	9.00	2.50

- ☐ 1 Title Card Checklist
- ☐ 2 Felipe Alou MG
- ☐ 3 Shooty Babbitt
- ☐ 4 Greg Bargar
- ☐ 5 Butch Benton
- ☐ 6 Tom Dixon
- ☐ 7 Mike Fuentes
- ☐ 8 Mike Gates
- ☐ 9 Gene Glynn
- ☐ 10 Dick Grapenthin
- ☐ 11 Bob James
- ☐ 12 Roy Johnson
- ☐ 13 Brad Mills
- ☐ 14 Eric Mustad
- ☐ 15 Luis Quintana
- ☐ 16 Rick Ramos
- ☐ 17 Bob Reece
- ☐ 18 Pat Rooney
- ☐ 19 Angel Salazar
- ☐ 20 Bill Sattler
- ☐ 21 Mike Stenhouse
- ☐ 22 Rennie Stennett
- ☐ 23 Tom Wieghaus
- ☐ 24 Roy Johnson 1982 Batting Title

1983 Wisconsin Rapids Twins Fritsch

	MINT	NRMT	EXC
COMPLETE SET (28)	5.00	2.20	.60

- ☐ 1 Coe Brier
- ☐ 2 Ronnie Scheer
- ☐ 3 Allan Anderson
- ☐ 4 Jeff Wilson
- ☐ 5 Joe Sain
- ☐ 6 Paul Felix
- ☐ 7 Carson Carroll
- ☐ 8 David Steinberg
- ☐ 9 Tim Graupmann
- ☐ 10 John Kearns
- ☐ 11 Bob Ferro
- ☐ 12 Mark Larcom
- ☐ 13 Johnny Salery
- ☐ 14 Bob Costello
- ☐ 15 Leo Cardenas Jr.
- ☐ 16 Danny Clay
- ☐ 17 Brian Hobaugh
- ☐ 18 Mike Maack
- ☐ 19 Luis Cruz
- ☐ 20 Jim Burnos
- ☐ 21 Ken Klump
- ☐ 22 Paul Mancuso
- ☐ 23 Brad Skoglund
- ☐ 24 Michael Moreno
- ☐ 25 David Baehr
- ☐ 26 John Marks GM
- ☐ 27 Charlie Manuel MG
- ☐ 28 Team Logo

1984 Albany A's TCMA

This 26-card standard-size set of the 1984 Albany A's, a Class AA Eastern League affiliate of the Oakland Athletics, features green-bordered posed color player shots on its fronts. The player's position, player's name and the team name are printed below the photo in white lettering. The white back carries the team name and year at the top, followed by the league, player's name, position, and biography.

	MINT	NRMT	EXC
COMPLETE SET (26)	30.00	13.50	3.70

- ☐ 1 Jim Bennett
- ☐ 2 Ron Arnold
- ☐ 3 Gene Gentile
- ☐ 4 Rodney Hobbs
- ☐ 5 Thad Reece
- ☐ 6 Brian Graham
- ☐ 7 Keith Lieppman
- ☐ 8 Rick Tronerud
- ☐ 9 Brian Thorson
- ☐ 10 John Liburdi
- ☐ 11 Tom Dozier
- ☐ 12 Todd Fischer
- ☐ 13 Bob Hallas
- ☐ 14 Pete Kendrick
- ☐ 15 Stan Kyles
- ☐ 16 Erik Bernard
- ☐ 17 Tim Lambert
- ☐ 18 Ed Myers
- ☐ 19 Les Straker
- ☐ 20 Tom Zmudosky
- ☐ 21 Mike Ashman
- ☐ 22 Mickey Tettleton
- ☐ 23 Bob Bathe
- ☐ 24 Jim Eppard
- ☐ 25 Greg Robles
- ☐ 26 Ray Thoma

1984 Albuquerque Dukes Cramer

This 27-card standard-size set of the 1984 Albuquerque Dukes, a Class AAA Pacific Coast League affiliate of the Los Angeles Dodgers, features white-bordered posed color player photos on its fronts. The player's name, position, and team name appear at the bottom. The gray horizontal back carries the player's name and position within a baseball bat icon at the top, followed below by biography and statistics, some enhanced by a cartoon.

	MINT	NRMT	EXC
COMPLETE SET (27)	5.00	2.20	.60

- ☐ 146 Jack Fimple
- ☐ 147 Rich Rodas
- ☐ 148 R.J. Reynolds
- ☐ 149 Sid Bream
- ☐ 150 Lemmie Miller
- ☐ 151 Franklin Stubbs
- ☐ 152 Dave Sax
- ☐ 153 Alex Taveras
- ☐ 154 Steve Perry
- ☐ 155 Don Smith
- ☐ 156 Robbie Allen
- ☐ 157 Greg Schultz
- ☐ 158 Larry White
- ☐ 159 Ernesto Borbon
- ☐ 160 Dean Rennicke
- ☐ 161 Tony Brewer
- ☐ 162 Larry See
- ☐ 163 Ed Amelung
- ☐ 164 John Debus
- ☐ 165 Ken Howell
- ☐ 166 Roberto Alexander
- ☐ 167 Terry Collins MGR
- ☐ 168 Brian Holton
- ☐ 169 Dick McLaughlin CO
- ☐ 245 Dave Wallace CO
- ☐ 246 Mark Sheehy CO

1984 Arizona Wildcats Police

	MINT	NRMT	EXC
COMPLETE SET (21)	12.00	5.50	1.50

- ☐ 1 Kevin Blankenship
- ☐ 2 Dave Cooper
- ☐ 3 Pat Coveney
- ☐ 4 Chip Dill
- ☐ 5 Scott Engle
- ☐ 6 Joe Estes
- ☐ 7 Chip Hale
- ☐ 8 Randy Hayes
- ☐ 9 Jerry Kindall CO
- ☐ 10 Lance Lincoln
- ☐ 11 John MacArthur
- ☐ 12 Joe Magrane
- ☐ 13 Gar Millay
- ☐ 14 Scott Nossek
- ☐ 15 Mike Ollom
- ☐ 16 Bobby Ralston
- ☐ 17 Jerry Stitt ACO
- ☐ 18 Todd Trafton
- ☐ 19 Tom Wieser MG
- ☐ 20 Jim Wing CO
- ☐ 21 Marc Wing

1984 Arkansas Travelers TCMA

This 26-card standard-size set of the 1984 Arkansas Travelers, a Class AA Texas League affiliate of the St. Louis Cardinals, features green-bordered posed color player shots on its fronts. The player's position, player's name and the team name are printed below the photo in white lettering. The white back carries the team name and year at the top, followed by the league, player's name, position, and biography. Approximately 3,000 sets were produced.

	MINT	NRMT	EXC
COMPLETE SET (26)	25.00	11.00	3.10

☐ 1 Eddie Tanner
☐ 2 Dave Clements
☐ 3 Dan Stryffeler
☐ 4 Deron Thomas
☐ 5 Tim Wallace
☐ 6 Todd Worrell
☐ 7 Bob Helsom
☐ 8 Al Morlock
☐ 9 Larry Reynolds
☐ 10 Greg Guin
☐ 11 Bob Geren
☐ 12 John Adams
☐ 13 Mark Schulte
☐ 14 Dave Bialas
☐ 15 Willie Hardwick
☐ 16 Curt Ford
☐ 17 John Martin
☐ 18 Pat Perry
☐ 19 Marty Mason
☐ 20 Joe Silkwood
☐ 21 Gotay Mills
☐ 22 John Young
☐ 23 Pete Stoll
☐ 24 Walt Pierce
☐ 25 Andy Hassler
☐ 26 Mike Harris

1984 Beaumont Golden Gators TCMA

This 25-card standard-size set of the 1984 Beaumont Golden Gators, a Class AA Texas League affiliate of the San Diego Padres, features green-bordered posed color player shots on its fronts. The player's position, player's name and the team name are printed below the photo in white lettering. The white back carries the team name and year at the top, followed by the league, player's name, position, and biography.

	MINT	NRMT	EXC
COMPLETE SET (25)	10.00	4.50	1.25

☐ 1 Jimmy Jones
☐ 2 Pete Kutsukos
☐ 3 James Steels
☐ 4 Al Newman
☐ 5 Mark Gillaspie
☐ 6 Ed Vosberg
☐ 7 Steve Murray
☐ 8 Mark Parent
☐ 9 Gene Walter
☐ 10 Kevin Towers
☐ 11 Bill Long
☐ 12 Tim Cook
☐ 13 Steve Schefsky
☐ 14 Jim Leopold
☐ 15 Jimmy Thomas
☐ 16 Pat Casey
☐ 17 Mark Wasinger
☐ 18 Steve Garcia
☐ 19 Jerry Johnson
☐ 20 Steve Johnson
☐ 21 Bobby Tolan
☐ 22 Chuck Kolotka
☐ 23 Todd Hutcheson
☐ 24 Ray Etchebarren
☐ 25 Jeff Ronk

1984 Buffalo Bisons TCMA

This 25-card standard-size set of the 1984 Buffalo Bisons, a Class AA Eastern League affiliate of the Cleveland Indians, features green-bordered posed color player shots on its fronts. The player's position, player's name and the team name are printed below the photo in white lettering. The white back carries the team name and year at the top, followed by the league, player's name, position, and biography.

	MINT	NRMT	EXC
COMPLETE SET (25)	10.00	4.50	1.25

☐ 1 Jeff Moronko
☐ 2 George Cecchetti
☐ 3 Tim Glass
☐ 4 Junior Naboa
☐ 5 Rene Quinones
☐ 6 Doug Simonic
☐ 7 Andy Allanson
☐ 8 Jose Roman
☐ 9 Jay Baller
☐ 10 Alec McCullock
☐ 11 Rich Doyle
☐ 12 Rich Thompson
☐ 13 Dave Szymczak
☐ 14 John Bohnet
☐ 15 Andy Ortiz
☐ 16 Ramon Romero
☐ 17 Steve Mardsen
☐ 18 Jack Aker
☐ 19 Ed Aponte
☐ 20 Randy Washington
☐ 21 Don Carter
☐ 22 Ed Saavedra
☐ 23 Pookie Bernstine
☐ 24 Robin Fuson
☐ 25 Doug Helmquist

1984 Butte Copper Kings TCMA

This 27-card standard-size set of the 1984 Butte Copper Kings, a Rookie Class Pioneer League affiliate of the Seattle Mariners, features green-bordered posed color player shots on its fronts. The player's position, player's name and the team name are printed below the photo in white lettering. The white back carries the team name and year at the top, followed by the league, player's name, position, and biography. Approximately 2,000 sets were produced.

	MINT	NRMT	EXC
COMPLETE SET (27)	10.00	4.50	1.25

☐ 1 Manny Estrada
☐ 2 John Anderson
☐ 3 James Bowden
☐ 4 Dan Clark
☐ 5 Mike Wood
☐ 6 Tom Osowski
☐ 7 Carl Moesche
☐ 8 Greg Brinkman
☐ 9 Tony Diaz
☐ 10 Charlie Fonville
☐ 11 Steve French
☐ 12 Richard Hayden
☐ 13 Brad Kinney
☐ 14 Dan Larson
☐ 15 Mark Machalec
☐ 16 Rafael Matos
☐ 17 Pablo Monceratt
☐ 18 Arvid Morfin
☐ 19 Kevin Ochs
☐ 20 Bill O'Leary
☐ 21 Bregg Ray
☐ 22 Paul Steinert
☐ 23 Gregg Thienpont
☐ 24 George Uribe
☐ 25 Nestor Valiente
☐ 26 Lazaro Vilella
☐ 27 Logan White

1984 Cedar Rapids Reds TCMA

This 28-card standard-size set of the 1984 Cedar Rapids Reds, a Class A Midwest League affiliate of the Cincinnati Reds, features green-bordered posed color player shots on its fronts. The player's position, player's name and the team name are printed below the photo in white lettering. The white back carries the team name and year at the top, followed by the league, player's name, position, and biography.

	MINT	NRMT	EXC
COMPLETE SET (28)	20.00	9.00	2.50

☐ 1 Robbie Phillips
☐ 2 Ted Langdon
☐ 3 Jim Pettibone
☐ 4 Doug Barba
☐ 5 Paul Kirsch
☐ 6 Brian Funk
☐ 7 Hugh Kemp
☐ 8 Virgil Conley
☐ 9 Mike Konderla
☐ 10 Jordan Berge
☐ 11 Tim Dodd
☐ 12 Jim Lett
☐ 13 Dexter Day
☐ 14 Joe Oliver
☐ 15 Tom Riley
☐ 16 Lanell Culver
☐ 17 Kurt Stillwell
☐ 18 Danny LaMar
☐ 19 Don Buchheister
☐ 20 Ronnie Giddens
☐ 21 Mike Manfre
☐ 22 Scott Loseke
☐ 23 Rod Lich
☐ 24 Mike Dowless
☐ 25 Lenny Harris
☐ 26 Gary Denbo
☐ 27 Ron Henika
☐ 28 Dave Haberle

1984 Charlotte O's TCMA

This 27-card standard-size set of the 1984 Charlotte O's, a Class AA Southern League affiliate of the Baltimore Orioles, features green-bordered posed color player shots on its fronts. The player's position, player's name and the team name are printed below the photo in white lettering. The white back carries the team name and year at the top, followed by the league, player's name, position, and biography.

	MINT	NRMT	EXC
COMPLETE SET (27)	10.00	4.50	1.25

☐ 1 Bob Hice
☐ 2 Terry Mauney
☐ 3 Charlie Frederick
☐ 4 Ronni Salcedo
☐ 5 Paul Cameron
☐ 6 Carlos Concepcion
☐ 7 Al Pardo
☐ 8 Jeff Kenaga
☐ 9 Peter Torrez
☐ 10 Grady Little
☐ 11 Chris Willsher
☐ 12 Bobby Mariano
☐ 13 Pat Dumouchelle
☐ 14 Jamie Reed
☐ 15 Bob Konopa
☐ 16 Dave Falcone
☐ 17 Kenny Dixon
☐ 18 Jeff Gilbert
☐ 19 Jesus Alfaro
☐ 20 Jeff Williams
☐ 21 Paul Bard
☐ 22 Ken Gerhart
☐ 23 Kurt Leiter
☐ 24 John Tutt
☐ 25 Jeff Summers
☐ 26 Tony Arnold
☐ 27 Herbie Oliveras

1984 Chattanooga Lookouts TCMA

This 29-card standard-size set of the 1984 Chattanooga Lookouts, a Class A California League affiliate of the Seattle Mariners, features green-bordered posed color player shots on its fronts. The player's position, player's name and the team name are printed below the photo in white lettering. The white back carries the team name and year at the top, followed by the league, player's name, position, and biography.

	MINT	NRMT	EXC
COMPLETE SET (29)	10.00	4.50	1.25

☐ 1A Mike Evans
☐ 1B Kevin King
☐ 2 Ramon Estepa
☐ 3 Dan Hanggle
☐ 4 Brick Smith
☐ 5 Ed Holtz
☐ 6 Clark Crist
☐ 7 Ross Grimsley
☐ 8 Bill Plummer
☐ 9 Tom Hunt
☐ 10 Donell Nixon
☐ 11 John Semprini
☐ 12 Paul Serna
☐ 13 Mike Johnson
☐ 14 Harry Landreth
☐ 15 Lee Guetterman
☐ 16 Joe Whitmer
☐ 18 Rick Luecken
☐ 19 Tom Rowe
☐ 20 A.J. Hill
☐ 21 Randy Ramirez
☐ 22 Ric Wilson
☐ 23 Rick Adair
☐ 24 John Moses
☐ 25 Mario Diaz
☐ 26 Mickey Brantley
☐ 27 Don Clay Hill
☐ 28 Jeff McDonald
☐ 29 Greg Bartley

1984 Columbus Clippers Police

	MINT	NRMT	EXC
COMPLETE SET (25)	5.00	2.20	.60

☐ 1 Curt Brown
☐ 2 Scott Bradley
☐ 3 Dan Briggs
☐ 4 George Cappuzzello
☐ 5 Clay Christiansen
☐ 6 Don Cooper
☐ 7 Joe Cowley
☐ 8 Pete Dalena
☐ 9 Brian Dayett
☐ 10 Don Fowler
☐ 11 Kelly Heath
☐ 12 Butch Hobson
☐ 13 Rex Hudler
☐ 14 Victor Mata
☐ 15 Stump Merrill MG
☐ 16 Mike O'Berry
☐ 17 Mike Pagliarulo
☐ 18 Scott Patterson
☐ 19 Dennis Rasmussen
☐ 20 Andre Robertson
☐ 21 Pat Rooney
☐ 22 Kelly Scott
☐ 23 George H. Sisler Jr.
General Manager
☐ 24 Matt Winters
☐ 25 Coaching Staff
Mark Connor CO
Mickey Vernon CO
Gil Patterson CO
Steve Donohue TR

1984 Columbus Clippers TCMA

This 25-card standard-size set of the 1984 Columbus Clippers, a Class AAA International League affiliate of the New York Yankees, features green-bordered posed color player shots on its fronts. The player's position, player's name and the team name are printed below the photo in white lettering. The white back carries the team name and year at the top, followed by the league, player's name, position, and biography.

	MINT	NRMT	EXC
COMPLETE SET (25)	15.00	6.75	1.85

☐ 1 Mike Pagliarulo
☐ 2 Kelly Heath
☐ 3 Pat Rooney
☐ 4 Brian Dayett
☐ 5 Dan Briggs
☐ 6 Don Fowler
☐ 7 George Cappuzzello
☐ 8 Rex Hudler
☐ 9 Andre Robertson
☐ 10 Victor Mata
☐ 11 Scott Bradley
☐ 12 Clay Christianson
☐ 13 Joe Cowley
☐ 14 Scott Patterson
☐ 15 Curt Brown
☐ 16 Butch Hobson
☐ 17 Don Cooper
☐ 18 Pete Dalena
☐ 19 Kelly Scott
☐ 20 Mike O'Berry
☐ 21 Steve Donahue TR
Mickey Vernon CO
Mark Conner CO
Gil Patterson CO
Stump Merrill MG
☐ 22 Matt Winters
☐ 23 Stump Merrill
☐ 24 George Sisler Jr. GM
☐ 25 Dennis Rasmussen

1984 Durham Bulls TCMA

This 30-card standard-size set of the 1984 Durham Bulls, a Class A Carolina League affiliate of the Atlanta Braves, features green-bordered posed color player shots on its fronts. The player's position, player's name and the team name are printed below the photo in white lettering. The white back carries the team name and year at the top, followed by the league, player's name, position, and biography.

	MINT	NRMT	EXC
COMPLETE SET (30)	15.00	6.75	1.85

☐ 1 Simon Rosario
☐ 2 Mark Lance
☐ 3 Mike Yastrzemski
☐ 4 Pat Hodge
☐ 5 Johnny Hatcher
☐ 6 Terry Cormack
☐ 7 Jeff Wagner
☐ 8 Dave Griffin
☐ 9 Leo Mazzone
☐ 10 Tim Alexander
☐ 11 Rafael Barbosa
☐ 12 Bob Tumpane
☐ 13 Chip Childress
☐ 14 Andres Thomas
☐ 15 Mike Knox
☐ 16 Tony Neuendorff
☐ 17 Scott Hood
☐ 18 Rich Leggatt
☐ 19 Todd Lamb
☐ 20 Paul Assenmacher
☐ 21 Paul Josephson
☐ 22 Jose Cano
☐ 23 Steve Ziem
☐ 24 John Mortillaro
☐ 25 Brian Aviles
☐ 26 Jim Rivera
☐ 27 Marty Schreiber
☐ 28 Brian Snitker
☐ 29 Randy Ingle
☐ 30 Sonny Jackson

1984 Edmonton Trappers Cramer

This 26-card standard-size set of the 1984 Edmonton Trappers, a Class AAA Pacific Coast League affiliate of the California Angels, features white-bordered posed color player photos on its fronts. The player's name, position, and team name appear at the bottom. The gray horizontal back carries the player's name and position within a baseball bat icon at the top, followed below by biography and statistics. .

	MINT	NRMT	EXC
COMPLETE SET (26)	5.00	2.20	.60

☐ 97 Moose Stubing MG
☐ 98 Tim Krauss
☐ 99 Angel Moreno
☐ 100 Marty Kain
☐ 101 Sap Randall
☐ 102 Rick Steirer
☐ 103 Dave W. Smith
☐ 104 Rick Adams
☐ 105 Craig Gerber
☐ 106 Steve Finch
☐ 107 Steve Liddle
☐ 108 Chris Clark
☐ 109 Darrell Miller
☐ 110 Bill Mooneyham
☐ 111 Doug Corbett
☐ 112 Steve Lubratich
☐ 113 Stu Cliburn
☐ 114 Mike Browning
☐ 115 Joe Simpson
☐ 116 Reggie West
☐ 117 Mike Brown
☐ 118 Pat Keedy
☐ 119 Jay Kibbe
☐ 120 Ed Ott CO
☐ 242 Frank Reberger CO
☐ 249 Steve Lubratich
(Action photo)

1984 El Paso Diablos TCMA

This 25-card standard-size set of the 1984 El Paso Diablos, a Class AA Texas League affiliate of the Milwaukee Brewers, features green-bordered posed color player shots on its fronts. The player's position, player's name and the team name are printed below the photo in white lettering. The white back carries the team name and year at the top, followed by the league, player's name, position, and biography.

	MINT	NRMT	EXC
COMPLETE SET (25)	20.00	9.00	2.50

☐ 1 Mark Effrig
☐ 2 Johnson Wood
☐ 3 Bob Schroeck
☐ 4 Steve Michael
☐ 5 Bryan Clutterbuck
☐ 6 Chuck Crim
☐ 7 Doug Jones
☐ 8 Mike Villegas
☐ 9 Mike Samuel
☐ 10 Tim Crews
☐ 11 Bryan Duquette
☐ 12 Terry Bevington
☐ 13 Kelvin Moore
☐ 14 Stan Davis
☐ 15 Ted Higuera
☐ 16 Juan Castillo
☐ 17 Dan Plants
☐ 18 Dave Klipstein
☐ 19 Alan Cartwright
☐ 20 Paul Hartzell
☐ 21 Joe Morales
☐ 22 Cam Walker
☐ 23 Mike Felder
☐ 24 Dale Sveum
☐ 25 Garrett Nago

1984 Evansville Triplets TCMA

This 22-card standard-size set of the 1984 Evansville Triplets, a Class AAA American Association affiliate of the Detroit Tigers, features green-bordered posed color player shots on its fronts. The player's position, player's name and the team name are printed below the photo in white lettering. The white back carries the team name and year at the top, followed by the league, player's name, position, and biography.

	MINT	NRMT	EXC
COMPLETE SET (22)	10.00	4.50	1.25

☐ 1 Juan Lopez
☐ 2 Howard Bailey
☐ 3 Rondal Rollin
☐ 4 Gordon McKenzie
☐ 5 Pat Larkin
☐ 6 Mark Dacko
☐ 7 Stan Younger
☐ 8 Dave Gumpert
☐ 9 Nelson Simmons
☐ 10 Len Faedo
☐ 11 Bob Melvin
☐ 12 Dallas Williams
☐ 13 Doug Baker
☐ 14 Scotty Earl
☐ 15 John Harris
☐ 16 Mike Laga
☐ 17 Randy O'Neal
☐ 18 Jeff Conner
☐ 19 Don Heinkel
☐ 20 Bill Armstrong
☐ 21 Roger Mason
☐ 22 Carl Willis

1984 Everett Giants Cramer

This 35-card standard-size set of the 1984 Everett Giants, a Class A Northwest League affiliate of the San Francisco Giants, features white-bordered posed color player photos on its fronts. The player's name, position, and team name appear at the bottom. The gray horizontal back carries the player's name and position within a baseball bat icon at the top, followed below by biography and statistics, some enhanced by a cartoon.

	MINT	NRMT	EXC
COMPLETE SET (35)	10.00	4.50	1.25

☐ 1 Greg Litton
☐ 2 Lyle Swepson
☐ 3 Mike Cicione
☐ 4 Joe Olker
☐ 5 Harry Davis
☐ 6A Greg Gilbert
☐ 6B Darin James
☐ 7 Kent Cooper
☐ 8 Steve Cottrell
☐ 9 Kevin Woodhouse
☐ 10A Keith Silver
☐ 10B Jim Ewing
☐ 11 Dave Hornsby
☐ 12 Stuart Tate
☐ 13A Rob Cosby
☐ 13B Rod Rush
☐ 14 Sixto Martes
☐ 15 Loren Hibbs
☐ 16 Dave Hinnrichs
☐ 17 Francisco Echevarria
☐ 18 Chris Stangel
☐ 19 Paul Blair
☐ 20 Terry Mulholland
☐ 21 Davis Tavarez
☐ 22A Brad Porter
☐ 22B T.J. McDonald
☐ 23 Francis Calzado
☐ 24 Jim Wasem
☐ 25 John Grimes
☐ 26 Todd Moriarty
☐ 27 John Ackerman
☐ 28 Rocky Bridges MG
☐ 29 Tom Wetzel
☐ 30A Tom Messier
☐ 30B Tony Perezchica

1984 Greensboro Hornets TCMA

This 26-card standard-size set of the 1984 Greensboro Hornets, a Class A South Atlantic League affiliate of the New York Yankees, features green-bordered posed color player shots on its fronts. The player's position, player's name and the team name are printed below the photo in white lettering. The white back carries the team name and year at the top, followed by the league, player's name, position, and biography.

	MINT	NRMT	EXC
COMPLETE SET (26)	30.00	13.50	3.70

☐ 1 Carlos Tosca
☐ 2 Ray Fortaleza
☐ 3 Brad Winkler
☐ 4 Roberto Kelly
☐ 5 Jeff Horne
☐ 6 Fredi Gonzales
☐ 7 Nattie George
☐ 8 Joey MacKay
☐ 9 Doug Carpenter
☐ 10 Brad Arnsberg
☐ 11 Chris Fedor
☐ 12 Bill Fulton
☐ 13 Dave Smalley
☐ 14 Tim Williams
☐ 15 Chuck Mathison
☐ 16 Eric Parent
☐ 17 Ricky Torres
☐ 18 Steve George
☐ 19 Mark Ferguson
☐ 20 Jonis Rodriguez
☐ 21 Bob Devlin
☐ 22 Moe Ching
☐ 23 Pedro Medina
☐ 24 Rich Mattocks
☐ 25 Mitch Seoane
☐ 26 Bill Englehart

1984 Hawaii Islanders Cramer

This 26-card standard-size set of the 1984 Hawaii Islanders, a Class AAA Pacific Coast League affiliate of the Pittsburgh Pirates, features white-bordered posed color player photos on its fronts. The player's name, position, and team name appear at the bottom. The gray horizontal back carries the player's name and position within a baseball bat icon at the top, followed below by biography and statistics, some enhanced by a cartoon.

	MINT	NRMT	EXC
COMPLETE SET (26)	5.00	2.20	.60

☐ 121 Al Pulido
☐ 122 Jeff Zaske
☐ 123 Kelly Paris
☐ 124 Larry Lamonde
☐ 125 Paul Semall
☐ 126 Dave Tomlin
☐ 127 Lorenzo Bundy
☐ 128 Ron Wotus
☐ 129 Ray Krawczyk
☐ 130 Denny Gonzales
☐ 131 Mike Bielecki
☐ 132 Stan Cliburn
☐ 133 Nelson Norman
☐ 134 Chuck Hartenstein CO
☐ 135 Mike Howard
☐ 136 Bob Miscik
☐ 137 Tom Sandt MG
☐ 138 Jim Winn
☐ 139 Trench Davis
☐ 140 Tim Wheeler
☐ 141 Bob Walk
☐ 142 Steve Herz
☐ 143 Carlos Ledezma
☐ 144 Benny Distefano
☐ 145 John Malkin
☐ 146 Jack Fimple

1984 Idaho Falls A's Team Issue

Less than 500 sets were produced and given away at the ballpark.

	MINT	NRMT	EXC
COMPLETE SET (30)	75.00	34.00	9.50

☐ 1 Russ Applegate
☐ 2 Eldridge Armstrong Jr.
☐ 3 Darren Balsley
☐ 4 Mickey Boyer
☐ 5 Adan Brito
☐ 6 Antonio Cabrera
☐ 7 Mike Cupples
☐ 8 Arturo Ferreira
☐ 9 Mark Gillespie
☐ 10 John Gonzalez
☐ 11 Bob Hassel
☐ 12 Jesus Hernaiz
☐ 13 James Jackson
☐ 14 Tony Johnson
☐ 15 Felix Jose
☐ 16 Mark Leonette
☐ 17 Scott LeVander
☐ 18 Jim Nettles
☐ 19 Ramon Nunez
☐ 20 Ken Patterson
☐ 21 Ted Polakowski
☐ 22 Basilo Reyes
☐ 23 Kevin Russ
☐ 24 Scott Sabo
☐ 25 David Sheriff
☐ 26 Bob Vantrease
☐ 27 Camilo Veras
☐ 28 Mike Walker
☐ 29 Mark Warren
☐ 30 James Wilridge

1984 Indianapolis Indians Team Issue

This 32-card set of the 1984 Indianapolis Indians, a Class AAA American Association affiliate of the Montreal Expos, features borderless posed color player shots on its fronts, and measures approximately 2 1/2" by 3 3/4". A blue arc above the photo carries the player's name, position, and team name. The white horizontal back carries the player's autograph facsimile at the top, followed by biography, statistics, and career highlights. 1,200 sets were produced.

	MINT	NRMT	EXC
COMPLETE SET (32)	10.00	4.50	1.25

☐ 1 Team Picture
☐ 2 Bob Rodgers MG
☐ 3 Leonel Carrion CO
☐ 4 Chris Welsh
☐ 5 Sal Butera
☐ 6 Joe Hesketh
☐ 7 Roy Johnson
☐ 8 Craig Eaton
☐ 9 Brad Mills
☐ 10 The Catchers
Sal Butera
George Bjorkman
Checklist
☐ 11 Eric Mustad
☐ 12 Mike Fuentes
☐ 13 Greg Bargar
☐ 14 Shooty Babitt
☐ 15 The Outfielders
Max Venable
Mike Fuentes
Roy Johnson
Shooty Babitt
☐ 16 Dick Grapenthin
☐ 17 Razor Shines
☐ 18 Starting Pitchers
Eric Mustad
Greg Bargar
Tim Burke
Joe Hesketh
☐ 19 Bill Sattler
☐ 20 George Bjorkman
☐ 21 The Relief Pitchers
Bill Sattler
Dick Grapenthin
Darren Dilks
Craig Eaton
☐ 22 Gene Glynn
☐ 23 Tim Burke
☐ 24 Ron Johnson
☐ 25 Rene Gonzales
☐ 26 The Infielders
Razor Shines
Rene Gonzales
Ron Johnson
Mike Gates
Gene Glynn
Brad Mills
☐ 27 Darren Dilks
☐ 28 Max Venable
☐ 29 Mike Gates
☐ 30 Mike Stenhouse
☐ 31 Jeff Porter TR
☐ 32 Bush Stadium

1984 Iowa Cubs TCMA

This 31-card standard-size set of the 1984 Iowa Cubs, a Class AAA American Association affiliate of the Chicago Cubs, features green-bordered posed color player shots on its fronts. The player's position, player's name and the team name are printed below the photo in white lettering. The white back carries the team name and year at the top, followed by the league, player's name, position, and biography. This issue includes a second year card of Joe Carter.

	MINT	NRMT	EXC
COMPLETE SET (31)	90.00	40.00	11.00

☐ 1 Ken Pryce
☐ 2 Bill Earley
☐ 3 Mascot (Cubby)
☐ 4 Dick Easter
☐ 5 Ken Grandquist
☐ 6 Jon Perlman
☐ 7 Thad Bosley
☐ 8 Don Rohn
☐ 9 Joe Hicks
☐ 10 Bill Holden
Frank Macy
☐ 11 Jim Napier
☐ 12 Pete MacKanin
☐ 13 Mark Schimming
Sam Bernabe
☐ 14 Trey Brooks
☐ 15 Bill Hayes
☐ 16 Don Werner
☐ 17 Tom Lombarski
☐ 18 Dave Owen
☐ 19 Carol McCullough
Bruce Bielenberg
☐ 20 Gil Carlos
☐ 21 Dick Cummings
☐ 22 Don Schulze
☐ 23 Porfirio Altamirano
☐ 24 Billy Hatcher
☐ 25 Joe Carter
☐ 27 Ron Meridith
☐ 28 Tom Filer
☐ 29 Bill Johnson
☐ 30 Tom Grant
☐ 31 Reggie Patterson
☐ NNO Derek Botelho

1984 Jackson Mets Feder

	MINT	NRMT	EXC
COMPLETE SET (15)	70.00	32.00	8.75

☐ 1 Neil Allen
☐ 2 Wally Backman
☐ 3 Hubie Brooks
☐ 4 Jody Davis
☐ 5 Brian Giles
☐ 6 Dave Johnson MG
☐ 7 Tim Leary
☐ 8 Lee Mazzilli
☐ 9 Jesse Orosco
☐ 10 Jeff Reardon
☐ 11 Doug Sisk
☐ 12 Darryl Strawberry
☐ 13 Mookie Wilson
☐ 14 Marvell Wynne
☐ 15 Ned Yost

1984 Jackson Mets TCMA

This 25-card standard-size set of the 1984 Jackson Mets, a Class AA Texas League affiliate of the New York Mets, features green-bordered posed color player shots on its fronts. The player's position, player's name and the team name are printed below the photo in white lettering. The white back carries the team name and year at the top, followed by the league, player's name, position, and biography.

	MINT	NRMT	EXC
COMPLETE SET (25)	40.00	18.00	5.00

☐ 1 DeWayne Vaughn
☐ 2 Rick Myles
☐ 3 Mark Lockenmeyer
☐ 4 Calvin Schiraldi
☐ 5 Reggie Jackson
☐ 6 Jeff Innis
☐ 7 Bill Fultz
☐ 8 Joe Graves
☐ 9 Jeff Bettendorf
☐ 10 Greg Pavlick
☐ 11 Staff Members
Bill Hetrick AGM
Rick Rainer TR
Stan Massengale CO
☐ 12 Bill Max
☐ 15 Floyd Youmans
☐ 16 Sam Perlozzo
☐ 17 Billy Beane
☐ 18 Lenny Dykstra
☐ 19 Daryl Denby
☐ 20 Mark Carreon
☐ 21 Dave Cochran
☐ 22 Steve Springer
☐ 23 Al Pedrique
☐ 24 Fermin Ubri
☐ 25 Randy Milligan
☐ NNO Ed Hearn
☐ NNO Greg Olson

1984 Las Vegas Stars Cramer

This 25-card standard-size set of the 1984 Las Vegas Stars, a Class AAA Pacific Coast League affiliate of the San Diego Padres, features white-bordered posed color player photos on its fronts. The player's name, position, and team name appear at the bottom. The gray horizontal back carries the player's name and position within a baseball bat icon at the top, followed below by biography and statistics, some enhanced by a cartoon.

	MINT	NRMT	EXC
COMPLETE SET (25)	18.00	8.00	2.20

☐ 218 Greg Booker
☐ 219 Ray Hayward
☐ 220 Joe Lansford
☐ 221 Bob Patterson
☐ 222 Jerry Davis
☐ 223 Jerry DeSimone
☐ 224 Fritz Connally
☐ 225 Bruce Bochy
☐ 226 Marty Decker
☐ 227 Mike Martin
☐ 228 John Kruk
☐ 229 Walt Vanderbush
☐ 230 Rick Lancellotti
☐ 231 Ed Wojna
☐ 232 Tom House CO
☐ 233 Feliz Oroz
☐ 234 George Hinshaw
☐ 235 Darren Burroughs
☐ 236 Ozzie Guillen
☐ 237 Ron Roenicke
☐ 238 Larry Brown
☐ 239 Bob Cluck MG
☐ 240 Ed Rodriguez
☐ 244 Larry Duensing TR
☐ 250 John Kruk

1984 Little Falls Mets TCMA

This 26-card standard-size set of the 1984 Little Falls Mets, a Class A New York-Penn League affiliate of the New York Mets, features green-bordered posed color player shots on its fronts. The player's position, player's name and the team name are printed below the photo in white lettering. The white back carries the team name and year at the top, followed by the league, player's name, position, and biography. Approximately 1,600 sets were produced.

	MINT	NRMT	EXC
COMPLETE SET (26)	15.00	6.75	1.85

☐ 1 Will Stiles
☐ 2 Keith Belcik
☐ 3 Mike Westbrock
☐ 4 Scott Little
☐ 5 Chuck Friedel
☐ 6 Ralph Adams
☐ 7 Jeff Karr
☐ 8 Ray Pereira
☐ 9 Keith Traylor
☐ 10 Shane Young
☐ 11 Owen Moreland III
☐ 12 Jeff Howes
☐ 13 Bud Harrelson
☐ 14 Terence Johnson
☐ 15 Craig Kiley
☐ 16 Jeff Ciszkowski
☐ 17 Hector Perez
☐ 18 Bucky Autry
☐ 19 Kevin Elster
☐ 20 Alan Wilson
☐ 21 Mauro Gozzo
☐ 22 Mark Davis
☐ 23 Lew Graham
☐ 24 David West
☐ 25 Rich Rodriguez
☐ 26 Ron Dominico

1984 Louisville Redbirds Riley's

	MINT	NRMT	EXC
COMPLETE SET (30)	20.00	9.00	2.50

☐ 1 Jim Fregosi
☐ 2 Gaylen Pitts
☐ 3 Jerry McKune
☐ 4 Dyar Miller
☐ 5 Gene Roof
☐ 6 Gary Rajsich
☐ 7 Doyle Harris
☐ 8 Tom Nieto
☐ 9 Dave Von Ohlen
☐ 10 Jed Smith
☐ 11 Kevin Hagen
☐ 12 Rod Booker
☐ 13 Jose Gonzalez
☐ 14 Bill Lyons
☐ 15 Terry Pendleton
☐ 16 Ralph Citarella
☐ 17 Kurt Kepshire
☐ 18 Vic Harris
☐ 19 Jim Adduci
☐ 20 Vince Coleman
☐ 21 Jack Ayer
☐ 22 Jeff Keener
☐ 23 Rick Ownbey
☐ 24 Terry Clark
☐ 25 Steve Baker
☐ 26 Jerry Johnson
☐ 27 Mark Salas
☐ 28 Mickey Mahler
☐ 29 Dave Kable
☐ 30 Dennis Werth

1984 Madison Muskies Police

	MINT	NRMT	EXC
COMPLETE SET (25)	25.00	11.00	3.10

☐ 1 Brad Fischer MG
☐ 2 Gary Lance CO
☐ 3 Dave Schober TR
☐ 4 Mike Wilder
☐ 5 Scotty Lee Whaley
☐ 6 Joe Odom
☐ 7 Luis Polonia
☐ 8 Al Heath
☐ 9 Tim Belcher
☐ 10 Terry Steinbach
☐ 11 Rob Nelson
☐ 12 John Marquardt
☐ 13 Bob Loscalzo
☐ 14 Jim Jones
☐ 15 Darel Hansen
☐ 16 Dennis Gonsalves
☐ 17 Shawn Gill
☐ 18 Wayne Giddings
☐ 19 Eric Garrett
☐ 20 Mike Fulmer
☐ 21 Kevin Coughlon
☐ 22 Maurice Castain
☐ 23 Rich Borowski
☐ 24 Larry Beardman
☐ 25 Darrel Akerfelds

1984 Maine Guides TCMA

This 23-card standard-size set of the 1984 Maine Guides, a Class AAA International League affiliate of the Cleveland Indians, features green-bordered posed color player shots on its fronts. The player's position, player's name and the team name are printed below the photo in white lettering. The white back carries the team name and year at the top, followed by the league, player's name, position, and biography.

	MINT	NRMT	EXC
COMPLETE SET (23)	10.00	4.50	1.25

☐ 1 Ramon Romero
☐ 2 Jerry Reed
☐ 3 Roy Smith
☐ 4 Steve Farr
☐ 5 Doug Simunic
☐ 6 Richard Barnes
☐ 7 Dave Gallagher
☐ 8 Bud Anderson
☐ 9 Vic Albury
☐ 10 Doc Edwards
☐ 11 Pichy DeLeon
☐ 12 Lorenzo Gray
☐ 13 Guy Elston
☐ 14 Wil Culmer
☐ 15 Jeff Barkley
☐ 16 Karl Pagel
☐ 17 Juan Espino
☐ 18 Dwight Taylor
☐ 19 Rod Craig
☐ 20 Luis Quinones
☐ 21 Keith MacWhorter
☐ 22 Ed Glynn
☐ 23 Shanie Dugas

1984 Memphis Chicks TCMA

This 25-card standard-size set of the 1984 Memphis Chicks, a Class AA Southern League affiliate of the Kansas City Royals, features green-bordered posed color player shots on its fronts. The player's position, player's name and the team name are printed below the photo in white lettering. The white back carries the team name and year at the top, followed by the league, player's name, position, and biography. This issue includes a second year minor league card of David Cone.

	MINT	NRMT	EXC
COMPLETE SET (25)	50.00	22.00	6.25

☐ 1 Rick Mathews
☐ 2 Rich Dubee
☐ 3 Rick Rizzo
☐ 4 Art Hartinez
☐ 5 Billy Best
☐ 6 Reggie Wyatt
☐ 7 Mike Kingery
☐ 8 Mitch Ashmore
☐ 9 Van Snider
☐ 10 Jeff Neuzil
☐ 11 Bill Wilder
☐ 12 Doug Cook
☐ 13 Bob Hegman
☐ 14 Lester Strode
☐ 15 Vinnie Yuhas
☐ 16 Jim Miner
☐ 17 Steve Reish
☐ 18 Roger Hansen
☐ 19 Doug Gilcrease
☐ 20 Hal Hatcher
☐ 21 Jose Reyes
☐ 22 Steve Morrow
☐ 23 Mark Pirruccello
☐ 24 Bill Pecota
☐ 25 David Cone

1984 Midland Cubs TCMA

This 24-card standard-size set of the 1984 Midland Cubs, a Class AA Texas League affiliate of the Chicago Cubs, features green-bordered posed color player shots on its fronts. The player's position, player's name and the team name are printed below the photo in white lettering. The white back carries the team name and year at the top, followed by the league, player's name, position, and biography.

	MINT	NRMT	EXC
COMPLETE SET (24)	30.00	13.50	3.70

☐ 1 Joe Henderson
☐ 2 Antonio Cordova
☐ 3 Don Hyman
☐ 4 Jim Boudreau
☐ 5 John Huey
☐ 6 Jorge Carpio
☐ 7 Joe Housey
☐ 8 Darryl Banks
☐ 9 Ray Soff
☐ 10 Mike Capel
☐ 11 Jeff Moscaret
☐ 12 Doug Petestio
☐ 13 Dennis Brogna
☐ 14 Glenn Gregson
☐ 15 George Enright
☐ 16 Darrin Jackson
☐ 17 Danny Norman
☐ 18 Ricky Baker
☐ 19 Jim Auten
☐ 20 Jeff Jones
☐ 21 Paul Noce
☐ 22 Shawon Dunston
☐ 23 Gary Varsho
☐ 24 Tony Woods

1984 Modesto A's Chong

	MINT	NRMT	EXC
COMPLETE SET (28)			

☐ 1 Eric Barry
☐ 2 Mark Bauer
☐ 3 Paul Bradley
☐ 4 Greg Cadaret
☐ 5 Jose Canseco
☐ 6 Chip Conklin
☐ 7 Ron Cummings
☐ 8 Rocky Coyle
☐ 9 Oscar De Chave
☐ 10 Brian Dorsett
☐ 11 Mark Ferguson
☐ 12 Eric Garret
☐ 13 Mike Gorman
☐ 14 Juan Cruz
☐ 15 Brian Guinn
☐ 16 Stan Hilton
☐ 17 Joe Law
☐ 18 Dave Leiper
☐ 19 Tony Moncrief
☐ 20 Doug Scherer
☐ 21 Keith Thrower
☐ 22 Jose Tolentino
☐ 23 George Mitterwald
☐ 24 Jeff Kobernus
☐ 25 Mark Doberenz
☐ 26 Dan Kiser
☐ 27 Dave Fry
☐ 28 Tom Zmudosky

1984 Nashville Sounds Team Issue

	MINT	NRMT	EXC
COMPLETE SET (25)	10.00	4.50	1.25

☐ 1 Johnny Baldwin
☐ 2 Tom Barrett
☐ 3 Ben Callahan
☐ 4 John Csefalvay
☐ 5 Pete Dalena
☐ 6 Pat Dempsey
☐ 7 Don Fowler
☐ 8 Randy Graham
☐ 9 Johnny Hawkins
☐ 10 Stan Javier
☐ 11 Mike King
☐ 12 Tim Knight
☐ 13 Jim Marshall MG
☐ 14 Don McGann TR
☐ 15 Scott Nielsen
☐ 16 Dan Pasqua
☐ 17 Erik Peterson
☐ 18 Jim Rasmussen
☐ 19 Jim Saul CO
☐ 20 Mark Shiflett
☐ 21 Keith Smith
☐ 22 Bob Tewksbury
☐ 23 Chuck Tomaselli
☐ 24 Hoyt Wilhelm CO
☐ 25 Bill Worden

1984 Newark Orioles TCMA

This 25-card standard-size set of the 1984 Newark Orioles, a Class A New York-Penn League affiliate of the Baltimore Orioles, features green-bordered posed color player shots on its fronts. The player's position, player's name and the team name are printed below the photo in white lettering. The white back carries the team name and year at the top, followed by the league, player's name, position, and biography.

	MINT	NRMT	EXC
COMPLETE SET (25)	10.00	4.50	1.25

☐ 1 Randy Riley
☐ 2 Eric Bell
☐ 3 Troy Howerton
☐ 4 David Dahse
☐ 5 Dan Mickan
☐ 6 Wayne Wilson
☐ 7 Dan Fitzpatrick
☐ 8 Alan Ennis
☐ 9 Rich Bair
☐ 10 Greg Wirth
☐ 11 David Smith
☐ 12 Mike Whalen
☐ 13 Dan Hayes
☐ 14 Tim Smith
☐ 15 Frank Velleggia
☐ 16 Jim Rooney
☐ 17 Rich Caldwell
☐ 18 Henry Gonzales
☐ 19 Larry Heise
☐ 20 Gerry Adams
☐ 21 Bob Gutierrez
☐ 22 Randy Wilson
☐ 23 Jim Hutto
☐ 24 Bob Kline
☐ 25 Jeff Arnold

1984 Oklahoma City 89ers TCMA

This 24-card standard-size set of the 1984 Oklahoma City 89ers, a Class AAA American Association affiliate of the Texas Rangers, features green-bordered posed color player shots on its fronts. The player's position, player's name and the team name are printed below the photo in white lettering. The white back carries the team name and year at the top, followed by the league, player's name, position, and biography.

	MINT	NRMT	EXC
COMPLETE SET (24)	20.00	9.00	2.50

☐ 1 Al Lachowicz
☐ 2 Rob Clark
☐ 3 Tommy Burgess
☐ 4 Cliff Wherry
☐ 5 Rusty Gerhardt
☐ 6 Dan Larson
☐ 7 Mike Griffin
☐ 8 Dave Stockstill
☐ 9 Mike Jirschele
☐ 10 Tom Henke
☐ 11 Nick Capra
☐ 12 Tony Fossas
☐ 13 Steve Buechele
☐ 14 Mike Rubel
☐ 15 Barry Brunkenkant
☐ 16 Kevin Buckley
☐ 17 Chuckie Canady
☐ 18 Tommy Dunbar
☐ 19 Don Scott
☐ 20 Victor Cruz
☐ 21 Mitch Zwolensky
☐ 22 Glenn Cook
☐ 23 Dan Murphy
☐ 24 German Barranca

1984 Omaha Royals TCMA

This 30-card standard-size set of the 1984 Omaha Royals, a Class AAA American Association League affiliate of the Kansas City Royals, features green-bordered posed color player shots on its fronts. The player's position, player's name and the team name are printed below the photo in white lettering. The white back carries the team name and year at the top, followed by the league, player's name, position, and biography.

	MINT	NRMT	EXC
COMPLETE SET (30)	15.00	6.75	1.85

☐ 1 Charlie Leibrandt
☐ 2 Gene Lamont
☐ 3 Tony Ferreira
☐ 4 Al Hargesheimer
☐ 5 Frank Wills
☐ 6 Rickey Keeton
☐ 7 Nick Swartz
☐ 8 John Morris
☐ 9 Mike Brewer
☐ 10 Steve Hammond
☐ 11 Mike Parrott
☐ 12 Marty Wilkerson
☐ 13 Jerry Cram
☐ 14 Bill Gorman
☐ 15 Keith Creel
☐ 16 Vinnie Yuhas
☐ 17 Theo Shaw
☐ 18 Dan St. Clair
☐ 19 Mike Alvarez
☐ 20 Mike Jones
☐ 21 Cliff Pastornicky
☐ 22 Dave Leeper
☐ 23 Brian Poldberg
☐ 24 Mark Ryal
☐ 25 Rondin Johnson
☐ 26 Russ Stephens
☐ 27 Jim Scranton
☐ 28 Frank Mancuso
☐ 29 Matt Bassett
☐ 30 Terry Wendlandt

1984 Pawtucket Red Sox TCMA

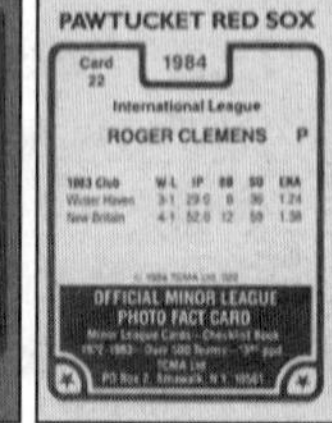

This 25-card standard-size set of the 1984 Pawtucket Red Sox, a Class AAA International League affiliate of the Boston Red Sox, features green-bordered posed color player shots on its fronts. The player's position, player's name and the team name are printed below the photo in white lettering. The white back carries the team name and year at the top, followed by the league, player's name, position, and biography. This issue includes the minor league card debut of Roger Clemens. Approximately 4,000 sets were produced.

	MINT	NRMT	EXC
COMPLETE SET (25)	225.00	100.00	28.00
COMPLETE SET (29)	250.00	110.00	31.00

☐ 1 Charlie Mitchell
☐ 2 Lee Graham
☐ 3A Tony Torchia
(Name incorrect)
☐ 3B Tony Torchia
(Name corrected)
☐ 4 Dale Robertson
☐ 5 Dennis Burtt
☐ 6 Jim Dorsey
☐ 7 Mike Davis
(Error pitcher)
☐ 8 Paul Gnacinski
☐ 9 Gus Burgess
☐ 10A Paul Hundhammer
(Name incorrect)
☐ 10B Paul Hundhammer
(Name corrected)
☐ 11A Tony Herron
(Name incorrect)
☐ 11B Tony Herron
(Name corrected)
☐ 12 Juan Pautt
☐ 13 Kevin Romine
☐ 14 Steve Crawford
☐ 15 Reggie Whittemore
☐ 16 Chico Walker
☐ 17 Dave Malpeso
☐ 18 Steve Lyons
☐ 19 Pat Dodson
☐ 20 Marc Sullivan
☐ 21 Mike Rochford
☐ 22 Roger Clemens
☐ 23 Rich Gale
☐ 24 Brian Denman
☐ 25 Juan Bustabad
☐ 26 Mike Davis
(Corrected infielder)

1984 Phoenix Giants Cramer

This 25-card standard-size set of the 1984 Phoenix Giants, a Class AAA Pacific Coast League affiliate of the San Francisco Giants, features white-bordered posed color player photos on its fronts. The player's name, position, and team name appear at the bottom. The gray horizontal back carries the player's name and position within a baseball bat icon at the top, followed below by biography and statistics, some enhanced by a cartoon.

	MINT	NRMT	EXC
COMPLETE SET (25)	10.00	4.50	1.25

☐ 1 Phil Ouellette
☐ 2 Mark Calvert
☐ 3 Mark Grant
☐ 4 Rob Deer
☐ 5 Scott Garrelts
☐ 6 Rich Murray
☐ 7 Mark Schuster
☐ 8 Alejandro Sanchez
☐ 9 Jim Farr
☐ 10 Herman Segelke
☐ 11 Tom O'Malley
☐ 12 Jeff Cornell
☐ 13 Joe Pettini
☐ 14 Tip Lefebvre
☐ 15 Brian Kingman
☐ 16 Alan Fowlkes
☐ 17 Dan Gladden
☐ 18 Randy Kutcher
☐ 19 Jeff Blobaum
☐ 20 Randy Gomez
☐ 21 Colin Ward
☐ 22 Guy Sularz
☐ 23 Chris Brown
☐ 24 Jack Mull
☐ 241 Tim Blackwell CO

1984 Portland Beavers Cramer

This 22-card standard-size set of the 1984 Portland Beavers, a Class AAA Pacific Coast League affiliate of the Philadelphia Phillies, features white-bordered posed color player photos on its fronts. The player's name, position, and team name appear at the bottom. The gray horizontal back carries the player's name and position within a baseball bat icon at the top, followed below by biography and statistics, some enhanced by a cartoon.

	MINT	NRMT	EXC
COMPLETE SET (22)	20.00	9.00	2.50

☐ 195 Dave Wehrmeister
☐ 196 Stephen Mura
☐ 197 Jeff Stone
☐ 198 Darren Daulton
☐ 199 Francisco Melendez
☐ 200 Lee Elia MG
☐ 201 Kelly Downs
☐ 202 Bobby Mitchell
☐ 203 Randy Salava
☐ 204 Don Carman
☐ 205 Steve Jeltz
☐ 206 George Riley
☐ 207 Jose Calderon
☐ 208 John Russell
☐ 209 Rick Schu
☐ 210 Ken Dowell
☐ 211 Willie Darkis
☐ 212 Richard Gaynor
☐ 213 Jay Davisson
☐ 214 Steve Fireovid
☐ 215 George Culver CO
☐ 216 Russ Hamric

1984 Prince William Pirates TCMA

This 34-card standard-size set of the 1984 Prince William Pirates, a Class A Carolina League affiliate of the Pittsburgh Pirates, features green-bordered posed color player shots on its fronts. The player's position, player's name and the team name are printed below the photo in white lettering. The white back carries the team name and year at the top, followed by the league, player's name, position, and biography.

	MINT	NRMT	EXC
COMPLETE SET (34)	12.00	5.50	1.50

☐ 1 Leon Roberts
☐ 2 Jim Buckmier
☐ 3 Sean Faherty
☐ 4 Shawn Holman
☐ 5 Jim Felt
☐ 6 Dorn Taylor
☐ 7 Mike Berger
☐ 8 Pete Piskol
☐ 9 John Pavlik
☐ 10 Brian Buckley
☐ 11 Eric Fink
☐ 12 Dorley Downs
☐ 13 Wilfrido Cordoba
☐ 14 Jim Aulenbach
☐ 15 Joe Charboneau
☐ 16 Felix Fermin
☐ 17 Jeff Patton
☐ 18 Scott Borland
☐ 19 Steve Lewis
☐ 20 Don Williams
☐ 21 Shawn Stone
☐ 22 Sam Haro
☐ 23 Rich Sauveur
☐ 24 Mitch McKelvey
☐ 25 Kim Christenson
☐ 26 Craig Brown
☐ 27 David Tumbas
☐ 28 Leo Sanchez
☐ 29 John Lipon
☐ 30 Dave Johnson
☐ 31 Nick Castaneda
☐ 32 Kerry Baker
☐ 33 George Borges
☐ 34 Stacy Pettis

1984 Richmond Braves TCMA

This 27-card standard-size set of the 1984 Richmond Braves, a Class AAA International League affiliate of the Atlanta Braves, features green-bordered posed color player shots on its fronts. The player's position, player's name and the team name are printed below the photo in white lettering. The white back carries the team name and year at the top, followed by the league, player's name, position, and biography.

	MINT	NRMT	EXC
COMPLETE SET (27)	10.00	4.50	1.25

☐ 1 Mike Reynolds
☐ 2 Rufino Linares
☐ 3 Ken Smith
☐ 4 Paul Boris
☐ 5 Larry Whisenton
☐ 6 Tom Hayes
☐ 7 Vic Lisi
☐ 8 Larry Owen
☐ 9 Tony Brizzolara
☐ 10 Brad Komminsk
Leo Vargas
☐ 11 Brad Komminsk
☐ 12 Leo Vargas
☐ 13 Craig Jones
☐ 14 Roger LaFrancois
☐ 15 Gary Reiter
☐ 16 Bob Galasso
☐ 17 Steve Shields
☐ 18 Randy Martz
☐ 19 Terry Leach
☐ 20 Brian Fisher
☐ 21 Joe Johnson
☐ 22 Sam Ayoub
☐ 23 Paul Zuvella
☐ 24 Paul Runge
☐ 25 Milt Thompson
☐ 26 Johnny Sain
☐ 27 Eddie Haas

1984 Rochester Red Wings TCMA

This 19-card standard-size set of the 1984 Rochester Red Wings, a Class AAA International League affiliate of the Baltimore Orioles, features green-bordered posed color player shots on its fronts. The player's position, player's name and the team name are printed below the photo in white lettering. The white back carries the team name and year at the top, followed by the league, player's name, position, and biography.

	MINT	NRMT	EXC
COMPLETE SET (19)	10.00	4.50	1.25

☐ 1 Larry Sheets
☐ 2 Rich Carlucci
☐ 3 Mark Wiley
☐ 4 Jim Hutto
☐ 5 Mike Calise
☐ 6 John Valle
☐ 7 Lee Granger
☐ 8 Ismael Oquendo
☐ 9 Frank Verdi
☐ 10 Jeff Shaefer
☐ 11 Glenn Gulliver
☐ 12 Luis Rosado
☐ 13 Bob Bonner
☐ 14 Don Welchel
☐ 15 Leo Hernandez
☐ 16 Allan Ramirez
☐ 17 Bill Swaggerty
☐ 18 Joe Kucharski
☐ 19 Mike Young

1984 Salt Lake City Gulls Cramer

This 24-card standard-size set of the 1984 Salt Lake City Gulls, a Class AAA Pacific Coast League affiliate of the Seattle Mariners, features white-bordered posed color player photos on its fronts. The player's name, position, and team name appear at the bottom. The gray horizontal back carries the player's name and position within a baseball bat icon at the top, followed below by biography and statistics, some enhanced by a cartoon.

	MINT	NRMT	EXC
COMPLETE SET (24)	20.00	9.00	2.50

☐ 170 Danny Tartabull
☐ 171 Brian Allard
☐ 172 Bill Crone
☐ 173 Ivan Calderon
☐ 174 Tito Nanni
☐ 175 Dave Geisel
☐ 176 Dave Valle
☐ 177 Jed Murray
☐ 178 Brian Snyder
☐ 179 Robert Long
☐ 180 Jim Lewis
☐ 181 Bill Nahorodny
☐ 182 Jamie Allen
☐ 183 Edwin Nunez
☐ 184 Jim Presley
☐ 185 Harold Reynolds
☐ 186 Jerry Gleaton
☐ 187 Glen Walker
☐ 188 Al Chambers
☐ 189 Karl Best
☐ 190 Darnell Coles
☐ 191 Bobby Floyd
☐ 192 Bubby Cuellar CO
☐ 193 Brad Boylan TR

1984 Savannah Cardinals TCMA

This 26-card standard-size set of the 1984 Savannah Cardinals, a Class A South Atlantic League affiliate of the St. Louis Cardinals, features green-bordered posed color player shots on its fronts. The player's position, player's name and the team name are printed below the photo in white lettering. The white back carries the team name and year at the top, followed by the league, player's name, position, and biography.

	MINT	NRMT	EXC
COMPLETE SET (26)	10.00	4.50	1.25

☐ 1 Sonny James
☐ 2 Jeff Lauck
☐ 3 Barry McPherson
☐ 4 John Costello
☐ 5 Kurt Kaull
☐ 6 Chuck McGrath
☐ 7 Ken Huth
☐ 8 Hans Herzog
☐ 9 Ted Milner
☐ 10 Jim Reboulet
☐ 11 Mark Angelo
☐ 12 Bob Kish
☐ 13 Jamie Brisco
☐ 14 Jeff Perry
☐ 15 Ernie Carrasco
☐ 16 Harry McCulla
☐ 17 Bill Packer
☐ 18 Glenn Harris
☐ 19 Victor Paulino
☐ 20 George Vogel
☐ 21 Lloyd Merritt
☐ 22 Sal Agostinelli
☐ 23 Ted Carson

☐ 24 Miguel Soto
☐ 25 Ken Sinclair
☐ 26 Mike Behrend

1984 Shreveport Captains First Base

	MINT	NRMT	EXC
COMPLETE SET (24)	15.00	6.75	1.85

☐ 1 Kevin Bates
☐ 2 Orlando Blackwell
☐ 3 Randy Bockus
☐ 4 Steve Cline CO
☐ 5 Larry Crews
☐ 6 Bob Cummings
☐ 7 Duane Espy MG
☐ 8 Bob Gendron
☐ 9 Mike Jones
☐ 10 Chuck Lusted
☐ 11 Kurt Mattson
☐ 12 Bobby Moore
☐ 13 Randy Morse
☐ 14 Matt Nokes
☐ 15 Bob O'Connor
☐ 16 Jessie Reid
☐ 17 Kernan Ronan
☐ 18 Steve Smith
☐ 19 Bryan Snyder
☐ 20 Van Sowards
☐ 21 Steve Stanicek
☐ 22 John Stevenson
☐ 23 Kelvin Torve
☐ 24 Dave Wilhelmi

1984 Syracuse Chiefs TCMA

This 32-card standard-size set of the 1984 Syracuse Chiefs, a Class AAA International League affiliate of the Toronto Blue Jays, features green-bordered posed color player shots on its fronts. The player's position, player's name and the team name are printed below the photo in white lettering. The white back carries the team name and year at the top, followed by the league, player's name, position, and biography.

	MINT	NRMT	EXC
COMPLETE SET (32)	35.00	16.00	4.40

☐ 1 Jim Beauchamp MG
☐ 2 Larry Hardy
☐ 3 Tommy Craig TR
☐ 4 Dennis Howard
☐ 5 Ron Shepherd
☐ 6 Rick Leach
☐ 7 Anthony Johnson
☐ 8 Augie Schmidt
☐ 9 Tony Fernandez
☐ 10 Jerry Keller
☐ 11 Matt Williams
☐ 12 Fred Manrique
☐ 13 Bobby Nandin
☐ 14 Al Woods
☐ 15 Toby Hernandez
☐ 16 Mike Proly
☐ 17 Tim Rodgers
☐ 18 Mark Eichhorn
☐ 19 Stan Clarke
☐ 20 Tom Lukish
☐ 21 David Walsh
☐ 22 Mike Morgan
☐ 23 Mark Bomback
☐ 24 Manny Castillo
☐ 25 Dave Shippanoff
☐ 26 Dave Stenhouse
☐ 27 Kelly Gruber
☐ 28 Dale Holman
☐ 29 Jim Baker
☐ 30 Tim Thompson
☐ 31 John Cerutti
☐ 32 Batboys

1984 Tacoma Tigers Cramer

This 25-card standard-size set of the 1984 Tacoma Tigers, a Class AAA Pacific Coast League affiliate of the Oakland Athletics, features white-bordered posed color player photos on its fronts. The player's name, position, and team name appear at the bottom. The gray horizontal back carries the player's name and position within a baseball bat icon at the top, followed below by biography and statistics, some enhanced by a cartoon.

	MINT	NRMT	EXC
COMPLETE SET (25)	5.00	2.20	.60

☐ 73 Bruce Robinson
☐ 74 Dave Hudgens
☐ 75 Ron Arnold
☐ 76 Ramon De Los Santos
☐ 77 Tom Romano
☐ 78 Steve Kiefer
☐ 79 Carlos Lezcano
☐ 80 Bill Bathe
☐ 81 Mike Gallego
☐ 82 Jeff Jones
☐ 83 Steve Ontiveros
☐ 84 Bill Krueger
☐ 85 Curt Young
☐ 86 Chuck Hensley
☐ 87 Tim Pyznarski
☐ 88 Phil Stephenson
☐ 89 Mark Wagner
☐ 90 Ed Nottle MG
☐ 91 Danny Goodwin
☐ 92 Bert Bradley
☐ 93 John Hotchkiss
☐ 94 Dave Ford
☐ 95 Gorman Heimueller
☐ 96 Dan Meyer
☐ 247 Ed Farmer

1984 Tidewater Tides TCMA

This 28-card standard-size set of the 1984 Tidewater Tides, a Class AAA International League affiliate of the New York Mets, features green-bordered posed color player shots on its fronts. The player's position, player's name and the team name are printed below the photo in white lettering. The white back carries the team name and year at the top, followed by the league, player's name, position, and biography. Approximately 4,000 sets were produced. Although it's not considered part of the set, a late issue card of Darryl Strawberry was released.

	MINT	NRMT	EXC
COMPLETE SET (28)	35.00	16.00	4.40
DARRYL STRAWBERRY SINGLE	25.00	11.00	3.10

☐ 1 Scott Holman
☐ 2 Sid Fernandez
☐ 3 Wes Gardner
☐ 4 John Christensen
☐ 5 Herman Winningham
☐ 6 Bill Latham
☐ 7 Gil Flores
☐ 8 Brent Gaff
☐ 9 Rusty Tillman
☐ 10 Bob Schaefer
☐ 11 Ed Olwine
☐ 12 Rich Pickett
☐ 13 Jeff Bittiger
☐ 14 Tom Gorman
☐ 15 Jay Tibbs
☐ 16 Rafael Santana
☐ 17 Bob Sikes
☐ 18 Ross Jones
☐ 19 Rick Anderson
☐ 20 Terry Blocker
☐ 21 Laschelle Tarver
☐ 22 Al Jackson
☐ 23 Kevin Mitchell
☐ 24 Brian Giles
☐ 25 Ronn Reynolds
☐ 26 Terry Leach
☐ 27 Kelvin Chapman
☐ 28 Clint Hurdle
☐ NNO Darryl Strawberry

1984 Toledo Mud Hens TCMA

This 24-card standard-size set of the 1984 Toledo Mud Hens, a Class AAA International League affiliate of the Minnesota Twins, features green-bordered posed color player shots on its fronts. The player's position, player's name and the team name are printed below the photo in white lettering. The white back carries the team name and year at the top, followed by the league, player's name, position, and biography.

	MINT	NRMT	EXC
COMPLETE SET (24)	10.00	4.50	1.25

☐ 1 Steve Lombardozzi
☐ 2 Jeffrey Reed
☐ 3 Alvaro Espinoza
☐ 4 Ray Smith
☐ 5 Rich Yett
☐ 6 Cal Ermer
☐ 7 Dan Schmitz
☐ 8 Brad Havens
☐ 9 Bob Mulligan
☐ 10 Bob Mitchell
☐ 11 Andre David
☐ 12 Scott Ullger
☐ 13 James Weaver
☐ 14 Tom Klawitter
☐ 15 Jack O'Connor
☐ 16 Keith Comstock
☐ 17 Eric Broersma
☐ 18 Greg Field
☐ 19 Tim Agan
☐ 20 Dave Baker
☐ 21 Jim Shellenback
☐ 22 Tack Wilson
☐ 23 Rick Lysander
☐ 24 Jay Pettibone

1984 Tucson Toros Cramer

This 25-card standard-size set of the 1984 Tucson Toros, a Class AAA Pacific Coast League affiliate of the Houston Astros, features white-bordered posed color player photos on its fronts. The player's name, position, and team name appear at the bottom. The gray horizontal back carries the player's name and position within a baseball bat icon at the top, followed below by biography and statistics, some enhanced by a cartoon.

	MINT	NRMT	EXC
COMPLETE SET (25)	5.00	2.20	.60

☐ 49 Eric Rasmussen
☐ 50 Matt Galante
☐ 51 Jose Alvarez
☐ 52 Chris Jones
☐ 53 Wes Clements
☐ 54 Greg Cypert
☐ 55 Dwight Bernard
☐ 56 Rex Jones TR
☐ 57 Tim Tolman
☐ 58 Jaime Williams
☐ 59 Manny Hernandez
☐ 60 Tye Waller
☐ 61 Jim Pankovits
☐ 62 Glenn Davis
☐ 63 Julio Solano
☐ 64 Eddie Bonine
☐ 65 Jeff Heathcock
☐ 66 Ruben Robles
☐ 67 Bert Pena
☐ 68 Mark Ross
☐ 69 Craig Minetto
☐ 70 Larry Ray
☐ 71 Luis Pujols
☐ 72 Ron Mathis
☐ 248 Gary Tuck CO

1984 Tulsa Drillers Team Issue

2,000 sets were produced.

	MINT	NRMT	EXC
COMPLETE SET (22)	20.00	9.00	2.50

☐ 4 Jorge Gomez
☐ 6 Keith Jones
☐ 7 Oscar Mejia
☐ 14 Greg Jemison CO
☐ 16 Dan Murphy
☐ 18 Randy Asadoor
☐ 19 Greg Tabor
☐ 20 Whitney Harry
☐ 22 Barry Bass
☐ 23 Orlando Gomez
☐ 24 Tim Meckes
☐ 26 Bob Gergen
☐ 27 John Buckley
☐ 28 Bill Hance
☐ 29 Jose Guzman
☐ 30 Steve Kordish
☐ 31 Javier Ortiz
☐ 32 Billy Taylor
☐ 34 Terry Johnson
☐ 36 Dwayne Henry
☐ 37 Tommy Joe Shimp
☐ NNO Greg Campbell TR

1984 Vancouver Canadians Cramer

Sponsored by Orange Crush, this 25-card standard-size set of the 1984 Vancouver Canadians, a Class AAA Pacific Coast League affiliate of the Milwaukee Brewers, features white-bordered posed color player photos on its fronts. The player's name, position, and team name appear at the bottom. The gray horizontal back carries the player's name and position within a baseball bat icon at the top, followed below by biography and statistics, some enhanced by a cartoon.

	MINT	NRMT	EXC
COMPLETE SET (25)	10.00	4.50	1.25

☐ 25 Ron Koenigsfeld
☐ 26 Andy Beene
☐ 27 Tony Muser MG
☐ 28 Doug Loman
☐ 29 Dan Davidsmeier
☐ 30 Ray Searage
☐ 31 Kelvin Moore
☐ 32 Tom Candiotti
☐ 33 Frank Thomas
☐ 34 Carlos Ponce
☐ 35 Earnie Riles
☐ 36 Dan Boone
☐ 37 Dave Huppert
☐ 38 Hosken Powell
☐ 39 Doug Jones
☐ 40 Bob Gibson
☐ 41 Eric Peyton
☐ 42 Scott Roberts
☐ 43 Jamie Nelson
☐ 44 Ed Irvine
☐ 45 Jim Koontz
☐ 46 Mike Anderson
☐ 47 Marshall Edwards
☐ 48 Jack Lazorko
☐ 243 Don Rowe CO

1984 Visalia Oaks TCMA

This 25-card standard-size set of the 1984 Visalia Oaks, a Class A California League affiliate of the Minnesota Twins, features green-bordered posed color player shots on its fronts. The player's position, player's name and the team name are printed below the photo in white lettering. The white back carries the team name and year at the top, followed by the league, player's name, position, and biography.

	MINT	NRMT	EXC
COMPLETE SET (25)	10.00	4.50	1.25

☐ 1 Bennie Richie
☐ 2 Curt Kindred
☐ 3 Erez Borowsky
☐ 4 Alexis Marte
☐ 5 Vincent Ferraro
☐ 6 Osvaldo Alfonzo
☐ 7 Corey Elliot
☐ 8 Phillip Sheppard
☐ 9 Leonard Braddy
☐ 10 John Hilton
☐ 11 Timothy Thompson
☐ 12 Brian Hobaugh
☐ 13 Tom Reed
☐ 14 Jeffrey Schugel
☐ 15 Carson Carroll
☐ 16 Tim Graupmann
☐ 17 Matthew Butcher
☐ 18 Paul Mancuso
☐ 19 Antonio Codinach
☐ 20 Allan Anderson
☐ 21 Ronald Scheer
☐ 22 Scott Gibson
☐ 23 Joseph Tarangelo
☐ 24 Steven Aragon
☐ 25 Dan Lindquist

1984 Wichita Aeros Rock's Dugout

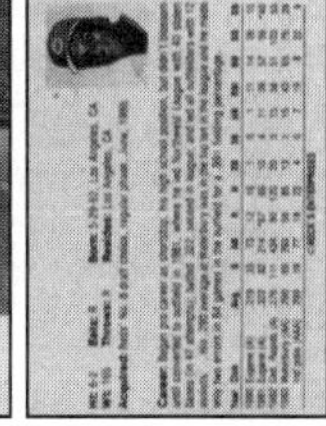

	MINT	NRMT	EXC
COMPLETE SET (23)	50.00	22.00	6.25

☐ 1 Charlie Puleo
☐ 2 Dave Miley
☐ 3 Hector Rincones
☐ 4 Leo Garcia
☐ 5 Tom Browning
☐ 6 Charlie Nail
☐ 7 Wayne Krenchicki
☐ 8 Ron Robinson
☐ 9 Curt Heidenreich
☐ 10 Dave Van Gorder
☐ 11 Tom Runnells
☐ 12 Mark Gilbert
☐ 13 Terry Bogener
☐ 14 Keefe Cato
☐ 15 Eric Davis
☐ 16 Skeeter Barnes
☐ 17 Bill Landrum
☐ 18 Alan Knicely
☐ 19 John Franco
☐ 20 Fred Toliver
☐ 21 Wade Rowdon
☐ 22 Gene Dusan
☐ NNO Checklist

1985 Albany Yankees TCMA

This 35-card standard-size set of the 1985 Albany Yankees, a Class AA Eastern League affiliate of the New York Yankees, features blue-bordered posed color player shots on its fronts. The team name is printed at the top with the player's name and position appearing vertically on the lower left edge. The white back carries the team name and league at the top, followed by the player's name, position, and biography.

	MINT	NRMT	EXC
COMPLETE SET (33)	40.00	18.00	5.00
COMPLETE SET W/LATE ISSUES (35)	50.00	22.00	6.25

☐ 1 Brad Arnsberg
☐ 2 Tim Byron
☐ 3 Darin Cloninger
☐ 4 Doug Drabek
☐ 5 Logan Easley
☐ 6 Mark Ferguson
☐ 7 Steve Frey
☐ 8 Randy Graham
☐ 9 Scott Nielsen
☐ 10 Scott Patterson

□ 11 Bob Tewksbury
□ 12 Bill Lindsey (Late Issue)
□ 13 Phil Lombardi
□ 14 Mark Blaser
□ 15 Ron Chapman
□ 16 Orestes Destrade
□ 17 Rafael Landestoy
□ 18 Jim Riggs
□ 19 Dick Scott
□ 20 Doug Carpenter
□ 21 Tony Russell
□ 22 Brad Winkler
□ 23 Barry Foote
□ 24 Dave LaRoche
□ 25 Jim Saul
□ 26 Mike Fennell
□ 27 Kevin Rand
□ 28 Bernard Bremer
□ 29 Erik Bernard
□ 30 Hayes and Lemperle
□ 31 Phil Pivnick
□ 32 John Hawkins
□ 33 Tim Knight
□ 34 John Liburdi
□ 35 Keith Hughes (Late Issue)

1985 Albuquerque Dukes Cramer

This 25-card standard-size set of the 1985 Albuquerque Dukes, a Class AAA Pacific Coast League affiliate of the Los Angeles Dodgers, features white-bordered posed color player photos on its fronts. The player's name, position, and team name appear at the bottom. The light blue horizontal back carries the player's name and position within a baseball bat icon at the top, followed below by biography and statistics, some enhanced by a cartoon.

	MINT	NRMT	EXC
COMPLETE SET (25)	5.00	2.20	.60

□ 151 Dean Rennicke
□ 152 Tony Brewer
□ 153 Joe Vavra
□ 154 Dennis Powell
□ 155 Craig Shipley
□ 156 Terry Collins MG
□ 157 Hector Rincones
□ 158 Ed Amelung
□ 159 Erik Sonberg
□ 160 Dick McLaughlin CO
□ 161 Ralph Bryant
□ 162 German Rivera
□ 163 Jack Fimple
□ 164 Brian Holton
□ 165 Lemmie Miller
□ 166 Bill Scudder
□ 167 Stu Pederson
□ 168 Larry White
□ 169 Tim Meeks
□ 170 Gil Reyes
□ 171 Don Smith
□ 172 Steve Martin
□ 173 Rafael Montalvo
□ 174 Rich Rodas
□ 175 Franklin Stubbs

1985 Beaumont Golden Gators TCMA

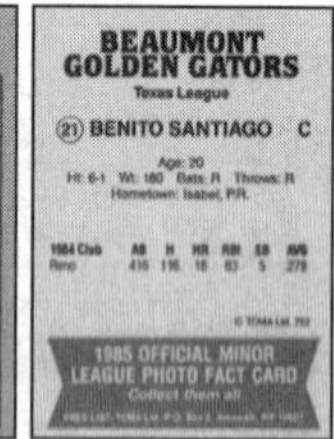

This 25-card standard-size set of the 1985 Beaumont Golden Gators, a Class AA Texas League affiliate of the San Diego Padres, features blue-bordered posed color player shots on its fronts. The team name is printed at the top with the player's name and position appearing vertically on the lower left edge. The white back carries the team name and league at the top, followed by the player's name, position, and biography.

	MINT	NRMT	EXC
COMPLETE SET (25)	25.00	11.00	3.10

□ 1 Jeffrey Childers
□ 2 Rickey Coleman
□ 3 Mark Williamson
□ 4 Shane Mack
□ 5 Edward Vosberg
□ 6 Gregory Smith
□ 7 Peter Kutsukos
□ 8 Jimmy Jones
□ 9 Ulises Sierra
□ 10 Rigo Rodriguez
□ 11 Steven Schefsky
□ 12 Michael McClain
□ 13 Edward Miller
□ 14 Thomas Brassil
□ 15 Frank Castro
□ 16 Mark Poston
□ 17 Michael Mills
□ 18 Gary Green
□ 19 Mark Wasinger
□ 20 Dave Corman
□ 21 Benito Santiago
□ 22 John Tutt
□ 23 Todd Hutcheson
□ 24 Jack Lamabe
□ 25 Bobby Tolan

1985 Beloit Brewers TCMA

This 26-card standard-size set of the 1985 Beloit Brewers, a Class A Midwest League affiliate of the Milwaukee Brewers, features blue-bordered posed color player shots on its fronts. The team name is printed at the top with the player's name and position appearing vertically on the lower left edge. The white back carries the team name and league at the top, followed by the player's name, position, and biography.

	MINT	NRMT	EXC
COMPLETE SET (26)	10.00	4.50	1.25

□ 1 Mike Samuel
□ 2 Walt Pohle
□ 3 Joe Mitchell
□ 4 Jim Rowe
□ 5 Mike Coin
□ 6 Bob Simonson
□ 7 Rob Dewolf
□ 8 Mike Gobbo
□ 9 Tom Steinbach
□ 10 Angel Rodriguez
□ 11 Frank Mattox
□ 12 Bernard Kent
□ 13 Darryel Walters
□ 14 Wes Clements
□ 15 Dean Freeland
□ 16 Mike Frew
□ 17 Greg Simmons
□ 18 Alex Madrid
□ 19 John Ludy
□ 20 Gary Kanwisher
□ 21 Alan Sadler
□ 22 Martin Montano
□ 23 Derek Diaz
□ 24 Miguel Alicea
□ 25 Rob Derksen
□ 26 Dave Machemer

1985 Bend Phillies Cramer

	MINT	NRMT	EXC
COMPLETE SET (24)	5.00	2.20	.60

□ 1 Dion Beck
□ 2 Ben Blackmun
□ 3 Steve Bowden
□ 4 Rodney Brunelle
□ 5 Tim Collins
□ 6 Luis Faccio
□ 7 Kenley Graves
□ 8 Nat Green
□ 9 Jason Grimsley
□ 10 Steve Harris
□ 11 Vince Holyfield
□ 12 Jose Hurtado
□ 13 Ron Jones
□ 14 Bruce Luttrull
□ 15 Trey McCall
□ 16 John McKinney
□ 17 Robert Nazabal
□ 18 Rich Parker
□ 19 Mario Perez
□ 20 Ernie Rodriguez
□ 21 Floyd Rossum
□ 22 Steve Sharts
□ 23 Clifton Walker
□ 24 Carlos Zayas

1985 Buffalo Bisons TCMA

This 26-card standard-size set of the 1985 Buffalo Bisons, a Class AAA American Association affiliate of the Chicago White Sox, features blue-bordered posed color player shots on its fronts. The team name is printed at the top with the player's name and position appearing vertically on the lower left edge. The white back carries the team name and league at the top, followed by the player's name, position, and biography.

	MINT	NRMT	EXC
COMPLETE SET (26)	10.00	4.50	1.25

□ 1 John Boles
□ 2 Nardi Contreras
□ 3 Greg Latta
□ 4 Steve Christmas
□ 5 Rick Sellheimer
□ 6 Joel Skinner
□ 7 Nelson Barrera
□ 8 Jose Castro
□ 9 Bryan Little
□ 10 Kelvin Moore
□ 11 Ramon Romero
□ 12 Alex Taveras
□ 13 Mark Gilbert
□ 14 Randy Johnson
□ 15 Mark Ryal
□ 16 Dave Yobs
□ 17 Bob Fallon
□ 18 Steve Fireovid
□ 19 Jerry Gleaton
□ 20 Jim Hickey
□ 21 Bill Long
□ 22 Joel McKeon
□ 23 Tom Mullen
□ 24 Scott Stranski
□ 25 Bruce Tanner
□ 26 Dave Wehrmeister

1985 Burlington Rangers TCMA

This 28-card standard-size set of the 1985 Burlington Rangers, a Class A Midwest League affiliate of the Texas Rangers, features blue-bordered posed color player shots on its fronts. The team name is printed at the top with the player's name and position appearing vertically on the lower left edge. The white back carries the team name and league at the top, followed by the player's name, position, and biography.

	MINT	NRMT	EXC
COMPLETE SET (28)	10.00	4.50	1.25

□ 1 Joe Grayston
□ 2 Mike Page
□ 3 Larry Klein
□ 4 Brad Hill
□ 5 Steve Cullers
□ 6 Neil Reilly
□ 7 Dale Lanok
□ 8 George Threadgill
□ 9 Dave Darretta
□ 10 Mike Bucci
□ 11 Steve Neilsen
□ 12 Sid Akins
□ 13 Angelo Vasquez
□ 14 Tim Owen
□ 15 Jim St. Laurent
□ 16 Bob O'Hearn
□ 17 Jim Jagnow
□ 18 Mark Kramer
□ 19 Carlos Hernandez
□ 20 Bryan Dial
□ 21 Ty Harden
□ 22 Robin Keathley
□ 23 Stu Rogers
□ 24 Darrell Whitaker
□ 25 Steve Daniel
□ 26 Ross Jones
□ 27 Jim Allison
□ 28 Jim Bridges

1985 Calgary Cannons Cramer

This 25-card standard-size set of the 1985 Calgary Cannons, a Class AAA Pacific Coast League affiliate of the Seattle Mariners, features white-bordered posed color player photos on its fronts. The player's name, position, and team name appear at the bottom. The blue horizontal back carries the player's name and position within a baseball bat icon at the top, followed below by biography and statistics.

	MINT	NRMT	EXC
COMPLETE SET (25)	18.00	8.00	2.20

□ 76 Karl Best
□ 77 Jim Lewis
□ 78 Bobby Floyd MG
□ 79 Paul Serna
□ 80 Al Chambers
□ 81 Don Scott
□ 82 Roy Thomas
□ 83 John Moses
□ 84 Bobby Cuellar CO
□ 85 Frank Wills
□ 86 Pat Casey
□ 87 Dave Tobik
□ 88 Mickey Brantley
□ 89 Paul Mirabella
□ 90 Bob Stoddard
□ 91 Ricky Nelson
□ 92 Brian Snyder
□ 93 Bill Crone
□ 94 Danny Tartabull
□ 95 Bob Long
□ 96 Darnell Coles
□ 97 Ron Tingley
□ 98 Rick Luecken
□ 99 Joe Whitmer
□ 100 Clay Hill

1985 Cedar Rapids Reds TCMA

This 32-card standard-size set of the 1985 Cedar Rapids Reds, a Class A Midwest League affiliate of the Cincinnati Reds, features blue-bordered posed color player shots on its fronts. The team name is printed at the top with the player's name and position appearing vertically on the lower left edge. The white back carries the team name and league at the top, followed by the player's name, position, and biography.

	MINT	NRMT	EXC
COMPLETE SET (32)	25.00	11.00	3.10

□ 1 John Boyles
□ 2 Mark Cieslak
□ 3 Mike Coffey
□ 4 Virgil Conley
□ 5 Clay Daniel
□ 6 Rob Dibble
□ 7 Barry Fick
□ 8 Mike Goedde
□ 9 Doug Kampsen
□ 10 Steve Oliverio
□ 11 Jim Pettibone
□ 12 Danny Smith
□ 13 Ozzio Soto
□ 14 Mark Berry
□ 15 Greg Toler
□ 16 Gary Denbo
□ 17 Greg Monda
□ 18 Carlos Porte
□ 19 Brian Robinson
□ 20 Eddie Williams
□ 21 Dan Boever
□ 22 Elvin Fulgencio
□ 23 Tubby Pace
□ 24 Darren Riley
□ 25 Allen Sigler
□ 26 Paul Kirsch
□ 27 Jay Ward
□ 28 Don Buchheister
□ 29 Rod Licht
□ 30 Bud Curron
□ 31 Tom Riley
□ 32 Scott Breeden

1985 Charlotte O's TCMA

This 31-card standard-size set of the 1985 Charlotte O's, a Class AA Southern League affiliate of the Baltimore Orioles, features blue-bordered posed color player shots on its fronts. The team name is printed at the top with the player's name and position appearing vertically on the lower left edge. The white back carries the team name and league at the top, followed by the player's name, position, and biography.

	MINT	NRMT	EXC
COMPLETE SET (29)	10.00	4.50	1.25
COMPLETE SET W/LATE ISSUES (31)	15.00	6.75	1.85

□ 1 Kenny Gerhart
□ 2 Lee Granger
□ 3 Jeff Jacobson
□ 4 Rick Lockwood
□ 5 John Stefero
□ 6 Dave Thielker
□ 7 Kelvin Torve
□ 8 Tony Arnold
□ 9 Carl Nichols (Late Issue)
□ 10 Mike Reddish
□ 11 Ron Salcedo
□ 12 Jeff Schaefer
□ 13 Dom Chiti
□ 14 John Hart
□ 15 Francisco Oliveras
□ 16 Jeff Summers
□ 17 Jeff Wood
□ 18 Bobby Mariano
□ 19 Rich Caldwell
□ 20 Jeff Gilbert (Late Issue)
□ 21 John Habyan
□ 22 John Hoover
□ 23 Ricky Jones
□ 24 John Flinn
□ 25 Alan Ramirez
□ 26 Jose Brito
□ 27 Bob Hice
□ 28 Terry Mauney
□ 29 Charlie Frederick
□ 30 Paul Cameron
□ 31 Mike Couche

1985 Columbus Clippers Police

	MINT	NRMT	EXC
COMPLETE SET (25)	5.00	2.20	.60

□ 1 Tom Barrett
□ 2 Bert Bradley
□ 3 Dan Briggs
□ 4 Curt Brown
□ 5 Clay Christiansen
□ 6 Don Cooper

- ☐ 7 Pete Dalena
- ☐ 8 Jim Deshaies
- ☐ 9 Juan Espino
- ☐ 10 Kelly Faulk
- ☐ 11 Brian Fisher
- ☐ 12 Kelly Heath
- ☐ 13 Butch Hobson
- ☐ 14 Rex Hudler
- ☐ 15 Tim Knight
- ☐ 16 Carl "Stump" Merrill MG
- ☐ 17 Dan Pasqua
- ☐ 18 Alphonso Pulido
- ☐ 19 Kelly Scott
- ☐ 20 Mark Silva
- ☐ 21 George H. Sisler Jr. General Manager
- ☐ 22 Keith Smith
- ☐ 23 Al Williams
- ☐ 24 Matt Winters
- ☐ 25 Coaching Staff Q.V. Lowe CO Jerry McNertney CO Mickey Vernon CO Steve Donohue TR

1985 Columbus Clippers TCMA

This 28-card standard-size set of the 1985 Columbus Clippers, a Class AAA International League affiliate of the New York Yankees, features blue-bordered posed color player shots on its fronts. The team name is printed at the top with the player's name and position appearing vertically on the lower left edge. The white back carries the team name and league at the top, followed by the player's name, position, and biography.

	MINT	NRMT	EXC
COMPLETE SET (26)	15.00	6.75	1.85
COMPLETE SET (28)	20.00	9.00	2.50

- ☐ 1 Vic Mata (Late Issue)
- ☐ 2 Bert Bradley
- ☐ 3 Curt Brown
- ☐ 4 Clay Christiansen
- ☐ 5 Don Cooper
- ☐ 6 Kelly Faulk
- ☐ 7 Brian Fisher
- ☐ 8 Alphonso Pulido
- ☐ 9 Kelly Scott
- ☐ 10 Al Williams
- ☐ 11 Juan Espino
- ☐ 12 Mike O'Berry
- ☐ 13 Tom Barrett
- ☐ 14 Dan Briggs
- ☐ 15 Pete Dalena
- ☐ 16 Kelly Heath
- ☐ 17 Butch Hobson
- ☐ 18 Rex Hudler
- ☐ 19 Keith Smith
- ☐ 20 Tim Knight
- ☐ 21 Dan Pasqua
- ☐ 22 Matt Winters
- ☐ 23 Jim Deshaies
- ☐ 24 Mark Silva
- ☐ 25 Doug Holmquist
- ☐ 26 Juan Bonilla (Late Issue)
- ☐ 29 George Sisler
- ☐ 30 Mickey Vernon CO Jerry McNertney CO Q.V. Lowe CO Steve Donohue TR

1985 Durham Bulls TCMA

This 31-card standard-size set of the 1985 Durham Bulls, a Class A Carolina League affiliate of the Atlanta Braves, features blue-bordered posed color player shots on its fronts. The team name is printed at the top with the player's name and position appearing vertically on the lower left edge. The white back carries the team name and league at the top, followed by the player's name, position, and biography.

	MINT	NRMT	EXC
COMPLETE SET (31)	15.00	6.75	1.85

- ☐ 1 Paul Assenmacher
- ☐ 2 Vince Barger
- ☐ 3 Kevin Blankenship
- ☐ 4 Mike Bormann
- ☐ 5 Kevin Coffman
- ☐ 6 Maximo Del Rosario
- ☐ 7 David Jones
- ☐ 8 Dave Morris
- ☐ 9 Mac Rogers
- ☐ 11 Mike Santiago
- ☐ 12 Marty Schrieber
- ☐ 13 Troy Tomsick
- ☐ 14 Harry Bright
- ☐ 15 Jim Grant
- ☐ 16 Bob Porter
- ☐ 17 Mike Delao
- ☐ 18 Flavio Alfaro
- ☐ 19 Chris Baird
- ☐ 20 Chip Childress
- ☐ 21 Terry Cormack
- ☐ 22 Sal D'Alessandro
- ☐ 23 Juan Fredymond
- ☐ 24 Dave Griffin
- ☐ 25 Wayne Harrison
- ☐ 26 Johnny Hatcher
- ☐ 27 Roger LaFrancois
- ☐ 28 Mike Nipper
- ☐ 29 Bob Posey
- ☐ 30 Mike Reynolds
- ☐ 31 Jeff Wagner
- ☐ 32 Mike Yastrzemski

1985 Edmonton Trappers Cramer

This 25-card standard-size set of the 1985 Edmonton Trappers, a Class AAA Pacific Coast League affiliate of the California Angels, features white-bordered posed color player photos on its fronts. The player's name, position, and team name appear at the bottom. The blue horizontal back carries the player's name and position within a baseball bat icon at the top, followed below by biography and statistics. This issue includes Wally Joyner's first and only minor league card appearance. Approximately 5,000 sets were produced.

	MINT	NRMT	EXC
COMPLETE SET (25)	20.00	9.00	2.50

- ☐ 1 Pat Keedy
- ☐ 2 Wally Joyner
- ☐ 3 Mike Madril
- ☐ 4 Don Groh
- ☐ 5 Scott Oliver
- ☐ 6 Tony Mack
- ☐ 7 Kirk McCaskill
- ☐ 8 Reggie West
- ☐ 9 Rafael Lugo
- ☐ 10 James Randall
- ☐ 11 Marty Kain
- ☐ 12 Gus Polidor
- ☐ 13 Steve Liddle
- ☐ 14 Winston Llenas MG
- ☐ 15 Bob Ramos
- ☐ 16 Dave Smith
- ☐ 17 Tim Krauss
- ☐ 18 Chris Clark
- ☐ 19 Stewart Cliburn
- ☐ 20 Curt Kaufman
- ☐ 21 Bob Bastian
- ☐ 22 Norman Carrasco
- ☐ 23 Frank Reberger CO
- ☐ 24 Jack Howell
- ☐ 25 Al Romero

1985 Elmira Pioneers TCMA

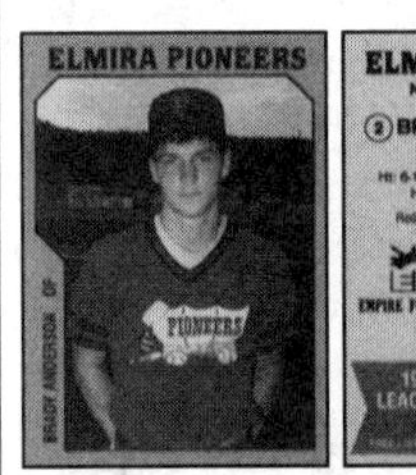

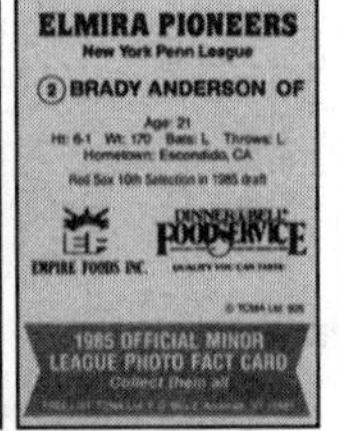

This 25-card standard-size set of the 1985 Elmira Pioneers, a Class A New York-Penn League affiliate of the Boston Red Sox, features blue-bordered posed color player shots on its fronts. The team name is printed at the top with the player's name and position appearing vertically on the lower left edge. The white back carries the team name and league at the top, followed by the player's name, position, and biography. This issue includes the minor league card debut of Brady Anderson.

	MINT	NRMT	EXC
COMPLETE SET (25)	90.00	40.00	11.00

- ☐ 1 John Abbot
- ☐ 2 Brady Anderson
- ☐ 3 Mike Carista
- ☐ 4 Dell Carter
- ☐ 5 Jim Cox
- ☐ 6 Roberto Fuentes
- ☐ 7 Dan Gabriele
- ☐ 8 Gary Gouldrup
- ☐ 9 Brock Knight
- ☐ 10 Eric Laseke
- ☐ 11 Derek Livernois
- ☐ 12 Greg Lotzar
- ☐ 13 Greg Magistri
- ☐ 14 Josias Manzanillo
- ☐ 15 Donnie McGowan
- ☐ 16 Bill Plante
- ☐ 17 Todd Pratt
- ☐ 18 Carlos Quintana
- ☐ 19 Marte Rogers
- ☐ 20 Victor Rosario
- ☐ 21 Tim Speakman
- ☐ 22 John Toale
- ☐ 23 Luis Vasquez
- ☐ 24 Kerman Williams
- ☐ 25 Bill Zupka

1985 Everett Giants Cramer

	MINT	NRMT	EXC
COMPLETE SET (24)	5.00	2.20	.60

- ☐ 1 David Blakely
- ☐ 2A George Bonilla (close up)
- ☐ 2B George Bonilla (arms over head)
- ☐ 3 Ty Dabney
- ☐ 4 Tom Ealy
- ☐ 5A Kim Flowers (close up)
- ☐ 5B Kim Flowers (showing glove)
- ☐ 6A George Jones (no bat showing)
- ☐ 6B George Jones (holding bat)
- ☐ 7 Joe Kmak
- ☐ 8 Alan Marr CO
- ☐ 9 Willie Mijares
- ☐ 10 Todd Miller
- ☐ 11A Rick Nelson (swinging)
- ☐ 11B Rick Nelson (bat in front)
- ☐ 12 Tom Osowski GM
- ☐ 13A Darren Pearson (showing teeth)
- ☐ 13B Darren Pearson (mouth closed)
- ☐ 14 Brian Petty
- ☐ 15 Steve Santora
- ☐ 16A Howard Townsend (without glove)
- ☐ 16B Howard Townsend (with glove)
- ☐ 17 John Verducci
- ☐ 18 Mike Whitt

1985 Everett Giants II Cramer

	MINT	NRMT	EXC
COMPLETE SET (24)	10.00	4.50	1.25

- ☐ 1 Jeff Carter
- ☐ 2 Mike Dandos
- ☐ 3 Bruce Graham TR
- ☐ 4 Dave Hornsby
- ☐ 5 Lloyd Jackson
- ☐ 6 Robert Jackson
- ☐ 7 Darrin James
- ☐ 8 Joe Jordan
- ☐ 9 Randy McCament
- ☐ 10 Timber Mead
- ☐ 11 Dave Morris
- ☐ 12 Curt Motton
- ☐ 13 Brian Ohnoutka
- ☐ 14 Doug Robertson
- ☐ 15 Darrell Rodgers
- ☐ 16 Steve Santora
- ☐ 17 Billy Smith
- ☐ 18 Joe Strain
- ☐ 19 Jach Uhey CO
- ☐ 20 John Van Kempen
- ☐ 21 Paul Van Stone
- ☐ 22 Mike Whitt
- ☐ 23 Rick Wilson
- ☐ 24 Trevor Wilson

1985 Fresno Giants Police

	MINT	NRMT	EXC
COMPLETE SET (32)	80.00	36.00	10.00

- ☐ 1 Wendell Kim MG
- ☐ 2 Marty DeMerritt CO
- ☐ 3 Charles Culberson
- ☐ 4 Angel Escobar
- ☐ 5 Dave Allen
- ☐ 6 Mike Jones
- ☐ 7 Jim Wasem
- ☐ 8 Mackey Sasser
- ☐ 9 Deron McCue
- ☐ 10 Greg Gilbert
- ☐ 11 Charlie Hayes
- ☐ 12 Greg Litton
- ☐ 13 Romy Cucjen
- ☐ 14 John Grimes
- ☐ 15 Ed Puikunas
- ☐ 16 Dan Winters
- ☐ 17 Charlie Corbell
- ☐ 18 Jay Reid
- ☐ 19 Stuart Tate
- ☐ 20 Al Candelaria
- ☐ 21 Todd Kuhn
- ☐ 22 John Burkett
- ☐ 23 Steve Smith
- ☐ 24 Rich Henning
- ☐ 25 Tommy Alexander
- ☐ 26 Todd Oakes
- ☐ 27 Don Wolfe CO
- ☐ 28 Paul Neff BB Paul Reyna BB
- ☐ 29 Bill Thompson GM
- ☐ 30 Curt Goldgrabe AGM
- ☐ 31 Mary Ellen Driscoll Sports Writer
- ☐ 32 Logo Card

1985 Ft. Myers Royals TCMA

This 30-card standard-size set of the 1985 Ft. Myers Royals, a Class A Florida State League affiliate of the Kansas City Royals, features blue-bordered posed color player shots on its fronts. The team name is printed at the top with the player's name and position appearing vertically on the lower left edge. The white back carries the team name and league at the top, followed by the player's name, position, and biography.

	MINT	NRMT	EXC
COMPLETE SET (30)	20.00	9.00	2.50

- ☐ 1 Ed Bass
- ☐ 2 Todd Mabe
- ☐ 3 Brad Davis
- ☐ 4 Craig Walter
- ☐ 5 Don Sparling
- ☐ 6 Tom Niemann
- ☐ 7 Angel Morris
- ☐ 8 Jeff Hull
- ☐ 9 Kevin Seitzer
- ☐ 10 Mark Van Blaricom
- ☐ 11 Phil George
- ☐ 12 Jose DeJesus
- ☐ 13 Jose Nunez
- ☐ 14 Jeff Brown
- ☐ 15 Israel Sanchez
- ☐ 16 Chito Martinez
- ☐ 17 Doug Gilcrease
- ☐ 18 Gary Thurman
- ☐ 19 Tommy Mohr
- ☐ 20 Theo Shaw
- ☐ 21 Mark Farnsworth
- ☐ 22 Steve DeSalvo
- ☐ 23 Mike Keckler
- ☐ 24 Jackie Blackburn
- ☐ 25 Jim Moore
- ☐ 26 Duane Gustavson
- ☐ 27 Mike Alvarez
- ☐ 28 Luis DeLosSantos
- ☐ 29 Derek Vanacore
- ☐ 30 Jose Rodiles

1985 Greensboro Hornets TCMA

This 28-card standard-size set of the 1985 Greensboro Hornets, a Class A South Atlantic League affiliate of the Boston Red Sox, features blue-bordered posed color player shots on its fronts. The team name is printed at the top with the player's name and position appearing vertically on the lower left edge. The white back carries the team name and league at the top, followed by the player's name, position, and biography.

	MINT	NRMT	EXC
COMPLETE SET (28)	10.00	4.50	1.25

- ☐ 1 Doug Camilli
- ☐ 2 Alan Ashikinazy
- ☐ 3 Tary Scott
- ☐ 4 Manuel Jose
- ☐ 5 Thomas Bonk
- ☐ 6 Bruce Lockhart
- ☐ 7 Christopher Moritz
- ☐ 8 Joseph Skripko
- ☐ 9 Zachary Crouch
- ☐ 10 Roberto Zambrano
- ☐ 11 Joseph Stephenson
- ☐ 12 Wayne Tremblay
- ☐ 13 Eduardo Zambrano
- ☐ 14 Pat Dewechter
- ☐ 15 Roy Hall
- ☐ 16 James Corsi
- ☐ 17 Daryl Irvine
- ☐ 18 Eric Hetzel
- ☐ 19 David Peterson
- ☐ 20 Daniel Gakeler
- ☐ 21 Ernest Abril
- ☐ 22 Patrick Jelks
- ☐ 23 Jose Flores
- ☐ 24 Eugene Barrios
- ☐ 25 Anthony DeFrancesco
- ☐ 26 Leverne Jackson
- ☐ 27 Bradley Mettler
- ☐ 28 John DePrimo

1985 Greenville Braves Team Issue

	MINT	NRMT	EXC
COMPLETE SET (26)	40.00	18.00	5.00

- ☐ 1 Rick Albert
- ☐ 2 Brian Aviles
- ☐ 3 Jim Beauchamp
- ☐ 4 Glen Bockhorn
- ☐ 5 Larry Bradford
- ☐ 6 Inocencio Guerrero

☐ 7 Tom Hayes
☐ 8 Randy Ingle
☐ 9 Joe Johnson
☐ 10 Mike Knox
☐ 11 Todd Lamb
☐ 12 Rich Leggatt
☐ 13 Bob Luzon
☐ 14 Simon Rosario
☐ 15 Matt Sinatro
☐ 16 Bill Slack
☐ 17 Jeff Taylor
☐ 18 Andre Thomas
☐ 19 Tommy Thompson
☐ 20 Freddie Tiburcio
☐ 21 Andre Treadway
☐ 22 Bob Tumpane
☐ 23 Leo Vargas
☐ 24 Duane Ward
☐ 25 Larry Whisenton
☐ 26 Steve Ziem

1985 Hawaii Islanders Cramer

This 25-card standard-size set of the 1985 Hawaii Islanders, a Class AAA Pacific Coast League affiliate of the Pittsburgh Pirates, features white-bordered posed color player photos on its fronts. The player's name, position, and team name appear at the bottom. The light blue horizontal back carries the player's name and position within a baseball bat icon at the top, followed below by biography and statistics, some enhanced by a cartoon.

	MINT	NRMT	EXC
COMPLETE SET (25)	5.00	2.20	.60

☐ 226 Jim Opie
☐ 227 Sam Khalifa
☐ 228 Scott Loucks
☐ 229 Denio Gonzales
☐ 230 Rick Reuschel
☐ 231 Benny Distefano
☐ 232 Paul Semall
☐ 233 Tommy Sandt MG
☐ 234 Mitchell Page
☐ 235 Steve Shirley
☐ 236 Hedi Vargas
☐ 237 Jim Winn
☐ 238 Trench Davis
☐ 239 Bobby Miscik
☐ 240 Chris Green
☐ 241 Dave Tomlin
☐ 242 Stan Cliburn
☐ 243 Bob Walk
☐ 244 Steve Herz
☐ 245 Ray Krawczyk
☐ 246 John Henry Johnson
☐ 247 John Malkin
☐ 248 Manny Sarmiento
☐ 249 Jeff Zaske
☐ 250 Jerry Dybzinski

1985 Huntsville Stars Jennings

	MINT	NRMT	EXC
COMPLETE SET (25)	12.00	5.50	1.50

☐ 11 Luis Polonia
☐ 14 Brian Graham
☐ 15 Tom Dozier
☐ 16 Terry Steinbach
☐ 17 Chip Conklin
☐ 18 John Marquardt
☐ 19 Ray Thoma
☐ 20 Stan Javier
☐ 21 Bill Mooneyham
☐ 22 Brian Dorsett
☐ 23 Scott Whaley
☐ 24 Gary Lance CO
☐ 25 Brad Fischer MG
☐ 26 Mark Bauer
☐ 30 Larry Smith
☐ 31 Tim Belcher
☐ 32 Darrel Akerfelds
☐ 33 Eric Plunk
☐ 34 Greg Cadaret
☐ 40 Joe Law
☐ 41 Rob Nelson
☐ 42 Wayne Giddings
☐ 43 Rick Stromer
☐ 44 Jose Canseco
☐ NNO Brian Thorson TR

1985 Indianapolis Indians Team Issue

Produced by Tom Aikens, this 36-card 10th Annual Set of the 1985 Indianapolis Indians, a Class AAA American Association affiliate of the Montreal Expos, features posed color player shots on its fronts, and measures approximately 2 1/2" by 3 5/8". A brown stripe above the photo carries the team name; another below the picture carries the player's name and position. The white horizontal back carries the player's autograph facsimile at the top, followed by biography, statistics, and career highlights. This issue includes Andres

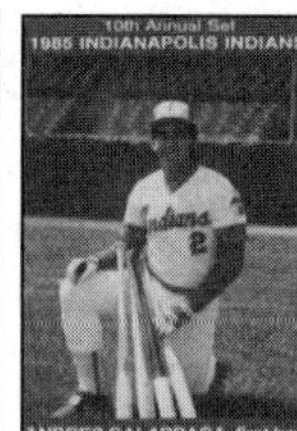

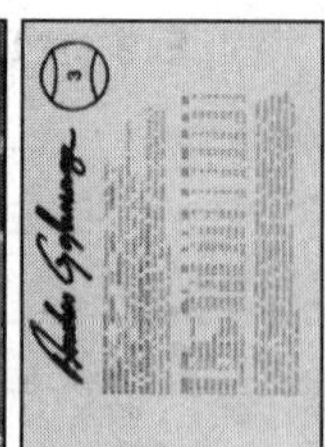

Galarraga's only minor league card appearance. The cards are numbered on the back. Cards 28-36 are authorized reproductions from each of the nine previous Indians sets. Each of these cards is denoted in the checklist below by the year of the set from which it was reproduced. 1,200 sets were produced.

	MINT	NRMT	EXC
COMPLETE SET (36)	60.00	27.00	7.50

☐ 1 Team Card
☐ 2 Felipe Alou MG
☐ 3 Andres Galarraga
☐ 4 Rich Stoll
☐ 5 Roy Johnson
☐ 6 Steve Baker
☐ 7 Mike Fuentes
☐ 8 Tim Cates
☐ 9 Max Venable
☐ 10 Fred Breining
☐ 11 Rene Gonzales
☐ 12 Fred Manrique
☐ 13 Greg Bargar
☐ 14 Al Newman
☐ 15 Sal Butera
☐ 16 Mickey Mahler
☐ 17 Dave Hostetler
☐ 18 Paul Hertzler
☐ 19 Randy St. Claire
☐ 20 George Bjorkman
☐ 21 Wally Johnson
☐ 22 Jack O'Conner
☐ 23 Dave Hoeksema
☐ 24 Steve Brown
☐ 25 Casey Candaele
☐ 26 They Also Serve
Gene Glynn CO
Lee Garrett TR
Rick Williams CO
☐ 27 Voices of the Indians
Howard Kellman ANN
Tom Akins ANN
☐ 28 Ray Knight '76
☐ 29 Dave Revering '77
☐ 30 Ron Oester '78
☐ 31 Mario Soto '79
☐ 32 Bruce Berenyi '80
☐ 33 Charlie Leibrandt '81
☐ 34 Gary Redus '82
☐ 35 Nick Esasky '83
☐ 36 Bob Rodgers MG '84

1985 International League All-Stars TCMA

Sets with cards #18, #44 and #45 demand a premium, since they were pulled from most sets. Approximately 2,500 sets were produced.

	MINT	NRMT	EXC
COMPLETE SET (42)	40.00	18.00	5.00
COMPLETE SET (45)	60.00	27.00	7.50

☐ 1 Bob Shaffer
☐ 2 Bob Tumpane
☐ 3 Miguel Sosa
☐ 4 Kevin Mitchell
☐ 5 Carlos Rios
☐ 6 Lashelle Tarver
☐ 7 Billy Beane
☐ 8 Doc Estes
☐ 9 Larry Owen
☐ 10 Ed Hearn
☐ 11 Tony Brizzolara
☐ 12 John Rabb
☐ 13 Billy "Steve" Springer
☐ 14 Al Pedrique
☐ 15 John Gibbons
☐ 16 Terry Blocker
☐ 17 Joe Johnson
☐ 18 Charlie Mitchell
☐ 19 Rick Anderson
☐ 20 Jeff Bittiger
☐ 21 Wes Gardner
☐ 22 Roy Majtyka
☐ 23 Bruce Dal Canton
☐ 24 Doc Edwards
☐ 25 Jim Wilson
☐ 26 Juan Bonilla
☐ 27 Scott Ullger
☐ 28 Kelly Paris
☐ 29 Rick Leach
☐ 30 Mike Hart
☐ 31 Kelly Heath
☐ 32 Juan Espino
☐ 33 Dan Briggs
☐ 34 Jim Deshaies
☐ 35 Dave Gallagher
☐ 36 Dan Rohn
☐ 37 Kelly Gruber
☐ 38 Jeff Reed
☐ 39 Dennis Burtt
☐ 40 Brad Havens
☐ 41 Tom Henke
☐ 42 Tom Rowe
☐ 43 Brian Allard
☐ 44 Mike Greenwell
☐ 45 Rac Slider

1985 Iowa Cubs TCMA

This 34-card standard-size set of the 1985 Iowa Cubs, a Class AAA American Association affiliate of the Chicago Cubs, features blue-bordered posed color player shots on its fronts. The team name is printed at the top with the player's name and position appearing vertically on the lower left edge. The white back carries the team name and league at the top, followed by the player's name, position, and biography.

	MINT	NRMT	EXC
COMPLETE SET (34)	15.00	6.75	1.85

☐ 1 Tony Castillo
☐ 2 Bill Hayes
☐ 3 Trey Brooks
☐ 4 Tom Lombarski
☐ 5 Paul Noce
☐ 6 Dave Owen
☐ 7 Julio Valdez
☐ 8 Brian Dayett
☐ 9 Tom Grant
☐ 10 Billy Hatcher
☐ 11 Chico Walker
☐ 12 Jay Baller
☐ 13 Derek Botelho
☐ 14 Dave Gumpert
☐ 15 Scott Holman
☐ 16 Bill Johnson
☐ 17 Ron Meridith
☐ 18 Sam Bernabe
☐ 19 Jon Perlman
☐ 20 Ken Pryce
☐ 21 Larry Rothschild
☐ 22 Mark Gillaspie
☐ 23 Dave Hostetler
☐ 24 Greg Hoffmann
☐ 25 Dick Cummings
☐ 26 Ken Grandquist
☐ 27 Don Silverman
☐ 28 Larry Cox
☐ 29 Jim Colborn
☐ 30 Steve Carroll
☐ 31 Steve Weck
☐ 33 Bruce Bielenberg
☐ 35 Danny Woolis
Cubby
Del Roy Smith
Batboys and Mascot
☐ 36 Steve Rodiles

1985 Kinston Blue Jays TCMA

This 26-card standard-size set of the 1985 Kinston Blue Jays, a Class A Carolina League affiliate of the Toronto Blue Jays, features blue-bordered posed color player shots on its fronts. The team name is printed at the top with the player's name and position appearing vertically on the lower left edge. The white back carries the team name and league at the top, followed by the player's name, position, and biography. The Howard and Carter Funeral Home sponsored the set. This issue includes the debuts of Pat Borders, Jose Mesa and Glenallen Hill.

	MINT	NRMT	EXC
COMPLETE SET (26)	30.00	13.50	3.70

☐ 1 Mark Clemons
☐ 2 Omar Bencomo
☐ 3 Tony Castillo
☐ 4 Mike Cullen
☐ 5 Mark Dickman
☐ 6 Perry Lychak
☐ 7 Alan McKay
☐ 8 Jose Mesa
☐ 9 Pablo Reyes
☐ 10 Jose Segura
☐ 11 Willie Shanks
☐ 12 Mark Cooper
☐ 13 Nelson Liriano
☐ 14 Randy Romagna
☐ 15 Pat Borders
☐ 16 Webster Garrison
☐ 17 Omar Malave
☐ 18 Joselito Reyes
☐ 19 Glenallen Hill
☐ 20 Drex Roberts
☐ 21 Geronimo Berroa
☐ 22 Ken Whitfield
☐ 23 Eric Yelding
☐ 24 Grady Little MG
☐ 25 Rocket Wheeler CO
☐ 26 Tex Drake (Batboy)

1985 Las Vegas Stars Cramer

This 25-card standard-size set of the 1985 Las Vegas Stars, a Class AAA Pacific Coast League affiliate of the San Diego Padres, features white-bordered posed color player photos on its fronts. The player's name, position, and team name appear at the bottom. The light blue horizontal back carries the player's name and position within a baseball bat icon at the top, followed below by biography and statistics, some enhanced by a cartoon.

	MINT	NRMT	EXC
COMPLETE SET (25)	20.00	9.00	2.50

☐ 101 Victor Rodriguez
☐ 102 Rusty Tillman
☐ 103 John Kruk
☐ 104 Ray Hayward
☐ 105 Mark Parent
☐ 106 Steve Lubratich
☐ 107 Marty Decker
☐ 108 Ed Rodriguez
☐ 109 Lance McCullers
☐ 110 Bob Cluck MG
☐ 111 Walt Vanderbush
☐ 112 Gene Walter
☐ 113 George Hinshaw
☐ 114 Ray Smith
☐ 115 Steve Garcia
☐ 116 Randy Asadoor
☐ 117 Bob Patterson
☐ 118 Keefe Cato
☐ 119 Jim Leopold
☐ 120 Ed Wojna
☐ 121 Sonny Siebert CO
☐ 122 Tim Pyznarski
☐ 123 Mike Couchee
☐ 124 Kevin Kristan
☐ 125 James Steels

1985 Little Falls Mets TCMA

This 27-card standard-size set of the 1985 Little Falls Mets, a Class A New York-Penn League affiliate of the New York Mets, features blue-bordered posed color player shots on its fronts. The team name is printed at the top with the player's name and position appearing vertically on the lower left edge. The white back carries the team name and league at the top, followed by the player's name, position, and biography.

	MINT	NRMT	EXC
COMPLETE SET (27)	10.00	4.50	1.25

☐ 1 Mike Anderson
☐ 2 Kevin Armstrong
☐ 3 Steve Brueggemann
☐ 4 Ron Dominico
☐ 5 Brian Givens
☐ 6 Lorin Jundy
☐ 7 Kelvin Page
☐ 8 Chris Rauth
☐ 9 Jeff Richardson
☐ 10 John Touzzo
☐ 11 Tom Wachs
☐ 12 Todd Welborn
☐ 13 Mark Brunswick
☐ 14 Ron Narcisse
☐ 15 Rob Colescott
☐ 16 Kurt DeLuca
☐ 17 Andres Espinoza
☐ 18 Dave Gelatt
☐ 19 T.J. Johnson
☐ 20 Luis Natera
☐ 21 Craig Repoz
☐ 22 Joaquin Contreras
☐ 23 Cliff Gonzales
☐ 24 Maury Gooden
☐ 25 Dean Johnson
☐ 26 Johnny Monell
☐ 27 Bryant Robertson

1985 Louisville Redbirds Riley's

	MINT	NRMT	EXC
COMPLETE SET (30)	15.00	6.75	1.85

☐ 1 Jim Fregosi MG
☐ 2 Joe Rigoli
☐ 3 Frank Evans
☐ 4 Jerry McKune
☐ 5 Vince Coleman
☐ 6 Andy Hassler
☐ 7 Kevin Hagen
☐ 8 Jeff Keener
☐ 9 Dave Kable
☐ 10 Jed Smith
☐ 11 Randy Hunt
☐ 12 Joe Pettini
☐ 13 Curt Ford
☐ 14 Dave Clements

- ☐ 15 Jose Oquendo
- ☐ 16 Matt Keough
- ☐ 17 Bill Lyons
- ☐ 18 Pat Perry
- ☐ 19 Willie Lozado
- ☐ 20 Fred Martinez
- ☐ 21 Jack Ayer
- ☐ 22 Mike LaValliere
- ☐ 23 John Morris
- ☐ 24 Mick Shade
- ☐ 25 Ben Hayes
- ☐ 26 Rick Ownbey
- ☐ 27 Casey Parsons
- ☐ 28 Todd Worrell
- ☐ 29 Mike Anderson
- ☐ 30 Ron Jackson

1985 Lynchburg Mets TCMA

This 27-card standard-size set of the 1985 Lynchburg Mets, a Class A Carolina League affiliate of the New York Mets, features blue-bordered posed color player shots on its fronts. The team name is printed at the top with the player's name and position appearing vertically on the lower left edge. The white back carries the team name and league at the top, followed by the player's name, position, and biography. Approximately 2,500 sets were produced.

	MINT	NRMT	EXC
COMPLETE SET (27)	10.00	4.50	1.25

- ☐ 1 Mike Cubbage
- ☐ 2 Jim Bibby
- ☐ 3 Dave Tresch
- ☐ 4 Jeff Innis
- ☐ 5 Reggie Dobie
- ☐ 6 Mickey Weston
- ☐ 7 Wray Bergendahl
- ☐ 8 Dave Jensen
- ☐ 9 Jose Bautista
- ☐ 10 David Wyatt
- ☐ 11 Tom Burns
- ☐ 12 Kyle Hartshorn
- ☐ 13 Joe Klink
- ☐ 14 Kevin Burrell
- ☐ 15 Al Carmichael
- ☐ 16 Steve Philips
- ☐ 17 Chris Maloney
- ☐ 18 Keith Miller
- ☐ 19 Kevin Elster
- ☐ 20 Frank Moscat
- ☐ 21 Wilmer Caraballo
- ☐ 22 Andy Lawrence
- ☐ 23 Rey Martinez
- ☐ 24 John Wilson
- ☐ 25 Shawn Abner
- ☐ 26 George Doggett
- ☐ 27 Scott Little

1985 Madison Muskies Police

	MINT	NRMT	EXC
COMPLETE SET (25)	25.00	11.00	3.10

- ☐ 1 Roy Anderson
- ☐ 2 Russ Applegate
- ☐ 3 Tony Arias
- ☐ 4 Greg Brake
- ☐ 5 Todd Burns
- ☐ 6 Brian Criswell
- ☐ 7 Mike Cupples
- ☐ 8 Brian Dorsett
- ☐ 9 P.J. Dietrick
- ☐ 10 Arturo Ferreira
- ☐ 11 Bob Gould
- ☐ 12 Darel Hansen
- ☐ 13 Mark Howie
- ☐ 14 Felix Jose
- ☐ 15 John Kanter
- ☐ 16 Russ Kibler
- ☐ 17 Joe Kramer
- ☐ 18 Andy Krause
- ☐ 19 Mark Leonette
- ☐ 20 Jim Nettles MG
- ☐ 21 Scott Sabo
- ☐ 22 Faustoe Santos
- ☐ 23 Dave Schober TR
- ☐ 24 Scotty Lee Whaley
- ☐ 25 Rick Wise CO

1985 Madison Muskies TCMA

This 25-card standard-size set of the 1985 Madison Muskies, a Class A Midwest League affiliate of the Oakland Athletics, features blue-bordered posed color player shots on its fronts. The team name is printed at the top with the player's name and position appearing vertically on the lower left edge. The white back carries the team name and league at the top, followed by the player's name, position, and biography.

	MINT	NRMT	EXC
COMPLETE SET (25)	25.00	11.00	3.10

- ☐ 1 Scott Sabo
- ☐ 2 Faustoe Santos
- ☐ 3 Scott Whaley
- ☐ 4 Roy Anderson
- ☐ 5 Russell Applegate
- ☐ 6 Antonio Arlas
- ☐ 7 Gregory Burns
- ☐ 8 Todd Burns
- ☐ 9 Brian Criswell
- ☐ 10 Michael Cupples
- ☐ 11 Brian Dorsett
- ☐ 12 Patrick Dietrick
- ☐ 13 Jose Ferreira
- ☐ 14 Robert Gould
- ☐ 15 Darel Hansen
- ☐ 16 Mark Howie
- ☐ 17 Domingo (Felix) Jose
- ☐ 18 John Kanter
- ☐ 19 Russell Kibler
- ☐ 20 Joseph Kramer
- ☐ 21 Andrew Krause
- ☐ 22 Mark Leonette
- ☐ 23 James Nettles
- ☐ 24 Richard Wise
- ☐ 25 David Schober

1985 Maine Guides TCMA

This 30-card standard-size set of the 1985 Maine Guides, a Class AAA International League affiliate of the Cleveland Indians, features blue-bordered posed color player shots on its fronts. The team name is printed at the top with the player's name and position appearing vertically on the lower left edge. The white back carries the team name and league at the top, followed by the player's name, position, and biography.

	MINT	NRMT	EXC
COMPLETE SET (30)	10.00	4.50	1.25

- ☐ 1 Jeff Barkley
- ☐ 2 Dave Beard
- ☐ 3 Jose Calderon
- ☐ 4 Mark Calvert
- ☐ 5 Bryan Clark
- ☐ 6 Keith Creel
- ☐ 8 Jerry Reed
- ☐ 9 Tommy Rowe
- ☐ 10 Roy Smith
- ☐ 11 Rich Thompson
- ☐ 12 Jim Siwy
- ☐ 13 Jose Roman
- ☐ 14 Pat Dempsey
- ☐ 15 Kevin Buckley
- ☐ 16 Geno Petralli
- ☐ 17 Shanie Dugas
- ☐ 18 Barry Evans
- ☐ 19 Jeff Moronko
- ☐ 20 Junior Noboa
- ☐ 21 Luis Quinones
- ☐ 22 Danny Rohn
- ☐ 23 Orlando Sanchez
- ☐ 24 Jim Wilson
- ☐ 26 Mike Brewer
- ☐ 27 Dave Gallagher
- ☐ 28 Dwight Taylor
- ☐ 29 Doc Edwards
- ☐ 30 Brian Allard
- ☐ 31 Steve Ciszczon
- ☐ 32 Scott Tellgren

1985 Mexico City Tigers TCMA

This 29-card standard-size set of the 1985 Mexico City Tigers, a Class AAA Mexican League Independent, features blue-bordered posed color player shots on its fronts. The team name is printed at the top with the player's name and position appearing vertically on the lower left edge. The white back carries the team name and league at the top, followed by the player's name, position, and biography.

	MINT	NRMT	EXC
COMPLETE SET (29)	10.00	4.50	1.25

- ☐ 1 Jesus Rios
- ☐ 2 Roberto Mendez
- ☐ 3 Maurillo Arangure
- ☐ 4 Oswaldo Alvarez
- ☐ 5 Martin Buitimea
- ☐ 6 Ramon Villegas
- ☐ 7 Rodolfo Dimas
- ☐ 8 Francisco Montano
- ☐ 9 Ildefonso Velazquel
- ☐ 10 Lorenzo Retes
- ☐ 11 Francisco Coto
- ☐ 12 Juan Palafox
- ☐ 13 Martin Torres
- ☐ 14 Jose Aguilar
- ☐ 15 Jose Alvarado
- ☐ 16 Ismael Jaime
- ☐ 17 Homar Rojas
- ☐ 18 Adulfo Camacho
- ☐ 19 Jose De Jesus
- ☐ 20 Manuel Morales
- ☐ 21 Amado Peralta
- ☐ 22 Ricardo Renteria
- ☐ 23 Nicolas Castaneda
- ☐ 24 Antionio Castro
- ☐ 25 Matias Caprillo
- ☐ 26 Javier Cruz
- ☐ 27 Juan Bellacetin
- ☐ 28 Luis Ibarra
- ☐ 29 Chano Chicken

1985 Miami Hurricanes

	MINT	NRMT	EXC
COMPLETE SET (16)	10.00	4.50	1.25

- ☐ 1 Dan Davies
- ☐ 2 Rusty DeBold
- ☐ 3 Frank Dominguez
- ☐ 4 Mike Fiore
- ☐ 5 Ron Fraser CO
- ☐ 6 Chris Hart
- ☐ 7 Calvin James
- ☐ 8 Jon Leake
- ☐ 9 Chris Magno
- ☐ 10 The Miami Maniac (Mascot)
- ☐ 11 Alain Patenaude
- ☐ 12 Ric Raether
- ☐ 13 Rick Richardi
- ☐ 14 Don Rowland
- ☐ 15 Kevin Sheary
- ☐ 16 Julio Solis

1985 Midland Angels TCMA

This 25-card standard-size set of the 1985 Midland Angels, a Class AA Texas League affiliate of the California Angels, features blue-bordered posed color player shots on its fronts. The team name is printed at the top with the player's name and position appearing vertically on the lower left edge. The white back carries the team name and league at the top, followed by the player's name, position, and biography.

	MINT	NRMT	EXC
COMPLETE SET (25)	25.00	11.00	3.10

- ☐ 1 Tito Nanni
- ☐ 2 Bryan Price
- ☐ 3 Greg Key
- ☐ 4 Fred Wilburn
- ☐ 5 Mark Bonner
- ☐ 6 David Heath
- ☐ 7 Doug McKenzie
- ☐ 8 Devon White
- ☐ 9 Dan Murphy
- ☐ 10 Joe Maddon
- ☐ 11 Tom Bryden
- ☐ 12 Don Timberlake
- ☐ 13 Steve Finch
- ☐ 14 Doug Davis
- ☐ 15 Ken Angulo
- ☐ 16 Spiro Psaltis
- ☐ 17 Mark McLemore
- ☐ 18 Kevin Davis
- ☐ 19 Billie Merrifield
- ☐ 20 Aurelio Monteagudo
- ☐ 21 Scott Suehr
- ☐ 22 Ed Delzer
- ☐ 23 Juan Cruz
- ☐ 24 Reggie Montgomery
- ☐ 25 Jullan Gonzales

1985 Modesto A's Chong

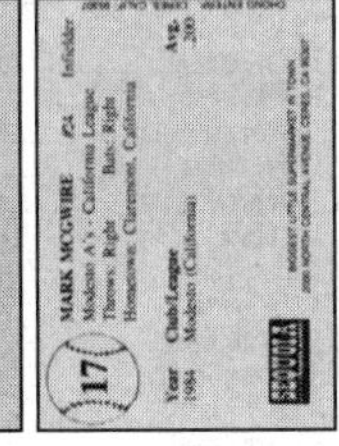

This 28-card set of the 1985 Modesto A's, a Class A California League affiliate of the Oakland Athletics, features white-bordered posed black-and-white player photos on its fronts. The player's name and position is printed at the bottom. The white back carries the player's name, position and biography. This issue includes the minor league card debut of Mark McGwire. Sets have either a correct spelling Mark McGwire or an error Mark McGuire.

	MINT	NRMT	EXC
COMPLETE COR SET (28)	120.00	55.00	15.00
COMPLETE ERR SET (28)	125.00	55.00	15.50

- ☐ 1 Kevin Stock
- ☐ 2 Paul Bradley
- ☐ 3 Antonio Cabrera
- ☐ 4 Twayne Harris
- ☐ 5 Oscar De Chavez
- ☐ 6 Eric Garrett
- ☐ 7 Brian Guinn
- ☐ 8 Allan Heath
- ☐ 9 Joe Strong
- ☐ 10 Mike Fulmer
- ☐ 11 Randy Harvey
- ☐ 12 Kevin Coughlon
- ☐ 13 Jim Eppard
- ☐ 14 Pete Kendrick
- ☐ 15 Jim Jones
- ☐ 16 Steve Howard
- ☐ 17A Mark McGwire ERR Sic, McGuire
- ☐ 17B Mark McGwire COR
- ☐ 18 Rick Rodriguez
- ☐ 19 Mark Bauer
- ☐ 20 Damon Farmar
- ☐ 21 Dave Wilder
- ☐ 22 Stan Hilton
- ☐ 23 Doug Scherer
- ☐ 24 Bob Loscalzo
- ☐ 25 Joe Odom
- ☐ 26 George Mitterwald MG
- ☐ 27 Rick Tronerud CO
- ☐ 28 John Cartelli TR

1985 Nashua Pirates TCMA

This 29-card standard-size set of the 1985 Nashua Pirates, a Class AA Eastern League affiliate of the Pittsburgh Pirates, features blue-bordered posed color player shots on its fronts. The team name is printed at the top with the player's name and position appearing vertically on the lower left edge. The white back carries the team name and league at the top, followed by the player's name, position, and biography.

	MINT	NRMT	EXC
COMPLETE SET (29)	15.00	6.75	1.85

- ☐ 1 Scott Bailes
- ☐ 2 Kerry Baker
- ☐ 3 Mike Berger
- ☐ 4 Craig Brown
- ☐ 5 Kim Christenson
- ☐ 6 Nelson DeLaRosa
- ☐ 7 Dorley Downs
- ☐ 8 Stan Fansler
- ☐ 9 Felix Fermin
- ☐ 10 Ken Ford
- ☐ 11 Sam Haro
- ☐ 12 Dave Johnson
- ☐ 13 Tony Laird
- ☐ 14 Larry Lamonde
- ☐ 15 Ravelo Manzanillo
- ☐ 16 Lee Marcheskie
- ☐ 17 Steve McAllister
- ☐ 18 Mitch McKelvy
- ☐ 19 Pete Rice
- ☐ 20 Leon Roberts
- ☐ 21 Ruben Rodriguez
- ☐ 22 Leo Sanchez
- ☐ 23 Rich Sauveur
- ☐ 24 Don Taylor
- ☐ 25 Dave Tumbas
- ☐ 26 Donald Williams
- ☐ 27 John Lipon
- ☐ 28 George Como
- ☐ 29 Jerome Mileur

1985 Nashville Sounds Team Issue

	MINT	NRMT	EXC
COMPLETE SET (25)	5.00	2.20	.60

- ☐ 1 Doug Baker
- ☐ 2 Darrell Brown
- ☐ 3 Chuck Cary
- ☐ 4 Jeff Conner
- ☐ 5 Brian Denman
- ☐ 6 Scott Earl
- ☐ 7 Bryan Kelly
- ☐ 8 Rusty Kuntz
- ☐ 9 Mike Laga
- ☐ 10 Dwight Lowry
- ☐ 11 Scotti Madison
- ☐ 12 Don McGann TR
- ☐ 13 Gordy McKenzie MG
- ☐ 14 Dan Meyer
- ☐ 15 Bobby Mitchell
- ☐ 16 Rich Monteleone
- ☐ 17 John Pacella
- ☐ 18 Chris Pittaro
- ☐ 19 Joe Pittman
- ☐ 20 Leon Roberts
- ☐ 21 Steve Shirley
- ☐ 22 Nelson Simmons
- ☐ 23 Robert Stoddard
- ☐ 24 Paul Voight
- ☐ 25 Don Werner

1985 Newark Orioles TCMA

This 25-card standard-size set of the 1985 Newark Orioles, a Class A New York-Penn League affiliate of the Baltimore Orioles, features blue-bordered posed color player shots on its fronts. The team name is printed at the top with the player's name and position appearing vertically on the lower left edge. The white back carries the team name and league at the top, followed by the player's name, position, and biography.

	MINT	NRMT	EXC
COMPLETE SET (25)	10.00	4.50	1.25

- ☐ 1 Scott Williams
- ☐ 2 Randy King
- ☐ 3 Ty Nichols
- ☐ 4 Greg Talamantez
- ☐ 5 Jeff Tackett
- ☐ 6 Hemmy McFarlane
- ☐ 7 Tony Rohan
- ☐ 8 Mike Holm
- ☐ 9 Gerald Adams
- ☐ 10 Henry Gonzalez
- ☐ 11 Wayne Wilson
- ☐ 12 Benny Bautista
- ☐ 13 Sherwin Cinjntje
- ☐ 14 Rico Rossy
- ☐ 15 Robert Gutierrez
- ☐ 16 Mark Schockman
- ☐ 17 Rob Dromerhauser
- ☐ 18 Ray Crone
- ☐ 19 Chris Gaeta
- ☐ 20 Pat Van Heyningen
- ☐ 21 Pete Mancini
- ☐ 22 Jesse Vazquez
- ☐ 23 Matt Skinner
- ☐ 24 Kevin Burke
- ☐ 25 Frank Bellino

1985 Oklahoma City 89ers TCMA

This 30-card standard-size set of the 1985 Oklahoma City 89ers, a Class AAA American Association affiliate of the Texas Rangers, features blue-bordered posed color player shots on its fronts. The team name is printed at the top with the player's name and position appearing vertically on the lower left edge. The white back carries the team name and league at the top, followed by the player's name, position, and biography. Approximately 2,500 sets were produced.

	MINT	NRMT	EXC
COMPLETE SET (30)	25.00	11.00	3.10

- ☐ 1 Orlando Mercado
- ☐ 2 Mitch Zwolensky
- ☐ 3 Jeff Kunkel
- ☐ 4 Mike Jirchele
- ☐ 5 Geno Petralli
- ☐ 6 Jim Anderson
- ☐ 7 Tommy Boggs
- ☐ 8 Glen Cook
- ☐ 9 Ricky Wright
- ☐ 10 Tony Fossas
- ☐ 11 Jose Guzman
- ☐ 12 Mike Parrott
- ☐ 13 Tommy Shimp
- ☐ 14 Greg Cambell
- ☐ 15 Dave Oliver
- ☐ 16 George Wright
- ☐ 17 Steve Buechele
- ☐ 18 Oddibe McDowell
- ☐ 19 Bob Sebra
- ☐ 20 Jim Maler
- ☐ 21 Bob Brower
- ☐ 22 Mike Rubel
- ☐ 23 Dave Stockstill
- ☐ 24 Rusty Gerhardt
- ☐ 25 Nick Capra
- ☐ 26 Dale Mohorcic
- ☐ 27 Dale Murray
- ☐ 28 Greg Tabor
- ☐ 29 Chuckie Canady
- ☐ 30 Bill Earley

1985 Omaha Royals TCMA

This 31-card standard-size set of the 1985 Omaha Royals, a Class AAA American Association affiliate of the Kansas City Royals, features blue-bordered posed color player shots on its fronts. The team name is printed at the top with the player's name and position appearing vertically on the lower left edge. The white back carries the team name and league at the top, followed by the player's name, position, and biography. This issue includes a third year minor league card of David Cone.

	MINT	NRMT	EXC
COMPLETE SET (31)	40.00	18.00	5.00

- ☐ 1 Bil Gorman
- ☐ 2 Matt Bassett
- ☐ 3 Nick Swartz
- ☐ 4 Frank Mancuso
- ☐ 5 Terry Wendlandt
- ☐ 6 Gus Cherry
- ☐ 7 Les Strode
- ☐ 8 Rich Murray
- ☐ 9 Pat Putnam
- ☐ 10 Tony Ferreira
- ☐ 11 Rich Dubee
- ☐ 12 Butch Davis
- ☐ 13 Mike Griffin
- ☐ 14 Renie Martin
- ☐ 15 Mark Huismann
- ☐ 16 Jamie Quirk
- ☐ 17 Jim Scranton
- ☐ 18 Mike Kinnunen
- ☐ 19 John Morris
- ☐ 20 Marty Wilkerson
- ☐ 21 Rondin Johnson
- ☐ 22 Gene Lamont
- ☐ 23 Mike Kingery
- ☐ 24 Dave Leeper
- ☐ 25 Dave Cone
- ☐ 26 Al Hargesheimer
- ☐ 27 Kenny Baker
- ☐ 28 Buster Keeton
- ☐ 29 Bill Pecota
- ☐ 30 Bob Hegman
- ☐ 31 Brian Pohlberg

1985 Orlando Twins TCMA

This 26-card standard-size set of the 1985 Orlando Twins, a Class AA Southern League affiliate of the Minnesota Twins, features blue-bordered posed color player shots on its fronts. The team name is printed at the top with the player's name and position appearing vertically on the lower left edge. The white back carries the team name and league at the top, followed by the player's name, position, and biography.

	MINT	NRMT	EXC
COMPLETE SET (26)	10.00	4.50	1.25

- ☐ 1 Steve Aragon
- ☐ 2 Erez Borowsky
- ☐ 3 Mark Davidson
- ☐ 4 Paul Felix
- ☐ 5 Mark Funderburk
- ☐ 6 Dan Hanggie
- ☐ 7 Alexis Marte
- ☐ 8 Mike Moreno
- ☐ 9 Greg Morhardt
- ☐ 10 Bobby Ralston
- ☐ 11 Sam Sorce
- ☐ 12 Jeff Trout
- ☐ 13 Mike Verkuilen
- ☐ 14 Ossie Alfonso
- ☐ 15 Al Cardwood
- ☐ 16 Danny Clay
- ☐ 17 Ken Klump
- ☐ 18 Paul Mancuso
- ☐ 19 Bob Mulligan
- ☐ 20 Les Straker
- ☐ 21 Tim Wiseman
- ☐ 22 Charlie Manuel
- ☐ 23 Wayne Hattaway
- ☐ 24 Dave Williams
- ☐ 25 Gorman Heimueller
- ☐ 26 Craig Henderson

1985 Osceola Astros Team Issue

This 30-card set of the 1985 Osceola Astros, a Class A Florida State League affiliate of the Houston Astros, features the minor league card debut of Ken Caminiti.

	MINT	NRMT	EXC
COMPLETE SET (30)	125.00	55.00	15.50

- ☐ 1 Dave Cripe
- ☐ 2 Charley Taylor
- ☐ 3 Mark Baker
- ☐ 4 Earl Cash
- ☐ 5 Mike Cerefin
- ☐ 6 Greg Dube
- ☐ 7 Mike Friederich
- ☐ 8 Arbrey Lucas
- ☐ 9 Rob Mallicoat
- ☐ 10 Mark Mangham
- ☐ 11 Chuck Mathews
- ☐ 12 Doug Shaab
- ☐ 13 Troy Afenir
- ☐ 14 Mark Reynolds
- ☐ 15 Glenn Sherlock
- ☐ 16 Karl Allaire
- ☐ 17 Ken Caminiti
- ☐ 18 Ryan Job
- ☐ 19 Clarke Lange
- ☐ 20 Jim O'Dell
- ☐ 21 Bob Parker
- ☐ 22 Curtis Burke
- ☐ 23 Tony Hampton
- ☐ 24 Scott Houp
- ☐ 25 Mike Stellern
- ☐ 26 Gerald Young
- ☐ 27 Larry Lasky TR
- ☐ 28 Kevin Jones Batboy
- ☐ 29 Kirk Jones Batboy
- ☐ 30 David Rosen Clubhouse Attendant

1985 Pawtucket Red Sox TCMA

This 20-card standard-size set of the 1985 Pawtucket Red Sox, a Class AAA International League affiliate of the Boston Red Sox, features blue-bordered posed color player shots on its fronts. The team name is printed at the top with the player's name and position appearing vertically on the lower left edge. The white back carries the team name and league at the top, followed by the player's name, position, and biography.

	MINT	NRMT	EXC
COMPLETE SET (20)	25.00	11.00	3.10

- ☐ 1 Gus Burgess
- ☐ 2 Juan Bustabad
- ☐ 3 Pat Dodson
- ☐ 4 Mike Greenwell
- ☐ 5 Paul Hundhammer
- ☐ 7 Dave Malpeso
- ☐ 8 Mike Mesh
- ☐ 9 Garry Miller-Jones
- ☐ 10 Sam Nattile
- ☐ 11 Kevin Romine
- ☐ 12 Danny Sheaffer
- ☐ 13 Robin Fuson
- ☐ 14 Rac Slider
- ☐ 15 Dave Sax
- ☐ 16 Tony Herron
- ☐ 17 Tom McCarthy
- ☐ 18 Kevin Kane
- ☐ 19 Mitch Johnson
- ☐ 20 Charlie Mitchell
- ☐ 21 George Mercerod

1985 Phoenix Giants Cramer

This 25-card standard-size set of the 1985 Phoenix Giants, a Class AAA Pacific Coast League affiliate of the San Francisco Giants, features white-bordered posed color player photos on its fronts. The player's name, position, and team name appear at the bottom. The light blue horizontal back carries the player's name and position within a baseball bat icon at the top, followed below by biography and statistics, some enhanced by a cartoon.

	MINT	NRMT	EXC
COMPLETE SET (25)	5.00	2.20	.60

- ☐ 176 Jack Lazorko
- ☐ 177 Randy Kutcher
- ☐ 178 Larry Crews
- ☐ 179 Randy Gomez
- ☐ 180 Fran Mullins
- ☐ 181 Mike Woodard
- ☐ 182 Phil Oullette
- ☐ 183 John Rabb
- ☐ 184 Jeff Robinson
- ☐ 185 Mark Schuster
- ☐ 186 Pat Adams
- ☐ 187 Jim Lefebvre MG
- ☐ 188 Ricky Adams
- ☐ 189 Kelly Downs
- ☐ 190 Roger Mason
- ☐ 191 Bob Lacey
- ☐ 192 Doug Mansolino CO
- ☐ 193 Kevin Rhomberg
- ☐ 194 Augie Schmidt
- ☐ 195 Tack Wilson
- ☐ 196 Greg Schultz
- ☐ 197 Bobby Cummings
- ☐ 198 Colin Ward
- ☐ 199 Mark Grant
- ☐ 200 Jeff Cornell

1985 Portland Beavers Cramer

This 25-card standard-size set of the 1985 Portland Beavers, a Class AAA Pacific Coast League affiliate of the Philadelphia Phillies, features white-bordered posed color player photos on its fronts. The player's name, position, and team name appear at the bottom. The light blue horizontal back carries the player's name and position within a baseball bat icon at the top, followed below by biography and statistics, some enhanced by a cartoon.

	MINT	NRMT	EXC
COMPLETE SET (25)	30.00	13.50	3.70

- ☐ 26 David Rucker
- ☐ 27 Gib Seibert
- ☐ 28 Dave Shipanoff
- ☐ 29 Chris James
- ☐ 30 Steve Moses
- ☐ 31 Rocky Childress
- ☐ 32 Alan LeBoeuf
- ☐ 33 Arturo Gonzalez
- ☐ 34 Rick Schu
- ☐ 35 Bill Dancy MG
- ☐ 36 Jim Olander
- ☐ 37 Randy Salava
- ☐ 38 Mike Maddux
- ☐ 39 Bill Nahorodny
- ☐ 40 Tony Ghelfi
- ☐ 41 Jay Davisson
- ☐ 42 Darren Daulton
- ☐ 43 Francisco Melendez
- ☐ 44 Ralph Citarella
- ☐ 45 Rodger Cole
- ☐ 46 Ken Dowell
- ☐ 47 Bob Tiefenauer CO
- ☐ 48 Greg Legg
- ☐ 49 Rick Surhoff
- ☐ 50 Mike Diaz

1985 Prince William Pirates TCMA

This 31-card standard-size set of the 1985 Prince William Pirates, a Class A Carolina League affiliate of the Pittsburgh Pirates, features blue-bordered posed color player shots on its fronts. The team name is printed at the top with the player's name and position appearing vertically on the lower left edge. The white back carries the team name and league at the top, followed by the player's name, position, and biography. This issue includes the minor league card debut of John Smiley.

	MINT	NRMT	EXC
COMPLETE SET (31)	20.00	9.00	2.50

- ☐ 1 Orlando Lind
- ☐ 2 Scott Neal
- ☐ 3 Barry Jones
- ☐ 4 Jose Melendez
- ☐ 5 Chip Cunningham
- ☐ 6 Terry Adkins
- ☐ 7 Robby Russell
- ☐ 8 Dimas Gutierrez
- ☐ 9 Steve Lewis
- ☐ 10 Jim Neidlinger
- ☐ 11 Steve Barnard
- ☐ 12 Mike Folga
- ☐ 13 Chris Lein
- ☐ 14 Lance Belen
- ☐ 15 Scott Borland
- ☐ 16 Shawn Holman
- ☐ 17 Jose Lind
- ☐ 18 Tony Blasucci
- ☐ 19 Gary Grudzinski
- ☐ 20 Reggie Barringer
- ☐ 21 Kevin Gordon
- ☐ 22 John Smiley
- ☐ 23 Ed Ott
- ☐ 24 Mike Stevens
- ☐ 25 Van Evans
- ☐ 26 Frank Klopp
- ☐ 27 J.B. Moore
- ☐ 28 Dave Butters
- ☐ 29 Scott Knox
- ☐ 30 Burk Goldthorn
- ☐ 31 Brian Jones

1985 Richmond Braves TCMA

This 26-card standard-size set of the 1985 Richmond Braves, a Class AAA International League affiliate of the Atlanta Braves, features blue-bordered posed color player shots on its fronts. The team name is printed at the top with the player's name and position appearing vertically on the lower left edge. The white back carries the team name and league at the top, followed by the player's name, position, and biography.

	MINT	NRMT	EXC
COMPLETE SET (26)	10.00	4.50	1.25

- ☐ 1 Tony Brizzolara
- ☐ 2 Marty Clary
- ☐ 3 David Clay
- ☐ 4 Jeff Dedmon
- ☐ 5 Dan Morogiello
- ☐ 6 Mike Payne
- ☐ 7 Gary Reiter
- ☐ 8 Dave Schuler
- ☐ 9 Steve Shields
- ☐ 10 Matt West
- ☐ 11 John Lickert
- ☐ 12 Larry Owen
- ☐ 13 Glenn Gulliver
- ☐ 14 Randy Johnson
- ☐ 15 Carlos Rios
- ☐ 16 Ken Smith
- ☐ 17 Miguel Sosa
- ☐ 18 Doc Estes
- ☐ 19 Lee Graham
- ☐ 20 Gene Roof
- ☐ 21 Milt Thompson
- ☐ 22 John Rabb
- ☐ 23 Bruce Dal Canton
- ☐ 24 Sam Ayoub
- ☐ 25 Sonny Jackson
- ☐ 26 Ray Majtyka

1985 Rochester Red Wings TCMA

This 31-card standard-size set of the 1985 Rochester Red Wings, a Class AAA International League affiliate of the Baltimore Orioles, features blue-bordered posed color player shots on its fronts. The team name is printed at the top with the player's name and position appearing vertically on the lower left edge. The white back carries the team name and league at the top, followed by the player's name, position, and biography.

	MINT	NRMT	EXC
COMPLETE SET (29)	10.00	4.50	1.25
COMPLETE SET W/LATE ISSUES (31)	15.00	6.75	1.85

- ☐ 1 Raymond Corbett
- ☐ 2 Al Pardo
- ☐ 3 Luis Rosado
- ☐ 4 Dave Falcone
- ☐ 5 Leonardo Hernandez
- ☐ 6 Ricky Jones
- ☐ 7 Nelson Norman
- ☐ 8 Kelly Paris
- ☐ 9 James Traber
- ☐ 10 Roderick Allen
- ☐ 11 Darrel Brown
- ☐ 12 Robert Molinaro
- ☐ 13 John Shelby
- ☐ 14 Gerald Augustine
- ☐ 15 Jose Brito
- ☐ 16 Bradley Havens
- ☐ 17 Phillip Huffman
- ☐ 18 Jerry Johnson
- ☐ 19 Odell Jones
- ☐ 20 Joseph Kucharski
- ☐ 21 David Rajsich
- ☐ 22 William Swaggerty
- ☐ 23 Donald Welchel
- ☐ 24 Frank Verdi
- ☐ 25 Sandy Valdespino
- ☐ 26 The Braintrust
- ☐ 27 Kurcharski and Gordon
- ☐ 28 Jamie Reed
- ☐ 29 Mark Wiley
- ☐ 30 Greg Biercevicz (Late Issue)
- ☐ 31 George Bjorkman (Late Issue)

1985 Spokane Indians Cramer

	MINT	NRMT	EXC
COMPLETE SET (24)	6.00	2.70	.75

- ☐ 1 Eric Bauer
- ☐ 2 Bill Blount
- ☐ 3 Jerald Clark
- ☐ 4 Joey Cora
- ☐ 5 Adam Ging
- ☐ 6 Greg Hall
- ☐ 7 Greg Harris
- ☐ 8 Nate Hill
- ☐ 9 Chris Knabenshue
- ☐ 10 Glen Kuiper
- ☐ 11 Joe Lynch
- ☐ 12 Jack Maloof MG
- ☐ 13 Matt Maysey
- ☐ 14 Tom Meagher
- ☐ 15 Maurice Morton
- ☐ 16 Jay Nieporte
- ☐ 17 Eric Nolte
- ☐ 18 Juan Paris
- ☐ 19 Jeff Parks
- ☐ 20 Ramon Rodriguez
- ☐ 21 Norm Sherry CO
- ☐ 22 Bill Stevenson
- ☐ 23 Jorge Suris
- ☐ 24 Jim Tatum

1985 Spokane Indians Greats Cramer

	MINT	NRMT	EXC
COMPLETE SET (24)	6.00	2.70	.75

- ☐ 1 Doyle Alexander
- ☐ 2 John Billingham
- ☐ 3 Bill Buckner
- ☐ 4 Willie Crawford
- ☐ 5 Jim Fairey
- ☐ 6 Alan Foster
- ☐ 7 Steve Garvey
- ☐ 8 Charlie Hough
- ☐ 9 Tommy Hutton
- ☐ 10 Von Joshua
- ☐ 11 Ray Lamb
- ☐ 12 Tom Lasorda MG
- ☐ 13 Dave Lopes
- ☐ 14 Joe Moeller
- ☐ 15 Tom Paciorek
- ☐ 16 John Purden
- ☐ 17 Bill Russell
- ☐ 18 Ted Sizemore
- ☐ 19 Gus Sposito
- ☐ 20 Jack Spring
- ☐ 21 Bob Stinson
- ☐ 22 Bob Valentine
- ☐ 23 Sandy Vance
- ☐ 24 Geoff Zahn

1985 Springfield Cardinals TCMA

This 25-card standard-size set of the 1985 Springfield Cardinals, a Class A Midwest League affiliate of the St. Louis Cardinals, features blue-bordered posed color player shots on its fronts. The team name is printed at the top with the player's name and position appearing vertically on the lower left edge. The white back carries the team name and league at the top, followed by the player's name, position, and biography. This issue includes the minor league card debut of Jeff Fassero.

	MINT	NRMT	EXC
COMPLETE SET (25)	15.00	6.75	1.85

- ☐ 1 John Rigos
- ☐ 2 Rich Embser
- ☐ 3 Jim Fregosi
- ☐ 4 Jim Van Houten
- ☐ 5 John Costello
- ☐ 6 Todd Demeter
- ☐ 7 John Di Gioia
- ☐ 8 Greg Dunn
- ☐ 9 John Fassero
- ☐ 10 Lloyd Merritt MG
- ☐ 11 Mike Fitzgerald
- ☐ 12 Craig Wilson
- ☐ 13 Mike Hartley
- ☐ 14 Matt Kinzer
- ☐ 15 Ron Leon
- ☐ 16 Brad Luther
- ☐ 17 Harry McCulla
- ☐ 18 Steve Turco
- ☐ 19 Steve Turgeon
- ☐ 20 Charles McGrath
- ☐ 21 Jay North
- ☐ 22 Angelo Nunley
- ☐ 23 Pete Stoll
- ☐ 25 Mike Robinson
- ☐ 30 Paul Wilmet

1985 Syracuse Chiefs TCMA

This 31-card standard-size set of the 1985 Syracuse Chiefs, a Class AAA International League affiliate of the Toronto Blue Jays, features blue-bordered posed color player shots on its fronts. The team name is printed at the top with the player's name and position appearing vertically on the lower left edge. The white back carries the team name and league at the top, followed by the player's name, position, and biography. This issue includes the minor league card debut of Fred McGriff. Approximately 3,000 sets were produced.

	MINT	NRMT	EXC
COMPLETE SET (31)	250.00	110.00	31.00

- ☐ 1 Gibson Alba
- ☐ 2 Fred McGriff
- ☐ 3 Gary Allenson
- ☐ 4 Stan Clarke
- ☐ 5 Dale Holman
- ☐ 6 Tom Filer
- ☐ 7 Keith Gilliam
- ☐ 8 Tom Henke
- ☐ 9 Dennis Howard
- ☐ 10 John Woodworth
- ☐ 11 Rick Leach
- ☐ 12 Matt Williams
- ☐ 13 Don Gordon
- ☐ 14 Alex Infante
- ☐ 15 Colin McLaughlin
- ☐ 16 Pat Rooney
- ☐ 17 Mark Poole
- ☐ 18 Jerry Keller
- ☐ 19 Mike Sharperson
- ☐ 20 John Mayberry
- ☐ 21 Doug Ault MG
- ☐ 22 Kelly Gruber
- ☐ 23 Vance McHenry
- ☐ 24 Red Coughlin TR
- ☐ 25 Fred McGriff
  Dale Holman
- ☐ 26 Batboys
- ☐ 27 John Cerutti
- ☐ 28 Dennis Homberg
- ☐ 29 Derwin McNealy
- ☐ 30 Cloyd Boyer
- ☐ 31 Dave Stegman

1985 Tacoma Tigers Cramer

This 25-card standard-size set of the 1985 Tacoma Tigers, a Class AAA Pacific Coast League affiliate of the Oakland Athletics, features white-bordered posed color player photos on its fronts. The player's name, position, and team name appear at the bottom. The light blue horizontal back carries the player's name and position within a baseball bat icon at the top, followed below by biography and statistics, some enhanced by a cartoon.

	MINT	NRMT	EXC
COMPLETE SET (25)	18.00	8.00	2.20

- ☐ 126 Keith Lieppman MG
- ☐ 127 Jose Tolentino
- ☐ 128 Keith Thrower
- ☐ 129 Chuck Estrada CO
- ☐ 130 Ricky Peters
- ☐ 131 Tom Romano
- ☐ 132 Phil Stephenson
- ☐ 133 Jose Rijo
- ☐ 134 Danny Goodwin
- ☐ 135 Thad Reece
- ☐ 136 Mike Ashman
- ☐ 137 Ron Harrison
- ☐ 138 Stan Kyles
- ☐ 139 Steve Kiefer
- ☐ 140 Tim Lambert
- ☐ 141 Doug Scherer
- ☐ 142 Steve Ontiveros
- ☐ 143 Bob Bathe
- ☐ 144 Bob Owchinko
- ☐ 145 Tom Dozier
- ☐ 146 Joe Lansford
- ☐ 147 Steve Mura
- ☐ 148 Bill Bathe
- ☐ 149 Mike Chris
- ☐ 150 Tom Tellman

1985 Tidewater Tides TCMA

This 28-card standard-size set of the 1985 Tidewater Tides, a Class AAA International League affiliate of the New York Mets, features blue-bordered posed color player shots on its fronts. The team name is printed at the top with the player's name and position appearing vertically on the lower left edge. The white back carries the team name and league at the top, followed by the player's name, position, and biography. Approximately 4,000 sets were produced.

	MINT	NRMT	EXC
COMPLETE SET (27)	60.00	27.00	7.50
COMPLETE SET W/COR (28)	70.00	32.00	8.75

- ☐ 1 Rick Lancellotti
- ☐ 2 Terry Leach
- ☐ 3 Sid Fernandez
- ☐ 4 Jeff Bettendorf
- ☐ 5 Calvin Schiraldi
- ☐ 6 Rick Anderson
- ☐ 7 Randy Niemann
- ☐ 8 Jeff Bittiger
- ☐ 9 Wes Gardner
- ☐ 10 Bill Latham
- ☐ 11 Rick Aguilera
- ☐ 12 Ed Olwine
- ☐ 13 Laschelle Tarver
- ☐ 14 Billy Beane
- ☐ 15 John Gibbons
- ☐ 16 Steve Springer COR (White Bat)
- ☐ 17 Steve Springer ERR (Black Bat)
- ☐ 18 Kevin Mitchell
- ☐ 19 Terry Blocker
- ☐ 20 Len Dykstra
- ☐ 21 Ed Hearn
- ☐ 22 Ross Jones
- ☐ 23 Mike Davis
- ☐ 24 Alfredo Pedrique
- ☐ 25 Mark Carreon
- ☐ 26 John Cumberland
- ☐ 27 Bob Schaefer
- ☐ 28 Rick Rainer

1985 Toledo Mud Hens TCMA

This 26-card standard-size set of the 1985 Toledo Mud Hens, a Class AAA International League affiliate of the Detroit Tigers, features blue-bordered posed color player shots on its fronts. The team name is printed at the top with the player's name and position appearing vertically on the lower left edge. The white back carries the team name and league at the top, followed by the player's name, position, and biography.

	MINT	NRMT	EXC
COMPLETE SET (25)	10.00	4.50	1.25
COMPLETE SET (26)	15.00	6.75	1.85

- ☐ 1 Allan Anderson
- ☐ 2 Eric Broersma
- ☐ 3 Mark Brown
- ☐ 4 Dennis Burtt
- ☐ 6 Frank Eufemia
- ☐ 8 Ed Hodge
- ☐ 10 Mark Portugal
- ☐ 11 Mike Walters
- ☐ 12 Len Whitehouse
- ☐ 13 Toby Hernandez
- ☐ 14 Jeff Reed
- ☐ 15 Alvaro Espinoze
- ☐ 16 Houston Jiminez
- ☐ 17 Steve Lombardozzi
- ☐ 18 Scott Ullger
- ☐ 19 Reggie Whittemore
- ☐ 20 Andre David
- ☐ 21 Mike Hart
- ☐ 22 Stan Holmes
- ☐ 23 Greg Howe
- ☐ 24 Jerry Lomastro
- ☐ 25 Al Woods
- ☐ 26 Cal Ermer
- ☐ 27 Jim Shellenback
- ☐ 30 Rich Yett
- ☐ 32 Floyd Cliffer

1985 Tucson Toros Cramer

This 25-card standard-size set of the 1985 Tucson Toros, a Class AAA Pacific Coast League affiliate of the Houston Astros, features white-bordered posed color player photos on its fronts. The player's name, position, and team name appear at the bottom. The light blue horizontal back carries the player's name and position within a baseball bat icon at the top, followed below by biography and statistics, some enhanced by a cartoon.

	MINT	NRMT	EXC
COMPLETE SET (25)	5.00	2.20	.60

- ☐ 51 Chris Jones
- ☐ 52 Eric Bullock
- ☐ 53 Jimmy Johnson MG
- ☐ 54 Mark Ross
- ☐ 55 Larry Acker
- ☐ 56 Manny Hernandez
- ☐ 57 Vern Followell
- ☐ 58 Larry Montgomery
- ☐ 59 Rick Colbert
- ☐ 60 Mark Knudson
- ☐ 61 Rafael Landestoy
- ☐ 62 Stan Hough
- ☐ 63 Mike Calise
- ☐ 64 Tye Waller
- ☐ 65 Glenn Davis
- ☐ 66 Randy Martz
- ☐ 67 Chuck Jackson
- ☐ 68 John Mizerock
- ☐ 69 Ty Gainey
- ☐ 70 Eddie Bonine
- ☐ 71 Pedro Hernandez
- ☐ 72 James Miner
- ☐ 73 Charlie Kerfeld
- ☐ 74 Rex Jones TR
- ☐ 75 Brad Mills

1985 Tulsa Drillers Team Issue

This issue includes the minor league card debut of Ruben Sierra.

	MINT	NRMT	EXC
COMPLETE SET (27)	70.00	32.00	8.75
COMP. SET W/SIERRA (28)	80.00	36.00	10.00

- ☐ 1 Ken Reitz
- ☐ 4 George Crum
- ☐ 6 George Foussianes
- ☐ 7 Oscar Mejia
- ☐ 9 Jamie Doughty
- ☐ 10 Mark Gile
- ☐ 12 Ruben Sierra
- ☐ 14 Barry Brunenkant
- ☐ 17 Larry Pott
- ☐ 18 Bobby Witt
- ☐ 20 Tony Hudson
- ☐ 22 Jeff Moronko
- ☐ 23 Orlando Gomez MGR
- ☐ 24 Jeff Mace
- ☐ 25 Bob Gergen
- ☐ 26 Barry Bass
- ☐ 27 Rob Clark
- ☐ 28 Bill Fahey CO
- ☐ 29 Duane James
- ☐ 29 Dwayne Henry
- ☐ 30 Terry Johnson
- ☐ 31 Javier Ortiz
- ☐ 32 Kirk Killingsworth
- ☐ 33 Scott Anderson
- ☐ 34 Bill Taylor
- ☐ 35 Otto L. Gonzalez
- ☐ 36 Al Lachowicz
- ☐ 37 Clyde Reichard

1985 Utica Blue Sox TCMA

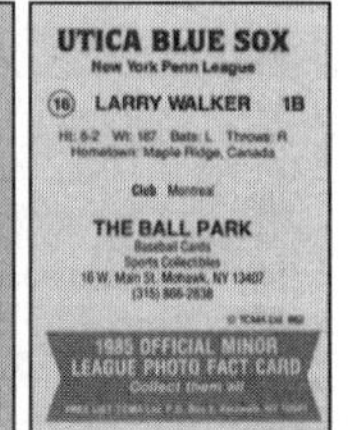

This 26-card standard-size set of the 1985 Utica Blue Sox, a Class A New York-Penn League Independent, features blue-bordered posed color player shots on its fronts. The team name is printed at the top with the player's name and position appearing vertically on the lower left edge. The white back carries the team name and league at the top, followed by the player's name, position, and biography. This issue includes the minor league card debut of Larry Walker.

	MINT	NRMT	EXC
COMPLETE SET (26)	50.00	22.00	6.25

- ☐ 1 Jim Allison
- ☐ 2 Ross Jones
- ☐ 3 Dave Linton
- ☐ 4 Paulino Paixao
- ☐ 5 Bob Sudo
- ☐ 6 Darren Travels
- ☐ 7 Sergio Valdez
- ☐ 8 Rob Williams
- ☐ 9 Roger Dean
- ☐ 10 Pancho Hedfelt
- ☐ 11 Al Hibbs
- ☐ 12 Esteban Beltre

☐ 13 Rodney Clark
☐ 14 Jeff Scheaffer
☐ 15 Alfonso Traverez
☐ 16 Larry Walker
☐ 17 Bob Brown
☐ 18 Andy Donatelli
☐ 19 Ray Garcia
☐ 20 Raymond Noble
☐ 21 Fred Perez
☐ 22 Troy Ricker
☐ 23 Steve St. Claire
☐ 24 Ken Brett
☐ 25 Gene Glynn
☐ 26 Dan Gazzilli

1985 Vancouver Canadians Cramer

This 25-card standard-size set of the 1985 Vancouver Canadians, a Class AAA Pacific Coast League affiliate of the Milwaukee Brewers, features white-bordered posed color player photos on its fronts. The player's name, position, and team name appear at the bottom. The light blue horizontal back carries the player's name and position within a baseball bat icon at the top, followed below by biography and statistics, some enhanced by a cartoon.

	MINT	NRMT	EXC
COMPLETE SET (25)	5.00	2.20	.60

☐ 201 Dan Davidsmeier
☐ 202 Brad Lesley
☐ 203 Tim Leary
☐ 204 Bobby Clark
☐ 205 Juan Castillo
☐ 206 Jim Adduci
Sic, Aducci
☐ 207 Earnie Riles
☐ 208 Mike Paul CO
☐ 209 Dale Sveum
☐ 210 Jamie Cocanower
☐ 211 Mike Felder
☐ 212 Brian Duquette
☐ 213 Jim Paciorek
☐ 214 Bob Skube
☐ 215 Tom Trebelhorn MG
☐ 216 Bill Wegman
☐ 217 Mike Martin
☐ 218 Scott Roberts
☐ 219 Rick Waits
☐ 220 Chuck Crim
☐ 221 Jamie Nelson
☐ 222 Bryan Clutterbuck
☐ 223 Garrett Nago
☐ 224 Carlos Ponce
☐ 225 Al Price TR

1985 Vero Beach Dodgers TCMA

This 27-card standard-size set of the 1985 Vero Beach Dodgers, a Class A Florida State League affiliate of the Los Angeles Dodgers, features blue-bordered posed color player shots on its fronts. The team name is printed at the top with the player's name and position appearing vertically on the lower left edge. The white back carries the team name and league at the top, followed by the player's name, position, and biography.

	MINT	NRMT	EXC
COMPLETE SET (27)	10.00	4.50	1.25

☐ 1 Bobby Hamilton
☐ 2 Tracy Woodson
☐ 3 John Schlichting
☐ 4 Gary Newsom
☐ 5 Manuel Francois
☐ 6 Joe Szekley
☐ 7 Felipe Gutierrez
☐ 8 Wayne Kirby
☐ 9 Gary Legumina
☐ 10 Ed Jacobo
☐ 11 Henry Gatewood
☐ 12 Norberto Flores
☐ 13 Harry Ritch
☐ 14 Joe Karmeris
☐ 15 William Brennan
☐ 16 Bob Jacobsen
☐ 17 Vince Beringhele
☐ 18 Mike Schweignoffer
☐ 19 Barry Wohler
☐ 20 Greg Mayberry
☐ 21 Luis Lopez
☐ 22 Mike Pesavento
☐ 23 Mike Cherry
☐ 24 Rob Giesecke
☐ 25 Dennis Lewallyn
☐ 26 Stan Wasiak
☐ 27 John Shoemaker

1985 Visalia Oaks TCMA

This 25-card standard-size set of the 1985 Visalia Oaks, a Class A California League affiliate of the Minnesota Twins, features blue-bordered posed color player shots on its fronts. The team name is printed at the top with the player's name and position appearing vertically on the lower left edge. The white back carries the team name and league at the top, followed by the player's name, position, and biography. This issue includes the minor league card debut of Jay Bell.

	MINT	NRMT	EXC
COMPLETE SET (25)	18.00	8.00	2.20

☐ 1 Phil Wilson
☐ 2 Doug Palmer
☐ 3 Perry Husband
☐ 4 Bill O'Connor
☐ 5 Sal Nicolosi
☐ 6 Jeff Schugel
☐ 7 Brad Bierley
☐ 8 Jay Bell
☐ 9 Chris Forgione
☐ 10 Robert Calley
☐ 11 Tom DiCeglio
☐ 12 Chris Calvert
☐ 13 Dave Vetsch
☐ 14 Gene Larkin
☐ 15 Bob Lee
☐ 16 Ray Velasquez
☐ 17 Todd Budke
☐ 18 Jeff Rojas
☐ 19 Wes Pierorazio
☐ 20 Neil Landmark
☐ 21 Tony Guerrero
☐ 22 Jose Dominquez
☐ 23 Scott Klingbeil
☐ 24 Troy Galloway
☐ 25 Danny Schmitz

1985 Waterbury Indians TCMA

This 25-card standard-size set of the 1985 Waterbury Indians, a Class AA Eastern League affiliate of the Cleveland Indians, features blue-bordered posed color player shots on its fronts. The team name is printed at the top with the player's name and position appearing vertically on the lower left edge. The white back carries the team name and league at the top, followed by the player's name, position, and biography.

	MINT	NRMT	EXC
COMPLETE SET (25)	18.00	8.00	2.20

☐ 1 Nelson Pedraza
☐ 2 Wilson Valera
☐ 3 Randy Washington
☐ 4 Winston Ficklin
☐ 5 Glenn Edwards
☐ 6 Richard Doyle
☐ 7 Mickey Street
☐ 8 John Miglio
☐ 9 Cal Santarelli
☐ 10 Wayne Johnson
☐ 11 Reggie Ritter
☐ 12 Doug Jones
☐ 13 Marty Leach
☐ 14 Jeff Arney
☐ 15 Dave Clark
☐ 16 Ron Wallenhaupt
☐ 17 German Barranca
☐ 18 Tim Glass
☐ 19 Jim Driscoll
☐ 20 George Cecchetti
☐ 21 John Farrell
☐ 22 Jack Aker
☐ 23 Cory Snyder
☐ 24 Andy Allanson
☐ 25 Dain Syverson

1986 Albany Yankees TCMA

This 32-card standard-size set of the 1986 Albany Yankees, a Class AA Eastern League affiliate of the New York Yankees, features white-bordered posed color player shots set on fuchsia backgrounds. The team name is printed within the fuchsia area below the photo. A black stripe at the bottom carries the player's name and position. The white back carries the team name and league at the top, followed by the player's name, positon, biography and statistics.

	MINT	NRMT	EXC
COMPLETE SET (32)	15.00	6.75	1.85

☐ 1 Jim Riggs
☐ 2 Roberto Kelly
☐ 3 Carson Carroll
☐ 4 Miguel Sosa
☐ 5 Tom Barrett
☐ 6 Ferdi Gonzalez
☐ 7 Keith Hughes
☐ 8 Bill Monbouquette
☐ 9 Carlos Martinez
☐ 10 Tony Russell
☐ 11 Mike Heifferon
☐ 12 Eric Bernard bb
☐ 13 John Liburdi
(Ground Crew)
☐ 14 Eric Dersin
☐ 15 Jeff Pries
☐ 16 Jim Saul MG
☐ 17 Logan Easley
☐ 18 Mo Ching
☐ 19 John Lemperle bb
☐ 20 Chuck Yaeger
☐ 21 Eric Schmidt
☐ 22 Bill Lindsey
☐ 23 Darren Reed
☐ 24 John Kennedy CO
☐ 25 Aris Tirado
☐ 26 Bill Fulton
☐ 27 Joe Impagliazzo
☐ 28 Clay Christiansen
Christenson
☐ 29 Steven George
☐ 30 Brent Blum
☐ 31 Bob Davidson
☐ 32 Bullpen Action
Bill Monbouquette
Logan Easley
Brent Blum

1986 Albuquerque Dukes ProCards

This 28-card standard-size set of the 1986 Albuquerque Dukes, a Class AAA Pacific Coast League affiliate of the Los Angeles Dodgers, features white-bordered posed color player photos on its fronts. The player's name, team, and position appear at the bottom. The white horizontal back carries the player's name and position at the top, followed by biography and statistics. The cards are unnumbered and checklisted below in alphabetical order.

	MINT	NRMT	EXC
COMPLETE SET (28)	6.00	2.70	.75

☐ 1 Ed Amelung
☐ 2 Ralph Bryant
☐ 3 Terry Collins MG
☐ 4 Lenny Currier TR
☐ 5 John Debus
☐ 6 Dave Eichhorn
☐ 7 Jack Fimple
☐ 8 Balvino Galvez
☐ 9 Jose Gonzalez
☐ 10 Jeff Hamilton
☐ 11 Mark Heller
☐ 12 Brian Holton
☐ 13 Dennis Livingston
☐ 14 Scott May
☐ 15 Dick McLaughlin CO
☐ 16 Adrian Meagher
☐ 17 Tim Meeks
☐ 18 Gary Newsom
☐ 19 Stu Pederson
☐ 20 Gil Reyes
☐ 21 Mike Schleighoffer
☐ 22 Larry See
☐ 23 Craig Shipley
☐ 24 Steve Shirley
☐ 25 Joe Vavra
☐ 26 Dave Wallace CO
☐ 27 Mike Watters
☐ 28 Reggie Williams

1986 Appleton Foxes ProCards

This 28-card standard-size set of the 1986 Appleton Foxes, a Class A Midwest League affiliate of the Chicago White Sox, features white-bordered posed color player photos on its fronts. The player's name, team, and position appear at the bottom. The white horizontal back carries the player's name and position at the top, followed by biography and statistics. The cards are unnumbered and checklisted below in alphabetical order.

	MINT	NRMT	EXC
COMPLETE SET (28)	6.00	2.70	.75

☐ 1 Tony Bartolomucci
☐ 2 John Boling
☐ 3 Glen Braxton
☐ 4 Kurt Brown
☐ 5 Buzz Capra CO
☐ 6 Tony Cento
☐ 7 William Eveline
☐ 8 James Filippi
☐ 9 Cornelio Garcia
☐ 10 Tom Hartley
☐ 11 Richard Issac
☐ 12 Scott Kershaw
☐ 13 William Magallanes
☐ 14 Steve McLaughlin TR
☐ 15 Eric Milholand
☐ 16 Steve Moran
☐ 17 Donn Pall
☐ 18 Luis Peraza
☐ 19 David Reynolds
☐ 20 Jesus Sandoval
☐ 21 Ron Scruggs
☐ 22 Dave Sheldon
☐ 23 Duke Sims MG
☐ 24 John Stein
☐ 25 George Stone
☐ 26 Randy Velarde
☐ 27 Aubrey Waggoner
☐ 28 Marty Warren

1986 Arizona Wildcats Police

	MINT	NRMT	EXC
COMPLETE SET (20)	10.00	4.50	1.25

☐ 1 David Carley
☐ 2 Joe Estes
☐ 3 Chip(Walter) Hale
☐ 4 Gilbert Heredia
☐ 5 Tommy Hinzo
☐ 6 Jeff Hird
☐ 7 Derek Huenneke
☐ 8 Chuck Johnson
☐ 9 Jerry Kindall CO
☐ 10 Jim McDonald
☐ 11 Gar Millay
☐ 12 David Rohde
☐ 13 Mike Senne
☐ 14 David Shermet
☐ 15 Jerry Stitt ACO
☐ 16 Steve Strong
☐ 17 David Taylor
☐ 18 Todd Trafton
☐ 19 Jim Wing CO
☐ 20 Mike Young

1986 Arkansas Travelers ProCards

This 26-card standard-size set of the 1986 Arkansas Travelers, a Class AA Texas League affiliate of the St. Louis Cardinals, features white-bordered posed color player photos on its fronts. The player's name, team, and position appear at the bottom. The white horizontal back carries the player's name and position at the top, followed by biography and statistics. The cards are unnumbered and checklisted below in alphabetical order. This issue includes the minor league card debut of Lance Johnson.

	MINT	NRMT	EXC
COMPLETE SET (26)	15.00	6.75	1.85

☐ 1 Tom Almante
☐ 2 Rod Booker
☐ 3 Ernie Carrasco
☐ 4 Paul Cherry
☐ 5 Dave Clements
☐ 6 Mark Dougherty
☐ 7 Rich Embser
☐ 8 Lance Johnson
☐ 9 Dave Kable
☐ 10 Jeff Kenner
☐ 11 Jeff Ledbetter
☐ 12 Joe Magrane
☐ 13 John Martin
☐ 14 Henry McCulla
☐ 15 Curt Metzger TR
☐ 16 Allen Morlock
☐ 17 Mike Rhodes
☐ 18 Mark Riggins CO
☐ 19 James Riggleman MG
☐ 20 Mike Robinson
☐ 21 Jose Rodriguez
☐ 22 Mark Schulte
☐ 23 Ray Soff
☐ 24 Eddie Tanner
☐ 25 Tim Wallace
☐ 26 Scott Young

1986 Asheville Tourists ProCards

This 29-card standard-size set of the 1986 Asheville Tourists, a Class A South Atlantic League affiliate of the Houston Astros, features white-bordered posed color player photos on its fronts. The player's name, team, and position appear at the bottom. The white horizontal back carries the player's name and position at the top, followed by biography and statistics. The cards are unnumbered and checklisted below in alphabetical order.

	MINT	NRMT	EXC
COMPLETE SET (29)	6.00	2.70	.75

☐ 1 Tim Arnsburg
☐ 2 Jeff Baldwin
☐ 3 Ken Bolek MG
☐ 4 Chris Clawson
☐ 5 Carlo Colombino
☐ 6 Todd Credeur
☐ 7 Pedro DeLeon
☐ 8 Cameron Drew
☐ 9 Jeff Edwards
☐ 10 John Elliot
☐ 11 Stan Fascher
☐ 12 Fred Gladding CO
☐ 13 Neder Horta
☐ 14 Bert Hunter
☐ 15 Blaise Ilsley
☐ 16 Richard Johnson
☐ 17 Larry Lasky TR
☐ 18 Scott Markley
☐ 19 David Meads
☐ 20 Tony Metoyer
☐ 21 Gary Murphy
☐ 22 Carlos Reyes
☐ 23 A. Rodriguez

☐ 24 Ron Roebuck
☐ 25 Wayne Rogalski
☐ 26 Joe Schulte
☐ 27 Shawn Talbott
☐ 28 Dan Walters
☐ 29 Terry Wells

1986 Auburn Astros ProCards

This 27-card standard-size set of the 1986 Auburn Astros, a Class A New York-Penn League affiliate of the Houston Astros, features white-bordered posed color player photos on its fronts. The player's name, team, and position appear at the bottom. The white horizontal back carries the player's name and position at the top, followed by biography and statistics. The cards are unnumbered and checklisted below in alphabetical order.

	MINT	NRMT	EXC
COMPLETE SET (27)	6.00	2.70	.75

☐ 1 Troy Aleshire
☐ 2 Dave Banks
☐ 3 Keith Bodie MG
☐ 4 Daven Bond
☐ 5 Bill Bonham CO
☐ 6 Damon Brooks
☐ 7 Gary Cooper
☐ 8 Jeff Edwards
☐ 9 Joel Estes
☐ 10 Scott Gray
☐ 11 Carl Grovom
☐ 12 Trent Hubbard
☐ 13 Bert Hunter
☐ 14 Gayron Jackson
☐ 15 Rusty Kryzandowski
☐ 16 Brian Meyer
☐ 17 Guy Normand
☐ 18 Jimmy Olson
☐ 19 Dave Potts
☐ 20 Ron Roebuck
☐ 21 Dave Rohde
☐ 22 Pedro Sanchez
☐ 23 Richie Simon
☐ 24 Matt Stennett
☐ 25 Kevin Wasilewski
☐ 26 Ed Whited
☐ 27 Jim Vike

1986 Bakersfield Dodgers ProCards

This 29-card standard-size set of the 1986 Bakersfield Dodgers, a Class A California League affiliate of the Los Angeles Dodgers, features white-bordered posed color player photos on its fronts. The player's name, team, and position appear at the bottom. The white horizontal back carries the player's name and position at the top, followed by biography and statistics. The cards are unnumbered and checklisted below in alphabetical order. This issue includes the minor league card debuts of Ramon Martinez and John Wetteland.

	MINT	NRMT	EXC
COMPLETE SET (29)	18.00	8.00	2.20

☐ 1 Dave Alario
☐ 2 Mike Batesole
☐ 3 Manuel Benitez
☐ 4 Mike Burke
☐ 5 Dave Carlucci
☐ 6 Jovon Edwards
☐ 7 Mike Fiala
☐ 8 Bert Flores
☐ 9 Rick Gahbrielson CO
☐ 10 Rene Garcia
☐ 11 Darryl Gilliam
☐ 12 Anthony Hardwick
☐ 13 Ted Holcomb
☐ 14 Jay Hornacek
☐ 15 Ron Jackson
☐ 16 Stan Johnston TR
☐ 17 Tim Kelly CO
☐ 18 Brian Kopetsky
☐ 19 Don "Ducky" LeJohn MG
☐ 20 Ramon Martinez
☐ 21 Andy Naworski
☐ 22 Jeff Nelson
☐ 23 Jay Ray
☐ 24 Jack Savage
☐ 25 Bryan Smith
☐ 26 Dan Smith
☐ 27 Walt Stull
☐ 28 John Wetteland
☐ 29 Mike White

1986 Beaumont Golden Gators ProCards

This 25-card standard-size set of the 1986 Beaumont Golden Gators, a Class AA Texas League affiliate of the San Diego Padres, features white-bordered posed color player photos on its fronts. The player's name, team, and position appear at the bottom. The white horizontal back carries the player's name and position at the top, followed by biography and statistics. The cards are unnumbered and checklisted below in alphabetical order. This issue includes the minor league card debut of Sandy Alomar Jr.

	MINT	NRMT	EXC
COMPLETE SET (25)	10.00	4.50	1.25

☐ 1 Santos Alomar
☐ 2 Joe Bitker
☐ 3 Tom Brass II
☐ 4 Randy Byers
☐ 5 Frank Castro
☐ 6 Joe Chavez TR
☐ 7 Joey Cora
☐ 8 Mike Costello
☐ 9 Mike Debutch
☐ 10 Rich Doyle
☐ 11 Rusty Ford
☐ 12 Brent Gjesdal
☐ 13 Eric Hardgrave
☐ 14 Steve Lubratich CO
☐ 15 Steve Luebber CO
☐ 16 Shane Mack
☐ 17 Paul Mancuso
☐ 18 Mike McClain
☐ 19 Mike Mills
☐ 20 Mark Poston
☐ 21 Candy Sierra
☐ 22 Todd Simmons
☐ 23 Steve Smith MG
☐ 24 Eric Varoz
☐ 25 Bill Wrona

1986 Bellingham Mariners Cramer

	MINT	NRMT	EXC
COMPLETE SET (29)	5.00	2.20	.60

☐ 101 David Hartnett
☐ 102 Jim Bowie Jr.
☐ 103 Michael McDonald
☐ 104 Jose Bennet
☐ 105 Deron Johnson Jr.
☐ 106 Wendell Bolar
☐ 107 Gregory Briley
☐ 108 Jose Tartabull Jr.
☐ 109 Thomas Little
☐ 110 Jerry Goff
☐ 111 Michael Thorpe
☐ 112 Brad Rohde
☐ 113 James Pritikin
☐ 114 Bret Simmermacher
☐ 115 Tim Fortugno
☐ 116 Arvid Morfin
☐ 117 Jody Ryan
☐ 118 Troy Williams
☐ 119 Randy Little
☐ 120 James Blueberg
☐ 121 Richard DeLucia
☐ 122 David Disher
☐ 123 Ted Williams
☐ 124 Raul Mendez
☐ 125 Fausto Ramirez
☐ 126 Clay Gunn
☐ 127 Rudy Webster
☐ 128 Patrick Lennon
☐ 129 Mark Wooden

1986 Beloit Brewers ProCards

This 26-card standard-size set of the 1986 Beloit Brewers, a Class A Midwest League affiliate of the Milwaukee Brewers, features white-bordered posed color player photos on its fronts. The player's name, team, and position appear at the bottom. The white horizontal back carries the player's name and position at the top, followed by biography and statistics. The cards are unnumbered and checklisted below in alphabetical order.

	MINT	NRMT	EXC
COMPLETE SET (26)	6.00	2.70	.75

☐ 1 Shon Ashley
☐ 2 Rich Bosley
☐ 3 Bob Caci
☐ 4 Isaiah Clark
☐ 5 Carlos Escalera
☐ 6 Frank Fazzini
☐ 7 Dan Fitzpatrick
☐ 8 Ed Greene
☐ 9 Joe Haney
☐ 10 Doug Henry
☐ 11 Gomer Hodge MG
☐ 12 Tom Kleean
☐ 13 Lance Lincoln
☐ 14 Rusty McGinnis
☐ 15 Charlie McGrew
☐ 16 Carl Moraw
☐ 17 Ray Ojeda
☐ 18 Warren Olson
☐ 19 Juan Reyes
☐ 20 Jim Rowe TR
☐ 21 Greg Simmons
☐ 22 Bob Simonson
☐ 23 Jeff Smith
☐ 24 Jose Ventura
☐ 25 Randy Veres
☐ 26 Larry Whitford

1986 Bend Phillies Cramer

This issue includes the minor league card debut of Andy Ashby.

	MINT	NRMT	EXC
COMPLETE SET (25)	8.00	3.60	1.00

☐ 130 Roderick Robertson
☐ 131 Quinn Williams
☐ 132 Al Hibbs
☐ 133 Scott Ruckman
☐ 134 Doug Hodo
☐ 135 Stephen Scarsone
☐ 136 Charles Malone
☐ 137 Keith Greene
☐ 138 Donald Church
☐ 139 Andrew Ashby
☐ 140 Elvis Romero
☐ 141 Glen Anderson
☐ 142 Kenny Miller
☐ 143 Fred Christopher
☐ 144 Brad Moore
☐ 145 Leroy Ventress
☐ 146 John Gianukakis
☐ 147 Chris Limbach
☐ 148 Tim Sossamon
☐ 149 Ryan Silva
☐ 150 Gary Berman
☐ 151 Bubba Allison
☐ 152 Juan Ascencio
☐ 153 Jeff Myaer
☐ 154 Garland Kiser

1986 Birmingham Barons Team Issue

	MINT	NRMT	EXC
COMPLETE SET (28)	40.00	18.00	5.00

☐ 1 Steve Oswald
☐ 2 Manny Salinas
☐ 3 Ken Reed
☐ 4 Dave White
☐ 5 Troy Thomas
☐ 6 Tony Menendez
☐ 7 Tom Moritz
☐ 8 Ron Karkovice
☐ 9 John Johnson
☐ 10 Mike Harris
☐ 11 Dave Cochrane
☐ 12 Rolando Pino
☐ 13 Mike Taylor
☐ 14 Rick Seilheimer
☐ 15 Tom Forrester
☐ 16 Jack Hardy
☐ 17 Mike Yastrzemski
☐ 18 Jim Hickey
☐ 19 Bobby Thigpen
☐ 20 Bob Bolin CO
☐ 21 Mark Williams
☐ 22 Kurt Walker
☐ 23 Marv Foley CO
☐ 24 Ken Koch TR
☐ 25 Tom Haller MG
☐ 26 Sam Hairston CO
☐ 27 Rich DeVincenzo
☐ 28 Rondal Rollin

1986 Buffalo Bisons ProCards

This 26-card standard-size set of the 1986 Buffalo Bisons, a Class AAA American Association affiliate of the Chicago White Sox, features white-bordered posed color player photos on its fronts. The player's name, team, and position appear at the bottom. The white horizontal back carries the player's name and position at the top, followed by biography and statistics. The cards are unnumbered and checklisted below in alphabetical order.

	MINT	NRMT	EXC
COMPLETE SET (26)	6.00	2.70	.75

☐ 1 Glen Bockhorn
☐ 2 Dick Bosman CO
☐ 3 Daryl Boston
☐ 4 Scott Bradley
☐ 5 Tony Brizzolara
☐ 6 Darren Burroughs
☐ 7 Nick Capra
☐ 8 Bryan Clark
☐ 9 Joe Cowley
☐ 10 Joe DeSa
☐ 11 Pete Filson
☐ 12 Jerry Don Gleaton
☐ 13 Al Jones
☐ 14 Tim Krauss
☐ 15 Greg Latta TR
☐ 16 Bill Long
☐ 17 Jim Marshall MG
☐ 18 Steve McCatty
☐ 19 Russ Morman
☐ 20 Chris Nyman
☐ 21 Bruce Tanner
☐ 22 Tom Thompson
☐ 23 Dave Wehrmeister
☐ 24 Ken Williams
☐ 25 Matt Winters
☐ 26 Dave Yobs

1986 Burlington Expos ProCards

This 28-card standard-size set of the 1986 Burlington Expos, a Class A Midwest League affiliate of the Montreal Expos, features white-bordered posed color player photos on its fronts. The player's name, team, and position appear at the bottom. The white horizontal back carries the player's name and position at the top, followed by biography and statistics. The cards are unnumbered and checklisted below in alphabetical order. This issue includes a second year card of Larry Walker.

	MINT	NRMT	EXC
COMPLETE SET (28)	30.00	13.50	3.70

☐ 1 Tom Arrington
☐ 2 Daryl Asbe
☐ 3 Luis Corcino
☐ 4 Matt Crouch
☐ 5 Geff Davis
☐ 6 Pat Dougherty
☐ 7 Fritz Fedor
☐ 8 Cesar Hernandez
☐ 9 Jim Hunter
☐ 10 Jeff Huson
☐ 11 Juan Jimenez CO
☐ 12 Tom Johnson
☐ 13 Frank Laureano
☐ 14 Tim Lemons
☐ 15 Andy Leonard
☐ 16 J.R. Miner MG
☐ 17 Melido Perez
☐ 18 Jose Rodriguez
☐ 19 Brad Shores TR
☐ 20 Joe Slotnick
☐ 21 Stuart Stauffacher
☐ 22 Bob Sudo
☐ 23 Scott Sundgren
☐ 24 Alfonso Tavarez
☐ 25 Larry Walker
☐ 26 Bob Williams
☐ 27 John Williams
☐ 28 1986 Burlington Expos (Team photo)

1986 Calgary Cannons ProCards

This 26-card standard-size police set of the 1986 Calgary Cannons, a Class AAA Pacific Coast League affiliate of the Seattle Mariners, features white-bordered posed color player photos on its fronts. The player's name, team, and position appear at the bottom. The white horizontal back carries the player's name at the top, followed by biography, statistics, and safety tips. The cards are unnumbered and checklisted below in alphabetical order.

	MINT	NRMT	EXC
COMPLETE SET (26)	6.00	2.70	.75

☐ 1 Greg Bartley
☐ 2 Mickey Brantley
☐ 3 Randy Braun
☐ 4 Pat Casey
☐ 5 Bill Crone
☐ 6 Mario Diaz
☐ 7 Jerry Dybzinski
☐ 8 Steve Fireovid
☐ 9 Dan Firova
☐ 10 Ross Grimsley CO
☐ 11 Dave Hengel
☐ 12 Clay Hill
☐ 13 Vic Martin
☐ 14 Doug Merrifield TR
☐ 15 Rich Monteleone
☐ 16 John Moses
☐ 17 Jed Murray
☐ 18 Ricky Nelson
☐ 19 Randy Newman
☐ 20 Jack O'Conner
☐ 21 Bill Plummer MG
☐ 22 Jerry Reed
☐ 23 Harold Reynolds
☐ 24 Dave Valle
☐ 25 Bill Wilkinson
☐ 26 Joe Witmer

1986 Cedar Rapids Reds TCMA

This 28-card standard-size set of the 1986 Cedar Rapids Reds, a Class A Midwest League affiliate of the Cincinnati Reds, features white-bordered posed color player photos on its fronts. The player's name, team, and position appear at the bottom. The white horizontal back carries the player's name and position at the top, followed by biography and statistics. The cards are unnumbered and checklisted below in alphabetical order.

	MINT	NRMT	EXC
COMPLETE SET (28)	7.00	3.10	.85

☐ 1 Dan Belinskas
☐ 2 Brad Brusky
☐ 3 Mike Converse
☐ 4 Mike Campbell
☐ 5 Tim Deitz
☐ 6 Curt Kindred
☐ 7 Gino Minutelli
☐ 8 Mike Roesler
☐ 9 Greg Simpson
☐ 10 Mike Smith
☐ 11 Greg Toler
☐ 12 Mike Vincent
☐ 13 Rod Zeratsky
☐ 14 Marty Brown
☐ 15 Joe Dunlap
☐ 16 Mark Germann
☐ 17 Scott Hilgenberg
☐ 18 Randy Hindman
☐ 19 Cal Cain
☐ 20 Mark Jackson
☐ 21 Chris Jones
☐ 22 Allen Sigler
☐ 23 John Bryant
☐ 24 Paul Kirsch CO
☐ 25 Gene Dusan MG
☐ 26 Neal Davenport TR
☐ 27 Bucky Buchheister GM
☐ 28 Lemar Mascot

1986 Charleston Rainbows ProCards

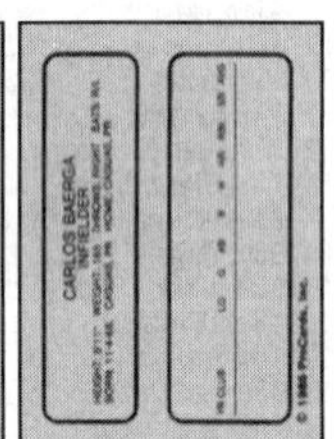

This 30-card standard-size set of the 1986 Charleston Rainbows, a Class A South Atlantic League affiliate of the San Diego Padres, features white-bordered posed color player photos on its fronts. The player's name, team, and position appear at the bottom. The white horizontal back carries the player's name and position at the top, followed by biography and statistics. The cards are unnumbered and checklisted below in alphabetical order. This issue includes the minor league card debut of Carlos Baerga.

	MINT	NRMT	EXC
COMPLETE SET (28)	50.00	22.00	6.25
COMPLETE SET (30)	60.00	27.00	7.50

☐ 1 Carlos Baerga (Baerega)
☐ 2A Miguel Batista (with bat)
☐ 2B Miguel Batista (with glove)
☐ 3 Billy Blount
☐ 4 Victor Cabrera
☐ 5 Rafael Chaves
☐ 6 Jeff Cisco
☐ 7 Roberto Clemente Jr.
☐ 8 Jim Daniel TR
☐ 9 Carl Ferraro
☐ 10 Greg Harris
☐ 11 Pat Kelly MG
☐ 12 Chris Knabenshue
☐ 13 Jim Lewis
☐ 14 Bill Marx
☐ 15 Matt Maysey
☐ 16 Rod McCray
☐ 17 Tom Meagher
☐ 18 Jaime Moreno
☐ 19 Eric Nolte
☐ 20 Juan Paris
☐ 21 Joe Pleasac
☐ 22 Ramon Rodriguez
☐ 23 Greg Sparks
☐ 24 Bill Stevenson
☐ 25 Jim Tatum
☐ 26 Kevin Towers
☐ 27 Rafael Valez
☐ 28A Jim Wasem (with bat)
☐ 28B Jim Wasem (with glove)

1986 Charlotte Orioles WBTV

Cards are unnumbered.

	MINT	NRMT	EXC
COMPLETE SET (30)	30.00	13.50	3.70

☐ 1 Kurt Beamesderfer
☐ 2 Eric Bell
☐ 3 Greg Biagini
☐ 4 Terry Bogener
☐ 5 Jim Boudreau
☐ 6 Mark Brown
☐ 7 Paul Cameron
☐ 8 Tom Dodd
☐ 9 Dave Falcone
☐ 10 John Flinn
☐ 11 Charlie Frederick
☐ 12 Lee Granger
☐ 13 Bob Hice
☐ 14 Jerry Holtz
☐ 15 John Hoover
☐ 16 Joe Kucharski
☐ 17 Terry Mauney
☐ 18 Carl Nichols
☐ 19 O's Fans
☐ 20 Francisco Oliveras
☐ 21 Chris Padget
☐ 22 Mike Raczka
☐ 23 Joe Redfield
☐ 24 Rich Rice
☐ 25 Bill Ripken
☐ 26 Rico Rossy
☐ 27 Ron Salcedo
☐ 28 Dave Smith
☐ 29 Scott Stranski
☐ 30 Jeff Wood TR

1986 Chattanooga Lookouts ProCards

This 25-card standard-size set of the 1986 Chattanooga Lookouts, a Class AA Southern League affiliate of the Seattle Mariners, features white-bordered posed color player photos on its fronts. The player's name, team, and position appear at the bottom. The white horizontal back carries the player's name and position at the top, followed by biography and statistics. The cards are unnumbered and checklisted below in alphabetical order. This issue includes the minor league card debut of Edgar Martinez.

	MINT	NRMT	EXC
COMPLETE SET (25)	25.00	11.00	3.10

☐ 1 Ben Amaya
☐ 2 Bob Baldrick
☐ 3 Brian Bargerhuff
☐ 4 Terry Bell
☐ 5 Jim Bryant
☐ 6 John Burden CO
☐ 7 Scott Buss
☐ 8 Brian David
☐ 9 John Duncun
☐ 10 Bob Gunnarson
☐ 11 Matt Hall
☐ 12 R.J. Harrison MG
☐ 13 Paul Hollins
☐ 14 Tom Hunt TR
☐ 15 Ross Jones
☐ 16 Rick Luecken
☐ 17 Edgar Martinez
☐ 18 Jeff McDonald
☐ 19 Rusty McNealy
☐ 20 Rick Moore
☐ 21 Dave Myers
☐ 22 Paul Schneider
☐ 23 Brick Smith
☐ 24 Terry Taylor
☐ 25 Mike Wishnevski

1986 Clearwater Phillies ProCards

This 26-card standard-size set of the 1986 Clearwater Phillies, a Class A Florida State League affiliate of the Philadelphia Phillies, features white-bordered posed color player photos on its fronts. The player's name, team, and position appear at the bottom. The white horizontal back carries the player's name and position at the top, followed by biography and statistics. The cards are unnumbered and checklisted below in alphabetical order.

	MINT	NRMT	EXC
COMPLETE SET (26)	6.00	2.70	.75

☐ 1 Carlos Arroyo CO
☐ 2 Bruce Carter
☐ 3 Travis Chambers
☐ 4 Ron Clark MG
☐ 5 Pat Coveney
☐ 6 Shawn Dantzler
☐ 7 Greg Edge
☐ 8 Jim Fortenberry
☐ 9 Todd Frohwirth
☐ 10 Billy Jester
☐ 11 Ronald Jones
☐ 12 Bart Kaiser
☐ 13 Jeff Kaye
☐ 14 Jeff Knox
☐ 15 Ken Kraft
☐ 16 Scott Madden
☐ 17 Mike Miller
☐ 18 Tom Newell
☐ 19 Segio Perez
☐ 20 Mark Pottinger
☐ 21 Wally Ritchie
☐ 22 Bob Scanlan
☐ 23 Scott Steen
☐ 24 Rodney Wheeler
☐ 25 Steven Williams
☐ 26 Ted Zipeto TR

1986 Clinton Giants ProCards

This 29-card standard-size set of the 1986 Clinton Giants, a Class A Midwest League affiliate of the San Francisco Giants, features white-bordered posed color player photos on its fronts. The player's name, team, and position appear at the bottom. The white horizontal back carries the player's name and position at the top, followed by biography and statistics. The cards are unnumbered and checklisted below in alphabetical order.

	MINT	NRMT	EXC
COMPLETE SET (29)	6.00	2.70	.75

☐ 1 John Barry
☐ 2 Dave Blakely
☐ 3 George Bonilla
☐ 4 Jeff Carter
☐ 5 Todd Cash
☐ 6 Tom Ealy
☐ 7 Bill Evers CO
☐ 8 Perry Flowers
☐ 9 Dean Freeland
☐ 10 Dave Hornsby
☐ 11 Lloyd Jackson
☐ 12 Timber Mead
☐ 13 Todd Miller
☐ 14 Dave Morris
☐ 15 Jack Mull MG
☐ 16 Rick Nelson
☐ 17 Eric Pawling
☐ 18 Darren Pearson
☐ 19 Jose Pena
☐ 20 C.L. Penigar
☐ 21 Eric Pilkington
☐ 22 Doug Robertson
☐ 23 Dobie Swepson
☐ 24 Howard Townsend
☐ 25 Paul Van Stone
☐ 26 Matt Walker
☐ 27 Mike Whitt
☐ 28 Trevor Wilson
☐ 29 1986 Clinton Giants

1986 Columbia Mets ProCards

This 29-card standard-size set of the 1986 Columbia Mets, a Class A South Atlantic League affiliate of the New York Mets, features white-bordered posed color player photos on its fronts. The player's name, team, and position appear at the bottom. The white horizontal back carries the player's name and position at the top, followed by biography and statistics. The cards are unnumbered and checklisted below in alphabetical order. This issue includes the minor league card debut of Gregg Jefferies.

	MINT	NRMT	EXC
COMPLETE SET (28)	30.00	13.50	3.70
COMPLETE SET (29)	40.00	18.00	5.00

☐ 1 Bob Apodaca CO
☐ 2 Jaime Archibald
☐ 3 Kevin Armstrong
☐ 4 Brandon Bailey
☐ 5 Chris Bayer
☐ 6 Mark Brunswick
☐ 7 Joaquin Contreras
☐ 8 Kurt DeLuca
☐ 9 Tom Doyle TR
☐ 10 Dave Gelatt
☐ 11A Brian Givens (blue jersey)
☐ 11B Brian Givens (white jersey)
☐ 12 Alan Hayden
☐ 13 Barry Hightower
☐ 14 Troy James
☐ 15 Scott Jaster
☐ 16 Gregg Jefferies
☐ 17 Geary Jones
☐ 18 Johnny Monell
☐ 19 Felix Perdomo
☐ 20 Chris Rauth
☐ 21 Craig Repoz
☐ 22 Robert Rinehart Jr.
☐ 23 Daniel Siblerud
☐ 24 William Stiles
☐ 25 John Tuozzo
☐ 26 Thomas Wachs
☐ 27A Mark Willoughby (blue jersey)
☐ 27B Mark Willoughby (white jersey)

1986 Columbus Astros ProCards

This 25-card standard-size set of the 1986 Columbus Astros, a Class AA Southern League affiliate of the Houston Astros, features white-bordered posed color player photos on its fronts. The player's name, team, and position appear at the bottom. The white horizontal back carries the player's name and position at the top, followed by biography and statistics. The cards are unnumbered and checklisted below in alphabetical order. This issue includes a second year card of Ken Caminiti.

	MINT	NRMT	EXC
COMPLETE SET (25)	25.00	11.00	3.10

☐ 1 Troy Afenir
☐ 2 Karl Allaire
☐ 3 Mark Baker
☐ 4 Jeff Bettendorf
☐ 5 Rich Bombard
☐ 6 Ken Caminiti
☐ 7 Mitch Cook
☐ 8 Dave Cripe MG
☐ 9 Jeff Datz
☐ 10 Juan Delgado
☐ 11 Ed Duke TR
☐ 12 Bobby Falls
☐ 13 Mike Friederich
☐ 14 Tom Funk
☐ 15 Ryan Job
☐ 16 Tony Kelley
☐ 17 Bob Mallicoat
☐ 18 Chuck Mathews
☐ 19 Joe Mikulik
☐ 20 Jim O'Dell
☐ 21 Bob Parker
☐ 22 Larry Ray
☐ 23 Roger Samuels
☐ 24 Chuck Taylor CO
☐ 25 Gerald Young

1986 Columbus Clippers Police

This 25-card standard-size set of the 1986 Columbus Clippers, a Class AAA International League affiliate of the New York Yankees.

	MINT	NRMT	EXC
COMPLETE SET (25)	10.00	4.50	1.25

☐ 1 Mike Armstrong
☐ 2 Brad Arnsberg
☐ 3 Clay Christiansen
☐ 4 Pete Dalena
☐ 5 Orestes Destrade
☐ 6 Doug Drabek
☐ 7 Juan Espino
☐ 8 Kelly Faulk
☐ 9 Randy Graham
☐ 10 Leo Hernandez
☐ 11 Al Holland
☐ 12 Phil Lombardi
☐ 13 Victor Mata
☐ 14 Derwin McNealy
☐ 15 Dan Pasqua
☐ 16 Scott Patterson
☐ 17 Jeff Pries
☐ 18 Alfonso Pulido
☐ 19 Andre Robertson
☐ 20 Mark Silva
☐ 21 Managers
Barry Clinton
Barry Foote
George H. Sisler Jr.
☐ 22 Keith Smith
☐ 23 Mike Soper
☐ 24 Dave Stegman
☐ 25 Coaching Staff
Dave LaRoche CO
Brian Butterfield CO
Kevin Rand TR

1986 Columbus Clippers ProCards

This 26-card standard-size set of the 1986 Columbus Clippers, a Class AAA International League affiliate of the New York Yankees, features white-bordered posed color player photos on its fronts. The player's name, team, and position appear at the bottom. The white horizontal back carries the player's name and position at the top, followed by biography and statistics. The cards are unnumbered and checklisted below in alphabetical order.

	MINT	NRMT	EXC
COMPLETE SET (26)	8.00	3.60	1.00

☐ 1 Mike Armstrong
☐ 2 Brad Arnsberg
☐ 3 Clay Christiansen
☐ 4 Pete Dalena
☐ 5 Orestes Destrade
☐ 6 Doug Drabek
☐ 7 Juan Espino
☐ 8 Kelly Faulk
☐ 9 Barry Foote MG
☐ 10 Randy Graham
☐ 11 Leo Hernandez
☐ 12 Al Holland
☐ 13 Dave Laroche CO
Brian Butterfield CO
Kevin Rand TR
☐ 14 Phil Lombardi
☐ 15 Victor Mata

☐ 16 Derwin McNealy
☐ 17 Dan Pasqua
☐ 18 Scott Patterson
☐ 19 Jeff Pries
☐ 20 Alfonso Pulido
☐ 21 Andre Robertson
☐ 22 Mark Silva
☐ 23 Keith Smith
☐ 24 Mike Soper
☐ 25 Miguel Sosa
☐ 26 Staff Members

1986 David Lipscomb Bisons

	MINT	NRMT	EXC
COMPLETE SET (24)	5.00	2.20	.60

☐ 1 Daron Akins
☐ 2 Al Austelee ACO
☐ 3 Jim Bailey
☐ 4 Neal Benson
☐ 5 Carmon Brown
☐ 6 Will Burks
☐ 7 Stan Cox
☐ 8 Derek Crownover
☐ 9 David Dinger
☐ 10 Ken Dugan CO
☐ 11 Mike Dugan
☐ 12 Scott Ford
☐ 13 Bobby Gilliam
☐ 14 Trey Hartman
☐ 15 Mark Johnson
☐ 16 John McPherson
☐ 17 Ritchie Pickens
☐ 18 Tommy Randolph
☐ 19 Jonathan Seamon
☐ 20 Chris Snoddy TR
☐ 21 Bryan True
☐ 22 Jon Williams
☐ 23 Michael Williams
☐ 24 Danny Wilson

1986 Daytona Beach Islanders ProCards

This 29-card standard-size set of the 1986 Daytona Beach Islanders, a Class A Florida State League Independent, features white-bordered posed color player photos on its fronts. The player's name, team, and position appear at the bottom. The white horizontal back carries the player's name and position at the top, followed by biography and statistics. The cards are unnumbered and checklisted below in alphabetical order.

	MINT	NRMT	EXC
COMPLETE SET (29)	6.00	2.70	.75

☐ 1 Jim Allison
☐ 2 Regan Bass
☐ 3 Warren Busick
☐ 4 Chino Cadahia MGR
☐ 5 Tony Clark
☐ 6 Rafael Cruz
☐ 7 Mike Dotzler
☐ 8 Darrin Garner
☐ 9 Otto Gonzalez
☐ 10 Ty Harden
☐ 11 David Hausterman TR
☐ 12 Perry W. Hill CO
☐ 13 Paul James
☐ 14 Ross Jones
☐ 15 Mark Kramer
☐ 16 Dave Linton
☐ 17 Carmen Losauro
☐ 18 Jimmy Meadows
☐ 19 Jeff Melrose
☐ 20 Tim Owen
☐ 21 Larry Pardo
☐ 22 Tom Petrizzo CHM
☐ 23 Dave Rolland
☐ 24 Ron Russell
☐ 25 Travis Sheffield
☐ 26 Ed Soto
☐ 27 Jim St.Laurent
☐ 28 George Threadgill
☐ 29 Tom West

1986 Durham Bulls ProCards

This 27-card standard-size set of the 1986 Durham Bulls, a Class A Carolina League affiliate of the Atlanta Braves, features white-bordered posed color player photos on its fronts. The player's name, team, and position appear at the bottom. The white horizontal back carries the player's name and position at the top, followed by biography and statistics. The cards are unnumbered and checklisted below in alphabetical order. This issue includes the minor league card debut of Ron Gant.

	MINT	NRMT	EXC
COMPLETE SET (27)	30.00	13.50	3.70

☐ 1 Buddy Bailey MG
☐ 2 Jeff Blauser
☐ 3 Johnny Cash
☐ 4 Bill Clossen
☐ 5 Kevin Coffman
☐ 6 Tim Criswell
☐ 7 Chris Cron
☐ 8 Maximo Del Rosario
☐ 9 Drew Denson
☐ 10 Todd Dewey
☐ 11 Juan Fredymond
☐ 12 Ronnie Gant
☐ 13 Wayne Harrison
☐ 14 Larry Jaster CO
☐ 15 Cesar Jimenez
☐ 16 John Kilner
☐ 17 Todd Lamb
☐ 18 Mike Merrill TR
☐ 19 Charlie Morelock
☐ 20 Mike Nipper
☐ 21 Bob Posey
☐ 22 Mike Reynolds
☐ 23 Jim Rockey
☐ 24 Mac Rogers
☐ 25 Rick Siebert
☐ 26 Gerald Wagner
☐ 27 Phil Wellman

1986 Edmonton Trappers ProCards

This 27-card standard-size set of the 1986 Edmonton Trappers, a Class AAA Pacific Coast League affiliate of the California Angels, features white-bordered posed color player photos on its fronts. The player's name, team, and position appear at the bottom. The white horizontal back carries the player's name and position at the top, followed by biography and statistics. The cards are unnumbered and checklisted below in alphabetical order.

	MINT	NRMT	EXC
COMPLETE SET (27)	10.00	4.50	1.25

☐ 1 Robert Bastien
☐ 2 Norman Carrasco
☐ 3 Ray Chadwick
☐ 4 Bobby Clark
☐ 5 Stan Cliburn
Stewart Cliburn
The Cliburn Brothers
☐ 6 Stan Cliburn
☐ 7 Stewart Cliburn
☐ 8 Steven Finch
☐ 9 Todd Fischer
☐ 10 Tony Fossas
☐ 11 Alan Fowlkes
☐ 12 Leonard Garcia TR
☐ 13 Craig Gerber
☐ 14 Chris Green
☐ 15 Jack Howell
☐ 16 Pat Keedy
☐ 17 Steven Liddle
☐ 18 Rufino Linares
☐ 19 Winston Llenas MG
☐ 20 Tony Lynn Mack
☐ 21 Reggie Montgomery
☐ 22 Gus Polidor
☐ 23 Frank Reberger CO
☐ 24 Al Romero
☐ 25 Mark Ryal
☐ 26 David Wayne Smith
☐ 27 Devon White

1986 El Paso Diablos ProCards

This 23-card standard-size set of the 1986 El Paso Diablos, a Class AA Texas League affiliate of the Milwaukee Brewers, features white-bordered posed color player photos on its fronts. The player's name, team, and position appear at the bottom. The white horizontal back carries the player's name and position at the top, followed by biography and statistics. The cards are unnumbered and checklisted below in alphabetical order.

	MINT	NRMT	EXC
COMPLETE SET (23)	6.00	2.70	.75

☐ 1 Jay Aldrich
☐ 2 Robby Allen
☐ 3 Jesus Alfaro
☐ 4 Bill Bates
☐ 5 Alan Cartwright
☐ 6 Dave Clay
☐ 7 Tim Crews
☐ 8 Derek Diaz
☐ 9 Duffy Dyer MG
☐ 10 Brian Finley
☐ 11 La Vel Freeman
Sic, Lavell
☐ 12 John Gibbons
☐ 13 Dave Huppert
☐ 14 Pete Hendrick
☐ 15 Pete Kolb TR
☐ 16 Dan Murphy
☐ 17 Garrett Nago
☐ 18 Bob Nandin
☐ 19 Steve Stanicek
☐ 20 Dave Stapleton
☐ 21 John Thorton
☐ 22 Jackson Todd CO
☐ 23 Cam Walker

1986 Elmira Pioneers ProCards

This 30-card standard-size set of the 1986 Elmira Pioneers, a Class A New York-Penn League affiliate of the Boston Red Sox, features white-bordered posed color player photos on its fronts. The player's name, team, and position appear at the bottom. The white horizontal back carries the player's name and position at the top, followed by biography and statistics. The cards are unnumbered and checklisted below in alphabetical order.

	MINT	NRMT	EXC
COMPLETE SET (30)	6.00	2.70	.75

☐ 1 Mike Baker
☐ 2 Steve Bast
☐ 3 Ken Bourne
☐ 4 Tim Buheller
☐ 5 Mike Coffey
☐ 6 Scott Cooper
☐ 7 Roger Haggerty
☐ 8 Bart Haley
☐ 9 Keith Harrison
☐ 10 Tony Hill
☐ 11 Joe Marchese
☐ 12 Dave Milstien
☐ 13 Jim Morrison
☐ 14 Glen O'Donnell
☐ 15 Lem Pilkinton
☐ 16 Chris Rawdon
☐ 17 Julio Rosario
☐ 18 Ken Ryan
☐ 19 Ed Sardinha
☐ 20 Curt Schilling
☐ 21 Thom Sepela
☐ 22 Scott Sommers
☐ 23 Joaquin Tejada
☐ 24 Al Thorton
☐ 25 David Walters
☐ 26 Ron Warren
☐ 27 Stuart Weidie
☐ 28 Mike Whiting
☐ 29 Kerman Williams
☐ 30 Paul Williams

1986 Erie Cardinals ProCards

This 31-card standard-size set of the 1986 Erie Cardinals, a Class A New York-Penn League affiliate of the St. Louis Cardinals, features white-bordered posed color player photos on its fronts. The player's name, team, and position appear at the bottom. The white horizontal back carries the player's name and position at the top, followed by biography and statistics. The cards are unnumbered and checklisted below in alphabetical order. The unnumbered William Hershman card is not included in all sets. This issue includes the minor league card debut of Todd Zeile.

	MINT	NRMT	EXC
COMPLETE SET (30)	15.00	6.75	1.85
COMPLETE SET (31)	25.00	11.00	3.10

☐ 1 Luis Alicea
☐ 2 Tom Baine
☐ 3 Mark Behny
☐ 4 Brad Bluestone TR
☐ 5 Randy Butts
☐ 6 Rick Christain
☐ 7 Bien Figueroa
☐ 8 Robert Glisson
☐ 9 Stephen Graff
☐ 10 Kerry Griffith
☐ 11 John Hackett
☐ 12 Scott Hamilton
☐ 13 Eric Hohn
☐ 14 Joe Hollinshed
☐ 15 David Horton
☐ 16 Glen Kuiper
☐ 17 Scott Lawrence
☐ 18 Roberto Marte
☐ 19 Steve Meyer
☐ 20 Carey Nemeth
☐ 21 Robert Nettles
☐ 22 Carrol Parker
☐ 23 Francisco Perez
☐ 24 Kyle Reese
☐ 25 Joe Rigoli MGR
☐ 26 Steve Shade
☐ 27 Greg Smith
☐ 28 Steve Turgeon CO
☐ 29 Stanley Zaltsman
☐ 30 Todd Zeile
☐ NNO William Hershman

1986 Eugene Emeralds Cramer

This issue includes the minor league card debut of Brian McRae.

	MINT	NRMT	EXC
COMPLETE SET (25)	12.00	5.50	1.50

☐ 26 Rob Wolkoys
☐ 27 David Tinkle
☐ 28 Brian McRae
☐ 29 Mike Oblesbee
☐ 30 Carlos Escalera
☐ 31 Pat Bailey
☐ 32 Tim Goff
☐ 33 Ondra Ford
☐ 34 Robert Bell
☐ 35 John Larios
☐ 36 Jim Larsen
☐ 37 Kenny Jackson
☐ 38 Sean Berry
☐ 39 Randy Goodenough
☐ 40 Mike Butcher
☐ 41 Kevin Karcher
☐ 42 Chuck Mount
☐ 43 Greg Hibbard
☐ 44 Boo Champagne
☐ 45 Gary Blouin
☐ 46 Ken Adams
☐ 47 Gus Jones
☐ 48 Joe Skodny
☐ 49 Mike Tresemer
☐ 50 Dennis Moeller

1986 Everett Giants Cramer

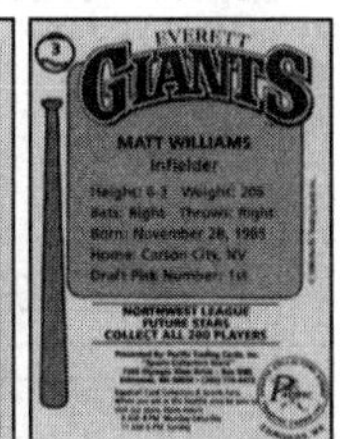

This issue includes the minor league card debut of Matt Williams.

	MINT	NRMT	EXC
COMPLETE SET (32)	50.00	22.00	6.25

☐ 1 Kevin Fitzgerald
☐ 2 Paul McClellan
☐ 3 Matt Williams
☐ 4 Brad Gambee
☐ 5 Gregg Ritchie
☐ 6 Kevin Redick
☐ 7 John Toal
☐ 8 Russ Swan
☐ 9 Drew Ricker
☐ 10 Jim McNamara
☐ 11 Andrew Dixon
☐ 12 David Patterson
☐ 13 Tim McCoy
☐ 14 James Pena
☐ 15 Marty Newton
☐ 16 Chuck Tate
☐ 17 Jim Massey
☐ 18 Chris Stubberfield
☐ 19 John Rannow
☐ 20 Shaun MacKenzie
☐ 21 Tod Ronson
☐ 22 Chris Shultis
☐ 23 Brock Birch
☐ 24 Keith Krafve
☐ 25 James Jones
☐ 180 Joe Strain MG
☐ 181 Todd Wilson
☐ 182 Mark Leonard
☐ 183 Robin Riemer
☐ 184 David Nash
☐ 185 Chuck Higson
☐ 186 Matt Walker

1986 Everett Giants Popcorn Cramer

	MINT	NRMT	EXC
COMPLETE SET (36)	10.00	4.50	1.25

☐ 1 James(Earl) Averill
☐ 2 Brock Birch
☐ 3 Andrew Dixon
☐ 4 Kevin Fitzgerald
☐ 5 Ricky Fleming
☐ 6 Brad Gambee
☐ 7 Bruce Graham
☐ 8 Chuck Higson
☐ 9 James Jones
☐ 10 Keith Krafve
☐ 11 Mark Leonard
☐ 12 Shaun MacKenzie
☐ 13 Jim Massey
☐ 14 Paul McClellan
☐ 15 Tim McCoy
☐ 16 Jim McNamara
☐ 17 Willie Mijares
☐ 18 Dave Nash
☐ 19 Marty Newton
☐ 20 Dave Patterson
☐ 21 James Pena
☐ 22 John Rannow
☐ 23 Kevin Redick
☐ 24 Drew Ricker

☐ 25 Robin Reimer
☐ 26 Gregg Ritchie
☐ 27 Tod Ronson
☐ 28 Chris Shultis
☐ 29 Damon Skyta
☐ 30 Joe Strain
☐ 31 Chris Stubberfield
☐ 32 Chuck Tate
☐ 33 John Toal
☐ 34 Jack Uhey
☐ 35 Matt Walker
☐ 36 Todd Wilson

1986 Florida State League All-Stars ProCards

This 50-card standard-size set of the 1986 Florida State League All-Stars features white-bordered posed color player photos on its fronts. The player's name, team, and position appear at the bottom. The white horizontal back carries the player's name and position at the top, followed by biography and statistics. The cards are unnumbered and checklisted below in alphabetical order. This issue includes a second year card of Brady Anderson.

	MINT	NRMT	EXC
COMPLETE SET (50)	80.00	36.00	10.00

☐ 1 Odie Abril
☐ 2 Julio Alcala
☐ 3 Chris Alvarez
☐ 4 Brady Anderson
☐ 5 Scott Arnold
☐ 6 Tim Arnold
☐ 7 Mark Berry
☐ 8 Dave Bialas MG
☐ 9 Marc Bombard CO
☐ 10 Norman Brock
☐ 11 Alex Cole
☐ 12 Rufus Ellis
☐ 13 Jeff Fassero
☐ 14 Jeff Fischer
☐ 15 John Fishel
☐ 16 Jim Fortenberry
☐ 17 Pete Geist
☐ 18 Otto Gonzalez
☐ 19 Maurice Guercio
☐ 20 Matt Harrison
☐ 21 John Hawkins
☐ 22 Brad Henderson TR
☐ 23 Ted Higgins
☐ 24 Dave Holt MG
☐ 25 Jim Jefferson
☐ 26 Ron Johns
☐ 27 Ron Jones
☐ 28 Dan Juenke
☐ 29 Tim Leiper
☐ 30 Joel Lond
☐ 31 Luis Lopez
☐ 32 Rob Lopez
☐ 33 Greg Lotzar
☐ 34 Walt McConnell
☐ 35 Jim Meadows
☐ 36 Chris Morgan
☐ 37 Max Oliveras CO
☐ 38 Ray Perkins
☐ 39 Dody Rather
☐ 40 Jim Reboulet
☐ 41 Darren Riley
☐ 42 Don Rowland
☐ 43 Tary Scott
☐ 44 Mike Sears TR
☐ 45 Doug Strange
☐ 46 George Threadgill
☐ 47 Shane Turner
☐ 48 Luis Vasquez
☐ 49 Tom West
☐ 50 John Wockenfuss

1986 Fresno Giants Police

This 32-card set features black and white photos framed with an orange lined border and a dark blue background. The team name and the player's last name appear across the top with the words "wildfire prevention" appearing across the bottom.

	MINT	NRMT	EXC
COMPLETE SET (32)	30.00	13.50	3.70

☐ 1 Tim Blackwell MG
☐ 2 Gary Davenport CO
☐ 3 Vince Sferrazza TR
☐ 4 Gary Jones
☐ 5 Felipe Gonzalez
☐ 6 Joe Kmak
☐ 7 Greg Gilbert
☐ 8 Sam Moore
☐ 9 Mike Villa
☐ 10 Tom Messier
☐ 11 Randy McCament
☐ 12 Joe Olker
☐ 13 Dave Hinnrichs
☐ 14 Eric Erickson
☐ 15 Darrell Rodgers
☐ 16 Dennis Cook
☐ 17 Steve Smith
☐ 18 Hector Quinones
☐ 19 Ty Dabney
☐ 20 Tony Perezchica
☐ 21 Scott Thompson
☐ 22 Tom Mathews
☐ 23 John Skurla
☐ 24 T.J. McDonald
☐ 25 Charles Culberson
☐ 26 Harry Davis
☐ 27 Kenny Compton bb
☐ 28 Tony Vitale Groundskeeper and Crew
☐ 29 Smokey Bear (with bat)
☐ 30 Smokey Bear (with ball)
☐ 31 Smokey Bear (looking up)
☐ 32 Title Card

1986 Ft. Lauderdale Yankees ProCards

This 23-card standard-size set of the 1986 Ft. Lauderdale Yankees, a Class A Florida State League affiliate of the New York Yankees, features white-bordered posed color player photos on its fronts. The player's name, team, and position appear at the bottom. The white horizontal back carries the player's name and position at the top, followed by biography and statistics. The cards are unnumbered and checklisted below in alphabetical order.

	MINT	NRMT	EXC
COMPLETE SET (23)	6.00	2.70	.75

☐ 1 Chris Alverez
☐ 2 Anthony Balabon
☐ 3 Douglas Carpenter
☐ 4 Chris Carroll
☐ 5 Gary Cathcart
☐ 6 Mike Christopher
☐ 7 Ysidro Giron
☐ 8 Fred Gonzalez
☐ 9 Robert Green
☐ 10 Maurice Guerico
☐ 11 Mathew Harrison
☐ 12 Johnny Hawkins
☐ 13 Theodore Higgins
☐ 14 Harvey Lee
☐ 15 Jason Maas
☐ 16 Michael McClear
☐ 17 Kenneth Patterson
☐ 18 Johnnie Pleicones
☐ 19 Norman Santiago
☐ 20 Robert Sepanek
☐ 21 Scott Shaw
☐ 22 Aristarco Tirado
☐ 23 Shane Turner

1986 Ft. Myers Royals ProCards

This 29-card standard-size set of the 1986 Ft. Myers Royals, a Class A Florida State League affiliate of the Kansas City Royals, features white-bordered posed color player photos on its fronts. The player's name, team, and position appear at the bottom. The white horizontal back carries the player's name and position at the top, followed by biography and statistics. The cards are unnumbered and checklisted below in alphabetical order.

	MINT	NRMT	EXC
COMPLETE SET (29)	6.00	2.70	.75

☐ 1 Julio Alcala
☐ 2 Mike Alvarez
☐ 3 Jeff Bedell
☐ 4 Stan Boroski
☐ 5 Pete Carey
☐ 6 Bob Davis
☐ 7 Jose DeJesus
☐ 8 Rafael DeLeon
☐ 9 Rufus Ellis
☐ 10 Mark Farnsworth TR
☐ 11 Phil George
☐ 12 Carlos Gonzalez
☐ 13 Duane Gustavson MG
☐ 14 Jeff Hull
☐ 15 Chris Jelic
☐ 16 Kevin Koslofski
☐ 17 Deric Ladnier
☐ 18 Mike Loggins
☐ 19 Mitch McKelvey
☐ 20 Bill Mulligan
☐ 21 Geoff Peterson
☐ 22 Henry Robinson
☐ 23 Ricky Rojas
☐ 24 Gregg Schmidt
☐ 25 Mark Van Blaricom
☐ 26 Bob Van Vuren
☐ 27 Troy Watkins
☐ 28 Dejon Watson
☐ 29 Don Woyce

1986 Geneva Cubs ProCards

This 27-card standard-size set of the 1986 Geneva Cubs, a Class A New York-Penn League affiliate of the Chicago Cubs, features white-bordered posed color player photos on its fronts. The player's name, team, and position appear at the bottom. The white horizontal back carries the player's name and position at the top, followed by biography and statistics. The cards are unnumbered and checklisted below in alphabetical order.

	MINT	NRMT	EXC
COMPLETE SET (27)	6.00	2.70	.75

☐ 1 Jim Bullinger
☐ 2 Todd Cloninger
☐ 3 Tony Collins
☐ 4 Mike Curtis
☐ 5 Sergio Espinal
☐ 6 Jimmie Gardner
☐ 7 John Green
☐ 8 Tony Hamza
☐ 9 Derrick Hardamon
☐ 10 Phil Harrison
☐ 11 Clint Warwick
☐ 12 Joe Housey
☐ 13 Ced Landrum
☐ 14 Jerry Lapenta
☐ 15 Tony Lapoint
☐ 16 Jay Loviglio MG
☐ 17 Kelly Mann
☐ 18 Jim Matas
☐ 19 Steve Melendez TR
☐ 20 Chuck Oertli
☐ 21 Brian Otten
☐ 22 Randy Penvose
☐ 23 Parnell Perry
☐ 24 Harry Shelton
☐ 25 Jose Soto
☐ 26 Bob Strickland
☐ 27 Fernando Zarranz

1986 Glen Falls Tigers ProCards

This 24-card standard-size set of the 1986 Glen Falls Tigers, a Class AA Eastern League affiliate of the Detroit Tigers, features white-bordered posed color player photos on its fronts. The player's name, team, and position appear at the bottom. The white horizontal back carries the player's name and position at the top, followed by biography and statistics. The cards are unnumbered and checklisted below in alphabetical order.

	MINT	NRMT	EXC
COMPLETE SET (24)	6.00	2.70	.75

☐ 1 Ricky Barlow
☐ 2 Willie Darkins
☐ 3 Allen Duffy
☐ 4 Paul Felix
☐ 5 Marty Freeman
☐ 6 Paul Gibson
☐ 7 Mike Gorman
☐ 8 Ruben Guzman
☐ 9 Jeff Herman
☐ 10 John Hiller CO
☐ 11 Al Labozzetta
☐ 12 Scott Lusader
☐ 13 Morris Madden
☐ 14 Frank Masters
☐ 15 Steve McInerney TR
☐ 16 Craig Mills
☐ 17 Rey Palacios
☐ 18 Roman Pena
☐ 19 Benny Ruiz
☐ 20 Bob Schaefer MG
☐ 21 Steve Searcy
☐ 22 Max Soto
☐ 23 James Walewander
☐ 24 Craig Weissmann

1986 Greensboro Hornets ProCards

This 27-card standard-size set of the 1986 Greensboro Hornets, a Class A South Atlantic League affiliate of the Boston Red Sox, features white-bordered posed color player photos on its fronts. The player's name, team, and position appear at the bottom. The white horizontal back carries the player's name and position at the top, followed by biography and statistics. The cards are unnumbered and checklisted below in alphabetical order.

	MINT	NRMT	EXC
COMPLETE SET (27)	6.00	2.70	.75

☐ 1 John Abbott
☐ 2 Alan Ashkinazy
☐ 3 Doug Camilli MG
☐ 4 Kevin Camilli
☐ 5 Jose Flores
☐ 6 Dan Gabriele
☐ 7 Chris Gaeckle
☐ 8 Dan Gakeler
☐ 9 Mike Goff
☐ 10 Dan Hale
☐ 11 Ray Hansen
☐ 12 Tom Kane
☐ 13 Derek Livernois
☐ 14 Don McGowan
☐ 15 Jim Orsag
☐ 16 Billy Plante
☐ 17 Todd Pratt
☐ 18 Carlos Quintana
☐ 19 Ray Revak
☐ 20 John Roberts
☐ 21 Victor Rosario
☐ 22 Larry Shikles
☐ 23 John Toale
☐ 24 Paul Toutsis
☐ 25 Pete Youngman TR
☐ 26 Eddie Zambrano
☐ 27 Bill Zupka

1986 Greenville Braves Team Issue

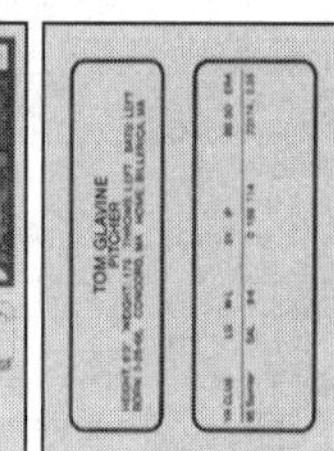

This 23-card standard-size set of the 1986 Greenville Braves, a Class AA Southern League affiliate of the Greenville Braves, features white-bordered posed color player photos on its fronts. The player's name, team, and position appear at the bottom. The white horizontal back carries the player's name and position at the top, followed by biography and statistics. The cards are unnumbered and checklisted below in alphabetical order. This issue includes the minor league card debut of Tom Glavine.

	MINT	NRMT	EXC
COMPLETE SET (23)	50.00	22.00	6.25

☐ 1 Rick Albert CO
☐ 2 Jose Alvarez
☐ 3 Jim Beauchamp MGR
☐ 4 Kevin Blankenship
☐ 5 Chip Childress
☐ 6 Steve Curry
☐ 7 Sal D'Alessandro
☐ 8 Darryl Denby
☐ 9 Tom Glavine
☐ 10 Paul Gnacinski
☐ 11 Dave Griffin
☐ 12 Jeff Groves
☐ 13 Inocencio Guerrero
☐ 14 Randy Ingle
☐ 15 Carlos Rios
☐ 16 Mike Scott
☐ 17 Bill Slack CO
☐ 18 Pete Smith
☐ 19 Thornton Stringfellow
☐ 20 Freddy Tiburcio
☐ 21 Greg Tubbs
☐ 22 Bob Tumpane
☐ 23 Steve Ziem

1986 Hagerstown Suns ProCards

This 29-card standard-size set of the 1986 Hagerstown Suns, a Class A Carolina League affiliate of the Baltimore Orioles, features white-bordered posed color player photos on its fronts. The player's name, team, and position appear at the bottom. The white horizontal back carries the player's name and position at the top, followed by biography and statistics. The cards are unnumbered and checklisted below in alphabetical order.

	MINT	NRMT	EXC
COMPLETE SET (29)	6.00	2.70	.75

☐ 1 Jeff Ballard
☐ 2 Frank Bellino
☐ 3 Mickey Billmeyer
☐ 4 Sherwin Clintje
☐ 5 Brian DuBois
☐ 6 Chris Eagelston
☐ 7 Glenn Gulliver
☐ 8 Scott Khoury
☐ 8 Tom Magrann
☐ 10 Paul McNeal CO
☐ 11 Bob Milacki
☐ 12 Bob Molinaro MG
☐ 13 Ty Nichols
☐ 14 Pete Palermo
☐ 15 Tim Richardson
☐ 16 Norman Roberts
☐ 17 Geraldo Sanchez
☐ 18 Dana Smith
☐ 19 Chuck Stanhope
☐ 20 Pete Stanicek

☐ 21 Earl Stephenson CO
☐ 22 Scott Stranski
☐ 23 Craig Strobel TR
☐ 24 Greg Talamantez
☐ 25 Paul Thorpe
☐ 26 Jesse Vasquez
☐ 27 Ted Wilborn
☐ 28 Wayne Wilson
☐ 29 Craig Worthington

1986 Hawaii Islanders ProCards

This 23-card standard-size set of the 1986 Hawaii Islanders, a Class AAA Pacific Coast League affiliate of the Pittsburgh Pirates, features white-bordered posed color player photos on its fronts. The player's name, team, and position appear at the bottom. The white horizontal back carries the player's name and position at the top, followed by biography and statistics. The cards are unnumbered and checklisted below in alphabetical order.

	MINT	NRMT	EXC
COMPLETE SET (23)	6.00	2.70	.75

☐ 1 Jackie Brown CO
☐ 2 Glenn Brummer
☐ 3 Trench Davis
☐ 4 Benny Distefano
☐ 5 Cecil Espy
☐ 6 Tom Sandt MG
☐ 7 Stan Fansler
☐ 8 Ed Farmer
☐ 9 Felix Fermin
☐ 10 Burk Goldthorn
☐ 11 Sam Haro
☐ 12 Dave Johnson
☐ 13 Barry Jones
☐ 14 Ray Krawczyk
☐ 15 Carlos Ledezma TR
☐ 16 Dave Leeper
☐ 17 Bobby Miscik
☐ 18 Scott Neal
☐ 19 Bob Patterson
☐ 20 Rick Renteria
☐ 21 Lee Tunnell
☐ 22 Ron Wotus
☐ 23 Jeff Zaske

1986 Huntsville Stars Jennings

This issue includes a second year card of Mark McGwire.

	MINT	NRMT	EXC
COMPLETE SET (25)	10.00	4.50	1.25

☐ 10 Amin David
☐ 11 Gary Jones
☐ 12 Dave Nix
☐ 14 Paul Wilder
☐ 15 Rocky Coyle
☐ 16 Terry Steinbach
☐ 18 Damon Farmar
☐ 19 Ray Thoma
☐ 20 Brian Guinn
☐ 21 Todd Burns
☐ 22 Stan Hilton
☐ 23 Wally Whitehurst
☐ 24 Jose Tolentino
☐ 25 Brad Fischer
☐ 26 Mark Leonette
☐ 30 Stan Kyles
☐ 31 Tim Belcher
☐ 32 Scott Whaley
☐ 33 Mark McGwire
☐ 34 Greg Cadaret
☐ 40 Doug Scherer
☐ 41 John Cox
☐ 42 Mirk McDonald
☐ 44 Rick Tronerud
☐ 45 Roy Johnson

1986 Indianapolis Indians Team Issue

This 36-card set of the 1986 Indianapolis Indians, a Class AAA American Association affiliate of the Montreal Expos, features posed color player shots on its fronts, and measures approximately 2 1/2" by 3 5/8". A gold stripe appears above and below the photo. The upper gold stripe carries the team name; the player's name and position are printed within a brown baseball bat icon in the bottom gold margin. The white horizontal back carries the player's autograph facsimile at the top, followed by biography, statistics, and career highlights. The cards are numbered on the back. Card nos. 2, 5, 8, 11, 14, 18, 21, 24 and 29 depict players or teams from the past.

	MINT	NRMT	EXC
COMPLETE SET (36)	8.00	3.60	1.00

☐ 1 Indians Are Coming
☐ 2 Owen J. Bush
☐ 3 Joe Sparks MG
☐ 4 Rich Stoll
☐ 5 Jack Glasscock
☐ 6 Randy Hunt
☐ 7 Tom Romano
☐ 8 Amos Rusie
☐ 9 Bob Owchinko
☐ 10 Rene Gonzales
☐ 11 Another League
Another Team
☐ 12 John Dopson
☐ 13 Derrell Baker
☐ 14 1928 Indians
☐ 15 Randy St. Claire
☐ 16 Skeeter Barnes
☐ 17 Rodger Cole
☐ 18 Bob(Lefty) Logan
☐ 19 Wally Johnson
☐ 20 Len Barker
☐ 21 Al Lopez MG 1948-50
☐ 22 Mike Hocutt
☐ 23 Bob Sebra
☐ 24 Herb Score
☐ 25 Curt Brown
☐ 26 Dallas Williams
☐ 27 Larry Groves
☐ 28 Luis Rivera
☐ 29 Don Buford
☐ 30 Tom Nieto
☐ 31 Dave Tomlin
☐ 32 Champ Summers
☐ 33 Casey Candaele
☐ 34 Tim Barrett
☐ 35 Billy Moore
☐ 36 A Little Help
Jerry Manuel CO
Lee Garrett TR
Rick Williams CO

1986 Iowa Cubs ProCards

This 26-card standard-size set of the 1986 Iowa Cubs, a Class AAA American Association affiliate of the Chicago Cubs, features white-bordered posed color player photos on its fronts. The player's name, team, and position appear at the bottom. The white horizontal back carries the player's name and position at the top, followed by biography and statistics. The cards are unnumbered and checklisted below in alphabetical order.

	MINT	NRMT	EXC
COMPLETE SET (26)	6.00	2.70	.75

☐ 1 Johnny Abrego
☐ 2 Bob Bathe
☐ 3 Pookie Bernstine
☐ 4 Trey Brooks
☐ 5 Mike Brumley
☐ 6 Steve Christmas
☐ 7 Jim Colborn CO
☐ 8 Jeff Cornell
☐ 9 Larry Cox MG
☐ 10 Steve Engel
☐ 11 Terry Francona
☐ 12 Dave Grossman TR
☐ 13 Dave Gumpert
☐ 14 Steve Hammond
☐ 15 Joe Hicks
☐ 16 Guy Hoffman
☐ 17 Dave Martinez
☐ 18 Ron Meridith
☐ 19 Brad Mills
☐ 20 Paul Noce
☐ 21 Gary Parmenter
☐ 22 Doug Potestio
☐ 23 Ken Pryce
☐ 24 Bobby Ramos
☐ 25 Julio Valdez
☐ 26 Chico Walker

1986 Jackson Mets TCMA

This 27-card standard-size set of the 1986 Jackson Mets, a Class AA Texas League affiliate of the New York Mets, features white-bordered posed color player shots set on fuchsia backgrounds. The team name is printed within the fuchsia area below the photo. A black stripe at the bottom carries the player's name and position. The white back carries the team name and league at the top, followed by the player's name, positon, biography and statistics.

	MINT	NRMT	EXC
COMPLETE SET (27)	8.00	3.60	1.00

☐ 1 Jim Adamczak
☐ 2 Reggie Dobie
☐ 3 Wray Bergendahl
☐ 4 Tom Edens
☐ 5 Kyle Hartshorn
☐ 6 Jeff Innis
☐ 7 Kurt Lundgren
☐ 8 Ed Pruitt
☐ 9 Mike Santiago
☐ 10 Mickey Weston
☐ 11 Doug Gwosdz
☐ 12 Greg Olson
☐ 13 Kevin Elster
☐ 14 Dennis Glynn
☐ 15 Paul Hertzler
☐ 16 Andy Lawrence
☐ 17 Jeff McKnight
☐ 18 Rick Lockwood
☐ 19 Shawn Abner
☐ 20 Jason Felice
☐ 21 Scott Little
☐ 22 Johnny Wilson
☐ 23 Sam McCrary TR
☐ 24 Mike Cubbage MG
☐ 25 Glenn Abbott
☐ 26 Randy Milligan
☐ 27 Keith Miller

1986 Jacksonville Expos TCMA

This 26-card standard-size set of the 1986 Jacksonville Expos, a Class AA Southern League affiliate of the Montreal Expos, features white-bordered posed color player shots set on fuchsia backgrounds. The team name is printed within the fuchsia area below the photo. A black stripe at the bottom carries the player's name and position. The white back carries the team name and league at the top, followed by the player's name, positon, biography and statistics. The set was sponsored by Golden Glove, a local sports card store.

	MINT	NRMT	EXC
COMPLETE SET (26)	8.00	3.60	1.00

☐ 1 Tony Nicometi
☐ 2 Johnny Paredes
☐ 3 Jim Cecchini
☐ 4 Armando Moreno
☐ 5 Tom Traen
☐ 6 Peter Camelo
☐ 7 John Trautwein
☐ 8 Nelson Santovenia
☐ 9 Leonel Carrion CO
☐ 10 Q.V. Lowe CO
☐ 11 Joe Graves
☐ 12 Greg Raymer
☐ 13 Matt Sferrazza
☐ 14 Kevin Price
☐ 15 Mark Gardner
☐ 16 Troy McKay
☐ 17 Gary Weinberger
☐ 18 Wilfredo Tejada
☐ 19 Tommy Thompson MG/CO
☐ 20 Mark Corey
☐ 21 Jeff Reynolds
☐ 22 Nelson Norman
☐ 23 Brian Holman
☐ 24 Bill Cutshall
☐ 25 Jack Daugherty
☐ 26 Tim McCormack TR

1986 Jamestown Expos ProCards

This 30-card standard-size set of the 1986 Jamestown Expos, a Class A New York-Penn League affiliate of the Montreal Expos, features white-bordered posed color player photos on its fronts. The player's name, team, and position appear at the bottom. The white horizontal back carries the player's name and position at the top, followed by biography and statistics. The cards are unnumbered and checklisted below in alphabetical order.

	MINT	NRMT	EXC
COMPLETE SET (30)	6.00	2.70	.75

☐ 1 Michael Blowers
☐ 2 Don Burke
☐ 3 Scott Clemo
☐ 4 William DeBoever
☐ 5 Kody Duey
☐ 6 Jerome Duke
☐ 7 Kenneth Fox
☐ 8 Paul Frye
☐ 9 Chan Galbato
☐ 10 Robert Gaylor
☐ 11 Michael Haines
☐ 12 Mark Hardy
☐ 13 Gene Harris
☐ 14 Steven King
☐ 15 Paul Peter Martineau
☐ 16 James McDonald
☐ 17 David Morrow
☐ 18 Jeffrey Oller
☐ 19 Troy Ricker
☐ 20 Michael Robertson
☐ 21 Dean Rockweiler
☐ 22 Robert Shannon
☐ 23 Joe Beely Sims
☐ 24 Steve St. Claire
☐ 25 Jeffrey Tabaka
☐ 26 Darren Travels
☐ 27 Sal Vaccaro
☐ 28 Jeffrey Wedvick
☐ 29 Frank Welborn
☐ 30 Yippee
Mascot

1986 Kenosha Twins ProCards

This 25-card standard-size set of the 1986 Kenosha Twins, a Class A Midwest League affiliate of the Minnesota Twins, features white-bordered posed color player photos on its fronts. The player's name, team, and position appear at the bottom. The white horizontal back carries the player's name and position at the top, followed by biography and statistics. The cards are unnumbered and checklisted below in alphabetical order.

	MINT	NRMT	EXC
COMPLETE SET (25)	6.00	2.70	.75

☐ 1 Paul Abbott
☐ 2 Larry Blackwell
☐ 3 Jeff Bumgarner
☐ 4 James Cook
☐ 5 Mark Davis
☐ 6 Tom DiCeglio
☐ 7 Julio Delancer
☐ 8 Rafael DeLima
☐ 9 Tom Fiore TR
☐ 10 Steven Gasser
☐ 11 Marty Lanoux
☐ 12 Bob Lee
☐ 13 Don Leppert MG
☐ 14 Jerry Mack
☐ 15 Howard Manzon
☐ 16 Ted Miller
☐ 17 Edgar Naveda
☐ 18 Tim O'Connor
☐ 19 Yorkis Perez
☐ 20 Bob Perry
☐ 21 Mike Redding
☐ 22 Bob Strube
☐ 23 Luis Tapais
☐ 24 Gary Thomason
☐ 25 Leonard Webster

1986 Kinston Eagles ProCards

This 25-card standard-size set of the 1986 Kinston Eagles, a Class A Carolina League Independent, features white-bordered posed color player photos on its fronts. The player's name, team, and position appear at the bottom. The white horizontal back carries the player's name and position at the top, followed by biography and statistics. The cards are unnumbered and checklisted below in alphabetical order.

	MINT	NRMT	EXC
COMPLETE SET (25)	6.00	2.70	.75

☐ 1 Howard Akers
☐ 2 Bubba Brevell
☐ 3 Scott Cannon
☐ 4 Ed Delzer
☐ 5 Tex Drake BB
☐ 6 Van Evans
☐ 7 Bruce Fischback TR
☐ 8 Gene Gentile
☐ 9 Al Heath
☐ 10 Mike Ingle
☐ 11 Lindsey Johnson
☐ 12 Roger Johnson
☐ 13 Randy Kramer
☐ 14 Dan Larsen
☐ 15 Perry Lychak
☐ 16 Scott Melvin
☐ 17 Paul Moralez
☐ 18 Marty Reed
☐ 19 Emmett Robinson
☐ 20 Gabriel Robles
☐ 21 Randy Romagna
☐ 22 Melvin Rosario
☐ 23 John Schofield
☐ 24 Dave Trembley MGR
☐ 25 Ken Whitfield

1986 Knoxville Blue Jays ProCards

Sponsored by Smokey Mountain Collectibles, this 27-card standard-size set of the 1986 Knoxville Blue Jays, a Class AA Southern League affiliate of the Toronto Blue Jays, features white-bordered posed color player photos on its fronts. The player's name, team, and position appear at the bottom. The white horizontal back carries the player's name and position at the top, followed by biography and statistics. The cards are unnumbered and checklisted below in alphabetical order.

	MINT	NRMT	EXC
COMPLETE SET (27)	6.00	2.70	.75

☐ 1 Kash Beauchamp
☐ 2 Jim Bishop
☐ 3 Pat Borders
☐ 4 Sil Campusano
☐ 5 J.J. Cannon CO
☐ 6 Eddie Dennis CO
☐ 7 Tim Englund
☐ 8 Keith Gilliam
☐ 9 Larry Hardy MG
☐ 10 Glenallen Hill
☐ 11 Randy Holland TR
☐ 12 Jim Howard
☐ 13 Tony Hudson
☐ 14 Manuel Lee
☐ 15 Nelson Liriano
☐ 16 Colin McLaughlin

☐ 17 Greg Moore
☐ 18 Oswald Peraza
☐ 19 Jose Segura
☐ 20 Chris Shaddy
☐ 21 Kevin Sliwinski
☐ 22 Matt Stark
☐ 23 Bernie Tatis
☐ 24 Norm Tonnucci
☐ 25 Dave Walsh
☐ 26 Mike Yearout
☐ 27 Cliff Young

1986 Lakeland Tigers ProCards

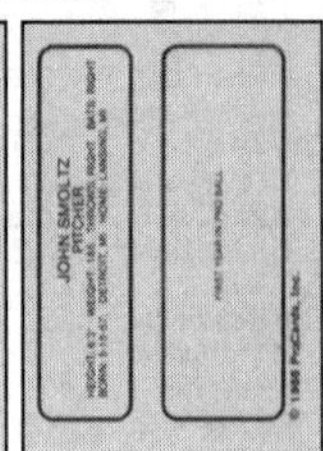

This 25-card standard-size set of the 1986 Lakeland Tigers, a Class A Florida State League affiliate of the Detroit Tigers, features white-bordered posed color player photos on its fronts. The player's name, team, and position appear at the bottom. The white horizontal back carries the player's name and position at the top, followed by biography and statistics. The cards are unnumbered and checklisted below in alphabetical order. This issue includes the minor league card debut of John Smoltz.

	MINT	NRMT	EXC
COMPLETE SET (25)	60.00	27.00	7.50

☐ 1 Jeff Agar
☐ 2 Bernie Anderson
☐ 3 Tommy Burgess MG
☐ 4 Bill Cooper
☐ 5 Steve Eagar
☐ 6 Ken Gohmann
☐ 7 Keith Hoskinson
☐ 8 Mark Lee
☐ 9 Tim Leiper
☐ 10 Al Liebert
☐ 11 Tony Long
☐ 12 Porfi Martinez
☐ 13 Chip McHugh
☐ 14 Jeff Minick
☐ 15 Dave Minnema
☐ 16 Chris Morgan
☐ 17 Rod Poissant
☐ 18 Laney Prioleau
☐ 19 Art Raubolt
☐ 20 Donnie Rowland
☐ 21 Joseph Slavic
☐ 22 Terry Smith TR
☐ 23 John Smoltz
☐ 24 Doug Strange
☐ 25 Mike York

1986 Las Vegas Stars ProCards

This 26-card standard-size set of the 1986 Las Vegas Stars, a Class AAA Pacific Coast League affiliate of the San Diego Padres, features white-bordered posed color player photos on its fronts. The player's name, team, and position appear at the bottom. The white horizontal back carries the player's name and position at the top, followed by biography and statistics. The cards are unnumbered and checklisted below in alphabetical order.

	MINT	NRMT	EXC
COMPLETE SET (24)	7.00	3.10	.85
COMPLETE SET W/Hutcheson (25)	8.00	3.60	1.00
COMPLETE SET W/Bowa (26)	12.00	5.50	1.50

☐ 1 Randy Asadoor
☐ 2 Greg Booker
☐ 3 Larry Bowa
☐ 4 Steve Garcia
☐ 5 Dick Grapenthin
☐ 6 Gary Green
☐ 7 Ray Hayward
☐ 8 Todd Hutcheson
☐ 9 Jimmy Jones
☐ 10 Steve Kemp
☐ 11 Steve Lubratich
☐ 12 Mark Parent
☐ 13 Tim Pyznarski
☐ 14 Edwin Rodriguez
☐ 15 Benito Santiago
☐ 16 James Siwy
☐ 17 Gregory Smith
☐ 18 Brian Snyder
☐ 19 James Steels
☐ 20 Bob Stoddard
☐ 21 John Tutt
☐ 22 Ed Vosberg

☐ 23 Mark Wasinger
☐ 24 Mark Williamson
☐ 25 Ed Wojna
☐ 26 Gary Woods

1986 Little Falls Mets ProCards

This 29-card standard-size set of the 1986 Little Falls Mets, a Class A New York-Penn League affiliate of the New York Mets, features white-bordered posed color player photos on its fronts. The player's name, team, and position appear at the bottom. The white horizontal back carries the player's name and position at the top, followed by biography and statistics. The cards are unnumbered and checklisted below in alphabetical order.

	MINT	NRMT	EXC
COMPLETE SET (29)	6.00	2.70	.75

☐ 1 Mike Anderson
☐ 2 Pete Bauer
☐ 3 Lou Berge
☐ 4 Rick Brown
☐ 5 Genaro Castro
☐ 6 Rob Colescott
☐ 7 Pat Crosby
☐ 8 Mark D'Vincenzo
☐ 9 Rich Duant
☐ 10 Ken Farmer
☐ 11 Mark Fiedler
☐ 12 Cliff Gonzalez
☐ 13 Cedric Hawkins
☐ 14 Rob Hernandez
☐ 15 Alex Jiminez
☐ 16 Lorin Jundy
☐ 17 Rich Lundahl
☐ 18 Dan McMurtrie
☐ 19 Rich Miller MG
☐ 20 Rodney Murrel
☐ 21 Ron Narcisse
☐ 22 Luis Natera
☐ 23 Fritz Polka
☐ 24 Jaime Roseboro
☐ 25 Joel Sklar
☐ 26 Heath Slocumb
☐ 27 Andy Taylor
☐ 28 Tony Thompson
☐ 29 Todd Welborn

1986 Louisville Redbirds Team Issue

	MINT	NRMT	EXC
COMPLETE SET (30)	12.00	5.50	1.50

☐ 1 Jim Fregosi MG
☐ 2 Dyar Miller CO
☐ 3 David"Hap' Hudson TR
☐ 4 Jack Ayer
☐ 5 Steve Braun
☐ 6 Joe Boever
☐ 7 Rod Booker
☐ 8 Rich Buonanthony
☐ 9 Ralph Citarella
☐ 10 Greg Dunn
☐ 11 Mike Dunne
☐ 12 Bill Earley
☐ 13 Curt Ford
☐ 14 Kurt Kepshire
☐ 15 Alan Knicely
☐ 16 Jim Lindeman
☐ 17 Bill Lyons
☐ 18 Fred Manrique
☐ 19 Fred Martinez
☐ 20 John Morris
☐ 21 Tom Pagnozzi
☐ 22 Casey Parsons
☐ 23 Joe Pettini
☐ 24 Marty Pevey
☐ 25 Dave Rajsich
☐ 26 Ray Soff
☐ 27 Dan Stryffeler
☐ 28 Tim Wallace
☐ 29 Jed Smith
☐ 30 The Redbird (Mascot)
Doyle Harris (Mascot)

1986 Lynchburg Mets ProCards

This 28-card standard-size set of the 1986 Lynchburg Mets, a Class A Carolina League affiliate of the New York Mets, features white-bordered posed color player photos on its fronts. The player's name, team, and position appear at the bottom. The white horizontal back carries the player's name and position at the top, followed by biography and statistics. The cards are unnumbered and checklisted below in alphabetical order.

	MINT	NRMT	EXC
COMPLETE SET (28)	6.00	2.70	.75

☐ 1 Ralph Adams
☐ 2 Jim Bibby CO
☐ 3 Desi Brooks
☐ 4 Kevin Brown
☐ 5 Wilmer Caraballo
☐ 6 Al Carmichael
☐ 7 Jeff Ciszkowski
☐ 8 Angelo Cuevas
☐ 9 Bobby Floyd
☐ 10 Jeff Gardner
☐ 11 Steve Gay
☐ 12 Ronnie Gideon
☐ 13 Mauro Gozzo
☐ 14 Marcus Lawton
☐ 15 Chuck Lynn
☐ 16 Hector Perez
☐ 17 Steve Phillips
☐ 18 Jeff Richardson
☐ 19 Rich Rodriguez
☐ 20 Zoilo Sanchez
☐ 21 Eric Stampel
☐ 22 Dave Tresch TR
☐ 23 Wilson Valera
☐ 24 Juan Villanueva
☐ 25 Dave West
☐ 26 Mike Westbrook
☐ 27 Dan Winters
☐ 28 Shane Young

1986 Macon Pirates ProCards

This 27-card standard-size set of the 1986 Macon Pirates, a Class A South Atlantic League affiliate of the Pittsburgh Pirates, features white-bordered posed color player photos on its fronts. The player's name, team, and position appear at the bottom. The white horizontal back carries the player's name and position at the top, followed by biography and statistics. The cards are unnumbered and checklisted below in alphabetical order. This issue includes the minor league card debut of Orlando Merced.

	MINT	NRMT	EXC
COMPLETE SET (27)	12.00	5.50	1.50

☐ 1 Ben Abner
☐ 2 Kevin Andersh
☐ 3 Kirk Berry
☐ 4 Dwight Bernard
☐ 5 Octavio Cepeda
☐ 6 Tony Chance
☐ 7 Jim Davins
☐ 8 Dorley Downs
☐ 9 Kevin Franchi
☐ 10 Ron Giddens
☐ 11 Andy Hall
☐ 12 Todd Hansen
☐ 13 Rob Hatfield
☐ 14 Guillermo Mercedes
☐ 15 Orlando Merced
☐ 16 Douglas Moreno
☐ 17 Rafael Muratti
☐ 18 Luis Pena
☐ 19 Julio Perez
☐ 20 Mike Quade MG
☐ 21 Gilbert Roca
☐ 22 Jeff Satzinger
☐ 23 Brian Stackhouse TR
☐ 24 Mike Stevanus
☐ 25 Keith Swartzlander
☐ 26 Jay Wollenburg
☐ 27 Joey Zellner

1986 Madison Muskies Police

	MINT	NRMT	EXC
COMPLETE SET (27)	10.00	4.50	1.25

☐ 1 Doug Ames
☐ 2 Tony Arias
☐ 3 Larry Arndt
☐ 4 Tony Cabrera
☐ 5 Ron Carter
☐ 6 Brian Criswell
☐ 7 Mike Cupples
☐ 8 Pat Dietrick
☐ 9 Bobby Gould
☐ 10 Marty Hall
☐ 11 Mark Howie
☐ 12 Andre Jacas
☐ 13 Russ Kibler
☐ 14 Kirk McDonald
☐ 15 Dave Nix
☐ 16 Dave Otto
☐ 17 Scott Sabo
☐ 18 Jeff Shaver
☐ 19 Nelson Silverio
☐ 20 Bob Stocker
☐ 21 Camilo Veras
☐ 22 Walt Weiss
☐ 23 Wally Whitehurst
☐ 24 Jim Nettles MG
☐ 25 Dave Schober TR
☐ 26 Dave Shillinglaw CO
☐ 27 Rick Wise CO

1986 Madison Muskies ProCards

This 28-card standard-size set of the 1986 Madison Muskies, a Class A Midwest League affiliate of the Oakland Athletics, features white-bordered posed color player photos on its fronts. The player's name, team, and position appear at the bottom. The white horizontal back carries the player's name and position at the top, followed by biography and statistics. The cards are unnumbered and checklisted below in alphabetical order.

	MINT	NRMT	EXC
COMPLETE SET (28)	6.00	2.70	.75

☐ 1 Douglas Ames
☐ 2 Tony Arias
☐ 3 Larry Arndt
☐ 4 Antonio Cabrera
☐ 5 Ron Carter
☐ 6 Brian Criswell
☐ 7 Michael Cupples
☐ 8 Patrick Dietrick
☐ 9 Bobby Gould
☐ 10 Marty Hall
☐ 11 Mark Howie
☐ 12 Andre Jacas
☐ 13 Russell Kibler
☐ 14 Kirk McDonald
☐ 15 James Nettles MG
☐ 16 Dave Nix
☐ 17 David Otis
☐ 18 Kevin Russ
☐ 19 Scott Sabo
☐ 20 Dave Schober TR
☐ 21 Jeffrey Shaver
☐ 22 Dave Shillinglaw CO
☐ 23 Nelson Silverio
☐ 24 Robert Stocker
☐ 25 Camilo Veras
☐ 26 Walter Weiss
☐ 27 Walter Whitehurst
☐ 28 Rich Wise CO

1986 Maine Guides ProCards

This 26-card standard-size set of the 1986 Maine Guides, a Class AAA International League affiliate of the Cleveland Indians, features white-bordered posed color player photos on its fronts. The player's name, team, and position appear at the bottom. The white horizontal back carries the player's name and position at the top, followed by biography and statistics. The cards are unnumbered and checklisted below in alphabetical order.

	MINT	NRMT	EXC
COMPLETE SET (26)	6.00	2.70	.75

☐ 1 Barry Bruenkant
☐ 2 Kevin Buckley
☐ 3 George Cecchetti
☐ 4 Steve Ciszczon TR
☐ 5 Dave Clark
☐ 6 Steve Comer CO
☐ 7 Keith Creel
☐ 8 Barry Evans
☐ 9 Dave Gallagher CO
☐ 10 Kevin Hagen
☐ 11 Doug Jones
☐ 12 Jim Napier MG
☐ 13 Junior Noboa
☐ 14 Bryan Oelkers
☐ 15 Craig Pippen
☐ 16 Reggie Ritter
☐ 17 Scott Roberts
☐ 18 Jose Roman
☐ 19 Tommy Rowe
☐ 20 Cory Snyder
☐ 21 Curt Wardle
☐ 22 Randy Washington
☐ 23 Jim Weaver
☐ 24 Frank Wills
☐ 25 Jim Wilson
☐ 26 Rich Yett

1986 Medford A's Cramer

	MINT	NRMT	EXC
COMPLETE SET (25)	8.00	3.60	1.00

☐ 51 William Savarino
☐ 52 James Reiser
☐ 53 David Veres
☐ 54 Mark Stancel
☐ 55 Mark Beavers
☐ 56 William Reynolds
☐ 57 Luis Martinez
☐ 58 Bill Coonan
☐ 59 Pat Gilbert
☐ 60 Larry Ritchey
☐ 61 Glenn Hoffinger
☐ 62 Robbie Gilbert
☐ 63 Todd Hartley
☐ 64 Kevin Tapani
☐ 65 Weston Weber
☐ 66 Jeff Kopyta
☐ 67 Dann P.J. Howitt

☐ 68 Jeff Glover
☐ 69 Lance Blankenship
☐ 70 Kevin Kunkel
☐ 71 James Carroll
☐ 72 Darrin Duffy
☐ 73 John"Bo' Kent
☐ 74 Vincent Teixeira
☐ 75 Keith Wentz

1986 Memphis Chicks Time Out Sports

This 26-card standard-size set of the 1986 Memphis Chicks features gold-bordered posed color player photos on its fronts. The player's name, team logo, and position appear at the bottom. The sets were produced by Time Out Sports Productions and come with a certificate of authenticity. 10,000 gold border and 5,000 silver border sets were produced. This issue includes the only minor league card of Bo Jackson.

	MINT	NRMT	EXC
COMPLETE GOLD SET (26)	15.00	6.75	1.85
COMPLETE SILVER SET (26)	25.00	11.00	3.10

☐ 1 Terry Bell
☐ 2 Ken Crew
☐ 3 Jimmy Daniel
☐ 4 John Davis
☐ 5 Luis De Los Santos
☐ 6 Rich Dubee CO
☐ 7 Phil George
☐ 8 Doug Gilcrease
☐ 9 Rick Goodin
☐ 10 Bo Jackson
☐ 11 Joe Jarrell
☐ 12 Tommy Jones MG
☐ 13 Jere Longenecker
☐ 14 Art Martinez
☐ 15 Chito Martinez
☐ 16 Mike Macfarlane
☐ 17 Mitch McKelvey
☐ 18 Mike Miller
☐ 19 Gene Morgan
☐ 20 Angel Morris
☐ 21 Steve Morrow TR
☐ 22 Hector Rincones
☐ 23 Jose Rodiles
☐ 24 Israel Sanchez
☐ 25 Van Snider
☐ 26 Gary Thurman

1986 Miami Marlins ProCards

This 29-card standard-size set of the 1986 Miami Marlins, a Class A Florida State League Independent, features white-bordered posed color player photos on its fronts. The player's name, team, and position appear at the bottom. The white horizontal back carries the player's name and position at the top, followed by biography and statistics. The cards are unnumbered and checklisted below in alphabetical order.

	MINT	NRMT	EXC
COMPLETE SET (29)	6.00	2.70	.75

☐ 1 German Bautista
☐ 2 Juan Bellver
☐ 3 Mike Browning
☐ 4 Rick Carrano TR
☐ 5 Tim Dulin
☐ 6 Todd Edwards
☐ 7 Marc Estes
☐ 8 John Harrington
☐ 9 Fred Hatfield MG
☐ 10 Tommy Hearn
☐ 11 Alan Hixon
☐ 12 Lance Hudson
☐ 13 Dan Juenke
☐ 14 Bob Latmore
☐ 15 Kurt Leiter
☐ 16 Pedro Llanes
☐ 17 Jerry Miller CO
☐ 18 Curt Morgan
☐ 19 Luis Ojeda
☐ 20 Ray Perkins
☐ 21 Eric Rasmussen
☐ 22 Elem Rossy
☐ 23 Todd Smith
☐ 24 Phil Taylor
☐ 25 Dave Van Ohlen
☐ 26 Greg Wallace
☐ 27 Phil Wielegman
☐ 28 Roger Wilson
☐ 29 John Wockenfuss

1986 Midland Angels ProCards

This 26-card standard-size set of the 1986 Midland Angels, a Class AA Texas League affiliate of the California Angels, features white-bordered posed color player photos on its fronts. The player's name, team, and position appear at the bottom. The white horizontal back carries the player's name and position at the top, followed by biography and statistics. The cards are unnumbered and checklisted below in alphabetical order.

	MINT	NRMT	EXC
COMPLETE SET (26)	6.00	2.70	.75

☐ 1 Doug Banning
☐ 2 Brian Brady
☐ 3 DeWayne Buice
☐ 4 Vinicio Cedeno
☐ 5 Terry Clark
☐ 6 Mike Cook
☐ 7 Sherman Corbett
☐ 8 Doug Davis
☐ 9 Brian Hartsock
☐ 10 Dave Heath
☐ 11 John Hotchkiss
☐ 12 Kevin King
☐ 13 Vance Lovelace
☐ 14 Joe Maddon MG
☐ 15 Mike Madril
☐ 16 Mark McLemore
☐ 17 Bill Merrifield
☐ 18 Aurelio Monteagudo
☐ 19 Rafael Pimental
☐ 20 James Randall
☐ 21 Jeff Schaffer
☐ 22 Don Timberlake
☐ 23 Raul Tovar
☐ 24 Phil Venturino
☐ 25 Glen Walker
☐ 26 Richard Zaleski TR

1986 Modesto A's Chong

	MINT	NRMT	EXC
COMPLETE SET (27)	15.00	6.75	1.85

☐ 1 Roy Anderson
☐ 2 Russ Applegate
☐ 3 Darren Balsley
☐ 4 Bo Kent
☐ 5 Tyler Brilinski
☐ 6 Pat Dietrick
☐ 7 Mike Duncan
☐ 8 Darel Hansen
☐ 9 Twayne Harris
☐ 10 Steve Howard
☐ 11 James Jones
☐ 12 Felix Jose
☐ 13 Lance Blankenship
☐ 14 Richard Martig
☐ 15 Shannon Mendenhall
☐ 16 Jerome Nelson
☐ 17 Jose Peguero
☐ 18 Bob Sharpnack
☐ 19 Mark Tortorice
☐ 20 Bruce Walton
☐ 21 Joe Xavier
☐ 22 Kevin Tapani
☐ 23 Mark Beavers
☐ 24 Butch Hughes
☐ 25 Tommie Reynolds
☐ 26 John Cartelli
☐ 27 Jeff Kopyta

1986 Modesto A's ProCards

This 27-card standard-size set of the 1986 Modesto A's, a Class A California League affiliate of the Oakland Athletics, features white-bordered posed color player photos on its fronts. The player's name, team, and position appear at the bottom. The white horizontal back carries the player's name and position at the top, followed by biography and statistics. The cards are unnumbered and checklisted below in alphabetical order.

	MINT	NRMT	EXC
COMPLETE SET (26)	6.00	2.70	.75
COMPLETE SET (27)	10.00	4.50	1.25

☐ 1A Roy Anderson (with bat)
☐ 1B Roy Anderson (catching)
☐ 2 Russell Applegate
☐ 3 Darren Balsley
☐ 4 Tyler Brilinski
☐ 5 John "Doc" Cartelli TR
☐ 6 Jerry Deguero
☐ 7 Mike Duncan
☐ 8 Vic Figueroa
☐ 9 Steve Gorey
☐ 10 Darel Hansen
☐ 11 Twayne Harris
☐ 12 Mike Hogan
☐ 13 Steve Howard
☐ 14 Butch Hughes
☐ 15 Jim Jones
☐ 16 Felix Jose
☐ 17 John Kanter
☐ 18 Joe Kramer
☐ 19 Rich Martig
☐ 20 Jerome Nelson
☐ 21 Tommie Reynolds MGR
☐ 22 Bob Sharpnack
☐ 23 Jim Strichek
☐ 24 Joe Strong
☐ 25 Mark Tortorice
☐ 26 Bruce Walton

1986 Nashua Pirates ProCards

This 28-card standard-size set of the 1986 Nashua Pirates, a Class AA Eastern League affiliate of the Pittsburgh Pirates, features white-bordered posed color player photos on its fronts. The player's name, team, and position appear at the bottom. The white horizontal back carries the player's name and position at the top, followed by biography and statistics. The cards are unnumbered and checklisted below in alphabetical order.

	MINT	NRMT	EXC
COMPLETE SET (28)	6.00	2.70	.75

☐ 1 Mike Ashman
☐ 2 Kerry Baker
☐ 3 Mike Berger
☐ 4 Craig Brown
☐ 5 Matias Carrillo
☐ 6 Scott Fiepke
☐ 7 Ken Ford
☐ 8 Kevin Gordon
☐ 9 Tommy Gregg
☐ 10 Dimas Gutierrez
☐ 11 Reggie Hammonds
☐ 12 Martin Hernandez
☐ 13 Shawn Holman
☐ 14 Tony Laird
☐ 15 Jim Leopold
☐ 16 Jose Lind
☐ 17 Orlando Lind
☐ 18 Steve McAllister
☐ 19 Jim Neidlinger
☐ 20 Jim Opie
☐ 21 Hipolito Pena
☐ 22 Pete Rice
☐ 23 Ruben Rodriguez
☐ 24 Dennis Rogers MG
☐ 25 Rich Sauveur
☐ 26 Dorn Taylor
☐ 27 Spin Williams CO
☐ 28 H.Williams TR

1986 Nashville Sounds Team Issue

	MINT	NRMT	EXC
COMPLETE SET (24)	8.00	3.60	1.00

☐ 1 Doug Baker
☐ 2 Fred Breining
☐ 3 Chuck Cary
☐ 4 Pedro Chavez
☐ 5 Jeff Conner
☐ 6 Brian Denman
☐ 7 Scott Earl
☐ 8 Bruce Fields
☐ 9 Paul Gibson
☐ 10 Brian Harper
☐ 11 Don Heinkel
☐ 12 Mike Henneman
☐ 13 Rodney Hobbs
☐ 14 Bryan Kelly
☐ 15 Jack Lazorko
☐ 16 Scotti Madison
☐ 17 Don McGann TR
☐ 18 Matt Nokes
☐ 19 Chris Nyman
☐ 20 German Rivera
☐ 21 Leon Roberts MG
☐ 22 Jeff Robinson
☐ 23 Gene Roof
☐ 24 Tim Tolman

1986 New Britain Red Sox ProCards

This 25-card standard-size set of the 1986 New Britain Red Sox, a Class AA Eastern League affiliate of the Boston Red Sox, features white-bordered posed color player photos on its fronts. The player's name, team, and position appear at the bottom. The white horizontal back carries the player's name and position at the top, followed by biography and statistics. The cards are unnumbered and checklisted below in alphabetical order. This issue includes the minor league card debut of Ellis Burks.

	MINT	NRMT	EXC
COMPLETE SET (25)	20.00	9.00	2.50

☐ 1 Andy Araujo
☐ 2 Tony Beal
☐ 3 Jose Birriel
☐ 4 Ellis Burks
☐ 5 Pete Cappadona
☐ 6 Robert Chadwick TR
☐ 7 Jim Corsi
☐ 8 Steve Curry
☐ 9 Chuck Davis
☐ 10 Steve Ellsworth
☐ 11 Eduardo Estrada
☐ 12 DeMarlo Hale
☐ 13 Sam Horn
☐ 14 Pat Jelks
☐ 15 Dana Kiecker
☐ 16 John Marzano
☐ 17 Bill McInnis
☐ 18 Mark Meleski
☐ 19 Sam Nattile
☐ 20 Dave Peterson
☐ 21 Jody Reed
☐ 22 Paul Slifko
☐ 23 Hector Steward
☐ 24 Tony Torchia MG
☐ 25 Scott Wade

1986 Oklahoma City 89ers ProCards

This 26-card standard-size set of the 1986 Oklahoma City 89ers, a Class AAA American Association affiliate of the Texas Rangers, features white-bordered posed color player photos on its fronts. The player's name, team, and position appear at the bottom. The white horizontal back carries the player's name and position at the top, followed by biography and statistics. The cards are unnumbered and checklisted below in alphabetical order.

	MINT	NRMT	EXC
COMPLETE SET (26)	8.00	3.60	1.00

☐ 1 Bob Brower
☐ 2 Greg Campbell TR
☐ 3 Rob Clark
☐ 4 Glen Cook
☐ 5 Tommy Dunbar
☐ 6 Dave Geisel
☐ 7 Rusty Gerhardt CO
☐ 8 Bobby Jones
☐ 9 Jeff Kunkel
☐ 10 Willie Lozado
☐ 11 Jim Maler
☐ 12 Orlando Mercado
☐ 13 Dale Mohoric
☐ 14 Jeff Moronko
☐ 15 Dave Oliver MG
☐ 16 Dave Owen
☐ 17 Mike Parrott
☐ 18 Luis Pujols
☐ 19 Jeff Russell
☐ 20 Tommy Joe Shimp
☐ 21 Ruben Sierra
☐ 22 Rick Surhoff
☐ 23 Greg Tabor
☐ 24 Don Welchel
☐ 25 Don Werner
☐ 26 Matt Williams

1986 Omaha Royals ProCards

This 29-card standard-size set of the 1986 Omaha Royals, a Class AAA American Association affiliate of the Kansas City Royals, features white-bordered posed color player photos on its fronts. The player's name, team, and position appear at the bottom. The white horizontal back carries the player's name and position at the top, followed by biography and statistics. The cards are unnumbered and checklisted below in alphabetical order.

	MINT	NRMT	EXC
COMPLETE SET (29)	20.00	9.00	2.50

☐ 1 Scott Bankhead
☐ 2 John Boles MG
☐ 3 Mike Brewer
☐ 4 Keefe Cato
☐ 5 Joe Citari
☐ 6 David Cone
☐ 7 Frank Funk CO
☐ 8 Mike Griffin
☐ 9 Roger Hansen
☐ 10 Bill Hayes
☐ 11 Bob Hegman
☐ 12 Rondin Johnson
☐ 13 Mike Kingery
☐ 14 Renie Martin
☐ 15 Mike Miller
☐ 16 Tom Mullen
☐ 17 Bill Pecota
☐ 18 Jose Reyes
☐ 19 Dave Schuler
☐ 20 Jeff Schulz
☐ 21 Jim Scranton
☐ 22 Kevin Seitzer
☐ 23 Theo Shaw
☐ 24 Russ Stephans
☐ 25 Lester Strode
☐ 26 Nick Swartz CO
☐ 27 Scott Taber
☐ 28 Mike Warren
☐ 29 Marty Wilkerson

1986 Omaha Royals TCMA

This 25-card standard-size set of the 1986 Omaha Royals, a Class AAA American Association affiliate of the Kansas City Royals, features white-bordered posed color player shots set on fuchsia backgrounds. The team name is printed within the fuchsia area below the photo. A black stripe at the bottom carries the player's name and position. The white back carries the team name and league at the top, followed by the player's name, positon, biography and statistics.

	MINT	NRMT	EXC
COMPLETE SET (25)	20.00	9.00	2.50

☐ 1 Bill Hayes
☐ 2 Ron Johnson
☐ 3 Kevin Seitzer
☐ 4 Mike Kingery
☐ 5 Roger Hansen
☐ 6 Jeff Schultz
☐ 7 Jim Scranton
☐ 8 Bob Hegman
☐ 9 Marty Wilkerson
☐ 10 Russ Stephans
☐ 11 Dwight Taylor
☐ 12 Bill Pecota
☐ 13 Mike Brewer
☐ 14 Joe Citari
☐ 15 Mike Griffin
☐ 16 Dave Cone
☐ 17 Scott Tabor
☐ 18 Jim Strode
☐ 19 Dave Schuler
☐ 20 Theo Shaw
☐ 21 Alan Hargesheimer
☐ 22 Tom Mullen
☐ 23 John Boles MGR
☐ 24 Frank Funk CO
☐ 25 Scott Bankhead

1986 Orlando Twins ProCards

This 24-card standard-size set of the 1986 Orlando Twins, a Class AA Southern League affiliate of the Minnesota Twins, features white-bordered posed color player photos on its fronts. The player's name, team, and position appear at the bottom. The white horizontal back carries the player's name and position at the top, followed by biography and statistics. The cards are unnumbered and checklisted below in alphabetical order.

	MINT	NRMT	EXC
COMPLETE SET (24)	6.00	2.70	.75

☐ 1 Steve Aragon
☐ 2 Brad Bierley
☐ 3 Todd Budke
☐ 4 Mark Clemons
☐ 5 Jose Dominguez
☐ 6 Troy Galloway
☐ 7 Steve Gomez
☐ 8 Stan Holmes
☐ 9 Joe Klink
☐ 10 Gene Larkin
☐ 11 John Marquardt
☐ 12 George Mitterwald MG
☐ 13 Greg Morhardt
☐ 14 Steve Padia
☐ 15 Doug Palmer
☐ 16 Ray Ramirez TR
☐ 17 Robbie Smith
☐ 18 Alan Sontag
☐ 19 Sam Sorce
☐ 20 Jeff Taylor
☐ 21 Jeff Trout
☐ 22 Dave Vetsch
☐ 23 Kevin Wiggins
☐ 24 Phil Wilson

1986 Osceola Astros ProCards

This 29-card standard-size set of the 1986 Osceola Astros, a Class A Florida State League affiliate of the Houston Astros, features white-bordered posed color player photos on its fronts. The player's name, team, and position appear at the bottom. The white horizontal back carries the player's name and position at the top, followed by biography and statistics. The cards are unnumbered and checklisted below in alphabetical order.

	MINT	NRMT	EXC
COMPLETE SET (29)	6.00	2.70	.75

☐ 1 Norman Brock
☐ 2 Mike Brown
☐ 3 Scott Camp
☐ 4 Jesus Carrion
☐ 5 Earl Cash
☐ 6 Don Dunster
☐ 7 Francois Durocher
☐ 8 John Fishel
☐ 9 Terry Green
☐ 10 Anthony Hampton
☐ 11 Geysi Heredia
☐ 12 Stan Hough CO
☐ 13 Ken Houston TR
☐ 14 Chris Hutchingson
☐ 15 Calvin James
☐ 16 Joe Kwolek
☐ 17 Jeff Livin
☐ 18 Dyrryl Menard
☐ 19 Pete Mueller
☐ 20 Randy Randle
☐ 21 Dody Rather
☐ 22 Marty Schreiber
☐ 23 Glenn Sherlock
☐ 24 Doug Snyder
☐ 25 Mel Stottlemyre
☐ 26 Gary Tuck CO
☐ 27 Jose Vargas
☐ 28 Tom Wiedenbauer MG
☐ 29 Jamie Williams

1986 Palm Springs Angels Police

	MINT	NRMT	EXC
COMPLETE SET (28)	20.00	9.00	2.50

☐ 1 Tom Osowski GM
☐ 2 Tom Kotchman MG
☐ 3 Chuck Hernandez CO
☐ 4 Paul Bilak TR
☐ 5 Bobby Bell
☐ 6 Eric Pappas
☐ 7 John DiGioia
☐ 8 Miguel Garcia
☐ 9 William Fraser
☐ 10 Mike Romanovsky
☐ 11 Larry Cook
☐ 12 Bryan Harvey
☐ 13 Scott Marrett
☐ 14 Richie Carter
☐ 15 Bryan Price
☐ 16 Todd Eggertsen
☐ 17 Mick Butler
☐ 18 Phil Venturino
☐ 19 Barry Dacus
☐ 20 Ty Van Burkleo
☐ 21 David Montanari
☐ 22 Pete Coachman
☐ 23 Billy Geivett
☐ 24 Mitch Seoane
☐ 25 Dario Nunez
☐ 26 Doug Jennings
☐ 27 Reggie Lambert
☐ NNO Title Card

1986 Palm Springs Angels ProCards

This 29-card standard-size set of the 1986 Palm Springs Angels, a Class A California League affiliate of the California Angels, features white-bordered posed color player photos on its fronts. The player's name, team, and position appear at the bottom. The white horizontal back carries the player's name and position at the top, followed by biography and statistics. The cards are unnumbered and checklisted below in alphabetical order. This issue includes the minor league card debut of Dante Bichette.

	MINT	NRMT	EXC
COMPLETE SET (29)	35.00	16.00	4.40

☐ 1 Kent Anderson
☐ 2 Bobby Bell
☐ 3 Dante Bichette
☐ 4 Paul Bilak TR
☐ 5 Mike Butler
☐ 6 Richie Carter
☐ 7 Pete Coachman
☐ 8 Larry Cook
☐ 9 Barry Dacus
☐ 10 John Digioia
☐ 11 Mark Doran
☐ 12 Todd Eggertsen
☐ 13 William Fraser
☐ 14 Miguel Garcia
☐ 15 Billy Geivett
☐ 16 Bryan Harvey
☐ 17 Chuck Hernandez CO
☐ 18 Doug Jennings
☐ 19 Tom Kotchman MG
☐ 20 Reggie Lambert
☐ 21 Scott Marrett
☐ 22 David Martinez
☐ 23 Dave Montanari
☐ 24 Dario Nunez
☐ 25 Erik Pappas
☐ 26 Stacey Pettis
☐ 27 Bryan Price
☐ 28 Mike Romanovsky
☐ 29 Ty Van Burkleo

1986 Pawtucket Red Sox ProCards

This 28-card standard-size set of the 1986 Pawtucket Red Sox, a Class AAA International League affiliate of the Boston Red Sox, features white-bordered posed color player photos on its fronts. The player's name, team, and position appear at the bottom. The white horizontal back carries the player's name and position at the top, followed by biography and statistics. The cards are unnumbered and checklisted below in alphabetical order.

	MINT	NRMT	EXC
COMPLETE SET (28)	7.00	3.10	.85

☐ 1 Dick Berardino CO
☐ 2 Todd Benzinger
☐ 3 Mike Brown
☐ 4 Chris Cannizzaro
☐ 5 John Christensen (glove right hand)
☐ 6 John Christensen (glove left hand)
☐ 7 Tony Cleary TR
☐ 8 Mike Dalton
☐ 9 Pat Dodson
☐ 10 Mike Greenwell
☐ 11 Mitch Johnson
☐ 12 John Leister
☐ 13 George McCerod
☐ 14 Mike Mesh
☐ 15 Gary Miller-Jones
☐ 16 Ed Nottle MG
☐ 17 Rey Quinonez
☐ 18 Mike Rochford
☐ 19 Kevin Romine
☐ 20 Calvin Schiraldi
☐ 21 Jeff Sellers
☐ 22 Danny Sheaffer
☐ 23 Mike Stenhouse
☐ 24 Laschelle Tarver
☐ 25 Gary Tremblay
☐ 26 Mike Trujillo
☐ 27 Dana Williams
☐ 28 Rob Woodard

1986 Peninsula White Sox ProCards

This 28-card standard-size set of the 1986 Peninsula White Sox, a Class A Carolina League affiliate of the Chicago White Sox, features white-bordered posed color player photos on its fronts. The player's name, team, and position appear at the bottom. The white horizontal back carries the player's name and position at the top, followed by biography and statistics. The cards are unnumbered and checklisted below in alphabetical order.

	MINT	NRMT	EXC
COMPLETE SET (28)	6.00	2.70	.75

☐ 1 Jorge Alcazar
☐ 2 Larry Allen
☐ 3 Jeff Anderson
☐ 4 Bob Bailey MG
☐ 5 Jerry Bertolani
☐ 6 Virgil Conley
☐ 7 Dan Cronkright
☐ 8 Tom Drees
☐ 9 Wayne Edwards
☐ 10 Duane Engram
☐ 11 Chuck Hartenstein CO
☐ 12 Mark Henry
☐ 13 Tom Hildebrand
☐ 14 Chris Jefts
☐ 15 Tom Lahrman
☐ 16 Jim Markert
☐ 17 Glen McElroy
☐ 18 Mike Moore
☐ 19 John Pawlowski
☐ 20 Adam Peterson
☐ 21 Darrell Pruitt
☐ 22 Kevin Renz
☐ 23 Ron Scheer
☐ 24 Ed Sedar
☐ 25 Pete Venturini
☐ 26 Dave Wallwork TR
☐ 27 Eric Wilson
☐ 28 Jim Winters

1986 Peoria Chiefs ProCards

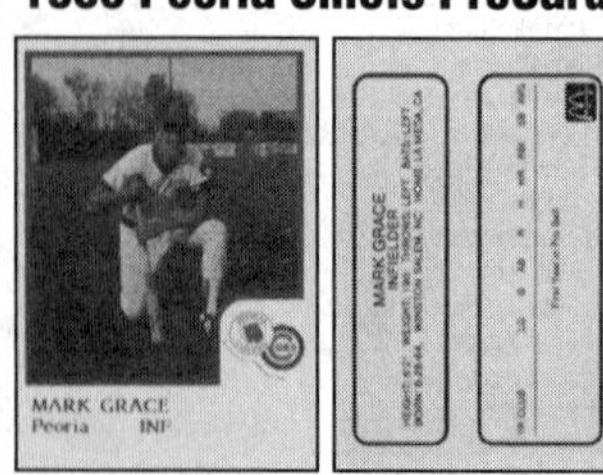

This 27-card standard-size set of the 1986 Peoria Chiefs, a Class A Midwest League affiliate of the Chicago Cubs, features white-bordered posed color player photos on its fronts. The player's name, team, and position appear at the bottom. The white horizontal back carries the player's name and position at the top, followed by biography and statistics. The cards are unnumbered and checklisted below in alphabetical order. This issue includes the minor league card debut of Mark Grace.

	MINT	NRMT	EXC
COMPLETE SET (27)	60.00	27.00	7.50

☐ 1 Scott Anders
☐ 2 Dick Canan
☐ 3 Tony Collins
☐ 4 Leonard Damian
☐ 5 Bill Danek
☐ 6 John Fierro TR
☐ 7 Jim Gardner
☐ 8 Mark Grace
☐ 9 John Green
☐ 10 Tony Hamza
☐ 11 Jeff Hirsch
☐ 12 Greg Kallevig
☐ 13 Joe Kraemer
☐ 14 John Lewis
☐ 15 Dave Liddell
☐ 16 Tom Lombarski
☐ 17 Pete MacKanin MG
☐ 18 Bob Mandeville
☐ 19 Bill Phillips
☐ 20 Kris Roth
☐ 21 Tad Slowik
☐ 22 Jeff Small
☐ 23 Dwight Smith
☐ 24 John Turner
☐ 25 Tim Wallace
☐ 26 Jim Wright CO
☐ 27 Fernando Zarranz

1986 Phoenix Firebirds ProCards

This 26-card standard-size set of the 1986 Phoenix Firebirds, a Class AAA Pacific Coast League affiliate of the San Francisco Giants, features white-bordered posed color player photos on its fronts. The player's name, team, and position appear at the bottom. The white horizontal back carries the player's name and position at the top, followed by biography and statistics. The cards are unnumbered and checklisted below in alphabetical order.

	MINT	NRMT	EXC
COMPLETE SET (26)	6.00	2.70	.75

☐ 1 Rick Adams
☐ 2 Mike Aldrete
☐ 3 Randy Bockus
☐ 4 Kelly Downs
☐ 5 Duane Espy CO
☐ 6 Randy Gomez
☐ 7 Everett Graham
☐ 8 Mark Grant
☐ 9 Chuck Hensley
☐ 10 Mike Jeffcoat
☐ 11 Randy Johnson
☐ 12 Cris Jones
☐ 13 Randy Kutcher
☐ 14 Rick Lancellotti
☐ 15 Jim Lefebvre MG
☐ 16 Jack McNight
☐ 17 Bob Moore
☐ 18 Terry Mulholland
☐ 19 Phil Ouellette
☐ 20 Jon Perlman
☐ 21 Luis Quinones
☐ 22 Jesse Reid
☐ 23 Cliff Shidawara TR
☐ 24 Frank Williams
☐ 25 Jack Wilson
☐ 26 Mike Woodard

1986 Pittsfield Cubs ProCards

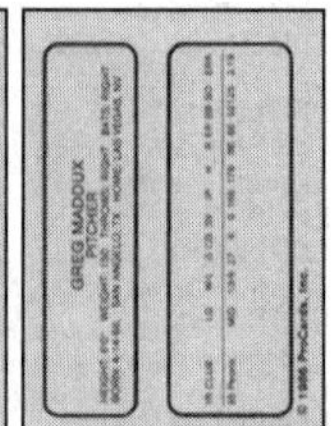

This 25-card standard-size set of the 1986 Pittsfield Cubs, a Class AA Eastern League affiliate of the Chicago Cubs, features white-bordered posed color player photos on its fronts. The player's name, team, and position appear at the bottom. The white horizontal back carries the player's name and position at the top, followed by biography and statistics. The cards are unnumbered and checklisted below in alphabetical order. This issue includes the minor league card debut of Greg Maddux and Rafael Palmeiro.

	MINT	NRMT	EXC
COMPLETE SET (25)	325.00	145.00	40.00

☐ 1 Rich Amaral
☐ 2 Damon Berryhill
☐ 3 Mike Capel
☐ 4 Bruce Crabbe

☐ 5 Luis Cruz
☐ 6 Jackie Davidson
☐ 7 Jim Dickerson
☐ 8 Drew Hall
☐ 9 Carl Hamilton
☐ 10 Darrin Jackson
☐ 11 Dave Kopf
☐ 12 Mike Lacer TR
☐ 13 Dave Lenderman
☐ 14 Greg Maddux
☐ 15 Mike Martin
☐ 16 Allen McKay
☐ 17 Jamie Moyer
☐ 18 Rafael Palmeiro
☐ 19 Dick Pole CO
☐ 20 Steve Roadcap
☐ 21 Jeff Rutledge
☐ 22 Tom Spencer MG
☐ 23 Phil Stephenson
☐ 24 Gary Varsho
☐ 25 Tony Woods

1986 Portland Beavers ProCards

This 23-card standard-size set of the 1986 Portland Beavers, a Class AAA Pacific Coast League affiliate of the Philadelphia Phillies, features white-bordered posed color player photos on its fronts. The player's name, team, and position appear at the bottom. The white horizontal back carries the player's name and position at the top, followed by biography and statistics. The cards are unnumbered and checklisted below in alphabetical order.

	MINT	NRMT	EXC
COMPLETE SET (23)	6.00	2.70	.75

☐ 1 Jeff Bittiger
☐ 2 Dave Bulls
☐ 3 Joe Cipolloni
☐ 4 Randy Day
☐ 5 Ken Dowell
☐ 6 Arturo Gonzalez
☐ 7 Tom Gorman
☐ 8 Kevin Hickey
☐ 9 Rob Hicks
☐ 10 Chris James
☐ 11 Greg Jelks
☐ 12 Tim Knight
☐ 13 Alan LeBoeuf
☐ 14 Randy Lerch
☐ 15 Mike Maddux
☐ 16 Francisco Melendez
☐ 17 Keith Miller
☐ 18 Kyle Money
☐ 19 Ronn Reynolds
☐ 20 Dave Shipanoff
☐ 21 Jeff Stone
☐ 22 Bobby Tiefenauer CO
☐ 23 Fred Toliver

1986 Prince William Pirates ProCards

This 27-card standard-size set of the 1986 Prince William Pirates, a Class A Carolina League affiliate of the Pittsburgh Pirates, features white-bordered posed color player photos on its fronts. The player's name, team, and position appear at the bottom. The white horizontal back carries the player's name and position at the top, followed by biography and statistics. The cards are unnumbered and checklisted below in alphabetical order.

	MINT	NRMT	EXC
COMPLETE SET (27)	7.00	3.10	.85

☐ 1 Reggie Barringer
☐ 2 Lance Belan
☐ 3 Tony Blasucci
☐ 4 Rocky Bridges MG
☐ 5 Tony Chance
☐ 6 Carey Cheek
☐ 7 Jeff Cook
☐ 8 Ron Delucchi
☐ 9 Tim Drummond
☐ 10 Sal Ferreiras
☐ 11 Brett Gideon
☐ 12 Mike Goodwin
☐ 13 Brian Jones
☐ 14 Bob Koopman
☐ 15 Tim McMillan
☐ 16 Jose Melendez
☐ 17 Larry Melton
☐ 18 Page Odle
☐ 19 Chris Pierce
☐ 20 Tom Prince
☐ 21 Chris Ritter
☐ 22 Dave Rooker
☐ 23 Rob Russell
☐ 24 John Smiley
☐ 25 Greg Stading
☐ 26 Mike Stevens
☐ 27 Kyle Todd

1986 Quad City Angels ProCards

This 33-card standard-size set of the 1986 Quad City Angels, a Class A Midwest League affiliate of the California Angels, features white-bordered posed color player photos on its fronts. The player's name, team, and position appear at the bottom. The white horizontal back carries the player's name and position at the top, followed by biography and statistics. The cards are unnumbered and checklisted below in alphabetical order. This issue includes the minor league card debut of Chuck Finley.

	MINT	NRMT	EXC
COMPLETE SET (33)	12.00	5.50	1.50

☐ 1 Edgar Alfonso
☐ 2 Tom Alfredson
☐ 3 Bob Auth
☐ 4 Gerald Baker
☐ 5 Mark Ban
☐ 6 Tim Burcham
☐ 7 Chris Collins
☐ 8 Frank Dimichele
☐ 9 Santiago Espinosha
☐ 10 Andres Esponisa
☐ 11 Chuck Finley
☐ 12 Ken Grant
☐ 13 Dan Grunard
☐ 14 Randy Harvey
☐ 15 Dave Johnson
☐ 16 Sam Joseph TR
☐ 17 Scott Kannenberg
☐ 18 Bill Lachemann MG
☐ 19 Jeff Manto
☐ 20 Mark Marino
☐ 21 Ed Marquez
☐ 22 Steve McGuire
☐ 23 Glenn Meyers
☐ 24 Richerd Morehouse
☐ 25 Gary Nalls
☐ 26 Giovanny Reyes
☐ 27 Elwin Rivera
☐ 28 Ed Rodriquez CO
☐ 29 Robert Rose
☐ 30 Mickey Saatzer CO
☐ 31 Glenn Washington
☐ 32 Roger Zottneck
☐ 33 1986 Quad City Angels

1986 Reading Phillies ProCards

This 26-card standard-size set of the 1986 Reading Phillies, a Class AA Eastern League affiliate of the Philadelphia Phillies, features white-bordered posed color player photos on its fronts. The player's name, team, and position appear at the bottom. The white horizontal back carries the player's name and position at the top, followed by biography and statistics. The cards are unnumbered and checklisted below in alphabetical order.

	MINT	NRMT	EXC
COMPLETE SET (26)	6.00	2.70	.75

☐ 1 Ramon Aviles CO
☐ 2 Shawn Barton
☐ 3 Mark Bowden
☐ 4 Tony Brown
☐ 5 Jose Cecena
☐ 6 George Culver MG
☐ 7 Steve DeAngelis
☐ 8 Marvin Freeman
☐ 9 Ramon Henderson
☐ 10 Ken Jackson
☐ 11 Michael Jackson
☐ 12 Rickey Jordan
☐ 13 Steve Labay
☐ 14 Jose Leiva
☐ 15 Bruce Long
☐ 16 Darren Loy
☐ 17 Keith Miller
☐ 18 Steve Moses
☐ 19 Howard Nichols Jr.
☐ 20 Barney Nugent TR
☐ 21 Jim Olander
☐ 22 Ray Ramon
☐ 23 Bruce Ruffin
☐ 24 Mike Shelton
☐ 25 Kevin Ward
☐ 26 Lenny Watts

1986 Richmond Braves ProCards

This 26-card standard-size set of the 1986 Richmond Braves, a Class AAA International League affiliate of the Atlanta Braves, features white-bordered posed color player photos on its fronts. The player's name, team, and position appear at the bottom. The white horizontal back carries the player's name and position at the top, followed by biography and statistics. The cards are unnumbered and checklisted below in alphabetical order.

	MINT	NRMT	EXC
COMPLETE SET (26)	6.00	2.70	.75

☐ 1 Sam Ayoub TR
☐ 2 Dave Beard
☐ 3 Steve Curry
☐ 4 Bruce Dal Canton CO
☐ 5 Juan Eichelberger
☐ 6 Doc Estes
☐ 7 Lee Graham
☐ 8 Al Hall
☐ 9 Kelly Heath
☐ 10 Mike Jones
☐ 11 Brad Komminsk
☐ 12 Robert Long
☐ 13 Roy Majtyka MG
☐ 14 Ed Olwine
☐ 15 Larry Owen
☐ 16 Gerald Perry
☐ 17 Charlie Puleo
☐ 18 John Rabb
☐ 19 Paul Runge
☐ 20 Steve Shields
☐ 21 Cliff Speck
☐ 22 Mark Strucher
☐ 23 Ron Tingley
☐ 24 Andre Treadway
☐ 25 Matt West
☐ 26 Paul Zuvella

1986 Rochester Red Wings ProCards

This 26-card standard-size set of the 1986 Rochester Red Wings, a Class AAA International League affiliate of the Baltimore Orioles, features white-bordered posed color player photos on its fronts. The player's name, team, and position appear at the bottom. The white horizontal back carries the player's name and position at the top, followed by biography and statistics. The cards are unnumbered and checklisted below in alphabetical order.

	MINT	NRMT	EXC
COMPLETE SET (26)	6.00	2.70	.75

☐ 1 Tony Arnold
☐ 2 Don Chiti CO
☐ 3 Ken Gerhart
☐ 4 Glenn Gulliver
☐ 5 John Habyan
☐ 6 John Hart MG
☐ 7 Moke Hart
☐ 8 Rex Hudler
☐ 9 Phil Huffman
☐ 10 Odell Jones
☐ 11 Rick Jones
☐ 12 Mick Kinnunen
☐ 13 Curt Motton CO
☐ 14 Tom O'Malley
☐ 15 Al Pardo
☐ 16 Kelly Paris
☐ 17 Eric Rasmussen
☐ 18 Mike Reddish
☐ 19 Don Scott
☐ 20 Silver Stadium
☐ 21 Nelson Simmons
☐ 22 Mike Skinner
☐ 23 Ken Smith
☐ 24 Kelvin Torve
☐ 25 Jim Traber
☐ 26 Jeff Williams

1986 Salem Angels Cramer

	MINT	NRMT	EXC
COMPLETE SET (25)	8.00	3.60	1.00

☐ 76 Colin Charland
☐ 77 Giovanny Reyes
☐ 78 Jeff Gay
☐ 79 Julio Granco
☐ 80 Brandy Vann
☐ 81 Alan Mills
☐ 82 Gary Gorski
☐ 83 Bobby Cabello
☐ 84 Bill Vanderwel
☐ 85 Greg Jackson
☐ 86 Scott Cerny
☐ 87 Michael Knapp
☐ 88 Daryl Green
☐ 89 Colby Ward
☐ 90 James Bisceglia
☐ 91 Greg Fix
☐ 92 Luis Merejo
☐ 93 Tony Bonura
☐ 94 David Grilione
☐ 95 Terence Carr
☐ 96 Lee Stevens
☐ 97 Michael Fetters
☐ 98 Santiaga Espinosa
☐ 99 Mike Spearnock
☐ 100 Roberto Hernandez

1986 Salem Red Birds ProCards

This 29-card standard-size set of the 1986 Salem Red Birds, a Class A Carolina League affiliate of the Texas Rangers, features white-bordered posed color player photos on its fronts. The player's name, team, and position appear at the bottom. The white horizontal back carries the player's name and position at the top, followed by biography and statistics. The cards are unnumbered and checklisted below in alphabetical order.

	MINT	NRMT	EXC
COMPLETE SET (29)	6.00	2.70	.75

☐ 1 Kevin Bootay
☐ 2 Mike Bucci MG
☐ 3 Joel Cartaya
☐ 4 Jeff Clay TR
☐ 5 Bryan Dial
☐ 6 Tom Duggan
☐ 7 Riley Epps
☐ 8 Al Farmer
☐ 9 Greg Ferlenda
☐ 10 Stephen Glasker
☐ 11 Tim Hallgren CO
☐ 12 Brad Hill
☐ 13 Duane James
☐ 14 Ron King
☐ 15 Steve Kordish
☐ 16 Chad Kreuter
☐ 17 Steve Lankard
☐ 18 Jeff Mays
☐ 19 Tim McLoughlin
☐ 20 Bob Mortimer
☐ 21 Dave Murray
☐ 22 Bob O'Hearn
☐ 23 Kevin Reimer
☐ 24 Dave Satnat
☐ 25 Mitch Thomas
☐ 26 Jose Vargas
☐ 27 Jim Vlcek
☐ 28 Darrell Whitaker
☐ 29 Mike Winbush

1986 San Jose Bees ProCards

This 25-card standard-size set of the 1986 San Jose Bees, a Class A California League Independent, features white-bordered posed color player photos on its fronts. The player's name, team, and position appear at the bottom. The white horizontal back carries the player's name and position at the top, followed by biography and statistics. The cards are unnumbered and checklisted below in alphabetical order.

	MINT	NRMT	EXC
COMPLETE SET (25)	6.00	2.70	.75

☐ 1 Freddie Arroyo
☐ 2 Shawn Barton
☐ 3 Mike Bigusiak
☐ 4 Randy Bispo
☐ 5 James Bolt
☐ 6 Darryl Cias
☐ 7 Ken Foster
☐ 8 Darren Garrick
☐ 9 Lorenzo Gray
☐ 10 Steven Howe
☐ 11 Brian Kubala
☐ 12 Edward McCarter
☐ 13 Ted Milner
☐ 14 Yoshi Nakashima
☐ 15 Mike Nittoli
☐ 16 Dave Okubo
☐ 17 Ken Reitz
☐ 18 Daryl Sconiers
☐ 19 Harry Steve
☐ 20 Nori Tanabe
☐ 21 Jim Tinkey
☐ 22 Mike Verdi CO
☐ 23 Hank Wada CO
☐ 24 Mickey Yamano
☐ 25 George Yokota

1986 Shreveport Captains ProCards

This 28-card standard-size set of the 1986 Shreveport Captains, a Class AA Texas League affiliate of the San Francisco Giants, features white-bordered posed color player photos on its fronts. The player's name, team, and position appear at the bottom. The white horizontal back carries the player's name and position at the top, followed by biography and statistics. The cards are unnumbered and checklisted below in alphabetical order.

	MINT	NRMT	EXC
COMPLETE SET (28)	8.00	3.60	1.00

☐ 1 Jeff Brantley
☐ 2 John Burkett
☐ 3 Kevin Burrell
☐ 4 Alan Cockrell
☐ 5 Charlie Corbell
☐ 6 Marty DeMerritt
☐ 7 Angel Escobar
☐ 8 George Ferran
☐ 9 John Grimes
☐ 10 Dean Hummel
☐ 11 Charlie Hayes
☐ 12 Mike Jones
☐ 13 Wendell Kim MG
☐ 14 Wendell Kim and Marty DeMerritt

☐ 15 Greg Litton
☐ 16 Daryl Masuyama TR
☐ 17 Deron McCue
☐ 18 Scott Medvin
☐ 19 Steve Miller
☐ 20 Brian Ohnoutka
☐ 21 Ed Puikunas
☐ 22 Mackey Sasser
☐ 23 Keith Silver
☐ 24 Stu Tate
☐ 25 Todd Thomas
☐ 26 John Verducci
☐ 27 Colin Ward
☐ 28 Shreveport Captains

1986 Southern League All-Stars Jennings

	MINT	NRMT	EXC
COMPLETE SET (25)	15.00	6.75	1.85

☐ 1 Bill Ripken
☐ 2 Mike Yastrzemski
☐ 3 Mark McGwire
☐ 4 Gary Thurman
☐ 5 Ron Karkovice
☐ 6 Jose Tolentino
☐ 7 Chris Padget
☐ 8 Brian Guinn
☐ 9 Luis De Los Santos
☐ 10 Terry Steinbach
☐ 11 Larry Ray
☐ 12 Tom Dodd
☐ 13 Bo Jackson
☐ 14 Jose Canseco
☐ 15 Alonzo Powell
☐ 16 Glenallen Hill
☐ 17 Brick Smith
☐ 18 Todd Burns
☐ 19 Dave White
☐ 20 Paul Schneider
☐ 21 Brian Holman
☐ 22 Anthony Kelly
☐ 23 Tom Glavine
☐ 24 Cliff Young
☐ 25 Kevin Price

1986 Spokane Indians Cramer

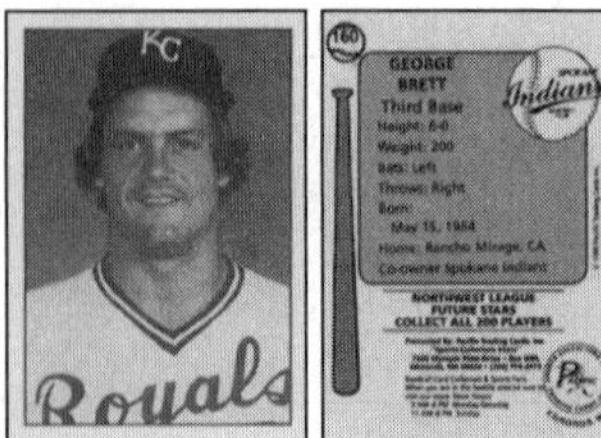

	MINT	NRMT	EXC
COMPLETE SET (24)	70.00	32.00	8.75

☐ 155 Brian Wood
☐ 156 Bob Lutticken
☐ 157 Jim Navilliat
☐ 158 Carl Holmes
☐ 159 Ronald Moore
☐ 160 George Brett
☐ 161 Greg Harris
☐ 162 Dave Brocail
Sic, Brockil
☐ 163 Ricky Bones
☐ 164 Brian Harrison
☐ 165 Paul Quinzer
☐ 166 Mark Sampson
☐ 167 Mike Basso
☐ 168 Craig Cooper
☐ 169 Tom LeVasseur
☐ 170 Terry McDevitt
☐ 171 Thomas Howard
☐ 172 Tony Pellegrino
☐ 173 Keith Harrison
☐ 174 Warren Newson
☐ 175 Kevin Coentopp
☐ 176 Jeff Yurtin
☐ 177 Rob Picciolo MG
☐ 178 James Austin
☐ 179 William Taylor

1986 St. Petersburg Cardinals ProCards

This 29-card standard-size set of the 1986 St. Petersburg Cardinals, a Class A Florida State League affiliate of the St. Louis Cardinals, features white-bordered posed color player photos on its fronts. The player's name, team, and position appear at the bottom. The white horizontal back carries the player's name and position at the top, followed by biography and statistics. The cards are unnumbered and checklisted below in alphabetical order.

	MINT	NRMT	EXC
COMPLETE SET (29)	8.00	3.60	1.00

☐ 1 Sal Agostinelli
☐ 2 Scott Arnold
☐ 3 Richard Arzola
☐ 4 David Bialis MG
☐ 5 Henry Carson
☐ 6 Alex Cole
☐ 7 John Costello
☐ 8 Jeff Fassero
☐ 9 Jim Fregosi Jr.
☐ 10 Brad Henderson TR
☐ 11 Hans Herzog
☐ 12 Stephen Hill
☐ 13 Howard Hilton
☐ 14 Ken Infante
☐ 15 Ronald Johns
☐ 16 Bill Jones
☐ 17 Matt Kinzer
☐ 18 Martin Mason CO
☐ 19 Charles McGrath
☐ 20 Jesus Mendez
☐ 21 Scott Murray
☐ 22 Jay North
☐ 23 Mauricio Nunez
☐ 24 Steven Petitt
☐ 25 Jim Puzey
☐ 26 Jim Reboulet
☐ 27 John Rigos
☐ 28 Roy Silver
☐ 29 Mike Theisen

1986 Stars of the Future TCMA

	MINT	NRMT	EXC
COMPLETE SET (40)	30.00	13.50	3.70

☐ 1 Cooper Stadium
☐ 2 Team Photo and Barry Foote MG
☐ 3 Pitchers: Alfonso Pulido
Doug Drabek
Mike Armstrong
Brad Arnsberg
☐ 4 Catchers: Juan Espino
Phil Lombardi
Outfielders: Darwin McNeely
Dave Stegman
☐ 5 1st Base: Orestes Destrade
2nd Base: Andre Robertson
Shortstop: Mike Soper
3rd Base: Leo Hernandez
☐ 6 Doug Potestio
☐ 7 Julio Valdez
☐ 8 Dave Martinez
Steve Hammond
Mike Brumley
Bobby Ramos
☐ 9 Dave Gumpert
Ken Price
☐ 10 Trey Brooks
☐ 11 Joe Hicks
☐ 12 Pookie Bernstine
☐ 13 Johnny Abrego
☐ 14 Dennis Livingston
☐ 15 Mike Watters
☐ 16 Stu Pederson
☐ 17 Ralph Bryant
☐ 18 Jeff Hamilton
☐ 19 Balvino Galvez
☐ 20 Ed Amelung
☐ 21 Alvis Woods
☐ 22 Scott Ullger
☐ 23 Andre David
☐ 24 Dennis Burtt
☐ 25 Geraldo Lomastro
☐ 26 Fred McGriff
☐ 27 Alex Infante
☐ 28 Stan Clarke
☐ 29 Chris Johnston
☐ 30 Jeff Hearron
☐ 31 Stan Jefferson
☐ 32 Dave Magadan
☐ 33 John Gibbons
☐ 34 John Mitchell
☐ 35 Tony Ferreira
☐ 36 Jesse Reid
☐ 37 Jim Lefebvre
☐ 38 Mike Aldrete
☐ 39 Terry Mulholland
☐ 40 Mark Grant

1986 Stockton Ports ProCards

This 26-card standard-size set of the 1986 Stockton Ports, a Class A California League affiliate of the Milwaukee Brewers, features white-bordered posed color player photos on its fronts. The player's name, team, and position appear at the bottom. The white horizontal back carries the player's name and position at the top, followed by biography and statistics. The cards are unnumbered and checklisted below in alphabetical order.

	MINT	NRMT	EXC
COMPLETE SET (26)	6.00	2.70	.75

☐ 1 John Beuerlein
☐ 2 Jamie Brisco
☐ 3 Todd Brown
☐ 4 Tim Casey
☐ 5 Rob Derksen CO
☐ 6 Rob DeWolf
☐ 7 Todd France TR
☐ 8 Mike Frew
☐ 9 Mike Fulmer
☐ 10 Mike Gobbo
☐ 11 Gary Kanwisher
☐ 12 Matt Kent
☐ 13 John Ludy
☐ 14 Dave Machemer MG
☐ 15 Joe Mitchell
☐ 16 Mario Monico
☐ 17 Martin Montano
☐ 18 Frank Mattox
☐ 19 Doug Norton
☐ 20 Jeff Peterek
☐ 21 Walter Pohle
☐ 22 Danny Ratliff
☐ 23 Jeff Reece
☐ 24 Alan Sadler
☐ 25 Darryel Walters
☐ 26 Fred Williams

1986 Sumter Braves ProCards

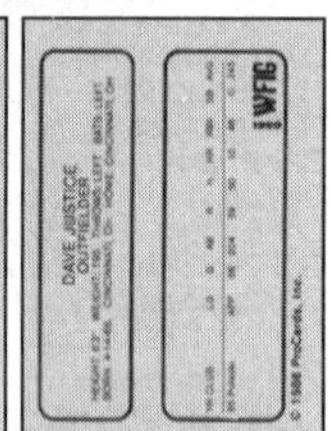

This 30-card standard-size set of the 1986 Sumter Braves, a Class A South Atlantic League affiliate of the Atlanta Braves, features white-bordered posed color player photos on its fronts. The player's name, team, and position appear at the bottom. The white horizontal back carries the player's name and position at the top, followed by biography and statistics. The cards are unnumbered and checklisted below in alphabetical order. This issue includes the minor league card debuts of Dave Justice and Al Martin.

	MINT	NRMT	EXC
COMPLETE SET (30)	40.00	18.00	5.00

☐ 1 Tom Abrell
☐ 2 John Alva
☐ 3 Ron Bianco
☐ 4 Johnny Cuevas
☐ 5 Shawn Frazier
☐ 6 Jeff Greene
☐ 7 Tom Green
☐ 8 Kevin Harmon TR
☐ 9 Mike Hennessy
☐ 10 Dennis Hood
☐ 11 Dodd Johnson
☐ 12 Barry Jones
☐ 13 Clarence Jones
☐ 14 David Jones
☐ 15 Dave Justice
☐ 16 Mark Lemke
☐ 17 Al Martin
☐ 18 Ed Mathews
☐ 19 Leo Mazzone CO
☐ 20 Bob McNally
☐ 21 Bob Pfaff
☐ 22 Ellis Roby
☐ 23 Matt Rowe
☐ 24 Jim Salisbury
☐ 25 David Seitz
☐ 26 Brian Snitker MG
☐ 27 Andy Tomberlin
☐ 28 Rob Tomberlain
☐ 29 Danny Weems
☐ 30 Jeff Wetherby

1986 Syracuse Chiefs ProCards

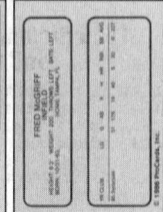

This 27-card standard-size set of the 1986 Syracuse Chiefs, a Class AAA International League affiliate of the Toronto Blue Jays, features white-bordered posed color player photos on its fronts. The player's name, team name, and position appear at the bottom. The white horizontal back carries the player's name and position at the top, followed by biography and statistics. The cards are unnumbered and checklisted below in alphabetical order. This issue includes a second year card of Fred McGriff.

	MINT	NRMT	EXC
COMPLETE SET (27)	40.00	18.00	5.00

☐ 1 Gibson Alba
☐ 2 Luis Aquino
☐ 3 Doug Ault MG
☐ 4 Joe Beckwith
☐ 5 Stan Clarke
☐ 6 Rich Carlucci
☐ 7 Jose Castro
☐ 8 John Cerutti
☐ 9 Don Cooper
☐ 10 Red Coughlin TR
☐ 11 Otis Green
☐ 12 Dale Holman
☐ 13 Dennis Howard
☐ 14 Alex Infante
☐ 15 Joe Johnston
☐ 16 Luis Leal
☐ 17 Manuel Lee
☐ 18 Fred McGriff
☐ 19 Steve Mingori CO
☐ 20 Ron Mussleman
☐ 21 Mark Poole
☐ 22 Mike Sharperson
☐ 23 Ron Shepherd
☐ 24 Dave Stenhouse
☐ 25 Lou Thornton
☐ 26 Rocket Wheeler CO
☐ 27 John Woodworth TR

1986 Tacoma Tigers ProCards

This 25-card standard-size set of the 1986 Tacoma Tigers, a Class AAA Pacific Coast League affiliate of the Oakland Athletics, features white-bordered posed color player photos on its fronts. The player's name, team, and position appear at the bottom. The white horizontal back carries the player's name and position at the top, followed by biography and statistics. The cards are unnumbered and checklisted below in alphabetical order.

	MINT	NRMT	EXC
COMPLETE SET (25)	6.00	2.70	.75

☐ 1 Darrel Ackerfelds
☐ 2 Ralph Citarella
☐ 3 Brian Dorsett
☐ 4 Tom Dozier
☐ 5 Jim Eppard
☐ 6 Chuck Estrada
☐ 7 Mike Gallego
☐ 8 Walt Horn TR
☐ 9 Stan Javier
☐ 10 Jeff Kaiser
☐ 11 Tim Lambert
☐ 12 Dave Leiper
☐ 13 Keith Lieppman MG
☐ 14 Joey McLaughlin
☐ 15 Rob Nelson
☐ 16 Eric Plunk
☐ 17 Luis Polonia
☐ 18 Thad Reece
☐ 19 Rick Rodriguez
☐ 20 Lenn Sakata
☐ 21 Ray Smith
☐ 22 Keith Thrower
☐ 23 Rusty Tillman
☐ 24 Jerry Willard
☐ 25 Curt Young

1986 Tampa Tarpons ProCards

This 27-card standard-size set of the 1986 Tampa Tarpons, a Class A Florida State League affiliate of the Cincinnati Reds, features white-bordered posed color player photos on its fronts. The player's name, team, and position appear at the bottom. The white horizontal back carries the player's name and position at the top, followed by biography and statistics. The cards are unnumbered and checklisted below in alphabetical order.

	MINT	NRMT	EXC
COMPLETE SET (27)	6.00	2.70	.75

☐ 1 Carlos Acosta
☐ 2 Tim Barker
☐ 3 Mark Berry
☐ 4 Phil Dale
☐ 5 Chuck Donahue
☐ 6 Jeff Hayward
☐ 7 Jim Jefferson
☐ 8 Dave Keller CO
☐ 9 Ted Langdon
☐ 10 Rod Lich TR
☐ 11 Joel Lono
☐ 12 Rob Lopez
☐ 13 Tim Mirabito

☐ 14 Angelo Nunley
☐ 15 Mike Ramsey
☐ 16 Darren Riley
☐ 17 Dusty Rogers
☐ 18 Isidro Rondon
☐ 19 Francisco Silverio
☐ 20 Jack Smith
☐ 21 Ozzie Soto
☐ 22 Tom Summers
☐ 23 Francisco Tenacen
☐ 24 Don Wakamatsu
☐ 25 Brant Weatherford
☐ 26 Jeff Wilson
☐ 27 Tom Wilson

1986 Tidewater Tides ProCards

This 28-card standard-size set of the 1986 Tidewater Tides, a Class AAA International League affiliate of the New York Mets, features white-bordered posed color player photos on its fronts. The player's name, team, and position appear at the bottom. The white horizontal back carries the player's name and position at the top, followed by biography and statistics. The cards are unnumbered and checklisted below in alphabetical order.

	MINT	NRMT	EXC
COMPLETE SET (28)	8.00	3.60	1.00

☐ 1 Richard Anderson
☐ 2 Terry Blocker
☐ 3 Tom Burns
☐ 4 Mark Carreon
☐ 5 Tim Corcoran
☐ 6 John Cumberland CO
☐ 7 Michael Davis
☐ 8 Tony Ferreira
☐ 9 Doug Frobel
☐ 10 Ronald Gardenhire
☐ 11 John Gibbons
☐ 12 Edward Glynn
☐ 13 Edward Hearn
☐ 14 Stanley Jefferson
☐ 15 Terry Leach
☐ 16 Barry Lyons
☐ 17 David Magadan
☐ 18 Marlin McPhail
☐ 19 Tom McCarthy
☐ 20 Randy Milligan
☐ 21 John Mitchell
☐ 22 Randy Myers
☐ 23 Sam Perlozzo MG
☐ 24 Alfredo Pedrique
☐ 25 Rick Rainer TR
☐ 26 Doug Sisk
☐ 27 Steven Springer
☐ 28 DeWayne Vaughn
☐ 29 David Wyatt

1986 Toledo Mud Hens ProCards

This 24-card standard-size set of the 1986 Toledo Mud Hens, a Class AAA International League affiliate of the Minnesota Twins, features white-bordered posed color player photos on its fronts. The player's name, team, and position appear at the bottom. The white horizontal back carries the player's name and position at the top, followed by biography and statistics. The cards are unnumbered and checklisted below in alphabetical order.

	MINT	NRMT	EXC
COMPLETE SET (24)	6.00	2.70	.75

☐ 1 Allen Anderson
☐ 2 Brad Boylan TR
☐ 3 Eric Broersma
☐ 4 Mark Brown
☐ 5 Danny Clay
☐ 6 Mark Davidson
☐ 7 Andre David
☐ 8 Pat Dempsey
☐ 9 Alvaro Espinosa
☐ 10 Frank Eufemia
☐ 11 Mark Funderburk
☐ 12 Gorman Heimueller
☐ 13 Richard Leggatt
☐ 14 Jerry Lomastro
☐ 15 Charlie Manuel MG
☐ 16 Alax Marte
☐ 17 Charlie Mitchell
☐ 18 Bob Ralston
☐ 19 Mario Ramirez
☐ 20 Ramon Romero
☐ 21 Les Straker
☐ 22 Scott Ullger
☐ 23 Ron Washington
☐ 24 Al Woods

1986 Tri-Cities Triplets Cramer

	MINT	NRMT	EXC
COMPLETE SET (14)	8.00	3.60	1.00

☐ 187 Andy Naworski
☐ 188 Kevin Brockway
☐ 189 Bruce Carter
☐ 190 Dan Adriance
☐ 191 Tony Rasmus
☐ 192 Kendall Walling
☐ 193 Eric Pawling
☐ 194 Joe Gioia
☐ 195 John Jaha
☐ 196 Daron Connelly
☐ 197 David Connelly
☐ 198 Andy Hall
☐ 199 Darryl Gilliam
☐ 200 Thomas Ealy

1986 Tucson Toros ProCards

This 26-card standard-size set of the 1986 Tucson Toros, a Class AAA Pacific Coast League affiliate of the Houston Astros, features white-bordered posed color player photos on its fronts. The player's name, team, and position appear at the bottom. The white horizontal back carries the player's name and position at the top, followed by biography and statistics. The cards are unnumbered and checklisted below in alphabetical order.

	MINT	NRMT	EXC
COMPLETE SET (26)	6.00	2.70	.75

☐ 1 Larry Acker
☐ 2 Carlos Alfonso MG
☐ 3 Don August
☐ 4 Glen Carpenter
☐ 5 Ty Gainey
☐ 6 Jeff Heathcock
☐ 7 Manny Hernandez
☐ 8 Chuck Jackson
☐ 9 Rex Jones TR
☐ 10 Mark Knudson
☐ 11 Rob Mallicoat
☐ 12 Ron Mathis
☐ 13 Louie Meadows
☐ 14 Jim Miner
☐ 15 John Mizerock
☐ 16 Rafael Montalvo
☐ 17 Ray Noble
☐ 18 Burt Pena
☐ 19 Nelson Rood
☐ 20 Mark Ross
☐ 21 Jim Sherman
☐ 22 Jim Thomas
☐ 23 Duane Walker
☐ 24 Tye Waller
☐ 25 Eddie Watt CO
☐ 26 Robbie Wine

1986 Tulsa Drillers Team Issue

	MINT	NRMT	EXC
COMPLETE SET (27)	15.00	6.75	1.85

☐ 1 Mark Poole
☐ 2 Tony Triplett
☐ 3 Kirk Killingsworth
☐ 4 Mike Couchee CO
☐ 5 Art Gardner CO
☐ 6 Bill Stearns MG
☐ 7 Tim Rodgers
☐ 8 Mike Loynd
☐ 9A Jerry Browne
☐ 9B Rick Knapp
☐ 10 Steve Wilson
☐ 11 Jamie Doughty
☐ 12 Benny Cadahia
☐ 14 Bob Gergen
☐ 15 Greg Ferlenda
☐ 16 Kevin Bootay
☐ 17 Javier Ortiz
☐ 18 Greg Bailey
☐ 19 Dan Olsson
☐ 20 Paul Kilgus
☐ 21 Jeff Melrose
☐ 22 Rich Raether
☐ 23 Randy Kramer
☐ 24 Larry Klein
☐ 25 Mike Stanley
☐ 26 Bob Bill TR
☐ 27 Jose Mota

1986 Vancouver Canadians ProCards

This 27-card standard-size set of the 1986 Vancouver Canadians, a Class AAA Pacific Coast League affiliate of Milwaukee Brewers, features white-bordered posed color player photos on its fronts. The player's name, team name, and position appear at the bottom. The white horizontal back carries the player's name and position at the top, followed by biography and statistics. There have been reports of scarce error cards of Steve Kiefer, Joe Meyer, Charlie O'Brien, and Rick Waits that carry Buffalo Bisons logos. The cards are unnumbered and checklisted below in alphabetical order. This issue includes the minor league card debut of B.J. Surhoff.

	MINT	NRMT	EXC
COMPLETE SET (27)	7.00	3.10	.85

☐ 1 Jim Adduci
☐ 2 Terry Bevington MG
☐ 3 Mike Birbeck
☐ 4 Chris Bosio
☐ 5 Glenn Braggs
☐ 6 Mark Ciardi
☐ 7 Bryan Clutterbuck
☐ 8 Chuck Crim
☐ 9 Dan Davidsmeier
☐ 10 Ed Diaz
☐ 11 Bryan Duguette
☐ 12 Bob Gibson
☐ 13 Dion James
☐ 14 John Johnson
☐ 15 Steve Kiefer
☐ 16 Dave Klipstein
☐ 17 Joe Meyer
☐ 18 Ed Myers
☐ 19 Charlie O'Brien
☐ 20 Jim Paciorek
☐ 21 Mike Paul CO
☐ 22 Chuck Porter
☐ 23 Ray Searage
☐ 24 B.J. Surhoff
☐ 25 Dale Sveum
☐ 26 Rich Thompson
☐ 27 Rick Waits

1986 Ventura Gulls ProCards

This 28-card standard-size set of the 1986 Ventura Gulls, a Class A affiliate of the Toronto Blue Jays, features white-bordered posed color player photos on its fronts. The player's name, team, and position appear at the bottom. The white horizontal back carries the player's name and position at the top, followed by biography and statistics. The cards are unnumbered and checklisted below in alphabetical order. This issue includes the minor league card debut of Todd Stottlemyre.

	MINT	NRMT	EXC
COMPLETE SET (28)	8.00	3.60	1.00

☐ 1 Geronimo Berroa
☐ 2 Hugh Brinson
☐ 3 Francisco Cabrera
☐ 4 Mark Dickman
☐ 5 Rob Ducey
☐ 6 Oscar Escobar
☐ 7 Glenn Ezell MG
☐ 8 Sandy Guerrero
☐ 9 Mike Jones
☐ 10 Ken Kinnard
☐ 11 Darryl Landrum
☐ 12 Omar Malave
☐ 13 Domingo Martinez
☐ 14 Jose Mesa
☐ 15 Steve Mumaw
☐ 16 Jeff Musselman
☐ 17 Greg Myers
☐ 18 Al Olsen TR
☐ 19 Alfredo Ortiz CO
☐ 20 Zack Paris
☐ 21 Todd Provence
☐ 22 Pablo Reyes
☐ 23 Luis Reyna
☐ 24 Willie Shanks
☐ 25 Todd Stottlemyre
☐ 26 Tom Wasilewski
☐ 27 Dave Wells
☐ 28 Eric Yelding

1986 Vermont Reds ProCards

This 24-card standard-size set of the 1986 Vermont Reds, a Class AA Eastern League affiliate of the Cincinnati Reds, features white-bordered posed color player photos on its fronts. The player's name, team, and position appear at the bottom. The white horizontal back carries the player's name and position at the top, followed by biography and statistics. The cards are unnumbered and checklisted below in alphabetical order.

	MINT	NRMT	EXC
COMPLETE SET (24)	6.00	2.70	.75

☐ 1 Jordan Berge
☐ 2 John Boyles
☐ 3 Norm Charlton
☐ 4 Jeff Cox
☐ 5 Clay Daniel
☐ 6 Gary Denbo
☐ 7 Rob Dibble
☐ 8 Jeff Gray
☐ 9 Lenny Harris
☐ 10 Billy Hawley
☐ 11 Ron Henika
☐ 12 Mike Manfre
☐ 13 Greg Monda
☐ 14 Steve Oliverio
☐ 15 Buddy Pryor
☐ 16 Brian Robinson
☐ 17 Jim Scott
☐ 18 Brooks Shumake
☐ 19 Mike Sims TR
☐ 20 Danny Smith
☐ 21 Glen Spagnola
☐ 22 Jeff Treadway
☐ 23 Jay Ward MG
☐ 24 Delwyn Young

1986 Vero Beach Dodgers ProCards

This 27-card standard-size set of the 1986 Vero Beach Dodgers, a Class A Florida State League affiliate of the Los Angeles Dodgers, features white-bordered posed color player photos on its fronts. The player's name, team, and position appear at the bottom. The white horizontal back carries the player's name and position at the top, followed by biography and statistics. The cards are unnumbered and checklisted below in alphabetical order. This issue includes the minor league card debut of Juan Guzman.

	MINT	NRMT	EXC
COMPLETE SET (27)	8.00	3.60	1.00

☐ 1 Andy Anthony
☐ 2 Kevin Ayers
☐ 3 Michael Cherry
☐ 4 Carl Cox
☐ 5 Kevin Devine
☐ 6 Peter Geist
☐ 7 Rob Giesecke TR
☐ 8 Juan Guzman
☐ 9 Jeff Hartman
☐ 10 Darren Holmes
☐ 11 Michael Huff
☐ 12 Ed Jacobo
☐ 13 Robert Jacobsen
☐ 14 Wayne Kirby
☐ 15 Ken Lampert
☐ 16 Luis Lopez
☐ 17 Walt McConnell
☐ 18 Domingo Michel
☐ 19 Jon Pequignot
☐ 20 Rod Rochie
☐ 21 John Schlichting
☐ 22 Jorge Sepulveda
☐ 23 John Shoemaker CO
☐ 24 Felix Tejeda
☐ 25 Bob Tucker
☐ 26 Jesus Vila
☐ 27 Stan Wasiak MG

1986 Visalia Oaks ProCards

This 24-card standard-size set of the 1986 Visalia Oaks, a Class A California League affiliate of the Minnesota Twins, features white-bordered posed color player photos on its fronts. The player's name, team, and position appear at the bottom. The white horizontal back carries the player's name and position at the top, followed by biography and statistics. The cards are unnumbered and checklisted below in alphabetical order.

	MINT	NRMT	EXC
COMPLETE SET (24)	6.00	2.70	.75

☐ 1 Mike Adams
☐ 2 Joey Aragon
☐ 3 Ben Bianchi
☐ 4 Gary Borg
☐ 5 Bob Calley
☐ 6 Alfredo Cardwood
☐ 7 DeWayne Coleman
☐ 8 Rob Cramer
☐ 9 Chris Forgione
☐ 10 Henry Gatewood
☐ 11 Donnie Iasparro
☐ 12 Chris Kroener
☐ 13 Sal Nicolosi
☐ 14 Bill O'Conner
☐ 15 Wes Pierorazio
☐ 16 Shannon Raybon TR
☐ 17 Scott Rohlof
☐ 18 Danny Schmitz MG
☐ 19 Tom Schwarz
☐ 20 Tim Senne
☐ 21 Bob Tabeling
☐ 22 Tom Thomas
☐ 23 Ray Velasquez
☐ 24 Eddie Yanes

1986 Waterbury Indians ProCards

This 26-card standard-size set of the 1986 Waterbury Indians, a Class AA Eastern League affiliate of the Cleveland Indians, features white-bordered posed color player photos on its fronts. The player's name, team, and position appear at the bottom. The white horizontal back carries the player's name and position at the top, followed by biography and statistics. The cards are unnumbered and checklisted below in alphabetical order.

	MINT	NRMT	EXC
COMPLETE SET (26)	6.00	2.70	.75

☐ 1 Jeff Arney
☐ 2 Chris Beasley
☐ 3 Mike Bellaman
☐ 4 Jay Bell
☐ 5 Bernardo Brito
☐ 6 George Crum
☐ 7 Jim Driscoll CO

☐ 8 Luis Encarnacion
☐ 9 John Farrell
☐ 10 Winston Ficklin
☐ 11 Orlando Gomez MG
☐ 12 Milt Harper
☐ 13 Rick Henke TR
☐ 14 Bob Link
☐ 15 Don Lovell
☐ 16 Oscar Mejia
☐ 17 Kent Murphy
☐ 18 Michael Murphy
☐ 19 Cliff Patornicky
☐ 20 Miguel Roman
☐ 21 Cal Santarelli
☐ 22 Craig Smajstra
☐ 23 Daryl Smith
☐ 24 Dain Syverson
☐ 25 Steve Whitmyer
☐ 26 Bill Worden

1986 Waterloo Indians ProCards

This 32-card standard-size set of the 1986 Waterloo Indians, a Class A Midwest League affiliate of the Cleveland Indians, features white-bordered posed color player photos on its fronts. The player's name, team, and position appear at the bottom. The white horizontal back carries the player's name and position at the top, followed by biography and statistics. The cards are unnumbered and checklisted below in alphabetical order.

	MINT	NRMT	EXC
COMPLETE SET (32)	6.00	2.70	.75

☐ 1 Brian Allard CO
☐ 2 David Alvis
☐ 3 Keith Bennett
☐ 4 Dave Bresnahan
☐ 5 Claudio Carrasco
☐ 6 Glen Fairchild
☐ 7 Mike Farr
☐ 8 Myron Gardner
☐ 9 Andy Ghelfi
☐ 10 John Githens
☐ 11 Mark Higgins
☐ 12 Trey Hillman
☐ 13 Steve Johnson
☐ 14 Scott Jordan
☐ 15 Greg Karpuk
☐ 16 Lee Kuntz TR
☐ 17 Greg LaFever
☐ 18 Luis Medina
☐ 19 Manny Mercado
☐ 20 Rod Nichols
☐ 21 Mike Poehl
☐ 22 John Power
☐ 23 Mike Rountree
☐ 24 Don Santo
☐ 25 Charles Scott
☐ 26 Rob Swain
☐ 27 Steve Swisher MG
☐ 28 Chuck Todd
☐ 29 Kevin Trudeau
☐ 30 Casey Webster
☐ 31 Greg Williamson
☐ 32 Mike Workman

1986 Watertown Pirates ProCards

This 27-card standard-size set of the 1986 Watertown Pirates, a Class A New York-Penn League affiliate of the Pittsburgh Pirates, features white-bordered posed color player photos on its fronts. The player's name, team, and position appear at the bottom. The white horizontal back carries the player's name and position at the top, followed by biography and statistics. The cards are unnumbered and checklisted below in alphabetical order. This issue includes the minor league card debut of Moises Alou.

	MINT	NRMT	EXC
COMPLETE SET (27)	20.00	9.00	2.50

☐ 1 Steve Adams
☐ 2 Moises Alou
☐ 3 Jeff Banister
☐ 4 Daryl Boyd
☐ 5 Lawrence Brady
☐ 6 Guy Conti CO
☐ 7 Bill Copp
☐ 8 Jeff Gurtcheff
☐ 9 Craig Heakins
☐ 10 Mike Khoury
☐ 11 Tim Kirk
☐ 12 Blain Lockley
☐ 13 Dino Moran
☐ 14 Douglas Moreno
☐ 15 Steve Moser
☐ 16 Ed Ott MG
☐ 17 Al Quintana
☐ 18 Randy Robicheaux
☐ 19 Carl Rose
☐ 20 Scott Runge
☐ 21 Bill Samen
☐ 22 Butch Schlopy
☐ 23 Tom Shields
☐ 24 Tracy Toy
☐ 25 Glenn Trudo TR
☐ 26 Miguel Varverde
☐ 27 Mike Walker

1986 Wausau Timbers ProCards

This 29-card standard-size set of the 1986 Wausau Timbers, a Class A Midwest League affiliate of the Seattle Mariners, features white-bordered posed color player photos on its fronts. The player's name, team, and position appear at the bottom. The white horizontal back carries the player's name and position at the top, followed by biography and statistics. The cards are unnumbered and checklisted below in alphabetical order. This issue includes the minor league card debut of Omar Vizquel.

	MINT	NRMT	EXC
COMPLETE SET (29)	7.00	3.10	.85

☐ 1 Robert Bernardo
☐ 2 Fremio Cabrera
☐ 3 John Clem
☐ 4 Don Cohoon
☐ 5 Bobby Cuellar MG
☐ 6 Mike Darby
☐ 7 Bret Davis
☐ 8 William Diaz
☐ 9 Tom Eccleston
☐ 10 Joe Georger CO
☐ 11 Bob Gibree
☐ 12 Dan Larson
☐ 13 Benito Malave
☐ 14 Brian McCann TR
☐ 15 Dave McCorkle
☐ 16 Tim McLain
☐ 17 Pablo Moncerratt
☐ 18 Clay Parker
☐ 19 Jeff Roberts
☐ 20 Brad Rohde
☐ 21 Mike Schooler
☐ 22 Rich Slominski
☐ 23 Paul Serna CO
☐ 24 Bob Siegel
☐ 25 Dave Snell
☐ 26 Jorge Uribe
☐ 27 Omar Vizquel
Sic, Visquel
☐ 28 Anthony Woods
☐ 29 Clint Zavaras

1986 West Palm Beach Expos ProCards

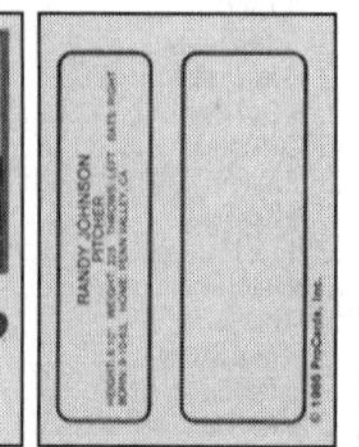

This 28-card standard-size set of the 1986 West Palm Beach Expos, a Class A Florida State League affiliate of the Montreal Expos, features white-bordered posed color player photos on its fronts. The player's name, team and position appear at the bottom. The white horizontal back carries the player's name, position and biography. This issue includes Randy Johnson's minor league card debut. The cards are unnumbered and checklisted below in alphabetical order.

	MINT	NRMT	EXC
COMPLETE SET (28)	35.00	16.00	4.40

☐ 1 Felipe Alou MG
☐ 2 Tim Arnold
☐ 3 Scott Ayers
☐ 4 Kent Bachman
☐ 5 Esteban Beltre
☐ 6 Mark Blaser
☐ 7 Edgar Caceres
☐ 8 Allen Collins
☐ 9 Kerry Cook
☐ 10 Bill Cunningham
☐ 11 Mike Day
☐ 12 Bob Devlin
☐ 13 Eddie Dixon
☐ 14 Kevin Dunton
☐ 15 Jeff Fischer
☐ 16 George Flower
☐ 17 Keith Foley
☐ 18 Gene Glynn CO
☐ 19 Sam Haley
☐ 20 Melvin Houston
☐ 21 Randy Johnson
☐ 22 Jim Kahmann TR
☐ 23 Scott Mann
☐ 24 Alonzo Powell
☐ 25 Iggy Rodriguez
☐ 26 Tim Thiessen
☐ 27 Gary Wayne
☐ 28 Bud Yanus CO

1986 Winston-Salem Spirits ProCards

This 29-card standard-size set of the 1986 Winston-Salem Spirits, a Class A Carolina League affiliate of the Chicago Cubs, features white-bordered posed color player photos on its fronts. The player's name, team, and position appear at the bottom. The white horizontal back carries the player's name and position at the top, followed by biography and statistics. The cards are unnumbered and checklisted below in alphabetical order.

	MINT	NRMT	EXC
COMPLETE SET (29)	6.00	2.70	.75

☐ 1 Greg Bell
☐ 2 Bob Bafia
☐ 3 Brent Casteel
☐ 4 Doug Dascenzo
Sic, Dacenzo
☐ 5 Ernie Shore Stadium
☐ 6 Ernie Shore Stadium
☐ 7 Jim Essian MG
☐ 8 Ron Ewart
☐ 9 Rick Hopkins
☐ 10 Brian House
☐ 11 Rick Kranitz CO
☐ 12 Lester Lancaster
☐ 13 Dave Masters
☐ 14 Steve Maye
☐ 15 Julius McDougal
☐ 16 Mark McMorris
☐ 17 William Menendez
☐ 18 David Pavlas
☐ 19 Jim Phillip
☐ 20 Jeff Pico
☐ 21 Cohen Renfroe
☐ 22 Tim Rice
☐ 23 Don Richardson
☐ 24 Rolando Roomes
☐ 25 Mike Tullier
☐ 26 Hector Villanueva
☐ 27 Darcy Walker
☐ 28 Rich Wrona
☐ 29 Winston-Salem Spirits

1986 Winter Haven Red Sox ProCards

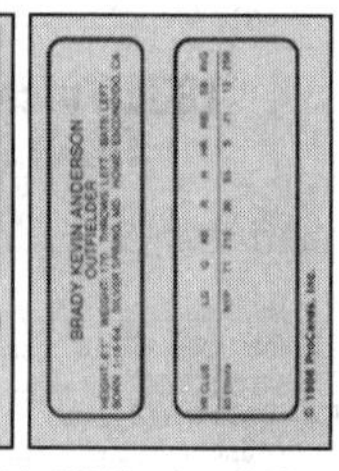

This 27-card standard-size set of the 1986 Winter Haven Red Sox, a Class A Florida State League affiliate of the Boston Red Sox, features white-bordered posed color player photos on its fronts. The player's name, team, and position appear at the bottom. The white horizontal back carries the player's name and position at the top, followed by biography and statistics. The cards are unnumbered and checklisted below in alphabetical order. This issue includes a second year card of Brady Anderson.

	MINT	NRMT	EXC
COMPLETE SET (27)	30.00	13.50	3.70

☐ 1 Odie Abril
☐ 2 Brady Anderson
☐ 3 Gregg Barrios
☐ 4 Greg Bochesa
☐ 5 Mike Carista
☐ 6 Mike Clarkin
☐ 7 Tony DeFrancesco
☐ 8 Robert Fuentes
☐ 9 Angel Gonzalez
☐ 10 Dave Holt MG
☐ 11 Daryl Irvine
☐ 12 LaVerne Jackson
☐ 13 Manny Jose
☐ 14 Eric Laseke
☐ 15 Bruce Lockhart
☐ 16 Greg Lotzar
☐ 17 Tim McGee
☐ 18 Chris Moritz
☐ 19 Rob Parkins
☐ 20 John Sanderski
☐ 21 Tary Scott
☐ 22 Mike Sears TR
☐ 23 Scott Skripko
☐ 24 Jim Snediker
☐ 25 Dan Sullivan
☐ 26 Luis Vasquez
☐ 27 Robert Zambrano

1987 Albany Yankees ProCards

This 23-card standard-size set of the 1987 Albany Yankees, a Class AA Eastern League affiliate of the New York Yankees, features white-bordered posed color player photos on its fronts. The player's name and position appear at the bottom. The white horizontal back is framed by a black line and carries the player's name at the top, followed by biography and statistics.

	MINT	NRMT	EXC
COMPLETE SET (23)	7.00	3.10	.85

☐ 1 Steve Rosenberg
☐ 2 Tony Russell
☐ 3 Bob Barker
☐ 4 Eric Schmidt
☐ 5 Robert Geren
☐ 6 Maurice Guercio
☐ 7 Randy Velarde
☐ 8 Ted Higgins
☐ 9 Gary Cathcart
☐ 10 Jerry McNertney
☐ 11 Tim Layana
☐ 12 Jim Howard
☐ 13 Matthew Harrison
☐ 14 Carson Carroll
☐ 15 Chris Alvarez
☐ 16 Darren Reed
☐ 17 Jeff Knox
☐ 18 Jeffrey Pries
☐ 19 Tommy Jones
☐ 20 Fredi Gonzalez
☐ 21 Hal Morris
☐ 22 Brent Blum
☐ 23 Steve Frey

1987 Albuquerque Dukes Police

Set was apparently produced and distributed by the team. At the bottom of the reverse on each card is an anti-drug message from the Dukes and the local police departments

	MINT	NRMT	EXC
COMPLETE SET (30)	8.00	3.60	1.00

☐ 1 Terry Collins MG
☐ 2 Ben Hines CO
☐ 3 Brent Strom CO
☐ 4 Lenny Currier TR
☐ 5 William Brennan
☐ 6 Dennis Burtt
☐ 7 Jaime Cocanower
☐ 8 Tim Crews
☐ 9 Jeff Edwards
☐ 10 Hector Heredia
☐ 11 Shawn Hillegas
☐ 12 Pete Ladd
☐ 13 Dennis Livingston
☐ 14 Tim Meeks
☐ 15 Jon Debus
☐ 16 Orlando Mercado
☐ 17 Gilberto Reyes
☐ 18 Shanie Dugas
☐ 19 Jeff Hamilton
☐ 20 Jack Perconte
☐ 21 Larry See
☐ 22 Craig Shipley
☐ 23 Brad Wellman
☐ 24 Tracy Woodson
☐ 25 Ralph Bryant
☐ 26 Jose Gonzalez
☐ 27 Chris Gwynn
☐ 28 George Hinshaw
☐ 29 Stu Pederson
☐ 30 Mike Ramsey

1987 Appleton Foxes ProCards

This 30-card standard-size set of the 1987 Appleton Foxes, a Class A Midwest League affiliate of the Kansas City Royals, features white-bordered posed color player photos on its fronts. The player's name and position appear at the bottom. The white horizontal back is framed by a black line and carries the player's name at the top, followed by biography and statistics.

	MINT	NRMT	EXC
COMPLETE SET (30)	5.00	2.20	.60

☐ 1 Chuck Mount
☐ 2 Bill Gilmore
☐ 3 John Larios
☐ 4 Pete Capello
☐ 5 D.J. Watson
☐ 6 Carlos Escalera
☐ 7 Frank Laureano
☐ 8 Deric Ladnier
☐ 9 Mike Tresemer
☐ 10 Mike Butcher
☐ 11 Joe Skodny
☐ 12 Darren Watkins
☐ 13 Ben Lee

☐ 14 Carlos Gonzalez
☐ 15 Charlie Eisenreich
☐ 16 Tom Gilles
☐ 17 Brian Poldberg
☐ 18 Mike Alvarez
☐ 19 Pat Bailey
☐ 20 Jose Rodriquez
☐ 21 Rob Wolkoys
☐ 22 Mike Leon
☐ 23 Tony Pickett
☐ 24 Ken Berry
☐ 25 Luke Nocas
☐ 26 Dennis Moeller
☐ 27 Greg Hibbard
☐ 28 Kenny Jackson
☐ 29 Phil McKinzie
☐ 30 Jim Willis

1987 Arizona Wildcats Police

	MINT	NRMT	EXC
COMPLETE SET (20)	12.00	5.50	1.50

☐ 1 Gary Alexander
☐ 2 Greg Fowble
☐ 3 Wayne Gilles
☐ 4 Frank Halcovich
☐ 5 Chip Hale
☐ 6 Gilbert Heredia
☐ 7 Jerry Kindall CO
☐ 8 Jason Klonoski
☐ 9 Heath Lane
☐ 10 David Martinez
☐ 11 Rich Schuman
☐ 12 Dave Shermet
☐ 13 J.T. Snow
☐ 14 Jerry Stitt ACO
☐ 15 Steve Strong
☐ 16 Mike Thorell
☐ 17 Pat Waid
☐ 18 Joe White
☐ 19 Jim Wing CO
☐ 20 Alan Zinter

1987 Arkansas Travelers ProCards

This 25-card standard-size set of the 1987 Arkansas Travelers, a Class AA Texas League affiliate of the St. Louis Cardinals, features white-bordered posed color player photos on its fronts. The player's name and position appear at the bottom. The white horizontal back is framed by a black line and carries the player's name at the top, followed by biography and statistics. This issue includes the minor league card debut of Ken Hill.

	MINT	NRMT	EXC
COMPLETE SET (25)	12.00	5.50	1.50

☐ 1 Dennis Carter
☐ 2 Mike Robinson
☐ 3 Charles McGrath
☐ 4 Jose Calderon
☐ 5 Kennedy Infante
☐ 6 Jeff Fassero
☐ 7 James Riggleman
☐ 8 Randall Champion
☐ 9 Steven Peters
☐ 10 Paul Wilmet
☐ 11 James Fregosi
☐ 12 Roy Silver
☐ 13 Scott Arnold
☐ 14 Tim Jones
☐ 15 Salvatore Agostinelli
☐ 16 Luis Alicea
☐ 17 Craig Weissmann
☐ 18 Jeff Oyster
☐ 19 Kenneth Hill
☐ 20 Alex Cole
☐ 21 Mike Fitzgerald
☐ 22 Ray Stevens
☐ 23 James Reboulet
☐ 24 Brad Henderson
☐ 25 John Costello

1987 Asheville Tourists ProCards

This 28-card standard-size set of the 1987 Asheville Tourists, a Class A South Atlantic League affiliate of the Houston Astros, features white-bordered posed color player photos on its fronts. The player's name and position appear at the bottom. The white horizontal back is framed by a black line and carries the player's name at the top, followed by biography and statistics.

	MINT	NRMT	EXC
COMPLETE SET (28)	5.00	2.20	.60

☐ 1 Karl Rhodes
☐ 2 Trent Hubbard
☐ 3 Gene Confreda
☐ 4 Keith Bodie
☐ 5 Ryan Bowen
☐ 6 Daven Bond
☐ 7 Lou Frazier
☐ 8 Doug Gonring
☐ 9 Jim Olson
☐ 10 Marty Hall
☐ 11 Charlie Taylor
☐ 12 Kevin Wasilewski
☐ 13 Guy Normand
☐ 14 Mike Stoker
☐ 15 Nedar Horta
☐ 16 Bert Hunter
☐ 17 Mike Simms
☐ 18 Shawn Talbott
☐ 19 Victor Hithe
☐ 20 Sam August
☐ 21 Todd McClure
☐ 22 Mike Oglesbee
☐ 23 Lou Deiley
☐ 24 Ed Whited
☐ 25 Jeff Edwards
☐ 26 Gorky Perez
☐ 27 Pedro Sanchez
☐ 28 John Sheehan

1987 Auburn Astros ProCards

This 25-card standard-size set of the 1987 Auburn Astros, a Class A New York-Penn affiliate of the Houston Astros, features white-bordered posed color player photos on its fronts. The player's name and position appear at the bottom. The white horizontal back is framed by a black line and carries the player's name at the top, followed by biography and statistics.

	MINT	NRMT	EXC
COMPLETE SET (25)	5.00	2.20	.60

☐ 1 John Massarelli
☐ 2 Rusty Harris
☐ 3 Todd McClure
☐ 5 Damon Brooks
☐ 6 Billy Paul Carver
☐ 7 Andres Mota
☐ 8 Dan Lewis
☐ 9 Steve Polverini
☐ 10 Randy Hennis
☐ 11 Chris Hawkins
☐ 12 Gary Tuck
☐ 13 Dan Nyssen
☐ 14 Carlos Laboy
☐ 15 Gorky Perez
☐ 16 Robert Romo
☐ 17 Todd Newman
☐ 18 Greg Johnson
☐ 19 Rick Aponte
☐ 20 Hector Herrera
☐ 21 Ken Dickson
☐ 22 Al Osuna
☐ 23 Edison Renteria
☐ 24 Dean Hartgraves
☐ 25 Richie Simon
☐ 26 Douglas Royalty

1987 Bakersfield Dodgers ProCards

This 29-card standard-size set of the 1987 Bakersfield Dodgers, a Class A California League affiliate of the Los Angeles Dodgers, features white-bordered posed color player photos on its fronts. The player's name and position appear at the bottom. The white horizontal back is framed by a black line and carries the player's name at the top, followed by biography and statistics.

	MINT	NRMT	EXC
COMPLETE SET (29)	5.00	2.20	.60

☐ 1 Mike Hartley
☐ 2 Dan Montgomery
☐ 3 Macario Gastelum
☐ 4 Miguel Mota
☐ 5 Juan Guzman
☐ 6 Billy Brooks
☐ 7 Juan Bell
☐ 8 Todd Kroll
☐ 9 John Stein
☐ 10 Luis Lopez
☐ 11 Jim Kating
☐ 12 Mike White
☐ 13 Doug Cox
☐ 14 Stan Johnston
☐ 15 Kevin Kennedy
☐ 16 Mark Hseehy
☐ 17 Rod Roche
☐ 18 Ted Holcomb
☐ 19 Eric Mangham
☐ 20 Fred Farwell
☐ 21 Dave Hansen
☐ 22 Tim Anderson
☐ 23 Wayne Kirby
☐ 24 Paul Moralez
☐ 25 Carlos Hernandez
☐ 26 Mike Siler
☐ 27 Mike Munoz
☐ 28 Mike Pitz
☐ 29 Willie Pinelli

1987 Bellingham Mariners Team Issue

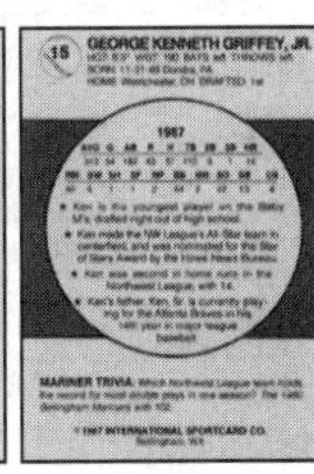

This 34-card standard-size set of the 1987 Bellingham Mariners, a Class A Northwest League affiliate of the Seattle Mariners, features white-bordered posed color player photos in a square yellow bordered box on its fronts. The player's name, position and team name appear across the bottom. The back carries the player's name at the top, followed by biography and statistics. This issue includes the minor league card debut of Ken Griffey Jr. 15,000 sets were produced.

	MINT	NRMT	EXC
COMPLETE SET (34)	75.00	34.00	9.50

☐ 1 Jeff Hooper
☐ 2 Erick Bryant
☐ 3 Brian Wilkinson
☐ 4 Dorian Daughtry
☐ 5 Kevin Reichardt
☐ 6 Keith Helton
☐ 7 John Hoffman
☐ 8 Victor Mangual
☐ 9 Chuck Carr
☐ 10 Tom Peters
☐ 11 Todd Haney
☐ 12 Joe Georger CO
☐ 13 Jeff Morrison
☐ 14 Wade Taylor
☐ 15 Ken Griffey Jr.
☐ 16 Spyder Webb TR
☐ 17 Otis Patrick
☐ 18 Mike Goff
☐ 19 Brian Baldwin
☐ 20 Tony Cayson
☐ 21 Mike Sisco
☐ 22 Mike McGuire
☐ 23 Ruben Gonzalez
☐ 24 Rick Sweet MG
☐ 25 Daryl Burrus
☐ 26 Scott Stoerck
☐ 27 Fausto Ramirez
☐ 28 Salty Parker CO
☐ 29 Steve Bieksha
☐ 30 Paul Togneri
☐ 31 Cory Paul
☐ 32 Chris VanBuren BB
Marty Reese BB
☐ 33 Team Photo CL
☐ NNO Title Card

1987 Beloit Brewers ProCards

This 26-card standard-size set of the 1987 Beloit Brewers, a Class A Midwest League affiliate of the Milwaukee Brewers, features white-bordered posed color player photos on its fronts. The player's name and position appear at the bottom. The white horizontal back is framed by a black line and carries the player's name at the top, followed by biography and statistics. This issue includes the minor league card debut of Greg Vaughn.

	MINT	NRMT	EXC
COMPLETE SET (26)	15.00	6.75	1.85

☐ 1 Randy Veres
☐ 2 Greg Vaughn
☐ 3 John Jaha
☐ 4 Shon Ashley
☐ 5 Steve Monson
☐ 6 Steve Kostickhka
☐ 7 Jamie Congemi
☐ 8 Robert Jones
☐ 9 Brian Stone
☐ 10 Brian Drahman
☐ 11 Jim Rowe
☐ 12 Doug Henry
☐ 13 Rusty McGinnis
☐ 14 Lance Lincoln
☐ 15 Terry Brown
☐ 16 Ron Harrison
☐ 17 Tim Barker
☐ 18 Gomer Hodge
☐ 19 Dave Carley
☐ 20 Hector Alberro
☐ 21 Rim Watkins
☐ 22 Ray Ojeda
☐ 23 Dan Adriance
☐ 24 Manny Chireno
☐ 25 Dave Taylor
☐ 26 Tim McIntosh

1987 Birmingham Barons Best

	MINT	NRMT	EXC
COMPLETE SET (28)	7.00	3.10	.85

☐ 1 Rico Petrocelli MG
☐ 2 Sam Hairston Sr. CO
☐ 3 Moe Drabowsky CO
☐ 4 James Wesley O'Dell
☐ 5 Marlin McPhail
☐ 6 Wil Caraballo
☐ 7 Rondal Rollin
☐ 8 Larry Acker
☐ 9 Jeff Bettendorf
☐ 10 Antonio G. Menendez
☐ 11 Richard Kent Gaynor
☐ 12 John Robert Boling
☐ 13 Adam Charles Peterson
☐ 14 Gardner C. Hall
☐ 15 Donn Steven Pall
☐ 16 James Joseph Hickey
☐ 17 John Pawlowski
☐ 18 John Graydon Hardy
☐ 19 Rolando Pino
☐ 20 Kenton Craig Torve
☐ 21 Darrell Ray Pruitt
☐ 22 Peter Paul Venturini
☐ 23 Manual Victor Salinas
☐ 24 James A. Winters
☐ 25 Troy Gene Thomas
☐ 26 Wm. Donald Lindsey
☐ 27 Jorge Enrique Alcazar
☐ 28 Rick DeHart TR

1987 Brigham Young Cougars

Produced by Utah Sports Card Co.

	MINT	NRMT	EXC
COMPLETE SET (21)	10.00	4.50	1.25

☐ 1 Checklist
☐ 2 Todd Newman
☐ 3 Mike Willes
☐ 4 Carl Kelipuleole
☐ 5 Chris Cooper
☐ 6 John DeSilva
☐ 7 Ron Masino
Kevin Nichols
Coray Tate
Rudy Pinon
☐ 8 Jason Jackson
☐ 9 Mike Littlewood
☐ 10 Darin Kracl
☐ 11 John Batina
☐ 12 John Sinclair
☐ 13 David Willes
☐ 14 Paul Cluff
Dave Wrape
Paul Herrera
Jeff Strong
☐ 15 Gary Young
☐ 16 Carter Cox
☐ 17 Gary Miner
☐ 18 Brad Eagar
☐ 19 Gary Schoonover
☐ 20 Bruce Ellis
☐ 21 Paul Prinz
Ed Zinter
Joe Smith
Ron Sisler

1987 Buffalo Bisons Pucko

5,000 sets were produced.

	MINT	NRMT	EXC
COMPLETE SET (29)	7.00	3.10	.85

☐ 1 Don Lovell
☐ 2 Kent Murphy
☐ 3 Andy Allanson
☐ 4 Jay Bell
☐ 5 Barry Brunenkant
☐ 6 Dave Clark
☐ 7 Doug Frobel
☐ 8 Junior Noboa
☐ 9 Casey Parsons
☐ 10 Craig Smajstria
☐ 11 Ron Tingley
☐ 12 Randy Washington
☐ 13 Eddie Williams
☐ 14 Gibson Alba
☐ 15 John Farrell
☐ 16 Jeff Kaiser
☐ 17 Mike Murphy
☐ 18 Bryan Oelkers
☐ 19 Reggie Ritter
☐ 20 Scott Roberts
☐ 21 Jose Roman
☐ 22 Don Schulze
☐ 23 Frank Wills
☐ 24 Rod Allen
☐ 25 Orlando Gomez

☐ 26 Mike Bucci
☐ 27 Mike Billoni
☐ 28 Donald Palmer
☐ 29 Pete Weber and John Murphy

1987 Burlington Expos ProCards

This 29-card standard-size set of the 1987 Burlington Expos, a Class A Midwest League affiliate of the Montreal Expos, features white-bordered posed color player photos on its fronts. The player's name and position appear at the bottom. The white horizontal back is framed by a black line and carries the player's name at the top, followed by biography and statistics. This issue includes the first team set appearance of Mel Rojas.

	MINT	NRMT	EXC
COMPLETE SET (29)	5.00	2.20	.60

☐ 1067 Leonard Kelly
☐ 1068 James Vincent Olson
☐ 1069 Nels Jacobsen
☐ 1070 Tony Welborn
☐ 1071 Kent Bottenfield
☐ 1072 Sal Vaccaro
☐ 1073 Doug Duke
☐ 1074 Jeff Oller
☐ 1075 Mike Dull
☐ 1076 Jose Alou
☐ 1077 Steven St.Claire
☐ 1078 Ben Spitale
☐ 1079 Kevin Finigan
☐ 1080 Russ Schueler
☐ 1081 Delwyn Young
☐ 1082 Jeff Wedvick
☐ 1083 David Morrow
☐ 1084 Bobby Gaylor
☐ 1085 Mike Ishmael
☐ 1086 Mark Haryd
☐ 1087 Buzz Capra CO
☐ 1088 John Howes
☐ 1089 Bobby Pate CO
☐ 1090 J.R. Miner MG
☐ 1091 Sean Cunningham TR
☐ 1092 Dan Larson
☐ 1093 Mel Rojas
☐ 1094 Robin DeYoung
☐ 1095 Doug Vontz

1987 Calgary Cannons ProCards

This 24-card standard-size set of the 1987 Calgary Cannons, a Class AAA Pacific Coast League affiliate of the Seattle Mariners, features white-bordered posed color player photos on its fronts. The player's name and position appear at the bottom. The white horizontal back is framed by a black line and carries the player's name at the top, followed by biography and statistics. This issue includes a second year card of Edgar Martinez.

	MINT	NRMT	EXC
COMPLETE SET (24)	12.00	5.50	1.50

☐ 2309 Edgar Martinez
☐ 2310 Mike Watters
☐ 2311 Jim Weaver
☐ 2312 Bill Plummer MG
☐ 2313 Ross Grimsley CO
☐ 2314 Dennis Powell
☐ 2315 Mike Brown
☐ 2316 Paul Schneider
☐ 2317 Dave Hengel
☐ 2318 Karl Best
☐ 2319 Mario Diaz
☐ 2320 Brick Smith
☐ 2321 Roy Thomas
☐ 2322 Mike Campbell
☐ 2323 Randy Braun
☐ 2324 Mike Wishnevski
☐ 2325 Terry Taylor
☐ 2326 Stan Clarke
☐ 2327 Donell Nixon
☐ 2328 Tony Ferreira
☐ 2329 Jerry Narron
☐ 2330 Dave Gallagher
☐ 2331 Doug Gwosdz
☐ 2332 Rich Monteleone

1987 Cedar Rapids Reds ProCards

This 28-card standard-size set of the 1987 Cedar Rapids Reds, a Class A Midwest League affiliate of the Cincinnati Reds, features white-bordered posed color player photos on its fronts. The player's name and position appear at the bottom. The white horizontal back is framed by a black line and carries the player's name at the top, followed by biography and statistics.

	MINT	NRMT	EXC
COMPLETE SET (28)	5.00	2.20	.60

☐ 1 Al Lobozzetta
☐ 2 Phil Dale
☐ 3 Scott Willis
☐ 4 Curt Kindred
☐ 5 Joe Lazor
☐ 6 Joel Lono
☐ 7 Scott Scudder
☐ 8 Ron Mullins
☐ 9 Mendy Espinal
☐ 10 Keith Brown
☐ 11 Dusty Rogers
☐ 12 Joe Bruno
☐ 13 Keith Lockhart
☐ 14 Reggie Jefferson
☐ 15 Greg Lonigro
☐ 16 Don Wakamatsu
☐ 17 Brian Robinson
☐ 18 Cal Cain
☐ 19 Mike Vincent
☐ 20 Ted Wilborn
☐ 21 John Stewart
☐ 22 Don Brown
☐ 23 Francisco Silverio
☐ 24 Paul Kirsch
☐ 25 Bernie Walker
☐ 26 Rich Bombard
☐ 27 Jim Knudtson
☐ 28 Lamar Mascot

1987 Charleston Rainbows ProCards

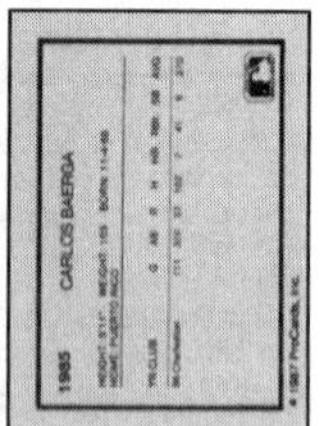

This 23-card standard-size set of the 1987 Charleston Rainbows, a Class A South Atlantic League affiliate of the San Diego Padres, features white-bordered posed color player photos on its fronts. The player's name and position appear at the bottom. The white horizontal back is framed by a black line and carries the player's name at the top, followed by biography and statistics. This issue includes a second year card of Carlos Baerga.

	MINT	NRMT	EXC
COMPLETE SET (23)	25.00	11.00	3.10

☐ 1 Brian Brooks
☐ 2 Carlos Baerga
☐ 3 Greg W. Harris Sic, Gregg S.
☐ 4 Michael J. King
☐ 5 Gregory Hall
☐ 6 William "Ooiee" Taylor
☐ 7 James "Bubba" Austin
☐ 8 Brian Lee Harrison
☐ 9 Gary Lance
☐ 10 Mike Young
☐ 11 James Navilliat
☐ 12 Terry McDevitt
☐ 13 Omar Olivares
☐ 14 Matt Maysey
☐ 15 Rafael Valdez
☐ 16 Warren "Newt" Newton
☐ 17 Tony Torchia
☐ 18 Jamie Morena
☐ 19 Jimmie Tatum Jr.
☐ 20 Michael A. Basso
☐ 21 Ricardo Bones
☐ 22 Keith Harrison
☐ 23 Doug Brocail

1987 Charleston Wheelers ProCards

This 28-card standard-size set of the 1987 Charleston Wheelers, a Class A South Atlantic League Independent, features white-bordered posed color player photos on its fronts. The player's name and position appear at the bottom. The white horizontal back is framed by a black line and carries the player's name at the top, followed by biography and statistics.

	MINT	NRMT	EXC
COMPLETE SET (28)	5.00	2.20	.60

☐ 1 William Melvin
☐ 2 James Hendrix
☐ 3 Gilbert Villavueva
☐ 4 Alan Wilson
☐ 5 Steven Scarsone
☐ 6 Peter Callas
☐ 7 Rodney Brunelle
☐ 8 Bob Gsellman
☐ 9 Steven Mehl
☐ 10 Gary Pifer
☐ 11 Larry Allen
☐ 12 John Knapp
☐ 13 Danny Weems
☐ 14 Hal Dyer
☐ 15 Carl Grovom
☐ 16 Kevin Main
☐ 17 Timothy McMillan
☐ 18 Robert Strickland
☐ 19 J. Anthony LaPoint
☐ 20 Jimmie Gardiver
☐ 21 Steven O'Quinn
☐ 22 Christopher Keshock
☐ 23 L. Timothy Sossamon
☐ 24 Jack Peel
☐ 25 Norberto Martin
☐ 26 Thomas Abrell
☐ 27 Randall Robinson
☐ 28 Doyle Balthazar

1987 Charlotte O's WBTV

	MINT	NRMT	EXC
COMPLETE SET (30)	8.00	3.60	1.00

☐ 1 Pete Stanicek
☐ 2 Sherwin Cijntje
☐ 5 Rico Rossy
☐ 7 Ricky Jones
☐ 8 Tom Dodd
☐ 9 Jack Tackett
☐ 10 Mike Raczka
☐ 11 Jim Daniel
☐ 12 Francisco Jav. Oliveras
☐ 13 Joe Jarrell
☐ 14 Robert Long
☐ 15 Matt Cimo
☐ 16 Miguel Alicea
☐ 17 Jerry Holtz
☐ 19 Kurt Beamesderfer
☐ 20 John Hoover
☐ 21 Brian Householder
☐ 24 Greg Biagini MG
☐ 25 John Flinn CO
☐ 30 Bob Milacki
☐ 30 Crockett Park (team logo on back)
☐ 31 Chester Durw. Stanhope
☐ 35 Greg Talamantez
☐ 36 Dave Falcone
☐ 37 Joe Kucharski
☐ NNO Paul Cameron (Sportscaster)
☐ NNO Charlie Frederick (Sportscaster)
☐ NNO Bob Hice (Sportscaster)
☐ NNO Terry Mauney (Sportscaster)
☐ NNO Jeff Wood TR

1987 Chattanooga Lookouts Best

	MINT	NRMT	EXC
COMPLETE SET (26)	8.00	3.60	1.00

☐ 1 Sal Rende MG
☐ 2 Dan Warthen CO
☐ 3 Gregory Bartley
☐ 4 James Parker
☐ 5 James Walker
☐ 6 Calvin Jones
☐ 7 James Bryant
☐ 8 Michael Schooler
☐ 9 Douglas Givler
☐ 10 Erik Hanson
☐ 11 Michael Christ
☐ 12 Kenneth Spratke
☐ 13 Robert Gunnarson
☐ 14 Roger Hansen
☐ 15 Bill McGuire
☐ 16 Eric Fox
☐ 17 Greg Briley
☐ 18 Gregory Fulton
☐ 19 Nesi Balelo
☐ 20 David Myers
☐ 21 Matthew Hall
☐ 22 John Gibbons
☐ 23 Brian David
☐ 24 William Mendek
☐ 25 Andre Robertson
☐ 26 Tom Hunt TR

1987 Clearwater Phillies ProCards

This 27-card standard-size set of the 1987 Philadelphia Phillies, a Class A Florida State League affiliate of the Philadelphia Phillies, features white-bordered posed color player photos on its fronts. The player's name and position appear at the bottom. The white horizontal back is framed by a black line and carries the player's name at the top, followed by biography and statistics.

	MINT	NRMT	EXC
COMPLETE SET (27)	5.00	2.20	.60

☐ 1 Rick Parker
☐ 2 Brad Moore
☐ 3 Curt Befort
☐ 4 Chuck Malone
☐ 5 Olen Parker
☐ 6 Carlos Zayas
☐ 7 Bobby Behnsch
☐ 8 Jeff Kaye
☐ 9 Harvey Brumfield
☐ 10 Shawn Dantzler
☐ 11 Ramon Caraballo
☐ 12 Eric Boudreaux
☐ 13 Garry Clark
☐ 14 Warren Magee
☐ 15 Carlos Arroyo
☐ 16 Steve Sharts
☐ 17 Gary White
☐ 18 Gary Berman
☐ 19 Roly DeArmas
☐ 20 Dave Brundage
☐ 21 Julio Machado
☐ 22 Juan Sanchez
☐ 23 Brad Brink
☐ 24 Allen Wisdom
☐ 25 Bart Kaiser
☐ 26 Todd Howey
☐ 27 Travis Warren

1987 Clinton Giants ProCards

This 29-card standard-size set of the 1987 Clinton Giants, a Class A Midwest League affiliate of the San Francisco Giants, features white-bordered posed color player photos on its fronts. The player's name and position appear at the bottom. The white horizontal back is framed by a black line and carries the player's name at the top, followed by biography and statistics.

	MINT	NRMT	EXC
COMPLETE SET (29)	5.00	2.20	.60

☐ 1 Doug Robertson
☐ 2 John Toal
☐ 3 Dave Patterson
☐ 4 Gregg Ritchie
☐ 5 Jim Anderson
☐ 6 Willie Mijares
☐ 7 Felipe Gonzalez
☐ 8 Tod Ronson
☐ 9 Jim McNamara
☐ 10 John Rannow
☐ 11 Bill Carlson
☐ 12 Tom Ealy
☐ 13 Kevin Redick
☐ 14 Mark Leonard
☐ 15 Dee Dixon
☐ 16 Kim Flowers
☐ 17 Bill Evers
☐ 18 Todd Oakes
☐ 19 Jim Pena
☐ 20 Brock Birch
☐ 21 Paul McClellan
☐ 22 Drew Ricker
☐ 23 Sam Moore
☐ 24 Daron Connelly
☐ 25 Bob Richmond
☐ 26 Ray Velasquez
☐ 27 Trevor Wilson
☐ 28 Brian Hickerson
☐ 29 Team Photo

1987 Columbia Mets ProCards

This 29-card standard-size set of the 1987 Columbia Mets, a Class A South Atlantic League affiliate of the New York Mets, features white-bordered posed color player photos on its fronts. The player's name and position appear at the bottom. The white horizontal back is framed by a black line and carries the player's name at the top, followed by biography and statistics.

	MINT	NRMT	EXC
COMPLETE SET (29)	5.00	2.20	.60

☐ 1 Barry Hightower
☐ 2 Bob Apodaca
☐ 3 Brandon Bailey
☐ 4 Cliff Gonzalez
☐ 5 David Lau
☐ 6 Jaime Roseboro
☐ 7 Rich Lundahl
☐ 8 Adam Ging
☐ 9 Johnny Monell
☐ 10 Butch Hobson
☐ 11 Steve Kenneley
☐ 12 Rick Brown
☐ 13 David Liddeu
☐ 14 Luis Natera
☐ 15 Bobby Hernandez
☐ 16 Victor Garcia
☐ 17 Scott Henion
☐ 18 Juan Marina
☐ 19 Danny Naughton
☐ 20 Mike Anderson
☐ 21 Fritz Polka
☐ 22 Rodney Murrell
☐ 23 Tom Doyle

☐ 24 Dan McMurtire
☐ 25 Rick Durant
☐ 26 Julio Valera
☐ 27 Rob Colescott
☐ 28 Alex Jiminez
☐ 29 Todd Welborn

1987 Columbus Astros ProCards

This 25-card standard-size set of the 1987 Columbus Astros, a Class AA Southern League affiliate of the Houston Astros, features white-bordered posed color player photos on its fronts. The player's name and position appear at the bottom. The white horizontal back is framed by a black line and carries the player's name at the top, followed by biography and statistics. This issue includes a third year card of Ken Caminiti.

	MINT	NRMT	EXC
COMPLETE SET (25)	15.00	6.75	1.85

☐ 1 Al Chambers
☐ 2 Jeff Datz
☐ 3 Fred Gladding
☐ 4 Troy Afenir
☐ 5 Jim Thomas
☐ 6 Mel Stottlemyre Jr.
☐ 7 Cameron Drew
☐ 8 Blaise Ilsley
☐ 9 Mitch Cook
☐ 10 Rob Parker
☐ 11 Jim Van Houten
☐ 12 John Fishel
☐ 13 Mark Baker
☐ 14 Karl Allaire
☐ 15 Joe Mikulik
☐ 16 Tom Wiedenbauer
☐ 17 Dody Rather
☐ 18 Jose Rodiles
☐ 19 Earl Cash
☐ 20 Jeff Livin
☐ 21 Larry Lasky
☐ 22 Rob Mallicoat
☐ 23 Rich Johnson
☐ 24 Norman Brock
☐ 25 Jeff Bumgarner

1987 Columbus Clippers Police

This 25-card standard-size set of the 1987 Columbus Clippers, a Class AAA International affiliate of the New York Yankees, features the minor league card debut of Jay Buhner.

	MINT	NRMT	EXC
COMPLETE SET (25)	20.00	9.00	2.50

☐ 1 Mike Armstrong
☐ 2 Brad Arnsberg
☐ 3 Rich Bordi
☐ 4 Jay Buhner
☐ 5 Pete Dalena
☐ 6 Bucky Dent MG
☐ 7 Orestes Destrade
☐ 8 Juan Espino
☐ 9 Pete Filson
☐ 10 Bill Fulton
☐ 11 Randy Graham
☐ 12 Al Holland
☐ 13 Keith Hughes
☐ 14 Roberto Kelly
☐ 15 Al Leiter
☐ 16 Bryan Little
☐ 17 Phil Lombardi
☐ 18 Mitch Lyden
☐ 19 Bobby Meacham
☐ 20 Alfonso Pulido
☐ 21 Ron Romanick
☐ 22 Glenn Sherlock
☐ 23 George Sisler Jr. GM
☐ 24 Shane Turner
☐ 25 Coaching Staff
Clete Boyer CO
Champ Summers CO
Jerry McNertney CO
Ken Rowe CO

1987 Columbus Clippers ProCards

This 27-card standard-size set of the 1987 Columbus Clippers, a Class AAA International affiliate of the New York Yankees, features white-bordered posed color player photos on its fronts. The player's name and position appear at the bottom. The white horizontal back is framed by a black line and carries the player's name at the top, followed by biography and statistics. This issue includes the minor league card debut of Jay Buhner.

	MINT	NRMT	EXC
COMPLETE SET (27)	20.00	9.00	2.50

☐ 1 Bucky Dent
☐ 2 Clete Boyer
Kevin Rand
Ken Rowe
Jerry McNertney
Champ Summers
☐ 3 Glenn Sherlock
☐ 4 Juan Espino
☐ 5 Mitch Lyden
☐ 6 Bobby Meacham
☐ 7 Pete Dalena
☐ 8 Orestes Destrade
☐ 9 Shane Turner
☐ 10 Bryan Little
☐ 11 Jeff Moronko
☐ 12 Phil Lombardi
☐ 13 Dick Scott
☐ 14 Roberto Kelly
☐ 15 Jay Buhner
☐ 16 Henry Cotto
☐ 17 Keith Hughes
☐ 18 Rich Bordi
☐ 19 Randy Graham
☐ 20 Alfonso Pulido
☐ 21 Mike Armstrong
☐ 22 Al Holland
☐ 23 Ron Romanick
☐ 24 Brad Arnsberg
☐ 25 Pete Filson
☐ 26 Al Leiter
☐ 27 Bill Fulton

1987 Columbus Clippers TCMA

This 25-card standard-size set of the 1987 Columbus Clippers, a Class AAA International affiliate of the New York Yankees, features the minor league card debut of Jay Buhner.

	MINT	NRMT	EXC
COMPLETE SET (25)	10.00	4.50	1.25

☐ 1 Brad Arnsberg
☐ 2 Rich Bordi
☐ 3 Pete Filson
☐ 4 Bill Fulton
☐ 5 Randy Graham
☐ 6 Al Holland
☐ 7 Alfonso Pulido
☐ 8 Ron Romanick
☐ 9 Bob Tewksbury
☐ 10 Juan Espino
☐ 11 Mitch Lyden
☐ 12 Pete Dalena
☐ 13 Orestes Destrade
☐ 14 Bryan Little
☐ 15 Phil Lombardi
☐ 16 Bobby Meacham
☐ 17 Jeff Moronko
☐ 18 Shane Turner
☐ 19 Jay Buhner
☐ 20 Henry Cotto
☐ 21 Keith Hughes
☐ 22 Roberto Kelly
☐ 23 Bucky Dent
☐ 24 Clete Boyer
Champ Summers
Jerry McNertney
Ken Rowe
☐ 25 Glenn Sherlock

1987 Daytona Beach Admirals ProCards

This 26-card standard-size set of the 1987 Daytona Beach Admirals, a Class A Florida State League affiliate of the Chicago White Sox, features white-bordered posed color player photos on its fronts. The player's name and position appear at the bottom. The white horizontal back is framed by a black line and carries the player's name at the top, followed by biography and statistics.

	MINT	NRMT	EXC
COMPLETE SET (26)	5.00	2.20	.60

☐ 1 Todd Trafton
☐ 2 Carl Sullivan
☐ 3 Eric Milholland
☐ 4 Tom Drees
☐ 5 Tony Blasucci
☐ 6 Carlos DeLaCruz
☐ 7 Ken Reed
☐ 8 Doug Little
☐ 9 James Brennen
☐ 10 Mark Henry
☐ 11 Francisco Abreu
☐ 12 Conde Cortez
☐ 13 Patrick Coveney
☐ 14 Matt Merullo
☐ 15 Wayne Edwards
☐ 16 Chris Jefts
☐ 17 Frank Potestio
☐ 18 Billy Eveline
☐ 19 Ed Sedar
☐ 20 Chris Cota
☐ 21 Graylyn Engram
☐ 22 Jerry Bertolani
☐ 23 Andy Nieto
☐ 24 Dave Cronkright
☐ 25 Mike Gellinger
☐ 26 Glen McElroy

1987 Denver Zephyrs ProCards

This 27-card standard-size set of the 1987 Denver Zephyrs, a Class AAA American Association affiliate of the Milwaukee Brewers, features white-bordered posed color player photos on its fronts. The player's name and position appear at the bottom. The white horizontal back is framed by a black line and carries the player's name at the top, followed by biography and statistics.

	MINT	NRMT	EXC
COMPLETE SET (27)	5.00	2.20	.60

☐ 1 David Clay
☐ 2 Tim Pyznarski
☐ 3 Al Price
☐ 4 Jay Aldrich
☐ 5 Joey Meyer
☐ 6 Brad Komminsk
☐ 7 Billy Bates
☐ 8 Ron Harrison
☐ 9 Paul Mirabella
☐ 10 Alex Madrid
☐ 11 Dave Schuler
☐ 12 Dave Klipstein
☐ 13 Terry Bevington
☐ 14 John Beuerlien
☐ 15 Dan Scarpetta
☐ 16 Jim Adduci
☐ 17 Don August
☐ 18 Steve Kiefer
☐ 19 Alan Cartwright
☐ 20 Mark Knudson
☐ 21 Jackson Todd
☐ 22 David Davidsmeier
☐ 23 Brian Clutterbuck
☐ 24 Charlie O'Brien
☐ 25 Keith Smith
☐ 26 Al Jones
☐ 27 Steve Stanicek

1987 Dunedin Blue Jays ProCards

This 29-card standard-size set of the 1987 Dunedin Blue Jays, a Class A Florida State League affiliate of the Toronto Blue Jays, features white-bordered posed color player photos on its fronts. The player's name and position appear at the bottom. The white horizontal back is framed by a black line and carries the player's name at the top, followed by biography and statistics.

	MINT	NRMT	EXC
COMPLETE SET (29)	5.00	2.20	.60

☐ 923 Carlos Diaz
☐ 924 Steve Cummings
☐ 925 Bob Watts
☐ 926 Mike Jones
☐ 927 Hugh Brinson
☐ 928 Bob Bailor MG
☐ 929 Dennis Holmberg CO
☐ 930 Dana Johnson
☐ 931 Darren Balsley
☐ 932 Steve Mumaw
☐ 933 Daryl Landrum
☐ 934 Tony Castillo
☐ 935 Steve Mingori
☐ 936 Ric Moreno TR
☐ 937 Webster Garrison
☐ 938 Hector Delacruz
☐ 939 Chris Jones
☐ 940 Ray Young
☐ 941 Kevin Batiste
☐ 942 Greg David
☐ 943 Shawn Jeter
☐ 944 Willie Blair
☐ 945 Domingo Martinez
☐ 946 Earl Sanders
☐ 947 Jerry Schunk
☐ 948 Pedro Munoz
☐ 949 Ken Rivers
☐ 950 Derek Ware
☐ 951 Pat Saitta

1987 Durham Bulls ProCards

This 28-card standard-size set of the 1987 Durham Bulls, a Class A Carolina League affiliate of the Atlanta Braves, features white-bordered posed color player photos on its fronts. The player's name and position appear at the bottom. The white horizontal back is framed by a black line and carries the player's name at the top, followed by biography and statistics.

	MINT	NRMT	EXC
COMPLETE SET (28)	5.00	2.20	.60

☐ 1 Cesar Jiminez
☐ 2 Barry Jones
☐ 3 Jeff Weiss
☐ 4 Bob Pfaff
☐ 5 Sid Akins
☐ 6 Brian G. Snitker
☐ 7 Tim Criswell
☐ 8 Johnny Cuevas
☐ 9 Gary Newsom
☐ 10 Ellis Roby
☐ 11 Dave Miller
☐ 12 Kent Mercker
☐ 13 John Stewart
☐ 14 Alex Smith
☐ 15 Bill Slack
☐ 16 Eddie Mathews
☐ 17 Mike Merrill
☐ 18 Rick Siebert
☐ 19 Gary Eave
☐ 20 Rick Morris
☐ 21 Juan Fredymond
☐ 22 Jeff Greene
☐ 23 D.J. Jones
☐ 24 Jim Salisbury
☐ 25 John Alva
☐ 26 Mark Lemke
☐ 27 Dennis Hood
☐ 28 Dodd Johnson

1987 Edmonton Trappers ProCards

This 23-card standard-size set of the 1987 Edmonton Trappers, a Class AAA Pacific Coast League affiliate of the California Angels, features white-bordered posed color player photos on its fronts. The player's name and position appear at the bottom. The white horizontal back is framed by a black line and carries the player's name at the top, followed by biography and statistics.

	MINT	NRMT	EXC
COMPLETE SET (23)	5.00	2.20	.60

☐ 2061 Jim Eppard
☐ 2062 Jack Lazorko
☐ 2063 David Heath
☐ 2064 Bobby Misick
☐ 2065 Dave Shipanoff UER
(Misspelled Shippanof
on front and back)
☐ 2066 Michael Ramsey CO
☐ 2067 Doug Banning
☐ 2068 Kevin King
☐ 2069 Allen Morelock
☐ 2070 Tack Wilson
☐ 2071 Ed Amelung
☐ 2072 Tom Kotchman MG
☐ 2073 Pete Coachman
☐ 2074 Bill Merrifield
☐ 2075 Richard Zaleski TR
☐ 2076 James Randall
☐ 2077 Frank Reberger CO
☐ 2078 Sherman Corbett
☐ 2079 Norm Carrasco
☐ 2080 Tony Fossas
☐ 2081 T.R. Bryden
☐ 2082 Terry Clark
☐ 2083 Jack Fimple

1987 El Paso Diablos ProCards

This 27-card standard-size set of the 1987 El Paso Diablos, a Class AA Texas League affiliate of the Milwaukee Brewers, features white-bordered posed color player photos on its fronts. The player's name and position appear at the bottom. The white horizontal back is framed by a black line and carries the player's name at the top, followed by biography and statistics.

	MINT	NRMT	EXC
COMPLETE SET (27)	5.00	2.20	.60

☐ 1 La Vell Freeman
Sic, Lavell
☐ 2 Joseph Mitchell
☐ 3 Donald Scott
☐ 4 Peter Kendrick
☐ 5 Garrett Nago
☐ 6 Robert DeWolf
☐ 7 Eric Hardgrave
☐ 8 Frank Mattox
☐ 9 Pete Kolb
☐ 10 Jamie Brisco
☐ 11 Mark Ambrose
☐ 12 John Miglio
☐ 13 Tim Casey
☐ 14 Duffy Dyer
☐ 15 Jesus Alfaro
☐ 16 Derek Diaz
☐ 17 Todd Brown
☐ 18 Cameron Walker
☐ 19 Walter Pohle
☐ 20 Paul Lindblad
☐ 21 Darryel Walters
☐ 22 Daniel Murphy Jr.
☐ 23 Jeffrey Peterek
☐ 24 Alan Sadler
☐ 25 Ramon Serna
☐ 26 Michael Gobbo
☐ 27 Barry Bass

1987 Elmira Pioneers (Black) Cain

This 34-card set of the 1987 Elmira Pioneers, a Class A New York-Penn League affiliate of the Boston Red Sox, features black and white player photos. The cards measure 41/2" x 3 1/2" and are horizontal. 2,500 sets were produced.

	MINT	NRMT	EXC
COMPLETE SET (34)	7.00	3.10	.85

☐ 1 Clyde Smoll
☐ 2 Bill Limoncelli
☐ 3 Dave Sullivan
☐ 4 Miguel Monegro
☐ 5 Larry Scanneli
☐ 6 Kendrick Bourne
☐ 7 Robert Echevarria
☐ 8 Julio Rosario
☐ 9 Brian Warfel
☐ 10 Terry Marrs
☐ 11 Sam Melton
☐ 12 Scott Powers
☐ 13 Al Thornton
☐ 14 Luis Dorante
☐ 15 Mike Kelly
☐ 16 Vicent Degifico
☐ 17 Tony Mosley
☐ 18 Craig Wilson
☐ 19 Stee Michael
☐ 20 Thom Sepela
☐ 21 Tony Romero
☐ 22 Johnny Diaz
☐ 23 Greg McCollum
☐ 24 Edward Banasiak
☐ 25 Joaquin Tejada
☐ 26 Jose Pemberton
☐ 27 Ronnie Richardson
☐ 28 Bernie Stento
☐ 29 Al Bumbry
☐ 30 Felix Maldonado
☐ 31 Frank Malzone
☐ 32 Eddie Popowski
☐ 33 Charlie Wagner
☐ 34 Paul Brown

1987 Elmira Pioneers (Red) Cain

This 35-card set of the 1987 Elmira Pioneers, a Class A New York-Penn League affiliate of the Boston Red Sox, features black and white player photos with a red border. The cards measure 3 3/4" x 2 1/2" and are horizontal. 1,500 sets were produced.

	MINT	NRMT	EXC
COMPLETE SET (35)	50.00	22.00	6.25

☐ 1 Clyde Smoll
President and GM
☐ 2 Bill Limoncelli MG
☐ 3 Dave Sullivan
Asst GM
☐ 4 Miguel Monegro
☐ 5 Larry Scanneli
☐ 6 Kendrick Bourne
☐ 7 Robert Echevarria
☐ 8 Julio Rosario
☐ 9 Brian Warfel
☐ 10 Terry Marrs
☐ 11 Sam Melton
☐ 12 Scott Powers
☐ 13 Al Thornton
☐ 14 Luis Dorante
☐ 15 Mike Kelly
☐ 16 Vincent Degifico
☐ 17 Tony Mosley
☐ 18 Craig Wilson
☐ 19 Steve Michael
☐ 20 Thom Sepela
☐ 21 Tony Romero
☐ 22 Jhonny Diaz
☐ 23 Greg McCollum
☐ 24 Edward Banasiak
☐ 25 Joaquin Tejada
☐ 26 Jose Pemberton
☐ 27 Ronnie Richardson
☐ 28 Bernie Stento
☐ 29 Al Bumbry
☐ 30 Reggie Harris
☐ 31 Bob Zupcic
☐ 32 Mike Dillard
☐ 33 Mickey Pina
☐ 34 Phillip Plantier
☐ NNO Checklist

1987 Erie Cardinals ProCards

This 29-card standard-size set of the 1987 Erie Cardinals, a Class A New York-Penn League affiliate of the St. Louis Cardinals, features white-bordered posed color player photos on its fronts. The player's name and position appear at the bottom. The white horizontal back is framed by a black line and carries the player's name at the top, followed by biography and statistics.

	MINT	NRMT	EXC
COMPLETE SET (29)	5.00	2.20	.60

☐ 1 Rick Christian
☐ 2 Opie Moran
☐ 3 Joe Rigoli
☐ 4 Reed Olmstead
☐ 5 Ron Leon
☐ 6 Steve Jeffers
☐ 7 Eddie Carter
☐ 8 Steve Jongewaard
☐ 9 Ernie Radcliffe
☐ 10 Roberto Marte
☐ 11 Gregg Smith
☐ 12 Antron Grier
☐ 13 Keith Bennett
☐ 14 Tim Meamber
☐ 15 Scott Broadfoot
☐ 16 Tony Russo
☐ 17 Mike Evans
☐ 18 Orlando Thomas
☐ 19 Brad Harvick
☐ 20 Kevin Robinson
☐ 21 Dave Payton
☐ 22 Scott Halama
☐ 23 Jerry Daniels
☐ 24 Chris Houser
☐ 25 Darren Nelson
☐ 26 Jeremy Hernandez
☐ 27 Pat Moore
☐ 28 Mike Hinkle
☐ 29 Rim Redman

1987 Eugene Emeralds Procards

This 30-card standard-size set of the 1987 Eugene Emeralds, a Class A Northwest League affiliate of the Kansas City Royals, features white-bordered posed color player photos on its fronts. The player's name and position appear at the bottom. The white horizontal back is framed by a black line and carries the player's name at the top, followed by biography and statistics. This issue includes the minor league card debuts of Kevin Appier and Tom Gordon.

	MINT	NRMT	EXC
COMPLETE SET (30)	15.00	6.75	1.85

☐ 2648 Darryl Robinson
☐ 2649 Antoine Pickett
☐ 2650 Doug Hupke
☐ 2651 Erv Houston
☐ 2652 Stu Cole
☐ 2653 Bob Moore
☐ 2654 James Campbell
☐ 2655 Archie Smith
☐ 2656 Doug Bock
☐ 2657 Doug Nelson
☐ 2658 Ben Pierce
☐ 2659 Keith Shibata
☐ 2660 Pete Alborano
☐ 2661 Brian McCormack
☐ 2662 Trey Gainous
☐ 2663 Derek Sholl
☐ 2664 Darren Watkins
☐ 2665 Bud Adams
☐ 2666 Luis Mallea
☐ 2667 Tony Clements
☐ 2668 Jorge Pedre
☐ 2669 Juan Berrios
☐ 2670 Montie Phillips
☐ 2671 Jim Hudson
☐ 2672 Kevin Appier
☐ 2673 Tom Gordon
☐ 2674 Terry Shumpert
☐ 2675 Don Wright
☐ 2676 Kevin Pickens
☐ 2677 Dennis Studeman

1987 Everett Giants Cramer

	MINT	NRMT	EXC
COMPLETE SET (34)	6.00	2.70	.75

☐ 1 Matt Walker
☐ 2 Gilbert Heredia
☐ 3 Scott Goins
☐ 4 Anthony Piazza
☐ 5 Lonnie Phillips
☐ 6 Richard Aldrete
☐ 7 Andy Rohn
☐ 8 Kip Southland
☐ 9 Jamie Cooper
☐ 10 Glen Abraham
☐ 11 Randy Lind
☐ 12 Joe Strain
☐ 13 Eric Gunderson
☐ 14 Chris Kooman
☐ 15 Tony Michalak
☐ 16 Tom Hostetler
☐ 17 Michael Ham
☐ 18 Todd Hawkins
☐ 19 Jimmy Terrill
☐ 20 Shaun MacKenzie
☐ 21 Jim Massey
☐ 22 Rob Willson
☐ 23 Donn Perno
☐ 24 Gary Geiger
☐ 25 Bill Bluhm
☐ 26 Jeff Morris
☐ 27 Brad Comstock
☐ 28 Dickens Benoit
☐ 29 Brad Gambee
☐ 30 Mark Owens
☐ 31 Mike Remlinger
☐ 32 Mark Dewey
☐ 33 Bruce Graham
☐ 34 Checklist

1987 Fayetteville Generals ProCards

This 27-card standard-size set of the 1987 Fayetteville Generals, a Class A South Atlantic League affiliate of the Detroit Tigers, features white-bordered posed color player photos on its fronts. The player's name and position appear at the bottom. The white horizontal back is framed by a black line and carries the player's name at the top, followed by biography and statistics.

	MINT	NRMT	EXC
COMPLETE SET (27)	5.00	2.20	.60

☐ 1 Hector Berrios
☐ 2 Jose Ramos
☐ 3 Dan O'Neill
☐ 4 Steve Parascand
☐ 5 Basilio Cabrera
☐ 6 Ramon Solano
☐ 7 Zach Doster
☐ 8 Milt Cuyler
☐ 9 Wade Phillips
☐ 10 Darryl Martin
☐ 11 Scott Aldred
☐ 12 Manny Mantrana
☐ 13 Darren Hursey
☐ 14 Carlos Rivera
☐ 15 Allen Liebert
☐ 16 Paul Foster
☐ 17 John Lipon
☐ 18 Juan Lopez
☐ 19 Arnie Beyeler
☐ 20 Marcos Gonzalez
☐ 21 Liliano Castro
☐ 22 Luis Melendez
☐ 23 Phil Clark
☐ 24 Ron Rightnowar
☐ 25 Ken Williams
☐ 26 Rob Friesen
☐ 27 Glenn Belcher

1987 Ft. Lauderdale Yankees ProCards

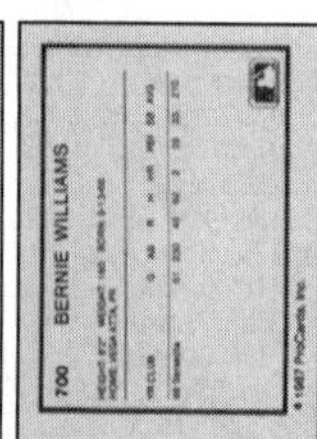

This 30-card standard-size set of the 1987 Ft,. Lauderdale Yankees, a Class A Florida State League affiliate of the New York Yankees, features white-bordered posed color player photos on its fronts. The player's name and position appear at the bottom. The white horizontal back is framed by a black line and carries the player's name at the top, followed by biography and statistics. This issue includes the minor league card debut of Bernie Williams.

	MINT	NRMT	EXC
COMPLETE SET (30)	40.00	18.00	5.00

☐ 1 Tim Becker
☐ 2 Marty Bystrom
☐ 3 Steve Frey
☐ 4 Troy Evers
☐ 5 Chris Carroll
☐ 6 Bob Green
☐ 7 Scott Shaw
☐ 8 Mike Christopher
☐ 9 Dana Ridenour
☐ 10 Andy Stankiewicz
☐ 11 George Berube
☐ 12 Max Ward
☐ 13 Dan Arendas
☐ 14 Paul Lassard
☐ 15 Ron Rub
☐ 16 Bill Voeltz
☐ 17 Scott Gay
☐ 18 Rich Scheid
☐ 19 Kevin Maas
☐ 20 Jose Laboy
☐ 21 Bernie Williams
☐ 22 Steve Adkins
☐ 23 John Johnson
☐ 24 Jim Leyritz
☐ 25 Jeff Hellman
☐ 26 Mel Rosario
☐ 27 Mark Manering
☐ 28 Steve Brow
☐ 29 Fred Carter
☐ 30 Ken Patterson

1987 Ft. Myers Royals ProCards

This 34-card standard-size set of the 1987 Ft. Myers Royals, a Class A Florida State League affiliate of the Kansas City Royals, features white-bordered posed color player photos on its fronts. The player's name and position appear at the bottom. The white horizontal back is framed by a black line and carries the player's name at the top, followed by biography and statistics. This issue includes the minor leagur card debut of Tom Gordon and a second year card of Brian McRae.

	MINT	NRMT	EXC
COMPLETE SET (34)	15.00	6.75	1.85

☐ 1 Bill Mulligan
☐ 2 Stan Boroski
☐ 3 Gary Blouin
☐ 4 Mike Trapp
☐ 5 David Tinkle
☐ 6 Greg Hibbard
☐ 7 Sean Berry
☐ 8 Boo Champagne
☐ 9 Andy Naworski
☐ 10 Tim Odom
☐ 11 Jesus DeLeon
☐ 12 Mark Schulte
☐ 13 Dennis Studeman
☐ 14 Gus Jones
☐ 15 Charles Culberson
☐ 16 Vasquez Aquedo
☐ 17 Tim Goff
☐ 18 Rufus Ellis
☐ 19 Tom Johnson
☐ 20 Ricky Rojas
☐ 21 Terry Jones
☐ 22 Luis Corcino
☐ 23 Randy Goodenough
☐ 24 Kevin Koslofski
☐ 25 Tom Gordon
☐ 26 Brian McRae
☐ 27 Kyle Reese
☐ 28 Ken Kravec
☐ 29 Jerry Terrell
☐ 30 Angel Morris
☐ 31 Mark Farnsworth
☐ 32 David Howard
☐ 33 Jacob Brumfield
☐ 34 Ron Johnson

1987 Gastonia Rangers ProCards

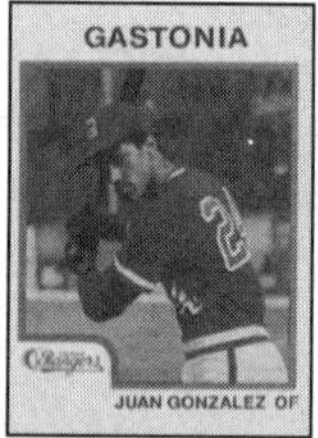

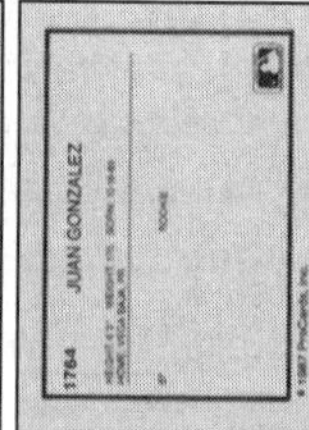

This 29-card standard-size set of the 1987 Gastonia Rangers, a Class A South Atlantic League affiliate of the Texas Rangers, features white-bordered posed color player photos on its fronts. The player's name and position appear at the bottom. The white horizontal back is framed by a black line and carries the player's name at the top, followed by biography and statistics. This issue includes the minor league card debuts of Juan Gonzalez, Sammy Sosa and Dean Palmer.

	MINT	NRMT	EXC
COMPLETE SET (29)	250.00	110.00	31.00

☐ 1 Felipe Castillo
☐ 2 Glenn Patterson
☐ 3 Aurelio Cadania
☐ 4 Juan Gonzalez
☐ 5 Bob Gross
☐ 6 Saul M. Barretto
☐ 7 Phil Bryant
☐ 8 Dean Palmer
☐ 9 Rivera Ortiz Lino
☐ 10 Allen Gerhardt
☐ 11 Bob Malloy
☐ 12 Gus Meizosa
☐ 13 Raphael Cruz
☐ 14 Ed Soto
☐ 15 Roger Pavlik
☐ 16 Paul Postier
☐ 17 Ross Jones
☐ 18 Wayne Rosenthal
☐ 19 Michael Scanlin
☐ 20 Ronald Jackson
☐ 21 James McCutcheon
☐ 22 Darrin Garner

☐ 23 Richard Ramirez
☐ 24 Art Gardner
☐ 25 Jose Velez
☐ 26 Darrell Whitaker
☐ 27 John Burgos
☐ 28 Francisco Sanchez
☐ 29 Samuel Sosa

1987 Geneva Cubs ProCards

This 26-card standard-size set of the 1987 Geneva Cubs, a Class A New York-Penn League affiliate of the Chicago Cubs, features white-bordered posed color player photos on its fronts. The player's name and position appear at the bottom. The white horizontal back is framed by a black line and carries the player's name at the top, followed by biography and statistics.

	MINT	NRMT	EXC
COMPLETE SET (26)	7.00	3.10	.85

☐ 1 Mike Aspray
☐ 2 Brett Robinson
☐ 3 Mark North
☐ 4 Tom Spencer MGR
☐ 5 Steve Melendez TR
☐ 6 Ken Reynolds CO
☐ 7 Rick Wilkins
☐ 8 Herberto Andrade
☐ 9 Ray Mullino
☐ 10 Fernando Ramsey
☐ 11 Derrick Moore
☐ 12 Mike Boswell
☐ 13 Marty Rivero
☐ 14 Mike Reeder
☐ 15 Gabby Rodriguez
☐ 16 Bill Melvin
☐ 17 Henry Gomez
☐ 18 Ed Caballero
☐ 19 Jeff Massicotte
☐ 20 Simeon Mejias
☐ 21 Kevin Main
☐ 22 Phil Hannon
☐ 23 Eddie Williams
☐ 24 Vaughn Williams
☐ 25 Glenn Sullivan
☐ 26 Steve Owens

1987 Glens Falls Tigers ProCards

This 25-card standard-size set of the 1987 Glens Falls Tigers, a Class AA Eastern League affiliate of the Detroit Tigers, features white-bordered posed color player photos on its fronts. The player's name and position appear at the bottom. The white horizontal back is framed by a black line and carries the player's name at the top, followed by biography and statistics. This issue includes the minor league card debut of Chris Hoiles and a second year card of John Smoltz.

	MINT	NRMT	EXC
COMPLETE SET (25)	25.00	11.00	3.10

☐ 1 Ruben Guzman
☐ 2 Chris Hoiles
☐ 3 Tom Burgess
☐ 4 Jeff Jones
☐ 5 Wes Clements
☐ 6 Kevin Ritz
☐ 7 Steve McInerney
☐ 8 Bill Cooper
☐ 9 Tim Leiper
☐ 10 Doug Strange
☐ 11 Ron Marigny
☐ 12 Jeff Agar
☐ 13 Matt Sferrazza
☐ 14 Benny Ruiz
☐ 15 Mark Lee
☐ 16 Rod Poissant
☐ 17 Chris Morgan
☐ 18 Jeff Hermann
☐ 19 Paul Felix
☐ 20 Ramon Pena
☐ 21 Pedro Chavez
☐ 22 Dan Dimascio
☐ 23 John Duffy
☐ 24 John Smoltz
☐ 25 Chip McHugh

1987 Greensboro Hornets ProCards

This 26-card standard-size set of the 1987 Greensboro Hornets, a Class A South Atlantic League affiliate of the Boston Red Sox, features white-bordered posed color player photos on its fronts. The player's name and position appear at the bottom. The white horizontal back is framed by a black line and carries the player's name at the top, followed by biography and statistics.

	MINT	NRMT	EXC
COMPLETE SET (26)	5.00	2.20	.60

☐ 1 Tom Kane
☐ 2 Curt Schilling
☐ 3 Dick Berardino
☐ 4 Pete Youngman
☐ 5 Mike Carista
☐ 6 Ken Ryan
☐ 7 Chuck Wacha
☐ 8 John Roberts
☐ 9 Scott Summers
☐ 10 Scott Cooper
☐ 11 Joe Marchese
☐ 12 Juan Paris
☐ 13 Juan Molero
☐ 14 Tony Hill
☐ 15 Gilberto Martinez
☐ 16 Tim McGee
☐ 17 Ray Hansen
☐ 18 Alex Flores
☐ 19 Victor Rosario
☐ 20 Dan Hale
☐ 21 Mike Baker
☐ 22 Jim Morrison
☐ 23 Lem Pilkinton
☐ 24 John Sanderski
☐ 25 Chris Gaeckle
☐ 26 David Walters

1987 Greenville Braves Best

This issue includes second year cards of Dave Justice and Ron Gant.

	MINT	NRMT	EXC
COMPLETE SET (28)	40.00	18.00	5.00

☐ 1 James Beauchamp MG
☐ 2 Leo D. Mazzone CO
☐ 3 Roland T. Jackson CO
☐ 4 Randy Ingle
☐ 5 Carlos Rafael Rios
☐ 6 Ronald Nipper
☐ 7 Andrew Denson
☐ 8 Adrian Charles Wills
☐ 9 David Justice
☐ 10 Todd Alan Dewey
☐ 11 Willie John Childress
☐ 12 Edgar Yost
☐ 13 Ronald Edwin Gant
☐ 14 John Steven Kilner
☐ 15 Brian Keith Aviles
☐ 16 Bryan Pierce Farmer
☐ 17 Inocencio Guerrero
☐ 18 Maximo Del Rosario
☐ 19 Kevin Blankenship
☐ 20 Kevin Reese Coffman
☐ 21 Jeffrey Wetherby
☐ 22 Larry Wayne Heise
☐ 23 Ira Thomas Greene
☐ 24 Peter John Smith
☐ 25 Johnny Hatcher
☐ 26 Gregory Alan Tubbs
☐ 27 Kenneth Joe Kinnard
☐ 28 Michael William Scott

1987 Hagerstown Suns ProCards

This 29-card standard-size set of the 1987 Hagerstown Suns, a Class A Carolina League affiliate of the Baltimore Orioles, features white-bordered posed color player photos on its fronts. The player's name and position appear at the bottom. The white horizontal back is framed by a black line and carries the player's name at the top, followed by biography and statistics.

	MINT	NRMT	EXC
COMPLETE SET (29)	5.00	2.20	.60

☐ 1 Mike Borgatti
☐ 2 Paul McNeal
☐ 3 Will George
☐ 4 Brian DuBois
☐ 5 Leo Gomez
☐ 6 Benny Bautista
☐ 7 Gerry Lomastro
☐ 8 Craig Strobel
☐ 9 Randy Struek
☐ 10 Tim Dulin
☐ 11 Glenn Gulliver
☐ 12 Blaine Beatty
☐ 13 John Posey
☐ 14 Louie Paulino
☐ 15 Steve Bowden
☐ 16 Wayne Wilson
☐ 17 Peter Palermo
☐ 18 Rick Carriger
☐ 19 Tim Richardson
☐ 20 Kevin Burke
☐ 21 Frank Bellino
☐ 22 Rafael Skeetl
☐ 23 Paul Thorpe
☐ 24 Mel Mallinak
☐ 25 Gordon Dillard
☐ 26 Scott Khoury
☐ 27 Ernie Young
☐ 28 Geraldo Sanchez
☐ 29 Doug Cinnella

1987 Harrisburg Senators ProCards

This 26-card standard-size set of the 1987 Harrisburg Senators, a Class AA Eastern League affiliate of the Pittsburgh Pirates, features white-bordered posed color player photos on its fronts. The player's name and position appear at the bottom. The white horizontal back is framed by a black line and carries the player's name at the top, followed by biography and statistics.

	MINT	NRMT	EXC
COMPLETE SET (26)	5.00	2.20	.60

☐ 1 Shawn Holman
☐ 2 Dave Trembley
☐ 3 Tom Prince
☐ 4 David Rooker
☐ 5 Jose Melendez
☐ 6 Felix Fermin
☐ 7 Phillip Wellman
☐ 8 Craig Brown
☐ 9 Scott Neal
☐ 10 Jeff Cook
☐ 11 Lance Belen
☐ 12 Rob Russell
☐ 13 Kyle Todd
☐ 14 Orlando Lind
☐ 15 Don"Spin' Williams
☐ 16 Dave Douglas
☐ 17 Brian Jones
☐ 18 Brett Gideon
☐ 19 Tommy Gregg
☐ 20 Jim Neidlinger
☐ 21 Gino Gentile
☐ 22 Dimas Gutierrez
☐ 23 Mike Walker
☐ 24 Rich Sauveur
☐ 25 Chris Ritter
☐ 26 Ben Abner

1987 Hawaii Rainbows

	MINT	NRMT	EXC
COMPLETE SET (30)	10.00	4.50	1.25

☐ 1 Les Murakami CO
☐ 2 Nelson Inabata
☐ 3 Mark Rasmussen
☐ 4 Cary Nagano
☐ 5 Richie Kibota
☐ 6 Jeff Vierra
☐ 7 Larry Gonzales
☐ 8 John Matias
☐ 9 Keith Ishibashi
☐ 10 Dan Snover
☐ 11 Ross Kagawa
☐ 12 Steve Morris
☐ 13 Mark Kawakami
☐ 14 Dan Nyssen
☐ 15 Steven Takara
☐ 16 Mark Furtak
☐ 17 Jeff Ball
☐ 18 Mark Reitzel
☐ 19 Markus Owens
☐ 20 Norman Holt
☐ 21 Joey Vierra
☐ 22 Greg Burlingame
☐ 23 Robert Muhammed
☐ 24 Rocky Ynclan
☐ 25 Jeff Howes
☐ 26 Randy Oyama
☐ 27 Ben Reitmeister
☐ 28 Paul Brown
☐ 29 Alan Higuchi
☐ 30 Don Robbs
Howard Dashefsky
Eric Tokunaga
(Radio broadcast team)

1987 Hawaii Islanders ProCards

This 27-card standard size set of the 1987 Hawaii Islanders, a Class AAA Pacific Coast League affiliate of the Chicago White Sox, features white-bordered posed color player photos on its fronts. The player's name and position appear at the bottom. The white horizontal back is framed by a black line and carries the player's name at the top, followed by biography and statistics.

	MINT	NRMT	EXC
COMPLETE SET (27)	5.00	2.20	.60

☐ 1 Mike Yastrzemski
☐ 2 Ken Williams
☐ 3 Jack Hardy
☐ 4 David White
☐ 5 Derek Tatsuno
☐ 6 Ralph Citarella
☐ 7 Tom Forrester
☐ 8 Brian Giles
☐ 9 Tommy Thompson
☐ 10 Don Rowe
☐ 11 Jim Rasmussen
☐ 12 Mike Taylor
☐ 13 Dave Cochrane
☐ 14 Tim Scott
☐ 15 Scott Nielsen
Sic, Nielson
☐ 16 Bill Long
☐ 17 Ray Krawczyk
☐ 18 Kevin Hickey
☐ 19 Joey McLaughlin
☐ 20 Kala Kaaihue
☐ 21 Carlos Martinez
☐ 22 Russ Norman
☐ 23 Tim Krauss
☐ 24 Randy Gomez
☐ 25 Greg Latta
☐ 26 Bob Bailey
☐ 27 Pat Keedy

1987 Huntsville Stars Team Issue

	MINT	NRMT	EXC
COMPLETE SET (25)	6.00	2.70	.75

☐ 1 Roy Anderson
☐ 2 Larry Arndt
☐ 3 Tim Birtsas
☐ 4 Lance Blankenship
☐ 5 Tyler Brilinski
☐ 6 Todd Burns
☐ 7 Jim Corsi
☐ 8 Brian Criswell
☐ 9 Pat Dietrick
☐ 10 Darrin Duffy
☐ 11 Brad Fischer MG
☐ 12 Scott Hemond
☐ 13 Steve Howard
☐ 14 Mark Howie
☐ 15 Jimmy Jones
☐ 16 Felix Jose
☐ 17 Russ Kibler
☐ 18 Joe Kramer
☐ 19 Reese Lambert
☐ 20 Doug Scherer
☐ 21 Jeff Shaver
☐ 22 Jose Tolentino
☐ 23 Walt Weiss
☐ 24 Wally Whitehurst
☐ 25 Joe Xavier

1987 Idaho Falls Braves ProCards

This 27-card standard-size set of the 1987 Idaho Falls Braves, a Rookie Class Pioneer League affiliate of the Atlanta Braves, features white-bordered posed color player photos on its fronts. The player's name and position appear at the bottom. The white horizontal back is framed by a black line and carries the player's name at the top, followed by biography and statistics.

	MINT	NRMT	EXC
COMPLETE SET (27)	5.00	2.20	.60

☐ 1 Mike Wilson
☐ 2 Anthony Ferrebee
☐ 3 Phillip Maldonado
☐ 4 Mark Martin
☐ 5 Jeff Allison
☐ 6 Richard Duke
☐ 7 Chuck Lavrusky
☐ 8 Kevin McNees
☐ 9 Rod Gilbreath
☐ 10 Teddy Williams
☐ 11 Walter Hawkins
☐ 12 Chris Bryant
☐ 13 A.J. Waznik
☐ 14 Mike Lomeli
☐ 15 Gregg Gilbert
☐ 16 Jim Procopio
☐ 17 Bill Wright
☐ 18 Herb Hippauf
☐ 19 Matthew Williams
☐ 20 Joe Koh
☐ 21 Darren Cox
☐ 22 Steve Glass
☐ 23 Frank Ramirez
☐ 24 John Mitchell
☐ 25 Jeff Dodig
☐ 26 Pat Abbatiello
☐ 27 Greg Ziegler

1987 Indianapolis Indians Team Issue

Sponsored by Pepsi, this 36-card set of the 1987 Indianapolis Indians, a Class AAA American Association affiliate of the Montreal Expos, features posed color player shots on its fronts, and measures approximately 2 1/2" by 3 5/8". The team name appears within the blue stripe across the top; in the blue stripe below the picture is the player's name and position. The white horizontal back carries the player's name at the top, followed by biography, statistics, and career highlights.

	MINT	NRMT	EXC
COMPLETE SET (36)	18.00	8.00	2.20

- ☐ 1 Team Photo Card
- ☐ 2 It Was Magic (Team celebration '86 AAA Playoffs)
- ☐ 3 The Magic Continues (Three championship rings)
- ☐ 4 Joe Sparks MGR
- ☐ 5 Jerry Manuel CO
- ☐ 6 Luis Pujols CO
- ☐ 7 Dave Tomlin CO
- ☐ 8 Razor Shines
- ☐ 9 Tim Barrett
- ☐ 10 Jack Daugherty
- ☐ 11 Ubaldo Heredia
- ☐ 12 Ron Shepherd
- ☐ 13 Curt Brown
- ☐ 14 Tom Romano
- ☐ 15 Jeff Fischer
- ☐ 16 Jeff Reynolds
- ☐ 17 Jeff Parrett
- ☐ 18 Billy Moore
- ☐ 19 Mark Gardner
- ☐ 20 Johnny Paredes
- ☐ 21 Sergio Valdez
- ☐ 22 Dallas Williams
- ☐ 23 Mike Smith
- ☐ 24 Kelly Faulk
- ☐ 25 Wilfredo Tejada
- ☐ 26 Pascual Perez
- ☐ 27 Luis Rivera
- ☐ 28 Scott Clemo
- ☐ 29 Nelson Norman
- ☐ 30 Mark Corey
- ☐ 31 Dennis Martinez
- ☐ 32 Tim McCormack TR
- ☐ 33 Alonzo Powell
- ☐ 34 Voices of the Indians
  Howard Kellman ANN
  Tom Akins ANN
  Bat Boys:Sean Schnaiter
  Kenny Akins
  Mark Schumacher
- ☐ 35 The Bat Boys
- ☐ 36 Bill Rowley

1987 International League All-Stars TCMA

	MINT	NRMT	EXC
COMPLETE SET (45)	10.00	4.50	1.25

- ☐ 1 Jeff Moronko
- ☐ 2 Jay Buhner
- ☐ 3 Brad Arnsberg
- ☐ 4 Roberto Kelly
- ☐ 5 Randy Milligan
- ☐ 6 Kevin Elster
- ☐ 7 Sam Horn
- ☐ 8 Nelson Liriano
- ☐ 9 Ed Nottle
- ☐ 10 Don Gordon
- ☐ 11 Rey Palacios
- ☐ 12 Mark Carreon
- ☐ 13 Randy Velarde
- ☐ 14 Bruce Fields
- ☐ 15 Mike Henneman
- ☐ 16 Scott Lusader
- ☐ 17 Jim Walewander
- ☐ 18 Keith Miller
- ☐ 19 John Marzano
- ☐ 20 Todd Benzinger
- ☐ 21 Jody Reed
- ☐ 22 Tom Bolton
- ☐ 23 Orestes Destrade
- ☐ 24 Sylvester Campusano
- ☐ 25 Todd Stottlemyre
- ☐ 26 Rob Ducey
- ☐ 27 Bill Ripken
- ☐ 28 Jeff Ballard
- ☐ 29 Pete Stanicek
- ☐ 30 Craig Worthington
- ☐ 31 Chris Padget
- ☐ 32 Tom Glavine
- ☐ 33 Jeff Blauser
- ☐ 34 Marty Clary
- ☐ 35 David Griffin
- ☐ 36 Keith Miller
- ☐ 37 Travis Chambers
- ☐ 38 Al Leiter
- ☐ 39 Columbus Clippers Team Card
- ☐ 40 Tidewater Tides Team Card
- ☐ 41 Pawtucket Red Sox Team Card
- ☐ 42 Syracuse Chiefs Team Card
- ☐ 43 Toledo Mud Hens Team Card
- ☐ 44 Rochester Red Wings Team Card
- ☐ 45 Maine Guides Team Card

1987 Iowa Cubs Team Issue

This issue includes a second year card of Rafael Palmeiro.

	MINT	NRMT	EXC
COMPLETE SET (25)	30.00	13.50	3.70

- ☐ 1 Carl Hamilton
- ☐ 2 Drew Hall
- ☐ 3 Jackie Davidson
- ☐ 4 Mike Capel
- ☐ 5 Jay Baller
- ☐ 6 Doug Potestio
- ☐ 7 Gary Permenter
- ☐ 8 Tom Layton
- ☐ 9 Joe Kraemer
- ☐ 10 Dave Kopf
- ☐ 11 Paul Noce
- ☐ 12 Bruce Crabbe
- ☐ 13 Mike Brumley
- ☐ 14 Bill Hayes
- ☐ 15 Damon Berryhill
- ☐ 16 Pookie Bernstine
- ☐ 17 Julio Valdez
- ☐ 18 Phil Stephenson
- ☐ 19 Wade Rowdon
- ☐ 20 Luis Quinones
- ☐ 21 Dick Pole CO
- ☐ 22 Larry Cox MGR
- ☐ 23 Gary Varsho
- ☐ 24 Rafael Palmeiro
- ☐ 25 Darrin Jackson

1987 Jackson Mets Feder

	MINT	NRMT	EXC
COMPLETE SET (25)	12.00	5.50	1.50

- ☐ 1 Dan Winters
- ☐ 2 Jeff McKnight
- ☐ 3 Jose Bautista
- ☐ 4 Tucker Ashford
- ☐ 5 Tom McCarthy
- ☐ 6 Zoilo Sanchez
- ☐ 7 Shane Young
- ☐ 8 Kurt Lundgren
- ☐ 9 Jeff Gardner
- ☐ 10 Mike Hocutt
- ☐ 11 Mickey Weston
- ☐ 12 Al Carmichael
- ☐ 13 Sam McCrary
- ☐ 14 Ed Pruitt
- ☐ 15 Joaquin Contreras
- ☐ 16 Marcus Lawton
- ☐ 17 Johnny Wilson
- ☐ 18 Steve Phillips
- ☐ 19 Kyle Hartshorn
- ☐ 20 Glenn Abbott
- ☐ 21 Tom Burns
- ☐ 22 Alan Hayden
- ☐ 23 Dave West
- ☐ 24 Gregg Jefferies
- ☐ 25 Mike Santiago

1987 Jacksonville Expos ProCards

This 29-card standard-size set of the 1987 Jacksonville Expos, a Class AA Southern League affiliate of the Montreal Expos, features white-bordered posed color player photos on its fronts. The player's name and position appear at the bottom. The white horizontal back is framed by a black line and carries the player's name at the top, followed by biography and statistics. This issue includes a second year card of Randy Johnson and a third year card of Larry Walker.

	MINT	NRMT	EXC
COMPLETE SET (29)	25.00	11.00	3.10

- ☐ 429 Larry Walker
- ☐ 430 Tim Arnold
- ☐ 431 Norm Santiago
- ☐ 432 Pete Camelo
- ☐ 433 Nelson Santovenia
- ☐ 434 Mike Berger
- ☐ 435 Andy Lawrence
- ☐ 436 Scott Mann
- ☐ 437 Edgar Caceres
- ☐ 438 Gary Weinberger
- ☐ 439 Esteban Beltre
- ☐ 440 Armando Moreno
- ☐ 441 James Opie
- ☐ 442 Mike Shade
- ☐ 443 Dave Graybill
- ☐ 444 Mike Payne
- ☐ 445 Bill Cunningham
- ☐ 446 Bob Devlin
- ☐ 447 Bob Sudo
- ☐ 448 Kevin Price
- ☐ 449 John Trautwein
- ☐ 450 Gary Wayne
- ☐ 451 Randy Johnson
- ☐ 452 Brian Holman
- ☐ 453 Tommy Thompson MG
- ☐ 454 Joe Kerrigan CO
- ☐ 455 Mike Quade CO
- ☐ 456 Jim Kahmann TR
- ☐ 457 Team Photo

1987 Jamestown Expos ProCards

Sponsored by Roach Photography, this 30-card standard-size set of the 1987 Jamestown Expos, a Class A New York-Penn League affiliate of the Montreal Expos, features white-bordered posed color player photos on its fronts. The player's name appears at the bottom. The white horizontal back is framed by a black line and carries the player's name at the top, followed by biography and the sponsor's logo.

	MINT	NRMT	EXC
COMPLETE SET (30)	5.00	2.20	.60

- ☐ 2538 Russ Martin
- ☐ 2539 Angelo Cianfrocco
- ☐ 2540 Michael Ishmael
- ☐ 2541 Scott McHugh
- ☐ 2542 Jeff Wedvick (Unnumbered)
- ☐ 2543 Jesus Paredes
- ☐ 2544 F. Boi Rodriguez
- ☐ 2545 Joe B. Sims
- ☐ 2546 Larry Doss
- ☐ 2547 Terrel E. Hansen
- ☐ 2548 Jorge Mitchell
- ☐ 2549 Kelvin Shepard
- ☐ 2550 Troy Ricker
- ☐ 2551 John Vander Wal
- ☐ 2552 Corey Viltz
- ☐ 2553 Gene Glynn
- ☐ 2554 Braden Brian
- ☐ 2555 Bob Natal
- ☐ 2556 Scott Ayers
- ☐ 2557 Mario Brito
- ☐ 2558 Bob Kerrigan
- ☐ 2559 Gilles Bergeron
- ☐ 2560 Danilo Leon
- ☐ 2561 Howard Farmer
- ☐ 2562 Matt Shiflett
- ☐ 2563 Kevin Cavalier
- ☐ 2564 Jeff Carter
- ☐ 2565 Chris Marchok
- ☐ 2678 Q.V. Lowe CO
- ☐ 2679 Chris Pollack

1987 Kenosha Twins ProCards

This 29-card standard-size set of the 1987 Kenosha Twins, a Class A Midwest League affiliate of the Minnesota Twins, features white-bordered posed color player photos on its fronts. The player's name and position appear at the bottom. The white horizontal back is framed by a black line and carries the player's name at the top, followed by biography and statistics.

	MINT	NRMT	EXC
COMPLETE SET (29)	5.00	2.20	.60

- ☐ 1 Jim Davins
- ☐ 2 Robert Hernandez
- ☐ 3 Michael Randle
- ☐ 4 Kendall Snuder
- ☐ 5 Edgar Naveda
- ☐ 6 Rafael DeLima
- ☐ 7 Buddy Buzzard
- ☐ 8 Burt Beattie
- ☐ 9 Rusty Kryzanowski
- ☐ 10 Michael Lexa
- ☐ 11 Mike Dyer
- ☐ 12 David Jacas
- ☐ 13 Robert Tinkey
- ☐ 14 Jarvis Brown
- ☐ 15 Dana Heinle
- ☐ 16 Dwight Bernard
- ☐ 17 Jeff Satzinger
- ☐ 18 Carl Thomas
- ☐ 19 Derek Parks
- ☐ 20 Lenny Webster
- ☐ 21 Scott Leius
- ☐ 22 Chris Forgione
- ☐ 23 Elvis Romero
- ☐ 24 Paul Abbott
- ☐ 25 Miguel Murphy
- ☐ 26 German Gonzalez
- ☐ 27 Don Leppert
- ☐ 28 John Skelton
- ☐ 29 Enrique Rios

1987 Kinston Indians ProCards

This 24-card standard-size set of the 1987 Kinston Indians, a Class A Carolina League affiliate of the Cleveland Indians, features white-bordered posed color player photos on its fronts. The player's name and position appear at the bottom. The white horizontal back is framed by a black line and carries the player's name at the top, followed by biography and statistics.

	MINT	NRMT	EXC
COMPLETE SET (24)	5.00	2.20	.60

- ☐ 1 Bill Shamblin
- ☐ 2 Kevin Wickander
- ☐ 3 Mark Gilles
- ☐ 4 Charles Soos
- ☐ 5 Scott Buss
- ☐ 6 Phillip Dillmore
- ☐ 7 Lewis Kent
- ☐ 8 Jim Grossman
- ☐ 9 Michael Poehl
- ☐ 10 Fritz Fedor
- ☐ 11 Brian Graham
- ☐ 12 Scott Jordan
- ☐ 13 Casey Webster
- ☐ 14 Michael Workman
- ☐ 15 Michael Farr
- ☐ 16 Andrew Ghelfi
- ☐ 17 James Bruske
- ☐ 18 Robert Swain
- ☐ 19 Trey Hillman
- ☐ 20 Doyle Wilson
- ☐ 21 Thomas Hinzo
- ☐ 22 Milton Harper
- ☐ 23 Kerry Richardson
- ☐ 24 Rodney Nichols

1987 Knoxville Blue Jays ProCards

This 27-card standard-size set of the 1987 Knoxville Blue Jays, a Class AA Southern League affiliate of the Toronto Blue Jays, features white-bordered posed color player photos on its fronts. The player's name and position appear at the bottom. The white horizontal back is framed by a black line and carries the player's name at the top, followed by biography and statistics.

	MINT	NRMT	EXC
COMPLETE SET (27)	5.00	2.20	.60

- ☐ 1494 Jose Mesa
- ☐ 1495 Chris Shaddy
- ☐ 1496 Mike Yearout
- ☐ 1497 Omar Malave
- ☐ 1498 Aurelio Monteagudo CO
- ☐ 1499 Rocky Coyle
- ☐ 1500 Troy Chestnut
- ☐ 1501 Tim Englund
- ☐ 1502 Luis Reyna
- ☐ 1503 Kevin Sliwinski
- ☐ 1504 Todd Provence
- ☐ 1505 Eric Yelding
- ☐ 1506 Keith Gilliam
- ☐ 1507 Omar Bencomo
- ☐ 1508 Geronimo Berroa
- ☐ 1509 Bernie Tatis
- ☐ 1510 Enrique Burgos
- ☐ 1511 Oswald Peraza
- ☐ 1512 Dave Walsh
- ☐ 1513 Pat Borders
- ☐ 1514 Jeff Hearron
- ☐ 1515 Randy Holland TR
- ☐ 1516 Glenn Ezell MG
- ☐ 1517 Kevin Kierst Equipment manager
- ☐ 1518 Norm Tonucci
- ☐ 1519 J.J. Cannon CO
- ☐ 1520 Cliff Young

1987 Lakeland Tigers ProCards

This 26-card standard-size set of the 1987 Lakeland Tigers, a Class A Florida State League affiliate of the Detroit Tigers, features white-bordered posed color player photos on its fronts. The player's name and position appear at the bottom. The white horizontal back is framed by a black line and carries the player's name at the top, followed by biography and statistics.

	MINT	NRMT	EXC
COMPLETE SET (26)	5.00	2.20	.60

- ☐ 1 Wayne Housie
- ☐ 2 Keith Nicholson
- ☐ 3 Craig Mills
- ☐ 4 Rich Wieligman
- ☐ 5 Scott Schultz
- ☐ 6 Donnie Rowland
- ☐ 7 Kevin Bradshaw
- ☐ 8 Doyle Balthazar
- ☐ 9 Ron Marigny
- ☐ 10 Bernie Anderson
- ☐ 11 Terry Smith
- ☐ 12 Rocky Cusack
- ☐ 13 Richard Carter
- ☐ 14 Rich Lacko
- ☐ 15 Wade Phillips
- ☐ 16 Mike Hansen
- ☐ 17 Mark Lee
- ☐ 18 Pat Austin
- ☐ 19 Bob Thompson
- ☐ 20 Mark Pottinger
- ☐ 21 Robinson Garces
- ☐ 22 Blane Fox
- ☐ 23 Dave Cooper
- ☐ 24 Adam Dempsay
- ☐ 25 Paul Wenson
- ☐ 26 Ken Gohmann

1987 Las Vegas Stars ProCards

This 27-card standard-size set of the 1987 Las Vegas Stars, a Class AAA Pacific Coast League affiliate of the San Diego Padres, features white-bordered posed color player photos on its fronts. The player's name and position appear at the bottom. The white horizontal back is framed by a black line and carries the player's name at the top, followed by biography and statistics.

	MINT	NRMT	EXC
COMPLETE SET (27)	5.00	2.20	.60

☐ 1 Joe Bitker
☐ 2 Shawn Abner
☐ 3 Jack Kroll
☐ 4 Joe Lansford
☐ 5 Scott Parsons
☐ 6 Sonny Seibert
☐ 7 Randy Asadoor
☐ 8 Kevin John Buckley
☐ 9 Rusty Ford
☐ 10 Mark Poston
☐ 11 Todd Simmons
☐ 12 Ray Hayward
☐ 13 Todd Hutcheson
☐ 14 Randell Byers
☐ 15 Brian Snyder
☐ 16 Bill Blount
☐ 17 Jimmy Jones
☐ 18 Shane Mack
☐ 19 Edwin Rodriguez
☐ 20 Steve Garcia
☐ 21 Craig Wiley
☐ 22 Gary Green
☐ 23 Leon "Bip" Roberts
☐ 24 Ed Vosberg
☐ 25 James Siwy
☐ 26 Rob Picciolo
☐ 27 Mark Wasinger

1987 Little Falls Mets ProCards

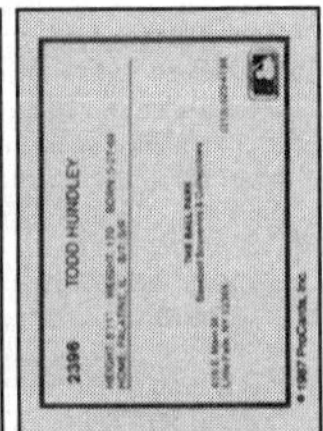

This 29-card standard-size set of the 1987 Little Falls Mets, a Class A New York-Penn affiliate of the New York Mets, features white-bordered posed color player photos on its fronts. The player's name and position appear at the bottom. The white horizontal back is framed by a black line and carries the player's name at the top, followed by biography and statistics. This issue includes the minor league card debut of Todd Hundley.

	MINT	NRMT	EXC
COMPLETE SET (29)	35.00	16.00	4.40

☐ 2382 Terry Bross
☐ 2383 Pat Disabato
☐ 2384 Terry Griffin
☐ 2385 Eric Hillman
☐ 2386 Lorin Jundy
☐ 2387 Steve LaRose
☐ 2388 Jim McAnarney
☐ 2389 Mike Miller
☐ 2390 Steve Newton
☐ 2391 Jeff Smith
☐ 2392 Dave Trautwein
☐ 2393 Butch Wallen
☐ 2394 Anthony Young
☐ 2395 Javier Gonzalez
☐ 2396 Todd Hundley
☐ 2397 Tim Bogar
☐ 2398 Ron Height
☐ 2399 Alex Jimenez UER (card misspelled Jiminez on front)
☐ 2400 Dave Joiner
☐ 2401 Bob Olah
☐ 2402 Radhames Polanco
☐ 2403 Rob Lemle
☐ 2404 Terry McDaniel
☐ 2405 Danny Naughton
☐ 2406 Titi Roche
☐ 2407 Jim Tesmer
☐ 2409 Rich Miller
☐ 2410 Al Jackson
☐ 2411 Rick McWane

1987 Louisville Redbirds Team Issue

	MINT	NRMT	EXC
COMPLETE SET (30)	15.00	6.75	1.85

☐ 1 Mike Jorgensen MG
☐ 2 Joe Pettini CO
☐ 3 Jack Ayer
☐ 4 Greg Bargar
☐ 5 Joe Boever
☐ 6 Rod Booker
☐ 7 Rich Buonantony
☐ 8 Jose Calderon
☐ 9 Paul Cherry
☐ 10 Rick Colbert
☐ 11 Mark Dougherty
☐ 12 Dan Driessen
☐ 13 Bill Earley
☐ 14 Dick Grapenthin
☐ 15 David Green
☐ 16 Lance Johnson
☐ 17 Tim Jones
☐ 18 Mickey Mahler
☐ 19 John A. Martin
☐ 20 John Morris
☐ 21 John Murphy
☐ 22 Tom Pagnozzi
☐ 23 Mike Laga
☐ 24 Bill Lyons
☐ 25 Joe Magrane
☐ 26 Victor Rodriguez
☐ 27 Ray Soff
☐ 28 Duane Walker
☐ 29 David "Hap" Hudson TR
☐ 30 Billy Johnson

1987 LSU Tigers Police

The cards are unnumbered and checklisted below in alphabetical order.

	MINT	NRMT	EXC
COMPLETE SET (8)	25.00	11.00	3.10

☐ 1 Joey Belle
☐ 2 Craig Faulkner
☐ 3 Mark Guthrie
☐ 4 Dan Kite
☐ 5 Stan Loewer
☐ 6 Barry Manuel
☐ 7 Mike Papajohn
☐ 8 Gregg Patterson

1987 Lynchburg Mets ProCards

This 28-card standard-size set of the 1987 Lynchburg Mets, a Class A Carolina League affiliate of the New York Mets, features white-bordered posed color player photos on its fronts. The player's name and position appear at the bottom. The white horizontal back is framed by a black line and carries the player's name at the top, followed by biography and statistics.

	MINT	NRMT	EXC
COMPLETE SET (28)	5.00	2.20	.60

☐ 1 Craig Repoz
☐ 2 Juan Villanueva
☐ 3 Tom Wachs
☐ 4 Chris Jelic
☐ 5 Kip Gross
☐ 6 Desi Brooks
☐ 7 Eric Erickson
☐ 8 Ron Gideon
☐ 9 Jamie Archibald
☐ 10 Hector Perez
☐ 11 Alan Hayden
☐ 12 Felix Perdomo
☐ 13 Jeff Ciszkowski
☐ 14 Pete Bauer
☐ 15 Chris Rauth
☐ 16 Bill Stiles
☐ 17 Geary Jones
☐ 18 Dave Gelatt
☐ 19 Rich Rodriguez
☐ 20 Jim Bibby
☐ 21 Scott Jaster
☐ 22 John Tamargo
☐ 23 Troy James
☐ 24 Jeff Richardson
☐ 25 Mark Brunswick
☐ 26 Wilson Valera
☐ 27 Scott Lawrenson
☐ 28 Brian Givens

1987 Macon Pirates ProCards

This 25-card standard-size set of the 1987 Macon Pirates, a Class A South Atlantic League affiliate of the Pittsburgh Pirates, features white-bordered posed color player photos on its fronts. The player's name and position appear at the bottom. The white horizontal back is framed by a black line and carries the player's name at the top, followed by biography and statistics.

	MINT	NRMT	EXC
COMPLETE SET (25)	5.00	2.20	.60

☐ 1 Ernesto Santana
☐ 2 Tracy Toy
☐ 3 Joel Forrest
☐ 4 Jeff Banister
☐ 5 Tony Mealy
☐ 6 John Love
☐ 7 Mike York
☐ 8 Tony Longmire
☐ 9 Tim Vaughn
☐ 10 Richard Reed
☐ 11 Pete Murphy
☐ 12 Blane Lockley
☐ 13 Steve Adams
☐ 14 Julio Perez
☐ 15 Doug Ellis
☐ 16 Julio Peguero
☐ 17 Stan Belinda
☐ 18 Damon Hansel
☐ 19 Craig Heakins
☐ 20 Ed Yacopino
☐ 21 Glenn Trudo
☐ 22 Scott Ruskin
☐ 23 Tony Cohen
☐ 24 Dennis Rogers
☐ 25 Dave Moharter

1987 Madison Muskies Police

	MINT	NRMT	EXC
COMPLETE SET (23)	8.00	3.60	1.00

☐ 1 Gerry Barragan
☐ 2 Mark Beavers
☐ 3 Ozzie Canseco
☐ 4 Jim Carroll
☐ 5 Mike Cupples
☐ 6 Blaine Deabenderfer
☐ 7 Pat Gilbert
☐ 8 Jeff Glover
☐ 9 Scott Hemond
☐ 10 Jeff Kopyta
☐ 11 Kevin Kunkel
☐ 12 Luis Martinez
☐ 13 Doug Ortman
☐ 14 Dave Otto
☐ 15 Jamie Reiser
☐ 16 Luis Salcedo
☐ 17 Bob Sharpnack
☐ 18 Bob Stocker
☐ 19 Vinnie Teixeira
☐ 20 Camilo Veras
☐ 21 Wes Weber
☐ 22 Jim Nettles MG
☐ 23 Dave Schober

1987 Madison Muskies ProCards

This 25-card standard-size set of the 1987 Madison Muskies, a Class A Midwest League affiliate of the Oakland Athletics, features white-bordered posed color player photos on its fronts. The player's name and position appear at the bottom. The white horizontal back is framed by a black line and carries the player's name at the top, followed by biography and statistics.

	MINT	NRMT	EXC
COMPLETE SET (25)	5.00	2.20	.60

☐ 1 Bert Bradley
☐ 2 David D. Schober
☐ 3 Scott Hemond
☐ 4 James Nettles
☐ 5 Vince Teixeira
☐ 6 Ozzie Canseco
☐ 7 Pat Gilbert
☐ 8 Luis Martinez
☐ 9 Doug Ortman
☐ 10 Jamie Reiser
☐ 11 Weston Weber
☐ 12 Gerry Barragan
☐ 13 Leland Maddox
☐ 14 Ken Jones
☐ 15 Camilo Veras
☐ 16 Mike Cupples
☐ 17 Jeffrey Glover
☐ 18 Jeff Kopyta
☐ 19 Kevin Kunkel
☐ 20 Mark Beavers
☐ 21 Jim Carroll
☐ 22 Blaine Deabenderfer
☐ 23 Reese Lambert
☐ 24 Luis Salcedo
☐ 25 Bob Sharpnack

1987 Maine Guides ProCards

This 23-card standard-size set of the 1987 Maine Guides, a Class AAA International League affiliate of the Philadelphia Phillies, features white-bordered posed color player photos on its fronts. The player's name and position appear at the bottom. The white horizontal back is framed by a black line and carries the player's name at the top, followed by biography and statistics.

	MINT	NRMT	EXC
COMPLETE SET (23)	5.00	2.20	.60

☐ 1 Jim Olander
☐ 2 Doug Bair
☐ 3 Len Watts
☐ 4 Greg Legg
☐ 5 Fred Tolliver
☐ 6 Shawn Barton
☐ 7 Ken Jackson
☐ 8 Keith Miller
☐ 9 Greg Jelks
☐ 10 Barney Nugent
☐ 11 Jeff Stone
☐ 12 Marvin Freeman
☐ 13 Steve DeAngelis
☐ 14 Jeff Calhoun
☐ 15 Gib Seibert
☐ 16 Ken Dowell
☐ 17 Wally Ritchie
☐ 18 Joe Cipolloni
☐ 19 Travis Owen Chambers
☐ 20 Tom Newell
☐ 21 Darren Loy
☐ 22 Alan LeBoeuf
☐ 23 Ron Jones

1987 Maine Guides TCMA

	MINT	NRMT	EXC
COMPLETE SET (25)	10.00	4.50	1.25

☐ 1 Shawn Barton
☐ 2 Jeff Calhoun
☐ 3 Travis Chambers
☐ 4 Marvin Freeman
☐ 5 Mike Maddux
☐ 6 Tom Newell
☐ 7 Fred Toliver
☐ 8 Joe Cipolloni
☐ 9 Darren Loy
☐ 10 Ken Dowell
☐ 11 Ken Jackson
☐ 12 Greg Jelks
☐ 13 Alan LeBoeuf
☐ 14 Greg Legg
☐ 15 Keith Miller
☐ 16 Gib Seibert
☐ 17 Ron Jones
☐ 18 Jim Olander
☐ 19 Jeff Stone
☐ 20 Len Watts
☐ 21 Darren Daulton
☐ 22 Kevin Ward
☐ 23 Bill Dancy
☐ 24 Tim Corcoran
☐ 25 Mike Willis

1987 Memphis Chicks Best

	MINT	NRMT	EXC
COMPLETE SET (27)	8.00	3.60	1.00

☐ 1 Bob Schaefer MG
☐ 2 Duane Gustavson CO
☐ 3 Rich Dubee CO
☐ 4 Jose Rivera
☐ 5 Julio Alcala
☐ 6 Mark Van Blaricom
☐ 7 Jim Bennett
☐ 8 Ken Crew
☐ 9 Jose DeJesus
☐ 10 Scott Stranski
☐ 11 Phil George
☐ 12 Theo Shaw
☐ 13 Mark Shiflett
☐ 14 Don Sparling
☐ 15 Mike Miller
☐ 16 Tim Lambert
☐ 17 Gene Morgan
☐ 18 Mike Loggins
☐ 19 Jere Longenecker
☐ 20 Mauro Gozza
☐ 21 Jim Eisenreich
☐ 22 Rick Luecken
☐ 23 Terry Bell
☐ 24 Matt Winters
☐ 25 Mike Fuentes
☐ 26 Jamie Nelson
☐ 27 Steve Morrow TR

1987 Memphis Chicks ProCards

This 27-card standard-size set of the 1987 Memphis Chicks, a Class AA Southern affiliate of the Kansas City Royals, features white-bordered posed color player photos on its fronts. The player's name and position appear at the bottom. The white horizontal back is framed by a black line and carries the player's name at the top, followed by biography and statistics.

	MINT	NRMT	EXC
COMPLETE SET (27)	5.00	2.20	.60

☐ 1 Mike Fuentes
☐ 2 Phil George
☐ 3 Mauro Gozzo
☐ 4 Mike Loggins

☐ 5 Jose DeJesus
☐ 6 Mark Shiflett
☐ 7 Matt Winters
☐ 8 Jamie Nelson
☐ 9 Jere Longenecker
☐ 10 Bob Schaefer
☐ 11 Rich Debee
☐ 12 Mark Van Blaricom
☐ 13 Tim Lambert
☐ 14 Scott Stranski
☐ 15 Theo Shaw
☐ 16 Gene Morgan
☐ 17 Terry Bell
☐ 18 Rick Luecken
☐ 19 Don Sparling
☐ 20 Ken Crew
☐ 21 Duane Gustavson
☐ 22 Mike Muller
☐ 23 Jose Rivera
☐ 24 Julio Alcala
☐ 25 Jim Bennett
☐ 26 Steve Morrow
☐ 27 Jim Eisenreich

1987 Miami Marlins ProCards

This 25-card standard-size set of the 1987 Miami Marlins, a Class A Florida State League Independent, features white-bordered posed color player photos on its fronts. The player's name and position appear at the bottom. The white horizontal back is framed by a black line and carries the player's name at the top, followed by biography and statistics.

	MINT	NRMT	EXC
COMPLETE SET (25)	5.00	2.20	.60

☐ 1 Kenny King
☐ 2 Jim Falzone
☐ 3 Stacey Burdick
☐ 4 Scott Evans
☐ 5 Tony Woods
☐ 7 Doug Carpenter
☐ 8 Rick Richardi
☐ 9 Tony Rohan
☐ 10 Bobby Latmore
☐ 11 Mickey Billmeyer
☐ 12 Masahito Watanabe
☐ 13 Shuji Inagaki
☐ 14 Scott Diez
☐ 15 Mike Browning
☐ 16 Frank Colston
☐ 18 Ken Adderly
☐ 19 Greg Daniels
☐ 20 John Harrington
☐ 21 Fred Dela Mata
☐ 22 Hideharu Matsuo
☐ 23 Larry Mims
☐ 24 Tom Magrann
☐ 25 Toshimitsu Suetsugu
☐ 26 Luis Ojeda
☐ 27 Mamoru Suigiura

1987 Midland Angels ProCards

This 30-card standard-size set of the 1987 Midland Angels, a Class AA Texas League affiliate of the California Angels, features white-bordered posed color player photos on its fronts. The player's name and position appear at the bottom. The white horizontal back is framed by a black line and carries the player's name at the top, followed by biography and statistics.

	MINT	NRMT	EXC
COMPLETE SET (30)	5.00	2.20	.60

☐ 1 Miguel Garcia
☐ 2 David Martinez
☐ 3 Bill Geivett
☐ 4 Chris Collins
☐ 5 Brian Brady
☐ 6 Doug Banning
☐ 7 Ty Van Burkleo
☐ 8 Vinicio Cedeno
☐ 9 Al Olson
☐ 10 Doug Davis
☐ 11 John Hotchkiss
☐ 12 Edwin Marquez
☐ 13 Joe Redfield
☐ 14 Damon Farmar
☐ 15 Max Oliveras
☐ 16 Doug Jennings
☐ 17 Stan Holmes
☐ 18 Chuck Hernandez
☐ 19 Toby Mack
☐ 20 Mitch Sedane
☐ 21 Mark Doran
☐ 22 Mike Romanovsky
☐ 23 Robbie Allen
☐ 24 Vance Lovelace
☐ 25 Brian Harvey
☐ 26 Steve McGuire
☐ 27 Marty Reed
☐ 28 Barry Dacus
☐ 29 Phil Venturino
☐ 30 Midland Angels Team

1987 Modesto A's Chong

The last four cards in the set feature Modesto A's alumni and are numbered 1-4; the prefix A has been added in the checklist below for clarity. Cards are black and white with green print on the back and are printed on thin card stock.

	MINT	NRMT	EXC
COMPLETE SET (32)	8.00	3.60	1.00

☐ 1 Mike Bordick
☐ 2 Pat Britt
☐ 3 Jim Corsi
☐ 4 David Gavin
☐ 5 Robert Gould
☐ 6 Scott Holcomb
☐ 7 Dann Howitt
☐ 8 Steve Iannini
☐ 9 Bo Kent
☐ 10 Joe Law
☐ 11 John Minch
☐ 12 Jerome Nelson
☐ 13 Jose Peguero
☐ 14 Bill Savarino
☐ 15 Kevin Tapani
☐ 16 David Veres
☐ 17 Bruce Walton
☐ 18 Kevin Williamson
☐ 19 Chris Hayes
☐ 20 Frank Masters
☐ 21 Jeff Whitney
☐ 22 Drew Stratton
☐ 23 Tommie Reynolds
☐ 24 Butch Hughes
☐ 25 John Cartelli
☐ 26 Bob Fingers
☐ 27 Gary Groski
☐ 28 Pro Sportsworld Team
☐ A1 Tony LaRussa
☐ A2 Joe Rudi
☐ A3 Dave Duncan
☐ A4 Dave Leiper

1987 Modesto A's ProCards

This 25-card standard-size set of the 1987 Modesto A's, a Class A California League affiliate of the Oakland Athletics, features white-bordered posed color player photos on its fronts. The player's name and position appear at the bottom. The white horizontal back is framed by a black line and carries the player's name at the top, followed by biography and statistics.

	MINT	NRMT	EXC
COMPLETE SET (25)	5.00	2.20	.60

☐ 1 John Kent
☐ 2 William Savarino
☐ 3 David Veres
☐ 4 Michael Duncan
☐ 5 Jerome Nelson
☐ 6 Michael Bordick
☐ 7 John Minch
☐ 8 Steve Gokey
☐ 9 Butch Hughes
☐ 10 Lance Blankenship
☐ 11 Robert Gould
☐ 12 Kevin Tapani
☐ 13 Chris Hayes
☐ 14 Bruce Walton
☐ 15 Steve Iannini
☐ 16 Kevin Williamson
☐ 17 Jerry Peguero
☐ 18 Bob Fingers
☐ 19 Joseph Law
☐ 20 Dann Howitt
☐ 21 Patrick Britt
☐ 22 John Cartelli
☐ 23 Tommie D. Reynolds
☐ 24 Scott Holcomb
☐ 25 Jim Corsi

1987 Myrtle Beach Blue Jays ProCards

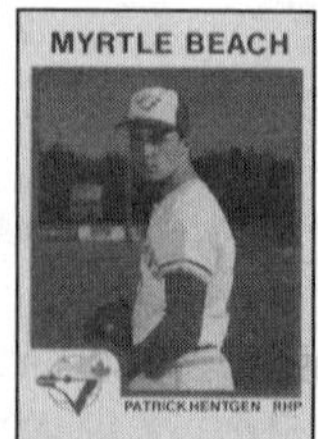

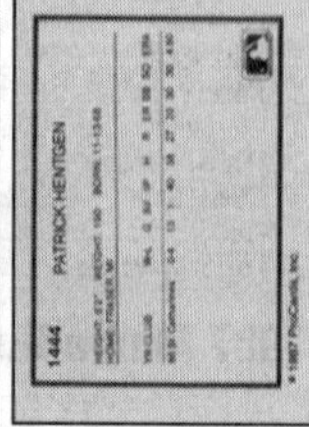

This 30-card standard-size set of the 1987 Myrtle Beach Blue Jays, a Class A South Atlantic League affiliate of the Toronto Blue Jays, features white-bordered posed color player photos on its fronts. The player's name and position appear at the bottom. The white horizontal back is framed by a black line and carries the player's name at the top, followed by biography and statistics. This issue includes the debut of Pat Hentgen.

	MINT	NRMT	EXC
COMPLETE SET (30)	25.00	11.00	3.10

☐ 1435 Julian Yan
☐ 1436 Oscar Escobar
☐ 1437 Jose Diaz
☐ 1438 Darren Hall
☐ 1439 Doug Linton
☐ 1440 Vince Horsman
☐ 1441 Barry Foote MG
☐ 1442 Mike Murray TR
☐ 1443 Leroy Stanton CO
☐ 1444 Pat Hentgen
☐ 1445 Tom Quinlan
☐ 1446 Randy Knorr
☐ 1447 Dennis Jones
☐ 1448 Secar Mejia
☐ 1449 Lindsay Foster
☐ 1450 Jim Tracy
☐ 1451 John Poloni CO
☐ 1452 John Shea
☐ 1453 Rocket Wheeler CO
☐ 1454 Wayne Davis
☐ 1455 Junior Felix
☐ 1456 Rich DePastino
☐ 1457 Victor Diaz
☐ 1458 Mark Whiten
☐ 1459 Joe Humphries
☐ 1460 Bob Guenther
☐ 1461 Andy Dziadkowiec
☐ 1462 Francisco Cabrera
☐ 1463 Luis Sojo
☐ 1464 Paul Rodgers

1987 Nashville Sounds Team Issue

	MINT	NRMT	EXC
COMPLETE SET (25)	7.00	3.10	.85

☐ 1 Mark Berry
☐ 2 Norm Charlton
☐ 3 Bill Cutshall
☐ 4 Rob Dibble
☐ 5 Leo Garcia
☐ 6 Wayne Garland CO
☐ 7 Orlando Gonzalez
☐ 8 Jeff Gray
☐ 9 Lenny Harris
☐ 10 Ron Henika
☐ 11 Hugh Kemp
☐ 12 Mike Konderla
☐ 13 Jack Lind MG
☐ 14 Mike Manfre
☐ 15 Jeff Montgomery
☐ 16 Pat Pacillo
☐ 17 Buddy Pryor
☐ 18 Chris Sabo
☐ 19 Eddie Tanner
☐ 20 Scott Terry
☐ 21 Jeff Treadway
☐ 22 Max Venable
☐ 23 Carl Willis
☐ 24 John Young
☐ 25 Bob Jamison and Duncan Stewart (Radio Broadcasters)

1987 New Britain Red Sox ProCards

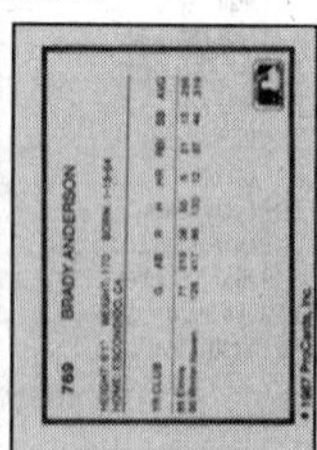

This 25-card standard-size set of the 1987 New Britain Red Sox, a Class AA Eastern League affiliate of the Boston Red Sox, features white-bordered posed color player photos on its fronts. The player's name and position appear at the bottom. The white horizontal back is framed by a black line and carries the player's name at the top, followed by biography and statistics. This issue includes a third year card of Brady Anderson.

	MINT	NRMT	EXC
COMPLETE SET (25)	18.00	8.00	2.20

☐ 1 Mike Clarkin
☐ 2 Zach Crouch
☐ 3 Bill Zupka
☐ 4 Angel Gonzalez
☐ 5 Luis Vasquez
☐ 6 Greg Lotzar
☐ 7 Brady Anderson
☐ 8 Bill McInnis
☐ 9 Bob Chadwick
☐ 10 Scott Skripko
☐ 11 Steve Bast
☐ 12 Carlos Quintana
☐ 13 Greg Bochesa
☐ 14 Daryl Irvine
☐ 15 Tony DeFrancesco
☐ 16 Dana Williams
☐ 17 Dana Kiecker
☐ 18 Dave Holt
☐ 19 Dan Gakeler
☐ 20 Roberto Aambrano
☐ 21 Josias Manzanillo
☐ 22 Tary Scott
☐ 23 Chris Moritz
☐ 24 Jose Birriel
☐ 25 Ed Estrada

1987 Newark Orioles ProCards

This 29-card standard-size set of the 1987 Newark Orioles, a Class A New York-Penn affiliate of the Baltimore Orioles, features white-bordered posed color player photos on its fronts. The player's name and position appear at the bottom. The white horizontal back is framed by a black line and carries the player's name at the top, followed by biography and statistics. This issue includes the minor league card debut of Steve Finley.

	MINT	NRMT	EXC
COMPLETE SET (29)	12.00	5.50	1.50

☐ 1 David Esquer
☐ 2 Mike Lehman
☐ 3 Mike Hart MGR
☐ 4 Earl Stephenson CO
☐ 5 John Oliphant TR
☐ 6 Gary Arnold AGM
☐ 7 Jack Voigt
☐ 8 Tom Michno
☐ 9 Frank Bryan
☐ 10 Craig Lopez
☐ 11 Steve Culkar
☐ 12 Mike Sander
☐ 13 Bob Shoulders
☐ 14 Joe Gast
☐ 15 Bob Williams
☐ 16 Mike Elmore
☐ 17 Chaun Wilson
☐ 18 Danny Hartline
☐ 19 Don Buford Jr.
☐ 20 Jeff Ahr
☐ 21 Steven Finley
☐ 22 Dickie Winzenread
☐ 23 Scott Evans
☐ 24 Mike Eberle
☐ 25 Ernie Young
☐ 26 Thomas Shannon GM
☐ 27 Randy Strijek
☐ 28 Tom Harms
☐ 29 Luis Pena

1987 Oklahoma City 89ers ProCards

This 27-card standard-size set of the 1987 Oklahoma City 89ers, a Class AAA American Association affiliate of the Texas Rangers, features white-bordered posed color player photos on its fronts. The player's name and position appear at the bottom. The white horizontal back is framed by a black line and carries the player's name at the top, followed by biography and statistics.

	MINT	NRMT	EXC
COMPLETE SET (27)	8.00	3.60	1.00

☐ 1 Paul Kilgus
☐ 2 Gary Wheelock
☐ 3 Dave Owen
☐ 4 Frank Pastore
☐ 5 Don Werner
☐ 6 Dave Meier
☐ 7 Keith Creel
☐ 8 Mike Stanley
☐ 9 Kirk Killingsworth
☐ 10 Mike Jeffcoat
☐ 11 Steve Kemp
☐ 12 Toby Harrah
☐ 13 Ron Meridith
☐ 14 Glen Cook
☐ 15 Javier Ortiz
☐ 16 Cecil Espy
☐ 17 Tim Rodgers
☐ 18 Dwayne Henry
☐ 19 Greg Smith
☐ 20 Tom O'Malley
☐ 21 Greg Tabor
☐ 22 Alan Knicely
☐ 23 Nick Capra
☐ 24 Ray Ramirez
☐ 25 Bill Taylor
☐ 26 Jeff Zaske
☐ 27 Dave Rucker

1987 Omaha Royals ProCards

This 26-card standard-size set of the 1987 Omaha Royals, a Class AAA American Association affiliate of the Kansas City Royals, features white-bordered posed color player photos on its fronts. The player's name and position appear at the bottom. The white horizontal back is framed by a black line and carries the player's name at the top, followed by biography and statistics.

	MINT	NRMT	EXC
COMPLETE SET (26)	5.00	2.20	.60

☐ 1 Frank Funk
☐ 2 Jose Angero
☐ 3 John Wathan
☐ 4 Van Snider
☐ 5 Nick Swartz
☐ 6 Gary Thurman
☐ 7 Chito Martinez
☐ 8 Dwight Taylor
☐ 9 Joe Citari
☐ 10 Derek Botelho
☐ 11 Rondin Johnson
☐ 12 Bob Stoddard
☐ 13 Al Hargesheimer
☐ 14 Steve Shirley
☐ 15 Craig Pippin
☐ 16 Adrian Garrett
☐ 17 Scotti Madison
☐ 18 Israel Sanchez
☐ 19 John Davis
☐ 20 Ron Wotus
☐ 21 Bobby Ramos
☐ 22 Rick Anderson
☐ 23 Jeff Schulz
☐ 24 MIke Macfarlane
☐ 25 Luis Delos Santos
☐ 26 Tom Muller

1987 Oneonta Yankees ProCards

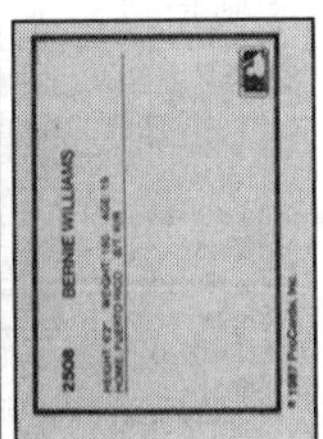

This 33-card standard-size set of the 1987 Oneonta Yankees, a Class A New York-Penn League affiliate of the New York Yankees, features white-bordered posed color player photos on its fronts. The player's name and position appear at the bottom. The white horizontal back is framed by a black line and carries the player's name at the top, followed by biography and statistics. This issue includes the minor league card debut of Bernie Williams.

	MINT	NRMT	EXC
COMPLETE SET (33)	40.00	18.00	5.00

☐ 1 Lew Hill
☐ 2 Anthony Morrison
☐ 3 Darrel Tingle
☐ 4 Bernie Williams
☐ 5 Hector Vargas
☐ 6 Gerald Williams
☐ 7 Dan Roman
☐ 8 Steve Erickson
☐ 9 Tom Popplewell
☐ 10 Doug Gogolewski
☐ 11 Bill DaCoste
☐ 12 David Turgeon
☐ 13 Tom Weeks
☐ 14 Brian Butterfield
☐ 15 Freddie Hailey
☐ 16 Julio Ramon
☐ 17 Dave Eiland
☐ 18 Jay Makemson
☐ 19 Bill Voeltz
☐ 20 Chris Byrnes
☐ 21 Randy Foster
☐ 22 Mark Mitchell
☐ 23 Ron Ehrhard
☐ 24 Gary Allenson
☐ 25 Rod Imes
☐ 26 Mark Marris
☐ 27 Bobby Dickerson
☐ 28 Tim Bishop
☐ 29 Dean Kelley
☐ 30 Ed Martel
☐ 31 Luc Berube
☐ 32 Jack Gills
☐ 33 Tom Cloninger

1987 Orlando Twins ProCards

This 26-card standard-size set of the 1987 Orlando Twins, a Class AA Southern League affiliate of the Minnnesota Twins, features white-bordered posed color player photos on its fronts. The player's name and position appear at the bottom. The white horizontal back is framed by a black line and carries the player's name at the top, followed by biography and statistics.

	MINT	NRMT	EXC
COMPLETE SET (26)	5.00	2.20	.60

☐ 1 Jeff Bumgarner
☐ 2 Robbie Smith
☐ 3 Dan Smith
☐ 4 John Eccles
☐ 5 Henry Gatewood
☐ 6 Bobby Ralston
☐ 7 Jim Shellenback
☐ 8 Ken Koch
☐ 9 George Mitterwald
☐ 10 Mark Clemons
☐ 11 Steve Gasser
☐ 12 Toby Nivens
☐ 13 Steve Gomez
☐ 14 Brad Bierley
☐ 15 Jeff Reboulet
☐ 16 Gary Borg
☐ 17 Doug Palmer
☐ 18 Tom Schwarz
☐ 19 Eddie Yanes
☐ 21 Jeff Bronkey
☐ 22 Wes Pierorazio
☐ 23 Allan Sontag
☐ 24 Darrel Higgs
☐ 25 Mark Funderburk
☐ 26 Larry Blackwell
☐ 27 Dave Vetsch

1987 Osceola Astros ProCards

This 29-card standard-size set of the 1987 Osceola Astros, a Class A Florida State League affiliate of the Houston Astros, features white-bordered posed color player photos on its fronts. The player's name and position appear at the bottom. The white horizontal back is framed by a black line and carries the player's name at the top, followed by biography and statistics.

	MINT	NRMT	EXC
COMPLETE SET (29)	5.00	2.20	.60

☐ 1 Terry Wells
☐ 2 Juan Lopez
☐ 3 Mike Brown
☐ 4 Carlo Colombino
☐ 5 Randy Randle
☐ 6 Ken Bolek
☐ 7 Calvin James
☐ 8 Dan Walters
☐ 9 Doug Snyder
☐ 10 Jeff Baldwin
☐ 11 Stan Fascher
☐ 12 Tony Metoyer
☐ 13 Brian Meyer
☐ 14 Joe Schulte
☐ 15 Jose Vargas
☐ 16 David Potts
☐ 17 John Elliott
☐ 18 Jack Billingham
☐ 19 Don Dunster
☐ 20 Joel Estes
☐ 21 Gary Cooper
☐ 22 Juan Delgado
☐ 23 Scot Markley
☐ 24 Ken Houston
☐ 25 Terry Green
☐ 26 Tim Arnsberg
☐ 27 Jose Cano
☐ 28 Todd Credeur
☐ 29 David Rohde

1987 Palm Springs ProCards

This 32-card standard-size set of the 1987 Palm Springs Angels, a Class A California League affiliate of the California Angels, features white-bordered posed color player photos on its fronts. The player's name and position appear at the bottom. The white horizontal back is framed by a black line and carries the player's name at the top, followed by biography and statistics.

	MINT	NRMT	EXC
COMPLETE SET (32)	7.00	3.10	.85

☐ 1 Mike Spearnock
☐ 2 Al Heath
☐ 3 David Johnson
☐ 4 Jeff Manto
☐ 5 Reggie Lambert
☐ 6 Paul Bilak
☐ 7 Kenny Grant
☐ 8 Dan Grunhard
☐ 9 Colin Charland
☐ 10 Mike Shull
☐ 11 Paul Sorrento
☐ 12 Lee Stevens
☐ 13 Bill Vanderwel
☐ 14 Colby Ward
☐ 15 Glenn Washington
☐ 16 Roger Zottneck
☐ 17 Bill Lachemann
☐ 18 Tim Kelly
☐ 19 Tom Alfredson
☐ 20 Edgar Alfonso
☐ 21 Tim Burcham
☐ 22 Dario Nunez
☐ 23 Erik Pappas
☐ 24 Michael Anderson
☐ 25 Bobby Bell
☐ 26 Mike Fetters
☐ 27 Frank Dimichele
☐ 28 Richard Morehouse
☐ 29 Todd Eggertsen
☐ 30 Mark Marino
☐ 31 Andres Espinoza
☐ 32 Gary Nalls

1987 Pan Am Team USA Blue INDEP

This issue includes the first card of Frank Thomas.

	MINT	NRMT	EXC
COMPLETE SET (34)	200.00	90.00	25.00
COMPLETE SET (35)	225.00	100.00	28.00

☐ 2 Larry Lamphere
☐ 4 Clyde Keller
☐ 5 Dave Silvestri
☐ 8 Jeff Mutis
☐ 9 Rick Hirtensteiner
☐ 10 Don Guillot
☐ 11 Ted Wood
☐ 14 Ty Griffin
☐ 15 Steve Hecht
☐ 18 Larry Gonzales
☐ 19 Tino Martinez
☐ 20 Mike Fiore
☐ 21 Longo Garcia
☐ 22 Bert Heffernan
☐ 23 Jim Poole
☐ 24 Joe Slusarski
☐ 25 Pat Combs
☐ 27 Chris Nichting
☐ 28 Scott Servais
☐ 30 Scott Livingstone
☐ 31 Gregg Olson
☐ 33 Ed Sprague
☐ 34A Cris Carpenter (w/glove)
☐ 34B Cris Carpenter (straight shot)
☐ 36 Frank Thomas
☐ 38 Jim Abbott
☐ NNO Ken Dominguez
☐ NNO Jerry Weinstein
☐ NNO Checklist
☐ NNO Bob Bensch
☐ NNO Millington Legion Field
☐ NNO Ron Fraser
☐ NNO Brad Kelley
☐ NNO Vinny Scavo
☐ NNO Jim Morris

1987 Pan Am Team USA Red BDK

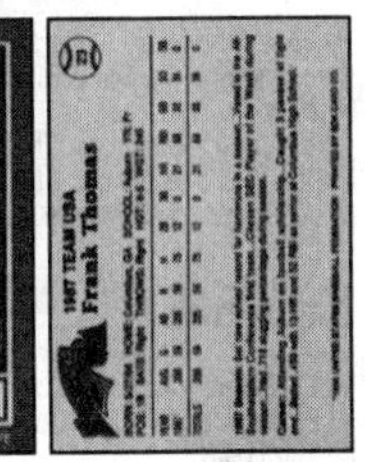

	MINT	NRMT	EXC
COMPLETE SET (26)	8.00	3.60	1.00

☐ 1 Tino Martinez
☐ 2 Ty Griffin
☐ 3 Scott Servais
☐ 4 Scott Livingstone
☐ 5 Pat Combs
☐ 6 Mike Fiore
☐ 7 Steve Hecht
☐ 8 Chris Nichting
☐ 9 Don Guillot
☐ 10 Larry Gonzales
☐ 11 Larry Lamphere
☐ 12 Gregg Olson
☐ 13 Jim Poole
☐ 14 Longo Garcia
☐ 15 Ted Wood
☐ 16 Jeff Mutis
☐ 17 Rick Hirtensteiner
☐ 18 Bert Heffernan
☐ 19 Cris Carpenter
☐ 20 Joe Slusarski
☐ 21 Clyde Keller
☐ 22 Ed Sprague
☐ 23 Frank Thomas
☐ 24 Dave Silvestri
☐ 25 Jim Abbott
☐ NNO Checklist

1987 Pawtucket Red Sox ProCards

This 27-card standard-size set of the 1987 Pawtucket Red Sox, a Class AAA International League affiliate of the Boston Red Sox, features white-bordered posed color player photos on its fronts. The player's name and position appear at the bottom. The white horizontal back is framed by a black line and carries the player's name at the top, followed by biography and statistics. This issue includes a second year card of Ellis Burks.

	MINT	NRMT	EXC
COMPLETE SET (27)	5.00	2.20	.60

☐ 51 John Marzano
☐ 52 Sam Horn
☐ 53 Stephen Curry
☐ 54 Kevin Romine
☐ 55 John Leister
☐ 56 Jody Reed
☐ 57 Todd Benzinger
☐ 58 Mitchell Johnson
☐ 59 Mike Rochford
☐ 60 LaSchelle Tarver
☐ 61 Hector Stewart
☐ 62 Tom Bolton
Sic, Bolten
☐ 63 Glenn Hoffman
☐ 64 Andy Araujo
☐ 65 Tony Cleary
☐ 66 Mike Dalton
☐ 67 Steve Ellsworth
☐ 68 Mike Mesh
☐ 69 Gary Miller-Jones
☐ 70 Gary Tremblay
☐ 71 Scott Wade
☐ 72 Ed Nottle
☐ 73 Ellis Burks
☐ 74 Chuck Davis
☐ 75 Mark Meleski
☐ 76 Dana Williams
☐ 77 Chris Cannizzaro

1987 Pawtucket Red Sox TCMA

	MINT	NRMT	EXC
COMPLETE SET (28)	4.00	1.80	.50

☐ 1 Andy Araujo
☐ 2 Chris Cannizzaro
☐ 3 Steve Curry
☐ 4 Mike Dalton
☐ 5 Chuck Davis
☐ 6 Steve Ellsworth
☐ 7 Mitch Johnson
☐ 8 Danny Sheaffer
☐ 9 Mike Rochford
☐ 10 Hector Stewart
☐ 11 John Marzano
☐ 12 Gary Tremblay
☐ 13 Todd Benzinger
☐ 14 Sam Horn
☐ 15 Mike Mesh
☐ 16 Gary Miller-Jones
☐ 17 Jody Reed
☐ 18 Kevin Romine
☐ 19 LaSchelle Tarver
☐ 20 Scott Wade
☐ 21 Ed Nottle
☐ 22 Ellis Burks
☐ 23 Rob Woodward
☐ 24 Pat Dodson
☐ 25 Dave Sax
☐ 26 John Leister
☐ 27 Tom Bolton
☐ 28 Mark Meleski

1987 Peninsula White Sox ProCards

This 29-card standard-size set of the 1987 Peninsula White Sox, a Class A Carolina affiliate of the Chicago White Sox, features white-bordered posed color player photos on its fronts. The player's name and position appear at the bottom. The white horizontal back is framed by a black line and carries the player's name at the top, followed by biography and statistics.

	MINT	NRMT	EXC
COMPLETE SET (29)	5.00	2.20	.60

☐ 1 Mark Davis
☐ 2 Kevin Renz
☐ 3 Chet Diemido
☐ 4 Mark Foley
☐ 5 Daniel Tauken
☐ 6 Joe Singley
☐ 7 Dewey Robinson
☐ 8 Aubrey Waggoner
☐ 9 Mike Ollom
☐ 10 Craig Grebeck
☐ 11 Dave Reynolds
☐ 12 Scott Radinsky
☐ 13 Miguel Audain

- ☐ 14 Bruce Hulstrom
- ☐ 15 Tom Sutryk
- ☐ 16 Glenn Braxton
- ☐ 17 Ron Scheer
- ☐ 18 Dave Wallwork
- ☐ 19 Tom Reichel
- ☐ 20 Jeff Greene
- ☐ 21 Kelsey Isa
- ☐ 22 Tom Lahrman
- ☐ 23 Bo Kennedy
- ☐ 24 Todd Hall
- ☐ 25 Ron Scruggs
- ☐ 26 Kurt Brown
- ☐ 27 Virgil Conley
- ☐ 28 Tony Cento
- ☐ 29 Dan Wagner

1987 Peoria Chiefs Pizza World

This 6-card promotional set was distributed through the Pizza World restaurant. One card per each Pizza World pizza ordered. The set was also sponsored by radio station WWCT 106. The cards measure 4'1/2" X 5'1/2" and feature black and white photos with blue borders.

	MINT	NRMT	EXC
COMPLETE SET (6)	25.00	11.00	3.10

- ☐ 1 Butch Garcia
- ☐ 2 Pat Gomez
- ☐ 3 John Green
- ☐ 4 Steve Hill
- ☐ 5 Jerome Walton
- ☐ 6 Chief Rainout

1987 Peoria Chiefs ProCards

This 29-card standard-size set of the 1987 Peoria Chiefs, a Class A Midwest League affiliate of the Chicago Cubs, features white-bordered posed color player photos on its fronts. The player's name and position appear at the bottom. The white horizontal back is framed by a black line and carries the player's name at the top, followed by biography and statistics.

	MINT	NRMT	EXC
COMPLETE SET (29)	5.00	2.20	.60

- ☐ 1 Ray Mullino
- ☐ 2 Butch Garcia
- ☐ 3 John Green
- ☐ 4 Sergio Espinal
- ☐ 5 Dick Canan
- ☐ 6 Jerry Lapenta
- ☐ 7 Steve Hill
- ☐ 8 Shawn Boskie
- ☐ 9 Greg Iaverone
- ☐ 10 John Berringer
- ☐ 11 Joe Housey
- ☐ 12 Derrick May
- ☐ 13 Pat Gomez
- ☐ 14 Greg Smith
- ☐ 15 Brian Otten
- ☐ 16 David Rosario
- ☐ 17 Elvin Paulino
- ☐ 18 Edward Williams
- ☐ 19 Harry Shelton
- ☐ 20 Jerome Walton
- ☐ 21 Simeon Mejias
- ☐ 22 Parnell Perry
- ☐ 23 Phil Harrison
- ☐ 24 Steve Parker
- ☐ 25 Kelly Mann
- ☐ 26 Mike Folga
- ☐ 27 Jim Tracy
- ☐ 28 William Kazmierczak
- ☐ 29 Fernando Zarranz

1987 Phoenix Firebirds ProCards

This 28-card standard-size set of the 1987 Phoenix Firebirds, a Class AAA Pacific Coast League affiliate of the San Francisco Giants, features white-bordered posed color player photos on its fronts. The player's name and position appear at the bottom. The white horizontal back is framed by a black line and carries the player's name at the top, followed by biography and statistics. This issue includes a second year card of Matt Williams.

	MINT	NRMT	EXC
COMPLETE SET (28)	15.00	6.75	1.85

- ☐ 1 Chris Jones
- ☐ 2 Matt Williams
- ☐ 3 Randy Bockus
- ☐ 4 George Ferran
- ☐ 5 Terry Mulholland
- ☐ 6 Charlie Corbell
- ☐ 7 Angel Escobar
- ☐ 8 Kevin Burrell
- ☐ 9 Colin Ward
- ☐ 10 Mike Woodard
- ☐ 11 Larry Hardy
- ☐ 12 Randy Kutcher
- ☐ 13 John Perlman
- ☐ 14 Jack McKnight
- ☐ 15 Alan Cockrell
- ☐ 16 Jessie Reid
- ☐ 17 Joe Price
- ☐ 18 John Verducci
- ☐ 19 Cliff Shidawara
- ☐ 20 Mackey Sasser
- ☐ 21 Pat Adams
- ☐ 22 Duane Espy
- ☐ 23 Wendell Kim
- ☐ 24 Atlee Hammaker
- ☐ 25 Francisco Melendez
- ☐ 26 Steve Miller
- ☐ 27 Mike Rubel
- ☐ 28 Jeff Brantley
  Sic, Brantley

1987 Pittsfield Cubs ProCards

This 26-card standard-size set of the 1987 Pittsfield Cubs, a Class AA Eastern League affiliate of the Chicago Cubs, features white-bordered posed color player photos on its fronts. The player's name and position appear at the bottom. The white horizontal back is framed by a black line and carries the player's name at the top, followed by biography and statistics. This issue includes a second year card of Mark Grace.

	MINT	NRMT	EXC
COMPLETE SET (26)	30.00	13.50	3.70

- ☐ 1 Ray Thoma
- ☐ 2 Greg Bell
- ☐ 3 Hector Villanueva
- ☐ 4 Jim Essian
- ☐ 5 Jim Wright
- ☐ 6 Brian McCann
- ☐ 7 Brian House
- ☐ 8 Laddie Renfroe
- ☐ 9 Mike Miller
- ☐ 10 Mark Grace
- ☐ 11 Brian Guinn
- ☐ 12 Jim Phillips
- ☐ 13 Leonard Damian
- ☐ 14 Dave Masters
- ☐ 15 Dave Pavlas
- ☐ 16 Make Leonette
- ☐ 17 Rick Wrona
- ☐ 18 David Wilder
- ☐ 19 Jeff Pico
- ☐ 20 Rick Hopkins
- ☐ 21 Roger Williams
- ☐ 22 Rich Amaral
- ☐ 23 Doug Dascenzo
- ☐ 24 Tim Rice
- ☐ 25 Rolando Roomes
- ☐ 26 Dwight Smith

1987 Pocatello Giants The Bon

The 32-card standard-szie set featuring the 1987 Pocatello Giants set was sponsored by The Bon clothing store. The fronts have posed player photos (from the waist up), with a stripe below the picture, as well as sponsor and team logos. The horizontally oriented backs have a picture of a bat and baseball at the top, with biography and career information below. Less than 1,000 sets were produced.

	MINT	NRMT	EXC
COMPLETE SET (32)	35.00	16.00	4.40

- ☐ 1 Doug Messer
- ☐ 2 Rafael Landestoy MG
- ☐ 3 Brett Lewis
- ☐ 4 Steve Connolly
- ☐ 5 Steve Lienhard
- ☐ 6 Kevin Meier
- ☐ 7 Jim Jones
- ☐ 8 Reid Gunter
- ☐ 9 Mike Greenwood
- ☐ 10 Jim Malseed
- ☐ 11 Domingo DeLaRosa
- ☐ 12 Matt Williams
- ☐ 13 Bill Carlson
- ☐ 14 John Vuz
- ☐ 15 Dominick Johnson
- ☐ 16 Jim Myers
- ☐ 17 Dave Edwards
- ☐ 18 Ron McLintock
- ☐ 19 Mike Williams
- ☐ 20 Mike Wandler
- ☐ 21 Karl Breitenbucher
- ☐ 22 Keith James
- ☐ 23 Andres Santana
- ☐ 24 Rocco Buffolino
- ☐ 25 Jesus Figueroa
- ☐ 26 Francisco Arias
- ☐ 27 Juan Guerrero
- ☐ 28 Jesus Laya
- ☐ 29 Erik Johnson
- ☐ 30 Diego Segui CO
- ☐ 31 Glenn Abraham
- ☐ 32 Jose Linarez

1987 Port Charlotte Rangers ProCards

This 27-card standard-size set of the 1987 Port Charlotte Rangers, a Class A Florida State League affiliate of the Texas Rangers, features white-bordered posed color player photos on its fronts. The player's name and position appear at the bottom. The white horizontal back is framed by a black line and carries the player's name at the top, followed by biography and statistics.

	MINT	NRMT	EXC
COMPLETE SET (27)	5.00	2.20	.60

- ☐ 1 Ken Clawson
- ☐ 2 John Schofield
- ☐ 3 Steve Lankard
- ☐ 4 Scott Morse
- ☐ 5 John Barfield
- ☐ 6 Mitch Thomas
- ☐ 7 Marty Cerny
- ☐ 8 Edwin Morales
- ☐ 9 Rick Raether
- ☐ 10 Steve Wilson
- ☐ 11 Jeff Mays
- ☐ 12 Jeff Andrews
- ☐ 13 Greg Harrell
- ☐ 14 Fred Samson
- ☐ 15 Stephen Glasker
- ☐ 16 Mick Billmeyer
- ☐ 17 Jose Vargas
- ☐ 18 Rick Bernardo
- ☐ 19 Mark Kramer
- ☐ 20 Julio DeLeon
- ☐ 21 Joel Cartaya
- ☐ 22 Cris Colon
- ☐ 23 Gar Millay
- ☐ 24 Jim Skaalen
- ☐ 25 Chad Kreuter
- ☐ 26 Kevin Reimer
- ☐ 27 Joe Pearn

1987 Portland Beavers ProCards

This 25-card standard-size set of the 1987 Portland Beavers, a Class AAA Pacific Coast League affiliate of the Minnesota Twins, features white-bordered posed color player photos on its fronts. The player's name and position appear at the bottom. The white horizontal back is framed by a black line and carries the player's name at the top, followed by biography and statistics.

	MINT	NRMT	EXC
COMPLETE SET (25)	5.00	2.20	.60

- ☐ 1 Jeff Bittiger
- ☐ 2 Pat Dempsey
- ☐ 3 Randy Niemann
- ☐ 4 Allan Anderson
- ☐ 5 Billy Beane
- ☐ 6 Chris Pittaro
- ☐ 7 Pat Casey
- ☐ 8 Roy Smith
- ☐ 9 Phil Wilson
- ☐ 10 Steve Liddle
- ☐ 11 Danny Clay
- ☐ 12 Julius McDougal
- ☐ 13 Kevin Hagen
- ☐ 14 Alvaro Espinosa
- ☐ 15 Kevin Trudeau
- ☐ 16 Ben Bianchi
- ☐ 17 Alex Marte
- ☐ 18 Bill Latham
- ☐ 19 Gene Larkin
- ☐ 20 Greg Morhardt
- ☐ 21 Ron Musselman
- ☐ 22 Charlie Manuel
- ☐ 23 Ken Silvestri
- ☐ 24 Brad Boylan
- ☐ 25 Ron Gardenhire

1987 Prince William Yankees ProCards

This 29-card standard-size set of the 1987 Prince William Yankees, a Class A Carolina League affiliate of the New York Yankees, features white-bordered posed color player photos on its fronts. The player's name and position appear at the bottom. The white horizontal back is framed by a black line and carries the player's name at the top, followed by biography and statistics.

	MINT	NRMT	EXC
COMPLETE SET (29)	5.00	2.20	.60

- ☐ 1 Hensley Meulens
- ☐ 2 Yanko Haurado
- ☐ 3 Bob Davidson
- ☐ 4 Ricky Torres
- ☐ 5 Ralph Kraus
- ☐ 6 Scott Kamieniecki
- ☐ 7 Alan Mills
- ☐ 8 Art Calvert
- ☐ 9 Rick Balabon
- ☐ 10 Rob Sepanek Jr.
- ☐ 11 Chris Howard
- ☐ 12 Micky Tresh
- ☐ 13 Chris Lombardozzi
- ☐ 14 Mike Heifferon
- ☐ 15 Bill Clossen
- ☐ 16 Bill Voeltz
- ☐ 17 Ysidro Giron
- ☐ 18 Aris Tirado
- ☐ 19 Amalio Carreno
- ☐ 20 Steve Adkins
- ☐ 21 Hector Vargas
- ☐ 22 Fernando Figuerda
- ☐ 23 Ramon Manon
- ☐ 24 Jason Maas
- ☐ 25 Rob Lambert
- ☐ 26 Joe Hicks
- ☐ 27 Tony Gwinn
- ☐ 28 John Ramos
- ☐ 29 William Morales

1987 Quad City Angels ProCards

This 31-card standard-size set of the 1987 Quad City Angels, a Class A Midwest League affiliate of the California Angels, features white-bordered posed color player photos on its fronts. The player's name and position appear at the bottom. The white horizontal back is framed by a black line and carries the player's name at the top, followed by biography and statistics.

	MINT	NRMT	EXC
COMPLETE SET (31)	7.00	3.10	.85

- ☐ 1 Terrence Carr
- ☐ 2 Troy Giles
- ☐ 3 Edgar Rodriguez
- ☐ 4 Santiago Espinosa
- ☐ 5 Giovanny Reyes
- ☐ 6 Lawrence Pardo
- ☐ 7 Jose Tapia
- ☐ 8 Roberto Hernandez
- ☐ 9 Scott Kannenberg
- ☐ 10 Daryl Green
- ☐ 11 Luis Merejo
- ☐ 12 Brandy Vann
- ☐ 13 Mike Kesler
- ☐ 14 Jim Bisceglia
- ☐ 15 Rafael Pineda
- ☐ 16 Elvin Rivera
- ☐ 17 Greg Fix
- ☐ 18 Eddie Rodriguez
- ☐ 19 Don Long
- ☐ 20 Gary Ruby
- ☐ 21 Jim McCollom
- ☐ 22 Chris Graves
- ☐ 23 Chris Cron
- ☐ 24 Scott Cernye
- ☐ 25 Kendall Walling
- ☐ 26 Jeff Gay
- ☐ 27 Michael Knapp
- ☐ 28 Ken Bandy
- ☐ 29 Dave Grilione
- ☐ 30 Greg Jackson
- ☐ 31 Luis Gallardo

1987 Reading Phillies ProCards

This 26-card standard-size set of the 1987 Reading Phillies, a Class AA Eastern League affiliate of the Philadelphia Phillies, features white-bordered posed color player photos on its fronts. The player's name and position appear at the bottom. The white horizontal back is framed by a black line and carries the player's name at the top, followed by biography and statistics.

	MINT	NRMT	EXC
COMPLETE SET (26)	5.00	2.20	.60

- ☐ 1 George Culver
- ☐ 2 Tony Brown
- ☐ 3 Joe Lefebvre
- ☐ 4 Greg Edge
- ☐ 5 Miguel Vargas
- ☐ 6 Dan Giesen
- ☐ 7 Tom Barrett
- ☐ 8 Dion Beck
- ☐ 9 Mike Shelton
- ☐ 10 Bruce Long
- ☐ 11 Ray Roman
- ☐ 12 Kevin Ward
- ☐ 13 Rick Lunblade
- ☐ 14 Howard Nichols
- ☐ 15 Ramon Henderson
- ☐ 16 Ricky Jordan
- ☐ 17 Mark Bowden
- ☐ 18 Steve Blackshear
- ☐ 19 Todd Frohwirth
- ☐ 20 Bob Scanlan
- ☐ 21 Jim Fortenberry
- ☐ 22 Jose Leiva
- ☐ 23 John McLarnan
- ☐ 24 Steve Williams
- ☐ 25 Michael Miller
- ☐ 26 Rob Hicks

1987 Richmond Braves Bob's Camera

This 29-card team set of the 1989 Richmond Braves, a Class AAA International League affiliate of the Atlanta Braves, was sponsored by Bob's Camera. The fronts feature borderless color player photos with sponsors' and team's logos in the wide bottom margin. The backs are blank. This issue includes a second year card of Tom Glavine. 500 sets were produced.

	MINT	NRMT	EXC
COMPLETE SET (24)	90.00	40.00	11.00

☐ 1 Chuck Cary
☐ 2 Floyd Chiffer
☐ 3 Marty Clary
☐ 4 Sal D'Alessandro
☐ 5 Trench Davis
☐ 6 Juan Eichelberger
☐ 7 Mike Fischlin
☐ 8 Tom Glavine
☐ 9 Dave Griffin
☐ 10 Inocencio Guerrero
☐ 11 Kelly Heath
☐ 12 Chuck Hensley
☐ 13 Dale Holman
☐ 14 John Mizerock
☐ 15 Darryl Motley
☐ 16 Ed Olwine
☐ 17 John Rabb
☐ 18 Paul Runge
☐ 19 Cliff Speck
☐ 20 Mark Strucher
☐ 21 Bob Tumpane
☐ 22 Matt West
☐ 23 Steve Ziem

1987 Richmond Braves Crown

This issue includes a second year card of Tom Glavine.

	MINT	NRMT	EXC
COMPLETE SET (30)	30.00	13.50	3.70

☐ 1 Kelly Heath
☐ 2 Jeff Blauser
☐ 5 Mark Strucher
☐ 6 Roy Majtyka MG
☐ 8 John Mizerock
☐ 9 Bob Tumpane
☐ 10 Sal D'Alessandro
☐ 12 Paul Runge
☐ 14 Tom Glavine
☐ 15 Juan Eichelberger
☐ 18 Mike Fischlin
☐ 19 Steve Ziem
☐ 20 John Rabb
☐ 24 David Griffin
☐ 25 Dale Holman
☐ 26 Rick Albert CO
☐ 28 Floyd Chiffer
☐ 29 Stan Cliburn
☐ 30 Darryl Motley
☐ 31 Bean Stringfellow
☐ 32 Trench Davis
☐ 34 Marty Clary
☐ 37 Chuck Hensley
☐ 39 Cliff Speck
☐ 42 Mike Brown
☐ 43 Nardi Contreras CO
☐ 45 Matt West
☐ 47 Chuck Cary
☐ NNO Sam Ayoub TR
☐ NNO Braves Logo
Title Card

1987 Richmond Braves TCMA

This issue includes a second year card of Tom Glavine.

	MINT	NRMT	EXC
COMPLETE SET (29)	12.00	5.50	1.50

☐ 1 Chuck Cary
☐ 2 Floyd Chiffer
☐ 3 Marty Clary
☐ 4 Juan Eichelberger
☐ 5 Tom Glavine
☐ 6 Chuck Hensley
☐ 7 Bean Stringfellow
☐ 8 Matt West
☐ 9 Steve Ziem
☐ 10 John Mizerock
☐ 11 Jeff Blauser
☐ 12 Mike Fischlin
☐ 13 David Griffin
☐ 14 Paul Runge
☐ 15 Mark Strucher
☐ 16 Bob Tumpane
☐ 17 Trench Davis
☐ 18 Kelly Heath
☐ 19 Darryl Motley
☐ 20 John Rabb
☐ 21 Roy Majtyka
☐ 22 Nardi Contreras
☐ 23 Dale Holman
☐ 24 Jim McManus
☐ 25 Cliff Speck
☐ 26 Rich Albert
☐ 27 Mike Brown
☐ 28 Stan Cliburn
☐ 29 Sam Ayoub

1987 Rochester Red Wings ProCards

This 27-card standard-size set of the 1987 Rochester Red Wings, a Class AAA International League affiliate of the Baltimore Orioles, features white-bordered posed color player photos on its fronts. The player's name and position appear at the bottom. The white horizontal back is framed by a black line and carries the player's name at the top, followed by biography and statistics.

	MINT	NRMT	EXC
COMPLETE SET (27)	5.00	2.20	.60

☐ 1 Phil Huffman
☐ 2 Dave Van Gorder
☐ 3 John Hart
☐ 4 Ron Salcedo
☐ 5 Mike Skinner
☐ 6 Chris Padget
☐ 7 Scott Ullger
☐ 8 Eric Rasmussen
☐ 9 Mike Griffin
☐ 10 Mike Hart
☐ 11 Carl Nichols
☐ 12 Bill Ripken
☐ 13 Curt Motton CO
☐ 14 D.L. Smith
☐ 15 Dom Chiti
☐ 16 Luis De Leon
☐ 17 Brad Havens
☐ 18 Nelson Simmons
☐ 19 Ron Washington
☐ 20 Jack O'Connor
☐ 21 Kelvin Torve
☐ 22 Jamie Reed
☐ 23 Craig Worthington
☐ 24 John Habyan
☐ 25 Jeff Ballard
☐ 26 Jim Traber
☐ 27 Bob Molinaro

1987 Rochester Red Wings TCMA

	MINT	NRMT	EXC
COMPLETE SET (29)	4.00	1.80	.50

☐ 1 Jeff Ballard
☐ 2 Luis DeLeon
☐ 3 Mike Griffin
☐ 4 John Habyan
☐ 5 Brad Havens
☐ 6 Phil Huffman
☐ 7 Jack O'Connor
☐ 8 Eric Rasmussen
☐ 9 Mike Skinner
☐ 10 Carl Nichols
☐ 11 Dave Van Gorder
☐ 12 Chris Padget
☐ 13 Bill Ripken
☐ 14 David Lee Smith
☐ 15 Kelvin Torve
☐ 16 Ron Washington
☐ 17 Craig Worthington
☐ 18 Mike Hart
☐ 19 Ron Salcedo
☐ 20 Jim Traber
☐ 21 Scott Ullger
☐ 22 Chris Green
☐ 23 Curt Motton
☐ 24 John Hart
☐ 25 Dom Chiti
☐ 26 Jerry Lomastro
☐ 27 Joe Kucharski
☐ 28 Rex Hudler
☐ 29 Don Gordon and
Joe Kucharski

1987 Salem Angels ProCards

This 34-card standard-size set of the 1987 Salem Angels, a Class A Northwest League affiliate of the California Angels, features white-bordered posed color player photos on its fronts. The player's name and position appear at the bottom. The white horizontal back is framed by a black line and carries the player's name at the top, followed by biography and statistics.

	MINT	NRMT	EXC
COMPLETE SET (34)	5.00	2.20	.60

☐ 1 Edgar Rodriguez
☐ 2 Gary Buckels
☐ 3 Jay Bobel Jr.
☐ 4 Troy Giles
☐ 5 Robert Wassenaar
☐ 6 John Orton
☐ 7 Mario Molina
☐ 8 Bill Robinson
☐ 9 Greg Jackson
☐ 10 Eric Reinholtz
☐ 11 Jorge Montero
☐ 12 Ramon Martinez
☐ 13 Reed Peters
☐ 14 Tony Rasmus
☐ 15 Jim Townsend
☐ 16 Frank Mutz
☐ 17 Ruben Amaro
☐ 18 Santiago Espinosa
☐ 19 Wiley Lee Jr.
☐ 20 Paul List
☐ 21 Rafael Pineda
☐ 22 Kevin Flora
☐ 23 Mikael Musolino
☐ 24 Mike Erb
☐ 25 Luis Gallardo
☐ 26 Cary Grubb
☐ 27 Lanny Abshier
☐ 28 Freddie Davis Jr.
☐ 29 Scott Randolph
☐ 30 Jeff Goettsch
☐ 31 Jesse Flores CO
☐ 32 Mark Weidemaier CO
☐ 33 Chris Smith MG
☐ 34 Derek Winchell TR

1987 Salem Buccaneers ProCards

This 30-card standard-size set of the 1987 Salem Buccaneers, a Class A Carolina League affiliate of the Pittsburgh Pirates, features white-bordered posed color player photos on its fronts. The player's name and position appear at the bottom. The white horizontal back is framed by a black line and carries the player's name at the top, followed by biography and statistics. This issue includes the minor league card debut of Jeff King.

	MINT	NRMT	EXC
COMPLETE SET (30)	12.00	5.50	1.50

☐ 1 Kevin Franchi
☐ 2 Mike Stevens
☐ 3 Larry Melton
☐ 4 Rob Hatfield
☐ 5 Octavio Cepeda
☐ 6 Greg Stading
☐ 7 Pete Rice
☐ 8 Tim Kirk
☐ 9 Ben Morrow
☐ 10 Matias Carrillo
☐ 11 Martin Hernandez
☐ 12 Mike Dotzher
☐ 13 Steve Moser
☐ 14 John Rigos
☐ 15 Harold Williams
☐ 16 Gilberto Roca
☐ 17 Rafael Muratti
☐ 18 Jim Thrift
☐ 19 Bill Copp
☐ 20 Bob Koopmann
☐ 21 Bill Sampen
☐ 22 Mike Stevanus
☐ 23 Reggie Barringer
☐ 24 Jeff King
☐ 25 Tony Chance
☐ 26 Todd Smith
☐ 27 Doug Pittman
☐ 28 Chris Lein
☐ 29 Steve Demeter
☐ 30 Kevin Davis

1987 Salinas Spurs Police

This issue includes a second year card of Omar Vizquel.

	MINT	NRMT	EXC
COMPLETE SET (32)	80.00	36.00	10.00

☐ 1 Keith Foley
☐ 2 Jorge Uribe
☐ 3 Dave Snell
☐ 4 Maryann Hudson GM
☐ 5 Mike Brandts
☐ 6 William Diaz
☐ 7 Andrea Fine AGM
☐ 8 Dave Mosley
☐ 9 John Clem
☐ 10 Rick Moore
☐ 11 Greg Brinkman
☐ 12 Dave McCorkle
☐ 13 Bob Bernardo
☐ 14 Tom Eccelston
☐ 15 Danny Larson
☐ 16 Jovan Edwards
☐ 17 Michael Darby
☐ 18 Buddy Meacham
☐ 19 Omar Vizquel
☐ 20 Robert Gibree
☐ 21 Tom Krause
☐ 22 Steve Murray
☐ 23 Pablo Moncerratt
☐ 24 Tom Newberg
☐ 25 Jeff Hull
☐ 26 Tim Fortugno
☐ 27 Jeff Nelson
☐ 28 Mike Kolovitz
☐ 29 John Burden CO
☐ 30 Clint Zavaras
☐ 31 Smokey Bear
☐ 32 Greg Mahlberg TR

1987 Salt Lake Trappers Taco Time

	MINT	NRMT	EXC
COMPLETE SET (30)	8.00	3.60	1.00

☐ 1 Kurt Stange
☐ 2 Michael Malinak
☐ 3 Kent Hetrick
☐ 4 Jon Beuder
☐ 5 Neil Reynolds
☐ 6 James Ferguson
☐ 7 Coach , Bat Boys
Rueben Rodriguez CO
Lance Bagshaw
Ryan Bagshaw
Andy Iacona
☐ 8 John Groennert
☐ 9 Isaac Alleyne
☐ 10 Todd Noonan
☐ 11 Jim Gilligan MGR
☐ 12 David Ward
☐ 13 Ed Citronnelli
☐ 14 Steve Pearson MGR ,
Glenn Seninger PR
☐ 15 Kouichi Ikeue
☐ 16 Mike Humphrey
☐ 17 Niles Creekmore
☐ 18 Frank Colston
☐ 19 Adam Ca
☐ 20 Yasuhiro Hiyama
☐ 21 Steve Fong TR ,
Randy Kerdoon ANN
☐ 22 Anthony Blackmon
☐ 23 Matt Huff
☐ 24 Jon Leake
☐ 25 Tim Peters
☐ 26 Steve Scott
☐ 27 David Poss
☐ 28 Team Checklist
☐ NNO Barry Moss CO
☐ NNO Kim Casey
Joie Casey
Baseball Card Etc.

1987 San Antonio Dodgers Team Issue

	MINT	NRMT	EXC
COMPLETE SET (24)	7.00	3.10	.85
COMPLETE SET W/LOGO (25)	8.00	3.60	1.00

☐ 1 Jeff Schaefer
☐ 2 Andres Mena
☐ 3 Jim Stoeckel CO
☐ 4 Tim Scott
☐ 5 Alonzo Tellez
☐ 6 Rob Rowen
☐ 7 Domingo Michel
☐ 8 Barry Wohler
☐ 9 Juan Bustabad
☐ 10 Mike Devereaux
☐ 11 Scott May
☐ 12 Jeff Brown
☐ 13 Mike Schweighoffer
☐ 14 Walt McConnell
☐ 15 Felix Tejeda
☐ 16 Mike Huff
☐ 17 Joe Szekely
☐ 18 Bob Hamilton
☐ 19 Jon Pequignot
☐ 20 Dave Eichhorn
☐ 21 Homar Rojas
☐ 22 Jack Savage
☐ 23 Ken Harvey
☐ 24 Mark Heuer
☐ NNO Logo Card

1987 San Bernardino Spirit ProCards

This 23-card standard-size set of the 1987 San Bernardino Spirit, a Class A California League Independent, features white-bordered posed color player photos on its fronts. The player's name and position appear at the bottom. The white horizontal back is framed by a black line and carries the player's name at the top, followed by biography and statistics.

	MINT	NRMT	EXC
COMPLETE SET (23)	5.00	2.20	.60

☐ 1 Steve Walker
☐ 2 Larry Smith
☐ 3 Jeff Edwards
☐ 4 Don Stearns

☐ 5 Randy Stearns
☐ 6 Stan Sanchez
☐ 7 Rich Dauer
☐ 8 Ron Carter
☐ 9 Mark Combs
☐ 10 James Filippi
☐ 11 Delwyn Young
☐ 12 Vince Shinholster
☐ 13 Brian Hartsock
☐ 14 Leon Baham
☐ 15 Scott Marrett
☐ 16 Mike Brocki
☐ 17 Brian Morrison
☐ 18 Walt Stull
☐ 19 Robert Greenlee
☐ 20 Todd Cruz
☐ 21 Tony Triplett
☐ 22 Todd Hayes
☐ 23 Tom Thompson

1987 San Jose Bees ProCards

This 30-card standard-size set of the 1987 San Jose Bees, a Class A California League Independent, features white-bordered posed color player photos on its fronts. The player's name and position appear at the bottom. The white horizontal back is framed by a black line and carries the player's name at the top, followed by biography and statistics.

	MINT	NRMT	EXC
COMPLETE SET (30)	5.00	2.20	.60

☐ 1 Sam Hirose CO
☐ 2 Hector Nakamura
☐ 3 Ken Rietz
☐ 4 Sal Vaccaro
☐ 5 Harvey Lee
☐ 6 Charlie Moore
☐ 7 Rocky Osaka
☐ 8 Kat Kamei
☐ 9 Frank Bryan
☐ 10 Ted Haraguchi
☐ 11 Mickey Yamano
☐ 12 Dan Mori
☐ 13 Tom Nabekawa
☐ 14 Ratoo Akimoto
☐ 15 David Rolland
☐ 16 Mark Seay
☐ 17 Paco Burgos
☐ 18 Elias Sosa
☐ 19 Mike Verdi MGR
☐ 20 Rick Tracy CO
☐ 21 Warren Brusstar
☐ 22 Lawrence Feola
☐ 23 Roger Erickson
☐ 24 Julian Gonzales
☐ 25 Eddie Gonzales
☐ 26 Steve McCatty
☐ 27 Rusty McNealy
☐ 28 Daryl Sconiers
☐ 29 Shawn Barton
☐ 30 Brian Kubala

1987 Savannah Cardinals ProCards

This 26-card standard-size set of the 1987 Savannah Cardinals, a Class A South Atlantic League affiliate of the St. Louis Cardinals, features white-bordered posed color player photos on its fronts. The player's name and position appear at the bottom. The white horizontal back is framed by a black line and carries the player's name at the top, followed by biography and statistics.

	MINT	NRMT	EXC
COMPLETE SET (26)	5.00	2.20	.60

☐ 1 Bobby DeLoach
☐ 2 Chuck Johnson
☐ 3 David Krebs
☐ 4 Geronimo Pena
☐ 5 Eric Hahn
☐ 6 Scott Nichols
☐ 7 Jay Martel
☐ 8 Greg Ward
☐ 9 Pat Hewes
☐ 10 Mike Henry
☐ 11 Mark Grater
☐ 12 Mark Davis
☐ 13 Pedro Llanes
☐ 14 Carroll Parker
☐ 15 Chico Singletary
☐ 16 Carey Nemeth
☐ 17 Reed Olmstead
☐ 18 Eddie Looper
☐ 19 Julian Martinez
☐ 20 Franklin Abreu
☐ 21 Don Dumas
☐ 22 Stan Zaltsman
☐ 23 Lenny Picota
☐ 24 Mark Behny
☐ 25 Scott Lawrence
☐ 26 Mark DeJohn

1987 Shreveport Captains ProCards

This 25-card standard-size set of the 1987 Shreveport Captains, a Class AA Texas League affiliate of the San Francisco Giants, features white-bordered posed color player photos on its fronts. The player's name and position appear at the bottom. The white horizontal back is framed by a black line and carries the player's name at the top, followed by biography and statistics.

	MINT	NRMT	EXC
COMPLETE SET (25)	7.00	3.10	.85

☐ 1 Everett Graham
☐ 2 Paul Meyers
☐ 3 Ty Dabney
☐ 4 Dennis Cook
☐ 5 Dean Freeland
☐ 6 Tony Perezchica
☐ 7 Scott Medvin
☐ 8 Greg Litton
☐ 9 Romy Cucjen
☐ 10 Kirt Manwaring
☐ 11 Todd Thomas
☐ 12 Brian Ohnoutka
☐ 13 Jeff Brantley
☐ 14 John Burkett
☐ 15 Ed Puikunas
☐ 16 Randy McCament
☐ 17 Charlie Hayes
☐ 18 T.J. McDonald
☐ 19 Deron McCue
☐ 20 Stuart Tate
☐ 21 Tom Wasilewski
☐ 22 John Grimes
☐ 23 Vince Sferazza
☐ 24 Marty DeMerritt
☐ 25 Jack Mull

1987 Southern League All-Stars Jennings

	MINT	NRMT	EXC
COMPLETE SET (25)	8.00	3.60	1.00

☐ 1 Dave Falcone
☐ 2 Rondal Rollin
☐ 3 Geronimo Berroa
☐ 4 Bernie Tatis
☐ 5 Nelson Santovenia
☐ 6 Tom Dodd
☐ 7 Cameron Drew
☐ 8 Larry Walker
☐ 9 Matt Winters
☐ 10 Ken Caminiti
☐ 11 Dave Myers
☐ 12 Jimmy Jones
☐ 13 Ronnie Gant
☐ 14 John Trautwein
☐ 15 Rob Mallicoat
☐ 16 Randy Johnson
☐ 17 Kevin Price
☐ 18 Steve Gasser
☐ 19 Kevin Coffman
☐ 20 Adam Peterson
☐ 21 Jeff Bettendorf
☐ 22 Jim Beauchamp MG
☐ 23 Rico Petrocelli CO
☐ 24 Greg Biagini CO
☐ 25 Leo Mazzone CO

1987 Spartanburg Phillies ProCards

This 28-card standard-size set of the 1987 Spartanburg Phillies, a Class A South Atlantic League affiliate of the Philadelphia Phillies, features white-bordered posed color player photos on its fronts. The player's name and position appear at the bottom. The white horizontal back is framed by a black line and carries the player's name at the top, followed by biography and statistics.

	MINT	NRMT	EXC
COMPLETE SET (28)	5.00	2.20	.60

☐ 1 Jim Platts
☐ 2 Peter Maldonado
☐ 3 Gene Bierscheid
☐ 4 Jeff Stark
☐ 5 Charles McElroy
☐ 6 Mark Sims
☐ 7 Garry Clark
☐ 8 Keith Greene
☐ 9 Kenny Miller
☐ 10 Michel LaMarche
☐ 11 Ramon Aviles
☐ 12 Ron Nelson
☐ 13 Andy Ashby
☐ 14 Trey McCall
☐ 15 Todd Crosby
☐ 16 Cliff Walker
☐ 17 Martin Foley
☐ 18 Luis Iglesias
☐ 19 Elbi Romero
☐ 20 Vince Holyfield
☐ 21 Jeff Grotewald
☐ 22 Bob Tiefenauer
☐ 23 Vladimir Perez
☐ 24 Cesar Dela Rosa
☐ 25 Phillip Price
☐ 26 Scott Hufford
☐ 27 Fred Christopher
☐ 28 Mike Colpitt

1987 Spokane Indians ProCards

This 25-card standard-size set of the 1987 Spokane Indians, a Class A Northwest League affiliate of the San Diego Padres, features white-bordered posed color player photos on its fronts. The player's name and position appear at the bottom. The white horizontal back is framed by a black line and carries the player's name at the top, followed by biography and statistics. This issue includes the minor league card debut of Jose Valentin.

	MINT	NRMT	EXC
COMPLETE SET (25)	8.00	3.60	1.00

☐ 1 Osvaldo Sanchez
☐ 2 Darrin Reichle
☐ 3 Tony Lewis
☐ 4 Saul Soltero
☐ 5 Jay Estrada
☐ 6 Rich Holsman
☐ 7 Andy Skeels
☐ 8 David Hollins
☐ 9 Charles Hilleman
☐ 10 Steve Lubratich
☐ 11 Reggie Farmer
☐ 12 Monte Brooks
☐ 13 Bobby Sheridan
☐ 14 Kevin Farmer
☐ 15 Francisco delaCruz
☐ 16 David Bond
☐ 17 Paul Faries
☐ 18 Bob Lutticken
☐ 19 Terry Gilmore
☐ 20 Pedro Aquino
☐ 21 Todd Torchia
☐ 22 Steve Hendricks
☐ 23 Jose Valentin
☐ 24 Mike Myers
☐ 25 Dustin Picciolo
☐ 26 Rob Picciolo

1987 Springfield Cardinals Best

This issue includes the minor league card debut of Bernard Gilkey and a second year card of Todd Zeile.

	MINT	NRMT	EXC
COMPLETE SET (28)	15.00	6.75	1.85

☐ 1 Gaylen R. Pitts MG
☐ 2 Mark A. Riggins CO
☐ 3 Alexander Ojea
☐ 4 Stephen W. Meyer
☐ 5 James W. Puzey
☐ 6 Ronald M. Johns
☐ 7 Tim Lemons
☐ 8 John T. Baine
☐ 9 Jeffrey L. Graham
☐ 10 William E. Bivens
☐ 11 Robert J. Faron
☐ 12 Stephen F. Hill
☐ 13 Howard Hilton
☐ 14 David Takach
☐ 15 Michael I. Perez
☐ 16 David J. Sala
☐ 17 Scott W. Hamilton
☐ 18 Robert A. Glisson
☐ 19 Michael Scott Raziano
☐ 20 Brian Farley
☐ 21 Larry R. Breedlove
☐ 22 Bienvenido Figueroa
☐ 23 Vincent L. Kindred
☐ 24 Scott Melvin
☐ 25 Otis Bernard Gilkey
☐ 26 Todd E. Zeile
☐ 27 Brad Bluestone TR
☐ 28 Scott Norman

1987 St. Petersburg Cardinals ProCards

This 27-card standard-size set of the 1987 St. Petersburg Cardinals, a Class A Florida State League affiliate of the St. Louis Cardinals, features white-bordered posed color player photos on its fronts. The player's name and position appear at the bottom. The white horizontal back is framed by a black line and carries the player's name at the top, followed by biography and statistics.

	MINT	NRMT	EXC
COMPLETE SET (27)	5.00	2.20	.60

☐ 1 Dave Osteen
☐ 2 Craig Wilson
☐ 3 Jesus Mendez
☐ 4 Mike Sassone
☐ 5 Mike Robertson
☐ 6 Mauricio Nunez
☐ 7 Brett Harrison
☐ 8 Joe Cunningham Jr.
☐ 9 Michael Senne
☐ 10 Tom Amante
☐ 11 Mike Fox
☐ 12 Dave Horton
☐ 13 John Murphy
☐ 14 David DeCordova
☐ 15 Chris Forrest
☐ 16 Hans Herzog
☐ 17 Tom Mauch
☐ 18 Dave Bialas
☐ 19 Marty Mason
☐ 20 Crucito Lara
☐ 21 William Hershmann
☐ 22 Benito Malave
☐ 23 Gregory Becker
☐ 24 Randy Butts
☐ 25 Jay North
☐ 26 Pete Fagan
☐ 27 Rob Livchak

1987 Stockton Ports ProCards

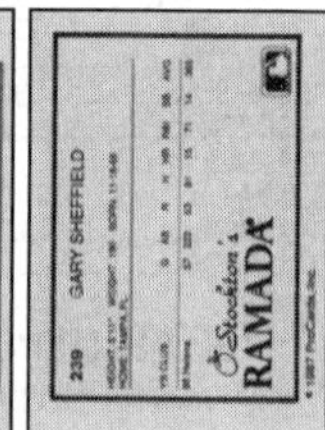

This 26-card standard-size set of the 1987 Stockton Ports, a Class A California League affiliate of the Milwaukee Brewers, features white-bordered posed color player photos on its fronts. The player's name and position appear at the bottom. The white horizontal back is framed by a black line and carries the player's name at the top, followed by biography and statistics. This issue includes the minor league card debut of Gary Sheffield.

	MINT	NRMT	EXC
COMPLETE SET (26)	40.00	18.00	5.00

☐ 1 Gary Sheffield
☐ 2 Rob Derksen
☐ 3 Dave Machemer
☐ 4 Sandy Guerrero
☐ 5 Todd France
☐ 6 Danny Fitzpatrick
☐ 7 Mario Monico
☐ 8 Daryl Hamilton
☐ 9 Renard Brown
☐ 10 Angel Rodriguez
☐ 11 Isaiah Clark
☐ 12 Charley McGrew
☐ 13 Martin Montano
☐ 14 Ruben Escalera
☐ 15 Mike Frew
☐ 16 John Ludy
☐ 17 Luis Castillo
☐ 18 Geroge Canale
☐ 19 Jim Hunter
☐ 20 Keith Fleming
☐ 21 Carl Moraw
☐ 22 Tim Torricelli
☐ 23 Jim Morris
☐ 25 Gary Kanwisher
☐ 26 Fred Williams
☐ 27 Ed Puig

1987 Sumter Braves ProCards

This 30-card standard-size set of the 1987 Sumter Braves, a Class A South Atlantic League affiliate of the Atlanta Braves, features white-bordered posed color player photos on its fronts. The player's name and position appear at the bottom. The white horizontal back is framed by a black line and carries the player's name at the top, followed by biography and statistics.

	MINT	NRMT	EXC
COMPLETE SET (30)	8.00	3.60	1.00

☐ 1 Jerald Frost
☐ 2 William "Matt" Turner
☐ 3 Miguel Sabino
☐ 4 Walt Williams
☐ 5 Bob McNally
☐ 6 Clarence Jones CO
☐ 7 Kevin Brown
☐ 8 Rusty Richards
☐ 9 Paul Marak
☐ 10 Buddy Bailey
☐ 11 Mark Clark
☐ 12 Kevin Harmon

☐ 13 David Plumb
☐ 14 Carl Jones
☐ 15 Rich Longuil
☐ 16 Mike Bell
☐ 17 Jesse Minton
☐ 18 Rich Maloney
☐ 19 Jim Czajkowski
☐ 20 Jim LeMasters
☐ 21 Larry Jaster CO
☐ 22 Danny Rogers
☐ 23 Ken Pennington
☐ 24 Al Martin
☐ 25 James Nowlin
☐ 26 Brian Deak
☐ 27 Sean Ross
☐ 28 Gerald Wagner
☐ 29 David Butts
☐ 30 Jay Johnson

1987 Syracuse Chiefs 10th Anniversary

1978-87 Souvenir Ticket set, unnumbered

	MINT	NRMT	EXC
COMPLETE SET (12)			

☐ 1 Lloyd Mosbey
☐ 2 Willie Upshaw
☐ 3 Dave Stieb
☐ 4 Garth Iorg
☐ 5 Ernie Whitt
☐ 6 Tom Henke
☐ 7 Rick Leach
☐ 8 Jimmy Key
☐ 9 John Cerutti
☐ 10 George Bell
☐ 11 Mark Eichhorn
☐ 12 Tony Fernandez

1987 Syracuse Chiefs ProCards

This 23-card standard-size set of the 1987 Syracuse Chiefs, a Class AAA International League affiliate of the Toronto Blue Jays, features white-bordered posed color player photos on its fronts. The player's name and position appear at the bottom. The white horizontal back is framed by a black line and carries the player's name at the top, followed by biography and statistics.

	MINT	NRMT	EXC
COMPLETE SET (23)	5.00	2.20	.60

☐ 1928 Sil Campusano
☐ 1929 Nelson Liriano
☐ 1930 Lou Thornton
☐ 1931 Greg Myers
☐ 1932 Don Gordon
☐ 1933 Steve Fireovid
(Misspelled Firevoid on front and back)
☐ 1934 Doug Ault MG
☐ 1935 Alex Infante
☐ 1936 Jose Segura
☐ 1937 Luis Aquino
☐ 1938 Todd Stottlemyre
☐ 1939 Tony Hudson
☐ 1940 Dave Stenhouse
☐ 1941 Manuel Lee
☐ 1942 Otis Green
☐ 1943 Rob Ducey
☐ 1944 Jose Escobar
☐ 1945 Jose Castro
☐ 1946 Dave LaRoche CO
☐ 1947 Hector Torres CO
☐ 1948 Steve Davis
☐ 1949 Doc Estes
☐ 1950 Glenallen Hill

1987 Syracuse Chiefs TCMA

This 33-card set of the 1987 Syracuse Chiefs, a Class AAA International League affiliate of the Toronto Blue Jays, measures about 2 1/2" by 3 3/4" and features white-bordered posed color player photos on its fronts. The player's name and position appear at the bottom. The white back carries the league and team names at the top, followed by the player's name, position, biography, and statistics.

	MINT	NRMT	EXC
COMPLETE SET (33)	4.00	1.80	.50

☐ 1 Luis Aquino
☐ 2 Steve Davis
☐ 3 Jeff Hearron
☐ 4 Don Gordon
☐ 5 Odell Jones
☐ 6 Colin McLaughlin
☐ 7 Jose Segura
☐ 8 Todd Stottlemyre
☐ 9 David Wells
☐ 10 Greg Myers
☐ 11 Dave Stenhouse
☐ 12 Jose Castro
☐ 13 Jose Escobar
☐ 14 Otis Green
☐ 15 Alex Infante
☐ 16 Manuel Lee
☐ 17 Nelson Liriano
☐ 18 Sil Campusano
☐ 19 Rob Ducey
☐ 20 Glenallen Hill
☐ 21 Lou Thornton
☐ 22 Doc Estes
☐ 23 Doug Ault MG
☐ 24 Dave LaRoche CO
☐ 25 Hector Torres CO
☐ 26 Don Gordon
Joe Kucharski
☐ 27 Rocky Coyle
☐ 28 Mel Queen CO
☐ 29 Kash Beauchamp
☐ 30 Steve Fireovid
☐ 31 Randy Day
☐ 32 Eddie Mahar
☐ 33 Red Coughlin TR

1987 Tacoma Tigers ProCards

This 23-card standard-size set of the 1987 Tacoma Tigers, a Class AAA Pacific Coast League affiliate of the Oakland Athletics, features white-bordered posed color player photos on its fronts. The player's name and position appear at the bottom. The white horizontal back is framed by a black line and carries the player's name at the top, followed by biography and statistics.

	MINT	NRMT	EXC
COMPLETE SET (23)	5.00	2.20	.60

☐ 1 Tim Dozier
☐ 2 Darrel Ackerfelds
☐ 3 Stan Kyles
☐ 4 Bobby Clark
☐ 5 Gary Jones
☐ 6 Wayne Krenchicki
☐ 7 Dave Van Ohlen
☐ 8 Bruce Tanner
☐ 9 Matt Sinatro
☐ 10 Thad Reece
☐ 11 Eric Broersma
☐ 12 Chuck Estrada
☐ 13 Steve Henderson
☐ 14 Keith Liepman
☐ 15 Roy Johnson
☐ 16 Dan Rohn
☐ 17 Jose Tolentino
☐ 18 Bill Mooneyham
☐ 19 Jerry Willard
☐ 20 Alejandro Sanchez
☐ 21 Tim Belcher
☐ 22 Brian Dorsett
☐ 23 Tim Birtsas

1987 Tampa Tarpons ProCards

This 30-card standard-size set of the 1987 Tampa Tarpons, a Class A Florida State League affiliate of the Cincinnati Reds, features white-bordered posed color player photos on its fronts. The player's name and position appear at the bottom. The white horizontal back is framed by a black line and carries the player's name at the top, followed by biography and statistics.

	MINT	NRMT	EXC
COMPLETE SET (30)	5.00	2.20	.60

☐ 1 Gary Denbo
☐ 2 Pete Carey
☐ 3 Mike Converse
☐ 4 Ken Huseby
☐ 5 Mike Roesler
☐ 6 Kevin Pearson
☐ 7 Juan Pinol
☐ 8 Marc Bombard
☐ 9 Tim Swob
☐ 10 Dwayne Williams
☐ 11 Tom Novak
☐ 12 Jeff Richardson
☐ 13 Bret Williamson
☐ 14 Jack Smith
☐ 15 Chris Hammond
☐ 16 Timber Mead
☐ 17 Kent Willis
☐ 18 Mark Jackson
☐ 19 Steve Davis
☐ 20 Gino Minutelli
☐ 21 Mike Campbell
☐ 22 Chris Fernandez
☐ 23 Neal Davenport
☐ 24 Scot Hilgenberg
☐ 25 Jeff Forney
☐ 26 Billy Hawley
☐ 27 Pete Beeler
☐ 28 Rod Zeratsky
☐ 29 Rich Sapienza
☐ 30 Mike Villa

1987 Texas League All-Stars Feder

	MINT	NRMT	EXC
COMPLETE SET (36)	25.00	11.00	3.10

☐ 1 Mike Debutch
☐ 2 Roy Silver
☐ 3 Joe Lynch
☐ 4 Doug Jennings
☐ 5 Brad Pounders
☐ 6 Jack Mull
☐ 7 Jeff Gardner
☐ 8 Roberto Alomar
☐ 9 Ed Jurak
☐ 10 Sandy Alomar Jr.
☐ 11 Gregg Jefferies
☐ 12 Joe Redfield
☐ 13 Steve Smith MG
☐ 14 Shane Young
☐ 15 Marty Reed
☐ 16 Joaquin Contreras
☐ 17 Jim St.Laurent
☐ 18 Thomas Howard
☐ 19 Steve Peters
☐ 20 John Miglio
☐ 21 Scott Arnold
☐ 22 Kirt Manwaring
☐ 23 Greg Harris
☐ 24 Marcus Lawton
☐ 25 LaVel Freeman
☐ 26 Mike Fitzgerald
☐ 27 Charlie Hayes
☐ 28 Mike Devereaux
☐ 29 David West
☐ 30 Jesus Alfaro
☐ 31 Ray Stephens
☐ 32 Ty Dabney
☐ 33 John Burkett
☐ 34 Jack Savage
☐ 35 Joe Szekely
☐ 36 Title/Logo Card
(blank back)

1987 Tidewater Tides ProCards

This 33-card standard-size set of the 1987 Tidewater Tides, a Class AAA International League affiliate of the New York Mets, features white-bordered posed color player photos on its fronts. The player's name and position appear at the bottom. The white horizontal back is framed by a black line and carries the player's name at the top, followed by biography and statistics.

	MINT	NRMT	EXC
COMPLETE SET (33)	8.00	3.60	1.00

☐ 1 Clint Hurdle
☐ 2 DeWayne Vaughn
☐ 3 Reggie Dobie
☐ 4 Jeff McKnight
☐ 5 Terry Blocker
☐ 6 John Gibbons
☐ 7 Jason Felice
☐ 8 Jeff Innis
☐ 9 Tom Edens
☐ 10 Keith Miller
☐ 11 Steve Springer
☐ 12 Mike Cubbage
☐ 13 Tom McCarthy
☐ 14 Dave Wyatt
☐ 15 Ed Glynn
☐ 16 Ricky Nelson
☐ 17 Tom Lombarski
☐ 18 John Cumberland
☐ 19 Greg Olson
☐ 20 John Mitchell
☐ 21 Mark Carreon
☐ 22 Bill Latham
☐ 23 Jose Roman
☐ 24 Andre David
☐ 25 Don Schulze
☐ 26 Bob Buchanan
☐ 27 Gene Walter
☐ 28 Randy Milligan
☐ 29 Rob Evans
☐ 30 Rick Rainer
☐ 31 Dwight Gooden
☐ 32 Kevin Elster
☐ 33 Bob Gibson

1987 Tidewater Tides TCMA

	MINT	NRMT	EXC
COMPLETE SET (30)	6.00	2.70	.75

☐ 1 Reggie Dobie
☐ 2 Tom Edens
☐ 3 Bob Gibson
☐ 4 Ed Glynn
☐ 5 Jeff Innis
☐ 6 Tom McCarthy
☐ 7 John Mitchell
☐ 8 DeWayne Vaughn
☐ 9 Dave Wyatt
☐ 10 John Gibbons
☐ 11 Greg Olson
☐ 12 Andre David
☐ 13 Kevin Elster
☐ 14 Tom Lombarski
☐ 15 Jeff McKnight
☐ 16 Keith Miller
☐ 17 Randy Milligan
☐ 18 Steve Springer
☐ 19 Terry Blocker
☐ 20 Mark Carreon
☐ 21 Gene Walter
☐ 22 Clint Hurdle
☐ 23 Mike Cubbage
☐ 24 John Cumberland
☐ 25 Rick Rainer
☐ 26 Don Schulze
☐ 27 Bob Buchanan
☐ 28 Bill Latham
☐ 29 Jose Roman
☐ 30 Dwight Gooden

1987 Toledo Mud Hens ProCards

This 30-card standard-size set of the 1987 Toledo Mud Hens, a Class AAA International League affiliate of the Detroit Tigers, features white-bordered posed color player photos on its fronts. The player's name and position appear at the bottom. The white horizontal back is framed by a black line and carries the player's name at the top, followed by biography and statistics.

	MINT	NRMT	EXC
COMPLETE SET (30)	6.00	2.70	.75

☐ 1 Scott Earl
☐ 2 Steve Searcy
☐ 3 Scott Lusader
☐ 4 German Rivera
☐ 5 Jim Walewander
☐ 6 Ricky Wright
☐ 7 Don Heinkel
☐ 8 John Pacella
☐ 9 Ricky Barlow
☐ 10 Paul Gibson
☐ 11 Fred Tiburcio
☐ 12 Tim Tolman
☐ 13 Jed Murray
☐ 14 Bruce Fields
☐ 15 Rey Palacios
☐ 16 Mike Henneman
☐ 17 Doug Baker
☐ 18 Morris Madden
☐ 19 Mike Stenhouse
☐ 20 Leon Roberts
☐ 21 Bill Laskey
☐ 22 Gene Roof
☐ 23 Don McGann
☐ 24 Jeff Ransom
☐ 25 John Hiller
☐ 26 Billy Bean
☐ 27 Willie Hernandez
☐ 28 Kirk Gibson
☐ 29 Bryan Kelly
☐ 30 Jerry Davis

1987 Toledo Mud Hens TCMA

	MINT	NRMT	EXC
COMPLETE SET (25)	4.00	1.80	.50

☐ 1 Rey Palacios
☐ 2 Don Heinkel
☐ 3 German Rivera
☐ 4 Bill Laskey
☐ 5 Mike Stenhouse
☐ 6 Fred Tiburcio
☐ 7 Jim Walewander
☐ 8 Scott Lusader
☐ 9 Bruce Fields
☐ 10 Scott Earl
☐ 11 Jeff Ransom
☐ 12 James R. Wright
☐ 13 Mike Henneman
☐ 14 John Pacella
☐ 15 Morris Madden
☐ 16 Steve Searcy
☐ 17 Paul Gibson
☐ 18 Jed Murray
☐ 19 Ricky Barlow
☐ 20 Doug Baker
☐ 21 Leon Roberts
☐ 22 Gene Roof
☐ 23 Tim Tolman
☐ 24 Jerry Davis
☐ 25 Dwight Lowry

1987 Tucson Toros ProCards

This 25-card standard-size set of the 1987 Tucson Toros, a Class AAA Pacific Coast League affiliate of the Houston Astros, features white-bordered posed color player photos on its fronts. The player's name and position appear at the bottom. The white horizontal back is framed by a black line and carries the player's name at the top, followed by biography and statistics.

	MINT	NRMT	EXC
COMPLETE SET (25)	5.00	2.20	.60

☐ 1 Juan Agosto
☐ 2 Glenn Carpenter
☐ 3 Robbie Wine
☐ 4 Bill Crone
☐ 5 Rafael Montalvo
☐ 6 Tye Waller
☐ 7 Manny Hernandez
☐ 8 Dale Berra
☐ 9 Louie Meadows
☐ 10 Rocky Childress
☐ 11 Gerald Young
☐ 12 Ray Fontenot
☐ 13 Jim Miner
☐ 14 Ron Mathis
☐ 15 Nelson Rood
☐ 16 Bert Pena
☐ 17 Kevin Hagen
☐ 18 Jeff Heathcock
☐ 19 Eric Bullock
☐ 20 Ronn Reynolds
☐ 21 Anthony Kelley
☐ 22 Eddie Watt
☐ 23 Ty Gainey
☐ 24 Bob Didier
☐ 25 Tom Funk

1987 Utica Blue Sox ProCards

This 33-card standard-size set of the 1987 Utica Blue Sox, a Class A New York-Penn League affiliate of the Philadelphia Phillies, features white-bordered posed color player photos on its fronts. The player's name and position appear at the bottom. The white horizontal back is framed by a black line and carries the player's name at the top, followed by biography and statistics.

	MINT	NRMT	EXC
COMPLETE SET (33)	5.00	2.20	.60

☐ 1 Manlio Perez
☐ 2 Leroy Ventress
☐ 3 Rafael Bustamante
☐ 4 Kim Batiste
☐ 5 Scott Ruckman
☐ 6 Shelby McDonald
☐ 7 Troy Zerb
☐ 8 Robert Jones
☐ 9 Jim Vatcher
☐ 10 Doug Lindsey
☐ 11 Jeffrey Scott
☐ 12 Gary White
☐ 13 Mark Cobb
☐ 14 Bob Chadwick
☐ 15 David Monterio
☐ 16 Marc Lopez
☐ 17 Rick Trlicek
☐ 18 Steve Kirkpatrick
☐ 19 Darrell Coulter
☐ 20 Scott Reaves
☐ 21 Joe Williams
☐ 22 Royal Thomas
☐ 23 John Larosa
☐ 24 Timothy Peek
☐ 25 Andy Ashby
☐ 26 Matt Rambo
☐ 27 Jaime Barragan
☐ 28 Robert Hurta
☐ 29 Phil Fagnano
☐ 30 Corey Smith
☐ 31 Ike Galloway
☐ 32 Dave Allen
☐ 33 Greg McCarthy

1987 Vancouver Canadians ProCards

This 25-card standard-size set of the 1987 Vancouver Canadians, a Class AAA Pacific Coast League affiliate of the Pittsburgh Pirates, features white-bordered posed color player photos on its fronts. The player's name and position appear at the bottom. The white horizontal back is framed by a black line and carries the player's name at the top, followed by biography and statistics.

	MINT	NRMT	EXC
COMPLETE SET (25)	5.00	2.20	.60

☐ 1598 Mike Bielecki
☐ 1599 Jackie Brown
☐ 1600 Jeff Cox
☐ 1601 Carlos LeDezma TR
☐ 1602 Mark Ross
☐ 1603 Tommy Dunbar
☐ 1604 Stan Fansler
☐ 1605 Rocky Bridges MG
☐ 1606 Dave Johnson
☐ 1607 Sammy Haro
☐ 1608 Sammy Khalifa
☐ 1609 Houston Jimenez
☐ 1610 Tim Drummond
☐ 1611 Dave Leeper
☐ 1612 Mike Dunne
☐ 1613 Randy Kramer
☐ 1614 Butch Davis
☐ 1615 Hipolito Pena
☐ 1616 Jose Lind
☐ 1617 Larry Ray
☐ 1618 Danny Bilardello
☐ 1619 Vincente Palacios
☐ 1620 Ruben Rodriquez
☐ 1621 Dorn Taylor
☐ 1622 U.L. Washington

1987 Vermont Reds ProCards

This 26-card standard-size set of the 1987 Vermont Reds, a Class AA Eastern League affiliate of the Cincinnati Reds, features white-bordered posed color player photos on its fronts. The player's name and position appear at the bottom. The white horizontal back is framed by a black line and carries the player's name at the top, followed by biography and statistics.

	MINT	NRMT	EXC
COMPLETE SET (26)	5.00	2.20	.60

☐ 1 Brad Brusky
☐ 2 Jim Jefferson
☐ 3 Ted Langdon
☐ 4 Francisco Tenacen
☐ 5 Marty Brown
☐ 6 Greg Simpson
☐ 7 Ramon Sambo
☐ 8 Tim Mirabito
☐ 9 Rob Lopez
☐ 10 Joe Dunlap
☐ 11 Don Dietz
☐ 12 Mike Smith
☐ 13 Angelo Nunley
☐ 14 Steve Oliverio
☐ 15 John Bryant
☐ 16 Tom Runnells
☐ 17 Dave Miley
☐ 18 Glenn Spagnola
☐ 19 Joe Oliver
☐ 20 Mark Germann
☐ 21 Greg Monita
☐ 22 Chris Jones
☐ 24 Mark Berry
☐ 25 Darren Riley
☐ 26 Marvin Haynes
☐ 27 Rod Lich

1987 Vero Beach Dodgers ProCards

This 31-card standard-size set of the 1987 Vero Beach Dodgers, a Class A Florida State League affiliate of the Los Angeles Dodgers, features white-bordered posed color player photos on its fronts. The player's name and position appear at the bottom. The white horizontal back is framed by a black line and carries the player's name at the top, followed by biography and statistics.

	MINT	NRMT	EXC
COMPLETE SET (31)	8.00	3.60	1.00

☐ 1 John Wetteland
☐ 2 Jose Tapia
☐ 3 Joe Spagnuolo
☐ 4 Dan Pena
☐ 5 Darren Holmes
☐ 6 Pete Geist
☐ 7 Ramon Martinez
☐ 8 Pat Zachry
☐ 9 Fred Gegan
☐ 10 Ken Lambert
☐ 11 Manny Francois
☐ 12 Mancy Benitez
☐ 13 Mike Garner
☐ 14 Tom Thomas
☐ 15 Mike Batesole
☐ 16 Jeff Brown
☐ 17 Kevin Campbell
☐ 18 Rob Giesecke
☐ 19 Joe Kellelmark
☐ 20 Jay Hornacek
☐ 21 Felipe Esteban
☐ 22 Tom Beyers
☐ 23 Kevin Devine
☐ 24 Bryan Smith
☐ 25 Mike Burke
☐ 26 Bill Bartels
☐ 27 Rene Garcia
☐ 28 Lee Langley
☐ 29 Kevin Shea
☐ 30 John Shoemaker
☐ 31 Phil Torres

1987 Visalia Oaks ProCards

This 27-card standard-size set of the 1987 Visalia Oaks, a Class A California League affiliate of the Minnesota Twins, features white-bordered posed color player photos on its fronts. The player's name and position appear at the bottom. The white horizontal back is framed by a black line and carries the player's name at the top, followed by biography and statistics.

	MINT	NRMT	EXC
COMPLETE SET (27)	5.00	2.20	.60

☐ 1 Jamie Williams
☐ 2 Glen Myers
☐ 3 Kenny Morgan
☐ 4 Tim Cota
☐ 5 Rob Strube
☐ 6 Bob Lee
☐ 7 Jeff Perry
☐ 8 Kurt Walker
☐ 9 Troy Galloway
☐ 10 Dave Blakely
☐ 11 Park Pittman
☐ 12 Ike Goldstein
☐ 13 Chris Calvert
☐ 14 Tim Senne
☐ 15 Kenny Davis
☐ 16 Mike Redding
☐ 17 Tim O'Conner
☐ 18 Todd Burke
☐ 19 Joey Aragon
☐ 20 Joey Zellner
☐ 21 John Pust
☐ 22 Mike Adams
☐ 23 Marty Lanoux
☐ 24 Gordon Heimueller
☐ 25 Dan Schatz
☐ 26 Clark Lange
☐ 27 Shannon Raybon

1987 Waterloo Indians ProCards

This 29-card standard-size set of the 1987 Waterloo Indians, a Class A Midwest League affiliate of the Cleveland Indians, features white-bordered posed color player photos on its fronts. The player's name and position appear at the bottom. The white horizontal back is framed by a black line and carries the player's name at the top, followed by biography and statistics.

	MINT	NRMT	EXC
COMPLETE SET (29)	5.00	2.20	.60

☐ 1 Fidel Compres
☐ 2 Manny Mercado
☐ 3 Jim Richardson
☐ 4 Steve Johnigan
☐ 5 Brad Wolten
☐ 6 Mark Pike
☐ 7 Dave Alvis
☐ 8 Tom Gamba
☐ 9 Scott Johnson
☐ 10 Glenn Adams
☐ 11 Todd Ganzales
☐ 12 Kevin Kuykendall
☐ 13 John Githens
☐ 14 Mike Walker
☐ 15 Bruce Egloff
☐ 16 Jeff Shaw
☐ 17 Carl Chambers
☐ 18 Rudy Seanez
☐ 19 Paul Kuzniar
☐ 20 Don Santos
☐ 21 Keith Seifert
☐ 22 Ray Williamson
☐ 23 Tom Lampkin
☐ 24 Riley Polk
☐ 25 Glenn Fairchild
☐ 26 Claudio Carrasco
☐ 27 Lenny Randle
☐ 28 Dan Redmond
☐ 29 Rick Adair

1987 Watertown Pirates ProCards

This 31-card standard-size set of the 1987 Watertown Pirates, a Class A New York-Penn League affiliate of the Pittsburgh Pirates, features white-bordered posed color player photos on its fronts. The player's name and position appear at the bottom. The white horizontal back is framed by a black line and carries the player's name at the top, followed by biography and statistics. This issue includes a second year card of Moises Alou.

	MINT	NRMT	EXC
COMPLETE SET (31)	15.00	6.75	1.85

☐ 1 Ben Webb
☐ 2 Rodger Castner
☐ 3 Robert Harris
☐ 4 Ed Shea
☐ 5 Scott Runge
☐ 6 Chip Duncan
☐ 7 Scott Barczi
☐ 8 Keith Raisanen
☐ 9 Pete Freeman
☐ 10 Steve Carter
☐ 11 Kevin Burdick
☐ 12 Wesley Chamberlain
☐ 13 Domingo Merejo
☐ 14 Junior Vizcaino
☐ 15 Keith Shepherd
☐ 16 Ed Hartman
☐ 17 Jose Acosta
☐ 18 Jim Garrison
☐ 19 Jody Williams
☐ 20 Mark Thomas
☐ 21 Rob Barnwell
☐ 22 Jeff Griffith
☐ 23 Joe Pacholec
☐ 24 Pete Murphy
☐ 25 Mark Koller
☐ 26 Joe Macavage
☐ 27 Moises Alou
☐ 28 Doug Torborg
☐ 29 Charlie Green
☐ 30 Jeff Cox
☐ 31 Mike Sandoval

1987 Wausau Timbers ProCards

This 28-card standard-size set of the 1987 Wausau Timbers, a Class A Midwest League affiliate of the Seattle Mariners, features white-bordered posed color player photos on its fronts. The player's name and position appear at the bottom. The white horizontal back is framed by a black line and carries the player's name at the top, followed by biography and statistics.

	MINT	NRMT	EXC
COMPLETE SET (28)	5.00	2.20	.60

☐ 1 Bobby Cuellar
☐ 2 Jim Blueberg
☐ 3 Jody Ryan
☐ 4 Dan Disher
☐ 5 Howard Townsend
☐ 6 Troy Williams
☐ 7 Patrick Lennon
☐ 8 Jose Tartabull
☐ 9 Wendell Bolar
☐ 10 Clay Gunn
☐ 11 Jose Bennett
☐ 12 Ted Williams
☐ 13 Anthony Woods
☐ 14 Drew Kosco
☐ 15 Jim Bowie
☐ 16 Mark Wooden
☐ 17 Jerry Goff
☐ 18 Deron Johnson
☐ 19 Mike Thorpe
☐ 20 Michael McDonald
☐ 21 Trent Intorcia
☐ 22 Dave Hartnett
☐ 23 Mark Gold
☐ 24 Pat Rice
☐ 25 Rudy Webster
☐ 27 Ric Wilson
☐ 28 Tim Erickson

1987 West Palm Beach Expos ProCards

This 28-card standard-size set of the 1987 West Palm Beach Expos, a Class A Florida State League affiliate of the Montreal Expos, features white-bordered posed color player photos on its fronts. The player's name and position appear at the bottom. The white horizontal back is framed by a black line and carries the player's name at the top, followed by biography and statistics.

	MINT	NRMT	EXC
COMPLETE SET (28)	5.00	2.20	.60

☐ 652 Rob Leary
☐ 653 Tim Touma
☐ 654 Paul Frye
☐ 655 Alfredo Cardwood
☐ 656 Jeff Tabaka
☐ 657 Rob Williams
☐ 658 Derrell Baker
☐ 659 Pat Sipe
☐ 660 Kevin Dean
☐ 661 Bob Caffrey
☐ 662 Bud Yanus CO
☐ 663 Don Burke
☐ 664 Mike Blowers
☐ 665 Cesar Hernandez
☐ 666 Al Collins
☐ 667 Yorkis Perez
☐ 668 Charlie Lea
☐ 669 Omer Munoz
☐ 670 Mel Houston
☐ 671 Tommy Traen
☐ 672 Eddie Dixon
☐ 673 Kevin Kristan
☐ 674 Jeff Huson
☐ 675 Don Burke
☐ 676 Steve Rousey
☐ 677 Gene Harris
☐ 678 Geff Davis
☐ 679 John Spinosa TR

1987 Wichita Pilots Rock's Dugout

This issue includes the minor league card debut of Roberto Alomar.

	MINT	NRMT	EXC
COMPLETE SET (25)	80.00	36.00	10.00

☐ 1 Mike DeButch
☐ 2 Kevin Armstrong

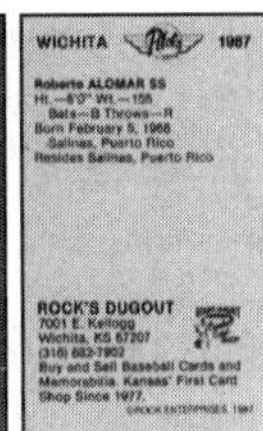

☐ 3 Tommy Alexander
☐ 4 Roberto Alomar
☐ 5 Sandy Alomar Jr.
☐ 6 Nate Colbert
☐ 7 Chris Knabenshue
☐ 8 Brad Pounders
☐ 9 Steve Smith
☐ 10 Joe Lynch
☐ 11 Greg Harris
☐ 12 Eric Nolte
☐ 13 Thomas Howard
☐ 14 Jeff Reece
☐ 15 Mike Costello
☐ 16 Scott Rainey
☐ 17 Jeff Stewart
☐ 18 Dave Cortez
☐ 19 Tom Brassil
☐ 20 Candy Sierra
☐ 21 Kevin Brown
☐ 22 Eric Bauer
☐ 23 Steve Luebber
☐ 24 Jerald Clark
☐ 25 Cam Walker

1987 Williamsport Bills ProCards

This 27-card standard-size set of the 1987 Williamsport Bills, a Class AA Eastern League affiliate of the Cleveland Indians, features white-bordered posed color player photos on its fronts. The player's name and position appear at the bottom. The white horizontal back is framed by a black line and carries the player's name at the top, followed by biography and statistics.

	MINT	NRMT	EXC
COMPLETE SET (27)	5.00	2.20	.60

☐ 1 Dain Syverson
☐ 2 Deith Bennett
☐ 3 Winston Ficklin
☐ 4 Oscar Mejia
☐ 5 Luis Encarnacion
☐ 6 Steve Moses
☐ 7 Bobby Link
☐ 8 Jim Bishop
☐ 9 Mark Higgins
☐ 10 Mike Bellaman
☐ 11 Ivan Murrell
☐ 12 Daryl Smith
☐ 13 Miguel Roman
☐ 14 Dave Breshnahan
☐ 15 Rick Henke
☐ 16 Brian Allard
☐ 17 Greg LaFever
☐ 18 Steve Swisher
☐ 19 Greg Dube
☐ 20 Scott Sabo
☐ 21 Roger Wilson
☐ 22 Chris Beasley
☐ 23 Bernardo Brito
☐ 24 Luis Medina
☐ 25 Turner Gill
☐ 26 Greg Karpuk
☐ 27 Joe Skalski

1987 Winston-Salem Spirits ProCards

This 27-card standard-size set of the 1987 Winston-Salem Spirits, a Class A Carolina League affiliate of the Chicago Cubs, features white-bordered posed color player photos on its fronts. The player's name and position appear at the bottom. The white horizontal back is framed by a black line and carries the player's name at the top, followed by biography and statistics.

	MINT	NRMT	EXC
COMPLETE SET (27)	5.00	2.20	.60

☐ 1 Mark McMorris
☐ 2 Greg Kallevig
☐ 3 Todd Cloninger
☐ 4 Cedric Landrum
☐ 5 Bill Danek
☐ 6 Phil Hannon
☐ 7 Heath Slocumb
☐ 8 Bob Bafia
☐ 9 Luiz Cruz
☐ 10 Jim Bullinger
☐ 11 Tad Slowik
☐ 12 Glenn Gregson
☐ 13 Jay Loviglio
☐ 14 Lee Grimes
☐ 15 Tim Wallace
☐ 16 John Lewis
☐ 17 Joe Girardi
☐ 18 Gabby Robles
☐ 19 Mike Tullier
☐ 20 Mike Miller
☐ 21 Chuck Dertli
☐ 22 Kris Roth
☐ 23 Jeff Hirsch
☐ 24 Jeff Small
☐ 25 Dewayne Coleman
☐ 26 Jim Matas
☐ 27 Mike Curtis

1987 Winter Haven Red Sox ProCards

This 30-card standard-size set of the 1987 Winter Haven Red Sox, a Class A Florida State league affiliate of the Boston Red Sox, features white-bordered posed color player photos on its fronts. The player's name and position appear at the bottom. The white horizontal back is framed by a black line and carries the player's name at the top, followed by biography and statistics.

	MINT	NRMT	EXC
COMPLETE SET (30)	5.00	2.20	.60

☐ 1 Tim Buheller
☐ 2 Felix Dedos
☐ 3 Livio Padilla
☐ 4 Larry Shikles
☐ 5 Donnie McGowan
☐ 6 Bart Haley
☐ 7 Erik Laseke
☐ 8 Leverne Jackson
☐ 9 Daniel Sullivan
☐ 10 Dan Gabriele
☐ 11 Mike Coffey
☐ 12 Stuart Weidie
☐ 13 Bruce Lockhart
☐ 14 David Milstien
☐ 15 Odie Abril
☐ 16 John Toale
☐ 17 Manny Jose
☐ 18 Wayne Murphy
☐ 19 Mike Sears
☐ 20 Paul Slifko
☐ 21 Eduardo Zambrano
☐ 22 Eric Hetzel
☐ 23 Derek Livernois
☐ 24 Doug Camilli
☐ 25 Mike Ickes
☐ 26 Roger Haggerty
☐ 27 Paul Thoutsis
☐ 28 Jim Orsag
☐ 29 Todd Pratt
☐ 30 Dana Gomez

1987 Wytheville Cubs ProCards

This 31-card standard-size set of the 1987 Wytheville Cubs, a Rookie Class Appalachian League affiliate of the Chicago Cubs, features white-bordered posed color player photos on its fronts. The player's name and position appear at the bottom. The white horizontal back is framed by a black line and carries the player's name at the top, followed by biography and statistics.

	MINT	NRMT	EXC
COMPLETE SET (31)	5.00	2.20	.60

☐ 1 Anthony Whitson
☐ 2 Matt Walbeck
☐ 3 Horace Tucker
☐ 4 Scott Taylor
☐ 5 Derek Stroud
☐ 6 Dave Sommer
☐ 7 Jossy Rosario
☐ 8 Victor Quiles
☐ 9 Eric Perry
☐ 10 Elvin Paulino
☐ 11 Nelson Nunex
☐ 12 Greg Jackson
☐ 13 John Gardner
☐ 14 Edgar Galarza
☐ 15 Henry Fleming
☐ 16 Matthew Franco
☐ 17 Francisco Espino
☐ 18 Darren Eggleston
☐ 19 Jay Eddings
☐ 20 Braz Davis
☐ 21 Frank Castillo
☐ 22 Danny Carpenter
☐ 23 Carlos Canino
☐ 24 Frank Campos
☐ 25 Matt Cakora
☐ 26 Warren Arrington
☐ 27 Alex Arias
☐ 28 Tom King TR
☐ 29 Rick Kranitz CO
☐ 30 Brad Mills MG
☐ 31 Team Photo

1988 Albany Yankees ProCards

This 27-card standard-size set of the 1988 Albany Yankees, a Class AA Eastern League affiliate of the New York Yankees, features silver-bordered posed color player photos on its fronts. The player's name, position, and team name appear at the bottom. The plain white back carries the player's name at the top, followed by biography and statistics.

	MINT	NRMT	EXC
COMPLETE SET (27)	5.00	2.20	.60

☐ 1329 Amalio Carreno
☐ 1330 Andy Stankiewicz
☐ 1331 Bob Green
☐ 1332 Rob Sepanek
☐ 1333 Tim Layana
☐ 1334 Bobby Davidson
☐ 1335 Gary Cathcart
☐ 1336 Dave Eiland
☐ 1337 Mike Christopher
☐ 1338 Rick Torres
☐ 1339 Tony Ferreira
☐ 1340 Troy Evers
☐ 1341 Tim Becker
☐ 1342 Dana Ridenour
☐ 1343 Melvin Rosario
☐ 1344 Jim Leyritz
☐ 1345 Scott Shaw
☐ 1346 Jason Maas
☐ 1347 Oscar Azocar
☐ 1348 Aris Tirado
☐ 1349 Hensley Meulens
☐ 1350 Dickie Scott
☐ 1351 Deron Johnson CO
☐ 1352 Tommy Jones MGR
☐ 1353 Tony Cloninger CO
☐ 1354 Mike Heifferon TR
☐ NNO Checklist

1988 Albuquerque Dukes CMC

10,000 sets were produced.

	MINT	NRMT	EXC
COMPLETE SET (25)	4.00	1.80	.50

☐ 1 Shawn Hillegas
☐ 2 Stan Kyles
☐ 3 Bill Krueger
☐ 4 Ray Searage
☐ 5 Tony Arnold
☐ 6 Bill Brennan
☐ 7 Dennis Burtt
☐ 8 Tim Crews
☐ 9 Mike Hartley
☐ 10 Chuck Hensley
☐ 11 Hector Heredia
☐ 12 Chris Gwynn
☐ 13 George Hinshaw
☐ 14 Mike Ramsey
☐ 15 Jon Debus
☐ 16 Mike Sharperson
☐ 17 Tracy Woodson
☐ 18 Mike Devereaux
☐ 19 Joe Gonzalez
☐ 20 John Gibbons
☐ 21 Gil Reyes
☐ 22 Shanie Dugas
☐ 23 Mariano Duncan
☐ 24 Steve Garcia
☐ 25 Terry Collins

1988 Albuquerque Dukes ProCards

This 29-card standard-size set of the 1988 Albuquerque Dukes, a Class AAA Pacific Coast League affiliate of the Los Angeles Dodgers, features bronze-bordered posed color player photos on its fronts. The player's name, position, and team name appear at the bottom. The plain white back carries the player's name at the top, followed by biography and statistics.

	MINT	NRMT	EXC
COMPLETE SET (29)	5.00	2.20	.60

☐ 249 Steve Garcia
☐ 250 Bill Brennan
☐ 251 Brent Strom
☐ 252 Mike Devereaux
☐ 253 Mike Sharperson
☐ 254 Von Joshua
☐ 255 Mariano Duncan
☐ 256 Tracy Woodson
☐ 257 Gilberto Reyes
☐ 258 Jose Gonzales
☐ 259 Chris Gwynn
☐ 260 John Gibbons
☐ 261 Tony Arnold
☐ 262 Ray Searage
☐ 263 Mike Hartley
☐ 264 Tim Crews
☐ 265 Shawn Hillegas
☐ 266 Shanie Dugas
☐ 267 Mike Ramsey
☐ 268 George Hinshaw
☐ 269 Jon Debus
☐ 270 Terry Collins
☐ 271 Bill Krueger
☐ 272 Lenny Currier
☐ 273 Chuck Hensley
☐ 274 Hector Heredia
☐ 275 Stan Kyles
☐ 276 Dennis Burtt
☐ NNO Checklist

1988 Appleton Foxes ProCards

This 30-card standard-size set of the 1988 Appleton Foxes, a Class A Midwest League affiliate of the Kansas City Royals, features bronze-bordered posed color player photos on its fronts. The player's name, position, and team name appear at the bottom. The plain white back carries the player's name at the top, followed by biography and statistics.

	MINT	NRMT	EXC
COMPLETE SET (30)	5.00	2.20	.60

☐ 137 Jorge Pedre
☐ 138 Luis Mallea
☐ 139 Brian Meyers
☐ 140 Kevin Shaw
☐ 141 Doug Nelson
☐ 142 Terry Shumpert
☐ 143 Linton Dyer
☐ 144 Darryl Robinson
☐ 145 Dave Howard
☐ 146 Don Wright
☐ 147 Bill Stonikas
☐ 148 Karl Drezek
☐ 149 Tom Gordon
☐ 150 Tim Odom
☐ 151 Trey Gainous
☐ 152 Brian McCormack
☐ 153 Keith Shibata
☐ 154 Frank Henderson
☐ 155 Jesus Deleon
☐ 156 Chris Gurchiek
☐ 157 Doug Bock
☐ 158 Jeff Baum
☐ 159 Andre Rabouin
☐ 160 Dennis Moeller
☐ 161 Bobby Knecht
☐ 162 Brian Poldberg
☐ 163 Mike Leon
☐ 164 Larry Dawson
☐ 165 Team Photo
☐ NNO Checklist

1988 Arizona Wildcats Police

	MINT	NRMT	EXC
COMPLETE SET (16)	10.00	4.50	1.25

☐ 1 Brian Callahan
☐ 2 Todd Devereaux
☐ 3 Greg Fowble
☐ 4 Frank Halcovich
☐ 5 Trevor Hoffman
☐ 6 Jerry Kindall CO
☐ 7 Jason Klonoski
☐ 8 Heath Lane
☐ 9 Rick Lantrip
☐ 10 Kevin Long
☐ 11 Dave Shermet
☐ 12 J.T. Snow
☐ 13 Jerry Stitt ACO
☐ 14 Mike Thorell
☐ 15 Jim Wing CO
☐ 16 Alan Zinter

1988 Arkansas Travelers Grand Slam

	MINT	NRMT	EXC
COMPLETE SET (25)	7.00	3.10	.85

☐ 1 Rick Colbert
☐ 2 Brad Henderson
☐ 3 Steve Engel
☐ 4 Jim Riggleman
☐ 5 Jeff Fassero
☐ 6 Bien Figueroa
☐ 7 Todd Zeile
☐ 8 Tom Blaine
☐ 9 Bob Faron
☐ 10 Mauricio Nunez
☐ 11 Ken Infante
☐ 12 Howard Hilton
☐ 13 Brett Harrison
☐ 14 Matt Kinzer
☐ 15 Jesus Mendez
☐ 16 Jim Fregosi
☐ 17 Benito Malave
☐ 18 Mike Sassone
☐ 19 Mike Robinson

☐ 20 Mike Robertson
☐ 21 Mike Perez
☐ 22 Jim Puzey
☐ 23 Dave Osteen
☐ 24 Jeff Oyster
☐ 25 Mike Senne

1988 Asheville Tourists ProCards

This 31-card standard-size set of the 1988 Asheville Tourists, a Class A South Atlantic League affiliate of the Houston Astros, features bronze-bordered posed color player photos on its fronts. The player's name, position, and team name appear at the bottom. The plain white back carries the player's name at the top, followed by biography and statistics.

	MINT	NRMT	EXC
COMPLETE SET (31)	5.00	2.20	.60

☐ 1049 Billy Carver
☐ 1050 Kenny Dickson
☐ 1051 Greg Johnson
☐ 1052 Andy Harter
☐ 1053 Ramon Cedeno
☐ 1054 Mike Beams
☐ 1055 Joe Charno
☐ 1056 Carlos Laboy
☐ 1057 Neder Horta
☐ 1058 Ed Renteria
☐ 1059 Chris Lee
☐ 1060 Harold Allen
☐ 1061 Dan Lewis
☐ 1062 Gorky Perez
☐ 1063 F. Costello
☐ 1064 Roger Dale Locke
☐ 1065 Doug Royalty
☐ 1066 Joe Ortiz
☐ 1067 Charley Taylor
☐ 1068 Gary Tuck
☐ 1069 Rickie Simon
☐ 1070 Dennis Tafoya
☐ 1071 Danny Newman
☐ 1072 Dean Hartgraves
☐ 1073 Mike Hook
☐ 1074 Carlos Henry
☐ 1075 Dave Cunningham
☐ 1076 Gene Confreda
☐ 1077 Ron McKee
☐ 1078 Todd Weber
☐ NNO Checklist

1988 Auburn Astros ProCards

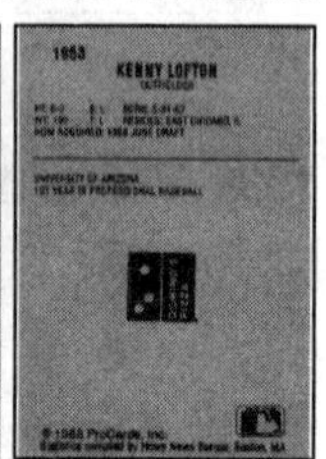

This 29-card standard-size set of the 1988 Auburn Astros, a Class A New York-Penn League affiliate of the Houston Astros, features bronze-bordered posed color player photos on its fronts. The player's name, position, and team name appear at the bottom. The plain white back carries the player's name at the top, followed by biography and statistics. This issue inlcudes the minor league card debut of Kenny Lofton.

	MINT	NRMT	EXC
COMPLETE SET (29)	40.00	18.00	5.00

☐ 1947 Larry Lamphere
☐ 1948 Scott Spurgeon
☐ 1949 Chris Small
☐ 1950 Wally Trice
☐ 1951 Dennis Tafoya
☐ 1952 Pat Penafeather
☐ 1953 Kenny Lofton
☐ 1954 Ron Porterfield
☐ 1955 Rodney Windes
☐ 1956 Harry Fuller
☐ 1957 Ken Morris
☐ 1958 Dave Shermet
☐ 1959 Bernie Jenkins
☐ 1960 Rod Scheckla
☐ 1961 John Massarelli
☐ 1962 Mike Beams
☐ 1963 Rick Wise
☐ 1964 Bob Neal
☐ 1965 Neder Horta
☐ 1966 Andy Mota
☐ 1967 Frank Cacciatore
☐ 1968 Jim DeSapio
☐ 1969 Rick Dunnum
☐ 1970 Gordy Farmer
☐ 1971 Johnny Graham
☐ 1972 David Klinefelter
☐ 1973 Luis Gonzalez
☐ 1974 Mica Lewis
☐ NNO Checklist

1988 Augusta Pirates ProCards

This 33-card standard-size set of the 1988 Augusta Pirates, a Class A South Atlantic League affiliate of the Pittsburgh Pirates, features bronze-bordered posed color player photos on its fronts. The player's name, position, and team name appear at the bottom. The plain white back carries the player's name at the top, followed by biography and statistics.

	MINT	NRMT	EXC
COMPLETE SET (33)	15.00	6.75	1.85

☐ 359 Wes Chamberlain
☐ 360 Moises Alou
☐ 361 Miguel Valverde
☐ 362 Mickey Peyton
☐ 363 Jeff Griffith
☐ 364 Orlando Merced
☐ 365 Carlos Garcia
☐ 366 Eddie Hartman
☐ 367 Pete Freeman
☐ 368 Scott Barczi
☐ 369 Jimmy Garrison
☐ 370 Ben Shelton
☐ 371 Jose Acosta
☐ 372 Joe Macavage
☐ 373 Joe Pacholec
☐ 374 Butch Schlopy
☐ 375 Keith Shepherd
☐ 376 Scott Runge
☐ 377 Willie Smith
☐ 378 Ron Downs
☐ 379 Tracy Toy
☐ 380 Tonny Cohen
☐ 381 Joel Forrest
☐ 382 Jeff Cox
☐ 383 Dave Moharter
☐ 384 Glenn Trudo
☐ 385 Steve Carter
☐ 386 Robert Harris
☐ 387 James Rhoades
☐ 388 Paul Day
☐ 389 Len Monheimer
☐ 1576 Mark Merchant
☐ NNO Checklist

1988 Bakersfield Dodgers Cal League Cards

	MINT	NRMT	EXC
COMPLETE SET (34)	5.00	2.20	.60

☐ 234 Jeff Brown
☐ 235 Dan Henley
☐ 236 John Knapp
☐ 237 Alan Lewis
☐ 238 Dan Montgomery
☐ 239 Jose Munoz
☐ 240 Jose Vizcaino
☐ 241 Amilcar Valdez
☐ 242 Adam Brown
☐ 243 Carlos Hernandez
☐ 244 Billy Argo
☐ 245 Jay Hornacek
☐ 246 John Beuder
☐ 247 Bruce Dostal
☐ 248 Steve Green
☐ 249 Wayne Kirby
☐ 250 Billy Brooks
☐ 251 Carlos Carrasco
☐ 252 Chris Cerny
☐ 253 Chris Gettler
☐ 254 Kenny King
☐ 255 Todd Kroll
☐ 256 Lee Langley
☐ 257 Dan Pena
☐ 258 Tim Scott
☐ 259 Zak Shinall
☐ 260 Dennis Springer
☐ 261 John Wanish
☐ 262 Gary LaRocque
☐ 263 Guy Conti
☐ 264 Stan Johnston
☐ 265 Tommy Davis
☐ 266 Jack Patton
☐ 267 Rick Smith

1988 Baseball America AA All-Stars Best

Produced by Best Cards and as selected by Baseball America. 7,000 sets were produced.

	MINT	NRMT	EXC
COMPLETE SET (30)	20.00	9.00	2.50

☐ 1 Hensley Meulens
☐ 2 Mike Harkey
☐ 3 Rob Ritchie
☐ 4 Omar Vizquel
☐ 5 Jerome Walton
☐ 6 Chuck Malone
☐ 7 Tom Lampkin
☐ 8 Joe Girardi
☐ 9 Kevin Wickander
☐ 10 Bill McGuire
☐ 11 Pete Harnisch
☐ 12 Derek Parks
☐ 13 Alex Sanchez
☐ 14 Jose DeJesus
☐ 15 Rafael DeLima
☐ 16 Mark Lemke
☐ 17 Chris Hammond
☐ 18 German Gonzalez
☐ 19 Dennis Jones
☐ 20 Francisco Cabrera
☐ 21 Ramon Martinez
☐ 22 Gary Sheffield
☐ 23 Juan Bell
☐ 24 Greg Vaughn
☐ 25 Kevin Brown
☐ 26 Mike Munoz
☐ 27 Trevor Wilson
☐ 28 John Wetteland
☐ 29 Jeff Manto
☐ 30 Buddy Bailey

1988 Baseball City Royals Star

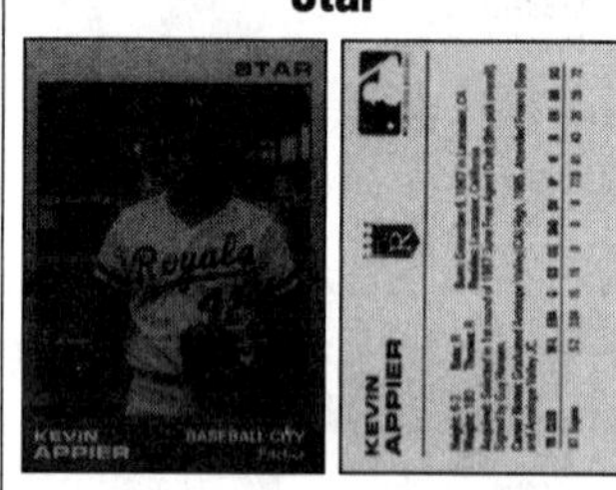

This issue includes the minor league card debut of Jeff Conine.

	MINT	NRMT	EXC
COMPLETE SET (25)	25.00	11.00	3.10

☐ 1 Bud Adams
☐ 2 Ken Adams
☐ 3 Jon Alexander
☐ 4 Jose Anglero
☐ 5 Kevin Appier
☐ 6 Sean Berry
☐ 7 Mike Butcher
☐ 8 Dera Clark
☐ 9 Tony Bridges-Clements
☐ 10 Jeff Conine
☐ 11 Carlos Escalera
☐ 12 Carlos Gonzalez
☐ 13 Dan Harlan
☐ 14 Kenny Jackson
☐ 15 Kevin Koslofski
☐ 16 Richie LeBlanc Jr.
☐ 17 Brian McRae
☐ 18 Bobby Moore
☐ 19 Harvey Pulliam Jr.
☐ 20 Tim Rice
☐ 21 Joe Skodny
☐ 22 Mike Tresemer
☐ 23 Aguedo Vasquez
☐ 24 Steve Walker
☐ 25 DeJon Watson

1988 Batavia Clippers ProCards

This 31-card standard-size set of the 1988 Batavia Clippers, a Class A New York-Penn League affiliate of the Philadelphia Phillies, features bronze-bordered posed color player photos on its fronts. The player's name, position, and team name appear at the bottom. The plain white back carries the player's name at the top, followed by biography and statistics.

	MINT	NRMT	EXC
COMPLETE SET (31)	5.00	2.20	.60

☐ 1662 Bob Tiefenauer
☐ 1663 Dave Cash
☐ 1664 Don McCormack
☐ 1665 Tony Trevino
☐ 1666 Leroy Ventress
☐ 1667 Nicio Martinez
☐ 1668 Scott Drury
☐ 1669 Wayne Fuller
☐ 1670 Rick Trlicek
☐ 1671 Eric Enos
☐ 1672 Mark Bradford
☐ 1673 Erik Bratlien
☐ 1674 Tim Dell
☐ 1675 Mike Owens
☐ 1676 Tom Marsh
☐ 1677 Chris Walker
☐ 1678 Nick Santa Cruz
☐ 1679 Joe Tenhunfeld
☐ 1680 Ike Galloway
☐ 1681 Rich Walker
☐ 1682 Todd Elam
☐ 1683 Matt Viggiano
☐ 1684 Dave Allen
☐ 1685 Rich Tracy
☐ 1686 Fred Felton
☐ 1687 Andy Barrick
☐ 1688 Gary Wilson
☐ 1689 Brain Cummings
☐ 1690 Troy Zerb
☐ 1691 Brad Rogers
☐ NNO Checklist

1988 Bellingham Mariners Legoe

	MINT	NRMT	EXC
COMPLETE SET (32)	7.00	3.10	.85

☐ 1 Ricky Canderlari
☐ 2 Dorian Daughtry
☐ 3 Tony Cayson
☐ 4 Ellerton Maynard
☐ 5 Mike McLaughlin
☐ 6 Tom McNamara
☐ 7 Greg Pirkl
☐ 8 Julio Reyan
☐ 9 Jeff Miller
☐ 10 Pete Schmidt
☐ 11 Tim Stargell
☐ 12 Gary Wheelock
☐ 13 Brian Wilkinson
☐ 14 Lee Hancock
☐ 15 John Kohli
☐ 16 Jim Kosnik
☐ 17 Tom Liss
☐ 18 Victor Mangual
☐ 19 Scott Pitcher
☐ 20 Keith Barrett
☐ 21 Scott Stoerck
☐ 22 Nick Felix
☐ 23 Ted Eldredge
☐ 24 Chris Doll
☐ 25 Erick Bryant
☐ 26 Mike Beiras
☐ 27 Otis Patrick
☐ 28 P.J. Carey
☐ 29 Donnie Reynolds
☐ 30 Spyder Webb
☐ 31 Batboys CL
☐ NNO Cover Card

1988 Beloit Brewers Grand Slam

	MINT	NRMT	EXC
COMPLETE SET (25)	7.00	3.10	.85

☐ 1 Gomer Hodge
☐ 2 Gary Robson
☐ 3 Jim Poulin
☐ 4 Frank Bolick
☐ 5 Tim Raley
☐ 6 Dan Adriance
☐ 7 Charlie McGrew
☐ 8 Juan Uribe
☐ 9 Bob Simonson
☐ 10 Mark Chapman
☐ 11 Bob Sobczyk
☐ 12 Bryan Foster
☐ 13 Kent Hetrick
☐ 14 Tim Torricelli
☐ 15 Mike Guerrero
☐ 16 Curt Krippner
☐ 17 Tim Wahl
☐ 18 Leonardo Perez
☐ 19 Dave Nilsson
☐ 20 Dan Peters
☐ 21 Randy Moore
☐ 22 Mike Whitlock
☐ 23 Chris Cassels
☐ 24 Steve Sparks
☐ 25 Chris Johnson

1988 Bend Bucks Legoe

This issue includes the minor league card debut of Jim Edmonds.

	MINT	NRMT	EXC
COMPLETE SET (36)	20.00	9.00	2.50

☐ 1 Angel Carrasquillo
☐ 2 Jeff Kipila
☐ 3 Shawn Cunningham
☐ 4 Jeff Oberdank
☐ 5 Ramon Martinez
☐ 6 Frank Brito
☐ 7 Gary DiSarcina
☐ 8 Steve Kirwin
☐ 9 Jeff Kelso
☐ 10 Jim Edmonds
☐ 11 Dave Partrick
☐ 12 Chris Threadgill

☐ 13 Huascar Mateo
☐ 14 Tim Taft
☐ 15 Dave Sturdivant
☐ 16 Enrique Tejeda
☐ 17 Miguel Batista
☐ 18 Bruce Vegely
☐ 19 Dave Neal
☐ 20 John Fritz
☐ 21 Glenn Carter
☐ 22 Mark Holzemer
☐ 23 Todd James
☐ 24 John Marchese
☐ 25 Justin Martin
☐ 26 Don Vidmar
☐ 27 Don Long MG
☐ 28 Howie Gershberg CO
☐ 29 Rick Ingalls CO
☐ 30 Derek Winchell TR
☐ 31 Gary Murphy
☐ 32 Paul List
☐ 33 Shawn Cunningham
Gary DiSarcina
Jeff Oberdank
Keystone Trio
☐ 34 Bucky Buck(Mascot) CL
☐ 35 Charles Phillips
☐ NNO Title Card

1988 Billings Mustangs ProCards

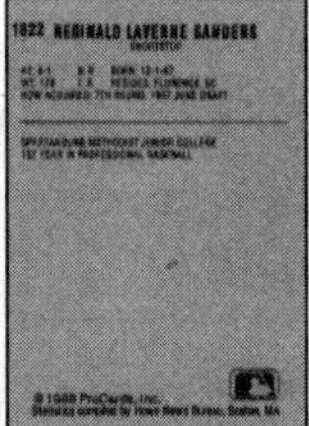

This 31-card standard-size set of the 1988 Billings Mustangs, a Rookie Class Pioneer League affiliate of the Cincinnati Reds, features bronze-bordered posed color player photos on its fronts. The player's name, position, and team name appear at the bottom. The plain white back carries the player's name at the top, followed by biography and statistics. This issue includes the minor league card debut of Reggie Sanders.

	MINT	NRMT	EXC
COMPLETE SET (31)	20.00	9.00	2.50

☐ 1802 David Keller
☐ 1803 Gerry Groninger
☐ 1804 Jim Brune
☐ 1805 Duane Mulville
☐ 1806 Glenn Sutko
☐ 1807 Scott Sellner
☐ 1808 Michael Mulvaney
☐ 1809 Doug Bond
☐ 1810 Steve Reyes
☐ 1811 Tony Terzarial
☐ 1812 Dante Johnson
☐ 1813 Danny Perozo
☐ 1814 Scott Economy
☐ 1815 John Groennert
☐ 1816 Tomas Rodriquez
☐ 1817 Steve McCarthy
☐ 1818 Steve Foster
☐ 1819 Brian Nichols
☐ 1820 Brian Landy
☐ 1821 Jerry Spradlin
☐ 1822 Reggie Sanders
☐ 1823 C.L. Thomas
☐ 1824 Vincente Javier
☐ 1825 Johnny Almaraz
☐ 1826 Carl Stewart
☐ 1827 Jim Hoff
☐ 1828 Kurt Dempster
☐ 1829 Michael Songini
☐ 1830 Benny Colvard
☐ 1831 Carl Nordstrom
☐ NNO Checklist

1988 Birmingham Barons Best

This 29-card standard-size set of the 1988 Birmingham Barons, a Class AA Southern League affiliate of the Chicago White Sox, features red and black bordered posed color player photos on its fronts. The team name appears at the top, and below the picture is the player's name and position. The horizontal gray back carries the player's name and position at the top, followed by biography, career highlights, and statistics. The set is printed on thin card stock.

	MINT	NRMT	EXC
COMPLETE SET (29)	5.00	2.20	.60

☐ 1 Wayne Edwards
☐ 2 Tony Blasucci
☐ 3 Tom Drees
☐ 4 Ray Chadwick
☐ 5 Jim Markert
☐ 6 Dave Wallwork
☐ 7 Moe Drabowsky
☐ 8 Rico Petrocelli
☐ 9 Todd Trafton
☐ 10 Tommy Thompson
☐ 11 Pete Venturini
☐ 12 Tom Forrester
☐ 13 Dan Wagner
☐ 14 Mark Davis
☐ 15 Rick Pollack
☐ 16 Carlos Martinez
☐ 17 Rich Gaynor
☐ 18 John Boling
☐ 19 Daryl Smith
☐ 20 Tony Menendez
☐ 21 Dan Conkright
☐ 22 Matt Merullo
☐ 23 Jerry Bertolani
☐ 24 Craig Grebeck
☐ 25 Willie Magallanes
☐ 26 Doug Little
☐ 27 Chuck Mount
☐ 28 Kevin Renz
☐ 29 Checklist

1988 Boise Hawks ProCards

This 29-card standard-size set of the 1988 Boise Hawks, a Class A Northwest League Independent, features bronze-bordered posed color player photos on its fronts. The player's name, position, and team name appear at the bottom. The plain white back carries the player's name at the top, followed by biography and statistics.

	MINT	NRMT	EXC
COMPLETE SET (29)	5.00	2.20	.60

☐ 1605 John Bilello
☐ 1606 Michael Tate
☐ 1607 Wendell Bolar
☐ 1608 Michael Moore
☐ 1609 Christopher Gurchiek
☐ 1610 James Qualls
☐ 1611 Mike Shambaugh
☐ 1612 Edward Holub
☐ 1613 Christopher Shultis
☐ 1614 Barry Griffin
☐ 1615 Larry Lundeen
☐ 1616 Jeff Mace
☐ 1617 Earl Malone
☐ 1618 Jerry Backus
☐ 1619 Randy Janikowski
☐ 1620 Michael Larson
☐ 1621 Chuck Lavrusky
☐ 1622 Michael Lomeli
☐ 1623 Bill Wenrick
☐ 1624 Charles Douglas
☐ 1625 Mark Krumback
☐ 1626 Joseph Mancini
☐ 1627 Daren De Pew
☐ 1628 Keven Bottenfield
☐ 1629 Tim MacKinnon
☐ 1630 Frank Jury
☐ 1631 Robert Winterburn
☐ 1632 Mal Fichman
☐ NNO Checklist

1988 Bristol Tigers ProCards

This 32-card standard-size set of the 1988 Bristol Tigers, a Rookie Class Appalachian League League affiliate of the Detroit Tigers, features bronze-bordered posed color player photos on its fronts. The player's name, position, and team name appear at the bottom. The plain white back carries the player's name at the top, followed by biography and statistics.

	MINT	NRMT	EXC
COMPLETE SET (32)	5.00	2.20	.60

☐ 1862 Rick Mag
☐ 1863 Carlos Maldonado
☐ 1864 Doug Biggs
☐ 1865 Tim Brader
☐ 1866 Juan Estevez
☐ 1867 Bob Frassa
☐ 1868 Rusty Meacham
☐ 1869 Julio Rosa
☐ 1870 Ron Howard
☐ 1871 Mike Davidson
☐ 1872 Rich Rowland
☐ 1873 Freddy Padilla
☐ 1874 Jimmy Hayes
☐ 1875 Chris Gollehon
☐ 1876 Eric Shoup
☐ 1877 Mike Rendina
☐ 1878 Duane Walker
☐ 1879 Blaine Rudolph
☐ 1880 Mike Koller
☐ 1881 Tom Aldrich
☐ 1882 Marcos Betances
☐ 1883 Mick Delas
☐ 1884 Bret Roach
☐ 1885 Rico Brogna
☐ 1886 Ed Ferm
☐ 1887 Kurt Shea
☐ 1888 Rob Thomas
☐ 1889 Mike Jones
☐ 1890 Paul Nozling
☐ 1891 Tookie Spann
☐ 1892 Benny Castillo
☐ NNO Checklist

1988 Buffalo Bisons CMC

10,000 sets were produced.

	MINT	NRMT	EXC
COMPLETE SET (25)	4.00	1.80	.50

☐ 1 Logan Easley
☐ 2 Stan Fansler
☐ 3 Brett Gideon
☐ 4 Dave Johnson
☐ 5 Randy Kramer
☐ 6 Morris Madden
☐ 7 Bob Patterson
☐ 8 Dave Rucker
☐ 9 Dorn Taylor
☐ 10 Scott Medvin
☐ 11 Benny Distefano
☐ 12 Tommy Gregg
☐ 13 Tom Romano
☐ 14 Bernie Tatis
☐ 15 Denny Gonzalez
☐ 16 Bryan Little
☐ 17 Jim Reboulet
☐ 18 Rico Rossy
☐ 19 Tom Prince
☐ 20 Orestes Destrade
☐ 21 Felix Fermin
☐ 22 Dave Sax
☐ 23 Skeeter Barnes
☐ 24 Stan Cliburn
☐ 25 Rocky Bridges

1988 Buffalo Bisons ProCards

This 31-card standard-size set of the 1988 Buffalo Bisons, a Class AAA American Association affiliate of the Pittsburgh Pirates, features gold-bordered posed color player photos on its fronts. The player's name, position, and team name appear at the bottom. The plain white back carries the player's name at the top, followed by biography and statistics.

	MINT	NRMT	EXC
COMPLETE SET (31)	5.00	2.20	.60

☐ 1464 Randy Kramer
☐ 1465 Felix Fermin
☐ 1466 Morris Madden
☐ 1467 Bob Patterson
☐ 1468 Dorn Taylor
☐ 1469 Stan Fansler
☐ 1470 Jim Reboulet
☐ 1471 Rico Rossy
☐ 1472 Dave Rucker
☐ 1473 Denny Gonzalez
☐ 1474 Tommy Gregg
☐ 1475 Bernie Tatis
☐ 1476 Dave Johnson
☐ 1477 The Butcher
☐ 1478 Rocky Bridges
☐ 1479 Jackie Brown
☐ 1480 Stan Cliburn
☐ 1481 Carlos Ledezma
☐ 1482 Kevin Hodge
☐ 1483 Dave Sax
☐ 1484 Scott Medvin
☐ 1485 Tom Romano
☐ 1486 Orestes Destrade
☐ 1487 Skeeter Barnes
☐ 1488 Tom Prince
☐ 1489 Benny Distefano
☐ 1490 Logan Easley
☐ 1491 Bryan Little
☐ 1492 Brett Gideon
☐ 1493 Pilot Field
☐ NNO Checklist

1988 Buffalo Bisons Team Issue

This 9-card set of the 1988 Buffalo Bisons, a Class AAA American Association affiliate of the Pittsburgh Pirates, features eight color player cards along with a team photo. The set was sponsored by Polaroid and distributed on a special promotional Polaroid Camera Day at the ballpark.

	MINT	NRMT	EXC
COMPLETE SET (9)	25.00	11.00	3.10

☐ 1 Rocky Bridges
☐ 2 Dave Johnson
☐ 3 Bryan Little
☐ 4 Tom Romano
☐ 5 Dorn Taylor
☐ 6 Benny Distefano
☐ 7 Jim Reboulet
☐ 8 Morris Madden
☐ 9 Team Photo

1988 Burlington Braves ProCards

This 31-card standard-size set of the 1988 Burlington Braves, a Class A Midwest League affiliate of the Atlanta Braves, features bronze-bordered posed color player photos on its fronts. The player's name, position, and team name appear at the bottom. The plain white back carries the player's name at the top, followed by biography and statistics.

	MINT	NRMT	EXC
COMPLETE SET (31)	7.00	3.10	.85

☐ 1 Lynn Robinson
☐ 2 Carl Pointer-Jones
☐ 3 Mike Stanton
☐ 4 Chad Smith
☐ 5 William Turner
☐ 6 Pat Tilmon
☐ 7 Brian Murphy
☐ 8 Jerald Frost
☐ 9 Steve Glass
☐ 10 Brian Champion
☐ 11 Grady Little
☐ 12 Brian Cummings
☐ 13 Jim LeMasters
☐ 14 Jeff Greene
☐ 15 Jim Nowlin
☐ 16 Dave Karasinski
☐ 17 Jamie Cuesta
☐ 18 Dave Grilone
☐ 19 Albert Martin
☐ 20 Sean Ross
☐ 21 Rich Casarotti
☐ 22 Rick Berg
☐ 23 Eduardo Perez
☐ 24 Andy Tomberlin
☐ 25 Brian Hunter
☐ 26 Gil Garrido
☐ 27 Brian Deak
☐ 28 John Mitchell
☐ 29 Jack Aker MG
☐ 30 Paul Egins III TR
☐ NNO Checklist

1988 Burlington Indians ProCards

This 31-card standard-size set of the 1988 Burlington Indians, a Rookie Class Appalachian League affiliate of the Cleveland Indians, features bronze-bordered posed color player photos on its fronts. The player's name, position, and team name appear at the bottom. The plain white back carries the player's name at the top, followed by biography and statistics. This issue includes the minor league card debut of Mark Lewis.

	MINT	NRMT	EXC
COMPLETE SET (31)	12.00	5.50	1.50

☐ 1772 Brent Roberts
☐ 1773 Rick Falkner
☐ 1774 Lenny Gilmore
☐ 1775 Martin Eddy
☐ 1776 Randy Mazey
☐ 1777 Vince Barranco
☐ 1778 Sean Baron
☐ 1779 Jeff Bonchek
☐ 1780 Rouglas Odor
☐ 1781 Axel Castillo
☐ 1782 Todd Butler
☐ 1783 Carlos Mota
☐ 1784 Scott Allen
☐ 1785 Charles Alexander
☐ 1786 Mike Bucci
☐ 1787 Pedro Arias
☐ 1788 Fabio Gomez
☐ 1789 David Oliveras
☐ 1790 Doug Piatt
☐ 1791 Barry Blundin
☐ 1792 Jeff Mutis
☐ 1793 Mike Ashworth
☐ 1794 Bob Kairis
☐ 1795 Brett Merriman
☐ 1796 Greg McMichael
☐ 1797 Andrew Halle
☐ 1798 Brian Johnson
☐ 1799 Dan Williams
☐ 1800 Mark Lewis
☐ 1801 Ray Borowicz
☐ NNO Checklist

1988 Butte Copper Kings Sports Pro

	MINT	NRMT	EXC
COMPLETE SET (29)	7.00	3.10	.85

☐ 1 Mike Hamilton
☐ 2 Jim Havizda
☐ 3 Greg Kuzma
☐ 4 Tim MacNeil
☐ 5 Robb Nen
☐ 6 Ken Penland
☐ 7 Carl Randle

- ☐ 8 Bill Schorr
- ☐ 9 Cedric Shaw
- ☐ 10 Kyle Spencer
- ☐ 11 Kenny Shiozaki
- ☐ 12 Denny Tomori
- ☐ 13 Bill Losa
- ☐ 14 Jeff Frye
- ☐ 15 Rob Maurer
- ☐ 16 Dom Pierce
- ☐ 17 Joe Wardlow
- ☐ 18 Trey McCoy
- ☐ 19 Rod Morris
- ☐ 20 Mike Spear
- ☐ 21 Thayer Swain
- ☐ 22 Monty Fariss
- ☐ 23 Travis Law
- ☐ 24 Brad Fontes
- ☐ 25 Jeff Hainline
- ☐ 26 Steve Allen
- ☐ 27 Ev Cunningham
- ☐ 28 Ernie Rodriguez CO
- ☐ 29 Bump Wills MGR

1988 California League All-Stars Cal League Cards

	MINT	NRMT	EXC
COMPLETE SET (50)	16.00	7.25	2.00

- ☐ 1 Dave Patterson
- ☐ 2 Gil Heredia
- ☐ 3 Mark Leonard
- ☐ 4 Paul Blair
- ☐ 5 Eric Gunderson
- ☐ 6 Doug Robertson
- ☐ 7 Rich Aldrete
- ☐ 8 Montie Phillips
- ☐ 9 Ron Coomer
- ☐ 10 David Veres
- ☐ 11 D. Fitzpatrick
- ☐ 12 Tim McIntosh
- ☐ 13 Robert Jones
- ☐ 14 Shon Ashley
- ☐ 15 Sandy Guerrero
- ☐ 16 Charlie Montoyo
- ☐ 17 Ruben Escalera
- ☐ 18 Rob Derksen
- ☐ 19 Dave Huppert
- ☐ 20 Joe Strong
- ☐ 21 Jamie Allison
- ☐ 22 Joe Ortiz
- ☐ 23 Matt Bohn
- ☐ 24 Dick Fossa
- ☐ 25 Joe Gagliardi
- ☐ 26 Ken Griffey Jr.
- ☐ 27 Jim Bowie Jr.
- ☐ 28 Ted Williams
- ☐ 29 Keith Helton
- ☐ 30 Jim Blueberg
- ☐ 31 Colin Charland
- ☐ 32 Ruben Amaro Jr.
- ☐ 33 Scott Cerny
- ☐ 34 Cris Cron
- ☐ 35 Bill Lachemann
- ☐ 36 Gary Ruby
- ☐ 37 Mike Randle
- ☐ 38 John Eccles
- ☐ 39 Marty Lanoux
- ☐ 40 Jim Williams
- ☐ 41 Ricky Bones
- ☐ 42 Rafael Chavez
- ☐ 43 Paul Faries
- ☐ 44 Dave Hollins
- ☐ 45 Warren Newson
- ☐ 46 Jeff Brown
- ☐ 47 Jose Vizcaino
- ☐ 48 Adam Brown
- ☐ 49 Ken Franek
- ☐ 50 Red Morrow

1988 Calgary Cannons CMC

This 25-card standard-size set of the 1988 Calgary Cannons, a Class AAA Pacific Coast League affiliate of the Seattle Mariners, features on its fronts black-bordered posed color player photos framed by a green line. The team's name, the player's name, and his position appear at the bottom. The white back is framed by a black line and carries the team's name and league at the top, followed by the player's name, biography and statistics.

	MINT	NRMT	EXC
COMPLETE SET (25)	6.00	2.70	.75

- ☐ 1 Darren Burroughs
- ☐ 2 Paul Schneider
- ☐ 3 Rich Monteleone
- ☐ 4 Dennis Powell
- ☐ 5 Jay Baller
- ☐ 6 Mike Christ
- ☐ 7 Jim Walker
- ☐ 8 Matt West
- ☐ 9 Mike Schooler
- ☐ 10 Rod Scurry
- ☐ 11 Donell Nixon
- ☐ 12 Phil Ouellette
- ☐ 13 Greg Briley
- ☐ 14 Dave Cochrane
- ☐ 15 Brian Giles
- ☐ 16 Edgar Martinez
- ☐ 17 John Christensen
- ☐ 18 Dave Hengel
- ☐ 19 Nelson Simmons
- ☐ 20 Mike Wishnevski
- ☐ 21 Roger Hansen
- ☐ 22 Doug Merrifield TR
- ☐ 23 Mike Watters
- ☐ 24 Bill Plummer MG
- ☐ 25 Dan Warthen CO

1988 Calgary Cannons ProCards

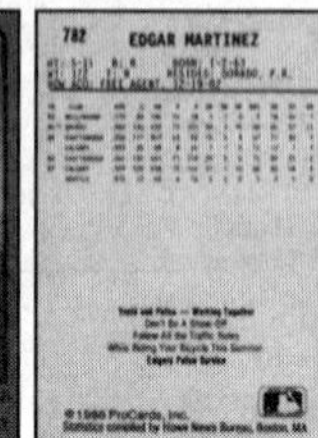

This 28-card standard-size set of the 1988 Calgary Cannons, a Class AAA Pacific Coast League affiliate of the Seattle Mariners, features gold-bordered posed color player photos on its fronts. The player's name, position, and team name appear at the bottom. The plain white back carries the player's name at the top, followed by biography and statistics.

	MINT	NRMT	EXC
COMPLETE SET (28)	8.00	3.60	1.00

- ☐ 779 Rod Scurry
- ☐ 780 Darren Burroughs
- ☐ 781 Terry Taylor
- ☐ 782 Edgar Martinez
- ☐ 783 Mike Wishnevski
- ☐ 784 Brian Giles
- ☐ 785 Dave Cochrane
- ☐ 786 Erik Hanson
- ☐ 787 Doug Merrifield TR
- ☐ 788 Matt West
- ☐ 789 Dan Warthen CO
- ☐ 790 Roger Hansen
- ☐ 791 Jim Walker
- ☐ 792 Jay Baller
- ☐ 793 Paul Schneider
- ☐ 794 John Christensen
- ☐ 795 Mike Schooler
- ☐ 796 Dennis Powell
- ☐ 797 Rich Monteleone
- ☐ 798 Mike Watters
- ☐ 799 Greg Briley
- ☐ 800 Bill Plummer MG
- ☐ 801 Phil Ouellette
- ☐ 802 Nelson Simmons
- ☐ 803 Brick Smith
- ☐ 804 Mario Diaz
- ☐ 1550 Dave Hengel
- ☐ NNO Checklist

1988 Cape Cod Prospects Ballpark

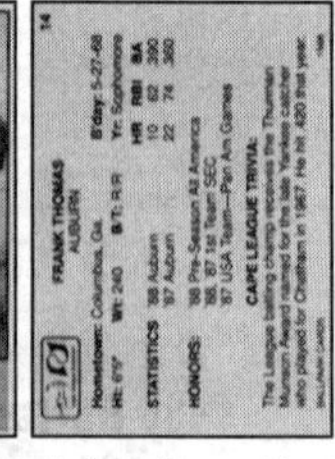

Issued and produced by collector/dealer Fred Suzman, this set features twenty of the Cape Cod League's top players and ten team cards. This issue includes first cards of Chuck Knoblauch, Jeff Bagwell and Mo Vaughn and a second card issue of Frank Thomas.

	MINT	NRMT	EXC
COMPLETE SET (30)	175.00	80.00	22.00

- ☐ 1 Tom Drell
- ☐ 2 Mark Johnson
- ☐ 3 Jimmie Jones
- ☐ 4 Jeff Bagwell
- ☐ 5 Robert Gralewski
- ☐ 6 Dennis Burbank
- ☐ 7 Brian Shabosky
- ☐ 8 Jeff Litzinger
- ☐ 9 Thomas Raffo
- ☐ 10 Bob Kiser
- ☐ 11 John Valentin
- ☐ 12 Kevin Morton
- ☐ 13 Jesse Levis
- ☐ 14 Frank Thomas
- ☐ 15 Chuck Knoblauch
- ☐ 16 Maurice Vaughn
- ☐ 17 Mike Mordecai
- ☐ 18 Stephen P. O'Donnell
- ☐ 19 Harry Ball
- ☐ 20 Brian Turang
- ☐ 21 Brewster Whitecaps
- ☐ 22 Orleans Cardinals
- ☐ 23 Chatham A's
- ☐ 24 Cotuit Ketleers
- ☐ 25 Wareham Gateman
- ☐ 26 Bourne Braves
- ☐ 27 Falmouth Commodores
- ☐ 28 Yarmouth-Dennis White Sox
- ☐ 29 Harwich Mariners
- ☐ 30 Hyannis Mets

1988 Cape Cod Prospects P & L Promotions

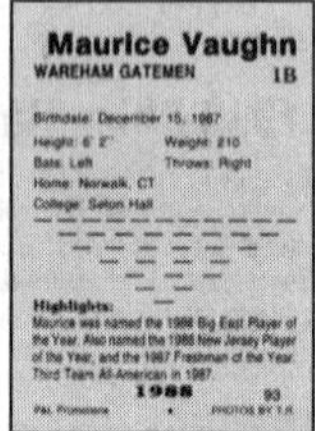

Issued by P and L Promotions. This set features 186 players from the Cape Cod league and includes first cards of Chuck Knoblauch, Jeff Bagwell, Tim Salmon and Mo Vaughn and a second card issue of Frank Thomas.

	MINT	NRMT	EXC
COMPLETE SET (186)	200.00	90.00	25.00

- ☐ 1 Mark Johnson
- ☐ 2 John Valente
- ☐ 3 Warren Sawkiw
- ☐ 4 Ed Therrien
- ☐ 5 Lenny Richardson
- ☐ 6 Paul Ciaglo
- ☐ 7 Alex Alvarez
- ☐ 8 Richard Cordani
- ☐ 9 Chris Snyder
- ☐ 10 Michael Kelly
- ☐ 11 Keith Wiley
- ☐ 12 Brian Moure
- ☐ 13 David Flynn
- ☐ 14 Ed Cooney
- ☐ 15 Joe Conti
- ☐ 16 Joseph Delli Carri
- ☐ 17 Eamon Kingman
- ☐ 18 Tom Drell
- ☐ 19 Joe Logan
- ☐ 20 Jeff Borgese
- ☐ 21 John Byington
- ☐ 22 Brian Turang
- ☐ 23 Travis Tarchione
- ☐ 24 Mike Truschke
- ☐ 25 Rick Hirtensteiner
- ☐ 26 Pete Tsotsos
- ☐ 27 Harry Ball
- ☐ 28 Larry Russell
- ☐ 29 Alan Zinter
- ☐ 30 Brian Ahern
- ☐ 31 Chris Schaefer
- ☐ 32 Mike McNary
- ☐ 33 Chris Ebright
- ☐ 34 Darryl Scott
- ☐ 35 Russell Springer
- ☐ 36 Rafael Novoa
- ☐ 37 Ron Raper
- ☐ 38 Brian Shehan
- ☐ 39 Dave Wrona
- ☐ 40 Doug Shields
- ☐ 41 Stephen O'Donnell
- ☐ 42 Mike Mordecai
- ☐ 43 Steven Parris
- ☐ 44 Mike Zimmerman
- ☐ 45 Mitch Hannahs
- ☐ 46 Nolan Lane
- ☐ 47 Kurt Olson
- ☐ 48 Peter Altenberger
- ☐ 49 Rick Strickland
- ☐ 50 Bill Klenoshek Jr.
- ☐ 51 Eric Wedge
- ☐ 52 Larry Owens
- ☐ 53 Dennis Neagle
- ☐ 54 Preston Woods
- ☐ 55 Jim Dougherty
- ☐ 56 John Davis
- ☐ 57 Jeff Bagwell
- ☐ 58 Tom Riginos
- ☐ 59 Mark Sweeney
- ☐ 60 Scott Odierno
- ☐ 61 Michael LeBlanc
- ☐ 62 Michael Hinde
- ☐ 63 Scott Shockey
- ☐ 64 Brian Dour
- ☐ 65 Matt Dunbar
- ☐ 66 David Swartzbaugh
- ☐ 67 Curry Harden
- ☐ 68 Don Hutchinson
- ☐ 69 Mike Gardella
- ☐ 70 James Jones
- ☐ 71 Colin Ryan
- ☐ 72 Robert Rivell
- ☐ 73 Duane O'Hara
- ☐ 74 Bobby Kiser
- ☐ 75 Mike Trombley
- ☐ 76 John Farrell
- ☐ 77 Mark LaRosa
- ☐ 78 Scott Erwin
- ☐ 79 Thomas G. Raffo Jr.
- ☐ 80 George Tsamis
- ☐ 81 Alan Botkin
- ☐ 82 Bob McCreary
- ☐ 83 Jeff Cerqueira
- ☐ 84 Jim Jimaki
- ☐ 85 Mike McNamara
- ☐ 86 Tom Hickox
- ☐ 87 Scott Miller
- ☐ 88 Gary Scott
- ☐ 89 Brian Specyalski
- ☐ 90 Ron Frazier
- ☐ 91 Marcelino Sellas
- ☐ 92 Craig A. Cala
- ☐ 93 Maurice Vaughn
- ☐ 94 Chuck Knoblauch
- ☐ 95 Dana Brown
- ☐ 96 Mike Weimerskirch
- ☐ 97 Darron Cox
- ☐ 98 Kevin Long
- ☐ 99 Kevin King
- ☐ 100 David Arendas
- ☐ 101 Burke Masters
- ☐ 102 Pat Leinan
- ☐ 103 Troy Bradford
- ☐ 104 Rich Samplinski
- ☐ 105 Sam Colarusso
- ☐ 106 John Thoden
- ☐ 107 Randy Pryor
- ☐ 108 John Kosenski
- ☐ 109 Keith Langston
- ☐ 110 Jody Hurst
- ☐ 111 Kevin Castleberry
- ☐ 112 Kyle Sanborn
- ☐ 113 Casey Waller
- ☐ 114 Brian Bark
- ☐ 115 Chris Barnes
- ☐ 116 Jesse Levis
- ☐ 117 George Sells
- ☐ 118 Tom Williams
- ☐ 119 Todd Mayo
- ☐ 120 Mathew Howard
- ☐ 121 Sam Taylor
- ☐ 122 Mike Grimes
- ☐ 123 Scott Centala
- ☐ 124 Drew Comeau
- ☐ 125 J.T. Snow
- ☐ 126 Frank Thomas
- ☐ 127 Jason Klonoski
- ☐ 128 Marty Durkin
- ☐ 129 Tim Lata
- ☐ 130 Brian Barnes
- ☐ 131 Sam Drake
- ☐ 132 Tom Hardgrove
- ☐ 133 Lance Jones
- ☐ 134 Kirk Dressendorfer
- ☐ 135 Brad Myers
- ☐ 136 Gordon Tipton
- ☐ 137 Terry Taylor
- ☐ 138 John Valentin
- ☐ 139 Kevin Morton
- ☐ 140 Ed Horowitz
- ☐ 141 Dave Tollison
- ☐ 142 Rick Kimball
- ☐ 143 Tim Williams
- ☐ 144 Tony Kounas
- ☐ 145 Jeromy Burnitz
- ☐ 146 Mark Smith
- ☐ 147 Brad Beanblossom
- ☐ 148 Stewart Keyes
- ☐ 149 Will Vespe
- ☐ 150 Henry Manning
- ☐ 151 Dennis Burbank
- ☐ 152 Darryl Vice
- ☐ 153 Eric Bennett
- ☐ 154 Bob Gralewski
- ☐ 155 Michael Boyan
- ☐ 156 F.P. Santangelo
- ☐ 157 Bob Allen
- ☐ 158 Michael S. Myers
- ☐ 159 Andrew Albrecht
- ☐ 160 Robert Fazekas
- ☐ 161 Chris Slattery
- ☐ 162 Scott Morehouse
- ☐ 163 Robbie Katzaroff
- ☐ 164 Chris L. Jones
- ☐ 165 Bret Donovan

- ☐ 166 Tucker Hammagren
- ☐ 167 David Staton
- ☐ 168 Joseph Bruett
- ☐ 169 Jeff Kent
- ☐ 170 Troy Buckley
- ☐ 171 Garett Teel
- ☐ 172 Mark Carper
- ☐ 173 Joseph Kelly
- ☐ 174 Michael Wiseman
- ☐ 175 Howard Prager
- ☐ 176 Timothy Salmon
- ☐ 177 Daniel Wilson
- ☐ 178 James Hoog
- ☐ 179 Trent Turner
- ☐ 180 David Krol
- ☐ 181 Steven Treadway
- ☐ 182 Patrick Varni
- ☐ 183 Troy Chacon
- ☐ 184 Roger Miller
- ☐ 185 Jeff Litzinger
- ☐ 186 Brian Shabosky

1988 Carolina League All-Stars Star

	MINT	NRMT	EXC
COMPLETE SET (40)	12.00	5.50	1.50

- ☐ 1 Jay Ward
- ☐ 2 Mike Hart
- ☐ 3 Stan Belinda
- ☐ 4 Royal Clayton
- ☐ 5 Scott Cooper
- ☐ 6 Brian DuBois
- ☐ 7 Mike Eberle
- ☐ 8 Andy Hall
- ☐ 9 Chris Howard
- ☐ 10 Dean Kelley
- ☐ 11 Tim Kirk
- ☐ 12 Joseph Marchese
- ☐ 13 Jim Orsag
- ☐ 14 Julio Peguero
- ☐ 15 John Ramos
- ☐ 16 Enrique Rios
- ☐ 17 Randy Strijek
- ☐ 18 Junior Vizcaino
- ☐ 19 Bernie Williams
- ☐ 20 Bob Zupcic
- ☐ 21 Glenn Adams
- ☐ 22 Pete Alborano
- ☐ 23 Beau Allred
- ☐ 24 Kevin Bearse
- ☐ 25 Mike Bell
- ☐ 26 Luis Cruz
- ☐ 27 Butch Garcia
- ☐ 28 Phil Harrison
- ☐ 29 Allen Liebert
- ☐ 30 Kelly Mann
- ☐ 31 Kent Mercker
- ☐ 32 Rick Morris
- ☐ 33 Charles Ogden
- ☐ 34 Dave Plumb
- ☐ 35 Greg Smith
- ☐ 36 Rob Swain
- ☐ 37 Theron Todd
- ☐ 38 Michael Twardoski
- ☐ 39 Danny Weems
- ☐ 40 Michael Westbrook

1988 Cedar Rapids Reds ProCards

This 31-card standard-size set of the 1988 Cedar Rapids Reds, a Class A Midwest League affiliate of the Cincinnati Reds, features bronze-bordered posed color player photos on its fronts. The player's name, position, and team name appear at the bottom. The plain white back carries the player's name at the top, followed by biography and statistics. .

	MINT	NRMT	EXC
COMPLETE SET (31)	5.00	2.20	.60

- ☐ 1136 Don Buchheister
- ☐ 1137 Greg Simpson
- ☐ 1138 Bill Dodd
- ☐ 1139 Mike Moscrey
- ☐ 1140 Sandy Krume
- ☐ 1141 Chico Fernandez
- ☐ 1142 Freddy Benavides
- ☐ 1143 Gary Denbo
- ☐ 1144 Marc Bombard
- ☐ 1145 Bruce Colson
- ☐ 1146 Reggie Jefferson
- ☐ 1147 Pete Beeler
- ☐ 1148 Rich Sapienza
- ☐ 1149 Ramon Sambo
- ☐ 1150 Steve Davis
- ☐ 1151 Jeff Forney
- ☐ 1152 Greg Lonigro
- ☐ 1153 Doug Eastman
- ☐ 1154 Jim Brune
- ☐ 1155 Eddie Rush
- ☐ 1156 Brad Brusky
- ☐ 1157 Scott Scudder
- ☐ 1158 Carl Nordstrom
- ☐ 1159 Butch Henry
- ☐ 1160 Sam Chavez
- ☐ 1161 Bud Curran
- ☐ 1162 Darrell Rogers
- ☐ 1163 Milton Hill
- ☐ 1164 Mike Malinak
- ☐ 1165 Jim Bishop
- ☐ NNO Checklist

1988 Charleston Rainbows ProCards

This 30-card standard-size set of the 1988 Charleston Rainbows, a Class A California League affiliate of the San Diego Padres, features bronze-bordered posed color player photos on its fronts. The player's name, position, and team name appear at the bottom. The plain white back carries the player's name at the top, followed by biography and statistics.

	MINT	NRMT	EXC
COMPLETE SET (30)	5.00	2.20	.60

- ☐ 1193 Willie Forbes
- ☐ 1194 Tony Pellegrino
- ☐ 1195 Jim Wasem
- ☐ 1196 David Bond
- ☐ 1197 Charles Hillemann
- ☐ 1198 Jose Valentin
- ☐ 1199 Mike Myers
- ☐ 1200 Osvaldo Sanchez
- ☐ 1201 Rafael Valdez
- ☐ 1202 Mike King
- ☐ 1203 Guillermo Velazquez
- ☐ 1204 Monte Brooks
- ☐ 1205 Mark Kleven
- ☐ 1206 Todd Hansen
- ☐ 1207 Keith Harrison
- ☐ 1208 Darrin Reichle
- ☐ 1209 Todd Torchia
- ☐ 1210 Omar Olivares
- ☐ 1211 Doug Brocail
- ☐ 1212 Gary Lance
- ☐ 1213 Jay Estrada
- ☐ 1214 Tony Lewis
- ☐ 1215 Saul Soltero
- ☐ 1216 Reggie Farmer
- ☐ 1217 Bob Lutticken
- ☐ 1218 Jaime Moreno
- ☐ 1219 Jack Krol
- ☐ 1220 Nelson Silverio
- ☐ 1221 Tim Barker
- ☐ NNO Checklist

1988 Charleston Wheelers Best

This 28-card standard-size set of the 1988 Charleston Wheelers, a Class A South Atlantic League affiliate of the Chicago Cubs, features blue and black bordered posed color player photos on its fronts. The team name appears at the top, and below the picture is the player's name and position. The horizontal gray back carries the player's name and position at the top, followed by biography, career highlights, and statistics. The set is printed on thin card stock.

	MINT	NRMT	EXC
COMPLETE SET (28)	5.00	2.20	.60

- ☐ 1 Matt Walbeck
- ☐ 2 Brad Mills
- ☐ 3 Greg Mahlberg
- ☐ 4 Scott Taylor
- ☐ 5 Mike Reeder
- ☐ 6 Lee Grimes
- ☐ 7 Eric Perry
- ☐ 8 Steve Owens
- ☐ 9 Alex Arias
- ☐ 10 Darren Eggleston
- ☐ 11 Vernon Duenas
- ☐ 12 Jay Eddings
- ☐ 13 Patrick Gomez
- ☐ 14 Henry Gomez
- ☐ 15 John Gardner
- ☐ 16 Marcos Lopez
- ☐ 17 Matt Cakora
- ☐ 18 Don Cohoon
- ☐ 19 Dewayne Coleman
- ☐ 20 Braz Davis
- ☐ 21 Harry Shelton
- ☐ 22 Fernando Ramsey
- ☐ 23 Elio Jose
- ☐ 24 Frank Campos
- ☐ 25 Ray Mullino
- ☐ 26 Nick Ramirez
- ☐ 27 Bob Grimes
- ☐ 28 Checklist

1988 Charlotte Knights Team Issue

	MINT	NRMT	EXC
COMPLETE SET (25)	12.00	5.50	1.50

- ☐ 1 Brian Householder
- ☐ 2 Bob Williams
- ☐ 3 Butch Davis
- ☐ 4 Kevin Price
- ☐ 5 Tim Dulin
- ☐ 6 Rob Walton
- ☐ 7 Jim O'Dell
- ☐ 8 Jeff Tackett
- ☐ 9 Joe Jarrell
- ☐ 10 Joe Wood
- ☐ 11 John Posey
- ☐ 12 Craig Chamberlain
- ☐ 13 Rocky Cusack
- ☐ 14 Mike Pazik
- ☐ 15 Rafael Skeete
- ☐ 16 Jim Daniel
- ☐ 17 Paul Thorpe
- ☐ 18 Pete Harnisch
- ☐ 19 Jerry Holtz
- ☐ 20 Gordon Dillard
- ☐ 21 Dana Smith
- ☐ 22 Ty Nichols
- ☐ 23 Greg Biagini
- ☐ 24 Curt Brown
- ☐ 25 Sherwin Cijntje

1988 Charlotte Rangers Star

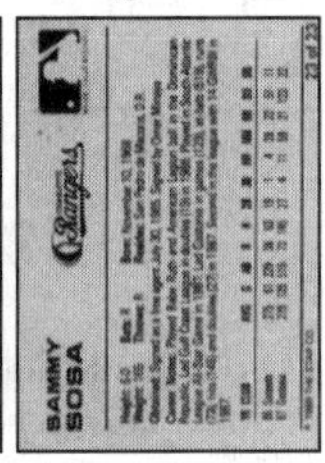

This 25-card standard-size set of the 1988 Charlotte Rangers, a Class A Florida State League affiliate of the Texas Rangers, features orange-bordered posed color player photos on its fronts. The player's name, team name, and position appear at the bottom. The yellowish horizontal back carries the player's name at the top, followed by biography, career highlights, and statistics. This issue inlcudes second year cards of Juan Gonzalez, Sammy Sosa and Dean Palmer.

	MINT	NRMT	EXC
COMPLETE SET (23)	120.00	55.00	15.00
COMPLETE SET W/JONES (24)	125.00	55.00	15.50
COMPLETE SET W/SANCHEZ (25)	130.00	57.50	16.00

- ☐ 1 Rick Bernardo
- ☐ 2 Brian Bohanon
- ☐ 3 Omar Brewer
- ☐ 4 Phil Bryant
- ☐ 5 Paco Burgos
- ☐ 6 Rufus Ellis
- ☐ 7 Darrin Garner
- ☐ 8 Juan Gonzalez
- ☐ 9 Bill Haselman
- ☐ 10 Jonathan Hurst
- ☐ 11 Mark Kramer
- ☐ 12 Adam Lamle
- ☐ 13 Darren Loy
- ☐ 14 Barry Manuel
- ☐ 14 Bobby Jones (Late Issue)
- ☐ 15 Terry Mathews
- ☐ 16 Jeff Mays
- ☐ 17 Darren Niethammer
- ☐ 18 Dean Palmer
- ☐ 19 Mark Petkovsek
- ☐ 20 Lino Rivera
- ☐ 21 Wayne Rosenthal
- ☐ 22 Tony Scruggs
- ☐ 23 Sammy Sosa
- ☐ NNO Rey Sanchez (Late Issue)

1988 Chattanooga Lookouts Best

This 26-card standard-size set of the 1988 Chattanooga Lookouts, a Class AA Southern League affiliate of the Cincinnati Reds, features red and black bordered posed color player photos on its fronts. The team name appears at the top, and below the picture is the player's name and position. The horizontal gray back carries the player's name and position at the top, followed by biography, career highlights, and statistics. The set is printed on thin card stock.

	MINT	NRMT	EXC
COMPLETE SET (26)	5.00	2.20	.60

- ☐ 1 Timber Mead
- ☐ 2 Chris Hammond
- ☐ 3 Keith Brown
- ☐ 4 Joe Lazor
- ☐ 5 Rich Bombard
- ☐ 6 Chris Jones
- ☐ 7 Tony DeFrancesco
- ☐ 8 Hedi Vargas
- ☐ 9 Keith Lockhart
- ☐ 10 Mark Germann
- ☐ 11 Darrell Pruitt
- ☐ 12 Don Wakamatsu
- ☐ 13 Brian Finley
- ☐ 14 Tom Runnells
- ☐ 15 Tim Deitz
- ☐ 16 Gino Minutelli
- ☐ 17 Joe Bruno
- ☐ 18 Phil Dale
- ☐ 19 Jim Jefferson
- ☐ 20 Lary Sorensen
- ☐ 21 Mike Smith
- ☐ 22 Jeff Richardson
- ☐ 23 Bernie Walker
- ☐ 24 Darren Riley
- ☐ 25 Angelo Nunley
- ☐ 26 Checklist

1988 Chattanooga Lookouts Legends Team Issue

	MINT	NRMT	EXC
COMPLETE SET (32)	25.00	11.00	3.10

- ☐ 1 Chris Bando
- ☐ 2 Juan G. Bonilla
- ☐ 3 Joe Charbonneau
- ☐ 4 Pat Corrales
- ☐ 5 Ellis Clary
- ☐ 6 Gilbert Coan
- ☐ 7 Jeff Cox
- ☐ 8 Sonny Dixon
- ☐ 9 Lee C. Elia
- ☐ 10 Joe Engel
- ☐ 11 Engel Stadium
- ☐ 12 Cal Ermer
- ☐ 13 Don Grate
- ☐ 14 Roy L. Hawes
- ☐ 15 Forrest Jacobs
- ☐ 16 Jim Kaat
- ☐ 17 Matt Keough
- ☐ 18 Harmon Killebrew
- ☐ 19 Rene Lachemann
- ☐ 20 Jesse Levan
- ☐ 21 Hillis Layne
- ☐ 22 Frank Lucchesi
- ☐ 23 Jackie Mitchell
- ☐ 24 Bobo Newsom
- ☐ 25 Sal Rende
- ☐ 26 Kevin Rhomberg
- ☐ 27 J. Costen Shockley
- ☐ 28 Al Sima
- ☐ 29 Buck Varner
- ☐ 30 Gene Verble
- ☐ 31 Junior Wooten
- ☐ 32 Checklist Card (blank back)

1988 Clearwater Phillies Star

	MINT	NRMT	EXC
COMPLETE SET (26)	5.00	2.20	.60

- ☐ 1 Steve Bates
- ☐ 2 Cliff Brantley
- ☐ 3 Rod Brunelle
- ☐ 4 Pete Callas
- ☐ 5 Chris Calvert
- ☐ 6 Ramon Caraballo
- ☐ 7 Fred Christopher
- ☐ 8 Garry Clark
- ☐ 9 Todd Crosby
- ☐ 10 Shawn Dantzler
- ☐ 11 Kevin Fynan
- ☐ 12 Jason Grimsley
- ☐ 13 Jeff Grotewold
- ☐ 14 Todd Howey
- ☐ 15 Luis Iglesias
- ☐ 16 Steve Kirkpatrick
- ☐ 17 Chris Limbach
- ☐ 18 Pete Maldonado
- ☐ 19 Trey McCall
- ☐ 20 Scott Reaves
- ☐ 21 Mark Sims
- ☐ 22 Steve Scarsone
- ☐ 23 Brad Smith
- ☐ 24 Tim Taft
- ☐ 25 Royal Thomas
- ☐ 26 Travis Walden

1988 Clinton Giants ProCards

This 29-card standard-size set of the 1988 Clinton Giants, a Class A Midwest League affiliate of the San Francisco Giants, features bronze-bordered posed color player photos on its fronts. The player's name, position, and team name appear at the bottom. The plain white back carries the player's name at the top, followed by biography and statistics.

	MINT	NRMT	EXC
COMPLETE SET (29)	6.00	2.70	.75

- ☐ 693 John Vuz
- ☐ 694 Steve Lienhard
- ☐ 695 Rod Beck
- ☐ 696 Steve Connolly
- ☐ 697 Tom Hostetler
- ☐ 698 Scott Nelson

☐ 699 Mark Poling
☐ 700 Bill Carlson
☐ 701 Juan Guerrero
☐ 702 Jimmy Terrill
☐ 703 Jim Anderson
☐ 704 Mark Owens
☐ 705 Andres Santana
☐ 706 Todd Miller
☐ 707 Craig Colbert
☐ 708 Erik Johnson
☐ 709 Mike Ham
☐ 710 Tony Michalak
☐ 711 Mark Dewey
☐ 712 Bill Evers
☐ 713 Mike Stanfield
☐ 714 Robert Lucero
☐ 715 Jamie Cooper
☐ 716 Elanis Westbrooks
☐ 717 Jeff Morris
☐ 718 Tom Ealy
☐ 719 Mike Villa
☐ 720 Lonnie Phillips
☐ NNO Checklist

1988 Colorado Springs Sky Sox CMC

10,000 sets were produced.

	MINT	NRMT	EXC
COMPLETE SET (25)	4.00	1.80	.50

☐ 1 Darrel Akerfelds
☐ 2 Mike Brown
☐ 3 Don Gordon
☐ 4 Jeff Kaiser
☐ 5 Ron Mathis
☐ 6 Jon Perlman
☐ 7 Reggie Ritter
☐ 8 Rick Rodriguez
Sic, Rodrigez
☐ 9 Charlie Scott
☐ 10 Joe Skalski
☐ 11 John Stefaro
☐ 12 Ron Tingley
☐ 13 Mark Higgins
☐ 14 Tommy Hinzo
☐ 15 Don Lovell
☐ 16 Domingo Ramos
☐ 17 Eddie Williams
☐ 18 Paul Zuvella
☐ 19 Rod Allen
☐ 20 Terry Francona
☐ 21 Luis Medina
☐ 22 Randy Washington
☐ 23 Reggie Williams
☐ 24 Steve Swisher
☐ 25 Aurelio Rodriguez
Sic, Rodrigues

1988 Colorado Springs Sky Sox ProCards

This 29-card standard-size set of the 1988 Colorado Springs Sky Sox, a Class AAA Pacific Coast League affiliate of the Cleveland Indians, features gold-bordered posed color player photos on its fronts. The player's name, position, and team name appear at the bottom. The plain white back carries the player's name at the top, followed by biography and statistics.

	MINT	NRMT	EXC
COMPLETE SET (29)	5.00	2.20	.60

☐ 1522 John Stefero
☐ 1523 Don Lovell
☐ 1524 Reggie Williams
☐ 1525 Randy Washington
☐ 1526 Mike Brown
☐ 1527 Tommy Hinzo
☐ 1528 Paul Zuvella
☐ 1529 Charles Scott
☐ 1530 Rick Peterson
☐ 1531 Jeff Kaiser
☐ 1532 Ron Tingley
☐ 1533 Joe Skalski
☐ 1534 Domingo Ramos
☐ 1535 Keith Bennett
☐ 1536 Aurelio Rodriguez
☐ 1537 Darrel Akerfelds
☐ 1538 Don Gordon
☐ 1539 Steve Ciszczon
☐ 1540 Reggie Ritter
☐ 1541 Terry Francona
☐ 1542 Jon Perlman
☐ 1543 Luis Medina
☐ 1544 Mark Higgins
☐ 1545 Rod Allen
☐ 1546 Steve Swisher
☐ 1547 Eddie Williams
☐ 1548 Ron Mathis
☐ 1549 Rick Rodriguez
☐ NNO Checklist

1988 Columbia Mets Grand Slam

	MINT	NRMT	EXC
COMPLETE SET (27)	5.00	2.20	.60

☐ 1 Butch Hobson
☐ 2 Pete Bauer
☐ 3 Rick Durant
☐ 4 Rocky Elli
☐ 5 Eric Hillman
☐ 6 Steve Larose
☐ 7 Juan Marina
☐ 8 James McAnarney
☐ 9 Mike Miller
☐ 10 Kevin Ponder
☐ 11 Julio Valera
☐ 12 Javier Gonzalez
☐ 13 David Lau
☐ 14 Alex Diaz
☐ 15 Alex Jimenez
☐ 16 David Joiner
☐ 17 Rodney Murrell
☐ 18 Fred Hina
☐ 19 Manny Mantrana
☐ 20 Scott Spoolstra
☐ 21 Rob Lemle
☐ 22 Terry McDaniel
☐ 23 Danny Naughton
☐ 24 Jaime Roseboro
☐ 25 Scott Jaster
☐ 26 Chris Donnels
☐ 28 Joel Horlen CO

1988 Columbus Astros Best

This 28-card standard-size set of the 1988 Columbus Astros, a Class AA Southern League affiliate of the Houston Astros, features orange and black bordered posed color player photos on its fronts. The team name appears at the top, and below the picture is the player's name and position. The horizontal gray back carries the player's name and position at the top, followed by biography, career highlights, and statistics. The set is printed on thin card stock.

	MINT	NRMT	EXC
COMPLETE SET (28)	5.00	2.20	.60

☐ 1 Charley Kerfeld
☐ 2 Don Dunster
☐ 3 Terry Wells
☐ 4 Glenn Spagnola
☐ 5 Brian Meyer
☐ 6 Ken Crew
☐ 7 Doug Givler
☐ 8 Jose Vargas
☐ 9 Kyle Todd
☐ 10 Juan Lopez
☐ 11 David Rohde
☐ 12 Dan Walters
☐ 13 John Elliott
☐ 14 Rich Johnson
☐ 15 Larry Lasky
☐ 16 Jeff Edwards
☐ 17 Blaise Ilsley
☐ 18 Tom Funk
☐ 19 Carlo Colombino
☐ 20 Fred Gladding
☐ 21 Gary Cooper
☐ 22 Terry Green
☐ 23 Troy Afenir
☐ 24 Dayton Preston
☐ 25 Tom Wiedenbauer
☐ 26 Calvin James
☐ 27 Norman Brock
☐ 28 Checklist

1988 Columbus Clippers CMC

10,000 sets were produced.

	MINT	NRMT	EXC
COMPLETE SET (26)	6.00	2.70	.75

☐ 1 Pat Clements
☐ 2 Clay Parker
☐ 3 Scott Nielsen
☐ 4 Bill Fulton
☐ 5 Matt Harrison
☐ 6 Steve Shields
☐ 7 Hipolito Pena
☐ 8 Eric Schimdt
☐ 9 Mike Kinnuenen
☐ 10 Rick Langford
☐ 11 Bob Geren
☐ 12 Jamie Nelson
☐ 13 Berto Pena
☐ 14 Rob Lambert
☐ 15 Alvaro Espinoza
☐ 16 Pete Dalena
☐ 17 Randy Velarde
☐ 18 Jeff Moronko
☐ 19 Turner Ward
☐ 20 Hal Morris
☐ 21 Casey Close
☐ 22 Cliff Speck
☐ 23 Jay Buhner
☐ 24 Chris Alvarez
☐ 25 Bucky Dent
☐ 26 Governors Cup

1988 Columbus Clippers Police

	MINT	NRMT	EXC
COMPLETE SET (25)	10.00	4.50	1.25

☐ 1 Pat Clements
☐ 2 Bill Fulton
☐ 3 Matt Harrison
☐ 4 Mike Kinnunen
☐ 5 Rick Langford
☐ 6 Scott Nielsen
☐ 7 Clay Parker
☐ 8 Hipolito Pena
☐ 9 Eric Schmidt
☐ 10 Steve Shields
☐ 11 Cliff Speck
☐ 12 Bob Geren
☐ 13 Chris Alvarez
☐ 14 Pete Dalena
☐ 15 Alvaro Espinoza
☐ 16 Bert Pena
☐ 17 Turner Ward
☐ 18 Jay Buhner
☐ 19 Casey Close
☐ 20 Jeff Moronko
☐ 21 Hal Morris
☐ 22 Randy Velarde
☐ 23 Jamie Nelson
☐ 24 Champ Summers CO
Kevin Rand TR
Ken Rowe CO
☐ 25 Bucky Dent MG
George Sisler GM

1988 Columbus Clippers ProCards

This 29-card standard-size set of the 1988 Columbus Clippers, a Class AAA International League affiliate of the New York Yankees, features gold-bordered posed color player photos on its fronts. The player's name, position, and team name appear at the bottom. The plain white back carries the player's name at the top, followed by biography and statistics. This issue includes a second year card of Jay Buhner.

	MINT	NRMT	EXC
COMPLETE SET (29)	10.00	4.50	1.25

☐ 303 Bob Geren
☐ 304 Glenn Sherlock
☐ 305 Jamie Nelson
☐ 306 Bucky Dent
☐ 307 Champ Summers CO
Ken Rowe CO
Bucky Dent MG
Kevin Rand TR
☐ 308 Rick Langford
☐ 309 Clay Parker
☐ 310 Scott Nielsen
☐ 311 Cliff Speck
☐ 312 Bill Fulton
☐ 313 Eric Schmidt
☐ 314 Steve Shields
☐ 315 Hipolito Pena
☐ 316 Mike Kinnunen
☐ 317 Matt Harrison
☐ 318 Pat Clements
☐ 319 Rob Lambert
☐ 320 Alvaro Espinoza
☐ 321 Pete Dalena
☐ 322 Berto Pena
☐ 323 Chris Alvarez
☐ 324 Randy Velarde
☐ 325 Casey Close
☐ 326 Max Ward
☐ 327 Hal Morris
☐ 328 Jeff Moronko
☐ 329 Jay Buhner
☐ 330 Team Photo
☐ NNO Checklist

1988 Denver Zephyrs CMC

10,000 sets were produced.

	MINT	NRMT	EXC
COMPLETE SET (25)	4.00	1.80	.50

☐ 1 Mark Knudson
☐ 2 Mike Konderla
☐ 3 Alex Madrid
☐ 4 John Miglio
☐ 5 Paul Mirabella
☐ 6 Tim Watkins
☐ 7 Jay Aldrich
☐ 8 Don August
☐ 9 Mark Ciardi
☐ 10 Tom Filer
☐ 11 Tim Pyznarski
☐ 12 German Rivera
☐ 13 Billy Jo Robidoux
☐ 14 Keith Smith
☐ 15 Charlie O'Brien
☐ 16 Ronn Reynolds
☐ 17 Billy Bates
☐ 18 Kiki Diaz
☐ 19 Todd Brown
☐ 20 La Vel Freeman
Sic, Lavell
☐ 21 Brad Komminsk
☐ 22 Steve Stanicek
☐ 23 Darryel Walters
☐ 24 Darryl Hamilton
☐ 25 Duffy Dyer

1988 Denver Zephyrs ProCards

This 30-card standard-size set of the 1988 Denver Zephyrs, a Class AAA American Association affiliate of the Milwaukee Brewers, features gold-bordered posed color player photos on its fronts. The player's name, position, and team name appear at the bottom. The plain white back carries the player's name at the top, followed by biography and statistics.

	MINT	NRMT	EXC
COMPLETE SET (30)	5.00	2.20	.60

☐ 1250 Jackson Todd
☐ 1251 Alex Madrid
☐ 1252 Peter Kolb
☐ 1253 German Rivera
☐ 1254 Bill Mooneyham
☐ 1255 Darryel Walters
☐ 1256 Kiki Diaz
☐ 1257 Tom Filer
☐ 1258 Paul Mirabella
☐ 1259 Don August
☐ 1260 John Miglio
☐ 1261 Keith Smith
☐ 1262 Ronn Reynolds
☐ 1263 Brad Komminsk
☐ 1264 Duffy Dyer
☐ 1265 Tim Watkins
☐ 1266 Steve Stanicek
☐ 1267 Billy Jo Robidoux
☐ 1268 Charlie O'Brien
☐ 1269 Pete Kendrick
☐ 1270 Jay Aldrich
☐ 1271 Billy Bates
☐ 1272 Mark Ciardi
☐ 1273 Tim Pyznarski
☐ 1274 Darryl Hamilton
☐ 1275 Mark Knudson
☐ 1276 Mike Konderla
☐ 1277 La Vel Freeman
Sic, Lavell
☐ 1278 Todd Brown
☐ NNO Checklist

1988 Dunedin Blue Jays Star

This 25-card standard-size set of the 1988 Dunedin Blue Jays, a Class A Florida State League affiliate of the Toronto Blue Jays, features blue-bordered posed color player photos on its fronts. The player's name, team name, and position appear at the bottom. The yellowish horizontal back carries the player's name at the top, followed by biography, career highlights, and statistics. Doug Ault's manager card (#25) was a late issue. This issue includes a second year card of Pat Hentgen.

	MINT	NRMT	EXC
COMPLETE SET (25)	15.00	6.75	1.85

☐ 1 Francisco Cabrera
☐ 2 Tony Castillo
☐ 3 Wayne Davis
☐ 4 Jose Diaz
☐ 5 Richard DePastino
☐ 6 Lindsay Foster
☐ 7 Peter Geist
☐ 8 Darren Hall
☐ 9 Pat Hentgen
☐ 10 Vince Horsman
☐ 11 Steve Mumaw
☐ 12 Shawn Jeter
☐ 13 Pedro Munoz
☐ 14 Paul Rodgers
☐ 15 Earl Sanders
☐ 16 Jerry Schunk
☐ 17 Jason Townley
☐ 18 Jim Tracy
☐ 19 Darrin Wade
☐ 20 Bob Watts
☐ 21 Mark Whiten
☐ 22 Bob Wishnevski
☐ 23 Julian Yan
☐ 24 Mark Young
☐ 25 Doug Ault MG

1988 Durham Bulls Star

	MINT	NRMT	EXC
COMPLETE SET (24)	5.00	2.20	.60
COMP. SET W/LATE ISSUES (27)	14.00	6.25	1.75
COMPLETE ORANGE SET (26)	12.00	5.50	1.50

☐ 1 Michael Bell
☐ 2 Scott Bohlke
☐ 3 David Butts
☐ 4A Jim Czajowski
☐ 4B Buddy Bailey (Late Issue)
☐ 5 Jeff Dodig
☐ 6 Mike Fowler
☐ 7 Ted Holcomb
☐ 8 Cesar Jimenez
☐ 9A Dodd Johnson
☐ 9B Kevin Costner (Gold/Late Issue)
☐ 10 Rich Longuil
☐ 11 Phil Maldonado
☐ 12 Rich Maloney
☐ 13 Paul Marak
☐ 14 Kent Mercker
☐ 15 Rick Morris
☐ 16 Kenneth Pennington
☐ 17 Dave Plumb
☐ 18 Ellis Roby
☐ 19 Doug Stockam
☐ 20 Mike Stoker
☐ 21 Theron Todd
☐ 22 Lee Upshaw
☐ 23 Danny Weems
☐ 24 Walt Williams
☐ NNO Kevin Costner (Blue/Late Issue)

1988 Eastern League All-Stars ProCards

	MINT	NRMT	EXC
COMPLETE SET (52)	8.00	3.60	1.00

☐ 1 Dave Eiland
☐ 2 Kevin Maas
☐ 3 Hensley Meulens
☐ 4 Dana Ridenour
☐ 5 Andy Stankiewicz
☐ 6 Dan Dimascio
☐ 7 Shawn Holman
☐ 8 Torey Lovullo
☐ 9 Julius McDougal
☐ 10 Cesar Mejia
☐ 11 Rob Richie
☐ 12 Delwyn Young
☐ 13 Jeff Cook
☐ 14 Kevin Davis
☐ 15 Dimas Gutierrez
☐ 16 Jeff King
☐ 17 Larry Melton
☐ 18 Paul Wilmet
☐ 19 Jose Birriel
☐ 20 Mike Carista
☐ 21 Ed Estrada
☐ 22 Todd Pratt
☐ 23 John Roberts
☐ 24 Luis Vasquez
☐ 25 Joe Girardi
☐ 26 Mike Harkey
☐ 27 Bryan House
☐ 28 Hector Villanueva
☐ 29 Jerome Walton
☐ 30 Dean Wilkins
☐ 31 Tony Brown
☐ 32 Greg Edge
☐ 33 Warren Magee
☐ 34 Chuck Malone
☐ 35 Jeff Hull
☐ 36 Ricky Rojas
☐ 37 Omar Vizquel
☐ 38 Jim Wilson
☐ 39 Mark Howie
☐ 40 Scott Jordan
☐ 41 Tom Lampkin
☐ 42 Mike Poehl
☐ 43 Casey Webster
☐ 44 Kevin Wickander
☐ 45 Dave Trembley
☐ 46 Harold Williams
☐ 47 Jim Essian
☐ 48 Grant Jackson
☐ 49 Brian McCann
☐ 50 Brian Allard
☐ 51 Brian Graham
☐ 52 Mike Hargrove

1988 Edmonton Trappers CMC

This 25-card standard-size set of the 1988 Edmonton Trappers, a Class AAA Pacific Coast League affiliate of the California Angels, features on its fronts black-bordered posed color player photos framed by a green line. The team's name, the player's name, and his position appear at the bottom. The white back is framed by a black line and carries the team's name and league at the top, followed by the player's name, position, biography and statistics. This issue includes a second year card of Dante Bichette. 10,000 sets were produced.

	MINT	NRMT	EXC
COMPLETE SET (25)	12.00	5.50	1.50

☐ 1 Terry Clark
☐ 2 Mike Cook
☐ 3 Jack Lazorko
☐ 4 Vance Lovelace
☐ 5 Bryan Harvey
☐ 6 Urbano Lugo
☐ 7 Joe Johnson
☐ 8 Philip Venturino
☐ 9 Marty Reed
☐ 10 Barry Dacus
☐ 11 Miguel Alicea
☐ 12 Darrell Miller
☐ 13 Pete Coachman
☐ 14 Stan Holmes
☐ 15 Bob Miscik
☐ 16 Brian Brady
☐ 17 Kent Anderson
☐ 18 Doug Davis
☐ 19 Edwin Marquez
☐ 20 Joe Redfield
☐ 21 Jim Eppard
☐ 22 Tom Kotchman MG
☐ 23 Dante Bichette
☐ 24 Mark Doran
☐ 25 Kevin King

1988 Edmonton Trappers ProCards

This 31-card standard-size set of the 1988 Edmonton Trappers, a Class AAA Pacific Coast League affiliate of the California Angels, features gold-bordered posed color player photos on its fronts. The player's name, position, and team name appear at the bottom. The plain white back carries the player's name at the top, followed by biography and statistics. This issue includes a second year card of Dante Bichette.

	MINT	NRMT	EXC
COMPLETE SET (31)	16.00	7.25	2.00

☐ 555 Joe Redfield
☐ 556 Jack Lazorko
☐ 557 Vance Lovelace
☐ 558 Jim Eppard
☐ 559 Doug Davis
☐ 560 Joe Johnson
☐ 561 Chico Walker
☐ 562 Marty Reed
☐ 563 Chuck Hernandez CO
☐ 564 Junior Noboa
☐ 565 Frank Dimechele
☐ 566 Phil Venturino
☐ 567 Mike Cook
☐ 568 Barry Dacus
☐ 569 Terry Clark
☐ 570 Mark Doran
☐ 571 Stan Holmes
☐ 572 Brian Brady
☐ 573 Kevin King
☐ 574 Kent Anderson
☐ 575 Edwin Marquez
☐ 576 Dante Bichette
☐ 577 Bobby Miscik
☐ 578 Pete Coachman
☐ 579 Darrell Miller
☐ 580 Tom Kotchman MG
☐ 581 Urbano Lugo
☐ 582 Miguel Alicea
☐ 583 Craig Gerber
☐ 584 Al Olson TR
☐ NNO Checklist

1988 El Paso Diablos Best

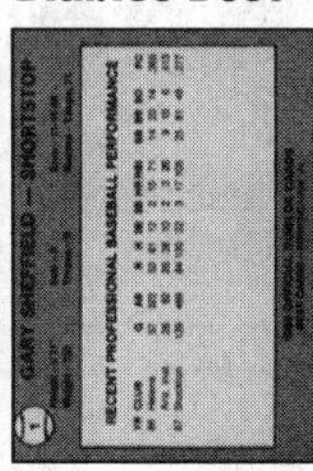

This 30-card standard-size set of the 1988 El Paso Diablos, a Class AA Texas League affiliate of the Milwaukee Brewers, features red and black bordered posed color player photos on its fronts. The team name appears at the top, and below the picture is the player's name and position. The horizontal gray back carries the player's name and position at the top, followed by biography, career highlights, and statistics. The set is printed on thin card stock. Only 1300 of the platinum version were produced. This issue includes second year cards of Gary Sheffield and Greg Vaughn.

	MINT	NRMT	EXC
COMPLETE SET (30)	35.00	16.00	4.40
COMPLETE PLATINUM SET (30)	60.00	27.00	7.50

☐ 1 Gary Sheffield
☐ 2 Donald Scott
☐ 3 Daniel Scarpetta
☐ 4 Jamie Brisco
☐ 5 George Canale
☐ 6 Dave Machemer
☐ 7 Ramon Serna
☐ 8 Luis Castillo
☐ 9 Bill Mooneyham
☐ 10 Paul Lindblad
☐ 11 Jim Rowe
☐ 12 Matias Carrillo
☐ 13 Alan Cartwright
☐ 14 Robert DeWolf
☐ 15 Mark Ambrose
☐ 16 Andy Anderson
☐ 17 Barry Bass
☐ 18 Bradley Wheeler
☐ 19 Fred Williams
☐ 20 Gregory Vaughn
☐ 21 Jeffrey Peterek
☐ 22 Edward Puig
☐ 23 Angel Rodriguez
☐ 24 Adrian Meagher
☐ 25 Joseph Mitchell
☐ 26 Mario Monico
☐ 27 Rob Hicks
☐ 28 James Hunter
☐ 29 Frankie Mattox
☐ 30 Checklist

1988 Elmira Pioneers 100th Cain

This 12-card set of the 1988 Elmira Pioneers, a Class A New York-Penn League affiliate of the Boston Red Sox, features black and white player photos with a blue star white border. 200 sets were produced.

	MINT	NRMT	EXC
COMPLETE SET (12)	30.00	13.50	3.70

☐ 1 Reggie Harris
☐ 2 Tony Mosley
☐ 3 Mickey Pina
☐ 4 Ronnie Richardson
☐ 5 Packy Rogers
☐ 6 Tony Romero
☐ 7 Julio Rosario
☐ 8 Brian Warfel
☐ 9 Bob Zupcic
☐ 10 Elmira Pioneers 1941
☐ 11 Elmira Pioneers 1967
☐ 12 Elmira Pioneers 1979

1988 Elmira Pioneers Cain

This 30-card set of the 1988 Elmira Pioneers, a Class A New York-Penn League affiliate of the Boston Red Sox, features black and white player photos with a red star white border. The cards measure 3 3/4" x 2 1/2" and are horizontal. This issue includes the minor league card debut of Tim Naehring. 4,800 sets were produced.

	MINT	NRMT	EXC
COMPLETE SET (30)	8.00	3.60	1.00

☐ 1 Logo Card
☐ 2 Alberto Pratts
☐ 3 Steve Michael
☐ 4 Scott Taylor
☐ 5 Bernie Dzafic
☐ 6 Dan Kite
☐ 7 John Dolan
☐ 8 Peter Estrada
☐ 9 Tim Stange
☐ 10 Al Sanders
☐ 11 Carlos Rivera
☐ 12 Luis Dorante
☐ 13 John Flaherty
☐ 14 Pedro Matilla
☐ 15 David Monegro
☐ 16 Lou Munoz
☐ 17 Tim Naehring
☐ 18 Julio Rosario
☐ 19 Willie Tatum
☐ 20 Al Thornton
☐ 21 Chris Whitehead
☐ 22 Terry Marrs
☐ 23 Mickey Rivers, Jr.
☐ 24 Larry Scannell
☐ 25 John Spencer
☐ 26 Brian Warfel
☐ 27 Bill Limoncelli MG
☐ 28 John Post TR
☐ 29 Dennis Robarge ASST
☐ 30 Clyde Smoll GM

1988 Eugene Emeralds Best

This 30-card standard-size set of the 1988 Eugene Emeralds, a Class A Northwest League affiliate of the Kansas City Royals, features blue and black bordered posed color player photos on its fronts. The team name appears at the top, and below the picture is the player's name and position. The horizontal gray back carries the player's name and position at the top, followed by biography, career highlights, and statistics. The set is printed on thin card stock.

	MINT	NRMT	EXC
COMPLETE SET (30)	5.00	2.20	.60

☐ 1 Bob Hamlin
Sic, Hamblin
☐ 2 Steve Hoeme
☐ 3 Greg Harvey
☐ 4 Steve Otto
☐ 5 Bill Drohan
☐ 6 Hector Wagner
☐ 7 Kyle Irvin
☐ 8 Jim Smith
☐ 9 Brad Hopper
☐ 10 Randy Vaughn
☐ 11 Joel Johnston
☐ 12 David Rolls
☐ 13 Rob Buchanan
☐ 14 Jeff Hulse
☐ 15 Fred Russell
☐ 16 Jeff Garber
☐ 17 Kelvin Davis
☐ 18 Ron Collins
☐ 19 Bill Gardner
☐ 20 Steve Preston
☐ 21 Karl Drezek
☐ 22 Bobby Holley
☐ 23 Frank Henderson
☐ 24 John Gilchrist
☐ 25 Derek Sholl
☐ 26 Gerald Ingram
☐ 27 Milt Richarson
☐ 28 Frankie Watson
☐ 29 Keith Shibata
☐ 30 Checklist

1988 Florida State League All-Stars Star

	MINT	NRMT	EXC
COMPLETE SET (52)	12.00	5.50	1.50

☐ 1 John Shoemaker MG
☐ 2 Felipe Alou CO
☐ 3 Keith Bodie
☐ 4 Doug Cinnella
☐ 5 Scott Diez
☐ 6 Kip Gross
☐ 7 Dave Hansen
☐ 8 Randy Hennis
☐ 9 Nels Jacobsen
☐ 10 Chris Limbach
☐ 11 Luis Martinez
☐ 12 Todd McClure
☐ 13 Brian Morrison
☐ 14 Bob Natal
☐ 15 Chris Nichting
☐ 16 Geronimo Pena
☐ 17 Fritz Polka
☐ 18 Karl Rhodes
☐ 19 Homar Rojas
☐ 20 Miguel Santana
☐ 21 Mike Simms
☐ 22 Greg Talamantez
☐ 23 John Vander Wal
☐ 24 Juan Villanueva
☐ 25 Mike White
☐ 26 Masahiro Yamamoto
☐ 27 Buck Showalter
☐ 28 John Lipon
☐ 29 Russ Meyer
☐ 30 Luis Silverio
☐ 31 Phil Clark
☐ 32 Milt Cuyler
☐ 33 Jose Diaz
☐ 34 Carlos Escalera
☐ 35 Greg Everson
☐ 36 Blane Fox
☐ 37 Cornelio Garcia
☐ 38 Darrin Garner
☐ 39 Mike Hansen
☐ 40 Brent Knackert
☐ 41 Adam Lamie
☐ 42 Richie LeBlanc
☐ 43 Ravelo Manzanillo
☐ 44 Kevin Mmahat
☐ 45 Tony Morrison
☐ 46 Livio Padilla
☐ 47 Dean Palmer
☐ 48 Dan Rohrmeier
☐ 49 Carl Sullivan
☐ 50 Aquedo Vasquez
☐ 51 Don Vesling
☐ 52 Julian Yan

1988 Fayetteville Generals ProCards

This 28-card standard-size set of the 1988 Fayetteville Generals, a Class A South Atlantic League affiliate of the Detroit Tigers, features bronze-bordered posed color player photos on its fronts. The player's name, position, and team name appear at the bottom. The plain white back carries the player's name at the top, followed by biography and statistics. This issue includes the minor league card debut of Travis Fryman.

	MINT	NRMT	EXC
COMPLETE SET (28)	30.00	13.50	3.70

☐ 1079 Keith Nicholson
☐ 1080 Glenn Belcher
☐ 1081 Steve Pegues

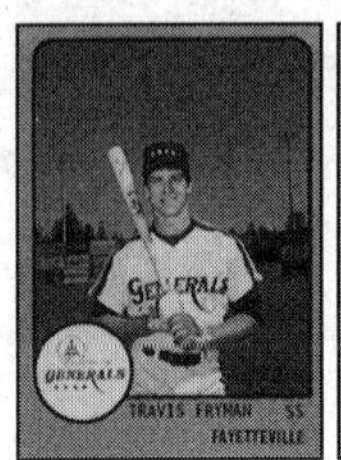

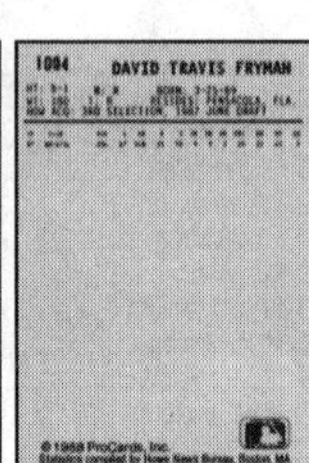

☐ 1082 Andy Toney
☐ 1083 Luis Melendez
☐ 1084 Larry Coker
☐ 1085 Mark Adler
☐ 1086 Jose Ramos
☐ 1087 Robinson Garces
☐ 1088 Steve Parascand
☐ 1089 Chuck Duquette
☐ 1090 Zack Doster
☐ 1091 Duben Bello
☐ 1092 Charles Steward
☐ 1093 Felix Liriano
☐ 1094 Travis Fryman
☐ 1095 Dave Richards
☐ 1096 Ron Cook
☐ 1097 Chris Schnurbusch
☐ 1098 Randy Luciani
☐ 1099 Kevin Camilli
☐ 1100 Miguel Murphy
☐ 1101 Liliano Castro
☐ 1102 Bill Henderson
☐ 1103 Michael Wilkins
☐ 1104 Leon Roberts
☐ 1105 Mike DeLao
☐ NNO Checklist

1988 Fresno Suns Cal League Cards

	MINT	NRMT	EXC
COMPLETE SET (27)	5.00	2.20	.60

☐ 1 Tony Triplett
☐ 2 Mark Combs
☐ 3 Joe Mancini
☐ 4 Jon Hobbs
☐ 5 Ernie Young
☐ 6 Dan Simonds
☐ 7 Tracy Pancoski
☐ 8 Frank Bellino
☐ 9 Todd Hawkins
☐ 10 John Barry
☐ 11 Kim Flowers
☐ 12 Jim Malseed
☐ 13 Dave Nash
☐ 14 Richard Yagi
☐ 15 Hector Miyauchi
☐ 16 Steve Bowden
☐ 17 Frank Bryan
☐ 18 John Bilello
☐ 19 Rob Rowen
☐ 20 Anthony Tagi
☐ 21 Bullet Manabe
☐ 22 Chuck Higson
☐ 23 Gary Geiger
☐ 24 Rocco Buffolino
☐ 25 Brad Comstock
☐ 26 Dean Treanor
☐ 27 Tom Bell

1988 Fresno Suns ProCards

This 29-card standard-size set of the 1988 Fresno Suns, a Class A California League Independent, features bronze-bordered posed color player photos on its fronts. The player's name, position, and team name appear at the bottom. The plain white back carries the player's name at the top, followed by biography and statistics.

	MINT	NRMT	EXC
COMPLETE SET (29)	5.00	2.20	.60

☐ 1222 Frank Bryan
☐ 1223 Kim Flowers
☐ 1224 John Bilello
☐ 1225 Chuck Higson
☐ 1226 Brad Comstock
☐ 1227 John Barry
☐ 1228 Dave Nash
☐ 1229 Gary Geiger
☐ 1230 Dan Simonds
☐ 1231 Rocco Buffolino
☐ 1232 Jim Malseed
☐ 1233 Hector Miyauchi
☐ 1234 Antony Tagi
☐ 1235 Bullet Manabe
☐ 1236 Dean Treanor
☐ 1237 Jon Hobbs
☐ 1238 Joe Ueda
☐ 1239 Richard Yagi
☐ 1240 Tracey Pancoski
☐ 1241 Ernie Young
☐ 1242 Todd Hawkins
☐ 1243 Tony Triplett
☐ 1244 Rob Rowen
☐ 1245 Marty Montano
☐ 1246 Geroge Omachi
☐ 1247 Joe Mancini
☐ 1248 Tom Bell
☐ 1249 Donna L. VanDuzer
☐ NNO Checklist

1988 Ft. Lauderdale Yankees Star

	MINT	NRMT	EXC
COMPLETE SET (24)	5.00	2.20	.60

☐ 1 Dan Arendas
☐ 2 Luc Berube
☐ 3 Art Calvert
☐ 4 Carrin Chapin
☐ 5 Bob Dickerson
☐ 6 Jim Ehrhard
☐ 7 Steve Erickson
☐ 8 Fernando Figueroa
☐ 9 Scott Gay
☐ 10 Doug Gogolewski
☐ 11 Fred Hailey
☐ 12 Rodney Imes
☐ 13 Scott Kamieniecki
☐ 14 Ralph Kraus
☐ 15 Mark Mitchell
☐ 16 Kevin Mmahat
☐ 17 Tony Morrison
☐ 18 Carlos Rodriguez
☐ 19 Gabriel Rodgriguez
☐ 20 Dan Roman
☐ 21 Wade Taylor
☐ 22 David Turgeon
☐ 23 Bill Voeltz
☐ 24 Thomas Weeks

1988 Gastonia Rangers ProCards

This 30-card standard-size set of the 1988 Gastonia Rangers, a Class A South Atlantic League affiliate of the Texas Rangers, features bronze-bordered posed color player photos on its fronts. The player's name, position, and team name appear at the bottom. The plain white back carries the player's name at the top, followed by biography and statistics.

	MINT	NRMT	EXC
COMPLETE SET (30)	10.00	4.50	1.25

☐ 995 Marv Rockman
☐ 996 Bob Lavender
☐ 997 Bill Findlay
☐ 998 Mike Taylor
☐ 999 Jay Baker
☐ 1000 Rick Knapp
☐ 1001 Chris Shiflett
☐ 1002 Luke Sable
☐ 1003 Robb Nen
☐ 1004 Jim McCutcheon
☐ 1005 Cris Colon
☐ 1006 Joe Pearn
☐ 1007 Brant Alyea
☐ 1008 Felipe Castillo
☐ 1009 Orlando Gomez
☐ 1010 Kevin Belcher
☐ 1011 Jose Velez
☐ 1012 Jeff Melrose
☐ 1013 Bill Losa
☐ 1014 Pat Garman
☐ 1015 Brad Meyer
☐ 1016 Marty Cerny
☐ 1017 Wilson Alvarez
☐ 1018 Brian Steiner
☐ 1019 Spencer Wilkinson
☐ 1020 Roger Pavlik
☐ 1021 Glenn Patterson
☐ 1022 Saul Barretto
☐ 1023 Chuck Marguardt
☐ NNO Checklist

1988 Geneva Cubs ProCards

This 30-card standard-size set of the 1988 Geneva Cubs, a Class A New York-Penn League affiliate of the Chicago Cubs, features bronze-bordered posed color player photos on its fronts. The player's name, position, and team name appear at the bottom. The plain white back carries the player's name at the top, followed by biography and statistics.

	MINT	NRMT	EXC
COMPLETE SET (30)	5.00	2.20	.60

☐ 1633 Eric Perry
☐ 1634 Nick Ramirez
☐ 1635 Eric Williams
☐ 1636 Gary Arnold
☐ 1637 Ray Figueroa
☐ 1638 Jim Murphy
☐ 1639 Skip Eggleston
☐ 1640 Rick Mundy
☐ 1641 Dave Goodwin
☐ 1642 Mike Sodders
☐ 1643 Tim Ellis
☐ 1644 Dan Johnston
☐ 1645 Matt Leonard
☐ 1646 Eligio Rodriguez
☐ 1647 Tracy Smith
☐ 1648 Francisco Espino
☐ 1649 Derek Stroud
☐ 1650 Bill St. Peter
☐ 1651 Scott Taylor
☐ 1652 Ben Shreve
☐ 1653 Chris Lutz
☐ 1654 Bill Hayes
☐ 1655 Carlos Canino
☐ 1656 Ken Shepard
☐ 1657 George Brzezinski
☐ 1658 Marty Owens
☐ 1659 Dave Oster
☐ 1660 Sheila Arnold
☐ 1661 Quinn's Cards
☐ NNO Checklist

1988 Glens Falls Tigers ProCards

This 27-card standard-size set of the 1988 Glens Falls Tigers, a Class AA Eastern League affiliate of the Detroit Tigers, features silver-bordered posed color player photos on its fronts. The player's name, position, and team name appear at the bottom. The plain white back carries the player's name at the top, followed by biography and statistics.

	MINT	NRMT	EXC
COMPLETE SET (27)	5.00	2.20	.60

☐ 913 Wayne Housie
☐ 914 Pat Austin
☐ 915 Eric Hardgrave
☐ 916 Delwyn Young
☐ 917 John Wockenfuss
☐ 918 Ken Williams
☐ 919 Julius McDougal
☐ 920 Rich Lacko
☐ 921 Paul Wenson
☐ 922 Rich Wieligman
☐ 923 Torey Lovullo
☐ 924 Cesar Mejia
☐ 925 Rob Richie
☐ 926 Kevin Ritz
☐ 927 Mike Schwabe
☐ 928 Bernie Anderson
☐ 929 Shawn Holman
☐ 930 Ken Gohmann
☐ 931 Dan Dimascio
☐ 932 Adam Dempsay
☐ 933 Bill Cooper
☐ 934 Kevin Bradshaw
☐ 935 Hector Berrios
☐ 936 Jeff Jones
☐ 937 Robert Link
☐ 938 Tim Leiper
☐ NNO Checklist

1988 Great Falls Dodgers Sports Pro

This issue includes the minor league card debut of Eric Karros. 4,000 sets were produced.

	MINT	NRMT	EXC
COMPLETE SET (27)	25.00	11.00	3.10

☐ 1 Bill Bene
☐ 2 Eric Karros
☐ 3 Brett Magnusson
☐ 4 Ernie Carr
☐ 5 Chris Morrow
☐ 6 Mike McHugh
☐ 7 Lance Rice
☐ 8 Jeff Castillo
☐ 9 Eddie Pye
☐ 10 Dan Opperman
☐ 11 Jerry Brooks
☐ 12 Don Carroll
☐ 13 Jim Wray
☐ 14 John Braase
☐ 15 Steve Finken
☐ 16 Brock McMurray
☐ 17 Bill Wengert
☐ 18 John Huebner
☐ 19 Bryan Beals
☐ 20 Sean Snedeker
☐ 21 Jeff Hartsock
☐ 22 Jose Offerman
Sic, Oferman
☐ 23 Mike James
☐ 24 Cam Biberdorf
☐ 25 Ramon Valdes
☐ 26 Tim Johnson MGR
☐ 27 Goose Gregson CO

1988 Greensboro Hornets ProCards

This 26-card standard-size set of the 1988 Greensboro Hornets, a Class A South Atlantic League affiliate of the Cincinnati Reds, features bronze-bordered posed color player photos on its fronts. The player's name, position, and team name appear at the bottom. The plain white back carries the player's name at the top, followed by biography and statistics.

	MINT	NRMT	EXC
COMPLETE SET (26)	5.00	2.20	.60

☐ 1551 Bill Risley
☐ 1552 Quinn Marsh
☐ 1553 Scott Jeffery
☐ 1554 Keith Thomas
☐ 1555 Brian Lane
☐ 1556 Shane Letterio
☐ 1557 Brad Robinson
☐ 1558 Eddie Taubensee
☐ 1559 Joe Turek
☐ 1560 Kevin Pearson
☐ 1561 Ron Mullins
☐ 1562 Adam Casillias
☐ 1563 Tony Mealy
☐ 1564 Ken Huseby
☐ 1565 Scott Westermann
☐ 1566 Mack Jenkins
☐ 1567 Rosario Rodriguez
☐ 1568 Andy Rickman
☐ 1569 Jack Smith
☐ 1570 Steve Hester
☐ 1571 Jimmy Mee
☐ 1572 Don Brown
☐ 1573 Keith Kaiser
☐ 1574 Joey Vierra
☐ 1575 Mark Berry
☐ NNO Checklist

1988 Greenville Braves Best

This 24-card standard-size set of the 1988 Greenville Braves, a Class AA Southern League affiliate of the Atlanta Braves, features blue and black bordered posed color player photos on its fronts. The team name appears at the top, and below the picture is the player's name and position. The horizontal gray back carries the player's name and position at the top, followed by biography, career highlights, and statistics. The set is printed on thin card stock.

	MINT	NRMT	EXC
COMPLETE SET (24)	5.00	2.20	.60

☐ 1 Ed Whited
☐ 2 Terry Bell
☐ 3 Sal D'Alessandro
☐ 4 Inocencio Guerrero
☐ 5 Dennis Hood
☐ 6 John Alva
☐ 7 Miguel Sabino
☐ 8 Barry Jones
☐ 9 Drew Denson
☐ 10 Mark Lemke
☐ 11 Jim Lovell
☐ 12 Dave Polley
☐ 13 Bryan Farmer
☐ 14 Dave Miller
☐ 15 Steve Ziem
☐ 16 Kevin Blankenship
☐ 17 Maximo Del Rosario
☐ 18 Tom Dozier
☐ 19 Andy Nezelek
☐ 20 John Kilner
☐ 21 Tom Dunbar
☐ 22 Eddie Mathews
☐ 23 Mike Fischlin
☐ 24 Checklist

1988 Hagerstown Suns Star

	MINT	NRMT	EXC
COMPLETE SET (25)	7.00	3.10	.85

☐ 1 Jeff Ahr
☐ 2 Dave Bettendorf
☐ 3 Don Buford Jr.
☐ 4 Mike Eberle
☐ 5 Scott Evans
☐ 6 Craig Faulkner
☐ 7 Steve Finley
☐ 8 Tom Harms
☐ 9 Walt Harris
☐ 10 Bob Latmore
☐ 11 Kevin McNees
☐ 12 Larry Mims

- ☐ 13 Chris Myers
- ☐ 14 Matt Nowak
- ☐ 15 Louie Paulino
- ☐ 16 Pete Palermo
- ☐ 17 Chris Pinder
- ☐ 18 Mike Sander
- ☐ 19 David Segui
  Sic, Secui
- ☐ 20 Steve Sonneberger
- ☐ 21 Randy Strijek
- ☐ 22 Anthony Telford
- ☐ 23 Jack Voigt
- ☐ 24 Chaun Wilson
- ☐ 25 Bob Williams

1988 Hamilton Redbirds ProCards

This 30-card standard-size set of the 1988 Hamilton Redbirds, a Class A New York-Penn League affiliate of the St. Louis Cardinals, features bronze-bordered posed color player photos on its fronts. The player's name, position, and team name appear at the bottom. The plain white back carries the player's name at the top, followed by biography and statistics.

	MINT	NRMT	EXC
COMPLETE SET (30)	5.00	2.20	.60

- ☐ 1719 Chris Houser
- ☐ 1720 Scott Halama
- ☐ 1721 John Cebuhar
- ☐ 1722 Brad DuVall
- ☐ 1723 Antron Grier
- ☐ 1724 Rick Christian
- ☐ 1725 Mark Battell
- ☐ 1726 Lee Plemel
- ☐ 1727 Mike Ross
- ☐ 1728 Dale Kisten
- ☐ 1729 Tim Redman
- ☐ 1730 Kevin Robinson
- ☐ 1731 Cory Saterfield
- ☐ 1732 Dan Radison
- ☐ 1733 Luis Melendez
- ☐ 1734 Mike Evans
- ☐ 1735 Randy Butts
- ☐ 1736 Mark Clark
- ☐ 1737 John Lepley
- ☐ 1738 Joe Federico
- ☐ 1739 Steve Fanning
- ☐ 1740 Rodney Brooks
- ☐ 1741 Tom Malchesky
- ☐ 1742 Ed Lampe
- ☐ 1743 Jean P. Gentleman
- ☐ 1744 Dean Weese
- ☐ 1745 Steve Graham
- ☐ 1746 Frank Moran
- ☐ 1747 Joe Hall
- ☐ NNO Checklist

1988 Harrisburg Senators ProCards

This 30-card standard-size set of the 1988 Harrisburg Senators, a Class AA Eastern Coast League affiliate of the Pittsburgh Pirates, features silver-bordered posed color player photos on its fronts. The player's name, position, and team name appear at the bottom. The plain white back carries the player's name at the top, followed by biography and statistics.

	MINT	NRMT	EXC
COMPLETE SET (30)	8.00	3.60	1.00

- ☐ 834 John Rigos
- ☐ 835 Jeff Cook
- ☐ 836 Tommy Shields
- ☐ 837 Kevin Davis
- ☐ 838 Scott Little
- ☐ 839 Spin Williams
- ☐ 840 Rick R. Redd
- ☐ 841 Dimas Gutierrez
- ☐ 842 Jim Neidlinger
- ☐ 843 Mike Curtis
- ☐ 844 Lance Belen
- ☐ 845 Chris Ritter
- ☐ 846 Dave Trembley
- ☐ 847 Orlando Lind
- ☐ 848 Jose Melendez
- ☐ 849 Ron Johns
- ☐ 850 Mike Walker
- ☐ 851 Gilberto Roca
- ☐ 852 Paul Wilmet
- ☐ 853 Bill Copp
- ☐ 854 Tony Chance
- ☐ 855 Jeff Banister
- ☐ 856 Gino Gentile
- ☐ 857 Larry Melton
- ☐ 858 Robby Russell
- ☐ 859 Jeff King
- ☐ 860 Clay Daniel
- ☐ 861 Harold Williams
- ☐ 862 Scott Kautz
- ☐ NNO Checklist

1988 Huntsville Stars Team Issue

	MINT	NRMT	EXC
COMPLETE SET (25)	5.00	2.20	.60

- ☐ 1 Mike Bordick
- ☐ 2 Scott Chiamparino
- ☐ 3 Brian Criswell
- ☐ 4 Pat Dietrick
- ☐ 5 DeMarlo Hale
- ☐ 6 Scott Hemond
- ☐ 7 Scott Holcomb
- ☐ 8 Steve Howard
- ☐ 9 Jimmy Jones
- ☐ 10 Bo Kent
- ☐ 11 Kirk McDonald
- ☐ 12 John Minch
- ☐ 13 Jerome Nelson
- ☐ 14 Jerry Peguero
- ☐ 15 Tommie Reynolds
- ☐ 16 Andre Robertson
- ☐ 17 Will Schock
- ☐ 18 Bob Sharpnack
- ☐ 19 Dave Shotkoski
- ☐ 20 Kevin Sliwinski
- ☐ 21 Greg Sparks
- ☐ 22 Bruce Tanner
- ☐ 23 Camilo Veras
- ☐ 24 Dave Veres
- ☐ 25 Bruce Walton

1988 Idaho Falls Braves ProCards

This 31-card standard-size set of the 1988 Idaho Falls Braves, a Rookie Class Pioneer League affiliate of the Atlanta Braves, features bronze-bordered posed color player photos on its fronts. The player's name, position, and team name appear at the bottom. The plain white back carries the player's name at the top, followed by biography and statistics.

	MINT	NRMT	EXC
COMPLETE SET (31)	5.00	2.20	.60

- ☐ 1832 The Clubhouse
- ☐ 1833 Team Photo
- ☐ 1834 Daryl Blanks
- ☐ 1835 Marco Paddy
- ☐ 1836 Gary Schoonover
- ☐ 1837 Glenn Mitchell
- ☐ 1838 Rodney Richey
- ☐ 1839 John Albertson
- ☐ 1840 Lamar Hall
- ☐ 1841 Dave Monteiro
- ☐ 1842 Matthew Williams
- ☐ 1843 Chris Jones
- ☐ 1844 Ramces Guerrero
- ☐ 1845 Donovan Campbell
- ☐ 1846 Kevin Henry
- ☐ 1847 Greg Harper
- ☐ 1848 Al Bacosa
- ☐ 1849 Pat Stivers
- ☐ 1850 Keith Leclair
- ☐ 1851 Eric Kuhlman
- ☐ 1852 Rai Henninger
- ☐ 1853 Jim Procopio
- ☐ 1854 Paul Opdyke
- ☐ 1855 Rudy Gardey
- ☐ 1856 Mark Eskins
- ☐ 1857 Daniel Lehnerz
- ☐ 1858 Jim Kortright
- ☐ 1859 Steve Lopez
- ☐ 1860 Herb Hippauf
- ☐ 1861 Rich Pohle
- ☐ NNO Checklist

1988 Indianapolis Indians CMC

10,000 sets were produced.

	MINT	NRMT	EXC
COMPLETE SET (25)	5.00	2.20	.60

- ☐ 1 Randy Johnson
- ☐ 2 Kurt Kepshire
- ☐ 3 Bob Sebra
- ☐ 4 Steve Shirley
- ☐ 5 Tim Barrett
- ☐ 6 Jeff Fischer
- ☐ 7 Mike Smith
- ☐ 8 Sergio Valdez
- ☐ 9 Brian Holman
- ☐ 10 Rex Hudler
- ☐ 11 Johnny Paredes
- ☐ 12 Razor Shines
- ☐ 13 Billy Moore
- ☐ 14 Otis Nixon
- ☐ 15 Alonzo Powell
- ☐ 16 Ron Shepherd
- ☐ 17 Tim Hulett
- ☐ 18 Nelson Santovenia
- ☐ 19 Wilfredo Tejada
- ☐ 20 Mike Berger
- ☐ 21 Jack Daugherty
- ☐ 22 Garrett Nago
- ☐ 23 Mel Houston
- ☐ 24 Joe Sparks
- ☐ 25 Joe Kerrigan CO
  Nelson Norman CO
  Mike Colbern CO

1988 Indianapolis Indians ProCards

This 31-card standard-size set of the 1988 Indianapolis Indians, a Class AAA American Association affiliate of the Montreal Expos, features gold-bordered posed color player photos on its fronts. The player's name, position, and team name appear at the bottom. The plain white back carries the player's name at the top, followed by biography and statistics.

	MINT	NRMT	EXC
COMPLETE SET (31)	10.00	4.50	1.25

- ☐ 496 Joe Sparks MG
- ☐ 497 Billy Moore
- ☐ 498 Tim McCormack TR
- ☐ 499 Joe Kerrigan CO
  Mike Colbern CO
- ☐ 500 Nelson Santovenia
- ☐ 501 Sergio Valdez
- ☐ 502 Tim Barrett
- ☐ 503 Jeff Fischer
- ☐ 504 Brian Holman
- ☐ 505 Steve Shirley
- ☐ 506 Kurt Kepshire
- ☐ 507 Mel Houston
- ☐ 508 Gary Wayne
- ☐ 509 Mike Smith
- ☐ 510 Randy Johnson
- ☐ 511 Bob Sebra
- ☐ 512 Joe Hesketh
- ☐ 513 Rex Hudler
- ☐ 514 Razor Shines
- ☐ 515 Garrett Nago
- ☐ 516 Johnny Paredes
- ☐ 517 Nelson Norman
- ☐ 518 Otis Nixon
- ☐ 519 Mike Berger
- ☐ 520 Alonzo Powell
- ☐ 521 Jack Daugherty
- ☐ 522 Tim Hulett
- ☐ 523 Will Tejada
- ☐ 524 Ron Shepherd
- ☐ 525 Howard Kellman ANN
  Tom Akins ANN
- ☐ NNO Checklist

1988 Iowa Cubs CMC

10,000 sets were produced.

	MINT	NRMT	EXC
COMPLETE SET (25)	8.00	3.60	1.00

- ☐ 1 Mike Capel
- ☐ 2 Len Damian
- ☐ 3 Jeff Pico
- ☐ 4 Laddie Renfroe
- ☐ 5 Bob Tewksbury
- ☐ 6 Jeff Hirsch
- ☐ 7 Joe Kraemer
- ☐ 8 Bill Landrum
- ☐ 9 Dave Masters
- ☐ 10 Rich Surhoff
- ☐ 11 Roger Williams
- ☐ 12 Damon Berryhill
- ☐ 13 Bruce Crabbe
- ☐ 14 Mark Grace
- ☐ 15 Brian Guinn
- ☐ 16 Paul Noce
- ☐ 17 Phil Stephenson
- ☐ 18 Greg Tabor
- ☐ 19 Doug Dascenzo
- ☐ 20 Dave Meier
- ☐ 21 Dwight Smith
- ☐ 22 Gary Varsho
- ☐ 23 Bill Bathe
- ☐ 24 Pete MacKanin
- ☐ 25 Jim Wright

1988 Iowa Cubs ProCards

This 30-card standard-size set of the 1988 Iowa Cubs, a Class AAA American Association affiliate of the Chicago Cubs, features gold-bordered posed color player photos on its fronts. The player's name, position, and team name appear at the bottom. The plain white back carries the player's name at the top, followed by biography and statistics.

	MINT	NRMT	EXC
COMPLETE SET (30)	10.00	4.50	1.25

- ☐ 526 Brian Guinn
- ☐ 527 Bill Bathe
- ☐ 528 Doug Dascenzo
- ☐ 529 Rick Surhoff

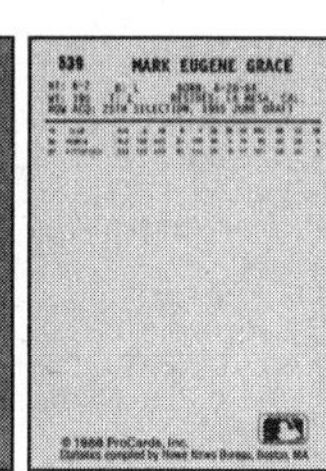

- ☐ 530 Dwight Smith
- ☐ 531 Dave Grossman
- ☐ 532 Jeff Hirsch
- ☐ 533 Dave Masters
- ☐ 534 Bob Tewksbury
- ☐ 535 Gary Varsho
- ☐ 536 Dave Meier
- ☐ 537 Damon Berryhill
- ☐ 538 Paul Noce
- ☐ 539 Mark Grace
- ☐ 540 Phil Stephenson
- ☐ 541 Bill Landrum
- ☐ 542 Jim Wright
- ☐ 543 Pete MacKanin
- ☐ 544 Leonard Damian
- ☐ 545 Roger Williams
- ☐ 546 Jeff Pico
- ☐ 547 Mike Capel
- ☐ 548 Greg Tabor
- ☐ 549 Joe Kraemer
- ☐ 550 Bruce Crabbe
- ☐ 551 Laddie Renfroe
- ☐ 552 Front Office
- ☐ 553 Front Office
- ☐ 554 Cubbie Bear
- ☐ NNO Checklist

1988 Jackson Mets Grand Slam

	MINT	NRMT	EXC
COMPLETE SET (25)	5.00	2.20	.60

- ☐ 1 Ron Gideon
- ☐ 2 Zoilo Sanchez
- ☐ 3 Geary Jones
- ☐ 4 Tucker Ashford
- ☐ 5 Glenn Abbott
- ☐ 6 Kyle Hartshorn
- ☐ 7 Tom Doyle
- ☐ 8 Chris Jelic
- ☐ 9 Mike Santiago
- ☐ 10 Jeff Gardner
- ☐ 11 Virgil Conley
- ☐ 12 Craig Shipley
- ☐ 13 Rich Rodriquez
- ☐ 14 Brian Givens
- ☐ 15 Blaine Beatty
- ☐ 16 Todd Welborn
- ☐ 17 Miguel Roman
- ☐ 18 Manny Salinas
- ☐ 19 Shawn Barton
- ☐ 20 Joaquin Contreras
- ☐ 21 Angelo Cuevas
- ☐ 22 Mickey Weston
- ☐ 23 Kevin Tapani
- ☐ 24 Felix Perdomo
- ☐ 25 Alan Hayden

1988 Jacksonville Expos Best

This 29-card standard-size set of the 1988 Jacksonville Expos, a Class AA Southern League affiliate of the Montreal Expos, features red and black bordered posed color player photos on its fronts. The team name appears at the top, and below the picture is the player's name and position. The horizontal gray back carries the player's name and position at the top, followed by biography, career highlights, and statistics. The set is printed on thin card stock.

	MINT	NRMT	EXC
COMPLETE SET (29)	5.00	2.20	.60

- ☐ 1 Rick Carriger
- ☐ 2 Mike Shade
- ☐ 3 Rich Sauveur
- ☐ 4 John Hoover
- ☐ 5 Gene Harris
- ☐ 6 Eddie Dixon
- ☐ 7 Mark Gardner
- ☐ 8 Mark Clemons
- ☐ 9 Tommy Alexander
- ☐ 10 Richie Lewis
- ☐ 11 Yorkis Perez
- ☐ 12 Orsino Hill
- ☐ 13 Kevin Dean
- ☐ 14 Derrell Baker
- ☐ 15 Bill Mann
- ☐ 16 Mike Blowers
- ☐ 17 Esteban Beltre
- ☐ 18 Jeff Huson

☐ 19 Andy Lawrence
☐ 20 Pat Sipe
☐ 21 Randy Braun
☐ 22 Doug Duke
☐ 23 Nardi Contreras CO
☐ 24 Tommy Thompson MG
☐ 25 Bob Caffrey
☐ 26 Jim Yahmann TR
☐ 27 Armando Moreno
☐ 28 Gary Engelkin CO
☐ 29 Sam W. Wolfson Stadium Checklist

1988 Jacksonville Expos ProCards

This 32-card standard-size set of the 1988 Jacksonville Expos, a Class AA Southern League affiliate of the Montreal Expos, features silver-bordered posed color player photos on its fronts. The player's name, position, and team name appear at the bottom. The plain white back carries the player's name at the top, followed by position, biography, and statistics. The set was sponsored by Golden Glove, a baseball card and sports memorablilia store.

	MINT	NRMT	EXC
COMPLETE SET (32)	5.00	2.20	.60

☐ 964 Scott Mann
☐ 965 Orsino Hill
☐ 966 Jeffrey Huson
☐ 967 Eddie Dixon
☐ 968 Derrell Baker P/CO
☐ 969 Nardi Contreras CO
☐ 970 Doug Duke
☐ 971 Tommy Thompson MG
☐ 972 Andy Lawrence
☐ 973 Yorkis Perez
☐ 974 Jim Kahmann TR
☐ 975 Mike Blowers
☐ 976 Randy Braun
☐ 977 Mark Clemons
☐ 978 Todd Soares
☐ 979 Bob Caffrey
☐ 980 Gene Harris
☐ 981 Pat Sipe
☐ 982 Tommy Alexander
☐ 983 Armando Moreno
☐ 984 Kevin Dean
☐ 985 Mike Shade
☐ 986 Rich Sauveur
☐ 987 Mark Gardner
☐ 988 Rick Carriger
☐ 989 John Hoover
☐ 990 Gary Engelkin Minor League Instructor
☐ 991 Esteban Beltre
☐ 992 Richie Lewis
☐ 993 Jacksonville Expos Team Photo Card
☐ 994 Sam Wolfson Park
☐ NNO Checklist

1988 Jamestown Expos ProCards

This 31-card standard-size set of the 1988 Jamestown Expos, a Class A New York-Penn League affiliate of the Montreal Expos, features copper-bordered posed color player photos on its fronts. The player's name, position, and team name appear at the bottom. The plain white back carries the player's name and position at the top, followed by biography and statistics. The set was sponsored by Roach Photography. This issue includes the first cards of Marquis Grissom and Wil Cordero.

	MINT	NRMT	EXC
COMPLETE SET (31)	25.00	11.00	3.10

☐ 1893 Kevin Malone CO
☐ 1894 Roger LaFrancois MG
☐ 1895 Wil Cordero UER (Wilfredo Nieva on front)
☐ 1896 Bryn Kosco
☐ 1897 Bret Davis
☐ 1898 Rob Kerrigan
☐ 1899 Daniel Freed
☐ 1900 Angel Rivera
☐ 1901 Jeff Atha
☐ 1902 Tim Piechowski
☐ 1903 Isaac Alleyne
☐ 1904 Tim Laker
☐ 1905 Rodney Boddie
☐ 1906 Idaiberto Echemendia
☐ 1907 Brian Sajonia
☐ 1908 Joe Siddall
☐ 1910 Marquis Grissom
☐ 1911 Keith Kaub
☐ 1912 Jose Solarte
☐ 1913 Danilo Leon
☐ 1914 Steve Overeem
☐ 1915 Kevin Finigan
☐ 1916 Jorge Mitchell
☐ 1917 Javan Reagans
☐ 1918 Darrin Winston
☐ 1919 Joe Klancnik
☐ 1919 Tim Stanley
☐ 1920 Dan Archibald
☐ 1921 Martin Robitaille
☐ 2039 Q.V. Lowe CO
☐ NNO Checklist

1988 Kenosha Twins ProCards

This 29-card standard-size set of the 1988 Kenosha Twins, a Class A Midwest League affiliate of the Minnesota Twins, features bronze-bordered posed color player photos on its fronts. The player's name, position, and team name appear at the bottom. The plain white back carries the player's name at the top, followed by biography and statistics.

	MINT	NRMT	EXC
COMPLETE SET (29)	5.00	2.20	.60

☐ 1379 Bob Tinkey
☐ 1380 Willie Banks
☐ 1381 Dwight Bernard
☐ 1382 Fred White
☐ 1383 Rusty Kryzanowski
☐ 1384 Steve Stowell
☐ 1385 Alex Perez
☐ 1386 Chad Swanson
☐ 1387 Tom Gilles
☐ 1388 Doug Pittman
☐ 1389 Dave Jacas
☐ 1390 Jarvis Brown
☐ 1391 David Smith
☐ 1392 Lenny Webster
☐ 1393 Frank Valdez
☐ 1394 Mark Ericson
☐ 1395 Michael Lexa
☐ 1396 Carlos Capellan
☐ 1397 Chris Martin
☐ 1398 Pete Delkus
☐ 1399 Don Leppert
☐ 1400 John Skelton
☐ 1401 Shane Jenny
☐ 1402 Ron Gardenhire
☐ 1403 Bob Lee
☐ 1404 Basil Meyer
☐ 1405 Tom Marten
☐ 1406 Pat Bangtson
☐ NNO Checklist

1988 Kinston Indians Star

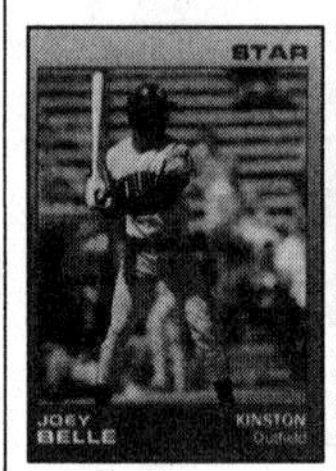

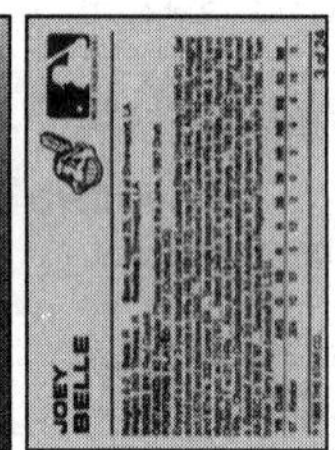

This issue includes the minor league card debut of Albert "Joey" Belle.

	MINT	NRMT	EXC
COMPLETE SET (24)	70.00	32.00	8.75

☐ 1 Beau Allread
☐ 2 Kevin Bearse
☐ 3 Joey Belle
☐ 4 Steven Bird
☐ 5 Glenn Fairchild
☐ 6 Greg Ferlinda
☐ 7 Mark Gilles
☐ 8 John Githens
☐ 9 Todd Gonzales
☐ 10 David Harwell
☐ 11 Christopher Isaacson
☐ 12 Scott Johnson
☐ 13 Carl Keliipuleole
☐ 14 Lewis Kent
☐ 15 Allen Liebert
☐ 16 Everado Magallanes
☐ 17 Mark Maloney
☐ 18 Charles Ogden
☐ 19 James Richardson
☐ 20 Charles Soos
☐ 21 Robert Swain
☐ 22 Michael Twardoski
☐ 23 Michael Westbrook
☐ 24 Raymond Williamson

1988 Knoxville Blue Jays Best

This 26-card standard-size set of the 1988 Knoxville Blue Jays, a Class AA Southern League affiliate of the Toronto Blue Jays, features blue- and black- bordered posed color player photos on its fronts. The team name appears at the top, and below the picture is the player's name and position. The horizontal gray back carries the player's name and position at the top, followed by biography, career highlights, and statistics. The set is printed on thin card stock.

	MINT	NRMT	EXC
COMPLETE SET (26)	5.00	2.20	.60

☐ 1 Alex Sanchez
☐ 2 Junior Felix
☐ 3 John Shea
☐ 4 Mike Jones
☐ 5 Jimy Kelly
☐ 6 Domingo Martinez
☐ 7 Kevin Batiste
☐ 8 Hector DeLaCruz
☐ 9 Kash Beauchamp
☐ 10 Darren Balsley
☐ 11 Doug Scherer
☐ 12 Carlos Diaz
☐ 13 Jose Escobar
☐ 14 Ken Rivers
☐ 15 Doug Linton
☐ 16 Chris Jones
☐ 17 Omar Bencomo
☐ 18 Juan Guzman
☐ 19 Dennis Jones
☐ 20 Steve Cummings
☐ 21 Gary McCune GM
☐ 22 Tim Ringler TR
☐ 23 John Poloni CO
☐ 24 Hugh Brinson
☐ 25 Tom Quinlan
☐ 26 Checklist

1988 Lakeland Tigers Star

	MINT	NRMT	EXC
COMPLETE SET (25)	5.00	2.20	.60

☐ 1 Scott Aldred
☐ 2 Doyle Balthazar
☐ 3 Arnie Beyeler
☐ 4 Basilio Cabrera
☐ 5 Luis Galindo
☐ 6 Richard Carter
☐ 7 Phil Clark
☐ 8 Milt Cuyler
☐ 9 Dean Decillis
☐ 10 Gregory Everson
☐ 11 Paul Foster
☐ 12 Blane Fox
☐ 13 Mike Hansen
☐ 14 Lance Hudson
☐ 15 Scott Hufford
☐ 16 Darren Hursey
☐ 17 Mark Lee
☐ 18 Randy Nosek
☐ 19 Dan O'Neill
☐ 20 Wade Phillips
☐ 21 Gary Pifer
☐ 22 Ron Rightnowar
☐ 23 Jospeh Slavik
☐ 24 Bob Thomson
☐ 25 Donald Vesling

1988 Las Vegas Stars CMC

This 25-card standard-size set of the 1988 Las Vegas Stars, a Class AAA Pacific Coast League affiliate of the San Diego Padres, features a second year card of Roberto Alomar. 10,000 sets were produced.

	MINT	NRMT	EXC
COMPLETE SET (25)	10.00	4.50	1.25

☐ 1 Joe Bitker
☐ 2 Keith Comstock
☐ 3 Greg Harris
☐ 4 Joel McKeon
☐ 5 Pete Roberts
☐ 6 Todd Simmons
☐ 7 Ed Vosberg
☐ 8 Kevin Towers
☐ 9 Joe Lynch
☐ 10 Shane Mack
☐ 11 Thomas Howard
☐ 12 Jerald Clark
☐ 13 Randy Byers
☐ 14 Bip Roberts
☐ 15 Brad Pounders
☐ 16 Rob Nelson
☐ 17 Gary Green
☐ 18 Joey Cora
☐ 19 Mike Brumley
☐ 20 Roberto Alomar
☐ 21 Bruce Bochy
☐ 22 Sandy Alomar Jr.
☐ 23 Tom Brassil
☐ 24 Steve Smith
☐ 25 Sonny Siebert

1988 Las Vegas Stars ProCards

This 28-card standard-size set of the 1988 Las Vegas Stars, a Class AAA Pacific Coast League affiliate of the San Diego Padres, features gold-bordered posed color player photos on its fronts. The player's name, position, and team name appear at the bottom. The plain white back carries the player's name at the top, followed by biography and statistics. This issue includes a second year card of Roberto Alomar.

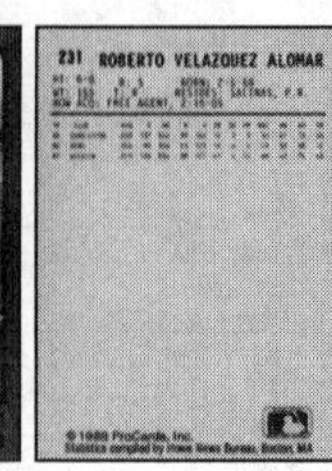

	MINT	NRMT	EXC
COMPLETE SET (28)	15.00	6.75	1.85

☐ 222 Edward Vosberg
☐ 223 Joe Lynch
☐ 224 Randell Byers
☐ 225 Joel McKeon
☐ 226 Todd Hutcheson
☐ 227 Greg Harris
☐ 228 Pete Roberts
☐ 229 Jerald Clark
☐ 230 Joe Bitker
☐ 231 Roberto Alomar
☐ 232 Gary Green
☐ 233 Shane Mack
☐ 234 Joey Cora
☐ 235 Mike Brumley
☐ 236 Sandy Alomar
☐ 237 Rob Nelson
☐ 238 Tom Brassil
☐ 239 Thomas Howard
☐ 240 Todd Simmons
☐ 241 Bruce Bochy
☐ 242 Kevin Towers
☐ 243 Steve Lubratich
☐ 244 Steve Smith
☐ 245 Bip Roberts
☐ 246 Keith Comstock
☐ 247 Brad Pounders
☐ 248 Sonny Siebert
☐ NNO Checklist

1988 Little Falls Mets Pucko

This issue includes a second year card of Todd Hundley. 3,500 sets produced.

	MINT	NRMT	EXC
COMPLETE SET (29)	16.00	7.25	2.00

☐ 1 Lee May Jr.
☐ 2 Kevin Baez
☐ 3 Tom Bales
☐ 4 Tom Becker
☐ 5 Ron Height
☐ 6 Todd Hundley
☐ 7 Michael Noelke
☐ 8 Bob Uhal
☐ 9 Steve Piskor
☐ 10 Radhames Polanco
☐ 11 Titi Roche
☐ 12 Sammye Sanchez
☐ 13 Greg Turtletaub
☐ 14 Lonnie Walker
☐ 15 Terry Bross
☐ 16 Terry Griffin
☐ 17 Chris Hill
☐ 18 Steve Newton
☐ 19 Vladimir Perez
☐ 20 Dale Plummer
☐ 21 Dave Proctor
☐ 22 Pete Schourek
☐ 23 John Wenrick
☐ 24 Anthony Young
☐ 25 Brian Zimmerman
☐ 26 Bill Stein
☐ 27 Al Jackson
☐ 28 Rick McWane
☐ 29 Frank Minissale

1988 Louisville Red Birds CMC

10,000 sets were produced.

	MINT	NRMT	EXC
COMPLETE SET (25)	4.00	1.80	.50

☐ 1 John Costello
☐ 2 Dick Grapenthin
☐ 3 John Martin
☐ 4 Randy O'Neal
☐ 5 Tim Conroy
☐ 6 Gibson Alba
☐ 7 Rich Buonantony
☐ 8 Cris Carpenter Sic, Chris
☐ 9 Dave Rajsich
☐ 10 Jim Leopold
☐ 11 Alex Cole
☐ 12 Bill Lyons
☐ 13 Tim Jones

☐ 14 David Green
☐ 15 Craig Wilson
☐ 16 John Murphy
☐ 17 Duane Walker
☐ 18 Mike Fitzgerald
☐ 19 Carl Ray Stephens
☐ 20 Luis Alicea
☐ 21 Sal Agostinelli
☐ 22 Roy Silver
☐ 23 Mark Dougherty
☐ 24 Joe Pettini
☐ 25 Mike Jorgensen
Sic, Jorgenson

1988 Louisville Red Birds ProCards

This 26-card standard-size set of the 1988 Louisville Red Birds, a Class AAA American Association affiliate of the St. Louis Cardinals, features gold-bordered posed color player photos on its fronts. The player's name, position, and team name appear at the bottom. The plain white back carries the player's name at the top, followed by biography and statistics.

	MINT	NRMT	EXC
COMPLETE SET (26)	5.00	2.20	.60

☐ 421 David Green
☐ 422 Carl Ray Stephens
☐ 423 John Martin
☐ 424 Sal Agostinelli
☐ 425 Duane Walker
☐ 426 Dick Grapenthin
☐ 427 Mike Fitzgerald
☐ 428 Cris Carpenter
Sic, Chris
☐ 429 John Murphy
☐ 430 Randy O'Neal
☐ 431 Roy Silver
☐ 432 Bill Lyons
☐ 433 Tim Jones
☐ 434 David Hudson
☐ 435 Joe Pettini
☐ 436 Luis Alicea
☐ 437 Jim Leopold
☐ 438 Alex Cole
☐ 439 Craig Wilson
☐ 440 John Costello
☐ 441 Mike Jorgensen
☐ 442 Gibson Alba
☐ 443 Dave Rajsich
☐ 444 Mark Dougherty
☐ 445 Rich Buonantony
☐ NNO Checklist

1988 Louisville Red Birds Team Issue

	MINT	NRMT	EXC
COMPLETE SET (54)	6.00	2.70	.75

☐ 1 Mike Jorgensen MG
☐ 2 Joe Pettini CO
☐ 3 Darold Knowles
☐ 4 Steve Braun
☐ 5 Sal Agostinelli
☐ 6 Gibson Alba
☐ 7 Luis Alicea
☐ 8 Scott Arnold
☐ 9 Greg Bargar
☐ 10 Rod Booker
☐ 11 Derek Botelho
☐ 12 Rich Buonantony
☐ 13 Cris Carpenter
☐ 14 Alex Cole
☐ 15 Tim Conroy
☐ 16 John Costello
☐ 17 Danny Cox
☐ 18 Mark Dougherty
☐ 19 Mike Fitzgerald
☐ 20 Dick Grapenthin
☐ 21 David Green
☐ 22 Mike Hocutt
☐ 23 Tim Jones
☐ 24 Matt Kinzer
☐ 25 Wayne Krenchicki
☐ 26 Mike Laga
☐ 27 Jim Leopold
☐ 28 Jim Lindeman
☐ 29 Rick Lockwood
☐ 30 Bill Lyons
☐ 31 Joe Magrane
☐ 32 John A. Martin
☐ 33 Greg Mathews
☐ 34 Ron Meridith
☐ 35 John Morris
☐ 36 John V. Murphy
☐ 37 Randy O'Neal
☐ 38 Jeff Oyster
☐ 39 Steve Peters
☐ 40 Jim Puzey
☐ 41 Dave Rajsich
☐ 42 Mike Robinson
☐ 43 Mark Ryal
☐ 44 Roy Silver
☐ 45 Carl Ray Stephens
☐ 46 Lester Strode
☐ 47 Scott Terry
☐ 48 Lee Tunnell
☐ 49 Duane Walker
☐ 50 Craig Wilson
☐ 51 Hap Hudson
☐ 52 Billy Bird'
☐ 53 Redbirds Bat Boys
☐ 54 Checklist

1988 Lynchburg Red Sox Star

	MINT	NRMT	EXC
COMPLETE SET (27)	5.00	2.20	.60

☐ 1 Billy Bartels
☐ 2 Paul Brown
☐ 3 Tim Buheller
☐ 4 Randy Cina
☐ 5 Scott Cooper
☐ 6 Paul Devlin
☐ 7 David Gray
☐ 8 Bart Haley
☐ 9 Reggie Harris
☐ 10 Joseph Marchese
☐ 11 Gilberto Martinez
☐ 12 Gregory McCollum
☐ 13 Timothy McGee
☐ 14 Shannon Mendenhall
☐ 15 Juan Molero
☐ 16 Jim Orsag
☐ 17 Mickey Pina
☐ 18 Jeffrey Plympton
☐ 19 Scott Powers
☐ 20 Ronnie Richardson
☐ 21 Enrique Rios
☐ 22 Kenneth Ryan
☐ 23 Scott Sommers
☐ 24 David Walters
☐ 25 Stuart Weidie
☐ 26 Craig Wilson
☐ 27 Robert Zupcic

1988 Madison Muskies Police

Set was sponsored by T and J Cards and WKOW-TV.

	MINT	NRMT	EXC
COMPLETE SET (25)	8.00	3.60	1.00

☐ 1 Rob Alexander
☐ 2 Bruce Arola
☐ 3 Pedro Baez
☐ 4 Bert Bradley
☐ 5 Scott Brosius
☐ 6 Nasusel Cabrera
☐ 7 Ozzie Canseco
☐ 8 Felix Caraballo
☐ 9 Jim Carroll
☐ 10 Jim Chenevey
☐ 11 Dave Gavin
☐ 12 Chris Gust
☐ 13 DeMarlo Hale
☐ 14 Fred Hanker
☐ 15 Frank Masters
☐ 16 Jim Nettles
☐ 17 Bob Parry
☐ 18 Jamie Reiser
☐ 19 Dion Reyna
☐ 20 Marteese Robinson
☐ 21 Will Schock
☐ 22 Matt Siuda
☐ 23 Bob Stocker
☐ 24 Brian Thorson
☐ 25 Pat Wernig

1988 Maine Phillies CMC

10,000 sets were produced.

	MINT	NRMT	EXC
COMPLETE SET (25)	4.00	1.80	.50

☐ 1 Marty Bystrom
☐ 2 Travis Chambers
☐ 3 Barney Nugent
☐ 4 Marvin Freeman
☐ 5 Brad Brink
☐ 6 John McLarnan
☐ 7 Mike Shelton
☐ 8 Tom Newell
☐ 9 Bob Scanlan
☐ 10 Todd Frohwirth
☐ 11 Ricky Jordan
☐ 12 John Russell
☐ 13 Shane Turner
☐ 14 Ron Jones
☐ 15 Rick Lundblade
☐ 16 Tommy Barrett
☐ 17 Kenny Jackson
☐ 18 Greg Jelks
☐ 19 Ramon Henderson
☐ 20 Keith Miller
☐ 21 Jim Olander
☐ 22 Kevin Ward
☐ 23 George Culver
☐ 24 Ramon Aviles
☐ 25 Joe Lefebvre

1988 Maine Phillies ProCards

This 27-card standard-size set of the 1988 Maine Phillies, a Class AAA International League affiliate of the Philadelphia Phillies, features gold-bordered posed color player photos on its fronts. The player's name, position, and team name appear at the bottom. The plain white back carries the player's name at the top, followed by biography and statistics.

	MINT	NRMT	EXC
COMPLETE SET (27)	5.00	2.20	.60

☐ 277 Jim Olander
☐ 278 Kevin Ward
☐ 279 Marvin Freeman
☐ 280 Ron Jones
☐ 281 John McLarnan
☐ 282 Mike Shelton
☐ 283 Travis Chambers
☐ 284 Tom Barrett
☐ 285 John Russell
☐ 286 Ricky Jordan
☐ 287 Ken Jackson
☐ 288 Shane Turner
☐ 289 Brad Brink
☐ 290 Keith Miller
☐ 291 Rick Lundblade
☐ 292 Marty Bystrom
☐ 293 Tom Newell
☐ 294 Bob Scanlan
☐ 295 Ramon Henderson
☐ 296 Todd Frohwirth
☐ 297 Danny Clay
☐ 298 Greg Jelks
☐ 299 Barney Nugent
☐ 300 George Culver
☐ 301 Joe LeFebvre
☐ 302 Ramon Aviles
☐ NNO Checklist

1988 Martinsville Phillies Star

	MINT	NRMT	EXC
COMPLETE SET (32)	5.00	2.20	.60

☐ 1 John Anderson
☐ 2 Kenneth Bean
☐ 3 Al Bennett
☐ 4 Toby Borland
☐ 5 Greg Breaux
☐ 6 Tim Churchill
☐ 7 Dan Coccia
☐ 8 Matt Current
☐ 9 Mike Dafforn
☐ 10 Roly DeArmas
☐ 11 Tom Doyle
☐ 12 Donnie Elliot
☐ 13 John Escobar
☐ 14 Paul Fletcher
☐ 15 Reggie Garcia
☐ 16 Brian Harper
☐ 17 Dennis Hoffman
☐ 18 Luther Johnson
☐ 19 Craig Johnston
☐ 20 Troy Kent
☐ 21 Darrell Lindsey
☐ 22 Antonio Linares
☐ 23 Aurelio Llanos
☐ 24 Chris Lowe
☐ 25 Nick Macaluso
☐ 26 John Marshall
☐ 27 Eulogio Perez
☐ 28 Edwin Rosado
☐ 29 Victor Rosario
☐ 30 Francisco Tejada
☐ 31 Chris Toney
☐ 32 Ray Walker

1988 Memphis Chicks Best

This 27-card standard-size set of the 1988 Memphis Chicks, a Class AA Southern League affiliate of the Kansas City Royals, features blue and black bordered posed color player photos on its fronts. The team name appears at the top, and below the picture is the player's name and position. The horizontal gray back carries the player's name and position at the top, followed by biography, career highlights, and statistics. The set is printed on thin card stock.

	MINT	NRMT	EXC
COMPLETE SET (27)	5.00	2.20	.60

☐ 1 Mel Stottlemyre Jr.
☐ 2 Rich Thompson
☐ 3 Mark Van Blaricom
☐ 4 Steve Morrow
☐ 5 Ken Bowen
☐ 6 Jacob Brumfield
☐ 7 Larry Acker
☐ 8 Matt Crouch
☐ 9 Casey Parson
☐ 10 Jim Campbell
☐ 11 Kevin Burrell
☐ 12 Luis Encarnacion
☐ 13 Mark Gillaspie
☐ 14 Ken Kraveo
☐ 15 Randy Hunt
☐ 16 Mauro Gozzo
☐ 17 Charlie Culberson
☐ 18 Jose DeJesus
☐ 19 Matt Winters
☐ 20 Rick Luecken
☐ 21 Chito Martinez
☐ 22 Mike Miller
☐ 23 Ken Spratke
☐ 24 Thad Reece
☐ 25 Jose Rivera
☐ 26 Sal Rende
☐ NNO Checklist

1988 Miami Marlins Star

	MINT	NRMT	EXC
COMPLETE SET (24)	5.00	2.20	.60

☐ 1 Jeff Allison
☐ 2 Mick Billmeyer
☐ 3 Ron Brevell
☐ 4 Mike Browning
☐ 5 Hector Cotto
☐ 6 Tony Diaz
☐ 7 Scott Diez
☐ 8 Orlando Gonzalez
☐ 9 Clay Hill
☐ 10 Matt Huff
☐ 11 Kanenori Tarumi
☐ 12 Shuji Inagaki
☐ 13 Trent Intorcia
☐ 14 Masao Kida
☐ 15 Brian Morrison
☐ 16 Rafael Muratii
☐ 17 Mitsuru Ogiwara
☐ 18 Julio Perez
☐ 19 Arnie Prieto
☐ 20 Rick Richardi
☐ 21 Sal Roldan
☐ 22 Tony Rohan
☐ 23 Motokuni Sano
☐ 24 Dave Van Ohlen

1988 Midland Angels Grand Slam

	MINT	NRMT	EXC
COMPLETE SET (25)	5.00	2.20	.60

☐ 1 Max Oliveras MG
☐ 2 Kurt Walker
☐ 3 Tim Kelly
☐ 4 Vinicio Cedeno
☐ 5 Shane Young
☐ 6 Tim Burcham
☐ 7 Chris Collins
☐ 8 Frank Dimichele
☐ 9 Todd Eggertsen
☐ 10 Mike Fetters
☐ 11 Colby Ward
☐ 12 Steve McGuire
☐ 13 Mike Knapp
☐ 14 Erik Pappas
☐ 15 Tom Alfredson
☐ 16 Danny Grunhard
☐ 17 C.L. Penigar
☐ 18 Lee Stevens
☐ 19 Jesus Alfaro
☐ 20 David Martinez
☐ 21 Jeff Manto
☐ 22 Jim McCollom
☐ 23 Jim Thomas
☐ 24 Craig Gerber
☐ 25 Norman Carrasco

1988 Midwest League All-Stars Grand Slam

	MINT	NRMT	EXC
COMPLETE SET (59)	12.00	5.50	1.50

☐ 1 Mark Owens
☐ 2 Andres Santana
☐ 3 Erik Johnson
☐ 4 Jamie Cooper
☐ 5 Rod Beck
☐ 6 Steve Connolly
☐ 7 Tom Hostetler
☐ 8 Pete Beeler
☐ 9 Greg Lonigro
☐ 10 Jeff Forney
☐ 11 Bill Dodd
☐ 12 Butch Henry
☐ 13 Darrell Rodgers
☐ 14 Scott Scudder
☐ 15 Marc Bombard

☐ 16 Brian Deak
☐ 17 Rich Casarotti
☐ 18 Brian Hunter
☐ 19 Al Martin
☐ 20 Jim Lemasters
☐ 21 Troy Neel
☐ 22 Tommy Kramer
☐ 23 Bob Rose
☐ 24 Wiley Lee
☐ 25 Gary Buckels
☐ 26 Ray Lankford
☐ 27 Greg Becker
☐ 28 Greg Kallevig
☐ 29 Fernando Zarranz
☐ 30 Steve Olin
☐ 31 Lenny Webster
☐ 32 Shawn Gilbert
☐ 33 Jarvis Brown
☐ 34 Pat Bangston
☐ 35 Pete Delkus
☐ 36 Ron Gardenhire
☐ 37 Jorge Pedre
☐ 38 Darryl Robinson
☐ 39 Jesus Deleon
☐ 40 Tom Gordon
☐ 41 Bobby Knecht
☐ 42 Greg Colbrunn
☐ 43 John Mello
☐ 44 Delino DeShields
☐ 45 Mario Brito
☐ 46 Howard Farmer
☐ 47 Tim Peters
☐ 48 Mike Maksudian
☐ 49 Ray Payton
☐ 50 Scott Brosius
☐ 51 Ozzie Canseco
☐ 52 Pat Wernig
☐ 53 Jim Chenevey
☐ 54 Will Schock
☐ 55 Mike McDonald
☐ 56 Chuck Carr
☐ 57 Mike Goff
☐ 58 Kurt Stange
☐ 59 Mark Chapman

1988 Mississippi State Bulldogs

	MINT	NRMT	EXC
COMPLETE SET (39)	12.00	5.50	1.50

☐ 1 Nelson Arriete
☐ 2 Darin Asbill
☐ 3 John Cohen
☐ 4 Chuck Daniel
☐ 5 Terry Ellis
☐ 6 Jimmy Gammill
☐ 7 Richie Grayum
☐ 8 Bob Griffin
☐ 9 Joey Hamilton
☐ 10 Jon Harden
☐ 11 Brad Hildreth
☐ 12 Chuck Holly
☐ 13 Jody Hurst
☐ 14 Tracy Jobes
☐ 15 Wes Johnson
☐ 16 Russ Mahan
☐ 17 Mike Martin
☐ 18 Burke Masters
☐ 19 David McMahon
☐ 20 Pat McMahon CO
☐ 21 David Mitchell
☐ 22 Scott Mitchell
☐ 23 Todd Nace
☐ 24 Rob Norman
☐ 25 Ron Polk CO
☐ 26 Steve Polk
☐ 27 Tommy Raffo
☐ 28 Bobby Reed
☐ 29 Jim Robinson
☐ 30 Jon Shave
☐ 31 Brian Shoop CO
☐ 32 Kent Walters
☐ 33 Barry Winford
☐ 34 Ron Winford
☐ 35 Ernie Wright
☐ 36 Pete Young
☐ 37 Assistant Coaches
Joe Hudak
Mike Hutcheon
Tommy Walker
☐ 38 Dudy Noble Field
☐ 39 Student Managers and Trainer
Bo McKinnis MG
Brooks Ayers MG
Rogers Smith MG
Carey Rial TR

1988 Modesto A's Cal League Cards

	MINT	NRMT	EXC
COMPLETE SET (28)	5.00	2.20	.60

☐ 56 David Veres
☐ 57 David Shotkoski
☐ 58 Ray Young
☐ 59 Kevin Williams
☐ 60 Jeff Glover
☐ 61 Mark Beavers
☐ 62 Gary Gorski
☐ 63 Jeff Kopyta
☐ 64 Scott Chiamparino
☐ 65 Mark Stancel
☐ 66 Steve Maye
☐ 67 Dann Howitt
☐ 68 Jorge Brito
☐ 69 Drew Stratton
☐ 70 David Finley
☐ 71 Keith Watkins
☐ 72 Ron Coomer
☐ 73 Gerry Barragan
☐ 74 Luis Martinez
☐ 75 Bill Savarino
☐ 76 Heriberto Done
☐ 77 Randy Randle
☐ 78 Francis Ciprian
☐ 79 Patrick Gilbert
☐ 80 Vince Teixeira
☐ 81 Jeff Newman
☐ 82 Pete Richert
☐ 83 David Hollenback

1988 Modesto A's Team Issue

	MINT	NRMT	EXC
COMPLETE SET (36)	6.00	2.70	.75

☐ 1 Jeff Newman MG
☐ 2 Pete Richert CO
☐ 3 Dave Hollenback TR
☐ 4 Rich Berg
☐ 5 Felix Caraballo
☐ 6 Jim Carroll
☐ 7 Jeff Childers
☐ 8 Scott Chiamparino
☐ 9 Jim Foley
☐ 10 Jeff Glover
☐ 11 Gary Gorski
☐ 12 Jeff Kopyta
☐ 13 Steve Maye
☐ 14 Mark Stancel
☐ 15 Weston Weber
☐ 16 Ray Young
☐ 17 Jorge Brito
☐ 18 Francis Ciprian
☐ 19 Tony Arias
☐ 20 Isaiah Clark
☐ 21 Ron Coomer
☐ 22 Darrin Duffy
☐ 23 Dave Finley
☐ 24 Angel Martinez
☐ 25 Dan Russell
☐ 26 Pat Gilbert
☐ 27 Dann Howitt
☐ 28 Antoine Pickett
☐ 29 Drew Stratton
☐ 30 Steve Gokey
☐ 31 Dave Shotkoski
☐ 32 David Veres
☐ 33 Mike Gallego
☐ 34 Walt Weiss
☐ 35 Greg Cadaret
☐ 36 Checklist Card

1988 Myrtle Beach Blue Jays ProCards

This 28-card standard-size set of the 1988 Myrtle Beach Blue Jays, a Class A South Atlantic League affiliate of the Toronto Blue Jays, features copper-bordered posed color player photos on its fronts. The player's name, position, and team name appear at the bottom. The plain white back carries the player's name at the top, followed by biography and statistics. The set was sponsored by Myrtle Beach Blue Jays Souvenir Store. This issue includes the first minor league card appearance of Derek Bell.

	MINT	NRMT	EXC
COMPLETE SET (28)	16.00	7.25	2.00

☐ 1166 Steve Wapnick
☐ 1167 Graeme Lloyd
☐ 1168 Denis Boucher
☐ 1169 Bernardino Nunez
☐ 1170 Edgar Marquez
☐ 1171 Derek Bell
☐ 1172 Steve Woide
☐ 1173 Chris Floyd
☐ 1174 Nate Cromwell
☐ 1175 Juan DeLaRosa
☐ 1176 Greg David
☐ 1177 Dan Etzweiler
☐ 1178 Xavier Hernandez
☐ 1179 Mike Murray TR
☐ 1180 Leroy Stanton CO
☐ 1181 Omar Malave
☐ 1182 Randy Knorr
☐ 1183 Greg Vella
☐ 1184 Mike Timlin
☐ 1185 Steve Towey
☐ 1186 William Suero
☐ 1187 Allan Silverstein
☐ 1188 Richie Hebner MG
☐ 1189 Luis Sojo
☐ 1190 Jimmy Rogers
☐ 1191 Bob MacDonald
☐ 1192 Todd Provence
☐ NNO Checklist

1988 Nashville Sounds CMC

10,000 sets were produced.

	MINT	NRMT	EXC
COMPLETE SET (25)	4.00	1.80	.50

☐ 1 Jack Armstrong
☐ 2 Tim Birtsas
☐ 3 Norm Charlton
☐ 4 Rob Dibble
☐ 5 Jeff Gray
☐ 6 Mike Jones
☐ 7 Hugh Kemp
☐ 8 Rob Lopez
☐ 9 Steve Oliverio
☐ 10 Pat Pacillo
☐ 11 Mike Roesler
☐ 12 Lenny Harris
☐ 13 Greg Monda
☐ 14 Luis Quinones
☐ 15 Dan Boever
☐ 16 Doug Gwosdz
☐ 17 Joe Oliver
☐ 18 Marty Brown
☐ 19 Scott Earl
☐ 20 Dave Klipstein
☐ 21 Ron Roenicke
☐ 22 Van Snider
☐ 23 Jack Lind
☐ 24 Wayne Garland
☐ 25 John Young

1988 Nashville Sounds ProCards

This 26-card standard-size set of the 1988 Nashville Sounds, a Class AAA American Association affiliate of the Cincinnati Reds, features gold-bordered posed color player photos on its fronts. The player's name, position, and team name appear at the bottom. The plain white back carries the player's name at the top, followed by biography and statistics.

	MINT	NRMT	EXC
COMPLETE SET (26)	5.00	2.20	.60

☐ 471 Scott Earl
☐ 472 Pat Pacillo
☐ 473 Van Snider
☐ 474 Dave Klipstein
☐ 475 Ron Roenicke
☐ 476 Dan Boever
☐ 477 Tim Birtsas
☐ 478 Jeff Gray
☐ 479 Hugh Kemp
☐ 480 Doug Gwosdz
☐ 481 Marty Brown
☐ 482 Steve Oliverio
☐ 483 Joe Oliver
☐ 484 Jack Armstrong
☐ 485 Mike Jones
☐ 486 Jack Lind
☐ 487 Rob Lopez
☐ 488 Norm Charlton
☐ 489 Lenny Harris
☐ 490 Luis Quinones
☐ 491 Greg Monda
☐ 492 Mike Roesler
☐ 493 Robbie Dibble
☐ 494 Wayne Garland
☐ 495 John R. Young
☐ NNO Checklist

1988 Nashville Sounds Team Issue

	MINT	NRMT	EXC
COMPLETE SET (25)	5.00	2.20	.60

☐ 1 Jack Armstrong
☐ 2 Skeeter Barnes
☐ 3 Dan Boever
☐ 4 Keith Brown
☐ 5 Marty Brown
☐ 6 Norm Charlton
☐ 7 Tony DeFrancesco
☐ 8 Rob Dibble
☐ 9 Scottie Earl
☐ 10 Jeff Gray
☐ 11 Doug Gwosdz
☐ 12 Lenny Harris
☐ 13 Jim Jefferson
☐ 14 Mike Jones
☐ 15 Hugh Kemp
☐ 16 Terry McGriff
☐ 17 Charlie Mitchell
☐ 18 Steve Oliverio
☐ 19 Luis Quinones
☐ 20 Ron Roenicke
☐ 21 Candy Sierra
☐ 22 Van Snider
☐ 23 Eddie Tanner
☐ 24 Hedi Vargas
☐ 25 Coaches
John Young TR
Frank Lucchesi MGR
Wayne Garland CO

1988 Nebraska Cornhuskers

	MINT	NRMT	EXC
COMPLETE SET (27)	10.00	4.50	1.25

☐ 1 Shawn Buchanan
☐ 2 Charlie Colon
☐ 3 Ron Crowe
☐ 4 Jeff Hausmann
☐ 5 Eric Helfand
☐ 6 Paul Henry
☐ 7 Dale Kistaitis
☐ 8 John Lepley
☐ 9 Tim Pettengill
☐ 10 Terrance Batiste
☐ 11 Bobby Benjamin
☐ 12 Rocky Johnson
☐ 13 Pat Leinen
☐ 14 Ken Ramos
☐ 15 Joel Sealer
☐ 16 Jeff Taylor
☐ 17 Doug Tegtmeier
☐ 18 Bruce Wobken
☐ 19 Mate Borgogno
☐ 20 Joe Federico
☐ 21 Phil Goguen
☐ 22 Marcel Johnson
☐ 23 John Kohli
☐ 24 Vinny Limon
☐ 25 McGraw Milhaven
☐ 26 Ken Sirak
☐ 27 Mike Zajeski CL

1988 New Britain Red Sox ProCards

This 25-card standard-size set of the 1988 New Britain Red Sox, a Class AA Eastern League affiliate of the Boston Red Sox, features silver-bordered posed color player photos on its fronts. The player's name, position, and team name appear at the bottom. The plain white back carries the player's name at the top, followed by biography and statistics.

	MINT	NRMT	EXC
COMPLETE SET (25)	5.00	2.20	.60

☐ 889 Luis Vasquez
☐ 890 Daryl Irvine
☐ 891 Mike Clarkin
☐ 892 Doug Palmer
☐ 893 Bob Chadwick
☐ 894 John Roberts
☐ 895 Eduardo Zambrano
☐ 896 Mike Dalton
☐ 897 Manny Jose
☐ 898 Dan Gabriele
☐ 899 Larry Shikles
☐ 900 Greg Bochesa
☐ 901 Tim McGee
☐ 902 Jose Birriel
☐ 903 Ed Estrada
☐ 904 Dan Gakeler
☐ 905 Tito Stewart
☐ 906 Todd Pratt
☐ 907 Chris Moritz
☐ 908 Curt Schilling
☐ 909 Mike Carista
☐ 910 Angel Gonzalez
☐ 911 Roberto Zambrano
☐ 912 Jason Jackson
☐ NNO Checklist

1988 Oklahoma Sooners

	MINT	NRMT	EXC
COMPLETE SET (24)	10.00	4.50	1.25

☐ 1 Jim Huslig
☐ 2 Mike Hensley
☐ 3 Chris Ebright
☐ 4 Jim Fleming CO
☐ 5 Stan Meek CO
☐ 6 Enos Semore CO
☐ 7 John Douglas
☐ 8 Kevin Castleberry
☐ 9 Matt Anderson
☐ 10 Mark Cole
☐ 11 Toby Walker
☐ 12 Darron Cox
☐ 13 John Kosenski
☐ 14 Korey Keling

☐ 15 Darin Cosby
☐ 16 Marvin Cobb
☐ 17 Todd Butler
☐ 18 Paul Oster
☐ 19 Diamond Girls
Paige Jackson
Donna Pearson
☐ 20 Kevin King
☐ 21 Wade Inman
☐ 22 Tom Lachmann
☐ 23 Mike Seal
☐ 24 Chris Burgen

1988 Oklahoma City 89ers CMC

10,000 sets were produced.

	MINT	NRMT	EXC
COMPLETE SET (25)	5.00	2.20	.60

☐ 1 Scott Anderson
☐ 2 Dwayne Henry
☐ 3 Scott May
☐ 4 Craig McMurtry
☐ 5 Gary Mielke
☐ 6 Ferguson Jenkins
☐ 7 Ray Hayward
☐ 8 Ed Vande Berg
☐ 9 Tony Fossas
☐ 10 Rick Odekirk
☐ 11 Darrell Whitaker
☐ 12 Otto Gonzalez
☐ 13 Gar Millay
☐ 14 Jose Tolentino
☐ 15 Bill Merrifield
☐ 16 Barbaro Garbey
☐ 17 Larry Klein
☐ 18 Jeff Kunkel
☐ 19 Tom O'Malley
☐ 20 Dan Rohn
☐ 21 Don Werner
☐ 22 Robby Wine
☐ 23 Jim St. Laurent
☐ 24 James Steels
☐ 25 Toby Harrah

1988 Oklahoma City 89ers ProCards

This 27-card standard-size set of the 1988 Oklahoma City 89ers, a Class AAA American Association affiliate of the Texas Rangers, features gold-bordered posed color player photos on its fronts. The player's name, position, and team name appear at the bottom. The plain white back carries the player's name at the top, followed by biography and statistics.

	MINT	NRMT	EXC
COMPLETE SET (27)	6.00	2.70	.75

☐ 27 Scott May
☐ 28 Bill Taylor
☐ 29 Rick Odekirk
☐ 30 Jeff Kunkel
☐ 31 Dan Rohn
☐ 32 Larry Klein
☐ 33 Dwayne Henry
☐ 34 Tony Fossas
☐ 35 Gary Mielke
☐ 36 Bill Merrifield
☐ 37 Don Werner
☐ 38 James Steels
☐ 39 Jim St. Laurent
☐ 40 Gar Millay
☐ 41 Jose Tolentino
☐ 42 Robbie Wine
☐ 43 Darrell Whitaker
☐ 44 Craig McMurtry
☐ 45 Barbaro Garbey
☐ 46 Toby Harrah
☐ 47 Otto Gonzalez
☐ 48 Tom O'Malley
☐ 49 Ray Hayward
☐ 50 Ferguson Jenkins
☐ 51 Ray Ramirez
☐ 52 Ed Vande Berg
☐ NNO Checklist

1988 Omaha Royals CMC

10,000 sets were produced.

	MINT	NRMT	EXC
COMPLETE SET (25)	5.00	2.20	.60

☐ 1 Rick Anderson
☐ 2 Luis Aquino
☐ 3 Bob Buchanan
☐ 4 Steve Fireovid
☐ 5 Jerry Don Gleaton
☐ 6 Al Hargesheimer
☐ 7 Jeff Montgomery
☐ 8 Tom Mullen
☐ 9 Bill Swaggerty
☐ 10 Rondin Johnson
☐ 11 Israel Sanchez
☐ 12 Nick Capra
☐ 13 Mike Loggins
☐ 14 Gary Thurman
☐ 15 Jeff Schulz
☐ 16 Dave Owen
☐ 17 Dann Bilardello
☐ 18 Larry Owen
☐ 19 Tom Dodd
☐ 20 Buddy Biancalana
☐ 21 Joe Citari
☐ 22 Luis De Los Santos
☐ 23 Rich Dubee
☐ 24 Jose Castro
☐ 25 Glenn Ezell

1988 Omaha Royals ProCards

This 29-card standard-size set of the 1988 Omaha Royals, a Class AAA American Association affiliate of the Kansas City Royals, features gold-bordered posed color player photos on its fronts. The player's name, position, and team name appear at the bottom. The plain white back carries the player's name at the top, followed by biography and statistics.

	MINT	NRMT	EXC
COMPLETE SET (29)	6.00	2.70	.75

☐ 1494 Rich Dubee
☐ 1495 Tom Poquette
☐ 1496 Israel Sanchez
☐ 1497 Jerry Don Gleaton
☐ 1498 Bill Swaggerty
☐ 1499 Nick Capra
☐ 1500 Nick Swartz
☐ 1501 Jeff Montgomery
☐ 1502 Buddy Biancalana
☐ 1503 Glenn Ezell
☐ 1504 Mike Loggins
☐ 1505 Tom Dodd
☐ 1506 Luis Delos Santos
☐ 1507 Tom Mullen
☐ 1508 Jeff Schulz
☐ 1509 Jose Castro
☐ 1510 Dave Owen
☐ 1511 Don Welchel
☐ 1512 Rick Anderson
☐ 1513 Steve Fireovid
☐ 1514 Bob Buchanan
☐ 1515 Ron Johnson
☐ 1516 Larry Owen
☐ 1517 Al Hargesheimer
☐ 1518 Dann Bilardello
☐ 1519 Joe Citari
☐ 1520 Luis Aquino
☐ 1521 Gary Thurman
☐ NNO Checklist

1988 Oneonta Yankees ProCards

This 34-card standard-size set of the 1988 Oneonta Yankees, a Class A New York-Penn League affiliate of the New York Yankees, features bronze-bordered posed color player photos on its fronts. The player's name, position, and team name appear at the bottom. The plain white back carries the player's name at the top, followed by biography and statistics.

	MINT	NRMT	EXC
COMPLETE SET (34)	5.00	2.20	.60

☐ 2040 Ed Martel
☐ 2041 Andy Cook
☐ 2042 Todd Brill
☐ 2043 Pat Kelly
☐ 2044 Bobby DeJardin
☐ 2045 Jason Bridges
☐ 2046 Herb Erhardt
☐ 2047 Ken Greer
☐ 2048 Skip Nelloms
☐ 2049 Hector Vargas
☐ 2050 John Seeburger
☐ 2051 Craig Brink
☐ 2052 Jeff Livesey
☐ 2053 Rey Fernandez
☐ 2054 Miguel Torres
☐ 2055 Jorge Candelaria
☐ 2056 Bob Hunter
☐ 2057 Jeff Hoffman
☐ 2058 Bob Zeihen
☐ 2059 Mike Draper
☐ 2060 Art Canestro
☐ 2061 Bruce Prybylinski
☐ 2062 Jerry Nielsen
☐ 2063 Jay Makemson
☐ 2064 Gary Allenson
☐ 2065 Tim Weston
☐ 2066 Alan Warren
☐ 2067 Jay Knoblauh
☐ 2068 Mark Martin
☐ 2069 Jeff Johnson
☐ 2070 Jeff Taylor
☐ 2071 Frank Seminara
☐ 2072 Rod Ehrhard
☐ NNO Checklist

1988 Orlando Twins Best

This 29-card standard-size set of the 1988 Orlando Twins, a Class AA Southern League affiliate of the Minnesota Twins, features red and black bordered posed color player photos on its fronts. The team name appears at the top, and below the picture is the player's name and position. The horizontal gray back carries the player's name and position at the top, followed by biography, career highlights, and statistics. The set is printed on thin card stock.

	MINT	NRMT	EXC
COMPLETE SET (29)	5.00	2.20	.60

☐ 1 Derek Parks
☐ 2 Tim O'Conner
☐ 3 Duane Gustavson
☐ 4 Eddie Yanes
☐ 5 Mark Funderburk
☐ 6 Toby Nivens
☐ 7 Steven Comer
☐ 8 James Pittman
☐ 9 Mike Dyer
☐ 10 Jaime Williams
☐ 11 Joey Aragon
☐ 12 Gary Borg
☐ 13 Jeff Satzinger
☐ 14 Kevin Trudeau
☐ 15 Terry Jorgensen
☐ 16 Chris Forgione
☐ 17 German Gonzalez
☐ 18 Chip Hale
☐ 19 Jeff Reboulet
☐ 20 Larry Gasian
☐ 21 Mike Dotzler
☐ 22 Rafael DeLima
☐ 23 Steve Gasser
☐ 24 Francisco Oliveras
☐ 25 Shannon Raybon
☐ 26 Wayne Hattaway
☐ 27 Bill Cutshall
☐ 28 Bernardo Brito
☐ 29 Checklist

1988 Osceola Astros Star

	MINT	NRMT	EXC
COMPLETE SET (25)	5.00	2.20	.60

☐ 1 Manuel Acta
☐ 2 Samuel August
☐ 3 Jeff Baldwin
☐ 4 Daven Bond
☐ 5 Ryan Bowen
☐ 6 Todd Credeur
☐ 7 Louis Deiley
☐ 8 Pedro DeLeon
☐ 9 Tony Eusebio
☐ 10 Lou Frazier
☐ 11 Carl Grovom
☐ 12 Rusty Harris
☐ 13 Randall Hennis
☐ 14 Victor Hithe
☐ 15 Trent Hubbard
☐ 16 Bert Hunter
☐ 17 Todd McClure
☐ 18 Guy Normand
☐ 19 Dan Nyssen
☐ 20 Alfonso Osuna
☐ 21 David Potts
☐ 22 Karl Rhodes
☐ 23 Pedro Sanchez
☐ 24 John Sheehan
☐ 25 Mike Simms

1988 Palm Springs Angels Cal League Cards

	MINT	NRMT	EXC
COMPLETE SET (31)	5.00	2.20	.60

☐ 85 Colin Charland
☐ 86 Mike Erb
☐ 87 John Fritz
☐ 88 Scott Kannenberg
☐ 89 James V. Long
☐ 90 Louis Merejo
☐ 91 Rich Morehouse
☐ 92 Jeff Richardson
☐ 93 Jose Tapia
☐ 94 Bill Vanderwel
☐ 95 Danny Ward
☐ 96 Edgar Alfonzo
☐ 97 Ruben Amaro Jr.
☐ 98 Mike Andeson
☐ 99 Mark A. Baca
☐ 100 Jeff Barns
☐ 101 Scott Cerny
☐ 102 Chris Cron
☐ 103 Ted Dyson
☐ 104 Jim McAnany
☐ 105 Mike Musolino
☐ 106 Gary Nalls
☐ 107 John Orton
☐ 108 Reed Peters
☐ 109 Giovanny Reyes
☐ 110 Paul Sorrento
☐ 111 Glenn Washington
☐ 112 Bill Lachemann
☐ 113 Reggie Lambert
☐ 114 Gary Ruby
☐ 115 Bill Durney

1988 Palm Springs Angels ProCards

This 32-card standard-size set of the 1988 Palm Springs Angels, a Class A California League affiliate of the California Angels, features bronze-bordered posed color player photos on its fronts. The player's name, position, and team name appear at the bottom. The plain white back carries the player's name at the top, followed by biography and statistics.

	MINT	NRMT	EXC
COMPLETE SET (32)	5.00	2.20	.60

☐ 1433 John Orton
☐ 1434 Ruben Amaro
☐ 1435 J. Gary Ruby
☐ 1436 Bill Lachemann
☐ 1437 Luis Merejo
☐ 1438 Mike Anderson
☐ 1439 Reed Peters
☐ 1440 Scott Cerny
☐ 1441 Chris Cron
☐ 1442 Dan Ward
☐ 1443 Mike Erb
☐ 1444 Scott Kannenberg
☐ 1445 John Fritz
☐ 1446 Jose Tapia
☐ 1447 Colin Charland
☐ 1448 Dario Nunez
☐ 1449 Richard Morehouse
☐ 1450 Paul Sorrento
☐ 1451 Jeff Barns
☐ 1452 Jim McAnany
☐ 1453 Tim Dyson
☐ 1454 Gary Nalls
☐ 1455 Glenn Washington
☐ 1456 Mark Baca
☐ 1457 Bill Vanderwel
☐ 1458 Jim Bisceglia
☐ 1459 Bobby Bell
☐ 1460 Jimmy Long
☐ 1461 Reggie Lambert
☐ 1462 Bill Durney
☐ 1463 Jeff Richardson
☐ NNO Checklist

1988 Pawtucket Red Sox CMC

10,000 sets were produced.

	MINT	NRMT	EXC
COMPLETE SET (25)	4.00	1.80	.50

☐ 1 Rob Woodward
☐ 2 Mike Rochford
☐ 3 Mitch Johnson
☐ 4 John Leister
☐ 5 Andy Araujo
☐ 6 Zack Crouch
☐ 7 Steve Curry
☐ 8 Eric Hetzel
☐ 9 Tom Bolton
☐ 10 Dana Kiecker
☐ 11 Randy Kutcher
☐ 12 Bill McInnis
☐ 13 Glenn Hoffman
☐ 14 Tony Cleary
☐ 15 Chris Cannizzaro
☐ 16 Pat Dodson
☐ 17 Angel Gonzalez
☐ 18 Mike Mesh
☐ 19 Gary Miller-Jones
☐ 20 Carlos Quintana
☐ 21 Dana Williams
☐ 22 Gary Tremblay
☐ 23 Scott Wade
☐ 24 Ed Nottle
☐ 25 Mark Meleski

1988 Pawtucket Red Sox ProCards

This 26-card standard-size set of the 1988 Pawtucket Red Sox, a Class AAA International League affiliate of the Boston Red Sox, features gold-bordered posed color player photos on its fronts. The player's name, position, and team name appear at the bottom. The plain white back carries the player's name at the top, followed by biography and statistics.

	MINT	NRMT	EXC
COMPLETE SET (26)	5.00	2.20	.60

☐ 446 Andy Araujo
☐ 447 Mike Rochford
☐ 448 Rob Woodward
☐ 449 Eric Hetzel

☐ 450 Gary Tremblay
☐ 451 Chris Cannizzaro
☐ 452 Tom Bolton
☐ 453 Carlos Quintana
☐ 454 Mark Meleski
☐ 455 Mitch Johnson
☐ 456 Bill McInnis
☐ 457 Zack Crouch
☐ 458 Scott Wade
☐ 459 Gary Miller-Jones
☐ 460 Dana Williams
☐ 461 Dana Kiecker
☐ 462 Angel Gonzalez
☐ 463 Mike Mesh
☐ 464 Randy Kutcher
☐ 465 Glenn Hoffman
☐ 466 Pat Dodson
☐ 467 Tony Cleary
☐ 468 Steve Curry
☐ 469 Ed Nottle
☐ 470 John Leister
☐ NNO Checklist

1988 Peoria Chiefs Team Issue

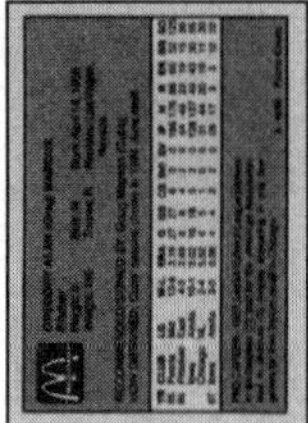

This issue includes third year cards of Mark Grace, Greg Maddux and Rafael Palmeiro. There is also a card of star Basketball player Hersey Hawkins, who attended Bradley University and led the nation in scoring.

	MINT	NRMT	EXC
COMPLETE SET (35)	90.00	40.00	11.00

☐ 1 Herbie Andrade
☐ 2 Warren Arrington
☐ 3 Mike Aspray
☐ 4 Lenny Bell
☐ 5 Pookie Bernstine
☐ 6 Mike Boswell
☐ 7 Ed Caballero
☐ 8 Harry Caray
☐ 9 Rusty Crockett
☐ 10 Sergio Espinal
☐ 11 Mark Grace
☐ 12 Phil Hannon
☐ 13 Carl Hamilton
☐ 14 Hersey Hawkins
☐ 15 Jeff Massicotte
☐ 16 Steve Melendez
☐ 17 Bill Melvin
☐ 18 Greg Kallevig
☐ 19 Rick Kranitz
☐ 20 Jerry Lapenta
☐ 21 Greg Maddux
☐ 22 Mark North
☐ 23 Rafael Palmeiro
☐ 24 Elvin Paulino
☐ 25 Jeff Pico
☐ 26 Marty Rivero
☐ 27 Brett Robinson
☐ 28 Gabby Rodriguez
☐ 29 Jim Tracy
☐ 30 Jerome Walton
☐ 31 Rick Wilkins
☐ 32 Eddie Williams
☐ 33 Fernando Zarranz
☐ 34 Mark Grace
Greg Maddux
Rafael Palmeiro
☐ 35 Mike Harkey
Derrick May
Pete Mackanin

1988 Phoenix Firebirds CMC

10,000 sets were produced.

	MINT	NRMT	EXC
COMPLETE SET (25)	10.00	4.50	1.25

☐ 1 Randy Bockus
☐ 2 John Burkett
☐ 3 Dennis Cook
☐ 4 Roger Mason
☐ 5 Jeff Brantley
☐ 6 Mike Hogan
☐ 7 Brian Ohnoutka
☐ 8 Roger Samuels
☐ 9 Randy McCament
☐ 10 Terry Mullholland
☐ 11 Ed Puikunas
☐ 12 Kirt Manwaring
☐ 13 Bobby Ramos
☐ 14 Angie Escobar
☐ 15 Charlie Hayes
☐ 16 Tony Perezchica
☐ 17 Mark Wasinger
☐ 18 Matt Williams
☐ 19 Alan Cockrell
☐ 20 Everett Graham
☐ 21 Rusty Tillman
☐ 22 Ty Dabney
☐ 23 Deron McCue
☐ 24 Wendell Kim
☐ 25 Marty DeMarrite
Tim Blackwell

1988 Phoenix Firebirds ProCards

This 29-card standard-size set of the 1988 Phoenix Firebirds, a Class AAA Pacific Coast League affiliate of the San Francisco Giants, features gold-bordered posed color player photos on its fronts. The player's name, position, and team name appear at the bottom. The plain white back carries the player's name at the top, followed by biography and statistics.

	MINT	NRMT	EXC
COMPLETE SET (29)	12.00	5.50	1.50

☐ 53 Tom Blackwell
☐ 54 Mark Wasinger
☐ 55 Randy Bockus
☐ 56 Matt Williams
☐ 57 Charlie Hayes
☐ 58 Deron McCue
☐ 59 Rusty Tillman
☐ 60 Everett Graham
☐ 61 Kirt Manwaring
☐ 62 Roger Mason
☐ 63 Angel Escobar
☐ 64 Francisco Melendez
☐ 65 Wendell Kim
☐ 66 Cliff Shidawara
☐ 67 Marty DeMerritt
☐ 68 Alan Cockrell
☐ 69 Bobby Ramos
☐ 70 Roger Samuels
☐ 71 Randy McCament
☐ 72 Ty Dabney
☐ 73 Mike Hogan
☐ 74 Ed Puikunas
☐ 75 Tony Perezchica
☐ 76 John Burkett
☐ 77 Terry Mulholland
☐ 78 Jeff Brantley
☐ 79 Brian Ohnoutka
☐ 80 Dennis Cook
☐ NNO Checklist

1988 Pittsfield Cubs ProCards

This 25-card standard-size set of the 1988 Pittsfield Cubs, a Class AA Eastern League affiliate of the Chicago Cubs, features silver-bordered posed color player photos on its fronts. The player's name, position, and team name appear at the bottom. The plain white back carries the player's name at the top, followed by biography and statistics.

	MINT	NRMT	EXC
COMPLETE SET (25)	5.00	2.20	.60

☐ 1355 Hector Villanueva
☐ 1356 Mitch Zwolensky
☐ 1357 Julio Valdez
☐ 1358 Ray Thoma
☐ 1359 Joe Girardi
☐ 1360 Jim Essian
☐ 1361 Bryan House
☐ 1362 Rich Amaral
☐ 1363 Bob Bafia
☐ 1364 Brian McCann
☐ 1365 Mike Tullier
☐ 1366 Jerry Lapenta
☐ 1367 Jim Bullinger
☐ 1368 Dean Wilkins
☐ 1369 Steve Parker
☐ 1370 Ced Landrum
☐ 1371 Mark Leonette
☐ 1372 Rich Scheid
☐ 1373 Dave Kopf
☐ 1374 Jerome Walton
☐ 1375 Jackie Davidson
☐ 1376 Kris Roth
☐ 1377 Mike Harkey
☐ 1378 Gary Parmenter
☐ NNO Checklist

1988 Pocatello Giants ProCards

This 31-card standard-size set of the 1988 Pocatello Giants, a Rookie Class Pioneer League affiliate of the San Francisco Giants, features bronze-bordered posed color player photos on its fronts. The player's name, position, and team name appear at the bottom. The plain white back carries the player's name at the top, followed by biography and statistics.

	MINT	NRMT	EXC
COMPLETE SET (31)	5.00	2.20	.60

☐ 2073 Don Brock
☐ 2074 David Wuthrich
☐ 2075 Andre George
☐ 2076 Jim Myers
☐ 2077 Carlos Sanchez
☐ 2078 Francisco Arias
☐ 2079 Sean Thompson
☐ 2080 Scott Ebert
☐ 2081 Adam Hilbert
☐ 2082 Steve Reed
☐ 2083 Lance Burnett
☐ 2084 Dave Edwards
☐ 2085 Marino Hernandez
☐ 2086 Greg Lee
☐ 2087 Reuben Smiley
☐ 2088 Daris Toussaint
☐ 2089 Victor Cruz
☐ 2090 B. Hewatt
☐ 2091 Kevin Rogers
Sic, Rodgers
☐ 2092 Adam Smith
☐ 2093 Kevin Hall
☐ 2094 David Slavin
☐ 2095 Dobie Swepson
☐ 2096 Jesus Laya
☐ 2097 Joey Speakes
☐ 2098 David Booth
☐ 2099 Carl Hanselman
☐ 2100 Diego Segui
☐ 2101 Jack Hiatt
☐ 2102 Jack Penrod
☐ NNO Checklist

1988 Portland Beavers CMC

10,000 sets were produced.

	MINT	NRMT	EXC
COMPLETE SET (25)	4.00	1.80	.50

☐ 1 Allan Anderson
Spelled Andy on card
☐ 2 Karl Best
☐ 3 T.R. Bryden
☐ 4 Jeff Bumgarner
☐ 5 Mark Portugal
☐ 6 Roy Smith
☐ 7 Ray Soff
☐ 8 Freddie Toliver
☐ 9 Jim Winn
☐ 10 Jim Davins
☐ 11 Brian Harper
☐ 12 Steve Liddle
☐ 13 Doug Baker
☐ 14 Ricky Jones
☐ 15 Kelvin Torve
☐ 16 Brad Bierley
☐ 17 Eric Bullock
☐ 18 Winston Ficklin
☐ 19 Chris Pittaro
☐ 20 Vic Rodriguez
☐ 21 Bobby Ralston
☐ 22 John Moses
☐ 23 Phil Wilson
☐ 24 Jim Mahoney
☐ 25 Jim Shellenback

1988 Portland Beavers ProCards

This 27-card standard-size set of the 1988 Portland Beavers, a Class AAA Pacific Coast League affiliate of the Minnesota Twins, features gold-bordered posed color player photos on its fronts. The player's name, position, and team name appear at the bottom. The plain white back carries the player's name at the top, followed by biography and statistics.

	MINT	NRMT	EXC
COMPLETE SET (27)	5.00	2.20	.60

☐ 639 Brad Bierley
☐ 640 Eric Bullock
☐ 641 Kelvin Torve
☐ 642 Jim Winn
☐ 643 John Moses
☐ 644 Jim Shellenback
☐ 645 Roy Smith
☐ 646 Karl Best
☐ 647 Doug Baker
☐ 648 Brad Boylan
☐ 649 Vic Rodriguez
☐ 650 Jim Mahoney
☐ 651 Brian Harper
☐ 652 Winston Ficklin
☐ 653 Chris Pittaro
☐ 654 Allan Anderson
☐ 655 Steve Liddle
☐ 656 Ricky Jones
☐ 657 Bobby Ralston
☐ 658 Mark Portugal
☐ 659 Jeff Bumgarner
☐ 660 Jim Davins
☐ 661 Phil Wilson
☐ 662 Ray Soff
☐ 663 T.R. Bryden
☐ 664 Fred Toliver
☐ NNO Checklist

1988 Prince William Yankees Star

This issue includes a second year card of Bernie Williams.

	MINT	NRMT	EXC
COMPLETE SET (25)	20.00	9.00	2.50

☐ 1 Steve Adkins
☐ 2 Tim Bishop
☐ 3 Brent Blum
☐ 4 Dennis Brow
☐ 5 Ken Brown
☐ 6 Royal Clayton
☐ 7 Bill Dacosta
☐ 8 Luis Faccio
☐ 9 Reynaldo Fernandez
☐ 10 Randy Foster
☐ 11 Victor Garcia
☐ 12 Chris Howard
☐ 13 Dean Kelly
☐ 14 Jose Laboy
☐ 15 Kevin Maas
☐ 16 Mark Marris
☐ 17 Alan Mills
☐ 18 Wiliam Morales
☐ 19 Tom Popplewell
☐ 20 John Ramos
☐ 21 Jerry Rub
☐ 22 Darrell Tingle
☐ 23 Mickey Tresh
☐ 24 Bernie Williams
☐ 25 Gerald Williams

1988 Pulaski Braves ProCards

This 25-card standard-size set of the 1988 Pulaski Braves, a Rookie Class Appalachian League affiliate of the Atlanta Braves, features bronze-bordered posed color player photos on its fronts. The player's name, position, and team name appear at the bottom. The plain white back carries the player's name at the top, followed by biography and statistics.

	MINT	NRMT	EXC
COMPLETE SET (25)	5.00	2.20	.60

☐ 1748 Phillip Wellman CO
☐ 1749 Fred Koenig
☐ 1750 Smoky Burgess
☐ 1751 Scott Goselin
☐ 1752 Scott Grove
☐ 1753 John Greenwood
☐ 1754 Tom Rizzo
☐ 1755 Steve Wendell
☐ 1756 Glen Gardner
☐ 1757 David Reis
☐ 1758 Errol Flynn
☐ 1759 Paul Reis
☐ 1760 Calvain Culberson
☐ 1761 Ricky Rigsby
☐ 1762 Brent McCoy
☐ 1763 Chris Mitta
☐ 1764 Mike Urman
☐ 1765 D. Piela
☐ 1766 Roger Hailey
☐ 1767 Robert Minaya
☐ 1768 Randy Simmons
☐ 1769 Ron Thomas
☐ 1770 Cloyd Boyer
☐ 1771 Don Bowman GM
☐ NNO Checklist

1988 Quad City Angels Grand Slam

	MINT	NRMT	EXC
COMPLETE SET (30)	5.00	2.20	.60

☐ 1 Eddie Rodriguez MG
☐ 2 Mike Couchee

☐ 3 Bill Zick
☐ 4 Wiley Lee
☐ 5 Kevin Flora
☐ 6 Larry Pardo
☐ 7 Edgal Rodriquez
☐ 8 Bill Robinson
☐ 9 Terence Carr
☐ 10 Steve Dunn
☐ 11 David Holdridge
☐ 12 Frank Mutz
☐ 13 Daryl Green
☐ 14 Bob Rose
☐ 15 Troy Giles
☐ 16 Rod Lung
☐ 17 Jim Townsend
☐ 18 Mario Molina
☐ 19 Edgar Alfonzo
☐ 20 Roberto Hernandez
☐ 21 Kenny Grant
☐ 22 Jim Aylward
☐ 23 Cesar Delarosa
☐ 24 Charlie Romero
☐ 25 Rob Wassenaar
☐ 26 Tim McKinnis
☐ 27 Chris Graves
☐ 28 Gary Buckels
☐ 29 Brandy Vann
☐ 30 Mike Musolino

1988 Reading Phillies ProCards

This 27-card standard-size set of the 1988 Reading Phillies, a Class AA Eastern League affiliate of the Philadelphia Phillies, features silver-bordered posed color player photos on its fronts. The player's name, position, and team name appear at the bottom. The plain white back carries the player's name at the top, followed by biography and statistics.

	MINT	NRMT	EXC
COMPLETE SET (27)	5.00	2.20	.60

☐ 863 Tom Schwarz
☐ 864 Alan LeBoeuf
☐ 865 Steve Sharts
☐ 866 Brad Moore
☐ 867 Tony Brown
☐ 868 Scott Service
☐ 869 Chuck Malone
☐ 870 Tim Sossamon
☐ 871 Warren Magee
☐ 872 Jeff Kaye
☐ 873 Gary Berman
☐ 874 Dan Giesen
☐ 875 Chuck McElroy
☐ 876 Tim Fortugno
☐ 877 Steve DeAngelis
☐ 878 Rick Parker
☐ 879 Howard Nichols
☐ 880 Greg Edge
☐ 881 Harvey Brumfield
☐ 882 Greg Legg
☐ 883 Vince Holyfield
☐ 884 Jose Leiva
☐ 885 Ray Roman
☐ 886 Chris Calvert
☐ 887 Tim Corcoran
☐ 888 Carlos Arroyo
☐ NNO Checklist

1988 Reno Silver Sox Cal League Cards

	MINT	NRMT	EXC
COMPLETE SET (24)	5.00	2.20	.60

☐ 268 Alan Fowlkes
☐ 269 Elvin Rivera
☐ 270 Tony La Cerra
☐ 271 Reggie Glover
☐ 272 Bill Shamblin
☐ 273 Scott Madden
☐ 274 Joe Strong
☐ 275 John Savage
☐ 276 Frank Mutz
☐ 277 Mike Garner
☐ 278 Kinney Sims
☐ 279 Jamie Allison
☐ 280 Jim Aylward
☐ 281 Cary Grubb
☐ 282 Chris Holmes
☐ 283 Robbie Rogers
☐ 284 Mike Rountree
☐ 285 Joe Ortiz
☐ 286 Gregg Ward
☐ 287 David Liddell
☐ 288 Jim Pace
☐ 289 Pete Houston
☐ 290 Fred Carter
☐ 291 Nate Oliver

1988 Richmond Braves Bob's Camera

This 29-card team set of the 1989 Richmond Braves, a Class AAA International League affiliate of the Atlanta Braves, was sponsored by Bob's Camera. The fronts feature borderless color player photos with sponsors' and team's logos in the wide bottom margin. The backs are blank. This issue includes third year cards of Dave Justice, Ron Gant and John Smoltz. 500 sets were produced.

	MINT	NRMT	EXC
COMPLETE SET (25)	100.00	45.00	12.50

☐ 1 Joe Boever
☐ 2 Bean Stringfellow
☐ 3 Carlos Rios
☐ 4 Sid Akins
☐ 5 Lonnie Smith
☐ 6 Todd Dewey
☐ 6 Jeff Blauser
☐ 7 Derek Lilliquist
☐ 8 John Smoltz
☐ 9 Juan Espino
☐ 10 John Mizerock
☐ 11 Marty Clary
☐ 12 Mike Fischlin
☐ 13 Dave Justice
☐ 14 Dave Griffin
☐ 15 Tommy Greene
☐ 16 Alex Smith
☐ 17 Jeff Wetherby
☐ 18 Gary Eave
☐ 19 Greg Tubbs
☐ 20 Dave Miller
☐ 21 Kevin Coffman
☐ 22 Tommy Dunbar
☐ 23 John Grubb
☐ 24 Barry Jones

1988 Richmond Braves CMC

This issue includes third year cards of Dave Justice, Ron Gant and John Smoltz.

	MINT	NRMT	EXC
COMPLETE SET (25)	14.00	6.25	1.75

☐ 1 Tommy Green
☐ 2 Derek Lilliquist
☐ 3 John Smoltz
☐ 4 Bean Stringfellow
☐ 5 Gary Eave
☐ 6 Juan Eichelberger
☐ 7 Sid Akins
☐ 8 Jose Alvarez
☐ 9 Joe Boever
☐ 10 Marty Clary
☐ 11 Todd Dewey
☐ 12 Ron Gant
☐ 13 Alex Smith
☐ 14 Lonnie Smith
☐ 15 Greg Tubbs
☐ 16 Jeff Wetherby
☐ 17 David Justice
☐ 18 Carlos Rios
☐ 19 Dave Griffin
☐ 20 Juan Espino
☐ 21 John Mizerock
☐ 22 Jeff Blauser
☐ 23 Jim Beauchamp
☐ 24 Leo Mazzone
☐ 25 Clarence Jones

1988 Richmond Braves ProCards

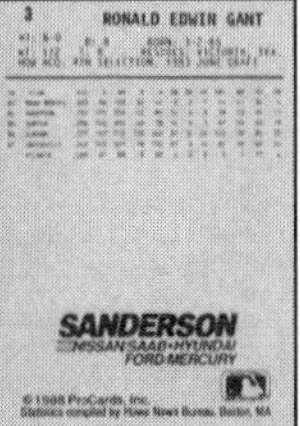

This 27-card standard-size set of the 1988 Richmond Braves, a Class AAA International League affiliate of the Atlanta Braves, features gold-bordered posed color player photos on its fronts. The player's name, position, and team name appear at the bottom. The plain white back carries the player's name at the top, followed by biography and statistics. This issue includes third year cards of Dave Justice, Ron Gant and John Smoltz.

	MINT	NRMT	EXC
COMPLETE SET (27)	30.00	13.50	3.70

☐ 1 Lonnie Smith
☐ 2 Tommy Greene
☐ 3 Ronnie Gant
☐ 4 Todd Dewey
☐ 5 Greg Tubbs
☐ 6 Sam Ayoub
☐ 7 Juan Espino
☐ 8 Carlos Rios
☐ 9 Jeff Wetherby
☐ 10 Juan Eichelberger
☐ 11 Marty Clary
☐ 12 Jose Alvarez
☐ 13 Bean Stringfellow
☐ 14 Sid Akins
☐ 15 Jim Beauchamp
☐ 16 Leo Mazzone
☐ 17 Clarence Jones
☐ 18 Jeff Blauser
☐ 19 John Mizerock
☐ 20 Dave Griffin
☐ 21 Derek Lilliquist
☐ 22 Joe Boever
☐ 23 John Smoltz
☐ 24 Dave Justice
☐ 25 Alex Smith
☐ 26 Gary Eave
☐ NNO Checklist

1988 Riverside Red Wave Cal League Cards

	MINT	NRMT	EXC
COMPLETE SET (28)	6.00	2.70	.75

☐ 206 Kevin Armstrong
☐ 207 James Austin
☐ 208 Ricky Bones
☐ 209 Rafael Chavez
☐ 210 Brian L. Harrison
☐ 211 Richard Holsman
☐ 212 James Lewis
☐ 213 Stephen Loubier
☐ 214 Bill Marx
☐ 215 Brian Wood
☐ 216 Brian Todd Brooks
☐ 217 Paul Faries
☐ 218 Kevin Farmer
☐ 219 Greg Hall
☐ 220 Kevin Garner
☐ 221 Steve Hendricks
☐ 222 Dave Hollins
☐ 223 Tom LeVasseur
☐ 224 Terry McDevitt
☐ 225 Warren Newson
☐ 226 Andy Skeels
☐ 227 William Taylor
☐ 228 Pat Jelks
☐ 229 Tony Torchia
☐ 230 Bill Blount
☐ 231 Jim Daniel
☐ 232 Ron Oglesby
☐ 233 Tye Waller

1988 Riverside Red Wave ProCards

This 27-card standard-size set of the 1988 Riverside Red Wave, a Class A California League affiliate of the San Diego Padres, features bronze-bordered posed color player photos on its fronts. The player's name, position, and team name appear at the bottom. The plain white back carries the player's name at the top, followed by biography and statistics.

	MINT	NRMT	EXC
COMPLETE SET (27)	5.00	2.20	.60

☐ 1407 Ron Oglesby
☐ 1408 Kevin Farmer
☐ 1409 Steve Hendricks
☐ 1410 Brian Brooks
☐ 1411 Pat Jelks
☐ 1412 Jim Daniel
☐ 1413 Tony Torchia
☐ 1414 Tye Waller
☐ 1415 Greg Hall
☐ 1416 Warren Newson
☐ 1417 Tom LeVasseur
☐ 1418 Dave Hollins
☐ 1419 Bill Taylor
☐ 1420 Brian Wood
☐ 1421 Bill Blount
☐ 1422 Paul Faries
☐ 1423 Jim Lewis
☐ 1424 Bill Marx
☐ 1425 Andy Skeels
☐ 1426 Ricky Bones
☐ 1427 Rich Holsman
☐ 1428 Brian Harrison
☐ 1429 Rafael Chavez
☐ 1430 Terry McDevitt
☐ 1431 Kevin Garner
☐ 1432 Steve Loubier
☐ NNO Checklist

1988 Rochester Red Wings CMC

10,000 sets were produced.

	MINT	NRMT	EXC
COMPLETE SET (25)	4.00	1.80	.50

☐ 1 Jeff Ballard
☐ 2 Eric Bell
☐ 3 Jose Mesa
☐ 4 Mark Bowden
☐ 5 Bob Gibson
☐ 6 John Habyan
☐ 7 Mike Griffin
☐ 8 Dickie Noles
☐ 9 Bill Scherrer
☐ 10 Jay Tibbs
☐ 11 Matt Cimo
☐ 12 Dale Berra
☐ 13 Chris Padget
☐ 14 Jerry Narron
☐ 15 Keith Hughes
☐ 16 Ron Salcedo
☐ 17 David Lee Smith
☐ 18 Pete Stanicek
☐ 19 Craig Worthington
☐ 20 Sherwin Cijntje
☐ 21 Mickey Tettleton
☐ 22 Tito Landrum
☐ 23 Vic Mata
☐ 24 Johnny Oates
☐ 25 Curt Motton

1988 Rochester Red Wings Governor's Cup Pucko

1,200 sets were produced.

	MINT	NRMT	EXC
COMPLETE SET (36)	15.00	6.75	1.85

☐ 1 Rochester Red Wings
☐ 2 Mark Bowden
☐ 3 Dale Berra
☐ 4 Curt Brown
☐ 5 Matt Cimo
☐ 6 Gordon Dillard
☐ 7 Steve Finley
☐ 8 Mike Griffin
☐ 9 John Habyan
☐ 10 Pete Harnisch
☐ 11 Kevin Hickey
☐ 12 Gerry Holtz
☐ 13 Keith Hughes
☐ 14 Ken Landreaux
☐ 15 Vic Mata
☐ 16 Bob Milacki
☐ 17 Jerry Narron
☐ 18 Carl Nichols
☐ 19 Dickie Noles
☐ 20 Chris Padget
☐ 21 Tim Pyznarski
☐ 22 Mike Raczka
☐ 23 Wade Rowdon
☐ 24 Ron Salcedo
☐ 25 Chuck Stanhope
☐ 26 Jeff Stone
☐ 27 Craig Worthington
☐ 28 Dom Chiti
☐ 29 Curt Motton
☐ 30 Johnny Oates
☐ 31 Jamie Reed
☐ 32 Bob Gougham
☐ 33 Rochester Red Wings
☐ 34 Rochester Red Wings
☐ 35 Rochester Red Wings
☐ 36 Rochester Red Wings

1988 Rochester Red Wings ProCards

This 30-card standard-size set of the 1988 Rochester Red Wings, a Class AAA International League affiliate of the Baltimore Orioles, features gold-bordered posed color player photos on its fronts. The player's name, position, and team name appear at the bottom. The plain white back carries the player's name at the top, followed by biography and statistics.

	MINT	NRMT	EXC
COMPLETE SET (30)	5.00	2.20	.60

☐ 193 Dale Berra
☐ 194 Eric Bell
☐ 195 Dave Smith
☐ 196 Bob Gibson
☐ 197 Vic Mata
☐ 198 Sherwin Cijntje
☐ 199 Jeff Ballard
☐ 200 Ron Salcedo
☐ 201 Jay Tibbs
☐ 202 Mickey Tettleton
☐ 203 Matt Cimo
☐ 204 Chris Padget

☐ 205 Pete Stanicek
☐ 206 Jose Mesa
☐ 207 Reg Montgomery
☐ 208 Mark Bowden
☐ 209 Bill Scherrer
☐ 210 Mike Griffin
☐ 211 Johnny Oates
☐ 212 Dom Chiti
☐ 213 Keith Hughes
☐ 214 Jamie Reed
☐ 215 John Habyan
☐ 216 Jerry Narron
☐ 217 Craig Worthington
☐ 218 Curt Motton
☐ 219 Dickie Noles
☐ 220 Jay Colley
☐ 221 Silver Stadium
☐ NNO Checklist

1988 Rochester Red Wings Team Issue

	MINT	NRMT	EXC
COMPLETE SET (26)	12.00	5.50	1.50

☐ 1 Jeff Ballard
☐ 2 Eric Bell
☐ 3 Dale Berra
☐ 4 Mark Bowden
☐ 5 Dom Chiti
☐ 6 Sherwin Cijntje
☐ 7 Matt Cimo
☐ 8 Bob Gibson
☐ 9 Mike Griffin
☐ 10 John Habyan
☐ 11 Keith Hughes
☐ 12 Vic Mata
☐ 13 Jose Mesa
☐ 14 Curt Motton
☐ 15 Jerry Narron
☐ 16 Dickie Noles
☐ 17 Johnny Oates
☐ 18 Chris Padget
☐ 19 Ron Salcedo
☐ 20 Bill Scherrer
☐ 21 Dave Smith
☐ 22 Pete Stanicek
☐ 23 Mickey Tettleton
☐ 24 Jay Tibbs
☐ 25 Jim Traber
☐ 26 Craig Worthington

1988 Rockford Expos Litho Center

Printed by Rockford Litho Center, this 34-card standard-size set of the 1988 Rockford Expos, a Class A Midwest League affiliate of the Montreal Expos, features on its white-bordered fronts posed color player photos set on red backgrounds. The player's name and position appear within a yellow diagonal stripe at the lower right. The white horizontal back is framed by a black line and carries the player's name and uniform number at the top, followed by biography and the name of the sponsor, Rockford Magazine. This issue includes Delino DeShields' first team set appearance. The cards are unnumbered and checklisted below in alphabetical order.

	MINT	NRMT	EXC
COMPLETE SET (34)	7.00	3.10	.85

☐ 1 Alan Bannister MG
☐ 2 Mario Brito
☐ 3 Scott Bromby
☐ 4 John Cain TR
☐ 5 Jeff Carter
☐ 6 Archi Cianfrocco
☐ 7 Dave Clark
☐ 8 Greg Colbrunn
☐ 9 Sean Cunningham TR
☐ 10 Delino DeShields
☐ 11 Dan Deweerdt TR
☐ 12 Howard Farmer
☐ 13 James Faulk
☐ 14 Paul Frye
☐ 15 Gene Glynn CO
☐ 16 Jeff Hauser TR
☐ 17 Cesar Hernandez
☐ 18 Rob Kerrigan
☐ 19 Scott Lane AGM
☐ 20 Chris Lariviere
☐ 21 Bill Larsen AGM
☐ 22 Rob Leary
☐ 23 Chris Marchok
☐ 24 John Mello
☐ 25 Nate Minchey
☐ 26 Jesus Paredes
☐ 27 Mike Parrott CO
☐ 28 Steve Pearse
☐ 29 Trevor Penn
☐ 30 Chris Pollack
☐ 31 Troy Ricker
☐ 32 Thomas Shannon GM
☐ 33 Kevin Sheary
☐ 34 Kent Willis

1988 South Atlantic League All-Stars Grand Slam

	MINT	NRMT	EXC
COMPLETE SET (28)	8.00	3.60	1.00

☐ 1 Richie Hebner MG
☐ 2 Mel Roberts
☐ 3 Ned Yost
☐ 4 Billy Paul Carver
☐ 5 Ron Downs
☐ 6 Eddie Taubensee
☐ 7 Brian Lane
☐ 8 Joe Turek
☐ 9 Ron Mullins
☐ 10 Omar Olivares
☐ 11 Darrin Reichle
☐ 12 Guillermo Velazquez
☐ 13 Alex Arias
☐ 14 Mike Miller
☐ 15 Anthony Toney
☐ 16 Brant Alyea
☐ 17 Williams Suero
☐ 18 Luis Sojo
☐ 19 Greg Vella
☐ 20 Derek Bell
☐ 21 Xavier Hernandez
☐ 22 Jimmy Rogers
☐ 23 Denis Boucher
☐ 24 Rob Colescott
☐ 25 John Sellick
☐ 26 James Vatcher
☐ 27 Andy Carter
☐ 28 Dennis Burlingame

1988 Salem Buccaneers Star

	MINT	NRMT	EXC
COMPLETE SET (25)	5.00	2.20	.60

☐ 1 Steve Adams
☐ 2 Stan Belinda
☐ 3 Kevin Burdick
☐ 4 Terry Crowley
☐ 5 Chip Duncan
☐ 6 Oscar Escobar
☐ 7 Andy Hall
☐ 8 Scott Henion
☐ 9 Tim Kirk
☐ 10 Tony Longmire
☐ 11 John Love
☐ 12 Tim McKinley
☐ 13 Tim McMillan
☐ 14 Pete Murphy
☐ 15 Julio Peguero
☐ 16 Keith Raisanen
☐ 17 Richard Reed
☐ 18 Scott Ruskin
☐ 19 Mike Stevanus
☐ 20 Dave Takach
☐ 21 Doug Torborg
☐ 22 Junior Vizcaino
☐ 23 Ben Webb
☐ 24 Ed Yacopino
☐ 25 Mike York

1988 Salt Lake City Trappers Team Issue

	MINT	NRMT	EXC
COMPLETE SET (31)	8.00	3.60	1.00

☐ 1 Patrick Waid
☐ 2 Brian Murray
Bill Murray
☐ 3 Rueben Rodriguez CO
Darren Garrick CO
Dan Shwan CO
Barry Moss CO
☐ 4 Glenn Seninger
Dave Baggott
Kurt Wilson
☐ 5 Chris Sloniger
☐ 6 Brent Terry CO
Andy Iacona BB
Ryan Bagshaw BB
☐ 7 Ray Karczewski
☐ 8 Kelly Zane
☐ 9 Jeff Allison
☐ 10 Tommy Boyce
☐ 11 Bobby Edwards
☐ 12 Rick Hurni
☐ 13 Will Ambos
☐ 14 Greg Ehmig
☐ 15 Michael Gibbons
☐ 16 Van Schley
Steve Pearson
☐ 17 Kerry Shaw
☐ 18 Barry Moss
☐ 19 Doug Howard
☐ 20 Myron Gardner
☐ 21 Fred Riscen
☐ 22 Martin Peralta
☐ 23 Terence Glover
☐ 24 Tim McKercher
☐ 25 Mando Verdugo
☐ 26 Bill Wenrick
☐ 27 Sal Roldan
☐ 28 Lee Carballo
☐ 29 Bill Murray
☐ 30 Sean Johnson
☐ NNO Joie Casey
Ed Anderson

1988 San Antonio Missions Best

This 28-card standard-size set of the 1988 San Antonio Missions, a Class AA Texas League affiliate of the Los Angeles Dodgers, features blue and black bordered posed color player photos on its fronts. The team name appears at the top, and below the picture is the player's name and position. The horizontal gray back carries the player's name and position at the top, followed by biography, career highlights, and statistics. The set is printed on thin card stock. Only 1300 platinum sets were produced.

	MINT	NRMT	EXC
COMPLETE SET (28)	7.00	3.10	.85
COMPLETE PLATINUM SET (28)	16.00	7.25	2.00

☐ 1 Ramon Martinez
☐ 2 Barry Wohler
☐ 3 Michael Pitz
☐ 4 Greg LaFever
☐ 5 Tony Mack
☐ 6 Domingo Michel
☐ 7 Michael Munoz
☐ 8 Wayne Kirby
☐ 9 Jim Kating
☐ 10 Mike Schweighoffer
☐ 11 Joe Kesselmark
☐ 12 Juan Bustabad
☐ 13 David Eichorn
☐ 14 Manuel Francois
☐ 15 Darrin Fletcher
☐ 16 Walter McConnell
☐ 17 Phil Torres
☐ 18 Jose Manuel
☐ 19 Mike Huff
☐ 20 Joe Humphries
☐ 21 John Wetteland
☐ 22 Javier Ortiz
☐ 23 Kevin Kennedy
☐ 24 Juan Bell
☐ 25 Mark Sheehy
☐ 26 Luis Lopez
☐ 27 Pat Zachry
☐ 28 Checklist

1988 San Bernadino Spirit Best

This 28-card standard-size set of the 1988 San Bernardino Spirit, a Class A California League affiliate of the Seattle Mariners, features blue and black bordered posed color player photos on its fronts. The team name appears at the top, and below the picture is the player's name and position. The horizontal gray back carries the player's name and position at the top, followed by biography, career highlights, and statistics. The set is printed on thin card stock. 5,000 sets were produced. Only 1300 platinum sets were produced. This issue includes a second year card of Ken Griffey Jr.

	MINT	NRMT	EXC
COMPLETE SET (28)	100.00	45.00	12.50
COMPLETE PLATINUM SET (28)	400.00	180.00	50.00

☐ 1 Ken Griffey Jr.
☐ 2 Don Reynolds
☐ 3 Lee Townsend
☐ 4 Ted Williams
☐ 5 Anthony Woods
☐ 6 Pat Rice
☐ 7 Jody Ryan
☐ 8 Rich DeLucia
☐ 9 William Diaz
☐ 10 Dan Disher
☐ 11 Ted Eldredge
☐ 12 Jerry Goff
☐ 13 Jose Tartabull
☐ 14 Ralph Dick
☐ 15 Jim Blueburg
☐ 16 Jim Bowie Jr.
☐ 17 Dave Burba
☐ 18 Clay Gunn
☐ 19 Keith Helton
☐ 20 Steve Hisey
☐ 21 Joe Kemp
☐ 22 Bryan King
☐ 23 Jeff Nelson
☐ 24 Rich Doyle
☐ 25 Todd Hayes
☐ 26 Mike Brocki
☐ 27 Bobby Cuellar
☐ 28 Checklist

1988 San Bernadino Spirit Cal League Cards

This 28-card standard-size set of the 1988 San Bernardino Spirit, a Class A California League affiliate of the Seattle Mariners, features a second year card of Ken Griffey Jr. 10,000 sets were produced.

	MINT	NRMT	EXC
COMPLETE SET (28)	16.00	7.25	2.00

☐ 28 Bryan King
☐ 29 Steve Murray
☐ 30 Jim Bowie Jr.
☐ 31 Dan Disher
☐ 32 Clay Gunn
☐ 33 Jerry Goff
☐ 34 Ken Griffey Jr.
☐ 35 Joe Kemp
☐ 36 Jose Tartabull
☐ 37 William Diaz
☐ 38 Ted Williams
☐ 39 Steve Hisey
☐ 40 Mike Brocki
☐ 41 Ted Eldredge
☐ 42 Jody Ryan
☐ 43 Pat Rice
☐ 44 Keith Helton
☐ 45 Howard Townsend
☐ 46 Tim McLain
☐ 47 Jim Blueberg
☐ 48 Jeff Nelson
☐ 49 David Burba
☐ 50 Rich DeLucia
☐ 51 Todd Hayes
☐ 52 Rich Doyle
☐ 53 Ralph Dick
☐ 54 Bobby Cuellar
☐ 55 Don Reynolds

1988 San Diego State Aztecs All-Time Greats

Honoring the best players from San Diego State, standard size, black inner border and white outer border with "SDSU" and school mascot in red at top. Cards are unnumbered but are ordered below alphabetically for reference.

	MINT	NRMT	EXC
COMPLETE SET (22)	20.00	9.00	2.50

☐ 1 Ed Amelung
☐ 2 John Andrews
☐ 3 Bud Black
(Headshot)
☐ 4 Bud Black
(Pitching)
☐ 5 Mike Couchee
☐ 6 Mark Grace
☐ 7 Chris Gwynn
☐ 8 Chris Gwynn
Tony Gwynn
☐ 9 Tony Gwynn
☐ 10 Chris Jones
☐ 11 Bob Meacham
(Batting)
☐ 12 Bob Meacham
(Fielding)
☐ 13 Graig Nettles
☐ 14 Jim Nettles
☐ 15 Al Newman
(Fielding)
☐ 16 Al Newman
(Batting)
☐ 17 Dave Robinson
☐ 18 Don Shaw
☐ 19 Dave Smith
☐ 20 Mark Williamson
☐ 21 Jim Wilson
☐ 22 Checklist Card

1988 San Jose Giants Cal League Cards

	MINT	NRMT	EXC
COMPLETE SET (29)	6.00	2.70	.75

☐ 116 Rich Aldrete
☐ 117 Paul Blair
☐ 118 Greg Conner
☐ 119 Tad Hanyuda
☐ 120 Daijiro Jodo
☐ 121 Gary Jones
☐ 122 Mark Leonard
☐ 123 James McNamara
☐ 124 Willie Mijares
☐ 125 Scott Murray
☐ 126 Dave Patterson
☐ 127 Gregg Ritchie
☐ 128 Tod Ronson
☐ 129 Ken Suzuki
☐ 130 Daron Connelly
☐ 131 Eric Gunderson
☐ 132 Gilbert Heredia
☐ 133 Koji Maeda

☐ 134 Tom Meagher
☐ 135 Kevin Meier
☐ 136 Eric Pilkington
☐ 137 Doug Robertson
☐ 138 Russell Swan
☐ 139 Ray Velasquez
☐ 140 Masa Yamamoto
☐ 141 Duane Espy
☐ 142 Sam Hirose
☐ 143 Todd Oakes
☐ 144 Lance Hutchins

1988 San Jose Giants ProCards

This 30-card standard-size set of the 1988 San Jose Giants, a Class A California League affiliate of the San Francisco Giants, features bronze-bordered posed color player photos on its fronts. The player's name, position, and team name appear at the bottom. The plain white back carries the player's name at the top, followed by biography and statistics.

	MINT	NRMT	EXC
COMPLETE SET (30)	5.00	2.20	.60

☐ 108 Koji Maeda
☐ 109 Paul Blair
☐ 110 Willie Mijares
☐ 111 Dave Patterson
☐ 112 Gary Jones
☐ 113 Scott Murray
☐ 114 Eric Gunderson
☐ 115 Doug Robertson
☐ 116 Ray Velasquez
☐ 117 Masa Yamamoto
☐ 118 Russ Swan
☐ 119 Rich Aldrete
☐ 120 Tom Meagher
☐ 121 Ken Suzuki
☐ 122 Todd Oakes
☐ 123 Sam Hirose
☐ 124 Lance Hutchins
☐ 125 Duane Espy
☐ 126 Tod Ronson
☐ 127 Eric Pilkington
☐ 128 Tad Hanyuda
☐ 129 Greg Conner
☐ 130 Gil Heredia
☐ 131 Gregg Ritchie
☐ 132 Kevin Meier
☐ 133 Jim McNamara
☐ 134 Mark Leonard
☐ 135 Daron Connelly
☐ 136 Joe Johdo
☐ NNO Checklist

1988 Savannah Cardinals ProCards

This 29-card standard-size set of the 1988 Savannah Cardinals, a Class A South Atlantic League affiliate of the St. Louis Cardinals, features bronze-bordered posed color player photos on its fronts. The player's name, position, and team name appear at the bottom. The plain white back carries the player's name at the top, followed by biography and statistics.

	MINT	NRMT	EXC
COMPLETE SET (29)	5.00	2.20	.60

☐ 331 Mike Hinkle
☐ 332 Ken Smith
☐ 333 Tony Russo
☐ 334 Tim Sherrill
☐ 335 Rob Colescott
☐ 336 Martin Mason
☐ 337 Keith Champion
☐ 338 Dave Krebs
☐ 339 Mark Behny
☐ 340 Bill Hershman
☐ 341 Roberto Marte
☐ 342 Hal Hempen
☐ 343 Clint Horsley
☐ 344 Tim Meamber
☐ 345 Brad Harvick
☐ 346 Reed Olmstead
☐ 347 John Sellick
☐ 348 Jim Ferguson
☐ 349 Stan Barrs
☐ 350 Eddie Looper
☐ 351 Kris Huffman
☐ 352 Ryan Johnston
☐ 353 Mike Alvarez
☐ 354 Eddie Carter
☐ 355 Antron Grier
☐ 356 Jean Gentleman
☐ 357 Greg Doss
☐ 358 Francisco Rosario
☐ NNO Checklist

1988 Shreveport Captains ProCards

This 25-card standard-size set of the 1988 Shreveport Captains, a Class AA Texas League affiliate of the San Francisco Giants, features silver-bordered posed color player photos on its fronts. The player's name, position, and team name appear at the bottom. The plain white back carries the player's name at the top, followed by biography and statistics.

	MINT	NRMT	EXC
COMPLETE SET (25)	5.00	2.20	.60

☐ 1279 Jack Mull MG
☐ 1280 Joe Kmak
☐ 1281 Jose Dominguez
☐ 1282 Joe Olker
☐ 1283 Mike Benjamin
☐ 1284 Vince Sferrazza
☐ 1285 Dean Freeland
☐ 1286 Steve Cline
☐ 1287 Andy Dixon
☐ 1288 Paul Meyers
☐ 1289 George Bonilla
☐ 1290 Paul McClellan
☐ 1291 Jeff Carter
☐ 1292 Jose Pena
☐ 1293 Romy Cucjen
☐ 1294 Rick Nelson
☐ 1295 Stuart Tate
☐ 1296 Mike Remlinger
☐ 1297 John Skurla
☐ 1298 Trevor Wilson
☐ 1299 Harry Davis
☐ 1300 Tim McCoy
☐ 1301 Ed Puikunas
☐ 1302 T.J. McDonald
☐ NNO Checklist

1988 South Bend White Sox Grand Slam

	MINT	NRMT	EXC
COMPLETE SET (28)	5.00	2.20	.60

☐ 1 Cesar Bernhardt
☐ 2 Larry Allen
☐ 3 Javier Ocasio
☐ 4 Kevin Murdock
☐ 5 Ed Smith
☐ 6 Ray Payton
☐ 7 Dwayne Hosey
☐ 8 Rod McCray
☐ 9 Kinnis Pledger
☐ 10 Mike Maksudian
☐ 11 Wilson Valera
☐ 12 Bernando Cruz
☐ 13 Kurt Brown
☐ 14 Don Cooper
☐ 15 Steve Dillard
☐ 16 Jim Reinebold
☐ 17 Ed Sedar
☐ 18 Argenis Conde
☐ 19 Mike Girouard
☐ 20 Julian Gonzalez
☐ 21 Curt Hasler
☐ 22 John Hudek
☐ 23 Bo Kennedy
☐ 24 Rob Resnikoff
☐ 25 Randy Robinson
☐ 26 Steve Schrenk
☐ 27 Mark Tortorice
☐ 28 Stanley Coveleski

1988 Southern League All-Stars Jennings

	MINT	NRMT	EXC
COMPLETE SET (40)	5.00	2.20	.60

☐ 1 Matt Winters
☐ 2 Kevin Burrell
☐ 3 Steve Howard
☐ 4 Mike Bordick
☐ 5 Keith Lockhart
☐ 6 Darrell Pruitt
☐ 7 Matt Merullo
☐ 8 Jerry Bertolani
☐ 9 Tim Dulin
☐ 10 Carlo Columbino
☐ 11 Rafael DeLima
☐ 12 Derek Parks
☐ 13 Bernardo Brito
☐ 14 Barry Jones
☐ 15 Mark Lemke
☐ 16 Ed Whited
☐ 17 Drew Denson
☐ 18 Jeff Huson
☐ 19 Bob Caffrey
☐ 20 Randy Braun
☐ 21 Armando Moreno
☐ 22 Francisco Cabrera
☐ 23 Webster Garrison
☐ 24 Junior Felix
☐ 25 Domingo Martinez
☐ 26 Alex Sanchez
☐ 27 Steve Cummings
☐ 28 Kevin Blankenship
☐ 29 Larry Casian
☐ 30 German Gonzalez
☐ 31 Brian Meyer
☐ 32 Pete Harnisch
☐ 33 Brian Householder
☐ 34 Tim Drees
☐ 35 Joe Lazor
☐ 36 Chris Hammond
☐ 37 Joe Bruno
☐ 38 Rico Petrocelli
☐ 39 Tommy Thompson
☐ 40 Nardi Contreres

1988 Southern Oregon A's ProCards

This 28-card standard-size set of the 1988 Southern Oregon A's, a Class A Northwest League affiliate of the Oakland Athletics, features bronze-bordered posed color player photos on its fronts. The player's name, position, and team name appear at the bottom. The plain white back carries the player's name at the top, followed by biography and statistics.

	MINT	NRMT	EXC
COMPLETE SET (28)	5.00	2.20	.60

☐ 1692 Jim Buccheri
☐ 1693 Tim Vannaman
☐ 1694 Richard Rozman
☐ 1695 Nick Venuto
☐ 1696 Tony Ariola
☐ 1697 Joel Smith
☐ 1698 DeWayne Jones
☐ 1699 Tom Carcione
☐ 1700 Josue Espinal
☐ 1701 Stan Royer
☐ 1702 Rod Correia
☐ 1703 Joel Chimelis
☐ 1704 Mike Messerly
☐ 1705 Dean Borelli
☐ 1706 Lee Tinsley
☐ 1707 Tony Floyd
☐ 1708 Greg Ferguson
☐ 1709 Kevin MacLeod
☐ 1710 Mike Mungin
☐ 1711 Dan Eskew
☐ 1712 Jim Lawson
☐ 1713 Ray Harris
☐ 1714 J.P. Ricciardi
☐ 1715 Jerry Rizza
☐ 1716 Joe Hillman
☐ 1717 Lenny Sakata
☐ 1718 Jesus Hernaiz
☐ NNO Checklist

1988 Spartanburg Phillies ProCards

This 26-card standard-size set of the 1988 Spartanburg Phillies, a Class A South Atlantic League affiliate of the Philadelphia Phillies, features bronze-bordered posed color player photos on its fronts. The player's name, position, and team name appear at the bottom. The plain white back carries the player's name at the top, followed by biography and statistics.

	MINT	NRMT	EXC
COMPLETE SET (26)	5.00	2.20	.60

☐ 1024 Jeff Stark
☐ 1025 Matt Rambo
☐ 1026 Bob Hurta
☐ 1027 Tim Peek
☐ 1028 Greg McCarthy
☐ 1029 Darrell Coulter
☐ 1030 Shelby McDonald
☐ 1031 John Larosa
☐ 1032 Phil Fagnano
☐ 1033 Mel Roberts
☐ 1034 Rod Robertson
☐ 1035 Kim Batiste
☐ 1036 Jaime Barragan
☐ 1037 Scott Ruckman
☐ 1038 Marty Foley
☐ 1039 Carlos Zayas
☐ 1040 Tony Trevino
☐ 1041 Gary Maasberg
☐ 1042 Doug Lindsey
☐ 1043 Todd Felton
☐ 1044 Gary White
☐ 1045 Jim Vatcher
☐ 1046 Bob Britt
☐ 1047 Buzz Capra
☐ 1048 Jim Platts
☐ NNO Checklist

1988 Spartanburg Phillies Star

2,500 sets produced.

	MINT	NRMT	EXC
COMPLETE SET (24)	5.00	2.20	.60

☐ 1 Scott Reaves
☐ 2 Rod Robertson
☐ 3 Scott Ruckman
☐ 4 Royal Thomas Jr.
☐ 5 James Vatcher
☐ 6 Mel Roberts
☐ 7 Buzz Capra
☐ 8 Bret Massie
☐ 9 Stephen Kirkpatrick
☐ 10 John Larosa
☐ 11 Doug Lindsey
☐ 12 Tim Mauser
☐ 13 Greg McCarthy
☐ 14 Sheebie McDonald
☐ 15 Timothy Peek
☐ 16 Matt Rambo
☐ 17 Jimmy Barragan
☐ 18 Kim Batiste
☐ 19 Andy Carter
☐ 20 Mark Cobb
☐ 21 Darrell Coulter
☐ 22 Paul Ellison
☐ 23 Martin Foley
☐ 24 Bobby Hurta

1988 Spokane Indians ProCards

This 26-card standard-size set of the 1988 Spokane Indians, a Class A Northwest League affiliate of the San Diego Padres, features bronze-bordered posed color player photos on its fronts. The player's name, position, and team name appear at the bottom. The plain white back carries the player's name at the top, followed by biography and statistics.

	MINT	NRMT	EXC
COMPLETE SET (26)	5.00	2.20	.60

☐ 1922 Greg Conley
☐ 1923 Tye Waller
☐ 1924 Rob Cantwell
☐ 1925 Kelly Lifgren
☐ 1926 Mike Humphreys
☐ 1927 Squeezer Thompson
☐ 1928 Steve Lubratich
☐ 1929 Pedro Aquino
☐ 1930 Luis Lopez
☐ 1931 Craig Bigham
☐ 1932 Greg Smith
☐ 1933 A.J. Sager
☐ 1934 John Kuehl
☐ 1935 Chad Kuhn
☐ 1936 Nikco Riesgo
☐ 1937 Brad Hoyer
☐ 1938 David Briggs
☐ 1939 Bob Curnow
☐ 1940 Brian Cisarik
☐ 1941 Renay Bryand
☐ 1942 Barry Hightower
☐ 1943 Mark Verstandig
☐ 1944 Craig Procter
☐ 1945 Chris Haslock
☐ 1946 Ron Morton
☐ NNO Checklist

1988 Springfield Cardinals Best

This 28-card standard-size set of the 1988 Springfield Cardinals, a Class A Midwest League affiliate of the St. Louis Cardinals, features red and black bordered posed color player photos on its fronts. The team name appears at the top, and below the picture is the player's name and position. The horizontal gray back carries the player's name and position at the top, followed by biography, career highlights, and statistics. The set is printed on thin card stock. This issue includes the minor league card debut of Ray Lankford and a second year card of Bernard Gilkey.

	MINT	NRMT	EXC
COMPLETE SET (28)	25.00	11.00	3.10

☐ 1 Robert Glisson
☐ 2 Mark Grater
☐ 3 Jeremy Hernandez
☐ 4 Michael Henry
☐ 5 Gregory Becker
☐ 6 Shawn Hathaway
☐ 7 William Bivens
☐ 8 Andrew Taylor
☐ 9 James Gibbs
☐ 10 Frank Potestio
☐ 11 Bob Sudo
☐ 12 Charles Johnson
☐ 13 Bernard Gilkey
☐ 14 Raymond Lankford
☐ 15 David Payton
☐ 16 Michael Raziano
☐ 17 Alex Ojea
☐ 18 Stephen Meyer
☐ 19 Rodney Brewer
☐ 20 Steven Jeffers
☐ 21 Franklin Abreu
☐ 22 John Murphy
☐ 23 Gary Nichols
☐ 24 Ed Fulton
☐ 25 Chris Maloney
☐ 26 Mark De John
☐ 27 Brad Bluestone
☐ 28 Checklist

1988 St. Catharines Blue Jays ProCards

Sponsored by The Standard, this 35-card standard-size set of the 1988 St. Catharines Blue Jays, a Class A New York-Penn League affiliate of the Toronto Blue Jays, features bronze-bordered posed color player photos on its fronts. The player's name, position, and team name appear at the bottom. The plain white back carries the player's name and position at the top, followed by biography and statistics.

	MINT	NRMT	EXC
COMPLETE SET (35)	5.00	2.20	.60

- ☐ 2005 Armando Pagliari TR
- ☐ 2006 Luis Salazar
- ☐ 2007 Timothy Brown
- ☐ 2008 Jose Villa
- ☐ 2009 Benigno Placeres
- ☐ 2010 Brad Evaschuk
- ☐ 2011 Jose Guarache
- ☐ 2012 Pablo Castro
- ☐ 2013 Donn Wolfe
- ☐ 2014 Eddie Dennis MG
- ☐ 2015 Mike McAlpin CO
- ☐ 2016 Timothy Hodge
- ☐ 2017 Nigel Wilson
- ☐ 2018 Daniel Dodd
- ☐ 2019 Greg Williams
- ☐ 2020 Greg McCutcheon
- ☐ 2021 Robert Montalvo
- ☐ 2022 Curtis Johnson
- ☐ 2023 David Weathers
- ☐ 2024 Jose Martinez
- ☐ 2025 Edgar Marquez
- ☐ 2026 Rafael Martinez
- ☐ 2027 Jason Townley
- ☐ 2028 Marcos Taveras
- ☐ 2029 Greg Harding
- ☐ 2030 Bryan Dixon
- ☐ 2031 Mike Jockish
- ☐ 2032 Mike Taylor
- ☐ 2033 Rick Vaughan
- ☐ 2034 Anthony Ward
- ☐ 2035 Ryan Thompson
- ☐ 2036 Darrin Wade
- ☐ 2037 Armando Serra
- ☐ 2038 Patrick Guerrero
  Batboy
- ☐ NNO Title Card
  Checklist

1988 St. Lucie Mets Star

	MINT	NRMT	EXC
COMPLETE SET (25)	5.00	2.20	.60

- ☐ 1 Brandon Bailey
- ☐ 2 Chris Bayer
- ☐ 3 Kevin Brown
- ☐ 4 Rick Brown
- ☐ 5 Jeff Ciszkowski
- ☐ 6 Chris Donnels
- ☐ 7 Jovon Edwards
- ☐ 8 Dave Gelatt
- ☐ 9 Adam Ging
- ☐ 10 Kip Gross
- ☐ 11 Rob Hernandez
- ☐ 12 Andre Jacas
- ☐ 13 Scott Jaster
- ☐ 14 Geary Jones
- ☐ 15 Manny Mantrana
- ☐ 16 Gus Meizoso
- ☐ 17 Doug Myres
- ☐ 18 Hector Perez
- ☐ 19 Fritz Polka
- ☐ 20 Craig Repoz
- ☐ 21 Bill Stiles
- ☐ 22 Greg Talamantez
- ☐ 23 John Toale
- ☐ 24 Dave Trautwein
- ☐ 25 Juan Villanueva

1988 St. Petersburg Cardinals Star

	MINT	NRMT	EXC
COMPLETE SET (25)	5.00	2.20	.60

- ☐ 1 John Balfanz
- ☐ 2 Scott Broadfoot
- ☐ 3 Dennis Carter
- ☐ 4 Joseph Cunningham Jr.
- ☐ 5 Jerry Daniels
- ☐ 6 Terry Elliot
- ☐ 7 James Fernandez
- ☐ 8 Scott Hamilton
- ☐ 9 Patrick Hewes
- ☐ 10 Stephen Hill
- ☐ 11 Crucito Lara
- ☐ 12 Scott Lawrence
- ☐ 13 Robert Livchak
- ☐ 14 Lonnie Maclin
- ☐ 15 Julian Martinez
- ☐ 16 Thomas Mauch
- ☐ 17 Kevin Maxey
- ☐ 18 Scott Melvin
- ☐ 19 Darren Nelson
- ☐ 20 Jay North
- ☐ 21 Geronimo Pena
- ☐ 22 Lenin Picota
- ☐ 23 Larry Pierson
- ☐ 24 Terrence Thomas
- ☐ 25 Stanley Zaltsman

1988 Stockton Ports Cal League Cards

	MINT	NRMT	EXC
COMPLETE SET (31)	5.00	2.20	.60

- ☐ 175 Steve Monson
- ☐ 176 Ron Romanick
- ☐ 177 Doug Henry
- ☐ 178 Brian Stone
- ☐ 179 Randy Veres
- ☐ 180 Angel Miranda
- ☐ 181 Alan Sadler
- ☐ 182 Jaime Navarro
- ☐ 183 Narcisco Elvira
- ☐ 184 Carl Moraw
- ☐ 185 Keith Fleming
- ☐ 186 Brian Drahman
- ☐ 187 Danny Fitzpatrick
- ☐ 188 Gilbert Villanueva
- ☐ 189 Tim McIntosh
- ☐ 190 Bobby Jones
- ☐ 191 Mark Aguilar
- ☐ 192 Rob Smith
- ☐ 193 John Jaha
- ☐ 194 Shon Ashley
- ☐ 195 Dave Taylor
- ☐ 196 Sandy "Epy" Guerrero
- ☐ 197 Bill Spiers
- ☐ 198 Angel Rodriguez
- ☐ 199 Charlie Montoyo
- ☐ 200 Ruben Escalera
- ☐ 201 Rob Derksen
- ☐ 202 Dave Huppert
- ☐ 203 Jay Williams
- ☐ 204 Don Miller
- ☐ 205 Dan Chapman

1988 Stockton Ports ProCards

This 33-card standard-size set of the 1988 Stockton Ports, a Class A California League affiliate of the Milwaukee Brewers, features bronze-bordered posed color player photos on its fronts. The player's name, position, and team name appear at the bottom. The plain white back carries the player's name at the top, followed by biography and statistics.

	MINT	NRMT	EXC
COMPLETE SET (33)	5.00	2.20	.60

- ☐ 721 Rob Derksen
- ☐ 722 Steve Monson
- ☐ 723 Mark Aguilar
- ☐ 724 Shon Ashley
- ☐ 725 Keith Fleming
- ☐ 726 Alan Sadler
- ☐ 727 Sandy Guerrero
- ☐ 728 Gil Villanueva
- ☐ 729 Dave Taylor
- ☐ 730 Randy Veres
- ☐ 731 Ron Romanick
- ☐ 732 Bobby Jones
- ☐ 733 Tim McIntosh
- ☐ 734 Brian Drahman
- ☐ 735 Ruben Escalera
- ☐ 736 Jaime Navarro
- ☐ 737 Charlie Montoyo
- ☐ 738 Bill Spiers
- ☐ 739 Brian Stone
- ☐ 740 Dave Hoppert
- ☐ 741 Rob Smith
- ☐ 742 Angel Rodriguez
- ☐ 743 John Jaha
- ☐ 744 Jay Williams
- ☐ 745 Danny Fitzpatrick
- ☐ 746 Carl Moraw
- ☐ 747 Doug Henry
- ☐ 748 Narciso Elvira
  Sic, Narcisso
- ☐ 749 Angel Miranda
- ☐ 750 Don Miller
- ☐ 751 Dan Chapman
- ☐ 752 Mike Conroy
  Mark Marino
- ☐ NNO Checklist

1988 Sumter Braves ProCards

This 32-card standard-size set of the 1988 Sumter Braves, a Class A South Atlantic League affiliate of the Atlanta Braves, features bronze-bordered posed color player photos on its fronts. The player's name, position, and team name appear at the bottom. The plain white back carries the player's name at the top, followed by biography and statistics.

	MINT	NRMT	EXC
COMPLETE SET (32)	5.00	2.20	.60

- ☐ 390 Keith Mitchell
- ☐ 391 Tony Baldwin
- ☐ 392 Bob Cole
- ☐ 393 Dennis Burlingame
- ☐ 394 John Reilley
- ☐ 395 Wes Currin
- ☐ 396 Mark Davis
- ☐ 397 Johnny Cuevas
- ☐ 398 Jesus Mendoza
- ☐ 399 Jose Valencia
- ☐ 400 Winnie Relaford
- ☐ 401 Greg Harper
- ☐ 402 Rick Siebert
- ☐ 403 Marcos Vazquez
- ☐ 404 Skipper Wright
- ☐ 405 Gregg Gilbert
- ☐ 406 Greg Cloninger
- ☐ 407 A.J. Waznik
- ☐ 408 Glenn Mitchell
- ☐ 409 Juan Fredymond
- ☐ 410 Ben Rivera
- ☐ 411 David Colon
- ☐ 412 Tom Redington
- ☐ 413 Dave Nied
- ☐ 414 Ned Yost
- ☐ 415 Larry Jaster
- ☐ 416 Rick Albert
- ☐ 417 Willy Johnson
- ☐ 418 Ralph Meister
- ☐ 419 Teddy Williams
- ☐ 420 Ed Holtz
- ☐ NNO Checklist

1988 Syracuse Chiefs CMC

This 25-card standard-size set of the 1988 Syracuse Chiefs, a Class AAA International League affiliate of the Toronto Blue Jays, features on its fronts black-bordered posed color player photos framed by a red line. The team's name, the player's name, and his position appear at the bottom. The white back is framed by a black line and carries the team's name and league at the top, followed by the player's name, biography and statistics. 10,000 sets were produced.

	MINT	NRMT	EXC
COMPLETE SET (25)	4.00	1.80	.50

- ☐ 1 Steve Davis
- ☐ 2 Randy Holland TR
- ☐ 3 Colin McLaughlin
- ☐ 4 Jose Nunez
- ☐ 5 Mark Ross
- ☐ 6 Norm Tonucci
- ☐ 7 Bob Shirley
- ☐ 8 Cliff Young
- ☐ 9 Doug Bair
- ☐ 10 Jack O'Connor
- ☐ 11 Frank Wills
- ☐ 12 Luis Reyna
- ☐ 13 Geronimo Berroa
- ☐ 14 Rob Ducey
- ☐ 15 Glenallen Hill
- ☐ 16 Sal Butera
- ☐ 17 Eric Yelding
- ☐ 18 Greg Myers
- ☐ 19 Otis Green
- ☐ 20 Kelly Heath
- ☐ 21 Alexis Infante
- ☐ 22 Chris Shaddy
- ☐ 23 Hector Torres CO
- ☐ 24 Bob Bailor MG
- ☐ 25 Galen Cisco CO

1988 Syracuse Chiefs ProCards

This 30-card standard-size set of the 1988 Syracuse Chiefs, a Class AAA International League affiliate of the Toronto Blue Jays, features gold-bordered posed color player photos on its fronts. The player's name, position, and team name appear at the bottom. The plain white back carries the player's name at the top, followed by biography and statistics.

	MINT	NRMT	EXC
COMPLETE SET (30)	5.00	2.20	.60

- ☐ 805 Jack O'Connor
- ☐ 806 Luis Leal
- ☐ 807 Cliff Young
- ☐ 808 Geronimo Berroa
- ☐ 809 Norm Tonucci
- ☐ 810 Luis Reyna
- ☐ 811 Kelly Heath
- ☐ 812 Glenallen Hill
- ☐ 813 Alexis Infante
- ☐ 814 Steve Davis
- ☐ 815 Enrique Burgos
- ☐ 816 Doug Bair
- ☐ 817 Bob Bailor MG
- ☐ 818 Galen Cisco CO
- ☐ 819 Red Coughlin TR
- ☐ 820 Jose Nunez
- ☐ 821 Greg Myers
- ☐ 822 Hector Torres CO
- ☐ 823 Colin McLaughlin
- ☐ 824 Mark Ross
- ☐ 825 Rob Ducey
- ☐ 826 Sal Butera
- ☐ 827 Bob Shirley
- ☐ 828 Marc DeBottis TR
- ☐ 829 Randy Holland TR
- ☐ 830 Frank Wills
- ☐ 831 Otis Green
- ☐ 832 Eric Yelding
- ☐ 833 Chris Shaddy
- ☐ NNO Title Card
  Checklist

1988 Tacoma Tigers CMC

10,000 sets were produced.

	MINT	NRMT	EXC
COMPLETE SET (25)	4.00	1.80	.50

- ☐ 1 Rich Bordi
- ☐ 2 Todd Burns
- ☐ 3 Charlie Corbell
- ☐ 4 Reese Lambert
- ☐ 5 Tim Meeks
- ☐ 6 Jeff Zaske
- ☐ 7 Jim Corsi
- ☐ 8 Jeff Shaver
- ☐ 9 Brian Snyder
- ☐ 10 Bob Stoddard
- ☐ 11 Lance Blakenship
- ☐ 12 Tyler Brilinski
- ☐ 13 Ed Jurak
- ☐ 14 Wayne Krenchicki
- ☐ 15 Roy Johnson
- ☐ 16 Luis Polonia
- ☐ 17 Alex Sanchez
- ☐ 18 Matt Sinatro
- ☐ 19 Andre Robertson
- ☐ 20 Kevin Sliwinski
- ☐ 21 Jimmy Jones
- ☐ 22 Orlando Mercado
- ☐ 23 Gary Jones
- ☐ 24 Felix Jose
- ☐ 25 Joe Xavier

1988 Tacoma Tigers ProCards

This 28-card standard-size set of the 1988 Tacoma Tigers, a Class AAA Pacific Coast League affiliate of the Oakland A's, features bronze-bordered posed color player photos on its fronts. The player's name, position, and team name appear at the bottom. The plain white back carries the player's name at the top, followed by biography and statistics.

	MINT	NRMT	EXC
COMPLETE SET (28)	5.00	2.20	.60

- ☐ 612 Gary Jones
- ☐ 613 Joe Xavier
- ☐ 614 Felix Jose
- ☐ 615 Eddie Jurak
- ☐ 616 Matt Sinatro
- ☐ 617 Tyler Brilinski
- ☐ 618 Jim Jones
- ☐ 619 Jeff Shaver
- ☐ 620 Stan Naccarato
- ☐ 621 Roy Johnson
- ☐ 622 Brad Fischer
- ☐ 623 Chuck Estrada
- ☐ 624 Orlando Mercado
- ☐ 625 Jim Corsi
- ☐ 626 Kevin Sliwinski
- ☐ 627 Rich Bordi
- ☐ 628 Bob Stoddard
- ☐ 629 Brian Snyder
- ☐ 630 Lance Blankenship
- ☐ 631 Reese Lambert
- ☐ 632 Todd Burns
- ☐ 633 Tim Meeks
- ☐ 634 Andre Robertson
- ☐ 635 Wayne Krenchicki
- ☐ 636 Charlie Corbell
- ☐ 637 Alex Sanchez
- ☐ 638 Luis Polonia
- ☐ NNO Checklist

1988 Tampa Tarpons Star

	MINT	NRMT	EXC
COMPLETE SET (24)	5.00	2.20	.60
COMPLETE SET (26)	7.00	3.10	.85

- ☐ 1 Hernan Adames
- ☐ 2 Leon Baham
- ☐ 3 Kurt Brown
- ☐ 4 Chris Cauley
- ☐ 5 Brian Davis

- ☐ 6 Bill Eveline
- ☐ 7 Cornelio Garcia
- ☐ 8 Jeff Greene
- ☐ 9 Buddy Groom
- ☐ 10A Todd Hall
- ☐ 10B Marv Foley
- ☐ 11 Brent Knackert
- ☐ 12 Jerry Kutzler
- ☐ 13 Tom Lahrman
- ☐ 14 Ravelo Manzanillo
- ☐ 15 Norberto Martin
- ☐ 16 Pat Mehrtens
- ☐ 17 Eric Milholland
- ☐ 18 Kevin Murdock
- ☐ 19 Mike Ollom
- ☐ 20 Jack Peel
- ☐ 21 Dave Reynolds
- ☐ 22 Dan Rohrmeier
- ☐ 23 Carl Sullivan
- ☐ 24 Tony Woods
- ☐ NNO Team Logo

1988 Texas League All-Stars Grand Slam

	MINT	NRMT	EXC
COMPLETE SET (39)	15.00	6.75	1.85

- ☐ 1 Jack Mull MG
- ☐ 2 Todd Zeile
- ☐ 3 Chad Kreuter
- ☐ 4 Gary Alexander
- ☐ 5 Steve Wilson
- ☐ 6 Dan Scarpetta
- ☐ 7 John Wetteland
- ☐ 8 Joe Olker
- ☐ 9 Kevin Bootay
- ☐ 10 Angelo Cuevas
- ☐ 11 Mike Benjamin
- ☐ 12 Scott Coolbaugh
- ☐ 13 Brett Harrison
- ☐ 14 Manny Salinas
- ☐ 15 John Skurla
- ☐ 16 Tom Baine
- ☐ 17 John Barfield
- ☐ 18 Blaine Beatty
- ☐ 19 Jose Dominguez
- ☐ 20 Scott Arnold
- ☐ 21 Dave Pavlas
- ☐ 22 Kevin Kennedy
- ☐ 23 Mike Basso
- ☐ 24 Mario Monico
- ☐ 25 Fred Williams
- ☐ 26 Gary Sheffield
- ☐ 27 Jim McCollom
- ☐ 28 Ramon Martinez
- ☐ 29 Terry Gilmore
- ☐ 30 Mike Munoz
- ☐ 31 Ed Puig
- ☐ 32 Carlos Baerga
- ☐ 33 Mike Huff
- ☐ 34 Chris Knabenshue
- ☐ 35 Greg Vaughn
- ☐ 36 Mike Knapp
- ☐ 37 Luis Lopez
- ☐ 38 Frank Mattox
- ☐ 39 Jeff Manto

1988 Tidewater Tides Candl

Set was produced as a perforated sheet with a team photo at the top.

	MINT	NRMT	EXC
COMPLETE SET (30)	15.00	6.75	1.85

- ☐ 1 Sam McCrary TR
- ☐ 2 John Cumberland PC
- ☐ 3 Mike Cubbage MGR
- ☐ 4 Rich Miller C
- ☐ 5 Dave Rosenfield GM
- ☐ 6 Greg Olson
- ☐ 7 Andre David
- ☐ 8 Ken Dowell
- ☐ 9 Gregg Jefferies
- ☐ 10 Phil Lombardi
- ☐ 11 Keith Miller
- ☐ 12 Steve Springer
- ☐ 13 Tim Tolman
- ☐ 14 Mark Carreon
- ☐ 15 Joaquin Contreras
- ☐ 16 Jeff McKnight
- ☐ 17 Darren Reed
- ☐ 18 Tim Drummond
- ☐ 19 Tom Edens
- ☐ 20 Steve Frey
- ☐ 21 Jeff Innis
- ☐ 22 Tom McCarthy
- ☐ 23 John Mitchell
- ☐ 24 Randy Niemann
- ☐ 25 Jose Roman
- ☐ 26 R.C. Reuteman AGM
- ☐ 27 Jack Savage
- ☐ 28 Dave West
- ☐ 29 Wally Whitehurst
- ☐ 30 Tony Mercurio Broadcaster

1988 Tidewater Tides CMC

10,000 sets were produced. Approximately, 2,000 of the sets contain the Gregg Jefferies error card.

	MINT	NRMT	EXC
COMPLETE SET (26)	8.00	3.60	1.00

- ☐ 1 Jack Savage
- ☐ 2 David West
- ☐ 3 Jeff Innis
- ☐ 4 Tim Drummond
- ☐ 5 Tom Edens
- ☐ 6 Steve Frey
- ☐ 7 Tom McCarthy
- ☐ 8 John Mitchell
- ☐ 9 Jose Roman
- ☐ 10 Randy Niemann
- ☐ 11 Wally Whitehurst
- ☐ 12 Phil Lombardi
- ☐ 13 Greg Olson
- ☐ 14 Ken Dowell
- ☐ 15A Gregg Jeffries ERR
- ☐ 15B Gregg Jefferies COR
- ☐ 16 Darren Reed
- ☐ 17 Joaquin Contreras
- ☐ 18 Andre David
- ☐ 19 Jeff McKnight
- ☐ 20 Keith Miller
- ☐ 21 Steve Springer
- ☐ 22 Mark Carreon
- ☐ 23 Tim Tolman
- ☐ 24 Mike Cubbage
- ☐ 25 John Cumberland
- ☐ 26 Rich Miller

1988 Tidewater Tides ProCards

This 29-card standard-size set of the 1988 Tidewater Tides, a Class AAA International League affiliate of the New York Mets, features gold-bordered posed color player photos on its fronts. The player's name, position, and team name appear at the bottom. The plain white back carries the player's name at the top, followed by biography and statistics.

	MINT	NRMT	EXC
COMPLETE SET (29)	8.00	3.60	1.00

- ☐ 1577 John Mitchell
- ☐ 1578 Phil Lombardi
- ☐ 1579 John Cumberland
- ☐ 1580 Sam McCrary
- ☐ 1581 Tom Edens
- ☐ 1582 Jeff Innis
- ☐ 1583 Jack Savage
- ☐ 1584 Tim Tolman
- ☐ 1585 Rich Miller
- ☐ 1586 Mike Cubbage
- ☐ 1587 Jeff McKnight
- ☐ 1588 Mark Carreon
- ☐ 1589 Wally Whitehurst
- ☐ 1590 Reggie Dobie
- ☐ 1591 Marcus Lawton
- ☐ 1592 Dave West
- ☐ 1593 Tim Drummond
- ☐ 1594 Al Pardo
- ☐ 1595 Ken Dowell
- ☐ 1596 Andre David
- ☐ 1597 Greg Olson
- ☐ 1598 Steve Springer
- ☐ 1599 Tom McCarthy
- ☐ 1600 Gregg Jefferies
- ☐ 1601 Jose Roman
- ☐ 1602 Steve Frey
- ☐ 1603 Darren Reed
- ☐ 1604 Keith Miller
- ☐ NNO Checklist

1988 Toledo Mud Hens CMC

10,000 sets were produced.

	MINT	NRMT	EXC
COMPLETE SET (25)	4.00	1.80	.50

- ☐ 1 Dave Beard
- ☐ 2 Stan Clarke
- ☐ 3 Don Schulze
- ☐ 4 Steve Searcy
- ☐ 5 Eric King
- ☐ 6 Roman Pena
- ☐ 7 Mike Trujillo
- ☐ 8 Dave Cooper
- ☐ 9 Paul Cherry
- ☐ 10 John Duffy
- ☐ 11 Mark Huismann
- ☐ 12 Billy Bean
- ☐ 13 Scott Lusader
- ☐ 14 Doug Strange
- ☐ 15 Jeff Reynolds
- ☐ 16 Benny Ruiz
- ☐ 17 Pedro Chavez
- ☐ 18 Rey Palacios
- ☐ 19 Chris Hoiles
- ☐ 20 Paul Felix
- ☐ 21 Tim Leiper
- ☐ 22 Donnie Rowland
- ☐ 23 Pete Rice
- ☐ 24 Mike Brown
- ☐ 25 Pat Corrales

1988 Toledo Mud Hens ProCards

This 28-card standard-size set of the 1988 Toledo Mud Hens, a Class AAA International League affiliate of the Detroit Tigers, features gold-bordered posed color player photos on its fronts. The player's name, position, and team name appear at the bottom. The plain white back carries the player's name at the top, followed by biography and statistics.

	MINT	NRMT	EXC
COMPLETE SET (28)	5.00	2.20	.60

- ☐ 585 Jeff Reynolds
- ☐ 586 Dave Beard
- ☐ 587 Doug Strange
- ☐ 588 Mark Huismann
- ☐ 589 Donnie Rowland
- ☐ 590 Pat Corrales
- ☐ 591 Paul Cherry
- ☐ 592 Eric King
- ☐ 593 Mike Trujillo
- ☐ 594 Scott Lusader
- ☐ 595 Billy Bean
- ☐ 596 John Duffy
- ☐ 597 Chris Hoiles
- ☐ 598 Pete Rice
- ☐ 599 Gene Roof
- ☐ 600 Paul Felix
- ☐ 601 Pedro Chavez
- ☐ 602 Benny Ruiz
- ☐ 603 Tim Leiper
- ☐ 604 Don Schulze
- ☐ 605 Rey Palacios
- ☐ 606 Don McGann
- ☐ 607 Stan Clarke
- ☐ 608 Dave Cooper
- ☐ 609 Steve Searcy
- ☐ 610 Ramon Pena
- ☐ 611 Mike Brown
- ☐ NNO Checklist

1988 Triple A All-Stars CMC

	MINT	NRMT	EXC
COMPLETE SET (45)	12.00	5.50	1.50

- ☐ 1 Bill Bathe
- ☐ 2 Luis De Los Santos
- ☐ 3 Johnny Paredes
- ☐ 4 Tom O'Malley
- ☐ 5 Felix Fermin
- ☐ 6 Billy Moore
- ☐ 7 Rolando Roomes
- ☐ 8 Van Snider
- ☐ 9 German Rivera
- ☐ 10 La Vel Freeman
- ☐ 11 Dorn Taylor
- ☐ 12 Norm Charlton
- ☐ 13 Randy Johnson
- ☐ 14 Gary Sheffield
- ☐ 15 Mike Harkey
- ☐ 16 Bob Geren
- ☐ 17 Dave Griffin
- ☐ 18 Tom Barrett
- ☐ 19 Craig Worthington
- ☐ 20 Randy Velarde
- ☐ 21 Steve Finley
- ☐ 22 Carlos Quintana
- ☐ 23 Mark Carreon
- ☐ 24 Lonnie Smith
- ☐ 25 Steve Searcy
- ☐ 26 Mark Huismann
- ☐ 27 Gregg Jefferies
- ☐ 28 Ricky Jordan
- ☐ 29 Dave West
- ☐ 30 John Smoltz
- ☐ 31 Sandy Alomar Jr.
- ☐ 32 Francisco Melendez
- ☐ 33 Mike Woodard
- ☐ 34 Edgar Martinez
- ☐ 35 Mike Brumley
- ☐ 36 Mike Devereaux
- ☐ 37 Cameron Drew
- ☐ 38 Luis Medina
- ☐ 39 Rod Allen
- ☐ 40 George Hinshaw
- ☐ 41 Bill Brennan
- ☐ 42 Bill Krueger
- ☐ 43 Karl Best
- ☐ 44 Juan Bell
- ☐ 45 Ramon Martinez

1988 Triple A All-Stars ProCards

	MINT	NRMT	EXC
COMPLETE SET (55)	10.00	4.50	1.25

- ☐ 1 Michael Devereaux
- ☐ 2 Chris Gwynn
- ☐ 3 Tracy Woodson
- ☐ 4 Benny Distefano
- ☐ 5 Tom Prince
- ☐ 6 Eddie Jurak
- ☐ 7 Phil Ouellette
- ☐ 8 Luis Medina
- ☐ 9 Bob Geren
- ☐ 10 Mike Kinnunen
- ☐ 11 Scott Nielsen
- ☐ 12 La Vel Freeman
- ☐ 13 Tim Pyznarski
- ☐ 14 German Rivera
- ☐ 15 Urbano Lugo
- ☐ 16 Bill Bathe
- ☐ 17 Bob Sebra
- ☐ 18 Mike Bielecki
- ☐ 19 Dwight Smith
- ☐ 20 Sandy Alomar
- ☐ 21 Mike Brumley
- ☐ 22 Joey Cora
- ☐ 23 Greg Harris
- ☐ 24 Dick Grapenthin
- ☐ 25 Mike Shelton
- ☐ 26 Marty Brown
- ☐ 27 Hugh Kemp
- ☐ 28 Tom O'Malley
- ☐ 29 Steve Finley
- ☐ 30 Luis Delos Santos
- ☐ 31 Steve Curry
- ☐ 32 Tony Perezchica
- ☐ 33 Roy Smith
- ☐ 34 Joe Boever
- ☐ 35 Bob Milacki
- ☐ 36 Geronimo Berroa
- ☐ 37 Eric Yelding
- ☐ 38 Lance Blankenship
- ☐ 39 Mark Carreon
- ☐ 40 Gregg Jefferies
- ☐ 41 David West
- ☐ 42 Mark Huismann
- ☐ 43 Rey Palacios
- ☐ 44 Cameron Drew
- ☐ 45 Donn Pall
- ☐ 46 Sap Randall
- ☐ 47 Terry Collins
- ☐ 48 Carlos Ledezma
- ☐ 49 Bill Plummer
- ☐ 50 Joe Sparks
- ☐ 51 Toby Harrah
- ☐ 52 Ed Nottle
- ☐ 53 Randy Holland
- ☐ 54 Mike Cubbage
- ☐ NNO Checklist

1988 Tucson Toros CMC

This issue includes the minor league card debut of Craig Biggio and a fourth year card of Ken Caminiti. 10,000 sets were produced.

	MINT	NRMT	EXC
COMPLETE SET (25)	8.00	3.60	1.00

- ☐ 1 Manny Hernandez
- ☐ 2 Anthony Kelley
- ☐ 3 Mike Loynd
- ☐ 4 Dave Meads
- ☐ 5 Kevin Hagan
- ☐ 6 Rafael Montalvo
- ☐ 7 Jose Cano
- ☐ 8 Rocky Childress
- ☐ 9 Jeff Datz
- ☐ 10 Luis DeLeon
- ☐ 11 Ken Caminiti
- ☐ 12 Glenn Carpenter
- ☐ 13 Nelson Rood
- ☐ 14 Cameron Drew
- ☐ 15 Craig Biggio
- ☐ 16 Alex Trevino
- ☐ 17 Karl Allaire
- ☐ 18 Joe Mikulik
- ☐ 19 John Fishel
- ☐ 20 Louie Meadows
- ☐ 21 Jim Weaver
- ☐ 22 Pat Keedy
- ☐ 23 Craig Smajstrla
- ☐ 24 Bob Didier
- ☐ 25 Eddie Watt

1988 Tucson Toros Jones Photo

Produced by Jones Photo. The cards are unnumbered so they are ordered below in alphabetical order. A complete set could only be obtained by attending all five promotional giveaway nights at the ballpark. The cards measure 5" by 7" and are full color photos of the players. This issue includes the minor league card debut of Craig Biggio and a fourth year card of Ken Caminiti. 400 sets were produced.

	MINT	NRMT	EXC
COMPLETE SET (24)	100.00	45.00	12.50

- ☐ 1 Karl Allaire
- ☐ 2 Craig Biggio
- ☐ 3 Ken Caminiti
- ☐ 4 Jose Cano
- ☐ 5 Glenn Carpenter
- ☐ 6 Rocky Childress
- ☐ 7 Jeff Datz
- ☐ 8 Luis DeLeon
- ☐ 9 Bob Didier
- ☐ 10 Cameron Drew
- ☐ 11 John Fishel
- ☐ 12 Kevin Hagen
- ☐ 13 Manny Hernandez
- ☐ 14 Pat Keedy
- ☐ 15 Anthony Kelley
- ☐ 16 Dave Meads
- ☐ 17 Joe Mikulik
- ☐ 18 Rafael Montalvo
- ☐ 19 Nelson Rood
- ☐ 20 Joe Sambito
- ☐ 21 Craig Smajstria
- ☐ 22 Alex Trevino
- ☐ 23 Eddie Watt
- ☐ 24 Jim Weaver

1988 Tucson Toros ProCards

This 28-card standard-size set of the 1988 Tucson Toros, a Class AAA Pacific Coast League affiliate of the Houston Astros, features gold-bordered posed color player photos on its fronts. The player's name, position, and team name appear at the bottom. The plain white back carries the player's name at the top, followed by biography and statistics. This issue includes the minor league card debut of Craig Biggio and a fourth year card of Ken Caminiti.

	MINT	NRMT	EXC
COMPLETE SET (28)	15.00	6.75	1.85

- ☐ 166 Craig Biggio
- ☐ 167 Karl Allaire
- ☐ 168 Craig Smajstrla
- ☐ 169 Manny Hernandez
- ☐ 170 Rafael Montalvo
- ☐ 171 Jose Cano
- ☐ 172 Jim Weaver
- ☐ 173 Glenn Carpenter
- ☐ 174 Luis DeLeon
- ☐ 175 Pat Keedy
- ☐ 176 Joe Mikulik
- ☐ 177 Louie Meadows
- ☐ 178 John Fishel
- ☐ 179 Clay Christiansen
- ☐ 180 Kevin Hagen
- ☐ 181 Rocky Childress
- ☐ 182 Ken Caminiti
- ☐ 183 Dave Meads
- ☐ 184 Eddie Watt
- ☐ 185 Mike Loynd
- ☐ 186 Anthony Kelley
- ☐ 187 Jeff Datz
- ☐ 188 Cameron Drew
- ☐ 189 Ernie Camacho
- ☐ 190 Bob Didier
- ☐ 191 Nelson Rood
- ☐ 192 Rex Jones
- ☐ NNO Checklist

1988 Tulsa Drillers Team Issue

	MINT	NRMT	EXC
COMPLETE SET (28)	15.00	6.75	1.85

- ☐ 1 Mike Scanlin
- ☐ 2 George Threadgill
- ☐ 3 Monty Fariss
- ☐ 4 Mitch Thomas
- ☐ 5 Efrain Valdez
- ☐ 6 Darrell Whitaker
- ☐ 7 Jose Vargas
- ☐ 8 Steve Wilson
- ☐ 9 Jeff Andrews CO
- ☐ 10 Jim Skaalen MG
- ☐ 11 Stan Hough CO
- ☐ 12 Gary Alexander
- ☐ 13 Kevin Bootay
- ☐ 14 John Barfield
- ☐ 15 Kevin Brown
- ☐ 16 Joel Cartaya
- ☐ 17 Bubba Jackson
- ☐ 18 Scott Coolbaugh
- ☐ 19 Chad Kreuter
- ☐ 20 Steve Lankard
- ☐ 21 Gar Millay
- ☐ 22 Bob Malloy
- ☐ 23 Dave Pavlas
- ☐ 24 Paul Postier
- ☐ 25 Kevin Reimer
- ☐ 26 Rick Raether
- ☐ 27 Greg Harrell TR
- ☐ 28 Kenny Rogers

1988 Utica Blue Sox Pucko

3,500 sets were produced.

	MINT	NRMT	EXC
COMPLETE SET (29)	6.00	2.70	.75

- ☐ 1 Rob Lukachyk
- ☐ 2 Clemente Alvarez
- ☐ 3 Brett Terry
- ☐ 4 Mark Chasey
- ☐ 5 Paul Fuller
- ☐ 6 Vince Harris
- ☐ 7 Derek Lee
- ☐ 8 Steve Mehl
- ☐ 9 Jesus Merejo
- ☐ 10 Eugenio Tejada
- ☐ 11 Marcus Trammell
- ☐ 12 Randy Warren
- ☐ 13 John Zaksek
- ☐ 14 John Chafin
- ☐ 15 Virgil Cooper
- ☐ 16 Fred Dabney
- ☐ 17 Carlos DeLaCruz
- ☐ 18 Keith Felden
- ☐ 19 Scott Fuller
- ☐ 20 Mike Galvan
- ☐ 21 Pat Mehrtens
- ☐ 22 Frank Merigliano
- ☐ 23 Jose Pena
- ☐ 24 Ron Stephens
- ☐ 25 Ed Walsh
- ☐ 26 Rick Patterson
- ☐ 27 Preston Douglas
- ☐ 28 Steve Jessup
- ☐ 29 Joanne Gerace

1988 Vancouver Canadians CMC

This 25-card standard-size set of the 1988 Vancouver Canadians, a Class AAA Pacific Coast League affiliate of the Chicago White Sox, features on its fronts black-bordered posed color player photos framed by a green line. The team's name, the player's name, and his position appear at the bottom. The white back is framed by a black line and carries the team's name and league at the top, followed by the player's name, biography and statistics. 10,000 sets were produced.

	MINT	NRMT	EXC
COMPLETE SET (25)	4.00	1.80	.50

- ☐ 1 Jeff Bittiger
- ☐ 2 Joel Davis
- ☐ 3 Steve Rosenberg
- ☐ 4 Carl Willis
- ☐ 5 Ed Wojna
- ☐ 6 Ken Patterson
- ☐ 7 Adam Peterson
- ☐ 8 Grady Hall
- ☐ 9 Donn Pall
- ☐ 10 Jack Hardy
- ☐ 11 Greg Hibbard
- ☐ 12 Kelly Paris
- ☐ 13 Santiago Garcia
- ☐ 14 Mike Woodard
- ☐ 15 Ron Karkovice
- ☐ 16 Bill Lindsey
- ☐ 17 Russ Morman
- ☐ 18 Troy Thomas
- ☐ 19 Mike Yastrzemski
- ☐ 20 James Randall
- ☐ 21 Jeff Schaefer
- ☐ 22 Daryl Sconiers
- ☐ 23 Jorge Alcazar
- ☐ 24 Dave Gallagher
- ☐ 25 Marlin McPhail

1988 Vancouver Canadians ProCards

This 27-card standard-size set of the 1988 Vancouver Canadians, a Class AAA Pacific Coast League affiliate of the Chicago White Sox, features gold-bordered posed color player photos on its fronts. The player's name, position, and team name appear at the bottom. The plain white back carries the player's name at the top, followed by biography and statistics.

	MINT	NRMT	EXC
COMPLETE SET (27)	5.00	2.20	.60

- ☐ 753 Jeff Schaefer
- ☐ 754 Steve Rosenberg
- ☐ 755 Jack Hardy
- ☐ 756 Edward Wojna
- ☐ 757 Ken Patterson
- ☐ 758 Bill Lindsey
- ☐ 759 Donn Pall
- ☐ 760 Russ Morman
- ☐ 761 Grady Hall
- ☐ 762 Carl Willis
- ☐ 763 Joel Davis
- ☐ 764 Santiago Garcia
- ☐ 765 James Randall
- ☐ 766 Daryl Sconiers
- ☐ 767 Mike Woodard
- ☐ 768 Ron Jackson CO
- ☐ 769 Eli Grba CO
- ☐ 770 Greg Hibbard
- ☐ 771 Dave Gallagher
- ☐ 772 Jorge Alcazar
- ☐ 773 Ron Karkovice
- ☐ 774 Mike Yastrzemski
- ☐ 775 Troy Thomas
- ☐ 776 Adam Peterson
- ☐ 777 Marlin McPhail
- ☐ 778 Terry Bevington MG
- ☐ NNO Title Card Checklist

1988 Vermont Mariners ProCards

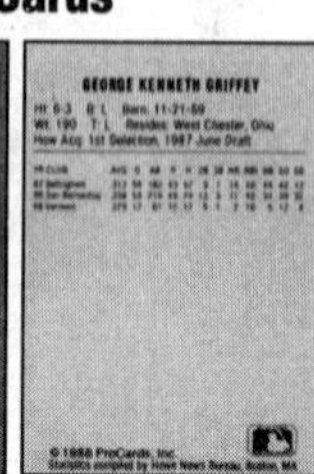

This 27-card standard-size set of the 1988 Vermont Mariners, a Class AA Eastern League affiliate of the Seattle Mariners, features silver-bordered posed color player photos on its fronts. The player's name, position, and team name appear at the bottom. The plain white back carries the player's name at the top, followed by biography and statistics. The cards are numbered on the back. A late issue promotional card of Ken Griffey Jr. was also produced by ProCards in 1988 but is not considered part of this set. The Griffey card has a red border.

	MINT	NRMT	EXC
COMPLETE SET (27)	5.00	2.20	.60
KEN GRIFFEY JR. PROMO	35.00	16.00	4.40

- ☐ 939 Mark Wooden
- ☐ 940 Bryan Price
- ☐ 941 Dave Schuler
- ☐ 942 Greg Fulton
- ☐ 943 Bill McGuire
- ☐ 944 Jim Wilson
- ☐ 945 Eric Fox
- ☐ 946 Omar Vizquel
- ☐ 947 Pat Lennon
- ☐ 948 Keith Foley
- ☐ 949 Nezi Balelo
- ☐ 950 John Gibbons
- ☐ 951 Dave Brundage
- ☐ 952 Dave Myers
- ☐ 953 Jorge Uribe
- ☐ 954 Rich Morales
- ☐ 955 Tom Newberg
- ☐ 956 Dave Snell
- ☐ 957 Greg Brinkman
- ☐ 958 Bill Mendek
- ☐ 959 Ricky Rojas
- ☐ 960 Clint Zavaras
- ☐ 961 Jeff Hull
- ☐ 962 Calvin Jones
- ☐ 963 Dave McCorkle
- ☐ NNO Checklist
- ☐ NNO Ken Griffey Jr.

1988 Vero Beach Dodgers Star

	MINT	NRMT	EXC
COMPLETE SET (26)	5.00	2.20	.60
COMPLETE SET (27)	7.00	3.10	.85

- ☐ 1 Michael Batesole
- ☐ 2 Kevin Campbell
- ☐ 3 Timothy Cash
- ☐ 4 Doug Cox
- ☐ 5 Thomas DeMerit
- ☐ 6 Felipe Esteban
- ☐ 7 Howard Freiling
- ☐ 8 Henry Goshay
- ☐ 9 David Hansen
- ☐ 10 Jeffrey Hartman
- ☐ 11 Gordon Hershiser
- ☐ 12 Carl Johnson
- ☐ 13 Eric Mangham
- ☐ 14 Angel Martinez
- ☐ 15 Gregory Mayberry
- ☐ 16 Frank Mustari
- ☐ 17 Jeffrey Mons
- ☐ 18A Christopher Nichting
- ☐ 18B John Shoemaker
- ☐ 19 Hioetsugu Nishimura
- ☐ 20 Douglas Noch
- ☐ 21 Jay Ray
- ☐ 22 Homar Rojas
- ☐ 23 Miquel Santana
- ☐ 24 Mike White
- ☐ 25 Stephen Wood
- ☐ 26 Masahiro Yamamoto

1988 Virginia Generals Star

	MINT	NRMT	EXC
COMPLETE SET (23)	5.00	2.20	.60

- ☐ 1 Pete Alborano
- ☐ 2 Mike Borgatti
- ☐ 3 Kevin Brooks
- ☐ 4 Pete Capello
- ☐ 5 Lee Carballo
- ☐ 6 Luis Corcino
- ☐ 7 Steve Culkar
- ☐ 8 Brian DuBois
- ☐ 9 Kent Headley
- ☐ 10 Jim Hendrix
- ☐ 11 Tom Johnson
- ☐ 12 John Joslyn
- ☐ 13 Frank Laureano
- ☐ 14 Carmelo Losauro
- ☐ 15 Pat McKinley
- ☐ 16 Angel Morris
- ☐ 17 Gregory Papageorge
- ☐ 18 Phil Price
- ☐ 19 Ruben Pujols
- ☐ 20 Ernest Radcliffe Jr.
- ☐ 21 Kyle Reese
- ☐ 22 Kent Willis
- ☐ xx Title Card (unnumbered) (ad on back)

1988 Visalia Oaks Cal League Cards

	MINT	NRMT	EXC
COMPLETE SET (30)	5.00	2.20	.60

- ☐ 145 Kenny Davis
- ☐ 146 Ken Morgan
- ☐ 147 Mike Randle
- ☐ 148 Joey Zellner
- ☐ 149 Tim Arnold
- ☐ 150 John Eccles
- ☐ 151 Shawn Gilbert
- ☐ 152 Kenny Grant
- ☐ 153 Marty Lanoux
- ☐ 154 Scott Leius
- ☐ 155 Jose Marzan
- ☐ 156 Edgar Naveda
- ☐ 157 A.J. Richardson
- ☐ 158 Doug Snyder
- ☐ 159 Larry Blackwell
- ☐ 160 Mike Redding
- ☐ 161 Steve Scanlon
- ☐ 162 Bob Strube
- ☐ 163 Jimmy Williams
- ☐ 164 Troy James
- ☐ 165 Paul Abbott
- ☐ 166 Jeff Bronkey
- ☐ 167 Mark Guthrie
- ☐ 168 Dana Heinle
- ☐ 169 Doug Kline
- ☐ 170 Scott Ullger
- ☐ 171 Bruce Bucz
- ☐ 172 Andy Seidensticker
- ☐ 173 Mark Jones
- ☐ 174 Gorman Heimueller

1988 Visalia Oaks ProCards

This 28-card standard-size set of the 1988 Visalia Oaks, a Class A California League affiliate of the Minnesota Twins, features bronze-bordered posed color player photos on its fronts. The player's name, position, and team name appear at the bottom. The plain white back carries the player's name at the top, followed by biography and statistics.

	MINT	NRMT	EXC
COMPLETE SET (28)	5.00	2.20	.60

- ☐ 81 Kenny Davis
- ☐ 82 Dana Heinle
- ☐ 83 Larry Blackwell
- ☐ 84 John Eccles
- ☐ 85 Mike Randle
- ☐ 86 Kenny Grant
- ☐ 87 A.J. Richardson
- ☐ 88 Troy James
- ☐ 89 Jose Marzan
- ☐ 90 Kenny Morgan
- ☐ 91 Shawn Gilbert
- ☐ 92 Paul Abbott
- ☐ 93 Mike Redding
- ☐ 94 Steve Scanlon
- ☐ 95 Jeff Bronkey
- ☐ 96 Slim Williams
- ☐ 97 Tim Arnold
- ☐ 98 Joey Zellner
- ☐ 99 Scott Ullger
- ☐ 100 Doug Snyder
- ☐ 101 Bob Strube

☐ 102 Scott Leius
☐ 103 Edgar Naveda
☐ 104 Marty Lanoux
☐ 105 Gorman Heimueller
☐ 106 Andy Seidensticker
☐ 107 Doug Kline
☐ NNO Checklist

1988 Waterloo Indians ProCards

This 29-card standard-size set of the 1988 Waterloo Indians, a Class A Midwest League League affiliate of the Cleveland Indians, features bronze-bordered posed color player photos on its fronts. The player's name, position, and team name appear at the bottom. The plain white back carries the player's name at the top, followed by biography and statistics.

	MINT	NRMT	EXC
COMPLETE SET (29)	5.00	2.20	.60

☐ 665 Tommy Kurczewski
☐ 666 Andy Casano
☐ 667 Angel Ortiz
☐ 668 Bill Bluhm
☐ 669 John Stitz
☐ 670 Willie Garza
☐ 671 Jim Baxter
☐ 672 Scott Khoury
☐ 673 T.J. Gamba
☐ 674 Bill Narleski
☐ 675 Julio Liriano
☐ 676 Ramon Bautista
☐ 677 Ivan McBride
☐ 678 Keith Seifert
☐ 679 Steve Colavito
☐ 680 Sam Ferretti
☐ 681 Troy Neel
☐ 682 Peter Kuld
☐ 683 Mark Pike
☐ 684 Keith Bennett
☐ 685 Roger Hill
☐ 686 Eric Rasmussen
☐ 687 Ken Bolek
☐ 688 Steve Olin
☐ 689 Tom Kramer
☐ 690 Tony Scaglione
☐ 691 Greg Roscoe
☐ 692 Rudy Seanez
☐ NNO Checklist

1988 Watertown Pirates Pucko

3,500 sets were produced.

	MINT	NRMT	EXC
COMPLETE SET (35)	6.00	2.70	.75

☐ 1 Keith Richardson
☐ 2 Joe Ausanio
☐ 3 Steven Buckholz
☐ 4 Rodger Castner
☐ 5 Joel Forrest
☐ 6 Tim Holmes
☐ 7 Mark Koller
☐ 8 Craig Lewis
☐ 9 Dan Nielsen
☐ 10 Ernesto Santana
☐ 11 Mike Stevanus
☐ 12 Randy Tomlin
☐ 13 Bobby Underwood
☐ 14 Bryan Arnold
☐ 15 Jay Bluthardt
☐ 16 Ken Buksa
☐ 17 Ralph Denkenberger
☐ 18 Chris Estep
☐ 19 Mike Huyler
☐ 20 Deron Johnson
☐ 21 Domingo Merejo
☐ 22 Steve Montejo
☐ 23 Darwin Pennye
☐ 24 Paul Spalt
☐ 25 Dave Stone
☐ 26 Mike Valla
☐ 27 Tim Wakefield
☐ 28 John Wehner
☐ 29 Flavio Williams
☐ 30 John Young
☐ 31 Stan Cliburn
☐ 32 Tom Barnard
☐ 33 Robert Bill
☐ 34 Gene Sunnen
☐ 35 Team Officials

1988 Wausau Timbers Grand Slam

	MINT	NRMT	EXC
COMPLETE SET (28)	5.00	2.20	.60

☐ 1 Rick Sweet
☐ 2 Chuck Kniffen
☐ 3 Fausto Ramirez
☐ 4 Chris Doll
☐ 5 Lorenzo Sisney
☐ 6 Ruben Gonzalez
☐ 7 Keith Frink
☐ 8 Chuck Carr
☐ 9 John Hoffman
☐ 10 Kurt Stange
☐ 11 Mike McDonald
☐ 12 Jim Pritikin
☐ 13 Ray Williams
☐ 14 Todd Haney
☐ 15 Todd Azar
☐ 16 Jeff Hooper
☐ 17 Rudy Webster
☐ 18 Steve Bieksha
☐ 19 Chuck Webb
☐ 20 Mike McGuire
☐ 21 Brian Baldwin
☐ 22 Tony Woods
☐ 23 Scott Stoerck
☐ 24 Frank Colston
☐ 25 Mike Gardner
☐ 26 Dru Kosco
☐ 27 Mike Goff
☐ 28 Randy Roetter

1988 West Palm Beach Expos Star

This 27-card standard-size set of the 1988 West Palm Beach Expos, a Class A Florida State League affiliate of the Montreal Expos, features turquoise-bordered posed color player photos on its fronts. The player's name, team name, and position appear at the bottom. The yellowish horizontal back carries the player's name at the top, followed by biography, career highlights, and statistics. The Felipe Alou card was a late issue.

	MINT	NRMT	EXC
COMPLETE SET (27)	5.00	2.20	.60

☐ 1 Pat Adams
☐ 2 Felipe Alou
☐ 3 Jose Alou
☐ 4 Kent Bottenfield
☐ 5 Kevin Cavalier
☐ 6 Doug Cinnella
☐ 7 Scott Clemo
☐ 8 Al Collins
☐ 9 Rob DeYoung
☐ 10 Mike Dull
☐ 11 Bobby Gaylor
☐ 12 John Howes
☐ 13 Nels Jacobsen
☐ 14 Ross Jones
☐ 15 Tyrone Kingwood
☐ 16 Danilo Leon
☐ 17 Quinn Mack
☐ 18 Rob Mason
☐ 19 Omer Munoz
☐ 20 Bob Natal
☐ 21 Jeff Oller
☐ 22 Boi Rodriguez
☐ 23 Norm Santiago
☐ 24 Jeff Tabaka
☐ 25 John Vander Wal
☐ 26 Cory Viltz
☐ 27 Tony Welborn

1988 Wichita Pilots Rock's Dugout

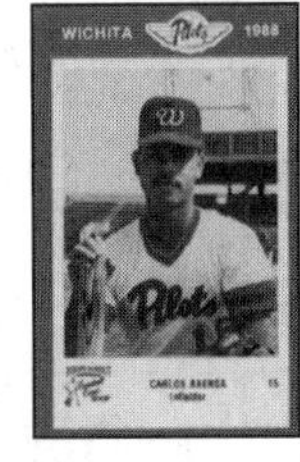

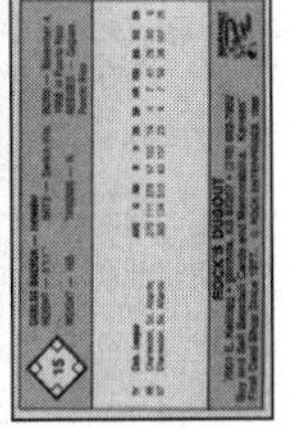

	MINT	NRMT	EXC
COMPLETE SET (30)	30.00	13.50	3.70

☐ 10 Mike DeButch
☐ 11 Jeff Yurtin
☐ 12 Craig Wiley
☐ 14 Chris Knabenshue
☐ 15 Carlos Baerga
☐ 16 Mike Basso
☐ 17 Nate Colbert CO
☐ 18 Jim Tatum
☐ 19 Gregg Harris
☐ 20 Terry Gilmore
☐ 21 Bill Wrona
☐ 22 Jimmy Lester
☐ 23 Paul Quinzer
☐ 24 Craig Cooper
☐ 25 James 'Bubba' Austin
☐ 26 Mike Costello
☐ 27 Jeff Hermann
☐ 28 Pat Jelks
☐ 29 Bill Stevenson
☐ 30 Jeff Childers
☐ 31 Mike Mills
☐ 32 Kevin Brown
☐ 33 Eric Bauer
☐ 40 Pat Kelly MG
☐ 41 Rusty Ford
☐ 42 Steve Luebber CO
☐ 43 Matt Maysey
☐ NNO Joe Chavez TR
☐ NNO Logo Card
☐ NNO Title Card

1988 Williamsport Bills ProCards

This 27-card standard-size set of the 1988 Williamsport Bills, a Class AA Eastern League affiliate of the Cleveland Indians, features silver-bordered posed color player photos on its fronts. The player's name, position, and team name appear at the bottom. The plain white back carries the player's name at the top, followed by biography and statistics.

	MINT	NRMT	EXC
COMPLETE SET (27)	5.00	2.20	.60

☐ 1303 Lee Kuntz
☐ 1304 Tom Lampkin
☐ 1305 Kent Murphy
☐ 1306 Mike Hargrove
☐ 1307 Mike Farr
☐ 1308 Andy Ghelfi
☐ 1309 Jeff Shaw
☐ 1310 Mike Walker
☐ 1311 Brian Allard
☐ 1312 Turner Gill
☐ 1313 Brian Graham
☐ 1314 Tony Ghelfi
☐ 1315 Kevin Wickander
☐ 1316 Stan Hilton
☐ 1317 Casey Webster
☐ 1318 Theo Shaw
☐ 1319 Darryl Landrum
☐ 1320 Claudio Carrasco
☐ 1321 Paul Kuzniar
☐ 1322 Mark Howie
☐ 1323 Jim Bruske
☐ 1324 Doyle Wilson
☐ 1325 Mike Poehl
☐ 1326 Scott Jordan
☐ 1327 Milt Harper
☐ 1328 Kerry Richardson
☐ NNO Checklist

1988 Winston-Salem Spirits Star

	MINT	NRMT	EXC
COMPLETE SET (22)	5.00	2.20	.60

☐ 1 John Berringer
☐ 2 Luis Cruz
☐ 3 Victor (Butch) Garcia
☐ 4 Henry Gatewood
☐ 5 Phil Harrison
☐ 6 Steve Hill
☐ 7 Bill Kazmierczak
☐ 8 John Lewis
☐ 9 Kelly Mann
☐ 10 Jim Matas
☐ 11 Derrick May
☐ 12 Tim Michno
☐ 13 Brian Otten
☐ 14 Gregg Patterson
☐ 15 David Rosario
☐ 16 Heath Slocumb
☐ 17 Greg Smith
☐ 18 Glen Sullivan
☐ 19 Jeff Schwarz
☐ 20 Francisco Tenacen
☐ 21 Tim Wallace
☐ 22 Eric Woods

1988 Winter Haven Red Sox Star

	MINT	NRMT	EXC
COMPLETE SET (27)	5.00	2.20	.60

☐ 1 John Abbott
☐ 2 Odie Abril
☐ 3 Mike Baker
☐ 4 Eddie Banasiak
☐ 5 Ken Bourne
☐ 6 Dale Burgo
☐ 7 Johnn Diaz
☐ 8 Donald Florence
☐ 9 Roger Haggerty
☐ 10 Michael Kelly
☐ 11 Jorge Kuilan
☐ 12 Donnie McGowan
☐ 13 David Milstien
☐ 14 Miguel Monegro
☐ 15 Tony Mosley
☐ 16 Luis Munoz
☐ 17 Warren Olson
☐ 18 Livio Padilla
☐ 19 Juan Paris
☐ 20 Phil Plantier
☐ 21 Carlos Rivera
☐ 22 Julio Rosario
☐ 23 Michael Thompson
☐ 24 Doug Treadway
☐ 25 Leslie Wallin
☐ 26 Brian Warfel
☐ 27 Paul Williams Jr.

1988 Wytheville Cubs ProCards

This 31-card standard-size set of the 1988 Wytheville Cubs, a Rookie Class Appalachian League affiliate of the Chicago Cubs, features bronze-bordered posed color player photos on its fronts. The player's name, position, and team name appear at the bottom. The plain white back carries the player's name at the top, followed by biography and statistics.

	MINT	NRMT	EXC
COMPLETE SET (31)	5.00	2.20	.60

☐ 1975 Milciades Uribe
☐ 1976 Rob Bonneau
☐ 1977 Wayne Weinheimer
☐ 1978 Kevin Roberson
☐ 1979 Brad Huff
☐ 1980 Victor Cancel
☐ 1981 Sean Reed
☐ 1982 Marvin Cole
☐ 1983 Bill Paynter
☐ 1984 Tony Whitson
☐ 1985 Daren Burns
☐ 1986 Roberto Smalls
☐ 1987 Bubba Browder
☐ 1988 Julio Valdez
☐ 1989 Bill Earley
☐ 1990 Woody Smith
☐ 1991 Steve Roadcap
☐ 1992 Benny Shreve
☐ 1993 Mike Gladu
☐ 1994 Kenny Holley
☐ 1995 Ivan Marteniz
☐ 1996 Matt Leonard
☐ 1997 Juan Adames
☐ 1998 Jason Doss
☐ 1999 Marc Carosielli
☐ 2000 Billy Gamble
☐ 2001 Ronnie Rasp
☐ 2002 Jerrone Williams
☐ 2003 Troy Bailey
☐ 2004 Wytheville Team
☐ NNO Checklist

1989 Albany Yankees Best

The 1989 Albany Yankees set contains 30 standard-size cards. The fronts have posed color player photos with white borders. The year "1989" and the city are written vertically on the left side of the card, and the player's name and position are given below the picture. In a horizontal format, the backs have biography, recent professional baseball performance summary (including statistics), and a color headshot, all in a yellow rectangular box. This issue includes the minor league card debut of Deion Sanders. The Platinum version sets were limited to a production run of 1,500.

	MINT	NRMT	EXC
COMPLETE SET (30)	20.00	9.00	2.50
COMP. LIMITED EDITION SET (30)	30.00	13.50	3.70

☐ 1 Deion Sanders
☐ 2 Jim Leyritz
☐ 3 Bob Davidson
☐ 4 Scott Shaw
☐ 5 Tim Layana
☐ 6 Royal Clayton
☐ 7 Glenn Sherlock
☐ 8 Buck Showalter MGR
☐ 9 Rob Sepanek
☐ 10 Bob Green
☐ 11 Ricky Torres
☐ 12 Jerry Rub
☐ 13 John Ramos
☐ 14 Mitch Lyden
☐ 15 Andy Stankiewicz
☐ 16 Bobby Dickerson
☐ 17 Hensley Meulens
☐ 18 Aris Tirado
☐ 19 Oscar Azocar
☐ 20 Tim Becker
☐ 21 Rodney Imes
☐ 22 Mike Christopher
☐ 23 Kevin Mmahat
☐ 24 Jason Maas
☐ 25 Scott Kamieniecki
☐ 26 Dale McConachie
Broadcaster

☐ 27 Russ Meyer CO
☐ 28 Bob Mariano CO
☐ 29 Tim Weston TR
☐ 30 Team logo
Checklist

1989 Albany Yankees ProCards

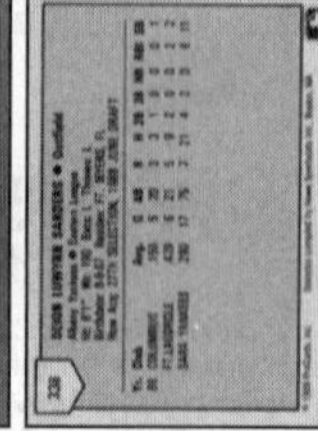

This 29-card standard-size set of the 1989 Albany Yankees, a Class AA Eastern League affiliate of the New York Yankees, features red-bordered posed color player photos on its fronts. The player's name, position, and team name appear at the bottom. The horizontal gray back carries the player's name and position at the top, followed by biography and statistics. This issue includes the minor league card debut of Deion Sanders.

	MINT	NRMT	EXC
COMPLETE SET (29)	20.00	9.00	2.50

☐ 313 Checklist
☐ 314 Rodney Imes
☐ 315 Tim Becker
☐ 316 Scott Kamieniecki
☐ 317 Scott Shaw
☐ 318 Royal Clayton
☐ 319 Bobby Dickerson
☐ 320 Mitch Lyden
☐ 321 Mike Christopher
☐ 322 Russ Meyer CO
☐ 323 Tim Weston TR
☐ 324 Bob Mariano CO
☐ 325 Jim Leyritz
☐ 326 Buck Showalter MGR
☐ 327 Bobby Davidson
☐ 328 Jerry Rub
☐ 329 Tim Layana
☐ 330 Rob Sepanek
☐ 331 Aris Tirado
☐ 332 Oscar Azocar
☐ 333 Andy Stankiewicz
☐ 334 Jason Maas
☐ 335 Ricky Torres
☐ 336 John Ramos
☐ 337 Hensley Meulens
☐ 338 Deion Sanders
☐ 339 Glenn Sherlock
☐ 340 Darrin Chapin
☐ 341 Kevin Mmahat

1989 Albany Yankees Star

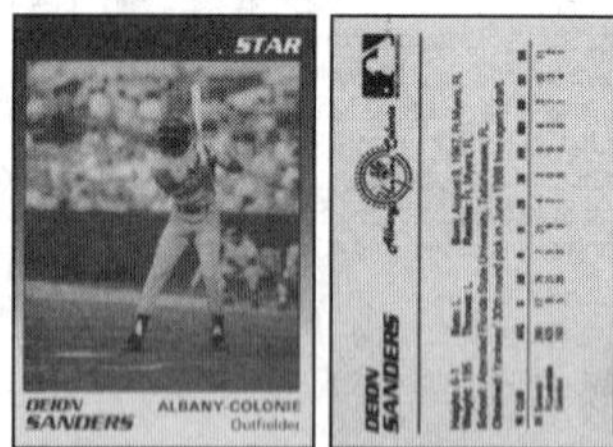

The 1989 Albany-Colonie Yankees set contains 23 standard-size cards. The fronts have posed color player photos, with purple borders on the top portion of the card fading to yellow as one moves down the card face. In purple print on a pale yellow background, the backs have biography and statistics. The Sanders card was not delivered with the original set; it has black in place of purple and appears out of alphabetical order. This issue includes the minor league card debut of Deion Sanders. 5,000 sets produced.

	MINT	NRMT	EXC
COMPLETE SET (23)	20.00	9.00	2.50

☐ 1 Oscar Azocar
☐ 2 Tim Becker
☐ 3 Darrin Chapin
☐ 4 Mike Christopher
☐ 5 Royal Clayton
☐ 6 Bobby Davidson
☐ 7 Bobby Dickerson
☐ 8 Rodney Imes
☐ 9 Tim Layana
☐ 10 Jim Leyritz
☐ 11 Mitch Lyden
☐ 12 Jason Maas
☐ 13 Hensley Meulens
☐ 14 Kevin Mmahat
☐ 15 John Ramos
☐ 16 Jerry Rub
☐ 17 Rob Sepanek
☐ 18 Scott Shaw
☐ 19 Andy Stankiewicz
☐ 20 Aris Tirado
☐ 21 Ricky Torres
☐ 22 Buck Showalter MGR
☐ 23 Deion Sanders

1989 Albuquerque Dukes CMC

	MINT	NRMT	EXC
COMPLETE SET (25)	6.00	2.70	.75

☐ 1 William Brennan
☐ 2 Dennis Burtt
☐ 3 Jeff Fischer
☐ 4 Mike Hartley
☐ 5 Hector Heredia
☐ 6 Dave Eichhorn
☐ 7 Ramon Martinez
☐ 8 Mike Munoz
☐ 9 Jim Neidlinger
☐ 10 Dave Walsh
☐ 11 John Wetteland
☐ 12 Jon Debus
☐ 13 Shanie Dugas
☐ 14 Mike Sharperson
☐ 15 Chris Gwynn
☐ 16 Tracy Woodson
☐ 17 Jose Gonzales
☐ 18 Darrin Fletcher
☐ 19 Joe Szekely
☐ 20 Juan Bustabad
☐ 21 Walt McConnell
☐ 22 Domingo Michel
☐ 23 Jose Vizcaino
☐ 24 Mike Huff
☐ 25 Javier Ortiz

1989 Albuquerque Dukes ProCards

This 30-card standard-size set of the 1989 Albuquerque Dukes, a Class AAA Pacific Coast League affiliate of the Los Angeles Dodgers, features blue-bordered posed color player photos on its fronts. The player's name, position, and team name appear at the bottom. The horizontal gray back carries the player's name and position at the top, followed by biography and statistics.

	MINT	NRMT	EXC
COMPLETE SET (30)	6.00	2.70	.75

☐ 58 Darrin Fletcher
☐ 59 Mike Sharperson
☐ 60 Brent Strom CO
☐ 61 Dave Eichhorn
☐ 62 Mike Munoz
☐ 63 John Wetteland
☐ 64 Chris Gwynn
☐ 65 William Brennan
☐ 66 Hector Heredia
☐ 67 Mike Hartley
☐ 68 Dennis Burtt
☐ 69 Ramon Martinez
☐ 70 Dave Walsh
☐ 71 Jim Neidlinger
☐ 72 Kevin Kennedy MGR
☐ 73 Von Joshua CO
☐ 74 Stan Johnston TR
☐ 75 Tracy Woodson
☐ 76 Jon Debus
☐ 77 Joe Szekely
☐ 78 Juan Bustabad
☐ 79 Mike Huff
☐ 80 Jose Gonzalez
☐ 81 Domingo Michel
☐ 82 Jose Vizcaino
☐ 83 Walt McConnell
☐ 84 Javier Ortiz
☐ 85 Shanie Dugas
☐ 86 Jeff Fischer
☐ 87 Checklist

1989 Appleton Foxes ProCards

This 31-card standard-size set of the 1989 Appleton Foxes, a Class A Midwest League affiliate of the Kansas City Royals, features orange-bordered posed color player photos on its fronts. The player's name, position, and team name appear at the bottom. The horizontal gray back carries the player's name and position at the top, followed by biography and statistics.

	MINT	NRMT	EXC
COMPLETE SET (31)	5.00	2.20	.60

☐ 848 Checklist
☐ 849 Hector Wagner
☐ 850 Randy Vaughn
☐ 851 Dennis Studeman
☐ 852 Steve Hoeme
☐ 853 Greg Harvey
☐ 854 Bill Drohan
☐ 855 Don Wright
☐ 856 Hugh Walker
☐ 857 Frank Henderson
☐ 858 Greg Prusia
☐ 859 Ondra Ford
☐ 860 Daryl Robinson
☐ 861 Steve Preston
☐ 862 Chris Caribaldo
☐ 863 Jeff Garber
☐ 864 Mike Beall
☐ 865 Pete Capello
☐ 866 Jeff Hulse
☐ 867 Linton Dyer
☐ 868 Rob Buchanan
☐ 869 Brad Shores TR
☐ 870 Allard Baird CO
☐ 871 Andre Rabouin CO
☐ 872 Brian Poldberg MGR
☐ 873 John McCormick
☐ 874 Ben Pierce
☐ 875 Mark Parnell
☐ 876 Steve Otto
☐ 877 Luke Nocas
☐ 878 John Hofer

1989 Arkansas Travelers Grand Slam

	MINT	NRMT	EXC
COMPLETE SET (25)	10.00	4.50	1.25

☐ 1 Gaylen Pitts MGR
☐ 2 Chris Maloney CO
☐ 3 Rod Brewer
☐ 4 Dennis Carter
☐ 5 Mike Fox
☐ 6 Bernard Gilkey
☐ 7 Steve Hill
☐ 8 Mike Hinkle
☐ 9 Ray Lankford
☐ 10 John Lepley
☐ 11 Julian Martinez
☐ 12 Chuck McGrath
☐ 13 Opie Moran
☐ 14 Steve Mumaw
☐ 15 Dave Osteen
☐ 16 Jeff Oyster
☐ 17 Mike Perez
☐ 18 Len Picota
☐ 19 Frank Potestio
☐ 20 Andy Rincon
☐ 21 Mike Robertson
☐ 22 Roy Silver
☐ 23 Ray Stephens
☐ 24 Craig Weissmann
☐ 25 Craig Wilson

1989 Asheville Tourists ProCards

This 30-card standard-size set of the 1989 Asheville Tourists, a Class A South Atlantic League affiliate of the Houston Astros, features orange-bordered posed color player photos on its fronts. The player's name, position, and team name appear at the bottom. The horizontal gray back carries the player's name and position at the top, followed by biography and statistics.

	MINT	NRMT	EXC
COMPLETE SET (30)	5.00	2.20	.60

☐ 939 Checklist
☐ 940 Matthew McKee
Batboy
☐ 941 Vitas Laniauskas
Asst GM
☐ 942 Ron McKee GM
☐ 943 Kevin Day TR
☐ 944 Charley Taylor CO
☐ 945 John Massarelli
☐ 946 Roddy Scheckla
☐ 947 Rodney Windes
☐ 948 Dave Shermet
☐ 949 Rafael Campos
☐ 950 Willie Ansley
☐ 951 Pedro Delossantos
☐ 952 Andujar Cedeno
☐ 953 Gordon Farmer
☐ 954 Brian Bennett
☐ 955 Brian Griffiths
☐ 956 Troy Dovey
☐ 957 Harry Fuller
☐ 958 Scott Spurgeon
☐ 959 Gregory Johnson
☐ 960 Dean Hartgraves
☐ 961 Jim Coveney MGR
☐ 962 Joe Charno
☐ 963 Francisco Perez
☐ 964 Rick Dunnum
☐ 965 Carlos Henry
☐ 966 Mica Lewis
☐ 967 Lawrence Lamphere
☐ 968 Mike Beams

1989 Auburn Astros ProCards

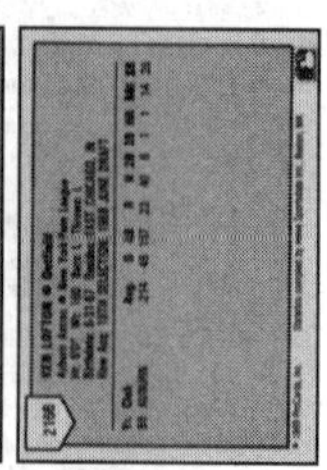

This 31-card standard-size set of the 1989 Auburn Astros, a Class A New York-Penn League affiliate of the Houston Astros, features orange-bordered posed color player photos on its fronts. The player's name, position, and team name appear at the bottom. The horizontal gray back carries the player's name and position at the top, followed by biography and statistics. This issue includes a second year card of Kenny Lofton.

	MINT	NRMT	EXC
COMPLETE SET (31)	25.00	11.00	3.10

☐ 2159 Checklist
☐ 2160 Edwin Valentin
☐ 2161 Shane Reynolds
☐ 2162 Teo Campusano
☐ 2163 Scott Makarewicz
☐ 2164 Lance Madsen
☐ 2165 Jose Santana
☐ 2166 Ken Lofton
☐ 2167 Toncie Reed
☐ 2168 Reggie Waller
☐ 2169 Brian Porter
☐ 2170 Cole Hyson
☐ 2171 Ben Gonzales
☐ 2172 Jim Desapio
☐ 2173 Mike McDowell
☐ 2174 Francisco Perez
☐ 2175 Howard Prager
☐ 2176 Luther Johnson
☐ 2177 John Graham MGR
☐ 2178 Bob Neal GM
☐ 2179 Darin Bruehl
☐ 2180 P.J. Riley
☐ 2181 Roger Marrero
☐ 2182 Donne Wall
☐ 2183 Kevin Scott
☐ 2184 Doug Simunic CO
☐ 2185 Dave Henderson
☐ 2186 Mica Lewis
☐ 2187 Rick Wise CO
☐ 2188 Mark Small
☐ 2189 Daryl Wooten TR

1989 Augusta Pirates ProCards

This 32-card standard-size set of the 1989 Augusta Pirates, a Class A South Atlantic League affiliate of the Pittsburgh Pirates, features orange-bordered posed color player photos on its fronts. The player's name, position, and team name appear at the bottom. The horizontal gray back carries the player's name and position at the top, followed by biography and statistics.

	MINT	NRMT	EXC
COMPLETE SET (32)	5.00	2.20	.60

☐ 490 Checklist
☐ 491 Jeff Kuder
☐ 492 Jose Acosta
☐ 493 Tim Odom
☐ 494 Jeff Osborne
☐ 495 Jeff Neely
☐ 496 Mark Merchant
☐ 497 Felix Antigua
☐ 498 Mandy Romero
☐ 499 Chris Estep
☐ 500 Bobby Underwood
☐ 501 Jeff Stout
☐ 502 Mike Stevanus
☐ 503 Ken Huseby
☐ 504 Darwin Pennye
☐ 505 Flavio Williams
☐ 506 Keith Raisanen
☐ 507 Mark Thomas
☐ 508 Glenn McNabb
☐ 509 Mike Huyler
☐ 510 Antonio Felix
☐ 511 Ben Shelton
☐ 512 Kevin Andersh
☐ 513 Bruce Klein TR
☐ 514 Stan Cliburn MGR
☐ 515 Terry Abbott CO
☐ 516 Pete Blohm
☐ 517 Greg Sims
☐ 518 Rod Byerly
☐ 519 Jay Snead
PR Director

☐ 520 Chris Scheuer GM
☐ 521 Kyle Fisher
Business MGR

1989 Bakersfield Dodgers Cal League Cards

This issue includes a second year card of Eric Karros.

	MINT	NRMT	EXC
COMPLETE SET (29)	6.00	2.70	.75

☐ 180 David Dawson
☐ 181 Sean Snedeker
☐ 182 Kevin Campbell
☐ 183 Jeff Hartsock
☐ 184 Bill Bene
☐ 185 Macario Gastelum
☐ 186 Mike James
☐ 187 Rob Piscetta
☐ 188 Bill Wengert
☐ 189 James Wray
☐ 190 Cam Biberdorf
☐ 191 Bill Parham
☐ 192 Lance Rice
☐ 193 Eric Boddie
☐ 194 Jose Offerman
☐ 195 Scott Marabell
☐ 196 John Huebner
☐ 197 Bryan Beals
☐ 198 Eddie Pye
☐ 199 K.G. White
☐ 200 Ernie Carr
☐ 201 Eric Karros
☐ 202 Braulio Castillo
☐ 203 Jerry Brooks
☐ 204 Chris Morrow
☐ 205 Steven Finken
☐ 206 Tim Johnson MGR
☐ 207 Guy Conti CO
☐ 208 Tim Terrio TR

1989 Baseball America AA Prospects Best

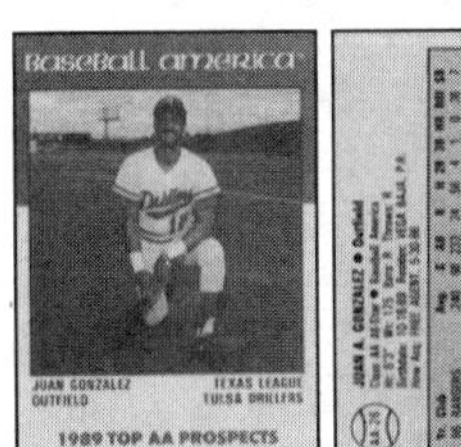

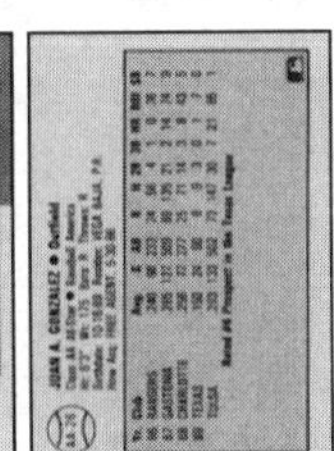

This 31-card standard-size set features top AA prospects from the Eastern League, the Southern League, and the Texas League. The fronts of the cards feature posed color player photos, with a red border on the top half of the card and a white border on the bottom half. Player information appears in black print below the picture. The words "1989 Top AA Prospects" in red lettering round out the card face at the bottom. The horizontally oriented backs have black print on gray and white, and present biography and statistics. Future major league stars in the set include Steve Avery, Robin Ventura, and Marquis Grissom.

	MINT	NRMT	EXC
COMPLETE SET (31)	35.00	16.00	4.40

☐ AA Title Card/Checklist
☐ AA1 Wes Chamberlain
☐ AA2 Travis Fryman
☐ AA3 Steve Adkins
☐ AA4 Jason Grimsley
☐ AA5 Bernie Williams
☐ AA6 Tino Martinez
☐ AA7 Beau Allred
☐ AA8 Rodney Imes
☐ AA9 Scott Cooper
☐ AA10 Pat Combs
☐ AA11 Eric Anthony
☐ AA12 Darryl Kile
☐ AA13 Steve Avery
☐ AA14 Marquis Grissom
☐ AA15 Delino DeShields
☐ AA16 Brian Lane
☐ AA17 Bob Hamelin
☐ AA18 Scott Leius
☐ AA19 Paul Sorrento
☐ AA20 Howard Farmer
☐ AA21 Robin Ventura
☐ AA22 Wayne Edwards
☐ AA23 Ray Lankford
☐ AA24 Andy Benes
☐ AA25 Jose Offerman
☐ AA26 Juan Gonzalez
☐ AA27 Dean Palmer
☐ AA28 Julio Valera
☐ AA29 Sammy Sosa
☐ AA30 Gary DiSarcina

1989 Baseball City Royals Star

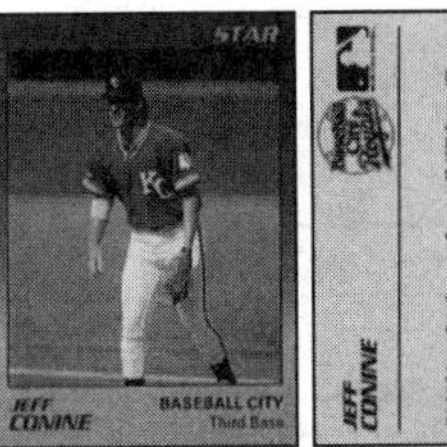

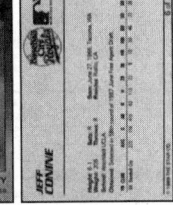

The 1989 Baseball City Royals set contains 26 standard-size cards. The fronts have posed color player photos, with purple borders on the top portion of the card fading to gray as one moves down the card face. In purple print on a gray background, the backs have biography and statistics. Card number 25 was never issued. This issue includes a second year card of Jeff Conine. 5,000 sets produced.

	MINT	NRMT	EXC
COMPLETE SET (26)	10.00	4.50	1.25

☐ 1 Ken Adams
☐ 2 Pete Alborano
☐ 3 Jon Alexander
☐ 4 Jose Anglero
☐ 5 Sean Berry
☐ 6 Jeff Conine
☐ 7 Carlos Gonzalez
☐ 8 Kevin Shaw
☐ 9 Dave Howard
☐ 10 Jim Hudson
☐ 11 Tom Johnson
☐ 12 Joel Johnston
☐ 13 Lorin Jundy
☐ 14 Kevin Koslofski
☐ 15 Francisco Laureano
☐ 16 Brian McCormack
☐ 17 Dennis Moeller
☐ 18 Bobby Moore
☐ 19 Doug Nelson
☐ 20 Jorge Pedre
☐ 21 Kevin Pickens
☐ 22 Ruben Pujols
☐ 23 Keith Shepherd
☐ 24 Bill Stonikas
☐ 26 DeJon Watson
☐ 27 Coaching Staff
Luis Silverio MGR
Ron Johnson CO
Mike Alvarez CO

1989 Batavia Clippers ProCards

This 31-card standard-size set of the 1989 Batavia Clippers, a Class A New York-Penn League affiliate of the Philadelphia Phillies, features orange-bordered posed color player photos on its fronts. The player's name, position, and team name appear at the bottom. The horizontal gray back carries the player's name and position at the top, followed by biography and statistics.

	MINT	NRMT	EXC
COMPLETE SET (31)	5.00	2.20	.60

☐ 1915 Checklist
☐ 1916 Tony Lozinski
☐ 1917 Jeff Etheredge
☐ 1918 Robert Mendonca
☐ 1919 Tim Churchill
☐ 1920 Albert Bennett
☐ 1921 Paul Fletcher
☐ 1922 Joe Millette
☐ 1923 Steve Parris
☐ 1924 Matt Stevens
☐ 1925 Donnie Elliott
☐ 1926 David Agado
☐ 1927 Todd Goergen
☐ 1928 Robert Gaddy
☐ 1929 Mike Sullivan
☐ 1930 Michael Owens
☐ 1931 Mickey Hyde
☐ 1932 Dana Brown
☐ 1933 Joe Urbon
☐ 1934 Steve Bieser
☐ 1935 Field Staff
Rich Walker TR
Don McCormack MGR
Tony Scott CO
Carlos Arroyo CO
☐ 1936 Pat Woodruff
☐ 1937 Sam Taylor
☐ 1938 Greg Gunderson
☐ 1939 Eduardo Ortega
☐ 1940 John Escobar
☐ 1941 Eric Bratlein
☐ 1942 Josh Lowery
☐ 1943 Brian Cummings
☐ 1944 Edwin Rosado
☐ 1945 Robby Corsaro

1989 Bellingham Mariners Legoe

The 1989 Bellingham Mariners set consists of 37 standard-size cards. The glossy color player photos are enframed by yellow and blue borders, while the card face itself is light blue. On a light blue background decorated with white baseballs across the top, the horizontally oriented backs have biography, complete Minor League record, and a "Did You Know?" trivia feature.

	MINT	NRMT	EXC
COMPLETE SET (37)	6.00	2.70	.75

☐ 1 Greg Pirkl
☐ 2 Julio Reyan
☐ 3 Keith Bryant
☐ 4 Jeff Darwin
☐ 5 Anthony Gordon
☐ 6 Jim Gutierrez
☐ 7 Michael LeBlanc
☐ 8 Tom Liss
☐ 9 Richard Lodding
☐ 10 Scott Lodgek
☐ 11 Darin Loe
☐ 12 Oscar Rivas
☐ 13 Roger Salkeld
☐ 14 Glenn Twardy
☐ 15 Johnny Wiggs
☐ 16 Kerry Woodson
☐ 17 Lash Bailey
☐ 18 Doug Davis
☐ 19 Pedro Roa
☐ 20 Brian Turang
☐ 21 Mark Brakebill
☐ 22 Jeremy Mathews
☐ 23 Bonel Chevalier
☐ 24 Alvin Rittman
☐ 25 Tony Cayson
☐ 26 Rich Hanlin
☐ 27 Corey Paul
☐ 28 Willie Romay
☐ 29 Dave Smith
☐ 30 P.J. Carey MGR
☐ 31 Mauro Mazzotti CO
☐ 32 Gary Wheelock CO
☐ 33 Spyder Webb TR
☐ 34 Bill Tucker
Owner
☐ 35 Jerry Walker
Owner
☐ 36 Bat Boys
Jeff Crnich
Mike Thompson
☐ NNO Title Card

1989 Beloit Brewers I Star

The 1989 Beloit Brewers set contains 26 standard-size cards. The fronts have posed color player photos, with blue borders on the top portion of the card fading to yellow as one moves down the card face. In blue print on a pale yellow background, the backs have biography and statistics. 5,000 sets produced.

	MINT	NRMT	EXC
COMPLETE SET (26)	7.00	3.10	.85

☐ 1 Frank Bolick
☐ 2 Kevin Carmody
☐ 3 Don Erickson
☐ 4 John Faccio
☐ 5 Dave Fitzgerald
☐ 6 Librado Garcia
☐ 7 Mike Grayson
☐ 8 Mike Guerrero
☐ 9 Bert Heffernan
☐ 10 Chris Johnson
☐ 11 Mark Kiefer
☐ 12 Ken Kremer
☐ 13 Greg Landry
☐ 14 Heath Lane
☐ 15 Oreste Marrero
☐ 16 Vilato Marrero
☐ 17 Don Meyett
☐ 18 Bob Muhammad
☐ 19 Troy O'Leary
☐ 20 Joe Ortiz
☐ 21 Joe Peguero
☐ 22 Rich Pfaff
☐ 23 Dave Voit
☐ 24 Tim Wahl
☐ 25 Bob Watts
☐ 26 Alex Taveras CO
Gary Robson CO

1989 Beloit Brewers II Star

The 1989 Beloit Brewers set contains 25 standard-size cards. The fronts have posed color player photos, with yellow borders on the top portion of the card fading to blue as one moves down the card face. In blue print on a pale yellow background, the backs have biography and statistics. 5,000 sets produced.

	MINT	NRMT	EXC
COMPLETE SET (25)	5.00	2.20	.60

☐ 1 Frank Bolick
☐ 2 Arthur Butcher
☐ 3 John Byington
☐ 4 Jamie Cangemi
☐ 5 Kevin Carmody
☐ 6 Larry Carter
☐ 7 Steve Diaz
☐ 8 Calvin Eldred
☐ 9 John Finn
☐ 10 Dave Fitzgerald
☐ 11 Librado Garcia
☐ 12 Ron Hanisch
☐ 13 Mitch Hannahs
☐ 14 Bert Heffernan
☐ 15 Kenny Jackson
☐ 16 Chris Johnson
☐ 17 Mark Kiefer
☐ 18 Ken Kremer
☐ 19 Curt Krippner
☐ 20 Vilato Marrero
☐ 21 Don Meyett
☐ 22 Angel Miranda
☐ 23 Rich Pfaff
☐ 24 Guillermo Sandoval
☐ 25 Alex Taveras MGR

1989 Bend Bucks Legoe

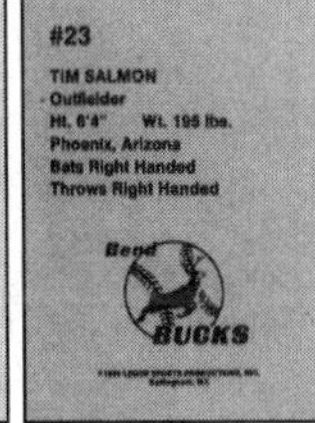

The 1989 Bend Bucks set consists of 30 standard-size cards. The front design features a mix of posed or action color player photos, with a thin black border on a white card face. In black print on a white card face, the backs have brief biographical information and the team logo. This issue includes the minor league card debut of Tim Salmon.

	MINT	NRMT	EXC
COMPLETE SET (30)	20.00	9.00	2.50

☐ 1 Erik Bennett
☐ 2 Marvin Cobb
☐ 3 Chris Cota
☐ 4 Wayne Helm
☐ 5 James Jones
☐ 6 Jaun Reyes
☐ 7 Fili Martinez
☐ 8 Marcus Moore
☐ 9 David Rice
☐ 10 Paul Swingle
☐ 11 Willie Warrecker
☐ 12 Joe Warren
☐ 13 David Neville
☐ 14 Richard Parker
☐ 15 Tom Rudstrom
☐ 16 Damion Easley
☐ 17 Corey Kapano
☐ 18 Jeff Kipila
☐ 19 Brian Specyalski
☐ 20 Rick Hirtensteiner
☐ 21 Bobby Jones
☐ 22 Jeff Kelso
☐ 23 Tim Salmon
☐ 24 Terry Taylor
☐ 25 Batboys
Jason Lundgren
Matt Russell
☐ 26 Don Long MGR
☐ 27 Howie Gershberg CO
☐ 28 Rick Ingalls CO
☐ 29 Bill Durney TR
☐ 30 Bucky
Mascot

1989 Billings Mustangs ProCards

This 31-card standard-size set of the 1989 Billings Mustangs, a Rookie Class Pioneer League affiliate of the Cincinnati Reds, features orange-bordered posed color player photos on its fronts. The player's name, position, and team name appear at the bottom. The horizontal gray back carries the player's name and position at the top, followed by biography and statistics.

	MINT	NRMT	EXC
COMPLETE SET (31)	7.00	3.10	.85

☐ 2038 Checklist
☐ 2039 Kevin Hudson TR
☐ 2040 Travis Teegarden
☐ 2041 Trey Wilburn
☐ 2042 K.C. Gillum
☐ 2043 Brian Nichols
☐ 2044 Tomas Rodriguez
☐ 2045 Rick Allen

□ 2046 Chris Gill
□ 2047 Kyle Reagan
□ 2048 David Keller MGR
□ 2049 Mike Goedde CO
□ 2050 Brian Parrotte
□ 2051 Brian Fry
□ 2052 Sean Doty
□ 2053 Kurt Dempster
□ 2054 Mark Cerny
□ 2055 Rob Dombrowski
□ 2056 Andy Duke
□ 2057 Steve Vondran
□ 2058 Danny Perozo
□ 2059 Harry Henderson IV
□ 2060 Bob Blenkenship
□ 2061 Eric Bates
□ 2062 Chris Keim
□ 2063 Scott Pose
□ 2064 Tim Pugh
□ 2065 Gill Galloway
□ 2066 Mark Borcherding
□ 2067 Darron Cox
□ 2068 Trevor Hoffman

1989 Birmingham Barons Best

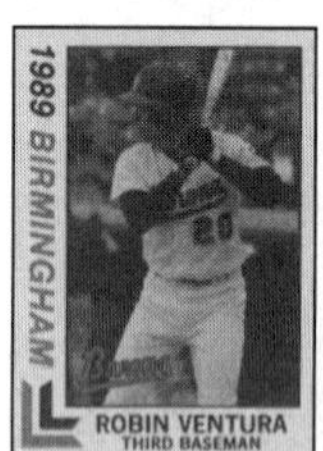

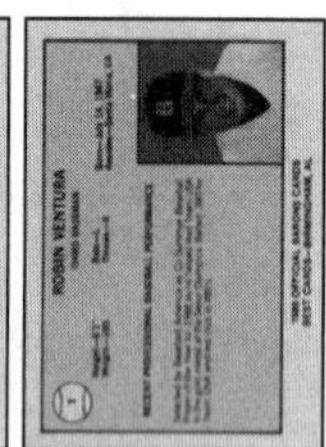

This 30-card standard-size set features the 1989 Birmingham Barons, a farm club for the Chicago White Sox. The fronts have posed color player photos with white borders. The year "1989" and the city are written vertically on the left side of the card, and the player's name and position are given below the picture. In a horizontal format, the backs have biography, recent professional baseball performance summary (including statistics), and a color headshot, all in a yellow rectangular box. The Platinum version sets were limited to a production run of 1,500.

	MINT	NRMT	EXC
COMPLETE SET (30)	20.00	9.00	2.50
COMP. LIMITED EDITION SET (30)	30.00	13.50	3.70

□ 1 Robin Ventura
□ 2 Mike Ollom
□ 3 Tony Menendez
□ 4 Victor Diaz
□ 5 Dan Wagner
□ 6 Kevin Davis
□ 7 Doug Frobel
□ 8 Aubrey Waggoner
□ 9 Chidez Garcia
□ 10 Tony Blasucci
□ 11 Grady Hall
□ 12 Jerry Bertolani
□ 13 Ravelo Manzanillo
□ 14 Rich Amaral
□ 15 Jerry Kutzler
□ 16 Don Wakamatsu
□ 17 Craig Grebeck
□ 18 Chuck Mount
□ 19 Todd Trafton
□ 20 Ken Berry MGR
□ 21 Wayne Edwards
□ 22 Doug Little
□ 23 C.L. Penigar
□ 24 Buddy Groom
□ 25 Dave Wallwork TR
□ 26 Ron Jackson CO
□ 27 Tommy Thompson CO
□ 28 Rick Peterson CO
□ 29 Sam Hairston CO
□ 30 Batboys
Nathan Sparks
Rhett White
Brad Reznik
Brian Picard
Jeremy Berry
Adam Power
Checklist

1989 Birmingham Barons ProCards

This 31-card standard-size set of the 1989 Birmingham Barons, a Class AA Southern League affiliate of the Chicago White Sox, features red-bordered posed color player photos on its fronts. The player's name, position, and team name appear at the bottom. The horizontal gray back carries the player's name and position at the top, followed by biography and statistics.

	MINT	NRMT	EXC
COMPLETE SET (31)	10.00	4.50	1.25

□ 88 Checklist
□ 89 Ken Berry MGR
□ 90 Dan Wagner
□ 91 Rich Amaral
□ 92 Chuck Mount
□ 93 Doug Little
□ 94 Tony Blasucci
□ 95 Mike Ollom
□ 96 Dave Wallwork TR ,
Fletch
□ 97 Todd Trafton
□ 98 Kevin Davis
□ 99 Rick Peterson CO
□ 100 Jerry Bertolani
□ 101 Victor Diaz
□ 102 Cornelio Garcia
□ 103 Tony Menendez
□ 104 Tommy Thompson
Player/Coach
□ 105 Doug Frobel
□ 106 Robin Ventura
□ 107 Don Wakamatsu
□ 108 Grady Hall
□ 109 Buddy Groom
□ 110 Wayne Edwards
□ 111 Craig Grebeck
□ 112 Sam Hairston Sr. CO
□ 113 Ron Jackson CO
□ 114 Aubrey Waggoner
□ 115 C.L. Penigar
□ 116 Glen McElroy
□ 117 Jerry Kutzler
□ 118 Hoover Metro Stadium

1989 Bluefield Orioles Star

The 1989 Bluefield Orioles set contains 30 standard-size cards. The fronts have posed color player photos, with black borders on the top portion of the card fading to orange as one moves down the card face. In black print on a pale orange background, the backs have brief biographical information. Card numbers 26-30 were issued later, and the color of their borders is reversed (orange at top fading to black). The cards are arranged alphabetically and numbered on the back "X of 31." Card number 31 was never issued. 5,000 sets produced.

	MINT	NRMT	EXC
COMPLETE SET (30)	5.00	2.20	.60

□ 1 Eric Alexander
□ 2 Manny Alexander
□ 3 Chris Batiste
□ 4 Mattie Belen
□ 5 Cristian Benitez
□ 6 Sergio Cairo
□ 7 Bo Davis
□ 8 Cesar Devares
□ 9 John Fowler
□ 10 Israel Frias
□ 11 Shawn Heiden
□ 12 Keith Kessinger
□ 13 T.R. Lewis
□ 14 John Marett
□ 15 Tom Martin
□ 16 Victor Medina
□ 17 Jimmy Roso
□ 18 Brad Pennington
□ 19 Arron Norwood
□ 20 Keith Schmidt
□ 21 Al Sieradzki
□ 22 Rob Stiegele
□ 23 Doug Sutton
□ 24 Tommy Taylor
□ 25 Joe Teixeira
□ 26 Mat Anderson
□ 27 Daryl Noore
□ 28 Bob Wheatcroft
□ 29 Earl Williams
□ 30 Mike Young MGR
Jose Soto CO
Chet Nichols CO

1989 Boise Hawks ProCards

This 31-card standard-size set of the 1989 Boise Hawks, a Class A Northwest League Independent, features orange-bordered posed color player photos on its fronts. The player's name, position, and team name appear at the bottom. The horizontal gray back carries the player's name and position at the top, followed by biography and statistics.

	MINT	NRMT	EXC
COMPLETE SET (31)	5.00	2.20	.60

□ 1976 Checklist
□ 1977 Jeff Mace CO
□ 1978 Batboys
J.D. Schmidt
Nick Baltes
Kevin Kuenzi
Bill Church
□ 1979 Chip Reese CO
□ 1980 Scott Jurgens
Clubhouse MGR
□ 1981 David Perry TR
□ 1982 Stan Cook
□ 1983 Eric Doucet
□ 1984 Tommy Griffith
□ 1985 Jeff Gyarmati
□ 1986 Darrell MacMillan
□ 1987 Rod Tafoya
□ 1988 Jeff Thrams
□ 1989 Steve Mattingly
□ 1990 Jack Malone
□ 1991 Joe Mancini
□ 1992 Ruben Rodriguez
□ 1993 Bob Sobczyk
□ 1994 Tim Wallace
□ 1995 Dan Olson
□ 1996 Bruce Arola
□ 1997 John Bilello
□ 1998 Jorge Candelaria
□ 1999 Chris Cerny
□ 2000 Brian Currie
□ 2001 Chris Forrest
□ 2002 Steve King
□ 2003 Michael Larson
□ 2004 Mike Lomeli
□ 2005 Garry Wurm
□ 2006 Paul Cluff

1989 Bristol Tigers Star

The 1989 Bristol Tigers set contains 31 standard-size cards. The fronts have posed color player photos, with blue borders on the top portion of the card fading to orange as one moves down the card face. In blue print on a pale orange background, the backs have biography and statistics. 5,000 sets produced.

	MINT	NRMT	EXC
COMPLETE SET (31)	5.00	2.20	.60

□ 1 Michael Bowman
□ 2 Jeff Braley
□ 3 Aurturo Caines
□ 4 Pedro Checo
□ 5 Matthew Coleman
□ 6 Lance Daniels
□ 7 Robert Davis
□ 8 Fredie Gamble
□ 9 Mike Garcia
□ 10 Jose Guzman
□ 11 Chris Hall
□ 12 Ricky Ibarguen
□ 13 Travis Kinyoun
□ 14 Ken Lewis
□ 15 Ron Maietta
□ 16 Steve Matchett
□ 17 Kasey McKeon
□ 18 Joe Neidinger
□ 19 Kelley O'Neal
□ 20 Rudy Pemberton
□ 21 Mike Rendina
□ 22 Juan Reyes
□ 23 Eddie Rodriguez
□ 24 Jose Rodriguez
□ 25 Brian Rountree
□ 26 Mac Siebert
□ 27 Mario Stefani
□ 28 Brad Wilson
□ 29 Ruben Amaro MGR
□ 30 Steve Webber TR
□ 31 Boyce Cox GM
and President

1989 Buffalo Bisons CMC

	MINT	NRMT	EXC
COMPLETE SET (25)	6.00	2.70	.75

□ 1 Mike Billoni VP/GM
□ 2 Bill Landrum
□ 3 Carlos Ledezma
□ 4 Jay Bell
□ 5 Dave Rucker
□ 6 Scott Medvin
□ 7 Miguel Garcia
□ 8 Larry Melton
□ 9 Rick Reed
□ 10 Andy Hall
□ 11 Benny Distefano
□ 12 Buster T. Bison
Mascot
□ 13 Dann Bilardello
□ 14 Steve Henderson
□ 15 Sammy Khalifa
□ 16 Jeff King
□ 17 Bobby Meacham
□ 18 Jim Pankovits
□ 19 Ron Krauza MGR
□ 20 Scott Little
□ 21 Tom Romano
□ 22 Lou Thornton
□ 23 Reggie Williams
□ 24 Terry Collins MGR
□ 25 Jackie Brown CO

1989 Buffalo Bisons ProCards

This 27-card standard-size set of the 1989 Buffalo Bisons, a Class AAA American Association affiliate of the Pittsburgh Pirates, features orange-bordered posed color player photos on its fronts. The player's name, position, and team name appear at the bottom. The horizontal gray back carries the player's name and position at the top, followed by biography and statistics.

	MINT	NRMT	EXC
COMPLETE SET (27)	7.00	3.10	.85

□ 1661 Checklist
□ 1662 Dave Rucker
□ 1663 Bobby Meacham
□ 1664 Jim Pankovits
□ 1665 Steve Carter
□ 1666 Buster T. Bison
Mascot
□ 1667 Sammy Khalifa
□ 1668 Terry Collins MGR
□ 1669 Lou Thornton
□ 1670 Tom Romano
□ 1671 Jeff King
□ 1672 Andy Hall
□ 1673 Larry Melton
□ 1674 Bill Landrum
□ 1675 Rick Reed
□ 1676 Steve Henderson
□ 1677 Dann Bilardello
□ 1678 Carlos Ledezma TR
□ 1679 Jay Bell
□ 1680 Scott Medvin
□ 1681 Scott Little
□ 1682 Benny Distefano
□ 1683 Jackie Brown CO
□ 1684 Bob Patterson
□ 1685 Reggie Williams
□ 1686 Miguel Garcia
□ 1687 Orestes Destrade

1989 Burlington Braves ProCards

This 32-card standard-size set of the 1989 Burlington Braves, a Class A Midwest League affiliate of the Atlanta Braves, features orange-bordered posed color player photos on its fronts. The player's name, position, and team name appear at the bottom. The horizontal gray back carries the player's name and position at the top, followed by biography and statistics.

	MINT	NRMT	EXC
COMPLETE SET (32)	5.00	2.20	.60

□ 1596 Checklist
□ 1597 Johnny Cuevas
□ 1598 Lee Upshaw
□ 1599 Mark Davis
□ 1600 Joe Saccomanno
□ 1601 Greg Cloninger
□ 1602 Gary Schoonover
□ 1603 Tom Kurczewski
□ 1604 Preston Watson
□ 1605 Jesus Mendoza
□ 1606 Bob Pfaff
□ 1607 Steve Glass
□ 1608 Tony Baldwin
□ 1609 Keith Mitchell
□ 1610 Tom Redington
□ 1611 Dave Karasinski
□ 1612 Allan Waznik
□ 1613 Steve Curry CO
□ 1614 Ross Grimsley CO
□ 1615 Jim Saul MGR
□ 1616 Steve Wendell
□ 1617 Chris Czarnik
□ 1618 Brian Cummings
□ 1619 Dave Reis
□ 1620 Don Campbell
□ 1621 Daryl Blanks
□ 1622 Teddy Williams
□ 1623 Kevin Kelly
□ 1624 Rich Longuil
□ 1625 Paul Egins III TR
□ 1626 Skipper Wright
□ 1627 Robert Cole

1989 Burlington Braves Star

The 1989 Burlington Braves set contains 29 standard-size cards. The fronts have posed color player photos, with red borders on the top portion of the card fading to purple as one moves down the card face. In purple print on a pale pink background, the backs have personal information, how the player was obtained, and statistics. Card numbers 26-29 have different color lettering on the fronts than the other cards. The cards are arranged alphabetically and numbered on the back "X of 30." Card number 30 was never issued. 5,000 sets produced.

	MINT	NRMT	EXC
COMPLETE SET (29)	5.00	2.20	.60

□ 1 Tony Baldwin
□ 2 Daryl Blanks
□ 3 Donovan Campbell
□ 4 Greg Cloninger
□ 5 Bob Cole
□ 6 Johnny Cuevas
□ 7 Brian Cummings

☐ 8 Chris Czarnik
☐ 9 Mark Davis
☐ 10 Steve Glass
☐ 11 Dave Karasinski
☐ 12 Kevin Kelly
☐ 13 Jesus Mendoza
☐ 14 Rich Longuil
☐ 15 Keith Mitchell
☐ 16 Bob Pfaff
☐ 17 Thomas Redington
☐ 18 David Reis
☐ 19 Joseph Saccomanno
☐ 20 Gary Schoonover
☐ 21 Lee Upshaw
☐ 22 Preston Watson
☐ 23 Allen Waznik
☐ 24 Steven Wendell
☐ 25 Teddy Williams
☐ 26 Skipper Wright
☐ 27 Jim Saul MGR
☐ 28 Ross Grimsley CO
☐ 29 Steve Curry CO

1989 Burlington Indians Star

The 1989 Burlington Indians set contains 29 standard-size cards. The fronts have posed color player photos, with blue borders on the top portion of the card fading to red as one moves down the card face. In blue print on a pink background, the backs have biography and statistics. 5,000 sets produced.

	MINT	NRMT	EXC
COMPLETE SET (29)	5.00	2.20	.60

☐ 1 Chad Allen
☐ 2 Andy Baker
☐ 3 Stacy Brown
☐ 4 Mark Charbonnet
☐ 5 Chris Cole
☐ 6 John Cotton
☐ 7 Mike Davis
☐ 8 Anthony Dela Cruz
☐ 9 Mark Delpiano
☐ 10 Carey Elston
☐ 11 Mike Gonzalez
☐ 12 Brian Hart
☐ 13 Avery Johnson
☐ 14 Tom Lachmann
☐ 15 Nolan Lane
☐ 16 Jesse Levis
☐ 17 Dean Meddaugh
☐ 18 David Nebraska
☐ 19 Ramon Ortiz
☐ 20 Cecil Pettiford
☐ 21 Clyde Pough
☐ 22 Roberto Rivera
☐ 23 Tommy Tillman
☐ 24 Ramon Torres
☐ 25 Reynaldo Ventura
☐ 26 Olonzo Woodfin
☐ 27 Jim Cabella
☐ 28 Coaching Staff
Mark Oestreich
Stan Hilton
☐ 29 Teddy Blackwell TR

1989 Butte Copper Kings Sports Pro

The 1989 Butte Copper Kings set consists of 30 standard-size cards. The front design has posed color player photos (shot from the waist up), with a thin black border on a white card face. The team logo adorns the card above the picture, and the player's name and position appear at the card bottom. In a horizontal format, the backs provide brief biographical information.

	MINT	NRMT	EXC
COMPLETE SET (30)	6.00	2.70	.75

☐ 1 Stacy Parker
☐ 2 David Perez
☐ 3 Brian Roper
☐ 4 Donald Harris
☐ 5 Eric Bickhardt
☐ 6 Brian Romero
☐ 7 Barry Winford
☐ 8 Brian Crowley
☐ 9 Jose Borges
☐ 10 Steve Rowley
☐ 11 Jim Clinton
☐ 12 Jose Oliva
☐ 13 Joe Eischen
☐ 14 Chris Shiflett
☐ 15 Geoff Flinn
☐ 16 Troy Eklund
☐ 17 Jay Franklin
☐ 18 Brian Steiner
☐ 19 Manny Garcia
☐ 20 Randy Marshall
☐ 21 John Graves
☐ 22 Mark Young
☐ 23 Darrin Hays
☐ 24 Bump Wills MGR
☐ 25 Buddy Micheu
☐ 26 Timmie Morrow
☐ 27 Dan Peltier
☐ 28 Ernie Rodriguez CO
☐ 29 Marvin White CO
☐ 30 Dave Freisleben CO

1989 California League All-Stars Cal League Cards

	MINT	NRMT	EXC
COMPLETE SET (56)	6.00	2.70	.75

☐ 1 Jose Offerman
☐ 2 Eric Karros
☐ 3 Mark Merchant
☐ 4 Willie Banks
☐ 5 Lance Rice
☐ 6 Carlos Capellan
☐ 7 Jose Valentin
☐ 8 David Jacas
☐ 9 Braulio Castillo
☐ 10 Mike Humphreys
☐ 11 Wiley Lee
☐ 12 Ruben Gonzalez
☐ 13 Johnny Ard
☐ 14 Mike Goff
☐ 15 Jeff Hartsock
☐ 16 James Wray
☐ 17 Doug Simons
☐ 18 Jerry Brooks
☐ 19 Eddie Pye
☐ 20 Andy Skeels
☐ 21 Sean Snedeker
☐ 22 Steve Finken
☐ 23 Tim Johnson MGR
☐ 24 Guy Conti CO
☐ 25 Scott Ullger CO
☐ 26 Tim Terrio TR
☐ 27 Bill Weiss
Statistican
☐ 28 Don Drysdale
Host
☐ 29 Charlie Montoyo
☐ 30 Jim Jones
☐ 31 Stan Royer
☐ 32 Bobby Jones
☐ 33 Darren Lewis
☐ 34 Gary Borg
☐ 35 Steve Hecht
☐ 36 Gary Nalls
☐ 37 John Balfanz
☐ 38 Chris George
☐ 39 Mike Ignasiak
☐ 40 Kevin Meier
☐ 41 Joe Strong
☐ 42 Shawn Barton
☐ 43 Mark Dewey
☐ 44 Bill Savarino
☐ 45 John Jaha
☐ 46 Joe Kmak
☐ 47 Steve Lienhard
☐ 48 Greg Sparks
☐ 49 Duane Espy MGR
☐ 50 Todd Oakes CO
☐ 51 Scott Wilson TR
☐ 52 Brent Howard UMP
☐ 53 Erik deSonnaville UMP
☐ 54 Bob Brooks UMP
☐ 55 George Ulrich UMP
☐ 56 Joe Gagliardi PRES

1989 Calgary Cannons CMC

This 25-card standard-size set of the 1989 Calgary Cannons, a Class AAA Pacific Coast League affiliate of the Seattle Mariners, features on its fronts white-bordered posed color player photos framed by a black line. The team's name, the player's name, and his position appear at the bottom. The white back is framed by a black line and carries the team's name and league at the top, followed by the player's name, biography and statistics. Cards 13, 24, and 25 bear incorrect copyright dates, 1988.

	MINT	NRMT	EXC
COMPLETE SET (25)	6.00	2.70	.75

☐ 1 Luis DeLeon
☐ 2 Chuck Hensley
☐ 3 Colin McLaughlin
☐ 4 Steve Oliverio
☐ 5 Reggie Dobie
☐ 6 Bill Wilkinson
☐ 7 Rich Doyle
☐ 8 Jeff Hull
☐ 9 Bryan Price
☐ 10 Glenn Spagnola
☐ 11 Clint Zavaras
☐ 12 Dan Boever
☐ 13 Jay Buhner
☐ 14 Dave Cochrane
☐ 15 Roger Hansen
☐ 16 Paul Noce
☐ 17 Jim Bowie
☐ 18 Joe Dunlap
☐ 19 Bruce Fields
☐ 20 Mike Kingery
☐ 21 Bill McGuire
☐ 22 Jim Wilson
☐ 23 Omar Vizquel
☐ 24 Rich Morales MG
☐ 25 Dan Warthen CO

1989 Calgary Cannons ProCards

This 24-card standard-size set of the 1989 Calgary Cannons, a Class AAA Pacific Coast League affiliate of the Seattle Mariners, features blue-bordered posed color player photos on its fronts. The player's name, position, and team name appear at the bottom. The horizontal gray back carries the player's name at the top, followed by biography and statistics.

	MINT	NRMT	EXC
COMPLETE SET (24)	8.00	3.60	1.00

☐ 522 Checklist
☐ 523 Dan Warthen CO
☐ 524 Greg Fulton
☐ 525 Jim Bowie
☐ 526 Jeff Hull
☐ 527 Glenn Spagnola
☐ 528 Reggie Dobie
☐ 529 Joe Dunlap
☐ 530 Roger Hansen
☐ 531 Chuck Hensley
☐ 532 Colin McLaughlin
☐ 533 Bill McGuire
☐ 534 Bruce Fields
☐ 535 Dan Boever
☐ 536 Jim Wilson
☐ 537 Omar Vizquel
☐ 538 Rich Morales MG
☐ 539 Paul Noce
☐ 540 Bryan Price
☐ 541 Rich Doyle
☐ 542 Dave Cochrane
☐ 543 Steve Oliverio
☐ 544 Jay Buhner
☐ 545 Mike Kingery

1989 Canton-Akron Indians Best

The 1989 Canton Indians set contains 28 standard-size cards. The fronts have posed color player photos with white borders. The year '1989' and the city are written vertically on the left side of the card, and the player's name and position are given below the picture. In a horizontal format, the backs have biography, recent professional baseball performance statistics, and a color headshot, all in a yellow rectangular box.

	MINT	NRMT	EXC
COMPLETE SET (28)	5.00	2.20	.60

☐ 1 Kevin Bearse
☐ 2 Julius McDougal
☐ 3 Jeff Shaw
☐ 4 Beau Allred
☐ 5 Casey Webster
☐ 6 Efrain Valdez
☐ 7 Dan Boever
☐ 8 William Williams CO
☐ 9 Dan Redmond TR
☐ 10 Tom Magrann
☐ 11 Eric Rasmussen CO
☐ 12 Michael Twardoski
☐ 13 Mark Gilles
☐ 14 Gregory Ferlenda
☐ 15 Lindsay Foster
☐ 16 Todd Gonzales
☐ 17 Bob Molinaro MGR
☐ 18 Carl Keliipuleole
☐ 19 Scott Khoury
☐ 20 Paul Kuzniar
☐ 21 Allen Liebert
☐ 22 Jose Leiva
☐ 23 Everado Magallanes
☐ 24 Gregory McMichael
☐ 25 Troy Neel
☐ 26 Robert Swain
☐ 27 Charles Ogden
☐ 28 Team logo
Checklist

1989 Canton-Akron Indians ProCards

This 28-card standard-size set of the 1989 Canton-Akron Indians, a Class AA Eastern League affiliate of the Cleveland Indians, features red-bordered posed color player photos on its fronts. The player's name, position, and team name appear at the bottom. The horizontal gray back carries the player's name and position at the top, followed by biography and statistics. .

	MINT	NRMT	EXC
COMPLETE SET (28)	5.00	2.20	.60

☐ 1297 Checklist
☐ 1298 Jeff Shaw
☐ 1299 Mike Twardoski
☐ 1300 Carl Keliipuleole
☐ 1302 Beau Allred
☐ 1303 Rob Swain
☐ 1304 Lindsay Foster
☐ 1305 Paul Kuzniar
☐ 1306 Kevin Bearse
☐ 1307 Sam Ferretti
☐ 1308 Eric Rasmussen CO
☐ 1309 Everardo Magallanes
☐ 1310 Scott Khoury
☐ 1311 Efrain Valdez
☐ 1312 Jose Leiva
☐ 1313 Tom Magrann
☐ 1314 Allen Liebert
☐ 1315 Greg McMichael
☐ 1316 Jeff Edwards
☐ 1317 Billy Williams CO
☐ 1318 Casey Webster
☐ 1319 Bob Molinaro MGR
☐ 1320 Todd Gonzales
☐ 1321 Julius McDougal
☐ 1322 Todd Ogden
☐ 1323 Mark Gilles
☐ 1324 Troy Neel
☐ 1325 Dan Boever

1989 Canton-Akron Indians Star

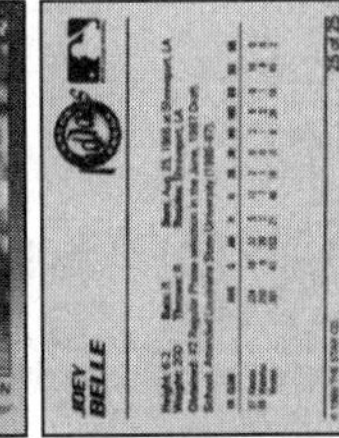

The 1989 Canton-Akron Indians set contains 25 standard-size cards. The fronts have posed color player photos, with purple borders on the top portion of the card fading to yellow as one moves down the card face. In purple print on a pale yellow background, the backs have biography and statistics. 5,000 sets produced. This issue includes a second year card of Albert 'Joey' Belle.

	MINT	NRMT	EXC
COMPLETE SET (25)	35.00	16.00	4.40

☐ 1 Beau Allred
☐ 2 Coaching Staff
Bob Molinaro MGR
Eric Rasmussen CO
Billy Williams CO
☐ 3 Dan Boever
☐ 4 Jeff Edwards
☐ 5 Greg Ferlenda
☐ 6 Lindsay Foster
☐ 7 Mark Gilles
☐ 8 Todd Gonzales
☐ 9 Carl Keliipuleole
☐ 10 Scott Khoury
☐ 11 Paul Kuzniar
☐ 12 Allen Liebert
☐ 13 Everardo Magallanes
☐ 14 Tom Magrann
☐ 15 Julius McDougal
☐ 16 Greg McMichael
☐ 17 Troy Neel
☐ 18 Todd Ogden
☐ 19 Jeff Shaw
☐ 20 Rob Swain
☐ 21 Mike Twardoski
☐ 22 Efrain Valdez
☐ 23 Casey Webster
☐ 24 Jose Leiva
☐ 25 Joey Belle

1989 Carson Newman Eagles

Sponsored by Havoline Motor Oil, this 27-card standard-size set features the 1989 Carson Newman Eagles. The cards measure the standard size. On a light blue card face, the fronts feature color action player photos with thin black borders. The player's name, number, position and the team logo appear below the photo. On a light blue background, the horizontal backs carry player biography and statistics.

	MINT	NRMT	EXC
COMPLETE SET (27)	10.00	4.50	1.25

☐ 1 Wesley Nokes
☐ 2 Steve Marshall
☐ 3 Brian Dean
☐ 4 Kevin Roach
☐ 5 Wayne Cabbage
☐ 6 Lee French
☐ 7 Jeff Taylor
☐ 8 Jay Howell
☐ 9 Joe Simpson
☐ 10 Rusty Bryan
☐ 11 Ryan Henry
☐ 12 Chad Silver

- ☐ 13 Brian Jevyak
- ☐ 14 Tony Patterson
- ☐ 15 Pete Lago
- ☐ 16 Greg Bishop
- ☐ 17 John Lee
- ☐ 18 Bob Badacour
- ☐ 19 Angel Segura
- ☐ 20 Tim Adams
- ☐ 21 Gary Rundles CO
- ☐ 22 Marty McDaniel ACO
- ☐ 23 Robbie Black
- ☐ 24 Freshmen
  Pitchers and Catchers
  Kirk Hembree
  Bryan Johnson
  Stacy Morrison
  Brian Overbay
  Barry Cesarz
  Bill Crawford
  Ryan Baker
- ☐ 25 Freshmen
  Infielders and Outfielders
  Jay Kynerd
  John Holland
  Fred Carr
  Cyrus Waters
  James Jeluso
  Steve Garland
- ☐ 26 Sports Promotion Office
  David W. Barger
  Steve Cotton
  Randy Winton
- ☐ NNO Team Photo
  (Havoline Motor Oil)

1989 Cedar Rapids Reds Best

The 1989 Cedar Rapids Reds set contains 30 standard-size cards. The fronts have posed color player photos with white borders. The year "1989" and the city are written vertically on the left side of the card, and the player's name and position are given below the picture. In a horizontal format, the backs have biography, recent professional baseball performance summary (including statistics), and a color headshot, all in a yellow rectangular box.

	MINT	NRMT	EXC
COMPLETE SET (30)	5.00	2.20	.60

- ☐ 1 Jeffery Branson
- ☐ 2 Stephen Foster
- ☐ 3 Scott Jeffery
- ☐ 4 Quinn Marsh
- ☐ 5 Michael Myers
- ☐ 6 William Risley
- ☐ 7 Joseph Turek
- ☐ 8 Joseph Vierra
- ☐ 9 Scott Economy
- ☐ 10 Steve McCarthy
- ☐ 11 Duane Mulville
- ☐ 12 Eddie Taubensee
- ☐ 13 Andy Rickman
- ☐ 14 Adam Casillas
- ☐ 15 Kennedy Infante
- ☐ 16 Chris Schnurbusch
- ☐ 17 Scott Sellner
- ☐ 18 Norman Brock
- ☐ 19 Benny Colvard
- ☐ 20 Douglas Eastman
- ☐ 21 Anthony Mealy
- ☐ 22 Dave Miley MGR
- ☐ 23 Gerry Groninger CO
- ☐ 24 Don Buchheister GM
- ☐ 25 Thomas Spencer TR
- ☐ 26 Larry Rothchild
  Pitching Instructor
- ☐ 27 Tony Vasquez
  Clubhouse Attendant
- ☐ 28 Chris Lombardozzi
- ☐ 29 Steve Hester
- ☐ 30 Team logo
  Checklist

1989 Cedar Rapids Reds ProCards

This 29-card standard-size set of the 1989 Cedar Rapids Reds, a Class A Midwest League affiliate of the Cincinnati Reds, features orange-bordered posed color player photos on its fronts. The player's name, position, and team name appear at the bottom. The horizontal gray back carries the player's name and position at the top, followed by biography and statistics.

	MINT	NRMT	EXC
COMPLETE SET (29)	5.00	2.20	.60

- ☐ 910 Checklist
- ☐ 911 Mike Malinak
- ☐ 912 Bill Risley
- ☐ 913 Scott Jeffery
- ☐ 914 Steve McCarthy
- ☐ 915 Joey Vierra
- ☐ 916 Benny Colvard
- ☐ 917 Tom Spencer TR
- ☐ 918 Mike Myers
- ☐ 919 Steve Hester
- ☐ 920 Joe Turek
- ☐ 921 Scott Economy
- ☐ 922 Adam Casillas
- ☐ 923 Doug Eastman
- ☐ 924 Duane Mulville
- ☐ 925 Scott Sellner
- ☐ 926 Tony Mealy
- ☐ 927 Dave Miley MGR
- ☐ 928 Jeff Branson
- ☐ 929 Quinn Marsh
- ☐ 930 Gerry Groninger CO
- ☐ 931 Don Buchheister GM
- ☐ 932 Andy Rickman
- ☐ 933 Larry Rothschild
  Pitching Instructor
- ☐ 934 Chris Schnurbusch
- ☐ 935 Chirs Lombardozzi
- ☐ 936 Steve Foster
- ☐ 937 Eddie Taubensee
- ☐ 938 Norm Brock

1989 Cedar Rapids Reds Star

The 1989 Cedar Rapids Reds set contains 30 standard-size cards. The fronts have posed color player photos, with red borders on the top portion of the card fading to yellow as one moves down the card face. In red print on a pale yellow background, the backs have biography and statistics. 5,000 sets produced.

	MINT	NRMT	EXC
COMPLETE SET (30)	5.00	2.20	.60

- ☐ 1 Jeff Branson
- ☐ 2 Norm Brock
- ☐ 3 Adam Casillas
- ☐ 4 Benny Colvard
- ☐ 5 Doug Eastman
- ☐ 6 Scott Economy
- ☐ 7 Steve Foster
- ☐ 8 Steve Hester
- ☐ 9 Scott Jeffery
- ☐ 10 Quinn Marsh
- ☐ 11 Steve McCarthy
- ☐ 12 Tony Mealy
- ☐ 13 Duane Mulville
- ☐ 14 Mike Myers
- ☐ 15 Andy Rickman
- ☐ 16 Bill Risley
- ☐ 17 Chris Schnurbusch
- ☐ 18 Scott Sellner
- ☐ 19 Eddie Taubensee
- ☐ 20 Joe Turek
- ☐ 21 Joey Vierra
- ☐ 22 Dave Miley MGR
- ☐ 23 Gerry Groninger CO
- ☐ 24 Tom Spencer TR
- ☐ 25 Pete Beeler
- ☐ 26 Don Brown
- ☐ 27 Steve Hester
- ☐ 28 Kennedy Infante
- ☐ 29 Mike Malinak
- ☐ 30 Ross Powell

1989 Charleston Rainbows ProCards

This 28-card standard-size set of the 1989 Charleston Rainbows, a Class A South Atlantic League affiliate of the San Diego Padres, features orange-bordered posed color player photos on its fronts. The player's name, position, and team name appear at the bottom. The horizontal gray back carries the player's name and position at the top, followed by biography and statistics.

	MINT	NRMT	EXC
COMPLETE SET (28)	5.00	2.20	.60

- ☐ 969 Checklist
- ☐ 970 Team Picture
- ☐ 971 A.J. Sager
- ☐ 972 Vance Tucker
- ☐ 973 Bob Brucato
- ☐ 974 Greg Conley
- ☐ 975 Brian Span
- ☐ 976 Vince Harris
- ☐ 977 Stan Tukes
- ☐ 978 Ron Oglesby CO
- ☐ 979 Greg Smith
- ☐ 980 Gerard Cirfarelli
- ☐ 981 Chris Haslock
- ☐ 982 Joe Murdock
- ☐ 983 Bryce Florie
- ☐ 984 Luis Lopez
- ☐ 985 Matt Witkowski
- ☐ 986 John Kuehl
- ☐ 987 Jeff Hart
- ☐ 988 Scot Welish
- ☐ 989 Jimmy Lester
- ☐ 990 Mark Verstandig
- ☐ 991 Jack Krol MGR
- ☐ 992 Pedro Martinez
- ☐ 993 David Bond
- ☐ 994 Dave Briggs
- ☐ 995 Nicko Riesgo
- ☐ 996 Renay Bryand

1989 Charleston Wheelers Best

This 27-card standard-size set features the 1989 Charleston Wheelers, a farm club for the Chicago Cubs. The fronts have posed color player photos with white borders. The year "1989" and the city are written vertically on the left side of the card, and the player's name and position are given below the picture. In a horizontal format, the backs have biography, recent professional baseball performance summary (including statistics), and a color headshot, all in a yellow rectangular box.

	MINT	NRMT	EXC
COMPLETE SET (27)	5.00	2.20	.60

- ☐ 1 Wayne Weinheimer
- ☐ 2 Eric Williams
- ☐ 3 Miliciades Uribe
- ☐ 4 Kraig Washington
- ☐ 5 Scott Taylor
- ☐ 6 William St. Peter
- ☐ 7 Kevin Roberson
- ☐ 8 Jossy Rosario
- ☐ 9 Mathew Leonard
- ☐ 10 James Murphy
- ☐ 11 Matthew Franco
- ☐ 12 Luis Benitez
- ☐ 13 Herberto Andrade
- ☐ 14 Anthony Whitson
- ☐ 15 Roberto Smalls
- ☐ 16 Sean Reed
- ☐ 17 Ronnie Rasp
- ☐ 18 David Goodwin
- ☐ 19 John Gardner
- ☐ 20 Jason Doss
- ☐ 21 Jay Eddings
- ☐ 22 Matthew Cakora
- ☐ 23 Frank Campos
- ☐ 24 William Earley CO
- ☐ 25 Greg Mahlberg MGR
- ☐ 26 Jim O'Reilly TR
- ☐ 27 Watt Powell Park
  Checklist

1989 Charleston Wheelers ProCards

This 28-card standard-size set of the 1989 Charleston Wheelers, a Class A South Atlantic League affiliate of the Chicago Cubs, features orange-bordered posed color player photos on its fronts. The player's name, position, and team name appear at the bottom. The horizontal gray back carries the player's name and position at the top, followed by biography and statistics.

	MINT	NRMT	EXC
COMPLETE SET (28)	5.00	2.20	.60

- ☐ 1743 Checklist
- ☐ 1744 Miliciades Uribe
- ☐ 1745 James Murphy
- ☐ 1746 Jim O'Reilly TR
- ☐ 1747 Kevin Roberson
- ☐ 1748 Matt Franco
- ☐ 1749 Luis Benitez
- ☐ 1750 Jossy Rosario
- ☐ 1751 Wayne Weinheimer
- ☐ 1752 Kraig Washington
- ☐ 1753 Bill St.Peter
- ☐ 1754 Bill Earley CO
- ☐ 1755 Greg Mahlberg MGR
- ☐ 1756 Eric Williams
- ☐ 1757 Scott Taylor
- ☐ 1758 Mathew Leonard
- ☐ 1759 Herberto Andrade
- ☐ 1760 Christopher Lutz
- ☐ 1761 Roberto Smalls
- ☐ 1762 Sean Reed
- ☐ 1763 Tony Whitson
- ☐ 1764 Ronnie Rasp
- ☐ 1765 Jason Doss
- ☐ 1766 Jay Eddings
- ☐ 1767 Frank Campos
- ☐ 1768 David Goodwin
- ☐ 1769 John Gardner
- ☐ 1770 Matt Cakora

1989 Charlotte Knights Team Issue

The 1989 Charlotte Knights set consists of 25 standard-size cards. The glossy color player photos are trimmed in black and have the player's name in a salmon-colored banner across the top of the picture. The team logo is superimposed at the lower right corner. In a horizontal format, the backs present biography and statistics.

	MINT	NRMT	EXC
COMPLETE SET (25)	6.00	2.70	.75

- ☐ 1 Laddie Renfroe
- ☐ 2 Jim Essian MGR
- ☐ 3 Grant Jackson CO
- ☐ 4 Ced Landrum
- ☐ 5 Derrick May
- ☐ 6 Jim Bullinger
- ☐ 7 Butch Garcia
- ☐ 8 Luis Cruz
- ☐ 9 Kelly Mann
- ☐ 10 Glenn Sullivan
- ☐ 11 Greg Smith
- ☐ 12 Erik Pappas
- ☐ 13 David Rosario
- ☐ 14 Ty Griffin
- ☐ 15 Tom Michno
- ☐ 16 Greg Kallevig
- ☐ 17 Shawn Boskie
- ☐ 18 Jeff Hirsch
- ☐ 19 Jackie Davidson
- ☐ 20 Matt Cakora
- ☐ 21 Phil Harrison
- ☐ 22 Bob Bafia
- ☐ 23 Brian McCann TR
- ☐ 24 Orsino Hill
- ☐ 25 Pablo Rivera

1989 Charlotte Rangers Star

The 1989 Charlotte Rangers set contains 28 standard-size cards. The fronts have posed color player photos, with blue borders on the top portion of the card fading to red as one moves down the card face. In blue print on a pink background, the backs have biography and statistics. The card numbers were inadvertently omitted from cards 10, 11, and 15. 5,000 sets produced.

	MINT	NRMT	EXC
COMPLETE SET (28)	7.00	3.10	.85

- ☐ 1 Wilson Alvarez
- ☐ 2 Rick Bernardo
- ☐ 3 Mick Billmeyer
- ☐ 4 Paco Burgos
- ☐ 5 Joel Cartaya
- ☐ 6 Felipe Castillo
- ☐ 7 Brian Evans
- ☐ 8 Pat Garman
- ☐ 9 Stephan Glasker
- ☐ 10 Jonathon Hurst
- ☐ 11 Rob Lavender
- ☐ 12 Travis Law
- ☐ 13 Bruce Lipscomb
- ☐ 14 Bill Losa
- ☐ 15 Rob Maurer
- ☐ 16 Rod Morris
- ☐ 17 Scott Morse
- ☐ 18 Ed Ohman
- ☐ 19 Roger Pavlik
- ☐ 20 Wayne Rosenthal
- ☐ 21 Luke Sable
- ☐ 22 Cedric Shaw
- ☐ 23 Jeff Shore
- ☐ 24 John Sipple
- ☐ 25 Mike Taylor
- ☐ 26 Bobby Jones MGR
- ☐ 27 Rusty Gerhardt CO
- ☐ 28 Jeff Hubbard CO

1989 Chattanooga Lookouts Best

This 26-card standard-size set features the 1989 Chattanooga Lookouts, a farm club for the Cincinnati Reds. The fronts have posed color player photos with white borders. The year "1989" and the city are written vertically on the left side of the card, and the player's name and position are given below the picture. In a horizontal format, the backs have biography, recent professional baseball performance summary (including statistics), and a color headshot, all in a yellow rectangular box.

	MINT	NRMT	EXC
COMPLETE SET (26)	5.00	2.20	.60

- ☐ 1 Reggie Jefferson
- ☐ 2 Keith Kaiser
- ☐ 3 Tony DeFrancesco
- ☐ 4 Brian Lane
- ☐ 5 Joe Lazor
- ☐ 6 Milton Hill
- ☐ 7 Jim Tracy MGR
- ☐ 8 Rich Bombard CO
- ☐ 9 Butch Henry
- ☐ 10 Terry Lee
- ☐ 11 Pete Beeler
- ☐ 12 Alfredo Benavides
- ☐ 13 Timber Mead
- ☐ 14 Bill Dodd
- ☐ 15 Darrell Rodgers
- ☐ 16 Greg Lonigro
- ☐ 17 Chris Lombardozzi
- ☐ 18 Kevin Pearson
- ☐ 19 Mike Moscrey
- ☐ 20 Bernie Walker
- ☐ 21 Joe Bruno
- ☐ 22 Don Brown
- ☐ 23 Jerome Nelson
- ☐ 24 Sandy Krum TR
- ☐ 25 Alan Hayden
- ☐ 26 Team logo
  Checklist

1989 Chattanooga Lookouts Grand Slam

	MINT	NRMT	EXC
COMPLETE SET (25)	5.00	2.20	.60

- ☐ 1 Jim Tracy MGR
- ☐ 2 Rich Bombard CO
- ☐ 3 Sandy Krum TR
- ☐ 4 Pete Beeler
- ☐ 5 Fred Benavides
- ☐ 6 Don Brown
- ☐ 7 Joe Bruno
- ☐ 8 Tony DeFrancesco
- ☐ 9 Bill Dodd
- ☐ 10 Milton Hill
- ☐ 11 Butch Henry
- ☐ 12 Reggie Jefferson
- ☐ 13 Keith Kaiser
- ☐ 14 Brian Lane
- ☐ 15 Joe Lazor
- ☐ 16 Terry Lee
- ☐ 17 Greg Lonigro
- ☐ 18 Mike Loscrey
- ☐ 19 Jerome Nelson
- ☐ 20 Kevin Pearson
- ☐ 21 Darrell Rodgers
- ☐ 22 Bernie Walker
- ☐ 23 Alan Hayden
- ☐ 24 Timber Mead
- ☐ 25 Chris Lombardozzi

1989 Chattanooga Lookouts Legends II Team Issue

This 33-card standard-size set features outstanding players who later went on to play in the Majors. The fronts have black and white mugshots, with red borders on a white card face. The words "Lookouts Legends II" and the Coke logo adorn the top of the front. The horizontally oriented backs present career summaries. The unnumbered checklist card has a photo of the Chatanooga Regional History Museum.

	MINT	NRMT	EXC
COMPLETE SET (33)	12.00	5.50	1.50

- ☐ 1 Ted Abernathy
- ☐ 2 Bob Allison
- ☐ 3 John Boozer
- ☐ 4 Jimmy Bragan MGR
- ☐ 5 Mickey Brantley
- ☐ 6 Keith Brown
- ☐ 7 Bob Costas ANN
- ☐ 8 Alvin Davis
- ☐ 9 Kid Elberfeld
- ☐ 10 Dave Gallagher
- ☐ 11 Erik Hanson
- ☐ 12 Dave Hengel
- ☐ 13 Grant Jackson
- ☐ 14 Ferguson Jenkins
- ☐ 15 Bill Lee GM
- ☐ 16 Charlie Letchas
- ☐ 17 Robert Long
- ☐ 18 Jim Morgan
- ☐ 19 Jeff Moronko
- ☐ 20 Al Neiger
- ☐ 21 Sammy Strang Nicklin Manager
- ☐ 22 Bob Oldis
- ☐ 23 Ernie Oravetz
- ☐ 24 Jim Presley
- ☐ 25 Tom Runnells MGR
- ☐ 26 Frank Sacka
- ☐ 27 Mike Schooler
- ☐ 28 Brick Smith
- ☐ 29 Danny Tartabull
- ☐ 30 Dave Valle
- ☐ 31 Hedi Vargas
- ☐ 32 Denny Walling
- ☐ NNO Checklist

1989 Clearwater Phillies Star

The 1989 Clearwater Phillies set contains 26 standard-size cards. The fronts have posed color player photos, with red borders on the top portion of the card fading to gray as one moves down the card face. In red print on a gray background, the backs have biography and statistics. The unnumbered Royal Thomas card was a late production; it has a different photo and a white background on the back. 5,000 sets produced.

	MINT	NRMT	EXC
COMPLETE SET (26)	5.00	2.20	.60

- ☐ 1 Jaime Barragan
- ☐ 2 Kim Batiste
- ☐ 3 Kendrick Bourne
- ☐ 4 Jim Carroll
- ☐ 5 Andy Carter
- ☐ 6 Fred Christopher
- ☐ 7 Mark Cobb
- ☐ 8 Pat Combs
- ☐ 9 Kevin Fynan
- ☐ 10 Jeff Grotewold
- ☐ 11 Dave Holdridge
- ☐ 12 Steve Kirkpatrick
- ☐ 13 Lee Langley
- ☐ 14 Tim Mauser
- ☐ 15 Trey McCall
- ☐ 16 Shelby McDonald
- ☐ 17 Matt Rambo
- ☐ 18 Scott Reaves
- ☐ 19 Rod Robertson
- ☐ 20 Mark Sims
- ☐ 21 Royal Thomas
- ☐ 22 Tony Trevino
- ☐ 23 Jim Vatcher
- ☐ 24 Chris Walker
- ☐ 25 Carlos Zayas
- ☐ NNO Royal Thomas

1989 Clinton Giants ProCards

This 31-card standard-size set of the 1989 Clinton Giants, a Class A Midwest League affiliate of the San Francisco Giants, features orange-bordered posed color player photos on its fronts. The player's name, position, and team name appear at the bottom. The horizontal gray back carries the player's name and position at the top, followed by biography and statistics.

	MINT	NRMT	EXC
COMPLETE SET (31)	7.00	3.10	.85

- ☐ 879 Checklist
- ☐ 880 Dave Bohnenkamp GM
- ☐ 881 Kevin Temperly GM
- ☐ 882 Adell Davenport
- ☐ 883 Adam Hilpert
- ☐ 884 Marino Hernandez
- ☐ 885 Chris Fye
- ☐ 886 Jimmy Myers
- ☐ 887 Gary Sharko
- ☐ 888 Kevin Breitenbucher
- ☐ 889 Shane Borchert TR
- ☐ 890 Chris Hancock
- ☐ 891 Kevin Rogers
- ☐ 892 Jeffry Bonner
- ☐ 893 Reggie Williams
- ☐ 894 Reuben Smiley
- ☐ 895 Royce Clayton
- ☐ 896 Robbie Kemper
- ☐ 897 Scooter Tucker
- ☐ 898 Keith Bodie MGR
- ☐ 899 Steve Gray
- ☐ 900 Julio Fernandez
- ☐ 901 Jeff Morris CO
- ☐ 902 Shannon Coppell
- ☐ 903 Carl Hanselman
- ☐ 904 Dominick Johnson
- ☐ 905 Domingo Delarosa
- ☐ 906 Steve Reed
- ☐ 907 Bill Gibbons
- ☐ 908 Steve Pratt
- ☐ 909 Dave Slavin

1989 Colorado Springs Sky Sox CMC

	MINT	NRMT	EXC
COMPLETE SET (25)	5.00	2.20	.60

- ☐ 1 Steve Davis
- ☐ 2 Don Gordon
- ☐ 3 Jeff Kaiser
- ☐ 4 Ed Wojna
- ☐ 5 Kevin Wickander
- ☐ 6 Neil Allen
- ☐ 7 Joel Davis
- ☐ 8 Charles Scott
- ☐ 9 Joe Skalski
- ☐ 10 Mike Hargrove
- ☐ 11 Ron Tingley
- ☐ 12 Pete Dalena
- ☐ 13 Brian Giles
- ☐ 14 Denny Gonzalez
- ☐ 15 Mark Higgins
- ☐ 16 Tommy Hinzo
- ☐ 17 Paul Zuvella
- ☐ 18 Dave Hengel
- ☐ 19 Dwight Taylor
- ☐ 20 Mark Salas
- ☐ 21 Danny Sheaffer
- ☐ 22 Ty Gainey
- ☐ 23 Rick Adair CO
- ☐ 24 Rich Dauer CO
- ☐ 25 Steve Ciczczon TR

1989 Colorado Springs Sky Sox ProCards

This 28-card standard-size set of the 1989 Colorado Springs Sky Sox, a Class AAA Pacific Coast League affiliate of the Cleveland Indians, features blue-bordered posed color player photos on its fronts. The player's name, position, and team name appear at the bottom. The horizontal gray back carries the player's name and position at the top, followed by biography and statistics.

	MINT	NRMT	EXC
COMPLETE SET (28)	5.00	2.20	.60

- ☐ 233 Checklist
- ☐ 234 Dwight Taylor
- ☐ 235 Pete Delena
- ☐ 236 Ed Wojna
- ☐ 237 Joel Davis
- ☐ 238 Kevin Wickander
- ☐ 239 Mike Walker
- ☐ 240 Mark Salas
- ☐ 241 Danny Sheaffer
- ☐ 242 Rich Dauer CO
- ☐ 243 Dave Hengel
- ☐ 244 Stan Hilton
- ☐ 245 Paul Zuvella
- ☐ 246 Mike Hargrove MGR
- ☐ 247 Rick Adair CO
- ☐ 248 Denny Gonzelez
- ☐ 249 Steve Davis
- ☐ 250 Steve Ciszczon TR
- ☐ 251 Mike Young
- ☐ 252 Steve Olin
- ☐ 253 Brian Giles
- ☐ 254 Tom Lampkin
- ☐ 255 Mark Higgins
- ☐ 256 Tommy Hinzo
- ☐ 257 Ton Tingley
- ☐ 258 Ty Gainey
- ☐ 259 Theo Shaw
- ☐ 260 Don Gordon

1989 Columbia Mets Best

The 1989 Columbia Mets set contains 30 standard-size cards. The fronts have posed color player photos with white borders. The year "1989" and the city are written vertically on the left side of the card, and the player's name and position are given below the picture. In a horizontal format, the backs have biography, recent professional baseball performance summary (including statistics), and a color headshot, all in a yellow rectangular box. This issue includes a third year card of Todd Hundley.

	MINT	NRMT	EXC
COMPLETE SET (30)	25.00	11.00	3.10

- ☐ 1 Todd Hundley
- ☐ 2 Vladimir Perez
- ☐ 3 Derrick Young
- ☐ 4 Rob Lemle
- ☐ 5 Archie Corbin
- ☐ 6 Dan Furmanik
- ☐ 7 Bob Olah
- ☐ 8 Dave Joiner
- ☐ 9 Michael Noelke
- ☐ 10 Lee May Jr.
- ☐ 11 Eric Hillman
- ☐ 12 Kevin Baez
- ☐ 13 Chris Hill
- ☐ 14 Pete Schourek
- ☐ 15 Jim Morrisette
- ☐ 16 Anthony Young
- ☐ 17 John Wenrick
- ☐ 18 Steve Newton
- ☐ 19 Andy Reich
- ☐ 20 Doug Saunders
- ☐ 21 Radhames Polanco
- ☐ 22 Bill Stein MGR
- ☐ 23 Jack Fisher CO
- ☐ 24 Pat Hyman Director of Broadcasting
- ☐ 25 Rich Bomgardner TR
- ☐ 26 Frank Harris
- ☐ 27 Lonnie Walker
- ☐ 28 Kevin Maloney Asst GM
- ☐ 29 Al Jimenez
- ☐ 30 Team logo Checklist

1989 Columbia Mets Grand Slam

The 1989 Columbia Mets set contains 29 cards measuring the standard size. This issue includes a third year card of Todd Hundley.

	MINT	NRMT	EXC
COMPLETE SET (29)	16.00	7.25	2.00

- ☐ 1 Bill Stein MGR
- ☐ 2 Jack Fisher CO
- ☐ 3 Rich Bomgardner TR
- ☐ 4 Skip Weisman GM
- ☐ 5 Kevin Maloney Asst GM
- ☐ 6 Kevin Baez
- ☐ 7 Archie Corbin
- ☐ 8 Dan Furmanik
- ☐ 9 Chris Hill
- ☐ 10 Eric Hillman
- ☐ 11 Todd Hundley
- ☐ 12 Alex Jimenez
- ☐ 13 Dave Joiner
- ☐ 14 Rob Lemle
- ☐ 15 Lee May Jr.
- ☐ 16 James Morrisette
- ☐ 17 Steve Newton
- ☐ 18 Mike Noelke
- ☐ 19 Bob Olah
- ☐ 20 Vladimir Perez
- ☐ 21 Radhames Polanco
- ☐ 22 Andy Reich
- ☐ 23 Doug Saunders
- ☐ 24 Pete Schourek
- ☐ 25 Julian Vasquez
- ☐ 26 Lonnie Walker
- ☐ 27 John Wenrick
- ☐ 28 Anthony Young
- ☐ 29 Derrick Young

1989 Columbus Clippers CMC

This 30-card standard-size set of the 1989 Columbus Clippers, a Class AAA International League affiliate of the New York Yankees, features a third year card of Bernie Williams.

	MINT	NRMT	EXC
COMPLETE SET (30)	8.00	3.60	1.00

- ☐ 1 Bill Fulton
- ☐ 2 Scott Nielsen
- ☐ 3 Dickie Noles
- ☐ 4 Clay Parker
- ☐ 5 Hipolito Pena
- ☐ 6 Don Schulze
- ☐ 7 Chuck Cary
- ☐ 8 Dave Eiland
- ☐ 9 Jimmy Jones
- ☐ 10 Balvino Galvez
- ☐ 11 Bob Geren
- ☐ 12 Mike Woodard
- ☐ 13 Randy Velarde
- ☐ 14 Brian Dorsett
- ☐ 15 Steve Kiefer
- ☐ 16 Hal Morris
- ☐ 17 Kevin Maas
- ☐ 18 John Fishel
- ☐ 19 Darrell Miller
- ☐ 20 Bob Green
- ☐ 21 Bernie Williams
- ☐ 22 Mark Wasinger
- ☐ 23 Dick Grapenthin
- ☐ 24 Coaches
  Ken Rowe
  Champ Summers
  Gary Tuck
  Mike Heifferon
- ☐ 25 Bucky Dent MGR
- ☐ 26 Dave Sax
- ☐ 27 Dave Griffin
- ☐ 28 Stanley Jefferson
- ☐ 29 Mark Leiter
- ☐ 30 Darrin Chapin

1989 Columbus Clippers Police

This 25-card standard-size set of the 1989 Columbus Clippers, a Class AAA International League affiliate of the New York Yankees, features a third year card of Bernie Williams.

	MINT	NRMT	EXC
COMPLETE SET (25)	6.00	2.70	.75

- ☐ 1 Chuck Cary
- ☐ 2 Dave Eiland
- ☐ 3 Bill Fulton
- ☐ 4 Balvino Galvez
- ☐ 5 Dick Grapenthin
- ☐ 6 Jimmy Jones
- ☐ 7 Scott Nielsen
- ☐ 8 Dickie Noles
- ☐ 9 Clay Parker
- ☐ 10 Hipolito Pena
- ☐ 11 Don Schulze
- ☐ 12 Brian Dorsett
- ☐ 13 Bob Geren
- ☐ 14 Darrell Miller
- ☐ 15 Steve Kiefer
- ☐ 16 Hal Morris
- ☐ 17 Randy Velarde
- ☐ 18 Mark Wasinger
- ☐ 19 Mike Woodard
- ☐ 20 John Fishel
- ☐ 21 Bobby Green
- ☐ 22 Kevin Maas
- ☐ 23 Bernie Williams
- ☐ 24 Coaches
  Ken Rowe
  Champ Summers

Mike Heifferon
Gary Tuck
☐ 25 Managers
George Sisler
Bucky Dent

1989 Columbus Clippers ProCards

This 28-card standard-size set of the 1989 Columbus Clippers, a Class AAA International League affiliate of the New York Yankees, features blue-bordered posed color player photos on its fronts. The player's name, position, and team name appear at the bottom. The horizontal gray back carries the player's name and position at the top, followed by biography and statistics.

	MINT	NRMT	EXC
COMPLETE SET (28)	10.00	4.50	1.25

☐ 732 Checklist
☐ 733 Darrell Miller
☐ 734 Bobby Green
☐ 735 John Fishel
☐ 736 Bernie Williams
☐ 737 Kevin Maas
☐ 738 Mark Wasinger
☐ 739 Chris Alvarez
☐ 740 Steve Keifer
☐ 741 Randy Velarde
☐ 742 Mike Woodard
☐ 743 Hal Morris
☐ 744 Hipolito Pena
☐ 745 Chuck Cary
☐ 746 Bill Fulton
☐ 747 Dick Grapenthin
☐ 748 Balvino Galvez
☐ 749 Dickie Noles
☐ 750 Dave Eiland
☐ 751 Clay Parker
☐ 752 Jimmy Jones
☐ 753 Don Schulze
☐ 754 Scott Nielsen
☐ 755 Field Staff
Bucky Dente
Mike Heifferon
Ken Rowe
Champ Summers
Gary Tuck
☐ 756 Dave Sax
Player/Coach
☐ 757 Bucky Dent MGR
☐ 758 Bob Geren
☐ 759 Brian Dorsett

1989 Columbus Mudcats Best

This 28-card standard-size set features the 1989 Columbus Mudcats, a farm club for the Houston Astros. The fronts have posed color player photos with white borders. The year "1989" and the city are written vertically on the left side of the card, and the player's name and position are given below the picture. In a horizontal format, the backs have biography, recent professional baseball performance summary (including statistics), and a color headshot, all in a yellow rectangular box. The Platinum version sets were limited to a production run of 1,500.

	MINT	NRMT	EXC
COMPLETE SET (28)	6.00	2.70	.75
COMP. LIMITED EDITION SET (28)	10.00	4.50	1.25

☐ 1 Eric Anthony
☐ 2 Manny Acta
☐ 3 Garrett Nago
Sic, Garret
☐ 4 Darryl Kile
☐ 5 David Salaiz
☐ 6 Pedro Sanchez
☐ 7 Michael Simms
☐ 8 Tom Wiedenbauer MGR
☐ 9 Randy Hennis
☐ 10 Fred Gladding CO
☐ 11 Doug Givler
☐ 12 Lou Frazier
☐ 13 Jeff Baldwin
☐ 14 Blane Fox
☐ 15 Tony Eusebio
☐ 16 Fred Costello
☐ 17 Mike Browning
☐ 18 Ryan Bowen
☐ 19 Jim Hickey
☐ 20 Bobby Ramos CO
☐ 21 David Rohde
☐ 22 Karl Rhodes
☐ 23 Billy Carver
☐ 24 Steve Oliverio
☐ 25 Jose Cano
☐ 26 Todd Credeur
☐ 27 Phil Torres
☐ 28 Team logo
Checklist

1989 Columbus Mudcats ProCards

This 31-card standard-size set of the 1989 Columbus Mudcats, a Class AA Southern League affiliate of the Houston Astros, features red-bordered posed color player photos on its fronts. The player's name, position, and team name appear at the bottom. The horizontal gray back carries the player's name and position at the top, followed by biography and statistics.

	MINT	NRMT	EXC
COMPLETE SET (31)	6.00	2.70	.75

☐ 119 Checklist
☐ 120 The Mudcat
Team Logo
☐ 121 Bobby Ramos
☐ 122 Mike Browning
☐ 123 Dave Rohde
☐ 124 Doug Givler
☐ 125 Tony Eusebio
☐ 126 Ryan Bowen
☐ 127 Pedro Sanchez
☐ 128 Joel Estes
☐ 129 Fred Costello
☐ 130 Tom Wiedenbauer MGR
☐ 131 Rob Millicoat
☐ 132 Trent Hubbard
☐ 133 Darryl Kile
☐ 134 Eric Anthony
☐ 135 Jeff Baldwin
☐ 136 Manny Acta
☐ 137 Randy Hennis
☐ 138 David Salaiz TR
☐ 139 Fred Gladding CO
☐ 140 Sam August
☐ 141 Mike Simms
☐ 142 Karl Rhodes
☐ 143 Blane Fox
☐ 144 Terry Wells
☐ 145 Lou Frazier
☐ 146 Garrett Nago
☐ 147 Mike Loynd
☐ 148 Bert Hunter
☐ 149 Team Picture

1989 Columbus Mudcats Star

This 24-card standard-size set features the 1989 Columbus Mudcats, a farm club for the Houston Astros. The fronts have posed color player photos, with red borders on the top portion of the card fading to gray as one moves down the card face. In red print on a gray background, the backs have biography and statistics. 5,000 sets produced.

	MINT	NRMT	EXC
COMPLETE SET (24)	7.00	3.10	.85

☐ 1 Manny Acta
☐ 2 Eric Anthony
☐ 3 Jeff Baldwin
☐ 4 Ryan Bowen
☐ 5 Mike Browning
☐ 6 Fred Costello
☐ 7 Joel Estes
☐ 8 Tony Eusebio
☐ 9 Blane Fox
☐ 10 Lou Frazier
☐ 11 Doug Givler
☐ 12 Randy Hennis
☐ 13 Trent Hubbard
☐ 14 Bert Hunter
☐ 15 Darryl Kile
☐ 16 Mike Loynd
☐ 17 Rob Mallicoat
☐ 18 Garrett Nago
Sic, Garret
☐ 19 Karl Rhodes
☐ 20 David Rohde
☐ 21 Pedro Sanchez
☐ 22 Mike Simms
☐ 23 Terry Wells
☐ 24 Coaching Staff
Tom Wiedenbauer MGR
Bobby Ramos CO
Fred Gladding CO

1989 Denver Zephrys CMC

	MINT	NRMT	EXC
COMPLETE SET (25)	5.00	2.20	.60

☐ 1 Jay Aldrich
☐ 2 Tim Watkins
☐ 3 Tony Fossas
☐ 4 Mike Kinnuenen
☐ 5 Mike Costello
☐ 6 Donnie Scott
☐ 7 Ray Krawczyk
☐ 8 Jeff Petarek
☐ 9 Al Sadler
☐ 10 Todd Simmons
☐ 11 Bob Stoddard
☐ 12 Kiki Diaz
☐ 13 Darryl Hamilton
☐ 14 La Vel Freeman
☐ 15 Billy Bates
☐ 16 Darryel Walters
☐ 17 Jimmy Jones
☐ 18 Ruben Rodriguez
☐ 19 George Canale
☐ 20 Joe Mitchell
☐ 21 Joe Xavier
☐ 22 Matias Carrillo
☐ 23 Greg Vaughn
☐ 24 Jackson Todd CO
☐ 25 Dave Machemer MGR

1989 Denver Zephyrs ProCards

This 28-card standard-size set of the 1989 Denver Zephyrs, a Class AAA Pacific Coast League affiliate of the Milwaukee Brewers, features blue-bordered posed color player photos on its fronts. The player's name, position, and team name appear at the bottom. The horizontal gray back carries the player's name and position at the top, followed by biography and statistics. .

	MINT	NRMT	EXC
COMPLETE SET (28)	5.00	2.20	.60

☐ 30 Todd Simmons
☐ 31 Bob Stoddard
☐ 32 Ray Krawczky
☐ 33 Mike Kinnunen
☐ 34 Ruben Rodriguez
☐ 35 George Canale
☐ 36 Greg Vaughn
☐ 37 Dave Machemer MGR
☐ 38 Billy Bates
☐ 39 Darryl Hamilton
☐ 40 Jim Jones
☐ 41 Tim Watkins
☐ 42 Jay Aldrich
☐ 43 Joe Mitchell
☐ 44 Alan Sadler
☐ 45 Mike Costello
☐ 46 Jeff Peterek
☐ 47 Kiki Diaz
☐ 48 Lavell Freeman
☐ 49 Matias Carrillo
☐ 50 Peter Kolb TR
☐ 51 Jackson Todd CO
☐ 52 Donnie Scott
☐ 53 Joe Xavier
☐ 54 Darryel Walters
☐ 55 Tony Fossas
☐ 56 Norm Jones ANN
☐ 57 Checklist

1989 Dunedin Blue Jays Star

This 26-card standard-size set of the 1989 Dunedin Blue Jays, a Class A Florida State League affiliate of the Toronto Blue Jays, features indigo-bordered posed color player photos on its fronts. The player's name, team name, and position appear at the bottom. The white horizontal back carries the player's name at the top, followed by biography and statistics. The coaching staff card (#26) was a late issue. 5,000 sets produced.

	MINT	NRMT	EXC
COMPLETE SET (25)	8.00	3.60	1.00
COMP. SET W/LATE ISSUE (26)	10.00	4.50	1.25

☐ 1 Denis Boucher
☐ 2 Enrique Burgos
☐ 3 Nate Cromwell
☐ 4 Andy Dziadkowiec
☐ 5 Henry Lee Goshay
☐ 6 Darren Hall
☐ 7 Pat Hentgen
☐ 8 Vince Horsman
☐ 9 Jimy Kelly
☐ 10 Randy Knorr
☐ 11 Mike Mills
☐ 12 Bernardino Nunez
☐ 13 Paul Rodgers
☐ 14 Earl Sanders
☐ 15 Al Silverstein
☐ 16 Ed Sprague
☐ 17 William Suero
☐ 18 Marcos Taveras
☐ 19 Mike Timlin
☐ 20 Relito Uribe
☐ 21 Greg Vella
☐ 22 Steve Wapnick
☐ 23 Woody Williams
☐ 24 Julian Yan
☐ 25 Mark Young
☐ 26 Coaching Staff
Doug Ault MG
Dennis Holmberg CO
Steve Mingori CO

1989 Durham Bulls I Star

This 29-card first series standard-size set features the 1989 Durham Bulls, a farm club for the Atlanta Braves. The fronts have posed color player photos, with aqua borders on the top portion of the card fading to orange as one moves down the card face. In blue print on a pale orange background, the backs have biography and statistics. Card numbers 26-29 have white backs; also Costner's card has an orange front border fading to blue. The cards are arranged alphabetically and numbered on the back. 5,000 sets produced.

	MINT	NRMT	EXC
COMPLETE SET (29)	15.00	6.75	1.85

☐ 1 Steve Avery
☐ 2 Dennis Burlingame
☐ 3 David Butts
☐ 4 Rich Casarotti
☐ 5 Brian Champion
☐ 6 Jamie Cuesta
☐ 7 Wes Currin
☐ 8 Jim Czajkowski
☐ 9 Brian Deak
☐ 10 Todd Dewey
☐ 11 Mike Fowler
☐ 12 Jerald Frost
☐ 13 Phil Maldonado
☐ 14 Rich Maloney
☐ 15 Al Martin
☐ 16 David Nied
☐ 17 Ken Pennington
☐ 18 Ben Rivera
☐ 19 Sean Ross
☐ 20 Mike Stoker
☐ 21 Pat Tilmon
☐ 22 Theron Todd
☐ 23 Andy Tomberlin
☐ 24 Matt Turner
☐ 25 Steve Ziem
☐ 26 Grady Little MGR
☐ 27 Larry Jaster CO
☐ 28 Inocencio Guerrero CO
☐ 29 Kevin Costner
Movie actor

1989 Durham Bulls II Star

This 29-card second series standard-size set features the 1989 Durham Bulls, a farm club for the Atlanta Braves. The fronts have the same posed color player photos as on the first series, but with orange borders on the top portion of the card fading to blue as one moves down the card face. In blue print on a white background, the backs have biography and statistics. The cards are arranged alphabetically and numbered on the back. 5,000 sets produced.

	MINT	NRMT	EXC
COMPLETE SET (29)	20.00	9.00	2.50

☐ 1 Steve Avery
☐ 2 Dennis Burlingame
☐ 3 David Butts
☐ 4 Rich Casarotti
☐ 5 Brian Champion
☐ 6 Jamie Cuesta
☐ 7 Wes Currin
☐ 8 Jim Czajkowski
☐ 9 Brian Deak
☐ 10 Todd Dewey
☐ 11 Mike Fowler
☐ 12 Jerald Frost
☐ 13 Phil Maldonado
☐ 14 Rich Maloney
☐ 15 Al Martin
☐ 16 David Nied
☐ 17 Ken Pennington
☐ 18 Ben Rivera
☐ 19 Sean Ross
☐ 20 Mike Stoker
☐ 21 Pat Tilmon
☐ 22 Theron Todd
☐ 23 Andy Tomberlin
☐ 24 Matt Turner
☐ 25 Steve Ziem
☐ 26 Grady Little MGR
☐ 27 Larry Jaster CO
☐ 28 Inocencio Guerrero CO
☐ 29 Kevin Costner
Movie actor

1989 Durham Bulls Team Issue

This 28-card second series set features the 1989 Durham Bulls, a farm club for the Atlanta Braves, was issued in one large sheet featuring six perforated strips with a large team photo in the wide top strip. Sponsored by Kodak, the fronts carry color player photos while the backs display player career statistics. The cards are unnumbered and checklisted below in alphabetical order.

	MINT	NRMT	EXC
COMPLETE SET (28)	20.00	9.00	2.50

☐ 1 Steve Avery
☐ 2 Dennis Burlingame
☐ 3 David Butts
☐ 4 Rich Casarotti
☐ 5 Brian Champion
☐ 6 Jaime Cuesta
☐ 7 Wes Currin
☐ 8 Jim Czajkowski
☐ 9 Brian Deak

☐ 10 Todd Dewey
☐ 11 Mike Fowler
☐ 12 Jerald Frost
☐ 13 Phil Maldonado
☐ 14 Rich Maloney
☐ 15 Al Martin
☐ 16 David Nied
☐ 17 Ken Pennington
☐ 18 Ben Rivera
☐ 19 Sean Ross
☐ 20 Mike Stoker
☐ 21 Pat Tilmon
☐ 22 Theron Todd
☐ 23 Andy Tomberlin
☐ 24 Matt Turner
☐ 25 Steve Ziem
☐ 26 Ino Guerrero CO
☐ 27 Larry Jaster CO
☐ 28 Grady Little MGR

1989 Eastern League All-Stars ProCards

	MINT	NRMT	EXC
COMPLETE SET (26)	15.00	6.75	1.85

☐ 1 Checklist
☐ 2 Andy Stankiewicz
☐ 3 Leo Gomez
☐ 4 Travis Fryman
☐ 5 Wes Chamberlain
☐ 6 Beau Allred
☐ 7 Troy Neel
☐ 8 Rob Sepanek
☐ 9 Jim Leyritz
☐ 10 Rodney Imes
☐ 11 Steve Adkins
☐ 12 Daryl Irvine
☐ 13 Dan Gabriele
☐ 14 Tim Layana
☐ 15 Scott Kamieniecki
☐ 16 Jason Grimsley
☐ 17 Josias Manzanillo
☐ 18 Tino Martinez
☐ 19 Casey Webster
☐ 20 Jack Smith
☐ 21 Victor Hithe
☐ 22 John Ramos
☐ 23 Jeff Banister
☐ 24 Tim Mauser
☐ 25 Rick Parker
☐ 26 Buck Showalter MG

1989 Eastern League Diamond Diplomacy ProCards

	MINT	NRMT	EXC
COMPLETE SET (50)	7.00	3.10	.85

☐ DD1 Checklist
☐ DD2 Vitalyi Romanov
☐ DD3 German Gulbit
☐ DD4 Sergey Korolev
☐ DD5 Vadim Kulakov
☐ DD6 Evgeny Puchkov
☐ DD7 Alexei Koshevoy
☐ DD8 Sergey Zhigalov
☐ DD9 Edmuntas Matusyavichus
☐ DD10 Alexander Dundik
☐ DD11 Sergei Onichuk
☐ DD12 Boris Rogascozv
☐ DD13 Andrei Fzelykovskyi
☐ DD14 Alexander Krupenchemkov
☐ DD15 Leonid Korneev
☐ DD16 Roman Stepanov
☐ DD17 Ilya Bogatyrev
☐ DD18 Alexander Kozyrez
☐ DD19 Timur Tritonenkov
☐ DD20 Igor Mahambitov
☐ DD21 Andrey Popov
☐ DD22 Kevin Burdick
☐ DD23 Dave Milstien
☐ DD24 Dave Walters
☐ DD25 Steve Scarsone
☐ DD26 Tommy Shields
☐ DD27 Steve Adams
☐ DD28 Jeff Banister
☐ DD29 Dan Simonds
☐ DD30 Joe Dunlap
☐ DD31 Leverne Jackson
☐ DD32 Rich Doyle
☐ DD33 Glenn Spagnola
☐ DD34 Chris Calvert
☐ DD35 Mike Twardoski
☐ DD36 Ted Williams
☐ DD37 Troy Neel
☐ DD38 Don Buford
☐ DD39 Frank Bellino
☐ DD40 Mike Sander
☐ DD41 Jeff Edwards
☐ DD42 Group Photo
☐ DD43 Rich Gale CO
☐ DD44 Stump Merrill Clinic Director
☐ DD45 Rob Thomson CO
☐ DD46 Dave Trembley MGR
☐ DD47 Dick Groch CO
☐ DD48 Umpires Scott Potter Mike Fitzpatrick Jeff Kellogg
☐ DD49 Kevin Rand TR
☐ DD50 David Hays Equipment MGR

1989 Edmonton Trappers CMC

This 25-card standard-size set of the 1989 Edmonton Trappers, a Class AAA Pacific Coast League affiliate of the California Angels, features on its fronts white-bordered posed color player photos framed by a black line. The team's name, the player's name, and his position appear at the bottom. The white back is framed by a black line and carries the team's name and league at the top, followed by the player's name, position, biography and statistics.

	MINT	NRMT	EXC
COMPLETE SET (25)	5.00	2.20	.60

☐ 1 Jack Lozorko
☐ 2 Rich Monteleone
☐ 3 Carl Willis
☐ 4 Cliff Young
☐ 5 Tim Burcham
☐ 6 Colin Charland
☐ 7 Stu Cliburn
☐ 8 Sherman Corbett
☐ 9 Mike Fetters
☐ 10 Colby Ward
☐ 11 Stan Holmes
☐ 12 Pete Coachman
☐ 13 Edwin Marquez
☐ 14 Jim Eppard
☐ 15 Doug Davis
☐ 16 Mike Ramsey
☐ 17 Kent Anderson
☐ 18 Mike Brown
☐ 19 Jamie Nelson
☐ 20 Jeff Manto
☐ 21 Lee Stevens
☐ 22 Jim Thomas
☐ 23 Max Venable
☐ 24 Chuck Hernandez CO
☐ 25 Tom Kotchman MG

1989 Edmonton Trappers ProCards

This 25-card standard-size set of the 1989 Edmonton Trappers, a Class AAA Pacific Coast League affiliate of the California Angels, features blue-bordered posed color player photos on its fronts. The player's name, position, and team name appear at the bottom. The horizontal gray back carries the player's name and position at the top, followed by biography and statistics.

	MINT	NRMT	EXC
COMPLETE SET (25)	5.00	2.20	.60

☐ 546 Checklist
☐ 547 Sherm Corbett
☐ 548 Jim Eppard
☐ 549 Tom Kotchman MG
☐ 550 Jim Thomas
☐ 551 Doug Davis
☐ 552 Edwin Marquez
☐ 553 Tim Burcham
☐ 554 Lee Stevens
☐ 555 Stan Holmes
☐ 556 Max Venable
☐ 557 Cliff Young
☐ 558 Mike Brown
☐ 559 Vance Lovelace
☐ 560 Don McGann TR
☐ 561 Mike Ramsey
☐ 562 Chuck Hernandez CO
☐ 563 Pete Coachman
☐ 564 Rich Monteleone
☐ 565 Colin Charland
☐ 566 Stewart Cliburn
☐ 567 Carl Willis
☐ 568 Colby Ward
☐ 569 Jamie Nelson
☐ 570 Jeff Manto

1989 El Paso Diablos Grand Slam

	MINT	NRMT	EXC
COMPLETE SET (30)	5.00	2.20	.60

☐ 1 Marc Bombard MGR
☐ 2 Paul Lindblad CO
☐ 3 James Austin
☐ 4 Mark Chapman
☐ 5 Mike Costello
☐ 6 Brian Drahman
☐ 7 Keith Fleming
☐ 8 Doug Henry
☐ 9 Jim Hunter
☐ 10 John Miglio
☐ 11 Steve Monson
☐ 12 Carl Moraw
☐ 13 Jaime Navarro
☐ 14 Ed Puig
☐ 15 Tim Watkins
☐ 16 Teddy Higuera
☐ 17 Randy Veres
☐ 18 Tim McIntosh
☐ 19 Tim Torricelli
☐ 20 Jesus Alfaro
☐ 21 Greg Edge
☐ 22 Sandy Guerrero
☐ 23 Frank Mattox
☐ 24 D.L. Smith
☐ 25 Shon Ashley
☐ 26 Andre David
☐ 27 Ruben Escalera
☐ 28 Ramon Sambo
☐ 29 Darryel Walters
☐ 30 Mario Monico

1989 Elizabethton Twins Star

The 1989 Elizabethton Twins set contains 31 standard-size cards. The fronts have posed color player photos, with purple borders on the top portion of the card fading to red as one moves down the card face. In purple print on a pink background, the backs have biography and statistics. Card numbers 26-31 have blue rather than purple borders. The cards are arranged alphabetically and numbered on the back. This issue includes the minor league card debuts of Marty Cordova and Denny Neagle. 5,000 sets produced.

	MINT	NRMT	EXC
COMPLETE SET (31)	30.00	13.50	3.70

☐ 1 Bryan Asp
☐ 2 Tom Benson
☐ 3 Jayson Best
☐ 4 David Bigham
☐ 5 Marty Cordova
☐ 6 Sandy Diaz
☐ 7 Steve Dunn
☐ 8 Rick Freeman
☐ 9 Randy Gentile
☐ 10 Jody Harrington
☐ 11 Mike Hinde
☐ 12 Mike House
☐ 13 Karl Johnson
☐ 14 Jose Leon
☐ 15 Mike Lloyd
☐ 16 Angel Lugo
☐ 17 Bob McCreary
☐ 18 Jeff Milene
☐ 19 Mike Misuraca
☐ 20 Steve Morris
☐ 21 Willie Mota
☐ 22 Dennis Neagle
☐ 23 Tim Nedin
☐ 24 Rex De La Nuez
☐ 25 Kerry Taylor
☐ 26 Amadeo Garcia
☐ 27 Wade Wacker
☐ 28 Phil Wiese
☐ 29 Ray Smith MGR
☐ 30 Coaching Staff Rick Tomlin Jim Lemon
☐ 31 Jeff Chambers TR

1989 Elmira Pioneers Pucko

The 1989 Elmira Pioneer set was first issued with 28 standard-size cards; later 4 cards (29-32) were added to the set, bringing the total to 32. The front design features color player photos bordered in red; the four update cards, however, have black and white photos. The team logo appears in a circle at the lower left corner of the picture. The back has biography and professional record (where appropriate). 3,750 sets were produced.

	MINT	NRMT	EXC
COMPLETE SET (32)	6.00	2.70	.75

☐ 1 Dave Alvarez
☐ 2 Jhonny Diaz
☐ 3 Luis Dorante
☐ 4 Chris Hanks
☐ 5 Pete Hoy
☐ 6 Garrett Jenkins
☐ 7 Steve Michael
☐ 8 Jim Morrison
☐ 9 Bart Moore
☐ 10 Frank Morelli
☐ 11 Tony Mosley
☐ 12 Lou Munoz
☐ 13 Ender Perozo
☐ 14 Ed Riley
☐ 15 Carlos Rivera
☐ 16 Julio Rosario
☐ 17 Chris Rosfelder
☐ 18 Andy Rush
☐ 19 Al Sanders
☐ 20 John Spencer
☐ 21 Richard Witherspoon
☐ 22 Mike Verdi MGR
☐ 23 Dave Kennedy TR
☐ 24 Dunn Field
☐ 25 Clyde Smoll MGR
☐ 26 Dennis Robarge MGR
☐ 27 Kevin Morton
☐ 28 Michael Thompson
☐ 29 John Locker
☐ 30 Jeff McNeely
☐ 31 Paul Quantrill
☐ 32 Eric Wedge

1989 Erie Orioles Star

The 1989 Erie Orioles set contains 29 standard-size cards. The fronts have posed color player photos, with black borders on the top portion of the card fading to orange as one moves down the card face. In black print on a pale orange background, the backs have biography and statistics. 5,000 sets produced.

	MINT	NRMT	EXC
COMPLETE SET (29)	5.00	2.20	.60

☐ 1 Tony Beasley
☐ 2 Dan Berthel
☐ 3 John Bowen
☐ 4 Dave Brown
☐ 5 Pat Hedge
☐ 6 John Hemmerly
☐ 7 Aman Hicks
☐ 8 Brad Hildreth
☐ 9 Ed Horowitz
☐ 10 Zack Kerr
☐ 11 Pat Leinen
☐ 12 Rich Meek
☐ 13 Carey Metts
☐ 14 Cary Moore
☐ 15 Steve Nicosia Not 80's Pirates Catcher
☐ 16 Mike Oquist
☐ 17 Jaime Pena
☐ 18 Doug Reynolds
☐ 19 Arthur Rhodes
☐ 20 Mike Richardson
☐ 21 David Riddle
☐ 22 Pete Rose Jr.
☐ 23 Mark Rupp
☐ 24 Gary Shingledecker
☐ 25 Melvin Wearing
☐ 26 Steve Williams
☐ 27 Bobby Tolan MGR
☐ 28 Mark Brown CO
☐ 29 Dave Werner TR

1989 Eugene Emeralds Best

This 25-card standard-size set features the 1989 Eugene Emeralds, a farm club for the Kansas City Royals. The fronts have posed color player photos with white borders. The year "1989" and the city are written vertically on the left side of the card, and the player's name and position are given below the picture. In a horizontal format, the backs have biography, recent professional baseball performance summary (including statistics), and a color headshot, all in a yellow rectangular box.

	MINT	NRMT	EXC
COMPLETE SET (25)	5.00	2.20	.60

☐ 1 Chris Schaefer
☐ 2 Mike Webster
☐ 3 Kirk Baldwin
☐ 4 Jake Jacobs
☐ 5 Don Lindsey
☐ 6 Matt Karchner
☐ 7 Scott Centala
☐ 8 Ben Pardo
☐ 9 Ed Pierce
☐ 10 Kirk Thompson
☐ 11 Dave Ritchie
☐ 12 David Solseth
☐ 13 Colin Ryan
☐ 14 Kevin Long
☐ 15 Javier Alvarez
☐ 16 Rich Tunison
☐ 17 Kerwin Moore
☐ 18 Milt Richardson
☐ 19 Fred Russell
☐ 20 Ron Collins
☐ 21 Rob Buchanan
☐ 22 John Gilcrist
☐ 23 Brian Ahern
☐ 24 Sean Collins
☐ 25 Team logo Checklist

1989 Everett Giants Star

The 1989 Everett Giants set contains 32 standard-size cards. The fronts have posed color player photos, with black borders on the top portion of the card fading to orange as one moves down the card face. In black print on a pale orange background, the backs have biographical information. 5,000 sets produced.

	MINT	NRMT	EXC
COMPLETE SET (32)	5.00	2.20	.60

- ☐ 1 Maximo Aleys
- ☐ 2 Clayton Bellinger
- ☐ 3 Steve Callahan
- ☐ 4 Teodoro Cespedes
- ☐ 5 Ron Crowe
- ☐ 6 Brian Dour
- ☐ 7 Scott Ebert
- ☐ 8 Mike Grahovac
- ☐ 9 Edward Gustafson
- ☐ 10 Kevin Hall
- ☐ 11 Chris Hancock
- ☐ 12 Carl Hanselman
- ☐ 13 Dan Hendrickson
- ☐ 14 David Hocking
- ☐ 15 Steve Hosey
- ☐ 16 Randy Johnson
- ☐ 17 Kevin Jones
- ☐ 18 Kevin Kasper
- ☐ 19 Jesus Laya
- ☐ 20 Mike McDonald
- ☐ 21 Troy Mentzer
- ☐ 22 Dan Montes
- ☐ 23 Vince Palyan
- ☐ 24 Ed Quesada
- ☐ 25 Jon Schiller
- ☐ 26 Greg Brummett
- ☐ 27 Greg Lund
- ☐ 28 Jason McFarlin
- ☐ 29 Glen Warren
- ☐ 30 Joe Strain MGR
- ☐ 31 Diego Segui CO
- ☐ 32 Bryce Welch

1989 Fayetteville Generals ProCards

This 29-card standard-size set of the 1989 Fayetteville Generals, a Class A South Atlantic League affiliate of the Detroit Tigers, features orange-bordered posed color player photos on its fronts. The player's name, position, and team name appear at the bottom. The horizontal gray back carries the player's name and position at the top, followed by biography and statistics.

	MINT	NRMT	EXC
COMPLETE SET (29)	5.00	2.20	.60

- ☐ 1567 Checklist
- ☐ 1568 Glenn Belcher
- ☐ 1569 Leo Torres
- ☐ 1570 Jeff Jones CO
- ☐ 1571 Rob Thomas
- ☐ 1572 Linty Ingram
- ☐ 1573 Lino Rivera
- ☐ 1574 Marcos Betances
- ☐ 1575 Rusty Meacham
- ☐ 1576 Mike Koller
- ☐ 1577 Gene Rood MGR
- ☐ 1578 Rich Rowland
- ☐ 1579 Blaine Rudolph
- ☐ 1580 Benny Castillo
- ☐ 1581 Randy Marshall
- ☐ 1582 Kurt Shea
- ☐ 1583 Tim Brader
- ☐ 1584 Mike Rendina
- ☐ 1585 Darryl Martin
- ☐ 1586 Jim Murphy
- ☐ 1587 Julio Rosa
- ☐ 1588 Freddy Torres
- ☐ 1589 Brett Roach
- ☐ 1590 Mickey Delas
- ☐ 1591 Paul Nozling
- ☐ 1592 Ron Howard
- ☐ 1593 Mike Davidson
- ☐ 1594 Steve Pegues
- ☐ 1595 Freddy Padilla

1989 Frederick Keys Star

This 27-card standard-size set features the 1989 Frederick Keys, a farm club for the Baltimore Orioles. The fronts have posed color player photos, with black borders on the top portion of the card fading to orange as one moves down the card face. In black print on a pale orange background, the backs have biography and statistics. Card numbers 26-27 were late productions; card number 26 has purple print on the reverse. 5,000 sets produced.

	MINT	NRMT	EXC
COMPLETE SET (27)	5.00	2.20	.60

- ☐ 1 Stacey Burdick
- ☐ 2 Mike Cavers
- ☐ 3 Andres Constant
- ☐ 4 Francisco Dela Rosa
- ☐ 5 Mike Deutsch
- ☐ 6 Oneri Fleita
- ☐ 7 Roy Gilbert
- ☐ 8 Ricky Gutierrez
- ☐ 9 Tom Harms
- ☐ 10 Paris Hayden
- ☐ 11 Stacy Jones
- ☐ 12 Mike Lehman
- ☐ 13 Mike Linskey
- ☐ 14 Rodney Lofton
- ☐ 15 Scott Meadows
- ☐ 16 Luis Mercedes
- ☐ 17 Dave Miller
- ☐ 18 Steve Mondile
- ☐ 19 Chris Myers
- ☐ 20 Luis Paulino
- ☐ 21 David Segui
- ☐ 22 Dan Simonds
- ☐ 23 Anthony Telford
- ☐ 24 Jack Voigt
- ☐ 25 Jerry Narron MGR
- ☐ 26 Mike Pazik CO
- ☐ 27 Pete Rose Jr.

1989 Fresno State Bulldogs Smokey

This 24-card standard-size set features the 1989 Fresno State Bulldog baseball team. The fronts feature either posed or action color player photos. Beneath the photo, the player's name, position, and "Bulldogs" is printed between the Smokey the Bear and team logos. The backs have biographical information and a fire prevention cartoon starring Smokey. The cards are unnumbered and checklisted below in alphabetical order.

	MINT	NRMT	EXC
COMPLETE SET (24)	10.00	4.50	1.25

- ☐ 1 Ken Baker
- ☐ 2 Bob Bennett CO
- ☐ 3 Bob Bennett CO
- ☐ 4 Eric Bridge
- ☐ 5 Mike Burton
- ☐ 6 Eddie Bustamante
- ☐ 7 Rich Crane
- ☐ 8 Terance Frazier
- ☐ 9 Tom Goodwin
- ☐ 10 Tom Goodwin
- ☐ 11 Steve Hosey
- ☐ 12 Tim Lockhart
- ☐ 13 Steve Lozano
- ☐ 14 Tony Mortensen
- ☐ 15 Mike Noel
- ☐ 16 Tim Painton ACO
- ☐ 17 Mike Rupcich ACO
- ☐ 18 Pat Ruth
- ☐ 19 Erik Schullstrom
- ☐ 20 Steve Vondran
- ☐ 21 Cary Windes
- ☐ 22 Steve Wolf
- ☐ 23 Eddie Zosky
- ☐ 24 Beiden Field

1989 Ft. Lauderdale Yankees Star

The 1989 Fort Lauderdale Yankees set contains 29 standard-size cards. The fronts have posed color player photos, with purple borders on the top portion of the card fading to gray as one moves down the card face. In purple print on a gray background, the backs have biography and statistics. Card numbers 26-29 have different colors and appear to be late productions. 5,000 sets produced.

	MINT	NRMT	EXC
COMPLETE SET (29)	6.00	2.70	.75

- ☐ 1 Steve Adkins
- ☐ 2 Russell Davis
- ☐ 3 Herb Erhardt
- ☐ 4 Steve Erickson
- ☐ 5 Victor Garcia
- ☐ 6 Doug Gogolewski
- ☐ 7 John Green
- ☐ 8 Freddie Hailey
- ☐ 9 Mike Hook
- ☐ 10 Chris Howard
- ☐ 11 Dean Kelly
- ☐ 12 Ralph Kraus
- ☐ 13 Mark Leiter
- ☐ 14 Ramon Manon
- ☐ 15 Ed Martel
- ☐ 16 Alan Mills
- ☐ 17 Red Morrison
- ☐ 18 Skip Nelloms
- ☐ 19 Tom Popplewell
- ☐ 20 Mike Rhodes
- ☐ 21 Carlos Rodriguez
- ☐ 22 Gabriel Rodriguez
- ☐ 23 Dan Roman
- ☐ 24 Melvin Rosario
- ☐ 25 John Seeburger
- ☐ 26 Bob Zeihen
- ☐ 27 Clete Boyer MGR
- ☐ 28 Jack Hubbard CO
- ☐ 29 David Schuler CO

1989 Gastonia Rangers ProCards

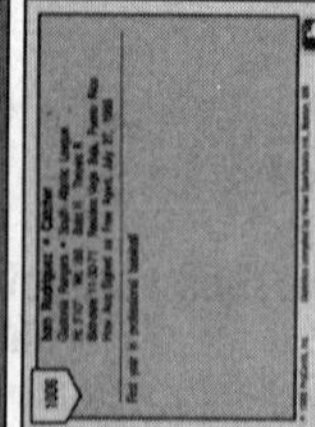

This 30-card standard-size set of the 1989 Gastonia Rangers, a Class A South Atlantic League affiliate of the Texas Rangers, features orange-bordered posed color player photos on its fronts. The player's name, position, and team name appear at the bottom. The horizontal gray back carries the player's name and position at the top, followed by biography and statistics. This issue includes the minor league card debut of Ivan Rodriguez.

	MINT	NRMT	EXC
COMPLETE SET (30)	30.00	13.50	3.70

- ☐ 997 Checklist
- ☐ 998 Joe Waldlow
- ☐ 999 Spencer Wilkinson
- ☐ 1000 Everett Cunningham
- ☐ 1001 Dominic Pierce
- ☐ 1002 Kyle Spencer
- ☐ 1003 Robb Nen
- ☐ 1004 Kevin Belcher
- ☐ 1005 Carl Randle
- ☐ 1006 Ivan Rodriguez
- ☐ 1007 Joe Lewis
- ☐ 1008 Eric McCray
- ☐ 1009 Anthony Berry
- ☐ 1010 Chuck Marquardt TR
- ☐ 1011 Jim McCutcheon
- ☐ 1012 Trey McCoy
- ☐ 1013 Doug Cronk
- ☐ 1014 Cris Colon
- ☐ 1015 Jim Crawford CO
- ☐ 1016 Ronaldo Romero
- ☐ 1017 Orlando Gomez MGR
- ☐ 1018 Jose Hernandez
- ☐ 1019 Jim Hvizda
- ☐ 1020 Francisco Valdez
- ☐ 1021 Darren Oliver
- ☐ 1022 Steve Allen
- ☐ 1023 Jeff Frye
- ☐ 1024 Tim MacNeil
- ☐ 1025 Oscar Acosta CO
- ☐ 1026 Mike Mendazona

1989 Gastonia Rangers Star

The 1989 Gastonia Rangers set contains 26 standard-size cards. The fronts have posed color player photos, with blue borders on the top portion of the card fading to gray as one moves down the card face. In blue print on a white background, the backs have biography and statistics. The cards are arranged alphabetically and numbered on the back. The Coaching Staff card has no number. This issue includes the minor league card debut of Ivan Rodriguez. 5,000 sets produced.

	MINT	NRMT	EXC
COMPLETE SET (26)	30.00	13.50	3.70

- ☐ 1 Steve Allen
- ☐ 2 Kevin Belcher
- ☐ 3 Tony Berry
- ☐ 4 Cris Colon
- ☐ 5 Doug Cronk
- ☐ 6 Everett Cunningham
- ☐ 7 Jeff Frye
- ☐ 8 Jose Hernandez
- ☐ 9 Jim Hvizda
- ☐ 10 Joe Lewis
- ☐ 11 Tim MacNeil
- ☐ 12 Trey McCoy
- ☐ 13 Eric McCray
- ☐ 14 Jim McCutchen
- ☐ 15 Mike Mendazona
- ☐ 16 Robb Nen
- ☐ 17 Darren Oliver
- ☐ 18 Dominic Pierce
- ☐ 19 Carl Randle
- ☐ 20 Ivan Rodriguez
- ☐ 21 Ronaldo Romero
- ☐ 22 Kyle Spencer
- ☐ 23 Frank Valdez
- ☐ 24 Joe Wardlow
- ☐ 25 Spencer Wilkinson
- ☐ NNO Coaching Staff
  Orlando Gomez MGR
  Jim Crawford CO
  Oscar Acosta CO

1989 Geneva Cubs ProCards

This 31-card standard-size set of the 1989 Geneva Cubs, a Class A New York-Penn League affiliate of the Chicago Cubs, features orange-bordered posed color player photos on its fronts. The player's name, position, and team name appear at the bottom. The horizontal gray back carries the player's name and position at the top, followed by biography and statistics.

	MINT	NRMT	EXC
COMPLETE SET (31)	5.00	2.20	.60

- ☐ 1856 Checklist
- ☐ 1857 Quinn's Cards
  Quinn Family
- ☐ 1858 Front Office Staff
  Tom Abernethy
  Gary Arnold
  Ken Burlew
  Kevin Heilbronner
  Dave Oster
  Ken Shepard
- ☐ 1859 Grounds Crew
  Dave Mungo
  Ed Smaldone III
- ☐ 1860 Frankie Espino
- ☐ 1861 Ed Smaldone
  Co-Owner
- ☐ 1862 Rene Francisco
- ☐ 1863 Darrin Beer
- ☐ 1864 Doug Welch
- ☐ 1865 Kevin Gore
- ☐ 1866 David Swartzbaugh
- ☐ 1867 Travis Willis
- ☐ 1868 Jeff Cesari
- ☐ 1869 Jeff Ludwig
- ☐ 1870 Luis Benitez
- ☐ 1871 Richie Grayum
- ☐ 1872 Kalani Bush
- ☐ 1873 Kim Sweeney
- ☐ 1874 Al Stacey
- ☐ 1875 Tony Colon
- ☐ 1876 Chris Ebright
- ☐ 1877 Gary Scott
- ☐ 1878 Mark Linden
- ☐ 1879 Pabla Delgado
- ☐ 1880 Micah Murphy
- ☐ 1881 Shannon Jones
- ☐ 1882 Gregg Patterson
- ☐ 1883 Rick Mundy
- ☐ 1884 Billy White
- ☐ 1885 Ken Reynolds CO
- ☐ 1886 Pookie Bernstine CO

1989 Georgia College Colonials

	MINT	NRMT	EXC
COMPLETE SET (36)	10.00	4.50	1.25

- ☐ 1 Jeff Besh
- ☐ 2 Kevin Blizzard
- ☐ 3 Monty Connell
- ☐ 4 Gary Diagostino
- ☐ 5 Mark Estes
- ☐ 6 Rick Evans
- ☐ 7 Matt Fincher ACO
- ☐ 8 Jay Flesher
- ☐ 9 Jim Frederick
- ☐ 10 Lee Henderson
- ☐ 11 Edgar Herrera
- ☐ 12 Angela Johnson MG
  Dan Barry TR
  Donna Kimsey MG
- ☐ 13 Jody Johnson
- ☐ 14 Rusty Kea
- ☐ 15 Ed Kiker
- ☐ 16 Eric Kobbe
- ☐ 17 John Kurtz CO
- ☐ 18 Ron Landy ACO
- ☐ 19 Skip Lindemann
- ☐ 20 Carlos Lopez
- ☐ 21 Chris Painter
- ☐ 22 James Parker
- ☐ 23 George Pearson
- ☐ 24 John Powell
- ☐ 25 Willard Riner MG
- ☐ 26 Rhett Robinson
- ☐ 27 Larry Schenck
- ☐ 28 Seniors
  Kevin Blizzard
  Rhett Robinson
  Skip Lindemann
  George Pearson
- ☐ 29 Mark Snider
- ☐ 30 Todd Staats
- ☐ 31 Crandall Stamps
- ☐ 32 Lee Stewart
- ☐ 33 Team Picture
- ☐ 34 Clay Vinson
- ☐ 35 Todd Ward
- ☐ 36 Stewart Whittaker

1989 Great Falls Dodgers Sports Pro

This 33-card standard-size set of the 1989 Great Falls Dodgers, a Rookie Class Pioneer League affiliate of the Los Angeles Dodgers, features posed color head-and-shoulders shots, with thin black borders on a white card face. The horizontally oriented backs have biographical information.

	MINT	NRMT	EXC
COMPLETE SET (33)	7.00	3.10	.85

☐ 1 Tom Goodwin
☐ 2 Michael Frame
☐ 3 Rich Crane
☐ 4 Michael Potthoff
☐ 5 Jamie McAndrew
☐ 6 Tony Helmick
☐ 7 Javier Loera
☐ 8 Audelle Cummings
☐ 9 Joe Vavra MGR
☐ 10 Jason Brosnan
☐ 11 Ray Bielanin
☐ 12 Michael Wismer
☐ 13 Yale Fowler
☐ 14 Tim Barker
☐ 15 Joey Seals
☐ 16 Lee DeLoach
☐ 17 John Deutsch
☐ 18 Kiki Jones
☐ 19 Bryan Baar
☐ 20 Barry Parisotto
☐ 21 Frank Humber
☐ 22 Anthony Collier
☐ 23 Mathew Howard
☐ 24 Erik Madsen
☐ 25 Steve O'Donnell
☐ 26 Rod Harvell
☐ 27 Bobby Fletcher
☐ 28 Mike Galle
☐ 29 Craig White
☐ 30 Ray Calhoun
☐ 31 Bill Miller
☐ 32 Matt Wilson
☐ 33 Goose Gregson

1989 Greensboro Hornets ProCards

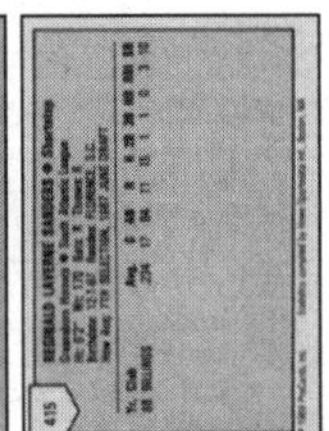

This 29-card standard-size set of the 1989 Greensboro Hornets, a Class A South Atlantic League affiliate of the Cincinnati Reds, features orange-bordered posed color player photos on its fronts. The player's name, position, and team name appear at the bottom. The horizontal gray back carries the player's name and position at the top, followed by biography and statistics. This issue includes a second year card of Reggie Sanders.

	MINT	NRMT	EXC
COMPLETE SET (29)	10.00	4.50	1.25

☐ 403 Checklist
☐ 404 Gary Denbo MGR
☐ 405 Mark Berry
☐ 406 Lavell Cudjo
☐ 407 Victor Garcia
☐ 408 Igor Baez
☐ 409 Danny Perozo
☐ 410 Mike Mulvaney
☐ 411 Dave McAuliffe
☐ 412 Brian Landy
☐ 413 Jerry Spradlin
☐ 414 Jason Satre
☐ 415 Reggie Sanders
☐ 416 Eugene Jones
☐ 417 Dante Johnson
☐ 418 Eddie Rush
☐ 419 Jim Wolfer
☐ 420 Glenn Sutko
☐ 421 Mike Songini
☐ 422 Vicente Javier
☐ 423 Mo Sanford
☐ 424 Mike Malley
☐ 425 Mark Krumback
☐ 426 Kurt Dempster
☐ 427 Phil Dale CO
☐ 428 Mike Anderson
☐ 429 Carl Nordstrom
☐ 430 Tom Iverson TR
☐ 431 Johnny Almaraz

1989 Greenville Braves Best

The 1989 Greenville Braves set contains 29 standard-size cards. The fronts have posed color player photos with white borders. The year "1989" and the city are written vertically on the left side of the card, and the player's name and position are given below the picture. In a horizontal format, the backs have biography, recent professional baseball performance summary (including statistics), and a color headshot, all in a yellow rectangular box. The Platinum version sets were limited to a production run of 1,500.

	MINT	NRMT	EXC
COMPLETE SET (29)	15.00	6.75	1.85
COMP. LIMITED EDITION SET (29)	25.00	11.00	3.10

☐ 1 Dennis Hood
☐ 2 Brian Hunter
☐ 3 Darrell Pruitt
☐ 4 Mike Bell
☐ 5 Rick Morris
☐ 6 Edwin Alicea
☐ 7 John Alva
☐ 8 Juan Pacho
☐ 9 Ellis Roby
☐ 10 Jim LeMasters
☐ 11 Maximo Del Rosario
☐ 12 Tim Deitz
☐ 13 Danny Weems
☐ 14 Mike Stanton
☐ 15 Dale Polley
☐ 16 Doug Stockam
☐ 17 Paul Marak
☐ 18 Bill Slack CO
☐ 19 Terry Bell
☐ 20 Buddy Bailey MGR
☐ 21 Randy Ingle CO
☐ 22 Jim Lovell TR
☐ 23 German Jimenez
☐ 24 Jimmy Kremers
☐ 25 Dave Plumb
☐ 26 Tommy Dunbar
☐ 27 Miguel Sabino
☐ 28 Steve Avery
☐ 29 Team logo
Checklist

1989 Greenville Braves ProCards

This 30-card standard-size set of the 1989 Greenville Braves, a Class AA Southern League affiliate of the Atlanta Braves, features red-bordered posed color player photos on its fronts. The player's name, position, and team name appear at the bottom. The horizontal gray back carries the player's name and position at the top, followed by biography and statistics.

	MINT	NRMT	EXC
COMPLETE SET (30)	5.00	2.20	.60

☐ 1150 Checklist
☐ 1151 Sid Akins
☐ 1152 Greg Tubbs
☐ 1153 German Jimenez
☐ 1154 John Alva
☐ 1155 Juan Pacho
☐ 1156 Edwin Alicea
☐ 1157 Danny Weems
☐ 1158 Brian Hunter
☐ 1159 Ellis Roby
☐ 1160 Dale Polley
☐ 1161 Maximo Delrosario
☐ 1162 Terry Bell
☐ 1163 Jimmy Kremers
☐ 1164 Dave Plumb
☐ 1165 Doug Stockam
☐ 1166 Mike Stanton
☐ 1167 Jim Lovell TR
☐ 1168 Bill Slack CO
☐ 1169 Dennis Hood
☐ 1170 Miguel Sabino
☐ 1171 Darrell Pruitt
☐ 1172 Rick Morris
☐ 1173 Mike Bell
☐ 1174 Paul Marak
☐ 1175 Tim Deitz
☐ 1176 Jim LeMasters
☐ 1177 Randy Ingle CO
☐ 1178 Buddy Bailey MGR
☐ 1179 Tommy Dunbar

1989 Greenville Braves Star

The 1989 Greenville Braves set contains 25 standard-size cards. The fronts have posed color player photos, with blue borders on the top portion of the card fading to red as one moves down the card face. In blue print on a pink background, the backs have biography and statistics. 5,000 sets produced.

	MINT	NRMT	EXC
COMPLETE SET (25)	5.00	2.20	.60

☐ 1 Edwin Alicea
☐ 2 John Alva
☐ 3 Mike Bell
☐ 4 Terry Bell
☐ 5 Tim Deitz
☐ 6 Maximo Del Rosario
☐ 7 Tommy Dunbar
☐ 8 Dennis Hood
☐ 9 Brian Hunter
☐ 10 German Jimenez
☐ 11 John Kilner
☐ 12 Jimmy Kremers
☐ 13 Jim LeMasters
☐ 14 Paul Marak
☐ 15 Rick Morris
☐ 16 Juan Pacho
☐ 17 Dave Plumb
☐ 18 Dale Polley
☐ 19 Darrell Pruitt
☐ 20 Ellis Roby
☐ 21 Miguel Sabino
☐ 22 Mike Stanton
☐ 23 Doug Stockam
☐ 24 Danny Weems
☐ 25 Coaching Staff
Buddy Bailey MGR
Bill Slack CO
Randy Ingle CO

1989 Hagerstown Suns Best

This 29-card standard-size set features the 1989 Hagerstown Suns, a farm club for the Baltimore Orioles. The fronts have posed color player photos with white borders. The year "1989" and the city are written vertically on the left side of the card, and the player's name and position are given below the picture. In a horizontal format, the backs have biography, recent professional baseball performance summary (including statistics), and a color headshot, all in a yellow rectangular box.

	MINT	NRMT	EXC
COMPLETE SET (29)	6.00	2.70	.75

☐ 1 Leo Gomez
☐ 2 John Githens
☐ 3 Jose Mesa
☐ 4 Robert Latmore
☐ 5 Victor Hithe
☐ 6 Maduro Garces
☐ 7 Sherwin Cijntje
☐ 8 Steve Culkar
☐ 9 Dave Bettendorf
☐ 10 Jimmie Schaffer MGR
☐ 11 Tom Brown CO
☐ 12 Mike Eberle
☐ 13 Brian DuBois
☐ 14 Craig Faulkner
☐ 15 Don Buford Jr.
☐ 16 Brian Ebel TR
☐ 17 Chuck Stanhope
☐ 18 Erik Sonberg
☐ 19 Paul Thorpe
☐ 20 Randy Strijek
☐ 21 Dana Smith
☐ 22 Rafael Skeete
☐ 23 Dan Simonds
☐ 24 Jeff Schwarz
☐ 25 Mike Sander
☐ 26 John Posey
☐ 27 Chris Pinder
☐ 28 Ty Nichols
☐ 29 Team logo
Checklist

1989 Hagerstown Suns ProCards

This 26-card standard-size set of the 1989 Hagerstown Suns, a Class AA Eastern League affiliate of the Baltimore Orioles, features red-bordered posed color player photos on its fronts. The player's name, position, and team name appear at the bottom. The horizontal gray back carries the player's name and position at the top, followed by biography and statistics.

	MINT	NRMT	EXC
COMPLETE SET (26)	5.00	2.20	.60

☐ 261 Checklist
☐ 262 John Githens
☐ 263 Jeff Schwarz
☐ 264 Larry Mims
☐ 265 Randy Strijek
☐ 266 Craig Faulkner
☐ 267 Erik Sonberg
☐ 268 Chris Pinder
☐ 269 Chuck Stanhope
☐ 270 Mike Eberle
☐ 271 Bob Latmore
☐ 272 Victor Hithe
☐ 273 Dave Bettendorf
☐ 274 Brian DuBois
☐ 275 Mike Sander
☐ 276 Steve Culkar
☐ 277 Don Buford Jr.
☐ 278 Rafael Skeete
☐ 279 Ty Nichols
☐ 280 Leo Gomez
☐ 281 Robinson Garces
☐ 282 Jim Schaffer MGR
☐ 283 Tom Brown CO
☐ 284 Brian Ebel TR
☐ 285 Paul Thorpe
☐ 286 Dana Smith

1989 Hagerstown Suns Star

This 22-card standard-size set features the 1989 Hagerstown Suns, a farm club of the Baltimore Orioles. The fronts have posed color player photos, with black borders on the top portion of the card fading to orange as one moves down the card face. In black print on a pale orange background, the backs have biography and statistics. 5,000 sets produced.

	MINT	NRMT	EXC
COMPLETE SET (22)	5.00	2.20	.60

☐ 1 Dave Bettendorf
☐ 2 Don Buford Jr.
☐ 3 Sherwin Cijntje
☐ 4 Steve Culkar
☐ 5 Brian DuBois
☐ 6 Mike Eberle
☐ 7 Craig Faulkner
☐ 8 Robinson Garces
☐ 9 John Githens
☐ 10 Leo Gomez
☐ 11 Victor Hithe
☐ 12 Bob Latmore
☐ 13 Ty Nichols
☐ 14 John Posey
☐ 15 Mike Sander
☐ 16 Jeff Schwarz
☐ 17 Rafael Skeete
☐ 18 Dana Smith
☐ 19 Randy Strijek
☐ 20 Pete Stanicek
☐ 21 Paul Thorpe
☐ 22 Coaching Staff
Jimmie Schaffer MGR
Tom Brown CO

1989 Hamilton Redbirds Star

This 29-card standard-size set features the 1989 Hamilton Redbirds, a farm club for the St. Louis Cardinals. The fronts have posed color player photos, with red borders on the top portion of the card fading to yellow as one moves down the card face. In red print on a pale yellow background, the backs have biography and statistics. 5,000 sets produced.

	MINT	NRMT	EXC
COMPLETE SET (29)	5.00	2.20	.60

☐ 1 Scott Banton
☐ 2 Mark Battell
☐ 3 Allan Biggers
☐ 4 Mark Bowlan
☐ 5 David Boss
☐ 6 Cliff Brannon
☐ 7 Mike Campas
☐ 8 John Cebuhar
☐ 9 David Cassidy
☐ 10 Tripp Cromer
☐ 11 Jose Fernandez
☐ 12 Randy Berlin
☐ 13 Steve Graham
☐ 14 Larry Gryskevich
☐ 15 Chris Gorton
☐ 16 Brian Golden
☐ 17 Sean Grubb
☐ 18 Don Green
☐ 19 Tom Infante
☐ 20 Tim Lata
☐ 21 Mike Milchin
☐ 22 Tim Redman
☐ 23 Dan Shannon
☐ 24 Jose Trujillo
☐ 25 Stan Tukes
☐ 26 Mark Wilson
☐ 27 Joseph Pettini MGR
☐ 28 Joseph Cunningham CO
☐ 29 Mike Evans TR

1989 Harrisburg Senators ProCards

This 26-card standard-size set of the 1989 Harrisburg Senators, a Class AA Eastern League affiliate of the Pittsburgh Pirates, features red-bordered posed color player photos on its fronts. The player's name, position, and team name appear at the bottom. The horizontal gray back carries the player's name and position at the top, followed by biography and statistics.

	MINT	NRMT	EXC
COMPLETE SET (26)	6.00	2.70	.75

☐ 287 Checklist
☐ 288 Tim Conroy
☐ 289 Rico Rossy
☐ 290 Bill Sampen
☐ 291 Ed Yacopino
☐ 292 Dave Trembley MGR
☐ 293 Junior Vizcaino
☐ 294 Julio Peguero
☐ 295 Steve Adams
☐ 296 Wes Chamberlain
☐ 297 Kevin Burdick
☐ 298 Tommy Shields
☐ 299 Orlando Merced

☐ 300 Orlando Lind
☐ 301 Chris Lein CO
☐ 302 Harold Williams TR
☐ 303 Robby Russell
☐ 304 Jeff Cook
☐ 305 Stan Belinda
☐ 306 Jeff Banister
☐ 307 Julio Perez
☐ 308 Pete Murphy
☐ 309 Jim Tracy
☐ 310 Mike York
☐ 311 Ben Webb
☐ 312 Tim McKinley

1989 Harrisburg Senators Star

This 23-card standard-size set features the 1989 Harrisburg Senators, a farm club for the Pittsburgh Pirates. The fronts have posed color player photos, with red borders on the top portion of the card fading to gray as one moves down the card face. In red print on a gray background, the backs have biography and statistics. 5,000 sets produced.

	MINT	NRMT	EXC
COMPLETE SET (23)	6.00	2.70	.75

☐ 1 Steve Adams
☐ 2 Jeff Banister
☐ 3 Stan Belinda
☐ 4 Kevin Burdick
☐ 5 Wes Chamberlain
☐ 6 Tim Conroy
☐ 7 Jeff Cook
☐ 8 Andy Hall
☐ 9 Orlando Lind
☐ 10 Orlando Merced
☐ 11 Tim McKinley
☐ 12 Pete Murphy
☐ 13 Julio Peguero
☐ 14 Julio Perez
☐ 15 Rico Rossy
☐ 16 Rob Russell
☐ 17 Bill Sampen
☐ 18 Tommy Shields
☐ 19 Jim Tracy
☐ 20 Junior Vizcaino
☐ 21 Ben Webb
☐ 22 Ed Yacopino
☐ 23 Mike York

1989 Helena Brewers Sports Pro

The 1989 Helena Brewers set consists of 27 standard-size cards. The front design has posed color head-and-shoulders shots, with thin black borders on a white card face. A black sticker with the words "1st Helena Set Ever!" is superimposed on the player photos and detracts from the cards' appearance. The horizontally oriented backs have brief biographical information.

	MINT	NRMT	EXC
COMPLETE SET (27)	7.00	3.10	.85

☐ 1 Joe Andrzejewski
☐ 2 Angel Diaz
☐ 3 Reggie Brown
☐ 4 Pat Rehwinkel
☐ 5 Tim Wilson
☐ 6 Rusty Rugg
☐ 7 Troy Haugen
☐ 8 Tony Diggs
☐ 9 Bill Brakeley
☐ 10 Greg Landry
☐ 11 Troy O'Leary
☐ 12 David Voit
☐ 13 Joe Roebuck
☐ 14 Gustavo Federico
☐ 15 Ramser Correa
☐ 16 Reed Charpia
☐ 17 Bo Dodson
☐ 18 Bob Vancho
☐ 19 Bob Kappesser
☐ 20 Eric Patton
☐ 21 David Weldin
☐ 22 Sam Drake
☐ 23 Kevin Tannahill
☐ 24 Scott Muscat
☐ 25 Darrin White
☐ 26 Ray Burris CO
☐ 27 Dusty Rhodes MGR

1989 High School Prospects Little Sun

This 23-card standard size set features color photos of some of the top senior high school players. The card backs contain complete high school career stats and biographical notes. 5,000 regular sets and 1,500 glossy sets were produced.

	MINT	NRMT	EXC
COMPLETE SET (23)	25.00	11.00	3.10
COMPLETE GLOSSY SET (23)	35.00	16.00	4.40

☐ 1 Checklist Card
☐ 2 Earl Cunningham
☐ 3 Tom Engle
☐ 4 Bill Lott
☐ 5 Tyler Houston
☐ 6 Rod Walker
☐ 7 Bub Maietta
☐ 8 Andy Fox
☐ 9 Steve Proffitt
☐ 10 Paul Coleman
☐ 11 Bo Dodson
☐ 12 Richard Greenwell
☐ 13 Javier Delahoya
☐ 14 Jason Robertson
☐ 15 Billy Kostlich
☐ 16 Brant McCreadie
☐ 17 Jorge Jaime
☐ 18 John Hope
☐ 19 Edward Gerald
☐ 20 Ryan Klesko
☐ 21 Greg Blosser
☐ 22 Don Sheppard
☐ 23 Billy Reed CO
Hillsborough High

1989 Huntsville Stars Best

This 29-card standard-size set features the 1989 Huntsville Stars, a farm club for the Oakland Athletics. The fronts have posed color player photos with white borders. The year "1989" and the city are written vertically on the left side of the card, and the player's name and position are given below the picture. In a horizontal format, the backs have biography, recent professional baseball performance summary (including statistics), and a color headshot, all in a yellow rectangular box.

	MINT	NRMT	EXC
COMPLETE SET (29)	7.00	3.10	.85

☐ 1 Scott Hemond
☐ 2 William Schock
☐ 3 Troy Afenir
☐ 4 William Savarino
☐ 5 David Veres
☐ 6 Jim Kating
☐ 7 Dann Howitt
☐ 8 Robert Stocker
☐ 9 Eric Fox
☐ 10 Stephen Maye
☐ 11 Robert Sharpnack
☐ 12 Scott Brosius
☐ 13 Weston Weber
☐ 14 Tim Casey
☐ 15 David Shotkoski
☐ 16 Scott Holcomb
☐ 17 Gary Jones P/CO
☐ 18 Rick Tronerud CO
☐ 19 Dave Schober TR
☐ 20 Jeffrey Newman MGR
☐ 21 Pat Gilbert
☐ 22 Kevin Ward
☐ 23 Patrick Wernig
☐ 24 Raymond Young
☐ 25 Angel Escobar
☐ 26 Jose Mota
☐ 27 Joe Klink
☐ 28 Ozzie Canseco
☐ 29 Team logo
Checklist

1989 Idaho Falls Braves ProCards

This 31-card standard-size set of the 1989 Idaho Falls Braves, a Rookie Class Pioneer League affiliate of the Atlanta Braves, features orange-bordered posed color player photos on its fronts. The player's name, position, and team name appear at the bottom. The horizontal gray back carries the player's name and position at the top, followed by biography and statistics.

	MINT	NRMT	EXC
COMPLETE SET (31)	5.00	2.20	.60

☐ 2007 Checklist
☐ 2008 Field Staff
Cloyd Boyer
Mike Boyer
Randy Smith
☐ 2009 Brian Wright
☐ 2010 Ramces Guerrero
☐ 2011 Jimmie Pullins
☐ 2012 Lionel Adams III
☐ 2013 Rickey Rigsby
☐ 2014 Ken Harring Jr.
☐ 2015 Jose Olmeda
☐ 2016 Fred Lopez
☐ 2017 Ricky Gore
☐ 2018 Daniel Sims Jr.
☐ 2019 Dave Waldenberger
☐ 2020 Billy Miller
☐ 2021 Tyler Houston
☐ 2022 Chris Burton
☐ 2023 Michael Sweeney
☐ 2024 Chris Sparrow
☐ 2025 Jim Baranoski
☐ 2026 Tony Valle
☐ 2027 Doug Rogers
☐ 2028 Eric Kuhlman
☐ 2029 Jeff Zona
☐ 2030 Tom Eckhardt
☐ 2031 Jim Kortright
☐ 2032 Scott Osmon
☐ 2033 Don Lemon
☐ 2034 Randy White
☐ 2035 Mike Parker
☐ 2036 Tom Newman
☐ 2037 Kevin Haeberle

1989 Indianapolis Indians CMC

This 25-card standard-size set of the 1989 Indianapolis Indians, a Class AAA American Association affiliate of the Montreal Expos, features on its fronts white-bordered posed color player photos framed by a black line. The team's name, the player's name, and his position appear at the bottom. The white back is framed by a black line and carries the team's name and league at the top, followed by the player's name, position, biography and statistics. Hook's and Pepsi co-sponsored the set.

	MINT	NRMT	EXC
COMPLETE SET (25)	8.00	3.60	1.00

☐ 1 Tim Barrett
☐ 2 Sergio Waldez
☐ 3 Steve Frey
☐ 4 Pat Pacillo
☐ 5 Brett Gideon
☐ 6 Scott Anderson
☐ 7 Jay Baller
☐ 8 Mark Gardner
☐ 9 Tim McCormack TR
☐ 10 Rich Thompson
☐ 11 Gil Reyes
☐ 12 Razor Shines
☐ 13 Billy Moore
☐ 14 Mike Blowers
☐ 15 Marty Pevey
☐ 16 Randy Braun
☐ 17 Lorenzo Bundy
☐ 18 Jeff Huson
☐ 19 Armondo Moreno
☐ 20 Junior Noboa
☐ 21 Kevin Dean
☐ 22 Darryl Motley
☐ 23 Larry Walker
☐ 24 Coaches
Dave Van Gorder CO
Joe Kerrigan CO
Nelson Norman CO
☐ 25 Tom Runnells MG

1989 Indianapolis Indians ProCards

This 32-card standard-size set of the 1989 Indianapolis Indians, a Class AAA American Association affiliate of the Montreal Expos, features blue-bordered posed color player photos on its fronts. The player's name, position, and team name appear at the bottom. The horizontal gray back carries the player's name and position at the top, followed by biography and statistics. The set was co-sponsored by Pepsi and Hook's.

	MINT	NRMT	EXC
COMPLETE SET (32)	7.00	3.10	.85

☐ 1209 Checklist
☐ 1210 Alonzo Powell
☐ 1211 Billy Moore
☐ 1212 Joel McKeon
☐ 1213 Randy Braun
☐ 1214 Jeff Dedmon
☐ 1215 Sergio Valdez
☐ 1216 Indians' Broadcasters
Tom Akins
Howard Kellman
☐ 1217 Marty Pevey
☐ 1218 Steve Frey
☐ 1219 Razor Shines
☐ 1220 Tom Runnells MG
☐ 1221 Mike Blowers
☐ 1222 Armando Moreno
☐ 1223 Lorenzo Bundy
☐ 1224 Mark Gardner
☐ 1225 Kevin Dean
☐ 1226 Tim McCormack TR
☐ 1227 Coaching Staff
Joe Kerrigan
Nelson Norman
Dave Van Gorder
☐ 1228 Rich Sauveur
☐ 1229 Tim Barrett
☐ 1230 Brett Gideon
☐ 1231 Jay Baller
☐ 1232 Urbano Lugo
☐ 1233 Jeffrey Huson
☐ 1234 Scott Anderson
☐ 1235 Junior Noboa
☐ 1236 Pat Pacillo
☐ 1237 Rich Thompson
☐ 1238 Darryl Motley
☐ 1239 Larry Walker
☐ 1240 Gilberto Reyes

1989 Iowa Cubs CMC

	MINT	NRMT	EXC
COMPLETE SET (25)	5.00	2.20	.60

☐ 1 Mike Capel
☐ 2 Len Damian
☐ 3 Joe Kraemer
☐ 4 Ed Vande Berg
☐ 5 Mike Harkey
☐ 6 Dave Masters
☐ 7 Kevin Blankenship
☐ 8 Lester Lancaster
☐ 9 Rich Scheid
☐ 10 Dean Wilkins
☐ 11 Butch Garcia
☐ 12 Lloyd McClendon
☐ 13 Hector Villanueva
☐ 14 Bruce Crabbe
☐ 15 Luis Cruz
☐ 16 Brian Guinn
☐ 17 Bryan House
☐ 18 Howard Nichols
☐ 19 Dave Owen
☐ 20 Doug Dascenzo
☐ 21 Winston Ficklin
☐ 22 Dwight Smith
☐ 23 Mike Tullier
☐ 24 Jim Wright CO
☐ 25 Pete MacKanin MGR

1989 Iowa Cubs ProCards

This 28-card standard-size set of the 1989 Iowa Cubs, a Class AAA American Association affiliate of the Chicago Cubs, features blue-bordered posed color player photos on its fronts. The player's name, position, and team name appear at the bottom. The horizontal gray back carries the player's name and position at the top, followed by biography and statistics.

	MINT	NRMT	EXC
COMPLETE SET (28)	5.00	2.20	.60

☐ 1688 Checklist
☐ 1689 Les Lancaster
☐ 1690 Dean Wilkins
☐ 1691 Roger Williams
☐ 1692 Luis Cruz
☐ 1693 Butch Garcia
☐ 1694 Dave Owen
☐ 1695 Lloyd McClendon
☐ 1696 Hector Vilanueva
☐ 1697 Jim Wright
☐ 1698 Dave Masters
☐ 1699 Kevin Blankenship
☐ 1700 Bryan House
☐ 1701 Mike Tullier
☐ 1702 Doug Dascenzo
☐ 1703 Dave Grossman TR
☐ 1704 Mike Harkey
☐ 1705 Len Damian
☐ 1706 Mike Capel
☐ 1707 Pete MacKanin MGR
☐ 1708 Dwight Smith
☐ 1709 Brian Guinn
☐ 1710 Ed Vande Berg
☐ 1711 Winston Ficklin
☐ 1712 Howard Nichols
☐ 1713 Rich Scheid
☐ 1714 Bruce Crabbe
☐ 1715 Joe Kraemer

1989 Jackson Mets Grand Slam

	MINT	NRMT	EXC
COMPLETE SET (30)	5.00	2.20	.60

☐ 1 Greg Talamantez
☐ 2 Chuck Carr
☐ 3 Tim Bogar
☐ 4 Craig Repoz
☐ 5 Chris Jelic
☐ 6 Toby Nivens
☐ 7 Todd Welborn
☐ 8 Dave Trautwein
☐ 9 Gus Meizoso
☐ 10 Jeff Bumgarner
☐ 11 Julio Machado
☐ 12 Juan Villanueva
☐ 13 Manny Salinas
☐ 14 Angelo Cuevas
☐ 15 Zoilo Sanchez
☐ 16 Johnny Monell
☐ 17 Gilberto Roca
☐ 18 Howie Freiling
☐ 19 Mike DeButch
☐ 20 Steve Swisher MGR
☐ 21 Bob Apodaca CO
☐ 22 Kip Gross
☐ 23 Pete Bauer

☐ 24 Chris Rauth
☐ 25 Dave Liddell
☐ 26 Kevin Brown
☐ 27 Brian Givens
☐ 28 Dale Plummer
☐ 29 Julio Valera
☐ 30 Alan Hayden

1989 Jacksonville Expos Best

This 29-card standard-size set of the 1989 Jacksonville Expos, a Class AA Southern League affiliate of the Montreal Expos, features white-bordered posed color player photos on its fronts. The year "1989" and the city are written vertically on the left side, and the player's name and position are given below the picture. In a horizontal format, the yellow backs carry the player's name and position at the top, followed by biography, career highlights, statistics, and a color headshot. A special "Platinum" set was issued, production for which was limited to 1,500 sets.

	MINT	NRMT	EXC
COMPLETE SET (29)	20.00	9.00	2.50
COMP. LIMITED EDITION SET (29)	30.00	13.50	3.70

☐ 1 Marquis Grissom
☐ 2 Alan Bannister MG
☐ 3 Mel Houston
☐ 4 Chris Marchok
☐ 5 Eddie Dixon
☐ 6 Doug Duke
☐ 7 Mike Dull
☐ 8 Pat Sipe
☐ 9 Kent Bottenfield
☐ 10 Travis Chambers
☐ 11 Archi Cianfrocco
☐ 12 Howard Farmer
☐ 13 Tim Peters
☐ 14 Quinn Mack
☐ 15 Delino DeShields
☐ 16 Boi Rodriguez
☐ 17 Rob Natal
☐ 18 Fred Williams
☐ 19 Rick Carriger
☐ 20 Gomer Hodge CO
☐ 21 Danilo Leon
☐ 22 Sean Cunningham TR
☐ 23 Peter Bragan GM
☐ 24 Dan Gakeler
☐ 25 John Vander Wal
☐ 26 Nardi Contreas CO
☐ 27 Gene Glynn CO
☐ 28 Mel Rojas
☐ 29 Team photo
Checklist

1989 Jacksonville Expos ProCards

This 29-card standard-size set of the 1989 Jacksonville Expos, a Class AA Southern League affiliate of the Montreal Expos, features red-bordered posed color player photos on its fronts. The player's name, position, and team name appear at the bottom. The horizontal gray back carries the player's name and position at the top, followed by biography and statistics. The set was sponsored by Kool-Aid.

	MINT	NRMT	EXC
COMPLETE SET (29)	12.00	5.50	1.50

☐ 150 Checklist
☐ 151 Alan Bannister MG
☐ 152 Delino DeShields
☐ 153 Quinn Mack
☐ 154 Tim Peters
☐ 155 Howard Farmer
☐ 156 Mel Rojas
☐ 157 Dan Gakeler
☐ 158 Sean Cunningham TR
☐ 159 Eddie Dixon
☐ 160 Archi Cianfrocco
☐ 161 John Vander Wal
☐ 162 Travis Chambers
☐ 163 Kent Bottenfield
☐ 164 Mike Dull
☐ 165 Pat Sipe
☐ 166 Chris Marchok
☐ 167 Doug Duke
☐ 168 Rick Carriger
☐ 169 Danilo Leon
☐ 170 Mel Houston
☐ 171 Phil Wilson
☐ 172 Fred Williams
☐ 173 Nardi Contreras CO
☐ 174 Gene Glynn CO
☐ 175 Marquis Grissom
☐ 176 Rob Natal
☐ 177 Boi Rodriguez
☐ 178 Team Picture

1989 Jamestown Expos ProCards

This 30-card standard-size set of the 1989 Jamestown Expos, a Class A New York-Penn League affiliate of the Montreal Expos, features orange-bordered posed color player photos on its fronts. The player's name, position, and team name appear at the bottom. The horizontal gray back carries the player's name and position at the top, followed by biography and statistics. The set was co-sponsored by McDonald's and Coca-Cola.

	MINT	NRMT	EXC
COMPLETE SET (30)	5.00	2.20	.60

☐ 2129 Checklist
☐ 2130 Dale Buzzard
☐ 2131 Buena Rodriguez
☐ 2132 F.P. Santangelo
☐ 2133 Robert Small
☐ 2134 Tyrone Woods
☐ 2135 Paul Ciaglo
☐ 2136 Pete Young
☐ 2137 Tim Laker
☐ 2138 Gary Pipik
☐ 2139 Troy Wessel
☐ 2140 Steve Whitehead
☐ 2141 Matt Stairs
☐ 2142 Dan Archibald
☐ 2143 Pat Heiderscheit
☐ 2144 David Sommer
☐ 2145 Scott Davison
☐ 2146 Todd Mayo
☐ 2147 Isaac Elder
☐ 2148 Ken Lake
☐ 2149 Gary Engelkin CO
☐ 2150 Don Werner MG
☐ 2151 Steve Mandl CO
☐ 2152 Q.V. Lowe CO
☐ 2153 Alejandro Tejada
☐ 2154 Gary Regira
☐ 2155 Joe Klancnik
☐ 2156 Rusty Kilgo
☐ 2157 John Thoden
☐ 2158 Joe Logan Jr.

1989 Johnson City Cardinals Star

The 1989 Johnson City Cardinals set contains 26 standard-size cards. The fronts have posed color player photos, with red borders on the top portion of the card fading to yellow as one moves down the card face. In red print on a pale yellow background, the backs have biography and statistics. The reverse of card number 26 is a slighter darker shade of yellow than the other cards. 5,000 sets produced.

	MINT	NRMT	EXC
COMPLETE SET (26)	5.00	2.20	.60

☐ 1 Jim Allen
☐ 2 Juan Andujar
☐ 3 Alan Botkin
☐ 4 Johnny Calzado
☐ 5 Frank Cimorelli
☐ 6 Paul Coleman
☐ 7 Ernie Baker
☐ 8 Steve Dixon
☐ 9 Chuck Edwards
☐ 10 Bryan Eversgerd
☐ 11 Willie Espinal
☐ 12 Bill Felitz
☐ 13 Jeff Fayne
☐ 14 Scott Halama
☐ 15 Mike Kraft
☐ 16 Tony Ochs
☐ 17 Al Pacheco
☐ 18 Ahmed Rodriguez
☐ 19 Odalis Savinon
☐ 20 Richard Shackle
☐ 21 John Stevens
☐ 22 Ron Weber
☐ 23 Denny Wiseman
☐ 24 Coaching Staff
Mark DeJohn MGR
Dick Sisler CO
☐ 25 Alfredo Ortiz CO
☐ 26 Robert Harrison TR

1989 Kenosha Twins ProCards

This 29-card standard-size set of the 1989 Kenosha Twins, a Class A Midwest League affiliate of the Minnesota Twins, features orange-bordered posed color player photos on its fronts. The player's name, position, and team name appear at the bottom. The horizontal gray back carries the player's name and position at the top, followed by biography and statistics.

	MINT	NRMT	EXC
COMPLETE SET (29)	5.00	2.20	.60

☐ 1057 Checklist
☐ 1058 Bob Lee
President/GM
☐ 1059 Mike Mathiot
☐ 1060 Steve Morris
☐ 1061 Mark North
☐ 1062 Brad Fontes
☐ 1063 Jay Kvasnicka
☐ 1064 Deryk Gross
☐ 1065 Carl Johnson
☐ 1066 Dom Rovasio
☐ 1067 Pat Mahomes
☐ 1068 Terry Brown
☐ 1069 Bryan Roskom
☐ 1070 Don Leppert
Field Coordinator
☐ 1071 Mike Misuraca
☐ 1072 J.P. Wright
☐ 1073 Steve Dunn
☐ 1074 J.T. Bruett
☐ 1075 Gary Resetar
☐ 1076 Rich Garces
☐ 1077 Rusty Kryzanowski
☐ 1078 Chad Swanson
☐ 1079 Steve Muh
☐ 1080 Brian Allard
☐ 1081 Mike Pomeranz
☐ 1082 Rolando Pino
☐ 1083 Cheo Garcia
☐ 1084 Steve Liddle MGR
☐ 1085 Dan Fox TR

1989 Kenosha Twins Star

The 1989 Kenosha Twins set contains 27 standard-size cards. The fronts have posed color player photos, with blue borders on the top portion of the card fading to red as one moves down the card face. In dark blue print on a medium blue background, the backs have biography and statistics. Card numbers 26-27 have a light blue background on the reverse. 5,000 sets produced.

	MINT	NRMT	EXC
COMPLETE SET (27)	5.00	2.20	.60

☐ 1 Tom Boyce
☐ 2 Terry Brown
☐ 3 J.T. Bruett
☐ 4 Steve Dunn
☐ 5 Brad Fontes
☐ 6 Rich Garces
☐ 7 Cheo Garcia
☐ 8 Deryk Gross
☐ 9 Carl Johnson
☐ 10 Rusty Kryzanowski
☐ 11 Jay Kvansnicka
☐ 12 Pat Mahomes
☐ 13 Mike Mathiot
☐ 14 Todd McClure
☐ 15 Mike Misuraca
☐ 16 Steve Morris
☐ 17 Steve Muh
☐ 18 Mark North
☐ 19 Rolando Pino
☐ 20 Mike Pomeranz
☐ 21 Gary Resetar
☐ 22 Bryan Roskom
☐ 23 Dom Ravasio
☐ 24 J.P. Wright
☐ 25 Steve Liddle MGR
☐ 26 Dan Fox TR
☐ 27 Brian Allard CO

1989 Kingsport Mets Star

The 1989 Kingsport Mets set contains 30 standard-size cards. The fronts have posed color player photos, with blue borders on the top portion of the card fading to orange as one moves down the card face. In blue print on a pale orange background, the backs have biography and statistics. The fronts of card numbers 26-30 have a lighter shade of orange than the other cards. 5,000 sets produced.

	MINT	NRMT	EXC
COMPLETE SET (30)	5.00	2.20	.60

☐ 1 Dan Auchard
☐ 2 Tim Buhe
☐ 3 Chris Butler
☐ 4 Hector Carrasco
☐ 5 Albert Castillo
☐ 6 Nick Davis
☐ 7 Alberto Diaz
☐ 8 Tom Engle
☐ 9 Andy Fidler
☐ 10 Brook Fordyce
☐ 11 Rob Guzik
☐ 12 James Harris
☐ 13 Reid Hartmann
☐ 14 Craig Johnston
☐ 15 Mike Lehnerz
☐ 16 Tim McClinton
☐ 17 Wallace Minnifield
☐ 18 Rich Ostopowicz
☐ 19 Nicolas Polanco
☐ 20 Deron Sample
☐ 21 Craig Scott
☐ 22 Jim Sheffler
☐ 23 Eric Thornton
☐ 24 Ed Vazquez
☐ 25 Kyle Washington
☐ 26 Jim Eschen MGR
☐ 27 Dan Norman CO
☐ 28 Mike Murray TR
☐ 29 Bat Boys
Tyler Hobbs
Josh Brickey
Ben Smith
Travis Nelson
☐ 30 Dottie Elsea GM
and President

1989 Kinston Indians Star

The 1989 Kinston Indians set contains 27 standard-size cards. The fronts have posed color player photos, with purple borders on the top portion of the card fading to yellow as one moves down the card face. In purple print on a pale yellow background, the backs have biography and statistics. This issue includes the minor league card debut of Charles Nagy. 5,000 sets produced.

	MINT	NRMT	EXC
COMPLETE SET (27)	15.00	6.75	1.85

☐ 1 Jamie Allison
☐ 2 Ramon Bautista
☐ 3 Barry Blackwell
☐ 4 Jim Bruske
☐ 5 Andy Casano
☐ 6 Daren Epley
☐ 7 Richard Falkner
☐ 8 Greg Ferlenda
☐ 9 Sam Ferretti
☐ 10 Brian Johnson
☐ 11 Tommy Kramer
☐ 12 Mark Lewis
☐ 13 Jeff Mutis
☐ 14 Charles Nagy
☐ 15 Rouglas Odor
☐ 16 David Oliveras
☐ 17 Angel Ortiz
☐ 18 Doug Piatt
☐ 19 Mark Pike
☐ 20 Jim Richardson
☐ 21 Greg Roscoe
☐ 22 Tony Scaglione
☐ 23 Rudy Seanez
☐ 24 Ken Whitfield
☐ 25 Ken Bolek MGR
☐ 26 Mike Brown CO
☐ 27 Will George CO

1989 Knoxville Blue Jays Best

This 31-card standard-size 10th Anniversary set of the 1989 Knoxville Blue Jays, a Class AA Southern League affiliate of the Toronto Blue Jays, features white-bordered posed and action color player photos on its fronts. The year "1989" and the city are written vertically on the left side of the card, and the player's name and position are given below the picture. In a horizontal format, the backs have biography, statistics, career highlights, and a color headshot, all in a yellow rectangular box. The backs of the Rogers and Schunk cards were reversed.

	MINT	NRMT	EXC
COMPLETE SET (31)	15.00	6.75	1.85

☐ 1 Derek Bell
☐ 2 Kevin Batiste
☐ 3 Darren Balsley
☐ 4 Carlos Diaz
☐ 5 Jose Diaz
☐ 6 Webster Garrison
☐ 7 Tom Gilles
☐ 8 Mauro Gozzo
☐ 9 Xavier Hernandez
☐ 10 Shawn Jeter
☐ 11 Chris Jones
☐ 12 Dennis Jones
☐ 13 Bob MacDonald
☐ 14 Omar Malave
☐ 15 Domingo Martinez
☐ 16 Mike Mills
☐ 17 Brian Morrison
☐ 18 Pedro Munoz
☐ 19 Joe Newcomb
☐ 20 Tom Quinlan
☐ 21 Ken Rivers
☐ 22 Jimmy Rogers
☐ 23 Jerry Schunk
☐ 24 John Shea
☐ 25 J.J. Cannon CO
☐ 26 Mark Whiten
☐ 27 Bob Wishnevski UER
(Misspelled Wishneuski
on front and back)
☐ 28 Barry Foote MG
☐ 29 John Poloni CO
☐ 30 Tim Ringler TR
☐ 31 Team logo
Checklist

1989 Knoxville Blue Jays ProCards

This 31-card standard-size set of the 1989 Knoxville Blue Jays, a Class AA Southern League affiliate of the Toronto Blue Jays, features red-bordered posed color player photos on its fronts. The player's name, position, and team name appear at the bottom. The horizontal gray back carries the player's name and position at the top, followed by biography and statistics. The set was sponsored by the Knoxville Coin Exchange.

	MINT	NRMT	EXC
COMPLETE SET (31)	10.00	4.50	1.25

☐ 1119 Checklist
☐ 1120 Bill Dyke
Asst GM
☐ 1121 Gary McCune GM
☐ 1122 Tim Ringler TR
☐ 1123 Tom Quinlan
☐ 1124 Kevin Batiste
☐ 1125 Carlos Diaz
☐ 1126 Pedro Munoz
☐ 1127 Omar Malave
☐ 1128 Barry Foote MG
☐ 1129 J.J. Cannon CO
☐ 1130 Shawn Jeter
☐ 1131 Webster Garrison
☐ 1132 Ken Rivers
☐ 1133 Jimmy Rogers
☐ 1134 Chris Jones
☐ 1135 Joe Newcomb
☐ 1136 Dennis Jones
☐ 1137 Darren Balsley
☐ 1138 Bob Wishnevski
☐ 1139 Bob MacDonald
☐ 1140 John Shea
☐ 1141 Mike Mills
☐ 1142 Jerry Schunk
☐ 1143 Tom Gilles
☐ 1144 Xavier Hernandez
☐ 1145 Goose Gozzo
☐ 1146 Brian Morrison
☐ 1147 John Paul Poloni CO
☐ 1148 Domingo Martinez
☐ 1149 Derek Bell

1989 Knoxville Blue Jays Star

This 25-card standard-size set of the 1989 Knoxville Blue Jays, a Class AA Southern League affiliate of the Toronto Blue Jays, features blue-bordered posed color player photos on its fronts. The player's name, team name, and position appear at the bottom. The light blue horizontal back carries the player's name at the top, followed by biography and statistics. 5,000 sets produced.

	MINT	NRMT	EXC
COMPLETE SET (25)	10.00	4.50	1.25

☐ 1 Derek Bell
☐ 2 Carlos Diaz
☐ 3 Jose Diaz
☐ 4 Webster Garrison
☐ 5 Darren Balsley
☐ 6 Goose Gozzo
☐ 7 Kevin Batiste
☐ 8 Shawn Jeter
☐ 9 Chris Jones
☐ 10 Dennis Jones
☐ 11 Bob MacDonald
☐ 12 Domingo Martinez
☐ 13 Omar Malave
☐ 14 Pedro Munoz
☐ 15 Joe Dean Newcomb
☐ 16 Tom Quinlan
☐ 17 Ken Rivers
☐ 18 Jimmy Rogers
☐ 19 Jerry Schunk
☐ 20 John Shea
☐ 21 Mark Whiten
☐ 22 Bob Wishnevski
☐ 23 Mike Mills
☐ 24 J.J. Cannon CO
☐ 25 John Poloni CO

1989 Lakeland Tigers Star

The 1989 Lakeland Tigers set contains 28 standard-size cards. The fronts have posed color player photos, with blue borders on the top portion of the card fading to orange as one moves down the card face. In blue print on a pale orange background, the backs have biography and statistics. The cards are arranged alphabetically and numbered on the back. 5,000 sets produced.

	MINT	NRMT	EXC
COMPLETE SET (28)	5.00	2.20	.60

☐ 1 Marcus Adler
☐ 2 Jim Baxter
☐ 3 Rico Brogna
☐ 4 Basilio Cabrera
☐ 5 Ron Cook
☐ 6 Luis Galindo
☐ 7 Dave Haas
☐ 8 Shawn Hare
☐ 9 Bill Henderson
☐ 10 Riccardo Ingram
☐ 11 Mike Jones
☐ 12 John Kiely
☐ 13 Kurt Knudsen
☐ 14 Mike Lumley
☐ 15 Ron Marigny
☐ 16 Dan O'Neill
☐ 17 Dan Raley
☐ 18 Dave Richards
☐ 19 Tookie Spann
☐ 20 Chuck Steward
☐ 21 Eric Stone
☐ 22 Steve Strong
☐ 23 Andy Toney
☐ 24 Mike Wilkins
☐ 25 Marty Willis
☐ 26 John Lipon
☐ 27 Kenn Cunningham
☐ 28 Ralph Treuel

1989 Las Vegas Stars CMC

	MINT	NRMT	EXC
COMPLETE SET (25)	10.00	4.50	1.25

☐ 1 Joe Bitker
☐ 2 Keith Comstock
☐ 3 Joe Lynch
☐ 4 Terry Gilmore
☐ 5 Tony Ghelfi
☐ 6 Matt Maysey
☐ 7 Dan Murphy
☐ 8 Eric Nolte
☐ 9 Pete Roberts
☐ 10 Bill Taylor
☐ 11 Sandy Alomar
☐ 12 Randy Byers
☐ 13 Jerald Clark
☐ 14 Joey Cora
☐ 15 Thomas Howard
☐ 16 Rob Nelson
☐ 17 Jeff Hearron
☐ 18 Carlos Baerga
☐ 19 Bill Wrona
☐ 20 Jeff Yurtin
☐ 21 Paul Runge
☐ 22 Shawn Abner
☐ 23 Chris Knabenshue
☐ 24 Steve Smith MGR
☐ 25 Coaches
Tony Torchia
Steve Luebber

1989 Las Vegas Stars ProCards

This 29-card standard-size set of the 1989 Las Vegas Stars, a Class AAA Pacific Coast League affiliate of the San Diego Padres, features blue-bordered posed color player photos on its fronts. The player's name, position, and team name appear at the bottom. The horizontal gray back carries the player's name and position at the top, followed by biography and statistics.

	MINT	NRMT	EXC
COMPLETE SET (29)	15.00	6.75	1.85

☐ 1 Tony Ghelfi
☐ 2 Dan Murphy
☐ 3 Billy Taylor
☐ 4 Joe Bitker
☐ 5 Matt Maysey
☐ 6 Randy Byers
☐ 7 Sandy Alomar
☐ 8 Thomas Howard
☐ 9 Carlos Baerga
☐ 10 Jerald Clark
☐ 11 Jeff Hearron
☐ 12 Eric Nolte
☐ 13 Pete Roberts
☐ 14 Keith Comstock
☐ 15 Pat Clements
☐ 16 Terry Gilmore
☐ 17 Roger Smithberg
☐ 18 Billy Wrona
☐ 19 Chris Knabenshue
☐ 20 Jeff Yurtin
☐ 21 Shawn Abner
☐ 22 Joe Lynch
☐ 23 Joey Cora
☐ 24 Rob Nelson
☐ 25 Steve Smith MGR
☐ 26 Steve Luebber CO
☐ 27 Tony Torchia CO
☐ 28 Todd Hutcheson TR
☐ 29 Checklist

1989 London Tigers ProCards

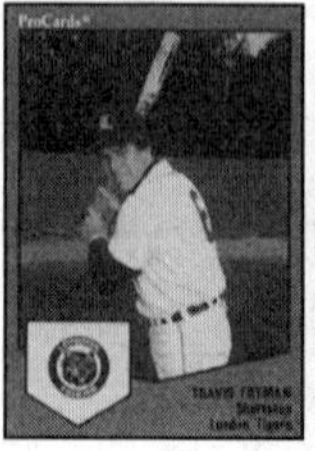
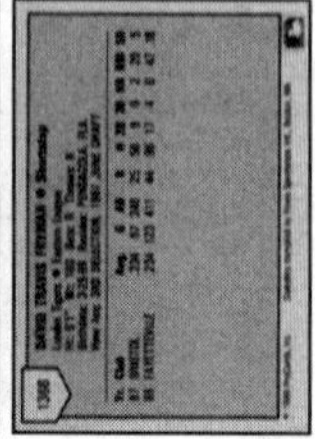

This 32-card standard-size set of the 1989 London Tigers, a Class AA Eastern League affiliate of the Detroit Tigers, features red-bordered posed color player photos on its fronts. The player's name, position, and team name appear at the bottom. The horizontal gray back carries the player's name and position at the top, followed by biography and statistics.

	MINT	NRMT	EXC
COMPLETE SET (32)	20.00	9.00	2.50

☐ 1356 Checklist
☐ 1357 Steve Howe
☐ 1358 Bob Gilson GM
☐ 1359 Bob Eaman
Director of Operations
☐ 1360 Bill Wilkinson
Asst GM
☐ 1361 Dan Ross
President
☐ 1362 Dave Cooper
☐ 1363 Donnie Rowland
☐ 1364 Bernie Anderson
☐ 1365 John Toale
☐ 1366 Travis Fryman
☐ 1367 Mike Delao TR
☐ 1368 Scott Aldred
☐ 1369 Ron Rightnowar
☐ 1370 Darren Hursey
☐ 1371 Arnie Beyeler
☐ 1372 Dean Decillis
☐ 1373 Tim Leiper
☐ 1374 Don Vesling
☐ 1375 Mike Schwabe
☐ 1376 Mike Hansen
☐ 1377 Randy Nosek
☐ 1378 Chris Chambliss MGR
☐ 1379 Rob Thomson CO
☐ 1380 Greg Everson
☐ 1381 Scott Livingstone
☐ 1382 Wayne Housie
☐ 1383 Phil Clark
☐ 1384 Doyle Balthazar
☐ 1385 Manny Jose
☐ 1386 Tom Aldrich
☐ 1387 Jose Ramos

1989 Louisville Red Birds CMC

	MINT	NRMT	EXC
COMPLETE SET (25)	5.00	2.20	.60

☐ 1 Gibson Alba
☐ 2 Scott Arnold
☐ 3 Roger Erickson
Sic, Erikson
☐ 4 Jeff Fassero
☐ 5 Hap Hudson TR
☐ 6 Howard Hilton
☐ 7 Matt Kinzer
☐ 8 Rod Booker
☐ 9 Steve Peters
☐ 10 Ted Power
☐ 11 Bob Tewksbury
☐ 12 Jim Puzey
☐ 13 Todd Zeile
☐ 14 Luis Alicea
☐ 15 Romy Cucjen
☐ 16 Leon Durham
☐ 17 Bien Figueroa
☐ 18 Mike Fitzgerald
☐ 19 Greg Jelks
☐ 20 Tom Baine
☐ 21 Alex Cole
☐ 22 Ron Shepherd
☐ 23 Randy Byers
☐ 24 Mark Riggins CO
☐ 25 Mike Jorgensen MGR

1989 Louisville Red Birds ProCards

This 28-card standard-size set of the 1989 Louisville Red Birds, a Class AAA American Association affiliate of the St. Louis Cardinals, features blue-bordered posed color player photos on its fronts. The player's name, position, and team name appear at the bottom. The horizontal gray back carries the player's name and position at the top, followed by biography and statistics. 7,500 sets were produced.

	MINT	NRMT	EXC
COMPLETE SET (28)	8.00	3.60	1.00

☐ 1241 Checklist
☐ 1242 Roger Erickson
☐ 1243 Jim Puzey
☐ 1244 Bryan Oelkers
☐ 1245 Randy Byers
☐ 1246 Jeff Fassero
☐ 1247 Steve Peters
☐ 1248 Scott Arnold
☐ 1249 Ted Power
☐ 1250 Bob Tewksbury
☐ 1251 Howard Hilton
☐ 1252 Gibson Alba
☐ 1253 David(Hap) Hudson TR
☐ 1254 Mark Riggins CO
☐ 1255 Matt Kinzer
☐ 1256 Mike Jorgensen MGR
☐ 1257 Romy Cucjen
☐ 1258 Greg Jelks
☐ 1259 Mike Fitzgerald
☐ 1260 Leon Durham
☐ 1261 Ron Shepherd
☐ 1262 Bien Figueroa
☐ 1263 Luis Alicea
☐ 1264 Rod Booker
☐ 1265 Tom Baine
☐ 1266 Alex Cole
☐ 1267 Todd Zeile
☐ 1268 Ken Hill

1989 Louisville Red Birds Team Issue

This set contains 38 standard-size cards. The color action player photos adorning the fronts have rounded corners and white borders. The team logo is superimposed at the lower left corner of the picture. The backs present biographical and statistical information.

	MINT	NRMT	EXC
COMPLETE SET (38)	10.00	4.50	1.25

☐ 1 Checklist
Billy Bird (Mascot)
☐ 2 Todd Zeile
Player of the Year
☐ 3 Todd Zeile
At bat
☐ 4 Todd Zeile
Awaiting throw
☐ 5 Todd Zeile
Looking over shoulder
☐ 6 Mike Jorgensen MGR
☐ 7 Gibson Alba
☐ 8 Luis Alicea
☐ 9 Scott Arnold
☐ 10 Tom Baine
☐ 11 Rod Booker
☐ 12 Randell Byers
☐ 13 Cris Carpenter
☐ 14 Alex Cole
☐ 15 Romy Cucjen
☐ 16 Leon Durham
☐ 17 Roger Erickson
☐ 18 Jeff Fassero
☐ 19 Bien Figueroa
☐ 20 Mike Fitzgerald
☐ 21 Don Heinkel
☐ 22 Ken Hill
☐ 23 Howard Hilton
☐ 24 Greg Jelks
☐ 25 Matt Kinzer
☐ 26 Jim Lindeman
☐ 27 Willie McGee
☐ 28 Chuck McGrath
☐ 29 Bryan Oelkers
☐ 30 Steve Peters
☐ 31 Frank Potestio
☐ 32 Ted Power
☐ 33 Jim Puzey
☐ 34 Ron Shepherd
☐ 35 Bob Tewksbury
☐ 36 Craig Wilson
☐ 37 Todd Worrell
☐ 38 Hap Hudson TR

1989 Lynchburg Red Sox Star

The 1989 Lynchburg Red Sox set contains 29 standard-size cards. The fronts have posed color player photos, with red borders on the top portion of the card fading to blue as one moves down the card face. In blue print on a pink background, the backs have biography and statistics. Card numbers 26-29 have blue background on the reverse. 5,000 sets produced.

	MINT	NRMT	EXC
COMPLETE SET (29)	6.00	2.70	.75

☐ 1 Mike Baker
☐ 2 Jose Birriel
☐ 3 Tim Buheller
☐ 4 Dale Burgo
☐ 5 Fred Davis
☐ 6 Paul Devlin
☐ 7 John Dolan
☐ 8 Tom Fischer
☐ 9 Dave Gray
☐ 10 Bart Haley
☐ 11 Mike Kelly
☐ 12 Derek Livernois
☐ 13 Gil Martinez
☐ 14 Juan Molero
☐ 15 Tim Naehring
☐ 16 David Owen
☐ 17 Juan Paris
☐ 18 Phil Plantier
☐ 19 Scott Powers
☐ 20 Leslie Wallin
☐ 21 Stu Weidie
☐ 22 Craig Wilson
☐ 23 Gary Allenson MGR
☐ 24 Jim Bibby CO
☐ 25 Scott Skripko
☐ 26 Roger Haggerty
☐ 27 Zack Dzafic
☐ 28 Ronnie Richardson
☐ 29 Rodney Taylor

1989 Madison Muskies Star

This 26-card standard-size set features the 1989 Madison Muskies, a farm club for the Oakland Athletics. The fronts have posed color player photos, with green borders on the top portion of the card fading to yellow as one moves down the card face. In green print on a pale yellow background, the backs have biography and statistics. Card numbers 23-25 were apparently never issued. 5,000 sets produced.

	MINT	NRMT	EXC
COMPLETE SET (26)	5.00	2.20	.60

- ☐ 1 Mark Aguilar
- ☐ 2 Tony Ariola
- ☐ 3 Rich Berg
- ☐ 4 Dean Borelli
- ☐ 5 James Buccheri
- ☐ 6 Tom Carcione
- ☐ 7 Mike Messerly
- ☐ 8 Jim Foley
- ☐ 9 Lorenzo Furcal
- ☐ 10 Apolinar Garcia
- ☐ 11 Dwayne Hosey
- ☐ 12 Jim Lawson
- ☐ 13 Will Love
- ☐ 14 Angel Martinez
- ☐ 15 Frank Masters
- ☐ 16 Luis Mateo
- ☐ 17 Jim Nettles MGR
- ☐ 18 Bronswell Patrick
- ☐ 19 Ed Ricks
- ☐ 20 Billy Taylor
- ☐ 21 Lee Tinsley
- ☐ 22 Tim Vannaman
- ☐ 26 Henry Mercedes
- ☐ 27 Marteese Robinson
- ☐ 28 Ray Harris
- ☐ 29 Van Golmont

1989 Martinsville Phillies Star

The 1989 Martinsville Phillies set contains 35 standard-size cards. The fronts have posed color player photos, with aqua borders on the top portion of the card fading to red as one moves down the card face. In red print on a white background, the backs have biography and statistics. 5,000 sets produced.

	MINT	NRMT	EXC
COMPLETE SET (35)	5.00	2.20	.60

- ☐ 1 Al Baur
- ☐ 2 Kenneth Bean
- ☐ 3 Luis Brito
- ☐ 4 Williams Carmona
- ☐ 5 Paul Carson
- ☐ 6 Cancio Casado
- ☐ 7 Jim Cosman
- ☐ 8 Ismael Cruz
- ☐ 9 Matt Current
- ☐ 10 Mike Dafforn
- ☐ 11 Lamar Foster
- ☐ 12 Darrell Goedhart
- ☐ 13 Elliott Gray
- ☐ 14 Tom Hardgrove
- ☐ 15 Charles Hurst
- ☐ 16 Jeff Jackson
- ☐ 17 Aurelio Llanos
- ☐ 18 Stewart Lovdal
- ☐ 19 Chris Lowe
- ☐ 20 Facanel Medina
- ☐ 21 Rick Meyer
- ☐ 22 Sixto Montero
- ☐ 23 Jeff Patterson
- ☐ 24 Eulogio Perez
- ☐ 25 Jimmy Phillips
- ☐ 26 Mark Randall
- ☐ 27 David Ross
- ☐ 28 Chuck Shive
- ☐ 29 Calvin Talford
- ☐ 30 Cory Thomas
- ☐ 31 Gil Valencia
- ☐ 32 Julio Vargas
- ☐ 33 Dan Welch
- ☐ 34 Scott Wiegandt
- ☐ 35 Coaching Staff
  Roly DeArmas MGR
  Al LeBoeuf CO
  John Martin CO

1989 Medford Athletics Best

The 1989 Medford Athletics set contains 31 standard-size cards. The fronts have posed color player photos with white borders. The year "1989" and the city are written vertically on the left side of the card, and the player's name and position are given below the picture. In a horizontal format, the backs have biography, recent professional baseball performance summary (including statistics), and a color headshot, all in a yellow rectangular box.

	MINT	NRMT	EXC
COMPLETE SET (31)	5.00	2.20	.60

- ☐ 1 Michael Conte
- ☐ 2 Scott Schockey
- ☐ 3 Frank Harris
- ☐ 4 James Gibbs
- ☐ 5 Scott Erwin
- ☐ 6 Mike Grimes
- ☐ 7 Brad Eagar
- ☐ 8 Scott Lydy
- ☐ 9 Fred Cooley
- ☐ 10 Dionini Guzman
- ☐ 11 Pedro Pena
- ☐ 12 Dave Latter
- ☐ 13 Darin Kracl
- ☐ 14 Nick Venuto
- ☐ 15 Ken Ritter
- ☐ 16 Trent Weaver
- ☐ 17 Lorenzo Furcal
- ☐ 18 Grady Fuson MGR
- ☐ 19 Steve Lemuth
- ☐ 20 Steve Chitren
- ☐ 21 Russ Cormier
- ☐ 22 Craig Paquette
- ☐ 23 Tim Annee
- ☐ 24 Marco Armas
- ☐ 25 Jimmy Waggoner
- ☐ 26 Enoch Simmons
- ☐ 27 Kurt Abbott
- ☐ 28 Dana Allison
- ☐ 29 Gavin Osteen
- ☐ 30 Todd Smith
- ☐ 31 Team logo
  Checklist

1989 Memphis Chicks Best

This 28-card standard-size set features the 1989 Memphis Chicks, a farm club for the Kansas City Royals. The fronts have posed color player photos with white borders. The year "1989" and the city are written vertically on the left side of the card, and the player's name and position are given below the picture. In a horizontal format, the backs have biography, recent professional baseball performance summary (including statistics), and a color headshot, all in a yellow rectangular box.

	MINT	NRMT	EXC
COMPLETE SET (28)	5.00	2.20	.60

- ☐ 1 Bob Hamelin
- ☐ 2 John Duffy
- ☐ 3 Jacob Brumfield
- ☐ 4 Mark Lee
- ☐ 5 Aguedo Vasquez
- ☐ 6 Julio Alcala
- ☐ 7 Tony Bridges-Clements
- ☐ 8 Kenny Bowen
- ☐ 9 Stewart Cole
- ☐ 10 Carlos Escalera
- ☐ 11 Deric Ladnier
- ☐ 12 Chito Martinez
- ☐ 13 Brian McRae
- ☐ 14 Angel Morris
- ☐ 15 Harvey Pulliam
- ☐ 16 Kyle Reese
- ☐ 17 Jim Campbell
- ☐ 18 Dera Clark
- ☐ 19 Victor Cole
- ☐ 20 Luis Encarnacion
- ☐ 21 Mike Magnante
- ☐ 22 Mike Tresemer
- ☐ 23 Steve Walker
- ☐ 24 Jeff Cox MGR
- ☐ 25 Joe Breeden CO
- ☐ 26 Guy Hansen CO
- ☐ 27 Mike Leon TR
- ☐ 28 Team logo
  Checklist

1989 Memphis Chicks ProCards

This 28-card standard-size set of the 1989 Memphis Chicks, a Class AA Southern League affiliate of the Kansas City Royals, features red-bordered posed color player photos on its fronts. The player's name, position, and team name appear at the bottom. The horizontal gray back carries the player's name and position at the top, followed by biography and statistics.

	MINT	NRMT	EXC
COMPLETE SET (28)	5.00	2.20	.60

- ☐ 1180 Checklist
- ☐ 1181 John Duffy
- ☐ 1182 Carlos Escalera
- ☐ 1183 Julio Alcala
- ☐ 1184 Stu Cole
- ☐ 1185 Victor Cole
- ☐ 1186 Aguedo Vasquez
- ☐ 1187 Luis Encarnacion
- ☐ 1188 Jacob Brumfield
- ☐ 1189 Deric Ladnier
- ☐ 1190 Mark Lee
- ☐ 1191 Mike Leon TR
- ☐ 1192 Guy Hansen CO
- ☐ 1193 Joe Breeden CO
- ☐ 1194 Jim Campbell
- ☐ 1195 Jeff Cox MGR
- ☐ 1196 Steve Walker
- ☐ 1197 Mike Tresemer
- ☐ 1198 Mike Magnante
- ☐ 1199 Dera Clark
- ☐ 1200 Chito Martinez
- ☐ 1201 Rob Hamelin
- ☐ 1202 Tony Bridges-Clements
- ☐ 1203 Angel Morris
- ☐ 1204 Harvey Pulliam
- ☐ 1205 Brian McRae
- ☐ 1206 Kyle Reese
- ☐ 1207 Ken Bowen

1989 Memphis Chicks Star

This 24-card standard-size set features the 1989 Memphis Chicks, a farm club for the Kansas City Royals. The fronts have posed color player photos, with blue borders on the top portion of the card fading to sky blue as one moves down the card face. In blue print on a pale blue background, the backs have biography and statistics. 5,000 sets produced.

	MINT	NRMT	EXC
COMPLETE SET (24)	5.00	2.20	.60

- ☐ 1 Julio Alcala
- ☐ 2 Kenny Bowen
- ☐ 3 Tony Bridges-Clements
- ☐ 4 Jacob Brumfield
- ☐ 5 Jim Campbell
- ☐ 6 Dera Clark
- ☐ 7 Stu Cole
- ☐ 8 Victor Cole
- ☐ 9 John Duffy
- ☐ 10 Luis Encarnacion
- ☐ 11 Carlos Escalera
- ☐ 12 Bob Hamelin
- ☐ 13 Deric Ladnier
- ☐ 14 Mark Lee
- ☐ 15 Mike Magnante
- ☐ 16 Chito Martinez
- ☐ 17 Brian McRae
- ☐ 18 Angel Morris
- ☐ 19 Harvey Pulliam
- ☐ 20 Kyle Reese
- ☐ 21 Mike Tresemer
- ☐ 22 Aguedo Vasquez
- ☐ 23 Steve Walker
- ☐ 24 Coaching Staff
  Jeff Cox MGR
  Guy Hansen CO
  Joe Breeden CO

1989 Miami Miracle I Star

The 1989 Miami Miracle I set contains 25 standard-size cards. The fronts have posed color player photos, with turquoise borders on the top portion of the card fading to yellow as one moves down the card face. In turquoise print on a pale yellow background, the backs have biography and statistics. 5,000 sets produced.

	MINT	NRMT	EXC
COMPLETE SET (25)	5.00	2.20	.60

- ☐ 1 Mike Barefoot
- ☐ 2 James Bishop
- ☐ 3 Jeff Bonchek
- ☐ 4 Marty Cerny
- ☐ 5 Zachery Doster
- ☐ 6 Keith Feldon
- ☐ 7 Longo Garcia
- ☐ 8 Dimas Gutierrez
- ☐ 9 Lindsey Johnson
- ☐ 10 Ken Lake
- ☐ 11 Shane Letterio
- ☐ 12 Scott Mackie
- ☐ 13 Randy Mazey
- ☐ 14 Brett Merriman
- ☐ 15 Javier Murillo
- ☐ 16 Kevin Ponder
- ☐ 17 John Rivard
- ☐ 18 Lawrence Smith
- ☐ 19 Marc Tepper
- ☐ 20 Mando Verdugo
- ☐ 21 Keith Kaub
- ☐ 22 Pete Kuld
- ☐ 23 Arnie Prieto
- ☐ 24 Duane Walker
- ☐ 25 Coaching Staff
  Jim Gattis MGR
  Dean Treanor CO
  Al Torres CO

1989 Miami Miracle II Star

The 1989 Miami Miracle II set contains 22 standard-size cards. The fronts have posed color player photos, with aqua borders on the top portion of the card fading to yellow as one moves down the card face. In blue print on a white background, the backs have biography and statistics. The card number was left off of card number 3. 5,000 sets produced.

	MINT	NRMT	EXC
COMPLETE SET (22)	5.00	2.20	.60

- ☐ 1 Rick Bernardo
- ☐ 2 Tommy Boyce
- ☐ 3 Marty Cerny
- ☐ 4 Fernando Figueroa
- ☐ 5 Longo Garcia
- ☐ 6 Jim Gattis
- ☐ 7 Lindsey Johnson
- ☐ 8 Randy Kotchman
- ☐ 9 Mark Kramer
- ☐ 10 Adam Lamle
- ☐ 11 Shane Letterio
- ☐ 12 Tony Mack
- ☐ 13 Tony Metoyer
- ☐ 14 Ronald Mullins
- ☐ 15 Michael Maksudian
- ☐ 16 Kevin Ponder
- ☐ 17 Chris Sloniger
- ☐ 18 Doug Torborg
- ☐ 19 Al Torres CO
- ☐ 20 Luis Verdugo
- ☐ 21 Front Office
  Seth Fogler TR
  Bruce Bielenberg GM
  Mark Booth Assistant GM
  Ben Creed (Sales MGR)
  Isabel DiAlberto (Office MGR)
  Paul Turbedsky TR
- ☐ 22 Team Photo

1989 Midland Angels Grand Slam

	MINT	NRMT	EXC
COMPLETE SET (30)	5.00	2.20	.60

- ☐ 1 Max Oliveras MGR
- ☐ 2 Nate Oliver CO
- ☐ 3 Gary Ruby CO
- ☐ 4 Tom Alfredson
- ☐ 5 Jeff Barns
- ☐ 6 Gary Buckels
- ☐ 7 Tim Burcham
- ☐ 8 Mike Butcher
- ☐ 9 Vinicio Cedeno
- ☐ 10 Scott Cerny
- ☐ 11 Chris Cron
- ☐ 12 Frank DiMichele
- ☐ 13 Gary DiSarcina
- ☐ 14 Mark Doran
- ☐ 15 Otto Gonzalez
- ☐ 16 Everett Graham
- ☐ 17 Danny Grunhard
- ☐ 18 Roberto Hernandez
- ☐ 19 Mark Howie
- ☐ 20 Mike Knapp
- ☐ 21 Scott Lewis
- ☐ 22 David Martinez
- ☐ 23 Luis Merejo
- ☐ 24 Rich Morehouse
- ☐ 25 John Orton
- ☐ 26 Reed Peters
- ☐ 27 Bobby Rose
- ☐ 28 Kevin Trudeau
- ☐ 29 Hediberto Vargas
- ☐ 30 Shane Young

1989 Mississippi State Bulldogs

	MINT	NRMT	EXC
COMPLETE SET (45)	10.00	4.50	1.25

- ☐ 1 Daryl Albro
- ☐ 2 Mike Alford
- ☐ 3 Nelson Arriete
- ☐ 4 Darin Asbill
- ☐ 5 Rex Buckner
- ☐ 6 Bart Carter
- ☐ 7 John Cohen
- ☐ 8 Scott Cooke
- ☐ 9 Chuck Daniel
- ☐ 10 Tracy Echols
- ☐ 11 Terry Fancher
- ☐ 12 Tim Fancher
- ☐ 13 Jimmy Gammill
- ☐ 14 Chris George
- ☐ 15 Richie Grayum
- ☐ 16 Joey Hamilton
- ☐ 17 Jon Harden
- ☐ 18 Tim Henderson
- ☐ 19 Brad Hildreth
- ☐ 20 Chuck Holly
- ☐ 21 Jody Hurst
- ☐ 22 Tracy Jobes
- ☐ 23 Russ Mahan
- ☐ 24 Burke Masters
- ☐ 25 Joel Matthews
- ☐ 26 David Mitchell
- ☐ 27 Scott Mitchell
- ☐ 28 Rob Norman
- ☐ 29 Ron Polk CO
- ☐ 30 Steve Polk
- ☐ 31 Tommy Raffo
- ☐ 32 Matthew Ramsey
- ☐ 33 Bobby Reed
- ☐ 34 Jim Robinson
- ☐ 35 Jon Shave

☐ 36 Rob Walsh
☐ 37 John Warburton
☐ 38 Barry Winford
☐ 39 Ron Winford
☐ 40 Ernie Wright
☐ 41 Pete Young
☐ 42 Assistant Coaches
Pat McMahon
Brian Shoop
☐ 43 Dudy Noble Field
☐ 44 Graduate Assistant
Coaches
Mike Hutcheon
Gary Murphy
Rusty McNickle
Gator Thiesen
☐ 45 Student Managers and
Trainers
Bo McKinnis MG
Brooks Ayers MG
Rogers Smith MG
Jeff Ainsworth MG
Cliff Rial TR

1989 Modesto A's Cal League Cards

	MINT	NRMT	EXC
COMPLETE SET (25)	5.00	2.20	.60

☐ 266 Joe Slusarski
☐ 267 Pedro Baez
☐ 268 Brian Veilleux
☐ 269 Steve Dye
☐ 270 Rob Alexander
☐ 271 Daryl Green
☐ 272 Jeff Kopyta
☐ 273 Kevin MacLeod
☐ 274 Kirk McDonald
☐ 275 Joe Hillman
☐ 276 Stan Royer
☐ 277 Rod Correia
☐ 278 Darren Lewis
☐ 279 Joel Chimelis
☐ 280 Joe Kemp
☐ 281 Ron Witmeyer
☐ 282 Jorge Brito
☐ 283 Francisco Matos
☐ 284 Charlie McGrew
☐ 285 Marteese Robinson
☐ 286 Bob Parry
☐ 287 Pete Richert CO
☐ 288 Lenn Sakata MGR
☐ 289 Steve Gokey CO
☐ 290 David Hollenback TR

1989 Modesto A's Chong

	MINT	NRMT	EXC
COMPLETE SET (35)	15.00	6.75	1.85

☐ 1 Ted Kubiak MGR
☐ 2 Pete Richert
☐ 3 Dave Hollenback TR
☐ 4 Dan Kiser GM
☐ 5 Mike Cobleigh
Asst GM
☐ 6 Steve Gokey
Special Team Asst
☐ 7 Rob Alexander
☐ 8 Pedro Baez
☐ 9 Steve Dye
☐ 10 Dan Eskew
☐ 11 Daryl Green
☐ 12 Gary Gorski
☐ 13 Kirk McDonald
☐ 14 William Perez
☐ 15 Joe Slusarski
☐ 16 Steve Towey
☐ 17 Brian Veilleux
☐ 18 Weston Weber
☐ 19 Tom Carcione
☐ 20 Henry Mercedes
☐ 21 Bill Savarino
☐ 22 Joel Chimelis
☐ 23 Rod Correia
☐ 24 Francisco Matos
☐ 25 Stan Royer
☐ 26 Daryl Vice
☐ 27 Ron Witmeyer
☐ 28 David Gavin
☐ 29 Joe Hillman
☐ 30 Darren Lewis
☐ 31 Bob Parry
☐ 32 Keith Thomas
☐ 33 Rickey Henderson
☐ 34 Jose Canseco
☐ 35 Mark McGwire
☐ NNO Checklist

1989 Myrtle Beach Blue Jays ProCards

This 30-card standard-size set of the 1989 Myrtle Beach Blue Jays, a Class A South Atlantic League affiliate of the Toronto Blue Jays, features orange-bordered posed color player photos on its fronts. The player's name, position, and team name appear at the bottom. The horizontal gray back carries the player's name and position at the top, followed by biography and statistics. The set was sponsored by the Myrtle Beach Blue Jays Souvenir Store.

	MINT	NRMT	EXC
COMPLETE SET (30)	5.00	2.20	.60

☐ 1450 Checklist
☐ 1451 Leroy Stanton CO
☐ 1452 Mark Young
☐ 1453 Eddie Mendez
☐ 1454 Greg David
☐ 1455 Todd Provence
☐ 1456 Domingo Cedeno
☐ 1457 Tom Hodge
☐ 1458 Juan DeLaRosa
☐ 1459 Jose Monzon
☐ 1460 Eric Brooks
☐ 1462 Mike Seal
☐ 1463 Mike Taylor
☐ 1464 Mike Ogliaruso
☐ 1465 Tim Brown
☐ 1466 Mike Fischlin MG
☐ 1467 Bill Monbouquette CO
☐ 1468 Rafael Martinez
☐ 1469 Greg Harding
☐ 1470 Ray Giannelli
☐ 1471 Curtis Johnson
☐ 1472 Dan Dodd
☐ 1473 Jose Olivares
☐ 1474 Jesse Cross
☐ 1475 Terry Wilson
☐ 1476 David Weathers
☐ 1477 Mike Brady
☐ 1628 Rich Depastino
☐ 1629 Rick Vaughan
☐ 1630 Anthony Ward

1989 Nashville Sounds CMC

	MINT	NRMT	EXC
COMPLETE SET (25)	5.00	2.20	.60

☐ 1 Charlie Mitchell
☐ 2 Keith Brown
☐ 3 Jeff Gray
☐ 4 Mike Griffin
☐ 5 Hugh Kemp
☐ 6 Rob Lopez
☐ 7 Mike Roesler
☐ 8 Scott Scudder
☐ 9 John Young TR
☐ 10 Luis Vasquez
☐ 11 Doug Gwosdz
☐ 12 Joe Oliver
☐ 13 Skeeter Barnes
☐ 14 Marty Brown
☐ 15 Mark Germann
☐ 16 Keith Lockhart
☐ 17 Luis Quinones
☐ 18 Jeff Richardson
☐ 19 Eddie Tanner
☐ 20 Chris Jones
☐ 21 Scotti Madison
☐ 22 Rolando Roomes
☐ 23 Van Snider
☐ 24 Ray Rippelmeyer CO
☐ 25 Frank Lucchesi MGR
Sic, Luccesi

1989 Nashville Sounds ProCards

This 28-card standard-size set of the 1989 Nashville Sounds, a Class AAA American Association affiliate of the Cincinnati Reds, features blue-bordered posed color player photos on its fronts. The player's name, position, and team name appear at the bottom. The horizontal gray back carries the player's name and position at the top, followed by biography and statistics.

	MINT	NRMT	EXC
COMPLETE SET (28)	5.00	2.20	.60

☐ 1269 Checklist
☐ 1270 Jeff Sellers
☐ 1271 Scotti Madison
☐ 1272 Luis Quinones
☐ 1273 Charlie Mitchell
☐ 1274 Mike Griffin
☐ 1275 Mark Germann
☐ 1276 John Young
☐ 1277 Doug Gwosdz
☐ 1278 Keith Lockhart
☐ 1279 Chris Hammond
☐ 1280 Ray Rippelmeyer CO
☐ 1281 Van Snider
☐ 1282 Mike Roesler
☐ 1283 Joe Oliver
☐ 1284 Frank Lucchesi MGR
☐ 1285 Luis Vasquez
☐ 1286 Rolando Roomes
☐ 1287 Eddie Tanner
☐ 1288 Jeff Gray
☐ 1289 Skeeter Barnes
☐ 1290 Chris Jones
☐ 1291 Jeff Richardson
☐ 1292 Marty Brown
☐ 1293 Scott Scudder
☐ 1294 Hugh Kemp
☐ 1295 Rob Lopez
☐ 1296 Keith Brown

1989 Nashville Sounds Team Issue

	MINT	NRMT	EXC
COMPLETE SET (30)	6.00	2.70	.75

☐ 1 Skeeter Barnes
☐ 2 Freddie Benavides
☐ 3 Keith Brown
☐ 4 Marty Brown
☐ 5 Jeff Gray
☐ 6 Mike Griffin
☐ 7 Doug Gwosdz
☐ 8 Chris Hammond
☐ 9 Alan Hayden
☐ 10 Hugh Kemp
☐ 11 Tito Landrum
☐ 12 Keith Lockhart
☐ 13 Rob Lopez
☐ 14 Scotti Madison
☐ 15 Terry McGriff
☐ 16 Charlie Mitchell
☐ 17 Joe Oliver
☐ 18 Kevin Pearson
☐ 19 Jeff Reynolds
☐ 20 Jeff Richardson
☐ 21 Mike Roesler
☐ 22 Scott Scudder
☐ 23 Van Snider
☐ 24 Eddie Tanner
☐ 25 Luis Vasquez
☐ 26 Bob Jamison ANN ,
Chip Walters COM
☐ 27 George Dyce Ex. VP
☐ 28 Larry Schmittou PRES
☐ 29 Ray Rippelmeyer CO ,
John Young TR
☐ 30 Frank Lucchesi MGR

1989 New Britain Red Sox ProCards

This 27-card standard-size set of the 1989 New Britain Red Sox, a Class AA Eastern League affiliate of the Boston Red Sox, features red-bordered posed color player photos on its fronts. The player's name, position, and team name appear at the bottom. The horizontal gray back carries the player's name and position at the top, followed by biography and statistics.

	MINT	NRMT	EXC
COMPLETE SET (27)	5.00	2.20	.60

☐ 598 Checklist
☐ 599 Ed Zambrano
☐ 600 Bob Zupcic
☐ 601 Pete Youngman TR
☐ 602 Rich Gale CO
☐ 603 Chris Moritz
☐ 604 Dan Gabriele
☐ 605 Mike Carista
☐ 606 Josias Manzanillo
☐ 607 Mike Dalton
☐ 608 Steve Bast
☐ 609 Scott Cooper
☐ 610 Jim Orsag
☐ 611 Daryl Irvine
☐ 612 Zach Crouch
☐ 613 Larry Shikles
☐ 614 Dave Walters
☐ 615 Leverne Jackson
☐ 616 Joe Marchese
☐ 617 Butch Hobson MGR
☐ 618 Randy Randle
☐ 619 Michey Pina
☐ 620 Livio Padilla
☐ 621 Dave Milstien
☐ 622 Jeff Plympton
☐ 623 Scott Sommers
☐ 624 Todd Pratt

1989 New Britain Red Sox Star

The 1989 New Britain Red Sox set contains 25 standard-size cards. The fronts have posed color player photos, with red borders on the top portion of the card fading to gray as one moves down the card face. In red print on a gray background, the backs have biography and statistics. 5,000 sets produced.

	MINT	NRMT	EXC
COMPLETE SET (25)	5.00	2.20	.60

☐ 1 Ed Estrada
☐ 2 Leverne Jackson
☐ 3 Scott Cooper
☐ 4 Zach Crouch
☐ 5 Tito Stewart
☐ 6 Dan Gabriele
☐ 7 Daryl Irvine
☐ 8 Josias Manzanillo
☐ 9 Joe Marchese
☐ 10 David Milstien
☐ 11 Chris Moritz
☐ 12 Jim Orsag
☐ 13 Livio Padilla
☐ 14 Mickey Pina
☐ 15 Todd Pratt
☐ 16 Jeff Plympton
☐ 17 Randy Randle
☐ 18 Larry Shikles
☐ 19 Scott Sommers
☐ 20 David Walters
☐ 21 Ed Zambrano
☐ 22 Robert Zupcic
☐ 23 Butch Hobson MGR
☐ 24 Rich Gale CO
☐ 25 Pete Youngman TR

1989 Niagara Falls Rapids Pucko

The 1989 Niagara Falls set contains 31 standard-size cards. The front features color action player photos bordered in red. The team name and player's name appear in white stripes above and below the picture respectively, with the team logo in the lower left corner. The backs have biography, the circumstances of the player's signing or drafting, and an advertisement for a baseball card shop. A peculiarity of the set is the two #5 cards. 3,750 sets were produced.

	MINT	NRMT	EXC
COMPLETE SET (31)	6.00	2.70	.75

☐ 1 Don Pedersen
☐ 2 Eric Albright
☐ 3 Marcos Betances
☐ 4 Brian Cornelius
☐ 5a Dave Keating
☐ 5b Ivan Cruz
☐ 6 John DeSilva
☐ 7 John Doherty
☐ 8 Mark Ettles
☐ 9 Jeff Goodale
☐ 10 Jim Heins
☐ 11 Tim Herrmann
☐ 12 Jody Hurst
☐ 13 Keith Kimberlin
☐ 14 Keith Langston
☐ 15 Matt Logue
☐ 16 Doug Marcero
☐ 17 Craig Middlekauff
☐ 18 Mario Moccia
☐ 19 Gustavo Pinto
☐ 20 Bob Reimink
☐ 21 Rick Sellers
☐ 22 Freddy Torres
☐ 23 Craig Wiley
☐ 24 David Wilson
☐ 25 Rick Magnante MGR
☐ 26 Juan Lopez CO
☐ 27 Ron Ross TR
☐ 28 Tom Prohaska GM
☐ 29 Sal Maglie Stadium
☐ 30 Fielder's Choice Ad
Jake Tierney
Larry Tierney (owner)
Erica Tierney

1989 Oklahoma Sooners

	MINT	NRMT	EXC
COMPLETE SET (24)	10.00	4.50	1.25

☐ 1 Enos Semore CO
☐ 2 Stan Meek ACO
☐ 3 Jim Fleming ACO
☐ 4 Joe Jordan ACO
☐ 5 L. Dale Mitchell Park
☐ 6 Brent Bohrofen
☐ 7 Kevin Castleberry
☐ 8 Andre Champagne
☐ 9 Marvin Cobb
☐ 10 Mark Cole
☐ 11 Darin Cosby
☐ 12 Darron Cox
☐ 13 John Douglas
☐ 14 Chris Ebright
☐ 15 Mike Hurley
☐ 16 Jim Huslig
☐ 17 Wade Inman
☐ 18 Korey Keling
☐ 19 Kevin King
☐ 20 John Kosenski
☐ 21 Paul Oster
☐ 22 Mike Ponio
☐ 23 Rich Samplinski
☐ 24 Rhett Smith

1989 Oklahoma City 89ers CMC

	MINT	NRMT	EXC
COMPLETE SET (25)	6.00	2.70	.75

☐ 1 Darrell Akerfelds
☐ 2 John Barfield
☐ 3 Bill Scherrer
☐ 4 Mike Jeffcoat
☐ 5 Scott May
☐ 6 Gary Mielke
☐ 7 Dave Miller
☐ 8 Dave Pavlas
☐ 9 Paul Wilmet
☐ 10 Darrell Whitaker
☐ 11 Mike Berger
☐ 12 John Gibbons
☐ 13 Jack Daugherty
☐ 14 Andre Robertson
☐ 15 Dan Rohn
☐ 16 Ron Roenicke
☐ 17 Jim St. Laurent
☐ 18 Rey Sanchez
☐ 19 Kevin Reimer
☐ 20 Darren Loy
☐ 21 Scott Coolbaugh
☐ 22 Tack Wilson
☐ 23 Jim Skaalen MGR
☐ 24 Stan Hough CO
☐ 25 Ferguson Jenkins CO

1989 Oklahoma City 89ers ProCards

This 29-card standard-size set of the 1989 Oklahoma City 89ers, a Class AAA American Association affiliate of the Texas Rangers, features blue-bordered posed color player photos on its fronts. The player's name, position, and team name appear at the bottom. The horizontal gray back carries the player's name and position at the top, followed by biography and statistics.

	MINT	NRMT	EXC
COMPLETE SET (29)	6.00	2.70	.75

☐ 1506 Checklist
☐ 1507 Abner 89er
Mascot
☐ 1508 Jim Skaalen MGR
☐ 1509 Paul Wilmet
☐ 1510 Jeff Stone
☐ 1511 Rey Sanchez
☐ 1512 Scott Coolbaugh
☐ 1513 Ferguson Jenkins CO
☐ 1514 Andre Robertson
☐ 1515 Mike Berger
☐ 1516 Darrell Whitaker
☐ 1517 Drew Hall
☐ 1518 John Barfield
☐ 1519 Ron Roenicke
☐ 1520 Mike Jeffcoat
☐ 1521 Stan Hough CO
☐ 1522 Dave Miller
☐ 1523 Scott May
☐ 1524 Jim St.Laurent
☐ 1525 Jack Daugherty
☐ 1526 Darren Loy
☐ 1527 Kevin Reimer
☐ 1528 Gary Mielke
☐ 1529 Dave Pavlas
☐ 1530 Dan Rohn
☐ 1531 John Gibbons
☐ 1532 Darrel Akerfelds
☐ 1533 Ray Ramirez TR
☐ 1534 Tack Wilson

1989 Omaha Royals CMC

	MINT	NRMT	EXC
COMPLETE SET (25)	8.00	3.60	1.00

☐ 1 Bob Buchanan
☐ 2 Stan Clarke
☐ 3 Steve Fireovid
☐ 4 Kevin Appier
☐ 5 Matt Crouch
☐ 6 Jose DeJesus
☐ 7 Rick Luecken
☐ 8 Ed Olwine
☐ 9 Ken Spratke
☐ 10 Kevin Burrell
☐ 11 Tom Dodd
☐ 12 Ed Hearn
☐ 13 Nick Castaneda
☐ 14 Jose Castro
☐ 15 Bill Pecota
☐ 16 Mike Mesh
☐ 17 Mike Jirschele
☐ 18 Terry Shumpert
☐ 19 Nick Capra
☐ 20 Mike Loggins
☐ 21 Matt Winters
☐ 22 Jeff Schulz
☐ 23 Sal Rende MGR
☐ 24 Steve Morrow TR
☐ 25 Coaches
Tom Poquette
Rich Cubee

1989 Omaha Royals ProCards

This 27-card standard-size set of the 1989 Omaha Royals, a Class AAA American Association affiliate of the Kansas City Royals, features blue-bordered posed color player photos on its fronts. The player's name, position, and team name appear at the bottom. The horizontal gray back carries the player's name and position at the top, followed by biography and statistics.

	MINT	NRMT	EXC
COMPLETE SET (27)	8.00	3.60	1.00

☐ 1716 Checklist
☐ 1717 Matt Crouch
☐ 1718 Steve Fireovid
☐ 1719 Ken Spratke
☐ 1720 Kevin Appier
☐ 1721 Terry Shumpert
☐ 1722 Nick Castaneda
☐ 1723 Steve Morrow TR
☐ 1724 Bob Buchanan
☐ 1725 Ed Olwine
☐ 1726 Tim Pyznarski
☐ 1727 Tom Dodd
☐ 1728 Matt Winters
☐ 1729 Luis de los Santos
☐ 1730 Mike Mesh
☐ 1731 Jose Castro
☐ 1732 Ed Hearn
☐ 1733 Kevin Burrell
☐ 1734 Rick Luecken
☐ 1735 Jose DeJesus
☐ 1736 Jeff Schulz
☐ 1737 Stan Clarke
☐ 1738 Mike Loggins
☐ 1739 Rich Debee
☐ 1740 Sal Rende MGR
☐ 1741 Tom Poquette CO
☐ 1742 Nick Capra

1989 Oneonta Yankees ProCards

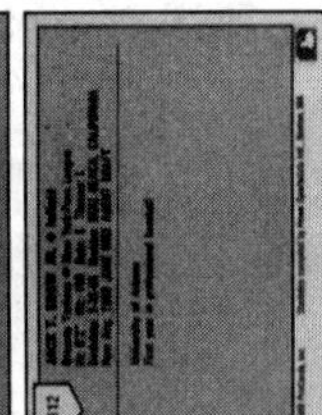

This 32-card standard-size set of the 1989 Oneonta Yankees, a Class A New York-Penn League affiliate of the New York Yankees, features orange-bordered posed color player photos on its fronts. The player's name, position, and team name appear at the bottom. The horizontal gray back carries the player's name and position at the top, followed by biography and statistics.

	MINT	NRMT	EXC
COMPLETE SET (32)	12.00	5.50	1.50

☐ 2097 Checklist
☐ 2098 Brian Butterfield MGR
☐ 2099 John Barrilleaux
Clubhouse Attendant
☐ 2100 Enrique Hernandez
☐ 2101 Jeff Taylor
☐ 2102 Sherman Obando
☐ 2103 Mike Gardella
☐ 2104 Art Canestro
☐ 2105 James Moody
☐ 2106 Larry Stanford
☐ 2107 Scott Chase
☐ 2108 Kelly Sharitt TR
☐ 2109 Russ Davis
☐ 2110 Brad Ausmus
☐ 2111 Lew Hill
☐ 2112 J.T. Snow
☐ 2113 David Howell
☐ 2114 Ken Juarbe
☐ 2115 Aaron Van Scoyoc
☐ 2116 Ricky Strickland
☐ 2117 Richard Varnwell
☐ 2118 Mark Hutton
☐ 2119 Dave Kent CO
☐ 2120 Rich Arena CO
☐ 2121 Frank Seminara
☐ 2122 Todd Malone
☐ 2123 Ricky Rhodes
☐ 2124 Orlando Miller
☐ 2125 Joe Ross
☐ 2126 Jose Vazquez
☐ 2127 Paul Oster
☐ 2128 John Brubaker

1989 Orlando Twins Best

The 1989 Orlando Twins set contains 31 standard-size cards. The fronts have posed color player photos with white borders. The year "1989" and the city are written vertically on the left side of the card, and the player's name and position are given below the picture. In a horizontal format, the backs have biography, recent professional baseball performance summary (including statistics), and a color headshot, all in a yellow rectangular box.

	MINT	NRMT	EXC
COMPLETE SET (31)	5.00	2.20	.60

☐ 1 Paul Sorrento
☐ 2 Jimmy Williams
☐ 3 Mark Funderburk CO
☐ 4 Dwight Bernard CO
☐ 5 Ron Gardenhire MGR
☐ 6 Jim Kahmann TR
☐ 7 Paul Abbott
☐ 8 Tim Arnold
☐ 9 Pat Bangston
☐ 10 Ben Bianchi
☐ 11 Larry Blackwell
☐ 12 Jeff Bronkey
☐ 13 Pete Delkus
☐ 14 Mark Guthrie
☐ 15 Terry Jorgensen
☐ 16 Scott Leius
☐ 17 Ken Morgan
☐ 18 Edgar Naveda
☐ 19 Derek Parks
☐ 20 Park Pittman
☐ 21 Mike Randle
☐ 22 Mike Redding
☐ 23 A.J. Richardson
☐ 24 Jeff Satzinger
☐ 25 Doug Snyder
☐ 26 Marty Lanoux
☐ 27 Wayne Hattaway MGR
☐ 28 Shereen Samonds
Public Relations Director
☐ 29 Jamie Lowe GM
☐ 30 Greg Brinkman
☐ 31 Team logo
Checklist

1989 Orlando Twins ProCards

This 30-card standard-size set of the 1989 Orlando Twins, a Class AA Southern League affiliate of the Minnesota Twins, features red-bordered posed color player photos on its fronts. The player's name, position, and team name appear at the bottom. The horizontal gray back carries the player's name and position at the top, followed by biography and statistics.

	MINT	NRMT	EXC
COMPLETE SET (30)	5.00	2.20	.60

☐ 1326 Checklist
☐ 1327 Doug Snyder
☐ 1328 Marty Lanoux
☐ 1329 Ben Bianchi
☐ 1330 Jeff Satzinger
☐ 1331 Pete Delkus
☐ 1332 Scott Leius
☐ 1333 Mike Redding
☐ 1334 Park Pittman
☐ 1335 Mark Guthrie
☐ 1336 Wayne Hattaway
Equipment Manager
☐ 1337 Jeff Bronkey
☐ 1338 Pat Bangtson
☐ 1339 Mike Randle
☐ 1340 Larry Blackwell
☐ 1341 Ken Morgan
☐ 1342 Dwight Bernard CO
☐ 1343 Paul Sorrento
☐ 1344 Mark Funderburk CO
☐ 1345 Jeff Reboulet
☐ 1346 A.J. Richardson
☐ 1347 Edgar Naveda
☐ 1348 Paul Abbott
☐ 1349 Jim Kahmann TR
☐ 1350 Derek Parks
☐ 1351 John Eccles
☐ 1352 Terry Jorgensen
☐ 1353 Tim Arnold
☐ 1354 Jimmy Williams
☐ 1355 Ron Gardenhire MGR

1989 Osceola Astros Star

The 1989 Osceola Astros set contains 27 standard-size cards. The fronts have posed color player photos, with orange borders on the top portion of the card fading to blue as one moves down the card face. In blue print on a pale yellow background, the backs have biography and statistics. 5,000 sets produced.

	MINT	NRMT	EXC
COMPLETE SET (27)	5.00	2.20	.60

☐ 1 Harold Allen
☐ 2 Daven Bond
☐ 3 Billy Paul Carver
☐ 4 Ramon Cedeno
☐ 5 Todd Credeur
☐ 6 Luis Gonzalez
☐ 7 Rusty Harris
☐ 8 Blaise Ilsley
☐ 9 Bernie Jenkins
☐ 10 Carlos Laboy
☐ 11 Dan Lewis
☐ 12 Andy Mota
☐ 13 Guy Normand
☐ 14 Dan Nyssen
☐ 15 Joe Ortiz
☐ 16 Al Osuna
☐ 17 Gorky Perez
☐ 18 David Potts
☐ 19 Ed Renteria
☐ 20 Scott Servais
☐ 21 John Sheehan
☐ 22 Dave Silvestri
☐ 23 Richie Simon
☐ 24 Dennis Tafoya
☐ 25 Wally Trice
☐ 26 Jose Vargas
☐ 27 Rick Sweet MGR

1989 Palm Springs Angels Cal League Cards

	MINT	NRMT	EXC
COMPLETE SET (32)	5.00	2.20	.60

☐ 32 Troy Giles
☐ 33 Dave Sturdivant
☐ 34 Jeff Gay
☐ 35 Ronnie Ortegon
☐ 36 Charlie Romero
☐ 37 Mario Marlina
☐ 38 Ramon Martinez
☐ 39 Wiley Lee
☐ 40 Christopher Graves
☐ 41 Ed Rodriguez
☐ 42 Christopher Threadgill
☐ 43 Cesar DeLaRosa
☐ 44 Edgar Alfonzo
☐ 45 Fred Carter
☐ 46 Jose Velez
☐ 47 Frank Bryan
☐ 48 James Townsend
☐ 49 David Neal
☐ 50 Donald Vidmar
☐ 51 Jeffrey Richardson
☐ 52 James Bisceglia
☐ 53 Brandy Vann
☐ 54 Steve McGuire
☐ 55 Miguel Alicia
☐ 56 Todd James
☐ 57 Tim McCoy
☐ 58 Chris Beardsley
☐ 59 David Graybill
☐ 60 Don Long CO
☐ 61 Al Olson TR
☐ 62 Kernan Ronan CO
☐ 63 Bill Lachemann MG
Sic, Lacheman

1989 Palm Springs Angels ProCards

This 28-card standard-size set of the 1989 Palm Springs Angels, a Class A California League affiliate of the California Angels, features orange-bordered posed color player photos on its fronts. The player's name, position, and team name appear at the bottom. The horizontal gray back carries the player's name and position at the top, followed by biography and statistics.

	MINT	NRMT	EXC
COMPLETE SET (28)	5.00	2.20	.60

☐ 462 Checklist
☐ 463 Jim Townsend
☐ 464 Edgar Alfonzo
☐ 465 Edgar Rodriguez
☐ 466 Jeff Gay
☐ 467 Ramon Martinez
☐ 468 Tim McCoy
☐ 469 Jeff Richardson
☐ 470 Charlie Romero
☐ 471 Brandy Vann
☐ 472 Chris Threadgill
☐ 473 Troy Giles
☐ 474 Dave Neal
☐ 475 Cesar De La Rosa
☐ 476 Don Long CO
☐ 477 Mario Molina
☐ 478 Ronnie Ortegon
☐ 479 Fred Carter
☐ 480 Al Olson TR
☐ 481 Keenan Ronan CO
☐ 482 Don Vidmar
☐ 483 Chris Graves
☐ 484 Jose Velez
☐ 485 Wiley Lee
☐ 486 Dave Sturdivant
☐ 487 Frank Bryan
☐ 488 Chris Beasley
☐ 489 Bill Lachemann MGR

1989 Pawtucket Red Sox CMC

	MINT	NRMT	EXC
COMPLETE SET (25)	5.00	2.20	.60

☐ 1 Tom Bolton
☐ 2 Steve Curry
☐ 3 Eric Hetzel
☐ 4 Dana Kiecker
☐ 5 John Leister
☐ 6 Mike Rochford
☐ 7 Steve Ellsworth
☐ 8 Andy Araujo
☐ 9 John Trautwein
☐ 10 Rob Woodward
☐ 11 Chris Cannizzaro
☐ 12 Gary Miller-Jones
☐ 13 Carlos Quintana
☐ 14 Gary Tremblay
☐ 15 Scott Wade
☐ 16 Dana Williams
☐ 17 John Marzano
☐ 18 Kevin Romine
☐ 19 Jackie Gutierrez
☐ 20 Luis Rivera
☐ 21 John Roberts
☐ 22 Angel Gonzales
☐ 23 Eduardo Estrade
☐ 24 Mark Meleski CO
☐ 25 Ed Nottle MGR

1989 Pawtucket Red Sox ProCards

This 28-card standard-size set of the 1989 Pawtucket Red Sox, a Class AAA International League affiliate of the Boston Red Sox, features blue-bordered posed color player photos on its fronts. The player's name, position, and team name appear at the bottom. The horizontal gray back carries the player's name and position at the top, followed by biography and statistics.

	MINT	NRMT	EXC
COMPLETE SET (28)	5.00	2.20	.60

☐ 677 Checklist
☐ 678 Ed Nottle MGR
☐ 679 Andy Araujo
☐ 680 Tom Bolton
☐ 681 John Leister
☐ 682 Kevin Romine
☐ 683 Tony Cleary TR
☐ 684 Angel Gonzalez
☐ 685 John Trautwein
☐ 686 Chris Cannizzaro
☐ 687 John Marzano
☐ 688 Carlos Quintana
☐ 689 Gary Miller-Jones
☐ 690 Dana Williams
☐ 691 Steve Curry
☐ 692 Lee Stange CO
☐ 693 John Roberts
☐ 694 Jackie Gutierrez
☐ 695 Scott Wade
☐ 696 Mark Meleski CO
☐ 697 Luis Rivera
☐ 698 Ed Estrada
☐ 699 Rob Woodward
☐ 700 Mike Rochford
☐ 701 Dana Kiecker
☐ 702 Gary Tremblay
☐ 703 Eric Hetzel
☐ 704 Steve Ellsworth

1989 Pawtucket Red Sox Dunkin' Donuts

This 30-card set of the Pawtucket Red Sox, a Class AAA International League affiliate of the Boston Red Sox, was issued in one large sheet featuring six perforated five-card strips with a large team photo in the wide top strip. Sponsored by Dunkin' Donuts, the fronts carry color player photos while the backs display player career statistics. The cards are unnumbered and checklisted below in alphabetical order. 5,000 sets were produced with the majority of them given away at the ballpark.

	MINT	NRMT	EXC
COMPLETE SET (29)	30.00	13.50	3.70

☐ 1 Andy Araujo
☐ 2 Steve Bast
☐ 3 Tom Bolton
☐ 4 Chris Cannizzaro
☐ 5 Tony Cleary TR
☐ 6 Steve Curry
☐ 7 Mike Dalton
☐ 8 Steve Ellsworth
☐ 9 Angel Gonzalez
☐ 10 Jackie Gutierrez
☐ 11 Eric Hetzel
☐ 12 Dana Kiecker
☐ 13 Rick Lancellotti
☐ 14 John Leister
☐ 15 John Marzano
☐ 16 Mark Meleski CO
☐ 17 Gary Miller-Jones
☐ 18 Ed Nottle MGR
☐ 19 Carlos Quintana
☐ 20 Luis Rivera
☐ 21 John Roberts
☐ 22 Mike Rochford
☐ 23 Kevin Romine
☐ 24 Lee Stange CO
☐ 25 John Trautwein
☐ 26 Gary Tremblay
☐ 27 Scott Wade
☐ 28 Dana Williams
☐ 29 Rob Woodward
☐ 30 Team Photo

1989 Peninsula Pilots Star

The 1989 Peninsula Pilots set contains 26 standard-size cards. The fronts have posed color player photos, with blue borders on the top portion of the card fading to sky blue as one moves down the card face. In blue print on a light blue background, the backs have biography and statistics. Card number 26 has blue-fading-to-red borders on the front and a pink background on the back. 5,000 sets produced.

	MINT	NRMT	EXC
COMPLETE SET (26)	5.00	2.20	.60

☐ 1 Dave Bauer
☐ 2 Chris Bushing
☐ 3 Jeff Champ
☐ 4 Hernan Cortes
☐ 5 Tom Fine
☐ 6 Joe Gast
☐ 7 Pat Hewes
☐ 8 Dodd Johnson
☐ 9 Tim Kirk
☐ 10 Jay Knoblauh
☐ 11 Al Lombardi
☐ 12 Julian Machado
☐ 13 Jay Makemson
☐ 14 Sam Manti
☐ 15 Matt Michael
Sic. Micheal
☐ 16 Rodney Murrell
☐ 17 Greg Papageorge
☐ 18 Hector Perez
☐ 19 Lem Pilkinton
☐ 20 Tad Powers
☐ 21 Clyde Reichard
☐ 22 Rick Seibert
☐ 23 Todd Stephan
☐ 24 Len Thigpen
☐ 25 Micky Tresh
☐ 26 Coaching Staff
Jim Thrift MGR
Clyde Reichard CO

1989 Peoria Chiefs Team Issue

This 35-card standard-size set was cosponsored by McDonald's restaurants and Kodak, and logos for these sponsors adorn the top of the card face. A coupon redeemable at McDonald's was included in the set. The front design features a mix of posed or action color player photos, with black borders on a white card face. A Chiefs' baseball hat and a baseball icon appear at the lower corners of the picture. In black print on gray and white, the horizontally oriented backs have biography, statistics, and a brief summary of the player's pro career (where appropriate). 7,000 regular sets and 3,000 Gold 200 sets were produced.

	MINT	NRMT	EXC
COMPLETE SET (35)	12.00	5.50	1.50
COMPLETE GOLD 200 SET (35)	18.00	8.00	2.20

☐ 1 Ty Griffin
☐ 2 Braz Davis
☐ 3 Frankie Espino
☐ 4 Marcos Lopez
☐ 5 Jeff Massicotte
☐ 6 Jay Eddings
☐ 7 Brett Robinson
☐ 8 John Salles
☐ 9 Heathcliff Slocumb
☐ 10 Mike Sodders
☐ 11 Derek Stroud
☐ 12 Rick Mundy
☐ 13 Billy Paynter
☐ 14 Team Photo
☐ 15 Matt Walbeck
☐ 16 Juan Adames
☐ 17 Alex Arias
☐ 18 Eddie Williams
☐ 19 Eric Perry
☐ 20 Tracy Smith
☐ 21 Olympic Stars
Fernando Ramsey
Ty Griffin
☐ 22 Woody Smith
☐ 23 Warren Arrington
☐ 24 Elvin Paulino
☐ 25 Fernando Ramsey
☐ 26 Harry Shelton
☐ 27 Greg Eberle MGR
☐ 28 Golf With The Stars
Jeff Pico
Greg Maddux
Paul Kilgus
☐ 29 Pookie Bernstine CO
☐ 30 Brad Mills MGR
☐ 31 Rick Kranitz CO
☐ 32 Bob Grimes TR
☐ 33 Clar Krusinski
Owner
☐ 34 Front Office Staff
Jeff Reeser
Mike Nelson
Mark Vonachen
John Butler
☐ NNO McDonald's Coupon

1989 Phoenix Firebirds CMC

	MINT	NRMT	EXC
COMPLETE SET (25)	12.00	5.50	1.50

☐ 1 John Burkett
☐ 2 Ed Puikunas
☐ 3 Dennis Cook
☐ 4 Terry Mullholland
☐ 5 Mark Leonard
☐ 6 Ernie Camacho
☐ 7 Marty DeMarrite CO
☐ 8 Joe Olker
☐ 9 Stu Tate
☐ 10 Trevor Wilson
☐ 11 Bill Bathe
☐ 12 Wil Tejeda
☐ 13 Charlie Hayes
☐ 14 Tony Perezchica
☐ 15 Rusty Tillman
☐ 16 Mike Benjamin
☐ 17 Mike Laga
☐ 18 Matt Williams
☐ 19 Ron Wotus
☐ 20 Ken Gerhart
☐ 21 Jack Mull CO
☐ 22 Paul Meyers
☐ 23 John Skurla
☐ 24 George Wright
☐ 25 Gordie McKenzie MGR

1989 Phoenix Firebirds ProCards

This 29-card standard-size set of the 1989 Phoenix Firebirds, a Class AAA Pacific Coast League affiliate of the San Francisco Giants, features blue-bordered posed color player photos on its fronts. The player's name, position, and team name appear at the bottom. The horizontal gray back carries the player's name and position at the top, followed by biography and statistics.

	MINT	NRMT	EXC
COMPLETE SET (29)	12.00	5.50	1.50

☐ 1477 Checklist
☐ 1478 Mike Ham
☐ 1479 Rusty Tillman
☐ 1480 Terry Mulholland
☐ 1481 Trevor Wilson
☐ 1482 Dennis Cook
☐ 1483 John Burkett
☐ 1484 George Wright
☐ 1485 Matt Williams
☐ 1486 Marty DeMerritt CO
☐ 1487 Charlie Hayes
☐ 1488 Bruce Graham TR
☐ 1489 Wil Tejada
☐ 1490 Paul Meyers
☐ 1491 Stu Tate
☐ 1492 Ed Puikunas
☐ 1493 Mike Laga
☐ 1494 Ernie Camacho
☐ 1495 Bill Bathe
☐ 1496 John Skurla
☐ 1497 Joe Olker
☐ 1498 Mark Leonard
☐ 1499 Ken Gerhart
☐ 1500 Mike Benjamin
☐ 1501 Ron Wotus
☐ 1502 Tony Perezchica
☐ 1503 Jack Mull
☐ 1504 Gordy MacKenzie
☐ 1505 Ron Davis

1989 Pittsfield Mets Star

The 1989 Pittsfield Mets set contains 29 standard-size cards. The fronts have posed color player photos, with blue borders on the top portion of the card fading to orange as one moves down the card face. In blue print on a pale orange background, the backs have biography and statistics. 5,000 sets produced.

	MINT	NRMT	EXC
COMPLETE SET (29)	5.00	2.20	.60

☐ 1 Chris Butterfield
☐ 2 Stanton Cameron
☐ 3 Joe Dellicarri
☐ 4 Chris Dorn
☐ 5 Steve Gasser
☐ 6 Dennis Harriger
☐ 7 Mike Hemmerich
☐ 8 Derek Henderson
☐ 9 Tim Hines
☐ 10 Tim Howard
☐ 11 Pat Howell
☐ 12 Paul Johnson
☐ 13 John Johnstone
☐ 14 Greg Langbehn
☐ 15 Medina Luciano
☐ 16 Lee May Jr.
☐ 17 Joe McCann
☐ 18 Norberto Navarro
☐ 19 Steve Piskor
☐ 20 Curtis Pride
☐ 21 Ryan Richmond
☐ 22 Dave Telgheder
☐ 23 Mark Willoughby
☐ 24 Tim Blackwell MGR
☐ 25 Dan Segui
☐ 26 Steve Jacobucci TR
☐ 27 Jamie Hoffner
☐ 28 Jim Tesmer
☐ 29 Alan Zinter

1989 Portland Beavers CMC

	MINT	NRMT	EXC
COMPLETE SET (25)	5.00	2.20	.60

☐ 1 Jim Davins
☐ 2 Manny Hernandez
☐ 3 Kurt Kepshire
☐ 4 Steve Shields
☐ 5 Ray Soff
☐ 6 Lee Tunnell
☐ 7 Larry Cadian
☐ 8 Mike Dyer
☐ 9 Francisco Oliveras
☐ 10 Les Straker
☐ 11 Randy St. Claire
☐ 12 Orlando Mercado
☐ 13 Greg Olson
☐ 14 Doug Baker
☐ 15 Bobby Ralston
☐ 16 Kelvin Torve
☐ 17 Vic Rodriguez
☐ 18 Brad Bierly
☐ 19 John Christensen
☐ 20 Alan Cockrell
☐ 21 Bernardo Brito
☐ 22 Mark Davidson
☐ 23 Rafael Delima
☐ 24 Chip Hale
☐ 25 Jim Shellenback CO

1989 Portland Beavers ProCards

This 26-card standard-size set of the 1989 Portland Beavers, a Class AAA Pacific Coast League affiliate of the Minnesota Twins, features blue-bordered posed color player photos on its fronts. The player's name, position, and team name appear at the bottom. The horizontal gray back carries the player's name and position at the top, followed by biography and statistics.

	MINT	NRMT	EXC
COMPLETE SET (26)	5.00	2.20	.60

☐ 207 Checklist
☐ 208 Chip Hale
☐ 209 Orlando Mercado
☐ 210 Victor Rodriguez
☐ 211 Jim Davins
☐ 212 Bernardo Brito
☐ 213 Randy St.Claire
☐ 214 John Christensen
☐ 215 Kurt Kepshire
☐ 216 Ray Soff
☐ 217 Lee Tunnell
☐ 218 Steve Shields
☐ 219 Lester Straker
☐ 220 Kelvin Torve
☐ 221 Manny Hernandez
☐ 222 Rafael Delima
☐ 223 Larry Casian
☐ 224 Alan Cockrell
☐ 225 Greg Olson
☐ 226 Jim Shellenback CO
☐ 227 Mark Davidson
☐ 228 Mike Dyer
☐ 229 Francisco Oliveras
☐ 230 Doug Baker
☐ 231 Brad Bierley
☐ 232 Bobby Ralston

1989 Prince William Cannons Star

This 29-card standard-size set features the 1989 Prince William Cannons, a farm club for the New York Yankees. The fronts have posed color player photos, with blue borders on the top portion of the card fading to red as one moves down the card face. In blue print on a pink background, the backs have biography and statistics. The backs of card numbers 26-29 are a lighter shade of pink than the other cards. 5,000 sets produced.

	MINT	NRMT	EXC
COMPLETE SET (29)	5.00	2.20	.60

☐ 1 Jason Bridges
☐ 2 Dennis Brow
☐ 3 Andy Cook
☐ 4 Bobby DeJardin
☐ 5 Pedro DeLeon
☐ 6 Mike Draper
☐ 7 Rob Ehrhard
☐ 8 Ken Greer
☐ 9 Jeff Johnson
☐ 10 Pat Kelly
☐ 11 Jeff Livesey
☐ 12 Mark Marris
☐ 13 Bill Masse
☐ 14 Gerald Nielsen
☐ 15 Mark Ohlms
☐ 16 Vince Phillips
☐ 17 Bruce Prybylinski
☐ 18 Frank Seminara
☐ 19 Don Sparks
☐ 20 Don Stanford
☐ 21 Wade Taylor
☐ 22 Dave Turgeon
☐ 23 Hector Vargas
☐ 24 Tom Weeks
☐ 25 Gerald Williams
☐ 26 Mauricio Zazueta
☐ 27 Mark Weidemaier MGR
☐ 28 Dave Jorn CO
☐ 29 Trey Hillman CO

1989 Princeton Pirates Star

The 1989 Princeton Pirates set contains 28 standard-size cards. The fronts have posed color player photos, with black borders on the top portion of the card fading to yellow as one moves down the card face. In black print on a pale yellow background, the backs have biography and statistics. 5,000 sets produced.

	MINT	NRMT	EXC
COMPLETE SET (28)	5.00	2.20	.60

☐ 1 Adrian Adkins
☐ 2 Felix Antigua
☐ 3 Tim Curley
☐ 4 John Curtis
☐ 5 Alberto De Los Santos
☐ 6 Marvin Dooley
☐ 7 Marc Giordano
☐ 8 Z.B. Hamilton
☐ 9 Bill Holmes
☐ 10 David Howard
☐ 11 Wade Lytle
☐ 12 Ramon Martinez
☐ 13 Troy Mooney
☐ 14 Eric Parkinson
☐ 15 Darryl Ratliff
☐ 16 Andre Redmond
☐ 17 Jose Rodriguez
☐ 18 Roman Rodriguez
☐ 19 Delvy Santiago
☐ 20 Bruce Schreiber
☐ 21 Jesse Torres
☐ 22 Ramon Valdez
☐ 23 Dave Watson
☐ 24 Bobby West
☐ 25 Kelly Woods
☐ 26 Julio Garcia MGR
☐ 27 Tom Dettore CO
☐ 28 Ken Crenshaw TR

1989 Pulaski Braves ProCards

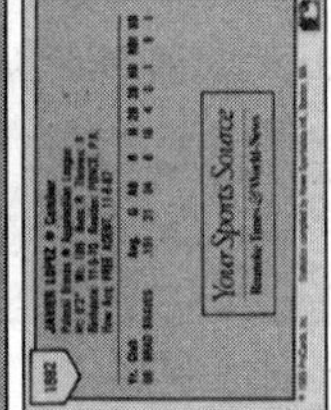

This 28-card standard-size set of the 1989 Pulaski Braves, a Rookie Class Appalachian League affiliate of the Atlanta Braves, features orange-bordered posed color player photos on its fronts. The player's name, position, and team name appear at the bottom. The horizontal gray back carries the player's name and position at the top, followed by biography and statistics. This issue includes the minor league card debuts of Javy Lopez and Melvin Nieves.

	MINT	NRMT	EXC
COMPLETE SET (28)	35.00	16.00	4.40

☐ 1887 Checklist
☐ 1888 Dave Dickman
☐ 1889 Ron Thomas
☐ 1890 Mike Pisacreta
☐ 1891 Batboys
Council Compton
Chris Dishon
☐ 1892 Javier Lopez
☐ 1893 Melvin Nieves
☐ 1894 Brent McCoy
☐ 1895 Don Strange
☐ 1896 Dan Snover
☐ 1897 Earl Jewett
☐ 1898 Shaun Sottile
☐ 1899 Tab Brown
☐ 1900 Fred Koenig MGR
☐ 1901 Phillip Wellman CO
☐ 1902 Matt West CO
☐ 1903 Mike Cerame TR
☐ 1904 Tony Tarasco
☐ 1905 Darren Ritter
☐ 1906 Jarrod Parker
☐ 1907 Roger Hailey
☐ 1908 Mark Wohlers
☐ 1909 Sean Hutchinson
☐ 1910 Jeff Clark
☐ 1911 Lee Heath
☐ 1912 Greg Arnold
☐ 1913 John Kupsey
☐ 1914 Steve Swail

1989 Quad City Angels Best

The 1989 Quad City Angels set contains 31 standard-size cards. The fronts have posed color player photos with white borders. The year "1989" and the city are written vertically on the left side of the card, and the player's name and position are given below the picture. In a horizontal format, the backs have biography, recent professional baseball performance summary (including statistics), and a color headshot, all in a yellow rectangular box. This issue includes a second year card of Jim Edmonds.

	MINT	NRMT	EXC
COMPLETE SET (31)	18.00	8.00	2.20

☐ 1 Glenn Carter
☐ 2 Eddie Rodriguez MGR
☐ 3 Joe Georger CO
☐ 4 Bill Zick TR
☐ 5 Jeff Oberdank
☐ 6 Kevin Flora
☐ 7 David Esquer
☐ 8 Jim Aylward
☐ 9 Mark Holzemer
☐ 10 Mike Erb
☐ 11 Justin Martin
☐ 12 Larry Pardo
☐ 13 Frank Mutz
☐ 14 Steve McGuire
☐ 15 Bill Vanderwel
☐ 16 Gary Murphy
☐ 17 Mark Zappelli
☐ 18 John Marchese
☐ 19 Bruce Vegely
☐ 20 Mike Musolino
☐ 21 Larry Gonzales
☐ 22 J.R. Phillips
☐ 23 Claudio Carrasco
☐ 24 Dave Partrick
☐ 25 Mitch Seoane CO
☐ 26 Bill Eveline
☐ 27 Jim Edmonds
☐ 28 Beban Perez
☐ 29 Steve De Angelis
☐ 30 Ruben Amaro Jr.
☐ 31 Team logo
Checklist

1989 Quad City Angels Grand Slam

	MINT	NRMT	EXC
COMPLETE SET (30)	15.00	6.75	1.85

☐ 1 Eddie Rodriguez MGR
☐ 2 Mitch Seoane CO
☐ 3 Joe Georger CO
☐ 4 Bill Zick TR
☐ 5 Mark Zappelli
☐ 6 Jim Edmonds
☐ 7 J.R. Phillips
☐ 8 Glenn Carter
☐ 9 Dave Partrick
☐ 10 John Marchese
☐ 11 Kevin Flora
☐ 12 Bruce Vegely
☐ 13 Kyle Abbott
☐ 14 Mike Erb
☐ 15 Mike Musolino
☐ 16 Bill Vanderwel
☐ 17 Steve McGuire
☐ 18 Ruben Amaro Jr.
☐ 19 Gary Murphy
☐ 20 Jeff Oberdank
☐ 21 Mark Holzemer
☐ 22 Frank Mutz
☐ 23 Beban Perez
☐ 24 Larry Pardo
☐ 25 David Esquer
☐ 26 Steve De Angelis
☐ 27 Jim Aylward
☐ 28 Larry Gonzales
☐ 29 Claudio Carrasco
☐ 30 Bill Eveline

1989 Reading Phillies Best

The 1989 Reading Phillies set contains 27 standard-size cards. The fronts have posed color player photos with white borders. The year "1989" and the city are written vertically on the left side of the card, and the player's name and position are given below the picture. In a horizontal format, the backs have biography, recent professional baseball performance summary (including statistics), and a color headshot, all in a yellow rectangular box.

	MINT	NRMT	EXC
COMPLETE SET (27)	5.00	2.20	.60

☐ 1 Chuck McElroy
☐ 2 Warren Magee
☐ 3 Chuck Malone
☐ 4 Steve Scarsone
☐ 5 Stephen Sharts
☐ 6 Scott Service
☐ 7 Jeff Tabaka
☐ 8 Bob Scanlan
☐ 9 Rick Parker
☐ 10 Jason Grimsley
☐ 11 Cliff Brantley
☐ 12 Shane Turner
☐ 13 Ramon Henderson
☐ 14 Vince Holyfield
☐ 15 Martin Foley
☐ 16 Gregory Edge
☐ 17 Bobby Joe Edmonds
☐ 18 Frank Bellino
☐ 19 Eric Boudreaux
☐ 20 Harvey Brumfield
☐ 21 Chris Calvert
☐ 22 Sal Agostinelli
☐ 23 Jeffrey Williams
☐ 24 Mark Ruffner TR
☐ 25 Ramon Aviles CO
☐ 26 Mike Hart MGR
☐ 27 Team logo
Checklist

1989 Reading Phillies ProCards

This 27-card standard-size set of the 1989 Reading Phillies, a Class AA Eastern League affiliate of the Philadelphia Phillies, features red-bordered posed color player photos on its fronts. The player's name, position, and team name appear at the bottom. The horizontal gray back carries the player's name and position at the top, followed by biography and statistics.

	MINT	NRMT	EXC
COMPLETE SET (27)	5.00	2.20	.60

☐ 650 Checklist
☐ 651 Steve Sharts
☐ 652 Bob Scanlan
☐ 653 Ramon Henderson
☐ 654 Sal Agostinelli
☐ 655 Shane Turner
☐ 656 Chuck Malone
☐ 657 Scott Service
☐ 658 Mike Hart MGR
☐ 659 Frank Bellino
☐ 660 Rick Parker
☐ 661 Vince Holyfield
☐ 662 Cliff Brantley
☐ 663 Jeff Tabaka
☐ 664 Chris Calvert
☐ 665 Steve Scarsone
☐ 666 Greg Edge
☐ 667 Harvey Brumfield
☐ 668 Eric Boudreaux
☐ 669 Chuck Mcelroy
☐ 670 Jason Grimsley
☐ 671 Ramon Aviles CO
☐ 672 Marty Foley
☐ 673 Bobby Joe Edmonds
☐ 674 Warren Magee
☐ 675 Jeff Williams
☐ 676 Pat Combs

1989 Reading Phillies Star

The 1989 Reading Phillies set contains 28 standard-size cards. The fronts have posed color player photos, with red borders on the top portion of the card fading to gray as one moves down the card face. In red print on a gray background, the backs have biography and statistics. Card number 27 has a white rather than a gray background, and there are two different cards with the number 26. 5,000 sets produced.

	MINT	NRMT	EXC
COMPLETE SET (28)	5.00	2.20	.60

☐ 1 Sal Agostinelli
☐ 2 Frank Bellino
☐ 3 Erik Bratlien
☐ 4 Harvey Brumfield
☐ 5 Chris Calvert
☐ 6 Amalio Carreno
☐ 7 Fred Christopher
☐ 8 Joe Citari
☐ 9 Pat Combs
☐ 10 Bobby Joe Edmonds
☐ 11 Marty Foley
☐ 12 Jason Grimsley
☐ 13 Ramon Henderson
☐ 14 Gerald Holtz
☐ 15 Vince Holyfield
☐ 16 Warren Magee
☐ 17 Chuck Malone
☐ 18 Chuck McElroy
☐ 19 Rick Parker
☐ 20 Victor Rosario
☐ 21 Bob Scanlan
☐ 22 Steve Scarsone
☐ 23 Scott Service
☐ 24 Shane Turner
☐ 25 Jeff Williams
☐ 26a Mike Hart MGR
☐ 26b Coaches
Ramon Aviles
George Culver
☐ 27 Steve Scarsone

1989 Reno Silver Sox Cal League Cards

	MINT	NRMT	EXC
COMPLETE SET (27)	5.00	2.20	.60

☐ 239 Mike Anderson
☐ 240 Bob Ayrault
☐ 241 John Bilello
☐ 242 Jorge Candelaria
☐ 243 Carlos Carrasco
☐ 244 Tim Fortugno
☐ 245 Joe Strong
☐ 246 Brian Sullivan
☐ 247 Gil Villanueva
☐ 248 Mike Warren
☐ 249 Brian Hartsock
☐ 250 Gary Nalls
☐ 251 Mike Westbrook
☐ 252 Joe Kmak
☐ 253 Mike Bosco
☐ 254 Doug Carpenter
☐ 255 Terence Carr
☐ 256 Frank Dominguez
☐ 257 Kaha Wong
☐ 258 Brian Palma
☐ 259 Claudio Carrasco
☐ 260 Shawn Barton
☐ 261 John Balfanz
☐ 262 Bill Bluhm
☐ 263 Jack Patton GM
☐ 264 Jerry Maldonado
Administrative Asst.
☐ 265 Eli Grba MGR

1989 Richmond Braves Bob's Camera

This 29-card team set of the 1989 Richmond Braves, a Class AAA International League affiliate of the Atlanta Braves, was sponsored by Bob's Camera. The fronts feature borderless color player photos with sponsors' and team's logos in the wide bottom margin. The backs are blank. 500 sets were produced.

	MINT	NRMT	EXC
COMPLETE SET (29)	70.00	32.00	8.75

☐ 1 Jim Beauchamp MGR
☐ 2 Kash Beauchamp
☐ 3 Terry Blocker
☐ 4 Drew Denson
☐ 5 Gary Eave
☐ 6 Bryan Farmer
☐ 7 Tommy Greene
☐ 8 John Grubb CO
☐ 9 Dwayne Henry
☐ 10 Sonny Jackson CO
☐ 11 Barry Jones
☐ 12 Dave Justice
☐ 13 Mark Lemke
☐ 14 Eddie Mathews
☐ 15 Leo Mazzone CO
☐ 16 Joel McKeon
☐ 17 Kent Mercker
☐ 18 John Mizerock
☐ 19 Andy Nezelek
☐ 20 Dave Plumb
☐ 21 Charlie Puleo
☐ 22 Rusty Richards
☐ 23 Carlos Rios
☐ 24 Chris Shaddy
☐ 25 Alex Smith
☐ 26 Greg Tubbs
☐ 27 Ed Whited

☐ 28 Robbie Wine
☐ 29 Steve Ziem

1989 Richmond Braves CMC

	MINT	NRMT	EXC
COMPLETE SET (25)	12.00	5.50	1.50

☐ 1 Marty Clary
☐ 2 Gary Eave
☐ 3 Tommy Greene
Sic, Green
☐ 4 Dwayne Henry
☐ 5 Kent Mercker
☐ 6 Andy Nezelek
☐ 7 Rusty Richards
☐ 8 Bryan Farmer
☐ 9 Bob Black ANN
☐ 10 Eddie Mathews
☐ 11 Robbie Wine
☐ 12 John Mizerock
☐ 13 Carlos Rios
☐ 14 Sam Ayoub TR
☐ 15 David Justice
☐ 16 Jeff Wetherby
☐ 17 Terry Blocker
☐ 18 Drew Denson
☐ 19 Mark Lemke
☐ 20 Barry Jones
☐ 21 Ed Whited
☐ 22 Chris Shaddy
☐ 23 Kash Beauchamp
☐ 24 Coaches
Leo Mazzone
Sonny Jackson
John Grubb
☐ 25 Jim Beauchamp MGR

1989 Richmond Braves ProCards

This 31-card standard-size set of the 1989 Richmond Braves, a Class AAA International League affiliate of the Atlanta Braves, features blue-bordered posed color player photos on its fronts. The player's name, position, and team name appear at the bottom. The horizontal gray back carries the player's name and position at the top, followed by biography and statistics.

	MINT	NRMT	EXC
COMPLETE SET (31)	15.00	6.75	1.85

☐ 817 Checklist
☐ 818 Team Picture
☐ 819 Clubhouse Managers
Steve Barden
Tex Drake
☐ 820 Sam Ayoub TR
☐ 821 John Grubb CO
☐ 822 Jim Beauchamp MGR
☐ 823 Greg Tubbs
☐ 824 Chris Shaddy
☐ 825 Mark Eichhorn
☐ 826 Marty Clary
☐ 827 John Mizerock
☐ 828 Gary Eave
☐ 829 Rusty Richards
☐ 830 Mark Lemke
☐ 831 Tommy Greene
☐ 832 Sonny Jackson CO
☐ 833 Leo Mazzone CO
☐ 834 Bryan Farmer
☐ 835 Kent Mercker
☐ 836 Kash Beauchamp
☐ 837 Ed Whited
☐ 838 Dave Justice
☐ 839 Andy Nezelek
☐ 840 Jeff Wetherby
☐ 841 Alex Smith
☐ 842 Carlos Rios
☐ 843 Robbie Wine
☐ 844 Dwayne Henry
☐ 845 Eddie Mathews
☐ 846 Barry Jones
☐ 847 Drew Denson

1989 Richmond Braves Team Issue

	MINT	NRMT	EXC
COMPLETE SET (25)	20.00	9.00	2.50

☐ 1 Jim Beauchamp
☐ 2 Kash Beauchamp
☐ 3 Terry Blocker
☐ 4 Marty Clary
☐ 5 Drew Denson
☐ 6 Gary Eave
☐ 7 Bryan Farmer
☐ 8 Tommy Greene
☐ 9 Dwayne Henry
☐ 10 Barry Jones
☐ 11 Dave Justice
☐ 12 John Kilner
☐ 13 Mark Lemke
☐ 14 Eddie Mathews
☐ 15 John Mizerock
☐ 16 Kent Mercker
☐ 17 Andy Nezelek
☐ 18 Rusty Richards
☐ 19 Carlos Rios
☐ 20 Chris Shaddy
☐ 21 Alex Smith
☐ 22 Jeff Wetherby
☐ 23 Ed Whited
☐ 24 Robbie Wine
☐ 25 Coaches and Trainer
John Grubb CO
Leo Mazzone CO
Sonny Jackson CO
Sam Ayoub TR

1989 Riverside Red Wave Best

This 30-card standard-size set features the 1989 Riverside Red Waves, a farm club for the San Diego Padres. The fronts have posed color player photos with white borders. The year "1989" and the city are written vertically on the left side of the card, and the player's name and position are given below the picture. In a horizontal format, the backs have biography, recent professional baseball performance summary (including statistics), and a color headshot, all in a yellow rectangular box.

	MINT	NRMT	EXC
COMPLETE SET (30)	5.00	2.20	.60

☐ 1 Bob Lutticken
☐ 2 Mark Beavers
☐ 3 Scott Bigham
☐ 4 Jay Estrada
☐ 5 Kevin Farmer
☐ 6 Todd Hansen
☐ 7 Brian Harrison
☐ 8 Mike Humphreys
☐ 9 Tony Lewis
☐ 10 Kelly Lifgren
☐ 11 Stephen Loubier
☐ 12 Bill Marx
☐ 13 Tim McWilliam
☐ 14 Darrin Reichle
☐ 15 Andy Skeels
☐ 16 Saul Soltero
☐ 17 William Taylor
☐ 18 Rafael Valdez
☐ 19 Jose Valentin
☐ 20 Guillermo Velasquez
☐ 21 Mike Young
☐ 22 Steve Lubratich MGR
☐ 23 Jon Matlack CO
☐ 24 Nate Colbert CO
☐ 25 Bruce Bochy CO
☐ 26 Greg Hall
Player/Coach
☐ 27 Monte Brooks
☐ 28 Jim Daniel TR
☐ 29 Isaiah Clark
☐ 30 Team logo
Checklist

1989 Riverside Red Wave Cal League Cards

	MINT	NRMT	EXC
COMPLETE SET (31)	5.00	2.20	.60

☐ 1 Scott Bigham
☐ 2 Tim McWilliam
☐ 3 Gil Valasquez
☐ 4 Rafael Valdez
☐ 5 Mike Humphreys
☐ 6 Greg Hall CO
☐ 7 Kevin Farmer
☐ 8 Jose Valentin
☐ 9 Isaiah Clark
☐ 10 Montie Brooks
☐ 11 Bob Lutticken
☐ 12 Andy Skeels
☐ 13 Will Taylor
☐ 14 Bill Marx
☐ 15 Darren Reichle
☐ 16 Kelly Lifgren
☐ 17 Brian Harrison
☐ 18 Mike Young
☐ 19 Bobby Sheridann
☐ 20 Steve Loubier
☐ 21 Jay Estrada
☐ 22 Todd Hansen
☐ 23 Mark Beavers
☐ 24 Tony Lewis
☐ 25 Steve Lubratich MGR
☐ 26 Jon Matlack
Pitching Instructor
☐ 27 Nate Colbert
Batting Instructor
☐ 28 Jim Daniels TR
☐ 29 Bruce Bochy CO
☐ 30 Tye Waller CO
☐ 31 Saul Soltero

1989 Riverside Red Wave ProCards

This 31-card standard-size set of the 1989 Riverside Red Wave, a Class A California League affiliate of the San Diego Padres, features orange-bordered posed color player photos on its fronts. The player's name, position, and team name appear at the bottom. The horizontal gray back carries the player's name and position at the top, followed by biography and statistics.

	MINT	NRMT	EXC
COMPLETE SET (31)	5.00	2.20	.60

☐ 1388 Checklist
☐ 1389 Steve Loubier
☐ 1390 Mark Beavers
☐ 1391 Nate Colbert CO
☐ 1392 Kelly Lifgren
☐ 1393 Darrin Reichle
☐ 1394 Guillermo Valezquez
☐ 1395 Tony Lewis
☐ 1396 Scott Bigham
☐ 1397 Greg Hall
☐ 1398 Rafael Valdez
☐ 1399 Mike Young
☐ 1400 Mike Humphreys
☐ 1401 Tim McWilliams
☐ 1402 Will Taylor
☐ 1403 Bob Lutticken
☐ 1404 Isaiah Clark
☐ 1405 Bruce Bochy CO
☐ 1406 Saul Soltero
☐ 1407 Jim Daniel TR
☐ 1408 Jon Matlack CO
☐ 1409 Jay Estrada
☐ 1410 Brian Harrison
☐ 1411 Steve Lubratich MGR
☐ 1412 Kevin Farmer
☐ 1413 Todd Hansen
☐ 1414 Andy Skeels
☐ 1415 Jose Valentin
☐ 1416 Bill Marx
☐ 1417 Monte Brooks
☐ 1418 Bobby Sheridan

1989 Rochester Red Wings CMC

	MINT	NRMT	EXC
COMPLETE SET (25)	5.00	2.20	.60

☐ 1 Mike Jones
☐ 2 Chuck Stanhope
☐ 3 Francisco Melendez
☐ 4 Cesar Mejia
☐ 5 Mike Raczka
☐ 6 Mickey Weston
☐ 7 Curt Shilling
☐ 8 Mike Smith
Mississippi
☐ 9 Mike Smith
Texas
☐ 10 Mark Huismann
☐ 11 Dave Johnson
☐ 12 John Posey
☐ 13 Keith Hughes
☐ 14 Chris Padget
☐ 15 Sherwin Cijntje
☐ 16 Tim Hulett
☐ 17 Jeff Tackett
☐ 18 Harold Perkins
☐ 19 Walt Harris
☐ 20 Tim Dulin
☐ 21 Juan Bell
☐ 22 Butch Davis
☐ 23 Rick Schu
☐ 24 Dick Bosman CO
☐ 25 Greg Biagini MGR

1989 Rochester Red Wings ProCards

This 30-card standard-size set of the 1989 Rochester Red Wings, a Class AAA International League affiliate of the Baltimore Orioles, features blue-bordered posed color player photos on its fronts. The player's name, position, and team name appear at the bottom. The horizontal gray back carries the player's name and position at the top, followed by biography and statistics.

	MINT	NRMT	EXC
COMPLETE SET (30)	7.00	3.10	.85

☐ 1631 Checklist
☐ 1632 Sherwin Cijntje
☐ 1633 Jay Tibbs
☐ 1634 Mike Smith
☐ 1635 Cesar Mejia
☐ 1636 Jose Mesa
☐ 1637 Mike Smith
Mississippi
☐ 1638 Mickey Weston
☐ 1639 Steve Finley
☐ 1640 Chris Hoiles
☐ 1641 Dick Bosman CO
☐ 1642 Rich Schu
☐ 1643 Harold Perkins
☐ 1644 Chris Padget
☐ 1645 Jeff Tackett
☐ 1646 Tim Dulin
☐ 1647 Billy Moore
☐ 1648 Mike Raczka
☐ 1649 Pete Harnisch
☐ 1650 Mark Huismann
☐ 1651 Walt Harris
☐ 1652 Butch Davis
☐ 1653 Tim Hulett
☐ 1654 Francisco Melendez
☐ 1655 Curt Schilling
☐ 1656 Dave Johnson
☐ 1657 Mike Jones
☐ 1658 Juan Bell
☐ 1659 Keith Hughes
☐ 1660 Greg Biagini MGR

1989 Rockford Expos /Litho Center

Printed by Rockford Litho Center, this 31-card standard-size set of the 1989 Rockford Expos, a Class A Midwest League affiliate of the Montreal Expos, features on its white-bordered fronts posed color player photos set on red backgrounds. The player's name and position appear within a yellow diagonal stripe at the lower right. The white horizontal back carries the player's name, uniform number, and position at the top, followed by biography and the name of the sponsor, Sports Wearhouse. The cards are unnumbered and checklisted below in alphabetical order.

	MINT	NRMT	EXC
COMPLETE SET (31)	7.00	3.10	.85

☐ 1 Isaac Alleyne
☐ 2 Derrell Baker CO
☐ 3 Esteban Beltre
☐ 4 Rod Boddie
☐ 5 Scott Bromby
☐ 6 Reid Cornelius
☐ 7 Bret Davis
☐ 8 Kevin Foster
☐ 9 Dan Freed
☐ 10 Michael Gibbons
☐ 11 Terrel Hansen
☐ 12 Dan Hargis
☐ 13 Ben Howze
☐ 14 Keith Kaub
☐ 15 Rob Kerrigan
☐ 16 Bryn Kosco
☐ 17 Rob Mason
☐ 18 Nate Minchey
☐ 19 Chris Nabholz
☐ 20 Dave Oropeza
☐ 21 Jesus Paredes
☐ 22 Mike Parrott CO
☐ 23 Mike Quade MG
☐ 24 Kelvin Shephard
☐ 25 Matt Shiflett
☐ 26 Joe Siddall
☐ 27 Joel Smith
☐ 28 Adam Terris
☐ 29 Jay Williams TR
☐ 30 Darrin Winston
☐ 31 Kelly Zane

1989 South Atlantic League All-Stars Grand Slam

	MINT	NRMT	EXC
COMPLETE SET (46)	15.00	6.75	1.85

☐ 1 Stan Cliburn
☐ 2 Orlando Gomez
☐ 3 Willie Ansley
☐ 4 Larry Lamphere
☐ 5 Greg Sims
☐ 6 Glen McNabb
☐ 7 Jeff Neely
☐ 8 Brian Wood
☐ 9 Keith Raisanen
☐ 10 Mandy Romero
☐ 11 Pedro Martinez
☐ 12 John Kuehl
☐ 13 Scott Taylor
☐ 14 Matt Franco
☐ 15 Chris Hill
☐ 16 Andy Reich
☐ 17 Todd Hundley
☐ 18 Bob Olah
☐ 19 Kevin Baez

- ☐ 20 James Morrisette
- ☐ 21 Lino Rivera
- ☐ 22 Anthony Young
- ☐ 23 Reggie Sanders
- ☐ 24 Darren Oliver
- ☐ 25 Jim Hvizka
- ☐ 26 Ivan Rodriguez
- ☐ 27 Jeff Frye
- ☐ 28 Trey McCoy
- ☐ 29 Doug Cronk
- ☐ 30 Kevin Belcher
- ☐ 31 Mo Sanford
- ☐ 32 Dave McAuliffe
- ☐ 33 Mike Mulvaney
- ☐ 34 Lavell Cudjo
- ☐ 35 Ray Giannelli
- ☐ 36 John Ericks
- ☐ 37 Gabriel Ozuna
- ☐ 38 Mauricio Nuinez
- ☐ 39 Darryl Martin
- ☐ 40 Francisco Valdez
- ☐ 41 Leroy Ventress
- ☐ 42 Glen Gardner
- ☐ 43 Everett Cunningham
- ☐ 44 Randy Simmons
- ☐ 45 Pete Blohm
- ☐ 46 Jeff Osborne

1989 Salem Buccaneers Star

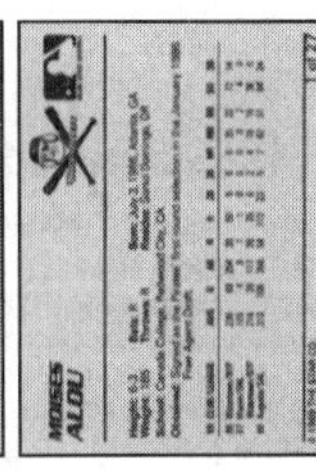

This 29-card standard-size set features the 1989 Salem Buccaneers, a farm club for the Pittsburgh Pirates. The fronts have posed color player photos, with black borders on the top portion of the card fading to yellow as one moves down the card face. In black print on a pale yellow background, the backs have biography and statistics. The Harris card is a late issue and has a white background on the reverse. 5,000 sets produced.

	MINT	NRMT	EXC
COMPLETE SET (29)	7.00	3.10	.85

- ☐ 1 Moises Alou
- ☐ 2 Fernando Arguelles
- ☐ 3 Joe Ausanio
- ☐ 4 Scott Barczi
- ☐ 5 Terry Crowley Jr.
- ☐ 6 Ron Downs
- ☐ 7 Chip Duncan
- ☐ 8 Mike Fortuna
- ☐ 9 Carlos Garcia
- ☐ 10 Ed Hartman
- ☐ 11 Trent Jewett
- ☐ 12 Domingo Merejo
- ☐ 13 Paul Miller
- ☐ 14 Blas Minor
- ☐ 15 Albert Molina
- ☐ 16 Joseph Pacholec
- ☐ 17 Keith Richardson
- ☐ 18 Scott Ruskin
- ☐ 19 Butch Schlopy
- ☐ 20 Winston Seymour
- ☐ 21 Willie Smith
- ☐ 22 Randy Tomlin
- ☐ 23 Miguel Valverde
- ☐ 24 John Wehner
- ☐ 25 Rocky Bridges MGR
- ☐ NNO Robert Harris
- ☐ NNO Julio Garcia
- ☐ NNO Spin Williams

1989 Salem Dodgers Team Issue

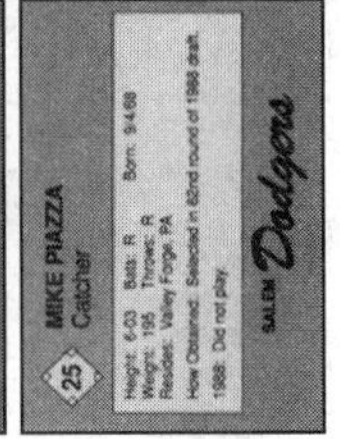

This 30-card set standard size set of the 1989 Salem Buccaneers, a farm club for the Los Angeles Dodgers, feature blue borders with color photos. 2,500 sets were produced. This issue includes the minor league card debut of Mike Piazza.

	MINT	NRMT	EXC
COMPLETE SET (30)	70.00	32.00	8.75

- ☐ 1 Tom Beyers MGR
- ☐ 2 Burt Hooton CO
- ☐ 3 Anthony Garcia TR
- ☐ 4 Geoff Clark TR
- ☐ 5 Jorge Alvarez
- ☐ 6 Garrett Beard
- ☐ 7 Bill Bene
- ☐ 8 Paul Branconier
- ☐ 9 Don Carroll
- ☐ 10 Clayton Enno
- ☐ 11 Gary Forrester
- ☐ 12 Larry Gonzalez
- ☐ 13 Sebastian Goodlow
- ☐ 14 John Kries
- ☐ 15 Ken Luckham
- ☐ 16 Brock McMurray
- ☐ 17 Bill Miller
- ☐ 18 Chris Morrow
- ☐ 19 Robin Nina
- ☐ 20 Hector Ortiz
- ☐ 21 Jorge Pascual
- ☐ 22 Jose Perez
- ☐ 23 Pedro Perez
- ☐ 24 Rex Peters
- ☐ 25 Mike Piazza
- ☐ 26 Rafael Rijo
- ☐ 27 Napoleon Robinson
- ☐ 28 Chris Sperry
- ☐ 29 Dan Stupur
- ☐ 30 Ramon Taveras

1989 Salinas Spurs Cal League Cards

	MINT	NRMT	EXC
COMPLETE SET (27)	5.00	2.20	.60

- ☐ 123 Ray Velasquez
- ☐ 124 Dan Adriance
- ☐ 125 Doug Messer
- ☐ 126 Larry Carter
- ☐ 127 Scott Nelson
- ☐ 128 Dave Horan
- ☐ 129 Dave Cantrell
- ☐ 130 Yuki Kaseda
- ☐ 131 Chikada Toyotoshi
- ☐ 132 Dragon Taguchi
- ☐ 133 Yuji Yamaguchi
- ☐ 134 Masa Kuoda
- ☐ 135 Yasu Suzuki
- ☐ 136 Yoshi Yoshinaga
- ☐ 137 Dickens Benoit
- ☐ 138 Pat Brady
- ☐ 139 Mark Standiford
- ☐ 140 Matt Williams
- ☐ 141 Greg Lee
- ☐ 142 Jeff Kaiser
- ☐ 143 Tod Ronson
- ☐ 144 Kerry Shaw
- ☐ 145 Jim McNamara
- ☐ 146 Tim Ireland MGR
- ☐ 147 Jerry Nyman CO
- ☐ 148 Ken Kajima CO
- ☐ 149 Brian Castello TR

1989 Salinas Spurs ProCards

This 30-card standard-size set of the 1989 Salinas Spurs, a Class A California League Independent, features orange-bordered posed color player photos on its fronts. The player's name, position, and team name appear at the bottom. The horizontal gray back carries the player's name and position at the top, followed by biography and statistics.

	MINT	NRMT	EXC
COMPLETE SET (30)	5.00	2.20	.60

- ☐ 1799 Checklist
- ☐ 1800 Dave Horan
- ☐ 1801 Mark Standiford
- ☐ 1802 Steve Gray
- ☐ 1803 Kerry Shaw
- ☐ 1804 Masa Kuoda
- ☐ 1805 Jeff Kaiser
- ☐ 1806 Greg Lee
- ☐ 1807 Ray Velasquez
- ☐ 1808 Yuki Kaseda
- ☐ 1809 Dragon Taguchi
- ☐ 1810 Yoshi Yoshinaga
- ☐ 1811 Jim McNamara
- ☐ 1812 Honen Chikida
- ☐ 1813 Yuji Yamaguchi
- ☐ 1814 Yasu Suzuki
- ☐ 1815 Pat Brady
- ☐ 1816 Larry Carter
- ☐ 1817 Doug Messer
- ☐ 1818 Dan Adriance
- ☐ 1819 Greg Sparks
- ☐ 1820 Jerry Nyman CO
- ☐ 1821 Tod Ronson
- ☐ 1822 Tim Ireland MGR
- ☐ 1823 Scott Gay
- ☐ 1824 Scott Nelson
- ☐ 1825 Matt Williams
- ☐ 1826 Dave Cantrell
- ☐ 1827 Dickens Benoit
- ☐ 1828 Brian Costello TR

1989 Salt Lake Trappers Team Issue

This 30-card standard-size set was sponsored by Baseball Cards, etc. and Magic 107.5 radio station. The fronts feature glossy posed color photos (some of which are rather comical), bordered in red on a white card face. The team name appears in red print on the card face, while player information is given in a yellow stripe below the picture. In black print on white and orange, the backs present biography, player profile, and a Baseball Cards, etc. advertisement. Card number 29 features Bill Murray, the well-known actor and comedian.

	MINT	NRMT	EXC
COMPLETE SET (30)	6.00	2.70	.75

- ☐ 1 Patrick Waid
- ☐ 2 Checklist
- ☐ 3 Coaches
Darren Garrick
Reuben Rodriguez
Dan Shwam
- ☐ 4 Dave Baggott GM
- ☐ 5 Mike Nyquist
- ☐ 6 Travis Tarchione
- ☐ 7 Ray Karczewski
- ☐ 8 Dan Ryan
- ☐ 9 Ed Garczyk
- ☐ 10 Holly Andretta MGR
John Stein MGR
Kurt Wilson ANN
- ☐ 11 J.D. Ramirez
- ☐ 12 Shingo Matsukubo
Akihiro Fukushima
Shigeki Taguchi
- ☐ 13 Mike Steinkamp
- ☐ 14 Mike Grace
- ☐ 15 Barry Moss MGR
- ☐ 16 Anthony St.John
- ☐ 17 Shaun Sanderson
- ☐ 18 Van Schley
Personnel Director
- ☐ 19 Chris Skryd
- ☐ 20 Max Tripodi
- ☐ 21 Mike Bible
- ☐ 22 Dave Alexander
- ☐ 23 Scott Bray
- ☐ 24 Joe Beaulac
- ☐ 25 Phil Evans
- ☐ 26 Gerard Giustino
- ☐ 27 James Troup
- ☐ 28 Michael Ashworth
- ☐ 29 Bill Murray
Team owner
- ☐ 30 John Stewart

1989 San Antonio Missions Best

This 28-card standard-size set features the 1989 San Antonio Missions, a farm club for the Los Angeles Dodgers. The fronts have posed color player photos with white borders. The year "1989" and the city are written vertically on the left side of the card, and the player's name and position are given below the picture. In a horizontal format, the backs have biography, recent professional baseball performance summary (including statistics), and a color headshot, all in a yellow rectangular box. The cards are numbered in a baseball icon on the back. The Platinum version sets were limited to a production run of 1,500.

	MINT	NRMT	EXC
COMPLETE SET (28)	6.00	2.70	.75
COMP. LIMITED EDITION SET (28)	8.00	3.60	1.00

- ☐ 1 Mike White
- ☐ 2 Manuel Fancois
- ☐ 3 Eric Mangham
- ☐ 4 Darren Holmes
- ☐ 5 Tony Arnold
- ☐ 6 Kevin Armstrong
- ☐ 7 Gordon Hershiser
- ☐ 8 Wayne Kirby
- ☐ 9 Joseph Kesselmark
- ☐ 10 Adam Brown
- ☐ 11 Brian Traxler
- ☐ 12 Dan Henley
- ☐ 13 Carlos Hernandez
- ☐ 14 Louie Martinez
- ☐ 15 Louie Lopez
- ☐ 16 Isidrio Marquez
- ☐ 17 Dave Hansen
- ☐ 18 Dan Scarpetta
- ☐ 19 Greg Mayberry
- ☐ 20 Dennis Springer
- ☐ 21 Homar Rojas
- ☐ 22 Chris Nichting
- ☐ 23 Michael Pitz
- ☐ 24 Tim Scott
- ☐ 25 John Shoemaker MGR
- ☐ 26 Claude Osteen CO
- ☐ 27 Jose Offerman UER
(Oferman on card)
- ☐ 28 Team photo
Checklist

1989 San Bernardino Spirit Best

This 29-card standard-size set features the 1989 San Bernardino Spirit, a farm club for the Seattle Mariners. The fronts have posed color player photos with white borders. The year "1989" and the city are written vertically on the left side of the card, and the player's name and position are given below the picture. In a horizontal format, the backs have biography, recent professional baseball performance summary (including statistics), and a color headshot, all in a yellow rectangular box. The owner of the team is Mark Harmon, the well-known actor.

	MINT	NRMT	EXC
COMPLETE SET (29)	6.00	2.70	.75

- ☐ 1 Jim Campanis
- ☐ 2 Dorian Daughtry
- ☐ 3 Richard Carter
- ☐ 4 Rick Balabon
- ☐ 5 Greg Burlingame
- ☐ 6 Jim Blueberg
- ☐ 7 Daniel Barbara
- ☐ 8 Brian Baldwin
- ☐ 9 Willie Ambos
- ☐ 10 Chuck Kniffin CO
- ☐ 11 Ralph Dick MGR
- ☐ 12 Jorge Uribe
- ☐ 13 Kurt Stange
- ☐ 14 Jim Pritikin
- ☐ 15 Steve Hill
- ☐ 16 Lee Hancock
- ☐ 17 Anthony Woods
- ☐ 18 Jose Tartabull Jr.
- ☐ 19 Scott Runge
- ☐ 20 Bryan King
- ☐ 21 Jody Ryan
- ☐ 22 Mike McDonald
- ☐ 23 Ruben Gonzalez
- ☐ 24 Mike Goff
- ☐ 25 Todd Haney
- ☐ 26 Stan Sanchez CO
- ☐ 27 Mark Merchant
- ☐ 28 Rich Dauer MGR
Mark Harmon (Owner)
- ☐ 29 Spirit (Mascot)
Checklist

1989 San Bernardino Spirit Cal League Cards

	MINT	NRMT	EXC
COMPLETE SET (32)	5.00	2.20	.60

- ☐ 64 Calvin Jones
- ☐ 65 Troy Evans
- ☐ 66 Will Ambos
- ☐ 67 Jody Ryan
- ☐ 68 Richard Carter
- ☐ 69 Kurt Strange
- ☐ 70 Greg Burlingame
- ☐ 71 Lee Hancock
- ☐ 72 Mike Goff
- ☐ 73 Brian Baldwin
- ☐ 74 Rick Balabon
- ☐ 75 Rodney Poissant
- ☐ 76 Dan Barbara
- ☐ 77 John Hoffman
- ☐ 78 Jorge Uribe
- ☐ 79 Jose Tartabull Jr.
- ☐ 80 Bryan King
- ☐ 81 Todd Haney
- ☐ 82 Ruben Gonzalez
- ☐ 83 Anthony Woods
- ☐ 84 Steve Hill
- ☐ 85 Jim Campanis
- ☐ 86 Jim Pritikin
- ☐ 87 Mike McDonald
- ☐ 88 Dorian Daughtry
- ☐ 89 Chuck Kniffen MGR
- ☐ 90 Ralph Dick MGR
- ☐ 91 Stan Sanchez CO
- ☐ 92 Chris Verna TR
- ☐ 93 Mark Merchant
- ☐ 94 The Bug
- ☐ 95 Smokey

1989 San Diego State Aztecs Smokey

	MINT	NRMT	EXC
COMPLETE SET (28)	10.00	4.50	1.25

- ☐ 1 Paul Austin
- ☐ 2 Jeff Barry
- ☐ 3 Mike Bitter
- ☐ 4 Dan Brown
- ☐ 5 Rob Brown
- ☐ 6 Eric Christopherson

☐ 7 Jim Dietz CO
☐ 8 Brian Dunn
☐ 9 Rusty Filter
☐ 10 Steve Goucher
☐ 11 Craig Harrison
☐ 12 John Hemmerly
☐ 13 Anthony Johnson
☐ 14 Bob Livingston
☐ 15 Brian Lutes
☐ 16 John Marshall
☐ 17 Kasey McKeon
☐ 18 Billy Miller
☐ 19 Rick Navarro
☐ 20 Kevin Nielsen
☐ 21 Andy Petersen
☐ 22 Lance Pinnell
☐ 23 Erik Plantenberg
☐ 24 Kelly Powell
☐ 25 Dave Riddle
☐ 26 Jack Skoog
☐ 27 Joe Valverde
☐ 28 Jim Vlcek

1989 San Jose Giants Best

The 1989 San Jose Giants set contains 31 standard-size cards. The fronts have posed color player photos with white borders. The year "1989" and the city are written vertically on the left side of the card, and the player's name and position are given below the picture. In a horizontal format, the backs have biography, recent professional baseball performance summary (including statistics), and a color headshot, all in a yellow rectangular box.

	MINT	NRMT	EXC
COMPLETE SET (31)	5.00	2.20	.60

☐ 1 Andres Santana
☐ 2 Rod Beck
☐ 3 Jamie Cooper
☐ 4 James Terrill
☐ 5 Lonnie Phillips
☐ 6 Don Brock
☐ 7 Mark Dewey
☐ 8 Dan Fernandez
☐ 9 Bill Carlson
☐ 10 David Booth
☐ 11 Steve Decker
☐ 12 Montie Phillips
☐ 13 Elanis Westbrook
☐ 14 Tom Ealy
☐ 15 Bryan Hickerson
☐ 16 James Pena
☐ 17 Scott Wilson
☐ 18 Kevin Meier
☐ 19 Tom Hostetler
☐ 20 Steve Lienhard
☐ 21 Juan Guerrero
☐ 22 James Malseed
☐ 23 Jim Jones
☐ 24 Steve Hecht
☐ 25 T.J. McDonald
☐ 26 Mike Ham
☐ 27 Scott Goins
☐ 28 Duanne Espy MGR
☐ 29 Todd Oakes CO
☐ 30 Ernie Sierra
☐ 31 Team logo
Checklist

1989 San Jose Giants Cal League Cards

	MINT	NRMT	EXC
COMPLETE SET (30)	5.00	2.20	.60

☐ 30 Dave Hilton
Instructor
☐ 209 Rod Beck
☐ 210 Don Brock
☐ 211 Mark Dewey
☐ 212 Bryan Hickerson
☐ 213 Tom Hostetler
☐ 214 Steve Lienhard
☐ 215 Kevin Meier
☐ 216 Jim Pena
☐ 217 Lonnie Phillips
☐ 218 Jim Terrill
☐ 219 Juan Guerrero
☐ 220 Mike Ham
☐ 221 Steve Hecht
☐ 222 Jim Jones
☐ 223 Jim Malseed
☐ 224 T.J. McDonald
☐ 225 Elanis Westbrooks
☐ 226 Andrew Santana
☐ 227 Steve Decker
☐ 228 David Booth
☐ 229 Bill Carlson
☐ 230 Jamie Cooper
☐ 231 Tom Ealy
☐ 232 Dan Fernandez
☐ 233 Scott Goins
☐ 234 Scott Wilson TR
☐ 235 Duane Espy MGR
☐ 236 Todd Oakes CO
☐ 237 Harry Steve GM

1989 San Jose Giants ProCards

This 30-card standard-size set of the 1989 San Jose Giants, a Class A California League affiliate of the San Francisco Giants, features orange-bordered posed color player photos on its fronts. The player's name, position, and team name appear at the bottom. The horizontal gray back carries the player's name and position at the top, followed by biography and statistics.

	MINT	NRMT	EXC
COMPLETE SET (30)	5.00	2.20	.60

☐ 432 Checklist
☐ 433 Montie Phillips
☐ 434 Tom Ealy
☐ 435 Elanis Westbrooks
☐ 436 T.J. McDonald
☐ 437 Jim Malseed
☐ 438 Scott Goins
☐ 439 Bill Carlson
☐ 440 David Booth
☐ 441 Dan Fernandez
☐ 442 Don Brock
☐ 443 Bryan Hickerson
☐ 444 Tom Hostetler
☐ 445 Jim Pena
☐ 446 Steve Decker
☐ 447 Kevin Meier
☐ 448 Mark Dewey
☐ 449 Jim Terrill
☐ 450 Andres Santana
☐ 451 Juan Guerrero
☐ 452 Lonnie Phillips
☐ 453 Duane Espy MGR
☐ 454 Scott Wilson TR
☐ 455 Todd Oakes CO
☐ 456 Steve Lienhard
☐ 457 Steve Hecht
☐ 458 Jamie Cooper
☐ 459 Rod Beck
☐ 460 Jim Jones
☐ 461 Mike Ham

1989 San Jose Giants Star

The 1989 San Jose Giants set contains 28 standard-size cards. The fronts have posed color player photos, with orange borders on the top portion of the card fading to black as one moves down the card face. In black print on a pale orange background, the backs have biography and statistics. The color scheme of the front borders on card numbers 26-28 is reversed; also these cards have blue instead of black print on the back. 5,000 sets produced.

	MINT	NRMT	EXC
COMPLETE SET (28)	5.00	2.20	.60

☐ 1 Rod Beck
☐ 2 Dave Booth
☐ 3 Don Brock
☐ 4 Bill Carlson
☐ 5 Jamie Cooper
☐ 6 Steve Decker
☐ 7 Mark Dewey
☐ 8 Tom Ealy
☐ 9 Dan Fernandez
☐ 10 Scott Goins
☐ 11 Juan Guerrero
☐ 12 Mike Ham
☐ 13 Steven Hecht
☐ 14 Bryan Hickerson
☐ 15 Tom Hostetler
☐ 16 Jim Jones
☐ 17 Steve Lienhard
☐ 18 James Malseed
☐ 19 T.J. McDonald
☐ 20 Kevin Meier
☐ 21 James Pena
☐ 22 Montie Phillips
☐ 23 Andres Santana
☐ 24 James Terrill
☐ 25 Elanis Westbrooks
☐ 26 Todd Oakes CO
☐ 27 Duane Espy MGR
☐ 28 Scott Wilson TR

1989 Sarasota White Sox Star

The 1989 Sarasota White Sox set contains 25 standard-size cards. The fronts have posed color player photos, with blue borders on the top portion of the card fading to red as one moves down the card face. In blue print on a light blue background, the backs have biography and statistics. 5,000 sets produced.

	MINT	NRMT	EXC
COMPLETE SET (25)	5.00	2.20	.60

☐ 1 Kurt Brown
☐ 2 Eddie Caceres
☐ 3 Darrin Campbell
☐ 4 Chris Cauley
☐ 5 Bob Fletcher
☐ 6 Paul Fuller
☐ 7 Ken Gohmann
☐ 8 Cliff Gonzalez
☐ 9 Todd Hall
☐ 10 Curt Hasler
☐ 11 John Hudek
☐ 12 Bo Kennedy
☐ 13 Brent Knackert
☐ 14 Rodney McCray
☐ 15 Jim Morris
☐ 16 Javier Ocasio
☐ 17 Raymond Payton
☐ 18 Jack Peel
☐ 19 Bob Resnikoff
☐ 20 Dave Reynolds
☐ 21 Dan Rohrmeier
☐ 22 Ron Stephens
☐ 23 Carl Sullivan
☐ 24 Scott Tedder
☐ 25 Coaching Staff
Tony Franklin MGR
Don Cooper CO
Pat Roessler CO

1989 Savannah Cardinals ProCards

This 30-card standard-size set of the 1989 Savannah Cardinals, a Class A South Atlantic affiliate of the St. Louis Cardinals, features orange-bordered posed color player photos on its fronts. The player's name, position, and team name appear at the bottom. The horizontal gray back carries the player's name and position at the top, followed by biography and statistics.

	MINT	NRMT	EXC
COMPLETE SET (30)	5.00	2.20	.60

☐ 342 Checklist
☐ 343 Jay North CO
☐ 344 Keith Champion MGR
☐ 345 Gabriel Ozuna
☐ 346 Bobby Deloach
☐ 347 Dan Doyel TR
☐ 348 Dean Weese
☐ 349 Orlando Thomas
☐ 350 Luis Martinez
☐ 351 John Burgos
☐ 352 Tim Pettengill
☐ 353 Ahmed Rodriguez
☐ 354 Jim Ferguson
☐ 355 Vince Kindred
☐ 356 Juan Belbru
☐ 357 Mauricio Nunez
☐ 358 Eddie Carter
☐ 359 Mateo Ozuna
☐ 360 Lorenzo Calzado
☐ 361 Julio Mendez
☐ 362 Al Biggers
☐ 363 Steve Fanning
☐ 364 Mike Hensley
☐ 365 Brad Harvick
☐ 366 Bill Hershman
☐ 367 David Sala
☐ 368 Andy Taylor
☐ 369 Dan Hitt
☐ 370 Mark Clark
☐ 371 John Ericks

1989 Scranton Red Barons CMC

	MINT	NRMT	EXC
COMPLETE SET (25)	5.00	2.20	.60

☐ 1 Marvin Freeman
☐ 2 Barney Nugent
☐ 3 John Martin
☐ 4 Bob Sebra
☐ 5 Alex Madrid
☐ 6 Dave Cash
☐ 7 Gordon Dillard
☐ 8 Brad Moore
☐ 9 Wally Ritchie
☐ 10 Randy O'Neal
☐ 11 Tommy Barrett
☐ 12 Steve Stanicek
☐ 13 Keith Miller
☐ 14 Matt Cimo
☐ 15 Jim Olander
☐ 16 Ron Salcedo
☐ 17 Ken Jackson
☐ 18 Joe LeFebvre
☐ 19 Greg Legg
☐ 20 Joe Redfield
☐ 21 Al Pardo
☐ 22 Floyd Rayford
☐ 23 Victor Rosario
☐ 24 Kevin Bootay
☐ 25 Bill Dancy

1989 Scranton Red Barons ProCards

This 28-card standard-size set of the 1989 Scranton Red Barons, a Class AAA International League affiliate of the Philadelphia Phillies, features blue-bordered posed color player photos on its fronts. The player's name, position, and team name appear at the bottom. The horizontal gray back carries the player's name and position at the top, followed by biography and statistics.

	MINT	NRMT	EXC
COMPLETE SET (28)	5.00	2.20	.60

☐ 705 Checklist
☐ 706 Danny Clay
☐ 707 Ron Salcedo
☐ 708 Greg Legg
☐ 709 Brad Moore
☐ 710 Victor Rosario
☐ 711 Al Pardo
☐ 712 Barney Nugent TR
☐ 713 Kevin Bootay
☐ 714 Gordon Dillard
☐ 715 Wally Ritchie
☐ 716 Keith Miller
☐ 717 Steve Stanicek
☐ 718 Bob Sebra
☐ 719 John Martin
☐ 720 Alex Madrid
☐ 721 Brad Brink
☐ 722 Joe Lefebvre CO
☐ 723 Jim Olander
☐ 724 George Culver CO
☐ 725 Tommy Barrett
☐ 726 Randy O'Neal
☐ 727 Floyd Rayford
☐ 728 Bruce Ruffin
☐ 729 Ken Jackson
☐ 730 Matt Cimo
☐ 731 Joe Redfield
☐ 1208 Bill Dancy MGR

1989 Shreveport Captains ProCards

This 27-card standard-size set of the 1989 Shreveport Captains, a Class AA Texas League affiliate of the San Francisco Giants, features red-bordered posed color player photos on its fronts. The player's name, position, and team name appear at the bottom. The horizontal gray back carries the player's name and position at the top, followed by biography and statistics.

	MINT	NRMT	EXC
COMPLETE SET (27)	5.00	2.20	.60

☐ 1829 Checklist
☐ 1830 Steve Connolly
☐ 1831 Russ Swan
☐ 1832 Mike Remlinger
☐ 1833 Eric Gunderson
☐ 1834 Paul Blair
☐ 1835 Jim Anderson TR
☐ 1836 Dee Dixon
☐ 1837 Steve Cline CO
☐ 1838 Bill Evers MGR
☐ 1839 Greg Conner
☐ 1840 Mike Senne
☐ 1841 Gregg Ritchie
☐ 1842 Ted Wood
☐ 1843 David Patterson
☐ 1844 Craig Colbert
☐ 1845 Erik Johnson
☐ 1846 Jeff Carter
☐ 1847 Rich Aldrete
☐ 1848 Jose Pena
☐ 1849 Markus Owens
☐ 1850 Paul McClellan
☐ 1851 Doug Robertson
☐ 1852 Dean Freeland
☐ 1853 Randy McCament
☐ 1854 Jose Dominguez
☐ 1855 George Bonilla

1989 South Bend White Sox Grand Slam

	MINT	NRMT	EXC
COMPLETE SET (30)	5.00	2.20	.60

☐ 1 Craig Wallin ANN
☐ 2 Rick Patterson MGR
☐ 3 Jim Reinebold CO
☐ 4 Roger LaFrancois
☐ 5 Kirk Champion CO
☐ 6 Scott Johnson TR
☐ 7 Scott Radinsky
☐ 8 Frank Merigliano
☐ 9 Sam Chavez
☐ 10 Virgil Cooper
☐ 11 Fred Dabney
☐ 12 Carlos DeLaCruz
☐ 13 Bret Marshall
☐ 14 Mike Mitchener
☐ 15 Steve Schrenck
☐ 16 Jose Venture
☐ 17 Randy Warren
☐ 18 Steve Mehl
☐ 19 Kinnis Pledger
☐ 20 John Zaksek
☐ 21 Mark Chasey
☐ 22 Rob Lukachyk
☐ 23 Wayne Busby

- ☐ 24 Cesar Bernhardt
- ☐ 25 Eugenio Tejada
- ☐ 26 Greg Roth
- ☐ 27 Derek Lee
- ☐ 28 Ed Smith
- ☐ 29 Jay Hornacek
- ☐ 30 Clemente Alvarez

1989 Southern League All-Stars Jennings

This 25-card standard-size set showcases Southern League All-Stars. The front design has a mix of posed or action color player photos, with white and purple borders on a light blue card face. The year "1989" appears in a row of stars at the card top, and the Southern League logo is superimposed at the lower left corner. The horizontally oriented backs have biography, statistics, and the player's regular team.

	MINT	NRMT	EXC
COMPLETE SET (25)	6.00	2.70	.75

- ☐ 1 Harvey Pulliam
- ☐ 2 Robin Ventura
- ☐ 3 Eric Anthony
- ☐ 4 Kelly Mann
- ☐ 5 Delino DeShields
- ☐ 6 Scott Leius
- ☐ 7 Bernie Walker
- ☐ 8 Jimmy Kremers
- ☐ 9 Bob Hamelin
- ☐ 10 Todd Trafton
- ☐ 11 Greg Smith
- ☐ 12 Terry Jorgensen
- ☐ 13 Paul Sorrento
- ☐ 14 Paul Abbott
- ☐ 15 Jerry Kutzler
- ☐ 16 Wayne Edwards
- ☐ 17 Buddy Groom
- ☐ 18 Joe Bruno
- ☐ 19 Mark Guthrie
- ☐ 20 Mel Rojas
- ☐ 21 Rob Wishnevski
- ☐ 22 Luis Encarnacion
- ☐ 23 Buddy Bailey MGR
- ☐ 24 Barry Foote CO
- ☐ 25 Jeff Newman CO

1989 Spartanburg Phillies ProCards

This 30-card standard-size set of the 1989 Spartanburg Phillies, a Class A South Atlantic League affiliate of the Philadelphia Phillies, features orange-bordered posed color player photos on its fronts. The player's name, position, and team name appear at the bottom. The horizontal gray back carries the player's name and position at the top, followed by biography and statistics.

	MINT	NRMT	EXC
COMPLETE SET (30)	5.00	2.20	.60

- ☐ 1027 Checklist
- ☐ 1028 Todd Elam
- ☐ 1029 Ed Rosado
- ☐ 1030 Mickey Morandini
- ☐ 1031 Jon Szynal
- ☐ 1032 Rick Jones CO
- ☐ 1033 Troy Kent
- ☐ 1034 Greg McCarthy
- ☐ 1035 Mike Carlin
- ☐ 1036 Gary Wilson
- ☐ 1037 Toby Borland
- ☐ 1038 Jason Backs
- ☐ 1039 Reggie Garcia
- ☐ 1040 Darrell Lindsey
- ☐ 1041 Paul Ellison
- ☐ 1042 Darrell Coulter
- ☐ 1043 Nick Santacruz
- ☐ 1044 Leroy Ventress
- ☐ 1045 John Marshall
- ☐ 1046 Antonio Lanares
- ☐ 1047 Tom Marsh
- ☐ 1048 Reed Olmstead
- ☐ 1049 Chris Sementelli TR
- ☐ 1050 Mel Roberts MGR
- ☐ 1051 Pedro Zayas
- ☐ 1052 Tim Dell
- ☐ 1053 Tim Churchill
- ☐ 1054 John Larosa
- ☐ 1055 Steve Keller
- ☐ 1056 Don(Moose) DeMuth Treasurer

1989 Spartanburg Phillies Star

The 1989 Spartanburg Phillies set contains 26 standard-size cards. The fronts have posed color player photos, with red borders on the top portion of the card fading to gray as one moves down the card face. In red print on a gray background, the backs have biography and statistics. The back of card number 26 has a white background. The cards are arranged alphabetically and numbered on the back. 5,000 sets produced.

	MINT	NRMT	EXC
COMPLETE SET (26)	5.00	2.20	.60

- ☐ 1 Jason Backs
- ☐ 2 Toby Borland
- ☐ 3 Mike Carlin
- ☐ 4 Tim Churchill
- ☐ 5 Darrell Coulter
- ☐ 6 Tim Dell
- ☐ 7 Todd Elam
- ☐ 8 Paul Ellison
- ☐ 9 Reggie Garcia
- ☐ 10 Steve Keller
- ☐ 11 Troy Kent
- ☐ 12 John LaRosa
- ☐ 13 Antonio Linares
- ☐ 14 Darrell Lindsey
- ☐ 15 Tom Marsh
- ☐ 16 John Marshall
- ☐ 17 Greg McCarthy
- ☐ 18 Mickey Morandini
- ☐ 19 Reed Olmstead
- ☐ 20 Ed Rosado
- ☐ 21 Nick Santa Cruz
- ☐ 22 Jon Szynal
- ☐ 23 Leroy Ventress
- ☐ 24 Gary Wilson
- ☐ 25 Pedro Zayas
- ☐ 26 Coaching Staff Mel Roberts MGR Rick Jones CO Buzz Capra CO

1989 Spokane Indians Sports Pro

The 1989 Spokane Indians set was sponsored by Sport Pro and University City. The 26 standard-size cards have on the fronts posed color player photos with white borders. The team name and logo appear in a black stripe at the top of the card. In a horizontal format, the backs have brief biographical information and sponsors' advertisements.

	MINT	NRMT	EXC
COMPLETE SET (26)	6.00	2.70	.75

- ☐ 1 Dave Staton
- ☐ 2 Eddie Zinter
- ☐ 3 Rod Billingsley
- ☐ 4 Bruce Bochy MGR
- ☐ 5 Tony McGee
- ☐ 6 John Phelan
- ☐ 7 Joe Buckley
- ☐ 8 Greg Hall CO
- ☐ 9 Terry Rupp
- ☐ 10 Dan Deville
- ☐ 11 Rick Davis
- ☐ 12 Bill Johnson
- ☐ 13 Tom Brassel CO
- ☐ 14 Kerry Knox
- ☐ 15 Brian Span
- ☐ 16 Scot Welish
- ☐ 17 Troy Cunningham
- ☐ 18 Steve Martin
- ☐ 19 Kevin Higgins
- ☐ 20 Chris Gollehon
- ☐ 21 Jeff Barton
- ☐ 22 Bobby Sheridan
- ☐ 23 Kevin Towers CO
- ☐ 24 Rico Coleman
- ☐ 25 Steve Bethea
- ☐ 26 Darrell Sherman

1989 Springfield Cardinals Best

The 1989 Springfield Cardinals set contains 30 standard-size cards. The fronts have posed color player photos with white borders. The year "1989" and the city are written vertically on the left side of the card, and the player's name and position are given below the picture. In a horizontal format, the backs have biography, recent professional baseball performance summary (including statistics), and a color headshot, all in a yellow rectangular box.

	MINT	NRMT	EXC
COMPLETE SET (30)	5.00	2.20	.60

- ☐ 1 Mike Fiore
- ☐ 2 Dave Grimes
- ☐ 3 Antron Grier
- ☐ 4 Brad DuVall
- ☐ 5 Bob Colescott
- ☐ 6 Scott Broadfoot
- ☐ 7 Luis Faccio
- ☐ 8 Winston Brown
- ☐ 9 Kris Huffman
- ☐ 10 Michael Ross
- ☐ 11 Lee Plemel
- ☐ 12 Jeff Shireman
- ☐ 13 Scott Lawrence
- ☐ 14 John Sellick
- ☐ 15 David Payton
- ☐ 16 David Richardson
- ☐ 17 Charlie White
- ☐ 18 Cory Satterfield
- ☐ 19 Tom Malchesky
- ☐ 20 Dale Kisten
- ☐ 21 Roberto Marte
- ☐ 22 Ti Meamber
- ☐ 23 Edward Looper
- ☐ 24 Fred Langiotti
- ☐ 25 Lonnie Maclin
- ☐ 26 Vince Sferrezza TR
- ☐ 27 Rick Colbert CO
- ☐ 28 Dan Moushon Asst GM
- ☐ 29 Dan Radison MGR
- ☐ 30 Team logo Checklist

1989 St. Catharines Blue Jays ProCards

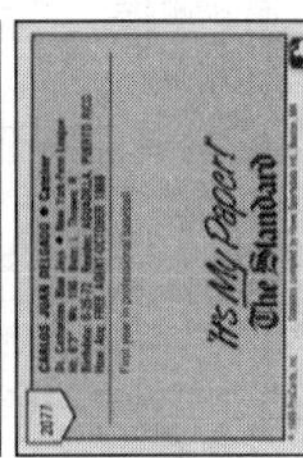

Sponsored by The Standard, this 28-card standard-size set of the 1989 St. Catharines Blue Jays, a Class A New York-Penn League affiliate of the Toronto Blue Jays, features orange-bordered posed color player photos on its fronts. The player's name, position, and team name appear at the bottom. The horizontal gray back carries the player's name and position at the top, followed by biography and statistics. This issue includes the minor league card debut of Carlos Delgado and Jeff Kent.

	MINT	NRMT	EXC
COMPLETE SET (28)	30.00	13.50	3.70

- ☐ 2069 Checklist
- ☐ 2070 Gregg Martin
- ☐ 2071 Bill Abare III
- ☐ 2072 Ryan Thompson
- ☐ 2073 Daren Brown
- ☐ 2074 Scott Hutson
- ☐ 2075 Oscar Garcia
- ☐ 2076 Daren Kizziah
- ☐ 2077 Carlos Delgado
- ☐ 2078 Mike Jockish
- ☐ 2079 Greg O'Halloran
- ☐ 2080 Hector Mercedes
- ☐ 2081 Nigel Wilson
- ☐ 2082 Billy Parese
- ☐ 2083 Gonzalo Vargas
- ☐ 2084 Anton Mobley
- ☐ 2085 Chris Beacom
- ☐ 2086 John Wanish
- ☐ 2087 Ernesto Santana
- ☐ 2088 Rob Blumberg
- ☐ 2089 Sterling Stock
- ☐ 2090 Greg Bicknell
- ☐ 2091 Jeff Kent
- ☐ 2092 Armando Pagliari TR
- ☐ 2093 Mike McAlpin CO
- ☐ 2094 Greg McCutcheon
- ☐ 2095 Bob Shirley MG
- ☐ 2096 Rick Holifield

1989 St. Lucie Mets Star

The 1989 St. Lucie Mets set contains 27 standard-size cards. The fronts have posed color player photos, with blue borders on the top portion of the card fading to orange as one moves down the card face. In blue print on a pale orange background, the backs have biography and statistics. The cards are arranged alphabetically and numbered on the back. 5,000 sets produced.

	MINT	NRMT	EXC
COMPLETE SET (27)	5.00	2.20	.60

- ☐ 1 Brant Alyea Jr.
- ☐ 2 Terry Bross
- ☐ 3 Alex Diaz
- ☐ 4 Tony Diaz
- ☐ 5 Chris Donnels
- ☐ 6 Clint Hurdle MGR
- ☐ 7 Ron Gideon
- ☐ 8 Terry Griffin
- ☐ 9 Rudy Hernandez
- ☐ 10 Tim Hines
- ☐ 11 Scott Jaster
- ☐ 12 Crucito Lara
- ☐ 13 Steve Larose
- ☐ 14 David Lau
- ☐ 15 Juan Marina
- ☐ 16 Terry McDaniel
- ☐ 17 Mike Miller
- ☐ 18 Danny Naughton
- ☐ 19 Dale Plummer
- ☐ 20 Dave Proctor
- ☐ 21 Titi Roche
- ☐ 22 Jaime Roseboro
- ☐ 23 Julio Valera
- ☐ 24 Mike Whitlock
- ☐ 25 Vince Zawaski
- ☐ 26 Joel Horlen CO
- ☐ 27 Fred Hina TR

1989 St. Petersburg Cardinals Star

The 1989 St. Petersburg Cardinals set contains 29 standard-size cards. The fronts have posed color player photos, with red borders on the top portion of the card fading to yellow as one moves down the card face. In red print on a pale yellow background, the backs have biography and statistics. 5,000 sets produced.

	MINT	NRMT	EXC
COMPLETE SET (29)	5.00	2.20	.60

- ☐ 1 Franklin Abreu
- ☐ 2 Greg Becker
- ☐ 3 Bill Bivens
- ☐ 4 Art Calvert
- ☐ 5 Greg Carmona
- ☐ 6 Ric Christian
- ☐ 7 Alex Cole
- ☐ 8 Rheal Cormier
- ☐ 9 Todd Crosby
- ☐ 10 Terry Elliot
- ☐ 11 Joe Federico
- ☐ 12 Joey Fernandez
- ☐ 13 Ed Fulton
- ☐ 14 Mark Grater
- ☐ 15 Joe Hall
- ☐ 16 Shawn Hathaway
- ☐ 17 Jeremy Hernandez
- ☐ 18 Rich Hoffman
- ☐ 19 Chuck Johnson
- ☐ 20 Scott Melvin
- ☐ 21 Scott Nichols
- ☐ 22 Larry Pierson
- ☐ 23 Tony Russo
- ☐ 24 Tim Sherrill
- ☐ 25 Ken Smith
- ☐ 26 Paul Thoutsis
- ☐ 27 Dave Bialas MGR
- ☐ 28 Marty Mason CO
- ☐ 29 Team Photo

1989 Star

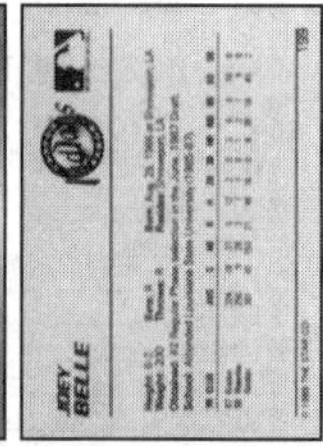

This 200-card set was issued wax packs in two series; the first series featured different color bordered while the second series featured just red posed color player photos on its fronts. The player's name, team name, and position appear at the bottom. The yellow series 1 and white series 2 horizontal back carries the player's name at the top, followed by biography, career highlights, and statistics.

	MINT	NRMT	EXC
COMPLETE SET (200)	15.00	6.75	1.85
COMPLETE SERIES 1 (100)	5.00	2.20	.60
COMPLETE SERIES 2 (100)	10.00	4.50	1.25
COMMON CARD (1-200)	.05	.02	.01
☐ 1 Eric Anthony	.05	.02	.01
☐ 2 David Rohde	.05	.02	.01
☐ 3 Mike Simms	.05	.02	.01
☐ 4 John Faccio	.05	.02	.01
☐ 5 Oreste Marrero	.05	.02	.01
☐ 6 Troy O'Leary	.10	.05	.01
☐ 7 Rob Maurer	.05	.02	.01
☐ 8 Rod Morris	.05	.02	.01
☐ 9 Ed Ohman	.05	.02	.01
☐ 10 Jim Byrd	.05	.02	.01
☐ 11 Mark Cobb	.05	.02	.01
☐ 12 Pat Combs	.05	.02	.01
☐ 13 Tim Mauser	.05	.02	.01
☐ 14 Jim Vatcher	.05	.02	.01
☐ 15 Luis Gonzalez	.10	.05	.01
☐ 16 Andres Mota	.05	.02	.01
☐ 17 Scott Servais	.10	.05	.01
☐ 18 David Silvestri	.05	.02	.01
☐ 19 Kevin Burdick	.05	.02	.01
☐ 20 Tommy Shields	.05	.02	.01
☐ 21 Mike York	.05	.02	.01
☐ 22 Mike Anaya	.05	.02	.01
☐ 23 Dale Plummer	.05	.02	.01
☐ 24 Titi Roche	.05	.02	.01
☐ 25 Vincent Zawaski	.05	.02	.01
☐ 26 Anthony Barron	.05	.02	.01
☐ 27 Rafael Bournigal	.05	.02	.01
☐ 28 Albert Bustillos	.05	.02	.01

Card			
☐ 29 Mark Griffin	.05	.02	.01
☐ 30 Brett Magnussn	.05	.02	.01
☐ 31 Mike Jones	.05	.02	.01
☐ 32 Bret Barberie	.10	.05	.01
☐ 33 Bert Echemendia	.05	.02	.01
☐ 34 Mike Bell	.05	.02	.01
☐ 35 Brian R. Hunter	.05	.02	.01
☐ 36 Jim Lemasters	.05	.02	.01
☐ 37 Rick Morris	.05	.02	.01
☐ 38 Dominic Pierce	.05	.02	.01
☐ 39 Joey Wardlow	.05	.02	.01
☐ 40 Dera Clark	.05	.02	.01
☐ 41 Stu Cole	.05	.02	.01
☐ 42 Bob Hamelin	.10	.05	.01
☐ 43 Deric Ladnier	.05	.02	.01
☐ 44 Brian McRae	.25	.11	.03
☐ 45 Mike Tresemer	.05	.02	.01
☐ 46 Steve Walker	.05	.02	.01
☐ 47 Greg Becker	.05	.02	.01
☐ 48 Art Calvert	.05	.02	.01
☐ 49 Todd Crosby	.05	.02	.01
☐ 50 Shawn Hathaway	.05	.02	.01
☐ 51 Rich Garces	.05	.02	.01
☐ 52 Todd McClure	.05	.02	.01
☐ 53 Steve Morris	.05	.02	.01
☐ 54 Tim Dell	.05	.02	.01
☐ 55 Antonio Linares	.05	.02	.01
☐ 56 John Marshall	.05	.02	.01
☐ 57 Mike Morandini	.05	.02	.01
☐ 58 Paul Fuller	.05	.02	.01
☐ 59 John Hudek	.10	.05	.01
☐ 60 Ron Stephens	.05	.02	.01
☐ 61 Scott Tedder	.05	.02	.01
☐ 62 Pete Alborano	.05	.02	.01
☐ 63 Kevin Shaw	.05	.02	.01
☐ 64 Antony Ariola	.05	.02	.01
☐ 65 James Buccheri	.05	.02	.01
☐ 66 William Love	.05	.02	.01
☐ 67 Steve Avery	.25	.11	.03
☐ 68 Rich Casarotti	.05	.02	.01
☐ 69 Brian Champion	.05	.02	.01
☐ 70 Wes Currin	.05	.02	.01
☐ 71 Biran Deak	.05	.02	.01
☐ 72 Ken Pennington	.05	.02	.01
☐ 73 Theron Todd	.05	.02	.01
☐ 74 Andy Tomberlin	.05	.02	.01
☐ 75 Richard Falkner	.05	.02	.01
☐ 76 Tommy Kramer	.05	.02	.01
☐ 77 Charles Nagy	.50	.23	.06
☐ 78 Chris Howard	.05	.02	.01
☐ 79 Mike Rhodes	.05	.02	.01
☐ 80 Gabriel Rodriguez	.05	.02	.01
☐ 81 Bob Zeihen	.05	.02	.01
☐ 82 Rod Beck	.15	.07	.02
☐ 83 Jamie Cooper	.05	.02	.01
☐ 84 Steve Decker	.05	.02	.01
☐ 85 Mark Dewey	.05	.02	.01
☐ 86 Juan Guerrero	.05	.02	.01
☐ 87 Andres Santana	.05	.02	.01
☐ 88 Pedro DeLeon	.05	.02	.01
☐ 89 Pat Kelly	.15	.07	.02
☐ 90 Bill Masse	.05	.02	.01
☐ 91 Jerry Neilson	.05	.02	.01
☐ 92 Mark Ohlms	.05	.02	.01
☐ 93 Moises Alou	.50	.23	.06
☐ 94 Ed Hartman	.05	.02	.01
☐ 95 Keith Richardson	.05	.02	.01
☐ 96 Royal Clayton	.05	.02	.01
☐ 97 Bobby Davidson	.05	.02	.01
☐ 98 Mitch Lyden	.05	.02	.01
☐ 99 Hensley Meulens	.05	.02	.01
☐ 100 John Ramos	.05	.02	.01
☐ 101 Robin Ventura	.75	.35	.09
☐ 102 Luis Mercedes	.05	.02	.01
☐ 103 Dave Miller	.05	.02	.01
☐ 104 Randy Berlin	.05	.02	.01
☐ 105 Mike Campas	.05	.02	.01
☐ 106 Jose Trujillo	.05	.02	.01
☐ 107 Lem Pilkenton	.05	.02	.01
☐ 108 Frank Bollick	.05	.02	.01
☐ 109 Bert Heffernan	.05	.02	.01
☐ 110 Chris Czarnik	.05	.02	.01
☐ 111 Andy Benes	.30	.14	.04
☐ 112 Skipper Wright	.05	.02	.01
☐ 113 Eric Alexander	.05	.02	.01
☐ 114 Manny Alexander	.15	.07	.02
☐ 115 Jimmy Roso	.05	.02	.01
☐ 116 Chris Donnels	.05	.02	.01
☐ 117 Jamie Roseboro	.05	.02	.01
☐ 118 Julian Yan	.05	.02	.01
☐ 119 Vicent Degifico	.05	.02	.01
☐ 120 Mickey Morandini	.15	.07	.02
☐ 121 Goose Gozzo	.05	.02	.01
☐ 122 Pedro Munoz	.15	.07	.02
☐ 123 Keith Helton	.05	.02	.01
☐ 124 Tino Martinez	.50	.23	.06
☐ 125 Sandy Alomar Jr.	.25	.11	.03
☐ 126 Scott Cooper	.05	.02	.01
☐ 127 Daryl Irvine	.05	.02	.01
☐ 128 Jim Orsag	.05	.02	.01
☐ 129 Mickey Pena	.05	.02	.01
☐ 130 Scott Sommers	.05	.02	.01
☐ 131 Ed Zambrano	.05	.02	.01
☐ 132 Dave Bettendorf	.05	.02	.01
☐ 133 Steve Allen	.05	.02	.01
☐ 134 Kevin Belcher	.05	.02	.01
☐ 135 Doug Cronk	.05	.02	.01
☐ 136 Tito Stewart	.05	.02	.01
☐ 137 Jeff Frye	.15	.07	.02
☐ 138 Trey McCoy	.05	.02	.01
☐ 139 Robb Nen	.15	.07	.02
☐ 140 Jim Hvizda	.05	.02	.01
☐ 141 Tommy Boyce	.05	.02	.01
☐ 142 Michael Maksudian	.05	.02	.01
☐ 143 Matt Current	.05	.02	.01
☐ 144 Tom Hardgrove	.05	.02	.01
☐ 145 Julio Vargas	.05	.02	.01
☐ 146 Dan Welch	.05	.02	.01
☐ 147 Steve Dunn	.15	.07	.02
☐ 148 Mike Misuraca	.05	.02	.01
☐ 149 Mike House	.05	.02	.01
☐ 150 Deion Sanders	2.50	1.10	.30
☐ 151 Willie Mota	.05	.02	.01
☐ 152 Tim Nedin	.05	.02	.01
☐ 153 Kerry Taylor	.05	.02	.01
☐ 154 Beau Allred	.05	.02	.01
☐ 155 Troy Neel	.05	.02	.01
☐ 156 Shawn Hare	.05	.02	.01
☐ 157 Chris Butterfield	.05	.02	.01
☐ 158 Tim Hines	.05	.02	.01
☐ 159 Pat Howell	.05	.02	.01
☐ 160 Paul Johnson	.05	.02	.01
☐ 161 Ryan Richmond	.05	.02	.01
☐ 162 Ernie Baker	.05	.02	.01
☐ 163 Pedro Castellano	.05	.02	.01
☐ 164 Eric Jaques	.05	.02	.01
☐ 165 Mark Willoughby	.05	.02	.01
☐ 166 Dan Segui	.05	.02	.01
☐ 167 Richard Shackle	.05	.02	.01
☐ 168 Mark Lewis	.15	.07	.02
☐ 169 John Johnstone	.05	.02	.01
☐ 170 Phil Plantier	.10	.05	.01
☐ 171 Wes Chamberlain	.05	.02	.01
☐ 172 James Harris	.05	.02	.01
☐ 173 Felix Antigua	.05	.02	.01
☐ 174 Bruce Schreiber	.05	.02	.01
☐ 175 Pete Rose Jr.	.05	.02	.01
☐ 176 Kelly Woods	.05	.02	.01
☐ 177 Anthony de la Cruz	.05	.02	.01
☐ 178 Charles Nagy	.50	.23	.06
☐ 179 Nolan Lane	.05	.02	.01
☐ 180 Fabio Gomez	.05	.02	.01
☐ 181 Chris Butler	.05	.02	.01
☐ 182 Brett Merriman	.05	.02	.01
☐ 183 Carlos Mota	.05	.02	.01
☐ 184 Doug Piatt	.05	.02	.01
☐ 185 Marc Tepper	.05	.02	.01
☐ 186 Dan Williams	.05	.02	.01
☐ 187 Maximo Aleys	.05	.02	.01
☐ 188 Ken Lewis	.05	.02	.01
☐ 189 Joey Vierra	.05	.02	.01
☐ 190 Ron Morton	.05	.02	.01
☐ 191 Brook Fordyce	.10	.05	.01
☐ 192 Steve McCarthy	.05	.02	.01
☐ 193 Steve Hosey	.05	.02	.01
☐ 194 Steve Foster	.05	.02	.01
☐ 195 Ron Crowe	.05	.02	.01
☐ 196 Steve Callahan	.05	.02	.01
☐ 197 Benny Colvard	.05	.02	.01
☐ 198 Adam Casillas	.05	.02	.01
☐ 199 Albert Belle	4.00	1.80	.50
☐ 200 Ben McDonald	.15	.07	.02

1989 Stockton Ports Best

This 32-card standard-size set features the 1989 Stockton Ports, a farm club for the Milwaukee Brewers. The fronts have posed color player photos with white borders. The year "1989" and the city are written vertically on the left side of the card, and the player's name and position are given below the picture. In a horizontal format, the backs have biography, recent professional baseball performance summary (including statistics), and a color headshot, all in a yellow rectangular box.

	MINT	NRMT	EXC
COMPLETE SET (32)	5.00	2.20	.60

☐ 1 Dave Nilsson
☐ 2 Chris George
☐ 3 Mike Ignasiak
☐ 4 Steve Monson
☐ 5 Carl Moraw
☐ 6 Jamie Cangemi
☐ 7 Richard Durant
☐ 8 Steve Sparks
☐ 9 Kent Hetrick
☐ 10 Mark Ambrose
☐ 11 Jeff Ciszkowski
☐ 12 Danny Fitzpatrick
☐ 13 Leo Perez
☐ 14 Carlie Montoyo
☐ 15 Larry Oedewaldt
☐ 16 John Jaha
☐ 17 Randy Snyder
☐ 18 Gary Borg
☐ 19 Chris Cassels
☐ 20 Tim Raley
☐ 21 Bryan Foster
☐ 22 Pat Listach
☐ 23 Rob Smith
☐ 24 Bobby Jones
☐ 25 Jim Poulin TR
☐ 26 Batboys
Chris Moreno
Mike Wickhan
☐ 27 Don Miller GM
☐ 28 Dan Chapman
Asst GM
☐ 29 Dave Huppert MGR
☐ 30 Rob Derksen CO
☐ 31 Mark Marion ,
Mike Conroy
Cardshop owners
☐ 32 Team logo
Checklist

1989 Stockton Ports Cal League Cards

	MINT	NRMT	EXC
COMPLETE SET (30)	5.00	2.20	.60

☐ 150 Jaime Cangemi
☐ 151 Dan Fitzpatrick
☐ 152 Steve Sparks
☐ 153 Chris George
☐ 154 Jeff Ciszkowski
☐ 155 Rick Durant
☐ 156 Carl Moraw
☐ 157 Mike Ignasiak
☐ 158 Leo Perez
☐ 159 Mark Ambrose
☐ 160 Steve Monson
☐ 161 Kent Hetrick
☐ 162 Dave Nilsson
☐ 163 Chris Cassels
☐ 164 Gary Borg
☐ 165 John Jaha
☐ 166 Bobby Jones
☐ 167 Larry Oedewaldt
☐ 168 Rob Smith
☐ 169 Tim Raley
☐ 170 Randy Snyder
☐ 171 Bryan Foster
☐ 172 Charlie Montoya
☐ 173 Pat Listach
☐ 174 Dan Chapman
Asst GM
☐ 175 Don(Killer) Miller GM
☐ 176 Dave Huppert MGR
☐ 177 Rob Derkson CO
☐ 178 Jim Poulin TR
☐ 179 Julio Cruz CO

1989 Stockton Ports ProCards

This 31-card standard-size set of the 1989 Stockton Ports, a Class A California League affiliate of the Milwaukee Brewers, features orange-bordered posed color player photos on its fronts. The player's name, position, and team name appear at the bottom. The horizontal gray back carries the player's name and position at the top, followed by biography and statistics. Card #376 Kent Hetrick has the wrong back. The card back is #466 Jeffrey Gay of the Palm Springs Angels. A second card in the set also has a wrong back. Card #372 Leo Perez has Palm Springs Angels player James Townsend #463 on the back.

	MINT	NRMT	EXC
COMPLETE SET (31)	5.00	2.20	.60

☐ 372 Checklist
☐ 373 Leo Perez
☐ 374 Dave Nilsson
☐ 375 Larry Oedewaldt
☐ 376 Kent Hetrick
☐ 377 Mark Ambrose
☐ 378 Carl Moraw
☐ 379 Pat Listach
☐ 380 John Jaha
☐ 381 Charlie Montoyo
☐ 382 Randy Snyder
☐ 383 Bobby Jones
☐ 384 Steve Monson
☐ 385 Rob Derksen CO
☐ 386 Dave Huppert MGR
☐ 387 Jim Poulin TR
☐ 388 Rick Durant
☐ 389 Jamie Cangemi
☐ 390 Steve Sparks
☐ 391 Chris George
☐ 392 Chris Cassels
☐ 393 Bryan Foster
☐ 394 Rob Smith
☐ 395 Dan Fitzpatrick
☐ 396 Gary Borg
☐ 397 Don Miller GM
☐ 398 Dan Chapman
Asst GM
☐ 399 Jeff Ciszkowski
☐ 400 Mike Ignasiak
☐ 401 Tim Raley
☐ 402 Mark Marino
Mike Conroy
Sports Shop Owners

1989 Stockton Ports Star

This 28-card standard-size set features the 1989 Stockton Ports, a farm club for the Milwaukee Brewers. The fronts have posed color player photos, with blue borders on the top portion of the card fading to yellow as one moves down the card face. In blue print on a pale yellow background, the backs have biography and statistics. 5,000 sets produced.

	MINT	NRMT	EXC
COMPLETE SET (28)	5.00	2.20	.60

☐ 1 Gary Borg
☐ 2 Larry Oedewaldt
☐ 3 John Jaha
☐ 4 Pat Listach
☐ 5 Mike Ignasiak
☐ 6 Narciso Elvira
☐ 7 Tim Fortugno
☐ 8 Chris George
☐ 9 Tim Raley
☐ 10 Kent Hetrick
☐ 11 Steve Sparks
☐ 12 Charlie Montoyo
☐ 13 Jamie Cangemi
☐ 14 Chris Cassels
☐ 15 Bobby Jones
☐ 16 Randy Snyder
☐ 17 Jeff Ciszkowski
☐ 18 Rob Smith
☐ 19 Richard Durant
☐ 20 Bryan Foster
☐ 21 Dave Nilsson
☐ 22 Dave Huppert MGR
☐ 23 Dan Chapman MGR
☐ 24 Don Miller GM
☐ 25 Rob Derksen CO
☐ 26 Batboys
Trent Marsh
Mike Wickham
☐ 27 Jim Poulin TR
☐ 28 Sponsors
Mark Marino
Mike Conroy

1989 Sumter Braves ProCards

This 33-card standard-size set of the 1989 Sumter Braves, a Class A South Atlantic League affiliate of the Atlanta Braves, features orange-bordered posed color player photos on its fronts. The player's name, position, and team name appear at the bottom. The horizontal gray back carries the player's name and position at the top, followed by biography and statistics.

	MINT	NRMT	EXC
COMPLETE SET (33)	5.00	2.20	.60

☐ 1086 Checklist
☐ 1087 Tom Rizzo
☐ 1088 Ed Holtz GM
☐ 1089 Billy Partin
Asst GM
☐ 1090 Paul Reis
☐ 1091 Ralph Rowe CO
☐ 1092 Willy Johnson TR
☐ 1093 Elias Sosa CO
☐ 1094 Gil Garrido CO
☐ 1095 Ned Yost MGR
☐ 1096 Steve Lopez
☐ 1097 Glen Gardner
☐ 1098 Lionel Adams
☐ 1099 Mark Wohlers
☐ 1100 Dave Dickman
☐ 1101 Calvain Culberson
☐ 1102 Judd Johnson
☐ 1103 Winnie Relaford
☐ 1104 Rod Richey
☐ 1105 Johnny Maldonado
☐ 1106 Lamar Hall
☐ 1107 Scott Goselin
☐ 1108 Chad Smith
☐ 1109 Mike Urman
☐ 1110 Randy Simmons
☐ 1111 Roberto Minaya
☐ 1112 Eduardo Perez
☐ 1113 Roberto DeLeon
☐ 1114 Scott Grove
☐ 1115 Marcos Vazquez
☐ 1116 Glenn Mitchell
☐ 1117 Greg Harper
☐ 1118 Jeff Meier

1989 Syracuse Chiefs CMC

This 25-card standard-size set of the 1989 Syracuse Chiefs, a Class AAA International League affiliate of the Toronto Blue Jays, features on its fronts white-bordered posed color player photos framed by a black line. The team's name, the player's name, and his position appear at the bottom. The white back is framed by a black line and carries the team's name and league at the top, followed by the player's name, biography and statistics.

	MINT	NRMT	EXC
COMPLETE SET (25)	5.00	2.20	.60

☐ 1 Doug Bair
☐ 2 Jose Nunez
☐ 3 Jack O'Connor
☐ 4 Mark Ross
☐ 5 Frank Wills
☐ 6 Willie Blair
☐ 7 Steve Cummings
☐ 8 DeWayne Buice
☐ 9 Juan Guzman
☐ 10 Alex Sanchez
☐ 11 Sal Butera
☐ 12 Otis Green
☐ 13 Randy Holland TR
☐ 14 Tim Tolman
☐ 15 Glenallen Hill
☐ 16 Stu Pederson
☐ 17 Kelly Heath
☐ 18 Hector De La Cruz
☐ 19 Junior Felix
☐ 20 Frank Cabrera
☐ 21 Sil Campusano
☐ 22 Luis Sojo
☐ 23 Chico Walker
☐ 24 Galen Cisco CO
Hector Torres CO
☐ 25 Bob Bailor MG

1989 Syracuse Chiefs Merchants Bank

Sponsored by Merchants Bank and WIXT Channel 9, this photo album features the 1989 Syracuse Chiefs, a Class AAA International League affiliate of the Toronto Blue Jays. The photo album unfolds to reveal three 11" by 8 1/4" sheets. The first sheet displays a color team photo, with player identification immediately below. The second panel carries fifteen player cards in three rows of five each. The third panel has ten player cards in its top two rows, with the third row consisting of Merchant Bank advertisements. The perforated player cards measure 2 1/4" by 2 1/2". The fronts display white-bordered color posed player portraits; player identification and sponsor logos are below the pictures. The horizontal backs carry biography and statistics. The cards are unnumbered and checklisted below in alphabetical order.

	MINT	NRMT	EXC
COMPLETE SET (25)	8.00	3.60	1.00

☐ 1 Doug Bair
☐ 2 Willie Blair
☐ 3 DeWayne Buice
☐ 4 Sal Butera
☐ 5 Francisco Cabrera
☐ 6 Sil Campusano
☐ 7 Steve Cummings
☐ 8 Hector De La Cruz
☐ 9 Jose Escobar
☐ 10 Junior Felix
☐ 11 Otis Green
☐ 12 Juan Guzman
☐ 13 Kelly Heath
☐ 14 Xavier Hernandez
☐ 15 Glenallen Hill
☐ 16 Jose Nunez
☐ 17 Jack O'Connor
☐ 18 Stu Pederson
☐ 19 Mark Ross
☐ 20 Alex Sanchez
☐ 21 Luis Sojo
☐ 22 Tim Tolman
☐ 23 Chico Walker
☐ 24 Frank Wills
☐ 25 Bob Bailor MG
Galen Cisco CO
Randy Holland TR
Hector Torres CO

1989 Syracuse Chiefs ProCards

This 27-card standard-size set of the 1989 Syracuse Chiefs, a Class AAA International League affiliate of the Toronto Blue Jays, features blue-bordered posed color player photos on its fronts. The player's name, position, and team name appear at the bottom. The horizontal gray back carries the player's name and position at the top, followed by biography and statistics.

	MINT	NRMT	EXC
COMPLETE SET (27)	5.00	2.20	.60

☐ 790 Checklist
☐ 791 Francisco Cabrera
☐ 792 Chico Walker
☐ 793 Otis Green
☐ 794 Frank Wills
☐ 795 Randy Holland TR
☐ 796 Bob Bailor MG
☐ 797 Juan Guzman
☐ 798 Stu Pederson
☐ 799 Galen Cisco CO
☐ 800 Kelly Heath
☐ 801 Hector Torres CO
☐ 802 Sal Butera
☐ 803 Steve Cummings
☐ 804 Glenallen Hill
☐ 805 Willie Blair
☐ 806 Jose Nunez
☐ 807 Doug Bair
☐ 808 Sil Campusano
☐ 809 Luis Sojo
☐ 810 Junior Felix
☐ 811 DeWayne Buice
☐ 812 Jack O'Connor
☐ 813 Alex Sanchez
☐ 814 Mark Ross
☐ 815 Tim Tolman
☐ 816 Hector De La Cruz

1989 Tacoma Tigers CMC

	MINT	NRMT	EXC
COMPLETE SET (25)	5.00	2.20	.60

☐ 1 Rich Bordi
☐ 2 Jim Corsi
☐ 3 Reese Lambert
☐ 4 Brian Snyder
☐ 5 Bill Dawley
☐ 6 Joe Law
☐ 7 Bryan Clark
☐ 8 Bruce Walton
☐ 9 Chuck Estrada CO
☐ 10 Dave Otto
☐ 11 Jeff Shaver
☐ 12 Lance Blankenship
☐ 13 Tyler Brilinski
☐ 14 Felix Jose
☐ 15 Buddy Pryor
☐ 16 Russ McGinnis
☐ 17 Jessie Reid
☐ 18 Donnie Hill
☐ 19 Doug Jennings
☐ 20 Dick Scott
☐ 21 Steve Howard
☐ 22 Larry Arndt
☐ 23 Mike Bordick
☐ 24 Pat Dietrick
☐ 25 Brad Fischer MGR

1989 Tacoma Tigers ProCards

This 32-card standard-size set of the 1989 Tacoma Tigers, a Class AAA Pacific Coast League affiliate of the Oakland Athletics, features blue-bordered posed color player photos on its fronts. The player's name, position, and team name appear at the bottom. The horizontal gray back carries the player's name and position at the top, followed by biography and statistics.

	MINT	NRMT	EXC
COMPLETE SET (32)	8.00	3.60	1.00

☐ 1535 Checklist
☐ 1536 Jose Canseco
☐ 1537 Mark McGwire
☐ 1538 Walt Weiss
☐ 1539 Lance Blankenship
☐ 1540 Bruce Tanner
☐ 1541 Doug Jennings
☐ 1542 Felix Jose
☐ 1543 Walt Horn TR
☐ 1544 Rich Bordi
☐ 1545 Brian Snyder
☐ 1546 Bruce Walton
☐ 1547 Dave Otto
☐ 1548 Reese Lambert
☐ 1549 Jessie Reid
☐ 1550 Joe Law
☐ 1551 Brad Fischer MGR
☐ 1552 Steve Howard
☐ 1553 Pat Dietrick
☐ 1554 Dickie Scott
☐ 1555 Bill Dawley
☐ 1556 Russ McGinnis
☐ 1557 Larry Arndt
☐ 1558 Buddy Pryor
☐ 1559 Jeff Shaver
☐ 1560 Jim Corsi
☐ 1561 Tyler Brilinski
☐ 1562 Donnie Hill
☐ 1563 Bryan Clark
☐ 1564 Chuck Estrada CO
☐ 1565 Mike Bordick
☐ 1566 Stan Naccarato
President/GM

1989 Tennessee Tech Golden Eagles

	MINT	NRMT	EXC
COMPLETE SET (36)	10.00	4.50	1.25

☐ 1 Steve Arnette
☐ 2 Matt Ballard
☐ 3 Scott Baerns
☐ 4 Terry Burton
☐ 5 Brent Carrier
☐ 6 Kevin Caroland
☐ 7 Steve Clapp
☐ 8 Mark Elkins
☐ 9 Moe Galbraith
☐ 10 Scott Hampton
☐ 11 Tim Horn
☐ 12 Randy Knight
☐ 13 Jeff Lavender
☐ 14 Troy Liggett
☐ 15 Don Maness
☐ 16 Kevin Mason
☐ 17 David Mays
☐ 18 Jay Mullin
☐ 19 Scott Norman
☐ 20 Johnny Orr
☐ 21 Rodney Przybylinski
☐ 22 Doug Rines
☐ 23 Bobby Roberts
☐ 24 Mike Schmittou
☐ 25 Harold Smith
☐ 26 Jeff Stallcup
☐ 27 J.C.Swafford
☐ 28 Scott Vick
☐ 29 Tony Wiggins
☐ 30 Chris West
☐ 31 David Wykle
☐ 32 Checklist
☐ 33 Kevin King MG
John Stout MG
☐ 34 Diamond 9 Batgirls
☐ 35 No Room On The Left
Brent Carrier
Kevin Mason
☐ 36 Team Photo

1989 Texas League All-Stars Grand Slam

	MINT	NRMT	EXC
COMPLETE SET (40)	20.00	9.00	2.50

☐ 1 Pat Kelly
☐ 2 Chris Cron
☐ 3 Bobby Rose
☐ 4 Gary DiSarcina
☐ 5 Scott Lewis
☐ 6 Luis Merejo
☐ 7 Paul Karies
☐ 8 Warren Newson
☐ 9 Charlie Hillemann
☐ 10 Andy Benes
☐ 11 Omar Olivares
☐ 12 Rich Holsman
☐ 13 Tim McIntosh
☐ 14 Shon Ashley
☐ 15 Ramon Sambo
☐ 16 D.L. Smith
☐ 17 Carlos Hernandez
☐ 18 Dennis Springer
☐ 19 Gaylen Pitts
Chris Mahoney
☐ 20 Julian Martinez
☐ 21 Ray Stephens
☐ 22 Ray Lankford
☐ 23 Dave Osteen
☐ 24 Mike Perez
☐ 25 Bill Bivens
☐ 26 Julio Valera
☐ 27 Dave Trautwein
☐ 28 Chuck Carr
☐ 29 Jeff Carter
☐ 30 Craig Colbert
☐ 31 Gary Alexander
☐ 32 Dean Palmer
☐ 33 Bill Haselman
☐ 34 Juan Gonzalez
☐ 35 Steve Lankard
☐ 36 Mark Petkovsek
☐ 37 Bob Malloy
☐ 38 Roy Silver
☐ 40 Carl Sawatski
☐ xx Title card

1989 Tidewater Tides Candl

	MINT	NRMT	EXC
COMPLETE SET (15)	10.00	4.50	1.25

☐ 1 Danny Frisella
☐ 2 Roy Foster
☐ 3 Jon Matlack
☐ 4 Amos Otis
☐ 5 Choo Choo Coleman
☐ 6 Mike Vail
☐ 7 Nino Espinosa
☐ 8 George Theodore
☐ 9 Craig Swan
☐ 10 Roy Staiger
☐ 11 Don Schulze
☐ 12 Clint Hurdle
☐ 13 Randy Milligan
☐ 14 Mark Carreon
☐ 15 Kevin Elster

1989 Tidewater Tides CMC

	MINT	NRMT	EXC
COMPLETE SET (29)	5.00	2.20	.60

☐ 1 Tim Drummond
☐ 2 Tom Edens
☐ 3 Jeff Innis
☐ 4 John Mitchell
☐ 5 Jack Savage
☐ 6 Wally Whitehurst
☐ 7 Dave West
☐ 8 Shawn Barton
☐ 9 Blaine Beatty
☐ 10 Kevin Tapini
☐ 11 Ken Dowell
☐ 12 Phil Lombardi
☐ 13 Jeff McKnight
☐ 14 Keith Miller
☐ 15 Tom O'Malley
☐ 16 Joaquin Contreras
☐ 17 Darren Reed
☐ 18 Dave Liddell
☐ 19 Rick Lundblade
☐ 20 Jeff Gardner
☐ 21 Mike Cubbage MGR
☐ 22 Craig Shipley
☐ 23 Marcus Lawton
☐ 24 Mark Carreon
☐ 25 Rich Miller CO
☐ 26 Glenn Abbott CO
☐ 27 Tony Brown
☐ 28 Sam McCrary TR
☐ 29 Mark Bailey

1989 Tidewater Tides ProCards

This 30-card standard-size set of the 1989 Tidewater Tides, a Class AAA International League affiliate of the New York Mets, features blue-bordered posed color player photos on its fronts. The player's name, position, and team name appear at the bottom. The horizontal gray back carries the player's name and position at the top, followed by biography and statistics.

	MINT	NRMT	EXC
COMPLETE SET (30)	5.00	2.20	.60

☐ 1946 Checklist
☐ 1947 Field Staff
Mike Cubbage
Glenn Abbott
Sam McCrary
Rich Miller
☐ 1948 Keith Miller
☐ 1949 Mark Bailey
☐ 1950 Jeff Innis
☐ 1951 Manny Salinas
☐ 1952 Tim Drummond
☐ 1953 Jeff McKnight
☐ 1954 Lou Thornton
☐ 1955 Bill Scherrer
☐ 1956 Tom Edens
☐ 1957 Darren Reed
☐ 1958 Wally Whitehurst
☐ 1959 Mike Debutch
☐ 1960 Joaquin Contreras
☐ 1961 Craig Shipley
☐ 1962 Kevin Brown
☐ 1963 Ken Dowell
☐ 1964 Blaine Beatty
☐ 1965 Tom O'Malley
☐ 1966 Jeff Gardner
☐ 1967 Marcus Lawton
☐ 1968 Rick Lundblade
☐ 1969 Shawn Barton
☐ 1970 John Mitchell
☐ 1971 Jack Savage
☐ 1972 Kevin Tapani
☐ 1973 Dave West
☐ 1974 Tony Brown
☐ 1975 Phil Lombardi

1989 Toledo Mud Hens CMC

	MINT	NRMT	EXC
COMPLETE SET (25)	5.00	2.20	.60

☐ 1 Randy Bockus
☐ 2 Ramon Pena
☐ 3 Mike Trujillo
☐ 4 Dave Palmer
☐ 5 Shawn Holman
☐ 6 Bob Link
☐ 7 Kevin Ritz
☐ 8 Paul Wenson
☐ 9 Kenny Williams
☐ 10 Dave Beard
☐ 11 Jeff Datz
☐ 12 Dave Griffin
☐ 13 Doug Strange
☐ 14 Larry See
☐ 15 Jim Walewander
☐ 16 Leo Garcia
☐ 17 Dan Dimascio
☐ 18 Pat Austin
☐ 19 Kevin Bradshaw
☐ 20 Norman Carrasco
☐ 21 Milt Cuyler
☐ 22 Delwyn Young
☐ 23 Rich Wieligman
☐ 24 Steve McInerney TR
☐ 25 John Wockenfuss MGR

1989 Toledo Mud Hens ProCards

This 30-card standard-size set of the 1989 Toledo Mud Hens, a Class AAA International League affiliate of the Detroit Tigers, features blue-bordered posed color player photos on its fronts. The player's name, position, and team name appear at the bottom. The horizontal gray back carries the player's name and position at the top, followed by biography and statistics.

	MINT	NRMT	EXC
COMPLETE SET (30)	5.00	2.20	.60

- ☐ 760 Checklist
- ☐ 761 Jeff Datz
- ☐ 762 Steve McInerney TR
- ☐ 763 Kenny Williams
- ☐ 764 Delwyn Young
- ☐ 765 Rob Richie
- ☐ 766 Pat Austin
- ☐ 767 Leo Garcia
- ☐ 768 Norman Carrasco
- ☐ 769 Randy Bockus
- ☐ 770 Jim Walewander
- ☐ 771 John Wockenfuss MGR
- ☐ 772 Billy Bean
- ☐ 773 Edwin Nunez
- ☐ 774 Ivan DeJesus CO
- ☐ 775 Rich Wieligman
- ☐ 776 Mike Trujillo
- ☐ 777 Dave Beard
- ☐ 778 Bob Link
- ☐ 779 Ramon Pena
- ☐ 780 Paul Wenson
- ☐ 781 Shawn Holman
- ☐ 782 Doug Strange
- ☐ 783 Kevin Bradshaw
- ☐ 784 Larry See
- ☐ 785 Dave Griffin
- ☐ 786 Kevin Ritz
- ☐ 787 Milt Cuyler
- ☐ 788 Dan Dimascio
- ☐ 789 Dave Palmer

1989 Triple A All-Stars CMC

	MINT	NRMT	EXC
COMPLETE SET (45)	10.00	4.50	1.25

- ☐ 1 Todd Zeile
- ☐ 2 Luis de Los Santos
- ☐ 3 Junior Noboa
- ☐ 4 Jeff Huson
- ☐ 5 Scott Coolbaugh
- ☐ 6 Skeeter Barnes
- ☐ 7 Larry Walker
- ☐ 8 Greg Vaughn
- ☐ 9 Steve Henderson
- ☐ 10 Mark Gardner
- ☐ 11 Morris Madden
- ☐ 12 Jack Armstrong
- ☐ 13 Stan Belinda
- ☐ 14 Alex Cole
- ☐ 15 Orlando Merced
- ☐ 16 Frank Cabrera
- ☐ 17 Hal Morris
- ☐ 18 Mark Lemke
- ☐ 19 Randy Velarde
- ☐ 20 Tom O'Malley
- ☐ 21 Butch Davis
- ☐ 22 Glenallen Hill
- ☐ 23 Greg Tubbs
- ☐ 24 Kevin Maas
- ☐ 25 Alex Sanchez
- ☐ 26 Mark Eichhorn
- ☐ 27 Mickey Pina
- ☐ 28 Julio Machado
- ☐ 29 Rob Richie
- ☐ 30 Tim Naehring
- ☐ 31 Sandy Alomar
- ☐ 32 Kelvin Torve
- ☐ 33 Joey Cora
- ☐ 34 Paul Zuvella
- ☐ 35 Matt Williams
- ☐ 36 Bruce Fields
- ☐ 37 Jerald Clark
- ☐ 38 Mike Huff
- ☐ 39 Jim Wilson
- ☐ 40 Ramon Martinez
- ☐ 41 Bryan Clark
- ☐ 42 Steve Olin
- ☐ 43 Andy Benes
- ☐ 44 Lee Stevens
- ☐ 45 Adam Peterson

1989 Triple A All-Stars ProCards

	MINT	NRMT	EXC
COMPLETE SET (55)	10.00	4.50	1.25

- ☐ AAA52 Stu Tate
- ☐ AAA1 Checklist
- ☐ AAA2 Scotti Madison
- ☐ AAA3 Mike Heifferon TR
- ☐ AAA4 Ed Hearn
- ☐ AAA5 Kent Mercker
- ☐ AAA6 Sandy Alomar
- ☐ AAA7 Jay Bell
- ☐ AAA8 Junior Noboa
- ☐ AAA9 Dorn Taylor
- ☐ AAA10 Mark Gardner
- ☐ AAA11 Jeff Huson
- ☐ AAA12 Hap Hudson TR
- ☐ AAA13 Tom O'Malley
- ☐ AAA14 Todd Zeile
- ☐ AAA15 Skeeter Barnes
- ☐ AAA16 Francisco Cabrera
- ☐ AAA17 Tom Bolton
- ☐ AAA18 Kevin Maas
- ☐ AAA19 Randy Velarde
- ☐ AAA20 Hal Morris
- ☐ AAA21 Bucky Dent MGR
- ☐ AAA22 Steve Henderson
- ☐ AAA23 Keith Hughes
- ☐ AAA24 Keith Miller
- ☐ AAA25 Mike Trujillo
- ☐ AAA26 Scott Coolbaugh
- ☐ AAA27 Terry Clark
- ☐ AAA28 Tom Kotchman CO
- ☐ AAA29 Tom Drees
- ☐ AAA30 Lance Johnson
- ☐ AAA31 Glenallen Hill
- ☐ AAA32 Jim Wilson
- ☐ AAA33 Paul Zuvella
- ☐ AAA34 Steve Olin
- ☐ AAA35 Tom Lampkin
- ☐ AAA36 Pete Delena
- ☐ AAA37 Sal Rende CO
- ☐ AAA38 Rick Luecken
- ☐ AAA39 Bryan Clark
- ☐ AAA40 Victor Rodriguez
- ☐ AAA41 Billy Bates
- ☐ AAA42 Greg Vaughn
- ☐ AAA43 Pete MacKanin MGR
- ☐ AAA44 Kevin Blankenship
- ☐ AAA45 Carl Nichols
- ☐ AAA46 Javier Ortiz
- ☐ AAA47 Ramon Martinez
- ☐ AAA48 Mike Huff
- ☐ AAA49 Jerald Clard
- ☐ AAA50 Steve Smith
- ☐ AAA51 Matt Williams
- ☐ AAA53 Jim Beauchamp CO
- ☐ AAA54 Tommy Greene
- ☐ AAA55 Mark Lemke

1989 Tucson Toros CMC

	MINT	NRMT	EXC
COMPLETE SET (25)	5.00	2.20	.60

- ☐ 1 Rocky Childress
- ☐ 2 Mitch Johnson
- ☐ 3 Anthony Kelley
- ☐ 4 Roger Mason
- ☐ 5 Dave Meads
- ☐ 6 Ed Vosberg
- ☐ 7 Jeff Heathcock
- ☐ 8 Charlie Kerfeld
- ☐ 9 Brian Meyer
- ☐ 10 Dan Schatzeder
- ☐ 11 Matt Sinatro
- ☐ 12 Craig Smajstrla
- ☐ 13 Jose Tolentino
- ☐ 14 Louie Meadows
- ☐ 15 Carl Nichols
- ☐ 16 Casey Candaele
- ☐ 17 Brick Smith
- ☐ 18 Harry Spillman
- ☐ 19 Ron Washington
- ☐ 20 Chuck Jackson
- ☐ 21 Carlo Columbino
- ☐ 22 Gary Cooper
- ☐ 23 Steve Lombardozzi
- ☐ 24 Coaches
  Eddie Watt
  Frank Cacciatore
- ☐ 25 Bob Skinner MGR

1989 Tucson Toros Jones Photo

Produced by Jones Photo. The cards are unnumbered so they are ordered below in alphabetical order. A complete set could only be obtained by attending all five promotional giveaway nights at the ballpark. The cards measure 5" by 7" and are full color photos of the players. 400 sets were produced. Less than 100 of each of the late issue cards exist.

	MINT	NRMT	EXC
COMPLETE SET (24)	40.00	18.00	5.00
COMP. SET W/LATE ISSUES	60.00	27.00	7.50

- ☐ 1 Eric Anthony (Late Issue)
- ☐ 2 Frank Cacciatore
- ☐ 3 Casey Candaele
- ☐ 4 Rocky Childress
- ☐ 5 Carlo Colombino
- ☐ 6 Gary Cooper
- ☐ 7 Jeff Heathcock
- ☐ 8 Chuck Jackson
- ☐ 9 Mitch Johnson
- ☐ 10 Anthony Kelley
- ☐ 11 Charley Kerfeld
- ☐ 12 Darryl Kile (Late Issue)
- ☐ 13 Steve Lombardozzi
- ☐ 14 Roger Mason
- ☐ 15 Louie Meadows
- ☐ 16 Dave Meads
- ☐ 17 Brian Meyer
- ☐ 18 Carl Nichols
- ☐ 19 Mark Portugal
- ☐ 20 Dave Rohde (Late Issue)
- ☐ 21 Dan Schatzeder
- ☐ 22 Craig Smajstrla
- ☐ 23 Brick Smith
- ☐ 24 Harry Spilman
- ☐ 25 Jose Tolentino
- ☐ 26 Ed Vosberg
- ☐ 27 Ron Washington

1989 Tucson Toros ProCards

This 28-card standard-size set of the 1989 Tucson Toros, a Class AAA Pacific Coast League affiliate of the Houston Astros, features blue-bordered posed color player photos on its fronts. The player's name, position, and team name appear at the bottom. The horizontal gray back carries the player's name and position at the top, followed by biography and statistics.

	MINT	NRMT	EXC
COMPLETE SET (28)	5.00	2.20	.60

- ☐ 179 Checklist
- ☐ 180 Dave Meads
- ☐ 181 Steve Lombardozzi
- ☐ 182 Larry Lasky TR
- ☐ 183 Jose Tolentino
- ☐ 184 Gary Cooper
- ☐ 185 Carl Nichols
- ☐ 186 Anthony Kelley
- ☐ 187 Mitch Johnson
- ☐ 188 Charley Kerfeld
- ☐ 189 Brian Meyer
- ☐ 190 Ron Washington
- ☐ 191 Louie Meadows
- ☐ 192 Ed Vosberg
- ☐ 193 Brick Smith
- ☐ 194 Rocky Childress
- ☐ 195 Roger Mason
- ☐ 196 Jeff Heathcock
- ☐ 197 Casey Candaele
- ☐ 198 Dan Schatzeder
- ☐ 199 Harry Spilman
- ☐ 200 Craig Smajstrla
- ☐ 201 Matt Sinatro
- ☐ 202 Frank Cacciatore CO
- ☐ 203 Bob Skinner MGR
- ☐ 204 Eddie Watt CO
- ☐ 205 Chuck Jackson
- ☐ 206 Carlo Colombino

1989 Tulsa Drillers Grand Slam

This issue includes third year cards of Juan Gonzalez, Dean Palmer and Sammy Sosa.

	MINT	NRMT	EXC
COMPLETE SET (26)	40.00	18.00	5.00

- ☐ 1 Tommy Thompson MGR
- ☐ 2 Walt Williams CO
- ☐ 3 Jeff Andrews CO
- ☐ 4 Greg Harrell TR
- ☐ 5 Gary Alexander
- ☐ 6 Phil Bryant
- ☐ 7 Felipe Castillo
- ☐ 8 Monty Fariss
- ☐ 9 Darrin Garner
- ☐ 10 Juan Gonzalez
- ☐ 11 Bill Haselman
- ☐ 12 Adam Lamle
- ☐ 13 Steve Lankard
- ☐ 14 David Lynch
- ☐ 15 Bob Malloy
- ☐ 16 Barry Manuel
- ☐ 17 Terry Mathews
- ☐ 18 Gar Millay
- ☐ 19 Dean Palmer
- ☐ 20 Mark Petkovsek
- ☐ 21 Paul Postier
- ☐ 22 Marv Rockman
- ☐ 23 Fred Samson
- ☐ 24 Tony Scruggs
- ☐ 25 Sammy Sosa
- ☐ 26 George Treadgill

1989 Tulsa Drillers Team Issue

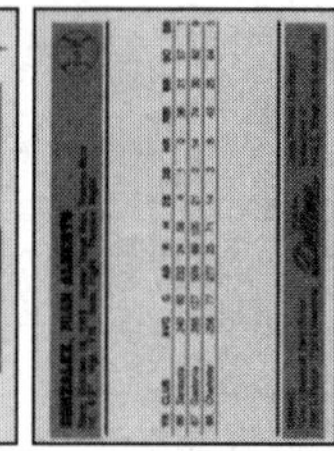

This issue includes third year cards of Juan Gonzalez, Dean Palmer and Sammy Sosa.

	MINT	NRMT	EXC
COMPLETE SET (27)	80.00	36.00	10.00

- ☐ 1 Gary Alexander
- ☐ 2 Wilson Alvarez
- ☐ 3 Jeff Andrews CO
- ☐ 4 Phil Bryant
- ☐ 5 Felipe Castillo
- ☐ 6 Monty Fariss
- ☐ 7 Darrin Garner
- ☐ 8 Juan Gonzalez
- ☐ 9 Greg Harrell TR
- ☐ 10 Bill Haselman
- ☐ 11 John Hoover
- ☐ 12 Darren Loy
- ☐ 13 Bob Malloy
- ☐ 14 Alex Marte
- ☐ 15 Terry Mathews
- ☐ 16 Gar Millay
- ☐ 17 Dean Palmer
- ☐ 18 Mark Petkovsek
- ☐ 19 Paul Postier
- ☐ 20 Marv Rockman
- ☐ 21 Wayne Rosenthal
- ☐ 22 Frederic Samson
- ☐ 23 Tony Scruggs
- ☐ 24 Sammy Sosa
- ☐ 25 Tommy Thompson MGR
- ☐ 26 Walt Williams CO
- ☐ 27 Ruben Sierra
  Past Star

1989 Utica Blue Sox Pucko

The 1989 Utica Blue Sox set contains 34 standard-size cards. The front design features glossy color player photos with purple borders. The team logo is superimposed at the lower left corner. The backs have brief biography, the circumstances under which the player was drafted, and statistics (where appropriate). Most of the players (2-27) are arranged alphabetically. 3,750 sets were produced.

	MINT	NRMT	EXC
COMPLETE SET (34)	6.00	2.70	.75

- ☐ 1 Dave Van Winkle
- ☐ 2 Glen Braxton
- ☐ 3 Kenny Burroughs
- ☐ 4 Ken Coleman
- ☐ 5 Mike Davino
- ☐ 6 Brian Davis
- ☐ 7 John Furch
- ☐ 8 Mike Galvan
- ☐ 9 Dave Gorman
- ☐ 10 Keith Harris
- ☐ 11 Jeff Ingram
- ☐ 12 Brian Keyser
- ☐ 13 Greg Kobza
- ☐ 14 Rich Long
- ☐ 15 Pat Mehrtens
- ☐ 16 Jesus Merejo
- ☐ 17 Greg Perschke
- ☐ 18 Ron Plemmons
- ☐ 19 Johnny Ruffin
- ☐ 20 Lance Sanders
- ☐ 21 Joe Singley
- ☐ 22 John Smith
- ☐ 23 Scott Stevens
- ☐ 24 Dean Tatarain
- ☐ 25 Rob Thompson
- ☐ 26 Dennis Walker
- ☐ 27 Jerry Wolak
- ☐ 28 Ron Vaughn MGR
- ☐ 29 Bill Ballou CO
- ☐ 30 Mike Gellinger CO
- ☐ 31 Rick Ray TR
- ☐ 32 Joanne Gerace GM
- ☐ 33 Strike-O
- ☐ 34 Murnane Field

1989 Vancouver Canadians CMC

This 25-card standard-size set of the 1989 Vancouver Canadians, a Class AAA Pacific Coast League affiliate of the Chicago White Sox, features on its fronts white-bordered posed color player photos framed by a black line. The team's name, the player's name, and his position appear at the bottom. The white back is framed by a black line and carries the team's name and league at the top, followed by the player's name, biography and statistics.

	MINT	NRMT	EXC
COMPLETE SET (25)	6.00	2.70	.75

☐ 1 Jeff Bittiger
☐ 2 Adam Peterson
☐ 3 Greg Hibbard
☐ 4 Tom McCarthy
☐ 5 Jack Hardy
☐ 6 Jose Segura
☐ 7 John Pawlowski
☐ 8 Rick Rodriguez
☐ 9 John Davis
☐ 10 Tom Drees
☐ 11 Kelly Paris
☐ 12 Steve Springer
☐ 13 Keith Smith
☐ 14 Jim Weaver
☐ 15 Marlin McPhail
☐ 16 Russ Morman
☐ 17 Carlos Martinez
☐ 18 Lance Johnson
☐ 19 Jerry Willard
☐ 20 Tom Forrester
☐ 21 Cal Emery CO
☐ 22 Mark Davis
☐ 23 Marv Foley MG
☐ 24 Jeff Schaefer
☐ 25 Moe Drabowsky CO

1989 Vancouver Canadians ProCards

This 27-card standard-size set of the 1989 Vancouver Canadians, a Class AAA Pacific Coast League affiliate of the Chicago White Sox, features blue-bordered posed color player photos on its fronts. The player's name, position, and team name appear at the bottom. The horizontal gray back carries the player's name and position at the top, followed by biography and statistics. This issue includes Jack McDowell's only minor league card.

	MINT	NRMT	EXC
COMPLETE SET (27)	12.00	5.50	1.50

☐ 571 Checklist
☐ 572 Cal Emery CO
☐ 573 Marv Foley MG
☐ 574 Greg Latta TR
☐ 575 Doug Mansolino CO
☐ 576 Lance Johnson
☐ 577 Jack McDowell
☐ 578 Keith Smith
☐ 579 Carlos Martinez
☐ 580 Rick Rodriguez
☐ 581 Moe Drabowsky CO
☐ 582 John Davis
☐ 583 Jim Weaver
☐ 584 Greg Hibbard
☐ 585 Mark Davis
☐ 586 Jack Hardy
☐ 587 Jerry Willard
☐ 588 Tom Drees
☐ 589 Adam Peterson
☐ 590 Russ Morman
☐ 591 Jose Segura
☐ 592 Steve Springer
☐ 593 Tom McCarthy
☐ 594 Kelly Paris
☐ 595 John Pawlowski
☐ 596 Marlin McPhail
☐ 597 Tom Forrester

1989 Vero Beach Dodgers Star

The 1989 Vero Beach set contains 29 standard-size cards. The fronts have posed color player photos, with blue borders on the top portion of the card fading to yellow as one moves down the card face. In blue print on a cream-colored background, the backs have biography and statistics. The backs of card numbers 26-29 have a pale yellow background. 5,000 sets produced.

	MINT	NRMT	EXC
COMPLETE SET (29)	20.00	9.00	2.50

☐ 1 William Argo
☐ 2 Anthony Barron
☐ 3 Rafael Bournigal
☐ 4 Albert Bustillos
☐ 5 J. Dale Coleman
☐ 6 Sherman Collins
☐ 7 Bruce Dostal
☐ 8 Dino Ebel
☐ 9 Stephen Green
☐ 10 Mark Griffin
☐ 11 Dana Heinle
☐ 12 Masaaki Kamanaka
☐ 13 Yasuhiro Kawabata
☐ 14 John Knapp
☐ 15 Alan Lewis
☐ 16 Brett Magnusson
☐ 17 Danny Montgomery
☐ 18 Jose Munoz
☐ 19 Douglas Noch
☐ 20 Daniel Opperman
☐ 21 Hector Ortiz
☐ 22 Jim Poole
☐ 23 Henry Rodriguez
☐ 24 Michael Sampson
☐ 25 Zakary Shinall
☐ 26 Jeff Van Zytveld
☐ 27 Joe Alvarez MGR
☐ 28 Dennis Lewallyn CO
☐ 29 Jun Irisawa CO

1989 Visalia Oaks Cal League Cards

	MINT	NRMT	EXC
COMPLETE SET (29)	5.00	2.20	.60

☐ 94 Basil Meyer
☐ 95 Doug Simons
☐ 96 Johnny Ard
☐ 97 Steve Stowell
☐ 98 Rob Wassenaar
☐ 99 Bob Strube
☐ 100 Howard Townsend
☐ 101 Willie Banks
☐ 102 Fred White
☐ 103 Kiyoshi Sagawa
☐ 104 Shawn Gilbert
☐ 105 Mike Dotzler
☐ 106 Jarvis Brown
☐ 107 Loy McBride
☐ 108 Frank Valdez
☐ 109 Dave Jacas
☐ 110 Lenny Webster
☐ 111 Jose Marzan
☐ 112 Carlos Capellan
☐ 113 Vince Teixeira
☐ 114 Kouichi Ozawa
☐ 115 Minoru Yojo
☐ 116 Ken Fujimoto
☐ 117 David Smith
☐ 118 Scott Ullger MGR
☐ 119 Gorman Heimueller CO
☐ 120 Takashi Yoshida CO
☐ 121 Acey Kohlogi
Administrative Asst.
☐ 122 Rick McWane TR

1989 Visalia Oaks ProCards

This 31-card standard-size set of the 1989 Visalia Oaks, a Class A Cal League affiliate of the Minnesota Twins, features orange-bordered posed color player photos on its fronts. The player's name, position, and team name appear at the bottom. The horizontal gray back carries the player's name and position at the top, followed by biography and statistics.

	MINT	NRMT	EXC
COMPLETE SET (31)	5.00	2.20	.60

☐ 1419 Checklist
☐ 1420 Gorman Heimueller CO
☐ 1421 Howard Townsend
☐ 1422 Kouichi Ozawa
☐ 1423 Vince Teixeira
☐ 1424 Minoru Yojo
☐ 1425 Rob Wassenaar
☐ 1426 Willie Banks
☐ 1427 Johnny Ard
☐ 1428 Greg Brinkman
☐ 1429 Bob Strube
☐ 1430 Takashi Yoshida CO
☐ 1431 Rick McWane TR
☐ 1432 Kenji Fujimoto
☐ 1433 Scott Ullger MGR
☐ 1434 Kiyoshi Sagawa
☐ 1435 Doug Simons
☐ 1436 Todd McClure
☐ 1437 Jarvis Brown
☐ 1438 Mike Dotzler
☐ 1439 Shawn Gilbert
☐ 1440 Frank Valdez
☐ 1441 Carlos Capellan
☐ 1442 Lenny Webster
☐ 1443 Jose Marzan
☐ 1444 Steve Stowell
☐ 1445 Basil Meyer
☐ 1446 Fred White
☐ 1447 David Jacas
☐ 1448 David Smith
☐ 1449 Loy McBride

1989 Waterloo Diamonds ProCards

This 28-card standard-size set of the 1989 Waterloo Diamonds, a Class A Midwest League Independent, features orange-bordered posed color player photos on its fronts. The player's name, position, and team name appear at the bottom. The horizontal gray back carries the player's name and position at the top, followed by biography and statistics.

	MINT	NRMT	EXC
COMPLETE SET (28)	5.00	2.20	.60

☐ 1771 Checklist
☐ 1772 Steve Hendricks
☐ 1773 Scott Meadows
☐ 1774 Alexis Figueroa
☐ 1775 Jose Lebron
☐ 1776 Dave Gavin
☐ 1777 Bob Curnow
☐ 1778 James Noland
☐ 1779 Tim Holland
☐ 1780 Rob Cantwell
☐ 1781 Jeff Hart
☐ 1782 Ron Morton
☐ 1783 Chuck Ricci
☐ 1784 Mark Littell CO
☐ 1785 Jaime Moreno MGR
☐ 1786 Osvaldo Sanchez
☐ 1787 Mike King
☐ 1788 Billy Reed
☐ 1789 Luis Galindez
☐ 1790 Pedro Lopez
☐ 1791 Ray Holbert
☐ 1792 Don Fowler
☐ 1793 Mike Borgatti
☐ 1794 Brad Hoyer
☐ 1795 Dave Cunningham
☐ 1796 Reggie Farmer
☐ 1797 Chad Kuhn
☐ 1798 Rich Slomkowski

1989 Waterloo Diamonds Star

The 1989 Waterloo Diamonds set contains 32 standard-size cards. The fronts have posed color player photos, with blue borders on the top portion of the card fading to sky blue as one moves down the card face. In blue print on a white background, the backs have biography and statistics. 5,000 sets produced.

	MINT	NRMT	EXC
COMPLETE SET (32)	5.00	2.20	.60

☐ 1 Mike Borgatti
☐ 2 Rob Cantwell
☐ 3 Dave Cunningham
☐ 4 Bob Curnow
☐ 5 Reggie Farmer
☐ 6 Alex Figueroa
☐ 7 Don Fowler
☐ 8 Luis Galindez
☐ 9 Dave Gavin
☐ 10 Darrin Hart
☐ 11 Steve Hendricks
☐ 12 Ray Holbert
☐ 13 Tim Holland
☐ 14 Brad Hoyer
☐ 15 Mike King
☐ 16 Chad Kuhn
☐ 17 Jose LeBron
☐ 18 Pedro Lopez
☐ 19 Rich Slomkowski
☐ 20 Scott Meadows
☐ 21 Ron Morton
☐ 22 James Noland
☐ 23 Billy Reed
☐ 24 Chuck Ricci
☐ 25 Osvaldo Sanchez
☐ 26 Jaime Moreno MGR
☐ 27 Mark Littell CO
☐ 28 George Paulis TR
☐ 29 Mark Gieseke
☐ 30 Darrin Hart
☐ 31 Terry McDevitt
☐ 32 Scott McNaney

1989 Watertown Indians Star

The 1989 Waterloo Diamonds set contains 29 standard-size cards. The fronts have posed color player photos, with blue borders on the top portion of the card fading to sky blue as one moves down the card face. In blue print on a pale blue background, the backs have biography and statistics. Card numbers 26-29 have a white background on the reverse. 5,000 sets produced.

	MINT	NRMT	EXC
COMPLETE SET (29)	5.00	2.20	.60

☐ 1 Chuck Alexander
☐ 2 Keith Bevenour
☐ 3 Jerry DiPoto
☐ 4 Martin Durkin
☐ 5 Bruce Egloff
☐ 6 Alex Ferran
☐ 7 Cornell Foggie
☐ 8 Fabio Gomez
☐ 9 Jeff Hancock
☐ 10 Joey James
☐ 11 Brian Graham
☐ 12 Garland Kiser
☐ 13 Ty Kovach
☐ 14 Brett Merriman
☐ 15 Carlos Mota
☐ 16 Scott Niell
☐ 17 Rouglas Odor
☐ 18 Doug Piatt
☐ 19 Tim Riemer
☐ 20 Greg Roscoe
☐ 21 Marc Tepper
☐ 22 Will Vespe
☐ 23 Dan Williams
☐ 24 Don Young
☐ 25 Erik Young
☐ 26 Ken Silvestri CO
Name misspelled
Silvertri
☐ 27 Frank Kelbe CO
☐ 28 Rich St. John TR
☐ 29 Brad DesJardins

1989 Wausau Timbers Grand Slam

	MINT	NRMT	EXC
COMPLETE SET (28)	5.00	2.20	.60

☐ 1 Mike McGuire
☐ 2 Tommy Jones MGR
☐ 3 Ernest Castro
☐ 4 Bob Burton TR
☐ 5 John Reilley
☐ 6 John Boyles
☐ 7 Ellerton Maynard
☐ 8 Scott Pitcher
☐ 9 Ted Eldridge
☐ 10 Ben Burnau
☐ 11 Scott Taylor
☐ 12 Mark Razook
☐ 13 Brian Wilkinson
☐ 14 Scott Stoerck
☐ 15 Jeremy Matthews
☐ 16 Nick Felix
☐ 17 Jim Bennett
☐ 18 Hunter Hoffman
☐ 19 Jorge Robles
☐ 20 Steve Murray
☐ 21 Rick Candelari
☐ 22 Kevin Kerkes
☐ 23 Jeff Miller
☐ 24 Jeff Keitges
☐ 25 Erick Bryant
☐ 26 Tim Stargell
☐ 27 Chris Howard
☐ 28 Mike Gardiner

1989 Welland Pirates Pucko

This 35-card standard-size set of the 1989 Welland Pirates, a Class A New York-Penn League affiliate of the Pittsburgh Pirates, features glossy player photos with mustard-colored borders on its fronts. The team name is printed in a white bar above the photo, while the player's name and position and the team logo appear on the bottom. The backs carry a brief biography, the circumstances under which the player was drafted, and statistics (where appropriate). 3,750 sets were produced.

	MINT	NRMT	EXC
COMPLETE SET (35)	6.00	2.70	.75

☐ 1 William Pennyfeather
☐ 2 Scott Arvesen
☐ 3 Robert Bailey Jr.
☐ 4 Angel Beltran
☐ 5 David Bird
☐ 6 Mike Brewington
☐ 7 Kim Broome
☐ 8 Rod Byerly
☐ 9 Nelson Caraballo
☐ 10 Tom Deller
☐ 11 Raymond Doss
☐ 12 Mike Fortuna
☐ 13 Valentine Henderson
☐ 14 Deron Johnson
☐ 15 Paul Keefer
☐ 16 Jeff Kuder
☐ 17 John Latham
☐ 18 Javier Magria
☐ 19 Erik Nelson
☐ 20 Rob Peterson
☐ 21 Winston Seymour
☐ 22 Garland Slaughter
☐ 23 Mark Thomas
☐ 24 Ken Trusky
☐ 25 Tom Tuholski
☐ 26 Paul Wagner
☐ 27 Tim Wakefield
☐ 28 Ron Way
☐ 29 Flavio Williams
☐ 30 U.L. Washington MG

☐ 31 Larry Smith CO
☐ 32 Paul Allen TR
☐ 33 Bill Kuehn GM
☐ 34 Bob Burgess GM
☐ 35 John Belford
Group Sales
Norma Chaney
Concessions Manager

1989 West Palm Beach Expos Star

This 31-card standard-size set of the 1989 West Palm Beach Expos, a Class A Florida State League affiliate of the Montreal Expos, features posed color player photos, with blue borders on the top portion of the card, fading to red as one moves down the card face. The player's name, team name, and position appear at the bottom. In blue print on a pink background, the backs carry biography and statistics. There are two cards numbered 26. The last seven cards listed below were late issues. 5,000 sets produced.

	MINT	NRMT	EXC
COMPLETE SET (31)	5.00	2.20	.60

☐ 1 Jose Alou
☐ 2 Bret Barberie
☐ 3 Chris Bennett
☐ 4 Daryl Boyd
☐ 5 Jeff Carter
☐ 6 Doug Cinnella
☐ 7 Greg Colbrunn
☐ 8 Wil Cordero
☐ 9 Rob DeYoung
☐ 10 Bert Echemendia
☐ 11 Jim Fregosi Jr.
☐ 12 Scott Henion
☐ 13 Ross Jones
☐ 14 Doug Kline
☐ 15 Rob Leary
☐ 16 John Mello
☐ 17 Yorkis Perez
☐ 18 Alonzo Powell
☐ 19 Troy Ricker
☐ 20 Hector Rivera
☐ 21 Trevor Penn
☐ 22 Matt Stairs
☐ 23 Corey Viltz
☐ 24 David Wainhouse
☐ 25 Pat Murphy ANN
☐ 26 Willie P. Bananas
Mascot
☐ 26 Luis Pujols CO
☐ 27 Felipe Alou MG
☐ 28 Dave Tomlin CO
☐ 29 Dave Jauss CO
☐ NNO Title Card
WPTV-5 Ad

1989 Wichita Bonus Rock

These two bonus cards were produced by Rock's Dugout. They are of the same size and design as the 1989 Wichita Champions regular issue, except they have orange borders on the front and red print on the back.

	MINT	NRMT	EXC
COMPLETE SET (2)	8.00	3.60	1.00

☐ B1 Bonus Card I
Preparing to pitch
☐ B2 Bonus Card II
After pitch

1989 Wichita Champions Rock

The 1989 Wichita Wranglers Champion Highlight set was produced by Rock's Dugout and contains 20 standard-size cards. The front features a glossy color player photo bordered in purple, with the team name and player's name in yellow lettering. The horizontally oriented backs have a caption printed in purple and a rope serving as a border.

	MINT	NRMT	EXC
COMPLETE SET (20)	8.00	3.60	1.00

☐ 1 Title Card
☐ 2 Warren Newson
Rob DeWolf
Brian Brooks
Kevin Garner
Home Run Threats
☐ 3 Wranglers Celebrate
☐ 4 Rich Rodriguez
Rich Holsman
Doug Brocail
Brian Wood
Omar Olivares
Rafael Chavez
Pitching Roundup
☐ 5 Paul Faries
☐ 6 Tribute to Giamatti
☐ 7 Jose Mota
☐ 8 Warren Newson
Brian Cisarik
Rob DeWolf
Tom LeVasseur
Paul Faries
.300 Club
☐ 9 Tom LeVasseur
☐ 10 Mike Basso
☐ 11 Dave Hollins
☐ 12 Warren Newson
☐ 13 Warren Newson
Scoring
☐ 14 Rich Holsman
Wind Up
☐ 15 Pat Kelly
Direction
☐ 16 Rafael Valdez
Pitching Sensation
☐ 17 Rob DeWolf
Grand Slam
☐ 18 Omar Olivares
☐ 19 Andy Benes
Delivers
☐ 20 Ricky Bones

1989 Wichita Stadium Rock

The 1989 Wichita Wranglers Stadium set was produced by Rock's Dugout and contains 30 standard-size cards. The front design of these cards is unique; it features color posed player photos cut out and superimposed on unfocused black and white shots of the baseball stadium. The lettering and numbering on the card fronts is in red. The backs are blank. The set also includes four advertisement cards for baseball card shops in Wichita. This set includes an early card of '88 Olympic star and San Diego Padre pitcher Andy Benes.

	MINT	NRMT	EXC
COMPLETE SET (30)	10.00	4.50	1.25

☐ 1 Rock's Dugout Ad
☐ 2 Warren Newson
☐ 3 Tony Pellegrino
☐ 4 Charlie Hillemann
☐ 5 Brian Cisarik
☐ 6 Larry Mims
☐ 7 Steve Hendricks
☐ 8 Andy Benes
☐ 9 Mike Basso
☐ 10 Game Day Ad
☐ 11 Omar Olivares
☐ 12 Dave Hollins
☐ 13 Doug Brocail
☐ 14 Jim Lewis
☐ 15 Pat Kelly
☐ 16 Ricky Bones
☐ 17 Kevin Garner
☐ 18 Paul Faries
☐ 19 Rich Rodriguez
☐ 20 Rich Holsman
☐ 21 Sports Collectibles Ad
☐ 22 Title Card
☐ 23 Saul Soltero
☐ 24 Steve Loubier
☐ 25 Rafael Chavez
☐ 26 Tom LeVasseur
☐ 27 Bryan Little
☐ 28 Gary Lance
☐ 29 Cookie
Mascot
☐ 30 Sportstuff Ad

1989 Wichita Update Rock

The 1989 Wichita Wranglers Update set was produced by Rock's Dugout and contains 20 standard-size cards. The front features a glossy color player photo bordered in red, with the team name and player's name in black lettering. The horizontally oriented backs have a caption printed in red and a rope serving as a border.

	MINT	NRMT	EXC
COMPLETE SET (20)	8.00	3.60	1.00

☐ 1 Title Card
☐ 2 Pat Kelly
☐ 3 Paul Faries
☐ 4 Omar Olivares
☐ 5 Andy Benes
☐ 6 Charlie Hillemann
☐ 7 Warren Newson
☐ 8 Craig Cooper
☐ 9 Saul Soltero
☐ 10 Rafael Valdez
☐ 11 Jose Mota
☐ 12 Brian Brooks
☐ 13 Larry Mims
☐ 14 Steve Loubier
☐ 15 Rob DeWolf
☐ 16 Paul Quinzer
☐ 17 Home Run Threats
Warren Newson
Rob DeWolf
Brian Brooks
Kevin Garner
☐ 18 Jose Valentin
☐ 19 Andy Benes
☐ 20 Rich Holsman

1989 Wichita Wranglers Rock

The 1989 Wichita Wranglers set was produced by Rock's Dugout and contains 30 standard-size cards. The fronts feature posed color player photos (from the waist up), with white borders on a red card face. In black lettering on gray and white, the horizontally oriented backs present biography, career record, and an advertisement for a baseball cardshop. The cards are skip-numbered on both sides by uniform number, and checklisted below accordingly.

	MINT	NRMT	EXC
COMPLETE SET (30)	10.00	4.50	1.25

☐ 4 Bryan Little CO
☐ 6 Pat Kelly MGR
☐ 7 David Hollins
☐ 9 Robert DeWolf
☐ 10 Ricky Bones
☐ 11 Dan Walters
☐ 12 Tony Pellegrino
☐ 14 Rafael Chavez
☐ 16 Mike Basso
☐ 17 Rich Holsman
☐ 18 Charlie Hillemann
☐ 19 Greg Harris
☐ 20 Jim Lewis
☐ 21 Tom LeVasseur
☐ 22 Paul Faries
☐ 23 Brian Wood
☐ 24 Warren Newson
☐ 25 Brian Brooks
☐ 26 Omar Olivares
☐ 27 Paul Quinzer
☐ 28 Doug Brocail
☐ 29 Rich Rodriguez
☐ 30 Andy Benes
☐ 32 Brian Cisarik
☐ 33 Kevin Garner
☐ 34 Craig Cooper
☐ 38 Gary Lance
☐ NNO Joe Chavez TR
☐ NNO Rock's Dugout Ad
☐ NNO Title Card

1989 Williamsport Bills ProCards

This 25-card standard-size set of the 1989 Williamsport Bills, a Class AA Eastern League affiliate of the Seattle Mariners, features red-bordered posed color player photos on its fronts. The player's name, position, and team name appear at the bottom. The horizontal gray back carries the player's name and position at the top, followed by biography and statistics. This issue includes the minor league card debut of Tino Martinez.

	MINT	NRMT	EXC
COMPLETE SET (25)	15.00	6.75	1.85

☐ 625 Checklist
☐ 626 Dru Kosco
☐ 627 Bobby Cuellar CO
☐ 628 Mark Wooden
☐ 629 Mike Brocki
☐ 630 David Burba
☐ 631 Jerry Goff
☐ 632 Pat Lennon
☐ 633 Jose Melendez
☐ 634 Randy Roetter TR
☐ 635 Tino Martinez
☐ 636 Ted Williams
☐ 637 Jeff Nelson
☐ 638 Scott Runge
☐ 639 Jeff Hooper
☐ 640 William Diaz
☐ 641 Harry Davis
☐ 642 Dave Brundage
☐ 643 Jack Smith
☐ 644 Brad Brusky
☐ 645 Keith Helton
☐ 646 Pat Rice
☐ 647 Dana Ridenour
☐ 648 Greg Fulton
☐ 649 Rich DeLucia

1989 Williamsport Bills Star

The 1989 Williamsport Bills set contains 25 standard-size cards. The fronts have posed color player photos, with blue borders on the top portion of the card fading to yellow as one moves down the card face. In blue print on a white background, the backs have biography and statistics. Card number 25 has a pale yellow background on the reverse. This issue includes the minor league card debut of Tino Martinez. 5,000 sets produced.

	MINT	NRMT	EXC
COMPLETE SET (25)	15.00	6.75	1.85

☐ 1 Dave Brundage
☐ 2 Brad Brusky
☐ 3 Bobby Cuellar CO
☐ 4 Harry Davis
☐ 5 Rich DeLucia
☐ 6 William Diaz
☐ 7 Jerry Goff
☐ 8 Todd Haney
☐ 9 Keith Helton
☐ 10 Jeff Hooper
☐ 11 Calvin Jones
☐ 12 Patrick Lennon
☐ 13 Tino Martinez
☐ 14 Jose Melendez
☐ 15 Jeff Nelson
☐ 16 Bryan Price
☐ 17 Mark Razook
☐ 18 Patrick Rice
☐ 19 Ricardo Rojas
☐ 20 Jack Smith
☐ 21 Glen Spagnola
☐ 22 Ted Williams
☐ 23 Mark Wooden
☐ 24 Jay Ward MGR
☐ 25 David Burba

1989 Winston-Salem Spirits Star

The 1989 Winston-Salem Spirits set contains 26 standard-size cards. The fronts have posed color player photos, with blue borders on the top portion of the card fading to green as one moves down the card face. In blue print on a pale green background, the backs have biography and statistics. The last four cards have white background on the reverse, and the front borders of the Julio Strauss card fade from blue to white. 5,000 sets produced.

	MINT	NRMT	EXC
COMPLETE SET (26)	5.00	2.20	.60

☐ 1 Lenny Bell
☐ 2 Ed Caballero
☐ 3 Dick Canan
☐ 4 Frank Castillo
☐ 5 Don Cohoon
☐ 6 Rusty Crockett
☐ 7 Darrin Duffy
☐ 8 Pat Gomez
☐ 9 Phillip Hannon
☐ 10 John Jensen
☐ 11 Dan Kennedy
☐ 12 Ray Mullino
☐ 13 Steve Parker
☐ 14 Marty Rivero
☐ 15 Bob Strickland
☐ 16 Francisco Tenacen
☐ 17 Rick Wilkins
☐ 18 Eric Woods
☐ 19 Jay Loviglio MGR
☐ 20 Joe Housey CO
☐ 21 Steve Melendez TR
☐ NNO Team Photo
☐ NNO Mike Aspray
☐ NNO Gabby Rodriguez
☐ NNO Bill Melvin
☐ NNO Julio Strauss

1989 Winter Haven Red Sox Star

The 1989 Winter Haven set contains 29 standard-size cards. The fronts have posed color player photos, with blue borders on the top portion of the card fading to gray as one moves down the card face. In blue print on a light gray background, the backs have biography and statistics. This issue includes the minor league card debut of John Valentin. 5,000 sets produced.

	MINT	NRMT	EXC
COMPLETE SET (29)	12.00	5.50	1.50

☐ 1 Odie Abril
☐ 2 Jim Byrd
☐ 3 Felix DeDos
☐ 4 Vincent Degifico
☐ 5 Bernie Dzafic
☐ 6 Peter Estrada
☐ 7 John Flaherty
☐ 8 Donald Florence
☐ 9 Chris Hanks
☐ 10 Reggie Harris
☐ 11 Howard Landry
☐ 12 Erik Laseke
☐ 13 Chris Leach
☐ 14 Terry Marrs
☐ 15 Pedro Matilla
☐ 16 Meredith Moore
☐ 17 Alfredo Pratts
☐ 18 Mickey Rivers Jr
☐ 19 Ken Ryan
☐ 20 Al Sanders
☐ 21 Larry Scannell
☐ 22 Hector Stewart
☐ 23 Willie Tatum
☐ 24 Mike Thompson
☐ 25 John Valentin
☐ 26 Charles Wacha
☐ 27 James Whitehead
☐ 28 Doug Camilli
☐ 29 David Holt

1989 Wytheville Cubs Star

The 1989 Wytheville Cubs set contains 30 standard-size cards. The fronts have posed color player photos, with blue borders on the top portion of the card fading to red as one moves down the card face. In blue print on a pink background, the backs have biography and statistics. 5,000 sets produced.

	MINT	NRMT	EXC
COMPLETE SET (30)	5.00	2.20	.60

- ☐ 1 Newlan Aponte
- ☐ 2 Troy Bailey
- ☐ 3 Ronnie Brown
- ☐ 4 Victor Cancel
- ☐ 5 Pedro Castellano
- ☐ 6 Amilcar Correa
- ☐ 7 Dale Craig
- ☐ 8 Earl Cunningham
- ☐ 9 Kevin Dalson
- ☐ 10 Eddie Fowler
- ☐ 11 Jac Gelb
- ☐ 12 Don Gillespie
- ☐ 13 Fred Hill
- ☐ 14 Brad Huff
- ☐ 15 Calvin Ford
- ☐ 16 Jessie Hollins
- ☐ 17 Eric Jacques
- ☐ 18 Dan Kennedy
- ☐ 19 Greg Kessler
- ☐ 20 Mike Little
- ☐ 21 Raymond Mack
- ☐ 22 Recardo Medina
- ☐ 23 Leo Perez
- ☐ 24 Randy Sodders
- ☐ 25 Aaron Taylor
- ☐ 26 Scott Teague
- ☐ 27 Paul Torres
- ☐ 28 Clinton White
- ☐ 29 Coaching Staff
  Les Strode CO
  Steve Roadcap MG
  Julio Valdez
  (Instructor)
- ☐ 30 Greg Keuter TR

1990 Albany Yankees All Decade Best

This 36-card standard-size set of the 1990 Albany Yankees, a Class AA Eastern League affiliate of the New York Yankees, features white-bordered posed and action color player photos on its fronts. The player's name and position appear vertically on the left side. The words "All Decade" appear across the top. The yellow horizontal back carries the player's name and years played at the top, followed by player's history, highlights, and statistics. 2,500 sets were produced.

	MINT	NRMT	EXC
COMPLETE SET (36)	12.00	5.50	1.50

- ☐ 1 Deion Sanders
- ☐ 2 Mike Ashman
- ☐ 3 Roberto Kelly
- ☐ 4 Bob Geren
- ☐ 5 Logan Easley
- ☐ 6 Jim Leyritz
- ☐ 7 Steve Ontiveros
- ☐ 8 Matt Harrison
- ☐ 9 Scott Nielsen
- ☐ 10 Royal Clayton
- ☐ 11 Tim Layana
- ☐ 12 Kevin Maas
- ☐ 13 Bob Tewksbury
- ☐ 14 Phil Stephenson
- ☐ 15 Tom Barrett
- ☐ 16 Rod Imes
- ☐ 17 Andy Stankiewicz
- ☐ 18 Hal Morris
- ☐ 19 Randy Velarde
- ☐ 20 Darren Reed
- ☐ 21 Orestes Destrade
- ☐ 22 Doug Drabek
- ☐ 23 Hensley Meulens
- ☐ 24 Tim Lambert
- ☐ 25 Kevin Mmahat
- ☐ 26 Dave Eiland
- ☐ 27 Brad Arnsberg
- ☐ 28 Steve Adkins
- ☐ 29 Rob Sepanek
- ☐ 30 Steve Rosenberg
- ☐ 31 Mickey Tettleton
- ☐ 32 Keith Hughes
- ☐ 33 Bernie Williams
- ☐ 34 Mitch Lyden
- ☐ 35 Thad Reece
- ☐ 36 Checklist

1990 Albany Yankees Best

This 26-card standard-size set of the 1990 Albany Yankees, a Class AA Eastern League affiliate of the New York Yankees, features white-bordered posed and action color player photos on its fronts. The player's name and position appear vertically on the left side. The yellow horizontal back carries the player's name and position at the top, followed by biography, career highlights, and statistics. A player head shot appears in the lower right corner.

	MINT	NRMT	EXC
COMPLETE SET (26)	10.00	4.50	1.25

- ☐ 1 Bernie Williams
- ☐ 2 Andy Cook
- ☐ 3 Ramon Manon
- ☐ 4 Tom Newell
- ☐ 5 Scott Kamieniecki
- ☐ 6 Russell Meyer CO
- ☐ 7 Willie Smith
- ☐ 8 Don Stanford
- ☐ 9 Wade Taylor
- ☐ 10 Ricky Torres
- ☐ 11 Mitch Lyden
- ☐ 12 John Ramos
- ☐ 13 Andy Skeels
- ☐ 14 Bobby DeJardin
- ☐ 15 Bobby Dickerson
- ☐ 16 Pat Kelly
- ☐ 17 Tim Weston
- ☐ 18 Donald Sparks
- ☐ 19 Greg Sparks
- ☐ 20 Freddie Hailey
- ☐ 21 Billy Masse
- ☐ 22 Vince Phillips
- ☐ 23 Royal Clayton
- ☐ 24 Robert Zeihen
- ☐ 25 Joseph Lefebvre CO
- ☐ 26 Checklist

1990 Albany Yankees ProCards

This 29-card standard-size set of the 1990 Albany Yankees, a Class AA Eastern League affiliate of the New York Yankees, features on its white-bordered fronts posed color player photos set on simulated wood-grain backgrounds. The player's name, position, and team appear within a gold-colored rectangle below the photo. The tan horizontal back is bordered in white and carries the player's name at the top, followed by biography and statistics.

	MINT	NRMT	EXC
COMPLETE SET (29)	8.00	3.60	1.00

- ☐ 1028 Checklist
- ☐ 1029 Darrin Chapin
- ☐ 1030 Royal Clayton
- ☐ 1031 Andy Cook
- ☐ 1032 Doug Gogolewski
- ☐ 1033 Chris Howard
- ☐ 1034 Scott Kamieniecki
- ☐ 1035 Jerry Rub
- ☐ 1036 Don Stanford
- ☐ 1037 Mitch Lyden
- ☐ 1038 Andy Skeels
- ☐ 1039 Bobby DeJardin
- ☐ 1040 Bobby Dickerson
- ☐ 1041 Pat Kelly
- ☐ 1042 Don Sparks
- ☐ 1043 Greg Sparks
- ☐ 1044 Freddie Hailey
- ☐ 1045 Billy Masse
- ☐ 1046 Vince Phillips
- ☐ 1047 Bob Zeihen
- ☐ 1175 Ramon Manon
- ☐ 1176 Wade Taylor
- ☐ 1177 John Ramos
- ☐ 1178 Carlos Rodriguez
- ☐ 1179 Bernie Williams
- ☐ 1180 Rick Down MGR
- ☐ 1181 Joe Lefebvre CO
- ☐ 1182 Russ Meyer CO
- ☐ 1183 Glenn Sherlock CO

1990 Albany Yankees Star

This 28-card standard-size set of the 1990 Albany Yankees, a Class AA Eastern League affiliate of the New York Yankees, features purple bordered posed color player photos on its fronts. The player's name, team name, and position appear at the bottom. The white horizontal back carries the player's name at the top, followed by biography, career highlights, and statistics.

	MINT	NRMT	EXC
COMPLETE SET (28)	8.00	3.60	1.00

- ☐ 1 Darrin Chapin
- ☐ 2 Royal Clayton
- ☐ 3 Andy Cook
- ☐ 4 Bobby Dickerson
- ☐ 5 Gogo Gogolewski
- ☐ 6 Freddie Hailey
- ☐ 7 Scott Kamieniecki
- ☐ 8 Pat Kelly
- ☐ 9 Mitch Lyden
- ☐ 10 Ramon Manon
- ☐ 11 Billy Masse
- ☐ 12 Vince Phillips
- ☐ 13 John Ramos
- ☐ 14 Carlos Rodriguez
- ☐ 15 Jerry Rub
- ☐ 16 Andy Skeels
- ☐ 17 Don Sparks
- ☐ 18 Greg Sparks
- ☐ 19 Don Stanford
- ☐ 20 Wade Taylor
- ☐ 21 Ricky Torres
- ☐ 22 Bernie Williams
- ☐ 23 Bob Zeihen
- ☐ 24 Rick Down MGR
- ☐ 25 Joe Lefebvre CO
- ☐ 26 Glenn Sherlock CO
- ☐ 27 Mark Shiflett CO
- ☐ 28 Tim Weston TR

1990 Albuquerque Dukes CMC

This 28-card standard-size set of the 1990 Albuquerque Dukes, a Class AAA Pacific Coast League affiliate of the Los Angeles Dodgers, features white-bordered posed color player photos on its fronts. The player's name and position appear at the bottom; the team name appears vertically on the left. The back carries the league emblem in the white area at the top, the team name in the green stripe below, and player's name, position, biography, and statistics in the yellow area at the bottom. 1,100 sets were produced.

	MINT	NRMT	EXC
COMPLETE SET (28)	5.00	2.20	.60

- ☐ 1 Mike Christopher
- ☐ 2 Jeff Bittiger
- ☐ 3 Jeff Fischer
- ☐ 4 Steve Davis
- ☐ 5 Morris Madden
- ☐ 6 Darren Holmes
- ☐ 7 Greg Mayberry
- ☐ 8 Mike Maddux
- ☐ 9 Tim Scott
- ☐ 10 Jim Neidlinger
- ☐ 11 Dave Walsh
- ☐ 12 Dennis Springer
- ☐ 13 Terry Wells
- ☐ 14 Adam Brown
- ☐ 15 Darrin Fletcher
- ☐ 16 Carlos Hernandez
- ☐ 17 Dave Hansen
- ☐ 18 Dan Henley
- ☐ 19 Jose Offerman
- ☐ 20 Jose Vizcaino
- ☐ 21 Luis Lopez
- ☐ 22 Butch Davis
- ☐ 23 Wayne Kirby
- ☐ 24 Mike Huff
- ☐ 25 Billy Bean
- ☐ 26 Glenn Hoffman
  Player/Coach
- ☐ 27 Kevin Kennedy MGR
- ☐ 28 Coaches
  Claude Osteen
  Von Joshua
  Walt McConnel

1990 Albuquerque Dukes ProCards

This 30-card standard-size set of the 1990 Albuquerque Dukes, a Class AAA Pacific Coast League affiliate of the Los Angeles Dodgers, features on its white-bordered fronts posed color player photos set on simulated wood-grain backgrounds. The player's name, position, and team appear within a gold-colored rectangle below the photo. The tan horizontal back is bordered in white and carries the player's name at the top, followed by biography and statistics.

	MINT	NRMT	EXC
COMPLETE SET (30)	5.00	2.20	.60

- ☐ 334 Checklist
- ☐ 335 Jeff Bittiger
- ☐ 336 Mike Christopher
- ☐ 337 Steve Davis
- ☐ 338 Jeff Fischer
- ☐ 339 Darren Holmes
- ☐ 340 Morris Madden
- ☐ 341 Mike Maddux
- ☐ 342 Greg Mayberry
- ☐ 343 Jim Neidlinger
- ☐ 344 Tim Scott
- ☐ 345 Dave Walsh
- ☐ 346 Terry Wells
- ☐ 347 Adam Brown
- ☐ 348 Darrin Fletcher
- ☐ 349 Carlos Hernandez
- ☐ 350 Dave Hansen
- ☐ 351 Dan Henley
- ☐ 352 Glenn Hoffman
- ☐ 353 Walt McConnell
- ☐ 354 Jose Offerman
- ☐ 355 Jose Vizcaino
- ☐ 356 Billy Bean
- ☐ 357 Butch Davis
- ☐ 358 Mike Huff
- ☐ 359 Wayne Kirby
- ☐ 360 Luis Lopez
- ☐ 361 Kevin Kennedy MGR
- ☐ 362 Von Joshua CO
- ☐ 363 Claude Osteen CO

1990 Albuquerque Dukes Tribune

This 31-card standard-size set was sponsored by the Albuquerque Tribune, and its logo appears at the bottom of the reverse. The cards feature on the observe a posed color player photo. No information is provided on the card fronts. The back lists biography and 1989 statistics. The cards are unnumbered and checklisted below in alphabetical order.

	MINT	NRMT	EXC
COMPLETE SET (31)	10.00	4.50	1.25

- ☐ 1 Billy Bean
- ☐ 2 Jeff Bittiger
- ☐ 3 Adam Brown
- ☐ 4 Mike Christopher
- ☐ 5 Butch Davis
- ☐ 6 Steve Davis
- ☐ 7 Jeff Fischer
- ☐ 8 Darrin Fletcher
- ☐ 9 Dave Hansen
- ☐ 10 Dan Henley
- ☐ 11 Carlos Hernandez
- ☐ 12 Glenn Hoffman
- ☐ 13 Darren Holmes
- ☐ 14 Mike Huff
- ☐ 15 Von Joshua CO
- ☐ 16 Kevin Kennedy MGR
- ☐ 17 Wayne Kirby
- ☐ 18 Luis Lopez
- ☐ 19 Morris Madden
- ☐ 20 Mike Maddux
- ☐ 21 Greg Mayberry
- ☐ 22 Walt McConnell
- ☐ 23 Jim Neidlinger
- ☐ 24 Jose Offerman
- ☐ 25 Claude Osteen CO
- ☐ 26 Tim Scott
- ☐ 27 Dennis Springer
- ☐ 28 Brian Traxler
- ☐ 29 Jose Vizcaino
- ☐ 30 Dave Walsh
- ☐ 31 Terry Wells

1990 Appleton Foxes Box Scores

	MINT	NRMT	EXC
COMPLETE SET (30)	7.00	3.10	.85

- ☐ 1 Checklist Card
- ☐ 2 Brian Ahern
- ☐ 3 Francisco Baez
- ☐ 4 Kirk Baldwin
- ☐ 5 Joe Breeden
- ☐ 6 Gary Caraballo
- ☐ 7 John Conner
- ☐ 8 Francisco Garcia
- ☐ 9 John Gilcrist
- ☐ 10 Grant Griesser
- ☐ 11 John Gross
- ☐ 12 Arned Hernandez
- ☐ 13 Jake Jacobs
- ☐ 14 Mike Jirschele
- ☐ 15 Matt Karchner
- ☐ 16 David King
- ☐ 17 Herb Milton
- ☐ 18 Giovanni Miranda
- ☐ 19 Kerwin Moore
- ☐ 20 Andre Rabouin
- ☐ 21 Fred Russell
- ☐ 22 Colin Ryan
- ☐ 23 Chris Schaefer
- ☐ 24 Steve Shifflett
- ☐ 25 Dave Solseth
- ☐ 26 Rod Stillwell
- ☐ 27 Louis Talbert
- ☐ 28 Rich Tunison
- ☐ 29 Pedro Vazquez
- ☐ 30 Skip Wiley

1990 Appleton Foxes ProCards

This 29-card standard-size set of the 1990 Appleton Foxes, a Class A Midwest League affiliate of the Kansas City Royals, features on its white-bordered fronts posed color player photos set on simulated wood-grain backgrounds. The player's name, position, and team appear within a gold-colored rectangle below the photo. The tan horizontal back is bordered in white and carries the player's name at the top, followed by biography and statistics.

	MINT	NRMT	EXC
COMPLETE SET (29)	5.00	2.20	.60

- ☐ 2085 Checklist
- ☐ 2086 Brian Ahern
- ☐ 2087 Francisco Baez
- ☐ 2088 Kirk Baldwin
- ☐ 2089 John Conner
- ☐ 2090 Jake Jacobs
- ☐ 2091 Matt Karchner
- ☐ 2092 Herb Milton

☐ 2093 Chris Schaefer
☐ 2094 Steve Shifflett
☐ 2095 Louis Talbert
☐ 2096 Skip Wiley
☐ 2097 Grant Griesser
☐ 2098 Colin Ryan
☐ 2099 Dave Solseth
☐ 2100 Gary Caraballo
☐ 2101 David King
☐ 2102 Giovanni Miranda
☐ 2103 Fred Russell
☐ 2104 Rod Stillwell
☐ 2105 Rich Tunison
☐ 2106 Pedro Vazquez
☐ 2107 Francisco Garcia
☐ 2108 John Gilcrist
☐ 2109 Kerwin Moore
☐ 2110 Arned Hernandez
☐ 2111 Joe Breeden MGR
☐ 2112 Mike Jirschele CO
☐ 2113 Andre Rabouin CO

1990 Arizona Wildcats Police

	MINT	NRMT	EXC
COMPLETE SET (18)	10.00	4.50	1.25

☐ 1 Troy Bradford
☐ 2 Lance Dickson
☐ 3 Phil Echeverria
☐ 4 Brian Eldridge
☐ 5 Matt Figueroa
☐ 6 Steve Gill
☐ 7 Jason Hisey
☐ 8 Barry Johnson
☐ 9 Jack Johnson
☐ 10 Jerry Kindall CO
☐ 11 Marc Lavoie
☐ 12 Damon Mashore
☐ 13 Robbie Moen
☐ 14 J.J. Northam
☐ 15 Billy Owens
☐ 16 Scott Stanley ACO
☐ 17 Jerry Stitt ACO
☐ 18 Jim Wing ACO

1990 Arkansas Razorbacks

	MINT	NRMT	EXC
COMPLETE SET (33)	10.00	4.50	1.25

☐ 1 Doug Bennett
☐ 2 Brent Birch
☐ 3 Danny Brown
☐ 4 Bubba Carpenter
☐ 5 Jay Carpenter
☐ 6 Brian Cook
☐ 7 Rob Dodd
☐ 8 Charles Downey
☐ 9 Scott Epps
☐ 10 Greg D'Alexander
☐ 11 The Razorback
☐ 12 Haden Etheridge
☐ 13 Tony Gilmore
☐ 14 Gary Harris
☐ 15 Todd Hobson
☐ 16 Jeff Houck
☐ 17 Dan Hreha
☐ 18 Mark Johnson
☐ 19 Greyson Liles
☐ 20 Ron Moore
☐ 21 Kirk Piskor
☐ 22 Peter Raether
☐ 23 Phil Stidham
☐ 24 Mark Swope
☐ 25 Tim Thomas
☐ 26 Doug Clark ACO
☐ 27 John Luedtke ACO
☐ 28 Norm DeBriyn CO
☐ 29 Graduate Coaches
Greg Boyd
Rod Moore
Kevin Smallwood
☐ 30 Promising Pitchers
Brian Dennison
Mark Coppock
Trent Nesmith
☐ 31 Team Photo
☐ 32 Promising Newcomers
Chris Pinson
Lance Lodes
David Cassinelli
Steve Taft
☐ 33 Promising Freshmen
Mike Troglin
Doug Mlicki
Allen Williams

1990 Arkansas Travelers Grand Slam

	MINT	NRMT	EXC
COMPLETE SET (30)	12.00	5.50	1.50

☐ 1 Dave Bialas MG
☐ 2 Marty Mason CO

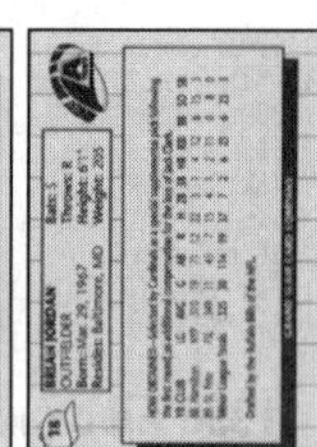

☐ 3 Dan Doyel TR
☐ 4 Frankie Abreu
☐ 5 Isaac Alleyne
☐ 6 John Burgos
☐ 7 Greg Carmona
☐ 8 Ric Christian
☐ 9 Rheal Cormier
☐ 10 John Ericks
☐ 11 Steve Fanning
☐ 12 Joey Fernandez
☐ 13 Mike Fitzgerald
☐ 14 Ed Fulton
☐ 15 Mark Grater
☐ 16 Joe Hall
☐ 17 Rich Hoffman
☐ 18 Brian Jordan
☐ 19 Dale Kisten
☐ 20 John Lepley
☐ 21 Scott Melvin
☐ 22 Dave Osteen
☐ 23 Gab Ozuna
☐ 24 Len Picota
☐ 25 Larry Pierson
☐ 26 Mike Ross
☐ 27 Brian Stone
☐ 28 Paul Thoutsis
☐ 29 Jose Vargas
☐ 30 Charlie White

1990 Asheville Tourists ProCards

This 28-card standard-size set of the 1990 Asheville Tourists, a Class A South Atlantic League affiliate of the Houston Astros, features on its white-bordered fronts posed color player photos set on simulated wood-grain backgrounds. The player's name, position, and team appear within a gold-colored rectangle below the photo. The tan horizontal back is bordered in white and carries the player's name at the top, followed by biography and statistics. This issue includes the minor league card debut of Brian L. Hunter.

	MINT	NRMT	EXC
COMPLETE SET (28)	10.00	4.50	1.25

☐ 2738 Checklist
☐ 2739 Troy Dovey
☐ 2740 Ben Gonzales
☐ 2741 Chris Gardner
☐ 2742 Anthony Gutierrez
☐ 2743 Mike McDowell
☐ 2744 Julio Munoz
☐ 2745 Francisco Perez
☐ 2746 Limbert Rivas
☐ 2747 Eliezel Rosario
☐ 2748 Mark Small
☐ 2749 Donne Wall
☐ 2750 Ken Wheeler
☐ 2751 Ed Beuerlein
☐ 2752 Kevin Scott
☐ 2753 Craig Curtis
☐ 2754 David Hajeck
☐ 2755 Brett Holum
☐ 2756 Justin McCray
☐ 2757 Orlando Miller
☐ 2758 Ed Quijada
☐ 2759 Gershon Dallas
☐ 2760 Juan Encarnacion
☐ 2761 Brian L. Hunter
☐ 2762 Luther Johnson
☐ 2763 Jose Santana
☐ 2764 Frank Cacciatore MGR
☐ 2765 Rick Aponte CO

1990 Auburn Astros Best

This 25-card standard-size set of the 1990 Auburn Astros, a Class A New York-Penn League affiliate of the Houston Astros, features white-bordered posed and action color player photos on its fronts. The player's name and position appear vertically on the left side. The yellow horizontal back carries the player's name and position at the top, followed by biography, career highlights, and statistics. A player head shot appears in the lower right corner.

	MINT	NRMT	EXC
COMPLETE SET (25)	5.00	2.20	.60

☐ 1 Manny Mota Jr.
☐ 2 Robert Hurta
☐ 3 Steve Veit
☐ 4 David Wilson
☐ 5 Efrain Barreiro
☐ 6 Jose Flores
☐ 7 Bob Hurlbutt
☐ 8 Doug Ketchen
☐ 9 Jeff Ball
☐ 10 Vince Roman
☐ 11 Steve Powers
☐ 12 Bryan Smith
☐ 13 Michael Irwin
☐ 14 Mark Hampton
☐ 15 Marty Jones
☐ 16 Dave Allen
☐ 17 Lincoln Gumbs Jr.
☐ 18 Fletcher Thompson
☐ 19 Tyrone Scott
☐ 20 John Graham MGR
☐ 21 Brian Porter CO
☐ 22 Marc Techman
Executive Assistant
☐ 23 Don Alexander CO
☐ 24 Mark Copeland TR
☐ 25 Checklist

1990 Auburn Astros ProCards

This 26-card standard-size set of the 1990 Auburn Astros, a Class A New York-Penn League affiliate of the Houston Astros, features on its white-bordered fronts posed color player photos set on simulated wood-grain backgrounds. The player's name, position, and team appear within a gold-colored rectangle below the photo. The tan horizontal back is bordered in white and carries the player's name at the top, followed by biography and statistics.

	MINT	NRMT	EXC
COMPLETE SET (26)	5.00	2.20	.60

☐ 3393 Checklist
☐ 3394 Ray Montgromery
☐ 3395 Chris Hatcher
☐ 3396 Layne Lambert
☐ 3397 Tony Gilmore
☐ 3398 Manny Mota Jr.
☐ 3399 Bob Hurta
☐ 3400 Steve Veit
☐ 3401 Mark Hampton
☐ 3402 Tyrone Scott
☐ 3403 Marty Jones
☐ 3404 David Wilson
☐ 3405 Vince Roman
☐ 3406 Bryan Smith
☐ 3407 Steve Powers
☐ 3408 Jeff Ball
☐ 3409 Lincoln Gumbs
☐ 3410 Fletcher Thompson
☐ 3411 Jose Flores
☐ 3412 Michael Irwin
☐ 3413 Efrain Barreiro
☐ 3414 Dave Allen
☐ 3415 J.B. Ketchen
☐ 3416 Robert Hurlbutt
☐ 3417 Ricky Peters MGR
☐ 3418 Don Alexander CO

1990 Augusta Pirates ProCards

This 27-card standard-size set of the 1990 Augusta Pirates, a Class A South Atlantic League affiliate of the Augusta Pirates, features on its white-bordered fronts posed color player photos set on simulated wood-grain backgrounds. The player's name, position, and team appear within a gold-colored rectangle below the photo. The tan horizontal back is bordered in white and carries the player's name at the top, followed by biography and statistics.

	MINT	NRMT	EXC
COMPLETE SET (27)	7.00	3.10	.85

☐ 2454 Checklist
☐ 2455 Scott Arvesen
☐ 2456 David Bird
☐ 2457 Brent Honeywell
☐ 2458 Ramon Martinez
☐ 2459 Wayne Masters
☐ 2460 Eric Parkinson
☐ 2461 Kevin Rychel
☐ 2462 Delvy Santiago
☐ 2463 Bobby Underwood
☐ 2464 Paul Wagner
☐ 2465 Ron Way
☐ 2466 Felix Antigua
☐ 2467 Jason Nixon
☐ 2468 Jessie Torres
☐ 2469 Rich Aude
☐ 2470 Willie Greene
☐ 2471 Bill Holmes
☐ 2472 Deron Johnson
☐ 2473 Austin Manahan
☐ 2474 Roman Rodriguez
☐ 2475 Winston Seymour
☐ 2476 Michael Brewington
☐ 2477 William Pennyfeather
☐ 2478 Daryl Ratliff
☐ 2479 Ken Trusky
☐ 2480 Lee Driggers MGR

1990 Bakersfield Dodgers Cal League Cards

	MINT	NRMT	EXC
COMPLETE SET (32)	6.00	2.70	.75

☐ 230 Kiki Jones
☐ 231 Fausto Tatis
☐ 232 Baltazar Mesa
☐ 233 Napoleon Robinson
☐ 234 Jason Brosnan
☐ 235 Rich Crane
☐ 236 Mike Frame
☐ 237 Jamie McAndrew
☐ 238 Tony Helmick
☐ 239 Frank Humber
☐ 240 Mike Potthoff
☐ 241 John Braase
☐ 242 Barry Parisotto
☐ 243 Craig Bishop
☐ 244 Tom Beyers
☐ 245 Anthony Garcia
☐ 246 Goose Gregson
☐ 247 Chris Morrow
☐ 248 Steve O'Donnell
☐ 249 John Deutsch
☐ 250 Brock McMurray
☐ 251 Gary Forrester
☐ 252 Garett Teel
☐ 253 Matt Howard
☐ 254 Brett Magnusson
☐ 255 Tim Barker
☐ 256 Bryan Baar
☐ 257 Bryan Beals
☐ 258 Jose Munoz
☐ 259 Bill Lott
☐ 260 Bill Ashley
☐ 261 Tom Goodwin

1990 Baseball City Royals Star

This 31-card standard-size set of the 1990 Baseball City Royals, a Class A Florida State League affiliate of the Kansas City Royals, features blue bordered posed color player photos on its fronts. The player's name, team name, and position appear at the bottom. The white horizontal back carries the player's name at the top, followed by biography, career highlights, and statistics.

	MINT	NRMT	EXC
COMPLETE SET (31)	5.00	2.20	.60

☐ 1 Jose Anglero
☐ 2 Mike Beall
☐ 3 Jacob Brumfield
☐ 4 Sean Collins
☐ 5 Huascar DeLeon
☐ 6 Bill Drohan
☐ 7 Linton Dyer
☐ 8 Jeff Garber
☐ 9 Chris Garibaldo
☐ 10 Greg Harvey
☐ 11 Steve Hoeme
☐ 12 Bobby Holley
☐ 13 Brad Hopper
☐ 14 Gary Koenig
☐ 15 Kevin Long
☐ 16 John McCormick
☐ 17 Steve Otto
☐ 18 Mark Parnell
☐ 19 Hipolito Pichardo
☐ 20 Ben Pierce
☐ 21 Darryl Robinson
☐ 22 Kevin Shaw
☐ 23 Randy Vaughn
☐ 24 Hugh Walker
☐ 25 Daren Watkins
☐ 26 Mike Webster
☐ 27 Don Wright
☐ 28 Brian Poldberg MGR
☐ 29 Mike Alzarez CO
☐ 30 Ron Johnson CO
☐ 31 Mark Farnsworth TR

1990 Batavia Clippers ProCards

This 30-card standard-size set of the 1990 Batavia Clippers, a Class A New York-Penn League affiliate of the Philadelphia Phillies, features on its white-bordered fronts posed color player photos set on simulated wood-grain backgrounds. The player's name, position, and team appear within a gold-colored rectangle below the photo. The tan horizontal back is bordered in white and carries the player's name at the top, followed by biography and statistics.

	MINT	NRMT	EXC
COMPLETE SET (30)	5.00	2.20	.60

☐ 3055 Checklist
☐ 3056 Al Baur
☐ 3057 Elliott Gray
☐ 3058 Eric Hill
☐ 3059 Charlie Hurst
☐ 3060 Tom Jones

☐ 3061 John Ingram
☐ 3062 Stewart Lovdal
☐ 3063 Steve McGovern
☐ 3064 Mike Montgomery
☐ 3065 Steve Parris
☐ 3066 Dave Ross
☐ 3067 Mike Williams
☐ 3068 Porfirio Pena
☐ 3069 Ryan Ridenour
☐ 3070 Willie Smith
☐ 3071 Ismael Cruz
☐ 3072 Erik Judson
☐ 3073 R.A. Neitzel
☐ 3074 Mike Owens
☐ 3075 Eulogio Perez
☐ 3076 Sean Ryan
☐ 3077 Jim Savage
☐ 3078 Steve Bieser
☐ 3079 Rob Hartwig
☐ 3080 Jeff Jackson
☐ 3081 Gary Morgan
Card front that
of #3084 Staff
☐ 3082 Tom Nuneville
☐ 3083 Gil Valencia
☐ 3084 Field Staff
Scott Hitting CO
Carlos Arroyo CO
Dave Cash MGR
Rich Walker TR
Card front that
of #3101 Morgan

1990 Beloit Brewers Best

This 27-card standard-size set of the 1990 Beloit Brewers, a Class A Midwest League affiliate of the Milwaukee Brewers, features white-bordered posed and action color player photos on its fronts. The player's name and position appear vertically on the left side. The yellow horizontal back carries the player's name and position at the top, followed by biography, career highlights, and statistics. A player head shot appears in the lower right corner.

	MINT	NRMT	EXC
COMPLETE SET (27)	5.00	2.20	.60

☐ 1 Ramser Correa
☐ 2 Bill Robertson
☐ 3 Joe Andrzejewski
☐ 4 Larry Carter
☐ 5 Troy O'Leary
☐ 6 Sam Drake
☐ 7 Tim Fortugno
☐ 8 Scott Kimball
☐ 9 Greg Landry
☐ 10 Scott Muscat
Sic, Muscatt
☐ 11 Brett Synder
☐ 12 Vilato Marrero
☐ 13 Randy Snyder
☐ 14 Darrin White
☐ 15 John Byington
☐ 16 Daren Cornell
☐ 17 Leon Glenn
☐ 18 Oreste Marrero
☐ 19 Henry Reynoso
☐ 20 Arthur Butcher
☐ 21 Jeff(Nikko) Na'te CO
☐ 22 Scooter Meissner TR
☐ 23 Bob Vancho
☐ 24 Troy Haugen
☐ 25 Keith Fleming
☐ 26 Robert Decksen MGR
☐ 27 Checklist

1990 Beloit Brewers Star

This 27-card standard-size set of the 1990 Beloit Brewers, a Class A Midwest League affiliate of the Milwaukee Brewers, features yellow bordered posed color player photos on its fronts. The player's name, team name, and position appear at the bottom. The white horizontal back carries the player's name at the top, followed by biography, career highlights, and statistics.

	MINT	NRMT	EXC
COMPLETE SET (27)	5.00	2.20	.60

☐ 1 Joe Andrezejewski
☐ 2 Arthur Butcher
☐ 3 John Byington
☐ 4 Larry Carter
☐ 5 Tim Clark
☐ 6 Sam Drake
☐ 7 Keith Fleming
☐ 8 Tim Fortugno
☐ 9 Leon Glenn
☐ 10 Troy Haugen
☐ 11 Scott Kimball
☐ 12 Oreste Marrero
☐ 13 Vilato Marrero
☐ 14 Tom McGraw
☐ 15 Scott Muscat
☐ 16 Troy O'Leary
☐ 17 Henry Reynoso
☐ 18 Bill Robertson
☐ 19 Rob Smith
☐ 20 Brett Snyder
☐ 21 Randy Snyder
☐ 22 Bob Vancho
☐ 23 Darrin White
☐ 24 Dave Wrona
☐ 25 Rob Derksen MGR
☐ 26 Jeff Nate CO
☐ 27 Scott Meissner TR

1990 Bend Bucks Legoe

	MINT	NRMT	EXC
COMPLETE SET (32)	6.00	2.70	.75

☐ 1 Buckey (Mascot)
☐ 2 Gene Dusan CO
☐ 3 Sean Krokroskia
☐ 4 Mickey Hyde
☐ 5 Marty Hunter CO
☐ 6 Kelley Ahrens
☐ 7 Bonell Chevalier
☐ 8 Mike Bubalo MG
☐ 9 Lonnie Potter
☐ 10 Jason Klonoski
☐ 11 Bob Blankenship
☐ 12 Dan Henrikson
☐ 13 Jose Reyes
☐ 14 Todd Russell
☐ 15 Russ Miller
☐ 16 Darrell Wagner
☐ 17 Glenn McCormick
☐ 18 Steve Avent
☐ 19 Chuck Wanke
☐ 20 Dan Vannell
☐ 21 Doug Twitty
☐ 22 Lee Sammons
☐ 23 Mario Lyons
☐ 24 Amner Reyes
☐ 25 Pedro Frias
☐ 26 Gary Ross
☐ 27 Pedro Roa
☐ 28 Shannon Hunt
☐ 29 Audy Mesa
☐ 30 Jim Gibbs
☐ 31 Matt Russell BB
Jason Lundgren BB
☐ NNO Title Card

1990 Best

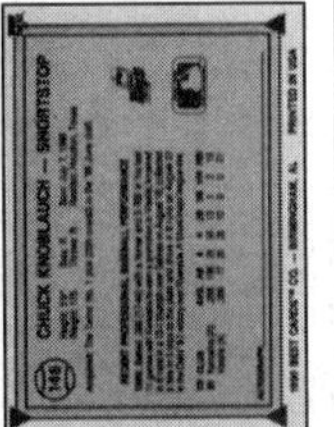

This 324-card set feature full color player shots with the player's name, team name and position appearing on the card fronts. The horizontal back carries the player's name and position at the top, followed by biography and statistics.

	MINT	NRMT	EXC
COMPLETE SET (324)	100.00	45.00	12.50
COMMON CARD (1-324)	.15	.07	.02
☐ 1 Frank Thomas	25.00	11.00	3.10
☐ 2 Eric Wedge	.15	.07	.02
☐ 3 Willie Ansley	.15	.07	.02
☐ 4 Mark Lewis	.60	.25	.07
☐ 5 Greg Colbrunn	.30	.14	.04
☐ 6 David Staton	.15	.07	.02
☐ 7 Ben McDonald	.40	.18	.05
☐ 8 Brent Mayne	.15	.07	.02
☐ 9 Ray Holbert	.15	.07	.02
☐ 10 T.R. Lewis	.15	.07	.02
☐ 11 Willie Banks	.30	.14	.04
☐ 12 Steve Dunn	.30	.14	.04
☐ 13 Juan Andujar	.15	.07	.02
☐ 14 Roger Salkeld	.15	.07	.02
☐ 15 Steve Hosey	.15	.07	.02
☐ 16 Tyler Houston	.30	.14	.04
☐ 17 David Holdridge	.15	.07	.02
☐ 18 Todd Malone	.15	.07	.02
☐ 19 Tony Scruggs	.15	.07	.02
☐ 20 Darron Cox	.15	.07	.02
☐ 21 Mike Linskey	.15	.07	.02
☐ 22 Darren Lewis	.40	.18	.05
☐ 23 Eddie Zosky	.15	.07	.02
☐ 24 Ramser Correa	.15	.07	.02
☐ 25 Lee Upshaw	.15	.07	.02
☐ 26 Bernie Williams	6.00	2.70	.75
☐ 27 Brian Harrison	.15	.07	.02
☐ 28 Len Brutcher	.15	.07	.02
☐ 29 Scott Centala	.15	.07	.02
☐ 30 Kenny Morgan	.15	.07	.02
☐ 31 Pedro Borbon Jr.	.15	.07	.02
☐ 32 Lee Hancock	.15	.07	.02
☐ 33 Clay Bellinger	.15	.07	.02
☐ 34 Chris Myers	.15	.07	.02
☐ 35 Russ Garside	.15	.07	.02
☐ 36 Ron Plemmons	.15	.07	.02
☐ 37 Jose LeBron	.15	.07	.02
☐ 38 Tom Hardgrove	.15	.07	.02
☐ 39 Alan Newman	.15	.07	.02
☐ 40 Ramonb Jimenez	.15	.07	.02
☐ 41 Ezequiel Herrera	.15	.07	.02
☐ 42 Jason Satre	.15	.07	.02
☐ 43 Bob Malloy	.15	.07	.02
☐ 44 William Suero	.15	.07	.02
☐ 45 Lenny Webster	.15	.07	.02
☐ 46 Andy Ashby	.40	.18	.05
☐ 47 Darren Ritter	.15	.07	.02
☐ 48 Andy Mota	.15	.07	.02
☐ 49 Pat Gomez	.15	.07	.02
☐ 50 Ron Stephens	.15	.07	.02
☐ 51 Daniel Eskew	.15	.07	.02
☐ 52 Joe Andrzejewski	.15	.07	.02
☐ 53 Doug Robbins	.15	.07	.02
☐ 54 Noel Velez	.15	.07	.02
☐ 55 Dana Ridenour	.15	.07	.02
☐ 56 Luis Martinez	.15	.07	.02
☐ 57 Dave Fleming	.15	.07	.02
☐ 58 Adell Davenport	.15	.07	.02
☐ 59 Brent McCoy	.15	.07	.02
☐ 60 Johnny Ard	.15	.07	.02
☐ 61 Cal Eldred	.30	.14	.04
☐ 62 Tab Brown	.15	.07	.02
☐ 63 Scott Kamieniecki	.15	.07	.02
☐ 64 Scott Bryant	.15	.07	.02
☐ 65 Brad Pennington	.15	.07	.02
☐ 66 Bernie Jenkins	.15	.07	.02
☐ 67 Frank Carey	.15	.07	.02
☐ 68 Matt Witkowski	.15	.07	.02
☐ 69 Checklist (1-48)	.15	.07	.02
☐ 70 Josias Manzanillo	.15	.07	.02
☐ 71 Checklist (49-96)	.15	.07	.02
☐ 72 Andujar Cedeno UER Andvjar	.30	.14	.04
☐ 73 Ricky Rojas	.15	.07	.02
☐ 74 Scott Brosius	1.00	.45	.12
☐ 75 Tom Redington	.15	.07	.02
☐ 76 Kevin Rogers	.15	.07	.02
☐ 77 Jerry Wolak	.15	.07	.02
☐ 78 Rick Davis	.15	.07	.02
☐ 79 Juan Guzman	.40	.18	.05
☐ 80 Cesar Bernhardt	.15	.07	.02
☐ 81 Randy Simmons	.15	.07	.02
☐ 82 Clyde Keller	.15	.07	.02
☐ 83 Anthony Manahan	.15	.07	.02
☐ 84 Tom Maynard	.15	.07	.02
☐ 85 Ed Gustafson	.15	.07	.02
☐ 86 Sean Berry	.50	.23	.06
☐ 87 Brian Boltz	.15	.07	.02
☐ 88 Shawn Gilbert	.15	.07	.02
☐ 89 Rafael Novoa	.15	.07	.02
☐ 90 Jon Vander Wal	.15	.07	.02
☐ 91 Scott Pose	.15	.07	.02
☐ 92 Don Stanford	.15	.07	.02
☐ 93 Joe Federico	.15	.07	.02
☐ 94 Todd Watson	.15	.07	.02
☐ 95 Luis Gonzalez	.30	.14	.04
☐ 96 Pat Leinen	.15	.07	.02
☐ 97 Joel Estes	.15	.07	.02
☐ 98 Troy O'Leary	.50	.23	.06
☐ 99 Matt Stark	.15	.07	.02
☐ 100 Tony Tarasco	.30	.14	.04
☐ 101 Marc Lipson	.15	.07	.02
☐ 102 Kevin Higgins	.15	.07	.02
☐ 103 Jack Voigt	.15	.07	.02
☐ 104 Steve Schrenk	.15	.07	.02
☐ 105 Jonathan Hurst	.15	.07	.02
☐ 106 Scott Erickson	.30	.14	.04
☐ 107 Javy Lopez	5.00	2.20	.60
☐ 108 Bob Zupcic	.15	.07	.02
☐ 109 Edwin Marquez	.15	.07	.02
☐ 110 Shawn Heiden	.15	.07	.02
☐ 111 Mike Maksudian	.15	.07	.02
☐ 112 Tony Eusebio	.15	.07	.02
☐ 113 Chris Hancock	.15	.07	.02
☐ 114 Royce Clayton	.50	.23	.06
☐ 115 Tim Mauser	.15	.07	.02
☐ 116 Checklist (97-144)	.15	.07	.02
☐ 117 Carlos Maldonado	.15	.07	.02
☐ 118 Rex De La Nunez	.15	.07	.02
☐ 119 Mike Curtis	.15	.07	.02
☐ 120 Roger Miller	.15	.07	.02
☐ 121 Daryl Moore	.15	.07	.02
☐ 122 Turk Wendell	.30	.14	.04
☐ 123 Dan Rambo	.15	.07	.02
☐ 124 Scott Kimball	.15	.07	.02
☐ 125 Willie Magallanes	.15	.07	.02
☐ 126 Dannie Ray Harris	.15	.07	.02
☐ 127 Joey James	.15	.07	.02
☐ 128 Wil Cordero	.50	.23	.06
☐ 129 Rob Taylor	.15	.07	.02
☐ 130 Bryce Florie	.15	.07	.02
☐ 131 Mike Mitchner	.15	.07	.02
☐ 132 Jeff Bagwell	12.00	5.50	1.50
☐ 133 Caesar Devares	.15	.07	.02
☐ 134 Tim Gillis	.15	.07	.02
☐ 135 Victor Hithe	.15	.07	.02
☐ 136 Earl Steinmetz	.15	.07	.02
☐ 137 Carl Keliipuleole	.15	.07	.02
☐ 138 Ted Williams	.15	.07	.02
☐ 139 Jorge Pedre	.15	.07	.02
☐ 140 Amalio Carreno	.15	.07	.02
☐ 141 Chris Gill	.15	.07	.02
☐ 142 Dennis Wiseman	.15	.07	.02
☐ 143 Checklist (145-192)	.15	.07	.02
☐ 144 Derek Lee	.15	.07	.02
☐ 145 Brett Synder	.15	.07	.02
☐ 146 Chuck Knoblauch	6.00	2.70	.75
☐ 147 Rafael Quirico	.15	.07	.02
☐ 148 Julian Yan	.15	.07	.02
☐ 149 John Thelen	.15	.07	.02
☐ 150 Checklist (193-240)	.15	.07	.02
☐ 151 Darrin Reichle	.15	.07	.02
☐ 152 John Ramos	.15	.07	.02
☐ 153 Patrick Lennon	.15	.07	.02
☐ 154 Wade Taylor	.15	.07	.02
☐ 155 Mike Twardoski	.15	.07	.02
☐ 156 Jeff Conine	2.00	.90	.25
☐ 157 Kelly Mann	.15	.07	.02
☐ 158 Gary Wilson	.15	.07	.02
☐ 159 Chris Fye	.15	.07	.02
☐ 160 Roger Hailey	.15	.07	.02
☐ 161 Harold Allen	.15	.07	.02
☐ 162 Ozzie Canseco	.15	.07	.02
☐ 163 Checklist (241-288)	.15	.07	.02
☐ 164 Rudy Seanez	.15	.07	.02
☐ 165 John Zaksek	.15	.07	.02
☐ 166 Roberto DeLeon	.15	.07	.02
☐ 167 Matt Merullo	.15	.07	.02
☐ 168 Checklist (289-324)	.15	.07	.02
☐ 169 Terrell Hansen	.15	.07	.02
☐ 170 Ron Crowe	.15	.07	.02
☐ 171 Luis Galindez	.15	.07	.02
☐ 172 Vilato Marrero	.15	.07	.02
☐ 173 Scott Cepicky	.15	.07	.02
☐ 174 Gary Resetar	.15	.07	.02
☐ 175 Rich Scheid	.15	.07	.02
☐ 176 Jimmy Rogers	.15	.07	.02
☐ 177 Ken Pennington	.15	.07	.02
☐ 178 Tom Martin	.15	.07	.02
☐ 179 Mitch Lyden	.15	.07	.02
☐ 180 Jorge Brito	.15	.07	.02
☐ 181 Chris Gorton	.15	.07	.02
☐ 182 Mark Sims	.15	.07	.02
☐ 183 Jose Olmeda	.15	.07	.02
☐ 184 Edward Taubensee	.30	.14	.04
☐ 185 Steve Morris	.15	.07	.02
☐ 186 Tim Pugh	.15	.07	.02
☐ 187 Barry Winford	.15	.07	.02
☐ 188 Allen Liebert	.15	.07	.02
☐ 189 Kurt Brown	.15	.07	.02
☐ 190 Kelly Lifgren	.15	.07	.02
☐ 191 Mike Kelly	.15	.07	.02
☐ 192 Roberto Munoz	.15	.07	.02
☐ 193 Judd Johnson	.15	.07	.02
☐ 194 Hector Wagner	.15	.07	.02
☐ 195 Dave Reis	.15	.07	.02
☐ 196 Isaiah Clark	.15	.07	.02
☐ 197 William Schock	.15	.07	.02
☐ 198 Ruben Gonzalez	.15	.07	.02
☐ 199 Mike Eberle	.15	.07	.02
☐ 200 Michael Arner	.15	.07	.02
☐ 201 Raphael Bustamante	.15	.07	.02
☐ 202 John Patterson	.15	.07	.02
☐ 203 Jose Slusarski	.15	.07	.02
☐ 204 Rodney McCray	.15	.07	.02
☐ 205 Wally Trice	.15	.07	.02
☐ 206 Edgar Caceres	.15	.07	.02
☐ 207 Eugene Jones	.15	.07	.02
☐ 208 Joey Wardlow	.15	.07	.02
☐ 209 Steve Martin	.15	.07	.02
☐ 210 Woody Williams	.15	.07	.02
☐ 211 Kevin Morton	.15	.07	.02
☐ 212 Bobby DeJardin	.15	.07	.02
☐ 213 Chris Bennett	.15	.07	.02
☐ 214 Brian Johnson	.15	.07	.02
☐ 215 Randy Snyder	.15	.07	.02
☐ 216 Roberto Hernandez	.40	.18	.05
☐ 217 Glen Gardner	.15	.07	.02
☐ 218 Fred Costello	.15	.07	.02
☐ 219 Melvin Nieves	.50	.23	.06
☐ 220 Al Martin UER All back information is wrong	.50	.23	.06
☐ 221 Kerry Knox	.15	.07	.02
☐ 222 Michael Eatinger	.15	.07	.02
☐ 223 Jim Myers	.15	.07	.02
☐ 224 Jay Owens	.15	.07	.02
☐ 225 Jayson Best	.15	.07	.02
☐ 226 Mike McDonald	.15	.07	.02
☐ 227 Kim Batiste	.15	.07	.02
☐ 228 Rich DeLucia	.15	.07	.02
☐ 229 Chris Delarwelle	.15	.07	.02
☐ 230 Jeff Hoffman	.15	.07	.02
☐ 231 Bobby Moore	.15	.07	.02
☐ 232 Dan Wilson	.40	.18	.05
☐ 233 Greg Pirkl	.15	.07	.02
☐ 234 Craig Newkirk	.15	.07	.02
☐ 235 Mike Hensley	.15	.07	.02
☐ 236 Ryan Klesko	8.00	3.60	1.00
☐ 237 Donald Sparks	.15	.07	.02
☐ 238 J.D. Noland	.15	.07	.02
☐ 239 Chris Howard	.15	.07	.02
☐ 240 Stan Royer	.15	.07	.02
☐ 241 Manny Alexander	.30	.14	.04

☐ 242 Jeff Plympton .15 .07 .02
☐ 243 Jeff Juden .15 .07 .02
☐ 244 Charles Nagy 2.50 1.10 .30
☐ 245 Ryan Bowen .15 .07 .02
☐ 246 Scott Taylor .15 .07 .02
☐ 247 Tom Quinlan .15 .07 .02
☐ 248 Royal Thomas .15 .07 .02
☐ 249 Ricky Rhodes .15 .07 .02
☐ 250 Alex Fernandez 1.25 .55 .16
☐ 251 Bruce Egloff .15 .07 .02
☐ 252 Greg Sparks .15 .07 .02
☐ 253 Brain Dour .15 .07 .02
☐ 254 John Byington .15 .07 .02
☐ 255 Stacey Burdick .15 .07 .02
☐ 256 Danny Matznick .15 .07 .02
☐ 257 Reed Olmstead .15 .07 .02
☐ 258 Jim Bowie .15 .07 .02
☐ 259 Jim Newlin .15 .07 .02
☐ 260 Ramon Caraballo .15 .07 .02
☐ 261 Brian Barnes .15 .07 .02
☐ 262 Mike Gardiner .15 .07 .02
☐ 263 Andy Fox .15 .07 .02
☐ 264 Brian McKeon .15 .07 .02
☐ 265 Andy Tomberlin .15 .07 .02
☐ 266 Frank Bellino .15 .07 .02
☐ 267 Tim Lata .15 .07 .02
☐ 268 Mike Burton .15 .07 .02
☐ 269 Jim Orsag .15 .07 .02
☐ 270 Scott Romano .15 .07 .02
☐ 271 Leon Glenn .15 .07 .02
☐ 272 Mike Misuraca .15 .07 .02
☐ 273 Randy Knorr .15 .07 .02
☐ 274 Eddie Tucker .15 .07 .02
☐ 275 Ken Powell .15 .07 .02
☐ 276 Brian McRae 1.25 .55 .16
☐ 277 Mark Merchant .15 .07 .02
☐ 278 Vinny Castilla 2.00 .90 .25
☐ 279 Stephen Chitren .15 .07 .02
☐ 280 Marteese Robinson .15 .07 .02
☐ 281 Osvaldo Sanchez .15 .07 .02
☐ 282 Michael Mongiello .15 .07 .02
☐ 283 John Valentin 1.50 .70 .19
☐ 284 Timmie Morrow .15 .07 .02
☐ 285 Matt Murray .15 .07 .02
☐ 286 Darrell Sherman .15 .07 .02
☐ 287 Royal Clayton .15 .07 .02
☐ 288 Jason Robertson .15 .07 .02
☐ 289 John Kilner .15 .07 .02
☐ 290 Jeff Mutis .15 .07 .02
☐ 291 Gary Alexander .15 .07 .02
☐ 292 Oreste Marrero .15 .07 .02
☐ 293 Melvin Wearing .15 .07 .02
☐ 294 Scott Meadows .15 .07 .02
☐ 295 Pat Hentgen 1.50 .70 .19
☐ 296 John Hudek .30 .14 .04
☐ 297 Tim Stargell .15 .07 .02
☐ 298 Tony Brown .15 .07 .02
☐ 299 Scott Plemmons .15 .07 .02
☐ 300 Chris Nabholz .15 .07 .02
☐ 301 Brian Romero .15 .07 .02
☐ 302 Vince Kindred .15 .07 .02
☐ 303 Robert Ayrault .15 .07 .02
☐ 304 Steve Stowell .15 .07 .02
☐ 305 Don Strange .15 .07 .02
☐ 306 Tim Nedin .15 .07 .02
☐ 307 Derek Livernois .15 .07 .02
☐ 308 Kerry Woodson .15 .07 .02
☐ 309 Sam Ferretti .15 .07 .02
☐ 310 Reuben Smiley .15 .07 .02
☐ 311 Jim Campbell .15 .07 .02
☐ 312 Al Osuna .15 .07 .02
☐ 313 Luis Mercedes .15 .07 .02
☐ 314 Billy Reed .15 .07 .02
☐ 315 Vince Harris .15 .07 .02
☐ 316 Jeff Carter .15 .07 .02
☐ 317 David Riddle .15 .07 .02
☐ 318 Frank Thomas BC 12.00 5.50 1.50
☐ 319 Eric Wedge BC .15 .07 .02
☐ 320 Mark Lewis BC .30 .14 .04
☐ 321 Alex Fernandez BC .60 .25 .07
☐ 322 Chuck Knoblauch BC 3.00 1.35 .35
☐ 323 Charles Nagy BC 1.25 .55 .16
☐ 324 Tyler Houston BC .30 .14 .04

1990 Billings Mustangs ProCards

This 30-card standard-size set of the 1990 Billings Mustangs, a Rookie Class Pioneer League affiliate of the Cincinnati Reds, features on its white-bordered fronts posed color player photos set on simulated wood-grain backgrounds. The player's name, position, and team appear within a gold-colored rectangle below the photo. The tan horizontal back is bordered in white and carries the player's name at the top, followed by biography and statistics.

	MINT	NRMT	EXC
COMPLETE SET (30)	5.00	2.20	.60

☐ 3210 Checklist
☐ 3211 Kevin Berry
☐ 3212 Sean Doty
☐ 3213 Scott Duff
☐ 3214 Mike Ferry
☐ 3215 Brian Fry
☐ 3216 Chris Keim
☐ 3217 Larry Luebbers
☐ 3218 Greg Margheim
☐ 3219 Ernesto Nieves
☐ 3220 Scott Robinson
☐ 3221 Carl Stewart
☐ 3222 Kevin Tatar
☐ 3223 Ryan Edwards
☐ 3224 Brian Nichols
☐ 3225 Roy Hammargren
☐ 3226 Dave Wheeler
☐ 3227 Bobby Filotei
☐ 3228 Keith Gordon
☐ 3229 Kevin Jones
☐ 3230 Rob Perna
☐ 3231 Kevin Riggs
☐ 3232 Todd Wilson
☐ 3233 Eric Burroughs
☐ 3234 Elliott Quinones
☐ 3235 Chris Vasquez
☐ 3236 Victor Perez
☐ 3237 K.C. Gillum
☐ 3238 Gerry Groninger MGR
☐ 3239 Mack Jenkins CO

1990 Birmingham Barons Best

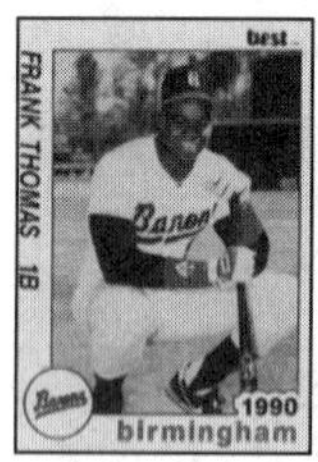

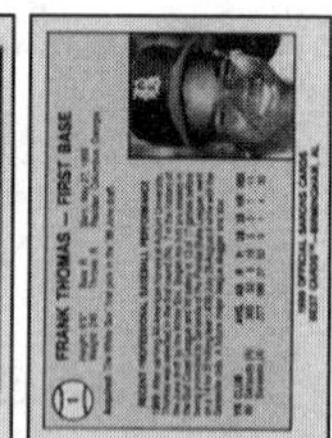

This 30-card standard-size set of the 1990 Birmingham Barons, a Class AA Southern League affiliate of the Chicago White Sox, features white-bordered posed and action color player photos on its fronts. The player's name and position appear vertically on the left side. The yellow horizontal back carries the player's name and position at the top, followed by biography, career highlights, and statistics. A player head shot appears in the lower right corner. This issue includes the minor league card debut of Frank Thomas.

	MINT	NRMT	EXC
COMPLETE SET (30)	90.00	40.00	11.00

☐ 1 Frank Thomas
☐ 2 Kurt Brown
☐ 3 Matt Merullo
☐ 4 Matt Stark
☐ 5 Tom Alfredson
☐ 6 Cesar Bernhardt
☐ 7 Edgar Caceres
☐ 8 Greg Roth
☐ 9 Cornelio Garcia
☐ 10 Derek Lee
☐ 11 Willie Magallanes
☐ 12 Rodney McCray
☐ 13 Aubrey Waggoner
☐ 14 Carlos Delacruz
☐ 15 Brian Drahman
☐ 16 Buddy Groom
☐ 17 Todd Hall
☐ 18 Roberto Hernandez
☐ 19 John Hudek
☐ 20 Bo Kennedy
☐ 21 Dave Reynolds
☐ 22 Rich Scheid
☐ 23 Ron Stephens
☐ 24 Mike Gellinger CO
☐ 25 Rick Peterson CO
☐ 26 Sam Hairston CO
☐ 27 Dave Wallwork
☐ 28 Ken Berry MGR
☐ 29 Pat Roessler CO
☐ 30 Checklist

1990 Birmingham Barons ProCards

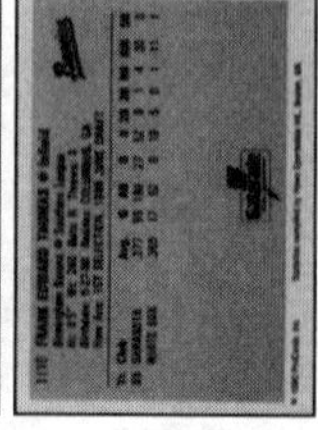

This 28-card standard-size set of the 1990 Birmingham Barons, a Class AA Southern League affiliate of the Chicago White Sox, features on its white-bordered fronts posed color player photos set on simulated wood-grain backgrounds. The player's name, position, and team appear within a gold-colored rectangle below the photo. The tan horizontal back is bordered in white and carries the player's name at the top, followed by biography and statistics. This issue includes the minor league card debut of Frank Thomas.

	MINT	NRMT	EXC
COMPLETE SET (28)	50.00	22.00	6.25

☐ 1101 Checklist
☐ 1102 Carlos Delacruz
☐ 1103 Brian Drahman
☐ 1104 Buddy Groom
☐ 1105 Todd Hall
☐ 1106 Roberto Hernandez
☐ 1107 John Hudek
☐ 1108 Bo Kennedy
☐ 1109 Dave Reynolds
☐ 1110 Rich Scheid
☐ 1111 Kurt Brown
☐ 1112 Matt Merullo
☐ 1113 Matt Stark
☐ 1114 Cesar Bernhardt
☐ 1115 Greg Roth
☐ 1116 Frank Thomas
☐ 1117 Cornelio Garcia
☐ 1118 Derek Lee
☐ 1119 Rodney McCray
☐ 1120 Aubrey Waggoner
☐ 1393 Ron Stephens
☐ 1394 Tom Alfredson
☐ 1395 Edgar Caceres
☐ 1396 Will Magallanes
☐ 1397 Ken Berry MGR
☐ 1398 Sam Hairston CO
☐ 1399 Pat Roessler CO
☐ 1400 Mike Gellinger CO

1990 Birmingham Barons All Decade Best

This 34-card standard-size set of the 1990 Birmingham Barons, a Class AA Southern League affiliate of the Chicago White Sox, features white-bordered posed and action color player photos on its fronts. The player's name and position appear vertically on the left side. The words "All Decade" appear across the top. The yellow horizontal back carries the player's name and years played at the top, followed by player's history, highlights, and statistics. 2,500 sets were produced.

	MINT	NRMT	EXC
COMPLETE SET (34)	8.00	3.60	1.00

☐ 1 Robin Ventura
☐ 2 Howard Johnson
☐ 3 Ken Berry MGR
☐ 4 Doug Baker
☐ 5 Keith Comstock
☐ 6 Ken Baker
☐ 7 Tom Drees
☐ 8 Scotty Earl
☐ 9 Wayne Edwards
☐ 10 Bruce Fields
☐ 11 Tom Forrester
☐ 12 George Foussianes
☐ 13 Barbaro Garbey
☐ 14 Paul Gibson
☐ 15 Craig Grebeck
☐ 16 Dave Gumpert
☐ 17 Don Heinkel
☐ 18 Mike Henneman
☐ 19 Ron Karkovice
☐ 20 Mike Laga
☐ 21 Roy Majtyka MGR
☐ 22 Carlos Martinez
☐ 23 Bob Melvin
☐ 24 Tony Menendez
☐ 25 Matt Merrullo
☐ 26 Donn Pall
☐ 27 Adam Peterson
☐ 28 Rico Petrocelli MGR
☐ 29 Rondall Rollin
☐ 30 Bobby Thigpen
☐ 31 Glenn Wilson
☐ 32 Mike Yastrzemski
☐ 33 Stan Younger
☐ 34 Checklist

1990 Boise Hawks ProCards

This 33-card standard-size set of the 1990 Boise Hawks, a Class A Northwest League affiliate of the California Angels, features on its white-bordered fronts posed color player photos set on simulated wood-grain backgrounds. The player's name, position, and team appear within a gold-colored rectangle below the photo. The tan horizontal back is bordered in white and carries the player's name at the top, followed by biography and statistics.

	MINT	NRMT	EXC
COMPLETE SET (33)	7.00	3.10	.85

☐ 3304 Checklist
☐ 3305 Randy Powers
☐ 3306 Phil Leftwich
☐ 3307 Todd McCray
☐ 3308 Ken Edenfield
☐ 3309 Louie Pakele
☐ 3310 Jeff Ball
☐ 3311 Hilly Hathaway
☐ 3312 Paul Swingle
☐ 3313 Darryl Scott
☐ 3314 Dan Stenz
☐ 3315 Wayne Helm
☐ 3316 Michael Search
☐ 3317 Bob Gamez
☐ 3318 Jose Santana
☐ 3319 J.R. Phillips
☐ 3320 P.J. Forbes
☐ 3321 Brian Grebeck
☐ 3322 Brian Specyalski
☐ 3323 Joe Williams
☐ 3324 Mark Dalesandro
☐ 3325 Randy Kotchman
☐ 3326 J.R. Showalter
☐ 3327 Dave Partrick
☐ 3328 Dave Staydohar
☐ 3329 Rich Shepperd
☐ 3330 Clifton Garrett
☐ 3331 Tom Kotchman MGR
☐ 3332 Orv Franchuk CO
☐ 3333 Howie Gershberg CO
☐ 3334 Fausto Tejero
☐ 3335 Troy Percival
☐ 3336 Danny Gil

1990 Bristol Tigers ProCards

This 29-card standard-size set of the 1990 Bristol Tigers, a Rookie Class Appalachian League affiliate of the Detroit Tigers, features on its white-bordered fronts posed color player photos set on simulated wood-grain backgrounds. The player's name, position, and team appear within a gold-colored rectangle below the photo. The tan horizontal back is bordered in white and carries the player's name at the top, followed by biography and statistics. This issue includes the minor league card debut of Tony Clark.

	MINT	NRMT	EXC
COMPLETE SET (29)	18.00	8.00	2.20

☐ 3148 Checklist
☐ 3149 Carlos Fermin
☐ 3150 Keith Roberts
☐ 3151 Kevin Miller
☐ 3152 Adrian Jordan
☐ 3153 Luis Hernandez
☐ 3154 Daniel Bautista
☐ 3155 Chris Hall
☐ 3156 Jose Lima
☐ 3157 Alex Ubinas
☐ 3158 Ron Maietta
☐ 3159 Greg Haeger
☐ 3160 Shannon Withem
☐ 3161 Robert Riker
☐ 3162 Daniel Cruz
☐ 3163 Brian DuBose
☐ 3164 Luis Salazar
☐ 3165 Felipe Lira
☐ 3166 Mike Guilfoyle
☐ 3167 Brian Warren
☐ 3168 Jimmy Alder
☐ 3169 Vince Bradford
☐ 3170 Paul Reinisch
☐ 3171 Jimmy Henry
☐ 3172 Brad Wilson
☐ 3173 Tony Clark
☐ 3174 Kenn Cunningham MGR
☐ 3175 Ruben Amaro CO
☐ 3176 Rich Henning CO

1990 Bristol Tigers Star

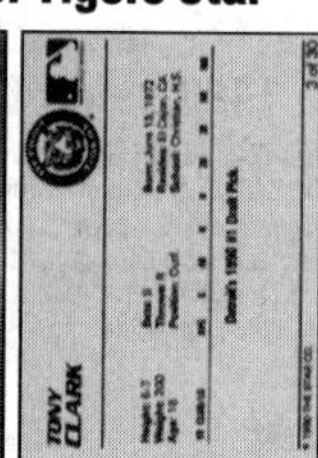

This 30-card standard-size set of the 1990 Bristol Tigers, a Rookie Class Appalachian League affiliate of the Detroit Tigers, features orange bordered posed color player photos on its fronts. The player's name, team name, and position appear at the bottom. The white horizontal back carries the player's name at the top, followed by biography, career highlights, and statistics. This issue includes the minor league card debut of Tony Clark.

	MINT	NRMT	EXC
COMPLETE SET (30)	18.00	8.00	2.20

☐ 1 Jimmy Adler
☐ 2 Vincent Bradford
☐ 3 Tony Clark
☐ 4 Danny Cruz
☐ 5 Brian DuBose
☐ 6 Carlos Fermin
☐ 7 Mike Guilfoyle
☐ 8 Greg Haeger

☐ 9 Chris Hall
☐ 10 Jimmy Henry
☐ 11 Luis Hernandez
☐ 12 Adrian Jordan
☐ 13 Dave Keating
☐ 14 Jose Lima
☐ 15 Felipe Lira
☐ 16 Ron Maietta
☐ 17 Mike Mauro
☐ 18 Kevin Miller
☐ 19 Paul Reinisch
☐ 20 Robert Riker
☐ 21 Keith Roberts
☐ 22 Luis Salazar
☐ 23 Randy Stokes
☐ 24 Alex Ubina
☐ 25 Brad Wilson
☐ 26 Shannon Withem
☐ 27 Kenn Cunningham MGR
☐ 28 Rich Henning CO
☐ 29 Steve Weber TR
☐ 30 Boyce Cox
President

1990 Buffalo Bisons CMC

This 25-card standard-size set of the 1990 Buffalo Bisons, a Class AAA American Association League affiliate of the Pittsburgh Pirates, features white-bordered posed color player photos on its fronts. The player's name and position appear at the bottom; the team name appears vertically on the left. The back carries the league emblem in the white area at the top, the team name in the green stripe below, and player's name, position, biography, and statistics in the yellow area at the bottom. 1,100 sets were produced.

	MINT	NRMT	EXC
COMPLETE SET (25)	5.00	2.20	.60

☐ 1 Stan Belinda
☐ 2 Gordon Dillard
☐ 3 Terry Collins MGR
☐ 4 Mark Huismann
☐ 5 Hugh Kemp
☐ 6 Scott Medvin
☐ 7 Vicente Palacios
☐ 8 Rick Reed
☐ 9 Mark Ross
☐ 10 Dorn Taylor
☐ 11 Mike York
☐ 12 Jeff Richardson
☐ 13 Dann Bilardello
☐ 14 Tom Prince
☐ 15 Danny Sheaffer
☐ 16 Kevin Burdick
☐ 17 Steve Kiefer
☐ 18 Orlando Merced
☐ 19 Armando Moreno
☐ 20 Mark Ryal
☐ 21 Tommy Shields
☐ 22 Steve Carter
☐ 23 Wes Chamberlain
☐ 24 Jeff Cook
☐ 25 Scott Little

1990 Buffalo Bisons ProCards

This 28-card standard-size set of the 1990 Buffalo Bisons, a Class AAA American Association League affiliate of the Pittsburgh Pirates, features on its white-bordered fronts posed color player photos set on simulated wood-grain backgrounds. The player's name, position, and team appear within a gold-colored rectangle below the photo. The tan horizontal back is bordered in white and carries the player's name at the top, followed by biography and statistics.

	MINT	NRMT	EXC
COMPLETE SET (28)	5.00	2.20	.60

☐ 364 Checklist
☐ 365 Stan Belinda
☐ 366 Gordon Dillard
☐ 367 Mark Huismann
☐ 368 Hugh Kemp
☐ 369 Scott Medvin
☐ 370 Vincente Palacios
☐ 371 Rick Reed
☐ 372 Mark Ross
☐ 373 Dorn Taylor
☐ 374 Mike York
☐ 375 Dann Bilardello
☐ 376 Tom Prince
☐ 377 Danny Sheaffer
☐ 378 Kevin Burdick
☐ 379 Steve Kiefer
☐ 380 Orlando Merced
☐ 381 Armando Moreno
☐ 382 Jeff Richardson
☐ 383 Mark Ryal
☐ 384 Tommy Shields
☐ 385 Steve Carter
☐ 386 Wes Chamberlain
☐ 387 Jeff Cook
☐ 388 Scott Little
☐ 389 Terry Collins MGR
☐ 390 Jackie Brown CO
☐ 391 Steve Henderson CO

1990 Buffalo Bisons Team Issue

	MINT	NRMT	EXC
COMPLETE SET (27)	10.00	4.50	1.25

☐ 1 Moises Alou
☐ 2 Dann Bilardello
☐ 3 Jackie Brown CO
☐ 4 Kevin Burdick
☐ 5 Steve Carter
☐ 6 Wes Chamberlain
☐ 7 Terry Collins MGR
☐ 8 Steve Henderson CO
☐ 9 Mark Huismann
☐ 10 Hugh Kemp
☐ 11 Steve Kiefer
☐ 12 Randy Kramer
☐ 13 Carlos Ledezma
☐ 14 Scott Little
☐ 15 Roger Mason
☐ 16 Orlando Merced
☐ 17 Armando Moreno
☐ 18 Vicente Palacios
☐ 19 Tom Prince
☐ 20 Jeff Richardson
☐ 21 Mike Roesler
☐ 22 Mark Ross
☐ 23 Mark Ryal
☐ 24 Dan Sheaffer
☐ 25 Tommy Shields
☐ 26 Dorn Taylor
☐ 27 Mike York

1990 Burlington Braves Best

This 30-card standard-size set of the 1990 Burlington Braves, a Class A Midwest League affiliate of the Atlanta Braves, features white-bordered posed and action color player photos on its fronts. The player's name and position appear vertically on the left side. The yellow horizontal back carries the player's name and position at the top, followed by biography, career highlights, and statistics. A player head shot appears in the lower right corner. This issue includes a second year card of Javy Lopez.

	MINT	NRMT	EXC
COMPLETE SET (30)	16.00	7.25	2.00

☐ 1 Pedro Borbon Jr.
☐ 2 Matt Murray
☐ 3 Glen Gardner
☐ 4 Ramon Caraballo
☐ 5 Tom Bruck
☐ 6 Oswaldo Apolinario
☐ 7 Dave Reis
☐ 8 Tony Valle
☐ 9 Steve Swail
☐ 10 Jeff Calderone
☐ 11 Roberto Deleon
☐ 12 Eddie Watt CO
☐ 13 Tim Gillis
☐ 14 Walt Roy
☐ 15 Dickey Marze
☐ 16 Jeff Clark
☐ 17 Paul Reis
☐ 18 Scott Grove
☐ 19 Tony Baldwin
☐ 20 Javy Lopez
☐ 21 Kevin Kelly
☐ 22 Greg Harper
☐ 23 Daryl Blanks
☐ 24 Randy Simmons
☐ 25 Darren Ritter
☐ 26 Rod Byerly
☐ 27 Brent McCoy
☐ 28 Jim Saul MGR
☐ 29 Gene Lane TR
☐ 30 Checklist

1990 Burlington Braves ProCards

This 30-card standard-size set of the 1990 Burlington Braves, a Class A Midwest League affiliate of the Atlanta Braves, features on its white-bordered fronts posed color player photos set on simulated wood-grain backgrounds. The player's name, position, and team appear within a gold-colored rectangle below the photo. The tan horizontal back is bordered in white and carries the player's name at the top, followed by biography and statistics. This issue includes a second year card of Javy Lopez.

	MINT	NRMT	EXC
COMPLETE SET (30)	14.00	6.25	1.75

☐ 2339 Checklist
☐ 2340 Pedro Borbon Jr.
☐ 2341 Tom Bruck
☐ 2342 Rod Byerly
☐ 2343 Jeff Calderone
☐ 2344 Scott Grove
☐ 2345 Kevin Kelly
☐ 2346 Matt Murray
☐ 2347 Dave Reis
☐ 2348 Darren Ritter
☐ 2349 Walt Roy
☐ 2350 Tony Valle
☐ 2351 Roberto Deleon
☐ 2352 Javier Lopez
☐ 2353 Steve Swail
☐ 2354 Oswaldo Apolinario
☐ 2355 Glen Gardner
☐ 2356 Tim Gillis
☐ 2357 Dickey Marze
☐ 2358 Brent McCoy
☐ 2359 Paulo Reis
☐ 2360 Ramon Caraballo
☐ 2361 Tony Baldwin
☐ 2362 Daryl Blanks
☐ 2363 Jeff Clark
☐ 2364 Randy Simmons
☐ 2365 Jim Saul MGR
☐ 2366 Gil Garrido CO
☐ 2367 Eddie Watt CO
☐ 2368 Phillip Wellman CO

1990 Burlington Braves Star

This 31-card standard-size set of the 1990 Burlington Braves, a Class A Midwest League affiliate of the Atlanta Braves, features red bordered posed color player photos on its fronts. The player's name, team name, and position appear at the bottom. The white horizontal back carries the player's name at the top, followed by biography, career highlights, and statistics. This issue includes a second year card of Javy Lopez.

	MINT	NRMT	EXC
COMPLETE SET (31)	16.00	7.25	2.00

☐ 1 Oswaldo Apolinario
☐ 2 Tony Baldwin
☐ 3 Daryl Blanks
☐ 4 Pedro Borbon Jr.
☐ 5 Tom Bruck
☐ 6 Rodney Byerly
☐ 7 Jeff Calderone
☐ 8 Ramon Caraballo
☐ 9 Jeff Clark
☐ 10 Roberto Deleon
☐ 11 Glen Gardner
☐ 12 Tim Gillis
☐ 13 Scott Grove
☐ 14 Greg Harper
☐ 15 Kevin Kelly
☐ 16 Javy Lopez
☐ 17 Dickey Marze
☐ 18 Brent McCoy
☐ 19 Matt Murray
☐ 20 Dave Reis
☐ 21 Paul Reis
☐ 22 Daren Ritter
☐ 23 Walt Roy
☐ 24 Randy Simmons
☐ 25 Steve Swail
☐ 26 Tony Valle
☐ 27 Jim Saul MGR
☐ 28 Gil Garrido CO
☐ 29 Eddie Watt CO
☐ 30 Phil Wellman CO
☐ 31 Gene Lane TR

1990 Burlington Indians ProCards

This 28-card standard-size set of the 1990 Burlington Indians, a Rookie Class Appalachian League affiliate of the Cleveland Indians, features on its white-bordered fronts posed color player photos set on simulated wood-grain backgrounds. The player's name, position, and team appear within a gold-colored rectangle below the photo. The tan horizontal back is bordered in white and carries the player's name at the top, followed by biography and statistics. This issue includes the minor league card debut of Jim Thome.

	MINT	NRMT	EXC
COMPLETE SET (28)	30.00	13.50	3.70

☐ 3000 Checklist
☐ 3001 Sam Baker
☐ 3002 Dickie Brown
☐ 3003 Shawn Bryant
☐ 3004 Alan Embree
☐ 3005 Steve Gajkowski
☐ 3006 Carl Johnson
☐ 3007 Shawn McElfish
☐ 3008 Tony Tillman
☐ 3009 Alan Walden
☐ 3010 Von Wechsberg
☐ 3011 Roberto Jimenez
☐ 3012 John Martinez
☐ 3013 Miguel Flores
☐ 3014 Matt Gilmore
☐ 3015 Frank Monastro
☐ 3016 Mike Pinckes
☐ 3017 Tim Thomas
☐ 3018 Jim Thome
☐ 3019 Jeff Brohm
☐ 3020 Sam Hence
☐ 3021 Pedro Henderson
☐ 3022 Ramon Ortiz
☐ 3023 Tracy Sanders
☐ 3024 Ramon Torres
☐ 3025 Darrell Whitmore
☐ 3026 David Keller
☐ 3027 Stan Hilton

1990 Butte Copper Kings Sports Pro

This 30-card standard-size set of the 1990 Butte Copper Kings, a Rookie Class A Pioneer League affiliate of the Texas Rangers, features posed color head-and-shoulders shots, with thin black borders on a white card face. The horizontally oriented backs have biographical information. This issue includes the minor league card debut of Rusty Greer.

	MINT	NRMT	EXC
COMPLETE SET (30)	15.00	6.75	1.85

☐ 1 Rodney Busha
☐ 2 Greg Blevins
☐ 3 Miguel Castellano
☐ 4 Rusty Greer
☐ 5 Terry Burrows
☐ 6 Gary Posey
☐ 7 Dan Smith
☐ 8 David Hulse
☐ 9 Jose Cardona
☐ 10 Steve Dreyer
Sic, Dryer
☐ 11 Paul Matachun
☐ 12 Malvin Matos
☐ 13 Scott Erickson
☐ 14 Shane Patterson
☐ 15 Brian Mercado
☐ 16 Keith Murray
☐ 17 Steve Ramharter
☐ 18 Bobby St. Pe
☐ 19 Brian Scheetz
☐ 20 Victor Reyes
☐ 21 Brian Mouton
☐ 22 Chris Geis
☐ 23 Steve Surico
☐ 24 Shannon Penn
☐ 25 Tyrone Washington
☐ 26 Jon Shave
☐ 27 Andy Watson
☐ 28 Tim Wells
☐ 29 Matt Whiteside
☐ 30 Todd Guggiana

1990 California League All-Stars Cal League Cards

	MINT	NRMT	EXC
COMPLETE SET (56)	8.00	3.60	1.00

☐ 1 Dave Staton
☐ 2 Brett Magnusson
☐ 3 John Deutsch
☐ 4 Jose Garcia
☐ 5 Vince Harris
☐ 6 Jim Edmonds
☐ 7 Steve Hendricks
☐ 8 Tim Barker
☐ 9 Carlos Capellan
☐ 10 Darrell Sherman
☐ 11 Frank Bolick
☐ 12 Chris Morrow
☐ 13 J.T. Bruett
☐ 14 Matt Howard
☐ 15 Troy Buckley
☐ 16 George Tsamis
☐ 17 Jason Brosnan
☐ 18 Rich Garces
☐ 19 Kerry Woodson
☐ 20 Kiki Jones
☐ 21 Roger Salkeld
☐ 22 Jamie McAndrew
☐ 23 Jim Newlin
☐ 24 Denny Neagle
☐ 25 Scott Ullger MGR
☐ 26 Brian Allard
☐ 27 Joe Gaglairdi PRES
☐ 28 Sal Artiaga COMM
☐ 29 Chris Bando MGR
☐ 30 Mitch Zwolensky
☐ 31 John Levenda ADMIN ,
Bill Weiss STAT
☐ 32 Kevin Dykstra UMP
☐ 33 Bob Brooks UMP
☐ 34 Brian Laxamana UMP
☐ 35 Brent Howard UMP
☐ 36 Pat Listach
☐ 37 Scooter Tucker
☐ 38 Bo Dodson
☐ 39 Tom Eiterman
☐ 40 Dan Lewis
☐ 41 Chris Cassels
☐ 42 Dwayne Hosey
☐ 43 Ron Witmeyer
☐ 44 Shikato Yanagida
☐ 45 Reuben Smiley
☐ 46 Mike Sarbaugh
☐ 47 Adell Davenport
☐ 48 Bob Kappesser
☐ 49 Royce Clayton

☐ 50 Kevin Rogers
☐ 51 Angel Miranda
☐ 52 Mike Soper
☐ 53 Dan Rambo
☐ 54 Dave Fitzgerald
☐ 55 Cecil Pettiford
☐ 56 Chris Johnson

1990 Calgary Cannons CMC

This 25-card standard-size set of the 1990 Calgary Cannons, a Class AAA Pacific Coast League affiliate of the Seattle Mariners, features white-bordered posed color player photos on its fronts. The player's name and position appear at the bottom; the team name appears vertically on the left. The back carries the league emblem in the white area at the top, the team name in the green stripe below, and player's name, position, biography, and statistics in the yellow area at the bottom. 1,100 sets were produced.

	MINT	NRMT	EXC
COMPLETE SET (25)	12.00	5.50	1.50

☐ 1 Pat Pacillo
☐ 2 Tony Blasucci
☐ 3 Mike Walker
☐ 4 Pat Rice
☐ 5 Terry Taylor
☐ 6 Dave Burba
☐ 7 Vance Lovelace
☐ 8 Ed Vande Berg
☐ 9 Greg Fulton
☐ 10 Ed Jurak
☐ 11 Dave Cochrane
☐ 12 Tino Martinez
☐ 13 Matt Sinatro
☐ 14 Bill McGuire
☐ 15 Mickey Brantley
☐ 16 Tom Dodd
☐ 17 Jim Weaver
☐ 18 Todd Haney
☐ 19 Casey Close
☐ 20 Theo Shaw
☐ 21 Keith Helton
☐ 22 Jose Melendez
☐ 23 Tom Jones MG
☐ 24 Dan Warthen CO
☐ 25 Randy Roetter TR

1990 Calgary Cannons ProCards

This 23-card standard-size set of the 1990 Calgary Cannons, a Class AAA Pacific Coast League affiliate of the Seattle Mariners, features on its white-bordered fronts posed color player photos set on simulated wood-grain backgrounds. The player's name, position, and team appear within a gold-colored rectangle below the photo. The tan horizontal back is bordered in white and carries the player's name at the top, followed by biography and statistics.

	MINT	NRMT	EXC
COMPLETE SET (23)	7.00	3.10	.85

☐ 643 Checklist
☐ 644 Tony Blasucci
☐ 645 Dave Burba
☐ 646 Keith Helton
☐ 647 Vance Lovelace
☐ 648 Jose Melendez
☐ 649 Pat Pacillo
☐ 650 Pat Rice
☐ 651 Terry Taylor
☐ 652 Mike Walker
☐ 653 Bill McGuire
☐ 654 Matt Sinatro
☐ 655 Mario Diaz
☐ 656 Greg Fulton
☐ 657 Todd Haney
☐ 658 Ed Jurak
☐ 659 Tino Martinez
☐ 660 Jeff Schaefer
☐ 661 Casey Close
☐ 662 Tom Dodd
☐ 663 Jim Weaver
☐ 664 Tommy Jones MG
☐ 665 Dan Warthen CO

1990 Canton-Akron Indians Best

This 28-card standard-size set of the 1990 Canton-Akron Indians, a Class AA Eastern League affiliate of the Cleveland Indians, features white-bordered posed and action color player photos on its fronts. The player's name and position appear vertically on the left side. The yellow horizontal back carries the player's name and position at the top, followed by biography, career highlights, and statistics. A player head shot appears in the lower right corner.

	MINT	NRMT	EXC
COMPLETE SET (28)	12.00	5.50	1.50

☐ 1 Mark Lewis
☐ 2 Will George CO
☐ 3 Lee Kuntz
☐ 4 Ken Bolek MGR
☐ 5 Darren Epley
☐ 6 Allen Liebert
☐ 7 Sam Ferretti
☐ 8 Manny Francois
☐ 9 Jim Orsag
☐ 10 Joe Kesselmark
☐ 11 Rob Swain
☐ 12 Jim Tatum
☐ 13 Lee Jackson
☐ 14 Delwyn Young
☐ 15 Miguel Sabino
☐ 16 Francisco Melendez
☐ 17 Rob Wine
☐ 18 Jim Bruske
☐ 19 Jeff Fassero
☐ 20 Bruce Egloff
☐ 21 Carl Keliipuleole
☐ 22 Jeff Mutis
☐ 23 Greg Roscoe
☐ 24 Rudy Seanez
☐ 25 Allen Collins
☐ 26 Mike Curtis
☐ 27 Charles Nagy
☐ 28 Checklist

1990 Canton-Akron Indians ProCards

This 27-card standard-size set of the 1990 Canton-Akron Indians, a Class AA Eastern League affiliate of the Cleveland Indians, features on its white-bordered fronts posed color player photos set on simulated wood-grain backgrounds. The player's name, position, and team appear within a gold-colored rectangle below the photo. The tan horizontal back is bordered in white and carries the player's name at the top, followed by biography and statistics.

	MINT	NRMT	EXC
COMPLETE SET (27)	8.00	3.60	1.00

☐ 1284 Checklist
☐ 1285 Jim Bruske
☐ 1286 Allen Collins
☐ 1287 Mike Curtis
☐ 1288 Bruce Egloff
☐ 1289 Jeff Fassero
☐ 1290 Carl Keliipuleole
☐ 1291 Jeff Mutis
☐ 1292 Charles Nagy
☐ 1293 Rudy Seanez
☐ 1294 Al Liebert
☐ 1295 Robbie Wine
☐ 1296 Daren Epley
☐ 1297 Sam Ferretti
☐ 1298 Manny Francois
☐ 1299 Mark Lewis
☐ 1300 Francisco Melendez
☐ 1301 Rob Swain
☐ 1302 Jimmy Tatum
☐ 1303 Leverne Jackson
☐ 1304 Joe Kesselmark
☐ 1305 Miguel Sabino
☐ 1306 Delwyn Young
☐ 1307 Roberto Zambrano
☐ 1308 Greg Roscoe
☐ 1309 Ken Bolek MGR
☐ 1363 Will George CO

1990 Canton-Akron Indians Star

This 21-card standard-size set of the 1990 Canton-Akron Indians, a Class AA Eastern League affiliate of the Cleveland Indians, features light purple bordered posed color player photos on its fronts. The player's name, team name, and position appear at the bottom. The white horizontal back carries the player's name at the top, followed by biography, career highlights, and statistics.

	MINT	NRMT	EXC
COMPLETE SET (21)	12.00	5.50	1.50

☐ 1 Jim Bruske
☐ 2 Allen Collins
☐ 3 Mike Curtis
☐ 4 Darren Epley
☐ 5 Jeff Fassero
☐ 6 Sam Ferretti
☐ 7 Jason Jackson
☐ 8 Carl Keliipuleole
☐ 9 Mark Lewis
☐ 10 Allen Leibert
☐ 11 Gregory McMichael
☐ 12 Francisco Melendez
☐ 13 Jeff Mutis
☐ 14 Charles Nagy
☐ 15 Greg Roscoe
☐ 16 Miguel Sabino
☐ 17 Casey Webster
☐ 18 Delwyn Young
☐ 19 Roberto Zambrano
☐ 20 Ken Bolek MGR
☐ 21 Lee Kuntz TR

1990 Carolina League All-Stars

	MINT	NRMT	EXC
COMPLETE SET (52)	7.00	3.10	.85

☐ 1 Zachary Kerr
☐ 2 Mike Oquist
☐ 3 Todd Stephan
☐ 4 Ricky Gutierrez
☐ 5 Tim Holland
☐ 6 Dan Berthel
☐ 7 Wally Moon MGR
☐ 8 Bill Murray TR
☐ 9 Brian Conroy
☐ 10 Freddie Davis
☐ 11 Paul Williams
☐ 12 Greg Blosser
☐ 13 James Byrd
☐ 14 Frank Seminara
☐ 15 Mike Gardella
☐ 16 Maurico Zazueta
☐ 17 J.T. Snow
☐ 18 Russ Davis
☐ 19 Gary Denbo
☐ 20 Mike Pomeranz
☐ 21 Mandy Romero
☐ 22 Mike Huyler
☐ 23 Bruce Schreiber
☐ 24 Darwin Pennye
☐ 25 Chris Estep
☐ 26 Paul Miller
☐ 27 Skipper Wright
☐ 28 Mike Mordecai
☐ 29 Keith Mitchell
☐ 30 Popeye Cole
☐ 31 Brian Champion
☐ 32 Brian Graham MGR
☐ 33 Dennis Noonan TR
☐ 34 Ty Kovach
☐ 35 Greg Ferlenda
☐ 36 Jerry DiPoto
☐ 37 Garland Kiser
☐ 38 Tommy Kramer
☐ 39 Jesse Levis
☐ 40 Brian Johnson
☐ 41 Rouglas Odor
☐ 42 Nolan Lane
☐ 43 Ken Ramos
☐ 44 Lem Pilkinton
☐ 45 Rick Balabon
☐ 46 Shannon Jones
☐ 47 John Salles
☐ 48 Elvin Paulino
☐ 49 Gary Scott
☐ 50 Billy White
☐ 51 Brad Mills CO
☐ 52 Steve DiBartolomeo

1990 Cedar Rapids Reds All Decade Best

This 36-card standard-size set of the 1990 Cedar Rapids Reds, a Class A Midwest League affiliate of the Cincinnati Reds, features white-bordered posed and action color player photos on its fronts. The player's name and position appear vertically on the left side. The words "All Decade" appear across the top. The yellow horizontal back carries the player's name and years played at the top, followed by player's history, highlights, and statistics. 2,500 sets were produced.

	MINT	NRMT	EXC
COMPLETE SET (36)	7.00	3.10	.85

☐ 1 Eric Davis
☐ 2 Kal Daniels
☐ 3 Lenny Harris
☐ 4 Chris Sabo
☐ 5 Paul O'Neill
☐ 6 Kurt Stillwell
☐ 7 Scott Terry
☐ 8 Joe Oliver
☐ 9 Reggie Jefferson
☐ 10 Eddie Williams
☐ 11 Eddie Taubensee
☐ 12 Keith Lockhart
☐ 13 Rob Murphy
☐ 14 Ron Robinson
☐ 15 Scott Scudder
☐ 16 Rob Dibble
☐ 17 Ron Henika
☐ 18 Adam Casillas
☐ 19 Jeff Jones
☐ 20 Jeff Branson
☐ 21 Brad Lesley
☐ 22 Phil Dale
☐ 23 Butch Henry
☐ 24 Rosario Rodriquez
☐ 25 Ray Corbett
☐ 26 Eski Viltz
☐ 27 Bruce Kimm MGR
☐ 28 Marc Bombard MGR
☐ 29 Marty Brown
☐ 30 Scott Bryant
☐ 31 Ross Powell
☐ 32 Keith Brown
☐ 33 Dan Boever
☐ 34 Don Buchheister GM
☐ 35 Lamar
Mascot
☐ 36 Checklist

1990 Cedar Rapids Reds Best

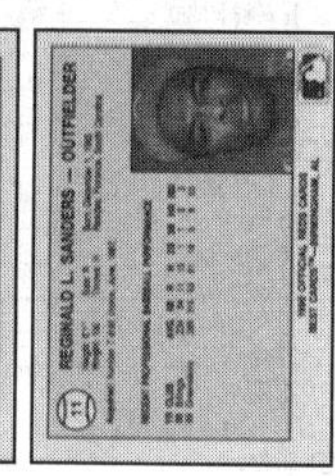

This 27-card standard-size set of the 1990 Cedar Rapids Reds, a Class A Midwest League affiliate of the Cincinnati Reds, features white-bordered posed and action color player photos on its fronts. The player's name and position appear vertically on the left side. The yellow horizontal back carries the player's name and position at the top, followed by biography, career highlights, and statistics. A player head shot appears in the lower right corner.

	MINT	NRMT	EXC
COMPLETE SET (27)	8.00	3.60	1.00

☐ 1 Scott Bryant
☐ 2 Glenn Sutko
☐ 3 Edward Taubensee
☐ 4 Vicente Javier
☐ 5 Terry Abbott CO
☐ 6 Edward Rush
☐ 7 Michael Mulvaney
☐ 8 Richard Allen
☐ 9 Lavell Cudjo
☐ 10 Anthony Terzarial
☐ 11 Reginald Sanders
☐ 12 Mark Krumback
☐ 13 Tom Spencer
☐ 14 William Risley
☐ 15 Robert Ayala
☐ 16 Victoriano Garcia
☐ 17 Ramon Manon
☐ 18 Joseph Turek
☐ 19 Dave Miley MGR
☐ 20 Michael Anderson
☐ 21 Douglas King
☐ 22 David McAuliffe
☐ 23 Meredith Sanford Jr.
☐ 24 Mark Borcherding
☐ 25 Scott Jeffery
☐ 26 Steve Hester
☐ 27 Checklist
Howard James GM

1990 Cedar Rapids Reds ProCards

This 27-card standard-size set of the 1990 Cedar Rapids Reds, a Class A Midwest League affiliate of the Cincinnati Reds, features on its white-bordered fronts posed color player photos set on simulated wood-grain backgrounds. The player's name, position, and team appear within a gold-colored rectangle below the photo. The tan horizontal back is bordered in white and carries the player's name at the top, followed by biography and statistics.

	MINT	NRMT	EXC
COMPLETE SET (27)	7.00	3.10	.85

☐ 2312 Checklist
☐ 2313 Bill Risley
☐ 2314 Bobby Ayala
☐ 2315 Victor Garcia
☐ 2316 Ramon Manon
☐ 2317 Scott Economy
☐ 2318 Mike Anderson
☐ 2319 Steve McCarthy
☐ 2320 Dave McAuliffe
☐ 2321 Mo Sanford
☐ 2322 Jerry Spradlin
☐ 2323 Steve Hester
☐ 2324 Frank Kremblas
☐ 2325 Eddie Taubensee
☐ 2326 Brian Nichols
☐ 2327 Vicente Javier
☐ 2328 Bob Dombrowski
☐ 2329 Eddie Rush
☐ 2330 Mike Mulvaney
☐ 2331 Rick Allen
☐ 2332 Lavell Cudjo
☐ 2333 Tony Terzarial
☐ 2334 Reggie Sanders
☐ 2335 Mark Krumback
☐ 2336 Scott Bryant
☐ 2337 Dave Miley MGR
☐ 2338 Terry Abbott CO

1990 Charleston Rainbows Best

This 28-card standard-size set of the 1990 Charleston Rainbows, a Class A South Atlantic League affiliate of the San Diego Padres, features white-bordered posed and action color player photos on its fronts. The player's name and position appear vertically on the left side. The yellow horizontal back carries the player's name and position at the top, followed by biography, career highlights, and statistics. A player head shot appears in the lower right corner.

	MINT	NRMT	EXC
COMPLETE SET (28)	5.00	2.20	.60

☐ 1 Russ Garside
☐ 2 Lance Banks
☐ 3 Jeff Barton
☐ 4 Brian Beck
☐ 5 Julio Bruno
☐ 6 Rico Coleman
☐ 7 Troy Cunningham
☐ 8 Bob Curnow
☐ 9 Roberto Arredono
☐ 10 Pedro Guzman
☐ 11 Lee Henderson
☐ 12 Bill Johnson
☐ 13 Pedro Lopez
☐ 14 Pablo Martinez
☐ 15 Jose Mateo
☐ 16 William Marx
☐ 17 Joe Murdock
☐ 18 Danny Pickett
☐ 19 Craig Pueschner
☐ 20 Rafael Santiago
☐ 21 Charles Thompson
☐ 22 William Thompson
☐ 23 Ed Zinter
☐ 24 John Maxwell
☐ 25 Mark Littell CO
☐ 26 Jack Krol MGR
☐ 27 Jimmy Lester CO
☐ 28 Checklist

1990 Charleston Rainbows ProCards

This 28-card standard-size set of the 1990 Charleston Rainbows, a Class A South Atlantic League affiliate of the San Diego Padres, features on its white-bordered fronts posed color player photos set on simulated wood-grain backgrounds. The player's name, position, and team appear within a gold-colored rectangle below the photo. The tan horizontal back is bordered in white and carries the player's name at the top, followed by biography and statistics.

	MINT	NRMT	EXC
COMPLETE SET (28)	5.00	2.20	.60

☐ 2029 Checklist
☐ 2030 Squeezer Thompson
☐ 2031 Rafael Santiago
☐ 2032 Lance Banks
☐ 2033 Danny Pickett
☐ 2034 Troy Cunningham
☐ 2035 Charles Thompson
☐ 2036 Joe Murdock
☐ 2037 Pete Guzman
☐ 2038 Russ Garside
☐ 2039 Ed Zinter
☐ 2040 Bill Johnson
☐ 2041 Lee Henderson
☐ 2042 Rob Curnow
☐ 2043 Pedro Lopez
☐ 2044 Pablo Martinez
☐ 2045 Roberto Arredondo
☐ 2046 Julio Bruno
☐ 2047 Jose Mateo
☐ 2048 Monte Brooks
☐ 2049 Scott Bream
☐ 2050 Brian Beck
☐ 2051 Jeff Barton
☐ 2052 Craig Pueschner
☐ 2053 Rico Coleman
☐ 2054 Jack Krol MGR
☐ 2055 Mark Littell CO
☐ 2056 Jimmy Lester CO

1990 Charleston Wheelers Best

This 29-card standard-size set of the 1990 Charleston Wheelers, a Class A South Atlantic League affiliate of the Cincinnati Reds, features white-bordered posed and action color player photos on its fronts. The player's name and position appear vertically on the left side. The yellow horizontal back carries the player's name and position at the top, followed by biography, career highlights, and statistics. A player head shot appears in the lower right corner.

	MINT	NRMT	EXC
COMPLETE SET (29)	7.00	3.10	.85

☐ 1 Darron Cox
☐ 2 Chris Hook
☐ 3 Mike Malley
☐ 4 Steve McCarthy
☐ 5 Ernie Nieves
☐ 6 Scott Pelmmons
☐ 7 Tim Pugh
☐ 8 Johnny Ray
☐ 9 Jason Satre
☐ 10 Jerry Spradlin
☐ 11 Trey Wilburn
☐ 12 Timothy Cecil
☐ 13 Brian Nichols
☐ 14 Raphael Bustamante
☐ 15 Chris Gill
☐ 16 Trevor Hoffman
☐ 17 Kevin Jones
☐ 18 Noel Velez
☐ 19 Todd Watson
☐ 20 Mark Arland
☐ 21 Jack Hollis
☐ 22 Eugene Jones
☐ 23 Danny Perozo
☐ 24 Scott Pose
☐ 25 Mary Berry CO
☐ 26 Jim Lett MGR
☐ 27 Mike Griffin CO
☐ 28 Tom Iverson TR
☐ 29 Checklist

1990 Charleston Wheelers ProCards

This 28-card standard-size set of the 1990 Charleston Wheelers, a Class A South Atlantic League affiliate of the Cincinnati Reds, features on its white-bordered fronts posed color player photos set on simulated wood-grain backgrounds. The player's name, position, and team appear within a gold-colored rectangle below the photo. The tan horizontal back is bordered in white and carries the player's name at the top, followed by biography and statistics.

	MINT	NRMT	EXC
COMPLETE SET (28)	6.00	2.70	.75

☐ 2231 Checklist
☐ 2232 Mark Borcherding
☐ 2233 Tim Cecil
☐ 2234 Chris Hook
☐ 2235 Doug King
☐ 2236 Mike Malley
☐ 2237 Ernesto Nieves
☐ 2238 Scott Plemmons
☐ 2239 Tim Pugh
☐ 2240 Johnny Ray
☐ 2241 Jason Satre
☐ 2242 Trey Wilburn
☐ 2243 Darron Cox
☐ 2244 Jon Fuller
☐ 2245 Rafael Bustamante
☐ 2246 Chris Gill
☐ 2247 Trevor Hoffman
☐ 2248 Noel Velez
☐ 2249 Todd Watson
☐ 2250 Mark Arland
☐ 2251 K.C. Gillum
☐ 2252 Jack Hollis
☐ 2253 Eugene Jones
☐ 2254 Danny Perozo
☐ 2255 Scott Pose
☐ 2256 Mark Berry
Player/Coach
☐ 2257 Jim Lett MGR
☐ 2258 Mike Griffin CO

1990 Charlotte Knights Team Issue

	MINT	NRMT	EXC
COMPLETE SET (25)	8.00	3.60	1.00

☐ 1 Lance Dickson
☐ 2 Phil Hannon
☐ 3 Dick Canan
☐ 4 Darrin Duffy
☐ 5 Alex Arias
☐ 6 Heathcliff Slocumb
☐ 7 Chico Walker
☐ 8 John Posey
☐ 9 John Stefaro
☐ 10 Butch Garcia
☐ 11 Glenn Sullivan
☐ 12 Fernando Zarranz
☐ 13 Bill Kazmierczak
☐ 14 Ty Griffin
☐ 15 Ray Mullino
☐ 16 Jay Loviglio
☐ 17 Brett Robinson
☐ 18 Chuck Mount
☐ 19 Tommy Helms MG
☐ 20 Frank Castillo
☐ 21 Rusty Crockett
☐ 22 Rick Wilkins
☐ 23 Richie Grayum
☐ 24 Bob Grimes TR
☐ 25 Rick Kranitz CO

1990 Charlotte Rangers Star

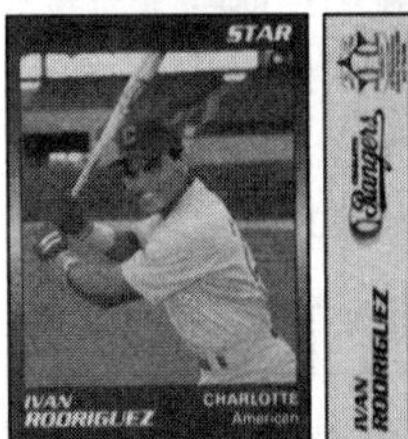

This 30-card standard-size set of the 1990 Charlotte Rangers, a Class A Florida State League affiliate of the Texas Rangers, features blue bordered posed color player photos on its fronts. The player's name, team name, and position appear at the bottom. The white horizontal back carries the player's name at the top, followed by biography, career highlights, and statistics.This issue includes a second year card of Ivan Rodriguez.

	MINT	NRMT	EXC
COMPLETE SET (30)	18.00	8.00	2.20

☐ 1 Gerald Alexander
☐ 2 Rob Brown
☐ 3 Cris Colon
☐ 4 Fidel Compres
☐ 5 Doug Cronk
☐ 6 Everett Cunningham
☐ 7 Jeff Frye
☐ 8 Bryan Gore
☐ 9 Daren Hays
☐ 10 Jose Hernandez
☐ 11 Jim Hvizda
☐ 12 Barry Manuel
☐ 13 Trey McCoy
☐ 14 Rod Morris
☐ 15 Robb Nen
☐ 16 Darren Niethammer
☐ 17 Darren Oliver
☐ 18 Jeff Oller
☐ 19 Roger Pavlik
☐ 20 Jack Peel
☐ 21 David Perez
☐ 22 Ivan Rodriguez
☐ 23 Bill Losa
☐ 24 Steve Rowley
☐ 25 Luke Sable
☐ 26 Fred Samson
☐ 27 Kyle Spencer
☐ 28 Thayer Swain
☐ 29 Bobby Jones MGR
☐ 30 Jeff Hubbard CO

1990 Chattanooga Lookouts Grand Slam

	MINT	NRMT	EXC
COMPLETE SET (27)	5.00	2.20	.60

☐ 1 Jim Tracy MG
☐ 2 Don Gullett CO
☐ 3 Gregg Grain TR
☐ 4 Doug Banning
☐ 5 Freddie Benavides
☐ 6 Jeff Branson
☐ 7 Joe Bruno
☐ 8 Adam Cassillas
☐ 9 Ben Colvard
☐ 10 Tony DeFrancesco
☐ 11 Bill Dodd
☐ 12 Brian Lee Finley
☐ 13 Jeff Forney
☐ 14 Steve Foster
☐ 15 Alan Hayden
☐ 16 Butch Henry
☐ 17 Keith Kaiser
☐ 18 Joe Lazor
☐ 19 Terry Lee
☐ 20 Greg Lonigro
☐ 21 Gino Minutelli
☐ 22 Mike Moscrey
☐ 23 Jerome Nelson
☐ 24 Ross Powell
☐ 25 Rosario Rodriguez
☐ 26 Melvin Rosario
☐ 27 Scott Sellner

1990 Classic Draft Picks

The 1990 Classic Draft Pick set is a standard-size 25-card set honoring the number one (first round) draft picks of 1990. According to the producer, the printing on this set was limited to 150,000 of each card. This was the first Classic set that was not a game set or trivia set. Card numbers 2 and 22 were not issued.

	MINT	NRMT	EXC
COMPLETE SET (25)	10.00	4.50	1.25
COMMON CARD (1-25)	.10	.05	.01
☐ 1 Chipper Jones	3.00	1.35	.35
☐ 3 Mike Lieberthal	.25	.11	.03

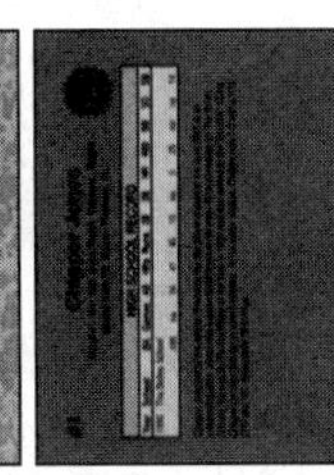

	MINT	NRMT	EXC
☐ 4 Alex Fernandez	.75	.35	.09
☐ 5 Kurt Miller	.10	.05	.01
☐ 6 Marc Newfield UER	.40	.18	.05
☐ 7 Dan Wilson	.20	.09	.03
☐ 8 Tim Costo	.10	.05	.01
☐ 9 Ron Walden	.10	.05	.01
☐ 10 Carl Everett UER Evertt	.20	.09	.03
☐ 11 Shane Andrews	.20	.09	.03
☐ 12 Todd Ritchie	.10	.05	.01
☐ 13 Donovan Osborne	.20	.09	.03
☐ 14 Todd Van Poppel	.10	.05	.01
☐ 15 Adam Hyzdu	.10	.05	.01
☐ 16 Dan Smith	.10	.05	.01
☐ 17 Jeromy Burnitz	.20	.09	.03
☐ 18 Aaron Holbert	.10	.05	.01
☐ 19 Eric Christopherson	.10	.05	.01
☐ 20 Mike Mussina	2.00	.90	.25
☐ 21 Tom Nevers	.10	.05	.01
☐ 23 Lance Dickson	.10	.05	.01
☐ 24 Rondell White	1.00	.45	.12
☐ 25 Robbie Beckett	.10	.05	.01
☐ 26 Don Peters	.10	.05	.01
☐ NNO Chipper Jones CL Rondell White CL	1.50	.70	.19

1990 Clearwater Phillies Star

This 27-card standard-size set of the 1990 Clearwater Phillies; a Class A Florida State League affiliate of the Philadelphia Phillies, features red bordered posed color player photos on its fronts. The player's name, team name, and position appear at the bottom. The white horizontal back carries the player's name at the top, followed by biography, career highlights, and statistics.

	MINT	NRMT	EXC
COMPLETE SET (27)	5.00	2.20	.60

☐ 1 Jimmy Barragan
☐ 2 Toby Borland
☐ 3 Cliff Brantley
☐ 4 Andy Carter
☐ 5 Tim Dell
☐ 6 Todd Elam
☐ 7 Kevin Fynan
☐ 8 Jeff Hulse
☐ 9 Kennedy Infante
☐ 10 Lee Langley
☐ 11 Darrell Lindsey
☐ 12 Tony Lozinski
☐ 13 Greg McCarthy
☐ 14 Terry McDevitt
☐ 15 Shelby McDonald
☐ 16 Joe Millette
☐ 17 Jeff Patterson
☐ 18 Mark Randall
☐ 19 Ed Rosado
☐ 20 Steve Scarsone
☐ 21 Joe Tenhunfeld
☐ 22 Tony Trevino
☐ 23 Leroy Ventress
☐ 24 Cary Williams
☐ 25 Pat Woodruff
☐ 26 Lee Elia MGR
☐ 27 Coaches
Al LeBoeuf
John Martin

1990 Clinton Giants Best

This 29-card standard-size set of the 1990 Clinton Giants, a Class A Midwest League affiliate of the San Francisco Giants, features white-bordered posed and action color player photos on its fronts. The player's name and position appear vertically on the left side. The yellow horizontal back carries the player's name and position at the top, followed by biography, career highlights, and statistics. A player head shot appears in the lower right corner.

	MINT	NRMT	EXC
COMPLETE SET (29)	5.00	2.20	.60

☐ 1 Clay Bellinger
☐ 2 Steve Callahan
☐ 3 Kelly Ahrens
☐ 4 Frank Carey
☐ 5 Jeff Bonner
☐ 6 Ed Gustafson
☐ 7 Greg Brummett
☐ 8 Chris Hancock
☐ 9 Jack Mull MGR
☐ 10 Steve Cline CO
☐ 11 Gus Vollmer
☐ 12 Brian Costello

- ☐ 13 Jason McFarlin
- ☐ 14 Carl Hanselman
- ☐ 15 Randy Johnson
- ☐ 16 Marino Hernandez
- ☐ 17 Kevin Kasper
- ☐ 18 Stewart Hillman
- ☐ 19 Rober Miller
- ☐ 20 Joey James
- ☐ 21 Ron Crowe
- ☐ 22 Maximo Aleys
- ☐ 23 Pat Rapp
- ☐ 24 Rafael Novoa
- ☐ 25 Steve Rolen
- ☐ 26 Vince Palyan
- ☐ 27 Rob Taylor
- ☐ 28 Jon Pattin
- ☐ 29 Checklist

1990 Clinton Giants ProCards

This 29-card standard-size set of the 1990 Clinton Giants, a Class A Midwest League affiliate of the San Francisco Giants, features on its white-bordered fronts posed color player photos set on simulated wood-grain backgrounds. The player's name, position, and team appear within a gold-colored rectangle below the photo. The tan horizontal back is bordered in white and carries the player's name at the top, followed by biography and statistics.

	MINT	NRMT	EXC
COMPLETE SET (29)	5.00	2.20	.60

- ☐ 2539 Checklist
- ☐ 2540 Carl Hanselman
- ☐ 2541 Rafael Novoa
- ☐ 2542 Stewart Hillman
- ☐ 2543 Chris Hancock
- ☐ 2544 Rob Taylor
- ☐ 2545 Steve Callahan
- ☐ 2546 Greg Brummett
- ☐ 2547 Pat Rapp
- ☐ 2548 Max Aleys
- ☐ 2549 Jim Foley
- ☐ 2550 Ed Gustafson
- ☐ 2551 Kelly Ahrens
- ☐ 2552 Jon Pattin
- ☐ 2553 Roger Miller
- ☐ 2554 Joey James
- ☐ 2555 Frank Carey
- ☐ 2556 Kevin Kasper
- ☐ 2557 Ron Crowe
- ☐ 2558 Clay Bellinger
- ☐ 2559 Steve Rolen
- ☐ 2560 Jeffry Bonner
- ☐ 2561 Randy Johnson
- ☐ 2562 Gus Vollmer
- ☐ 2563 Jason McFarlin
- ☐ 2564 Vince Palyan
- ☐ 2565 Jack Mull MGR
- ☐ 2566 Steve Cline CO
- ☐ 2567 Ron Wotus CO

1990 Clinton Giants Update Team Issue

This 12-card standard-size update set of the 1990 Clinton Giants, a Class A Midwest League affiliate of the San Francisco Giants, features white-bordered posed and action color player photos on its fronts. The player's name and position appear vertically on the left side. The yellow horizontal back carries the player's name and position at the top, followed by biography, career highlights, and statistics. A player head shot appears in the lower right corner. 1,000 sets were produced.

	MINT	NRMT	EXC
COMPLETE SET (12)	6.00	2.70	.75

- ☐ U11 Chris Hancock
  Roger Miller
  Rafael Novoa
  Frank Carey
  Joey James
  Rob Taylor
  All-Stars
- ☐ U1 Mate Borgogno
- ☐ U2 Courtney Davis
- ☐ U3 Scott Ebert
- ☐ U4 Dan Flanagan
- ☐ U5 Mike Grahovac
- ☐ U6 Rick Huisman
- ☐ U7 Jim Huslig
- ☐ U8 Pete Weber
- ☐ U9 Fred Whatley
- ☐ U10 Jason Young
- ☐ U12 Checklist

1990 CMC

This 880-card set features Triple A cards of CMC and lower classification cards from ProCards. Both the CMC and ProCards, feature color player shots with the player's name, team name and position appearing on the card fronts. The CMC cards hve a green and yellow combination border with the team logo in the lower corner while the ProCards feature a wood grain border with the words ProCards in the upper corner of the card. On the card backs, the CMC cards carries the league name, team name and affiliation followed by

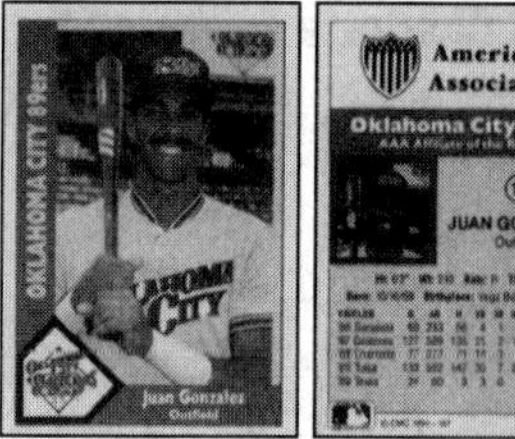

the player's name, position, biography and statistics. The ProCards cards carries the player's name, position, biography and statistics.

	MINT	NRMT	EXC
COMPLETE SET (880)	90.00	40.00	11.00
COMMON PLAYER (1-880)	.10	.05	.01
☐ 1 Stan Belinda	.10	.05	.01
☐ 2 Gordon Dillard	.10	.05	.01
☐ 3 Terry Collins MG	.10	.05	.01
☐ 4 Mark Huismann	.10	.05	.01
☐ 5 Hugh Kemp	.10	.05	.01
☐ 6 Scott Medvin	.10	.05	.01
☐ 7 Vicente Palacios	.10	.05	.01
☐ 8 Rick Reed	.10	.05	.01
☐ 9 Mark Ross	.10	.05	.01
☐ 10 Dorn Taylor	.10	.05	.01
☐ 11 Mike York	.10	.05	.01
☐ 12 Jeff Richardson	.10	.05	.01
☐ 13 Dann Bilardello	.10	.05	.01
☐ 14 Tom Prince	.10	.05	.01
☐ 15 Danny Sheaffer	.10	.05	.01
☐ 16 Kevin Burdick	.10	.05	.01
☐ 17 Steve Kiefer	.10	.05	.01
☐ 18 Orlando Merced	.10	.05	.01
☐ 19 Armando Moreno	.10	.05	.01
☐ 20 Mark Ryal	.10	.05	.01
☐ 21 Tommy Shields	.10	.05	.01
☐ 22 Steve Carter	.10	.05	.01
☐ 23 Wes Chamberlain	.10	.05	.01
☐ 24 Jeff Cook	.10	.05	.01
☐ 25 Scott Little	.10	.05	.01
☐ 26 Jeff Peterek	.10	.05	.01
☐ 27 Ed Puig	.10	.05	.01
☐ 28 Tim Watkins	.10	.05	.01
☐ 29 Tom Edens	.10	.05	.01
☐ 30 Mike Capel	.10	.05	.01
☐ 31 Darryel Walters	.10	.05	.01
☐ 32 Joe Xavier	.10	.05	.01
☐ 33 Tim Torricelli	.10	.05	.01
☐ 34 Joe Redfield	.10	.05	.01
☐ 35 D.L. Smith	.10	.05	.01
☐ 36 Billy Moore	.10	.05	.01
☐ 37 Joe Mitchell	.10	.05	.01
☐ 38 Mario Monico	.10	.05	.01
☐ 39 Frank Mattox	.10	.05	.01
☐ 40 Tim McIntosh	.10	.05	.01
☐ 41 Mark Higgins	.10	.05	.01
☐ 42 George Canale	.10	.05	.01
☐ 43 Don Gordon	.10	.05	.01
☐ 44 Al Sadler	.10	.05	.01
☐ 45 Don August	.10	.05	.01
☐ 46 Mike Birkbeck	.10	.05	.01
☐ 47 Dennis Powell	.10	.05	.01
☐ 48 Chuck McGrath	.10	.05	.01
☐ 49 Ruben Escalera	.10	.05	.01
☐ 50 Dave Machemer MG	.10	.05	.01
☐ 51 Steve Fireovid	.10	.05	.01
☐ 52 Danny Clay	.10	.05	.01
☐ 53 Howard Farmer	.10	.05	.01
☐ 54 Travis Chambers	.10	.05	.01
☐ 55 Chris Marchok	.10	.05	.01
☐ 56 Dan Gakeler	.10	.05	.01
☐ 57 Scott Anderson	.10	.05	.01
☐ 58 Dale Mohorcic	.10	.05	.01
☐ 59 Richard Thompson	.10	.05	.01
☐ 60 Eddie Dixon	.10	.05	.01
☐ 61 Jim Davins	.10	.05	.01
☐ 62 Edwin Marquez	.10	.05	.01
☐ 63 Jerry Goff	.10	.05	.01
☐ 64 Dwight Lowry	.10	.05	.01
☐ 65 Jim Steels	.10	.05	.01
☐ 66 Quinn Mack	.10	.05	.01
☐ 67 Eric Bullock	.10	.05	.01
☐ 68 Otis Green	.10	.05	.01
☐ 69 Randy Braun	.10	.05	.01
☐ 70 Mel Houston	.10	.05	.01
☐ 71 Jesus Paredes	.10	.05	.01
☐ 72 Romy Cucjen	.10	.05	.01
☐ 73 Jose Castro	.10	.05	.01
☐ 74 Esteban Beltre	.10	.05	.01
☐ 75 Tim Johnson MG	.10	.05	.01
☐ 76 Shawn Boskie	.10	.05	.01
☐ 77 Dave Masters	.10	.05	.01
☐ 78 Kevin Blankenship	.10	.05	.01
☐ 79 Greg Kallevig	.10	.05	.01
☐ 80 Steve Parker	.10	.05	.01
☐ 81 David Pavlas	.10	.05	.01
☐ 82 Jeff Pico	.10	.05	.01
☐ 83 Laddie Renfroe	.10	.05	.01
☐ 84 Dean Wilkins	.10	.05	.01
☐ 85 Paul Wilmet	.10	.05	.01
☐ 86 Bob Bafia	.10	.05	.01
☐ 87 Brian Guinn	.10	.05	.01
☐ 88 Greg Smith	.10	.05	.01
☐ 89 Derrick May	.10	.05	.01
☐ 90 Glenn Sullivan	.10	.05	.01
☐ 91 Bill Wrona	.10	.05	.01
☐ 92 Erik Pappas	.10	.05	.01
☐ 93 Hector Villanueva	.10	.05	.01
☐ 94 Ced Landrum	.10	.05	.01
☐ 95 Jeff Small	.10	.05	.01
☐ 96 Gary Varsho	.10	.05	.01
☐ 97 Brad Bierly	.10	.05	.01
☐ 98 Jeff Hearron	.10	.05	.01
☐ 99 Jim Essian MG	.10	.05	.01
☐ 100 Brian McCann TR	.10	.05	.01
☐ 101 Scott Arnold	.10	.05	.01
☐ 102 Gibson Alba	.10	.05	.01
☐ 103 Cris Carpenter	.10	.05	.01
☐ 104 Stan Clarke	.10	.05	.01
☐ 105 Mike Hinkle	.10	.05	.01
☐ 106 Howard Hilton	.10	.05	.01
☐ 107 Dave Osteen	.10	.05	.01
☐ 108 Mike Perez	.10	.05	.01
☐ 109 Bernard Gilkey	1.25	.55	.16
☐ 110 Dennis Carter	.10	.05	.01
☐ 111 Julian Martinez	.10	.05	.01
☐ 112 Rod Brewer	.10	.05	.01
☐ 113 Ray Stephens	.10	.05	.01
☐ 114 Ray Lankford	1.25	.55	.16
☐ 115 Craig Wilson	.10	.05	.01
☐ 116 Roy Silver	.10	.05	.01
☐ 117 Bien Figueroa	.10	.05	.01
☐ 118 Jesus Mendez	.10	.05	.01
☐ 119 Geronimo Pena	.10	.05	.01
☐ 120 Omar Olivares	.10	.05	.01
☐ 121 Mark Grater	.10	.05	.01
☐ 122 Tim Sherrill	.10	.05	.01
☐ 123 Pat Austin	.10	.05	.01
☐ 124 Todd Crosby	.10	.05	.01
☐ 125 Gary Nichols	.10	.05	.01
☐ 126 Milt Hill	.10	.05	.01
☐ 127 Robert Moore	.10	.05	.01
☐ 128 Joey Vierra	.10	.05	.01
☐ 129 Terry McGriff	.10	.05	.01
☐ 130 Chris Hammond	.10	.05	.01
☐ 131 Charlie Mitchell	.10	.05	.01
☐ 132 Rodney Imes	.10	.05	.01
☐ 133 Rob Lopez	.10	.05	.01
☐ 134 Keith Brown	.10	.05	.01
☐ 135 Scott Scudder	.10	.05	.01
☐ 136 Bob Sebra	.10	.05	.01
☐ 137 Donnie Scott	.10	.05	.01
☐ 138 Skeeter Barnes	.10	.05	.01
☐ 139 Paul Noce	.10	.05	.01
☐ 140 Leo Garcia	.10	.05	.01
☐ 141 Chris Jones	.10	.05	.01
☐ 142 Kevin Pearson	.10	.05	.01
☐ 143 Darryl Motley	.10	.05	.01
☐ 144 Keith Lockhart	.10	.05	.01
☐ 145 Brian Lane	.10	.05	.01
☐ 146 Eddie Tanner	.10	.05	.01
☐ 147 Reggie Jefferson	.20	.09	.03
☐ 148 Neil Allen	.10	.05	.01
☐ 149 Pete MacKanin MG	.10	.05	.01
☐ 150 Ray Rippelmeyer CO	.10	.05	.01
☐ 151 Jack Hardy	.10	.05	.01
☐ 152 Steve Lankard	.10	.05	.01
☐ 153 John Hoover	.10	.05	.01
☐ 154 David Lynch	.10	.05	.01
☐ 155 Mark Petkovsek	.10	.05	.01
☐ 156 David Miller	.10	.05	.01
☐ 157 Brad Arnsberg	.10	.05	.01
☐ 158 Jeff Satzinger	.10	.05	.01
☐ 159 John Barfield	.10	.05	.01
☐ 160 Mike Berger	.10	.05	.01
☐ 161 John Russell	.10	.05	.01
☐ 162 Pat Garman	.10	.05	.01
☐ 163 Gary Green	.10	.05	.01
☐ 164 Brian House	.10	.05	.01
☐ 165 Ron Washington	.10	.05	.01
☐ 166 Nick Capra	.10	.05	.01
☐ 167 Juan Gonzalez	12.00	5.50	1.50
☐ 168 Gar Millay	.10	.05	.01
☐ 169 Kevin Reimer	.10	.05	.01
☐ 170 Bernie Tatis	.10	.05	.01
☐ 171 Steve Smith MG	.10	.05	.01
☐ 172 Dick Egan CO	.10	.05	.01
☐ 173 Stan Hough CO	.10	.05	.01
☐ 174 Ray Ramirez TR	.10	.05	.01
☐ 175 Moe Drabowsky CO	.10	.05	.01
☐ 176 Jay Baller	.10	.05	.01
☐ 177 Ray Chadwick	.10	.05	.01
☐ 178 Dera Clark	.10	.05	.01
☐ 179 Luis Encarnacion	.10	.05	.01
☐ 180 Jim LeMasters	.10	.05	.01
☐ 181 Mike Magnante	.10	.05	.01
☐ 182 Mel Stottlemyre	.10	.05	.01
☐ 183 Tony Ferreira	.10	.05	.01
☐ 184 Pete Filson	.10	.05	.01
☐ 185 Andy McGaffigan	.10	.05	.01
☐ 186 Luis de los Santos	.10	.05	.01
☐ 187 Mike Loggins	.10	.05	.01
☐ 188 Chito Martinez	.10	.05	.01
☐ 189 Bobby Meacham	.10	.05	.01
☐ 190 Russ Morman	.10	.05	.01
☐ 191 Bill Pecota	.10	.05	.01
☐ 192 Harvey Pulliam	.10	.05	.01
☐ 193 Jeff Schulz	.10	.05	.01
☐ 194 Gary Thurman	.10	.05	.01
☐ 195 Thad Reece	.10	.05	.01
☐ 196 Tim Spehr	.10	.05	.01
☐ 197 Paul Zuvella	.10	.05	.01
☐ 198 Tom Poquette CO UER	.10	.05	.01
Rich Dubee CO			
(Card misnumbered			
199 on back)			
☐ 199 Bob Hamelin	.15	.07	.02
☐ 200 Sal Rende	.10	.05	.01
☐ 201 Steve Adkins	.10	.05	.01
☐ 202 Dave Eiland	.10	.05	.01
☐ 203 John Habyan	.10	.05	.01
☐ 204 Mark Leiter	.10	.05	.01
☐ 205 Kevin Mmahat	.10	.05	.01
☐ 206 Hipolito Pena	.10	.05	.01
☐ 207 Willie Smith	.10	.05	.01
☐ 208 Rich Monteleone	.10	.05	.01
☐ 209 Hensley Meulens	.10	.05	.01
☐ 210 Andy Stankiewicz	.10	.05	.01
☐ 211 Jim Leyritz	.20	.09	.03
☐ 212 Jim Walewander	.10	.05	.01
☐ 213 Oscar Azocar	.10	.05	.01
☐ 214 John Fishel	.10	.05	.01
☐ 215 Jason Maas	.10	.05	.01
☐ 216 Van Snider	.10	.05	.01
☐ 217 Kevin Maas	.10	.05	.01
☐ 218 Ricky Torres	.10	.05	.01
☐ 219 Dave Sax	.10	.05	.01
☐ 220 Darrin Chapin	.10	.05	.01
☐ 221 Rob Sepanek	.10	.05	.01
☐ 222 Mark Wasinger	.10	.05	.01
☐ 223 Jimmy Jones	.10	.05	.01
☐ 224 Ken Rowe CO	.10	.05	.01
Stump Merrill MG			
Clete Boyer CO			
Mike Heifferon TR			
Troy Hillman CO			
☐ 225 Carl(Stump) Merrill MG	.10	.05	.01
☐ 226 Bob Davidson	.10	.05	.01
☐ 227 Eric Boudreaux	.10	.05	.01
☐ 228 Marvin Freeman	.20	.09	.03
☐ 229 Jason Grimsley	.10	.05	.01
☐ 230 Chuck Malone	.10	.05	.01
☐ 231 Dickie Noles	.10	.05	.01
☐ 232 Wally Ritchie	.10	.05	.01
☐ 233 Bob Scanlan	.10	.05	.01
☐ 234 Scott Service	.10	.05	.01
☐ 235 Steve Sharts	.10	.05	.01
☐ 236 John Gibbons	.10	.05	.01
☐ 237 Sal Agostinelli	.10	.05	.01
☐ 238 Jim Adduci	.10	.05	.01
☐ 239 Kelly Heath	.10	.05	.01
☐ 240 Mickey Morandini	.20	.09	.03
☐ 241 Victor Rosario	.10	.05	.01
☐ 242 Steve Stanicek	.10	.05	.01
☐ 243 Jim Vatcher	.10	.05	.01
☐ 244 Bill Dancy MG	.10	.05	.01
☐ 245 Ron Jones	.10	.05	.01
☐ 246 Chris Knabenshue	.10	.05	.01
☐ 247 Keith Miller	.10	.05	.01
☐ 248 Floyd Rayford CO	.10	.05	.01
☐ 249 Jim Wright CO	.10	.05	.01
☐ 250 Todd Frohwirth	.10	.05	.01
☐ 251 Barney Nugent TR	.10	.05	.01
☐ 252 Tito Stewart	.10	.05	.01
☐ 253 John Trautwein	.10	.05	.01
☐ 254 Mike Rochford	.10	.05	.01
☐ 255 Larry Shikles	.10	.05	.01
☐ 256 Daryl Irvine	.10	.05	.01
☐ 257 John Leister	.10	.05	.01
☐ 258 Joe Johnson	.10	.05	.01
☐ 259 Mark Meleski CO	.10	.05	.01
☐ 260 Steven Bast	.10	.05	.01
☐ 261 Ed Nottle MG	.10	.05	.01
☐ 262 John Flaherty	.10	.05	.01
☐ 263 John Marzano	.10	.05	.01
☐ 264 Gary Tremblay	.10	.05	.01
☐ 265 Scott Cooper	.10	.05	.01
☐ 266 Angel Gonzalez	.10	.05	.01
☐ 267 Julius McDougal	.10	.05	.01
☐ 268 Tim Naehring	.50	.23	.06
☐ 269 Jim Pankovits	.10	.05	.01
☐ 270 Rick Lancellotti	.10	.05	.01
☐ 271 Mickey Pina	.10	.05	.01
☐ 272 Phil Plantier	.20	.09	.03
☐ 273 Jeff Stone	.10	.05	.01
☐ 274 Scott Wade	.10	.05	.01
☐ 275 Mike Dalton	.10	.05	.01
☐ 276 Jeff Gray	.10	.05	.01
☐ 277 Steve Avery	.75	.35	.09
☐ 278 Leo Mazzone CO	.10	.05	.01
Sonny Jackson CO			
John Grubb CO			
☐ 279 Dale Polley	.10	.05	.01
☐ 280 Rusty Richards	.10	.05	.01
☐ 281 Andy Nezelek	.10	.05	.01
☐ 282 Ed Olwine	.10	.05	.01
☐ 283 Jim Beauchamp MG	.10	.05	.01
☐ 284 Paul Marak	.10	.05	.01
☐ 285 Dave Justice	4.00	1.80	.50
☐ 286 Jimmy Kremers	.10	.05	.01

Card			
☐ 287 Drew Denson	.10	.05	.01
☐ 288 Barry Jones	.10	.05	.01
☐ 289 Francisco Cabrera	.10	.05	.01
☐ 290 Bruce Crabbe	.10	.05	.01
☐ 291 Dennis Hood	.10	.05	.01
☐ 292 Geronimo Berroa	.75	.35	.09
☐ 293 Ed Whited	.10	.05	.01
☐ 294 Sam Ayoub TR	.10	.05	.01
☐ 295 Brian R. Hunter	.10	.05	.01
☐ 296 Tommy Greene	.20	.09	.03
☐ 297 John Mizerock	.10	.05	.01
☐ 298 Ken Dowell	.10	.05	.01
☐ 299 John Alva	.10	.05	.01
☐ 300 Bill Laskey	.10	.05	.01
☐ 301 Brian Snyder	.10	.05	.01
☐ 302 Ben McDonald	.25	.11	.03
☐ 303 Rob Woodward	.10	.05	.01
☐ 304 Mickey Weston	.10	.05	.01
☐ 305 Mike Jones	.10	.05	.01
☐ 306 Curtis Schilling	.25	.11	.03
☐ 307 Jay Aldrich	.10	.05	.01
☐ 308 Paul Blair CO	.10	.05	.01
☐ 309 Mike Smith	.10	.05	.01
☐ 310 Jack Tackett	.10	.05	.01
☐ 311 Leo Gomez	.10	.05	.01
☐ 312 Juan Bell	.10	.05	.01
☐ 313 Chris Hoiles	.25	.11	.03
☐ 314 Donell Nixon	.10	.05	.01
☐ 315 Steve Stanicek	.10	.05	.01
☐ 316 Tim Dulin	.10	.05	.01
☐ 317 Chris Padget	.10	.05	.01
☐ 318 Greg Walker	.10	.05	.01
☐ 319 Tony Chance	.10	.05	.01
☐ 320 Jeff McKnight	.10	.05	.01
☐ 321 J.J. Bautista	.10	.05	.01
☐ 322 John Mitchell	.10	.05	.01
☐ 323 Vic Hithe	.10	.05	.01
☐ 324 Darrell Miller	.10	.05	.01
☐ 325 Shane Turner	.10	.05	.01
☐ 326 Greg Biagini	.10	.05	.01
☐ 327 Alex Sanchez	.10	.05	.01
☐ 328 Mauro Gozzo	.10	.05	.01
☐ 329 Steve Cummings	.10	.05	.01
☐ 330 Tom Gilles	.10	.05	.01
☐ 331 Doug Linton	.10	.05	.01
☐ 332 Mike Loynd	.10	.05	.01
☐ 333 Bob Shirley	.10	.05	.01
☐ 334 John Shea	.10	.05	.01
☐ 335 Paul Kilgus	.10	.05	.01
☐ 336 Carlos Diaz	.10	.05	.01
☐ 337 Joe Szekely	.10	.05	.01
☐ 338 Rick Lysander	.10	.05	.01
☐ 339 Jim Eppard	.10	.05	.01
☐ 340 Derek Bell	1.25	.55	.16
☐ 341 Jose Escobar	.10	.05	.01
☐ 342 Webster Garrison	.10	.05	.01
☐ 343 Paul Runge	.10	.05	.01
☐ 344 Luis Sojo	.10	.05	.01
☐ 345 Ed Sprague	.20	.09	.03
☐ 346 Hector DeLaCruz	.10	.05	.01
☐ 347 Rob Ducey	.10	.05	.01
☐ 348 Ozzie Virgil	.10	.05	.01
☐ 349 Stu Pederson	.10	.05	.01
☐ 350 Mark Whiten	.20	.09	.03
☐ 351 Andy Dziadkowiec	.10	.05	.01
☐ 352 Shawn Barton	.10	.05	.01
☐ 353 Kevin Brown	.10	.05	.01
☐ 354 Rocky Childress	.10	.05	.01
☐ 355 Brian Givens	.10	.05	.01
☐ 356 Manny Hernandez	.10	.05	.01
☐ 357 Jeff Innis	.10	.05	.01
☐ 358 Cesar Mejia	.10	.05	.01
☐ 359 Scott Nielsen	.10	.05	.01
☐ 360 Dale Plummer	.10	.05	.01
☐ 361 Ray Soff	.10	.05	.01
☐ 362 Lou Thornton	.10	.05	.01
☐ 363 Dave Trautwein	.10	.05	.01
☐ 364 Julio Valera	.10	.05	.01
☐ 365 Tim Bogar	.10	.05	.01
☐ 366 Mike DeButch	.10	.05	.01
☐ 367 Jeff Gardner	.10	.05	.01
☐ 368 Denny Gonzalez	.10	.05	.01
☐ 369 Chris Jelic	.10	.05	.01
☐ 370 Roger Samuels	.10	.05	.01
☐ 371 Dave Liddell	.10	.05	.01
☐ 372 Orlando Mercado	.10	.05	.01
☐ 373 Kelvin Torve	.10	.05	.01
☐ 374 Alex Diaz	.10	.05	.01
☐ 375 Keith Hughes	.10	.05	.01
☐ 376 Darren Reed	.10	.05	.01
☐ 377 Zolio Sanchez	.10	.05	.01
☐ 378 Don Vesling	.10	.05	.01
☐ 379 Scott Aldred	.10	.05	.01
☐ 380 Dennis Burtt	.10	.05	.01
☐ 381 Shawn Holman	.10	.05	.01
☐ 382 Matt Kinzer	.10	.05	.01
☐ 383 Randy Nosek	.10	.05	.01
☐ 384 Jose Ramos	.10	.05	.01
☐ 385 Kevin Ritz	.25	.11	.03
☐ 386 Mike Schwabe	.10	.05	.01
☐ 387 Steve Searcy	.10	.05	.01
☐ 388 Eric Stone	.10	.05	.01
☐ 389 Domingo Michel	.10	.05	.01
☐ 390 Phil Ouellette	.10	.05	.01
☐ 391 Shawn Hare	.10	.05	.01
☐ 392 Jim Lindeman	.10	.05	.01
☐ 393 Scott Livingstone	.10	.05	.01
☐ 394 La Vel Freeman	.10	.05	.01
☐ 395 Travis Fryman	3.00	1.35	.35
☐ 396 Scott Lusader	.10	.05	.01
☐ 397 Dean Decillis	.10	.05	.01
☐ 398 Milt Cuyler	.10	.05	.01
☐ 399 Jeff Jones CO UER (Card misnumbered 691 on back)	.10	.05	.01
☐ 400 Phil Clark	.10	.05	.01
☐ 401 Torey Lovullo	.10	.05	.01
☐ 402 Aurelio Rodriguez CO	.10	.05	.01
☐ 403 Mike Christopher	.10	.05	.01
☐ 404 Jeff Bittiger	.10	.05	.01
☐ 405 Jeff Fischer	.10	.05	.01
☐ 406 Steve Davis	.10	.05	.01
☐ 407 Morris Madden	.10	.05	.01
☐ 408 Darren Holmes	.10	.05	.01
☐ 409 Greg Mayberry	.10	.05	.01
☐ 410 Mike Maddux	.10	.05	.01
☐ 411 Tim Scott	.10	.05	.01
☐ 412 Jim Neidlinger	.10	.05	.01
☐ 413 Dave Walsh	.10	.05	.01
☐ 414 Dennis Springer	.10	.05	.01
☐ 415 Terry Wells	.10	.05	.01
☐ 416 Adam Brown	.10	.05	.01
☐ 417 Darrin Fletcher	.10	.05	.01
☐ 418 Carlos Hernandez	.10	.05	.01
☐ 419 Dave Hansen	.10	.05	.01
☐ 420 Dan Henley	.10	.05	.01
☐ 421 Jose Offerman	.20	.09	.03
☐ 422 Jose Vizcaino	.20	.09	.03
☐ 423 Luis Lopez	.10	.05	.01
☐ 424 Butch Davis	.10	.05	.01
☐ 425 Wayne Kirby	.15	.07	.02
☐ 426 Mike Huff	.10	.05	.01
☐ 427 Billy Bean	.10	.05	.01
☐ 428 Pat Pacillo	.10	.05	.01
☐ 429 Tony Blasucci	.10	.05	.01
☐ 430 Mike Walker	.10	.05	.01
☐ 431 Pat Rice	.10	.05	.01
☐ 432 Terry Taylor	.10	.05	.01
☐ 433 David Burba	.20	.09	.03
☐ 434 Vance Lovelace	.10	.05	.01
☐ 435 Ed Vande Berg	.10	.05	.01
☐ 436 Greg Fulton	.10	.05	.01
☐ 437 Ed Jurak	.10	.05	.01
☐ 438 Dave Cochrane	.10	.05	.01
☐ 439 Edgar Martinez	1.50	.70	.19
☐ 440 Matt Sinatro	.10	.05	.01
☐ 441 Bill McGuire	.10	.05	.01
☐ 442 Mickey Brantley	.10	.05	.01
☐ 443 Tom Dodd	.10	.05	.01
☐ 444 Jim Weaver	.10	.05	.01
☐ 445 Todd Haney	.10	.05	.01
☐ 446 Casey Close	.10	.05	.01
☐ 447 Theo Shaw	.10	.05	.01
☐ 448 Keith Helton	.10	.05	.01
☐ 449 Jose Melendez	.10	.05	.01
☐ 450 Tom Jones MG	.10	.05	.01
☐ 451 Dan Warthen CO	.10	.05	.01
☐ 452 Randy Roetter TR	.10	.05	.01
☐ 453 Mike Walker	.10	.05	.01
☐ 454 Colby Ward	.10	.05	.01
☐ 455 Joe Skalski	.10	.05	.01
☐ 456 Efrain Valdez	.10	.05	.01
☐ 457 Doug Robertson	.10	.05	.01
☐ 458 Jeff Edwards	.10	.05	.01
☐ 459 Greg McMichael	.10	.05	.01
☐ 460 Carl Willis	.10	.05	.01
☐ 461 Beau Allred	.10	.05	.01
☐ 462 Jeff Kaiser	.10	.05	.01
☐ 463 Ty Gainey	.10	.05	.01
☐ 464 Tom Lampkin	.10	.05	.01
☐ 465 Ever Magallanes	.10	.05	.01
☐ 466 Tom Magrann	.10	.05	.01
☐ 467 Jeff Manto	.10	.05	.01
☐ 468 Luis Medina	.10	.05	.01
☐ 469 Troy Neel	.10	.05	.01
☐ 470 Steve Springer	.10	.05	.01
☐ 471 Rick Adair CO UER (Card misnumbered 476 on back)	.10	.05	.01
☐ 472 Turner Ward	.10	.05	.01
☐ 473 Casey Webster	.10	.05	.01
☐ 474 Jeff Wetherby	.10	.05	.01
☐ 475 Alan Cockrell	.10	.05	.01
☐ 476 Steve McInerney TR	.10	.05	.01
☐ 477 Bobby Molinaro MG	.10	.05	.01
☐ 478 Cliff Young	.10	.05	.01
☐ 479 Mike Arner	.10	.05	.01
☐ 480 Gary Buckels	.10	.05	.01
☐ 481 Timothy Burcham	.10	.05	.01
☐ 482 Sherman Corbett	.10	.05	.01
☐ 483 Mike Erb	.10	.05	.01
☐ 484 Mike Fetters	.10	.05	.01
☐ 485 Chuck Hernandez CO	.10	.05	.01
☐ 486 Jeff Heathcock	.10	.05	.01
☐ 487 Scott Lewis	.10	.05	.01
☐ 488 Rafael Montalvo	.10	.05	.01
☐ 489 John Skurla	.10	.05	.01
☐ 490 Lee Stevens	.15	.07	.02
☐ 491 Nelson Rood	.10	.05	.01
☐ 492 Bobby Rose	.10	.05	.01
☐ 493 Dan Grunhard	.10	.05	.01
☐ 494 Reed Peters	.10	.05	.01
☐ 495 Doug Davis	.10	.05	.01
☐ 496 Gary DiSarcina	.20	.09	.03
☐ 497 Pete Coachman	.10	.05	.01
☐ 498 Chris Cron	.10	.05	.01
☐ 499 Karl Allaire	.10	.05	.01
☐ 500 Ron Tingley	.10	.05	.01
☐ 501 Chris Beasley	.10	.05	.01
☐ 502 Max Oliveras MG	.10	.05	.01
☐ 503 Roger Smithberg	.10	.05	.01
☐ 504 Steve Peters	.10	.05	.01
☐ 505 Matt Maysey	.10	.05	.01
☐ 506 Terry Gilmore	.10	.05	.01
☐ 507 Jeff Datz	.10	.05	.01
☐ 508 Eric Nolte	.10	.05	.01
☐ 509 Jim Lewis	.10	.05	.01
☐ 510 Pete Roberts	.10	.05	.01
☐ 511 Dan Murphy	.10	.05	.01
☐ 512 Rich Rodriguez	.10	.05	.01
☐ 513 Joe Lynch	.10	.05	.01
☐ 514 Mike Basso	.10	.05	.01
☐ 515 Ronn Reynolds	.10	.05	.01
☐ 516 Jose Mota	.10	.05	.01
☐ 517 Paul Faries	.10	.05	.01
☐ 518 Warren Newson	.15	.07	.02
☐ 519 Alex Cole	.10	.05	.01
☐ 520 Tom LeVasseur	.10	.05	.01
☐ 521 Charles Hillemann	.10	.05	.01
☐ 522 Jeff Yurtin	.10	.05	.01
☐ 523 Rafael Valdez	.10	.05	.01
☐ 524 Brian Ohnoutka	.10	.05	.01
☐ 525 Pat Kelly MG	.10	.05	.01
☐ 526 Gary Lance CO	.10	.05	.01
☐ 527 Tony Torchia CO	.10	.05	.01
☐ 528 Paul McClellan	.10	.05	.01
☐ 529 Randy McCament	.10	.05	.01
☐ 530 Gil Heredia	.10	.05	.01
☐ 531 George Bonilla	.10	.05	.01
☐ 532 Russ Swan	.10	.05	.01
☐ 533 Ed Vosberg	.10	.05	.01
☐ 534 Eric Gunderson	.10	.05	.01
☐ 535 Trevor Wilson	.10	.05	.01
☐ 536 Greg Booker	.10	.05	.01
☐ 537 Kirt Manwaring	.10	.05	.01
☐ 538 Mike Kingery	.10	.05	.01
☐ 539 Brian Brady	.10	.05	.01
☐ 540 Mark Bailey	.10	.05	.01
☐ 541 Gregg Ritchie	.10	.05	.01
☐ 542 George Hinshaw	.10	.05	.01
☐ 543 Craig Colbert	.10	.05	.01
☐ 544 Kash Beauchamp	.10	.05	.01
☐ 545 Jeff Carter	.10	.05	.01
☐ 546 Mark Leonard	.10	.05	.01
☐ 547 Tony Perezchica	.10	.05	.01
☐ 548 Mike Laga	.10	.05	.01
☐ 549 Mike Benjamin	.10	.05	.01
☐ 550 Timber Mead	.10	.05	.01
☐ 551 Duane Espy MG	.10	.05	.01
☐ 552 Tim Ireland CO	.10	.05	.01
☐ 553 Paul Abbott	.10	.05	.01
☐ 554 Pat Bangtson	.10	.05	.01
☐ 555 Larry Casian	.10	.05	.01
☐ 556 Mike Cook	.10	.05	.01
☐ 557 Pete Delkus	.10	.05	.01
☐ 558 Mike Dyer	.10	.05	.01
☐ 559 Charles Scott	.10	.05	.01
☐ 560 Francisco Oliveras	.10	.05	.01
☐ 561 Park Pittman	.10	.05	.01
☐ 562 Jimmy Williams	.10	.05	.01
☐ 563 Rich Yett	.10	.05	.01
☐ 564 Vic Rodriguez	.10	.05	.01
☐ 565 Jamie Nelson	.10	.05	.01
☐ 566 Derek Parks	.10	.05	.01
☐ 567 Ed Naveda	.10	.05	.01
☐ 568 Scott Leius	.20	.09	.03
☐ 569 Terry Jorgensen	.10	.05	.01
☐ 570 Doug Baker	.10	.05	.01
☐ 571 Chip Hale	.10	.05	.01
☐ 572 Dave Jacas	.10	.05	.01
☐ 573 Jim Shellenback CO	.10	.05	.01
☐ 574 Rafael DeLima	.10	.05	.01
☐ 575 Bernardo Brito	.10	.05	.01
☐ 576 J.T. Bruett	.10	.05	.01
☐ 577 Paul Sorrento	.50	.23	.06
☐ 578 Ray Young	.10	.05	.01
☐ 579 Dave Veres	.10	.05	.01
☐ 580 Scott Chiamparino	.10	.05	.01
☐ 581 Tony Ariola	.10	.05	.01
☐ 582 Weston Weber	.10	.05	.01
☐ 583 Bruce Walton	.10	.05	.01
☐ 584 Dave Otto	.10	.05	.01
☐ 585 Reese Lambert	.10	.05	.01
☐ 586 Joe Bitker	.10	.05	.01
☐ 587 Joe Law	.10	.05	.01
☐ 588 Ed Wojna	.10	.05	.01
☐ 589 Timothy Casey	.10	.05	.01
☐ 590 Patrick Dietrick	.10	.05	.01
☐ 591 Bruce Fields	.10	.05	.01
☐ 592 Eric Fox	.10	.05	.01
☐ 593 Scott Hemond	.10	.05	.01
☐ 594 Steve Howard	.10	.05	.01
☐ 595 Doug Jennings	.10	.05	.01
☐ 596 Al Pedrique	.10	.05	.01
☐ 597 Dann Howitt	.10	.05	.01
☐ 598 Russ McGinnis	.10	.05	.01
☐ 599 Troy Afenir	.10	.05	.01
☐ 600 Larry Arndt	.10	.05	.01
☐ 601 Dickie Scott CO	.10	.05	.01
☐ 602 Kevin Ward	.10	.05	.01
☐ 603 Ryan Bowen	.10	.05	.01
☐ 604 Brian Meyer	.10	.05	.01
☐ 605 Terry Clark	.10	.05	.01
☐ 606 Darryl Kile	.10	.05	.01
☐ 607 Randy St. Claire	.10	.05	.01
☐ 608 Randy Hennis	.10	.05	.01
☐ 609 Lee Tunnell	.10	.05	.01
☐ 610 William Brennan	.10	.05	.01
☐ 611 Craig Smajstra	.10	.05	.01
☐ 612 Gary Cooper	.10	.05	.01
☐ 613 Carl Nichols	.10	.05	.01
☐ 614 Louie Meadows	.10	.05	.01
☐ 615 Josse Tolentino	.10	.05	.01
☐ 616 Harry Spillman	.10	.05	.01
☐ 617 Javier Ortiz	.10	.05	.01
☐ 618 Doug Strange	.10	.05	.01
☐ 619 Jim Olander	.10	.05	.01
☐ 620 Karl Rhodes	.10	.05	.01
☐ 621 Dave Rohde	.10	.05	.01
☐ 622 Mike Simms	.10	.05	.01
☐ 623 Scott Servais	.50	.23	.06
☐ 624 Pedro Sanchez	.10	.05	.01
☐ 625 Kevin Dean	.10	.05	.01
☐ 626 Brian Fisher	.10	.05	.01
☐ 627 Bob Skinner MG	.10	.05	.01
☐ 628 Wilson Alvarez	.75	.35	.09
☐ 629 Adam Peterson	.10	.05	.01
☐ 630 Tom Drees	.10	.05	.01
☐ 631 Ravelo Manzanillo	.10	.05	.01
☐ 632 Marv Foley MG	.10	.05	.01
☐ 633 Grady Hall	.10	.05	.01
☐ 634 Mike Campbell	.10	.05	.01
☐ 635 Shawn Hillegas	.10	.05	.01
☐ 636 C.L. Penigar	.10	.05	.01
☐ 637 John Pawlowski	.10	.05	.01
☐ 638 Steve Rosenberg	.10	.05	.01
☐ 639 Jose Segura	.10	.05	.01
☐ 640 Rich Amaral	.10	.05	.01
☐ 641 Pete Dalena	.10	.05	.01
☐ 642 Ramon Sambo	.10	.05	.01
☐ 643 Marcus Lawton	.10	.05	.01
☐ 644 Orsino Hill	.10	.05	.01
☐ 645 Marlin McPhail	.10	.05	.01
☐ 646 Keith Smith	.10	.05	.01
☐ 647 Todd Trafton	.10	.05	.01
☐ 648 Norberto Martin	.10	.05	.01
☐ 649 Don Wakamatsu	.10	.05	.01
☐ 650 Jerry Willard	.10	.05	.01
☐ 651 Dana Williams	.10	.05	.01
☐ 652 Tracy Woodson	.10	.05	.01
☐ 653 Glenn Hoffman CO	.10	.05	.01
☐ 654 Tony Scruggs	.10	.05	.01
☐ 655 Reggie Sanders	1.00	.45	.12
☐ 656 Rick Luecken	.10	.05	.01
☐ 657 Kent Mercker	.20	.09	.03
☐ 658 Claude Osteen CO / Von Joshua CO / Walt McConnel CO	.10	.05	.01
☐ 659 Scott Shockey	.10	.05	.01
☐ 660 Mario Brito	.10	.05	.01
☐ 660 Brian Barnes	.10	.05	.01
☐ 662 Ed Quijada	.10	.05	.01
☐ 663 Steve Wapnick	.10	.05	.01
☐ 664 Kevin Tahan	.10	.05	.01
☐ 665 Johnny Guzman	.10	.05	.01
☐ 666 Bronswell Patrick	.10	.05	.01
☐ 667 Kevin Kennedy MG	.10	.05	.01
☐ 668 Orlando Miller	.10	.05	.01
☐ 669 Mauricio Nunez	.10	.05	.01
☐ 670 Hector Rivera	.10	.05	.01
☐ 671 Roger LaFrancois CO	.10	.05	.01
☐ 672 Jackson Todd CO	.10	.05	.01
☐ 673 John Young TR	.10	.05	.01
☐ 674 Bob Bailor MG	.10	.05	.01
☐ 675 David Hajeck	.10	.05	.01
☐ 676 Ralph Wheeler CO	.10	.05	.01
☐ 677 Anthony Gutierrez	.10	.05	.01
☐ 678 Gaylen Pitts MG	.10	.05	.01
☐ 679 Mark Riggins CO	.10	.05	.01
☐ 680 Brad Bluestone TR	.10	.05	.01
☐ 681 Dick Bosman CO	.10	.05	.01
☐ 682 Wil Cordero	.30	.14	.04
☐ 683 Todd Hutcheson TR	.10	.05	.01
☐ 684 Steve Swisher MG	.10	.05	.01
☐ 685 John Cumberland CO	.10	.05	.01
☐ 686 Rich Miller CO	.10	.05	.01
☐ 687 Scott Lawrenson TR	.10	.05	.01
☐ 688 Larry Hardy CO	.10	.05	.01
☐ 689 Danny Boone	.10	.05	.01
☐ 690 Terrel Hansen	.10	.05	.01
☐ 691 Tom Gamboa MG	.10	.05	.01
☐ 692 Gavin Osteen	.10	.05	.01
☐ 693 Dave Riddle	.10	.05	.01
☐ 694 Tim Pugh	.10	.05	.01
☐ 695 Eugene Jones	.10	.05	.01
☐ 696 Scott Pose	.10	.05	.01
☐ 697 Ramon Jimenez	.10	.05	.01
☐ 698 Fred Russell	.10	.05	.01
☐ 699 Louis Talbert	.10	.05	.01
☐ 700 J.D. Noland	.10	.05	.01

☐ 701 Osvaldo Sanchez .10 .05 .01
☐ 702 David Colon .10 .05 .01
☐ 703 Jeff Hart .10 .05 .01
☐ 704 Jeff Hoffman .10 .05 .01
☐ 705 Sean Gilliam .10 .05 .01
☐ 706 Al Pacheco .10 .05 .01
☐ 707 Jason Satre .10 .05 .01
☐ 708 Tim Cecil .10 .05 .01
☐ 709 Phil Weise .10 .05 .01
☐ 710 Larry Pardo .10 .05 .01
☐ 711 Clemente Acosta .10 .05 .01
☐ 712 Chris Johnson .10 .05 .01
☐ 713 Frank Bolick .10 .05 .01
☐ 714 Jose Garcia .10 .05 .01
☐ 715 Adell Davenport .10 .05 .01
☐ 716 Kevin Rogers .10 .05 .01
☐ 717 Dan Rambo .10 .05 .01
☐ 718 Vince Harris .10 .05 .01
☐ 719 Darrell Sherman .10 .05 .01
☐ 720 Isaiah Clark .10 .05 .01
☐ 721 Miguel Sabino .10 .05 .01
☐ 722 Frank Valdez .10 .05 .01
☐ 723 Giovanni Miranda .10 .05 .01
☐ 724 Dary Ratliff .10 .05 .01
☐ 725 Michael Brewington .10 .05 .01
☐ 726 Eric Parkinson .10 .05 .01
☐ 727 Vinicio Castilla 1.25 .55 .16
☐ 728 Roger Hailey .10 .05 .01
☐ 729 Earl Steinmetz .10 .05 .01
☐ 730 Doug Gogolewski .10 .05 .01
☐ 731 Andy Cook .10 .05 .01
☐ 732 John Toale .10 .05 .01
☐ 733 Mike Curtis .10 .05 .01
☐ 734 Delwyn Young .10 .05 .01
☐ 735 Scott Meadows .10 .05 .01
☐ 736 Don Sparks .10 .05 .01
☐ 737 Gary Wilson .10 .05 .01
☐ 738 Blas Minor .10 .05 .01
☐ 739 Jeff Bagwell 8.00 3.60 1.00
☐ 740 Phil Bryant .10 .05 .01
☐ 741 Felipe Castillo .10 .05 .01
☐ 742 Craig Faulkner .10 .05 .01
☐ 743 Jeff Conine 1.25 .55 .16
☐ 744 Kevin Belcher .10 .05 .01
☐ 745 Bill Haselman .15 .07 .02
☐ 746 Matt Stark .10 .05 .01
☐ 747 Todd Hall .10 .05 .01
☐ 748 Scott Centala .10 .05 .01
☐ 749 Doug Simons .10 .05 .01
☐ 750 Shawn Gilbert .10 .05 .01
☐ 751 Kenny Morgan .10 .05 .01
☐ 752 Andy Mota .10 .05 .01
☐ 753 Jeff Baldwin .10 .05 .01
☐ 754 Reed Olmstead .10 .05 .01
☐ 755 Basil Meyer .10 .05 .01
☐ 756 Mark Razook .10 .05 .01
☐ 757 Ken Pennington .10 .05 .01
☐ 758 Shane Letterio .10 .05 .01
☐ 759 Ted Williams .10 .05 .01
☐ 760 Luis Gonzalez .20 .09 .03
☐ 761 Carlos Garcia .10 .05 .01
☐ 762 Terry Crowley .10 .05 .01
☐ 763 Julio Peguero .10 .05 .01
☐ 764 Francisco DeLaRosa .10 .05 .01
☐ 765 Rodney Lofton .10 .05 .01
☐ 766 Eric McCray .10 .05 .01
☐ 767 Michael Wilkins .10 .05 .01
☐ 768 John Kiely .10 .05 .01
☐ 769 Derek Lee .10 .05 .01
☐ 770 Bo Kennedy .10 .05 .01
☐ 771 John Hudek .15 .07 .02
☐ 772 Bernie Nunez .10 .05 .01
☐ 773 Tom Quinlan .10 .05 .01
☐ 774 Jimmy Tatum .10 .05 .01
☐ 775 Casey Waller .10 .05 .01
☐ 776 Doug Lindsey .10 .05 .01
☐ 777 Roberto Zambrano .10 .05 .01
☐ 778 Wade Taylor .10 .05 .01
☐ 779 Carlos Maldonado .10 .05 .01
☐ 780 Brent Mayne .10 .05 .01
☐ 781 Jerry Rub .10 .05 .01
☐ 782 Vince Phillips .10 .05 .01
☐ 783 Eric Wedge .10 .05 .01
☐ 784 Andy Ashby .20 .09 .03
☐ 785 Royal Clayton .10 .05 .01
☐ 786 Jeffrey Osborne .10 .05 .01
☐ 787 Pat Kelly .15 .07 .02
☐ 788 John Wehner .10 .05 .01
☐ 789 Bernie Williams 4.00 1.80 .50
☐ 790 Moises Alou 1.50 .70 .19
☐ 791 Mark Merchant .10 .05 .01
☐ 792 Chris Myers .10 .05 .01
☐ 793 Donald Harris .10 .05 .01
☐ 794 Mike McDonald .10 .05 .01
☐ 795 Jim Blueberg .10 .05 .01
☐ 796 Jim Bowie .10 .05 .01
☐ 797 Ruben Gonzalez .10 .05 .01
☐ 798 Rob Maurer .10 .05 .01
☐ 799 Monty Fariss .10 .05 .01
☐ 800 Bob Ayrault .10 .05 .01
☐ 801 Tim Mauser .10 .05 .01
☐ 802 David Holdridge .10 .05 .01
☐ 803 Kim Batiste .10 .05 .01
☐ 804 Dan Peltier .10 .05 .01
☐ 805 Derek Livernois .10 .05 .01
☐ 806 Tom Fischer .10 .05 .01
☐ 807 Chuck Knoblauch 4.00 1.80 .50
☐ 808 Willie Banks .20 .09 .03
☐ 809 Johnny Ard .10 .05 .01
☐ 810 Willie Ansley .10 .05 .01
☐ 811 Andujar Cedeno .20 .09 .03
☐ 812 Eddie Zosky .10 .05 .01
☐ 813 Randy Knorr .10 .05 .01
☐ 814 Juan Guzman .20 .09 .03
☐ 815 Jimmy Rogers .10 .05 .01
☐ 816 Nate Cromwell .10 .05 .01
☐ 817 Aubrey Waggoner .10 .05 .01
☐ 818 Frank Thomas 15.00 6.75 1.85
☐ 819 Matt Merullo .10 .05 .01
☐ 820 Roberto Hernandez .20 .09 .03
☐ 821 Cesar Bernhardt .10 .05 .01
☐ 822 Sterling Hitchcock .30 .14 .04
☐ 823 Ricky Rhodes .10 .05 .01
☐ 824 Todd Malone .10 .05 .01
☐ 825 Andy Fox .10 .05 .01
☐ 826 Ryan Klesko 5.00 2.20 .60
☐ 827 Tyler Houston .25 .11 .03
☐ 828 Tab Brown .10 .05 .01
☐ 829 Brian McRae .75 .35 .09
☐ 830 Victor Cole .10 .05 .01
☐ 831 Mark Lewis .40 .18 .05
☐ 832 Rudy Seanez .10 .05 .01
☐ 833 Charles Nagy 1.50 .70 .19
☐ 834 Jeff Mutis .10 .05 .01
☐ 835 Carl Keliipuleole .10 .05 .01
☐ 836 Steve Pegues .10 .05 .01
☐ 837 Mike Lumley .10 .05 .01
☐ 838 Tim Leiper .10 .05 .01
☐ 839 Dave Evans .10 .05 .01
☐ 840 Darron Cox .10 .05 .01
☐ 841 Tony Ochs .10 .05 .01
☐ 842 Paul Coleman .10 .05 .01
☐ 843 Rafael Novoa .10 .05 .01
☐ 844 Clay Bellinger .10 .05 .01
☐ 845 Jason McFarlin .10 .05 .01
☐ 846 Craig Paquette .20 .09 .03
☐ 847 Timmie Morrow .10 .05 .01
☐ 848 Brian R. Hunter .10 .05 .01
☐ 849 Willie Greene .25 .11 .03
☐ 850 Austin Manahan .10 .05 .01
☐ 851 Rich Aude .10 .05 .01
☐ 852 Luis Lopez .10 .05 .01
☐ 853 Darrin Reichle .10 .05 .01
☐ 854 Tim Salmon 4.00 1.80 .50
☐ 855 Royce Clayton .25 .11 .03
☐ 856 Steve Hosey .10 .05 .01
☐ 857 Kerry Woodson .10 .05 .01
☐ 858 Roger Salkeld .10 .05 .01
☐ 859 Tim Stargell .10 .05 .01
☐ 860 Greg Pirkl .10 .05 .01
☐ 861 Pat Mahomes .10 .05 .01
☐ 862 Denny Neagle 1.25 .55 .16
☐ 863 Troy Buckley .10 .05 .01
☐ 864 Ray Ortiz .10 .05 .01
☐ 865 Leo Perez .10 .05 .01
☐ 866 Calvin Eldred .25 .11 .03
☐ 867 Darin Kracl .10 .05 .01
☐ 868 Lee Tinsley .20 .09 .03
☐ 869 T.R. Lewis .10 .05 .01
☐ 870 Jimmy Roso .10 .05 .01
☐ 871 Tom Taylor .10 .05 .01
☐ 872 Matt Anderson .10 .05 .01
☐ 873 Kerwin Moore .10 .05 .01
☐ 874 Rich Tunison .10 .05 .01
☐ 875 Brian Ahern .10 .05 .01
☐ 876 Eddie Taubensee .20 .09 .03
☐ 877 Scott Bryant .10 .05 .01
☐ 878 Steve Martin .10 .05 .01
☐ 879 Josias Manzanillo .10 .05 .01
☐ 880 Bob Zupcic .10 .05 .01

1990 Colorado Springs Sky Sox CMC

This 24-card standard-size set of the 1990 Colorado Springs Sky Sox, a Class AAA Pacific Coast League affiliate of the Cleveland Indians, features white-bordered posed color player photos on its fronts. The player's name and position appear at the bottom; the team name appears vertically on the left. The back carries the league emblem in the white area at the top, the team name in the green stripe below, and player's name, position, biography, and statistics in the yellow area at the bottom. 1,100 sets were produced.

	MINT	NRMT	EXC
COMPLETE SET (24)	5.00	2.20	.60

☐ 1 Mike Walker
☐ 2 Colby Ward
☐ 3 Joe Skalski
☐ 4 Efrain Valdez
☐ 5 Doug Robertson
☐ 6 Jeff Edwards
☐ 7 Greg McMichael
☐ 8 Carl Willis
☐ 9 Beau Allred
☐ 10 Jeff Kaiser
☐ 11 Ty Gainey
☐ 12 Tom Lampkin
☐ 13 Ever Magallanes
☐ 14 Tom Magrann
☐ 15 Jeff Manto
☐ 16 Luis Medina
☐ 17 Troy Neel
☐ 18 Steve Springer
☐ 19 Rick Adair CO
☐ 20 Turner Ward
☐ 21 Casey Webster
☐ 22 Jeff Wetherby
☐ 23 Alan Cockrell
☐ 24 Bobby Molinaro MGR

1990 Colorado Springs Sky Sox ProCards

This 27-card standard-size set of the 1990 Colorado Springs Sky Sox, a Class AAA Pacific Coast League affiliate of the Cleveland Indians, features on its white-bordered fronts posed color player photos set on simulated wood-grain backgrounds. The player's name, position, and team appear within a gold-colored rectangle below the photo. The tan horizontal back is bordered in white and carries the player's name at the top, followed by biography and statistics.

	MINT	NRMT	EXC
COMPLETE SET (27)	5.00	2.20	.60

☐ 30 Checklist
☐ 31 Greg McMichael
☐ 32 Doug Robertson
☐ 33 Jeff Shaw
☐ 34 Joe Skalski
☐ 35 Efrain Valdez
☐ 36 Mike Walker
☐ 37 Colby Ward
☐ 38 Carl Willis
☐ 39 Tom Lampkin
☐ 40 Tom Magrann
☐ 41 Juan Castillo
☐ 42 Ever Magallanes
☐ 43 Jeff Manto
☐ 44 Luis Medina
☐ 45 Troy Neel
☐ 46 Steve Springer
☐ 47 Casey Webster
☐ 48 Beau Allred
☐ 49 Alan Cockrell
☐ 50 Ty Gainey
☐ 51 Dwight Taylor
☐ 52 Turner Ward
☐ 53 Jeff Wetherby
☐ 54 Bobby Molinaro MGR
☐ 55 Buddy Bell CO
☐ 56 Rick Adair CO

1990 Columbia Mets Grand Slam

	MINT	NRMT	EXC
COMPLETE SET (30)	5.00	2.20	.60

☐ 1 Bill Stein MG
☐ 2 Jack Fisher CO
☐ 3 Tim McClinton
☐ 4 Jarrod Parker
☐ 5 Nick Davis
☐ 6 Joe McCann
☐ 7 James Harris
☐ 8 Reid Hartmann
☐ 9 Pat Howell
☐ 10 Deron Sample
☐ 11 Tim Howard
☐ 12 Brian Davis
☐ 13 Tito Navarro
☐ 14 Alberto Diaz
☐ 15 Julian Vasquez
☐ 16 Greg Langbehn
☐ 17 Art Emm
☐ 18 Ryan Richmond
☐ 19 Alberto Castillo
☐ 20 Chris Dorn
☐ 21 Joe Vitko
☐ 22 Brook Fordyce
☐ 23 Kevin Carroll
☐ 24 Mark Thomas
☐ 25 Stanton Cameron
☐ 26 Dave Telgheder
☐ 27 Bob Burton TR
☐ 28 Tim Marting GM
☐ 29 Jay Brazeau AMG
☐ 30 Team Photo

1990 Columbia Mets Postcards Play II

This 27-card set was issued in 4 series, with 7 cards in Series I, III-IV, and 6 in Series II. Play II produced 2,000 sets and 100 uncut sheets; 500 sets were given away at Mets games during the summer of '90. The cards measure 3 1/2" by 5" and are in the postcard format. The front design has posed glossy color player photos, with interlocking orange and navy blue borders. The player's name and team logo appear in blue and white stripes respectively below the picture. The backs are printed in dark blue. On the left half appears biography and player profile, while the right half has space for the address and stamp. The cards are numbered on the back within each series.

	MINT	NRMT	EXC
COMPLETE SET (27)	16.00	7.25	2.00

☐ 1 Bill Stein MGR
☐ 1 Deron Sample
☐ 1 Art Emm
☐ 1 David Telgheder
☐ 2 Alberto Castillo
☐ 2 Kevin Carroll
☐ 2 Alberto Diaz
☐ 2 Jarrod Parker
☐ 3 Joe Vitko
☐ 3 Julian Vasquez
☐ 3 Ryan Richmond
☐ 3 Pat Howell
☐ 4 Reid Hartmann
☐ 4 Stanton Cameron
☐ 4 Mark Thomas
☐ 4 Brook Fordyce
☐ 5 Joe McCann
☐ 5 Brian Davis
☐ 5 Chris Dorn
☐ 5 James Harris
☐ 6 Tim Howard
☐ 6 Tito Navarro
☐ 6 Nick Davis
☐ 6 Jack Fisher
☐ 7 Gregg Langbehn
☐ 7 Tim McClinton
☐ 7 1990 Columbia Mets Team Photo

1990 Columbus Clippers CMC

This 27-card standard-size set of the 1990 Columbus Clippers, a Class AAA International League affiliate of the New York Yankees, features white-bordered posed color player photos on its fronts. The player's name and position appear at the bottom; the team name appears vertically on the left. The back carries the league emblem in the white area at the top, the team name in the green stripe below, and player's name, position, biography, and statistics in the yellow area at the bottom. 1,100 sets were produced.

	MINT	NRMT	EXC
COMPLETE SET (27)	5.00	2.20	.60

☐ 1 Steve Adkins
☐ 2 Dave Eiland
☐ 3 John Habyan
☐ 4 Mark Leiter
☐ 5 Kevin Mmahat
☐ 6 Hipolito Pena
☐ 7 Willie Smith
☐ 8 Rich Monteleone
☐ 9 Hensley Meulens
☐ 10 Andy Stankiewicz
☐ 11 Jim Leyritz
☐ 12 Jim Walewander
☐ 13 Oscar Azocar
☐ 14 John Fishel
☐ 15 Jason Maas
☐ 16 Van Snider
☐ 17 Kevin Maas
☐ 18 Ricky Torres
☐ 19 Dave Sax
☐ 19 Jeff Datz
☐ 20 Darrin Chapin
☐ 21 Rob Sepanek
☐ 22 Mark Wasinger
☐ 23 Jimmy Jones
☐ 24 Coaches
Ken Rowe
Stump Merrill
Clete Boyer
Mike Heifferon
Troy Hillman
☐ 25 Carl Merrill MGR
☐ 26 Bob Davidson

1990 Columbus Clippers Police

	MINT	NRMT	EXC
COMPLETE SET (25)	5.00	2.20	.60

☐ 1 Ken Rowe CO
☐ 2 Clete Boyer CO
☐ 3 Stump Merrill MG
☐ 4 Kevin Maas
☐ 5 Jim Leyritz
☐ 6 John Fishel
☐ 7 Dave Sax
☐ 8 Jason Maas
☐ 9 Ron Davis
☐ 10 Bob Davidson
☐ 11 Mark Leiter
☐ 12 Oscar Azocar
☐ 13 Dave Eiland
☐ 14 Willie Smith
☐ 15 Van Snider
☐ 16 John Habyan
☐ 17 Steve Adkins
☐ 18 Brian Dorsett
☐ 19 Jimmy Jones
☐ 20 Kevin Mmahat

☐ 21 Jim Walewander
☐ 22 Rob Sepanek
☐ 23 Hensley Meulens
☐ 24 Andy Stankiewicz
☐ 25 Mark Wasinger

1990 Columbus Clippers ProCards

This 28-card standard-size set of the 1990 Columbus Clippers, a Class AAA International League affiliate of the New York Yankees, features on its white-bordered fronts posed color player photos set on simulated wood-grain backgrounds. The player's name, position, and team appear within a gold-colored rectangle below the photo. The tan horizontal back is bordered in white and carries the player's name at the top, followed by biography and statistics.

	MINT	NRMT	EXC
COMPLETE SET (28)	5.00	2.20	.60

☐ 666 Checklist
☐ 667 Steve Adkins
☐ 668 Darrin Chapin
☐ 669 Bob Davidson
☐ 670 Dave Eiland
☐ 671 John Habyan
☐ 672 Jimmy Jones
☐ 673 Mark Leiter
☐ 674 Kevin Mmahat
☐ 675 Rich Monteleone
☐ 676 Willie Smith
☐ 677 Ricky Torres
☐ 678 Jeff Datz
☐ 679 Brian Dorsett
☐ 680 Dave Sax
☐ 681 Jim Leyritz
☐ 682 Hensley Meulens
☐ 683 Carlos Rodriguez
☐ 684 Rob Sepanek
☐ 685 Andy Stankiewicz
☐ 686 Jim Walewander
☐ 687 Mark Wasinger
☐ 688 Oscar Azocar
☐ 689 John Fishel
☐ 690 Jason Maas
☐ 691 Kevin Maas
☐ 692 Van Snider
☐ 693 Field Staff
Clete Boyer
Stump Merrill MGR
Ken Row
Trey Hillman
Mike Heifferon

1990 Columbus Mudcats Best

This 26-card standard-size set of the 1990 Columbus Mudcats, a Class AA Southern League affiliate of the Houston Astros, features white-bordered posed and action color player photos on its fronts. The player's name and position appear vertically on the left side. The yellow horizontal back carries the player's name and position at the top, followed by biography, career highlights, and statistics. A player head shot appears in the lower right corner.

	MINT	NRMT	EXC
COMPLETE SET (26)	8.00	3.60	1.00

☐ 1 Willie Ansley
☐ 2 Andy Mota
☐ 3 Andujar Cedeno
☐ 4 Luis Gonzalez
☐ 5 Tony Eusebio
☐ 6 Dean Hartgraves
☐ 7 Rusty Harris
☐ 8 Burt Hunter
☐ 9 Jeff Baldwin
☐ 10 Bernie Jenkins
☐ 11 Harold Allen
☐ 12 Shane Reynolds
☐ 13 Rich Simon
☐ 14 Daven Bond
☐ 15 Wally Trice
☐ 16 Fred Costello
☐ 17 Todd Credeur
☐ 18 John Sheehan
☐ 19 Al Osuna
☐ 20 Mike Browning
☐ 21 Charley Taylor CO
☐ 22 Joe Mikulik
☐ 23 Ed Renteria
☐ 24 Dennis Tafoya
☐ 25 Jose Cano
☐ 26 Checklist

1990 Columbus Mudcats ProCards

This 27-card standard-size set of the 1990 Columbus Mudcats, a Class AA Southern League affiliate of the Houston Astros, features on its white-bordered fronts posed color player photos set on simulated wood-grain backgrounds. The player's name, position, and team appear within a gold-colored rectangle below the photo. The tan horizontal back is bordered in white and carries the player's name at the top, followed by biography and statistics.

	MINT	NRMT	EXC
COMPLETE SET (27)	7.00	3.10	.85

☐ 1336 Checklist
☐ 1337 Harold Allen
☐ 1338 Daven Bond
☐ 1339 Mike Browning
☐ 1340 Jose Cano
☐ 1341 Fred Costello
☐ 1342 Todd Credeur
☐ 1343 Dean Hartgraves
☐ 1344 Al Osuna
☐ 1345 Shane Reynolds
☐ 1346 John Sheehan
☐ 1347 Richie Simon
☐ 1348 Dennis Tafoya
☐ 1349 Wally Trice
☐ 1350 Tony Eusebio
☐ 1351 Andujar Cedeno
☐ 1352 Luis Gonzalez
☐ 1353 Rusty Harris
☐ 1354 Andy Nota
☐ 1355 Ed Renteria
☐ 1356 Willie Ansley
☐ 1357 Jeff Baldwin
☐ 1358 Bert Hunter
☐ 1359 Bernie Jenkins
☐ 1360 Joe Mikulik
☐ 1361 Rick Sweet MGR
☐ 1362 Charley Taylor CO

1990 Columbus Mudcats Star

This 29-card standard-size set of the 1990 Columbus Mudcats, a Class AA Southern League affiliate of the Houston Astros, features red bordered posed color player photos on its fronts. The player's name, team name, and position appear at the bottom. The white horizontal back carries the player's name at the top, followed by biography, career highlights, and statistics.

	MINT	NRMT	EXC
COMPLETE SET (29)	5.00	2.20	.60

☐ 1 Harold Allen
☐ 2 Willie Ansley
☐ 3 Eric Anthony
☐ 4 Jeff Baldwin
☐ 5 Daven Bond
☐ 6 Mike Browning
☐ 7 Andujar Cedeno
☐ 8 Fred Costello
☐ 9 Todd Credeur
☐ 10 Tony Eusebio
☐ 11 Luis Gonzalez
☐ 12 Rusty Harris
☐ 13 Dean Hartgraves
☐ 14 Bert Hunter
☐ 15 Bernie Jenkins
☐ 16 Joe Mikulik
☐ 17 Andy Mota
☐ 18 Joe Ortiz
☐ 19 Al Osuna
☐ 20 Ed Renteria
☐ 21 John Sheehan
☐ 22 Rich Simon
☐ 23 Dennis Tafoya
☐ 24 Wally Trice
☐ 25 Coaching Staff
Rick Sweet MGR
Carley Taylor
Bob Robertson
☐ 26 Ron Porterfield TR
☐ 27 Diamond Jim
☐ 28 Mason Dixon
☐ 29 Belinda Kay

1990 Denver Zephyrs CMC

This 26-card standard-size set of the 1990 Denver Zephyrs, a Class AAA American Association affiliate of the Milwaukee Brewers, features white-bordered posed color player photos on its fronts. The player's name and position appear at the bottom; the team name appears vertically on the left. The back carries the league emblem in the white area at the top, the team name in the green stripe below, and player's name, position, biography, and statistics in the yellow area at the bottom. 1,100 sets were produced.

	MINT	NRMT	EXC
COMPLETE SET (26)	5.00	2.20	.60

☐ 1 Jeff Peterek
☐ 2 Ed Puig
☐ 3 Tim Watkins
☐ 4 Tom Edens
☐ 5 Mike Capel
☐ 6 Darryel Walters
☐ 7 Joe Xavier
☐ 8 Tim Torricelli
☐ 9 Joe Redfield
☐ 10 D.L. Smith
☐ 11 Billy Moore
☐ 12 Joe Mitchell
☐ 13 Mario Monico
☐ 14 Frank Mattox
☐ 15 Tim McIntosh
☐ 16 Mark Higgins
☐ 17 George Canale
☐ 18 Don Gordon
☐ 19 Al Sadler
☐ 20 Don August
☐ 21 Mike Birkbeck
☐ 22 Dennis Powell
☐ 23 Chuck McGrath
☐ 24 Ruben Escalera
☐ 25 Dave Machemer MGR
☐ 26 Jackson Todd CO

1990 Denver Zephyrs ProCards

This 28-card standard-size set of the 1990 Denver Zephyrs, a Class AAA American Association affiliate of the Milwaukee Brewers, features on its white-bordered fronts posed color player photos set on simulated wood-grain backgrounds. The player's name, position, and team appear within a gold-colored rectangle below the photo. The tan horizontal back is bordered in white and carries the player's name at the top, followed by biography and statistics.

	MINT	NRMT	EXC
COMPLETE SET (28)	5.00	2.20	.60

☐ 615 Checklist
☐ 616 Don August
☐ 617 Mike Birkbeck
☐ 618 Mike Capel
☐ 619 Logan Easley
☐ 620 Tom Edens
☐ 621 Don Gordon
☐ 622 Chuck McGrath
☐ 623 Jeff Peterek
☐ 624 Dennis Powell
☐ 625 Ed Puig
☐ 626 Al Sadler
☐ 627 Tim Watkins
☐ 628 Tim McIntosh
☐ 629 Tim Torricelli
☐ 630 George Canale
☐ 631 Mark Higgins
☐ 632 Frank Mattox
☐ 633 Joe Mitchell
☐ 634 Joe Redfield
☐ 635 D.L. Smith
☐ 636 Joe Xavier
☐ 637 Ruben Escalera
☐ 638 Mario Monico
☐ 639 Billy Moore
☐ 640 Darryel Walters
☐ 641 Dave Machemer MGR
☐ 642 Jackson Todd CO

1990 Dunedin Blue Jays Star

This 28-card standard-size set of the 1990 Dunedin Blue Jays, a Class A Florida State League affiliate of the Toronto Blue Jays, features blue bordered posed color player photos on its fronts. The player's name, team name, and position appear at the bottom. The white horizontal back carries the player's name at the top, followed by biography, career highlights, and statistics.

	MINT	NRMT	EXC
COMPLETE SET (28)	5.00	2.20	.60

☐ 1 Chris Beacom
☐ 2 Denis Boucher
☐ 3 Pete Blohm
☐ 4 Tim Brown
☐ 5 Domingo Cedeno
☐ 6 Jesse Cross
☐ 7 Juan DeLaRosa
☐ 8 Rich DePastino
☐ 9 Ray Giannelli
☐ 10 Tim Hodge
☐ 11 Vince Horsman
☐ 12 Jeff Irish
☐ 13 Jeff Kent
☐ 14 Greg O'Halloran
☐ 15 Blaine Rudolph
☐ 16 Al Silverstein
☐ 17 Marcos Taveras
☐ 18 Mike Taylor
☐ 19 Ryan Thompson
☐ 20 Mike Timlin
☐ 21 Jason Townley
☐ 22 Rick Trlicek
☐ 23 Anthony Ward
☐ 24 Dave Weathers
☐ 25 Mark Young
☐ 26 Dennis Holmberg MG
☐ 27 Bill Monbouquette CO
☐ 28 Jon Woodworth TR

1990 Durham Bulls Team Issue

This 29-card set of the 1990 Durham Bulls, a Class A Carolina League affiliate of the Atlanta Braves, features team colors with classic head shots of each player. The set was sponsored by the Herald Sun and printed by SportsPrint in Atlanta on a high-gloss 14 pt. card stock and measure 2 3/8" X 3 1/2". This issue includes a first year minor league card of Ryan Klesko.

	MINT	NRMT	EXC
COMPLETE SET (29)	7.00	3.10	.85

☐ 1 Team Photo
☐ 2 Keith Mitchell
☐ 3 Brian Champion
☐ 4 Brian Deak
☐ 5 Ken Harring
☐ 6 Kevin Castleberry
☐ 7 Mike Mordecai
☐ 8 D.C. Campbell
☐ 9 Chris Czarnik
☐ 10 Marcos Vasquez
☐ 11 Skipper Wright
☐ 12 Popeye Cole
☐ 13 Edwin Alicea
☐ 14 Pat Tilmon
☐ 15 Theron Todd
☐ 16 Johnny Cuevas
☐ 17 David Nied
☐ 18 Josman Robles
☐ 19 Brian Cummings
☐ 20 Dave Brust
☐ 21 Rich Longuil
☐ 22 Phil Maldonado
☐ 23 Chad Smith
☐ 24 Rod Richey
☐ 25 Todd Dewey
☐ 26 Dave Karasinski
☐ 27 Nate Minchey
☐ 28 Larry Jaster
☐ 29 Grady Little

1990 Durham Bulls Update Team Issue

This 8-card update set of the 1990 Durham Bulls, a Class A Carolina League affiliate of the Atlanta Braves, features team colors with classic head shots of each player. The set was sponsored by the Herald Sun and printed by SportsPrint in Atlanta on a high-gloss 14 pt. card stock and measure 2 3/8" X 3 1/2". This issue includes a first year minor league card of Ryan Klesko.

	MINT	NRMT	EXC
COMPLETE SET (8)	30.00	13.50	3.70

☐ 1 Lee Johnson
☐ 2 Pedro Borbon Jr.
☐ 3 Scott Diez
☐ 4 Ben Rivera
☐ 5 Rod Byerly
☐ 6 Dan Snover
☐ 7 Ryan Klesko
☐ 8 Title Card

1990 Eastern League All-Stars ProCards

	MINT	NRMT	EXC
COMPLETE SET (48)	20.00	9.00	2.50

☐ EL1 Checklist
☐ EL2 Don Sparks
☐ EL3 John Toale
☐ EL4 Rico Brogna
☐ EL5 Tim Leiper
☐ EL6 Rusty Meacham
☐ EL7 Arnie Beyeler
☐ EL8 Jack Voigt
☐ EL9 Scott Meadows
☐ EL10 Paul Thorpe
☐ EL11 Butch Hobson MGR
☐ EL12 Wade Taylor
☐ EL13 Royal Clayton
☐ EL14 Greg Sparks
☐ EL15 Mitch Lyden
☐ EL16 Ken Pennington
☐ EL17 Mike Gardiner
☐ EL18 Dana Ridenour
☐ EL19 Gary Alexander
☐ EL20 Kim Batiste
☐ EL21 Pat Kelly
☐ EL22 Mark Sims
☐ EL23 Vince Holyfield
☐ EL24 Julio Peguero
☐ EL25 Carlos Garcia
☐ EL26 John Wehner
☐ EL27 Jim Tracy
☐ EL28 Spin Williams CO
☐ EL29 Marc Bombard MGR
☐ EL30 Steve Adams
☐ EL31 Bob Ayrault
☐ EL32 Kevin Morton
☐ EL33 Jeff Plympton
☐ EL34 Bobby Latmore
☐ EL35 Al Liebert
☐ EL36 Mark Lewis
☐ EL37 Charles Nagy
☐ EL38 Mike Curtis
☐ EL39 Mike Kelly
☐ EL40 Jeff Bagwell
☐ EL41 Eric Wedge
☐ EL42 John Ramos
☐ EL43 Stacey Burdick
☐ EL44 Luis Mercedes

☐ EL45 Bernie Williams
☐ EL46 Mike Wilkins
☐ EL47 Gordon Hurlbert TR
☐ EL48 Mike DeLao TR

1990 Edmonton Trappers CMC

This 24-card standard-size set of the 1990 Edmonton Trappers, a Class AAA Pacific Coast League affiliate of the California Angels, features white-bordered posed color player photos on its fronts. The player's name and position appear at the bottom; the team name appears vertically on the left. The back carries the league emblem in the white area at the top, the team name in the green stripe below, and player's name, position, biography, and statistics in the yellow area at the bottom. 1,100 sets were produced.

	MINT	NRMT	EXC
COMPLETE SET (24)	5.00	2.20	.60

☐ 1 Cliff Young
☐ 2 Max Oliveras MG
☐ 3 Gary Buckels
☐ 4 Chris Beasley
☐ 4 Timothy Burcham
2nd #4 in team
☐ 5 Sherman Corbett
☐ 6 Mike Erb
☐ 7 Mike Fetters
☐ 8 Chuck Hernandez CO
☐ 9 Jeff Heathcock
☐ 10 Scott Lewis
☐ 11 Rafael Montalvo
☐ 12 John Skurla
☐ 13 Lee Stevens
☐ 14 Nelson Rood
☐ 15 Bobby Rose
☐ 16 Dan Grunhard
☐ 17 Reed Peters
☐ 18 Doug Davis
☐ 19 Gary DiSarcina
☐ 20 Pete Coachman
☐ 21 Chris Cron
☐ 22 Karl Allaire
☐ 23 Ron Tingley

1990 Edmonton Trappers ProCards

This 25-card standard-size set of the 1990 Edmonton Trappers, a Class AAA Pacific Coast League affiliate of the California Angels, features on its white-bordered fronts posed color player photos set on simulated wood-grain backgrounds. The player's name, position, and team appear within a gold-colored rectangle below the photo. The tan horizontal back is bordered in white and carries the player's name and position at the top, followed by biography and statistics.

	MINT	NRMT	EXC
COMPLETE SET (25)	5.00	2.20	.60

☐ 508 Checklist
☐ 509 Chris Beasley
☐ 510 Gary Buckels
☐ 511 Tim Burcham
☐ 512 Sherman Corbett
☐ 513 Mike Erb
☐ 514 Mike Fetters
☐ 515 Jeff Heathcock
☐ 516 Scott Lewis
☐ 517 Rafael Montalvo
☐ 518 Cliff Young
☐ 519 Doug Davis
☐ 520 Ron Tingley
☐ 521 Karl Allaire
☐ 522 Pete Coachman
☐ 523 Chris Cron
☐ 524 Gay DiSarcina
☐ 525 Nelson Rood
☐ 526 Bobby Rose
☐ 527 Lee Stevens
☐ 528 Dan Grunhard
☐ 529 Reed Peters
☐ 530 John Skurla
☐ 531 Max Oliveras MG
☐ 532 Chuck Hernandez CO

1990 El Paso Diablos All-Time Greats Team Issue

	MINT	NRMT	EXC
COMPLETE SET (45)			

☐ 1 Billy Bates
☐ 2 Chris Bosio
☐ 3 Glenn Braggs
☐ 4 Jesus Alfaro
☐ 5 Dan Plesac
☐ 6 Teddy Higuera
☐ 7 Chuck Crim
☐ 8 Dale Sveum
☐ 9 Ernie Riles
☐ 10 Carlos Ponce
☐ 11 Jim Paciorek
☐ 12 Mike Felder
☐ 13 Randy Ready
☐ 14 Dion James
☐ 15 Doug Jones
☐ 16 Edgar Diaz
☐ 17 Tony Muser MGR
☐ 18 Bill Schroeder
☐ 19 Buck Rodgers
☐ 20 Duffy Dyer
☐ 21 Chris George
☐ 22 James Austin
☐ 23 Jaime Navarro
☐ 24 Tim McIntosh
☐ 25 Greg Vaughn
☐ 26 Bill Spiers
☐ 27 Gary Sheffield
☐ 28 George Canale
☐ 29 Tim Crews
☐ 30 Charlie O'Brien
☐ 31 La Vel Freeman
☐ 32 Tom Candiotti
☐ 33 Mike Witt
☐ 34 Tom Brunansky
☐ 35 Brian Harper
☐ 36 Ken Schrom
☐ 37 Mark Clear
☐ 38 Dan Boone
☐ 39 Floyd Rayford
☐ 40 Carney Lansford
☐ 41 Ken Landreaux
☐ 42 Rance Mulliniks
☐ 43 Willie Mays Aikens
☐ 44 Bobby Knoop MGR
☐ NNO Team Logo

1990 El Paso Diablos Grand Slam

	MINT	NRMT	EXC
COMPLETE SET (25)	5.00	2.20	.60

☐ 1 Dave Huppert MG
☐ 2 Paul Lindblad CO
☐ 3 Jesus Alfaro
☐ 4 Shon Ashley
☐ 5 James Austin
☐ 6 Mark Chapman
☐ 7 Craig Cooper
☐ 8 Dee Dixon
☐ 9 Greg Edge
☐ 10 Cal Eldred
☐ 11 Ruben Escalera
☐ 12 Dean Freeland
☐ 13 Robinson Garces
☐ 14 Chris George
☐ 15 Sandy Guerrero
☐ 16 Mitch Hannahs
☐ 17 Bert Heffernan
☐ 18 Mike Ignasiak
☐ 19 Joe Kmak
☐ 20 Scott May
☐ 21 Charles McGrath
☐ 22 Steve Monson
☐ 23 Charlie Montoyo
☐ 24 Ed Puig
☐ 25 Rafael Skeete

1990 Elizabethton Twins Star

This 26-card standard-size set of the 1990 Elizabethton Twins, a Rookie Class Appalachian League affiliate of the Minnesota Twins, features blue bordered posed color player photos on its fronts. The player's name, team name, and position appear at the bottom. The white horizontal back carries the player's name at the top, followed by biography, career highlights, and statistics.

	MINT	NRMT	EXC
COMPLETE SET (26)	6.00	2.70	.75

☐ 1 Rich Becker
☐ 2 Tom Benson
☐ 3 Jose Bethancourt
☐ 4 David Bigham
☐ 5 Todd Blakeman
☐ 6 Brent Brede
☐ 7 Matt Brown
☐ 8 Sandy Diaz
☐ 9 Roger Dixon
☐ 10 Tom Gavin
☐ 11 John Gumpf
☐ 12 Jon Henry
☐ 13 Damian Miller
☐ 14 Matt Morse
☐ 15 Devin Peppers
☐ 16 Tim Pershing
☐ 17 Kurt Pfeffer
☐ 18 Cisco Pichardo
☐ 19 Todd Ritchie
☐ 20 Paul Russo
☐ 21 Tony Spaan
☐ 22 Steve Taylor
☐ 23 Chris Wallgren
☐ 24 Ray Smith CO
☐ 25 Coaches
Jim Lemon MGR
Rick Tomlin
☐ 26 Joe Hubbard TR

1990 Elmira Pioneers Pucko

	MINT	NRMT	EXC
COMPLETE SET (27)	7.00	3.10	.85

☐ 1 Tim Graham
☐ 2 Dave Alvarez
☐ 3 Randy Brown
☐ 4 Tim Davis
☐ 5 Jason Friedman
☐ 6 Larry Grant
☐ 7 Jeff Limoncelli
☐ 8 Shea Wardwell
☐ 9 Willie Dukes
☐ 10 Jose Lora
☐ 11 Jose Malave
☐ 12 Jeff McNeeley
☐ 13 Joe Demus
☐ 14 John Lammon
☐ 15 Chris Davis
☐ 16 Jim Dennison
☐ 17 Gar Finnvold
☐ 18 John Locker
☐ 19 Erik Plantenberg
☐ 20 Dave Ring
☐ 21 Silverio Santa Maria
☐ 22 Cedric Santiago
☐ 23 Tim Smith
☐ 24 Brian Young
☐ 25 Mike Verdi MGR
☐ 26 Mike Quatrine TR
☐ 27 Checklist
Old Pioneer , Friend

1990 Erie Sailors Star

This 31-card standard-size set of the 1990 Erie Sailors, a Class A New York-Penn League Independent, features purple bordered posed color player photos on its fronts. The player's name, team name, and position appear at the bottom. The white horizontal back carries the player's name at the top, followed by biography, career highlights, and statistics.

	MINT	NRMT	EXC
COMPLETE SET (31)	5.00	2.20	.60

☐ 1 Joe Boyce
☐ 2 Mark Cerny
☐ 3 Stan Cook
☐ 4 Brian Currie
☐ 5 Gary Daniels
☐ 6 D.J. Floyd
☐ 7 Brian Golden
☐ 8 Van Golmont
☐ 9 Mike Holland
☐ 10 Mike Jockish
☐ 11 Robbie Kemper
☐ 12 Mike Larson
☐ 13 Mike Lomeli
☐ 14 Darryll MacMillan
☐ 15 Greg McCutcheon
☐ 16 Linc Mikkelson
☐ 17 Thomas Mitchell
☐ 18 Andy Postema
☐ 19 Brian Reimsnyder
☐ 20 Jerry Rizza
☐ 21 Ruben Rodriguez
☐ 22 Joe Roebuck
☐ 23 Shaun Sanderson
☐ 24 Mike Songini
☐ 25 Al Stacey
☐ 26 Rod Tafoya
☐ 27 Steve Woide
☐ 28 Gary Wurm
☐ 29 Mal Fichman MGR
☐ 30 David Voit
☐ 31 Brad Weitzel CO

1990 Eugene Emeralds Grand Slam

	MINT	NRMT	EXC
COMPLETE SET (30)	5.00	2.20	.60

☐ 1 Javier Alvarez
☐ 2 Francisco Baez
☐ 3 Ramy Brooks
☐ 4 Jay Carballo
☐ 5 Scott Davis
☐ 6 Weddison Ebanks
☐ 7 Sean Franceschi
☐ 8 Chuck Frederick
☐ 9 Harry Guanchez
☐ 10 Rafael Gutierrez
☐ 11 Dave Haber
☐ 12 Donny Harrel
☐ 13 Doug Harris
☐ 14 Phil Hiatt
☐ 15 Dave Hierholzer
☐ 16 Brad Holman
☐ 17 Darron Johnson
☐ 18 Tony Long
☐ 19 Giovanni Miranda
☐ 20 Ricky Moser
☐ 21 Gabriel Pineda
☐ 22 Doug Peters
☐ 23 Damon Pollard
☐ 24 Shayne Rea
☐ 25 Dave Rolls
☐ 26 Arnie Sambel
☐ 27 Doug Shields
☐ 28 Vernon Slater
☐ 29 Brady Stewart
☐ 30 Shannon Strong

1990 Everett Giants Best

This 28-card standard-size set of the 1990 Everett Giants, a Class A Northwest League affiliate of the San Francisco Giants, features white-bordered posed and action color player photos on its fronts. The player's name and position appear vertically on the left side. The yellow horizontal back carries the player's name and position at the top, followed by biography, career highlights, and statistics. A player head shot appears in the lower right corner.

	MINT	NRMT	EXC
COMPLETE SET (28)	5.00	2.20	.60

☐ 1 Adam Hyzdu
☐ 2 Dan Varnell
☐ 3 Dan Carlson
☐ 4 Dan Flanagan
☐ 5 Frank Gould
☐ 6 Jim Huslig
☐ 7 The Walker
☐ 8 Brian McLeod
☐ 9 Mike Myers
☐ 10 Kurt Peltzer
☐ 11 Joe Rosselli
☐ 12 Mark Yockey
☐ 13 Eric Christopherson
☐ 14 Marcus Jensen
☐ 15 Jason Sievers
☐ 16 Mate Borgogno
☐ 17 Brian Dakin
☐ 18 Mike Helms
☐ 19 Tony Spires
☐ 20 Ricky Ward
☐ 21 Jason Young
☐ 22 Courtney Davis
☐ 23 Shelby Hard
☐ 24 Lenny Ayres
☐ 25 John Jackson
☐ 26 Derek Reid
☐ 27 Keith Ringgold
☐ 28 Dave Edwards

1990 Everett Giants ProCards

This 32-card standard-size set of the 1990 Everett Giants, a Class A Northwest League affiliate of the San Francisco Giants, features on its white-bordered fronts posed color player photos set on simulated wood-grain backgrounds. The player's name, position, and team appear within a gold-colored rectangle below the photo. The tan horizontal back is bordered in white and carries the player's name at the top, followed by biography and statistics.

	MINT	NRMT	EXC
COMPLETE SET (32)	5.00	2.20	.60

☐ 3116 Checklist
☐ 3117 Lenny Ayres
☐ 3118 Scott Ebert
☐ 3119 Dan Carlson
☐ 3120 Dan Flanagan
☐ 3121 Frank Gould
☐ 3122 James Huslig
☐ 3123 Kevin McGehee
☐ 3124 Brian McLeod
☐ 3125 Mike Myers
☐ 3126 Kurt Peltzer
☐ 3127 Joe Rosselli
☐ 3128 Mark Yockey
☐ 3129 Eric Christopherson
☐ 3130 Marcus Jensen
☐ 3131 Jason Sievers
☐ 3132 Mate Borgono
☐ 3133 Brian Dakin
☐ 3134 Mike Helms
☐ 3135 Tony Spires
☐ 3136 Rick Ward
☐ 3137 Jason Young
☐ 3138 Courtney Davis
☐ 3139 Shelby Hart
☐ 3140 Adam Hyzdu
☐ 3141 John Jackson
☐ 3142 Derek Reid
☐ 3143 Keith Ringgold
☐ 3144 Dan Varnell
☐ 3145 Deron McCue MGR
☐ 3146 Diego Segui CO
☐ 3147 Juan Lopez CO

1990 Florida State League All-Stars Star

	MINT	NRMT	EXC
COMPLETE SET (50)	18.00	8.00	2.20

☐ 1 Cam Biberdorf
☐ 2 Bobby DeLoach

☐ 3 Bruce Dostal
☐ 4 D.J. Dozier
☐ 5 Jim Faulk
☐ 6 Dan Freed
☐ 7 John Johnstone
☐ 8 Jeff Juden
☐ 9 Anthony Kelley
☐ 10 George Kerfut
☐ 11 Kenny Lofton
☐ 12 Scott Makarewicz
☐ 13 John Massarelli
☐ 14 John Mello
☐ 15 Joe Millette
☐ 16 Nikco Riesgo
☐ 17 Roman Taveras
☐ 18 Tony Trevino
☐ 19 Jeff Vanzytveld
☐ 20 Eric Young
☐ 21 Pete Young
☐ 22 Alan Zinter
☐ 23 Felipe Alou
☐ 24 Tim Blackwell
☐ 25 Doyle Balthazar
☐ 26 Jacob Brumfield
☐ 27 Jesse Cross
☐ 28 Ivan Cruz
☐ 29 Everett Cunningham
☐ 30 John DeSilva
☐ 31 Greg Harvey
☐ 32 Garrett Jenkins
☐ 33 Jeff Kent
☐ 34 Keith Kimberlin
☐ 35 Jay Knoblauh
☐ 36 Barry Manuel
☐ 37 Javier Ocasio
☐ 38 Greg O'Halloran
☐ 39 David Perez
☐ 40 Tom Popplewell
☐ 41 Ivan Rodriguez
☐ 42 Fred Samson
☐ 43 Larry Stanford
☐ 44 Scott Tedder
☐ 45 Mike Timlin
☐ 46 Jason Townley
☐ 47 Anthony Ward
☐ 48 Dennis Holmberg
☐ 49 John Lipon
☐ 50 Bobby Jones

1990 Fayetteville Generals ProCards

This 28-card standard-size set of the 1990 Fayetteville Generals, a Class A South Atlantic League affiliate of the Detroit Tigers, features on its white-bordered fronts posed color player photos set on simulated wood-grain backgrounds. The player's name, position, and team appear within a gold-colored rectangle below the photo. The tan horizontal back is bordered in white and carries the player's name at the top, followed by biography and statistics.

	MINT	NRMT	EXC
COMPLETE SET (28)	5.00	2.20	.60

☐ 2396 Checklist
☐ 2397 Jeffrey Braley
☐ 2398 Michael Garcia
☐ 2399 Frank Gonzales
☐ 2400 Jose Guzman
☐ 2401 Tim Herrmann
☐ 2402 Linty Ingram
☐ 2403 Mike Koller
☐ 2404 Randy Marshall
☐ 2405 Brian Rountree
☐ 2406 Mal Seibert
☐ 2407 Marino Stefany
☐ 2408 Leo Torres
☐ 2409 Mike Gillette
☐ 2410 Hunter Hoffman
☐ 2411 Kasey McKeon
☐ 2412 Rick Sellers
☐ 2413 Ron Howard
☐ 2414 Don Pedersen
☐ 2415 Patrick Pesavento
☐ 2416 Mike Rendina
☐ 2417 Gino Tagliaferri
☐ 2418 Freddy Torres
☐ 2419 Art Caines
☐ 2420 Brian Cornelius
☐ 2421 Rudy Pemberton
☐ 2422 Team Picture
☐ 2423 Gene Roof MGR

1990 Frederick Keys Team Issue

	MINT	NRMT	EXC
COMPLETE SET (30)	6.00	2.70	.75

☐ 1 Wally Moon
☐ 2 Mike Pazik
☐ 3 Bobby Miscik
☐ 4 Tony Beasley
☐ 5 Mike Deutach
☐ 6 Mike Richardson
☐ 7 Steve Mondile
☐ 8 Rich Slomkowaki
☐ 9 Doug Reynolds
☐ 10 Zachary Kerr
☐ 11 Anthony Telford
☐ 12 Stacy Jones
☐ 13 Paris Hayden
☐ 14 Roy Gilbert
☐ 15 Tim Holland
☐ 16 Mike Lehman
☐ 17 Ken Shamburg
☐ 18 Ricky Gutierrez
☐ 19 Dan Berthel
☐ 20 Pete Rose Jr.
☐ 21 Ed Horowitz
☐ 22 Mike Oquist
☐ 23 Bob Stiegele
☐ 24 Todd Stephan
☐ 25 Andres Constant
☐ 26 Chuck Riccitant
☐ 27 Jeff Bumgarner
☐ 28 Pat Hedgearner
☐ 29 Art Rhodes
☐ 30 Brad Hildreth

1990 Ft. Lauderdale Yankees Star

This 27-card standard-size set of the 1990 Ft. Lauderdale Yankees, a Class A Florida State League affiliate of the New York Yankees, features purple bordered posed color player photos on its fronts. The player's name, team name, and position appear at the bottom. The white horizontal back carries the player's name at the top, followed by biography, career highlights, and statistics.

	MINT	NRMT	EXC
COMPLETE SET (27)	5.00	2.20	.60

☐ 1 Rich Barnwell
☐ 2 John Brubaker
☐ 3 Hernan Cortes
☐ 4 Todd Devereaux
☐ 5 Mike Draper
☐ 6 Kirk Dulom
☐ 7 Rod Ehrhard
☐ 8 Victor Garcia Jr.
☐ 9 Ken Greer
☐ 10 Jeff Johnson
☐ 11 Jay Knoblauh
☐ 12 Jeff Livesey
☐ 13 Skip Nelloms
☐ 14 Tom Newell
☐ 15 Rey Noriega
☐ 16 Mark Ohlms
☐ 17 Ed Pimentel
☐ 18 Tom Popplewell
☐ 19 Larry Stanford
☐ 20 Dave Turgeon
☐ 21 Hector Vargas
☐ 22 Gerald Williams
☐ 23 Mike Hart MGR
☐ 24 Dave Schuler CO
☐ 25 Rob Thomson CO
☐ 26 Mark Zettelmeyer GM
☐ 27 Adam Wagner TR

1990 Gastonia Rangers Best

This 30-card standard-size set of the 1990 Gastonia Rangers, a Class A South Atlantic League affiliate of the Texas Rangers, features white-bordered posed and action color player photos on its fronts. The player's name and position appear vertically on the left side. The yellow horizontal back carries the player's name and position at the top, followed by biography, career highlights, and statistics. A player head shot appears in the lower right corner.

	MINT	NRMT	EXC
COMPLETE SET (30)	5.00	2.20	.60

☐ 1 Tony Scruggs
☐ 2 Ronaldo Romero
☐ 3 Carl Randle
☐ 4 Travis Buckley
☐ 5 Ken Powell
☐ 6 Joey Eischen
☐ 7 Brian Romero
☐ 8 Buddy Micheu
☐ 9 Jonathan Hurst
☐ 10 Joey Wardlow
☐ 11 Jay Franklin
☐ 12 Troy Eklund
☐ 13 Brian Evans
☐ 14 Eric Bickhardt
☐ 15 Brian Steiner
☐ 16 Barry Winford
☐ 17 Timmie Morrow
☐ 18 Randy Marshall
☐ 19 Michael Arner
☐ 20 Joe Lewis
☐ 21 Jose Oliva
☐ 22 Craig Newkirk
☐ 23 John Graves
☐ 24 James Clinton
☐ 25 Orlando Gomez
☐ 26 Marvin White CO
☐ 27 Randy Whisler CO
☐ 28 Tom Tisdale
☐ 29 Ramon Stantiago MGR
☐ 30 Checklist

1990 Gastonia Rangers ProCards

This 29-card standard-size set of the 1990 Gastonia Rangers, a Class A South Atlantic League affiliate of the Texas Rangers, features on its white-bordered fronts posed color player photos set on simulated wood-grain backgrounds. The player's name, position, and team appear within a gold-colored rectangle below the photo. The tan horizontal back is bordered in white and carries the player's name at the top, followed by biography and statistics.

	MINT	NRMT	EXC
COMPLETE SET (29)	5.00	2.20	.60

☐ 2510 Checklist
☐ 2511 Mike Arner
☐ 2512 Eric Bickhardt
☐ 2513 Travis Buckley
☐ 2514 Joey Eischen
☐ 2515 Brian Evans
☐ 2516 Jay Franklin
☐ 2517 John Graves
☐ 2518 Jonathan Hurst
☐ 2519 Carl Randle
☐ 2520 Brian Romero
☐ 2521 Ronaldo Romero
☐ 2522 Brian Steiner
☐ 2523 Joe Lewis
☐ 2524 Buddy Micheu
☐ 2525 Barry Winford
☐ 2526 Mike Burton
☐ 2527 Jim Clinton
☐ 2528 Randy Marshall
☐ 2529 Craig Newkirk
☐ 2530 Jose Oliva
☐ 2531 Joey Wardlow
☐ 2532 Troy Eklund
☐ 2533 Timmie Morrow
☐ 2534 Kenny Powell
☐ 2535 Tony Scruggs
☐ 2536 Orlando Gomez MGR
☐ 2537 Randy Whisler CO
☐ 2538 Marvin White CO

1990 Gastonia Rangers Star

This 29-card standard-size set of the 1990 Gastonia Rangers, a Class A South Atlantic League affiliate of the Texas Rangers, features blue bordered posed color player photos on its fronts. The player's name, team name, and position appear at the bottom. The white horizontal back carries the player's name at the top, followed by biography, career highlights, and statistics.

	MINT	NRMT	EXC
COMPLETE SET (29)	5.00	2.20	.60

☐ 1 Michael Arner
☐ 2 Eric Bickhardt
☐ 3 Travis Buckley
☐ 4 Michael Burton
☐ 5 James Clinton
☐ 6 Joey Eischen
☐ 7 Troy Eklund
☐ 8 Brian Evans
☐ 9 Jay Franklin
☐ 10 John Graves
☐ 11 Jonathan Hurst
☐ 12 Joe Lewis
☐ 13 Randy Marshall
☐ 14 Bubby Micheu
☐ 15 Timmie Morrow
☐ 16 Craig Newkirk
☐ 17 Jose Oliva
☐ 18 Ken Powell
☐ 19 Carl Randle
☐ 20 Brian Romero
☐ 21 Ronaldo Romero
☐ 22 Tony Scruggs
☐ 23 Brian Steiner
☐ 24 Joey Wardlow
☐ 25 Barry Winford
☐ 26 Orlando Gomez MGR
☐ 27 Marvin White CO
☐ 28 Perry Hill
Hitting Instructor
☐ 29 Randy Whisler CO

1990 Gate City Pioneers ProCards

This 27-card standard-size set of the 1990 Gate City Pioneers, a Rookie Class Pioneer League Independent, features on its white-bordered fronts posed color player photos set on simulated wood-grain backgrounds. The player's name, position, and team appear within a gold-colored rectangle below the photo. The tan horizontal back is bordered in white and carries the player's name at the top, followed by biography and statistics.

	MINT	NRMT	EXC
COMPLETE SET (27)	5.00	2.20	.60

☐ 3337 Checklist
☐ 3338 Keith Casey
Card # says 3337
☐ 3339 Akihiko Chiyomaru
☐ 3340 Hiroyuki Satoh
☐ 3341 Hector Ortega
☐ 3342 Hideki Masuzawa
☐ 3343 Carlos Espinoza
☐ 3344 William Martinez
☐ 3345 Itsuki Asai
☐ 3346 Jim Heilgeist
☐ 3347 Tony Marabella
☐ 3348 Tyrone Horne
☐ 3349 Hector Rivera
☐ 3350 Mike Fier
☐ 3351 Paul Hutto
☐ 3352 Gary Adams
☐ 3353 Buck Atwater
☐ 3354 Angelo Santiago
☐ 3355 Trey Wilburn
☐ 3356 Doug Noce
☐ 3357 Chris Emerick
☐ 3358 Takashi Maema
☐ 3359 Kelly Frederiksen
☐ 3360 Perry Sanchez
☐ 3361 David Carter
☐ 3362 Keiji Abe CO
☐ 3363 Eddie Bonine CO

1990 Gate City Pioneers Sports Pro

This 30-card standard-size set of the 1990 Gate City Pioneers, a Rookie Class A Pioneer League Independent, features posed color head-and-shoulders shots, with thin black borders on a white card face. The horizontally oriented backs have biographical information.

	MINT	NRMT	EXC
COMPLETE SET (24)	6.00	2.70	.75

☐ 1 Gary Adams
☐ 2 Itsuki Asai
☐ 3 Tyrone Atwater
☐ 4 David Carter
☐ 5 Keith Casey
☐ 6 Akihiko Chiyomaru
☐ 7 Chris Emerick
☐ 8 Trey Wilburn
☐ 9 Mike Fier
☐ 10 Kelly Frederiksen
☐ 11 Jim Heilgeist
☐ 12 Tyrone Horne
☐ 13 Paul Hutto
☐ 14 Takashi Maema
☐ 15 Tony Marabella
☐ 16 Angelo Santiago
☐ 17 Hideki Mizusawa
☐ 18 Doug Noce
☐ 19 Hiroyuki Satoh
☐ 20 Hector Rivera
☐ 21 Perry Sanchez
☐ 22 Ed Bonine CO
☐ 23 Keiji Abe CO
☐ 24 Ed Creech MG

1990 Geneva Cubs ProCards

This 27-card standard-size set of the 1990 Geneva Cubs, a Class A New York-Penn League affiliate of the Chicago Cubs, features on its white-bordered fronts posed color player photos set on simulated wood-grain backgrounds. The player's name, position, and team appear within a gold-colored rectangle below the photo. The tan horizontal back is bordered in white and carries the player's name at the top, followed by biography and statistics.

	MINT	NRMT	EXC
COMPLETE SET (27)	5.00	2.20	.60

☐ 3028 Checklist
☐ 3029 Lance Dickson
☐ 3030 Troy Bradford
☐ 3031 Ricardo Medina
☐ 3032 Brad Huff
☐ 3033 Brad Erdman
☐ 3034 Victor Cancel
☐ 3035 Charlie Fiacco
☐ 3036 Phil Dauphin
☐ 3037 Greg Kessler
☐ 3038 Joe Porcelli
☐ 3039 German Diaz
☐ 3040 Bill Paynter
☐ 3041 Jessie Hollins
☐ 3042 Clinton White
☐ 3043 John DeRicco
☐ 3044 Andrew Hartung
☐ 3045 Tim Delgado
☐ 3046 Mike Young
☐ 3047 Stephen Coffey
☐ 3048 Paul Torres
☐ 3049 Tim Parker
☐ 3050 Luis Benitez
☐ 3051 Amilcar Correa
☐ 3052 Roberto Smalls
☐ 3053 Bill Hayes MGR
☐ 3054 Joe Housey CO

1990 Geneva Cubs Star

This 26-card standard-size set of the 1990 Geneva Cubs, a Class A New York-Penn League affiliate of the Chicago Cubs, features light orange bordered posed color player photos on its fronts. The player's name, team name, and position appear at the bottom. The white horizontal back carries the player's name at the top, followed by biography, career highlights, and statistics.

	MINT	NRMT	EXC
COMPLETE SET (26)	5.00	2.20	.60

☐ 1 Luis Benitez
☐ 2 Troy Bradford
☐ 3 Victor Cancel
☐ 4 Stephen Coffey
☐ 5 Amilcar Correa
☐ 6 Phil Dauphin Jr.
☐ 7 Paul Torres
☐ 8 John DeRicco
☐ 9 German Diaz
☐ 10 Lance Dickson
☐ 11 Brad Erdman
☐ 12 Charlie Fiacco
☐ 13 Andrew Hartung
☐ 14 Jessie Hollins
☐ 15 Brad Huff
☐ 16 Greg Kessler
☐ 17 Ricardo Medina
☐ 18 Tim Parker
☐ 19 Bill Paynter
☐ 20 Joe Porcelli
☐ 21 Gabby Rodriguez
☐ 22 Roberto Smalls
☐ 23 Carl Stanley
☐ 24 Clinton White
☐ 25 Michael Young
☐ 26 Bill Hayes
Field Manager

1990 Georgia College Colonials

	MINT	NRMT	EXC
COMPLETE SET (35)	10.00	4.50	1.25

☐ 1 Ryan Butcher
☐ 2 Mark Estes
☐ 3 Matt Fincher
☐ 4 Larry Flowers
☐ 5 Andry Gentry
☐ 6 Craig Griner
☐ 7 Lee Henderson
☐ 8 Edgar Herrera
☐ 9 Mark Hightower
☐ 10 Doug Jones
☐ 11 Chad Jubyna
☐ 12 Rusty Kea
☐ 13 Bill Kemp
☐ 14 John King
☐ 15 Eric Kobbe
☐ 16 John Kurtz CO
☐ 17 Kevin Laudenslager
☐ 18 Anthony Leatherwood
☐ 19 Carlos Lopez
☐ 20 Greg Manley
☐ 21 Darrell McMillin
☐ 22 Michael Murrell
☐ 23 James Parker
☐ 24 Chad Payne
☐ 25 Willard Riner MG
☐ 26 Larry Schenck
☐ 27 Jeff Silvey
☐ 28 Mark Snider
☐ 29 Crandall Stamps
☐ 30 Eugene Tuggle
☐ 31 Clay Vinson
☐ 32 Todd Ward
☐ 33 Larry Schenck
Lee Henderson
Todd Ward
☐ 34 Carlos Lopez
Edgar Herrera
☐ 35 Dan Barry TR
Angela Johnson MG

1990 Great Falls Dodgers Sports Pro

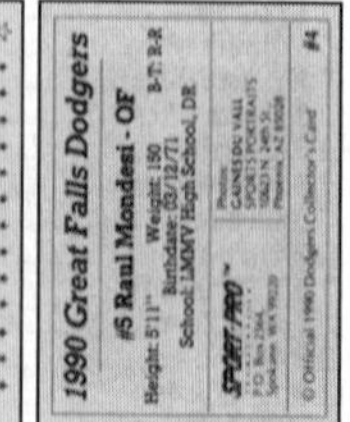

This 30-card standard-size set of the 1990 Great Falls Dodgers, a Rookie Class A Pioneer League affiliate of the Los Angeles Dodgers, features posed color head-and-shoulders shots, with thin black borders on a white card face. The horizontally oriented backs have biographical information. This issue includes the minor league card debuts of Pedro J. Martinez and Raul Mondesi.

	MINT	NRMT	EXC
COMPLETE SET (30)	40.00	18.00	5.00

☐ 1 Ron Walden
☐ 2 Dan Gray
☐ 3 Mike Busch
☐ 4 Ed Lund
☐ 5 James Daspit
☐ 6 Raul Mondesi
☐ 7 Lonnie Webb
☐ 8 Keoki Farrish
☐ 9 Mark Mimbs
☐ 10 Mike Mimbs
☐ 11 Burgess Watts
☐ 12 Pedro J. Martinez
☐ 13 David Baumann
☐ 14 Eric Blackwell
☐ 15 Jason Derr
☐ 16 Junior Perez
☐ 17 Don Meyers
☐ 18 Garey Ingram
☐ 19 Ken Hamilton
☐ 20 Gordon Tipton
☐ 21 Mike Frauenhoffer
☐ 22 Dan Andrews
☐ 23 Brain Piotrowicz
☐ 24 John Dejarld
☐ 25 Tim Griffin
☐ 26 Ed Stryker
☐ 27 Ron Mauer
☐ 28 Ira Smith
☐ 29 Guy Conti CO
☐ 30 Joe Vavra MG

1990 Greensboro Hornets Best

This 30-card standard-size set of the 1990 Greensboro Hornets, a Class A South Atlantic League affiliate of the New York Yankees, features white-bordered posed and action color player photos on its fronts. The player's name and position appear vertically on the left side. The yellow horizontal back carries the player's name and position at the top, followed by biography, career highlights, and statistics. A player head shot appears in the lower right corner.

	MINT	NRMT	EXC
COMPLETE SET (30)	6.00	2.70	.75

☐ 1 Todd Malone
☐ 2 Sterling Hitchcock
☐ 3 Jeff Hoffman
☐ 4 Mark Hutton
☐ 5 Dan Johnston
☐ 6 Ken Juarbe
☐ 7 Jim Haller
☐ 8 Roberto Munoz
☐ 9 Cesar Perez
☐ 10 Rafael Quirico
☐ 11 Ricky Rhodes
☐ 12 Steve Tucker
☐ 13 Brian Johnson
☐ 14 John Jarvis
☐ 15 Larry Walker
☐ 16 Andy Fox
☐ 17 Ramon Jimenez
☐ 18 Scott Romano
☐ 19 Daniel Sanchez
☐ 20 Aaron Van Scoyoc
☐ 21 Tim Garland
☐ 22 Sean Gilliam
☐ 23 Lew Hill
☐ 24 Michael Rhodes
☐ 25 Jason Robertson
☐ 26 Brian Turner
☐ 27 Brian Butterfield MGR
☐ 28 Ted Uhlaender CO
☐ 29 Rich Arena CO
☐ 30 Dave Jorn CO

1990 Greensboro Hornets ProCards

This 31-card standard-size set of the 1990 Greensboro Hornets, a Class A South Atlantic League affiliate of the New York Yankees, features on its white-bordered fronts posed color player photos set on simulated wood-grain backgrounds. The player's name, position, and team appear within a gold-colored rectangle below the photo. The tan horizontal back is bordered in white and carries the player's name at the top, followed by biography and statistics. .

	MINT	NRMT	EXC
COMPLETE SET (31)	6.00	2.70	.75

☐ 2652 Checklist
☐ 2653 Jim Haller
☐ 2654 Sterling Hitchcock
☐ 2655 Jeff Hoffman
☐ 2656 Mark Hutton
☐ 2657 Dan Johnston
☐ 2658 Ken Juarbe
☐ 2659 Todd Malone
☐ 2660 Roberto Munoz
☐ 2661 Cesar Perez
☐ 2662 Rafael Quirico
☐ 2663 Ricky Rhodes
☐ 2664 Steve Tucker
☐ 2665 Brian Johnson
☐ 2666 John Jarvis
☐ 2667 Larry Walker
☐ 2668 Andy Fox
☐ 2669 Ramon Jimenez
☐ 2670 Scott Romano
☐ 2671 Daniel Sanchez
☐ 2672 Aaron Van Scoyoc
☐ 2673 Tim Garland
☐ 2674 Sean Gilliam
☐ 2675 Lew Hill
☐ 2676 Mike Rhodes
☐ 2677 Jason Robertson
☐ 2678 Brian Turner
☐ 2679 Brian Butterfield MGR
☐ 2680 Dave Jorn CO
☐ 2681 Rich Arena CO
☐ 2682 Ted Uhlaender CO

1990 Greensboro Hornets Star

This 26-card standard-size set of the 1990 Greensboro Hornets, a Class A South Atlantic League affiliate of the New York Yankees, features green bordered posed color player photos on its fronts. The player's name, team name, and position appear at the bottom. The white horizontal back carries the player's name at the top, followed by biography, career highlights, and statistics.

	MINT	NRMT	EXC
COMPLETE SET (26)	6.00	2.70	.75

☐ 1 Andy Fox
☐ 2 Tim Garland
☐ 3 Sean Gilliam
☐ 4 Jim Haller
☐ 5 Sterling Hitchcock
☐ 6 Jeff Hoffman
☐ 7 Mark Hutton
☐ 8 John Jarvis
☐ 9 Ramon Jimenez
☐ 10 Brian Johnson
☐ 11 Dan Johnston
☐ 12 Ken Juarbe
☐ 13 Todd Malone
☐ 14 Roberto Munoz
☐ 15 Cesar Perez
☐ 16 Rafael Quirico
☐ 17 Mike Rhodes
☐ 18 Ricky Rhodes
☐ 19 Jason Robertson
☐ 20 Scott Romano
☐ 21 Daniel Sanchez
☐ 22 Tuck Tucker
☐ 23 Brian Turner
☐ 24 Aaron Van Scoyoc
☐ 25 Larry Walker
☐ 26 Field Personnel
Brian Butterfield MGR
Dave Jorn CO
Ted Uhlaender CO
Rich Arena CO
Kelly Sharitt TR

1990 Greenville Braves Best

This 22-card standard-size set of the 1990 Greenville Braves, a Class AA Southern League affiliate of the Atlanta Braves, features white-bordered posed and action color player photos on its fronts. The player's name and position appear vertically on the left side. The yellow horizontal back carries the player's name and position at the top, followed by biography, career highlights, and statistics. A player head shot appears in the lower right corner.

	MINT	NRMT	EXC
COMPLETE SET (22)	5.00	2.20	.60

☐ 1 Lee Upshaw
☐ 2 David Plumb
☐ 3 Brian Champion
☐ 4 Pat Gomez
☐ 5 Tom Redington
☐ 6 Ben Rivera
☐ 7 Brian Boltz
☐ 8 Turk Wendell
☐ 9 Kelly Mann
☐ 10 Rich Casarotti
☐ 11 Rick Morris
☐ 12 Matt Turner
☐ 13 Judd Johnson
☐ 14 Rich Maloney
☐ 15 Doug Stockam
☐ 16 Dan Weems
☐ 17 Al Martin
☐ 18 Kevin Bastiste
☐ 19 Andy Tomberlin
☐ 20 Rolando Pino
☐ 21 John Kilner
☐ 22 Checklist

1990 Greenville Braves ProCards

This 26-card standard-size set of the 1990 Greenville Braves, a Class AA Southern League affiliate of the Atlanta Braves, features on its white-bordered fronts posed color player photos set on simulated wood-grain backgrounds. The player's name, position, and team appear within a gold-colored rectangle below the photo. The tan horizontal back is bordered in white and carries the player's name at the top, followed by biography and statistics. The cards are numbered on the back.

	MINT	NRMT	EXC
COMPLETE SET (26)	5.00	2.20	.60

☐ 1121 Checklist
☐ 1122 Brian Boltz
☐ 1123 Maximo Del Rosario
☐ 1124 Lee Johnson
☐ 1125 John Kilner
☐ 1126 Ben Rivera
Bien
☐ 1127 Doug Stockam
☐ 1128 Matt Turner
☐ 1129 Preston Watson
☐ 1130 Danny Weems
☐ 1131 Turk Wendell
☐ 1132 Kelly Mann
☐ 1133 Dave Plumb
☐ 1134 Mike Bell
☐ 1135 Rich Casarotti
☐ 1136 Rick Morris
☐ 1137 Tom Redington
☐ 1138 Rico Rossy
☐ 1139 Rich Maloney
☐ 1140 Kevin Batiste
☐ 1141 Al Martin
☐ 1142 Andy Tomberlin
☐ 1143 Buddy Bailey MGR
☐ 1144 Bill Slack CO
☐ 1145 Terry Harper CO
☐ 1146 Randy Ingle CO

1990 Greenville Braves Star

This 24-card standard-size set of the 1990 Greenville Braves, a Class AA Southern League affiliate of the Atlanta Braves, features blue bordered posed color player photos on its fronts. The player's name, team name, and position appear at the bottom. The white horizontal back carries the player's name at the top, followed by biography, career highlights, and statistics.

	MINT	NRMT	EXC
COMPLETE SET (24)	5.00	2.20	.60

☐ 1 John Alva
☐ 2 Kevin Batiste
☐ 3 Michael Bell
☐ 4 Brian Boltz
☐ 5 Rich Casarotti
☐ 6 Kevin Dean
☐ 7 Maximo Del Rosario
☐ 8 Judd Johnson
☐ 9 Lee Johnson
☐ 10 John Kilner
☐ 11 Rich Maloney
☐ 12 Kelly Mann
☐ 13 Gene Martin
☐ 14 Rich Morris
☐ 15 David Plumb
☐ 16 Thomas Redington
☐ 17 Ben Rivera
☐ 18 Doug Stockam
☐ 19 Andy Tomberlin
☐ 20 Matt Turner
☐ 21 Preston Watson
☐ 22 Danny Weems
☐ 23 Steven Wendell
☐ 24 Coaching Staff
Buddy Bailet MGR
Randy Ingle CO
Bill Slack CO
Terry Harper CO

1990 Hagerstown Suns All Decade Best

This 36-card standard-size set of the 1990 Hagerstown Suns, a Class AA Eastern League affiliate of the Baltimore Orioles,features white-bordered posed and action color player photos on its fronts. The player's name and position appear vertically on the left side. The words "All Decade" appear across the top. The yellow horizontal back carries the player's name and years played at the top, followed by player's history, highlights, and statistics. 2,500 sets were produced.

	MINT	NRMT	EXC
COMPLETE SET (36)	6.00	2.70	.75

☐ 1 Jeff Ballard
☐ 2 Blaine Beatty
☐ 3 Eric Bell
☐ 4 Dave Bettendorf
☐ 5 Dave Corman
☐ 6 Paul Croft
☐ 7 Brian Dubois

☐ 8 Pat Dumouchelle
☐ 9 Dave Falcone
☐ 10 Steve Finley
☐ 11 Ken Gerhart
☐ 12 Leo Gomez
☐ 13 Ed Hook
☐ 14 Bob Konopa
☐ 15 Mike Linskey
☐ 16 Grady Little MGR
☐ 17 Bob Molinaro MGR
☐ 18 Chris Myers
☐ 19 Gregg Olson
☐ 20 Al Pardo
☐ 21 Tim Richardson
☐ 22 Bill Ripken
☐ 23 Ramon Romero
☐ 24 Ron Salcedo
☐ 25 Mike Sander
☐ 26 Dave Segui
☐ 27 Larry Sheets
☐ 28 Chuck Stanhope
☐ 29 Pete Stanicek
☐ 30 John Stefaro
☐ 31 Scott Stranski
☐ 32 Andy Timko
☐ 33 Jim Traber
☐ 34 Matt Tyner
☐ 35 Craig Worthington
☐ 36 Checklist

1990 Hagerstown Suns Best

This 30-card standard-size set of the 1990 Hagerstown Suns, a Class AA Eastern League affiliate of the Baltimore Orioles, features white-bordered posed and action color player photos on its fronts. The player's name and position appear vertically on the left side. The yellow horizontal back carries the player's name and position at the top, followed by biography, career highlights, and statistics. A player head shot appears in the lower right corner.

	MINT	NRMT	EXC
COMPLETE SET (30)	7.00	3.10	.85

☐ 1 Ben McDonald
☐ 2 Dan Simonds
☐ 3 Doug Robbins
☐ 4 Mike Eberle
☐ 5 Tom Brown CO
☐ 6 Joe Durham CO
☐ 7 Bobby Latmore
☐ 8 Ty Nichols
☐ 9 Rodney Lofton
☐ 10 Craig Faulkner
☐ 11 Paris Haden
☐ 12 Luis Mercedes
☐ 13 Scott Meadows
☐ 14 Victor Hithe
☐ 15 Jack Voigt
☐ 16 Steve Culkar
☐ 17 Stacey Burdick
☐ 18 Chris Myers
☐ 19 Mike Borgatti
☐ 20 Mike Linskey
☐ 21 Mike Sander
☐ 22 Joel McKeon
☐ 23 Francisco de la Rosa
☐ 24 Dave Miller
☐ 25 Mike Cavers
☐ 26 Paul Thorpe
☐ 27 Ozzie Peraza
☐ 28 Jose Mesa
☐ 29 Jerry Narron MGR
☐ 30 Checklist

1990 Hagerstown Suns ProCards

This 33-card standard-size set of the 1990 Hagerstown Suns, a Class AA Eastern League affiliate of the Baltimore Orioles, features on its white-bordered fronts posed color player photos set on simulated wood-grain backgrounds. The player's name, position, and team appear within a gold-colored rectangle below the photo. The tan horizontal back is bordered in white and carries the player's name at the top, followed by biography and statistics.

	MINT	NRMT	EXC
COMPLETE SET (33)	7.00	3.10	.85

☐ 1401 Checklist
☐ 1402 Mike Borgatti
☐ 1403 Stacey Burdick
☐ 1404 Mike Cavers
☐ 1405 Steve Culkar
☐ 1406 Francisco de la Rosa
☐ 1407 Mike Linskey
☐ 1408 Ben McDonald
☐ 1409 Joel McKeon
☐ 1410 Jose Mesa
☐ 1411 Dave Miller
☐ 1412 Chris Myers
☐ 1413 Mike Sander
☐ 1414 Paul Thorpe
☐ 1415 Mike Eberle
☐ 1416 Doug Robbins
☐ 1417 Dan Simonds
☐ 1418 Pat Austin
☐ 1419 Dave Bettendorf
☐ 1420 Don Buford
☐ 1421 Craig Faulkner
☐ 1422 Bobby Latmore
☐ 1423 Rodney Lofton
☐ 1424 Rick Lundblade
☐ 1425 Ty Nichols
☐ 1426 Victor Hithe
☐ 1427 Paris Hayden
☐ 1428 Scott Meadows
☐ 1429 Luis Mercedes
☐ 1430 Jack Voight
☐ 1431 Jerry Narron MGR
☐ 1432 Tom Brown CO
☐ 1433 Joe Durham CO

1990 Hagerstown Suns Star

This 28-card standard-size set of the 1990 Hagerstown Suns, a Class AA Eastern League affiliate of the Baltimore Orioles, features blue bordered posed color player photos on its fronts. The player's name, team name, and position appear at the bottom. The white horizontal back carries the player's name at the top, followed by biography, career highlights, and statistics.

	MINT	NRMT	EXC
COMPLETE SET (28)	5.00	2.20	.60

☐ 1 Pat Austin
☐ 2 Mike Borgatti
☐ 3 Don Buford
☐ 4 Stacey Burdick
☐ 5 Mike Cavers
☐ 6 Steve Culkar
☐ 7 Francisco de la Rosa
☐ 8 Mike Eberle
☐ 9 Craig Faulkner
☐ 10 Walt Harris
☐ 11 Paris Hayden
☐ 12 Bobby Latmore
☐ 13 Rod Lofton
☐ 14 Joel McKeon
☐ 15 Scott Meadows
☐ 16 Luis Mercedes
☐ 17 Jose Mesa
☐ 18 Dave Miller
☐ 19 Chris Myers
☐ 20 Ty Nichols
☐ 21 Doug Robbins
☐ 22 Mike Sander
☐ 23 Tony Telford
☐ 24 Paul Thorpe
☐ 25 Jack Voigt
☐ 26 Jerry Narron MGR
☐ 27 Tom Brown CO
☐ 28 Joe Durham CO

1990 Hamilton Redbirds Best

This 28-card standard-size set of the 1990 Hamilton Redbirds, a Class A New York-Penn League affiliate of the St. Louis Cardinals, features white-bordered posed and action color player photos on its fronts. The player's name and position appear vertically on the left side. The yellow horizontal back carries the player's name and position at the top, followed by biography, career highlights, and statistics. A player head shot appears in the lower right corner.

	MINT	NRMT	EXC
COMPLETE SET (28)	5.00	2.20	.60

☐ 1 Donovan Osborne
Sic, Donavan
☐ 2 Roy Bailey
☐ 3 Marcos Betances
☐ 4 Chris Maloney CO
☐ 5 Tom Fusco
☐ 6 Kevin McLeod
☐ 7 Mark Smith
☐ 8 David Boss
☐ 9 George Sells
☐ 10 Troy Salvior
☐ 11 Mike Newby
☐ 12 Rich Rupkey
☐ 13 Paul Ellis
☐ 14 Marc Ronan
☐ 15 Joe Turvey
☐ 16 Wander Pimentel
☐ 17 Ahmed Rodriguez
☐ 18 Ozzie Perez
☐ 19 Gary Cooper
☐ 20 Rodney Eldridge
☐ 21 Mark MacArthur
☐ 22 Chris Alesio
☐ 23 Terry Bradshaw
☐ 24 John Thomas
☐ 25 Jeff Payne
☐ 26 Juan Belru
☐ 27 Luis Melendez MGR
☐ 28 Checklist

1990 Hamilton Redbirds Star

This 28-card standard-size set of the 1990 Hamilton Redbirds, a Class A New York-Penn League affiliate of the St. Louis Cardinals, features yellow bordered posed color player photos on its fronts. The player's name, team name, and position appear at the bottom. The white horizontal back carries the player's name at the top, followed by biography, career highlights, and statistics.

	MINT	NRMT	EXC
COMPLETE SET (28)	5.00	2.20	.60

☐ 1 Chris Alesio
☐ 2 Jose Arias
☐ 3 Roy Bailey
☐ 4 Andy Beasly
☐ 5 Juan Belbru
☐ 6 Marcos Betances
☐ 7 David Boss
☐ 8 Alan Botkin
☐ 9 Gary Cooper
☐ 10 Rodney Eldridge
☐ 11 Paul Ellis
☐ 12 Jeff Fayne
☐ 13 Tom Fusco
☐ 14 Chris Lowe
☐ 15 Mark MacArthur
☐ 16 Kevin McLeod
☐ 17 Mike Newby
☐ 18 Ozzie Perez
☐ 19 Wander Pimentel
☐ 20 Ahmed Rodriguez
☐ 21 Rich Rupkey
☐ 22 Troy Salvior
☐ 23 George Sells
☐ 24 Mark Smith
☐ 25 John Thomas
☐ 26 Luis Melendez MGR
☐ 27 Chris Maloney CO
☐ 28 Robert Harrison TR

1990 Harrisburg Senators ProCards

This 26-card standard-size set of the 1990 Harrisburg Senators, a Class AA Eastern League affiliate of the Pittsburgh Pirates, features on its white-bordered fronts posed color player photos set on simulated wood-grain backgrounds. The player's name, position, and team appear within a gold-colored rectangle below the photo. The tan horizontal back is bordered in white and carries the player's name at the top, followed by biography and statistics.

	MINT	NRMT	EXC
COMPLETE SET (26)	7.00	3.10	.85

☐ 1184 Checklist
☐ 1185 Steve Adams
☐ 1186 Joe Ausanio
☐ 1187 Jim Czajkowski
☐ 1188 Miguel Garcia
☐ 1189 Blas Minor
☐ 1190 Pete Murphy
☐ 1191 Keith Richardson
☐ 1192 Randy Tomlin
☐ 1193 Jim Tracy
☐ 1194 Ben Webb
☐ 1195 Jeff Banister
☐ 1196 Scott Barczi
☐ 1197 Trent Jewett
☐ 1198 Terry Crowley Jr.
☐ 1199 Carlos Garcia
☐ 1200 Jeffrey Osborne
☐ 1201 Julio Perez
☐ 1202 Junior Vizcaino
☐ 1203 John Wehner
☐ 1204 Moises Alou
☐ 1205 Robert Harris
☐ 1206 Julio Peguero
☐ 1207 Ed Yacopino
☐ 1208 Marc Bombard MGR
☐ 1209 Spin Williams CO

1990 Harrisburg Senators Star

This 25-card standard-size set of the 1990 Harrisburg Senators, a Class AA Eastern League affiliate of the Pittsburgh Pirates, features red bordered posed color player photos on its fronts. The player's name, team name, and position appear at the bottom. The white horizontal back carries the player's name at the top, followed by biography, career highlights, and statistics.

	MINT	NRMT	EXC
COMPLETE SET (25)	7.00	3.10	.85

☐ 1 Steve Adams
☐ 2 Moises Alou
☐ 3 Jeff Banister
☐ 4 Scott Barczi
☐ 5 Terry Crowley Jr.
☐ 6 Jim Czajkowski
☐ 7 Carlos Garcia
☐ 8 Miguel Garcia
☐ 9 Robert Harris
☐ 10 Trent Jewett
☐ 11 Blas Minor
☐ 12 Pete Murphy
☐ 13 Jeffrey Osborne
☐ 14 Julio Peguero
☐ 15 Julio Perez
☐ 16 Keith Richardson
☐ 17 Randy Tomlin
☐ 18 Jim Tracy
☐ 19 Junior Vizcaino
☐ 20 Ben Webb
☐ 21 John Wehner
☐ 22 Ed Yacopino
☐ 23 Marc Bombard MGR
☐ 24 Spin Williams CO
☐ 25 Mike Sandoval TR

1990 Helena Brewers Sports Pro

This 29-card standard-size set of the 1990 Helena Brewers, a Rookie Class Pioneer League affiliate of the Milwaukee Brewers, features posed color head-and-shoulders shots, with thin black borders on a white card face. The horizontally oriented backs have biographical information. The cards are numbered on the back.

	MINT	NRMT	EXC
COMPLETE SET (29)	6.00	2.70	.75

☐ 1 Tim Carter
☐ 2 Mike Hooper
☐ 3 Juan Flores
☐ 4 Tony Coble
☐ 5 Kevin McDonald
☐ 6 Chris Wheat
☐ 7 Pat Miller
☐ 8 Scott Moseley
☐ 9 Tony Diggs
☐ 10 Jason Zimbauer
☐ 11 Mike Couture
☐ 12 Gordon Powell
☐ 13 Larue Baber
☐ 14 Mark Stephens
☐ 15 Kurt Archer
☐ 16 Vince Castaldo
☐ 17 Geoffery Kellogg
☐ 18 Eric Patten
☐ 19 Todd Edwards
☐ 20 Don Pruitt
☐ 21 Mark Rupp
☐ 22 Charles Rambadt
☐ 23 Tim Wilson
☐ 24 Mike Carter
☐ 25 Brian Souza
☐ 26 Mike Norris
☐ 27 Bill Brakeley
☐ 28 Mike Coombs CO
☐ 29 Gary Calhoun MG

1990 High School Prospects Little Sun

This 24-card standard size set features color photos of some of the top senior high school players. The card backs contain complete high school career stats and biographical notes. 6,000 regular sets and 1,500 glossy sets were produced.

	MINT	NRMT	EXC
COMPLETE SET (24)	12.00	5.50	1.50
COMPLETE GLOSSY SET (24)	15.00	6.75	1.85

☐ 1 Checklist
☐ 2 Mike Lieberthal
☐ 3 Lamar Cherry
☐ 4 Aaron Holbert
☐ 5 Sean Cheetham
☐ 6 Charles Poe
☐ 7 Gabriel White
☐ 8 Daniel Hernandez
☐ 9 Mark Anthony
☐ 10 Keith Tobey
☐ 11 Ronald Caridad
☐ 12 John Schulte
☐ 13 Carl Everett
☐ 14 Shawn Wooten
☐ 15 Gary Hust
☐ 16 Vincent Bradford
☐ 17 Mark Lambert
☐ 18 Dan Tobin
☐ 19 Garret Anderson
☐ 20 Michael Hampton
☐ 21 David Mowry
☐ 22 Jim Converse
☐ 23 Wade Fyock
☐ 24 Clyde Metcalf CO

1990 Huntington Cubs ProCards

This 32-card standard-size set of the 1990 Huntington Cubs, a Rookie Class Appalachian League affiliate of the Chicago Cubs, features on its white-bordered fronts posed color player photos set on simulated wood-grain backgrounds. The player's name, position, and team appear within a gold-colored rectangle below the photo. The tan horizontal back is bordered in white and carries the player's name at the top, followed by biography and statistics.

	MINT	NRMT	EXC
COMPLETE SET (32)	5.00	2.20	.60

☐ 3271 Checklist
☐ 3272 Miguel Camarena

☐ 3273 Sean Cheetham
☐ 3274 Scott Gardner
☐ 3275 Tyson Godfrey
☐ 3276 Ryan Hawblitzel
☐ 3277 Chuck Kirk
☐ 3278 Ken Krahenbuhl
☐ 3279 Tom Mann
☐ 3280 Nelson Ramirez
☐ 3281 Adrian Sanchez
☐ 3282 Dave Stevens
☐ 3283 Aaron Taylor
☐ 3284 Mike Gabbani
☐ 3285 Matt Walbeck
☐ 3286 Jim Wolff
☐ 3287 Morris Craig
☐ 3289 Cesar Montero
☐ 3290 Tim Moore
☐ 3291 Micah Murphy
☐ 3292 J.P. Postiff
☐ 3293 Humberto Saa
☐ 3294 Rafael Soto
☐ 3295 Jose Viera
☐ 3296 Pablo Delgado
☐ 3297 Rolando Fernandez
☐ 3298 Calvin Ford
☐ 3299 Willie Gardner
☐ 3300 Ed Larregui
☐ 3301 Mike Little
☐ 3302 Jason Sehorn
☐ 3303 Steve Roadcap MGR

1990 Huntsville Stars Best

This 27-card standard-size set of the 1990 Huntsville Stars, a Class AA Southern League affiliate of the Oakland A's, features white-bordered posed and action color player photos on its fronts. The player's name and position appear vertically on the left side. The yellow horizontal back carries the player's name and position at the top, followed by biography, career highlights, and statistics. A player head shot appears in the lower right corner.

	MINT	NRMT	EXC
COMPLETE SET (27)	5.00	2.20	.60

☐ 1 Darren Lewis
☐ 2 Richard Berg
☐ 3 Samuel Chavez
☐ 4 Stephen Chitren
☐ 5 Daniel Eskew
☐ 6 Daryl Green
☐ 7 Dannie Harris
☐ 8 Kevin MacLeod
☐ 9 William Schock
☐ 10 Joe Slusarski
☐ 11 Mark Stancel
☐ 12 Brian Veilleux
☐ 13 Jorge Brito
☐ 14 Peter Kuld
☐ 15 Scott Brosius
☐ 16 Ronald Coomer
☐ 17 Jim Kating
☐ 18 Robert Ralston
☐ 19 Stan Royer
☐ 20 Tony Brown
☐ 21 Ozzie Canceco
☐ 22 Nelson Simmons
☐ 23 Tack Wilson
☐ 24 Jeff Newman MGR
☐ 25 Glenn Abbott CO
☐ 26 Brian Thorson
☐ 27 Checklist

1990 Idaho Falls Braves ProCards

This 31-card standard-size set of the 1990 Idaho Falls Braves, a Rookie Class Pioneer League affiliate of the Atlanta Braves, features on its white-bordered fronts posed color player photos set on simulated wood-grain backgrounds. The player's name, position, and team appear within a gold-colored rectangle below the photo. The tan horizontal back is bordered in white and carries the player's name at the top, followed by biography and statistics.

	MINT	NRMT	EXC
COMPLETE SET (31)	5.00	2.20	.60

☐ 3240 Checklist
☐ 3241 Brian Dare
☐ 3242 Steve Hodges
☐ 3243 Tom Newman
☐ 3244 Michael Hoog
☐ 3245 Scott Ryder
☐ 3246 Tom Rizzo
☐ 3247 Don'l Dease
☐ 3248 Tommy Owen
☐ 3249 John Wood
☐ 3250 John Surane
☐ 3251 Grant Brittain
☐ 3252 Geoff Orr
☐ 3253 Joe Markulike
☐ 3254 Paul DiPino
☐ 3255 Rick Karcher
☐ 3256 Corby Fister
☐ 3257 Kevin O'Connor
☐ 3258 Michael Sweeney
☐ 3259 Chris Burton
☐ 3260 Nathan Fults
☐ 3261 Stu McMillan
☐ 3262 Steve Curry (MGR)
☐ 3263 Randy Smith CO
☐ 3264 Doc Halliday
☐ 3265 Bill Bates
☐ 3266 Shawn Rohrwild
☐ 3267 Bill Kooiman
☐ 3268 Marek Brabinski
☐ 3269 Ed Giovanola
☐ 3270 Loren Gress

Last seven cards are misnumbered. #3262 was repeated after #3263 and so on.

1990 Indianapolis Indians CMC

This 25-card standard-size set of the 1990 Indianapolis Indians, a Class AAA American Association affiliate of the Montreal Expos, features white-bordered posed color player photos on its fronts. The player's name and position appear at the bottom; the team name appears vertically on the left. The back carries the league emblem in the white area at the top, the team name in the green stripe below, and player's name, position, biography, and statistics in the yellow area at the bottom. 1,100 sets were produced.

	MINT	NRMT	EXC
COMPLETE SET (25)	5.00	2.20	.60

☐ 1 Steve Fireovid
☐ 2 Danny Clay
☐ 3 Howard Farmer
☐ 4 Travis Chambers
☐ 5 Chris Marchok
☐ 6 Dan Gakeler
☐ 7 Scott Anderson
☐ 8 Dale Mohorcic
☐ 9 Richard Thompson
☐ 10 Eddie Dixon
☐ 11 Jim Davins
☐ 12 Edwin Marquez
☐ 13 Jerry Goff
☐ 14 Dwight Lowry
☐ 15 Jim Steels
☐ 16 Quinn Mack
☐ 17 Eric Bullock
☐ 18 Otis Green
☐ 19 Randy Braun
☐ 20 Mel Houston
☐ 21 Jesus Paredes
☐ 22 Romy Cucjen
☐ 23 Jose Castro
☐ 24 Esteban Beltre
☐ 25 Tim Johnson MG

1990 Indianapolis Indians ProCards

This 31-card standard-size set of the 1990 Indianapolis Indians, a Class AAA American Association affiliate of the Montreal Expos, features on its white-bordered fronts posed color player photos set on simulated wood-grain backgrounds. The player's name, position, and team appear within a gold-colored rectangle below the photo. The tan horizontal back is bordered in white and carries the player's name and position at the top, followed by biography and statistics. The set was co-sponsored by Pepsi and Hook's.

	MINT	NRMT	EXC
COMPLETE SET (31)	5.00	2.20	.60

☐ 279 Checklist
☐ 280 Scott Anderson
☐ 281 Esteban Beltre
☐ 282 Travis Chambers
☐ 283 Randy Braun
☐ 284 Danny Clay
☐ 285 Eric Bullock
☐ 286 Jim Davins
☐ 287 Jose Castro
☐ 288 Eddie Dixon
☐ 289 Romy Cucjen
☐ 290 Howard Farmer
☐ 291 Jerry Goff
☐ 292 Steve Fireovid
☐ 293 Otis Green
☐ 294 Dan Gakeler
☐ 295 Mel Houston
☐ 296 Balvino Galvez
☐ 297 Dwight Lowry
☐ 298 Dale Mohorcic
☐ 299 Quinn Mack
☐ 300 Chris Marchok
☐ 301 Edwin Marquez
☐ 302 Mel Rojas
☐ 303 Johnny Paredes
☐ 304 Rich Thompson
☐ 305 German Rivera
☐ 306 James Steels
☐ 307 Tim Johnson MG
☐ 308 Gomer Hodge CO
☐ 309 Joe Kerrigan CO

1990 Iowa Cubs CMC

This 25-card standard-size set of the 1990 Iowa Cubs, a Class AAA American Association affiliate of the Chicago Cubs, features white-bordered posed color player photos on its fronts. The player's name and position appear at the bottom; the team name appears vertically on the left. The back carries the league emblem in the white area at the top, the team name in the green stripe below, and player's name, position, biography, and statistics in the yellow area at the bottom. 1,100 sets were produced.

	MINT	NRMT	EXC
COMPLETE SET (25)	5.00	2.20	.60

☐ 1 Shawn Boskie
☐ 2 Dave Masters
☐ 3 Kevin Blankenship
☐ 4 Greg Kallevig
☐ 5 Steve Parker
☐ 6 David Pavlas
☐ 7 Jeff Pico
☐ 8 Laddie Renfroe
☐ 9 Dean Wilkins
☐ 10 Paul Wilmet
☐ 11 Bob Bafia
☐ 12 Brian Guinn
☐ 13 Greg Smith
☐ 14 Derrick May
☐ 15 Glenn Sullivan
☐ 16 Bill Wrona
☐ 17 Erik Pappas
☐ 18 Hector Villanueva
☐ 19 Ced Landrum
☐ 20 Jeff Small
☐ 21 Gary Varsho
☐ 22 Brad Bierly
☐ 23 Jeff Hearron
☐ 24 Jim Essian MGR
☐ 25 Brian McCann TR

1990 Iowa Cubs ProCards

This 24-card standard-size set of the 1990 Iowa Cubs, a Class AAA American Association affiliate of the Chicago Cubs, features on its white-bordered fronts posed color player photos set on simulated wood-grain backgrounds. The player's name, position, and team appear within a gold-colored rectangle below the photo. The tan horizontal back is bordered in white and carries the player's name at the top, followed by biography and statistics.

	MINT	NRMT	EXC
COMPLETE SET (24)	5.00	2.20	.60

☐ 310 Checklist
☐ 311 Kevin Blankenship
☐ 312 Shawn Boskie
☐ 313 Mark Bowden
☐ 314 Greg Kallevig
☐ 315 Dave Masters
☐ 316 Steve Parker
☐ 317 Dave Pavlas
☐ 318 Laddie Renfroe
☐ 319 Paul Wilmet
☐ 320 Jeff Hearron
☐ 321 Erik Pappas
☐ 322 Hector Villanueva
☐ 323 Bob Bafia
☐ 324 Brian Guinn
☐ 325 Jeff Small
☐ 326 Greg Smith
☐ 327 Glenn Sullivan
☐ 328 Bill Wrona
☐ 329 Brad Bierley
☐ 330 Cedric Landrum
☐ 331 Derrick May
☐ 332 Gary Varsho
☐ 333 Jim Essian

1990 Jackson Mets Grand Slam

	MINT	NRMT	EXC
COMPLETE SET (29)	8.00	3.60	1.00

☐ 1 Todd Hundley
☐ 2 Doug Kline
☐ 3 Alex Jimenez
☐ 4 Bob Apodaca CO
☐ 5 Clint Hurdle MG
☐ 6 Fred Hina TR
☐ 7 Terry Bross
☐ 8 Steve Larose
☐ 9 Joe Delli Carri
☐ 10 Jaime Roseboro
☐ 11 Howie Freiling
☐ 12 Chris Donnels
☐ 13 Javier Gonzalez
☐ 14 Dave Proctor
☐ 15 Doug Cinnella
☐ 16 Kevin Baez
☐ 17 Toby Nivens
☐ 18 Mike Miller
☐ 19 Aguedo Vasquez
☐ 20 Joe Whipps
☐ 21 Rudy Hernandez
☐ 22 Rocky Elli
☐ 23 Ron Gideon
☐ 24 Chuck Carr
☐ 25 Crucito Lara
☐ 26 Anthony Young
☐ 27 Terry McDaniel
☐ 28 Steve Davis
☐ NNO Title Card

1990 Jacksonville Expos Best

This 30-card standard-size set of the 1990 Jacksonville Expos, a Class AA Southern League affiliate of the Montreal Expos, features white-bordered posed and action color player photos on its fronts. The player's name and position appear vertically on the left side. The yellow horizontal back carries the player's name and position at the top, followed by biography, career highlights, and statistics. A player head shot appears in the lower right corner.

	MINT	NRMT	EXC
COMPLETE SET (30)	5.00	2.20	.60

☐ 1 Greg Colbrunn
☐ 2 Rob Natal
☐ 3 Bret Barberie
☐ 4 Archi Cianfrocco
☐ 5 Wilfredo Cordero
☐ 6 Bryn Kosco
☐ 7 Omer Munoz
☐ 8 Boi Rodriguez
☐ 9 Terrel Hansen
☐ 10 Cesar Hernandez
☐ 11 Trevor Penn
☐ 12 Miguel Santana
☐ 13 John Vander Wal
☐ 14 Brian Barnes
☐ 15 Chris Bennett
☐ 16 Kent Bottenfield
☐ 17 Mario Brito
☐ 18 Jeff Carter
☐ 19 Bob Malloy
☐ 20 Richie Lewis
☐ 21 Chris Nabholz
☐ 22 Yorkis Perez
☐ 23 Hector Rivera
☐ 24 Darrin Winston
☐ 25 Jerry Manuel MG
☐ 26 Nardi Contreras CO
☐ 27 Lorenzo Bundy CO
☐ 28 Jay Williams TR
☐ 29 Edwin Marquez
☐ 30 Team Photo
Checklist

1990 Jacksonville Expos ProCards

This 29-card standard-size set of the 1990 Jacksonville Expos, a Class AA Southern League affiliate of the Montreal Expos, features on its white-bordered fronts posed color player photos set on simulated wood-grain backgrounds. The player's name, position, and team appear within a gold-colored rectangle below the photo. The tan horizontal back is bordered in white and carries the player's name and position at the top, followed by biography and statistics.

	MINT	NRMT	EXC
COMPLETE SET (29)	5.00	2.20	.60

☐ 1364 Checklist
☐ 1365 Brian Barnes
☐ 1366 Chris Bennett
☐ 1367 Kent Bottenfield
☐ 1368 Mario Brito
☐ 1369 Jeff Carter
☐ 1370 Bob Malloy
☐ 1371 Chris Nabholz
☐ 1372 Yorkis Perez
☐ 1373 Tim Peters
☐ 1374 Hector Rivera
☐ 1375 Tim Sossamon
☐ 1376 Darrin Winston
☐ 1377 Greg Colbrunn
☐ 1378 Rob Natal
☐ 1379 Bret Barberie
☐ 1380 Archi Cianfrocco
☐ 1381 Wil Cordero
☐ 1382 Bryn Kosco
☐ 1383 Omer Munoz
☐ 1384 Terrel Hansen
☐ 1385 Cesar Hernandez
☐ 1386 Trevor Penn
☐ 1387 Miguel Santana
☐ 1388 John Vander Wal
☐ 1389 Lorenzo Bundy
Player/Coach
☐ 1390 Team Picture
☐ 1391 Jerry Manuel MG
☐ 1392 Nardi Contreras CO

1990 Jamestown Expos Pucko

This 34-card standard-size set of the 1990 Jamestown Expos, a Class A New York-Penn League affiliate of the Montreal Expos, features gray-bordered posed color player shots on its fronts. A red stripe below the photo carries the team name; a white stripe above, the player's name and position. The white back carries the player's name at the top, followed by biography, player profile, and statistics. This issue includes the first minor league card of Glenn Murray.

	MINT	NRMT	EXC
COMPLETE SET (34)	7.00	3.10	.85

- ☐ 1 Theodore Ciesla
- ☐ 2 Robert Fitzpatrick
- ☐ 3 Domingo Matos
- ☐ 4 Abimael Rodriguez
- ☐ 5 Marc Tsitouris
- ☐ 6 Randon Wilstead
- ☐ 7 Jeff Barry
- ☐ 8 Robert Katzaroff
- ☐ 9 Glenn Murray
- ☐ 10 Jerry Nyman
- ☐ 11 Todd Samples
- ☐ 12 Michael Friedland
- ☐ 13 Derek Aucoin
- ☐ 14 Robert Baxter
- ☐ 15 Billy Brewer
- ☐ 16 Ralph Diaz
- ☐ 17 Ranbir Grewal
- ☐ 18 Chris Haney
- ☐ 19 Darrin Kotch
- ☐ 20 Steve Long
- ☐ 21 Michael Mathile
- ☐ 22 Felix Moya
- ☐ 23 Joe Morris
- ☐ 24 John Polasek
- ☐ 25 Troy Ricker
- ☐ 26 Troy Wessel
- ☐ 27 Pat Daugherty MG
- ☐ 28 Q.V. Lowe CO
- ☐ 29 Jose Castro CO
- ☐ 30 Scott Yurcisin
- ☐ 31 Tom O'Reilley and Staff
  Andy Barlow
  Tom Glick
- ☐ 32 Yuppi
  Mascot
- ☐ 33 College Stadium
  Checklist
- ☐ 34 Dan Hargis

1990 Johnson City Cardinals Star

This 30-card standard-size set of the 1990 Johnson City Cardinals, a Rookie Class Appalachian League affiliate of the St. Louis Cardinals, features red bordered posed color player photos on its fronts. The player's name, team name, and position appear at the bottom. The white horizontal back carries the player's name at the top, followed by biography, career highlights, and statistics.

	MINT	NRMT	EXC
COMPLETE SET (30)	5.00	2.20	.60

- ☐ 1 Hector Alberro
- ☐ 2 Joe Aversa
- ☐ 3 Scott Baker
- ☐ 4 Harrison Ball
- ☐ 5 Duff Brumley
- ☐ 6 Kevin Carpenter
- ☐ 7 Jerry Davis
- ☐ 8 John Dempsey
- ☐ 9 Tremayne Donald
- ☐ 10 Tracey Ealy
- ☐ 11 Ben Ellsworth
- ☐ 12 Ron French
- ☐ 13 Cecilio Gonzalez
- ☐ 14 Aaron Holbert
- ☐ 15 Tim Jordan
- ☐ 16 John Kelly
- ☐ 17 Jose Lopez
- ☐ 18 Jeremy McGarity
- ☐ 19 David Norris
- ☐ 20 Sean Page
- ☐ 21 Beto Rodriguez
- ☐ 22 Manuel Rodriguez
- ☐ 23 Craig Ruyak
- ☐ 24 Frank Speek
- ☐ 25 Jim Spivey
- ☐ 26 Brian Sullivan
- ☐ 27 Tom Urbani
- ☐ 28 Coaching Staff
  Mark DeJohn MGR
  George Kissell
  Bob Milliken
- ☐ 29 Joe Cunningham Jr. CO
- ☐ 30 Mike Gaddie TR

1990 Kenosha Twins Best

This 30-card standard-size set of the 1990 Kenosha Twins, a Class A Midwest League affiliate of the Minnesota Twins, features white-bordered posed and action color player photos on its fronts. The player's name and position appear vertically on the left side. The yellow horizontal back carries the player's name and position at the top, followed by biography, career highlights, and statistics. A player head shot appears in the lower right corner.

	MINT	NRMT	EXC
COMPLETE SET (30)	5.00	2.20	.60

- ☐ 1 Steve Dunn
- ☐ 2 Rex DeLaNuez
- ☐ 3 Randy Gentile
- ☐ 4 Deryk Gross
- ☐ 5 Troy Heorner
- ☐ 6 Mike Lloyd
- ☐ 7 Mike Mathiot
- ☐ 8 Jeff Milene
- ☐ 9 Steve Morris
- ☐ 10 Willi Mota
- ☐ 11 Alex Nunex
- ☐ 12 Francisco Pichardo
- ☐ 13 Rob Schiel
- ☐ 14 Joe Siwa
- ☐ 15 Bryan Roskom
- ☐ 16 Darren Musselwhite
- ☐ 17 Jayson Best
- ☐ 18 Sandy Diaz
- ☐ 19 Jody Harrington
- ☐ 20 Marc Lipson
- ☐ 21 Mike Misuraca
- ☐ 22 Tim Nedin
- ☐ 23 Alan Newman
- ☐ 24 Carlos Pulido
- ☐ 25 Scott Robles
- ☐ 26 Jeff Thelen
- ☐ 27 Steve Liddle MGR
- ☐ 28 Rick Anderson CO
- ☐ 29 Dan Fox TR
- ☐ 30 Checklist

1990 Kenosha Twins ProCards

This 27-card standard-size set of the 1990 Kenosha Twins, a Class A Midwest League affiliate of the Minnesota Twins, features on its white-bordered fronts posed color player photos set on simulated wood-grain backgrounds. The player's name, position, and team appear within a gold-colored rectangle below the photo. The tan horizontal back is bordered in white and carries the player's name at the top, followed by biography and statistics.

	MINT	NRMT	EXC
COMPLETE SET (27)	5.00	2.20	.60

- ☐ 2285 Checklist
- ☐ 2286 Jayson Best
- ☐ 2287 Sandy Diaz
- ☐ 2288 Jody Harrington
- ☐ 2289 Marc Lipson
- ☐ 2290 Mike Misuraca
- ☐ 2291 Tim Nedin
- ☐ 2292 Alan Newman
- ☐ 2293 Carlos Pulido
- ☐ 2294 Scott Robles
- ☐ 2295 Jeff Thelen
- ☐ 2296 Jeff Milene
- ☐ 2297 Willie Mota
- ☐ 2298 Joe Siwa
- ☐ 2299 Steve Dunn
- ☐ 2300 Randy Gentile
- ☐ 2301 Mike Lloyd
- ☐ 2302 Mike Mathiot
- ☐ 2303 Alex Nunez
- ☐ 2304 Rob Schiel
- ☐ 2305 Rex DeLaNuez
- ☐ 2306 Deryk Gross
- ☐ 2307 Troy Hoerner
- ☐ 2308 Steve Morris
- ☐ 2309 Francisco Pichardo
- ☐ 2310 Steve Liddle MGR
- ☐ 2311 Rich Anderson CO

1990 Kenosha Twins Star

This 29-card standard-size set of the 1990 Kenosha Twins, a Class A Midwest League affiliate of the Minnesota Twins, features purple bordered posed color player photos on its fronts. The player's name, team name, and position appear at the bottom. The white horizontal back carries the player's name at the top, followed by biography, career highlights, and statistics.

	MINT	NRMT	EXC
COMPLETE SET (29)	5.00	2.20	.60

- ☐ 1 Jayson Best
- ☐ 2 Sandy Diaz
- ☐ 3 Steve Dunn
- ☐ 4 Randy Gentile
- ☐ 5 Deryk Gross
- ☐ 6 Jody Harrington
- ☐ 7 Troy Hoerner
- ☐ 8 Rex DeLa Nuez
- ☐ 9 Marc Lipson
- ☐ 10 Mike Lloyd
- ☐ 11 Mike Mathiot
- ☐ 12 Jeff Milene
- ☐ 13 Mike Misuraca
- ☐ 14 Steve Morris
- ☐ 15 Willi Mota
- ☐ 16 Tim Nedin
- ☐ 17 Alan Newman
- ☐ 18 Alex Nunez
- ☐ 19 Francisco Pichardo
- ☐ 20 Carlos Pulido
- ☐ 21 Scott Robles
- ☐ 22 Rob Schiel
- ☐ 23 Joe Siwa
- ☐ 24 Jeffrey Thelen
- ☐ 25 Steve Liddle MGR
- ☐ 26 Rick Anderson CO
- ☐ 27 Dan Fox TR
- ☐ 28 Darren Musselwhite
- ☐ 29 Bryan Roskom

1990 Kingsport Mets Best

This 28-card standard-size set of the 1990 Kingsport Mets, a Rookie Class Appalachian League affiliate of the New York Mets, features white-bordered posed and action color player photos on its fronts. The player's name and position appear vertically on the left side. The yellow horizontal back carries the player's name and position at the top, followed by biography, career highlights, and statistics. A player head shot appears in the lower right corner.

	MINT	NRMT	EXC
COMPLETE SET (28)	5.00	2.20	.60

- ☐ 1 Aaron Ledesma
- ☐ 2 Darian Lindsay
- ☐ 3 Gerrod Davis
- ☐ 4 Wayne Mathis
- ☐ 5 Bernie Millan
- ☐ 6 Mason Rudolph
- ☐ 7 Micah Franklin
- ☐ 8 Rey Martinez
- ☐ 9 Tony Moore
- ☐ 10 Rob Carpenter
- ☐ 11 Edward Fully
- ☐ 12 Nicholas Polanco
- ☐ 13 Omar Garcia
- ☐ 14 Rob Rees
- ☐ 15 Mike Anaya
- ☐ 16 Hector Carrasco
- ☐ 17 Tim Sandy
- ☐ 18 Nate Benson
- ☐ 19 Casper Van Rybach
- ☐ 20 Tom Wegmann
- ☐ 21 Rich Bristow
- ☐ 22 Tom Engle
- ☐ 23 Marcel Johnson
- ☐ 24 Charlie Williams
- ☐ 25 Jim Thrift MGR
- ☐ 26 Gil Randon CO
- ☐ 27 Dan Norman CO
- ☐ 28 Dave Fricke
  Checklist

1990 Kingsport Mets Star

This 30-card standard-size set of the 1990 Kingsport Mets, a Rookie Class Appalachian League affiliate of the New York Mets, features orange bordered posed color player photos on its fronts. The player's name, team name, and position appear at the bottom. The white horizontal back carries the player's name at the top, followed by biography, career highlights, and statistics.

	MINT	NRMT	EXC
COMPLETE SET (30)	10.00	4.50	1.25

- ☐ 1 Mike Anaya
- ☐ 2 Nate Benson
- ☐ 3 Richie Bristow
- ☐ 4 Rob Carpenter
- ☐ 5 Hector Carrasco
- ☐ 6 Jay Davis
- ☐ 7 Tom Engle
- ☐ 8 Micah Franklin
- ☐ 9 Edward Fully
- ☐ 10 Omar Garcia
- ☐ 11 Butch Huskey
- ☐ 12 Marcel Johnson
- ☐ 13 Aaron Ledesma
- ☐ 14 Darian Lindsay
- ☐ 15 Rey Martinez
- ☐ 16 Wayne Mathis
- ☐ 17 Bernie Millan
- ☐ 18 Tony Moore
- ☐ 19 Nicolas Polanco
- ☐ 20 Rob Rees
- ☐ 21 Mason Rudolph
- ☐ 22 Tim Sandy
- ☐ 23 Casper Van Rybach
- ☐ 24 Tom Wegmann
- ☐ 25 Charlie Williams
- ☐ 26 Jim Thrift MGR
- ☐ 27 Gil Rondon CO
- ☐ 28 Dave Fricke TR
- ☐ 29 Dottie Elsea GM
- ☐ 30 Bat Boys
  Jason Adams
  Josh Brickey
  Ben Smith

1990 Kinston Indians Team Issue

NNO Tim Costo was a late addition to the set.

	MINT	NRMT	EXC
COMPLETE SET (30)	6.00	2.70	.75
COMPLETE SET (31)	7.00	3.10	.85

- ☐ 1 Jerry DiPoto
- ☐ 2 Tommy Dramer
- ☐ 3 Rouglas Odor
- ☐ 4 Ty Kovach
- ☐ 5 Curtis Leskanic
- ☐ 6 Brian Johnson
- ☐ 7 Fabio Gomez
- ☐ 8 Jessie Levis
- ☐ 9 Ken Ramos
- ☐ 10 Nolan Lane
- ☐ 11 Marc Tepper
- ☐ 12 Garland Kiser
- ☐ 13 Jamie Allison
- ☐ 14 Lindsay Foster
- ☐ 15 Will Vespe
- ☐ 16 Ramon Bautista
- ☐ 17 David Oliveras
- ☐ 18 Rick Falkner
- ☐ 19 Greg Ferlenda
- ☐ 20 Chris Pinder
- ☐ 21 Mando Verdugo
- ☐ 22 Dan Williams
- ☐ 23 Robert Person
- ☐ 24 Scott Neill
- ☐ 25 Eddie Zambrano
- ☐ 26 Tim Ellis
- ☐ 27 Fred Gladding
- ☐ 28 Brian Graham
- ☐ 29 Dennis Noonan
- ☐ NNO Checklist
- ☐ NNO Tim Costo

1990 Kissimmee Dodgers Diamond

	MINT	NRMT	EXC
COMPLETE SET (29)	5.00	2.20	.60

- ☐ 1 Henry Blanco
- ☐ 2 Jake Botts
- ☐ 3 Jimmy Brown
- ☐ 4 Jason Broyles
- ☐ 5 Donnie Carroll
- ☐ 6 Nelson Castro
- ☐ 7 Jose Cruz
- ☐ 8 Keith Daniel
- ☐ 9 Greg Davis
- ☐ 10 Andres Diaz
- ☐ 11 Ross Farnsworth
- ☐ 12 Dirk Gorman
- ☐ 13 Randy Graves
- ☐ 14 Rob Hoffman
- ☐ 15 Andres Macu
- ☐ 16 Al Maldonado
- ☐ 17 Tom Matthews
- ☐ 18 Domingo Mota
- ☐ 19 Peter Nurre
- ☐ 20 Jose Parra
- ☐ 21 Jose Perez
- ☐ 22 Alton Pinkney
- ☐ 23 Javier Puchales
- ☐ 24 Mike Racobaldo
- ☐ 25 Frank Smith
- ☐ 26 Rob Sweeney
- ☐ 27 Jose Valdez
- ☐ 28 Leroy Williams
- ☐ 29 Ivan DeJesus MGR

1990 Knoxville Blue Jays Best

This 28-card standard-size set of the 1990 Knoxville Blue Jays, a Class AA Southern League affiliate of the Toronto Blue Jays, features white-bordered posed and action color player photos on its fronts. The player's name and position appear vertically on the left side. The yellow horizontal back carries the player's name and position at the top, followed by biography and statistics. A player head shot appears in the lower right corner.

	MINT	NRMT	EXC
COMPLETE SET (28)	8.00	3.60	1.00

- ☐ 1 Eddie Zosky
- ☐ 2 Jimmy Rogers
- ☐ 3 Pete Blohm
- ☐ 4 Pat Hentgen
- ☐ 5 William Suero
- ☐ 6 Shawn Jeter
- ☐ 7 Doug Merrifield
- ☐ 8 Juan Guzman
- ☐ 9 John Stearns MG
- ☐ 10 J.J. Cannon CO
- ☐ 11 Mike Maksudian
- ☐ 12 Paul Rodgers
- ☐ 13 Julian Yan
- ☐ 14 Bernie Nunez
- ☐ 15 Domingo Martinez
- ☐ 16 Chris Rauth
- ☐ 17 Andy Dziadkowiec
- ☐ 18 Woody Williams
- ☐ 19 John Poloni CO
- ☐ 20 Chris Jones
- ☐ 21 Darren Hall
- ☐ 22 Tom Quinlan

- ☐ 23 Earl Sanders
- ☐ 24 Dennis Jones
- ☐ 25 Jerry Schunk
- ☐ 26 Randy Knorr
- ☐ 27 Nate Cromwell
- ☐ 28 Checklist

1990 Knoxville Blue Jays ProCards

This 25-card standard-size set of the 1990 Knoxville Smokies, a Class AA Southern League affiliate of the Toronto Blue Jays, features on its white-bordered fronts posed color player photos set on simulated wood-grain backgrounds. The player's name, position, and team appear within a gold-colored rectangle below the photo. The tan horizontal back is bordered in white and carries the player's name at the top, followed by biography and statistics.

	MINT	NRMT	EXC
COMPLETE SET (25)	8.00	3.60	1.00

- ☐ 1237 Checklist
- ☐ 1238 Nate Cromwell
- ☐ 1239 Woody Williams
- ☐ 1240 Pat Hentgen
- ☐ 1241 Jimmy Rogers
- ☐ 1242 Juan Guzman
- ☐ 1243 Chris Jones
- ☐ 1244 Darren Hall
- ☐ 1245 Earl Sanders
- ☐ 1246 Pete Blohm
- ☐ 1247 Bob MacDonald
- ☐ 1248 Randy Knorr
- ☐ 1249 William Suero
- ☐ 1250 Jerry Schunk
- ☐ 1251 Eddie Zosky
- ☐ 1252 Tom Quinlan
- ☐ 1253 Julian Yan
- ☐ 1254 Domingo Martinez
- ☐ 1255 Paul Rodgers
- ☐ 1256 Bernie Nunez
- ☐ 1257 Shawn Jeter
- ☐ 1258 Mike Maksudian
- ☐ 1259 John Stearns MGR
- ☐ 1260 J.J. Cannon CO
- ☐ 1261 John Poloni CO

1990 Knoxville Blue Jays Star

This 26-card standard-size set of the 1990 Knoxville Blue Jays, a Class AA Southern League affiliate of the Toronto Blue Jays, features yellow-bordered posed color player photos on its fronts. The player's name, team name, and position appear at the bottom. The white horizontal back carries the player's name at the top, followed by biography and statistics.

	MINT	NRMT	EXC
COMPLETE SET (26)	8.00	3.60	1.00

- ☐ 1 Pete Blohm
- ☐ 2 Nate Cromwell
- ☐ 3 Andy Dziadkowiec
- ☐ 4 Darren Hall
- ☐ 5 Pat Hentgen
- ☐ 6 Shawn Jeter
- ☐ 7 Chris Jones
- ☐ 8 Dennis Jones
- ☐ 9 Randy Knorr
- ☐ 10 Bob MacDonald
- ☐ 11 Mike Maksudian
- ☐ 12 Domingo Martinez
- ☐ 13 Bernie Nunez
- ☐ 14 Tom Quinlan
- ☐ 15 Paul Rodgers
- ☐ 16 Jimmy Rogers
- ☐ 17 Earl Sanders
- ☐ 18 Jerry Schunk
- ☐ 19 William Suero
- ☐ 20 Woody Williams
- ☐ 21 Rob Wishnevski
- ☐ 22 Julian Yan
- ☐ 23 Eddie Zosky
- ☐ 24 John Stearns MG
- ☐ 25 J.J. Cannon CO
- ☐ 26 John Poloni CO

1990 Lakeland Tigers Star

This 28-card standard-size set of the 1990 Lakeland Tigers, a Class A Florida State League affiliate of the Detroit Tigers, features orange bordered posed color player photos on its fronts. The player's name, team name, and position appear at the bottom. The white horizontal back carries the player's name at the top, followed by biography, career highlights, and statistics.

	MINT	NRMT	EXC
COMPLETE SET (28)	5.00	2.20	.60

- ☐ 1 Eric Albright
- ☐ 2 Doyle Balthazar
- ☐ 3 Hector Berrios
- ☐ 4 Mark Cole
- ☐ 5 Ron Cook
- ☐ 6 Ivan Cruz
- ☐ 7 John Doherty
- ☐ 8 John DeSilva
- ☐ 9 Mark Ettles
- ☐ 10 Ed Ferm
- ☐ 11 Greg Gohr
- ☐ 12 Jeff Goodale
- ☐ 13 Darren Hursey
- ☐ 14 Jody Hurst
- ☐ 15 Keith Kimberlin
- ☐ 16 Kurt Knudsen
- ☐ 17 Todd Krum
- ☐ 18 Ron Marigny
- ☐ 19 Darryl Martin
- ☐ 20 Dan Raley
- ☐ 21 Robert Reimink
- ☐ 22 Lino Rivera
- ☐ 23 Tookie Spann
- ☐ 24 Mike Tresh
- ☐ 25 Marty Willis
- ☐ 26 John Lipon MGR
- ☐ 27 Doug Carpenter CO
- ☐ 28 Terry Smith TR

1990 Las Vegas Stars CMC

This 25-card standard-size set of the 1990 Las Vegas Stars, a Class AAA Pacific Coast League affiliate of the San Diego Padres, features white-bordered posed color player photos on its fronts. The player's name and position appear at the bottom; the team name appears vertically on the left. The back carries the league emblem in the white area at the top, the team name in the green stripe below, and player's name, position, biography, and statistics in the yellow area at the bottom. 1,100 sets were produced.

	MINT	NRMT	EXC
COMPLETE SET (25)	5.00	2.20	.60

- ☐ 1 Roger Smithberg
- ☐ 2 Steve Peters
- ☐ 3 Matt Maysey
- ☐ 4 Terry Gilmore
- ☐ 5 Eric Nolte
- ☐ 6 Jim Lewis
- ☐ 7 Pete Roberts
- ☐ 8 Dan Murphy
- ☐ 9 Rich Rodriguez
- ☐ 10 Joe Lynch
- ☐ 11 Mike Basso
- ☐ 12 Ronn Reynolds
- ☐ 13 Jose Mota
- ☐ 14 Paul Faries
- ☐ 15 Warren Newson
- ☐ 16 Alex Cole
- ☐ 17 Tom LeVasseur
- ☐ 18 Charles Hillemann
- ☐ 19 Jeff Yurtin
- ☐ 20 Rafael Valdez
- ☐ 21 Brian Ohnoutka
- ☐ 22 Pat Kelly MGR
- ☐ 23 Gary Lance CO
- ☐ 24 Tony Torchia CO
- ☐ 25 Todd Hutcheson TR

1990 Las Vegas Stars ProCards

This 28-card standard-size set of the 1990 Las Vegas Stars, a Class AAA Pacific Coast League affiliate of the San Diego Padres, features on its white-bordered fronts posed color player photos set on simulated wood-grain backgrounds. The player's name, position, and team appear within a gold-colored rectangle below the photo. The tan horizontal back is bordered in white and carries the player's name at the top, followed by biography and statistics.

	MINT	NRMT	EXC
COMPLETE SET (28)	5.00	2.20	.60

- ☐ 112 Checklist
- ☐ 113 Terry Gilmore
- ☐ 114 Jim Lewis
- ☐ 115 Joe Lynch
- ☐ 116 Matt Maysey
- ☐ 117 Dan Murphy
- ☐ 118 Eric Nolte
- ☐ 119 Brian Ohnoutka
- ☐ 120 Steve Peters
- ☐ 121 Paul Quinzer
- ☐ 122 Pete Roberts
- ☐ 123 Rich Rodriguez
- ☐ 124 Roger Smithberg
- ☐ 125 Rafael Valdez
- ☐ 126 Mike Basso
- ☐ 127 Ronn Reynolds
- ☐ 128 Paul Faries
- ☐ 129 Tom LeVasseur
- ☐ 130 Jose Mota
- ☐ 131 Eddie Williams
- ☐ 132 Jeff Yurtin
- ☐ 133 Alex Cole
- ☐ 134 Charles Hillemann
- ☐ 135 Tom Howard
- ☐ 136 Warren Newson
- ☐ 136 Pat Kelly MGR
- ☐ 138 Gary Lance CO
- ☐ 139 Tony Torchia CO

1990 London Tigers ProCards

This 22-card standard-size set of the 1990 London Tigers, a Class AA Eastern League affiliate of the Detroit Tigers, features on its white-bordered fronts posed color player photos set on simulated wood-grain backgrounds. The player's name, position, and team appear within a gold-colored rectangle below the photo. The tan horizontal back is bordered in white and carries the player's name at the top, followed by biography and statistics.

	MINT	NRMT	EXC
COMPLETE SET (22)	5.00	2.20	.60

- ☐ 1262 Checklist
- ☐ 1263 David Haas
- ☐ 1264 John Kiely
- ☐ 1265 Mike Lumley
- ☐ 1266 Rusty Meacham
- ☐ 1267 Dave Richards
- ☐ 1268 Ron Rightnowar
- ☐ 1269 Mike Wilkins
- ☐ 1270 Ken Williams
- ☐ 1271 Rich Rowland
- ☐ 1272 Tom Aldrich
- ☐ 1273 Chris Alvarez
- ☐ 1274 Arnie Beyeler
- ☐ 1275 Rico Brogna
- ☐ 1276 Lou Frazier
- ☐ 1277 Luis Galindo
- ☐ 1278 Basilio Cabrera
- ☐ 1279 Steve Green
- ☐ 1280 Riccardo Ingram
- ☐ 1281 Tim Leiper
- ☐ 1282 Steve Pegues
- ☐ 1283 John Toale

1990 Louisville Red Birds CMC

This 29-card standard-size set of the 1990 Louisville Red Birds, a Class AAA American Association affiliate of the St. Louis Cardinals, features white-bordered posed color player photos on its fronts. The player's name and position appear at the bottom; the team name appears vertically on the left. The back carries the league emblem in the white area at the top, the team name in the green stripe below, and player's name, position, biography, and statistics in the yellow area at the bottom. 1,100 sets were produced.

	MINT	NRMT	EXC
COMPLETE SET (29)	10.00	4.50	1.25

- ☐ 1 Scott Arnold
- ☐ 2 Gibson Alba
- ☐ 3 Cris Carpenter
- ☐ 4 Stan Clarke
- ☐ 5 Mike Hinkle
- ☐ 6 Howard Hilton
- ☐ 7 Dave Osteen
- ☐ 8 Mike Perez
- ☐ 9 Bernard Gilkey
- ☐ 10 Dennis Carter
- ☐ 11 Julian Martinez
- ☐ 12 Rod Brewer
- ☐ 13 Ray Stephens
- ☐ 14 Ray Lankford
- ☐ 15 Craig Wilson
- ☐ 16 Roy Silver
- ☐ 17 Bien Figueroa
- ☐ 18 Jesus Mendez
- ☐ 19 Geronimo Pena
- ☐ 20 Omar Olivares
- ☐ 21 Mark Grater
- ☐ 22 Tim Sherrill
- ☐ 23 Pat Austin
- ☐ 24 Todd Crosby
- ☐ 25 Gary Nichols
- ☐ 26 Mauricio Nunez
- ☐ 27 Gaylen Pitts
- ☐ 28 Mark Riggins CO
- ☐ 29 Brad Bluestone TR

1990 Louisville Red Birds Louisville Baseball Club

	MINT	NRMT	EXC
COMPLETE SET (42)	12.00	5.50	1.50

- ☐ 1 Checklist
- ☐ 2 Bernard Gilkey
  1990 MVP
- ☐ 3 Gaylen Pitts MG
- ☐ 4 Mark Riggins CO
- ☐ 5 Gibson Alba
- ☐ 6 Luis Alicea
- ☐ 7 Scott Arnold
- ☐ 8 Rod Brewer
- ☐ 9 Ernie Camacho
- ☐ 10 Cris Carpenter
- ☐ 11 Stan Clarke
- ☐ 12 Rheal Cormier
- ☐ 13 Danny Cox
- ☐ 14 Todd Crosby
- ☐ 15 Bien Figueroa
- ☐ 16 Terry Francona
- ☐ 17 Ed Fulton
- ☐ 18 Bernard Gilkey
- ☐ 19 Ken Hill
- ☐ 20 Howard Hilton
- ☐ 21 Mike Hinkle
- ☐ 22 Dale Kisten
- ☐ 23 Ray Lankford
- ☐ 24 Lonnie Maclin
- ☐ 25 Julian Martinez
- ☐ 26 Greg Mathews
- ☐ 27 Jesus Mendez
- ☐ 28 Scott Nichols
- ☐ 29 Tom Niedenfuer
- ☐ 30 Mauricio Nunez
- ☐ 31 Omar Olivares
- ☐ 32 Dave Osteen
- ☐ 33 Geronimo Pena
- ☐ 34 Mike Perez
- ☐ 35 Dave Richardson
- ☐ 36 Stan Royer
- ☐ 37 Tim Sherrill
- ☐ 38 Roy Silver
- ☐ 39 Ray Stephens
- ☐ 40 Bob Tewksbury
- ☐ 41 Steve Trout
- ☐ 42 Craig Wilson

1990 Louisville Red Birds ProCards

This 29-card standard-size set of the 1990 Louisville Red Birds, a Class AAA American Association affiliate of the St. Louis Cardinals, features on its white-bordered fronts posed color player photos set on simulated wood-grain backgrounds. The player's name, position, and team appear within a gold-colored rectangle below the photo. The tan horizontal back is bordered in white and carries the player's name at the top, followed by biography and statistics.

	MINT	NRMT	EXC
COMPLETE SET (29)	8.00	3.60	1.00

- ☐ 392 Checklist
- ☐ 393 Gibson Alba
- ☐ 394 Scott Arnold
- ☐ 395 Cris Carpenter
- ☐ 396 Stan Clarke
- ☐ 397 Mark Grater
- ☐ 398 Howard Hilton
- ☐ 399 Mike Hinkle
- ☐ 400 Omar Olivares
- ☐ 401 Dave Osteen
- ☐ 402 Mike Perez
- ☐ 403 Tim Sherrill
- ☐ 404 Scott Nichols
- ☐ 405 Ray Stephens
- ☐ 406 Pat Austin
- ☐ 407 Rod Brewer
- ☐ 408 Todd Crosby
- ☐ 409 Bien Figueroa
- ☐ 410 Julian Martinez
- ☐ 411 Jesus Mendez
- ☐ 412 Geronimo Pena
- ☐ 413 Craig Wilson
- ☐ 414 Dennis Carter
- ☐ 415 Bernard Gilkey
- ☐ 416 Ray Lankford
- ☐ 417 Mauricio Nunez
- ☐ 418 Roy Silver
- ☐ 419 Gaylen Pitts MGR
- ☐ 420 Mark Riggins CO

1990 LSU Tigers Anheuser-Busch

Sponsored by Anheuser-Busch, this 16-card set measures the standard size. On a white card face, the fronts feature color action player photos with rounded corners. The team and sponsor logos appear above the photo, while the player's name and position are printed inside a baseball in the lower left corner. The backs carry player profiles and a message from Anheuser-Busch to drink responsibly.

	MINT	NRMT	EXC
COMPLETE SET (16)	12.00	5.50	1.50

- ☐ 1 Title Card
- ☐ 2 Wes Grisham
- ☐ 3 Paul Byrd
- ☐ 4 Keith Osik
- ☐ 5 Tookie Johnson
- ☐ 6 Chad Ogea
- ☐ 7 Brad Stuart
- ☐ 8 Alan Barnard
- ☐ 9 Dirk Wilner
- ☐ 10 Bo Loftin
- ☐ 11 Brian Stevens
- ☐ 12 Darryl Gilevich
- ☐ 13 Rob Gerdes
- ☐ 14 Bryan Brown
- ☐ 15 Darrin Dares
- ☐ 16 Henri Saunders

1990 LSU Tigers Ben McDonald McDag

This 16-card standard-size set was produced by McDag Productions in honor of LSU All-American baseball pitcher Ben McDonald. Ten thousand sets were produced. The color photos on the card fronts capture various moments in McDonald's career, from childhood to his college days. The pictures are bordered in white. In blue print, the horizontally oriented backs summarize McDonald's career and present a "question and answer" trivia feature. A drawing of the Big Ben clock appears on both sides of the card.

	MINT	NRMT	EXC
COMPLETE SET (16)	5.00	2.20	.60

☐ 1 Ben McDonald
LSU All-American
☐ 2 Ben McDonald
The U.S.A. Experience
☐ 3 Ben McDonald
The Olympic Gold
☐ 4 Ben McDonald
Tiger Waiting to Roar
☐ 5 Ben McDonald
Upcoming Star
☐ 6 Ben McDonald
USA in Korea
☐ 7 Ben McDonald
On the Mound
☐ 8 Ben McDonald
Football
☐ 9 Ben McDonald
High School Fireballer
☐ 10 Ben McDonald
All-State Hoopster
☐ 11 Ben McDonald
LSU Basketball
☐ 12 Ben McDonald
To the Hoop
☐ 13 Ben McDonald
A Stellar College Career
☐ 14 Ben McDonald
LSU "K" Leader
☐ 15 Ben McDonald
The No. 1 Draft Pick
☐ 16 Ben McDonald
Two Sport Star

1990 LSU Tigers Greats McDag

	MINT	NRMT	EXC
COMPLETE SET (16)	10.00	4.50	1.25

☐ 1 Skip Bertman CO
☐ 2 Mark Howie
☐ 3 Dan Kite
☐ 4 Jeff Reboulet
☐ 5 Eric Hetzel
☐ 6 Graig Faulkner
☐ 7 Ben McDonald
☐ 8 Rob Leary
☐ 9 Mark Guthrie
☐ 10 Jeff Yurtin
☐ 11 Clay Parker
☐ 12 Joe Bill Adcock
☐ 13 Mike Miley
☐ 14 Gregg Patterson
☐ 15 Russell Springer
☐ 16 Barry Manuel

1990 LSU Tigers Police

	MINT	NRMT	EXC
COMPLETE SET (16)	10.00	4.50	1.25

☐ 1 Skip Bertman CO
☐ 2 Wes Grisham
☐ 3 Pat Garrity
☐ 4 Paul Byrd
☐ 5 Keith Osik
☐ 6 Rich Cordani
☐ 7 Gary Hymel
☐ 8 Chad Ogea
☐ 9 John Tellechea
☐ 10 Scott Bethea
☐ 11 Jason Wall
☐ 12 Ron Lim
☐ 13 Luis Garcia
☐ 14 Tim Clark
☐ 15 John O'Donoghue
☐ 16 Tookie Johnson

1990 Lynchburg Red Sox Team Issue

	MINT	NRMT	EXC
COMPLETE SET (27)	7.00	3.10	.85

☐ 1 Greg Blosser
☐ 2 Chris Leach
☐ 3 Ed Perozo
☐ 4 Mickey Rivers Jr.
☐ 5 James Byrd
☐ 6 Miguel Monegro
☐ 7 Scott Powers
☐ 8 Willie Tatum
☐ 9 Les Wallin
☐ 10 Chris Whitehead
☐ 11 Luis Dorante
☐ 12 Chris Hanks
☐ 13 Paul Williams
☐ 14 Odie Abril
☐ 15 Paul Brown
☐ 16 Brian Conroy
☐ 17 Freddie Davis
☐ 18 Peter Estrada
☐ 19 Howard Landry
☐ 20 Tato Pratts
☐ 21 Ken Ryan
☐ 22 Rennie Scott
☐ 23 Tim Stange
☐ 24 Scott Taylor
☐ 25 David Duchin
☐ 26 Jim Bibby
☐ 27 Gary Allenson

1990 Madison Muskies Best

This 29-card standard-size set of the 1990 Madison Muskies, a Class A Midwest League affiliate of the Oakland Athletics, features white-bordered posed and action color player photos on its fronts. The player's name and position appear vertically on the left side. The yellow horizontal back carries the player's name and position at the top, followed by biography, career highlights, and statistics. A player head shot appears in the lower right corner.

	MINT	NRMT	EXC
COMPLETE SET (29)	5.00	2.20	.60

☐ 1 Todd Van Poppel
☐ 2 Ed Tredway
☐ 3 Kurt Abbott
☐ 4 Marcos Armas
☐ 5 Eric Campa
☐ 6 Fred Cooley
☐ 7 Scott Henry
☐ 8 Glenn Osinski
☐ 9 Jim Waggoner
☐ 10 Enoch Simmons
☐ 11 Keith Thomas
☐ 12 Lee Tinsley
☐ 13 Leandro Mejia
☐ 14 Gerbacio Deleon
☐ 15 Jim Gibbs
☐ 16 Hugh Gulledge
☐ 17 Chad Kuhn
☐ 18 Dave Latter
☐ 19 Jim Lawson
☐ 20 Mike Mohler
☐ 21 Gavin Osteen
☐ 22 Bronswell Patrick
☐ 23 Timothy Peek
☐ 24 Bill Taylor
☐ 25 Casey Parson MGR
☐ 26 Bert Bradley CO
☐ 27 Shane Borchert TR
☐ 28 Wynn Beck
☐ 29 Checklist

1990 Madison Muskies ProCards

This 26-card standard-size set of the 1990 Madison Muskies, a Class A Midwest League affiliate of the Oakland Athletics, features on its white-bordered fronts posed color player photos set on simulated wood-grain backgrounds. The player's name, position, and team appear within a gold-colored rectangle below the photo. The tan horizontal back is bordered in white and carries the player's name at the top, followed by biography and statistics.

	MINT	NRMT	EXC
COMPLETE SET (26)	5.00	2.20	.60

☐ 2259 Checklist
☐ 2260 Brad Brimhall
☐ 2261 Matthew Grott
☐ 2262 Darin Kracl
☐ 2263 Chad Kuhn
☐ 2264 Dave Latter
☐ 2265 Rey Martinez
☐ 2266 Leandro Mejia
☐ 2267 Mike Mohler
☐ 2268 Gavin Osteen
☐ 2269 Steve Peck
☐ 2270 Pedro Pena
☐ 2271 Wynn Beck
☐ 2272 Henry Mercedes
☐ 2273 Ed Tredway
☐ 2274 Kurt Abbott
☐ 2275 Fred Cooley
☐ 2276 Mike Conte
☐ 2277 Glenn McCormick
☐ 2278 Scott Shockey
☐ 2279 Carlos Tamarez
☐ 2280 Darryl Vice
☐ 2281 Enoch Simmons
☐ 2282 Lee Tinsley
☐ 2283 Casey Parsons
☐ 2284 Bert Bradley

1990 Martinsville Phillies ProCards

This 34-card standard-size set of the 1990 Martinsville Phillies, a Rookie Class Appalachian League affiliate of the Philadelphia Phillies, features on its white-bordered fronts posed color player photos set on simulated wood-grain backgrounds. The player's name, position, and team appear within a gold-colored rectangle below the photo. The tan horizontal back is bordered in white and carries the player's name at the top, followed by biography and statistics.

	MINT	NRMT	EXC
COMPLETE SET (34)	5.00	2.20	.60

☐ 3177 Checklist
☐ 3178 Rick Meyer
☐ 3179 Lamar Foster
☐ 3180 Facanel Medina
☐ 3181 Willimas Carmona
☐ 3182 Mike Farmer
☐ 3183 Darren Hedley
☐ 3184 Bill Higgins
☐ 3185 Winston Wheeler
☐ 3186 Patrico Medina
☐ 3187 Maurice Hines
☐ 3188 David Croak
☐ 3189 Bob Badacour
☐ 3190 Gary Bennett
☐ 3191 Gary Lance
☐ 3192 Ray Domecq
☐ 3193 Pete Freeman
☐ 3194 Francisco Rosario
☐ 3195 Antonio Grossom
☐ 3196 J.J. Munoz
☐ 3197 Mike Lieberthal
☐ 3198 Mike Murphy
☐ 3199 Robbie Kamerschen
☐ 3200 Darren Cooper
☐ 3201 Jeff Borgese
☐ 3202 Terry Tewell
☐ 3203 Jorge Pascual
☐ 3204 David Agado
☐ 3205 Chad Anderson
☐ 3206 Domingo Tejada
☐ 3207 German Arias
☐ 3208 Dagoberto Tapia
☐ 3209 Derek Botelho CO ,
Roly Dearmas MGR
☐ 3419 Alberto Vicente

1990 Medicine Hat Blue Jays Best

This 28-card standard-size set of the 1990 Medicine Hat Blue Jays, a Class A Pioneer League affiliate of the Toronto Blue Jays, features white-bordered posed color player photos on its fronts. The player's name and position appear vertically on the left side. The yellow horizontal back carries the player's name and position at the top, followed by biography. A player head shot appears in the lower right corner.

	MINT	NRMT	EXC
COMPLETE SET (28)	5.00	2.20	.60

☐ 1 Mike Coolbaugh
☐ 2 Jason Reese
☐ 3 Tim Hyers
☐ 4 Travis Burley
☐ 5 Kyle Duey
☐ 6 Mark Choate
☐ 7 Richard Orman
☐ 8 Greg Wilcox
☐ 9 Lonell Roberts
☐ 10 Brent Bowers
☐ 11 Felix Septino UER
(Name misspelled Septimo)
☐ 12 Ned Barley
☐ 13 Anastacio Garcia
☐ 14 Keith Hines
☐ 15 Scott Miller
☐ 16 Morgan Adams
☐ 17 David Fletcher
☐ 18 Dale Kistaitis
☐ 19 John Gilligan
☐ 20 Kris Harmes
☐ 21 Lee Daniel
☐ 22 Ronald Reams
☐ 23 Thomas Hotchkiss
☐ 24 Marc Loeb TR
☐ 25 Raphael Garcia
☐ 26 Howard Battle
☐ 27 Hector Tavarez
☐ 28 Checklist

1990 Memphis Chicks Best

This 29-card standard-size set of the 1990 Memphis Chicks, a Class AA Southern League affiliate of the Kansas City Royals, features white-bordered posed and action color player photos on its fronts. The player's name and position appear vertically on the left side. The yellow horizontal back carries the player's name and position at the top, followed by biography, career highlights, and statistics. A player head shot appears in the lower right corner.

	MINT	NRMT	EXC
COMPLETE SET (29)	8.00	3.60	1.00

☐ 1 Brent Mayne
☐ 2 Jorge Pedre
☐ 3 Pete Alborano
☐ 4 Stu Cole
☐ 5 David Howard
☐ 6 Sean Berry
☐ 7 Frank Laureano
☐ 8 Jeff Conine
☐ 9 Bobby Moore
☐ 10 Kevin Koslofski
☐ 11 Tommy Dunbar
☐ 12 Kyle Reese
☐ 13 Brian McRae
☐ 14 Scott Centala
☐ 15 Greg Everson
☐ 16 Richie LeBlanc
☐ 17 Joel Johnston
☐ 18 Hector Wagner
☐ 19 Brian McCormack
☐ 20 Victor Cole
☐ 21 Carlos Maldonado
☐ 22 Jim Campbell
☐ 23 Andres Cruz
☐ 24 Doug Nelson
☐ 25 Guy Hansen CO
☐ 26 Jeff Cox MGR
☐ 27 Mike Leon TR
☐ 28 Brian Peterson CO
☐ 29 Checklist

1990 Memphis Chicks ProCards

This 28-card standard-size set of the 1990 Memphis Chicks, a Class AA Southern League affiliate of the Kansas City Royals, features on its white-bordered fronts posed color player photos set on simulated wood-grain backgrounds. The player's name, position, and team appear within a gold-colored rectangle below the photo. The tan horizontal back is bordered in white and carries the player's name at the top, followed by biography and statistics.

	MINT	NRMT	EXC
COMPLETE SET (28)	7.00	3.10	.85

☐ 1000 Checklist
☐ 1001 Scott Centala
☐ 1002 Jim Campbell
☐ 1003 Andres Cruz
☐ 1004 Doug Nelson
☐ 1005 Greg Everson
☐ 1006 Victor Cole
☐ 1007 Carlos Maldonado
☐ 1008 Hector Wagner
☐ 1009 Brian McCormack
☐ 1010 Joel Johnston
☐ 1011 Kyle Reese
☐ 1012 Brent Mayne
☐ 1013 Jorge Pedre
☐ 1014 Stu Cole
☐ 1015 Dave Howard
☐ 1016 Sean Berry
☐ 1017 Jeff Conine
☐ 1018 Frank Laureano
☐ 1019 Bobby Moore
☐ 1020 Pete Alborano
☐ 1021 Kevin Koslofski
☐ 1022 Brian McRae
☐ 1023 Tommy Dunbar
☐ 1024 Richie LeBlance
☐ 1025 Jeff Cox MGR
☐ 1026 Guy Hansen CO
☐ 1027 Brian Peterson CO

1990 Memphis Chicks Star

This 27-card standard-size set of the 1990 Memphis Chicks, a Class AA Southern League affiliate of the Kansas City Royals, features blue bordered posed color player photos on its fronts. The player's name, team name, and position appear at the bottom. The white horizontal back carries the player's name at the top, followed by biography, career highlights, and statistics.

	MINT	NRMT	EXC
COMPLETE SET (27)	7.00	3.10	.85

☐ 1 Pete Alborano
☐ 2 Sean Berry
☐ 3 Jim Campbell
☐ 4 Scott Centala
☐ 5 Stu Cole
☐ 6 Victor Cole
☐ 7 Jeff Conine
☐ 8 Andres Cruz
☐ 9 Tommy Dunbar
☐ 10 Chuck Everson
☐ 11 David Howard
☐ 12 Kevin Koslofski
☐ 13 Frank Laureano

☐ 14 Richie LeBlanc
☐ 15 Carlos Maldonado
☐ 16 Brent Mayne
☐ 17 Brian McCormack
☐ 18 Brian McRae
☐ 19 Dennis Moeller
☐ 20 Bobby Moore
☐ 21 Doug Nelson
☐ 22 Jorge Pedre
☐ 23 Kyle Reese
☐ 24 Daryl Smith
☐ 25 Hector Wagner
☐ 26 Coaching Staff
Jeff Cox MGR
Guy Hansen CO
Brian Peterson CO
☐ 27 Mike Leon TR

1990 Miami Miracle I Star

This 31-card standard-size set of the 1990 Miami Miracle, a Class A Florida State League Independent, features yellow bordered posed color player photos on its fronts. The player's name, team name, and position appear at the bottom. The white horizontal back carries the player's name at the top, followed by biography, career highlights, and statistics.

	MINT	NRMT	EXC
COMPLETE SET (31)	8.00	3.60	1.00

☐ 1 Miah Bradbury
☐ 2 Matt Cakora
☐ 3 Paul Carey
☐ 4 Greg D'Alexander
☐ 5 Clay Daniel
☐ 6 Marty Durkin
☐ 7 Mike Ericson
☐ 8 Librado Garcia
☐ 9 Marc Giordano
☐ 10 Brad Gregory
☐ 11 Jackie Gutierrez
☐ 12 Dennis Kidd
☐ 13 Anthony Kelley
☐ 14 George Kerfut
☐ 15 Tito Landrum
☐ 16 Mike Lansing
☐ 17 Tom Mincho
☐ 18 Bill Miller
☐ 19 Jorge Pascual
☐ 20 Tom Raffo
☐ 21 Tim Rigsby
☐ 22 Charlie Rogers
☐ 23 Rich Sauveur
☐ 24 Harry Shelton
☐ 25 Chad Smith
☐ 26 Tim Rigsby
☐ 27 Charlie Rogers
☐ 28 Coaching Staff
Mike Easler MGR
Bob Fralick CO
Fredi Gonzalez CO
☐ 29 Michael Veeck GM
☐ 30 Jericho
Mascot
☐ 31 Team Picture

1990 Miami Miracle II Star

This 31-card standard-size set of the 1990 Miami Miracle, a Class A Florida State League Independent, features green bordered posed color player photos on its fronts. The player's name, team name, and position appear at the bottom. The white horizontal back carries the player's name at the top, followed by biography, career highlights, and statistics.

	MINT	NRMT	EXC
COMPLETE SET (31)	5.00	2.20	.60

☐ 1 Dave Alexander
☐ 2 Joe Beaulac
☐ 3 Tommy Boyce
☐ 4 Tim Delgado
☐ 5 Marty Durkin
☐ 6 Eddie Garczyk
☐ 7 Marc Giordano
☐ 8 Pierre Gomez
☐ 9 Jackie Gutierrez
☐ 10 Lance Hudson
☐ 11 Anthony Kelley
☐ 12 George Kerfut
☐ 13 Dennis Kidd
☐ 14 Angel Lugo
☐ 15 Tim MacNeil
☐ 16 Javier Magria
☐ 17 Tim McKinley
☐ 18 Bill Miller
☐ 19 Angel Morris
☐ 20 Jorge Pascual
☐ 21 Kevin Ponder
☐ 22 Mike Reitzel
☐ 23 Harry Shelton
☐ 24 Dave Taylor
☐ 25 Pat Varni
☐ 26 Mike Easler MGR
☐ 27 Bob Fralick CO
☐ 28 Fredi Gonzalez CO
☐ 29 Seth Fogler TR
☐ 30 Office Personnel
Bruce Bielenberg
Bennett Creed
Sherri clemans
Rhonda Miller
Leslie Smith
Seth Fogler
☐ 31 Jericho
Mascot

1990 Midland Angels Grand Slam

	MINT	NRMT	EXC
COMPLETE SET (30)	5.00	2.20	.60

☐ 1 Eddie Rodriguez MG
☐ 2 Gary Ruby CO
☐ 3 Steve DeAngelis
☐ 4 Ruben Amaro Jr.
☐ 5 Kyle Abbott
☐ 6 Mark Zappelli
☐ 7 Mark Howie
☐ 8 Scott Cerny
☐ 9 Jeff Barns
☐ 10 Mark Davis
☐ 11 Wiley Lee
☐ 12 Joe Grahe
☐ 13 Mike Knapp
☐ 14 Jim Aylward
☐ 15 Mike Butcher
☐ 16 Mark Holzemer
☐ 17 Carl Hamilton
☐ 18 Glenn Carter
☐ 19 Kevin Trudeau
☐ 20 Dan Wagner
☐ 21 Andy Hall
☐ 22 Frank DiMichele
☐ 23 Luis Merejo
☐ 24 Kevin Flora
☐ 25 Scott Sowell TR
☐ NNO Juice the Moose
Mascot
☐ NNO Joshua Rodriguez
☐ NNO Monty Hoppel MG
☐ NNO Title Card
☐ NNO Advertisement Card

1990 Mississippi State Bulldogs

	MINT	NRMT	EXC
COMPLETE SET (44)	10.00	4.50	1.25

☐ 1 Daryl Albro
☐ 2 Mike Alford
☐ 3 Charlie Anderson
☐ 4 Craig Bane
☐ 5 Rex Buckner
☐ 6 John Cohen
☐ 7 Chuck Daniel
☐ 8 Corbin Davis
☐ 9 Tracy Echols
☐ 10 Park Evans
☐ 11 Justin Ewing
☐ 12 Jimmy Gammill
☐ 13 Damon Gardner
☐ 14 Chris George
☐ 15 Joey Hamilton
☐ 16 Jon Harden
☐ 17 Steve Hegan
☐ 18 Carl Henderson
☐ 19 Tim Henderson
☐ 20 Tripp Hill
☐ 21 Chuck Holly
☐ 22 Tracy Jobes
☐ 23 Eddie Lyons
☐ 24 Jeff Mackin
☐ 25 Burke Masters
☐ 26 Joel Matthews
☐ 27 David Mitchell
☐ 28 Rob Norman
☐ 29 David Perkins
☐ 30 Ron Polk CO
☐ 31 Steve Polk
☐ 32 Tom Quinn
☐ 33 Tommy Raffo
☐ 34 Matt Ramsey
☐ 35 Bobby Reed
☐ 36 Jim Robinson
☐ 37 Scott Mitchell
☐ 38 Jon Shave
☐ 39 B.J. Wallace
☐ 40 John Warburton
☐ 41 Assistant Coaches
Joe Hudak
Steve Smith
☐ 42 Checklist
☐ 43 Dudy Noble Field
☐ 44 Student Managers and Trainers
Jay McKinney MG
John Mooney MG
Rogers Smith MG
Scott Walters MG
Bruce Langston TR

1990 Modesto A's Cal League Cards

	MINT	NRMT	EXC
COMPLETE SET (25)	5.00	2.20	.60

☐ 149 Scott Erwin
☐ 150 John Briscoe
Sic, Briscoa
☐ 151 Todd Smith
☐ 152 James Lawson
☐ 153 Dana Allison
☐ 154 William Taylor
☐ 155 Bronswell Patrick
☐ 156 Timothy McCoy
☐ 157 William Love
☐ 158 Joseph Ortiz
☐ 159 Timothy Vannaman
☐ 160 Michael Messerly
☐ 161 Keith Thomas
☐ 162 James Buccheri
☐ 163 Ronald Correia
☐ 164 Dean Borelli
☐ 165 Ronald Witmeyer
☐ 166 James Waggoner
☐ 167 Thomas Carcione
☐ 168 Francisco Matos
☐ 169 Dwayne Hosey
☐ 170 Kevin Lofthus
☐ 171 Ted Kubiak MGR
☐ 172 Pete Richert CO
☐ 173 Dave Hollenback TR

1990 Modesto A's Chong

	MINT	NRMT	EXC
COMPLETE SET (35)	6.00	2.70	.75

☐ 1 Dean Borelli
☐ 2 John Briscoe
☐ 3 Jim Buccheri
☐ 4 Tom Carcione
☐ 5 Joel Chimelis
☐ 6 Mike Conte
☐ 7 Russell Cormier
☐ 8 Rod Correia
☐ 9 Scott Erwin
☐ 10 Apolinar Garcia
☐ 11 Matt Grott
☐ 12 Johnny Guzman
☐ 13 Brett Hendley
☐ 14 Dave Hollenback
☐ 15 Dwayne Hosey
☐ 16 Mike Kennedy
☐ 17 Ruben Lardizabal
☐ 18 William Love
☐ 19 Francisco Matos
☐ 20 Tim McCoy
☐ 21 Mike Messerly
☐ 22 Craig Paquette
☐ 23 Bob Parry
☐ 24 Bronswell Patrick
☐ 25 Steve Peck
☐ 26 Pedro Pena
☐ 27 Richard Shockey
☐ 28 Todd Smith
☐ 29 Rick Strebeck
☐ 30 Darryl Vice
☐ 31 James Waggoner
☐ 32 Ron Witmeyer
☐ 33 Ted Kubiak MG
☐ 34 Pete Richert CO
☐ NNO Title Card

1990 Modesto A's ProCards

This 29-card standard-size set of the 1990 Modesto A's, a Class A California League affiliate of the Oakland Athletics, features on its white-bordered fronts posed color player photos set on simulated wood-grain backgrounds. The player's name, position, and team appear within a gold-colored rectangle below the photo. The tan horizontal back is bordered in white and carries the player's name at the top, followed by biography and statistics.

	MINT	NRMT	EXC
COMPLETE SET (29)	5.00	2.20	.60

☐ 2202 Checklist
☐ 2203 Dana Allison
☐ 2204 John Briscoe
☐ 2205 Scott Erwin
☐ 2206 Apolinar Garcia
☐ 2207 Johnny Guzman
☐ 2208 Tim McCoy
☐ 2209 Jim Lawson
☐ 2210 Will Love
☐ 2211 Bronswell Patrick
☐ 2212 Todd Smith
☐ 2213 Bill Taylor
☐ 2214 Dean Borrelli
☐ 2215 Tom Carcione
☐ 2216 Joe Ortiz
☐ 2217 James Buccheri
☐ 2218 Rod Correia
☐ 2219 Kevin Lofthus
☐ 2220 Francisco Matos
☐ 2221 Mike Messerly
☐ 2222 Craig Paquette
☐ 2223 James Waggoner
☐ 2224 Ron Witmeyer
☐ 2225 Dwayne Hosey
☐ 2226 Keith Thomas
☐ 2227 Tim Vannaman
☐ 2228 Bob Parry
☐ 2229 Ted Kubiak MGR
☐ 2230 Pete Richert CO

1990 Midwest League All-Stars Grand Slam

	MINT	NRMT	EXC
COMPLETE SET (58)	10.00	4.50	1.25

☐ 1 Kurt Abbott
☐ 2 Joe Andrzejewski
☐ 3 Jayson Best
☐ 4 Doug Bochtler
☐ 5 Len Brutcher
☐ 6 John Byington
☐ 7 Scott Cepicky
☐ 8 Fred Cooley
☐ 9 Steve Dunn
☐ 10 Mike Eatinger
☐ 11 Rusty Kilgo
☐ 12 Scott Kimball
☐ 13 Tim Laker
☐ 14 Marc Lipson
☐ 15 Danny Matznick
☐ 16 Henry Mercedes
☐ 17 Alan Newman
☐ 18 Randy Snyder
☐ 19 Tom Taylor
☐ 20 Lee Tinsley
☐ 21 Rich Tunison
☐ 22 Bob Vancho
☐ 23 Jerry Wolak
☐ 24 Tryon Woods
☐ 25 John Zaksek
☐ 26 Casey Parsons MG
Bert Bradley CO
☐ 27 Ramon Caraballo
☐ 28 Frank Carey
☐ 29 Pedro Castellano
☐ 30 Chad Curtis
☐ 31 Damion Easley
☐ 32 Luis Galindez
☐ 33 Victor Garcia
☐ 34 Chris Hancock
☐ 35 Mike Hook
☐ 36 Joey James
☐ 37 Clyde Keller
☐ 38 Javy Lopez
☐ 39 Chris Lutz
☐ 40 Fili Martinez
☐ 41 Dave McAuliffe
☐ 42 Brent McCoy
☐ 43 Roger Miller
☐ 44 Mike Mulvaney
☐ 45 Matt Murray
☐ 46 J.D. Noland
☐ 47 Dave Reis
☐ 48 Reggie Sanders
☐ 49 Mo Sanford
☐ 50 Ed Taubensee
☐ 51 Rob Taylor
☐ 52 Matt Witkowski
☐ 53 Terry Abbott CO
Robert Horowitz TR
Davey Miley MG
Tom Spencer TR
☐ 54 Matt Grott
☐ 55 Darin Kracl
☐ 56 Pedro Pena
☐ 57 Rafael Novoa
☐ 58 Pedro Borbon Jr.

1990 Myrtle Beach Blue Jays ProCards

This 29-card standard-size set of the 1990 Myrtle Beach Blue Jays, a Class A South Atlantic League affiliate of the Toronto Blue Jays, features on its white-bordered fronts posed color player photos set on simulated wood-grain backgrounds. The player's name, position, and team appear within a gold-colored rectangle below the photo. The tan horizontal back is bordered in white and carries the player's name and position at the top, followed by biography and statistics.

	MINT	NRMT	EXC
COMPLETE SET (29)	5.00	2.20	.60

☐ 2766 Checklist
☐ 2767 Greg Bicknell
☐ 2768 Rob Blumberg
☐ 2769 Eric Bradley
☐ 2770 Daren Brown
☐ 2771 Jason Hutson
☐ 2772 Daren Kizziah

- ☐ 2773 Gregg Martin
- ☐ 2774 Rick Nowak
- ☐ 2775 Mike Ogliaruso
- ☐ 2776 Jose Olivares
- ☐ 2777 Aaron Small
- ☐ 2778 John Wanish
- ☐ 2779 Ken Rivers
- ☐ 2780 Juan Jaime
- ☐ 2781 Bill Abare
- ☐ 2782 Brad Mengel
- ☐ 2783 Hector Mercedes
- ☐ 2784 Scott Miller
- ☐ 2786 Bill Parese
- ☐ 2787 Rickey Holifield
- ☐ 2788 Shawn Holtzclaw
- ☐ 2789 Anton Mobley
- ☐ 2790 Todd Provence
- ☐ 2791 Nigel Wilson
- ☐ 2792 Mike Fischlin MG
- ☐ 2793 Steve Mingori CO
- ☐ 2794 Leroy Stanton CO
- ☐ 2875 Robert Montalvo

1990 Nashville Sounds CMC

This 26-card standard-size set of the 1990 Nashville Sounds, a Class AAA American Association affiliate of the Cincinnati Reds, features white-bordered posed color player photos on its fronts. The player's name and position appear at the bottom; the team name appears vertically on the left. The back carries the league emblem in the white area at the top, the team name in the green stripe below, and player's name, position, biography, and statistics in the yellow area at the bottom. 1,100 sets were produced.

	MINT	NRMT	EXC
COMPLETE SET (26)	5.00	2.20	.60

- ☐ 1 Milt Hill
- ☐ 2 Robert Moore
- ☐ 3 Joey Vierra
- ☐ 4 Terry McGriff
- ☐ 5 Chris Hammond
- ☐ 6 Charlie Mitchell
- ☐ 7 Rodney Imes
- ☐ 8 Rob Lopez
- ☐ 9 Keith Brown
- ☐ 10 Scott Scudder
- ☐ 11 Bob Sebra
- ☐ 12 Donnie Scott
- ☐ 13 Skeeter Barnes
- ☐ 14 Paul Noce
- ☐ 15 Leo Garcia
- ☐ 16 Chris Jones
- ☐ 17 Kevin Pearson
- ☐ 18 Darryl Motley
- ☐ 19 Keith Lockhart
- ☐ 20 Brian Lane
- ☐ 21 Eddie Tanner
- ☐ 22 Reggie Jefferson
- ☐ 23 Neil Allen
- ☐ 24 Pete MacKanin MGR
- ☐ 25 Ray Rippelmeyer CO
- ☐ 26 John Young TR

1990 Nashville Sounds ProCards

This 29-card standard-size set of the 1990 Nashville Sounds, a Class AAA American Association affiliate of the Cincinnati Reds, features on its white-bordered fronts posed color player photos set on simulated wood-grain backgrounds. The player's name, position, and team appear within a gold-colored rectangle below the photo. The tan horizontal back is bordered in white and carries the player's name at the top, followed by biography and statistics.

	MINT	NRMT	EXC
COMPLETE SET (29)	5.00	2.20	.60

- ☐ 222 Checklist
- ☐ 223 Neil Allen
- ☐ 224 Keith Brown
- ☐ 225 Chris Hammond
- ☐ 226 Milton Hill
- ☐ 227 Rodney Imes
- ☐ 228 Rob Lopez
- ☐ 229 Charlie Mitchell
- ☐ 230 Robert Moore
- ☐ 231 Rosario Rodriguez
- ☐ 232 Scott Scudder
- ☐ 233 Bob Sebra
- ☐ 234 Joey Vierra
- ☐ 235 Tony DeFrancesco
- ☐ 236 Terry McGriff
- ☐ 237 Donnie Scott
- ☐ 238 Reggie Jefferson
- ☐ 239 Brian Lane
- ☐ 240 Chris Lombardozzi
- ☐ 241 Paul Noce
- ☐ 242 Kevin Pearson
- ☐ 243 Eddie Tanner
- ☐ 244 Skeeter Barnes
- ☐ 245 Leo Garcia
- ☐ 246 Chris Jones
- ☐ 247 Keith Lockhart
- ☐ 248 Darryl Motley
- ☐ 249 Pete MacKanin MGR
- ☐ 250 Ray Rippelmeyer CO

1990 Nebraska Cornhuskers

	MINT	NRMT	EXC
COMPLETE SET (28)	10.00	4.50	1.25

- ☐ 1 Eddie Anderson
- ☐ 2 Brian Arntzen
- ☐ 3 Bobby Benjamin
- ☐ 4 Aaron Bilyeu
- ☐ 5 Shawn Buchanan
- ☐ 6 Josh Bullock
- ☐ 7 Charlie Colon
- ☐ 8 Vince Di Grandi
- ☐ 9 Craig Fairley
- ☐ 10 Paul Fanucchi
- ☐ 11 Kevin French
- ☐ 12 Armando Garza
- ☐ 13 Kevin Jordan
- ☐ 14 Jerry Madison
- ☐ 15 Brian McArn
- ☐ 16 Shaun McGinn
- ☐ 17 Sean McKenna
- ☐ 18 Dave Matranga
- ☐ 19 Todd Mosser
- ☐ 20 John Ofstun
- ☐ 21 Joe Shapley
- ☐ 22 Dirk Skillicorn
- ☐ 23 Gary Tackett
- ☐ 24 Doug Tegtmeier
- ☐ 25 Greg Thorell
- ☐ 26 Billy Thorell
- ☐ 27 Bill Vosik
- ☐ 28 Mike Zajeski

1990 New Britain Red Sox Best

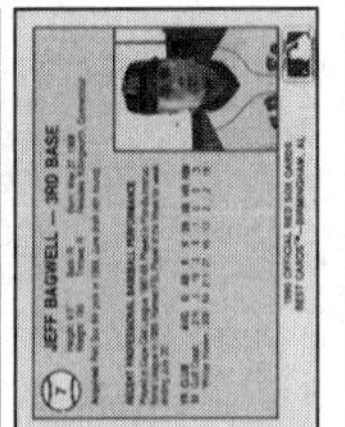

This 29-card standard-size set of the 1990 New Britain Red Sox, a Class AA Eastern League affiliate of the Boston Red Sox, features white-bordered posed and action color player photos on its fronts. The player's name and position appear vertically on the left side. The yellow horizontal back carries the player's name and position at the top, followed by biography, career highlights, and statistics. A player head shot appears in the lower right corner. This issue includes the minor league card debut of Jeff Bagwell.

	MINT	NRMT	EXC
COMPLETE SET (29)	35.00	16.00	4.40

- ☐ 1 Eric Wedge
- ☐ 2 Tom Fischer
- ☐ 3 Julius McDougal
- ☐ 4 Josias Manzanillo
- ☐ 5 Dave Milstien
- ☐ 6 Bob Zupcic
- ☐ 7 Jeff Bagwell
- ☐ 8 Craig Wilson
- ☐ 9 Mike Twardoski
- ☐ 10 Donald Florence
- ☐ 11 Mike Kelly
- ☐ 12 Mike Carista
- ☐ 13 Stu Weidie
- ☐ 14 Kevin Morton
- ☐ 15 Gordon Hurlbert TR
- ☐ 16 Vince Degifico
- ☐ 17 Juan Paris
- ☐ 18 Dave Owen
- ☐ 19 Randy Randle
- ☐ 20 Jeff Plympton
- ☐ 21 John Valentin
- ☐ 22 Todd Pratts
- ☐ 23 Butch Hobson MGR
- ☐ 24 Derek Livernois
- ☐ 25 David Walters
- ☐ 26 Rich Gale CO
- ☐ 27 Bob Spencer
- ☐ 28 The Staff
- ☐ 29 Checklist

1990 New Britain Red Sox ProCards

This 26-card standard-size set of the 1990 New Britain Red Sox, a Class AA Eastern League affiliate of the Boston Red Sox, features on its white-bordered fronts posed color player photos set on simulated wood-grain backgrounds. The player's name, position, and team appear within a gold-colored rectangle below the photo. The tan horizontal back is bordered in white and carries the player's name at the top, followed by biography and statistics. This issue includes the minor league card debut of Jeff Bagwell.

	MINT	NRMT	EXC
COMPLETE SET (26)	25.00	11.00	3.10

- ☐ 1310 Checklist
- ☐ 1311 Mike Carista
- ☐ 1312 Tom Fischer
- ☐ 1313 Don Florence
- ☐ 1314 Derek Livernois
- ☐ 1315 Josias Manzanillo
- ☐ 1316 Kevin Morton
- ☐ 1317 Dan O'Neill
- ☐ 1318 Dave Owen
- ☐ 1319 Jeff Plympton
- ☐ 1320 Dave Walters
- ☐ 1321 Todd Pratt
- ☐ 1322 Eric Wedge
- ☐ 1323 Craig Wilson
- ☐ 1324 Jeff Bagwell
- ☐ 1325 Vinnie Degifico
- ☐ 1326 Julius McDougal
- ☐ 1327 Dave Milstien
- ☐ 1328 Randy Randle
- ☐ 1329 Mike Twardoski
- ☐ 1330 Mike Kelly
- ☐ 1331 Juan Paris
- ☐ 1332 Stu Weidie
- ☐ 1333 Bob Zupcic
- ☐ 1334 Butch Hobson
- ☐ 1335 Rich Gale CO

1990 New Britain Red Sox Star

This 27-card standard-size set of the 1990 New Britain Red Sox, a Class AA Eastern League affiliate of the Boston Red Sox, features blue bordered posed color player photos on its fronts. The player's name, team name, and position appear at the bottom. The white horizontal back carries the player's name at the top, followed by biography, career highlights, and statistics. This issue includes the minor league card debut of Jeff Bagwell.

	MINT	NRMT	EXC
COMPLETE SET (27)	25.00	11.00	3.10

- ☐ 1 Jeff Bagwell
- ☐ 2 Mike Carista
- ☐ 3 Vinnie Degifico
- ☐ 4 Tom Fischer
- ☐ 5 Donald Florence
- ☐ 6 Michael Kelly
- ☐ 7 Kooz Kuzniar
- ☐ 8 Derek Livernois
- ☐ 9 Josias Manzanillo
- ☐ 10 Julius McDougal
- ☐ 11 David Milstien
- ☐ 12 Kevin Morton
- ☐ 13 David Owen
- ☐ 14 Juan Paris
- ☐ 15 Jeff Plympton
- ☐ 16 Todd Pratt
- ☐ 17 Randy Randle
- ☐ 18 Mike Twardoski
- ☐ 19 John Valentin
- ☐ 20 David Walters
- ☐ 21 Eric Wedge
- ☐ 22 Stuart Weidie
- ☐ 23 Craig Wilson
- ☐ 24 Robert Zupcic
- ☐ 25 Butch Hobson MGR
- ☐ 26 Rich Gale CO
- ☐ 27 Gordon Hurlbert TR

1990 Niagara Falls Rapids Pucko

	MINT	NRMT	EXC
COMPLETE SET (33)	6.00	2.70	.75

- ☐ 1 Danny Rogers
- ☐ 2 Doug Kimbler
- ☐ 3 Tim Kirt
- ☐ 4 Denny McNamara
- ☐ 5 Dave Mastropietro
- ☐ 6 Kirk Mendenhall
- ☐ 7 Mario Moccia
- ☐ 8 Kelley O'Neal
- ☐ 9 Brian Saltzgaber
- ☐ 10 Warren Sawkiw
- ☐ 11 Gino Tagliaferri
- ☐ 12 Genaro DeBrand
- ☐ 13 Gregg Radachowsky
- ☐ 14 Sean Sadler
- ☐ 15 Francisco Alcantara
- ☐ 16 Greg Coppeta
- ☐ 17 Tom Drell
- ☐ 18 Rob Fazekas
- ☐ 19 Kevin Keon
- ☐ 20 Eric Leimeister
- ☐ 21 Doug Marcero
- ☐ 22 Brian Nelson
- ☐ 23 Eddy Rodriguez
- ☐ 24 Brian Schubert
- ☐ 25 Arthur Thigpen
- ☐ 26 Bob Undorf
- ☐ 27 Steve Wolf
- ☐ 28 Juan Lopez MGR
- ☐ 29 Joe Decker CO
- ☐ 30 Chris Rogaliner TR
- ☐ 31 Joe DeDario
  Official Game Host
- ☐ 32 Fielder's Choice
- ☐ 33 Checklist
  Dinger the Duck

1990 Oklahoma Sooners

	MINT	NRMT	EXC
COMPLETE SET (24)	10.00	4.50	1.25

- ☐ 1 Bryan Grejtak
- ☐ 2 Brian Cavalli
- ☐ 3 Matt Burke
- ☐ 4 Andre Champagne
- ☐ 5 Joey Green
- ☐ 6 Mike Hickey
- ☐ 7 Rich Samplinski
- ☐ 8 Scott Campbell
- ☐ 9 Pat Tozier
- ☐ 10 Steve Dean
- ☐ 11 Byron Mathews
- ☐ 12 Brent Bohrofen
- ☐ 13 Kevin King
- ☐ 14 Jim Huslig
- ☐ 15 John Kosenski
- ☐ 16 Bert Inman
- ☐ 17 Clint Whitworth
- ☐ 18 Matt Ruebel
- ☐ 19 Rick Bennett
- ☐ 20 Lance Yates
- ☐ 21 Greg McKitrick
- ☐ 22 Casey Mendenhall
- ☐ 23 Korey Keling
- ☐ 24 Stan Meek CO

1990 Oklahoma City 89ers CMC

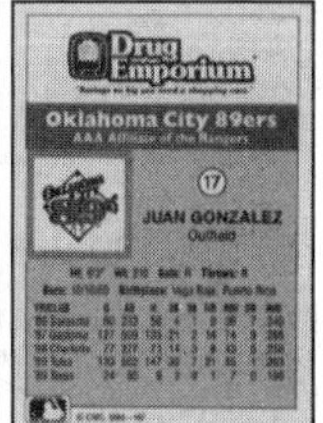

This 24-card standard-size set of the 1990 Oklahoma City 89ers, a Class AAA American Association affiliate of the Texas Rangers, features white-bordered posed color player photos on its fronts. The player's name and position appear at the bottom; the team name appears vertically on the left. The back carries the league emblem in the white area at the top, the team name in the green stripe below, and player's name, position, biography, and statistics in the yellow area at the bottom. This issue includes a fourth year card of Juan Gonzalez. 1,100 sets were produced.

	MINT	NRMT	EXC
COMPLETE SET (24)	40.00	18.00	5.00

- ☐ 1 Jack Hardy
- ☐ 2 Steve Lankard
- ☐ 3 John Hoover
- ☐ 4 David Lynch
- ☐ 5 Mark Petkovsek
- ☐ 6 David Miller
- ☐ 7 Brad Arnsberg
- ☐ 8 Jeff Satzinger
- ☐ 9 John Barfield
- ☐ 10 Mike Berger
- ☐ 11 John Russell
- ☐ 12 Pat Garman
- ☐ 13 Gary Green
- ☐ 14 Bryan House
- ☐ 15 Ron Washington
- ☐ 16 Nick Capra
- ☐ 17 Juan Gonzalez
- ☐ 18 Gar Millay
- ☐ 19 Kevin Reimer
- ☐ 20 Bernie Tatis
- ☐ 21 Steve Smith MGR
- ☐ 22 Dick Egan CO
- ☐ 23 Stan Hough CO
- ☐ 24 Ray Ramirez TR

1990 Oklahoma City 89ers ProCards

This 30-card standard-size set of the 1990 Oklahoma City 89ers, a Class AAA American Association affiliate of the Texas Rangers, features on its white-bordered fronts posed color player photos set on simulated wood-grain backgrounds. The player's name, position, and

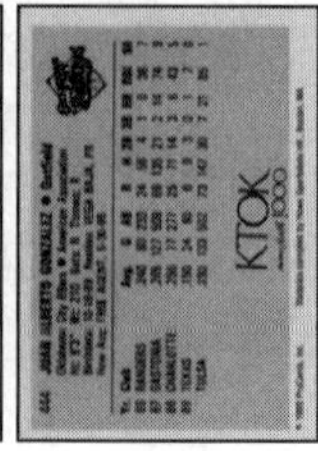

team appear within a gold-colored rectangle below the photo. The tan horizontal back is bordered in white and carries the player's name at the top, followed by biography and statistics. This issue includes fourth year cards of Juan Gonzalez and Dean Palmer.

	MINT	NRMT	EXC
COMPLETE SET (30)	35.00	16.00	4.40

- ☐ 421 Checklist
- ☐ 422 Gerald Alexander
- ☐ 423 Brad Arnsberg
- ☐ 424 John Barfield
- ☐ 425 Jack Hardy
- ☐ 426 Ray Hayward
- ☐ 427 John Hoover
- ☐ 428 Steve Lankard
- ☐ 429 David Lynch
- ☐ 430 Craig McMurtry
- ☐ 431 David Miller
- ☐ 432 Mark Petkovsek
- ☐ 433 Jeff Satzinger
- ☐ 434 Mike Berger
- ☐ 435 Dave Engle
- ☐ 436 John Russell
- ☐ 437 Pat Dodson
- ☐ 438 Pat Garman
- ☐ 439 Gary Green
- ☐ 440 Bryan House
- ☐ 441 Dean Palmer
- ☐ 442 Ron Washington
- ☐ 443 Nick Capra
- ☐ 444 Juan Gonzalez
- ☐ 445 Gar Millay
- ☐ 446 Kevin Reimer
- ☐ 447 Bernie Tatis
- ☐ 448 Steve Smith MGR
- ☐ 449 Dick Egan CO
- ☐ 450 Stan Hough CO

1990 Omaha Royals CMC

This 25-card standard-size set of the 1990 Omaha Royals, a Class AAA American Association affiliate of the Kansas City Royals, features white-bordered posed color player photos on its fronts. The player's name and position appear at the bottom; the team name appears vertically on the left. The back carries the league emblem in the white area at the top, the team name in the green stripe below, and player's name, position, biography, and statistics in the yellow area at the bottom. 1,100 sets were produced.

	MINT	NRMT	EXC
COMPLETE SET (25)	5.00	2.20	.60

- ☐ 1 Jay Baller
- ☐ 2 Ray Chadwick
- ☐ 3 Dera Clark
- ☐ 4 Luis Encarnacion
- ☐ 5 Jim LeMasters
- ☐ 6 Mike Magnante
- ☐ 7 Mel Stottlemyre Jr.
- ☐ 8 Tony Ferreira
- ☐ 9 Pete Filson
- ☐ 10 Andy McGaffigan
- ☐ 11 Luis de los Santos
- ☐ 12 Mike Loggins
- ☐ 13 Chito Martinez
- ☐ 14 Bobby Meacham
- ☐ 15 Russ Morman
- ☐ 16 Bill Pecota
- ☐ 17 Harvey Pulliam
- ☐ 18 Jeff Schulz
- ☐ 19 Gary Thurman
- ☐ 20 Thad Reece
- ☐ 21 Tim Spehr
- ☐ 22 Paul Zuvella
- ☐ 23 Coaches
  Tom Poquette
  Rich Debee
  Card # says 24
- ☐ 24 Bob Hamelin
- ☐ 25 Sal Rende MGR

1990 Omaha Royals ProCards

This 26-card standard-size set of the 1990 Omaha Royals, a Class AAA American Association affiliate of the Kansas City Royals, features on its white-bordered fronts posed color player photos set on simulated wood-grain backgrounds. The player's name, position, and team appear within a gold-colored rectangle below the photo. The tan horizontal back is bordered in white and carries the player's name at the top, followed by biography and statistics.

	MINT	NRMT	EXC
COMPLETE SET (26)	5.00	2.20	.60

- ☐ 57 Checklist
- ☐ 58 Ray Chadwick
- ☐ 59 Dera Clark
- ☐ 60 Luis Encarnacion
- ☐ 61 Tony Ferreira
- ☐ 62 Pete Filson
- ☐ 63 Jim LeMasters
- ☐ 64 Mike Magnante
- ☐ 65 Mike Tresemer
- ☐ 66 Mel Stottlemyre Jr.
- ☐ 67 Bill Wilkinson
- ☐ 68 Kevin Burrell
- ☐ 69 Tim Spehr
- ☐ 70 Luis de los Santos
- ☐ 71 Bob Hamelin
- ☐ 72 Bobby Meacham
- ☐ 73 Russ Morman
- ☐ 74 Thad Reece
- ☐ 75 Paul Zuvella
- ☐ 76 Mike Loggins
- ☐ 77 Chito Martinez
- ☐ 78 Harvey Pulliam
- ☐ 79 Jeff Schulz
- ☐ 80 Sal Rende MGR
- ☐ 81 Tom Poquette CO
- ☐ 82 Rich Dubee CO

1990 Oneonta Yankees ProCards

This 29-card standard-size set of the 1990 Oneonta Yankees, a Class A New York-Penn League affiliate of the New York Yankees, features on its white-bordered fronts posed color player photos set on simulated wood-grain backgrounds. The player's name, position, and team appear within a gold-colored rectangle below the photo. The tan horizontal back is bordered in white and carries the player's name at the top, followed by biography and statistics.

	MINT	NRMT	EXC
COMPLETE SET (29)	5.00	2.20	.60

- ☐ 3365 Checklist
- ☐ 3366 Luis Gallardo
- ☐ 3367 Adin Lohry
- ☐ 3368 Todd Malone
- ☐ 3369 Cesar Perez
- ☐ 3370 Steve Perry
- ☐ 3371 Rafael Quirico
- ☐ 3372 Dedrick Strickland
- ☐ 3373 Scott Romano
- ☐ 3374 Brian Turner
- ☐ 3375 Jovina Carvajal
- ☐ 3376 Ron Frazier
- ☐ 3377 Darren Hodges
- ☐ 3378 Sam Militello
- ☐ 3379 Pat Morphy
- ☐ 3380 Kirt Ojala
- ☐ 3381 Bo Siberz
- ☐ 3382 Matt Dunbar
- ☐ 3383 Doug Demetre
- ☐ 3384 Robert Eenhoorn
- ☐ 3385 Mike Hankins
- ☐ 3386 Kevin Jordan
- ☐ 3387 Rich Lantrip
- ☐ 3388 Bob Deller
- ☐ 3389 Trey Hillman MGR
- ☐ 3390 Ken Dominguez CO
- ☐ 3391 Mark Shiflett CO
- ☐ 3392 Brian Milner CO
- ☐ 3420 Jalal Leach

1990 Orlando Sun Rays Best

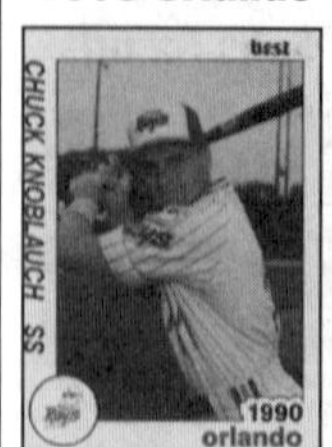

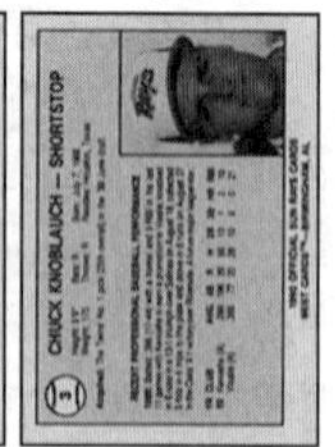

This 30-card standard-size set of the 1990 Orlando Sun Rays, a Class AA Southern League affiliate of the Minnesota Twins, features white-bordered posed and action color player photos on its fronts. The player's name and position appear vertically on the left side. The yellow horizontal back carries the player's name and position at the top, followed by biography, career highlights, and statistics. A player head shot appears in the lower right corner. This issue includes the minor league card debuts of Chuck Knoblauch and Scott Erickson.

	MINT	NRMT	EXC
COMPLETE SET (30)	20.00	9.00	2.50

- ☐ 1 Willie Banks
- ☐ 2 John Eccles
- ☐ 3 Chuck Knoblauch
- ☐ 4 Shawn Gilbert
- ☐ 5 Ed Naveda
- ☐ 6 Jose Marzan
- ☐ 7 Reed Olmstead
- ☐ 8 Jeff Hull
- ☐ 9 Jarvis Brown
- ☐ 10 Kenny Morgan
- ☐ 11 Mike Randle
- ☐ 12 Gary Resetar
- ☐ 13 Lenny Webster
- ☐ 14 Frank Valdez
- ☐ 15 Greg Johnson
- ☐ 16 Scott Erickson
- ☐ 17 Basil Meyer
- ☐ 18 Rob Wassenaar
- ☐ 19 Mike Redding
- ☐ 20 Steve Muh
- ☐ 21 Doug Simons
- ☐ 22 Steve Stowell
- ☐ 23 Johnny Ard
- ☐ 24 Gorman Heimueller CO
- ☐ 25 Rick McWane
- ☐ 26 Wayne Hattaway
- ☐ 27 Jeff Reboulet
- ☐ 28 Ron Gardenhire MGR
- ☐ 29 Mark Funderburk CO
- ☐ 30 Checklist

1990 Orlando Sun Rays ProCards

This 27-card standard-size set of the 1990 Orlando Sun Rays, a Class AA Southern League affiliate of the Minnesota Twins, features on its white-bordered fronts posed color player photos set on simulated wood-grain backgrounds. The player's name, position, and team appear within a gold-colored rectangle below the photo. The tan horizontal back is bordered in white and carries the player's name at the top, followed by biography and statistics. This issue includes the minor league card debuts of Chuck Knoblauch and Scott Erickson.

	MINT	NRMT	EXC
COMPLETE SET (27)	15.00	6.75	1.85

- ☐ 1074 Checklist
- ☐ 1075 Johnny Ard
- ☐ 1076 Willie Banks
- ☐ 1077 Scott Erickson
- ☐ 1078 Greg Johnson
- ☐ 1079 Basil Meyer
- ☐ 1080 Steve Muh
- ☐ 1081 Mike Redding
- ☐ 1082 Doug Simons
- ☐ 1083 Steve Stowell
- ☐ 1084 Rob Wassenaar
- ☐ 1085 Jeff Hull
- ☐ 1086 John Eccles
- ☐ 1087 Gary Resetar
- ☐ 1088 Lenny Webster
- ☐ 1089 Shawn Gilbert
- ☐ 1090 Chuck Knoblauch
- ☐ 1091 Jose Marzan
- ☐ 1092 Reed Olmstead
- ☐ 1093 Jeff Reboulet
- ☐ 1094 Frank Valdez
- ☐ 1095 Jarvis Brown
- ☐ 1096 Kenny Morgan
- ☐ 1097 Mike Randle
- ☐ 1098 Ron Gardenhire MGR
- ☐ 1099 Mark Funderburk CO
- ☐ 1100 Gorman Heimueller CO

1990 Orlando Sun Rays Star

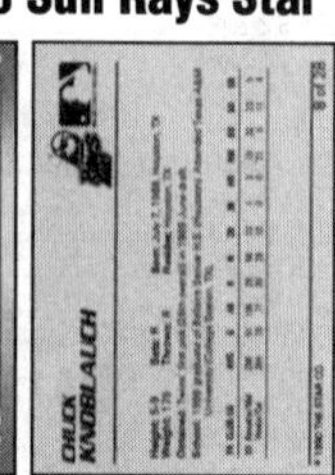

This 28-card standard-size set of the 1990 Orlando Sun Rays, a Class AA Southern League affiliate of the Minnesota Twins, features blue bordered posed color player photos on its fronts. The player's name, team name, and position appear at the bottom. The white horizontal back carries the player's name at the top, followed by biography, career highlights, and statistics. This issue includes the minor league card debuts of Chuck Knoblauch and Scott Erickson.

	MINT	NRMT	EXC
COMPLETE SET (28)	20.00	9.00	2.50

- ☐ 1 Johnny Ard
- ☐ 2 Willie Banks
- ☐ 3 Jarvis Brown
- ☐ 4 John Eccles
- ☐ 5 Scott Erickson
- ☐ 6 Shawn Gilbert
- ☐ 7 Greg Johnson
- ☐ 8 Chuck Knoblauch
- ☐ 9 Orlando Lind
- ☐ 10 Jose Marzan
- ☐ 11 Basil Meyer
- ☐ 12 Kenny Morgan
- ☐ 13 Denny Neagle
- ☐ 14 Reed Olmstead
- ☐ 15 Mike Randle
- ☐ 16 Jeff Reboulet
- ☐ 17 Mike Redding
- ☐ 18 Gary Resetar
- ☐ 19 Doug Simons
- ☐ 20 Steve Stowell
- ☐ 21 Frank Valdez
- ☐ 22 Rob Wassenaar
- ☐ 23 Lenny Webster
- ☐ 24 Ron Gardenhire MGR
- ☐ 25 Mark Funderburk CO
- ☐ 26 Gorman Heimueller CO
- ☐ 27 Rick McWane TR
- ☐ 28 Wayne Hattaway
  Equipment Manager

1990 Osceola Astros Star

This 30-card standard-size set of the 1990 Osceola Astros, a Class A Florida State League affiliate of the Houston Astros, features orange bordered posed color player photos on its fronts. The player's name, team name, and position appear at the bottom. The white horizontal back carries the player's name at the top, followed by biography, career highlights, and statistics. This issue includes a third year card of Kenny Lofton.

	MINT	NRMT	EXC
COMPLETE SET (30)	15.00	6.75	1.85

- ☐ 1 Manny Acta
- ☐ 2 Donald Angotti
- ☐ 3 Peter Bauer
- ☐ 4 Michael Beams
- ☐ 5 Chris Colombino
- ☐ 6 Troy Dovey
- ☐ 7 Rick Dunnum
- ☐ 8 Brian Griffiths
- ☐ 9 David Henderson
- ☐ 10 Cole Hyson
- ☐ 11 Jeff Juden
- ☐ 12 Todd Jones
- ☐ 13 Frank Kellner
- ☐ 14 Lawrence Lamphere
- ☐ 15 Mica Lweis
- ☐ 16 Kenny Lofton
- ☐ 17 Ken Luckham
- ☐ 18 Lance Madsen
- ☐ 19 Scott Makarewicz
- ☐ 20 John Massarelli
- ☐ 21 Dan Nyssen
- ☐ 22 Edward Ponte
- ☐ 23 Howard Prager
- ☐ 24 Toncie Reed
- ☐ 25 Gabriel Rodriguez
- ☐ 26 Rodney Windes
- ☐ 27 Sal Butera MGR
- ☐ 28 Jack Billingham CO
- ☐ 29 Bobby Ramos CO
- ☐ 30 Gene Confreda TR

1990 Palm Springs Angels Cal League Cards

	MINT	NRMT	EXC
COMPLETE SET (27)	10.00	4.50	1.25

- ☐ 203 Terence Carr
- ☐ 204 David Esquer
- ☐ 205 Jeff Kipila
- ☐ 206 Jeff Oberdank
- ☐ 207 J.R. Phillips
- ☐ 208 Terry Taylor
- ☐ 209 Frank Dominguez
- ☐ 210 Richard Parker
- ☐ 211 David Sturdivant
- ☐ 212 Dave Partrick
- ☐ 213 Beban Perez
- ☐ 214 Jeff Kelso
- ☐ 215 Tim Salmon
- ☐ 216 Tim Wallace
- ☐ 217 David Martinez
- ☐ 218 Brandy Vann
- ☐ 219 Marvin Cobb
- ☐ 220 Stephen Dunn
- ☐ 221 John Fritz
- ☐ 222 Michael Shull
- ☐ 223 Michael Search
- ☐ 224 William Warrecker
- ☐ 225 Donald Vidmar
- ☐ 226 Clemente Acosta
- ☐ 227 Tim Meeks
- ☐ 228 Nate Oliver MGR
- ☐ 229 Kernan Ronan CO

1990 Palm Springs Angels ProCards

This 28-card standard-size set of the 1990 Palm Springs Angels, a Class A California League affiliate of the California Angels, features on its white-bordered fronts posed color player photos set on simulated

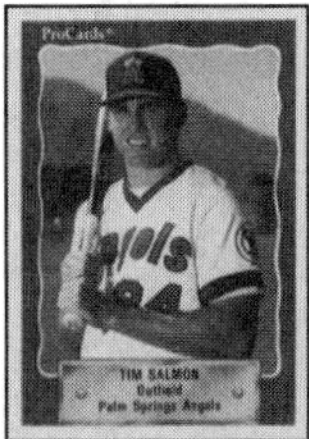
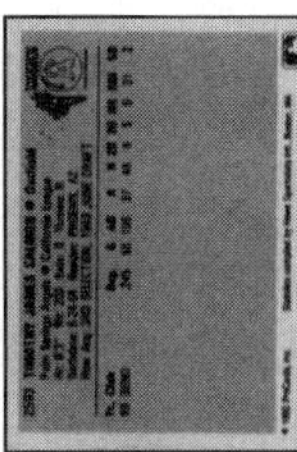

wood-grain backgrounds. The player's name, position, and team appear within a gold-colored rectangle below the photo. The tan horizontal back is bordered in white and carries the player's name at the top, followed by biography and statistics.

	MINT	NRMT	EXC
COMPLETE SET (28)	18.00	8.00	2.20

☐ 2568 Checklist
☐ 2569 Clemente Acosta
☐ 2570 Marvin Cobb
☐ 2571 Steve Dunn
☐ 2572 John Fritz
☐ 2573 David Martinez
☐ 2574 Brett Merriman
☐ 2575 Larry Pardo
☐ 2576 Michael Search
☐ 2577 Brandy Vann
☐ 2578 Don Vidmar
☐ 2579 Willy Warrencker
☐ 2580 Frank Dominguez
☐ 2581 Richard Parker
☐ 2582 Dave Strudivant
☐ 2583 Dave Esquer
☐ 2584 Jeff Kipila
☐ 2585 Jeff Oberdank
☐ 2586 J.R. Phillips
☐ 2587 Terry Taylor
☐ 2588 Tim Wallace
☐ 2589 Terry Carr
☐ 2590 Jeff Kelso
☐ 2591 Dave Partrick
☐ 2592 Beban Perez
☐ 2593 Tim Salmon
☐ 2594 Nate Oliver MGR
☐ 2595 Kernan Ronan CO

1990 Pawtucket Red Sox CMC

This 31-card set of the Pawtucket Red Sox, a Class AAA International League affiliate of the Boston Red Sox, features white-bordered posed color player photos on its fronts. The player's name and position appear at the bottom; the team name appears vertically on the left. The back carries the league emblem in the white area at the top, the team name in the green stripe below, and player's name, position, biography, and statistics in the yellow area at the bottom. 1,100 sets were produced.

	MINT	NRMT	EXC
COMPLETE SET (25)	5.00	2.20	.60

☐ 1 Tito Stewart
☐ 2 John Trautwein
☐ 3 Mike Rochford
☐ 4 Larry Shikles
☐ 5 Daryl Irvine
☐ 6 John Leister
☐ 7 Joe Johnson
☐ 8 Mark Meleski
☐ 9 Steven Bast
☐ 10 Ed Nottle MGR
☐ 11 John Flaherty
☐ 12 John Marzano
☐ 13 Gary Tremblay
☐ 14 Scott Cooper
☐ 15 Angel Gonzalez
☐ 16 Julius McDougal
☐ 17 Tim Naehring
☐ 18 Jim Pankovits
☐ 19 Rick Lancellotti
☐ 20 Mickey Pina
☐ 21 Phil Plantier
☐ 22 Jeff Stone
☐ 23 Scott Wade
☐ 24 Mike Dalton
☐ 25 Jeff Gray

1990 Pawtucket Red Sox Dunkin' Donuts

This 31-card set of the Pawtucket Red Sox, a Class AAA International League affiliate of the Boston Red Sox, was issued in one large sheet featuring six perforated five-card strips with a large team photo in the wide top strip. Sponsored by Dunkin' Donuts, the fronts carry color player photos while the backs display player career statistics. The cards are unnumbered and checklisted below in alphabetical order. This issue includes the minor league card debut of Mo Vaughn.

	MINT	NRMT	EXC
COMPLETE SET (31)	60.00	27.00	7.50

☐ 1 Steve Bast
☐ 2 Tom Bolton
☐ 3 Scott Cooper
☐ 4 Steve Curry
☐ 5 Mike Dalton
☐ 6 John Flaherty
☐ 7 Angel Gonzalez
☐ 8 Jeff Gray
☐ 9 Eric Hetzel
☐ 10 Daryl Irvine
☐ 11 Joe Johnson
☐ 12 Rick Lancellotti
☐ 13 John Leister
☐ 14 Julius McDougal
☐ 15 Mark Meleski
☐ 16 Tim Naehring
☐ 17 Ed Nottle
☐ 18 Jim Pankovits
☐ 19 Mickey Pina
☐ 20 Phil Plantier
☐ 21 Mike Rochford
☐ 22 Larry Shikles
☐ 23 Tito Stewart
☐ 24 Jeff Stone
☐ 25 Lee Strange
☐ 26 John Trautwein
☐ 27 Gary Tremblay
☐ 28 Mo Vaughn
☐ 29 Scott Wade
☐ 30 Peter Youngman
☐ 31 Team Photo

1990 Pawtucket Red Sox ProCards

This 29-card standard-size set of the 1990 Pawtucket Red Sox, a Class AAA International League affiliate of the Boston Red Sox, features on its white-bordered fronts posed color player photos set on simulated wood-grain backgrounds. The player's name, position, and team appear within a gold-colored rectangle below the photo. The tan horizontal back is bordered in white and carries the player's name at the top, followed by biography and statistics. This issue includes the minor league card debut of Mo Vaughn.

	MINT	NRMT	EXC
COMPLETE SET (29)	25.00	11.00	3.10

☐ 451 Checklist
☐ 452 Steve Bast
☐ 453 Tom Bolton
☐ 454 Steve Curry
☐ 455 Mike Dalton
☐ 456 Jeff Gray
☐ 457 Daryl Irvine
☐ 458 Joe Johnson
☐ 459 John Leister
☐ 460 Mike Rochford
☐ 461 Larry Shikles
☐ 462 Tito Stewart
☐ 463 John Trautwein
☐ 464 John Flaherty
☐ 465 John Marzano
☐ 466 Gary Tremblay
☐ 467 Scott Cooper
☐ 468 Angel Gonzalez
☐ 469 Tim Naehring
☐ 470 Jim Pankovits
☐ 471 Mo Vaughn
☐ 472 Rick Lancellotti
☐ 473 Mickey Pina
☐ 474 Phil Plantier
☐ 475 Jeff Stone
☐ 476 Scott Wade
☐ 477 Ed Nottle MGR
☐ 478 Mark Meleski CO
☐ 479 Lee Stange CO

1990 Peninsula Pilots Star

This 27-card standard-size set of the 1990 Peninsula Pilots, a Class A Carolina League affiliate of the Seattle Mariners, features red bordered posed color player photos on its fronts. The player's name, team name, and position appear at the bottom. The white horizontal back carries the player's name at the top, followed by biography, career highlights, and statistics.

	MINT	NRMT	EXC
COMPLETE SET (27)	5.00	2.20	.60

☐ 1 Lash Bailey
☐ 2 Rick Balabon
☐ 3 Dan Barbara
☐ 4 Mark Brakebill
☐ 5 Jimmy Campanis
☐ 6 Jeff Darwin
☐ 7 Kyle Duke
☐ 8 Marcos Garcia
☐ 9 Anthony Gordon
☐ 10 Jim Gutierrez
☐ 11 Scott Lodgek
☐ 12 Darin Loe
☐ 13 Ron Mullins
☐ 14 Ron Pezzoni
☐ 15 Lem Pilkington
☐ 16 Rod Poissant
☐ 17 Oscar Rivas
☐ 18 Jorge Robles
☐ 19 Damon Saetre
☐ 20 Ruben Santana
☐ 21 Jesus Tavarez
☐ 22 Delvin Thomas
☐ 23 Kelvin Thomas
☐ 24 Landon Williams
☐ 25 Jim Nettles MGR
☐ 26 Ross Grimsley CO
☐ 27 Allan Lovinger TR

1990 Peoria Chiefs Earl Cunningham Team Issue

	MINT	NRMT	EXC
COMPLETE SET (4)	12.00	5.50	1.50

☐ 1 Earl Cunningham
(Batting pose, middle of swing
☐ 2 Earl Cunningham
(Sitting on white sports car)
☐ 3 Earl Cunningham
(Follow-through, bat behind shoulders)
☐ 4 Earl Cunningham
(Front pose, arms folded)

1990 Peoria Chiefs Team Issue

	MINT	NRMT	EXC
COMPLETE SET (38)	10.00	4.50	1.25

☐ 1 Earl Cunningham
With Glove
☐ 2 Earl Cunningham
Posed with Car
☐ 3 Front Office Staff
John Butler GM
Michael Nelson Asst. GM
Jeffrey Reeser Asst. GM
Ralph Rashid Sr. Acct. EX
Norm Jenkins DIR
☐ 4 Brad Erdman
☐ 5 Bill Paynter
☐ 6 Rick Mundy
☐ 7 Kraig Washington
☐ 8 Pete Castellano
☐ 9 Top Prospects
Earl Cunningham
Pete Castellano
☐ 10 Curley'Boo' Johnson
☐ 11 Matt Franco
☐ 12 Bill St. Peter
☐ 13 Woody Smith
☐ 14 Paul Torres
☐ 15 Victor Cancel
☐ 16 Chris Ebright
☐ 17 Rene Francisco
☐ 18 Jerrone Williams
☐ 19 Jason Doss
☐ 20 Famous Five
Greg Maddux
Jeff Hirsch
Mike Harkey
Shawn Boskie
Jeff Pico
☐ 21 Jay Eddings
☐ 22 Jac Gelb
☐ 23 Henry Gomez
☐ 24 Eric Jaques
☐ 25 Chris Lutz
☐ 26 Ray Mullino
☐ 27 Ronnie Rasp
☐ 28 Dave Swartzbaugh
☐ 29 Travis Willis
☐ 30 Mark Young
☐ 31 Greg Mahlberg MGR
☐ 32 Lester Strode CO
☐ 33 Jim O'Reilly TR
☐ 34 Bill Harford VP
☐ 35 Richie Zisk
Hitting Instructor
☐ 36 Sully's Pub
☐ 37 Joseph Bosco
Author
☐ NNO Checklist

1990 Peoria Chiefs Update Team Issue

	MINT	NRMT	EXC
COMPLETE SET (7)	6.00	2.70	.75

☐ U1 Lance Dickson
☐ U2 Jim Robinson
☐ U3 Damon Berryhill
☐ U4 Matt Walbeck
☐ U5 Marvin Cole
☐ U6 Jim Sweeney
☐ U7 Jim Murphy

1990 Phoenix Firebirds CMC

This 26-card standard-size set of the 1990 Phoenix Firebirds, a Class AAA Pacific Coast League affiliate of the San Francisco Giants, features white-bordered posed color player photos on its fronts. The player's name and position appear at the bottom; the team name appears vertically on the left. The back carries the league emblem in the white area at the top, the team name in the green stripe below, and player's name, position, biography, and statistics in the yellow area at the bottom. 1,100 sets were produced.

	MINT	NRMT	EXC
COMPLETE SET (26)	5.00	2.20	.60

☐ 1 Paul McClellan
☐ 2 Randy McCament
☐ 3 Gill Heredia
☐ 4 George Bonilla
☐ 5 Russ Swan
☐ 6 Ed Vosberg
☐ 7 Eric Gunderson
☐ 8 Trevor Wilson
☐ 9 Greg Booker
☐ 10 Kirt Manwaring
☐ 11 Mike Kingery
☐ 12 Brian Brady
☐ 13 Mark Bailey
☐ 14 Gregg Ritchie
☐ 15 George Hinshaw
☐ 16 Craig Colbert
☐ 17 Kash Beauchamp
☐ 18 Jeff Carter
☐ 19 Mark Leonard
☐ 20 Tony Perezchica
☐ 21 Mike Laga
☐ 22 Mike Benjamin
☐ 23 Timber Mead
☐ 24 Duane Espy MGR
☐ 25 Tim Ireland CO
☐ 26 Larry Hardy CO

1990 Phoenix Firebirds ProCards

This 29-card standard-size set of the 1990 Phoenix Firebirds, a Class AAA Pacific Coast League affiliate of the San Francisco Giants, features on its white-bordered fronts posed color player photos set on simulated wood-grain backgrounds. The player's name, position, and team appear within a gold-colored rectangle below the photo. The tan horizontal back is bordered in white and carries the player's name at the top, followed by biography and statistics.

	MINT	NRMT	EXC
COMPLETE SET (29)	5.00	2.20	.60

☐ 1 Checklist
☐ 2 George Bonilla
☐ 3 Greg Booker
☐ 4 Rich Bordi
☐ 5 John Burkett
☐ 6 Gil Heredia
☐ 7 Bob Knepper
☐ 8 Randy McCament
☐ 9 Paul McClellan
☐ 10 Timber Mead
☐ 11 Ed Vosberg
☐ 12 Trevor Wilson
☐ 13 Mark Bailey
☐ 14 Kirt Manwaring
☐ 15 Mike Benjamin
☐ 16 Brian Brady
☐ 17 Jeff Carter
☐ 18 Craig Colbert
☐ 19 Erik Johnson
☐ 20 Greg Litton
☐ 21 Kash Beauchamp
☐ 22 George Hinshaw
☐ 23 Mike Kingery
☐ 24 Mark Leonard
☐ 25 Gregg Ritchie
☐ 26 Rick Parker
☐ 27 Duane Espy MGR
☐ 28 Tim Ireland CO
☐ 29 Larry Hardy CO

1990 Pittsfield Mets Pucko

	MINT	NRMT	EXC
COMPLETE SET (32)	7.00	3.10	.85

☐ 1 Phillip Scott
☐ 2 Kyle Washington
☐ 3 Eric Thornton
☐ 4 Wallace Minnifield
☐ 5 Robbi Guzik
☐ 6 Joe Arrendondo
☐ 7 Jarrod Parker
☐ 8 Jason King
☐ 9 Tim Buhe
☐ 10 Tim McClinton
☐ 11 Nicky Davis
☐ 12 Brian Dunn
☐ 13 Todd Douma
☐ 14 Steve Thomas
☐ 15 Mike Sciortino

□ 16 Peter Walker
□ 17 Tom Wilson
□ 18 Mike Thomas
□ 19 Andy Fidler
□ 20 Juan Castillo
□ 21 Jim Scheffler
□ 22 Ed Vazquez
□ 23 Alberto Castillo
□ 24 Mike Freitas
□ 25 Jim Eschen MGR
□ 26 Randy Neimann CO
□ 27 Billy Gardner Jr. CO
□ 28 Joe Hawkins TR
□ 29 Clubhouse Boys
Bill Bird
Dave Tarjick
□ 30 Checklist
□ 31 Jeromy Burnitz
□ 32 Tommy Allison

1990 Portland Beavers CMC

This 25-card standard-size set of the 1990 Portland Beavers, a Class AAA Pacific Coast League affiliate of the Minnesota Twins, features white-bordered posed color player photos on its fronts. The player's name and position appear at the bottom; the team name appears vertically on the left. The back carries the league emblem in the white area at the top, the team name in the green stripe below, and player's name, position, biography, and statistics in the yellow area at the bottom. 1,100 sets were produced.

	MINT	NRMT	EXC
COMPLETE SET (25)	5.00	2.20	.60

□ 1 Paul Abbott
□ 2 Pat Bangtson
□ 3 Larry Casian
□ 4 Mike Cook
□ 5 Pete Delkus
□ 6 Mike Dyer
□ 7 Charles Scott
□ 8 Francisco Oliveras
□ 9 Park Pittman
□ 10 Jimmy Williams
□ 11 Rich Yett
□ 12 Vic Rodriguez
□ 13 Jamie Nelson
□ 14 Derek Parks
□ 15 Ed Naveda
□ 16 Scott Leius
□ 17 Terry Jorgensen
□ 18 Doug Baker
□ 19 Chip Hale
□ 20 Dave Jacas
□ 21 Jim Shellenback CO
□ 22 Rafael DeLima
□ 23 Bernardo Brito
□ 24 J.T. Bruett
□ 25 Paul Sorrento

1990 Portland Beavers ProCards

This 28-card standard-size set of the 1990 Portland Beavers, a Class AAA Pacific Coast League affiliate of the Minnesota Twins, features on its white-bordered fronts posed color player photos set on simulated wood-grain backgrounds. The player's name, position, and team appear within a gold-colored rectangle below the photo. The tan horizontal back is bordered in white and carries the player's name at the top, followed by biography and statistics.

	MINT	NRMT	EXC
COMPLETE SET (28)	5.00	2.20	.60

□ 167 Checklist
□ 168 Paul Abbott
□ 169 Pat Bangtson
□ 170 Larry Casian
□ 171 Mike Cook
□ 172 Pete Delkus
□ 173 Mike Dyer
□ 174 Mark Guthrie
□ 175 Orlando Lind
□ 176 Francisco Oliveras
□ 177 Park Pittman
□ 178 Charles Scott
□ 179 Jimmy Williams
□ 180 Jamie Nelson
□ 181 Derek Parks
□ 182 Doug Baker
□ 183 Chip Hale
□ 184 Terry Jorgensen
□ 185 Scott Leius
□ 186 Marty Lanoux
□ 187 Ed Naveda
□ 188 Victor Rodriguez
□ 189 Paul Sorrento
□ 190 Bernardo Brito
□ 191 Rafael DeLima
□ 192 Dave Jacas
□ 193 Alonzo Powell
□ 194 Jim Shellenback MGR

1990 Prince William Cannons Team Issue

	MINT	NRMT	EXC
COMPLETE SET (30)	7.00	3.10	.85

□ 1 Mike Brown
□ 2 Gary Denbo
□ 3 Darren London
□ 4 Bob Marinaro
□ 5 Brad Ausmus
□ 6 Jason Bridges
□ 7 Art Canestro
□ 8 Russ Davis
□ 9 Herb Erhardt
□ 10 Mike Gardella
□ 11 Cullen Hartzog
□ 12 Enrique Hernandez
□ 13 Dave Howell
□ 14 Ed Martel
□ 15 James Moody
□ 16 Gerald Nielson
□ 17 Sherman Obando
□ 18 Paul Oster
□ 19 Rich Polak
□ 20 Bruce Prybylinski
□ 21 Curtis Ralph
□ 22 Andres Rodriquez
□ 23 Frank Seminara
□ 24 Dave Silvestri
□ 25 J.T. Snow
□ 26 John Viera
□ 27 Tom Weeks
□ 28 Jim Wiley
□ 29 Mauricio Zazueta
□ 30 Team Photo

1990 Princeton Patriots Diamond

	MINT	NRMT	EXC
COMPLETE SET (30)	7.00	3.10	.85

□ 1 Joel Adamson
□ 2 Ron Blazier
□ 3 Luis Brito
□ 4 Patrick Cheek
□ 5 Jerome Edwards
□ 6 Samuel Edwards
□ 7 Jesus Garces
□ 8 Mario Garcia
□ 9 Jeffrey Gunn
□ 10 David Hammond
□ 11 Brad Hassinger
□ 12 Steve Hollins
□ 13 Aurelio Llanos
□ 14 Ron Lockett
□ 15 Bryan Manicchia
□ 16 Jeff Repoz
□ 17 Troy Rusk
□ 18 Chad Silver
□ 19 Terry Smith
□ 20 Chris Snyder
□ 21 Jose Sosa
□ 22 Mark Steffens
□ 23 Bill Stohr
□ 24 Francisco Tejada
□ 25 Julio Vargas
□ 26 Juan Villareal
□ 27 Matt Whisenant
□ 28 Eli Grba MGR
□ 29 Ramon Henderson CO
□ 30 Brent Leiby TR

1990 ProCards A and AA

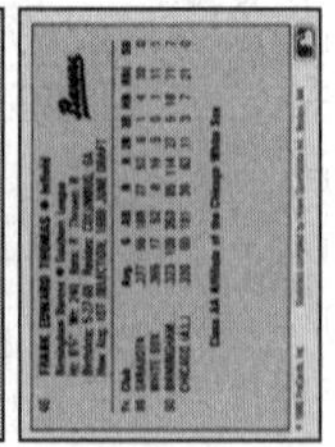

This 200-card set was issued wax packs and features orange bordered color player photos on its fronts. The player's name, position and team name appear at the bottom. The horizontal back carries the player's name and position at the top, followed by biography and statistics.

	MINT	NRMT	EXC
COMPLETE SET (200)	15.00	6.75	1.85
COMMON CARD (1-200)	.05	.02	.01
□ 1 Mike Linskey	.05	.02	.01
□ 2 Ben McDonald	.10	.05	.01
□ 3 Francisco DeLaRosa	.05	.02	.01
□ 4 Jose Mesa	.10	.05	.01
□ 5 Kevin Morton	.05	.02	.01
□ 6 Dan O'Neill	.05	.02	.01
□ 7 Dave Owen	.05	.02	.01
□ 8 Jeff Plympton	.05	.02	.01
□ 9 Charles Nagy	.15	.07	.02
□ 10 Rudy Seanez	.05	.02	.01
□ 11 Bruce Egloff	.05	.02	.01
□ 12 Joe Ausanio	.05	.02	.01
□ 13 Jim Tracy	.05	.02	.01
□ 14 Randy Tomlin	.05	.02	.01
□ 15 Jim Campbell	.05	.02	.01
□ 16 Mike Gardiner	.05	.02	.01
□ 17 Rusty Meacham	.05	.02	.01
□ 18 John Kiely	.05	.02	.01
□ 19 Darrin Chapin	.05	.02	.01
□ 20 Wade Taylor	.05	.02	.01
□ 21 Don Stanford	.05	.02	.01
□ 22 Andy Ashby	.10	.05	.01
□ 23 Bob Ayrault	.05	.02	.01
□ 24 Luis Mercedes	.05	.02	.01
□ 25 Scott Meadows	.05	.02	.01
□ 26 Jeff Bagwell	2.50	1.10	.30
□ 27 Mark Lewis	.10	.05	.01
□ 28 Carlos Garcia	.10	.05	.01
□ 29 Moises Alou	.50	.23	.06
□ 30 Rico Brogna	.10	.05	.01
□ 31 Bernie Williams	1.25	.55	.16
□ 32 Pat Kelly	.10	.05	.01
□ 33 Mitch Lyden	.05	.02	.01
□ 34 Hector Wagner	.05	.02	.01
□ 35 Carlos Maldonado	.05	.02	.01
□ 36 Brian Barnes	.05	.02	.01
□ 37 Chris Nabholz	.05	.02	.01
□ 38 Jeff Carter	.05	.02	.01
□ 39 Johnny Ard	.05	.02	.01
□ 40 Willie Banks	.05	.02	.01
□ 41 Scott Erickson	.10	.05	.01
□ 42 Greg Johnson	.05	.02	.01
□ 43 Al Osuna	.05	.02	.01
□ 44 Bob MacDonald	.05	.02	.01
□ 45 Pat Hentgen	.20	.09	.03
□ 46 Frank Thomas	5.00	2.20	.60
□ 47 Matt Stark	.05	.02	.01
□ 48 Jeff Conine	.40	.18	.05
□ 49 Sean Berry	.20	.09	.03
□ 50 Brian McRae	.25	.11	.03
□ 51 Bobby Moore	.05	.02	.01
□ 52 Brent Mayne	.05	.02	.01
□ 53 Greg Colbrunn	.05	.02	.01
□ 54 Terrel Hansen	.05	.02	.01
□ 55 Lenny Webster	.05	.02	.01
□ 56 Chuck Knoblauch	1.25	.55	.16
□ 57 Willie Ansley	.05	.02	.01
□ 58 Andujar Cedeno	.05	.02	.01
□ 59 Luis Gonzalez	.05	.02	.01
□ 60 Eddie Zosky	.05	.02	.01
□ 61 William Suero	.05	.02	.01
□ 62 Tom Quinlan	.05	.02	.01
□ 63 Kelly Mann	.05	.02	.01
□ 64 Mike Bell	.05	.02	.01
□ 65 Mark Dewey	.05	.02	.01
□ 66 Tom Hostetler	.05	.02	.01
□ 67 Kevin Belcher	.05	.02	.01
□ 68 Bill Haselman	.05	.02	.01
□ 69 Rob Maurer	.05	.02	.01
□ 70 Dan Rohrmeier	.05	.02	.01
□ 71 Dan Peltier	.05	.02	.01
□ 72 Steve Decker	.05	.02	.01
□ 73 Dave Patterson	.05	.02	.01
□ 74 Ed Zinter	.05	.02	.01
□ 75 David Bird	.05	.02	.01
□ 76 Willie Espinal	.05	.02	.01
□ 77 Dennis Fletcher	.05	.02	.01
□ 78 Travis Buckley	.05	.02	.01
□ 79 Brian Romero	.05	.02	.01
□ 80 Mike Arner	.05	.02	.01
□ 81 Brian Evans	.05	.02	.01
□ 82 John Graves	.05	.02	.01
□ 83 Randy Marshall	.05	.02	.01
□ 84 Mike Garcia	.05	.02	.01
□ 85 Jeff Braley	.05	.02	.01
□ 86 Ricky Rhodes	.05	.02	.01
□ 87 Jim Haller	.05	.02	.01
□ 88 Sterling Hitchcock	.05	.02	.01
□ 89 Rob Blumberg	.05	.02	.01
□ 90 Mike Ogliaruso	.05	.02	.01
□ 91 Gregg Martin	.05	.02	.01
□ 92 Tim Pugh	.05	.02	.01
□ 93 Roger Hailey	.05	.02	.01
□ 94 Don Strange	.05	.02	.01
□ 95 Robert Gaddy	.05	.02	.01
□ 96 Willie Greene	.10	.05	.01
□ 97 Austin Manahan	.05	.02	.01
□ 98 Tony Scruggs	.05	.02	.01
□ 99 Mike Burton	.05	.02	.01
□ 100 Shawn Holtzclaw	.05	.02	.01
□ 101 Orlando Miller	.05	.02	.01
□ 102 David Hajek	.05	.02	.01
□ 103 Scott Pose	.05	.02	.01
□ 104 Tyler Houston	.10	.05	.01
□ 105 Melvin Nieves	.10	.05	.01
□ 106 Ryan Klesko	1.50	.70	.19
□ 107 Daryl Moore	.05	.02	.01
□ 108 Skip Wiley	.05	.02	.01
□ 109 Brian McKeon	.05	.02	.01
□ 110 Rusty Kilgo	.05	.02	.01
□ 111 Chris Bushing	.05	.02	.01
□ 112 Alan Newman	.05	.02	.01
□ 113 Marc Lipson	.05	.02	.01
□ 114 Darin Karol	.05	.02	.01
□ 115 Matt Grott	.05	.02	.01
□ 116 Rafael Novoa	.05	.02	.01
□ 117 Pat Rapp	.10	.05	.01
□ 118 Ed Gustafson	.05	.02	.01
□ 119 Chris Hancock	.05	.02	.01
□ 120 Mo Sanford	.05	.02	.01
□ 121 Bill Risley	.05	.02	.01
□ 122 Victor Garcia	.05	.02	.01
□ 123 Dave McAuliffe	.05	.02	.01
□ 124 Pedro Borbon Jr.	.05	.02	.01
□ 125 Rich Tunison	.05	.02	.01
□ 126 Fred Cooley	.05	.02	.01
□ 127 Joey James	.05	.02	.01
□ 128 Reggie Sanders	.30	.14	.04
□ 129 Scott Bryant	.05	.02	.01
□ 130 Brent McCoy	.05	.02	.01
□ 131 Ramon Caraballo	.05	.02	.01
□ 132 Javy Lopez	1.00	.45	.12
□ 133 Brian Harrison	.05	.02	.01
□ 134 Rich DeLucia	.05	.02	.01
□ 135 Roger Salkeld	.05	.02	.01
□ 136 Kerry Woodson	.05	.02	.01
□ 137 Chris Johnson	.05	.02	.01
□ 138 Cal Eldred	.10	.05	.01
□ 139 Angel Miranda	.05	.02	.01
□ 140 Rich Garces	.05	.02	.01
□ 141 Pat Mahomes	.05	.02	.01
□ 142 Denny Neagle	.15	.07	.02
□ 143 George Tsamis	.05	.02	.01
□ 144 Johnny Guzman	.05	.02	.01
□ 145 Dan Rambo	.05	.02	.01
□ 146 Jim Myers	.05	.02	.01
□ 147 Darrell Sherman	.05	.02	.01
□ 148 Dave Staton	.05	.02	.01
□ 149 Brian Turang	.05	.02	.01
□ 150 Bo Dodson	.05	.02	.01
□ 151 Dave Nilsson	.10	.05	.01
□ 152 Frank Bolick	.05	.02	.01
□ 153 Ray Ortiz	.05	.02	.01
□ 154 J.T. Bruett	.05	.02	.01
□ 155 John Patterson	.05	.02	.01
□ 156 Royce Clayton	.10	.05	.01
□ 157 Hilly Hathaway	.05	.02	.01
□ 158 Phil Leftwich	.05	.02	.01
□ 159 Randy Powers	.05	.02	.01
□ 160 Todd Van Poppel	.05	.02	.01
□ 161 Don Peters	.05	.02	.01
□ 162 Dave Zancanaro	.05	.02	.01
□ 163 Kirk Dressendorfer	.05	.02	.01
□ 164 Curtis Shaw	.05	.02	.01
□ 165 Joe Rosselli	.05	.02	.01
□ 166 Mark Dalesandro	.05	.02	.01
□ 167 Eric Helfand	.05	.02	.01
□ 168 Eric Booker	.05	.02	.01
□ 169 Adam Hyzdu	.05	.02	.01
□ 170 Eric Christopherson	.05	.02	.01
□ 171 Marcus Jensen	.05	.02	.01
□ 172 Derek Reid	.05	.02	.01
□ 173 Lance Dickson	.05	.02	.01
□ 174 Tim Parker	.05	.02	.01
□ 175 Jessie Hollins	.05	.02	.01
□ 176 Sam Militello	.05	.02	.01
□ 177 Darren Hodges	.05	.02	.01
□ 178 Kirt Ojala	.05	.02	.01
□ 179 Steve Karsay	.10	.05	.01
□ 180 Andrew Hartung	.05	.02	.01
□ 181 Kevin Jordan	.05	.02	.01
□ 182 Robert Eenhoorn	.05	.02	.01
□ 183 Jalal Leach	.05	.02	.01
□ 184 Carlos Delgado	1.00	.45	.12
□ 185 Sean Cheetham	.05	.02	.01
□ 186 J.J. Munoz	.05	.02	.01
□ 187 Jim Thome	2.50	1.10	.30
□ 188 Tracy Sanders	.05	.02	.01
□ 189 Tony Clark	1.00	.45	.12
□ 190 Jose Viera	.05	.02	.01
□ 191 Pat Dando	.05	.02	.01
□ 192 Brian Kowitz	.05	.02	.01
□ 193 Mike Lieberthal	.10	.05	.01
□ 194 Jeff Borgese	.05	.02	.01
□ 195 Mike Ferry	.05	.02	.01
□ 196 K.C. Gillum	.05	.02	.01
□ 197 Elliott Quinones	.05	.02	.01
□ 198 Grant Brittain	.05	.02	.01
□ 199 Checklist	.05	.02	.01
□ 200 Checklist	.05	.02	.01

1990 ProCards AAA

This 700-card set was issued wax packs and features white bordered color player photos on its fronts. The player's name, position and team name appear at the bottom. The horizontal back carries the player's name and position at the top, followed by biography and statistics.

	MINT	NRMT	EXC
COMPLETE SET (700)	40.00	18.00	5.00
COMMON CARD (1-700)	.05	.02	.01
□ 1 Terry Gilmore	.05	.02	.01
□ 2 Jim Lewis	.05	.02	.01
□ 3 Joe Lynch	.05	.02	.01

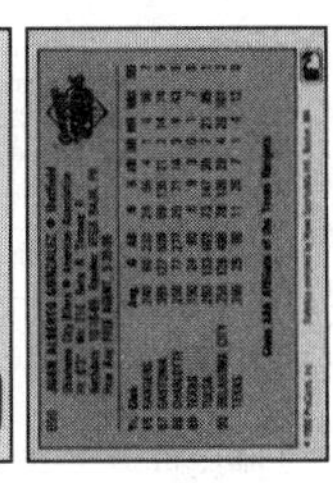

☐ 4 Matt Maysey .05 .02 .01
☐ 5 Dan Murphy .05 .02 .01
☐ 6 Eric Nolte .05 .02 .01
☐ 7 Brian Ohnoutka .05 .02 .01
☐ 8 Steve Peters .05 .02 .01
☐ 9 Paul Quinzer .05 .02 .01
☐ 10 Pete Roberts .05 .02 .01
☐ 11 Rich Rodriguez .05 .02 .01
☐ 12 Roger Smithberg .05 .02 .01
☐ 13 Rafael Valdez .05 .02 .01
☐ 14 Mike Basso .05 .02 .01
☐ 15 Ronn Reynolds .05 .02 .01
☐ 16 Paul Faries .05 .02 .01
☐ 17 Tom LeVasseur .05 .02 .01
☐ 18 Jose Mota .05 .02 .01
☐ 19 Eddie Williams .05 .02 .01
☐ 20 Jeff Yurtin .05 .02 .01
☐ 21 Alex Cole .05 .02 .01
☐ 22 Charles Hillemann .05 .02 .01
☐ 23 Tom Howard .05 .02 .01
☐ 24 Warren Newson .05 .02 .01
☐ 25 Pat Kelly MG .05 .02 .01
☐ 26 Gary Lance CO .05 .02 .01
☐ 27 Tony Torchia CO .05 .02 .01
☐ 28 George Bonilla .05 .02 .01
☐ 29 Greg Booker .05 .02 .01
☐ 30 Rich Bordi .05 .02 .01
☐ 31 John Burkett .10 .05 .01
☐ 32 Gil Heredia .05 .02 .01
☐ 33 Bob Knepper .05 .02 .01
☐ 34 Randy McCament .05 .02 .01
☐ 35 Paul McClellan .05 .02 .01
☐ 36 Timber Mead .05 .02 .01
☐ 37 Ed Vosberg .05 .02 .01
☐ 38 Trevor Wilson .05 .02 .01
☐ 39 Mark Bailey .05 .02 .01
☐ 40 Kirt Manwaring .05 .02 .01
☐ 41 Mike Benjamin .05 .02 .01
☐ 42 Brian Brady .05 .02 .01
☐ 43 Jeff Carter .05 .02 .01
☐ 44 Craig Colbert .05 .02 .01
☐ 45 Erik Johnson .05 .02 .01
☐ 46 Greg Litton .05 .02 .01
☐ 47 Kash Beauchamp .05 .02 .01
☐ 48 George Hinshaw .05 .02 .01
☐ 49 Mike Kingery .05 .02 .01
☐ 50 Mark Leonard .05 .02 .01
☐ 51 Gregg Ritchie .05 .02 .01
☐ 52 Rick Parker .05 .02 .01
☐ 53 Duane Espy MG .05 .02 .01
☐ 54 Tim Ireland CO .05 .02 .01
☐ 55 Larry Hardy CO .05 .02 .01
☐ 56 Jeff Bittiger .05 .02 .01
☐ 57 Mike Christopher .05 .02 .01
☐ 58 Steve Davis .05 .02 .01
☐ 59 Jeff Fischer .05 .02 .01
☐ 60 Darren Holmes .05 .02 .01
☐ 61 Morris Madden .05 .02 .01
☐ 62 Mike Maddux .05 .02 .01
☐ 63 Greg Mayberry .05 .02 .01
☐ 64 Jim Neidlinger .05 .02 .01
☐ 65 Tim Scott .05 .02 .01
☐ 66 Dave Walsh .05 .02 .01
☐ 67 Terry Wells .05 .02 .01
☐ 68 Adam Brown .05 .02 .01
☐ 69 Darrin Fletcher .05 .02 .01
☐ 70 Carlos Hernandez .05 .02 .01
☐ 71 Dave Hansen .05 .02 .01
☐ 72 Dan Henley .05 .02 .01
☐ 73 Glenn Hoffman .05 .02 .01
☐ 74 Walt McConnell .05 .02 .01
☐ 75 Jose Offerman .15 .07 .02
☐ 76 Jose Vizcaino .15 .07 .02
☐ 77 Billy Bean .05 .02 .01
☐ 78 Butch Davis .05 .02 .01
☐ 79 Mike Huff .05 .02 .01
☐ 80 Wayne Kirby .10 .05 .01
☐ 81 Luis Lopez .05 .02 .01
☐ 82 Kevin Kennedy MG .05 .02 .01
☐ 83 Claude Osteen CO .05 .02 .01
☐ 84 Von Joshua CO .05 .02 .01
☐ 85 Chris Beasley .05 .02 .01
☐ 85 Gary Buckels .05 .02 .01
☐ 87 Tim Burcham .05 .02 .01
☐ 88 Sherman Corbett .05 .02 .01
☐ 89 Mike Erb .05 .02 .01
☐ 90 Mike Fetters .05 .02 .01
☐ 91 Jeff Heathcock .05 .02 .01
☐ 92 Scott Lewis .05 .02 .01
☐ 93 Rafael Montalvo .05 .02 .01
☐ 94 Cliff Young .05 .02 .01
☐ 95 Doug Davis .05 .02 .01
☐ 96 Ron Tingley .05 .02 .01
☐ 97 Karl Allaire .05 .02 .01
☐ 98 Pete Coachman .05 .02 .01
☐ 99 Chris Cron .05 .02 .01
☐ 100 Gary DiSarcina .15 .07 .02
☐ 101 Nelson Rood .05 .02 .01
☐ 102 Bobby Rose .05 .02 .01
☐ 103 Lee Stevens .10 .05 .01
☐ 104 Dan Grunhard .05 .02 .01
☐ 105 Reed Peters .05 .02 .01
☐ 106 John Skurla .05 .02 .01
☐ 107 Max Oliveras .05 .02 .01
☐ 108 Chuck Hernandez .05 .02 .01
☐ 109 Tony Blasucci .05 .02 .01
☐ 110 Dave Burba .15 .07 .02
☐ 111 Keith Helton .05 .02 .01
☐ 112 Vance Lovelace .05 .02 .01
☐ 113 Jose Melendez .05 .02 .01
☐ 114 Pat Pacillo .05 .02 .01
☐ 115 Pat Rice .05 .02 .01
☐ 116 Terry Taylor .05 .02 .01
☐ 117 Mike Walker .05 .02 .01
☐ 118 Bill McGuire .05 .02 .01
☐ 119 Matt Sinatro .05 .02 .01
☐ 120 Mario Diaz .05 .02 .01
☐ 121 Greg Fulton .05 .02 .01
☐ 122 Todd Haney .05 .02 .01
☐ 123 Ed Jurak .05 .02 .01
☐ 124 Tino Martinez 1.00 .45 .12
☐ 125 Jeff Schaefer .05 .02 .01
☐ 126 Casey Close .05 .02 .01
☐ 127 Tom Dodd .05 .02 .01
☐ 128 Jim Weaver .05 .02 .01
☐ 129 Tommy Jones .05 .02 .01
☐ 130 Dan Warthen CO .05 .02 .01
☐ 131 Tony Ariola .05 .02 .01
☐ 132 Joe Bitker .05 .02 .01
☐ 133 Scott Chiamparino .05 .02 .01
☐ 134 Reese Lambert .05 .02 .01
☐ 135 Joe Law .05 .02 .01
☐ 136 Dave Otto .05 .02 .01
☐ 137 Dave Veres .05 .02 .01
☐ 138 Bruce Walton .05 .02 .01
☐ 139 Wes Weber .05 .02 .01
☐ 140 Ed Wojna .05 .02 .01
☐ 141 Ray Young .05 .02 .01
☐ 142 Troy Afenir .05 .02 .01
☐ 143 Russ McGinnis .05 .02 .01
☐ 144 Larry Arndt .05 .02 .01
☐ 145 Mike Bordick .15 .07 .02
☐ 146 Scott Hemond .05 .02 .01
☐ 147 Dann Howitt .05 .02 .01
☐ 148 Doug Jennings .05 .02 .01
☐ 149 Al Pedrique .05 .02 .01
☐ 150 Dick Scott .05 .02 .01
☐ 151 Tim Casey .05 .02 .01
☐ 152 Pat Dietrick .05 .02 .01
☐ 153 Bruce Fields .05 .02 .01
☐ 154 Eric Fox .05 .02 .01
☐ 155 Steve Howard .05 .02 .01
☐ 156 Kevin Ward .05 .02 .01
☐ 157 Brad Fischer MG .05 .02 .01
☐ 158 Chuck Estrada CO .05 .02 .01
☐ 159 Wilson Alvarez .25 .11 .03
☐ 160 Mike Campbell .05 .02 .01
☐ 161 Tom Drees .05 .02 .01
☐ 162 Grady Hall .05 .02 .01
☐ 163 Shawn Hillegas .05 .02 .01
☐ 164 Ravelo Manzanillo .05 .02 .01
☐ 165 John Pawlowski .05 .02 .01
☐ 166 Adam Peterson .05 .02 .01
☐ 167 Steve Rosenberg .05 .02 .01
☐ 168 Jose Segura .05 .02 .01
☐ 169 Don Wakamatsu .05 .02 .01
☐ 170 Jerry Willard .05 .02 .01
☐ 171 Rich Amaral .05 .02 .01
☐ 172 Pete Dalena .05 .02 .01
☐ 173 Norberto Martin .05 .02 .01
☐ 174 Keith Smith .05 .02 .01
☐ 175 Todd Trafton .05 .02 .01
☐ 176 Tracy Woodson .05 .02 .01
☐ 177 Orsino Hill .05 .02 .01
☐ 178 Marcus Lawton .05 .02 .01
☐ 179 Marlin McPhail .05 .02 .01
☐ 180 C.L. Penigar .05 .02 .01
☐ 181 Ramon Sambo .05 .02 .01
☐ 182 Dana Williams .05 .02 .01
☐ 183 Marv Foley .05 .02 .01
☐ 184 Moe Drabowsky CO .05 .02 .01
☐ 185 Roger LaFrancois CO .05 .02 .01
☐ 186 Ryan Bowen .05 .02 .01
☐ 187 William Brennan .05 .02 .01
☐ 188 Terry Clark .05 .02 .01
☐ 189 Brian Fisher .05 .02 .01
☐ 190 Randy Hennisaire .05 .02 .01
☐ 191 Darryl Kile .15 .07 .02
☐ 192 Brian Meyer .05 .02 .01
☐ 193 Randy St. Claire .05 .02 .01
☐ 194 Lee Tunnell .05 .02 .01
☐ 195 Carl Nichols .05 .02 .01
☐ 196 Scott Servais .15 .07 .02
☐ 197 Pedro Sanchez .05 .02 .01
☐ 198 Mike Simms .05 .02 .01
☐ 199 Craig Smajstra .05 .02 .01
☐ 200 Harry Spilman .05 .02 .01
☐ 201 Doug Strange .05 .02 .01
☐ 202 Jose Tolentino .05 .02 .01
☐ 203 Gary Cooper .05 .02 .01
☐ 204 Kevin Dean .05 .02 .01
☐ 205 Louie Meadows .05 .02 .01
☐ 206 Jim Olander .05 .02 .01
☐ 207 Javier Ortiz .05 .02 .01
☐ 208 Karl Rhodes .05 .02 .01
☐ 209 Bob Skinner MG .05 .02 .01
☐ 210 Brent Strom CO .05 .02 .01
☐ 211 Tim Tolman CO .05 .02 .01
☐ 212 Greg McMichael .05 .02 .01
☐ 213 Doug Robertson .05 .02 .01
☐ 214 Jeff Shaw .05 .02 .01
☐ 215 Joe Skalski .05 .02 .01
☐ 216 Efrain Valdez .05 .02 .01
☐ 217 Mike Walker .05 .02 .01
☐ 218 Colby Ward .05 .02 .01
☐ 219 Carl Willis .05 .02 .01
☐ 220 Tom Lampkin .05 .02 .01
☐ 221 Tom Magrann .05 .02 .01
☐ 222 Juan Castillo .05 .02 .01
☐ 223 Ever Magallanes .05 .02 .01
☐ 224 Jeff Manto .05 .02 .01
☐ 225 Luis Medina .05 .02 .01
☐ 226 Troy Neel .05 .02 .01
☐ 227 Steve Springer .05 .02 .01
☐ 228 Casey Webster .05 .02 .01
☐ 229 Beau Allred .05 .02 .01
☐ 230 Alan Cockrell .05 .02 .01
☐ 231 Ty Gainey .05 .02 .01
☐ 232 Dwight Taylor .05 .02 .01
☐ 233 Turner Ward .05 .02 .01
☐ 234 Jeff Wetherby .05 .02 .01
☐ 235 Bobby Molinaro MG .05 .02 .01
☐ 236 Buddy Bell CO .05 .02 .01
☐ 237 Rick Adair CO .05 .02 .01
☐ 238 Paul Abbott .05 .02 .01
☐ 239 Pat Bangtson .05 .02 .01
☐ 240 Larry Casian .05 .02 .01
☐ 241 Mike Cook .05 .02 .01
☐ 242 Pete Delkus .05 .02 .01
☐ 243 Mike Dyer .05 .02 .01
☐ 244 Mark Guthrie .05 .02 .01
☐ 245 Orlando Lind .05 .02 .01
☐ 246 Francisco Oliveras .05 .02 .01
☐ 247 Park Pittman .05 .02 .01
☐ 248 Charles Scott .05 .02 .01
☐ 249 Jimmy Williams .05 .02 .01
☐ 250 Jamie Nelson .05 .02 .01
☐ 251 Derek Parks .05 .02 .01
☐ 252 Doug Baker .05 .02 .01
☐ 253 Chip Hale .05 .02 .01
☐ 254 Terry Jorgensen .05 .02 .01
☐ 255 Scott Leius .15 .07 .02
☐ 256 Marty Lanoux .05 .02 .01
☐ 257 Ed Naveda .05 .02 .01
☐ 258 Victor Rodriguez .05 .02 .01
☐ 259 Paul Sorrento .20 .09 .03
☐ 260 Bernardo Brito .05 .02 .01
☐ 261 Rafael Delima .05 .02 .01
☐ 262 David Jacas .05 .02 .01
☐ 263 Alonzo Powell .05 .02 .01
☐ 264 Jim Shellenback MG .05 .02 .01
☐ 265 Shawn Barton .05 .02 .01
☐ 266 Kevin Brown .05 .02 .01
☐ 267 Rocky Childress .05 .02 .01
☐ 268 Brian Givens .05 .02 .01
☐ 269 Manny Hernandez .05 .02 .01
☐ 270 Jeff Innis .05 .02 .01
☐ 271 Cesar Mejia .05 .02 .01
☐ 272 Scott Nielsen .05 .02 .01
☐ 273 Dale Plummer .05 .02 .01
☐ 274 Roger Samuels .05 .02 .01
☐ 275 Ray Soff .05 .02 .01
☐ 276 Dave Trautwein .05 .02 .01
☐ 277 Julio Valera .05 .02 .01
☐ 278 Dave Liddell .05 .02 .01
☐ 279 Orlando Mercado .05 .02 .01
☐ 280 Tim Bogar .05 .02 .01
☐ 281 Mike Debutch .05 .02 .01
☐ 282 Jeff Gardner .05 .02 .01
☐ 283 Denny Gonzalez .05 .02 .01
☐ 284 Chris Jelic .05 .02 .01
☐ 285 Kelvin Torve .05 .02 .01
☐ 286 Alex Diaz .05 .02 .01
☐ 287 Keith Hughes .05 .02 .01
☐ 288 Darren Reed .05 .02 .01
☐ 289 Zoilo Sanchez .05 .02 .01
☐ 290 Lou Thornton .05 .02 .01
☐ 291 Steve Swisher MG .05 .02 .01
☐ 292 John Cumberland CO .05 .02 .01
☐ 293 Rich Miller CO .05 .02 .01
☐ 294 Jose DeJesus .05 .02 .01
☐ 295 Marvin Freeman .10 .05 .01
☐ 296 Todd Frohwirth .05 .02 .01
☐ 297 Jason Grimsley .05 .02 .01
☐ 298 Chuck Malone .05 .02 .01
☐ 299 Brad Moore .05 .02 .01
☐ 300 Wally Ritchie .05 .02 .01
☐ 301 Bob Scanlan .05 .02 .01
☐ 302 Scott Service .05 .02 .01
☐ 303 Steve Sharts .05 .02 .01
☐ 304 John Gibbons .05 .02 .01
☐ 305 Tom Nieto .05 .02 .01
☐ 306 Jim Adduci .05 .02 .01
☐ 307 Kelly Heath .05 .02 .01
☐ 308 Mickey Morandini .05 .02 .01
☐ 309 Victor Rosario .05 .02 .01
☐ 310 Steve Stanicek .05 .02 .01
☐ 311 Greg Legg .05 .02 .01
☐ 312 Ron Jones .05 .02 .01
☐ 313 Chris Knabenshue .05 .02 .01
☐ 314 Keith Miller .05 .02 .01
☐ 315 Jim Vatcher .05 .02 .01
☐ 316 Jim Wright CO .05 .02 .01
☐ 317 Steve Adkins .05 .02 .01
☐ 318 Darrin Chapin .05 .02 .01
☐ 319 Bob Davidson .05 .02 .01
☐ 320 Dave Eiland .05 .02 .01
☐ 321 John Habyan .05 .02 .01
☐ 322 Jimmy Jones .05 .02 .01
☐ 323 Mark Leiter .05 .02 .01
☐ 324 Kevin Mmahat .05 .02 .01
☐ 325 Rich Monteleone .05 .02 .01
☐ 326 Willie Smith .05 .02 .01
☐ 327 Ricky Torres .05 .02 .01
☐ 328 Jeff Datz .05 .02 .01
☐ 329 Brian Dorsett .05 .02 .01
☐ 330 Dave Sax .05 .02 .01
☐ 331 Jim Leyritz .15 .07 .02
☐ 332 Hensley Meulens .05 .02 .01
☐ 333 Carlos Rodriguez .05 .02 .01
☐ 334 Rob Sepanek .05 .02 .01
☐ 335 Andy Stankiewicz .05 .02 .01
☐ 336 Jim Walewander .05 .02 .01
☐ 337 Mark Wasinger .05 .02 .01
☐ 338 Oscar Azocar .05 .02 .01
☐ 339 John Fishel .05 .02 .01
☐ 340 Jason Maas .05 .02 .01
☐ 341 Kevin Maas .05 .02 .01
☐ 342 Van Snider .05 .02 .01
☐ 343 Field Staff .05 .02 .01
Clete Boyer
Stump Merrill MG
Ken Rowe
Trey Hillman
Mike Heifferon
☐ 344 Tom Gilles .05 .02 .01
☐ 345 Maurio Gozzo .05 .02 .01
☐ 346 Paul Kilgus .05 .02 .01
☐ 347 Doug Linton .05 .02 .01
☐ 348 Mike Loynd .05 .02 .01
☐ 349 Rick Lysander .05 .02 .01
☐ 350 Alex Sanchez .05 .02 .01
☐ 351 John Shea .05 .02 .01
☐ 352 Steve Wapnick .05 .02 .01
☐ 353 Andy Dziadkowiec .05 .02 .01
☐ 354 Joe Szekely .05 .02 .01
☐ 355 Ozzie Virgil .05 .02 .01
☐ 356 Jim Eppard .05 .02 .01
☐ 357 Jose Escobar .05 .02 .01
☐ 358 Webster Garrison .05 .02 .01
☐ 359 Paul Runge .05 .02 .01
☐ 360 Luis Sojo .05 .02 .01
☐ 361 Ed Sprague .25 .11 .03
☐ 362 Derek Bell .60 .25 .07
☐ 363 Hector DeLaCruz .05 .02 .01
☐ 364 Rob Ducey .05 .02 .01
☐ 365 Pedro Munoz .10 .05 .01
☐ 366 Stu Pederson .05 .02 .01
☐ 367 Mark Whiten .15 .07 .02
☐ 368 Bob Bailor MG .05 .02 .01
☐ 369 Bob Shirley CO .05 .02 .01
☐ 370 Rocket Wheeler CO .05 .02 .01
☐ 371 Scott Aldred .05 .02 .01
☐ 372 Dennis Burtt .05 .02 .01
☐ 373 Shawn Holman .05 .02 .01
☐ 374 Matt Kinzer .05 .02 .01
☐ 375 Randy Nosek .05 .02 .01
☐ 376 Jose Ramos .05 .02 .01
☐ 377 Kevin Ritz .20 .09 .03
☐ 378 Mike Schwabe .05 .02 .01
☐ 379 Steve Searcy .05 .02 .01
☐ 380 Eric Stone .05 .02 .01
☐ 381 Don Vesling .05 .02 .01
☐ 382 Phil Clark .05 .02 .01
☐ 383 Phil Ouellette .05 .02 .01
☐ 384 Dean DeCillis .05 .02 .01
☐ 385 Travis Fryman 1.50 .70 .19
☐ 386 Jim Lindeman .05 .02 .01
☐ 387 Scott Livingstone .05 .02 .01
☐ 388 Torey Lovullo .05 .02 .01
☐ 389 Domingo Michel .05 .02 .01
☐ 390 Milt Cuyler .05 .02 .01
☐ 391 La Vel Freeman .05 .02 .01
☐ 392 Shawn Hare .05 .02 .01
☐ 393 Scott Lusader .05 .02 .01
☐ 394 Tom Gamboa MG .05 .02 .01
☐ 395 Jeff Jones CO .05 .02 .01
☐ 396 Aurelio Rodriguez CO .05 .02 .01
☐ 397 Steve Avery .40 .18 .05
☐ 398 Tommy Greene .10 .05 .01
☐ 399 Bill Laskey .05 .02 .01
☐ 400 Paul Marak .05 .02 .01
☐ 401 Andy Nezelek .05 .02 .01
☐ 402 Ed Olwine .05 .02 .01
☐ 403 Dale Polley .05 .02 .01
☐ 404 Rusty Richards .05 .02 .01
☐ 405 Brian Snyder .05 .02 .01

☐ 406 Jimmy Kremers .05 .02 .01
☐ 407 John Mizerock .05 .02 .01
☐ 408 John Alva .05 .02 .01
☐ 409 Francisco Cabrera .05 .02 .01
☐ 410 Bruce Crabbe .05 .02 .01
☐ 411 Drew Denson .05 .02 .01
☐ 412 Ken Dowell .05 .02 .01
☐ 413 Ed Whited .05 .02 .01
☐ 414 Geronimo Berroa .25 .11 .03
☐ 415 Dennis Hood .05 .02 .01
☐ 416 Brian R. Hunter .05 .02 .01
☐ 417 Barry Jones .05 .02 .01
☐ 418 Dave Justice 2.00 .90 .25
☐ 419 Jim Beauchamp MG .05 .02 .01
☐ 420 John Grubb CO .05 .02 .01
☐ 421 Leo Mazzone CO .05 .02 .01
☐ 422 Sonny Jackson CO .05 .02 .01
☐ 423 Rick Berg CO .05 .02 .01
☐ 424 Steve Bast .05 .02 .01
☐ 425 Tom Bolton .05 .02 .01
☐ 426 Steve Curry .05 .02 .01
☐ 427 Mike Dalton .05 .02 .01
☐ 428 Jeff Gray .05 .02 .01
☐ 429 Daryl Irvine .05 .02 .01
☐ 430 Joe Johnson .05 .02 .01
☐ 431 John Leister .05 .02 .01
☐ 432 Mike Rochford .05 .02 .01
☐ 433 Larry Shikles .05 .02 .01
☐ 434 Tito Stewart .05 .02 .01
☐ 435 John Trautwein .05 .02 .01
☐ 436 John Flaherty .05 .02 .01
☐ 437 John Marzano .05 .02 .01
☐ 438 Gary Tremblay .05 .02 .01
☐ 439 Scott Cooper .05 .02 .01
☐ 440 Angel Gonzalez .05 .02 .01
☐ 441 Tim Naehring .25 .11 .03
☐ 442 Jim Pankovits .05 .02 .01
☐ 443 Mo Vaughn 5.00 2.20 .60
☐ 444 Rick Lancellotti .05 .02 .01
☐ 445 Mickey Pina .05 .02 .01
☐ 446 Phil Plantier .15 .07 .02
☐ 447 Jeff Stone .05 .02 .01
☐ 448 Scott Wade .05 .02 .01
☐ 449 Ed Nottle MG .05 .02 .01
☐ 450 Mark Meleski CO .05 .02 .01
☐ 451 Lee Stange CO .05 .02 .01
☐ 452 Jay Aldrich .05 .02 .01
☐ 453 Jose Bautista .05 .02 .01
☐ 454 Eric Bell .05 .02 .01
☐ 455 Dan Boone .05 .02 .01
☐ 456 Ben McDonald .15 .07 .02
☐ 457 John Mitchell .05 .02 .01
☐ 458 Curt Schilling .25 .11 .03
☐ 459 Mike Smith .05 .02 .01
☐ 460 Rob Woodward .05 .02 .01
☐ 461 Chris Hoiles .15 .07 .02
☐ 462 Darrell Miller .05 .02 .01
☐ 463 Jack Tackett .05 .02 .01
☐ 464 Juan Bell .05 .02 .01
☐ 465 Tim Dulin .05 .02 .01
☐ 466 Leo Gomez .05 .02 .01
☐ 467 Jeff McKnight .05 .02 .01
☐ 468 Shane Turner .05 .02 .01
☐ 469 Greg Walker .05 .02 .01
☐ 470 Tony Chance .05 .02 .01
☐ 471 Victor Hithe .05 .02 .01
☐ 472 Donell Nixon .05 .02 .01
☐ 473 Chris Padget .05 .02 .01
☐ 474 Pete Stanicek .05 .02 .01
☐ 475 Mike Linskey .05 .02 .01
☐ 476 Joaquin Contreras .05 .02 .01
☐ 477 Greg Biagini .05 .02 .01
☐ 478 Dick Bosman .05 .02 .01
☐ 479 Paul Blair CO .05 .02 .01
☐ 480 Stan Belinda .05 .02 .01
☐ 481 Gordon Dillard .05 .02 .01
☐ 482 Mark Huismann .05 .02 .01
☐ 483 Hugh Kemp .05 .02 .01
☐ 484 Scott Medvin .05 .02 .01
☐ 485 Vincente Palacios .05 .02 .01
☐ 486 Rick Reed .05 .02 .01
☐ 487 Mark Ross .05 .02 .01
☐ 488 Dorn Taylor .05 .02 .01
☐ 489 Mike York .05 .02 .01
☐ 490 Dann Bilardello .05 .02 .01
☐ 491 Tom Prince .05 .02 .01
☐ 492 Danny Sheaffer .05 .02 .01
☐ 493 Kevin Burdick .05 .02 .01
☐ 494 Steve Kiefer .05 .02 .01
☐ 495 Orlando Merced .20 .09 .03
☐ 496 Armando Moreno .05 .02 .01
☐ 497 Jeff Richardson .05 .02 .01
☐ 498 Mark Ryal .05 .02 .01
☐ 499 Tommy Shields .05 .02 .01
☐ 500 Steve Carter .05 .02 .01
☐ 501 Wes Chamberlain .05 .02 .01
☐ 502 Jeff Cook .05 .02 .01
☐ 503 Scott Little .05 .02 .01
☐ 504 Terry Collins MG .05 .02 .01
☐ 505 Jackie Brown CO .05 .02 .01
☐ 506 Steve Henderson CO .05 .02 .01
☐ 507 Gibson Alba .05 .02 .01
☐ 508 Scott Arnold .05 .02 .01
☐ 509 Cris Carpenter .05 .02 .01
☐ 510 Stan Clarke .05 .02 .01
☐ 511 Mark Grater .05 .02 .01
☐ 512 Howard Hilton .05 .02 .01
☐ 513 Mike Hinkle .05 .02 .01
☐ 514 Omar Olivares .05 .02 .01
☐ 515 Dave Osteen .05 .02 .01
☐ 516 Mike Perez .05 .02 .01
☐ 517 Tim Sherrill .05 .02 .01
☐ 518 Scott Nichols .05 .02 .01
☐ 519 Ray Stephens .05 .02 .01
☐ 520 Pat Austin .05 .02 .01
☐ 521 Red Brewer .05 .02 .01
☐ 522 Todd Crosby .05 .02 .01
☐ 523 Bien Figueroa .05 .02 .01
☐ 524 Julian Martinez .05 .02 .01
☐ 525 Jesus Mendez .05 .02 .01
☐ 526 Geronimo Pena .05 .02 .01
☐ 527 Craig Wilson .05 .02 .01
☐ 528 Dennis Carter .05 .02 .01
☐ 529 Bernard Gilkey .30 .14 .04
☐ 530 Ray Lankford .60 .25 .07
☐ 531 Mauricio Nunez .05 .02 .01
☐ 532 Roy Silver .05 .02 .01
☐ 533 Gaylen Pitts MG .05 .02 .01
☐ 534 Mark Riggins CO .05 .02 .01
☐ 535 Neil Allen .05 .02 .01
☐ 536 Keith Brown .05 .02 .01
☐ 537 Chris Hammond .05 .02 .01
☐ 538 Milton Hill .05 .02 .01
☐ 539 Rodney Imes .05 .02 .01
☐ 540 Rob Lopez .05 .02 .01
☐ 541 Charlie Mitchell .05 .02 .01
☐ 542 Robert Moore .05 .02 .01
☐ 543 Rosario Rodriguez .05 .02 .01
☐ 544 Scott Scudder .05 .02 .01
☐ 545 Bob Sebra .05 .02 .01
☐ 546 Joey Vierra .05 .02 .01
☐ 547 Tony DeFrancesco .05 .02 .01
☐ 548 Terry McGriff .05 .02 .01
☐ 549 Donnie Scott .05 .02 .01
☐ 550 Reggie Jefferson .15 .07 .02
☐ 551 Brian Lane .05 .02 .01
☐ 552 Chris Lombardozzi .05 .02 .01
☐ 553 Paul Noce .05 .02 .01
☐ 554 Kevin Pearson .05 .02 .01
☐ 555 Eddie Tanner .05 .02 .01
☐ 556 Skeeter Barnes .05 .02 .01
☐ 557 Leo Garcia .05 .02 .01
☐ 558 Chris Jones .05 .02 .01
☐ 559 Keith Lockhart .05 .02 .01
☐ 560 Darryl Motley .05 .02 .01
☐ 561 Pete MacKanin MG .05 .02 .01
☐ 562 Ray Rippelmeyer CO .05 .02 .01
☐ 563 Scott Anderson .05 .02 .01
☐ 564 Esteban Beltre .05 .02 .01
☐ 565 Travis Chambers .05 .02 .01
☐ 566 Randy Braun .05 .02 .01
☐ 567 Danny Clay .05 .02 .01
☐ 568 Eric Bullock .05 .02 .01
☐ 569 Jim Davins .05 .02 .01
☐ 570 Jose Castro .05 .02 .01
☐ 571 Eddie Dixon .05 .02 .01
☐ 572 Romy Cucjen .05 .02 .01
☐ 573 Howard Farmer .05 .02 .01
☐ 574 Jerry Goff .05 .02 .01
☐ 575 Steve Fireovid .05 .02 .01
☐ 576 Otis Green .05 .02 .01
☐ 577 Dan Gakeler .05 .02 .01
☐ 578 Mel Houston .05 .02 .01
☐ 579 Balvino Galvez .05 .02 .01
☐ 580 Dwight Lowry .05 .02 .01
☐ 581 Dale Mohorcic .05 .02 .01
☐ 582 Quinn Mack .05 .02 .01
☐ 583 Chris Marchok .05 .02 .01
☐ 584 Edwin Marquez .05 .02 .01
☐ 585 Mel Rojas .15 .07 .02
☐ 586 Johnny Paredes .05 .02 .01
☐ 587 Rich Thompson .05 .02 .01
☐ 588 German Rivera .05 .02 .01
☐ 589 James Steels .05 .02 .01
☐ 590 Tim Johnson MG .05 .02 .01
☐ 591 Gomer Hodge CO .05 .02 .01
☐ 592 Joe Kerrigan CO .05 .02 .01
☐ 593 Ray Chadwick .05 .02 .01
☐ 594 Dera Clark .05 .02 .01
☐ 595 Luis Encarnacion .05 .02 .01
☐ 596 Tony Ferreira .05 .02 .01
☐ 597 Pete Filson .05 .02 .01
☐ 598 Jim LeMasters .05 .02 .01
☐ 599 Mike Magnante .05 .02 .01
☐ 600 Mike Tresemer .05 .02 .01
☐ 601 Mel Stottlemyre Jr. .05 .02 .01
☐ 602 Bill Wilkinson .05 .02 .01
☐ 603 Kevin Burrell .05 .02 .01
☐ 604 Tim Spehr .05 .02 .01
☐ 605 Luis de los Santos .05 .02 .01
☐ 606 Bob Hamelin .10 .05 .01
☐ 607 Bobby Meacham .05 .02 .01
☐ 608 Russ Morman .05 .02 .01
☐ 609 Thad Reece .05 .02 .01
☐ 610 Paul Zuvella .05 .02 .01
☐ 611 Mike Loggins .05 .02 .01
☐ 612 Chito Martinez .05 .02 .01
☐ 613 Harvey Pulliam .05 .02 .01
☐ 614 Jeff Schulz .05 .02 .01
☐ 615 Sal Rende MG .05 .02 .01
☐ 616 Tom Poquette CO .05 .02 .01
☐ 617 Rich Dubee CO .05 .02 .01
☐ 618 Kevin Blankenship .05 .02 .01
☐ 619 Shawn Boskie .05 .02 .01
☐ 620 Mark Bowden .05 .02 .01
☐ 621 Greg Kallevig .05 .02 .01
☐ 622 Dave Masters .05 .02 .01
☐ 623 Steve Parker .05 .02 .01
☐ 624 Dave Pavlas .05 .02 .01
☐ 625 Laddie Renfroe .05 .02 .01
☐ 626 Paul Wilmet .05 .02 .01
☐ 627 Jeff Hearron .05 .02 .01
☐ 628 Erik Pappas .05 .02 .01
☐ 629 Hector Villanueva .05 .02 .01
☐ 630 Bob Bafia .05 .02 .01
☐ 631 Brian Guinn .05 .02 .01
☐ 632 Jeff Small .05 .02 .01
☐ 633 Greg Smith .05 .02 .01
☐ 634 Glenn Sullivan .05 .02 .01
☐ 635 Bill Wrona .05 .02 .01
☐ 636 Brad Bierley .05 .02 .01
☐ 637 Cedric Landrum .05 .02 .01
☐ 638 Derrick May .05 .02 .01
☐ 639 Gary Varsho .05 .02 .01
☐ 640 Jim Essian MG .05 .02 .01
☐ 641 Don August .05 .02 .01
☐ 642 Mike Birkbeck .05 .02 .01
☐ 643 Mike Capel .05 .02 .01
☐ 644 Logan Easley .05 .02 .01
☐ 645 Tom Edens .05 .02 .01
☐ 646 Don Gordon .05 .02 .01
☐ 647 Chuck McGrath .05 .02 .01
☐ 648 Jeff Peterek .05 .02 .01
☐ 649 Dennis Powell .05 .02 .01
☐ 650 Ed Puig .05 .02 .01
☐ 651 Al Sadler .05 .02 .01
☐ 652 Tim Watkins .05 .02 .01
☐ 653 Tim McIntosh .05 .02 .01
☐ 654 Tim Torricelli .05 .02 .01
☐ 655 George Canale .05 .02 .01
☐ 656 Mark Higgins .05 .02 .01
☐ 657 Frank Mattox .05 .02 .01
☐ 658 Joe Mitchell .05 .02 .01
☐ 659 Joe Redfield .05 .02 .01
☐ 660 D.L. Smith .05 .02 .01
☐ 661 Joe Xavier .05 .02 .01
☐ 662 Ruben Escalera .05 .02 .01
☐ 663 Mario Monico .05 .02 .01
☐ 664 Billy Moore .05 .02 .01
☐ 665 Darryel Walters .05 .02 .01
☐ 666 Dave Machemer MG .05 .02 .01
☐ 667 Jackson Todd CO .05 .02 .01
☐ 668 Gerald Alexander .05 .02 .01
☐ 669 Brad Arnsberg .05 .02 .01
☐ 670 John Barfield .05 .02 .01
☐ 671 Jack Hardy .05 .02 .01
☐ 672 Ray Hayward .05 .02 .01
☐ 673 John Hoover .05 .02 .01
☐ 674 Steve Lankard .05 .02 .01
☐ 675 David Lynch .05 .02 .01
☐ 676 Craig McMurtry .05 .02 .01
☐ 677 David Miller .05 .02 .01
☐ 678 Mark Petkovsek .05 .02 .01
☐ 679 Jeff Satzinger .05 .02 .01
☐ 680 Mike Berger .05 .02 .01
☐ 681 Dave Engle .05 .02 .01
☐ 682 John Russell .05 .02 .01
☐ 683 Pat Dodson .05 .02 .01
☐ 684 Pat Garman .05 .02 .01
☐ 685 Gary Green .05 .02 .01
☐ 686 Brian House .05 .02 .01
☐ 687 Dean Palmer 1.50 .70 .19
☐ 688 Ron Washington .05 .02 .01
☐ 689 Nick Capra .05 .02 .01
☐ 690 Juan Gonzalez 8.00 3.60 1.00
☐ 691 Gar Millay .05 .02 .01
☐ 692 Kevin Reimer .05 .02 .01
☐ 693 Bernie Tatis .05 .02 .01
☐ 694 Checklist .05 .02 .01
☐ 695 Checklist .05 .02 .01
☐ 696 Checklist .05 .02 .01
☐ 697 Checklist .05 .02 .01
☐ 698 Checklist .05 .02 .01
☐ 699 Checklist .05 .02 .01
☐ 700 Checklist .05 .02 .01

1990 Pulaski Braves Best

This 29-card standard-size set of the 1990 Pulaski Braves, a Rookie Class Appalachian League affiliate of the Atlanta Braves, features white-bordered posed and action color player photos on its fronts. The player's name and position appear vertically on the left side. The yellow horizontal back carries the player's name and position at the top, followed by biography, career highlights, and statistics. A player head shot appears in the lower right corner

	MINT	NRMT	EXC
COMPLETE SET (29)	5.00	2.20	.60

☐ 1 Brian Bark
☐ 2 Barry Chiles
☐ 3 Travis Dunlap
☐ 4 Stewart Ford
☐ 5 Brett Grebe
☐ 6 Keith Morrison
☐ 7 Larry Owens
☐ 8 Mike Place
☐ 9 Joe Roa
☐ 10 Mike Shepherd
☐ 11 Henry Werland
☐ 12 David Williams
☐ 13 Wallace Gonzalez
☐ 14 Vincent Jiminez
☐ 15 Jamie Crump
☐ 16 Patrick Dando
☐ 17 Hector Roa
☐ 18 Karl Rudison
☐ 19 George Virgilio
☐ 20 Troy Hughes
☐ 21 Anthony Johnson
☐ 22 Brian Kowitz
☐ 23 Jimmie Pullins
☐ 24 Armando Rodriquez
☐ 25 Juan Williams
☐ 26 Randy Ingle MGR
☐ 27 Randy Phillips CO
☐ 28 Cloyd Boyer CO
☐ 29 Mike Cerame
Checklist

1990 Pulaski Braves ProCards

This 31-card standard-size set of the 1990 Pulaski Braves, a Rookie Class Appalachian League affiliate of the Atlanta Braves, features on its white-bordered fronts posed color player photos set on simulated wood-grain backgrounds. The player's name, position, and team appear within a gold-colored rectangle below the photo. The tan horizontal back is bordered in white and carries the player's name at the top, followed by biography and statistics.

	MINT	NRMT	EXC
COMPLETE SET (31)	5.00	2.20	.60

☐ 3085 Checklist
☐ 3086 Anthony Johnson
☐ 3087 Brian Kowitz
☐ 3088 Troy Hughes
☐ 3089 George Virgilio
☐ 3090 Raymond Mack
☐ 3091 David Williams
☐ 3092 Vincent Jiminez
☐ 3093 Wallace Gonzalez
☐ 3094 Karl Rudison
☐ 3095 Jamie Crump
☐ 3096 Pat Dando
☐ 3097 Hector Roa
☐ 3098 Stewart Ford
☐ 3099 Travis Dunlap
☐ 3100 Barry Chiles
☐ 3101 Brian Bark
☐ 3102 Larry Owens
☐ 3103 Brett Grebe
☐ 3104 Keith Morrison
☐ 3105 Mike Shepherd
☐ 3106 Michael Place
☐ 3107 Joe Roa
☐ 3108 Henry Werland
☐ 3109 Armondo Rodriguez
☐ 3110 Jimmie Pullins
☐ 3111 Juan Williams
☐ 3112 Johnny Walker
☐ 3113 Coaches
Cloyd Boyer
Randy Philips
☐ 3114 Randy Ingle MGR
☐ 3115 Team Photo

1990 Quad City Angels Grand Slam

	MINT	NRMT	EXC
COMPLETE SET (30)	6.00	2.70	.75

☐ 1 Don Long MG
☐ 2 Joe Georger CO
☐ 3 Mitch Seoane CO
☐ 4 Robert Horowitz TR
☐ 5 Dave Neal
☐ 6 Mike Hook
☐ 7 Bruce Vegely
☐ 8 Roberto Castillo
☐ 9 Justin Martin
☐ 10 Steve King
☐ 11 Les Haffner
☐ 12 Dave Adams
☐ 13 Marcus Moore
☐ 14 Erik Bennett
☐ 15 John Marchese
☐ 16 Jeff Gay
☐ 17 Larry Gonzales
☐ 18 Mick Billmeyer
☐ 19 Corey Kapano
☐ 20 Henry Threadgill
☐ 21 Chad Curtis
☐ 22 Ron Ortegon
☐ 23 Rey Martinez
☐ 24 Damion Easley
☐ 25 Fili Martinez
☐ 26 Reggie Williams
☐ 27 Rick Hirtensteiner

☐ 28 Edgal Rodriguez
☐ 29 Chris Treadgill
☐ 30 Bobby Jones

1990 Reading Phillies Best

This 26-card standard-size set of the 1990 Reading Phillies, a Class AA Eastern League affiliate of the Philadelphia Phillies, features white-bordered posed and action color player photos on its fronts. The player's name and position appear vertically on the left side. The yellow horizontal back carries the player's name and position at the top, followed by biography, career highlights, and statistics. A player head shot appears in the lower right corner

	MINT	NRMT	EXC
COMPLETE SET (26)	5.00	2.20	.60

☐ 1 David Holdridge
☐ 2 Robert Ayrault
☐ 3 Eric Boudreaux
☐ 4 John McLarnan
☐ 5 Amalio Carreno
☐ 6 Ramon Aviles CO
☐ 7 Andy Ashby
☐ 8 Timothy Mauser
☐ 9 Warren Magee
☐ 10 Mark Sims
☐ 11 Gary Wilson
☐ 12 Douglas Lindsey
☐ 13 Sal Agostinalli
☐ 14 Gary Alexander
☐ 15 Kim Batiste
☐ 16 Martin Foley
☐ 17 Jeff Grotewold
☐ 18 Roderick Robertson
☐ 19 Casey Lee Waller
☐ 20 Frank Bellino
☐ 21 Vince Holyfield
☐ 22 Stephen Kirkpatrick
☐ 23 Thomas Marsh
☐ 24 Don McCormack MGR
☐ 25 George Culver CO
☐ 26 Checklist

1990 Reading Phillies ProCards

This 27-card standard-size set of the 1990 Reading Phillies, a Class AA Eastern League affiliate of the Philadelphia Phillies, features on its white-bordered fronts posed color player photos set on simulated wood-grain backgrounds. The player's name, position, and team appear within a gold-colored rectangle below the photo. The tan horizontal back is bordered in white and carries the player's name at the top, followed by biography and statistics.

	MINT	NRMT	EXC
COMPLETE SET (27)	5.00	2.20	.60

☐ 1210 Checklist
☐ 1211 Andy Ashby
☐ 1212 Bob Ayrault
☐ 1213 Amalio Carreno
☐ 1214 Eric Boudreaux
☐ 1215 Fred Christopher
☐ 1216 David Holdridge
☐ 1217 Tim Mauser
☐ 1218 Warren Magee
☐ 1219 John McLarnan
☐ 1220 Mark Sims
☐ 1221 Gary Wilson
☐ 1222 Sal Agostinelli
☐ 1223 Doug Lindsey
☐ 1224 Gary Alexander
☐ 1225 Kim Batiste
☐ 1226 Marty Foley
☐ 1227 Jeff Grotewold
☐ 1228 Rod Robertson
☐ 1229 Casey Waller
☐ 1230 Frank Bellino
☐ 1231 Vince Holyfield
☐ 1232 Steve Kirkpatrick
☐ 1233 Tom Marsh
☐ 1234 Don McCormack MGR
☐ 1235 George Culver CO
☐ 1236 Ramon Aviles CO

1990 Reading Phillies Star

This 28-card standard-size set of the 1990 Reading Phillies, a Class AA Eastern League affiliate of the Philadelphia Phillies, features blue bordered posed color player photos on its fronts. The player's name, team name, and position appear at the bottom. The white horizontal back carries the player's name at the top, followed by biography, career highlights, and statistics.

	MINT	NRMT	EXC
COMPLETE SET (28)	5.00	2.20	.60

☐ 1 Sal Agostinelli
☐ 2 Gary Alexander
☐ 3 Andy Ashby
☐ 4 Bob Ayrault
☐ 5 Kim Batiste
☐ 6 Frank Bellino
☐ 7 Eric Boudreaux
☐ 8 Cliff Brantley
☐ 9 Richard Buonantony
☐ 10 Jeff Grotewold
☐ 11 Amalio Carreno
☐ 12 Marty Foley
☐ 13 David Holdridge
☐ 14 Vince Holyfield
☐ 15 Steve Kirkpatrick
☐ 16 Doug Lindsey
☐ 17 Warren Magee
☐ 18 Tom Marsh
☐ 19 Tim Mauser
☐ 20 John McLarnan
☐ 21 Rod Robertson
☐ 22 Mark Sims
☐ 23 Casey Waller
☐ 24 Gary Wilson
☐ 25 Floyd Youmans
☐ 26 Don McCormack MGR
☐ 27 Ramon Aviles CO
☐ 28 George Culver CO

1990 Reno Silver Sox Cal League Cards

	MINT	NRMT	EXC
COMPLETE SET (31)	5.00	2.20	.60

☐ 262 Ken Whitfield
☐ 263 Tom Eiterman
☐ 264 Clyde Pough
☐ 265 Alex Ferran
☐ 266 Mike Easley
☐ 267 Joel Chimelis
☐ 268 Todd Blackwell
☐ 269 Mark Charbonnet
☐ 270 Tim Donahue
☐ 271 Carlos Mota
☐ 272 Shawn Barton
☐ 273 Kaha Wong
☐ 274 Gary Nalls
☐ 275 Milt Harper
☐ 276 Keith Shepherd
☐ 277 Michael Soper
☐ 278 Jeff Whitney
☐ 279 Cecil Pettiford
☐ 280 William Wertz
☐ 281 Felix Caraballo
☐ 282 Greg Paxton
☐ 283 Howard Cole
☐ 284 Garry Clark
☐ 285 Tad Powers
☐ 286 Mike Brown MGR
☐ 287 Ben Gallo CO
☐ 288 Dean Treanor CO
☐ 289 Rich St. John TR
☐ 290 Jerry Maldonado AGM
☐ 291 Todd Karli ANN
☐ 292 Jack Patton GM

1990 Richmond Braves 25th Anniversary Team Issue

	MINT	NRMT	EXC
COMPLETE SET (23)	20.00	9.00	2.50

☐ 1 Tommie Aaron MGR
☐ 2 Sam Ayoub TR
☐ 3 Dusty Baker
☐ 4 Jim Beauchamp
☐ 5 Tony Brizzolara
☐ 6 Brett Butler
☐ 7 Ken Dayley
Sic, Daley
☐ 8 Darrell Evans
☐ 9 Ralph Garr
☐ 10 Tom House
☐ 11 Glenn Hubbard
☐ 12 Brook Jacoby
☐ 13 Jerry Keller
☐ 14 Brad Komminsk
☐ 15 Rick Mahler
☐ 16 Larry Marie
☐ 17 Dale Murphy
☐ 18 Larry Owen
☐ 19 Gerald Perry
☐ 20 Ron Reed
☐ 21 Chico Ruiz
☐ 22 Pablo Torrealba
☐ 23 Paul Zuvella

1990 Richmond Braves Bob's Camera

This 22-card team set of the 1990 Richmond Braves, a Class AAA International League affiliate of the Atlanta Braves, was sponsored by Bob's Camera. The fronts feature borderless color player photos with sponsors' and team's logos in the wide bottom margin. The backs are blank. 500 sets were produced.

	MINT	NRMT	EXC
COMPLETE SET (22)	60.00	27.00	7.50

☐ 1 Ed Olwine
☐ 2 Steve Ziem
☐ 3 Bill Laskey
☐ 4 Brian Snyder
☐ 5 Bruce Crabbe
☐ 6 John Mizerock
☐ 7 Steve Avery
☐ 8 Kent Mercker
☐ 9 Tommy Greene
☐ 10 Paul Marak
☐ 11 Barry Jones
☐ 12 Jimmy Kremers
☐ 13 Andy Nezelek
☐ 14 Dale Polley
☐ 15 Geronimo Berroa
☐ 16 Ed Whited
☐ 17 Rusty Richards
☐ 18 Dennis Hood
☐ 19 Rico Rossy
☐ 20 Andy Tomberlin
☐ 21 Kelly Mann
☐ 22 Rick Berg CO

1990 Richmond Braves CMC

This 27-card standard-size set of the 1990 Richmond Braves, a Class AAA International League affiliate of the Atlanta Braves, features white-bordered posed color player photos on its fronts. The player's name and position appear at the bottom; the team name appears vertically on the left. The back carries the league emblem in the white area at the top, the team name in the green stripe below, and player's name, position, biography, and statistics in the yellow area at the bottom. 1,100 sets were produced.

	MINT	NRMT	EXC
COMPLETE SET (27)	15.00	6.75	1.85

☐ 1 Steve Avery
☐ 2 Coaches
Leo Mazzone
Sonny Jackson
John Grubb
☐ 3 Dale Polley
☐ 4 Rusty Richards
☐ 5 Andy Nezelek
☐ 6 Ed Olwine
☐ 7 Jim Beauchamp MGR
☐ 8 Paul Marak
☐ 9 Dave Justice
☐ 10 Jimmy Kremers
☐ 11 Drew Denson
☐ 12 Barry Jones
☐ 13 Francisco Cabrera
☐ 14 Bruce Crabbe
☐ 15 Dennis Hood
☐ 16 Geronimo Berroa
☐ 17 Ed Whited
☐ 18 Sam Ayoub TR
☐ 19 Brian R. Hunter
☐ 20 Tommy Greene
☐ 21 John Mizerock
☐ 22 Ken Dowell
☐ 23 John Alva
☐ 24 Bill Laskey
☐ 25 Brian Snyder
☐ 26 Rick Luecken
☐ 27 Kent Mercker

1990 Richmond Braves ProCards

This 28-card standard-size set of the 1990 Richmond Braves, a Class AAA International League affiliate of the Atlanta Braves, features on its white-bordered fronts posed color player photos set on simulated wood-grain backgrounds. The player's name, position, and team appear within a gold-colored rectangle below the photo. The tan horizontal back is bordered in white and carries the player's name at the top, followed by biography and statistics.

	MINT	NRMT	EXC
COMPLETE SET (28)	12.00	5.50	1.50

☐ 251 Checklist
☐ 252 Steve Avery
☐ 253 Tommy Greene
☐ 254 Bill Laskey
☐ 255 Paul Marak
☐ 256 Andy Nezelek
☐ 257 Ed Olwine
☐ 258 Dale Polley
☐ 259 Rusty Richards
☐ 260 Brian Snyder
☐ 261 Jimmy Kremers
☐ 262 John Mizerock
☐ 263 John Alva
☐ 264 Francisco Cabrera
☐ 265 Bruce Crabbe
☐ 266 Drew Denson
☐ 267 Ken Dowell
☐ 268 Ed Whited
☐ 269 Geronimo Berroa
☐ 270 Dennis Hood
☐ 271 Brian R. Hunter
☐ 272 Barry Jones
☐ 273 Dave Justice
☐ 274 Jim Beauchamp MGR
☐ 275 John Grubb CO
☐ 276 Leo Mazzone CO
☐ 277 Sonny Jackson CO
☐ 278 Rick Berg CO

1990 Richmond Braves Team Issue

This 30-card set of the Richmond Braves, a Class AAA International League affiliate of the Atlanta Braves, was issued in one large sheet featuring six perforated five-card strips with a large team photo in the wide top strip. Sponsored by Richmond Comix and Cards and WRNL Radio, the fronts carry color player photos. 5,000 sets were produced with 3,000 of them given away on a promotional night at the ballpark.

	MINT	NRMT	EXC
COMPLETE SET (30)	20.00	9.00	2.50

☐ 1 Steve Avery
☐ 2 Sam Ayoub TR
☐ 3 Jim Beauchamp
☐ 4 Rick Berg
☐ 5 Geronimo Berroa
☐ 6 Francisco Cabrera
☐ 7 Bruce Crabbe
☐ 8 Drew Denson
☐ 9 Ken Dowell
☐ 10 Tommy Greene
☐ 11 John Grubb
☐ 12 Dennis Hood
☐ 13 Brian Hunter
☐ 14 Sonny Jackson
☐ 15 Barry Jones
☐ 16 David Justice
☐ 17 Jimmy Kremers
☐ 18 Bill Laskey
☐ 19 Rick Luecken
☐ 20 Paul Marak
☐ 21 Leo Mazzone
☐ 22 Kent Mercker
☐ 23 John Mizerock
☐ 24 Andy Nezelek
☐ 25 Ed Olwine
☐ 26 Dale Polley
☐ 27 Rusty Richards
☐ 28 Brian Snyder
☐ 29 Ed Whited
☐ 30 25th Anniversary

1990 Riverside Red Wave Best

This 27-card standard-size set of the 1990 Riverside Red Wave, a Class A California League affiliate of the San Diego Padres, features white-bordered posed and action color player photos on its fronts. The player's name and position appear vertically on the left side. The yellow horizontal back carries the player's name and position at the top, followed by biography, career highlights, and statistics. A player head shot appears in the lower right corner

	MINT	NRMT	EXC
COMPLETE SET (27)	5.00	2.20	.60

☐ 1 David Staton
☐ 2 Steve Bethea
☐ 3 Scott Bigham
☐ 4 Renay Bryand
☐ 5 Rick Davis
☐ 6 Dan Deville
☐ 7 Jay Estrada
☐ 8 Reggie Farmer
☐ 9 Vince Harris
☐ 10 Brian Harrison
☐ 11 Chris Haslock
☐ 12 Steve Hendricks
☐ 13 Kevin Higgins
☐ 14 Kerry Knox
☐ 15 Kelly Lifgren
☐ 16 Tony McGee
☐ 17 Darrell Sherman
☐ 18 Greg Smith
☐ 19 Nate Colbert CO
☐ 20 Steve Luebber CO
☐ 21 Jim Daniel TR
☐ 22 Bruce Bochy MGR
☐ 23 Candy Sierra
☐ 24 Darrin Reichle
☐ 25 Royal Thomas
☐ 26 Heath Lane
☐ 27 Checklist

1990 Riverside Red Wave Cal League Cards

	MINT	NRMT	EXC
COMPLETE SET (27)	5.00	2.20	.60

☐ 1 Dave Staton
☐ 2 Greg Smith
☐ 3 Darrell Sherman
☐ 4 Tony McGee
☐ 5 Luis Lopez
☐ 6 Kevin Higgins
☐ 7 Steve Bethea
☐ 8 Scott Bigham

- ☐ 9 Reggie Farmer
- ☐ 10 Mark Geiske
- ☐ 11 Steve Hendricks
- ☐ 12 Vince Harris
- ☐ 13 Renay Bryand
- ☐ 14 Rick Davis
- ☐ 15 Dan Deville
- ☐ 16 Jay Estrada
- ☐ 17 Brian Harrison
- ☐ 18 Chris Haslock
- ☐ 19 Heath Lane
- ☐ 20 Bill Marx
- ☐ 21 Royal Thomas
- ☐ 22 Kelly Lifgren
- ☐ 23 Darrin Reichele
- ☐ 24 Bruce Bochy MGR
- ☐ 25 Steve Luebber CO
- ☐ 26 Nate Colbert CO
- ☐ 27 Tye Waller CO

1990 Riverside Red Wave ProCards

This 28-card standard-size set of the 1990 Riverside Red Wave, a Class A California League affiliate of the San Diego Padres, features on its white-bordered fronts posed color player photos set on simulated wood-grain backgrounds. The player's name, position, and team appear within a gold-colored rectangle below the photo. The tan horizontal back is bordered in white and carries the player's name at the top, followed by biography and statistics.

	MINT	NRMT	EXC
COMPLETE SET (28)	5.00	2.20	.60

- ☐ 2596 Checklist
- ☐ 2597 Renay Bryand
- ☐ 2598 Rick Davis
- ☐ 2599 Danny DeVille
- ☐ 2600 Jay Estrada
- ☐ 2601 Brian Harrison
- ☐ 2602 Chris Haslock
- ☐ 2603 Kerry Knox
- ☐ 2604 Heath Lane
- ☐ 2605 Kelly Lifgren
- ☐ 2606 Bill Marx
- ☐ 2607 Darrin Reichle
- ☐ 2608 Royal Thomas
- ☐ 2609 Candy Sierra
- ☐ 2610 Kevin Higgins
- ☐ 2611 Tony McGee
- ☐ 2612 Steve Bethea
- ☐ 2613 Scott Bigham
- ☐ 2614 Mark Gieseke
- ☐ 2615 Steve Hendricks
- ☐ 2616 Luis Lopez
- ☐ 2617 Dave Staton
- ☐ 2618 Reggie Farmer
- ☐ 2619 Vince Harris
- ☐ 2620 Darrell Sherman
- ☐ 2621 Greg Smith
- ☐ 2622 Nate Colbert CO
- ☐ 2623 Steve Luebber CO

1990 Rochester Red Wings CMC

This 27-card standard-size set of the 1990 Rochester Red Wings, a Class AAA International League affiliate of the Baltimore Orioles, features white-bordered posed color player photos on its fronts. The player's name and position appear at the bottom; the team name appears vertically on the left. The back carries the league emblem in the white area at the top, the team name in the green stripe below, and player's name, position, biography, and statistics in the yellow area at the bottom. 1,100 sets were produced.

	MINT	NRMT	EXC
COMPLETE SET (27)	8.00	3.60	1.00

- ☐ 1 Ben McDonald
- ☐ 2 Rob Woodward
- ☐ 3 Mickey Weston
- ☐ 4 Mike Jones
- ☐ 5 Curtis Schilling
- ☐ 6 Jay Aldrich
- ☐ 7 Paul Blair CO
- ☐ 8 Mike Smith
- ☐ 9 Jack Tackett
- ☐ 10 Leo Gomez
- ☐ 11 Donell Nixon
- ☐ 12 Jeff McKnight
- ☐ 13 Juan Bell
- ☐ 14 Chris Hoiles
- ☐ 15 Steve Stanicek
- ☐ 16 Tim Dulin
- ☐ 17 Chris Padget
- ☐ 18 Greg Walker
- ☐ 19 Tony Chance
- ☐ 20 J.J. Bautista
- ☐ 21 John Mitchell
- ☐ 22 Vic Hithe
- ☐ 23 Darrell Miller
- ☐ 24 Shane Turner
- ☐ 25 Greg Biagini MGR
- ☐ 26 Dick Bosman CO
- ☐ 27 Danny Boone

1990 Rochester Red Wings Governor's Cup

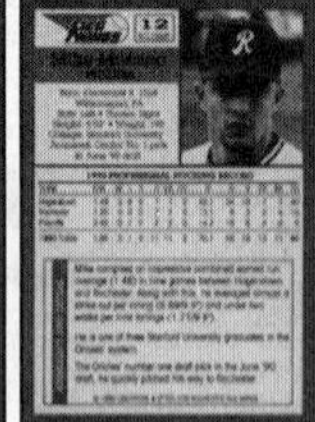

This issue includes the minor league card debut of Mike Mussina. 2,000 sets were produced.

	MINT	NRMT	EXC
COMPLETE SET (36)	40.00	18.00	5.00

- ☐ 1 1990 Governors' Cup Champions
- ☐ 2 David Segui
- ☐ 3 Ben McDonald
- ☐ 4 Chris Hoiles
- ☐ 5 Tim Dulin
- ☐ 6 Leo Gomez
- ☐ 7 Jeff McKnight
- ☐ 8 Donell Nixon
- ☐ 9 Juan Bell
- ☐ 10 Mickey Weston
- ☐ 11 Sam Horn
- ☐ 12 Mike Mussina
- ☐ 13 Jack Tackett
- ☐ 14 Curt Schilling
- ☐ 15 Dan Boone
- ☐ 16 Eric Bell
- ☐ 17 Marty Brown
- ☐ 18 Rob Woodward
- ☐ 19 Tony Chance
- ☐ 20 Mike Linskey
- ☐ 21 Chris Padget
- ☐ 22 Shane Turner
- ☐ 23 Mike Smith
- ☐ 24 Victor Hithe
- ☐ 25 Joaquin Contreras
- ☐ 26 Joel McKeon
- ☐ 27 Brad Komminsk
- ☐ 28 Jose Bautista
- ☐ 29 Francisco de la Rosa
- ☐ 30 Anthony Kelley
- ☐ 31 Ken Shamburg
- ☐ 32 Brian Holton
- ☐ 33 Dan Lunetta GM
- ☐ 34 Greg Biagini MG
- ☐ 35 Dick Bosman CO
- ☐ 36 Jeff Wood TR

1990 Rochester Red Wings ProCards

This 29-card standard-size set of the 1990 Rochester Red Wings, a Class AAA International League affiliate of the Baltimore Orioles, features on its white-bordered fronts posed color player photos set on simulated wood-grain backgrounds. The player's name, position, and team appear within a gold-colored rectangle below the photo. The tan horizontal back is bordered in white and carries the player's name at the top, followed by biography and statistics.

	MINT	NRMT	EXC
COMPLETE SET (29)	7.00	3.10	.85

- ☐ 694 Checklist
- ☐ 695 Jay Aldrich
- ☐ 696 Jose Bautista
- ☐ 697 Eric Bell
- ☐ 698 Dan Boone
- ☐ 699 Ben McDonald
- ☐ 700 John Mitchell
- ☐ 701 Curt Schilling
- ☐ 702 Mike Smith
- ☐ 703 Rob Woodward
- ☐ 704 Chris Hoiles
- ☐ 705 Darrell Miller
- ☐ 706 Jack Tackett
- ☐ 707 Juan Bell
- ☐ 708 Tim Dulin
- ☐ 709 Leo Gomez
- ☐ 710 Jeff McKnight
- ☐ 711 Shane Turner
- ☐ 712 Greg Walker
- ☐ 713 Tony Chance
- ☐ 714 Victor Hithe
- ☐ 715 Donell Nixon
- ☐ 716 Chris Padget
- ☐ 717 Pete Stanicek
- ☐ 718 Mike Linskey
- ☐ 719 Joaquin Contreras
- ☐ 720 Greg Biagini
- ☐ 721 Dick Bosman
- ☐ 722 Paul Blair

1990 Rockford Expos ProCards

This 29-card standard-size set of the 1990 Rockford Expos, a Class A Midwest League affiliate of the Montreal Expos, features on its white-bordered fronts posed color player photos set on simulated wood-grain backgrounds. The player's name, position, and team appear within a gold-colored rectangle below the photo. The tan horizontal back is bordered in white and carries the player's name and position at the top, followed by biography and statistics.

	MINT	NRMT	EXC
COMPLETE SET (29)	5.00	2.20	.60

- ☐ 2683 Checklist
- ☐ 2684 Dan Archibald
- ☐ 2685 Rusty Kilgo
- ☐ 2686 John Thoden
- ☐ 2687 Steve Whitehead
- ☐ 2688 Gary Regira
- ☐ 2689 Joe Logan
- ☐ 2690 Brian Sullivan
- ☐ 2691 Jim Eddy
- ☐ 2692 Brian Wilkinson
- ☐ 2693 Martin Martinez
- ☐ 2694 Doug Bochtler
- ☐ 2695 Chris Bushing
- ☐ 2696 Tim Laker
- ☐ 2697 Rob Leary P/CO
- ☐ 2698 Bill Cramer
- ☐ 2699 Scott Davison
- ☐ 2700 Ron Krause
- ☐ 2701 Deryk Hudson
- ☐ 2702 Michael Grace
- ☐ 2703 J.D. Ramirez
- ☐ 2704 Keith Kaub
- ☐ 2705 Buena Rodriguez
- ☐ 2706 Isaac Elder
- ☐ 2707 Jeff Ramsey
- ☐ 2708 Troy Ricker
- ☐ 2709 Tyrone Woods
- ☐ 2710 Mike Quade MG
- ☐ 2711 Sid Monge CO

1990 Rockford Expos Litho Center

Printed by Rockford Litho Center, this 30-card standard-size (2 1/2" by 3 1/2") set of the 1990 Rockford Expos, a Class A Midwest League affiliate of the Montreal Expos, features on its white-bordered fronts posed color player photos set on red backgrounds. The player's name and position appear within a yellow diagonal stripe at the lower right. The white horizontal back is framed by a black line and carries the player's name, uniform number, and position at the top, followed by biography and the names of the sponsors, WROK radio and Tomorrow is Yesterday. The cards are unnumbered and checklisted below in alphabetical order.

	MINT	NRMT	EXC
COMPLETE SET (30)	6.00	2.70	.75

- ☐ 1 Dan Archibald
- ☐ 2 Doug Bochtler
- ☐ 3 Chris Bushing
- ☐ 4 John Cain TR
- ☐ 5 Bill Cramer
- ☐ 6 Scotty Davison
- ☐ 7 Jim Eddy
- ☐ 8 Isaac Charles Elder
- ☐ 9 Michael Grace
- ☐ 10 Ben Howze
- ☐ 11 Deryk Hudson
- ☐ 12 Rusty Kilgo
- ☐ 13 Ron Krause
- ☐ 14 Tim Laker
- ☐ 15 Rob Leary P/CO
- ☐ 16 Joe Logan
- ☐ 17 Martin Martinez
- ☐ 18 Sid Monge CO
- ☐ 19 Mike Quade MG
- ☐ 20 J.D. Ramirez
- ☐ 21 Jeff Ramsey
- ☐ 22 Gary Regira
- ☐ 23 Troy Ricker
- ☐ 24 Buena Ventura Rodriguez
- ☐ 25 C.L. Smith
- ☐ 26 John Thoden
- ☐ 27 Steve Whitehead
- ☐ 28 Brian Wilkinson
- ☐ 29 Tyrone Woods
- ☐ 30 Team Card

1990 South Atlantic League All-Stars Star

	MINT	NRMT	EXC
COMPLETE SET (48)	10.00	4.50	1.25

- ☐ 1 Mike Arner
- ☐ 2 Jeff Braley
- ☐ 3 Mike Burton
- ☐ 4 Cris Colon
- ☐ 5 Darron Cox
- ☐ 6 Andy Fox
- ☐ 7 Bob Gaddy
- ☐ 8 Mike Garcia
- ☐ 9 John Graves
- ☐ 10 David Hajeck
- ☐ 11 Jeff Hoffman
- ☐ 12 Jonathan Hurst
- ☐ 13 Ramon Jimenez
- ☐ 14 Brian Johnson
- ☐ 15 Chris Limbach
- ☐ 16 Orlando Miller
- ☐ 17 Rudy Pemberton
- ☐ 18 Pat Pesavento
- ☐ 19 Scott Pose
- ☐ 20 Mike Rendina
- ☐ 21 Brian Romero
- ☐ 22 Tony Scruggs
- ☐ 23 Gene Roof MGR
- ☐ 24 Orlando Gomez CO
- ☐ 25 Kelly Sharitt TR
- ☐ 26 Felix Antigua
- ☐ 27 Rob Blumberg
- ☐ 28 Vinicio Castilla
- ☐ 29 Brian Davis
- ☐ 30 Brook Fordyce
- ☐ 31 Roger Hailey
- ☐ 32 James Harris
- ☐ 33 Shawn Holtzclaw
- ☐ 34 Tim Howard
- ☐ 35 Pat Howell
- ☐ 36 Austin Manahan
- ☐ 37 Tito Navarro
- ☐ 38 Mike Ogliaruso
- ☐ 39 William Pennyfeather
- ☐ 40 Craig Pueschner
- ☐ 41 Deron Sample
- ☐ 42 Rick Shackle
- ☐ 43 Don Strange
- ☐ 44 Ken Trusky
- ☐ 45 Joe Vitko
- ☐ 46 Bill Stein MGR
- ☐ 47 Mike Fischlin CO
- ☐ 48 Bob Burton TR

1990 Salem Buccaneers Star

This 27-card standard-size set of the 1990 Salem Buccaneers, a Class A Carolina League affiliate of the Pittsburgh Pirates, features yellow bordered posed color player photos on its fronts. The player's name, team name, and position appear at the bottom. The white horizontal back carries the player's name at the top, followed by biography, career highlights, and statistics.

	MINT	NRMT	EXC
COMPLETE SET (27)	5.00	2.20	.60

- ☐ 1 Robert Bailey
- ☐ 2 Steve Buckholz
- ☐ 3 Tom Deller
- ☐ 4 Chip Duncan
- ☐ 5 Chris Estep
- ☐ 6 Antonio Felix
- ☐ 7 Tim Hines
- ☐ 8 Mike Huyler
- ☐ 9 John Latham
- ☐ 10 Tim McDowell
- ☐ 11 Glen McNabb
- ☐ 12 Domingo Merejo
- ☐ 13 Paul Miller
- ☐ 14 Brian Morrison
- ☐ 15 Darwin Pennye
- ☐ 16 Mike Pomeranz
- ☐ 17 Keith Raisanen
- ☐ 18 Mandy Romero
- ☐ 19 Butch Schlopy
- ☐ 20 Bruce Schreiber
- ☐ 21 Ben Shelton
- ☐ 22 Greg Sims
- ☐ 23 Tim Wakefield
- ☐ 24 Flavio Williams
- ☐ 25 Stan Cliburn MGR
- ☐ 26 Chris Lein CO
- ☐ 27 Sandy Krum TR

1990 Salinas Spurs Cal League Cards

	MINT	NRMT	EXC
COMPLETE SET (32)	5.00	2.20	.60

- ☐ 117 Steve Howe
- ☐ 118 Shigehi Sasaki
- ☐ 119 Seiichi Murakami
- ☐ 120 Kenichi Ootsuka
- ☐ 121 Kouichi Emoto
- ☐ 122 Kenichi Uchiyama
- ☐ 123 Rudy Gardey
- ☐ 124 Quinn Marsh
- ☐ 125 Ray Velasquez
- ☐ 126 Greg Page
- ☐ 127 Carlos Carrasco
- ☐ 128 Steve Maye
- ☐ 129 John Reilly
- ☐ 130 Ed Landphere

☐ 131 Bill Carlson
☐ 132 Greg Mannion
☐ 133 Paul Alegre
☐ 134 Brent Hahn
☐ 135 Jerry Peguero
☐ 136 Steve Meredith
☐ 137 Sean Thompson
☐ 138 Jim Shevlin
☐ 139 Shikato Yanagida
☐ 140 Kenichi Yamanouchi
☐ 141 Yoshiki Ootsuka
☐ 142 Hide Koga MGR
☐ 143 Takayuki Kohno CO
☐ 144 John Jonas GM
☐ 145 Mike Spiers CO
☐ 146 Pete Rowe CO
☐ 147 Yoshi Okamoto OP MGR
☐ 148 Masahiro Kuboto TR

1990 Salinas Spurs ProCards

This 26-card standard-size set of the 1990 Salinas Spurs, a Class A California League Independent, features on its white-bordered fronts posed color player photos set on simulated wood-grain backgrounds. The player's name, position, and team appear within a gold-colored rectangle below the photo. The tan horizontal back is bordered in white and carries the player's name at the top, followed by biography and statistics.

	MINT	NRMT	EXC
COMPLETE SET (26)	5.00	2.20	.60

☐ 2712 Checklist
☐ 2713 Kenichi Uchiyama
☐ 2714 Greg Page
☐ 2715 Kouichi Emoto
☐ 2716 Kenichi Ohtsuka
☐ 2717 Seiichi Murakami
☐ 2718 Carlos Carrasco
☐ 2719 Sigeki Sasaki
☐ 2720 John Reilley
☐ 2721 Quinn Marsh
☐ 2722 Yoshiki Ohtsuka
☐ 2723 Shikato Yanagita
☐ 2724 Kenichi Yamanouchi
☐ 2725 Brent Hahn
☐ 2726 Jose Peguero
☐ 2727 Jim Shevlin
☐ 2728 Ed Landphere
☐ 2729 Paul Alegre
☐ 2730 Bill Carlson
☐ 2731 Wayne Housie
☐ 2732 Scott Jaster
☐ 2733 Corey Paul
☐ 2734 Sean Thompson
☐ 2735 Hide Koga MGR
☐ 2736 Takayuki Kohno
Player/Coach
☐ 2737 Pete Rowe
Player/Coach

1990 San Antonio Missions Grand Slam

	MINT	NRMT	EXC
COMPLETE SET (30)	10.00	4.50	1.25

☐ 1 John Shoemaker MG
☐ 2 Burton Hooton CO
☐ 3 Jon Debus CO
☐ 4 Rob Giesecke TR
☐ 5 Rafael Bournigal
☐ 6 Jerry Brooks
☐ 7 Adam Brown
☐ 8 Kevin Campbell
☐ 9 Ernie Carr
☐ 10 Braulio Castillo
☐ 11 Dale Coleman
☐ 12 Steve Finken
☐ 13 Tom Goodwin
☐ 14 Jeff Hartsock
☐ 15 Mike James
☐ 16 Eric Karros
☐ 17 Isidrio Marquez
☐ 18 Luis Martinez
☐ 19 Dan Opperman
☐ 20 Mike Pitz
☐ 21 Jim Poole
☐ 22 Eddie Pye
☐ 23 Lance Rice
☐ 24 Henry Rodriguez
☐ 25 Homar Rojas
☐ 26 Zak Shinall
☐ 27 Dennis Springer
☐ 28 Mica Valdez
☐ 29 Mike White
☐ 30 James Wray

1990 San Bernardino Spirit Best

This 28-card standard-size set of the 1990 San Bernardino Spirit, a Class A California League affiliate of the Seattle Mariners, features white-bordered posed and action color player photos on its fronts. The player's name and position appear vertically on the left side. The yellow horizontal back carries the player's name and position at the top, followed by biography, career highlights, and statistics. A player head shot appears in the lower right corner

	MINT	NRMT	EXC
COMPLETE SET (28)	5.00	2.20	.60

☐ 1 Roger Salkeld
☐ 2 Rich DeLucia
☐ 3 Calvin Jones
☐ 4 Jim Bennett
☐ 5 Dave Evans
☐ 6 Jeff Keitges
☐ 7 Isaiah Clark
☐ 8 Chuck Kniffin CO
☐ 9 Patrick Lennon
☐ 10 Roberto Del Pozo
☐ 11 Manuel Furcal
☐ 12 Bob Magallanes
☐ 13 Tom Maynard
☐ 14 Greg Pirki
☐ 15 Scott Taylor
☐ 16 Fernando Arguelles
☐ 17 Scott Pitcher
☐ 18 Brian Turang
☐ 19 Steve Murray
Player/Coach
☐ 20 David Smith
☐ 21 Johnny Wiggs
☐ 22 Ray Williams
☐ 23 Jim Newlin
☐ 24 Tim Stargell
☐ 25 Kerry Woodson
☐ 26 Keith Bodie MGR
☐ 27 The Bug
Mascot
☐ 28 Checklist

1990 San Bernardino Spirit Cal League Cards

	MINT	NRMT	EXC
COMPLETE SET (32)	5.00	2.20	.60

☐ 87 Roger Salkeld
☐ 88 Rich Delucia
☐ 89 Jim Newlin
☐ 90 Kerry Woodson
☐ 91 Jim Bennett
☐ 92 Nick Felix
☐ 93 Scott Taylor
☐ 94 Johnny Wiggs
☐ 95 Scott Pitcher
☐ 96 Calvin Jones
☐ 97 Dave Evans
☐ 98 Manuel Furcal
☐ 99 Dave Smith
☐ 100 Fernando Arguelles
☐ 101 Pat Lennon
☐ 102 Tyrone Kingwood
☐ 103 Isaiah Clark
☐ 104 Roberto Del Pozo
☐ 105 Greg Pirkl
☐ 106 Brian Turang
☐ 107 Bobby Magallenes
☐ 108 Tim Stargell
☐ 109 Rich Morales
☐ 110 Jeff Keitges
☐ 111 Ellerton Maynard
☐ 112 Ray Williams
☐ 113 Steve Murray CO
☐ 114 Keith Bodie MGR
☐ 115 Chuck Kniffin CO
☐ 116 Lance Bland TR
☐ xxx The Bug
☐ xxx Robert Harvey
Batboy

1990 San Bernardino Spirit ProCards

This 28-card standard-size set of the 1990 San Bernardino Spirit, a Class A California League affiliate of the Seattle Mariners, features on its white-bordered fronts posed color player photos set on simulated wood-grain backgrounds. The player's name, position, and team appear within a gold-colored rectangle below the photo. The tan horizontal back is bordered in white and carries the player's name at the top, followed by biography and statistics.

	MINT	NRMT	EXC
COMPLETE SET (28)	5.00	2.20	.60

☐ 2624 Checklist
☐ 2625 Jim Bennett
☐ 2626 Rich DeLucia
☐ 2627 Dave Evans
☐ 2628 Manuel Furcal
☐ 2629 Calvin Jones
☐ 2630 Jim Newlin
☐ 2631 Scott Pitcher
☐ 2632 Roger Salkeld
☐ 2633 Scott Taylor
☐ 2634 Johnny Wiggs
☐ 2635 Kerry Woodson
☐ 2636 Fernando Arguelles
☐ 2637 Greg Pirkl
☐ 2638 Isaiah Clark
☐ 2639 Jeff Keitges
☐ 2640 Bob Magallanes
☐ 2641 Tim Stargell
☐ 2642 Brian Turang
☐ 2643 Roberto Del Pozo
☐ 2644 Tyrone Kingwood
☐ 2645 Patrick Lennon
☐ 2646 Ellerton Maynard
☐ 2647 Dave Smith
☐ 2648 Bo Williams
☐ 2649 Keith Bodie MGR
☐ 2650 Chuck Kniffin CO
☐ 2651 Steve Murray CO

1990 San Diego State Aztecs 3D/Autograph Pro Image

	MINT	NRMT	EXC
COMPLETE SET (10)	50.00	22.00	6.25

☐ 1 Kurt Archer
☐ 2 Jeff Barry
☐ 3 Eric Christopherson
☐ 4 Rusty Filter
☐ 5 Brian Grebeck
☐ 6 Kevin Nielsen
☐ 7 Andy Pettersen
☐ 8 Erik Plantenberg
☐ 9 Title Card
☐ 10 3D Poster
3D Glasses

1990 San Jose Giants Best

This 30-card standard-size set of the 1990 San Jose Giants, a Class A California League affiliate of the San Francisco Giants, features white-bordered posed and action color player photos on its fronts. The player's name and position appear vertically on the left side. The yellow horizontal back carries the player's name and position at the top, followed by biography, career highlights, and statistics. A player head shot appears in the lower right corner

	MINT	NRMT	EXC
COMPLETE SET (30)	5.00	2.20	.60

☐ 1 Steve Hosey
☐ 2 Kerry Shaw
☐ 3 Reuben Smiley
☐ 4 Pat Brady
☐ 5 Jeff Brauning
☐ 6 Craig Cala
☐ 7 Royce Clayton
☐ 8 Adell Devenport
☐ 9 John Patterson
☐ 10 Troy Mentzer
☐ 11 Jim Jones
☐ 12 Dan Fernandez
☐ 13 Eddie Tucker
☐ 14 Elanis Westbrook
☐ 15 Jim Myers
☐ 16 Chris Fye
☐ 17 Joel Estes
☐ 18 Don Brock
☐ 19 Gary Sharko
☐ 20 Vince Herring
☐ 21 Brian Dour
☐ 22 John Vuz
☐ 23 Dan Rambo
☐ 24 Kevin Rogers
☐ 25 Dom Johnson
☐ 26 Jeff Morris CO
☐ 27 Scott Wilson
☐ 28 Dick Dietz CO
☐ 29 Tom Spencer MGR
☐ 30 Checklist

1990 San Jose Giants Cal League Cards

	MINT	NRMT	EXC
COMPLETE SET (28)	6.00	2.70	.75

☐ 28 Steve Hosey
☐ 29 Kerry Shaw
☐ 30 Rueben Smiley
☐ 31 Pat Brady
☐ 32 Elanis Westbrooks
☐ 33 John Patterson
☐ 34 Jeff Brauning
☐ 35 Craig Cala
☐ 36 Royce Clayton
☐ 37 Scooter Tucker
☐ 38 Jim Jones
☐ 39 Adell Davenport
☐ 40 Dan Fernandez
☐ 41 Troy Mentzer
☐ 42 Brian Dour
☐ 43 Chris Fye
☐ 44 Dan Rambo
☐ 45 Joel Estes
☐ 46 Gary Sharko
☐ 47 Dominic Johnson
☐ 48 Vince Herring
☐ 49 Jim Myers
☐ 50 Don Brock
☐ 51 Kevin Rogers
☐ 52 John Vuz
☐ 53 Tom Spencer MGR
☐ 54 Jeff Morris CO
☐ 55 Scott Wilson TR

1990 San Jose Giants ProCards

This 30-card standard-size set of the 1990 San Jose Giants, a Class A California League affiliate of the San Francisco Giants, features on its white-bordered fronts posed color player photos set on simulated wood-grain backgrounds. The player's name, position, and team appear within a gold-colored rectangle below the photo. The tan horizontal back is bordered in white and carries the player's name at the top, followed by biography and statistics.

	MINT	NRMT	EXC
COMPLETE SET (30)	5.00	2.20	.60

☐ 2000 Checklist
☐ 2001 John Vuz
☐ 2002 Chris Fye
☐ 2003 Kevin Rogers
☐ 2004 Don Brock
☐ 2005 Gary Sharko
☐ 2006 Dan Rambo
☐ 2007 Joel Estes
☐ 2008 Jim Myers
☐ 2009 Brian Dour
☐ 2010 Vince Herring
☐ 2011 Dom Johnson
☐ 2012 Dan Fernandez
☐ 2013 Troy Mentzer
☐ 2014 Eddie Tucker
☐ 2015 Jeff Brauning
☐ 2016 Jim Jones
☐ 2017 John Patterson
☐ 2018 Royce Clayton
☐ 2019 Adell Davenport
☐ 2020 Kerry Shaw
☐ 2021 Elanis Westbrooks
☐ 2022 Craig Cala
☐ 2023 Pat Brady
☐ 2024 Rueben Smiley
☐ 2025 Steve Hosey
☐ 2026 Tom Spencer MGR
☐ 2027 Dick Dietz CO
☐ 2028 Jeff Morris CO
☐ 2172 Chris Fye
Kevin Rogers

1990 San Jose Giants Star

This 30-card standard-size set of the 1990 San Jose Giants, a Class A California League affiliate of the San Francisco Giants, features orange bordered posed color player photos on its fronts. The player's name, team name, and position appear at the bottom. The white horizontal back carries the player's name at the top, followed by biography, career highlights, and statistics.

	MINT	NRMT	EXC
COMPLETE SET (30)	7.00	3.10	.85

☐ 1 Pat Brady
☐ 2 Jeff Brauning
☐ 3 Don Brock
☐ 4 Craig Cala
☐ 5 Royce Clayton
☐ 6 Adell Davenport
☐ 7 Brian Dour
☐ 8 Joel Estes
☐ 9 Dan Fernandez
☐ 10 Chris Fye
☐ 11 Vince Herring
☐ 12 Steve Hosey
☐ 13 Dominic Johnson
☐ 14 Jim Jones
☐ 15 Troy Mentzer
☐ 16 Jim Myers
☐ 17 John Patterson
☐ 18 Dan Rambo
☐ 19 Kevin Rogers
☐ 20 Gary Sharko
☐ 21 Kerry Shaw
☐ 22 Reuben Smiley
☐ 23 Scooter Tucker
☐ 24 John Vuz
☐ 25 Elanis Westbrooks
☐ 26 San Jose Outfielders
Steve Hosey
Pat Brady
Reuben Smiley
☐ 27 Tom Spencer MGR
☐ 28 Dick Dietz CO
☐ 29 Jeff Morris CO
☐ 30 Scott Wilson TR

1990 Sarasota White Sox Star

This 30-card standard-size set of the 1990 Sarasota White Sox, a Class A Florida State League affiliate of the Chicago White Sox, features blue bordered posed color player photos on its fronts. The player's name, team name, and position appear at the bottom. The white horizontal back carries the player's name at the top, followed by biography, career highlights, and statistics.

	MINT	NRMT	EXC
COMPLETE SET (30)	5.00	2.20	.60

☐ 1 Clemente Alvarez
☐ 2 Wayne Busby
☐ 3 Darrin Campbell
☐ 4 Mark Chasey
☐ 5 Nandi Cruz
☐ 6 Fred Dabney
☐ 7 Mike Davino
☐ 8 Horace Gaither
☐ 9 Mike Galvan
☐ 10 Ramon Garcia
☐ 11 Cliff Gonzalez
☐ 12 Jay Hornacek
☐ 13 Brian Keyser
☐ 14 Rob Lukachyk
☐ 15 Frank Merigliano
☐ 16 Scott Middaugh
☐ 17 Javier Ocasio
☐ 18 Ray Payton
☐ 19 Greg Perschke
☐ 20 Kinnis Pledger
☐ 21 Rob Resnikoff
☐ 22 Ed Smith
☐ 23 Carl Sullivan
☐ 24 Scott Tedder
☐ 25 Jose Ventura
☐ 26 Tony Franklin MGR
☐ 27 Don Cooper CO
☐ 28 Ron Jackson CO
☐ 29 Steve Davis TR
☐ 30 Batboys
Scott Serbin
Daniel Flath

1990 Savannah Cardinals ProCards

This 28-card standard-size set of the 1990 Savannah Cardinals, a Class A South Atlantic League affiliate of the St. Louis Cardinals, features on its white-bordered fronts posed color player photos set on simulated wood-grain backgrounds. The player's name, position, and team appear within a gold-colored rectangle below the photo. The tan horizontal back is bordered in white and carries the player's name at the top, followed by biography and statistics.

	MINT	NRMT	EXC
COMPLETE SET (28)	5.00	2.20	.60

☐ 2057 Checklist
☐ 2058 Jose Arias
☐ 2059 Ernie Baker
☐ 2060 Marcos Betances
☐ 2061 Steve Dixon
☐ 2062 Bill Espinal
☐ 2063 Luis Faccio
☐ 2064 Dennis Fletcher
☐ 2065 Russ Gaston
☐ 2066 Donald Green
☐ 2067 Al Pacheco
☐ 2068 Rick Shackle
☐ 2069 Mark Tolbert
☐ 2070 Tony Ochs
☐ 2071 Joe Turvey
☐ 2072 Ignacio Duran
☐ 2073 Larry Gryskevich
☐ 2074 Mike Keating
☐ 2075 Jim Ferguson
☐ 2076 Nicio Martinez
☐ 2077 Mateo Ozuna
☐ 2078 Kevin Tahan
☐ 2079 Scott Banton
☐ 2080 Cliff Brannon
☐ 2081 Johnny Calzado
☐ 2082 Paul Coleman
☐ 2083 Anthony Lewis
☐ 2084 Field Staff
Rick Colbert MGR
Mark O'Neal TR
Andy Rincon CO

1990 Scranton Red Barons CMC

This 25-card standard-size set of the 1990 Scranton Red Barons, a Class AAA International League affiliate of the Philadelphia Phillies, features white-bordered posed color player photos on its fronts. The player's name and position appear at the bottom; the team name appears vertically on the left. The back carries the league emblem in the white area at the top, the team name in the green stripe below, and player's name, position, biography, and statistics in the yellow area at the bottom. 1,100 sets were produced.

	MINT	NRMT	EXC
COMPLETE SET (25)	5.00	2.20	.60

☐ 1 Eric Boudreaux
☐ 2 Marvin Freeman
☐ 3 Jason Grimsley
☐ 4 Chuck Malone
☐ 5 Dickie Noles
☐ 6 Wally Ritchie
☐ 7 Bob Scanlan
☐ 8 Scott Service
☐ 9 Steve Sharts
☐ 10 John Gibbons
☐ 11 Sal Agostinelli
☐ 12 Jim Adduci
☐ 13 Kelly Heath
☐ 14 Mickey Morandini
☐ 15 Victor Rosario
☐ 16 Steve Stanicek
☐ 17 Jim Vatcher
☐ 18 Bill Dancy MGR
☐ 19 Ron Jones
☐ 20 Chris Knabenshue
☐ 21 Keith Miller
☐ 22 Floyd Rayford CO
☐ 23 Jim Wright CO
☐ 24 Todd Frohwirth
☐ 25 Barney Nugent TR

1990 Scranton Red Barons ProCards

This 24-card standard-size set of the 1990 Scranton Red Barons, a Class AAA International League affiliate of the Philadelphia Phillies, features on its white-bordered fronts posed color player photos set on simulated wood-grain backgrounds. The player's name, position, and team appear within a gold-colored rectangle below the photo. The tan horizontal back is bordered in white and carries the player's name at the top, followed by biography and statistics.

	MINT	NRMT	EXC
COMPLETE SET (24)	5.00	2.20	.60

☐ 591 Checklist
☐ 592 Jose DeJesus
☐ 593 Marvin Freeman
☐ 594 Todd Frohwirth
☐ 595 Jason Grimsley
☐ 596 Chuck Malone
☐ 597 Brad Moore
☐ 598 Wally Ritchie
☐ 599 Bob Scanlan
☐ 600 Scott Service
☐ 601 Steve Sharts
☐ 602 John Gibbons
☐ 603 Tom Nieto
☐ 604 Jim Adduci
☐ 605 Kelly Heath
☐ 606 Mickey Morandini
☐ 607 Victor Rosario
☐ 608 Steve Stanicek
☐ 609 Greg Legg
☐ 610 Ron Jones
☐ 611 Chris Knabenshue
☐ 612 Keith Miller
☐ 613 Jim Vatcher
☐ 614 Jim Wright CO

1990 Shreveport Captains ProCards

This 27-card standard-size set of the 1990 Shreveport Captains, a Class AA Texas League affiliate of the San Francisco Giants, features on its white-bordered fronts posed color player photos set on simulated wood-grain backgrounds. The player's name, position, and team appear within a gold-colored rectangle below the photo. The tan horizontal back is bordered in white and carries the player's name at the top, followed by biography and statistics.

	MINT	NRMT	EXC
COMPLETE SET (27)	5.00	2.20	.60

☐ 1434 Checklist
☐ 1435 Rod Beck
☐ 1436 Mark Dewey
☐ 1437 Steve Connolly
☐ 1438 Bryan Hickerson
☐ 1439 Tom Hostetler
☐ 1440 Steve Lienhard
☐ 1441 Kevin Meier
☐ 1442 Jim Pena
☐ 1443 Steve Reed
☐ 1444 Mike Remlinger
☐ 1445 Steve Decker
☐ 1446 Mark Owens
☐ 1447 Mike Ham
☐ 1448 Rich Aldrete
☐ 1449 Andres Santana
☐ 1450 Juan Guerrero
☐ 1451 Steve Hecht
☐ 1452 Randy Strijek
☐ 1453 Dave Patterson
☐ 1454 Tom Ealy
☐ 1455 Rick Nelson
☐ 1456 Ted Wood
☐ 1457 Jamie Cooper
☐ 1458 Bill Evers MGR
☐ 1459 Tony Taylor CO
☐ 1460 Todd Oakes CO

1990 Shreveport Captains Star

This 27-card standard-size set of the 1990 Shreveport Captains, a Class AA Texas League affiliate of the San Francisco Giants, features purple bordered posed color player photos on its fronts. The player's name, team name, and position appear at the bottom. The white horizontal back carries the player's name at the top, followed by biography, career highlights, and statistics.

	MINT	NRMT	EXC
COMPLETE SET (27)	5.00	2.20	.60

☐ 1 Rich Aldrete
☐ 2 Rod Beck
☐ 3 Steve Connolly
☐ 4 Jamie Cooper
☐ 5 Steve Decker
☐ 6 Mark Dewey
☐ 7 Tom Ealy
☐ 8 Juan Guerrero
☐ 9 Mike Ham
☐ 10 Steve Hecht
☐ 11 Bryan Hickerson
☐ 12 Tom Hostetler
☐ 13 Erik Johnson
☐ 14 Steve Leinhard
☐ 15 Kevin Meier
☐ 16 Rick Nelson
☐ 17 Mark Owens
☐ 18 Dave Patterson
☐ 19 Jim Pena
☐ 20 Steve Reed
☐ 21 Mike Remlinger
☐ 22 Andres Santana
☐ 23 Randy Strijek
☐ 24 Ted Wood
☐ 25 Bill Evers MGR
☐ 26 Todd Oakes CO
☐ 27 Tony Taylor CO

1990 Southern Cal Trojans Smokey

This 12-card set was sponsored by the USDA Forest Service in conjunction with other federal agencies. The standard-size cards have on their fronts black and white photos of outstanding players (except for legendary coach Rod Dedeaux) from past USC baseball teams who went on to play in the major Leagues. The team name and player information appear in maroon stripes above and below the picture. A yellow stripe on the bottom and right side of the picture serve as a shadow border. School and Smokey logos superimposed on the picture round out the card face. In black lettering on white, each back has career summary and a fire prevention cartoon starring Smokey. The cards are unnumbered and checklisted below in alphabetical order, with the player's number after the name. The set was also issued as a an uncut sheet, with three rows of four cards each. The card sets were given away to the first 1,000 fans who attended any game during a series between USC and Stanford, February 23-25, at Dedeaux Field.

	MINT	NRMT	EXC
COMPLETE SET (12)	10.00	4.50	1.25

☐ 1 Don Buford
☐ 2 Steve Busby
☐ 3 Rich Dauer
☐ 4 Rod Dedeaux CO
☐ 5 Ron Fairly
☐ 6 Steve Kemp
☐ 7 Dave Kingman
☐ 8 Bill Lee
☐ 9 Fred Lynn
☐ 10 Mark McGwire
☐ 11 Tom Seaver
☐ 12 Roy Smalley

1990 South Bend White Sox Best

This 29-card standard-size set of the 1990 South Bend White Sox, a Class A Midwest League affiliate of the Chicago White Sox,features white-bordered posed and action color player photos on its fronts. The player's name and position appear vertically on the left side. The yellow horizontal back carries the player's name and position at the top, followed by biography, career highlights, and statistics. A player head shot appears in the lower right corner

	MINT	NRMT	EXC
COMPLETE SET (29)	5.00	2.20	.60

☐ 1 Len Brutcher
☐ 2 Scott Cepicky
☐ 3 John Hairston
☐ 4 David Vanwinkle
☐ 5 Jeff Ingram
☐ 6 Leo Tejada
☐ 7 Ron Plemmons
☐ 8 Jorge Ramos
☐ 9 Joe Singley
☐ 10 Richard Long
☐ 11 Craig Teter
☐ 12 Dennis Walker
☐ 13 Jerry Wolak
☐ 14 John Zaksek
☐ 15 Greg Kobza
☐ 16 Steve Schrenk
☐ 17 Mike Mitchner
☐ 18 Michael Eatinger
☐ 19 Thomas Forrester
☐ 20 Danny Matznick
☐ 21 Michael Mongiello
☐ 22 Scott Stevens
☐ 23 Bill Vanderwel
☐ 24 Rick Patterson MGR
☐ 25 Scott Johnson TR
☐ 26 Mike Barnett CO
☐ 27 Kirk Champion CO
☐ 28 Robert Wickman
☐ 29 Jim Reinebold
Checklist

1990 South Bend White Sox Grand Slam

	MINT	NRMT	EXC
COMPLETE SET (30)	5.00	2.20	.60

☐ 1 Lenny Brutcher
☐ 2 Scott Cepicky
☐ 3 Mike Eatinger
☐ 4 Tom Forrester
☐ 5 John Hairston
☐ 6 Jeff Ingram
☐ 7 Earnie Johnson
☐ 8 Scott Johnson TR
☐ 9 Rich Long
☐ 10 Dan Matznick
☐ 11 Mike Mitchener
☐ 12 Mike Mongiello
☐ 13 Ron Plemmons
☐ 14 Jorge Ramos
☐ 15 Johnny Ruffin
☐ 16 Steve Schrenk
☐ 17 Scott Stevens
☐ 18 Eugenio Tejada
☐ 19 Dave Vanwinkle
☐ 20 Dennis Walker
☐ 21 Jerry Wolak
☐ 22 John Zaksek
☐ 23 Frank Campos
☐ 24 Greg Kobza
☐ 25 Joe Singley
☐ 26 Craig Teter
☐ 27 Rick Patterson MG
☐ 28 Kirk Champion CO
☐ 29 Jim Reinebold CO
☐ 30 Mike Barnett CO

1990 Southern Oregon A's Best

This 30-card standard-size set of the 1990 Southern Oregon A's, a Class A South Atlantic League affiliate of the Oakland Athletics, features white-bordered posed and action color player photos on its fronts. The player's name and position appear vertically on the left side. The yellow horizontal back carries the player's name and position at the top, followed by biography, career highlights, and statistics. A player head shot appears in the lower right corner

	MINT	NRMT	EXC
COMPLETE SET (30)	5.00	2.20	.60

☐ 1 Todd Van Poppel
☐ 2 Eric Helfand
☐ 3 Kirk Dressendorfer
☐ 4 Kevin Dattaola
☐ 5 Doug Johns
☐ 6 Luis Lan Franco
☐ 7 Bill Picketts
☐ 8 Todd Revenig
☐ 9 Craig Sudbury
☐ 10 Eric Booker
☐ 11 Jim Dillon
☐ 12 Manny Martinez
☐ 13 Jeff Clifford
☐ 14 Chaon Garland
☐ 15 Ernie Young
☐ 16 Mark Craft
☐ 17 Curtis Shaw
☐ 18 Chris Hart
☐ 19 Carlos Salazar
☐ 20 Craig Connolly
☐ 21 Dan Vizzini
☐ 22 Brad Brimhall
☐ 23 Dave Tripp
☐ 24 Dave Zancanaro
☐ 25 Don Peters
☐ 26 Mike Muhlethaler
☐ 27 Eric Myers
☐ 28 Glen Osinski
☐ 29 Scott Henry
☐ 30 Checklist
Grady Fuson MGR
Scott Budner

1990 Southern Oregon A's ProCards

This 30-card standard-size set of the 1990 Southern Oregon A's, a Class A South Atlantic League affiliate of the Oakland Athletics, features on its white-bordered fronts posed color player photos set on simulated wood-grain backgrounds. The player's name, position, and team appear within a gold-colored rectangle below the photo. The tan horizontal back is bordered in white and carries the player's name at the top, followed by biography and statistics.

	MINT	NRMT	EXC
COMPLETE SET (30)	5.00	2.20	.60

☐ 3421 Checklist
☐ 3422 Todd Van Poppel
☐ 3423 Dave Zancanaro
☐ 3424 Don Peters
☐ 3425 Kirk Dressendorfer
☐ 3426 Eric Helfand
☐ 3427 Curtis Shaw
☐ 3428 Chaon Garland
☐ 3429 Eric Booker
☐ 3430 Craig Sudbury
☐ 3431 Chris Hart
☐ 3432 Luis Lan Franco
☐ 3433 Manny Martinez
☐ 3434 Rafael Mercado
☐ 3435 Bill Picketts
☐ 3436 Carlos Salazar
☐ 3437 Carlos Tamarez
☐ 3438 Ernie Young
☐ 3439 Brad Brimhall
☐ 3440 Jeff Clifford
☐ 3441 Craig Connolly
☐ 3442 Mark Craft
☐ 3443 Jim Dillon
☐ 3444 Eric Myers
☐ 3445 Todd Revenig
☐ 3446 Dave Tripp
☐ 3447 Dan Vizzini
☐ 3448 Mike Muhlethaler
☐ 3449 Grady Fuson MGR
☐ 3450 Scott Budner CO

1990 Spartanburg Phillies Best

This 30-card standard-size set of the 1990 Spartanburg Phillies, a Class A South Atlantic League affiliate of the Philadelphia Phillies, features white-bordered posed and action color player photos on its fronts. The player's name and position appear vertically on the left side. The yellow horizontal back carries the player's name and position at the top, followed by biography, career highlights, and statistics. A player head shot appears in the lower right corner

	MINT	NRMT	EXC
COMPLETE SET (30)	5.00	2.20	.60

☐ 1 Tom Hardgrove
☐ 2 Paul Fletcher
☐ 3 Robert Gaddy
☐ 4 Darrell Goedhart
☐ 5 Todd Goergen
☐ 6 Greg Gunderson
☐ 7 Chris Limbach
☐ 8 Matt Stevens
☐ 9 Michael Sullivan
☐ 10 Bob Wells
☐ 11 Scott Wiegandt
☐ 12 Brian Adams
☐ 13 Matt Current
☐ 14 Tim Churchill
☐ 15 John Escobar
☐ 16 Donnie Elliott
☐ 17 Eduardo Ortega
☐ 18 Nick Santa Cruz
☐ 19 Dana Brown
☐ 20 Antonio Linares
☐ 21 Dan Shannon
☐ 22 Joe Urbon
☐ 23 Gil Valencia
☐ 24 Dan Welch
☐ 25 Mel Roberts MGR
☐ 26 Buzz Capra CO
☐ 27 Rick Jones CO
☐ 28 Tom Marsh
☐ 29 Rick Zolzer MGR
☐ 30 Craig Strobel
Checklist

1990 Spartanburg Phillies ProCards

This 29-card standard-size set of the 1990 Spartanburg Phillies, a Class A South Atlantic League affiliate of the Philadelphia Phillies, features on its white-bordered fronts posed color player photos set on simulated wood-grain backgrounds. The player's name, position, and team appear within a gold-colored rectangle below the photo. The tan horizontal back is bordered in white and carries the player's name at the top, followed by biography and statistics.

	MINT	NRMT	EXC
COMPLETE SET (29)	5.00	2.20	.60

☐ 2481 Checklist
☐ 2482 Donnie Elliott
☐ 2483 Paul Fletcher
☐ 2484 Robert Gaddy
☐ 2485 Darrell Goedhart
☐ 2486 Todd Goergen
☐ 2487 Greg Gunderson
☐ 2488 Chris Limbach
☐ 2489 Matt Stevens
☐ 2490 Mike Sullivan
☐ 2491 Bob Wells
☐ 2492 Scott Wiegandt
☐ 2493 Brian Adams
☐ 2494 Matt Current
☐ 2495 Tom Marsh
☐ 2496 Tim Churchill
☐ 2497 John Escobar
☐ 2498 Tom Hardgrove
☐ 2499 Eduardo Ortega
☐ 2500 Eulogio Perez
☐ 2501 Nick Santa Cruz
☐ 2502 Dana Brown
☐ 2503 Antonio Linares
☐ 2504 Dan Shannon
☐ 2505 Joe Urbon
☐ 2506 Gil Valencia
☐ 2507 Dan Welch
☐ 2508 Mel Roberts MGR ,
Buzz Capra CO
☐ 2509 Rick Jones CO

1990 Spartanburg Phillies Star

This 29-card standard-size set of the 1990 Spartanburg Phillies, a Class A South Atlantic League affiliate of the Philadelphia Phillies, features red bordered posed color player photos on its fronts. The player's name, team name, and position appear at the bottom. The white horizontal back carries the player's name at the top, followed by biography, career highlights, and statistics.

	MINT	NRMT	EXC
COMPLETE SET (29)	5.00	2.20	.60

☐ 1 Brian Adams
☐ 2 Dana Brown
☐ 3 Tim Churchill
☐ 4 Matt Current
☐ 5 Donnie Elliott
☐ 6 John Escobar
☐ 7 Paul Fletcher
☐ 8 Robert Gaddy
☐ 9 Darrell Goedhart
☐ 10 Todd Goergen
☐ 11 Greg Gunderson
☐ 12 Tom Hardgrove
☐ 13 Chris Limbach
☐ 14 Antonio Linares
☐ 15 Tom Marsh
☐ 16 Eduardo Ortega
☐ 17 Eulogio Perez
☐ 18 Nick Santa Cruz
☐ 19 Dan Shannon
☐ 20 Matt Stevens
☐ 21 Michael Sullivan
☐ 22 Joe Urbon
☐ 23 Gil Valencia
☐ 24 Dan Welch
☐ 25 Bob Wells
☐ 26 Scott Wiegandt
☐ 27 Coaching Staff
Mel Roberts MGR
Buzz Capra CO
Rick Jones CO
☐ 28 Craig Strobeo TR
☐ 29 Rick Zulzer GM

1990 Spokane Indians Sports Pro

This 28-card standard-size set of the 1990 Spokane Indians, a Class A Northwest League affiliate of the San Diego Padres, features posed color head-and-shoulders shots, with thin black borders on a white card face. The horizontally oriented backs have biographical information. The cards are numbered on the back.

	MINT	NRMT	EXC
COMPLETE SET (28)	6.00	2.70	.75

☐ 1 Keith McKoy
☐ 2 Jeff Ordway
☐ 3 Rusty Silcox
☐ 4 Tony Mortensen
☐ 5 Larry Hawks
☐ 6 Bill Ostermeyer
☐ 7 Russ Garside
☐ 8 Dave Adams
☐ 9 Rob Hays
☐ 10 Brent Bish
☐ 11 Jim Elliott
☐ 12 Jay Gainer
☐ 13 Steve Siebert
☐ 14 Scott Sanders
☐ 15 Jim West
☐ 16 Scott Fredrickson
☐ 17 Jeff Pearce
☐ 18 Mike Bradley
☐ 19 Matt Mieske
☐ 20 Julio Bruno
☐ 21 Lance Painter
☐ 22 Bruce Bensching
☐ 23 Kevin Farlow
☐ 24 Darius Gash
☐ 25 Ryan Thibault
☐ 26 Gene Glynn MG
☐ 27 Bruce Tanner CO
☐ 28 Kevin Towers CO

1990 Springfield Cardinals Best

This 29-card standard-size set of the 1990 Springfield Cardinals, a Class A Midwest League affiliate of the St. Louis Cardinals, features white-bordered posed and action color player photos on its fronts. The player's name and position appear vertically on the left side. The yellow horizontal back carries the player's name and position at the top, followed by biography, career highlights, and statistics. A player head shot appears in the lower right corner

	MINT	NRMT	EXC
COMPLETE SET (29)	5.00	2.20	.60

☐ 1 Juan Andujar
☐ 2 Alvin Rittman
☐ 3 David Bell
☐ 4 Randy Berlin
☐ 5 Alan Botkin
☐ 6 Mike Campas
☐ 7 Troy Clemens
☐ 8 Joe Federico
☐ 9 Ezequiel Herrera
☐ 10 Vince Kindred
☐ 11 Mike Kraft
☐ 12 Carlos Landinez
☐ 13 Fred Langiotti
☐ 14 Luis Martinez
☐ 15 Orlando Thomas
☐ 16 Tim Lata
☐ 17 Tom Infante
☐ 18 Clyde Keller
☐ 19 Mike Hensley
☐ 20 Chris Gorton
☐ 21 Steve Gewecke
☐ 22 John Corona
☐ 23 Frank Cimorelli
☐ 24 Ron Weber
☐ 25 Dennis Wiseman
☐ 26 Keith Champion MGR
☐ 27 Roger Erickson CO
☐ 28 Mike Evans TR
☐ 29 Checklist

1990 Springfield Cardinals All Decade Best

This 36-card standard-size set of the 1990 Springfield Cardinals, a Class A Midwest League affiliate of the St. Louis Cardinals, features white-bordered posed and action color player photos on its fronts. The player's name and position appear vertically on the left side. The words "All Decade" appear across the top. The yellow horizontal back carries the player's name and years played at the top, followed by player's history, highlights, and statistics. 2,500 sets were produced.

	MINT	NRMT	EXC
COMPLETE SET (36)	8.00	3.60	1.00

☐ 1 Todd Zeile
☐ 2 Craig Wilson
☐ 3 Harry McCulla
☐ 4 Tom Amante
☐ 5 Frankie Batista
☐ 6 Ed Tanner
☐ 7 Alan Hunsinger
☐ 8 Tom Dozier
☐ 9 Danny Cox
☐ 10 John Costello
☐ 11 Jeff Oyster
☐ 12 John Young
☐ 13 Matt Kinzer
☐ 14 Joe Boever
☐ 15 Mike Hartley
☐ 16 Paul Wilmet
☐ 17 Pat Perry
☐ 18 Scott Arnold
☐ 19 Dale Kisten
☐ 20 Steve Peters
☐ 21 Robert Faron
☐ 22 Dave Bialas MGR
☐ 23 Tom Baine
☐ 24 Ray Lankford
☐ 25 Mike Perez
☐ 26 Mike Milchin
☐ 27 Gaylen Pitts MGR
☐ 28 Bob Geren
☐ 29 Jim Lindeman
☐ 30 Curt Ford
☐ 31 Vince Coleman
☐ 32 Bill Lyons
☐ 33 Randy Hunt
☐ 34 Mike Fitzgerald
☐ 35 Tom Pagnozzi
☐ 36 Checklist

1990 St. Catharines Blue Jays ProCards

This 34-card standard-size set of the 1990 St. Catharines Blue Jays, a Class A New York-Penn League affiliate of the Toronto Blue Jays, features on its white-bordered fronts posed color player photos set on simulated wood-grain backgrounds. The player's name, position, and team appear within a gold-colored rectangle below the photo. The tan horizontal back is bordered in white and carries the player's name and position at the top, followed by biography and statistics. This issue includes Steve Karsay's minor league team set debut.

	MINT	NRMT	EXC
COMPLETE SET (34)	14.00	6.25	1.75

☐ 3451 Checklist
☐ 3452 Matt Hudik
☐ 3453 Juan Querecuto
☐ 3454 Carlos Delgado
☐ 3455 Edgar Marquez
☐ 3456 Robert Perez
☐ 3457 Tom Singer
☐ 3458 Scott Brow
☐ 3459 Sam Mandia
☐ 3460 Matt Watson
☐ 3461 Joe Ganote
☐ 3462 Frank Kowar
☐ 3463 Dave Marcon
☐ 3464 Paul Menhart
☐ 3465 Bobby Aylmer
☐ 3466 Rob Montalvo
☐ 3467 Ciro Ambrosio
☐ 3468 Rusty Filter
☐ 3469 Allen Rhea
☐ 3470 Huck Flener
☐ 3471 David Tollison
☐ 3472 Steve Karsay
☐ 3473 Rick Steed
☐ 3474 Mike Taylor
☐ 3475 Jeff Irish
☐ 3476 Andy Carlton
☐ 3477 Wally Heckel
☐ 3478 Wilberto Rojas
☐ 3479 Anton Mobley
☐ 3480 Shawn Scott
☐ 3481 Jacinto Yorro
☐ 3482 Doug Ault MG
☐ 3483 Mike McAlpin CO
☐ 3484 Darren Balsley CO

1990 St. Lucie Mets Star

This 31-card standard-size set of the 1990 St. Lucie Mets, a Class A Florida State League affiliate of the New York Mets, features blue bordered posed color player photos on its fronts. The player's name, team name, and position appear at the bottom. The white horizontal back carries the player's name at the top, followed by biography, career highlights, and statistics.

	MINT	NRMT	EXC
COMPLETE SET (31)	5.00	2.20	.60

☐ 1 Mike Brady
☐ 2 Kevin Brown
☐ 3 Chris Butterfield
☐ 4 Archie Corbin
☐ 5 Joe Dellicarri
☐ 6 D.J. Dozier
☐ 7 Dan Furmanik
☐ 8 Kenny Graves
☐ 9 Denny Harriger
☐ 10 Chris Hill
☐ 11 Paul Johnson
☐ 12 John Johnstone
☐ 13 Jim Kelly
☐ 14 Vega Marina
☐ 15 Lee May Jr.
☐ 16 Loy McBride
☐ 17 Jim Morrisette
☐ 18 Steve Newton
☐ 19 Bob Olah
☐ 20 Vladimir Perez
☐ 21 Andy Reich
☐ 22 Nikco Reisgo
☐ 23 Bryan Rogers
☐ 24 Doug Saunders
☐ 25 Pete Schourek
☐ 26 Derrick Young
☐ 27 Alan Zinter
Sic, Mike
☐ 28 Tim Blackwell
☐ 29 Joel Horlen
☐ 30 Steve Jacobucci
☐ 31 Marc Goldberg

1990 St. Pete Cardinals Star

This 26-card standard-size set of the 1990 St. Pete Cardinals, a Class A Florida State League affiliate of the St. Louis Cardinals, features red bordered posed color player photos on its fronts. The player's name, team name, and position appear at the bottom. The white horizontal back carries the player's name at the top, followed by biography, career highlights, and statistics.

	MINT	NRMT	EXC
COMPLETE SET (26)	5.00	2.20	.60

☐ 1 Ed Carter
☐ 2 Mark Clark
☐ 3 Tripp Cromer
☐ 4 Bobby DeLoach
☐ 5 Brad DuVall
☐ 6 John Ericks
☐ 7 Jose Fernandez
☐ 8 Mike Fiore
☐ 9 Steve Graham
☐ 10 Antron Grier
☐ 11 David Grimes
☐ 12 Henry Hernandez
☐ 13 Daniel Hitt
☐ 14 Lonnie Maclin
☐ 15 Steffen Majer
☐ 16 Tim Meamber
☐ 17 Mike Milchin
☐ 18 Lee Plemel
☐ 19 Tim Redman
☐ 20 Dave Richardson
☐ 21 Cory Satterfield
☐ 22 John Sellick
☐ 23 Jeff Shireman
☐ 24 Jose Trujillo
☐ 25 Dean Weese
☐ 26 Coaches
Joe Pettini
Jay North

1990 Star

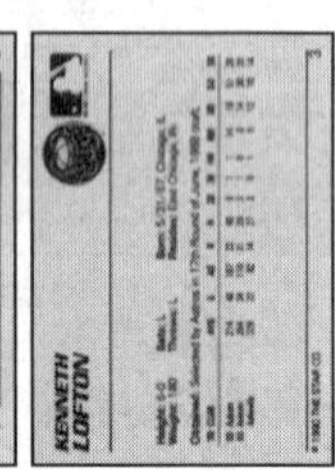

This 100-card set was issued wax packs and features yellow bordered color player photos on its fronts. The player's name, team name, and position appear at the bottom. The yellow horizontal back carries the player's name and team name at the top, followed by biography, career highlights, and statistics.

	MINT	NRMT	EXC
COMPLETE SET (100)	10.00	4.50	1.25
COMMON CARD (1-100)	.05	.02	.01
☐ 1 Bruce Schreiber	.05	.02	.01
☐ 2 Jeff Juden	.05	.02	.01
☐ 3 Kenny Lofton	1.25	.55	.16
☐ 4 Scott Makarewicz	.05	.02	.01
☐ 5 Al Sanders	.05	.02	.01
☐ 6 Rod Boddie	.05	.02	.01
☐ 7 Jim Faulk	.05	.02	.01
☐ 8 Dan Freed	.05	.02	.01
☐ 9 D.J. Dozier	.05	.02	.01
☐ 10 Nikco Riesgo	.05	.02	.01
☐ 11 Alan Zinter	.05	.02	.01
☐ 12 Jim Bruske	.05	.02	.01
☐ 13 Mark Lewis	.10	.05	.01
☐ 14 Willie Ansley	.05	.02	.01
☐ 15 Tony Eusebio	.05	.02	.01
☐ 16 Luis Gonzalez	.10	.05	.01
☐ 17 Andy Mota	.05	.02	.01
☐ 18 Tony Barron	.05	.02	.01
☐ 19 Kevin Maas	.05	.02	.01
☐ 20 Anthony Collier	.05	.02	.01
☐ 21 Ramon Taveras	.05	.02	.01
☐ 22 Eric Young	.10	.05	.01
☐ 23 Earl Cunningham	.05	.02	.01
☐ 24 Barry Manuel	.05	.02	.01
☐ 25 David Perez	.05	.02	.01
☐ 26 Ivan Rodriguez	1.25	.55	.16
☐ 27 Fred Samson	.05	.02	.01
☐ 28 Ben McDonald	.10	.05	.01
☐ 29 Blas Minor	.05	.02	.01
☐ 30 Jeff Bagwell	2.50	1.10	.30
☐ 31 Mike Twardoski	.05	.02	.01
☐ 32 T.R. Lewis	.05	.02	.01
☐ 33 Ron Cook	.05	.02	.01
☐ 34 Ivan Cruz	.05	.02	.01
☐ 35 Jody Hurst	.05	.02	.01
☐ 36 Keith Kimberlin	.05	.02	.01
☐ 37 Lino Rivera	.05	.02	.01
☐ 38 Mike Tresh	.05	.02	.01
☐ 39 Hernan Cortes	.05	.02	.01
☐ 40 Jay Knoblauh	.05	.02	.01
☐ 41 Larry Stanford	.05	.02	.01
☐ 42 Hector Vargas	.05	.02	.01
☐ 43 Jacob Brumfield	.05	.02	.01
☐ 44 Mark Parnell	.05	.02	.01
☐ 45 Willie Banks	.05	.02	.01
☐ 46 Reed Olmstead	.05	.02	.01
☐ 47 Mike Redding	.05	.02	.01
☐ 48 Rich DeLucia	.05	.02	.01
☐ 49 Mike Gardiner	.05	.02	.01
☐ 50 Royal Clayton	.05	.02	.01
☐ 51 Darrin Chapin	.05	.02	.01
☐ 52 Mitch Lyden	.05	.02	.01
☐ 53 Don Sparks	.05	.02	.01
☐ 54 Bernie Williams	1.25	.55	.16
☐ 55 Steve Dunn	.10	.05	.01
☐ 56 Alan Newman	.05	.02	.01
☐ 57 Brent McCoy	.05	.02	.01
☐ 58 Mike Galvan	.05	.02	.01
☐ 59 Greg Perschke	.05	.02	.01
☐ 60 Rob Resnikoff	.05	.02	.01
☐ 61 Sammy Sosa	2.00	.90	.25
☐ 62 Bobby DeLoach	.05	.02	.01
☐ 63 Jesse Cross	.05	.02	.01
☐ 64 Ray Giannelli	.05	.02	.01
☐ 65 Jeff Kent	.15	.07	.02
☐ 66 Greg O'Halloran	.05	.02	.01
☐ 67 Mike Timlin	.05	.02	.01
☐ 68 Brian McRae	.25	.11	.03
☐ 69 Anthony Ward	.05	.02	.01
☐ 70 Toby Borland	.05	.02	.01
☐ 71 Joe Millette	.05	.02	.01
☐ 72 Tony Trevino	.05	.02	.01
☐ 73 Anthony Kelley	.05	.02	.01
☐ 74 George Kerfut	.05	.02	.01
☐ 75 Scott Meadows	.05	.02	.01
☐ 76 Luis Mercedes	.05	.02	.01
☐ 77 Dan Barbara	.05	.02	.01
☐ 78 Rod Poissant	.05	.02	.01
☐ 79 Gary Alexander	.05	.02	.01
☐ 80 Bob Ayrault	.05	.02	.01
☐ 81 Kim Batiste	.05	.02	.01
☐ 82 Pete Alborano	.05	.02	.01
☐ 83 Scott Centala	.05	.02	.01
☐ 84 Stu Cole	.05	.02	.01
☐ 85 Jeff Conine	.40	.18	.05
☐ 86 Bobby Moore	.05	.02	.01
☐ 87 Jorge Pedre	.05	.02	.01
☐ 88 Mike Muksudian	.05	.02	.01
☐ 89 Jerry Schunk	.05	.02	.01
☐ 90 William Suero	.05	.02	.01
☐ 91 Eddie Zosky	.05	.02	.01
☐ 92 Jeff Holman	.05	.02	.01
☐ 93 Ramon Jimenez	.05	.02	.01
☐ 94 Michael Bell	.05	.02	.01
☐ 95 Thomas Redington	.05	.02	.01
☐ 96 Mike Arner	.05	.02	.01
☐ 97 Brian Romero	.05	.02	.01
☐ 98 Tony Scruggs	.05	.02	.01
☐ 99 James Harris	.05	.02	.01
☐ 100 Tito Navarro	.05	.02	.01

1990 Stockton Ports Best

This 29-card standard-size set of the 1990 Stockton Ports, a Class A California League affiliate of the Milwaukee Brewers, features white-bordered posed and action color player photos on its fronts. The player's name and position appear vertically on the left side. The yellow horizontal back carries the player's name and position at the top, followed by biography, career highlights, and statistics. A player head shot appears in the lower right corner

	MINT	NRMT	EXC
COMPLETE SET (29)	5.00	2.20	.60

☐ 1 Cal Eldred
☐ 2 Dave Nilsson
☐ 3 Steve Diaz
☐ 4 Bob Kappesser
☐ 5 Pat Listach
☐ 6 Remigio Diaz
☐ 7 Frank Bolick
☐ 8 Mike Guerrero
☐ 9 Sylvester Love
☐ 10 Jim Sass
☐ 11 John Finn
☐ 12 Ken Jackson
☐ 13 Tim Raley
☐ 14 Chris Cassels
☐ 15 Chris Johnson
☐ 16 Mike Ignasiak
☐ 17 Dave Fitzgerald
☐ 18 Juan Uribe
☐ 19 Scott Hamilton
☐ 20 Kevin Carmody
☐ 21 Jamie Cangemi
☐ 22 Guillermo Sandoval
☐ 23 Ron Hanisch
☐ 24 Leo Perez
☐ 25 Angel Miranda
☐ 26 Bo Dodson
☐ 27 Chris Bando MGR
☐ 28 Mitch Zwolensky CO
☐ 29 Checklist

1990 Stockton Ports Cal League Cards

	MINT	NRMT	EXC
COMPLETE SET (29)	5.00	2.20	.60

☐ 170 Juan Uribe
☐ 174 Cal Eldred
☐ 175 Angel Miranda
☐ 176 Chris Johnson
☐ 177 Mike Ignasiak
☐ 178 Dave Fitzgerald
☐ 180 Scott Hamilton
☐ 181 Kevin Carmody
☐ 182 Jamie Cangemi
☐ 183 Guillermo Sandoval
☐ 184 Doug Henry
☐ 185 Curt Krippner
☐ 186 Leo Perez
☐ 187 Dave Nilsson
☐ 188 Steve Diaz
☐ 189 Bob Kappesser
☐ 190 Bo Dodson
☐ 191 Pat Listach
☐ 192 Remigio Diaz
☐ 193 Frank Bolick
☐ 194 Sylvester Love
☐ 195 Jim Sass
☐ 196 John Finn
☐ 197 Ken Jackson
☐ 198 Tim Raley
☐ 199 Chris Cassels
☐ 200 Chris Bando
☐ 201 Mitch Zwolensky
☐ 202 Ron Hanisch

1990 Stockton Ports ProCards

This 29-card standard-size set of the 1990 Stockton Ports, a Class A California League affiliate of the Milwaukee Brewers, features on its white-bordered fronts posed color player photos set on simulated wood-grain backgrounds. The player's name, position, and team appear within a gold-colored rectangle below the photo. The tan horizontal back is bordered in white and carries the player's name at the top, followed by biography and statistics.

	MINT	NRMT	EXC
COMPLETE SET (29)	5.00	2.20	.60

☐ 2173 Checklist
☐ 2174 Chris Johnson
☐ 2175 Angel Miranda
☐ 2176 Mike Ignasiak
☐ 2177 Dave Fitzgerald
☐ 2178 Calvin Eldred
☐ 2179 Juan Uribe
☐ 2180 Scott Hamilton
☐ 2181 Kevin Carmody
☐ 2182 Jamie Cangemi
☐ 2183 Guillermo Sandoval
☐ 2184 Curt Krippner
☐ 2185 Leo Perez
☐ 2186 Dave Nilsson
☐ 2187 Steve Diaz
☐ 2188 Bob Kappesser
☐ 2189 Bo Dodson
☐ 2190 Pat Listach
☐ 2191 Remigio Diaz
☐ 2192 Frank Bolick
☐ 2193 Mike Guerrero
☐ 2194 Sylvester Love
☐ 2195 James Sass
☐ 2196 John Finn
☐ 2197 Kenny Jackson
☐ 2198 Tim Raley
☐ 2199 Chris Cassels
☐ 2200 Chris Bando MGR
☐ 2201 Mitch Zwolensky CO

1990 Sumter Braves Best

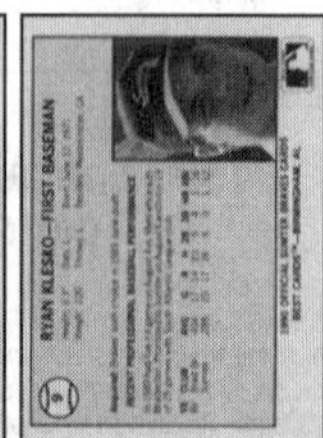

This 30-card standard-size set of the 1990 Sumter Braves, a Class A South Atlantic League affiliate of the Atlanta Braves, features white-bordered posed and action color player photos on its fronts. The player's name and position appear vertically on the left side. The yellow horizontal back carries the player's name and position at the top, followed by biography, career highlights, and statistics. A player head shot appears in the lower right corner. This issue includes the minor league card debuts of Ryan Klesko and Vinny Castilla.

	MINT	NRMT	EXC
COMPLETE SET (30)	30.00	13.50	3.70

☐ 1 Tyler Houston
☐ 2 Tab Brown
☐ 3 Mike Gabriele
☐ 4 Roger Hailey
☐ 5 Lee Heath
☐ 6 Ron Thomas
☐ 7 Earl Jewett
☐ 8 Pat Kelly
☐ 9 Ryan Klesko
☐ 10 John Kupsey
☐ 11 Gene Martin
☐ 12 Eddie Mathews
☐ 13 Miguel Mendez
☐ 14 Tom Newman
☐ 15 Melvin Nieves
☐ 16 Jose Olmeda
☐ 17 Eduardo Perez
☐ 18 Bill Schafer
☐ 19 Fred Lopez
☐ 20 Dan Sims
☐ 21 Shawn Sottile
☐ 22 Earl Steinmetz
☐ 23 Tony Tarasco
☐ 24 Don Strange
☐ 25 Mark Wohlers
☐ 26 Willy Johnson TR
☐ 27 Kevin Haeberle
☐ 28 Vinicio Castilla
☐ 29 Steve Glass CO
☐ 30 Ned Yost MGR
Checklist

1990 Sumter Braves ProCards

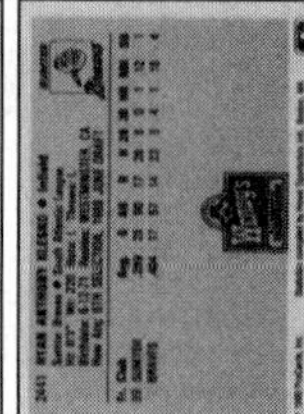

This 30-card standard-size set of the 1990 Sumter Braves, a Class A South Atlantic League affiliate of the Atlanta Braves, features on its white-bordered fronts posed color player photos set on simulated wood-grain backgrounds. The player's name, position, and team appear within a gold-colored rectangle below the photo. The tan horizontal back is bordered in white and carries the player's name at the top, followed by biography and statistics. This issue includes the minor league card debuts of Ryan Klesko and Vinny Castilla.

	MINT	NRMT	EXC
COMPLETE SET (30)	30.00	13.50	3.70

☐ 2424 Checklist
☐ 2425 Tab Brown
☐ 2426 Mike Gabriele
☐ 2427 Kevin Haeberle
☐ 2428 Roger Hailey
☐ 2429 Earl Jewett
☐ 2430 Bill Schafer
☐ 2431 Shaun Sottile
☐ 2432 Earl Steinmetz
☐ 2433 Don Strange
☐ 2434 Ron Thomas
☐ 2435 Mark Wohlers
☐ 2436 Tyler Houston
☐ 2437 Fred Lopez
☐ 2438 Eduardo Perez
☐ 2439 Vinicio Castilla
☐ 2440 Pat Kelly
☐ 2441 Ryan Klesko
☐ 2442 John Kupsey
☐ 2443 Miguel Mendez
☐ 2444 Jose Olmeda
☐ 2445 Lee Heath
☐ 2446 Gene Martin
☐ 2447 Melvin Nieves
☐ 2448 Dan Sims
☐ 2449 Tony Tarasco
☐ 2450 Ned Yost MGR
☐ 2451 Matt West CO
☐ 2452 Steve Glass
Player/Coach
☐ 2453 Ralph Rowe CO

1990 Syracuse Chiefs CMC

This 28-card standard-size set of the 1990 Syracuse Chiefs, a Class AAA International League affiliate of the Toronto Blue Jays, features white-bordered posed color player photos on its fronts. The player's name and position appear at the bottom; the team name appears vertically on the left. The back carries the league emblem in the white area at the top, the team name in the green stripe below, and player's name, position, biography, and statistics in the yellow area at the bottom. 1,100 sets were produced.

	MINT	NRMT	EXC
COMPLETE SET (28)	10.00	4.50	1.25

☐ 1 Alex Sanchez
☐ 2 Mauro Gozzo
☐ 3 Steve Cummings
☐ 4 Tom Gilles
☐ 5 Doug Linton
☐ 6 Mike Loynd

☐ 7 Bob Shirley CO
☐ 8 John Shea
☐ 9 Paul Kilgus
☐ 10 Carlos Diaz
☐ 11 Joe Szekely
☐ 12 Rick Lysander
☐ 13 Jim Eppard
☐ 14 Derek Bell
☐ 15 Jose Escobar
☐ 16 Webster Garrison
☐ 17 Paul Runge
☐ 18 Luis Sojo
☐ 19 Ed Sprague
☐ 20 Hector De La Cruz
☐ 21 Rob Ducey
☐ 22 Ozzie Virgil
☐ 23 Stu Pederson
☐ 24 Mark Whiten
☐ 25 Andy Dziadkowiec
☐ 26 Bob Bailor MG
☐ 27 Steve Wapnick
☐ 28 Ralph Wheeler CO

1990 Syracuse Chiefs Merchants Bank

Sponsored by Merchants Bank and WIXT Channel 9, this photo album features the 1990 Syracuse Chiefs, a Class AAA International League affiliate of the Toronto Blue Jays. The photo album unfolds to reveal three 11" by 9 1/2" sheets. The first sheet displays a color team photo, with player identification and a Merchants Bank advertisement beneath the picture. The second and third panels each consist of three rows with five cards per row. The perforated player cards measure roughly 2 1/4" by 3 1/4". The fronts display white-bordered color posed player pictures shot from the waist up; player identification and sponsor logos are below the pictures. In blue lettering, the horizontal backs carry biography and statistics. A facsimile autograph in red ink rounds out the back. The cards are unnumbered and checklisted below in alphabetical order.

	MINT	NRMT	EXC
COMPLETE SET (30)	10.00	4.50	1.25

☐ 1 Bob Bailor MG
☐ 2 Derek Bell
☐ 3 Steve Cummings
☐ 4 Hector De La Cruz
☐ 5 Carlos Diaz
☐ 6 Rob Ducey
☐ 7 Jim Eppard
☐ 8 Jose Escobar
☐ 9 Webster Garrison
☐ 10 Tom Gilles
☐ 11 Mauro Gozzo
☐ 12 Randy Holland
☐ 13 Paul Kilgus
☐ 14 Doug Linton
☐ 15 Mike Loynd
☐ 16 Rick Lysander
☐ 17 Pedro Munoz
☐ 18 Stu Pederson
☐ 19 Paul Runge
☐ 20 Alex Sanchez
☐ 21 John Shea
☐ 22 Bob Shirley CO
☐ 23 Luis Sojo
☐ 24 Ed Sprague
☐ 25 Joe Szekely
☐ 26 Ozzie Virgil
☐ 27 Steve Wapnick
☐ 28 Rocket Wheeler CO
☐ 29 Mark Whiten
☐ 30 Bob Wishnevski

1990 Syracuse Chiefs ProCards

This 28-card standard-size set of the 1990 Syracuse Chiefs, a Class AAA International League affiliate of the Toronto Blue Jays, features on its white-bordered fronts posed color player photos set on simulated wood-grain backgrounds. The player's name, position, and team appear within a gold-colored rectangle below the photo. The tan horizontal back is bordered in white and carries the player's name at the top, followed by biography and statistics.

	MINT	NRMT	EXC
COMPLETE SET (28)	8.00	3.60	1.00

☐ 563 Checklist
☐ 564 Tom Gilles
☐ 565 Mauro Gozzo
☐ 566 Paul Kilgus
☐ 567 Doug Linton
☐ 568 Mike Loynd
☐ 569 Rick Lysander
☐ 570 Alex Sanchez
☐ 571 John Shea
☐ 572 Steve Wapnick
☐ 573 Andy Dziadkowiec
☐ 574 Joe Szekely
☐ 575 Ozzie Virgil
☐ 576 Jim Eppard
☐ 577 Jose Escobar
☐ 578 Webster Garrison
☐ 579 Paul Runge
☐ 580 Luis Sojo
☐ 581 Ed Sprague
☐ 582 Derek Bell
☐ 583 Hector De La Cruz
☐ 584 Rob Ducey
☐ 585 Pedro Munoz
☐ 586 Stu Pederson
☐ 587 Mark Whiten
☐ 588 Bob Bailor MG
☐ 589 Bob Shirley CO
☐ 590 Rocket Wheeler CO

1990 Tacoma Tigers CMC

This 25-card standard-size set of the 1990 Tacoma Tigers, a Class AAA Pacific Coast League affiliate of the Oakland Athletics, features white-bordered posed color player photos on its fronts. The player's name and position appear at the bottom; the team name appears vertically on the left. The back carries the league emblem in the white area at the top, the team name in the green stripe below, and player's name, position, biography, and statistics in the yellow area at the bottom. 1,100 sets were produced.

	MINT	NRMT	EXC
COMPLETE SET (25)	5.00	2.20	.60

☐ 1 Ray Young
☐ 2 Dave Veres
☐ 3 Scott Chiamparino
☐ 4 Tony Ariola
☐ 5 Weston Weber
☐ 6 Bruce Walton
☐ 7 Dave Otto
☐ 8 Reese Lambert
☐ 9 Joe Bitker
☐ 10 Joe Law
☐ 11 Ed Wojna
☐ 12 Timothy Casey
☐ 13 Patrick Dietrick
☐ 14 Bruce Fields
☐ 15 Eric Fox
☐ 16 Scott Hemond
☐ 17 Steve Howard
☐ 18 Doug Jennings
☐ 19 Al Pedrique
☐ 20 Dann Howitt
☐ 21 Russ McGinnis
☐ 22 Troy Afenir
☐ 23 Larry Arndt
☐ 24 Dickie Scott
Player/Coach
☐ 25 Kevin Ward

1990 Tacoma Tigers ProCards

This 29-card standard-size set of the 1990 Tacoma Tigers, a Class AAA Pacific Coast League affiliate of the Oakland Athletics, features on its white-bordered fronts posed color player photos set on simulated wood-grain backgrounds. The player's name, position, and team appear within a gold-colored rectangle below the photo. The tan horizontal back is bordered in white and carries the player's name at the top, followed by biography and statistics.

	MINT	NRMT	EXC
COMPLETE SET (29)	5.00	2.20	.60

☐ 83 Checklist
☐ 84 Tony Ariola
☐ 85 Joe Bitker
☐ 86 Scott Chiamparino
☐ 87 Reese Lambert
☐ 88 Joe Law
☐ 89 Dave Otto
☐ 90 Dave Veres
☐ 91 Bruce Walton
☐ 92 Wes Weber
☐ 93 Ed Wojna
☐ 94 Ray Young
☐ 95 Troy Afenir
☐ 96 Russ McGinnis
☐ 97 Larry Arndt
☐ 98 Mike Bordick
☐ 99 Scott Hemond
☐ 100 Dann Howitt
☐ 101 Doug Jennings
☐ 102 Al Pedrique
☐ 103 Dick Scott
☐ 104 Tim Casey
☐ 105 Pat Dietrick
☐ 106 Bruce Fields
☐ 107 Eric Fox
☐ 108 Steve Howard
☐ 109 Kevin Ward
☐ 110 Brad Fischer MGR
☐ 111 Chuck Estrada CO

1990 Tampa Yankees Diamond

	MINT	NRMT	EXC
COMPLETE SET (28)	15.00	6.75	1.85

☐ 1 Tim Cooper
☐ 2 Abdiel Cumberbatch
☐ 3 Tim Demerson
☐ 4 Ryan Eberly
☐ 5 Carl Everett
☐ 6 Brian Faw
☐ 7 Nathanael Felix
☐ 8 Michael Figga
☐ 9 Brent Gilbert
☐ 10 Adoldo Harris
☐ 11 Jim Hayes
☐ 12 Richard Hines
☐ 13 Frank Laviano
☐ 14 Ricardo Ledee
☐ 15 Johnny Leon
☐ 16 Jeff Matouzas
☐ 17 Mariano Rivera
☐ 18 Tim Rumer
☐ 19 Edwin Salcedo
☐ 20 Alexis Santaella
☐ 21 Sandi Santiago
☐ 22 Tate Seefried
☐ 23 Keith Seiler
☐ 24 Michael Smith
☐ 25 Shane Spencer
☐ 26 John Thibert
☐ 27 Rich Turrentine
☐ 28 Coaching Staff
Rich Arena CO
Glenn Sherlock MGR
Mark Rose CO
Hop Cassady CO

1990 Texas League All-Stars Grand Slam

	MINT	NRMT	EXC
COMPLETE SET (38)	12.00	5.50	1.50

☐ 1 Eric Karros
☐ 2 Eddie Pye
☐ 3 David Greg
☐ 4 Charlie Montoya
☐ 5 Bert Heffernan
☐ 6 Mike Knapp
☐ 7 Mike Humphreys
☐ 8 Henry Rodriguez
☐ 9 Dee Dixon
☐ 10 Jesus Alfaro
☐ 11 Jeff Barns
☐ 12 Ricky Bones
☐ 13 Jeremy Hernandez
☐ 14 Mike James
☐ 15 Dennis Springer
☐ 16 Kevin Campbell
☐ 17 Chris George
☐ 18 Dave Huppert MG
☐ 19 Rob Giesecke TR
☐ 20 Rob Maurer
☐ 21 Rudy Hernandez
☐ 22 Dave Patterson
☐ 23 Andres Santana
☐ 24 Steve Decker
☐ 25 Bill Haselman
☐ 26 Kevin Belcher
☐ 27 Ted Wood
☐ 28 Terry McDaniel
☐ 29 Dan Rohrmeier
☐ 30 Joe Hall
☐ 31 Anthony Young
☐ 32 Terry Bross
☐ 33 Peter Schourek
☐ 34 Dave Osteen
☐ 35 Jim Pena
☐ 36 Steve Allen
☐ 37 Bill Evers MG
☐ 38 Greg Harrell TR

1990 Tidewater Tides CMC

This 30-card standard-size set of the 1990 Tidewater Tides, a Class AAA International League affiliate of the New York Mets, features white-bordered posed color player photos on its fronts. The player's name and position appear at the bottom; the team name appears vertically on the left. The back carries the league emblem in the white area at the top, the team name in the green stripe below, and player's name, position, biography, and statistics in the yellow area at the bottom. 1,100 sets were produced.

	MINT	NRMT	EXC
COMPLETE SET (30)	5.00	2.20	.60

☐ 1 Shawn Barton
☐ 2 Kevin Brown
☐ 3 Rocky Childress
☐ 4 Brian Givens
☐ 5 Manny Hernandez
☐ 6 Jeff Innis
☐ 7 Cesar Mejia
☐ 8 Scott Nielsen
☐ 9 Dale Plummer
☐ 10 Ray Soff
☐ 11 Lou Thornton
☐ 12 Dave Trautwein
☐ 13 Julio Valera
☐ 14 Tim Bogar
☐ 15 Mike DeButch
☐ 16 Jeff Gardner
☐ 17 Denny Gonzalez
☐ 18 Chris Jelic
☐ 19 Roger Samuels
☐ 20 Dave Liddell
☐ 21 Orlando Mercado
☐ 22 Kelvin Torve
☐ 23 Alex Diaz
☐ 24 Keith Hughes
☐ 25 Darren Reed
☐ 26 Zolio Sanchez
☐ 27 Steve Swisher MGR
☐ 28 John Cumberland CO
☐ 29 Rich Miller CO
☐ 30 Scott Lawrenson TR

1990 Tidewater Tides ProCards

This 30-card standard-size set of the 1990 Tidewater Tides, a Class AAA International League affiliate of the New York Mets, features on its white-bordered fronts posed color player photos set on simulated wood-grain backgrounds. The player's name, position, and team appear within a gold-colored rectangle below the photo. The tan horizontal back is bordered in white and carries the player's name at the top, followed by biography and statistics.

	MINT	NRMT	EXC
COMPLETE SET (30)	5.00	2.20	.60

☐ 533 Checklist
☐ 534 Shawn Barton
☐ 535 Kevin Brown
☐ 536 Rocky Childress
☐ 537 Brian Givens
☐ 538 Manny Hernandez
☐ 539 Jeff Innis
☐ 540 Cesar Mejia
☐ 541 Scott Nielsen
☐ 542 Dale Plummer
☐ 543 Roger Samuels
☐ 544 Ray Soff
☐ 545 Dave Trautwein
☐ 546 Julio Valera
☐ 547 Dave Liddell
☐ 548 Orlando Mercado
☐ 549 Tim Bogar
☐ 550 Mike Debutch
☐ 551 Jeff Gardner
☐ 552 Denny Gonzalez
☐ 553 Chris Jelic
☐ 554 Kelvin Torve
☐ 555 Alex Diaz
☐ 556 Keith Hughes
☐ 557 Darren Reed
☐ 558 Zoilo Sanchez
☐ 559 Lou Thornton
☐ 560 Steve Swisher MGR
☐ 561 John Cumberland CO
☐ 562 Rich Miller CO

1990 Toledo Mud Hens CMC

This 27-card standard-size set of the 1990 Toledo Mud Hens, a Class AAA International League affiliate of the Detroit Tigers, features white-bordered posed color player photos on its fronts. The player's name and position appear at the bottom; the team name appears vertically on the left. The back carries the league emblem in the white area at the top, the team name in the green stripe below, and player's name, position, biography, and statistics in the yellow area at the bottom. 1,100 sets were produced.

	MINT	NRMT	EXC
COMPLETE SET (27)	12.00	5.50	1.50

☐ 1 Don Vesling
☐ 2 Scott Aldred
☐ 3 Dennis Burtt
☐ 4 Shawn Holman
☐ 5 Matt Kinzer
☐ 6 Randy Nosek
☐ 7 Jose Ramos
☐ 8 Kevin Ritz
☐ 9 Mike Schwabe
☐ 10 Steve Searcy
☐ 11 Eric Stone
☐ 12 Domingo Michel
☐ 13 Phil Ouellette
☐ 14 Shawn Hare
☐ 15 Jim Lindeman
☐ 16 Scott Livingstone
☐ 17 La Vel Freeman
☐ 18 Travis Fryman
☐ 19 Scott Lusader
☐ 20 Dean Decillis
☐ 21 Milt Cuyler
☐ 22 Tom Gamboa MGR
☐ 23 Phil Clark
☐ 24 Torey Lovullo
☐ 25 Aurelio Rodriguez CO
☐ 26 Jeff Jones CO
☐ 27 Steve McInerney TR

1990 Toledo Mud Hens ProCards

This 27-card standard-size set of the 1990 Toledo Mud Hens, a Class AAA International League affiliate of the Detroit Tigers, features on its white-bordered fronts posed color player photos set on simulated wood-grain backgrounds. The player's name, position, and team appear within a gold-colored rectangle below the photo. The tan horizontal back is bordered in white and carries the player's name at the top, followed by biography and statistics.

	MINT	NRMT	EXC
COMPLETE SET (27)	18.00	8.00	2.20

- ☐ 140 Checklist
- ☐ 141 Scott Alfred
- ☐ 142 Dennis Burtt
- ☐ 143 Shawn Holman
- ☐ 144 Matt Kinzer
- ☐ 145 Randy Nosek
- ☐ 146 Jose Ramos
- ☐ 147 Kevin Ritz
- ☐ 148 Mike Schwabe
- ☐ 149 Steve Searcy
- ☐ 150 Eric Stone
- ☐ 151 Don Vesling
- ☐ 152 Phil Clark
- ☐ 153 Phil Ouellette
- ☐ 154 Dean DeCillis
- ☐ 155 Travis Fryman
- ☐ 156 Jim Lindeman
- ☐ 157 Scott Livingstone
- ☐ 158 Torey Lovullo
- ☐ 159 Domingo Michel
- ☐ 160 Milt Cuyler
- ☐ 161 La Vel Freeman
- ☐ 162 Shawn Hare
- ☐ 163 Scott Lusader
- ☐ 164 Tom Gamboa MGR
- ☐ 165 Jeff Jones CO
- ☐ 166 Aurelio Rodriguez

1990 Triple A All-Stars CMC

	MINT	NRMT	EXC
COMPLETE SET (45)	8.00	3.60	1.00

- ☐ 1 Todd Zeile
- ☐ 2 Luis de los Santos
- ☐ 3 Junior Noboa
- ☐ 4 Jeff Huson
- ☐ 5 Scott Coolbaugh
- ☐ 6 Skeeter Barnes
- ☐ 7 Larry Walker
- ☐ 8 Greg Vaughn
- ☐ 9 Steve Henderson
- ☐ 10 Mark Gardner
- ☐ 11 Morris Madden
- ☐ 12 Jack Armstrong
- ☐ 13 Stan Belinda
- ☐ 14 Alex Cole
- ☐ 15 Orlando Merced
- ☐ 16 Frank Cabrera
- ☐ 17 Hal Morris
- ☐ 18 Mark Lemke
- ☐ 19 Randy Velarde
- ☐ 20 Tom O'Malley
- ☐ 21 Butch Davis
- ☐ 22 Glenallen Hill
- ☐ 23 Greg Tubbs
- ☐ 24 Kevin Maas
- ☐ 25 Alex Sanchez
- ☐ 26 Mark Eichhorn
- ☐ 27 Mickey Pina
- ☐ 28 Julio Machado
- ☐ 29 Rob Richie
- ☐ 30 Tim Naehring
- ☐ 31 Sandy Alomar Jr.
- ☐ 32 Kelvin Torve
- ☐ 33 Joey Cora
- ☐ 34 Paul Zuvella
- ☐ 35 Matt Williams
- ☐ 36 Bruce Fields
- ☐ 37 Jerald Clark
- ☐ 38 Mike Huff
- ☐ 39 Jim Wilson
- ☐ 40 Ramon Martinez
- ☐ 41 Bryan Clark
- ☐ 42 Steve Olin
- ☐ 43 Andy Benes
- ☐ 44 Lee Stevens
- ☐ 45 Adam Peterson

1990 Triple A All-Stars ProCards

	MINT	NRMT	EXC
COMPLETE SET (54)	20.00	9.00	2.50

- ☐ AAA1 Checklist
- ☐ AAA2 Mark Whiten
- ☐ AAA3 Luis Sojo
- ☐ AAA4 Dale Polley
- ☐ AAA5 Kelvin Torve
- ☐ AAA6 Keith Hughes
- ☐ AAA7 Keith Miller
- ☐ AAA8 Paul Faries
- ☐ AAA9 German Rivera
- ☐ AAA10 Leo Gomez
- ☐ AAA11 Bob Bailor MGR
- ☐ AAA12 Juan Gonzalez
- ☐ AAA13 Hensley Meulens
- ☐ AAA14 Brian Dorsett
- ☐ AAA15 Kevin Mmahat
- ☐ AAA16 Tim Naehring
- ☐ AAA17 Steve Carter
- ☐ AAA18 Terry Gilmore
- ☐ AAA19 Bernard Gilkey
- ☐ AAA20 Steve Searcy
- ☐ AAA21 Mike Cook
- ☐ AAA22 Dorn Taylor
- ☐ AAA23 Pete Filson
- ☐ AAA24 Tim McIntosh
- ☐ AAA25 Joe Redfield
- ☐ AAA26 Dave Machemer MGR
- ☐ AAA27 Bill Dancy MGR
- ☐ AAA28 Eddie Williams
- ☐ AAA29 Mike Perez
- ☐ AAA30 Travis Fryman
- ☐ AAA31 Jose Offerman
- ☐ AAA32 Kevin Kennedy MGR
- ☐ AAA33 Dave Walsh
- ☐ AAA34 Erik Pappas
- ☐ AAA35 Jeff Small
- ☐ AAA36 Terry Collins MGR
- ☐ AAA37 Jerry Willard
- ☐ AAA38 Tom Drees
- ☐ AAA39 Marv Foley
- ☐ AAA40 Craig Smajstra
- ☐ AAA41 Orsino Hill
- ☐ AAA42 Lee Stevens
- ☐ AAA43 Todd Haney
- ☐ AAA44 Darrin Fletcher
- ☐ AAA45 Dave Hansen
- ☐ AAA46 Mike Huff
- ☐ AAA47 Joe Bitker
- ☐ AAA48 Ray Young
- ☐ AAA49 Scott Chiamparino
- ☐ AAA50 Alan Cockrell
- ☐ AAA51 Chris Hammond
- ☐ AAA52 Mark Leonard
- ☐ AAA53 Ken Hill
- ☐ AAA54 David Segui

1990 Tucson Toros CMC

This 25-card standard-size set of the 1990 Tucson Toros, a Class AAA Pacific Coast League affiliate of the Houston Astros, features white-bordered posed color player photos on its fronts. The player's name and position appear at the bottom; the team name appears vertically on the left. The back carries the league emblem in the white area at the top, the team name in the green stripe below, and player's name, position, biography, and statistics in the yellow area at the bottom. 1,100 sets were produced.

	MINT	NRMT	EXC
COMPLETE SET (25)	5.00	2.20	.60

- ☐ 1 Ryan Bowen
- ☐ 2 Brian Meyer
- ☐ 3 Terry Clark
- ☐ 4 Darryl Kile
- ☐ 5 Randy St. Claire
- ☐ 6 Randy Hennis
- ☐ 7 Lee Tunnell
- ☐ 8 William Brennan
- ☐ 9 Craig Smajstra
- ☐ 10 Gary Cooper
- ☐ 11 Carl Nichols
- ☐ 12 Louie Meadows
- ☐ 13 Jose Tolentino
- ☐ 14 Harry Spillman
- ☐ 15 Javier Ortiz
- ☐ 16 Doug Strange
- ☐ 17 Jim Olander
- ☐ 18 Karl Rhodes
- ☐ 19 David Rohde
- ☐ 20 Mike Simms
- ☐ 21 Scott Servais
- ☐ 22 Pedro Sanchez
- ☐ 23 Kevin Dean
- ☐ 24 Brian Fisher
- ☐ 25 Bob Skinner MGR

1990 Tucson Toros ProCards

This 27-card standard-size set of the 1990 Tucson Toros, a Class AAA Pacific Coast League affiliate of the Houston Astros, features on its white-bordered fronts posed color player photos set on simulated wood-grain backgrounds. The player's name, position, and team appear within a gold-colored rectangle below the photo. The tan horizontal back is bordered in white and carries the player's name at the top, followed by biography and statistics.

	MINT	NRMT	EXC
COMPLETE SET (27)	5.00	2.20	.60

- ☐ 195 Checklist
- ☐ 196 Ryan Bowen
- ☐ 197 William Brennan
- ☐ 198 Terry Clark
- ☐ 199 Brian Fisher
- ☐ 200 Randy Hennis
- ☐ 201 Darryl Kile
- ☐ 202 Brian Meyer
- ☐ 203 Randy St. Claire
- ☐ 204 Lee Tunnell
- ☐ 205 Carl Nichols
- ☐ 206 Scott Servais
- ☐ 207 Pedro Sanchez
- ☐ 208 Mike Simms
- ☐ 209 Craig Smajstra
- ☐ 210 Harry Spilman
- ☐ 211 Doug Strange
- ☐ 212 Jose Tolentino
- ☐ 213 Gary Cooper
- ☐ 214 Kevin Dean
- ☐ 215 Louie Meadows
- ☐ 216 Jim Olander
- ☐ 217 Javier Ortiz
- ☐ 218 Karl Rhodes
- ☐ 219 Bob Skinner MGR
  Card # is 1219
- ☐ 220 Brent Strom CO
- ☐ 221 Tim Tolman CO

1990 Tulsa Drillers All Decade Best

This 28-card standard-size set of the 1990 Tulsa Drillers, a Class AA Texas League affiliate of the Texas Rangers, features white-bordered posed and action color player photos on its fronts. The player's name and position appear vertically on the left side. The words "All Decade" appear across the top. The yellow horizontal back carries the player's name and years played at the top, followed by player's history, highlights, and statistics. 2,500 sets were produced.

	MINT	NRMT	EXC
COMPLETE SET (36)	25.00	11.00	3.10

- ☐ 1 Scott Coolbaugh
- ☐ 2 Chuckie Canady
- ☐ 3 Wayne Tolleson
- ☐ 4 Pete O'Brien
- ☐ 5 Dean Palmer
- ☐ 6 Mike Stanley
- ☐ 7 Jim St. Laurent
- ☐ 8 Bob Sebra
- ☐ 9 Steve Wilson
- ☐ 10 Rick Raether
- ☐ 11 Walt Terrell
- ☐ 12 Mike Rubel
- ☐ 13 Jack Lazorko
- ☐ 14 Kevin Buckley
- ☐ 15 Steve Buechele
- ☐ 16 David Lynch
- ☐ 17 Jerry Gleaton
- ☐ 18 Ron Darling
- ☐ 19 Tom Henke
- ☐ 20 Mike Jirschele
- ☐ 21 Eddie Jurak
- ☐ 22 Phil Klimas
- ☐ 23 Chad Kreuter
- ☐ 24 Tommy Dunbar
- ☐ 25 Juan Gonzalez
- ☐ 26 Mel Barrow
- ☐ 27 Jerry Browne
- ☐ 28 Tom Burgess MGR
- ☐ 29 Jim Skaalen MGR
- ☐ 30 Kevin Reimer
- ☐ 31 Sammy Sosa
- ☐ 32 Kevin Brown
- ☐ 33 Rob Clark
- ☐ 34 Marty Scott
- ☐ 35 Ruben Sierra
- ☐ 36 Checklist

1990 Tulsa Drillers ProCards

This 28-card standard-size set of the 1990 Tulsa Drillers, a Class AA Texas League affiliate of the Texas Rangers, features on its white-bordered fronts posed color player photos set on simulated wood-grain backgrounds. The player's name, position, and team appear within a gold-colored rectangle below the photo. The tan horizontal back is bordered in white and carries the player's name at the top, followed by biography and statistics.

	MINT	NRMT	EXC
COMPLETE SET (28)	8.00	3.60	1.00

- ☐ 1147 Checklist
- ☐ 1148 Steve Allen
- ☐ 1149 Phil Bryant
- ☐ 1150 Felipe Castillo
- ☐ 1151 Eric McCray
- ☐ 1152 Marv Rockman
- ☐ 1153 Wayne Rosenthal
- ☐ 1154 Cedric Shaw
- ☐ 1155 Chris Shiflett
- ☐ 1156 Mike Taylor
- ☐ 1157 Mitch Thomas
- ☐ 1158 Bill Haselman
- ☐ 1159 Greg Iavarone
- ☐ 1160 Paco Burgos
- ☐ 1161 Monty Fariss
- ☐ 1162 Darrin Garner
- ☐ 1163 Rob Maurer
- ☐ 1164 Paul Postier
- ☐ 1165 Brant Alyea
- ☐ 1166 Kevin Belcher
- ☐ 1167 Donald Harris
- ☐ 1168 Dan Peltier
- ☐ 1169 Dan Rohrmeier
- ☐ 1170 Dean Palmer
- ☐ 1171 Terry Mathews
- ☐ 1172 Tommy Thompson MGR
- ☐ 1173 Walt Williams CO
- ☐ 1174 Jeff Andrews CO

1990 Tulsa Drillers Team Issue

	MINT	NRMT	EXC
COMPLETE SET (28)	10.00	4.50	1.25

- ☐ 1 Steve Allen
- ☐ 2 Jeff Andrews
- ☐ 3 Kevin Belcher
- ☐ 4 Paco Burgos
- ☐ 5 Felipe Castillo
- ☐ 6 Everett Cunningham
- ☐ 7 Monty Fariss
- ☐ 8 Darrin Garner
- ☐ 9 Greg Harrell TR
- ☐ 10 Donald Harris
- ☐ 11 Bill Haselman
- ☐ 12 Jim Hvizda
- ☐ 13 Greg Iavarone
- ☐ 14 David Lynch
- ☐ 15 Terry Mathews
- ☐ 16 Rob Maurer
- ☐ 17 Eric McCray
- ☐ 18 Roger Pavlik
- ☐ 19 Dan Peltier
- ☐ 20 Paul Postier
- ☐ 21 Marv Rockman
- ☐ 22 Dan Rohrmeier
- ☐ 23 Cedric Shaw
- ☐ 24 Mike Taylor
- ☐ 25 Tommy Thompson MG
- ☐ 26 George Threadgill
- ☐ 27 Walt Williams CO
- ☐ 28 Tom Henke
  Past Star '81 and '82

1990 Utica Blue Sox Pucko

	MINT	NRMT	EXC
COMPLETE SET (30)	6.00	2.70	.75

- ☐ 1 Kevin Coughlin
- ☐ 2 Todd Martin
- ☐ 3 Dan Monzon
- ☐ 4 Rogelio Nunez
- ☐ 5 Rafael Ochoa
- ☐ 6 Adam Sanders
- ☐ 7 Joe Solimine
- ☐ 8 Chris Sparrow
- ☐ 9 Keith Strange
- ☐ 10 Dean Tatarian
- ☐ 11 Craig Teter
- ☐ 12 Kerry Valrie
- ☐ 13 Barry Williams
- ☐ 14 Rodney Bolton
- ☐ 15 Frank Campos
- ☐ 16 Rolando Caridad
- ☐ 17 Chris Fruge
- ☐ 18 Dave Gorman
- ☐ 19 Todd Hotz
- ☐ 20 Pat Hulme
- ☐ 21 Jonathan Jenkins
- ☐ 22 Ernesto Santana
- ☐ 23 John Smith
- ☐ 24 Kevin Tolar
- ☐ 25 Tommy Thompson
- ☐ 26 Bill Ballou CO
  Charlie Lau Jr. CO
  Ron McKay CO
  Rick Ray TR
  Thompson's Staff
- ☐ 27 Morganna
  Sic, Morgana
- ☐ 28 Murnane Field
- ☐ 29 Mike Bradish
- ☐ 30 Lee Dorsey

1990 Vancouver Canadians CMC

This 27-card standard-size set of the 1990 Vancouver Canadians, a Class AAA Pacific Coast League affiliate of the Chicago White Sox, features white-bordered posed color player photos on its fronts. The player's name and position appear at the bottom; the team name appears vertically on the left. The back carries the league emblem in the white area at the top, the team name in the green stripe below, and player's name, position, biography, and statistics in the yellow area at the bottom. 1,100 sets were produced.

	MINT	NRMT	EXC
COMPLETE SET (27)	7.00	3.10	.85

☐ 1 Wilson Alvarez
☐ 2 Adam Peterson
☐ 3 Tom Drees
☐ 4 Ravelo Manzanillo
☐ 5 Marv Foley MG
☐ 6 Grady Hall
☐ 7 Mike Campbell
☐ 7 Shawn Hillegas
(Second #7 in set)
☐ 9 C.L. Penigar
☐ 10 John Pawlowski
☐ 11 Steve Rosenberg
☐ 12 Jose Segura
☐ 13 Rich Amaral
☐ 14 Pete Dalena
☐ 15 Ramon Sambo
☐ 16 Marcus Lawton
☐ 17 Orsino Hill
☐ 18 Marlin McPhail
☐ 19 Keith Smith
☐ 20 Todd Trafton
☐ 21 Norberto Martin
☐ 22 Don Wakamatsu
☐ 23 Jerry Willard
☐ 24 Dana Williams
☐ 25 Tracy Woodson
☐ 26 Moe Drabowsky CO
☐ 27 Roger LaFrancois CO

1990 Vancouver Canadians ProCards

This 28-card standard-size set of the 1990 Vancouver Canadians, a Class AAA Pacific Coast League affiliate of the White Sox, features on its white-bordered fronts posed color player photos set on simulated wood-grain backgrounds. The player's name, position, and team appear within a gold-colored rectangle below the photo. The tan horizontal back is bordered in white and carries the player's name and position at the top, followed by biography and statistics.

	MINT	NRMT	EXC
COMPLETE SET (28)	7.00	3.10	.85

☐ 480 Checklist
☐ 481 Wilson Alvarez
☐ 482 Mike Campbell
☐ 483 Tom Drees
☐ 484 Grady Hall
☐ 485 Shawn Hillegas
☐ 486 Ravelo Manzanillo
☐ 487 John Pawlowski
☐ 488 Adam Peterson
☐ 489 Steve Rosenberg
☐ 490 Jose Segura
☐ 491 Don Wakamatsu
☐ 492 Jerry Willard
☐ 493 Rich Amaral
☐ 494 Pete Dalena
☐ 495 Norberto Martin
☐ 496 Keith Smith
☐ 497 Todd Trafton
☐ 498 Tracy Woodson
☐ 499 Orsino Hill
☐ 500 Marcus Lawton
☐ 501 Marlin McPhail
☐ 502 C.L. Penigar
☐ 503 Ramon Sambo
☐ 504 Dana Williams
☐ 505 Marv Foley MG
☐ 506 Moe Drabowsky CO
☐ 507 Roger LaFrancois CO

1990 Vero Beach Dodgers Star

This 31-card standard-size set of the 1990 Vero Beach Dodgers, a Class A Florida State League affiliate of the Los Angeles Dodgers, features blue bordered posed color player photos on its fronts. The player's name, team name, and position appear at the bottom. The white horizontal back carries the player's name at the top, followed by biography, career highlights, and statistics. This issue includes a second year card of Mike Piazza.

	MINT	NRMT	EXC
COMPLETE SET (31)	110.00	50.00	14.00

☐ 1 Jorge Alvarez
☐ 2 Pedro Astacio
☐ 3 Tony Barron
☐ 4 Bill Bene
☐ 5 Cam Biberdorf
☐ 6 Eric Boddie
☐ 7 Ray Calhoun
☐ 8 Anthony Collier
☐ 9 Edwin Correa
☐ 10 Javier Delahoya
☐ 11 Bruce Dostal
☐ 12 Dino Ebel
☐ 13 Bob Fletcher
☐ 14 Freddy Gonzalez
☐ 15 Pete Gonzalez
☐ 16 Marc Griffin
☐ 17 John Knapp
☐ 18 Alan Lewis
☐ 19 Scott Marabell
☐ 20 Robin Nina
☐ 21 Tim Patrick
☐ 22 Pedro Perez
☐ 23 Rex Peters
☐ 24 Mike Piazza
☐ 25 Ramon Taveras
☐ 26 Jeff Vanzytveld
☐ 27 Bill Wengert
☐ 28 Mike Wismer
☐ 29 Eric Young
☐ 30 Coaches
Joe Alvarez
Dennis Lewallyn
☐ 31 Matt Wilson TR

1990 Visalia Oaks Cal League Cards

	MINT	NRMT	EXC
COMPLETE SET (30)	5.00	2.20	.60

☐ 57 Chad Swanson
☐ 58 Mike Trombley
☐ 59 Mike Aspray
☐ 60 Pat Mohomes
☐ 61 Tom Fine
☐ 62 Richard Garces
☐ 63 Fred White
☐ 64 Phil Wiese
☐ 65 George Tsamis
☐ 66 Carl Fraticelli
☐ 67 Dan Masteller
☐ 68 Ramon Cedeno
☐ 69 Bob McCreary
☐ 70 Ray Ortiz
☐ 71 Carlos Capellan
☐ 72 Jay Kausnicka
☐ 73 Mike House
☐ 74 J.T. Bruett
☐ 75 Troy Buckley
☐ 76 Todd Logan
☐ 77 Daniel Segui
☐ 78 Jose Garcia
☐ 79 Scott Ullger MGR
☐ 80 Brian Allard CO
☐ 81 Bruce Bucz GM
☐ 82 Joel Safly TR
☐ 83 Joseph Bucz
Opeations
☐ 84 Jason Elick
Bat Boy
☐ 85 Robert Spurlock
Bat Boy
☐ 86 Darren Holt
Groundskeeper

1990 Visalia Oaks ProCards

This 26-card standard-size set of the 1990 Visalia Oaks, a Class A California League affiliate of the Minnesota Twins, features on its white-bordered fronts posed color player photos set on simulated wood-grain backgrounds. The player's name, position, and team appear within a gold-colored rectangle below the photo. The tan horizontal back is bordered in white and carries the player's name at the top, followed by biography and statistics.

	MINT	NRMT	EXC
COMPLETE SET (26)	7.00	3.10	.85

☐ 2146 Checklist
☐ 2147 Tom Fine
☐ 2148 Richard Garces
☐ 2149 Pat Mahomes
☐ 2150 Denny Neagle
☐ 2151 Mike Aspray
☐ 2152 Chad Swanson
☐ 2153 Mike Trombley
☐ 2154 Geroge Tsamis
☐ 2155 Fred White
☐ 2156 Phil Wiese
☐ 2157 Troy Buckley
☐ 2157 Todd Logan
☐ 2159 Carlos Capellan
☐ 2160 Carl Fraticelli
☐ 2161 Jose Garcia
☐ 2162 Dan Masteller
☐ 2163 Bob McCreary
☐ 2164 Dan Segui
☐ 2165 J.T. Bruett
☐ 2166 Ramon Cedeno
☐ 2167 Mike House
☐ 2168 Jay Kvasnicka
☐ 2169 Ray Ortiz
☐ 2170 Scott Ullger MGR
☐ 2171 Brian Allard CO

1990 Waterloo Diamonds Best

This 28-card standard-size set of the 1990 Waterloo Diamonds, a Class A Midwest League affiliate of the San Diego Padres, features white-bordered posed and action color player photos on its fronts. The player's name and position appear vertically on the left side. The yellow horizontal back carries the player's name and position at the top, followed by biography, career highlights, and statistics. A player head shot appears in the lower right corner.

	MINT	NRMT	EXC
COMPLETE SET (28)	5.00	2.20	.60

☐ 1 Ray Holbert
☐ 2 David Colon
☐ 3 Bryce Florie
☐ 4 Todd Embry
☐ 5 Luis Galindez
☐ 6 Jeff Hart
☐ 7 Rod Billingsley
☐ 8 Brad Hoyer
☐ 9 Tony Lewis
☐ 10 Steven Martin
☐ 11 Brian McKeon
☐ 12 Ron Morton
☐ 13 J.D. Noland
☐ 14 Billy Reed
☐ 15 Terry Rupp
☐ 16 Osvaldo Sanchez
☐ 17 Shawn Whalen
☐ 18 Matt Witkowski
☐ 19 Bryan Little MGR
☐ 20 Ron Oglesby CO
☐ 21 George Poulis
☐ 22 Greg Conley
☐ 23 Gene Glynn CO
☐ 24 Matt Toole
☐ 25 Mark Verstanding
☐ 26 Tom Doyle
☐ 27 Jose Lebron
☐ 28 Checklist

1990 Waterloo Diamonds ProCards

This 27-card standard-size set of the 1990 Waterloo Diamonds, a Class A Midwest League affiliate of the San Diego Padres, features on its white-bordered fronts posed color player photos set on simulated wood-grain backgrounds. The player's name, position, and team appear within a gold-colored rectangle below the photo. The tan horizontal back is bordered in white and carries the player's name at the top, followed by biography and statistics.

	MINT	NRMT	EXC
COMPLETE SET (27)	5.00	2.20	.60

☐ 2369 Checklist
☐ 2370 Todd Embry
☐ 2371 Bryce Florie
☐ 2372 Luis Galindez
☐ 2373 Jeff Hart
☐ 2374 Brad Hoyer
☐ 2375 Jose LeBron
☐ 2376 Tony Lewis
☐ 2377 Brian McKeon
☐ 2378 Ron Morton
☐ 2379 Billy Reed
☐ 2380 Rod Billingsley
☐ 2381 Greg Conley
☐ 2382 Mark Verstandig
☐ 2383 Tom Doyle
☐ 2384 Ray Holbert
☐ 2385 Steve Martin
☐ 2386 Terry Rupp
☐ 2387 Matt Toole
☐ 2388 Matt Witkowski
☐ 2389 David Colon
☐ 2390 J.D. Noland
☐ 2391 Osvaldo Sanchez
☐ 2392 Shawn Whelan
☐ 2393 Bryan Little MGR
☐ 2394 Ron Oglesby CO
☐ 2395 Gene Glynn CO

1990 Watertown Indians Star

This 28-card standard-size set of the 1990 Watertown Indians, a Class A New York-Penn League affiliate of the Cleveland Indians, features red bordered posed color player photos on its fronts. The player's name, team name, and position appear at the bottom. The white horizontal back carries the player's name at the top, followed by biography, career highlights, and statistics.

	MINT	NRMT	EXC
COMPLETE SET (28)	5.00	2.20	.60

☐ 1 Chad Allen
☐ 2 William Canate
☐ 3 Mark Charbonnet
☐ 4 Brian Cofer
☐ 5 John Cotton
☐ 6 Mike Davis
☐ 7 Marc Del Piano
☐ 8 Tim Ellis
☐ 9 Brian Giles
☐ 10 Mike Gonzalez
☐ 11 Dane Kallevig
☐ 12 Dennis Kluss
☐ 13 John Lorms
☐ 14 Oscar Munoz
☐ 15 Joe Perez
☐ 16 Clyde Pough
☐ 17 Roberto Rivera
☐ 18 Bobby Ryan
☐ 19 Keith Shepherd
☐ 20 Kelly Stinnett
☐ 21 Paulino Tena
☐ 22 Ken Welch
☐ 23 Bill Wertz
☐ 24 Jim Gabella MGR
☐ 25 Ken Silvestri CO
☐ 26 Teddy Blackwell TR
☐ 27 Tom Van Schaack GM
☐ 28 Tracey Richardson

1990 Wausau Timbers Best

This 28-card standard-size set of the 1990 Wausau Timbers, a Class A Midwest League affiliate of the Baltimore Orioles, features white-bordered posed and action color player photos on its fronts. The player's name and position appear vertically on the left side. The yellow horizontal back carries the player's name and position at the top, followed by biography, career highlights, and statistics. A player head shot appears in the lower right corner.

	MINT	NRMT	EXC
COMPLETE SET (28)	5.00	2.20	.60

☐ 1 T.R. Lewis
☐ 2 Steven Williams
☐ 3 Pat Leinen
☐ 4 Tom Martin
☐ 5 Daryl Moore
☐ 6 Matt Anderson
☐ 7 Richard Smith
☐ 8 Brad Pennington
☐ 9 Thomas Taylor
☐ 10 Bob Wheatcroft
☐ 11 Joe Teixeira
☐ 12 David Riddle
☐ 13 Shawn Heiden
☐ 14 Sergio Cairo
☐ 15 Greg Zaun
☐ 16 Jim Roso
☐ 17 Caesar Devares
☐ 18 Keith Kessinger
☐ 19 Gary Shingledecker
☐ 20 Manuel Alexander
☐ 21 John Fowler
☐ 22 Christian Benitez
☐ 23 Melvin Wearing Jr.
☐ 24 Aman Hicks
☐ 25 Hector Bautista
☐ 26 Allen(Bo) Davis
☐ 27 Keith Schmidt
☐ 28 Checklist
Checklist # on card is 29

1990 Wausau Timbers ProCards

This 32-card standard-size set of the 1990 Wausau Timbers, a Class A Midwest League affiliate of the Baltimore Orioles, features on its white-bordered fronts posed color player photos set on simulated wood-grain backgrounds. The player's name, position, and team appear within a gold-colored rectangle below the photo. The tan horizontal back is bordered in white and carries the player's name at the top, followed by biography and statistics.

	MINT	NRMT	EXC
COMPLETE SET (32)	5.00	2.20	.60

☐ 2114 Checklist
☐ 2115 Steve Williams
☐ 2116 Pat Leinen
☐ 2117 Tom Martin
☐ 2118 Daryl Moore
☐ 2119 Matt Anderson
☐ 2120 Rich Smith
☐ 2121 Brad Pennington
☐ 2122 Tom Taylor
☐ 2123 Rob Wheatcroft
☐ 2124 Joe Teixeira
☐ 2125 Dave Riddle
☐ 2126 Shawn Heiden
☐ 2127 John Marett
☐ 2128 Greg Zaun
☐ 2129 Jimmy Roso
☐ 2130 Cesar Devares
☐ 2131 Keith Kessinger
☐ 2132 Gary Shingledecker
☐ 2133 T.R. Lewis
☐ 2134 John Fowler
☐ 2135 Manny Alexander

☐ 2136 Christian Benitez
☐ 2137 Melvin Wearing
☐ 2138 Aman Hicks
☐ 2139 Hector Bautista
☐ 2140 Bo Davis
☐ 2141 Keith Schmidt
☐ 2142 Sergio Cairo
☐ 2143 Mike Young MGR
☐ 2144 Chet Nichols CO
☐ 2145 Oneri Fleita CO

1990 Wausau Timbers Star

This 29-card standard-size set of the 1990 Wausau Timbers, a Class A Midwest League affiliate of the Baltimore Orioles, features orange bordered posed color player photos on its fronts. The player's name, team name, and position appear at the bottom. The white horizontal back carries the player's name at the top, followed by biography, career highlights, and statistics.

	MINT	NRMT	EXC
COMPLETE SET (29)	5.00	2.20	.60

☐ 1 Matthew Anderson
☐ 2 Hector Bautista
☐ 3 Christian Benitez
☐ 4 John Boothby
☐ 5 Sergio Cairo
☐ 6 Bo Davis
☐ 7 Cesar Devares
☐ 8 John Fowler
☐ 9 Shawn Heiden
☐ 10 Aman Hicks
☐ 11 Brad Hildreth
☐ 12 Keith Kessinger
☐ 13 Michael Leinen
☐ 14 T.R. Lewis
☐ 15 John Marett
☐ 16 Thomas Martin
☐ 17 John Moore
☐ 18 Brad Pennington
☐ 19 David Riddle
☐ 20 James Roso
☐ 21 Keith Schmidt
☐ 22 Richard Smith
☐ 23 Tommy Taylor
☐ 24 Melvin Wearing
☐ 25 Robert Wheatcroft
☐ 26 Steven Williams
☐ 27 Gregory Zaun
☐ 28 Coaching Staff
Mike Young MGR
Chet Nichols CO
Oneri Fleita CO
☐ 29 Mitch Bibb TR

1990 Welland Pirates Pucko

This 36-card standard-size set of the 1990 Welland Pirates, a Class A New York-Penn League affiliate of the Pittsburgh Pirates, features posed color player photos on a gray background with black and white dots. The player's name and position are printed in a white bar above the photo, while the team name and logo appear on the bottom. The backs carry a brief biography, the circumstances under which the player was drafted, and statistics (where appropriate). The set was sponsored by Farr and Fuss Lincoln Mercury in Welland.

	MINT	NRMT	EXC
COMPLETE SET (36)	6.00	2.70	.75

☐ 1 Kurt Miller
☐ 2 Michael Brown
☐ 3 Genaro Campusano
☐ 4 Jon Martin
☐ 5 Janiero Feliz
☐ 6 Ben Johnson
☐ 7 Steve Polewski
☐ 8 Kevin Young
☐ 9 John Schulte
☐ 10 Anthony Brown
☐ 11 Scott Bullett
Sic, Bullet
☐ 12 John Curtis
☐ 13 Thomas Green
☐ 14 Joe Ronca
☐ 15 Wes Grisham
☐ 16 Tim Edge
☐ 17 Marcus Hanel
☐ 18 Rob Peterson
☐ 19 Lynn Carlson
☐ 20 Steve Cooke
☐ 21 Mark Futrell
☐ 22 Jeff Lyle
☐ 23 Troy Mooney
☐ 24 Alex Pacheco
☐ 25 Andre Redmond
☐ 26 Richard Robertson
☐ 27 Steve Roeder
☐ 28 Brian Shouse
☐ 29 Shelton Simpson
☐ 30 David Tellers
☐ 31 Michael Zimmerman
☐ 32 Jim Mallon MG
☐ 33 Mallon's Staff
Jerry Nyman CO
Rocky Bridges CO
☐ 34 Bob Burgess GM
☐ 35 Farr and Fuss
(Sponsor)
☐ 36 Welland Sports Complex
Checklist

1990 West Palm Beach Expos Star

This 32-card standard-size set of the 1990 West Palm Beach Expos, a Class A Florida State League affiliate of the Montreal Expos, features red-bordered posed color player photos on its fronts. The player's name, team name, and position appear at the bottom. In red letters on a white background, the horizontal back carries the player's name at the top, followed by biography, career highlights, and statistics.

	MINT	NRMT	EXC
COMPLETE SET (32)	5.00	2.20	.60

☐ 1 Rod Boddie
☐ 2 Paul Ciaglo
☐ 3 Reid Cornelius
☐ 4 Bret Davis
☐ 5 Jim Faulk
☐ 6 Rob Fletcher
☐ 7 Kevin Foster
☐ 8 Dan Freed
☐ 9 Dan Gakeler
☐ 10 Eddie Gonzalez
☐ 11 Rob Kerrigan
☐ 12 Ken Lake
☐ 13 Richie Lewis
☐ 14 Rob Mason
☐ 15 Todd Mayo
☐ 16 John Mello
☐ 17 Doug Piatt
☐ 18 Chris Pollack
☐ 19 F.P. Santangelo
☐ 20 Joe Siddall
☐ 21 David Sommer
☐ 22 Joel Smith
☐ 23 Matt Stairs
☐ 24 Adam Terris
☐ 25 David Wainhouse
☐ 26 John Wenrick
☐ 27 Fred Williams
☐ 28 Pete Young
☐ 29 Felipe Alou MG
☐ 30 Dave Jauss CO
☐ 31 Sean Cunningham TR
☐ NNO Team Logo

1990 Wichita State Shockers Game Day

	MINT	NRMT	EXC
COMPLETE SET (46)	20.00	9.00	2.50

☐ 1 1990 Title Card
(past post-season
record on back)
☐ 2 Spike Anderson
☐ 3 Matt Arst
☐ 4 Jim Audley
☐ 5 Jeff Bluma
☐ 6 Brian Buzard
☐ 7 Joe Carter
(Shocker Flashback)
☐ 8 Matt Criss
☐ 9 Todd Dreifort
☐ 10 Rodney Escobar
☐ 11 P.J. Forbes
☐ 12 Charlie Giaudrone
☐ 13 Tyler Green
☐ 14 Don Heinkel
(Shocker Flashback)
☐ 15 Jay Haffley
☐ 16 Billy Hall
☐ 17 Carl Hall
☐ 18 Mike Jones
☐ 19 Matt Klusener
☐ 20 Mike Lansing
☐ 21 Russ Morman
(Shocker Flashback)
☐ 22 Morgan LeClair
☐ 23 Scot McCloughan
☐ 24 Pat Meares
☐ 25 Tony Mills
☐ 26 Doug Mirabelli
☐ 27 Brian Morrow
☐ 28 Charlie O'Brien
(Shocker Flashback)
☐ 29 Darrin Paxton
☐ 30 Jose Ramos
☐ 31 Steve Smith
☐ 32 Kennie Steenstra
☐ 33 Jamey Tarrh
☐ 34 Tommy Tilma
☐ 35 Phil Stephenson
(Shocker Flashback)
☐ 36 Jamie Williams
☐ 37 Jeff Williams
☐ 38 Chris Wimmer
☐ 39 Bryant Winslow
☐ 40 Loren Hibbs
☐ 41 Brent Kemnitz
☐ 42 '89 Championship Team
(Shocker Flashback)
☐ 43 Gregg Miller
☐ 44 Gene Stephenson
☐ 45 All-Americans
(list on back)
☐ 46 Game Day Sponsor Card
(set checklist on back)

1990 Wichita Wranglers Rock's Dugout

	MINT	NRMT	EXC
COMPLETE SET (28)	6.00	2.70	.75

☐ 1 Checklist
☐ 2 Ricky Bones
☐ 3 Doug Brocail
☐ 4 Rafael Chavez
☐ 5 Brian Cisarik
☐ 6 Gregory David
☐ 7 Todd Hansen
☐ 8 Jeremy Hernandez
☐ 9 Charles Hillemann
☐ 10 Richard Holsmann
☐ 11 Mike Humphreys
☐ 12 Dean Alan Kelley
☐ 13 Stephen H. Loubier
☐ 14 Bob Lutticken
☐ 15 Pedro Martinez
☐ 16 Tim McWilliam
☐ 17 Craig Repoz
☐ 18 A.J. Sager
☐ 19 William Taylor
☐ 20 Jose Valentin
☐ 21 Guillermo Velasquez
☐ 22 Juan Villanueva
☐ 23 Dan Walters
☐ 24 Brian S. Wood
☐ 25 Steve Lubratich MGR
☐ 26 Lonnie Keeter CO
☐ 27 Jon Matlack CO
☐ 28 Cookie
Mascot

1990 Williamsport Bills Best

This 27-card standard-size set of the 1990 Williamsport Bills, a Class AA Eastern League affiliate of the Seattle Mariners, features white-bordered posed and action color player photos on its fronts. The player's name and position appear vertically on the left side. The yellow horizontal back carries the player's name and position at the top, followed by biography, career highlights, and statistics. A player head shot appears in the lower right corner.

	MINT	NRMT	EXC
COMPLETE SET (27)	5.00	2.20	.60

☐ 1 Lee Hancock
☐ 2 Jim Blueberg
☐ 3 Jim Bowie
☐ 4 Troy Evers
☐ 5 Fernando Figueroa
☐ 6 Mike Gardiner
☐ 7 Mike Goff
☐ 8 Ruben Gonzalez
☐ 9 Chuck Hensley
☐ 10 Jeff Hooper
☐ 11 Chris Howard
☐ 12 Bryan King
☐ 13 Dru Kosco
☐ 14 Shane Letterio
☐ 15 Mike McDonald
☐ 16 Mark Merchant
☐ 17 Jeff Nelson
☐ 18 Ken Pennington
☐ 19 Mark Razook
☐ 20 Dana Ridenour
☐ 21 Ricky Rojas
☐ 22 Ted Williams
☐ 23 Mark Wooden
☐ 24 Chris Verna
☐ 25 Rich Morales MGR
☐ 26 Bobby Cuellar CO
☐ 27 Checklist

1990 Williamsport Bills ProCards

This 26-card standard-size set of the 1990 Williamsport Bills, a Class AA Eastern League affiliate of the Seattle Mariners, features on its white-bordered fronts posed color player photos set on simulated wood-grain backgrounds. The player's name, position, and team appear within a gold-colored rectangle below the photo. The tan horizontal back is bordered in white and carries the player's name at the top, followed by biography and statistics.

	MINT	NRMT	EXC
COMPLETE SET (26)	5.00	2.20	.60

☐ 1048 Checklist
☐ 1049 Jim Blueberg
☐ 1050 Troy Evers
☐ 1051 Fernando Figueroa
☐ 1052 Mike Gardiner
☐ 1053 Mike Goff
☐ 1054 Lee Hancock
☐ 1055 Chuck Hensley
☐ 1056 Jeff Nelson
☐ 1057 Dana Ridenour
☐ 1058 Ricky Rojas
☐ 1059 Mark Wooden
☐ 1060 Jeff Hooper
☐ 1061 Chris Howard
☐ 1062 Ruben Gonzalez
☐ 1063 Bryan King
☐ 1064 Shane Letterio
☐ 1065 Ken Pennington
☐ 1066 Mark Razook
☐ 1067 Jim Bowie
☐ 1068 Dru Kosco
☐ 1069 Mike McDonald
☐ 1070 Mark Merchant
☐ 1071 Ted Willimas
☐ 1072 Rich Morales MGR
☐ 1073 Bobby Cuellar CO

1990 Williamsport Bills Star

This 27-card standard-size set of the 1990 Williamsport Bills, a Class AA Eastern League affiliate of the Seattle Mariners, features blue bordered posed color player photos on its fronts. The player's name, team name, and position appear at the bottom. The white horizontal back carries the player's name at the top, followed by biography, career highlights, and statistics.

	MINT	NRMT	EXC
COMPLETE SET (27)			

☐ 1 Jim Blueberg
☐ 2 Jim Bowie
☐ 3 Dave Brundage
☐ 4 Rich DeLucia
☐ 5 Troy Evers
☐ 6 Fernando Figueroa
☐ 7 Mike Gardiner
☐ 8 Mike Goff
☐ 9 Lee Hancock
☐ 10 Chuck Hensley
☐ 11 Jeff Hooper
☐ 12 Chris Howard
☐ 13 Bryan King
☐ 14 Dru Kosco
☐ 15 Shane Letterio
☐ 16 Mike McDonald
☐ 17 Mark Merchant
☐ 18 Jeff Nelson
☐ 19 Ken Pennington
☐ 20 Mark Razook
☐ 21 Dana Ridenour
☐ 22 Ricky Rojas
☐ 23 Ted Williams
☐ 24 Mark Wooden
☐ 25 Rich Morales MGR
☐ 26 Bobby Cuellar CO
☐ 27 Chris Verna TR

1990 Winston-Salem Spirits Team Issue

	MINT	NRMT	EXC
COMPLETE SET (30)	6.00	2.70	.75

☐ 1 Gary Scott
☐ 2 Billy White
☐ 3 John Salles
☐ 4 Paul Blair
☐ 5 Bill Melvin
☐ 6 John Gardner
☐ 7 Doug Welch
☐ 8 Dale Craig
☐ 9 Derek Stroud
☐ 10 Kevin Roberson
☐ 11 Fernando Ramsey
☐ 12 Shannon Jones
☐ 13 Ronnie Rasp
☐ 14 Jim Murphy
☐ 15 John Jensen
☐ 16 Steve DiBartolomeo
☐ 17 Jim Bullinger
☐ 18 Ed Caballero
☐ 19 Tim Moore
☐ 20 Jeff Massicotte
☐ 21 Tracy Smith
☐ 22 Scott Taylor
☐ 23 Julio Strauss
☐ 24 Elvin Paulino
☐ 25 Eddie Williams
☐ 26 Lickety Split
☐ 27 Steve Melendez
☐ 28 Bill Earley
☐ 29 Brad Mills
☐ 30 1990 Spirits

1990 Winter Haven Red Sox Star

This 28-card standard-size set of the 1990 Winter Haven Red Sox, a Class A Florida State League affiliate of the Boston Red Sox, features blue bordered posed color player photos on its fronts. The player's name, team name, and position appear at the bottom. The white horizontal back carries the player's name at the top, followed by biography, career highlights, and statistics.

	MINT	NRMT	EXC
COMPLETE SET (28)	5.00	2.20	.60

- ☐ 1 Tracy Allen
- ☐ 2 Felix Colon
- ☐ 3 Freddie Davis
- ☐ 4 Alex Delgado
- ☐ 5 Jim Dennison
- ☐ 6 Colin Dixon
- ☐ 7 Willie Dukes
- ☐ 8 Ray Fagnant
- ☐ 9 Jason Friedman
- ☐ 10 Greg Hansell
- ☐ 11 Pete Hoy
- ☐ 12 Garrett Jenkins
- ☐ 13 Dan Kite
- ☐ 14 Pedro Matilla
- ☐ 15 Jeff McNeely
- ☐ 16 Steve Michael
- ☐ 17 Bart Moore
- ☐ 18 Boo Moore
- ☐ 19 Tony Mosley
- ☐ 20 Lou Munoz
- ☐ 21 Paul Quantrill
- ☐ 22 Ed Riley
- ☐ 23 Andy Rush
- ☐ 24 Al Sanders
- ☐ 25 Richard Witherspoon
- ☐ 26 Dave Holt MGR
- ☐ 27 Doug Camilli CO
- ☐ 28 Jim Stricek TR

1990 Yakima Bears Team Issue

	MINT	NRMT	EXC
COMPLETE SET (37)	6.00	2.70	.75

- ☐ 1 Garrett Beard
- ☐ 2 Javier Delahoya
- ☐ 3 Mike Sampson
- ☐ 4 Helms Borhinger
- ☐ 5 Juan Bustabad
- ☐ 6 Kurt Olson
- ☐ 7 Jeff Brummer
- ☐ 8 Ken Burroughs
- ☐ 9 Erik Madsen
- ☐ 10 Daniel Cardenas
- ☐ 11 Hector Ortiz
- ☐ 12 Pedro Astacio
- ☐ 13 Rafael Rijo
- ☐ 14 Tim Patrick
- ☐ 15 Scott Doffek
- ☐ 16 Ben O'Connor
- ☐ 17 Joe Kelly
- ☐ 18 Billy Lott
- ☐ 19 Tony Arnold CO
- ☐ 20 Steve Ford VP/GM
- ☐ 21 Trainers
  Scott Faurot
  Eric Moen Asst.
- ☐ 22 Sean Sena
- ☐ 23 Jerry Royster MGR
- ☐ 24 Craig White
- ☐ 25 Nolberton Troncoso
- ☐ 26 Mike Galle
- ☐ 27 Craig Bishop
- ☐ 28 Scott Freeman
- ☐ 29 Steve Mintz
- ☐ 30 Eric Blackwell
- ☐ 31 Paul Branconier
- ☐ 32 Yale Fowler
- ☐ 33 Fausto Tatis
- ☐ 34 Jose Perez
- ☐ 35 Jorge Cantres
- ☐ 36 Pedro Perez
- ☐ NNO Team Picture

1991 Albany Yankees Classic/Best Kraft

This 6-card set features white-bordered posed color player photos on its fronts. The player's name, team, and position appear at the bottom. A Classic and Kraft logo also appear on the front of the card. The white back is framed by a thin black line and carries the player's name and position at the top, followed by biography, statistics and team logos.

	MINT	NRMT	EXC
COMPLETE SET (6)	8.00	3.60	1.00

- ☐ 1 Pat Kelly
- ☐ 2 Wade Taylor
- ☐ 3 Bernie Williams
- ☐ 4 John Ramos
- ☐ 5 Willie Smith
- ☐ 6 Coupon Card

1991 Albany Yankees Line Drive

	MINT	NRMT	EXC
COMPLETE SET (26)	5.00	2.20	.60

- ☐ 1 Andy Cook
- ☐ 2 Russell Davis
- ☐ 3 Bobby DeJardin
- ☐ 4 Mike Draper
- ☐ 5 Victor Garcia
- ☐ 6 Mike Gardella
- ☐ 7 Cullen Hartzog
- ☐ 8 Jay Knoblauh
- ☐ 9 Billy Masse
- ☐ 10 Jeff Livesey
- ☐ 11 Edward Martel
- ☐ 12 Vince Phillips
- ☐ 13 Tom Popplewell
- ☐ 14 Jerry Rub
- ☐ 15 Dave Silvestri
- ☐ 16 Tom Newell
- ☐ 17 Willie Smith
- ☐ 18 J.T Snow
- ☐ 19 Don Stanford
- ☐ 20 Larry Stanford
- ☐ 21 John Toale
- ☐ 22 Hector Vargas
- ☐ 23 Gerald Williams
- ☐ 24 Dan Radison MG
- ☐ 25 Dave Jorn CO
  Bob Mariano CO
- ☐ NNO Checklist

1991 Albany Yankees ProCards

This 28-card standard-size set of the 1991 Albany Yankees, a Class AA Eastern League affiliate of the New York Yankees, features on its white-bordered fronts posed color player photos set on simulated spiral-bound yellow notebooks. The player's name, position, and team appear within a green rectangle below the photo. The yellow horizontal back is bordered in white and carries the player's name at the top, followed by biography and statistics.

	MINT	NRMT	EXC
COMPLETE SET (28)	5.00	2.20	.60

- ☐ 999 Andy Cook
- ☐ 1000 Mike Draper
- ☐ 1001 Victor Garcia
- ☐ 1002 Mike Gardella
- ☐ 1003 Cullen Hartzog
- ☐ 1004 Ed Martel
- ☐ 1005 Tom Newell
- ☐ 1006 Tom Popplewell
- ☐ 1007 Jerry Rub
- ☐ 1008 Willie Smith
- ☐ 1009 Don Stanford
- ☐ 1010 Larry Stanford
- ☐ 1011 Jeff Livesey
- ☐ 1012 Andy Skeels
- ☐ 1013 John Toale
- ☐ 1014 Russ Davis
- ☐ 1015 Bobby DeJardin
- ☐ 1016 Dave Silvestri
- ☐ 1017 J.T. Snow
- ☐ 1018 Hector Vargas
- ☐ 1019 Jay Knoblauh
- ☐ 1020 Billy Masse
- ☐ 1021 Vince Phillips
- ☐ 1022 Gerald Williams
- ☐ 1023 Dan Radison MGR
- ☐ 1024 Dave Jorn CO
- ☐ 1025 Bob Mariano CO
- ☐ 1026 Checklist

1991 Albuquerque Dukes Line Drive

	MINT	NRMT	EXC
COMPLETE SET (26)	10.00	4.50	1.25

- ☐ 1 Billy Bean
- ☐ 2 Jerry Brooks
- ☐ 3 Mike Cristopher
- ☐ 4 Dennis Cook
- ☐ 5 Butch Davis
- ☐ 6 Tom Goodwin
- ☐ 7 Dave Hansen
- ☐ 8 Jeff Hartsock
- ☐ 9 Bert Heffernan
- ☐ 10 Carlos Hernandez
- ☐ 11 Chris Jones
- ☐ 12 Eric Karros
- ☐ 13 Dave Lynch
- ☐ 14 Luis Martinez
- ☐ 15 Jamie McAndrew
- ☐ 16 Jim Neidlinger
- ☐ 17 Jose Offerman
- ☐ 18 Eddie Pye
- ☐ 19 Henry Rodriguez
- ☐ 20 Greg Smith
- ☐ 21 Dave Veres
- ☐ 22 Dave Walsh
- ☐ 23 John Wetteland
- ☐ 24 Kevin Kennedy MGR
- ☐ 25 Von Joshua CO
  Claude Osteen CO
- ☐ NNO Checklist

1991 Albuquerque Dukes ProCards

This 27-card standard-size set of the 1991 Albuquerque Dukes, a Class AAA Pacific Coast League affiliate of the Los Angeles Dodgers, features on its white-bordered fronts posed color player photos set on simulated spiral-bound yellow notebooks. The player's name, position, and team appear within a green rectangle below the photo. The yellow horizontal back is bordered in white and carries the player's name at the top, followed by biography and statistics. This issue includes a third year card of Henry Rodriguez and a fourth year card of Eric Karros.

	MINT	NRMT	EXC
COMPLETE SET (27)	10.00	4.50	1.25

- ☐ 1134 Mike Christopher
- ☐ 1135 Jeff Hartsock
- ☐ 1136 Chris Jones
- ☐ 1137 Dave Lynch
- ☐ 1138 Jamie McAndrew
- ☐ 1139 Jim Neidlinger
- ☐ 1140 Dan Opperman
- ☐ 1141 Dave Veres
- ☐ 1142 John Wetteland
- ☐ 1143 Bert Heffernan
- ☐ 1144 Carlos Hernandez
- ☐ 1145 Dave Hansen
- ☐ 1146 Eric Harros
- ☐ 1147 Luis Martinez
- ☐ 1148 Walt McConnell
- ☐ 1149 Jose Offerman
- ☐ 1150 Eddie Pye
- ☐ 1151 Greg Smith
- ☐ 1152 Billy Bean
- ☐ 1153 Jerry Brooks
- ☐ 1154 Butch Davis
- ☐ 1155 Tom Goodwin
- ☐ 1156 Henry Rodriguez
- ☐ 1157 Kevin Kennedy MGR
- ☐ 1158 Von Joshua CO
- ☐ 1159 Claude Osteen CO
- ☐ 1160 Checklist

1991 Appleton Foxes Classic/Best

This 29-card standard-size set of the 1991 Appleton Foxes, a Class A Midwest League affiliate of the Kansas City Royals, features white-bordered posed color player photos on its fronts. The player's name, team, and position appear at the bottom. The white back is framed by a thin black line and carries the player's name and position at the top, followed by biography, statistics and team logos.

	MINT	NRMT	EXC
COMPLETE SET (29)	5.00	2.20	.60

- ☐ 1 Francisco Baez
- ☐ 2 Jim Chrisman
- ☐ 3 Wade Fyock
- ☐ 4 Doug Harris
- ☐ 5 David Hierholzer
- ☐ 6 Herb Milton
- ☐ 7 Vernon Slater
- ☐ 8 Dario Perez
- ☐ 9 Gabriel Pineda
- ☐ 10 Damon Pollard
- ☐ 11 Shayne Rea
- ☐ 12 Donny Harrel
- ☐ 13 Lance Jennings
- ☐ 14 Chad Strickland
- ☐ 15 Gary Caraballo
- ☐ 16 Jeff Clarke
- ☐ 17 George Day
- ☐ 18 Harry Guanchez
- ☐ 19 Giovanni Miranda
- ☐ 20 Brady Stewart
- ☐ 21 Brad Shores TR
- ☐ 22 Darren Burton
- ☐ 23 Butch Cole
- ☐ 24 Ed Gerald
- ☐ 25 Tom Smith
- ☐ 26 Joe Breeden MGR
- ☐ 27 Mike Jirschele CO
- ☐ 28 Mike Mason
  Pitching Instructor
- ☐ 29 Checklist

1991 Appleton Foxes ProCards

This 28-card standard-size set of the 1991 Appleton Foxes, a Class A Midwest League affiliate of the Kansas City Royals, features on its white-bordered fronts posed color player photos set on simulated spiral-bound yellow notebooks. The player's name, position, and team appear within a green rectangle below the photo. The yellow horizontal back is bordered in white and carries the player's name at the top, followed by biography and statistics.

	MINT	NRMT	EXC
COMPLETE SET (28)	5.00	2.20	.60

- ☐ 1707 Francisco Baez
- ☐ 1708 Jim Chrisman
- ☐ 1709 Wade Fyock
- ☐ 1710 Doug Harris
- ☐ 1711 Dave Hierholzer
- ☐ 1712 Herb Milton
- ☐ 1713 Rodney Myers
- ☐ 1714 Dario Perez
- ☐ 1715 Gabriel Pineda
- ☐ 1716 Damon Pollard
- ☐ 1717 Shayne Rea
- ☐ 1718 Donny Harrel
- ☐ 1719 Lance Jennings
- ☐ 1720 Chad Strickland
- ☐ 1721 Gary Caraballo
- ☐ 1722 Jeff Clarke
- ☐ 1723 George Day
- ☐ 1724 Harry Guanchez
- ☐ 1725 Giovanni Miranda
- ☐ 1726 Brady Stewart
- ☐ 1727 Darren Burton
- ☐ 1728 Butch Cole
- ☐ 1729 Ed Gerald
- ☐ 1730 Tom Smith
- ☐ 1731 Joe Breeden MGR
- ☐ 1732 Mike Jirschele CO
- ☐ 1733 Mike Mason CO
- ☐ 1734 Checklist

1991 Arkansas Travelers Line Drive

	MINT	NRMT	EXC
COMPLETE SET (26)	5.00	2.20	.60

- ☐ 26 Frank Abreu
- ☐ 27 Cliff Brannon
- ☐ 28 Greg Carmona
- ☐ 29 Ric Christian
- ☐ 30 John Ericks
- ☐ 31 Steve Fanning
- ☐ 32 Joey Fernandez
- ☐ 33 Jose Fernandez
- ☐ 34 Mike Fiore
- ☐ 35 David Grimes
- ☐ 36 Dale Kisten
- ☐ 37 John Lepley
- ☐ 38 Luis Martinez
- ☐ 39 Mike Milchin
- ☐ 40 Donovan Osborne
- ☐ 41 Gabriel Ozuna
- ☐ 42 Lee Plemel
- ☐ 43 Don Prybylinski
- ☐ 44 John Sellick
- ☐ 45 Jeff Shireman
- ☐ 46 Brian Stone
- ☐ 47 Charlie White
- ☐ 48 Dennis Wiseman
- ☐ 49 Joe Pettini MGR
- ☐ 50 Scott Melvin CO
  Marty Mason CO
- ☐ NNO Title card

1991 Arkansas Travelers ProCards

This 29-card standard-size set of the 1991 Arkansas Travelers, a Class AA Texas League affiliate of the St. Louis Cardinals, features on its white-bordered fronts posed color player photos set on simulated spiral-bound yellow notebooks. The player's name, position, and team appear within a green rectangle below the photo. The yellow horizontal back is bordered in white and carries the player's name at the top, followed by biography and statistics.

	MINT	NRMT	EXC
COMPLETE SET (29)	5.00	2.20	.60

- ☐ 1276 Fidel Compres
- ☐ 1277 John Ericks
- ☐ 1278 David Grimes
- ☐ 1279 Dale Kisten
- ☐ 1280 John Lepley
- ☐ 1281 Steffen Majer
- ☐ 1282 Mike Milchin
- ☐ 1283 Donovan Osborne
- ☐ 1284 Gabriel Ozuna
- ☐ 1285 Lee Plemel
- ☐ 1286 Dean Weese
- ☐ 1287 Dennis Wiseman
- ☐ 1288 Jose Fernandez
- ☐ 1289 Don Prybylinski
- ☐ 1290 Tim Redman
- ☐ 1291 Greg Carmona
- ☐ 1292 Steve Fanning
- ☐ 1293 Joey Fernandez
- ☐ 1294 Mike Fiore
- ☐ 1295 Scott Melvin
- ☐ 1296 John Sellick
- ☐ 1297 Jeff Shireman
- ☐ 1298 Cliff Brannon
- ☐ 1299 Rick Christian
- ☐ 1300 Luis Martinez

- ☐ 1301 Charlie White
- ☐ 1302 Joe Pettini MGR
- ☐ 1303 Marty Mason CO
- ☐ 1304 Checklist

1991 Asheville Tourists Classic/Best

This 29-card standard-size set of the 1991 Asheville Tourists, a Class A South Atlantic League affiliate of the Houston Astros, features white-bordered posed color player photos on its fronts. The player's name, team, and position appear at the bottom. The white back is framed by a thin black line and carries the player's name and position at the top, followed by biography, statistics and team logos.

	MINT	NRMT	EXC
COMPLETE SET (29)	5.00	2.20	.60

- ☐ 1 Efrain Barreiro
- ☐ 2 Paul Branconier
- ☐ 3 Duane Brown
- ☐ 4 Jim Daugherty
- ☐ 5 Javier Hernandez
- ☐ 6 Douglas Ketchen
- ☐ 7 Fionel Nieves
- ☐ 8 Steve Powers
- ☐ 9 Mario Prts
- ☐ 10 Dennis Reed
- ☐ 11 David Wilson
- ☐ 12 Nicky Davis
- ☐ 13 Jose Flores
- ☐ 15 Alberto Montero
- ☐ 16 Tom Nevers
- ☐ 17 Steve Veit
- ☐ 18 Bob Hurlbutt
- ☐ 19 Raphael Lanfranco
- ☐ 20 Lance Smith
- ☐ 21 John Gonzales
- ☐ 22 Vince Roman
- ☐ 23 Jermaine Swinton
- ☐ 24 David Wallace
- ☐ 25 Jimmy White
- ☐ 26 Frank Cacciatore MGR
- ☐ 27 Rick Aponte CO
- ☐ 28 Bob Robertson CO
- ☐ 29 Ron Hanishch TR Checklist

1991 Asheville Tourists ProCards

This 29-card standard-size set of the 1991 Asheville Tourists, a Class A South Atlantic League affiliate of the Houston Astros, features on its white-bordered fronts posed color player photos set on simulated spiral-bound yellow notebooks. The player's name, position, and team appear within a green rectangle below the photo. The yellow horizontal back is bordered in white and carries the player's name at the top, followed by biography and statistics.

	MINT	NRMT	EXC
COMPLETE SET (29)	5.00	2.20	.60

- ☐ 559 Efrain Barreiro
- ☐ 560 Paul Branconier
- ☐ 561 Duane Brown
- ☐ 562 Jim Daugherty
- ☐ 563 Javier Hernandez
- ☐ 564 Doug Ketchen
- ☐ 565 Fionel Nieves
- ☐ 566 Steve Powers
- ☐ 567 Mario Prats
- ☐ 568 Dennis Reed
- ☐ 569 Dave Wilson
- ☐ 570 Bob Hurlbutt
- ☐ 571 Rafael LanFranco
- ☐ 572 Lance Smith
- ☐ 573 Nick Davis
- ☐ 574 Jose Flores
- ☐ 575 Al Harley
- ☐ 576 Alberto Montero
- ☐ 577 Tom Nevers
- ☐ 578 Steve Veit
- ☐ 579 John Gonzales
- ☐ 580 Vince Roman
- ☐ 581 Jermaine Swinton
- ☐ 582 David Wallace
- ☐ 583 Jimmy White
- ☐ 584 Frank Cacciatore MGR
- ☐ 585 Ricardo Aponte CO
- ☐ 586 Bob Robertson CO
- ☐ 587 Checklist

1991 Auburn Astros Classic/Best

This 29-card standard-size set of the 1991 Auburn Astros, a Class A New York-Penn League affiliate of the Houston Astros, features white-bordered posed color player photos on its fronts. The player's name, team, and position appear at the bottom. The white back is framed by a thin black line and carries the player's name and position at the top, followed by biography, statistics and team logos.

	MINT	NRMT	EXC
COMPLETE SET (29)	5.00	2.20	.60

- ☐ 1 Mark Loughlin
- ☐ 2 Tony Miller
- ☐ 3 Jim Lewis
- ☐ 4 Rod Biehl
- ☐ 5 Chris White
- ☐ 6 Louie Martinez
- ☐ 7 Jamie Evans
- ☐ 8 Tom Anderson
- ☐ 9 Joe Sewell
- ☐ 10 Rich Schulte
- ☐ 11 Ron Calini
- ☐ 12 Don Angotti
- ☐ 13 Eric Martinez
- ☐ 14 Mike Murphy
- ☐ 15 Mario Linares
- ☐ 16 Bryant Winslow
- ☐ 17 James Mouton
- ☐ 18 Todd Hobson
- ☐ 19 Chris Durkin
- ☐ 20 Brian McGione
- ☐ 21 Brian Thompson
- ☐ 22 Jim Waring
- ☐ 23 Mick Matuszak TR
- ☐ 24 Clar Crist CO
- ☐ 25 Don Alexander CO
- ☐ 26 Steve Dillard MGR
- ☐ 27 Kory Finzer Dir. Special Events
- ☐ 28 Marc Techman Asst GM
- ☐ 29 John Garham GM Checklist

1991 Auburn Astros ProCards

This 26-card standard-size set of the 1991 Auburn Astros, a Class A New York-Penn League affiliate of the Houston Astros, features on its white-bordered fronts posed color player photos set on simulated spiral-bound yellow notebooks. The player's name, position, and team appear within a green rectangle below the photo. The yellow horizontal back is bordered in white and carries the player's name at the top, followed by biography and statistics.

	MINT	NRMT	EXC
COMPLETE SET (26)	5.00	2.20	.60

- ☐ 4267 Rod Biehl
- ☐ 4268 Jamie Evans
- ☐ 4269 Jim Lewis
- ☐ 4270 Mark Loughlin
- ☐ 4271 Louie Martinez
- ☐ 4272 Tony Miller
- ☐ 4273 Joe Sewell
- ☐ 4274 Jim Waring
- ☐ 4275 Chris White
- ☐ 4276 Don Angotti
- ☐ 4277 Mario Linares
- ☐ 4278 Mike Murphy
- ☐ 4279 Ron Cacini
- ☐ 4280 Eric Martinez
- ☐ 4281 Brian McGlone
- ☐ 4282 James Mouton
- ☐ 4283 Bryant Winslow
- ☐ 4284 Miguel Cabrera
- ☐ 4285 Chris Durkin
- ☐ 4286 Todd Hobson
- ☐ 4287 Rich Schulte
- ☐ 4288 Brian Thompson
- ☐ 4289 Steve Dillard MGR
- ☐ 4290 Don Alexander CO
- ☐ 4291 Clark Crist CO
- ☐ 4292 Checklist

1991 Augusta Pirates Classic/Best

This 30-card standard-size set of the 1991 Augusta Pirates, a Class A South Atlantic League affiliate of the Pittsburgh Pirates, features white-bordered posed color player photos on its fronts. The player's name, team, and position appear at the bottom. The white back is framed by a thin black line and carries the player's name and position at the top, followed by biography, statistics and team logos.

	MINT	NRMT	EXC
COMPLETE SET (30)	5.00	2.20	.60

- ☐ 1 Julio Garcia CO
- ☐ 2 Scott Arvesen
- ☐ 3 Lynn Garlson
- ☐ 4 Steve Cooke
- ☐ 5 Hector Fajardo
- ☐ 6 Mark Futrell
- ☐ 7 Donnie Gobel
- ☐ 8 Bobby Hunter
- ☐ 9 John Latham
- ☐ 10 Troy Mooney
- ☐ 11 Brian Shouse
- ☐ 12 Rick White
- ☐ 13 Marcus Hanel
- ☐ 14 Jessie Torres
- ☐ 15 Mark Johnson
- ☐ 16 Ramon Martinez
- ☐ 17 Steve Polewski
- ☐ 18 Hector Rodriguez
- ☐ 19 Pasquale Arace
- ☐ 20 Tom Green
- ☐ 21 Paul List
- ☐ 22 Joe Ronca
- ☐ 23 Tony Brown
- ☐ 24 Mike Brown
- ☐ 25 Scott Bullett
- ☐ 26 Joe Sondrini
- ☐ 27 Rick Keeton CO
- ☐ 28 Kurt Miller
- ☐ 29 Genaro Campusano
- ☐ 30 Don Werner MGR Checklist

1991 Augusta Pirates ProCards

This 31-card standard-size set of the 1991 Augusta Pirates, a Class A South Atlantic League affiliate of the Pittsburgh Pirates, features on its white-bordered fronts posed color player photos set on simulated spiral-bound yellow notebooks. The player's name, position, and team appear within a green rectangle below the photo. The yellow horizontal back is bordered in white and carries the player's name at the top, followed by biography and statistics.

	MINT	NRMT	EXC
COMPLETE SET (31)	5.00	2.20	.60

- ☐ 795 Scott Arvesen
- ☐ 796 Lynn Carlson
- ☐ 797 Steve Cooke
- ☐ 798 Hector Fajardo
- ☐ 799 Mark Futrell
- ☐ 800 Donnie Gobel
- ☐ 801 John Latham
- ☐ 802 Jeff Lyle
- ☐ 803 Kurt Miller
- ☐ 804 Troy Mooney
- ☐ 805 Andre Redmond
- ☐ 806 Rick White
- ☐ 807 Mark Hanel
- ☐ 808 Jessie Torres
- ☐ 809 Mike Brown
- ☐ 810 Genaro Campusano
- ☐ 811 Mark Johnson
- ☐ 812 Ramon Martinez
- ☐ 813 Steve Polewski
- ☐ 814 Hector Rodriguez
- ☐ 815 Joe Sondrini
- ☐ 816 Pasquale Arace
- ☐ 817 Anthony Brown
- ☐ 818 Scott Bullett
- ☐ 819 Tom Green
- ☐ 820 Paul List
- ☐ 821 Joe Ronca
- ☐ 822 Don Werner MGR
- ☐ 823 Julio Garcia CO
- ☐ 824 Rick Keeton CO
- ☐ 825 Checklist

1991 Bakersfield Dodgers Cal League Cards

This issue includes a second year card of Raul Mondesi and a third year card of Mike Piazza.

	MINT	NRMT	EXC
COMPLETE SET (32)	16.00	7.25	2.00

- ☐ 1 Raul Mondesi
- ☐ 2 Ron Maurer
- ☐ 3 Fausto Tatis
- ☐ 4 Gordon Tipton
- ☐ 5 Ed Stryker
- ☐ 6 Rex Peters
- ☐ 7 Mike Piazza
- ☐ 8 Brian Piotrowicz
- ☐ 9 Alan Lewis
- ☐ 10 Domingo Mota
- ☐ 11 Steve Mintz
- ☐ 12 Mark Mimbs
- ☐ 13 Ed Lund
- ☐ 14 Garey Ingram
- ☐ 15 Billy Lott
- ☐ 16 Mike Galle
- ☐ 17 Greg Hansell
- ☐ 18 Javier DeLaHoya
- ☐ 19 Dino Ebel
- ☐ 20 Anthony Collier
- ☐ 21 James Daspit
- ☐ 22 Dan Cardenas
- ☐ 23 Garrett Beard
- ☐ 24 Helms Bohringer
- ☐ 25 Mike Busch
- ☐ 26 Al Bustillos
- ☐ 27 Don Carroll
- ☐ 28 Tom Beters
- ☐ 29 Glenn Gregson
- ☐ 30 Glenn Hoffman
- ☐ 31 Terry McFarlin
- ☐ 32 Pedro Martinez

1991 Baseball City Royals Classic/Best

This 30-card standard-size set of the 1991 Baseball City Royals, a Class A Florida State League affiliate of the Kansas City Royals, features white-bordered posed color player photos on its fronts. The player's name, team, and position appear at the bottom. The white back is framed by a thin black line and carries the player's name and position at the top, followed by biography, statistics and team logos.

	MINT	NRMT	EXC
COMPLETE SET (30)	5.00	2.20	.60

- ☐ 1 Andres Berumen
- ☐ 2 John Conner
- ☐ 3 Bubba Dunn
- ☐ 4 John Gross
- ☐ 5 Greg Harvey
- ☐ 6 Brad Hopper
- ☐ 7 Jake Jacobs
- ☐ 8 Matt Karchner
- ☐ 9 Tony Long
- ☐ 10 John McCormick
- ☐ 11 Kevin Shaw
- ☐ 12 Skip Wiley
- ☐ 13 Huascar DeLeon
- ☐ 14 Travis Kinyoun
- ☐ 15 Colin Ryan
- ☐ 16 Dave Solseth
- ☐ 17 Phil Hiatt
- ☐ 18 David King
- ☐ 19 Cesar Morillo
- ☐ 20 Fred Russell
- ☐ 21 John Schreiner
- ☐ 22 Pedro Vazquez
- ☐ 23 Jay Andrews III
- ☐ 24 John Gilcrist
- ☐ 25 Scott Hennessey
- ☐ 26 Kerwin Moore
- ☐ 27 Doug Shields
- ☐ 28 Carlos Tosca MGR
- ☐ 29 Ron Johnson CO
- ☐ 30 Pete Filson CO

1991 Baseball City Royals ProCards

This 29-card standard-size set of the 1991 Baseball City Royals, a Class A Florida State League affiliate of the Kansas City Royals, features on its white-bordered fronts posed color player photos set on simulated spiral-bound yellow notebooks. The player's name, position, and team appear within a green rectangle below the photo. The yellow horizontal back is bordered in white and carries the player's name at the top, followed by biography and statistics.

	MINT	NRMT	EXC
COMPLETE SET (29)	5.00	2.20	.60

- ☐ 1388 Andres Berumen
- ☐ 1389 John Conner
- ☐ 1390 Bubba Dunn
- ☐ 1391 John Gross
- ☐ 1392 Greg Harvey
- ☐ 1393 Brad Hopper
- ☐ 1394 Jake Jacobs
- ☐ 1395 Matt Karchner
- ☐ 1396 Tony Long
- ☐ 1397 John McCormick
- ☐ 1398 Kevin Shaw
- ☐ 1399 Skip Wiley
- ☐ 1400 Travis Kinyoun
- ☐ 1401 Colin Ryan
- ☐ 1402 Dave Solseth
- ☐ 1403 Phil Hiatt
- ☐ 1404 David King
- ☐ 1405 Cesar Morillo
- ☐ 1406 Fred Russell
- ☐ 1407 John Schreiner
- ☐ 1408 Pedro Vazquez
- ☐ 1409 Jay Andrews
- ☐ 1410 John Gilcrist
- ☐ 1411 Scott Hennessey
- ☐ 1412 Kerwin Moore
- ☐ 1413 Doug Shields
- ☐ 1414 Pete Filson CO
- ☐ 1415 Ron Johnson CO
- ☐ 1416 Checklist

1991 Batavia Clippers Classic/Best

This 30-card standard-size set of the 1991 Batavia Clippers, a Class A New York-Penn League affiliate of the Philadelphia Phillies, features white-bordered posed color player photos on its fronts. The player's name, team, and position appear at the bottom. The white back is framed by a thin black line and carries the player's name and position at the top, followed by biography, statistics and team logos.

	MINT	NRMT	EXC
COMPLETE SET (30)	5.00	2.20	.60

- ☐ 1 Rob Nash
- ☐ 2 Gene Schall
- ☐ 3 Tommy Eason

☐ 4 Pat Ruth
☐ 5 Julio Vargas
☐ 6 Craig Billeci
☐ 7 Patrick Cheek
☐ 8 Lamar Foster
☐ 9 Jesus Garces
☐ 10 David Hayden
☐ 11 Bruce Smolen
☐ 12 Jerome Edwards
☐ 13 Antonio Grissom
☐ 14 Facaner Medina
☐ 15 Tom Vilet
☐ 16 Bryan Manicchia
☐ 17 Matt Whisenant
☐ 18 Carlos Arroyo CO
☐ 19 Glenn Nevill
☐ 20 Tyler Green
☐ 21 Pat Bojcun
☐ 22 Mike Grace
☐ 23 John Whisonant
☐ 24 Greg Brown
☐ 25 Ron Allen
☐ 26 Ron Blazier
☐ 27 Ramon Aviles MGR
☐ 28 Craig Holman
☐ 29 Chipper the Clipper Mascot
☐ 30 Gary Beatty TR Checklist

1991 Batavia Clippers ProCards

This 30-card standard-size set of the 1991 Batavia Clippers, a Class A New York-Penn League affiliate of the Philadelphia Phillies, features on its white-bordered fronts posed color player photos set on simulated spiral-bound yellow notebooks. The player's name, position, and team appear within a green rectangle below the photo. The yellow horizontal back is bordered in white and carries the player's name at the top, followed by biography and statistics.

	MINT	NRMT	EXC
COMPLETE SET (30)	5.00	2.20	.60

☐ 3474 Ron Allen
☐ 3475 Ron Blazier
☐ 3476 Pat Bojcun
☐ 3477 Greg Brown
☐ 3478 Mike Grace
☐ 3479 Tyler Green
☐ 3480 Craig Holman
☐ 3481 Bryan Manicchia
☐ 3482 Glenn Nevill
☐ 3483 Matt Whisenant
☐ 3484 John Whisonant
☐ 3485 Tommy Eason
☐ 3486 Pat Ruth
☐ 3487 Julio Vargas
☐ 3488 Craig Billeci
☐ 3489 Pat Cheek
☐ 3490 Lamar Foster
☐ 3491 Jesus Garces
☐ 3492 David Hayden
☐ 3493 Gene Schall
☐ 3494 Bruce Smolen
☐ 3495 Jerome Edwards
☐ 3496 Antonio Grissom
☐ 3497 Facaner Medina
☐ 3498 Rob Nash
☐ 3499 Tom Vilet
☐ 3500 Ramon Aviles MGR
☐ 3501 Carlos Arroyo CO
☐ 3502 Tony Scott CO
☐ 3503 Checklist

1991 Bellingham Mariners Classic/Best

This 30-card standard-size set of the 1991 Bellingham Mariners, a Class A Northwest League affiliate of the Seattle Mariners, features white-bordered posed color player photos on its fronts. The player's name, team, and position appear at the bottom. The white back is framed by a thin black line and carries the player's name and position at the top, followed by biography, statistics and team logos.

	MINT	NRMT	EXC
COMPLETE SET (30)	5.00	2.20	.60

☐ 1 Clem Barlow
☐ 2 Clay Klavitter
☐ 3 Tommy Boudreau
☐ 4 Jon Halland
☐ 5 Eddy Diaz
☐ 6 James Terrell
☐ 7 Sean Twitty
☐ 8 Todd Walles
☐ 9 Barney Erhard
☐ 10 Erik O'Donnell
☐ 11 Michael Bond
☐ 12 Charles Smith
☐ 13 Craig Clayton
☐ 14 Willie Speakman
☐ 15 Scott Bosarge
☐ 16 Tommy Adams
☐ 17 Julio Fernandez
☐ 18 Trey Witte
☐ 19 Doug Anderson
☐ 20 Pete Weinbaum
☐ 21 Toby Foreman
☐ 22 David Lisiecki
☐ 23 Jeff Borski
☐ 24 Charles Wiley
☐ 25 Todd Youngblood
☐ 26 Giovanni Polanco
☐ 27 Staff
Dave Myers MGR
Spyder Webb TR
Gary Wheelock CO
☐ 28 LaGrande Russell
☐ 29 Shawn Estes
☐ 30 Checklist

1991 Bellingham Mariners ProCards

This 32-card standard-size set of the 1991 Bellingham Mariners, a Class A Northwest League affiliate of the Seattle Mariners, features on its white-bordered fronts posed color player photos set on simulated spiral-bound yellow notebooks. The player's name, position, and team appear within a green rectangle below the photo. The yellow horizontal back is bordered in white and carries the player's name at the top, followed by biography and statistics

	MINT	NRMT	EXC
COMPLETE SET (32)	5.00	2.20	.60

☐ 3654 Doug Anderson
☐ 3655 Jeff Borski
☐ 3656 Shawn Estes
☐ 3657 Toby Foreman
☐ 3658 David Lisiecki
☐ 3659 Erik O'Donnell
☐ 3660 Giovanni Polanco
☐ 3661 Julio Reyan
☐ 3662 Richard Russell
☐ 3663 Pete Weinbaum
☐ 3664 Charles Wiley
☐ 3665 Trey Witte
☐ 3666 Todd Youngblood
☐ 3667 Scott Bosarge
☐ 3668 Clay Klavitter
☐ 3669 Willie Speakman
☐ 3670 Michael Bond
☐ 3671 Craig Clayton
☐ 3672 Eddy Diaz
☐ 3673 Barney Erhard
☐ 3674 Jon Halland
☐ 3675 Bubba Smith
☐ 3676 Todd Walles
☐ 3677 Tommy Adams
☐ 3678 Clem Barlow
☐ 3679 Tommy Boudreau
☐ 3680 Julio Fernandez
☐ 3681 James Terrell
☐ 3682 Sean Twitty
☐ 3683 Dave Myers MGR
☐ 3684 Gary Wheelock CO
☐ 4174 Checklist

1991 Beloit Brewers Classic/Best

This 28-card standard-size set of the 1991 Beloit Brewers, a Class A Midwest League affiliate of the Milwaukee Brewers, features white-bordered posed color player photos on its fronts. The player's name, team, and position appear at the bottom. The white back is framed by a thin black line and carries the player's name and position at the top, followed by biography, statistics and team logos.

	MINT	NRMT	EXC
COMPLETE SET (28)	5.00	2.20	.60

☐ 1 William Brakeley
☐ 2 Larry Carter
☐ 3 Francisco Gamez
☐ 4 Geoffrey Kellogg
☐ 5 Pat Miller
☐ 6 Donald Pruitt
☐ 7 Brian Souze
☐ 8 Mark Stephens
☐ 9 James Sass
☐ 10 Jason Zimbauer
☐ 11 Steve Diaz
☐ 12 Darrin White
☐ 13 Juan Cabrera
☐ 14 Tim Carter
☐ 15 Gordon Powell Jr.
☐ 16 Julian Salazar
☐ 17 Bobby Benjamin
☐ 18 Tony Diggs
☐ 19 Todd Edwards
☐ 20 Graciano Enriquez
☐ 21 Chris Ervin
☐ 22 Michael Carter
☐ 23 Dave Wrona
☐ 24 Leon Glenn
☐ 25 Mike Hooper
☐ 26 Dave Rajsich CO
☐ 27 Rob Derksen MGR
☐ 28 James Hvizda Checklist

1991 Beloit Brewers ProCards

This 28-card standard-size set of the 1991 Beloit Brewers, a Class A Midwest League affiliate of the Milwaukee Brewers, features on its white-bordered fronts posed color player photos set on simulated spiral-bound yellow notebooks. The player's name, position, and team appear within a green rectangle below the photo. The yellow horizontal back is bordered in white and carries the player's name at the top, followed by biography and statistics.

	MINT	NRMT	EXC
COMPLETE SET (28)	5.00	2.20	.60

☐ 2094 William Brakeley
☐ 2095 Larry Carter
☐ 2096 Francisco Gamez
☐ 2097 Mike Hooper
☐ 2098 Jim Hvizda
☐ 2099 Geoffrey Kellogg
☐ 2100 Pat Miller
☐ 2101 Donald Pruitt
☐ 2102 Brian Souza
☐ 2103 Mark Stephens
☐ 2104 Jason Zimbauer
☐ 2105 Steve Diaz
☐ 2106 Darrin White
☐ 2107 Juan Cabrera
☐ 2108 Michael Carter
☐ 2109 Tim Carter
☐ 2110 Leon Glenn
☐ 2111 Gordon Powell
☐ 2112 Julian Salazar
☐ 2113 Dave Wrona
☐ 2114 Bobby Benjamin
☐ 2115 Tony Diggs
☐ 2116 Todd Edwards
☐ 2117 Graciano Enriquez
☐ 2118 James Sass
☐ 2119 Rob Derksen MGR
☐ 2120 Dave Rajsich CO
☐ 2121 Checklist

1991 Bend Bucks Classic/Best

This 29-card standard-size set of the 1991 Bend Bucks, a Class A Northwest League Independent, features white-bordered posed color player photos on its fronts. The player's name, team, and position appear at the bottom. The white back is framed by a thin black line and carries the player's name and position at the top, followed by biography, statistics and team logos.

	MINT	NRMT	EXC
COMPLETE SET (29)	5.00	2.20	.60

☐ 1 J.R. Cock
☐ 2 Tim Cain
☐ 3 Stan Kyles CO
☐ 4 Kyle Duke
☐ 5 Mark Finney
☐ 6 Steve Goucher
☐ 7 Darren Haddock
☐ 8 Tim Minik
☐ 9 Robert Person
☐ 10 Geoff Samuels
☐ 11 Mike Boker
☐ 12 Jim Fregosi Jr. CO
☐ 13 Jim Savage
☐ 14 Jerry Schoen
☐ 15 Frank Turco
☐ 16 Ryan Turner
☐ 17 Clifford Williams
☐ 18 Anthony Pritchett
☐ 19 Keith Ringgold
☐ 20 Scott Ollison
☐ 21 Stacy Parker
☐ 22 Brian McGee
☐ 23 Ed Lightner
☐ 24 Larry Hawks
☐ 25 Leon Glenn
☐ 26 Michael Bard
☐ 27 Eric Moen TR
☐ 28 Bill Stein MGR
☐ 29 Checklist

1991 Bend Bucks ProCards

This 29-card standard-size set of the 1991 Bend Bucks, a Class A Northwest League Independent, features on its white-bordered fronts posed color player photos set on simulated spiral-bound yellow notebooks. The player's name, position, and team appear within a green rectangle below the photo. The yellow horizontal back is bordered in white and carries the player's name at the top, followed by biography and statistics.

	MINT	NRMT	EXC
COMPLETE SET (29	5.00	2.20	.60

☐ 3685 Mike Boker
☐ 3686 Tim Cain
☐ 3687 Robbie Castaneda
☐ 3688 J.R. Cock
☐ 3689 Kyle Duke
☐ 3690 Mark Finney
☐ 3691 Steve Goucher
☐ 3692 Darin Haddock
☐ 3693 Tim Minik
☐ 3694 Robert Person
☐ 3695 Geoff Samuels
☐ 3696 Larry Hawks
☐ 3697 Brian McGee
☐ 3698 Cliff Williams
☐ 3699 Mike Bard
☐ 3700 Leon Glenn
☐ 3701 Ed Lightner
☐ 3702 Scott Ollison
☐ 3703 Jim Savage
☐ 3704 Jerry Schoen
☐ 3705 Frank Turco
☐ 3706 Stacy Parker
☐ 3707 Tony Pritchett
☐ 3708 Keith Ringgold
☐ 3709 Ryan Turner
☐ 3710 Bill Stein MGR
☐ 3711 Jim Fregosi Jr. CO
☐ 3712 Stan Kyles CO
☐ 3713 Checklist

1991 Billings Mustangs ProCards

This 28-card standard-size set of the 1991 Billings Mustangs, a Rookie Class Pioneer League affiliate of the Cincinnati Reds, features on its white-bordered fronts posed color player photos set on simulated spiral-bound yellow notebooks. The player's name, position, and team appear within a green rectangle below the photo. The yellow horizontal back is bordered in white and carries the player's name at the top, followed by biography and statistics.

	MINT	NRMT	EXC
COMPLETE SET (28)	5.00	2.20	.60

☐ 3745 Mike Coletti
☐ 3746 John Courtright
☐ 3747 Scott Dodd
☐ 3748 Phil Kendall
☐ 3749 Rich Langford
☐ 3750 Charles McClain
☐ 3751 Dave Reeves
☐ 3752 Dan Tobin
☐ 3753 Domingo Vivas
☐ 3754 Chuck Wyatt
☐ 3755 Rich Zastoupil
☐ 3756 Mike Harrison
☐ 3757 Bo Loftin
☐ 3758 Trey Wilburn
☐ 3759 Joe DeBerry
☐ 3760 Ramon Hernandez
☐ 3761 Mike Jones
☐ 3762 Brian Koelling
☐ 3763 Matt Martin
☐ 3764 Scott Snead
☐ 3765 Pierre Burris
☐ 3766 Derick Graham
☐ 3767 Bob Jesperson
☐ 3768 Damin Montgomery
☐ 3769 Gene Taylor
☐ 3770 P.J. Carey MGR
☐ 3771 Mack Jenkins CO
☐ 3772 Checklist

1991 Billings Mustangs Sports Pro

This 30-card standard-size set of the 1991 Billings Mustangs, a Rookie Class Pioneer League affiliate of the Cincinnati Reds, features posed color head-and-shoulders shots, with thin black borders on a white card face. The horizontally oriented backs have biographical information.

	MINT	NRMT	EXC
COMPLETE SET (30)	6.00	2.70	.75

☐ 1 Charles McClain
☐ 2 Pierre Burris
☐ 3 Scott Snead
☐ 4 Dan Tobin
☐ 5 Bo Loftin
☐ 6 Trey Wilburn
☐ 7 Domingo Vivas
☐ 8 Matt Martin
☐ 9 Derrick Graham
☐ 10 Chuck Wyatt
☐ 11 Scott Dodd
☐ 12 Damin Montgomery
☐ 13 John Coletti
☐ 14 Joe DeBerry
☐ 15 John Courtright
☐ 16 Gene Taylor
☐ 17 Ramon Hernandez
☐ 18 Mike Jones
☐ 19 Rich Langford
☐ 20 Brian Koelling
☐ 21 Mike Harrison
☐ 22 Dave Reeves
☐ 23 Rich Zastoupil
☐ 24 Bob Jesperson
☐ 25 Phil Kendall
☐ 26 Kevin Hudson TR

☐ 27 Mack Jenkins CO
☐ 28 Paul'P.J.' Carey MGR
☐ 29 Blank Card
☐ 30 Blank Card

1991 Birmingham Barons Line Drive

	MINT	NRMT	EXC
COMPLETE SET (26)	6.00	2.70	.75

☐ 51 Wilson Alvarez
☐ 52 Wayne Busby
☐ 53 Darrin Campbell
☐ 54 Mark Chasey
☐ 55 Ron Coomer
☐ 56 Argenis Cortez
☐ 57 Mike Davino
☐ 58 Lindsay Foster
☐ 59 Ramon Garcia
☐ 60 Kevin Garner
☐ 61 Jeff Gay
☐ 62 Chris Howard
☐ 63 John Hudek
☐ 64 Scott Jaster
☐ 65 Bo Kennedy
☐ 66 Derek Lee
☐ 67 Frank Merigliano
☐ 68 Scott Middaugh
☐ 69 Javier Ocasio
☐ 70 Kinnis Pledger
☐ 71 Greg Roth
☐ 72 Aubrey Waggoner
☐ 73 Jose Ventura
☐ 74 Tony Franklin MGR
☐ 75 Rick Peterson CO
Pat Roessler CO
Sam Hairston CO
☐ NNO Title card

1991 Birmingham Barons ProCards

This 28-card standard-size set of the 1991 Birmingham Barons, a Class AA Southern League affiliate of the Chicago White Sox, features on its white-bordered fronts posed color player photos set on simulated spiral-bound yellow notebooks. The player's name, position, and team appear within a green rectangle below the photo. The yellow horizontal back is bordered in white and carries the player's name at the top, followed by biography and statistics. This issue includes a fourth year card of Wilson Alvarez.

	MINT	NRMT	EXC
COMPLETE SET (28)	6.00	2.70	.75

☐ 1446 Wilson Alvarez
☐ 1447 Conde Cortez
☐ 1448 Mike Davino
☐ 1449 Ramon Garcia
☐ 1450 Chris Howard
☐ 1451 John Hudek
☐ 1452 Bo Kennedy
☐ 1453 Frank Merigliano
☐ 1454 Scott Middaugh
☐ 1455 Jose Ventura
☐ 1456 Darrin Campbell
☐ 1457 Jeff Gay
☐ 1458 Wayne Busby
☐ 1459 Mark Chasey
☐ 1460 Ron Coomer
☐ 1461 Lindsay Foster
☐ 1462 Kevin Garner
☐ 1463 Javier Ocasio
☐ 1464 Greg Roth
☐ 1465 Scott Jaster
☐ 1466 Derek Lee
☐ 1467 Kinnis Pledger
☐ 1468 Aubrey Waggoner
☐ 1469 Tony Franklin MGR
☐ 1470 Sam Hairston CO
☐ 1471 Rick Peterson CO
☐ 1472 Pat Roessler CO
☐ 1473 Checklist

1991 Bluefield Orioles Classic/Best

This 26-card standard-size set of the 1991 Bluefield Orioles, a Rookie Class Appalachian League affiliate of the Baltimore Orioles, features white-bordered posed color player photos on its fronts. The player's name, team, and position appear at the bottom. The white back is framed by a thin black line and carries the player's name and position at the top, followed by biography, statistics and team logos.

	MINT	NRMT	EXC
COMPLETE SET (26)	5.00	2.20	.60

☐ 1 Kris Gresham
☐ 2 Gordie Graham
☐ 3 Stewart Ruiz
☐ 4 Terry Farrar
☐ 5 Mike Thomas
☐ 6 Juan Mercedes
☐ 7 Vaughn Eshelman
☐ 8 Brad Seitzer
☐ 9 Basilio Ortiz
☐ 10 Mike Coss
☐ 11 Eric Alexander
☐ 12 Derek Adams
☐ 13 Bryan Grejtak
☐ 14 Glenn Coleman
☐ 15 Doug McConathy
☐ 16 Mat Sanders
☐ 17 Kevin Ryan
☐ 18 Rick Krivda
☐ 19 Allen Plaster
☐ 20 Steve Firsich
☐ 21 Chris Lemp
☐ 22 Brett Benge
☐ 23 Shawn O'Connell
☐ 24 Mike Tullier CO
☐ 25 Chris Lein CO
☐ 26 Checklist

1991 Bluefield Orioles ProCards

This 26-card standard-size set of the 1991 Bluefield Orioles, a Rookie Class Appalachian League affiliate of the Baltimore Orioles, features on its white-bordered fronts posed color player photos set on simulated spiral-bound yellow notebooks. The player's name, position, and team appear within a green rectangle below the photo. The yellow horizontal back is bordered in white and carries the player's name at the top, followed by biography and statistics.

	MINT	NRMT	EXC
COMPLETE SET (26)	5.00	2.20	.60

☐ 4119 Brett Benge
☐ 4120 Vaughn Eshelman
☐ 4121 Terry Farrar
☐ 4122 Stevie Firsich
☐ 4123 Ricky Krivda
☐ 4124 Chris Lemp
☐ 4125 Juan Mercedes
☐ 4126 Shawn O'Connor
☐ 4127 Al Plaster
☐ 4128 Kevin Ryan
☐ 4129 Matt Sanders
☐ 4130 Bryan Grejtak
☐ 4131 Kris Gresham
☐ 4132 Derk Adams
☐ 4133 Mike Coss
☐ 4134 Gordie Graham
☐ 4135 Doug McConathy
☐ 4136 Stu Ruiz
☐ 4137 Brad Seitzer
☐ 4138 Eric Alexander
☐ 4139 Glenn Coleman
☐ 4140 Basil Ortiz
☐ 4141 Mike Thomas
☐ 4142 Chris Lein CO
☐ 4143 Mike Tullier CO
☐ 4144 Checklist

1991 Boise Hawks Classic/Best

This 30-card standard-size set of the 1991 Boise Hawks, a Class A Northwest League affiliate of the California Angels, features white-bordered posed color player photos on its fronts. The player's name, team, and position appear at the bottom. The white back is framed by a thin black line and carries the player's name and position at the top, followed by biography, statistics and team logos.

	MINT	NRMT	EXC
COMPLETE SET (30)	5.00	2.20	.60

☐ 1 Todd Claus
☐ 2 Chris Prichett
☐ 3 Luis Raven
☐ 4 Chance Gledhill
☐ 5 Tyrone Boykin
☐ 6 James Ruocchio
☐ 7 Rod Van Dyke
☐ 8 Eduardo Perez
☐ 9 Orlando Palmeiro
☐ 10 Elgin Bobo
☐ 11 Jose Stein
☐ 12 Shawn Purdy
☐ 13 Mark Mammola
☐ 14 John Wylie
☐ 15 Mark Sweeney
☐ 16 Ron Tallent
☐ 17 Chris Turner
☐ 18 Brando Markiewicz
☐ 19 Gary Hagy
☐ 20 Jim Sears
☐ 21 Carlos Polanco
☐ 22 Ron Watson
☐ 23 Troy Percival
☐ 24 Eric Martinez
☐ 25 Korey Keling
☐ 26 Rob Dodd
☐ 27 Chris Robinson
☐ 28 Mark Ratekin
☐ 29 Julian Heredia
☐ 30 Alan Russell TR
Checklist

1991 Boise Hawks ProCards

This 35-card standard-size set of the 1991 Boise Hawks, a Class A Northwest League affiliate of the California Angels, features on its white-bordered fronts posed color player photos set on simulated spiral-bound yellow notebooks. The player's name, position, and team appear within a green rectangle below the photo. The yellow horizontal back is bordered in white and carries the player's name at the top, followed by biography and statistics.

	MINT	NRMT	EXC
COMPLETE SET (35)	5.00	2.20	.60

☐ 3869 Rob Dodd
☐ 3870 Chance Gledhill
☐ 3871 Julian Heredia
☐ 3872 Korey Keling
☐ 3873 Mark Mammola
☐ 3874 Eric Martinez
☐ 3875 Troy Percival
☐ 3876 Shawn Purdy
☐ 3877 Mark Ratekin
☐ 3878 Chris Robinson
☐ 3879 Rod Van Dyke
☐ 3880 Ron Watson
☐ 3881 John Wylie
☐ 3882 Elgin Bobo
☐ 3883 Jose Stela
☐ 3884 Chris Turner
☐ 3885 Todd Claus
☐ 3886 Gary Hagy
☐ 3887 Brandon Markiewicz
☐ 3888 Carlos Polanco
☐ 3889 Chris Pritchett
☐ 3890 James Ruocchio
☐ 3891 Jimmy Sears
☐ 3892 Ron Tallent
☐ 3893 Ty Boykin
☐ 3894 Robby Cannon
☐ 3895 Orlando Palmeiro
☐ 3896 Eduardo Perez
☐ 3897 Luis Raven
☐ 3898 Mark Sweeney
☐ 3899 Tom Kotchman MGR
☐ 3900 Joe Caro CO
☐ 3901 Orv Franchuk CO
☐ 3902 Howie Gershberg CO
☐ 3903 Checklist

1991 Bristol Tigers Classic/Best

This 30-card standard-size set of the 1991 Bristol Tigers, a Rookie Class Appalachian League affiliate of the Detroit Tigers, features white-bordered posed color player photos on its fronts. The player's name, team, and position appear at the bottom. The white back is framed by a thin black line and carries the player's name and position at the top, followed by biography, statistics and team logos.

	MINT	NRMT	EXC
COMPLETE SET (30)	6.00	2.70	.75

☐ 1 James Givens
☐ 2 Jorge Caro
☐ 3 Justin Mashore
☐ 4 Tom Mezzanotte
☐ 5 Luis Hernandez
☐ 6 Tarrick Brock
☐ 7 Rob Yelton
☐ 8 Brian Prichard
☐ 9 Alex Ubina
☐ 10 John Sutey
☐ 11 Jose Sanjurjo
☐ 12 Keith Kimsey
☐ 13 Jorge Moreno
☐ 14 Trevor Miller
☐ 15 Vince Bradford
☐ 16 Greg Raffo
☐ 17 Clint Sadowsky
☐ 18 Carlos Diaz
☐ 19 Blas Cedeno
☐ 20 Juan Lopez MGR
☐ 21 Matt Bauer
☐ 22 Brian Nelson
☐ 23 Tom Schwarber
☐ 24 Dan Ruff
☐ 25 Justin Thompson
☐ 26 Brian Edmondson
☐ 27 Paul Magrini
☐ 28 Nelson Perpetuo
☐ 29 Art Adams
☐ 30 Kevin Bradshaw CO
Checklist

1991 Bristol Tigers ProCards

This 30-card standard-size set of the 1991 Bristol Tigers, a Rookie Class Appalachian League affiliate of the Detroit Tigers, features on its white-bordered fronts posed color player photos set on simulated spiral-bound yellow notebooks. The player's name, position, and team appear within a green rectangle below the photo. The yellow horizontal back is bordered in white and carries the player's name at the top, followed by biography and statistics. This issue includes the minor league card debut of Justin Thompson.

	MINT	NRMT	EXC
COMPLETE SET (30)	6.00	2.70	.75

☐ 3594 Art Adams
☐ 3595 Matt Bauer
☐ 3596 Blas Cedeno
☐ 3597 Brian Edmondson
☐ 3598 Paul Magrini
☐ 3599 Trever Miller
☐ 3600 Brian Nelson
☐ 3601 Nelson Perpetuo
☐ 3602 Henry Quiles
☐ 3603 Greg Raffo
☐ 3604 Clint Sadowsky
☐ 3605 Tom Schwarber
☐ 3606 Justin Thompson
☐ 3607 Tom Mezzanotte
☐ 3608 Brian Prichard
☐ 3609 Alex Ubina
☐ 3610 Rob Yelton
☐ 3611 Jorge Caro
☐ 3612 Carlos Diaz
☐ 3613 James Givens
☐ 3614 Luis Hernandez
☐ 3615 Jorge Moreno
☐ 3616 Dan Ruff
☐ 3617 Vince Bradford
☐ 3618 Keith Kimsey
☐ 3619 Justin Mashore
☐ 3620 Jose Sanjurjo
☐ 3621 John Sutey
☐ 3622 Juan Lopez
☐ 3623 Checklist

1991 Buffalo Bisons Line Drive

	MINT	NRMT	EXC
COMPLETE SET (26)	5.00	2.20	.60

☐ 26 Jeff Banister
☐ 27 Cecil Espy
☐ 28 Steve Fireovid
☐ 29 Carlos Garcia
☐ 30 Mark Huismann
☐ 31 Scott Little
☐ 32 Tom Magrann
☐ 33 Roger Mason
☐ 34 Tim Meeks
☐ 35 Orlando Merced
☐ 36 Joey Meyer
☐ 37 Keith Miller
☐ 38 Blas Minor
☐ 39 Armando Moreno
☐ 40 Jeff Neely
☐ 41 Joe Redfield
☐ 42 Rick Reed
☐ 43 Jeff Richardson
☐ 44 Rosario Rodriguez
☐ 45 Jeff Schulz
☐ 46 Jim Tracy
☐ 47 Greg Tubbs
☐ 48 Mike York
☐ 49 Terry Collins MGR
☐ 50 Jackie Brown CO
☐ NNO Title card

1991 Buffalo Bisons ProCards

This 26-card standard-size set of the 1991 Buffalo Bisons, a Class AAA American Association affiliate of the Pittsburgh Pirates, features on its white-bordered fronts posed color player photos set on simulated spiral-bound yellow notebooks. The player's name, position, and team appear within a green rectangle below the photo. The yellow horizontal back is bordered in white and carries the player's name at the top, followed by biography and statistics.

	MINT	NRMT	EXC
COMPLETE SET (26)	5.00	2.20	.60

☐ 533 Kevin Blankenship
☐ 534 Steve Fireovid
☐ 535 Mark Huismann
☐ 536 Roger Mason
☐ 537 Tim Meeks
☐ 538 Blas Minor
☐ 539 Jeff Neely
☐ 540 Rick Reed
☐ 541 Rosario Rodriguez
☐ 542 Jim Tracy
☐ 543 Mike York
☐ 544 Jeff Banister
☐ 545 Tom Magrann
☐ 546 Carlos Garcia
☐ 547 Joey Meyer
☐ 548 Armando Moreno
☐ 549 Joe Redfield
☐ 550 Jeff Richardson
☐ 551 Cecil Espy
☐ 552 Scott Little
☐ 553 Keith Miller
☐ 554 Jeff Schulz
☐ 555 Greg Tubbs
☐ 556 Terry Collins MGR

☐ 557 Jackie Brown CO
☐ 558 Checklist

1991 Burlington Astros Classic/Best

This 29-card standard-size set of the 1991 Burlington Astros, a Class A Midwest League affiliate of the Houston Astros, features white-bordered posed color player photos on its fronts. The player's name, team, and position appear at the bottom. The white back is framed by a thin black line and carries the player's name and position at the top, followed by biography, statistics and team logos.

	MINT	NRMT	EXC
COMPLETE SET (29)	5.00	2.20	.60

☐ 1 David Allen
☐ 2 Troy Dovey
☐ 3 Benjamin Gonzales
☐ 4 Anthony Gutierrez
☐ 5 Robert Hurta
☐ 6 Kevin Lane
☐ 7 Michael McDowell
☐ 8 Tyrone Scott
☐ 9 Walter Trice
☐ 10 Donne Wall
☐ 11 Kenneth Wheeler Jr.
☐ 12 Manuel Acta
☐ 13 Raul Chavez
☐ 14 Gary Christopherson
☐ 15 David Henderson
☐ 16 Layne Lambert
☐ 17 Roberto Petagine
☐ 18 Fletcher Thompson
☐ 19 Ruben Cruz
☐ 20 Christopher Hatcher
☐ 21 Raymond Montgomery
☐ 22 Bryan Smith
☐ 23 Jeffery Bennington
☐ 24 Michael Burns
☐ 25 Tony Gilmore
☐ 26 Jim Hickey CO
☐ 27 Tim Tolman MGR
☐ 28 Chris Correnti TR
☐ 29 Checklist

1991 Burlington Astros ProCards

This 28-card standard-size set of the 1991 Burlington Astros, a Class A Midwest League affiliate of the Houston Astros, features on its white-bordered fronts posed color player photos set on simulated spiral-bound yellow notebooks. The player's name, position, and team appear within a green rectangle below the photo. The yellow horizontal back is bordered in white and carries the player's name at the top, followed by biography and statistics.

	MINT	NRMT	EXC
COMPLETE SET (28)	5.00	2.20	.60

☐ 2792 Dave Allen
☐ 2793 Troy Dovey
☐ 2794 Benny Gonzales
☐ 2795 Anthony Gutierrez
☐ 2796 Bob Hurta
☐ 2797 Kevin Lane
☐ 2798 Mike McDowell
☐ 2799 Tyrone Scott
☐ 2800 Wally Trice
☐ 2801 Donne Wall
☐ 2802 Ken Wheeler
☐ 2803 Jeff Bennington
☐ 2804 Mike Burns
☐ 2805 Tony Gilmore
☐ 2806 Manuel Acta
☐ 2807 Raul Chavez
☐ 2808 Gary Christopherson
☐ 2809 Dave Henderson
☐ 2810 Layne Lambert
☐ 2811 Roberto Petagine
☐ 2812 Fletcher Thompson
☐ 2813 Ruben Cruz
☐ 2814 Chris Hatcher
☐ 2815 Ray Montgomery
☐ 2816 Bryan Smith
☐ 2817 Tim Tolman MGR
☐ 2818 Jim Hickey CO
☐ 2819 Checklist

1991 Burlington Indians ProCards

This 34-card standard-size set of the 1991 Burlington Indians, a Rookie Class Appalachian League affiliate of the Cleveland Indians, features on its white-bordered fronts posed color player photos set on simulated spiral-bound yellow notebooks. The player's name, position, and team appear within a green rectangle below the photo. The yellow horizontal back is bordered in white and carries the player's name at the top, followed by biography and statistics. This issue includes the minor league card debut of Manny Ramirez.

	MINT	NRMT	EXC
COMPLETE SET (34)	25.00	11.00	3.10

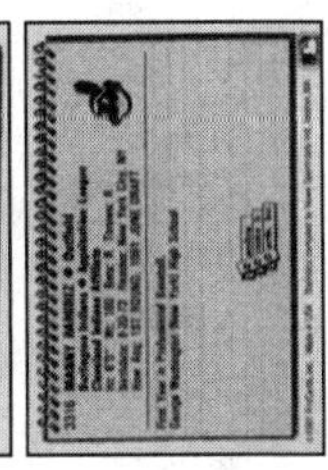

☐ 3290 Brandon Bluhm
☐ 3291 Jose Colon
☐ 3292 Chris Coulter
☐ 3293 Carlos Crawford
☐ 3294 Ian Doyle
☐ 3295 Jesus Gonzalez
☐ 3296 Pep Harris
☐ 3297 Fernando Hernandez
☐ 3298 Denny Key
☐ 3299 Rodney Koller
☐ 3300 Albie Lopez
☐ 3301 Chris Maffett
☐ 3302 Oscar Resendez
☐ 3303 Pete Guerra
☐ 3304 Cale Lawson
☐ 3305 Mike Taylor
☐ 3306 Dave Chisum
☐ 3307 Felipe Duran
☐ 3308 Rodd Hairston
☐ 3309 Javier Robles
☐ 3310 Jorge Santiago
☐ 3311 Jeff Whitaker
☐ 3312 Todd Whitehurst
☐ 3313 Mike Zollars
☐ 3314 Ronnie Coleman
☐ 3315 Sam Hence
☐ 3316 Manny Ramirez
☐ 3317 Bobby Schultz
☐ 3318 Mike Shirley
☐ 3319 Andre White
☐ 3320 David Keller MGR
☐ 3321 Stan Hilton CO
☐ 3322 Don Jacoby CO
☐ 3323 Checklist

1991 Butte Copper Kings Sports Pro

This 30-card standard-size set of the 1991 Butte Copper Kings, a Rookie Class Pioneer League affiliate of the Texas Rangers, features posed color head-and-shoulders shots, with thin black borders on a white card face. The horizontally oriented backs have biographical information.

	MINT	NRMT	EXC
COMPLETE SET (30)	6.00	2.70	.75

☐ 1 James Koehler
☐ 2 Jason Ayala
☐ 3 Chris Starr
☐ 4 Terrell Berthau
☐ 5 Andy Watson
☐ 6 Paul Dalzachio
☐ 7 Michael Crespo
☐ 8 Dave Giberti
☐ 9 Mike Edwards
☐ 10 Chris Curtis
☐ 11 Lanny Williams
☐ 12 Shawn Kennedy
☐ 13 Todd Gates
☐ 14 Kerry Lacey
☐ 15 Eric Vargas
☐ 16 Lance Schueremann
☐ 17 Terrell Lowery
☐ 18 Victor Madrigal
☐ 19 Charlie Sullivan
☐ 20 Franklin Parra
☐ 21 Kevin Sisk
☐ 22 Bo Magee
☐ 23 Greg Wiseman
☐ 24 Keith McGough
☐ 25 Brian Roberts
☐ 26 Jose Texidor
☐ 27 Doug Sisson
☐ 28 Chuck Marquardt
☐ 29 Jim Benedict
☐ 30 Dick Egan

1991 California League All-Stars

The 1991 California League All-Stars contains 56 standard-size cards. The fronts feature mostly posed color player photos with silver borders. The words "All Star" are printed in red across the bottom of the picture, with the player's name below and to the right. In black print on white background, the horizontally oriented backs present biography and career statistics.

	MINT	NRMT	EXC
COMPLETE SET (56)	12.00	5.50	1.50

☐ 1 Marc Newfield
☐ 2 Pedro Martinez
☐ 3 Raul Mondesi
☐ 4 Matt Mieske
☐ 5 Dave Van Winkle
☐ 6 Mike Piazza
☐ 7 Jay Gainer
☐ 8 Brian Raabe
☐ 9 Terry McFarlin
☐ 10 Ed Zinter
☐ 11 Jesus Tavarez
☐ 12 Garey Ingram
☐ 13 Alan Newman
☐ 14 Greg Hansell
☐ 15 Mick Billmeyer
☐ 16 Corey Kapano
☐ 17 Anthony Collier
☐ 18 J.D. Noland
☐ 19 Rex Peters
☐ 20 Mark Gieseke
☐ 21 Ron Maurer
☐ 22 Marcos Garcia
☐ 23 Tom Beyers
☐ 24 Goose Gregson
☐ 25 Matt Wilson
☐ 26 Joe Gagliardi
☐ 27 John Lavenda
Administrator and
Rick Smith
Vice President
☐ 28 Bob Brooks
☐ 29 Adell Davenport
☐ 30 John Finn
☐ 31 Rick Huisman
☐ 32 Hideyuki Mifune
☐ 33 Joey James
☐ 34 Mark Krumback
☐ 35 Gary Sharko
☐ 36 Troy O'Leary
☐ 37 Kevin McGehee
☐ 38 Henry Mercedes
☐ 39 Pat Rapp
☐ 40 Hideyuki Yasuda
☐ 41 Clay Bellinger
☐ 42 Mike Mohler
☐ 43 Jason McFarlin
☐ 44 Manny Martinez
☐ 45 Carl Hanselman
☐ 46 Cliff Gonzalez
☐ 47 Ron Wotus
☐ 48 Gary Lucas
☐ 49 Scott Wilson
☐ 50 Brian Laxamana
☐ 51 Todd Whitty
☐ 52 Mike Stetson
☐ 53 Ray Dimuro
☐ 54 Dave Littimer
☐ 55 Bo Dodson
☐ 56 Timber Mead

1991 Calgary Cannons Line Drive

This 26-card standard-size set of the 1991 Calgary Cannons, a Class AAA Pacific Coast League affiliate of the Seattle Mariners, features posed color player photos on its white-bordered fronts. The player's name appears in red lettering at the top; his position and team name appear in red lettering below the photo. The back carries the player's name within a red stripe at the top, followed by position, team name and affiliation, biography and statistics.

	MINT	NRMT	EXC
COMPLETE SET (26)	5.00	2.20	.60

☐ 51 Rich Amaral
☐ 52 Rick Balabon
☐ 53 Dave Brundage
☐ 54 Dave Burba
☐ 55 Dave Cochrane
☐ 56 Alan Cockrell
☐ 57 Mike Cook
☐ 58 Keith Helton
☐ 59 Dennis Hood
☐ 60 Chris Howard
☐ 61 Chuck Jackson
☐ 62 Calvin Jones
☐ 63 Pat Lennon
☐ 64 Shane Letterio
☐ 65 Vance Lovelace
☐ 66 Tino Martinez
☐ 67 John Mitchell
☐ 68 Dennis Powell
☐ 69 Alonzo Powell
☐ 70 Pat Rice
☐ 71 Ricky Rojas
☐ 72 Steve Springer
☐ 73 Ed Vande Berg
☐ 74 Keith Bodie MG
☐ 75 Ross Grimsley CO
☐ NNO Title card

1991 Calgary Cannons ProCards

This 25-card standard-size set of the 1991 Calgary Cannons, a Class AAA Pacific Coast League affiliate of the Seattle Mariners, features on its white-bordered fronts posed color player photos set on simulated spiral-bound yellow notebooks. The player's name, position, and team appear within a green rectangle below the photo. The yellow horizontal back is bordered in white and carries the player's name at the top, followed by biography and statistics.

	MINT	NRMT	EXC
COMPLETE SET (25)	5.00	2.20	.60

☐ 508 Rick Balabon
☐ 509 Dave Burba
☐ 510 Keith Helton
☐ 511 Calvin Jones
☐ 512 Vance Lovelace
☐ 513 John Mitchell
☐ 514 Dennis Powell
☐ 515 Pat Rice
☐ 516 Ricky Rojas
☐ 517 Ed Vande Berg
☐ 518 Dave Cochrane
☐ 519 Chris Howard
☐ 520 Rich Amaral
☐ 521 Chuck Jackson
☐ 522 Shane Letterio
☐ 523 Tino Martinez
☐ 524 Steve Springer
☐ 525 Dave Brundage
☐ 526 Alan Cockrell
☐ 527 Dennis Hood
☐ 528 Pat Lennon
☐ 529 Alonzo Powell
☐ 530 Keith Bodie MG UER
(Card misnumbered
as no. 2649)
☐ 531 Ross Grimsley CO
☐ 532 Checklist

1991 Canton-Akron Indians Line Drive

	MINT	NRMT	EXC
COMPLETE SET (26)	10.00	4.50	1.25

☐ 76 Ramon Bautista
☐ 77 Eric Bell
☐ 78 Jim Bruske
☐ 79 Tim Costo
☐ 80 Mike Curtis
☐ 81 Jerry DiPoto
☐ 82 Daren Epley
☐ 83 Sam Ferretti
☐ 84 Garland Kiser
☐ 85 Ty Kovach
☐ 86 Tom Kramer
☐ 87 Nolan Lane
☐ 88 Jesse Levis
☐ 89 Carlos Martinez
☐ 90 Jeff Mutis
☐ 91 Rouglas Odor
☐ 92 Gary Resetar
☐ 93 Greg Roscoe
☐ 94 Miguel Sabino
☐ 95 Bernie Tatis
☐ 96 Jim Thome
☐ 97 Ken Ramos
☐ 98 Ken Whitfield
☐ 99 Ken Bolek MGR
☐ 100 Dave Keller CO
☐ NNO Title card

1991 Canton-Akron Indians ProCards

This 28-card standard-size set of the 1991 Canton-Akron Indians, a Class AA Eastern League affiliate of the Cleveland Indians, features on its white-bordered fronts posed color player photos set on simulated spiral-bound yellow notebooks. The player's name, position, and team appear within a green rectangle below the photo. The yellow horizontal back is bordered in white and carries the player's name at the top, followed by biography and statistics. This issue includes Jim Thome's second year minor league card.

	MINT	NRMT	EXC
COMPLETE SET (28)	8.00	3.60	1.00

☐ 971 Eric Bell
☐ 972 Mike Birkbeck
☐ 973 Jim Bruske
☐ 974 Mike Curtis
☐ 975 Jerry DiPoto
☐ 976 Garland Kiser
☐ 977 Ty Kovach
☐ 978 Tom Kramer
☐ 979 Jeff Mutis
☐ 980 Greg Roscoe
☐ 981 Jesse Levis

☐ 982 Gary Resetar
☐ 983 Ramon Bautista
☐ 984 Tim Costo
☐ 985 Daren Epley
☐ 986 Sam Ferretti
☐ 987 Carlos Martinez
☐ 988 Rouglas Odor
☐ 989 Jim Thome
☐ 990 Nolan Lane
☐ 991 Ken Ramos
☐ 992 Miguel Sabino
☐ 993 Bernie Tatis
☐ 994 Ken Whitfield
☐ 995 Ken Bolek MGR
☐ 996 Will George CO
☐ 997 Dave Keller CO
☐ 998 Checklist

1991 Carolina League All-Stars ProCards

	MINT	NRMT	EXC
COMPLETE SET (47)	8.00	3.60	1.00

☐ CAR1 Tim Gillis
☐ CAR2 Javy Lopez
☐ CAR3 Scott Taylor
☐ CAR4 Manny Alexander
☐ CAR5 Tony Beasley
☐ CAR6 Sergio Cairo
☐ CAR7 Cesar Devares
☐ CAR8 Ed Horowitz
☐ CAR9 Mel Wearing
☐ CAR10 Kip Yaughn
☐ CAR11 Chad Allen
☐ CAR12 Mike Easley
☐ CAR13 Tom Eiterman
☐ CAR14 Miguel Flores
☐ CAR15 Brian Giles
☐ CAR16 Brian Graham MGR
☐ CAR17 Garland Kiser
☐ CAR18 Scott Neill
☐ CAR19 Tracy Sanders
☐ CAR20 Mike Soper
☐ CAR21 Buddy Bailey MGR
☐ CAR22 Bruce Chick
☐ CAR23 Jeff McNeely
☐ CAR24 Boo Moore
☐ CAR25 Bill Norris
☐ CAR26 Erik Plantenberg
☐ CAR27 Tim Smith
☐ CAR28 Bobby Holley
☐ CAR29 Ron Pezzoni
☐ CAR30 Andy Fox
☐ CAR31 Mike Hankins
☐ CAR32 Mike Hart MGR
☐ CAR33 Darren Hodges
☐ CAR34 Sam Militello
☐ CAR35 Mark Ohlms
☐ CAR36 Daryl Ratliff
☐ CAR37 Dave Tellers
☐ CAR38 Paul Wagner
☐ CAR39 Troy Bradford
☐ CAR40 Pete Castellano
☐ CAR41 Chris Ebright
☐ CAR42 Ryan Hawblitzel
☐ CAR43 John Jensen
☐ CAR44 Brad Mills MGR
☐ CAR45 Matt Walbeck
☐ CAR46 Travis Willis
☐ CAR47 Checklist

1991 Carolina Mudcats Line Drive

	MINT	NRMT	EXC
COMPLETE SET (26)	5.00	2.20	.60

☐ 101 Steve Adams
☐ 102 Stan Fansler
☐ 103 Mandy Romero
☐ 104 Terry Crowley Jr.
☐ 105 Chip Duncan
☐ 106 Greg Edge
☐ 107 Chris Estep
☐ 108 Carl Hamilton
☐ 109 Lee Hancock
☐ 110 Tim Hines
☐ 111 Mike Huyler
☐ 112 Paul Miller
☐ 113 Pete Murphy
☐ 114 Darwin Pennye
☐ 115 Mike Roesler
☐ 116 Bruce Schreiber
☐ 117 Greg Sparks
☐ 118 Dennis Tafoya
☐ 119 Tim Wakefield
☐ 120 Ben Webb
☐ 121 John Wehner
☐ 122 Ed Yacopino
☐ 123 Eddie Zambrano
☐ 124 Marc Bombard MGR
☐ 125 Trent Jewett CO
Spin Williams CO
☐ NNO Title card

1991 Carolina Mudcats ProCards

This 26-card standard-size set of the 1991 Carolina Mudcats, a Class AA Southern League affiliate of the Pittsburgh Pirates, features on its white-bordered fronts posed color player photos set on simulated spiral-bound yellow notebooks. The player's name, position, and team appear within a green rectangle below the photo. The yellow horizontal back is bordered in white and carries the player's name at the top, followed by biography and statistics.

	MINT	NRMT	EXC
COMPLETE SET (26)	5.00	2.20	.60

☐ 1078 Steve Adams
☐ 1079 Chip Duncan
☐ 1080 Stan Fansler
☐ 1081 Carl Hamilton
☐ 1082 Lee Hancock
☐ 1083 Paul Miller
☐ 1084 Pete Murphy
☐ 1085 Mike Roesler
☐ 1086 Dennis Tafoya
☐ 1087 Tim Wakefield
☐ 1088 Ben Webb
☐ 1089 Tim Hines
☐ 1090 Mandy Romero
☐ 1091 Terry Crowley
☐ 1092 Greg Edge
☐ 1093 Mike Huyler
☐ 1094 Bruce Schreiber
☐ 1095 Greg Sparks
☐ 1096 John Wehner
☐ 1097 Chris Estep
☐ 1098 Darwin Pennye
☐ 1099 Ed Yacopino
☐ 1100 Eddie Zambrano
☐ 1101 Marc Bombard MGR
☐ 1102 Spin Williams CO
☐ 1103 Checklist

1991 Cedar Rapids Reds Classic/Best

This 30-card standard-size set of the 1991 Cedar Rapids Reds, a Class A Midwest League affiliate of the Cincinnati Reds, features white-bordered posed color player photos on its fronts. The player's name, team, and position appear at the bottom. The white back is framed by a thin black line and carries the player's name and position at the top, followed by biography, statistics and team logos.

	MINT	NRMT	EXC
COMPLETE SET (30)	5.00	2.20	.60

☐ 1 Kevin Berry
☐ 2 Mark Borcherding
☐ 3 Ryan Edwards
☐ 4 Mike Ferry
☐ 5 Leonard Griffen
☐ 6 Trevor Hoffman
☐ 7 Rich Langford
☐ 8 Larry Luebbers
☐ 9 Ramon Manon
☐ 10 Greg Margheim
☐ 11 Scott Robinson
☐ 12 Jason Satre
☐ 13 Darron Cox
☐ 14 Jon Fuller
☐ 15 Matt Giegling
☐ 16 Amadoz Arias
☐ 17 Jamie Dismuke
☐ 18 Vicente Javier
☐ 19 Kevin Riggs
☐ 20 Steve Vondran
☐ 21 Todd Wilson
☐ 22 Eugene Jones
☐ 23 Danny Perozo
☐ 24 Noel Velez
☐ 25 K.C. Gillum
☐ 26 Frank Funk MGR
☐ 27 Mark Berry CO
☐ 28 Mack Jenkins CO
☐ 29 Gregg Crain TR
☐ 30 Checklist

1991 Cedar Rapids Reds ProCards

This 30-card standard-size set of the 1991 Cedar Rapids Reds, a Class A Midwest League affiliate of the Cincinnati Reds, features on its white-bordered fronts posed color player photos set on simulated spiral-bound yellow notebooks. The player's name, position, and team appear within a green rectangle below the photo. The yellow horizontal back is bordered in white and carries the player's name at the top, followed by biography and statistics.

	MINT	NRMT	EXC
COMPLETE SET (30)	5.00	2.20	.60

☐ 2709 Kevin Berry
☐ 2710 Mark Borcherding
☐ 2711 Ryan Edwards
☐ 2712 Mike Ferry
☐ 2713 Leonard Griffen
☐ 2714 Trevor Hoffman
☐ 2715 Rich Langford
☐ 2716 Larry Luebbers
☐ 2717 Greg Margheim
☐ 2718 Scott Robinson
☐ 2719 Jason Satre
☐ 2720 Darron Cox
☐ 2721 Jon Fuller
☐ 2722 Matt Giegling
☐ 2723 Steve Vondran
☐ 2724 Amadoz Arias
☐ 2725 Jamie Dismuke
☐ 2726 Bob Filotei
☐ 2727 Vincent Javier
☐ 2728 Kevin Riggs
☐ 2729 Eddie Rush
☐ 2730 Todd Wilson
☐ 2731 K.C. Gillum
☐ 2732 Eugene Jones
☐ 2733 Danny Perozo
☐ 2734 Noel Velez
☐ 2735 Frank Funk MGR
☐ 2736 Mark Berry CO
☐ 2737 Mack Jenkins CO
☐ 2738 Checklist

1991 Charleston Rainbows Classic/Best

This 29-card standard-size set of the 1991 Charleston Rainbows, a Class A South Atlantic League affiliate of the San Diego Padres, features white-bordered posed color player photos on its fronts. The player's name, team, and position appear at the bottom. The white back is framed by a thin black line and carries the player's name and position at the top, followed by biography, statistics and team logos.

	MINT	NRMT	EXC
COMPLETE SET (29)	5.00	2.20	.60

☐ 1 Robbie Beckett
☐ 2 Mike Bradley
☐ 3 Jeff Brown
☐ 4 Cameron Cairncross
☐ 5 Ted Devore
☐ 6 Craig Eubanks
☐ 7 Jeff Huber
☐ 8 Bill Johnson
☐ 9 Steve Newton
☐ 10 Charles Thompson
☐ 11 Joe Waldron
☐ 12 Adan Ayala
☐ 13 Jerrey Thurston
☐ 14 Dave Adams
☐ 15 Brent Bish
☐ 16 Scott Bream
☐ 17 Craig Bullock
☐ 18 Tom Doyle
☐ 19 Pablo Martinez
☐ 20 Brian Beck
☐ 21 Ray McDavid
☐ 22 Keith McKoy
☐ 23 Jeff Pearce
☐ 24 Dave Trembley MGR
☐ 25 Bruce Tanner CO
☐ 26 Jaime Moreno CO
☐ 27 Tom Ivie
☐ 28 John Maxwell TR
☐ 29 Checklist

1991 Charleston Rainbows ProCards

This 27-card standard-size set of the 1991 Charleston Rainbows, a Class A South Atlantic League affiliate of the San Diego Padres, features on its white-bordered fronts posed color player photos set on simulated spiral-bound yellow notebooks. The player's name, position, and team appear within a green rectangle below the photo. The yellow horizontal back is bordered in white and carries the player's name at the top, followed by biography and statistics.

	MINT	NRMT	EXC
COMPLETE SET (27)	5.00	2.20	.60

☐ 87 Robbie Beckett
☐ 88 Mike Bradley
☐ 89 Jeff Brown
☐ 90 Cameron Cairncross
☐ 91 Ted Devore
☐ 92 Craig Eubanks
☐ 93 Jeff Huber
☐ 94 Bill Johnson
☐ 95 Charles Thompson
☐ 96 Joe Waldron
☐ 97 Adan Ayala
☐ 98 Jerrey Thurston
☐ 99 Dave Adams
☐ 100 Brent Bish
☐ 101 Scott Bream
☐ 102 Craig Bullock
☐ 103 Tom Doyle
☐ 104 Pablo Martinez
☐ 105 Bill Ostermeyer
☐ 106 Brian Beck
☐ 107 Ray McDavid
☐ 108 Keith McKoy
☐ 109 Jeff Pearce
☐ 110 Dave Trembley MGR
☐ 111 Jaime Moreno CO
☐ 112 Bruce Tanner CO
☐ 113 Checklist

1991 Charleston Wheelers Classic/Best

This 28-card standard-size set of the 1991 Charleston Wheelers, a Class A South Atlantic League affiliate of the Cincinnati Reds, features white-bordered posed color player photos on its fronts. The player's name, team, and position appear at the bottom. The white back is framed by a thin black line and carries the player's name and position at the top, followed by biography, statistics and team logos.

	MINT	NRMT	EXC
COMPLETE SET (28)	6.00	2.70	.75

☐ 1 Tim Cecil
☐ 2 Sean Doty
☐ 3 Scott Duff
☐ 4 Chris Hook
☐ 5 Doug King
☐ 6 Reggie Leslie
☐ 7 Ernie Nieves
☐ 8 Johnny Ray
☐ 9 John Roper
☐ 10 Carl Stewart
☐ 11 Kevin Tatar
☐ 12 Roy Hammargren
☐ 13 Greg Hammond
☐ 14 Dan Wilson
☐ 15 Rafael Bustamante
☐ 16 Herb Erhardt
☐ 17 Chris Gill
☐ 18 Bobby Perna
☐ 19 Tom Raffo
☐ 20 Lenny Wentz
☐ 21 Mark Arland
☐ 22 Steve Gibralter
☐ 23 Keith Gordon
☐ 24 Tom Spencer TR
☐ 25 Elliot Quinones
☐ 26 Chris Vasquez
☐ 27 Derek Botelho CO
☐ 28 Checklist

1991 Charleston Wheelers ProCards

This 27-card standard-size set of the 1991 Charleston Wheelers, a Class A South Atlantic League affiliate of the Cincinnati Reds, features on its white-bordered fronts posed color player photos set on simulated spiral-bound yellow notebooks. The player's name, position, and team appear within a green rectangle below the photo. The yellow horizontal back is bordered in white and carries the player's name at the top, followed by biography and statistics. This issue includes the minor league card debut of Steve Gibralter.

	MINT	NRMT	EXC
COMPLETE SET (27)	6.00	2.70	.75

☐ 2878 Tim Cecil
☐ 2879 Sean Doty
☐ 2880 Scott Duff
☐ 2881 Chris Hook
☐ 2882 Doug King
☐ 2883 Reggie Leslie
☐ 2884 Ernie Nieves
☐ 2885 Johnny Ray
☐ 2886 John Roper
☐ 2887 Carl Stewart
☐ 2888 Kevin Tatar
☐ 2889 Roy Hammargren
☐ 2890 Greg Hammond
☐ 2891 Dan Wilson
☐ 2892 Rafael Bustamante
☐ 2893 Herb Erhardt
☐ 2894 Chris Gill
☐ 2895 Bobby Perna
☐ 2896 Tom Raffo
☐ 2897 Lenny Wentz
☐ 2898 Mark Arland
☐ 2899 Steve Gibralter
☐ 2900 Elliott Quinones
☐ 2901 Chris Vasquez
☐ 2902 Dave Miley MGR
☐ 2903 Derek Botelho
☐ 2904 Checklist

1991 Charlotte Knights Line Drive

	MINT	NRMT	EXC
COMPLETE SET (26)	5.00	2.20	.60

☐ 126 Alex Arias
☐ 127 Paul Blair
☐ 128 Jim Bullinger
☐ 129 Dick Canan
☐ 130 Rusty Crockett

- ☐ 131 Steve DiBartolomeo
- ☐ 132 John Gardner
- ☐ 133 Henry Gomez
- ☐ 134 Ty Griffin
- ☐ 135 Shannon Jones
- ☐ 136 Mike Knapp
- ☐ 137 Tim Parker
- ☐ 138 Elvin Paulino
- ☐ 139 Fernando Ramsey
- ☐ 140 Kevin Roberson
- ☐ 141 John Salles
- ☐ 142 Mike Sodders
- ☐ 143 Bill St. Peter
- ☐ 144 Julio Strauss
- ☐ 145 Scott Taylor
- ☐ 146 Tim Watkins
- ☐ 147 Doug Welch
- ☐ 148 Billy White
- ☐ 149 Jay Loviglio MGR
- ☐ 150 Rick Kranitz CO
- ☐ NNO Title card

1991 Charlotte Knights ProCards

This 26-card standard-size set of the 1991 Charlotte Knights, a Class AA Southern League affiliate of the Chicago Cubs, features on its white-bordered fronts posed color player photos set on simulated spiral-bound yellow notebooks. The player's name, position, and team appear within a green rectangle below the photo. The yellow horizontal back is bordered in white and carries the player's name at the top, followed by biography and statistics.

	MINT	NRMT	EXC
COMPLETE SET (26)	5.00	2.20	.60

- ☐ 1681 Jim Bullinger
- ☐ 1682 Steve DiBartolomeo
- ☐ 1683 John Gardner
- ☐ 1684 Henry Gomez
- ☐ 1685 Shannon Jones
- ☐ 1686 Tim Parker
- ☐ 1687 John Salles
- ☐ 1688 Mike Sodders
- ☐ 1689 Julio Strauss
- ☐ 1690 Tim Watkins
- ☐ 1691 Michael Knapp
- ☐ 1692 Scott Taylor
- ☐ 1693 Alex Arias
- ☐ 1694 Paul Blair
- ☐ 1695 Dick Canan
- ☐ 1696 Rusty Crockett
- ☐ 1697 Elvin Paulino
- ☐ 1698 Bill St. Peter
- ☐ 1699 Billy White
- ☐ 1700 Ty Griffin
- ☐ 1701 Fernando Ramsey
- ☐ 1702 Kevin Roberson
- ☐ 1703 Doug Welch
- ☐ 1704 Jay Loviglio MGR
- ☐ 1705 Rick Kranitz CO
- ☐ 1706 Checklist

1991 Charlotte Rangers Classic/Best

This 30-card standard-size set of the 1991 Charlotte Rangers, a Class A Florida State League affiliate of the Texas Rangers, features white-bordered posed color player photos on its fronts. The player's name, team, and position appear at the bottom. The white back is framed by a thin black line and carries the player's name and position at the top, followed by biography, statistics and team logos.

	MINT	NRMT	EXC
COMPLETE SET (30)	5.00	2.20	.60

- ☐ 1 Michael Arner
- ☐ 2 Eric Bickhardt
- ☐ 3 Travis Buckley
- ☐ 4 Joey Eischen
- ☐ 5 Nick Felix
- ☐ 6 Barry Goetz
- ☐ 7 Darren Oliver
- ☐ 8 Juan Quero
- ☐ 9 Carl Randle
- ☐ 10 Steve Rowley
- ☐ 11 Kyle Spencer
- ☐ 12 Brian Steiner
- ☐ 13 Darren Niethammer
- ☐ 14 Kevin Tannahill
- ☐ 15 Barry Winford
- ☐ 16 James Glinton
- ☐ 17 Cris Colon
- ☐ 18 Todd Guggiana
- ☐ 19 Craig Newkirk
- ☐ 20 Jose Oliva
- ☐ 21 Rusty Greer
- ☐ 22 David Hulse
- ☐ 23 Timmie Morrow
- ☐ 24 Ken Powell
- ☐ 25 Jose Texidor
- ☐ 26 Donna Van Duzer TR
- ☐ 27 Bob Molinaro MGR
- ☐ 28 Marvin White CO
- ☐ 29 Walt Williams CO
- ☐ 30 Checklist

1991 Charlotte Rangers ProCards

This 28-card standard-size set of the 1991 Charlotte Rangers, a Class A Florida State League affiliate of the Texas Rangers, features on its white-bordered fronts posed color player photos set on simulated spiral-bound yellow notebooks. The player's name, position, and team appear within a green rectangle below the photo. The yellow horizontal back is bordered in white and carries the player's name at the top, followed by biography and statistics.

	MINT	NRMT	EXC
COMPLETE SET (28)	5.00	2.20	.60

- ☐ 1305 Michael Arner
- ☐ 1306 Eric Bickhardt
- ☐ 1307 Travis Buckley
- ☐ 1308 Joey Eischen
- ☐ 1309 Nick Felix
- ☐ 1310 Barry Goetz
- ☐ 1311 Darren Oliver
- ☐ 1312 Juan Quero
- ☐ 1313 Carl Randle
- ☐ 1314 Stephen Rowley
- ☐ 1315 Kyle Spencer
- ☐ 1316 Brian Steiner
- ☐ 1317 Darren Niethammer
- ☐ 1318 Kevin Tannahill
- ☐ 1319 Barry Winford
- ☐ 1320 Jim Clinton
- ☐ 1321 Cris Colon
- ☐ 1322 Todd Guggiana
- ☐ 1323 Craig Newkirk
- ☐ 1324 Jose Oliva
- ☐ 1325 Rusty Greer
- ☐ 1326 David Hulse
- ☐ 1327 Timmie Morrow
- ☐ 1328 Kenny Powell
- ☐ 1329 Jose Texidor
- ☐ 1330 Bobby Molinaro MGR
- ☐ 1331 Marvin White CO
- ☐ 1332 Checklist

1991 Chattanooga Lookouts Line Drive

	MINT	NRMT	EXC
COMPLETE SET (26)	6.00	2.70	.75

- ☐ 151 Rick Allen
- ☐ 152 Mike Anderson
- ☐ 153 Bobby Ayala
- ☐ 154 Pete Beeler
- ☐ 155 Jeff Branson
- ☐ 156 Scott Bryant
- ☐ 157 Bill Dodd
- ☐ 158 Steve Foster
- ☐ 159 Victor Garcia
- ☐ 160 Frank Kremblas
- ☐ 161 Greg Lonigro
- ☐ 162 Dave McAuliffe
- ☐ 163 Steve McCarthy
- ☐ 164 Scott Pose
- ☐ 165 Tim Pugh
- ☐ 166 Bill Risley
- ☐ 167 Reggie Sanders
- ☐ 168 Mo Sanford
- ☐ 169 Scott Sellner
- ☐ 170 Jerry Spradlin
- ☐ 171 Glenn Sutko
- ☐ 172 Todd Trafton
- ☐ 173 Bernie Walker
- ☐ 174 Jim Tracy MGR
- ☐ 175 Mike Griffin CO
- ☐ NNO Title card

1991 Chattanooga Lookouts ProCards

This 27-card standard-size set of the 1991 Chattanooga Lookouts, a Class AA Southern League affiliate of the Cincinnati Reds, features on its white-bordered fronts posed color player photos set on simulated spiral-bound yellow notebooks. The player's name, position, and team appear within a green rectangle below the photo. The yellow horizontal back is bordered in white and carries the player's name at the top, followed by biography and statistics. This issue includes a fourth year card of Reggie Sanders.

	MINT	NRMT	EXC
COMPLETE SET (27)	6.00	2.70	.75

- ☐ 1950 Mike Anderson
- ☐ 1951 Bobby Ayala
- ☐ 1952 Bill Dodd
- ☐ 1953 Steve Foster
- ☐ 1954 Victor Garcia
- ☐ 1955 Scott Jeffery
- ☐ 1956 Dave McAuliffe
- ☐ 1957 Steve McCarthy
- ☐ 1958 Tim Pugh
- ☐ 1959 Bill Risley
- ☐ 1960 Mo Sanford
- ☐ 1961 Jerry Spradlin
- ☐ 1962 Joe Turek
- ☐ 1963 Glenn Sutko
- ☐ 1964 Rick Allen
- ☐ 1965 Jeff Branson
- ☐ 1966 Frank Kremblas
- ☐ 1967 Greg Lonigro
- ☐ 1968 Scott Sellner
- ☐ 1969 Todd Trafton
- ☐ 1970 Scott Bryant
- ☐ 1971 Ben Colvard
- ☐ 1972 Scott Pose
- ☐ 1973 Reggie Sanders
- ☐ 1974 Jim Tracy MGR
- ☐ 1975 Mike Griffin CO
- ☐ 1976 Checklist

1991 Classic Draft Picks

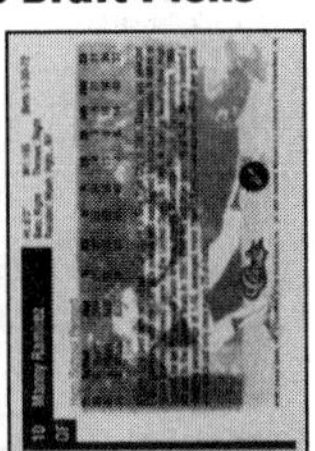

The premier edition of the 1991 Classic Draft Picks set contains 50 standard-size cards, plus a bonus card featuring Frankie Rodriguez. The production run was distributed between 330,000 hobby sets, 165,000 non-hobby sets, and 1,500 test sets. Each set includes a certificate of limited edition with a unique set number. The fronts display glossy color player photos, with maroon borders and a gray card face. The draft pick number, player's name, and position appear in the maroon border at the bottom of the picture. The horizontal backs have biography and maroon border stripes intersecting at the upper corner. Also high school or college statistics and player profile are printed over a washed-out picture of a batter and catcher at home plate. This set includes Brien Taylor, the first pick of the '91 draft. The Frankie Rodriguez bonus card was only included in hobby sets. Cards were checklisted by Classic based on draft order.

	MINT	NRMT	EXC
COMPLETE SET (50)	4.00	1.80	.50
COMMON CARD (1-50)	.05	.02	.01
☐ 1 Brien Taylor	.05	.02	.01
☐ 2 Mike Kelly	.05	.02	.01
☐ 3 David McCarty	.05	.02	.01
☐ 4 Dmitri Young	.50	.23	.06
☐ 5 Joe Vitiello	.05	.02	.01
☐ 6 Mark Smith	.05	.02	.01
☐ 7 Tyler Green	.05	.02	.01
☐ 8 Shawn Estes	.15	.07	.02
☐ 9 Doug Glanville	.05	.02	.01
☐ 10 Manny Ramirez	2.00	.90	.25
☐ 11 Cliff Floyd	.15	.07	.02
☐ 12 Tyrone Hill	.05	.02	.01
☐ 13 Eduardo Perez	.05	.02	.01
☐ 14 Al Shirley	.05	.02	.01
☐ 15 Benji Gil	.15	.07	.02
☐ 16 Calvin Reese	.15	.07	.02
☐ 17 Allen Watson	.05	.02	.01
☐ 18 Brian Barber	.05	.02	.01
☐ 19 Aaron Sele	.15	.07	.02
☐ 20 John Farrell	.05	.02	.01
☐ 21 Scott Ruffcorn	.05	.02	.01
☐ 22 Brent Gates	.05	.02	.01
☐ 23 Scott Stahoviak	.05	.02	.01
☐ 24 Tom McKinnon	.05	.02	.01
☐ 25 Shawn Livsey	.05	.02	.01
☐ 26 Jason Pruitt	.05	.02	.01
☐ 27 Greg Anthony	.05	.02	.01
☐ 28 Justin Thompson	.15	.07	.02
☐ 29 Steve Whitaker	.05	.02	.01
☐ 30 Jorge Fabregas	.05	.02	.01
☐ 31 Jeff Ware	.05	.02	.01
☐ 32 Bobby Jones	.25	.11	.03
☐ 33 J.J. Johnson	.05	.02	.01
☐ 34 Mike Rossiter	.05	.02	.01
☐ 35 Dan Cholowsky	.05	.02	.01
☐ 36 Jimmy Gonzalez	.05	.02	.01
☐ 37 Trevor Miller	.05	.02	.01
☐ 38 Scott Hatteberg	.05	.02	.01
☐ 39 Mike Groppuso	.05	.02	.01
☐ 40 Ryan Long	.05	.02	.01
☐ 41 Eddie Williams	.05	.02	.01
☐ 42 Mike Durant	.05	.02	.01
☐ 43 Buck McNabb	.05	.02	.01
☐ 44 Jimmy Lewis	.05	.02	.01
☐ 45 Eddie Ramos	.05	.02	.01
☐ 46 Terry Horn	.05	.02	.01
☐ 47 Jon Barnes	.05	.02	.01
☐ 48 Shawn Curran	.05	.02	.01
☐ 49 Tommy Adams	.05	.02	.01
☐ 50 Trevor Mallory	.05	.02	.01
☐ NNO Frank Rodriguez BC	.30	.14	.04

1991 Classic/Best

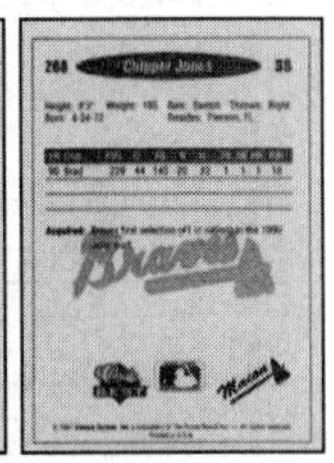

The 1991 Classic/Best baseball card set contains 450 standard-size cards. The cards were sold in factory sets and 12-card wax packs. A total of 2,100 autographed Mike Schmidt cards were randomly inserted in the wax packs only. The front design features action or posed color player photos, with a dotted black line to the left and bottom of the picture on a white card face. The backs contain basic player data and a washed-out major league logo of each player's team.

	MINT	NRMT	EXC
FACTORY SET (450)	15.00	6.75	1.85
COMPLETE SET (396)	10.00	4.50	1.25
COMMON CARD (1-450)	.05	.02	.01
☐ 1 Mike Schmidt	.30	.14	.04
☐ 2 Kevin Roberson	.05	.02	.01
☐ 3 Paul Rodgers	.05	.02	.01
☐ 4 Marc Newfield	.15	.07	.02
☐ 5 Marc Ronan	.05	.02	.01
☐ 6 Marty Willis	.05	.02	.01
☐ 7 Jason Hardtke	.05	.02	.01
☐ 8 Matt Mieske	.10	.05	.01
☐ 9 Brian Johnson	.10	.05	.01
☐ 10 Alex Arias	.05	.02	.01
☐ 11 Eric Young	.10	.05	.01
☐ 12 Donald Harris	.05	.02	.01
☐ 13 Bruce Chick	.05	.02	.01
☐ 14 Brian Williams	.05	.02	.01
☐ 15 Brian Cornelius	.05	.02	.01
☐ 16 Brian Giles	.05	.02	.01
☐ 17 Brad Ausmus	.05	.02	.01
☐ 18 Ivan Cruz	.05	.02	.01
☐ 19 Kevin Flora	.05	.02	.01
☐ 20 Robie Katzaroff	.05	.02	.01
☐ 21 Randy Knorr	.05	.02	.01
☐ 22 Micky Henson	.05	.02	.01
☐ 23 Chris Haney	.05	.02	.01
☐ 24 Jeff Mutis	.05	.02	.01
☐ 25 Barry Winford	.05	.02	.01
☐ 26 Ray Giannelli	.05	.02	.01
☐ 27 Donovan Osborne	.15	.07	.02
☐ 28 Ruben Gonzalez	.05	.02	.01
☐ 29 Howard Battle	.10	.05	.01
☐ 30 Greg O'Halloran	.05	.02	.01
☐ 31 Ben Vanryn	.05	.02	.01
☐ 32 Rick Huisman	.05	.02	.01
☐ 33 Jose Valentin	.15	.07	.02
☐ 34 Jose Zambrano	.05	.02	.01
☐ 35 John Gross	.05	.02	.01
☐ 36 Jessie Hollins	.05	.02	.01
☐ 37 Kevin Scott	.05	.02	.01
☐ 38 Kerwin Moore	.05	.02	.01
☐ 39 Eric Albright	.05	.02	.01
☐ 40 Ernesto Rodriguez	.05	.02	.01
☐ 41 Reggie Sanders	.40	.18	.05
☐ 42 Henry Werland	.05	.02	.01
☐ 43 Boo Moore	.05	.02	.01
☐ 44 Mike Messerly	.05	.02	.01
☐ 45 Mike Lansing	.15	.07	.02
☐ 46 Mike Gardella	.05	.02	.01
☐ 47 Mo Sanford	.05	.02	.01
☐ 48 Tavo Alvarez	.05	.02	.01
☐ 49 Nick Davis	.05	.02	.01
☐ 50 Charlie Hillemann	.05	.02	.01
☐ 51 Jeff Darwin	.05	.02	.01
☐ 52 Reid Cornelius	.05	.02	.01
☐ 53 Matt Rambo	.05	.02	.01
☐ 54 Rich Batchelor	.05	.02	.01
☐ 55 Ricky Gutierrez	.05	.02	.01
☐ 56 Rod Bolton	.05	.02	.01
☐ 57 Pat Bryant	.05	.02	.01
☐ 58 Hugh Walker	.05	.02	.01
☐ 59 Keith Schmidt	.05	.02	.01
☐ 60 Cesar Morillo	.05	.02	.01
☐ 61 Gabe White	.05	.02	.01
☐ 62 Javy Lopez UER	1.25	.55	.16
☐ 63 Carlos Delgado	1.25	.55	.16
☐ 64 John Johnstone	.05	.02	.01
☐ 65 Andres Berumen	.05	.02	.01
☐ 66 Brian Kowitz	.05	.02	.01
☐ 67 Shane Reynolds	.15	.07	.02
☐ 68 Jeromy Burnitz	.10	.05	.01
☐ 69 Scott Bryant	.05	.02	.01
☐ 70 Jason McFarlin	.05	.02	.01
☐ 71 John Conner	.05	.02	.01
☐ 72 Garrett Jenkins	.05	.02	.01
☐ 73 Greg Kobza	.05	.02	.01
☐ 74 Mark Swope	.05	.02	.01
☐ 75 Jeronne Williams	.05	.02	.01
☐ 76 Jeff Bonner	.05	.02	.01

☐ 77 Jermaine Swinton	.05	.02	.01
☐ 78 John Cohen	.05	.02	.01
☐ 79 Johnny Calzado	.05	.02	.01
☐ 80 Juan Andujar	.05	.02	.01
☐ 81 Paul Ellis	.05	.02	.01
☐ 82 Paul Gonzalez	.05	.02	.01
☐ 83 Scott Taylor	.05	.02	.01
☐ 84 Stan Spencer	.05	.02	.01
☐ 85 Steve Martin	.05	.02	.01
☐ 86 Scott Cepicky	.05	.02	.01
☐ 87 Max Aleys	.05	.02	.01
☐ 88 Michael Brown	.05	.02	.01
☐ 89 Jim Waggoner	.05	.02	.01
☐ 90 Mickey Rivers Jr.	.05	.02	.01
☐ 91 Nate Cromwell	.05	.02	.01
☐ 92 Carlos Perez	.15	.07	.02
☐ 93 Matt Brown	.05	.02	.01
☐ 94 Jose Hernandez	.05	.02	.01
☐ 95 Johnny Ruffin	.05	.02	.01
☐ 96 Kevin Jordan	.05	.02	.01
☐ 97 Manny Alexander	.10	.05	.01
☐ 98 Tony Longmire	.05	.02	.01
☐ 99 Lonell Roberts	.05	.02	.01
☐ 100 Doug Lindsey	.05	.02	.01
☐ 101 Al Harley	.05	.02	.01
☐ 102 Jerrey Thurston	.05	.02	.01
☐ 103 Mike Williams	.05	.02	.01
☐ 104 David Bell	.05	.02	.01
☐ 105 Greg Johnson	.05	.02	.01
☐ 106 Roger Salkeld	.05	.02	.01
☐ 107 Mike Milchin	.05	.02	.01
☐ 108 Jeff Kent	.15	.07	.02
☐ 109 Tim Stargell	.05	.02	.01
☐ 110 Miah Bradbury	.05	.02	.01
☐ 111 Paul Fletcher	.05	.02	.01
☐ 112 Steve Rolen	.05	.02	.01
☐ 113 Tony Spires	.05	.02	.01
☐ 114 Kevin Tolar	.05	.02	.01
☐ 115 Kevin Dattola	.05	.02	.01
☐ 116 Sherman Obando	.05	.02	.01
☐ 117 Sean Ryan	.05	.02	.01
☐ 118 Carlos Mota	.05	.02	.01
☐ 119 Steve Karsay	.10	.05	.01
☐ 120 Kelly Lifgren	.05	.02	.01
☐ 121 Damion Easley	.10	.05	.01
☐ 122 Fred Russell	.05	.02	.01
☐ 123 Freddie Davis Jr.	.05	.02	.01
☐ 124 Dave Zancanaro	.05	.02	.01
☐ 125 Jeff Jackson	.05	.02	.01
☐ 126 Steve Pegues	.05	.02	.01
☐ 127 Gerald Williams	.05	.02	.01
☐ 128 Eric Helfand	.05	.02	.01
☐ 129 Gary Painter	.05	.02	.01
☐ 130 Colin Ryan	.05	.02	.01
☐ 131 Randy Brown	.05	.02	.01
☐ 132 Andy Fox	.05	.02	.01
☐ 133 Mike Ogliaruso	.05	.02	.01
☐ 134 Matt Franco	.05	.02	.01
☐ 135 Willie Ansley	.05	.02	.01
☐ 136 Ivan Rodriguez	1.50	.70	.19
☐ 137 Anthony Lewis	.05	.02	.01
☐ 138 Bill Wertz	.05	.02	.01
☐ 139 Tom Kinney	.05	.02	.01
☐ 140 Brad Hassinger	.05	.02	.01
☐ 141 Elliot Gray	.05	.02	.01
☐ 142 Clemente Alvarez	.05	.02	.01
☐ 143 Mike Hankins	.05	.02	.01
☐ 144 Jim Haller	.05	.02	.01
☐ 145 Manuel Martinez	.05	.02	.01
☐ 146 Nilson Rolbedo	.05	.02	.01
☐ 147 Rex De La Nuez	.05	.02	.01
☐ 148 Steve Bethea	.05	.02	.01
☐ 149 Oscar Munoz	.05	.02	.01
☐ 150 Sam Militello Jr.	.05	.02	.01
☐ 151 Phil Hiatt	.05	.02	.01
☐ 152 Alberto DeLos Santos	.05	.02	.01
☐ 153 Darrell Sherman	.05	.02	.01
☐ 154 Henry Mercedes	.05	.02	.01
☐ 155 David Holdridge	.05	.02	.01
☐ 156 Sean Ross	.05	.02	.01
☐ 157 Brandon Wilson	.05	.02	.01
☐ 158 William Pennyfeather	.05	.02	.01
☐ 159 Derek Parks	.05	.02	.01
☐ 160 Troy O'Leary	.10	.05	.01
☐ 161 Genaro Capusano	.05	.02	.01
☐ 162 Robbie Beckett	.05	.02	.01
☐ 163 Chris Burton	.05	.02	.01
☐ 164 Jeff Williams	.05	.02	.01
☐ 165 John Massarelli	.05	.02	.01
☐ 166 John Kelly	.05	.02	.01
☐ 167 Jim Wiley	.05	.02	.01
☐ 168 Mark Mitchelson	.05	.02	.01
☐ 169 Jeff McNeely	.05	.02	.01
☐ 170 Keith Kimberlin	.05	.02	.01
☐ 171 Mike DeKneef	.05	.02	.01
☐ 172 Rusty Greer	.25	.11	.03
☐ 173 Pete Castellano	.05	.02	.01
☐ 174 Paul Torres	.05	.02	.01
☐ 175 Rod McCall	.05	.02	.01
☐ 176 Jim Bullinger	.05	.02	.01
☐ 177 Brian Champion	.05	.02	.01
☐ 178 Greg Hunter	.05	.02	.01
☐ 179 Luis Galindez	.05	.02	.01
☐ 180 Rodney Eldridge	.05	.02	.01
☐ 181 Rudy Pemberton	.05	.02	.01
☐ 182 Russ Davis	.10	.05	.01
☐ 183 Cristobal Colon	.05	.02	.01
☐ 184 Scott Bream	.05	.02	.01
☐ 185 Tim Nedin	.05	.02	.01
☐ 186 Joe Ausanio	.05	.02	.01
☐ 187 Shannon Withem	.05	.02	.01
☐ 188 Mike Oquist	.05	.02	.01
☐ 189 Pete Young	.05	.02	.01
☐ 190 Paul Carey	.05	.02	.01
☐ 191 Chris Gies	.05	.02	.01
☐ 192 Gar Finnvold	.05	.02	.01
☐ 193 Greg Martin	.05	.02	.01
☐ 194 Oreste Marrero	.05	.02	.01
☐ 195 Jim Thome	3.00	1.35	.35
☐ 196 Bill Ostermeyer	.05	.02	.01
☐ 197 David Hulse	.05	.02	.01
☐ 198 Damon Buford	.05	.02	.01
☐ 199 Jonathan Hurst	.05	.02	.01
☐ 200 Rich Tunison	.05	.02	.01
☐ 201 Tom Nevers	.05	.02	.01
☐ 202 Tracy Sanders	.05	.02	.01
☐ 203 Troy Buckley	.05	.02	.01
☐ 204 Todd Guggiana	.05	.02	.01
☐ 205 Tim Laker	.05	.02	.01
☐ 206 Dean Locklear	.05	.02	.01
☐ 207 Lee Tinsley	.05	.02	.01
☐ 208 Jose Velez	.05	.02	.01
☐ 209 Greg Zaun	.05	.02	.01
☐ 210 Billy Ashley	.15	.07	.02
☐ 211 Gary Caraballo	.05	.02	.01
☐ 212 Kiki Jones	.05	.02	.01
☐ 213 Dave Wrona	.05	.02	.01
☐ 214 Michael Carter	.05	.02	.01
☐ 215 Leon Glenn Jr.	.05	.02	.01
☐ 216 Glenn Sutko	.05	.02	.01
☐ 217 Pat Howell	.05	.02	.01
☐ 218 Austin Manahan	.05	.02	.01
☐ 219 Jon Jenkins	.05	.02	.01
☐ 220 Brook Fordyce	.05	.02	.01
☐ 221 Kevin Rogers	.05	.02	.01
☐ 222 David Allen	.05	.02	.01
☐ 223 Kurt Archer	.05	.02	.01
☐ 224 Keith Mitchell	.05	.02	.01
☐ 225 Bruce Schreiber	.05	.02	.01
☐ 226 Greg Blosser	.05	.02	.01
☐ 227 Dave Nilsson	.10	.05	.01
☐ 228 Fred Cooley	.05	.02	.01
☐ 229 Marc Lipson	.05	.02	.01
☐ 230 Jay Gainer	.05	.02	.01
☐ 231 Sean Cheetham	.05	.02	.01
☐ 232 Tim Howard	.05	.02	.01
☐ 233 Steve Hosey	.05	.02	.01
☐ 234 Javier Ocasio	.05	.02	.01
☐ 235 Ricky Rhodes	.05	.02	.01
☐ 236 Mark Griffin	.05	.02	.01
☐ 237 Scott Shockey	.05	.02	.01
☐ 238 T.R. Lewis	.05	.02	.01
☐ 239 Kevin Young	.05	.02	.01
☐ 240 Robb Nen	.10	.05	.01
☐ 241 Steve Dunn	.10	.05	.01
☐ 242 Tommy Taylor	.05	.02	.01
☐ 243 Keith Valrie	.05	.02	.01
☐ 244 Mateo Ozuna	.05	.02	.01
☐ 245 Scott Bullett	.05	.02	.01
☐ 246 Anthony Brown	.05	.02	.01
☐ 247 Phil Leftwich	.05	.02	.01
☐ 248 Cliff Garrett	.05	.02	.01
☐ 249 Wade Fyock	.05	.02	.01
☐ 250 Shayne Rea	.05	.02	.01
☐ 251 Royce Clayton	.05	.02	.01
☐ 252 Martin Martinez	.05	.02	.01
☐ 253 Dave Patterson	.05	.02	.01
☐ 254 Robert Fitzpatrick	.05	.02	.01
☐ 255 John Jackson	.05	.02	.01
☐ 256 Enoch Simmons	.05	.02	.01
☐ 257 Dave Proctor	.05	.02	.01
☐ 258 Garret Anderson	.75	.35	.09
☐ 259 Mark Dalesandro	.05	.02	.01
☐ 260 Ken Edenfield	.05	.02	.01
☐ 261 Tom Raffo	.05	.02	.01
☐ 262 Tim Cecil	.05	.02	.01
☐ 263 Bobby Magallanes	.05	.02	.01
☐ 264 Vince Castaldo	.05	.02	.01
☐ 265 Terry Burrows	.05	.02	.01
☐ 266 Victor Madrigal	.05	.02	.01
☐ 267 Tyler Houston	.10	.05	.01
☐ 268 Chipper Jones	4.00	1.80	.50
☐ 269 Terry Bradshaw	.05	.02	.01
☐ 270 Jalal Leach	.05	.02	.01
☐ 271 Jose Ventura	.05	.02	.01
☐ 272 Derek Lee	.05	.02	.01
☐ 273 Derek Reid	.05	.02	.01
☐ 274 David Wilson	.05	.02	.01
☐ 275 Pat Rapp	.10	.05	.01
☐ 276 John Roper	.05	.02	.01
☐ 277 Rogelio Nunez	.05	.02	.01
☐ 278 Fred White	.05	.02	.01
☐ 279 J.T. Snow	.25	.11	.03
☐ 280 Pedro Astacio	.15	.07	.02
☐ 281 Carey Thomas	.05	.02	.01
☐ 282 Chris Johnson	.05	.02	.01
☐ 283 Ignacio Duran	.05	.02	.01
☐ 284 Dave Fleming	.05	.02	.01
☐ 285 Wilson Alvarez	.15	.07	.02
☐ 286 Eric Booker	.05	.02	.01
☐ 287 John Ericks	.05	.02	.01
☐ 288 Don Peters	.05	.02	.01
☐ 289 Ed Ferm	.05	.02	.01
☐ 290 Mike Lieberthal	.15	.07	.02
☐ 291 John Jaha	.15	.07	.02
☐ 292 Bryan Baar	.05	.02	.01
☐ 293 Archie Corbin	.05	.02	.01
☐ 294 Kevin Tatar	.05	.02	.01
☐ 295 Shea Wardwell	.05	.02	.01
☐ 296 Hipolito Pichardo	.05	.02	.01
☐ 297 Curtis Leskanic	.05	.02	.01
☐ 298 Sam August	.05	.02	.01
☐ 299 Tim Pugh	.05	.02	.01
☐ 300 Mike Huyler	.05	.02	.01
☐ 301 Mark Parnell	.05	.02	.01
☐ 302 Jeff Juden	.05	.02	.01
☐ 303 Carl Sullivan	.05	.02	.01
☐ 304 Tyrone Kingwood	.05	.02	.01
☐ 305 Glenn Carter	.05	.02	.01
☐ 306 Tom Fischer	.05	.02	.01
☐ 307 Braulio Castillo	.05	.02	.01
☐ 308 Bob McCreary	.05	.02	.01
☐ 309 Ty Kovach	.05	.02	.01
☐ 310 Troy Salvior	.05	.02	.01
☐ 311 Mike Weimerskirch	.05	.02	.01
☐ 312 Christopher Hatcher	.05	.02	.01
☐ 313 Bryan Smith	.05	.02	.01
☐ 314 John Patterson	.05	.02	.01
☐ 315 Scooter Tucker	.05	.02	.01
☐ 316 Ray Callari	.05	.02	.01
☐ 317 Mike Moberg	.05	.02	.01
☐ 318 Midre Cummings	.05	.02	.01
☐ 319 Todd Ritchie	.05	.02	.01
☐ 320 Eric Christopherson	.05	.02	.01
☐ 321 Adam Hyzdu	.05	.02	.01
☐ 322 Andres Duncan	.05	.02	.01
☐ 323 Mike Myers	.05	.02	.01
☐ 324 Salomon Torres	.05	.02	.01
☐ 325 Tony Gilmore	.05	.02	.01
☐ 326 Walter Trice	.05	.02	.01
☐ 327 Tom Redington	.05	.02	.01
☐ 328 Terry Taylor	.05	.02	.01
☐ 329 Tim Salmon	1.50	.70	.19
☐ 330 Dan Masteller	.05	.02	.01
☐ 331 Mark Wohlers	.40	.18	.05
☐ 332 Willie Smith	.05	.02	.01
☐ 333 Todd Jones	.05	.02	.01
☐ 334 Alan Zinter	.05	.02	.01
☐ 335 Arthur Rhodes	.05	.02	.01
☐ 336 Toby Borland	.05	.02	.01
☐ 337 Shawn Whalen	.05	.02	.01
☐ 338 Scott Sanders	.10	.05	.01
☐ 339 Bill Meury	.05	.02	.01
☐ 340 Amadoz Arias	.05	.02	.01
☐ 341 Denny Hoppe	.05	.02	.01
☐ 342 Dave Telgheder	.05	.02	.01
☐ 343 Paul Bruno	.05	.02	.01
☐ 344 Paul Russo	.05	.02	.01
☐ 345 Rich Becker	.20	.09	.03
☐ 346 Steve Vondran	.05	.02	.01
☐ 347 Rich Langford	.05	.02	.01
☐ 348 Ron Lockett	.05	.02	.01
☐ 349 Sam Taylor	.05	.02	.01
☐ 350 Willie Greene	.10	.05	.01
☐ 351 Tom Houk	.05	.02	.01
☐ 352 Lance Painter	.05	.02	.01
☐ 353 Dan Wilson	.10	.05	.01
☐ 354 John Keuhl	.05	.02	.01
☐ 355 Pedro J. Martinez	.40	.18	.05
☐ 356 John Byington	.05	.02	.01
☐ 357 Scott Freeman	.05	.02	.01
☐ 358 Bo Dodson	.05	.02	.01
☐ 359 Julian Vasquez	.05	.02	.01
☐ 360 Rondell White	.75	.35	.09
☐ 361 Aaron Small	.05	.02	.01
☐ 362 Doug Fitzer	.05	.02	.01
☐ 363 Billy White	.05	.02	.01
☐ 364 Jeff Tuss	.05	.02	.01
☐ 365 Jeff Barry	.05	.02	.01
☐ 366 Craig Pueschner	.05	.02	.01
☐ 367 Julio Bruno	.05	.02	.01
☐ 368 Jamie Dismuke	.05	.02	.01
☐ 369 K.C. Gillum	.05	.02	.01
☐ 370 Jason Klonoski	.05	.02	.01
☐ 371 Tim Persing	.05	.02	.01
☐ 372 Mark Borcherding	.05	.02	.01
☐ 373 Larry Luebbers	.05	.02	.01
☐ 374 Carlos Fermin	.05	.02	.01
☐ 375 Charlie Rogers	.05	.02	.01
☐ 376 Ramon Caraballo	.05	.02	.01
☐ 377 Orlando Miller	.05	.02	.01
☐ 378 Joey James	.05	.02	.01
☐ 379 Dan Rogers	.05	.02	.01
☐ 380 Jon Shave	.05	.02	.01
☐ 381 Frank Bolick	.05	.02	.01
☐ 382 Frank Seminara	.05	.02	.01
☐ 383 Mel Wearing Jr.	.05	.02	.01
☐ 384 Zak Shinall	.05	.02	.01
☐ 385 Sterling Hitchcock	.10	.05	.01
☐ 386 Todd Van Poppel	.05	.02	.01
☐ 387 D.J. Dozier	.05	.02	.01
☐ 388 Ryan Klesko	2.00	.90	.25
☐ 389 Tim Costo	.05	.02	.01
☐ 390 Brad Pennington	.05	.02	.01
☐ 391 Checklist	.05	.02	.01
☐ 392 Checklist	.05	.02	.01
☐ 393 Checklist	.05	.02	.01
☐ 394 Checklist	.05	.02	.01
☐ 395 Checklist	.05	.02	.01
☐ 396 Checklist	.05	.02	.01
☐ 397 Frank Rodriquez	.10	.05	.01
☐ 398 Frank Jacobs	.05	.02	.01
☐ 399 Mike Kelly	.05	.02	.01
☐ 400 David McCarty	.05	.02	.01
☐ 401 Scott Stahoviak	.10	.05	.01
☐ 402 Doug Glanville	.05	.02	.01
☐ 403 Curt Krippner	.05	.02	.01
☐ 404 Joe Vitiello	.10	.05	.01
☐ 405 Justin Thompson	.15	.07	.02
☐ 406 Trevor Miller	.05	.02	.01
☐ 407 Tarrick Brock	.05	.02	.01
☐ 408 Eddie Williams	.05	.02	.01
☐ 409 Scott Ruffcorn	.05	.02	.01
☐ 410 Chris Durkin	.05	.02	.01
☐ 411 Jim Lewis	.05	.02	.01
☐ 412 Calvin Reese	.15	.07	.02
☐ 413 Toby Rumfield	.05	.02	.01
☐ 414 Brent Gates	.10	.05	.01
☐ 415 Mike Neill	.05	.02	.01
☐ 416 Tyler Green	.10	.05	.01
☐ 417 Ron Allen	.05	.02	.01
☐ 418 Larry Thomas Jr.	.05	.02	.01
☐ 419 Chris Weinke	.05	.02	.01
☐ 420 Matt Brewer	.05	.02	.01
☐ 421 Dax Jones	.05	.02	.01
☐ 422 Jon Farrell	.05	.02	.01
☐ 423 Dan Jones	.05	.02	.01
☐ 424 Eduardo Perez	.05	.02	.01
☐ 425 Rodney Pedraza	.05	.02	.01
☐ 426 Tom McKinnon	.05	.02	.01
☐ 427 Al Watson	.05	.02	.01
☐ 428 Herbert Perry	.05	.02	.01
☐ 429 Shawn Estes	.15	.07	.02
☐ 430 Tommy Adams	.05	.02	.01
☐ 431 Mike Grace	.05	.02	.01
☐ 432 Tyson Godfrey	.05	.02	.01
☐ 433 Andy Hartung	.05	.02	.01
☐ 434 Shawn Livsey	.05	.02	.01
☐ 435 Earl Cunningham	.05	.02	.01
☐ 436 Scott Lydy	.05	.02	.01
☐ 437 Aaron Sele	.15	.07	.02
☐ 438 Tim Costo	.05	.02	.01
☐ 439 Tanyon Sturtze	.05	.02	.01
☐ 440 Ed Ramos	.05	.02	.01
☐ 441 Buck McNabb	.05	.02	.01
☐ 442 Scott Hatteberg	.05	.02	.01
☐ 443 Brian Barber	.05	.02	.01
☐ 444 Julian Heredia	.05	.02	.01
☐ 445 Chris Pritchett	.05	.02	.01
☐ 446 Bubba Smith	.05	.02	.01
☐ 447 Shawn Purdy	.05	.02	.01
☐ 448 Jeff Borski	.05	.02	.01
☐ 449 Jamie Gonzalez	.05	.02	.01
☐ 450 Checklist (397-450)	.05	.02	.01
☐ AU1 Mike Schmidt AU/2100	175.00	80.00	22.00

1991 Classic/Best Gold Bonus

The 1991 Classic/Best Gold Bonus card set contains 20 standard-size cards. These cards were inserted at a rate of one per jumbo pack. The card design is the same as the 1991 Classic/Best regular issued set except for the gold foil stamp on the player's name.

	MINT	NRMT	EXC
COMPLETE SET (20)	12.00	5.50	1.50
COMMON CARD (BC1-BC20)	.20	.09	.03
☐ BC1 Mike Schmidt	.75	.35	.09
☐ BC2 Marc Newfield	.30	.14	.04
☐ BC3 Matt Mieske	.20	.09	.03
☐ BC4 Reggie Sanders	.75	.35	.09
☐ BC5 Jeromy Burnitz	.30	.14	.04
☐ BC6 Todd Van Poppel	.20	.09	.03
☐ BC7 Ivan Rodriguez	3.00	1.35	.35
☐ BC8 Sam Militello	.20	.09	.03
☐ BC9 Jim Thome	6.00	2.70	.75
☐ BC10 Brook Fordyce	.20	.09	.03
☐ BC11 Dave Nilsson	.30	.14	.04
☐ BC12 Royce Clayton	.30	.14	.04
☐ BC13 Mark Wohlers	.30	.14	.04
☐ BC14 Arthur Rhodes	.20	.09	.03
☐ BC15 Ryan Klesko	4.00	1.80	.50
☐ BC16 Mike Kelly	.20	.09	.03
☐ BC17 Frank Rodriguez	.30	.14	.04
☐ BC18 David McCarty	.20	.09	.03
☐ BC19 Tyler Green	.20	.09	.03
☐ BC20 Eduardo Perez	.20	.09	.03

1991 Clearwater Phillies Classic/Best

This 27-card standard-size set of the 1991 Clearwater Phillies, a Class A Florida State League affiliate of the Philadelphia Phillies, features white-bordered posed color player photos on its fronts. The player's name, team, and position appear at the bottom. The white back is framed by a thin black line and carries the player's name and position at the top, followed by biography, statistics and team logos.

	MINT	NRMT	EXC
COMPLETE SET (27)	5.00	2.20	.60

☐ 1 Elliott Gray
☐ 2 Paul Fletcher
☐ 3 Bob Gaddy
☐ 4 Darrell Goedhart
☐ 5 Ramon Henderson CO
☐ 6 Chris Limbach
☐ 7 Steve Parris
☐ 8 Matt Stevens
☐ 9 Mike Sullivan
☐ 10 Darold Knowles
☐ 11 Scott Wiegandt
☐ 12 Mike Williams
☐ 13 Matt Current
☐ 14 Terry Tewell
☐ 15 Pat Brady
☐ 16 John Escobar
☐ 17 Ron Lockett
☐ 18 Lee Elia MGR
☐ 19 R.A. Neitzel
☐ 20 Troy Paulsen
☐ 21 Mickey Hyde
☐ 22 Tom Nuneviller
☐ 23 Stacy Parker
☐ 24 Sam Taylor
☐ 25 Joe Urbon
☐ 26 Leroy Ventress
☐ 27 Checklist

1991 Clearwater Phillies ProCards

This 29-card standard-size set of the 1991 Clearwater Phillies, a Class A Florida State League affiliate of the Philadelphia Phillies, features on its white-bordered fronts posed color player photos set on simulated spiral-bound yellow notebooks. The player's name, position, and team appear within a green rectangle below the photo. The yellow horizontal back is bordered in white and carries the player's name at the top, followed by biography and statistics.

	MINT	NRMT	EXC
COMPLETE SET (29)	5.00	2.20	.60

☐ 1613 Paul Fletcher
☐ 1614 Bob Gaddy
☐ 1615 Darrell Goedhart
☐ 1616 Elliott Gray
☐ 1617 Chris Limbach
☐ 1618 Steve Parris
☐ 1619 Matt Stevens
☐ 1620 Mike Sullivan
☐ 1621 Bob Wells
☐ 1622 Scott Wiegandt
☐ 1623 Mike Williams
☐ 1624 Matt Current
☐ 1625 Terry Tewell
☐ 1626 Pat Brady
☐ 1627 John Escobar
☐ 1628 Ron Lockett
☐ 1629 Joe Millette
☐ 1630 R.A. Neitzel
☐ 1631 Troy Paulsen
☐ 1632 Mickey Hyde
☐ 1633 Tom Nuneviller
☐ 1634 Stacy Parker
☐ 1635 Sam Taylor
☐ 1636 Joe Urbon
☐ 1637 Leroy Ventress
☐ 1638 Lee Elia MGR
☐ 1639 Ramon Henderson CO
☐ 1640 Darold Knowles CO
☐ 1641 Checklist

1991 Clinton Giants Classic/Best

This 29-card standard-size set of the 1991 Clinton Giants, a Class A Midwest League affiliate of the San Francisco Giants, features white-bordered posed color player photos on its fronts. The player's name, team, and position appear at the bottom. The white back is framed by a thin black line and carries the player's name and position at the top, followed by biography, statistics and team logos.

	MINT	NRMT	EXC
COMPLETE SET (29)	5.00	2.20	.60

☐ 1 Dan Carlson
☐ 2 Dan Flanagan
☐ 3 Dan Henrikson
☐ 4 Brett McGonnigal
☐ 5 Rod Huffman
☐ 6 Joe Rosselli
☐ 7 Kurt Peltzer
☐ 8 Salomon Torres
☐ 9 Jose Reyes
☐ 10 Mark Yockey
☐ 11 Mate Borgogno
☐ 12 Matt Davis
☐ 13 Andres Duncan
☐ 14 Eric Christopherson
☐ 15 Gary Mayse
Asst GM
☐ 16 Bill Carpine TR
☐ 17 Shelby Hart
☐ 18 Pepe Frias
☐ 19 Teodulo Mujias
☐ 20 Adam Hyzdu
☐ 21 Barry Miller
☐ 22 Rikkert Faneyte
☐ 23 Greg Brummett
☐ 24 Ricky Ward
☐ 25 Jason Young
☐ 26 Jack Mull MGR
☐ 27 Steve Cline CO
☐ 28 Deron McCue CO
☐ 29 Checklist

1991 Clinton Giants ProCards

This 29-card standard-size set of the 1991 Clinton Giants, a Class A Midwest League affiliate of the San Francisco Giants, features on its white-bordered fronts posed color player photos set on simulated spiral-bound yellow notebooks. The player's name, position, and team appear within a green rectangle below the photo. The yellow horizontal back is bordered in white and carries the player's name at the top, followed by biography and statistics.

	MINT	NRMT	EXC
COMPLETE SET (29)	5.00	2.20	.60

☐ 826 Dan Carlson
☐ 827 Dan Flanagan
☐ 828 Dan Henrikson
☐ 829 Rod Huffman
☐ 830 Brian McLeod
☐ 831 Mike Myers
☐ 832 Kurt Peltzer
☐ 833 Jose Reyes
☐ 834 Salomon Torres
☐ 835 Mark Yockey
☐ 836 Eric Christopherson
☐ 837 Mike Grahovac
☐ 838 Teodulo Mejias
☐ 839 Mate Borgogno
☐ 840 Matt Davis
☐ 841 Andres Duncan
☐ 842 Carlos Lak
☐ 843 Barry Miller
☐ 844 Ricky Ward
☐ 845 Courtney Davis
☐ 846 Shelby Hart
☐ 847 Adam Hyzdu
☐ 848 Roberto Ramirez
☐ 849 Dan Rumsey
☐ 850 Jason Young
☐ 851 Jack Mull MGR
☐ 852 Deron McCue CO
☐ 853 Steve Cline CO
☐ 854 Checklist

1991 Colorado Springs Sky Sox Line Drive

	MINT	NRMT	EXC
COMPLETE SET (26)	5.00	2.20	.60

☐ 76 Eddie Taubensee
☐ 77 Jeff Bittiger
☐ 78 Willie Blair
☐ 79 Marty Brown
☐ 80 Kevin Burdick
☐ 81 Steve Cummings
☐ 82 Mauro Gozzo
☐ 83 Ricky Horton
☐ 84 Stan Jefferson
☐ 85 Brian Johnson
☐ 86 Barry Jones
☐ 87 Wayne Kirby
☐ 88 Mark Lewis
☐ 89 Rudy Seanez
☐ 90 Luis Lopez
☐ 91 Ever Magallanes
☐ 92 Lius Medina
☐ 93 Dave Otto
☐ 94 Roberto Zambrano
☐ 95 Jeff Shaw
☐ 96 Efrain Valdez
☐ 97 Sergio Valdez
☐ 98 Kevin Wickander
☐ 99 Charlie Manuel MGR
☐ 100 Rick Adair CO
Jim Gabella CO
☐ NNO Title card

1991 Colorado Springs Sky Sox ProCards

This 28-card standard-size set of the 1991 Colorado Springs Sky Sox, a Class AAA Pacific Coast League affiliate of the Cleveland Indians, features on its white-bordered fronts posed color player photos set on simulated spiral-bound yellow notebooks. The player's name, position, and team appear within a green rectangle below the photo. The yellow horizontal back is bordered in white and carries the player's name at the top, followed by biography and statistics.

	MINT	NRMT	EXC
COMPLETE SET (28)	5.00	2.20	.60

☐ 2176 Jeff Bittiger
☐ 2177 Willie Blair
☐ 2178 Steve Cummings
☐ 2179 Mauro Gozzo
☐ 2180 Dave Otto
☐ 2181 Rudy Seanez
☐ 2182 Jeff Shaw
☐ 2183 Efrain Valdez
☐ 2184 Sergio Valdez
☐ 2185 Kevin Wickander
☐ 2186 Brian Johnson
☐ 2187 Eddie Taubensee
☐ 2188 Marty Brown
☐ 2189 Kevin Burdick
☐ 2190 Mark Lewis
☐ 2191 Luis Lopez
☐ 2192 Ever Magallanes
☐ 2193 Luis Medina
☐ 2194 Bernie Tatis
☐ 2195 Geronimo Berroa
☐ 2196 Barry Jones
☐ 2197 Wayne Kirby
☐ 2198 John Moses
☐ 2199 Roberto Zambrano
☐ 2200 Charlie Manuel MGR
☐ 2201 Rick Adair CO
☐ 2202 Jim Gabella CO
☐ 2203 Checklist

1991 Columbia Mets Play II

The 32 cards in this Columbia Mets set measure 2 3/8" by 3 1/2". Play II produced 3,000 sets; 1,000 sets were intended for distribution by the Columbia Mets at the ballpark in late August. In addition, 150 uncut sheets were made. The fronts feature posed color player photos with rounded corners. The card face is primarily white, with diagonal blue streaks visible at the top and bottom of the card. Player information is given in the lower left corner, and the Mets' team logo appears in the lower right corner. The horizontally oriented backs are printed in black and gray on white, and present biographical as well as statistical information.

	MINT	NRMT	EXC
COMPLETE SET (33)	15.00	6.75	1.85

☐ 1 Tim Blackwell MGR
☐ 2 Bill Latham CO
☐ 3 Howie Freiling CO
☐ 4 Bob Burton
Trainer
☐ 5 Tom Engle
☐ 6 Ed Perozo
☐ 7 Tom Allison
☐ 8 Rob Rees
☐ 9 Omar Garcia
☐ 10 Alberto Castillo
☐ 11 Edward Fully
☐ 12 Richie Bristow
☐ 13 Aaron Ledesma
☐ 14 Juan Castillo
☐ 15 Fernando Vina
☐ 16 Mike Thomas
☐ 17 Bernie Millan
☐ 18 Jake King
☐ 19 Brian Dunn
☐ 20 Danilo Mompres
☐ 21 Tim McClinton
☐ 22 Robbi Guzik
☐ 23 Mike Freitas
☐ 24 Jay Davis
☐ 25 Mason Rudolph
☐ 26 Rob Carpenter
☐ 27 Tom Wegman
☐ 27 Tom Wegmann
☐ 28 Jose Martinez
☐ 29 Butch Huskey
☐ 30 Met Maulers
Omar Garcia
Butch Huskey
☐ 31 Strike Force
Tom Wegmann
Mike Thomas
Tom Engle
Jose Martinez
☐ 32 Tito Navarro
Flashback

1991 Columbia Mets Postcards Play II

This 28-card set was issued in 4 series, with 7 cards per series. Play II produced 1,500 sets and 150 uncut sheets; 500 sets were given out at Mets park. The cards measure 5" by 3 9/16" and are in the postcard format. The front design has posed color player photos, with thin red borders in purple, white, and red on a black card face. The player's name is written vertically in yellow block lettering in a purple stripe on the left side of the picture. The backs are printed in dark blue. On the left half appears biography and player profile, while the right half has space for the address and stamp. The cards are numbered on the back 1-7 within series I-IV.

	MINT	NRMT	EXC
COMPLETE SET (28)	25.00	11.00	3.10

☐ 1 Jay Davis
☐ 1 Tim McClinton
☐ 1 Andy Fidler
☐ 1 Rob Carpentier
☐ 2 Robert Guzik
☐ 2 Mike Freitas
☐ 2 Mason Rudolph
☐ 2 Richie Bristow
☐ 3 Bernie Millan
☐ 3 Juan Castillo
☐ 3 Danilo Mompres
☐ 3 Edward Fully
☐ 4 Robert Rees
☐ 4 Fernando Vina
☐ 4 Ed Perozo
☐ 4 Tom Wegmann
☐ 5 Mike Thomas
☐ 5 Tom Allison
☐ 5 Tom Engle
☐ 5 Butch Huskey
☐ 6 Aaron Ledesma
☐ 6 Omar Garcia
☐ 6 Jose Martinez
☐ 6 Aaron Ledesma
Fernando Vina
Double Trouble
☐ 7 Tim Blackwell MGR
☐ 7 Brian Dunn
☐ 7 Alberto Castillo
☐ 7 Brook Fordyce
Flashback

1991 Columbus Clippers Line Drive

	MINT	NRMT	EXC
COMPLETE SET (26)	7.00	3.10	.85

☐ 101 Steve Adkins
☐ 102 Daven Bond
☐ 103 Darrin Chapin
☐ 104 Royal Clayton
☐ 105 Steve Howe
☐ 106 Keith Hughes
☐ 107 Mike Humphreys
☐ 108 Jeff Johnson
☐ 109 Scott Kamieniecki
☐ 110 Pat Kelly
☐ 111 Jason Maas
☐ 112 Alan Mills
☐ 113 Rich Monteleone
☐ 114 Hipolito Pena
☐ 115 John Ramos
☐ 116 Carlos Rodriguez
☐ 117 Dave Sax
☐ 118 Van Snider
☐ 119 Don Sparks
☐ 120 Andy Stankiewicz
☐ 121 Wade Taylor
☐ 122 Jim Walewander
☐ 123 Bernie Williams
☐ 124 Rick Down MGR
☐ 125 Gary Denbo CO
Clete Boyer CO
Russ Meyer CO
☐ NNO Title card

1991 Columbus Clippers Police

	MINT	NRMT	EXC
COMPLETE SET (24)	7.00	3.10	.85

☐ 1 Steve Adkins
☐ 2 Daven Bond
☐ 3 Darrin Chapin
☐ 4 Royal Clayton
☐ 5 Steve Howe
☐ 6 Keith Hughes
☐ 7 Mike Humphreys
☐ 8 Jeff Johnson
☐ 9 Scott Kamieniecki
☐ 10 Pat Kelly
☐ 11 Jason Maas
☐ 12 Alan Mills
☐ 13 Kevin Mmahat
☐ 14 Rich Monteleone
☐ 15 John Ramos
☐ 16 Carlos Rodriguez
☐ 17 Dave Sax
☐ 18 Van Snider
☐ 19 Don Sparks
☐ 20 Andy Stankiewicz

☐ 21 Wade Taylor
☐ 22 Jim Walewander
☐ 23 Bernie Williams
☐ NNO Clete Boyer
Gary Denbo
Monk Meyer
Rick Down
Ken Schnacks

1991 Columbus Clippers ProCards

This 29-card standard-size set of the 1991 Columbus Clippers, a Class AAA International League affiliate of the New York Yankees, features on its white-bordered fronts posed color player photos set on simulated spiral-bound yellow notebooks. The player's name, position, and team appear within a green rectangle below the photo. The yellow horizontal back is bordered in white and carries the player's name at the top, followed by biography and statistics. This issue includes a fifth year card of Bernie Williams.

	MINT	NRMT	EXC
COMPLETE SET (29)	7.00	3.10	.85

☐ 588 Steve Adkins
☐ 589 Daven Bond
☐ 590 Darrin Chapin
☐ 591 Royal Clayton
☐ 592 Steve Howe
☐ 593 Jeff Johnson
☐ 594 Scott Kamieniecki
☐ 595 Alan Mills
☐ 596 Rich Monteleone
☐ 597 Hipolito Pena
☐ 598 Wade Taylor
☐ 599 John Ramos
☐ 600 Dave Sax
☐ 601 Keith Hughes
☐ 602 Pat Kelly
☐ 603 Tory Lovullo
☐ 604 Carlos Rodriguez
☐ 605 Don Sparks
☐ 606 Andy Stankiewicz
☐ 607 Jim Walewander
☐ 608 Mike Humphreys
☐ 609 Jason Maas
☐ 610 Pat Sheridan
☐ 611 Van Snider
☐ 612 Bernie Williams
☐ 613 Team Picture
☐ 614 Rick Down MGR
☐ 615 Field Staff
☐ 616 Checklist

1991 Columbus Indians Classic/Best

This 30-card standard-size set of the 1991 Columbus Indians, a Class A South Atlantic League affiliate of the Cleveland Indians, features white-bordered posed color player photos on its fronts. The player's name, team, and position appear at the bottom. The white back is framed by a thin black line and carries the player's name and position at the top, followed by biography, statistics and team logos.

	MINT	NRMT	EXC
COMPLETE SET (30)	5.00	2.20	.60

☐ 1 Raymond Harvey
☐ 2 Victor Jones
☐ 3 Joe Perez
☐ 4 Kyle Washington
☐ 5 Mike Pinckes
☐ 6 David Mlicki
☐ 7 Mark Charbonnet
☐ 8 Andy Baker
☐ 9 Sam Baker
☐ 10 Dickie Brown
☐ 11 Brain Cofer
☐ 12 Alan Embree
☐ 13 Steve Gajkowski
☐ 14 Mike McLochlin
☐ 15 Robert Rivera
☐ 16 Delvy Santiago
☐ 17 Alan Walden
☐ 18 Bill Wertz
☐ 19 Chip Winiarski
☐ 20 John Lorms
☐ 21 Kelly Stinnett
☐ 22 David Bell
☐ 23 John Cotton
☐ 24 Tim Donahue
☐ 25 Jason Hardtke
☐ 26 Rod McCall
☐ 27 Fabio Gamez
☐ 28 Robbie Smith
☐ 29 Pat Bryant
☐ 30 Teddy Blackwell TR
Checklist

1991 Columbus Indians ProCards

This 32-card standard-size set of the 1991 Columbus Indians, a Class A South Atlantic League affiliate of the Cleveland Indians, features on its white-bordered fronts posed color player photos set on simulated spiral-bound yellow notebooks. The player's name, position, and team appear within a green rectangle below the photo. The yellow horizontal back is bordered in white and carries the player's name at the top, followed by biography and statistics.

	MINT	NRMT	EXC
COMPLETE SET (32)	5.00	2.20	.60

☐ 1475 Andy Baker
☐ 1476 Sam Baker
☐ 1477 Dickie Brown
☐ 1478 Brian Cofer
☐ 1479 Alan Embree
☐ 1480 Steve Gajkowski
☐ 1481 Mike McClochlin
☐ 1482 Roberto Rivera
☐ 1483 Delvy Santiago
☐ 1484 Alan Walden
☐ 1485 Bill Wertz
☐ 1486 Chip Winiarski
☐ 1487 John Lorms
☐ 1488 Kelly Stinnett
☐ 1489 David Bell
☐ 1490 John Cotton
☐ 1491 Tim Donahue
☐ 1492 Jason Hardtke
☐ 1493 Rod McCall
☐ 1494 Mike Pinckes
☐ 1495 Robbie Smith
☐ 1496 Patrick Bryant
☐ 1497 Mark Charbonnet
☐ 1498 Raymond Harvey
☐ 1499 Pedro Henderson
☐ 1500 Victor Jones
☐ 1501 Joe Perez
☐ 1502 Ramon Torres
☐ 1503 Kyle Washington
☐ 1504 Mike Brown MGR
☐ 1505 Dyar Miller CO
☐ 1506 Checklist

1991 Denver Zephyrs Line Drive

	MINT	NRMT	EXC
COMPLETE SET (26)	5.00	2.20	.60

☐ 126 D.L. Smith
☐ 127 James Austin
☐ 128 Esteban Beltre
☐ 129 Mickey Brantley
☐ 130 George Canale
☐ 131 Matias Carrillo
☐ 132 Juan Castillo
☐ 133 Jim Davins
☐ 134 Carlos Diaz
☐ 135 Cal Eldred
☐ 136 Narciso Elvira
☐ 137 Brian Fisher
☐ 138 Chris George
☐ 139 Sandy Guerrero
☐ 140 Doug Henry
☐ 141 Darren Holmes
☐ 142 Mike Ignasiak
☐ 143 Jeff Kaiser
☐ 144 Joe Kmak
☐ 145 Tim McIntosh
☐ 146 Charlie Montoyo
☐ 147 Jim Olander
☐ 148 Ed Puig
☐ 149 Tony Muser MGR
☐ 150 Lamar Johnson CO
Don Rowe CO
☐ NNO Title card

1991 Denver Zephyrs ProCards

This 27-card standard-size set of the 1991 Denver Zephyrs, a Class AAA American Association affiliate of the Milwaukee Brewers, features on its white-bordered fronts posed color player photos set on simulated spiral-bound yellow notebooks. The player's name, position, and team appear within a green rectangle below the photo. The yellow horizontal back is bordered in white and carries the player's name at the top, followed by biography and statistics.

	MINT	NRMT	EXC
COMPLETE SET (27)	5.00	2.20	.60

☐ 114 Jim Austin
☐ 115 Jim Davins
☐ 116 Cal Eldred
☐ 117 Narciso Elvira
☐ 118 Brian Fisher
☐ 119 Chris George
☐ 120 Doug Henry
☐ 121 Mike Ignasiak
☐ 122 Jeff Kaiser
☐ 123 Ed Puig
☐ 124 Carlos Diaz
☐ 125 Joe Kmak
☐ 126 Tim McIntosh
☐ 127 Esteban Beltre
☐ 128 George Canale
☐ 129 Juan Castillo
☐ 130 Sandy Guerrero
☐ 131 Charlie Montoyo
☐ 132 D.L. Smith
☐ 133 Mickey Brantley
☐ 134 Matias Carrillo
☐ 135 Jim Olander
☐ 136 Rolando Roomes
☐ 137 Tony Muser MGR
☐ 138 Lamar Johnson CO
☐ 139 Don Rowe CO
☐ 140 Checklist

1991 Dunedin Blue Jays Classic/Best

This 30-card standard-size set of the 1991 Dunedin Blue Jays, a Class A Florida State League affiliate of the Toronto Blue Jays, features white-bordered posed color player photos on its fronts. The player's name, position, and team name appear within a black stripe below the photo. The white back is framed by a black line and carries the player's name and position at the top, followed by biography and statistics.

	MINT	NRMT	EXC
COMPLETE SET (30)	5.00	2.20	.60

☐ 1 Scott Brow
☐ 2 Daren Brown
☐ 3 Tim Brown
☐ 4 Daren Kizziah
☐ 5 Graeme Lloyd
☐ 6 Gregg Martin
☐ 7 Paul Menhart
☐ 8 Marcus Moore
☐ 9 Mike Ogliaruso
☐ 10 Aaron Small
☐ 11 John Wanish
☐ 12 Eric Brooks
☐ 13 Anastacio Garcia
☐ 14 Greg O'Halloran
☐ 15 Bill Abare
☐ 16 Nandi Cruz
☐ 17 Brad Mengel
☐ 18 Billy Parese
☐ 19 David Tollison
☐ 20 Tim Hodge
☐ 21 Shawn Holtzclaw
☐ 22 Robert Perez
☐ 23 Shawn Scott
☐ 24 Nigel Wilson
☐ 25 Dennis Holmberg MG
☐ 26 Bill Monbouquette CO
☐ 27 Pete Rowe CO
☐ 28 Rob Montalvo
☐ 29 Kris Harmes
☐ 30 Jon Woodworth TR
Checklist

1991 Dunedin Blue Jays ProCards

This 29-card standard-size set of the 1991 Dunedin Blue Jays, a Class A Florida State League affiliate of the Toronto Blue Jays, features on its white-bordered fronts posed color player photos set on simulated spiral-bound yellow notebooks. The player's name, position, and team appear within a green rectangle below the photo. The yellow horizontal back is bordered in white and carries the player's name at the top, followed by biography and statistics.

	MINT	NRMT	EXC
COMPLETE SET (29)	5.00	2.20	.60

☐ 197 Scott Brow
☐ 198 Daren Brown
☐ 199 Tim Brown
☐ 200 Daren Kizziah
☐ 201 Graeme Lloyd
☐ 202 Gregg Martin
☐ 203 Paul Menhart
☐ 204 Marcus Moore
☐ 205 Mike Ogliaruso
☐ 206 Aaron Small
☐ 207 John Wanish
☐ 208 Eric Brooks
☐ 209 Anastacio Garcia
☐ 210 Kris Harmes
☐ 211 Greg O'Halloran
☐ 212 Bill Abare
☐ 213 Nandi Cruz
☐ 214 Brad Mengel
☐ 215 Robert Montalvo
☐ 216 Billy Parese
☐ 217 David Tollison
☐ 218 Tim Hodge
☐ 219 Shawn Holtzclaw
☐ 220 Robert Perez
☐ 221 Shawn Scott
☐ 222 Nigel Wilson
☐ 223 Dennis Holmberg MG
☐ 224 Bill Monbouquette CO
☐ 225 Checklist

1991 Durham Bulls Classic/Best

This 26-card standard-size set of the 1991 Durham Bulls, a Class A Carolina League affiliate of the Atlanta Braves, features white-bordered posed color player photos on its fronts. The player's name, team, and position appear at the bottom. The white back is framed by a thin black line and carries the player's name and position at the top, followed by biography, statistics and team logos. This issue includes a third year card of Javy Lopez.

	MINT	NRMT	EXC
COMPLETE SET (26)	10.00	4.50	1.25

☐ 1 Matt Shiflett
☐ 2 Brian Bark
☐ 3 David Nied
☐ 4 Matt Murray
☐ 5 Jeff Cronin
☐ 6 Mike Kelly
☐ 7 Dennis Burlingame
☐ 8 Dave Brust
☐ 9 Earl Steinmetz
☐ 10 Pedro Borbon Jr.
☐ 11 Steve Swail
☐ 12 Eddie Perez
☐ 13 Mike Mordecai
☐ 14 Ed Giovanola
☐ 15 Grady Little
☐ 16 Larry Jaster
☐ 17 Tim Gillis
☐ 18 Pat Dando
☐ 19 Javy Lopez
☐ 20 Jeff Clark
☐ 21 Tony Tarasco
☐ 22 Shawan Sottile
☐ 23 Brent McCoy
☐ 24 Ramon Caraballo
☐ 25 Brian Kowitz
☐ 26 Phillip Wellman CO
Checklist

1991 Durham Bulls ProCards

This 26-card standard-size set of the 1991 Durham Bulls, a Class A Carolina League affiliate of the Atlanta Braves, features on its white-bordered fronts posed color player photos set on simulated spiral-bound yellow notebooks. The player's name, position, and team appear within a green rectangle below the photo. The yellow horizontal back is bordered in white and carries the player's name at the top, followed by biography and statistics. This issue includes a third year card of Javy Lopez.

	MINT	NRMT	EXC
COMPLETE SET (33)	8.00	3.60	1.00

☐ 1535 Brian Bark
☐ 1536 Pedro Borbon Jr.
☐ 1537 Dennis Burlingame
☐ 1538 Jeff Cronin
☐ 1539 Roger Hailey
☐ 1540 Matt Murray
☐ 1541 David Nied
☐ 1542 Walt Roy
☐ 1543 Matt Shiflett
☐ 1544 Earl Steinmetz
☐ 1545 Don Strange
☐ 1546 Scott Taylor
☐ 1547 Javy Lopez
☐ 1548 Eddie Perez
☐ 1549 Steve Swail
☐ 1550 Dave Brust
☐ 1551 Ramon Caraballo
☐ 1552 Pat Dando
☐ 1553 Tim Gillis
☐ 1554 Ed Giovanola
☐ 1555 Pat Kelly
☐ 1556 Brent McCoy
☐ 1557 Mike Mordecai
☐ 1558 Jeff Clark
☐ 1559 Brian Kowitz
☐ 1560 Melvin Nieves
☐ 1561 Randy Simmons
☐ 1675 Tony Tarasco
☐ 1676 Grady Little MGR
☐ 1677 Gil Garrido CO
☐ 1678 Larry Jaster CO
☐ 1679 Phil Wellman CO
☐ 1680 Checklist

1991 Durham Bulls Update ProCards

This 9-card standard-size set of the 1991 Durham Bulls, a Class A Carolina League affiliate of the Atlanta Braves, features on its white-bordered fronts posed color player photos set on simulated spiral-bound yellow notebooks. The player's name, position, and team appear within a green rectangle below the photo. The yellow horizontal back is bordered in white and carries the player's name at the top, followed by biography and statistics.

	MINT	NRMT	EXC
COMPLETE SET (9)	5.00	2.20	.60

☐ 1 Mike Kelly

☐ 2 Hank Werland
☐ 3 Rob Mattson
☐ 4 Marcos Vazquez
☐ 5 Nate Minchey
☐ 6 Darren Ritter
☐ 7 Greg McMichael
☐ 8 Darren Watkins
☐ 9 Checklist

1991 Edmonton Trappers Line Drive

This 26-card standard-size set of the 1991 Edmonton Trappers, a Class AAA Pacific Coast League affiliate of the California Angels, features posed color player photos on its white-bordered fronts. The player's name appears in red lettering at the top; his position and team name appear in red lettering below the photo. The back carries the player's name within a red stripe at the top, followed by position, team name and affiliation, biography and statistics.

	MINT	NRMT	EXC
COMPLETE SET (26)	5.00	2.20	.60

☐ 151 Kyle Abbott
☐ 152 Ruben Amaro
☐ 153 Kent Anderson
☐ 154 Mike Erb
☐ 155 Randy Bockus
☐ 156 Gary Buckels
☐ 157 Tim Burcham
☐ 158 Chris Cron
☐ 159 Chad Curtis
☐ 160 Doug Davis
☐ 161 Mark Davis
☐ 162 Gary DiSarcina
☐ 163 Mike Fetters
☐ 164 Joe Grahe
☐ 165 Dan Grunhard
☐ 166 Dave Leiper
☐ 167 Rafael Montalvo
☐ 168 Reed Peters
☐ 169 Bobby Rose
☐ 170 Lee Stevens
☐ 171 Ron Tingley
☐ 172 Ed Vosberg
☐ 173 Mark Wasinger
☐ 174 Max Oliveras MG
☐ 175 Lenn Sakata CO
Gary Ruby CO
☐ NNO Title card

1991 Edmonton Trappers ProCards

This 28-card standard-size set of the 1991 Edmonton Trappers, a Class AAA Pacific Coast League affiliate of the California Angels, features on its white-bordered fronts posed color player photos set on simulated spiral-bound yellow notebooks. The player's name, position, and team appear within a green rectangle below the photo. The yellow horizontal back is bordered in white and carries the player's name at the top, followed by biography and statistics.

	MINT	NRMT	EXC
COMPLETE SET (28)	5.00	2.20	.60

☐ 1507 Kyle Abbott
☐ 1508 Chris Beasley
☐ 1509 Gary Buckels
☐ 1510 Tim Burcham
☐ 1511 Mike Erb
☐ 1512 Mike Fetters
☐ 1513 Joe Grahe
☐ 1514 Dave Leiper
☐ 1515 Rafael Montalvo
☐ 1516 Ed Vosberg
☐ 1517 Cliff Young
☐ 1518 Doug Davis
☐ 1519 Ron Tingley
☐ 1520 Kent Anderson
☐ 1521 Chris Cron
☐ 1522 Chad Curtis
☐ 1523 Gary DiSarcina
☐ 1524 Bobby Rose
☐ 1525 Mark Wasinger
☐ 1526 Ruben Amaro
☐ 1527 Mark Davis
☐ 1528 Dan Grunhard
☐ 1529 Reed Peters
☐ 1530 Lee Stevens
☐ 1531 Max Oliveras MG
☐ 1532 Gary Ruby CO
☐ 1533 Lenn Sakata CO
☐ 1534 Checklist

1991 El Paso Diablos Line Drive

	MINT	NRMT	EXC
COMPLETE SET (26)	5.00	2.20	.60

☐ 176 Shon Ashley
☐ 177 John Byington
☐ 178 Mark Chapman
☐ 179 Jim Czajkowski
☐ 180 Ruben Escalera
☐ 181 Craig Faulkner
☐ 182 Tim Fortugno
☐ 183 Don Gordon
☐ 184 Mitch Hannahs
☐ 185 Steve Lienhard
☐ 186 Dave Jacas
☐ 187 Kenny Jackson
☐ 188 John Jaha
☐ 189 Chris Johnson
☐ 190 Mark Kiefer
☐ 191 Pat Listach
☐ 192 Tom McGraw
☐ 193 Angel Miranda
☐ 194 Dave Nilsson
☐ 195 Jeff Schwarz
☐ 196 Steve Sparks
☐ 197 Jim Tatum
☐ 198 Brandy Vann
☐ 199 Dave Huppert MGR
☐ 200 Paul Lindblad CO
☐ NNO Title card

1991 El Paso Diablos ProCards

This 26-card standard-size set of the 1991 El Paso Diablos, a Class AA Texas League affiliate of the Milwaukee Brewers, features on its white-bordered fronts posed color player photos set on simulated spiral-bound yellow notebooks. The player's name, position, and team appear within a green rectangle below the photo. The yellow horizontal back is bordered in white and carries the player's name at the top, followed by biography and statistics.

	MINT	NRMT	EXC
COMPLETE SET (26)	5.00	2.20	.60

☐ 2739 Mark Chapman
☐ 2740 Jim Czajkowski
☐ 2741 Tim Fortugno
☐ 2742 Don Gordon
☐ 2743 Chris Johnson
☐ 2744 Mark Kiefer
☐ 2745 Steve Lienhard
☐ 2746 Tom McGraw
☐ 2747 Angel Miranda
☐ 2748 Jeff Schwarz
☐ 2749 Steve Sparks
☐ 2750 Craig Faulkner
☐ 2751 Dave Nilsson
☐ 2752 John Byington
☐ 2753 Pat Listach
☐ 2754 Mike Guerrero
☐ 2755 Mitch Hannahs
☐ 2756 John Jaha
☐ 2757 Jim Tatum
☐ 2758 Shon Ashley
☐ 2759 Ruben Escalera
☐ 2760 Dave Jacas
☐ 2761 Kenny Jackson
☐ 2762 Dave Huppert MGR
☐ 2763 Paul Lindblad CO
☐ 2764 Checklist

1991 Elizabethton Twins ProCards

This 26-card standard-size set of the 1991 Elizabethton Twins, a Rookie Class Appalachian League affiliate of the Minnesota Twins, features on its white-bordered fronts posed color player photos set on simulated spiral-bound yellow notebooks. The player's name, position, and team appear within a green rectangle below the photo. The yellow horizontal back is bordered in white and carries the player's name at the top, followed by biography and statistics.

	MINT	NRMT	EXC
COMPLETE SET (26)	5.00	2.20	.60

☐ 4293 Ron Caridad
☐ 4294 Bob Carlson
☐ 4295 Sandy Diaz
☐ 4296 Eddie Guardado
☐ 4297 Melanio Mieses
☐ 4298 Rafael Pina
☐ 4299 Dave Sartain
☐ 4300 Dave Schwartz
☐ 4301 Dennis Sweeney
☐ 4302 Alvin Brown
☐ 4303 Pedro Grifol
☐ 4304 Francisco Ramirez
☐ 4305 Mike Fernandez
☐ 4306 Craig Hawkins
☐ 4307 Steve Hazlett
☐ 4308 Scott Shell
☐ 4309 Ramon Valette
☐ 4310 Merritt Bowden
☐ 4311 Brent Brede
☐ 4312 Tim Moore
☐ 4313 Kenny Norman
☐ 4314 Kevin Strong
☐ 4315 Ray Smith MGR
☐ 4316 Jim Lemon CO
☐ 4317 Rick Tomlin CO
☐ 4318 Checklist

1991 Elmira Pioneers Classic/Best

This 30-card standard-size set of the 1991 Elmira Pioneers, a Class A New York-Penn League affiliate of the Boston Red Sox, features white-bordered posed color player photos on its fronts. The player's name, team, and position appear at the bottom. The white back is framed by a thin black line and carries the player's name and position at the top, followed by biography, statistics and team logos. This issue includes the minor league card debut of Frank Rodriguez.

	MINT	NRMT	EXC
COMPLETE SET (30)	7.00	3.10	.85

☐ 1 Brian Bright
☐ 2 Felix Colon
☐ 3 Jim Crowley
☐ 4 John Eierman
☐ 5 Jason Fridman
☐ 6 Tim Graham
☐ 7 John Lammon
☐ 8 Dana LeVangie
☐ 9 Jose Lora
☐ 10 Bill Madril
☐ 11 Jose Marin
☐ 12 Paul Rappoli
☐ 13 Tony Rodriguez
☐ 14 Frank Rodriguez
☐ 15 Emison Sotoy
☐ 16 Corey Bailey
☐ 17 Timothy Budrewicz
☐ 18 Chris Davis
☐ 19 Richard Delgado
☐ 20 Rob Henkel
☐ 21 Melvin Gonzalez
☐ 22 Mark Konopki
☐ 23 John Chafin
☐ 24 Todd Miller
☐ 25 Mark Mitchelson
☐ 26 Alberto Pratts
☐ 27 Dave Holt MGR
☐ 28 Garry Roggenburk CO
☐ 29 Phil Ksenich
Michael Ksenich
K.K. Cards
☐ 30 Steve Jacobucci TR

1991 Elmira Pioneers ProCards

This 29-card standard-size set of the 1991 Elmira Pioneers, a Class A New York-Penn League affiliate of the Boston Red Sox, features on its white-bordered fronts posed color player photos set on simulated spiral-bound yellow notebooks. The player's name, position, and team appear within a green rectangle below the photo. The yellow horizontal back is bordered in white and carries the player's name at the top, followed by biography and statistics. This issue includes the minor league card debut of Frank Rodriguez.

	MINT	NRMT	EXC
COMPLETE SET (29)	6.00	2.70	.75

☐ 3261 Cory Bailey
☐ 3262 Tim Bubrewicz
☐ 3263 John Chafin
☐ 3264 Chris Davis
☐ 3265 Richard Delgado
☐ 3266 Melvin Gonzales
☐ 3267 Rob Henkel
☐ 3268 Mark Konopki
☐ 3269 Todd Miller
☐ 3270 Mark Mitchelson
☐ 3271 Alberto Pratts
☐ 3272 John Lammon
☐ 3273 Dana Levangie
☐ 3274 Bill Madril
☐ 3275 Felix Colon
☐ 3276 Jim Crowley
☐ 3277 Jason Friedman
☐ 3278 Jose Marin
☐ 3279 Frank Rodriguez
☐ 3280 Tony Rodriguez
☐ 3281 Brian Bright
☐ 3282 John Eierman
☐ 3283 Tim Graham
☐ 3284 Jose Lora
☐ 3285 Paul Rappoli
☐ 3286 Emison Soto
☐ 3287 Dave Holt MGR
☐ 3288 Garry Roggenburk
☐ 3289 Checklist

1991 Erie Sailors Classic/Best

This 29-card standard-size set of the 1991 Erie Sailors, a Class A New York-Penn League Independent, features white-bordered posed color player photos on its fronts. The player's name, team, and position appear at the bottom. The white back is framed by a thin black line and carries the player's name and position at the top, followed by biography, statistics and team logos.

	MINT	NRMT	EXC
COMPLETE SET (29)	5.00	2.20	.60

☐ 1 Amador Arias
☐ 2 Rafael Astacio
☐ 3 Irene Cabral
☐ 4 J.J. Cruz
☐ 5 Steve DiMarco
☐ 6 Rick Juday
☐ 7 Dan Mahony
☐ 8 Kenny Marrero
☐ 9 Scott Sprick
☐ 10 Jeff Stenta
☐ 11 Kelvin Thomas
☐ 12 Noel Velez
☐ 13 Jim Whitman
☐ 14 David Carter
☐ 15 Joe Andrzejewski
☐ 16 Matt Connolly
☐ 17 Dominic Konieczki
☐ 18 Jeff Letourneau
☐ 19 Mike Lynch
☐ 20 Edwin Millerick
☐ 21 Tom Paskievitch
☐ 22 Scott Pudio
☐ 23 Tim Roberts
☐ 24 Roosevelt Smith
☐ 25 Bob Zeihen CO
☐ 26 Roberto Marte CO
☐ 27 Ray Korn CO
☐ 28 Barry Moss MGR
☐ 29 WJEE News Team
Checklist

1991 Erie Sailors ProCards

This 30-card standard-size set of the 1991 Erie Sailors, a Class A New York-Penn League Independent, features on its white-bordered fronts posed color player photos set on simulated spiral-bound yellow notebooks. The player's name, position, and team appear within a green rectangle below the photo. The yellow horizontal back is bordered in white and carries the player's name at the top, followed by biography and statistics.

	MINT	NRMT	EXC
COMPLETE SET (30)	5.00	2.20	.60

☐ 4059 Joe Andrzejewski
☐ 4060 David Carter
☐ 4061 Matt Connolly
☐ 4062 Dominic Konieczki
☐ 4063 Curt Krippner
☐ 4064 Jeff Letourneau
☐ 4065 Mike Lynch
☐ 4066 Edwin Millerick
☐ 4067 Tom Paskievitch
☐ 4068 Scott Pudlo
☐ 4069 Tim Roberts
☐ 4070 Roosevelt Smith
☐ 4071 J.J. Cruz
☐ 4072 Dan Mahony
☐ 4073 Ken Marrero
☐ 4074 Amador Arias
☐ 4075 Rafael Astacio
☐ 4076 Rich Juday
☐ 4077 Steve DiMarco
☐ 4078 Scott Sprick
☐ 4079 Jeff Stenta
☐ 4080 Irene Cabral
☐ 4081 Kelvin Thomas
☐ 4082 Noel Velez
☐ 4083 Jim Whitman
☐ 4084 Barry Moss MGR
☐ 4085 Ray Korn CO
☐ 4086 Roberto Marte CO
☐ 4087 Bob Zeihen CO
☐ 4088 Checklist

1991 Eugene Emeralds Classic/Best

This 30-card standard-size set of the 1991 Eugene Emeralds, a Class A Northwest League affiliate of the Kansas City Royals, features white-bordered posed color player photos on its fronts. The player's name, team, and position appear at the bottom. The white back is framed by a thin black line and carries the player's name and position at the top, followed by biography, statistics and team logos.

	MINT	NRMT	EXC
COMPLETE SET (30)	5.00	2.20	.60

☐ 1 Tony Castro
☐ 2 Dave Haber
☐ 3 Andy Brookens
☐ 4 Shane Halter
☐ 5 Troy Babbit
☐ 6 Nick Kaiser
☐ 7 Ramie Brooks
☐ 8 Paul Sanders
☐ 9 Steve Hinton
☐ 10 Vernon Slater
☐ 11 Mark Johnson
☐ 12 Dan Servello
☐ 13 Les Norman
☐ 14 Joe Randa
☐ 15 Joe Vitiello
☐ 16 Kevin Kobetitsch
☐ 17 Dave Farsaci

- ☐ 18 John Medrick
- ☐ 19 Angel Macias
- ☐ 20 Jeff Smith
- ☐ 21 Danny Miceli
- ☐ 22 John Downs
- ☐ 23 Thomas Lee
- ☐ 24 Roger Landress
- ☐ 25 Mike Bailey
- ☐ 26 Joel Johnson
- ☐ 27 Jason Bryans
- ☐ 28 Kris Glaser
- ☐ 29 Chris Connolly
- ☐ 30 Checklist

1991 Eugene Emeralds ProCards

This 30-card standard-size set of the 1991 Eugene Emeralds, a Class A Northwest League affiliate of the Kansas City Royals, features on its white-bordered fronts posed color player photos set on simulated spiral-bound yellow notebooks. The player's name, position, and team appear within a green rectangle below the photo. The yellow horizontal back is bordered in white and carries the player's name at the top, followed by biography and statistics.

	MINT	NRMT	EXC
COMPLETE SET (30)	5.00	2.20	.60

- ☐ 3714 Mike Bailey
- ☐ 3715 Jason Bryans
- ☐ 3716 Chris Connolly
- ☐ 3717 J.D. Downs
- ☐ 3718 Dave Farsaci
- ☐ 3719 Kris Glaser
- ☐ 3720 Joel Johnson
- ☐ 3721 Kevin Kobetitsch
- ☐ 3722 Roger Landress
- ☐ 3723 Thomas Lee
- ☐ 3724 Angel Macias
- ☐ 3725 John Medrick
- ☐ 3726 Danny Miceli
- ☐ 3727 Jeff Smith
- ☐ 3728 Rayme Brooks
- ☐ 3729 Paul Sanders
- ☐ 3730 Troy Babbitt
- ☐ 3731 Andy Brookens
- ☐ 3732 Dave Haber
- ☐ 3733 Shane Halter
- ☐ 3734 Steve Hinton
- ☐ 3735 Nick Kaiser
- ☐ 3736 Joe Randa
- ☐ 3737 Tony Castro
- ☐ 3738 Mark Johnson
- ☐ 3739 Les Norman
- ☐ 3740 Dan Servello
- ☐ 3741 Vernon Slater
- ☐ 3742 Joe Vitiello
- ☐ 3743 Checklist

1991 Everett Giants Classic/Best

This 30-card standard-size set of the 1991 Everett Giants, a Class A Northwest League affiliate of the San Francisco Giants, features white-bordered posed color player photos on its fronts. The player's name, team, and position appear at the bottom. The white back is framed by a thin black line and carries the player's name and position at the top, followed by biography, statistics and team logos.

	MINT	NRMT	EXC
COMPLETE SET (30)	5.00	2.20	.60

- ☐ 1 D.J. Thielen
- ☐ 2 Doug VanderWeele
- ☐ 3 Al Rodriquez
- ☐ 4 Randy Swank
- ☐ 5 Brett McGonnigal
- ☐ 6 Don Montgomery
- ☐ 7 Ray Jackson
- ☐ 8 Dax Jones
- ☐ 9 Ken Feist
- ☐ 10 Tim Florez
- ☐ 11 Frank Charles
- ☐ 12 Derek Dana
- ☐ 13 Tim Casper
- ☐ 14 Jarod Juelsgaard
- ☐ 15 Tim Luther
- ☐ 16 Shawn Henrichs
- ☐ 17 Rich Wyde
- ☐ 18 Ken Grundt
- ☐ 19 Ken Henderson
- ☐ 20 Moose Adams
- ☐ 21 Matt Brewer
- ☐ 22 Lenny Ayers
- ☐ 23 Eric Stonecipher
- ☐ 24 Bill VanLandingham
- ☐ 25 Chuck Wanke
- ☐ 26 Darren Wittcke
- ☐ 27 Roberto Ramirez
- ☐ 28 Kevin Bellomo
- ☐ 29 Paul Eckard TR
- ☐ 30 Checklist

1991 Everett Giants ProCards

This 33-card standard-size set of the 1991 Everett Giants, a Class A Northwest League affiliate of the San Francisco Giants, features on its white-bordered fronts posed color player photos set on simulated spiral-bound yellow notebooks. The player's name, position, and team appear within a green rectangle below the photo. The yellow horizontal back is bordered in white and carries the player's name at the top, followed by biography and statistics.

	MINT	NRMT	EXC
COMPLETE SET (33)	5.00	2.20	.60

- ☐ 3904 Moose Adams
- ☐ 3905 Lenny Ayres
- ☐ 3906 Ken Grundt
- ☐ 3907 Shawn Henrichs
- ☐ 3908 Rich Hyde
- ☐ 3909 Jarod Juelsgaard
- ☐ 3910 Tim Luther
- ☐ 3911 Eric Stonecipher
- ☐ 3912 Doug Vander Weele
- ☐ 3913 William VanLandingham
- ☐ 3914 Chuck Wanke
- ☐ 3915 Darren Wittcke
- ☐ 3916 Dan Calcagno
- ☐ 3917 Frank Charles
- ☐ 3918 Derek Dana
- ☐ 3919 Don Montgomery
- ☐ 3920 Tim Casper
- ☐ 3921 Tim Florez
- ☐ 3922 Roberto Ramirez
- ☐ 3923 Al Rodriguez
- ☐ 3924 Randy Swank
- ☐ 3925 D.J. Thielen
- ☐ 3926 Kevin Bellomo
- ☐ 3927 Matt Brewer
- ☐ 3928 Ken Feist
- ☐ 3929 Ken Henderson
- ☐ 3930 Ray Jackson
- ☐ 3931 Dax Jones
- ☐ 3932 Brett McGonnigal
- ☐ 3933 Rob Ellis MGR
- ☐ 3934 Mike Bubalo
- ☐ 3935 Dan Spillner CO
- ☐ 3936 Checklist

1991 Florida State League All-Stars ProCards

	MINT	NRMT	EXC
COMPLETE SET (46)	6.00	2.70	.75

- ☐ FSL1 Phil Hiatt
- ☐ FSL2 Tony Long
- ☐ FSL3 Kevin Shaw
- ☐ FSL4 Rusty Greer
- ☐ FSL5 Darren Niethammer
- ☐ FSL6 Pat Brady
- ☐ FSL7 Ron Lockett
- ☐ FSL8 Troy Paulsen
- ☐ FSL9 Paul Menhart
- ☐ FSL10 Nigel Wilson
- ☐ FSL11 Rich Batchelor
- ☐ FSL12 Jovino Carvajal
- ☐ FSL13 Mark Hutton
- ☐ FSL14 Brian Johnson
- ☐ FSL15 Kevin Jordan
- ☐ FSL16 Bob Munoz
- ☐ FSL17 Rey Noriega
- ☐ FSL18 Russ Springer
- ☐ FSL19 Jeff Braley
- ☐ FSL20 Brian Cornelius
- ☐ FSL21 Kirk Mendenhall
- ☐ FSL22 Parish Hayden
- ☐ FSL23 Jonathan Hurst
- ☐ FSL24 Mike Lansing
- ☐ FSL25 Tom Michno
- ☐ FSL26 Montie Phillips
- ☐ FSL27 Rod Bolton
- ☐ FSL28 Scott Cepicky
- ☐ FSL29 Rob Lukachyk
- ☐ FSL30 Todd Douma
- ☐ FSL31 Brook Fordyce
- ☐ FSL32 Pat Howell
- ☐ FSL33 Curtis Pride
- ☐ FSL34 Paul Ellis
- ☐ FSL35 Rick Shackle
- ☐ FSL36 Adam Brown
- ☐ FSL37 Ray Calhoun
- ☐ FSL38 Marc Griffin
- ☐ FSL39 Matt Howard
- ☐ FSL40 Michael Mimbs
- ☐ FSL41 Chris Morrow
- ☐ FSL42 Reid Cornelius
- ☐ FSL43 Rusty Kilgo
- ☐ FSL44 Joe Logan
- ☐ FSL45 Gary Painter
- ☐ FSL46 Checklist

1991 Fayetteville Generals Classic/Best

This 30-card standard-size set of the 1991 Fayetteville Generals, a Class A South Atlantic League affiliate of the Detroit Tigers, features white-bordered posed color player photos on its fronts. The player's name, team, and position appear at the bottom. The white back is framed by a thin black line and carries the player's name and position at the top, followed by biography, statistics and team logos.

	MINT	NRMT	EXC
COMPLETE SET (30)	5.00	2.20	.60

- ☐ 1 Greg Coppeta
- ☐ 2 Mike Guilfoyle
- ☐ 3 Greg Haeger
- ☐ 4 John Kosenski
- ☐ 5 Seth Stephens
  #1 Fan
- ☐ 6 Joe Neidinger
- ☐ 7 Corey Reincke
- ☐ 8 Eddy Rodriguez
- ☐ 9 Bob Fazekas
- ☐ 10 Brad Wilson
- ☐ 11 Dwight Lowry
- ☐ 12 Rich Bombard
- ☐ 13 Shannon Withem
- ☐ 14 Gerry Groninger MGR
- ☐ 15 Sean Sadler
- ☐ 16 Brian Saltzgaber
- ☐ 17 Jimmy Alder
- ☐ 18 Carlos Fermin
- ☐ 19 Doug Kimbler
- ☐ 20 Carlos Maldonado
- ☐ 21 Kelley O'Neal
- ☐ 22 Dan Rogers
- ☐ 23 Dan Bautista
- ☐ 24 Steve Looney
- ☐ 25 Aaron Beja
- ☐ 26 Mike Weinberg
- ☐ 27 Robert Undorf
- ☐ 28 Randall Stokes
- ☐ 29 Brian Warren
- ☐ 30 Mike Delao TR
  Checklist

1991 Fayetteville Generals ProCards

This 29-card standard-size set of the 1991 Fayetteville Generals, a Class A South Atlantic League affiliate of the Detroit Tigers, features on its white-bordered fronts posed color player photos set on simulated spiral-bound yellow notebooks. The player's name, position, and team appear within a green rectangle below the photo. The yellow horizontal back is bordered in white and carries the player's name at the top, followed by biography and statistics.

	MINT	NRMT	EXC
COMPLETE SET (29)	5.00	2.20	.60

- ☐ 1161 Greg Coppeta
- ☐ 1162 Bob Fazekas
- ☐ 1163 Mike Guilfoyle
- ☐ 1164 Greg Haeger
- ☐ 1165 John Kosenski
- ☐ 1166 Joe Neidinger
- ☐ 1167 Corey Reincke
- ☐ 1168 Eddy Rodriguez
- ☐ 1169 Randy Stokes
- ☐ 1170 Bob Undorf
- ☐ 1171 Brian Warren
- ☐ 1172 Shannon Withem
- ☐ 1173 Sean Sadler
- ☐ 1174 Brian Saltzgaber
- ☐ 1175 Brad Wilson
- ☐ 1176 Jimmy Alder
- ☐ 1177 Carlos Fermin
- ☐ 1178 Doug Kimbler
- ☐ 1179 Carlos Maldonado
- ☐ 1180 Kelley O'Neal
- ☐ 1181 Dan Rogers
- ☐ 1182 Dan Bautista
- ☐ 1183 Steve Looney
- ☐ 1184 Aaron Seja
- ☐ 1185 Mike Weinberg
- ☐ 1186 Gerry Groninger MGR
- ☐ 1187 Rich Rombard CO
- ☐ 1188 Dwight Lowry CO
- ☐ 1189 Checklist

1991 Frederick Keys Classic/Best

This 30-card standard-size set of the 1991 Frederick Keys, a Class A Carolina League affiliate of the Baltimore Orioles, features white-bordered posed color player photos on its fronts. The player's name, team, and position appear at the bottom. The white back is framed by a thin black line and carries the player's name and position at the top, followed by biography, statistics and team logos.

	MINT	NRMT	EXC
COMPLETE SET (30)	5.00	2.20	.60

- ☐ 1 Mark Carper
- ☐ 2 Andres Constant
- ☐ 3 Shane Hale
- ☐ 4 Mike Hook
- ☐ 5 Zachary Kerr
- ☐ 6 John O'Donoghue Jr.
- ☐ 7 Chuck Ricci
- ☐ 8 David Riddle
- ☐ 9 Jeff Williams
- ☐ 10 Steve Williams
- ☐ 11 Kip Yaughn
- ☐ 12 Cesar Devares
- ☐ 13 Ed Horowitz
- ☐ 14 Doug Reynolds
- ☐ 15 Manny Alexander
- ☐ 16 Tony Beasley
- ☐ 17 Randy Berlin
- ☐ 18 T.R. Lewis
- ☐ 19 Scott Sprick
- ☐ 20 Mel Wearing Jr.
- ☐ 21 Jason Alstead
- ☐ 22 Dan Berthel
- ☐ 23 Damon Buford
- ☐ 24 Sergio Cairo
- ☐ 25 Pat Hedge
- ☐ 26 Wally Moon MGR
- ☐ 27 John O'Donoghue Sr.CO
- ☐ 28 Joel Youngblood CO
- ☐ 29 Keith Kessinger
- ☐ 30 Mitch Bibb TR

1991 Frederick Keys ProCards

This 29-card standard-size set of the 1991 Frederick Keys, a Class A Carolina League affiliate of the Baltimore Orioles, features on its white-bordered fronts posed color player photos set on simulated spiral-bound yellow notebooks. The player's name, position, and team appear within a green rectangle below the photo. The yellow horizontal back is bordered in white and carries the player's name at the top, followed by biography and statistics.

	MINT	NRMT	EXC
COMPLETE SET (29)	5.00	2.20	.60

- ☐ 2355 Mark Carper
- ☐ 2356 Andres Constant
- ☐ 2357 Shane Hale
- ☐ 2358 Mike Hook
- ☐ 2359 Pat Leinen
- ☐ 2360 Daryl Moore
- ☐ 2361 John O'Donoghue
- ☐ 2362 Chuck Ricci
- ☐ 2363 David Riddle
- ☐ 2364 Jeff Williams
- ☐ 2365 Kip Yaughn
- ☐ 2366 Cesar Devares
- ☐ 2367 Ed Horowitz
- ☐ 2368 Doug Reynolds
- ☐ 2369 Manny Alexander
- ☐ 2370 Tony Beasley
- ☐ 2371 Randy Berlin
- ☐ 2372 T.R. Lewis
- ☐ 2373 Scott Sprick
- ☐ 2374 Mel Wearing
- ☐ 2375 Jason Alstead
- ☐ 2376 Dan Berthel
- ☐ 2377 Damon Buford
- ☐ 2378 Sergio Cairo
- ☐ 2379 Roy Gilbert
- ☐ 2380 Pat Hedge
- ☐ 2381 Wally Moon MGR
- ☐ 2382 Don Buford
  Director Field Operations
- ☐ 2383 Checklist

1991 Fresno State Bulldogs Smokey

The Fresno State Bulldogs set was sponsored by Grandy's in cooperation USDA Forest Service and other agencies. The set was issued as a unperforated sheet with four rows of four cards each. If the cards were cut, they would measure the standard size (2 1/2" by 3 1/2"). The fronts feature glossy color player photos, with blue borders on a red card face. Player information appears below the picture, between the Smokey and Grandy's logos. The backs present college statistics and a fire prevention cartoon starring Smokey. The cards are unnumbered and checklisted below in alphabetical order.

	MINT	NRMT	EXC
COMPLETE SET (16)	12.00	5.50	1.50

- ☐ 1 Bob Bennett CO
- ☐ 2 Kelly Champlin
- ☐ 3 Tim Costic
- ☐ 4 Chris Falco
- ☐ 5 Steve Griffin
- ☐ 6 Todd Johnson
- ☐ 7 Bobby Jones
- ☐ 8 Mike Noel
- ☐ 9 Jim Patterson
- ☐ 10 Philip Romero
- ☐ 11 Robbie Saitz
- ☐ 12 Steve Soderstrom
- ☐ 13 Martin Togher
- ☐ 14 James Wheaton
- ☐ 15 Jason Wood
- ☐ 16 Coaches
  Tim Painton
  Mike Rupcich

1991 Front Row Draft Picks

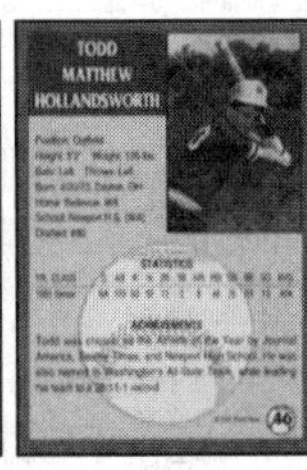

This 50-card premier edition set includes 27 of the top 40 eligible players from the 1991 Baseball Draft. The cards measure the standard size and 240,000 sets were produced. Each set contains a numbered card registering the set and one card from a limited Draft Pick subset as a bonus card. In exchange for returning the bonus card, the collector received card number 50 (Benji Gil), a mini-update set (51-54; sent to the first 120,000 respondents), and one card from a five-card Frankie Rodriguez bonus set. The photos on both sides of the card are highlighted with an ultra violet finish. The obverse has glossy color player photos bordered in gray, with the player's name in black lettering below the picture. The words "Front Row" appear in a baseball in the upper right corner, while the words "91 Draft Pick" appear in a diamond in the lower left corner. The reverse has a color photo of the player in little league, biography, statistics, and career achievements.

	MINT	NRMT	EXC
COMPLETE SET (50)	4.00	1.80	.50
COMMON CARD (1-49)	.05	.02	.01
*GOLD: 4X VALUE			
*SILVER: 2X VALUE			
□ 1 Frank Rodriguez	.40	.18	.05
□ 2 Aaron Sele	.15	.07	.02
□ 3 Chad Schoenvogel	.05	.02	.01
□ 4 Scott Ruffcorn	.05	.02	.01
□ 5 Dan Cholowski	.05	.02	.01
□ 6 Gene Schall	.05	.02	.01
□ 7 Trever Miller	.05	.02	.01
□ 8 Chris Durkin	.05	.02	.01
□ 9 Mike Neill	.05	.02	.01
□ 10 Kevin Stocker	.05	.02	.01
□ 11 Bobby Jones	.25	.11	.03
□ 12 Jon Farrell	.05	.02	.01
□ 13 Ron Allen	.05	.02	.01
□ 14 Mike Rossiter	.05	.02	.01
□ 15 Scott Hatteberg	.05	.02	.01
□ 16 Rod Pedraza	.05	.02	.01
□ 17 Mike Durant	.05	.02	.01
□ 18 Ryan Long	.05	.02	.01
□ 19 Greg Anthony	.05	.02	.01
□ 20 Jon Barnes	.05	.02	.01
□ 21 Brian Barber	.05	.02	.01
□ 22 Brent Gates	.05	.02	.01
□ 23 Calvin Reese	.15	.07	.02
□ 24 Terry Horn	.05	.02	.01
□ 25 Scott Stahoviak	.05	.02	.01
□ 26 Jason Pruitt	.05	.02	.01
□ 27 Shawn Curran	.05	.02	.01
□ 28 Jimmy Lewis	.05	.02	.01
□ 29 Alex Ochoa	.60	.25	.07
□ 30 Joe DeBerry	.05	.02	.01
□ 31 Justin Thompson	.15	.07	.02
□ 32 Jimmy Gonzalez	.05	.02	.01
□ 33 Edward Ramos	.05	.02	.01
□ 34 Tyler Green	.05	.02	.01
□ 35 Toby Rumfield	.05	.02	.01
□ 36 Dave Doorneweerd	.05	.02	.01
□ 37 Jeff Hostetler	.05	.02	.01
□ 38 Shawn Livsey	.05	.02	.01
□ 39 Mike Groppuso	.05	.02	.01
□ 40 Steve Whitaker	.05	.02	.01
□ 41 Tom McKinnon	.05	.02	.01
□ 42 Buck McNabb	.05	.02	.01
□ 43 Al Shirley	.05	.02	.01
□ 44 Allan Watson	.05	.02	.01
□ 45 Bill Bliss	.05	.02	.01
□ 46 Todd Hollandsworth	.60	.25	.07
□ 47 Manny Ramirez	2.00	.90	.25
□ 48 J.J. Johnson	.05	.02	.01
□ 49 Cliff Floyd	.15	.07	.02
□ 50 Benji Gil	.15	.07	.02
□ 51 Herbert Perry	.05	.02	.01
□ 52 Tarrik Brock	.05	.02	.01
□ 53 Trevor Mallory	.05	.02	.01
□ 54 Chris Pritchett	.05	.02	.01

1991 Ft. Lauderdale Yankees Classic/Best

This 30-card standard-size set of the 1991 Ft. Lauderdale Yankees, a Class A Florida State League affiliate of the New York Yankees, features white-bordered posed color player photos on its fronts. The player's name, team, and position appear at the bottom. The white back is framed by a thin black line and carries the player's name and position at the top, followed by biography, statistics and team logos.

	MINT	NRMT	EXC
COMPLETE SET (30)	5.00	2.20	.60

□ 1 Rich Batchelor
□ 2 Art Canestro
□ 3 Glenn Sherlock MGR
□ 4 Ken Greer
□ 5 Mark Hutton
□ 6 Ramon Manon
□ 7 Moose Marris
□ 8 Ted Uhlaender CO
□ 9 Bob Munoz
□ 10 Jerry Nielsen
□ 11 Rich Polak
□ 12 Bruce Prybylinski
□ 13 Tim Rumer
□ 14 Russ Springer
□ 15 Jim Wiley
□ 16 Brian Johnson
□ 17 Jose Pineda
□ 18 Larry Walker
□ 19 Juan Blackwell
□ 20 Dave Howell
□ 21 Kevin Jordan
□ 22 Rey Noriega
□ 23 Andres Rodriguez
□ 24 Rich Barnwell
□ 25 Jovino Carvajal
□ 26 Nookie Garland
□ 27 Jay Leach
□ 28 Rick Strickland
□ 29 Mike Brown CO
□ 30 Checklist

1991 Ft. Lauderdale Yankees ProCards

This 31-card standard-size set of the 1991 Ft. Lauderdale Yankees, a Class A Florida State League affiliate of the New York Yankees, features on its white-bordered fronts posed color player photos set on simulated spiral-bound yellow notebooks. The player's name, position, and team appear within a green rectangle below the photo. The yellow horizontal back is bordered in white and carries the player's name at the top, followed by biography and statistics.

	MINT	NRMT	EXC
COMPLETE SET (31)	5.00	2.20	.60

□ 2416 Rich Batchelor
□ 2417 Art Canestro
□ 2418 Ken Greer
□ 2419 Mark Hutton
□ 2420 Ramon Manon
□ 2421 Mark Marris
□ 2422 Bob Munoz
□ 2423 Jerry Nielsen
□ 2424 Rich Polak
□ 2425 Bruce Prybylinski
□ 2426 Tim Rumer
□ 2427 Russ Springer
□ 2428 Jim Wiley
□ 2429 Brian Johnson
□ 2430 Jose Pineda
□ 2431 Larry Walker
□ 2432 Juan Blackwell
□ 2433 Dave Howell
□ 2434 Kevin Jordan
□ 2435 Rey Noriega
□ 2436 Andres Rodriguez
□ 2437 Aaron Van Scoyoc
□ 2438 Rich Barnwell
□ 2439 Jovino Carvajal
□ 2440 Tim Garland
□ 2441 Jalal Leach
□ 2442 Rick Strickland
□ 2443 Glenn Sherlock MGR
□ 2444 Mike Brown CO
□ 2445 Ted Uhlaender CO
□ 2446 Checklist

1991 Gastonia Rangers Classic/Best

This 30-card standard-size set of the 1991 Gastonia Rangers, a Class A South Atlantic League affiliate of the Texas Rangers, features white-bordered posed color player photos on its fronts. The player's name, team, and position appear at the bottom. The white back is framed by a thin black line and carries the player's name and position at the top, followed by biography, statistics and team logos. Both Dell Curry, the NBA 6th Man Award winner of 1994; and Muggsy Bogues, star NBA guard; are also included in this set.

	MINT	NRMT	EXC
COMPLETE SET (30)	7.00	3.10	.85

□ 1 Tony Bouton
□ 2 Terry Burrows
□ 3 Jose Cardona
□ 4 Steve Dreyer
□ 5 Scott Erickson
□ 6 Chris Gies
□ 7 Micky Henson
□ 8 Victor Madrigal
□ 9 Keith McGough
□ 10 Tyrone Washington
□ 11 Tim Wells
□ 12 Matt Whiteside
□ 13 Greg Blevins
□ 14 Michael Crespo
□ 15 Tom Hernandez
□ 16 Miguel Castellano
□ 17 Bump Wills
□ 18 David Lowery
□ 19 Randy Marshall
□ 20 Paul Matachun
□ 21 Shannon Penn
□ 22 Jon Shave
□ 23 Sid Holland
□ 24 Malvin Matos
□ 25 Keith Murray
□ 26 Marty Posey
□ 27 Dell Curry
□ 28 Tom Tisdale TR
□ 29 Muggsy Bogues
□ 30 Rowdy Ranger
Checklist

1991 Gastonia Rangers ProCards

This 31-card standard-size set of the 1991 Gastonia Rangers, a Class A South Atlantic League affiliate of the Texas Rangers, features on its white-bordered fronts posed color player photos set on simulated spiral-bound yellow notebooks. The player's name, position, and team appear within a green rectangle below the photo. The yellow horizontal back is bordered in white and carries the player's name at the top, followed by biography and statistics.

	MINT	NRMT	EXC
COMPLETE SET (31)	5.00	2.20	.60

□ 2678 Tony Bouton
□ 2679 Terry Burrows
□ 2680 Jose Cardona
□ 2681 Steve Dreyer
□ 2682 Scott Erickson
□ 2683 Chris Gies
□ 2684 Mickey Henson
□ 2685 Victor Madrigal
□ 2686 Keith McGough
□ 2687 Tyrone Washington
□ 2688 Tim Wells
□ 2689 Matt Whiteside
□ 2690 Greg Blevins
□ 2691 Mike Crespo
□ 2692 Tom Hernandez
□ 2693 Miguel Castellanos
□ 2694 Pete Laake
□ 2695 David Lowery
□ 2696 Randy Marshall
□ 2697 Paul Matachun
□ 2698 Shannon Penn
□ 2699 Jon Shave
□ 2700 Sid Holland
□ 2701 Malvin Matos
□ 2702 Keith Murray
□ 2703 Marty Posey
□ 2704 Bump Wills MGR
□ 2705 Perry Hill
Fielding Instructor
□ 2706 Jackson Todd CO
□ 2707 Randy Whisler CO
□ 2708 Checklist

1991 Geneva Cubs Classic/Best

This 30-card standard-size set of the 1991 Geneva Cubs, a Class A New York-Penn League affiliate of the Chicago Cubs, features white-bordered posed color player photos on its fronts. The player's name, team, and position appear at the bottom. The white back is framed by a thin black line and carries the player's name and position at the top, followed by biography, statistics and team logos.

	MINT	NRMT	EXC
COMPLETE SET (30)	5.00	2.20	.60

□ 1 Bill Bliss
□ 2 Ben Burlingame
□ 3 Dale Craig
□ 4 Morris Craig
□ 5 Steve Davis
□ 6 Serge Doiron
□ 7 Willie Gardner
□ 8 Rudy Gomez
□ 9 Pat Huston
□ 10 Brian Kenny
□ 11 Ed Larregui
□ 12 Ricardo Medina
□ 13 Tim Moore
□ 14 Leo Perez
□ 15 Pedro Perez
□ 16 Jim Robinson
□ 17 Humberto Saa DeLaCruz
□ 18 Joe Sarcia
□ 19 Greg Mahlberg
□ 20 Joe Szczepanski
□ 21 Joey Terilli
□ 22 Mike Tidwell
□ 23 Ozzie Timmons
□ 24 Doug Glanville
□ 25 Scott Weiss
□ 26 Mike Young
□ 27 Carl Schramm
□ 28 Joe Housey CO
□ 29 Phil Hannon CO
□ NNO Checklist

1991 Geneva Cubs ProCards

This 30-card standard-size set of the 1991 Geneva Cubs, a Class A New York-Penn League affiliate of the Chicago Cubs, features on its white-bordered fronts posed color player photos set on simulated spiral-bound yellow notebooks. The player's name, position, and team appear within a green rectangle below the photo. The yellow horizontal back is bordered in white and carries the player's name at the top, followed by biography and statistics.

	MINT	NRMT	EXC
COMPLETE SET (30)	5.00	2.20	.60

□ 4207 Bill Bliss
□ 4208 Ben Burlingame
□ 4209 Steve Davis
□ 4210 Brian Kenny
□ 4211 Leo Perez
□ 4212 Pedro Perez
□ 4213 Carl Schramm
□ 4214 Dave Stevens
□ 4215 Joe Szczepanski
□ 4216 Mike Tidwell
□ 4217 Steve Trachsel
□ 4218 Scott Weiss
□ 4219 Mike Young
□ 4220 Dale Craig
□ 4221 Serge Doiron
□ 4222 Jim Robinson
□ 4223 Rudy Gomez
□ 4224 Pat Huston
□ 4225 Ricardo Medina
□ 4226 Tim Moore
□ 4227 Humberto Saa
□ 4228 Joe Sarcia
□ 4229 Willie Gardner
□ 4230 Doug Glanville
□ 4231 Ed Larregui
□ 4232 Joey Terilli
□ 4233 Ozzie Timmons
□ 4234 Greg Mahlberg MGR
□ 4235 Phil Hannon CO
□ 4236 Checklist

1991 Great Falls Dodgers Sports Pro

This 30-card standard-size set of the 1991 Great Falls Dodgers, a Rookie Class Pioneer League affiliate of the Los Angeles Dodgers, features posed color head-and-shoulders shots, with thin black borders on a white card face. The horizontally oriented backs have biographical information.

	MINT	NRMT	EXC
COMPLETE SET (30)	6.00	2.70	.75

□ 1 Frank Smith
□ 2 Albert Maldonado
□ 3 Mike Brown
□ 4 Nelson Castro
□ 5 Henry Blanco
□ 6 Jose Parra
□ 7 Robert Mejia
□ 8 Larry Jacinto
□ 9 Jacob Botts
□ 10 Joe Seals
□ 11 Ross Farnsworth
□ 12 Mike Boyzuick
□ 13 Stewart Strong
□ 14 Willis Otanez
□ 15 Greg Davis
□ 16 Randall Graves
□ 17 Ken Huckaby
□ 18 Jay Kirkpatrick
□ 19 Daniel Andrews
□ 20 Erik Zammarchi
□ 21 Chris Sinacori
□ 22 Cam Aronetz
□ 23 Mike Walkden
□ 24 Rick Gorecki
□ 25 Todd Williams
□ 26 Juan Castro
□ 27 Patrick Reed
□ 28 Tito Landrum
□ 29 Javier Puchales
□ 30 Alton Pinkney

1991 Greensboro Hornets ProCards

This 29-card standard-size set of the 1991 Greensboro Hornets, a Class A South Atlantic League affiliate of the New York Yankees, features on its white-bordered fronts posed color player photos set on simulated spiral-bound yellow notebooks. The player's name, position, and team appear within a green rectangle below the photo. The yellow horizontal back is bordered in white and carries the player's name at the top, followed by biography and statistics. This issue includes the minor league card debut of Mariano Rivera.

	MINT	NRMT	EXC
COMPLETE SET (29)	8.00	3.60	1.00

☐ 3050 Matt Dunbar
☐ 3051 Bryan Faw
☐ 3052 Ron Frazier
☐ 3053 Rich Hines
☐ 3054 Todd Malone
☐ 3055 Pat Morphy
☐ 3056 Cesar Perez
☐ 3057 Rafael Quirico
☐ 3058 Mariano Rivera
☐ 3059 Keith Seiler
☐ 3060 Bo Siberz
☐ 3061 Shad Smith
☐ 3062 Kiki Hernandez
☐ 3063 Kevin McMullen
☐ 3064 Tim Cooper
☐ 3065 Luis Gallardo
☐ 3066 Rick Lantrip
☐ 3067 Scott Romano
☐ 3068 Philip Scott
☐ 3069 Brian Turner
☐ 3070 Richard Turrentine
☐ 3071 Bob Deller
☐ 3072 Carl Everett
☐ 3073 Sean Gilliam
☐ 3074 Lew Hill
☐ 3075 Trey Hillman MGR
☐ 3076 Brian Milner
☐ 3077 Mark Shiflett CO
☐ 3078 Checklist

1991 Greenville Braves Classic/Best

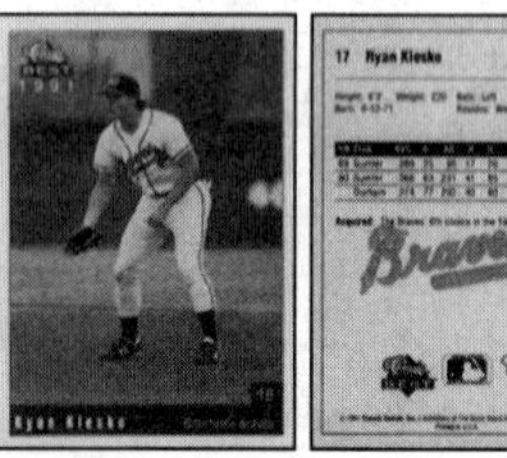

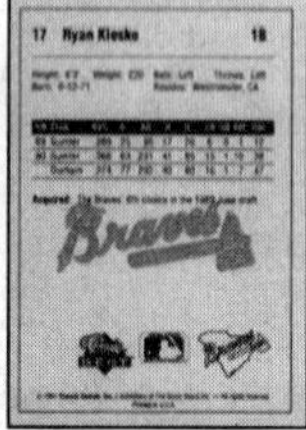

This 29-card standard-size set of the 1991 Greenville Braves, a Class AA Southern League affiliate of the Atlanta Braves, features white-bordered posed color player photos on its fronts. The player's name, team, and position appear at the bottom. The white back is framed by a thin black line and carries the player's name and position at the top, followed by biography, statistics and team logos.

	MINT	NRMT	EXC
COMPLETE SET (29)	12.00	5.50	1.50

☐ 1 Pat Gomez
☐ 2 Judd Johnson
☐ 3 Ben Rivera
☐ 4 Napoleon Robinson
☐ 5 Earl Sanders
☐ 6 Bill Taylor
☐ 7 Lee Upshaw
☐ 8 Preston Watson
☐ 9 Turk Wendell
☐ 10 Mark Wohlers
☐ 11 Johnny Cuevas
☐ 12 Brian Deak
☐ 13 Fred Lopez
☐ 14 Rich Casarotti
☐ 15 Vinnie Castilla
☐ 16 Brian Champion
☐ 17 Ryan Klesko
☐ 18 Rich Maloney
☐ 19 Rick Morris
☐ 20 Popeye Cole
☐ 21 Keith Mitchell
☐ 22 Sean Ross
☐ 23 Al Martin
☐ 24 Boi Rodriguez
☐ 25 Chris Chambliss MGR
☐ 26 Bill Slack CO
☐ 27 Terry Harper CO
☐ 28 Randy Ingle CO
☐ 29 Jim Lovell TR
Checklist

1991 Greenville Braves Line Drive

	MINT	NRMT	EXC
COMPLETE SET (26)	12.00	5.50	1.50

☐ 201 Rich Casarotti
☐ 202 Vinnie Castilla
☐ 203 Brian Champion
☐ 204 Popeye Cole
☐ 205 Johnny Cuevas
☐ 206 Brian Deak
☐ 207 Pat Gomez
☐ 208 Judd Johnson
☐ 209 Ryan Klesko
☐ 210 Rich Maloney
☐ 211 Al Martin
☐ 212 Keith Mitchell
☐ 213 Rick Morris
☐ 214 Ben Rivera
☐ 215 Napoleon Robinson
☐ 216 Boi Rodriguez
☐ 217 Sean Ross
☐ 218 Earl Sanders
☐ 219 Scott Taylor
☐ 220 Lee Upshaw
☐ 221 Preston Watson
☐ 222 Steven Wendell
☐ 223 Mark Wohlers
☐ 224 Chris Chambliss MGR
☐ 225 Terry Harper CO
Bill Slack CO
Randy Nagle CO
☐ NNO Title card

1991 Greenville Braves ProCards

This 27-card standard-size set of the 1991 Greenville Braves, a Class AA Southern League affiliate of the Atlanta Braves, features on its white-bordered fronts posed color player photos set on simulated spiral-bound yellow notebooks. The player's name, position, and team appear within a green rectangle below the photo. The yellow horizontal back is bordered in white and carries the player's name at the top, followed by biography and statistics. This issue includes a third year card of Ryan Klesko.

	MINT	NRMT	EXC
COMPLETE SET (27)	10.00	4.50	1.25

☐ 2995 Pat Gomez
☐ 2996 Judd Johnson
☐ 2997 Ben Rivera
☐ 2998 Napoleon Robinson
☐ 2999 Earl Sanders
☐ 3000 Bill Taylor
☐ 3001 Lee Upshaw
☐ 3002 Preston Watson
☐ 3003 Steven Wendell
☐ 3004 Mark Wohlers
☐ 3005 Johnny Cuevas
☐ 3006 Brian Deak
☐ 3007 Fred Lopez
☐ 3008 Rich Casarotti
☐ 3009 Vinny Castilla
☐ 3010 Brian Champion
☐ 3011 Ryan Klesko
☐ 3012 Rich Maloney
☐ 3013 Rick Morris
☐ 3014 Popeye Cole
☐ 3015 Al Martin
☐ 3016 Keith Mitchell
☐ 3017 Sean Ross
☐ 3018 Chris Chambliss MGR
☐ 3019 Terry Harper CO
☐ 3020 Bill Slack CO
☐ 3021 Checklist

1991 Gulf Coast Rangers Sports Pro

This 30-card standard-size set of the 1991 Gulf Coast Rangers, a Rookie Class Gulf Coast League affiliate of the Texas Rangers, features posed color head-and-shoulders shots, with thin black borders on a white card face. The horizontally oriented backs have biographical information.

	MINT	NRMT	EXC
COMPLETE SET (30)	6.00	2.70	.75

☐ 1 Mike McCollough
☐ 2 Jose Alberrro
☐ 3 Keith Nalepka
☐ 4 David Gandolph
☐ 5 Eric Strovink
☐ 6 Wilson Heredia
☐ 7 Jamie Bethke
☐ 8 Mark O'Brien
☐ 9 Paul Paramo
☐ 10 Kevin Woodall
☐ 11 Danny Patterson
☐ 12 James Kennedy
☐ 13 Billy Seaton
☐ 14 Trevor Haughney
☐ 15 Pat Underhill
☐ 16 Jon Lindsay
☐ 17 Jeff Carew
☐ 18 Marty Davis
☐ 19 George Evangelista
☐ 20 Miguel Ubiera
☐ 21 Bert Gerhart
☐ 22 Daryl Henderson
☐ 23 Steve Burton
☐ 24 Joey Vallot
☐ 25 Reynaldo Tolentino
Roberto Troncoso
☐ 26 Heath Vaughn
☐ 27 Miguel Soto
☐ 28 Bryan Wilson
☐ 29 H.B. Awkard
☐ 30 Chino Cadahia MG
Rick Knapp CO
Victor Ramirez CO

1991 Hagerstown Suns Line Drive

This 26-card standard-size set of the 1991 Hagerstown Suns, a Class AA Eastern League affiliate of the Baltimore Orioles, features posed color player photos on its white-bordered fronts. The player's name appears in blue lettering at the top; his position and team name appear in blue lettering below the photo. The back carries the player's name within a blue stripe at the top, followed by position, team name and affiliation, biography and statistics.

	MINT	NRMT	EXC
COMPLETE SET (26)	5.00	2.20	.60

☐ 226 Jeff Baumgarner
☐ 227 Stacey Burdick
☐ 228 Paul Carey
☐ 229 Bobby Dickerson
☐ 230 Roy Bilbert
☐ 231 Ricky Gutierrez
☐ 232 Tim Holland
☐ 233 Stacy Jones
☐ 234 Tyrone Kingwood
☐ 235 Mike Lehman
☐ 236 Rod Lofton
☐ 237 Kevin Hickey
☐ 238 Joel McKeon
☐ 239 Scott Meadows
☐ 240 Steve Luebber
☐ 241 Mike Oquist
☐ 242 Ozzie Peraza
☐ 243 Tim Raley
☐ 244 Arthur Rhodes
☐ 245 Doug Robbins
☐ 246 Ken Shamburg
☐ 247 Todd Stephan
☐ 248 Jack Voigt
☐ 249 Jerry Narron MGR
☐ 250 Joe Durham CO
☐ NNO Title card

1991 Hagerstown Suns ProCards

This 28-card standard-size set of the 1991 Hagerstown Suns, a Class AA Eastern League affiliate of the Baltimore Orioles, features on its white-bordered fronts posed color player photos set on simulated spiral-bound yellow notebooks. The player's name, position, and team appear within a green rectangle below the photo. The yellow horizontal back is bordered in white and carries the player's name at the top, followed by biography and statistics.

	MINT	NRMT	EXC
COMPLETE SET (28)	5.00	2.20	.60

☐ 2447 Jeff Bumgarner
☐ 2448 Stacey Burdick
☐ 2449 Steve Culkar
☐ 2450 Kevin Hickey
☐ 2451 Stacy Jones
☐ 2452 Pat Leinen
☐ 2453 Joel McKeon
☐ 2454 Bob Milacki
☐ 2455 Mike Oquist
☐ 2456 Ozzie Peraza
☐ 2457 Arthur Rhodes
☐ 2458 Todd Stephan
☐ 2459 Mike Lehman
☐ 2460 Doug Robbins
☐ 2461 Bobby Dickerson
☐ 2462 Ricky Gutierrez
☐ 2463 Tim Holland
☐ 2464 Rod Lofton
☐ 2465 Ken Shamburg
☐ 2466 Paul Carey
☐ 2467 Tyrone Kingwood
☐ 2468 Scott Meadows
☐ 2469 Tim Raley
☐ 2470 Jack Voigt
☐ 2471 Jerry Narron MGR
☐ 2472 Joe Durham CO
☐ 2473 Steve Leubber CO
☐ 2474 Checklist

1991 Hamilton Redbirds Classic/Best

This 30-card standard-size set of the 1991 Hamilton Redbirds, a Class A New York-Penn League affiliate of the St. Louis Cardinals, features white-bordered posed color player photos on its fronts. The player's name, team, and position appear at the bottom. The white back is framed by a thin black line and carries the player's name and position at the top, followed by biography, statistics and team logos. This set features the minor league card debut of John Mabry.

	MINT	NRMT	EXC
COMPLETE SET (30)	8.00	3.60	1.00

☐ 1 Joe Castaldo
☐ 2 Tim DeGrasse
☐ 3 John Frascatore
☐ 4 Kevin Lucero
☐ 5 Mike Badorek
☐ 6 Rigo Beltran
☐ 7 Al Watson
☐ 8 Jeff Pasquale
☐ 9 Scott Longaker
☐ 10 Duff Brumley
☐ 11 Jason Hisey
☐ 12 Jeff Tanderys
☐ 13 Antonio Boone
☐ 14 Gary Taylor
☐ 15 Mike DiFelice
☐ 16 Garrett Blanton
☐ 17 John Mabry
☐ 18 John O'Brien
☐ 19 Mike Cantu
☐ 20 Joe Turvey
☐ 21 Ron Warner
☐ 22 Brent Bohrofen
☐ 23 Keith Black
☐ 24 Jim Davenport
☐ 25 Ben Ellsworth
☐ 26 Rick Mediavilla
☐ 27 Ronnie French
☐ 28 Larry Meza
☐ 29 Rick Colbert MGR
☐ 30 Steve Turco CO
Checklist

1991 Hamilton Redbirds ProCards

This 33-card standard-size set of the 1991 Hamilton Redbirds, a Class A New York-Penn League affiliate of the St. Louis Cardinals, features on its white-bordered fronts posed color player photos set on simulated spiral-bound yellow notebooks. The player's name, position, and team appear within a green rectangle below the photo. The yellow horizontal back is bordered in white and carries the player's name at the top, followed by biography and statistics. This issue includes the minor league card debut of John Mabry. .

	MINT	NRMT	EXC
COMPLETE SET (33)	7.00	3.10	.85

☐ 4026 Mike Baddrek
☐ 4027 Rigo Beltran
☐ 4028 Antonio Boone
☐ 4029 Duff Brumley
☐ 4030 Joe Castaldo
☐ 4031 Doug Creek
☐ 4032 Tim DeGrasse
☐ 4033 John Frascatore
☐ 4034 Jason Hisey
☐ 4035 Scott Longaker
☐ 4036 Kevin Lucero
☐ 4037 Jeff Pasquale
☐ 4038 Scott Simmons
☐ 4039 Jeff Tanderys
☐ 4040 Allen Watson
☐ 4041 Mike DiFelice
☐ 4042 Joe Turvey
☐ 4043 Keith Black
☐ 4044 Mike Cantu
☐ 4045 Ben Ellsworth
☐ 4046 Larry Meza
☐ 4047 John O'Brien
☐ 4048 Ron Warner
☐ 4049 Garrett Blanton
☐ 4050 Brent Bohrofen
☐ 4051 Jim Davenport
☐ 4052 Ronnie French
☐ 4053 John Mabry
☐ 4054 Rick Mediavilla
☐ 4055 Gary Taylor
☐ 4056 Rick Colbert MGR
☐ 4057 Steve Turco CO
☐ 4058 Checklist

1991 Harrisburg Senators Line Drive

This 26-card standard-size set of the 1991 Harrisburg Senators, a Class AA Eastern League affiliate of the Montreal Expos, features posed color player photos on its white-bordered fronts. The player's name appears in blue lettering at the top; his position and team name appear in blue lettering below the photo. The back carries the player's name within a blue stripe at the top, followed by position, team name and affiliation, biography and statistics.

	MINT	NRMT	EXC
COMPLETE SET (26)	5.00	2.20	.60

☐ 251 Chris Cassels
☐ 252 Archi Cianfrocco
☐ 253 Dan Freed
☐ 254 Greg Fulton
☐ 255 Chris Haney
☐ 256 Cesar Hernandez
☐ 257 Richard Holsman
☐ 258 Rob Katzaroff
☐ 259 Bryn Kosco UER
(Misspelled Bryan
on front and back)

- ☐ 260 Ken Lake
- ☐ 261 Hector Rivera
- ☐ 262 Chris Marchok
- ☐ 263 Chris Martin
- ☐ 264 Matt Maysey
- ☐ 265 Omer Munoz
- ☐ 266 Bob Natal
- ☐ 267 Chris Pollack
- ☐ 268 F.P. Santangelo
- ☐ 269 Joe Siddall
- ☐ 270 Stan Spencer
- ☐ 271 Matt Stairs
- ☐ 272 David Wainhouse
- ☐ 273 Pete Young
- ☐ 274 Mike Quade MG
- ☐ 275 Joe Kerrigan CO
  Pete Delena CO
- ☐ NNO Title card

1991 Harrisburg Senators ProCards

This 29-card standard-size set of the 1991 Harrisburg Senators, a Class AA Eastern League affiliate of the Montreal Expos, features on its white-bordered fronts posed color player photos set on simulated spiral-bound yellow notebooks. The player's name, position, and team appear within a green rectangle below the photo. The yellow horizontal back is bordered in white and carries the player's name and position at the top, followed by biography and statistics.

	MINT	NRMT	EXC
COMPLETE SET (29)	5.00	2.20	.60

- ☐ 617 Dan Freed
- ☐ 618 Chris Haney
- ☐ 619 Rich Holsman
- ☐ 620 Carl Keliipuleole
- ☐ 621 Richie Lewis
- ☐ 622 Chris Marchok
- ☐ 623 Matt Maysey
- ☐ 624 Chris Pollack
- ☐ 625 Hector Rivera
- ☐ 626 Stan Spencer
- ☐ 627 David Wainhouse
- ☐ 628 Pete Young
- ☐ 629 Greg Fulton
- ☐ 630 Bob Natal
- ☐ 631 Joe Siddall
- ☐ 632 Archi Cianfrocco
- ☐ 633 Bryn Kosco
- ☐ 634 Chris Martin
- ☐ 635 Omer Munoz
- ☐ 636 F.P. Santangelo
- ☐ 637 Matt Stairs
- ☐ 638 Chris Cassels
- ☐ 639 Cesar Hernandez
- ☐ 640 Rob Katzaroff
- ☐ 641 Ken Lake
- ☐ 642 Mike Quade MG
- ☐ 643 Pete Dalena P/CO
- ☐ 644 Joe Kerrigan CO
- ☐ 645 Checklist

1991 Helena Brewers Sports Pro

This 30-card standard-size set of the 1991 Helena Brewers, a Rookie Class Pioneer League affiliate of the Milwaukee Brewers, features posed color head-and-shoulders shots, with thin black borders on a white card face. The horizontally oriented backs have biographical information.

	MINT	NRMT	EXC
COMPLETE SET (30)	6.00	2.70	.75

- ☐ 1 John Trisler
- ☐ 2 Derek Ghostlaw
- ☐ 3 Matt Benson
- ☐ 4 Mike Lawn
- ☐ 5 Marshall Boze
- ☐ 6 Scott Lucas
- ☐ 7 Larry Winawer
- ☐ 8 Tyrone Hill
- ☐ 9 LaRue Baber
- ☐ 10 Joe Gmitter
- ☐ 11 Mike Matheny
- ☐ 12 Jeff Cirillo
- ☐ 13 James Wilkie
- ☐ 14 Dave Preikszas
- ☐ 15 Brian Dennison
- ☐ 16 Andy Fairman
- ☐ 17 Todd Iwema
- ☐ 18 Dave Fitzgerald
- ☐ 19 Rusty Rugg
- ☐ 20 Chris Wheat
- ☐ 21 Tom Hickox
- ☐ 22 Robert Tucker
- ☐ 23 Randy Hood
- ☐ 24 Brian Souza
- ☐ 25 Mike Basse
- ☐ 26 Chuck Bush
- ☐ 27 Eric Wilford
- ☐ 28 Roger Caplinger TR
- ☐ 29 Dusty Rhodes CO
- ☐ 30 Harry Dunlop MG

1991 High Desert Mavericks Classic/Best

This 30-card standard-size set of the 1991 High Desert Mavericks, a Class A California League affiliate of the San Diego Padres, features white-bordered posed color player photos on its fronts. The player's name, team, and position appear at the bottom. The white back is framed by a thin black line and carries the player's name and position at the top, followed by biography, statistics and team logos.

	MINT	NRMT	EXC
COMPLETE SET (30)	5.00	2.20	.60

- ☐ 1 Renay Bryand
- ☐ 2 Dan Deville
- ☐ 3 Jay Estrada
- ☐ 4 Luis Galindez
- ☐ 5 Chris Haslock
- ☐ 6 Jose LeBron
- ☐ 7 Kelly Lifgren
- ☐ 8 Brian McKeon
- ☐ 9 Billy Reed
- ☐ 10 Rusty Silcox
- ☐ 11 Roger Smithberg
- ☐ 12 Royal Thomas Jr.
- ☐ 13 Ed Zinter
- ☐ 14 John Abercrombie Jr.
- ☐ 15 Greg Conely
- ☐ 16 Bob Luttichen
- ☐ 17 Mark Verstandig
- ☐ 18 Steve Bethea
- ☐ 19 Jay Gainer
- ☐ 20 Mark Gieseke
- ☐ 21 Paul Gonzalez
- ☐ 22 Ray Holbert
- ☐ 23 Mat Witkowski
- ☐ 24 Reggie Farmer
- ☐ 25 Steve Martin
- ☐ 26 Matt Mieske
- ☐ 27 J.D. Noland
- ☐ 28 Osvaldo Sanchez
- ☐ 29 Bruce Bochy MGR
- ☐ 30 Mark Littel CO
  Checklist

1991 High Desert Mavericks ProCards

This 32-card standard-size set of the 1991 High Desert Mavericks, a Class A California League affiliate of the San Diego Padres, features on its white-bordered fronts posed color player photos set on simulated spiral-bound yellow notebooks. The player's name, position, and team appear within a green rectangle below the photo. The yellow horizontal back is bordered in white and carries the player's name at the top, followed by biography and statistics.

	MINT	NRMT	EXC
COMPLETE SET (32)	5.00	2.20	.60

- ☐ 2384 Renay Bryand
- ☐ 2385 Dan Deville
- ☐ 2386 Jay Estrada
- ☐ 2387 Luis Galindez
- ☐ 2388 Chris Haslock
- ☐ 2389 Jose Lebron
- ☐ 2390 Kelly Lifgren
- ☐ 2391 Brian McKeon
- ☐ 2392 Billy Reed
- ☐ 2393 Rusty Silcox
- ☐ 2394 Roger Smithberg
- ☐ 2395 Royal Thomas
- ☐ 2396 Ed Zinter
- ☐ 2397 John Abercrombie
- ☐ 2398 Greg Conley
- ☐ 2399 Bob Lutticken
- ☐ 2400 Mark Verstandig
- ☐ 2401 Steve Bethea
- ☐ 2402 Jay Gainer
- ☐ 2403 Mark Gieseke
- ☐ 2404 Paul Gonzalez
- ☐ 2405 Ray Holbert
- ☐ 2406 Matt Witkowski
- ☐ 2407 Reggie Farmer
- ☐ 2408 Steve Martin
- ☐ 2409 Matt Mieske
- ☐ 2410 J.D. Noland
- ☐ 2411 Osvaldo Sanchez
- ☐ 2412 Bruce Bochy MGR
- ☐ 2413 Lonnie Keeter CO
- ☐ 2414 Mark Littell CO
- ☐ 2415 Checklist

1991 High School Prospects Little Sun

This 36-card, standard-size set highlights outstanding high school prospects for 1991 that were drafted by major league teams. According to the first card, only 10,000 sets were produced. Each picture is framed by a thin purple border stripe and the card faces exhibit various shades of tan, purple, mustard and cranberry. The player's name appears in turquoise lettering beneath the picture. In black print on a yellowish-orange background, the backs present player profiles. The set also included a coupon that could be redeemed for an 8" X 10" uncut sheet featuring the four players included in Little Sun's 1991 Gold Prospects Club, Al Shirley, Benji Gil, Shawn Estes and Cliff Floyd. Glossy sets were also produced and contained one autograph of either Al Shirley, Shawn Estes, Cliff Floyd or Benji Gil.

	MINT	NRMT	EXC
COMPLETE SET (36)	12.00	5.50	1.50
COMP. GLOSSY SET W/ESTES AU	18.00	8.00	2.20
COMP. GLOSSY SET W/FLOYD AU	20.00	9.00	2.50
COMP. GLOSSY SET W/GIL AU	18.00	8.00	2.20
COMP. GLOSSY SET W/SHIRLEY AU	15.00	6.75	1.85

- ☐ 1 Title Card
- ☐ 2 Al Shirley
- ☐ 3 Tyrone Hill
- ☐ 4 Justin Thompson
- ☐ 5 Mike Sweeney
- ☐ 6 Jimmy Haynes
- ☐ 7 Manny Ramirez
- ☐ 8 Tarrik Brock
- ☐ 9 Vince Jackson
- ☐ 10 John Barnes
- ☐ 11 Shawn Estes
- ☐ 12 Johnny Walker
- ☐ 13 O'Brian Cunningham
- ☐ 14 Mike Busby
- ☐ 15 Khary Heidelberg
- ☐ 16 Tom McKinnon
- ☐ 17 Billy Stephens
- ☐ 18 John Barnes
  Pep Harris
- ☐ 19 Cliff Floyd
- ☐ 20 Rick Gorecki
- ☐ 21 Mike Rossiter
- ☐ 22 Mike Walkden
- ☐ 23 Dwayne Gerald
- ☐ 24 Terry Horn
- ☐ 25 Shawn Curran
- ☐ 26 Pep Harris
- ☐ 27 Benji Gil
- ☐ 28 Jon Pitts
- ☐ 29 Maceo Houston
- ☐ 30 Ryan Long
- ☐ 31 Jason Pruitt
- ☐ 32 Eddie Williams
- ☐ 33 Steve Mandl CO
- ☐ 34 Al Berry CO
- ☐ 35 George Genovese SC
- ☐ 36 Checklist
  Prep Baseball
  Facts and Figures

1991 Huntington Cubs Classic/Best

This 30-card standard-size set of the 1991 Huntington Cubs, a Rookie Class Appalachian League affiliate of the Chicago Cubs, features white-bordered posed color player photos on its fronts. The player's name, team, and position appear at the bottom. The white back is framed by a thin black line and carries the player's name and position at the top, followed by biography, statistics and team logos.

	MINT	NRMT	EXC
COMPLETE SET (30)	5.00	2.20	.60

- ☐ 1 Terry Adams
- ☐ 2 Perry Amos
- ☐ 3 Ken Arnold
- ☐ 4 Randy Belyeu
- ☐ 5 Joaquin Cabral
- ☐ 6 Miguel Camarena
- ☐ 7 Devin Chavez
- ☐ 8 Jose Fernandez
- ☐ 9 Mario Garcia
- ☐ 10 Scott Gardner
- ☐ 11 Kirk Goodson
- ☐ 12 Krandall Hernandez
- ☐ 13 Maceo Houston
- ☐ 14 Jay Meyer
- ☐ 15 Geno Morones
- ☐ 16 Jose Pacheo
- ☐ 17 Richard Perez
- ☐ 18 Mickey Reeves
- ☐ 19 Sergio Reyes
- ☐ 20 Chris Rodriguez
- ☐ 21 Mitchell Root
- ☐ 22 Frank Sample
- ☐ 23 Adrian Sanchez
- ☐ 24 Calvin Smith
- ☐ 25 Darren Tillman
- ☐ 26 Jim Wolff
- ☐ 27 Pedro Valdez
- ☐ 28 Steve Walker
- ☐ 29 Tom Walker
- ☐ 30 Steve Roadcap MGR
  Checklist

1991 Huntington Cubs ProCards

This 32-card standard-size set of the 1991 Huntington Cubs, a Rookie Class Appalachian League affiliate of the Chicago Cubs, features on its white-bordered fronts posed color player photos set on simulated spiral-bound yellow notebooks. The player's name, position, and team appear within a green rectangle below the photo. The yellow horizontal back is bordered in white and carries the player's name at the top, followed by biography and statistics.

	MINT	NRMT	EXC
COMPLETE SET (32)	5.00	2.20	.60

- ☐ 3324 Terry Adams
- ☐ 3325 Perry Amos
- ☐ 3326 Miguel Camareno
- ☐ 3327 Mario Garcia
- ☐ 3328 Scott Gardner
- ☐ 3329 Kirk Goodson
- ☐ 3330 Jay Meyer
- ☐ 3331 Geno Morones
- ☐ 3332 Jose Pacheo
- ☐ 3333 Chris Rodriguez
- ☐ 3334 Frank Sample
- ☐ 3335 Adrian Sanchez
- ☐ 3336 Randy Belyeu
- ☐ 3337 Krandall Hernandez
- ☐ 3338 Jim Wolff
- ☐ 3339 Ken Arnold
- ☐ 3340 Joaquin Cabral
- ☐ 3341 Devon Chavez
- ☐ 3342 Richard Perez
- ☐ 3343 Mitchell Root
- ☐ 3344 Calvin Smith
- ☐ 3345 Tom Walker
- ☐ 3346 Jose Fernanadez
- ☐ 3347 Maceo Houston
- ☐ 3348 Mickey Reeves
- ☐ 3349 Sergio Reyes
- ☐ 3350 Darren Tillman
- ☐ 3351 Pedro Valdez
- ☐ 3352 Steven Walker
- ☐ 3353 Steve Roadcap MGR
- ☐ 3354 Gil Kubski Co
- ☐ 3355 Checklist

1991 Huntsville Stars Classic/Best

This 26-card standard-size set of the 1991 Huntsville Stars, a Class AA Southern League affiliate of the Oakland Athletics, features white-bordered posed color player photos on its fronts. The player's name, team, and position appear near the bottom. The white back is framed by a black line and carries the player's name and position at the top, followed by biography and statistics.

	MINT	NRMT	EXC
COMPLETE SET (26)	5.00	2.20	.60

- ☐ 1 Marcos Armas
- ☐ 2 Bob Bafia
- ☐ 3 Dean Borrelli
- ☐ 4 Mike Conte
- ☐ 5 James Buccheri
- ☐ 6 Tom Carcione
- ☐ 7 Joel Chimelis
- ☐ 8 Fred Cooley
- ☐ 9 Russ Cormier
- ☐ 10 Doc Thorson
- ☐ 11 Matt Grott
- ☐ 12 Dwayne Hosey
- ☐ 13 Chad Kuhn
- ☐ 14 Dave Latter
- ☐ 15 Francisco Matos
- ☐ 16 Gavin Osteen
- ☐ 17 Bert Bradley CO
- ☐ 18 Tim Peek
- ☐ 19 Don Peters
- ☐ 20 Dave Zancanaro
- ☐ 21 Scott Shockey
- ☐ 22 Casey Parsons MGR
- ☐ 23 Lee Tinsley
- ☐ 24 Todd Van Poppel
- ☐ 25 Darryl Vice
- ☐ 26 Pat Gomez
  Checklist

1991 Huntsville Stars Line Drive

	MINT	NRMT	EXC
COMPLETE SET (26)	5.00	2.20	.60

- ☐ 276 Marco Armas
- ☐ 277 Bob Bafia
- ☐ 278 Dean Borrelli
- ☐ 279 John Briscoe
- ☐ 280 James Buccheri
- ☐ 281 Tom Carcione
- ☐ 282 Joel Chimelis
- ☐ 283 Fred Cooley
- ☐ 284 Russ Cormier
- ☐ 285 Matt Grott
- ☐ 286 Dwayne Hosey
- ☐ 287 Chad Kuhn
- ☐ 288 Dave Latter
- ☐ 289 Francisco Matos
- ☐ 290 Gavin Osteen
- ☐ 291 Tim Peek
- ☐ 292 Don Peters
- ☐ 293 Scott Shockey
- ☐ 294 Will Tejada

- ☐ 295 Lee Tinsley
- ☐ 296 Todd Van Poppel
- ☐ 297 Darryl Vice
- ☐ 298 Dave Zancanaro
- ☐ 299 Casey Parsons MGR
- ☐ 300 Bert Bradley CO
- ☐ NNO Title card

1991 Huntsville Stars ProCards

This 26-card standard-size set of the 1991 Huntsville Stars, a Class AA Southern League affiliate of the Oakland Athletics, features on its white-bordered fronts posed color player photos set on simulated spiral-bound yellow notebooks. The player's name, position, and team appear within a green rectangle below the photo. The yellow horizontal back is bordered in white and carries the player's name at the top, followed by biography and statistics.

	MINT	NRMT	EXC
COMPLETE SET (26)	5.00	2.20	.60

- ☐ 1788 Russ Cormier
- ☐ 1789 Matt Grott
- ☐ 1790 Chad Kuhn
- ☐ 1791 Dave Latter
- ☐ 1792 Gavin Osteen
- ☐ 1793 Tim Peek
- ☐ 1794 Don Peters
- ☐ 1795 Todd Van Poppel
- ☐ 1796 Weston Weber
- ☐ 1797 Dave Zancanaro
- ☐ 1798 Dean Borrelli
- ☐ 1799 Tom Carcione
- ☐ 1800 Bob Bafia
- ☐ 1801 James Buccheri
- ☐ 1802 Joel Chimelis
- ☐ 1803 Fred Cooley
- ☐ 1804 Francisco Matos
- ☐ 1805 Scott Shockey
- ☐ 1806 Darryl Vice
- ☐ 1807 Marcos Armas
- ☐ 1808 Mike Conte
- ☐ 1809 Dwayne Hosey
- ☐ 1810 Lee Tinsley
- ☐ 1811 Casey Parsons MGR
- ☐ 1812 Bert Bradley CO
- ☐ 1813 Checklist

1991 Huntsville Stars Team Issue

	MINT	NRMT	EXC
COMPLETE SET (25)	7.00	3.10	.85

- ☐ 1 Kurt Abbott
- ☐ 2 Dean Borrelli
- ☐ 3 Jorge Brito
- ☐ 4 James Buccheri
- ☐ 5 Joel Chimelis
- ☐ 6 Mike Conte
- ☐ 7 Rod Correia
- ☐ 8 Kevin Dattola
- ☐ 9 Dan Eskew
- ☐ 10 Apolinar Garcia
- ☐ 11 Matt Grott
- ☐ 12 Chad Kuhn
- ☐ 13 Dave Latter
- ☐ 14 Troy Neel
- ☐ 15 Gavin Osteen
- ☐ 16 Craig Paquette
- ☐ 17 Tim Peek
- ☐ 18 Don Peters
- ☐ 19 Scott Shockey
- ☐ 20 Lee Tinsley
- ☐ 21 Darryl Vice
- ☐ 22 Weston Weber
- ☐ 23 Dave Zancanaro
- ☐ 24 Bert Bradley CO
- ☐ 25 Casey Parsons MG

1991 Idaho Falls Braves ProCards

This 29-card standard-size set of the 1991 Idaho Falls Braves, a Rookie Class Pioneer League affiliate of the Atlanta Braves, features on its white-bordered fronts posed color player photos set on simulated spiral-bound yellow notebooks. The player's name, position, and team appear within a green rectangle below the photo. The yellow horizontal back is bordered in white and carries the player's name at the top, followed by biography and statistics.

	MINT	NRMT	EXC
COMPLETE SET (29)	5.00	2.20	.60

- ☐ 4319 Jimmy Armstrong
- ☐ 4320 Scott Behrens
- ☐ 4321 Doug Cook
- ☐ 4322 Wayne Koklys
- ☐ 4323 Jerry Koller
- ☐ 4324 Shannon Ledwick
- ☐ 4325 Carl Majeski
- ☐ 4326 Ricardo Petit
- ☐ 4327 Craig Rapp
- ☐ 4328 Matt Viarengo
- ☐ 4329 Brent Weber
- ☐ 4330 Ben Weeks
- ☐ 4331 Brad Woodall
- ☐ 4332 Paul Kelliher
- ☐ 4333 Brad Rippelmeyer
- ☐ 4334 Dave Toth
- ☐ 4335 Anthony Graffagnino
- ☐ 4336 Loren Gress
- ☐ 4337 Kevin Grijak
- ☐ 4338 Dario Paulino
- ☐ 4339 Thomas Coates
- ☐ 4340 Armando Rodriguez
- ☐ 4341 Pedro Swann
- ☐ 4342 Dominic Therrien
- ☐ 4343 Tom Tierney
- ☐ 4344 Steve Curry MGR
- ☐ 4345 Pail Dale CO
- ☐ 4346 Randy Smith CO
- ☐ 4347 Checklist

1991 Idaho Falls Braves Sports Pro

This 30-card standard-size set of the 1991 Idaho Falls Braves, a Rookie Class Pioneer League affiliate of the Atlanta Braves, features posed color head-and-shoulders shots, with thin black borders on a white card face. The horizontally oriented backs have biographical information.

	MINT	NRMT	EXC
COMPLETE SET (30)	7.00	3.10	.85

- ☐ 1 Ronald York
- ☐ 2 Michael Place
- ☐ 3 Brad Rippelmeyer
- ☐ 4 Amando Rodriguez
- ☐ 5 Anthony Graffignino
- ☐ 6 Tom Coates
- ☐ 7 Richard O'Neil
- ☐ 8 Ben Weeks
- ☐ 9 Greg Reinert
- ☐ 10 Jim Armstrong
- ☐ 11 Travis Dunlap
- ☐ 12 Julio Vasquez
- ☐ 13 Gary Stanton
- ☐ 14 Johnny Walker
- ☐ 15 David Toth
- ☐ 16 Shannon Ledwick
- ☐ 17 Kevin Grijak
- ☐ 18 Cristobal Santoya
- ☐ 19 Wayne Simoneaux
- ☐ 20 Craig Rapp
- ☐ 21 Vincent Jimenez
- ☐ 22 Carl Majeski
- ☐ 23 Dario Paulino
- ☐ 24 Jason Kempfer
- ☐ 25 Pedro Swann
- ☐ 26 Brad Woodall
- ☐ 27 Blank card
- ☐ 28 Blank card
- ☐ 29 Blank card
- ☐ 30 Blank card

1991 Indianapolis Indians Line Drive

This 26-card standard-size set of the 1991 Indianapolis Indians, a Class AAA American Association affiliate of the Montreal Expos, features posed color player photos on its white-bordered fronts. The player's name appears in red lettering at the top; his position and team name appear in red lettering below the photo. The back carries the player's name within a red stripe at the top, followed by position, team name and affiliation, biography and statistics.

	MINT	NRMT	EXC
COMPLETE SET (26)	5.00	2.20	.60

- ☐ 176 Bret Barberie
- ☐ 177 Kevin Bearse
- ☐ 178 Kent Bottenfield
- ☐ 179 Wil Cordero
- ☐ 180 Mike Davis
- ☐ 181 Alex Diaz
- ☐ 182 Eddie Dixon
- ☐ 183 Jeff Fassero
- ☐ 184 Jerry Goff
- ☐ 185 Todd Haney
- ☐ 186 Steve Hecht
- ☐ 187 Jimmy Kremers
- ☐ 188 Quinn Mack
- ☐ 189 David Masters
- ☐ 190 Marlin McPhail
- ☐ 191 Doug Piatt
- ☐ 192 Dana Ridenour
- ☐ 193 Scott Service
- ☐ 194 Razor Shines
- ☐ 195 Tito Stewart
- ☐ 196 Mel Houston
- ☐ 197 John Vander Wal
- ☐ 198 Darrin Winston
- ☐ 199 Jerry Manuel MG
- ☐ 200 Gomer Hodge CO
  Nardi Contreras CO
- ☐ NNO Title card

1991 Indianapolis Indians ProCards

This 28-card standard-size set of the 1991 Indianapolis Indians, a Class AAA American Association affiliate of the Montreal Expos, features on its white-bordered fronts posed color player photos set on simulated spiral-bound yellow notebooks. The player's name, position, and team appear within a green rectangle below the photo. The yellow horizontal back is bordered in white and carries the player's name and position at the top, followed by biography and statistics. The logos for Pepsi and Hook's Drug Stores round out the back. .

	MINT	NRMT	EXC
COMPLETE SET (28)	5.00	2.20	.60

- ☐ 453 Kevin Bearse
- ☐ 454 Chris Bennett
- ☐ 455 Kent Bottenfield
- ☐ 456 Eddie Dixon
- ☐ 457 Jeff Fassero
- ☐ 458 Dave Masters
- ☐ 459 Doug Piatt
- ☐ 460 Dana Ridenour
- ☐ 461 Scott Service
- ☐ 462 Tito Stewart
- ☐ 463 Darrin Winston
- ☐ 464 Jimmy Kremers
- ☐ 465 Bret Barberie
- ☐ 466 Wil Cordero
- ☐ 467 Jerry Goff
- ☐ 468 Todd Haney
- ☐ 469 Mel Houston
- ☐ 470 Marlin McPhail
- ☐ 471 Razor Shines
- ☐ 472 Mike Davis
- ☐ 473 Alex Diaz
- ☐ 474 Steve Hecht
- ☐ 475 Quinn Mack
- ☐ 476 John Vander Wal
- ☐ 477 Jerry Manuel MG
- ☐ 478 Nardi Contreras CO
- ☐ 479 Gomer Hodge CO
- ☐ 480 Checklist

1991 Iowa Cubs Line Drive

	MINT	NRMT	EXC
COMPLETE SET (26)	5.00	2.20	.60

- ☐ 201 Brad Bierley
- ☐ 202 Steve Carter
- ☐ 203 Frank Castillo
- ☐ 204 Lance Dickson
- ☐ 205 Craig Smajstra
- ☐ 206 Brian Guinn
- ☐ 207 Joe Kraemer
- ☐ 208 Cedric Landrum
- ☐ 209 Derrick May
- ☐ 210 Scott May
- ☐ 211 Russ McGinnis
- ☐ 212 Chuck Mount
- ☐ 213 Dave Pavlas
- ☐ 214 Laddie Renfroe
- ☐ 215 David Rosario
- ☐ 216 Rey Sanchez
- ☐ 217 Dan Simonds
- ☐ 218 Jeff Small
- ☐ 219 Doug Strange
- ☐ 220 Glenn Sullivan
- ☐ 221 Rick Wilkins
- ☐ 222 Steve Wilson
- ☐ 223 Bob Scanlan
- ☐ 224 Jim Essian MGR
- ☐ 225 Grant Jackson CO
- ☐ NNO Title card

1991 Iowa Cubs ProCards

This 26-card standard-size set of the 1991 Iowa Cubs, a Class AAA American Association affiliate of the Chicago Cubs, features on its white-bordered fronts posed color player photos set on simulated spiral-bound yellow notebooks. The player's name, position, and team appear within a green rectangle below the photo. The yellow horizontal back is bordered in white and carries the player's name at the top, followed by biography and statistics.

	MINT	NRMT	EXC
COMPLETE SET (26)	5.00	2.20	.60

- ☐ 1053 Lance Dickson
- ☐ 1054 Joe Kraemer
- ☐ 1055 Scott May
- ☐ 1056 Chuck Mount
- ☐ 1057 Jose Nunez
- ☐ 1058 Dave Pavlas
- ☐ 1059 Laddie Renfroe
- ☐ 1060 David Rosario
- ☐ 1061 Bob Scanlan
- ☐ 1062 Steve Wilson
- ☐ 1063 Russ McGinnis
- ☐ 1064 Dan Simonds
- ☐ 1065 Rick Wilkins
- ☐ 1066 Brian Guinn
- ☐ 1067 Rey Sanchez
- ☐ 1068 Gary Scott
- ☐ 1069 Craig Smajstra
- ☐ 1070 Jeff Small
- ☐ 1071 Doug Strange
- ☐ 1072 Glenn Sullivan
- ☐ 1073 Brad Bierley
- ☐ 1074 Steve Carter
- ☐ 1075 Cedric Landrum
- ☐ 1076 Jim Essian MGR
- ☐ 1077 Grant Jackson CO
- ☐ 2233 Checklist

1991 Jackson Generals Line Drive

	MINT	NRMT	EXC
COMPLETE SET (26)	5.00	2.20	.60

- ☐ 551 Willie Ansley
- ☐ 552 Sam August
- ☐ 553 Jeff Baldwin
- ☐ 554 Pete Bauer
- ☐ 555 Kevin Coffman
- ☐ 556 Kevin Dean
- ☐ 557 Tony Eusebio
- ☐ 558 Dean Freeland
- ☐ 559 Rusty Harris
- ☐ 560 Dean Hartgraves
- ☐ 561 Trent Hubbard
- ☐ 562 Bert Hunter
- ☐ 563 Bernie Jenkins
- ☐ 564 Jeff Juden
- ☐ 565 Keith Kaiser
- ☐ 566 Steve Larose
- ☐ 567 Lance Madsen
- ☐ 568 Scott Makarewicz
- ☐ 569 Rob Mallicoat
- ☐ 570 Joe Mikulik
- ☐ 571 Orlando Miller
- ☐ 572 Shane Reynolds
- ☐ 573 Richie Simon
- ☐ 574 Rick Sweet MGR
- ☐ 575 Don Reynolds CO
  Charles Taylor CO
- ☐ NNO Title card

1991 Jackson Generals ProCards

This 28-card standard-size set of the 1991 Jackson Generals, a Class AA Texas League affiliate of the Houston Astros, features on its white-bordered fronts posed color player photos set on simulated spiral-bound yellow notebooks. The player's name, position, and team appear within a green rectangle below the photo. The yellow horizontal back is bordered in white and carries the player's name at the top, followed by biography and statistics.

	MINT	NRMT	EXC
COMPLETE SET (28)	5.00	2.20	.60

- ☐ 916 Sam August
- ☐ 917 Pete Bauer
- ☐ 918 Kevin Coffman
- ☐ 919 Chris Gardner
- ☐ 920 Carl Grovom
- ☐ 921 Dean Hartgraves
- ☐ 922 Jeff Juden
- ☐ 923 Keith Kaiser
- ☐ 924 Steve Larose
- ☐ 925 Rob Mallicoat
- ☐ 926 Shane Reynolds
- ☐ 927 Richie Simon
- ☐ 928 Tony Eusebio
- ☐ 929 Scott Makarewicz
- ☐ 930 Jeff Baldwin
- ☐ 931 Rusty Harris
- ☐ 932 Trent Hubbard
- ☐ 933 Lance Madsen
- ☐ 934 Orlando Miller
- ☐ 935 Willie Ansley
- ☐ 936 Kevin Dean
- ☐ 937 Bert Hunter
- ☐ 938 Bernie Jenkins
- ☐ 939 Joe Mikulik
- ☐ 940 Rick Sweet MGR
- ☐ 941 Don Reynolds CO
- ☐ 942 Charlie Taylor CO
- ☐ 943 Checklist

1991 Jacksonville Suns Line Drive

	MINT	NRMT	EXC
COMPLETE SET (26)	5.00	2.20	.60

- ☐ 326 Fernando Arguelles
- ☐ 327 Shawn Barton
- ☐ 328 Jim Blueberg
- ☐ 329 Frank Bolick
- ☐ 330 Bret Boone
- ☐ 331 Jim Bowie
- ☐ 332 Jim Campanis
- ☐ 333 Gary Eave
- ☐ 334 David Evans

☐ 335 Fernando Figueroa
☐ 336 Dave Fleming
☐ 337 Ruben Gonzalez
☐ 338 Mike McDonald
☐ 339 Jeff Nelson
☐ 340 Jim Newlin
☐ 341 Ken Pennington
☐ 342 Mike Pitz
☐ 343 Dave Richards
☐ 344 Roger Salkeld
☐ 345 Jack Smith
☐ 346 Tim Stargell
☐ 347 Brian Turang
☐ 348 Ted Williams
☐ 349 Jim Nettles MGR
☐ 350 Bobby Cuellar CO
Lem Pilkinton CO
☐ NNO Title card

1991 Jacksonville Suns ProCards

This 29-card standard-size set of the 1991 Jacksonville Suns, a Class AA Southern League affiliate of the Seattle Mariners, features on its white-bordered fronts posed color player photos set on simulated spiral-bound yellow notebooks. The player's name, position, and team appear within a green rectangle below the photo. The yellow horizontal back is bordered in white and carries the player's name at the top, followed by biography and statistics.

	MINT	NRMT	EXC
COMPLETE SET (29)	5.00	2.20	.60

☐ 141 Shawn Barton
☐ 142 Jim Bleuberg
☐ 143 Gary Eave
☐ 144 David Evans
☐ 145 Fernando Figueroa
☐ 146 Dave Fleming
☐ 147 Jeff Nelson
☐ 148 Jim Newlin
☐ 149 Michael Pitz
☐ 150 Dave Richards
☐ 151 Roger Salkeld
☐ 152 Fernando Arguelles
☐ 153 Jim Campanis
☐ 154 Frank Bolick
☐ 155 Bret Boone
☐ 156 Jim Bowie
☐ 157 Ruben Gonzalez
☐ 158 Tony Manahan
☐ 159 Ken Pennington
☐ 160 Jack Smith
☐ 161 Brian Turang
☐ 162 Mike McDonald
☐ 163 Tim Stargell
☐ 164 Ted Williams
☐ 165 Team Picture
☐ 166 Jim Nettles MGR
☐ 167 Bobby Cuellar CO
☐ 168 Lem Pilkinton
Player/Coach
☐ 169 Checklist

1991 Jamestown Expos Classic/Best

This 30-card standard-size set of the 1991 Jamestown Expos, a Class A New York-Penn League affiliate of the Montreal Expos, features white-bordered posed color player photos on its fronts. The player's name, team, and position appear near the bottom. The white back is framed by a black line and carries the player's name and position at the top, followed by biography and statistics. This issue includes the minor league card debut of Mark Grudzielanek.

	MINT	NRMT	EXC
COMPLETE SET (30)	8.00	3.60	1.00

☐ 1 John White
☐ 2 Blake Babki
☐ 3 Derrick White
☐ 4 Mark Grudzielanek
☐ 5 Jim Austin
☐ 6 Mike Daniel UER
(Misspelled Danrel
on front and back)
☐ 7 Matt Allen
☐ 8 Scott Campbell
☐ 9 Chris Falco
☐ 10 Scott Dennison
☐ 11 Douglas O'Neill
☐ 12 Mitch Simons
☐ 13 Tommy Owen
☐ 14 Domingo Matos
☐ 15 Mark LaRosa UER
(Misspelled LoRosa
on front and back)
☐ 16 Duane Ashley
☐ 17 Brian Looney
☐ 18 Jim Wynne
☐ 19 Nick Sproviero
☐ 20 Jeff Hostetler
☐ 21 Buddy Jenkins Jr.
☐ 22 Matt Figueroa
☐ 23 James Ferguson
☐ 24 Darek Braunecker
☐ 25 Heath Haynes
☐ 26 Pete Tarutis
☐ 27 Rodney Pedraza
☐ 28 Coaching Staff
Ed Creech MG
Q.V. Lowe CO
Jim Fleming CO
Lee Slagle TR
☐ 29 Front Office
Tom O'Reilly GM
Scott Daniel AGM
Neal Hunington AGM
☐ 30 Checklist

1991 Jamestown Expos ProCards

This 29-card standard-size set of the 1991 Jamestown Expos, a Class A New York-Penn League affiliate of the Montreal Expos, features on its white-bordered fronts posed color player photos set on simulated spiral-bound yellow notebooks. The player's name, position, and team appear within a green rectangle below the photo. The yellow horizontal back is bordered in white and carries the player's name and position at the top, followed by biography and statistics. This issue includes the minor league card debut of Mark Grudzielanek.

	MINT	NRMT	EXC
COMPLETE SET (29)	7.00	3.10	.85

☐ 3534 Duane Ashley
☐ 3535 Darek Braunecker
☐ 3536 James Ferguson
☐ 3537 Matt Figueroa
☐ 3538 Heath Haynes
☐ 3539 Jeff Hostetler
☐ 3540 Buddy Jenkins Jr.
☐ 3541 Mark LaRosa
☐ 3542 Brian Looney
☐ 3543 Rodney Pedraza
☐ 3544 Nick Sproviero
☐ 3545 Pete Tarutis
☐ 3546 Jim Wynne
☐ 3547 Matt Allen
☐ 3548 Mike Daniel
☐ 3549 Tommy Owen
☐ 3550 Scott Campbell
☐ 3551 Scott Dennison
☐ 3552 Chris Falco
☐ 3553 Mark Grudzielanek
☐ 3554 Domingo Matos
☐ 3555 Mitch Simons
☐ 3556 Derrick White
☐ 3557 Jim Austin
☐ 3558 Blake Babki
☐ 3559 Doug O'Neill
☐ 3560 Johnny White
☐ 3561 Field Staff
Ed Creech MG
Q.V. Lowe CO
Jim Fleming CO
Lee Slagle TR
☐ 3562 Checklist

1991 Johnson City Cardinals Classic/Best

This 30-card standard-size set of the 1991 Johnson City Cardinals, a Rookie Class Appalachian League affiliate of the St. Louis Cardinals, features white-bordered posed color player photos on its fronts. The player's name, team, and position appear at the bottom. The white back is framed by a thin black line and carries the player's name and position at the top, followed by biography, statistics and team logos. This issue includes the minor league card debut of Dmitri Young.

	MINT	NRMT	EXC
COMPLETE SET (30)	12.00	5.50	1.50

☐ 1 Eddie Williams
☐ 2 John Dempsey
☐ 3 Aaire Borzello
☐ 4 Pat Murray
☐ 5 Andy Bruce
☐ 6 Darrel Deak
☐ 7 Larry Gilligan
☐ 8 Doug Radziewicz
☐ 9 Steve Dudek
☐ 10 Jesus Ugueto
☐ 11 Dmitri Young
☐ 12 DaRond Stoval
☐ 13 Chris Vlasis
☐ 14 Hector Colon
☐ 15 Basil Shabazz
☐ 16 Keith Jones
☐ 17 Jamie Cochran
☐ 18 Brian Barber
☐ 19 Russell Gaston
☐ 20 Dennis Slininger
☐ 21 Gerald Santos
☐ 22 David Chasin
☐ 23 Brian Avram
☐ 24 Manuel Rodriguez
☐ 25 Steve Jones
☐ 26 Cecilio Gonzalez
☐ 27 Jose Arias
☐ 28 Tom McKinnon
☐ 29 Chris Maloney
☐ 30 Joe Cunningham Jr. CO
Checklist

1991 Johnson City Cardinals ProCards

This 29-card standard-size set of the 1991 Johnson City Cardinals, a Rookie Class Appalachian League affiliate of the St. Louis Cardinals, features on its white-bordered fronts posed color player photos set on simulated spiral-bound yellow notebooks. The player's name, position, and team appear within a green rectangle below the photo. The yellow horizontal back is bordered in white and carries the player's name at the top, followed by biography and statistics. This issue includes the minor league card debut of Dmitri Young.

	MINT	NRMT	EXC
COMPLETE SET (29)	12.00	5.50	1.50

☐ 3968 Brian Avram
☐ 3969 Brian Barber
☐ 3970 David Chajin
☐ 3971 Jamie Cochran
☐ 3972 Cecilio Gonzalez
☐ 3973 Bill Hurst
☐ 3974 Steve Jones
☐ 3975 Tom McKinnon
☐ 3976 Manuel Rodriguez
☐ 3977 Jerry Santos
☐ 3978 Dennis Slininger
☐ 3979 John Dempsey
☐ 3980 Eddie Williams
☐ 3981 Andy Bruce
☐ 3982 Darrel Deak
☐ 3983 Steve Dudek
☐ 3984 Larry Gilligan
☐ 3985 Pat Murray
☐ 3986 Doug Radziewicz
☐ 3987 Jesus Ugueto
☐ 3988 Hector Colon
☐ 3989 Keith Jones
☐ 3990 Basis Shabazz
☐ 3991 DaRond Stovall
☐ 3992 Chris Vlasis
☐ 3993 Dmitri Young
☐ 3994 Chris Maloney MGR
☐ 4172 Joe Cunningham Jr. CO
☐ 4273 Checklist

1991 Kane County Cougars Team Issue

This 27-card set measures the standard size. On a black card face, the glossy color action player photos are bordered in white and green. The player's name and position appear in white lettering above the picture, with the team name on a diagonal stripe in the lower right corner. In a horizontal format,the back has biography, statistics, and a question-and-answer trivia feature. The cards are unnumbered and checklisted below in alphabetical order, with the uniform number after the name.

	MINT	NRMT	EXC
COMPLETE SET (27)	6.00	2.70	.75

☐ 1 Matthew Anderson
☐ 2 Jim Audley
☐ 3 Joe Borowski
☐ 4 James Dedrick
☐ 5 Vaughn Eshelman
☐ 6 Terry Farrar
☐ 7 Manny Garcia
☐ 8 Steve Godin
☐ 9 Michael Hebb
☐ 10 Aman Hicks
☐ 11 Shaun Hrabar
☐ 12 Tom Martin
☐ 13 Jose Millares
☐ 14 Brent Miller
☐ 15 David Paveloff
☐ 16 Daniel Ramirez
☐ 17 Doug Reynolds
☐ 18 Jimmy Roso
☐ 19 Brad Seitzer
☐ 20 Thomas Taylor
☐ 21 Bradley Tippitt
☐ 22 Michael Wiley
☐ 23 Todd Unrein
☐ 24 Gregory Zaun
☐ 25 Mark Zello TR
☐ 26 Coaching Staff
Bob Miscik MGR
Larry McCall CO
Oneri Fleita CO
☐ 27 Ozzie
Mascot

1991 Kane County Cougars Classic/Best

This 30-card standard-size set of the 1991 Kane County Cougars, a Class A Midwest League affiliate of the Baltimore Orioles, features white-bordered posed color player photos on its fronts. The player's name, team, and position appear at the bottom. The white back is framed by a thin black line and carries the player's name and position at the top, followed by biography, statistics and team logos.

	MINT	NRMT	EXC
COMPLETE SET (30)	5.00	2.20	.60

☐ 1 Shaun Hrabar
☐ 2 Joe Borowski
☐ 3 Matt Anderson
☐ 4 Rob Blumberg Jr.
☐ 5 James Dedrick
☐ 6 Michael Hebb
☐ 7 Thomas Martin
☐ 8 David Paveloff
☐ 9 Brad Pennington
☐ 10 Tommy Taylor
☐ 11 Todd Unrein
☐ 12 Michael Wiley
☐ 13 Jimmy Roso
☐ 14 Greg Zaun
☐ 15 Steven DiMarco
☐ 16 Manny Garcia
☐ 17 Jose Millares
☐ 18 Brent Miller
☐ 19 Daniel Ramirez
☐ 20 Brad Tyler
☐ 21 Bo Davis
☐ 22 Steven Godin
☐ 23 Aman Hicks
☐ 24 German Paredes
☐ 25 Keith Schmidt
☐ 26 Bob Miscik MGR
☐ 27 Larry McCall CO
☐ 28 Oneri Fleita CO
☐ 29 Doug Flowers
☐ 30 Mark Zello TR
Checklist

1991 Kane County Cougars ProCards

This 28-card standard-size set of the 1991 Kane County Cougars, a Class A Midwest League affiliate of the Baltimore Orioles, features on its white-bordered fronts posed color player photos set on simulated spiral-bound yellow notebooks. The player's name, position, and team appear within a green rectangle below the photo. The yellow horizontal back is bordered in white and carries the player's name at the top, followed by biography and statistics.

	MINT	NRMT	EXC
COMPLETE SET (28)	5.00	2.20	.60

☐ 2650 Matt Anderson
☐ 2651 Rob Blumberg
☐ 2652 Joe Borowski
☐ 2653 Jim Dedrick
☐ 2654 Mike Hebb
☐ 2655 Thomas Martin
☐ 2656 Dave Paveloff
☐ 2657 Brad Pennington
☐ 2658 Todd Unrein
☐ 2659 Mike Wiley
☐ 2660 Jimmy Roso
☐ 2661 Greg Zaun
☐ 2662 Steve Dimarco
☐ 2663 Manny Garcia
☐ 2664 Jose Millares
☐ 2665 Brent Miller
☐ 2666 Daniel Ramirez
☐ 2667 Brad Tyler
☐ 2668 Allen Davis
☐ 2669 Steven Godin
☐ 2670 Aman Hicks
☐ 2671 Shaun Hrabar
☐ 2672 German Paredes
☐ 2673 Keith Schmidt
☐ 2674 Bob Miscik MGR
☐ 2675 Oneri Fleita CO
☐ 2676 Larry McCall CO
☐ 2677 Checklist

1991 Kenosha Twins Classic/Best

This 28-card standard-size set of the 1991 Kenosha Twins, a Class A Midwest League affiliate of the Minnesota Twins, features white-bordered posed color player photos on its fronts. The player's name, team, and position appear at the bottom. The white back is framed by a thin black line and carries the player's name and position at the top, followed by biography, statistics and team logos.

	MINT	NRMT	EXC
COMPLETE SET (28)	5.00	2.20	.60

☐ 1 Alvin Brown
☐ 2 Willie Mota
☐ 3 Todd Blakeman
☐ 4 Denny Hocking
☐ 5 Matt Morse
☐ 6 David Rivera
☐ 7 Brent Brede
☐ 8 Tim Persing
☐ 9 John Gumpf
☐ 10 Denny Hoppe
☐ 11 Kurt Pfeffer

- ☐ 12 Dave Bigham
- ☐ 13 Dickie Dixon
- ☐ 14 Bart Peterson
- ☐ 15 Pat Russo
- ☐ 16 Kerry Taylor
- ☐ 17 Steve Taylor
- ☐ 18 Jeff Thelen
- ☐ 19 Joel Lepel MGR
- ☐ 20 Rick Anderson CO
- ☐ 21 Dan Fox TR
- ☐ 22 Todd Ritchie
- ☐ 23 Paul Bruno
- ☐ 24 Midre Cummings
- ☐ 25 Rich Becker
- ☐ 26 Tom Houk
- ☐ 27 Jason Klonoski
- ☐ 28 Checklist

1991 Kenosha Twins ProCards

This 28-card standard-size set of the 1991 Kenosha Twins, a Class A Midwest League affiliate of the Minnesota Twins, features on its white-bordered fronts posed color player photos set on simulated spiral-bound yellow notebooks. The player's name, position, and team appear within a green rectangle below the photo. The yellow horizontal back is bordered in white and carries the player's name at the top, followed by biography and statistics.

	MINT	NRMT	EXC
COMPLETE SET (28)	5.00	2.20	.60

- ☐ 2066 Dave Bigham
- ☐ 2067 Dickie Dixon
- ☐ 2068 Denny Hoppe
- ☐ 2069 Jason Klonoski
- ☐ 2070 Tim Persing
- ☐ 2071 Bart Peterson
- ☐ 2072 Todd Ritchie
- ☐ 2073 Pat Russo
- ☐ 2074 Kerry Taylor
- ☐ 2075 Steve Taylor
- ☐ 2076 Jeff Thelen
- ☐ 2077 Alvin Brown
- ☐ 2078 Paul Bruno
- ☐ 2079 Willie Motz
- ☐ 2080 Todd Blakeman
- ☐ 2081 Denny Hocking
- ☐ 2082 Tom Houk
- ☐ 2083 Matt Morse
- ☐ 2084 David Rivera
- ☐ 2085 Paul Russo
- ☐ 2086 Rich Becker
- ☐ 2087 Brent Brede
- ☐ 2088 Midre Cummings
- ☐ 2089 John Gumpf
- ☐ 2090 Kurt Pfeffer
- ☐ 2091 Joel Lepel MGR
- ☐ 2092 Rick Anderson CO
- ☐ 2093 Checklist

1991 Kingsport Mets Classic/Best

This 29-card standard-size set of the 1991 Kingsport Mets, a Rookie Class Appalachian League affiliate of the New York Mets, features white-bordered posed color player photos on its fronts. The player's name, team, and position appear at the bottom. The white back is framed by a thin black line and carries the player's name and position at the top, followed by biography, statistics and team logos.

	MINT	NRMT	EXC
COMPLETE SET (29)	5.00	2.20	.60

- ☐ 1 Jeff Henderson
- ☐ 2 Bemond Smith
- ☐ 3 Darwin Davis
- ☐ 4 Mike Patrizi
- ☐ 5 Suliban Luciano
- ☐ 6 Brian Daubach
- ☐ 7 Ty Quillin
- ☐ 8 Ricky Otero
- ☐ 9 Paul Meyer
- ☐ 10 Quilvio Veras
- ☐ 11 Rafael Hernandez
- ☐ 12 Brett Rossler
- ☐ 13 Randy Farmer
- ☐ 14 Guillermo Garcia
- ☐ 15 Todd Fiegel
- ☐ 16 Joe Crawford
- ☐ 17 Eric Corbell
- ☐ 18 Shaun Watson
- ☐ 19 Hector Ramirez
- ☐ 20 Steve Seymour
- ☐ 21 Mark Hokanson
- ☐ 22 Bradley Schorr
- ☐ 23 Jason Jacome
- ☐ 24 Andre David MGR
- ☐ 25 L.D. Bennese TR
- ☐ 26 Jesus Hernaiz CO
- ☐ 27 Cesar Diaz
- ☐ 28 Andrew Cotner
- ☐ 29 Checklist

1991 Kingsport Mets ProCards

This 28-card standard-size set of the 1991 Kingsport Mets, a Rookie Class Appalachian League affiliate of the New York Mets, features on its white-bordered fronts posed color player photos set on simulated spiral-bound yellow notebooks. The player's name, position, and team appear within a green rectangle below the photo. The yellow horizontal back is bordered in white and carries the player's name at the top, followed by biography and statistics.

	MINT	NRMT	EXC
COMPLETE SET (28)	5.00	2.20	.60

- ☐ 3804 Eric Corbell
- ☐ 3805 Andrew Cotner
- ☐ 3806 Joe Crawford
- ☐ 3807 Todd Fiegel
- ☐ 3808 Jeff Henderson
- ☐ 3809 Mark Hokanson
- ☐ 3810 Jason Jacome
- ☐ 3811 Hector Ramirez
- ☐ 3812 Brad Schorr
- ☐ 3813 Steve Seymour
- ☐ 3814 Shaun Watson
- ☐ 3815 Cesar Diaz
- ☐ 3816 Mike Patrizi
- ☐ 3817 Ross Rossler
- ☐ 3818 Brian Daubach
- ☐ 3819 Darwin Davis
- ☐ 3820 Randy Farmer
- ☐ 3821 Guillermo Garcia
- ☐ 3822 Rafael Hernandez
- ☐ 3823 Paul Meyer
- ☐ 3824 Quilvio Veras
- ☐ 3825 Suliban Luciano
- ☐ 3826 Ricky Otero
- ☐ 3827 Ty Quillin
- ☐ 3828 Demond Smith
- ☐ 3829 Andre David MGR
- ☐ 3830 Jesus Hernaiz CO
- ☐ 3831 Checklist

1991 Kinston Indians Classic/Best

This 30-card standard-size set of the 1991 Kinston Indians, a Class A Carolina League affiliate of the Cleveland Indians, features white-bordered posed color player photos on its fronts. The player's name, team, and position appear at the bottom. The white back is framed by a thin black line and carries the player's name and position at the top, followed by biography, statistics and team logos.

	MINT	NRMT	EXC
COMPLETE SET (30)	5.00	2.20	.60

- ☐ 1 Chad Allen
- ☐ 2 Shawn Bryant
- ☐ 3 Carl Johnson
- ☐ 4 Tim Langdon
- ☐ 5 Curtis Leskanic
- ☐ 6 Mike Malley
- ☐ 7 Scott Morgan
- ☐ 8 Oscar Munoz
- ☐ 9 Scott Neill
- ☐ 10 Robert Person
- ☐ 11 Cecil Pettiford
- ☐ 12 Mike Soper
- ☐ 13 Carlos Mota
- ☐ 14 Bill Losa
- ☐ 15 Mike Easley
- ☐ 16 Miguel Flores
- ☐ 17 Fred Gladding CO
- ☐ 18 Clyde Pough
- ☐ 19 Tim Rigsby
- ☐ 20 Mike Sarbaugh
- ☐ 21 Paulino Tena
- ☐ 22 Marc Tepper
- ☐ 23 William Canate
- ☐ 24 Danny Williams CO
- ☐ 25 Tom Eiterman
- ☐ 26 Brian Giles
- ☐ 27 Tracy Sanders
- ☐ 28 Brian Graham MGR
- ☐ 29 Dan Devoe TR
- ☐ 30 North Johnson Checklist

1991 Kinston Indians ProCards

This 31-card standard-size set of the 1991 Kinston Indians, a Class A Carolina League affiliate of the Cleveland Indians, features on its white-bordered fronts posed color player photos set on simulated spiral-bound yellow notebooks. The player's name, position, and team appear within a green rectangle below the photo. The yellow horizontal back is bordered in white and carries the player's name at the top, followed by biography and statistics.

	MINT	NRMT	EXC
COMPLETE SET (31)	5.00	2.20	.60

- ☐ 313 Chad Allen
- ☐ 314 Shawn Bryant
- ☐ 315 Carl Johnson
- ☐ 316 Tim Langdon
- ☐ 317 Curtis Leskanic
- ☐ 318 Mike Malley
- ☐ 319 Scott Morgan
- ☐ 320 Oscar Munoz
- ☐ 321 Scott Neill
- ☐ 322 Robert Person
- ☐ 323 Cecil Pettiford
- ☐ 324 Mike Soper
- ☐ 325 Bill Losa
- ☐ 326 Carlos Mota
- ☐ 327 Mike Easley
- ☐ 328 Miguel Flores
- ☐ 329 Fabio Gomez
- ☐ 330 Clyde Pough
- ☐ 331 Tim Rigsby
- ☐ 332 Mike Sarbaugh
- ☐ 333 Paulino Tena
- ☐ 334 Marc Tepper
- ☐ 335 William Canate
- ☐ 336 Brad DeJardin
- ☐ 337 Tom Eiterman
- ☐ 338 Brian Giles
- ☐ 339 Tracy Sanders
- ☐ 340 Brian Graham MGR
- ☐ 341 Fred Gladding CO
- ☐ 342 Dan Williams Player/Coach
- ☐ 343 Checklist

1991 Kissimmee Dodgers ProCards

This 32-card standard-size set of the 1991 Kissimmee Dodgers, a Rookie Class Gulf Coast League affiliate of the Los Angeles Dodgers, features on its white-bordered fronts posed color player photos set on simulated spiral-bound yellow notebooks. The player's name, position, and team appear within a green rectangle below the photo. The yellow horizontal back is bordered in white and carries the player's name at the top, followed by biography and statistics. This issue includes the minor league card debut of Ismael Valdes.

	MINT	NRMT	EXC
COMPLETE SET (32)	8.00	3.60	1.00

- ☐ 4175 Gary Cope
- ☐ 4176 John Davidson
- ☐ 4177 Dave Fitzpatrick
- ☐ 4178 Michael Iglesias
- ☐ 4179 Martin Lavigne
- ☐ 4180 Clint Minear
- ☐ 4181 Antonio Osuna
- ☐ 4182 Jose Salcedo
- ☐ 4183 Kevin Smith
- ☐ 4184 Young Chul Sohn
- ☐ 4185 Robert Sweeney
- ☐ 4186 Ismael Valdez
- ☐ 4187 Brandon Watts
- ☐ 4188 Chad Zerbe
- ☐ 4189 Anthony Rodriguez
- ☐ 4190 Felix Rodriguez
- ☐ 4191 Carlo Walton
- ☐ 4192 Brent Williams
- ☐ 4193 German Gonzalez
- ☐ 4194 Chris Latham
- ☐ 4195 Sandy Martinez
- ☐ 4196 Todd Soares
- ☐ 4197 Bill Stephens
- ☐ 4198 Dennis Winicki
- ☐ 4199 Gustavo Zapata
- ☐ 4200 Angel Dotelson
- ☐ 4201 Lonnie Jackson
- ☐ 4202 Vince Jackson
- ☐ 4203 Clarence Richmond
- ☐ 4204 Mel Warren
- ☐ 4205 Field Staff
  Charlie Hamilton TR
  Doug Simunic CO
  Ivan DeJesus MGR
  Dennis Burtt CO
- ☐ 4206 Checklist

1991 Knoxville Blue Jays Line Drive

This 26-card standard-size set of the 1991 Knoxville Blue Jays, a Class AA Southern League affiliate of the Toronto Blue Jays, features posed color player photos on its white-bordered fronts. The player's name appears in blue lettering at the top; his position and team name appear in blue lettering below the photo. The back carries the player's name within a blue stripe at the top, followed by position, team name and affiliation, biography and statistics.

	MINT	NRMT	EXC
COMPLETE SET (26)	5.00	2.20	.60

- ☐ 351 Pete Blohm
- ☐ 352 Domingo Cedeno
- ☐ 353 Nate Cromwell
- ☐ 354 Jesse Cross
- ☐ 355 Juan DeLaRosa
- ☐ 356 Bobby Deloach
- ☐ 357 Ray Giannelli
- ☐ 358 Darren Hall
- ☐ 359 Mark Young
- ☐ 360 Jeff Kent
- ☐ 361 Randy Knorr
- ☐ 362 Jose Monzon
- ☐ 363 Bernie Nunez
- ☐ 364 Paul Rodgers
- ☐ 365 Jimmy Rogers
- ☐ 366 Mike Taylor
- ☐ 367 Ryan Thompson
- ☐ 368 Jason Townley
- ☐ 369 Rick Trlicek
- ☐ 370 Anthony Ward
- ☐ 371 Dave Weathers
- ☐ 372 Woody Williams
- ☐ 373 Julian Yan
- ☐ 374 John Stearns MG
- ☐ 375 Mike McAlpin CO
  Steve Mingori CO
- ☐ NNO Title card

1991 Knoxville Blue Jays ProCards

This 28-card standard-size set of the 1991 Knoxville Blue Jays, a Class AA Southern League affiliate of the Toronto Blue Jays, features on its white-bordered fronts posed color player photos set on simulated spiral-bound yellow notebooks. The player's name, position, and team appear within a green rectangle below the photo. The yellow horizontal back is bordered in white and carries the player's name and position at the top, followed by biography and statistics.

	MINT	NRMT	EXC
COMPLETE SET (28)	5.00	2.20	.60

- ☐ 1760 Nathaniel Cromwell
- ☐ 1761 Jesse Cross
- ☐ 1762 Darren Hall
- ☐ 1763 Vince Horsman
- ☐ 1764 Jimmy Rogers
- ☐ 1765 Rick Trlicek
- ☐ 1766 Anthony Ward
- ☐ 1767 Dave Weathers
- ☐ 1768 Woody Williams
- ☐ 1769 Rob Wishnevski
- ☐ 1770 Randy Knorr
- ☐ 1771 Jose Monzon
- ☐ 1772 Jason Townley
- ☐ 1773 Domingo Cedeno
- ☐ 1774 Ray Giannelli
- ☐ 1775 Jeff Kent
- ☐ 1776 Mike Taylor
- ☐ 1777 Julian Yan
- ☐ 1778 Mark Young
- ☐ 1779 Juan DeLaRosa
- ☐ 1780 Bobby DeLoach
- ☐ 1781 Bernie Nunez
- ☐ 1782 Paul Rodgers
- ☐ 1783 Ryan Thompson
- ☐ 1784 John Stearns MG
- ☐ 1785 Mike McAlpin CO
- ☐ 1786 Steve Mingori CO
- ☐ 1787 Checklist

1991 Lakeland Tigers Classic/Best

This 30-card standard-size set of the 1991 Lakeland Tigers, a Class A Florida State League affiliate of the Detroit Tigers, features white-bordered posed color player photos on its fronts. The player's name, team, and position appear at the bottom. The white back is framed by a thin black line and carries the player's name and position at the top, followed by biography, statistics and team logos.

	MINT	NRMT	EXC
COMPLETE SET (30)	5.00	2.20	.60

- ☐ 1 Jeff Braley
- ☐ 2 Tom Drell
- ☐ 3 Mark Ettles
- ☐ 4 Ed Ferm
- ☐ 5 Mike Garcia
- ☐ 6 Frank Gonzales
- ☐ 7 Eric Leimeister
- ☐ 8 Steve Carter
- ☐ 9 Mike Lumley
- ☐ 10 Doug Carpenter CO
- ☐ 11 Lino Rivera
- ☐ 12 Leonardo Torres
- ☐ 13 Steve Wolf
- ☐ 14 Eric Albright
- ☐ 15 Mike Gillette
- ☐ 16 Rick Sellers
- ☐ 17 Fernando Arroyo
- ☐ 18 Jose Anglero
- ☐ 19 Ron Howard
- ☐ 20 Ron Marigny
- ☐ 21 Kirt Mendenhall
- ☐ 22 Mike Rendina
- ☐ 23 Brian Cornelius
- ☐ 24 Jeff Goodale
- ☐ 25 Dennis McNamara
- ☐ 26 Rudy Pemberton
- ☐ 27 Warren Sawkiw
- ☐ 28 Pat Woodruff

☐ 29 John Lipon MGR
☐ 30 Checklist

1991 Lakeland Tigers ProCards

This 29-card standard-size set of the 1991 Lakeland Tigers, a Class A Florida State League affiliate of the Detroit Tigers, features on its white-bordered fronts posed color player photos set on simulated spiral-bound yellow notebooks. The player's name, position, and team appear within a green rectangle below the photo. The yellow horizontal back is bordered in white and carries the player's name at the top, followed by biography and statistics.

	MINT	NRMT	EXC
COMPLETE SET (29)	5.00	2.20	.60

☐ 257 Jeff Braley
☐ 258 Tom Drell
☐ 259 Mark Ettles
☐ 260 Ed Ferm
☐ 261 Mike Garcia
☐ 262 Frank Gonzales
☐ 263 Eric Leimeister
☐ 264 Mike Lumley
☐ 265 Doug Marcero
☐ 266 Lino Rivera
☐ 267 Leonardo Torres
☐ 268 Steve Wolf
☐ 269 Mike Gillette
☐ 270 Brad Wilson
☐ 271 Jose Anglero
☐ 272 Ron Howard
☐ 273 Ron Marigny
☐ 274 Kirk Mendenhall
☐ 275 Mike Rendina
☐ 276 Warren Sawkiw
☐ 277 Brian Cornelius
☐ 278 Jeff Goodale
☐ 279 Denny McNamara
☐ 280 Rudy Pemberton
☐ 281 Pat Woodruff
☐ 282 John Lipon MGR
☐ 283 Fernando Arroyo CO
☐ 284 Doug Carpenter CO
☐ 285 Checklist

1991 Las Vegas Stars Line Drive

	MINT	NRMT	EXC
COMPLETE SET (26)	5.00	2.20	.60

☐ 276 Oscar Azocar
☐ 277 Dann Bilardello
☐ 278 Ricky Bones
☐ 279 Brian Dorsett
☐ 280 Scott Coolbaugh
☐ 281 John Costello
☐ 282 Terry Gilmore
☐ 283 Jeremy Hernandez
☐ 284 Kevin Higgins
☐ 285 Chris Jelic
☐ 286 Dean Kelley
☐ 287 Derek Lilliquist
☐ 288 Jose Melendez
☐ 289 Jose Mota
☐ 290 Adam Peterson
☐ 291 Ed Romero
☐ 292 Steven Rosenberg
☐ 293 Tim Scott
☐ 294 Dave Staton
☐ 295 Will Taylor
☐ 296 Jim Vatcher
☐ 297 Dan Walters
☐ 298 Kevin Ward
☐ 299 Jim Riggleman MGR
☐ 300 Jon Matlack CO
Tony Torchia CO
☐ NNO Title card

1991 Las Vegas Stars ProCards

This 31-card standard-size set of the 1991 Las Vegas Stars, a Class AAA Pacific Coast League affiliate of the San Diego Padres, features on its white-bordered fronts posed color player photos set on simulated spiral-bound yellow notebooks. The player's name, position, and team appear within a green rectangle below the photo. The yellow horizontal back is bordered in white and carries the player's name at the top, followed by biography and statistics.

	MINT	NRMT	EXC
COMPLETE SET (31)	5.00	2.20	.60

☐ 226 Ricky Bones
☐ 227 Pat Clements
☐ 228 John Costello
☐ 229 Terry Gilmore
☐ 230 Jeremy Hernandez
☐ 231 Derek Lilliquist
☐ 232 Jose Melendez
☐ 233 Adam Peterson
☐ 234 Steve Rosenberg
☐ 235 Tim Scott
☐ 236 Rafael Valdez
☐ 237 Dann Bilardello
☐ 238 Brian Dorsett
☐ 239 Kevin Higgins
☐ 240 Dan Walters
☐ 241 Scott Coolbaugh
☐ 242 Dean Kelley
☐ 243 Jose Mota
☐ 244 Ed Romero
☐ 245 Craig Shipley
☐ 246 Dave Staton
☐ 247 Oscar Azocar
☐ 248 Thomas Howard
☐ 249 Chris Jelic
☐ 250 Will Taylor
☐ 251 Jim Vatcher
☐ 252 Kevin Ward
☐ 253 Jim Riggleman MGR
☐ 254 Jon Matlack CO
☐ 255 Tony Torchia CO
☐ 256 Checklist

1991 Line Drive AA

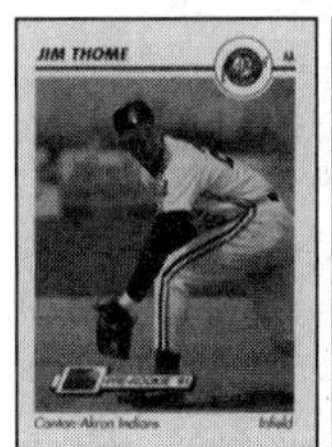

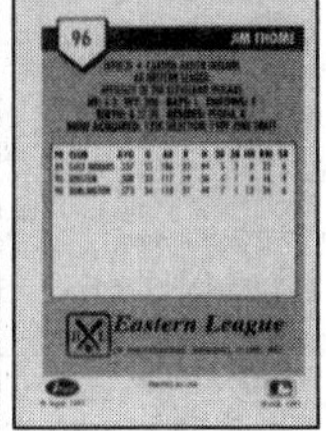

This 650-card standard-size set has glossy color action player photos bordered in white. The player's name appears in either red or blue lettering at the card top, with team logo in the upper right corner. The team name and position are given below the picture. The backs are printed in black on either blue and white or red and white, and feature biography and statistics. The cards are numbered in the upper left corner.

	MINT	NRMT	EXC
COMPLETE SET (650)	25.00	11.00	3.10
COMMON CARD (1-650)	.05	.02	.01
☐ 1 Andy Cook	.05	.02	.01
☐ 2 Russ Davis	.10	.05	.01
☐ 3 Bobby DeJardin	.05	.02	.01
☐ 4 Mike Draper	.05	.02	.01
☐ 5 Victor Garcia	.05	.02	.01
☐ 6 Mike Gardella	.05	.02	.01
☐ 7 Cullen Hartzog	.05	.02	.01
☐ 8 Jay Knoblauh	.05	.02	.01
☐ 9 Billy Masse	.05	.02	.01
☐ 10 Jeff Livesey	.05	.02	.01
☐ 11 Edward Martel	.05	.02	.01
☐ 12 Vince Phillips	.05	.02	.01
☐ 13 Tom Popplewell	.05	.02	.01
☐ 14 Jerry Rub	.05	.02	.01
☐ 15 Dave Silvestri	.05	.02	.01
☐ 16 Tom Newell	.05	.02	.01
☐ 17 Willie Smith	.05	.02	.01
☐ 18 J.T. Snow	.30	.14	.04
☐ 19 Don Stanford	.05	.02	.01
☐ 20 Larry Stanford	.05	.02	.01
☐ 21 John Toale	.05	.02	.01
☐ 22 Hector Vargas	.05	.02	.01
☐ 23 Gerald Williams	.05	.02	.01
☐ 24 Dan Radison MGR	.05	.02	.01
☐ 25 Coaches	.05	.02	.01
Dave Jorn			
Bob Mariano			
☐ 26 Frank Abreau	.05	.02	.01
☐ 27 Cliff Brannon	.05	.02	.01
☐ 28 Greg Carmona	.05	.02	.01
☐ 29 Ric Christian	.05	.02	.01
☐ 30 John Ericks	.05	.02	.01
☐ 31 Steve Fanning	.05	.02	.01
☐ 32 Joey Fernandez	.05	.02	.01
☐ 33 Jose Fernandez	.05	.02	.01
☐ 34 Mike Fiore	.05	.02	.01
☐ 35 David Grimes	.05	.02	.01
☐ 36 Dale Kisten	.05	.02	.01
☐ 37 John Lepley	.05	.02	.01
☐ 38 Luis Martinez	.05	.02	.01
☐ 39 Mike Milchin	.05	.02	.01
☐ 40 Donovan Osborne	.15	.07	.02
☐ 41 Gabriel Ozuna	.05	.02	.01
☐ 42 Lee Plemel	.05	.02	.01
☐ 43 Don Prybylinski	.05	.02	.01
☐ 44 John Sellick	.05	.02	.01
☐ 45 Jeff Shireman	.05	.02	.01
☐ 46 Brian Stone	.05	.02	.01
☐ 47 Charlie White	.05	.02	.01
☐ 48 Dennis Wiseman	.05	.02	.01
☐ 49 Joe Pettini MGR	.05	.02	.01
☐ 50 Coaches	.05	.02	.01
Scott Melvin			
Marty Mason			
☐ 51 Wilson Alvarez	.15	.07	.02
☐ 52 Wayne Busby	.05	.02	.01
☐ 53 Darrin Campbell	.05	.02	.01
☐ 54 Mark Chasey	.05	.02	.01
☐ 55 Ron Coomer	.10	.05	.01
☐ 56 Argenis Cortez	.05	.02	.01
☐ 57 Mike Davino	.05	.02	.01
☐ 58 Lindsay Foster	.05	.02	.01
☐ 59 Ramon Garcia	.05	.02	.01
☐ 60 Kevin Garner	.05	.02	.01
☐ 61 Jeff Gay	.05	.02	.01
☐ 62 Chris Howard	.05	.02	.01
☐ 63 John Hudek	.05	.02	.01
☐ 64 Scott Jaster	.05	.02	.01
☐ 65 Bo Kennedy	.05	.02	.01
☐ 66 Derek Lee	.05	.02	.01
☐ 67 Frank Merigliano	.05	.02	.01
☐ 68 Scott Middaugh	.05	.02	.01
☐ 69 Javier Ocasio	.05	.02	.01
☐ 70 Kinnis Pledger	.05	.02	.01
☐ 71 Greg Roth	.05	.02	.01
☐ 72 Aubrey Waggoner	.05	.02	.01
☐ 73 Jose Ventura	.05	.02	.01
☐ 74 Tony Franklin MGR	.05	.02	.01
☐ 75 Coaches	.05	.02	.01
Rick Peterson			
Pat Roessler			
Sam Hairston			
☐ 76 Ramon Bautista	.05	.02	.01
☐ 77 Eric Bell	.05	.02	.01
☐ 78 Jim Bruske	.05	.02	.01
☐ 79 Tim Costo	.05	.02	.01
☐ 80 Mike Curtis	.05	.02	.01
☐ 81 Jerry DiPoto	.05	.02	.01
☐ 82 Daren Epley	.05	.02	.01
☐ 83 Sam Ferretti	.05	.02	.01
☐ 84 Garland Kiser	.05	.02	.01
☐ 85 Ty Kovach	.05	.02	.01
☐ 86 Tom Kramer	.05	.02	.01
☐ 87 Nolan Lane	.05	.02	.01
☐ 88 Jesse Levis	.05	.02	.01
☐ 89 Carlos Martinez	.05	.02	.01
☐ 90 Jeff Mutis	.05	.02	.01
☐ 91 Rouglas Odor	.05	.02	.01
☐ 92 Gary Resetar	.05	.02	.01
☐ 93 Greg Roscoe	.05	.02	.01
☐ 94 Miguel Sabino	.05	.02	.01
☐ 95 Bernie Tatis	.05	.02	.01
☐ 96 Jim Thome	4.00	1.80	.50
☐ 97 Ken Ramos	.05	.02	.01
☐ 98 Ken Whitfield	.05	.02	.01
☐ 99 Ken Bolek MGR	.05	.02	.01
☐ 100 Dave Keller CO	.05	.02	.01
☐ 101 Steve Adams	.05	.02	.01
☐ 102 Stan Fansler	.05	.02	.01
☐ 103 Mandy Romero	.05	.02	.01
☐ 104 Terry Crowley Jr.	.05	.02	.01
☐ 105 Chip Duncan	.05	.02	.01
☐ 106 Greg Edge	.05	.02	.01
☐ 107 Chris Estep	.05	.02	.01
☐ 108 Carl Hamilton	.05	.02	.01
☐ 109 Lee Hancock	.05	.02	.01
☐ 110 Tim Hines	.05	.02	.01
☐ 111 Mike Huyler	.05	.02	.01
☐ 112 Paul Miller	.05	.02	.01
☐ 113 Pete Murphy	.05	.02	.01
☐ 114 Darwin Pennye	.05	.02	.01
☐ 115 Mike Roesler	.05	.02	.01
☐ 116 Bruce Schreiber	.05	.02	.01
☐ 117 Greg Sparks	.05	.02	.01
☐ 118 Dennis Tafoya	.05	.02	.01
☐ 119 Tim Wakefield	.10	.05	.01
☐ 120 Ben Webb	.05	.02	.01
☐ 121 John Wehner	.05	.02	.01
☐ 122 Ed Yacopino	.05	.02	.01
☐ 123 Eddie Zambrano	.05	.02	.01
☐ 124 Marc Bombard MGR	.05	.02	.01
☐ 125 Coaches	.05	.02	.01
Trent Jewett			
Spin Williams			
☐ 126 Alex Arias	.05	.02	.01
☐ 127 Paul Blair	.05	.02	.01
☐ 128 Jim Bullinger	.05	.02	.01
☐ 129 Dick Canan	.05	.02	.01
☐ 130 Rusty Crockett	.05	.02	.01
☐ 131 Steve DiBartolomeo	.05	.02	.01
☐ 132 John Gardner	.05	.02	.01
☐ 133 Henry Gomez	.05	.02	.01
☐ 134 Ty Griffin	.05	.02	.01
☐ 135 Shannon Jones	.05	.02	.01
☐ 136 Mike Knapp	.05	.02	.01
☐ 137 Tim Parker	.05	.02	.01
☐ 138 Elvin Paulino	.05	.02	.01
☐ 139 Fernando Ramsey	.05	.02	.01
☐ 140 Kevin Roberson	.05	.02	.01
☐ 141 John Salles	.05	.02	.01
☐ 142 Mike Sodders	.05	.02	.01
☐ 143 Bill St. Peter	.05	.02	.01
☐ 144 Julio Strauss	.05	.02	.01
☐ 145 Scott Taylor	.05	.02	.01
☐ 146 Tim Watkins	.05	.02	.01
☐ 147 Doug Welch	.05	.02	.01
☐ 148 Billy White	.05	.02	.01
☐ 149 Jay Loviglio MGR	.05	.02	.01
☐ 150 Rick Kranitz CO	.05	.02	.01
☐ 151 Rick Allen	.05	.02	.01
☐ 152 Mike Anderson	.05	.02	.01
☐ 153 Bobby Ayala	.05	.02	.01
☐ 154 Pete Beeler	.05	.02	.01
☐ 155 Jeff Branson	.05	.02	.01
☐ 156 Scott Bryant	.05	.02	.01
☐ 157 Bill Dodd	.05	.02	.01
☐ 158 Steve Foster	.05	.02	.01
☐ 159 Victor Garcia	.05	.02	.01
☐ 160 Frank Kremblas	.05	.02	.01
☐ 161 Greg Lonigro	.05	.02	.01
☐ 162 Dave Mcauliffe	.05	.02	.01
☐ 163 Steve McCarthy	.05	.02	.01
☐ 164 Scott Pose	.05	.02	.01
☐ 165 Tim Pugh	.05	.02	.01
☐ 166 Bill Risley	.05	.02	.01
☐ 167 Reggie Sanders	.50	.23	.06
☐ 168 Mo Sanford	.05	.02	.01
☐ 169 Scott Sellner	.05	.02	.01
☐ 170 Jerry Spradlin	.05	.02	.01
☐ 171 Glenn Sutko	.05	.02	.01
☐ 172 Todd Trafton	.05	.02	.01
☐ 173 Bernie Walker	.05	.02	.01
☐ 174 Jim Tracy MGR	.05	.02	.01
☐ 175 Mike Griffin CO	.05	.02	.01
☐ 176 Shon Ashley	.05	.02	.01
☐ 177 John Byington	.05	.02	.01
☐ 178 Mark Chapman	.05	.02	.01
☐ 179 Jim Czajkowski	.05	.02	.01
☐ 180 Ruben Escalera	.05	.02	.01
☐ 181 Craig Faulkner	.05	.02	.01
☐ 182 Tim Fortugno	.05	.02	.01
☐ 183 Don Gordon	.05	.02	.01
☐ 184 Mitch Hannahs	.05	.02	.01
☐ 185 Steve Lienhard	.05	.02	.01
☐ 186 Dave Jacas	.05	.02	.01
☐ 187 Kenny Jackson	.05	.02	.01
☐ 188 John Jaha	.15	.07	.02
☐ 189 Chris Johnson	.05	.02	.01
☐ 190 Mark Kiefer	.05	.02	.01
☐ 191 Pat Listach	.10	.05	.01
☐ 192 Tom McGraw	.05	.02	.01
☐ 193 Angel Miranda	.05	.02	.01
☐ 194 Dave Nilsson	.15	.07	.02
☐ 195 Jeff Schwarz	.05	.02	.01
☐ 196 Steve Sparks	.05	.02	.01
☐ 197 Jim Tatum	.05	.02	.01
☐ 198 Brandy Vann	.05	.02	.01
☐ 199 Dave Huppert MGR	.05	.02	.01
☐ 200 Paul Lindblad CO	.05	.02	.01
☐ 201 Rich Casarotti	.05	.02	.01
☐ 202 Vinny Castilla	.60	.25	.07
☐ 203 Brian Champion	.05	.02	.01
☐ 204 Popeye Cole	.05	.02	.01
☐ 205 Johnny Cuevas	.05	.02	.01
☐ 206 Brian Deak	.05	.02	.01
☐ 207 Pat Gomez	.05	.02	.01
☐ 208 Judd Johnson	.05	.02	.01
☐ 209 Ryan Klesko	2.50	1.10	.30
☐ 210 Rich Maloney	.05	.02	.01
☐ 211 Al Martin	.15	.07	.02
☐ 212 Keith Mitchell	.05	.02	.01
☐ 213 Rick Morris	.05	.02	.01
☐ 214 Ben Rivera	.05	.02	.01
☐ 215 Napoleon Robinson	.05	.02	.01
☐ 216 Boi Rodriguez	.05	.02	.01
☐ 217 Sean Ross	.05	.02	.01
☐ 218 Earl Sanders	.05	.02	.01
☐ 219 Scott Taylor	.05	.02	.01
☐ 220 Lee Upshaw	.05	.02	.01
☐ 221 Preston Watson	.05	.02	.01
☐ 222 Steven Wendell	.05	.02	.01
☐ 223 Mark Wohlers	.25	.11	.03
☐ 224 Chris Chambliss MGR	.05	.02	.01
☐ 225 Coaches	.05	.02	.01
Terry Harper			
Bill Slack			
Randy Ingle			
☐ 226 Jeff Bumgarner	.05	.02	.01
☐ 227 Stacey Burdick	.05	.02	.01
☐ 228 Paul Carey	.05	.02	.01
☐ 229 Bobby Dickerson	.05	.02	.01
☐ 230 Roy Gilbert	.05	.02	.01
☐ 231 Ricky Gutierrez	.05	.02	.01
☐ 232 Tim Holland	.05	.02	.01
☐ 233 Stacy Jones	.05	.02	.01
☐ 234 Tyrone Kingwood	.05	.02	.01
☐ 235 Mike Lehman	.05	.02	.01
☐ 236 Rod Lofton	.05	.02	.01
☐ 237 Kevin Hickey	.05	.02	.01
☐ 238 Joel McKeon	.05	.02	.01
☐ 239 Scott Meadows	.05	.02	.01
☐ 240 Steve Luebber CO	.05	.02	.01
☐ 241 Mike Oquist	.05	.02	.01
☐ 242 Ozzie Peraza	.05	.02	.01
☐ 243 Tim Raley	.05	.02	.01
☐ 244 Arthur Rhodes	.05	.02	.01
☐ 245 Doug Robbins	.05	.02	.01
☐ 246 Ken Shamburg	.05	.02	.01
☐ 247 Todd Stephan	.05	.02	.01
☐ 248 Jack Voigt	.05	.02	.01
☐ 249 Jerry Narron MGR	.05	.02	.01
☐ 250 Joe Durham CO	.05	.02	.01
☐ 251 Chris Cassels	.05	.02	.01
☐ 252 Arcie Cianfrocco	.05	.02	.01
☐ 253 Dan Freed	.05	.02	.01

☐ 254 Greg Fulton .05 .02 .01
☐ 255 Chris Haney .05 .02 .01
☐ 256 Cesar Hernandez .05 .02 .01
☐ 257 Richard Holsman .05 .02 .01
☐ 258 Rob Katzaroff .05 .02 .01
☐ 259 Bryn Kosco .05 .02 .01
☐ 260 Ken Lake .05 .02 .01
☐ 261 Hector Rivera .05 .02 .01
☐ 262 Chris Marchok .05 .02 .01
☐ 263 Chris Martin .05 .02 .01
☐ 264 Matt Maysey .05 .02 .01
☐ 265 Omer Munoz .05 .02 .01
☐ 266 Bob Natal .05 .02 .01
☐ 267 Chris Pollack .05 .02 .01
☐ 268 F.P. Santangelo .05 .02 .01
☐ 269 Joe Siddall .05 .02 .01
☐ 270 Stan Spencer .05 .02 .01
☐ 271 Matt Stairs .05 .02 .01
☐ 272 David Wainhouse .05 .02 .01
☐ 273 Pete Young .05 .02 .01
☐ 274 Mike Quade MGR .05 .02 .01
☐ 275 Coaches .05 .02 .01
Joe Kerrigan
Pete Dalena
☐ 276 Marco Armas .05 .02 .01
☐ 277 Bob Bafia .05 .02 .01
☐ 278 Dean Borrelli .05 .02 .01
☐ 279 John Briscoe .05 .02 .01
☐ 280 James Buccheri .05 .02 .01
☐ 281 Tom Carcione .05 .02 .01
☐ 282 Joel Chimelis .05 .02 .01
☐ 283 Fred Cooley .05 .02 .01
☐ 284 Russ Cormier .05 .02 .01
☐ 285 Matt Grott .05 .02 .01
☐ 286 Dwayne Hosey .05 .02 .01
☐ 287 Chad Kuhn .05 .02 .01
☐ 288 Dave Latter .05 .02 .01
☐ 289 Francisco Matos .05 .02 .01
☐ 290 Gavin Osteen .05 .02 .01
☐ 291 Tim Peek .05 .02 .01
☐ 292 Don Peters .05 .02 .01
☐ 293 Scott Shockey .05 .02 .01
☐ 294 Will Tejada .05 .02 .01
☐ 295 Lee Tinsley .05 .02 .01
☐ 296 Todd Van Poppel .05 .02 .01
☐ 297 Darryl Vice .05 .02 .01
☐ 298 Dave Zancanaro .05 .02 .01
☐ 299 Casey Parsons MGR .05 .02 .01
☐ 300 Bert Bradley CO .05 .02 .01
☐ 301 Frank Carey .05 .02 .01
☐ 302 Larry Carter .05 .02 .01
☐ 303 Jim McNamara .05 .02 .01
☐ 304 Tom Ealy .05 .02 .01
☐ 305 Juan Guerrero .05 .02 .01
☐ 306 Bryan Hickerson .05 .02 .01
☐ 307 Steve Hosey .05 .02 .01
☐ 308 Tom Hostetler .05 .02 .01
☐ 309 Erik Johnson .05 .02 .01
☐ 310 Dan Lewis .05 .02 .01
☐ 311 Paul McClellan .05 .02 .01
☐ 312 Jim McNamara .05 .02 .01
☐ 313 Kevin Meier .05 .02 .01
☐ 314 Jim Myers .05 .02 .01
☐ 315 Dave Patterson .05 .02 .01
☐ 316 John Patterson .05 .02 .01
☐ 317 Jim Pena .05 .02 .01
☐ 318 Dan Rambo .05 .02 .01
☐ 319 Steve Reed .05 .02 .01
☐ 320 Kevin Rogers .05 .02 .01
☐ 321 Reuben Smiley .05 .02 .01
☐ 322 Scooter Tucker .05 .02 .01
☐ 323 Pete Weber .05 .02 .01
☐ 324 Bill Evers MGR .05 .02 .01
☐ 325 Coaches .05 .02 .01
Tony Taylor
Todd Oakes
☐ 326 Fernando Arguelles .05 .02 .01
☐ 327 Shawn Barton .05 .02 .01
☐ 328 Jim Blueberg .05 .02 .01
☐ 329 Frank Bolick .05 .02 .01
☐ 330 Bret Boone .15 .07 .02
☐ 331 Jim Bowie .05 .02 .01
☐ 332 Jim Campanis .05 .02 .01
☐ 333 Gary Eave .05 .02 .01
☐ 334 David Evans .05 .02 .01
☐ 335 Fernando Figueroa .05 .02 .01
☐ 336 Dave Fleming .05 .02 .01
☐ 337 Ruben Gonzalez .05 .02 .01
☐ 338 Mike McDonald .05 .02 .01
☐ 339 Jeff Nelson .05 .02 .01
☐ 340 Jim Newlin .05 .02 .01
☐ 341 Ken Pennington .05 .02 .01
☐ 342 Mike Pitz .05 .02 .01
☐ 343 Dave Richards .05 .02 .01
☐ 344 Roger Salkeld .05 .02 .01
☐ 345 Jack Smith .05 .02 .01
☐ 346 Tim Stargell .05 .02 .01
☐ 347 Brian Turang .05 .02 .01
☐ 348 Ted Williams .05 .02 .01
☐ 349 Jim Nettles MGR .05 .02 .01
☐ 350 Coaches .05 .02 .01
Bobby Cuellar
Lem Pilkinton
☐ 351 Pete Blohm .05 .02 .01
☐ 352 Domingo Cedeno .05 .02 .01
☐ 353 Nate Cromwell .05 .02 .01
☐ 354 Jesse Cross .05 .02 .01
☐ 355 Juan DeLaRosa .05 .02 .01
☐ 356 Bobby Deloach .05 .02 .01
☐ 357 Ray Giannelli .05 .02 .01
☐ 358 Darren Hall .05 .02 .01
☐ 359 Mark Young .05 .02 .01
☐ 360 Jeff Kent .25 .11 .03
☐ 361 Randy Knorr .05 .02 .01
☐ 362 Jose Monzon .05 .02 .01
☐ 363 Bernie Nunez .05 .02 .01
☐ 364 Paul Rodgers .05 .02 .01
☐ 365 Jimmy Rogers .05 .02 .01
☐ 366 Mike Taylor .05 .02 .01
☐ 367 Ryan Thompson .05 .02 .01
☐ 368 Jason Townley .05 .02 .01
☐ 369 Rick Trlicek .05 .02 .01
☐ 370 Anthony Ward .05 .02 .01
☐ 371 Dave Weathers .05 .02 .01
☐ 372 Woody Williams .05 .02 .01
☐ 373 Julian Yan .05 .02 .01
☐ 374 John Stearns MGR .05 .02 .01
☐ 375 Coaches .05 .02 .01
Mike McAlpin
Steve Mingori
☐ 376 Doyle Balthazar .05 .02 .01
☐ 377 Basilio Cabrera .05 .02 .01
☐ 378 Ron Cook .05 .02 .01
☐ 379 Ivan Cruz .05 .02 .01
☐ 380 Dean Decillis .05 .02 .01
☐ 381 John DeSilva .05 .02 .01
☐ 382 John Doherty .05 .02 .01
☐ 383 Lou Frazier .05 .02 .01
☐ 384 Luis Galindo .05 .02 .01
☐ 385 Greg Gohr .05 .02 .01
☐ 386 Bud Groom .05 .02 .01
☐ 387 Darren Hursey .05 .02 .01
☐ 388 Riccardo Ingram .05 .02 .01
☐ 389 Keith Kimberlin .05 .02 .01
☐ 390 Todd Krumm .05 .02 .01
☐ 391 Randy Marshall .05 .02 .01
☐ 392 Domingo Michel .05 .02 .01
☐ 393 Steve Pegues .05 .02 .01
☐ 394 Jose Ramos .05 .02 .01
☐ 395 Bob Reimink .05 .02 .01
☐ 396 Ruben Rodriguez .05 .02 .01
☐ 397 Eric Stone .05 .02 .01
☐ 398 Marty Willis .05 .02 .01
☐ 399 Gene Roof MGR .05 .02 .01
☐ 400 Coaches .05 .02 .01
Jeff Jones
Dan Raley
☐ 401 Pete Alborano .05 .02 .01
☐ 402 Jim Baxter .05 .02 .01
☐ 403 Tony Clements .05 .02 .01
☐ 404 Archie Corbin .05 .02 .01
☐ 405 Andres Cruz .05 .02 .01
☐ 406 Jeff Garber .05 .02 .01
☐ 407 David Gonzalez .05 .02 .01
☐ 408 Kevin Koslofski .05 .02 .01
☐ 409 Deric Ladnier .05 .02 .01
☐ 410 Mark Parnell .05 .02 .01
☐ 411 Jorge Pedre .05 .02 .01
☐ 412 Doug Peters .05 .02 .01
☐ 413 Hipolito Pichardo .05 .02 .01
☐ 414 Eddie Pierce .05 .02 .01
☐ 415 Mike Poehl .05 .02 .01
☐ 416 Darryl Robinson .05 .02 .01
☐ 417 Steve Shifflett .05 .02 .01
☐ 418 Jim Smith .05 .02 .01
☐ 419 Lou Talbert .05 .02 .01
☐ 420 Terry Taylor .05 .02 .01
☐ 421 Rich Tunison .05 .02 .01
☐ 422 Hugh Walker .05 .02 .01
☐ 423 Darren Watkins .05 .02 .01
☐ 424 Jeff Cox MGR .05 .02 .01
☐ 425 Coaches .05 .02 .01
Brian Peterson
Mike Alvarez
☐ 426 Clemente Acosta .05 .02 .01
☐ 427 Jeff Barns .05 .02 .01
☐ 428 Mike Butcher .05 .02 .01
☐ 429 Glenn Carter .05 .02 .01
☐ 430 Marvin Cobb .05 .02 .01
☐ 431 Sherman Corbett .05 .02 .01
☐ 432 Kevin Davis .05 .02 .01
☐ 433 Damion Easley .15 .07 .02
☐ 434 Kevin Flora .05 .02 .01
☐ 435 Larry Gonzalez .05 .02 .01
☐ 436 Mark Howie .05 .02 .01
☐ 437 Todd James .05 .02 .01
☐ 438 Bobby Jones .05 .02 .01
☐ 439 Steve King .05 .02 .01
☐ 440 Marcus Lawton .05 .02 .01
☐ 441 Ken Rivers .05 .02 .01
☐ 442 Doug Robertson .05 .02 .01
☐ 443 Tim Salmon 2.00 .90 .25
☐ 444 Ramon Sambo .05 .02 .01
☐ 445 Daryl Sconiers .05 .02 .01
☐ 446 Dave Shotkoski .05 .02 .01
☐ 447 Terry Taylor .05 .02 .01
☐ 448 Mark Zappelli .05 .02 .01
☐ 449 Don Long MGR .05 .02 .01
☐ 450 Coaches .05 .02 .01
Kernan Ronan
Gene Richards
☐ 451 Michael Beams .05 .02 .01
☐ 452 Greg Blosser .05 .02 .01
☐ 453 Brian Conroy .05 .02 .01
☐ 454 Freddie Davis .05 .02 .01
☐ 455 Colin Dixon .05 .02 .01
☐ 456 Peter Estrada .05 .02 .01
☐ 457 Ray Fagnant .05 .02 .01
☐ 458 Tom Fischer .05 .02 .01
☐ 459 John Flaherty .05 .02 .01
☐ 460 Donald Florence .05 .02 .01
☐ 461 Blane Fox .05 .02 .01
☐ 462 Steve Hendricks .05 .02 .01
☐ 463 Wayne Housie .05 .02 .01
☐ 464 Peter Hoy .05 .02 .01
☐ 465 Thomas Kane .05 .02 .01
☐ 466 David Milstien .05 .02 .01
☐ 467 Juan Paris .05 .02 .01
☐ 468 Scott Powers .05 .02 .01
☐ 469 Paul Quantrill .05 .02 .01
☐ 470 Randy Randle .05 .02 .01
☐ 471 Al Sanders .05 .02 .01
☐ 472 Scott Taylor .05 .02 .01
☐ 473 John Valentin .50 .23 .06
☐ 474 Gary Allenson MGR .05 .02 .01
☐ 475 Rick Wise CO .05 .02 .01
☐ 476 Pat Bangtson .05 .02 .01
☐ 477 Carlos Capellan .05 .02 .01
☐ 478 Rafael DeLima .05 .02 .01
☐ 479 Frank Valdez .05 .02 .01
☐ 480 Cheo Garcia .05 .02 .01
☐ 481 Shawn Gilbert .05 .02 .01
☐ 482 Greg Johnson .05 .02 .01
☐ 483 Jay Kvasnicka .05 .02 .01
☐ 484 Orlando Lind .05 .02 .01
☐ 485 Pat Mahomes .05 .02 .01
☐ 486 Jose Marzan .05 .02 .01
☐ 487 Dan Masteller .05 .02 .01
☐ 488 Bob McCreary .05 .02 .01
☐ 489 Steve Muh .05 .02 .01
☐ 490 Reed Olmstead .05 .02 .01
☐ 491 Ray Ortiz .05 .02 .01
☐ 492 Derek Parks .05 .02 .01
☐ 493 Joe Siwa .05 .02 .01
☐ 494 Steve Stowell .05 .02 .01
☐ 495 Mike Trombley .05 .02 .01
☐ 496 Jim Shellenback CO .05 .02 .01
☐ 497 Rob Wassenaar .05 .02 .01
☐ 498 Phil Wiese .05 .02 .01
☐ 499 Scott Ullger MGR .05 .02 .01
☐ 500 Mark Funderburk CO .05 .02 .01
☐ 501 Jason Backs .05 .02 .01
☐ 502 Toby Borland .05 .02 .01
☐ 503 Cliff Brantley .05 .02 .01
☐ 504 Dana Brown .05 .02 .01
☐ 505 John Burgos .05 .02 .01
☐ 506 Andy Carter .05 .02 .01
☐ 507 Bruce Dostal .05 .02 .01
☐ 508 Rick Dunnum .05 .02 .01
☐ 509 John Martin CO .05 .02 .01
☐ 510 David Holdridge .05 .02 .01
☐ 511 Darrell Lindsey .05 .02 .01
☐ 512 Doug Lindsey .05 .02 .01
☐ 513 Tony Longmire .05 .02 .01
☐ 514 Tom Marsh .05 .02 .01
☐ 515 Rod Robertson .05 .02 .01
☐ 516 Edwin Rosado .05 .02 .01
☐ 517 Sean Ryan .05 .02 .01
☐ 518 Steve Scarsone .05 .02 .01
☐ 519 Mark Sims .05 .02 .01
☐ 520 Jeff Tabaka .05 .02 .01
☐ 521 Tony Trevino .05 .02 .01
☐ 522 Casey Waller .05 .02 .01
☐ 523 Cary Williams .05 .02 .01
☐ 524 Don McCormack MGR .05 .02 .01
☐ 525 Al LeBoeuf CO .05 .02 .01
☐ 526 Steve Allen .05 .02 .01
☐ 527 Jorge Alvarez .05 .02 .01
☐ 528 Bryan Baar .05 .02 .01
☐ 529 Tim Barker .05 .02 .01
☐ 530 Tony Barron .05 .02 .01
☐ 531 Cam Biberdorf .05 .02 .01
☐ 532 Jason Brosnan .05 .02 .01
☐ 533 Braulio Castillo .05 .02 .01
☐ 534 Steve Finken .05 .02 .01
☐ 535 Freddy Gonzalez .05 .02 .01
☐ 536 Mike James .05 .02 .01
☐ 537 Brett Magnusson .05 .02 .01
☐ 538 Jose Munoz .05 .02 .01
☐ 539 Lance Rice .05 .02 .01
☐ 540 Zak Shinall .05 .02 .01
☐ 541 Dennis Springer .05 .02 .01
☐ 542 Ramon Taveras .05 .02 .01
☐ 543 Jimmy Terrill .05 .02 .01
☐ 544 Brian Taxler .05 .02 .01
☐ 545 Jody Treadwell .05 .02 .01
☐ 546 Mike White .05 .02 .01
☐ 547 Mike Wilkins .05 .02 .01
☐ 548 Eric Young .05 .02 .01
☐ 549 John Shoemaker MGR .05 .02 .01
☐ 550 James Wray .05 .02 .01
☐ 551 Willie Ansley .05 .02 .01
☐ 552 Sam August .05 .02 .01
☐ 553 Jeff Baldwin .05 .02 .01
☐ 554 Pete Bauer .05 .02 .01
☐ 555 Kevin Coffman .05 .02 .01
☐ 556 Kevin Dean .05 .02 .01
☐ 557 Tony Eusebio .05 .02 .01
☐ 558 Dean Freeland .05 .02 .01
☐ 559 Rusty Harris .05 .02 .01
☐ 560 Dean Hartgraves .05 .02 .01
☐ 561 Trent Hubbard .05 .02 .01
☐ 562 Bert Hunter .05 .02 .01
☐ 563 Bernie Jenkins .05 .02 .01
☐ 564 Richie Simon .05 .02 .01
☐ 565 Keith Kaiser .05 .02 .01
☐ 566 Steve Larose .05 .02 .01
☐ 567 Lance Madsen .05 .02 .01
☐ 568 Scott Makarewicz .05 .02 .01
☐ 569 Rob Mallicoat .05 .02 .01
☐ 570 Joe Mikulik .05 .02 .01
☐ 571 Orlando Miller .05 .02 .01
☐ 572 Shane Reynolds .50 .23 .06
☐ 573 Richie Simon .05 .02 .01
☐ 574 Rick Sweet MGR .05 .02 .01
☐ 575 Coaches .05 .02 .01
Don Reynolds
Charlie Taylor
☐ 576 Rob Brown .05 .02 .01
☐ 577 Mike Burton .05 .02 .01
☐ 578 Everett Cunningham .05 .02 .01
☐ 579 Jeff Frye .05 .02 .01
☐ 580 Pat Garman .05 .02 .01
☐ 581 Bryan Gore .05 .02 .01
☐ 582 David Green .05 .02 .01
☐ 583 Donald Harris .05 .02 .01
☐ 584 Jose Hernandez .05 .02 .01
☐ 585 Greg Iavarone .05 .02 .01
☐ 586 Barry Manuel .05 .02 .01
☐ 587 Trey McCoy .05 .02 .01
☐ 588 Rod Morris .05 .02 .01
☐ 589 Robb Nen .15 .07 .02
☐ 590 David Perez .05 .02 .01
☐ 591 Bobby Reed .05 .02 .01
☐ 592 Ivan Rodriguez 2.00 .90 .25
☐ 593 Dan Rohrmeier .05 .02 .01
☐ 594 Brian Romero .05 .02 .01
☐ 595 Luke Sable .05 .02 .01
☐ 596 Frederic Samson .05 .02 .01
☐ 597 Cedric Shaw .05 .02 .01
☐ 598 Chris Shiflett .05 .02 .01
☐ 599 Bobby Jones MGR .05 .02 .01
☐ 600 Coaches .05 .02 .01
Oscar Acosta
Jeff Hubbard
☐ 601 Mike Basso .05 .02 .01
☐ 602 Doug Brocail .05 .02 .01
☐ 603 Rafael Chavez .05 .02 .01
☐ 604 Brian Cisarik .05 .02 .01
☐ 605 Greg David .05 .02 .01
☐ 606 Rick Davis .05 .02 .01
☐ 607 Vince Harris .05 .02 .01
☐ 608 Charles Hillemann .05 .02 .01
☐ 609 Kerry Knox .05 .02 .01
☐ 610 Pete Kuld .05 .02 .01
☐ 611 Jim Lewis .05 .02 .01
☐ 612 Luis Lopez .05 .02 .01
☐ 613 Pedro Martinez .05 .02 .01
☐ 614 Tim McWilliam .05 .02 .01
☐ 615 Tom Redington .05 .02 .01
☐ 616 Darrin Reichle .05 .02 .01
☐ 617 A.J. Sager .05 .02 .01
☐ 618 Frank Seminara .05 .02 .01
☐ 619 Darrell Sherman .05 .02 .01
☐ 620 Jose Valentin .15 .07 .02
☐ 621 Guillermo Velasquez .05 .02 .01
☐ 622 Tim Wallace .05 .02 .01
☐ 623 Brian Wood .05 .02 .01
☐ 624 Steve Lubratich MGR .05 .02 .01
☐ 625 Coaches .05 .02 .01
John Cumberland
Jack Maloof
☐ 626 Tim Bogar .05 .02 .01
☐ 627 Jeromy Burnitz .15 .07 .02
☐ 628 Hernan Cortes .05 .02 .01
☐ 629 Steve Davis .05 .02 .01
☐ 630 Joe Delli Carri .05 .02 .01
☐ 631 D.J. Dozier .05 .02 .01
☐ 632 Javier Gonzalez .05 .02 .01
☐ 633 Rudy Hernandez .05 .02 .01
☐ 634 Chris Hill .05 .02 .01
☐ 635 John Johnstone .05 .02 .01
☐ 636 Doug Kline .05 .02 .01
☐ 637 Loy McBride .05 .02 .01
☐ 638 Joel Horlen CO .05 .02 .01
☐ 639 Tito Navarro .05 .02 .01
☐ 640 Toby Nivens .05 .02 .01
☐ 641 Bryan Rogers .05 .02 .01
☐ 642 David Sommer .05 .02 .01
☐ 643 Greg Talamantez .05 .02 .01
☐ 644 Dave Telgheder .05 .02 .01
☐ 645 Jose Vargas .05 .02 .01
☐ 646 Aguedo Vasquez .05 .02 .01
☐ 647 Paul Williams .05 .02 .01
☐ 648 Alan Zinter .05 .02 .01
☐ 649 Clint Hurdle MGR .05 .02 .01
☐ 650 Jim Eschen CO .05 .02 .01

1991 Line Drive AAA

This 650-card standard-size set has glossy color action player photos bordered in white. The player's name appears in either red or blue

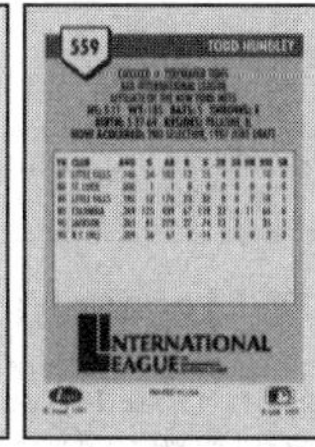

lettering at the card top, with team logo in the upper right corner. The team name and position are given below the picture. The backs are printed in black on either blue and white or red and white, and feature biography and statistics. The cards are numbered in the upper left corner.

	MINT	NRMT	EXC
COMPLETE SET (650)	25.00	11.00	3.10
COMMON CARD (1-650)	.05	.02	.01
☐ 1 Billy Bean	.05	.02	.01
☐ 2 Jerry Brooks	.05	.02	.01
☐ 3 Mike Christopher	.05	.02	.01
☐ 4 Dennis Cook	.05	.02	.01
☐ 5 Butch Davis	.05	.02	.01
☐ 6 Tom Goodwin	.15	.07	.02
☐ 7 Dave Hansen	.05	.02	.01
☐ 8 Jeff Hartsock	.05	.02	.01
☐ 9 Bert Heffernan	.05	.02	.01
☐ 10 Carlos Hernandez	.05	.02	.01
☐ 11 Chris Jones	.05	.02	.01
☐ 12 Eric Karros	1.25	.55	.16
☐ 13 Dave Lynch	.05	.02	.01
☐ 14 Luis Martinez	.05	.02	.01
☐ 15 Jamie McAndrew	.05	.02	.01
☐ 16 Jim Neidlinger	.05	.02	.01
☐ 17 Jose Offerman	.15	.07	.02
☐ 18 Eddie Pye	.05	.02	.01
☐ 19 Henry Rodriguez	1.25	.55	.16
☐ 20 Greg Smith	.05	.02	.01
☐ 21 Dave Veres	.05	.02	.01
☐ 22 Dave Walsh	.05	.02	.01
☐ 23 John Wetteland	.30	.14	.04
☐ 24 Kevin Kennedy MGR	.05	.02	.01
☐ 25 Coaches	.05	.02	.01
Von Joshua			
Claude Osteen			
☐ 26 Jeff Banister	.05	.02	.01
☐ 27 Cecil Espy	.05	.02	.01
☐ 28 Steve Fireovid	.05	.02	.01
☐ 29 Carlos Garcia	.05	.02	.01
☐ 30 Mark Huismann	.05	.02	.01
☐ 31 Scott Little	.05	.02	.01
☐ 32 Tom Magrann	.05	.02	.01
☐ 33 Roger Mason	.05	.02	.01
☐ 34 Tim Meeks	.05	.02	.01
☐ 35 Orlando Merced	.15	.07	.02
☐ 36 Joey Meyer	.05	.02	.01
☐ 37 Keith Miller	.05	.02	.01
☐ 38 Blas Minor	.05	.02	.01
☐ 39 Armando Moreno	.05	.02	.01
☐ 40 Jeff Neely	.05	.02	.01
☐ 41 Joe Redfield	.05	.02	.01
☐ 42 Rick Reed	.05	.02	.01
☐ 43 Jeff Richardson	.05	.02	.01
☐ 44 Rosario Rodriguez	.05	.02	.01
☐ 45 Jeff Schulz	.05	.02	.01
☐ 46 Jim Tracy	.05	.02	.01
☐ 47 Greg Tubbs	.05	.02	.01
☐ 48 Mike York	.05	.02	.01
☐ 49 Terry Collins MGR	.05	.02	.01
☐ 50 Jackie Brown CO	.05	.02	.01
☐ 51 Rich Amaral	.05	.02	.01
☐ 52 Rick Balabon	.05	.02	.01
☐ 53 Dave Brundage	.05	.02	.01
☐ 54 Dave Burba	.15	.07	.02
☐ 55 Dave Cochrane	.05	.02	.01
☐ 56 Alan Cockrell	.05	.02	.01
☐ 57 Mike Cook	.05	.02	.01
☐ 58 Keith Helton	.05	.02	.01
☐ 59 Dennis Hood	.05	.02	.01
☐ 60 Chris Howard	.05	.02	.01
☐ 61 Chuck Jackson	.05	.02	.01
☐ 62 Calvin Jones	.05	.02	.01
☐ 63 Pat Lennon	.05	.02	.01
☐ 64 Shane Letterio	.05	.02	.01
☐ 65 Vance Lovelace	.05	.02	.01
☐ 66 Tino Martinez	.75	.35	.09
☐ 67 John Mitchell	.05	.02	.01
☐ 68 Dennis Powell	.05	.02	.01
☐ 69 Alonzo Powell	.05	.02	.01
☐ 70 Pat Rice	.05	.02	.01
☐ 71 Ricky Rojas	.05	.02	.01
☐ 72 Steve Springer	.05	.02	.01
☐ 73 Ed Vande Berg	.05	.02	.01
☐ 74 Keith Bodie MGR	.05	.02	.01
☐ 75 Ross Grimsley CO	.05	.02	.01
☐ 76 Eddie Taubensee	.10	.05	.01
☐ 77 Jeff Bittiger	.05	.02	.01
☐ 78 Willie Blair	.05	.02	.01
☐ 79 Marty Brown	.05	.02	.01
☐ 80 Kevin Burdick	.05	.02	.01
☐ 81 Steve Cummings	.05	.02	.01
☐ 82 Mauro Gozzo	.05	.02	.01
☐ 83 Ricky Horton	.05	.02	.01
☐ 84 Stan Jefferson	.05	.02	.01
☐ 85 Brian Johnson	.05	.02	.01
☐ 86 Barry Jones	.05	.02	.01
☐ 87 Wayne Kirby	.05	.02	.01
☐ 88 Mark Lewis	.15	.07	.02
☐ 89 Rudy Seanez	.05	.02	.01
☐ 90 Luis Lopez	.05	.02	.01
☐ 91 Ever Magallanes	.05	.02	.01
☐ 92 Luis Medina	.05	.02	.01
☐ 93 Dave Otto	.05	.02	.01
☐ 94 Roberto Zambrano	.05	.02	.01
☐ 95 Jeff Shaw	.05	.02	.01
☐ 96 Efrain Valdez	.05	.02	.01
☐ 97 Sergio Valdez	.05	.02	.01
☐ 98 Kevin Wickander	.05	.02	.01
☐ 99 Charlie Manuel MGR	.05	.02	.01
☐ 100 Coaches	.05	.02	.01
Rick Adair			
Jim Gabella			
☐ 101 Steve Adkins	.05	.02	.01
☐ 102 Daven Bond	.05	.02	.01
☐ 103 Darrin Chapin	.05	.02	.01
☐ 104 Royal Clayton	.05	.02	.01
☐ 105 Steve Howe	.05	.02	.01
☐ 106 Keith Hughes	.05	.02	.01
☐ 107 Mike Humphreys	.05	.02	.01
☐ 108 Jeff Johnson	.05	.02	.01
☐ 109 Scott Kamieniecki	.05	.02	.01
☐ 110 Pat Kelly	.10	.05	.01
☐ 111 Jason Maas	.05	.02	.01
☐ 112 Alan Mills	.05	.02	.01
☐ 113 Rich Monteleone	.05	.02	.01
☐ 114 Hipolito Pena	.05	.02	.01
☐ 115 John Ramos	.05	.02	.01
☐ 116 Carlos Rodriguez	.05	.02	.01
☐ 117 Dave Sax	.05	.02	.01
☐ 118 Van Snider	.05	.02	.01
☐ 119 Don Sparks	.05	.02	.01
☐ 120 Andy Stankiewicz	.05	.02	.01
☐ 121 Wade Taylor	.05	.02	.01
☐ 122 Jim Walewander	.05	.02	.01
☐ 123 Bernie Williams	2.00	.90	.25
☐ 124 Rick Down MGR	.05	.02	.01
☐ 125 Coaches	.05	.02	.01
Gary Denbo			
Clete Boyer			
Russ Meyer			
☐ 126 D.L. Smith	.05	.02	.01
☐ 127 James Austin	.05	.02	.01
☐ 128 Esteban Beltre	.05	.02	.01
☐ 129 Mickey Brantley	.05	.02	.01
☐ 130 George Canale	.05	.02	.01
☐ 131 Matias Carrillo	.05	.02	.01
☐ 132 Juan Castillo	.05	.02	.01
☐ 133 Jim Davins	.05	.02	.01
☐ 134 Carlos Diaz	.05	.02	.01
☐ 135 Cal Eldred	.15	.07	.02
☐ 136 Narciso Elvira	.05	.02	.01
☐ 137 Brian Fisher	.05	.02	.01
☐ 138 Chris George	.05	.02	.01
☐ 139 Sandy Guerrero	.05	.02	.01
☐ 140 Doug Henry	.05	.02	.01
☐ 141 Darren Holmes	.05	.02	.01
☐ 142 Mike Ignasiak	.05	.02	.01
☐ 143 Jeff Kaiser	.05	.02	.01
☐ 144 Joe Kmak	.05	.02	.01
☐ 145 Tim McIntosh	.05	.02	.01
☐ 146 Charlie Montoyo	.05	.02	.01
☐ 147 Jim Olander	.05	.02	.01
☐ 148 Ed Puig	.05	.02	.01
☐ 149 Tony Muser MGR	.05	.02	.01
☐ 150 Coaches	.05	.02	.01
Lamar Johnson			
Don Rowe			
☐ 151 Kyle Abbott	.05	.02	.01
☐ 152 Ruben Amaro	.05	.02	.01
☐ 153 Kent Anderson	.05	.02	.01
☐ 154 Mike Erb	.05	.02	.01
☐ 155 Randy Bockus	.05	.02	.01
☐ 156 Gary Buckels	.05	.02	.01
☐ 157 Tim Burcham	.05	.02	.01
☐ 158 Chris Cron	.05	.02	.01
☐ 159 Chad Curtis	.15	.07	.02
☐ 160 Doug Davis	.05	.02	.01
☐ 161 Mark Davis	.05	.02	.01
☐ 162 Gary DiSarcina	.15	.07	.02
☐ 163 Mike Fetters	.05	.02	.01
☐ 164 Joe Grahe	.05	.02	.01
☐ 165 Dan Grunhard	.05	.02	.01
☐ 166 Dave Leiper	.05	.02	.01
☐ 167 Rafael Montalvo	.05	.02	.01
☐ 168 Reed Peters	.05	.02	.01
☐ 169 Bobby Rose	.05	.02	.01
☐ 170 Lee Stevens	.10	.05	.01
☐ 171 Ron Tingley	.05	.02	.01
☐ 172 Ed Vosberg	.05	.02	.01
☐ 173 Mark Wasinger	.05	.02	.01
☐ 174 Max Oliveras MGR	.05	.02	.01
☐ 175 Coaches	.05	.02	.01
Lenn Sakata			
Gary Ruby			
☐ 176 Bret Barberie	.05	.02	.01
☐ 177 Kevin Bearse	.05	.02	.01
☐ 178 Kent Bottenfield	.05	.02	.01
☐ 179 Wil Cordero	.20	.09	.03
☐ 180 Mike Davis	.05	.02	.01
☐ 181 Alex Diaz	.05	.02	.01
☐ 182 Eddie Dixon	.05	.02	.01
☐ 183 Jeff Fassero	.25	.11	.03
☐ 184 Jerry Goff	.05	.02	.01
☐ 185 Todd Haney	.05	.02	.01
☐ 186 Steve Hecht	.05	.02	.01
☐ 187 Jimmy Kremers	.05	.02	.01
☐ 188 Quinn Mack	.05	.02	.01
☐ 189 David Masters	.05	.02	.01
☐ 190 Marlin McPhail	.05	.02	.01
☐ 191 Doug Piatt	.05	.02	.01
☐ 192 Dana Ridenour	.05	.02	.01
☐ 193 Scott Service	.05	.02	.01
☐ 194 Razor Shines	.05	.02	.01
☐ 195 Tito Stewart	.05	.02	.01
☐ 196 Mel Houston	.05	.02	.01
☐ 197 John Vander Wal	.05	.02	.01
☐ 198 Darrin Winston	.05	.02	.01
☐ 199 Jerry Manuel MGR	.05	.02	.01
☐ 200 Coaches	.05	.02	.01
Gomer Hodge			
Nardi Contreras			
☐ 201 Brad Bierley	.05	.02	.01
☐ 202 Steve Carter	.05	.02	.01
☐ 203 Frank Castillo	.05	.02	.01
☐ 204 Lance Dickson	.05	.02	.01
☐ 205 Craig Smajstra	.05	.02	.01
☐ 206 Brian Guinn	.05	.02	.01
☐ 207 Joe Kraemer	.05	.02	.01
☐ 208 Cedric Landrum	.05	.02	.01
☐ 209 Derrick May	.05	.02	.01
☐ 210 Scott May	.05	.02	.01
☐ 211 Russ McGinnis	.05	.02	.01
☐ 212 Chuck Mount	.05	.02	.01
☐ 213 Dave Pavlas	.05	.02	.01
☐ 214 Laddie Renfroe	.05	.02	.01
☐ 215 David Rosario	.05	.02	.01
☐ 216 Rey Sanchez	.05	.02	.01
☐ 217 Dan Simonds	.05	.02	.01
☐ 218 Jeff Small	.05	.02	.01
☐ 219 Doug Strange	.05	.02	.01
☐ 220 Glenn Sullivan	.05	.02	.01
☐ 221 Rick Wilkins	.15	.07	.02
☐ 222 Steve Wilson	.05	.02	.01
☐ 223 Bob Scanlan	.05	.02	.01
☐ 224 Jim Essian	.05	.02	.01
☐ 225 Grant Jackson	.05	.02	.01
☐ 226 Luis Alicea	.05	.02	.01
☐ 227 Rob Brewer	.05	.02	.01
☐ 228 Nick Castaneda	.05	.02	.01
☐ 229 Stan Clarke	.05	.02	.01
☐ 230 Marty Clary	.05	.02	.01
☐ 231 Fidel Compres	.05	.02	.01
☐ 232 Todd Crosby	.05	.02	.01
☐ 233 Bob Davidson	.05	.02	.01
☐ 234 Bien Figueroa	.05	.02	.01
☐ 235 Ed Fulton	.05	.02	.01
☐ 236 Mark Grater	.05	.02	.01
☐ 237 Omar Olivares	.05	.02	.01
☐ 238 Brian Jordan	1.50	.70	.19
☐ 239 Lonnie Maclin	.05	.02	.01
☐ 240 Julian Martinez	.05	.02	.01
☐ 241 Al Nipper	.05	.02	.01
☐ 242 Dave Osteen	.05	.02	.01
☐ 243 Leny Picota	.05	.02	.01
☐ 244 Dave Richardson	.05	.02	.01
☐ 245 Mike Ross	.05	.02	.01
☐ 246 Stan Royer	.05	.02	.01
☐ 247 Tim Sherrill	.05	.02	.01
☐ 248 Carl Ray Stephens	.05	.02	.01
☐ 249 Mark DeJohn MGR	.05	.02	.01
☐ 250 Mark Riggins CO	.05	.02	.01
☐ 251 Billy Bates	.05	.02	.01
☐ 252 Freddie Benavides	.05	.02	.01
☐ 253 Keith Brown	.05	.02	.01
☐ 254 Adam Casillas	.05	.02	.01
☐ 255 Tony DeFrancesco	.05	.02	.01
☐ 256 Leo Garcia	.05	.02	.01
☐ 257 Angel Gonzalez	.05	.02	.01
☐ 258 Denny Gonzalez	.05	.02	.01
☐ 259 Kip Gross	.05	.02	.01
☐ 260 Charlie Mitchell	.05	.02	.01
☐ 261 Milton Hill	.05	.02	.01
☐ 262 Rodney Imes	.05	.02	.01
☐ 263 Reggie Jefferson	.10	.05	.01
☐ 264 Kieth Lockhart	.05	.02	.01
☐ 265 Manny Jose	.05	.02	.01
☐ 266 Terry Lee	.05	.02	.01
☐ 267 Rob Lopez	.05	.02	.01
☐ 268 Gino Minutelli	.05	.02	.01
☐ 269 Kevin Pearson	.05	.02	.01
☐ 270 Ross Powell	.05	.02	.01
☐ 271 Donnie Scott	.05	.02	.01
☐ 272 Luis Vasquez	.05	.02	.01
☐ 273 Joey Vierra	.05	.02	.01
☐ 274 Pete MacKanin MGR	.05	.02	.01
☐ 275 Coaches	.05	.02	.01
Don Gullett			
Jim Lett			
☐ 276 Oscar Azocar	.05	.02	.01
☐ 277 Dann Bilardello	.05	.02	.01
☐ 278 Ricky Bones	.15	.07	.02
☐ 279 Brian Dorsett	.05	.02	.01
☐ 280 Scott Coolbaugh	.05	.02	.01
☐ 281 John Costello	.05	.02	.01
☐ 282 Terry Gilmore	.05	.02	.01
☐ 283 Jeremy Hernandez	.05	.02	.01
☐ 284 Kevin Higgins	.05	.02	.01
☐ 285 Chris Jelic	.05	.02	.01
☐ 286 Dean Kelley	.05	.02	.01
☐ 287 Derek Lilliquist	.05	.02	.01
☐ 288 Jose Melendez	.05	.02	.01
☐ 289 Jose Mota	.05	.02	.01
☐ 290 Adam Peterson	.05	.02	.01
☐ 291 Ed Romero	.05	.02	.01
☐ 292 Steven Rosenberg	.05	.02	.01
☐ 293 Tim Scott	.05	.02	.01
☐ 294 Dave Staton	.05	.02	.01
☐ 295 Will Taylor	.05	.02	.01
☐ 296 Jim Vatcher	.05	.02	.01
☐ 297 Dan Walters	.05	.02	.01
☐ 298 Kevin Ward	.05	.02	.01
☐ 299 Jim Riggleman MGR	.05	.02	.01
☐ 300 Coaches	.05	.02	.01
Jon Matlack			
Tony Torchia			
☐ 301 Gerald Alexander	.05	.02	.01
☐ 302 Kevin Belcher	.05	.02	.01
☐ 303 Jeff Andrews	.05	.02	.01
☐ 304 Tony Scruggs	.05	.02	.01
☐ 305 Jeff Bronkey	.05	.02	.01
☐ 306 Paco Burgos	.05	.02	.01
☐ 307 Nick Capra	.05	.02	.01
☐ 308 Monty Fariss	.05	.02	.01
☐ 309 Darrin Garner	.05	.02	.01
☐ 310 Bill Haselman	.10	.05	.01
☐ 311 Terry Mathews	.05	.02	.01
☐ 312 Rob Maurer	.05	.02	.01
☐ 313 Gar Millay	.05	.02	.01
☐ 314 Dean Palmer	1.50	.70	.19
☐ 315 Roger Pavlik	.10	.05	.01
☐ 316 Dan Peltier	.05	.02	.01
☐ 317 Steve Peters	.05	.02	.01
☐ 318 Mark Petkovsek	.05	.02	.01
☐ 319 Jim Poole	.05	.02	.01
☐ 320 Paul Postier	.05	.02	.01
☐ 321 Wayne Rosenthal	.05	.02	.01
☐ 322 Dan Smith	.05	.02	.01
☐ 323 Terry Wells	.05	.02	.01
☐ 324 Tommy Thompson MGR	.05	.02	.01
☐ 325 Stan Hough CO	.05	.02	.01
☐ 326 Sean Berry	.15	.07	.02
☐ 327 Jacob Brumfield	.05	.02	.01
☐ 328 Bob Buchanan	.05	.02	.01
☐ 329 Kevin Burrell	.05	.02	.01
☐ 330 Stu Cole	.05	.02	.01
☐ 331 Victor Cole	.05	.02	.01
☐ 332 Jeff Conine	.60	.25	.07
☐ 333 Tommy Dunbar	.05	.02	.01
☐ 334 Luis Encarnacion	.05	.02	.01
☐ 335 Greg Everson	.05	.02	.01
☐ 336 Bob Hamelin	.10	.05	.01
☐ 337 Joel Johnston	.05	.02	.01
☐ 338 Frank Laureano	.05	.02	.01
☐ 339 Jim LeMasters	.05	.02	.01
☐ 340 Mike Magnante	.05	.02	.01
☐ 341 Carlos Maldonado	.05	.02	.01
☐ 342 Andy McGaffigan	.05	.02	.01
☐ 343 Bobby Moore	.05	.02	.01
☐ 344 Harvey Pulliam	.05	.02	.01
☐ 345 Daryl Smith	.05	.02	.01
☐ 346 Tim Spehr	.05	.02	.01
☐ 347 Hector Wagner	.05	.02	.01
☐ 348 Paul Zuvella	.05	.02	.01
☐ 349 Sal Rende MGR	.05	.02	.01
☐ 350 Coaches	.05	.02	.01
Brian Poldberg			
Guy Hansen			
☐ 351 Luis Aguayo	.05	.02	.01
☐ 352 Tom Barrett	.05	.02	.01
☐ 353 Mike Brumley	.05	.02	.01
☐ 354 Scott Cooper	.05	.02	.01
☐ 355 Mike Gardiner	.05	.02	.01
☐ 356 Eric Hetzel	.05	.02	.01
☐ 357 Mike Twardoski	.05	.02	.01
☐ 358 Rick Lancellotti	.05	.02	.01
☐ 359 Derek Livernois	.05	.02	.01
☐ 360 Mark Meleski	.05	.02	.01
☐ 361 Kevin Morton	.05	.02	.01
☐ 362 Dan O'Neill	.05	.02	.01
☐ 363 Jim Pankovits	.05	.02	.01
☐ 364 Mickey Pina	.05	.02	.01
☐ 365 Phil Plantier	.10	.05	.01
☐ 366 Jeff Plympton	.05	.02	.01
☐ 367 Todd Pratt	.05	.02	.01
☐ 368 Larry Shikles	.05	.02	.01
☐ 369 Jeff Stone	.05	.02	.01
☐ 370 Mo Vaughn	5.00	2.20	.60
☐ 371 David Walters	.05	.02	.01
☐ 372 Eric Wedge	.05	.02	.01
☐ 373 Bob Zupcic	.05	.02	.01
☐ 374 Butch Hobson MGR	.05	.02	.01
☐ 375 Rich Gale	.05	.02	.01
☐ 376 Rich Aldrete	.05	.02	.01
☐ 377 Mark Bailey	.05	.02	.01
☐ 378 Rod Beck	.15	.07	.02

- ☐ 379 Jeff Carter .05 .02 .01
- ☐ 380 Craig Colbert .05 .02 .01
- ☐ 381 Darnell Coles .05 .02 .01
- ☐ 382 Mark Dewey .05 .02 .01
- ☐ 383 Gil Heredia .05 .02 .01
- ☐ 384 Darren Lewis .15 .07 .02
- ☐ 385 Johnny Ard .05 .02 .01
- ☐ 386 Rafael Novoa .05 .02 .01
- ☐ 387 Francisco Oliveras .05 .02 .01
- ☐ 388 Tony Perezchica .05 .02 .01
- ☐ 389 Mark Thurmond .05 .02 .01
- ☐ 390 Mike Remlinger .05 .02 .01
- ☐ 391 Greg Ritchie .05 .02 .01
- ☐ 392 Rick Rodriguez .05 .02 .01
- ☐ 393 Andres Santana .05 .02 .01
- ☐ 394 Jose Segura .05 .02 .01
- ☐ 395 Stuart Tate .05 .02 .01
- ☐ 396 Jimmy Williams .05 .02 .01
- ☐ 397 Jim Wilson .05 .02 .01
- ☐ 398 Ted Wood .05 .02 .01
- ☐ 399 Duane Espy MGR .05 .02 .01
- ☐ 400 Coaches .05 .02 .01
  Alan Bannister
  Larry Hardy
- ☐ 401 Paul Abbott .05 .02 .01
- ☐ 402 Willie Banks .05 .02 .01
- ☐ 403 Bernardo Brito .05 .02 .01
- ☐ 404 Jarvis Brown .05 .02 .01
- ☐ 405 J.T. Bruett .05 .02 .01
- ☐ 406 Tim Drummond .05 .02 .01
- ☐ 407 Tom Edens .05 .02 .01
- ☐ 408 Rich Garces .05 .02 .01
- ☐ 409 Chip Hale .05 .02 .01
- ☐ 410 Terry Jorgensen .05 .02 .01
- ☐ 411 Kenny Morgan .05 .02 .01
- ☐ 412 Pedro Munoz .05 .02 .01
- ☐ 413 Edgar Naveda .05 .02 .01
- ☐ 414 Denny Neagle .25 .11 .03
- ☐ 415 Jeff Reboulet .05 .02 .01
- ☐ 416 Victor Rodriguez .05 .02 .01
- ☐ 417 Jack Savage .05 .02 .01
- ☐ 418 Dan Sheaffer .05 .02 .01
- ☐ 419 Charles Scott .05 .02 .01
- ☐ 420 Paul Sorento .15 .07 .02
- ☐ 421 George Tsamis .05 .02 .01
- ☐ 422 Lenny Webster .05 .02 .01
- ☐ 423 Carl Willis .05 .02 .01
- ☐ 424 Russ Nixon MGR .05 .02 .01
- ☐ 425 Coaches .05 .02 .01
  Jim Dwyer
  Gorman Heimueller
  Paul Kirsch
- ☐ 426 John Alva .05 .02 .01
- ☐ 427 Mike Bell .05 .02 .01
- ☐ 428 Tony Castillo .05 .02 .01
- ☐ 429 Bruce Crabbe .05 .02 .01
- ☐ 430 John Davis .05 .02 .01
- ☐ 431 Brian R. Hunter .05 .02 .01
- ☐ 432 Randy Kramer .05 .02 .01
- ☐ 433 Mike Loggins .05 .02 .01
- ☐ 434 Kelly Mann .05 .02 .01
- ☐ 435 Tom McCarthy .05 .02 .01
- ☐ 436 Yorkis Perez .05 .02 .01
- ☐ 437 Dale Polley .05 .02 .01
- ☐ 438 Armando Reynoso .05 .02 .01
- ☐ 439 Rusty Richards .05 .02 .01
- ☐ 440 Victor Rosario .05 .02 .01
- ☐ 441 Mark Ross .05 .02 .01
- ☐ 442 Rico Rossy .05 .02 .01
- ☐ 443 Randy St. Claire .05 .02 .01
- ☐ 444 Joe Szekely .05 .02 .01
- ☐ 445 Andy Tomberlin .05 .02 .01
- ☐ 446 Matt Turner .05 .02 .01
- ☐ 447 Glenn Wilson .05 .02 .01
- ☐ 448 Tracy Woodson .05 .02 .01
- ☐ 449 Phil Niekro MGR .05 .02 .01
- ☐ 450 Coaches .05 .02 .01
  Bruce Dal Canton
  Sonny Jackson
- ☐ 451 Tony Chance .05 .02 .01
- ☐ 452 Joaquin Contreras .05 .02 .01
- ☐ 453 Francisco DeLaRosa .05 .02 .01
- ☐ 454 Benny Distefano .05 .02 .01
- ☐ 455 Mike Eberle .05 .02 .01
- ☐ 456 Todd Frohwirth .05 .02 .01
- ☐ 457 Steve Jeltz .05 .02 .01
- ☐ 458 Chito Martinez .05 .02 .01
- ☐ 459 Dave Martinez .05 .02 .01
- ☐ 460 Jeff McKnight .05 .02 .01
- ☐ 461 Luis Mercedes .05 .02 .01
- ☐ 462 Mike Mussina 1.50 .70 .19
- ☐ 463 Chris Myers .05 .02 .01
- ☐ 464 Joe Price .05 .02 .01
- ☐ 465 Israel Sanchez .05 .02 .01
- ☐ 466 David Segui .10 .05 .01
- ☐ 467 Tommy Shields .05 .02 .01
- ☐ 468 Mike Linskey .05 .02 .01
- ☐ 469 Jack Tackett .05 .02 .01
- ☐ 470 Anthony Telford .05 .02 .01
- ☐ 471 Shane Turner .05 .02 .01
- ☐ 472 Jeff Wetherby .05 .02 .01
- ☐ 473 Rob Woodward .05 .02 .01
- ☐ 474 Greg Biagini MGR .05 .02 .01
- ☐ 475 Coaches .05 .02 .01
  Mike Young
  Dick Bosman
- ☐ 476 Sal Agostinelli .05 .02 .01
- ☐ 477 Gary Alexander .05 .02 .01
- ☐ 478 Andy Ashby .10 .05 .01
- ☐ 479 Bob Ayrault .05 .02 .01
- ☐ 480 Kim Batiste .05 .02 .01
- ☐ 481 Amalio Carreno .05 .02 .01
- ☐ 482 Rocky Elli .05 .02 .01
- ☐ 483 Darrin Fletcher .05 .02 .01
- ☐ 484 Jeff Grotewold .05 .02 .01
- ☐ 485 Chris Knabenshue .05 .02 .01
- ☐ 486 Greg Legg .05 .02 .01
- ☐ 487 Jim Lindeman .05 .02 .01
- ☐ 488 Chuck Malone .05 .02 .01
- ☐ 489 Tim Mauser .05 .02 .01
- ☐ 490 Louie Meadows .05 .02 .01
- ☐ 491 Mickey Morandini .10 .05 .01
- ☐ 492 Julio Peguero .05 .02 .01
- ☐ 493 Wally Ritchie .05 .02 .01
- ☐ 494 Bruce Ruffin .05 .02 .01
- ☐ 495 Rick Schu .05 .02 .01
- ☐ 496 Ray Searage .05 .02 .01
- ☐ 497 Scott Wade .05 .02 .01
- ☐ 498 Gary Wilson .05 .02 .01
- ☐ 499 Bill Dancy MGR .05 .02 .01
- ☐ 500 Coaches .05 .02 .01
  Floyd Rayford
  Jim Wright
- ☐ 501 Derek Bell .60 .25 .07
- ☐ 502 Rob Ducey .05 .02 .01
- ☐ 503 Julius McDougal .05 .02 .01
- ☐ 504 Juan Guzman .20 .09 .03
- ☐ 505 Pat Hentgen .25 .11 .03
- ☐ 506 Shawn Jeter .05 .02 .01
- ☐ 507 Doug Linton .05 .02 .01
- ☐ 508 Bob MacDonald .05 .02 .01
- ☐ 509 Mike Maksudian .05 .02 .01
- ☐ 510 Ravelo Manzanillo .05 .02 .01
- ☐ 511 Domingo Martinez .05 .02 .01
- ☐ 512 Stu Pederson .05 .02 .01
- ☐ 513 Marty Pevey .05 .02 .01
- ☐ 514 Tom Quinlan .05 .02 .01
- ☐ 515 Alex Sanchez .05 .02 .01
- ☐ 516 Jerry Schunk .05 .02 .01
- ☐ 517 John Shea .05 .02 .01
- ☐ 518 Ed Sprague .15 .07 .02
- ☐ 519 William Suero .05 .02 .01
- ☐ 520 Steve Wapnick .05 .02 .01
- ☐ 521 Mickey Weston .05 .02 .01
- ☐ 522 John Poloni .05 .02 .01
- ☐ 523 Eddie Zosky .05 .02 .01
- ☐ 524 Bob Bailor MGR .05 .02 .01
- ☐ 525 Rocket Wheeler CO .05 .02 .01
- ☐ 526 Troy Afenir .05 .02 .01
- ☐ 527 Mike Bordick .10 .05 .01
- ☐ 528 Jorge Brito .05 .02 .01
- ☐ 529 Scott Brosius .10 .05 .01
- ☐ 530 Kevin Campbell .05 .02 .01
- ☐ 531 Pete Coachman .05 .02 .01
- ☐ 532 Dan Eskew .05 .02 .01
- ☐ 533 Eric Fox .05 .02 .01
- ☐ 534 Apolinar Garcia .05 .02 .01
- ☐ 535 Webster Garrison .05 .02 .01
- ☐ 536 Johnny Guzman .05 .02 .01
- ☐ 537 Jeff Pico .05 .02 .01
- ☐ 538 Dann Howitt .05 .02 .01
- ☐ 539 Doug Jennings .05 .02 .01
- ☐ 540 Brad Komminsk .05 .02 .01
- ☐ 541 Tim McCoy .05 .02 .01
- ☐ 542 Jeff Musselman .05 .02 .01
- ☐ 543 Troy Neel .05 .02 .01
- ☐ 544 Will Schock .05 .02 .01
- ☐ 545 Nelson Simmons .05 .02 .01
- ☐ 546 Bruce Walton .05 .02 .01
- ☐ 547 Pat Wernig .05 .02 .01
- ☐ 548 Ron Witmeyer .05 .02 .01
- ☐ 549 Jeff Newman MGR .05 .02 .01
- ☐ 550 Glenn Abbott CO .05 .02 .01
- ☐ 551 Kevin Baez .05 .02 .01
- ☐ 552 Blaine Beatty .05 .02 .01
- ☐ 553 Doug Cinnella .05 .02 .01
- ☐ 554 Chris Donnels .05 .02 .01
- ☐ 555 Jeff Gardner .05 .02 .01
- ☐ 556 Terrel Hansen .05 .02 .01
- ☐ 557 Manny Hernandez .05 .02 .01
- ☐ 558 Eric Hillman .05 .02 .01
- ☐ 559 Todd Hundley 2.00 .90 .25
- ☐ 560 Alex Jimenez .05 .02 .01
- ☐ 561 Tim Leiper .05 .02 .01
- ☐ 562 Lee May Jr. .05 .02 .01
- ☐ 563 Orlando Mercado .05 .02 .01
- ☐ 564 Brad Moore .05 .02 .01
- ☐ 565 Al Pedrique .05 .02 .01
- ☐ 566 Dale Plummer .05 .02 .01
- ☐ 567 Rich Sauveur .05 .02 .01
- ☐ 568 Ray Soff .05 .02 .01
- ☐ 569 Kelvin Torve .05 .02 .01
- ☐ 570 Dave Trautwein .05 .02 .01
- ☐ 571 Julio Valera .05 .02 .01
- ☐ 572 Robbie Wine .05 .02 .01
- ☐ 573 Anthony Young .05 .02 .01
- ☐ 574 Steve Swisher MGR .05 .02 .01
- ☐ 575 Coaches .05 .02 .01
  Ron Washington
  Bob Apodaca
- ☐ 576 Scott Aldred .05 .02 .01
- ☐ 577 Karl Allaire .05 .02 .01
- ☐ 578 Skeeter Barnes .05 .02 .01
- ☐ 579 Arnie Beyeler .05 .02 .01
- ☐ 580 Rico Brogna .10 .05 .01
- ☐ 581 Phil Clark .05 .02 .01
- ☐ 582 Mike Dalton .05 .02 .01
- ☐ 583 Curt Ford .05 .02 .01
- ☐ 584 Dan Gakeler .05 .02 .01
- ☐ 585 David Haas .05 .02 .01
- ☐ 586 Shawn Hare .05 .02 .01
- ☐ 587 John Kiely .05 .02 .01
- ☐ 588 Mark Leiter .05 .02 .01
- ☐ 589 Scott Livingstone .05 .02 .01
- ☐ 590 Mitch Lyden .05 .02 .01
- ☐ 591 Eric Mangham .05 .02 .01
- ☐ 592 Rusty Meacham .05 .02 .01
- ☐ 593 Mike Munoz .05 .02 .01
- ☐ 594 Randy Nosek .05 .02 .01
- ☐ 595 Johnny Paredes .05 .02 .01
- ☐ 596 Kevin Ritz .15 .07 .02
- ☐ 597 Rich Rowland .05 .02 .01
- ☐ 598 Don Vesling .05 .02 .01
- ☐ 599 Joe Sparks .05 .02 .01
- ☐ 600 Coaches .05 .02 .01
  Mark Wagner
  Ralph Treuel
- ☐ 601 Harold Allen .05 .02 .01
- ☐ 602 Eric Anthony .05 .02 .01
- ☐ 603 Doug Baker .05 .02 .01
- ☐ 604 Ryan Bowen .05 .02 .01
- ☐ 605 Mike Capel .05 .02 .01
- ☐ 606 Andujar Cedeno .05 .02 .01
- ☐ 607 Terry Clark .05 .02 .01
- ☐ 608 Carlo Colombino .05 .02 .01
- ☐ 609 Gary Cooper .05 .02 .01
- ☐ 610 Calvin Schiraldi .05 .02 .01
- ☐ 611 Randy Hennis .05 .02 .01
- ☐ 612 Butch Henry .05 .02 .01
- ☐ 613 Blaise Ilsley .05 .02 .01
- ☐ 614 Kenny Lofton 1.50 .70 .19
- ☐ 615 Terry McGriff .05 .02 .01
- ☐ 616 Andy Mota .05 .02 .01
- ☐ 617 Javier Ortiz .05 .02 .01
- ☐ 618 Scott Servais .05 .02 .01
- ☐ 619 Mike Simms .05 .02 .01
- ☐ 620 Jose Tolentino .05 .02 .01
- ☐ 621 Lee Tunnell .05 .02 .01
- ☐ 622 Brent Strom .05 .02 .01
- ☐ 623 Gerald Young .05 .02 .01
- ☐ 624 Bob Skinner MGR .05 .02 .01
- ☐ 625 Dave Engle CO .05 .02 .01
- ☐ 626 Cesar Bernhardt .05 .02 .01
- ☐ 627 Mario Brito .05 .02 .01
- ☐ 628 Kurt Brown .05 .02 .01
- ☐ 629 John Cangelosi .05 .02 .01
- ☐ 630 Jeff Carter .05 .02 .01
- ☐ 631 Tom Drees .05 .02 .01
- ☐ 632 Grady Hall .05 .02 .01
- ☐ 633 Joe Hall .05 .02 .01
- ☐ 634 Curt Hasler .05 .02 .01
- ☐ 635 Danny Heep .05 .02 .01
- ☐ 636 Dan Henley .05 .02 .01
- ☐ 637 Roberto Hernandez .10 .05 .01
- ☐ 638 Orsino Hill .05 .02 .01
- ☐ 639 Jerry Kutzler .05 .02 .01
- ☐ 640 Norberto Martin .05 .02 .01
- ☐ 641 Rod McCray .05 .02 .01
- ☐ 642 Rob Nelson .05 .02 .01
- ☐ 643 Warren Newson .05 .02 .01
- ☐ 644 Greg Perschke .05 .02 .01
- ☐ 645 Rich Scheid .05 .02 .01
- ☐ 646 Matt Stark .05 .02 .01
- ☐ 647 Ron Stephens .05 .02 .01
- ☐ 648 Don Wakamatsu .05 .02 .01
- ☐ 649 Marv Foley MGR .05 .02 .01
- ☐ 650 Coaches .05 .02 .01
  Roger LaFrancois
  Moe Drabowsky

1991 London Tigers Line Drive

	MINT	NRMT	EXC
COMPLETE SET (26)	5.00	2.20	.60

- ☐ 376 Doyle Balthazar
- ☐ 377 Basilio Cabrera
- ☐ 378 Ron Cook
- ☐ 379 Ivan Cruz
- ☐ 380 Dean Decillis
- ☐ 381 John DeSilva
- ☐ 382 John Doherty
- ☐ 383 Lou Frazier
- ☐ 384 Luis Galindo
- ☐ 385 Greg Gohr
- ☐ 386 Bud Groom
- ☐ 387 Darren Hursey
- ☐ 388 Riccardo Ingram
- ☐ 389 Keith Kimberlin
- ☐ 390 Todd Krumm
- ☐ 391 Randy Marshall
- ☐ 392 Domingo Michel
- ☐ 393 Steve Pegues
- ☐ 394 Jose Ramos
- ☐ 395 Bob Reimink
- ☐ 396 Ruben Rodriguez
- ☐ 397 Eric Stone
- ☐ 398 Marty Willis
- ☐ 399 Gene Roof MGR
- ☐ 400 Jeff Jones CO
  Dan Raley CO
- ☐ NNO Title card

1991 London Tigers ProCards

This 27-card standard-size set of the 1991 London Tigers, a Class AA Eastern League affiliate of the Detroit Tigers, features on its white-bordered fronts posed color player photos set on simulated spiral-bound yellow notebooks. The player's name, position, and team appear within a green rectangle below the photo. The yellow horizontal back is bordered in white and carries the player's name at the top, followed by biography and statistics.

	MINT	NRMT	EXC
COMPLETE SET (27)	5.00	2.20	.60

- ☐ 1869 John DeSilva
- ☐ 1870 John Doherty
- ☐ 1871 Greg Gohr
- ☐ 1872 Buddy Groom
- ☐ 1873 Darren Hursey
- ☐ 1874 Kurt Knudsen
  Card numbered #2232
- ☐ 1875 Todd Krumm
- ☐ 1876 Randy Marshall
- ☐ 1877 Jose Ramos
- ☐ 1878 Eric Stone
- ☐ 1879 Marty Willis
- ☐ 1880 Doyle Balthazar
- ☐ 1881 Ruben Rodriguez
- ☐ 1882 Ivan Cruz
- ☐ 1883 Dean Decillis
- ☐ 1884 Luis Galindo
- ☐ 1885 Keith Kimberlin
- ☐ 1886 Domingo Michel
- ☐ 1887 Bob Reimink
- ☐ 1888 Basilio Cabrera
- ☐ 1889 Lou Frazier
- ☐ 1890 Riccardo Ingram
- ☐ 1891 Steve Pegues
- ☐ 1892 Gene Roof MGR
- ☐ 1893 Jeff Jones CO
- ☐ 1894 Dan Raley CO
- ☐ 2232 Checklist

1991 Louisville Redbirds Line Drive

	MINT	NRMT	EXC
COMPLETE SET (26)	10.00	4.50	1.25

- ☐ 226 Luis Alicea
- ☐ 227 Rod Brewer
- ☐ 228 Nick Castaneda
- ☐ 229 Stan Clarke
- ☐ 230 Marty Clary
- ☐ 231 Fidel Compres
- ☐ 232 Todd Crosby
- ☐ 233 Bob Davidson
- ☐ 234 Bien Figueroa
- ☐ 235 Ed Fulton
- ☐ 236 Mark Grater
- ☐ 237 Omar Olivares
- ☐ 238 Brian Jordan
- ☐ 239 Lonnie Maclin
- ☐ 240 Julian Martinez
- ☐ 241 Al Nipper
- ☐ 242 Dave Osteen
- ☐ 243 Leny Picota
- ☐ 244 Dave Richardson
- ☐ 245 Mike Ross
- ☐ 246 Stan Royer
- ☐ 247 Tim Sherrill
- ☐ 248 Carl Ray Stephens
- ☐ 249 Mark DeJohn MGR
- ☐ 250 Mark Riggins CO
- ☐ NNO Title card

1991 Louisville Redbirds ProCards

This 29-card standard-size set of the 1991 Louisville Redbirds, a Class AAA American Association affiliate of the Louisville Redbirds, features on its white-bordered fronts posed color player photos set on simulated spiral-bound yellow notebooks. The player's name, position, and team appear within a green rectangle below the photo. The yellow horizontal back is bordered in white and carries the player's name at the top, followed by biography and statistics. This issue includes the second year card of Brian Jordan.

	MINT	NRMT	EXC
COMPLETE SET (29)	10.00	4.50	1.25

- ☐ 2906 Marty Clary
- ☐ 2907 Rheal Cormier
- ☐ 2908 Bob Davidson
- ☐ 2909 Mark Grater
- ☐ 2910 Mike Milchin
- ☐ 2911 Al Nipper
- ☐ 2912 Omar Olivares

☐ 2913 Dave Osteen
☐ 2914 Len Picota
☐ 2915 Dave Richardson
☐ 2916 Ed Fulton
☐ 2917 Scott Nichols
☐ 2918 Ray Stephens
☐ 2919 Luis Alicea
☐ 2920 Greg Carmona
☐ 2921 Nick Castaneda
☐ 2922 Todd Crosby
☐ 2923 Bien Figueroa
☐ 2924 Stan Royer
☐ 2925 Rod Brewer
☐ 2926 Joey Fernandez
☐ 2927 Brian Jordan
☐ 2928 Lonnie Maclin
☐ 2929 Julian Martinez
☐ 2930 Jesus Mendez
☐ 2931 Mike Ross
☐ 2932 Mark DeJohn MGR
☐ 2933 Mark Riggins CO
☐ 2934 Checklist

1991 Louisville Redbirds Team Issue

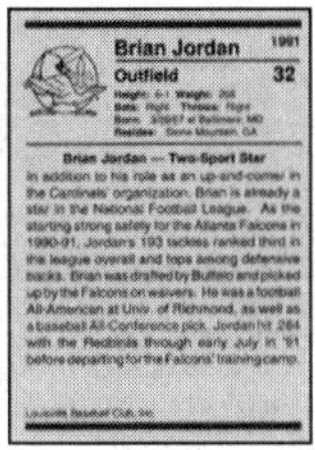

	MINT	NRMT	EXC
COMPLETE SET (34)	40.00	18.00	5.00

☐ 1 Checklist
Billy Bird (Mascot)
☐ 2 Mark Clark
☐ 3 Omar Olivares
☐ 4 Ken Hill
☐ 5 Rheal Cormier
☐ 6 Tim Sherrill
☐ 7 Mark Grater
☐ 8 Jamie Moyer
☐ 9 Mike Milchin
☐ 10 Mike Hinkle
☐ 11 Mike Loynd
☐ 12 Mike Perez
☐ 13 Todd Worrell
☐ 14 Rod Brewer
☐ 15 Joey Fernandez
☐ 16 Pedro Guerrero
☐ 17 Luis Alicea
☐ 18 Todd Crosby
☐ 19 Tim Jones
☐ 20 Bien Figueroa
☐ 21 Greg Carmona
☐ 22 Stan Royer
☐ 23 Bernard Gilkey
☐ 24 Brian Jordan
☐ 25 Lonnie Maclin
☐ 26 Julian Martinez
☐ 27 Ray Stephens
☐ 28 Ed Fulton
☐ 29 Scott Nichols
☐ 30 Mark DeJohn
☐ 31 Mark Riggins
☐ 32 Brian Jordan
☐ 33 1991 Triple-A All Stars
National League
☐ 34 1991 Triple-A All Stars
American League

1991 LSU Tigers Police

This 16-card standard-size set was sponsored by law enforcement agencies in conjunction with other sponsors in honor of the 1991 NCAA National Champion LSU Tigers. Production quantities were limited to 5,000 sets. The fronts have color action photos, accented in purple on mustard-colored borders. A banner with the words "National Champions" overlays the upper left corner of the picture, and the sponsors' logos appear across the card bottom. The backs have either a caption to the picture or player profile, as well as "Tips from the National Champions" in the form of anti-drug and alcohol messages.

	MINT	NRMT	EXC
COMPLETE SET (16)	10.00	4.50	1.25

☐ 1 NCAA Championship
Rosenblatt Stadium
June 8, 1991
☐ 2 Team Celebration
☐ 3 Skip Bertman CO
☐ 4 Pat Garrity
☐ 5 Tookie Johnson
☐ 6 Johnny Tellechea
☐ 7 Gary Hymel
☐ 8 Rich Cordani
☐ 9 Mark LaRosa
☐ 10 The Tiger Fans
☐ 11 1991 NCAA South
Regional Game
☐ 12 Bayou Bombers
Gary Hymel
Lyle Mouton
☐ 13 Lyle Mouton
☐ 14 Paul Byrd
☐ 15 Chad Ogea
☐ 16 College World Series
May 31, 1991

1991 Lynchburg Red Sox Classic/Best

This 29-card standard-size set of the 1991 Lynchburg Red Sox, a Class A Carolina League affiliate of the Boston Red Sox, features white-bordered posed color player photos on its fronts. The player's name, team, and position appear at the bottom. The white back is framed by a thin black line and carries the player's name and position at the top, followed by biography, statistics and team logos.

	MINT	NRMT	EXC
COMPLETE SET (29)	5.00	2.20	.60

☐ 1 Dale Brugo
☐ 2 Jim Dennison
☐ 3 Gar Finnvold
☐ 4 Brad Hoyer
☐ 5 Tony Mosley
☐ 6 Erik Plantenberg
☐ 7 Ed Riley
☐ 8 Rennie Scott
☐ 9 Tim Smith
☐ 10 Kevin Uhrhan
☐ 11 Denny Berni
☐ 12 Joe Luis
☐ 13 Craig Wilson
☐ 14 Scott Bethea
☐ 15 James Byrd
☐ 16 Alex Delgado
☐ 17 Bill Norris
☐ 18 Willie Tatum
☐ 19 Gary Villalobos
☐ 20 Bruce Chick
☐ 21 Chris Leach
☐ 22 Jeff McNeely
☐ 23 Boo Moore
☐ 24 Jose Zambrano
☐ 25 Buddy Bailey MGR
☐ 26 Jim Bibby CO
☐ 27 David Duchin TR
☐ 28 Andy Rush
☐ 29 Checklist

1991 Lynchburg Red Sox ProCards

This 28-card standard-size set of the 1991 Lynchburg Red Sox, a Class A Carolina League affiliate of the Boston Red Sox, features on its white-bordered fronts posed color player photos set on simulated spiral-bound yellow notebooks. The player's name, position, and team appear within a green rectangle below the photo. The yellow horizontal back is bordered in white and carries the player's name at the top, followed by biography and statistics.

	MINT	NRMT	EXC
COMPLETE SET (28)	5.00	2.20	.60

☐ 1190 Dale Burgo
☐ 1191 Jim Dennison
☐ 1192 Gar Finnvold
☐ 1193 Brad Hoyer
☐ 1194 Tony Mosley
☐ 1195 Erik Plantenberg
☐ 1196 Ed Riley
☐ 1197 Andy Rush
☐ 1198 Rennie Scott
☐ 1199 Tim Smith
☐ 1200 Kevin Uhrhan
☐ 1201 Denny Berni
☐ 1202 Joe Luis
☐ 1203 Craig Wilson
☐ 1204 Scott Bethea
☐ 1205 Jim Byrd
☐ 1206 Alex Delgado
☐ 1207 Bill Norris
☐ 1208 Willie Tatum
☐ 1209 Gary Villalobos
☐ 1210 Bruce Chick
☐ 1211 Chris Leach
☐ 1212 Jeff McNeely
☐ 1213 Boo Moore
☐ 1214 Jose Zambrano
☐ 1215 Buddy Bailey MGR
☐ 1216 Jim Bibby CO
☐ 1217 Checklist

1991 Macon Braves Classic/Best

This 30-card standard-size set of the 1991 Macon Braves, a Class A South Atlantic League affiliate of the Atlanta Braves, features white-

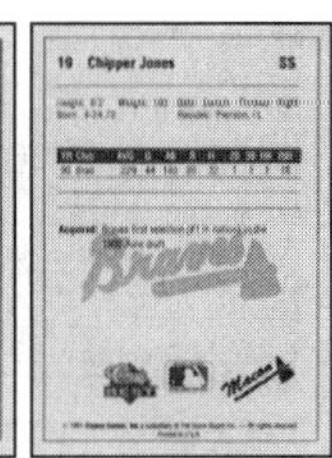

bordered posed color player photos on its fronts. The player's name, team, and position appear near the bottom. The white back is framed by a black line and carries the player's name and position at the top, followed by biography and statistics. This issue includes the minor league card debut of Chipper Jones.

	MINT	NRMT	EXC
COMPLETE SET (30)	30.00	13.50	3.70

☐ 1 Barry Chiles
☐ 2 Earl Jewett
☐ 3 Thomas Leahy
☐ 4 Ray Mack
☐ 5 Don Mattson
☐ 6 Keith Morrison
☐ 7 Darren Ritter
☐ 8 Joe Roa
☐ 9 Shawn Rohrwild
☐ 10 Glenn Hubbard CO
☐ 11 Marcos Vazquez
☐ 12 Henry Werland
☐ 13 David Williams
☐ 14 Marek Drabinski
☐ 15 Wallace Gonzalez
☐ 16 Tyler Houston
☐ 17 Grant Brittain
☐ 18 Brian Snitker CO
☐ 19 Chipper Jones
☐ 20 Rick Karcher
☐ 21 Jose Dimeda
☐ 22 Geoff Orr
☐ 23 Lee Heath
☐ 24 Troy Hughes
☐ 25 Kevin O'Connor
☐ 26 Raul Robinson
☐ 27 Juan Williams
☐ 28 Roy Majtyka MGR
☐ 29 Matt West CO
☐ 30 Checklist

1991 Macon Braves ProCards

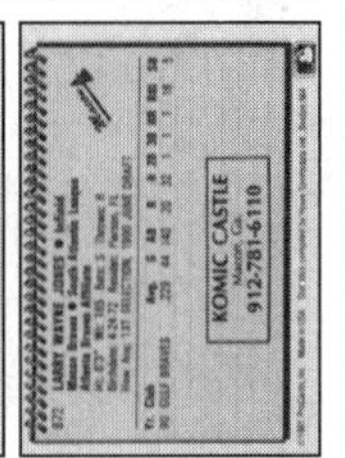

This 31-card standard-size set of the 1991 Macon Braves, a Class A South Atlantic League affiliate of the Atlanta Braves, features on its white-bordered fronts posed color player photos set on simulated spiral-bound yellow notebooks. The player's name, position, and team appear within a green rectangle below the photo. The yellow horizontal back is bordered in white and carries the player's name and position at the top, followed by biography and statistics. This issue includes the minor league card debut of Chipper Jones.

	MINT	NRMT	EXC
COMPLETE SET (31)	25.00	11.00	3.10

☐ 855 Barry Chiles
☐ 856 Earl Jewett
☐ 857 Tom Leahy
☐ 858 Ray Mack
☐ 859 Rob Mattson
☐ 860 Keith Morrison
☐ 861 Darren Ritter
☐ 862 Joe Roa
☐ 863 Shawn Rohrwild
☐ 864 Marcos Vazquez
☐ 865 Henry Werland
☐ 866 David Williams
☐ 867 Marek Drabinski
☐ 868 Wallace Gonzalez
☐ 869 Tyler Houston
☐ 870 Grant Brittain
☐ 871 Loren Gress
☐ 872 Chipper Jones
☐ 873 Rick Karcher
☐ 874 Jose Olmeda
☐ 875 Geoff Orr
☐ 876 Lee Heath
☐ 877 Troy Hughes
☐ 878 Kevin O'Connor
☐ 879 Raul Robinson
☐ 880 Juan Williams
☐ 881 Roy Majtyka MGR
☐ 882 Glenn Hubbard CO
☐ 883 Brian Snitker CO
☐ 884 Matt West CO
☐ 885 Checklist

1991 Madison Muskies Classic/Best

This 30-card standard-size set of the 1991 Madison Muskies, a Class A Midwest League affiliate of the Oakland Athletics, features white-bordered posed color player photos on its fronts. The player's name, team, and position appear at the bottom. The white back is framed by a thin black line and carries the player's name and position at the top, followed by biography, statistics and team logos.

	MINT	NRMT	EXC
COMPLETE SET (30)	5.00	2.20	.60

☐ 1 Todd Russell
☐ 2 Tanyon Sturtze
☐ 3 Craig Sudbury
☐ 4 Michael Grimes
☐ 5 Bradley Brimhall
☐ 6 Craig Connolly
☐ 7 James Dillon
☐ 8 William Gulledge
☐ 9 Douglas Johns
☐ 10 Scott McCarty
☐ 11 Leandro Mejia
☐ 12 Eric Myers
☐ 13 Scott Budner
☐ 14 Malcolm Shaw
☐ 15 Brett Hendley
☐ 16 Islay Molina
☐ 17 Scott Henry
☐ 18 Ernest Young
☐ 19 Gregory Reid
☐ 20 Donald Lydy
☐ 21 Shane Borchert
☐ 22 Gary Jones MGR
☐ 23 Luis Lanfranco
☐ 24 Carlos Hernandez
☐ 25 Robert Carisen
☐ 26 William Picketts
☐ 27 Rafael Mercado
☐ 28 Lee Sammons
☐ 29 Checklist
☐ NNO Team Logo

1991 Madison Muskies ProCards

This 27-card standard-size set of the 1991 Madison Muskies, a Class A Midwest League affiliate of the Oakland Athletics, features on its white-bordered fronts posed color player photos set on simulated spiral-bound yellow notebooks. The player's name, position, and team appear within a green rectangle below the photo. The yellow horizontal back is bordered in white and carries the player's name at the top, followed by biography and statistics.

	MINT	NRMT	EXC
COMPLETE SET (27)	5.00	2.20	.60

☐ 2122 Brad Brimhall
☐ 2123 Craig Connolly
☐ 2124 Jim Dillon
☐ 2125 Hugh Gulledge
☐ 2126 Doug Johns
☐ 2127 Scott McCarty
☐ 2128 Leandro Mejia
☐ 2129 Eric Myers
☐ 2130 Todd Revenig
☐ 2131 Gary Ross
☐ 2132 Curt Shaw
☐ 2133 Tanyon Sturtze
☐ 2134 Brett Hendley
☐ 2135 Scott Henry
☐ 2136 Islay Molina
☐ 2137 Robert Carlsen
☐ 2138 Carlos Hernandez
☐ 2139 Luis Lanfranco
☐ 2140 Rafael Mercado
☐ 2141 Bill Picketts
☐ 2142 Scott Lydy
☐ 2143 Greg Reid
☐ 2144 Keith Thomas
☐ 2145 Ernie Young
☐ 2146 Gary Jones MGR
☐ 2147 Scott Budner CO
☐ 2148 Checklist

1991 Martinsville Phillies Classic/Best

This 30-card standard-size set of the 1991 Martinsville Phillies, a Rookie Class Appalachian League affiliate of the Philadelphia Phillies, features white-bordered posed color player photos on its fronts. The player's name, team, and position appear at the bottom. The white back is framed by a thin black line and carries the player's name and position at the top, followed by biography, statistics and team logos.

	MINT	NRMT	EXC
COMPLETE SET (30)	5.00	2.20	.60

☐ 1 Mike Murphy
☐ 2 Eric Mauldin
☐ 3 Dan Larson
☐ 4 Wayne Johnson
☐ 5 Reynaldo DeLosSantos
☐ 6 Jason Urbanek
☐ 7 Andy Sallee
☐ 8 Johnny Mallee
☐ 9 Joey Jelinek
☐ 10 Carlton Hardy
☐ 11 Phillip Geisler
☐ 12 Lamar Cherry
☐ 13 Luis Brito
☐ 14 Brent Bell
☐ 15 Porfirio Pena
☐ 16 Gary Bennett
☐ 17 Dean Hopp
☐ 18 John Salamon
☐ 19 Thane Page
☐ 20 Robert Mitchell
☐ 21 Fernando Mejias
☐ 22 John Ingram
☐ 23 Sam Edwards
☐ 24 Dominic De Santis
☐ 25 Scott Coleman
☐ 26 Dan Brown
☐ 27 Chad Anderson
☐ 28 Juan Alexis
☐ 29 Roly DeArmas MGR
☐ 30 Mike Townsend TR
Checklist

1991 Martinsville Phillies ProCards

This 31-card standard-size set of the 1991 Martinsville Phillies, a Rookie Class Appalachian League affiliate of the Philadelphia Phillies, features on its white-bordered fronts posed color player photos set on simulated spiral-bound yellow notebooks. The player's name, position, and team appear within a green rectangle below the photo. The yellow horizontal back is bordered in white and carries the player's name at the top, followed by biography and statistics.

	MINT	NRMT	EXC
COMPLETE SET (31)	5.00	2.20	.60

☐ 3442 Juan Alexi
☐ 3443 Chad Anderson
☐ 3444 Dan Brown
☐ 3445 Scott Coleman
☐ 3446 Dominic DeSantis
☐ 3447 Sam Edwards
☐ 3448 Joel Gilmore
☐ 3449 John Ingram
☐ 3450 Fernando Mejias
☐ 3451 Robert Mitchell
☐ 3452 Thane Page
☐ 3453 John Salamon
☐ 3454 Gary Bennett
☐ 3455 Dean Hopp
☐ 3456 Porfirio Pena
☐ 3457 Brent Bell
☐ 3458 Luis Brito
☐ 3459 Lamar Cherry
☐ 3460 Phil Geisler
☐ 3461 Carlton Hardy
☐ 3462 Joey Jelinek
☐ 3463 Johnny Mallee
☐ 3464 Andy Salee
☐ 3465 Jason Urbanek
☐ 3466 Reynaldo DeLosSantos
☐ 3467 Wayne Johnson
☐ 3468 Danny Larson
☐ 3469 Eric Mauldin
☐ 3470 Mike Murphy
☐ 3471 Eli Grba CO
☐ 3472 Checklist

1991 Medicine Hat Blue Jays ProCards

This 31-card standard-size set of the 1991 Medicine Hat Blue Jays, a Class A Pioneer League affiliate of the Toronto Blue Jays, features on its white-bordered fronts posed color player photos set on simulated spiral-bound yellow notebooks. The player's name, position, and team appear within a green rectangle below the photo. The yellow horizontal back is bordered in white and carries the player's name and position at the top, followed by biography. This issue includes the minor league card debut of Jose Herrera.

	MINT	NRMT	EXC
COMPLETE SET (31)	6.00	2.70	.75

☐ 4089 Travis Baptist
☐ 4090 Isbel Cardona
☐ 4091 Ned Darley
☐ 4092 Andrew Dolson
☐ 4093 Chris Ermis
☐ 4094 Allen Ford
☐ 4095 Freddy Lopez
☐ 4096 Jose Manuare
☐ 4097 Albert Montoya
☐ 4098 Mike O'Halloran
☐ 4099 Ken Robinson
☐ 4100 Steve Sinclair
☐ 4101 Mike Taylor
☐ 4102 John Lombardi
☐ 4103 Brent Lutz
☐ 4104 Angel Martinez
☐ 4105 D.J. Boston
☐ 4106 Felipe Crespo
☐ 4107 Ted Langowski
☐ 4108 Gabriel Rosario
☐ 4109 Hector Tavarez
☐ 4110 John Tsoukalas
☐ 4111 Matt Wilke
☐ 4112 Emenegilda Alvarez
☐ 4113 Stoney Briggs
☐ 4114 Lee Daniels
☐ 4115 Jose Herrera
☐ 4116 Jairo Ramos
☐ 4117 J.J. Cannon MG
☐ 4118 Gilbert Rondon CO
☐ 4119 Checklist

1991 Medicine Hat Blue Jays Sports Pro

This 30-card standard-size set of the 1991 Medicine Hat Blue Jays, a Class A Pioneer League affiliate of the Toronto Blue Jays, features white-bordered posed color player photos on its fronts. The team name appears above the picture; the player's name appears below. The white horizontal back is framed by a black line and carries the player's name and position followed by biography. The set was sponsored by Monarch Cable TV Ltd. and printed on thin card stock. This issue includes the minor league card debut of Jose Herrera.

	MINT	NRMT	EXC
COMPLETE SET (30)	7.00	3.10	.85

☐ 1 D.J. Boston
☐ 2 Angel Martinez
☐ 3 Jose Manuare
☐ 4 John Tsoukalas
☐ 5 Chris Ermis
☐ 6 Hector Tavarez
☐ 7 Michael Taylor
☐ 8 Jairo Ramos
☐ 9 Jose Herrera
☐ 10 Travis Baptist
☐ 11 Isbel Cardona UER
(Name misspelled Isabel on front and back)
☐ 12 Steve Sinclair
☐ 13 Freddy Lopez
☐ 14 Lee Daniels
☐ 15 Gabriel Rosario
☐ 16 Albert Montoya
☐ 17 Andrew Dolson
☐ 18 Matt Wilke
☐ 19 Ned Darley
☐ 20 William Briggs
☐ 21 Emenegilda Alvarez
☐ 22 Felipe Crespo
☐ 23 Mike O'Halloran
☐ 24 Gilbert Rondon CO
☐ 25 Geoff Horne TR
☐ 26 J.J. Cannon MG
☐ 27 Blank card
☐ 28 Blank card
☐ 29 Blank card
☐ 30 Blank card

1991 Memphis Chicks Line Drive

	MINT	NRMT	EXC
COMPLETE SET (26)	5.00	2.20	.60

☐ 401 Pete Alborano
☐ 402 Jim Baxter
☐ 403 Tony Clements
☐ 404 Archie Corbin
☐ 405 Andres Cruz
☐ 406 Jeff Garber
☐ 407 David Gonzalez
☐ 408 Kevin Koslofski
☐ 409 Deric Ladnier
☐ 410 Mark Parnell
☐ 411 Jorge Pedre
☐ 412 Doug Peters
☐ 413 Hipolito Pichardo
☐ 414 Eddie Pierce
☐ 415 Mike Poehl
☐ 416 Darryl Robinson
☐ 417 Steve Shiffett
☐ 418 Jim Smith
☐ 419 Lou Talbert
☐ 420 Terry Taylor
☐ 421 Rich Tunison
☐ 422 Hugh Walker
☐ 423 Darren Watkins
☐ 424 Jeff Cox MGR
☐ 425 Brian Peterson CO
Mike Alvarez CO
☐ NNO Title card

1991 Memphis Chicks ProCards

This 27-card standard-size set of the 1991 Memphis Chicks, a Class AA Southern League affiliate of the Kansas City Royals, features on its white-bordered fronts posed color player photos set on simulated spiral-bound yellow notebooks. The player's name, position, and team appear within a green rectangle below the photo. The yellow horizontal back is bordered in white and carries the player's name at the top, followed by biography and statistics.

	MINT	NRMT	EXC
COMPLETE SET (27)	5.00	2.20	.60

☐ 646 Archie Corbin
☐ 647 Andres Cruz
☐ 648 Mark Parnell
☐ 649 Doug Peters
☐ 650 Hipolito Richardo
☐ 651 Eddie Pierce
☐ 652 Mike Poehl
☐ 653 Steve Shifflett
☐ 654 Jim Smith
☐ 655 Lou Talbert
☐ 656 Terry Taylor
☐ 657 Jim Baxter
☐ 658 Jorge Pedre
☐ 659 Tony Bridges-Clements
☐ 660 Jeff Garber
☐ 661 David Gonzalez
☐ 662 Deric Ladnier
☐ 663 Darryl Robinson
☐ 664 Rich Tunison
☐ 665 Pete Alborano
☐ 666 Kevin Koslofski
☐ 667 Hugh Walker
☐ 668 Darren Watkins
☐ 669 Jeff Cox MGR
☐ 670 Mike Alvarez CO
☐ 671 Brian Peterson CO
☐ 672 Checklist

1991 Miami Hurricanes Bumble Bee

The University of Miami Hurricane baseball team is featured on this sheet measuring approximately 10" by 10 1/2". After perforation, the cards measure the standard size. The fronts have color action player photos, with orange borders on a green card face. The school and team name appear above in white lettering, while player information appears between the logos beneath the picture. The backs have player profile (in English and Spanish), statistics, and a "Hurricanes Just Say No to Drugs" public service message. The cards are unnumbered and checklisted below in alphabetical order.

	MINT	NRMT	EXC
COMPLETE SET (12)	12.00	5.50	1.50

☐ 1 Jeff Alkire
☐ 2 Chris Anderson
☐ 3 Todd Bush
☐ 4 Gino DiMare
☐ 5 Jorge Fabregas
☐ 6 Ron Fraser CO
☐ 7 Charles Johnson
☐ 8 Greg Knowles
☐ 9 Miami Maniac
Team Mascot
☐ 10 Jose Prado
☐ 11 Shawn Purdy
☐ 12 Mike Tosar

1991 Miami Miracle Classic/Best

This 30-card standard-size set of the 1991 Miami Miracles, a Class A Florida State League Independent, features white-bordered posed color player photos on its fronts. The player's name, team, and position appear at the bottom. The white back is framed by a thin black line and carries the player's name and position at the top, followed by biography, statistics and team logos.

	MINT	NRMT	EXC
COMPLETE SET (30)	5.00	2.20	.60

☐ 1 Fredi Gonzalez MGR
☐ 2 Will McEnaney CO
☐ 3 Rodney Nettnin
☐ 4 Billy Walker
☐ 5 Scott Asche
☐ 6 Mike Ericson
☐ 7 John Fritz
☐ 8 Jonathan Hurst
☐ 9 Tom Michno
☐ 10 Nate Minchey
☐ 11 Charlie Rodgers
☐ 12 Ken Whitworth
☐ 13 Ken Williams
☐ 14 Lee Langley
☐ 15 George Kerfut
☐ 16 Miah Bradbury
☐ 17 Andy Dziadkowiec
☐ 18 Kevin Castleberry
☐ 19 Greg D'Alexander
☐ 20 Marc Giordano
☐ 21 Mike Lansing
☐ 22 Ray Ledinsky
☐ 23 Hector Roa
☐ 24 John Urcioli
☐ 25 James Morrisette
☐ 26 Edwin Alicea
☐ 27 Chris Burton
☐ 28 Paris Hayden
☐ 29 Dennis Kidd
☐ 30 Bob Fralick CO
Checklist

1991 Miami Miracles ProCards

This 27-card standard-size set of the 1991 Miami Miracles, a Class A Florida State League Independent, features on its white-bordered fronts posed color player photos set on simulated spiral-bound yellow notebooks. The player's name, position, and team appear within a green rectangle below the photo. The yellow horizontal back is bordered in white and carries the player's name at the top, followed by biography and statistics.

	MINT	NRMT	EXC
COMPLETE SET (27)	5.00	2.20	.60

☐ 399 Scott Asche
☐ 400 Mike Ericson
☐ 401 John Fritz
☐ 402 Jonathan Hurst
☐ 403 George Kerfut
☐ 404 Lee Langley
☐ 405 Tom Michno
☐ 406 Nate Minchey
☐ 407 Charlie Rogers
☐ 408 Ken Whitworth
☐ 409 Ken Williams
☐ 410 Miah Bradbury
☐ 411 Andy Dziadkowiec
☐ 412 Kevin Castleberry
☐ 413 Greg D'Alexander
☐ 414 Marc Giordano
☐ 415 Mike Lansing
☐ 416 Ray Ledinsky
☐ 417 Hector Roa
☐ 418 John Urcioli
☐ 419 Edwin Alicea
☐ 420 Chris Burton
☐ 421 Paris Hayden
☐ 422 Dennis Kidd
☐ 423 Fredi Gonzalez MGR
☐ 424 Coaches
Bob Fralick
Will McEnaney
☐ 425 Checklist

1991 Midland Angels Line Drive

	MINT	NRMT	EXC
COMPLETE SET (26)	8.00	3.60	1.00

☐ 426 Clemente Acosta
☐ 427 Jeff Barns
☐ 428 Mike Butcher
☐ 429 Glenn Carter
☐ 430 Marvin Cobb
☐ 431 Sherman Corbett
☐ 432 Kevin Davis
☐ 433 Damion Easley
☐ 434 Kevin Flora
☐ 435 Larry Gonzales
☐ 436 Mark Howie
☐ 437 Todd James
☐ 438 Bobby Jones
☐ 439 Steve King
☐ 440 Marcus Lawton
☐ 441 Ken Rivers
☐ 442 Doug Robertson
☐ 443 Tim Salmon
☐ 444 Ramon Sambo
☐ 445 Daryl Sconiers
☐ 446 Dave Shotkoski
☐ 447 Terry Taylor
☐ 448 Mark Zappelli
☐ 449 Don Long MGR
☐ 450 Kernan Ronan CO
Gene Richards CO
☐ NNO Title card

1991 Midland Angels One Hour Photo

This 32-card set of the 1991 Midland Angels, a Class AA Texas League affiliate of the California Angels, features color player photos. The set measures approximately 5 1/2" by 5". The backs are blank. The cards are unnumbered and checklisted below in alphabetical order. 500 sets were produced.

	MINT	NRMT	EXC
COMPLETE SET (32)	70.00	32.00	8.75

☐ 1 Edgar Alfonzo

☐ 2 Don Barbara
☐ 3 Jeff Barnes
☐ 4 Hector Berrios
☐ 5 Mick Billmeyer
☐ 6 Mike Butcher
☐ 7 Marvin Cobb
☐ 8 Sherman Corbett
☐ 9 Kevin Davis
☐ 10 Damion Easley
☐ 11 Kevin Flora
☐ 12 Larry Gonzales
☐ 13 Mark Howie
☐ 14 Bobby Jones
☐ 15 Steve King
☐ 16 Marcus Lawton
☐ 17 Don Long
☐ 18 Fili Martinez
☐ 19 Walt McConnell
☐ 20 Rafael Montazvo
☐ 21 Gene Richards
☐ 22 Ken Rivers
☐ 23 Doug Robertson
☐ 24 Kernan Ronan
☐ 25 Tim Salmon
☐ 26 Ramon Sambo
☐ 27 Dave Shotkoski
☐ 28 Alan Sontag
☐ 29 Terry Taylor
☐ 30 Don Vidmar
☐ 31 Reggie Williams
☐ 32 Mark Zapelli

1991 Midland Angels ProCards

This 27-card standard-size set of the 1991 Midland Angels, a Class AA Texas League affiliate of the California Angels, features on its white-bordered fronts posed color player photos set on simulated spiral-bound yellow notebooks. The player's name, position, and team appear within a green rectangle below the photo. The yellow horizontal back is bordered in white and carries the player's name at the top, followed by biography and statistics. This issue includes the fourth year card of Tim Salmon.

	MINT	NRMT	EXC
COMPLETE SET (27)	8.00	3.60	1.00

☐ 426 Clemente Acosta
☐ 427 Mike Butcher
☐ 428 Glenn Carter
☐ 429 Marvin Cobb
☐ 430 Sherman Corbett
☐ 431 Todd James
☐ 432 Steve King
☐ 433 Doug Robertson
☐ 434 Dave Shotkoski
☐ 435 Mark Zappelli
☐ 436 Larry Gonzales
☐ 437 Ken Rivers
☐ 438 Jeff Barns
☐ 439 Kevin Davis
☐ 440 Damion Easley
☐ 441 Kevin Flora
☐ 442 Mark Howie
☐ 443 Daryl Sconiers
☐ 444 Terry Taylor
☐ 445 Bobby Jones
☐ 446 Marcus Lawton
☐ 447 Tim Salmon
☐ 448 Ramon Sambo
☐ 449 Don Long MGR
☐ 450 Gene Richards CO
☐ 451 Kernan Ronan CO
☐ 452 Checklist

1991 Midwest League All-Stars ProCards

	MINT	NRMT	EXC
COMPLETE SET (51)	7.00	3.10	.85

☐ MWL1 Darren Burton
☐ MWL2 Gary Caraballo
☐ MWL3 Eric Christopherson
☐ MWL4 Rod Huffman
☐ MWL5 Mike Myers
☐ MWL6 Salomon Torres
☐ MWL7 Phil Dauphin
☐ MWL8 Brad Erdman
☐ MWL9 Jose Vierra
☐ MWL10 Domingo Jean
☐ MWL11 Rogelio Nunez
☐ MWL12 Kevin Tolar
☐ MWL13 Brandon Wilson
☐ MWL14 Clyde Keller
☐ MWL15 Tony Gilmore
☐ MWL16 Chris Hatcher
☐ MWL17 Fletcher Thompson
☐ MWL18 Wally Trice
☐ MWL19 Donne Wall
☐ MWL20 Ken Wheeler
☐ MWL21 Mark Borcherding
☐ MWL22 Larry Luebbers
☐ MWL23 Eddie Rush
☐ MWL24 Don Barbara
☐ MWL25 Mark Dalesandro
☐ MWL26 Cliff Garrett
☐ MWL27 Phil Leftwich
☐ MWL28 Billy Minnis
☐ MWL29 Roberto Arredondo
☐ MWL30 John Kuehl
☐ MWL31 Tim Worrell
☐ MWL32 Larry Carter
☐ MWL33 Mike Carter
☐ MWL34 Don Pruitt
☐ MWL35 Brad Tyler
☐ MWL36 Greg Zaun
☐ MWL37 Denny Hocking
☐ MWL38 Tim Pershing
☐ MWL39 Todd Ritchie
☐ MWL40 Jim Dillon
☐ MWL41 Brett Hendley
☐ MWL42 Rafael Mercado
☐ MWL43 Islay Molina
☐ MWL44 Tanyon Sturtze
☐ MWL45 Ranbir Grewal
☐ MWL46 Shaun Murphy
☐ MWL47 Glenn Murray
☐ MWL48 Corey Powell
☐ MWL49 Mike Weimerskirch
☐ MWL50 Randy Wilstead
☐ MWL51 Checklist

1991 Mississippi State Bulldogs

	MINT	NRMT	EXC
COMPLETE SET (55)	12.00	5.50	1.50

☐ 1 Daryl Albro
☐ 2 Clint Allen
☐ 3 Charlie Anderson
☐ 4 Craig Bane
☐ 5 Jeff Brantley
☐ 6 Ron Brown
☐ 7 Rex Buckner
☐ 8 Brad Burckel
☐ 9 Gary Butterworth
☐ 10 Matt Carpenter
☐ 11 Will Clark
☐ 12 Chuck Daniel
☐ 13 Corbin Davis
☐ 14 Jim Ellis
☐ 15 Park Evans
☐ 16 Hap Fleming
☐ 17 Jimmy Gammill
☐ 18 Damon Gardner
☐ 19 Chris George
☐ 20 Joey Hamilton
☐ 21 Jon Harden
☐ 22 Robbie Hayes
☐ 23 Steve Hegan
☐ 24 Carl Henderson
☐ 25 Tripp Hill
☐ 26 Scot Hollingsworth
☐ 27 Chuck Holly
☐ 28 Tom Howe
☐ 29 Joe Hudak CO
☐ 30 Eddie Lyons
☐ 31 Jeff Mackin
☐ 32 Joel Matthews
☐ 33 Doug Newman
☐ 34 Rob Norman
☐ 35 Rafael Palmeiro
☐ 36 David Perkins
☐ 37 Paul Petrulis
☐ 38 Ron Polk CO
☐ 39 Jay Powell
☐ 40 Tom Quinn
☐ 41 Ricky Joe Redd
☐ 42 Steve Smith CO
☐ 43 Bobby Thigpen
☐ 44 Larry Tomkins
☐ 45 Scott Tribolet
☐ 46 Bryan Triche
☐ 47 B.J. Wallace
☐ 48 John Warburton
☐ 49 Drew Williams
☐ 50 Jason Williams
☐ 51 Checklist
☐ 52 Diamond Girls
☐ 53 Dudy Noble Field
☐ 54 Graduate Assistant
Coaches
Mitch Thompson
Rob McDonald
Paul Wyczawski
John Cedarburg
☐ 55 Student Managers and
Trainers
Rogers Smith MG
John Mooney MG
Lance Vining MG
Jay McKinney MG
John Bergstrom TR
Phillip Page TR

1991 Modesto A's Classic/Best

This 27-card standard-size set of the 1991 Modesto A's, a Class A California League affiliate of the Oakland Athletics, features white-bordered posed color player photos on its fronts. The player's name, team, and position appear at the bottom. The white back is framed by a thin black line and carries the player's name and position at the top, followed by biography, statistics and team logos.

	MINT	NRMT	EXC
COMPLETE SET (27)	5.00	2.20	.60

☐ 1 Kurt Abbott
☐ 2 Trent Weaver
☐ 3 Craig Sudbury
☐ 4 Rob Fletcher
☐ 5 Chaon Garland
☐ 6 Ken Hokul
☐ 7 Ruben Lardizabal
☐ 8 Rick Miller
☐ 9 Mike Mohler
☐ 10 Glenn Osinski
☐ 11 Bronswell Patrick
☐ 12 Delfino Mejia
☐ 13 Scott Rose
☐ 14 Todd Smith
☐ 15 Rick Strebeck
☐ 16 Eric Booker
☐ 17 Ted Kubiak MGR
☐ 18 Pete Richert CO
☐ 19 Dave Hollenback TR
☐ 20 Mike Messerly
☐ 21 Eric Helfand
☐ 22 Henry Mercedes
☐ 23 Enoch Simmons
☐ 24 Manuel Martinez
☐ 25 Kevin Dattola
☐ 26 Jim Waggoner
☐ 27 Checklist

1991 Modesto A's ProCards

This 30-card standard-size set of the 1991 Modesto A's, a Class A California League affiliate of the Oakland Athletics, features on its white-bordered fronts posed color player photos set on simulated spiral-bound yellow notebooks. The player's name, position, and team appear within a green rectangle below the photo. The yellow horizontal back is bordered in white and carries the player's name at the top, followed by biography and statistics.

	MINT	NRMT	EXC
COMPLETE SET (30)	5.00	2.20	.60

☐ 3079 Scott Erwin
☐ 3080 Chaon Garland
☐ 3081 Ken Hokuf
☐ 3082 Ruben Lardizabal
☐ 3083 Will Love
☐ 3084 Mike Mohler
☐ 3085 Bronswell Patrick
☐ 3086 Steve Phoenix
☐ 3087 Scott Rose
☐ 3088 Todd Smith
☐ 3089 Craig Sudbury
☐ 3090 Don Keathley
☐ 3091 Henry Mercedes
☐ 3092 Kurt Abbott
☐ 3093 Marcos Armas
☐ 3094 Fred Cooley
☐ 3095 Fausto Cruz
☐ 3096 Rob Fletcher
☐ 3097 Mike Messerly
☐ 3098 Glenn Osinski
☐ 3099 Carlos Salazar
☐ 3100 Jim Waggoner
☐ 3101 Eric Booker
☐ 3102 Kevin Dattola
☐ 3103 Chris Hart
☐ 3104 Manuel Martinez
☐ 3105 Enoch Simmons
☐ 3106 Ted Kubiak MGR
☐ 3107 Pete Richert CO
☐ 3108 Checklist

1991 Myrtle Beach Hurricanes Classic/Best

This 30-card standard-size set of the 1991 Myrtle Beach Hurricanes, a Class A South Atlantic League affiliate of the Toronto Blue Jays, features white-bordered posed color player photos on its fronts. The player's name, team, and position appear near the bottom. The white back is framed by a black line and carries the player's name and position at the top, followed by biography and statistics. This issue includes the third year card of Carlos Delgado.

	MINT	NRMT	EXC
COMPLETE SET (30)	8.00	3.60	1.00

☐ 1 Bobby Aylmer
☐ 2 Greg Bicknell
☐ 3 Kyle Duey
☐ 4 Huck Flener
☐ 5 Joe Ganote
☐ 6 Raphael Garcia
☐ 7 Ricardo Jordan
☐ 8 Steve Karsay
☐ 9 Sam Mandia
☐ 10 Tom Singer
☐ 11 Rick Steed
☐ 12 Carlos Delgado
☐ 13 Juan Jaime
☐ 14 Marc Loeb
☐ 15 Ciro Ambrosio
☐ 16 Howard Battle
☐ 17 Andy Carlton
☐ 18 Mark Choate
☐ 19 Mariano Dotel
☐ 20 Tim Hyers
☐ 21 Scott Miller
☐ 22 Ernesto Rodriquez
☐ 23 Brent Bowers
☐ 24 Rickey Holifield
☐ 25 Ronald Reams
☐ 26 Lonell Roberts
☐ 27 Garth Iorg MG
☐ 28 Darren Balsley CO
☐ 29 Leroy Stanton CO
☐ 30 Armando Pagliari TR
Checklist

1991 Myrtle Beach Hurricanes ProCards

This 30-card standard-size set of the 1991 Myrtle Beach Hurricanes, a Class A South Atlantic League affiliate of the Toronto Blue Jays, features on its white-bordered fronts posed color player photos set on simulated spiral-bound yellow notebooks. The player's name, position, and team appear within a green rectangle below the photo. The yellow horizontal back is bordered in white and carries the player's name and position at the top, followed by biography and statistics. This issue includes the third year card of Carlos Delgado.

	MINT	NRMT	EXC
COMPLETE SET (30)	7.00	3.10	.85

☐ 2935 Bobby Aylmer
☐ 2936 Greg Bicknell
☐ 2937 Kyle Duey
☐ 2938 Huck Flener
☐ 2939 Joe Ganote
☐ 2940 Raphael Garcia
☐ 2941 Ricardo Jordan
☐ 2942 Steve Karsay
☐ 2943 Sam Mandia
☐ 2944 Tom Singer
☐ 2945 Rick Steed
☐ 2946 Carlos Delgado
☐ 2947 Juan Jaime
☐ 2948 Marc Loeb
☐ 2949 Ciro Ambrosio
☐ 2950 Howard Battle
☐ 2951 Andy Carlton
☐ 2952 Mark Choate
☐ 2953 Mariano Dotel
☐ 2954 Tim Hyers
☐ 2955 Scott Miller
☐ 2956 Ernesto Rodriguez
☐ 2957 Brent Bowers
☐ 2958 Rickey Holifield
☐ 2959 Ron Reams
☐ 2960 Lonell Roberts
☐ 2961 Garth Iorg MG
☐ 2962 Darren Balsley CO
☐ 2963 Leroy Stanton CO
☐ 2964 Checklist

1991 Nashville Sounds Line Drive

	MINT	NRMT	EXC
COMPLETE SET (26)	5.00	2.20	.60

☐ 251 Billy Bates
☐ 252 Freddie Benavides
☐ 253 Keith Brown
☐ 254 Adam Casillas
☐ 255 Tony DeFrancesco
☐ 256 Leo Garcia
☐ 257 Angel Gonzalez
☐ 258 Denny Gonzalez
☐ 259 Kip Gross
☐ 260 Charlie Mitchell
☐ 261 Milton Hill
☐ 262 Rodney Imes
☐ 263 Reggie Jefferson
☐ 264 Keith Lockhart
☐ 265 Manny Jose
☐ 266 Terry Lee
☐ 267 Rob Lopez
☐ 268 Gino Minutelli
☐ 269 Kevin Pearson
☐ 270 Ross Powell
☐ 271 Donnie Scott
☐ 272 Luis Vasquez
☐ 273 Joey Vierra
☐ 274 Pete MacKanin MGR
☐ 275 Don Gullett CO
Jim Lett CO
☐ NNO Title card

1991 Nashville Sounds ProCards

This 27-card standard-size set of the 1991 Nashville Sounds, a Class AAA American Association affiliate of the Cincinnati Reds, features on its white-bordered fronts posed color player photos set on simulated spiral-bound yellow notebooks. The player's name, position, and team appear within a green rectangle below the photo. The yellow horizontal back is bordered in white and carries the player's name at the top, followed by biography and statistics.

	MINT	NRMT	EXC
COMPLETE SET (27)	5.00	2.20	.60

☐ 2149 Keith Brown
☐ 2150 Kip Gross
☐ 2151 Milton Hill
☐ 2152 Rodney Imes
☐ 2153 Gino Minutelli
☐ 2154 Charlie Mitchell
☐ 2155 Ross Powell
☐ 2156 Luis Vasquez
☐ 2157 Joey Vierra
☐ 2158 Pete Beeler
☐ 2159 Tony DeFrancesco
☐ 2160 Donnie Scott
☐ 2161 Freddie Benavides
☐ 2162 Angel Gonzalez
☐ 2163 Denny Gonzalez
☐ 2164 Reggie Jefferson
☐ 2165 Terry Lee
☐ 2166 Keith Lockhart
☐ 2167 Kevin Pearson
☐ 2168 Adam Casillas
☐ 2169 Leo Garcia
☐ 2170 Manny Jose
☐ 2171 Bernie Walker
☐ 2172 Pete MacKanin MGR
☐ 2173 Don Gullett CO
☐ 2174 Jim Lett CO
☐ 2175 Checklist

1991 New Britain Red Sox Line Drive

	MINT	NRMT	EXC
COMPLETE SET (26)	5.00	2.20	.60

☐ 451 Michael Beams
☐ 452 Greg Blosser
☐ 453 Brian Conroy
☐ 454 Freddie Davis
☐ 455 Colin Dixon
☐ 456 Peter Estrada
☐ 457 Ray Fagnant
☐ 458 Tom Fischer
☐ 459 John Flaherty
☐ 460 Donald Florence
☐ 461 Blane Fox
☐ 462 Steve Hendricks
☐ 463 Wayne Housie
☐ 464 Peter Hoy
☐ 465 Thomas Kane
☐ 466 David Milstien
☐ 467 Juan Paris
☐ 468 Scott Powers
☐ 469 Paul Quantrill
☐ 470 Randy Randle
☐ 471 Al Sanders
☐ 472 Scott Taylor
☐ 473 John Valentin
☐ 474 Gary Allenson MGR
☐ 475 Rick Wise CO
☐ NNO Title card

1991 New Britain Red Sox ProCards

This 26-card standard-size set of the 1991 New Britain Red Sox, a Class AA Eastern League affiliate of the Boston Red Sox, features on its white-bordered fronts posed color player photos set on simulated spiral-bound yellow notebooks. The player's name, position, and team appear within a green rectangle below the photo. The yellow horizontal back is bordered in white and carries the player's name at the top, followed by biography and statistics.

	MINT	NRMT	EXC
COMPLETE SET (26)	5.00	2.20	.60

☐ 344 Brian Conroy
☐ 345 Freddie Davis
☐ 346 Pete Estrada
☐ 347 Tom Fischer
☐ 348 Don Florence
☐ 349 Peter Hoy
☐ 350 Tom Kane
☐ 351 Paul Quantrill
☐ 352 Al Sanders
☐ 353 Scott Taylor
☐ 354 Ray Fagnant
☐ 355 John Flaherty
☐ 356 Colin Dixon
☐ 357 Steve Hendricks
☐ 358 Dave Milstien
☐ 359 Scott Powers
☐ 360 Randy Randle
☐ 361 John Valentin
☐ 362 Mike Beams
☐ 363 Greg Blosser
☐ 364 Blane Fox
☐ 365 Wayne Housie
☐ 366 Juan Paris
☐ 367 Gary Allenson MGR
☐ 368 Rick Wise CO
☐ 369 Checklist

1991 Niagara Falls Rapids Classic/Best

This 30-card standard-size set of the 1991 Niagara Falls Rapids, a Class A New York-Penn League affiliate of the Detroit Tigers, features white-bordered posed color player photos on its fronts. The player's name, team, and position appear at the bottom. The white back is framed by a thin black line and carries the player's name and position at the top, followed by biography, statistics and team logos. This issue includes the second year card of Tony Clark.

	MINT	NRMT	EXC
COMPLETE SET (30)	7.00	3.10	.85

☐ 1 Kevin Morgan
☐ 2 Jimmy Brown
☐ 3 Arthur Johnson
☐ 4 Thomas Gibson
☐ 5 Ryan Haley
☐ 6 Jim Van Scoyoc CO
☐ 7 Aaron Seja
☐ 8 Clarke Rea
☐ 9 Brian Sullivan
☐ 10 Brian DuBose
☐ 11 Kevin Miller
☐ 12 Evan Pratte
☐ 13 Tony Clark
☐ 14 Rob Grable
☐ 15 Robin Higginbotham
☐ 16 Peter Feeley
☐ 17 Carlos Burguillos
☐ 18 Rich Kelley
☐ 19 Ben Blomdahl
☐ 20 John Reid
☐ 21 Dennis Walsh
☐ 22 Shawn Turri
☐ 23 Doug Martin
☐ 24 Sean Bergman
☐ 25 Jim Henry
☐ 26 Shannon Withem
☐ 27 Bob Lemay
☐ 28 Corey Reincke
☐ 29 Gary Calhoun MGR
☐ 30 Stan Luketich CO
Checklist

1991 Niagara Falls Rapids ProCards

This 30-card standard-size set of the 1991 Niagara Falls Rapids, a Class A New York-Penn League affiliate of the Detroit Tigers, features on its white-bordered fronts posed color player photos set on simulated spiral-bound yellow notebooks. The player's name, position, and team appear within a green rectangle below the photo. The yellow horizontal back is bordered in white and carries the player's name at the top, followed by biography and statistics. This issue includes the second year card of Tony Clark.

	MINT	NRMT	EXC
COMPLETE SET (30)	7.00	3.10	.85

☐ 3624 Sean Bergman
☐ 3625 Ben Blomdahl
☐ 3626 Scott DuRussel
☐ 3627 Jimmy Henry
☐ 3628 Rich Kelley
☐ 3629 Bob LeMay
☐ 3630 Doug Martin
☐ 3631 Corey Reincke
☐ 3632 Shawn Turri
☐ 3633 Dennis Walsh
☐ 3634 Shonnon Withem
☐ 3635 Ryan Haley
☐ 3636 Kevin Miller
☐ 3637 Gregg Radachowsky
☐ 3638 Clarke Rea
☐ 3639 Jimmy Brown
☐ 3640 Brian DuBose
☐ 3641 Rob Grable
☐ 3642 Kevin Morgan
☐ 3643 Evan Pratte
☐ 3644 Carlos Burguillos
☐ 3645 Tony Clark
☐ 3646 Peter Feeley
☐ 3647 Robin Higginbotham
☐ 3648 Aaron Seja
☐ 3649 Brian Sullivan
☐ 3650 Gary Calhoun MGR
☐ 3651 Stan Luketich CO
☐ 3652 Jim Van Scoyoc CO
☐ 3653 Checklist

1991 Oklahoma City 89ers Line Drive

	MINT	NRMT	EXC
COMPLETE SET (26)	7.00	3.10	.85

☐ 301 Gerald Alexander
☐ 302 Kevin Belcher
☐ 303 Jeff Andrews
☐ 304 Tony Scruggs
☐ 305 Jeff Bronkey
☐ 306 Paco Burgos
☐ 307 Nick Capra
☐ 308 Monty Fariss
☐ 309 Darrin Garner
☐ 310 Bill Haselman
☐ 311 Terry Mathews
☐ 312 Rob Maurer
☐ 313 Gar Millay
☐ 314 Dean Palmer
☐ 315 Roger Pavlik
☐ 316 Dan Peltier
☐ 317 Steve Peters
☐ 318 Mark Petkovsek
☐ 319 Jim Poole
☐ 320 Paul Postier
☐ 321 Wayne Rosenthal
☐ 322 Dan Smith
☐ 323 Terry Wells
☐ 324 Tommy Thompson MGR
☐ 325 Stan Hough CO
☐ NNO Title card

1991 Oklahoma City 89ers ProCards

This 27-card standard-size set of the 1991 Oklahoma City 89ers, a Class AAA American Association affiliate of the Texas Rangers, features on its white-bordered fronts posed color player photos set on simulated spiral-bound yellow notebooks. The player's name, position, and team appear within a green rectangle below the photo. The yellow horizontal back is bordered in white and carries the player's name at the top, followed by biography and statistics. This issue includes the fifth year card of Dean Palmer.

	MINT	NRMT	EXC
COMPLETE SET (27)	7.00	3.10	.85

☐ 170 Gerald Alexander
☐ 171 Joe Bitker
☐ 172 Jeff Bronkey
☐ 173 Terry Mathews
☐ 174 Roger Pavlik
☐ 175 Steve Peters
☐ 176 Jim Poole
☐ 177 Mark Petkovsek
☐ 178 Wayne Rosenthal
☐ 179 Dan Smith
☐ 180 Terry Wells
☐ 181 Mike Berger
☐ 182 Bill Haselman
☐ 183 Paco Burgos
☐ 184 Monty Fariss
☐ 185 Darrin Garner
☐ 186 Rob Maurer
☐ 187 Dean Palmer
☐ 188 Paul Postier
☐ 189 Kevin Belcher
☐ 190 Nick Capra
☐ 191 Gar Millay
☐ 192 Dan Peltier
☐ 193 Tommy Thompson MGR
☐ 194 Jeff Andrews CO
☐ 195 Stan Hough CO
☐ 196 Checklist

1991 Oklahoma State Cowboys

	MINT	NRMT	EXC
COMPLETE SET (32)	12.00	5.50	1.50

☐ 1 Derek Brandow
☐ 2 Dennis Burbank
☐ 3 Lee Cantrelle
☐ 4 John Castor
☐ 5 Scott Cunningham
☐ 6 Steve Dailey
☐ 7 Michael Daniel
☐ 8 Brad Dolejsi
☐ 9 Manny Gagliano
☐ 10 Brad Gore
☐ 11 Tom Holliday ACO
☐ 12 Chip Johnson
☐ 13 Billy Kanwisher
☐ 14 Rob Linfante
☐ 15 Lou Lucca
☐ 16 Paul Meador
☐ 17 Ritchie Moody
☐ 18 Danny Perez
☐ 19 Kelly Reavis
☐ 20 Bryon Remo
☐ 21 Ryan Richards
☐ 22 Jim Schwanke ACO
☐ 23 Mitchel Simons
☐ 24 Todd Smith
☐ 25 John Swanson
☐ 26 Neil Szeryk
☐ 27 Darren Tawwater
☐ 28 Joe Wallace
☐ 29 Gary Ward CO
☐ 30 Scott Watkins
☐ 31 Earl Wheeler
☐ 32 Scott Wolfenbarger

1991 Omaha Royals Line Drive

	MINT	NRMT	EXC
COMPLETE SET (26)	7.00	3.10	.85

☐ 326 Sean Berry
☐ 327 Jacob Brumfield
☐ 328 Bob Buchanan
☐ 329 Kevin Burrell
☐ 330 Stu Cole
☐ 331 Victor Cole
☐ 332 Jeff Conine
☐ 333 Tommy Dunbar
☐ 334 Luis Encarnacion
☐ 335 Greg Everson
☐ 336 Bob Hamelin
☐ 337 Joel Johnston
☐ 338 Frank Laureano
☐ 339 Jim LeMasters
☐ 340 Mike Magnante
☐ 341 Carlos Maldonado
☐ 342 Andy McGaffigan
☐ 343 Bobby Moore
☐ 344 Harvey Pulliam
☐ 345 Daryl Smith
☐ 346 Tim Spehr
☐ 347 Hector Wagner
☐ 348 Paul Zuvella
☐ 349 Sal Rende MGR
☐ 350 Brian Poldberg CO
Guy Hansen CO
☐ NNO Title card

1991 Omaha Royals ProCards

This 26-card standard-size set of the 1991 Omaha Royals, a Class AAA American Association affiliate of the Kansas City Royals, features on its white-bordered fronts posed color player photos set on simulated spiral-bound yellow notebooks. The player's name, position, and team appear within a green rectangle below the photo. The yellow horizontal back is bordered in white and carries the player's name at the top, followed by biography and statistics. This issue includes the fourth year card of Jeff Conine.

	MINT	NRMT	EXC
COMPLETE SET (26)	7.00	3.10	.85

☐ 1027 Bob Buchanan
☐ 1028 Victor Cole
☐ 1029 Luis Encarnacion
☐ 1030 Greg Everson
☐ 1031 Joel Johnston
☐ 1032 Jim LeMasters
☐ 1033 Mike Magnante
☐ 1034 Carlos Maldonado
☐ 1035 Daryl Smith
☐ 1036 Hector Wagner
☐ 1037 Kevin Burrell
☐ 1038 Tim Spehr
☐ 1039 Sean Berry
☐ 1040 Stu Cole
☐ 1041 Jeff Conine
☐ 1042 Bob Hamelin
☐ 1043 Frank Laureano
☐ 1044 Paul Zuvella
☐ 1045 Jacob Brumfield
☐ 1046 Tommy Dunbar
☐ 1047 Bobby Moore
☐ 1048 Harvey Pulliam
☐ 1049 Sal Rende MGR
☐ 1050 Guy Hansen CO
☐ 1051 Brian Poldberg CO
☐ 1052 Checklist

1991 Oneonta Yankees ProCards

This 27-card standard-size set of the 1991 Oneonta Yankees, a Class A New York-Penn League affiliate of the New York Yankees, features on its white-bordered fronts posed color player photos set on simulated spiral-bound yellow notebooks. The player's name, position, and team appear within a green rectangle below the photo. The yellow horizontal back is bordered in white and carries the player's name at the top, followed by biography and statistics.

	MINT	NRMT	EXC
COMPLETE SET (27)	5.00	2.20	.60

☐ 4145 Dennis Burbank
☐ 4146 Billy Coleman
☐ 4147 Andy Croghan
☐ 4148 Keith Garagozzo
☐ 4149 Scott Gully

☐ 4150 Bert Inman
☐ 4151 Frank Laviano
☐ 4152 Steve Munda
☐ 4153 Sandi Santiago
☐ 4154 Ben Short
☐ 4155 Grant Sullivan
☐ 4156 Jorge Posada
☐ 4157 John Quintell
☐ 4158 Tom Wilson
☐ 4159 Steve Anderson
☐ 4160 Roger Burnett
☐ 4161 Tim Flannelly
☐ 4162 Steve Livesey
☐ 4163 Tate Seefried
☐ 4164 Andrew Albrecht
☐ 4165 Mark Hubbard
☐ 4166 Lyle Mouton
☐ 4167 Steve Phillips
☐ 4168 Jack Gillis MGR
☐ 4169 Mark Rose CO
☐ 4170 Bill Schmidt CO
☐ 4171 Checklist

1991 Orlando Sun Rays Line Drive

	MINT	NRMT	EXC
COMPLETE SET (26)	5.00	2.20	.60

☐ 476 Pat Bangston
☐ 477 Carlos Capellan
☐ 478 Rafael DeLima
☐ 479 Frank Valdez
☐ 480 Cheo Garcia
☐ 481 Shawn Gilbert
☐ 482 Greg Johnson
☐ 483 Jay Kvasnicka
☐ 484 Orlando Lind
☐ 485 Pat Mahomes
☐ 486 Jose Marzan
☐ 487 Dan Masteller
☐ 488 Bob McCreary
☐ 489 Steve Muh
☐ 490 Reed Olmstead
☐ 491 Ray Ortiz
☐ 492 Derek Parks
☐ 493 Joe Siwa
☐ 494 Steve Stowell
☐ 495 Mike Trombley
☐ 496 Jim Shellenback
☐ 497 Rob Wassenaar
☐ 498 Phil Wiese
☐ 499 Scott Ullger MGR
☐ 500 Mark Funderburk CO
☐ NNO Title card

1991 Orlando Sun Rays ProCards

This 27-card standard-size set of the 1991 Orlando Sun Rays, a Class AA Southern League affiliate of the Minnesota Twins, features on its white-bordered fronts posed color player photos set on simulated spiral-bound yellow notebooks. The player's name, position, and team appear within a green rectangle below the photo. The yellow horizontal back is bordered in white and carries the player's name at the top, followed by biography and statistics.

	MINT	NRMT	EXC
COMPLETE SET (27)	5.00	2.20	.60

☐ 1842 Pat Bangtson
☐ 1843 Pete Delkus
☐ 1844 Greg Johnson
☐ 1845 Orlando Lind
☐ 1846 Pat Mahomes
☐ 1847 Steve Muh
☐ 1848 Steve Stowell
☐ 1849 Mike Trombley
☐ 1850 Rob Wassenaar
☐ 1851 Phil Wiese
☐ 1852 Derek Parks
☐ 1853 Joe Siwa
☐ 1854 Carlos Capellan
☐ 1855 Cheo Garcia
☐ 1856 Shawn Gilbert
☐ 1857 Jose Marzan
☐ 1858 Dan Masteller
☐ 1859 Bob McCreary
☐ 1860 Reed Olmstead
☐ 1861 Rafael DeLima
☐ 1862 Jay Kvasnicka
☐ 1863 Ray Ortiz
☐ 1864 Frank Valdez
☐ 1865 Scott Ullger MGR
☐ 1866 Mark Funderburk CO
☐ 1867 Jim Shellenback CO
☐ 1868 Checklist

1991 Osceola Astros Classic/Best

This 29-card standard-size set of the 1991 Osceola Astros, a Class A Florida State League affiliate of the Houston Astros, features white-bordered posed color player photos on its fronts. The player's name, team, and position appear at the bottom. The white back is framed by a thin black line and carries the player's name and position at the top, followed by biography, statistics and team logos.

	MINT	NRMT	EXC
COMPLETE SET (29)	6.00	2.70	.75

☐ 1 Fred Costello
☐ 2 Gordon Farmer
☐ 3 Brian Griffiths
☐ 4 Cole Hyson
☐ 5 Lee Johnson
☐ 6 Todd Jones
☐ 7 Ken Luckham
☐ 8 Montie Phillips
☐ 9 Ed Ponte
☐ 10 Matt Rambo
☐ 11 Mark Small
☐ 12 Brian Williams
☐ 13 Rodney Windes
☐ 14 Ed Beuerlein
☐ 15 John Massarelli
☐ 16 Jeff Ball
☐ 17 Perry Berry
☐ 18 David Hajeck
☐ 19 Frank Kellner
☐ 20 Bobby Ramos CO
☐ 21 Ed Renteria
☐ 22 Craig Curtis
☐ 23 Gershon Dallas
☐ 24 Brian L. Hunter
☐ 25 Luther Johnson
☐ 26 Sal Butera MGR
☐ 27 Mike Freer TR
☐ 28 Kevin Scott
☐ 29 Checklist

1991 Osceola Astros ProCards

This 29-card standard-size set of the 1991 Osceola Astros, a Class A Florida State League affiliate of the Houston Astros, features on its white-bordered fronts posed color player photos set on simulated spiral-bound yellow notebooks. The player's name, position, and team appear within a green rectangle below the photo. The yellow horizontal back is bordered in white and carries the player's name at the top, followed by biography and statistics. This issue includes the second year card of Brian L. Hunter.

	MINT	NRMT	EXC
COMPLETE SET (29)	6.00	2.70	.75

☐ 673 Fred Costello
☐ 674 Gordon Farmer
☐ 675 Brian Griffiths
☐ 676 Cole Hyson
☐ 677 Lee Johnson
☐ 678 Todd Jones
☐ 679 Ken Luckham
☐ 680 Montie Phillips
☐ 681 Ed Ponte
☐ 682 Matt Rambo
☐ 683 Robert Resnikoff
☐ 684 Mark Small
☐ 685 Brian Williams
☐ 686 Rodney Windes
☐ 688 John Massarelli
☐ 689 Kevin Scott
☐ 690 Jeff Ball
☐ 691 Perry Berry
☐ 692 David Hajeck
☐ 693 Frank Kellner
☐ 694 Howard Prager
☐ 695 Ed Renteria
☐ 696 Craig Curtis
☐ 697 Gershon Dallas
☐ 698 Brian L. Hunter
☐ 699 Luther Johnson
☐ 700 Coaching Staff
Sal Butera MGR
Jack Billingham CO
Bobby Ramos CO
☐ 701 Checklist
☐ 867 Ed Beuerlein

1991 Palm Springs Angels ProCards

This 30-card standard-size set of the 1991 Palm Springs Angels, a Class A California League affiliate of the California Angels, features on its white-bordered fronts posed color player photos set on simulated spiral-bound yellow notebooks. The player's name, position, and team appear within a green rectangle below the photo. The yellow horizontal back is bordered in white and carries the player's name at the top, followed by biography and statistics. This issue includes the fourth year card of Jim Edmonds.

	MINT	NRMT	EXC
COMPLETE SET (30)	8.00	3.60	1.00

☐ 2007 Hector Berrios
☐ 2008 Steve Loubier
☐ 2009 Brett Merriman
☐ 2010 Louis Pakele
☐ 2011 Steve Peck
☐ 2012 Randy Powers
☐ 2013 Alan Sontag
☐ 2014 Paul Swingle
☐ 2015 Dave Van Winkle
☐ 2016 Bruce Vegely
☐ 2017 Don Vidmar
☐ 2018 Mick Billmeyer
☐ 2019 Frank Dominguez
☐ 2020 Danny Gil
☐ 2021 Edgar Alfonzo
☐ 2022 P.J. Forbes
☐ 2023 Corey Kapano
☐ 2024 Ramon Martinez
☐ 2025 J.R. Phillips
☐ 2026 J.R. Showalter
☐ 2027 Davie Colon
☐ 2028 Jim Edmonds
☐ 2029 Carlos Laboy
☐ 2030 Dave Partrick
☐ 2031 Beban Perez
☐ 2032 Edgal Rodriguez
☐ 2033 Nate Oliver MGR
☐ 2034 Stu Cliburn CO
☐ 2035 Mario Mendoza CO
☐ 2036 Checklist

1991 Pawtucket Red Sox Dunkin' Donuts

This 31-card set of the Pawtucket Red Sox, a Class AAA International League affiliate of the Boston Red Sox, was issued in one large sheet featuring six perforated five-card strips with a large team photo in the wide top strip. Sponsored by Channel 10 and Dunkin' Donuts, the fronts carry color player photos while the backs display player career statistics. The cards are unnumbered and checklisted below in alphabetical order. This issue includes a third year card of Mo Vaughn.

	MINT	NRMT	EXC
COMPLETE SET (31)	60.00	27.00	7.50

☐ 1 Luis Aguayo
☐ 2 Tom Barrett
☐ 3 Scott Cooper
☐ 4 John Flaherty
☐ 5 Rich Gale
☐ 6 Mike Gardiner
☐ 7 Eric Hetzel
☐ 8 Butch Hobson
☐ 9 Daryl Irvine
☐ 10 Rick Lancellotti
☐ 11 Derek Livernois
☐ 12 Mark Meleski
☐ 13 Kevin Morton
☐ 14 Dan O'Neill
☐ 15 Jim Pankovitz
☐ 16 Mickey Pina
☐ 17 Phil Plantier
☐ 18 Jeff Plympton
☐ 19 Todd Pratt
☐ 20 Paul Quantrill
☐ 21 Larry Shikles
☐ 22 Jeff Stone
☐ 23 Scott Taylor
☐ 24 Mike Twardoski
☐ 25 John Valentin
☐ 26 Mo Vaughn
☐ 27 Gene Walter
☐ 28 Dave Walters
☐ 29 Eric Wedge
☐ 30 Bob Zupcic
☐ 31 Team Photo

1991 Pawtucket Red Sox Line Drive

	MINT	NRMT	EXC
COMPLETE SET (26)	10.00	4.50	1.25

☐ 351 Luis Aguayo
☐ 352 Tom Barrett
☐ 353 Mike Brumley
☐ 354 Scott Cooper
☐ 355 Mike Gardiner
☐ 356 Eric Hetzel
☐ 357 Mike Twardoski
☐ 358 Rick Lancellotti
☐ 359 Derek Livernois
☐ 360 Mark Meleski
☐ 361 Kevin Morton
☐ 362 Dan O'Neill
☐ 363 Jim Pankovits
☐ 364 Mickey Pina
☐ 365 Phil Plantier
☐ 366 Jeff Plympton
☐ 367 Todd Pratt
☐ 368 Larry Shikles
☐ 369 Jeff Stone
☐ 370 Mo Vaughn
☐ 371 David Walters
☐ 372 Eric Wedge
☐ 373 Bob Zupcic
☐ 374 Butch Hobson MGR
☐ 375 Rich Gale CO
☐ NNO Title card

1991 Pawtucket Red Sox ProCards

This 27-card standard-size set of the 1991 Pawtucket Red Sox, a Class AAA International League affiliate of the Boston Red Sox, features on its white-bordered fronts posed color player photos set on simulated spiral-bound yellow notebooks. The player's name, position, and team appear within a green rectangle below the photo. The yellow horizontal back is bordered in white and carries the player's name at the top, followed by biography and statistics. This issue includes the second year minor league card of Mo Vaughn.

	MINT	NRMT	EXC
COMPLETE SET (27)	10.00	4.50	1.25

☐ 31 Mike Gardiner
☐ 32 Eric Hetzel
☐ 33 Daryl Irvine
☐ 34 Derek Livernois
☐ 35 Josias Manzanillo
☐ 36 Kevin Morton
☐ 37 Dan O'Neill
☐ 38 Jeff Plympton
☐ 39 Larry Shikles
☐ 40 David Walters
☐ 41 Todd Pratt
☐ 42 Eric Wedge
☐ 43 Luis Aguayo
☐ 44 Tom Barrett
☐ 45 Mike Brumley
☐ 46 Scott Cooper
☐ 47 Rick Lancellotti
☐ 48 Jim Pankovits
☐ 49 Mo Vaughn
☐ 50 Mickey Pina
☐ 51 Phil Plantier
☐ 52 Jeff Stone
☐ 53 Bob Zupcic
☐ 54 Butch Hobson MGR
☐ 55 Rich Gale CO
☐ 56 Mark Meleski CO
☐ 57 Checklist

1991 Peninsula Pilots Classic/Best

This 25-card standard-size set of the 1991 Peninsula Pilots, a Class A Carolina League affiliate of the Seattle Mariners, features white-bordered posed color player photos on its fronts. The player's name, team, and position appear at the bottom. The white back is framed by a thin black line and carries the player's name and position at the top, followed by biography, statistics and team logos.

	MINT	NRMT	EXC
COMPLETE SET (25)	5.00	2.20	.60

☐ 1 Greg Pirkl
☐ 2 Jim Converse
☐ 3 Kelvin Thomas
☐ 4 Manuel Furcal
☐ 5 Brad Holman
☐ 6 Kevin King
☐ 7 Bill Kostitch
☐ 8 Richard Lodding
☐ 9 Paul Perkins
☐ 10 Scott Schanz
☐ 11 Doug Tegtmeier
☐ 12 Salvy Urso
☐ 13 Johnny Wiggs
☐ 14 Tony Kounas
☐ 15 Jorge Morales
☐ 16 Damon Saetre
☐ 17 Willie Romay
☐ 18 Mark Brakebill
☐ 19 Mike Fermaint
☐ 20 Ron Pezzoni
☐ 21 Bobby Holley
☐ 22 Israel Seda
☐ 23 Roberto Del Pozo
☐ 24 Mark Merchant
☐ 25 Checklist

1991 Peninsula Pilots ProCards

This 28-card standard-size set of the 1991 Peninsula Pilots, a Class A Carolina League affiliate of the Seattle Mariners, features on its white-bordered fronts posed color player photos set on simulated spiral-bound yellow notebooks. The player's name, position, and team appear within a green rectangle below the photo. The yellow horizontal back is bordered in white and carries the player's name at the top, followed by biography and statistics.

	MINT	NRMT	EXC
COMPLETE SET (28)	5.00	2.20	.60

☐ 370 Manuel Furcal
☐ 371 Brad Holman
☐ 372 Kevin King
☐ 373 Bill Kostich
☐ 374 Richard Lodding
☐ 375 Paul Perkins
☐ 376 Scott Schanz
☐ 377 Doug Tegtmeier

☐ 378 Sal Urso
☐ 379 Johnny Wiggs
☐ 380 Tony Kounas
☐ 381 Jorge Morales
☐ 382 Glen Raasch
☐ 383 Mark Brakebill
☐ 384 Mike Fermaint
☐ 385 Jon Halland
☐ 386 Bobby Holley
☐ 387 Israel Seda
☐ 388 Roberto Del Pozo
☐ 389 Mark Merchant
☐ 390 Ron Pezzoni
☐ 391 Willie Romay
☐ 392 Damon Saetre
☐ 393 Kelvin Thomas
☐ 394 Steve Smith MGR
☐ 395 Carlos Lezcano CO
☐ 396 Bryan Price CO
☐ 397 Checklist

1991 Peoria Chiefs Classic/Best

This 29-card standard-size set of the 1991 Peoria Cubs, a Class A Midwest League affiliate of the Chicago Cubs, features white-bordered posed color player photos on its fronts. The player's name, team, and position appear at the bottom. The white back is framed by a thin black line and carries the player's name and position at the top, followed by biography, statistics and team logos.

	MINT	NRMT	EXC
COMPLETE SET (29)	5.00	2.20	.60

☐ 1 Dave Ross
☐ 2 Pedro Alicano
☐ 3 Amilcar Correa
☐ 4 Tim Delgado
☐ 5 Jason Doss
☐ 6 Chuck Kirk
☐ 7 Tom Mann
☐ 8 Earl Cunningham
☐ 9 Aaron Taylor
☐ 10 Brad Erdman
☐ 11 Rick Mundy
☐ 12 Tyson Godfrey
☐ 13 Paul Torres
☐ 14 Jose Viera
☐ 15 Bryan Wilson
☐ 16 German Diaz
☐ 17 Tim Moore
☐ 18 Victor Cancel
☐ 19 Rolando Fernandez
☐ 20 Willie Gardner
☐ 21 Mike Little
☐ 22 Bill Hayes MGR
☐ 23 Lester Strode CO
☐ 24 Jim O'Reilly TR
☐ 25 Philip Dauphin
☐ 26 Kenneth Krahenbuhl
☐ 27 Rafael Soto
☐ 28 Andy Hartung
☐ 29 Checklist

1991 Peoria Chiefs ProCards

This 29-card standard-size set of the 1991 Peoria Cubs, a Class A Midwest League affiliate of the Chicago Cubs, features on its white-bordered fronts posed color player photos set on simulated spiral-bound yellow notebooks. The player's name, position, and team appear within a green rectangle below the photo. The yellow horizontal back is bordered in white and carries the player's name at the top, followed by biography and statistics.

	MINT	NRMT	EXC
COMPLETE SET (29)	5.00	2.20	.60

☐ 1333 Pedro Alicano
☐ 1334 Amilcar Correa
☐ 1335 Tim Delgado
☐ 1336 Jason Doss
☐ 1337 Tyson Godfrey
☐ 1338 Chuck Kirk
☐ 1339 Tom Mann
☐ 1340 Pedro Perez
☐ 1341 Dave Ross
☐ 1342 Dave Swartzbaugh
☐ 1343 Aaron Taylor
☐ 1344 Brad Erdman
☐ 1345 Rick Mundy
☐ 1346 Steve Coffey
☐ 1347 Morris Craig
☐ 1348 German Diaz
☐ 1349 Andy Hartung
☐ 1350 Tim Moore
☐ 1351 Rafael Soto
☐ 1352 Jose Vierra
☐ 1353 Danny Cancel
☐ 1354 Earl Cunningham
☐ 1355 Phil Dauphin
☐ 1356 Rolando Fernandez
☐ 1357 Willie Gardner
☐ 1358 Mike Little
☐ 1359 Bill Hayes MGR
☐ 1360 Lester Strode CO
☐ 1361 Checklist

1991 Peoria Chiefs Team Issue

	MINT	NRMT	EXC
COMPLETE SET (34)	6.00	2.70	.75

☐ 1 Bill Hayes MG
☐ 2 Lester Strode CO
☐ 3 Jim O'Reilly TR
☐ 4 Pedro Alicano
☐ 5 Amilcar Correa
☐ 6 Tim Delgado
☐ 7 Jason Doss
☐ 8 Tyson Godfrey
☐ 9 Chuck Kirk
☐ 10 Ken Krahenbuhl
☐ 11 Tom Mann
☐ 12 David Ross
☐ 13 Aaron Taylor
☐ 14 Brad Erdman
☐ 15 Rick Mundy
☐ 16 German Diaz
☐ 17 Andy Hartung
☐ 18 Tim Moore
☐ 19 Rafael Soto
☐ 20 Paul Torres
☐ 21 Jose Viera
☐ 22 Bryan Wilson
☐ 23 Victor Cancel
☐ 24 Earl Cunningham
☐ 25 Phil Dauphin
☐ 26 Rolando Fernandez
☐ 27 Mike Little
☐ 28 John Davis CO
☐ 29 Acro
(Mascot)
☐ 30 Staff
Ted Cox
Mike Nelson
Mark Krusinski
Norm Jenkins
Ralph Rashid
Greg Ayers
Tom Nichols
☐ 31 Rick Sutcliffe
☐ 32 Scott Weiss
☐ 33 Darrin Duffy
☐ 34 Bill Bliss

1991 Phoenix Firebirds Line Drive

	MINT	NRMT	EXC
COMPLETE SET (26)	5.00	2.20	.60

☐ 376 Rich Aldrete
☐ 377 Mark Bailey
☐ 378 Rod Beck
☐ 379 Jeff Carter
☐ 380 Craig Colbert
☐ 381 Darnell Coles
☐ 382 Mark Dewey
☐ 383 Gil Heredia
☐ 384 Darren Lewis
☐ 385 Johnny Ard
☐ 386 Rafael Novoa
☐ 387 Francisco Oliveras
☐ 388 Tony Perezchica
☐ 389 Mark Thurmond
☐ 390 Mike Remlinger
☐ 391 Greg Ritchie
☐ 392 Rick Rodriguez
☐ 393 Andres Santana
☐ 394 Jose Segura
☐ 395 Stuart Tate
☐ 396 Jimmy Williams
☐ 397 Jim Wilson
☐ 398 Ted Wood
☐ 399 Duane Espy MGR
☐ 400 Alan Bannister CO
Larry Hardy CO
☐ NNO Title card

1991 Phoenix Firebirds ProCards

This 29-card standard-size set of the 1991 Phoenix Firebirds, a Class AAA Pacific Coast League affiliate of the San Francisco Giants, features on its white-bordered fronts posed color player photos set on simulated spiral-bound yellow notebooks. The player's name, position, and team appear within a green rectangle below the photo. The yellow horizontal back is bordered in white and carries the player's name at the top, followed by biography and statistics.

	MINT	NRMT	EXC
COMPLETE SET (29)	5.00	2.20	.60

☐ 58 Johnny Ard
☐ 59 Rod Beck
☐ 60 Mark Dewey
☐ 61 Gil Heredia
☐ 62 Rafael Novoa
☐ 63 Francisco Oliveras
☐ 64 Mike Remlinger
☐ 65 Rick Rodriguez
☐ 66 Jose Segura
☐ 67 Stuart Tate
☐ 68 Jimmy Williams
☐ 69 Mark Bailey
☐ 70 Craig Colbert
☐ 71 Jeff Carter
☐ 72 Paul Noce
☐ 73 Rick Parker
☐ 74 Tony Perezchica
☐ 75 Ken Phelps
☐ 76 Andres Santana
☐ 77 Jim Wilson
☐ 78 Rich Aldrete
☐ 79 Darnell Coles
☐ 80 Darren Lewis
☐ 81 Gregg Ritchie
☐ 82 Ted Wood
☐ 83 Duane Espy MGR
☐ 84 Alan Bannister CO
☐ 85 Larry Hardy CO
☐ 86 Checklist

1991 Pittsfield Mets Classic/Best

This 28-card standard-size set of the 1991 Pittsfield Mets, a Class A New York-Penn League affiliate of the New York Mets, features white-bordered posed color player photos on its fronts. The player's name, team, and position appear at the bottom. The white back is framed by a thin black line and carries the player's name and position at the top, followed by biography, statistics and team logos.

	MINT	NRMT	EXC
COMPLETE SET (28)	5.00	2.20	.60

☐ 1 Tony Tijerina
☐ 2 Greg Beals
☐ 3 Dwight Robinson
☐ 4 Frank Jacobs
☐ 5 Todd Nace
☐ 6 Randy Curtis
☐ 7 Jerome Tolliver
☐ 8 Tim Sandy
☐ 9 Michael Sciortino
☐ 10 Danilo Mompres
☐ 11 Bernie Millan
☐ 12 Micah Franklin
☐ 13 Joe Arredondo
☐ 14 Casper Van Rynbach
☐ 15 Ottis Smith
☐ 16 Chris Shanahan
☐ 17 Jim Scheffler
☐ 18 Jim Manfred
☐ 19 Darian Lindsay
☐ 20 Mike Lehnerz
☐ 21 Hector Carrasco
Sic, Carraso
☐ 22 Mike Anaya
☐ 23 Chris George
☐ 24 Eric Reichenbach
☐ 25 Jim Thrift MGR
☐ 26 Jerry Koosman CO
☐ 27 Billy Gardner CO
☐ 28 Checklist

1991 Pittsfield Mets ProCards

This 28-card standard-size set of the 1991 Pittsfield Mets, a Class A New York-Penn League affiliate of the New York Mets, features on its white-bordered fronts posed color player photos set on simulated spiral-bound yellow notebooks. The player's name, position, and team appear within a green rectangle below the photo. The yellow horizontal back is bordered in white and carries the player's name at the top, followed by biography and statistics.

	MINT	NRMT	EXC
COMPLETE SET (28)	5.00	2.20	.60

☐ 3414 Mike Anaya
☐ 3415 Hector Carrasco
☐ 3416 Chris George
☐ 3417 Mike Lehnerz
☐ 3418 Darian Lindsay
☐ 3419 Jim Manfred
☐ 3420 Eric Reichenbach
☐ 3421 Jim Scheffler
☐ 3422 Chris Shanahan
☐ 3423 Ottis Smith
☐ 3424 Caspar Van Rynbach
☐ 3425 Greg Beals
☐ 3426 Tony Tijerina
☐ 3427 Joe Arredondo
☐ 3428 Micah Franklin
☐ 3429 Frank Jacobs
☐ 3430 Bernie Millan
☐ 3431 Danilo Mompres
☐ 3432 Dwight Robinson
☐ 3433 Mike Sciortino
☐ 3434 Randy Curtis
☐ 3435 Todd Nace
☐ 3436 Tim Sandy
☐ 3437 Jerome Tolliver
☐ 3438 Jim Thrift MGR
☐ 3439 Billy Gardner CO
☐ 3440 Jerry Koosman CO
☐ 3441 Checklist

1991 Pocatello Pioneers ProCards

This 31-card standard-size set of the 1991 Pocatello Pioneers, a Rookie Class Pioneer League Independent, features on its white-bordered fronts posed color player photos set on simulated spiral-bound yellow notebooks. The player's name, position, and team appear within a green rectangle below the photo. The yellow horizontal back is bordered in white and carries the player's name at the top, followed by biography and statistics.

	MINT	NRMT	EXC
COMPLETE SET (31)	5.00	2.20	.60

☐ 3773 Derek Atwood
☐ 3774 Robby Callistro
☐ 3775 Rich Ekman
☐ 3776 Monty Gibson
☐ 3777 Steve Grennan
☐ 3778 Steve Mill
☐ 3779 Steve Patterson
☐ 3780 Jason Reese
☐ 3781 Bruce Schenck
☐ 3782 Dale Stevens
☐ 3783 Von Wechsberg
☐ 3784 James Joyce
☐ 3785 John Martinez
☐ 3786 Marc Morris
☐ 3787 Buck Atwater
☐ 3788 Dean Banks
☐ 3789 Kris Kaelin
☐ 3790 Audy Mesa
☐ 3791 Jeff Scholzen
☐ 3792 Paul Weldon
☐ 3793 Kevin Wong
☐ 3794 Todd Anderson
☐ 3795 William Carmona
☐ 3796 Stacy Hamm
☐ 3797 Larry Minter
☐ 3798 Dino Philyaw
☐ 3799 Terry Robinson
☐ 3800 Rich Morales Jr.
☐ 3801 Rick Rodriguez CO
☐ 3802 Eddie Sedar CO
☐ 3803 Checklist

1991 Pocatello Pioneers Sports Pro

This 30-card standard-size set of the 1991 Pocatello Pioneers, a Rookie Class Pioneer League Independent, features posed color head-and-shoulders shots, with thin black borders on a white card face. The horizontally oriented backs have biographical information.

	MINT	NRMT	EXC
COMPLETE SET (30)	6.00	2.70	.75

☐ 1 Larry Minter
☐ 2 Rob Callistro
☐ 3 Steve Mill
☐ 4 Richard Joyce
☐ 5 Terry Robinson
☐ 6 Bruce Schenck
☐ 7 Von Wechsberg
☐ 8 John Martinez
☐ 9 Rich Ekman
☐ 10 Dean Banks
☐ 11 Jason Reese
☐ 12 Marc Morris
☐ 13 Derick Atwood
☐ 14 Kevin Wong
☐ 15 Steve Patterson
☐ 16 Todd Anderson
☐ 17 Dale Stevens
☐ 18 Monty Gibson
☐ 19 Steve Grennan
☐ 20 Kris Kaelin
☐ 21 Paul Weldon
☐ 22 Jeffrey Scholzen
☐ 23 Tyrone Atwater
☐ 24 Audy Mesa
☐ 25 Dino Philyaw
☐ 26 Stacy Hamm
☐ 27 William Carmona
☐ 28 Eddie Sedar CO
☐ 29 Rick Rodriguez CO
☐ 30 Rich Morales Jr. MG

1991 Portland Beavers Line Drive

	MINT	NRMT	EXC
COMPLETE SET (26)	5.00	2.20	.60

☐ 401 Paul Abbott
☐ 402 Willie Banks
☐ 403 Bernardo Brito
☐ 404 Jarvis Brown
☐ 405 J.T. Bruett
☐ 406 Tim Drummond

☐ 407 Tom Edens
☐ 408 Rich Garces
☐ 409 Chip Hale
☐ 410 Terry Jorgensen
☐ 411 Kenny Morgan
☐ 412 Pedro Munoz
☐ 413 Edgar Naveda
☐ 414 Denny Neagle
☐ 415 Jeff Reboulet
☐ 416 Victor Rodriguez
☐ 417 Jack Savage
☐ 418 Dan Sheaffer
☐ 419 Charles Scott
☐ 420 Paul Sorrento
☐ 421 George Tsamis
☐ 422 Lenny Webster
☐ 423 Carl Willis
☐ 424 Russ Nixon MGR
☐ 425 Jim Dwyer CO
Gorman Heimueller CO
Paul Kirsch CO
☐ NNO Title card

1991 Portland Beavers ProCards

This 28-card standard-size set of the 1991 Portland Beavers, a Class AAA Pacific Coast League affiliate of the Minnesota Twins, features on its white-bordered fronts posed color player photos set on simulated spiral-bound yellow notebooks. The player's name, position, and team appear within a green rectangle below the photo. The yellow horizontal back is bordered in white and carries the player's name at the top, followed by biography and statistics.

	MINT	NRMT	EXC
COMPLETE SET (28)	5.00	2.20	.60

☐ 1558 Paul Abbott
☐ 1559 Willie Banks
☐ 1560 Tim Drummond
☐ 1561 Tom Edens
☐ 1562 Richard Garces
☐ 1563 Denny Neagle
☐ 1564 Jack Savage
☐ 1565 Charles Scott
☐ 1566 George Tsamis
☐ 1567 Carl Willis
☐ 1568 Danny Sheaffer
☐ 1569 Lenny Webster
☐ 1570 Chip Hale
☐ 1571 Terry Jorgensen
☐ 1572 Jeff Reboulet
☐ 1573 Victor Rodriguez
☐ 1574 Paul Sorrento
☐ 1575 Bernardo Brito
☐ 1576 Jarvis Brown
☐ 1577 J.T. Bruett
☐ 1578 Kenny Morgan
☐ 1579 Pedro Munoz
☐ 1580 Edgar Naveda
☐ 1581 Russ Nixon MGR
☐ 1582 Jim Swyer CO
☐ 1583 Gorman Heimueller CO
☐ 1584 Paul Kirsch CO
☐ 1585 Checklist

1991 Prince William Cannons Classic/Best

This 30-card standard-size set of the 1991 Prince William Cannons, a Class A Carolina League affiliate of the New York Yankees, features white-bordered posed color player photos on its fronts. The player's name, team, and position appear at the bottom. The white back is framed by a thin black line and carries the player's name and position at the top, followed by biography, statistics and team logos.

	MINT	NRMT	EXC
COMPLETE SET (30)	5.00	2.20	.60

☐ 1 Brent Gilbert
☐ 2 Sterling Hitchcock
☐ 3 Darren Hodges
☐ 4 Jeff Hoffman
☐ 5 Mike Hankins
☐ 6 Dan Johnston
☐ 7 Sam Militello Jr.
☐ 8 Mark Ohlms
☐ 9 Kirt Ojala
☐ 10 Curtis Ralph
☐ 11 Rocky Rhodes
☐ 12 Stephen Tucker
☐ 13 Brad Ausmus
☐ 14 Michael Figga
☐ 15 John Jarvis
☐ 16 Robert Eenhoorn
☐ 17 Andy Fox
☐ 18 Ramon Jimenez
☐ 19 Daniel Sanchez
☐ 20 Joey Wardlow
☐ 21 Paul Oster
☐ 22 Jason Robertson
☐ 23 John Viera
☐ 24 Mike Hart
☐ 25 Dave Schuler CO
☐ 26 Rob Thomson CO
☐ 27 Adam Wagner TR
☐ 28 Sherman Obando
☐ 29 Jim Haller
☐ 30 Prince Willie
Checklist

1991 Prince William Cannons ProCards

This 29-card standard-size set of the 1991 Prince William Cannons, a Class A Carolina League affiliate of the New York Yankees, features on its white-bordered fronts posed color player photos set on simulated spiral-bound yellow notebooks. The player's name, position, and team appear within a green rectangle below the photo. The yellow horizontal back is bordered in white and carries the player's name at the top, followed by biography and statistics.

	MINT	NRMT	EXC
COMPLETE SET (29)	5.00	2.20	.60

☐ 1417 Brent Gilbert
☐ 1418 Jim Haller
☐ 1419 Sterling Hitchcock
☐ 1420 Darren Hodges
☐ 1421 Jeff Hoffman
☐ 1422 Dan Johnston
☐ 1423 Sam Militello
☐ 1424 Mark Ohlms
☐ 1425 Kirt Ojala
☐ 1426 Curtis Ralph
☐ 1427 Ricky Rhodes
☐ 1428 Stephen Tucker
☐ 1429 Brad Ausmus
☐ 1430 Michael Figga
☐ 1431 John Jarvis
☐ 1432 Robert Eenhoorn
☐ 1433 Andy Fox
☐ 1434 Mike Hankins
☐ 1435 Ramon Jimenez
☐ 1436 Daniel Sanchez
☐ 1437 Joe Wardlow
☐ 1438 Sherman Obando
☐ 1439 Paul Oster
☐ 1440 Jason Robertson
☐ 1441 John Viera
☐ 1442 Mike Hart MGR
☐ 1443 Dave Schuler CO
☐ 1444 Rob Thomson CO
☐ 1445 Checklist

1991 Princeton Reds Classic/Best

This 30-card standard-size set of the 1991 Princeton Reds, a Rookie Class Appalachian League affiliate of the Cincinnati Reds, features white-bordered posed color player photos on its fronts. The player's name, team, and position appear at the bottom. The white back is framed by a thin black line and carries the player's name and position at the top, followed by biography, statistics and team logos.

	MINT	NRMT	EXC
COMPLETE SET (30)	5.00	2.20	.60

☐ 1 Kevin Aubin
☐ 2 Juan Loyola
☐ 3 Omar Malpice
☐ 4 John Gast
☐ 5 Ken Cavazzoni
☐ 6 Chris Reed
☐ 7 James Miller
☐ 8 John Hrusovsky
☐ 9 Rodney Steph
☐ 10 Rossi Morris
☐ 11 Armando Morales
☐ 12 Bill Dreisbach
☐ 13 Toby Rumfield
☐ 14 Dee Jenkins
☐ 15 Calvin Reese
☐ 16 Rodney Thomas
☐ 17 Eli Robinson
☐ 18 Jeff Murphy
☐ 19 Yamil Concepcion
☐ 20 Blake Bentley
Sic, Bently
☐ 21 Wayne Wilkerson
☐ 22 Rory Rhodriguez
☐ 23 Kevin Jarvis
☐ 24 Bryant Balentine
☐ 25 John Brothers
☐ 26 Jimmy Wiggins
☐ 27 Fermin Garcia
☐ 28 Sam Mejias MGR
☐ 29 Jim Arendt
☐ 30 Tom Iverson TR
Checklist

1991 Princeton Reds ProCards

This 30-card standard-size set of the 1991 Princeton Reds, a Rookie Class Appalachian League affiliate of the Cincinnati Reds, features on its white-bordered fronts posed color player photos set on simulated spiral-bound yellow notebooks. The player's name, position, and team appear within a green rectangle below the photo. The yellow horizontal back is bordered in white and carries the player's name at the top, followed by biography and statistics.

	MINT	NRMT	EXC
COMPLETE SET (30)	5.00	2.20	.60

☐ 3504 Bryant Balentine
☐ 3505 John Brothers
☐ 3506 Fermin Garcia
☐ 3507 John Hrusovsky
☐ 3508 Kevin Jarvis
☐ 3509 Jim Miller
☐ 3510 Armando Morales
☐ 3511 Jeff Murphy
☐ 3512 Chris Reed
☐ 3513 Rory Rhodriguez
☐ 3514 Rodney Steph
☐ 3515 Jim Wiggins
☐ 3516 Kevin Aubin
☐ 3517 Bill Dreisbach
☐ 3518 Toby Rumfield
☐ 3519 Ken Cavazzoni
☐ 3520 Yamil Concepcion
☐ 3521 John Gast
☐ 3522 Dee Jenkins
☐ 3523 Calvin Reese
☐ 3524 Eli Robinson
☐ 3525 Blake Bentley
☐ 3526 Juan Loyola
☐ 3527 Omar Malpica
☐ 3528 Rossi Morris
☐ 3529 Rodney Thomas
☐ 3530 Wayne Wilkerson
☐ 3531 Sam Mejias MGR
☐ 3532 Doc Rodgers CO
☐ 3533 Checklist

1991 Pulaski Braves Classic/Best

This 30-card standard-size set of the 1991 Pulaski Braves, a Rookie Class Appalachian League affiliate of the Atlanta Braves, features white-bordered posed color player photos on its fronts. The player's name, team, and position appear at the bottom. The white back is framed by a thin black line and carries the player's name and position at the top, followed by biography, statistics and team logos.

	MINT	NRMT	EXC
COMPLETE SET (30)	5.00	2.20	.60

☐ 1 Joe Ayrault
☐ 2 Paul Keliher
☐ 3 Carlos Lara
☐ 4 Carl Archer
☐ 5 Keith Chaney
☐ 6 Cory Crosnoe
☐ 7 Manuel Jimenez
☐ 8 Jason Keeline
☐ 9 Lansing Marks
☐ 10 George Virgilio
☐ 11 Mark Chambers
☐ 12 Andre Johnson
☐ 13 Don Robinson
☐ 14 Randy Ingle MGR
☐ 15 Javier Rivas
☐ 16 Scott Behrens
☐ 17 Dirk Blair
☐ 18 Stewart Ford
☐ 19 Dwayne Fowler
☐ 20 Cloyd Boyer CO
☐ 21 Jason Butler
☐ 22 Scott Francis
☐ 23 Fred Koening CO
☐ 24 Eric Lairsey
☐ 25 Ricardo Petit
☐ 26 Scott Ryder
☐ 27 John Wilder
☐ 28 Matt Viarengo
☐ 29 Kevin Saulter
☐ 30 Mike Cerame TR
Checklist

1991 Pulaski Braves ProCards

This 31-card standard-size set of the 1991 Pulaski Braves, a Rookie Class Appalachian League affiliate of the Atlanta Braves, features on its white-bordered fronts posed color player photos set on simulated spiral-bound yellow notebooks. The player's name, position, and team appear within a green rectangle below the photo. The yellow horizontal back is bordered in white and carries the player's name at the top, followed by biography and statistics.

	MINT	NRMT	EXC
COMPLETE SET (31)	5.00	2.20	.60

☐ 3995 Scott Behrens
☐ 3996 Dirk Blair
☐ 3997 Jason Butler
☐ 3998 Stewart Ford
☐ 3999 Dwayne Fowler
☐ 4000 Scott Francis
☐ 4001 Eric Lairsey
☐ 4002 Ricardo Petit
☐ 4003 Scott Ryder
☐ 4004 Kevin Saulter
☐ 4005 Matt Viarengo
☐ 4006 John Wilder
☐ 4007 Joe Ayrault
☐ 4008 Paul Kelliher
☐ 4009 Carlos Lara
☐ 4010 Carl Archer
☐ 4011 Keith Chaney
☐ 4012 Cory Crosnoe
☐ 4013 Manuel Jimenez
☐ 4014 Jason Keeline
☐ 4015 Lance Marks
☐ 4016 George Virgilio
☐ 4017 Mark Chambers
☐ 4018 Andre Johnson
☐ 4019 Javier Rivas
☐ 4020 Don Robinson
☐ 4021 Dominic Therrien
☐ 4022 Randy Ingle MGR
☐ 4023 Cloyd Boyer CO
☐ 4024 Fred Koenig CO
☐ 4025 Checklist

1991 Quad City Angels Classic/Best

This 29-card standard-size set of the 1991 Quad City Angels, a Class A Midwest League affiliate of the California Angels, features white-bordered posed color player photos on its fronts. The player's name, team, and position appear at the bottom. The white back is framed by a thin black line and carries the player's name and position at the top, followed by biography, statistics and team logos. This issue includes the minor league card debut of Garret Anderson.

	MINT	NRMT	EXC
COMPLETE SET (29)	8.00	3.60	1.00

☐ 1 Dave Adams
☐ 2 Britt Craven
☐ 3 Ken Edenfield
☐ 4 Bobby Gamez
☐ 5 Matt Hyde CO
☐ 6 Bret Lacheman
☐ 7 Phil Leftwich
☐ 8 Justin Martin
☐ 9 Norm Montoya
☐ 10 Darryl Scott
☐ 11 Victor Silverio
☐ 12 Tom Dodge
☐ 13 Jose Stela
☐ 14 Fausto Tejero
☐ 15 Don Barbara
☐ 16 Mark Dalesandro
☐ 17 Brian Grebeck
☐ 18 Jeff Kipila
☐ 19 Billy Minnis
☐ 20 Jeff Oberdank
☐ 21 Carlos Polanco
☐ 22 Garret Anderson
☐ 23 Emmitt Cohick
☐ 24 Cliff Garrett
☐ 25 Dan Pieratt TR
☐ 26 Rafael Muratti
☐ 27 Mitch Seoane MGR
☐ 28 Joe Georger CO
☐ 29 Checklist

1991 Quad City Angels ProCards

This 31-card standard-size set of the 1991 Quad City Angels, a Class A Midwest League affiliate of the California Angels, features on its white-bordered fronts posed color player photos set on simulated spiral-bound yellow notebooks. The player's name, position, and team appear within a green rectangle below the photo. The yellow horizontal back is bordered in white and carries the player's name at the top, followed by biography and statistics. This issue includes the minor league card debut of Garret Anderson.

	MINT	NRMT	EXC
COMPLETE SET (31)	7.00	3.10	.85

☐ 2618 Dave Adams
☐ 2619 Britt Craven
☐ 2620 Ken Edenfield
☐ 2621 Bobby Gamez
☐ 2622 Joe Klancnik
☐ 2623 Bret Lachemann
☐ 2624 Phil Leftwich
☐ 2625 Justin Martin
☐ 2626 Norman Montoya
☐ 2627 Darryl Scott
☐ 2628 Victor Silverio
☐ 2629 Jon Anderson
☐ 2630 Tom Dodge
☐ 2631 Jose Stela
☐ 2632 Fausto Tejero
☐ 2633 Don Barbara
☐ 2634 Mark Dalesandro
☐ 2635 Gary Forrester
☐ 2636 Brian Grebeck
☐ 2637 Jeff Kipila
☐ 2638 Billy Minnis
☐ 2639 Jeff Oberdank
☐ 2640 Carlos Polanco

☐ 2641 Garret Anderson
☐ 2642 Emmitt Cohick
☐ 2643 Cliff Garrett
☐ 2644 Rafael Muratti
☐ 2645 Mitch Seoane MGR
☐ 2646 Joe Georger CO
☐ 2647 Matt Hyde CO
☐ 2648 Checklist

1991 Reading Phillies Line Drive

	MINT	NRMT	EXC
COMPLETE SET (26)	5.00	2.20	.60

☐ 501 Jason Backs
☐ 502 Toby Borland
☐ 503 Cliff Brantley
☐ 504 Dana Brown
☐ 505 John Burgos
☐ 506 Andy Carter
☐ 507 Bruce Dostal
☐ 508 Rick Dunnum
☐ 509 John Martin
☐ 510 David Holdridge
☐ 511 Darrell Lindsey
☐ 512 Doug Lindsey
☐ 513 Tony Longmire
☐ 514 Tom Marsh
☐ 515 Rod Robertson
☐ 516 Edwin Rosado
☐ 517 Sean Ryan
☐ 518 Steve Scarsone
☐ 519 Mark Sims
☐ 520 Jeff Tabaka
☐ 521 Tony Trevino
☐ 522 Casey Waller
☐ 523 Cary Williams
☐ 524 Don McCormack MGR
☐ 525 Al LeBoeuf CO
☐ NNO Title card

1991 Reading Phillies ProCards

This 27-card standard-size set of the 1991 Reading Phillies, a Class AA Eastern League affiliate of the Philadelphia Phillies, features on its white-bordered fronts posed color player photos set on simulated spiral-bound yellow notebooks. The player's name, position, and team appear within a green rectangle below the photo. The yellow horizontal back is bordered in white and carries the player's name at the top, followed by biography and statistics.

	MINT	NRMT	EXC
COMPLETE SET (27)	5.00	2.20	.60

☐ 398 Checklist
☐ 1362 Jason Backs
☐ 1363 Toby Borland
☐ 1364 Cliff Brantley
☐ 1365 John Burgos
☐ 1366 Andy Carter
☐ 1367 Rick Dunnum
☐ 1368 David Holdridge
☐ 1369 Darrell Lindsey
☐ 1370 Mark Sims
☐ 1371 Jeff Tabaka
☐ 1372 Doug Lindsey
☐ 1373 Edwin Rosado
☐ 1374 Joe Millette
☐ 1375 Nikco Riesgo
☐ 1376 Rod Robertson
☐ 1377 Sean Ryan
☐ 1378 Tony Trevino
☐ 1379 Casey Waller
☐ 1380 Dana Brown
☐ 1381 Bruce Dostal
☐ 1382 Tony Longmire
☐ 1383 Tom Marsh
☐ 1384 Cary Williams
☐ 1385 Don McCormack MGR
☐ 1386 Al LeBoeuf CO
☐ 1387 John Martin CO

1991 Reno Silver Sox Cal League Cards

	MINT	NRMT	EXC
COMPLETE SET (29)	6.00	2.70	.75

☐ 1 John Rabb
☐ 2 Mark Krumback
☐ 3 Lonnie Phillips
☐ 4 Frank Turco
☐ 5 Jim Jones
☐ 6 Dom Johnson
☐ 7 Cliff Williams
☐ 8 Rick Odekirk
☐ 9 Andy Postema
☐ 10 Joe Warren
☐ 11 Doug Messer
☐ 12 Cliff Gonzalez
☐ 13 Joe Roebuck
☐ 14 Tom Mitchell
☐ 15 Mike Norris
☐ 16 Tom Gilles
☐ 17 Troy Clemens
☐ 18 Todd McCray
☐ 19 Rich Buonantony
☐ 20 Francisco Alcantara
☐ 21 Mike Songini
☐ 22 Dodd Johnson
☐ 23 Dion Beck
☐ 24 Brian Stephens
☐ 25 Joe Olker
☐ 26 David Voit
☐ 27 Bill Murray TR
☐ 28 Dean Treanor CO
☐ 29 Mal Fichman MG

1991 Richmond Braves Bob's Camera

This 42-card team set of the 1991 Richmond Braves, a Class AAA International League affiliate of the Atlanta Braves, was sponsored by Bob's Camera. The fronts feature borderless color player photos with sponsors' and team's logos in the wide bottom margin. The backs are blank. 500 sets were produced.

	MINT	NRMT	EXC
COMPLETE SET (42)	75.00	34.00	9.50

☐ 1 Andy Tomberlin
☐ 2 Bruce Crabbe
☐ 3 Kelly Mann
☐ 4 Rusty Richards
☐ 5 Gibson Alba
☐ 6 John Davis
☐ 7 Tony Castillo
☐ 8 Randy Kramer
☐ 10 Tom McCarthy
☐ 11 Andy Nezelek
☐ 12 Yorkis Perez
☐ 13 Dale Polley
☐ 14 Armando Reynoso
☐ 15 Mark Ross
☐ 16 Randy St. Claire
☐ 17 Matt Turner
☐ 18 Joe Szekely
☐ 19 John Alva
☐ 20 Mike Bell
☐ 21 Victor Rosario
☐ 22 Rico Rossy
☐ 23 Tracy Woodson
☐ 24 Bruce Fields
☐ 25 Brian R. Hunter
☐ 26 Mike Loggins
☐ 27 Al Martin
☐ 28 Rich Casarotti
☐ 29 Vinny Castilla
☐ 30 Mark Wohlers
☐ 31 Jerome Nelson
☐ 32 Jeff Parrett
☐ 33 Keith Mitchell
☐ 34 Pat Gomez
☐ 35 Boi Rodriguez
☐ 36 Jerry Willard
☐ 37 Deion Sanders
☐ 38 Phil Niekro MG
☐ 39 Sonny Jackson CO
☐ 40 Bruce Dal Canton CO
☐ 41 Johnny Grubb CO
☐ 42 Rick Berg CO
☐ 43 Steve Curry CO

1991 Richmond Braves Line Drive

	MINT	NRMT	EXC
COMPLETE SET (26)	5.00	2.20	.60

☐ 426 John Alva
☐ 427 Mike Bell
☐ 428 Tony Castillo
☐ 429 Bruce Crabbe
☐ 430 John Davis
☐ 431 Brian R. Hunter
☐ 432 Randy Kramer
☐ 433 Mike Loggins
☐ 434 Kelly Mann
☐ 435 Tom McCarthy
☐ 436 Yorkis Perez
☐ 437 Dale Polley
☐ 438 Armando Reynoso
☐ 439 Rusty Richards
☐ 440 Victor Rasario
☐ 441 Mark Ross
☐ 442 Rico Rossy
☐ 443 Randy St. Claire
☐ 444 Joe Szekely
☐ 445 Andy Tomberlin
☐ 446 Matt Turner
☐ 447 Glenn Wilson
☐ 448 Tracy Woodson
☐ 449 Phil Niekro MGR
☐ 450 Bruce Dal Canton CO
Sonny Jackson CO
☐ NNO Title card

1991 Richmond Braves ProCards

This 30-card standard-size set of the 1991 Richmond Braves, a Class AAA International League affiliate of the Atlanta Braves, features on its white-bordered fronts posed color player photos set on simulated spiral-bound yellow notebooks. The player's name, position, and team appear within a green rectangle below the photo. The yellow horizontal back is bordered in white and carries the player's name at the top, followed by biography and statistics.

	MINT	NRMT	EXC
COMPLETE SET (30)	5.00	2.20	.60

☐ 2559 Gibson Alba
☐ 2560 Tony Castillo
☐ 2561 Randy Kramer
☐ 2562 Paul Marak
☐ 2563 Tom McCarthy
☐ 2564 Yorkis Perez
☐ 2565 Dale Polley
☐ 2566 Armando Reynoso
☐ 2567 Mark Ross
☐ 2568 Randy St. Claire
☐ 2569 Matt Turner
☐ 2570 Randy Veres
☐ 2571 Kelly Mann
☐ 2572 Joe Szekely
☐ 2573 Jerry Willard
☐ 2574 John Alva
☐ 2575 Mike Bell
☐ 2576 Bruce Crabbe
☐ 2577 Victor Rosario
☐ 2578 Rico Rossy
☐ 2579 Tracy Woodson
☐ 2580 Bruce Fields
☐ 2581 Brian R. Hunter
☐ 2582 Glenn Wilson
☐ 2583 Phil Niekro MGR
☐ 2584 Rick Berg CO
☐ 2585 Bruce Dal Canton CO
☐ 2586 John Grubb CO
☐ 2587 Sonny Jackson CO
☐ 2588 Checklist

1991 Richmond Braves Team Issue

This 28-card standard-size set of the 1991 Richmond Braves, a Class AAA International League affiliate of the Atlanta Braves, was issued in seven strips that included four cards and a Pepsi coupon. The set was sponsored by Ukrop's. One strip was inserted in every 24 packs of Pepsi.

	MINT	NRMT	EXC
COMPLETE SET (28)	6.00	2.70	.75

☐ 1 Armando Reynoso
☐ 2 Mike Loggins
☐ 3 Rico Rossy
☐ 4 Phil Niekro MGR
☐ 5 Bruce Fields
☐ 6 Tony Castillo
☐ 7 Gibson Alba
☐ 8 Mike Bell
☐ 9 Rusty Richards
☐ 10 Randy St. Claire
☐ 11 Victor Rosario
☐ 12 Joe Szekely
☐ 13 John Alva
☐ 14 Tom McCarthy
☐ 15 Tracy Woodson
☐ 16 Yorkis Perez
☐ 17 Randy Kramer
☐ 18 Brian R. Hunter
☐ 19 Andy Tomberlin
☐ 20 Jerry Willard
☐ 21 Bruce Crabbe
☐ 22 John Davis
☐ 23 Dale Polley
☐ 24 Kelly Mann
☐ 25 Matt Turner
☐ 26 Glenn Wilson
☐ 27 Diamond Duck
Mascot
☐ 28 Mark Ross

1991 Rochester Red Wings Line Drive

	MINT	NRMT	EXC
COMPLETE SET (26)	7.00	3.10	.85

☐ 451 Tony Chance
☐ 452 Joaquin Contreras
☐ 453 Francisco Delarosa
☐ 454 Benny Distefano
☐ 455 Mike Eberle
☐ 456 Todd Frohwirth
☐ 457 Steve Jeltz
☐ 458 Chito Martinez
☐ 459 Dave Martinez
☐ 460 Jeff McKnight
☐ 461 Luis Mercedes
☐ 462 Mike Mussina
☐ 463 Chris Myers
☐ 464 Joe Price
☐ 465 Israel Sanchez
☐ 466 David Segui
☐ 467 Tommy Shields
☐ 468 Mike Linskey
☐ 469 Jack Tackett
☐ 470 Anthony Telford
☐ 471 Shane Turner
☐ 472 Jeff Wetherby
☐ 473 Rob Woodward
☐ 474 Greg Biagini MGR
☐ 475 Mike Young CO
Dick Bosman CO
☐ NNO Title card

1991 Rochester Red Wings ProCards

This 27-card standard-size set of the 1991 Rochester Red Wings, a Class AAA International League affiliate of the Baltimore Orioles, features on its white-bordered fronts posed color player photos set on simulated spiral-bound yellow notebooks. The player's name, position, and team appear within a green rectangle below the photo. The yellow horizontal back is bordered in white and carries the player's name at the top, followed by biography and statistics. This issue includes the second year card of Mike Mussina.

	MINT	NRMT	EXC
COMPLETE SET (27)	8.00	3.60	1.00

☐ 1895 Francisco De La Rosa
☐ 1896 Todd Frohwirth
☐ 1897 Mike Linskey
☐ 1898 Dave Martinez
☐ 1899 Mike Mussina
☐ 1900 Chris Myers
☐ 1901 Israel Sanchez
☐ 1902 Roy Smith
☐ 1903 Anthony Telford
☐ 1904 Rob Woodward
☐ 1905 Mike Eberle
☐ 1906 Jack Tackett
☐ 1907 Benny Distefano
☐ 1908 Steve Jeltz
☐ 1909 Jeff McKnight
☐ 1910 David Segui
☐ 1911 Tommy Shields
☐ 1912 Shane Turner
☐ 1913 Tony Chance
☐ 1914 Chito Martinez
☐ 1915 Obbibe McDowell
☐ 1916 Luis Mercedes
☐ 1917 Jeff Wetherby
☐ 1918 Greg Biagini MGR
☐ 1919 Dick Bosman CO
☐ 1920 Mike Young CO
☐ 1921 Checklist

1991 Rockford Expos Classic/Best

This 30-card standard-size set of the 1991 Rockford Expos, a Class A Midwest League affiliate of the Montreal Expos, features white-bordered posed color player photos on its fronts. The player's name, team, and position appear at the bottom. The white back is framed by a thin black line and carries the player's name and position at the top, followed by biography, statistics and team logos.

	MINT	NRMT	EXC
COMPLETE SET (30)	5.00	2.20	.60

☐ 1 Bob Baxter
☐ 2 Jim Young TR
☐ 3 Stacey Collins
☐ 4 Ralph Diaz
☐ 5 Ranbir Grewal
☐ 6 Ben Howze
☐ 7 Pat Jurado
☐ 8 Martin Martinez
☐ 9 Mike Mathile
☐ 10 Corey Powell
☐ 11 Rafael Reyes
☐ 12 Bobby Ryan
☐ 13 Jose Castro CO
☐ 14 Robert Fitzpatrick
☐ 15 Steve Keighley
☐ 16 Rich Dubee CO
☐ 17 Ray Callari
☐ 18 Ted Ciesla
☐ 19 Mike Friedland
☐ 20 Chris Malinoski
☐ 21 Dan Smith
☐ 22 Randy Wilstead
☐ 23 Mike Moberg
☐ 24 Shaun Murphy
☐ 25 Glenn Murray
☐ 26 Mike Weimerskirch
☐ 27 Pat Kelly MG
☐ 28 Steve Whitehead
☐ 29 Steve Hargis
☐ 30 Checklist

1991 Rockford Expos ProCards

This 29-card standard-size set of the 1991 Rockford Expos, a Class A Midwest League affiliate of the Montreal Expos, features on its white-bordered fronts posed color player photos set on simulated spiral-bound yellow notebooks. The player's name, position, and team appear within a green rectangle below the photo. The yellow horizontal back is bordered in white and carries the player's name and position at the top, followed by biography and statistics.

	MINT	NRMT	EXC
COMPLETE SET (29)	5.00	2.20	.60

☐ 2037 Bob Baxter
☐ 2038 Stacey Collins
☐ 2039 Ralph Diaz
☐ 2040 Ranbir Grewal
☐ 2041 Ben Howze
☐ 2042 Pat Jurado
☐ 2043 Martin Martinez
☐ 2044 Mike Mathile
☐ 2045 Corey Powell
☐ 2046 Rafael Reyes
☐ 2047 Bobby Ryan
☐ 2048 Steve Whitehead
☐ 2049 Robert Fitzpatrick
☐ 2050 Dan Hargis
☐ 2051 Steve Keighley
☐ 2052 Ray Callari
☐ 2053 Ted Ciesla
☐ 2054 Mike Friedland
☐ 2055 Chris Malinoski
☐ 2056 Randy Smith
☐ 2057 Randy Wilstead
☐ 2058 Mike Moberg
☐ 2059 Shaun Murphy
☐ 2060 Glenn Murray
☐ 2061 Mike Weimerskirch
☐ 2062 Pat Kelly MG
☐ 2063 Jose Castro CO
☐ 2064 Rich Dubee CO
☐ 2065 Checklist

1991 Salem Buccaneers Classic/Best

This 26-card standard-size set of the 1991 Salem Buccaneers, a Class A Carolina League affiliate of the Pittsburgh Pirates, features white-bordered posed color player photos on its fronts. The player's name, team, and position appear at the bottom. The white back is framed by a thin black line and carries the player's name and position at the top, followed by biography, statistics and team logos.

	MINT	NRMT	EXC
COMPLETE SET (26)	5.00	2.20	.60

☐ 1 Tim Edge
☐ 2 Rick Osik
☐ 3 Rich Aude
☐ 4 Rob Bailey
☐ 5 Alberto De Los Santos
☐ 6 Austin Manahan
☐ 7 Roman Rodriguez
☐ 8 Ben Shelton
☐ 9 Kevin Young
☐ 10 Mike Brewington
☐ 11 William Pennyfeather
☐ 12 Daryl Ratliff
☐ 13 Ken Trusky
☐ 14 David Bird
☐ 15 Bobby Underwood
☐ 16 Tim McDowell
☐ 17 Eric Parkinson
☐ 18 Rich Robertson
☐ 19 Kevin Rychel
☐ 20 Dave Tellers
☐ 21 Paul Wagner
☐ 22 Dave Watson
☐ 23 Ron Way
☐ 24 Sandy Krum
☐ 25 Stan Cliburn MGR
☐ 26 Checklist

1991 Salem Buccaneers ProCards

This 27-card standard-size set of the 1991 Salem Buccaneers, a Class A Carolina League affiliate of the Pittsburgh Pirates, features on its white-bordered fronts posed color player photos set on simulated spiral-bound yellow notebooks. The player's name, position, and team appear within a green rectangle below the photo. The yellow horizontal back is bordered in white and carries the player's name at the top, followed by biography and statistics.

	MINT	NRMT	EXC
COMPLETE SET (27)	5.00	2.20	.60

☐ 944 David Bird
☐ 945 Steve Buckholz
☐ 946 Tim McDowell
☐ 947 Eric Parkinson
☐ 948 Rich Robertson
☐ 949 Kevin Rychel
☐ 950 Dave Tellers
☐ 951 Paul Wagner
☐ 952 Dave Watson
☐ 953 Ron Way
☐ 954 Mike Zimmerman
☐ 955 Tim Edge
☐ 956 Keith Osik
☐ 957 Rich Aude
☐ 958 Rob Bailey
☐ 959 Alberto De Los Santos
☐ 960 Austin Manahan
☐ 961 Roman Rodriguez
☐ 962 Ben Shelton
☐ 963 Kevin Young
☐ 964 Mike Brewington
☐ 965 William Pennyfeather
☐ 966 Daryl Ratliff
☐ 967 Ken Trusky
☐ 968 Stan Cliburn MGR
☐ 969 Tom Dettore CO
☐ 970 Checklist

1991 Salinas Spurs Classic/Best

This 30-card standard-size set of the 1991 Salinas Spurs, a Class A California League Independent, features white-bordered posed color player photos on its fronts. The player's name, team, and position appear at the bottom. The white back is framed by a thin black line and carries the player's name and position at the top, followed by biography, statistics and team logos.

	MINT	NRMT	EXC
COMPLETE SET (30)	5.00	2.20	.60

☐ 1 Ken Briggs
☐ 2 Rafael Rivera
☐ 3 Hideyuki Yasuda
☐ 4 Hideyuki Mifune
☐ 5 Todd Cruz
☐ 6 Tommy Griffith
☐ 7 Kenichi Ramanouchi
☐ 8 Brant McCreadie
☐ 9 James Bishop
☐ 10 Arihito Muramatsu
☐ 11 Rye Kawano
☐ 12 Brian Palma
☐ 13 Richard Shepperd
☐ 14 Katsumasa Ohta
☐ 15 Yukitoshi Oka
☐ 16 Kukio Ohsubo
☐ 17 Steve Maye
☐ 18 Tsuyoshi Nichioka
☐ 19 John Stewart
☐ 20 Dave Karaskinski
☐ 21 Kazutaka Ikesue
☐ 22 Bruce Arola
☐ 23 Carlos Carrasco
☐ 24 Hide Koga MGR
☐ 25 Dick Little CO
☐ 26 Takayuki Kohno CO
☐ 27 Shuzo Arita CO
☐ 28 Dee Marge Goshgarian
☐ 29 Greg Swim
☐ 30 Bill Carlson
Checklist

1991 Salinas Spurs ProCards

This 31-card standard-size set of the 1991 Salinas Spurs, a Class A California League Independent, features on its white-bordered fronts posed color player photos set on simulated spiral-bound yellow notebooks. The player's name, position, and team appear within a green rectangle below the photo. The yellow horizontal back is bordered in white and carries the player's name at the top, followed by biography and statistics.

	MINT	NRMT	EXC
COMPLETE SET (31)	5.00	2.20	.60

☐ 2234 Bruce Arola
☐ 2235 Carlos Carrasco
☐ 2236 Kazutaka Ikesue
☐ 2237 Dave Karasinski
☐ 2238 Steve Maye
☐ 2239 Brant McCreadie
☐ 2240 Ken Olson
☐ 2241 Tsuyoshi Nishioka
☐ 2242 Katsumasa Ohta
☐ 2243 Yukio Ohtsubo
☐ 2244 Yukitoshi Oka
☐ 2245 John Stewart
☐ 2246 Ken Briggs
☐ 2247 Rafael Rivera
☐ 2248 Hideyuki Yasuda
☐ 2249 Jim Bishop
☐ 2250 Bill Carlson
☐ 2251 Todd Cruz
☐ 2252 Hideyuki Mifune
☐ 2253 Greg Swim
☐ 2254 Kenichi Ramanouchi
☐ 2255 Tommy Griffith
☐ 2256 Ryo Kawano
☐ 2257 Arihito Mauramatsu
☐ 2258 Brian Palma
☐ 2259 Rich Shepperd
☐ 2260 Hide Koga MGR
☐ 2261 Shuzo Arita CO
☐ 2262 Takayuki Kohno CO
☐ 2263 Dick Little CO
☐ 2264 Checklist

1991 Salt Lake Trappers ProCards

This 30-card standard-size set of the 1991 Salt Lake Trappers, a Rookie Class Pioneer League Independent, features on its white-bordered fronts posed color player photos set on simulated spiral-bound yellow notebooks. The player's name, position, and team appear within a green rectangle below the photo. The yellow horizontal back is bordered in white and carries the player's name at the top, followed by biography and statistics.

	MINT	NRMT	EXC
COMPLETE SET (30)	5.00	2.20	.60

☐ 3202 Willie Ambox
☐ 3203 Dan Furmanik
☐ 3204 John Gilligan
☐ 3205 Jim Guidi
☐ 3206 Dave Marcon
☐ 3207 Kevin McDonald
☐ 3208 Geno Mirabella
☐ 3209 Tad Powers
☐ 3210 Chris Sultea
☐ 3211 Mark Stephens
☐ 3212 Jon Willard
☐ 3213 David Rolls
☐ 3214 Willie Smith
☐ 3215 Mike Aranzullo
☐ 3216 Brian Biggers
☐ 3217 Jeff Cooper
☐ 3218 Eric Macrina
☐ 3219 Eddie Ortega
☐ 3220 Keith Rader
☐ 3221 Todd Stefan
☐ 3222 Ben Castillo
☐ 3223 Steve Cunha
☐ 3224 Todd Edwards
☐ 3225 Rick Hirtensteiner
☐ 3226 Jim Martin
☐ 3227 Nick Belmonte MGR
☐ 3228 Mark Brewer CO
☐ 3229 Dan Shwan CO
☐ 3230 Team Picture
☐ 3231 Checklist

1991 Salt Lake Trappers Sports Pro

This 30-card standard-size set of the 1991 Salt Late Trappers, a Rookie Class Pioneer League Independent, features posed color head-and-shoulders shots, with thin black borders on a white card face. The horizontally oriented backs have biographical information.

	MINT	NRMT	EXC
COMPLETE SET (30)	6.00	2.70	.75

☐ 1 Keith Radar
☐ 2 Dan Furmanik
☐ 3 Tad Powers
☐ 4 Todd Edwards
☐ 5 Kevin McDonald
☐ 6 Rick Hirtensteiner
☐ 7 Mike Aranzullo
☐ 8 Brian Biggers
☐ 9 David Rolls
☐ 10 Jon Willard
☐ 11 Steve Cunha
☐ 12 John Gilligan
☐ 13 Eric Mecrina
☐ 14 Jim Martin
☐ 15 Willie Smith
☐ 16 Ben Castillo
☐ 17 Geno Mirabella
☐ 18 Eddie Ortega
☐ 19 Chris Shultea
☐ 20 Mark Stephens
☐ 21 Todd Stefan
☐ 22 Jeff Copper
☐ 23 David Marcon
☐ 24 Jim Guidi
☐ 25 Willie Ambos CO
☐ 26 Mark Brewer CO
☐ 27 Dan Shwan ACO
☐ 28 Nick Belmonte MG
☐ 29 Kelly O'Brien TR
☐ 30 Blank card

1991 San Antonio Missions Line Drive

	MINT	NRMT	EXC
COMPLETE SET (26)	5.00	2.20	.60

☐ 526 Steve Allen
☐ 527 Jorge Alvarez
☐ 528 Bryan Baar
☐ 529 Tim Barker
☐ 530 Tony Barron
☐ 531 Cam Biberdorf
☐ 532 Jason Brosnan
☐ 533 Braulio Castillo
☐ 534 Steve Finken
☐ 535 Freddy Gonzalez
☐ 536 Mike James
☐ 537 Brett Magnusson
☐ 538 Joe Munoz
☐ 539 Lance Rice
☐ 540 Zak Shinall
☐ 541 Dennis Springer
☐ 542 Ramon Taveras
☐ 543 Jimmy Terrill
☐ 544 Brian Traxler
☐ 545 Jody Treadwell
☐ 546 Mike White
☐ 547 Mike Wilkins
☐ 548 Eric Young
☐ 549 John Shoemaker MGR
☐ 550 James Wray
☐ NNO Title card

1991 San Antonio Missions ProCards

This 30-card standard-size set of the 1991 San Antonio Missions, a Class AA Texas League affiliate of the Los Angeles Dodgers, features on its white-bordered fronts posed color player photos set on simulated spiral-bound yellow notebooks. The player's name, position, and team appear within a green rectangle below the photo. The yellow horizontal back is bordered in white and carries the player's name at the top, followed by biography and statistics. This issue includes the second year card of Pedro J. Martinez.

	MINT	NRMT	EXC
COMPLETE SET (30)	7.00	3.10	.85

☐ 2965 Steve Allen
☐ 2966 Pedro Astacio
☐ 2967 Dale Coleman
☐ 2968 Orel Hershiser
☐ 2969 Mike James
☐ 2970 Isidrio Marquez
☐ 2971 Pedro J. Martinez
☐ 2972 Zak Shinall
☐ 2973 Dennis Springer
☐ 2974 Jimmy Terrill
☐ 2975 Jody Treadwell
☐ 2976 Mike Wilkins
☐ 2977 James Wray
☐ 2978 Bryan Baar
☐ 2979 Lance Rice
☐ 2980 Timothy Barker
☐ 2981 Dino Ebel
☐ 2982 Steve Finken
☐ 2983 Jose Munoz
☐ 2984 Brian Traxler
☐ 2985 Eric Young
☐ 2986 Tony Barron
☐ 2987 Braulio Castillo
☐ 2988 Brett Magnusson
☐ 2989 Scott Marabell
☐ 2990 Mike White
☐ 2991 John Shoemaker MGR
☐ 2992 Burt Hooton CO
☐ 2993 Ron Roenicke CO
☐ 2994 Checklist

1991 San Bernardino Spirit Classic/Best

This 28-card standard-size set of the 1991 San Bernardino Spirit, a Class A California League affiliate of the Seattle Mariners, features white-bordered posed color player photos on its fronts. The player's name, team, and position appear at the bottom. The white back is framed by a thin black line and carries the player's name and position at the top, followed by biography, statistics and team logos. This issue includes the minor league card debuts of Marc Newfield and Mike Hampton.

	MINT	NRMT	EXC
COMPLETE SET (28)	8.00	3.60	1.00

☐ 1 John Cummings
☐ 2 Jeff Darwin
☐ 3 Doug Fitzer
☐ 4 Marcos Garcia
☐ 5 Jim Gutierrez
☐ 6 Mike Hampton
☐ 7 Troy Kent
☐ 8 Darin Loe
☐ 9 Dave McDonald
☐ 10 Antonio Pena
☐ 11 Scott Pitcher
☐ 12 Steve Murray CO
☐ 13 Clay Klavitter
☐ 14 Greg Pirkl
☐ 15 Greg Hunter
☐ 16 Jeff Keitges
☐ 17 Bryan King
☐ 18 Bobby Magallanes
☐ 19 Lipso Nava
☐ 20 Ruben Santana
☐ 21 Delvin Thomas

☐ 22 Tow Maynard
☐ 23 Marc Newfield
☐ 24 Jesus Tavarez
☐ 25 Derrick Young
☐ 26 Chuck Kniffin CO
☐ 27 Tommy Jones MGR
☐ 28 Sam Vranjes
Checklist

1991 San Bernardino Spirit ProCards

This 30-card standard-size set of the 1991 San Bernardino Spirit, a Class A California League affiliate of the Seattle Mariners, features on its white-bordered fronts posed color player photos set on simulated spiral-bound yellow notebooks. The player's name, position, and team appear within a green rectangle below the photo. The yellow horizontal back is bordered in white and carries the player's name at the top, followed by biography and statistics. This issue includes the minor league card debuts of Marc Newfield and Mike Hampton.

	MINT	NRMT	EXC
COMPLETE SET (30)	7.00	3.10	.85

☐ 1977 John Cummings
☐ 1978 Jeff Darwin
☐ 1979 Doug Fitzer
☐ 1980 Marcos Garcia
☐ 1981 Jim Gutierrez
☐ 1982 Mike Hampton
☐ 1983 Troy Kent
☐ 1984 Darin Loe
☐ 1985 Dave McDonald
☐ 1986 Antonio Pena
☐ 1987 Scott Pitcher
☐ 1988 Oscar Rivas
☐ 1989 Clay Klavitter
☐ 1990 Greg Pirkl
☐ 1991 Sam Vranjes
☐ 1992 Greg Hunter
☐ 1993 Jeff Keitges
☐ 1994 Bryan King
☐ 1995 Bobby Magallanes
☐ 1996 Lipso Nava
☐ 1997 Reben Santana
☐ 1998 Delvin Thomas
☐ 1999 Ellerton Maynard
☐ 2000 Marc Newfield
☐ 2001 Jesus Tavarez
☐ 2002 Derrick Young
☐ 2003 Tommy Jones MGR
☐ 2004 Chuck Kniffin CO
☐ 2005 Steve Murray CO
☐ 2006 Checklist

1991 San Jose Giants Classic/Best

This 30-card standard-size set of the 1991 San Jose Giants, a Class A California League affiliate of the San Francisco Giants, features white-bordered posed color player photos on its fronts. The player's name, team, and position appear at the bottom. The white back is framed by a thin black line and carries the player's name and position at the top, followed by biography, statistics and team logos.

	MINT	NRMT	EXC
COMPLETE SET (30)	5.00	2.20	.60

☐ 1 Dan Fernandez
☐ 2 Roger Miller
☐ 3 Jon Pattin
☐ 4 Clay Bellinger
☐ 5 Ron Crowe
☐ 6 Adell Davenport
☐ 7 Kevin Kasper
☐ 8 Tony Spires
☐ 9 Jeffry Bonner
☐ 10 Jason McFarlin
☐ 11 Steven Rolen
☐ 12 Eddie Williams
☐ 13 Max Aleys
☐ 14 Steve Callahan
☐ 15 Brian Dour
☐ 16 Carl Hanselman
☐ 17 Vince Herring
☐ 18 Kevin McGehee
☐ 19 Pedro Pena
☐ 20 Parick Rapp
☐ 21 Gary Sharko
☐ 22 Rob Taylor
☐ 23 Ron Wotus MGR
☐ 24 Gary Lucas CO
☐ 25 Dick Dietz CO
☐ 26 John Jackson
☐ 27 Rick Huisman
☐ 28 Derek Reid
☐ 29 Joey James
☐ 30 Scott Wilson TR
Checklist

1991 San Jose Giants ProCards

This 30-card standard-size set of the 1991 San Jose Giants, a Class A California League affiliate of the San Francisco Giants, features on its white-bordered fronts posed color player photos set on simulated spiral-bound yellow notebooks. The player's name, position, and team appear within a green rectangle below the photo. The yellow horizontal back is bordered in white and carries the player's name at the top, followed by biography and statistics.

	MINT	NRMT	EXC
COMPLETE SET (30)	5.00	2.20	.60

☐ 1 Max Aleys
☐ 2 Steve Callahan
☐ 3 Brian Dour
☐ 4 Carl Hanselman
☐ 5 Vince Herring
☐ 6 Rick Huisman
☐ 7 Kevin McGehee
☐ 8 Pedro Pena
☐ 9 Pat Rapp
☐ 10 Gary Sharko
☐ 11 Rob Taylor
☐ 12 Dan Fernandez
☐ 13 Roger Miller
☐ 14 Jon Pattin
☐ 15 Clay Bellinger
☐ 16 Ron Crowe
☐ 17 Adell Davenport
☐ 18 Joey James
☐ 19 Kevin Kasper
☐ 20 Steve Rolen
☐ 21 Tony Spires
☐ 22 Jeff Bonner
☐ 23 John Jackson
☐ 24 Jason McFarlin
☐ 25 Derek Reid
☐ 26 Outfield Stars
John Jackson
Jason McFarlin
Derek Reid
☐ 27 Ron Wotus MGR
☐ 28 Dick Dietz CO
☐ 29 Gary Lucas CO
☐ 30 Checklist

1991 Sarasota White Sox Classic/Best

This 29-card standard-size set of the 1991 Sarasota White Sox, a Class A Florida State League affiliate of the Chicago White Sox, features white-bordered posed color player photos on its fronts. The player's name, team, and position appear at the bottom. The white back is framed by a thin black line and carries the player's name and position at the top, followed by biography, statistics and team logos.

	MINT	NRMT	EXC
COMPLETE SET (29)	5.00	2.20	.60

☐ 1 Rod Bolton
☐ 2 Lenny Brutcher
☐ 3 Fred Dabney
☐ 4 Mike Galvan
☐ 5 Earnie Johnson
☐ 6 Brian Keyser
☐ 7 Dan Matznick
☐ 8 Mike Mongiello
☐ 9 Johnny Ruffin
☐ 10 Scott Stevens
☐ 11 Robert Wickman
☐ 12 Clemente Alvarez
☐ 13 Greg McGough
☐ 14 Greg Kobza
☐ 15 Scott Cepicky
☐ 16 Don Cooper CO
☐ 17 Justin McCray
☐ 18 Peter Rose II
☐ 19 Ed Smith
☐ 20 Dean Tatarian
☐ 21 Leo Tejada
☐ 22 Jerry Wolak
☐ 23 Rob Lukachyk
☐ 24 Ron Plemmons
☐ 25 Carl Sullivan
☐ 26 Scott Tedder
☐ 27 Rick Patterson MGR
☐ 28 Mike Barnett CO
☐ 29 Checklist

1991 Sarasota White Sox ProCards

This 30-card standard-size set of the 1991 Sarasota White Sox, a Class A Florida State League affiliate of the Chicago White Sox, features on its white-bordered fronts posed color player photos set on simulated spiral-bound yellow notebooks. The player's name, position, and team appear within a green rectangle below the photo. The yellow horizontal back is bordered in white and carries the player's name at the top, followed by biography and statistics.

	MINT	NRMT	EXC
COMPLETE SET (30)	5.00	2.20	.60

☐ 1104 Rod Bolton
☐ 1105 Len Brutcher
☐ 1106 Fred Dabney
☐ 1107 Mike Galvan
☐ 1108 Earnie Johnson
☐ 1109 Brian Keyser
☐ 1110 Danny Matznick
☐ 1111 Mike Mongiello
☐ 1112 Johnny Ruffin
☐ 1113 Scott Stevens
☐ 1114 Bob Wickman
☐ 1115 Clemente Alvarez
☐ 1116 Greg Kobza
☐ 1117 Greg McGough
☐ 1118 Scott Cepicky
☐ 1119 Justin McCray
☐ 1120 Pete Rose Jr.
☐ 1121 Ed Smith
☐ 1122 Dean Tatarian
☐ 1123 Leo Tejada
☐ 1124 Rob Lukachyk
☐ 1125 Ron Plemmons
☐ 1126 Carl Sullivan
☐ 1127 Scott Tedder
☐ 1128 Jerry Wolak
☐ 1129 Rick Patterson MGR
☐ 1130 Mike Barnett CO
☐ 1131 Don Cooper CO
☐ 1132 Chet Diemidio CO
☐ 1133 Checklist

1991 Savannah Cardinals Classic/Best

This 29-card standard-size set of the 1991 Savannah Cardinals, a Class A South Atlantic League affiliate of the St. Louis Cardinals, features white-bordered posed color player photos on its fronts. The player's name, team, and position appear at the bottom. The white back is framed by a thin black line and carries the player's name and position at the top, followed by biography, statistics and team logos.

	MINT	NRMT	EXC
COMPLETE SET (29)	5.00	2.20	.60

☐ 1 Roy Bailey
☐ 2 Roy Silver CO
☐ 3 Bryan Eversgerd
☐ 4 Pete Fagan TR
☐ 5 Russell Gaston
☐ 6 Mike Jolley
☐ 7 John Kelly
☐ 8 Tom Kinney
☐ 9 Jose Lopez
☐ 10 Jeremy McGarity
☐ 11 Frank Speek
☐ 12 Matt Tomso
☐ 13 Jim Spivey
☐ 14 Marc Ronan
☐ 15 Mark Taylor
☐ 16 Rodney Eldridge
☐ 17 Miccal Jackson
☐ 18 Carlos Landinez
☐ 19 Mark MacArthur
☐ 20 Sean Page
☐ 21 Ozzie Perez
☐ 22 Wander Pimentel
☐ 23 Terry Bradshaw
☐ 24 Tracey Ealy
☐ 25 Anthony Jenkins
☐ 26 Tim Jordan
☐ 27 Larry Milbourne MGR
☐ 28 John Stuper CO
☐ 29 Checklist

1991 Savannah Cardinals ProCards

This 29-card standard-size set of the 1991 Savannah Cardinals, a Class A South Atlantic League affiliate of the St. Louis Cardinals, features on its white-bordered fronts posed color player photos set on simulated spiral-bound yellow notebooks. The player's name, position, and team appear within a green rectangle below the photo. The yellow horizontal back is bordered in white and carries the player's name at the top, followed by biography and statistics.

	MINT	NRMT	EXC
COMPLETE SET (29)	5.00	2.20	.60

☐ 1642 Roy Bailey
☐ 1643 Scott Baker
☐ 1644 Bryan Eversgerd
☐ 1645 Thomas Fusco
☐ 1646 Russ Gaston
☐ 1647 Mike Jolley
☐ 1648 John Kelly
☐ 1649 Tom Kinney
☐ 1650 Jose Lopez
☐ 1651 Jeremy McGarity
☐ 1652 Frank Speek
☐ 1653 Matt Tomso
☐ 1654 Marc Ronan
☐ 1655 Jim Spivey
☐ 1656 Mark Taylor
☐ 1657 Rodney Eldridge
☐ 1658 Miccal Jackson
☐ 1659 Carlos Landinez
☐ 1660 Mark MacArthur
☐ 1661 Sean Page
☐ 1662 Ozzie Perez
☐ 1663 Wander Pimentel
☐ 1664 Terry Bradshaw
☐ 1665 Tracey Ealy
☐ 1666 Anthony Jenkins
☐ 1667 Tim Jordan
☐ 1668 Larry Milbourne MGR
☐ 1669 Coaches
John Stuper
Roy Silver
☐ 1670 Checklist

1991 Scranton Red Barons Line Drive

	MINT	NRMT	EXC
COMPLETE SET (26)	5.00	2.20	.60

☐ 476 Sal Agostinelli
☐ 477 Gary Alexander
☐ 478 Andy Ashby
☐ 479 Bob Ayrault
☐ 480 Kim Batiste
☐ 481 Amalio Carreno
☐ 482 Rocky Elli
☐ 483 Darrin Fletcher
☐ 484 Jeff Grotewold
☐ 485 Chris Knabenshue
☐ 486 Greg Legg
☐ 487 Jim Lindeman
☐ 488 Chuck Malone
☐ 489 Tim Mauser
☐ 490 Louie Meadows
☐ 491 Mickey Morandini
☐ 492 Julio Peguero
☐ 493 Wally Ritchie
☐ 494 Bruce Ruffin
☐ 495 Rick Schu
☐ 496 Ray Searage
☐ 497 Scott Wade
☐ 498 Gary Wilson
☐ 499 Bill Dancy MGR
☐ 500 Floyd Rayford CO
Jim Wright CO
☐ NNO Title card

1991 Scranton Red Barons ProCards

This 29-card standard-size set of the 1991 Scranton Red Barons, a Class AAA International League affiliate of the Philadelphia Phillies, features on its white-bordered fronts posed color player photos set on simulated spiral-bound yellow notebooks. The player's name, position, and team appear within a green rectangle below the photo. The yellow horizontal back is bordered in white and carries the player's name at the top, followed by biography and statistics.

	MINT	NRMT	EXC
COMPLETE SET (29)	5.00	2.20	.60

☐ 2530 Andy Ashby
☐ 2531 Bob Ayrault
☐ 2532 Amalio Carreno
☐ 2533 Rocky Elli
☐ 2534 Chuck Malone
☐ 2535 Tim Mauser
☐ 2536 Wally Ritchie
☐ 2537 Bruce Ruffin
☐ 2538 Ray Searage
☐ 2539 Gary Wilson
☐ 2540 Sal Agostinelli
☐ 2541 Darrin Fletcher
☐ 2542 Gary Alexander
☐ 2543 Kim Batiste
☐ 2544 Jeff Grotewold
☐ 2545 Dave Hollins
☐ 2546 Greg Legg
☐ 2547 Rick Schu
☐ 2548 Steve Scarsone
☐ 2549 Sil Campusano
☐ 2550 Wes Chamberlain
☐ 2551 Chris Knabenshue
☐ 2552 Louie Meadows
☐ 2553 Julio Peguero
☐ 2554 Scott Wade
☐ 2555 Bill Dancy MGR
☐ 2556 Floyd Rayford CO
☐ 2557 Jim Wright CO
☐ 2558 Checklist

1991 Shreveport Captains Line Drive

	MINT	NRMT	EXC
COMPLETE SET (26)	5.00	2.20	.60

☐ 301 Frank Carey
☐ 302 Larry Carter
☐ 303 Royce Clayton
☐ 304 Tom Ealy
☐ 305 Juan Guerrero
☐ 306 Bryan Hickerson
☐ 307 Steve Hosey
☐ 308 Tom Hostetler
☐ 309 Erik Johnson
☐ 310 Dan Lewis

☐ 311 Paul McClellan
☐ 312 Jim McNamara
☐ 313 Kevin Meier
☐ 314 Jim Myers
☐ 315 Dave Patterson
☐ 316 John Patterson
☐ 317 Jim Pena
☐ 318 Dan Rambo
☐ 319 Steve Reed
☐ 320 Kevin Rogers
☐ 321 Reuben Smiley
☐ 322 Scooter Tucker
☐ 323 Peter Weber
☐ 324 Bill Evers MGR
☐ 325 Tony Taylor CO
Todd Oakes CO
☐ NNO Title card

1991 Shreveport Captains ProCards

This 28-card standard-size set of the 1991 Shreveport Captains, a Class AA Texas League affiliate of the San Francisco Giants, features on its white-bordered fronts posed color player photos set on simulated spiral-bound yellow notebooks. The player's name, position, and team appear within a green rectangle below the photo. The yellow horizontal back is bordered in white and carries the player's name at the top, followed by biography and statistics.

	MINT	NRMT	EXC
COMPLETE SET (28)	5.00	2.20	.60

☐ 1814 Larry Carter
☐ 1815 Bryan Kickerson
☐ 1816 Tom Hostetler
☐ 1817 Paul McClellan
☐ 1818 Kevin Meier
☐ 1819 Jim Myers
☐ 1820 Jim Pena
☐ 1821 Dan Rambo
☐ 1822 Steve Reed
☐ 1823 Kevin Rogers
☐ 1824 Jim McNamara
☐ 1825 Scooter Tucker
☐ 1826 Frank Carey
☐ 1827 Royce Clayton
☐ 1828 Juan Guerrero
☐ 1829 Erik Johnson
☐ 1830 Dan Lewis
☐ 1831 Dave Patterson
☐ 1832 John Patterson
☐ 1833 Jamie Cooper
☐ 1834 Tom Ealy
☐ 1835 Steve Hosey
☐ 1836 Reuben Smiley
☐ 1837 Pete Weber
☐ 1838 Bill Evers MGR
☐ 1839 Todd Oakes CO
☐ 1840 Tony Taylor CO
☐ 1841 Checklist

1991 South Atlantic League All-Stars ProCards

	MINT	NRMT	EXC
COMPLETE SET (48)	15.00	6.75	1.85

☐ SAL1 Jim Daugherty
☐ SAL2 Tom Nevers
☐ SAL3 Scott Bullett
☐ SAL4 Hector Fajardo
☐ SAL5 Bill Ostermeyer
☐ SAL6 Bruce Tanner CO
☐ SAL7 Steve Gibralter
☐ SAL8 Dave Miley MGR
☐ SAL9 Bobby Perna
☐ SAL10 Tom Raffo
☐ SAL11 John Roper
☐ SAL12 Tim Blackwell MGR
☐ SAL13 Juan Castillo
☐ SAL14 Jay Davis
☐ SAL15 Edward Fully
☐ SAL16 Butch Huskey
☐ SAL17 Jose Martinez
☐ SAL18 Rod McCall
☐ SAL19 Kyle Washington
☐ SAL20 Kelley O'Neal
☐ SAL21 Brian Saltzgaber
☐ SAL22 Steve Dreyer
☐ SAL23 David Lowery
☐ SAL24 Marty Posey
☐ SAL25 Carl Everett
☐ SAL26 Kiki Hernandez
☐ SAL27 Trey Hillman MGR
☐ SAL28 Rich Hines
☐ SAL29 Rafael Quirico
☐ SAL30 Mark Shiflett CO
☐ SAL31 Greg Spratt TR
☐ SAL32 Tyler Houston
☐ SAL33 Chipper Jones
☐ SAL34 Roy Majtyka MGR
☐ SAL35 Jose Olmeda
☐ SAL36 Howard Battle
☐ SAL37 Carlos Delgado
☐ SAL38 Joe Ganote
☐ SAL39 Ernesto Rodriguez
☐ SAL40 Rick Steed
☐ SAL41 Terry Bradshaw
☐ SAL42 John Kelly
☐ SAL43 Michael Farmer
☐ SAL44 Mike Lieberthal
☐ SAL45 Corey Thomas
☐ SAL46 William Martinez
☐ SAL47 Todd Samples
☐ SAL48 Checklist

1991 South Bend White Sox Classic/Best

This 29-card standard-size set of the 1991 South Bend White Sox, a Class A Midwest League affiliate of the Chicago White Sox, features white-bordered posed color player photos on its fronts. The player's name, team, and position appear at the bottom. The white back is framed by a thin black line and carries the player's name and position at the top, followed by biography, statistics and team logos.

	MINT	NRMT	EXC
COMPLETE SET (29)	6.00	2.70	.75

☐ 1 Kevin Tolar
☐ 2 Horace Gaither
☐ 3 Dan Monzon
☐ 4 Jorege Ramos
☐ 5 Keith Strange
☐ 6 Dennis Walker
☐ 7 Brandon Wilson
☐ 8 John Hairston
☐ 9 Kevin Coughlin
☐ 10 Charles Poe
☐ 11 Don Sheppard
☐ 12 Todd Altaffer
☐ 13 Jason Bere
☐ 14 Frank Campos
☐ 15 Rolando Caridad
☐ 16 Domingo Jean
☐ 17 Jon Jenkins
☐ 18 Dean Locklear
☐ 19 Don Perigny
☐ 20 Keith Shepherd
☐ 21 Greg Young
☐ 22 Rogelio Nunez
☐ 23 Mark Haley CO
☐ 24 Nilson Robledo
☐ 25 Keith Valrie
☐ 26 Kirk Champion CO
☐ 27 Tommy Thompson MGR
☐ 28 John Hawkins
☐ 29 Checklist

1991 South Bend White Sox ProCards

This 30-card standard-size set of the 1991 South Bend White Sox, a Class A Midwest League affiliate of the Chicago White Sox, features on its white-bordered fronts posed color player photos set on simulated spiral-bound yellow notebooks. The player's name, position, and team appear within a green rectangle below the photo. The yellow horizontal back is bordered in white and carries the player's name at the top, followed by biography and statistics. This issue includes the minor league card debut of Jason Bere.

	MINT	NRMT	EXC
COMPLETE SET (30)	6.00	2.70	.75

☐ 2848 Todd Altaffer
☐ 2849 Jason Bere
☐ 2850 Frank Campos
☐ 2851 Rolando Caridad
☐ 2852 Domingo Jean
☐ 2853 Jon Jenkins
☐ 2854 Dean Locklear
☐ 2855 Don Perigny
☐ 2856 Keith Shepherd
☐ 2857 Kevin Tolar
☐ 2858 Greg Young
☐ 2859 Rogelio Nunez
☐ 2860 Nilson Robledo
☐ 2861 Joe Solimine
☐ 2862 Horace Gaither
☐ 2863 John Hairston
☐ 2864 Jorge Ramos
☐ 2865 Keith Strange
☐ 2866 Dennis Walker
☐ 2867 Brandon Wilson
☐ 2868 Kevin Coughlin
☐ 2869 Ty Hawkins
☐ 2870 Charles Poe
☐ 2871 Don Sheppard
☐ 2872 Kerry Valrie
☐ 2873 Tommy Thompson MGR
☐ 2874 Kirk Champion CO
☐ 2875 Mark Haley CO
☐ 2876 Jim Reinebold CO
☐ 2877 Checklist

1991 Southern Oregon A's Classic/Best

This 30-card standard-size set of the 1991 Southern Oregon A's, a Class A Northwest League affiliate of the Oakland Athletics, features white-bordered posed color player photos on its fronts. The player's name, team, and position appear at the bottom. The white back is framed by a thin black line and carries the player's name and position at the top, followed by biography, statistics and team logos.

	MINT	NRMT	EXC
COMPLETE SET (30)	5.00	2.20	.60

☐ 1 Joel Wolfe
☐ 2 Damon Mashore
☐ 3 Tim Smith
☐ 4 Tim Doyle
☐ 5 George Williams
☐ 6 Ricky Kimball
☐ 7 Chris Thomsen
☐ 8 Rick Norton
☐ 9 Todd Ingram
☐ 10 Russell Brock
☐ 11 Brent Cookson
☐ 12 Jason Wood
☐ 13 Scott Sheldon
☐ 14 Miguel Jimenez
☐ 15 Mike Neill
☐ 16 Gary Hust
☐ 17 Santiago Morillo
☐ 18 Michael Evans
☐ 19 Tony Scharff
☐ 20 Dan Vizzini
☐ 21 Mike Kennedy
☐ 22 Vicente Francisco
☐ 23 Creighton Cubanich
☐ 24 Brent Gates
☐ 25 Kirt Endebrock
☐ 26 Michael Thees
☐ 27 Dan Nerat
☐ 28 Joe Misa
☐ 29 Steve Wojciechowski
☐ 30 Checklist

1991 Southern Oregon A's ProCards

This 37-card standard-size set of the 1991 Southern Oregon A's, a Class A Northwest League affiliate of the Oakland Athletics, features on its white-bordered fronts posed color player photos set on simulated spiral-bound yellow notebooks. The player's name, position, and team appear within a green rectangle below the photo. The yellow horizontal back is bordered in white and carries the player's name at the top, followed by biography and statistics.

	MINT	NRMT	EXC
COMPLETE SET (37)	5.00	2.20	.60

☐ 3832 Russell Brock
☐ 3833 Tim Doyle
☐ 3834 Michael Evans
☐ 3835 Todd Ingram
☐ 3836 Jeff Jenson
☐ 3837 Miguel Jimenez
☐ 3838 Ricky Kimball
☐ 3839 Joe Misa
☐ 3840 Santiago Morillo
☐ 3841 Dan Nerat
☐ 3842 Tony Scharff
☐ 3843 Tim Smith
☐ 3844 Brad Stowell
☐ 3845 Michael Thees
☐ 3846 Dan Vizzini
☐ 3847 Steve Wojciechowski
☐ 3848 Tod Frick
☐ 3849 Mike Kennedy
☐ 3850 Creighton Gubanich
☐ 3851 George Williams
☐ 3852 Juan Cabrera
☐ 3853 Kurt Endebrock
☐ 3854 Vicente Francisco
☐ 3855 Brent Gates
☐ 3856 Rick Norton
☐ 3857 Scott Sheldon
☐ 3858 Chris Thomsen
☐ 3859 Jason Wood
☐ 3860 Brent Cookson
☐ 3861 Chris Hart
☐ 3862 Gary Hust
☐ 3863 Damon Mashore
☐ 3864 Mike Neill
☐ 3865 Joel Wolfe
☐ 3866 Grady Fuson MGR
☐ 3867 Jim Slaton CO
☐ 3868 Checklist

1991 Spartanburg Phillies Classic/Best

This 30-card standard-size set of the 1991 Spartanburg Phillies, a Class A South Atlantic League affiliate of the Philadelphia Phillies, features white-bordered posed color player photos on its fronts. The player's name, team, and position appear at the bottom. The white back is framed by a thin black line and carries the player's name and position at the top, followed by biography, statistics and team logos.

	MINT	NRMT	EXC
COMPLETE SET (30)	5.00	2.20	.60

☐ 1 Scott Carlton
☐ 2 Ray Donecq
☐ 3 Donnie Elliott
☐ 4 Todd Goergen
☐ 5 Brad Hassinger
☐ 6 Eric Hill
☐ 7 Charlie Hurst
☐ 8 Bryan Manicchia
☐ 9 J.J. Munoz
☐ 10 Mike Owens
☐ 11 Jeff Patterson
☐ 12 Mark Randall
☐ 13 Stephen Avent
☐ 14 Mike Lieberthal
☐ 15 Troy Rusk
☐ 16 Erik Judson
☐ 17 Eulogio Perez
☐ 18 Jim Savage
☐ 19 Kenny Sirak
☐ 20 Corey Thomas
☐ 21 Al Bennett
☐ 22 Steve Bieser
☐ 23 Michael Farmer
☐ 24 Antonio Grissom
☐ 25 Rob Hartwig
☐ 26 Jeff Jackson
☐ 27 Mark Steffens
☐ 28 Mel Roberts MGR
☐ 29 Buzz Capra CO
☐ 30 Brent Leiby TR
Checklist

1991 Spartanburg Phillies ProCards

This 30-card standard-size set of the 1991 Spartanburg Phillies, a Class A South Atlantic League affiliate of the Philadelphia Phillies, features on its white-bordered fronts posed color player photos set on simulated spiral-bound yellow notebooks. The player's name, position, and team appear within a green rectangle below the photo. The yellow horizontal back is bordered in white and carries the player's name at the top, followed by biography and statistics.

	MINT	NRMT	EXC
COMPLETE SET (30)	5.00	2.20	.60

☐ 886 Scott Carlton
☐ 887 Ray Domecq
☐ 888 Donnie Elliott
☐ 889 Todd Goergen
☐ 890 Brad Hassinger
☐ 891 Eric Hill
☐ 892 Chuck Hurst
☐ 893 Bryan Manicchia
☐ 894 J.J. Munoz
☐ 895 Mike Owens
☐ 896 Jeff Patterson
☐ 897 Mark Randall
☐ 898 Steve Avent
☐ 899 Mike Lieberthal
☐ 900 Erik Judson
☐ 901 Eulogio Perez
☐ 902 Troy Rusk
☐ 903 Jim Savage
☐ 904 Kenny Sirak
☐ 905 Corey Thomas
☐ 906 Al Bennett
☐ 907 Steve Bieser
☐ 908 Michael Farmer
☐ 909 Antonio Grissom
☐ 910 Rob Hartwig
☐ 911 Jeff Jackson
☐ 912 Mark Steffens
☐ 913 Mel Roberts MGR
☐ 914 Buzz Capra CO
☐ 915 Checklist

1991 Spokane Indians Classic/Best

This 30-card standard-size set of the 1991 Spokane Indians, a Class A Northwest League affiliate of the San Diego Padres, features white-bordered posed color player photos on its fronts. The player's name, team, and position appear at the bottom. The white back is framed by a thin black line and carries the player's name and position at the top, followed by biography, statistics and team logos.

	MINT	NRMT	EXC
COMPLETE SET (30)	5.00	2.20	.60

☐ 1 Eric Ciocca
☐ 2 Joey Long
☐ 3 Jim Campbell
☐ 4 Mike Grohs
☐ 5 Scotty Pugh
☐ 6 Kyle Moody
☐ 7 David Leback
☐ 8 Derek Vaughn
☐ 9 Reggie Stephens
☐ 10 Shawn Robertson
☐ 11 Jerrold Rountree
☐ 12 Mark Anthony
☐ 13 Tim Ploeger
☐ 14 Drew Overholser
☐ 15 Craig Hanson
☐ 16 Joe Grygiel
☐ 17 Scott Eggleston

☐ 18 Jose Davila
☐ 19 Cord Corbitt
☐ 20 Kevin Johnson
☐ 21 Jerrey Thurston
☐ 22 John Biancamano
☐ 23 Scott Bream
☐ 24 Chris Benhardt
☐ 25 Alvaro Samboy
☐ 26 Tim Hall
☐ 27 Joe Frias
☐ 28 Danny Garcia CO
☐ 29 Gene Glynn MGR
☐ 30 Keith Dugger TR
Checklist

1991 Spokane Indians ProCards

This 31-card standard-size set of the 1991 Spokane Indians, a Class A Northwest League affiliate of the San Diego Padres, features on its white-bordered fronts posed color player photos set on simulated spiral-bound yellow notebooks. The player's name, position, and team appear within a green rectangle below the photo. The yellow horizontal back is bordered in white and carries the player's name at the top, followed by biography and statistics.

	MINT	NRMT	EXC
COMPLETE SET (31)	5.00	2.20	.60

☐ 3937 Chris Benhardt
☐ 3938 Jimbo Campbell
☐ 3939 Eric Ciocca
☐ 3940 Cord Corbitt
☐ 3941 J.D. DaVila
☐ 3942 Scott Eggleston
☐ 3943 Mike Grohs
☐ 3944 Joe Grygiel
☐ 3945 Craig Hanson
☐ 3946 Joe Long
☐ 3947 Drew Overholser
☐ 3948 Tim Ploeger
☐ 3949 Alvaro Samboy
☐ 3950 Tim Hall
☐ 3951 Kevin Johnson
☐ 3952 Jerrey Thurston
☐ 3953 Juice Biancamano
☐ 3954 Scott Bream
☐ 3955 Mel Edwards
☐ 3956 Joe Frias
☐ 3957 Kyle Moody
☐ 3958 Scotty Pugh
☐ 3959 Mark Anthony
☐ 3960 David Lebak
☐ 3961 Shawn Robertson
☐ 3962 Jerrold Rountree
☐ 3963 Reggie Stephens
☐ 3964 Derek Vaughn
☐ 3965 Gene Glynn MGR
☐ 3966 Danny Garcia CO
☐ 3967 Checklist

1991 Springfield Cardinals Classic/Best

This 30-card standard-size set of the 1991 Springfield Cardinals, a Class A Midwest League affiliate of the St. Louis Cardinals, features white-bordered posed color player photos on its fronts. The player's name, team, and position appear at the bottom. The white back is framed by a thin black line and carries the player's name and position at the top, followed by biography, statistics and team logos.

	MINT	NRMT	EXC
COMPLETE SET (30)	5.00	2.20	.60

☐ 1 Paul Anderson
☐ 2 Juan Andujar
☐ 3 Joe Aversa
☐ 4 Scott Banton
☐ 5 Fernando Barreiro
☐ 6 Andy Beasley
☐ 7 Alan Botkin
☐ 8 Mark Bowlan
☐ 9 Johnny Calzado
☐ 10 Frank Cimorelli
☐ 11 Mike Ramsey MGR
☐ 12 John Dempsey
☐ 13 Ignacio Duran
☐ 14 Dann Eaton
☐ 15 Bill Espinal
☐ 16 Jeff Fayne
☐ 17 Dennis Fletcher
☐ 18 Clyde Keller
☐ 19 Kevin Nielsen
☐ 20 Dave Norris
☐ 21 Mateo Ozuna
☐ 22 Ahmed Rodriguez
☐ 23 Beto Rodriguez
☐ 24 Odalis Savinon
☐ 25 Kevin Tahan
☐ 26 Orlando Thomas
☐ 27 Tom Urbani
☐ 28 Jose Velez
☐ 29 Roger Erickson CO
☐ 30 Mike Evans TR
Checklist

1991 Springfield Cardinals ProCards

This 31-card standard-size set of the 1991 Springfield Cardinals, a Class A Midwest League affiliate of the St. Louis Cardinals, features on its white-bordered fronts posed color player photos set on simulated spiral-bound yellow notebooks. The player's name, position, and team appear within a green rectangle below the photo. The yellow horizontal back is bordered in white and carries the player's name at the top, followed by biography and statistics.

	MINT	NRMT	EXC
COMPLETE SET (31)	5.00	2.20	.60

☐ 731 Paul Anderson
☐ 732 Fernando Barreiro
☐ 733 Alan Botkin
☐ 734 Mark Bowlan
☐ 735 Frank Cimorelli
☐ 736 Dann Eaton
☐ 737 Willie Espinal
☐ 738 Dennis Fletcher
☐ 739 Clyde Keller
☐ 740 Kevin Nielsen
☐ 741 Dave Norris
☐ 742 Tom Urbani
☐ 743 Andy Beasley
☐ 744 John Dempsey
☐ 745 Orlando Thomas
☐ 746 Juan Andujar
☐ 747 Joe Aversa
☐ 748 Ignacio Duran
☐ 749 Mateo Ozuna
☐ 750 Ahmed Rodriguez
☐ 751 Beto Rodriguez
☐ 752 Kevin Tahan
☐ 753 Scott Banton
☐ 754 Johnny Calzado
☐ 755 Paul Coleman
☐ 756 Jeff Fayne
☐ 757 Odalis Savinon
☐ 758 Jose Velez
☐ 759 Mike Ramsey MGR
☐ 760 Roger Erickson CO
☐ 761 Checklist

1991 St. Catharines Blue Jays Classic/Best

This 30-card standard-size set of the 1991 St. Catharines Blue Jays, a Class A New York-Penn League affiliate of the Montreal Expos, features white-bordered posed color player photos on its fronts. The player's name, team, and position appear at the bottom. The white back is framed by a thin black line and carries the player's name and position at the top, followed by biography, statistics and team logos.

	MINT	NRMT	EXC
COMPLETE SET (30)	5.00	2.20	.60

☐ 1 Mike Morland
☐ 2 Keiver Campbell
☐ 3 Lou Benbow Jr.
☐ 4 Kris Harmes
☐ 5 Sharnol Adriana
☐ 6 Chris Weinke
☐ 7 Mike Coolbaugh
☐ 8 Robert Butler
☐ 9 Joe Lis Jr.
☐ 10 Craig Quinlan
☐ 11 Kurt Heble
☐ 12 Keith Hines
☐ 13 Giovanni Carrara
☐ 14 James O'Connor
☐ 15 Gary Miller
☐ 16 Dennis Gray Jr.
☐ 17 Chris Kotes
☐ 18 Paul Barton
☐ 19 Ben Weber
☐ 20 Paul Spoljaric
☐ 21 Tim Lindsay
☐ 22 Darin Nolan
☐ 23 Angel Lugo
☐ 24 Scott Shannon TR
☐ 25 Coco Divison CO
☐ 26 Doug Ault MG
☐ 27 Checklist
☐ NNO MLB Licensee Card
☐ NNO St. Catharines Logo
☐ NNO Toronto Logo

1991 St. Catharines Blue Jays ProCards

This 28-card standard-size set of the 1991 St. Catharines Blue Jays, a Class A New York-Penn League affiliate of the Toronto Blue Jays, features on its white-bordered fronts posed color player photos set on simulated spiral-bound yellow notebooks. The player's name, position, and team appear within a green rectangle below the photo. The yellow horizontal back is bordered in white and carries the player's name and position at the top, followed by biography and statistics.

	MINT	NRMT	EXC
COMPLETE SET (28)	5.00	2.20	.60

☐ 3386 Paul Barton
☐ 3387 Giovanni Carrara
☐ 3388 Dennis Gray
☐ 3389 Chris Kotes
☐ 3390 Tim Lindsay
☐ 3391 Angel Lugo
☐ 3392 Gary Miller
☐ 3393 Darin Nolan
☐ 3394 Jim O'Connor
☐ 3395 Paul Spoljaric
☐ 3396 Ben Weber
☐ 3397 Kris Harmes
☐ 3398 Mike Morland
☐ 3399 Craig Quinlan
☐ 3400 Sharnol Adriana
☐ 3401 Lou Benbow
☐ 3402 Mike Coolbaugh
☐ 3403 Kurt Heble
☐ 3404 Joe Lis Jr.
☐ 3405 Chris Weinke
☐ 3406 Robert Butler
☐ 3407 Keiver Campbell
☐ 3408 Keith Hines
☐ 3409 Felix Septimo
☐ 3410 Jacinto Yorro
☐ 3411 Doug Ault MG
☐ 3412 Julio Divison CO
☐ 3413 Checklist

1991 St. Lucie Mets Classic/Best

This 30-card standard-size set of the 1991 St. Lucie Mets, a Class A Florida State League affiliate of the New York Mets, features white-bordered posed color player photos on its fronts. The player's name, team, and position appear at the bottom. The white back is framed by a thin black linc and carries the player's name and position at the top, followed by biography, statistics and team logos.

	MINT	NRMT	EXC
COMPLETE SET (30)	5.00	2.20	.60

☐ 1 Mark Thomas
☐ 2 Curtis Pride
☐ 3 James Morrisette
☐ 4 Stanton Cameron
☐ 5 Doug Saunders
☐ 6 Jamie Hoffner
☐ 7 Derek Henderson
☐ 8 James Harris
☐ 9 Alberto Diaz
☐ 10 Chris Butterfield
☐ 11 Brook Fordyce
☐ 12 Kevin Carroll
☐ 13 Tom Wegmann
☐ 14 Pete Walker
☐ 15 Joe Vitko
☐ 16 Julian Vasquez
☐ 17 Deron Sample
☐ 18 Andy Reich
☐ 19 Joe McCann
☐ 20 Gregg Langbehn
☐ 21 Denny Harriger
☐ 22 Chris Dorn
☐ 23 Tim Howard
☐ 24 Todd Douma
☐ 25 Pat Howell
☐ 26 John Tamargo MGR
☐ 27 Ron Gideon CO
☐ 28 Randy Niemann CO
☐ 29 Marc Goldberg
Sports Director
☐ 30 Joe Hawkins TR

1991 St. Lucie Mets ProCards

This 29-card standard-size set of the 1991 St. Lucie Mets, a Class A Florida State League affiliate of the New York Mets, features on its white-bordered fronts posed color player photos set on simulated spiral-bound yellow notebooks. The player's name, position, and team appear within a green rectangle below the photo. The yellow horizontal back is bordered in white and carries the player's name at the top, followed by biography and statistics.

	MINT	NRMT	EXC
COMPLETE SET (29)	5.00	2.20	.60

☐ 702 Mike Brady
☐ 703 Chris Dorn
☐ 704 Todd Douma
☐ 705 Gregg Langbehn
☐ 706 Joe McCann
☐ 707 David Proctor
☐ 708 Andy Reich
☐ 709 Deron Sample
☐ 710 Julian Vasquez
☐ 711 Joe Vitko
☐ 712 Pete Walker
☐ 713 Kevin Carroll
☐ 714 Brook Fordyce
☐ 715 Chris Butterfield
☐ 716 Al Diaz
☐ 717 James Harris
☐ 718 Derek Henderson
☐ 719 Jamie Hoffner
☐ 720 Tim Howard
☐ 721 Doug Saunders
☐ 722 Stanton Cameron
☐ 723 Brian Davis
☐ 724 Pat Howell
☐ 725 Curtis Pride
☐ 726 Mark Thomas
☐ 727 John Tamargo MGR
☐ 728 Ron Gideon CO
☐ 729 Randy Niemann CO
☐ 730 Checklist

1991 St. Petersburg Cardinals Classic/Best

This 30-card standard-size set of the 1991 St. Petersburg Cardinals, a Class A Florida State League affiliate of the St. Louis Cardinals, features white-bordered posed color player photos on its fronts. The player's name, team, and position appear at the bottom. The white back is framed by a thin black line and carries the player's name and position at the top, followed by biography, statistics and team logos.

	MINT	NRMT	EXC
COMPLETE SET (30)	5.00	2.20	.60

☐ 1 Ernie Baker
☐ 2 Mike Cassidy
☐ 3 John Corona
☐ 4 Steve Dixon
☐ 5 John Thomas
☐ 6 Luis Faccio
☐ 7 Chris Gorton
☐ 8 Daryl Green
☐ 9 Dave Bialas MGR
☐ 10 Troy Salvior
☐ 11 Jay North CO
☐ 12 Rick Shackle
☐ 13 Mark Smith
☐ 14 Ron Weber
☐ 15 Paul Ellis
☐ 16 Fred Langiotti
☐ 17 Brad Beanblossom
☐ 18 Mike Campas
☐ 19 Tripp Cromer
☐ 20 Joe Federico
☐ 21 Jonas Hamlin
☐ 22 Tony Ochs
☐ 23 Jose Trujillo
☐ 24 Bill Gate
☐ 25 Rich Gonzales
☐ 26 Ezequiel Herrera
☐ 27 Anthony Lewis
☐ 28 Mauricio Nunez
☐ 29 Tim Lata
☐ 30 Dan Doyel TR
Checklist

1991 St. Petersburg Cardinals ProCards

This 30-card standard-size set of the 1991 St. Petersburg Cardinals, a Class A Florida State League affiliate of the St. Louis Cardinals, features on its white-bordered fronts posed color player photos set on simulated spiral-bound yellow notebooks. The player's name, position, and team appear within a green rectangle below the photo. The yellow horizontal back is bordered in white and carries the player's name at the top, followed by biography and statistics.

	MINT	NRMT	EXC
COMPLETE SET (30)	5.00	2.20	.60

☐ 2265 Ernie Baker
☐ 2266 Dave Cassidy
☐ 2267 John Corona
☐ 2268 Steve Dixon
☐ 2269 Luis Faccio
☐ 2270 Chris Gorton
☐ 2271 Daryl Green
☐ 2272 Mike Hensley
☐ 2273 Tim Lata
☐ 2274 Troy Salvior
☐ 2275 George Sells
☐ 2276 Rick Shackle
☐ 2277 Ron Weber
☐ 2278 Paul Ellis
☐ 2279 Fred Langiotti
☐ 2280 Brad Beanblossom
☐ 2281 Mike Campas
☐ 2282 Tripp Cromer
☐ 2283 Joe Federico
☐ 2284 Jonas Hamlin
☐ 2285 Tony Ochs
☐ 2286 Jose Trujillo
☐ 2287 Bill Gale
☐ 2288 Rich Gonzalez
☐ 2289 Ezequiel Herrera
☐ 2290 Anthony Lewis
☐ 2291 Skeets Thomas
☐ 2292 Dave Bialas MGR
☐ 2293 Jay North CO
☐ 2294 Checklist

1991 Stockton Ports Classic/Best

This 26-card standard-size set of the 1991 Stockton Ports, a Class A California League affiliate of the Milwaukee Brewers, features white-bordered posed color player photos on its fronts. The player's name, team, and position appear at the bottom. The white back is framed by a thin black line and carries the player's name and position at the top, followed by biography, statistics and team logos.

	MINT	NRMT	EXC
COMPLETE SET (26)	5.00	2.20	.60

- ☐ 1 Jamie Cangemi
- ☐ 2 Otis Green
- ☐ 3 Steve Monson
- ☐ 4 Robert Vancho
- ☐ 5 Linc Mikkelsen
- ☐ 6 Oreste Marrero
- ☐ 7 Richard Berg
- ☐ 8 Kurt Archer
- ☐ 9 Sam Drake
- ☐ 10 Guillermo Sandoval
- ☐ 11 Dave Fitzgerald
- ☐ 12 Troy Haugen
- ☐ 13 Remigio Diaz
- ☐ 14 Randy Snyder
- ☐ 15 Michael Couturo
- ☐ 16 Randy Hood
- ☐ 17 Troy O'Leary
- ☐ 18 John Finn
- ☐ 19 Vince Castaldo
- ☐ 20 Bo Dodson
- ☐ 21 Vilato Marrero
- ☐ 22 Juan Flores
- ☐ 23 Tim Clark
- ☐ 24 Chris Bando MGR
- ☐ 25 Mitch Zwolensky CO
- ☐ 26 Checklist

1991 Stockton Ports ProCards

This 27-card standard-size set of the 1991 Stockton Ports, a Class A California League affiliate of the Milwaukee Brewers, features on its white-bordered fronts posed color player photos set on simulated spiral-bound yellow notebooks. The player's name, position, and team appear within a green rectangle below the photo. The yellow horizontal back is bordered in white and carries the player's name at the top, followed by biography and statistics.

	MINT	NRMT	EXC
COMPLETE SET (27)	5.00	2.20	.60

- ☐ 3023 Kurt Archer
- ☐ 3024 Rich Berg
- ☐ 3025 Jamie Cangemi
- ☐ 3026 Tim Dell
- ☐ 3027 Sam Drake
- ☐ 3028 Otis Green
- ☐ 3029 Lincoln Mikkelsen
- ☐ 3030 Mo Monson
- ☐ 3031 Steve Sparks
- ☐ 3032 Bob Vancho
- ☐ 3033 Brandy Vann
- ☐ 3034 Juan Flores
- ☐ 3035 Randy Snyder
- ☐ 3036 Vince Castaldo
- ☐ 3036 Remigio Diaz
- ☐ 3038 Bo Dodson
- ☐ 3039 Troy Haugen
- ☐ 3040 Oreste Marrero
- ☐ 3041 Vilato Marrero
- ☐ 3042 Tim Clark
- ☐ 3043 Mike Couture
- ☐ 3044 John Finn
- ☐ 3045 Randy Hood
- ☐ 3046 Troy O'Leary
- ☐ 3047 Chris Bando MGR
- ☐ 3048 Mitch Zwolensky CO
- ☐ 3049 Checklist

1991 Sumter Flyers Classic/Best

This 30-card standard-size set of the 1991 Sumter Flyers, a Class A South Atlantic League affiliate of the Montreal Expos, features white-bordered posed color player photos on its fronts. The player's name, team, and position appear at the bottom. The white back is framed by a thin black line and carries the player's name and position at the top, followed by biography, statistics and team logos. This issue includes the team set debuts of Rondell White and Shane Andrews.

	MINT	NRMT	EXC
COMPLETE SET (30)	8.00	3.60	1.00

- ☐ 1 Tavo Alvarez
- ☐ 2 Derek Aucoin
- ☐ 3 Matt Conley
- ☐ 4 Kevin Foster
- ☐ 5 Ron Gerstein
- ☐ 6 Darrin Kotch
- ☐ 7 Steve Long
- ☐ 8 William Martinez
- ☐ 9 Joe Norris
- ☐ 10 Shane Andrews
- ☐ 11 Ben VanRyn
- ☐ 12 Gabe White
- ☐ 13 Chris Hirsch
- ☐ 14 Doug Noce
- ☐ 15 Raul Santana
- ☐ 16 Tony Marabella
- ☐ 17 Hector Ortega
- ☐ 18 Claudio Ozario
- ☐ 19 Abimael Rodriguez
- ☐ 20 Gus Santiago
- ☐ 21 Marc Tsitouris
- ☐ 22 Gary Adams
- ☐ 23 Tyrone Horne
- ☐ 24 Todd Samples
- ☐ 25 Rondell White
- ☐ 26 Lorenzo Bundy MG
- ☐ 27 Gary Lance CO
- ☐ 28 Carlos Ponce CO
- ☐ 29 Bill Slosson TR
- ☐ 30 Checklist

1991 Sumter Flyers ProCards

This 31-card standard-size set of the 1991 Sumter Flyers, a Class A South Atlantic League affiliate of the Montreal Expos, features on its white-bordered fronts posed color player photos set on simulated spiral-bound yellow notebooks. The player's name, position, and team appear within a green rectangle below the photo. The yellow horizontal back is bordered in white and carries the player's name and position at the top, followed by biography and statistics. This issue includes the team set debuts of Rondell White and Shane Andrews.

	MINT	NRMT	EXC
COMPLETE SET (31)	7.00	3.10	.85

- ☐ 2324 Tavo Alvarez
- ☐ 2325 Derek Aucoin
- ☐ 2326 Matt Conley
- ☐ 2327 Kevin Foster
- ☐ 2328 Ron Gerstein
- ☐ 2329 Darrin Kotch
- ☐ 2330 Steve Long
- ☐ 2331 William Martinez
- ☐ 2332 Joe Norris
- ☐ 2333 Carlos Perez
- ☐ 2334 Ben VanRyn
- ☐ 2335 Gabe White
- ☐ 2336 Chris Hirsch
- ☐ 2337 Doug Noce
- ☐ 2338 Raul Santana
- ☐ 2339 Shane Andrews
- ☐ 2340 Jolbert Cabrera
- ☐ 2341 Tony Marabella
- ☐ 2342 Hector Ortega
- ☐ 2343 Claudio Ozario
- ☐ 2344 Abimael Rodriguez
- ☐ 2345 Gus Santiago
- ☐ 2346 Marc Tsitouris
- ☐ 2347 Gary Adams
- ☐ 2348 Tyrone Horne
- ☐ 2349 Todd Samples
- ☐ 2350 Rondell White
- ☐ 2351 Lorenzo Bundy MG
- ☐ 2352 Gary Lance CO
- ☐ 2353 Carlos Ponce CO
- ☐ 2354 Checklist

1991 Syracuse Chiefs Kraft

This 5-card set of the 1991 Syracuse Chiefs, a Class AAA International League affiliate of the Toronto Blue Jays, measures 2 3/8" by 3 1/2" and features on its white-bordered fronts posed color player photos set on backgrounds consisting of diagonal blue lines. The player's name, team name, and uniform number appear within a blue diamond at the lower right. The white horizontal back carries the player's name, uniform number, and position at the top, followed by biography and statistics. The cards are unnumbered and checklisted below in alphabetical order.

	MINT	NRMT	EXC
COMPLETE SET (5)	10.00	4.50	1.25

- ☐ 1 Derek Bell
- ☐ 2 Pat Hentgen
- ☐ 3 Alex Sanchez
- ☐ 4 Ed Sprague
- ☐ 5 Eddie Zosky

1991 Syracuse Chiefs Line Drive

This 26-card standard-size set of the 1991 Syracuse Chiefs, a Class AAA International League affiliate of the Toronto Blue Jays, features posed color player photos on its white-bordered fronts. The player's name appears in red lettering at the top; his position and team name appear in red lettering below the photo. The back carries the player's name within a red stripe at the top, followed by position, team name and affiliation, biography and statistics.

	MINT	NRMT	EXC
COMPLETE SET (26)	7.00	3.10	.85

- ☐ 501 Derek Bell
- ☐ 502 Rob Ducey
- ☐ 503 Julius McDougal
- ☐ 504 Juan Guzman
- ☐ 505 Pat Hentgen
- ☐ 506 Shawn Jeter
- ☐ 507 Doug Linton
- ☐ 508 Bob MacDonald
- ☐ 509 Mike Maksudian
- ☐ 510 Ravelo Manzanillo
- ☐ 511 Domingo Martinez
- ☐ 512 Stu Pederson
- ☐ 513 Marty Pevey
- ☐ 514 Tom Quinlan
- ☐ 515 Alex Sanchez
- ☐ 516 Jerry Schunk
- ☐ 517 John Shea
- ☐ 518 Ed Sprague
- ☐ 519 William Suero
- ☐ 520 Steve Wapnick
- ☐ 521 Mickey Weston
- ☐ 522 John Poloni CO
- ☐ 523 Eddie Zosky
- ☐ 524 Bob Bailor MG
- ☐ 525 Rocket Wheeler CO
- ☐ NNO Title card

1991 Syracuse Chiefs Merchants Bank

Sponsored by Merchants Bank and WIXT Channel 9, this photo album features the 1991 Syracuse Chiefs, a Class AAA International League affiliate of the Toronto Blue Jays. The photo album unfolds to reveal three 9 3/8 by 10 5/8" sheets. The first sheet displays a montage of five color action player photos, with a Merchants Bank advertisement beneath the picture. The second and third panels each consist of five rows with three cards per row. The perforated player cards are horizontally oriented and measure 3 1/8" by 2 1/8". Inside a light blue border, the fronts display white-bordered color posed or action player pictures, with player identification immediately below. Sponsor logos and the team logo appear to the right of the photos on a wide white stripe. In blue print, the horizontal backs carry biography and statistics. A facsimile autograph in red ink rounds out the back. The cards are unnumbered and checklisted below in alphabetical order.

	MINT	NRMT	EXC
COMPLETE SET (30)	10.00	4.50	1.25

- ☐ 1 Bob Bailor MG
- ☐ 2 Derek Bell
- ☐ 3 Pete Blohm
- ☐ 4 Denis Boucher
- ☐ 5 Rob Ducey
- ☐ 6 Juan Guzman
- ☐ 7 Pat Hentgen
- ☐ 8 Randy Holland TR
- ☐ 9 Shawn Jeter
- ☐ 10 Randy Knorr
- ☐ 11 Doug Linton
- ☐ 12 Mike Maksudian
- ☐ 13 Ravelo Manzanilla
- ☐ 14 Domingo Martinez
- ☐ 15 Robert MacDonald
- ☐ 16 Julius McDougal
- ☐ 17 Stu Pederson
- ☐ 18 Marty Pevey
- ☐ 19 John Poloni CO
- ☐ 20 Tom Quinlan
- ☐ 21 Alex Sanchez
- ☐ 22 Jerry Schunk
- ☐ 23 John Shea
- ☐ 24 Ed Sprague
- ☐ 25 William Suero
- ☐ 26 Steve Wapnick
- ☐ 27 Mickey Weston
- ☐ 28 Rocket Wheeler CO
- ☐ 29 Frank Wills
- ☐ 30 Eddie Zosky

1991 Syracuse Chiefs ProCards

This 25-card standard-size set of the 1991 Syracuse Chiefs, a Class AAA International League affiliate of the Toronto Blue Jays, features on its white-bordered fronts posed color player photos set on simulated spiral-bound yellow notebooks. The player's name, position, and team appear within a green rectangle below the photo. The yellow horizontal back is bordered in white and carries the player's name and position at the top, followed by biography and statistics. This issue includes the fourth year card of Derek Bell.

	MINT	NRMT	EXC
COMPLETE SET (25)	6.00	2.70	.75

- ☐ 2475 Pete Blohm
- ☐ 2476 Juan Guzman
- ☐ 2477 Pat Hentgen
- ☐ 2478 Doug Linton
- ☐ 2479 Alex Sanchez
- ☐ 2480 John Shea
- ☐ 2481 Steve Wapnick
- ☐ 2482 Mickey Weston
- ☐ 2483 Marty Pevey
- ☐ 2484 Ed Sprague
- ☐ 2485 Domingo Martinez
- ☐ 2486 Julius McDougal
- ☐ 2487 Tom Quinlan
- ☐ 2488 Jerry Schunk
- ☐ 2489 William Suero
- ☐ 2490 Eddie Zosky
- ☐ 2491 Derek Bell
- ☐ 2492 Rob Ducey
- ☐ 2493 Shawn Jeter
- ☐ 2494 Mike Maksudian
- ☐ 2495 Stu Pederson
- ☐ 2496 Bob Bailor MG
- ☐ 2497 John Poloni CO
- ☐ 2498 Rocket Wheeler CO
- ☐ 2499 Checklist

1991 Tacoma Tigers Line Drive

	MINT	NRMT	EXC
COMPLETE SET (26)	5.00	2.20	.60

- ☐ 526 Troy Afenir
- ☐ 527 Mike Bordick
- ☐ 528 Jorge Brito
- ☐ 529 Scott Brosius
- ☐ 530 Kevin Campbell
- ☐ 531 Pete Coachman
- ☐ 532 Dan Eskew
- ☐ 533 Eric Fox
- ☐ 534 Apolinar Garcia
- ☐ 535 Webster Garrison
- ☐ 536 Johnny Guzman
- ☐ 537 Jeff Pico
- ☐ 538 Dann Howitt
- ☐ 539 Doug Jennings
- ☐ 540 Brad Komminsk
- ☐ 541 Tim McCoy
- ☐ 542 Jeff Musselman
- ☐ 543 Troy Neel
- ☐ 544 Will Schock
- ☐ 545 Nelson Simmons
- ☐ 546 Bruce Walton
- ☐ 547 Pat Wernig
- ☐ 548 Ron Witmeyer
- ☐ 549 Jeff Newman MGR
- ☐ 550 Glenn Abbott CO
- ☐ NNO Title card

1991 Tacoma Tigers ProCards

This 29-card standard-size set of the 1991 Tacoma Tigers, a Class AAA Pacific Coast League affiliate of the Oakland Athletics, features on its white-bordered fronts posed color player photos set on simulated spiral-bound yellow notebooks. The player's name, position, and team appear within a green rectangle below the photo. The yellow horizontal back is bordered in white and carries the player's name at the top, followed by biography and statistics.

	MINT	NRMT	EXC
COMPLETE SET (29)	5.00	2.20	.60

- ☐ 2295 Dana Allison
- ☐ 2296 Kevin Campbell
- ☐ 2297 Dan Eskew
- ☐ 2298 Apolinar Garcia
- ☐ 2299 Johnny Guzman
- ☐ 2300 Reggie Harris
- ☐ 2301 Jeff Musselman
- ☐ 2302 Clay Parker
- ☐ 2303 Jeff Pico
- ☐ 2304 Will Schock
- ☐ 2305 Joe Slusarski
- ☐ 2306 Bruce Walton
- ☐ 2307 Pat Wernig
- ☐ 2308 Troy Afenir
- ☐ 2309 Jorge Brito
- ☐ 2310 Scott Brosius
- ☐ 2311 Pete Coachman
- ☐ 2312 Rod Correia
- ☐ 2313 Webster Garrison
- ☐ 2314 Scott Hemond
- ☐ 2315 Dann Howitt
- ☐ 2316 Ron Witmeyer
- ☐ 2317 Eric Fox
- ☐ 2318 Troy Neel
- ☐ 2319 Lee Sammons
- ☐ 2320 Nelson Simmons
- ☐ 2321 Jeff Newman MGR
- ☐ 2322 Glenn Abbott CO
- ☐ 2323 Checklist

1991 Tidewater Tides Line Drive

	MINT	NRMT	EXC
COMPLETE SET (26)	8.00	3.60	1.00

- ☐ 551 Kevin Baez
- ☐ 552 Blaine Beatty
- ☐ 553 Doug Cinnella
- ☐ 554 Chris Donnels
- ☐ 555 Jeff Gardner
- ☐ 556 Terrel Hansen

- ☐ 557 Manny Hernandez
- ☐ 558 Eric Hillman
- ☐ 559 Todd Hundley
- ☐ 560 Alex Jimenez
- ☐ 561 Tim Leiper
- ☐ 562 Lee May Jr.
- ☐ 563 Orlando Mercado
- ☐ 564 Brad Moore
- ☐ 565 Al Pedrique
- ☐ 566 Dale Plummer
- ☐ 567 Rich Sauveur
- ☐ 568 Ray Soff
- ☐ 569 Kelvin Torve
- ☐ 570 Dave Trautwein
- ☐ 571 Julio Valera
- ☐ 572 Robbie Wine
- ☐ 573 Anthony Young
- ☐ 574 Steve Swisher MGR
- ☐ 575 Ron Washington CO
  Bob Apodaca CO
- ☐ NNO Title card

1991 Tidewater Tides ProCards

This 30-card standard-size set of the 1991 Tidewater Tides, a Class AAA International League affiliate of the New York Mets, features on its white-bordered fronts posed color player photos set on simulated spiral-bound yellow notebooks. The player's name, position, and team appear within a green rectangle below the photo. The yellow horizontal back is bordered in white and carries the player's name at the top, followed by biography and statistics. This issue includes the fourth year card of Todd Hundley.

	MINT	NRMT	EXC
COMPLETE SET (30)	5.00	2.20	.60

- ☐ 2500 Blaine Beatty
- ☐ 2501 Terry Bross
- ☐ 2502 Doug Cinnella
- ☐ 2503 Mark Dewey
- ☐ 2504 Manny Hernandez
- ☐ 2505 Eric Hillman
- ☐ 2506 Brad Moore
- ☐ 2507 Dale Plummer
- ☐ 2508 Rich Sauveur
- ☐ 2509 Ray Soff
- ☐ 2510 Dave Trautwein
- ☐ 2511 Julio Valera
- ☐ 2512 Anthony Young
- ☐ 2513 Todd Hundley
- ☐ 2514 Orlando Mercado
- ☐ 2515 Kevin Baez
- ☐ 2516 Chris Donnels
- ☐ 2517 Jeff Gardner
- ☐ 2518 Alex Jimenez
- ☐ 2519 Al Pedrique
- ☐ 2520 Kelvin Torve
- ☐ 2521 Chuck Carr
- ☐ 2522 Terrel Hansen
- ☐ 2523 Tim Leiper
- ☐ 2524 Terry McDaniel
- ☐ 2525 Jaime Roseboro
- ☐ 2526 Steve Swisher MGR
- ☐ 2527 Bob Apodaca CO
- ☐ 2528 Ron Washington CO
- ☐ 2529 Checklist

1991 Toledo Mud Hens Line Drive

	MINT	NRMT	EXC
COMPLETE SET (26)	5.00	2.20	.60

- ☐ 576 Scott Aldred
- ☐ 577 Karl Allaire
- ☐ 578 Skeeter Barnes
- ☐ 579 Arnie Beyeler
- ☐ 580 Rico Brogna
- ☐ 581 Phil Clark
- ☐ 582 Mike Dalton
- ☐ 583 Curt Ford
- ☐ 584 Dan Gakeler
- ☐ 585 David Haas
- ☐ 586 Shawn Hare
- ☐ 587 John Kiely
- ☐ 588 Mark Leiter
- ☐ 589 Scott Livingstone
- ☐ 590 Mitch Lyden
- ☐ 591 Eric Mangham
- ☐ 592 Rusty Meacham
- ☐ 593 Mike Munoz
- ☐ 594 Randy Nosek
- ☐ 595 Johnny Paredes
- ☐ 596 Kevin Ritz
- ☐ 597 Rich Rowland
- ☐ 598 Don Vesling
- ☐ 599 Joe Sparks MGR
- ☐ 600 Mark Wagner CO
  Ralph Treuel CO
- ☐ NNO Title card

1991 Toledo Mud Hens ProCards

This 28-card standard-size set of the 1991 Toledo Mud Hens, a Class AAA International League affiliate of the Detroit Tigers, features on its white-bordered fronts posed color player photos set on simulated spiral-bound yellow notebooks. The player's name, position, and team appear within a green rectangle below the photo. The yellow horizontal back is bordered in white and carries the player's name at the top, followed by biography and statistics.

	MINT	NRMT	EXC
COMPLETE SET (28)	5.00	2.20	.60

- ☐ 1922 Scott Alfred
- ☐ 1923 Mike Dalton
- ☐ 1924 Dan Gakeler
- ☐ 1925 Greg Gohr
- ☐ 1926 Dave Haas
- ☐ 1927 John Kiely
- ☐ 1928 Rusty Meacham
- ☐ 1929 Mike Munoz
- ☐ 1930 Randy Nosek
- ☐ 1931 Ron Rightnowar
- ☐ 1932 Kevin Ritz
- ☐ 1933 Don Vesling
- ☐ 1934 Phil Clark
- ☐ 1935 Mitch Lyden
- ☐ 1936 Rich Rowland
- ☐ 1937 Karl Allaire
- ☐ 1938 Arnie Beyeler
- ☐ 1939 Rico Brogna
- ☐ 1940 Scott Livingstone
- ☐ 1941 Johnny Paredes
- ☐ 1942 Skeeter Barnes
- ☐ 1943 Curt Ford
- ☐ 1944 Shawn Hare
- ☐ 1945 Eric Mangham
- ☐ 1946 Joe Sparks MGR
- ☐ 1947 Ralph Treuel CO
- ☐ 1948 Mark Wagner CO
- ☐ 1949 Checklist

1991 Triple A All-Stars ProCards

	MINT	NRMT	EXC
COMPLETE SET (55)	12.00	5.50	1.50

- ☐ AAA17 John Vander Wal
- ☐ AAA1 Jerry Brooks
- ☐ AAA2 Carlos Hernandez
- ☐ AAA3 Roger Mason
- ☐ AAA4 Rick Reed
- ☐ AAA5 Tino Martinez
- ☐ AAA6 Luis Medina
- ☐ AAA7 Rich Monteleone
- ☐ AAA8 Bernie Williams
- ☐ AAA9 Doug Henry
- ☐ AAA10 Tim McIntosh
- ☐ AAA11 Jim Olander
- ☐ AAA12 Ruben Amaro
- ☐ AAA13 Chad Curtis
- ☐ AAA14 Max Oliveras MGR
- ☐ AAA15 Lee Stevens
- ☐ AAA16 Dana Ridenour
- ☐ AAA18 Russ McGinnis
- ☐ AAA19 Laddie Renfroe
- ☐ AAA20 Rey Sanchez
- ☐ AAA21 Kevin Ward
- ☐ AAA22 Ray Stephens
- ☐ AAA23 Terry Lee
- ☐ AAA24 Pete MacKanin MGR
- ☐ AAA25 Monty Fariss
- ☐ AAA26 Rob Maurer
- ☐ AAA27 Sal Rende MGR
- ☐ AAA28 Tim Spehr
- ☐ AAA29 Scott Cooper
- ☐ AAA30 Daryl Irvine
- ☐ AAA31 Phil Plantier
- ☐ AAA32 Mo Vaughn
- ☐ AAA33 Darren Lewis
- ☐ AAA34 Andres Santana
- ☐ AAA35 Tom Edens
- ☐ AAA36 Denny Neagle
- ☐ AAA37 Gary Wayne
- ☐ AAA38 Armando Reynoso
- ☐ AAA39 Greg Biagini MGR
- ☐ AAA40 Chito Martinez
- ☐ AAA41 Steve Scarsone
- ☐ AAA42 Derek Bell
- ☐ AAA43 Rob Ducey
- ☐ AAA44 Eddie Zosky
- ☐ AAA45 Kevin Campbell
- ☐ AAA46 Scott Livingstone
- ☐ AAA47 Chris Donnels
- ☐ AAA48 Jeff Gardner
- ☐ AAA49 Todd Hundley
- ☐ AAA50 Steve Swisher MGR
- ☐ AAA51 Gary Cooper
- ☐ AAA52 Kenny Lofton
- ☐ AAA53 Bob Skinner MGR
- ☐ AAA54 Dean Wilkins
- ☐ AAA55 Checklist

1991 Tucson Toros Line Drive

	MINT	NRMT	EXC
COMPLETE SET (26)	8.00	3.60	1.00

- ☐ 601 Harold Allen
- ☐ 602 Eric Anthony
- ☐ 603 Doug Baker
- ☐ 604 Ryan Bowen
- ☐ 605 Mike Capel
- ☐ 606 Andujar Cedeno
- ☐ 607 Terry Clark
- ☐ 608 Carlo Colombino
- ☐ 609 Gary Cooper
- ☐ 610 Calvin Schiraldi
- ☐ 611 Randy Hennis
- ☐ 612 Butch Henry
- ☐ 613 Blaise Ilsley
- ☐ 614 Kenny Lofton
- ☐ 615 Terry McGriff
- ☐ 616 Andy Mota
- ☐ 617 Javier Ortiz
- ☐ 618 Scott Servais
- ☐ 619 Mike Simms
- ☐ 620 Jose Tolentino
- ☐ 621 Lee Tunnell
- ☐ 622 Brent Strom
- ☐ 623 Gerald Young
- ☐ 624 Bob Skinner MGR
- ☐ 625 Dave Engle CO
- ☐ NNO Title card

1991 Tucson Toros ProCards

This 28-card standard-size set of the 1991 Tucson Toros, a Class AAA Pacific Coast League affiliate of the Houston Astros, features on its white-bordered fronts posed color player photos set on simulated spiral-bound yellow notebooks. The player's name, position, and team appear within a green rectangle below the photo. The yellow horizontal back is bordered in white and carries the player's name at the top, followed by biography and statistics. This issue includes the fourth year card of Kenny Lofton.

	MINT	NRMT	EXC
COMPLETE SET (28)	8.00	3.60	1.00

- ☐ 2204 Harold Allen
- ☐ 2205 Ryan Bowen
- ☐ 2206 Mike Capel
- ☐ 2207 Terry Clark
- ☐ 2208 Dean Freeland
- ☐ 2209 Randy Hennis
- ☐ 2210 Butch Henry
- ☐ 2211 Blaise Ilsley
- ☐ 2212 Calvin Schiraldi
- ☐ 2213 Lee Tunnell
- ☐ 2214 Dean Wilkins
- ☐ 2215 Terry McGriff
- ☐ 2216 Scott Servais
- ☐ 2217 Doug Baker
- ☐ 2218 Andujar Cedeno
- ☐ 2219 Carlo Colombino
- ☐ 2220 Andy Mota
- ☐ 2221 Mike Simms
- ☐ 2222 Jose Tolentino
- ☐ 2223 Eric Anthony
- ☐ 2224 Gary Cooper
- ☐ 2225 Kenny Lofton
- ☐ 2226 Javier Ortiz
- ☐ 2227 Gerald Young
- ☐ 2228 Bob Skinner MGR
- ☐ 2229 Dave Engle CO
- ☐ 2230 Brent Strom CO
- ☐ 2231 Checklist

1991 Tulsa Drillers Line Drive

	MINT	NRMT	EXC
COMPLETE SET (26)	10.00	4.50	1.25

- ☐ 576 Rob Brown
- ☐ 577 Mike Burton
- ☐ 578 Everett Cunningham
- ☐ 579 Jeff Frye
- ☐ 580 Pat Garman
- ☐ 581 Bryan Gore
- ☐ 582 David Green
- ☐ 583 Donald Harris
- ☐ 584 Jose Hernandez
- ☐ 585 Greg Iavarone
- ☐ 586 Barry Manuel
- ☐ 587 Trey McCoy
- ☐ 588 Rod Morris
- ☐ 589 Robb Nen
- ☐ 590 David Perez
- ☐ 591 Bobby Reed
- ☐ 592 Ivan Rodriguez
- ☐ 593 Dan Rohrmeier
- ☐ 594 Brian Romero
- ☐ 595 Luke Sable
- ☐ 596 Frederic Samson
- ☐ 597 Cedric Shaw
- ☐ 598 Chris Shiflett
- ☐ 599 Bobby Jones MGR
- ☐ 600 Oscar Acosta CO
  Jeff Hubbard CO
- ☐ NNO Title card

1991 Tulsa Drillers ProCards

This 27-card standard-size set of the 1991 Tulsa Drillers, a Class AA Texas League affiliate of the Texas Rangers, features on its white-bordered fronts posed color player photos set on simulated spiral-bound yellow notebooks. The player's name, position, and team appear within a green rectangle below the photo. The yellow horizontal back is bordered in white and carries the player's name at the top, followed by biography and statistics. This issue includes the third year card of Ivan Rodriguez.

	MINT	NRMT	EXC
COMPLETE SET (27	8.00	3.60	1.00

- ☐ 2765 Rob Brown
- ☐ 2766 Everett Cunningham
- ☐ 2767 Bryan Gore
- ☐ 2768 Barry Manuel
- ☐ 2769 Robb Nen
- ☐ 2770 David Perez
- ☐ 2771 Bobby Reed
- ☐ 2772 Brian Romero
- ☐ 2773 Cedric Shaw
- ☐ 2774 Chris Shiflett
- ☐ 2775 Greg Iavarone
- ☐ 2776 Ivan Rodriguez
- ☐ 2777 Mike Burton
- ☐ 2778 Jeff Frye
- ☐ 2779 Pat Garman
- ☐ 2780 Jose Hernandez
- ☐ 2781 Trey McCoy
- ☐ 2782 Luke Sable
- ☐ 2783 Frederic Samson
- ☐ 2784 David Green
- ☐ 2785 Donald Harris
- ☐ 2786 Rod Morris
- ☐ 2787 Dan Rohrmeier
- ☐ 2788 Bobby Jones MGR
- ☐ 2789 Oscar Acosta CO
- ☐ 2790 Jeff Hubbard CO
- ☐ 2791 Checklist

1991 Tulsa Drillers Team Issue

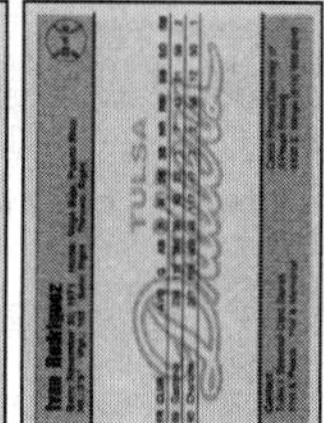

	MINT	NRMT	EXC
COMPLETE SET (30)	20.00	9.00	2.50

- ☐ 1 Oscar Acosta CO
- ☐ 2 Rob Brown
- ☐ 3 Paco Burgos
- ☐ 4 Mike Burton
- ☐ 5 Mike Campbell
- ☐ 6 Everett Cunningham
- ☐ 7 Jeff Frye
- ☐ 8 Bryan Gore
- ☐ 9 David Green
- ☐ 10 Greg Harrell
- ☐ 11 Donald Harris
- ☐ 12 Jose Hernandez
- ☐ 13 Jeff Hubbard CO
- ☐ 14 Greg Iavarone
- ☐ 15 Bobby Jones
- ☐ 16 Barry Manuel
- ☐ 17 Trey McCoy
- ☐ 18 Eric McCray
- ☐ 19 Rod Morris
- ☐ 20 Robb Nen
- ☐ 21 David Perez
- ☐ 22 Bobby Reed
- ☐ 23 Ivan Rodriguez
- ☐ 24 Dan Rohrmeier
- ☐ 25 Brian Romero
- ☐ 26 Steve Rowley
- ☐ 27 Luke Sable
- ☐ 28 Frederic Samson
- ☐ 29 Cedric Shaw
- ☐ 30 Juan Gonzalez
  Past Star

1991 Utica Blue Sox Classic/Best

This 30-card standard-size set of the 1991 Utica Blue Sox, a Class A New York-Penn League affiliate of the Chicago White Sox, features white-bordered posed color player photos on its fronts. The player's name, team, and position appear at the bottom. The white back is framed by a thin black line and carries the player's name and position at the top, followed by biography, statistics and team logos.

	MINT	NRMT	EXC
COMPLETE SET (30)	8.00	3.60	1.00

☐ 1 Marc Kubiki
☐ 2 Doug Brady
☐ 3 John Herrholtz
☐ 4 Mike Bertotti
☐ 5 Shawn Buchanan
☐ 6 Ray Durham
☐ 7 Rob Ellis
☐ 8 Mike Heathcott
☐ 9 Greg Young
☐ 10 Matt Hattabaugh
☐ 11 Dean Haase
☐ 12 Dave Martorana
☐ 13 Jeff Pierce
☐ 14 Jonathan Story
☐ 15 Steve Siebert
☐ 16 Glenn DiSarcina
☐ 17 Tommy Helms
☐ 18 Harold Henry
☐ 19 Greg Fritz
☐ 20 Larry Thomas Jr.
☐ 21 Al Levine
☐ 22 Bill Ballou CO
☐ 23 Mike Gellinger MGR
☐ 24 Charlie Culberson CO
☐ 25 Rick Ray TR
☐ 26 Hank Tagle
☐ 27 Troy Fryman
☐ 28 Patrick Rollins
☐ 29 Rafael Ochoa
☐ 30 Checklist

1991 Utica Blue Sox ProCards

This 29-card standard-size set of the 1991 Utica Blue Sox, a Class A New York-Penn League affiliate of the Chicago White Sox, features on its white-bordered fronts posed color player photos set on simulated spiral-bound yellow notebooks. The player's name, position, and team appear within a green rectangle below the photo. The yellow horizontal back is bordered in white and carries the player's name at the top, followed by biography and statistics. This issue includes the minor league card debut of Ray Durham.

	MINT	NRMT	EXC
COMPLETE SET (29)	7.00	3.10	.85

☐ 3232 Mike Bertotti
☐ 3233 Bull Ellis
☐ 3234 Greg Fritz
☐ 3235 Mike Heathcott
☐ 3236 John Herrholtz
☐ 3237 Marc Kubicki
☐ 3238 Al Levine
☐ 3239 Hank Tagle
☐ 3240 Larry Thomas
☐ 3241 Greg Young
☐ 3242 Dean Haase
☐ 3243 Matt Hattabaugh
☐ 3244 Doug Brady
☐ 3245 Glenn DiSarcina
☐ 3246 Ray Durham
☐ 3247 Troy Fryman
☐ 3248 Tommy Helms
☐ 3249 Mutta Martorana
☐ 3250 Pep Rollins
☐ 3251 Steve Siebert
☐ 3252 Shawn Buchanan
☐ 3253 Harold Henry
☐ 3254 Rafael Ochoa
☐ 3255 Jeff Pierce
☐ 3256 Jonathan Story
☐ 3257 Mike Gellinger MGR
☐ 3258 Bill Ballou CO
☐ 3259 Charlie Culberson
☐ 3260 Checklist

1991 Vancouver Canadians Line Drive

This 26-card standard-size set of the 1991 Vancouver Canadians, a Class AAA Pacific Coast League affiliate of the Chicago White Sox, features posed color player photos on its white-bordered fronts. The player's name appears in red lettering at the top; his position and team name appear in red lettering below the photo. The back carries the player's name within a red stripe at the top, followed by position, team name and affiliation, biography and statistics.

	MINT	NRMT	EXC
COMPLETE SET (26)	5.00	2.20	.60

☐ 626 Cesar Bernhardt
☐ 627 Mario Brito
☐ 628 Kurt Brown
☐ 629 John Cangelosi
☐ 630 Jeff Carter
☐ 631 Tom Drees
☐ 632 Grady Hall
☐ 633 Joe Hall
☐ 634 Curt Hasler
☐ 635 Danny Heep
☐ 636 Dan Henley
☐ 637 Roberto Hernandez
☐ 638 Orsino Hill
☐ 639 Jerry Kutzler
☐ 640 Norberto Martin
☐ 641 Rod McCray
☐ 642 Rob Nelson
☐ 643 Warren Newson
☐ 644 Greg Perschke
☐ 645 Rich Scheid
☐ 646 Matt Stark
☐ 647 Ron Stephens
☐ 648 Don Wakamatsu
☐ 649 Marv Foley MG
☐ 650 Roger LaFrancois CO
Moe Drabowsky CO
☐ NNO Title card

1991 Vancouver Canadians ProCards

This 27-card standard-size set of the 1991 Vancouver Canadians, a Class AAA Pacific Coast League affiliate of the Chicago White Sox, features on its white-bordered fronts posed color player photos set on simulated spiral-bound yellow notebooks. The player's name, position, and team appear within a green rectangle below the photo. The yellow horizontal back is bordered in white and carries the player's name and position at the top, followed by biography and statistics.

	MINT	NRMT	EXC
COMPLETE SET (27)	5.00	2.20	.60

☐ 1586 Mario Brito
☐ 1587 Jeff Carter
☐ 1588 Tom Drees
☐ 1589 Grady Hall
☐ 1590 Curt Hasler
☐ 1591 Roberto Hernandez
☐ 1592 Jerry Kutzler
☐ 1593 Greg Perschke
☐ 1594 Rich Scheid
☐ 1595 Ron Stephens
☐ 1596 Kurt Brown
☐ 1597 Matt Stark
☐ 1598 Don Wakamatsu
☐ 1599 Cesar Bernhardt
☐ 1600 Joe Hall
☐ 1601 Danny Heep
☐ 1602 Dan Henley
☐ 1603 Norberto Martin
☐ 1604 Rob Nelson
☐ 1605 John Cangelosi
☐ 1606 Orsino Hill
☐ 1607 Rod McCray
☐ 1608 Warren Newson
☐ 1609 Marv Foley MG
☐ 1610 Moe Drabowsky CO
☐ 1611 Roger LaFrancois CO
☐ 1612 Checklist

1991 Vero Beach Dodgers Classic/Best

This 30-card standard-size set of the 1991 Vero Beach Dodgers, a Class A Florida State League affiliate of the Los Angeles Dodgers, features white-bordered posed color player photos on its fronts. The player's name, team, and position appear at the bottom. The white back is framed by a thin black line and carries the player's name and position at the top, followed by biography, statistics and team logos.

	MINT	NRMT	EXC
COMPLETE SET (30)	5.00	2.20	.60

☐ 1 Pedro Astacio
☐ 2 Dave Baumann
☐ 3 Bill Bene
☐ 4 Mike Brady
☐ 5 Ray Calhoun
☐ 6 Dale Coleman
☐ 7 Scott Freeman
☐ 8 Kiki Jones
☐ 9 Mike Mimbs
☐ 10 Tim Patrick
☐ 11 Mike Sampson
☐ 12 Sean Snedeker
☐ 13 Bill Wengert
☐ 14 Adam Brown
☐ 15 Pedro Gonzalez
☐ 16 Hector Ortiz Jr.
☐ 17 Rafael Bournigal
☐ 18 John Deutsch
☐ 19 Scott Boffek
☐ 20 Tim Griffin
☐ 21 Matt Howard
☐ 22 Sean McKamie
☐ 23 Steve O'Donnell
☐ 24 Bill Ashley
☐ 25 Rafael Rijo
☐ 26 Jeffrey Vanzytveld
☐ 27 Mark Griffin
☐ 28 Brock McMurray
☐ 29 Chris Morrow
☐ 30 Jerry Royster MGR
Checklist

1991 Vero Beach Dodgers ProCards

This 33-card standard-size set of the 1991 Vero Beach Dodgers, a Class A Florida State League affiliate of the Los Angeles Dodgers, features on its white-bordered fronts posed color player photos set on simulated spiral-bound yellow notebooks. The player's name, position, and team appear within a green rectangle below the photo. The yellow horizontal back is bordered in white and carries the player's name at the top, followed by biography and statistics.

	MINT	NRMT	EXC
COMPLETE SET (33)	5.00	2.20	.60

☐ 762 Pedro Astacio
☐ 763 Dave Baumann
☐ 764 Bill Bene
☐ 765 Mike Brady
☐ 766 Ray Calhoun
☐ 767 Dale Coleman
☐ 768 Scott Freeman
☐ 769 Kiki Jones
☐ 770 Michael Mimbs
☐ 771 Tim Patrick
☐ 772 Mike Sampson
☐ 773 Sean Snedeker
☐ 774 Bill Wengert
☐ 775 Adam Brown
☐ 776 Pedro Gonzalez
☐ 777 Hector Ortiz
☐ 778 Rafael Bournigal
☐ 779 John Deutsch
☐ 780 Scott Doffek
☐ 781 Tim Griffin
☐ 782 Matt Howard
☐ 783 Sean McKamie
☐ 784 Steve O'Donnell
☐ 785 Billy Ashley
☐ 786 Eric Blackwell
☐ 787 Mark Griffin
☐ 788 Brock McMurray
☐ 789 Chris Morrow
☐ 790 Rafael Rijo
☐ 791 Jerry Royster MGR
☐ 792 Jon Debus CO
☐ 793 Dennis Lewallyn CO
☐ 794 Checklist

1991 Visalia Oaks Classic/Best

This 27-card standard-size set of the 1991 Visalia Oaks, a Class A California League affiliate of the Minnesota Twins, features white-bordered posed color player photos on its fronts. The player's name, team, and position appear at the bottom. The white back is framed by a thin black line and carries the player's name and position at the top, followed by biography, statistics and team logos.

	MINT	NRMT	EXC
COMPLETE SET (27)	5.00	2.20	.60

☐ 1 Jayson Best
☐ 2 Ed Gustafson
☐ 3 Jon Henry
☐ 4 Marc Lipson
☐ 5 Mike Misuraca
☐ 6 Darren Musselwhite
☐ 7 Tim Nedin
☐ 8 Al Newman
☐ 9 Carlos Pulido
☐ 10 Mark Swope
☐ 11 Fred White
☐ 12 Matt Brown
☐ 13 Troy Buckley
☐ 14 Chris Delarwelle
☐ 15 Steve Dunn
☐ 16 Mica Lewis
☐ 17 Pat Meares
☐ 18 Alex Nunez
☐ 19 Brian Raabe
☐ 20 John Cohen
☐ 21 Rex De La Nuez
☐ 22 Tom Gavin
☐ 23 Derrell Rumsey
☐ 24 Steve Liddle MGR
☐ 25 Bob Kappesser
☐ 26 Brian Allard CO
☐ 27 Joel Sefly TR
Checklist

1991 Visalia Oaks ProCards

This 25-card standard-size set of the 1991 Visalia Oaks, a Class A California League affiliate of the Minnesota Twins, features on its white-bordered fronts posed color player photos set on simulated spiral-bound yellow notebooks. The player's name, position, and team appear within a green rectangle below the photo. The yellow horizontal back is bordered in white and carries the player's name at the top, followed by biography and statistics.

	MINT	NRMT	EXC
COMPLETE SET (25)	5.00	2.20	.60

☐ 1735 Jayson Best
☐ 1736 Ed Gustafson
☐ 1737 Jon Henry
☐ 1738 Marc Lipson
☐ 1739 Mike Misuraca
☐ 1740 Darren Musselwhite
☐ 1741 Mark Swope
☐ 1742 Fred White
☐ 1743 Matt Brown
☐ 1744 Troy Buckley
☐ 1745 Bob Kappeser
☐ 1746 Chris Delarwelle
☐ 1747 Steve Dunn
☐ 1748 Mica Lewis
☐ 1749 Pat Meares
☐ 1750 Alex Nunez
☐ 1751 Brian Raabe
☐ 1752 John Cohen
☐ 1753 Rex DeLaNuez
☐ 1754 Tom Gavin
☐ 1755 Derrell Rumsey
☐ 1756 Greg Sims
☐ 1757 Steve Liddle MGR
☐ 1758 Brian Allard CO
☐ 1759 Checklist

1991 Visalia Oaks Update ProCards

This 3-card standard-size set of the 1991 Visalia Oaks, a Class A California League affiliate of the Minnesota Twins, features on its white-bordered fronts posed color player photos set on simulated spiral-bound yellow notebooks. The player's name, position, and team appear within a green rectangle below the photo. The yellow horizontal back is bordered in white and carries the player's name at the top, followed by biography and statistics.

	MINT	NRMT	EXC
COMPLETE SET (3)	5.00	2.20	.60

☐ 1 David McCarty
☐ 2 Scott Stahoviak
☐ 3 David McCarty
Scott Stahoviak

1991 Waterloo Diamonds Classic/Best

This 29-card standard-size set of the 1991 Waterloo Diamonds, a Class A Midwest League affiliate of the San Diego Padres, features white-bordered posed color player photos on its fronts. The player's name, team, and position appear at the bottom. The white back is framed by a thin black line and carries the player's name and position at the top, followed by biography, statistics and team logos.

	MINT	NRMT	EXC
COMPLETE SET (29)	5.00	2.20	.60

☐ 1 Lance Banks
☐ 2 Bruce Bensching
☐ 3 Bryce Florie
☐ 4 Scott Fredrickson
☐ 5 Rob Hays
☐ 6 Tony Mortensen
☐ 7 Lance Painter
☐ 8 Scott Sanders
☐ 9 Ryan Thibault
☐ 10 Tim Worrell
☐ 11 Jimmy Lester
☐ 12 Lee Henderson
☐ 13 Jim West
☐ 14 Roberto Arredondo
☐ 15 Julio Bruno
☐ 16 Kevin Farlow
☐ 17 John Kuehl
☐ 18 Bill Meury
☐ 19 Bill Rivell
☐ 20 Darius Gash
☐ 21 Steve Gill
☐ 22 Craig Peuschner
☐ 23 Reggie Stephens
☐ 24 Shawn Whalen
☐ 25 Bryan Little MGR
☐ 26 Sonny Siebert CO
☐ 27 George Poulis TR
☐ 28 Larry Hawks
☐ 29 Checklist

1991 Waterloo Diamonds ProCards

This 28-card standard-size set of the 1991 Waterloo Diamonds, a Class A Midwest League affiliate of the San Diego Padres, features on its white-bordered fronts posed color player photos set on simulated spiral-bound yellow notebooks. The player's name, position, and team appear within a green rectangle below the photo. The yellow horizontal back is bordered in white and carries the player's name at the top, followed by biography and statistics.

	MINT	NRMT	EXC
COMPLETE SET (28)	5.00	2.20	.60

☐ 1248 Lance Banks
☐ 1249 Bruce Bensching
☐ 1250 Bryce Florie
☐ 1251 Scott Fredrickson

☐ 1252 Rob Hays
☐ 1253 Tony Mortensen
☐ 1254 Lance Painter
☐ 1255 Scott Sanders
☐ 1256 Ryan Thibault
☐ 1257 Tim Worrell
☐ 1258 Larry Hawks
☐ 1259 Lee Henderson
☐ 1260 Jim West
☐ 1261 Roberto Arredondo
☐ 1262 Julio Bruno
☐ 1263 Kevin Farlow
☐ 1264 John Kuehl
☐ 1265 Bill Meury
☐ 1266 Bob Rivell
☐ 1267 Darius Gash
☐ 1268 Steve Gill
☐ 1269 Craig Pueschner
☐ 1270 Reggie Stephens
☐ 1271 Shawn Whalen
☐ 1272 Bryan Little MGR
☐ 1273 Jimmy Lester CO
☐ 1274 Sonny Siebert
☐ 1275 Checklist

1991 Watertown Indians Classic/Best

This 30-card standard-size set of the 1991 Watertown Indians, a Class A New York-Penn League affiliate of the Cleveland Indians, features white-bordered posed color player photos on its fronts. The player's name, team, and position appear at the bottom. The white back is framed by a thin black line and carries the player's name and position at the top, followed by biography, statistics and team logos.

	MINT	NRMT	EXC
COMPLETE SET (30)	5.00	2.20	.60

☐ 1 Sam Baker
☐ 2 Brian Buzard
☐ 3 Grady Davidson
☐ 4 Joe Fleet
☐ 5 Jason Fronio
☐ 6 Steve Gajkowski
☐ 7 Mike Jewell
☐ 8 Greg Knapland
☐ 9 Kevin Logsdon
☐ 10 Mike Malley
☐ 11 Andy Stemler
☐ 12 Gary Taterson
☐ 13 Ryan Martindale
☐ 14 Mike Moore
☐ 15 Jose Moreno
☐ 16 Hector Andujar
☐ 17 Tommy Bates
☐ 18 Brad Kantor
☐ 19 Aaron Morris
☐ 20 Pat Maxwell
☐ 21 Herbert Perry
☐ 22 Scott Sharts
☐ 23 Bill Vosik
☐ 24 Jeff Brohm
☐ 25 Ottis Edwards
☐ 26 Pedro Henderson
☐ 27 Omar Ramirez
☐ 28 Tim Thomas
☐ 29 Tom Van Tiger
☐ 30 Checklist

1991 Watertown Indians ProCards

This 31-card standard-size set of the 1991 Watertown Indians, a Class A New York-Penn League affiliate of the Cleveland Indians, features on its white-bordered fronts posed color player photos set on simulated spiral-bound yellow notebooks. The player's name, position, and team appear within a green rectangle below the photo. The yellow horizontal back is bordered in white and carries the player's name at the top, followed by biography and statistics.

	MINT	NRMT	EXC
COMPLETE SET (31)	5.00	2.20	.60

☐ 3356 Sam Baker
☐ 3357 Brian Buzard
☐ 3358 Grady Davidson
☐ 3359 Joe Fleet
☐ 3360 Jason Fronio
☐ 3361 Steve Gajkowski
☐ 3362 Mike Jewell
☐ 3363 Greg Knapland
☐ 3364 Kevin Logsdon
☐ 3365 Mike Malley
☐ 3366 Andy Stemler
☐ 3367 Gary Tatterson
☐ 3368 Ryan Martindale
☐ 3369 Mike Moore
☐ 3370 Jose Moreno
☐ 3371 Hector Andujar
☐ 3372 Tommy Bates
☐ 3373 Brad Kantor
☐ 3374 Pat Maxwell
☐ 3375 Aaron Morris
☐ 3376 Herbert Perry
☐ 3377 Scott Sharts
☐ 3378 Bill Vosik
☐ 3379 Jeff Brohm
☐ 3380 Otis Edwards
☐ 3381 Pedro Henderson
☐ 3382 Omar Ramirez
☐ 3383 Tim Thomas
☐ 3384 Tom Van Tiger
☐ 3385 Darrell Whitmore
☐ 3386 Checklist

1991 Welland Pirates Classic/Best

This 30-card standard-size set of the 1991 Welland Pirates, a Class A New York-Penn League affiliate of the Pittsburgh Pirates, features white-bordered posed color player photos on its fronts. The player's name, team, and position appear at the bottom. The white back is framed by a thin black line and carries the player's name and position at the top, followed by biography, statistics and team logos.

	MINT	NRMT	EXC
COMPLETE SET (30)	5.00	2.20	.60

☐ 1 Jon Farrell
☐ 2 Tony Womack
☐ 3 Todd Schroeder
☐ 4 Don Garvey
☐ 5 Tony Mitchell
☐ 6 James Cardona
☐ 7 Mitch House
☐ 8 James Krevokuch
☐ 9 Dean Hinson II
☐ 10 Angelo Encarnacion
☐ 11 Chuck Touch
☐ 12 Gregg Leavell
☐ 13 Joe McLin Jr.
☐ 14 Trace Ragland
☐ 15 Craig Sholton
☐ 16 Marty Neff
☐ 17 Jeff Leatherman
☐ 18 Deon Danner
☐ 19 Steven Roeder
☐ 20 Matt Ruebel
☐ 21 John Douris
☐ 22 Mike Maguire
☐ 23 David Bradley
☐ 24 Roberto Ramirez
☐ 25 Glenn Coombs
☐ 26 John Hope
☐ 27 Mike Teich
☐ 28 Jason Bullard
☐ 29 Dan Jones
☐ 30 Checklist

1991 Welland Pirates ProCards

This 31-card standard-size set of the 1991 Welland Pirates, a Class A New York-Penn League affiliate of the Pittsburgh Pirates, features on its white-bordered fronts posed color player photos set on simulated spiral-bound yellow notebooks. The player's name, position, and team appear within a green rectangle below the photo. The yellow horizontal back is bordered in white and carries the player's name and position at the top, followed by biography and statistics.

	MINT	NRMT	EXC
COMPLETE SET (31)	5.00	2.20	.60

☐ 3563 Jason Bullard
☐ 3564 Glenn Coombs
☐ 3565 Deon Danner
☐ 3566 J.D. Douris
☐ 3567 John Hope
☐ 3568 Dan Jones
☐ 3569 Mike Maguire
☐ 3570 Marc Pisciotta
☐ 3571 Roberto Ramirez
☐ 3572 Matt Ruebel
☐ 3573 Mike Teich
☐ 3574 Angelo Encarnacion
☐ 3575 Jon Farrell
☐ 3576 Dean Hinson
☐ 3577 Don Garvey
☐ 3578 Mitch House
☐ 3579 Krev Krevokuch
☐ 3580 Jeff Leatherman
☐ 3581 Joe McLin
☐ 3582 Todd Schroeder
☐ 3583 Chuck Tooch
☐ 3584 Tony Womack
☐ 3585 James Cardona
☐ 3586 Gregg Leavell
☐ 3587 Tony Mitchell
☐ 3588 Marty Neff
☐ 3589 Trace Ragland
☐ 3590 Craig Shotton
☐ 3591 Lee Driggers MG
☐ 3592 Jerry Nyman CO
☐ 3593 Checklist

1991 West Palm Beach Expos Classic/Best

This 30-card standard-size set of the 1991 West Palm Beach Expos, a Class A Florida State League affiliate of the Montreal Expos, features white-bordered posed color player photos on its fronts. The player's name, team, and position appear at the bottom. The white back is framed by a thin black line and carries the player's name and position at the top, followed by biography, statistics and team logos.

	MINT	NRMT	EXC
COMPLETE SET (30)	5.00	2.20	.60

☐ 1 Felipe Alou MG
☐ 2 Doug Bochtler
☐ 3 Chris Bushing
☐ 4 Reid Cornelius
☐ 5 Jim Eddy
☐ 6 Rusty Kilgo
☐ 7 Joe Logan
☐ 8 Felix Moya
☐ 9 John Polasek
☐ 10 Gary Regira
☐ 11 Steve Renko Jr.
☐ 12 John Thoden
☐ 13 Jeff Tuss
☐ 14 Brian Wilkinson
☐ 15 Bill Cramer
☐ 16 Tim Laker
☐ 17 Perry Sanchez
☐ 18 Rob Bargas
☐ 19 Scott Davison
☐ 20 Willie Greene
☐ 21 Ron Krause
☐ 22 Chad McDonald
☐ 23 J.D. Ramirez
☐ 24 Jeff Barry
☐ 25 Marty Durkin
☐ 26 Todd Mayo
☐ 27 Dave Jauss CO
☐ 28 Troy Ricker
☐ 29 Tyrone Woods
☐ 30 Sean Cunningham TR Checklist

1991 West Palm Beach Expos ProCards

This 30-card standard-size set of the 1991 West Palm Beach Expos, a Class A Florida State League affiliate of the Montreal Expos, features on its white-bordered fronts posed color player photos set on simulated spiral-bound yellow notebooks. The player's name, position, and team appear within a green rectangle below the photo. The yellow horizontal back is bordered in white and carries the player's name and position at the top, followed by biography and statistics.

	MINT	NRMT	EXC
COMPLETE SET (30)	5.00	2.20	.60

☐ 1218 Doug Bochtler
☐ 1219 Chris Bushing
☐ 1220 Reid Cornelius
☐ 1221 Jim Eddy
☐ 1222 Rusty Kilgo
☐ 1223 Joe Logan
☐ 1224 Felix Moya
☐ 1225 John Polasek
☐ 1226 Gary Regira
☐ 1227 Steve Renko Jr.
☐ 1228 John Thoden
☐ 1229 Jeff Tuss
☐ 1230 Brian Wilkinson
☐ 1231 Bill Cramer
☐ 1232 Tim Laker
☐ 1233 Perry Sanchez
☐ 1234 Rob Bargas
☐ 1235 Scott Davison
☐ 1236 Willie Greene
☐ 1237 Chad McDonald
☐ 1238 J.D. Ramirez
☐ 1239 Jeff Barry
☐ 1240 Marty Durkin
☐ 1241 Todd Mayo
☐ 1242 Troy Ricker
☐ 1243 Tyrone Woods
☐ 1244 Felipe Alou MG
☐ 1245 Dave Jauss CO
☐ 1246 Mike Parrott CO
☐ 1247 Checklist

1991 Wichita Wranglers Line Drive

	MINT	NRMT	EXC
COMPLETE SET (26)	5.00	2.20	.60

☐ 601 Mike Basso
☐ 602 Doug Brocail
☐ 603 Rafael Chavez
☐ 604 Brian Cisarik
☐ 605 Greg David
☐ 606 Rick Davis
☐ 607 Vince Harris
☐ 608 Charles Hillemann
☐ 609 Kerry Knox
☐ 610 Pete Kuld
☐ 611 Jim Lewis
☐ 612 Luis Lopez
☐ 613 Pedro Martinez
☐ 614 Tim McWilliam
☐ 615 Tom Redington
☐ 616 Darrin Reichle
☐ 617 A.J. Sager
☐ 618 Frank Seminara
☐ 619 Darrell Sherman
☐ 620 Jose Valentin
☐ 621 Guillermo Velasquez
☐ 622 Tim Wallace
☐ 623 Brian Wood
☐ 624 Steve Lubratich MGR
☐ 625 John Cumberland CO Jeff Maloof CO
☐ NNO Title card

1991 Wichita Wranglers ProCards

This 28-card standard-size set of the 1991 Wichita Wranglers, a Class AA Texas League affiliate of the San Diego Padres, features on its white-bordered fronts posed color player photos set on simulated spiral-bound yellow notebooks. The player's name, position, and team appear within a green rectangle below the photo. The yellow horizontal back is bordered in white and carries the player's name at the top, followed by biography and statistics.

	MINT	NRMT	EXC
COMPLETE SET (28)	5.00	2.20	.60

☐ 2590 Doug Brocail
☐ 2591 Renay Bryand
☐ 2592 Rafael Chavez
☐ 2593 Rick Davis
☐ 2594 Kerry Knox
☐ 2595 Pedro Martinez
☐ 2596 Darrin Reichle
☐ 2597 A.J. Sager
☐ 2598 Frank Seminara
☐ 2599 Roger Smithberg
☐ 2600 Brian Wood
☐ 2601 Mike Basso
☐ 2602 Pete Kuld
☐ 2603 Greg David
☐ 2604 Luis Lopez
☐ 2605 Tom Redington
☐ 2606 Jose Valentin
☐ 2607 Guillermo Valasquez
☐ 2608 Tim Wallace
☐ 2609 Brian Cisarik
☐ 2610 Vince Harris
☐ 2611 Charlie Hillemann
☐ 2612 Tim McWilliam
☐ 2613 Darrell Sherman
☐ 2614 Steve Lubratich MGR
☐ 2615 John Cumberland CO
☐ 2616 Jack Maloof CO
☐ 2617 Checklist

1991 Wichita Wranglers Rock's Dugout

	MINT	NRMT	EXC
COMPLETE SET (27)	6.00	2.70	.75

☐ 1 Doug Brocail
☐ 2 Rafael Chavez
☐ 3 Rick Davis
☐ 4 Kerry Knox
☐ 5 Jim Lewis
☐ 6 Pedro Martinez
☐ 7 Darrin Reichle
☐ 8 A.J. Sager
☐ 9 Frank Seminara
☐ 10 Brian Wood
☐ 11 Mike Basso
☐ 12 Pete Kuld
☐ 13 Greg David
☐ 14 Luis Lopez
☐ 15 Tom Redington
☐ 16 Jose Valentin
☐ 17 Guillermo Velasquez
☐ 18 Tim Wallace
☐ 19 Brian Cisarik
☐ 20 Vince Harris
☐ 21 Charlie Hillerman
☐ 22 Tim McWilliam
☐ 23 Darrell Sherman
☐ 24 Steve Lubratich MG
☐ 25 John Cumberland CO
☐ 26 Jack Maloof CO
☐ 27 Title Card CL

1991 Williamsport Bills Line Drive

	MINT	NRMT	EXC
COMPLETE SET (26)	5.00	2.20	.60

☐ 626 Tim Bogar
☐ 627 Jeromy Burnitz
☐ 628 Hernan Cortes
☐ 629 Steve Davis
☐ 630 Joe Delli Carri
☐ 631 D.J. Dozier

- ☐ 632 Javier Gonzalez
- ☐ 633 Rudy Hernandez
- ☐ 634 Chris Hill
- ☐ 635 John Johnstone
- ☐ 636 Doug Kline
- ☐ 637 Loy McBride
- ☐ 638 Joel Horlen
- ☐ 639 Tito Navarro
- ☐ 640 Toby Nivens
- ☐ 641 Bryan Rogers
- ☐ 642 David Sommer
- ☐ 643 Greg Talamantez
- ☐ 644 Dave Telgheder
- ☐ 645 Jose Vargas
- ☐ 646 Aguedo Vasquez
- ☐ 647 Paul Williams
- ☐ 648 Alan Zinter
- ☐ 649 Clint Hurdle MGR
- ☐ 650 Jim Eschen
- ☐ NNO Title card

1991 Williamsport Bills ProCards

This 27-card standard-size set of the 1991 Williamsport Bills, a Class AA Eastern League affiliate of the New York Mets, features on its white-bordered fronts posed color player photos set on simulated spiral-bound yellow notebooks. The player's name, position, and team appear within a green rectangle below the photo. The yellow horizontal back is bordered in white and carries the player's name at the top, followed by biography and statistics.

	MINT	NRMT	EXC
COMPLETE SET (27)	5.00	2.20	.60

- ☐ 286 Chris Hill
- ☐ 287 John Johnstone
- ☐ 288 Doug Kline
- ☐ 289 Toby Nivens
- ☐ 290 Bryan Rogers
- ☐ 291 David Sommer
- ☐ 292 Greg Talamantez
- ☐ 293 Dave Telgheder
- ☐ 294 Jose Vargas
- ☐ 295 Aguedo Vasquez
- ☐ 296 Javier Gonzalez
- ☐ 297 Alan Zinter
- ☐ 298 Tim Bogar
- ☐ 299 Hernan Cortes
- ☐ 300 Joe DelliCarri
- ☐ 301 Rudy Hernandez
- ☐ 302 Tito Navarro
- ☐ 303 Paul Williams
- ☐ 304 Jeromy Burnitz
- ☐ 305 Steve Davis
- ☐ 306 D.J. Dozier
- ☐ 307 Lee May Jr.
- ☐ 308 Loy McBride
- ☐ 309 Clint Hurdle MGR
- ☐ 310 Jim Eschen CO
- ☐ 311 Joel Horlen CO
- ☐ 312 Checklist

1991 Winston-Salem Spirits Classic/Best

This 29-card standard-size set of the 1991 Winston Salem Spirits, a Class A Carolina League affiliate of the Chicago Cubs, features white-bordered posed color player photos on its fronts. The player's name, team, and position appear at the bottom. The white back is framed by a thin black line and carries the player's name and position at the top, followed by biography, statistics and team logos.

	MINT	NRMT	EXC
COMPLETE SET (29)	5.00	2.20	.60

- ☐ 1 Troy Bradford
- ☐ 2 Ed Caballero
- ☐ 3 Sean Cheetham
- ☐ 4 Ryan Hawblitzel
- ☐ 5 Jessie Hollins
- ☐ 6 Eric Jaques
- ☐ 7 Billy Melvin
- ☐ 8 Leo Perez
- ☐ 9 Chris Lutz
- ☐ 10 Joe Porcelli
- ☐ 11 Travis Willis
- ☐ 12 Brad Mills MGR
- ☐ 13 Mike Gabbani
- ☐ 14 Brad Huff
- ☐ 15 Matt Walbeck
- ☐ 16 Joe Biasucci
- ☐ 17 Pete Castellano
- ☐ 18 Marvin Cole
- ☐ 19 Matt Franco
- ☐ 20 Mike Grace
- ☐ 21 Bill Earley
- ☐ 22 Bryan Wilson
- ☐ 23 Chris Ebright
- ☐ 24 Richie Grayum
- ☐ 25 John Jensen
- ☐ 26 Paul Torres
- ☐ 27 Jerrone Williams
- ☐ 28 Steve Melendez TR
- ☐ 29 Checklist

1991 Winston-Salem Spirits ProCards

This 28-card standard-size set of the 1991 Winston Salem Spirits, a Class A Carolina League affiliate of the Chicago Cubs, features on its white-bordered fronts posed color player photos set on simulated spiral-bound yellow notebooks. The player's name, position, and team appear within a green rectangle below the photo. The yellow horizontal back is bordered in white and carries the player's name at the top, followed by biography and statistics.

	MINT	NRMT	EXC
COMPLETE SET (28)	5.00	2.20	.60

- ☐ 2820 Troy Bradford
- ☐ 2821 Ed Caballero
- ☐ 2822 Sean Cheetham
- ☐ 2823 Ryan Hawblitzel
- ☐ 2824 Jessie Hollins
- ☐ 2825 Eric Jacques
- ☐ 2826 Bill Melvin
- ☐ 2827 Leo Perez
- ☐ 2828 Joe Porcelli
- ☐ 2829 Dave Swartzbaugh
- ☐ 2830 Travis Willis
- ☐ 2831 Mike Gabbani
- ☐ 2832 Matt Walbeck
- ☐ 2833 Joe Biasucci
- ☐ 2834 Pete Castellano
- ☐ 2835 Marvin Cole
- ☐ 2836 Matt Franco
- ☐ 2837 Mike Grace
- ☐ 2838 J.P. Postiff
- ☐ 2839 Bryan Wilson
- ☐ 2841 Richie Grayum
- ☐ 2842 John Jensen
- ☐ 2843 Paul Torres
- ☐ 2844 Jerrone Williams
- ☐ 2845 Brad Mills MGR
- ☐ 2846 Bill Earley CO
- ☐ 2847 Checklist
- ☐ 3840 Chris Ebright

1991 Winter Haven Red Sox Classic/Best

This 30-card standard-size set of the 1991 Winter Haven Red Sox, a Class A Florida State League affiliate of the Boston Red Sox, features white-bordered posed color player photos on its fronts. The player's name, team, and position appear at the bottom. The white back is framed by a thin black line and carries the player's name and position at the top, followed by biography, statistics and team logos.

	MINT	NRMT	EXC
COMPLETE SET (30)	5.00	2.20	.60

- ☐ 1 Tracy Allen
- ☐ 2 Paul Brown
- ☐ 3 Dan Kite
- ☐ 4 Mark Mitchelson
- ☐ 5 Mike Verdi MGR
- ☐ 6 Gary Painter
- ☐ 7 Terry Powers
- ☐ 8 Kenny Ryan Jr.
- ☐ 9 Silverio Santa Maria
- ☐ 10 Brian Young
- ☐ 11 Joe Demus
- ☐ 12 Lou Dorante
- ☐ 13 Willie Dukes Jr.
- ☐ 14 Pedro Matilla
- ☐ 15 Randy Brown
- ☐ 16 Lee Stange CO
- ☐ 17 Mike DeKneef
- ☐ 18 Greg Graham
- ☐ 19 Larry Grant
- ☐ 20 John Malzone
- ☐ 21 Les Wallin
- ☐ 22 Garrett Jenkins
- ☐ 23 Jim Morrison
- ☐ 24 Mickey Rivers Jr.
- ☐ 25 Shea Wardwell
- ☐ 26 Joe Marchese CO
- ☐ 27 Jim Stricek TR
- ☐ 28 Jose Lora
- ☐ 29 Richard Delgado
- ☐ 30 Checklist

1991 Winter Haven Red Sox ProCards

This 27-card standard-size set of the 1991 Winter Haven Red Sox, a Class A Florida State League affiliate of the Boston Red Sox, features on its white-bordered fronts posed color player photos set on simulated spiral-bound yellow notebooks. The player's name, position, and team appear within a green rectangle below the photo. The yellow horizontal back is bordered in white and carries the player's name at the top, followed by biography and statistics.

	MINT	NRMT	EXC
COMPLETE SET (27)	5.00	2.20	.60

- ☐ 481 Tracy Allen
- ☐ 482 Paul Brown
- ☐ 483 Dan Kite
- ☐ 484 Mark Mitchelson
- ☐ 485 Tommy Niles
- ☐ 486 Gary Painter
- ☐ 487 Terry Powers
- ☐ 488 Kenny Ryan
- ☐ 489 Silverio Santa Maria
- ☐ 490 Brian Young
- ☐ 491 Joe Demus
- ☐ 492 Lou Dorante
- ☐ 493 Willie Dukes
- ☐ 494 Bill Madril
- ☐ 495 Randy Brown
- ☐ 496 Mike DeKneef
- ☐ 497 Greg Graham
- ☐ 498 Larry Grant
- ☐ 499 John Malzone
- ☐ 500 Les Wallin
- ☐ 501 Garrett Jenkins
- ☐ 502 Jim Morrison
- ☐ 503 Mickey Rivers Jr.
- ☐ 504 Shea Wardwell
- ☐ 505 Mike Verdi MGR
- ☐ 506 Joe Marchese CO
- ☐ 507 Checklist

1991 Yakima Bears Classic/Best

This 30-card standard-size set of the 1991 Yakima Bears, a Class A Northwest League affiliate of the Los Angeles Dodgers, features white-bordered posed color player photos on its fronts. The player's name, team, and position appear at the bottom. The white back is framed by a thin black line and carries the player's name and position at the top, followed by biography, statistics and team logos.

	MINT	NRMT	EXC
COMPLETE SET (30)	5.00	2.20	.60

- ☐ 1 Vernon Spearman
- ☐ 2 Eric Vorbeck
- ☐ 3 Marc Tramuta
- ☐ 4 Ron Richard
- ☐ 5 Murph Proctor
- ☐ 6 J.J. Johnson
- ☐ 7 Chris Demetral
- ☐ 8 Eric Blackwell
- ☐ 9 Keoki Farrish
- ☐ 10 Dan Gray
- ☐ 11 Tim Griffin
- ☐ 12 Don Meyers
- ☐ 13 Kevin Van DeBrake
- ☐ 14 Burgess Watts
- ☐ 15 Ben O'Connor
- ☐ 16 Jason Kerr
- ☐ 17 Ken Hamilton
- ☐ 18 Don Carroll
- ☐ 19 Jason Broyles
- ☐ 20 Brad Boggetto
- ☐ 21 David Bauman
- ☐ 22 Doug Bennett
- ☐ 23 Carlos Castillo
- ☐ 24 Chris Crabtree
- ☐ 25 Rob Legendre
- ☐ 26 Mike Sharp
- ☐ 27 Jo Jo Smith
- ☐ 28 Carlos Thomas
- ☐ 29 Joe Vavra MGR
- ☐ 30 Geoff Clark TR Checklist

1991 Yakima Bears ProCards

This 30-card standard-size set of the 1991 Yakima Bears, a Class A Northwest League affiliate of the Los Angeles Dodgers, features on its white-bordered fronts posed color player photos set on simulated spiral-bound yellow notebooks. The player's name, position, and team appear within a green rectangle below the photo. The yellow horizontal back is bordered in white and carries the player's name at the top, followed by biography and statistics.

	MINT	NRMT	EXC
COMPLETE SET (30)	5.00	2.20	.60

- ☐ 4237 Doug Bennett
- ☐ 4238 Brad Boggetto
- ☐ 4239 Jason Broyles
- ☐ 4240 Don Carroll
- ☐ 4241 Carlos Castillo
- ☐ 4242 Chris Crabtree
- ☐ 4243 Kenny Hamilton
- ☐ 4244 Jason Kerr
- ☐ 4245 Rob Legendre
- ☐ 4246 Ben O'Connor
- ☐ 4247 Mike Sharp
- ☐ 4248 Jo Jo Smith
- ☐ 4249 Carlos Thomas
- ☐ 4250 Dan Gray
- ☐ 4251 Don Meyers
- ☐ 4252 Chris Demetral
- ☐ 4253 Tim Griffin
- ☐ 4254 Murph Proctor
- ☐ 4255 Ron Richard
- ☐ 4256 Marc Tramuta
- ☐ 4257 Kevin Van de Brake
- ☐ 4258 Burgess Watts
- ☐ 4259 Eric Blackwell
- ☐ 4260 Keoki Farrish
- ☐ 4261 Vernon Spearman
- ☐ 4262 Roger Sweeney
- ☐ 4263 Eric Vorbeck
- ☐ 4264 Joe Vavra MGR
- ☐ 4265 Tony Arnold CO
- ☐ 4266 Checklist

1992 Triple A All-Stars SkyBox

	MINT	NRMT	EXC
COMPLETE SET (38)	15.00	6.75	1.85

- ☐ 13 Pedro Martinez
- ☐ 19 Henry Rodriguez
- ☐ 33 Carlos Garcia
- ☐ 48 Eddie Zambrano
- ☐ 55 Bret Boone
- ☐ 87 Wayne Kirby
- ☐ 104 Mike Draper
- ☐ 111 Hensley Meulens
- ☐ 112 Sam Militello
- ☐ 122 Gerald Williams
- ☐ 123 Bernie Williams
- ☐ 145 Jim Tatum
- ☐ 165 Tim Salmon
- ☐ 189 Bob Natal
- ☐ 230 Paul Faries
- ☐ 241 Dave Staton
- ☐ 245 Guillermo Velasquez
- ☐ 251 Rene Arocha
- ☐ 253 Rod Brewer
- ☐ 284 Geronimo Berroa
- ☐ 296 Joey Vierra
- ☐ 329 Jeff Conine
- ☐ 338 Dennis Moeller
- ☐ 369 Mike Twardoski
- ☐ 381 Steve Decker
- ☐ 404 Larry Casian
- ☐ 435 David Nied
- ☐ 442 Pete Smith
- ☐ 462 Mark Parent
- ☐ 492 Steve Scarsone
- ☐ 493 Rick Schu
- ☐ 503 Butch Davis
- ☐ 517 Ed Sprague
- ☐ 562 Randy Marshall
- ☐ 590 Jeff Kaiser
- ☐ 605 Gary Cooper
- ☐ 628 Rod Bolton
- ☐ NNO Title Card

1992 Albany Polecats Classic/Best

This 30-card standard-size set of the 1992 Albany Polecats, a Class A South Atlantic League affiliate of the Montreal Expos, features white-bordered posed color player photos on its fronts. The player's name, position, and team name appear at the lower right. The white back is framed by a red line and carries the player's name and position at the top, followed by biography and statistics. This issue includes the first Classic/Best team set appearances of Cliff Floyd, Yamil Benitez, and Ugueth Urbina.

	MINT	NRMT	EXC
COMPLETE SET (30)	12.00	5.50	1.50

- ☐ 1 Shane Andrews
- ☐ 2 Jim Ferguson
- ☐ 3 Darrin Paxton
- ☐ 4 Claudio Ozario
- ☐ 5 Matt Allen
- ☐ 6 Rodney Pedraza
- ☐ 7 Jolbert Cabrera
- ☐ 8 Chris Hmielewski
- ☐ 9 Mark LaRosa
- ☐ 10 Robbie Carabba
- ☐ 11 Javier Pages
- ☐ 12 Mark Respondek
- ☐ 13 Jim Wynne
- ☐ 14 Rick Clelland
- ☐ 15 Rick Dehart
- ☐ 16 Vince Fultz
- ☐ 17 Yamil Benitez
- ☐ 18 Matt Conley
- ☐ 19 Alberto Reyes
- ☐ 20 Keith Morrison
- ☐ 21 Ugueth Urbina
- ☐ 22 Cliff Floyd
- ☐ 23 Stan Robertson
- ☐ 24 Gary Hymel
- ☐ 25 Mitch Simons
- ☐ 26 Antonio Grissom
- ☐ 27 Lorenzo Bundy MG
- ☐ 28 Jeff Kinlaw TR
- ☐ 29 Gary Lance CO
- ☐ 30 Checklist

1992 Albany Polecats Fleer/ProCards

This 27-card standard-size set of the 1992 Albany Polecats, a Class A South Atlantic League affiliate of the Montreal Expos, features brown-bordered posed color player photos on its fronts. The player's name appears in an upper corner; his team and position appear in a lower corner. The white back is framed by a black line and carries the player's name at the top, followed by biography and statistics. This issue includes the first Fleer/ProCards team set appearances of Cliff Floyd and Ugueth Urbina. Z

	MINT	NRMT	EXC
COMPLETE SET (27)	10.00	4.50	1.25

☐ 2297 Rick Clelland
☐ 2298 Matt Conley
☐ 2299 Rick DeHart
☐ 2300 Mark LaRosa
☐ 2301 Keith Morrison
☐ 2302 Darrin Paxton
☐ 2303 Rodney Pedraza
☐ 2304 Mark Respondek
☐ 2305 Alberto Reyes
☐ 2306 Ugueth Urbina
☐ 2307 Jim Wynne
☐ 2308 Matt Allen
☐ 2309 Gary Hymel
☐ 2310 Javier Pages
☐ 2311 Shane Andrews
☐ 2312 Jolbert Cabrera
☐ 2313 Robb Carabba
☐ 2314 Cliff Floyd
☐ 2315 Mitch Simmons
☐ 2316 Antonio Grissom
☐ 2317 Chris Hmielewski
☐ 2318 Doug O'Neal
☐ 2319 Claudio Ozario
☐ 2320 Stan Robertson
☐ 2321 Lorenzo Bundy MG
☐ 2322 Gary Lance CO
☐ 2323 Checklist

1992 Albany Yankees Fleer/ProCards

This 28-card standard-size set of the 1992 Albany Yankees, a Class AA Eastern League affiliate of the New York Yankees, features brown-bordered posed color player photos on its fronts. The player's name appears in an upper corner; his team and position appear in a lower corner. The white back is framed by a black line and carries the player's name at the top, followed by biography and statistics.

	MINT	NRMT	EXC
COMPLETE SET(28)	5.00	2.20	.60

☐ 2217 Richard Batchelor
☐ 2218 Mark Carper
☐ 2219 Ken Greer
☐ 2220 Sterling Hitchcock
☐ 2221 Darren Hodges
☐ 2222 Jeff Hoffman
☐ 2223 Mark Hutton
☐ 2224 Bobby Munoz
☐ 2225 Gerald Nielson
☐ 2226 Kirt Ojala
☐ 2227 Tom Popplewell
☐ 2228 Kiki Hernandez
☐ 2229 Jeff Livesey
☐ 2230 Juan Blackwell
☐ 2231 Russell Davis
☐ 2232 Sherman Obando
☐ 2233 Carlos Rodriguez
☐ 2234 Don Sparks
☐ 2235 Hector Vargas
☐ 2236 Rich Barnwell
☐ 2237 Bubba Carpenter
☐ 2238 Jay Knoblauh
☐ 2239 Rick Strickland
☐ 2240 John Viera
☐ 2348 Dan Radison
☐ 2349 Dave Jorn
☐ 2350 Rob Thomson
☐ 2351 Checklist

1992 Albany Yankees SkyBox

	MINT	NRMT	EXC
COMPLETE SET(26)	5.00	2.20	.60

☐ 1 Sherman Obando
☐ 2 Rich Barnwell
☐ 3 Richard Batchelor
☐ 4 Juan Blackwell
☐ 5 Bubba Carpenter
☐ 6 Russell Davis
☐ 7 Mike Gardella
☐ 8 Sterling Hitchcock
☐ 9 Darren Hodges
☐ 10 Jeff Hoffman
☐ 11 Scott Holcomb
☐ 12 Mark Hutton
☐ 13 Bobby Munoz
☐ 14 Jerry Nielsen
☐ 15 Rey Noriega
☐ 16 Tom Popplewell
☐ 17 John Quintell
☐ 18 Carlos Rodriguez
☐ 19 Don Sparks
☐ 20 Rick Strickland
☐ 21 Hector Vargas
☐ 22 John Viera
☐ 23 Kiki Hernandez
☐ 24 Dan Radison
☐ 25 Dave Jorn
Rob Thompson
☐ NNO Checklist

1992 Albuquerque Dukes SkyBox

	MINT	NRMT	EXC
COMPLETE SET (26)	12.00	5.50	1.50

☐ 1 Dave Anderson
☐ 2 Pedro Astacio
☐ 3 Bryan Baar
☐ 4 Hector Berrios
☐ 5 Rafael Bournigal
☐ 6 Jerry Brooks
☐ 7 Jason Brosnan
☐ 8 Tom Goodwin
☐ 9 Eddie Pye
☐ 10 Jeff Hamilton
☐ 11 Mike James
☐ 12 Luis Martinez
☐ 13 Pedro Martinez
☐ 14 Jamie McAndrew
☐ 15 Mark Mimbs
☐ 16 Raul Mondesi
☐ 17 Jose Munoz
☐ 18 Jim Neidlinger
☐ 19 Henry Rodriguez
☐ 20 Zak Shinall
☐ 21 Brian Traxler
☐ 22 Don Wakamatsu
☐ 23 Eric Young
☐ 24 Bill Russell MG
☐ 25 Von Joshua CO
Claude Osteen CO
Mickey Hatcher CO
☐ NNO Checklist

1992 Alburquerque Dukes Fleer/ProCards

This 32-card standard-size set of the 1992 Alburquerque Dukes, a Class AAA Pacific Coast League affiliate of the Los Angeles Dodgers, features brown-bordered posed color player photos on its fronts. The player's name appears in an upper corner; his team and position appear in a lower corner. The white back is framed by a black line and carries the player's name at the top, followed by biography and statistics. This set includes a fourth year card of Mike Piazza.

	MINT	NRMT	EXC
COMPLETE SET(32)	20.00	9.00	2.50

☐ 710 Pedro Astacio
☐ 711 Albert Bustillos
☐ 712 Omar Daal
☐ 713 Grady Hall
☐ 714 Greg Hansell
☐ 715 Brian Holton
☐ 716 Pedro Martinez
☐ 717 Mark Mimbs
☐ 718 Jim Neidlinger
☐ 719 Chris Nichting
☐ 720 Dan Opperman
☐ 721 Zak Shinall
☐ 722 Mike Wilkins
☐ 723 Mike Piazza
☐ 724 Don Wakamatsu
☐ 725 Rafael Bournigal
☐ 726 Jeff Hamilton
☐ 727 Luis Martinez
☐ 728 Jose Munoz
☐ 729 Eddie Pye
☐ 730 Brian Traxler
☐ 731 Billy Ashley
☐ 732 Tony Barron
☐ 733 Jerry Brooks
☐ 734 Tom Goodwin
☐ 735 Henry Rodriguez
☐ 736 Eric Young
☐ 737 Bill Russell
☐ 738 Mickey Hatcher
☐ 739 Von Joshua
☐ 740 Claude Osteen
☐ 741 Checklist

1992 Appleton Foxes Classic/Best

This 30-card standard-size set of the 1992 Appleton Foxes, a Class A Midwest League affiliate of the Kansas City Royals, features white-bordered posed color player photos on its fronts. The player's name, team, and position appear at the bottom. The white back is framed by a thin red line and carries the player's name and position at the top, followed by biography, statistics and team logos.

	MINT	NRMT	EXC
COMPLETE SET (30)	5.00	2.20	.60

☐ 1 Joe Randa
☐ 2 Andres Berumen
☐ 3 Andre Newhouse
☐ 4 Chad Strickland
☐ 5 Roger Landress
☐ 6 Danny Miceli
☐ 7 Anthony Lee
☐ 8 Shane Halter
☐ 9 Brian Bevil
☐ 10 Mark Johnson
☐ 11 Francisco Baez
☐ 12 Paco Burgos
☐ 13 Jeff Clarke
☐ 14 Les Norman
☐ 15 Robert Toth
☐ 16 Yobanne DeLeon
☐ 17 Shayne Rea
☐ 18 Michael Bovee
☐ 19 Raul Gonzalez
☐ 20 Dan Servello
☐ 21 Jeff Smith
☐ 22 Kevin Kobetitsch
☐ 23 Steve Hinton
☐ 24 Juan Indriago
☐ 25 Ed Gerald
☐ 26 Jason Pruitt
☐ 27 Tom Poquette
☐ 28 Mike Mason
☐ 29 Jeff Stevenson
☐ 30 Checklist

1992 Appleton Foxes Fleer/ProCards

This 32-card standard-size set of the 1992 Appleton Foxes, a Class A Midwest League affiliate of the Kansas City Royals, features brown-bordered posed color player photos on its fronts. The player's name appears in an upper corner; his team and position appear in a lower corner. The white back is framed by a black line and carries the player's name at the top, followed by biography and statistics.

	MINT	NRMT	EXC
COMPLETE SET (32)	5.00	2.20	.60

☐ 974 Francisco Baez
☐ 975 Andres Berumen
☐ 976 Brian Bevil
☐ 977 Mike Bovee
☐ 978 Chris Connolly
☐ 979 Brian Harrison
☐ 980 Roger Landress
☐ 981 Anthony Lee
☐ 982 Danny Micelli
☐ 983 Jason Pruitt
☐ 984 Shayne Rea
☐ 985 Robert Toth
☐ 986 Carlos Burgos
☐ 987 Yobanne de Leon
☐ 988 Chad Strickland
☐ 989 Troy Babbitt
☐ 990 Jeff Clarke
☐ 991 Shane Halter
☐ 992 Steve Hinton
☐ 993 Juan Indriago
☐ 994 Mark Johnson
☐ 995 Joe Randa
☐ 996 Ed Gerald
☐ 997 Raul Gonzalez
☐ 998 Andre Newhouse
☐ 999 Les Norman
☐ 1000 Dan Servello
☐ 1001 Tom Poquette
☐ 1002 Mike Mason
☐ 1003 Checklist
☐ 1091 Jeff Smith
☐ 3105 Sean Delaney

1992 Arizona Wildcats Police

	MINT	NRMT	EXC
COMPLETE SET (20)	10.00	4.50	1.25

☐ 1 Jason Bates
☐ 2 Tony Bouie
☐ 3 Phil Echeverria
☐ 4 Billy Grajeda
☐ 5 Chris Gump
☐ 6 Rob Ippolito
☐ 7 Jerry Kindall CO
☐ 8 Richard Lemons
☐ 9 Robbie Moen
☐ 10 Willie Morales
☐ 11 Ron Oelschlager
☐ 12 Billy Owens
☐ 13 Don Parker
☐ 14 Carlos Rico
☐ 15 Mike Schiefelbein
☐ 16 Tim Schweitzer
☐ 17 Scott Stanley ACO
☐ 18 Jerry Stitt ACO
☐ 19 John Tejcek
☐ 20 Jim Wing ACO

1992 Arkansas Travelers Fleer/ProCards

This 27-card standard-size set of the 1992 Arkansas Travelers, a Class AA Texas League affiliate of the St. Louis Cardinals, features brown-bordered posed color player photos on its fronts. The player's name appears in an upper corner; his team and position appear in a lower corner. The white back is framed by a black line and carries the player's name at the top, followed by biography and statistics.

	MINT	NRMT	EXC
COMPLETE SET(27)	5.00	2.20	.60

☐ 1120 Paul Anderson
☐ 1121 Dave Cassidy
☐ 1122 Fidel Compres
☐ 1123 Steve Dixon
☐ 1124 John Ericks
☐ 1125 Steffen Majer
☐ 1126 Kevin Meier
☐ 1127 Gabriel Ozuna
☐ 1128 Lee Plemel
☐ 1129 Dave Richards
☐ 1130 Rick Shackle
☐ 1131 Dennis Wiseman
☐ 1132 Jose Fernandez
☐ 1133 Don Prybylinski
☐ 1134 Brad Beanblossom
☐ 1135 Tripp Cromer
☐ 1136 Steve Fanning
☐ 1137 David Howell
☐ 1138 Jesus Mendez
☐ 1139 Mike Ross
☐ 1140 John Sellick
☐ 1141 Cliff Brannon
☐ 1142 Julian Martinez
☐ 1143 Skeets Thomas
☐ 1144 Joe Pettini
☐ 1145 Marty Mason
☐ 1146 Checklist

1992 Arkansas Travelers SkyBox

	MINT	NRMT	EXC
COMPLETE SET (26)	5.00	2.20	.60

☐ 26 Rich Aldrete
☐ 27 Brad Beanblossom
☐ 28 Cliff Brannon
☐ 29 Chuck Carr
☐ 30 Fidel Compres
☐ 31 Tripp Cromer
☐ 32 Steve Dixon
☐ 33 John Ericks
☐ 34 Steve Fanning
☐ 35 Dennis Wiseman
☐ 36 Steffen Majer
☐ 37 Julian Martinez
☐ 38 Kevin Meier
☐ 39 Jesus Mendez
☐ 40 Gabby Ozuna
☐ 41 Lee Plemel
☐ 42 Don Prybylinski
☐ 43 Lino Rivera
☐ 44 Mike Ross
☐ 45 John Sellick
☐ 46 Rick Shackle
☐ 47 John Thomas
☐ 48 Tom Urbani
☐ 49 Joe Pettini MG
☐ 50 Marty Mason CO
☐ NNO Checklist

1992 Asheville Tourists Classic/Best

This 30-card standard-size set of the 1992 Asheville Tourists, a Class A South Atlantic League affiliate of the Houston Astros, features white-bordered posed color player photos on its fronts. The player's name, team, and position appear at the bottom. The white back is framed by a thin red line and carries the player's name and position at the top, followed by biography, statistics and team logos. This issue includes the minor league card debut of Bob Abreu.

	MINT	NRMT	EXC
COMPLETE SET (30)	10.00	4.50	1.25

☐ 1 Gary Mota
☐ 2 Jose Flores
☐ 3 Henry Centeno
☐ 4 Tom Anderson
☐ 5 Ed Beuerlein
☐ 6 Todd Hobson
☐ 7 Kevin Webb
☐ 8 Raul Chavez
☐ 9 Eric Martinez
☐ 10 Duane Brown
☐ 11 Roy Nieto
☐ 12 Jamie Evans
☐ 13 Ron Cacini
☐ 14 Chris White
☐ 15 Eddie Ramos
☐ 16 Danny Young

☐ 17 Miguel Cabrera
☐ 18 Craig Bjornson
☐ 19 Bob Abreu
☐ 20 Alvin Morman
☐ 21 Chris Durkin
☐ 22 Mario Linares
☐ 23 Chuck Smith
☐ 24 Hector Carrasco
☐ 25 Mark Loughlin
☐ 26 Tim Tolman
☐ 27 Bob Robertson
☐ 28 Jim Hickey
☐ 29 Manny Acta
☐ 30 Ron Harnisch CL

1992 Auburn Astros Classic/Best

This 30-card standard-size set of the 1992 Auburn Astros, a Class A New York-Penn League affiliate of the Houston Astros, features white-bordered posed color player photos on its fronts. The player's name, team, and position appear at the bottom. The white back is framed by a thin red line and carries the player's name and position at the top, followed by biography, statistics and team logos.

	MINT	NRMT	EXC
COMPLETE SET (30)	5.00	2.20	.60

☐ 1 Chris Holt
☐ 2 Greg Elliot
☐ 3 Chris Thomas
☐ 4 Jeffrey Tenbarge
☐ 5 Bill Minnich
☐ 6 Donovan Mitchell
☐ 7 Jeff Rhein
☐ 8 Mike Aubel
☐ 9 Brian Thompson
☐ 10 Bryant Winslow
☐ 11 Jose Santana
☐ 12 Ernest Martinez
☐ 13 Kirk Larson
☐ 14 Todd Winston
☐ 15 Brett Wyngarden
☐ 16 Alan Probst
☐ 17 Jamie Walker
☐ 18 Doug Mlicki
☐ 19 Derrick Bottoms
☐ 20 Dwayne Dawson
☐ 21 Destry Westbrook
☐ 22 Craig Bjoprnson
☐ 23 Wayne Cupit
☐ 24 Zak Krislock
☐ 25 Juan Holleday
☐ 26 Jorge Correa
☐ 27 Steve Dillard
☐ 28 Clark Crist
☐ 29 Bill Kelso
☐ 30 Team Photo CL

1992 Auburn Astros Fleer/ProCards

This 31-card standard-size set of the 1992 Auburn Astros, a Class A New York-Penn League affiliate of the Houston Astros, features brown-bordered posed color player photos on its fronts. The player's name appears in an upper corner; his team and position appear in a lower corner. The white back is framed by a black line and carries the player's name at the top, followed by biography and statistics.

	MINT	NRMT	EXC
COMPLETE SET(31)	5.00	2.20	.60

☐ 1344 Craig Bjornson
☐ 1345 Derrick Bottoms
☐ 1346 Jorge Correa
☐ 1347 Wayne Cupit
☐ 1348 Dwayne Dawson
☐ 1349 Juan Holleday
☐ 1350 Chris Holt
☐ 1351 Zak Krislock
☐ 1352 Doug Mlicki
☐ 1353 Jeffrey Tenbarge
☐ 1354 Jamie Walker
☐ 1355 Destry Westbrook
☐ 1356 Alan Probst
☐ 1357 Todd Winston
☐ 1358 Brett Wyngarden
☐ 1359 Greg Elliot
☐ 1360 Kirk Larson
☐ 1361 Ernest Martinez
☐ 1362 Don Mitchell
☐ 1363 Jose Santana
☐ 1364 Bryant Winslow
☐ 1365 Mike Aubel
☐ 1366 Bill Minnich
☐ 1367 Jeff Rhein
☐ 1368 Chris Thomas
☐ 1369 Brian Thompson
☐ 1370 Steve Dillard
☐ 1371 Bill Kelso
☐ 1372 Clark Crist
☐ 1373 Team Picture
☐ 1735 Checklist

1992 Augusta Pirates Classic/Best

This 28-card standard-size set of the 1992 Augusta Pirates, a Class A South Atlantic League affiliate of the Pittsburgh Pirates, features white-bordered posed color player photos on its fronts. The player's name, team, and position appear at the bottom. The white back is framed by a thin red line and carries the player's name and position at the top, followed by biography, statistics and team logos.

	MINT	NRMT	EXC
COMPLETE SET (28)	5.00	2.20	.60

☐ 1 John Farrell
☐ 2 Shane Sparks
☐ 3 Jim Krevokuch
☐ 4 Steve Loaiza
☐ 5 Mike Teich
☐ 6 Todd Schroeder
☐ 7 Jason Christiansen
☐ 8 Deon Danner
☐ 9 Kevin Rychel
☐ 10 Sean Evans
☐ 11 Ramon Zapata
☐ 12 Matt Ruebel
☐ 13 Antonio Mitchell
☐ 14 Mariano De Los Santos
☐ 15 John Schulte
☐ 16 Marty Neff
☐ 17 Jeff McCurry
☐ 18 Ken Bonifay
☐ 19 Jose Sosa
☐ 20 Kevin Maguire
☐ 21 Brian Beck
☐ 22 Jeff Leatherman
☐ 23 Joe Calder
☐ 24 Jeff Conger
☐ 25 Scott Little
☐ 26 Julio Garcia
☐ 27 Rod Lich
☐ 30 Checklist

1992 Augusta Pirates Fleer/ProCards

This 29-card standard-size set of the 1992 Augusta Pirates, a Class A South Atlantic League affiliate of the Pittsburgh Pirates, features brown-bordered posed color player photos on its fronts. The player's name appears in an upper corner; his team and position appear in a lower corner. The white back is framed by a black line and carries the player's name at the top, followed by biography and statistics.

	MINT	NRMT	EXC
COMPLETE SET(29)	5.00	2.20	.60

☐ 229 Glenn Coombs
☐ 230 Deon Danner
☐ 231 Mariano De Los Santos
☐ 232 Dave Doorneweerd
☐ 233 Steve Loaiza
☐ 234 Jim Martin
☐ 235 Jeff McCurry
☐ 236 Marc Pisciotta
☐ 237 Matt Ruebel
☐ 238 Jose Sosa
☐ 239 Shane Sparks
☐ 240 Mike Teich
☐ 241 Angelo Encarnacion
☐ 242 Kevin Maguire
☐ 243 Michael Brown
☐ 244 Joe Calder
☐ 245 Don Garvey
☐ 246 Jim Krevokuch
☐ 247 Tony Womack
☐ 248 Ramon Zapata
☐ 249 Brian Beck
☐ 250 Jeff Conger
☐ 251 Jon Farrell
☐ 252 Antonio Mitchell
☐ 253 Marty Neff
☐ 254 John Schulte
☐ 255 Scott Little
☐ 256 Dave Rajsich
☐ 257 Checklist

1992 Bakersfield Dodgers Cal League Cards

This issue includes the minor league card debut of Todd Hollandsworth.

	MINT	NRMT	EXC
COMPLETE SET(32)	8.00	3.60	1.00

☐ 1 Todd Hollandsworth
☐ 2 Cam Aronetz
☐ 3 Henry Blanco
☐ 4 Mike Boyzuick
☐ 5 Carlos Castillo
☐ 6 Juan Castro
☐ 7 Nelson Castro
☐ 8 Chris Demetral
☐ 9 Angel Dotel
☐ 10 Ross Farnsworth
☐ 11 Scott Freeman
☐ 12 Rick Gorecki
☐ 13 Jack Johnson
☐ 14 Steve Kliafas
☐ 15 Al Maldonado
☐ 16 Brock McMurray
☐ 17 Don Meyers
☐ 18 Hector Ortiz
☐ 19 Jose Parra
☐ 20 Murph Proctor
☐ 21 Mike Sharp
☐ 22 Ira Smith
☐ 23 Joe Smith
☐ 24 Robert Sweeney
☐ 25 Gordon Tipton
☐ 26 Eric Vorbeck
☐ 27 Mike Walkden
☐ 28 Lonnie Webb
☐ 29 Todd Williams
☐ 30 Tom Beyers
☐ 31 Dino Ebel
Goose Gregson
☐ 32 Matt Wilson

1992 Baseball City Royals Classic/Best

This 30-card standard-size set of the 1992 Baseball City Royals, a Class A Florida State League affiliate of the Kansas City Royals, features white-bordered posed color player photos on its fronts. The player's name, team, and position appear at the bottom. The white back is framed by a thin red line and carries the player's name and position at the top, followed by biography, statistics and team logos.

	MINT	NRMT	EXC
COMPLETE SET (30)	5.00	2.20	.60

☐ 1 Joe Vitiello
☐ 2 Kevin Shaw
☐ 3 Pat Dando
☐ 4 Dean Tatarian
☐ 5 Lance Jennings
☐ 6 Damon Pollard
☐ 7 Tom Smith
☐ 8 Brady Stewart
☐ 9 John Gross
☐ 10 Jim Chrisman
☐ 11 Huascar de Leon
☐ 12 Cesar Morillo
☐ 13 Andy Stewart
☐ 14 Kerwin Moore
☐ 15 Butch Cole
☐ 16 Anthony Gordon
☐ 17 Dario Perez
☐ 18 Giovanni Miranda
☐ 19 Gary Caraballo
☐ 20 Vladimir Perez
☐ 21 Mike Fyhrie
☐ 22 Scott Stevens
☐ 23 Darren Burton
☐ 24 Ron Johnson MG
☐ 25 Rafael Santana CO
☐ 26 Pete Filson CO
☐ 27 Frank Kyte TR
☐ 28 Advertising Card
☐ 29 Advertising Card
☐ 30 Checklist

1992 Baseball City Royals Fleer/ProCards

This 27-card standard-size set of the 1992 Baseball City Royals, a Class A Florida State League affiliate of the Kansas City Royals, features brown-bordered posed color player photos on its fronts. The player's name appears in an upper corner; his team and position appear in a lower corner. The white back is framed by a black line and carries the player's name at the top, followed by biography and statistics.

	MINT	NRMT	EXC
COMPLETE SET(27)	5.00	2.20	.60

☐ 3837 Jim Chrisman
☐ 3838 Mike Fyhrie
☐ 3839 John Gross
☐ 3840 Doug Harris
☐ 3841 Kevin Kobetitsch
☐ 3842 Roger Landress
☐ 3843 Tony Long
☐ 3844 Dario Perez
☐ 3845 Damon Pollard
☐ 3846 Alex Sanchez
☐ 3847 Kevin Shaw
☐ 3848 Yobanne De Leon
☐ 3849 Andy Stewart
☐ 3850 Tony Bridges
☐ 3851 Pat Dando
☐ 3852 Joe Randa
☐ 3853 Brady Stewart
☐ 3854 Dean Tatarian
☐ 3855 Joe Vitiello
☐ 3856 Darren Burton
☐ 3857 Butch Cole
☐ 3858 Tom Smith
☐ 3859 Hugh Walker
☐ 3860 Ron Johnson
☐ 3861 Rafael Santana
☐ 3862 Pete Filson
☐ 3863 Checklist

1992 Batavia Clippers Classic/Best

This 30-card standard-size set of the 1992 Batavia Clippers, a Class A New York-Penn League affiliate of the Philadelphia Phillies, features white-bordered posed color player photos on its fronts. The player's name, team, and position appear at the bottom. The white back is framed by a thin red line and carries the player's name and position at the top, followed by biography, statistics and team logos.

	MINT	NRMT	EXC
COMPLETE SET (30)	5.00	2.20	.60

☐ 1 Jamie Sepeda
☐ 2 Michael Murphy
☐ 3 Chad Anderson
☐ 4 Gary Bennett
☐ 5 Lamar Cherry
☐ 6 J.J. Cruz
☐ 7 Patrick Bojcun
☐ 8 Reynaldo DeLosSantos
☐ 9 Wayne Johnson
☐ 10 Alan Burke
☐ 11 Shawn Wills
☐ 12 Eric Smith
☐ 13 Gary Herrmann
☐ 14 Glenn Nevill
☐ 15 Ron Kratz
☐ 16 Laurence Heisler
☐ 17 Steve Solomon
☐ 18 Mike Gomez
☐ 19 Joseph McIntyre
☐ 20 Ryan McWilliams
☐ 21 Thane Page
☐ 22 Mark Tranberg
☐ 23 Jon Zuber
☐ 24 Dean Hopp
☐ 25 Blake Doolan
☐ 26 Tom Vilet
☐ 27 Tom Irwin
☐ 28 Andrew Sallee
☐ 29 Floyd Rayford CO
Ramon Aviles MG
John Martin CO
☐ 30 Checklist

1992 Batavia Clippers Fleer/ProCards

This 32-card standard-size set of the 1992 Batavia Clippers, a Class A New York-Penn League affiliate of the Philadelphia Phillies, features brown-bordered posed color player photos on its fronts. The player's name appears in an upper corner; his team and position appear in a lower corner. The white back is framed by a black line and carries the player's name at the top, followed by biography and statistics.

	MINT	NRMT	EXC
COMPLETE SET(32)	5.00	2.20	.60

☐ 3254 Chad Anderson
☐ 3255 Pat Bojcun
☐ 3256 Blake Doolan
☐ 3257 Laurence Heisler
☐ 3258 Gary Herrmann
☐ 3259 Tom Irwin
☐ 3260 Joe McIntyre
☐ 3261 Ryan McWilliams
☐ 3262 Glenn Nevill
☐ 3263 Thane Page
☐ 3264 Jamie Sepeda
☐ 3265 Eric Smith
☐ 3266 Mark Tranberg
☐ 3267 Gary Bennett
☐ 3268 J.J.Cruz
☐ 3269 Dean Hopp
☐ 3270 Alan Burke
☐ 3271 Lamar Cherry
☐ 3272 Mike Gomez
☐ 3273 Ron Kratz
☐ 3274 Andy Sallee
☐ 3275 Jon Zuber
☐ 3276 Reynaldo DeLosSantos
☐ 3277 Wayne Johnson
☐ 3278 Mike Murphy
☐ 3279 Steven Solomon
☐ 3280 Tom Vilet
☐ 3281 Shawn Wills
☐ 3282 Ramon Aviles
☐ 3283 John Martin
☐ 3284 Floyd Rayford
☐ 3285 Checklist

1992 Bellingham Mariners Classic/Best

This 30-card standard-size set of the 1992 Bellingham Mariners, a Class A Northwest League affiliate of the Seattle Mariners, features white-bordered posed color player photos on its fronts. The player's name, team, and position appear at the bottom. The white back is framed by a thin red line and carries the player's name and position at the top, followed by biography, statistics and team logos.

	MINT	NRMT	EXC
COMPLETE SET (30)	5.00	2.20	.60

☐ 1 Shawn Estes
☐ 2 Greg Shockey
☐ 3 Derrick Warren
☐ 4 Jerry Aschoff
☐ 5 Rich Graham
☐ 6 Fred McNair
☐ 7 Jamon Deal
☐ 8 Ron Cody
☐ 9 Tim Harikkala
☐ 10 Kelly Hartman
☐ 11 Derek Lowe
☐ 12 Joe Mountain
☐ 13 Kevin Stock
☐ 14 Ryan Smith
☐ 15 Oscar Rivera
☐ 16 Jackie Nickell
☐ 17 Bob Worley
☐ 18 James Bonnici
☐ 19 Mark Calvi
☐ 20 Chris Widger
☐ 21 Mike Bond
☐ 22 James Clifford
☐ 23 Barney Erhard
☐ 24 David Lawson
☐ 25 Craig Griffey
☐ 26 Renaldo Bullock
☐ 27 Brian Wallace
☐ 28 Mike Hickey
☐ 29 Bobby Llanos
☐ 30 Checklist

1992 Bellingham Mariners Fleer/ProCards

This 33-card standard-size set of the 1992 Bellingham Mariners, a Class A Northwest League affiliate of the Seattle Mariners, features brown-bordered posed color player photos on its fronts. The player's name appears in an upper corner; his team and position appear in a lower corner. The white back is framed by a black line and carries the player's name at the top, followed by biography and statistics.

	MINT	NRMT	EXC
COMPLETE SET(33)	5.00	2.20	.60

☐ 1432 Jerry Aschoff
☐ 1433 William Cody
☐ 1434 Jamon Deal
☐ 1435 Shawn Estes
☐ 1436 Richard Graham
☐ 1437 Tim Harikkala
☐ 1438 Kelly Hartman
☐ 1439 Derek Lowe
☐ 1440 Joe Mountain
☐ 1441 Jackie Nickell
☐ 1442 Oscar Rivera
☐ 1443 Ryan Smith
☐ 1444 Kevin Stock
☐ 1445 Bob Worley
☐ 1446 James Bonnici
☐ 1447 Mark Calui
☐ 1448 Chris Widger
☐ 1449 Mike Bond
☐ 1450 James Clifford
☐ 1451 Barney Erhard
☐ 1452 Michael Hickey
☐ 1453 Bobby Llanos
☐ 1454 Brian Wallace
☐ 1455 Renaldo Bullock
☐ 1456 Craig Griffey
☐ 1457 David Lawson
☐ 1458 Fred McNair
☐ 1459 Greg Shockey
☐ 1460 Derrick Warren
☐ 1461 Dave Myers
☐ 1462 Lem Pilkinton
☐ 1463 Bryan Price
☐ 1464 Checklist

1992 Beloit Brewers Classic/Best

This 30-card standard-size set of the 1992 Beloit Brewers, a Class A Midwest League affiliate of the Milwaukee Brewers, features white-bordered posed color player photos on its fronts. The player's name, team, and position appear at the bottom. The white back is framed by a thin red line and carries the player's name and position at the top, followed by biography, statistics and team logos.

	MINT	NRMT	EXC
COMPLETE SET (30)	5.00	2.20	.60

☐ 1 Tyrone Hill
☐ 2 Scott VonDerleith
☐ 3 Terry Christopher
☐ 4 Byron Browne
☐ 5 Sam Rutter
☐ 6 Marshall Boze
☐ 7 Scott Talanoa
☐ 8 Brian Souza
☐ 9 Don Pruitt
☐ 10 Mike Couture
☐ 11 Chad O'Laughlin
☐ 12 Brian Dennison
☐ 13 Francisco Mendoza
☐ 14 Trini House
☐ 15 Tim Albert
☐ 16 Mike Stefanski
☐ 17 Granciano Enriquez
☐ 18 Derek Wachter
☐ 19 Bill Dobrolsky
☐ 20 Andy Fairman
☐ 21 LaRue Baber
☐ 22 Gordon Powell
☐ 23 Pat Fetty
☐ 24 Rick Zurn
☐ 25 Jeff Cirillo
☐ 26 Mike Huyler
☐ 27 Kerry Knox
☐ 28 Wayne Krenchicki MG
☐ 29 Steve Foucault CO
☐ 30 Brian Jaqutte TR
Checklist

1992 Beloit Brewers Fleer/ProCards

This 30-card standard-size set of the 1992 Beloit Brewers, a Class A Midwest League affiliate of the Milwaukee Brewers, features brown-bordered posed color player photos on its fronts. The player's name appears in an upper corner; his team and position appear in a lower corner. The white back is framed by a black line and carries the player's name at the top, followed by biography and statistics.

	MINT	NRMT	EXC
COMPLETE SET(30)	5.00	2.20	.60

☐ 395 Marshall Boze
☐ 396 Bryon Browne
☐ 397 Terry Christopher
☐ 398 John Criminger
☐ 399 Brian Dennison
☐ 400 Pat Fetty
☐ 401 Tyrone Hill
☐ 402 Kerry Knox
☐ 403 Don Pruitt
☐ 404 Sam Rutter
☐ 405 John Trisler
☐ 406 Rick Zurn
☐ 407 Bill Dobrolsky
☐ 408 Mike Stefanski
☐ 409 Jeff Cirillo
☐ 410 Andy Fairman
☐ 411 Mike Huyler
☐ 412 Jason Imperial
☐ 413 Fransisco Mendoza
☐ 414 Gordon Powell
☐ 415 Scott Talanoa
☐ 416 Tim Albert
☐ 417 Larue Baber
☐ 418 Mike Couture
☐ 419 Graciano Enriquez
☐ 420 Trini House
☐ 421 Derek Wachter
☐ 422 Wayne Krenchicki
☐ 423 Steve Foucault
☐ 424 Checklist

1992 Bend Rockies Classic/Best

This 30-card standard-size set of the 1992 Bend Rockies, a Class A Northwest League affiliate of the Colorado Rockies, features white-bordered posed color player photos on its fronts. The player's name, team, and position appear at the bottom. The white back is framed by a thin red line and carries the player's name and position at the top, followed by biography, statistics and team logos.

	MINT	NRMT	EXC
COMPLETE SET (30)	5.00	2.20	.60

☐ 1 John Burke
☐ 2 Roger Bailey
☐ 3 Mark Voisard
☐ 4 Ryan Freeburg
☐ 5 Garvin Alston
☐ 6 Jason Bates
☐ 7 Mark Thompson
☐ 8 Mike Case
☐ 9 Craig Counsell
☐ 10 Angel Echevarria
☐ 11 Michael Eiffert
☐ 12 Chris Henderson
☐ 13 Jay Holland
☐ 14 James Hovey
☐ 15 Jason Hutchins
☐ 16 Mike Kotarski
☐ 17 Keith Krenke
☐ 18 Quinton McCracken
☐ 19 Mike Oakland
☐ 20 Will Scalzitti
☐ 21 Tom Schmidt
☐ 22 Tim Scott
☐ 23 Mark Strittmatter
☐ 24 Gene Glynn MG
☐ 25 Joe Niekro CO
☐ 26 Johnny Zizzo CO
☐ 27 Thomas Probst TR
☐ 28 John Dusan BB
☐ 29 Logo Card
☐ 30 Checklist

1992 Bend Rockies Fleer/ProCards

This 27-card standard-size set of the 1992 Bend Rockies, a Class A Northwest League affiliate of the Colorado Rockies, features brown-bordered posed color player photos on its fronts. The player's name appears in an upper corner; his team and position appear in a lower corner. The white back is framed by a black line and carries the player's name at the top, followed by biography and statistics.

	MINT	NRMT	EXC
COMPLETE SET (27)	5.00	2.20	.60

☐ 1465 Garvin Alston
☐ 1466 Roger Bailey
☐ 1467 John Burke
☐ 1468 Mike Eiffert
☐ 1469 Chris Henderson
☐ 1470 Jay Holland
☐ 1471 Jamie Hovey
☐ 1472 Jason Hutchins
☐ 1473 Mike Kotarski
☐ 1474 Mark Thompson
☐ 1475 Mark Voisard
☐ 1476 Will Scalzitti
☐ 1477 Mark Strittmatter
☐ 1478 Jason Bates
☐ 1479 Craig Counsell
☐ 1480 Quinton McCracken
☐ 1481 Mike Garland
☐ 1482 Tom Schmidt
☐ 1483 Tim Scott
☐ 1484 Mike Case
☐ 1485 Angel Echevarria
☐ 1486 Ryan Freeburg
☐ 1487 Keith Krenke
☐ 1488 Gene Glynn
☐ 1489 Johnny Zizzo
☐ 1490 Joe Niekro
☐ 1491 Checklist

1992 Billings Mustangs Fleer/ProCards

This 30-card standard-size set of the 1992 Billings Mustangs, a Rookie Class Pioneer League affiliate of the Cincinnati Reds, features brown-bordered posed color player photos on its fronts. The player's name appears in an upper corner; his team and position appear in a lower corner. The white back is framed by a black line and carries the player's name at the top, followed by biography and statistics.

	MINT	NRMT	EXC
COMPLETE SET(30)	5.00	2.20	.60

☐ 3346 Jason Angel
☐ 3347 Fermin Garcia
☐ 3348 Jason Kummerfeldt
☐ 3349 Rich Langford
☐ 3350 Martin Lister
☐ 3351 Bo Loftin
☐ 3352 Jeff Murphy
☐ 3353 Ricky Pickett
☐ 3354 Chris Reed
☐ 3355 William Sullivan
☐ 3356 Dan Tobin
☐ 3357 Bill Dreisbach
☐ 3358 Jeff Ramey
☐ 3359 Toby Rumfield
☐ 3360 Tim Belk
☐ 3361 Mike Collins
☐ 3362 Derick Graham
☐ 3363 Dee Jenkins
☐ 3364 Brad Keenan
☐ 3365 Matt Martin
☐ 3366 Eric Owens
☐ 3367 Micah Franklin
☐ 3368 Jeff Manship
☐ 3369 Mike Meggers
☐ 3370 Chad Mottola
☐ 3371 Jeff Nagy
☐ 3372 Wayne Wilkerson
☐ 3373 Donnie Scott
☐ 3374 Terry Abbott
☐ 3375 Checklist

1992 Billings Mustangs Sports Pro

	MINT	NRMT	EXC
COMPLETE SET (30)	7.00	3.10	.85

☐ 1 Bo Loftin
☐ 2 Chad Mottola
☐ 3 Brad Keenan
☐ 4 Jason Angel
☐ 5 Wayne Wilkerson
☐ 6 Toby Rumfield
☐ 7 Ricky Pickett
☐ 8 Mike Meggers
☐ 9 Rich Langford
☐ 10 Micah Franklin
☐ 11 Jason Kummerfeldt
☐ 12 Dee Jenkins
☐ 13 Dan Tobin
☐ 14 Mike Collins
☐ 15 Chris Reed
☐ 16 Eric Owens
☐ 17 Jeff Ramey
☐ 18 Martin Lister
☐ 19 Jeff Manship
☐ 20 Derick Graham
☐ 21 Jeff Murphy
☐ 22 Bill Dreisbach
☐ 23 Fermin Garcia
☐ 24 Tim Belk
☐ 25 Jeff Nagy
☐ 26 William Sullivan
☐ 27 Matthew Martin
☐ 28 Damon Montgomery
☐ 29 Terry Abbott
☐ 30 Donnie Scott

1992 Binghamton Mets Fleer/ProCards

This 28-card standard-size set of the 1992 Binghamton Mets, a Class AA Eastern League affiliate of the New York Mets, features brown-bordered posed color player photos on its fronts. The player's name appears in an upper corner; his team and position appear in a lower corner. The white back is framed by a black line and carries the player's name at the top, followed by biography and statistics. This set includes Bobby Jones' first team set card.

	MINT	NRMT	EXC
COMPLETE SET(28)	7.00	3.10	.85

☐ 508 Chris Dorn
☐ 509 Todd Douma
☐ 510 John Johnstone
☐ 511 Bobby Jones
☐ 512 Gregg Langbehn
☐ 513 Andy Reich
☐ 514 Bryan Rogers
☐ 515 Julian Vasquez
☐ 516 Joe Vitko
☐ 517 Pete Walker
☐ 518 Tom Wegmann
☐ 519 Andy Dziadkowiec
☐ 520 Brook Fordyce
☐ 521 Tom Allison
☐ 522 Chris Butterfield
☐ 523 Joe Dellicarri
☐ 524 Jamie Hoffner
☐ 525 Doug Saunders
☐ 526 Alan Zinter
☐ 527 Tim Howard
☐ 528 Bert Hunter
☐ 529 Rob Katzaroff
☐ 530 Curtis Pride
☐ 531 Mike White
☐ 532 Steve Swisher
☐ 533 Ron Gideon
☐ 534 Randy Niemann
☐ 535 Checklist

1992 Binghamton Mets SkyBox

This issue includes the minor league card debut of Bobby Jones.

	MINT	NRMT	EXC
COMPLETE SET (26)	7.00	3.10	.85

☐ 51 Tom Allison
☐ 52 Chris Butterfield
☐ 53 Joe Delli Carri
☐ 54 Chris Dorn
☐ 55 Todd Douma
☐ 56 Andy Dziadkowiec
☐ 57 Brook Fordyce
☐ 58 Jamie Hoffner
☐ 59 Tim Howard
☐ 60 Bert Hunter
☐ 61 John Johnstone
☐ 62 Bobby Jones
☐ 63 Rob Katzaroff
☐ 64 Gregg Langbehn
☐ 65 Curtis Pride
☐ 66 Bryan Rogers
☐ 67 Doug Saunders
☐ 68 Julian Vasquez
☐ 69 Joe Vitko
☐ 70 Pete Walker
☐ 71 Tom Wegmann
☐ 72 Mike White
☐ 73 Alan Zinter
☐ 74 Steve Swisher MG
☐ 75 Randy Niemann CO
Ron Gideon CO
☐ NNO Checklist

1992 Birmingham Barons Fleer/ProCards

This 28-card standard-size set of the 1992 Birmingham Barons, a Class AA Southern League affiliate of the Chicago White Sox, features brown-bordered posed color player photos on its fronts. The player's name appears in an upper corner; his team and position appear in a lower corner. The white back is framed by a black line and carries the player's name at the top, followed by biography and statistics.

	MINT	NRMT	EXC
COMPLETE SET(28)	5.00	2.20	.60

- ☐ 2574 Frank Campos
- ☐ 2575 Fred Dabney
- ☐ 2576 Earnie Johnson
- ☐ 2577 Bo Kennedy
- ☐ 2578 Brian Keyser
- ☐ 2579 Frank Merigliano
- ☐ 2580 Mike Mongiello
- ☐ 2581 Jeff Schwarz
- ☐ 2582 Keith Shepherd
- ☐ 2583 Larry Thomas
- ☐ 2584 Jose Ventura
- ☐ 2585 Clemete Alvarez
- ☐ 2586 Al Liebert
- ☐ 2587 James Bishop
- ☐ 2588 Wayne Busby
- ☐ 2589 Kevin Castleberry
- ☐ 2590 Scott Cepicky
- ☐ 2591 Lindsay Foster
- ☐ 2592 Kevin Garner
- ☐ 2593 Tom Redington
- ☐ 2594 Robert Harris
- ☐ 2595 Scott Jaster
- ☐ 2596 Scott Tedder
- ☐ 2597 Charlie White
- ☐ 2598 Tony Franklin
- ☐ 2599 Pat Roessler
- ☐ 2600 Don Cooper
- ☐ 2601 Checklist

1992 Birmingham Barons SkyBox

	MINT	NRMT	EXC
COMPLETE SET (26)	5.00	2.20	.60

- ☐ 76 Clemente Alvarez
- ☐ 77 Cesar Bernhardt
- ☐ 78 James Bishop
- ☐ 79 Wayne Busby
- ☐ 80 Scott Cepicky
- ☐ 81 Fred Dabney
- ☐ 82 Lindsay Foster
- ☐ 83 Robert Harris
- ☐ 84 John Hudek
- ☐ 85 Scott Jaster
- ☐ 86 Bo Kennedy
- ☐ 87 Tom Redington
- ☐ 88 Allen Liebert
- ☐ 89 Frank Merigliano
- ☐ 90 Mike Mongiello
- ☐ 91 Kinnis Pledger
- ☐ 92 Greg Roth
- ☐ 93 Johnny Ruffin
- ☐ 94 Jeff Schwarz
- ☐ 95 Keith Shepherd
- ☐ 96 Scott Tedder
- ☐ 97 Jose Ventura
- ☐ 98 Charlie White
- ☐ 99 Tony Franklin MG
- ☐ 100 Don Cooper CO
  Sam Hairston CO
- ☐ NNO Checklist

1992 Bluefield Orioles Classic/Best

This 30-card standard-size set of the 1992 Bluefield Orioles, a Rookie Class Appalachian League affiliate of the Baltimore Orioles, features white-bordered posed color player photos on its fronts. The player's name, team, and position appear at the bottom. The white back is framed by a thin red line and carries the player's name and position at the top, followed by biography, statistics and team logos.

	MINT	NRMT	EXC
COMPLETE SET (30)	5.00	2.20	.60

- ☐ 1 Garrett Stephenson
- ☐ 2 Kyle Yeske
- ☐ 3 Mike Thomas
- ☐ 4 Dan Fregoso
- ☐ 5 Mike Porter
- ☐ 6 Ishovany Marquez
- ☐ 7 Francisco Saneaux
- ☐ 8 Jose Serra
- ☐ 9 Feliciano Mercedes
- ☐ 10 Scott Metcalf
- ☐ 11 Duane Thomas
- ☐ 12 Roy Hodge
- ☐ 13 Keith Eaddy
- ☐ 14 Christopher Chatterton
- ☐ 15 Scott Emerson
- ☐ 16 Joe Lantrip
- ☐ 17 Matt Riemer
- ☐ 18 Paul Jones
- ☐ 19 Marco Manrique
- ☐ 20 George Freeberger
- ☐ 21 Armando Benitez
- ☐ 22 Carlos Chavez
- ☐ 23 Mike O'Berry
- ☐ 24 Len Johnston CO
- ☐ 25 Frank Neville TR
- ☐ 26 Logo Card
- ☐ 27 Logo Card
- ☐ 28 Logo Card
- ☐ 29 Logo Card
- ☐ 30 Checklist

1992 Bluefield Orioles Fleer/ProCards

This 26-card standard-size set of the 1992 Bluefield Orioles, a Rookie Class Appalachian League affiliate of the Baltimore Orioles, features brown-bordered posed color player photos on its fronts. The player's name appears in an upper corner; his team and position appear in a lower corner. The white back is framed by a black line and carries the player's name at the top, followed by biography and statistics.

	MINT	NRMT	EXC
COMPLETE SET(26)	5.00	2.20	.60

- ☐ 2352 Armando Benitez
- ☐ 2353 Chris Chatterton
- ☐ 2354 Carlos Chavez
- ☐ 2355 Scott Emerson
- ☐ 2356 Dan Fregoso
- ☐ 2357 Joe Lantrip
- ☐ 2358 Ishovany Marquez
- ☐ 2359 Mike Porter
- ☐ 2360 Francisco Saneaux
- ☐ 2361 Garrett Stephenson
- ☐ 2362 George Freberger
- ☐ 2363 Marco Manrique
- ☐ 2364 Eric Chavez
- ☐ 2365 Paul Jones
- ☐ 2366 Feliciano Mercedes
- ☐ 2367 Scott Metcalf
- ☐ 2368 Matt Riemer
- ☐ 2369 Jose Serra
- ☐ 2370 Keith Eaddy
- ☐ 2371 Roy Hodge
- ☐ 2372 Duane Thomas
- ☐ 2373 Mike Thomas
- ☐ 2374 Kyle Yeske
- ☐ 2375 Mike O'Leary
- ☐ 2376 Charlie Puleo
- ☐ 2377 Checklist

1992 Boise Hawks Classic/Best

This 30-card standard-size set of the 1992 Boise Hawks, a Class A Northwest League affiliate of the California Angels, features white-bordered posed color player photos on its fronts. The player's name, team, and position appear at the bottom. The white back is framed by a thin red line and carries the player's name and position at the top, followed by biography, statistics and team logos.

	MINT	NRMT	EXC
COMPLETE SET (30)	5.00	2.20	.60

- ☐ 1 Marquis Riley
- ☐ 2 Max Valennia
- ☐ 3 Joe Hardwick
- ☐ 4 Joel Smith
- ☐ 5 Dave Kessler
- ☐ 6 Dave Partrick
- ☐ 7 Mark Simmons
- ☐ 8 Michael Pineiro
- ☐ 9 Lyall Barwick
- ☐ 10 Jay Simpson
- ☐ 11 Bill Blanchette
- ☐ 12 John Wylie
- ☐ 13 Mickey Kerns
- ☐ 14 Lino Connell
- ☐ 15 Chris Anderson
- ☐ 16 Javier Martinez
- ☐ 17 Joe Urso
- ☐ 18 John Pricher
- ☐ 19 Anthony Chavez
- ☐ 20 Mike Butler
- ☐ 21 Dallas Rinehart
- ☐ 22 Daron Sutton
- ☐ 23 Bill Dunkel
- ☐ 24 Elgin Bobo
- ☐ 25 Paxton Briley
- ☐ 26 Chris Smith
- ☐ 27 Jeff Schmidt
- ☐ 28 Michael Wolf
- ☐ 29 Bill Simas
- ☐ 30 Larry Hingle CL

1992 Boise Hawks Fleer/ProCards

This 33-card standard-size set of the 1992 Boise Hawks, a Class A Northwest League affiliate of the California Angels, features brown-bordered posed color player photos on its fronts. The player's name appears in an upper corner; his team and position appear in a lower corner. The white back is framed by a black line and carries the player's name at the top, followed by biography and statistics.

	MINT	NRMT	EXC
COMPLETE SET(33)	5.00	2.20	.60

- ☐ 3616 Bill Blanchette
- ☐ 3617 Paxton Briley
- ☐ 3618 Mike Butler
- ☐ 3619 Anthony Chavez
- ☐ 3620 Larry Hingel
- ☐ 3621 Dave Partrick
- ☐ 3622 Beban Perez
- ☐ 3623 John Pricher
- ☐ 3624 Dallas Rhinehart
- ☐ 3625 Jeff Schmidt
- ☐ 3626 Kyle Sebach
- ☐ 3627 Bill Simas
- ☐ 3628 Daron Sutton
- ☐ 3629 John Wylie
- ☐ 3630 Chris Hunt
- ☐ 3631 Dave Kessler
- ☐ 3632 Mike Pineiro
- ☐ 3633 Joel Smith
- ☐ 3634 Chris Anderson
- ☐ 3635 Elgin Bobo
- ☐ 3636 Lino Connell
- ☐ 3637 Mickey Kerns
- ☐ 3638 Javier Martinez
- ☐ 3639 Mark Simmons
- ☐ 3640 Chris Smith
- ☐ 3641 Lyall Barwick
- ☐ 3642 Bill Dunckel
- ☐ 3643 Joe Hardwick
- ☐ 3644 Marquis Riley
- ☐ 3645 Michael Wolf
- ☐ 3646 Tom Kotchman
- ☐ 3647 Howie Gershberg
- ☐ 3648 Checklist

1992 Bristol Tigers Classic/Best

This 30-card standard-size set of the 1992 Bristol Tigers, a Rookie Class Appalachian League affiliate of the Detroit Tigers, features white-bordered posed color player photos on its fronts. The player's name, team, and position appear at the bottom. The white back is framed by a thin red line and carries the player's name and position at the top, followed by biography, statistics and team logos.

	MINT	NRMT	EXC
COMPLETE SET (30)	5.00	2.20	.60

- ☐ 1 Mike Berlin
- ☐ 2 Jeff Brown
- ☐ 3 Blas Cedeno
- ☐ 4 Paul Magrini
- ☐ 5 Brian Maxcy
- ☐ 6 Toby McFarland
- ☐ 7 Trever Miller
- ☐ 8 Riccardo Munoz
- ☐ 9 John Rosengren
- ☐ 10 Henry Santos
- ☐ 11 Clint Sodowsky
- ☐ 12 John Grimm
- ☐ 13 Tim Jones
- ☐ 14 David Rodriguez
- ☐ 15 Moises Ayala
- ☐ 16 Del Marine
- ☐ 17 Kenny Marrero
- ☐ 18 Matt Evans
- ☐ 19 Roberto Ortega
- ☐ 20 Yuri Sanchez
- ☐ 21 Tim Thomas
- ☐ 22 Jorge Valeandia
- ☐ 23 Bart Greene
- ☐ 24 Johnny Lamar
- ☐ 25 Darren Milne
- ☐ 26 John Sutey
- ☐ 27 Mark Wagner MG
- ☐ 28 Jim Van Scoyoc CO
- ☐ 29 Mike Quinn TR
- ☐ 30 Checklist

1992 Bristol Tigers Fleer/ProCards

This 33-card standard-size set of the 1992 Bristol Tigers, a Rookie Class Appalachian League affiliate of the Detroit Tigers, features brown-bordered posed color player photos on its fronts. The player's name appears in an upper corner; his team and position appear in a lower corner. The white back is framed by a black line and carries the player's name at the top, followed by biography and statistics.

	MINT	NRMT	EXC
COMPLETE SET(33)	5.00	2.20	.60

- ☐ 1399 Mike Berlin
- ☐ 1400 Jeff Brown
- ☐ 1401 Blas Cedeno
- ☐ 1402 John Grimm
- ☐ 1403 Tim Jones
- ☐ 1404 Paul Magrini
- ☐ 1405 Brian Maxcy
- ☐ 1406 Toby McFarland
- ☐ 1407 Trever Miller
- ☐ 1408 Ricky Munoz
- ☐ 1409 Dave Rodriguez
- ☐ 1410 Rosey Rosengren
- ☐ 1411 Henry Santos
- ☐ 1412 Clint Sodowsky
- ☐ 1413 Moises Ayala
- ☐ 1414 Kevin Lidle
- ☐ 1415 Del Marine
- ☐ 1416 Kenny Marrero
- ☐ 1417 Matt Evans
- ☐ 1418 Luis Hernandez
- ☐ 1419 Art Johnson
- ☐ 1420 Roberto Ortega
- ☐ 1421 Yuri Sanchez
- ☐ 1422 Tim Thomas
- ☐ 1423 Jorge Velandia
- ☐ 1424 Bart Greene
- ☐ 1425 Johnny Lamar
- ☐ 1426 Darren Milne
- ☐ 1427 Jorge Moreno
- ☐ 1428 Roberto Rojas
- ☐ 1429 John Sutey
- ☐ 1430 Ken Valdez
- ☐ 1431 Checklist

1992 Buffalo Bisons Blue Shield

This 28-card set subtitled "Stars of the Future" is sponsored by Blue Shield of Western New York,.and is produced on a tri-fold sheet containing perforated cards. The first panel displays a Blue Shield logo, the second panel contains four rows of 4 cards, and the third panel contains four rows of 3 cards. The cards measure approximately 2 1/2" x 3 7/16" and are edged in royal blue. The fronts display a color action shot of the player with the Buffalo Bison's team logo in the upper left corner, the Blue Shield logo in a white box on the lower left corner and to the side, a gold box with the player's name and team number. The horizontal backs contain biography and career statistics printed in black on a white background. The cards are unnumbered and checklisted below alphabetically.

	MINT	NRMT	EXC
COMPLETE SET (28)	10.00	4.50	1.25

- ☐ 1 Joe Ausanio
- ☐ 2 Marc Bombard
- ☐ 3 Dave Clark
- ☐ 4 Steve Cooke
- ☐ 5 Danny Cox
- ☐ 6 Mike Dalton
- ☐ 7 Brian Dorsett
- ☐ 8 Doc Edwards CO
- ☐ 9 Carlos Garcia
- ☐ 10 Tom Green
- ☐ 11 Al Martin
- ☐ 12 Blas Minor
- ☐ 13 Paul Miller
- ☐ 14 Mark Petkovsek
- ☐ 15 Tom Prince
- ☐ 15 Spin Williams CO
- ☐ 16 Joe Redfield
- ☐ 17 Jeff Richardson
- ☐ 18 Rosario Rodriguez
- ☐ 19 Mike Roesler
- ☐ 20 Mike Sandoval TR
- ☐ 21 Jose Tolentino
- ☐ 22 Jim Tracy
- ☐ 23 Greg Tubbs
- ☐ 24 Tim Wakefield
- ☐ 26 Kevin Young
- ☐ 27 Eddie Zambrano
- ☐ 28 Buster T. Bison
  (Mascot)

1992 Buffalo Bisons Fleer/ProCards

This 27-card standard-size set of the 1992 Buffalo Bisons, a Class AAA American Association affiliate of the Pittsburgh Pirates, features brown-bordered posed color player photos on its fronts. The player's name appears in an upper corner; his team and position appear in a lower corner. The white back is framed by a black line and carries the player's name at the top, followed by biography and statistics.

	MINT	NRMT	EXC
COMPLETE SET(27)	5.00	2.20	.60

- ☐ 315 Joe Ausanio
- ☐ 316 Victor Cole
- ☐ 317 Mike Dalton
- ☐ 318 Eddie Dixon
- ☐ 319 Paul Miller
- ☐ 320 Blas Minor
- ☐ 321 Mark Petkovsek
- ☐ 322 Mike Roesler
- ☐ 323 Jim Tracy
- ☐ 324 Tim Wakefield
- ☐ 325 Pete Beeler
- ☐ 326 Brian Dorsett
- ☐ 327 Carlos Garcia
- ☐ 328 Jeff Richardson
- ☐ 329 Jose Tolentino

☐ 330 John Wehner
☐ 331 Kevin Young
☐ 332 Dave Clark
☐ 333 Al Martin
☐ 334 Will Pennyfeather
☐ 335 Joe Redfield
☐ 336 Greg Tubbs
☐ 337 Eddie Zambrano
☐ 338 Marc Bombard
☐ 339 Doc Edwards
☐ 340 Spin Williams
☐ 341 Checklist

1992 Buffalo Bisons SkyBox

	MINT	NRMT	EXC
COMPLETE SET (26)	5.00	2.20	.60

☐ 26 Joe Ausanio
☐ 27 Pete Beeler
☐ 28 Dave Clark
☐ 29 Victor Cole
☐ 30 Mike Dalton
☐ 31 Eddie Dixon
☐ 32 Brian Dorsett
☐ 33 Carlos Garcia
☐ 34 Rosario Rodriguez
☐ 35 Albert Martin
☐ 36 Blas Minor
☐ 37 William Pennyfeather
☐ 38 Mark Petkovsek
☐ 39 Joe Redfield
☐ 40 Jeff Richardson
☐ 41 Mike Roesler
☐ 42 Jose Tolentino
☐ 43 Jim Tracy
☐ 44 Greg Tubbs
☐ 45 Tim Wakefield
☐ 46 John Wehner
☐ 47 Kevin Young
☐ 48 Eddie Zambrano
☐ 49 Marc Bombard MG
☐ 50 Doc Edwards CO
Spin Williams CO
☐ NNO Checklist

1992 Burlington Astros Classic/Best

This 30-card standard-size set of the 1992 Burlington Astros, a Class A Midwest League affiliate of the Houston Astros, features white-bordered posed color player photos on its fronts. The player's name, team, and position appear at the bottom. The white back is framed by a thin red line and carries the player's name and position at the top, followed by biography, statistics and team logos.

	MINT	NRMT	EXC
COMPLETE SET (30)	5.00	2.20	.60

☐ 1 David Wallace
☐ 2 Fernando Mercedes
☐ 3 Jeff Miller
☐ 4 Jimmy White
☐ 5 Jermaine Swinton
☐ 6 Jim Waring
☐ 7 Joe Sewell
☐ 8 Raphael Lanfranco
☐ 9 Tyrone Scott
☐ 10 Lance Smith
☐ 11 Dennis Reed
☐ 12 Rod Biehl
☐ 13 Steve Powers
☐ 14 Ed Quijada
☐ 15 Brian Holliday
☐ 16 Brian McGlone
☐ 17 Alberto Montero
☐ 18 Craig Curtis
☐ 19 Dennis Colon
☐ 20 Perry Berry
☐ 21 Pat Murphy
☐ 22 Jim Gonzalez
☐ 23 Al Harley
☐ 24 Rich Schulte
☐ 25 Buck McNabb
☐ 26 Steve Curry MG
☐ 27 Rick Aponte CO
☐ 28 Rick Peters CO
☐ 29 Chris Correnti TR
☐ 30 Checklist

1992 Burlington Astros Fleer/ProCards

This 30-card standard-size set of the 1992 Burlington Astros, a Class A Midwest League affiliate of the Houston Astros, features brown-bordered posed color player photos on its fronts. The player's name appears in an upper corner; his team and position appear in a lower corner. The white back is framed by a black line and carries the player's name at the top, followed by biography and statistics.

	MINT	NRMT	EXC
COMPLETE SET(30)	5.00	2.20	.60

☐ 536 Rod Biehl
☐ 537 Kevin Gallaher
☐ 538 Brian Holliday
☐ 539 Fernando Mercedes
☐ 540 Jeff Miller
☐ 541 Pat Murphy
☐ 542 Steve Powers
☐ 543 Ed Quijada
☐ 544 Dennis Reed
☐ 545 Heath Rose
☐ 546 Tyrone Scott
☐ 547 Joe Sewell
☐ 548 Jim Waring
☐ 549 Jim Gonzales
☐ 550 Raphael Lanfranco
☐ 551 Lance Smith
☐ 552 Perry Berry
☐ 553 Dennis Colon
☐ 554 Craig Curtis
☐ 555 Al Harley
☐ 556 Brian McGlone
☐ 557 Alberto Montero
☐ 558 Buck McNabb
☐ 559 Rich Schulte
☐ 560 Jermaine Swinton
☐ 561 David Wallace
☐ 562 Jimmy White
☐ 563 Steve Curry
☐ 564 Rick Aponte
☐ 565 Checklist

1992 Burlington Indians Classic/Best

This 30-card standard-size set of the 1992 Burlington Indians, a Rookie Class Appalachian League affiliate of the Cleveland Indians, features white-bordered posed color player photos on its fronts. The player's name, team, and position appear at the bottom. The white back is framed by a thin red line and carries the player's name and position at the top, followed by biography, statistics and team logos. This issue includes the minor league card debut of Damian Jackson.

	MINT	NRMT	EXC
COMPLETE SET (30)	6.00	2.70	.75

☐ 1 John Lewandowski
☐ 2 Jeff Whitaker
☐ 3 Damian Jackson
☐ 4 Germaine Mayberry
☐ 5 Craig Sides
☐ 6 Brandon Bluhm
☐ 7 Rodney Koller
☐ 8 Mike Burritt
☐ 9 Jose Cabrera
☐ 10 Leroy Thompson
☐ 11 Jon Zubiri
☐ 12 Chris Maffett
☐ 13 Greg Sinner
☐ 14 Greg Rideau
☐ 15 R.W. Augustine
☐ 16 Roberto Garza
☐ 17 Allen Gallagher
☐ 18 Julian Tavares
☐ 19 Damian Leyva
☐ 20 Michael Moyle
☐ 21 Patricio Claudin
☐ 22 Mitch Meluskey
☐ 23 Huascar Genao
☐ 24 Terry Miller
☐ 25 Chad Townsend
☐ 26 Ronnie Coleman
☐ 27 Brian Holter
☐ 28 Einar Diaz
☐ 29 Eric White
☐ 30 Maximo De La Rosa
Checklist

1992 Burlington Indians Fleer/ProCards

This 32-card standard-size set of the 1992 Burlington Indians, a Rookie Class Appalachian League affiliate of the Cleveland Indians, features brown-bordered posed color player photos on its fronts. The player's name appears in an upper corner; his team and position appear in a lower corner. The white back is framed by a black line and carries the player's name at the top, followed by biography and statistics. This set includes the minor league card debut of Damian Jackson.

	MINT	NRMT	EXC
COMPLETE SET(32)	6.00	2.70	.75

☐ 1644 Rob Augustine
☐ 1645 Brandon Bluhn
☐ 1646 Mike Burritt
☐ 1647 Jose Cabrera
☐ 1648 Allen Gallagher
☐ 1649 Roberto Garza
☐ 1650 Brian Holter
☐ 1651 Rod Koller
☐ 1652 Damian Leyva
☐ 1653 Chris Maffett
☐ 1654 Greg Rideau
☐ 1655 Craig Sides
☐ 1656 Greg Sinnor
☐ 1657 Julian Tavares
☐ 1658 Jon Zubiri
☐ 1659 John Lewandowski
☐ 1660 Mitch Meluskey
☐ 1661 Michael Moyle
☐ 1662 Einar Diaz
☐ 1663 Huascar Genao
☐ 1664 Damian Jackson
☐ 1665 Chad Townsend
☐ 1666 Jeff Whitaker
☐ 1667 Eric White
☐ 1668 Patricio Claudio
☐ 1669 Ronnie Coleman
☐ 1670 Maximo De La Rosa
☐ 1671 Germaine Mayberry
☐ 1672 Terry Miller
☐ 1673 Leroy Thompson
☐ 1674 Team Picture
☐ 1675 Checklist

1992 Butte Copper Kings Sports Pro

	MINT	NRMT	EXC
COMPLETE SET (30)	6.00	2.70	.75

☐ 1 Dan Mascia
☐ 2 Scott Malone
☐ 3 Jeff Carew
☐ 4 David Manning
☐ 5 Jamie Bethke
☐ 6 Richard Aurilia
☐ 7 Todd Gates
☐ 8 Mark Brandenburg
☐ 9 Wes Shook
☐ 10 Brent Evans
☐ 11 Jack Kimel
☐ 12 Terry Rosenkranz
☐ 13 Franklin Parra
☐ 14 Chris Newcomb
☐ 15 Charlie Sullivan
☐ 16 Desi Wilson
☐ 17 David Chavarria
☐ 18 Scott Eyre
☐ 19 Mark O'Brien
☐ 20 Mike Welch
☐ 21 Victor Madrigal
☐ 22 Earl Heib
☐ 23 Chris Kelley
☐ 24 Wayne Eggleston
☐ 25 Kevin Woodall
☐ 26 Chad Wiley
☐ 27 Keith Nalepka
☐ 28 Efrain Gonzalez
☐ 29 Paul Lesch
☐ 30 Victor Ramirez Sr. MG

1992 Calgary Cannons Fleer/ProCards

This 22-card standard-size set of the 1992 Calgary Cannons, a Class AAA Pacific Coast League affiliate of the Seattle Mariners, features brown-bordered posed color player photos on its fronts. The player's name appears in an upper corner; his team and position appear in a lower corner. The white back is framed by a black line and carries the player's name and position at the top, followed by biography and statistics.

	MINT	NRMT	EXC
COMPLETE SET (22)	5.00	2.20	.60

☐ 3726 Kevin Brown
☐ 3727 Mark Grant
☐ 3728 Jim Newlin
☐ 3729 Mike Remlinger
☐ 3730 Pat Rice
☐ 3731 Ed Vande Berg
☐ 3732 Mike Walker
☐ 3733 Kerry Woodson
☐ 3734 Bill Haselman
☐ 3735 Chris Howard
☐ 3736 Greg Pirkl
☐ 3737 Rich Amaral
☐ 3738 Kent Anderson
☐ 3739 Mike Blowers
☐ 3740 Bret Boone
☐ 3741 Shane Turner
☐ 3742 Dave Brundage
☐ 3743 John Moses
☐ 3744 Jeff Wetherby
☐ 3745 Keith Bodie MG
☐ 3746 Ross Grimsley CO
☐ 3747 Checklist

1992 Calgary Cannons SkyBox

This 26-card standard-size set of the 1992 Calgary Cannons, a Class AAA Pacific Coast League affiliate of the Seattle Mariners, features white-bordered posed color player photos on its fronts. The player's name appears at the top; his team and position appear at the bottom. The white back carries the player's name, team name, and position at the top, followed by biography and statistics.

	MINT	NRMT	EXC
COMPLETE SET (26)	5.00	2.20	.60

☐ 51 Roger Salkeld
☐ 52 Kevin Brown
☐ 53 Shawn Barton
☐ 54 Mike Blowers
☐ 55 Bret Boone
☐ 56 Jim Bowie
☐ 57 Dave Brundage
☐ 58 Mario Diaz
☐ 59 Andy Hawkins
☐ 60 Bert Heffernan
☐ 61 Chris Howard
☐ 62 Randy Kramer
☐ 63 John Moses
☐ 64 Pat Lennon
☐ 65 Jose Nunez
☐ 66 Alonzo Powell
☐ 67 Clay Parker
☐ 68 Mike Remlinger
☐ 69 Pat Rice
☐ 70 Dave Schmidt
☐ 71 Shane Turner
☐ 72 Jim Newlin
☐ 73 Clint Zavaras
☐ 74 Keith Bodie MG
☐ 75 Ross Grimsley CO
☐ NNO Checklist

1992 California League All-Stars Cal League Cards

	MINT	NRMT	EXC
COMPLETE SET (53)	8.00	3.60	1.00

☐ 1 Brent Gates
☐ 2 Fabio Gamez
☐ 3 Eric Helfand
☐ 4 Mike Neill
☐ 5 Adam Hyzdu
☐ 6 Dave Wrona
☐ 7 Dan Flanagan
☐ 8 Tanyon Sturtze
☐ 9 Fausto Cruz
☐ 10 Barry Miller
☐ 11 Enoch Simmons
☐ 12 Damon Mashore
☐ 13 Tsutomu Yamada
☐ 14 Matt Davis
☐ 15 Mike Farrell
☐ 16 Islay Molina
☐ 17 Joe Rosselli
☐ 18 Mike Basse
☐ 19 Curtis Shaw
☐ 20 Jim Waggoner
☐ 21 Ted Kubiak
☐ 22 Pete Richert
☐ 23 Dave Hollenback
☐ 24 Paul Schreiber
☐ 25 Bill Miller
☐ 26 Ian Lamplugh
☐ 27 Jeff Paterson
☐ 28 George Glinatsis
☐ 29 Ray McDavid
☐ 30 Murph Proctor
☐ 31 Korey Keling
☐ 32 Marty Cordova
☐ 33 Bob McCreary
☐ 34 Mike Sharp
☐ 35 Troy Richer
☐ 36 Brent Bish
☐ 37 Rich Becker
☐ 38 Mark Dalesandro
☐ 39 Billy Hall
☐ 40 Mike Hampton
☐ 41 Scott Stahoviak
☐ 42 Joey Hamilton
☐ 43 Edgar Alfonzo
☐ 44 Hector Ortiz
☐ 45 Tommy Adams
☐ 46 Garret Anderson
☐ 47 Mike Durant
☐ 48 Eduardo Perez
☐ 49 Mario Mendoza
☐ 50 Derek Winchell
☐ 51 Stu Cliburn
☐ 52 Gene Richards
☐ NNO Checklist

1992 Canton-Akron Indians Fleer/ProCards

This 28-card standard-size set of the 1992 Canton-Akron Indians, a Class AA Eastern League affiliate of the Cleveland Indians, features brown-bordered posed color player photos on its fronts. The player's name appears in an upper corner; his team and position appear in a lower corner. The white back is framed by a black line and carries the player's name at the top, followed by biography and statistics. .

	MINT	NRMT	EXC
COMPLETE SET(28)	5.00	2.20	.60

☐ 682 Paul Byrd
☐ 683 Colin Charland
☐ 684 Victor Garcia
☐ 685 Mike Gardella
☐ 686 Brett Gideon

☐ 687 Garland Kiser
☐ 688 David Mlicki
☐ 689 Willie Smith
☐ 690 Wally Trice
☐ 691 Joe Turek
☐ 692 Bill Wertz
☐ 693 Carlos Mota
☐ 694 Kelly Stinnett
☐ 695 Carlo Colombino
☐ 696 Terry Crowley
☐ 697 Miguel Flores
☐ 698 Jose Hernandez
☐ 699 Mike Sarbaugh
☐ 700 Tom Eiterman
☐ 701 Brian Giles
☐ 702 Ken Ramos
☐ 703 Tracy Sanders
☐ 704 Lee Tinsley
☐ 705 Kyle Washington
☐ 706 Brian Graham
☐ 707 Jim Gabella
☐ 708 Ken Rowe
☐ 709 Checklist

1992 Canton-Akron Indians SkyBox

	MINT	NRMT	EXC
COMPLETE SET (26)	5.00	2.20	.60

☐ 101 Chad Allen
☐ 102 Paul Byrd
☐ 103 Carlo Colombino
☐ 104 Craig Cooper
☐ 105 Tom Eiterman
☐ 106 Miguel Flores
☐ 107 Victor Garcia
☐ 108 Brian Giles
☐ 109 Jose Hernandez
☐ 110 Colin Charland
☐ 111 Nolan Lane
☐ 112 David Mlicki
☐ 113 Scott Morgan
☐ 114 Carlos Mota
☐ 115 Ken Ramos
☐ 116 Tracy Sanders
☐ 117 Mike Sarbaugh
☐ 118 Mike Soper
☐ 119 Kelly Stinnett
☐ 120 Willie Smith
☐ 121 Joe Turek
☐ 122 Kyle Washington
☐ 123 Bill Wertz
☐ 124 Brian Graham MG
☐ 125 Ken Rowe CO
Jim Gabella CO
☐ NNO Checklist

1992 Carolina Mudcats Fleer/ProCards

This 26-card standard-size set of the 1992 Carolina Mudcats, a Class AA Southern League affiliate of the Pittsburgh Pirates, features brown-bordered posed color player photos on its fronts. The player's name appears in an upper corner; his team and position appear in a lower corner. The white back is framed by a black line and carries the player's name at the top, followed by biography and statistics.

	MINT	NRMT	EXC
COMPLETE SET(26)	5.00	2.20	.60

☐ 1172 Dave Bird
☐ 1173 Steve Buckholz
☐ 1174 Jason Bullard
☐ 1175 Stan Fansler
☐ 1176 Lee Hancock
☐ 1177 Bobby Hunter
☐ 1178 Rich Robertson
☐ 1179 Brian Shouse
☐ 1180 Dave Teller
☐ 1181 Paul Wagner
☐ 1182 Ben Webb
☐ 1183 Mike Zimmerman
☐ 1184 Keith Osik
☐ 1185 Mandy Romero
☐ 1186 Jessie Torres
☐ 1187 Mark Johnson
☐ 1188 Austin Manahan
☐ 1189 Bruce Schreiber
☐ 1190 Ben Shelton
☐ 1191 Scott Bullett
☐ 1192 Alberto De Los Santos
☐ 1193 Tom Green
☐ 1194 Daryl Ratliff
☐ 1195 Don Werner
☐ 1196 Rich Chiles
☐ 1197 Checklist

1992 Carolina Mudcats SkyBox

	MINT	NRMT	EXC
COMPLETE SET (26)	5.00	2.20	.60

☐ 126 Dave Bird
☐ 127 Steve Buckholz
☐ 128 Jason Bullard
☐ 129 Scott Bullett
☐ 130 Steve Cooke
☐ 131 Alberto de los Santos
☐ 132 Greg Edge
☐ 133 Chris Estep
☐ 134 Stan Fansler
☐ 135 Lee Hancock
☐ 136 Mark Johnson
☐ 137 Austin Manahan
☐ 138 Keith Osik
☐ 139 Daryl Ratliff
☐ 140 Roman Rodriguez
☐ 141 Mandy Romero
☐ 142 Ben Shelton
☐ 143 Brian Shouse
☐ 144 Dennis Tafoya
☐ 145 Jessie Torres
☐ 146 Paul Wagner
☐ 147 Ben Webb
☐ 148 Mike Zimmerman
☐ 149 Don Werner MG
☐ 150 Rich Chiles CO
☐ NNO Checklist

1992 Cedar Rapids Reds Classic/Best

This 31-card standard-size set of the 1992 Cedar Rapids Reds, a Class A Midwest League affiliate of the Cincinnati Reds, features white-bordered posed color player photos on its fronts. The player's name, team, and position appear at the bottom. The white back is framed by a thin red line and carries the player's name and position at the top, followed by biography, statistics and team logos.

	MINT	NRMT	EXC
COMPLETE SET (31)	5.00	2.20	.60

☐ 1 Keith Gordon
☐ 2 Gene Taylor
☐ 3 Leonard Griffen
☐ 4 Johnny Ray
☐ 5 Tom Raffo
☐ 6 Matt Giegling
☐ 7 Mike Ferry
☐ 8 Keith Kessinger
☐ 9 Reggie Leslie
☐ 10 Chris Hook
☐ 11 Larry Luebbers
☐ 12 Jon Fuller
☐ 13 Rodney Steph
☐ 14 Joe DeBerry
☐ 15 Rusty Kilgo
☐ 16 Mike Jones
☐ 17 Steve Gibralter
☐ 18 Kevin Riggs
☐ 19 Chris Vasquez
☐ 20 Willie Greene
☐ 21 Craig Pueschner
☐ 22 Scott Plemmons
☐ 23 Scott Duff
☐ 24 Calvain Culberson
☐ 25 Sean Doty
☐ 26 Brian Koelling
☐ 27 Ryan Edwards
☐ 28 Mark Berry MG
☐ 29 Mack Jenkins CO
☐ 30 Tom Iverson TR
Checklist
☐ 31 Logo Card

1992 Cedar Rapids Reds Fleer/ProCards

This 30-card standard-size set of the 1992 Cedar Rapids Reds, a Class A Midwest League affiliate of the Cincinnati Reds, features brown-bordered posed color player photos on its fronts. The player's name appears in an upper corner; his team and position appear in a lower corner. The white back is framed by a black line and carries the player's name at the top, followed by biography and statistics.

	MINT	NRMT	EXC
COMPLETE SET(30)	5.00	2.20	.60

☐ 1061 Calvain Culberson
☐ 1062 Scott Dodd
☐ 1063 Sean Doty
☐ 1064 Scott Duff
☐ 1065 Ryan Edwards
☐ 1066 Mike Ferry
☐ 1067 Leonard Griffen
☐ 1068 Chris Hook
☐ 1069 Rusty Kilgo
☐ 1070 Reggie Leslie
☐ 1071 Larry Luebbers
☐ 1072 Scott Plemmons
☐ 1073 Rodney Steph
☐ 1074 Jon Fuller
☐ 1075 Matt Giegling
☐ 1076 Joe DeBerry
☐ 1077 Mike Jones
☐ 1078 Keith Kessinger
☐ 1079 Brian Koelling
☐ 1080 Tom Raffo
☐ 1081 Kevin Riggs
☐ 1082 Chris Estep
☐ 1083 Steve Gibralter
☐ 1084 Keith Gordon
☐ 1085 Bernie Jenkins
☐ 1086 Craig Pueschner
☐ 1087 Chris Vasquez
☐ 1088 Gene Taylor
☐ 1089 Mark Berry
☐ 1090 Checklist

1992 Charleston (WV) Wheelers Classic/Best

This 30-card standard-size set of the 1992 Charleston Wheelers, a Class A South Atlantic League affiliate of the Cincinnati Reds, features white-bordered posed color player photos on its fronts. The player's name, team, and position appear at the bottom. The white back is framed by a thin red line and carries the player's name and position at the top, followed by biography, statistics and team logos.

	MINT	NRMT	EXC
COMPLETE SET (30)	5.00	2.20	.60

☐ 1 Calvin Reese
☐ 2 Charles McClain
☐ 3 John Hrusovsky
☐ 4 Fermin Garcia
☐ 5 Ernie Nieves
☐ 6 Richard Zastoupil
☐ 7 Tucker Hammargren
☐ 8 Mike Harrison
☐ 9 Rich Langford
☐ 10 Motorboat Jones
☐ 11 Elliott Quinones
☐ 12 Kevin Jarvis
☐ 13 Armando Morales
☐ 14 John Courtright
☐ 15 K.C. Gillum
☐ 16 Jamie Dismuke
☐ 17 Greg Hammond
☐ 18 Scott Robinson
☐ 19 Carl Stewart
☐ 20 Amador Arias
☐ 21 Bobby Perna
☐ 22 Lenny Wentz
☐ 23 P.J. Carey MG
☐ 24 Tom Spencer TR
☐ 25 Logo Card
☐ 26 Logo Card
☐ 27 Logo Card
☐ 28 Logo Card
☐ 29 Logo Card
☐ 30 Checklist

1992 Charleston Rainbows Classic/Best

This 30-card standard-size set of the 1992 Charleston Rainbows, a Class A South Atlantic League affiliate of the San Diego Padres, features white-bordered posed color player photos on its fronts. The player's name, team, and position appear at the bottom. The white back is framed by a thin red line and carries the player's name and position at the top, followed by biography, statistics and team logos. This issue includes the minor league card debut of Joey Hamilton.

	MINT	NRMT	EXC
COMPLETE SET (30)	8.00	3.60	1.00

☐ 1 Manny Cora
☐ 2 Adan Ayala
☐ 3 Mark Anthony
☐ 4 Stacy Hamm
☐ 5 J.J. Burns
☐ 6 Greg Mucerino
☐ 7 John Roberts
☐ 8 Brian D'Amato
☐ 9 Marcelino DeLaCruz
☐ 10 Jeff Huber
☐ 11 Juan Cruz
☐ 12 Charlie Greene
☐ 13 Richard Loiselle
☐ 14 David Lebak
☐ 15 German Carrion
☐ 16 Homer Bush
☐ 17 Clint Compton
☐ 18 John Barnes
☐ 19 Saul Soltero
☐ 20 Dave Mowry
☐ 21 Joey Hamilton
☐ 22 Dave Trembley MG
☐ 23 Jack Lamabe CO
☐ 24 Jaime Moreno CO
☐ 25 Logo Card
☐ 26 Logo Card
☐ 27 Logo Card
☐ 28 Logo Card
☐ 29 Logo Card
☐ 30 Checklist

1992 Charleston Rainbows Fleer/ProCards

This 28-card standard-size set of the 1992 Charleston Rainbows, a Class A South Atlantic League affiliate of the San Diego Padres, features brown-bordered posed color player photos on its fronts. The player's name appears in an upper corner; his team and position appear in a lower corner. The white back is framed by a black line and carries the player's name at the top, followed by biography and statistics.

	MINT	NRMT	EXC
COMPLETE SET(28)	5.00	2.20	.60

☐ 111 Greg Anthony
☐ 112 Jon Barnes
☐ 113 Jerry Burns
☐ 114 Eric Ciocca
☐ 115 Brian D'Amato
☐ 116 Richard Loiselle
☐ 117 Michael Grohs
☐ 118 Craig Hanson
☐ 119 Jeff Huber
☐ 120 Saul Soltero
☐ 121 Adan Ayala
☐ 122 Charlie Greene
☐ 123 Tim Hall
☐ 124 Homer Bush
☐ 125 German Carrion
☐ 126 Manny Cora
☐ 127 Kyle Moody
☐ 128 David Mowry
☐ 129 Greg Mucerino
☐ 130 Bill Ostermeyer
☐ 131 Mark Anthony
☐ 132 Stacy Hamm
☐ 133 David Lebak
☐ 134 John Roberts
☐ 135 Dave Trembley
☐ 136 Jack Lamabe
☐ 137 Jaime Moreno
☐ 138 Checklist

1992 Charleston Wheelers Fleer/ProCards

This 25-card standard-size set of the 1992 Charleston Wheelers, a Class A South Atlantic League affiliate of the Cincinnati Reds, features brown-bordered posed color player photos on its fronts. The player's name appears in an upper corner; his team and position appear in a lower corner. The white back is framed by a black line and carries the player's name at the top, followed by biography and statistics.

	MINT	NRMT	EXC
COMPLETE SET(25)	5.00	2.20	.60

☐ 1 John Courtright
☐ 2 Fermin Garcia
☐ 3 John Hrusovsky
☐ 4 Kevin Jarvis
☐ 5 Rich Langford
☐ 6 Charles McClain
☐ 7 Armando Morales
☐ 8 Ernie Nieves
☐ 9 Richard Zastoupil
☐ 10 Roy Hammargren
☐ 11 Greg Hammond
☐ 12 Mike Harrison
☐ 13 Amador Arias
☐ 14 Robert Carlsen
☐ 15 Jamie Dismuke
☐ 16 Bobby Perna
☐ 17 Calvin Reese
☐ 18 Lenny Wentz
☐ 19 K.C. Gillum
☐ 20 Bob Jesperson
☐ 21 Eugene Jones
☐ 22 Elliott Quinones
☐ 23 P.J.Carey
☐ 24 Derek Botelho
☐ 25 Checklist

1992 Charlotte Knights Fleer/ProCards

This 25-card standard-size set of the 1992 Charlotte Knights, a Class AA Southern League affiliate of the Chicago Cubs, features brown-bordered posed color player photos on its fronts. The player's name appears in an upper corner; his team and position appear in a lower corner. The white back is framed by a black line and carries the player's name at the top, followed by biography and statistics.

	MINT	NRMT	EXC
COMPLETE SET(25)	5.00	2.20	.60

☐ 2764 Troy Bradford
☐ 2765 Ryan Hawblitzel
☐ 2766 Jessie Hollins
☐ 2767 Eric Jaques
☐ 2768 Paul Marak
☐ 2769 Bill Melvin
☐ 2770 Mike Sodders
☐ 2771 Dave Swartzbaugh
☐ 2772 Steve Trachsel

☐ 2773 Travis Willis
☐ 2774 Jim Robinson
☐ 2775 Matt Walbeck
☐ 2776 Rich Casarotti
☐ 2777 Rusty Crockett
☐ 2778 Chris Ebright
☐ 2779 Matt Franco
☐ 2780 Mike Grace
☐ 2781 Billy White
☐ 2782 Phil Dauphin
☐ 2783 Richie Grayum
☐ 2784 John Jensen
☐ 2785 Doug Welch
☐ 2786 Marv Foley
☐ 2787 Bill Earley
☐ 2788 Checklist

1992 Charlotte Knights SkyBox

	MINT	NRMT	EXC
COMPLETE SET (26)	5.00	2.20	.60

☐ 151 Rusty Crockett
☐ 152 Phil Dauphin
☐ 153 Darrin Duffy
☐ 154 Chris Ebright
☐ 155 Matt Franco
☐ 156 Mike Grace
☐ 157 Richie Grayum
☐ 158 Ryan Hawblitzel
☐ 159 Jessie Hollins
☐ 160 Eric Jaques
☐ 161 John Jensen
☐ 162 Bill Melvin
☐ 163 Tim Parker
☐ 164 Jimmy Robinson
☐ 165 Mike Sodders
☐ 166 Dave Stevens
☐ 167 Julio Strauss
☐ 168 Dave Swartzbaugh
☐ 169 Steve Trachsel
☐ 170 Matt Walbeck
☐ 171 Doug Welch
☐ 172 Billy White
☐ 173 Jerrone Williams
☐ 174 Marv Foley MG
☐ 175 Bill Earley CO
☐ NNO Checklist

1992 Charlotte Rangers Classic/Best

This 30-card standard-size set of the 1992 Charlotte Rangers, a Class A Florida State League affiliate of the Texas Rangers, features white-bordered posed color player photos on its fronts. The player's name, team, and position appear at the bottom. The white back is framed by a thin red line and carries the player's name and position at the top, followed by biography, statistics and team logos.

	MINT	NRMT	EXC
COMPLETE SET (30)	5.00	2.20	.60

☐ 1 David Lowery
☐ 2 Michael Burton
☐ 3 Benigno Castillo
☐ 4 Roger Luce
☐ 5 Frank Turco
☐ 6 Craig Newkirk
☐ 7 James Hurst
☐ 8 Joseph Roebuck
☐ 9 Albert Felix
☐ 10 Christopher Gies
☐ 11 Anthony Bouton
☐ 12 Lawrence Hanlon
☐ 13 David Rolls
☐ 14 Miguel Castellano
☐ 15 James Clinton
☐ 16 Sid Holland
☐ 17 James Vleck
☐ 18 David Geeve
☐ 19 Darren Oliver
☐ 20 Barry Goetz
☐ 21 Kurt Miller
☐ 22 Shelby Shaw
☐ 23 Steven Dreyer
☐ 24 Michael Arner
☐ 25 Terry Burrows
☐ 26 Bump Wills MG
☐ 27 Marvin White CO
☐ 28 Doug Sisson CO
☐ 29 Kevin Blaske TR
☐ 30 Checklist

1992 Charlotte Rangers Fleer/ProCards

This 27-card standard-size set of the 1992 Charlotte Rangers, a Class A Florida State League affiliate of the Texas Rangers, features brown-bordered posed color player photos on its fronts. The player's name appears in an upper corner; his team and position appear in a lower corner. The white back is framed by a black line and carries the player's name at the top, followed by biography and statistics.

	MINT	NRMT	EXC
COMPLETE SET(27)	5.00	2.20	.60

☐ 2043 Checklist
☐ 2217 Jose Alberro
☐ 2218 Tony Bouton
☐ 2219 Joe Brownholtz
☐ 2220 Steven Dreyer
☐ 2221 David Geeve
☐ 2222 Barry Goetz
☐ 2223 James Hurst
☐ 2224 David Perez
☐ 2225 Steve Sadecki
☐ 2226 Shelby Shaw
☐ 2227 Roger Luce
☐ 2228 David Rolls
☐ 2229 Mike Burton
☐ 2230 Miguel Castellanos
☐ 2231 James Clinton
☐ 2232 Larry Hanlon
☐ 2233 David Lowery
☐ 2234 Craig Newkirk
☐ 2235 Frank Turco
☐ 2236 Benigno Castillo
☐ 2237 Sid Holland
☐ 2238 Timmie Morrow
☐ 2239 Joe Roebuck
☐ 2240 Bump Wills
☐ 2241 Doug Sisson
☐ 2242 Marvin White

1992 Chattanooga Lookouts Fleer/ProCards

This 27-card standard-size set of the 1992 Chattanooga Lookouts, a Class AA Southern League affiliate of the Cincinnati Reds, features brown-bordered posed color player photos on its fronts. The player's name appears in an upper corner; his team and position appear in a lower corner. The white back is framed by a black line and carries the player's name at the top, followed by biography and statistics.

	MINT	NRMT	EXC
COMPLETE SET(27)	5.00	2.20	.60

☐ 3810 Mike Anderson
☐ 3811 Bobby Ayala
☐ 3812 Matt Grott
☐ 3813 Rodney Imes
☐ 3814 Rusty Kilgo
☐ 3815 Larry Luebbers
☐ 3816 David Lynch
☐ 3817 Johnny Ray
☐ 3818 Scott Robinson
☐ 3819 John Roper
☐ 3820 Jason Satre
☐ 3821 Jerry Spradlin
☐ 3822 Darron Cox
☐ 3823 Glenn Sutko
☐ 3824 Tim Costo
☐ 3825 Kevin Garner
☐ 3826 Willie Greene
☐ 3827 Ty Griffin
☐ 3828 Frank Kremblas
☐ 3829 Ben Colvard
☐ 3830 Chris Estep
☐ 3831 Scott Pose
☐ 3832 Todd Trafton
☐ 3833 Ron Oester
☐ 3834 Mike Griffin
☐ 3835 Tom Nieto
☐ 3836 Checklist

1992 Chattanooga Lookouts SkyBox

	MINT	NRMT	EXC
COMPLETE SET (26)	5.00	2.20	.60

☐ 176 Rick Allen
☐ 177 Mike Anderson
☐ 178 Bobby Ayala
☐ 179 Ben Colvard
☐ 180 Tim Costo
☐ 181 Darron Cox
☐ 182 Kiki Diaz
☐ 183 Ty Griffin
☐ 184 Matt Grott
☐ 185 Cesar Hernandez
☐ 186 Trevor Hoffman
☐ 187 Rodney Imes
☐ 188 Frank Kremblas
☐ 189 Brian Lane
☐ 190 Reggie Leslie
☐ 191 David Lynch
☐ 192 Scott Pose
☐ 193 Johnny Ray
☐ 194 John Roper
☐ 195 Jerry Spradlin
☐ 196 Glenn Sutko
☐ 197 Kevin Tatar
☐ 198 Dwight Taylor
☐ 199 Dave Miley MG
☐ 200 Tom Nieto CO
Mike Griffin CO
☐ NNO Checklist

1992 Classic/Best

The 1992 Classic/Best Minor League set features top prospects from Double-A and Single-A teams. The cards were sold in a reusable card box initially containing 12 cards but capable of holding a larger quantity. According to Classic, 14,000 numbered and autographed cards of five different superstars were randomly inserted in packs; the players and their quantities are Nolan Ryan (3,000), Mike Schmidt (4,000), Ken Griffey Jr. (3,000), Brien Taylor (3,000) and David McCarty (1,000). The sixth autograph card, that of Royce Clayton (2,000) was randomingly in white jumbo packs. Classic issued a transferable Certificate of Registration to owners mailing in pictures taken showing their autograph card. Classic announced a production run of 20,000 numbered cases. The standard size cards feature on fronts either color or black and white player photos bordered in white. The Classic/Best logo and several red and white lines cut across the bottom of the card; the player's name, position and team appear immediately below. The horizontally oriented backs have biography, statistics and a close-up photo.

	MINT	NRMT	EXC
FACTORY SET (450)	15.00	6.75	1.85
COMPLETE SET (400)	10.00	4.50	1.25
COMPLETE HI SET (50)	5.00	2.20	.60
COMMON CARD (1-450)	.05	.02	.01
☐ 1 Nolan Ryan	1.00	.45	.12
☐ 2 Darius Gash	.05	.02	.01
☐ 3 Brad Ausmus	.05	.02	.01
☐ 4 Mike Gardella	.05	.02	.01
☐ 5 Mark Hutton	.05	.02	.01
☐ 6 Bobby Munoz	.05	.02	.01
☐ 7 Don Sparks	.05	.02	.01
☐ 8 Shane Andrews	.05	.02	.01
☐ 9 Gary Hymel	.05	.02	.01
☐ 10 Roberto Arredondo	.05	.02	.01
☐ 11 Joe Randa	.10	.05	.01
☐ 12 Pedro Grifol	.05	.02	.01
☐ 13 Steve Dixon	.05	.02	.01
☐ 14 John Thomas	.05	.02	.01
☐ 15 Chris Durkin	.05	.02	.01
☐ 16 Jeff Conger	.05	.02	.01
☐ 17 John Farrell	.05	.02	.01
☐ 18 Antonio Mitchell	.05	.02	.01
☐ 19 Matt Ruebel	.05	.02	.01
☐ 20 Darren Burton	.05	.02	.01
☐ 21 Lance Jennings	.05	.02	.01
☐ 22 Kerwin Moore	.05	.02	.01
☐ 23 Julio Bruno	.05	.02	.01
☐ 24 Joe Vitiello	.05	.02	.01
☐ 25 Brook Fordyce	.05	.02	.01
☐ 26 Rob Katzaroff	.05	.02	.01
☐ 27 Julian Vasquez	.05	.02	.01
☐ 28 Alan Zinter	.05	.02	.01
☐ 29 Clemente Alvarez	.05	.02	.01
☐ 30 Scott Cepicky	.05	.02	.01
☐ 31 Mike Mongiello	.05	.02	.01
☐ 32 Tom Redington	.05	.02	.01
☐ 33 Johnny Ruffin	.05	.02	.01
☐ 34 Eric Booker	.05	.02	.01
☐ 35 Manny Martinez	.05	.02	.01
☐ 36 Mike Grimes	.05	.02	.01
☐ 37 Paul Byrd	.05	.02	.01
☐ 38 Brian Giles	.05	.02	.01
☐ 39 David Mlicki	.05	.02	.01
☐ 40 Tracy Sanders	.05	.02	.01
☐ 41 Kyle Washington	.05	.02	.01
☐ 42 Scott Bullett	.05	.02	.01
☐ 43 Steve Cooke	.05	.02	.01
☐ 44 Austin Manahan	.05	.02	.01
☐ 45 Ben Shelton	.05	.02	.01
☐ 46 Joe DeBerry	.05	.02	.01
☐ 47 Steve Gibralter	.10	.05	.01
☐ 48 Willie Greene	.10	.05	.01
☐ 49 Brian Koelling	.05	.02	.01
☐ 50 Larry Luebbers	.05	.02	.01
☐ 51 Greg Pepper Anthony	.05	.02	.01
☐ 52 Homer Bush	.05	.02	.01
☐ 53 Manny Cora	.05	.02	.01
☐ 54 Joey Hamilton	.40	.18	.05
☐ 55 David Mowry	.05	.02	.01
☐ 56 Bobby Perna	.05	.02	.01
☐ 57 Jamie Dismuke	.05	.02	.01
☐ 58 Kenneth Gillum	.05	.02	.01
☐ 59 Calvin Reese	.10	.05	.01
☐ 60 Phil Dauphin	.05	.02	.01
☐ 61 Ryan Hawblitzel	.05	.02	.01
☐ 62 Tim Parker	.05	.02	.01
☐ 63 Dave Swartzbaugh	.05	.02	.01
☐ 64 Billy White	.05	.02	.01
☐ 65 Terry Burrows	.05	.02	.01
☐ 66 Chris Gies	.05	.02	.01
☐ 67 Kurt Miller	.05	.02	.01
☐ 68 Timmie Morrow	.05	.02	.01
☐ 69 Benny Colvard	.05	.02	.01
☐ 70 Tim Costo	.05	.02	.01
☐ 71 Mica Lewis	.05	.02	.01
☐ 72 John Roper	.05	.02	.01
☐ 73 Kevin Tatar	.05	.02	.01
☐ 74 Joel Adamson	.05	.02	.01
☐ 75 Mike Farmer	.05	.02	.01
☐ 76 Kevin Stocker	.15	.07	.02
☐ 77 David Tokheim	.05	.02	.01
☐ 78 Ray Jackson	.05	.02	.01
☐ 79 Dax Jones	.05	.02	.01
☐ 80 Randy Curtis	.05	.02	.01
☐ 81 Eric Reichenbach	.05	.02	.01
☐ 82 Jerome Tolliver	.05	.02	.01
☐ 83 Quilvio Veras	.15	.07	.02
☐ 84 George Evangelista	.05	.02	.01
☐ 85 Pat Bryant	.05	.02	.01
☐ 86 Willie Canate	.05	.02	.01
☐ 87 Brian Lane	.05	.02	.01
☐ 88 Howard Battle	.05	.02	.01
☐ 89 Rob Butler	.05	.02	.01
☐ 90 Carlos Delgado	1.25	.55	.16
☐ 91 Tyler Houston	.05	.02	.01
☐ 92 Troy Hughes	.05	.02	.01
☐ 93 Chipper Jones	4.00	1.80	.50
☐ 94 Mel Nieves	.10	.05	.01
☐ 95 Jose Olmeda	.05	.02	.01
☐ 96 John Finn	.05	.02	.01
☐ 97 Mike Guerrero	.05	.02	.01
☐ 98 Troy O'Leary	.10	.05	.01
☐ 99 Ben Blomdahl	.05	.02	.01
☐ 100 Mike Schmidt	.30	.14	.04
☐ 101 Carlos Burguillos	.05	.02	.01
☐ 102 Kiki Hernandez	.05	.02	.01
☐ 103 Brian DuBose	.05	.02	.01
☐ 104 Kevin Morgan	.05	.02	.01
☐ 105 Justin Thompson	.10	.05	.01
☐ 106 Jason Alstead	.05	.02	.01
☐ 107 Matt Anderson	.05	.02	.01
☐ 108 Brad Pennington	.05	.02	.01
☐ 109 Brad Tyler	.05	.02	.01
☐ 110 Jovino Carvajal	.05	.02	.01
☐ 111 Roger Luce	.05	.02	.01
☐ 112 Ken Powell	.05	.02	.01
☐ 113 Steve Sadecki	.05	.02	.01
☐ 114 Craig Clayton	.05	.02	.01
☐ 115 Russell Davis	.10	.05	.01
☐ 116 Mike Kelly	.05	.02	.01
☐ 117 Javy Lopez	1.25	.55	.16
☐ 118 Doug Piatt	.05	.02	.01
☐ 119 Manny Alexander	.05	.02	.01
☐ 120 Damon Buford	.05	.02	.01
☐ 121 Erik Schullstrom	.05	.02	.01
☐ 122 Mark Smith	.05	.02	.01
☐ 123 Jeff Williams	.05	.02	.01
☐ 124 Reid Cornelius	.05	.02	.01
☐ 125 Tim Laker	.05	.02	.01
☐ 126 Chris Martin	.05	.02	.01
☐ 127 Mike Mathile	.05	.02	.01
☐ 128 Derrick White	.05	.02	.01
☐ 129 Luis Galindez	.05	.02	.01
☐ 130 John Kuehl	.05	.02	.01
☐ 131 Ray McDavid	.05	.02	.01
☐ 132 Sean Mulligan	.05	.02	.01
☐ 133 Tookie Spann	.05	.02	.01
☐ 134 Marcos Armas	.05	.02	.01
☐ 135 Scott Erwin	.05	.02	.01
☐ 136 Johnny Guzman	.05	.02	.01
☐ 137 Mike Mohler	.05	.02	.01
☐ 138 Craig Paquette	.05	.02	.01
☐ 139 Dean Tatarian	.05	.02	.01
☐ 140 Orlando Miller	.05	.02	.01
☐ 141 Tow Maynard	.05	.02	.01
☐ 142 Marc Newfield	.10	.05	.01
☐ 143 Greg Pirkl	.05	.02	.01
☐ 144 Jesus Tavarez	.05	.02	.01
☐ 145 Tom Smith	.05	.02	.01
☐ 146 Brad Seitzer	.05	.02	.01
☐ 147 Brent Brede	.05	.02	.01
☐ 148 Elston Hansen	.05	.02	.01
☐ 149 Jamie Ogden	.05	.02	.01
☐ 150 Rogelio Nunez	.05	.02	.01
☐ 151 Manny Cervantes	.05	.02	.01
☐ 152 David Sartain	.05	.02	.01
☐ 153 Shawn Bryant	.05	.02	.01
☐ 154 Chad Ogea	.05	.02	.01
☐ 155 Manny Ramirez	3.00	1.35	.35
☐ 156 Darrell Whitmore	.05	.02	.01
☐ 157 Greg O'Halloran	.05	.02	.01
☐ 158 Tim Brown	.05	.02	.01
☐ 159 Curtis Pride	.05	.02	.01
☐ 160 Marcus Moore	.05	.02	.01
☐ 161 Robert Perez	.05	.02	.01
☐ 162 Aaron Small	.05	.02	.01
☐ 163 David Tollison	.05	.02	.01
☐ 164 Nigel Wilson	.05	.02	.01
☐ 165 Jim Givens	.05	.02	.01
☐ 166 Dennis McNamara	.05	.02	.01
☐ 167 Kelley O'Neal	.05	.02	.01
☐ 168 Rudy Pemberton	.05	.02	.01
☐ 169 Joe Perona	.05	.02	.01
☐ 170 Brian Warren	.05	.02	.01
☐ 171 Ivan Cruz	.05	.02	.01

☐ 172 Frank Gonzales	.05	.02	.01
☐ 173 Mike Lumley	.05	.02	.01
☐ 174 Brian Warren	.05	.02	.01
☐ 175 Aaron Sele	.10	.05	.01
☐ 176 Gary Carballo	.05	.02	.01
☐ 177 Creighton Gubanich	.05	.02	.01
☐ 178 Brad Parker	.05	.02	.01
☐ 179 Scott Sheldon	.05	.02	.01
☐ 180 Archie Corbin	.05	.02	.01
☐ 181 Phil Hiatt	.05	.02	.01
☐ 182 Domingo Mota	.05	.02	.01
☐ 183 Dan Carlson	.05	.02	.01
☐ 184 Hugh Walker	.05	.02	.01
☐ 185 Joe Ciccarella	.05	.02	.01
☐ 186 John Jackson	.05	.02	.01
☐ 187 Brent Gates	.05	.02	.01
☐ 188 Eric Helfand	.05	.02	.01
☐ 189 Damon Mashore	.05	.02	.01
☐ 190 Curtis Shaw	.05	.02	.01
☐ 191 Jason Wood	.05	.02	.01
☐ 192 Terry Powers	.05	.02	.01
☐ 193 Steve Karsay	.10	.05	.01
☐ 194 Greg Blosser	.05	.02	.01
☐ 195 Gar Finnvold	.05	.02	.01
☐ 196 Scott Hatteberg	.05	.02	.01
☐ 197 Derek Livernois	.05	.02	.01
☐ 198 Jeff McNeely	.05	.02	.01
☐ 199 Rex DeLaNuez	.05	.02	.01
☐ 200 Ken Griffey Jr.	1.00	.45	.12
☐ 201 Pat Meares	.05	.02	.01
☐ 202 Alan Newman	.05	.02	.01
☐ 203 Paul Russo	.05	.02	.01
☐ 204 Anthony Collier	.05	.02	.01
☐ 205 Roberto Petagine	.05	.02	.01
☐ 206 Brian L. Hunter	.50	.23	.06
☐ 207 James Mouton	.10	.05	.01
☐ 208 Tom Nevers	.05	.02	.01
☐ 209 Garret Anderson	.75	.35	.09
☐ 210 Clifton Garrett	.05	.02	.01
☐ 211 Eduardo Perez	.05	.02	.01
☐ 212 Shawn Purdy	.05	.02	.01
☐ 213 Darren Bragg	.05	.02	.01
☐ 214 Glenn Murray	.05	.02	.01
☐ 215 Ruben Santana	.05	.02	.01
☐ 216 Charles(Bubba) Smith	.05	.02	.01
☐ 217 Terry Adams	.05	.02	.01
☐ 218 William(Bill) Bliss	.05	.02	.01
☐ 219 German Diaz	.05	.02	.01
☐ 220 Willie Gardner	.05	.02	.01
☐ 221 Ed Larregui	.05	.02	.01
☐ 222 Tim Garland	.05	.02	.01
☐ 223 Kevin Jordan	.05	.02	.01
☐ 224 Tim Rumer	.05	.02	.01
☐ 225 Jason Robertson	.05	.02	.01
☐ 226 Todd Claus	.05	.02	.01
☐ 227 Julian Heredia	.05	.02	.01
☐ 228 Mark Sweeney	.05	.02	.01
☐ 229 Robert Eenhoorn	.05	.02	.01
☐ 230 Tyler Green	.05	.02	.01
☐ 231 Mike Lieberthal	.10	.05	.01
☐ 232 Ron Lockett	.05	.02	.01
☐ 233 Tom Nuneviller	.05	.02	.01
☐ 234 Sean Ryan	.05	.02	.01
☐ 235 Alvaro Benavides	.05	.02	.01
☐ 236 Kevin Bellomo	.05	.02	.01
☐ 237 Tony Bridges	.05	.02	.01
☐ 238 Eric Whitford	.05	.02	.01
☐ 239 James Bishop	.05	.02	.01
☐ 240 Midre Cummings	.10	.05	.01
☐ 241 Tom Green	.05	.02	.01
☐ 242 Marcus Hanel	.05	.02	.01
☐ 243 Billy Ashley	.10	.05	.01
☐ 244 Matt Howard	.05	.02	.01
☐ 245 Tommy Adams	.05	.02	.01
☐ 246 Craig Bryant	.05	.02	.01
☐ 247 Ron Pezzoni	.05	.02	.01
☐ 248 Barry Miller	.05	.02	.01
☐ 249 Jason McFarlin	.05	.02	.01
☐ 250 Joe Rosselli	.05	.02	.01
☐ 251 Billy Van Landingham	.05	.02	.01
☐ 252 Christopher Seelbach	.05	.02	.01
☐ 253 Jason Bere	.10	.05	.01
☐ 254 Eric Christopherson	.05	.02	.01
☐ 255 Rick Huisman	.05	.02	.01
☐ 256 Kevin McGehee	.05	.02	.01
☐ 257 Salomon Torres	.05	.02	.01
☐ 258 Brian Boehringer	.05	.02	.01
☐ 259 Glenn DiSarcina	.05	.02	.01
☐ 260 Jason Schmidt	.25	.11	.03
☐ 261 Charles Poe	.05	.02	.01
☐ 262 Ricky Bottalico	.10	.05	.01
☐ 263 Tommy Eason	.05	.02	.01
☐ 264 Joel Gilmore	.05	.02	.01
☐ 265 Pat Ruth	.05	.02	.01
☐ 266 Gene Schall	.05	.02	.01
☐ 267 Jim Campbell	.05	.02	.01
☐ 268 Brian Barber	.05	.02	.01
☐ 269 Allen Battle	.05	.02	.01
☐ 270 Marc Ronan	.05	.02	.01
☐ 271 Scott Simmons	.05	.02	.01
☐ 272 Dmitri Young	.20	.09	.03
☐ 273 Butch Huskey	.25	.11	.03
☐ 274 Frank Jacobs	.05	.02	.01
☐ 275 Aaron Ledesma	.05	.02	.01
☐ 276 Jose Martinez	.05	.02	.01
☐ 277 Andy Beasley	.05	.02	.01
☐ 278 Paul Ellis	.05	.02	.01
☐ 279 John Kelly	.05	.02	.01
☐ 280 Jeremy McGarity	.05	.02	.01
☐ 281 Mateo Ozuna	.05	.02	.01
☐ 282 Allen Watson	.05	.02	.01
☐ 283 Francisco Gamez	.05	.02	.01
☐ 284 Leon Glenn	.05	.02	.01
☐ 285 Duane Singleton	.05	.02	.01
☐ 286 Andy Pettitte	2.50	1.10	.30
☐ 287 Donald Harris	.05	.02	.01
☐ 288 Robb Nen	.10	.05	.01
☐ 289 Jose Oliva	.05	.02	.01
☐ 290 Keith Garagozzo	.05	.02	.01
☐ 291 Dan Smith	.05	.02	.01
☐ 292 Kiki Jones	.05	.02	.01
☐ 293 Rich Becker	.15	.07	.02
☐ 294 Mike Durant	.05	.02	.01
☐ 295 Denny Hocking	.05	.02	.01
☐ 296 Mike Lewis	.05	.02	.01
☐ 297 Troy Ricker	.05	.02	.01
☐ 298 Todd Ritchie	.05	.02	.01
☐ 299 Scott Stahoviak	.10	.05	.01
☐ 300 Brien Taylor	.05	.02	.01
☐ 301 Jim Austin	.05	.02	.01
☐ 302 Mike Daniel	.05	.02	.01
☐ 303 Joseph Eischen	.05	.02	.01
☐ 304 Ranbir Grewal	.05	.02	.01
☐ 305 Rondell White	.75	.35	.09
☐ 306 Mark Hubbard	.05	.02	.01
☐ 307 Tate Seefried	.05	.02	.01
☐ 308 Tom Wilson	.05	.02	.01
☐ 309 Benji Gil	.10	.05	.01
☐ 310 Mike Edwards	.05	.02	.01
☐ 311 J.D. Noland	.05	.02	.01
☐ 312 Jay Gainer	.05	.02	.01
☐ 313 Lance Painter	.05	.02	.01
☐ 314 Tim Worrell	.10	.05	.01
☐ 315 Sean Cheetham	.05	.02	.01
☐ 316 Earl Cunningham	.05	.02	.01
☐ 317 Brad Erdman	.05	.02	.01
☐ 318 Paul Torres	.05	.02	.01
☐ 319 Jose Vierra	.05	.02	.01
☐ 320 Chris Gambs	.05	.02	.01
☐ 321 Brandon Wilson	.05	.02	.01
☐ 322 Bret Donovan	.05	.02	.01
☐ 323 Larry Thomas	.05	.02	.01
☐ 324 Brian Griffiths	.05	.02	.01
☐ 325 Chad Schoenvogel	.05	.02	.01
☐ 326 Mandy Romero	.05	.02	.01
☐ 327 Chris Curtis	.05	.02	.01
☐ 328 Jim Campanis	.05	.02	.01
☐ 329 Anthony Manahan	.05	.02	.01
☐ 330 Jason Townley	.05	.02	.01
☐ 331 Fidel Compres	.05	.02	.01
☐ 332 John Ericks	.05	.02	.01
☐ 333 Don Prybylinski	.05	.02	.01
☐ 334 Jason Best	.05	.02	.01
☐ 335 Rob Wishnevski	.05	.02	.01
☐ 336 John Byington	.05	.02	.01
☐ 337 Omar Garcia	.05	.02	.01
☐ 338 Tony Eusebio	.05	.02	.01
☐ 339 Paul Swingle	.05	.02	.01
☐ 340 Mark Zappelli	.05	.02	.01
☐ 341 Bobby Jones	.25	.11	.03
☐ 342 J.R. Phillips	.05	.02	.01
☐ 343 Jim Edmonds	2.00	.90	.25
☐ 344 Greg Hansell	.05	.02	.01
☐ 345 Mike Piazza	4.00	1.80	.50
☐ 346 Mike Busch	.05	.02	.01
☐ 347 Darrell Sherman	.05	.02	.01
☐ 348 Shawn Green	.30	.14	.04
☐ 349 Willie Mota	.05	.02	.01
☐ 350 David McCarty	.05	.02	.01
☐ 351 James Dougherty	.05	.02	.01
☐ 352 Fernando Vina	.05	.02	.01
☐ 353 Ken Huckaby	.05	.02	.01
☐ 354 Joe Vitko	.05	.02	.01
☐ 355 Roberto(Diaz) Mejia	.05	.02	.01
☐ 356 Willis Otanez	.05	.02	.01
☐ 357 Billy Lott	.05	.02	.01
☐ 358 Jason Pruitt	.05	.02	.01
☐ 359 Jorge Fabregas	.05	.02	.01
☐ 360 Mike Stefanski	.05	.02	.01
☐ 361 Robert Saitz	.05	.02	.01
☐ 362 Scott Talanoa	.05	.02	.01
☐ 363 LaRue Baber	.05	.02	.01
☐ 364 Tyrone Hill	.05	.02	.01
☐ 365 Rick Mediavilla	.05	.02	.01
☐ 366 Eddie Williams	.05	.02	.01
☐ 367 Rigo Beltran	.05	.02	.01
☐ 368 Doug VanderWeele	.05	.02	.01
☐ 369 Donnie Elliott	.05	.02	.01
☐ 370 Dan Cholowsky	.05	.02	.01
☐ 371 Derrell Rumsey	.05	.02	.01
☐ 372 Anthony Graffagnino	.05	.02	.01
☐ 373 Scott Ruffcorn	.05	.02	.01
☐ 374 Mike Rossiter	.05	.02	.01
☐ 375 Mike Robertson	.05	.02	.01
☐ 376 P.J. Forbes	.05	.02	.01
☐ 377 Doug Brady	.05	.02	.01
☐ 378 Rick Clelland	.05	.02	.01
☐ 379 Ugueth Urbina	.05	.02	.01
☐ 380 Cliff Floyd	.15	.07	.02
☐ 381 Danny Young	.05	.02	.01
☐ 382 Eddie Ramos	.05	.02	.01
☐ 383 Bob Abreu	1.00	.45	.12
☐ 384 Gary Mota	.05	.02	.01
☐ 385 Tony Womack	.05	.02	.01
☐ 386 Jeff Motuzas	.05	.02	.01
☐ 387 Desi Relaford	.05	.02	.01
☐ 388 John Elerman	.05	.02	.01
☐ 389 Walt McKeel	.05	.02	.01
☐ 390 Tim VanEgmond	.05	.02	.01
☐ 391 Frank Rodriguez	.10	.05	.01
☐ 392 Paul Carey	.05	.02	.01
☐ 393 Michael Matheny	.05	.02	.01
☐ 394 George Glinatsis	.05	.02	.01
☐ 395 Checklist 1-69	.05	.02	.01
☐ 396 Checklist 70-138	.05	.02	.01
☐ 397 Checklist 139-207	.05	.02	.01
☐ 398 Checklist 208-276	.05	.02	.01
☐ 399 Checklist 277-345	.05	.02	.01
☐ 400 Checklist 346-400	.05	.02	.01
☐ 401 Paul Shuey	.05	.02	.01
☐ 402 Derek Jeter	3.00	1.35	.35
☐ 403 Derek Wallace	.05	.02	.01
☐ 404 Sean Lowe	.05	.02	.01
☐ 405 Jim Pittsley	.15	.07	.02
☐ 406 Shannon Stewart	.15	.07	.02
☐ 407 Jamie Arnold	.05	.02	.01
☐ 408 Jason Kendall	1.00	.45	.12
☐ 409 Eddie Pearson	.05	.02	.01
☐ 410 Todd Steverson	.05	.02	.01
☐ 411 Dan Serafini	.25	.11	.03
☐ 412 John Burke	.05	.02	.01
☐ 413 Jeff Schmidt	.05	.02	.01
☐ 414 Sherard Clinkscales UER (Name misspelled Sherrard on both sides)	.05	.02	.01
☐ 415 Shon Walker	.15	.07	.02
☐ 416 Brandon Cromer	.05	.02	.01
☐ 417 Johnny Damon	1.25	.55	.16
☐ 418 Michael Moore	.05	.02	.01
☐ 419 Michael Matthews	.05	.02	.01
☐ 420 Brian Sackinsky	.05	.02	.01
☐ 421 Jon Lieber	.15	.07	.02
☐ 422 Danny Clyburn	.50	.23	.06
☐ 423 Chris Smith	.05	.02	.01
☐ 424 Dwain Bostic	.05	.02	.01
☐ 425 Bob Wolcott	.15	.07	.02
☐ 426 Mike Gulan	.05	.02	.01
☐ 427 Yuri Sanchez	.05	.02	.01
☐ 428 Tony Sheffield	.05	.02	.01
☐ 429 Ritchie Moody	.05	.02	.01
☐ 430 Andy Hartung	.05	.02	.01
☐ 431 Trey Beamon	.60	.25	.07
☐ 432 Tim Crabtree	.05	.02	.01
☐ 433 Mark Thompson	.10	.05	.01
☐ 434 John Lynch	.05	.02	.01
☐ 435 Adell Davenport	.05	.02	.01
☐ 436 Juan DeLaRosa	.05	.02	.01
☐ 437 Ben Gonzalez	.05	.02	.01
☐ 438 Lew Hill	.05	.02	.01
☐ 439 Tavo Alvarez	.05	.02	.01
☐ 440 Kevin Meier	.05	.02	.01
☐ 441 Troy Penix	.05	.02	.01
☐ 442 Scott Pose	.05	.02	.01
☐ 443 Scott Samuels	.05	.02	.01
☐ 444 Mark Voisard	.05	.02	.01
☐ 445 Jon Shave	.05	.02	.01
☐ 446 Joel Chimelis	.05	.02	.01
☐ 447 Jesus Martinez	.10	.05	.01
☐ 448 Elgin Bobo	.05	.02	.01
☐ 449 Chad Fonville	.05	.02	.01
☐ 450 Checklist (401-450)	.05	.02	.01

1992 Classic/Best Autographs

	MINT	NRMT	EXC
COMPLETE SET (6)	600.00	275.00	75.00
COMMON CARD (AU1-AU6)	15.00	6.75	1.85
☐ AU1 Ken Griffey Jr. AU/3100	200.00	90.00	25.00
☐ AU2 David McCarty AU/1000	15.00	6.75	1.85
☐ AU3 Nolan Ryan AU/3100	250.00	110.00	31.00
☐ AU4 Mike Schmidt AU/4100	125.00	55.00	15.50
☐ AU5 Brien Taylor AU/3100	15.00	6.75	1.85
☐ AU6 Royce Clayton AU/2000	25.00	11.00	3.10

1992 Classic/Best Blue Bonus

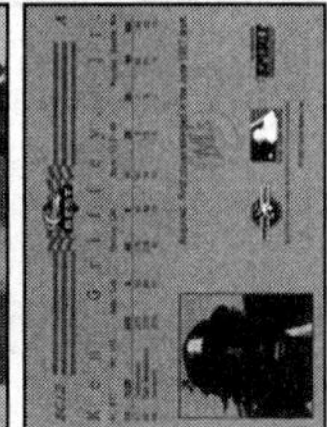

The 30 standard-size cards were inserted one per 1992 Classic/Best Black Jumbo Packs. These borderless cards feature action color player photos. A light-gray stripe at the bottom contains the player's name and team. The Classic/Best logo is superimposed on the bottom of the picture. Three wavy blue stripes emanate from the logo to the card edge. The horizontally oriented backs are light gray and have biographical and statistical information printed in black. A small mugshot is in the lower left corner. The Classic/Best logo and blue stripes appear at the top. The cards are numbered on the back with a "BC" prefix.

	MINT	NRMT	EXC
COMPLETE SET (30)	25.00	11.00	3.10
COMMON CARD (BC1-BC30)	.15	.07	.02
☐ BC1 Nolan Ryan	3.00	1.35	.35
☐ BC2 Mark Hutton	.15	.07	.02
☐ BC3 Shane Andrews	.40	.18	.05
☐ BC4 Scott Bullett	.15	.07	.02
☐ BC5 Kurt Miller	.15	.07	.02
☐ BC6 Carlos Delgado	2.50	1.10	.30
☐ BC7 Chipper Jones	8.00	3.60	1.00
☐ BC8 Dmitri Young	.50	.23	.06
☐ BC9 Mike Kelly	.15	.07	.02
☐ BC10 Javy Lopez	2.50	1.10	.30
☐ BC11 Aaron Sele	.40	.18	.05
☐ BC12 Ken Griffey Jr.	3.00	1.35	.35
☐ BC13 Midre Cummings	.40	.18	.05
☐ BC14 Salomon Torres	.15	.07	.02
☐ BC15 Brien Taylor	.15	.07	.02
☐ BC16 Mike Piazza	8.00	3.60	1.00
☐ BC17 David McCarty	.15	.07	.02
☐ BC18 Scott Ruffcorn	.15	.07	.02
☐ BC19 Cliff Floyd	.40	.18	.05
☐ BC20 Frank Rodriguez	.40	.18	.05
☐ BC21 Paul Shuey	.15	.07	.02
☐ BC22 Derek Jeter	6.00	2.70	.75
☐ BC23 Derek Wallace	.15	.07	.02
☐ BC24 Shannon Stewart	.40	.18	.05
☐ BC25 Jamie Arnold	.15	.07	.02
☐ BC26 Jason Kendall	2.00	.90	.25
☐ BC27 Todd Steverson	.15	.07	.02
☐ BC28 Dan Serafini	.50	.23	.06
☐ BC29 John Burke	.15	.07	.02
☐ BC30 Michael Moore	.15	.07	.02

1992 Classic/Best Red Bonus

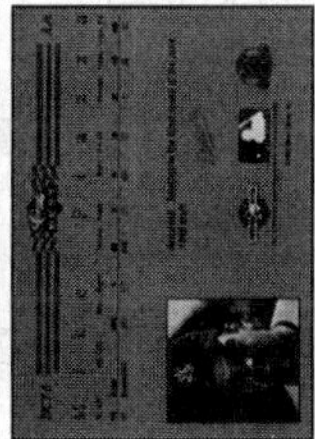

The 20 standard-size cards in this set were inserted one per 1992 Classic/Best Black Jumbo Packs. These borderless cards feature action color player photos. A light-gray stripe at the bottom contains the player's name and team. The Classic/Best logo is superimposed on the bottom of the picture. Three wavy red stripes emanate from the logo to the card edge. The horizontally oriented backs are light gray and have biographical and statistical information printed in black. A small mugshot is in the lower left corner. The Classic/ Best logo and red stripes appear at the top. The cards are numbered on the back with a "BC" prefix.

	MINT	NRMT	EXC
COMPLETE SET (20)	20.00	9.00	2.50
COMMON CARD (BC1-BC20)	.15	.07	.02
☐ BC1 Nolan Ryan	3.00	1.35	.35
☐ BC2 Mark Hutton	.15	.07	.02
☐ BC3 Shane Andrews	.40	.18	.05
☐ BC4 Scott Bullett	.15	.07	.02
☐ BC5 Kurt Miller	.15	.07	.02
☐ BC6 Carlos Delgado	2.50	1.10	.30
☐ BC7 Chipper Jones	8.00	3.60	1.00
☐ BC8 Dmitri Young	.50	.23	.06
☐ BC9 Mike Kelly	.15	.07	.02
☐ BC10 Javy Lopez	2.50	1.10	.30
☐ BC11 Aaron Sele	3.00	1.35	.35
☐ BC12 Ken Griffey Jr.	3.00	1.35	.35
☐ BC13 Midre Cummings	.40	.18	.05
☐ BC14 Salomon Torres	.15	.07	.02
☐ BC15 Brien Taylor	.15	.07	.02
☐ BC16 Mike Piazza	8.00	3.60	1.00
☐ BC17 David McCarty	.15	.07	.02
☐ BC18 Scott Ruffcorn	.15	.07	.02
☐ BC19 Cliff Floyd	.40	.18	.05
☐ BC20 Frank Rodriguez	.40	.18	.05

1992 Classic Draft Picks Previews

These five baseball draft preview standard-size cards were inserted into Classic basketball draft pick foil packs. According to the backs, only 11,200 of each card were produced. The fronts display glossy color action player photos with white borders. The player's name appears in a teal stripe beneath the picture. This stripe intersects the Classic logo at the lower left corner, and the word "Preview" wraps around the top of the logo. The brightly colored backs display a drawing of a batter clad in a red-and-purple uniform with a stadium in the background. This picture is accented by two series of short purple diagonal stripes on the left and right. The picture is overprinted with silver foil lettering.

	MINT	NRMT	EXC
COMPLETE SET (5)	6.00	2.70	.75
COMMON CARD (BB1-BB5)	1.00	.45	.12
☐ BB1 Phil Nevin	1.00	.45	.12
☐ BB2 Paul Shuey	1.00	.45	.12
☐ BB3 B.J. Wallace	1.00	.45	.12
☐ BB4 Jeffrey Hammonds	4.00	1.80	.50
☐ BB5 Chad Mottola	1.00	.45	.12

1992 Classic Draft Picks

The 1992 Classic Draft Picks set consists of 125 standard-size cards. The set was sold in 16-card jumbo packs only to the hobby and periodical industries. The production run was reported to be 5,000 individually number cases, and no factory sets were produced. The fronts display color action player photos bordered in white. The player's name appears in a forest green stripe beneath the picture, and his position is printed in a small black bar. On a forest green background with white lettering, the backs present 1991 and 1992 college (and/or high school) statistics, player profile, and biography on the upper portion and a second color player photo on the lower portion. A ten-card flashback subset (cards 86-95) features Mike Mussina, Brien Taylor, and Mike Kelly.

	MINT	NRMT	EXC
COMPLETE SET (125)	8.00	3.60	1.00
COMMON CARD (1-125)	.05	.02	.01
☐ 1 Phil Nevin	.05	.02	.01
☐ 2 Paul Shuey	.05	.02	.01
☐ 3 B.J. Wallace	.05	.02	.01
☐ 4 Jeffrey Hammonds	.25	.11	.03
☐ 5 Chad Mottola	.05	.02	.01
☐ 6 Derek Jeter	2.00	.90	.25
☐ 7 Michael Tucker	.30	.14	.04
☐ 8 Derek Wallace	.05	.02	.01
☐ 9 Kenny Felder	.05	.02	.01
☐ 10 Chad McConnell	.05	.02	.01
☐ 11 Sean Lowe	.05	.02	.01
☐ 12 Ricky Greene	.05	.02	.01
☐ 13 Chris Roberts	.05	.02	.01
☐ 14 Shannon Stewart	.10	.05	.01
☐ 15 Benji Grigsby	.05	.02	.01
☐ 16 Jamie Arnold	.05	.02	.01
☐ 17 Rick Helling	.05	.02	.01
☐ 18 Jason Kendall	.75	.35	.09
☐ 19 Todd Steverson	.05	.02	.01
☐ 20 Dan Serafini	.10	.05	.01
☐ 21 Jeff Schmidt	.05	.02	.01
☐ 22 Sherard Clinkscales	.05	.02	.01
☐ 23 Ryan Luzinski	.05	.02	.01
☐ 24 Shon Walker	.10	.05	.01
☐ 25 Brandon Cromer	.05	.02	.01
☐ 26 Dave Landaker	.05	.02	.01
☐ 27 Mike Mathews	.05	.02	.01
☐ 28 Brian Sackinsky	.05	.02	.01
☐ 29 Jon Lieber	.05	.02	.01
☐ 30 Jim Rosenbohm	.05	.02	.01
☐ 31 DeShawn Warren	.05	.02	.01
☐ 32 Danny Clyburn	.40	.18	.05
☐ 33 Chris Smith	.05	.02	.01
☐ 34 Dwain Bostic	.05	.02	.01
☐ 35 Bobby Hughes	.05	.02	.01
☐ 36 Ricky Magdellano	.05	.02	.01
☐ 37 Bob Wolcott	.05	.02	.01
☐ 38 Mike Gulan	.05	.02	.01
☐ 39 Yuri Sanchez	.05	.02	.01
☐ 40 Tony Sheffield	.05	.02	.01
☐ 41 Dan Melendez	.05	.02	.01
☐ 42 Jason Giambi	1.00	.45	.12
☐ 43 Ritchie Moody	.05	.02	.01
☐ 44 Trey Beamon	.50	.23	.06
☐ 45 Tim Crabtree	.05	.02	.01
☐ 46 Chad Roper	.05	.02	.01
☐ 47 Mark Thompson	.05	.02	.01
☐ 48 Marquis Riley	.05	.02	.01
☐ 49 Tom Knauss	.05	.02	.01
☐ 50 Chris Holt	.15	.07	.02
☐ 51 Jon Nunnally	.05	.02	.01
☐ 52 Everett Stull	.05	.02	.01
☐ 53 Billy Owens	.05	.02	.01
☐ 54 Todd Etler	.05	.02	.01
☐ 55 Benji Simonton	.05	.02	.01
☐ 56 Dwight Maness	.05	.02	.01
☐ 57 Chris Eddy	.05	.02	.01
☐ 58 Brant Brown	.05	.02	.01
☐ 59 Trevor Humphrey	.05	.02	.01
☐ 60 Chris Widger	.05	.02	.01
☐ 61 Steve Montgomery	.05	.02	.01
☐ 62 Chris Gomez	.05	.02	.01
☐ 63 Jared Baker	.05	.02	.01
☐ 64 Doug Hecker	.05	.02	.01
☐ 65 David Spykstra	.05	.02	.01
☐ 66 Scott Miller	.05	.02	.01
☐ 67 Carey Paige	.05	.02	.01
☐ 68 Dave Manning	.05	.02	.01
☐ 69 James Keefe	.05	.02	.01
☐ 70 Levon Largusa	.05	.02	.01
☐ 71 Roger Bailey	.05	.02	.01
☐ 72 Rich Ireland	.05	.02	.01
☐ 73 Matt Williams	.05	.02	.01
☐ 74 Scott Gentile	.05	.02	.01
☐ 75 Hut Smith	.05	.02	.01
☐ 76 Rod Henderson	.05	.02	.01
☐ 77 Mike Buddie	.05	.02	.01
☐ 78 Steve Lyons	.05	.02	.01
☐ 79 John Burke	.05	.02	.01
☐ 80 Jim Pittsley	.15	.07	.02
☐ 81 Donnie Leshnock	.05	.02	.01
☐ 82 Cory Pearson	.05	.02	.01
☐ 83 Kurt Ehmann	.05	.02	.01
☐ 84 Bobby Bonds Jr.	.05	.02	.01
☐ 85 Steve Cox	.40	.18	.05
☐ 86 Brien Taylor	.05	.02	.01
☐ 87 Mike Kelly	.05	.02	.01
☐ 88 David McCarty	.05	.02	.01
☐ 89 Dmitri Young	.15	.07	.02
☐ 90 Joey Hamilton	.05	.02	.01
☐ 91 Mark Smith	.05	.02	.01
☐ 92 Doug Glanville	.05	.02	.01
☐ 93 Mike Lieberthal	.15	.07	.02
☐ 94 Joe Vitiello	.10	.05	.01
☐ 95 Mike Mussina FLB	.40	.18	.05
☐ 96 Derek Hacopian	.05	.02	.01
☐ 97 Ted Corbin	.05	.02	.01
☐ 98 Carlton Fleming	.05	.02	.01
☐ 99 Aaron Rounsifer	.05	.02	.01
☐ 100 Chad Fox	.05	.02	.01
☐ 101 Chris Sheff	.05	.02	.01
☐ 102 Ben Jones	.05	.02	.01
☐ 103 David Post	.05	.02	.01
☐ 104 Johnie Gendron	.05	.02	.01
☐ 105 Bob Juday	.05	.02	.01
☐ 106 David Becker	.05	.02	.01
☐ 107 Brandon Pico	.05	.02	.01
☐ 108 Tom Evans	.15	.07	.02
☐ 109 Jeff Faino	.05	.02	.01
☐ 110 Shawn Wills	.05	.02	.01
☐ 111 Derrick Cantrell	.05	.02	.01
☐ 112 Steve Rodriguez	.05	.02	.01
☐ 113 Ray Suplee	.05	.02	.01
☐ 114 Pat Leahy	.05	.02	.01
☐ 115 Matt Luke	.05	.02	.01
☐ 116 Jon McMullen	.05	.02	.01
☐ 117 Preston Wilson	.40	.18	.05
☐ 118 Gus Gandarillas	.05	.02	.01
☐ 119 Pete Janicki	.05	.02	.01
☐ 120 Byron Mathews	.05	.02	.01
☐ 121 Eric Owens	.05	.02	.01
☐ 122 John Lynch	.05	.02	.01
☐ 123 Mike Hickey	.05	.02	.01
☐ 124 Checklist 1-64	.05	.02	.01
☐ 125 Checklist 65-125	.05	.02	.01

1992 Classic Draft Picks Foil Bonus

One of these twenty foil bonus standard-size cards was inserted in each 1992 Classic Draft Picks jumbo pack. The photos and text of these bonus cards are identical to the regular issues, except that a silver foil coating has created a metallic sheen on the front, and the forest green backs have a faded look. A three-card flashback subset (cards BC18-BC20) features Brien Taylor, Mike Kelly, and Mike Mussina.

	MINT	NRMT	EXC
COMPLETE SET (20)	8.00	3.60	1.00
COMMON CARD (BC1-BC20)	.20	.09	.03
☐ BC1 Phil Nevin	.20	.09	.03
☐ BC2 Paul Shuey	.20	.09	.03
☐ BC3 B.J. Wallace	.20	.09	.03
☐ BC4 Jeffrey Hammonds	.50	.23	.06
☐ BC5 Chad Mottola	.20	.09	.03
☐ BC6 Derek Jeter	3.00	1.35	.35
☐ BC7 Michael Tucker	.60	.25	.07
☐ BC8 Derek Wallace	.20	.09	.03
☐ BC9 Kenny Felder	.20	.09	.03
☐ BC10 Chad McConnell	.20	.09	.03
☐ BC11 Sean Lowe	.20	.09	.03
☐ BC12 Chris Roberts	.20	.09	.03
☐ BC13 Shannon Stewart	.60	.25	.07
☐ BC14 Benji Grigsby	.20	.09	.03
☐ BC15 Jamie Arnold	.20	.09	.03
☐ BC16 Ryan Luzinski	.20	.09	.03
☐ BC17 Bobby Bonds Jr.	.20	.09	.03
☐ BC18 Brien Taylor	.20	.09	.03
☐ BC19 Mike Kelly	.20	.09	.03
☐ BC20 Mike Mussina FLB	1.00	.45	.12

1992 Clearwater Phillies Classic/Best

This 30-card standard-size set of the 1992 Clearwater Phillies, a Class A Florida State League affiliate of the Philadelphia Phillies, features white-bordered posed color player photos on its fronts. The player's name, team, and position appear at the bottom. The white back is framed by a thin red line and carries the player's name and position at the top, followed by biography, statistics and team logos.

	MINT	NRMT	EXC
COMPLETE SET (30)	5.00	2.20	.60

☐ 1 Jeff Jackson
☐ 2 Eric Hill
☐ 3 Darrell Goedhart
☐ 4 Rob Gaddy
☐ 5 Steve Bieser
☐ 6 Mickey Hyde
☐ 7 Jeff Patterson
☐ 8 Michael Farmer
☐ 9 David Tokheim
☐ 10 Kenny Sirak
☐ 11 Lee Langley
☐ 12 Elliott Gray
☐ 13 Bob Wells
☐ 14 Joel Adamson
☐ 15 Terry Tewell
☐ 16 Tony Trevino
☐ 17 J.J. Munoz
☐ 18 Phillip Geisler
☐ 19 Kevin Stocker
☐ 20 Duane Mulville
☐ 21 Rick Meyer
☐ 22 Pat Brady
☐ 23 Ronnie Allen
☐ 24 Ramon Henderson CO
☐ 25 Darold Knowles CO
☐ 26 Craig Strobel TR
☐ 27 Logo Card
☐ 28 Logo Card
☐ 29 Logo Card
☐ 30 Checklist

1992 Clearwater Phillies Fleer/ProCards

This 32-card standard-size set of the 1992 Clearwater Phillies, a Class A Florida State League affiliate of the Philadelphia Phillies, features brown-bordered posed color player photos on its fronts. The player's name appears in an upper corner; his team and position appear in a lower corner. The white back is framed by a black line and carries the player's name at the top, followed by biography and statistics.

	MINT	NRMT	EXC
COMPLETE SET(32)	5.00	2.20	.60

☐ 2045 Joel Adamson
☐ 2046 Ronnie Allen
☐ 2047 Dan Brown
☐ 2048 Andy Carter
☐ 2049 Rocky Elli
☐ 2050 Robert Gaddy
☐ 2051 Joel Gilmore
☐ 2052 Todd Goergen
☐ 2053 Elliot Gray
☐ 2054 Lee Langley
☐ 2055 Darrell Lindsey
☐ 2056 J.J.Munoz
☐ 2057 Mark Randall
☐ 2058 Steve Bieser
☐ 2059 Duane Mulville
☐ 2060 Terry Tewell
☐ 2061 Luis Brito
☐ 2062 Phil Geisler
☐ 2063 Rick Meyer
☐ 2064 Ron Ollison
☐ 2065 Troy Rusk
☐ 2066 Ken Sirak
☐ 2067 Corey Thomas
☐ 2068 Pat Brady
☐ 2069 Mike Farmer
☐ 2070 Jeff Jackson
☐ 2071 Mark Steffens
☐ 2072 David Tokheim
☐ 2073 Bill Dancy
☐ 2074 Ramon Henderson
☐ 2075 Darold Knowles
☐ 2076 Checklist

1992 Clinton Giants Classic/Best

This 30-card standard-size set of the 1992 Clinton Giants, a Class A Midwest League affiliate of the San Francisco Giants, features white-bordered posed color player photos on its fronts. The player's name, team, and position appear at the bottom. The white back is framed by a thin red line and carries the player's name and position at the top, followed by biography, statistics and team logos.

	MINT	NRMT	EXC
COMPLETE SET (30)	5.00	2.20	.60

☐ 1 Dax Jones
☐ 2 Rich Hyde
☐ 3 Angel Ortiz
☐ 4 Mike Boker
☐ 5 Brent Cookson
☐ 6 Ken Feist
☐ 7 Roberto Delgado
☐ 8 Lenny Ayres
☐ 9 Ray Jackson
☐ 10 Andre Keene
☐ 11 Eric Stonecipher
☐ 12 Kurt Peltzer
☐ 13 Chris Gambs
☐ 14 Derek Dana
☐ 15 Jarod Juelsgaard
☐ 16 Chuck Wanke
☐ 17 Doug VanderWeele
☐ 18 Al Rodriguez
☐ 19 Charles Alimena
☐ 20 Adame Tamarez
☐ 21 D.J. Thielen
☐ 22 Tim Florez
☐ 23 Ken Grundt
☐ 24 Marcus Jensen
☐ 25 C.L. Dotolo
☐ 26 Bill Stein MG
☐ 27 Nelson Rood CO
☐ 28 Gary Lucas CO
☐ 29 Bill Carpine Tr
☐ 30 Kevin Temperly
Lorie Baran
Gary Mayse
Administrative Staff
Checklist

1992 Clinton Giants Fleer/ProCards

This 29-card standard-size set of the 1992 Clinton Giants, a Class A Midwest League affiliate of the San Francisco Giants, features brown-bordered posed color player photos on its fronts. The player's name appears in an upper corner; his team and position appear in a lower corner. The white back is framed by a black line and carries the player's name at the top, followed by biography and statistics.

	MINT	NRMT	EXC
COMPLETE SET(29)	5.00	2.20	.60

☐ 3588 Lenny Ayres
☐ 3589 Mike Boker
☐ 3590 Chris Gambs
☐ 3591 Ken Grundt
☐ 3592 Jarod Juelsgaard
☐ 3593 Jeff Locklear
☐ 3594 John Lowery
☐ 3595 Mike McLain
☐ 3596 Angel Ortiz
☐ 3597 Denny Szczechowski
☐ 3598 Bill VanLandingham
☐ 3599 Chuck Wanke
☐ 3600 Dan Calcagno
☐ 3601 Derek Dana
☐ 3602 Marcus Jensen
☐ 3603 C.L.Dotolo
☐ 3604 Andre Keene
☐ 3605 Tom O'Neill
☐ 3606 Adame Tamarez
☐ 3607 D.J.Thielen
☐ 3608 Ken Feist
☐ 3609 Ray Jackson
☐ 3610 Dax Jones
☐ 3611 Brett McGonnigal
☐ 3612 Bill Stein
☐ 3613 Nelson Rood
☐ 3614 Gary Lucas
☐ 3615 Team Picture
☐ 3779 Checklist

1992 Colorado Springs Sky Sox Fleer/ProCards

This 28-card standard-size set of the 1992 Colorado Springs Sky Sox, a Class AAA Pacific Coast League affiliate of the Cleveland Indians, features brown-bordered posed color player photos on its fronts. The player's name appears in an upper corner; his team and position appear in a lower corner. The white back is framed by a black line and carries the player's name at the top, followed by biography and statistics.

	MINT	NRMT	EXC
COMPLETE SET(28)	5.00	2.20	.60

☐ 742 Brad Arnsberg
☐ 743 Eric Bell
☐ 744 Mike Christopher
☐ 745 Terry Clark
☐ 746 Jerry DiPoto
☐ 747 Bruce Egloff
☐ 748 Tom Kramer
☐ 749 Jeff Mutis
☐ 750 Greg Roscoe
☐ 751 Jeff Shaw
☐ 752 Willie Smith
☐ 753 Alan Cockrell
☐ 754 Brian Johnson
☐ 755 Jesse Levis

☐ 756 Mike Aldrete
☐ 757 Alvaro Espinoza
☐ 758 Nelson Liriano
☐ 759 Tony Perezchica
☐ 760 Dave Rohde
☐ 761 Craig Worthington
☐ 762 Beau Allred
☐ 763 Mark Davidson
☐ 764 Wayne Kirby
☐ 765 Donell Nixon
☐ 766 Charlie Manuel
☐ 767 Luis Isaac
☐ 768 Dyar Miller
☐ 769 Checklist

1992 Colorado Springs Sky Sox SkyBox

	MINT	NRMT	EXC
COMPLETE SET (26)	5.00	2.20	.60

☐ 76 Mike Aldrete
☐ 77 Beau Allred
☐ 78 Denis Boucher
☐ 79 Craig Worthington
☐ 80 Mike Christopher
☐ 81 Terry Clark
☐ 82 Alan Cockrell
☐ 83 Mark Davidson
☐ 84 Jerry DiPoto
☐ 85 Daren Epley
☐ 86 Alvaro Espinoza
☐ 87 Wayne Kirby
☐ 88 Tom Kramer
☐ 89 Terry Lee
☐ 90 Jesse Levis
☐ 91 Nelson Liriano
☐ 92 Jeff Mutis
☐ 93 Donell Nixon
☐ 94 Greg Roscoe
☐ 95 Jeff Shaw
☐ 96 D.L. Smith
☐ 97 Lee Tinsley
☐ 98 Kevin Wickander
☐ 99 Charlie Manuel MG
☐ 100 Luis Isaac CO
Dyar Miller CO
☐ NNO Checklist

1992 Columbia Mets Classic/Best

This 30-card standard-size set of the 1992 Columbia Mets, a Class A South Atlantic League affiliate of the New York Mets, features white-bordered posed color player photos on its fronts. The player's name, team, and position appear at the bottom. The white back is framed by a thin red line and carries the player's name and position at the top, followed by biography, statistics and team logos.

	MINT	NRMT	EXC
COMPLETE SET (30)	7.00	3.10	.85

☐ 1 Jerome Tolliver
☐ 2 Hector Ramirez
☐ 3 Ottis Smith
☐ 4 Mike Patrizi
☐ 5 Brad Schorr
☐ 6 Jim Manfred
☐ 7 Greg Beals
☐ 8 Darian Lindsay
☐ 9 Steve Thomas
☐ 10 Jason Jacome
☐ 11 Todd Fiegel
☐ 12 Ricky Otero
☐ 13 Rob Guzik
☐ 14 Randy Farmer
☐ 15 Ed Perozo
☐ 16 Danilo Mompres
☐ 17 Juan Moreno
☐ 18 Craig Bullock
☐ 19 Raul Casanova
☐ 20 Dwight Robinson
☐ 21 Omar Garcia
☐ 22 Jim McCready
☐ 23 Eric Reichenbach
☐ 24 Randy Curtis
☐ 25 Quilvio Veras
☐ 26 Tim Blackwell MG
☐ 27 Jerry Koosman CO
☐ 28 Marlin McPhail CO
☐ 29 David Fricke TR
☐ 30 Checklist

1992 Columbia Mets Fleer/ProCards

This 27-card standard-size set of the 1992 Columbia Mets, a Class A South Atlantic League affiliate of the New York Mets, features brown-bordered posed color player photos on its fronts. The player's name appears in an upper corner; his team and position appear in a lower corner. The white back is framed by a black line and carries the player's name at the top, followed by biography and statistics. This includes the first team set card of Raul Casanova.

	MINT	NRMT	EXC
COMPLETE SET(27)	7.00	3.10	.85

☐ 288 Todd Fiegel
☐ 289 Rob Guzik
☐ 290 Darian Lindsay
☐ 291 Jim Manfred
☐ 292 Jim McCready
☐ 293 Hector Ramirez
☐ 294 Rob Rees
☐ 295 Eric Reichenbach
☐ 296 Brad Schorr
☐ 297 Steve Thomas
☐ 298 Greg Beals
☐ 299 Raul Casanova
☐ 300 Mike Patrizi
☐ 301 Craig Bullock
☐ 302 Randy Farmer
☐ 303 Omar Garcia
☐ 304 Danilo Mompres
☐ 305 Dwight Robinson
☐ 306 Quilvio Veras
☐ 307 Randy Curtis
☐ 308 Juan Moreno
☐ 309 Ricky Otero
☐ 310 Ed Perozo
☐ 311 Jerome Tolliver
☐ 312 Tim Blackwell
☐ 313 Marlin McPhail
☐ 314 Checklist

1992 Columbia Mets PLAY II

1,500 sets were produced.

	MINT	NRMT	EXC
COMPLETE SET(42)	35.00	16.00	4.40

☐ 1 Tim Blackwell
☐ 2 Jerry Koosman
☐ 3 Marlin McPhail
☐ 4 Steve Thomas
☐ 5 Danilo Mompres
☐ 6 Randy Farmer
☐ 7 Omar Garcia
☐ 8 Greg Beals
☐ 9 Ed Perozo
☐ 10 Juan Moreno
☐ 11 Cesar Diaz
☐ 12 Darian Lindsay
☐ 13 Randy Curtis
☐ 14 Jerome Tolliber
☐ 15 Robbie Guzik
☐ 16 Jim McCready
☐ 17 Eric Reichenbach
☐ 18 Todd Fiegel
☐ 19 Ottis Smith
☐ 20 Brad Schorr
☐ 21 Quilvio Veras
☐ 22 Dwight Robinson
☐ 23 Mike Patrizi
☐ 24 Ricky Otero
☐ 25 Craig Bullock
☐ 26 Jim Manfred
☐ 27 Hector Ramirez
☐ 28 Jason Jacome
☐ 29 Tom Engle
☐ 30 Todd Fiegel
Robbie Guzik
Jason Jacome
Brad Schorr
☐ 31 Randy Curtis
Quilvio Veras
Ricky Otero
Randy Farmer
☐ 32 David Fricke
☐ 33 David Williams C/S
Bomber the Mouse
Mascot
☐ 34 Dr.Eric Margenau OW
☐ 35 Bill Shanahan MG
☐ 36 Team Photo Bombers
☐ 37 Team Photo The Spirit
☐ 38 Mark Harmon
☐ 39 Joe Crawford
☐ 40 Bobby Jones
☐ 41 Jose Martinez FB
☐ 42 Butch Huskey FB

1992 Columbia Mets Insert Set PLAY II

Inserted one per 1992 Columbia Mets PLAY II sets. 250 sets were produced.

	MINT	NRMT	EXC
COMPLETE SET(9)	125.00	55.00	15.50

☐ 1 Jose Martinez
☐ 2 Butch Huskey
Chipper Jones
☐ 3 Jose Martinez
☐ 4 Butch Huskey
☐ 5 Bobby Jones
☐ 6 Ricky Otero
☐ 7 Quilvio Veras
☐ 8 Omar Garcia
☐ 9 Jason Jacome

1992 Columbus Clippers Fleer/ProCards

This 28-card standard-size set of the 1992 Columbus Clippers, a Class AAA International League affiliate of the New York Yankees, features brown-bordered posed color player photos on its fronts. The player's name appears in an upper corner; his team and position appear in a lower corner. The white back is framed by a black line and carries the player's name at the top, followed by biography and statistics. This set includes a sixth year card of Bernie Williams.

	MINT	NRMT	EXC
COMPLETE SET(28)	5.00	2.20	.60

☐ 342 Andy Cook
☐ 343 Royal Clayton
☐ 344 Francisco De La Rosa
☐ 345 Mike Draper
☐ 346 Shawn Hillegas
☐ 347 Ed Martel
☐ 348 Sam Militello
☐ 349 David Rosario
☐ 350 Russ Springer
☐ 351 Don Stanford
☐ 352 Larry Stanford
☐ 353 Wade Taylor
☐ 354 Bob Wickman
☐ 355 Brad Ausmus
☐ 356 John Ramos
☐ 357 Dave Sax
☐ 358 Bobby DeJardin
☐ 359 Torey Lovullo
☐ 360 Hensley Meulens
☐ 361 Dave Silvestri
☐ 362 J.T.Snow
☐ 363 Mike Humphreys
☐ 364 Billy Masse
☐ 365 Bernie Williams
☐ 366 Gerald Williams
☐ 367 Rick Down
☐ 368 Mike Heifferon TR
Mike Brown CO
Ted Uhlaender CO
Howard Cassado CO
Coaching Staff
☐ 369 Checklist

1992 Columbus Clippers Police

	MINT	NRMT	EXC
COMPLETE SET (25)	6.00	2.70	.75

☐ 1 Ken Schnacke
Executive
Rick Down
☐ 2 Coaches
Ted Uhlaender
Mike Brown
Hop Cassady
Mike Heifferon TR
☐ 3 Royal Clayton
☐ 4 Francisco de la Rosa
☐ 5 Mike Draper
☐ 6 Ed Martel
☐ 7 Sam Militello
☐ 8 David Rosario
☐ 9 Russ Springer
☐ 10 Don Stanford
☐ 11 Jeff Johnson
☐ 12 Wade Taylor
☐ 13 Bob Wickman
☐ 14 John Ramos
☐ 15 Dave Sax
☐ 16 Bobby DeJardin
☐ 17 Torey Lovullo
☐ 18 Hensley Meulens
☐ 19 David Silvestri
☐ 20 J.T. Snow
☐ 21 Mike Humphreys
☐ 22 Bernie Williams
☐ 23 Billy Masse
☐ 24 Gerald Williams
☐ 25 Chief Jackson
(Police Chief)

1992 Columbus Clippers SkyBox

	MINT	NRMT	EXC
COMPLETE SET (26)	5.00	2.20	.60

☐ 101 Royal Clayton
☐ 102 Bobby DeJardin
☐ 103 Francisco De La Rosa
☐ 104 Mike Draper
☐ 105 Mike Humphreys
☐ 106 Jay Knoblauh
☐ 107 Jeff Livesey
☐ 108 Torey Lovullo
☐ 109 Ed Martel
☐ 110 Billy Masse
☐ 111 Hensley Meulens
☐ 112 Sam Militello
☐ 113 John Ramos
☐ 114 David Rosario
☐ 115 Dave Sax
☐ 116 David Silvestri
☐ 117 J.T. Snow
☐ 118 Russ Springer
☐ 119 Don Stanford
☐ 120 Larry Stanford
☐ 121 Wade Taylor
☐ 122 Gerald Williams
☐ 123 Bernie Williams
☐ 124 Rick Down MG
☐ 125 Mike Brown CO
Hop Cassady CO
Ted Uhlaender CO
☐ NNO Checklist

1992 Columbus Redstixx Fleer/ProCards

This 32-card standard-size set of the 1992 Columbus Redstixx, a Class A South Atlantic League affiliate of the Cleveland Indians, features brown-bordered posed color player photos on its fronts. The player's name appears in an upper corner; his team and position appear in a lower corner. The white back is framed by a black line and carries the player's name at the top, followed by biography and statistics.

	MINT	NRMT	EXC
COMPLETE SET(32)	5.00	2.20	.60

☐ 2378 Andy Baker
☐ 2379 Sam Baker
☐ 2380 Dickie Brown
☐ 2381 Carlos Crawford
☐ 2382 Ian Doyle
☐ 2383 Kenyatta Fleet
☐ 2384 Pep Harris
☐ 2385 Fernando Hernandez
☐ 2386 Joel Johnson
☐ 2387 Kevin Logsdon
☐ 2388 Albie Lopez
☐ 2389 Oscar Resendez
☐ 2390 Paul Shuey
☐ 2391 Alan Waldin
☐ 2392 David Welch
☐ 2393 Mike Crosby
☐ 2394 Nick Sued
☐ 2395 Mark Carbonnet
☐ 2396 Felipe Duran
☐ 2397 Pat Maxwell
☐ 2398 Rod McCall
☐ 2399 Paul Meade
☐ 2401 Robbie Smith
☐ 2402 Pat Bryant
☐ 2403 Willie Canate
☐ 2404 Gershon Dallas
☐ 2405 Sam Hence
☐ 2406 Marc Marini
☐ 2407 Mike Brown
☐ 2408 Fred Gladding
☐ 2409 Checklist
☐ 2420 Pete Rose Jr.

1992 Columbus RedStixx Classic/Best

This 30-card standard-size set of the 1992 Columbus Redstixx, a Class A South Atlantic League affiliate of the Cleveland Indians, features white-bordered posed color player photos on its fronts. The player's name, team, and position appear at the bottom. The white back is framed by a thin red line and carries the player's name and position at the top, followed by biography, statistics and team logos.

	MINT	NRMT	EXC
COMPLETE SET (30)	5.00	2.20	.60

☐ 1 Pete Rose Jr.
☐ 2 Dickie Brown
☐ 3 Pat Bryant
☐ 4 Willie Canate
☐ 5 Pat Maxwell
☐ 6 Carlos Crawford
☐ 7 Sam Hence
☐ 8 Mark Sweeney
☐ 9 Michael Crosby
☐ 10 Marc Marini
☐ 11 Kevin Logsdon
☐ 12 Paul Meade
☐ 13 Mark Charbonnett
☐ 14 Gershon Dallas
☐ 15 Pep Harris
☐ 16 Fernando Hernandez
☐ 17 Nick Sued
☐ 18 Ian Doyles
☐ 19 Albie Lopez
☐ 20 Andy Baker
☐ 21 Alan Walden
☐ 22 Rod McCall
☐ 23 Robbie Smith
☐ 24 Felipe Duran

☐ 25 Brian Buzard
☐ 26 Kenyatta Fleet
☐ 27 Mike Brown MG
☐ 28 Dan Norman CO
☐ 29 Ted Blackwell TR
☐ 30 Checklist

1992 David Lipscomb Bisons

	MINT	NRMT	EXC
COMPLETE SET (25)	10.00	4.50	1.25

☐ 1 Matt Alexander
☐ 2 Al Austelle CO
☐ 3 Randy Bell
Paul Bobo
☐ 4 John Boatman
Chris Lewis
☐ 5 Stephan Britt
☐ 6 Brad Buher
☐ 7 Kerry Coker
☐ 8 Kyle Coker
☐ 9 Jeff Colvin
Bryan Skelton
☐ 10 Ken Dugan CO
☐ 11 Kurt Dugan
Chad Estep
☐ 12 Trent Green
☐ 13 Bailey Heflin
☐ 14 Joey Henson
☐ 15 Kolin Holladay CO
☐ 16 Gary Johnson
☐ 17 Brian Mast
☐ 18 Brent McNutt
☐ 19 Bubba Moneypenny MG
Wally Hitchcox TR
☐ 20 Brent Oliver TR
☐ 21 Michael Rollins
Jeremy Graham
☐ 22 Troy Rorex
☐ 23 Seniors
Kyle Coker
Brent McNutt
Stephan Britt
☐ 24 Kerry Summitt
Alex Irons
☐ 25 Brian Womble

1992 Denver Zephyrs Fleer/ProCards

This 28-card standard-size set of the 1992 Denver Zephyrs, a Class AAA American Association affiliate of the Milwaukee Brewers, features brown-bordered posed color player photos on its fronts. The player's name appears in an upper corner; his team and position appear in a lower corner. The white back is framed by a black line and carries the player's name at the top, followed by biography and statistics.

	MINT	NRMT	EXC
COMPLETE SET(28)	5.00	2.20	.60

☐ 2631 Cal Eldred
☐ 2632 Chris George
☐ 2633 Otis Green
☐ 2634 Jim Hunter
☐ 2635 Mike Ignasiak
☐ 2636 Mark Kiefer
☐ 2637 Mark Lee
☐ 2638 Angel Miranda
☐ 2639 Eric Nolte
☐ 2640 Efrain Valdez
☐ 2641 Rob Wishnevski
☐ 2642 Andy Allanson
☐ 2643 Joe Kmak
☐ 2644 Dave Liddell
☐ 2645 Alex Diaz
☐ 2646 Sandy Guerrero
☐ 2647 John Jaha
☐ 2648 Jeff Kunkel
☐ 2649 Charlie Montoyo
☐ 2650 William Suero
☐ 2651 Jim Tatum
☐ 2652 Jose Valentin
☐ 2653 Kenny Jackson
☐ 2654 Matt Mieske
☐ 2655 Tony Muser
☐ 2656 Bill Campbell
☐ 2657 Lamar Johnson
☐ 2658 Checklist

1992 Denver Zephyrs SkyBox

	MINT	NRMT	EXC
COMPLETE SET (26)	5.00	2.20	.60

☐ 126 Alex Diaz
☐ 127 Cal Eldred
☐ 128 Chris George
☐ 129 Otis Green
☐ 130 Darren Holmes
☐ 131 Mike Ignasiak
☐ 132 Kenneth Jackson
☐ 133 John Jaha
☐ 134 Mark Kiefer
☐ 135 Joe Kmak
☐ 136 Jeff Kunkel
☐ 137 Mark Lee
☐ 138 Dave Liddell
☐ 139 Matt Mieske
☐ 140 Angel Miranda
☐ 141 Charlie Montoyo
☐ 142 Dave Nilsson
☐ 143 Eric Nolte
☐ 144 Jim Olander
☐ 145 Jim Tatum
☐ 146 Efrain Valdez
☐ 147 Jose Valentin
☐ 148 Jim Hunter
☐ 149 Tony Muser MG
☐ 150 Lamar Johnson CO
Bill Campbell CO
☐ NNO Checklist

1992 Dunedin Blue Jays Classic/Best

This 30-card standard-size set of the 1992 Dunedin Blue Jays, a Class A Florida State League affiliate of the Toronto Blue Jays, features white-bordered posed color player photos on its fronts. The player's name, position, and team name appear at the lower right. The white back is framed by a red line and carries the player's name and position at the top, followed by biography and statistics. This issue includes Shawn Green's first Classic/Best team set appearance.

	MINT	NRMT	EXC
COMPLETE SET (30)	14.00	6.25	1.75

☐ 1 Steve Karsay
☐ 2 Jeff Ware
☐ 3 Scott Brow
☐ 4 Eric Brooks
☐ 5 Howard Battle
☐ 6 Brent Bowers
☐ 7 Rob Butler
☐ 8 Shawn Green
☐ 9 Kris Harmes
☐ 10 Tim Hyers
☐ 11 Ricardo Jordan
☐ 12 Mariano Dotel
☐ 13 Scott Grove
☐ 14 Raphael Garcia
☐ 15 Tim Hodge
☐ 16 Tom Singer
☐ 17 Giovanni Carrara
☐ 18 Rick Steed
☐ 19 Ernesto Rodriguez
☐ 20 Carlos Delgado
☐ 21 Hector Tavarez
☐ 22 Kyle Duey
☐ 23 Tom Hotchkiss
☐ 24 Huck Flener
☐ 25 Scott Miller
☐ 26 Dennis Holmberg MG
☐ 27 Hector Torres CO
☐ 28 John Woodworth TR
☐ 29 Bill Monbouquette CO
☐ 30 Kenny Holmberg
Bat Boy
Checklist

1992 Dunedin Blue Jays Fleer/ProCards

This 27-card standard-size set of the 1992 Dunedin Blue Jays, a Class A Florida State League affiliate of the Toronto Blue Jays, features brown-bordered posed color player photos on its fronts. The player's name appears in an upper corner; his team and position appear in a lower corner. The white back is framed by a black line and carries the player's name and position at the top, followed by biography and statistics. This issue includes Shawn Green's first team set card appearance and a fourth year card of Carlos Delgado.

	MINT	NRMT	EXC
COMPLETE SET (27)	14.00	6.25	1.75

☐ 1990 Scott Brow
☐ 1991 Kyle Duey
☐ 1992 Huck Flener
☐ 1993 Joe Ganote
☐ 1994 Scott Grove
☐ 1995 Tom Hotchkiss
☐ 1996 Ricardo Jordan
☐ 1997 Steve Karsay
☐ 1998 Mike Ogliaruso
☐ 1999 Tom Singer
☐ 2000 Rick Steed
☐ 2001 Jeff Ware
☐ 2002 Eric Brooks
☐ 2003 Carlos Delgado
☐ 2004 Sharnol Adriana
☐ 2005 Howard Battle
☐ 2006 Mariano Dotel
☐ 2007 Tim Hyers
☐ 2008 Ernesto Rodriguez
☐ 2009 Brent Bowers
☐ 2010 Rob Butler
☐ 2011 Shawn Green
☐ 2012 Tim Hodge
☐ 2013 Dennis Holmberg MG
☐ 2014 Hector Torres CO
☐ 2015 Bill Monbouquette CO
☐ 2016 Checklist

1992 Durham Bulls Classic/Best

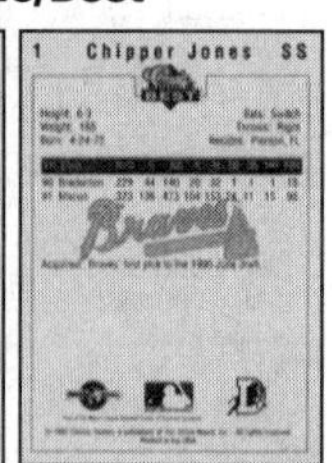

This 30-card standard-size set of the 1992 Durham Bulls, a Class A Carolina League affiliate of the Atlanta Braves, features white-bordered posed color player photos on its fronts. The player's name, team, and position appear at the bottom. The white back is framed by a thin red line and carries the player's name and position at the top, followed by biography, statistics and team logos. This issue includes a second year card of Chipper Jones.

	MINT	NRMT	EXC
COMPLETE SET (30)	20.00	9.00	2.50

☐ 1 Chipper Jones
☐ 2 Johnny Cuevas
☐ 3 Rick Karcher
☐ 4 Scott Ryder
☐ 5 Hector Roa
☐ 6 Osvaldo Sanchez
☐ 7 Lee Heath
☐ 8 Kevin Lomon
☐ 9 Darren Ritter
☐ 10 Grant Brittain
☐ 11 Tim Gillis
☐ 12 Earl Steinmetz
☐ 13 Brad Rippelmeyer
☐ 14 Kevin O'Connor
☐ 15 Troy Hughes
☐ 16 Tyler Houston
☐ 17 Mike Hostetler
☐ 18 Thomas Leahy
☐ 19 Marcos Vasquez
☐ 20 Barry Chiles
☐ 21 Mike Potts
☐ 22 Melvin Nieves
☐ 23 Brad Woodall
☐ 24 David Williams
☐ 25 Leon Roberts MG
☐ 26 Matt West CO
☐ 27 George Threadgill CO
☐ 28 Logo Card
☐ 29 Logo Card
☐ 30 Checklist

1992 Durham Bulls Fleer/ProCards

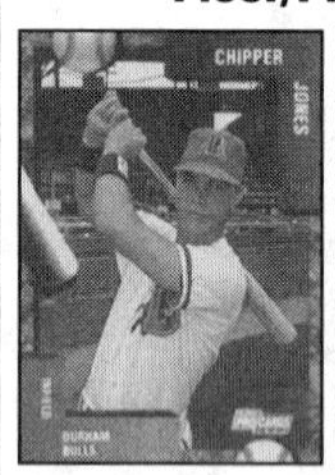

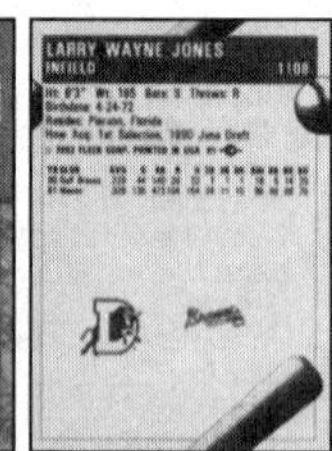

This 28-card standard-size set of the 1992 Durham Bulls, a Class A Carolina League affiliate of the Atlanta Braves, features brown-bordered posed color player photos on its fronts. The player's name appears in an upper corner; his team and position appear in a lower corner. The white back is framed by a black line and carries the player's name at the top, followed by biography and statistics. This set includes a second year card of Chipper Jones.

	MINT	NRMT	EXC
COMPLETE SET(28)	20.00	9.00	2.50

☐ 1092 Barry Chiles
☐ 1093 Roger Hailey
☐ 1094 Mike Hostetler
☐ 1095 Tom Leahy
☐ 1096 Mike Potts
☐ 1097 Darren Ritter
☐ 1098 Scott Ryder
☐ 1099 Blase Sparma
☐ 1100 Earl Steinmetz
☐ 1101 David Williams
☐ 1102 Brad Woodall
☐ 1103 Johnny Cuevas
☐ 1104 Tyler Houston
☐ 1105 Brad Rippelmeyer
☐ 1106 Steve Swail
☐ 1107 Tim Gillis
☐ 1108 Chipper Jones
☐ 1109 Rick Karcher
☐ 1110 Hector Roa
☐ 1111 Ozzie Sanchez
☐ 1112 Lee Heath
☐ 1113 Troy Hughes
☐ 1114 Brian Kowitz
☐ 1115 Leon Roberts
☐ 1116 Doug Baker
☐ 1117 George Threadgrill
☐ 1118 Matt West
☐ 1119 Checklist

1992 Durham Bulls Team Issue

This 28-card standard-size set of the 1992 Durham Bulls, a Class A Carolina League affiliate of the Atlanta Braves features a second year card of Chipper Jones.

	MINT	NRMT	EXC
COMPLETE SET(29)	20.00	9.00	2.50

☐ 2 Hector Roa
☐ 5 Mike Potts
☐ 7 Leon Roberts
☐ 9 Grant Brittain
☐ 10 Chipper Jones
☐ 11 Brad Woodall
☐ 12 Kevin O'Connor
☐ 13 Jose Olmeda
☐ 14 Kevin Lomon
☐ 15 Brad Rippelmeyer
☐ 17 Ozzie Sanchez
☐ 18 Tim Gillis
☐ 19 Tyler Houston
☐ 20 Marcos Vasquez
☐ 21 Melvin Nieves
☐ 22 Rick Karcher
☐ 23 Earl Steinmetz
☐ 24 Mike Hostetler
☐ 25 Tom Leahy
☐ 26 Scott Ryder
☐ 27 Troy Hughes
☐ 28 Johnny Cuevas
☐ 30 Matt West
☐ 31 Darren Ritter
☐ 32 Roger Hailey
☐ 33 Lee Heath
☐ 34 Barry Chiles
☐ 35 David Williams
☐ NNO Team Photo

1992 Edmonton Trappers Fleer/ProCards

This 24-card standard-size set of the 1992 Edmonton Trappers, a Class AAA Pacific Coast League affiliate of the California Angels, features brown-bordered posed color player photos on its fronts. The player's name appears in an upper corner; his team and position appear in a lower corner. The white back is framed by a black line and carries the player's name and position at the top, followed by biography and statistics. This set inlcudes a fifth year card of Tim Salmon.

	MINT	NRMT	EXC
COMPLETE SET (24)	8.00	3.60	1.00

☐ 3533 Chris Beasley
☐ 3534 Mike Butcher
☐ 3535 Tim Fortugno
☐ 3536 Willie Fraser
☐ 3537 Scott Lewis
☐ 3538 John Pawlowski
☐ 3539 Ray Searage
☐ 3540 Don Vidmar
☐ 3541 Mick Billmeyer
☐ 3542 Larry Gonzalez
☐ 3543 Don Barbara
☐ 3544 Damion Easley
☐ 3545 Kevin Flora
☐ 3546 Ramon Martinez
☐ 3547 Ken Oberkfell
☐ 3548 Ty Van Burkleo
☐ 3549 Mark Wasinger
☐ 3550 Phil Bradley
☐ 3551 Tim Salmon
☐ 3552 Reggie Williams
☐ 3553 Max Oliveras MG
☐ 3554 Gary Ruby CO
☐ 3555 Lenn Sakata CO
☐ 3556 Checklist

1992 Edmonton Trappers SkyBox

This 26-card standard-size set of the 1992 Edmonton Trappers, a Class AAA Pacific Coast League affiliate of the California Angels, features white-bordered posed color player photos on its fronts. The player's name appears at the top; his team and position appear at the bottom. The white back carries the player's name at the top, followed by biography and statistics. This set includes a fifth year card of Tim Salmon.

	MINT	NRMT	EXC
COMPLETE SET (26)	8.00	3.60	1.00

☐ 151 Don Barbara
☐ 152 Chris Beasley
☐ 153 Mike Butcher
☐ 154 Damion Easley
☐ 155 John Orton
☐ 156 Kevin Flora
☐ 157 Tim Fortugno
☐ 158 Willie Fraser
☐ 159 Larry Gonzalez
☐ 160 Jose Gonzalez
☐ 161 Todd James
☐ 162 Dave Johnson
☐ 163 Oddibe McDowell
☐ 164 John Pawlowski
☐ 165 Tim Salmon
☐ 166 Ray Soff
☐ 167 Luis Sojo
☐ 168 Mick Billmeyer
☐ 169 Ty Van Burkleo
☐ 170 Don Vidmar
☐ 171 Mark Wasinger
☐ 172 Reggie Williams
☐ 173 Cliff Young
☐ 174 Max Oliveras MG
☐ 175 Lenn Sakata CO
Gary Ruby CO
☐ NNO Checklist

1992 El Paso Diablos Fleer/ProCards

This 27-card standard-size set of the 1992 El Paso Diablos, a Class AA Texas League affiliate of the Milwaukee Brewers, features brown-bordered posed color player photos on its fronts. The player's name appears in an upper corner; his team and position appear in a lower corner. The white back is framed by a black line and carries the player's name at the top, followed by biography and statistics.

	MINT	NRMT	EXC
COMPLETE SET(27)	5.00	2.20	.60

☐ 3913 Jim Czajkowski
☐ 3914 Tim Dell
☐ 3915 Mike Farrell
☐ 3916 Dave Martinez
☐ 3917 Tom McGraw
☐ 3918 Rafael Novoa
☐ 3919 Dave Richards
☐ 3920 Steve Sparks
☐ 3921 Jeff Tabaka
☐ 3922 Scott Taylor
☐ 3923 Brandy Vann
☐ 3924 Craig Faulkner
☐ 3925 Bob Kappesser
☐ 3926 John Byington
☐ 3927 Edgar Caceres
☐ 3928 Bo Dodson
☐ 3929 John Finn
☐ 3930 Mike Guerrero
☐ 3931 Alan Lewis
☐ 3932 Ed Smith
☐ 3933 Michael Carter
☐ 3934 Vince Castaldo
☐ 3935 Tony Diggs
☐ 3936 Troy O'Leary
☐ 3937 Chris Bando
☐ 3938 Rob Derksen
☐ 3939 Checklist

1992 El Paso Diablos SkyBox

	MINT	NRMT	EXC
COMPLETE SET (26)	5.00	2.20	.60

☐ 201 John Byington
☐ 202 Edgar Caceres
☐ 203 Vince Castaldo
☐ 204 Jim Czajkowski
☐ 205 Tim Dell
☐ 206 Tony Diggs
☐ 207 Bo Dodson
☐ 208 Craig Faulkner
☐ 209 John Finn
☐ 210 Dave Fitzgerald
☐ 211 Mike Guerrero
☐ 212 Sandy Guerrero
☐ 213 Rob Wishnevski
☐ 214 Jim Hunter
☐ 215 Bob Kappesser
☐ 216 Alan Lewis
☐ 217 Steve Lienhard
☐ 218 Orestes Marrero
☐ 219 Dave Martinez
☐ 220 Troy O'Leary
☐ 221 Steve Sparks
☐ 222 Jeff Tabaka
☐ 223 Brandy Vann
☐ 224 Chris Bando MG
☐ 225 Rob Derksen CO
☐ NNO Checklist

1992 Elizabethton Twins Classic/Best

This 30-card standard-size set of the 1992 Elizabethton Twins, a Rookie Class Appalachian League affiliate of the Minnesota Twins, features white-bordered posed color player photos on its fronts. The player's name, team, and position appear at the bottom. The white back is framed by a thin red line and carries the player's name and position at the top, followed by biography, statistics and team logos.

	MINT	NRMT	EXC
COMPLETE SET (30)	5.00	2.20	.60

☐ 1 Shawn Miller
☐ 2 Keith Linebarger
☐ 3 Craig Saccavino
☐ 4 Scott Moten
☐ 5 Tim Costic
☐ 6 Thomas Horincewich
☐ 7 Henry Burrough
☐ 8 Kevin Legault
☐ 9 Ken Tirpack
☐ 10 Jeff Horn
☐ 11 Marlon Nava
☐ 12 Rafael Pina
☐ 13 Blanco Pedro
☐ 14 Craig Hawkins
☐ 15 Cory Lidle
☐ 16 Jose Correa
☐ 17 Kenny Norman
☐ 18 Ramon Valette
☐ 19 Glen Evans
☐ 20 Jason Baker
☐ 21 Ronald Caridad
☐ 22 Joey Miller
☐ 23 Ray Smith MG
☐ 24 Rick Tomlin CO
☐ 25 Lanning H. Tucker TR
☐ 26 Logo Card
☐ 27 Logo Card
☐ 28 Logo Card
☐ 29 Logo Card
☐ 30 Checklist

1992 Elizabethton Twins Fleer/ProCards

This 28-card standard-size set of the 1992 Elizabethton Twins, a Rookie Class Appalachian League affiliate of the Minnesota Twins, features brown-bordered posed color player photos on its fronts. The player's name appears in an upper corner; his team and position appear in a lower corner. The white back is framed by a black line and carries the player's name at the top, followed by biography and statistics.

	MINT	NRMT	EXC
COMPLETE SET(28)	5.00	2.20	.60

☐ 3672 Ron Caridad
☐ 3673 Jose Correa
☐ 3674 Gus Gandarillas
☐ 3675 Kevin Legault
☐ 3676 Cory Lidle
☐ 3677 Keith Linebarger
☐ 3678 Shawn Miller
☐ 3679 Scott Moten
☐ 3680 Rafael Pina
☐ 3681 Craig Saccavino
☐ 3682 Jeff Horn
☐ 3683 Todd Taylor
☐ 3684 Pedro Blanco
☐ 3685 Tom Horencewich
☐ 3686 Keith Legree
☐ 3687 Marlo Nava
☐ 3688 Ken Tirpack
☐ 3689 Ramon Vallette
☐ 3690 Jason Baker
☐ 3691 Butch Burrough
☐ 3692 Tim Costic
☐ 3693 Glenn Evans
☐ 3694 Craig Hawkins
☐ 3695 Joey Miller
☐ 3696 Kenny Norman
☐ 3697 Ray Smith
☐ 3698 Rick Tomlin
☐ 3699 Checklist

1992 Elmira Pioneers Classic/Best

This 30-card standard-size set of the 1992 Elmira Pioneers, a Class A New York-Penn League affiliate of the Boston Red Sox, features white-bordered posed color player photos on its fronts. The player's name, team, and position appear at the bottom. The white back is framed by a thin red line and carries the player's name and position at the top, followed by biography, statistics and team logos.

	MINT	NRMT	EXC
COMPLETE SET (30)	5.00	2.20	.60

☐ 1 George Scott
☐ 2 Dan Collier
☐ 3 Bret Donovan
☐ 4 Michael Canton
☐ 5 Craig Bush
☐ 6 Jason Smith
☐ 7 Randy Lawrence
☐ 8 John Crimmins
☐ 9 Todd Carey
☐ 10 Thomas Niles
☐ 11 Quinn Feno
☐ 12 Cesar Martinez
☐ 13 Jose Malave
☐ 14 Leif McKinley
☐ 15 Gerald David
☐ 16 Douglas MacNeil
☐ 17 Mark Senkowitz
☐ 18 Joe Hudson
☐ 19 Bill Selby
☐ 20 Gettys Glaze
☐ 21 Jeff Fanio
☐ 22 Andrew Moore
☐ 23 Bob Juday
☐ 24 Dave Holt MG
☐ 25 Garry Roggenburk CO
☐ 26 James Love TR
☐ 27 Logo Card
☐ 28 Logo Card
☐ 29 Logo Card
☐ 30 Checklist

1992 Elmira Pioneers Fleer/ProCards

This 25-card standard-size set of the 1992 Elmira Pioneers, a Class A New York-Penn League affiliate of the Boston Red Sox, features brown-bordered posed color player photos on its fronts. The player's name appears in an upper corner; his team and position appear in a lower corner. The white back is framed by a black line and carries the player's name at the top, followed by biography and statistics.

	MINT	NRMT	EXC
COMPLETE SET(25)	5.00	2.20	.60

☐ 1374 Craig Bush
☐ 1375 Bret Donovan
☐ 1376 Jeffrey Faino
☐ 1377 Gettys Glaze
☐ 1378 Joe Hudson
☐ 1379 Randy Lawrence
☐ 1380 Doug MacNeil
☐ 1381 Cesar Martinez
☐ 1382 Leif McKinley
☐ 1383 Tom Niles
☐ 1384 John Crimmins
☐ 1385 Mark Senkowitz
☐ 1386 Jason Smith
☐ 1387 Michael Canton
☐ 1388 Todd Carey
☐ 1389 Bob Juday
☐ 1390 Jose Malave
☐ 1391 Andy Moore
☐ 1392 George Scott
☐ 1393 Bill Selby
☐ 1394 Dan Collier
☐ 1395 Gerald Davis
☐ 1396 Quinn Feno
☐ 1397 Garry Roggenburk
☐ 1398 Checklist

1992 Erie Sailors Classic/Best

This 30-card standard-size set of the 1992 Erie Sailors, a Class A New York-Penn League affiliate of the Florida Marlins, features white-bordered posed color player photos on its fronts. The player's name, team, and position appear at the bottom. The white back is framed by a thin red line and carries the player's name and position at the top, followed by biography, statistics and team logos.

	MINT	NRMT	EXC
COMPLETE SET (30)	5.00	2.20	.60

☐ 1 Willie Brown
☐ 2 Matt Peterson
☐ 3 Brad Frazier
☐ 4 Freddie Gamble
☐ 5 Donald Lemon
☐ 6 Tim North
☐ 7 Deron Sample
☐ 8 Mark Skeels
☐ 9 Ryan Whitman
☐ 10 Reynol Mendoza
☐ 11 Dan Roman
☐ 12 Scott Englehart
☐ 13 Scott Samuels
☐ 14 Pat Leahy
☐ 15 Kenny Kendrena
☐ 16 Lou Lucca
☐ 17 John Lynch
☐ 18 Sean Gousha
☐ 19 Doug Pettit
☐ 20 Todd Pridy
☐ 21 Rick Freehling
☐ 22 Ray Cervantes
☐ 23 Brad Clem
☐ 24 Michael Taylor
☐ 25 Luis Cordova
☐ 26 Jerry Stafford
☐ 27 Matt Donahue
☐ 28 Jim Patterson
☐ 29 Tony Torres
☐ 30 Fredi Gonzalez MG
Checklist

1992 Erie Sailors Fleer/ProCards

This 33-card standard-size set of the 1992 Erie Sailors, a Class A New York-Penn League affiliate of the Florida Marlins, features brown-bordered posed color player photos on its fronts. The player's name appears in an upper corner; his team and position appear in a lower corner. The white back is framed by a black line and carries the player's name at the top, followed by biography and statistics.

	MINT	NRMT	EXC
COMPLETE SET(33)	5.00	2.20	.60

☐ 1611 Matt Donahue
☐ 1612 Scott Englehart
☐ 1613 Brad Frazier
☐ 1614 Kenny Kendrena
☐ 1615 Pat Leahy
☐ 1616 Donald Lemon
☐ 1617 John Lynch
☐ 1618 Reynol Mendoza
☐ 1619 Jim Patterson
☐ 1620 Matt Petersen
☐ 1621 Doug Petit
☐ 1622 Dan Roman
☐ 1623 Deron Sample
☐ 1624 Jerry Stafford
☐ 1625 Ryan Whitman
☐ 1626 Sean Gousha
☐ 1627 Mark Skeels
☐ 1628 Mike Taylor
☐ 1629 Raymond Cervantes
☐ 1630 Freddie Gamble
☐ 1631 Lou Lucca
☐ 1632 Tim North
☐ 1633 Todd Pridy
☐ 1634 Tony Torres
☐ 1635 Willie Brown
☐ 1636 Brad Clem
☐ 1637 Luis Cordova
☐ 1638 Rick Freehling
☐ 1639 Scott Samuels
☐ 1640 Fredi Gonzalez
☐ 1643 Jose Castro
☐ 1643 Marty DeMerritt
☐ 1643 Checklist

1992 Eugene Emeralds Classic/Best

This 30-card standard-size set of the 1992 Eugene Emeralds, a Class A Northwest League affiliate of the Kansas City Royals, features white-bordered posed color player photos on its fronts. The player's name, team, and position appear at the bottom. The white back is framed by a thin red line and carries the player's name and position at the top, followed by biography, statistics and team logos.

	MINT	NRMT	EXC
COMPLETE SET (30)	12.00	5.50	1.50

☐ 1 Sherard Clinkscales
☐ 2 Ryan Long
☐ 3 Jeff Haas
☐ 4 Scott Abell
☐ 5 Jeff Antoon
☐ 6 Dave Bladow
☐ 7 Ramy Brooks
☐ 8 Bryan Currier
☐ 9 John Dickens
☐ 10 Aaron Dorlarque
☐ 11 Tracey Ealy
☐ 12 Chris Eddy
☐ 13 Bart Evans
☐ 14 Paul Fletcher
☐ 15 Tom Heming
☐ 16 Jon Lieber
☐ 17 Jason Marshall
☐ 18 Troy McAllister
☐ 19 Darrell McMillin
☐ 20 Cesar Morillo
☐ 21 Jason Pruitt
☐ 22 Chris Sheehan
☐ 23 Steve Sisco
☐ 24 Larry Sutton
☐ 25 Mike Sweeney
☐ 26 Brian Teeters
☐ 27 John Weglarz
☐ 28 Logo Card
☐ 29 Logo Card
☐ 30 Team Photo
Checklist

1992 Eugene Emeralds Fleer/ProCards

This 30-card standard-size set of the 1992 Eugene Emeralds, a Class A Northwest League affiliate of the Kansas City Royals, features brown-bordered posed color player photos on its fronts. The player's name appears in an upper corner; his team and position appear in a lower corner. The white back is framed by a black line and carries the player's name at the top, followed by biography and statistics. This set inlcudes the first team set card of Mike Sweeney.

	MINT	NRMT	EXC
COMPLETE SET(30)	12.00	5.50	1.50

☐ 3017 Dave Bladow
☐ 3018 Sherard Clinkscales
☐ 3019 Bryan Currier
☐ 3020 John Dickens
☐ 3021 Aaron Dorlarque
☐ 3022 Chris Eddy
☐ 3023 Bart Evans
☐ 3024 Paul Fletcher
☐ 3025 Jeff Haas
☐ 3026 Tom Heming
☐ 3027 Jon Lieber
☐ 3028 Jason Pruitt
☐ 3029 Chris Sheehan
☐ 3030 John Weglarz
☐ 3031 Scott Abell
☐ 3032 Ramy Brooks
☐ 3033 Mike Sweeney
☐ 3034 Jeff Antoon
☐ 3035 Ryan Long
☐ 3036 Jason Marshall
☐ 3037 Troy McAllister
☐ 3038 Cesar Morillo
☐ 3039 Steve Sisco
☐ 3040 Larry Sutton
☐ 3041 David Cornell
☐ 3042 Tracey Ealy
☐ 3043 Darrell McMillin
☐ 3044 Brian Teeters
☐ 3649 Team Picture
☐ 3650 Checklist

1992 Everett Giants Classic/Best

This 30-card standard-size set of the 1992 Everett Giants, a Class A Northwest League affiliate of the San Francisco Giants, features white-bordered posed color player photos on its fronts. The player's name, team, and position appear at the bottom. The white back is framed by a thin red line and carries the player's name and position at the top, followed by biography, statistics and team logos.

	MINT	NRMT	EXC
COMPLETE SET (30)	5.00	2.20	.60

☐ 1 Mark Saugsrad
☐ 2 Petie Roach
☐ 3 Tim Luther
☐ 4 Marvin Benard
☐ 5 Blair Hanneman
☐ 6 Ken Henderson
☐ 7 Kenny Woods
☐ 8 Scott Stroth
☐ 9 Benji Simonton
☐ 10 Mike McLain
☐ 11 Shelby Hart
☐ 12 Jeff Myers
☐ 13 Butter Jones
☐ 14 Clay King
☐ 15 Mark Peterson
☐ 16 Jim Riley
☐ 17 Papo Ramos
☐ 18 Jamie Brewington
☐ 19 Tom O'Neill
☐ 20 Jeff Richey
☐ 21 Michael Cavanagh
☐ 22 Dennis Szczechowski
☐ 23 Kurt Ehmann
☐ 24 David Baine
☐ 25 Bobby Gorham
☐ 26 Craig Mayes
☐ 27 Charlie Hicks
☐ 28 Chad Fonville
☐ 29 Andy Heckman
☐ 30 Norm Sherry MG
Checklist

1992 Everett Giants Fleer/ProCards

This 32-card standard-size set of the 1992 Everett Giants, a Class A Northwest League affiliate of the San Francisco Giants, features brown-bordered posed color player photos on its fronts. The player's name appears in an upper corner; his team and position appear in a lower corner. The white back is framed by a black line and carries the player's name at the top, followed by biography and statistics.

	MINT	NRMT	EXC
COMPLETE SET(32)	5.00	2.20	.60

☐ 1676 David Baine
☐ 1677 Jamie Brewington
☐ 1678 Bobby Gorham
☐ 1679 Blair Henneman
☐ 1680 Andy Heckman
☐ 1681 Ken Henderson
☐ 1682 Charlie Hicks
☐ 1683 Tim Luther
☐ 1684 Mike McLain
☐ 1685 Jeff Myers
☐ 1686 Mark Peterson
☐ 1687 Jeff Richey
☐ 1688 Jim Riley
☐ 1689 Scott Stroth
☐ 1690 Dennis Szczechowski
☐ 1691 Carlos Valdez
☐ 1692 Michael Cavanagh
☐ 1693 Craig Mayes
☐ 1694 Jason Sievers
☐ 1695 Chad Fonville
☐ 1696 Shelby Hart
☐ 1697 Clay King
☐ 1698 Tom O'Neill
☐ 1699 Petie Roach
☐ 1700 Mark Saugstad
☐ 1701 Kenny Woods
☐ 1702 Marvin Benard
☐ 1703 Butter Jones
☐ 1704 Papo Ramos
☐ 1705 Benji Simonton
☐ 1706 Norm Sherry
☐ 1707 Checklist

1992 Fayetteville Generals Classic/Best

This 30-card standard-size set of the 1992 Fayetteville Generals, a Class A South Atlantic League affiliate of the Detroit Tigers, features white-bordered posed color player photos on its fronts. The player's name, team, and position appear at the bottom. The white back is framed by a thin red line and carries the player's name and position at the top, followed by biography, statistics and team logos.

	MINT	NRMT	EXC
COMPLETE SET (30)	5.00	2.20	.60

☐ 1 Justin Thompson
☐ 2 Ben Blomdahl
☐ 3 Brian Edmondson
☐ 4 John Reid
☐ 5 Brian DuBose
☐ 6 Tarrick Brock
☐ 7 Kevin Miller
☐ 8 Bob Lemany
☐ 9 Greg Haeger
☐ 10 James Merriweather
☐ 11 Todd Bussa
☐ 12 Steve Waite
☐ 13 Dan Bautista
☐ 14 Rich Kelly
☐ 15 Rob Yelton
☐ 16 Art Adams
☐ 17 Justin Mashore
☐ 18 Bob Grable
☐ 19 Tom Schwarber
☐ 20 Pedro Gonzalez
☐ 21 Dave Leonhardt
☐ 22 Evan Pratte
☐ 23 Dennis Walsh
☐ 24 Gerry Groninger MG
☐ 25 Dwight Lowry CO
☐ 26 Sid Monge CO
☐ 27 Bryan Goike TR
☐ 28 Logo Card
☐ 29 Logo Card
☐ 30 Checklist

1992 Fayetteville Generals Fleer/ProCards

This 29-card standard-size set of the 1992 Fayetteville Generals, a Class A South Atlantic League affiliate of the Detroit Tigers, features brown-bordered posed color player photos on its fronts. The player's name appears in an upper corner; his team and position appear in a lower corner. The white back is framed by a black line and carries the player's name at the top, followed by biography and statistics.

	MINT	NRMT	EXC
COMPLETE SET(29)	5.00	2.20	.60

☐ 2159 Ben Blomdahl
☐ 2160 Todd Bussa
☐ 2161 Ken Carlyle
☐ 2162 Brian Edmondson
☐ 2163 Greg Haeger
☐ 2164 Rich Kelley
☐ 2165 Bob Lemay
☐ 2166 John Reid
☐ 2167 Tom Schwarber
☐ 2168 Justin Thompson
☐ 2169 Dennis Walsh
☐ 2170 Shannon Withem
☐ 2171 Tim McConnell
☐ 2172 Kevin Miller
☐ 2173 Rob Yelton
☐ 2174 Brian DuBose
☐ 2175 Dave Leonhardt
☐ 2176 James Merriweather
☐ 2177 Kevin Morgan
☐ 2178 Evan Pratte
☐ 2179 Danny Bautista
☐ 2180 Tarrik Brock
☐ 2181 Carlos Burguillos
☐ 2182 Justin Mashore
☐ 2183 Brian Sullivan
☐ 2184 Gerry Groninger
☐ 2185 Dwight Lowry
☐ 2186 Sid Monge
☐ 2187 Checklist

1992 Frederick Keys Classic/Best

This 30-card standard-size set of the 1992 Frederick Keys, a Class A Carolina League affiliate of the Baltimore Orioles, features white-bordered posed color player photos on its fronts. The player's name, team, and position appear at the bottom. The white back is framed by a thin red line and carries the player's name and position at the top, followed by biography, statistics and team logos.

	MINT	NRMT	EXC
COMPLETE SET (30)	5.00	2.20	.60

☐ 1 Paul Carey
☐ 2 Jim Audley
☐ 3 David Paveloff
☐ 4 Mike Cross
☐ 5 Brad Tippitt
☐ 6 Brad Tyler
☐ 7 Greg Zaun
☐ 8 Stanton Cameron
☐ 9 Jason Alstead
☐ 10 Jim Wawruck
☐ 11 Brad Seitzer
☐ 12 Allen Plaster
☐ 13 Steve Godin
☐ 14 John Polasek
☐ 15 Jim Dedrick
☐ 16 Basilio Ortiz
☐ 17 Jose Millares
☐ 18 Terry Farrar
☐ 19 Matt Anderson
☐ 20 Brad Pennington
☐ 21 Doug McConathy
☐ 22 Tommy Taylor
☐ 23 Joe Borowski
☐ 24 Jimmy Roso
☐ 25 Stacy Jones
☐ 26 Kevin Ryan
☐ 27 Dan Ramirez
☐ 28 Oneri Fleita CO
☐ 29 Logo Card
☐ 30 Checklist

1992 Frederick Keys Fleer/ProCards

This 29-card standard-size set of the 1992 Frederick Keys, a Class A Carolina League affiliate of the Baltimore Orioles, features brown-bordered posed color player photos on its fronts. The player's name appears in an upper corner; his team and position appear in a lower corner. The white back is framed by a black line and carries the player's name at the top, followed by biography and statistics.

	MINT	NRMT	EXC
COMPLETE SET(29)	5.00	2.20	.60

☐ 1797 Matt Anderson
☐ 1798 Joe Borowski
☐ 1799 Tim Dedrick
☐ 1800 Terry Farrar
☐ 1801 Stacy Jones
☐ 1802 Dave Paveloff
☐ 1803 Allen Plaster
☐ 1804 John Polasek
☐ 1805 Kevin Ryan
☐ 1806 Tom Taylor
☐ 1807 Brad Tippitt
☐ 1808 Jimmy Roso
☐ 1809 Greg Zaun
☐ 1810 Mike Coss
☐ 1811 T.R.Lewis
☐ 1812 Doug McConathy
☐ 1813 Jose Millares
☐ 1814 Dan Ramirez
☐ 1815 Brad Seitzer
☐ 1816 Jason Alstead
☐ 1817 Jim Audley
☐ 1818 Stanton Cameron
☐ 1819 Steven Godin
☐ 1820 Basilio Ortiz
☐ 1821 Jim Wawruck
☐ 1822 Bob Miscik
☐ 1823 Oneri Fleita
☐ 1824 John O'Donoghue
☐ 1825 Checklist

1992 Fort Lauderdale Yankees Classic/Best

This 30-card standard-size set of the 1992 Fort Lauderdale Yankees, a Class A Florida State League affiliate of the New York Yankees, features white-bordered posed color player photos on its fronts. The player's name, team, and position appear at the bottom. The white back is framed by a thin red line and carries the player's name and position at the top, followed by biography, statistics and team logos.

	MINT	NRMT	EXC
COMPLETE SET (30)	5.00	2.20	.60

☐ 1 Brien Taylor
☐ 2 Jovino Carvajal
☐ 3 Doug Gogolewski
☐ 4 Robert Eenhoorn
☐ 5 Andres Rodriguez
☐ 6 Jose Pineda
☐ 7 Cesar Perez
☐ 8 Dan Johnston
☐ 9 Tom Carter
☐ 10 Michael Figga
☐ 11 Luis Gallardo
☐ 12 Curtis Ralph
☐ 13 Elston Hansen
☐ 14 Scott Kamieniecki
☐ 15 Scott Romano
☐ 16 Larry Walker
☐ 17 Pat Morphy
☐ 18 Bo Gilliam
☐ 19 Brian Faw
☐ 20 Brian Turner
☐ 21 Tim Demerson
☐ 22 Ricky Rhodes
☐ 23 Brian Butterfield MG
☐ 24 Mark Shiflett CO
☐ 25 Bob Marino CO
☐ 26 Logo Cards
☐ 27 Logo Cards
☐ 28 Logo Cards
☐ 29 Logo Cards
☐ 30 Checklist

1992 Fort Lauderdale Yankees Fleer/ProCards

This 31-card standard-size set of the 1992 Fort Lauderdale Yankees, a Class A Florida State League affiliate of the New York Yankees, features brown-bordered posed color player photos on its fronts. The player's name appears in an upper corner; his team and position appear in a lower corner. The white back is framed by a black line and carries the player's name at the top, followed by biography and statistics. This set includes a second year card of Mariano Rivera.

	MINT	NRMT	EXC
COMPLETE SET(31)	8.00	3.60	1.00

☐ 2602 Dennis Burbank
☐ 2603 Tom Carter
☐ 2604 Brian Faw
☐ 2605 Doug Gogolewski
☐ 2606 Jim Haller
☐ 2607 Domingo Jean
☐ 2608 Dan Johnston
☐ 2609 Pat Morphy
☐ 2610 Ricky Rhodes
☐ 2611 Mariano Rivera
☐ 2612 Brien Taylor
☐ 2613 Cesar Perez
☐ 2614 Mike Figga
☐ 2615 John Quintell
☐ 2616 Larry Walker
☐ 2617 Robert Eenhoorn
☐ 2618 Greg Erikson
☐ 2619 Luis Gallardo
☐ 2620 Mike Hankins
☐ 2621 Andres Rodriguez
☐ 2622 Scott Romano
☐ 2623 Brian Turner
☐ 2624 Jovino Carvajal
☐ 2625 Robert Deller
☐ 2626 Carl Everett
☐ 2627 Bo Gilliam
☐ 2628 Rey Noriega
☐ 2629 Brian Bottenfield
☐ 2630 Bob Mariano
☐ 3010 Mark Shiflett
☐ 3011 Checklist

1992 Fort Lauderdale Yankees Team Issue

	MINT	NRMT	EXC
COMPLETE SET (32)	5.00	2.20	.60

☐ 1 Sam Arena EQMG
☐ 2 Dennis Burbank
☐ 3 Brian J. Butterfield MG
☐ 4 Tom Carter
☐ 5 Jovino Carvajal
☐ 6 Tim Demerson
☐ 7 Robert Eenhorn
☐ 8 Greg Erickson
☐ 9 Carl Everett
☐ 10 Brian Faw
☐ 11 Michael Figga
☐ 12 Luis Gallardo
☐ 13 Bo Gilliam
☐ 14 Doug Gogolewski
☐ 15 Jim Haller
☐ 16 Elston Hansen
☐ 17 Kiki Hernandez
☐ 18 Domingo Jean
☐ 19 Dan Johnston

- ☐ 20 Bob Joseph Mariano CO
- ☐ 21 Pat Morphy
- ☐ 22 Cesar Perez
- ☐ 23 Jose Pineda
- ☐ 24 Curtis Ralph
- ☐ 25 Tom Raynor TR
- ☐ 26 Ricky Rhodes
- ☐ 27 Andres Rodriguez
- ☐ 28 Scott Romano
- ☐ 29 Mark Winston Shiflett CO
- ☐ 30 Brien Taylor
- ☐ 31 Brian Turner
- ☐ 32 Larry Walker

1992 Fort Myer Miracle Classic/Best

This 30-card standard-size set of the 1992 Fort Myers Miracle, a Class A Florida State League Independent, features white-bordered posed color player photos on its fronts. The player's name, team, and position appear at the bottom. The white back is framed by a thin red line and carries the player's name and position at the top, followed by biography, statistics and team logos.

	MINT	NRMT	EXC
COMPLETE SET (30)	5.00	2.20	.60

- ☐ 1 Jayson Best
- ☐ 2 Ted Corbin
- ☐ 3 George Evangelista
- ☐ 4 Brian Roberts
- ☐ 5 Apolinar Garcia
- ☐ 6 Pedro Grifol
- ☐ 7 Mike Shirley
- ☐ 8 Brian Raabe
- ☐ 9 Mark Ringkamp
- ☐ 10 Willie Mota
- ☐ 11 Mark Swope
- ☐ 12 Derrell Rumsey
- ☐ 13 Carlos Estevez
- ☐ 14 Tim Nedin
- ☐ 15 David Giberti
- ☐ 16 Tyrone Washington
- ☐ 17 Bart Peterson
- ☐ 18 Mike Misuraca
- ☐ 19 Troy Buckley
- ☐ 20 Nolan Lane
- ☐ 21 Denny Hoppe
- ☐ 22 John Gumpf
- ☐ 23 Greg Wiseman
- ☐ 24 Lance Schuermann
- ☐ 25 Jim Kohn
- ☐ 26 Dan Rohn MG
- ☐ 27 Dennis Burtt CO
- ☐ 28 Mark Stoughton TR
- ☐ 29 Logo Card
- ☐ 30 Checklist

1992 Fort Myers Miracle Fleer/ProCards

This 27-card standard-size set of the 1992 Fort Myers Miracle, a Class A Florida State League Independent, features brown-bordered posed color player photos on its fronts. The player's name appears in an upper corner; his team and position appear in a lower corner. The white back is framed by a black line and carries the player's name at the top, followed by biography and statistics.

	MINT	NRMT	EXC
COMPLETE SET(27)	5.00	2.20	.60

- ☐ 2737 Jayon Best
- ☐ 2738 Apolinar Garcia
- ☐ 2739 Dave Giberti
- ☐ 2740 Denny Hoppe
- ☐ 2741 Jim Kohl
- ☐ 2742 Mike Misuraca
- ☐ 2743 Tim Persing
- ☐ 2744 Bart Peterson
- ☐ 2745 Mark Ringkamp
- ☐ 2746 Lance Schuermann
- ☐ 2747 Mark Swope
- ☐ 2748 Troy Buckley
- ☐ 2749 Pedro Grifol
- ☐ 2750 Brian Roberts
- ☐ 2751 Ted Corbin
- ☐ 2752 Carlos Estevez
- ☐ 2753 George Evangelista
- ☐ 2754 Willie Mota
- ☐ 2755 Brian Raabe
- ☐ 2756 John Gumpf
- ☐ 2757 Derrell Rumsey
- ☐ 2758 Mike Shirley
- ☐ 2759 Greg Wiseman
- ☐ 2760 Dan Rohn
- ☐ 2761 Bob Zeihen
- ☐ 2762 Dennis Burtt
- ☐ 2763 Checklist

1992 Front Row Draft Picks

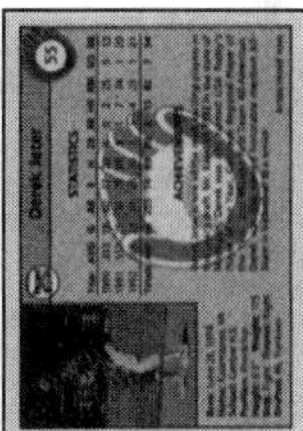

This 100-card standard-size set features color action player photos. According to Front Row, the production run was 10,000 wax cases and 2,500 30-set factory cases (both were individually numbered). Gold and silver foil stamped cards were randomly inserted into wax packs. Also randomly inserted were pure gold cards of Ken Griffey Jr. and Frank Thomas and HOFer signature cards of Brooks Robinson, Yogi Berra, Whitey Ford and others. The fronts feature color action player photos with blue borders that fade as one moves down the card face. The words "Draft Pick '92" appear in a yellow stripe that cuts across the card top, intersecting the Front Row logo at the upper right corner. The player's name in a yellow bar toward the bottom complete the front. On a tan panel featuring the Front Row logo, the horizontally oriented backs carry a color photo of the player in little league, biography, complete amateur statistics, and career achievements.

	MINT	NRMT	EXC
COMPLETE SET (100)	8.00	3.60	1.00
COMMON CARD (1-100)	.05	.02	.01
*GOLD: 4X VALUE			
*SILVER: 2X VALUE			
☐ 1 Dan Melendez	.05	.02	.01
☐ 2 Billy Owens	.05	.02	.01
☐ 3 Sherard Clinkscales	.05	.02	.01
☐ 4 Tim Moore	.05	.02	.01
☐ 5 Mike Hickey	.05	.02	.01
☐ 6 Ken Carlyle	.05	.02	.01
☐ 7 Todd Steverson	.05	.02	.01
☐ 8 Ted Corbin	.05	.02	.01
☐ 9 Tim Crabtree	.05	.02	.01
☐ 10 Jason Angel	.05	.02	.01
☐ 11 Mike Gulan	.05	.02	.01
☐ 12 Jared Baker	.05	.02	.01
☐ 13 Mike Buddie	.05	.02	.01
☐ 14 Brandon Pico	.05	.02	.01
☐ 15 Jon Nunnally	.05	.02	.01
☐ 16 Scott Patton	.05	.02	.01
☐ 17 Tony Sheffield	.05	.02	.01
☐ 18 Danny Clyburn	.40	.18	.05
☐ 19 Tom Knauss	.05	.02	.01
☐ 20 Carey Paige	.05	.02	.01
☐ 21 Keith Johnson	.05	.02	.01
☐ 22 Larry Mitchell	.05	.02	.01
☐ 23 Tim Leger	.05	.02	.01
☐ 24 Doug Hecker	.05	.02	.01
☐ 25 Aaron Thatcher	.05	.02	.01
☐ 26 Marquis Riley	.05	.02	.01
☐ 27 Jamie Taylor	.05	.02	.01
☐ 28 Don Wengert	.05	.02	.01
☐ 29 Jason Moler	.05	.02	.01
☐ 30 Kevin Kloek	.05	.02	.01
☐ 31 Kevin Pearson	.05	.02	.01
☐ 32 David Mysel	.05	.02	.01
☐ 33 Chris Holt	.15	.07	.02
☐ 34 Chris Gomez	.05	.02	.01
☐ 35 Joe Hamilton	.05	.02	.01
☐ 36 Brandon Cromer	.05	.02	.01
☐ 37 Lloyd Peever	.05	.02	.01
☐ 38 Gordon Sanchez	.05	.02	.01
☐ 39 Bonus Card	.05	.02	.01
☐ 40 Jason Giambi	1.00	.45	.12
☐ 41 Sean Runyan	.05	.02	.01
☐ 42 Jamie Keefe	.05	.02	.01
☐ 43 Scott Gentile	.05	.02	.01
☐ 44 Michael Tucker	.30	.14	.04
☐ 45 Scott Klingenbeck	.05	.02	.01
☐ 46 Ed Christian	.05	.02	.01
☐ 47 Scott Miller	.05	.02	.01
☐ 48 Rick Navarro	.05	.02	.01
☐ 49 Bill Selby	.05	.02	.01
☐ 50 Chris Roberts	.05	.02	.01
☐ 51 John Dillinger	.05	.02	.01
☐ 52 Keith Johns	.05	.02	.01
☐ 53 Matt Williams	.05	.02	.01
☐ 54 Garvin Alston	.05	.02	.01
☐ 55 Derek Jeter	2.00	.90	.25
☐ 56 Chris Eddy	.05	.02	.01
☐ 57 Jeff Schmidt	.05	.02	.01
☐ 58 Chris Petersen	.05	.02	.01
☐ 59 Chris Sheff	.05	.02	.01
☐ 60 Chad Roper	.05	.02	.01
☐ 61 Rich Ireland	.05	.02	.01
☐ 62 Tibor Brown	.05	.02	.01
☐ 63 Todd Etler	.05	.02	.01
☐ 64 John Turlais	.05	.02	.01
☐ 65 Shawn Holcomb	.05	.02	.01
☐ 66 Ben Jones	.05	.02	.01
☐ 67 Marcel Galligani	.05	.02	.01
☐ 68 Troy Penix	.05	.02	.01
☐ 69 Matt Luke	.05	.02	.01
☐ 70 David Post	.05	.02	.01
☐ 71 Mike Warner	.05	.02	.01
☐ 72 Alexis Aranzamendi	.05	.02	.01
☐ 73 Larry Hingle	.05	.02	.01
☐ 74 Shon Walker	.10	.05	.01
☐ 75 Mark Thompson	.05	.02	.01
☐ 76 Jon Lieber	.15	.07	.02
☐ 77 Wes Weger	.05	.02	.01
☐ 78 Mike Smith	.05	.02	.01
☐ 79 Ritchie Moody	.05	.02	.01
☐ 80 B.J. Wallace	.05	.02	.01
☐ 81 Rick Helling	.05	.02	.01
☐ 82 Chad Mottola	.05	.02	.01
☐ 83 Brant Brown	.05	.02	.01
☐ 84 Steve Rodriguez	.05	.02	.01
☐ 85 John Vanhof	.05	.02	.01
☐ 86 Brian Wolf	.05	.02	.01
☐ 87 Steve Montgomery	.05	.02	.01
☐ 88 Eric Owens	.05	.02	.01
☐ 89 Jason Kendall	.75	.35	.09
☐ 90 Bob Bennett	.05	.02	.01
☐ 91 Joe Petcka	.05	.02	.01
☐ 92 Jim Rosenbohm	.05	.02	.01
☐ 93 David Manning	.05	.02	.01
☐ 94 David Landaker	.05	.02	.01
☐ 95 Dan Kyslinger	.05	.02	.01
☐ 96 Roger Bailey	.05	.02	.01
☐ 97 Jon Zuber	.05	.02	.01
☐ 98 Steve Cox	.40	.18	.05
☐ 99 Chris Widger	.05	.02	.01
☐ 100 Checklist 1-100	.05	.02	.01

1992 Gastonia Rangers Classic/Best

This 30-card standard-size set of the 1992 Gastonia Rangers, a Class A South Atlantic League affiliate of the Texas Rangers, features white-bordered posed color player photos on its fronts. The player's name, team, and position appear at the bottom. The white back is framed by a thin red line and carries the player's name and position at the top, followed by biography, statistics and team logos.

	MINT	NRMT	EXC
COMPLETE SET (30)	5.00	2.20	.60

- ☐ 1 Benji Gil
- ☐ 2 Steve Sadecki
- ☐ 3 Michael Crespo
- ☐ 4 Bert Gerhart
- ☐ 5 Mark Hampton
- ☐ 6 Jose Alberro
- ☐ 7 Wilson Heredia
- ☐ 8 Joe Brownholtz
- ☐ 9 Jose Texidor
- ☐ 10 Daryl Henderson
- ☐ 11 Darryl Kennedy
- ☐ 12 Mike Edwards
- ☐ 13 Kevin Woodall
- ☐ 14 Bo Magee
- ☐ 15 Kerry Lacy
- ☐ 16 David Gandolph
- ☐ 17 Franklin Parra
- ☐ 18 Paul Matachun
- ☐ 19 Chris Curtis
- ☐ 20 Lanny Williams
- ☐ 21 Steve Burton
- ☐ 22 Mike McCollough
- ☐ 23 Malvin Matos
- ☐ 24 Danny Patterson
- ☐ 25 Walt Williams MG
- ☐ 26 Stan Cliburn CO
- ☐ 27 Andy Graziano TR
- ☐ 28 Logo Card
- ☐ 29 Logo Card
- ☐ 30 Checklist

1992 Gastonia Rangers Fleer/ProCards

This 29-card standard-size set of the 1992 Gastonia Rangers, a Class A South Atlantic League affiliate of the Texas Rangers, features brown-bordered posed color player photos on its fronts. The player's name appears in an upper corner; his team and position appear in a lower corner. The white back is framed by a black line and carries the player's name at the top, followed by biography and statistics.

	MINT	NRMT	EXC
COMPLETE SET(29)	5.00	2.20	.60

- ☐ 2044 Checklist
- ☐ 2243 Chris Curtis
- ☐ 2244 John Dettmer
- ☐ 2245 Jay Franklin
- ☐ 2246 David Gandolph
- ☐ 2247 Mark Hampton
- ☐ 2248 Daryl Henderson
- ☐ 2249 Wilson Heredia
- ☐ 2250 Kerry Lacy
- ☐ 2251 Bo Magee
- ☐ 2252 Ritchie Moody
- ☐ 2253 Danny Patterson
- ☐ 2254 Heath Vaughn
- ☐ 2255 Mike Crespo
- ☐ 2256 Scot Sealy
- ☐ 2257 Lanny Williams
- ☐ 2258 Steve Burton
- ☐ 2259 Mike Edwards
- ☐ 2260 Benji Gil
- ☐ 2261 Paul Matachun
- ☐ 2262 Mike Smith
- ☐ 2263 John Tomasello
- ☐ 2264 Paul List
- ☐ 2265 Malvin Matos
- ☐ 2266 Kenny Powell
- ☐ 2267 Jose Texidor
- ☐ 2268 Walt Williams
- ☐ 2269 Stan Cliburn
- ☐ 2270 Gary Mielke

1992 Geneva Cubs Classic/Best

This 30-card standard-size set of the 1992 Geneva Cubs, a Class A New York-Penn League affiliate of the Chicago Cubs, features white-bordered posed color player photos on its fronts. The player's name, team, and position appear at the bottom. The white back is framed by a thin red line and carries the player's name and position at the top, followed by biography, statistics and team logos.

	MINT	NRMT	EXC
COMPLETE SET (30)	5.00	2.20	.60

- ☐ 1 Pedro Valdez
- ☐ 2 Jose Trujillo
- ☐ 3 Hector Trinidad
- ☐ 4 Chad Tredaway
- ☐ 5 Paul Stojsavljevic
- ☐ 6 Kennie Steenstra
- ☐ 7 Adam Schulhofer
- ☐ 8 Chris Rodriguez
- ☐ 9 Chris Peterson
- ☐ 10 Geno Morones
- ☐ 11 Dan Madsen
- ☐ 12 Collin Kerley
- ☐ 13 Robin Jennings
- ☐ 14 Jonathan Jarolimek
- ☐ 15 Mike Hubbard
- ☐ 16 Scott Gardner
- ☐ 17 Pat Fairly
- ☐ 18 Todd Edwards
- ☐ 19 Darren Dreyer
- ☐ 20 German Diaz
- ☐ 21 Dave DeMoss
- ☐ 22 David Dark
- ☐ 23 Chuck Daniel
- ☐ 24 Darren Tillman
- ☐ 25 London Bradley
- ☐ 26 Greg Mahlberg MG
- ☐ 27 Stan Kyles CO
- ☐ 28 Brad Bierley CO
- ☐ 29 Dick Cummings TR
- ☐ 30 Checklist

1992 Geneva Cubs Fleer/ProCards

This 28-card standard-size set of the 1992 Geneva Cubs, a Class A New York-Penn League affiliate of the Chicago Cubs, features brown-bordered posed color player photos on its fronts. The player's name appears in an upper corner; his team and position appear in a lower corner. The white back is framed by a black line and carries the player's name at the top, followed by biography and statistics.

	MINT	NRMT	EXC
COMPLETE SET(28)	5.00	2.20	.60

- ☐ 1551 Chuck Daniel
- ☐ 1552 David Dark
- ☐ 1553 Darren Dreyer
- ☐ 1554 Todd Edwards
- ☐ 1555 Scott Gardner
- ☐ 1556 Jonathan Jarolimek
- ☐ 1557 Collin Kerley
- ☐ 1558 Geno Morones
- ☐ 1559 Chris Rodriguez
- ☐ 1560 Adam Schulhofer
- ☐ 1561 Kennie Steenstra
- ☐ 1562 Hector Trinidad
- ☐ 1563 Mike Hubbard
- ☐ 1564 Paul Stojsavljevic
- ☐ 1565 Byron Bradley
- ☐ 1566 German Diaz
- ☐ 1567 Pat Fairly
- ☐ 1568 Chris Petersen
- ☐ 1569 Chad Tredaway
- ☐ 1570 Jose Trujillo
- ☐ 1571 Dave DeMoss
- ☐ 1572 Robin Jennings
- ☐ 1573 Dan Madsen
- ☐ 1574 Darren Tillman
- ☐ 1575 Pedro Valdez
- ☐ 1576 Brad Bierley
- ☐ 1577 Stan Kyles
- ☐ 1578 Checklist

1992 Great Falls Dodgers Sports Pro

This issue includes the minor league card debut of Roger Cedeno.

	MINT	NRMT	EXC
COMPLETE SET (30)	10.00	4.50	1.25

- ☐ 1 Ryan Luzinski
- ☐ 2 Vince Jackson
- ☐ 3 Nathan Dunn

☐ 4 Chad Zerbe
☐ 5 Gary Cope
☐ 6 Felix Rodriguez
☐ 7 Chris Latham
☐ 8 Roger Sweeney
☐ 9 David Pyc
☐ 10 Jesus Martinez
☐ 11 Reginald Johnson
☐ 12 Kevin Pincavitch
☐ 13 Craig Watts
☐ 14 Franz Groot
☐ 15 Eddie Rodriguez
☐ 16 David Fitzpatrick
☐ 17 Ryan Henderson
☐ 18 Doug Kimball
☐ 19 Roger Cedeno
☐ 20 Dennis Winicki
☐ 21 Dustin Rennspies
☐ 22 Jason Butcher
☐ 23 Angel Jaime
☐ 24 Brandon Watts
☐ 25 James Martin
☐ 26 German Gonzalez
☐ 27 Frank Smith
☐ 28 Joe Vogelgesang
☐ 29 John Debus CO
☐ 30 Guy Conti CO

1992 Greensboro Hornets Classic/Best

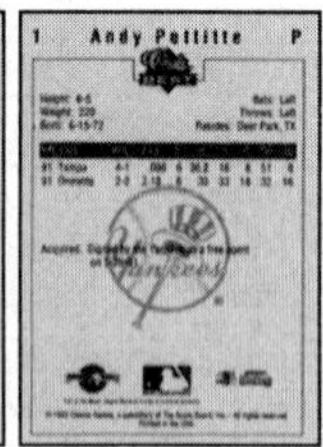

This 30-card standard-size set of the 1992 Greensboro Hornets, a Class A South Atlantic League affiliate of the New York Yankees, features white-bordered posed color player photos on its fronts. The player's name, team, and position appear at the bottom. The white back is framed by a thin red line and carries the player's name and position at the top, followed by biography, statistics and team logos. This issue includes the minor league card debut of Andy Pettitte.

	MINT	NRMT	EXC
COMPLETE SET (30)	25.00	11.00	3.10

☐ 1 Andy Pettitte
☐ 2 Keith Garagozza
☐ 3 Tim Flannelly
☐ 4 Shane Spencer
☐ 5 Andrew Croghan
☐ 6 Frank Laviano
☐ 7 Jorge Posada
☐ 8 Sean Smith
☐ 9 Ben Short
☐ 10 John Thibert
☐ 11 Thomas Wilson
☐ 12 Steve Phillips
☐ 13 Scott Gully
☐ 14 Billy Coleman
☐ 15 Rick Lantrip
☐ 16 Peter Gietzen
☐ 17 Bert Inman
☐ 18 Steve Anderson
☐ 19 Grant Sullivan
☐ 20 Lew Hill
☐ 21 Tim Cooper
☐ 22 Steve Munda
☐ 23 Rich Turrentine
☐ 24 Mark Hubbard
☐ 25 Tate Seefried
☐ 26 Trey Hillman MG
☐ 27 Mark Rose CO
☐ 28 Brian Milner CO
☐ 29 Logo Card
☐ 30 Checklist

1992 Greensboro Hornets Fleer/ProCards

This 30-card standard-size set of the 1992 Greensboro Hornets, a Class A South Atlantic League affiliate of the New York Yankees, features brown-bordered posed color player photos on its fronts. The player's name appears in an upper corner; his team and position appear in a lower corner. The white back is framed by a black line and carries the player's name at the top, followed by biography and statistics. This set inlcudes the first team set card of Andy Pettitte.

	MINT	NRMT	EXC
COMPLETE SET(30)	25.00	11.00	3.10

☐ 770 Billy Coleman
☐ 771 Andy Croghan
☐ 772 Keith Garagozzo
☐ 773 Peter Gietzen
☐ 774 Scott Gully
☐ 775 Bert Inman
☐ 776 Steve Munda
☐ 777 Andy Pettitte
☐ 778 Ben Short
☐ 779 Sean Smith
☐ 780 Grant Sullivan
☐ 781 Jose Pineda
☐ 782 Jorge Posada
☐ 783 Tom Wilson
☐ 784 Steve Anderson
☐ 785 Tim Cooper
☐ 786 Tim Flannelly
☐ 787 Elston Hansen
☐ 788 Rick Lantrip
☐ 789 Tate Seefried
☐ 790 Richard Turrentine
☐ 791 Tim Demerson
☐ 792 Lew Hill
☐ 793 Mark Hubbard
☐ 794 Steve Phillips
☐ 795 Shane Spencer
☐ 796 Trey Hillman
☐ 797 Brian Milner
☐ 798 Mark Rose
☐ 799 Checklist

1992 Greenville Braves Fleer/ProCards

This 25-card standard-size set of the 1992 Greenville Braves, a Class AA Southern League affiliate of the Atlanta Braves, features brown-bordered posed color player photos on its fronts. The player's name appears in an upper corner; his team and position appear in a lower corner. The white back is framed by a black line and carries the player's name at the top, followed by biography and statistics. This set includes a fourth year card of Javy Lopez.

	MINT	NRMT	EXC
COMPLETE SET(25)	8.00	3.60	1.00

☐ 1147 Brian Bark
☐ 1148 Pedro Borbon Jr.
☐ 1149 Dennis Burlingame
☐ 1150 Donnie Elliott
☐ 1151 Judd Johnson
☐ 1152 Don Strange
☐ 1153 Scott Taylor
☐ 1154 Marcos Vasquez
☐ 1155 Preston Watson
☐ 1156 Javy Lopez
☐ 1157 Eduardo Perez
☐ 1158 Mike Bell
☐ 1159 Ed Giovanola
☐ 1160 Pat Kelly
☐ 1161 Mike Mordecai
☐ 1162 Jose Olmeda
☐ 1163 Edwin Alicea
☐ 1164 Mike Kelly
☐ 1165 Melvin Nieves
☐ 1166 Tony Tarasco
☐ 1167 Aubrey Waggoner
☐ 1168 Grady Little
☐ 1169 Mark Ross
☐ 1170 Bill Slack
☐ 1171 Checklist

1992 Greenville Braves SkyBox

	MINT	NRMT	EXC
COMPLETE SET (26)	8.00	3.60	1.00

☐ 226 Edwin Alicea
☐ 227 Brian Bark
☐ 228 Mike Bell
☐ 229 Pedro Borbon Jr.
☐ 230 Dennis Burlingame
☐ 231 Ramon Caraballo
☐ 232 Kevin Coffman
☐ 233 Ed Giovanola
☐ 234 Judd Johnson
☐ 235 Mike Kelly
☐ 236 Pat Kelly
☐ 237 Brian Kowitz
☐ 238 Javier Lopez
☐ 239 Greg McMichael
☐ 240 Nate Minchey
☐ 241 Mike Mordecai
☐ 242 Andy Nezelek
☐ 243 Eduardo Perez
☐ 244 Don Strange
☐ 245 Tony Tarasco
☐ 246 Scott Taylor
☐ 247 Aubrey Waggoner
☐ 248 Preston Watson
☐ 249 Grady Little MG
☐ 250 Randy Ingle CO
Mark Ross CO
☐ NNO Checklist

1992 Gulf Coast Dodgers Fleer/ProCards

This 31-card standard-size set of the 1992 Gulf Coast Dodgers, a Rookie Class A Gulf Coast League affiliate of the Los Angeles Dodgers, features brown-bordered posed color player photos on its fronts. The player's name appears in an upper corner; his team and position appear in a lower corner. The white back is framed by a black line and carries the player's name at the top, followed by biography and statistics. This set includes the first team set cards of Jesus Martinez, Juan Hernaiz and Brian Richardson.

	MINT	NRMT	EXC
COMPLETE SET(31)	15.00	6.75	1.85

☐ 3557 Jason Bobb
☐ 3558 Kenny Cook
☐ 3559 Chris Costello
☐ 3560 Roberto Duran
☐ 3561 Kacy Hendricks
☐ 3562 Dan Markham
☐ 3563 Jesus Martinez
☐ 3564 Jayson Perez
☐ 3565 Danny Sarmiento
☐ 3566 Kevin Smith
☐ 3567 Bill Stephens
☐ 3568 Gavin Edmondson
☐ 3569 Anthony Rodriguez
☐ 3570 Paul Wittig
☐ 3571 Dwain Bostic
☐ 3572 Miguel Cairo
☐ 3573 Eduardo Lantigua
☐ 3574 Tyrone Lewis
☐ 3575 Brian Richardson
☐ 3576 Fausto Urena
☐ 3577 Ervan Wingate
☐ 3578 Paul Flagg
☐ 3579 Eduardo Garcia
☐ 3580 Juan Hernaiz
☐ 3581 Dwight Maness
☐ 3582 Clarence Richmond
☐ 3583 John Shoemakere
☐ 3584 John Knapp
☐ 3585 Luis Tiant
☐ 3586 Doug Simunic
☐ 3587 Checklist

1992 Gulf Coast Mets Fleer/ProCards

This 31-card standard-size set of the 1992 Gulf Coast Mets, a Rookie Class Gulf Coast League affiliate of the New York Mets, features brown-bordered posed color player photos on its fronts. The player's name appears in an upper corner; his team and position appear in a lower corner. The white back is framed by a black line and carries the player's name at the top, followed by biography and statistics. This set includes the first team set card of Jason Isringhausen.

	MINT	NRMT	EXC
COMPLETE SET(31)	15.00	6.75	1.85

☐ 3470 Derek Baker
☐ 3471 Bobby Carr
☐ 3472 John Harris
☐ 3473 Brent Hayward
☐ 3474 Jason Isringhausen
☐ 3475 James Knott
☐ 3476 Justin Krablin
☐ 3477 Allen McDill
☐ 3478 Mark McGinn
☐ 3479 Rafael Roque
☐ 3480 Tyril Sherman
☐ 3481 R.J. Spang
☐ 3482 Ramon Tatis
☐ 3483 Chad Epperson
☐ 3484 Al Hammell
☐ 3485 Heriberto Morales
☐ 3486 Thomas Arvelo
☐ 3487 Bob Daly
☐ 3488 Jose Espinoza
☐ 3489 Mike Farrell
☐ 3490 Josh Haggas
☐ 3491 Stephen Lackey
☐ 3492 Sandy Pichardo
☐ 3493 Rafael Guerrero
☐ 3494 Jerry Hiraldo
☐ 3495 Randy Warner
☐ 3496 Ty Young
☐ 3497 Junior Roman
☐ 3498 Felix Millan
☐ 3499 Jeff Edwards
☐ 3500 Checklist

1992 Gulf Coast Rangers Sports Pro

	MINT	NRMT	EXC
COMPLETE SET (30)	6.00	2.70	.75

☐ 1 Rod Seip
☐ 2 Chris Burr
☐ 3 Jon Pitts
☐ 4 Kevin Dunivan
☐ 5 Luis Perez
☐ 6 Ramino Martinez
☐ 7 Deshon Brown
☐ 8 Jerry Martin
☐ 9 Miguel Ubiera
☐ 10 Leo Perez
☐ 11 Brian Wilson
☐ 12 Hanley Frias
☐ 13 Billy Jo Seaton
☐ 14 Craig Anderson
☐ 15 Luis Garcia
☐ 16 Domingo Delzine
☐ 17 Mario Gonzalez
☐ 18 Jorge Melendez
☐ 19 Guillermo Mercedes
☐ 20 Joey Vallot
☐ 21 Brian Seesz
☐ 22 Corey Pearson
☐ 23 Querbin Reynozo
☐ 24 Jeff Runion
☐ 25 Ray Williams
☐ 26 Tony Riggs
☐ 27 Tom Tisdale TR
☐ 28 Darren Garner CO
☐ 29 Rick Knapp CO
☐ 30 Chino Cadahia MG

1992 Gulf Coast Yankees Fleer/ProCards

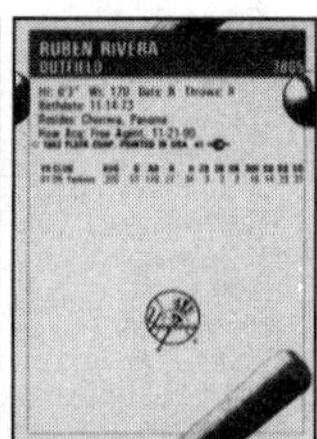

This 30-card standard-size set of the 1992 Gulf Coast Yankees, a Rookie Class Gulf Coast League affiliate of the New York Yankees, features brown-bordered posed color player photos on its fronts. The player's name appears in an upper corner; his team and position appear in a lower corner. The white back is framed by a black line and carries the player's name at the top, followed by biography and statistics. This issue includes the first year cards of Derek Jeter, Ruben Rivera, Ricky Ledee and Marty Janzen.

	MINT	NRMT	EXC
COMPLETE SET(30)	60.00	27.00	7.50

☐ 3701 Glenn Delafield
☐ 3702 Ricky Ledee
☐ 3703 Brian Lewis
☐ 3704 Travion Nelson
☐ 3705 Ruben Rivera
☐ 3706 Gary Denbo
☐ 3707 Rich Arena
☐ 3708 Team Picture
☐ 3709 Checklist
☐ 3780 Charlie Brown
☐ 3781 Jeff Calcaterra
☐ 3782 Tyron Christopher
☐ 3783 Jeff Cindrich
☐ 3784 Shane Ferguson
☐ 3785 Mike Gordon
☐ 3786 Marty Janzen
☐ 3787 Kory Kiper
☐ 3788 Joe Long
☐ 3789 Randall McDermott
☐ 3790 Luis Parra
☐ 3791 Chad Plonk
☐ 3792 Luis Ramirez
☐ 3793 Marcus Gipner
☐ 3794 Jaime Torres
☐ 3795 Cody Beason-Samuels
☐ 3796 Chris Heaps
☐ 3797 Derek Jeter
☐ 3798 Orangel Lopez
☐ 3799 David Renteria
☐ 3800 Jason Wuerch

1992 Hagerstown Suns Fleer/ProCards

This 25-card standard-size set of the 1992 Hagerstown Suns, a Class AA Eastern League affiliate of the Baltimore Orioles, features brown-bordered posed color player photos on its fronts. The player's name appears in an upper corner; his team and position appear in a lower corner. The white back is framed by a black line and carries the player's name at the top, followed by biography and statistics.

	MINT	NRMT	EXC
COMPLETE SET (25)	5.00	2.20	.60

☐ 2549 Jeff Baumgarner
☐ 2550 Tim Drummond
☐ 2551 David Miller
☐ 2552 John O'Donoghue
☐ 2553 John Polasek
☐ 2554 Chuck Ricci

☐ 2555 Erik Schullstrom
☐ 2556 Jeff Williams
☐ 2557 Brian Wood
☐ 2558 Kip Yaughn
☐ 2559 Cesar Devares
☐ 2560 Manny Alexander
☐ 2561 Sam Ferretti
☐ 2562 Tim Holland
☐ 2563 Brent Miller
☐ 2564 Greg Roth
☐ 2565 Brad Tyler
☐ 2566 Mel Wearing
☐ 2567 Damond Buford
☐ 2568 Sergio Cairo
☐ 2569 Mark Smith
☐ 2570 Don Buford MG
☐ 2571 Joe Durham CO
☐ 2572 Moe Drabowsky CO
☐ 2573 Checklist

1992 Hagerstown Suns SkyBox

	MINT	NRMT	EXC
COMPLETE SET (26)	5.00	2.20	.60

☐ 251 Manny Alexander
☐ 252 Rob Blumberg
☐ 253 Damon Buford
☐ 254 Jeff Bumgarner
☐ 255 Sergio Cairo
☐ 256 Mark Carper
☐ 257 Cesar Devares
☐ 258 Sam Ferretti
☐ 259 Tim Holland
☐ 260 Mike Hook
☐ 261 Ed Horowitz
☐ 262 Rodney Lofton
☐ 263 Steve Martin
☐ 264 Brent Miller
☐ 265 David Miller
☐ 266 Daryl Moore
☐ 267 John O'Donoghue
☐ 268 Erik Schullstrom
☐ 269 Mark Smith
☐ 270 Mel Wearing
☐ 271 Jeff Williams
☐ 272 Paul Williams
☐ 273 Kip Yaughn
☐ 274 Don Buford MG
☐ 275 Moe Drabowsky CO
Joe Durham CO
☐ NNO Checklist

1992 Hamilton Redbirds Classic/Best

This 30-card standard-size set of the 1992 Hamilton Redbirds, a Class A New York-Penn League affiliate of the St. Louis Cardinals, features white-bordered posed color player photos on its fronts. The player's name, team, and position appear at the bottom. The white back is framed by a thin red line and carries the player's name and position at the top, followed by biography, statistics and team logos.

	MINT	NRMT	EXC
COMPLETE SET (30)	5.00	2.20	.60

☐ 1 Jeff Tanderys
☐ 2 Kirk Bullinger
☐ 3 Chad Smith
☐ 4 Blaine Milne
☐ 5 Jamie Cochran
☐ 6 Donnie Bellum
☐ 7 Ron French
☐ 8 Duff Brumley
☐ 9 Antonio Boone
☐ 10 Steve Jones
☐ 11 Andrew Martin
☐ 12 Keith Johns
☐ 13 Dennis Milius
☐ 14 Al Beavers
☐ 15 Tim DeGrasse
☐ 16 Ken Britt
☐ 17 Trey Ritz
☐ 18 Larry Gilligan
☐ 19 Tim Mathews
☐ 20 Tim Jordan
☐ 21 Alan Robinson
☐ 22 Darren Doucette
☐ 23 Mike Difelice
☐ 24 Keith Black
☐ 25 Jeff Murphy
☐ 26 Mike Gulan
☐ 27 Todd Henderson
☐ 28 Brad Owens
☐ 29 DeLynn Corry
☐ 30 Scott Melvin CL
Chris Maloney CL

1992 Hamilton Redbirds Fleer/ProCards

This 32-card standard-size set of the 1992 Hamilton Redbirds, a Class A New York-Penn League affiliate of the St. Louis Cardinals, features brown-bordered posed color player photos on its fronts. The player's name appears in an upper corner; his team and position appear in a lower corner. The white back is framed by a black line and carries the player's name at the top, followed by biography and statistics.

	MINT	NRMT	EXC
COMPLETE SET (32)	5.00	2.20	.60

☐ 1579 Alan Beavers
☐ 1580 Antonio Boone
☐ 1581 Ken Britt
☐ 1582 Puff Brumley
☐ 1583 Kirk Bullinger
☐ 1584 Jamie Cochran
☐ 1585 DeLynn Corry
☐ 1586 Tim DeGrasse
☐ 1587 Steve Jones
☐ 1588 T.J. Mathews
☐ 1589 Dennis Milius
☐ 1590 David Oehrlein
☐ 1591 Chad Smith
☐ 1592 Jeff Tanderys
☐ 1593 Mike Difelice
☐ 1594 Blaine Milne
☐ 1595 Jeff Murphy
☐ 1596 Keith Black
☐ 1597 Mike Gulan
☐ 1598 Darren Doucette
☐ 1599 Larry Gilligan
☐ 1600 Keith Johns
☐ 1601 Andy Martin
☐ 1602 Brad Owens
☐ 1603 Trey Ritz
☐ 1604 Donnie Bellum
☐ 1605 Ronnie French
☐ 1606 Todd Henderson
☐ 1607 Timmy Jordan
☐ 1608 Alan Robinson
☐ 1609 Field Staff
Scott Melvin CO
Dave Novak TR
Chris Maloney MG
☐ 1610 Checklist

1992 Harrisburg Senators Fleer/ProCards

This 27-card standard-size set of the 1992 Harrisburg Senators, a Class AA Eastern League affiliate of the Montreal Expos, features brown-bordered posed color player photos on its fronts. The player's name appears in an upper corner; his team and position appear in a lower corner. The white back is framed by a black line and carries the player's name at the top, followed by biography and statistics.

	MINT	NRMT	EXC
COMPLETE SET (27)	5.00	2.20	.60

☐ 452 Doug Bochtler
☐ 453 Mario Brito
☐ 454 Travis Buckley
☐ 455 Mark Chapman
☐ 456 Chris Johnson
☐ 457 Chris Marchok
☐ 458 Mike Mathile
☐ 459 Chris Myers
☐ 460 Doug Piatt
☐ 461 Len Picota
☐ 462 Chris Pollack
☐ 463 Tim Laker
☐ 464 Joe Siddall
☐ 465 Bryn Kosco
☐ 466 Mike Lansing
☐ 467 Chris Martin
☐ 468 Chad McDonald
☐ 469 Derrick White
☐ 470 Steve Hecht
☐ 471 Rick Hirtensteiner
☐ 472 Jerome Nelson
☐ 473 Darwin Pennye
☐ 474 Jaime Roseboro
☐ 475 Mike Quade MG
☐ 476 Mike Parrott CO
☐ 477 Checklist
☐ NNO Jay Williams TR

1992 Harrisburg Senators SkyBox

This 26-card standard-size set of the 1992 Harrisburg Senators, a Class AA Eastern League affiliate of the Montreal Expos, features white-bordered posed color player photos on its fronts. The player's name appears at the top; his team and position appear at the bottom. The white back carries the player's name at the top, followed by team name, position, biography, and statistics.

	MINT	NRMT	EXC
COMPLETE SET (26)	5.00	2.20	.60

☐ 276 Doug Bochtler
☐ 277 Mario Brito
☐ 278 Travis Buckley
☐ 279 Mark Chapman
☐ 280 Reid Cornelius
☐ 281 Greg Fulton
☐ 282 Steve Hecht
☐ 283 Rick Hirtensteiner
☐ 284 Chris Johnson
☐ 285 Bryn Kosco
☐ 286 Tim Laker
☐ 287 Mike Lansing
☐ 288 Chris Marchok
☐ 289 Chris Martin
☐ 290 Mike Mathile
☐ 291 Todd Mayo
☐ 292 Chad McDonald
☐ 293 Derrick White
☐ 294 Darwin Pennye
☐ 295 Doug Piatt
☐ 296 Len Picota
☐ 297 Chris Pollack
☐ 298 Joe Siddall
☐ 299 Mike Quade MG
☐ 300 Mike Parrott
☐ NNO Checklist CO

1992 Helena Brewers Fleer/ProCards

This 27-card standard-size set of the 1992 Helena Brewers, a Rookie Class Pioneer League affiliate of the Milwaukee Brewers, features brown-bordered posed color player photos on its fronts. The player's name appears in an upper corner; his team and position appear in a lower corner. The white back is framed by a black line and carries the player's name at the top, followed by biography and statistics.

	MINT	NRMT	EXC
COMPLETE SET (27)	5.00	2.20	.60

☐ 1708 Jeff Droll
☐ 1709 Dave England
☐ 1710 Bobby Jones
☐ 1711 Scott Karl
☐ 1712 Dan Kyslinger
☐ 1713 Chris Petrocella
☐ 1714 Ron Rico
☐ 1715 Tom Schenbeck
☐ 1716 Rafael Torres
☐ 1717 Bill Dobrolsky
☐ 1718 Brian Hostetler
☐ 1719 George Behr
☐ 1720 Sean Holub
☐ 1721 Mark Kingston
☐ 1722 Robert Powers
☐ 1723 Scott Richardson
☐ 1724 Tim Unroe
☐ 1725 Wes Weger
☐ 1726 Kenny Felder
☐ 1727 Dana Hughes
☐ 1728 Shane Lay
☐ 1729 Danny Perez
☐ 1730 Cecil Rodriques
☐ 1731 Jackie Ross
☐ 1732 Harry Dunlop MG
☐ 1733 Mike Caldwell CO
☐ 1734 Checklist

1992 Helena Brewers Sports Pro

	MINT	NRMT	EXC
COMPLETE SET (30)	6.00	2.70	.75

☐ 1 Dan Kyslinger
☐ 2 Kenny Felder
☐ 3 Mark Kingston
☐ 4 David England
☐ 5 Bill Dobrolsky
☐ 6 Shane Lay
☐ 7 Bobby Jones
☐ 8 George Behr
☐ 9 Jeff Droll
☐ 10 Wes Weger
☐ 11 Robert Powers
☐ 12 Sean Holub
☐ 13 Jackie Ross
☐ 14 Chris Petrocella
☐ 15 Brian Hostetler
☐ 16 Scott Karl
☐ 17 Dana Hughes
☐ 18 Tim Unroe
☐ 19 Ron Rico
☐ 20 Cecil Rodriquez
☐ 21 Scott Richardson
☐ 22 Tom Schenbeck
☐ 23 Danny Perez
☐ 24 Mike Caldwell CO
☐ 25 Scott Meissner TR
☐ 26 Harry Dunlop MG
☐ 27 Blank Card
☐ 28 Blank Card
☐ 29 Blank Card
☐ 30 Blank Card

1992 High Desert Mavericks Classic/Best

This 30-card standard-size set of the 1992 High Desert Mavericks, a Class A California League affiliate of the San Diego Padres, features white-bordered posed color player photos on its fronts. The player's name, team, and position appear at the bottom. The white back is framed by a thin red line and carries the player's name and position at the top, followed by biography, statistics and team logos.

	MINT	NRMT	EXC
COMPLETE SET (30)	5.00	2.20	.60

☐ 1 Rusty Silcox
☐ 2 Steve Gill
☐ 3 Brent Bish
☐ 4 Bill Meury
☐ 5 Pablo Martinez
☐ 6 Roberto Arrendondo
☐ 7 Billy Hall
☐ 8 Kelly Lifgren
☐ 9 Ray McDavid
☐ 10 Linty Ingram
☐ 11 Tony Mortensen
☐ 12 Ed Zinter
☐ 13 Tookie Spann
☐ 14 Ted Devore
☐ 15 John Kuehl
☐ 16 Luis Galindez
☐ 17 Sean Mulligan
☐ 18 Geoff Kellogg
☐ 19 Bill Ostermeyer
☐ 20 Bryce Florie
☐ 21 Ryan Thibault
☐ 22 Jose LeBron
☐ 23 Rafael Chaves
☐ 24 Tom Martin
☐ 25 Julio Bruno
☐ 26 Lee Henderson
☐ 27 Darius Gash
☐ 28 Brian McKeon
☐ 29 Bryan Little MG
☐ 30 Bruce Tanner CO
Checklist

1992 High School Prospects Little Sun

This card set includes first year cards of Derek Jeter and Jason Kendall. Autograph cards of Jeter, Kendall, Landaker and Roper were randomingly inserted into sets. Each player signed 250 cards. 3,000 sets were produced.

	MINT	NRMT	EXC
COMPLETE SET (30)	18.00	8.00	2.20
COMPLETE SET W/JETER AU	80.00	36.00	10.00
COMPLETE SET W/KENDALL AU	50.00	22.00	6.25
COMPLETE SET W/LANDAKER AU	20.00	9.00	2.50
COMPLETE SET W/ROPER AU	25.00	11.00	3.10

☐ 1 Logo Card
☐ 2 Derek Jeter
☐ 3 William Urbina
☐ 4 Mike Rennhack
☐ 5 Tony Sheffield
☐ 6 Ryan Wilson
☐ 7 Todd Etler
☐ 8 Brendan Hause
☐ 9 Carey Paige
☐ 10 Chris Dean
☐ 11 Jason Kendall
☐ 12 Scott Patton
☐ 13 John Bowles
☐ 14 Sean Runyan
☐ 15 Jason Lowe
☐ 16 David Post
☐ 17 Rick Talbott
☐ 18 Hut Smith
☐ 19 Dave Landaker
☐ 20 Tim Adkins
☐ 21 Tray Nelson
☐ 22 Chad Roper
☐ 23 Steve Lackey
☐ 24 Tom Evans
☐ 25 Damon Hollins
☐ 26 Jeff Patzke
☐ 27 Preston Wilson
☐ 28 Tyrone Domingo
☐ 29 Rich Hofman
☐ 30 Did You Know

1992 Huntington Cubs Classic/Best

This 30-card standard-size set of the 1992 Huntsville Stars, a Class AA Southern League affiliate of the Oakland Athletics, features white-bordered posed color player photos on its fronts. The player's name, team, and position appear at the bottom. The white back is framed by a thin red line and carries the player's name and position at the top, followed by biography, statistics and team logos.

	MINT	NRMT	EXC
COMPLETE SET (30)	6.00	2.70	.75

☐ 1 Brandon Pico
☐ 2 Robert Nutting
☐ 3 Jason Boehlow
☐ 4 Danny Montero
☐ 5 Andre Nelson
☐ 6 Ricky Perez
☐ 7 Roque Colon

☐ 8 Kevin Booker
☐ 9 Maceo Houston
☐ 10 Josh Simmons
☐ 11 Scott Barton
☐ 12 Micky Reeves
☐ 13 Dan Gustavson
☐ 14 Matt Lawrence
☐ 15 Jose Pacheco
☐ 16 Andy Elsbecker
☐ 17 Coleman Smith
☐ 18 Steven Walker
☐ 19 Mitch Root
☐ 20 William Latimer
☐ 21 Jon Waite
☐ 22 Patrick Kendrick
☐ 23 Chris Plonk
☐ 24 Tim Stutheit
☐ 25 Jay Hassel
☐ 26 Daryle Gavlick
☐ 27 Amaury Telemaco
☐ 28 Phillip Hannon
☐ 29 Gil Kubski
☐ 30 Greg Keuter CL

1992 Huntington Cubs Fleer/ProCards

This 32-card standard-size set of the 1992 Huntington Cubs, a Rookie Class A Appalachian League affiliate of the Chicago Cubs, features brown-bordered posed color player photos on its fronts. The player's name appears in an upper corner; his team and position appear in a lower corner. The white back is framed by a black line and carries the player's name at the top, followed by biography and statistics. This set includes the first team set card of Amaury Telemaco.

	MINT	NRMT	EXC
COMPLETE SET (32)	7.00	3.10	.85

☐ 3137 Billy Childress
☐ 3138 Andy Elsbecker
☐ 3139 Mario Garcia
☐ 3140 Daryle Gavlick
☐ 3141 Dan Gustavson
☐ 3142 Jay Hassel
☐ 3143 Patrick Kendrick
☐ 3144 William Latimer
☐ 3145 Matt Lawrence
☐ 3146 Luis Matos
☐ 3147 Jose Pacheco
☐ 3148 Amaury Telemaco
☐ 3149 Jon Waite
☐ 3150 Scott Barton
☐ 3151 Danny Montero
☐ 3152 Francisco Morales
☐ 3153 Jason Boehlow
☐ 3154 Robert Nutting
☐ 3155 Richard Perez
☐ 3156 Chris Plonk
☐ 3157 Mitch Root
☐ 3158 Josh Simmons
☐ 3159 Tim Stutheit
☐ 3160 Kevin Booker
☐ 3161 Roque Colon
☐ 3162 Maceo Houston
☐ 3163 Andre Nelson
☐ 3164 Brandon Pico
☐ 3165 Mickey Reeves
☐ 3166 Coleman Smith
☐ 3167 Steven Walker
☐ 3168 Checklist

1992 Huntsville Stars Fleer/ProCards

This 27-card standard-size set of the 1992 Huntsville Stars, a Class AA Southern League affiliate of the Oakland Athletics, features brown-bordered posed color player photos on its fronts. The player's name appears in an upper corner; his team and position appear in a lower corner. The white back is framed by a black line and carries the player's name at the top, followed by biography and statistics.

	MINT	NRMT	EXC
COMPLETE SET (27)	5.00	2.20	.60

☐ 3940 Dana Allison
☐ 3941 Jeff Bittiger
☐ 3942 Scott Erwin
☐ 3943 Johnny Guzman
☐ 3944 Chad Kuhn
☐ 3945 Dave Latter
☐ 3946 Mike Mohler
☐ 3947 Gavin Osteen
☐ 3948 Bronswell Patrick
☐ 3949 Steve Phoenix
☐ 3950 Todd Revenig
☐ 3951 Rick Strebeck
☐ 3952 Dean Borrelli
☐ 3953 Jorge Brito
☐ 3954 Kurt Abbott
☐ 3955 Marcos Armas
☐ 3956 Webster Garrison
☐ 3957 Craig Paquette
☐ 3958 Darryl Vice
☐ 3959 Mike Conte
☐ 3960 Kevin Dattola
☐ 3961 Eric Fox
☐ 3962 Dave Jacas
☐ 3963 Scott Lydy
☐ 3964 Casey Parsons MG
☐ 3965 Bert Bradley CO
☐ 3966 Checklist

1992 Huntsville Stars SkyBox

	MINT	NRMT	EXC
COMPLETE SET (26)	5.00	2.20	.60

☐ 301 Kurt Abbott
☐ 302 Marcos Armas
☐ 303 Jeff Bittiger
☐ 304 Dean Borrelli
☐ 305 James Buccheri
☐ 306 Tom Carcione
☐ 307 Mike Conte
☐ 308 Kevin Dattola
☐ 309 Scott Erwin
☐ 310 Johnny Guzman
☐ 311 David Jacas
☐ 312 Chris Knabenshue
☐ 313 Dave Latter
☐ 314 Francisco Matos
☐ 315 Mike Mohler
☐ 316 Craig Paquette
☐ 317 Bronswell Patrick
☐ 318 Steve Phoenix
☐ 319 Todd Revenig
☐ 320 Todd Smith
☐ 321 Rick Strebeck
☐ 322 Darryl Vice
☐ 323 Bill Wilkinson
☐ 324 Casey Parsons MG
☐ 325 Bert Bradley CO
☐ NNO Checklist

1992 Idaho Falls Gems Fleer/ProCards

This 32-card standard-size set of the 1992 Idaho Falls Gems, a Rookie Class Pioneer League affiliate of the Atlanta Braves, features brown-bordered posed color player photos on its fronts. The player's name appears in an upper corner; his team and position appear in a lower corner. The white back is framed by a black line and carries the player's name at the top, followed by biography and statistics. This set includes the first team set card of Terrell Wade.

	MINT	NRMT	EXC
COMPLETE SET (32)	6.00	2.70	.75

☐ 3501 Scott Behrens
☐ 3502 Craig Bradshaw
☐ 3503 Chris Brock
☐ 3504 Burke Cromer
☐ 3505 Stewart Ford
☐ 3506 Ken Giard
☐ 3507 Eric Lairsey
☐ 3508 Bill Maitland
☐ 3509 Yves Martineau
☐ 3510 David Pike
☐ 3511 Chris Rusciano
☐ 3512 John Simmons
☐ 3513 Tony Stoecklin
☐ 3514 Terrell Wade
☐ 3515 Ben Lavigne
☐ 3516 Kevin Schula
☐ 3517 Miguel Soto
☐ 3518 Kevin Nalls
☐ 3519 Rob Newman
☐ 3520 Van Torian
☐ 3521 Gerald Trevino
☐ 3522 Tom Waldrop
☐ 3523 Doug Wollenburg
☐ 3524 David Bingham
☐ 3525 Miguel Correa
☐ 3526 Ralph Garr
☐ 3527 Andre Johnson
☐ 3528 Sherton Saturnino
☐ 3529 Michael Warner
☐ 3530 Byron Woods
☐ 3531 Dave Hilton MG
☐ 3532 Checklist

1992 Idaho Falls Gems Sports Pro

This 30-card standard-size set of the 1992 Idaho Falls Gems, a Rookie Class Pioneer League affiliate of the Atlanta Braves, features the minor league card debut of Terrell Wade.

	MINT	NRMT	EXC
COMPLETE SET (30)	8.00	3.60	1.00

☐ 1 John Simmons
☐ 2 David Bingham
☐ 3 Kevin Nalls
☐ 4 Chris Rusciano
☐ 5 Kenneth Giard
☐ 6 William Maitland
☐ 7 Andre Johnson
☐ 8 Tom Waldrop
☐ 9 Terrell Wade
☐ 10 Douglas Wollenburg
☐ 11 Smerton Saturnino
☐ 12 David Pike
☐ 13 Van Torian
☐ 14 Scott Bahrens
☐ 15 Ralph Garr
☐ 16 Miguel Correa
☐ 17 Rob Newman
☐ 18 Anthony Stoecklin
☐ 19 Chris Brock
☐ 20 Michael Warner
☐ 21 Burke Cromer
☐ 22 Gerald Trevino
☐ 23 Miguel Soto
☐ 24 Byron Woods
☐ 25 Stewart Ford
☐ 26 Eric Lairsey
☐ 27 Yves Martineau
☐ 28 Craig Bradshaw
☐ 29 Blank Card
☐ 30 Blank Card

1992 Indianapolis Indians Fleer/ProCards

This 29-card standard-size set of the 1992 Indianapolis Indians, a Class AAA American Association affiliate of the Montreal Expos, features brown-bordered posed color player photos on its fronts. The player's name appears in an upper corner; his team and position appear in a lower corner. The white back is framed by a black line and carries the player's name and position at the top, followed by biography and statistics.

	MINT	NRMT	EXC
COMPLETE SET (29)	5.00	2.20	.60

☐ 1852 Blaine Beatty
☐ 1853 Kent Bottenfield
☐ 1854 Howard Farmer
☐ 1855 Matt Maysey
☐ 1856 Dana Ridenour
☐ 1857 Bill Risley
☐ 1858 Doug Simons
☐ 1859 Sergio Valdez
☐ 1860 David Wainhouse
☐ 1861 Darrin Fletcher
☐ 1862 Jim Kremers
☐ 1863 Bob Natal
☐ 1864 Greg Colbrunn
☐ 1865 Wil Cordero
☐ 1866 Greg Fulton
☐ 1867 Jerry Goff
☐ 1868 Omer Munoz
☐ 1869 F.P. Santangelo
☐ 1870 Razor Shines
☐ 1871 Shon Ashley
☐ 1872 Eric Bullock
☐ 1873 Jim Eppard
☐ 1874 Quinn Mack
☐ 1875 Pat Kelly MG
☐ 1876 Rich Dubee CO
☐ 1877 Gomer Hodge CO
☐ 1878 Checklist
☐ NNO Ball Boys
Nick Hodge
Christopher Kelly
Michael Dubee
☐ NNO John Spinosa TR

1992 Indianapolis Indians SkyBox

This 26-card standard-size set of the 1992 Indianapolis Indians, a Class AAA American Association affiliate of the Montreal Expos, features white-bordered posed color player photos on its fronts. The player's name appears at the top; his team and position appear at the bottom. The white back carries the player's name at the top, followed by his team's name, position, biography and statistics. The set was co-sponsored by Pepsi and Hood's Drug Stores.

	MINT	NRMT	EXC
COMPLETE SET (26)	5.00	2.20	.60

☐ 176 Shon Ashley
☐ 177 Brian Barnes
☐ 178 Kent Bottenfield
☐ 179 Wil Cordero
☐ 180 Jim Eppard
☐ 181 Howard Farmer
☐ 182 Jerry Goff
☐ 183 Blaine Beatty
☐ 184 Jonathan Hurst
☐ 185 Jim Kremers
☐ 186 Quinn Mack
☐ 187 Matt Maysey
☐ 188 Omer Munoz
☐ 189 Bob Natal
☐ 190 Dana Ridenour
☐ 191 Mel Rojas
☐ 192 F.P. Santangelo
☐ 193 Scott Service
☐ 194 Razor Shines
☐ 195 Matt Stairs
☐ 196 Sergio Valdez
☐ 197 David Wainhouse
☐ 198 Pete Young
☐ 199 Pat Kelly MG
☐ 200 Gomer Hodge CO
Rich Dubee CO
☐ NNO Checklist

1992 Iowa Cubs Fleer/ProCards

This 24-card standard-size set of the 1992 Iowa Cubs, a Class AAA American Association affiliate of the Chicago Cubs, features brown-bordered posed color player photos on its fronts. The player's name appears in an upper corner; his team and position appear in a lower corner. The white back is framed by a black line and carries the player's name at the top, followed by biography and statistics.

	MINT	NRMT	EXC
COMPLETE SET (24)	5.00	2.20	.60

☐ 4044 Steve Adkins
☐ 4045 Brad Arnsberg
☐ 4046 Hector Berrios
☐ 4047 John Gardner
☐ 4048 Jeff Hartsock
☐ 4049 Scott May
☐ 4050 Laddie Renfroe
☐ 4051 Bob Sebra
☐ 4052 Julio Strauss
☐ 4053 Mike Knapp
☐ 4054 Jorge Pedre
☐ 4055 Alex Arias
☐ 4056 Billy Bates
☐ 4057 Pedro Castellano
☐ 4058 Darrin Duffy
☐ 4059 Scott Bryant
☐ 4060 Tony Chance
☐ 4061 Fernando Ramsey
☐ 4062 Kevin Roberson
☐ 4063 Jeff Schulz
☐ 4064 Scott Wade
☐ 4065 Brad Mills MG
☐ 4066 Rick Kranitz CO
☐ 4067 Checklist

1992 Iowa Cubs SkyBox

	MINT	NRMT	EXC
COMPLETE SET (26)	5.00	2.20	.60

☐ 201 Steve Adkins
☐ 202 Alex Arias
☐ 203 Scott Bryant
☐ 204 Jim Bullinger
☐ 205 Pedro Castellano
☐ 206 Tony Chance
☐ 207 Lance Dickson
☐ 208 John Gardner
☐ 209 Jeff Hartsock
☐ 210 Mike Knapp
☐ 211 Ced Landrum
☐ 212 Derrick May
☐ 213 Scott May
☐ 214 Elvin Paulino
☐ 215 George Pedre
☐ 216 Fernando Ramsey
☐ 217 Laddie Renfroe
☐ 218 Kevin Roberson
☐ 219 Jeff Robinson
☐ 220 John Salles
☐ 221 Rey Sanchez
☐ 222 Doug Strange
☐ 223 Turk Wendell
☐ 224 Brad Mills MG
☐ 225 Rick Kranitz CO
☐ NNO Checklist

1992 Jackson Generals Fleer/ProCards

This 27-card standard-size set of the 1992 Jackson Generals, a Class AA Texas League affiliate of the Houston Astros, features brown-bordered posed color player photos on its fronts. The player's name appears in an upper corner; his team and position appear in a lower corner. The white back is framed by a black line and carries the player's name at the top, followed by biography and statistics.

	MINT	NRMT	EXC
COMPLETE SET (27)	5.00	2.20	.60

☐ 3991 Harold Allen
☐ 3992 Jim Bruske
☐ 3993 Fred Costello
☐ 3994 Brian Griffiths
☐ 3995 Dean Hartgraves
☐ 3996 Keith Helton
☐ 3997 Bob Hurta
☐ 3998 Todd Jones
☐ 3999 Jim Lewis
☐ 4000 Richie Simon
☐ 4001 Scott Makarewicz
☐ 4002 Jeff Ball
☐ 4003 David Hajeck
☐ 4004 Rusty Harris
☐ 4005 Frank Kellner
☐ 4006 Lance Madsen

- ☐ 4007 Joe Mikulik
- ☐ 4008 Roberto Petagine
- ☐ 4009 Howard Prager
- ☐ 4010 Willie Ansley
- ☐ 4011 Jeff Baldwin
- ☐ 4012 Ray Montgomery
- ☐ 4013 Lee Sammons
- ☐ 4014 Rick Sweet MG
- ☐ 4015 Charley Taylor CO
- ☐ 4016 Don Reynolds CO
- ☐ 4017 Checklist

1992 Jackson Generals SkyBox

	MINT	NRMT	EXC
COMPLETE SET (26)	5.00	2.20	.60

- ☐ 326 Harold Allen
- ☐ 327 Sam August
- ☐ 328 Jeff Baldwin
- ☐ 329 Jeff Ball
- ☐ 330 Kevin Dean
- ☐ 331 Tony Eusebio
- ☐ 332 Brian Griffiths
- ☐ 333 Rusty Harris
- ☐ 334 Bob Hurta
- ☐ 335 Todd Jones
- ☐ 336 Frank Kellner
- ☐ 337 Steve Larose
- ☐ 338 Ken Luckham
- ☐ 339 Lance Madsen
- ☐ 340 Scott Makarewicz
- ☐ 341 John Massarelli
- ☐ 342 Orlando Miller
- ☐ 343 Richie Simon
- ☐ 344 Ed Ponte
- ☐ 345 Howard Prager
- ☐ 346 Matt Rambo
- ☐ 347 Lee Sammons
- ☐ 348 Rodney Windes
- ☐ 349 Rick Sweet MG
- ☐ 350 Charley Taylor CO
  Don Reynolds CO
- ☐ NNO Checklist

1992 Jacksonville Suns Fleer/ProCards

This 26-card standard-size set of the 1992 Jacksonville Suns, a Class AA Southern League affiliate of the Seattle Mariners, features brown-bordered posed color player photos on its fronts. The player's name appears in an upper corner; his team and position appear in a lower corner. The white back is framed by a black line and carries the player's name at the top, followed by biography and statistics.

	MINT	NRMT	EXC
COMPLETE SET (26)	5.00	2.20	.60

- ☐ 3700 Jeff Borski
- ☐ 3701 Jim Converse
- ☐ 3702 Mark Czarkowski
- ☐ 3703 Fernando Figueroa
- ☐ 3704 Brad Holman
- ☐ 3705 Troy Kent
- ☐ 3706 Scott Pitcher
- ☐ 3707 Kerry Woodson
- ☐ 3708 Clint Zavaras
- ☐ 3709 Jim Campanis
- ☐ 3710 Greg Pirkl
- ☐ 3711 Craig Wilson
- ☐ 3712 Frank Bolick
- ☐ 3713 Mike Bond
- ☐ 3714 Jim Bowie
- ☐ 3715 Bobby Holley
- ☐ 3716 Shane Letterio
- ☐ 3717 Anthony Manahan
- ☐ 3718 Brian Turang
- ☐ 3719 Ellerton Maynard
- ☐ 3720 Mike McDonald
- ☐ 3721 Mark Merchant
- ☐ 3722 Marc Newfield
- ☐ 3723 Jesus Tavarez
- ☐ 3724 Bob Hartsfield MG
- ☐ 3725 Checklist

1992 Jacksonville Suns SkyBox

	MINT	NRMT	EXC
COMPLETE SET (26)	5.00	2.20	.60

- ☐ 351 Frank Bolick
- ☐ 352 Daven Bond
- ☐ 353 Jim Campanis
- ☐ 354 Jim Converse
- ☐ 355 Fernando Figueroa
- ☐ 356 Marcos Garcia
- ☐ 357 Eric Gunderson
- ☐ 358 Brian Turang
- ☐ 359 Bobby Holley
- ☐ 360 Troy Kent
- ☐ 361 Shane Letterio
- ☐ 362 Anthony Manahan
- ☐ 363 Tow Maynard
- ☐ 364 Mike McDonald
- ☐ 365 Marc Newfield
- ☐ 366 Mark Merchant
- ☐ 367 Greg Pirkl
- ☐ 368 Jesus Tavarez
- ☐ 369 Mike Erb
- ☐ 370 Mike Walker
- ☐ 371 Craig Wilson
- ☐ 372 Brent Knackert
- ☐ 373 Kerry Woodson
- ☐ 374 Bob Hartsfield MG
- ☐ 375 Jeff Andrews CO
  Mike Goff CO
- ☐ NNO Checklist

1992 Jamestown Expos Classic/Best

This 30-card standard-size set of the 1992 Jamestown Expos, a Class A New York-Penn League affiliate of the Montreal Expos, features white-bordered posed color player photos on its fronts. The player's name, team, and position appear near the bottom. The white back is framed by a orange line and carries the player's name and position at the top, followed by biography and statistics. This issue includes the minor league card debut of Yamil Benitez.

	MINT	NRMT	EXC
COMPLETE SET (30)	6.00	2.70	.75

- ☐ 1 Rodney Henderson
- ☐ 2 Jim Henderson
- ☐ 3 Tom Doyle
- ☐ 4 Steve Falteisek
- ☐ 5 Alex Pacheco
- ☐ 6 Matt Rundels
- ☐ 7 Todd Dreifort
- ☐ 8 Robert Campillo
- ☐ 9 Scott Pisciotta
- ☐ 10 James Ferguson
- ☐ 11 Alfred Kermode
- ☐ 12 Charles Lee
- ☐ 13 Everett Stull
- ☐ 14 Danny Lane
- ☐ 15 Brad Aurila
- ☐ 16 Matt Allen
- ☐ 17 Scott Gentile
- ☐ 18 Curt Schmidt
- ☐ 19 Yamil Benitez
- ☐ 20 Scott Harrison
- ☐ 21 Edgar Tovar
- ☐ 22 Jim Rushworth
- ☐ 23 Matt Raleigh
- ☐ 24 Kevin Northrup
- ☐ 25 David Eggert
- ☐ 26 Q.V. Lowe MG
- ☐ 27 Jim Fleming CO
- ☐ 28 Martin Robitaille CO
- ☐ 29 Lee Slagle TR
- ☐ 30 Checklist

1992 Jamestown Expos Fleer/ProCards

This 28-card standard-size set of the 1992 Jamestown Expos, a Class A New York-Penn League affiliate of the Montreal Expos, features brown-bordered posed color player photos on its fronts. The player's name appears in an upper corner; his team and position appear in a lower corner. The white back is framed by a black line and carries the player's name and position at the top, followed by biography and statistics. This issue includes the minor league card debut of Yamil Benitez.

	MINT	NRMT	EXC
COMPLETE SET (28)	7.00	3.10	.85

- ☐ 1492 David Eggert
- ☐ 1493 Steven Falteisik
- ☐ 1494 Jim Ferguson
- ☐ 1495 Scott Gentile
- ☐ 1496 Scott Harrison
- ☐ 1497 Rodney Henderson
- ☐ 1498 Al Kermode
- ☐ 1499 Alex Pacheco
- ☐ 1500 Scott Pisciotta
- ☐ 1501 Jim Rushworth
- ☐ 1502 Curt Schmidt
- ☐ 1503 Everett Stull
- ☐ 1504 Matt Allen
- ☐ 1505 Robert Campillo
- ☐ 1506 Brad Aurila
- ☐ 1507 Danny Lane
- ☐ 1508 Matt Raleigh
- ☐ 1509 Matt Rundels
- ☐ 1510 Edgar Tovar
- ☐ 1511 Yamil Benitez
- ☐ 1512 Todd Dreifort
- ☐ 1513 Charles Lee
- ☐ 1514 Kevin Northrup
- ☐ 1515 Stan Robertson
- ☐ 1516 Q.V. Lowe MG
- ☐ 1517 Jim Fleming CO
- ☐ 1518 Martin Robitaille CO
- ☐ 1519 Checklist

1992 Johnson City Cardinals Classic/Best

This 30-card standard-size set of the 1992 Johnson City Cardinals, a Rookie Class Appalachian League affiliate of the St. Louis Cardinals, features white-bordered posed color player photos on its fronts. The player's name, team, and position appear at the bottom. The white back is framed by a thin red line and carries the player's name and position at the top, followed by biography, statistics and team logos.

	MINT	NRMT	EXC
COMPLETE SET (30)	5.00	2.20	.60

- ☐ 1 Basil Shabazz
- ☐ 2 Derek Stanley
- ☐ 3 Douglas Goodman
- ☐ 4 Steven Dudek
- ☐ 5 Rongie Dicken
- ☐ 6 Juan Ballara
- ☐ 7 Charles Anderson
- ☐ 8 Jose Vazquez
- ☐ 9 Jesus Uqueto
- ☐ 10 Aldo Pecorilli
- ☐ 11 Santo Mota
- ☐ 12 Antoine Henry
- ☐ 13 Chad Sumner
- ☐ 14 Charles Pittman
- ☐ 15 Jose Lopez
- ☐ 16 Joe Larson
- ☐ 17 Don Slattery
- ☐ 18 Eric Miller
- ☐ 19 Darryl Meek
- ☐ 20 Jeffrey Matulevich
- ☐ 21 James Marchesi
- ☐ 22 Hector Colon
- ☐ 23 Duffy Guyton
- ☐ 24 Joe Carrillo
- ☐ 25 Todd Blake
- ☐ 26 Steve Turco MG
- ☐ 27 Orlando Thomas CO
- ☐ 28 Mike Gaddie
- ☐ 29 Logo Card
- ☐ 30 Checklist

1992 Johnson City Cardinals Fleer/ProCards

This 31-card standard-size set of the 1992 Johnson City Cardinals, a Rookie Class Appalachian League affiliate of the St. Louis Cardinals, features brown-bordered posed color player photos on its fronts. The player's name appears in an upper corner; his team and position appear in a lower corner. The white back is framed by a black line and carries the player's name at the top, followed by biography and statistics.

	MINT	NRMT	EXC
COMPLETE SET (31)	5.00	2.20	.60

- ☐ 3106 Todd Blake
- ☐ 3107 Joe Carrillo
- ☐ 3108 Doug Goodman
- ☐ 3109 Duffy Guyton
- ☐ 3110 Joe Larson
- ☐ 3111 Jose Lopez
- ☐ 3112 Jim Marchesi
- ☐ 3113 Jeff Matranga
- ☐ 3114 Jeff Matulevich
- ☐ 3115 Darryl Meek
- ☐ 3116 Eric Miller
- ☐ 3117 Chuck Pittman
- ☐ 3118 Juan Ballara
- ☐ 3119 Aldo Pecorilli
- ☐ 3120 Mark Williams
- ☐ 3121 Charlie Anderson
- ☐ 3122 Rongie Dicken
- ☐ 3123 Steve Dudek
- ☐ 3124 Santo Mota
- ☐ 3125 Don Slattery
- ☐ 3126 John Stutz
- ☐ 3127 Chad Sumner
- ☐ 3128 Jesus Ugueto
- ☐ 3129 Hector Colon
- ☐ 3130 Antoine Henry
- ☐ 3131 Basil Shabazz
- ☐ 3132 Derek Stanley
- ☐ 3133 Jose Vazquez
- ☐ 3134 Steve Turco MG
- ☐ 3135 Orlando Thomas CO
- ☐ 3136 Checklist

1992 Kane County Cougars Team Issue

This 30-card standard-size set of the 1992 Kane County Cougars, a Class A Midwest League affiliate of the Baltimore Orioles, features the minor league card debut of Alex Ochoa.

	MINT	NRMT	EXC
COMPLETE SET (30)	12.00	5.50	1.50

- ☐ 1 Derek Adams
- ☐ 2 Brad Brimhall
- ☐ 3 Clayton Byrne
- ☐ 4 Gregg Castaldo
- ☐ 5 Bobby Chouinard
- ☐ 6 Rich Dauer CO
- ☐ 7 Eugenio Delgado
- ☐ 8 Steve Firsich
- ☐ 9 Rick Forney
- ☐ 10 Don Gilbert
- ☐ 11 Curtis Goodwin
- ☐ 12 Kris Gresham
- ☐ 13 Jimmy Haynes
- ☐ 14 Peter Howell TR
- ☐ 15 Matt Jarvis
- ☐ 16 Drew Johnson
- ☐ 17 Scott Klingenbeck
- ☐ 18 Rick Krivda
- ☐ 19 Chris Lemp
- ☐ 20 Larry McCall CO
- ☐ 21 Scott McClain
- ☐ 22 Juan Mercedes
- ☐ 23 Alex Ochoa
- ☐ 24 Billy Owens
- ☐ 25 Ozzie
  (Mascot)
- ☐ 26 Estuar Ruiz
- ☐ 27 Mat Sanders
- ☐ 28 Keith Schmidt
- ☐ 29 B.J. Waszgis
- ☐ 30 Joel Youngblood MG

1992 Kane County Cougars Classic/Best

This 30-card standard-size set of the 1992 Kane County Cougars, a Class A Midwest League affiliate of the Baltimore Orioles, features white-bordered posed color player photos on its fronts. The player's name, team, and position appear at the bottom. The white back is framed by a thin red line and carries the player's name and position at the top, followed by biography, statistics and team logos. This issue includes the minor league card debut of Alex Ochoa.

	MINT	NRMT	EXC
COMPLETE SET (30)	12.00	5.50	1.50

- ☐ 1 B.J. Waszgis
- ☐ 2 Drew Johnson
- ☐ 3 Roy Hodge
- ☐ 4 Don Gilbert
- ☐ 5 Curtis Goodwin
- ☐ 6 Matt Jarvis
- ☐ 7 Mat Sanders
- ☐ 8 T.R. Lewis
- ☐ 9 Kris Gresham
- ☐ 10 Scott McClain
- ☐ 11 Chris Lemp
- ☐ 12 Troy Tallman
- ☐ 13 Alex Ochoa
- ☐ 14 Rick Krivda
- ☐ 15 Keith Schmidt
- ☐ 16 Juan Mercedes
- ☐ 17 Feliciano Mercedes
- ☐ 18 Jimmy Haynes
- ☐ 19 Shawn O'Connell
- ☐ 20 Bobby Chouinard
- ☐ 21 Derek Adams
- ☐ 22 Rick Forney
- ☐ 23 Ishovany Marquez
- ☐ 24 Steve Firsich
- ☐ 25 Clayton Byrne
- ☐ 26 Joel Youngblood MG
- ☐ 27 Larry McCall CO
- ☐ 28 Peter Howell TR
- ☐ 29 Logo Card
- ☐ 30 Checklist

1992 Kane County Cougars Fleer/ProCards

This 29-card standard-size set of the 1992 Kane County Cougars, a Class A Midwest League affiliate of the Baltimore Orioles, features brown-bordered posed color player photos on its fronts. The player's name appears in an upper corner; his team and position appear in a lower corner. The white back is framed by a black line and carries the player's name at the top, followed by biography and statistics. This issue includes the minor league card debut of Alex Ochoa.

	MINT	NRMT	EXC
COMPLETE SET (29)	12.00	5.50	1.50

- ☐ 82 Bobby Chouinard
- ☐ 83 Steve Firsich
- ☐ 84 Rick Forney
- ☐ 85 Jimmy Haynes
- ☐ 86 Matt Jarvis
- ☐ 87 Rick Krivda
- ☐ 88 Chris Lemp
- ☐ 89 Ishovany Marquez
- ☐ 90 Juan Mercedes
- ☐ 91 Shawn O'Connell
- ☐ 92 Mat Sanders
- ☐ 93 Kris Gresham
- ☐ 94 Troy Tallman
- ☐ 95 B.J. Waszgis
- ☐ 96 Derek Adams
- ☐ 97 Donald Gilbert
- ☐ 98 Drew Johnson
- ☐ 99 T.R. Lewis

☐ 100 Scott McClain
☐ 101 Feliciano Mercedes
☐ 102 Stewart Ruiz
☐ 103 Clayton Byrne
☐ 104 Curtis Goodwin
☐ 105 Roy Hodge
☐ 106 Alex Ochoa
☐ 107 Keith Schmidt
☐ 108 Joel Youngblood MG
☐ 109 Larry McCall CO
☐ 110 Checklist

1992 Kenosha Twins Classic/Best

This 27-card standard-size set of the 1992 Kenosha Twins, a Class A Midwest League affiliate of the Minnesota Twins, features white-bordered posed color player photos on its fronts. The player's name, team, and position appear at the bottom. The white back is framed by a thin red line and carries the player's name and position at the top, followed by biography, statistics and team logos.

	MINT	NRMT	EXC
COMPLETE SET (27)	6.00	2.70	.75

☐ 1 Jamie Ogden
☐ 2 Jeee Mansur
☐ 3 Eddie Guardado
☐ 4 David Sartain
☐ 5 Glenn Evans
☐ 6 Carlos Estevez
☐ 7 Tim Moore
☐ 8 Todd Blakeman
☐ 9 A.J. Johnson
☐ 10 Greg Johnson
☐ 11 Steve Hazlett
☐ 12 Damian Miller
☐ 13 Marlo Nava
☐ 14 Kerry Taylor
☐ 15 Ken Norman
☐ 16 Luis Garcia
☐ 17 David Garrow
☐ 18 Bill Wissler
☐ 19 Brent Brede
☐ 20 Monte Dufault
☐ 21 Bob Carlson
☐ 22 Brad Radke
☐ 23 Dom Konieczki
☐ 24 Michael Fernandez
☐ 25 Jim Dwyer
☐ 26 Rick Anderson
☐ 27 Dan Fox

1992 Kenosha Twins Fleer/ProCards

This 28-card standard-size set of the 1992 Kenosha Twins, a Class A Midwest League affiliate of the Minnesota Twins, features brown-bordered posed color player photos on its fronts. The player's name appears in an upper corner; his team and position appear in a lower corner. The white back is framed by a black line and carries the player's name at the top, followed by biography and statistics. This issue includes the minor league card debut of Brad Radke.

	MINT	NRMT	EXC
COMPLETE SET (28)	6.00	2.70	.75

☐ 595 Sandy Diaz
☐ 596 Luis Garcia
☐ 597 Sean Gavaghan
☐ 598 Eddie Guardado
☐ 599 Dominic Konieczki
☐ 600 Dan Naulty
☐ 601 Brad Radke
☐ 602 David Sartain
☐ 603 Dennis Sweeney
☐ 604 Kerry Taylor
☐ 605 Scott Watkins
☐ 606 Bill Wissler
☐ 607 Kyle Caple
☐ 608 Damian Miller
☐ 609 Marc Claus
☐ 610 Monte Dufault
☐ 611 Mike Fernandez
☐ 612 David Garrow
☐ 613 Greg Johnson
☐ 614 Andrew Kontorinis
☐ 615 Brent Brede
☐ 616 Anthony Byrd
☐ 617 Steve Hazlett
☐ 618 Tim Moore
☐ 619 Jamie Ogden
☐ 620 Jim Dwyer MG
☐ 621 Rick Anderson CO
☐ 622 Checklist

1992 Kingsport Mets Classic/Best

This 30-card standard-size set of the 1992 Kingsport Mets, a Rookie Class Appalachian League affiliate of the New York Mets, features white-bordered posed color player photos on its fronts. The player's name, team, and position appear at the bottom. The white back is framed by a thin red line and carries the player's name and position at the top, followed by biography, statistics and team logos.

	MINT	NRMT	EXC
COMPLETE SET (30)	7.00	3.10	.85

☐ 1 Tom Pinson
☐ 2 Kenny Bradley
☐ 3 Jared Osentowski
☐ 4 Travis Shaffer
☐ 5 David Swanson
☐ 6 Jeff Kiraly
☐ 7 Steve Grennan
☐ 8 Eric Harris
☐ 9 Al Shirley
☐ 10 Raul Casanova
☐ 11 Steven Steele
☐ 12 Allen McDill
☐ 13 Erik Hiljus
☐ 14 Mark Wipf
☐ 15 Terrell Williams
☐ 16 Scottie Williams
☐ 17 Eddy Beltre
☐ 18 Marc Kroon
☐ 19 Pedro Belmonte
☐ 20 Ervin Collier
☐ 21 Jose Flores
☐ 22 Andrew Cotner
☐ 23 Andre David MG
☐ 24 Jesus Hernaiz CO
☐ 25 Kevin Culpepper TR
☐ 26 Geary Jones CO
☐ 27 Logo Card
☐ 28 Logo Card
☐ 29 Logo Card
☐ 30 Checklist

1992 Kingsport Mets Fleer/ProCards

This 31-card standard-size set of the 1992 Kingsport Mets, a Rookie Class Appalachian League affiliate of the New York Mets, features brown-bordered posed color player photos on its fronts. The player's name appears in an upper corner; his team and position appear in a lower corner. The white back is framed by a black line and carries the player's name at the top, followed by biography and statistics. This issue includes the minor league card debut of Raul Casanova.

	MINT	NRMT	EXC
COMPLETE SET (31)	7.00	3.10	.85

☐ 1520 Bill Bellman
☐ 1521 Pedro Belmonte
☐ 1522 Chris Berg
☐ 1523 Ervin Collier
☐ 1524 Andrew Cotner
☐ 1525 Steve Grennan
☐ 1526 Erik Hiljus
☐ 1527 Marc Kroon
☐ 1528 Allen McDill
☐ 1529 Tom Pinson
☐ 1530 Travis Shaffer
☐ 1531 Dave Swanson
☐ 1532 Scott Williams
☐ 1533 Raul Casanova
☐ 1534 Eric Harris
☐ 1535 Steve Steele
☐ 1536 Eddy Beltre
☐ 1537 Kenny Bradley
☐ 1538 Joe Flores
☐ 1539 Jeff Kiraly
☐ 1540 Jim Mrowka
☐ 1541 Ozzie Osentowski
☐ 1542 Terrell Williams
☐ 1543 Don Parker
☐ 1544 Al Shirley
☐ 1545 Donnie White
☐ 1546 Mark Wipf
☐ 1547 Andre David MG
☐ 1548 Geary Jones CO
☐ 1549 Jesus Hernaiz CO
☐ 1550 Checklist

1992 Kinston Indians Classic/Best

This 30-card standard-size set of the 1992 Kinston Indians, a Class A Carolina League affiliate of the Cleveland Indians, features white-bordered posed color player photos on its fronts. The player's name, team, and position appear at the bottom. The white back is framed by a thin red line and carries the player's name and position at the top, followed by biography, statistics and team logos.

	MINT	NRMT	EXC
COMPLETE SET (30)	5.00	2.20	.60

☐ 1 Shawn Bryant
☐ 2 Ryan Martindale
☐ 3 Brian Cofer
☐ 4 Omar Ramirez
☐ 5 Dickie Brown
☐ 6 Ty Kovach
☐ 7 Tommy Bates
☐ 8 Gary Tatterson
☐ 9 Rouglas Odor
☐ 10 John Lorms
☐ 11 Tim Donahue
☐ 12 Raymond Harvey
☐ 13 Carl Johnson
☐ 14 Chip Winiarski
☐ 15 Roberto Rivera
☐ 16 John Cotton
☐ 17 Alan Embree
☐ 18 David Bell
☐ 19 Eric Stone
☐ 20 Clyde Pough
☐ 21 Greg McCarthy
☐ 22 Darrell Whitmore
☐ 23 Herbert Perry
☐ 24 Tom Van Tiger
☐ 25 Chad Ogea
☐ 26 Dave Keller CO
☐ 27 Rick Horton CO
☐ 28 Rob Swain CO
☐ 29 Dan DeVoe TR
☐ 30 Checklist

1992 Kinston Indians Fleer/ProCards

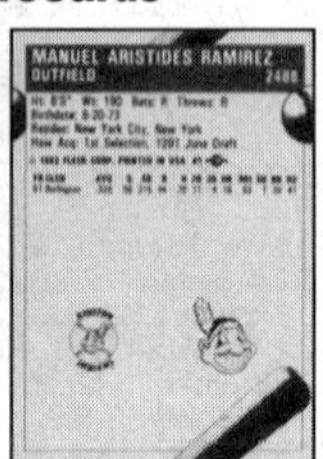

This 29-card standard-size set of the 1992 Kinston Indians, a Class A Carolina League affiliate of the Cleveland Indians, features brown-bordered posed color player photos on its fronts. The player's name appears in an upper corner; his team and position appear in a lower corner. The white back is framed by a black line and carries the player's name at the top, followed by biography and statistics. This issue includes a second year card of Manny Ramirez.

	MINT	NRMT	EXC
COMPLETE SET (29)	25.00	11.00	3.10

☐ 2466 Chad Allen
☐ 2467 Shawn Bryant
☐ 2468 Brian Cofer
☐ 2469 Alan Embree
☐ 2470 Ty Kovach
☐ 2471 Greg McCarthy
☐ 2472 Scott Morgan
☐ 2473 Chad Ogea
☐ 2474 Roberto Rivera
☐ 2475 Mark Sweeney
☐ 2476 Eric Stone
☐ 2477 Chip Winiarski
☐ 2478 John Lorms
☐ 2479 Ryan Martindale
☐ 2480 Tommy Bates
☐ 2481 David Bell
☐ 2482 John Cotton
☐ 2483 Tim Donahue
☐ 2484 Ray Harvey
☐ 2485 Rouglas Odor
☐ 2486 Herbert Perry
☐ 2487 Clyde Pough
☐ 2488 Manny Ramirez
☐ 2489 Victor Ramirez
☐ 2490 Darell Whitmore
☐ 2491 David Keller MG
☐ 2492 Rick Horton CO
☐ 2493 Rob Swain CO
☐ 2494 Checklist

1992 Knoxville Blue Jays Fleer/ProCards

This 29-card standard-size set of the 1992 Knoxville Blue Jays, a Class AA Southern League affiliate of the Toronto Blue Jays, features brown-bordered posed color player photos on its fronts. The player's name appears in an upper corner; his team and position appear in a lower corner. The white back is framed by a black line and carries the player's name and position at the top, followed by biography and statistics.

	MINT	NRMT	EXC
COMPLETE SET (29)	5.00	2.20	.60

☐ 2981 Daren Brown
☐ 2982 Tim Brown
☐ 2983 Nate Cromwell
☐ 2984 Jesse Cross
☐ 2985 Daren Kizziah
☐ 2986 Graeme Lloyd
☐ 2987 Paul Menhart
☐ 2988 Marcus Moore
☐ 2989 Mike Ogliaruso
☐ 2990 Mark Ohlms
☐ 2991 Aaron Small
☐ 2992 Jose Monzon
☐ 2993 Greg O'Halloran
☐ 2994 Jason Townley
☐ 2995 Domingo Cedeno
☐ 2996 Derek Henderson
☐ 2997 Brad Mengel
☐ 2998 Rob Montalvo
☐ 2999 Rance Mulliniks
☐ 3000 David Tollison
☐ 3001 Julian Yan
☐ 3002 Juan DeLaRosa
☐ 3003 Robert Perez
☐ 3004 Shawn Scott
☐ 3005 Nigel Wilson
☐ 3006 Garth Iorg MG
☐ 3007 Mike McAlpin CO
☐ 3008 Steve Mingori CO
☐ 3009 Checklist

1992 Knoxville Blue Jays SkyBox

This 26-card standard-size set of the 1992 Knoxville Blue Jays, a Class AA Southern League affiliate of the Toronto Blue Jays, features white-bordered posed color player photos on its fronts. The player's name appears at the top; his team and position appear at the bottom. The white back carries the player's name at the top, followed by biography and statistics.

	MINT	NRMT	EXC
COMPLETE SET (26)	5.00	2.20	.60

☐ 376 Daren Brown
☐ 377 Tim Brown
☐ 378 Domingo Cedeno
☐ 379 Nate Cromwell
☐ 380 Juan DeLaRosa
☐ 381 Derek Henderson
☐ 382 Daren Kizziah
☐ 383 Graeme Lloyd
☐ 384 Paul Menhart
☐ 385 Rob Montalvo
☐ 386 Jose Monzon
☐ 387 Marcus Moore
☐ 388 Mike Ogliaruso
☐ 389 Greg O'Halloran
☐ 390 Mark Ohlms
☐ 391 Robert Perez
☐ 392 Shawn Scott
☐ 393 Aaron Small
☐ 394 Mike Taylor
☐ 395 David Tollison
☐ 396 Jason Townley
☐ 397 Nigel Wilson
☐ 398 Julian Yan
☐ 399 Garth Iorg MG
☐ 400 Steve Mingori CO
Mike McAlpin CO
☐ NNO Checklist

1992 Lakeland Tigers Classic/Best

This 30-card standard-size set of the 1992 Lakeland Tigers, a Class A Florida State League affiliate of the Detroit Tigers, features white-bordered posed color player photos on its fronts. The player's name, team, and position appear at the bottom. The white back is framed by a thin red line and carries the player's name and position at the top, followed by biography, statistics and team logos.

	MINT	NRMT	EXC
COMPLETE SET (30)	5.00	2.20	.60

☐ 1 Bob Undorf
☐ 2 Mike Rendina
☐ 3 Eric Albright
☐ 4 Dan Ruff
☐ 5 Joe Perona
☐ 6 Ron Howard
☐ 7 Kelley O'Neal
☐ 8 Denny McNamara
☐ 9 Jose Lima
☐ 10 Brian Saltzgaber
☐ 11 Jimmy Alder
☐ 12 Greg Coppeta
☐ 13 Mike Guilfoyle
☐ 14 John Kosenski
☐ 15 Matt Bauer
☐ 16 Felipe Lira
☐ 17 Jimmy Henry
☐ 18 Jason Pfaff
☐ 19 Sean Bergman
☐ 20 Phil Stidham
☐ 21 Tom Drell
☐ 22 Jim Givens
☐ 23 Tom Ealy
☐ 24 Warren Sawkiw
☐ 25 Eddy Rodriguez
☐ 26 Rudy Pemberton
☐ 27 John Lipon MG
☐ 28 Rich Bombard CO
☐ 29 Dan Raley CO
☐ 30 Checklist

1992 Lakeland Tigers Fleer/ProCards

This 26-card standard-size set of the 1992 Lakeland Tigers, a Class A Florida State League affiliate of the Detroit Tigers, features brown-bordered posed color player photos on its fronts. The player's name appears in an upper corner; his team and position appear in a lower corner. The white back is framed by a black line and carries the player's name at the top, followed by biography and statistics.

	MINT	NRMT	EXC
COMPLETE SET (26)	5.00	2.20	.60

- ☐ 2271 Pat Ahearne
- ☐ 2272 Mike Guilfoyle
- ☐ 2273 John Kosenski
- ☐ 2274 Jose Lima
- ☐ 2275 Felipe Lira
- ☐ 2276 Jason Pfaff
- ☐ 2277 John Reid
- ☐ 2278 Eddy Rodriguez
- ☐ 2279 Phillip Stidham
- ☐ 2280 Bob Undorf
- ☐ 2281 Pedro Gonzalez
- ☐ 2282 Joe Perona
- ☐ 2283 Brian Saltzgaber
- ☐ 2284 Jimmy Alder
- ☐ 2285 Jim Givens
- ☐ 2286 Ron Howard
- ☐ 2287 Kelley O'Neal
- ☐ 2288 Mike Rendina
- ☐ 2289 Dan Ruff
- ☐ 2290 Tom Ealy
- ☐ 2291 Denny McNamara
- ☐ 2292 Rudy Pemberton
- ☐ 2293 John Lipon MG
- ☐ 2294 Rich Bombard CO
- ☐ 2295 Dan Raley CO
- ☐ 2296 Checklist

1992 Las Vegas Stars Fleer/ProCards

This 24-card standard-size set of the 1992 Las Vegas Stars, a Class AAA Pacific Coast League affiliate of the San Diego Padres, features brown-bordered posed color player photos on its fronts. The player's name appears in an upper corner; his team and position appear in a lower corner. The white back is framed by a black line and carries the player's name at the top, followed by biography and statistics.

	MINT	NRMT	EXC
COMPLETE SET (24)	5.00	2.20	.60

- ☐ 2789 Doug Brocail
- ☐ 2790 Rick Davis
- ☐ 2791 Jim Deshaies
- ☐ 2792 Jeremy Hernandez
- ☐ 2793 Mark Knudson
- ☐ 2794 Adam Peterson
- ☐ 2795 A.J. Sager
- ☐ 2796 Tim Scott
- ☐ 2797 Rafael Valdez
- ☐ 2798 Mike Basso
- ☐ 2799 Paul Faries
- ☐ 2800 Jeff Gardner
- ☐ 2801 Kevin Higgins
- ☐ 2802 Chris Jelic
- ☐ 2803 Luis Lopez
- ☐ 2804 Phil Stephenson
- ☐ 2805 Guillermo Velasquez
- ☐ 2806 Steve Pegues
- ☐ 2807 Dave Staton
- ☐ 2808 Jim Vatcher
- ☐ 2809 Jim Riggleman MG
- ☐ 2810 Tony Torchia CO
- ☐ 2811 Jon Matlack CO
- ☐ 2812 Checklist

1992 Las Vegas Stars SkyBox

	MINT	NRMT	EXC
COMPLETE SET (26)	5.00	2.20	.60

- ☐ 226 Doug Brocail
- ☐ 227 Terry Bross
- ☐ 228 Scott Coolbaugh
- ☐ 229 Rick Davis
- ☐ 230 Paul Faries
- ☐ 231 Jeff Gardner
- ☐ 232 Kevin Higgins
- ☐ 233 Mark Knudson
- ☐ 234 Tom Lampkin
- ☐ 235 Luis Lopez
- ☐ 236 Steve Pegues
- ☐ 237 Adam Peterson
- ☐ 238 A.J. Sager
- ☐ 239 Tim Scott
- ☐ 240 Frank Seminara
- ☐ 241 Dave Staton
- ☐ 242 Linty Ingram
- ☐ 243 Will Taylor
- ☐ 244 Jim Vatcher
- ☐ 245 Guillermo Velasquez
- ☐ 246 Dan Walters
- ☐ 247 Pat Wernig
- ☐ 248 Mike York
- ☐ 249 Jim Riggleman MG
- ☐ 250 Tony Torchia CO
  Jon Matlack CO
- ☐ NNO Checklist

1992 Lethbridge Mounties Sports Pro

	MINT	NRMT	EXC
COMPLETE SET (30)	6.00	2.70	.75

- ☐ 1 Todd Hudson
- ☐ 2 Milton Acevedo
- ☐ 3 Giovanni Polanco
- ☐ 4 Dan Ruhl
- ☐ 5 Anibal Campusano
- ☐ 6 Dale Ballance
- ☐ 7 Chris Edmendsen
- ☐ 8 Thomathon Good
- ☐ 9 Ross Urshan
- ☐ 10 Clark Rea
- ☐ 11 Jim Bennett CO
- ☐ 12 Blake Babki
- ☐ 13 Marcus Ponder
- ☐ 14 Paul West
- ☐ 15 Rodney Williams
- ☐ 16 Mitchell House
- ☐ 17 Mike Kimler
- ☐ 18 Thomas Lee
- ☐ 19 Matthew Scales
- ☐ 20 Lavell Cudjo
- ☐ 21 O'Brien Cunningham
- ☐ 22 Steve Lampkin
- ☐ 23 Rodney Myers
- ☐ 24 Ron Matthews
- ☐ 25 Robert Stefanik
- ☐ 26 Jim Procopio CO
- ☐ 27 Blank Card
- ☐ 28 Blank Card
- ☐ 29 Blank Card
- ☐ 30 Blank Card

1992 London Tigers Fleer/ProCards

This 29-card standard-size set of the 1992 London Tigers, a Class AA Eastern League affiliate of the Detroit Tigers, features brown-bordered posed color player photos on its fronts. The player's name appears in an upper corner; his team and position appear in a lower corner. The white back is framed by a black line and carries the player's name at the top, followed by biography and statistics.

	MINT	NRMT	EXC
COMPLETE SET (29)	5.00	2.20	.60

- ☐ 623 Don August
- ☐ 624 Jeff Braley
- ☐ 625 Sherman Corbett
- ☐ 626 Dan Freed
- ☐ 627 Mike Garcia
- ☐ 628 Frank Gonzales
- ☐ 629 Jimmy Henry
- ☐ 630 Mike Lumley
- ☐ 631 Rick Rojas
- ☐ 632 Don Vesling
- ☐ 633 Brian Warren
- ☐ 634 Marty Willis
- ☐ 635 Steve Wolf
- ☐ 636 Mike Gillette
- ☐ 637 Rick Sellers
- ☐ 638 Ivan Cruz
- ☐ 639 Mike DeButch
- ☐ 640 Kirk Mendenhall
- ☐ 641 Bob Reimink
- ☐ 642 Rod Robertson
- ☐ 643 Basilio Cabrera
- ☐ 644 Brian Cornelius
- ☐ 645 Lou Frazier
- ☐ 646 Tyrone Kingwood
- ☐ 647 Greg Sparks
- ☐ 648 Mark DeJohn MG
- ☐ 649 Bruce Fields CO
- ☐ 650 Jeff Jones CO
- ☐ 651 Checklist

1992 London Tigers SkyBox

	MINT	NRMT	EXC
COMPLETE SET (26)	5.00	2.20	.60

- ☐ 401 Jeff Braley
- ☐ 402 Basilio Cabrera
- ☐ 403 Brian Carnelius
- ☐ 404 Ivan Cruz
- ☐ 405 Mike Debutch
- ☐ 406 Lou Frazier
- ☐ 407 Dan Freed
- ☐ 408 Mike Garcia
- ☐ 409 Mike Gillete
- ☐ 410 Frank Gonzalez
- ☐ 411 Tyrone Kingwood
- ☐ 412 Mike Lumley
- ☐ 413 Kirk Mendenhall
- ☐ 414 Jose Ramos
- ☐ 415 Robert Reimink
- ☐ 416 Rod Robertson
- ☐ 417 Ricky Rojas
- ☐ 418 Rick Sellers
- ☐ 419 Greg Sparks
- ☐ 420 Leo Torres
- ☐ 421 Don Vesling
- ☐ 422 Brian Warren
- ☐ 423 Marty Willis
- ☐ 424 Mark DeJohn MG
- ☐ 425 Bruce Fields CO
- ☐ NNO Checklist

1992 Louisville Redbirds Fleer/ProCards

This 26-card standard-size set of the 1992 Louisville Redbirds, a Class AAA American Association affiliate of the St. Louis Cardinals, features brown-bordered posed color player photos on its fronts. The player's name appears in an upper corner; his team and position appear in a lower corner. The white back is framed by a black line and carries the player's name at the top, followed by biography and statistics.

	MINT	NRMT	EXC
COMPLETE SET (26)	5.00	2.20	.60

- ☐ 1879 Rene Arocha
- ☐ 1880 Jeff Ballard
- ☐ 1881 Mike Cook
- ☐ 1882 Mark Grater
- ☐ 1883 Mike Hinkle
- ☐ 1884 Blaise Ilsley
- ☐ 1885 Paul Kilgus
- ☐ 1886 Mike Loynd
- ☐ 1887 Tim Sherrill
- ☐ 1888 Tom Urbani
- ☐ 1889 Ed Fulton
- ☐ 1890 Tim Redman
- ☐ 1891 Alex Trevino
- ☐ 1892 Greg Carmona
- ☐ 1893 Bien Figueroa
- ☐ 1894 Stan Royer
- ☐ 1895 Jeff Shireman
- ☐ 1896 Tracy Woodson
- ☐ 1897 Rod Brewer
- ☐ 1898 Ozzie Canseco
- ☐ 1899 Chuck Carr
- ☐ 1900 Curt Ford
- ☐ 1901 Lonnie Maclin
- ☐ 1902 Jack Krol MG
- ☐ 1903 Mark Riggins CO
- ☐ 1904 Checklist

1992 Louisville Redbirds SkyBox

	MINT	NRMT	EXC
COMPLETE SET (26)	5.00	2.20	.60

- ☐ 251 Rene Arocha
- ☐ 252 Jeff Ballard
- ☐ 253 Rod Brewer
- ☐ 254 Ozzie Canseco
- ☐ 255 Greg Carmona
- ☐ 256 Rico Christian
- ☐ 257 Mark Clark
- ☐ 258 Mike Cook
- ☐ 259 Mike Loynd
- ☐ 260 Joey Fernandez
- ☐ 261 Jose Fernandez
- ☐ 262 Bien Figueroa
- ☐ 263 Mark Grater
- ☐ 264 Mike Hinkle
- ☐ 265 Blaise Ilsley
- ☐ 266 Paul Kilgus
- ☐ 267 Lonnie Maclin
- ☐ 268 Stan Royer
- ☐ 269 Tim Sherrill
- ☐ 270 Jeff Shireman
- ☐ 271 Alex Trevino
- ☐ 272 Tracy Woodson
- ☐ 273 Mike Milchin
- ☐ 274 Jack Krol MG
- ☐ 275 Mark Reggins CO
- ☐ NNO Checklist

1992 LSU Tigers McDag

	MINT	NRMT	EXC
COMPLETE SET (16)	15.00	6.75	1.85

- ☐ 1 Skip Bertman CO
- ☐ 2 Adrian Antonini
- ☐ 3 Chris Moock
- ☐ 4 Harry Berrios
- ☐ 5 Rick Greene
- ☐ 6 Scott Schultz
- ☐ 7 Mike Neal
- ☐ 8 Lloyd Peever
- ☐ 9 Armando Rios
- ☐ 10 Andy Sheets
- ☐ 11 Mike Sirotka
- ☐ 12 Todd Walker
- ☐ 13 Kenny Jackson
- ☐ 14 Russ Johnson
- ☐ 15 David Herry
- ☐ 16 Jared Mula

1992 Lynchburg Red Sox Classic/Best

This 30-card standard-size set of the 1992 Lynchburg Red Sox, a Class A Carolina League affiliate of the Boston Red Sox, features white-bordered posed color player photos on its fronts. The player's name, team, and position appear at the bottom. The white back is framed by a thin red line and carries the player's name and position at the top, followed by biography, statistics and team logos. This issue includes the minor league card debut of Aaron Sele.

	MINT	NRMT	EXC
COMPLETE SET (30)	6.00	2.70	.75

- ☐ 1 Frank Rodriguez
- ☐ 2 John Eierman
- ☐ 3 Pete Estrada
- ☐ 4 Jose Marin
- ☐ 5 Cory Bailey
- ☐ 6 Jason Friedman
- ☐ 7 Tony Rodriguez
- ☐ 8 Denny Berni
- ☐ 9 Walt McKeel
- ☐ 10 Paul Rappoli
- ☐ 11 Luis Ortiz
- ☐ 12 Tim Graham
- ☐ 13 Erik Plantenberg
- ☐ 14 Andy Rush
- ☐ 15 David Klvac
- ☐ 16 Aaron Sele
- ☐ 17 Kevin Carroll
- ☐ 18 Jim Crowley
- ☐ 19 Boo Moore
- ☐ 20 Joe Caruso
- ☐ 21 Mark Konopki
- ☐ 22 John Malzone
- ☐ 23 Tim VanEgmond
- ☐ 24 Jim Dennison
- ☐ 25 Jim Morrison
- ☐ 26 Buddy Bailey MG
- ☐ 27 David Duchin TR
- ☐ 28 Logo Card
- ☐ 29 Logo Card
- ☐ 30 Checklist

1992 Lynchburg Red Sox Fleer/ProCards

This 26-card standard-size set of the 1992 Lynchburg Red Sox, a Class A Carolina League affiliate of the Boston Red Sox, features brown-bordered posed color player photos on its fronts. The player's name appears in an upper corner; his team and position appear in a lower corner. The white back is framed by a black line and carries the player's name at the top, followed by biography and statistics. This issue includes the minor league card debut of Aaron Sele and a second year card of Frank Rodriguez.

	MINT	NRMT	EXC
COMPLETE SET (26)	6.00	2.70	.75

- ☐ 2898 Cory Bailey
- ☐ 2899 Joe Caruso
- ☐ 2900 Jim Dennison
- ☐ 2901 Pete Estrada
- ☐ 2902 Dave Klvac
- ☐ 2903 Mark Konopki
- ☐ 2904 Erik Plantenberg
- ☐ 2905 Frank Rodriguez
- ☐ 2906 Andy Rush
- ☐ 2907 Aaron Sele
- ☐ 2908 Tim Vanegmond
- ☐ 2909 Denny Berni
- ☐ 2910 Kevin Carroll
- ☐ 2911 Walt McKeel
- ☐ 2912 Jim Crowley
- ☐ 2913 Jason Friedman
- ☐ 2914 John Malzone
- ☐ 2915 Jose Marin
- ☐ 2916 Luis Ortiz
- ☐ 2917 Tony Rodriguez
- ☐ 2918 John Eierman
- ☐ 2919 Tim Graham
- ☐ 2920 Boo Moore
- ☐ 2921 Jim Morrison
- ☐ 2922 Paul Rappoli
- ☐ 2923 Checklist

1992 Macon Braves Classic/Best

This 30-card standard-size set of the 1992 Macon Braves, a Class A South Atlantic League affiliate of the Atlanta Braves, features white-bordered posed color player photos on its fronts. The player's name, team, and position appear at the bottom. The white back is framed by a thin red line and carries the player's name and position at the top, followed by biography, statistics and team logos.

	MINT	NRMT	EXC
COMPLETE SET (30)	6.00	2.70	.75

☐ 1 Anthony Graffagnino
☐ 2 Dirk Blair
☐ 3 Lansing Marks
☐ 4 David Toth
☐ 5 George Virgilio
☐ 6 Dario Paulino
☐ 7 Steve Swail
☐ 8 Manuel Jimenez
☐ 9 Joe Ayrault
☐ 10 Travis Dunlap
☐ 11 Cory Crosnoe
☐ 12 John Wilder
☐ 13 Blase Sparma
☐ 14 Kevin Saulter
☐ 15 Jason Butler
☐ 16 Michael Josephina
☐ 17 Juan Williams
☐ 18 Vincent Moore
☐ 19 Jason Keeline
☐ 20 Carlos Reyes
☐ 21 Michael Place
☐ 22 Christopher Seelbach
☐ 23 Kurt Burgess
☐ 24 Don Robinson
☐ 25 Jason Schmidt
☐ 26 Brian Snitker MG
☐ 27 Glenn Hubbard CO
☐ 28 Larry Jaster CO
☐ 29 Logo Card
☐ 30 Checklist

1992 Macon Braves Fleer/ProCards

This 30-card standard-size set of the 1992 Macon Braves, a Class A South Atlantic League affiliate of the Atlanta Braves, features brown-bordered posed color player photos on its fronts. The player's name appears in an upper corner; his team and position appear in a lower corner. The white back is framed by a black line and carries the player's name at the top, followed by biography and statistics. This issue includes the minor league card debut of Jason Schmidt.

	MINT	NRMT	EXC
COMPLETE SET (30)	6.00	2.70	.75

☐ 258 Dirk Blair
☐ 259 Kurt Burgess
☐ 260 Jason Butler
☐ 261 Travis Dunlap
☐ 262 Scott Francis
☐ 263 Jerry Koller
☐ 264 Mike Place
☐ 265 Carlos Reyes
☐ 266 Kevin Saulter
☐ 267 Jason Schmidt
☐ 268 Chris Seelbach
☐ 269 John Wilder
☐ 270 Joe Ayrault
☐ 271 David Toth
☐ 272 Cory Crosnoe
☐ 273 Anthony Graffagnino
☐ 274 Manny Jimenez
☐ 275 Jason Keeline
☐ 276 Lance Marks
☐ 277 Dominic Therrien
☐ 278 George Virgilio
☐ 279 Mike Josephina
☐ 280 Vince Moore
☐ 281 Richard Paulino
☐ 282 Don Robinson
☐ 283 Juan Williams
☐ 284 Brian Snitker MG
☐ 285 Glenn Hubbard CO
☐ 286 Larry Jaster CO
☐ 287 Checklist

1992 Madison Muskies Classic/Best

This 30-card standard-size set of the 1992 Madison Muskies, a Class A Midwest League affiliate of the Oakland Athletics, features white-bordered posed color player photos on its fronts. The player's name, team, and position appear at the bottom. The white back is framed by a thin red line and carries the player's name and position at the top, followed by biography, statistics and team logos.

	MINT	NRMT	EXC
COMPLETE SET (30)	5.00	2.20	.60

☐ 1 Creighton Gubanich
☐ 2 Ramon Fermin
☐ 3 Jeff Duncan
☐ 4 Dane Walker
☐ 5 Greg Reid
☐ 6 Rob Leary
☐ 7 Miguel Jimenez
☐ 8 Tom Havens
☐ 9 Gary Hust
☐ 10 Ricardo Mendez
☐ 11 Eric Booker
☐ 12 Steve Shoemaker
☐ 13 Lee Cusey
☐ 14 Luinis Aracena
☐ 15 Scott Sheldon
☐ 16 George Williams
☐ 17 Brad Parker
☐ 18 Brad Stowell
☐ 19 Ray Sutch
☐ 20 Mike Rossiter
☐ 21 Tom Myers
☐ 22 Robert Pierce
☐ 23 Scott Rose
☐ 24 Tony Scharff
☐ 25 Vincente Francisco
☐ 26 Dick Scott MG
☐ 27 Gil Patterson CO
☐ 28 Brian Thorson TR
☐ 29 Logo Card
☐ 30 Checklist

1992 Madison Muskies Fleer/ProCards

This 29-card standard-size set of the 1992 Madison Muskies, a Class A Midwest League affiliate of the Oakland Athletics, features brown-bordered posed color player photos on its fronts. The player's name appears in an upper corner; his team and position appear in a lower corner. The white back is framed by a black line and carries the player's name at the top, followed by biography and statistics.

	MINT	NRMT	EXC
COMPLETE SET (29)	5.00	2.20	.60

☐ 1226 Lee Cusey
☐ 1227 Ramon Fermin
☐ 1228 Miguel Jimenez
☐ 1229 Keith Millay
☐ 1230 Tim Minik
☐ 1231 Tom Myers
☐ 1232 Rob Pierce
☐ 1233 Scott Rose
☐ 1234 Mike Rossiter
☐ 1235 Steve Shoemaker
☐ 1236 Brad Stowell
☐ 1237 Ray Sutch
☐ 1238 Creighton Gubanich
☐ 1239 George Williams
☐ 1240 Jeff Duncan
☐ 1241 Vicente Francisco
☐ 1242 Tom Havens
☐ 1243 Rob Leary
☐ 1244 Ricardo Mendez
☐ 1245 Brad Parker
☐ 1246 Scott Sheldon
☐ 1247 Luinis Aracena
☐ 1248 Eric Booker
☐ 1249 Gary Hust
☐ 1250 Greg Reid
☐ 1251 Dane Walker
☐ 1252 Dickie Scott MG
☐ 1253 Gil Patterson CO
☐ 1254 Checklist

1992 Martinsville Phillies Classic/Best

This 30-card standard-size set of the 1992 Martinsville Phillies, a Rookie Class Appalachian League affiliate of the Philadelphia Phillies, features white-bordered posed color player photos on its fronts. The player's name, team, and position appear at the bottom. The white back is framed by a thin red line and carries the player's name and position at the top, followed by biography, statistics and team logos.

	MINT	NRMT	EXC
COMPLETE SET (30)	5.00	2.20	.60

☐ 1 Larry Mitchell
☐ 2 Michael Crouwel
☐ 3 Sean Boldt
☐ 4 Charlton Moore
☐ 5 Michael Thompson
☐ 6 Tony Costa
☐ 7 Ben Martinez
☐ 8 Joey Jelinek
☐ 9 Phillip Romero
☐ 10 Rickey Bush
☐ 11 Jason Urbanek
☐ 12 Rob Mitchell
☐ 13 Scott Coleman
☐ 14 Tim Cornish
☐ 15 Jeremey Kendall
☐ 16 Scott Haws
☐ 17 Tim Pugh
☐ 18 Brent Bell
☐ 19 Mike Shipman
☐ 20 David Fisher
☐ 21 William Carmona
☐ 22 Tony Fiore
☐ 23 Sam Edwards
☐ 24 Kevin Alger
☐ 25 E.J. Brophy
☐ 26 Dell Allen
☐ 27 Fernando Mejias
☐ 28 Steve Nutt
☐ 29 Stanley Evans
☐ 30 Roly DeArmas MG
Checklist

1992 Martinsville Phillies Fleer/ProCards

This 32-card standard-size set of the 1992 Martinsville Phillies, a Rookie Class Appalachian League affiliate of the Philadelphia Phillies, features brown-bordered posed color player photos on its fronts. The player's name appears in an upper corner; his team and position appear in a lower corner. The white back is framed by a black line and carries the player's name at the top, followed by biography and statistics.

	MINT	NRMT	EXC
COMPLETE SET (32)	5.00	2.20	.60

☐ 3045 Kevin Alger
☐ 3046 Sean Boldt
☐ 3047 Scott Coleman
☐ 3048 Tim Costa
☐ 3049 Sam Edwards
☐ 3050 Tony Fiore
☐ 3051 Trevor Humphry
☐ 3052 Fernando Mejias
☐ 3053 Larry Mitchell
☐ 3054 Rob Mitchell
☐ 3055 Steven Nutt
☐ 3056 Tim Pugh
☐ 3057 E.J. Brophy
☐ 3058 Ricky Bush
☐ 3059 Mike Crouwel
☐ 3060 Scott Haws
☐ 3061 Mike Shipman
☐ 3062 Dell Allen
☐ 3063 Brent Bell
☐ 3064 David Fisher
☐ 3065 Joey Jelinek
☐ 3066 Philip Romero
☐ 3067 Jason Urbanek
☐ 3068 William Carmona
☐ 3069 Tim Cornish
☐ 3070 Stanley Evans
☐ 3071 Jeremy Kendall
☐ 3072 Ben Martinez
☐ 3073 Charlton Moore
☐ 3074 Michael Thompson
☐ 3075 Roly DeArmas MG
☐ 3076 Checklist

1992 Medicine Hat Blue Jays Fleer/ProCards

This 24-card standard-size set of the 1992 Medicine Hat Blue Jays, a Class A Pioneer League affiliate of the Toronto Blue Jays, features brown-bordered posed color player photos on its fronts. The player's name appears in an upper corner; his team and position appear in a lower corner. The white back is framed by a black line and carries the player's name and position at the top, followed by biography and statistics.

	MINT	NRMT	EXC
COMPLETE SET (24)	5.00	2.20	.60

☐ 3201 Alonso Beltran
☐ 3202 Walter Bills
☐ 3203 Chad Brown
☐ 3204 Pat Crema
☐ 3205 Andrew Dolson
☐ 3206 Harry Muir
☐ 3207 Mike O'Halloran
☐ 3208 Randy Phillips
☐ 3209 Gabriel Reynoso
☐ 3210 Angel Martinez
☐ 3211 Pete Polis
☐ 3212 Carlos Colmenares
☐ 3213 Emanuel Hayes
☐ 3214 Matt Johnson
☐ 3215 Alexis Luna
☐ 3216 Wade Norris
☐ 3217 Matt Wilke
☐ 3218 Rickey Cradle
☐ 3219 Sean Hearn
☐ 3220 Jose Herrera
☐ 3221 Kadir Villalona
☐ 3222 Jim Nettles MG
☐ 3223 Scott Miller CO
☐ 3224 Checklist

1992 Medicine Hat Blue Jays Sports Pro

This 29-card standard-size set of the 1992 Medicine Hat Blue Jays, a Class A Pioneer League affiliate of the Toronto Blue Jays, features on its fronts white-bordered posed color player photos framed by double black lines. The white-on-black team name appears at the top. The white back is framed by double black lines and carries the year and team name at the top, followed by the player's name, uniform number, position, and biography. The sponsor's name, Safeway, appears near the bottom.

	MINT	NRMT	EXC
COMPLETE SET (29)	6.00	2.70	.75

☐ 1 Matt Johnson
☐ 2 Chad Brown
☐ 3 Sean Hearn
☐ 4 Pat Crema
☐ 5 Emanuel Hayes
☐ 6 Angel Martinez
☐ 7 Alonso Beltran
☐ 8 Andrew Dolson
☐ 9 Jose Herrera
☐ 10 Harry Muir
☐ 11 Randy Phillips
☐ 12 Pascuel Herrera
☐ 13 Wade Norris
☐ 14 Walter Bills
☐ 15 Rickey Cradle
☐ 16 Pete Polis
☐ 17 Alexis Luna
☐ 18 Carlos Colmenares
☐ 19 Kadir Villalona
☐ 20 Mike O'Halloran
☐ 21 Gabriel Reynoso
☐ 22 Michael Taylor
☐ 23 Jeff Patzke
☐ 24 Tom Evans
☐ 25 Rob Patterson
☐ 26 Mike Wirsta TR
☐ 27 Scott Miller CO
☐ 28 Gilbert Rondon CO
☐ 29 Jim Nettles MG

1992 Memphis Chicks Fleer/ProCards

This 29-card standard-size set of the 1992 Memphis Chicks, a Class AA Southern League affiliate of the Kansas City Royals, features brown-bordered posed color player photos on its fronts. The player's name appears in an upper corner; his team and position appear in a lower corner. The white back is framed by a black line and carries the player's name and position at the top, followed by biography and statistics.

	MINT	NRMT	EXC
COMPLETE SET (29)	5.00	2.20	.60

☐ 2410 Archie Corbin
☐ 2411 Steve Curry
☐ 2412 Chip Duncan
☐ 2413 Greg Harvey
☐ 2414 Matt Karchner
☐ 2415 Danny Miceli
☐ 2416 Mark Parnell
☐ 2417 Vladimir Perez
☐ 2418 Ed Pierce
☐ 2419 Ed Puig
☐ 2420 Skip Wiley
☐ 2421 Greg David
☐ 2422 Carlos Diaz
☐ 2423 Lance Jennings
☐ 2424 Paco Burgos
☐ 2425 Jeff Garber
☐ 2426 Phil Hiatt
☐ 2427 Domingo Mota
☐ 2428 Darryl Robinson
☐ 2429 Rich Tunison
☐ 2430 Tony Bridges
☐ 2431 Tim Leiper
☐ 2432 Les Norman
☐ 2433 Dan Rohrmeier
☐ 2434 Doug Shields
☐ 2435 Brian Poldberg MG
☐ 2436 Mike Alvarez CO
☐ 2437 U.L. Washington CO
☐ 2438 Checklist

1992 Memphis Chicks SkyBox

	MINT	NRMT	EXC
COMPLETE SET (26)	5.00	2.20	.60

☐ 426 Brian Ahern
☐ 427 Tony Bridges
☐ 428 Paco Burgos
☐ 429 Josias Manzanillo
☐ 430 Adam Casillas
☐ 431 Archie Corbin
☐ 432 Steve Curry
☐ 433 Greg David
☐ 434 Carlos Diaz
☐ 435 Jeff Garber
☐ 436 Phil Hiatt
☐ 437 Matt Karchner
☐ 438 Marcus Lawton
☐ 439 Domingo Mota
☐ 440 Mark Parnell
☐ 441 Tim Leiper
☐ 442 Ed Pierce
☐ 443 Ed Puig
☐ 444 Darryl Robinson
☐ 445 Dan Rohrmeier
☐ 446 Rich Tunison
☐ 447 Hugh Walker
☐ 448 Skip Wiley
☐ 449 Brian Poldberg MG
☐ 450 U.L. Washington CO
Mike Alvarez CO
☐ NNO Checklist

1992 Midland Angels One Hour Photo

This 28-card set of the 1992 Midland Angels, a Class AA Texas League affiliate of the California Angels, features color player photos. The set measures approximately 5 1/2" by 5". The backs are blank. The cards are unnumbered and checklisted below in alphabetical order. 500 sets were produced.

	MINT	NRMT	EXC
COMPLETE SET (28)	75.00	34.00	9.50

- ☐ 1 Dave Adams
- ☐ 2 Garret Anderson
- ☐ 3 Tony Brown
- ☐ 4 Rod Correia
- ☐ 5 Ken Edenfield
- ☐ 6 Jim Edmonds
- ☐ 7 Hilly Hathaway
- ☐ 8 John Jackson
- ☐ 9 Todd James
- ☐ 10 Bobby Jones
- ☐ 11 Corey Kapano
- ☐ 12 Jeff Kipila
- ☐ 13 Joe Kraemer
- ☐ 14 Marcus Lawton
- ☐ 15 Rey Martinez
- ☐ 16 Brett Merriman
- ☐ 17 Nate Oliver
- ☐ 18 Steve Peck
- ☐ 19 Troy Percival
- ☐ 20 Eduardo Perez
- ☐ 21 J.R. Phillips
- ☐ 22 Darryl Scott
- ☐ 23 Paul Swingle
- ☐ 24 Terry Taylor
- ☐ 25 Fausto Tejero
- ☐ 26 Don Vidmar
- ☐ 27 Mark Wasinger
- ☐ 28 Mark Zappelli

1992 Midland Angels Fleer/ProCards

This 26-card standard-size set of the 1992 Midland Angels, a Class AA Texas League affiliate of the California Angels, features brown-bordered posed color player photos on its fronts. The player's name appears in an upper corner; his team and position appear in a lower corner. The white back is framed by a black line and carries the player's name and position at the top, followed by biography and statistics. This issue includes a fifth year card of Jim Edmonds.

	MINT	NRMT	EXC
COMPLETE SET (26)	8.00	3.60	1.00

- ☐ 4018 Dave Adams
- ☐ 4019 Marvin Cobb
- ☐ 4020 Ken Edenfield
- ☐ 4021 Mark Holzemer
- ☐ 4022 Todd James
- ☐ 4023 Joe Kraemer
- ☐ 4024 Phil Leftwich
- ☐ 4025 Brett Merriman
- ☐ 4026 Steve Peck
- ☐ 4027 Darryl Scott
- ☐ 4028 Paul Swingle
- ☐ 4029 Mark Zappelli
- ☐ 4030 Mick Billmeyer
- ☐ 4031 Fausto Tejero
- ☐ 4032 Rod Correia
- ☐ 4033 Walt McConnell
- ☐ 4034 Jonathan Romero
- ☐ 4035 Terry Taylor
- ☐ 4036 Tony Brown
- ☐ 4037 Jim Edmonds
- ☐ 4038 Jeff Kipila
- ☐ 4039 Dan Rumsey
- ☐ 4040 Don Long MG
- ☐ 4041 Nate Oliver CO
- ☐ 4042 Kernan Ronan CO
- ☐ 4043 Checklist

1992 Midland Angels SkyBox

	MINT	NRMT	EXC
COMPLETE SET (26)	8.00	3.60	1.00

- ☐ 451 Clemente Acosta
- ☐ 452 Dave Adams
- ☐ 453 Mick Billmeyer
- ☐ 454 Fausto Tejero
- ☐ 455 Tony Brown
- ☐ 456 Marvin Cobb
- ☐ 457 Rod Correia
- ☐ 458 Jim Edmonds
- ☐ 459 John Jackson
- ☐ 460 Bobby Jones
- ☐ 461 Corey Kapano
- ☐ 462 Jeff Kipila
- ☐ 463 Joe Kraemer
- ☐ 464 Rey Martinez
- ☐ 465 Walt McConnell
- ☐ 466 Brett Merriman
- ☐ 467 Steve Peck
- ☐ 468 J.R. Phillips
- ☐ 469 Darryl Scott
- ☐ 470 Matt Stark
- ☐ 471 Paul Swingle
- ☐ 472 Terry Taylor
- ☐ 473 Mark Zappelli
- ☐ 474 Don Long MG
- ☐ 475 Nate Oliver CO
  Kernan Ronan CO
- ☐ NNO Checklist

1992 Midwest League All-Stars Team Issue

	MINT	NRMT	EXC
COMPLETE SET (54)	12.00	5.50	1.50

- ☐ 1 Mike Badorek
- ☐ 2 James Baldwin
- ☐ 3 Allen Battle
- ☐ 4 Brian Bevil
- ☐ 5 Bobby Chouinard
- ☐ 6 Frank Cimorelli
- ☐ 7 Jeff Cirillo
- ☐ 8 Mike Couture
- ☐ 9 Mike Ferry
- ☐ 10 Rick Forney
- ☐ 11 Jon Fuller
- ☐ 12 Steve Gibralter
- ☐ 13 Ken Grundt
- ☐ 14 Gary Hagy
- ☐ 15 Shane Halter
- ☐ 16 Jason Hardtke
- ☐ 17 Heath Haynes
- ☐ 18 Steve Hazlett
- ☐ 19 Tyrone Hill
- ☐ 20 Steve Hinton
- ☐ 21 Tyrone Horne
- ☐ 22 Mark Johnson
- ☐ 23 Andre Keene
- ☐ 24 Brian Kenny
- ☐ 25 Brian Koelling
- ☐ 26 Rick Krivda
- ☐ 27 Ed Larregui
- ☐ 28 Buck McNabb
- ☐ 29 Ricardo Medina
- ☐ 30 Alex Ochoa
- ☐ 31 Orlando Palmeiro
- ☐ 32 Jeff Pierce
- ☐ 33 Chris Pritchett
- ☐ 34 Joe Randa
- ☐ 35 Kevin Riggs
- ☐ 36 Mike Rossiter
- ☐ 37 Adrian Sanchez
- ☐ 38 Jerry Santos
- ☐ 39 Scott Sheldon
- ☐ 40 Scott Simmons
- ☐ 41 Mike Stefanski
- ☐ 42 Jose Stela
- ☐ 43 Chad Strickland
- ☐ 44 Scott Talanoa
- ☐ 45 Joey Terilli
- ☐ 46 Kerry Valrie
- ☐ 47 Jim Waring
- ☐ 48 B.J. Waszgis
- ☐ 49 Gabe White
- ☐ 50 Steve Whitehead
- ☐ 51 Jim Wolff
- ☐ 52 Tyrone Woods
- ☐ 53 Shad Williams
- ☐ 54 Dmitri Young

1992 Mississippi State Bulldogs

	MINT	NRMT	EXC
COMPLETE SET (50)	10.00	4.50	1.25

- ☐ 1 Daryl Albro
- ☐ 2 Clint Allen
- ☐ 3 Charlie Anderson
- ☐ 4 Craig Bane
- ☐ 5 Ron Brown
- ☐ 6 Rex Buckner
- ☐ 7 Matt Carpenter
- ☐ 8 Bubba Carter
- ☐ 9 Brian Clark
- ☐ 10 Chuck Daniel
- ☐ 11 Logan DeFord
- ☐ 12 Jim Ellis
- ☐ 13 Brent Deweese
- ☐ 14 Park Evans
- ☐ 15 Hap Fleming
- ☐ 16 Jon Harden
- ☐ 17 Nat Harden
- ☐ 18 Robbie Hayes
- ☐ 19 Steve Hegan
- ☐ 20 Carl Henderson
- ☐ 21 Tripp Hill
- ☐ 22 Tom Howe
- ☐ 23 Steve Johnigan
- ☐ 24 Kyle Kennedy
- ☐ 25 Carlton Loewer
- ☐ 26 Eddie Lyons
- ☐ 27 Jeff Mackin
- ☐ 28 Joel Matthews
- ☐ 29 Blake Mayo
- ☐ 30 Doug Newman
- ☐ 31 David Perkins
- ☐ 32 Paul Petrulis
- ☐ 33 Ron Polk CO
- ☐ 34 Jay Powell
- ☐ 35 Tom Quinn
- ☐ 36 Gary Rath
- ☐ 37 Ricky Joe Redd
- ☐ 38 Brian Roundtree
- ☐ 39 Steve Smith CO
- ☐ 40 Mitch Thompson CO
- ☐ 41 Larry Tomkins
- ☐ 42 Scott Tribolet
- ☐ 43 Bryan Triche
- ☐ 44 B.J. Wallace
- ☐ 45 Drew Williams
- ☐ 46 Checklist
- ☐ 47 Diamond Girls
- ☐ 48 Dudy Noble Field
- ☐ 49 Graduate Assistant
  Coaches
  Paul Wyczawski
  Rob McDonald
  Marty Lamb
  Pat Olmi
- ☐ 50 Managers - Trainers
  Greg Bishop TR
  Phil Page Tr
  Jay Bailey MG
  Jason Ayers MG
  John Mooney MG
  Lance Vining MG

1992 Modesto A's Classic/Best

This 30-card standard-size set of the 1992 Modesto A's, a Class A California League affiliate of the Oakland Athletics, features white-bordered posed color player photos on its fronts. The player's name, team, and position appear at the bottom. The white back is framed by a thin red line and carries the player's name and position at the top, followed by biography, statistics and team logos.

	MINT	NRMT	EXC
COMPLETE SET (30)	5.00	2.20	.60

- ☐ 1 Jason Wood
- ☐ 2 Curtis Shaw
- ☐ 3 Eric Helfand
- ☐ 4 Damon Mashore
- ☐ 5 Chris Hart
- ☐ 6 Steve Wojciechowski
- ☐ 7 Garrett Beard
- ☐ 8 Tanyon Sturtze
- ☐ 9 Eric Booker
- ☐ 10 Ernie Young
- ☐ 11 Chaon Garland
- ☐ 12 Jeff Barnes
- ☐ 13 Steve Callahan
- ☐ 14 Craig Sudbury
- ☐ 15 Brent Gates
- ☐ 16 Brett Hendley
- ☐ 17 Manny Martinez
- ☐ 18 Mike Raczka
- ☐ 19 Carlos Salazar
- ☐ 20 Mike Grimes
- ☐ 21 Jim Dillon
- ☐ 22 Ken Hokuf
- ☐ 23 Jose Martinez
- ☐ 24 Tom Carcione
- ☐ 25 Ted Kubiak MG
- ☐ 26 Pete Richart CO
  Sic, Riechart
- ☐ 27 Dave Hollenback TR
- ☐ 28 Logo Card
- ☐ 29 Logo Card
- ☐ 30 Checklist

1992 Modesto A's Fleer/ProCards

This 22-card standard-size set of the 1992 Modesto A's, a Class A California League affiliate of the Oakland Athletics, features brown-bordered posed color player photos on its fronts. The player's name appears in an upper corner; his team and position appear in a lower corner. The white back is framed by a black line and carries the player's name and position at the top, followed by biography and statistics.

	MINT	NRMT	EXC
COMPLETE SET (22)	5.00	2.20	.60

- ☐ 3891 Steve Callahan
- ☐ 3892 Jim Dillon
- ☐ 3893 Chaon Garland
- ☐ 3894 Mike Grimes
- ☐ 3895 Ken Hokuf
- ☐ 3896 Joe Martinez
- ☐ 3897 Dan Nerat
- ☐ 3898 Curtis Shaw
- ☐ 3899 Craig Sudbury
- ☐ 3900 Steve Wojciechowski
- ☐ 3901 Garrett Beard
- ☐ 3902 Tom Carcione
- ☐ 3903 Eric Helfand
- ☐ 3904 Jeff Barns
- ☐ 3905 Brent Gates
- ☐ 3906 Brett Hendley
- ☐ 3907 Carlos Salazar
- ☐ 3908 Jason Wood
- ☐ 3909 Damon Mashore
- ☐ 3910 Ted Kubiak MG
- ☐ 3911 Pete Richert CO
- ☐ 3912 Checklist

1992 Myrtle Beach Hurricanes Classic/Best

]This 30-card standard-size set of the 1992 Myrtle Beach Hurricanes, a Class A South Atlantic League affiliate of the Toronto Blue Jays, features white-bordered posed color player photos on its fronts. The player's name, team, and position appear near the bottom. The white back is framed by an orange line and carries the player's name and position at the top, followed by biography and statistics. This issue includes the minor league debut of Alex Gonzalez.

	MINT	NRMT	EXC
COMPLETE SET (30)	7.00	3.10	.85

- ☐ 1 Chris Weinke
- ☐ 2 John Tsoukalas
- ☐ 3 Trevor Mallory
- ☐ 4 Rob Adkins
- ☐ 5 Anastacio Garcia
- ☐ 6 Ben Weber
- ☐ 7 Dennis Gray
- ☐ 8 Mike Morland
- ☐ 9 Ronald Reams
- ☐ 10 Chris Stynes
- ☐ 11 Alex Gonzalez
- ☐ 12 Rich Butler
- ☐ 13 Rick Holifield
- ☐ 14 Chris Kotes
- ☐ 15 Joe Lis Jr.
- ☐ 16 Stoney Briggs
- ☐ 17 Darin Nolan
- ☐ 18 Tim Lindsay
- ☐ 19 Felipe Crespo
- ☐ 20 Mike Taylor
- ☐ 21 Brent Lutz
- ☐ 22 Gabriel Rosario
- ☐ 23 Paul Spoljaric
- ☐ 24 Albert Montoya
- ☐ 25 Giovanni Carrara
- ☐ 26 Kurt Heble
- ☐ 27 Doug Ault MG
- ☐ 28 Leroy Stanton CO
- ☐ 29 Darren Balsley CO
- ☐ 30 Dennis Brogna TR
  Checklist

1992 Myrtle Beach Hurricanes Fleer/ProCards

This 29-card standard-size set of the 1992 Myrtle Beach Hurricanes, a Class A South Atlantic League affiliate of the Toronto Blue Jays, features brown-bordered posed color player photos on its fronts. The player's name appears in an upper corner; his team and position appear in a lower corner. The white back is framed by a black line and carries the player's name and position at the top, followed by biography and statistics. This issue includes the minor league card debut of Alex Gonzalez.

	MINT	NRMT	EXC
COMPLETE SET (29)	7.00	3.10	.85

- ☐ 2188 Travis Baptist
- ☐ 2189 Raphael Garcia
- ☐ 2190 Dennis Gray
- ☐ 2191 Kurt Heble
- ☐ 2192 Chris Kotes
- ☐ 2193 Tim Lindsay
- ☐ 2194 Gregg Martin
- ☐ 2195 Albert Montoya
- ☐ 2196 Ken Robinson
- ☐ 2197 Paul Spoljaric
- ☐ 2198 Ben Weber
- ☐ 2199 Anastacio Garcia
- ☐ 2200 Brent Lutz
- ☐ 2201 Mike Morland
- ☐ 2202 Felipe Crespo
- ☐ 2203 Alex Gonzalez
- ☐ 2204 Joe Lis Jr.
- ☐ 2205 Gabriel Rosario
- ☐ 2206 Chris Stynes
- ☐ 2207 John Tsoukalas
- ☐ 2208 Chris Weinke
- ☐ 2209 Stoney Briggs
- ☐ 2210 Rich Butler
- ☐ 2211 Rick Holifield
- ☐ 2212 Ron Reams
- ☐ 2213 Doug Ault MG
- ☐ 2214 Darren Balsley CO
- ☐ 2215 Leroy Stanton CO
- ☐ 2216 Checklist

1992 Nashville Sounds Fleer/ProCards

This 26-card standard-size set of the 1992 Nashville Sounds, a Class AAA American Association affiliate of the Cincinnati Reds, features brown-bordered posed color player photos on its fronts. The player's name appears in an upper corner; his team and position appear in a lower corner. The white back is framed by a black line and carries the player's name and position at the top, followed by biography and statistics.

	MINT	NRMT	EXC
COMPLETE SET (26)	5.00	2.20	.60

☐ 1826 Brian Fisher
☐ 1827 Steve Foster
☐ 1828 Milton Hill
☐ 1829 Trevor Hoffman
☐ 1830 Tony Menendez
☐ 1831 Gino Minutelli
☐ 1832 Tim Pugh
☐ 1833 Joey Vierra
☐ 1834 Dan Wilson
☐ 1835 Rick Wrona
☐ 1836 Jeff Branson
☐ 1837 Gary Green
☐ 1838 Mark Howie
☐ 1839 Brian Lane
☐ 1840 Russ Morman
☐ 1841 Jeff Small
☐ 1842 Todd Trafton
☐ 1843 Geronimo Berroa
☐ 1844 Jacob Brumfield
☐ 1845 Nick Capra
☐ 1846 Jeff Stone
☐ 1847 Dwight Taylor
☐ 1848 Pete MacKanin MG
☐ 1849 Frank Funk CO
☐ 1850 Jim Lett CO
☐ 1851 Checklist

1992 Nashville Sounds SkyBox

	MINT	NRMT	EXC
COMPLETE SET (26)	5.00	2.20	.60

☐ 276 Troy Afenir
☐ 277 Bob Buchanan
☐ 278 Brian Fisher
☐ 279 Keith Brown
☐ 280 Nick Capra
☐ 281 Darnell Coles
☐ 282 Milton Hill
☐ 283 Ruben Escalera
☐ 284 Geronimo Berroa
☐ 285 Mark Howie
☐ 286 Tony Menendez
☐ 287 Gino Minutelli
☐ 288 Kiki Diaz
☐ 289 Tim Pugh
☐ 290 Mo Sanford
☐ 291 Jeff Schulz
☐ 292 Jose Segura
☐ 293 Jeff Small
☐ 294 Jeff Stone
☐ 295 Todd Trafton
☐ 296 Joey Vierra
☐ 297 Dan Wilson
☐ 298 Rick Wrona
☐ 299 Pete MacKanin MG
☐ 300 Frank Funk CO
Jim Left CO
John Young CO
☐ NNO Checklist

1992 New Britain Red Sox Fleer/ProCards

This 27-card standard-size set of the 1992 New Britain Red Sox, a Class AA Eastern League affiliate of the Boston Red Sox, features brown-bordered posed color player photos on its fronts. The player's name appears in an upper corner; his team and position appear in a lower corner. The white back is framed by a black line and carries the player's name and position at the top, followed by biography and statistics.

	MINT	NRMT	EXC
COMPLETE SET (27)	5.00	2.20	.60

☐ 425 Brian Conroy
☐ 426 Gar Finnvold
☐ 427 Don Florence
☐ 428 Derek Livernois
☐ 429 Tony Mosley
☐ 430 Gary Painter
☐ 431 Ed Riley
☐ 432 Kenny Ryan
☐ 433 Al Sanders
☐ 434 Tim Smith
☐ 435 Kevin Uhrhan
☐ 436 Joe Demus
☐ 437 Scott Hatteberg
☐ 438 Scott Bethea
☐ 439 Colin Dixon
☐ 440 Mike DeKneef
☐ 441 Greg Graham
☐ 442 Bill Norris
☐ 443 Willie Tatum
☐ 444 Mike Beams
☐ 445 Greg Blosser
☐ 446 Bruce Chick
☐ 447 Jeff McNeely
☐ 448 Paul Thoutsis
☐ 449 Jim Pankovits MG
☐ 450 Rick Wise CO
☐ 451 Checklist

1992 New Britain Red Sox SkyBox

	MINT	NRMT	EXC
COMPLETE SET (26)	5.00	2.20	.60

☐ 476 Michael Beams
☐ 477 Scott Bethea
☐ 478 Greg Blosser
☐ 479 Kevin Uhrhan
☐ 480 Bruce Chick
☐ 481 Mike Dekneef
☐ 482 Joe Demus
☐ 483 Colin Dixon
☐ 484 Gar Finnvold
☐ 485 Don Florence
☐ 486 Gregg Graham
☐ 487 Scott Hatteberg
☐ 488 Derek Livernois
☐ 489 Jeff McNeely
☐ 490 Tony Mosley
☐ 491 Bill Norris
☐ 492 Gary Painter
☐ 493 Ed Riley
☐ 494 Ken Ryan
☐ 495 Al Sanders
☐ 496 Tim Smith
☐ 497 Willie Tatum
☐ 498 Paul Thoutsis
☐ 499 Jim Pankovits MG
☐ 500 DeMarlo Hale CO
Rick Wise CO
☐ NNO Checklist

1992 Niagara Falls Rapids Classic/Best

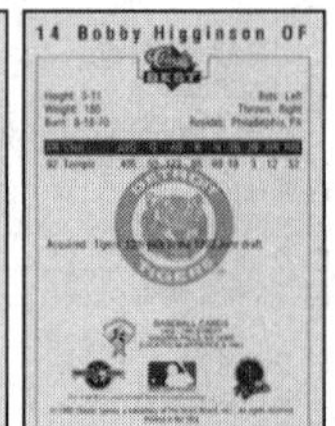

This 30-card standard-size set of the 1992 Niagara Falls , a Class A New York-Penn League affiliate of the Detroit Tigers, features white-bordered posed color player photos on its fronts. The player's name, team, and position appear at the bottom. The white back is framed by a thin red line and carries the player's name and position at the top, followed by biography, statistics and team logos. This issue includes the minor league card debut of Bobby Higginson and a third year card of Tony Clark.

	MINT	NRMT	EXC
COMPLETE SET (30)	15.00	6.75	1.85

☐ 1 Tony Clark
☐ 2 David Robson
☐ 3 Scott Pagano
☐ 4 Malvin De Jesus
☐ 5 Peter Feeley
☐ 6 Rick Martinez
☐ 7 Kazuharu Yamazaki
☐ 8 Rick Navarro
☐ 9 Robert Dickerson
☐ 10 Yoshitaro Ban
☐ 11 Mike Lopez
☐ 12 David Mysel
☐ 13 Corey Parker
☐ 14 Bobby Higginson
☐ 15 Casey Mendenhall
☐ 16 Shannon Penn
☐ 17 Carlos Fermin
☐ 18 Scott DuRussel
☐ 19 Kevin Crombie
☐ 20 John Timko
☐ 21 Sean Whiteside
☐ 22 Keith Kimsey
☐ 23 Brent Killen
☐ 24 Curt Bell
☐ 25 Dave Verduzco
☐ 26 Greg Raffo
☐ 27 Larry Parrish MG
☐ 28 Shigeyuki Takahashi CO
☐ 29 Stan Luketich CO
☐ 30 Mike Twomey TR
Checklist

1992 Niagara Falls Rapids Fleer/ProCards

This 32-card standard-size set of the 1992 Niagara Falls , a Class A New York-Penn League affiliate of the Detroit Tigers, features brown-bordered posed color player photos on its fronts. The player's name appears in an upper corner; his team and position appear in a lower corner. The white back is framed by a black line and carries the player's name and position at the top, followed by biography and statistics. This issue inlcudes the minor league card debut of Bobby Higginson and a third year card of Tony Clark.

	MINT	NRMT	EXC
COMPLETE SET (32)	15.00	6.75	1.85

☐ 3314 Yoshitaro Ban
☐ 3315 Matt Bauer
☐ 3316 Kevin Crombie
☐ 3317 Scott DuRussel
☐ 3318 Mike Lopez
☐ 3319 Doug Martin
☐ 3320 Casey Mendenhall
☐ 3321 David Mysel
☐ 3322 Greg Raffo
☐ 3323 Dave Verduzco
☐ 3324 Sean Whiteside
☐ 3325 Kazu Yamazaki
☐ 3326 Curt Bell
☐ 3327 David Robson
☐ 3328 John Timko
☐ 3329 Malvin DeJesus
☐ 3330 Peter Feeley
☐ 3331 Carlos Fermin
☐ 3332 Brent Killen
☐ 3333 Rick Martinez
☐ 3334 Corey Parker
☐ 3335 Shannon Penn
☐ 3336 Tony Clark
☐ 3337 Robert Dickerson
☐ 3338 Robin Higginbotham
☐ 3339 Bobby Higginson
☐ 3340 Keith Kimsey
☐ 3341 Scott Pagano
☐ 3342 Larry Parrish MG
☐ 3343 Stan Luketich CO
☐ 3344 Shige Takahashi CO
☐ 3345 Checklist

1992 Oklahoma City 89ers Fleer/ProCards

This 28-card standard-size set of the 1992 Oklahoma City 89ers, a Class AAA American Association League affiliate of the Texas Rangers, features brown-bordered posed color player photos on its fronts. The player's name appears in an upper corner; his team and position appear in a lower corner. The white back is framed by a black line and carries the player's name and position at the top, followed by biography and statistics.

	MINT	NRMT	EXC
COMPLETE SET (28)	5.00	2.20	.60

☐ 1905 Gerald Alexander
☐ 1906 John Barfield
☐ 1907 Kevin Blankenship
☐ 1908 Brian Bohanon
☐ 1909 Mike Campbell
☐ 1910 Don Carman
☐ 1911 Narciso Elvira
☐ 1912 Steve Fireovid
☐ 1913 Barry Manuel
☐ 1914 Roger Pavlik
☐ 1915 Wayne Rosenthal
☐ 1916 Doug Davis
☐ 1917 Ray Stephens
☐ 1918 Steve Balboni
☐ 1919 Mario Diaz
☐ 1920 Jeff Frye
☐ 1921 Chuck Jackson
☐ 1922 Rob Maurer
☐ 1923 Keith Miller
☐ 1924 Jim Presley
☐ 1925 Bob Brower
☐ 1926 Monty Fariss
☐ 1927 Dan Peltier
☐ 1928 Tony Scruggs
☐ 1929 Tommy Thompson MG
☐ 1930 Oscar Acosta CO
☐ 1931 Mike Berger P/CO
☐ 1932 Checklist

1992 Oklahoma City 89ers SkyBox

	MINT	NRMT	EXC
COMPLETE SET (26)	5.00	2.20	.60

☐ 301 Gerald Alexander
☐ 302 Steve Balboni
☐ 303 Kevin Blankenship
☐ 304 Wayne Rosenthal
☐ 305 Bob Brower
☐ 306 Todd Burns
☐ 307 Mike Campbell
☐ 308 Doug Davis
☐ 309 Tom Drees
☐ 310 Jeff Frye
☐ 311 Chuck Jackson
☐ 312 Mike Jeffcoat
☐ 313 Darrel Akerfelds
☐ 314 Rob Maurer
☐ 315 Lance McCullers
☐ 316 Russ McGinnis
☐ 317 Roger Pavlik
☐ 318 Dan Peltier
☐ 319 Paul Postier
☐ 320 Jim Presley
☐ 321 Tony Scruggs
☐ 322 Bob Sebra
☐ 323 Narciso Elvira
☐ 324 Tommy Thompson MG
☐ 325 Mike Berger CO
Oscar Acosta CO
☐ NNO Checklist

1992 Oklahoma State Cowboys

	MINT	NRMT	EXC
COMPLETE SET (32)	10.00	4.50	1.25

☐ 1 Derek Brandow
☐ 2 Jay Canizaro
☐ 3 Brian Cavalli
☐ 4 Chabon Childers
☐ 5 Coaches
Tom Holliday
Jim Schwanke
☐ 6 Scott Cunningham
☐ 7 Steve Dailey
☐ 8 Manny Gagliano
☐ 9 Rob Gaiko
☐ 10 Brad Gore
☐ 11 Jason Heath
☐ 12 Sean Hugo
☐ 13 Traver Hunter
☐ 14 Billy Kanwisher
☐ 15 Rob Linfante
☐ 16 Robert Lopez
☐ 17 Lou Lucca
☐ 18 Mark Lukasiewicz
☐ 19 James Martin
☐ 20 Paul Meador
☐ 21 Ritchie Moody
☐ 22 Fredy Ocasio
☐ 23 Peter Prodanov
☐ 24 Joe Raineri
☐ 25 Ernesto Rivera
☐ 26 Darren Tawwater
☐ 27 Hunter Triplett
☐ 28 Joe Wallace
☐ 29 Gary Ward CO
☐ 30 Scott Watkins
☐ 31 Earl Wheeler
☐ 32 Todd Wodraska

1992 Omaha Royals Fleer/ProCards

This 29-card standard-size set of the 1992 Omaha Royals, a Class AAA American Association affiliate of the Kansas City Royals, features brown-bordered posed color player photos on its fronts. The player's name appears in an upper corner; his team and position appear in a lower corner. The white back is framed by a black line and carries the player's name and position at the top, followed by biography and statistics. This issue includes a fifth year card of Jeff Conine.

	MINT	NRMT	EXC
COMPLETE SET (29)	6.00	2.70	.75

☐ 2952 Brian Ahern
☐ 2953 Jose Bautista
☐ 2954 Jim Campbell
☐ 2955 Dera Clark
☐ 2956 Mark Huismann
☐ 2957 Reese Lambert
☐ 2958 Carlos Maldonado
☐ 2959 Josias Manzanillo
☐ 2960 Dennis Moeller
☐ 2961 Steve Shifflett
☐ 2962 Rich Sauveur
☐ 2963 Carlos Diaz
☐ 2964 Erik Pappas
☐ 2965 Tim Spehr
☐ 2966 Sean Berry
☐ 2967 Stu Cole
☐ 2968 Jeff Conine
☐ 2969 Luis Medina
☐ 2970 Jose Mota
☐ 2971 Al Pedrique
☐ 2972 Terry Shumpert
☐ 2973 Adam Casillas
☐ 2974 Leo Garcia
☐ 2975 Kevin Koslofski
☐ 2976 Kevin Long

- ☐ 2977 Jeff Cox MG
- ☐ 2978 Bob Herold CO
- ☐ 2979 Joel Horlen CO
- ☐ 2980 Checklist

1992 Omaha Royals SkyBox

This set incleds a fifth year card of Jeff Conine.

	MINT	NRMT	EXC
COMPLETE SET (26)	6.00	2.70	.75

- ☐ 326 Jose Bautista
- ☐ 327 Sean Berry
- ☐ 328 Stu Cole
- ☐ 329 Jeff Conine
- ☐ 330 Leo Garcia
- ☐ 331 Mark Huismann
- ☐ 332 Kevin Koslofski
- ☐ 333 Reese Lambert
- ☐ 334 Kevin Long
- ☐ 335 Carlos Maldonado
- ☐ 336 Josias Manzanillo
- ☐ 337 Luis Medina
- ☐ 338 Dennis Moeller
- ☐ 339 Jose Mota
- ☐ 340 Erik Pappas
- ☐ 341 Al Pedrique
- ☐ 342 Harvey Pulliam
- ☐ 343 Rick Reed
- ☐ 344 Rico Rossy
- ☐ 345 Rich Sauveur
- ☐ 346 Steve Shifflett
- ☐ 347 Tim Spehr
- ☐ 348 Curt Young
- ☐ 349 Jeff Cox MG
- ☐ 350 Bob Herold CO
  Joel Horlen CO
- ☐ NNO Checklist

1992 Oneonta Yankees Classic/Best

This 30-card standard-size set of the 1992 Oneonta Yankees, a Class A New York-Penn League affiliate of the New York Yankees, features white-bordered posed color player photos on its fronts. The player's name, team, and position appear at the bottom. The white back is framed by a thin red line and carries the player's name and position at the top, followed by biography, statistics and team logos.

	MINT	NRMT	EXC
COMPLETE SET (30)	5.00	2.20	.60

- ☐ 1 Matt Luke
- ☐ 2 Mike Buddie
- ☐ 3 Ernie Yaroshuk
- ☐ 4 Abdiel Cumberbatch
- ☐ 5 Carlton Fleming
- ☐ 6 Gordon Sanchez
- ☐ 7 Ryan Karp
- ☐ 8 Don Leshnock
- ☐ 9 Jim Thomforde
- ☐ 10 Derek Shelton
- ☐ 11 Bert Inman
- ☐ 12 John Sutherland
- ☐ 13 Sandi Santiago
- ☐ 14 Robert Hinds
- ☐ 15 R.D. Long
- ☐ 16 John Thibert
- ☐ 17 Ray Suplee
- ☐ 18 Mike DeJean
- ☐ 19 Nick DelVecchio
- ☐ 20 Bill Underwood
- ☐ 21 Blaise Kozeniewski
- ☐ 22 Kent Wallace
- ☐ 23 Bruce Pool
- ☐ 24 Eric Knowles
- ☐ 25 Kraig Hawkins
- ☐ 26 Jeff Antolick
- ☐ 27 Jack Gillis MG
- ☐ 28 Bill Schmidt CO
- ☐ 29 Fernando Arango CO
- ☐ 30 Checklist

1992 Orlando Sun Rays Fleer/ProCards

This 26-card standard-size set of the 1992 Orlando Sun Rays, a Class AA Southern League affiliate of the Minnesota Twins, features brown-bordered posed color player photos on its fronts. The player's name appears in an upper corner; his team and position appear in a lower corner. The white back is framed by a black line and carries the player's name and position at the top, followed by biography and statistics.

	MINT	NRMT	EXC
COMPLETE SET (26)	5.00	2.20	.60

- ☐ 2840 Rich Garces
- ☐ 2841 Ed Gustafson
- ☐ 2842 Jon Henry
- ☐ 2843 Jason Klonoski
- ☐ 2844 Curtis Leskanic
- ☐ 2845 Marc Lipson
- ☐ 2846 Bob McCreary
- ☐ 2847 Oscar Munoz
- ☐ 2848 Carlos Pulido
- ☐ 2849 Jay Owens
- ☐ 2850 Joe Siwa
- ☐ 2851 Rick Allen
- ☐ 2852 Chris Delarwelle
- ☐ 2853 Cheo Garcia
- ☐ 2854 Dan Masteller
- ☐ 2855 Pat Meares
- ☐ 2856 Paul Russo
- ☐ 2857 Rex De La Nuez
- ☐ 2858 Mica Lewis
- ☐ 2859 Jay Kvasnicka
- ☐ 2860 David McCarty
- ☐ 2861 Ray Ortiz
- ☐ 2862 Phil Roof MG
- ☐ 2863 Mark Funderburk CO
- ☐ 2864 Jim Shellenback CO
- ☐ 2865 Checklist

1992 Orlando Sun Rays SkyBox

	MINT	NRMT	EXC
COMPLETE SET (26)	5.00	2.20	.60

- ☐ 501 Cheo Garcia
- ☐ 502 Fred Cooley
- ☐ 503 Rex De La Nuez
- ☐ 504 Rafael de Lima
- ☐ 505 Rich Garces
- ☐ 506 Ed Gustafson
- ☐ 507 Jon Henry
- ☐ 508 Jason Klonoski
- ☐ 509 Curtis Leskanic
- ☐ 510 Mica Lewis
- ☐ 511 Dan Masteller
- ☐ 512 David McCarty
- ☐ 513 Pat Meares
- ☐ 514 Alan Newman
- ☐ 515 Ray Ortiz
- ☐ 516 J. Owens
- ☐ 517 Carlos Pulido
- ☐ 518 Rusty Richards
- ☐ 519 Paul Russo
- ☐ 520 Joe Siwa
- ☐ 521 Jack Smith
- ☐ 522 Oscar Munoz
- ☐ 523 Fred White
- ☐ 524 Phil Roof MG
- ☐ 526 Mark Funderburk CO
  Jim Shellenback CO
- ☐ NNO Checklist

1992 Osceola Astros Classic/Best

This 30-card standard-size set of the 1992 Osceola Astros, a Class A Florida State League affiliate of the Houston Astros, features white-bordered posed color player photos on its fronts. The player's name, team, and position appear at the bottom. The white back is framed by a thin red line and carries the player's name and position at the top, followed by biography, statistics and team logos. This issue includes a third year card of Brian L. Hunter.

	MINT	NRMT	EXC
COMPLETE SET (30)	6.00	2.70	.75

- ☐ 1 Tom Nevers
- ☐ 2 Tony Gilmore
- ☐ 3 Chris Hill
- ☐ 4 Kenneth Wheeler Jr.
- ☐ 5 Mike Burns
- ☐ 6 Chris Hatcher
- ☐ 7 Bryant Winslow
- ☐ 8 Gary Christopherson
- ☐ 9 Brian L. Hunter
- ☐ 10 Doug Ketchen
- ☐ 11 Fred Costello
- ☐ 12 Mark Small
- ☐ 13 Mike Groppuso
- ☐ 14 Kevin Scott
- ☐ 15 Layne Lambert
- ☐ 16 Ben Gonzales
- ☐ 17 James Dougherty
- ☐ 18 Anthony Gutierrez
- ☐ 19 Donne Wall
- ☐ 20 Jim Lewis
- ☐ 21 James Mouton
- ☐ 22 Ruben Cruz
- ☐ 23 Roberto Petagine
- ☐ 24 Vince Roman
- ☐ 25 Kevin Lane
- ☐ 26 Sal Butera MG
- ☐ 27 Mike Freer TR
- ☐ 28 James Billingham CO
- ☐ 29 Frank Cacciatore CO
- ☐ 30 Checklist

1992 Osceola Astros Fleer/ProCards

This 28-card standard-size set of the 1992 Osceola Astros, a Class A Florida State League affiliate of the Houston Astros, features brown-bordered posed color player photos on its fronts. The player's name appears in an upper corner; his team and position appear in a lower corner. The white back is framed by a black line and carries the player's name and position at the top, followed by biography and statistics. This issue includes a third year card of Brian L. Hunter.

	MINT	NRMT	EXC
COMPLETE SET (28)	6.00	2.70	.75

- ☐ 2521 Jim Dougherty
- ☐ 2522 Troy Dovey
- ☐ 2523 Ben Gonzales
- ☐ 2524 Anthony Gutierrez
- ☐ 2525 Javier Hernandez
- ☐ 2526 Chris Hill
- ☐ 2527 Doug Ketchen
- ☐ 2528 Kevin Lane
- ☐ 2529 Jim Lewis
- ☐ 2530 Mark Small
- ☐ 2531 Kenny Wheeler
- ☐ 2532 Mike Burns
- ☐ 2533 Tony Gilmore
- ☐ 2534 Kevin Scott
- ☐ 2535 Gary Christopherson
- ☐ 2536 Tim Evans
- ☐ 2537 Mike Groppuso
- ☐ 2538 James Mouton
- ☐ 2539 Tom Nevers
- ☐ 2540 Roberto Petagine
- ☐ 2541 Ruben Cruz
- ☐ 2542 Chris Hatcher
- ☐ 2543 Brian Hunter
- ☐ 2544 Vince Roman
- ☐ 2545 Sal Butera MG
- ☐ 2546 Frank Cacciatore CO
- ☐ 2547 Jack Billingham CO
- ☐ 2548 Checklist

1992 Palm Springs Angels Classic/Best

This 30-card standard-size set of the 1992 Palm Springs Angels, a Class A California League affiliate of the California Angels, features white-bordered posed color player photos on its fronts. The player's name, team, and position appear at the bottom. The white back is framed by a thin red line and carries the player's name and position at the top, followed by biography, statistics and team logos. This issue includes a third year card of Garret Anderson.

	MINT	NRMT	EXC
COMPLETE SET (30)	7.00	3.10	.85

- ☐ 1 Eduardo Perez
- ☐ 2 Robbie Saitz
- ☐ 3 Norm Montoya
- ☐ 4 Chris Robinson
- ☐ 5 Victor Silverio
- ☐ 6 Jonathan Romero
- ☐ 7 John Wylie
- ☐ 8 Bobby Gamez
- ☐ 9 David Holdridge
- ☐ 10 Korey Keling
- ☐ 11 Brian Grebeck
- ☐ 12 Garret Anderson
- ☐ 13 Ken Edenfield
- ☐ 14 Orlando Munoz
- ☐ 15 Luis Raven
- ☐ 16 Shawn Purdy
- ☐ 17 Rod Van Dyke
- ☐ 18 Jorge Fabregas
- ☐ 19 Tom Dodge
- ☐ 20 Mark Dalesandro
- ☐ 21 Emmitt Cohick
- ☐ 22 Mike Musolino
- ☐ 23 Edgar Alfonzo
- ☐ 24 David Colon
- ☐ 25 Clifton Garrett
- ☐ 26 Dan Rumsey
- ☐ 27 Mark Holzemer
- ☐ 28 Mario Mendoza MG
- ☐ 29 Gene Richards CO
- ☐ 30 Stewart Cliburn CO
  Checklist

1992 Palm Springs Angels Fleer/ProCards

This 29-card standard-size set of the 1992 Palm Springs Angels, a Class A California League affiliate of the California Angels, features brown-bordered posed color player photos on its fronts. The player's name appears in an upper corner; his team and position appear in a lower corner. The white back is framed by a black line and carries the player's name and position at the top, followed by biography and statistics. This issue includes a third year card of Garret Anderson.

	MINT	NRMT	EXC
COMPLETE SET (29)	7.00	3.10	.85

- ☐ 830 Bobby Gamez
- ☐ 831 Hilly Hathaway
- ☐ 832 David Holdridge
- ☐ 833 Dominick Johnson
- ☐ 834 Korey Keling
- ☐ 835 Norman Montoya
- ☐ 836 Shawn Purdy
- ☐ 837 Chris Robinson
- ☐ 838 Robbie Saitz
- ☐ 839 Victor Silverio
- ☐ 840 Derek Stroud
- ☐ 841 Rod Van Dyke
- ☐ 842 Tom Dodge
- ☐ 843 Jorge Fabregas
- ☐ 844 Mike Musolino
- ☐ 845 Edgar Alfonzo
- ☐ 846 Mark Dalesandro
- ☐ 847 Brian Grebeck
- ☐ 848 Orlando Munoz
- ☐ 849 Eduardo Perez
- ☐ 850 Luis Raven
- ☐ 851 Garret Anderson
- ☐ 852 Emmit Cohick
- ☐ 853 David Colon
- ☐ 854 Clifton Garrett
- ☐ 855 Mario Mendoza MG
- ☐ 856 Stewart Cliburn CO
- ☐ 857 Gene Richards CO
- ☐ 858 Checklist

1992 Pawtucket Red Sox Dunkin' Donuts

This 31-card set of the Pawtucket Red Sox, a Class AAA International League affiliate of the Boston Red Sox, was issued in one large sheet featuring six perforated five-card strips with a large team photo in the wide top strip. Sponsored by Channel 10 and Dunkin' Donuts, the fronts carry color player photos while the backs display player career statistics. The cards are unnumbered and checklisted below in alphabetical order. This issue includes a fourth year card of Mo Vaughn.

	MINT	NRMT	EXC
COMPLETE SET (31)	60.00	27.00	7.50

- ☐ 1 Luis Aguayo
- ☐ 2 Tom Barrett
- ☐ 3 Mike Brumley
- ☐ 4 John Cerutti
- ☐ 5 Brian Conroy
- ☐ 6 Colin Dixon
- ☐ 7 John Dopson
- ☐ 8 Tom Fischer
- ☐ 9 Bob Geren
- ☐ 10 Wayne Housie
- ☐ 11 Peter Hoy
- ☐ 12 Daryl Irvine
- ☐ 13 Mark Meleski
- ☐ 14 Dave Milstien
- ☐ 15 Kevin Morton
- ☐ 16 Juan Paris
- ☐ 17 Rico Petrocelli
- ☐ 18 Jeff Plympton
- ☐ 19 Dick Pole
- ☐ 20 Paul Quantrill
- ☐ 21 John Shelby
- ☐ 22 Larry Shikles
- ☐ 23 Van Snider
- ☐ 24 Scott Taylor
- ☐ 25 Mike Twardoski
- ☐ 26 John Valentin
- ☐ 27 Mo Vaughn
- ☐ 28 Dave Walters
- ☐ 29 Eric Wedge
- ☐ 30 Bob Zupcic
- ☐ 31 Team Photo

1992 Pawtucket Red Sox Fleer/ProCards

This 28-card standard-size set of the 1992 Pawtucket Red Sox, a Class AAA International League affiliate of the Boston Red Sox, features brown-bordered posed color player photos on its fronts. The player's name appears in an upper corner; his team and position appear in a lower corner. The white back is framed by a black line and carries the player's name and position at the top, followed by biography and statistics. This issue includes a fourth year card of Mo Vaughn.

	MINT	NRMT	EXC
COMPLETE SET (28)	10.00	4.50	1.25

- ☐ 915 John Cerutti
- ☐ 916 Tom Fischer
- ☐ 917 Peter Hoy
- ☐ 918 Daryl Irvine
- ☐ 919 Kevin Morton
- ☐ 920 Jeff Plympton
- ☐ 921 Paul Quantrill
- ☐ 922 Larry Shikles
- ☐ 923 Scott Taylor
- ☐ 924 David Walters
- ☐ 925 Bob Geren
- ☐ 926 Ruben Rodriguez
- ☐ 927 Eric Wedge
- ☐ 928 Tom Barrett
- ☐ 929 Mike Brumley
- ☐ 930 Jim Byrd
- ☐ 931 Dave Milstien
- ☐ 932 Mike Twardoski
- ☐ 933 John Valentin
- ☐ 934 Mo Vaughn
- ☐ 935 Wayne Housie

☐ 936 Juan Paris
☐ 937 John Shelby
☐ 938 Van Snider
☐ 939 Rico Petrocelli MG
☐ 940 Mark Meleski CO
☐ 941 Dick Pole CO
☐ 942 Checklist

1992 Pawtucket Red Sox SkyBox

	MINT	NRMT	EXC
COMPLETE SET (26)	5.00	2.20	.60

☐ 351 Luis Aguayo
☐ 352 Tom Barrett
☐ 353 Mike Brumley
☐ 354 John Cerutti
☐ 355 Brian Conroy
☐ 356 Tom Fischer
☐ 357 Wayne Housie
☐ 358 Daryl Irvine
☐ 359 Dave Milstien
☐ 360 John Dopson
☐ 361 Juan Paris
☐ 362 Jeff Plympton
☐ 363 Paul Quantrill
☐ 364 Ruben Rodriguez
☐ 365 John Shelby
☐ 366 Larry Shikles
☐ 367 Van Snider
☐ 368 Scott Taylor
☐ 369 Mike Twardoski
☐ 370 John Valentin
☐ 371 David Walters
☐ 372 Eric Wedge
☐ 373 Bob Zupcic
☐ 374 Rico Petrocelli MG
☐ 375 Dick Pole CO
Mark Meleski CO
☐ NNO Checklist

1992 Peninsula Pilots Classic/Best

This 30-card standard-size set of the 1992 Peninsula Pilots, a Class A Carolina League affiliate of the Seattle Mariners, features white-bordered posed color player photos on its fronts. The player's name, team, and position appear at the bottom. The white back is framed by a thin red line and carries the player's name and position at the top, followed by biography, statistics and team logos.

	MINT	NRMT	EXC
COMPLETE SET (30)	5.00	2.20	.60

☐ 1 Bubba Smith
☐ 2 Chuck Wiley
☐ 3 Miah Bradbury
☐ 4 Lipso Nava
☐ 5 Erik O'Donnell
☐ 6 Jorge Morales
☐ 7 Sean Rees
☐ 8 Desi Relaford
☐ 9 Scott Pitcher
☐ 10 Raul Rodarte
☐ 11 Doug Fitzer
☐ 12 LaGrande Russell
☐ 13 Will Speakman
☐ 14 Ruben Santana
☐ 15 Sean Twitty
☐ 16 Jeff Darwin
☐ 17 John Cummings
☐ 18 Willie Wilder
☐ 19 Greg Hunter
☐ 20 Greg Bicknell
☐ 21 Bill Kostich
☐ 22 Dan Sullivan
☐ 23 Darren Bragg
☐ 24 Brad Holman
☐ 25 Todd Youngblood
☐ 26 James Terrell
☐ 27 Marc Hill MG
☐ 28 Tommy Cruz CO
☐ 29 Paul Lindblad CO
☐ 30 Paul Harker TR
Checklist

1992 Peninsula Pilots Fleer/ProCards

This 28-card standard-size set of the 1992 Peninsula Pilots, a Class A Carolina League affiliate of the Seattle Mariners, features brown-bordered posed color player photos on its fronts. The player's name appears in an upper corner; his team and position appear in a lower corner. The white back is framed by a black line and carries the player's name and position at the top, followed by biography and statistics.

	MINT	NRMT	EXC
COMPLETE SET (28)	5.00	2.20	.60

☐ 2924 Greg Bicknell
☐ 2925 John Cummings
☐ 2926 Jeff Darwin
☐ 2927 Doug Fitzer
☐ 2928 Bill Kostich
☐ 2929 Erik O'Donnell
☐ 2930 Sean Rees
☐ 2931 LaGrande Russell
☐ 2932 Dan Sullivan
☐ 2933 Chuck Wiley
☐ 2934 Todd Youngblood
☐ 2935 Miah Bradbury
☐ 2936 Jorge Morales
☐ 2937 Craig Wilson
☐ 2938 Greg Hunter
☐ 2939 Bob Magallanes
☐ 2940 Lipso Nava
☐ 2941 Desi Relaford
☐ 2942 Raul Rodarte
☐ 2943 Ruben Santana
☐ 2944 Bubba Smith
☐ 2945 Darren Bragg
☐ 2946 James Terrell
☐ 2947 Willie Wilder
☐ 2948 Marc Hill MG
☐ 2949 Tommy Cruz CO
☐ 2950 Paul Lindblad CO
☐ 2951 Checklist

1992 Peoria Chiefs Classic/Best

This 30-card standard-size set of the 1992 Peoria Chiefs, a Class A Midwest League affiliate of the Chicago Cubs, features white-bordered posed color player photos on its fronts. The player's name, team, and position appear at the bottom. The white back is framed by a thin red line and carries the player's name and position at the top, followed by biography, statistics and team logos.

	MINT	NRMT	EXC
COMPLETE SET (30)	5.00	2.20	.60

☐ 1 Earl Cunningham
☐ 2 Darren Tillman
☐ 3 Mike Tidwell
☐ 4 Bill Bliss
☐ 5 Jose Trujillo
☐ 6 Joey Terilli
☐ 7 Brian Kenny
☐ 8 Carl Schramm
☐ 9 Todd Stefan
☐ 10 German Diaz
☐ 11 Tim Moore
☐ 12 Ricardo Medina
☐ 13 Ed Larregui
☐ 14 Willie Garner
☐ 15 Yogi Pacheco
☐ 16 Esmili Guerra
☐ 17 Tyson Godfrey
☐ 18 Adrian Sanchez
☐ 19 Terry Adams
☐ 20 J.P. Postiff
☐ 21 Pedro Valdez
☐ 22 Jay Meyer
☐ 23 Morris Craig
☐ 24 Troy Bradford
☐ 25 Jim Wolff
☐ 26 Brian McGee
☐ 27 Ken Arnold
☐ 28 Steve Roadcap MG
☐ 29 Bill McGuire CO
☐ 30 Jim O'Reilly TR
Checklist

1992 Peoria Chiefs Team Issue

	MINT	NRMT	EXC
COMPLETE SET (31)	6.00	2.70	.75

☐ 1 Terry Adams
☐ 2 Ken Arnold
☐ 3 Joe Biasucci
☐ 4 Bill Bliss
☐ 5 Brant Brown
☐ 6 Earl Cunningham
☐ 7 Willie Gardner
☐ 8 Tyson Godfrey
☐ 9 Brian Kenny
☐ 10 Ken Krahenbuhl
☐ 11 Ed Larregui
☐ 12 Brian McGee
☐ 13 Bill McGuire
☐ 14 Ricardo Medina
☐ 15 Jay Meyer
☐ 16 Chris Moock
☐ 17 Tim Moore
☐ 18 Jim O'Reilly TR
☐ 19 Ken Patterson
☐ 20 J.P. Postiff
☐ 21 Steve Roadcap MG
☐ 22 Ray Sadecki
☐ 23 Adrian Sanchez
☐ 24 Carl Schramm
☐ 25 Kennie Steenstra
☐ 26 Todd Stefan
☐ 27 Joey Terilli
☐ 28 Mike Tidwell
☐ 29 Derek Wallace
☐ 30 Jim Wolff
☐ 31 All-Stars
Adam Sanchez
Brian Kenny
Jim Wolff
Joey Terilli
Ricardo Medina
Ed Larregui

1992 Phoenix Firebirds Fleer/ProCards

This 26-card standard-size set of the 1992 Phoenix Firebirds, a Class AAA Pacific Coast League affiliate of the San Francisco Giants, features brown-bordered posed color player photos on its fronts. The player's name appears in an upper corner; his team and position appear in a lower corner. The white back is framed by a black line and carries the player's name and position at the top, followed by biography and statistics.

	MINT	NRMT	EXC
COMPLETE SET (26)	5.00	2.20	.60

☐ 2814 Johnny Ard
☐ 2815 Larry Carter
☐ 2816 Dave Masters
☐ 2817 Paul McClellan
☐ 2818 Craig McMurtry
☐ 2819 Jim Pena
☐ 2820 Dan Rambo
☐ 2821 Pat Rapp
☐ 2822 Steve Reed
☐ 2823 Mark Bailey
☐ 2824 Steve Decker
☐ 2825 Mike Benjamin
☐ 2826 Craig Colbert
☐ 2827 Erik Johnson
☐ 2828 Dan Lewis
☐ 2829 Dave Patterson
☐ 2830 John Patterson
☐ 2831 Andres Santana
☐ 2832 Steve Hosey
☐ 2833 Mark Leonard
☐ 2834 Reed Peters
☐ 2835 Greg Ritchie
☐ 2836 Ted Wood
☐ 2837 Bill Evers MG
☐ 2838 Todd Oakes CO
☐ 2839 Checklist

1992 Phoenix Firebirds SkyBox

	MINT	NRMT	EXC
COMPLETE SET (26)	5.00	2.20	.60

☐ 376 Johnny Ard
☐ 377 Mark Bailey
☐ 378 Larry Carter
☐ 379 John Patterson
☐ 380 Jamie Cooper
☐ 381 Steve Decker
☐ 382 Dave Hengel
☐ 383 Steve Hosey
☐ 384 Erik Johnson
☐ 385 Dan Lewis
☐ 386 Greg Litton
☐ 387 Dave Masters
☐ 388 Paul McClellan
☐ 389 Craig McMurtry
☐ 390 Jim Myers
☐ 391 Francisco Oliveras
☐ 392 Dave Patterson
☐ 393 Jim Pena
☐ 394 Pat Rapp
☐ 395 Greg Ritchie
☐ 396 Andres Thomas
☐ 397 Randy Veres
☐ 398 Ted Wood
☐ 399 Bill Evers MG
☐ 400 Tony Taylor CO
Todd Oakes CO
☐ NNO Checklist

1992 Pittsfield Mets Classic/Best

This 28-card standard-size set of the 1992 Pittsfield Mets, a Class A New York-Penn League affiliate of the New York Mets, features white-bordered posed color player photos on its fronts. The player's name, team, and position appear at the bottom. The white back is framed by a thin red line and carries the player's name and position at the top, followed by biography, statistics and team logos.

	MINT	NRMT	EXC
COMPLETE SET (30)	10.00	4.50	1.25

☐ 1 Bill Pulsipher
☐ 2 Demond Smith
☐ 3 Tripp Keister
☐ 4 Ty Quillin
☐ 5 Andy Beckerman
☐ 6 Guillermo Garcia
☐ 7 Steve Seymour
☐ 8 Rafael Hernandez
☐ 9 Brett Rossler
☐ 10 Edgardo Alfonzo
☐ 11 Cesar Diaz
☐ 12 Shaun Watson
☐ 13 Gregg Stark
☐ 14 Mark Fuller
☐ 15 Brian Daubach
☐ 16 Chris George
☐ 17 Cliff Jones
☐ 18 Jim Thrift MG
☐ 19 Jeff Morris CO
☐ 20 Howie Freiling CO
☐ 21 Larry Bennesse TR
☐ 22 Logo Card
☐ 23 Logo Card
☐ 24 Logo Card
☐ 25 Logo Card
☐ 26 Logo Card
☐ 27 Logo Card
☐ 28 Logo Card
☐ 29 Logo Card
☐ 30 Checklist

1992 Pittsfield Mets Fleer/ProCards

This 28-card standard-size set of the 1992 Pittsfield Mets, a Class A New York-Penn League affiliate of the New York Mets, features brown-bordered posed color player photos on its fronts. The player's name appears in an upper corner; his team and position appear in a lower corner. The white back is framed by a black line and carries the player's name and position at the top, followed by biography and statistics. This issue includes the minor league card debuts of Bill Pulsipher and Edgardo Alfonzo.

	MINT	NRMT	EXC
COMPLETE SET (28)	10.00	4.50	1.25

☐ 3286 Andy Beckerman
☐ 3287 Mark Fuller
☐ 3288 Chris George
☐ 3289 Mark Hokanson
☐ 3290 Cliff Jones
☐ 3291 Joe Petcka
☐ 3292 Jim Popoff
☐ 3293 Bill Pulsipher
☐ 3294 Steve Seymour
☐ 3295 Greg Stark
☐ 3296 David Teske
☐ 3297 Shaun Watson
☐ 3298 Cesar Diaz
☐ 3299 Guillermo Garcia
☐ 3300 Brett Rossler
☐ 3301 Edgardo Alfonzo
☐ 3302 Brian Daubach
☐ 3303 Jose Flores
☐ 3304 Rafael Hernandez
☐ 3305 Chris Saunders
☐ 3306 Tripp Keister
☐ 3307 Ty Quillin
☐ 3308 Demond Smith
☐ 3309 John Smith
☐ 3310 Jim Thrift MG
☐ 3311 Howie Freiling CO
☐ 3312 Jeff Morris CO
☐ 3313 Checklist

1992 Portland Beavers Fleer/ProCards

This 26-card standard-size set of the 1992 Portland Beavers, a Class AAA Pacific Coast League affiliate of the Minnesota Twins, features brown-bordered posed color player photos on its fronts. The player's name appears in an upper corner; his team and position appear in a lower corner. The white back is framed by a black line and carries the player's name and position at the top, followed by biography and statistics.

	MINT	NRMT	EXC
COMPLETE SET (26)	5.00	2.20	.60

☐ 2659 Willie Banks
☐ 2660 Larry Casian
☐ 2661 Mauro Gozzo
☐ 2662 Greg Johnson
☐ 2663 Orlando Lind
☐ 2664 Pat Mahomes
☐ 2665 Mike Schwabe
☐ 2666 Mike Trombley
☐ 2667 George Tsamis
☐ 2668 Rob Wassenaar
☐ 2669 David West
☐ 2670 Derek Parks
☐ 2671 Danny Sheaffer
☐ 2672 Shawn Gilbert
☐ 2673 Chip Hale
☐ 2674 Keith Hughes
☐ 2675 Terry Jorgensen
☐ 2676 Luis Quinones
☐ 2677 Bernardo Brito
☐ 2678 J.T. Bruett
☐ 2679 Jay Kvasnicka
☐ 2680 Edgar Naveda

☐ 2681 Scott Ullger MG
☐ 2682 Paul Kirsch CO
☐ 2683 Gorman Heimueller CO
☐ 2684 Checklist

1992 Portland Beavers SkyBox

	MINT	NRMT	EXC
COMPLETE SET (26)	5.00	2.20	.60

☐ 401 Willie Banks
☐ 402 Bernardo Bito
☐ 403 J.T. Bruett
☐ 404 Larry Casian
☐ 405 Luis Quinones
☐ 406 Shawn Gilbert
☐ 407 Mauro Gozzo
☐ 408 Chip Hale
☐ 409 Keith Hughes
☐ 410 Greg Johnson
☐ 411 Terry Jorgensen
☐ 412 Jay Kvasnicka
☐ 413 Orlando Lind
☐ 414 Edgar Naveda
☐ 415 Rob Nelson
☐ 416 Derek Parks
☐ 417 Jeff Reboulet
☐ 418 Mike Schwabe
☐ 419 Danny Sheaffer
☐ 420 Mike Trombley
☐ 421 George Tsamis
☐ 422 Rob Wassenaar
☐ 423 David West
☐ 424 Scott Ullger MG
☐ 425 Paul Kirsch CO
Gorman Heimueller CO
☐ NNO Checklist

1992 Prince William Cannons Classic/Best

This 30-card standard-size set of the 1992 Prince William Cannons, a Class A Carolina League affiliate of the New York Yankees, features white-bordered posed color player photos on its fronts. The player's name, team, and position appear at the bottom. The white back is framed by a thin red line and carries the player's name and position at the top, followed by biography, statistics and team logos.

	MINT	NRMT	EXC
COMPLETE SET (30)	5.00	2.20	.60

☐ 1 Bruce Prybylinski
☐ 2 Andy Fox
☐ 3 Ramon Manon
☐ 4 Mike Hankins
☐ 5 Jalal Leach
☐ 6 Richard Hines
☐ 7 Andy Albrecht
☐ 8 Adin Lohry
☐ 9 Matt Dunbar
☐ 10 Jeff Motuzas
☐ 11 Ramon Jimenez
☐ 12 Roger Burnett
☐ 13 Tim Rumer
☐ 14 Edwin Salcedo
☐ 15 Tim Garland
☐ 16 Lyle Mouton
☐ 17 Rich Polak
☐ 18 Shad Smith
☐ 19 Steve Livesey
☐ 20 Keith Seiler
☐ 21 Ron Frazier
☐ 22 Kevin Jordan
☐ 23 Todd Malone
☐ 24 Jason Robertson
☐ 25 Curtis Ralph
☐ 26 Mike Hart MG
☐ 27 Dave Shuler CO
☐ 28 Ken Dominguez CO
☐ 29 Adam Wagner TR
☐ 30 Checklist

1992 Prince William Cannons Fleer/ProCards

This 29-card standard-size set of the 1992 Prince William Cannons, a Class A Carolina League affiliate of the New York Yankees, features brown-bordered posed color player photos on its fronts. The player's name appears in an upper corner; his team and position appear in a lower corner. The white back is framed by a black line and carries the player's name and position at the top, followed by biography and statistics.

	MINT	NRMT	EXC
COMPLETE SET (29)	5.00	2.20	.60

☐ 139 Matt Dunbar
☐ 140 Ron Frazier
☐ 141 Richard Hines
☐ 142 Todd Malone
☐ 143 Ramon Manon
☐ 144 Rich Polak
☐ 145 Bruce Prybylinski
☐ 146 Rafael Quirico
☐ 147 Curtis Ralph
☐ 148 Tim Rumer
☐ 149 Keith Seiler
☐ 150 Shad Smith
☐ 151 Adin Lohry
☐ 152 Jeff Motuzas
☐ 153 Edwin Salcedo
☐ 154 Roger Burnett
☐ 155 Andy Fox
☐ 156 Ramon Jimenez
☐ 157 Kevin Jordan
☐ 158 Steve Livesey
☐ 159 Andrew Albrecht
☐ 160 Tim Garland
☐ 161 Jalal Leach
☐ 162 Lyle Mouton
☐ 163 Jason Robertson
☐ 164 Mike Hart MG
☐ 165 Ken Dominguez CO
☐ 166 Dave Schuler CO
☐ 167 Checklist

1992 Princeton Reds Classic/Best

This 30-card standard-size set of the 1992 Princeton Reds, a Rookie Class Appalachian League affiliate of the Cincinnati Reds, features white-bordered posed color player photos on its fronts. The player's name, team, and position appear at the bottom. The white back is framed by a thin red line and carries the player's name and position at the top, followed by biography, statistics and team logos. This issue includes the minor league card debuts of Curt Lyons and Justin Towle.

	MINT	NRMT	EXC
COMPLETE SET (30)	7.00	3.10	.85

☐ 1 Todd Etler
☐ 2 Eli Robinson
☐ 3 Jeff Ashton
☐ 4 Cleveland Ladell
☐ 5 Ray Moon
☐ 6 Yamil Concepcion
☐ 7 Sam Mullins
☐ 8 Jim Miller
☐ 9 Roger Etheridge
☐ 10 Johnny Bess
☐ 11 Curtis Lyons
☐ 12 Todd Ruyak
☐ 13 Chad Fox
☐ 14 Will Brunson
☐ 15 Denny Fussell
☐ 16 James Nix
☐ 17 Louis Maberry
☐ 18 Brian Silvia
☐ 19 Rodney Thomas
☐ 20 Rossi Morris
☐ 21 Rod Sanders
☐ 22 Ramon Hernandez
☐ 23 Dan Frye
☐ 24 Justin Towle
☐ 25 Dan Kopriva
☐ 26 Dan Oyas
☐ 27 Glen Cullop
☐ 28 Darrell Rodgers CO
☐ 29 Billy Maxwell TR
☐ 30 Checklist

1992 Princeton Reds Fleer/ProCards

This 29-card standard-size set of the 1992 Princeton Reds, a Rookie Class Appalachian League affiliate of the Cincinnati Reds, features brown-bordered posed color player photos on its fronts. The player's name appears in an upper corner; his team and position appear in a lower corner. The white back is framed by a black line and carries the player's name and position at the top, followed by biography and statistics. This issue includes the minor league card debuts of Curt Lyons and Justin Towle.

	MINT	NRMT	EXC
COMPLETE SET (29)	7.00	3.10	.85

☐ 2685 Glen Cullop
☐ 3077 Bill Brunson
☐ 3078 Yamil Concepcion
☐ 3079 Roger Etheridge
☐ 3080 Todd Etler
☐ 3081 Chad Fox
☐ 3082 Denny Fussell
☐ 3083 Curt Lyons
☐ 3084 Louis Maberry
☐ 3085 Jim Miller
☐ 3086 Sam Mullins
☐ 3087 James Nix
☐ 3088 Todd Ruyak
☐ 3089 Johnny Bess
☐ 3090 Brian Silvia
☐ 3091 Justin Towle
☐ 3092 Jeff Ashton
☐ 3093 Dan Frye
☐ 3094 Ramon Hernandez
☐ 3095 Dan Kopriva
☐ 3096 Eli Robinson
☐ 3097 Rod Sanders
☐ 3098 Cleveland Ladell
☐ 3099 Ray Moon
☐ 3100 Rossi Morris
☐ 3101 Danny Oyas
☐ 3102 Rodney Thomas
☐ 3103 Doc Rodgers CO
☐ 3104 Checklist

1992 ProCards

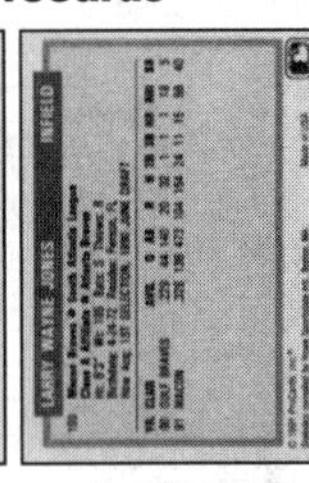

This 360-card standard size set features white bordered color player photos of the minor league top prospects. The player's name, position, and team name appear at the bottom. The back carries the player's name and position, followed by biography and statistics. The cards were issued in 12-card wax packs. 1,009 cases were produced.

	MINT	NRMT	EXC
COMPLETE SET (360)	100.00	45.00	12.50
COMMON CARD (1-360)	.10	.05	.01
☐ 1 Mike Mussina	3.00	1.35	.35
☐ 2 Luis Mercedes	.10	.05	.01
☐ 3 Todd Frohwirth	.10	.05	.01
☐ 4 Chito Martinez	.10	.05	.01
☐ 5 David Segui	.25	.11	.03
☐ 6 Arthur Rhodes	.10	.05	.01
☐ 7 Stacy Jones	.10	.05	.01
☐ 8 Darryl Moore	.10	.05	.01
☐ 9 Manny Alexander	.20	.09	.03
☐ 10 Jeff Williams	.10	.05	.01
☐ 11 Matt Anderson	.10	.05	.01
☐ 12 Chris Lemp	.10	.05	.01
☐ 13 Rick Krivda	.10	.05	.01
☐ 14 Phil Plantier	.10	.05	.01
☐ 15 Mo Vaughn	10.00	4.50	1.25
☐ 16 Scott Cooper	.10	.05	.01
☐ 17 Mike Gardiner	.10	.05	.01
☐ 18 Kevin Morton	.10	.05	.01
☐ 19 Jeff Plympton	.10	.05	.01
☐ 20 Jeff McNeely	.10	.05	.01
☐ 21 Willie Tatum	.10	.05	.01
☐ 22 Tim Smith	.10	.05	.01
☐ 23 Frank Rodriguez	.40	.18	.05
☐ 24 Chris Davis	.10	.05	.01
☐ 25 Cory Bailey	.10	.05	.01
☐ 26 Rob Henkel	.10	.05	.01
☐ 27 Kyle Abbott	.10	.05	.01
☐ 28 Lee Stevens	.20	.09	.03
☐ 29 Chad Curtis	.20	.09	.03
☐ 30 Ruben Amaro	.10	.05	.01
☐ 31 Mark Howie	.10	.05	.01
☐ 32 Tim Salmon	4.00	1.80	.50
☐ 33 Kevin Flora	.10	.05	.01
☐ 34 Garret Anderson	2.00	.90	.25
☐ 35 Darryl Scott	.10	.05	.01
☐ 36 Don Vidmar	.10	.05	.01
☐ 37 Korey Keling	.10	.05	.01
☐ 38 Troy Percival	.30	.14	.04
☐ 39 Eduardo Perez	.10	.05	.01
☐ 40 Julian Heredia	.10	.05	.01
☐ 41 Wilson Alvarez	.75	.35	.09
☐ 42 Ramon Garcia	.10	.05	.01
☐ 43 Johnny Ruffin	.10	.05	.01
☐ 44 Scott Cepicky	.10	.05	.01
☐ 45 Rod Bolton	.10	.05	.01
☐ 46 Rogelio Nunez	.10	.05	.01
☐ 47 Brandon Wilson	.10	.05	.01
☐ 48 Marc Kubicki	.10	.05	.01
☐ 49 Mark Lewis	.40	.18	.05
☐ 50 Jim Thome	8.00	3.60	1.00
☐ 51 Tim Costo	.10	.05	.01
☐ 52 Jeff Mutis	.10	.05	.01
☐ 53 Tracy Sanders	.10	.05	.01
☐ 54 Mike Soper	.10	.05	.01
☐ 55 Miguel Flores	.10	.05	.01
☐ 56 Brian Giles	.10	.05	.01
☐ 57 Curtis Leskanic	.10	.05	.01
☐ 58 Kyle Washington	.10	.05	.01
☐ 59 Jason Hardtke	.10	.05	.01
☐ 60 Albie Lopez	.10	.05	.01
☐ 61 Oscar Resendez	.10	.05	.01
☐ 62 Manny Ramirez	8.00	3.60	1.00
☐ 63 Rico Brogna	.20	.09	.03
☐ 64 Scott Livingstone	.10	.05	.01
☐ 65 Greg Gohr	.10	.05	.01
☐ 66 Scott Aldred	.10	.05	.01
☐ 67 Brian Warren	.10	.05	.01
☐ 68 Bob Undorf	.10	.05	.01
☐ 69 Rob Grable	.10	.05	.01
☐ 70 Tom Mezzanotte	.10	.05	.01
☐ 71 Justin Thompson	.40	.18	.05
☐ 72 Trever Miller	.10	.05	.01
☐ 73 Joel Johnston	.10	.05	.01
☐ 74 Kevin Koslofski	.10	.05	.01
☐ 75 Archie Corbin	.10	.05	.01
☐ 76 Phil Hiatt	.10	.05	.01
☐ 77 Danny Miceli	.10	.05	.01
☐ 78 Joe Randa	.20	.09	.03
☐ 79 Mark Johnson	.10	.05	.01
☐ 80 Joe Vitiello	.20	.09	.03
☐ 81 Cal Eldred	.20	.09	.03
☐ 82 Doug Henry	.10	.05	.01
☐ 83 Dave Nilsson	.20	.09	.03
☐ 84 John Jaha	.25	.11	.03
☐ 85 Shon Ashley	.10	.05	.01
☐ 86 Jim Tatum	.10	.05	.01
☐ 87 Bo Dodson	.10	.05	.01
☐ 88 Otis Green	.10	.05	.01
☐ 89 Denny Neagle	1.25	.55	.16
☐ 90 Checklist (1-90)	.10	.05	.01
☐ 91 Pedro Munoz	.10	.05	.01
☐ 92 Jarvis Brown	.10	.05	.01
☐ 93 Pat Mahomes	.10	.05	.01
☐ 94 Cheo Garcia	.10	.05	.01
☐ 95 David McCarty	.10	.05	.01
☐ 96 Chris Delawelle	.10	.05	.01
☐ 97 Scott Stahoviak	.20	.09	.03
☐ 98 Midre Cummings	.20	.09	.03
☐ 99 Todd Ritchie	.10	.05	.01
☐ 100 Dave Sartain	.10	.05	.01
☐ 101 Pedro Grifol	.10	.05	.01
☐ 102 Eddie Guardado	.10	.05	.01
☐ 103 Bob Carlson	.10	.05	.01
☐ 104 Sandy Diaz	.10	.05	.01
☐ 105 John Ramos	.10	.05	.01
☐ 106 Bernie Williams	4.00	1.80	.50
☐ 107 Wade Taylor	.10	.05	.01
☐ 108 Pat Kelly	.15	.07	.02
☐ 109 Jeff Johnson	.10	.05	.01
☐ 110 Scott Kamieniecki	.10	.05	.01
☐ 111 Dave Silvestri	.10	.05	.01
☐ 112 Ed Martel	.10	.05	.01
☐ 113 Willie Smith	.10	.05	.01
☐ 114 J.T. Snow	.60	.25	.07
☐ 115 Gerald Williams	.15	.07	.02
☐ 116 Larry Stanford	.10	.05	.01
☐ 117 Bruce Prybylinski	.10	.05	.01
☐ 118 Rey Noriega	.10	.05	.01
☐ 119 Rich Batchelor	.10	.05	.01
☐ 120 Brad Ausmus	.20	.09	.03
☐ 121 Robert Eenhoorn	.10	.05	.01
☐ 122 Sam Militello	.10	.05	.01
☐ 123 Jason Robertson	.10	.05	.01
☐ 124 Carl Everett	.20	.09	.03
☐ 125 Kiki Hernandez	.10	.05	.01
☐ 126 Rafael Quirico	.10	.05	.01
☐ 127 Lyle Mouton	.10	.05	.01
☐ 128 Tim Flannelly	.10	.05	.01
☐ 129 Todd Van Poppel	.10	.05	.01
☐ 130 Tim Peek	.10	.05	.01
☐ 131 Henry Mercedes	.10	.05	.01
☐ 132 Todd Smith	.10	.05	.01
☐ 133 Brent Gates	.15	.07	.02
☐ 134 Gary Hust	.10	.05	.01
☐ 135 Mike Neill	.10	.05	.01
☐ 136 Russ Brock	.10	.05	.01
☐ 137 Ricky Kimball	.10	.05	.01
☐ 138 Tino Martinez	1.00	.45	.12
☐ 139 Calvin Jones	.10	.05	.01
☐ 140 Roger Salked	.10	.05	.01
☐ 141 Dave Fleming	.10	.05	.01
☐ 142 Bret Boone	.20	.09	.03
☐ 143 Jim Campanis	.10	.05	.01
☐ 144 Marc Newfield	.50	.23	.06
☐ 145 Mike Hampton	.25	.11	.03
☐ 146 Shawn Estes	.25	.11	.03
☐ 147 David Lisiecki	.10	.05	.01
☐ 148 Dean Palmer	3.00	1.35	.35
☐ 149 Rob Maurer	.10	.05	.01
☐ 150 Jim Poole	.10	.05	.01
☐ 151 Terry Mathews	.10	.05	.01
☐ 152 Monty Fariss	.10	.05	.01
☐ 153 Ivan Rodriguez	4.00	1.80	.50
☐ 154 Barry Manuel	.10	.05	.01
☐ 155 Donald Harris	.10	.05	.01
☐ 156 Rusty Greer	1.50	.70	.19
☐ 157 Matt Whiteside	.10	.05	.01
☐ 158 Derek Bell	1.25	.55	.16
☐ 159 Eddie Zosky	.10	.05	.01
☐ 160 Domingo Martinez	.10	.05	.01
☐ 161 Juan Guzman	.25	.11	.03
☐ 162 Ed Sprague	.25	.11	.03
☐ 163 Rob Ducey	.10	.05	.01
☐ 164 Vince Horsman	.10	.05	.01
☐ 165 Darren Hall	.10	.05	.01
☐ 166 Rick Trlicek	.10	.05	.01
☐ 167 Dave Weathers	.10	.05	.01
☐ 168 Robert Perez	.10	.05	.01
☐ 169 Nigel Wilson	.10	.05	.01
☐ 170 Carlos Delgado	3.00	1.35	.35
☐ 171 Steve Karsay	.20	.09	.03
☐ 172 Howard Battle	.20	.09	.03
☐ 173 Huck Flener	.10	.05	.01
☐ 174 Robert Butler	.10	.05	.01
☐ 175 Giovanni Carrara	.10	.05	.01
☐ 176 Michael Taylor	.10	.05	.01

Card	MINT	NRMT	EXC
177 Brian R. Hunter	.10	.05	.01
178 Turk Wendell	.10	.05	.01
179 Mark Wohlers	.40	.18	.05
180 Checklist (91-180)	.10	.05	.01
181 Ryan Klesko	5.00	2.20	.60
182 Keith Mitchell	.10	.05	.01
183 Vinny Castilla	1.25	.55	.16
184 Napoleon Robinson	.10	.05	.01
185 Mike Kelly	.10	.05	.01
186 Javy Lopez	3.00	1.35	.35
187 Ramon Caraballo	.10	.05	.01
188 David Nied	.10	.05	.01
189 Don Strange	.10	.05	.01
190 Chipper Jones	10.00	4.50	1.25
191 Troy Hughes	.10	.05	.01
192 Don Robinson	.10	.05	.01
193 Lance Marks	.10	.05	.01
194 Manuel Jimenez	.10	.05	.01
195 Tony Graffanino	.10	.05	.01
196 Brad Woodall	.10	.05	.01
197 Kevin Grijak	.10	.05	.01
198 Dario Paulino	.10	.05	.01
199 Lance Dickson	.10	.05	.01
200 Rey Sanchez	.10	.05	.01
201 Elvin Paulino	.10	.05	.01
202 Alex Arias	.10	.05	.01
203 Fernando Ramsey	.10	.05	.01
204 Pete Castellano	.10	.05	.01
205 Ryan Hawblitzel	.10	.05	.01
206 John Jensen	.10	.05	.01
207 Jerrone Williams	.10	.05	.01
208 Earl Cunningham	.10	.05	.01
209 Phil Dauphin	.10	.05	.01
210 Doug Glanville	.10	.05	.01
211 Jim Robinson	.10	.05	.01
212 Ken Arnold	.10	.05	.01
213 Reggie Jefferson	.20	.09	.03
214 Reggie Sanders	1.00	.45	.12
215 Mo Sanford	.10	.05	.01
216 Steve Foster	.10	.05	.01
217 Dan Wilson	.15	.07	.02
218 John Roper	.10	.05	.01
219 Trevor Hoffman	.10	.05	.01
220 Calvin Reese	.20	.09	.03
221 John Hrusovsky	.10	.05	.01
222 Andy Mota	.10	.05	.01
223 Kenny Lofton	3.00	1.35	.35
224 Andujar Cedeno	.10	.05	.01
225 Ryan Bowen	.10	.05	.01
226 Jeff Juden	.10	.05	.01
227 Chris Gardner	.10	.05	.01
228 Brian Williams	.10	.05	.01
229 Ed Ponte	.10	.05	.01
230 Chris Hatcher	.10	.05	.01
231 Fletcher Thompson	.10	.05	.01
232 Wally Trice	.10	.05	.01
233 Donne Wall	.10	.05	.01
234 Tom Nevers	.10	.05	.01
235 Jim Daugherty	.10	.05	.01
236 Mark Loughlin	.10	.05	.01
237 Jose Offerman	.20	.09	.03
238 Dave Hansen	.10	.05	.01
239 Carlos Hernandez	.10	.05	.01
240 Eric Karros	2.50	1.10	.30
241 Henry Rodriguez	2.50	1.10	.30
242 Jamie McAndrew	.10	.05	.01
243 Tom Goodwin	.20	.09	.03
244 Pedro J. Martinez	1.00	.45	.12
245 Braulio Castillo	.10	.05	.01
246 Matt Howard	.10	.05	.01
247 Michael Mimbs	.10	.05	.01
248 Murph Proctor	.10	.05	.01
249 Vernon Spearman	.10	.05	.01
250 Jason Kerr	.10	.05	.01
251 Mike Sharp	.10	.05	.01
252 Pedro Osuna	.10	.05	.01
253 Doug Piatt	.10	.05	.01
254 Wil Cordero	.30	.14	.04
255 John Vander Wal	.10	.05	.01
256 Bret Barberie	.10	.05	.01
257 Todd Haney	.10	.05	.01
258 Chris Haney	.10	.05	.01
259 Matt Stairs	.10	.05	.01
260 David Wainhouse	.10	.05	.01
261 Bob Natal	.10	.05	.01
262 Rob Katzaroff	.10	.05	.01
263 Willie Greene	.20	.09	.03
264 Reid Cornelius	.10	.05	.01
265 Glenn Murray	.10	.05	.01
266 Rondell White	2.00	.90	.25
267 Tavo Alvarez	.10	.05	.01
268 Gabe White	.10	.05	.01
269 Brian Looney	.10	.05	.01
270 Checklist (181-270)	.10	.05	.01
271 Derrick White	.10	.05	.01
272 Heath Haynes	.10	.05	.01
273 Mike Daniel	.10	.05	.01
274 Jim Austin	.10	.05	.01
275 Chris Donnels	.10	.05	.01
276 Julio Valera	.10	.05	.01
277 Todd Hundley	4.00	1.80	.50
278 Anthony Young	.10	.05	.01
279 Jeff Gardner	.10	.05	.01
280 Jeromy Burnitz	.20	.09	.03
281 Tito Navarro	.10	.05	.01
282 D.J. Dozier	.10	.05	.01
283 Julian Vasquez	.10	.05	.01
284 Pat Howell	.10	.05	.01
285 Brook Fordyce	.15	.07	.02
286 Todd Douma	.10	.05	.01
287 Jose Martinez	.10	.05	.01
288 Ricky Otero	.10	.05	.01
289 Quilvio Veras	.20	.09	.03
290 Joe Crawford	.10	.05	.01
291 Todd Fiegel	.10	.05	.01
292 Jason Jacome	.10	.05	.01
293 Kim Batiste	.10	.05	.01
294 Andy Ashby	.20	.09	.03
295 Wes Chamberlain	.10	.05	.01
296 Dave Hollins	.10	.05	.01
297 Tony Longmire	.10	.05	.01
298 Nikco Riesgo	.10	.05	.01
299 Cliff Brantley	.10	.05	.01
300 Troy Paulsen	.10	.05	.01
301 Elliott Gray	.10	.05	.01
302 Mike Lieberthal	.25	.11	.03
303 Tyler Green	.15	.07	.02
304 Dan Brown	.10	.05	.01
305 Carlos Garcia	.15	.07	.02
306 John Wehner	.10	.05	.01
307 Paul Miller	.10	.05	.01
308 Tim Wakefield	.10	.05	.01
309 Kurt Miller	.10	.05	.01
310 Joe Sondrini	.10	.05	.01
311 Hector Fajardo	.10	.05	.01
312 Scott Bullett	.10	.05	.01
313 Jon Farrell	.10	.05	.01
314 Marc Pisciotta	.10	.05	.01
315 Rheal Cormier	.10	.05	.01
316 Omar Olivares	.10	.05	.01
317 Donovan Osborne	.20	.09	.03
318 Clyde Keller	.10	.05	.01
319 John Kelly	.10	.05	.01
320 Terry Bradshaw	.10	.05	.01
321 Brian Eversgerd	.10	.05	.01
322 Dmitri Young	2.00	.90	.25
323 Eddie Williams	.10	.05	.01
324 Brian Barber	.10	.05	.01
325 Andy Bruce	.10	.05	.01
326 Tom McKinnon	.10	.05	.01
327 Jamie Cochran	.10	.05	.01
328 Steve Jones	.10	.05	.01
329 Jerry Santos	.10	.05	.01
330 Allen Watson	.15	.07	.02
331 John Mabry	.25	.11	.03
332 Jose Melendez	.10	.05	.01
333 Dave Staton	.10	.05	.01
334 Frank Seminara	.10	.05	.01
335 Matt Mieske	.20	.09	.03
336 Jay Gainer	.10	.05	.01
337 J.D. Noland	.10	.05	.01
338 Roberto Arredondo	.10	.05	.01
339 Lance Painter	.10	.05	.01
340 Darren Lewis	.10	.05	.01
341 Ted Wood	.10	.05	.01
342 Johnny Ard	.10	.05	.01
343 Royce Clayton	.20	.09	.03
344 Paul McClellan	.10	.05	.01
345 John Patterson	.10	.05	.01
346 Steve Hosey	.10	.05	.01
347 Larry Carter	.10	.05	.01
348 Juan Guerrero	.10	.05	.01
349 Bryan Hickerson	.10	.05	.01
350 Rich Huisman	.10	.05	.01
351 Kevin McGehee	.10	.05	.01
352 Gary Sharko	.10	.05	.01
353 Salomon Torres	.10	.05	.01
354 Eric Christopherson	.10	.05	.01
355 Rod Huffman	.10	.05	.01
356 Will VanLandingham	.10	.05	.01
357 Frank Charles	.10	.05	.01
358 Ken Grundt	.10	.05	.01
359 Matt Brewer	.10	.05	.01
360 Checklist (271-360)	.10	.05	.01

1992 Pulaski Braves Classic/Best

This 30-card standard-size set of the 1992 Pulaski Braves, a Rookie Class Appalachian League affiliate of the Atlanta Braves, features white-bordered posed color player photos on its fronts. The player's name, team, and position appear at the bottom. The white back is framed by a thin red line and carries the player's name and position at the top, followed by biography, statistics and team logos.

	MINT	NRMT	EXC
COMPLETE SET (30)	5.00	2.20	.60

☐ 1 Theodore Hassan
☐ 2 John Avery
☐ 3 Jay Noel
☐ 4 Kian Sly
☐ 5 Mark Chambers
☐ 6 Mark St.Claire
☐ 7 Thomas Coates
☐ 8 Raymond Nunez
☐ 9 Marcel Johnson
☐ 10 Phil Zimmerman
☐ 11 Adrian Garcia
☐ 12 Ben Weeks
☐ 13 Brad Clontz
☐ 14 Aaron Turnier
☐ 15 Will Havens
☐ 16 Jason Kempfer
☐ 17 Kevin Grijak
☐ 18 Augie Vivenzio
☐ 19 Bryan Spetter
☐ 20 Jason Wendt
☐ 21 Pedro Swann
☐ 22 Billy Paragin
☐ 23 Steve Roeder
☐ 24 Bill Shafer
☐ 25 Mike D'Andrea
☐ 26 Nelson Paulino
☐ 27 Randy Ingle MG
☐ 28 Douglas Baker CO
☐ 29 Cloyd Boyer CO
☐ 30 Team Photo CL

1992 Pulaski Braves Fleer/ProCards

This 32-card standard-size set of the 1992 Pulaski Braves, a Rookie Class Appalachian League affiliate of the Atlanta Braves, features brown-bordered posed color player photos on its fronts. The player's name appears in an upper corner; his team and position appear in a lower corner. The white back is framed by a black line and carries the player's name and position at the top, followed by biography and statistics.

	MINT	NRMT	EXC
COMPLETE SET (32)	5.00	2.20	.60

☐ 3169 John Avery
☐ 3170 Brad Clontz
☐ 3171 Mike D'Andrea
☐ 3172 Theodore Hassan
☐ 3173 Will Havens
☐ 3174 Jason Kempfer
☐ 3175 Steve Roeder
☐ 3176 Bill Shafer
☐ 3177 Aaron Turnier
☐ 3178 Ben Weeks
☐ 3179 Jason Wendt
☐ 3180 Adrian Garcia
☐ 3181 Billy Paragin
☐ 3182 Mark St.Claire
☐ 3183 Augie Vivenzio
☐ 3184 Marcel Johnson
☐ 3185 Raymond Nunez
☐ 3186 Nelson Paulino
☐ 3187 Bryan Spetter
☐ 3188 Phil Zimmerman
☐ 3189 Mark Chambers
☐ 3190 Thomas Coates
☐ 3191 Kevin Grijak
☐ 3192 Jay Noel
☐ 3193 Kian Sly
☐ 3194 Pedro Swann
☐ 3195 Randy Ingle MG
☐ 3196 Doug Baker CO
☐ 3197 Cloyd Boyer CO
☐ 3198 Fred Koenig CO
☐ 3199 Team Picture
☐ 3200 Checklist

1992 Quad City River Bandits Classic/Best

This 30-card standard-size set of the 1992 Quad City River Bandits, a Class A Midwest League affiliate of the California Angels, features white-bordered posed color player photos on its fronts. The player's name, team, and position appear at the bottom. The white back is framed by a thin red line and carries the player's name and position at the top, followed by biography, statistics and team logos.

	MINT	NRMT	EXC
COMPLETE SET (30)	5.00	2.20	.60

☐ 1 Julian Heredia
☐ 2 Todd Claus
☐ 3 Orlando Palmeiro
☐ 4 Mark Ratekin
☐ 5 Brandon Markiewicz
☐ 6 Chris Turner
☐ 7 Shad Williams
☐ 8 Beban Perez
☐ 9 Eric Martinez
☐ 10 John Fritz
☐ 11 Glenn Mitchell
☐ 12 Jose Musset
☐ 13 Ron Watson
☐ 14 Chance Gledhill
☐ 15 Jose Stela
☐ 16 Dennis McCaffery
☐ 17 Elgin Bobo
☐ 18 P.J. Forbes
☐ 19 Mark Mammola
☐ 20 Kyle Sebach
☐ 21 Mark Sweeney
☐ 22 Gary Hagy
☐ 23 Tyrone Boykin
☐ 24 Mark Brakebill
☐ 25 David Staydohar
☐ 26 Chris Pritchett
☐ 27 Mitch Seoane MG
☐ 28 Matt Hyde CO
☐ 29 Joe Georger CO
☐ 30 Dan Pieratt TR
Checklist

1992 Quad City River Bandits Fleer/ProCards

This 30-card standard-size set of the 1992 Quad City River Bandits, a Class A Midwest League affiliate of the California Angels, features brown-bordered posed color player photos on its fronts. The player's name appears in an upper corner; his team and position appear in a lower corner. The white back is framed by a black line and carries the player's name and position at the top, followed by biography and statistics.

	MINT	NRMT	EXC
COMPLETE SET (30)	5.00	2.20	.60

☐ 800 Erik Bennett
☐ 801 John Fritz
☐ 802 Chance Gledhill
☐ 803 Julian Heredia
☐ 804 Eric Martinez
☐ 805 Glenn Mitchell
☐ 806 Jose Musset
☐ 807 Beban Perez
☐ 808 Mark Ratekin
☐ 809 Kyle Sebach
☐ 810 Ron Watson
☐ 811 Shad Williams
☐ 812 Elgin Bobo
☐ 813 Jose Stela
☐ 814 Chris Turner
☐ 815 Mark Brakebill
☐ 816 Todd Claus
☐ 817 P.J. Forbes
☐ 818 Gary Hagy
☐ 819 Brandon Markiewicz
☐ 820 Chris Pritchett
☐ 821 Tyrone Boykin
☐ 822 Dennis McCaffery
☐ 823 Orlando Palmeiro
☐ 824 Dave Staydohar
☐ 825 Mark Sweeney
☐ 826 Mitch Seoane MG
☐ 827 Joe Georger CO
☐ 828 Matt Hyde CO
☐ 829 Checklist

1992 Reading Phillies Fleer/ProCards

This 29-card standard-size set of the 1992 Reading Phillies, a Class AA Eastern League affiliate of the Philadelphia Phillies, features brown-bordered posed color player photos on its fronts. The player's name appears in an upper corner; his team and position appear in a lower corner. The white back is framed by a black line and carries the player's name and position at the top, followed by biography and statistics.

	MINT	NRMT	EXC
COMPLETE SET (29)	5.00	2.20	.60

☐ 566 Chris Bushing
☐ 567 Paul Fletcher
☐ 568 Darrell Goedhart
☐ 569 Tyler Green
☐ 570 Eric Hill
☐ 571 Chris Limbach
☐ 572 Steve Parris
☐ 573 Jeff Patterson
☐ 574 Matt Stevens
☐ 575 Mike Sullivan
☐ 576 Bob Wells
☐ 577 Scott Wiegandt
☐ 578 Mike Lieberthal
☐ 579 Edwin Rosado
☐ 580 Juan Escobar
☐ 581 R.A. Neitzel
☐ 582 Troy Paulsen
☐ 583 Sean Ryan
☐ 584 Tony Trevino
☐ 585 Pete Alborano
☐ 586 Bruce Dostal
☐ 587 Mickey Hyde
☐ 588 Ron Lockett
☐ 589 Tom Nuneviller
☐ 590 Sam Taylor
☐ 591 Don McCormack MG
☐ 592 Carlos Arroyo CO
☐ 593 Kelly Heath CO
☐ 594 Checklist

1992 Reading Phillies SkyBox

	MINT	NRMT	EXC
COMPLETE SET (26)	5.00	2.20	.60

☐ 526 Pete Alborano
☐ 527 Brad Brink
☐ 528 Chris Bushing

☐ 529 Andy Carter
☐ 530 John Escobar
☐ 531 Tyler Green
☐ 532 Mike Lieberthal
☐ 533 Chris Limbach
☐ 534 Ron Lockett
☐ 535 Paul Fletcher
☐ 536 R.A. Neitzel
☐ 537 Tom Nuneviller
☐ 538 Steve Parris
☐ 539 Troy Paulsen
☐ 540 Todd Pratt
☐ 541 Ed Rosado
☐ 542 Sean Ryan
☐ 543 Matt Stevens
☐ 544 Mike Sullivan
☐ 545 Sam Taylor
☐ 546 Casey Waller
☐ 547 Scott Wiegandt
☐ 548 Mike Williams
☐ 549 Don McCormack MG
☐ 550 Carlos Arroyo CO
Kelly Heath CO
☐ NNO Checklist

1992 Reno Silver Sox Cal League Cards

	MINT	NRMT	EXC
COMPLETE SET (29)	6.00	2.70	.75

☐ 34 Scott Lydy
☐ 35 Mike Neill
☐ 36 Mark Acre
☐ 37 Craig Connolly
☐ 38 Fausto Cruz
☐ 39 Tony DeFrancesco
☐ 40 Fabio Gomez
☐ 41 Hugh Gulledge
☐ 42 Scott Henry
☐ 43 Todd Ingram
☐ 44 Doug Johns
☐ 45 Will Love
☐ 46 Russ Brock
☐ 47 Delfino Mejia
☐ 48 Rafael Mercado
☐ 49 Islay Molina
☐ 50 Tom Myers
☐ 51 Bill Picketts
☐ 52 Rob Pierce
☐ 53 Enoch Simmons
☐ 54 Tim Smith
☐ 55 Jim Waggoner
☐ 56 Joel Wolfe
☐ 57 Joe Misa
☐ 58 Greg Smock
☐ 59 Gary Jones MG
☐ 60 Scott Budner CO
☐ 61 Jim Slaton CO
☐ 62 Shane Borchert TR

1992 Richmond Braves Bleacher Bums

3,500 sets were produced. This set includes a fourth year card of Ryan Klesko.

	MINT	NRMT	EXC
COMPLETE SET (26)	20.00	9.00	2.50

☐ 1 Jeff Manto
☐ 2 Vinny Castilla
☐ 3 Keith Smith
☐ 4 Ryan Klesko
☐ 5 Chris Chambliss
☐ 6 Mark Wohlers
☐ 7 Armando Reynoso
☐ 8 Andy Tomberlin
☐ 9 Bobby Moore
☐ 10 Keith Mitchell
☐ 11 Ramon Caraballo
☐ 12 Billy Taylor
☐ 13 Brian Deak
☐ 14 Randy St.Claire
☐ 15 Pat Gomez
☐ 16 Joe Szekely
☐ 17 Dale Polley
☐ 18 Pete Smith
☐ 19 Sean Ross
☐ 20 Napoleon Robinson
☐ 21 Francisco Cabrera
☐ 22 David Nied
☐ 23 Sonny Jackson
Bruce Dal Canton
☐ 24 Tom McCarthy
☐ 25 Boi Rodriguez
☐ 26 Team Photo

1992 Richmond Braves Bob's Camera

This 26-card team set of the 1992 Richmond Braves, a Class AAA International League affiliate of the Atlanta Braves, was sponsored by Bob's Camera and measures approximately 4" by 4 7/8". The fronts feature borderless color player photos with sponsors' and team's logos in the wide bottom margin. This issue includes a fourth year card of Ryan Klesko The backs are blank. 500 sets were produced.

	MINT	NRMT	EXC
COMPLETE SET (26)	70.00	32.00	8.75

☐ 1 Keith Mitchell
☐ 2 Armando Reynoso
☐ 3 Ryan Klesko
☐ 4 Vinny Castilla
☐ 5 Sean Ross
☐ 6 Mark Wohlers
☐ 7 David Nied
☐ 8 Brian Deak
☐ 9 Pat Gomez
☐ 10 Pete Smith
☐ 11 Boi Rodriguez
☐ 12 Jeff Manto
☐ 13 Ramon Caraballo
☐ 14 Francisco Cabrera
☐ 15 Tom McCarthy
☐ 16 Andy Tomberlin
☐ 17 Dale Polley
☐ 18 Napoleon Robinson
☐ 19 Bobby Moore
☐ 20 Randy St. Claire
☐ 21 Billy Taylor
☐ 22 Tommy Gregg
☐ 23 Kevin Coffman
☐ 24 Nick Esasky
☐ 25 Ryan Klesko
☐ 26 Chris Chambliss

1992 Richmond Braves Fleer/ProCards

This 28-card standard-size set of the 1992 Richmond Braves, a Class AAA International League affiliate of the Atlanta Braves, features brown-bordered posed color player photos on its fronts. The player's name appears in an upper corner; his team and position appear in a lower corner. The white back is framed by a black line and carries the player's name and position at the top, followed by biography and statistics. This issue includes a fourth year card of Ryan Klesko.

	MINT	NRMT	EXC
COMPLETE SET (28)	8.00	3.60	1.00

☐ 370 Kevin Coffman
☐ 371 Pat Gomez
☐ 372 Tom McCarthy
☐ 373 David Nied
☐ 374 Dale Polley
☐ 375 Armando Reynoso
☐ 376 Napoleon Robinson
☐ 377 Randy St. Claire
☐ 378 Bill Taylor
☐ 379 Francisco Cabrera
☐ 380 Brian Deak
☐ 381 Joe Szekely
☐ 382 Vinny Castilla
☐ 383 Ryan Klesko
☐ 384 Jeff Manto
☐ 385 Boi Rodriguez
☐ 386 Keith Smith
☐ 387 Keith Mitchell
☐ 388 Bobby Moore
☐ 389 Sean Ross
☐ 390 Andy Tomberlin
☐ 391 Chris Chambliss MG
☐ 392 Bruce Dal Canton CO
☐ 393 Sonny Jackson CO
☐ 394 Checklist
☐ 3014 Pete Smith
☐ 3015 Mark Wohlers
☐ 3016 Eddie Williams

1992 Richmond Braves Richmond Comix

	MINT	NRMT	EXC
COMPLETE SET (26)	25.00	11.00	3.10

☐ 1 Francisco Cabrera
☐ 2 Vinny Castilla
☐ 3 Chris Chambliss MG
☐ 4 Bruce Dal Canton CO
☐ 5 Brian Deak
☐ 6 Pat Gomez
☐ 7 Sonny Jackson
☐ 8 Ryan Klesko
☐ 9 Jeff Manto
☐ 10 Tom McCarthy
☐ 11 Keith Mitchell
☐ 12 Bobby Moore
☐ 13 David Nied
☐ 14 Dale Polley
☐ 15 Armando Reynoso
☐ 16 Napoleon Robinson
☐ 17 Boi Rodriguez
☐ 18 Sean Ross
☐ 19 Randy St.Claire
☐ 20 Keith Smith
☐ 21 Pete Smith
☐ 22 Joe Szekely
☐ 23 Billy Taylor
☐ 24 Andy Tomberlin
☐ 25 Eddie Williams
☐ 26 Mark Wohlers

1992 Richmond Braves SkyBox

	MINT	NRMT	EXC
COMPLETE SET (26)	8.00	3.60	1.00

☐ 426 Steve Howard
☐ 427 Vinny Castilla
☐ 428 Brian Deak
☐ 429 Pat Gomez
☐ 430 Ryan Klesko
☐ 431 Jeff Manto
☐ 432 Tom McCarthy
☐ 433 Keith Mitchell
☐ 434 Bobby Moore
☐ 435 David Nied
☐ 436 Dale Polley
☐ 437 Armando Reynoso
☐ 438 Napoleon Robinson
☐ 439 Boi Rodriguez
☐ 440 Sean Ross
☐ 441 Keith Smith
☐ 442 Pete Smith
☐ 443 Randy St.Claire
☐ 444 Joe Szekely
☐ 445 Billy Taylor
☐ 446 Andy Tomberlin
☐ 447 Eddie Williams
☐ 448 Mark Wohlers
☐ 449 Chris Chambliss MG
☐ 450 Bruce Dal Canton CO
Sonny Jackson CO
☐ NNO Checklist

1992 Rochester Red Wings Fleer/ProCards

This 26-card standard-size set of the 1992 Rochester Red Wings, a Class AAA International League affiliate of the Baltimore Orioles, features brown-bordered posed color player photos on its fronts. The player's name appears in an upper corner; his team and position appear in a lower corner. The white back is framed by a black line and carries the player's name and position at the top, followed by biography and statistics.

	MINT	NRMT	EXC
COMPLETE SET (26)	5.00	2.20	.60

☐ 1933 Tim Layana
☐ 1934 Pat Leinen
☐ 1935 Jim Lewis
☐ 1936 Richie Lewis
☐ 1937 Daryl Moore
☐ 1938 Mike Oquist
☐ 1939 Arthur Rhodes
☐ 1940 Todd Stephan
☐ 1941 Anthony Telford
☐ 1942 Mark Parent
☐ 1943 Doug Robbins
☐ 1944 Bobby Dickerson
☐ 1945 Ricky Gutierrez
☐ 1946 Rodney Lofton
☐ 1947 Ken Shamburg
☐ 1948 Tommy Shields
☐ 1949 Paul Carey
☐ 1950 Doug Jennings
☐ 1951 Scott Meadows
☐ 1952 Luis Mercedes
☐ 1953 Jack Voigt
☐ 1954 Ed Yacopino
☐ 1955 Jerry Narron MG
☐ 1956 Steve Luebber CO
☐ 1957 Mike Young CO
☐ 1958 Checklist

1992 Rochester Red Wings SkyBox

	MINT	NRMT	EXC
COMPLETE SET (26)	5.00	2.20	.60

☐ 451 Juan Bell
☐ 452 Bobby Dickerson
☐ 453 Ricky Gutierrez
☐ 454 Doug Jennings
☐ 455 Mike Lehman
☐ 456 Pat Leinen
☐ 457 Jim Lewis
☐ 458 Richie Lewis
☐ 459 Scott Meadows
☐ 460 Tim Layana
☐ 461 Mike Oquist
☐ 462 Mark Parent
☐ 463 Dennis Rasmussen
☐ 464 Arthur Rhodes
☐ 465 Doug Robbins
☐ 466 Greg Roth
☐ 467 Israel Sanchez
☐ 468 Ken Shamburg
☐ 469 Tommy Shields
☐ 470 Todd Stephan
☐ 471 Anthony Telford
☐ 472 Jack Voigt
☐ 473 Ed Yacopino
☐ 474 Jerry Narron MG
☐ 475 Steve Luebber CO
Mike Young CO
☐ NNO Checklist

1992 Rockford Expos Classic/Best

This 30-card standard-size set of the 1992 Rockford Expos, a Class A Midwest League affiliate of the Montreal Expos, features white-bordered posed color player photos on its fronts. The player's name, team, and position appear at the bottom. The white back is framed by a thin red line and carries the player's name and position at the top, followed by biography, statistics and team logos.

	MINT	NRMT	EXC
COMPLETE SET (30)	5.00	2.20	.60

☐ 1 Mike Thomas
☐ 2 Scott Dennison
☐ 3 Raul Santana
☐ 4 Rusty Kilgo
☐ 5 Darrin Kotch
☐ 6 Mike Hardge
☐ 7 Derek Aucoin
☐ 8 Ron Gerstein
☐ 9 Tyrone Woods
☐ 10 Domingo Matos
☐ 11 Gabe White
☐ 12 Doug O'Neill
☐ 13 Kirk Rueter
☐ 14 Derek Dehdashtion
(Name misspelled on
both sides Dehdashtian)
☐ 15 Carlos Perez
☐ 16 Hector Ortega
☐ 17 Steve Whitehead
☐ 18 Brian Looney
☐ 19 William Martinez
☐ 20 Mark Grudzielanek
☐ 21 Heath Haynes
☐ 22 Joe Norris
☐ 23 Chris Falco
☐ 24 Tyrone Horne
☐ 25 Todd Samples
☐ 26 Dusty Freitag
☐ 27 Rafael Rijo
☐ 28 Rob Leary MG
☐ 29 Herm Starrette CO
☐ 30 Jim Young TR
Checklist

1992 Rockford Expos Fleer/ProCards

This 28-card standard-size set of the 1992 Rockford Expos, a Class A Midwest League affiliate of the Montreal Expos, features brown-bordered posed color player photos on its fronts. The player's name appears in an upper corner; his team and position appear at a lower corner. The white back is framed by a black line and carries the player's name and position at the top, followed by biography and statistics.

	MINT	NRMT	EXC
COMPLETE SET (28)	5.00	2.20	.60

☐ 2106 Derek Aucoin
☐ 2107 Vince Fultz
☐ 2108 Ron Gerstein
☐ 2109 Heath Haynes
☐ 2110 Darrin Kotch
☐ 2111 Brian Looney
☐ 2112 Bill Martinez
☐ 2113 Joe Norris
☐ 2114 Kirk Rueter
☐ 2115 Mike Thomas
☐ 2116 Gabe White
☐ 2117 Steve Whitehead
☐ 2118 Derek Dehdashtion
☐ 2119 Dusty Freitag
☐ 2120 Raul Santana
☐ 2121 Scott Dennison
☐ 2122 Chris Falco
☐ 2123 Mark Grudzielanek
☐ 2124 Mike Hardge
☐ 2125 Domingo Matos
☐ 2126 Hector Ortega
☐ 2127 Tyrone Horne
☐ 2128 Rafael Rijo
☐ 2129 Todd Samples
☐ 2130 Tyrone Woods
☐ 2131 Rob Leary MG
☐ 3012 Tim Torricelli CO
☐ 3013 Checklist

1992 Salem Buccaneers Classic/Best

This 30-card standard-size set of the 1992 Salem Buccaneers, a Class A Carolina League affiliate of the Pittsburgh Pirates, features white-bordered posed color player photos on its fronts. The player's name, team, and position appear at the bottom. The white back is framed by a thin red line and carries the player's name and position at the top, followed by biography, statistics and team logos.

	MINT	NRMT	EXC
COMPLETE SET (30)	5.00	2.20	.60

☐ 1 Midre Cummings
☐ 2 Ramon Martinez
☐ 3 Rich Aude
☐ 4 Eric Parkinson
☐ 5 Bruce Schreiber
☐ 6 Doug Harrah
☐ 7 Dave Tellers
☐ 8 Pasquale Arace
☐ 9 Genaro Campusano
☐ 10 Keith Thomas
☐ 11 Jason Christiansen
☐ 12 Jose Alvarez
☐ 13 Bobby Hunter
☐ 14 Marcus Hanel
☐ 15 John Hope
☐ 16 Joe Sondrini
☐ 17 Tom Green
☐ 18 Rob Bailey
☐ 19 Tim Edge
☐ 20 Todd Schroeder
☐ 21 Dan Jones
☐ 22 Troy Mooney
☐ 23 Dave Watson
☐ 24 Rick White
☐ 25 Rony Beasley
☐ 26 John Wockenfuss MG
☐ 27 Rick Keeton CO
☐ 28 Bill Zick TR
☐ 29 Logo Card
☐ 30 Checklist

1992 Salem Buccaneers Fleer/ProCards

This 28-card standard-size set of the 1992 Salem Buccaneers, a Class A Carolina League affiliate of the Pittsburgh Pirates, features brown-bordered posed color player photos on its fronts. The player's name appears in an upper corner; his team and position appear in a lower corner. The white back is framed by a black line and carries the player's name and position at the top, followed by biography and statistics.

	MINT	NRMT	EXC
COMPLETE SET (28)	5.00	2.20	.60

☐ 54 Jose Alvarez
☐ 55 Jason Christiansen
☐ 56 Sean Evans
☐ 57 Doug Harrah
☐ 58 John Hope
☐ 59 Bobby Hunter
☐ 60 Dan Jones
☐ 61 Troy Mooney
☐ 62 Eric Parkinson
☐ 63 Kevin Rychel
☐ 64 Dave Watson
☐ 65 Rick White
☐ 66 Tim Edge
☐ 67 Marcus Hanel
☐ 68 Rich Aude
☐ 69 Tony Beasley
☐ 70 Ken Bonifay
☐ 71 Ramon Martinez
☐ 72 Todd Schroeder
☐ 73 Joe Sondrini
☐ 74 Pasquale Arace
☐ 75 Rob Bailey
☐ 76 Midre Cummings
☐ 77 Joe Ronca
☐ 78 Keith Thomas
☐ 79 John Wockenfuss MG
☐ 80 Rick Keeton CO
☐ 81 Checklist

1992 Salinas Spurs Classic/Best

This 30-card standard-size set of the 1992 Salinas Spurs, a Class A California League Independent, features white-bordered posed color player photos on its fronts. The player's name, team, and position appear at the bottom. The white back is framed by a thin red line and carries the player's name and position at the top, followed by biography, statistics and team logos.

	MINT	NRMT	EXC
COMPLETE SET (30)	5.00	2.20	.60

☐ 1 Kiyoshi Arai
☐ 2 Greg Fritz
☐ 3 Geoff Samuels
☐ 4 Dave Trautwein
☐ 5 Randy Powers
☐ 6 Marc Kubicki
☐ 7 Takayuki Nishijima
☐ 8 Mike Lawn
☐ 9 Rafael Rivera
☐ 10 Hideki Kato
☐ 11 Alan Sontag
☐ 12 Tommy Helms
☐ 13 Don Sheppard
☐ 14 Greg McGough
☐ 15 Kevin Wong
☐ 16 Kevin Tolar
☐ 17 Arthur Butcher
☐ 18 Hidefumi Hara
☐ 19 Tsutomu Yamada
☐ 20 Cliff Gonzalez
☐ 21 Dave DuPlessis
☐ 22 Carlos Laboy
☐ 23 Mike Bradish
☐ 24 Takashi Uchinokura
☐ 25 Hide Koga
☐ 26 Takayuki Hohno CO
☐ 27 Dick Little CO
☐ 28 Kelly Luse TR
☐ 29 Keishi Asano CO
☐ 30 Rich Morales CO Checklist

1992 Salinas Spurs Fleer/ProCards

This 31-card standard-size set of the 1992 Salinas Spurs, a Class A California League Independent, features brown-bordered posed color player photos on its fronts. The player's name appears in an upper corner; his team and position appear in a lower corner. The white back is framed by a black line and carries the player's name and position at the top, followed by biography and statistics.

	MINT	NRMT	EXC
COMPLETE SET (31)	5.00	2.20	.60

☐ 3748 Bruce Arola
☐ 3749 Rick Green
☐ 3750 Mike Hooper
☐ 3751 Troy Hooper
☐ 3752 Geoff Samuels
☐ 3753 Alan Sontag
☐ 3754 Mark Stephens
☐ 3755 Fred Toliver
☐ 3756 Dave Trautwein
☐ 3757 Tsutoma Yamada
☐ 3758 Greg McGough
☐ 3759 Rafael Rivera
☐ 3760 Andy Skeels
☐ 3761 Kiyoshi Arai
☐ 3762 Kevin Davis
☐ 3763 Dave DuPlessis
☐ 3764 Hideki Kato
☐ 3765 Tokashi Uchinokura
☐ 3766 Kevin Wong
☐ 3767 Cliff Gonzalez
☐ 3768 Hidefumi Hara
☐ 3769 Carlos Laboy
☐ 3770 Mike Lawn
☐ 3771 Takayuki Nishijima
☐ 3772 Don Sheppard
☐ 3773 Hide Koga MG
☐ 3774 Keishi Asano CO
☐ 3775 Takayuki Kohno CO
☐ 3776 Dick Little CO
☐ 3777 Rich Morales CO
☐ 3778 Checklist

1992 Salt Lake Trappers Sports Pro

	MINT	NRMT	EXC
COMPLETE SET (30)	6.00	2.70	.75

☐ 1 Richard Licursi
☐ 2 Bill Vosik
☐ 3 Andrew Jackson
☐ 4 Jeff DeVaughan
☐ 5 Barry Parisotto
☐ 6 Tim Rigsby
☐ 7 John Gilligan
☐ 8 Tim Clark
☐ 9 Willie Smith
☐ 10 Shannon Jones
☐ 11 Todd Rosenthal
☐ 12 Chris Schultea
☐ 13 Pookie Wilson
☐ 14 Randy Snyder
☐ 15 Cecil Pettiford
☐ 16 Ken Folger
☐ 17 George Kerfut
☐ 18 John Thoden
☐ 19 Eddie Ortega
☐ 20 Jon Harden
☐ 21 Richard Palumbo
☐ 22 Bobby Ryan
☐ 23 John Calarco
☐ 24 Bobby Benjamin
☐ 25 George Baker
☐ 26 Jim Guidi
☐ 27 Les Jennette
☐ 28 Art Canestro
☐ 29 Brian Peterson CO
☐ 30 Nick Belmonte MG

1992 San Antonio Missions Fleer/ProCards

This 24-card standard-size set of the 1992 San Antonio Missions, a Class AA Texas League affiliate of the Los Angeles Dodgers, features brown-bordered posed color player photos on its fronts. The player's name appears in an upper corner; his team and position appear in a lower corner. The white back is framed by a black line and carries the player's name and position at the top, followed by biography and statistics. This issue includes a third year card of Raul Mondesi.

	MINT	NRMT	EXC
COMPLETE SET (24)	14.00	6.25	1.75

☐ 3967 Steve Allen
☐ 3968 Ray Calhoun
☐ 3969 Balvino Galvez
☐ 3970 Mike James
☐ 3971 Jamie McAndrew
☐ 3972 Michael Mimbs
☐ 3973 Dennis Springer
☐ 3974 Jody Treadwell
☐ 3975 Bill Wengert
☐ 3976 Todd Williams
☐ 3977 Adam Brown
☐ 3978 Lance Rice
☐ 3979 Jorge Alvarez
☐ 3980 Tim Barker
☐ 3981 John Deutsch
☐ 3982 Scott Doffek
☐ 3983 Matt Howard
☐ 3984 Steve Kliafas
☐ 3985 Ron Maurer
☐ 3986 Garey Ingram
☐ 3987 Raul Mondesi
☐ 3988 Jerry Royster MG
☐ 3989 Darrell Evans CO
☐ 3990 Checklist

1992 San Antonio Missions SkyBox

	MINT	NRMT	EXC
COMPLETE SET (26)	18.00	8.00	2.20

☐ 551 Steve Allen
☐ 552 Jorge Alvarez
☐ 553 Billy Ashley
☐ 554 Tim Barker
☐ 555 Tony Barron
☐ 556 Bill Bene
☐ 557 Adam Brown
☐ 558 Mike Busch
☐ 559 Albert Bustillos
☐ 560 Ray Calhoun
☐ 561 Omar Daal
☐ 562 John Deutsch
☐ 563 Scott Doffek
☐ 564 Balvino Galvez
☐ 565 Freddy Gonzalez
☐ 566 Greg Hansell
☐ 567 Matt Howard
☐ 568 Dennis Springer
☐ 569 Ron Maurer
☐ 570 Mike Mimbs
☐ 571 Chris Morrow
☐ 572 Chris Nichting
☐ 573 Mike Piazza
☐ 574 Jerry Royster MG
☐ 575 Rudy Seanez
☐ NNO Checklist

1992 San Bernardino Classic/Best

This 30-card standard-size set of the 1992 San Bernardino Spirit, a Class A California League affiliate of the Seattle Mariners, features white-bordered posed color player photos on its fronts. The player's name, team, and position appear at the bottom. The white back is framed by a thin red line and carries the player's name and position at the top, followed by biography, statistics and team logos.

	MINT	NRMT	EXC
COMPLETE SET (30)	5.00	2.20	.60

☐ 1 Tommy Adams
☐ 2 Ron Pezzoni
☐ 3 Pat Garrigan
☐ 4 Kyle Duke
☐ 5 Matt Kluge
☐ 6 Rich Lodding
☐ 7 Jeff Borski
☐ 8 Tony Kounas
☐ 9 Marc Rosenbalm
☐ 10 Tommy Robertson
☐ 11 Jim Mecir
☐ 12 Scott Schanz
☐ 13 Craig Bryant
☐ 14 Doyle Balthazar
☐ 15 George Glinatsis
☐ 16 Manny Cervantes
☐ 17 Mike Hampton
☐ 18 David Adam
☐ 19 Julio Fernandez
☐ 20 Ed Diaz
☐ 21 Craig Clayton
☐ 22 Kevin King
☐ 23 Salvy Urso
☐ 24 Paul Perkins
☐ 25 Paul Brannon
☐ 26 David Waldenberger
☐ 27 Ivan De Jesus MG
☐ 28 Gary Wheelock CO
☐ 29 Lem Pilkinton CO
☐ 30 Rory Riddoch TR Checklist

1992 San Bernardino Spirit Fleer/ProCards

This 33-card standard-size set of the 1992 San Bernardino Spirit, a Class A California League affiliate of the Seattle Mariners, features brown-bordered posed color player photos on its fronts. The player's name appears in an upper corner; his team and position appear in a lower corner. The white back is framed by a black line and carries the player's name and position at the top, followed by biography and statistics.

	MINT	NRMT	EXC
COMPLETE SET (33)	5.00	2.20	.60

☐ 228 Ivan DeJesus MG
☐ 943 Dave Adam
☐ 944 Jeff Borski
☐ 945 Kyle Duke
☐ 946 George Glinatsis
☐ 947 Mike Hampton
☐ 948 Kevin King
☐ 949 Rich Lodding
☐ 950 Jim Mecir
☐ 951 Paul Perkins
☐ 952 Anthony Phillips
☐ 953 Scott Schanz
☐ 954 Sal Urso
☐ 955 Trey Witte
☐ 956 Doyle Balthazar
☐ 957 Matt Kluge
☐ 958 Tony Kounas
☐ 959 Alex Sutherland
☐ 960 Paul Brannon
☐ 961 Craig Bryant
☐ 962 Manny Cervantes
☐ 963 Craig Clayton
☐ 964 Ed Diaz
☐ 965 Pat Garrigan
☐ 966 David Henderson
☐ 967 Arquimedez Pozo
☐ 968 Dave Waldenberger
☐ 969 Tommy Adams
☐ 970 Ken Pennington
☐ 971 Ron Pezzoni
☐ 972 Tommy Robertson
☐ 973 Sean Twitty
☐ 3437 Checklist

1992 San Jose Giants Classic/Best

This 30-card standard-size set of the 1992 San Jose Giants, a Class A California League affiliate of the San Francisco Giants, features white-bordered posed color player photos on its fronts. The player's name, team, and position appear at the bottom. The white back is framed by a thin red line and carries the player's name and position at the top, followed by biography, statistics and team logos.

	MINT	NRMT	EXC
COMPLETE SET (30)	5.00	2.20	.60

☐ 1 Matt Brewer
☐ 2 Jose Rosselli
☐ 3 Steven Rolen
☐ 4 Billy VanLandingham
☐ 5 Steve Whitaker
☐ 6 Brian McLeod
☐ 7 Rikkert Faneyte
☐ 8 Adam Hyzdu
☐ 9 Barry Miller
☐ 10 Andres Duncan
☐ 11 Dan Calcagno
☐ 12 Dan Flanagan
☐ 13 Troy Clemens
☐ 14 Don Montgomery
☐ 15 Jason McFarlin
☐ 16 Greg Brummett
☐ 17 Ricky Ward
☐ 18 Carl Hanselman
☐ 19 Chris Hancock
☐ 20 Rod Huffman
☐ 21 Pepe Frias
☐ 22 Vince Herring
☐ 23 Matt Davis
☐ 24 Brett McGonnigal
☐ 25 Al Benavides
☐ 26 Ron Wotus MG
☐ 27 Rick Miller CO
☐ 28 Frank Reberger CO
☐ 29 Brian Costello TR
☐ 30 Mark Wilson MG Checklist

1992 Sarasota White Sox Fleer/ProCards

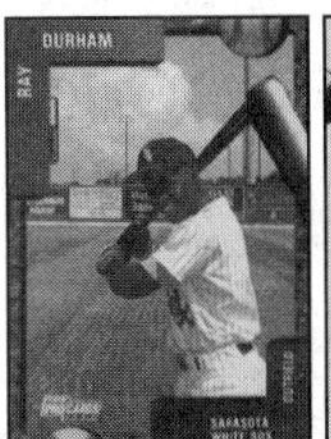

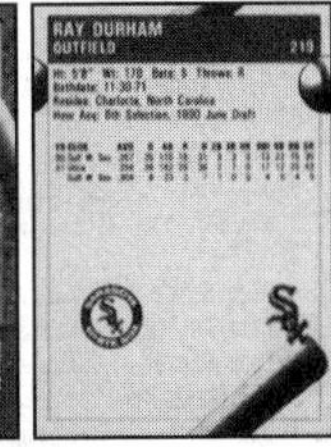

This 30-card standard-size set of the 1992 Sarasota White Sox, a Class A Florida State League affiliate of the Chicago White Sox, features brown-bordered posed color player photos on its fronts. The player's name appears in an upper corner; his team and position appear in a lower corner. The white back is framed by a black line and carries the player's name and position at the top, followed by biography and statistics. This issue includes the second year card of Ray Durham.

	MINT	NRMT	EXC
COMPLETE SET (30)	7.00	3.10	.85

☐ 198 Jason Bere
☐ 199 Rolando Caridad
☐ 200 Tony Gordon
☐ 201 Dean Locklear
☐ 202 Steve Olsen
☐ 203 Don Perigny
☐ 204 Robert Person
☐ 205 Scott Ruffcorn
☐ 206 Johnny Ruffin
☐ 207 Steve Schrenk
☐ 208 Rogelio Nunez
☐ 209 Nilson Robledo
☐ 210 Keith Strange
☐ 211 Doug Brady
☐ 212 Ken Coleman
☐ 213 Mike Eatinger
☐ 214 Giovanni Miranda
☐ 215 Mike Robertson
☐ 216 Dennis Walker
☐ 217 Brandon Wilson
☐ 218 Shawn Buchanan
☐ 219 Ray Durham
☐ 220 Randall Hood
☐ 221 Kinnis Pledger
☐ 222 Ron Plemmons
☐ 223 Jerry Wolak
☐ 224 Rick Patterson MG
☐ 225 Mike Barnett CO
☐ 226 Kirk Champion CO
☐ 227 Checklist

1992 Sarasota White Sox Classic/Best

This 30-card standard-size set of the 1992 Sarasota White Sox, a Class A Florida State League affiliate of the Chicago White Sox, features white-bordered posed color player photos on its fronts. The player's name, team, and position appear at the bottom. The white back is framed by a thin red line and carries the player's name and position at the top, followed by biography, statistics and team logos.

	MINT	NRMT	EXC
COMPLETE SET (30)	5.00	2.20	.60

☐ 1 Scott Ruffcorn
☐ 2 Ken Coleman
☐ 3 Rogelio Nunez
☐ 4 Brandon Wilson
☐ 5 Keith Strange
☐ 6 Jason Bere
☐ 7 Dean Locklear
☐ 8 Kevin Castleberry
☐ 9 Mike Eatinger
☐ 10 Dean Haase
☐ 11 Rolando Caridad
☐ 12 Don Perigny
☐ 13 Dennis Walker
☐ 14 Jerry Wolak
☐ 15 Steve Schrenk
☐ 16 Randall Hood
☐ 17 Shawn Buchanan
☐ 18 Frank Campos
☐ 19 Kevin Coughlin
☐ 20 Mike Robertson
☐ 21 Steve Olsen
☐ 22 Larry Thomas
☐ 23 Monte Mathis
☐ 24 Anthony Gordon
☐ 25 Doug Brady
☐ 26 Mike Hooper
☐ 27 Rick Patterson MG
☐ 28 Kirk Champion CO
☐ 29 Mike Barnett CO
☐ 30 Scott Johnson TR
Checklist

1992 Savannah Cardinals Classic/Best

This 30-card standard-size set of the 1992 Savannah Cardinals, a Class A South Atlantic League affiliate of the St. Louis Cardinals, features white-bordered posed color player photos on its fronts. The player's name, team, and position appear at the bottom. The white back is framed by a thin red line and carries the player's name and position at the top, followed by biography, statistics and team logos.

	MINT	NRMT	EXC
COMPLETE SET (30)	5.00	2.20	.60

☐ 1 Eddie Williams
☐ 2 Mike Jolley
☐ 3 Kevin Lucero
☐ 4 Larry Lucchetti
☐ 5 Ben Ellsworth
☐ 6 Ron Warner
☐ 7 Clint Davis
☐ 8 John Frascatore
☐ 9 Steve Johnson
☐ 10 Curtis Underwood
☐ 11 DaRond Stovall
☐ 12 Jonas Hamlin
☐ 13 John Dempsey
☐ 14 Gary Taylor
☐ 15 Joe Turvey
☐ 16 Jason Hisey
☐ 17 Rigo Beltran
☐ 18 Dan Cholowsky
☐ 19 Allan Hammond
☐ 20 Tom Fusco
☐ 21 Aarom Holbert
☐ 22 Derron Spiller
☐ 23 Mike Ramsey MG
☐ 24 Ramon Ortiz CO
☐ 25 Pete Fagan TR
☐ 26 Logo Card
☐ 27 Logo Card
☐ 28 Logo Card
☐ 29 Logo Card
☐ 30 Checklist

1992 Savannah Cardinals Fleer/ProCards

This 30-card standard-size set of the 1992 Savannah Cardinals, a Class A South Atlantic League affiliate of the St. Louis Cardinals, features brown-bordered posed color player photos on its fronts. The player's name appears in an upper corner; his team and position appear in a lower corner. The white back is framed by a black line and carries the player's name and position at the top, followed by biography and statistics.

	MINT	NRMT	EXC
COMPLETE SET (30)	5.00	2.20	.60

☐ 652 Rigo Beltran
☐ 653 Mike Busby
☐ 654 Clint Davis
☐ 655 John Frascatore
☐ 656 Tom Fusco
☐ 657 Allan Hammond
☐ 658 Jason Hisey
☐ 659 Steve Johnson
☐ 660 Mike Jolley
☐ 661 Greg Knowles
☐ 662 Kevin Lucero
☐ 663 Larry Lucchetti
☐ 664 Derron Spiller
☐ 665 Joe Turvey
☐ 666 Eddie Williams
☐ 667 Dan Cholowsky
☐ 668 Ignacio Duran
☐ 669 Ben Ellsworth
☐ 670 Jonas Hamlin
☐ 671 Aaron Holbert
☐ 672 Curtis Underwood
☐ 673 Ron Warner
☐ 674 Brent Bohrofen
☐ 675 Rick Mediavilla
☐ 676 DaRond Stovall
☐ 677 Gary Taylor
☐ 678 Jose Velez
☐ 679 Mike Ramsey MG
☐ 680 Ramon Ortiz CO
☐ 681 Checklist

1992 Scranton-Wilkes-Barre Red Barons SkyBox

This 26-card standard-size set of the 1992 Scranton/Wilkes-Barre Red Barons, a Class AAA International League affiliate of the Philadelphia Phillies, features white-bordered posed color player photos on its fronts. The player's name, team, and position appear at the bottom. The white back is framed by a thin red line and carries the player's name and position at the top, followed by biography, statistics and team logos.

	MINT	NRMT	EXC
COMPLETE SET (26)	5.00	2.20	.60

☐ 476 Gary Alexander
☐ 477 Bob Ayrault
☐ 478 Jay Baller
☐ 479 Toby Borland
☐ 480 Braulio Castillo
☐ 481 Darrin Chapin
☐ 482 Pat Combs
☐ 483 Bruce Dostal
☐ 484 Brad Brink
☐ 485 Mike Hartley
☐ 486 Greg Legg
☐ 487 Doug Lindsey
☐ 488 Tom Marsh
☐ 489 Greg Mathews
☐ 490 Tim Mauser
☐ 491 Joe Millette
☐ 492 Steve Scarsone
☐ 493 Rick Schu
☐ 494 Mark Sims
☐ 495 Ray Stephens
☐ 496 Mickey Weston
☐ 497 Cary Williams
☐ 498 Julio Peguero
☐ 499 Lee Elia MG
☐ 500 Jim Wright CO
Al LeBoeuf CO
☐ NNO Checklist

1992 Scranton/Wilkes-Barre Red Barons Fleer/ProCards

This 27-card standard-size set of the 1992 Scranton/Wilkes-Barre Red Barons, a Class AAA International League affiliate of the Philadelphia Phillies, features brown-bordered posed color player photos on its fronts. The player's name appears in an upper corner; his team and position appear in a lower corner. The white back is framed by a black line and carries the player's name and position at the top, followed by biography and statistics.

	MINT	NRMT	EXC
COMPLETE SET (27)	5.00	2.20	.60

☐ 2439 Jay Baller
☐ 2440 Toby Borland
☐ 2441 Darrin Chapin
☐ 2442 Pat Combs
☐ 2443 Greg Mathews
☐ 2444 Tim Mauser
☐ 2445 Steve Searcy
☐ 2446 Mark Sims
☐ 2447 Mickey Weston
☐ 2448 Mike Williams
☐ 2449 Doug Lindsey
☐ 2450 Todd Pratt
☐ 2451 Gary Alexander
☐ 2452 Greg Legg
☐ 2453 Joe Millette
☐ 2454 Vic Rodriguez
☐ 2455 Steve Scarsone
☐ 2456 Rick Schu
☐ 2457 Casey Waller
☐ 2458 Braulio Castillo
☐ 2459 Wes Chamberlain
☐ 2460 Julio Peguero
☐ 2461 Cary Williams
☐ 2462 Lee Elia MG
☐ 2463 Al LeBoeuf CO
☐ 2464 Jim Wright CO
☐ 2465 Checklist

1992 Shreveport Captains Fleer/ProCards

This 27-card standard-size set of the 1992 Shreveport Captains, a Class AA Texas League affiliate of the San Francisco Giants, features brown-bordered posed color player photos on its fronts. The player's name appears in an upper corner; his team and position appear in a lower corner. The white back is framed by a black line and carries the player's name and position at the top, followed by biography and statistics.

	MINT	NRMT	EXC
COMPLETE SET (27)	5.00	2.20	.60

☐ 3864 Dan Carlson
☐ 3865 Rick Huisman
☐ 3866 Kevin McGehee
☐ 3867 Lou Pote
☐ 3868 Dan Rambo
☐ 3869 Steve Reed
☐ 3870 Kevin Rogers
☐ 3871 Rob Taylor
☐ 3872 Salomon Torres
☐ 3873 Mark Yockey
☐ 3874 Eric Christopherson
☐ 3875 Ron Crowe
☐ 3876 Dan Fernandez
☐ 3877 Clay Bellinger
☐ 3878 Joel Chimelis
☐ 3879 Todd Crosby
☐ 3880 Adell Davenport
☐ 3881 Mike Easley
☐ 3882 Kevin Kasper
☐ 3883 Reed Peters
☐ 3884 Derek Reid
☐ 3885 Reuben Smiley
☐ 3886 Pete Weber
☐ 3887 Bill Robinson MG
☐ 3888 Steve Cline CO
☐ 3889 Dick Dietz CO
☐ 3890 Checklist

1992 Shreveport Captains SkyBox

	MINT	NRMT	EXC
COMPLETE SET (26)	5.00	2.20	.60

☐ 576 Clay Bellinger
☐ 577 Dan Carlson
☐ 578 Joel Chimelis
☐ 579 Eric Christopherson
☐ 580 Todd Crosby
☐ 581 Ron Crowe
☐ 582 Adell Davenport
☐ 583 Mike Easley
☐ 584 Dan Fernandez
☐ 585 Rick Huisman
☐ 586 Kevin Kasper
☐ 587 Kevin McGehee
☐ 588 Reed Peters
☐ 589 Lou Pote
☐ 590 Dan Rambo
☐ 591 Steve Reed
☐ 592 Steve Finken
☐ 593 Kevin Rogers
☐ 594 Rueben Smiley
☐ 595 Rob Taylor
☐ 596 Salomon Torres
☐ 597 Pete Weber
☐ 598 Mark Yockey
☐ 599 Bill Robinson MG
☐ 600 Dick Dietz CO
Steve Cline CO
☐ NNO Checklist

1992 SkyBox AA

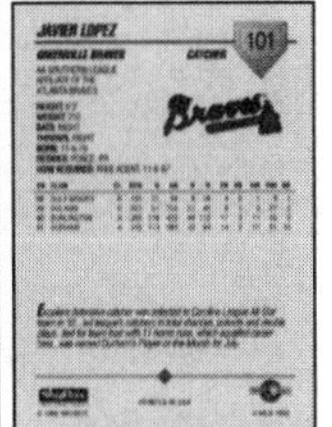

This 310-card standard-size set has glossy color action player photos bordered in white. The player's name appears in black lettering at the top of the card top, with team logo in the upper right corner. The team name and position are given below the photo. The white back carries the player's name at the top, followed by biography and statistics.

	MINT	NRMT	EXC
COMPLETE SET (310)	15.00	6.75	1.85
COMMON CARD (1-310)	.05	.02	.01
☐ 1 Rich Batchelor	.05	.02	.01
☐ 2 Russ Davis	.10	.05	.01
☐ 3 Kiki Hernandez	.05	.02	.01
☐ 4 Sterling Hitchcock	.15	.07	.02
☐ 5 Darren Hodges	.05	.02	.01
☐ 6 Jeff Hoffman	.05	.02	.01
☐ 7 Mark Hutton	.05	.02	.01
☐ 8 Bobby Munoz	.05	.02	.01
☐ 9 Rey Noriega	.05	.02	.01
☐ 10 Sherman Obando	.05	.02	.01
☐ 11 John Viera	.05	.02	.01
☐ 12 Cliff Brannon	.05	.02	.01
☐ 13 Chuck Carr	.05	.02	.01
☐ 14 Fidel Compres	.05	.02	.01
☐ 15 Tripp Cromer	.05	.02	.01
☐ 16 John Ericks	.05	.02	.01
☐ 17 Gabby Ozuna	.05	.02	.01
☐ 18 Don Prybylinski	.05	.02	.01
☐ 19 John Sellick	.05	.02	.01
☐ 20 John Thomas	.05	.02	.01
☐ 21 Tom Urbani	.05	.02	.01
☐ 22 Chris Butterfield	.05	.02	.01
☐ 23 Todd Douma	.05	.02	.01
☐ 24 Brook Fordyce	.05	.02	.01
☐ 25 Tim Howard	.05	.02	.01
☐ 26 John Johnstone	.05	.02	.01
☐ 27 Bobby Jones	.25	.11	.03
☐ 28 Rob Katzaroff	.05	.02	.01
☐ 29 Gregg Langbehn	.05	.02	.01
☐ 30 Curtis Pride	.05	.02	.01
☐ 31 Julian Vasquez	.05	.02	.01
☐ 32 Joe Vitko	.05	.02	.01
☐ 33 Tom Wegmann	.05	.02	.01
☐ 34 Mike White	.05	.02	.01
☐ 35 Alan Zinter	.05	.02	.01
☐ 36 Clemente Alvarez	.05	.02	.01
☐ 37 Cesar Bernhardt	.05	.02	.01
☐ 38 Wayne Busby	.05	.02	.01
☐ 39 Scott Cepicky	.05	.02	.01
☐ 40 John Hudek	.05	.02	.01
☐ 41 Scott Jaster	.05	.02	.01

Card	Mint	NRMT	EXC
☐ 42 Bo Kennedy	.05	.02	.01
☐ 43 Mike Mongiello	.05	.02	.01
☐ 44 Kinnis Pledger	.05	.02	.01
☐ 45 Johnny Ruffin	.05	.02	.01
☐ 46 Jose Ventura	.05	.02	.01
☐ 47 Paul Byrd	.05	.02	.01
☐ 48 Colin Charland	.05	.02	.01
☐ 49 Miguel Flores	.05	.02	.01
☐ 50 Brian Giles	.05	.02	.01
☐ 51 Jose Hernandez	.05	.02	.01
☐ 52 Nolan Lane	.05	.02	.01
☐ 53 David Mlicki	.05	.02	.01
☐ 54 Tracy Sanders	.05	.02	.01
☐ 55 Mike Soper	.05	.02	.01
☐ 56 Kelly Stinnett	.05	.02	.01
☐ 57 Joe Turek	.05	.02	.01
☐ 58 Kyle Washington	.05	.02	.01
☐ 59 Dave Bird	.05	.02	.01
☐ 60 Scott Bullett	.05	.02	.01
☐ 61 Steve Cooke	.05	.02	.01
☐ 62 Alberto De Los Santos	.05	.02	.01
☐ 63 Stan Fansler	.05	.02	.01
☐ 64 Austin Manahan	.05	.02	.01
☐ 65 Daryl Ratliff	.05	.02	.01
☐ 66 Mandy Romero	.05	.02	.01
☐ 67 Ben Shelton	.05	.02	.01
☐ 68 Paul Wagner	.05	.02	.01
☐ 69 Mike Zimmerman	.05	.02	.01
☐ 70 Phil Dauphin	.05	.02	.01
☐ 71 Chris Ebright	.05	.02	.01
☐ 72 Mike Grace	.05	.02	.01
☐ 73 Ryan Hawblitzel	.05	.02	.01
☐ 74 Jessie Hollins	.05	.02	.01
☐ 75 Tim Parker	.05	.02	.01
☐ 76 Dave Swartzbaugh	.05	.02	.01
☐ 77 Steve Trachsel	.05	.02	.01
☐ 78 Billy White	.05	.02	.01
☐ 79 Bobby Ayala	.05	.02	.01
☐ 80 Tim Costo	.05	.02	.01
☐ 81 Ty Griffin	.05	.02	.01
☐ 82 Cesar Hernandez	.05	.02	.01
☐ 83 Trevor Hoffman	.15	.07	.02
☐ 84 Brian Lane	.05	.02	.01
☐ 85 Scott Pose	.05	.02	.01
☐ 86 Johnny Ray	.05	.02	.01
☐ 87 John Roper	.05	.02	.01
☐ 88 Glenn Sutko	.05	.02	.01
☐ 89 Kevin Tatar	.05	.02	.01
☐ 90 John Byington	.05	.02	.01
☐ 91 Tony Diggs	.05	.02	.01
☐ 92 Bo Dodson	.05	.02	.01
☐ 93 Craig Faulkner	.05	.02	.01
☐ 94 Jim Hunter	.05	.02	.01
☐ 95 Oreste Marrero	.05	.02	.01
☐ 96 Troy O'Leary	.15	.07	.02
☐ 97 Brian Bark	.05	.02	.01
☐ 98 Dennis Burlingame	.05	.02	.01
☐ 99 Ramon Caraballo	.05	.02	.01
☐ 100 Mike Kelly	.05	.02	.01
☐ 101 Javy Lopez	1.25	.55	.16
☐ 102 Don Strange	.05	.02	.01
☐ 103 Tony Tarasco	.15	.07	.02
☐ 104 Manny Alexander	.10	.05	.01
☐ 105 Damon Buford	.05	.02	.01
☐ 106 Cesar Devares	.05	.02	.01
☐ 107 Rodney Lofton	.05	.02	.01
☐ 108 Brent Miller	.05	.02	.01
☐ 109 David Miller	.05	.02	.01
☐ 110 Daryl Moore	.05	.02	.01
☐ 111 John O'Donoghue	.05	.02	.01
☐ 112 Erik Schullstrom	.05	.02	.01
☐ 113 Mark Smith	.05	.02	.01
☐ 114 Mel Wearing	.05	.02	.01
☐ 115 Jeff Williams	.05	.02	.01
☐ 116 Kip Yaughn	.05	.02	.01
☐ 117 Doug Bochtler	.05	.02	.01
☐ 118 Travis Buckley	.05	.02	.01
☐ 119 Reid Cornelius	.05	.02	.01
☐ 120 Chris Johnson	.05	.02	.01
☐ 121 Tim Laker	.05	.02	.01
☐ 122 Chris Martin	.05	.02	.01
☐ 123 Mike Mathile	.05	.02	.01
☐ 124 Darwin Pennye	.05	.02	.01
☐ 125 Doug Piatt	.05	.02	.01
☐ 126 Kurt Abbott	.10	.05	.01
☐ 127 Marcos Armas	.05	.02	.01
☐ 128 James Buccheri	.05	.02	.01
☐ 129 Kevin Dettola	.05	.02	.01
☐ 130 Scott Erwin	.05	.02	.01
☐ 131 Johnny Guzman	.05	.02	.01
☐ 132 David Jacas	.05	.02	.01
☐ 133 Francisco Matos	.05	.02	.01
☐ 134 Mike Mohler	.05	.02	.01
☐ 135 Craig Paquette	.10	.05	.01
☐ 136 Todd Revenig	.05	.02	.01
☐ 137 Todd Smith	.05	.02	.01
☐ 138 Ricky Strebeck	.05	.02	.01
☐ 139 Sam August	.05	.02	.01
☐ 140 Tony Eusebio	.05	.02	.01
☐ 141 Brian Griffiths	.05	.02	.01
☐ 142 Todd Jones	.05	.02	.01
☐ 143 Orlando Miller	.05	.02	.01
☐ 144 Howard Prager	.05	.02	.01
☐ 145 Matt Rambo	.05	.02	.01
☐ 146 Lee Sammons	.05	.02	.01
☐ 147 Richie Simon	.05	.02	.01
☐ 148 Frank Bolick	.05	.02	.01
☐ 149 Jim Campanis	.05	.02	.01
☐ 150 Jim Converse	.05	.02	.01
☐ 151 Bobby Holley	.05	.02	.01
☐ 152 Troy Kent	.05	.02	.01
☐ 153 Brent Knackert	.05	.02	.01
☐ 154 Anthony Manahan	.05	.02	.01
☐ 155 Tow Maynard	.05	.02	.01
☐ 156 Mike McDonald	.05	.02	.01
☐ 157 Marc Newfield	.15	.07	.02
☐ 158 Greg Pirkl	.05	.02	.01
☐ 159 Jesus Tavarez	.05	.02	.01
☐ 160 Kerry Woodson	.05	.02	.01
☐ 161 Graeme Lloyd	.05	.02	.01
☐ 162 Paul Menhart	.05	.02	.01
☐ 163 Marcus Moore	.05	.02	.01
☐ 164 Greg O'Halloran	.05	.02	.01
☐ 165 Mark Ohlms	.05	.02	.01
☐ 166 Robert Perez	.05	.02	.01
☐ 167 Aaron Small	.05	.02	.01
☐ 168 Nigel Wilson	.05	.02	.01
☐ 169 Julian Yan	.05	.02	.01
☐ 170 Jeff Braley	.05	.02	.01
☐ 171 Brian Cornelius	.05	.02	.01
☐ 172 Ivan Cruz	.05	.02	.01
☐ 173 Lou Frazier	.05	.02	.01
☐ 174 Frank Gonzalez	.05	.02	.01
☐ 175 Tyrone Kingwood	.05	.02	.01
☐ 176 Leo Torres	.05	.02	.01
☐ 177 Brian Warren	.05	.02	.01
☐ 178 Brian Ahern	.05	.02	.01
☐ 179 Tony Bridges	.05	.02	.01
☐ 180 Paco Burgos	.05	.02	.01
☐ 181 Adam Casillas	.05	.02	.01
☐ 182 Archie Corbin	.05	.02	.01
☐ 183 Phil Hiatt	.05	.02	.01
☐ 184 Marcus Lawton	.05	.02	.01
☐ 185 Domingo Mota	.05	.02	.01
☐ 186 Mark Parnell	.05	.02	.01
☐ 187 Ed Pierce	.05	.02	.01
☐ 188 Rich Tunison	.05	.02	.01
☐ 189 Hugh Walker	.05	.02	.01
☐ 190 Skip Wiley	.05	.02	.01
☐ 191 Dave Adams	.05	.02	.01
☐ 192 Mick Billmeyer	.05	.02	.01
☐ 193 Marvin Cobb	.05	.02	.01
☐ 194 Jim Edmonds	2.00	.90	.25
☐ 195 Corey Kapano	.05	.02	.01
☐ 196 Jeff Kipila	.05	.02	.01
☐ 197 Joe Kraemer	.05	.02	.01
☐ 198 Rey Martinez	.05	.02	.01
☐ 199 J.R. Phillips	.05	.02	.01
☐ 200 Darryl Scott	.05	.02	.01
☐ 201 Paul Swingle	.05	.02	.01
☐ 202 Mark Zapelli	.05	.02	.01
☐ 203 Greg Blosser	.05	.02	.01
☐ 204 Bruce Chick	.05	.02	.01
☐ 205 Colin Dixon	.05	.02	.01
☐ 206 Gar Finnvold	.05	.02	.01
☐ 207 Scott Hatteberg	.05	.02	.01
☐ 208 Derek Livernois	.05	.02	.01
☐ 209 Jeff McNeely	.05	.02	.01
☐ 210 Tony Mosley	.05	.02	.01
☐ 211 Bill Norris	.05	.02	.01
☐ 212 Ed Riley	.05	.02	.01
☐ 213 Ken Ryan	.05	.02	.01
☐ 214 Tim Smith	.05	.02	.01
☐ 215 Willie Tatum	.05	.02	.01
☐ 216 Rex De La Nuez	.05	.02	.01
☐ 217 Rich Garces	.05	.02	.01
☐ 218 Curtis Leskanic	.05	.02	.01
☐ 219 Mica Lewis	.05	.02	.01
☐ 220 David McCarty	.05	.02	.01
☐ 221 Pat Meares	.05	.02	.01
☐ 222 Alan Newman	.05	.02	.01
☐ 223 J. Owens	.05	.02	.01
☐ 224 Carlos Pulido	.05	.02	.01
☐ 225 Rusty Richards	.05	.02	.01
☐ 226 Paul Russo	.05	.02	.01
☐ 227 Brad Brink	.05	.02	.01
☐ 228 Andy Carter	.05	.02	.01
☐ 229 Tyler Green	.05	.02	.01
☐ 230 Mike Lieberthal	.15	.07	.02
☐ 231 Chris Limbech	.05	.02	.01
☐ 232 Ron Lockett	.05	.02	.01
☐ 233 Tom Nuneviller	.05	.02	.01
☐ 234 Troy Paulson	.05	.02	.01
☐ 235 Todd Pratt	.05	.02	.01
☐ 236 Sean Ryan	.05	.02	.01
☐ 237 Matt Stevens	.05	.02	.01
☐ 238 Sam Taylor	.05	.02	.01
☐ 239 Casey Waller	.05	.02	.01
☐ 240 Mike Williams	.05	.02	.01
☐ 241 Jorge Alvarez	.05	.02	.01
☐ 242 Billy Ashley	.15	.07	.02
☐ 243 Tim Barker	.05	.02	.01
☐ 244 Bill Bene	.05	.02	.01
☐ 245 John Deutsch	.05	.02	.01
☐ 246 Greg Hansell	.05	.02	.01
☐ 247 Matt Howard	.05	.02	.01
☐ 248 Ron Maurer	.05	.02	.01
☐ 249 Mike Mimbs	.05	.02	.01
☐ 250 Chris Morrow	.05	.02	.01
☐ 251 Mike Piazza	4.00	1.80	.50
☐ 252 Dennis Springer	.05	.02	.01
☐ 253 Clay Bellinger	.05	.02	.01
☐ 254 Dan Carlson	.05	.02	.01
☐ 255 Eric Christopherson	.05	.02	.01
☐ 256 Adell Davenport	.05	.02	.01
☐ 257 Steve Finken	.05	.02	.01
☐ 258 Rick Huisman	.05	.02	.01
☐ 259 Kevin McGehee	.05	.02	.01
☐ 260 Dan Rambo	.05	.02	.01
☐ 261 Steve Reed	.05	.02	.01
☐ 262 Kevin Rogers	.05	.02	.01
☐ 263 Salomon Torres	.05	.02	.01
☐ 264 Pete Weber	.05	.02	.01
☐ 265 Brian Romero	.05	.02	.01
☐ 266 Cris Colon	.05	.02	.01
☐ 267 Rusty Greer	.20	.09	.03
☐ 268 Donald Harris	.05	.02	.01
☐ 269 David Hulse	.05	.02	.01
☐ 270 Pete Kidd	.05	.02	.01
☐ 271 Robb Nen	.10	.05	.01
☐ 272 Jose Oliva	.05	.02	.01
☐ 273 Steve Rowley	.05	.02	.01
☐ 274 Jon Shave	.05	.02	.01
☐ 275 Cedric Shaw	.05	.02	.01
☐ 276 Dan Smith	.05	.02	.01
☐ 277 Matt Whiteside	.05	.02	.01
☐ 278 Scott Fredrickson	.05	.02	.01
☐ 279 Jay Gainer	.05	.02	.01
☐ 280 Paul Gonzalez	.05	.02	.01
☐ 281 Vince Harris	.05	.02	.01
☐ 282 Ray Holbert	.05	.02	.01
☐ 283 Dwayne Hosey	.05	.02	.01
☐ 284 J.D. Noland	.05	.02	.01
☐ 285 Lance Painter	.05	.02	.01
☐ 286 Scott Sanders	.10	.05	.01
☐ 287 Darrell Sherman	.05	.02	.01
☐ 288 Brian Wood	.05	.02	.01
☐ 289 Tim Worrell	.10	.05	.01
☐ 290 John Jaha	.20	.09	.03
☐ 291 Jim Bowie	.05	.02	.01
☐ 292 Mark Howie	.05	.02	.01
☐ 293 Matt Stairs	.05	.02	.01
☐ 294 Larry Carter	.05	.02	.01
☐ 295 Pat Mahomes	.05	.02	.01
☐ 296 Jeff Mutis	.05	.02	.01
☐ 297 Municipal Stadium	.05	.02	.01
☐ 298 Knights Castle	.05	.02	.01
☐ 299 Engel Stadium	.05	.02	.01
☐ 300 Tim McCarver Stadium	.05	.02	.01
☐ 301 Beehive Field	.05	.02	.01
☐ 302 Tinker Field	.05	.02	.01
☐ 303 Checklist Alpha 1	.05	.02	.01
☐ 304 Checklist Alpha 2	.05	.02	.01
☐ 305 Checklist Alpha 3	.05	.02	.01
☐ 306 Checklist Alpha 4	.05	.02	.01
☐ 307 Checklist Numeric 1	.05	.02	.01
☐ 308 Checklist Numeric 2	.05	.02	.01
☐ 309 Checklist Numeric 3	.05	.02	.01
☐ 310 Checklist Numeric 4	.05	.02	.01

1992 SkyBox AAA

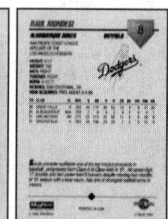

This 310-card standard-size set has glossy color action player photos bordered in white. The player's name appears in black lettering at the card top, with team logo in the upper right corner. The team name and position are given below the photo. The white back carries the player's name at the top, followed by biography and statistics.

	MINT	NRMT	EXC
COMPLETE SET (310)	15.00	6.75	1.85
COMMON CARD (1-310)	.05	.02	.01
☐ 1 Pedro Astacio	.15	.07	.02
☐ 2 Bryan Baar	.05	.02	.01
☐ 3 Tom Goodwin	.15	.07	.02
☐ 4 Jeff Hamilton	.05	.02	.01
☐ 5 Pedro J. Martinez	.40	.18	.05
☐ 6 Jamie McAndrew	.05	.02	.01
☐ 7 Mark Mimbs	.05	.02	.01
☐ 8 Raul Mondesi	1.50	.70	.19
☐ 9 Jose Munoz	.05	.02	.01
☐ 10 Henry Rodriguez	1.00	.45	.12
☐ 11 Eric Young	.15	.07	.02
☐ 12 Joe Ausanio	.05	.02	.01
☐ 13 Victor Cole	.05	.02	.01
☐ 14 Carlos Garcia	.10	.05	.01
☐ 15 Blas Minor	.05	.02	.01
☐ 16 William Pennyfeather	.05	.02	.01
☐ 17 Mark Petkovsek	.05	.02	.01
☐ 18 Jeff Richardson	.05	.02	.01
☐ 19 Rosario Rodriguez	.05	.02	.01
☐ 20 Tim Wakefield	.10	.05	.01
☐ 21 John Wehner	.05	.02	.01
☐ 22 Kevin Young	.05	.02	.01
☐ 23 Mike Blowers	.05	.02	.01
☐ 24 Bret Boone	.10	.05	.01
☐ 25 Jim Bowie	.05	.02	.01
☐ 26 Dave Brundage	.05	.02	.01
☐ 27 Randy Kramer	.05	.02	.01
☐ 28 Patrick Lennon	.05	.02	.01
☐ 29 Jim Newlin	.05	.02	.01
☐ 30 Jose Nunez	.05	.02	.01
☐ 31 Mike Remlinger	.05	.02	.01
☐ 32 Pat Rice	.05	.02	.01
☐ 33 Roger Salkeld	.05	.02	.01
☐ 34 Beau Allred	.05	.02	.01
☐ 35 Denis Boucher	.05	.02	.01
☐ 36 Mike Christopher	.05	.02	.01
☐ 37 Daren Epley	.05	.02	.01
☐ 38 Tom Kramer	.05	.02	.01
☐ 39 Jerry DiPoto	.05	.02	.01
☐ 40 Jeff Mutis	.05	.02	.01
☐ 41 Jeff Shaw	.05	.02	.01
☐ 42 Lee Tinsley	.05	.02	.01
☐ 43 Kevin Wickander	.05	.02	.01
☐ 44 Royal Clayton	.05	.02	.01
☐ 45 Bobby DeJardin	.05	.02	.01
☐ 46 Mike Draper	.05	.02	.01
☐ 47 Mike Humphreys	.05	.02	.01
☐ 48 Torey Lovullo	.05	.02	.01
☐ 49 Ed Martel	.05	.02	.01
☐ 50 Billy Masse	.05	.02	.01
☐ 51 Hensley Meulens	.05	.02	.01
☐ 52 Sam Militello	.05	.02	.01
☐ 53 John Ramos	.05	.02	.01
☐ 54 David Rosario	.05	.02	.01
☐ 55 David Silvestri	.05	.02	.01
☐ 56 J.T. Snow	.25	.11	.03
☐ 57 Russ Springer	.05	.02	.01
☐ 58 Larry Stanford	.05	.02	.01
☐ 59 Wade Taylor	.05	.02	.01
☐ 60 Gerald Williams	.05	.02	.01
☐ 61 Cal Eldred	.20	.09	.03
☐ 62 Chris George	.05	.02	.01
☐ 63 Otis Green	.05	.02	.01
☐ 64 Mike Ignasiak	.05	.02	.01
☐ 65 John Jaha	.20	.09	.03
☐ 66 Mark Kiefer	.05	.02	.01
☐ 67 Matt Mieske	.20	.09	.03
☐ 68 Angel Miranda	.05	.02	.01
☐ 69 Dave Nilsson	.20	.09	.03
☐ 70 Jim Olander	.05	.02	.01
☐ 71 Jim Tatum	.05	.02	.01
☐ 72 Jose Valentin	.15	.07	.02
☐ 73 Don Barbara	.05	.02	.01
☐ 74 Chris Beasley	.05	.02	.01
☐ 75 Mike Butcher	.05	.02	.01
☐ 76 Damion Easley	.10	.05	.01
☐ 77 Kevin Flora	.05	.02	.01
☐ 78 Tim Fortugno	.05	.02	.01
☐ 79 Larry Gonzalez	.05	.02	.01
☐ 80 Todd James	.05	.02	.01
☐ 81 Tim Salmon	1.50	.70	.19
☐ 82 Don Vidmar	.05	.02	.01
☐ 83 Cliff Young	.05	.02	.01
☐ 84 Shon Ashley	.05	.02	.01
☐ 85 Brian Barnes	.05	.02	.01
☐ 86 Blaine Beatty	.05	.02	.01
☐ 87 Kent Bottenfield	.05	.02	.01
☐ 88 Wil Cordero	.10	.05	.01
☐ 89 Jerry Goff	.05	.02	.01
☐ 90 Jon Hurst	.05	.02	.01
☐ 91 Jim Kremers	.05	.02	.01
☐ 92 Matt Maysey	.05	.02	.01
☐ 93 Rob Natal	.05	.02	.01
☐ 94 Matt Stairs	.05	.02	.01
☐ 95 David Wainhouse	.05	.02	.01
☐ 96 Alex Arias	.05	.02	.01
☐ 97 Scott Bryant	.05	.02	.01
☐ 98 Jim Bullinger	.05	.02	.01
☐ 99 Pedro Castellano	.05	.02	.01
☐ 100 Lance Dickson	.05	.02	.01
☐ 101 John Gardner	.05	.02	.01
☐ 102 Jeff Hartsock	.05	.02	.01
☐ 103 Elvin Paulino	.05	.02	.01
☐ 104 Fernando Ramsey	.05	.02	.01
☐ 105 Laddie Renfroe	.05	.02	.01
☐ 106 Kevin Roberson	.05	.02	.01
☐ 107 John Salles	.05	.02	.01
☐ 108 Derrick May	.05	.02	.01
☐ 109 Turk Wendell	.10	.05	.01
☐ 110 Doug Brocail	.05	.02	.01
☐ 111 Terry Bross	.05	.02	.01
☐ 112 Scott Coolbaugh	.05	.02	.01
☐ 113 Rick Davis	.05	.02	.01
☐ 114 Jeff Gardner	.05	.02	.01
☐ 115 Steve Pegues	.05	.02	.01
☐ 116 Frank Seminara	.05	.02	.01
☐ 117 Dave Staton	.05	.02	.01
☐ 118 Will Taylor	.05	.02	.01
☐ 119 Jim Vatcher	.05	.02	.01
☐ 120 Guillermo Velasquez	.05	.02	.01
☐ 121 Dan Walters	.05	.02	.01
☐ 122 Rene Arocha	.05	.02	.01
☐ 123 Rod Brewer	.05	.02	.01
☐ 124 Ozzie Canseco	.05	.02	.01
☐ 125 Mark Clark	.15	.07	.02

Card	MINT	NRMT	EXC
☐ 126 Joey Fernandez	.05	.02	.01
☐ 127 Lonnie Maclin	.05	.02	.01
☐ 128 Mike Milchin	.05	.02	.01
☐ 129 Stan Royer	.05	.02	.01
☐ 130 Tracy Woodson	.05	.02	.01
☐ 131 Bob Buchanan	.05	.02	.01
☐ 132 Mark Howie	.05	.02	.01
☐ 133 Tony Menendez	.05	.02	.01
☐ 134 Gino Minutelli	.05	.02	.01
☐ 135 Tim Pugh	.05	.02	.01
☐ 136 Mo Sanford	.05	.02	.01
☐ 137 Joey Vierra	.05	.02	.01
☐ 138 Dan Wilson	.10	.05	.01
☐ 139 Kevin Blankenship	.05	.02	.01
☐ 140 Todd Burns	.05	.02	.01
☐ 141 Tom Drees	.05	.02	.01
☐ 142 Jeff Frye	.05	.02	.01
☐ 143 Chuck Jackson	.05	.02	.01
☐ 144 Rob Maurer	.05	.02	.01
☐ 145 Russ McGinnis	.05	.02	.01
☐ 146 Dan Peltier	.05	.02	.01
☐ 147 Wayne Rosenthal	.05	.02	.01
☐ 148 Bob Sebra	.05	.02	.01
☐ 149 Sean Berry	.10	.05	.01
☐ 150 Stu Cole	.05	.02	.01
☐ 151 Jeff Conine	.50	.23	.06
☐ 152 Kevin Koslofski	.05	.02	.01
☐ 153 Kevin Long	.05	.02	.01
☐ 154 Carlos Maldonado	.05	.02	.01
☐ 155 Dennis Moeller	.05	.02	.01
☐ 156 Harvey Pulliam	.05	.02	.01
☐ 157 Luis Medina	.05	.02	.01
☐ 158 Steve Shifflett	.05	.02	.01
☐ 159 Tim Spehr	.05	.02	.01
☐ 160 Brian Conroy	.05	.02	.01
☐ 161 Wayne Housie	.05	.02	.01
☐ 162 Daryl Irvine	.05	.02	.01
☐ 163 Dave Milstien	.05	.02	.01
☐ 164 Jeff Plympton	.05	.02	.01
☐ 165 Paul Quantrill	.05	.02	.01
☐ 166 Larry Shikles	.05	.02	.01
☐ 167 Scott Taylor	.05	.02	.01
☐ 168 Mike Twardoski	.05	.02	.01
☐ 169 John Valentin	.40	.18	.05
☐ 170 David Walters	.05	.02	.01
☐ 171 Eric Wedge	.05	.02	.01
☐ 172 Bob Zupcic	.05	.02	.01
☐ 173 Johnny Ard	.05	.02	.01
☐ 174 Larry Carter	.05	.02	.01
☐ 175 Steve Decker	.05	.02	.01
☐ 176 Steve Hosey	.05	.02	.01
☐ 177 Paul McClellan	.05	.02	.01
☐ 178 Jim Myers	.05	.02	.01
☐ 179 Jamie Cooper	.05	.02	.01
☐ 180 Pat Rapp	.10	.05	.01
☐ 181 Ted Wood	.05	.02	.01
☐ 182 Willie Banks	.05	.02	.01
☐ 183 Bernardo Brito	.05	.02	.01
☐ 184 J.T. Bruett	.05	.02	.01
☐ 185 Larry Casian	.05	.02	.01
☐ 186 Shawn Gilbert	.05	.02	.01
☐ 187 Greg Johnson	.05	.02	.01
☐ 188 Terry Jorgensen	.05	.02	.01
☐ 189 Edgar Naveda	.05	.02	.01
☐ 190 Derek Parks	.05	.02	.01
☐ 191 Danny Sheaffer	.05	.02	.01
☐ 192 Mike Trombley	.05	.02	.01
☐ 193 George Tsamis	.05	.02	.01
☐ 194 Rob Wessenaar	.05	.02	.01
☐ 195 Vinny Castilla	.50	.23	.06
☐ 196 Pat Gomez	.05	.02	.01
☐ 197 Ryan Klesko	2.00	.90	.25
☐ 198 Keith Mitchell	.05	.02	.01
☐ 199 Bobby Moore	.05	.02	.01
☐ 200 David Nied	.05	.02	.01
☐ 201 Armando Reynoso	.05	.02	.01
☐ 202 Napoleon Robinson	.05	.02	.01
☐ 203 Boi Rodriguez	.05	.02	.01
☐ 204 Randy St. Claire	.05	.02	.01
☐ 205 Mark Wohlers	.15	.07	.02
☐ 206 Ricky Gutierrez	.05	.02	.01
☐ 207 Mike Lehman	.05	.02	.01
☐ 208 Richie Lewis	.05	.02	.01
☐ 209 Scott Meadows	.05	.02	.01
☐ 210 Mike Oquist	.05	.02	.01
☐ 211 Arthur Rhodes	.05	.02	.01
☐ 212 Ken Shamburg	.05	.02	.01
☐ 213 Todd Stephan	.05	.02	.01
☐ 214 Anthony Telford	.05	.02	.01
☐ 215 Jack Voigt	.05	.02	.01
☐ 216 Bob Ayrault	.05	.02	.01
☐ 217 Toby Borland	.05	.02	.01
☐ 218 Braulio Castillo	.05	.02	.01
☐ 219 Darrin Chapin	.05	.02	.01
☐ 220 Bruce Dostal	.05	.02	.01
☐ 221 Tim Mauser	.05	.02	.01
☐ 222 Steve Scarsone	.05	.02	.01
☐ 223 Rick Schu	.05	.02	.01
☐ 224 Butch Davis	.05	.02	.01
☐ 225 Ray Gianelli	.05	.02	.01
☐ 226 Randy Knorr	.05	.02	.01
☐ 227 Al Leiter	.25	.11	.03
☐ 228 Doug Linton	.05	.02	.01
☐ 229 Domingo Martinez	.05	.02	.01
☐ 230 Tom Quinlan	.05	.02	.01
☐ 231 Jerry Schunk	.05	.02	.01
☐ 232 Ed Sprague	.15	.07	.02
☐ 233 David Weathers	.05	.02	.01
☐ 234 Eddie Zosky	.05	.02	.01
☐ 235 John Briscoe	.05	.02	.01
☐ 236 Kevin Campbell	.05	.02	.01
☐ 237 Jeff Carter	.05	.02	.01
☐ 238 Steve Chitren	.05	.02	.01
☐ 239 Reggie Harris	.05	.02	.01
☐ 240 Dann Howitt	.05	.02	.01
☐ 241 Troy Neel	.05	.02	.01
☐ 242 Gavin Osteen	.05	.02	.01
☐ 243 Tim Peek	.05	.02	.01
☐ 244 Todd Van Poppel	.05	.02	.01
☐ 245 Ron Witmeyer	.05	.02	.01
☐ 246 David Zancanaro	.05	.02	.01
☐ 247 Kevin Baez	.05	.02	.01
☐ 248 Jeromy Burnitz	.15	.07	.02
☐ 249 Chris Donnels	.05	.02	.01
☐ 250 D.J. Dozier	.05	.02	.01
☐ 251 Terrel Hansen	.05	.02	.01
☐ 252 Eric Hillman	.05	.02	.01
☐ 253 Pat Howell	.05	.02	.01
☐ 254 Lee May Jr.	.05	.02	.01
☐ 255 Pete Schourek	.20	.09	.03
☐ 256 David Telgheder	.05	.02	.01
☐ 257 Julio Valera	.05	.02	.01
☐ 258 Rico Brogna	.10	.05	.01
☐ 259 Steve Carter	.05	.02	.01
☐ 260 Steve Cummings	.05	.02	.01
☐ 261 Greg Gohr	.05	.02	.01
☐ 262 David Haas	.05	.02	.01
☐ 263 Shawn Hare	.05	.02	.01
☐ 264 Riccardo Ingram	.05	.02	.01
☐ 265 John Kiely	.05	.02	.01
☐ 266 Kurt Knudsen	.05	.02	.01
☐ 267 Victor Rosario	.05	.02	.01
☐ 268 Rich Rowland	.05	.02	.01
☐ 269 John DeSilva	.05	.02	.01
☐ 270 Gary Cooper	.05	.02	.01
☐ 271 Chris Gardner	.05	.02	.01
☐ 272 Jeff Juden	.05	.02	.01
☐ 273 Rob Mallicoat	.05	.02	.01
☐ 274 Andy Mota	.05	.02	.01
☐ 275 Shane Reynolds	.40	.18	.05
☐ 276 Mike Simms	.05	.02	.01
☐ 277 Scooter Tucker	.05	.02	.01
☐ 278 Brian Williams	.05	.02	.01
☐ 279 Rod Bolton	.05	.02	.01
☐ 280 Ron Coomer	.05	.02	.01
☐ 281 Chris Cron	.05	.02	.01
☐ 282 Ramon Garcia	.05	.02	.01
☐ 283 Chris Howard	.05	.02	.01
☐ 284 Roberto Hernandez	.10	.05	.01
☐ 285 Derek Lee	.05	.02	.01
☐ 286 Ever Magallanes	.05	.02	.01
☐ 287 Norberto Martin	.05	.02	.01
☐ 288 Greg Perschke	.05	.02	.01
☐ 289 Ron Stephens	.05	.02	.01
☐ 290 Derek Bell POY	.10	.05	.01
☐ 291 Rich Amaral	.05	.02	.01
☐ 292 Derek Bell BC	.10	.05	.01
☐ 293 Jim Olander	.05	.02	.01
☐ 294 Gil Heredia	.05	.02	.01
☐ 295 Rick Reed	.05	.02	.01
☐ 296 Armando Reynoso	.05	.02	.01
☐ 297 Charlotte NC	.05	.02	.01
☐ 298 Ottawa Ontario	.05	.02	.01
☐ 299 Pilot Field	.05	.02	.01
☐ 300 Harold Cooper Stadium	.05	.02	.01
☐ 301 Bush Stadium	.05	.02	.01
☐ 302 Silver Stadium	.05	.02	.01
☐ 303 Checklist Alpha 1	.05	.02	.01
☐ 304 Checklist Alpha 2	.05	.02	.01
☐ 305 Checklist Alpha 3	.05	.02	.01
☐ 306 Checklist Alpha 4	.05	.02	.01
☐ 307 Checklist Numeric 1	.05	.02	.01
☐ 308 Checklist Numeric 2	.05	.02	.01
☐ 309 Checklist Numeric 3	.05	.02	.01
☐ 310 Checklist Numeric 4	.05	.02	.01

1992 South Bend White Sox Classic/Best

This 30-card standard-size set of the 1992 South Bend White Sox, a Class A Midwest League affiliate of the Chicago White Sox, features white-bordered posed color player photos on its fronts. The player's name, team, and position appear at the bottom. The white back is framed by a thin red line and carries the player's name and position at the top, followed by biography, statistics and team logos.

	MINT	NRMT	EXC
COMPLETE SET (30)	5.00	2.20	.60

☐ 1 Brian Boehringer
☐ 2 Don Culberson
☐ 3 Robert Ellis
☐ 4 Luis Andujar
☐ 5 Jeff Pierce
☐ 6 Julio Vinas
☐ 7 Kerry Valrie
☐ 8 Corie Austin
☐ 9 Doug Brady
☐ 10 Mike Vogel
☐ 11 Mike Bertotti
☐ 12 Jonathan Jenkins
☐ 13 Olmedo Saenz
☐ 14 Brian Filosa
☐ 15 Glenn DiSarcina
☐ 16 Harold Henry
☐ 17 Chris Woodfin
☐ 18 Alan Levine
☐ 19 Ramon Guzman
☐ 20 Essex Burton
☐ 21 Troy Fryman
☐ 22 Henry Manning
☐ 23 Hank Tagle
☐ 24 Terry Francona MG
☐ 25 Mark Haley CO
☐ 26 Jamie Garcia CO
☐ 27 Scott Takao TR
☐ 28 Logo Card
☐ 29 Logo Card
☐ 30 Checklist

1992 South Bend White Sox Fleer/ProCards

This 30-card standard-size set of the 1992 South Bend White Sox, a Class A Midwest League affiliate of the Chicago White Sox, features brown-bordered posed color player photos on its fronts. The player's name appears in an upper corner; his team and position appear in a lower corner. The white back is framed by a black line and carries the player's name and position at the top, followed by biography and statistics. This issue includes the minor league card debut of James Baldwin.

	MINT	NRMT	EXC
COMPLETE SET (30)	5.00	2.20	.60

☐ 168 Luis Andujar
☐ 169 James Baldwin
☐ 170 Mike Bertotti
☐ 171 Brian Boehringer
☐ 172 Don Culberson
☐ 173 John Herrholtz
☐ 174 Alan Levine
☐ 175 Jeff Pierce
☐ 176 Hank Tagle
☐ 177 Kevin Tolar
☐ 178 Chris Woodfin
☐ 179 Dean Haase
☐ 180 Henry Manning
☐ 181 Julio Vinas
☐ 182 Essex Burton
☐ 183 Glenn DiSarcina
☐ 184 Brian Filosa
☐ 185 Troy Fryman
☐ 186 Dave Martorana
☐ 187 Olmedo Saenz
☐ 188 Corey Austin
☐ 189 Harold Henry
☐ 190 Rafael Ochoa
☐ 191 Charles Poe
☐ 192 Kerry Valrie
☐ 193 Terry Francona MG
☐ 194 Jaime Garcia CO
☐ 195 Mark Haley CO
☐ 196 Jim Reinebold CO
☐ 197 Checklist

1992 Southern Oregon A's Classic/Best

This 30-card standard-size set of the 1992 Southern Oregon A's, a Class A Northwest League affiliate of the Oakland Athletics, features white-bordered posed color player photos on its fronts. The player's name, team, and position appear at the bottom. The white back is framed by a thin red line and carries the player's name and position at the top, followed by biography, statistics and team logos.

	MINT	NRMT	EXC
COMPLETE SET (30)	5.00	2.20	.60

☐ 1 Troy Penix
☐ 2 Bob Bennett
☐ 3 Marcel Galligani
☐ 4 Steve Lemke
☐ 5 Mark Sobolewski
☐ 6 Brian Lesher
☐ 7 David Cromer
☐ 8 Terance Frazier
☐ 9 Mark Moore
☐ 10 Geoff Loomis
☐ 11 Jason White
☐ 12 Tim Killeen
☐ 13 Jason Geis
☐ 14 Craig Gienger
☐ 15 Steve Griffin
☐ 16 Jeff Post
☐ 17 Gary Haught
☐ 18 Jim Byerly
☐ 19 Tim Bojan
☐ 20 James Banks
☐ 21 John MacCauley
☐ 22 Don Wengert
☐ 23 Herman Johnson
☐ 24 Clifton Foster
☐ 25 Stan Payne
☐ 26 Sean Scott
☐ 27 Kurt Endebrock
☐ 28 Chris Pittaro MG
☐ 29 Jim Slaton CO
☐ 30 Tony DeFrancesco CO
Checklist

1992 Southern Oregon A's Fleer/ProCards

This 33-card standard-size set of the 1992 Southern Oregon A's, a Class A Northwest League affiliate of the Oakland Athletics, features brown-bordered posed color player photos on its fronts. The player's name appears in an upper corner; his team and position appear in a lower corner. The white back is framed by a black line and carries the player's name and position at the top, followed by biography and statistics.

	MINT	NRMT	EXC
COMPLETE SET (33)	5.00	2.20	.60

☐ 3404 James Banks
☐ 3405 Bob Bennett
☐ 3406 Tim Bojan
☐ 3407 Jim Byerly
☐ 3408 Clifton Foster
☐ 3409 Craig Gienger
☐ 3410 Steve Griffin
☐ 3411 Gary Haught
☐ 3412 Richard King
☐ 3413 Steve Lemke
☐ 3414 John MacCauley
☐ 3415 Stan Payne
☐ 3416 Jeff Post
☐ 3417 Don Wengert
☐ 3418 Herman Johnson
☐ 3419 Tim Killeen
☐ 3420 Mark Moore
☐ 3421 Rick Norton
☐ 3422 Roberto Ramirez
☐ 3423 Terance Frazier
☐ 3424 Marcel Galligani
☐ 3425 Geoff Loomis
☐ 3426 Ricardo Mendez
☐ 3427 Troy Penix
☐ 3428 Mark Sobolewski UER
(Name misspelled
Sobolewsk)
☐ 3429 Chris Thomsen
☐ 3430 Jason White
☐ 3431 D.T. Cromer
☐ 3432 Kurt Endebrock
☐ 3433 Jason Geis
☐ 3434 Brian Lesher
☐ 3435 Sean Scott
☐ 3436 Checklist

1992 Spartanburg Phillies Classic/Best

This 30-card standard-size set of the 1992 Spartanburg Phillies, a Class A South Atlantic League affiliate of the Philadelphia Phillies, features white-bordered posed color player photos on its fronts. The player's name, team, and position appear at the bottom. The white back is framed by a thin red line and carries the player's name and position at the top, followed by biography, statistics and team logos.

	MINT	NRMT	EXC
COMPLETE SET (30)	5.00	2.20	.60

☐ 1 Craig Holman
☐ 2 Jerome Edwards
☐ 3 John Mallee
☐ 4 Troy Rusk
☐ 5 Jesus Garces
☐ 6 Mike Juhl
☐ 7 Bryan Manicchia
☐ 8 Francisco Tejada
☐ 9 Dominic Desantis
☐ 10 Ron Blazier
☐ 11 John Kupsey
☐ 12 Al Bennett
☐ 13 Charlie Hurst
☐ 14 Mark Randall
☐ 15 Lamar Cherry
☐ 16 Jeff Bigler
☐ 17 Luis Brito
☐ 18 David Hayden
☐ 19 Mark Steffens
☐ 20 Matt Whisenant
☐ 21 Logo Card
☐ 22 Roy Majtyka MG
☐ 23 Tony Scott CO
☐ 24 Buzz Capra CO
☐ 25 Gary Beatty TR
☐ 26 Logo Card
☐ 27 Logo Card
☐ 28 Logo Card
☐ 29 Logo Card
☐ 30 Checklist

1992 Spartanburg Phillies Fleer/ProCards

This 29-card standard-size set of the 1992 Spartanburg Phillies, a Class A South Atlantic League affiliate of the Philadelphia Phillies, features brown-bordered posed color player photos on its fronts. The player's name appears in an upper corner; his team and position appear in a lower corner. The white back is framed by a black line and carries the player's name and position at the top, followed by biography and statistics.

	MINT	NRMT	EXC
COMPLETE SET (29)	5.00	2.20	.60

☐ 1255 Ron Blazier
☐ 1256 Rick Bottalico
☐ 1257 Greg Brown
☐ 1258 Dominic DeSantis
☐ 1259 Brad Hassinger
☐ 1260 Craig Holman
☐ 1261 Charlie Hurst
☐ 1262 Mike Juhl
☐ 1263 Bryan Manicchia
☐ 1264 Matt Whisenant
☐ 1265 Tommy Eason
☐ 1266 Francisco Tejada
☐ 1267 Luis Brito
☐ 1268 Jesus Garces
☐ 1269 David Hayden
☐ 1270 John Kupsey
☐ 1271 John Mallee
☐ 1272 Troy Rusk
☐ 1273 Al Bennett
☐ 1274 Jeff Bigler
☐ 1275 Lamar Cherry
☐ 1276 Jerome Edwards
☐ 1277 Pat Ruth
☐ 1278 Gene Schall
☐ 1279 Mark Steffens
☐ 1280 Roy Majtyka MG
☐ 1281 Buzz Capra CO
☐ 1282 Tony Scott CO
☐ 1283 Checklist

1992 Spokane Indians Classic/Best

This 30-card standard-size set of the 1992 Spokane Indians, a Class A Northwest League affiliate of the San Diego Padres, features white-bordered posed color player photos on its fronts. The player's name, team, and position appear at the bottom. The white back is framed by a thin red line and carries the player's name and position at the top, followed by biography, statistics and team logos.

	MINT	NRMT	EXC
COMPLETE SET (30)	5.00	2.20	.60

☐ 1 Jared Baker
☐ 2 Kenneth Grzelaczyk
☐ 3 Britton Scheibe
☐ 4 Kyle White
☐ 5 Bill Robbs
☐ 6 Todd Marshall
☐ 7 Todd Schmitt
☐ 8 Tom Kindler
☐ 9 Mike Hermanson
☐ 10 Christen Murphy
☐ 11 Marcelino Garcia
☐ 12 Roberto De Leon
☐ 13 Kevin Minchk
☐ 14 Melvin Rosario
☐ 15 Sean Drinkwater
☐ 16 Kraig Constantino
☐ 17 Manny Gagliano
☐ 18 Von Wechsberg
☐ 19 Adrian Hollinger
☐ 20 Scott Eggleston
☐ 21 Arthur Vazquez
☐ 22 Tim Ploeger
☐ 23 Stacy Hamm
☐ 24 Rafael Perez
☐ 25 Juan Cruz
☐ 26 Marcelino DeLaCruz
☐ 27 Ed Romero MG
☐ 28 Fred Cambria CO
☐ 29 Barry Moss CO
☐ 30 Jason Perry BB
Eddie Romero BB

1992 Spokane Indians Fleer/ProCards

This 30-card standard-size set of the 1992 Spokane Indians, a Class A Northwest League affiliate of the San Diego Padres, features brown-bordered posed color player photos on its fronts. The player's name appears in an upper corner; his team and position appear in a lower corner. The white back is framed by a black line and carries the player's name and position at the top, followed by biography and statistics.

	MINT	NRMT	EXC
COMPLETE SET (30)	5.00	2.20	.60

☐ 1284 Jared Baker
☐ 1285 Scott Eggleston
☐ 1286 Ken Grzelaczylc
☐ 1287 Mike Hermanson
☐ 1288 Adrian Hollinger
☐ 1289 Tom Kindler
☐ 1290 Todd Marshall
☐ 1291 Chris Murphy
☐ 1292 Tim Ploeger
☐ 1293 Todd Schmitt
☐ 1294 Archie Vazquez
☐ 1295 Von Wechsberg
☐ 1296 Marcelino Garcia
☐ 1297 Melvin Rosario
☐ 1298 Kraig Constantino
☐ 1299 Marcelino DeLaCruz
☐ 1300 Robert DeLeon
☐ 1301 Sean Drinkwater
☐ 1302 Manny Gagliano
☐ 1303 Kevin Minchk
☐ 1304 Kyle White
☐ 1305 Juan Cruz
☐ 1306 Stacy Hamm
☐ 1307 Ralph Perez
☐ 1308 Bill Robbs
☐ 1309 Britton Scheibe
☐ 1310 Ed Romero MG
☐ 1311 Fred Cambria CO
☐ 1312 Barry Moss CO
☐ 1313 Checklist

1992 Springfield Cardinals Classic/Best

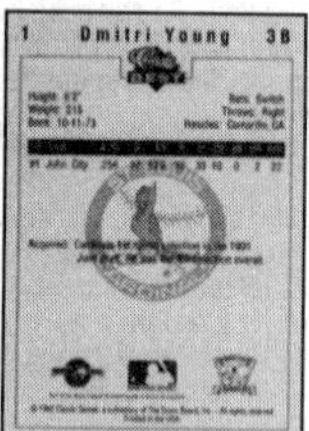

This 30-card standard-size set of the 1992 Springfield Cardinals, a Class A Midwest League affiliate of the St. Louis Cardinals, features white-bordered posed color player photos on its fronts. The player's name, team, and position appear at the bottom. The white back is framed by a thin red line and carries the player's name and position at the top, followed by biography, statistics and team logos.

	MINT	NRMT	EXC
COMPLETE SET (30)	6.00	2.70	.75

☐ 1 Dmitri Young
☐ 2 Marc Ronan
☐ 3 Frank Speek
☐ 4 Brian Barber
☐ 5 Doug Radziewicz
☐ 6 Allen Battle
☐ 7 Paul Romanoli
☐ 8 Wander Pimentel
☐ 9 Mike Badorek
☐ 10 Keith Jones
☐ 11 Frank Martinez
☐ 12 Troy Konemann
☐ 13 Chris Vlasis
☐ 14 Mark Smith
☐ 15 Dennis Slininger
☐ 16 Mark Tranbarger
☐ 17 Mike Eicher
☐ 18 Darrel Deak
☐ 19 John Mabry
☐ 20 Kevin Tahan
☐ 21 John O'Brien
☐ 22 Scott Simmons
☐ 23 Frank Cimorelli
☐ 24 Gerald Santos
☐ 25 Steve Cerio
☐ 26 Lorenzo Meza
☐ 27 Rick Colbert MG
☐ 28 Roy Silver CO
☐ 29 Mike Evans TR
☐ 30 Checklist

1992 Springfield Cardinals Fleer/ProCards

This 29-card standard-size set of the 1992 Springfield Cardinals, a Class A Midwest League affiliate of the St. Louis Cardinals, features brown-bordered posed color player photos on its fronts. The player's name appears in an upper corner; his team and position appear in a lower corner. The white back is framed by a black line and carries the player's name and position at the top, followed by biography and statistics. This issue includes a second year card of Dmitri Young.

	MINT	NRMT	EXC
COMPLETE SET (29)	6.00	2.70	.75

☐ 859 Mike Badorek
☐ 860 Brian Barber
☐ 861 Frank Cimorelli
☐ 862 Troy Konemann
☐ 863 Frank Martinez
☐ 864 Paul Romanoli
☐ 865 Gerry Santos
☐ 866 Scott Simmons
☐ 867 Dennis Slininger
☐ 868 Mark Smith
☐ 869 Frank Speek
☐ 870 Mark Tranbarger
☐ 871 Steve Cerio
☐ 872 Marc Ronan
☐ 873 Kevin Tahan
☐ 874 Larry Meza
☐ 875 John O'Brien
☐ 876 Wander Pimentel
☐ 877 Doug Radziewicz
☐ 878 Ahmed Rodriguez
☐ 879 Dmitri Young
☐ 880 Allen Battle
☐ 881 Mike Eicher
☐ 882 Keith Jones
☐ 883 John Mabry
☐ 884 Chris Vlasis
☐ 885 Rick Colbert MG
☐ 886 Roy Silver CO
☐ 887 Checklist

1992 St. Catharines Blue Jays Classic/Best

This 30-card standard-size set of the 1992 St. Catharines Blue Jays, a Class A New York-Penn League affiliate of the Montreal Expos, features white-bordered posed color player photos on its fronts. The player's name, team, and position appear at the bottom. The white back is framed by a thin red line and carries the player's name and position at the top, followed by biography, statistics and team logos.

	MINT	NRMT	EXC
COMPLETE SET (30)	5.00	2.20	.60

☐ 1 Todd Steverson
☐ 2 Keith Hines
☐ 3 Mike Coolbaugh
☐ 4 Juan Querecuto
☐ 5 Adam Meinershagen
☐ 6 Trevor Mallory
☐ 7 Roger Doman
☐ 8 Ned Darley
☐ 9 Lee Daniels
☐ 10 Santiago Henry
☐ 11 D.J. Boston
☐ 12 Lou Benbow
☐ 13 Mark Choate
☐ 14 Keiver Campbell
☐ 15 Rob Adkins
☐ 16 Kris Harmes
☐ 17 Lonell Roberts
☐ 18 Jeff Ladd
☐ 19 Gary Miller
☐ 20 Scot McCloughan
☐ 21 Chris Chandler
☐ 22 Brad Cornett
☐ 23 Timothy Crabtree
☐ 24 Derek Brandow
☐ 25 Levon Largusa
☐ 26 Aaron Jersild
☐ 27 J.J. Cannon MG
☐ 28 Reggie Cleveland CO
☐ 29 Scott Shannon TR
☐ 30 Rolando Pino CO
Checklist

1992 St. Catharines Blue Jays Fleer/ProCards

This 29-card standard-size set of the 1992 St. Catharines Blue Jays, a Class A New York-Penn League affiliate of the Toronto Blue Jays, features brown-bordered posed color player photos on its fronts. The player's name appears in an upper corner; his team and position appear in a lower corner. The white back is framed by a black line and carries the player's name and position at the top, followed by biography and statistics.

	MINT	NRMT	EXC
COMPLETE SET (29)	5.00	2.20	.60

☐ 2813 Checklist
☐ 3376 Rob Adkins
☐ 3377 Derek Brandow
☐ 3378 Brad Cornett
☐ 3379 Tim Crabtree
☐ 3380 Lee Daniels
☐ 3381 Ned Darley
☐ 3382 Roger Doman
☐ 3383 Aaron Jersild
☐ 3384 Levon Largusa
☐ 3385 Trevor Mallory
☐ 3386 Adam Meinershagen
☐ 3387 Gary Miller
☐ 3388 Kris Harmes
☐ 3389 Jeff Ladd
☐ 3390 Juan Querecuto
☐ 3391 Lou Benbow
☐ 3392 D.J. Boston
☐ 3393 Chris Chandler
☐ 3394 Mark Choate
☐ 3395 Mike Coolbaugh
☐ 3396 Santiago Henry
☐ 3397 Keiver Campbell
☐ 3398 Scot McCloughan
☐ 3399 Lonell Roberts
☐ 3400 Todd Steverson
☐ 3401 J.J. Cannon MG
☐ 3402 Rolando Pino CO
☐ 3403 Team Picture

1992 St. Lucie Mets Classic/Best

This 30-card standard-size set of the 1992 St. Lucie Mets, a Class A Florida State League affiliate of the New York Mets, features white-bordered posed color player photos on its fronts. The player's name, team, and position appear at the bottom. The white back is framed by a thin red line and carries the player's name and position at the top, followed by biography, statistics and team logos.

	MINT	NRMT	EXC
COMPLETE SET (30)	5.00	2.20	.60

☐ 1 Butch Huskey
☐ 2 Bernie Millan
☐ 3 Tim Sandy
☐ 4 Chris Shanahan
☐ 5 Joe Crawford
☐ 6 James Harris
☐ 7 Mike Freitas
☐ 8 Denny Harriger
☐ 9 Joe McCann
☐ 10 Joe Roa
☐ 11 Clyde Keller
☐ 12 Rob Carpentier
☐ 13 Juan Castillo
☐ 14 Jose Martinez
☐ 15 Alberto Castillo
☐ 16 Mason Rudolph
☐ 17 Aaron Ledesma
☐ 18 Fernando Vina
☐ 19 Gerrod Davis
☐ 20 Edward Fully
☐ 21 Tim McClinton
☐ 22 Tony Tijerina
☐ 23 Jason King
☐ 24 Frank Jacobs
☐ 25 Chris George
☐ 26 John Tamargo MG
☐ 27 Bill Gardner CO
☐ 28 Bill Latham CO
☐ 29 Bob Burton TR
☐ 30 Checklist

1992 St. Lucie Mets Fleer/ProCards

This 30-card standard-size set of the 1992 St. Lucie Mets, a Class A Florida State League affiliate of the New York Mets, features brown-bordered posed color player photos on its fronts. The player's name appears in an upper corner; his team and position appear in a lower corner. The white back is framed by a black line and carries the player's name and position at the top, followed by biography and statistics.

	MINT	NRMT	EXC
COMPLETE SET (30)	5.00	2.20	.60

☐ 1737 Rob Carpentier
☐ 1738 Juan Castillo
☐ 1739 Joe Crawford
☐ 1740 Mike Freitas
☐ 1741 Denny Harriger
☐ 1742 Jason Jacome
☐ 1743 Jose Martinez
☐ 1744 Joe McCann
☐ 1745 David Proctor
☐ 1746 Joe Roa
☐ 1747 Chris Shanahan
☐ 1748 Alberto Castillo
☐ 1749 Mason Rudolph
☐ 1750 Tony Tijerina
☐ 1751 James Harris
☐ 1752 Butch Huskey
☐ 1753 Frank Jacobs
☐ 1754 Jason King
☐ 1755 Aaron Ledesma
☐ 1756 Tim McClinton
☐ 1757 Bernie Millan
☐ 1758 Fernando Vina
☐ 1759 Jeff Barry
☐ 1760 Jay Davis
☐ 1761 Edward Fully
☐ 1762 Tim Sandy
☐ 1763 John Tamargo
☐ 1764 Bill Gardner
☐ 1765 Bill Latham
☐ 1766 Checklist

1992 St. Petersburg Cardinals Classic/Best

This 30-card standard-size set of the 1992 St. Petersburg Cardinals, a Class A Florida State League affiliate of the St. Louis Cardinals, features white-bordered posed color player photos on its fronts. The player's name, team, and position appear at the bottom. The white back is framed by a thin red line and carries the player's name and position at the top, followed by biography, statistics and team logos.

	MINT	NRMT	EXC
COMPLETE SET (30)	5.00	2.20	.60

- ☐ 1 Allen Watson
- ☐ 2 Dennis Fletcher
- ☐ 3 Andy Beasley
- ☐ 4 Roy Bailey
- ☐ 5 Paul Ellis
- ☐ 6 Juan Andujar
- ☐ 7 Donovan Campbell
- ☐ 8 Franklin Abreau
- ☐ 9 Ron Weber
- ☐ 10 Scott Baker
- ☐ 11 Dave Howell
- ☐ 12 Bryan Eversgerd
- ☐ 13 Kevin Nielsen
- ☐ 14 Joe Aversa
- ☐ 15 Rod Eldridge
- ☐ 16 Jeremy McGarity
- ☐ 17 Anthony Lewis
- ☐ 18 Mateo Ozuna
- ☐ 19 Tremayne Donald
- ☐ 20 John Kelly
- ☐ 21 Odalis Savinon
- ☐ 22 Ezequiel Herrera
- ☐ 23 Ernie Baker
- ☐ 24 Alan Botkin
- ☐ 25 Greg Rudolph
- ☐ 26 Logo Card
- ☐ 27 Dave Bialas MG
- ☐ 28 John Stuper CO
- ☐ 29 Dan Doyel TR
- ☐ 30 Checklist

1992 St. Petersburg Cardinals Fleer/ProCards

This 26-card standard-size set of the 1992 St. Petersburg Cardinals, a Class A Florida State League affiliate of the St. Louis Cardinals, features brown-bordered posed color player photos on its fronts. The player's name appears in an upper corner; his team and position appear in a lower corner. The white back is framed by a black line and carries the player's name and position at the top, followed by biography and statistics.

	MINT	NRMT	EXC
COMPLETE SET (26)	5.00	2.20	.60

- ☐ 2017 Roy Bailey
- ☐ 2018 Ernie Baker
- ☐ 2019 Scott Baker
- ☐ 2020 Brian Barber
- ☐ 2021 Alan Botkin
- ☐ 2022 Bryan Eversgerd
- ☐ 2023 Dennis Fletcher
- ☐ 2024 John Kelly
- ☐ 2025 Jeremy McGarity
- ☐ 2026 Kevin Nielsen
- ☐ 2027 Troy Salvior
- ☐ 2028 Ron Weber
- ☐ 2029 Andy Beasley
- ☐ 2030 Paul Ellis
- ☐ 2031 Frank Abreu
- ☐ 2032 Juan Andujar
- ☐ 2033 Andy Bruce
- ☐ 2034 Mike Cantu
- ☐ 2035 Carlos Landinez
- ☐ 2036 Mateo Ozuna
- ☐ 2037 Greg Rudolph
- ☐ 2038 Tremayne Donald
- ☐ 2039 Ezequiel Herrera
- ☐ 2040 Anthony Lewis
- ☐ 2041 Dave Bialas MG
- ☐ 2042 Checklist

1992 Stockton Ports Classic/Best

This 30-card standard-size set of the 1992 Stockton Ports, a Class A California League affiliate of the Milwaukee Brewers, features white-bordered posed color player photos on its fronts. The player's name, team, and position appear at the bottom. The white back is framed by a thin red line and carries the player's name and position at the top, followed by biography, statistics and team logos.

	MINT	NRMT	EXC
COMPLETE SET (30)	5.00	2.20	.60

- ☐ 1 Larry Carter
- ☐ 2 Chuck Bush
- ☐ 3 Bobby Benjamin
- ☐ 4 Ed Smith
- ☐ 5 Michael Baase
- ☐ 6 Tim Carter
- ☐ 7 Duane Singleton
- ☐ 8 Dave Wrona
- ☐ 9 Lincoln Mikkelsen
- ☐ 10 Greg Kobza
- ☐ 11 Charlie Rogers
- ☐ 12 Leon Glenn
- ☐ 13 Bob Lukachyk
- ☐ 14 Michael Hancock
- ☐ 15 Michael Matheny
- ☐ 16 Francisco Gamez
- ☐ 17 Eric Whitford
- ☐ 18 Pat Miller
- ☐ 19 Michael Cater
- ☐ 20 Mark Cole
- ☐ 21 Mike Farrell
- ☐ 22 Kurt Archer
- ☐ 23 Tim Ireland MG
- ☐ 24 Mark Littell CO
- ☐ 25 Greg Calhoon TR
- ☐ 26 Logo Card
- ☐ 27 Logo Card
- ☐ 28 Logo Card
- ☐ 29 Logo Card
- ☐ 30 Checklist

1992 Stockton Ports Fleer/ProCards

This 28-card standard-size set of the 1992 Stockton Ports, a Class A California League affiliate of the Milwaukee Brewers, features brown-bordered posed color player photos on its fronts. The player's name appears in an upper corner; his team and position appear in a lower corner. The white back is framed by a black line and carries the player's name and position at the top, followed by biography and statistics.

	MINT	NRMT	EXC
COMPLETE SET (28)	5.00	2.20	.60

- ☐ 26 Kurt Archer
- ☐ 27 Chuck Bush
- ☐ 28 Ramser Correa
- ☐ 29 Mike Farrell
- ☐ 30 Francisco Gamez
- ☐ 31 Michael Hancock
- ☐ 32 Tom McGraw
- ☐ 33 Lincoln Mikkelsen
- ☐ 34 Pat Miller
- ☐ 35 Charlie Rogers
- ☐ 36 Greg Kobza
- ☐ 37 Mike Matheny
- ☐ 38 Tim Carter
- ☐ 39 Mark Cole
- ☐ 40 Leon Glenn
- ☐ 41 Oreste Marrero
- ☐ 42 Julian Salazar
- ☐ 43 Ed Smith
- ☐ 44 Eric Whitford
- ☐ 45 Dave Wrona
- ☐ 46 Mike Basse
- ☐ 47 Mike Carter
- ☐ 48 Michael Harris
- ☐ 49 Mike Lawn
- ☐ 50 Rob Lukachyk
- ☐ 51 Tim Ireland MG
- ☐ 52 Mark Littell CO
- ☐ 53 Checklist

1992 Syracuse Chiefs Fleer/ProCards

This 31-card standard-size set of the 1992 Syracuse Chiefs, a Class AAA International League affiliate of the Toronto Blue Jays, features brown-bordered posed color player photos on its fronts. The player's name appears in an upper corner; his team and position appear in a lower corner. The white back is framed by a black line and carries the player's name and position at the top, followed by biography and statistics. This issue includes a sixth year card of Pat Hentgen.

	MINT	NRMT	EXC
COMPLETE SET (31)	5.00	2.20	.60

- ☐ 1959 Pete Blohm
- ☐ 1960 Wayne Edwards
- ☐ 1961 Darren Hall
- ☐ 1962 Pat Hentgen
- ☐ 1963 Al Leiter
- ☐ 1964 Doug Linton
- ☐ 1965 John Shea
- ☐ 1966 Rick Trlicek
- ☐ 1967 Gene Walter
- ☐ 1968 Anthony Ward
- ☐ 1969 David Weathers
- ☐ 1970 Woody Williams
- ☐ 1971 Jose Monzon
- ☐ 1972 Ed Sprague
- ☐ 1973 Bruce Crabbe
- ☐ 1974 Ray Giannelli
- ☐ 1975 Domingo Martinez
- ☐ 1976 Rob Montalvo
- ☐ 1977 Tom Quinlan
- ☐ 1978 Jerry Schunk
- ☐ 1979 Eddie Zosky
- ☐ 1980 Butch Davis
- ☐ 1981 Randy Knorr
- ☐ 1982 Mike Maksudian
- ☐ 1983 Stu Pederson
- ☐ 1984 Ryan Thompson
- ☐ 1985 Turner Ward
- ☐ 1986 Nick Leyva MG
- ☐ 1987 John Poloni CO
- ☐ 1988 Rocket Wheeler CO
- ☐ 1989 Checklist

1992 Syracuse Chiefs Merchants Bank

This set includes a sixth year card of Pat Hentgen.

	MINT	NRMT	EXC
COMPLETE SET (30)	10.00	4.50	1.25

- ☐ 1 Pete Blohm
- ☐ 2 Bruce Crabbe
- ☐ 3 Butch Davis
- ☐ 4 Carlos Delgado
- ☐ 5 Wayne Edwards
- ☐ 6 Ray Giannelli
- ☐ 7 Darren Hall
- ☐ 8 Pat Hentgen
- ☐ 9 Randy Knorr
- ☐ 10 Al Leiter
- ☐ 11 Nick Leyva MG
- ☐ 12 Doug Linton
- ☐ 13 Mike Maksudian
- ☐ 14 Domingo Martinez
- ☐ 15 Stu Pederson
- ☐ 16 John Poloni CO
- ☐ 17 Tom Quinlan
- ☐ 18 Jerry Schunk
- ☐ 19 Scooch (Mascot)
- ☐ 20 John Shea
- ☐ 21 Ed Sprague
- ☐ 22 Ryan Thompson
- ☐ 23 Mike Timlin
- ☐ 24 Rick Trlicek
- ☐ 25 Gene Walters
- ☐ 26 Anthony Ward
- ☐ 27 Turner Ward
- ☐ 28 David Weathers
- ☐ 29 Rocket Wheeler CO
- ☐ 30 Eddie Zosky
- ☐ 31 Team Photo

1992 Syracuse Chiefs SkyBox

This 26-card standard-size set of the 1992 Syracuse Chiefs, a Class AAA International League affiliate of the Toronto Blue Jays, features white-bordered posed color player photos on its fronts. The player's name appears at the top; his team and position appear at the bottom. The white back carries the player's name at the top, followed by biography and statistics.

	MINT	NRMT	EXC
COMPLETE SET (26)	5.00	2.20	.60

- ☐ 501 Pete Blohm
- ☐ 502 Bruce Crabbe
- ☐ 503 Jesse Cross
- ☐ 504 Butch Davis
- ☐ 505 Wayne Edwards
- ☐ 506 Ray Giannelli
- ☐ 507 Darren Hall
- ☐ 508 Randy Knorr
- ☐ 509 Al Leiter
- ☐ 510 Doug Linton
- ☐ 511 Mike Maksudian
- ☐ 512 Domingo Martinez
- ☐ 513 Stu Pederson
- ☐ 514 Tom Quinlan
- ☐ 515 Jerry Schunk
- ☐ 516 John Shea
- ☐ 517 Ed Sprague
- ☐ 518 Ryan Thompson
- ☐ 519 Scott Wade
- ☐ 520 Gene Walter
- ☐ 521 Anthony Ward
- ☐ 522 David Weathers
- ☐ 523 Eddie Zosky
- ☐ 524 Nick Leyva MG
- ☐ 525 John Poloni CO
Rocket Wheeler CO
- ☐ NNO Checklist

1992 Syracuse Chiefs Tallmadge Tire

Printed on thin card stock, this 5-card set features former Syracuse Chiefs who've gone on to major league careers. Each card measures about 2 3/8" by 3 1/2" and features on its front a posed color player photo with a white outer border and blue inner border. The player's name appears within a baseball diamond design at the lower right; below is the sponsor's name, Tallmadge Tire, and the set's subtitle, Former Chiefs Collectibles. The horizontal white back carries the player's name and position at the top, followed by biography and statistics, all in blue lettering. The cards are unnumbered and checklisted below in alphabetical order. Several coupon cards for Tallmadge Tire's products and services were also issued with the set.

	MINT	NRMT	EXC
COMPLETE SET (5)	15.00	6.75	1.85

- ☐ 1 Danny Ainge
- ☐ 2 Derek Bell
- ☐ 3 Juan Guzman
- ☐ 4 Tom Henke
- ☐ 5 Fred McGriff

1992 Tacoma Tigers Fleer/ProCards

This 26-card standard-size set of the 1992 Tacoma Tigers, a Class AAA Pacific Coast League affiliate of the Oakland Athletics, features brown-bordered posed color player photos on its fronts. The player's name appears in an upper corner; his team and position appear in a lower corner. The white back is framed by a black line and carries the player's name and position at the top, followed by biography and statistics.

	MINT	NRMT	EXC
COMPLETE SET (26)	5.00	2.20	.60

- ☐ 2495 John Briscoe
- ☐ 2496 Steve Chitren
- ☐ 2497 Reggie Harris
- ☐ 2498 Jeff Musselman
- ☐ 2499 Tim Peek
- ☐ 2500 Mike Raczka
- ☐ 2501 Todd Van Poppel
- ☐ 2502 Bruce Walton
- ☐ 2503 Weston Weber
- ☐ 2504 Bill Wilkinson
- ☐ 2505 Dave Zancanaro
- ☐ 2506 Mike Heath
- ☐ 2507 Henry Mercedes
- ☐ 2508 Scott Brosius
- ☐ 2509 Jeff Carter
- ☐ 2510 Keith Lockhart
- ☐ 2511 Gus Polidor
- ☐ 2512 Jack Smith
- ☐ 2513 Ron Witmeyer
- ☐ 2514 Dan Grunhard
- ☐ 2515 Orsino Hill
- ☐ 2516 Mike Kingery
- ☐ 2517 Troy Neel
- ☐ 2518 Glenn Abbott CO
- ☐ 2519 Mitchell Page CO
- ☐ 2520 Checklist

1992 Tacoma Tigers SkyBox

	MINT	NRMT	EXC
COMPLETE SET (26)	5.00	2.20	.60

- ☐ 526 Dana Allison
- ☐ 527 Jorge Brito
- ☐ 528 Kevin Campbell
- ☐ 529 Jeff Carter
- ☐ 530 Steve Chitren
- ☐ 531 Jim Corsi
- ☐ 532 Eric Fox
- ☐ 533 Webster Garrison
- ☐ 534 Dan Grunhard
- ☐ 535 Reggie Harris
- ☐ 536 Orsino Hill
- ☐ 537 Dann Howitt
- ☐ 538 Keith Lockhart
- ☐ 539 John Briscoe
- ☐ 540 Jeff Musselman
- ☐ 541 Troy Neel
- ☐ 542 Gavin Osteen
- ☐ 543 Tim Peek
- ☐ 544 Gus Polidor
- ☐ 545 Todd Van Poppel
- ☐ 546 Weston Weber
- ☐ 547 Ron Witmeyer
- ☐ 548 David Zancanaro
- ☐ 549 Bob Boone MG
- ☐ 550 Mitchell Page CO
Glenn Abbott CO
- ☐ NNO Checklist

1992 Texas Longhorns

This set features leading players in University of Texas history. The first 41 cards feature players and they are sequenced in alphabetical order. The last four cards highlight special events.

	MINT	NRMT	EXC
COMPLETE SET (45)	15.00	6.75	1.85

- ☐ 1 Jim Acker
- ☐ 2 Max Alvis
- ☐ 3 Tony Arnold
- ☐ 4 Billy Bates
- ☐ 5 Bill Bethea
- ☐ 6 Mike Brumley
- ☐ 7 Mike Capel
- ☐ 8 Roger Clemens
- ☐ 9 Jack Conway
- ☐ 10 Dennis Cook
- ☐ 11 Scott Coolbaugh
- ☐ 12 Melvin Deutsch
- ☐ 13 Kirk Dressendorfer
- ☐ 14 Ronnie Gardenhire
- ☐ 15 Jim Gideon
- ☐ 16 Jerry Don Gleaton
- ☐ 17 Charley Gorin
- ☐ 18 Wayne Graham
- ☐ 19 Cliff Gustafson
- ☐ 20 Larry Hardy
- ☐ 21 Tommy Harmon
- ☐ 22 Chuck Hartenstein

☐ 23 Grady Hatton
☐ 24 Burt Hooton
☐ 25 Tex Hughson
☐ 26 Ransom Jackson
☐ 27 Bob Kearney
☐ 28 Ernie Koy
☐ 29 Keith Moreland
☐ 30 Spike Owen
☐ 31 Ken Pape
☐ 32 Mark Petkovsek
☐ 33 Rusty Richards
☐ 34 Andre Robertson
☐ 35 Bruce Ruffin
☐ 36 Calvin Schiraldi
☐ 37 Bart Shirley
☐ 38 Greg Swindell
☐ 39 Harry Taylor
☐ 40 Richard Wortham
☐ 41 Ricky Wright
☐ 42 Baseball Players in the Hall of Honor
☐ 43 First Team All-Americans
☐ 44 Longhorns in the Major Leagues
☐ 45 Checklist

1992 Tidewater Tides Fleer/ProCards

This 28-card standard-size set of the 1992 Tidewater Tides, a Class AAA International League affiliate of the New York Mets, features brown-bordered posed color player photos on its fronts. The player's name appears in an upper corner; his team and position appear in a lower corner. The white back is framed by a black line and carries the player's name and position at the top, followed by biography and statistics.

	MINT	NRMT	EXC
COMPLETE SET (28)	5.00	2.20	.60

☐ 888 Mike Birkbeck
☐ 889 Mark Dewey
☐ 890 Tom Filer
☐ 891 Eric Hillman
☐ 892 Randy Marshall
☐ 893 Brad Moore
☐ 894 Dale Plummer
☐ 895 Chris Rauth
☐ 896 Dave Telgheder
☐ 897 Julio Valera
☐ 898 Julian Vasquez
☐ 899 Javier Gonzalez
☐ 900 Orlando Mercado
☐ 901 Mitch Lyden
☐ 902 Kevin Baez
☐ 903 Tim Bogar
☐ 904 Chris Donnels
☐ 905 Terrel Hansen
☐ 906 Jeff McKnight
☐ 907 Steve Springer
☐ 908 Jeromy Burnitz
☐ 909 D.J. Dozier
☐ 910 Pat Howell
☐ 911 Lee May Jr.
☐ 912 Clint Hurdle MG
☐ 913 Bob Apodaca CO
☐ 914 Ron Washington CO
☐ 1736 Checklist

1992 Tidewater Tides SkyBox

	MINT	NRMT	EXC
COMPLETE SET (26)	5.00	2.20	.60

☐ 551 Kevin Baez
☐ 552 Mike Birkbeck
☐ 553 Tim Bogar
☐ 554 Jeromy Burnitz
☐ 555 Chris Donnels
☐ 556 D.J. Dozier
☐ 557 Terrel Hansen
☐ 558 Eric Hillman
☐ 559 Pat Howell
☐ 560 Javier Gonzalez
☐ 561 Mitch Lyden
☐ 562 Randy Marshall
☐ 563 Lee May Jr.
☐ 564 Mark Dewey
☐ 565 Jeff McKnight
☐ 566 Orlando Mercado
☐ 567 Brad Moore
☐ 568 Dale Plummer
☐ 569 Chris Rauth
☐ 570 Pete Schourek
☐ 571 Steve Springer
☐ 572 David Telgheder
☐ 573 Julio Valera
☐ 574 Clint Hurdle MG
☐ 575 Ron Washington CO Bob Apodaca CO
☐ NNO Checklist

1992 Toledo Mud Hens Fleer/ProCards

This 29-card standard-size set of the 1992 Toledo Mud Hens, a Class AAA International League affiliate of the Detroit Tigers, features brown-bordered posed color player photos on its fronts. The player's name appears in an upper corner; his team and position appear in a lower corner. The white back is framed by a black line and carries the player's name and position at the top, followed by biography and statistics.

	MINT	NRMT	EXC
COMPLETE SET (29)	5.00	2.20	.60

☐ 1032 William Brennan
☐ 1033 Tony Castillo
☐ 1034 Steve Cummings
☐ 1035 John DeSilva
☐ 1036 Greg Gohr
☐ 1037 Buddy Groom
☐ 1038 David Haas
☐ 1039 Jeff Kaiser
☐ 1040 John Kiely
☐ 1041 Vance Lovelace
☐ 1042 Jamie Moyer
☐ 1043 Ron Rightnowar
☐ 1044 Mike Walker
☐ 1045 Pedro Gonzalez
☐ 1046 Marty Pevey
☐ 1047 Rich Rowland
☐ 1048 Karl Allaire
☐ 1049 Rico Brogna
☐ 1050 Dean DeCillis
☐ 1051 Victor Rosario
☐ 1052 Greg Smith
☐ 1053 Steve Carter
☐ 1054 Jody Hurst
☐ 1055 Riccardo Ingram
☐ 1056 Johnny Paredes
☐ 1057 Joe Sparks MG
☐ 1058 Kevin Bradshaw CO
☐ 1059 Ralph Treuel
☐ 1060 Checklist

1992 Toledo Mud Hens SkyBox

	MINT	NRMT	EXC
COMPLETE SET (26)	5.00	2.20	.60

☐ 576 Karl Allaire
☐ 577 William Brennan
☐ 578 Rico Brogna
☐ 579 Steve Carter
☐ 580 Tony Castillo
☐ 581 Phil Clark
☐ 582 Steve Cummings
☐ 583 Dean Decillis
☐ 584 Greg Gohr
☐ 585 Buddy Groom
☐ 586 David Haas
☐ 587 Shawn Hare
☐ 588 Jody Hurst
☐ 589 Riccardo Ingram
☐ 590 Jeff Kaiser
☐ 591 John Kiely
☐ 592 Kurt Knudsen
☐ 593 Vance Lovelace
☐ 594 Mike Walker
☐ 595 Victor Rosario
☐ 596 Rich Rowland
☐ 597 Greg Smith
☐ 598 John Desilva
☐ 599 Joe Sparks MG
☐ 600 Kevin Bradshaw CO Ralph Treuel CO
☐ NNO Checklist

1992 Tucson Toros Fleer/ProCards

This 30-card standard-size set of the 1992 Tucson Toros, a Class AAA Pacific Coast League affiliate of the Houston Astros, features brown-bordered posed color player photos on its fronts. The player's name appears in an upper corner; his team and position appear in a lower corner. The white back is framed by a black line and carries the player's name and position at the top, followed by biography and statistics.

	MINT	NRMT	EXC
COMPLETE SET (30)	5.00	2.20	.60

☐ 478 Willie Blair
☐ 479 Ryan Bowen
☐ 480 Mike Capel
☐ 481 Chris Gardner
☐ 482 Jason Grimsley
☐ 483 Bobby Hurta
☐ 484 Jeff Juden
☐ 485 Shane Reynolds
☐ 486 Richie Simon
☐ 487 Matt Turner
☐ 488 Dave Veres
☐ 489 Brian Williams
☐ 490 Barry Lyons
☐ 491 John Massarelli
☐ 492 Scooter Tucker
☐ 493 Rod Booker
☐ 494 Andujar Cedeno
☐ 495 Gary Cooper
☐ 496 Trent Hubbard
☐ 497 Andy Mota
☐ 498 Ernest Riles
☐ 499 Joe Mikulik
☐ 500 Rick Parker
☐ 501 Mike Simms
☐ 502 Eric Yelding
☐ 503 Bob Skinner MG
☐ 504 Don Angotti CO
☐ 505 Dave Engle CO
☐ 506 Brent Strom CO
☐ 507 Checklist

1992 Tucson Toros SkyBox

	MINT	NRMT	EXC
COMPLETE SET (26)	5.00	2.20	.60

☐ 601 Willie Blair
☐ 602 Rod Booker
☐ 603 Mickey Brantley
☐ 604 Mike Capel
☐ 605 Gary Cooper
☐ 606 Benny Distefano
☐ 607 Chris Gardner
☐ 608 Jason Grimsley
☐ 609 Dean Hartgraves
☐ 610 Trent Hubbard
☐ 611 Jeff Juden
☐ 612 Barry Lyons
☐ 613 Rob Mallicoat
☐ 614 Joe Mikulik
☐ 615 Andy Mota
☐ 616 Rick Parker
☐ 617 Shane Reynolds
☐ 618 Karl Rhodes
☐ 619 Mike Simms
☐ 620 Scoter Tucker
☐ 621 Matt Turner
☐ 622 Brian Williams
☐ 623 Eric Yelding
☐ 624 Bob Skinner MG
☐ 625 Brent Strom CO Dave Engle CO
☐ NNO Checklist

1992 Tulsa Drillers Fleer/ProCards

This 27-card standard-size set of the 1992 Tulsa Drillers, a Class AA Texas League affiliate of the Texas Rangers, features brown-bordered posed color player photos on its fronts. The player's name appears in an upper corner; his team and position appear in a lower corner. The white back is framed by a black line and carries the player's name and position at the top, followed by biography and statistics.

	MINT	NRMT	EXC
COMPLETE SET (27)	5.00	2.20	.60

☐ 2686 Brian Bohanon
☐ 2687 Jeff Bronkey
☐ 2688 Rob Brown
☐ 2689 Don Carman
☐ 2690 Bryan Gore
☐ 2691 Danilo Leon
☐ 2692 Robb Nen
☐ 2693 Brian Romero
☐ 2694 Jeff Sellers
☐ 2695 Cedric Shaw
☐ 2696 Dan Smith
☐ 2697 Matt Whiteside
☐ 2698 Darren Niethammer
☐ 2699 John Russell
☐ 2700 Chris Colon
☐ 2701 Rusty Greer
☐ 2702 Trey McCoy
☐ 2703 Jose Oliva
☐ 2704 Luke Sable
☐ 2705 Jon Shave
☐ 2706 Kevin Belcher
☐ 2707 David Hulse
☐ 2708 Rod Morris
☐ 2709 Bobby Jones MG
☐ 2710 Randy Whisler CO
☐ 2711 Jackson Todd CO
☐ 2712 Checklist

1992 Tulsa Drillers SkyBox

	MINT	NRMT	EXC
COMPLETE SET (26)	5.00	2.20	.60

☐ 601 Brian Romero
☐ 602 Kevin Belcher
☐ 603 Jeff Bronkey
☐ 604 Rob Brown
☐ 605 Cris Colon
☐ 606 Bryan Gore
☐ 607 Rusty Greer
☐ 608 Donald Harris
☐ 609 David Hulse
☐ 610 Pete Kuld
☐ 611 Trey McCoy
☐ 612 Robb Nen
☐ 613 Darren Niethammer
☐ 614 Jose Oliva
☐ 615 David Perez
☐ 616 Don Carman
☐ 617 Steve Rowley
☐ 618 John Russell
☐ 619 Luke Sable
☐ 620 Jon Shave
☐ 621 Cedric Shaw
☐ 622 Dan Smith
☐ 623 Matt Whiteside
☐ 624 Bobby Jones MG
☐ 625 Randy Whisler CO Jackson Todd CO
☐ NNO Checklist

1992 Upper Deck

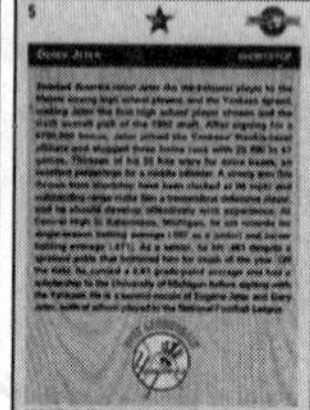

The 1992 Upper Deck Minor League set consists of 330 standard-size cards highlighting top prospects and stand out players from Triple-A, Double-A and Single-A teams. No factory sets were produced and the foil packs featured a 26-card Organizational Players of the Year insert set and a 9-card Top Prospect Holograms insert set. The set commences with three subsets: 1992 Draft Picks (1-23), Team Checklists (24-49) and Diamond Skills (50-70). The remainder of the set (260 cards) highlights the top ten players in each of the 26 minor league organizations. The fronts features shadow-bordered action color player photos on a white face. The backs feature posed and action color player photos on the right portion of the card while biography, statistics and player profile run horizontally along the left side of the photo. The back carries a Major League Rating in which each player is graded in five skill categories. Upper Deck's traditional anti-counterfeiting hologram is star-shaped on these cards.

	MINT	NRMT	EXC
COMPLETE SET (330)	100.00	45.00	12.50
COMMON CARD (1-330)	.10	.05	.01
☐ 1 Johnny Damon CL Michael Tucker FDP CL	.50	.23	.06
☐ 2 B.J. Wallace FDP	.10	.05	.01
☐ 3 Jeffrey Hammonds FDP	.75	.35	.09
☐ 4 Chad Mottola FDP	.10	.05	.01
☐ 5 Derek Jeter FDP	15.00	6.75	1.85
☐ 6 Michael Tucker FDP	2.00	.90	.25
☐ 7 Derek Wallace FDP	.10	.05	.01
☐ 8 Chad McConnell FDP	.10	.05	.01
☐ 9 Rick Greene FDP	.10	.05	.01
☐ 10 Shannon Stewart FDP	.75	.35	.09
☐ 11 Benji Grigsby FDP	.10	.05	.01
☐ 12 Jamie Arnold FDP	.10	.05	.01
☐ 13 Rick Helling FDP	.10	.05	.01
☐ 14 Jason Kendall FDP	4.00	1.80	.50
☐ 15 Eddie Pearson FDP	.20	.09	.03
☐ 16 Todd Steverson FDP	.10	.05	.01
☐ 17 John Burke FDP	.10	.05	.01
☐ 18 Brandon Cromer FDP	.10	.05	.01
☐ 19 Johnny Damon FDP	5.00	2.20	.60
☐ 20 Jason Giambi FDP	4.00	1.80	.50
☐ 21 John Lynch FDP	.10	.05	.01
☐ 22 Jared Baker FDP	.10	.05	.01
☐ 23 Roger Bailey FDP	.20	.09	.03
☐ 24 Eduardo Perez TC	.10	.05	.01
☐ 25 Gary Mota TC	.10	.05	.01
☐ 26 Mike Neill TC	.10	.05	.01
☐ 27 Howard Battle TC	.10	.05	.01
☐ 28 Mike Kelly TC	.10	.05	.01
☐ 29 Tyrone Hill TC	.10	.05	.01
☐ 30 Dmitri Young TC	.25	.11	.03
☐ 31 Ryan Hawblitzel TC	.10	.05	.01
☐ 32 Raul Mondesi TC	.40	.18	.05
☐ 33 Rondell White TC	.25	.11	.03
☐ 34 Salomon Torres TC	.10	.05	.01
☐ 35 Manny Ramirez TC	.75	.35	.09
☐ 36 Marc Newfield TC	.10	.05	.01
☐ 37 Butch Huskey TC	.10	.05	.01
☐ 38 Mark Smith TC	.10	.05	.01
☐ 39 Joey Hamilton TC	.10	.05	.01
☐ 40 Tyler Green TC	.10	.05	.01
☐ 41 Midre Cummings TC	.10	.05	.01
☐ 42 Kurt Miller TC	.10	.05	.01
☐ 43 Frank Rodriguez TC	.10	.05	.01
☐ 44 John Roper TC	.10	.05	.01
☐ 45 Phil Hiatt TC	.10	.05	.01
☐ 46 Justin Thompson TC	.10	.05	.01
☐ 47 David McCarty TC	.10	.05	.01
☐ 48 Mike Robertson TC	.10	.05	.01

Card	MINT	NRMT	EXC
☐ 49 Brien Taylor TC	.10	.05	.01
☐ 50 Carlos Delgado CL Rondell White CL	.75	.35	.09
☐ 51 Damon Buford DS	.10	.05	.01
☐ 52 Mike Neill DS	.10	.05	.01
☐ 53 Carlos Delgado DS	1.25	.55	.16
☐ 54 Frank Rodriguez DS	.10	.05	.01
☐ 55 Manny Ramirez DS	3.00	1.35	.35
☐ 56 Carl Everett DS	.10	.05	.01
☐ 57 Brien Taylor DS	.10	.05	.01
☐ 58 Kurt Miller DS	.10	.05	.01
☐ 59 Alex Ochoa DS	1.00	.45	.12
☐ 60 Alex Gonzalez DS	.25	.11	.03
☐ 61 Darrell Sherman DS	.10	.05	.01
☐ 62 Dmitri Young DS	.75	.35	.09
☐ 63 Cliff Floyd DS	.25	.11	.03
☐ 64 Ray McDavid DS	.10	.05	.01
☐ 65 Rondell White DS	.75	.35	.09
☐ 66 Chipper Jones DS	4.00	1.80	.50
☐ 67 Allen Watson DS	.10	.05	.01
☐ 68 Tyler Green DS	.10	.05	.01
☐ 69 Steve Gibralter DS	.10	.05	.01
☐ 70 Calvin Reese DS	.10	.05	.01
☐ 71 Scott Burrell	.50	.23	.06
☐ 72 Julian Vasquez	.10	.05	.01
☐ 73 Juan Delarosa	.10	.05	.01
☐ 74 Lance Dickson	.10	.05	.01
☐ 75 Todd Van Poppel	.10	.05	.01
☐ 76 Joey Hamilton	1.50	.70	.19
☐ 77 Mark Mimbs	.10	.05	.01
☐ 78 Austin Manahan	.10	.05	.01
☐ 79 Mike Milchin	.10	.05	.01
☐ 80 David Bell	.10	.05	.01
☐ 81 Terrell Lowery	.10	.05	.01
☐ 82 Tony Tarasco	.25	.11	.03
☐ 83 Shon Walker	.25	.11	.03
☐ 84 Robb Nen	.15	.07	.02
☐ 85 Turk Wendell	.15	.07	.02
☐ 86 John Byington	.10	.05	.01
☐ 87 Derek Reid	.10	.05	.01
☐ 88 Lee Heath	.10	.05	.01
☐ 89 Matt Anderson	.10	.05	.01
☐ 90 Joe Perona	.10	.05	.01
☐ 91 Tito Navarro	.10	.05	.01
☐ 92 Scott Erwin	.10	.05	.01
☐ 93 Jim Pittsley	.60	.25	.07
☐ 94 Chris Seelbach	.10	.05	.01
☐ 95 Skeets Thomas	.10	.05	.01
☐ 96 Kevin Flora	.10	.05	.01
☐ 97 Scott Pose	.10	.05	.01
☐ 98 Jason Hardtke	.10	.05	.01
☐ 99 Joe Ciccarella	.10	.05	.01
☐ 100 Les Norman	.10	.05	.01
☐ 101 Joe Calder	.10	.05	.01
☐ 102 Willie Otanez	.10	.05	.01
☐ 103 Ray Holbert	.10	.05	.01
☐ 104 Dan Serafini	1.00	.45	.12
☐ 105 Trevor Hoffman	.50	.23	.06
☐ 106 Todd Ritchier	.10	.05	.01
☐ 107 Lance Jennings	.10	.05	.01
☐ 108 Jon Farrell	.10	.05	.01
☐ 109 Rick Gorecki	.10	.05	.01
☐ 110 Kevin Stocker	.25	.11	.03
☐ 111 Joe Caruso	.10	.05	.01
☐ 112 Tom Nuneviller	.10	.05	.01
☐ 113 Matt Mieske	.10	.05	.01
☐ 114 Luis Ortiz	.10	.05	.01
☐ 115 Marty Cordova	5.00	2.20	.60
☐ 116 Rikkert Faneyte	.10	.05	.01
☐ 117 Rodney Bolton	.10	.05	.01
☐ 118 Steve Trachsel	.40	.18	.05
☐ 119 Sean Lowe	.10	.05	.01
☐ 120 Sean Ryan	.10	.05	.01
☐ 121 Tim Vanegmond	.10	.05	.01
☐ 122 Craig Paquette	.15	.07	.02
☐ 123 Andre Keene	.10	.05	.01
☐ 124 Kevin Roberson	.10	.05	.01
☐ 125 Mark Anthony	.10	.05	.01
☐ 126 Joe DeBerry	.10	.05	.01
☐ 127 Tracy Sanders	.10	.05	.01
☐ 128 Eric Christopherson	.10	.05	.01
☐ 129 Steve Dreyer	.10	.05	.01
☐ 130 Jeromy Burnitz	.25	.11	.03
☐ 131 Mike Lansing	.50	.23	.06
☐ 132 Russ Davis	.50	.23	.06
☐ 133 Pedro Castellano	.10	.05	.01
☐ 134 Troy Percival	.40	.18	.05
☐ 135 Tyrone Hill	.10	.05	.01
☐ 136 Rene Arocha	.10	.05	.01
☐ 137 John DeSilva	.10	.05	.01
☐ 138 Donne Wall	.15	.07	.02
☐ 139 Justin Mashore	.10	.05	.01
☐ 140 Miguel Flores	.10	.05	.01
☐ 141 John Finn	.10	.05	.01
☐ 142 Paul Shuey	.10	.05	.01
☐ 143 Gabby Martinez	.10	.05	.01
☐ 144 Ryan Luzinski	.10	.05	.01
☐ 145 Brent Gates	.10	.05	.01
☐ 146 Manny Ramirez	12.00	5.50	1.50
☐ 147 Mark Hutton	.10	.05	.01
☐ 148 Derek Lee	.10	.05	.01
☐ 149 Scott Pisciotta	.10	.05	.01
☐ 150 Greg Hansell	.10	.05	.01
☐ 151 Tyler Houston	.10	.05	.01
☐ 152 Chris Pritchett	.10	.05	.01
☐ 153 Allen Watson	.10	.05	.01
☐ 154 Steve Karsay	.10	.05	.01
☐ 155 Carl Everett	.15	.07	.02
☐ 156 Mike Robertson	.10	.05	.01
☐ 157 Fausto Cruz	.10	.05	.01
☐ 158 Kiki Hernandez	.10	.05	.01
☐ 159 Bill Bliss	.10	.05	.01
☐ 160 Todd Hollandsworth	4.00	1.80	.50
☐ 161 Justin Thompson	.60	.25	.07
☐ 162 Ozzie Timmons	.20	.09	.03
☐ 163 Raul Mondesi	6.00	2.70	.75
☐ 164 Shawn Estes	.40	.18	.05
☐ 165 Chipper Jones	15.00	6.75	1.85
☐ 166 Kurt Miller	.10	.05	.01
☐ 167 Tyler Green	.15	.07	.02
☐ 168 Jimmy Haynes	.10	.05	.01
☐ 169 Dave Doorneweerd	.10	.05	.01
☐ 170 Bubba Smith	.10	.05	.01
☐ 171 Scott Lydy	.10	.05	.01
☐ 172 Aaron Holbert	.10	.05	.01
☐ 173 Doug Glanville	.10	.05	.01
☐ 174 Benji Gil	.20	.09	.03
☐ 175 Eddie Williams	.10	.05	.01
☐ 176 Phil Hiatt	.10	.05	.01
☐ 177 Chris Durkin	.10	.05	.01
☐ 178 Brian Barber	.10	.05	.01
☐ 179 John Cummings	.10	.05	.01
☐ 180 Frank Campos	.10	.05	.01
☐ 181 Tim Worrell	.20	.09	.03
☐ 182 Tony Clark	5.00	2.20	.60
☐ 183 T.R. Lewis	.10	.05	.01
☐ 184 Mike Lieberthal	.25	.11	.03
☐ 185 Keith Mitchell	.10	.05	.01
☐ 186 Rick Huisman	.10	.05	.01
☐ 187 Quilvio Veras	.20	.09	.03
☐ 188 Brian Hancock	.10	.05	.01
☐ 189 Tarrik Brock	.10	.05	.01
☐ 190 Herbert Perry	.10	.05	.01
☐ 191 Dave Staton	.10	.05	.01
☐ 192 Derek Lowe	.10	.05	.01
☐ 193 Joel Wolfe	.10	.05	.01
☐ 194 Lyle Mouton	.10	.05	.01
☐ 195 Greg Gohr	.10	.05	.01
☐ 196 Duane Singleton	.10	.05	.01
☐ 197 Jamie McAndrew	.10	.05	.01
☐ 198 Brad Pennington	.10	.05	.01
☐ 199 Pork Chop Pough	.10	.05	.01
☐ 200 Boo Moore	.10	.05	.01
☐ 201 Henry Blanco	.10	.05	.01
☐ 202 Gabe White	.10	.05	.01
☐ 203 Manny Cora	.10	.05	.01
☐ 204 Keith Gordon	.10	.05	.01
☐ 205 John Jackson	.10	.05	.01
☐ 206 Mike Hostetler	.10	.05	.01
☐ 207 Jeff McCurry	.10	.05	.01
☐ 208 Steve Olsen	.10	.05	.01
☐ 209 Roberto Mejia	.10	.05	.01
☐ 210 Ramon Caraballo	.10	.05	.01
☐ 211 Matt Whisenant	.10	.05	.01
☐ 212 Mike Bovee	.10	.05	.01
☐ 213 Riccardo Ingram	.10	.05	.01
☐ 214 Mike Rossiter	.10	.05	.01
☐ 215 Andres Duncan	.10	.05	.01
☐ 216 Steve Dunn	.20	.09	.03
☐ 217 Mike Grace	.10	.05	.01
☐ 218 Tim Howard	.10	.05	.01
☐ 219 Todd Jones	.10	.05	.01
☐ 220 Tyrone Kingwood	.10	.05	.01
☐ 221 Damon Buford	.10	.05	.01
☐ 222 Bobby Munoz	.10	.05	.01
☐ 223 Jim Campanis	.10	.05	.01
☐ 224 Johnny Ruffin	.10	.05	.01
☐ 225 Shawn Green	1.25	.55	.16
☐ 226 Calvin Reese	.20	.09	.03
☐ 227 Kevin McGehee	.10	.05	.01
☐ 228 J.R.Phillips	.10	.05	.01
☐ 229 Rafael Quirico	.10	.05	.01
☐ 230 Mike Zimmerman	.10	.05	.01
☐ 231 Ron Lockett	.10	.05	.01
☐ 232 Bobby Reed	.10	.05	.01
☐ 233 John Roper	.10	.05	.01
☐ 234 John Mabry	1.00	.45	.12
☐ 235 Chris Martin	.10	.05	.01
☐ 236 Ricky Otero	.10	.05	.01
☐ 237 Orlando Miller	.10	.05	.01
☐ 238 Scott Hatteberg	.10	.05	.01
☐ 239 Toby Borland	.10	.05	.01
☐ 240 Alan Newman	.10	.05	.01
☐ 241 Ivan Cruz	.10	.05	.01
☐ 242 Paul Byrd	.10	.05	.01
☐ 243 Daryl Henderson	.10	.05	.01
☐ 244 Adam Hyzdu	.10	.05	.01
☐ 245 Rich Becker	.75	.35	.09
☐ 246 Scott Ruffcorn	.10	.05	.01
☐ 247 Tommy Adams	.10	.05	.01
☐ 248 Jose Martinez	.10	.05	.01
☐ 249 Darrell Sherman	.10	.05	.01
☐ 250 Tom Nevers	.10	.05	.01
☐ 251 Brandon Wilson	.10	.05	.01
☐ 252 Mike Hampton	.75	.35	.09
☐ 253 Mo Sanford	.10	.05	.01
☐ 254 Alex Ochoa	4.00	1.80	.50
☐ 255 David McCarty	.10	.05	.01
☐ 256 Ray McDavid	.10	.05	.01
☐ 257 Roger Salkeld	.10	.05	.01
☐ 258 Jeff McNeely	.10	.05	.01
☐ 259 Jim Converse	.10	.05	.01
☐ 260 Greg Blosser	.10	.05	.01
☐ 261 Salomon Torres	.10	.05	.01
☐ 262 Tavo Alvarez	.10	.05	.01
☐ 263 Marc Newfield	.75	.35	.09
☐ 264 Carlos Delgado	5.00	2.20	.60
☐ 265 Brien Taylor	.10	.05	.01
☐ 266 Frank Rodriguez	.60	.25	.07
☐ 267 Cliff Floyd	.75	.35	.09
☐ 268 Troy O'Leary	.50	.23	.06
☐ 269 Butch Huskey	1.00	.45	.12
☐ 270 Micahel Carter	.10	.05	.01
☐ 271 Eduardo Perez	.10	.05	.01
☐ 272 Gary Mota	.10	.05	.01
☐ 273 Mike Neill	.10	.05	.01
☐ 274 Dmitri Young	3.00	1.35	.35
☐ 275 Mike Kelly	.10	.05	.01
☐ 276 Rondell White	3.00	1.35	.35
☐ 277 Midre Cummings	.20	.09	.03
☐ 278 Kerwin Moore	.10	.05	.01
☐ 279 Derrick White	.10	.05	.01
☐ 280 Howard Battle	.15	.07	.02
☐ 281 Mark Smith	.10	.05	.01
☐ 282 Ben Shelton	.10	.05	.01
☐ 283 Jose Oliva	.10	.05	.01
☐ 284 Steve Gibralter	.30	.14	.04
☐ 285 Billy Hall	.10	.05	.01
☐ 286 Nigel Wilson	.10	.05	.01
☐ 287 Brook Fordyce	.10	.05	.01
☐ 288 Mike Durant	.10	.05	.01
☐ 289 Gary Caraballo	.10	.05	.01
☐ 290 Shane Andrews	.40	.18	.05
☐ 291 Aaron Sele	.50	.23	.06
☐ 292 Garret Anderson	3.00	1.35	.35
☐ 293 Oscar Munoz	.10	.05	.01
☐ 294 Bobby Jones	1.00	.45	.12
☐ 295 Joe Rosselli	.10	.05	.01
☐ 296 Chad Ogea	.10	.05	.01
☐ 297 Ugueth Urbina	1.00	.45	.12
☐ 298 Ryan Hawblitzel	.10	.05	.01
☐ 299 Dennis Burlingame	.10	.05	.01
☐ 300 Damon Mashore	.10	.05	.01
☐ 301 Jeff Jackson	.10	.05	.01
☐ 302 Glenn Murray	.10	.05	.01
☐ 303 Darren Burton	.10	.05	.01
☐ 304 Scott Cepicky	.10	.05	.01
☐ 305 Phil Dauphin	.10	.05	.01
☐ 306 Kevin Tatar	.10	.05	.01
☐ 307 Domingo Jean	.10	.05	.01
☐ 308 Darren Oliver	.10	.05	.01
☐ 309 Joe Vitiello	.15	.07	.02
☐ 310 John Johnstone	.10	.05	.01
☐ 311 Bo Dodson	.10	.05	.01
☐ 312 Jon Shave	.10	.05	.01
☐ 313 Roberto Petagine	.10	.05	.01
☐ 314 Clifton Garrett	.10	.05	.01
☐ 315 Rob Butler	.10	.05	.01
☐ 316 Jermaine Swinton	.10	.05	.01
☐ 317 Alex Gonzalez	1.00	.45	.12
☐ 318 Jeff Williams	.10	.05	.01
☐ 319 James Baldwin	1.25	.55	.16
☐ 320 Scott Stahoviak	.20	.09	.03
☐ 321 John Cotton	.10	.05	.01
☐ 322 Jim Wawruck	.10	.05	.01
☐ 323 Jeff Ware	.10	.05	.01
☐ 324 Brian L. Hunter	2.00	.90	.25
☐ 325 Joe Randa	.20	.09	.03
☐ 326 Robert Eenhoorn	.10	.05	.01
☐ 327 Rod Lofton	.10	.05	.01
☐ 328 Buck McNabb	.10	.05	.01
☐ 329 Jorge Fabregas	.10	.05	.01
☐ 330 Brian Koelling	.10	.05	.01

1992 Upper Deck Player of the Year

These twenty-six standard-size Player of the Year cards were randomly inserted in 1992 Upper Deck Minor League foil packs and features each Major League club's minor league player of the year. The card front displays a full color player shot with the player's name in white leters across the top. The back of the cards feature another color photo along with some background information about the player.

	MINT	NRMT	EXC
COMPLETE SET (26)	150.00	70.00	19.00
COMMON CARD (PY1-PY26)	2.50	1.10	.30
☐ PY1 Garret Anderson	10.00	4.50	1.25
☐ PY2 Gary Mota	2.50	1.10	.30
☐ PY3 Scott Lydy	2.50	1.10	.30
☐ PY4 Carlos Delgado	15.00	6.75	1.85
☐ PY5 Chipper Jones	40.00	18.00	5.00
☐ PY6 Troy O'Leary	4.00	1.80	.50
☐ PY7 Dmitri Young	12.00	5.50	1.50
☐ PY8 Ozzie Timmons	3.00	1.35	.35
☐ PY9 Todd Hollandsworth	15.00	6.75	1.85
☐ PY10 Cliff Floyd	4.00	1.80	.50
☐ PY11 Joe Rosselli	2.50	1.10	.30
☐ PY12 Chad Ogea	3.00	1.35	.35
☐ PY13 Tommy Adams	2.50	1.10	.30
☐ PY14 Bobby Jones	5.00	2.20	.60
☐ PY15 Mark Smith	2.50	1.10	.30
☐ PY16 Ray McDavid	2.50	1.10	.30
☐ PY17 Mike Lieberthal	3.00	1.35	.35
☐ PY18 Midre Cummings	3.00	1.35	.35
☐ PY19 Kurt Miller	2.50	1.10	.30
☐ PY20 Aaron Sele	3.00	1.35	.35
☐ PY21 Steve Gibralter	3.00	1.35	.35
☐ PY22 Phil Hiatt	2.50	1.10	.30
☐ PY23 Ivan Cruz	2.50	1.10	.30
☐ PY24 Marty Cordova	15.00	6.75	1.85
☐ PY25 Brandon Wilson SP	2.50	1.10	.30
☐ PY26 Brien Taylor SP	3.00	1.35	.35

1992 Upper Deck Top Prospect Holograms

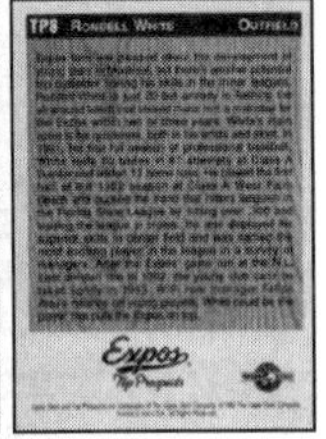

These nine standard-size hologram cards were randomly inserted in 1992 Upper Deck Minor League foil packs. Using a four-color lithography/hologram process, the fronts display a color player photo cut out and superimposed on a holographic background consisting of an action shot. The player's name and his minor league team name appear in a gray banner at the bottom that is edged in red and blue. With a royal blue stripe at the top, the backs present a player profile on a tan wood-grained panel.

	MINT	NRMT	EXC
COMPLETE SET (9)	50.00	22.00	6.25
COMMON CARD (TP1-TP9)	2.00	.90	.25
☐ TP1 Midre Cummings	2.50	1.10	.30
☐ TP2 Cliff Floyd	2.50	1.10	.30
☐ TP3 Chipper Jones	25.00	11.00	3.10
☐ TP4 Mike Kelly	2.00	.90	.25
☐ TP5 David McCarty	2.00	.90	.25
☐ TP6 Frank Rodriguez	5.00	2.20	.60
☐ TP7 Brien Taylor	2.00	.90	.25
☐ TP8 Rondell White	8.00	3.60	1.00
☐ TP9 Dmitri Young	8.00	3.60	1.00

1992 Utica Blue Sox Classic/Best

This 26-card standard-size set of the 1992 Utica Blue Sox, a Class A New York-Penn League affiliate of the Chicago White Sox, features white-bordered posed color player photos on its fronts. The player's name, team, and position appear at the bottom. The white back is framed by a thin red line and carries the player's name and position at the top, followed by biography, statistics and team logos. This issue includes the minor league card debut of Mike Cameron.

	MINT	NRMT	EXC
COMPLETE SET (26)	15.00	6.75	1.85

☐ 1 Tim Moore
☐ 2 Jason Pierson
☐ 3 Chris Snopek
☐ 4 Jimmy Hurst
☐ 5 Carmine Cappuccio
☐ 6 Mike Cameron
☐ 7 Byron Mathews
☐ 8 Jason Ogden
☐ 9 Julio Foster
☐ 10 Ted Rich
☐ 11 Jason Evans
☐ 12 Brian Filosa
☐ 13 Ricky Bowrosen
☐ 14 Robert Machado
☐ 15 Julio Vinas
☐ 16 Chris Tremie
☐ 17 Jason Watkins
☐ 18 Doug McGraw
☐ 19 Jim McDermont
☐ 20 Wayne Linemann
☐ 21 Sean Johnston
☐ 22 Steve Gajkowski
☐ 23 David Elsbernd
☐ 24 Ty Lynch
☐ 25 Mike Bertotti
☐ 26 John Herrolz

1992 Vancouver Canadians Fleer/ProCards

This 24-card standard-size set of the 1992 Vancouver Canadians, a Class AAA Pacific Coast League affiliate of the Chicago White Sox, features brown-bordered posed color player photos on its fronts. The player's name appears in an upper corner; his team and position appear in a lower corner. The white back is framed by a black line and carries the player's name and position at the top, followed by biography and statistics.

	MINT	NRMT	EXC
COMPLETE SET (24)	5.00	2.20	.60

☐ 2713 Rodney Bolton
☐ 2714 Jeff Carter
☐ 2715 Mike Dunne
☐ 2716 Ramon Garcia
☐ 2717 Chris Howard
☐ 2718 John Hudek
☐ 2719 Bo Kennedy
☐ 2720 Greg Perschke
☐ 2721 Rich Scheid
☐ 2722 Jeff Schwarz
☐ 2723 Ron Stephens
☐ 2724 Steve Wapnick
☐ 2725 Matt Merullo
☐ 2726 Nelson Santovenia
☐ 2727 Ron Coomer
☐ 2728 Chris Cron
☐ 2729 Drew Denson
☐ 2730 Joe Hall
☐ 2731 Ever Magallanes
☐ 2732 Norberto Martin
☐ 2733 Derek Lee
☐ 2734 Rick Renick MG
☐ 2735 Roger LaFrancois CO
☐ 2736 Checklist

1992 Vancouver Canadians SkyBox

This 26-card standard-size set of the 1992 Vancouver Canadians, a Class AAA Pacific Coast League affiliate of the Chicago White Sox, features white-bordered posed color player photos on its fronts. The player's name appears at the top; his team and position appear at the bottom. The white back carries the player's name at the top, followed by biography and statistics.

	MINT	NRMT	EXC
COMPLETE SET (26)	5.00	2.20	.60

☐ 626 Shawn Abner
☐ 627 Steve Wapnick
☐ 628 Rod Bolton
☐ 629 Brian Guinn
☐ 630 Jeff Carter
☐ 631 Ron Coomer
☐ 632 Chris Cron
☐ 633 Brian Drahman
☐ 634 Mike Dunne
☐ 635 Ramon Garcia
☐ 636 Joe Hall
☐ 637 Drew Denson
☐ 638 Chris Howard
☐ 639 Shawn Jeter
☐ 640 Roberto Hernandez
☐ 641 John Hudek
☐ 642 Derek Lee
☐ 643 Ever Magallanes
☐ 644 Norberto Martin
☐ 645 Greg Perschke
☐ 646 Nelson Santovenia
☐ 647 Rich Scheid
☐ 648 Ron Stephens
☐ 649 Rick Renick MG
☐ 650 Roger LaFrancois CO
☐ NNO Checklist

1992 Vero Beach Dodgers Classic/Best

This 30-card standard-size set of the 1992 Vero Beach Dodgers, a Class A Florida State League affiliate of the Los Angeles Dodgers, features white-bordered posed color player photos on its fronts. The player's name, team, and position appear at the bottom. The white back is framed by a thin red line and carries the player's name and position at the top, followed by biography, statistics and team logos.

	MINT	NRMT	EXC
COMPLETE SET (30)	5.00	2.20	.60

☐ 1 Kiki Jones
☐ 2 Keoki Farrish
☐ 3 Roberto Mejia
☐ 4 Alton Pinkney
☐ 5 Ken Hamilton
☐ 6 Tim Griffin
☐ 7 Jay Kirkpatrick
☐ 8 Willis Otanez
☐ 9 Jason Kerr
☐ 10 Sean McKamie
☐ 11 Anthony Collier
☐ 12 Vernon Spearman
☐ 13 Billy Lott
☐ 14 Brian Piotrowicz
☐ 15 James Wray
☐ 16 Chris Sinacori
☐ 17 Ed Stryker
☐ 18 Jamie Daspit
☐ 19 Steve O'Donnell
☐ 20 Dan Gray
☐ 21 Mike Brady
☐ 22 Javier DeLaHoya
☐ 23 Rafael Gutierrez
☐ 24 Bill Wengert
☐ 25 Steve Mintz
☐ 26 Ben Van Ryn
☐ 27 Ken Huckaby
☐ 28 Kazushige Nagashima
☐ 29 Glenn Hoffman MG
☐ 30 Dennis Lewallyn CO Checklist

1992 Vero Beach Dodgers Fleer/ProCards

This 32-card standard-size set of the 1992 Vero Beach Dodgers, a Class A Florida State League affiliate of the Los Angeles Dodgers, features brown-bordered posed color player photos on its fronts. The player's name appears in an upper corner; his team and position appear in a lower corner. The white back is framed by a black line and carries the player's name and position at the top, followed by biography and statistics.

	MINT	NRMT	EXC
COMPLETE SET (32)	5.00	2.20	.60

☐ 2866 Jason Brosnan
☐ 2867 Jim Daspit
☐ 2868 Javier DeLaHoya
☐ 2869 Ken Hamilton
☐ 2870 Jason Kerr
☐ 2871 Steve Mintz
☐ 2872 Brian Piotrowicz
☐ 2873 Chris Sinacori
☐ 2874 Ed Stryker
☐ 2875 Ben Van Ryn
☐ 2876 James Weaver
☐ 2877 James Wray
☐ 2878 Ken Huckaby
☐ 2879 Ed Lund
☐ 2880 Jonathon Taylor
☐ 2881 Mike Boyzuick
☐ 2882 Jay Kirkpatrick
☐ 2883 Steve Kliafas
☐ 2884 Sean McKamie
☐ 2885 Roberto Mejia
☐ 2886 Steve O'Donnell
☐ 2887 Willis Otanez
☐ 2888 Anthony Collier
☐ 2889 Freddy Gonzalez
☐ 2890 Keoki Farrish
☐ 2891 Billy Lott
☐ 2892 Vernon Spearman
☐ 2893 Glenn Hoffman MG
☐ 2894 Bo Chun CO
☐ 2895 Garrett Teel CO
☐ 2896 Dennis Lewallyn CO
☐ 2897 Checklist

1992 Visalia Oaks Classic/Best

This 30-card standard-size set of the 1992 Visalia Oaks, a Class A California League affiliate of the Minnesota Twins, features white-bordered posed color player photos on its fronts. The player's name, team, and position appear at the bottom. The white back is framed by a thin red line and carries the player's name and position at the top, followed by biography, statistics and team logos.

	MINT	NRMT	EXC
COMPLETE SET (30)	12.00	5.50	1.50

☐ 1 Scott Stahoviak
☐ 2 Rich Becker
☐ 3 Dickie Dixon
☐ 4 Matt Conolly
☐ 5 Marc Morris
☐ 6 Dave Bigham
☐ 7 Tim Persing
☐ 8 Mike Ericson
☐ 9 Jeff Thelen
☐ 10 Bob Robinson
☐ 11 Mark MacArthur
☐ 12 Tom Houk
☐ 13 Todd Logan
☐ 14 Marty Cordova
☐ 15 Mike Lewis
☐ 16 Matt Brown
☐ 17 Ryan Turner
☐ 18 David Rivera
☐ 19 Steve Dunn
☐ 20 Denny Hocking
☐ 21 Mike Durant
☐ 22 Troy Ricker
☐ 23 Todd Ritchie
☐ 24 Steve Liddle MG
☐ 25 Brian Allard CO
☐ 26 Joel Safly TR
☐ 27 Logo Card
☐ 28 Logo Card
☐ 29 Logo Card
☐ 30 Checklist

1992 Visalia Oaks Fleer/ProCards

This 28-card standard-size set of the 1992 Visalia Oaks, a Class A California League affiliate of the Minnesota Twins, features brown-bordered posed color player photos on its fronts. The player's name appears in an upper corner; his team and position appear in a lower corner. The white back is framed by a black line and carries the player's name and position at the top, followed by biography and statistics. This issue includes Marty Cordova's second minor league team set card.

	MINT	NRMT	EXC
COMPLETE SET (28)	12.00	5.50	1.50

☐ 1004 Dave Bigham
☐ 1005 Carlos Castillo
☐ 1006 Matt Connolly
☐ 1007 Dickie Dixon
☐ 1008 Mike Ericson
☐ 1009 Mike Lewis
☐ 1010 Jeff Mansur
☐ 1011 Bob McCreary
☐ 1012 Marc Morris
☐ 1013 Tim Persing
☐ 1014 Todd Ritchie
☐ 1015 Bob Robinson
☐ 1016 Jeff Thelen
☐ 1017 Matt Brown
☐ 1018 Mike Durant
☐ 1019 Steve Dunn
☐ 1020 Denny Hocking
☐ 1021 Tom Houk
☐ 1022 Mark MacArthur
☐ 1023 David Rivera
☐ 1024 Scott Stahoviak
☐ 1025 Rich Becker
☐ 1026 Marty Cordova
☐ 1027 Troy Ricker
☐ 1028 Ryan Turner
☐ 1029 Steve Liddle MG
☐ 1030 Brian Allard CO
☐ 1031 Checklist

1992 Waterloo Diamonds Classic/Best

This 30-card standard-size set of the 1992 Waterloo Diamonds, a Class A Midwest League affiliate of the San Diego Padres, features white-bordered posed color player photos on its fronts. The player's name, team, and position appear at the bottom. The white back is framed by a thin red line and carries the player's name and position at the top, followed by biography, statistics and team logos.

	MINT	NRMT	EXC
COMPLETE SET (30)	5.00	2.20	.60

☐ 1 Kevin Farlow
☐ 2 Joe Waldron
☐ 3 Scott Bream
☐ 4 Scott Pugh
☐ 5 Billy Johnson
☐ 6 Bruce Benshing
☐ 7 Ryan Ivie
☐ 8 Jeff Brown
☐ 9 Steve Hoeme
☐ 10 Jose Davila
☐ 11 Jerrey Thurston UER (misnumbered #1 on back)
☐ 12 Cameron Cairncross
☐ 13 Tom Paskievitch
☐ 14 Robbie Beckett
☐ 15 Tim Goins
☐ 16 Derek Vaughn
☐ 17 Todd Altaffer
☐ 18 Shawn Robertson
☐ 19 John Abercrombie Jr
☐ 20 Keith McKoy
☐ 21 Jason Hardtke
☐ 22 Shawn Whalen
☐ 23 Jeff Pearce
☐ 24 Dave Adams
☐ 25 Cole Hyson
☐ 26 Keith Champion MG
☐ 27 Dean Treanor CO
☐ 28 John Maxwell TR
☐ 29 Jack Grandy MG
☐ 30 Checklist

1992 Waterloo Diamonds Fleer/ProCards

This 27-card standard-size set of the 1992 Waterloo Diamonds, a Class A Midwest League affiliate of the San Diego Padres, features brown-bordered posed color player photos on its fronts. The player's name appears in an upper corner; his team and position appear in a lower corner. The white back is framed by a black line and carries the player's name and position at the top, followed by biography and statistics.

	MINT	NRMT	EXC
COMPLETE SET (27)	5.00	2.20	.60

☐ 2132 Todd Altaffer
☐ 2133 Robbie Beckett UER (First and last name reversed on front)
☐ 2134 Chris Benhardt
☐ 2135 Bruce Bensching
☐ 2136 Jeff Brown
☐ 2137 Cameron Cairncross
☐ 2138 Jose Davila
☐ 2139 Ryan Ivie
☐ 2140 Tom Martin
☐ 2141 Tom Paskievitch
☐ 2142 Joe Waldron
☐ 2143 Tim Goins
☐ 2144 Sean Mulligan
☐ 2145 Jerrey Thurston
☐ 2146 John Abercrombie
☐ 2147 Dave Adams
☐ 2148 Scott Bream
☐ 2149 Kevin Farlow
☐ 2150 Jason Hardtke
☐ 2151 Scott Pugh
☐ 2152 Keith McKoy
☐ 2153 Jeff Pearce
☐ 2154 Shawn Robertson
☐ 2155 Derek Vaughn
☐ 2156 Keith Champion MG
☐ 2157 Dean Treanor CO
☐ 2158 Checklist

1992 Watertown Indians Classic/Best

This 30-card standard-size set of the 1992 Watertown Indians, a Class A New York-Penn League affiliate of the Cleveland Indians, features white-bordered posed color player photos on its fronts. The player's name, team, and position appear at the bottom. The white back is framed by a thin red line and carries the player's name and position at the top, followed by biography, statistics and team logos.

	MINT	NRMT	EXC
COMPLETE SET (30)	5.00	2.20	.60

☐ 1 Jamie Taylor
☐ 2 Paul Gibbs
☐ 3 Jason Fronio
☐ 4 Scott Sharts
☐ 5 Denny Key
☐ 6 Mike Jewel
☐ 7 Oscar Resendez
☐ 8 Ben Blake
☐ 9 Charles York
☐ 10 Matt Williams
☐ 11 Mike Neilson
☐ 12 Noe Najera
☐ 13 Fred Smith
☐ 14 Epi Cardenas
☐ 15 Brian Arntzen
☐ 16 David Chisum
☐ 17 Jonathan Nunnally
☐ 18 Pat Bryant
☐ 19 Mike Lockhart
☐ 20 Brad Kantor
☐ 21 Mike Zollars
☐ 22 Curtis George
☐ 23 Mike Moore
☐ 24 Derek Hacopian
☐ 25 Kevin DiGiacomo
☐ 26 Shawn Pender
☐ 27 Greg Ferlenda
☐ 28 Ed Stabile
☐ 29 Rick Jameyson
☐ 30 Checklist

1992 Watertown Indians Fleer/ProCards

This 29-card standard-size set of the 1992 Watertown Indians, a Class A New York-Penn League affiliate of the Cleveland Indians, features brown-bordered posed color player photos on its fronts. The player's name appears in an upper corner; his team and position appear in a lower corner. The white back is framed by a black line and carries the player's name and position at the top, followed by biography and statistics.

	MINT	NRMT	EXC
COMPLETE SET (29)	5.00	2.20	.60

☐ 3225 Ben Blake
☐ 3226 Jason Fronio
☐ 3227 Paul Gibbs
☐ 3228 Mike Jewell
☐ 3229 Denny Key
☐ 3230 Noe Najera
☐ 3231 Mike Neilson
☐ 3232 Oscar Resendez
☐ 3233 Scott Sharts

- □ 3234 Fred Smith
- □ 3235 Matt Williams
- □ 3236 Charles York
- □ 3237 Brian Arntzen
- □ 3238 Mike Lockhart
- □ 3239 Mike Moore
- □ 3240 Epi Cardenas
- □ 3241 Kevin DiGiacomo
- □ 3242 Curtis George
- □ 3243 Brad Kantor
- □ 3244 Jamie Taylor
- □ 3245 Pat Bryant
- □ 3246 Dave Chisum
- □ 3247 Sam Hence
- □ 3248 Jon Nunnally
- □ 3249 Mike Zollars
- □ 3250 Shawn Pender MG
- □ 3251 Greg Ferlenda CO
- □ 3252 Derek Hacopian CO
- □ 3253 Checklist

1992 Welland Pirates Classic/Best

This 30-card standard-size set of the 1992 Welland Pirates, a Class A New York-Penn League affiliate of the Pittsburgh Pirates, features white-bordered posed color player photos on its fronts. The player's name, team, and position appear at the bottom. The white back is framed by a thin red line and carries the player's name and position at the top, followed by biography, statistics and team logos. This issue includes the debut of John Carter.

	MINT	NRMT	EXC
COMPLETE SET (30)	5.00	2.20	.60

- □ 1 Jacob Austin
- □ 2 Miguel Bonilla
- □ 3 Aaron Cannaday
- □ 4 John Carter
- □ 5 John Cranford
- □ 6 Angel Colon
- □ 7 Ramon Espinosa
- □ 8 Frank Garcia-Luna
- □ 9 Rico Gholston
- □ 10 Riegal Hunt UER (Name misspelled Riegel)
- □ 11 Matt Jones
- □ 12 Erskine Kelly
- □ 13 Dennis Konuszewski
- □ 14 Ted Klamm
- □ 15 Michel LaPlante UER (Name misspelled Michael on both sides)
- □ 16 Sean Lawrence
- □ 17 Pat Lussier
- □ 18 Dave Maize
- □ 19 Gil Perez
- □ 20 Chance Sanford
- □ 21 Craig Shotton
- □ 22 Larry Stahlhoefer
- □ 23 Chuck Tooch
- □ 24 Richard Townsend
- □ 25 Marc Wilkins
- □ 26 Gary Wilson
- □ 27 Stanley Wiltz
- □ 28 Trent Jewett MG
- □ 29 Julio Garcia CO
- □ 30 Tom Barnard CO Checklist

1992 Welland Pirates Fleer/ProCards

This 30-card standard-size set of the 1992 Welland Pirates, a Class A New York-Penn League affiliate of the Pittsburgh Pirates, features brown-bordered posed color player photos on its fronts. The player's name appears in an upper corner; his team and position appear in a lower corner. The white back is framed by a black line and carries the player's name and position at the top, followed by biography and statistics. This issue includes the debut of John Carter.

	MINT	NRMT	EXC
COMPLETE SET (30)	5.00	2.20	.60

- □ 1314 Miguel Bonilla
- □ 1315 John Carter
- □ 1316 Frank Garcia-Luna
- □ 1317 Ted Klamm
- □ 1318 Michel LaPlante
- □ 1319 Sean Lawrence
- □ 1320 Mark Mesewicz
- □ 1321 Gil Perez
- □ 1322 Richard Townsend
- □ 1323 Marc Wilkins
- □ 1324 Gary Wilson
- □ 1325 Aaron Cannaday
- □ 1326 Dave Maize
- □ 1327 Larry Stahlhoefer
- □ 1328 Angel Colon
- □ 1329 John Cranford
- □ 1330 Rico Gholston
- □ 1331 Matt Jones
- □ 1332 Kevin Polcovich
- □ 1333 Chance Sanford
- □ 1334 Chuck Tooch
- □ 1335 Stanley Wiltz
- □ 1336 Ramon Espinosa
- □ 1337 Riegal Hunt UER (Name misspelled Riegel)
- □ 1338 Erskine Kelley
- □ 1339 Pat Lussier
- □ 1340 Trent Jewett MG
- □ 1341 Tom Barnard CO
- □ 1342 Julio Garcia CO
- □ 1343 Checklist

1992 West Palm Beach Expos Classic/Best

This 30-card standard-size set of the 1992 West Palm Beach Expos, a Class A Florida State League affiliate of the Montreal Expos, features white-bordered posed color player photos on its fronts. The player's name, team, and position appear at the bottom. The white back is framed by a thin red line and carries the player's name and position at the top, followed by biography, statistics and team logos. This issue includes a second year card of Rondell White.

	MINT	NRMT	EXC
COMPLETE SET (30)	7.00	3.10	.85

- □ 1 Rondell White
- □ 2 Ron Krause
- □ 3 Tavo Alvarez
- □ 4 Rob Fitzpatrick
- □ 5 James Austin
- □ 6 Steve Keighley
- □ 7 Jeff Tuss
- □ 8 Kevin McDonald
- □ 9 Miguel Batista
- □ 10 Scott Campbell
- □ 11 Steve Long
- □ 12 Ranbir Grewal
- □ 13 Shaun Murphy
- □ 14 Rafael Diaz
- □ 15 Chris Malinoski
- □ 16 Bob Baxter
- □ 17 Corey Powell
- □ 18 Joey Eischen
- □ 19 Glenn Murray
- □ 20 Billy Brewer
- □ 21 Brett Jenkins
- □ 22 Randy Wilstead
- □ 23 Mike Daniel
- □ 24 Felix Moya
- □ 25 Mike Weimerskirch
- □ 26 Dave Jauss MG
- □ 27 Marc Golberg Sports Director
- □ 28 Nancy Graham Mayor
- □ 29 John Picano ANN
- □ 30 Chuck Kniffin CO Checklist

1992 West Palm Beach Expos Fleer/ProCards

This 29-card standard-size set of the 1992 West Palm Beach Expos, a Class A Florida State League affiliate of the Montreal Expos, features brown-bordered posed color player photos on its fronts. The player's name appears in an upper corner; his team and position appear in a lower corner. The white back is framed by a black line and carries the player's name and position at the top, followed by biography and statistics. This issue includes a second year card of Rondell White.

	MINT	NRMT	EXC
COMPLETE SET (29)	7.00	3.10	.85

- □ 2077 Tavo Alvarez
- □ 2078 Miguel Batista
- □ 2079 Bob Baxter
- □ 2080 Billy Brewer
- □ 2081 Rafael Diaz
- □ 2082 Joey Eischen
- □ 2083 Kevin Foster
- □ 2084 Ranbir Grewal
- □ 2085 Steve Long
- □ 2086 Kevin McDonald
- □ 2087 Felix Moya
- □ 2088 Corey Powell
- □ 2089 Jeff Tuss
- □ 2090 Mike Daniel
- □ 2091 Rob Fitzpatrick
- □ 2092 Steve Keighley
- □ 2093 Scott Campbell
- □ 2094 Brett Jenkins
- □ 2095 Ron Krause
- □ 2096 Chris Malinoski
- □ 2097 Randy Wilstead
- □ 2098 Jim Austin
- □ 2099 Shaun Murphy
- □ 2100 Glenn Murray
- □ 2101 Mike Weimerskirch
- □ 2102 Rondell White
- □ 2103 Dave Jauss MG
- □ 2104 Chuck Kniffin CO
- □ 2105 Checklist

1992 Wichita Wranglers Fleer/ProCards

This 21-card standard-size set of the 1992 Wichita Wrnaglers, a Class AA Texas League affiliate of the San Diego Padres, features brown-bordered posed color player photos on its fronts. The player's name appears in an upper corner; his team and position appear in a lower corner. The white back is framed by a black line and carries the player's name and position at the top, followed by biography and statistics.

	MINT	NRMT	EXC
COMPLETE SET (21)	5.00	2.20	.60

- □ 3651 Renay Bryand
- □ 3652 Mark Ettles
- □ 3653 Scott Fredrickson
- □ 3654 Steve Hoeme
- □ 3655 Mike Linskey
- □ 3656 Pedro Martinez
- □ 3657 Lance Painter
- □ 3658 Royal Thomas
- □ 3659 Brian Johnson
- □ 3660 Steve Bethea
- □ 3661 Jay Gainer
- □ 3662 Mark Gieseke
- □ 3663 Paul Gonzalez
- □ 3664 Ray Holbert
- □ 3665 Matt Witkowski
- □ 3666 Vince Harris
- □ 3667 Dwayne Hosey
- □ 3668 Steve Martin
- □ 3669 Bruce Bochy MG
- □ 3670 Danny Garcia CO
- □ 3671 Checklist

1992 Wichita Wranglers SkyBox

	MINT	NRMT	EXC
COMPLETE SET (26)	5.00	2.20	.60

- □ 626 Steve Bethea
- □ 627 Renay Bryand
- □ 628 Mark Ettles
- □ 629 Scott Fredrickson
- □ 630 Jay Gainer
- □ 631 Tim Worrell
- □ 632 Paul Gonzalez
- □ 633 Vince Harris
- □ 634 Ray Holbert
- □ 635 Dwayne Hosey
- □ 636 Chris Jelic
- □ 637 Brian Johnson
- □ 638 Mike Linskey
- □ 639 Pedro Lopez
- □ 640 Pedro Martinez
- □ 641 Tim McWilliam
- □ 642 J.D. Noland
- □ 643 Lance Painter
- □ 644 Scott Sanders
- □ 645 Darrell Sherman
- □ 646 Royal Thomas
- □ 647 Mat Witkowski
- □ 648 Brian Wood
- □ 649 Bruce Bochy MG
- □ 650 Sonny Siebert CO Danny Garcia CO
- □ NNO Checklist

1992 Winston-Salem Spirits Classic/Best

This 29-card standard-size set of the 1992 Winston-Salem Spirits, a Class A Carolina League affiliate of the Chicago Cubs, features white-bordered posed color player photos on its fronts. The player's name, team, and position appear at the bottom. The white back is framed by a thin red line and carries the player's name and position at the top, followed by biography, statistics and team logos.

	MINT	NRMT	EXC
COMPLETE SET (29)	5.00	2.20	.60

- □ 1 Doug Glanville
- □ 2 Earl Cunningham
- □ 3 Rafael Soto
- □ 4 Jose Viera
- □ 5 Rich Juday
- □ 6 Sean Cheetham
- □ 7 Paul Torres
- □ 8 Scott Taylor
- □ 9 Jason Doss
- □ 10 Marc Little
- □ 11 Brad Erdman
- □ 12 Rolando Fernandez
- □ 13 Andrew Hartung
- □ 14 Tim Delgado
- □ 15 Ken Krahenbuhl
- □ 16 Amilcar Correa
- □ 17 Chuck Kirk
- □ 18 Rudy Gomez
- □ 19 Joe Biasucci
- □ 20 Mike Gabbani
- □ 21 Pedro Alicano
- □ 22 Joe Szczepanski
- □ 23 Aaron Taylor
- □ 24 Ben Burlingame
- □ 25 Tim Budrewicz
- □ 26 Bill Hayes
- □ 27 Lester Strode
- □ 28 Steve Melendez
- □ 30 Checklist

1992 Winston-Salem Spirits Fleer/ProCards

This 28-card standard-size set of the 1992 Winston-Salem Spirits, a Class A Carolina League affiliate of the Chicago Cubs, features brown-bordered posed color player photos on its fronts. The player's name appears in an upper corner; his team and position appear in a lower corner. The white back is framed by a black line and carries the player's name and position at the top, followed by biography and statistics.

	MINT	NRMT	EXC
COMPLETE SET (28)	5.00	2.20	.60

- □ 1198 Pedro Alicano
- □ 1199 Tim Budrewicz
- □ 1200 Ben Burlingame
- □ 1201 Sean Cheetham
- □ 1202 Amilcar Correa
- □ 1203 Tim Delgado
- □ 1204 Jason Doss
- □ 1205 Chuck Kirk
- □ 1206 Pedro Perez
- □ 1207 Joe Szczepanski
- □ 1208 Aaron Taylor
- □ 1209 Scott Weiss
- □ 1210 Brad Erdman
- □ 1211 Mike Gabbani
- □ 1212 Scott Taylor
- □ 1213 Rudy Gomez
- □ 1214 Andy Hartung
- □ 1215 Rich Juday
- □ 1216 Rafael Soto
- □ 1217 Jose Vierra
- □ 1218 Rolando Fernandez
- □ 1219 Doug Glanville
- □ 1220 Corey Kapano
- □ 1221 Mike Little
- □ 1222 Paul Torres
- □ 1223 Bill Hayes MG
- □ 1224 Lester Strode CO
- □ 1225 Checklist

1992 Winter Haven Red Sox Classic/Best

This 30-card standard-size set of the 1992 Winter Haven Red Sox, a Class A Florida State League affiliate of the Boston Red Sox, features white-bordered posed color player photos on its fronts. The player's name, team, and position appear at the bottom. The white back is framed by a thin red line and carries the player's name and position at the top, followed by biography, statistics and team logos.

	MINT	NRMT	EXC
COMPLETE SET (30)	5.00	2.20	.60

- □ 1 Chris Davis
- □ 2 Joe Ciccarella
- □ 3 Randy Brown
- □ 4 David Schmidt
- □ 5 Bill Madril
- □ 6 Diogenes Baez
- □ 7 Tony Ferreira
- □ 8 Gary Villalobos
- □ 9 Jim Byrd
- □ 10 Terry Powers
- □ 11 Doug MacNeil
- □ 12 Joe Luis
- □ 13 Silverio Santa Maria
- □ 14 Ron Mahay
- □ 15 Joel Bennett
- □ 16 Chad Schoenvogel
- □ 17 Ryan Maloney
- □ 18 Bryan Brown
- □ 19 Bob Pickett
- □ 20 Dana Levangie
- □ 21 Les Wallin
- □ 22 Bret Donovan
- □ 23 Brian Bright
- □ 24 Todd Miller
- □ 25 Mark Mitchelson
- □ 26 Felix Maldonado
- □ 27 Jim Stricek
- □ 28 Joe Marchese
- □ 29 Steve Braun
- □ 30 Lee Strange Checklist

1992 Winter Haven Red Sox Fleer/ProCards

This 30-card standard-size set of the 1992 Winter Haven Red Sox, a Class A Florida State League affiliate of the Boston Red Sox, features brown-bordered posed color player photos on its fronts. The player's name appears in an upper corner; his team and position appear in a lower corner. The white back is framed by a black line and carries the player's name and position at the top, followed by biography and statistics.

	MINT	NRMT	EXC
COMPLETE SET (30)	5.00	2.20	.60

- ☐ 1767 Joel Bennett
- ☐ 1768 Joe Ciccarella
- ☐ 1769 Bernie Dzafic
- ☐ 1770 Rob Henkel
- ☐ 1771 Mike Lynch
- ☐ 1772 Ryan Maloney
- ☐ 1773 Todd Miller
- ☐ 1774 Dave Owen
- ☐ 1775 Terry Powers
- ☐ 1776 Steve Renko
- ☐ 1777 Chad Schoenvogel
- ☐ 1778 Brian Young
- ☐ 1779 Alex Delgado
- ☐ 1780 Joe Demus
- ☐ 1781 Dana LeVangie
- ☐ 1782 Emison Soto
- ☐ 1783 Randy Brown
- ☐ 1784 Felix Colon
- ☐ 1785 Marty Durkin
- ☐ 1786 Tony Ferreira
- ☐ 1787 David Schmidt
- ☐ 1788 Gary Villalobos
- ☐ 1789 Les Wallin
- ☐ 1790 Diogenes Baez
- ☐ 1791 Brian Bright
- ☐ 1792 Bryan Brown
- ☐ 1793 Jose Zambrano
- ☐ 1794 Felix Maldonado MG
- ☐ 1795 Joe Marchese CO
- ☐ 1796 Checklist

1992 Yakima Bears Classic/Best

This 27-card standard-size set of the 1992 Yakima Bears, a Class A Northwest League affiliate of the Los Angeles Dodgers, features white-bordered posed color player photos on its fronts. The player's name, team, and position appear at the bottom. The white back is framed by a thin red line and carries the player's name and position at the top, followed by biography, statistics and team logos.

	MINT	NRMT	EXC
COMPLETE SET (27)	5.00	2.20	.60

- ☐ 1 Doug Bennett
- ☐ 2 John Graves
- ☐ 3 Alton Pinkney
- ☐ 4 Dan Gray
- ☐ 5 Burgess Watts
- ☐ 6 Keith Johnson
- ☐ 7 Patrick Reed
- ☐ 8 Clint Minear
- ☐ 9 Kevin Zahner
- ☐ 10 Robert Legendre
- ☐ 11 Tito Landrum
- ☐ 12 Ken Chapman
- ☐ 13 Tory Miran
- ☐ 14 Cliff Anderson
- ☐ 15 Matt Herges
- ☐ 16 Todd Rizzo
- ☐ 17 Todd LaValley
- ☐ 18 Erik Zammarchi
- ☐ 19 Keith Trautman
- ☐ 20 John Callihan
- ☐ 21 Rafael Gutierrez
- ☐ 22 Matt Filson
- ☐ 23 Joe Barbein
- ☐ 24 Joe Varva
- ☐ 25 Brett Magnusson
- ☐ 26 Tony Arnold
- ☐ NNO Checklist

1992 Yakima Bears Fleer/ProCards

This 32-card standard-size set of the 1992 Yakima Bears, a Class A Northwest League affiliate of the Los Angeles Dodgers, features brown-bordered posed color player photos on its fronts. The player's name appears in an upper corner; his team and position appear in a lower corner. The white back is framed by a black line and carries the player's name and position at the top, followed by biography and statistics.

	MINT	NRMT	EXC
COMPLETE SET (32)	5.00	2.20	.60

- ☐ 3438 Joe Barbeln
- ☐ 3439 Doug Bennett
- ☐ 3440 Brent Colson
- ☐ 3441 John Graves
- ☐ 3442 Rafael Gutierrez
- ☐ 3443 Matt Herges
- ☐ 3444 Todd LaValley
- ☐ 3445 Rob Legendre
- ☐ 3446 Clint Minear
- ☐ 3447 Todd Rizzo
- ☐ 3448 Carlos Thomas
- ☐ 3449 Keith Troutman
- ☐ 3450 Burgess Watts
- ☐ 3451 Chris Abbe
- ☐ 3452 Mike Brown
- ☐ 3453 Dan Gray
- ☐ 3454 Kevin Zahner
- ☐ 3455 Cliff Anderson
- ☐ 3456 John Callihan
- ☐ 3457 Ken Chapman
- ☐ 3458 Keith Johnson
- ☐ 3459 Sandy Martinez
- ☐ 3460 Mike Serbalik
- ☐ 3461 Matt Filson
- ☐ 3462 Tito Landrum
- ☐ 3463 Tory Miran
- ☐ 3464 Michael Moore
- ☐ 3465 Alton Pinkney
- ☐ 3466 Pat Reed
- ☐ 3467 Erik Zammarchi
- ☐ 3468 Joe Vavra MG
- ☐ 3469 Checklist

1993 Albany Polecats Classic/Best

This 30-card standard-size set of the 1993 Albany Polecats, a Class A South Atlantic League affiliate of the Baltimore Orioles, features white-bordered posed color player shots on its fronts. A team-color-coded stripe below the photo carries the player's name; another above, his position and team name. On a ghosted team-logo, the white back carries the player's name at the top, followed by biography and statistics..

	MINT	NRMT	EXC
COMPLETE SET (30)	5.00	2.20	.60

- ☐ 1 Billy Owens
- ☐ 2 Myles Barnden
- ☐ 3 Juan Bautista
- ☐ 4 Armando Benitez
- ☐ 5 Clayton Byrne
- ☐ 6 Christopher Chatterton
- ☐ 7 Carlos Chavez
- ☐ 8 Eric Chavez
- ☐ 9 Howie Clark
- ☐ 10 Scott Conner
- ☐ 11 Geno Delgado
- ☐ 12 Charles Devereux
- ☐ 13 Keith Eaddy
- ☐ 14 Scott Emerson
- ☐ 15 Matt Jarvis
- ☐ 16 Marco Manrique
- ☐ 17 Scott Metcalf
- ☐ 18 Matt Reimer
- ☐ 19 Jose Serra
- ☐ 20 Garrett Stephenson
- ☐ 21 B.J. Waszgis
- ☐ 22 Kyle Yeske
- ☐ 23 Mike O'Berry MG
- ☐ 24 Charlie Puleo CO
- ☐ 25 Peter Howell TR
- ☐ 26 Larry Shenk
- ☐ 27 Scott Skadan GM
- ☐ 28 Mike Kardamis AGM
- ☐ 29 Brad Sparesus ANN
- ☐ 30 Pepper (Mascot) Checklist

1993 Albany Polecats Fleer/ProCards

This 28-card standard-size set of the 1993 Albany Polecats, a Class A South Atlantic League affiliate of the Baltimore Orioles, features white-bordered posed color player photos on its fronts. The player's name, team, and position appear near the bottom. The white horizontal back is framed by a blue line and carries the player's name at the top, followed by biography and statistics. A drawing of a ballplayer in action appears on the left.

	MINT	NRMT	EXC
COMPLETE SET (28)	5.00	2.20	.60

- ☐ 2017 Armando Benitez
- ☐ 2018 Chris Chatterton
- ☐ 2019 Carlos Chavez
- ☐ 2020 Scott Conner
- ☐ 2021 Lee Cusey
- ☐ 2022 Scott Emerson
- ☐ 2023 Matt Jarvis
- ☐ 2024 Aaron Lane
- ☐ 2025 Brian Sackinsky
- ☐ 2026 Larry Shenk
- ☐ 2027 Garrett Stephenson
- ☐ 2028 Marco Manrique
- ☐ 2029 B.J. Waszgis
- ☐ 2030 Juan Bautista
- ☐ 2031 Eric Chavez
- ☐ 2032 Geno Delgado
- ☐ 2033 Scott Metcalf
- ☐ 2034 Billy Owens
- ☐ 2035 Jose Serra
- ☐ 2036 Clayton Byrne
- ☐ 2037 Keith Eaddy
- ☐ 2038 Roy Hodge
- ☐ 2039 Keith Schmidt
- ☐ 2040 Duane Thomas
- ☐ 2041 Kyle Yeske
- ☐ 2042 Mike O'Berry MG
- ☐ 2043 Charlie Puleo CO
- ☐ 2127 Checklist

1993 Albany Yankees Fleer/ProCards

This 29-card standard-size set of the 1993 Albany Yankees, a Class AA Eastern League affiliate of the New York Yankees, features white-bordered posed color player photos on its fronts. The player's name, team, and position appear near the bottom. The white horizontal back is framed by a blue line and carries the player's name at the top, followed by biography and statistics. A drawing of a ballplayer in action appears on the left.

	MINT	NRMT	EXC
COMPLETE SET (29)	5.00	2.20	.60

- ☐ 2153 Richard Batchelor
- ☐ 2154 Mark Carper
- ☐ 2155 Brian Faw
- ☐ 2156 Doug Gogolewski
- ☐ 2157 Jim Haller
- ☐ 2158 Richard Hines
- ☐ 2159 Darren Hodges
- ☐ 2160 Domingo Jean
- ☐ 2161 Rich Polak
- ☐ 2162 Tom Popplewell
- ☐ 2163 Rafael Quirico
- ☐ 2164 Brien Taylor
- ☐ 2165 Jeff Livesey
- ☐ 2166 Jose Pineda
- ☐ 2167 Bubba Carpenter
- ☐ 2168 Joe DeBerry
- ☐ 2169 Robert Eenhoorn
- ☐ 2170 Andy Fox
- ☐ 2171 Mike Hankins
- ☐ 2172 Kevin Jordan
- ☐ 2173 Rich Barnwell
- ☐ 2174 Lyle Mouton
- ☐ 2175 Paul Oster
- ☐ 2176 Jason Robertson
- ☐ 2177 Mike Hart MG
- ☐ 2178 Brian Butterfield CO
- ☐ 2179 Dave Schuler CO
- ☐ 2180 Rob Thomson CO
- ☐ 2181 Checklist

1993 Albuquerque Dukes Fleer/ProCards

This 31-card standard-size set of the 1993 Albuquerque Dukes, a Class AAA Pacific Coast League affiliate of the Los Angeles Dodgers, features white-bordered posed color player photos on its fronts. The player's name, team, and position appear near the bottom. The white horizontal back is framed by a blue line and carries the player's name at the top, followed by biography and statistics. A drawing of a ballplayer in action appears on the left.

	MINT	NRMT	EXC
COMPLETE SET (31)	12.00	5.50	1.50

- ☐ 1451 Steve Allen
- ☐ 1452 Albert Bustillos
- ☐ 1453 Omar Daal
- ☐ 1454 Greg Hansell
- ☐ 1455 Mike James
- ☐ 1456 Jerry Kutzler
- ☐ 1457 Rod Nichols
- ☐ 1458 Greg Perschke
- ☐ 1459 Dennis Springer
- ☐ 1460 Jody Treadwell
- ☐ 1461 Joey Vierra
- ☐ 1462 Todd Williams
- ☐ 1463 Jerry Brooks
- ☐ 1464 Lance Parrish
- ☐ 1465 Don Wakamatsu
- ☐ 1466 Rafael Bournigal
- ☐ 1467 Mike Busch
- ☐ 1468 Matt Howard
- ☐ 1469 Ron Maurer
- ☐ 1470 Jose Munoz
- ☐ 1471 Eddie Pye
- ☐ 1472 Brian Traxler
- ☐ 1473 Billy Ashley
- ☐ 1474 Tony Barron
- ☐ 1475 Raul Mondesi
- ☐ 1476 Chris Morrow
- ☐ 1477 Henry Rodriguez
- ☐ 1478 Bill Russell MG
- ☐ 1479 Tom Beyers CO
- ☐ 1480 Glenn Gregson CO
- ☐ 1481 Checklist

1993 Appleton Foxes Classic/Best

This 30-card standard-size set of the 1993 Appleton Foxes, a Class A Midwest League affiliate of the Seattle Mariners, features white-bordered posed color player shots on its fronts. A team-color-coded stripe below the photo carries the player's name; another above, his position and team name. On a ghosted team-logo, the white back carries the player's name at the top, followed by biography and statistics.

	MINT	NRMT	EXC
COMPLETE SET (30)	5.00	2.20	.60

- ☐ 1 Shawn Estes
- ☐ 2 Jerry Aschoff
- ☐ 3 Enrique Atencio
- ☐ 4 Craig Bryant
- ☐ 5 Ron Cody
- ☐ 6 Tim Davis
- ☐ 7 Jamon Deal
- ☐ 8 Charles Gipson
- ☐ 9 Richard Graham
- ☐ 10 Craig Griffey
- ☐ 11 Mike Hickey
- ☐ 12 Raul Ibanez
- ☐ 13 Bill Kostich
- ☐ 14 David Lawson
- ☐ 15 Bobby Llanos
- ☐ 16 Jesus Marquez
- ☐ 17 Jorge Morales
- ☐ 18 Jackie Nickell
- ☐ 19 Erik O'Donnell
- ☐ 20 Robby Robertson
- ☐ 21 Jose Sanchez
- ☐ 22 Alex Sutherland
- ☐ 23 Brian Wallace
- ☐ 24 Trey Witte
- ☐ 25 Rob Worley
- ☐ 26 Carlos Lezcano MG
- ☐ 27 Orlando Gomez CO
- ☐ 28 Paul Lindblad CO
- ☐ 29 Jim Skaalen CO
- ☐ 30 Allen Wirtala TR Checklist

1993 Appleton Foxes Fleer/ProCards

This 29-card standard-size set of the 1993 Appleton Foxes, a Class A Midwest League affiliate of the Seattle Mariners, features white-bordered posed color player photos on its fronts. The player's name, team, and position appear near the bottom. The white horizontal back is framed by a blue line and carries the player's name at the top, followed by biography and statistics. A drawing of a ballplayer in action appears on the left.

	MINT	NRMT	EXC
COMPLETE SET (29)	5.00	2.20	.60

- ☐ 2451 Jerry Aschoff
- ☐ 2452 Ron Cody
- ☐ 2453 Tim Davis
- ☐ 2454 Jamon Deal
- ☐ 2455 Shawn Estes
- ☐ 2456 Richard Graham
- ☐ 2457 Bil Kostich
- ☐ 2458 Jackie Nickell
- ☐ 2459 Jose Sanchez
- ☐ 2460 Trey Witte
- ☐ 2461 Rob Worley
- ☐ 2462 Raul Ibanez
- ☐ 2463 Jorge Morales
- ☐ 2464 Alex Sutherland
- ☐ 2465 Enrique Atencio
- ☐ 2466 Craig Bryant
- ☐ 2467 Eddy Diaz
- ☐ 2468 Charles Gipson
- ☐ 2469 Mike Hickey
- ☐ 2470 Brian Wallace
- ☐ 2471 Craig Griffey
- ☐ 2472 David Lawson
- ☐ 2473 Bobby Llanos
- ☐ 2474 Jesus Marquez
- ☐ 2475 Robbie Robertson
- ☐ 2476 Carlos Lezcano MG
- ☐ 2477 Orlando Gomez CO
- ☐ 2478 Steve Smith CO
- ☐ 2479 Checklist

1993 Arkansas Travelers Fleer/ProCards

This 27-card standard-size set of the 1993 Arkansas Travelers, a Class AA Texas League affiliate of the St. Louis Cardinals, features white-bordered posed color player photos on its fronts. The player's name, team, and position appear near the bottom. The white horizontal back is framed by a blue line and carries the player's name at the top, followed by biography and statistics. A drawing of a ballplayer in action appears on the left.

	MINT	NRMT	EXC
COMPLETE SET (27)	5.00	2.20	.60

- ☐ 2803 Paul Anderson
- ☐ 2804 Brian Barber
- ☐ 2805 Rigo Beltran
- ☐ 2806 Frank Cimorelli
- ☐ 2807 Doug Creek
- ☐ 2808 Bryan Eversgerd
- ☐ 2809 Luis Faccio
- ☐ 2810 John Kelly
- ☐ 2811 Kerry Knox
- ☐ 2812 Gerald Santos
- ☐ 2813 Rick Shackle
- ☐ 2814 Paul Ellis

☐ 2815 Kevin Tahan
☐ 2816 Joe Aversa
☐ 2817 Darrel Deak
☐ 2818 Steve Fanning
☐ 2819 Craig Faulkner
☐ 2820 Wander Pimentel
☐ 2821 Jeff Shireman
☐ 2822 Allen Battle
☐ 2823 Anthony Lewis
☐ 2824 John Mabry
☐ 2825 Howard Prager
☐ 2826 Odalis Savinon
☐ 2827 Joe Pettini MG
☐ 2828 Marty Mason CO
☐ 2829 Checklist

1993 Asheville Tourists Classic/Best

This 30-card standard-size set of the 1993 Asheville Tourists, a Class A South Atlantic League affiliate of the Houston Astros, features white-bordered posed color player shots on its fronts. A team-color-coded stripe below the photo carries the player's name; another above, his position and team name. On a ghosted team-logo, the white back carries the player's name at the top, followed by biography and statistics. This issue includes the minor league card debut of Richard Hidalgo.

	MINT	NRMT	EXC
COMPLETE SET (30)	8.00	3.60	1.00

☐ 1 Richard Hidalgo
☐ 2 Randy Albaladejo
☐ 3 Marvin Billingsley
☐ 4 Eduardo Cedeno
☐ 5 Jose Centeno
☐ 6 Greg Elliott
☐ 7 Sean Fesh
☐ 8 Oscar Henriquez
☐ 9 Todd Hobson
☐ 10 Zak Krislock
☐ 11 Shawn Livsey
☐ 12 Victor Madrigal
☐ 13 James McCutchen
☐ 14 Melvin Mora
☐ 15 Tyrone Narcisse
☐ 16 Alan Probst
☐ 17 Mike Rennhack
☐ 18 Noel Rodriguez
☐ 19 Jose Santana
☐ 20 Jeff Tenbarge
☐ 21 Victor Valdez
☐ 22 Kevin Webb
☐ 23 Clifford Williams
☐ 24 Danny Young
☐ 25 Bobby Ramos MG
☐ 26 Jim Coveney CO
☐ 27 Don Alexander CO
☐ 28 Ron Hanisch TR
☐ 29 Title Card
☐ 30 Checklist

1993 Asheville Tourists Fleer/ProCards

This 30-card standard-size set of the 1993 Asheville Tourists, a Class A South Atlantic League affiliate of the Houston Astros, features white-bordered posed color player photos on its fronts. The player's name, team, and position appear near the bottom. The white horizontal back is framed by a blue line and carries the player's name at the top, followed by biography and statistics. A drawing of a ballplayer in action appears on the left. This set includes Richard Hidalgo's first team set card.

	MINT	NRMT	EXC
COMPLETE SET (30)	8.00	3.60	1.00

☐ 2267 Marvin Billingsley
☐ 2268 Jose Centeno
☐ 2269 Sean Fesh
☐ 2270 Oscar Henriquez
☐ 2271 Zak Krislock
☐ 2272 Victor Madrigal
☐ 2273 Jim McCutchen
☐ 2274 Tyrone Narcisse
☐ 2275 Jeff Tenbarge
☐ 2276 Victor Valdez
☐ 2277 Danny Young
☐ 2278 Randy Albaladejo
☐ 2279 Alan Probst
☐ 2280 Clifford Williams
☐ 2281 Ed Cedeno
☐ 2282 Greg Elliott
☐ 2283 Dan Grapethien
☐ 2284 Melvin Mora
☐ 2285 Jose Santana
☐ 2286 Jermaine Swinton
☐ 2287 Kevin Webb
☐ 2288 Richard Hidalgo
☐ 2289 Todd Hobson
☐ 2290 Shawn Livsey
☐ 2291 Mike Rennhack
☐ 2292 Noel Rodriguez
☐ 2293 Bobby Ramos MG
☐ 2294 Don Alexander CO
☐ 2295 Jim Coveney CO
☐ 2296 Checklist

1993 Auburn Astros Classic/Best

This 30-card standard-size set of the 1993 Auburn Astros, a Class A New York-Penn League affiliate of the Houston Astros, features white-bordered posed color player shots on its fronts. A team-color-coded stripe below the photo carries the player's name; another above, his position and team name. On a ghosted team-logo, the white back carries the player's name at the top, followed by biography and statistics. This issue includes the minor league card debut of Billy Wagner.

	MINT	NRMT	EXC
COMPLETE SET (30)	8.00	3.60	1.00

☐ 1 Billy Wagner
☐ 2 Marsalis Basey
☐ 3 Brett Callan
☐ 4 Eduardo Cedeno
☐ 5 Carlos Crispin
☐ 6 Tom Czanstkowski
☐ 7 Raymond Dault
☐ 8 Mike Diorio
☐ 9 Tim Forkner
☐ 10 Tevor Froschaner
☐ 11 Daniel Grapenthien
☐ 12 Michael Grzanich
☐ 13 Bill Hartnett
☐ 14 Richard Humphrey
☐ 15 Tim Kester
☐ 16 Klinton Klass
☐ 17 Arquimedes Lugo
☐ 18 Nathan Peterson
☐ 19 Kendall Rhine
☐ 20 Noel Rodriguez
☐ 21 Troy Schulte
☐ 22 Kevin Smith
☐ 23 Joshua Spring
☐ 24 Steve Verduzco
☐ 25 John Vindivich
☐ 26 Chad White
☐ 27 Ted Wieczorek
☐ 28 Manny Acta MG
☐ 29 Tad Slowik CO
☐ 30 Michael Ra TR Checklist

1993 Auburn Astros Fleer/ProCards

This 30-card standard-size set of the 1993 Auburn Astros, a Class A New York-Penn League affiliate of the Houston Astros, features white-bordered posed color player photos on its fronts. The player's name, team, and position appear near the bottom. The white horizontal back is framed by a blue line and carries the player's name at the top, followed by biography and statistics. A drawing of a ballplayer in action appears on the left. This set includes Billy Wagner's first team set card.

	MINT	NRMT	EXC
COMPLETE SET (30)	8.00	3.60	1.00

☐ 3433 Tom Czanstkowski
☐ 3434 Donnie Dault
☐ 3435 Mike Diorio
☐ 3436 Mike Grzanich
☐ 3437 Bill Hartnett
☐ 3438 Richard Humphrey
☐ 3439 Tim Kester
☐ 3440 Arquimedes Lugo
☐ 3441 Kendall Rhine
☐ 3442 Troy Schulte
☐ 3443 Kevin Smith
☐ 3444 Josh Spring
☐ 3445 Billy Wagner
☐ 3446 Brett Callan
☐ 3447 Trevor Froschauer
☐ 3448 Nate Peterson
☐ 3449 Marsalis Basey
☐ 3450 Eduardo Cedeno
☐ 3451 Carlos Crispin
☐ 3452 Tim Forkner
☐ 3453 Dan Grapenthien
☐ 3454 Steve Verduzco
☐ 3455 Klint Klaas
☐ 3456 Noel Rodriguez
☐ 3457 John Vindivich
☐ 3458 Chad White
☐ 3459 Ted Wieczorek
☐ 3460 Manny Acta MG
☐ 3461 Ted Slowik CO
☐ 3462 Checklist

1993 Augusta Pirates Classic/Best

This 30-card standard-size set of the 1993 Augusta Pirates, a Class A South Atlantic League affiliate of the Pittsburgh Pirates, features white-bordered posed color player shots on its fronts. A team-color-coded stripe below the photo carries the player's name; another above, his position and team name. On a ghosted team-logo, the white back carries the player's name at the top, followed by biography and statistics. This issue includes the minor league card debuts of Jason Kendall, Danny Clyburn and Trey Beamon.

	MINT	NRMT	EXC
COMPLETE SET (30)	15.00	6.75	1.85

☐ 1 Jason Kendall
☐ 2 Jake Austin
☐ 3 Trey Beamon
☐ 4 Miguel Bonilla
☐ 5 Danny Clyburn
☐ 6 Jay Cranford
☐ 7 Ramon Espinosa
☐ 8 Rico Gholston
☐ 9 G.G. Harris
☐ 10 Ted Klamm
☐ 11 Michel Laplante
☐ 12 Sean Lawrence
☐ 13 Mark Mesewicz
☐ 14 Marc Pisciotta
☐ 15 Kevin Polcovich
☐ 16 Matt Pontbriant
☐ 17 John Salamon
☐ 18 Manuel Santana
☐ 19 Reed Secrist
☐ 20 Jose Sosa
☐ 21 Larry Stahlhoefer
☐ 22 Chuck Tooch
☐ 23 Rich Townsend
☐ 24 Shon Walker
☐ 25 Marc Wilkins
☐ 26 Ramon Zapata
☐ 27 Wayne Garland CO
☐ 28 Rod Lich TR
☐ 29 Title Card
☐ 30 Checklist

1993 Augusta Pirates Fleer/ProCards

This 27-card standard-size set of the 1993 Augusta Pirates, a Class A South Atlantic League affiliate of the Pittsburgh Pirates, features white-bordered posed color player photos on its fronts. The player's name, team, and position appear near the bottom. The white horizontal back is framed by a blue line and carries the player's name at the top, followed by biography and statistics. A drawing of a ballplayer in action appears on the left. This set includes the first minor league team set cards of Jason Kendall, Trey Beamon and Danny Clyburn.

	MINT	NRMT	EXC
COMPLETE SET (27)	15.00	6.75	1.85

☐ 1390 Checklist
☐ 1536 Miguel Bonilla
☐ 1537 Ted Klamm
☐ 1538 Michel LaPlante
☐ 1539 Mark Mesewicz
☐ 1540 Marc Pisciotta
☐ 1541 Matt Pontbriant
☐ 1542 John Salamon
☐ 1543 Manuel Santana
☐ 1544 Jose Sosa
☐ 1545 Rich Townsend
☐ 1546 Marc Wilkins
☐ 1547 Jason Kendall
☐ 1548 Larry Stahlhoefer
☐ 1549 Jake Austin
☐ 1550 Jay Cranford
☐ 1551 Rico Gholston
☐ 1552 G.G. Harris
☐ 1553 Kevin Polcovich
☐ 1554 Reed Secrist
☐ 1555 Chuck Tooch
☐ 1556 Ramon Zapata
☐ 1557 Trey Beamon
☐ 1558 Danny Clyburn
☐ 1559 Ramon Espinosa
☐ 1560 Shon Walker
☐ 1561 Wayne Garland CO

1993 Bakersfield Dodgers Cal League Cards

This issue includes the minor league card debut of Karim Garcia.

	MINT	NRMT	EXC
COMPLETE SET (32)	10.00	4.50	1.25

☐ 1 Mike Moore
☐ 2 Ryan Luzinski
☐ 3 Nelson Castro
☐ 4 Brent Colson
☐ 5 Bubba Costello
☐ 6 Gavin Edmondson
☐ 7 Matt Filson
☐ 8 Jose Garcia
☐ 9 Karim Garcia
☐ 10 Matt Herges
☐ 11 Mike Iglesias
☐ 12 Angel Jaime
☐ 13 Jason Kenady
☐ 14 Jay Kirkpatrick
☐ 15 Ty Lewis
☐ 16 Ed Lund
☐ 17 Jimmy Martin
☐ 18 Jesus Martinez
☐ 19 Sean McKamie
☐ 20 Tory Miran
☐ 21 Willis Otanez
☐ 22 Frank Smith
☐ 23 Carlos Thomas
☐ 24 Burgess Watts
☐ 25 Eric Weaver
☐ 26 Leroy Williams
☐ 27 Chad Zerbe
☐ 28 Rick Dempsey MG
☐ 29 Guy Conti CO
☐ 30 Dino Ebel CO
☐ 31 Bart Dugger TR
☐ 32 Checklist

1993 Batavia Clippers Classic/Best

This 30-card standard-size set of the 1993 Batavia Clippers, a Class A New York-Penn League affiliate of the Philadelphia Phillies, features white-bordered posed color player shots on its fronts. A team-color-coded stripe below the photo carries the player's name; another above, his position and team name. On a ghosted team-logo, the white back carries the player's name at the top, followed by biography and statistics.

	MINT	NRMT	EXC
COMPLETE SET (30)	5.00	2.20	.60

☐ 1 Tom Franek
☐ 2 Pete Agostinelli
☐ 3 Doug Angeli
☐ 4 Brent Bell
☐ 5 Mathew Brainard
☐ 6 Silvio Censale
☐ 7 Tony Costa
☐ 8 Scott Eggleston
☐ 9 Tony Fiore
☐ 10 Jeff Gyselman
☐ 11 Dan Held
☐ 12 Ramon Hernandez
☐ 13 Tommy Irwin
☐ 14 Jeremey Kendall
☐ 15 Kris Kirkland
☐ 16 Joey Madden
☐ 17 Dan McDonald
☐ 18 Shaun McGinn
☐ 19 Jon McMullen
☐ 20 Michael Metheney
☐ 21 Charlton Moore
☐ 22 Neil Murphy
☐ 23 Bruce Petillo
☐ 24 Timothy Pugh
☐ 25 Kevin Sefcik
☐ 26 Tyrone Swan
☐ 27 Michael Thompson
☐ 28 Mike Wood
☐ 29 Alan LeBoeuf MG
☐ 30 Checklist

1993 Batavia Clippers Fleer/ProCards

This 30-card standard-size set of the 1993 Batavia Clippers, a Class A New York-Penn League affiliate of the Philadelphia Phillies, features white-bordered posed color player photos on its fronts. The player's name, team, and position appear near the bottom. The white horizontal back is framed by a blue line and carries the player's name at the top, followed by biography and statistics. A drawing of a ballplayer in action appears on the left.

	MINT	NRMT	EXC
COMPLETE SET (30)	5.00	2.20	.60

☐ 3135 Pete Agostinelli
☐ 3136 Silvio Censale
☐ 3137 Tony Costa
☐ 3138 Scott Eggleston
☐ 3139 Tony Fiore
☐ 3140 Tom Franek
☐ 3141 Tom Irwin
☐ 3142 Kris Kirkland
☐ 3143 Nelson Methenthy
☐ 3144 Tim Pugh
☐ 3145 Tyrone Swan
☐ 3146 Mike Wood
☐ 3147 Jeff Gyselman
☐ 3148 Dan Held
☐ 3149 Neil Murphy

☐ 3150 Bruce Petillo
☐ 3151 Doug Angeli
☐ 3152 Matt Brainard
☐ 3153 Shaun McGinn
☐ 3154 Jon McMullen
☐ 3155 Kevin Sefcik
☐ 3156 Brent Bell
☐ 3157 Ramon Hernandez
☐ 3158 Jeremey Kendall
☐ 3159 Joey Madden
☐ 3160 Dan McDonald
☐ 3161 Charlton Moore
☐ 3162 Mike Thompson
☐ 3163 Al LeBoeuf MG
☐ 3164 Checklist

1993 Bellingham Mariners Classic/Best

This 30-card standard-size set of the 1993 Bellingham Mariners, a Class A Northwest League affiliate of the Seattle Mariners, features white-bordered posed color player shots on its fronts. A team-color-coded stripe below the photo carries the player's name; another above, his position and team name. On a ghosted team-logo, the white back carries the player's name at the top, followed by biography and statistics.

	MINT	NRMT	EXC
COMPLETE SET (30)	5.00	2.20	.60

☐ 1 Mike Collett
☐ 2 Matt Apana
☐ 3 Mike Barger
☐ 4 Joe Henry Berube
☐ 5 Tim Bruce
☐ 6 Antonio Cabrera
☐ 7 Johnny Cardenas
☐ 8 Rafael Carmona
☐ 9 James Clifford
☐ 10 Dean Crow
☐ 11 Brian Doughty
☐ 12 Chad Dunavan
☐ 13 Ryan Franklin
☐ 14 Giomar Guevara
☐ 15 Raul Ibanez
☐ 16 Randy Jorgensen
☐ 17 Matthew Mantei
☐ 18 Eduard Martinez
☐ 19 Roy Miller
☐ 20 Ivan Montane
☐ 21 Manish Patel
☐ 22 Keifer Rackley
☐ 23 Marino Santana
☐ 24 Nestor Serrano
☐ 25 Brian Sosa
☐ 26 Marcus Sturdivant
☐ 27 Greg Theron
☐ 28 John Thompson
☐ 29 Bob Wolcott
☐ 30 The Staff Checklist

1993 Bellingham Mariners Fleer/ProCards

This 30-card standard-size set of the 1993 Bellingham Mariners, a Class A Northwest League affiliate of the Seattle Mariners, features white-bordered posed color player photos on its fronts. The player's name, team, and position appear near the bottom. The white horizontal back is framed by a blue line and carries the player's name at the top, followed by biography and statistics. A drawing of a ballplayer in action appears on the left.

	MINT	NRMT	EXC
COMPLETE SET (30)	5.00	2.20	.60

☐ 3196 Matt Arana
☐ 3197 Tim Bruce
☐ 3198 Rafael Carmona
☐ 3199 Mike Collett
☐ 3200 Dean Crow
☐ 3201 Brian Doughty
☐ 3202 Ryan Franklin
☐ 3203 Tim Harikkala
☐ 3204 Matt Mantei
☐ 3205 Ivan Montane
☐ 3206 Marino Santana
☐ 3207 Brian Sosa
☐ 3208 Greg Theron
☐ 3209 John Thompson
☐ 3210 Bob Wolcott
☐ 3211 Joe Berube
☐ 3212 Johnny Cardenas
☐ 3213 Raul Ibanez
☐ 3214 Antonio Cabera
☐ 3215 James Clifford
☐ 3216 Giomar Guevara
☐ 3217 Randy Jorgensen
☐ 3218 Jaime Martinez
☐ 3219 Roy Miller
☐ 3220 Manny Patel
☐ 3221 Mike Barger
☐ 3222 Chad Dunavan
☐ 3223 Keifer Rackley
☐ 3224 Nestor Serrano
☐ 3225 Marcus Sturdivant
☐ 3226 Checklist

1993 Beloit Brewers Classic/Best

This 30-card standard-size set of the 1993 Beloit Brewers, a Class A Midwest League affiliate of the Milwaukee Brewers, features white-bordered posed color player shots on its fronts. A team-color-coded stripe below the photo carries the player's name; another above, his position and team name. On a ghosted team-logo, the white back carries the player's name at the top, followed by biography and statistics.

	MINT	NRMT	EXC
COMPLETE SET (30)	5.00	2.20	.60

☐ 1 Cameron Aronetz
☐ 2 Donny Blair
☐ 3 Mike Boyzuick
☐ 4 Kirk Demyan
☐ 5 Jeff Droll
☐ 6 Michael Dumas
☐ 7 Kenny Felder
☐ 8 Tom Froning
☐ 9 Brad Gay
☐ 10 Bobby Hughes
☐ 11 Jaosn Imperial
☐ 12 Bobby Jones
☐ 13 Dan Kyslinger
☐ 14 Gabby Martinez
☐ 15 Darryl Meek
☐ 16 Francisco Mendoza
☐ 17 Danny Perez
☐ 18 Scott Richardson
☐ 19 Cecil Rodriques
☐ 20 Jackie Ross
☐ 21 Al Sadler
☐ 22 T.J. Schenbeck
☐ 23 Scott Talanoa
☐ 24 Ryan Thibault
☐ 25 Rafael Torres
☐ 26 Wayne Krenchicki MG
☐ 27 Steve Foucault CO
☐ 28 Bob Mariano CO
☐ 29 Bryan Jaquette TR
☐ 30 Checklist

1993 Beloit Brewers Fleer/ProCards

This 30-card standard-size set of the 1993 Beloit Brewers, a Class A Midwest League affiliate of the Milwaukee Brewers, features white-bordered posed color player photos on its fronts. The player's name, team, and position appear near the bottom. The white horizontal back is framed by a blue line and carries the player's name at the top, followed by biography and statistics. A drawing of a ballplayer in action appears on the left.

	MINT	NRMT	EXC
COMPLETE SET (30)	5.00	2.20	.60

☐ 1700 Cameron Aronetz
☐ 1701 Donny Blair
☐ 1702 Kirk Demyan
☐ 1703 Jeff Droll
☐ 1704 Tom Froning
☐ 1705 Bobby Jones
☐ 1706 Dan Kyslinger
☐ 1707 Darryl Meek
☐ 1708 Al Sadler
☐ 1709 Thomas Sehenbeck
☐ 1710 Ryan Thibault
☐ 1711 Rafael Torres
☐ 1712 Brad Gay
☐ 1713 Brian Hostetler
☐ 1714 Bobby Hughes
☐ 1715 Michael Boyzuick
☐ 1716 Michael Dumas
☐ 1717 Jason Imperial
☐ 1718 Gabby Martinez
☐ 1719 Francisco Mendoza
☐ 1720 Scott Richardson
☐ 1721 Scott Talanoa
☐ 1722 Kenny Felder
☐ 1723 Danny Perez
☐ 1724 Cecil Rodriques
☐ 1725 Jackie Ross
☐ 1726 Wayne Krenchicki MG
☐ 1727 Steve Foucault CO
☐ 1728 Bob Mariano CO
☐ 1729 Checklist

1993 Bend Rockies Classic/Best

This 30-card standard-size set of the 1993 Bend Rockies, a Class A Northwest League affiliate of the Colorado Rockies, features white-bordered posed color player shots on its fronts. A team-color-coded stripe below the photo carries the player's name; another above, his position and team name. On a ghosted team-logo, the white back carries the player's name at the top, followed by biography and statistics. This issue includes the minor league card debut of Neifi Perez.

	MINT	NRMT	EXC
COMPLETE SET (30)	8.00	3.60	1.00

☐ 1 Bryan Rekar
☐ 2 Steve Bernhardt
☐ 3 Greg Boyd
☐ 4 Derrick Calvin
☐ 5 Curt Conley
☐ 6 Carlos Cristopher
☐ 7 Mike Eiffert
☐ 8 John Giudice
☐ 9 Jon Goodrich
☐ 10 Chris Henderson
☐ 11 Mike Higgins
☐ 12 Nate Holdren
☐ 13 Jason Johnson
☐ 14 Terry Jones
☐ 15 Robert Lasbury
☐ 16 Patrick McClinton
☐ 17 Joel Moore
☐ 18 Mario Munoz
☐ 19 Chris Neier
☐ 20 Benjamin Ortman
☐ 21 Neifi Perez
☐ 22 Michael Pineiro
☐ 23 Philip Schneider
☐ 24 Jason Smith
☐ 25 Jeff Sobkoviak
☐ 26 Kevin Wehn
☐ 27 Howie Bedell MG
☐ 28 Bill McGuire CO
☐ 29 Bill Champion CO
☐ 30 Keith Dugger TR Checklist

1993 Bend Rockies Fleer/ProCards

This 30-card standard-size set of the 1993 Bend Rockies, a Class A Northwest League affiliate of the Colorado Rockies, features white-bordered posed color player photos on its fronts. The player's name, team, and position appear near the bottom. The white horizontal back is framed by a blue line and carries the player's name at the top, followed by biography and statistics. A drawing of a ballplayer in action appears on the left. This set includes Neifi Perez first team set card.

	MINT	NRMT	EXC
COMPLETE SET (30)	8.00	3.60	1.00

☐ 3257 Derrick Calvin
☐ 3258 Curt Conley
☐ 3259 Mike Eiffert
☐ 3260 Jon Goodrich
☐ 3261 Chris Henderson
☐ 3262 Jason Johnson
☐ 3263 Bob Lasbury
☐ 3264 Patrick McClinton
☐ 3265 Joel Moore
☐ 3266 Chris Neier
☐ 3267 Bryan Rekar
☐ 3268 Phil Schneider
☐ 3269 Jeff Sobkoviak
☐ 3270 Kevin Wehn
☐ 3271 Mike Higgins
☐ 3272 Michael Pineiro
☐ 3273 Jason Smith
☐ 3274 Steve Bernhardt
☐ 3275 Greg Boyd
☐ 3276 Carlos Cristopher
☐ 3277 Nate Holdren
☐ 3278 Mario Munoz
☐ 3279 Neifi Perez
☐ 3280 John Giudice
☐ 3281 Terry Jones
☐ 3282 Ben Ortman
☐ 3283 Howie Bedell MG
☐ 3284 Bill Champion CO
☐ 3285 Bill McGuire CO
☐ 3286 Checklist

1993 Billings Mustangs Fleer/ProCards

This 30-card standard-size set of the 1993 Billings Mustangs, a Rookie Class Pioneer League affiliate of the Cincinnati Reds, features white-bordered posed color player photos on its fronts. The player's name, team, and position appear near the bottom. The white horizontal back is framed by a blue line and carries the player's name at the top, followed by biography and statistics. A drawing of a ballplayer in action appears on the left. This set includes Pat Watkins' first team set card.

	MINT	NRMT	EXC
COMPLETE SET (30)	6.00	2.70	.75

☐ 3935 Chad Connors
☐ 3936 Todd Etler
☐ 3937 Denny Fussell
☐ 3938 Pete Harvell
☐ 3939 Jon Hebel
☐ 3940 Curt Lyons
☐ 3941 Pete Magre
☐ 3942 David McKenzie
☐ 3943 Mike Moses
☐ 3944 Scott Sullivan
☐ 3945 Brad Tweedlie
☐ 3946 Steve Wilkerson
☐ 3947 Shane Witzel
☐ 3948 Paul Bako
☐ 3949 Justin Towle
☐ 3950 Chad Akers
☐ 3951 Jeff Ashton
☐ 3952 Steve Eddie
☐ 3953 Steve Gann
☐ 3954 Doug Durrwachter
☐ 3955 Eli Robinson
☐ 3956 Chris Sexton
☐ 3957 Jason Baker
☐ 3958 Ray Moon
☐ 3959 Danny Oyas
☐ 3960 Rodney Thomas
☐ 3961 Pat Watkins
☐ 3962 Donnie Scott MG
☐ 3963 Terry Abbott CO
☐ 3964 Checklist

1993 Billings Mustangs Sports Pro

This issue includes the minor league card debut of Pat Watkins.

	MINT	NRMT	EXC
COMPLETE SET (28)	8.00	3.60	1.00

☐ 1 Chad Connors
☐ 2 Chris Sexton
☐ 3 Ray Moon
☐ 4 Justin Towle
☐ 5 Todd Etler
☐ 6 Curt Lyons
☐ 7 Steve Eddle
☐ 8 Danny Oyas
☐ 9 Pete Harvell
☐ 10 Denny Fussell
☐ 11 Eli Robinson
☐ 12 Pat Watkins
☐ 13 Paul Bako
☐ 14 Shane Witzel
☐ 15 Pete Marge
☐ 16 Chad Akers
☐ 17 Scott Sullivan
☐ 18 Steve Gann
☐ 19 Rodney Thomas
☐ 20 Michael Moses
☐ 21 Jason Baker
☐ 22 Jon Hebel
☐ 23 Brad Tweedlie
☐ 24 Steve Wilkerson
☐ 25 David McKenzie
☐ 26 Mark Mann TR
☐ 27 Donnie Scott MG
☐ 28 Terry Abbott CO

1993 Binghamton Mets Fleer/ProCards

This 26-card standard-size set of the 1993 Binghamton Mets, a Class AA Eastern League affiliate of the New York Mets, features white-bordered posed color player photos on its fronts. The player's name, team, and position appear near the bottom. The white horizontal back is framed by a blue line and carries the player's name at the top, followed by biography and statistics. A drawing of a ballplayer in action appears on the left.

	MINT	NRMT	EXC
COMPLETE SET (26)	5.00	2.20	.60

☐ 2326 Juan Castillo
☐ 2327 Chris Dorn
☐ 2328 Todd Douma
☐ 2329 Denny Harriger
☐ 2330 Steve Long
☐ 2331 Andy Reich
☐ 2332 Joe Roa
☐ 2333 Bryan Rogers
☐ 2334 Rusty Silcox
☐ 2335 Pete Walker
☐ 2336 Andy Dziadkowiec
☐ 2337 Javier Gonzalez
☐ 2338 Alan Zinter
☐ 2339 Tom Allison
☐ 2340 Butch Huskey
☐ 2341 Frank Jacobs
☐ 2342 Aaron Ledesma
☐ 2343 David Lowery
☐ 2344 Quilvio Veras
☐ 2345 Chris Butterfield
☐ 2346 Jay Davis
☐ 2347 Ricky Otero
☐ 2348 Tim Sandy
☐ 2349 Steve Swisher MG
☐ 2350 Randy Niemann CO
☐ 2351 Checklist

1993 Birmingham Barons Fleer/ProCards

This 27-card standard-size set of the 1993 Birmingham Barons, a Class AA Southern League affiliate of the Chicago White Sox, features white-bordered posed color player photos on its fronts. The player's name, team, and position appear near the bottom. The white horizontal back is framed by a blue line and carries the player's name at the top, followed by biography and statistics. A drawing of a ballplayer in action appears on the left. This set includes a second year team set card of Ray Durham.

	MINT	NRMT	EXC
COMPLETE SET (27)	6.00	2.70	.75

☐ 1185 James Baldwin
☐ 1186 Frank Campos
☐ 1187 Ramon Manon
☐ 1188 Frank Merigliano
☐ 1189 Mike Mongiello
☐ 1190 Steve Olsen
☐ 1191 Don Perigny
☐ 1192 Jeff Pierce
☐ 1193 Scott Ruffcorn
☐ 1194 Johnny Ruffin
☐ 1195 Clemente Alvarez
☐ 1196 Rogelio Nunez
☐ 1197 Ron Coomer
☐ 1198 Ray Durham
☐ 1199 Giovanni Miranda
☐ 1200 Mike Robertson
☐ 1201 Dennis Walker
☐ 1202 Brandon Wilson
☐ 1203 Kevin Belcher
☐ 1204 Sergio Cairo
☐ 1205 Kinnis Pledger
☐ 1206 Jerry Wolak
☐ 1207 Terry Francona MG
☐ 1208 Mike Barnett CO
☐ 1209 Kirk Champion CO
☐ 1210 Mike Rojas CO
☐ 1211 Checklist

1993 Bluefield Orioles Classic/Best

This 30-card standard-size set of the 1993 Bluefield Orioles, a Rookie Class Appalachian League affiliate of the Baltimore Orioles, features white-bordered posed color player shots on its fronts. A team-color-coded stripe below the photo carries the player's name; another above, his position and team name. On a ghosted team-logo, the white back carries the player's name at the top, followed by biography and statistics.

	MINT	NRMT	EXC
COMPLETE SET (30)	5.00	2.20	.60

☐ 1 Matt Riemer
☐ 2 Bill Asermely
☐ 3 Myles Barnden
☐ 4 Kimera Bartee
☐ 5 Brian Brewer
☐ 6 Brandon Bridgers
☐ 7 Cory Brown
☐ 8 Hector Castaneda
☐ 9 Carlos Chavez
☐ 10 Howie Clark
☐ 11 Joey Dawley
☐ 12 Andy Etchebarren
☐ 13 Jim Foster
☐ 14 P.J. Jones
☐ 15 Shawn Knott
☐ 16 Bryan Link
☐ 17 Calvin Maduro
☐ 18 Lincoln Martin
☐ 19 Billy Percibel
☐ 20 Mike Porter
☐ 21 Kenny Reed
☐ 22 Ron Shankle
☐ 23 Mike Trimarco
☐ 24 Shane Ziegler
☐ 25 Len Johnston Co
☐ 26 Jeff Morris CO
☐ 27 Frank Neville TR
☐ 28 Brien Taylor
Classic Best
Advertisement
☐ 29 Title Card
☐ 30 Checklist

1993 Bluefield Orioles Fleer/ProCards

This 27-card standard-size set of the 1993 Bluefield Orioles, a Rookie Class Appalachian League affiliate of the Baltimore Orioles, features white-bordered posed color player photos on its fronts. The player's name, team, and position appear near the bottom. The white horizontal back is framed by a blue line and carries the player's name at the top, followed by biography and statistics. A drawing of a ballplayer in action appears on the left.

	MINT	NRMT	EXC
COMPLETE SET (27)	5.00	2.20	.60

☐ 4115 Rick Barnett
☐ 4116 Brian Brewer
☐ 4117 Cory Brown
☐ 4118 Carlos Chavez
☐ 4119 Joe Dawley
☐ 4120 Ron Kitchen
☐ 4121 Calvin Maduro
☐ 4122 William Percibel
☐ 4123 Mike Porter
☐ 4124 Bob Rinderknecht
☐ 4125 Mike Trimarco
☐ 4126 Shane Ziegler
☐ 4127 Hector Castaneda
☐ 4128 Jim Foster
☐ 4129 Ken Reed
☐ 4130 Myles Barnden
☐ 4131 Howie Clark
☐ 4132 Bryan Link
☐ 4133 Lincoln Martin
☐ 4134 Matt Riemer
☐ 4135 Ron Shankle
☐ 4136 Bill Asermely
☐ 4137 Kimera Bartee
☐ 4138 Brandon Bridgers
☐ 4139 Wes Hawkins
☐ 4140 Jarvis White
☐ 4141 Checklist

1993 Boise Hawks Classic/Best

This 30-card standard-size set of the 1993 Boise Hawks, a Class A Northwest League affiliate of the California Angels, features white-bordered posed color player shots on its fronts. A team-color-coded stripe below the photo carries the player's name; another above, his position and team name. On a ghosted team-logo, the white back carries the player's name at the top, followed by biography and statistics. This issue includes the minor league card debut of Todd Greene.

	MINT	NRMT	EXC
COMPLETE SET (30)	8.00	3.60	1.00

☐ 1 Todd Greene
☐ 2 Lyall Barwick
☐ 3 Bill Blanchette
☐ 4 Willard Brown
☐ 5 Jamie Burke
☐ 6 Brian Cavalli
☐ 7 Freddie Diaz
☐ 8 John Donati
☐ 9 Derrin Doty
☐ 10 Geoff Edsell
☐ 11 Brian Fontes
☐ 12 Geoff Grenert
☐ 13 Bryan Harris
☐ 14 Aaron Iatarola
☐ 15 Mike Kane
☐ 16 David Kennedy
☐ 17 Bobby Kim
☐ 18 Hank King
☐ 19 Johnny Lloyd
☐ 20 Matt Myers
☐ 21 John Nedeau
☐ 22 Aaron Puffer
☐ 23 Rudolf Razjigaev
☐ 24 Shawn Slade
☐ 25 Wil Speakman
☐ 26 Julian Vizcaino
☐ 27 Tom Kotchman MG
☐ 28 Orv Franchuk CO
☐ 29 Zeke Zimmerman CO
☐ 30 Alan Russell TR
Checklist

1993 Boise Hawks Fleer/ProCards

This 31-card standard-size set of the 1993 Boise Hawks, a Class A Northwest League affiliate of the California Angels, features white-bordered posed color player photos on its fronts. The player's name, team, and position appear near the bottom. The white horizontal back is framed by a blue line and carries the player's name at the top, followed by biography and statistics. A drawing of a ballplayer in action appears on the left. This set includes Todd Greene's first team set card.

	MINT	NRMT	EXC
COMPLETE SET (31)	8.00	3.60	1.00

☐ 3904 Bill Blanchette
☐ 3905 Willard Brown
☐ 3906 Jamie Burke
☐ 3907 Geoff Edsell
☐ 3908 Brian Fontes
☐ 3909 Geoff Grenert
☐ 3910 Bryan Harris
☐ 3911 Mike Kane
☐ 3912 Johnny Lloyd
☐ 3913 Matt Myers
☐ 3914 John Nedeau
☐ 3915 Aaron Puffer
☐ 3916 Rodolf Razjigaev
☐ 3917 Andy Runzi
☐ 3918 Shawn Slade
☐ 3919 Brian Cavalli
☐ 3920 Will Speakman
☐ 3921 Freddie Diaz
☐ 3922 John Donati
☐ 3923 David Kennedy
☐ 3924 Hank King
☐ 3925 Julian Vizcaino
☐ 3926 Lyall Barwick
☐ 3927 Derrin Doty
☐ 3928 Todd Greene
☐ 3929 Aaron Iatarola
☐ 3930 Bobby Kim
☐ 3931 Mark Simmons
☐ 3932 Zeke Zimmerman CO
☐ 3933 Orv Franchuk CO
☐ 3934 Checklist

1993 Bowie Baysox Fleer/ProCards

This 24-card standard-size set of the 1993 Bowie Baysox, a Class AA Eastern League affiliate of the Baltimore Orioles, features white-bordered posed color player photos on its fronts. The player's name, team, and position appear near the bottom. The white horizontal back is framed by a blue line and carries the player's name at the top, followed by biography and statistics. A drawing of a ballplayer in action appears on the left. This set includes Jeffrey Hammonds' first team set card.

	MINT	NRMT	EXC
COMPLETE SET (24)	7.00	3.10	.85

☐ 2182 Rafael Chaves
☐ 2183 Jim Dedrick
☐ 2184 Terry Farrar
☐ 2185 Jose Mercedes
☐ 2186 Chuck Ricci
☐ 2187 Kevin Ryan
☐ 2188 Jason Satre
☐ 2189 Erik Schullstrom
☐ 2190 Tommy Taylor
☐ 2191 Jimmy Roso
☐ 2192 Gregg Zaun
☐ 2193 Edgar Alfonzo
☐ 2194 Sam Ferretti
☐ 2195 Tim Holland
☐ 2196 T.R. Lewis
☐ 2197 Brent Miller
☐ 2198 Brad Tyler
☐ 2199 Stanton Cameron
☐ 2200 Jeffrey Hammonds
☐ 2201 Kyle Washington
☐ 2202 Jim Wawruck
☐ 2203 Don Buford MG
☐ 2204 John O'Donoghue CO
☐ 2205 Checklist

1993 Bristol Tigers Classic/Best

This 30-card standard-size set of the 1993 Bristol Tigers, a Rookie Class Appalachian League affiliate of the Detroit Tigers, features white-bordered posed color player shots on its fronts. A team-color-coded stripe below the photo carries the player's name; another above, his position and team name. On a ghosted team-logo, the white back carries the player's name at the top, followed by biography and statistics.

	MINT	NRMT	EXC
COMPLETE SET (30)	5.00	2.20	.60

☐ 1 Cameron Smith
☐ 2 Moises Ayala
☐ 3 Jason Bass
☐ 4 Alvin Brown
☐ 5 Frank Catalanotto
☐ 6 Drew Christmon
☐ 7 Edward Cordero
☐ 8 Chris Facione
☐ 9 Luis Garcia
☐ 10 Ismael Guzman
☐ 11 Jason Hamilton
☐ 12 Bobby Jones
☐ 13 Chris Keenan
☐ 14 Lonny Landry
☐ 15 Dalvis Martinez
☐ 16 Scott Norman
☐ 17 Willie Roberts
☐ 18 Jose Sanjurjo
☐ 19 Jose Severino
☐ 20 Matt Skrmetta
☐ 21 John Timko
☐ 22 Craig Tupper
☐ 23 Kenny Valdez
☐ 24 Eric Weber
☐ 25 Mike Wilson
☐ 26 Chris Wyrick
☐ 27 Ruben Amaro MG
☐ 28 Basilio Cabrera CO
☐ 29 Jim Van Scoyoc CO
☐ 30 Checklist

1993 Bristol Tigers Fleer/ProCards

This 30-card standard-size set of the 1993 Bristol Tigers, a Rookie Class Appalachian League affiliate of the Detroit Tigers, features white-bordered posed color player photos on its fronts. The player's name, team, and position appear near the bottom. The white horizontal back is framed by a blue line and carries the player's name at the top, followed by biography and statistics. A drawing of a ballplayer in action appears on the left.

	MINT	NRMT	EXC
COMPLETE SET (30)	5.00	2.20	.60

☐ 3639 Candido Brazoban
☐ 3640 Alvin Brown
☐ 3641 Tony Fuduric
☐ 3642 Yasutara Fursato
☐ 3643 Greg Granger
☐ 3644 Will Hunt
☐ 3645 Ryan Meredith
☐ 3646 Shinya Nakagawa
☐ 3647 Steve Nowak
☐ 3648 Adam Rodriguez
☐ 3649 Shawn Wooten
☐ 3650 Edward Cordero
☐ 3651 Bryan Corey
☐ 3652 Luis Garcia
☐ 3653 Jason Hamilton
☐ 3654 Dalvis Martinez
☐ 3655 Kenny Valdez
☐ 3656 Chris Wyrick
☐ 3657 Frank Catalanotto
☐ 3658 Jason Bass
☐ 3659 Drew Christmon
☐ 3660 Chris Facione
☐ 3661 Ismael Guzman
☐ 3662 Bobby Jones
☐ 3663 Chris Keenan
☐ 3664 Lonny Landry
☐ 3665 Jose Sanjurjo
☐ 3666 Ruben Amaro MG
☐ 3667 Shigeyuki
Takahaski CO
☐ 3668 Checklist

1993 Buffalo Bisons Fleer/ProCards

This 27-card standard-size set of the 1993 Buffalo Bisons, a Class AAA American Association affiliate of the Pittsburgh Pirates, features white-bordered posed color player photos on its fronts. The player's name, team, and position appear near the bottom. The white horizontal back is framed by a blue line and carries the player's name at the top, followed by biography and statistics. A drawing of a ballplayer in action appears on the left.

	MINT	NRMT	EXC
COMPLETE SET (27)	5.00	2.20	.60

☐ 508 Brett Backlund
☐ 509 Victor Cole
☐ 510 Mike Dalton
☐ 511 Daryl Irvine
☐ 512 Joel Johnston
☐ 513 Tony Menendez
☐ 514 Mark Petkovsek
☐ 515 Rich Robertson
☐ 516 Brian Shouse
☐ 517 Roy Smith
☐ 518 Jim Tracy
☐ 519 Mike Zimmerman
☐ 520 Jerry Goff
☐ 521 Mandy Romero
☐ 522 Mike Bell
☐ 523 Gary Cooper
☐ 524 Russ Morman
☐ 525 Omer Munoz
☐ 526 Dave Rohde
☐ 527 Jose Sandoval
☐ 528 Ben Shelton
☐ 529 Scott Bullett
☐ 530 William Pennyfeather
☐ 531 Andy Tomberlin
☐ 532 Glenn Wilson
☐ 533 Tom Dettore CO
☐ 534 Checklist

1993 Burlington Bees Classic/Best

This 30-card standard-size set of the 1993 Burlington Bees, a Class A Midwest League affiliate of the Montreal Expos, features white-bordered posed color player shots on its fronts. A team-color-coded stripe below the photo carries the player's name; another above, his position and team name. The white back carries the player's name at the top, followed by biography and statistics. This set includes Jose Vidro's first team set card.

	MINT	NRMT	EXC
COMPLETE SET (30)	6.00	2.70	.75

☐ 1 Yamil Benitez
☐ 2 Isreal Alcantara
☐ 3 Ivan Arteaga
☐ 4 Jolbert Cabrera
☐ 5 Rick Clelland
☐ 6 Fernando DaSilva
☐ 7 Tom Doyle
☐ 8 David Eggert
☐ 9 Antonio Grissom
☐ 10 Chris Hmielewski

☐ 11 Jeff Hostetler
☐ 12 Gary Hymel
☐ 13 Shane McCubbin
☐ 14 Doug O'Neill
☐ 15 Javier Pages
☐ 16 Darrin Paxton
☐ 17 Carlos Perez
☐ 18 Tom Phelps
☐ 19 Scott Pisciotta
☐ 20 Corey Powell
☐ 21 Alberto Reyes
☐ 22 Matt Rundels
☐ 23 Jim Rushworth
☐ 24 Ugueth Urbina
☐ 25 Jose Vidro
☐ 26 Lorenzo Bundy MG
☐ 27 Pete Dalena CO
☐ 28 Jeff Fischer CO
☐ 29 Alex Ochoa TR
☐ 30 Checklist

1993 Burlington Bees Fleer/ProCards

This 28-card standard-size set of the 1993 Burlington Bees, a Class A Midwest League affiliate of the Montreal Expos, features white-bordered posed color player photos on its fronts. The player's name, team, and position appear near the bottom. The white horizontal back is framed by a blue line and carries the player's name at the top, followed by biography and statistics. A drawing of a ballplayer in action appears on the left. This issue includes the minor league card debut of Jose Vidro.

	MINT	NRMT	EXC
COMPLETE SET (28)	6.00	2.70	.75

☐ 148 Ivan Arteaga
☐ 149 Rick Clelland
☐ 150 Fernando DaSilva
☐ 151 Dave Eggert
☐ 152 Jeff Hostetler
☐ 153 Darrin Paxton
☐ 154 Carlos Perez
☐ 155 Tom Phelps
☐ 156 Scott Pisciotta
☐ 157 Alberto Reyes
☐ 158 Jim Rushworth
☐ 159 Ugueth Urbina
☐ 160 Gary Hymel
☐ 161 Shane McCubbin
☐ 162 Javier Pages
☐ 163 Isreal Alcantara
☐ 164 Jolbert Cabrera
☐ 165 Tom Doyle
☐ 166 Chris Hmielewski
☐ 167 Matt Rundels
☐ 168 Jose Vidro
☐ 169 Yamil Benitez
☐ 170 Antonio Grissom
☐ 171 Doug O'Neill
☐ 172 Corey Powell
☐ 173 Lorenzo Bundy MG
☐ 174 Jeff Fischer CO
☐ 175 Checklist

1993 Burlington Indians Classic/Best

This 30-card standard-size set of the 1993 Burlington Indians, a Rookie Class Appalachian League affiliate of the Cleveland Indians, features white-bordered posed color player shots on its fronts. A team-color-coded stripe below the photo carries the player's name; another above, his position and team name. On a ghosted team-logo, the white back carries the player's name at the top, followed by biography and statistics. This issue includes the minor league card debuts of Alex Ramirez and Richie Sexson.

	MINT	NRMT	EXC
COMPLETE SET (30)	10.00	4.50	1.25

☐ 1 Matt Hobbie
☐ 2 Jesus Azuaje
☐ 3 Darnell Batiste
☐ 4 Todd Betts
☐ 5 Daniel Brabant
☐ 6 Camp Campbell
☐ 7 Mack Chambers
☐ 8 Ronnie Coleman
☐ 9 Maximo De La Rosa
☐ 10 Einar Diaz
☐ 11 Kevin Dinnen
☐ 12 Derrick Hritz
☐ 13 Todd Johnson
☐ 14 Steven Kline
☐ 15 Richard Lemons
☐ 16 Damian Leyva
☐ 17 Jason Mackey
☐ 18 Johnny Martinez
☐ 19 Michael Moyle
☐ 20 Brett Palmer
☐ 21 Alex Ramirez
☐ 22 Richard Ramirez
☐ 23 Cesar Ramos
☐ 24 Richie Sexson
☐ 25 Leroy Thompson
☐ 26 Eric White
☐ 27 Norman Williams
☐ 28 Brian Wisler
☐ 29 Jon Zubiri
☐ 30 James Gabella MG Checklist

1993 Burlington Indians Fleer/ProCards

This 31-card standard-size set of the 1993 Burlington Indians, a Rookie Class Appalachian League affiliate of the Cleveland Indians, features white-bordered posed color player photos on its fronts. The player's name, team, and position appear near the bottom. The white horizontal back is framed by a blue line and carries the player's name at the top, followed by biography and statistics. A drawing of a ballplayer in action appears on the left. This set includes the first team set cards of Richie Sexson and Alex Ramirez.

	MINT	NRMT	EXC
COMPLETE SET (31)	10.00	4.50	1.25

☐ 3287 Dan Brabanmt
☐ 3288 Camp Campbell
☐ 3289 Maximo DeLaRosa
☐ 3290 Kevin Dinnen
☐ 3291 Derrick Hritz
☐ 3292 Steve Kline
☐ 3293 Damian Leyva
☐ 3294 Jason Mackey
☐ 3295 Johnny Martinez
☐ 3296 Brett Palmer
☐ 3297 Cesar Ramos
☐ 3298 Brian Wisler
☐ 3299 Jon Zubiri
☐ 3300 Einar Diar
☐ 3301 Todd Johnson
☐ 3302 Mike Moyle
☐ 3303 Jesus Azuaje
☐ 3304 Darnell Batiste
☐ 3305 Todd Betts
☐ 3306 Mack Chambers
☐ 3307 Richard Ramirez
☐ 3308 Richie Sexson
☐ 3309 Eric White
☐ 3310 Ronnie Coleman
☐ 3311 Matt Hobbie
☐ 3312 Rich Lemons
☐ 3313 Alex Ramirez
☐ 3314 Leroy Thompson
☐ 3315 Norman Williams
☐ 3316 Jim Gabella MG
☐ 3317 Checklist

1993 Butte Copper Kings Sports Pro

	MINT	NRMT	EXC
COMPLETE SET (24)	6.00	2.70	.75

☐ 1 Dom Gatti
☐ 2 Jason Sievers
☐ 3 Tiger King
☐ 4 Chris Starr
☐ 5 Jeff Derosa
☐ 6 Shane McCubbin
☐ 7 John Mahalik
☐ 8 Matt Huff
☐ 9 Steve Cook
☐ 10 Kacy Hendricks
☐ 11 Ben Week
☐ 12 Chris Kelley
☐ 13 Marty Watson
☐ 14 John Tomasello
☐ 15 Rod Holland
☐ 16 Jeff Carew
☐ 17 Craig Morrill
☐ 18 Jason Bobb
☐ 19 Reggie Ignash
☐ 20 Clint Minear
☐ 21 Jon Pitts
☐ 22 John Shelby MG
☐ 23 Billy Gardner CO
☐ 24 Tim Conroy CO

1993 Calgary Cannons Fleer/ProCards

This 29-card standard-size set of the 1993 Calgary Cannons, a Class AAA Pacific Coast League affiliate of the Seattle Mariners, features white-bordered posed color player photos on its fronts. The player's name, team, and position appear near the bottom. The white horizontal back is framed by a blue line and carries the player's name at the top, followed by biography and statistics. A drawing of a ballplayer in action appears on the left.

	MINT	NRMT	EXC
COMPLETE SET (29)	5.00	2.20	.60

☐ 1156 Shawn Barton
☐ 1157 Kevin Coffman
☐ 1158 Jim Converse
☐ 1159 Mark Czarkowski
☐ 1160 Eric Gunderson
☐ 1161 Brad Holman
☐ 1162 Troy Kent
☐ 1163 Lance McCullers
☐ 1164 Rob Parkins
☐ 1165 Dennis Powell
☐ 1166 Mike Remlinger
☐ 1167 Mike Walker
☐ 1168 Brian Deak
☐ 1169 Bert Heffernan
☐ 1170 Chris Howard
☐ 1171 Greg Litton
☐ 1172 Anthony Manahan
☐ 1173 Greg Pirkl
☐ 1174 Jack Smith
☐ 1175 Brian Turang
☐ 1176 Shane Turner
☐ 1177 Dann Howitt
☐ 1178 Carmelo Martinez
☐ 1179 Tow Maynard
☐ 1180 Aubrey Waggoner
☐ 1181 Keith Bodie MG
☐ 1182 Dave Brundage CO
☐ 1183 Ross Grimsley CO
☐ 1184 Checklist

1993 Canton-Akron Indians Fleer/ProCards

This 26-card standard-size set of the 1993 Canton-Akron Indians, a Class AA Eastern League affiliate of the Cleveland Indians, features white-bordered posed color player photos on its fronts. The player's name, team, and position appear near the bottom. The white horizontal back is framed by a blue line and carries the player's name at the top, followed by biography and statistics. A drawing of a ballplayer in action appears on the left. This set includes a third year team set card of Manny Ramirez.

	MINT	NRMT	EXC
COMPLETE SET (26)	18.00	8.00	2.20

☐ 2830 Paul Abbott
☐ 2831 Chad Allen
☐ 2832 Shawn Bryant
☐ 2833 Apolinar Garcia
☐ 2834 Mike Gardella
☐ 2835 Albie Lopez
☐ 2836 Greg McCarthy
☐ 2837 Roberto Rivera
☐ 2838 Paul Shuey
☐ 2839 Mike Soper
☐ 2840 Eric Stone
☐ 2841 Joe Turek
☐ 2842 Ryan Martindale
☐ 2843 Carlos Mota
☐ 2844 David Bell
☐ 2845 Miguel Flores
☐ 2846 Luis Lopez
☐ 2847 Rouglas Odor
☐ 2848 Brian Giles
☐ 2849 Manny Ramirez
☐ 2850 Omar Ramirez
☐ 2851 Tracy Sanders
☐ 2852 Brian Graham MG
☐ 2853 Rick Colbert CO
☐ 2854 Ken Rowe CO
☐ 2855 Checklist

1993 Capital City Bombers Classic/Best

This 30-card standard-size set of the 1993 Capital City Bombers, a Class A South Atlantic League affiliate of the New York Mets, features white-bordered posed color player shots on its fronts. A team-color-coded stripe below the photo carries the player's name; another above, his position and team name. On a ghosted team-logo, the white back carries the player's name at the top, followed by biography and statistics.

	MINT	NRMT	EXC
COMPLETE SET (30)	5.00	2.20	.60

☐ 1 Al Shirley
☐ 2 Andy Beckerman
☐ 3 Craig Bullock
☐ 4 Tom Engle
☐ 5 Joe Flores
☐ 6 Guillermo Garcia
☐ 7 Erik Hiljus
☐ 8 Mark Hokanson
☐ 9 Jeff Kiraly
☐ 10 Marc Kroon
☐ 11 Steve Lyons
☐ 12 Jacen Martinez
☐ 13 Danilo Mompres
☐ 14 Juan Moreno
☐ 15 Jared Osentowski
☐ 16 Mike Patrizi
☐ 17 Joe Petcka
☐ 18 Eric Reichenbach
☐ 19 Dwight Robinson
☐ 20 Chris Shanahan
☐ 21 Greg Stark
☐ 22 Tony Tijerina
☐ 23 Donnie White
☐ 24 Mark Wipf
☐ 25 Ron Washington MG
☐ 26 David Jorn CO
☐ 27 Michael Herbst TR
☐ 28 Brien Taylor Classic Best Advertisement
☐ 29 Title Card
☐ 30 Checklist

1993 Capital City Bombers Fleer/ProCards

This 26-card standard-size set of the 1993 Capital City Bombers, a Class A South Atlantic League affiliate of the New York Mets, features white-bordered posed color player photos on its fronts. The player's name, team, and position appear near the bottom. The white horizontal back is framed by a blue line and carries the player's name at the top, followed by biography and statistics. A drawing of a ballplayer in action appears on the left.

	MINT	NRMT	EXC
COMPLETE SET (26)	5.00	2.20	.60

☐ 451 Andy Beckerman
☐ 452 Craig Bullock
☐ 453 Tom Engle
☐ 454 Erik Hijus
☐ 455 Mark Hokanson
☐ 456 Marc Kroon
☐ 457 Steve Lyons
☐ 458 Joe Petcka
☐ 459 Eric Reichenbach
☐ 460 Chris Shanahan
☐ 461 Greg Stark
☐ 462 Gullermo Garcia
☐ 463 Mike Patrizi
☐ 464 Tony Tijerina
☐ 465 Jose Flores
☐ 466 Jeff Kiraly
☐ 467 Jacen Martinez
☐ 468 Danilo Mompres
☐ 469 Jared Osentowski
☐ 470 Dwight Robinson
☐ 471 Juan Moreno
☐ 472 Al Shirley
☐ 473 Demond Smith
☐ 474 Don White
☐ 475 Mark Wipf
☐ 476 Checklist

1993 Carolina League All-Stars Fleer/ProCards

	MINT	NRMT	EXC
COMPLETE SET (52)	12.00	5.50	1.50

☐ 1 Rick Forney
☐ 2 Curtis Goodwin
☐ 3 Scott McClain
☐ 4 Alex Ochoa
☐ 5 Joel Bennett
☐ 6 Randy Brown
☐ 7 Doug Hecker
☐ 8 Rob Henkel
☐ 9 Bob Juday
☐ 10 Jose Malave
☐ 11 Raul Gonzalez
☐ 12 Brian Harrison
☐ 13 Ron Johnson
☐ 14 Gary Lance
☐ 15 Jon Lieber
☐ 16 Jeff Smith
☐ 17 Chad Strickland
☐ 18 Robert Toth
☐ 19 Matt Dunbar
☐ 20 Greg Erickson
☐ 21 Carlton Fleming
☐ 22 Ron Frazier
☐ 23 Jorge Posada
☐ 24 Tate Seefried
☐ 25 Juan Andujar
☐ 26 Greg Booker
☐ 27 John Cotton
☐ 28 Dan Devoe
☐ 29 Ian Doyle
☐ 30 Jason Fronio
☐ 31 Dave Keller
☐ 32 Pat Maxwell
☐ 33 Dan Norman
☐ 34 Julian Tavarez
☐ 35 Joe Ayrault
☐ 36 Dirk Blair
☐ 37 Anthony Graffagnino
☐ 38 Vince Moore
☐ 39 Dominic Therrien
☐ 40 Tim Belk
☐ 41 John Hrusovsky
☐ 42 Motorboat Jones
☐ 43 Cleveland Ladell
☐ 44 Chad Mottola
☐ 45 Ken Bonifay
☐ 46 Mike Brown
☐ 47 Jason Christiansen
☐ 48 Mariano DeLosSantos
☐ 49 Angelo Encarnacion

□ 50 Jeff McCurry
□ 51 Tony Womack
□ 52 Checklist

1993 Carolina Mudcats Fleer/ProCards

This 30-card standard-size set of the 1993 Carolina Mudcats, a Class AA Southern League affiliate of the Pittsburgh Pirates, features white-bordered posed color player photos on its fronts. The player's name, team, and position appear near the bottom. The white horizontal back is framed by a blue line and carries the player's name at the top, followed by biography and statistics. A drawing of a ballplayer in action appears on the left.

	MINT	NRMT	EXC
COMPLETE SET (30)	5.00	2.20	.60

□ 2044 Blaine Beatty
□ 2045 Jose Cecena
□ 2046 Alex Garza
□ 2047 Lee Hancock
□ 2048 Doug Harrah
□ 2049 John Hope
□ 2050 Bobby Hunter
□ 2051 Dan Jones
□ 2052 Eric Parkinson
□ 2053 Dennis Tafoya
□ 2054 Freddie Toliver
□ 2055 Rick White
□ 2056 Jeff Banister
□ 2057 Tim Edge
□ 2058 Keith Osik
□ 2059 Rich Aude
□ 2060 Tony Beasley
□ 2061 Mark Johnson
□ 2062 Jim Krevokuch
□ 2063 Tim Leiper
□ 2064 Bruce Schreiber
□ 2065 Joe Sondrini
□ 2066 Midre Cummings
□ 2067 Alberto DeLosSantos
□ 2068 Tom Green
□ 2069 Daryl Ratliff
□ 2070 Keith Thomas
□ 2071 Joe Lonnett CO
□ 2072 Spin Williams CO
□ 2073 Checklist

1993 Carolina Mudcats Team Issue

	MINT	NRMT	EXC
COMPLETE SET (24)	6.00	2.70	.75

□ 1 Timothy Edge
□ 2 Keith Osik
□ 3 Richard Aude
□ 4 Anthony Beasley
□ 5 Bruce Schreiber
□ 6 Keith Thomas
□ 7 Alejandro Garza
□ 8 Eric Parkinson
□ 9 Daniel Jones
□ 10 Doug Harrah
□ 11 John Hope
□ 12 Blaine Beatty
□ 13 Dennis Tofoya
□ 14 Tom Green
□ 15 Jose Cecena
□ 16 Daryl Ratliff
□ 17 Mark Johnson
□ 18 James Krevokuch
□ 19 Lee Hancock
□ 20 Bobby Hunter
□ 21 Freddie Lee Toliver
□ 22 Midre Cummings
□ 23 Timothy Leiper
□ 24 Alberto de Los Santos

1993 Cedar Rapids Kernels Classic/Best

This 30-card standard-size set of the 1993 Cedar Rapids Kernels, a Class A Midwest League affiliate of the California Angels, features white-bordered posed color player shots on its fronts. A team-color-coded stripe below the photo carries the player's name; another above, his position and team name. On a ghosted team-logo, the white back carries the player's name at the top, followed by biography and statistics.

	MINT	NRMT	EXC
COMPLETE SET (30)	5.00	2.20	.60

□ 1 Clifton Garrett
□ 2 Antonio Castro
□ 3 Tony Chavez
□ 4 Lino Connell
□ 5 Morisse Daniels
□ 6 Miguel Fermin
□ 7 Brian Guzik
□ 8 Joseph Hardwick
□ 9 Larry Hingle
□ 10 Mickey Kerns
□ 11 David Kessler
□ 12 Dave Marcon
□ 13 Brandon Markiewicz
□ 14 Dallas Rinehart
□ 15 Jeff Schmidt
□ 16 Kyle Sebach
□ 17 Billy Simas
□ 18 Mark Simmons
□ 19 Chris Smith
□ 20 José Stela
□ 21 Robert Tucker
□ 22 Max Valencia
□ 23 Steve White
□ 24 Brian Williard
□ 25 Michael Wolff
□ 26 Mitch Seoane MG
□ 27 Matt Hyde CO
□ 28 Joe Georger CO
□ 29 Douglas Baker TR
□ 30 Ronald Plein
Checklist

1993 Cedar Rapids Kernels Fleer/ProCards

This 28-card standard-size set of the 1993 Cedar Rapids Kernels, a Class A Midwest League affiliate of the California Angels, features white-bordered posed color player photos on its fronts. The player's name, team, and position appear near the bottom. The white horizontal back is framed by a blue line and carries the player's name at the top, followed by biography and statistics. A drawing of a ballplayer in action appears on the left.

	MINT	NRMT	EXC
COMPLETE SET (28)	5.00	2.20	.60

□ 1730 Tony Chavez
□ 1731 Miguel Fermin
□ 1732 Larry Hingle
□ 1733 Dave Marcon
□ 1734 Jeff Schmidt
□ 1735 Kyle Sebach
□ 1736 Billy Simas
□ 1737 Max Valencia
□ 1738 Rod Van Dyke
□ 1739 Steve White
□ 1740 Brian Williard
□ 1741 Chris Hirsch
□ 1742 David Kessler
□ 1743 Robert Tucker
□ 1744 Antonio Castro
□ 1745 Lino Connell
□ 1746 Brian Guzik
□ 1747 Brandon Markiewicz
□ 1748 Mark Simmons
□ 1749 Chris Smith
□ 1750 Morisse Daniels
□ 1751 Joseph Hardwick
□ 1752 Mickey Kerns
□ 1753 Michael Wolff
□ 1754 Mitch Seoane MG
□ 1755 Joe Georger CO
□ 1756 Matt Hyde CO
□ 1757 Checklist

1993 Central Valley Rockies Classic/Best

This 30-card standard-size set of the 1993 Central Valley Rockies, a Class A California League affiliate of the Colorado Rockies, features white-bordered posed color player shots on its fronts. A team-color-coded stripe below the photo carries the player's name; another above, his position and team name. On a ghosted team-logo, the white back carries the player's name at the top, followed by biography and statistics.

	MINT	NRMT	EXC
COMPLETE SET (30)	5.00	2.20	.60

□ 1 Mark Thompson
□ 2 Juan Acevedo
□ 3 Garvin Alston
□ 4 Roger Bailey
□ 5 John Burke
□ 6 Mike Case
□ 7 Craig Counsell
□ 8 Angel Echevarria
□ 9 Mike Eiffert
□ 10 Mike Ericson
□ 11 Mauricio Gonzalez
□ 12 Mike Grimes
□ 13 Jim Hovey
□ 14 Jason Hutchins
□ 15 Mike Kotarski
□ 16 Keith Krenke
□ 17 Darryl Martin
□ 18 Quinton McCracken
□ 19 Marcus Moore
□ 20 Mike Oakland
□ 21 Will Scalzitti
□ 22 Tom Schmidt
□ 23 Mark Strittmatter
□ 24 Ryan Turner
□ 25 Mark Voisard
□ 26 Paul Zuvella MG
□ 27 Jack Lamabe CO
□ 28 Bili Borowski TR
□ 29 Title Card
□ 30 Checklist

1993 Central Valley Rockies Fleer/ProCards

This 29-card standard-size set of the 1993 Central Valley Rockies, a Class A California League affiliate of the Colorado Rockies, features white-bordered posed color player photos on its fronts. The player's name, team, and position appear near the bottom. The white horizontal back is framed by a blue line and carries the player's name at the top, followed by biography and statistics. A drawing of a ballplayer in action appears on the left.

	MINT	NRMT	EXC
COMPLETE SET (29)	5.00	2.20	.60

□ 2883 Garvin Alston
□ 2884 Roger Bailey
□ 2885 John Burke
□ 2886 Mike Eiffert
□ 2887 Mike Ericson
□ 2888 Mike Grimes
□ 2889 Jim Hovey
□ 2890 Jason Hutchins
□ 2891 Mike Kotarski
□ 2892 Marcus Moore
□ 2893 Mark Thompson
□ 2894 Mark Voisard
□ 2895 Will Scalzitti
□ 2896 Mark Strittmatter
□ 2897 Craig Counsell
□ 2898 Mauricio Gonzalez
□ 2899 Quinton McCracken
□ 2900 Mike Oakland
□ 2901 LaMarr Rogers
□ 2902 Tom Schmidt
□ 2903 Mike Case
□ 2904 Angel Echevarria
□ 2905 Kieth Krenke
□ 2906 Darryl Martin
□ 2907 Ryan Turner
□ 2908 Paul Zuvella MG
□ 2909 P.J. Carey CO
□ 2910 Jack Lamabe CO
□ 2911 Checklist

1993 Charleston Rainbows Classic/Best

This 30-card standard-size set of the 1993 Charleston Rainbows, a Class A South Atlantic League affiliate of the Texas Rangers, features white-bordered posed color player shots on its fronts. A team-color-coded stripe below the photo carries the player's name; another above, his position and team name. On a ghosted team-logo, the white back carries the player's name at the top, followed by biography and statistics.

	MINT	NRMT	EXC
COMPLETE SET (30)	5.00	2.20	.60

□ 1 Scott Eyre
□ 2 Mike Anderson
□ 3 Jamie Bethke
□ 4 Mark Brandenburg
□ 5 Steve Burton
□ 6 Wayne Eggleston
□ 7 Hanley Frias
□ 8 Jack Kimel
□ 9 Kerry Lacy
□ 10 David Manning
□ 11 Jerry Martin
□ 12 Ramiro Martinez
□ 13 Malvin Matos
□ 14 Guillermo Mercedes
□ 15 Paulino Perez
□ 16 Querbin Reynoso
□ 17 Jeff Runion
□ 18 Scot Sealy
□ 19 Brian Seesz
□ 20 Bob Simonson
□ 21 Heath Vaughn
□ 22 Mike Welch
□ 23 Chad Wiley
□ 24 Kevin Woodall
□ 25 Scott Malone
□ 26 Chris Burr
□ 27 Walt Williams MG
□ 28 George Threadgill CO
□ 29 Sponsor Card
□ 30 Andy Graziano TR
Checklist

1993 Charleston Rainbows Fleer/ProCards

This 31-card standard-size set of the 1993 Charleston Rainbows, a Class A South Atlantic League affiliate of the Texas Rangers, features white-bordered posed color player photos on its fronts. The player's name, team, and position appear near the bottom. The white horizontal back is framed by a blue line and carries the player's name at the top, followed by biography and statistics. A drawing of a ballplayer in action appears on the left.

	MINT	NRMT	EXC
COMPLETE SET (31)	5.00	2.20	.60

□ 1900 Mike Anderson
□ 1901 Mark Brandenburg
□ 1902 Scott Eyre
□ 1903 Jack Kimel
□ 1904 Kerry Lacy
□ 1905 David Manning
□ 1906 Jerry Martin
□ 1907 Ramiro Martinez
□ 1908 Paulino Perez
□ 1909 Querbin Reynoso
□ 1910 Jeff Runion
□ 1911 Heath Vaughn
□ 1912 Chad Wiley
□ 1913 Jamie Bethke
□ 1914 Scot Sealy
□ 1915 Brian Seesz
□ 1916 Chris Burr
□ 1917 Steve Burton
□ 1918 Wayne Eggleston
□ 1919 Hanley Frias
□ 1920 Scott Malone
□ 1921 Guillermo Mercedes
□ 1922 Franklin Parra
□ 1923 Kevin Woodall
□ 1924 Malvin Matos
□ 1925 Bob Simonson
□ 1926 Mike Welch
□ 1927 Walt Williams MG
□ 1928 Gary Mielke CO
□ 1929 George Threadgill CO
□ 1930 Checklist

1993 Charlotte Knights Fleer/ProCards

This 28-card standard-size set of the 1993 Charlotte Knights, a Class AAA International League affiliate of the Cleveland Indians, features white-bordered posed color player photos on its fronts. The player's name, team, and position appear near the bottom. The white horizontal back is framed by a blue line and carries the player's name at the top, followed by biography and statistics. A drawing of a ballplayer in action appears on the left. This set includes Jim Thome's third team set card.

	MINT	NRMT	EXC
COMPLETE SET (28)	7.00	3.10	.85

□ 535 Paul Byrd
□ 536 Jerry DiPoto
□ 537 Jason Grimsley
□ 538 Tom McCarthy
□ 539 Bob Milacki
□ 540 Chad Ogea
□ 541 Zak Shinall
□ 542 Terry Wells
□ 543 Bill Wertz
□ 544 Cliff Young
□ 545 Matt Young
□ 546 Jesse Levis
□ 547 Kelly Stinnett
□ 548 George Canale
□ 549 Sam Horn
□ 550 Jeff Kunkel
□ 551 Mark Lewis
□ 552 Jeff Schaefer
□ 553 Jim Thome
□ 554 Beau Allred
□ 555 Alan Cockrell
□ 556 Mark Davidson
□ 557 Wayne Kirby
□ 558 Ken Ramos
□ 559 Charlie Manuel MG
□ 560 Luis Isaac CO
□ 561 Dyar Miller CO
□ 562 Checklist

1993 Charlotte Rangers Classic/Best

This 30-card standard-size set of the 1993 Charlotte Rangers, a Class A Florida State League affiliate of the Texas Rangers, features white-bordered posed color player shots on its fronts. A team-color-coded stripe below the photo carries the player's name; another above, his position and team name. On a ghosted team-logo, the white back carries the player's name at the top, followed by biography and statistics.

	MINT	NRMT	EXC
COMPLETE SET (30)	5.00	2.20	.60

□ 1 Terrell Lowery
□ 2 Rich Aurilia
□ 3 Joe Brownholtz
□ 4 Jim Clinton
□ 5 Michael Crespo
□ 6 Chris Curtis
□ 7 John Dettmer
□ 8 Mike Edwards
□ 9 George Evangelista
□ 10 Dave Gandolph
□ 11 Dave Geeve
□ 12 Dave Giberti

☐ 13 Todd Guggiana
☐ 14 Daryl Henderson
☐ 15 Wilson Heredia
☐ 16 Daryl Kennedy
☐ 17 Bo Magee
☐ 18 Danny Patterson
☐ 19 Steve Sadecki
☐ 20 Lance Schuermann
☐ 21 Mike Smith
☐ 22 Jose Texidor
☐ 23 Tyrone Washington
☐ 24 Lanny Williams
☐ 25 Desi Wilson
☐ 26 Tommy Thompson MG
☐ 27 Darrin Garner CO
☐ 28 Title Card
☐ 29 Marvin White CO
☐ 30 Greg Kersgeiter TR
Checklist

1993 Charlotte Rangers Fleer/ProCards

This 28-card standard-size set of the 1993 Charlotte Rangers, a Class A Florida State League affiliate of the Texas Rangers, features white-bordered posed color player photos on its fronts. The player's name, team, and position appear near the bottom. The white horizontal back is framed by a blue line and carries the player's name at the top, followed by biography and statistics. A drawing of a ballplayer in action appears on the left.

	MINT	NRMT	EXC
COMPLETE SET (28)	5.00	2.20	.60

☐ 1931 Joe Brownholtz
☐ 1932 John Dettmer
☐ 1933 Dave Gandolph
☐ 1934 Dave Geeve
☐ 1935 Dave Giberti
☐ 1936 Daryl Henderson
☐ 1937 Wilson Heredia
☐ 1938 Bo Magee
☐ 1939 Danny Patterson
☐ 1940 Steve Sadecki
☐ 1941 Lance Schuermann
☐ 1942 Tyrone Washington
☐ 1943 Michael Crespo
☐ 1944 Daryl Kennedy
☐ 1945 Lanny Williams
☐ 1946 Rich Aurilia
☐ 1947 Mike Edwards
☐ 1948 George Evangelista
☐ 1949 Todd Guggiana
☐ 1950 Mike Smith
☐ 1951 Desi Wilson
☐ 1952 Terrell Lowery
☐ 1953 Ken Powell
☐ 1954 Jose Texidor
☐ 1955 Tommy Thompson MG
☐ 1956 Darrin Garner CO
☐ 1957 Marvin White CO
☐ 1958 Checklist

1993 Chattanooga Lookouts Fleer/ProCards

This 26-card standard-size set of the 1993 Chattanooga Lookouts, a Class AA Southern League affiliate of the Cincinnati Reds, features white-bordered posed color player photos on its fronts. The player's name, team, and position appear near the bottom. The white horizontal back is framed by a blue line and carries the player's name at the top, followed by biography and statistics. A drawing of a ballplayer in action appears on the left.

	MINT	NRMT	EXC
COMPLETE SET (26)	5.00	2.20	.60

☐ 2352 Mike Anderson
☐ 2353 Chris Bushing
☐ 2354 John Courtright
☐ 2355 Calvain Culberson
☐ 2356 Mike Ferry
☐ 2357 Victor Garcia
☐ 2358 Scott Holcomb
☐ 2359 Chris Hook
☐ 2360 Rusty Kilgo
☐ 2361 Johnny Ray
☐ 2362 Scott Robinson
☐ 2363 Darron Cox
☐ 2364 Jon Fuller
☐ 2365 Jamie Dismuke
☐ 2366 Keith Kessinger
☐ 2367 Brian Koelling
☐ 2368 Brian Lane
☐ 2369 Calvin Reese
☐ 2370 Steve Gibralter
☐ 2371 K.C. Gillum
☐ 2372 Keith Gordon
☐ 2373 Bernie Jenkins
☐ 2374 Mark Merchant
☐ 2375 Pat Kelly MG
☐ 2376 Grant Jackson CO
☐ 2377 Checklist

1993 Classic/Best

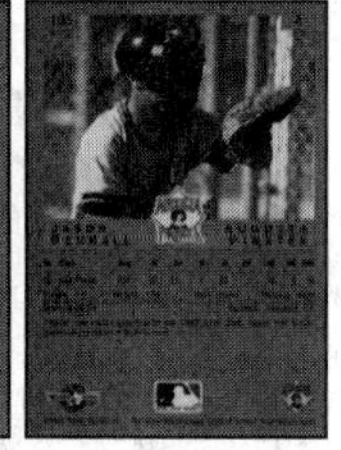

The 1993 Classic/Best Minor League set features top prospects from Double-A and Single-A teams. According to Classic, 9,600 numbered and autographed cards of eight different prospects were randomly inserted in packs with each player signing 1,200 cards; the players are Carlos Delgado, Cliff Floyd, Jeffrey Hammonds, Derek Jeter, Mike Kelly, Phil Nevin, Paul Shuey and Dmitri Young. The standard size cards feature on fronts a color player photo bordered in gray. The Classic/Best logo, the player's name, position and team name also appear. The backs have biography, statistics and a photo.

	MINT	NRMT	EXC
COMPLETE SET (300)	10.00	4.50	1.25
COMMON CARD (1-300)	.05	.02	.01
☐ 1 Paul Shuey	.05	.02	.01
☐ 2 Brad Clontz	.05	.02	.01
☐ 3 Phil Dauphin	.05	.02	.01
☐ 4 Kevin Flora	.05	.02	.01
☐ 5 Doug Glanville	.05	.02	.01
☐ 6 Hilly Hathaway	.05	.02	.01
☐ 7 Scott Hatteberg	.05	.02	.01
☐ 8 Ryan Hawblitzel	.05	.02	.01
☐ 9 Bob Henkel	.05	.02	.01
☐ 10 Mike Kelly	.05	.02	.01
☐ 11 Jose Malave	.05	.02	.01
☐ 12 Jeff McNeely	.05	.02	.01
☐ 13 Roberto Mejia	.05	.02	.01
☐ 14 Kevin Roberson	.05	.02	.01
☐ 15 Chad Roper	.05	.02	.01
☐ 16 John Roper	.05	.02	.01
☐ 17 Pete Rose Jr.	.05	.02	.01
☐ 18 Paul Russo	.05	.02	.01
☐ 19 John Salles	.05	.02	.01
☐ 20 Tracy Sanders	.05	.02	.01
☐ 21 Chris Saunders	.05	.02	.01
☐ 22 Jason Schmidt	.05	.02	.01
☐ 23 Aaron Sele	.10	.05	.01
☐ 24 Bob Abreu	.15	.07	.02
☐ 25 Don Sparks	.05	.02	.01
☐ 26 Scott Stahoviak	.05	.02	.01
☐ 27 Matt Stairs	.05	.02	.01
☐ 28 Todd Steverson	.05	.02	.01
☐ 29 Ozzie Timmons	.05	.02	.01
☐ 30 Michael Tucker	.20	.09	.03
☐ 31 Jose Viera	.05	.02	.01
☐ 32 B.J. Wallace	.05	.02	.01
☐ 33 Mark Wohlers	.10	.05	.01
☐ 34 Gabe White	.05	.02	.01
☐ 35 Rick White	.05	.02	.01
☐ 36 Rondell White	.40	.18	.05
☐ 37 Gerald Williams	.05	.02	.01
☐ 38 Mike Williams	.05	.02	.01
☐ 39 Todd Williams	.05	.02	.01
☐ 40 Desi Wilson	.05	.02	.01
☐ 41 Johnny Ard	.05	.02	.01
☐ 42 Jamie Arnold	.05	.02	.01
☐ 43 Howard Battle	.05	.02	.01
☐ 44 Greg Blosser	.05	.02	.01
☐ 45 Rob Butler	.05	.02	.01
☐ 46 Dan Carlson	.05	.02	.01
☐ 47 Joe Caruso	.05	.02	.01
☐ 48 Bobby Chouinard	.05	.02	.01
☐ 49 Adell Davenport	.05	.02	.01
☐ 50 Juan De La Rosa	.05	.02	.01
☐ 51 Alex Gonzalez	.10	.05	.01
☐ 52 Steve Hosey	.05	.02	.01
☐ 53 Rick Krivda	.05	.02	.01
☐ 54 T.R. Lewis	.05	.02	.01
☐ 55 Jose Mercedes	.05	.02	.01
☐ 56 Melvin Nieves	.10	.05	.01
☐ 57 Luis Ortiz	.05	.02	.01
☐ 58 Joe Rosselli	.05	.02	.01
☐ 59 Brian Sackinsky	.05	.02	.01
☐ 60 Salomon Torres	.05	.02	.01
☐ 61 James Baldwin	.10	.05	.01
☐ 62 Travis Baptist	.05	.02	.01
☐ 63 Bret Boone	.05	.02	.01
☐ 64 Mike Buddie	.05	.02	.01
☐ 65 Paul Carey	.05	.02	.01
☐ 66 Tim Crabtree	.05	.02	.01
☐ 67 Tony Longmire	.05	.02	.01
☐ 68 Robert Eenhoorn	.05	.02	.01
☐ 69 Paul Ellis	.05	.02	.01
☐ 70 Shawn Estes	.10	.05	.01
☐ 71 Andy Fox	.05	.02	.01
☐ 72 Shawn Green UER Front photo is Alex Gonzalez	.10	.05	.01
☐ 73 Jimmy Haynes	.05	.02	.01
☐ 74 Sterling Hitchcock	.05	.02	.01
☐ 75 Mark Hutton	.05	.02	.01
☐ 76 Domingo Jean	.05	.02	.01
☐ 77 Kevin Jordan	.05	.02	.01
☐ 78 Steve Karsay	.05	.02	.01
☐ 79 Paul Fletcher	.05	.02	.01
☐ 80 Mike Milchin	.05	.02	.01
☐ 81 Lyle Mouton	.05	.02	.01
☐ 82 Bobby Munoz	.05	.02	.01
☐ 83 Alex Ochoa	.10	.05	.01
☐ 84 Steve Olsen	.05	.02	.01
☐ 85 Billy Owens	.05	.02	.01
☐ 86 Eddie Pearson	.05	.02	.01
☐ 87 Mike Robertson	.05	.02	.01
☐ 88 Johnny Ruffin	.05	.02	.01
☐ 89 Mark Smith	.05	.02	.01
☐ 90 Brandon Wilson	.05	.02	.01
☐ 91 Derek Jeter	1.50	.70	.19
☐ 92 Edgardo Alfonzo	.10	.05	.01
☐ 93 Jeff Alkire	.05	.02	.01
☐ 94 Roger Bailey	.05	.02	.01
☐ 95 Jeff Barry	.05	.02	.01
☐ 96 Terrell Buckley	.05	.02	.01
☐ 97 Hector Carrasco	.05	.02	.01
☐ 98 Danny Clyburn	.25	.11	.03
☐ 99 Darren Burton	.05	.02	.01
☐ 100 Scott Eyre	.05	.02	.01
☐ 101 Chad Fox	.05	.02	.01
☐ 102 Joe Hudson	.05	.02	.01
☐ 103 Jason Hutchins	.05	.02	.01
☐ 104 Bobby Jones	.10	.05	.01
☐ 105 Jason Kendall	.50	.23	.06
☐ 106 Ricky Magdaleno	.05	.02	.01
☐ 107 Buck McNabb	.05	.02	.01
☐ 108 Doug Mlicki	.05	.02	.01
☐ 109 Chris Eddy	.05	.02	.01
☐ 110 Jon Lieber	.05	.02	.01
☐ 111 Ken Powell	.05	.02	.01
☐ 112 Todd Pridy	.05	.02	.01
☐ 113 Marquis Riley	.05	.02	.01
☐ 114 Steve Rodriguez	.05	.02	.01
☐ 115 Brian Rupp	.05	.02	.01
☐ 116 Yuri Sanchez	.05	.02	.01
☐ 117 Al Shirley	.05	.02	.01
☐ 118 Paul Spoljaric	.05	.02	.01
☐ 119 Amaury Telemaco	.25	.11	.03
☐ 120 Shon Walker	.05	.02	.01
☐ 121 Tavo Alvarez	.05	.02	.01
☐ 122 Shane Andrews	.05	.02	.01
☐ 123 Billy Ashley	.05	.02	.01
☐ 124 Brian Barber	.05	.02	.01
☐ 125 Trey Beamon	.30	.14	.04
☐ 126 Scott Bryant	.05	.02	.01
☐ 127 Scott Bullett	.05	.02	.01
☐ 128 Ozzie Canseco	.05	.02	.01
☐ 129 Brian Carpenter	.05	.02	.01
☐ 130 Roger Cedeno	.20	.09	.03
☐ 131 Randy Curtis	.05	.02	.01
☐ 132 Alberto De Los Santos	.05	.02	.01
☐ 133 Steve Dixon	.05	.02	.01
☐ 134 Joey Eischen	.05	.02	.01
☐ 135 Brook Fordyce	.05	.02	.01
☐ 136 Rick Gorecki	.05	.02	.01
☐ 137 Lee Hancock	.05	.02	.01
☐ 138 Todd Hollandsworth	.15	.07	.02
☐ 139 Frank Jacobs	.05	.02	.01
☐ 140 Mark Johnson	.05	.02	.01
☐ 141 Albie Lopez	.05	.02	.01
☐ 142 Dan Melendez	.05	.02	.01
☐ 143 William Pennyfeather	.05	.02	.01
☐ 144 Scott Lydy	.05	.02	.01
☐ 145 Chris Snopek	.05	.02	.01
☐ 146 Quilvio Veras	.05	.02	.01
☐ 147 Jose Vidro	.05	.02	.01
☐ 148 Allen Watson	.05	.02	.01
☐ 149 Matt Whisenant	.05	.02	.01
☐ 150 Craig Wilson	.05	.02	.01
☐ 151 Rich Becker	.05	.02	.01
☐ 152 Mike Durant	.05	.02	.01
☐ 153 Brad Ausmus	.05	.02	.01
☐ 154 Robbie Beckett	.05	.02	.01
☐ 155 Steve Dunn	.05	.02	.01
☐ 156 Paul Byrd	.05	.02	.01
☐ 157 Jason Bere	.05	.02	.01
☐ 158 Ben Blomdahl	.05	.02	.01
☐ 159 John Brothers	.05	.02	.01
☐ 160 Tim Costo	.05	.02	.01
☐ 161 Joel Chimelis	.05	.02	.01
☐ 162 Kenny Carlyle	.05	.02	.01
☐ 163 Garvin Alston	.05	.02	.01
☐ 164 Sean Bergman	.05	.02	.01
☐ 165 Marshall Boze	.05	.02	.01
☐ 166 Terry Burrows	.05	.02	.01
☐ 167 Danny Bautista	.05	.02	.01
☐ 168 Jason Bates	.05	.02	.01
☐ 169 Brent Bowers	.05	.02	.01
☐ 170 Rico Brogna	.05	.02	.01
☐ 171 Armann Brown	.05	.02	.01
☐ 172 Brant Brown	.05	.02	.01
☐ 173 Julio Bruno	.05	.02	.01
☐ 174 Mike DeJean	.05	.02	.01
☐ 175 Nick Delvecchio	.05	.02	.01
☐ 176 Bobby Bonds Jr.	.05	.02	.01
☐ 177 Miguel Castellano	.05	.02	.01
☐ 178 Tommy Adams	.05	.02	.01
☐ 179 Alan Burke	.05	.02	.01
☐ 180 John Burke	.05	.02	.01
☐ 181 Ivan Cruz	.05	.02	.01
☐ 182 Johnny Damon	.60	.25	.07
☐ 183 Carl Everett	.05	.02	.01
☐ 184 Jorge Fabregas	.05	.02	.01
☐ 185 John Fantauzzi	.05	.02	.01
☐ 186 Mike Farmer	.05	.02	.01
☐ 187 Mike Farrell	.05	.02	.01
☐ 188 Omar Garcia	.05	.02	.01
☐ 189 Brent Gates	.05	.02	.01
☐ 190 Jason Giambi	.15	.07	.02
☐ 191 K.C. Gillum	.05	.02	.01
☐ 192 Chris Gomez	.05	.02	.01
☐ 193 Ricky Greene	.05	.02	.01
☐ 194 Willie Greene	.05	.02	.01
☐ 195 Benji Grigsby	.05	.02	.01
☐ 196 Mike Groppuso	.05	.02	.01
☐ 197 Johnny Guzman	.05	.02	.01
☐ 198 Bob Hamelin	.05	.02	.01
☐ 199 Joey Hamilton	.05	.02	.01
☐ 200 Chris Haney	.05	.02	.01
☐ 201 Donald Harris	.05	.02	.01
☐ 202 Andy Hartung	.05	.02	.01
☐ 203 Chris Hatcher	.05	.02	.01
☐ 204 Rick Helling	.05	.02	.01
☐ 205 Edgar Herrera	.05	.02	.01
☐ 206 Aaron Holbert	.05	.02	.01
☐ 207 Ray Holbert	.05	.02	.01
☐ 208 Tyler Houston	.05	.02	.01
☐ 209 Brian L. Hunter	.25	.11	.03
☐ 210 Miguel Jiminez	.05	.02	.01
☐ 211 Charles Johnson	.50	.23	.06
☐ 212 Corey Kapano	.05	.02	.01
☐ 213 Tom Knauss	.05	.02	.01
☐ 214 Brian Koelling	.05	.02	.01
☐ 215 Brian Lane	.05	.02	.01
☐ 216 Kevin Legault	.05	.02	.01
☐ 217 Mark Lewls	.05	.02	.01
☐ 218 Luis Lopez	.05	.02	.01
☐ 219 Jose Martinez	.05	.02	.01
☐ 220 Mitch Meluskey	.05	.02	.01
☐ 221 Casey Mendenhall	.05	.02	.01
☐ 222 Danny Miceli	.05	.02	.01
☐ 223 Tony Mitchell	.05	.02	.01
☐ 224 Ritchie Moody	.05	.02	.01
☐ 225 James Mouton	.05	.02	.01
☐ 226 Steve Murphy	.05	.02	.01
☐ 227 Mike Neill	.05	.02	.01
☐ 228 Tom Nevers	.05	.02	.01
☐ 229 Alan Newman	.05	.02	.01
☐ 230 Tom Neneviller	.05	.02	.01
☐ 231 Jon Nunnally	.05	.02	.01
☐ 232 Chad Ogea	.05	.02	.01
☐ 233 Ray Ortiz	.05	.02	.01
☐ 234 Orlando Palmeiro	.05	.02	.01
☐ 235 Criag Paquette	.05	.02	.01
☐ 236 Troy Percival	.05	.02	.01
☐ 237 Bobby Perna	.05	.02	.01
☐ 238 John Pricher	.05	.02	.01
☐ 239 Ken Ramos	.05	.02	.01
☐ 240 Joe Randa	.05	.02	.01
☐ 241 Ron Blazier	.05	.02	.01
☐ 242 Terry Bradshaw	.05	.02	.01
☐ 243 Jason Hisey	.05	.02	.01
☐ 244 Sean Lowe	.05	.02	.01
☐ 245 Chad McConnell	.05	.02	.01
☐ 246 Jackie Nickell	.05	.02	.01
☐ 247 Pat Rapp	.05	.02	.01
☐ 248 Calvin Reese	.05	.02	.01
☐ 249 Desi Relaford	.05	.02	.01
☐ 250 Troy Ricker	.05	.02	.01
☐ 251 Todd Ritchie	.05	.02	.01
☐ 252 Chris Roberts	.05	.02	.01
☐ 253 Scott Sanders	.05	.02	.01
☐ 254 Ruben Santana	.05	.02	.01
☐ 255 Chris Seelbach	.05	.02	.01
☐ 256 Dan Serafini	.05	.02	.01
☐ 257 Curtis Shaw	.05	.02	.01
☐ 258 Kennie Steenstra	.05	.02	.01
☐ 259 Kevin Stocker	.05	.02	.01
☐ 260 Tanyon Sturtze	.05	.02	.01
☐ 261 Tim Stutheit	.05	.02	.01
☐ 262 Jamie Taylor	.05	.02	.01
☐ 263 Chad Townsend	.05	.02	.01
☐ 264 Steve Trachsel	.05	.02	.01
☐ 265 Jose Valentin	.05	.02	.01
☐ 266 K.C. Waller	.05	.02	.01
☐ 267 Chris Weinke	.05	.02	.01
☐ 268 Darrell Whitmore	.05	.02	.01
☐ 269 Juan Williams	.05	.02	.01
☐ 270 Tim Worrell	.05	.02	.01
☐ 271 Tim Belk	.05	.02	.01
☐ 272 London Bradley	.05	.02	.01
☐ 273 Tilson Brito	.05	.02	.01
☐ 274 Felipe Crespo	.05	.02	.01
☐ 275 Kenny Felder	.05	.02	.01
☐ 276 Billy Hall	.05	.02	.01
☐ 277 Terrell Hansen	.05	.02	.01
☐ 278 Rod Henderson	.05	.02	.01
☐ 279 Bobby Holley	.05	.02	.01
☐ 280 Bobby Hughes	.05	.02	.01
☐ 281 Rick Huisman	.05	.02	.01
☐ 282 Jack Johnson	.05	.02	.01
☐ 283 Gabby Martinez	.05	.02	.01
☐ 284 Jose Millares	.05	.02	.01
☐ 285 Jason Moler	.05	.02	.01

☐ 286 Willie Mota	.05	.02	.01
☐ 287 Marty Neff	.05	.02	.01
☐ 288 Eric Owens	.05	.02	.01
☐ 289 Daryl Ratliff	.05	.02	.01
☐ 290 Ozzie Sanchez	.05	.02	.01
☐ 291 Dave Silvestri	.05	.02	.01
☐ 292 Chris Stynes	.05	.02	.01
☐ 293 Aubrey Waggoner	.05	.02	.01
☐ 294 Jimmy White	.05	.02	.01
☐ 295 Jim Campanis	.05	.02	.01
☐ 296 Tony Womack	.05	.02	.01
☐ 297 Checklist	.05	.02	.01
☐ 298 Checklist	.05	.02	.01
☐ 299 Checklist	.05	.02	.01
☐ 300 Checklist	.05	.02	.01
☐ AU1 Carlos Delgado AU/1200	40.00	18.00	5.00
☐ AU2 Cliff Floyd AU/1200	20.00	9.00	2.50
☐ AU3 Jeffrey Hammonds AU/1200	20.00	9.00	2.50
☐ AU4 Derek Jeter AU/1200	90.00	40.00	11.00
☐ AU5 Mike Kelly AU/1200	10.00	4.50	1.25
☐ AU6 Phil Nevin AU/1200	10.00	4.50	1.25
☐ AU7 Paul Shuey AU/1200	15.00	6.75	1.85
☐ AU8 Dmitri Young AU/1200	40.00	18.00	5.00

1993 Classic/Best Expansion #1 Picks

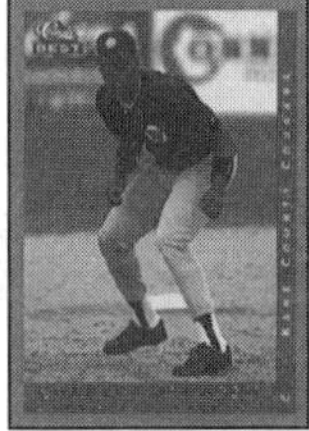

These two standard-size cards depict 1992 #1 draft picks for the 1993 expansion teams Colorado Rockies and Florida Marlins. The cards were randomly inserted in 1993 Classic/Best foil packs. The fronts display color action player photos bordered in light green with the player's name, team and position along the bottom and right edge. On a green background, a second color photo appears on the back with player profile. The player's name and team appear below the picture on a team color-coded stripe. The cards are numbered on the back with the prefix "EP."

	MINT	NRMT	EXC
COMPLETE SET (2)	4.00	1.80	.50
COMMON CARD (EP1-EP2)	.50	.23	.06
☐ EP1 John Burke	.50	.23	.06
☐ EP2 Charles Johnson	4.00	1.80	.50

1993 Classic/Best MVPs

This ten-card standard-size set features minor league MVPs in color photos framed on the lower and right side by a team color-coded stripe. The player's name, team and position are printed on the stripe with the lettering "Classic/Best MVP." On a silver background with the backs carry close-up player pictures with the name, team logo and team name printed on a team color-coded stripe below. Statistics, player profile and biography are located in the lower section. The cards are numbered on the back with an "MVP" prefix. The cards were randomly inserted in 1993 Classic/Best foil packs.

	MINT	NRMT	EXC
COMPLETE SET (10)	8.00	3.60	1.00
COMMON CARD (1-10)	.40	.18	.05
☐ 1 Bubba Smith	.40	.18	.05
☐ 2 Javy Lopez	2.50	1.10	.30
☐ 3 Marty Cordova	2.50	1.10	.30
☐ 4 Troy O'Leary	.50	.23	.06
☐ 5 Steve Gibralter	.50	.23	.06
☐ 6 Gary Mota	.40	.18	.05
☐ 7 Larry Sutton	.40	.18	.05
☐ 8 Dan Frye	.40	.18	.05
☐ 9 Russ Davis	.50	.23	.06
☐ 10 Carlos Delgado	2.50	1.10	.30

1993 Classic/Best Player and Manager of the Year

This set of two standard-size cards displays Manager of the Year Marc Hill and Player of the Year Carlos Delgado holding their trophies in waist up color portraits. The cards are outlined in light green with their names printed across the bottom and their position and team along the right side. The backs carry a close-up photo on a light green background. The player's name and team appear below the picture on a team color-coded stripe. The cards are numbered on the back with a "PM" prefix. The cards were randomly inserted in 1993 Classic/Best foil packs.

	MINT	NRMT	EXC
COMPLETE SET (2)	2.50	1.10	.30
COMMON CARD (PM1-PM2)	.50	.23	.06
☐ PM1 Carlos Delgado	2.50	1.10	.30
☐ PM2 Marc Hill	.50	.23	.06

1993 Classic/Best Young Guns

This set consists of 28 standard-size cards featuring high-gloss full-action photos enclosed by silver foil borders. The player's name appears on a team color-coded stripe across the bottom and his position and team are printed on a stripe along the right side. The logo "Young Guns 1993" is stamped in gold above the player's name. On a silver background, the backs carry close-up pictures with the name, team logo and team name printed on a team color-coded stripe below. Statistics, player profile and biography are located in the lower section. The cards are numbered on the back with a "YG" prefix. The cards were randomly inserted in 1993 Classic/Best foil packs at an average of two or three per box.

	MINT	NRMT	EXC
COMPLETE SET (28)	50.00	22.00	6.25
COMMON CARD (YG1-YG28)	.40	.18	.05
☐ YG1 Midre Cummings	.50	.23	.06
☐ YG2 Carlos Delgado	5.00	2.20	.60
☐ YG3 Cliff Floyd	.75	.35	.09
☐ YG4 Jeffrey Hammonds	.75	.35	.09
☐ YG5 Tyrone Hill	.40	.18	.05
☐ YG6 Butch Huskey	1.00	.45	.12
☐ YG7 Chipper Jones	15.00	6.75	1.85
☐ YG8 Mike Lieberthal	.50	.23	.06
☐ YG9 David McCarty	.40	.18	.05
☐ YG10 Ray McDavid	.40	.18	.05
☐ YG11 Kurt Miller	.40	.18	.05
☐ YG12 Raul Mondesi	6.00	2.70	.75
☐ YG13 Chad Mottola	.40	.18	.05
☐ YG14 Calvin Murray	.40	.18	.05
☐ YG15 Phil Nevin	.40	.18	.05
☐ YG16 Marc Newfield	.75	.35	.09
☐ YG17 Eduardo Perez	.40	.18	.05
☐ YG18 Manny Ramirez	12.00	5.50	1.50
☐ YG19 Edgar Renteria	5.00	2.20	.60
☐ YG20 Frank Rodriguez	.60	.25	.07
☐ YG21 Scott Ruffcorn	.40	.18	.05
☐ YG22 Brien Taylor	.40	.18	.05
☐ YG23 Justin Thompson	.60	.25	.07
☐ YG24 Mark Thompson	.50	.23	.06
☐ YG25 Todd Van Poppel	.40	.18	.05
☐ YG26 Joe Vitiello	.50	.23	.06
☐ YG27 Derek Wallace	.40	.18	.05
☐ YG28 Dmitri Young	3.00	1.35	.35

1993 Classic/Best Gold

The 1993 Classic/Best Minor League Gold set consists of 220 standard-size cards featuring 216 cards of players in Double A, Class A and Rookie Leagues plus four checklist cards. The production run was 6,000 sequentially numbered ten-box cases. The foil packs included randomly inserted autograph cards of Barry Bonds and Gary Sheffield. The fronts feature glossy color player photos tilted slightly to the right so that the picture's corners extend off the card edges. The color of the front border varies from card to card. The player's name and team name are printed in gold foil lettering and the oversized first letter of the player's name is scripted. The backs have a larger version of the player's name in gold foil and display two smaller player photos, biography and in a color-coded bar statistics.

	MINT	NRMT	EXC
COMPLETE SET (220)	20.00	9.00	2.50
COMMON CARD (1-220)	.05	.02	.01
☐ 1 Barry Bonds	.75	.35	.09
☐ 2 Mark Hutton	.05	.02	.01
☐ 3 Lyle Mouton	.05	.02	.01
☐ 4 Don Sparks	.05	.02	.01
☐ 5 Joe Randa	.05	.02	.01
☐ 6 Dave Mlicki	.05	.02	.01
☐ 7 Ken Ramos	.05	.02	.01
☐ 8 Bill Wertz	.05	.02	.01
☐ 9 Jon Shave	.05	.02	.01
☐ 10 Dan Smith	.05	.02	.01
☐ 11 William Canate	.05	.02	.01
☐ 12 Albie Lopez	.05	.02	.01
☐ 13 Rod McCall	.05	.02	.01
☐ 14 Paul Shuey	.05	.02	.01
☐ 15 Ian Doyle	.05	.02	.01
☐ 16 Marc Marini	.05	.02	.01
☐ 17 Brien Taylor	.05	.02	.01
☐ 18 Mike Kelly	.05	.02	.01
☐ 19 Andy Nezelek	.05	.02	.01
☐ 20 Marcos Armas	.05	.02	.01
☐ 21 Chad Ogea	.05	.02	.01
☐ 22 Frank Rodriguez	.05	.02	.01
☐ 23 Aaron Sele	.05	.02	.01
☐ 24 Tim Vanegmond	.05	.02	.01
☐ 25 Phil Hiatt	.05	.02	.01
☐ 26 Dan Rohrmeier	.05	.02	.01
☐ 27 Greg Blosse	.05	.02	.01
☐ 28 Scott Hatteberg	.05	.02	.01
☐ 29 Ed Riley	.05	.02	.01
☐ 30 Edgar Alfonzo	.05	.02	.01
☐ 31 Jorge Fabregas	.05	.02	.01
☐ 32 Eduardo Perez	.05	.02	.01
☐ 33 John Cummings	.05	.02	.01
☐ 34 Bubba Smith	.05	.02	.01
☐ 35 Kevin Jordan	.05	.02	.01
☐ 36 Tyler Green	.05	.02	.01
☐ 37 Heath Haynes	.05	.02	.01
☐ 38 Gabe White	.05	.02	.01
☐ 39 Doug Glanville	.05	.02	.01
☐ 40 Jose Viera	.05	.02	.01
☐ 41 Rich Becker	.05	.02	.01
☐ 42 Marty Cordova	1.25	.55	.16
☐ 43 Mike Durant	.05	.02	.01
☐ 44 Todd Ritchie	.05	.02	.01
☐ 45 Scott Stahoviak	.05	.02	.01
☐ 46 Tavo Alvarez	.05	.02	.01
☐ 47 Chris Malinoski	.05	.02	.01
☐ 48 Rondell White	.75	.35	.09
☐ 49 Tim Worrell	.05	.02	.01
☐ 50 Benji Gil	.05	.02	.01
☐ 51 Ben Blomdahl	.05	.02	.01
☐ 52 Rich Kelly	.05	.02	.01
☐ 53 Justin Thompson	.05	.02	.01
☐ 54 Scott Pose	.05	.02	.01
☐ 55 John Roper	.05	.02	.01
☐ 56 Rafael Chaves	.05	.02	.01
☐ 57 Billy Hall	.05	.02	.01
☐ 58 Ray McDavid	.05	.02	.01
☐ 59 Mark Smith	.05	.02	.01
☐ 60 Jeff Williams	.05	.02	.01
☐ 61 Bobby Jones	.25	.11	.03
☐ 62 Stanton Cameron	.05	.02	.01
☐ 63 Mike Lumley	.05	.02	.01
☐ 64 Troy Buckley	.05	.02	.01
☐ 65 James Dougherty	.05	.02	.01
☐ 66 Chris Hill	.05	.02	.01
☐ 67 Tom Nevers	.05	.02	.01
☐ 68 Joe Rosselli	.05	.02	.01
☐ 69 Steve Whitaker	.05	.02	.01
☐ 70 Butch Huskey	.25	.11	.03
☐ 71 Shane Andrews	.05	.02	.01
☐ 72 Cliff Floyd	.20	.09	.03
☐ 73 Alex Ochoa	1.00	.45	.12
☐ 74 Brent Gates	.05	.02	.01
☐ 75 Curtis Shaw	.05	.02	.01
☐ 76 Midre Cummings	.05	.02	.01
☐ 77 Steve Olsen	.05	.02	.01
☐ 78 Mike Robertson	.05	.02	.01
☐ 79 Scott Ruffcorn	.05	.02	.01
☐ 80 Brandon Wilson	.05	.02	.01
☐ 81 Darren Burton	.05	.02	.01
☐ 82 Kerwin Moore	.05	.02	.01
☐ 83 Joe Vitiello	.05	.02	.01
☐ 84 Hugh Walker	.05	.02	.01
☐ 85 Howard Battle	.05	.02	.01
☐ 86 Rob Butler	.05	.02	.01
☐ 87 Carlos Delgado	1.25	.55	.16
☐ 88 Jeff Ware	.05	.02	.01
☐ 89 Mike Hostetler	.05	.02	.01
☐ 90 Brian Kowitz	.05	.02	.01
☐ 91 Ryan Hawblitzel	.05	.02	.01
☐ 92 Juan De La Rosa	.05	.02	.01
☐ 93 David McCarty	.05	.02	.01
☐ 94 Paul Russo	.05	.02	.01
☐ 95 Dan Cholowsky	.05	.02	.01
☐ 96 Dmitri Young	.25	.11	.03
☐ 97 Paul Ellis	.05	.02	.01
☐ 98 Jay Kirkpatrick	.05	.02	.01
☐ 99 Jeff Jackson	.05	.02	.01
☐ 100 Duane Singleton	.05	.02	.01
☐ 101 Kiki Hernandez	.05	.02	.01
☐ 102 Raul Herrera	.05	.02	.01
☐ 103 Brian Bevil	.05	.02	.01
☐ 104 Mark Johnson	.05	.02	.01
☐ 105 Bob Abreu	1.00	.45	.12
☐ 106 Gary Mota	.05	.02	.01
☐ 107 Jose Cabrera	.05	.02	.01
☐ 108 Jeff Runion	.05	.02	.01
☐ 109 B.J. Wallace	.05	.02	.01
☐ 110 Jim Arnold	.05	.02	.01
☐ 111 Dwight Maness	.05	.02	.01
☐ 112 Fernando DaSilva	.05	.02	.01
☐ 113 Chris Burr	.05	.02	.01
☐ 114 Dan Serafini	.25	.11	.03
☐ 115 Derek Jeter	3.00	1.35	.35
☐ 116 Lew Hill	.05	.02	.01
☐ 117 Andy Pettitte	2.50	1.10	.30
☐ 118 Keith Johns	.05	.02	.01
☐ 119 Sean Lowe	.05	.02	.01
☐ 120 T.J. Mathews	.05	.02	.01
☐ 121 Ricardo Medina	.05	.02	.01
☐ 122 Scott Gentile	.05	.02	.01
☐ 123 Everett Stull	.05	.02	.01
☐ 124 Manny Ramirez	3.00	1.35	.35
☐ 125 Archie Corbin	.05	.02	.01
☐ 126 Matt Karchner	.05	.02	.01
☐ 127 Domingo Mota	.05	.02	.01
☐ 128 Alex Gonzalez	.25	.11	.03
☐ 129 Joe Lis Jr.	.05	.02	.01
☐ 130 Paul Spoljaric	.05	.02	.01
☐ 131 Clifton Garrett	.05	.02	.01
☐ 132 Marc Hill	.05	.02	.01
☐ 133 Jesus Martinez	.05	.02	.01
☐ 134 Salomon Torres	.05	.02	.01
☐ 135 Tommy Eason	.05	.02	.01
☐ 136 Matt Whisenant	.05	.02	.01
☐ 137 Jon Zuber	.05	.02	.01
☐ 138 Luis Martinez	.05	.02	.01
☐ 139 Glenn Murray	.05	.02	.01
☐ 140 John Saffer	.05	.02	.01
☐ 141 Tommy Adams	.05	.02	.01
☐ 142 Manny Cervantes	.05	.02	.01
☐ 143 George Glinatsis	.05	.02	.01
☐ 144 Chris Dessellier	.05	.02	.01
☐ 145 Joe Pomierski	.05	.02	.01
☐ 146 John Vanhof	.05	.02	.01
☐ 147 Matt Williams	.05	.02	.01
☐ 148 Maurice Christmas	.05	.02	.01
☐ 149 Damon Hollins	.30	.14	.04
☐ 150 Sean Smith	.05	.02	.01
☐ 151 Doug Hecker	.05	.02	.01
☐ 152 Jamie Sepeda	.05	.02	.01
☐ 153 Steve Solomon	.05	.02	.01
☐ 154 Jeff Tabaka	.05	.02	.01
☐ 155 Greg Elliott	.05	.02	.01
☐ 156 Jim Waring	.05	.02	.01
☐ 157 Omar Garcia	.05	.02	.01
☐ 158 Ricky Otero	.05	.02	.01
☐ 159 Jamie Brewington	.05	.02	.01
☐ 160 Chad Fonville	.05	.02	.01
☐ 161 Sean Runyan	.05	.02	.01
☐ 162 Jim Givens	.05	.02	.01
☐ 163 Dennis McNamara	.05	.02	.01
☐ 164 Rudy Pemberton	.05	.02	.01
☐ 165 Brian Raabe	.05	.02	.01
☐ 166 Jeffrey Hammonds	.20	.09	.03
☐ 167 Chris Hatcher	.05	.02	.01
☐ 168 Chris Saunders	.05	.02	.01
☐ 169 Aaron Fultz	.05	.02	.01
☐ 170 Mike Freitas	.05	.02	.01
☐ 171 Tim Adkins	.05	.02	.01
☐ 172 Chipper Jones	4.00	1.80	.50
☐ 173 Brandon Cromer	.05	.02	.01
☐ 174 Shannon Stewart	.10	.05	.01
☐ 175 David Tollison	.05	.02	.01
☐ 176 Rob Adkins	.05	.02	.01
☐ 177 Todd Steverson	.05	.02	.01
☐ 178 Dennis Konuszewski	.05	.02	.01
☐ 179 Marty Neff	.05	.02	.01
☐ 180 Vernon Spearman	.05	.02	.01
☐ 181 Don Wengert	.05	.02	.01
☐ 182 Allen Battle	.05	.02	.01
☐ 183 Michael Moore	.05	.02	.01
☐ 184 Sherard Clinkscales	.05	.02	.01
☐ 185 Jamie Dismuke	.05	.02	.01
☐ 186 Tucker Hammargren	.05	.02	.01
☐ 187 John Hrusovsky	.05	.02	.01
☐ 188 Elliott Quinones	.05	.02	.01
☐ 189 Calvin Reese	.05	.02	.01
☐ 190 Rich Ireland	.05	.02	.01
☐ 191 Shawn Estes	.10	.05	.01
☐ 192 Greg Shockey	.05	.02	.01
☐ 193 Mike Zimmerman	.05	.02	.01
☐ 194 Danny Clyburn	.50	.23	.06
☐ 195 Jason Kendall	1.00	.45	.12
☐ 196 Shon Walker	.05	.02	.01
☐ 197 Gary Wilson	.05	.02	.01
☐ 198 John Dillinger	.05	.02	.01
☐ 199 Jim Keefe	.05	.02	.01
☐ 200 Eddie Pearson	.05	.02	.01
☐ 201 Johnny Damon	1.25	.55	.16
☐ 202 Jim Pittsley	.10	.05	.01
☐ 203 Jason Bere	.05	.02	.01
☐ 204 James Baldwin	.10	.05	.01
☐ 205 John Burke	.05	.02	.01
☐ 206 Scot Sealy	.05	.02	.01
☐ 207 Ken Carlyle	.05	.02	.01
☐ 208 Tim Crabtree	.05	.02	.01
☐ 209 Quilvio Veras	.05	.02	.01
☐ 210 Edgardo Alfonzo	.05	.02	.01

☐ 211 Adell Davenport	.05	.02	.01
☐ 212 Dan Frye	.05	.02	.01
☐ 213 Derek Lowe	.05	.02	.01
☐ 214 Steve Gibralter	.05	.02	.01
☐ 215 Troy O'Leary	.05	.02	.01
☐ 216 Gary Sheffield	.40	.18	.05
☐ 217 Checklist (1-55)	.05	.02	.01
☐ 218 Checklist (56-110)	.05	.02	.01
☐ 219 Checklist (111-165)	.05	.02	.01
☐ 220 Checlklist (166-220)	.05	.02	.01
☐ AU1 Barry Bonds AU/2050	90.00	40.00	11.00
☐ AU2 Gary Sheffield AU/2050	60.00	27.00	7.50

1993 Classic/Best Gold LPs

Randomly inserted in 1992 Classic/Best retail white jumbo packs, this limited-print five-card set measures the standard size. The fronts are identical to the regular series featuring glossy color player photos tilted slightly to the right so that the picture's corners extend off the card edges. The color of the front border varies from card to card. The player's name and team name are printed in gold foil lettering and the oversized first letter of the player's name is scripted. The background of the full-bleed photo on the horizontal back is out of focus to make the player stand out. Each card has a message congratulating the collector on receiving this limited print card.

	MINT	NRMT	EXC
COMPLETE SET(5)	20.00	9.00	2.50
COMMON CARD (1-5)	4.00	1.80	.50
☐ 1 David McCarty	4.00	1.80	.50
☐ 2 Brien Taylor	4.00	1.80	.50
☐ 3 Joe Vitiello	5.00	2.20	.60
☐ 4 Mike Kelly	4.00	1.80	.50
☐ 5 Carlos Delgado	8.00	3.60	1.00

1993 Clearwater Phillies Classic/Best

This 30-card standard-size set of the 1993 Clearwater Phillies, a Class A Florida State League affiliate of the Philadelphia Phillies, features white-bordered posed color player shots on its fronts. A team-color-coded stripe below the photo carries the player's name; another above, his position and team name. On a ghosted team-logo, the white back carries the player's name at the top, followed by biography and statistics.

	MINT	NRMT	EXC
COMPLETE SET (30)	5.00	2.20	.60

☐ 1 Jason Moler
☐ 2 Jeff Bigler
☐ 3 Ron Blazier
☐ 4 Ricky Bottalico
☐ 5 Greg Brown
☐ 6 Dominic Desantis
☐ 7 Jerome Edwards
☐ 8 David Fisher
☐ 9 Phil Geisler
☐ 10 Joel Gilmore
☐ 11 Mike Gomez
☐ 12 Rob Grable
☐ 13 David Hayden
☐ 14 Craig Holman
☐ 15 Dean Hopp
☐ 16 Mike Juhl
☐ 17 J.J. Munoz
☐ 18 Mark Randall
☐ 19 Troy Rusk
☐ 20 Jamie Sepeda
☐ 21 Ken Sirak
☐ 22 David Tokheim
☐ 23 John Trisler
☐ 24 Tom Vilet
☐ 25 Jon Zuber
☐ 26 Bil Dancy MG
☐ 27 Roly Dearmas CO
☐ 28 Darold Knowles CO
☐ 29 Troy Hoffert TR
☐ 30 Checklist

1993 Clearwater Phillies Fleer/ProCards

This 27-card standard-size set of the 1993 Clearwater Phillies, a Class A Florida State League affiliate of the Philadelphia Phillies, features white-bordered posed color player photos on its fronts. The player's name, team, and position appear near the bottom. The white horizontal back is framed by a blue line and carries the player's name at the top, followed by biography and statistics. A drawing of a ballplayer in action appears on the left.

	MINT	NRMT	EXC
COMPLETE SET (27)	5.00	2.20	.60

☐ 2675 Ron Blazier
☐ 2676 Ricky Bottalico
☐ 2677 Greg Brown
☐ 2678 Dominic DeSantis
☐ 2679 Joel Gilmore
☐ 2680 Mike Juhl
☐ 2681 J.J. Munoz
☐ 2682 Mark Randall
☐ 2683 Jamie Sepeda
☐ 2684 John Trisler
☐ 2685 Dean Hopp
☐ 2686 Jason Moler
☐ 2687 Troy Rusk
☐ 2688 David Fisher
☐ 2689 Mike Gomez
☐ 2690 Rob Grable
☐ 2691 David Hayden
☐ 2692 Ken Sirak
☐ 2693 Jon Zuber
☐ 2694 Jay Edwards
☐ 2695 Phil Geisler
☐ 2696 Chad McConnell
☐ 2697 David Tokheim
☐ 2698 Tom Vilet
☐ 2699 Bill Dancy MG
☐ 2700 Darold Knowles CO
Roly DeArmas CO
☐ 2701 Checklist

1993 Clinton Giants Classic/Best

This 30-card standard-size set of the 1993 Clinton Giants, a Class A Midwest League affiliate of the San Francisco Giants, features white-bordered posed color player shots on its fronts. A team-color-coded stripe below the photo carries the player's name; another above, his position and team name. On a ghosted team-logo, the white back carries the player's name at the top, followed by biography and statistics.

	MINT	NRMT	EXC
COMPLETE SET (30)	5.00	2.20	.60

☐ 1 Jim Rosenbohm
☐ 2 Charles Alimena
☐ 3 David Baine
☐ 4 Marvin Benard
☐ 5 Jamie Brewington
☐ 6 Marino Castillo
☐ 7 Mike Cavanagh
☐ 8 Ron Crowe
☐ 9 Tracey Ealy
☐ 10 Aaron Fultz
☐ 11 Chris Gambs
☐ 12 Andy Heckman
☐ 13 Marcus Jensen
☐ 14 Clay King
☐ 15 Jeff Locklear
☐ 16 Craig Mayes
☐ 17 Tom O'Neill
☐ 18 Papo Ramos
☐ 19 Jeff Richey
☐ 20 Petie Roach
☐ 21 Mark Saugstad
☐ 22 D.J. Thielen
☐ 23 Carlos Valdez
☐ 24 Kevin Wong
☐ 25 Kenny Woods
☐ 26 Jack Mull MG
☐ 27 Frank Cacciatore CO
☐ 28 Steve Lienhard CO
☐ 29 Steve Dietzman TR
☐ 30 Checklist

1993 Clinton Giants Fleer/ProCards

This 28-card standard-size set of the 1993 Clinton Giants, a Class A Midwest League affiliate of the San Francisco Giants, features white-bordered posed color player photos on its fronts. The player's name, team, and position appear near the bottom. The white horizontal back is framed by a blue line and carries the player's name at the top, followed by biography and statistics. A drawing of a ballplayer in action appears on the left.

	MINT	NRMT	EXC
COMPLETE SET (28)	5.00	2.20	.60

☐ 2480 Jamie Brewington
☐ 2481 Marino Castillo
☐ 2482 Ron Crowe
☐ 2483 Aaron Fultz
☐ 2484 Chris Gambs
☐ 2485 Andy Heckman
☐ 2486 Jeff Locklear
☐ 2487 Jeff Myers
☐ 2488 Jeff Richey
☐ 2489 Jim Rosembohm
☐ 2490 Carlos Valdez
☐ 2491 Mike Cavanagh
☐ 2492 Marcus Jensen
☐ 2493 Craig Mayes
☐ 2494 Charles Alimena
☐ 2495 Chad Fonville
☐ 2496 Tom O'Neill
☐ 2497 D.J. Thielen
☐ 2498 Kevin Wong
☐ 2499 Marvin Benard
☐ 2500 Tracey Ealy
☐ 2501 Petie Roach
☐ 2502 Benji Simonton
☐ 2503 Kenny Woods
☐ 2504 Jack Mull MG
☐ 2505 Frank Cacciatore CO
☐ 2506 Steve Lienhard CO
☐ 2507 Checklist

1993 Colorado Springs Sky Sox Fleer/ProCards

This 25-card standard-size set of the 1993 Colorado Springs Sky Sox, a Class AAA Pacific Coast League affiliate of the Colorado Rockies, features white-bordered posed color player photos on its fronts. The player's name, team, and position appear near the bottom. The white horizontal back is framed by a blue line and carries the player's name at the top, followed by biography and statistics. A drawing of a ballplayer in action appears on the left.

	MINT	NRMT	EXC
COMPLETE SET (25)	5.00	2.20	.60

☐ 3080 Steve Allen
☐ 3081 Ryan Hawbitzel
☐ 3082 Curt Leskanic
☐ 3083 Mike Munoz
☐ 3084 Lance Painter
☐ 3085 Dana Ridenour
☐ 3086 Mo Sanford
☐ 3087 Mark Thompson
☐ 3088 Brad Ausmus
☐ 3089 Gilberto Reyes
☐ 3090 Jason Bates
☐ 3091 Pedro Castellano
☐ 3092 Stu Cole
☐ 3093 Jay Gainer
☐ 3094 Trent Hubbard
☐ 3095 Nelson Liriano
☐ 3096 Roberto Mejia
☐ 3097 Andy Mota
☐ 3098 Edwin Alicea
☐ 3099 Jim Olander
☐ 3100 Sean Ross
☐ 3101 Brad Mills MG
☐ 3102 Frank Funk CO
☐ 3103 Bobby Meacham CO
☐ 3104 Checklist

1993 Columbus Clippers Police

	MINT	NRMT	EXC
COMPLETE SET (25)	6.00	2.70	.75

☐ 1 Royal Clayton
☐ 2 Andy Cook
☐ 3 Francisco de la Rosa
☐ 4 Kenny Greer
☐ 5 Sterling Hitchcock
☐ 6 Kirt Ojala
☐ 7 Don Stanford
☐ 8 Mark Hutton
☐ 9 Sam Militello
☐ 10 Bobby Munoz
☐ 11 Kiki Hernandez
☐ 12 Gordon Sanchez
☐ 13 Russ Davis
☐ 14 Stump Merrill MG
☐ 15 Carlos Rodriguez
☐ 16 Dave Silvestri
☐ 17 Don Sparks
☐ 18 Andy Stankiewicz
☐ 19 Hensley Meulens
☐ 20 Gerald Williams
☐ 21 Mike Humphreys
☐ 22 Jay Knoblauh
☐ 23 Billy Masse
☐ 24 Stump Merrill CO
Hop Cassady CO
Ted Uhlaender CO
Darren London TR
Mike Brown CO
☐ 25 Ken Schnacke MG

1993 Columbus Clippers Fleer/ProCards

This 27-card standard-size set of the 1993 Columbus Clippers, a Class AAA International League affiliate of the New York Yankees, features white-bordered posed color player photos on its fronts. The player's name, team, and position appear near the bottom. The white horizontal back is framed by a blue line and carries the player's name at the top, followed by biography and statistics. A drawing of a ballplayer in action appears on the left.

	MINT	NRMT	EXC
COMPLETE SET (27)	5.00	2.20	.60

☐ 1102 Royal Clayton
☐ 1103 Andy Cook
☐ 1104 Francisco DeLaRosa
☐ 1105 Kenny Greer
☐ 1106 Sterling Hitchcock
☐ 1107 Mark Hutton
☐ 1108 Jeff Johnson
☐ 1109 Sam Militello
☐ 1110 Bobby Munoz
☐ 1111 Kirt Ojala
☐ 1112 Don Stanford
☐ 1113 Kiki Hernandez
☐ 1114 Gordon Sanchez
☐ 1115 Russ Davis
☐ 1116 Bobby DeJardin
☐ 1117 Carlos Rodriguez
☐ 1118 Dave Silvestri
☐ 1119 Don Sparks
☐ 1120 Andy Stankiewicz
☐ 1121 Mike Humphreys
☐ 1122 Jay Knoblauh
☐ 1123 Billy Masse
☐ 1124 Hensley Meulens
☐ 1125 Gerald Williams
☐ 1126 Stump Merrill MG
☐ 1127 Field Staff Card
☐ 1128 Checklist

1993 Columbus RedStixx Classic/Best

This 30-card standard-size set of the 1993 Columbus RedStixx, a Class A South Atlantic League affiliate of the Cleveland Indians, features white-bordered posed color player shots on its fronts. A team-color-coded stripe below the photo carries the player's name; another above, his position and team name. On a ghosted team-logo, the white back carries the player's name at the top, followed by biography and statistics.

	MINT	NRMT	EXC
COMPLETE SET (30)	5.00	2.20	.60

☐ 1 Derek Hacopian
☐ 2 Brian Arntzen
☐ 3 Jim Beauchamp
☐ 4 Pat Bryant
☐ 5 Jose Cabrera
☐ 6 Epi Cardenas
☐ 7 John Carter
☐ 8 Patricio Claudio
☐ 9 Felipe Duran
☐ 10 Paul Gibbs
☐ 11 Pep Harris
☐ 12 Sam Hence
☐ 13 Damian Jackson
☐ 14 Rod Koller
☐ 15 Mitch Meluskey
☐ 16 Rafael Mercado
☐ 17 Jon Nunnally
☐ 18 Jeff Williams
☐ 19 Oscar Resendez
☐ 20 Scott Sharts
☐ 21 Fred Smith
☐ 22 Jamie Taylor
☐ 23 J.J. Thobe
☐ 24 Chad Townsend
☐ 25 Andre White
☐ 26 Charles York
☐ 27 Mike Brown MG
☐ 28 Dan Williams CO
☐ 29 Fred Gladding CO
☐ 30 Ted Blackwell TR
Checklist

1993 Columbus RedStixx Fleer/ProCards

This 30-card standard-size set of the 1993 Columbus RedStixx, a Class A South Atlantic League affiliate of the Cleveland Indians, features white-bordered posed color player photos on its fronts. The player's name, team, and position appear near the bottom. The white horizontal back is framed by a blue line and carries the player's name at the top, followed by biography and statistics. A drawing of a ballplayer in action appears on the left.

	MINT	NRMT	EXC
COMPLETE SET (30)	5.00	2.20	.60

☐ 588 Jim Beauchamp
☐ 589 Jose Cabera
☐ 590 John Carter
☐ 591 Paul Gibbs
☐ 592 Pep Harris
☐ 593 Rod Koller
☐ 594 Oscar Resendez
☐ 595 Scott Sharts
☐ 596 Fred Smith
☐ 597 J.J. Thobe
☐ 598 Jeff Williams
☐ 599 Charles York
☐ 600 Brian Arntzen
☐ 601 Mitch Meluskey
☐ 602 Epi Cardenas
☐ 603 Felipe Duran
☐ 604 Damian Jackson
☐ 605 Rafael Mercado
☐ 606 Jonathan Nunnally
☐ 607 Jamie Taylor
☐ 608 Chad Townsend
☐ 609 Pat Bryant
☐ 610 Patricio Claudio
☐ 611 Derek Hacopian
☐ 612 Sam Hence
☐ 613 Andre White
☐ 614 Mike Brown MG
☐ 615 Fred Gladding CO
☐ 616 Dan Williams CO
☐ 617 Checklist

1993 Danville Braves Classic/Best

This 30-card standard-size set of the 1993 Danville Braves, a Rookie Class Appalachian League affiliate of the Atlanta Braves, features white-bordered posed color player shots on its fronts. A team-color-coded stripe below the photo carries the player's name; another above, his position and team name. On a ghosted team-logo, the white back carries the player's name at the top, followed by biography and statistics. This issue includes the minor league card debuts of Damon Hollins and Randall Simon.

	MINT	NRMT	EXC
COMPLETE SET (30)	8.00	3.60	1.00

☐ 1 Andre King
☐ 2 Fernando Benitez
☐ 3 Jeff Bock
☐ 4 Craig Bradshaw
☐ 5 Shawn Brennan
☐ 6 Darold Brown
☐ 7 Matt Byrd
☐ 8 Maurice Christmas
☐ 9 Jose Columna
☐ 10 Chris Cox
☐ 11 Burke Cromer
☐ 12 Jason Dailey
☐ 13 Will Havens
☐ 14 Damon Hollins
☐ 15 Feliberto Selmo
☐ 16 Ryan Jacobs
☐ 17 Carey Paige
☐ 18 Billy Paragin
☐ 19 John Reece
☐ 20 Sherton Saturnino
☐ 21 Carl Schutz Jr.
☐ 22 Bill Shafer
☐ 23 Jason Shelley
☐ 24 Randall Simon
☐ 25 Sean Smith
☐ 26 Angelo Stutts
☐ 27 Kenneth Warner
☐ 28 Mike Wieser
☐ 29 Esteban Yan
☐ 30 Bruce Benedict MG
Checklist

1993 Danville Braves Fleer/ProCards

This 31-card standard-size set of the 1993 Danville Braves, a Rookie Class Appalachian League affiliate of the Atlanta Braves, features white-bordered posed color player photos on its fronts. The player's name, team, and position appear near the bottom. The white horizontal back is framed by a blue line and carries the player's name at the top, followed by biography and statistics. A drawing of a ballplayer in action appears on the left. This set includes the first team set cards of Damon Hollins and Randall Simon.

	MINT	NRMT	EXC
COMPLETE SET (31)	8.00	3.60	1.00

☐ 3608 Jeff Bock
☐ 3609 Craig Bradshaw
☐ 3610 Darold Brown
☐ 3611 Matt Byrd
☐ 3612 Maurice Christmas
☐ 3613 Burke Cromer
☐ 3614 Will Havens
☐ 3615 Ryan Jacobs
☐ 3616 Carey Paige
☐ 3617 Carl Schultz
☐ 3618 Bill Shafer
☐ 3619 Esteban Yan
☐ 3620 Fernando Benitez
☐ 3621 Billy Paragin
☐ 3622 Sean Smith
☐ 3623 Jose Columna
☐ 3624 Chris Cox
☐ 3625 Feliberto Selmo
☐ 3626 Randall Simon
☐ 3627 Kenneth Warner
☐ 3628 Mike Wieser
☐ 3629 Shawn Brennan
☐ 3630 Jason Dailey
☐ 3631 Damon Hollins
☐ 3632 Andre King
☐ 3633 John Reece
☐ 3634 Sherton Saturnino
☐ 3635 Jason Shelley
☐ 3636 Angelo Stutts
☐ 3637 Bruce Benedict MG
☐ 3638 Checklist

1993 David Lipscomb Bisons

	MINT	NRMT	EXC
COMPLETE SET (25)	10.00	4.50	1.25

☐ 1 Matt Alexander
☐ 2 John Boatman
☐ 3 Paul Bobo
☐ 4 Brad Buher
☐ 5 Kerry Coker
☐ 6 Ken Dugan CO
☐ 7 Kurt Dugan
☐ 8 Chad Estep
☐ 9 Chris Gainer
Adam Sullivan
☐ 10 Jeremy Graham
☐ 11 Bailey Heflin
☐ 12 Joey Henson
☐ 13 Alex Irons
☐ 14 Gary Johnson
☐ 15 Chris Lewis
☐ 16 Brian Mast
☐ 17 Joey McDaniel
Brent High
☐ 18 Michael Rollins
☐ 19 Troy Rorex
☐ 20 Bryan Skelton
☐ 21 Brian Womble
☐ 22 Chris Young
Brian Fann
☐ 23 Assistant Coaches
Lynn Griffith
Roy Pardue
Kolin Holladay
☐ 24 Managers - Trainers
Bubba Moneypenny
Wally Hitchcox
Brent Oliver
Craig Portwood
☐ 25 Redshirt Players
Aaron Bronson
Brett Shackelford
Jake Wolaver
Hunter Henson

1993 Daytona Cubs Classic/Best

This 30-card standard-size set of the 1993 Daytona Cubs, a Class A Florida State League affiliate of the Chicago Cubs, features white-bordered posed color player shots on its fronts. A team-color-coded stripe below the photo carries the player's name; another above, his position and team name. On a ghosted team-logo, the white back carries the player's name at the top, followed by biography and statistics.

	MINT	NRMT	EXC
COMPLETE SET (30)	5.00	2.20	.60

☐ 1 Andrew Hartung
☐ 2 Terry Adams
☐ 3 Adam Brown
☐ 4 Ben Burlingame
☐ 5 Tim Delgado
☐ 6 Lance Dickson
☐ 7 Jay Franklin
☐ 8 Doug Glanville
☐ 9 Rudy Gomez
☐ 10 Mike Hubbard
☐ 11 Chuck Kirk
☐ 12 Ed Larregui
☐ 13 Danny Montero
☐ 14 Bernardino Nunez
☐ 15 Chris Petersen
☐ 16 Carl Schramm
☐ 17 Daniel Smith
☐ 18 Kennie Steenstra
☐ 19 Joe Terilli
☐ 20 Mike Tidwell
☐ 21 Paul Torres
☐ 22 Derek Wallace
☐ 23 Frederick White
☐ 24 Bill Hayes
☐ 25 Les Strode
☐ 26 Joe Tanner CO
☐ 27 Steve Melendez TR
☐ 28 Brien Taylor
Classic Best
Advertisement
☐ 29 Title Card
☐ 30 Checklist

1993 Daytona Cubs Fleer/ProCards

This 26-card standard-size set of the 1993 Daytona Cubs, a Class A Florida State League affiliate of the Chicago Cubs, features white-bordered posed color player photos on its fronts. The player's name, team, and position appear near the bottom. The white horizontal back is framed by a blue line and carries the player's name at the top, followed by biography and statistics. A drawing of a ballplayer in action appears on the left.

	MINT	NRMT	EXC
COMPLETE SET (26)	5.00	2.20	.60

☐ 850 Terry Adams
☐ 851 Ben Burlingame
☐ 852 Tim Delgado
☐ 853 Lance Dickson
☐ 854 Jay Franklins
☐ 855 Chuck Kirk
☐ 856 Carl Schramm
☐ 857 Ken Steenstra
☐ 858 Mike Tidwell
☐ 859 Derek Wallace
☐ 860 Fred White
☐ 861 Adam Brown
☐ 862 Mike Hubbard
☐ 863 Danny Montero
☐ 864 Andy Hartung
☐ 865 Chris Peterson
☐ 866 Dan Smith
☐ 867 Tim Stutheit
☐ 868 Doug Glavnille
☐ 869 Ed Larregui
☐ 870 Bernardino Nunez
☐ 871 Joe Terilli
☐ 872 Paul Torres
☐ 873 Bill Hayes MG
☐ 874 Les Strode CO
☐ 875 Checklist

1993 Dunedin Blue Jays Classic/Best

This 30-card standard-size set of the 1993 Dunedin Blue Jays, a Class A Florida State League affiliate of the Toronto Blue Jays, features white-bordered posed color player shots on its fronts. A team-color-coded stripe below the photo carries the player's name; another above, his position and team name. The white back carries the player's name at the top, followed by biography and statistics.

	MINT	NRMT	EXC
COMPLETE SET (30)	5.00	2.20	.60

☐ 1 Todd Steverson
☐ 2 Tilson Brito
☐ 3 Eric Brooks
☐ 4 Rich Butler
☐ 5 Giovanni Carrara
☐ 6 Felipe Crespo
☐ 7 Dennis Gray
☐ 8 Scott Grove
☐ 9 Kurt Heble
☐ 10 Rick Holifield
☐ 11 Tom Hotchkiss
☐ 12 Matt Johnson
☐ 13 Chris Kotes
☐ 14 Tim Lindsay
☐ 15 Marc Loeb
☐ 16 Brent Lutz
☐ 17 Al Montoya
☐ 18 Gabriel Rosario
☐ 19 Don Sheppard
☐ 20 Tom Singer
☐ 21 Paul Spoljaric
☐ 22 Rick Steed
☐ 23 Chris Stynes
☐ 24 Ben Weber
☐ 25 Chris Weinke
☐ 26 Dennis Holmberg MG
☐ 27 Bill Monbouquette CO
☐ 28 John Woodworth TR
☐ 29 Kenny Holmberg BB
☐ 30 Chris Nega BB
Checklist

1993 Dunedin Blue Jays Family Fun Night

	MINT	NRMT	EXC
COMPLETE SET (30)	20.00	9.00	2.50

☐ 1 Doug Ault
☐ 2 Tilson Brito
☐ 3 Eric Brooks
☐ 4 Rich Butler
☐ 5 Giovanni Carrara
☐ 6 Felipe Crespo
☐ 7 Dennis Gray
☐ 8 Scott Grove
☐ 9 Kurt Heble
☐ 10 Rick Holifield
☐ 11 Dennis Holmberg
☐ 12 Tom Hotchkiss
☐ 13 Matt Johnson
☐ 14 Chris Kotes
☐ 15 Tim Lindsay
☐ 16 Marc Loeb
☐ 17 Brent Lutz
☐ 18 Bill Monbouquette
☐ 19 Al Montoya
☐ 20 Gabriel Rosario
☐ 21 Don Sheppard
☐ 22 Tom Singer
☐ 23 Paul Spoljaric
☐ 24 Rick Steed
☐ 25 Todd Steverson
☐ 26 Chris Stynes
☐ 27 Ben Weber
☐ 28 Chris Weinke
☐ 29 Jon Woodworth
☐ 30 Team Photo CL

1993 Dunedin Blue Jays Fleer/ProCards

This 27-card standard-size set of the 1993 Dunedin Blue Jays, a Class A Florida State League affiliate of the Toronto Blue Jays, features white-bordered posed color player photos on its fronts. The player's name, team, and position appear near the bottom. The white horizontal back is framed by a blue line and carries the player's name at the top, followed by biography and statistics. A drawing of a ballplayer in action appears on the left.

	MINT	NRMT	EXC
COMPLETE SET (27)	5.00	2.20	.60

☐ 1787 Giovanni Carrara
☐ 1788 Dennis Gray
☐ 1789 Scott Grove
☐ 1790 Kurt Heble
☐ 1791 Tom Hotchkiss
☐ 1792 Chris Kotes
☐ 1793 Al Montoya
☐ 1794 Randy Phillips
☐ 1795 Tom Singer
☐ 1796 Rick Steed
☐ 1797 Ben Weber
☐ 1798 Eric Brooks
☐ 1799 Marc Loeb
☐ 1800 Brent Lutz
☐ 1801 Tilson Brito
☐ 1802 Carlos Cabrera
☐ 1803 Felipe Crespo
☐ 1804 Matt Johnson
☐ 1805 Chris Stynes
☐ 1806 Chris Weinke
☐ 1807 Rich Butler
☐ 1808 Ronald Helsel
☐ 1809 Rick Holifield
☐ 1810 Todd Steverson
☐ 1811 Dennis Holmberg MG
☐ 1812 Bill Monbouquette CO
☐ 1813 Checklist

1993 Durham Bulls Classic/Best

This 30-card standard-size set of the 1993 Durham Bulls, a Class A Carolina League affiliate of the Atlanta Braves, features white-bordered posed color player shots on its fronts. A team-color-coded stripe below the photo carries the player's name; another above, his position and team name. On a ghosted team-logo, the white back carries the player's name at the top, followed by biography and statistics.

	MINT	NRMT	EXC
COMPLETE SET (30)	5.00	2.20	.60

☐ 1 Vince Moore
☐ 2 Joe Ayrault
☐ 3 Dirk Blair
☐ 4 Kurt Burgess
☐ 5 Barry Chiles
☐ 6 Brad Clontz
☐ 7 Tom Coates
☐ 8 Tony Graffanino
☐ 9 Manny Jimenez
☐ 10 Pat Kelly
☐ 11 Jerry Koller
☐ 12 Tom Leahy
☐ 13 Lance Marks
☐ 14 Don Robinson
☐ 15 Scott Ryder
☐ 16 Ozzie Sanchez
☐ 17 Jason Schmidt
☐ 18 Chris Seelbach
☐ 19 Steve Swail
☐ 20 Pedro Swann
☐ 21 Dominic Therrien
☐ 22 Mike Warner
☐ 23 John Wilder
☐ 24 Juan Williams
☐ 25 Doug Wollenburg
☐ 26 Leon Roberts MG
☐ 27 Rick Albert CO
☐ 28 Tack Wilson CO
☐ 29 Matt West CO
☐ 30 Dave Tomchek TR
Checklist

1993 Durham Bulls Fleer/ProCards

This 31-card standard-size set of the 1993 Durham Bulls, a Class A Carolina League affiliate of the Atlanta Braves, features white-bordered posed color player photos on its fronts. The player's name, team, and position appear near the bottom. The white horizontal back is framed by a blue line and carries the player's name at the top, followed by biography and statistics. A drawing of a ballplayer in action appears on the left.

	MINT	NRMT	EXC
COMPLETE SET (31)	5.00	2.20	.60

☐ 477 Dirk Blair
☐ 478 Kurt Burgess
☐ 479 Barry Chiles
☐ 480 Brad Clontz
☐ 481 Jerry Koller
☐ 482 Tom Leahy
☐ 483 Kevin Lomon
☐ 484 Scott Ryder
☐ 485 Jason Schmidt

☐ 486 Chris Seelbach
☐ 487 John Wilder
☐ 488 Joe Ayrault
☐ 489 Steve Swail
☐ 490 Anthony Graffagnino
☐ 491 Manny Jimenez
☐ 492 Pat Kelly
☐ 493 Lance Marks
☐ 494 Dominic Therrien
☐ 495 Doug Wollenburg
☐ 496 Tom Coates
☐ 497 Vince Moore
☐ 498 Don Robinson
☐ 499 Ozzie Sanchez
☐ 500 Pedro Swann
☐ 501 Mike Warner
☐ 502 Juan Williams
☐ 503 Leon Roberts MG
☐ 504 Rick Albert CO
☐ 505 Matt West CO
☐ 506 Tack Wilson CO
☐ 507 Checklist

1993 Durham Bulls Team Issue

	MINT	NRMT	EXC
COMPLETE SET (31)	6.00	2.70	.75

☐ 1 Leon Roberts MG
☐ 2 Michael(Tack) Wilson CO
☐ 3 Matt West CO
☐ 4 Dave Tomchek TR
☐ 5 Team Photo
☐ 6 Durham Athletic Park
☐ 7 The Famous Bull
☐ 8 Mike Warner
☐ 10 Manny Jimenez
☐ 11 Pat Kelly
☐ 12 Kurt Burgess
☐ 13 Dominic Therrien
☐ 14 Brad Clontz
☐ 15 Pedro Swann
☐ 16 Doug Wollenburg
☐ 17 Juan Williams
☐ 18 John Wilder
☐ 19 Tom Coates
☐ 20 Tom Leahy
☐ 21 Kevin Lomon
☐ 22 Anthony Graffanino
☐ 23 Lance Marks
☐ 24 Vince Moore
☐ 27 Jerry Koller
☐ 28 Steve Swail
☐ 29 Jason Schmidt
☐ 31 Chris Seelbach
☐ 32 Don Robinson
☐ 33 Joe Ayrault
☐ 34 Barry Chiles
☐ 35 Dirk Blair

1993 Edmonton Trappers Fleer/ProCards

This 27-card standard-size set of the 1993 Edmonton Trappers, a Class AAA Pacific Coast League affiliate of the Florida Marlins, features white-bordered posed color player photos on its fronts. The player's name, team, and position appear near the bottom. The white horizontal back is framed by a blue line and carries the player's name at the top, followed by biography and statistics. A drawing of a ballplayer in action appears on the left..

	MINT	NRMT	EXC
COMPLETE SET (27)	5.00	2.20	.60

☐ 1129 Scott Anderson
☐ 1130 Jerry Don Gleaton
☐ 1131 John Johnstone
☐ 1132 Randy Kramer
☐ 1133 Jose Martinez
☐ 1134 Pat Rapp
☐ 1135 Rich Scheid
☐ 1136 Matt Turner
☐ 1137 Gene Walter
☐ 1138 Dave Weathers
☐ 1139 Mitch Lyden
☐ 1140 Terry McGriff
☐ 1141 Bob Natal
☐ 1142 Luis de los Santos
☐ 1143 Chuck Jackson
☐ 1144 Al Pedrique
☐ 1145 Gus Polidor
☐ 1146 Jeff Small
☐ 1147 Geronimo Berroa
☐ 1148 Nick Capra
☐ 1149 Mark Ryal
☐ 1150 Darrell Whitmore
☐ 1151 Nigel Wilson
☐ 1152 Sal Rende MG
☐ 1153 Fernando Arroyo CO
☐ 1154 Adrian Garrett CO
☐ 1155 Checklist

1993 El Paso Diablos Fleer/ProCards

This 30-card standard-size set of the 1993 El Paso Brewers, a Class AA Texas Laegue League affiliate of the Milwaukee Brewers, features white-bordered posed color player photos on its fronts. The player's name, team, and position appear near the bottom. The white horizontal back is framed by a blue line and carries the player's name at the top, followed by biography and statistics. A drawing of a ballplayer in action appears on the left.

	MINT	NRMT	EXC
COMPLETE SET (30)	5.00	2.20	.60

☐ 2940 Kurt Archer
☐ 2941 Glenn Carter
☐ 2942 Tim Dell
☐ 2943 Francisco Gamez
☐ 2944 Brian Hancock
☐ 2945 Dane Johnston
☐ 2946 Scott Karl
☐ 2947 Mark Kiefer
☐ 2948 Kevin Kloek
☐ 2949 Dave Richards
☐ 2950 Charlie Rogers
☐ 2951 Scott Taylor
☐ 2952 Bob Kappesser
☐ 2953 Mike Matheny
☐ 2954 Kevin Castleberry
☐ 2955 Jeff Cirillo
☐ 2956 Bo Dodson
☐ 2957 Al Lewis
☐ 2958 Rodney Lofton
☐ 2959 Ed Smith
☐ 2960 Wes Weger
☐ 2961 Mike Basse
☐ 2962 Michael Carter
☐ 2963 Steve Gill
☐ 2964 Rob Lukachyk
☐ 2965 Duane Singleton
☐ 2966 Tim Ireland MG
☐ 2967 Rob Derksen CO
☐ 2968 Ben Oglivie CO
☐ 2969 Checklist

1993 Elizabethton Twins Classic/Best

This 30-card standard-size set of the 1993 Elizabethton Twins, a Rookie Class Appalachian League affiliate of the Minnesota Twins, features white-bordered posed color player shots on its fronts. A team-color-coded stripe below the photo carries the player's name; another above, his position and team name. On a ghosted team-logo, the white back carries the player's name at the top, followed by biography and statistics. This issue includes the minor league card debut of Enrique Wilson.

	MINT	NRMT	EXC
COMPLETE SET (30)	7.00	3.10	.85

☐ 1 Dan Perkins
☐ 2 Jesus Acevedo
☐ 3 Jason Baker
☐ 4 Pedro Blanco
☐ 5 Shane Bowers
☐ 6 Armann Brown
☐ 7 Troy Carrasco
☐ 8 Trevor Cobb
☐ 9 Javier DeJesus
☐ 10 Deron Downhower
☐ 11 Edgar Herrera
☐ 12 Benjamin Jones
☐ 13 Tom Knauss
☐ 14 Russell Lehoisky
☐ 15 Shawn Miller
☐ 16 James Motte
☐ 17 Brian O'Brien
☐ 18 David Oiler
☐ 19 Chad Rupp
☐ 20 Scott Stricklin
☐ 21 Danny Venezia
☐ 22 Enrique Wilson
☐ 23 Stewart Cliburn CO
☐ 24 Brad Olson TR
☐ 25 Bill Crow PRES
☐ 26 David McQueen MG
☐ 27 Chipper Jones
Classic Best
Advertisement
☐ 28 Brien Taylor
Classic Best
Advertisement
☐ 29 Title Card
☐ 30 Checklist

1993 Elizabethton Twins Fleer/ProCards

This 25-card standard-size set of the 1993 Elizabethton Twins, a Rookie Class Appalachian League affiliate of the Minnesota Twins, features white-bordered posed color player photos on its fronts. The player's name, team, and position appear near the bottom. The white horizontal back is framed by a blue line and carries the player's name at the top, followed by biography and statistics. A drawing of a ballplayer in action appears on the left. This set includes Enrique Wilson's first team set card.

	MINT	NRMT	EXC
COMPLETE SET (25)	7.00	3.10	.85

☐ 3408 Shane Bowers
☐ 3409 Troy Carrasco
☐ 3410 Trevor Cobb
☐ 3411 Javier DeJesus
☐ 3412 Deron Dowher
☐ 3413 Russell Lahoisky
☐ 3414 Shawn Miller
☐ 3415 Brian O'Brien
☐ 3416 David Oiler
☐ 3417 Dan Perkins
☐ 3418 Jesus Acevedo
☐ 3419 Scott Stricklin
☐ 3420 Tom Knauss
☐ 3421 James Motte
☐ 3422 Chad Rupp
☐ 3423 Danny Venezia
☐ 3424 Ewligul Wilson
☐ 3425 Jason Baker
☐ 3426 Pedro Blanco
☐ 3427 Armann Brown
☐ 3428 Edgar Herrera
☐ 3429 Benjamin Jones
☐ 3430 Ray Smith MG
☐ 3431 Stu Cliburn CO
☐ 3432 Checklist

1993 Elmira Pioneers Classic/Best

This 30-card standard-size set of the 1993 Elmira Pioneers, a Class A New York-Penn League affiliate of the Florida Marlins, features white-bordered posed color player shots on its fronts. A team-color-coded stripe below the photo carries the player's name; another above, his position and team name. On a ghosted team-logo, the white back carries the player's name at the top, followed by biography and statistics. Erick Strickland, who went on to become an NBA player, is also in this set.

	MINT	NRMT	EXC
COMPLETE SET (30)	6.00	2.70	.75

☐ 1 Clemente Nunez
☐ 2 David Berg
☐ 3 Mitch Bowen
☐ 4 Ron Brown
☐ 5 Dan Chergey
☐ 6 Johnny Dominguez
☐ 7 Ryan Filbeck
☐ 8 Phil Gomez
☐ 9 Andy Larkin
☐ 10 Matt Martinez
☐ 11 Wiliam McMillon
☐ 12 Sam Minyard
☐ 13 Greg Mix
☐ 14 Robbie Moen
☐ 15 Andrew Prater
☐ 16 Sergio Sanchez
☐ 17 Rich Seminoff
☐ 18 Mike Sims
☐ 19 Andru Small
☐ 20 Scott Southard
☐ 21 Erick Strickland
☐ 22 Paul Thornton
☐ 23 Anthony Turnbull
☐ 24 Jon Van Zandt
☐ 25 Alan Walania
☐ 26 Bryan Ward
☐ 27 Lynn Jones MG
☐ 28 Bernie Flaherty CO
☐ 29 Title Card
☐ 30 Checklist

1993 Elmira Pioneers Fleer/ProCards

This 29-card standard-size set of the 1993 Elmira Pioneers, a Class A New York-Penn League affiliate of the Florida Marlins, features white-bordered posed color player photos on its fronts. The player's name, team, and position appear near the bottom. The white horizontal back is framed by a blue line and carries the player's name at the top, followed by biography and statistics. A drawing of a ballplayer in action appears on the left. This set includes the first team set cards of Andy Larkin and Billy McMillon. Erick Strickland, who went on to become an NBA player, is also in this set.

	MINT	NRMT	EXC
COMPLETE SET (29)	6.00	2.70	.75

☐ 3814 Mitch Bowen
☐ 3815 Dan Chergey
☐ 3816 Ryan Filbeck
☐ 3817 Phil Gomez
☐ 3818 Andy Larkin
☐ 3819 Sam Minyard
☐ 3820 Greg Mix
☐ 3821 Clemente Nunez
☐ 3822 Paul Thornton
☐ 3823 Jon VanZandt
☐ 3824 Al Walania
☐ 3825 Bryan Ward
☐ 3826 Andrew Prater
☐ 3827 Mike Sims
☐ 3828 Tony Turnbull
☐ 3829 Dave Berg
☐ 3830 Matt Martinez
☐ 3831 Sergio Sanchez
☐ 3832 Rich Seminoff
☐ 3833 Andru Small
☐ 3834 Scott Southard
☐ 3835 Ron Brown
☐ 3836 Billy McMillon
☐ 3837 Rob Moen
☐ 3838 Erick Strickland
☐ 3839 Lynn Jones MG
☐ 3840 Bernie Flaherty CO
☐ 3841 Jeff Pentland CO
☐ 3842 Checklist

1993 Erie Sailors Classic/Best

This 30-card standard-size set of the 1993 Erie Sailors, a Class A New York-Penn League affiliate of the Texas Rangers, features white-bordered posed color player shots on its fronts. A team-color-coded stripe below the photo carries the player's name; another above, his position and team name. On a ghosted team-logo, the white back carries the player's name at the top, followed by biography and statistics.

	MINT	NRMT	EXC
COMPLETE SET (30)	5.00	2.20	.60

☐ 1 Wes Shook
☐ 2 Brian Blair
☐ 3 Tim Cossins
☐ 4 Jeffrey Davis
☐ 5 Ray Desimone
☐ 6 Eric Dominow
☐ 7 James Franklin
☐ 8 Bert Gerhart III
☐ 9 Lonnie Goldberg
☐ 10 Pete Hartmann
☐ 11 Mike Hill
☐ 12 Rob Kell
☐ 13 Devin Kunz
☐ 14 Jr Lesch
☐ 15 Jorge Melendez
☐ 16 Eric Moody
☐ 17 Joe Morvay
☐ 18 Mark O'Brien
☐ 19 Cory Pearson
☐ 20 Marc Sagmoen
☐ 21 Rodney Seip
☐ 22 Wesley Sims
☐ 23 Scotty Smith
☐ 24 Alfred Triplett
☐ 25 Gregory Willming
☐ 26 Kevin Wozney
☐ 27 Doug Sisson MG
☐ 28 Marc Del Piano CO
☐ 29 Jim Benedict CO
☐ 30 Check Marquardt TR
Checklist

1993 Erie Sailors Fleer/ProCards

This 30-card standard-size set of the 1993 Erie Sailors, a Class A New York-Penn League affiliate of the Texas Rangers, features white-bordered posed color player photos on its fronts. The player's name, team, and position appear near the bottom. The white horizontal back is framed by a blue line and carries the player's name at the top, followed by biography and statistics. A drawing of a ballplayer in action appears on the left.

	MINT	NRMT	EXC
COMPLETE SET (30)	5.00	2.20	.60

☐ 3105 Jeff Davis
☐ 3106 Jim Franklins
☐ 3107 Bert Gerhart
☐ 3108 Peter Hartmann
☐ 3109 Rob Kell
☐ 3110 Devin Kunz
☐ 3111 Paul Lesch
☐ 3112 Eric Moody
☐ 3113 Joe Morvay
☐ 3114 Mark O'Brien
☐ 3115 Rodney Seip
☐ 3116 Scotty Smith
☐ 3117 Greg Willming
☐ 3118 Kevin Wozney
☐ 3119 Tim Cossins
☐ 3120 Jorge Melendez
☐ 3121 Wes Shook
☐ 3122 Ray DeSimone
☐ 3123 Eric Dominow
☐ 3124 Lonnie Goldberg
☐ 3125 Wes Sims
☐ 3126 Alfred Triplett
☐ 3127 Brian Blair
☐ 3128 Mike Hill
☐ 3129 Cory Pearson

☐ 3130 Marc Sagmoen
☐ 3131 Doug Sisson MG
☐ 3132 Jim Benedict CO
☐ 3133 Marc DelPiano CO
☐ 3134 Checklist

1993 Eugene Emeralds Classic/Best

This 30-card standard-size set of the 1993 Eugene Emeralds, a Class A Northwest League affiliate of the Kansas City Royals, features white-bordered posed color player shots on its fronts. A team-color-coded stripe below the photo carries the player's name; another above, his position and team name. On a ghosted team-logo, the white back carries the player's name at the top, followed by biography and statistics.

	MINT	NRMT	EXC
COMPLETE SET (30)	5.00	2.20	.60

☐ 1 Phil Grundy
☐ 2 Matthew Aminoff
☐ 3 Neil Atkinson
☐ 4 Rick Bacon
☐ 5 Phil Brassington
☐ 6 Nevin Brewer
☐ 7 Rick Burley
☐ 8 Jimmie Byington
☐ 9 Jeremy Carr
☐ 10 Malcolm Cepeda
☐ 11 Lino Diaz
☐ 12 Mike Evans
☐ 13 Sal Fasano
☐ 14 Pat Flury
☐ 15 Dwayne Gerald
☐ 16 Braxton Hickman
☐ 17 Oscar Jimenez
☐ 18 Cody Kosman
☐ 19 Andres Lopez
☐ 20 Luke Oglesby
☐ 21 Kris Ralston
☐ 22 O.J. Rhone
☐ 23 Juan Santos
☐ 24 Carlos Subero
☐ 25 Mike Sweeney
☐ 26 Ryan Towns
☐ 27 Stephen Wojtkowski
☐ 28 Brien Taylor
Classic Best
Advertisement
☐ 29 Title Card
☐ 30 Checklist

1993 Eugene Emeralds Fleer/ProCards

This 29-card standard-size set of the 1993 Eugene Emeralds, a Class A Northwest League affiliate of the Kansas City Royals, features white-bordered posed color player photos on its fronts. The player's name, team, and position appear near the bottom. The white horizontal back is framed by a blue line and carries the player's name at the top, followed by biography and statistics. A drawing of a ballplayer in action appears on the left.

	MINT	NRMT	EXC
COMPLETE SET (29)	5.00	2.20	.60

☐ 3844 Matthew Aminoff
☐ 3845 Neil Atkinson
☐ 3846 Rick Bacon
☐ 3847 Phil Brassington
☐ 3848 Nevin Brewer
☐ 3849 Rick Burley
☐ 3850 Pat Flury
☐ 3851 Phil Grundy
☐ 3852 Cody Kosman
☐ 3853 Andres Lopez
☐ 3854 Kris Ralson
☐ 3855 Kevin Rawitzer
☐ 3856 Juan Santos
☐ 3857 Ryan Towns
☐ 3858 Sal Fasano
☐ 3859 Mike Sweeney
☐ 3860 Jeremy Carr
☐ 3861 Lino Diaz
☐ 3862 Dwayne Gerald
☐ 3863 Braxton Hickman
☐ 3864 Carlos Subero
☐ 3865 Steve Wojkowski
☐ 3866 Jimmie Byington
☐ 3867 Mike Evans
☐ 3868 Thomathan Good
☐ 3869 Oscar Jimenez
☐ 3870 Luke Oglesby
☐ 3871 O.J. Rhone
☐ 3872 Checklist

1993 Everett Giants Classic/Best

This 30-card standard-size set of the 1993 Everett Giants, a Class A Northwest League affiliate of the San Francisco Giants, features white-bordered posed color player shots on its fronts. A team-color-coded stripe below the photo carries the player's name; another above, his position and team name. On a ghosted team-logo, the white back carries the player's name at the top, followed by biography and statistics.

	MINT	NRMT	EXC
COMPLETE SET (30)	5.00	2.20	.60

☐ 1 Heath Altman
☐ 2 Clark Anderson
☐ 3 Scott Barrett
☐ 4 Matt Baumann
☐ 5 Steve Bourgeois
☐ 6 Mike Cecere
☐ 7 Melvin Davis
☐ 8 Steve Day
☐ 9 Doug Drumm
☐ 10 Kris Franko
☐ 11 Marc Grande
☐ 12 Mark Gulseth
☐ 13 Chris Gump
☐ 14 Blair Hanneman
☐ 15 Brett King
☐ 16 Brian Lootens
☐ 17 Jeff Martin
☐ 18 Andy Mason
☐ 19 Bill Mueller
☐ 20 Gary Phillips
☐ 21 Chance Reynolds
☐ 22 Petie Roach
☐ 23 Mark Saugstad
☐ 24 Brent Smith
☐ 25 Brook Smith
☐ 26 Mitch Stafford
☐ 27 David Tessicini
☐ 28 Gene Thomas
☐ 29 Keith Williams
☐ 30 Brian Zaletel
Checklist

1993 Everett Giants Fleer/ProCards

This 31-card standard-size set of the 1993 Everett Giants, a Class A Northwest League affiliate of the San Francisco Giants, features white-bordered posed color player photos on its fronts. The player's name, team, and position appear near the bottom. The white horizontal back is framed by a blue line and carries the player's name at the top, followed by biography and statistics. A drawing of a ballplayer in action appears on the left.

	MINT	NRMT	EXC
COMPLETE SET (31)	5.00	2.20	.60

☐ 3756 Heath Altman
☐ 3757 Clark Anderson
☐ 3758 David Baine
☐ 3759 Matt Baumann
☐ 3760 Steven Bourgeis
☐ 3761 Steve Day
☐ 3762 Doug Drumm
☐ 3763 Kris Franko
☐ 3764 Marc Grande
☐ 3765 Blair Hanneman
☐ 3766 Jeff Martin
☐ 3767 Mark Saugstad
☐ 3768 Brent Smith
☐ 3769 Brook Smith
☐ 3770 Scott Barrett
☐ 3771 Mike Cecere
☐ 3772 Chance Reynolds
☐ 3773 Mark Gulseth
☐ 3774 Chris Gump
☐ 3775 Brett King
☐ 3776 Bill Mueller
☐ 3777 Gary Phillips
☐ 3778 Petie Roach
☐ 3779 Mitch Stafford
☐ 3780 David Tessicini
☐ 3781 Brian Zaletel
☐ 3782 Melvin Davis
☐ 3783 Brian Lootens
☐ 3784 Andy Mason
☐ 3785 Keith Williams
☐ 3786 Checklist

1993 Excel

The 1993 Excel Minor League set consists of 250 cards featuring minor league players from AAA, AA and A teams. The fronts display color player photos bordered in white. The player's name, the team's city, and his position appear in a gold foil bar superimposed at the bottom of the picture. The backs carry a large color close-up photo with the team logo superimposed at the upper left corner. Overlaying the photo toward the bottom is a colorful player information panel displaying biographical and statistical information. The cards are numbered on the back and checklisted below alphabetically within and according to major league teams for the NL and AL.

	MINT	NRMT	EXC
COMPLETE SET (250)	50.00	22.00	6.25
COMMON CARD (1-250)	.10	.05	.01
☐ 1 Mike D'Andrea	.10	.05	.01
☐ 2 Chipper Jones	10.00	4.50	1.25
☐ 3 Mike Kelly	.10	.05	.01
☐ 4 Brian Kowitz	.10	.05	.01
☐ 5 Napoleon Robinson	.10	.05	.01
☐ 6 Tony Tarasco	.10	.05	.01
☐ 7 Pedro Castellano	.10	.05	.01
☐ 8 Doug Glanville	.10	.05	.01
☐ 9 Andy Hartung	.10	.05	.01
☐ 10 Jay Hassel	.10	.05	.01
☐ 11 Ryan Hawblitzel	.10	.05	.01
☐ 12 Kevin Roberson	.10	.05	.01
☐ 13 Chad Tredaway	.10	.05	.01
☐ 14 Jose Vierra	.10	.05	.01
☐ 15 Matt Wallbeck	.10	.05	.01
☐ 16 Tim Belk	.10	.05	.01
☐ 17 Jamie Dismuke	.10	.05	.01
☐ 18 Chad Fox	.10	.05	.01
☐ 19 Micah Franklin	.10	.05	.01
☐ 20 Dan Frye	.10	.05	.01
☐ 21 Steve Gibralter	.15	.07	.02
☐ 22 Demetrish Jenkins	.10	.05	.01
☐ 23 Jason Kummerfeldt	.10	.05	.01
☐ 24 Bo Loftin	.10	.05	.01
☐ 25 Chad Mottola	.10	.05	.01
☐ 26 Bobby Perna	.10	.05	.01
☐ 27 Scott Pose	.10	.05	.01
☐ 28 Calvin Reese	.15	.07	.02
☐ 29 John Roper	.10	.05	.01
☐ 30 Jerry Spradin	.10	.05	.01
☐ 31 Roger Bailey	.10	.05	.01
☐ 32 Jason Bates	.10	.05	.01
☐ 33 John Burke	.10	.05	.01
☐ 34 Jason Hutchins	.10	.05	.01
☐ 35 Troy Ricker	.10	.05	.01
☐ 36 Mark Thompson	.10	.05	.01
☐ 37 Lou Lucca	.10	.05	.01
☐ 38 John Lynch	.10	.05	.01
☐ 39 Todd Pridy	.10	.05	.01
☐ 40 Gary Cooper	.10	.05	.01
☐ 41 Jim Dougherty	.10	.05	.01
☐ 42 Tony Eusebio	.10	.05	.01
☐ 43 Chris Hatcher	.10	.05	.01
☐ 44 Chris Hill	.10	.05	.01
☐ 45 Trent Hubbard	.10	.05	.01
☐ 46 Todd Jones	.10	.05	.01
☐ 47 Jeff Juden	.10	.05	.01
☐ 48 James Mouton	.10	.05	.01
☐ 49 Tom Nevers	.10	.05	.01
☐ 50 Jim Waring	.10	.05	.01
☐ 51 Chris Abbe	.10	.05	.01
☐ 52 Jay Kirkpatrick	.10	.05	.01
☐ 53 Raul Mondesi	3.00	1.35	.35
☐ 54 Vernon Spearman	.10	.05	.01
☐ 55 Tavo Alvarez	.10	.05	.01
☐ 56 Shane Andrews	.10	.05	.01
☐ 57 Yamil Benitez	.20	.09	.03
☐ 58 Cliff Floyd	.50	.23	.06
☐ 59 Antonio Grissom	.10	.05	.01
☐ 60 Tyrone Horne	.10	.05	.01
☐ 61 Mike Lansing	.15	.07	.02
☐ 62 Edgar Tovar	.10	.05	.01
☐ 63 Ugueth Urbina	.20	.09	.03
☐ 64 David Wainhouse	.10	.05	.01
☐ 65 Derrick White	.10	.05	.01
☐ 66 Gabe White	.10	.05	.01
☐ 67 Rondell White	2.00	.90	.25
☐ 68 Edgardo Alfonzo	.50	.23	.06
☐ 69 Jeromy Burnitz	.10	.05	.01
☐ 70 Jay Davis	.10	.05	.01
☐ 71 Cesar Diaz	.10	.05	.01
☐ 72 Todd Douma	.10	.05	.01
☐ 73 Brook Fordyce	.10	.05	.01
☐ 74 Butch Huskey	.60	.25	.07
☐ 75 Bobby Jones	.60	.25	.07
☐ 76 Jose Martinez	.10	.05	.01
☐ 77 Ricky Otero	.10	.05	.01
☐ 78 Jim Popoff	.10	.05	.01
☐ 79 Al Shirley	.10	.05	.01
☐ 80 Julian Vasquez	.10	.05	.01
☐ 81 Quilvio Veras	.20	.09	.03
☐ 82 Fernando Vina	.10	.05	.01
☐ 83 Ron Blazier	.10	.05	.01
☐ 84 Tommy Eason	.10	.05	.01
☐ 85 Tyler Green	.10	.05	.01
☐ 86 Mike Lieberthal	.20	.09	.03
☐ 87 Tom Nuneviller	.10	.05	.01
☐ 88 Matt Whisenant	.10	.05	.01
☐ 89 Jon Zuber	.10	.05	.01
☐ 90 Midre Cummings	.15	.07	.02
☐ 91 Jon Farrell	.10	.05	.01
☐ 92 Ramon Martinez	.10	.05	.01
☐ 93 Antonio Mitchell	.10	.05	.01
☐ 94 Keith Thomas	.10	.05	.01
☐ 95 Rene Arocha	.10	.05	.01
☐ 96 Brian Barber	.10	.05	.01
☐ 97 Jamie Cochran	.10	.05	.01
☐ 98 Mike Gulan	.10	.05	.01
☐ 99 Keith Johns	.10	.05	.01
☐ 100 John Kelly	.10	.05	.01
☐ 101 Anthony Lewis	.10	.05	.01
☐ 102 T.J. Mathews	.10	.05	.01
☐ 103 Kevin Meier	.10	.05	.01
☐ 104 David Oehrlein	.10	.05	.01
☐ 105 Gerry Santos	.10	.05	.01
☐ 106 Basil Shabazz	.10	.05	.01
☐ 107 Eddie Williams	.10	.05	.01
☐ 108 Dmitri Young	2.00	.90	.25
☐ 109 Jay Gainer	.10	.05	.01
☐ 110 Pedro Martinez	.10	.05	.01
☐ 111 Dave Staton	.10	.05	.01
☐ 112 Tim Worrell	.10	.05	.01
☐ 113 Dan Carlson	.10	.05	.01
☐ 114 Joel Chimelis	.10	.05	.01
☐ 115 Eric Christopherson	.10	.05	.01
☐ 116 Adell Davenport	.10	.05	.01
☐ 117 Ken Grundt	.10	.05	.01
☐ 118 Rick Huisman	.10	.05	.01
☐ 119 Andre Keene	.10	.05	.01
☐ 120 Kevin McGehee	.10	.05	.01
☐ 121 Salomon Torres	.10	.05	.01
☐ 122 Damon Buford	.10	.05	.01
☐ 123 Stanton Cameron	.10	.05	.01
☐ 124 Rick Krivda	.10	.05	.01
☐ 125 Alex Ochoa	2.50	1.10	.30
☐ 126 Brad Pennington	.10	.05	.01
☐ 127 Mark Smith	.10	.05	.01
☐ 128 Mel Wearing	.10	.05	.01
☐ 129 Cory Bailey	.10	.05	.01
☐ 130 Greg Blosser	.10	.05	.01
☐ 131 Joe Caruso	.10	.05	.01
☐ 132 Jason Friedman	.10	.05	.01
☐ 133 Jose Malave	.10	.05	.01
☐ 134 Jeff McNeely	.10	.05	.01
☐ 135 Luis Ortiz	.10	.05	.01
☐ 136 Ed Riley	.10	.05	.01
☐ 137 Frank Rodriguez	.40	.18	.05
☐ 138 Aaron Sele	.30	.14	.04
☐ 139 Garret Anderson	2.00	.90	.25
☐ 140 Ron Correia	.10	.05	.01
☐ 141 Jim Edmonds	5.00	2.20	.60
☐ 142 John Fritz	.10	.05	.01
☐ 143 Brian Grebeck	.10	.05	.01
☐ 144 Jeff Kipila	.10	.05	.01
☐ 145 Orlando Palmeiro	.10	.05	.01
☐ 146 Eduardo Perez	.10	.05	.01
☐ 147 John Pricher	.10	.05	.01
☐ 148 Chris Pritchett	.10	.05	.01
☐ 149 James Baldwin	.20	.09	.03
☐ 150 Rod Bolton	.10	.05	.01
☐ 151 Essex Burton	.10	.05	.01
☐ 152 Scott Cepicky	.10	.05	.01
☐ 153 Steve Olsen	.10	.05	.01
☐ 154 Scott Ruffcorn	.10	.05	.01
☐ 155 Steve Schrenk	.10	.05	.01
☐ 156 Larry Thomas	.10	.05	.01
☐ 157 Brandon Wilson	.10	.05	.01
☐ 158 Paul Byrd	.10	.05	.01
☐ 159 Willie Canate	.10	.05	.01
☐ 160 Marc Marini	.10	.05	.01
☐ 161 Jon Nunnally	.10	.05	.01
☐ 162 Chad Ogea	.10	.05	.01
☐ 163 Herb Perry	.10	.05	.01
☐ 164 Manny Ramirez	8.00	3.60	1.00
☐ 165 Omar Ramirez	.10	.05	.01
☐ 166 Ken Ramos	.10	.05	.01
☐ 167 Tracy Sanders	.10	.05	.01
☐ 168 Paul Shuey	.10	.05	.01
☐ 169 Kyle Washington	.10	.05	.01
☐ 170 Ivan Cruz	.10	.05	.01
☐ 171 Lou Frazier	.10	.05	.01
☐ 172 Brian Bevil	.10	.05	.01
☐ 173 Shane Halter	.10	.05	.01
☐ 174 Phil Hiatt	.10	.05	.01
☐ 175 Lance Jennings	.10	.05	.01
☐ 176 Les Norman	.10	.05	.01
☐ 177 Joe Randa	.15	.07	.02
☐ 178 Dan Rohmeier	.10	.05	.01
☐ 179 Larry Sutton	.10	.05	.01
☐ 180 Joe Vitiello	.10	.05	.01
☐ 181 John Byington	.10	.05	.01
☐ 182 Edgar Caceres	.10	.05	.01
☐ 183 Jeff Cirillo	.15	.07	.02
☐ 184 Mike Farrell	.10	.05	.01
☐ 185 Kenny Felder	.10	.05	.01
☐ 186 Tyrone Hill	.10	.05	.01
☐ 187 Brian Hostetler	.10	.05	.01
☐ 188 Danan Hughes	.10	.05	.01
☐ 189 Scott Karl	.10	.05	.01
☐ 190 Joe Kmak	.10	.05	.01
☐ 191 Rob Lukachyk	.10	.05	.01
☐ 192 Matt Mieske	.15	.07	.02
☐ 193 Troy O'Leary	.30	.14	.04
☐ 194 Cecil Rodriguez	.10	.05	.01
☐ 195 Tim Unroe	.10	.05	.01
☐ 196 Wes Weger	.10	.05	.01
☐ 197 Rich Becker	.20	.09	.03
☐ 198 Marty Cordova	3.00	1.35	.35
☐ 199 Steve Dunn	.15	.07	.02
☐ 200 Mike Durant	.10	.05	.01
☐ 201 Denny Hocking	.10	.05	.01

☐ 202 David McCarty	.10	.05	.01
☐ 203 Orlando Miller	.10	.05	.01
☐ 204 Scott Stahoviak	.15	.07	.02
☐ 205 Russ Davis	.40	.18	.05
☐ 206 Mike Draper	.10	.05	.01
☐ 207 Carl Everett	.15	.07	.02
☐ 208 Lew Hill	.10	.05	.01
☐ 209 Mark Hutton	.10	.05	.01
☐ 210 Derek Jeter	10.00	4.50	1.25
☐ 211 Kevin Jordan	.10	.05	.01
☐ 212 Lyle Mouton	.10	.05	.01
☐ 213 Bobby Munoz	.10	.05	.01
☐ 214 Andy Pettitte	6.00	2.70	.75
☐ 215 Brien Taylor	.10	.05	.01
☐ 216 Brent Gates	.10	.05	.01
☐ 217 Eric Helfand	.10	.05	.01
☐ 218 Curtis Shaw	.10	.05	.01
☐ 219 Todd Van Poppel	.10	.05	.01
☐ 220 Miah Bradbury	.10	.05	.01
☐ 221 Darren Bragg	.10	.05	.01
☐ 222 Jim Converse	.10	.05	.01
☐ 223 John Cummings	.10	.05	.01
☐ 224 Shawn Estes	.20	.09	.03
☐ 225 Mike Hampton	.15	.07	.02
☐ 226 Derek Lowe	.10	.05	.01
☐ 227 Ellerton Maynard	.10	.05	.01
☐ 228 Fred McNair	.10	.05	.01
☐ 229 Marc Newfield	.50	.23	.06
☐ 230 Desi Relaford	.10	.05	.01
☐ 231 Ruben Santana	.10	.05	.01
☐ 232 Bubba Smith	.10	.05	.01
☐ 233 Brian Turang	.10	.05	.01
☐ 234 Benji Gil	.10	.05	.01
☐ 235 Jose Oliva	.10	.05	.01
☐ 236 Jon Shave	.10	.05	.01
☐ 237 Travis Baptist	.10	.05	.01
☐ 238 Howard Battle	.15	.07	.02
☐ 239 Rob Butler	.10	.05	.01
☐ 240 Tim Crabtree	.10	.05	.01
☐ 241 Juan DeLaRosa	.10	.05	.01
☐ 242 Carlos Delgado	3.00	1.35	.35
☐ 243 Alex Gonzalez	.60	.25	.07
☐ 244 Steve Karsay	.15	.07	.02
☐ 245 Paul Spoljaric	.10	.05	.01
☐ 246 Todd Steverson	.10	.05	.01
☐ 247 Nigel Wilson	.10	.05	.01
☐ 248 Checklist (1-82)	.10	.05	.01
☐ 249 Checklist (83-164)	.10	.05	.01
☐ 250 Checklist (165-250)	.10	.05	.01

1993 Excel All-Stars

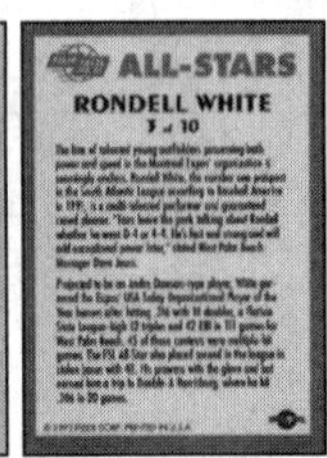

	MINT	NRMT	EXC
COMPLETE SET (10)	40.00	18.00	5.00
COMMON CARD (1-10)	2.00	.90	.25
☐ 1 Brien Taylor	2.00	.90	.25
☐ 2 Chipper Jones	25.00	11.00	3.10
☐ 3 Rondell White	6.00	2.70	.75
☐ 4 Mike Lieberthal	2.50	1.10	.30
☐ 5 Bobby Jones	2.50	1.10	.30
☐ 6 Carlos Delgado	8.00	3.60	1.00
☐ 7 Aaron Sele	2.00	.90	.25
☐ 8 Brent Gates	2.00	.90	.25
☐ 9 Phil Hiatt	2.00	.90	.25
☐ 10 Brandon Wilson	2.00	.90	.25

1993 Excel League Leaders

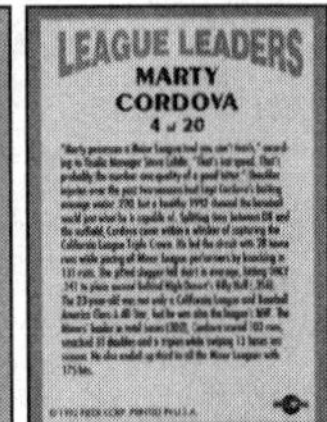

	MINT	NRMT	EXC
COMPLETE SET (20)	8.00	3.60	1.00
COMMON CARD (1-20)	.25	.11	.03
☐ 1 Travis Baptist	.25	.11	.03
☐ 2 Bubba Smith	.25	.11	.03
☐ 3 Rob Butler	.30	.14	.04
☐ 4 Marty Cordova	3.00	1.35	.35
☐ 5 John Fritz	.25	.11	.03
☐ 6 Quilvio Veras	.30	.14	.04
☐ 7 Cliff Floyd	.50	.23	.06
☐ 8 Denny Hocking	.25	.11	.03
☐ 9 Rich Becker	.50	.23	.06
☐ 10 Jim Popoff	.25	.11	.03
☐ 11 John Kelly	.25	.11	.03
☐ 12 Tavo Alvarez	.25	.11	.03
☐ 13 Scott Pose	.25	.11	.03
☐ 14 Steve Gibralter	.30	.14	.04
☐ 15 Joe Caruso	.25	.11	.03
☐ 16 Chad Ogea	.30	.14	.04
☐ 17 Troy O'Leary	.30	.14	.04
☐ 18 Russ Davis	.30	.14	.04
☐ 19 John Cummings	.25	.11	.03
☐ 20 Ken Ramos	.25	.11	.03

1993 Fayetteville Generals Classic/Best

This 30-card standard-size set of the 1993 Fayetteville Generals, a Class A South Atlantic League affiliate of the Detroit Tigers, features white-bordered posed color player shots on its fronts. A team-color-coded stripe below the photo carries the player's name; another above, his position and team name. On a ghosted team-logo, the white back carries the player's name at the top, followed by biography and statistics.

	MINT	NRMT	EXC
COMPLETE SET (30)	5.00	2.20	.60

☐ 1 Yuri Sanchez
☐ 2 Matt Bauer
☐ 3 Curt Bell
☐ 4 Mike Berlin
☐ 5 Tarrik Brock
☐ 6 Todd Bussa
☐ 7 Blas Cedeno
☐ 8 Kevin Crombie
☐ 9 Malvin DeJesus
☐ 10 Matt Evans
☐ 11 Peter Feeley
☐ 12 Keith Kimsey
☐ 13 Kevin Lidle
☐ 14 Brian Maxcy
☐ 15 Trever Miller
☐ 16 Jorge Moreno
☐ 17 David Mysel
☐ 18 Rick Navarro
☐ 19 Corey Parker
☐ 20 Clarke Rea
☐ 21 Roberto Rojas
☐ 22 Clint Sodowsky
☐ 23 Jorge Velandia
☐ 24 Sean Whiteside
☐ 25 Mark Wagner MG
☐ 26 Dwight Lowry CO
☐ 27 Brian Allard CO
☐ 28 Doug Teter TR
☐ 29 Jamzy (Mascot)
☐ 30 Checklist

1993 Fayetteville Generals Fleer/ProCards

This 29-card standard-size set of the 1993 Fayetteville Generals, a Class A South Atlantic League affiliate of the Detroit Tigers, features white-bordered posed color player photos on its fronts. The player's name, team, and position appear near the bottom. The white horizontal back is framed by a blue line and carries the player's name at the top, followed by biography and statistics. A drawing of a ballplayer in action appears on the left.

	MINT	NRMT	EXC
COMPLETE SET (29)	5.00	2.20	.60

☐ 119 Art Adams
☐ 120 Matt Bauer
☐ 121 Mike Berlin
☐ 122 Todd Bussa
☐ 123 Blas Cedeno
☐ 124 Kevin Crombie
☐ 125 Brian Maxcy
☐ 126 Trever Miller
☐ 127 David Mysel
☐ 128 Rick Navarro
☐ 129 Clint Sodowsky
☐ 130 Sean Whiteside
☐ 131 Curt Bell
☐ 132 Kevin Lidle
☐ 133 Clarke Rea
☐ 134 Malvin DeJesus
☐ 135 Matt Evans
☐ 136 Peter Feeley
☐ 137 Corey Parker
☐ 138 Yuri Sanchez
☐ 139 Jorge Velandia
☐ 140 Tarrick Brock
☐ 141 Keith Kimsey
☐ 142 Jorge Moreno
☐ 143 Roberto Rojas
☐ 144 Mark Wagner MG
☐ 145 Brian Allard CO
☐ 146 Dwight Lowry CO
☐ 147 Checklist

1993 Florida State League All-Stars Fleer/ProCards

	MINT	NRMT	EXC
COMPLETE SET (51)	12.00	5.50	1.50

☐ 1 Rich Aurilia
☐ 2 Todd Guggiana
☐ 3 Daryl Henderson
☐ 4 Wilson Heredia
☐ 5 Daryl Kennedy
☐ 6 Terrell Lowery
☐ 7 Rich Butler
☐ 8 Felipe Crespo
☐ 9 Randy Phillips
☐ 10 Chris Stynes
☐ 11 Ben Weber
☐ 12 Chris Weinke
☐ 13 Brian Bright
☐ 14 Brent Brede
☐ 15 Steve Hazlett
☐ 16 Damian Miller
☐ 17 Brian Edmondson
☐ 18 Rich Kelley
☐ 19 Phil Stidham
☐ 20 Justin Thompson
☐ 21 Brian Boehringer
☐ 22 Glenn DiSarcina
☐ 23 Robert Ellis
☐ 24 Nilson Robledo
☐ 25 Greg Brown
☐ 26 Rob Grable
☐ 27 Mike Juhl
☐ 28 Jason Moler
☐ 29 Jon Zuber
☐ 30 Tim Delgado
☐ 31 Mike Hubbard
☐ 32 Bernardino Nunez
☐ 33 Ken Steenstra
☐ 34 Tom Anderson
☐ 35 Kevin Lane
☐ 36 Buck McNabb
☐ 37 Chris White
☐ 38 Edgardo Alfonzo
☐ 39 Randy Curtis
☐ 40 Bernie Millan
☐ 41 Chris Roberts
☐ 42 Duff Brumley
☐ 43 Michael Cantu
☐ 44 Clint Davis
☐ 45 Jason Hisey
☐ 46 Chris Demetral
☐ 47 Ken Huckaby
☐ 48 Rich Linares
☐ 49 Rod Henderson
☐ 50 Tyrone Horne
☐ 51 Checklist

1993 Fort Lauderdale Red Sox Classic/Best

This 30-card standard-size set of the 1993 Ft. Lauderdale Red Sox, a Class A Florida State League affiliate of the Boston Red Sox, features white-bordered posed color player shots on its fronts. A team-color-coded stripe below the photo carries the player's name; another above, his position and team name. On a ghosted team-logo, the white back carries the player's name at the top, followed by biography and statistics.

	MINT	NRMT	EXC
COMPLETE SET (30)	5.00	2.20	.60

☐ 1 Brent Hansen
☐ 2 Chad Amos
☐ 3 Brian Bright
☐ 4 Bryan Brown
☐ 5 Todd Carey
☐ 6 Chris Davis
☐ 7 Tim Davis
☐ 8 Alex Delgado
☐ 9 Gino Dimare
☐ 10 Marty Durkin
☐ 11 Tony Ferreira
☐ 12 Melvin Gonzalez
☐ 13 Pete Hoy
☐ 14 Jeff Johnson
☐ 15 David Klvac
☐ 16 Randy Lawrence
☐ 17 Dana Levangie
☐ 18 Cesar Martinez
☐ 19 Nick Ortiz
☐ 20 Ken Osterkamp
☐ 21 Hilario Perez
☐ 22 Ed Perozo
☐ 23 Silverio Santa Maria
☐ 24 Emison Soto
☐ 25 Derek Vinyard
☐ 26 Jose Zambrano
☐ 27 DeMarlo Hale MG
☐ 28 Luis Doprante CO
☐ 29 Lee Stange CO
☐ 30 Jim Love TR
Checklist

1993 Fort Myers Miracle Classic/Best

This 30-card standard-size set of the 1993 Fort Myers Miracle, a Class A Florida State League affiliate of the Minnesota Twins, features white-bordered posed color player shots on its fronts. A team-color-coded stripe below the photo carries the player's name; another above, his position and team name. On a ghosted team-logo, the white back carries the player's name at the top, followed by biography and statistics.

	MINT	NRMT	EXC
COMPLETE SET (30)	5.00	2.20	.60

☐ 1 Chad Roper
☐ 2 Dave Bigham
☐ 3 Brent Brede
☐ 4 Matt Brown
☐ 5 Ted Corbin
☐ 6 Dickie Dixon
☐ 7 Mike Fernandez
☐ 8 Luis Garcia
☐ 9 David Garrow
☐ 10 Steve Hazlett
☐ 11 Tom Horincewich
☐ 12 Jim Kohl
☐ 13 Andrew Kontorinis
☐ 14 Damian Miller
☐ 15 Tim Moore
☐ 16 Willie Mota
☐ 17 Dan Naulty
☐ 18 Ken Norman
☐ 19 Jamie Ogden
☐ 20 Brad Radke
☐ 21 Brett Roberts
☐ 22 Bob Robinson
☐ 23 Craig Saccavino
☐ 24 Dennis Sweeney
☐ 25 Jeff Thelen
☐ 26 Steve Liddle MG
☐ 27 Jim Shellenback CO
☐ 28 Joel Safly TR
☐ 29 Kenny Agacinski BB
☐ 30 Checklist

1993 Fort Myers Miracle Fleer/ProCards

This 28-card standard-size set of the 1993 Fort Myers Miracle, a Class A Florida State League affiliate of the Minnesota Twins, features white-bordered posed color player photos on its fronts. The player's name, team, and position appear near the bottom. The white horizontal back is framed by a blue line and carries the player's name at the top, followed by biography and statistics. A drawing of a ballplayer in action appears on the left..

	MINT	NRMT	EXC
COMPLETE SET (28)	5.00	2.20	.60

☐ 2647 Dave Bigham
☐ 2648 Dickie Dixon
☐ 2649 Luis Garcia
☐ 2650 Jim Kohl
☐ 2651 Dan Naulty
☐ 2652 Brad Radke
☐ 2653 Brett Roberts
☐ 2654 Craig Saccavino
☐ 2655 Dennis Sweeney
☐ 2656 Mark Swope
☐ 2657 Jeff Thelen
☐ 2658 Matt Brown
☐ 2659 Damian Miller
☐ 2660 Ted Corbin
☐ 2661 Mike Fernandez
☐ 2662 Dave Garrow
☐ 2663 Tom Horincewich
☐ 2664 Andrew Kontorinis
☐ 2665 Chad Roper
☐ 2666 Brent Brede
☐ 2667 Butch Burrough
☐ 2668 Steve Hazlett
☐ 2669 Tim Moore
☐ 2670 Ken Norman
☐ 2671 Jamie Ogden
☐ 2672 Steve Liddle MG
☐ 2673 Jim Shellenback CO
☐ 2674 Checklist

1993 Fort Wayne Wizards Classic/Best

This 30-card standard-size set of the 1993 Fort Wayne Wizards, a Class A Midwest League affiliate of the Minnesota Twins, features white-bordered posed color player shots on its fronts. A team-color-coded stripe below the photo carries the player's name; another above, his position and team name. On a ghosted team-logo, the white back carries the player's name at the top, followed by biography and statistics.

	MINT	NRMT	EXC
COMPLETE SET (30)	7.00	3.10	.85

☐ 1 Dan Serafini
☐ 2 Armann Brown

☐ 3 Anthony Byrd
☐ 4 Ron Caridad
☐ 5 Marc Claus
☐ 6 Jose Correa
☐ 7 Tim Costic
☐ 8 Gus Gandarillas
☐ 9 Sean Gavaghan
☐ 10 LaTroy Hawkins
☐ 11 Edgar Herrera
☐ 12 Jeff Horn
☐ 13 Tom Knauss
☐ 14 Matt Lawton
☐ 15 Kevin Legault
☐ 16 Keith Linebarger
☐ 17 Rene Lopez
☐ 18 Joey Miller
☐ 19 Shawn Miller
☐ 20 Scott Moten
☐ 21 Marlo Nava
☐ 22 Todd Taylor
☐ 23 Ken Tirpack
☐ 24 Ramon Valette
☐ 25 Scott Watkins
☐ 26 Jim Dwyer MG
☐ 27 Rick Tomlin CO
☐ 28 Dan Fox TR
☐ 29 Eric Margenau OW
☐ 30 Wayne The Wizard (Mascot) Checklist

1993 Fort Wayne Wizards Fleer/ProCards

This 28-card standard-size set of the 1993 Fort Wayne Wizards, a Class A Midwest League affiliate of the Minnesota Twins, features white-bordered posed color player photos on its fronts. The player's name, team, and position appear near the bottom. The white horizontal back is framed by a blue line and carries the player's name at the top, followed by biography and statistics. A drawing of a ballplayer in action appears on the left. This set includes Dan Serafini's first team set card.

	MINT	NRMT	EXC
COMPLETE SET (28)	7.00	3.10	.85

☐ 1959 Ron Caridad
☐ 1960 Jose Correa
☐ 1961 Gus Gandarillas
☐ 1962 Sean Gavaghan
☐ 1963 LaTroy Hawkins
☐ 1964 Kevin Legault
☐ 1965 Keith Linebarger
☐ 1966 Shawn Miller
☐ 1967 Scott Moten
☐ 1968 Dan Serafini
☐ 1969 Todd Taylor
☐ 1970 Scott Watkins
☐ 1971 Jeff Horn
☐ 1972 Rene Lopez
☐ 1973 Marc Claus
☐ 1974 Tom Knauss
☐ 1975 Marlo Nava
☐ 1976 Ken Tirpack
☐ 1977 Ramon Valette
☐ 1978 Armann Brown
☐ 1979 Anthony Byrd
☐ 1980 Tim Costic
☐ 1981 Edgar Herrera
☐ 1982 Matt Lawton
☐ 1983 Joey Miller
☐ 1984 Jim Dwyer
☐ 1985 Rick Tomlin
☐ 1986 Checklist

1993 Frederick Keys Classic/Best

This 30-card standard-size set of the 1993 Frederick Keys, a Class A Carolina League affiliate of the Baltimore Orioles, features white-bordered posed color player shots on its fronts. A team-color-coded stripe below the photo carries the player's name; another above, his position and team name. On a ghosted team-logo, the white back carries the player's name at the top, followed by biography and statistics. This issue includes a second year card of Alex Ochoa.

	MINT	NRMT	EXC
COMPLETE SET (30)	7.00	3.10	.85

☐ 1 Brian DuBois
☐ 2 Jason Alstead
☐ 3 Al Benavides
☐ 4 Joe Borowski
☐ 5 Cesar Devarez
☐ 6 Vaughn Eshelman
☐ 7 Rick Forney
☐ 8 Curtis Goodwin
☐ 9 Kris Gresham
☐ 10 Jimmy Haynes
☐ 11 Stacy Jones
☐ 12 Scott Klingenbeck
☐ 13 Chris Lemp
☐ 14 Scott McClain
☐ 15 Doug McConathy
☐ 16 Feliciano Mercedes
☐ 17 Jose Millares
☐ 18 Alex Ochoa
☐ 19 Bo Ortiz
☐ 20 Dave Paveloff
☐ 21 John Polasek
☐ 22 Dan Ramirez
☐ 23 Brad Seitzer
☐ 24 Mark Smith
☐ 25 Troy Tallman
☐ 26 Pete MacKanin MG
☐ 27 Joe Durham CO
☐ 28 Larry McCall CO
☐ 29 Rudy Higgins TR
☐ 30 Key-Ote (Mascot) Checklist

1993 Frederick Keys Fleer/ProCards

This 30-card standard-size set of the 1993 Frederick Keys, a Class A Carolina League affiliate of the Baltimore Orioles, features white-bordered posed color player photos on its fronts. The player's name, team, and position appear near the bottom. The white horizontal back is framed by a blue line and carries the player's name at the top, followed by biography and statistics. A drawing of a ballpark in action appears on the left. This set includes a second year issue of Alex Ochoa.

	MINT	NRMT	EXC
COMPLETE SET (30)	7.00	3.10	.85

☐ 1016 Al Benadvides
☐ 1017 Joe Borowski
☐ 1018 Brian DuBois
☐ 1019 Vaughn Eshelman
☐ 1020 Rick Forney
☐ 1021 Jimmy Haynes
☐ 1022 Stacy Jones
☐ 1023 Scott Klingenbeck
☐ 1024 Chris Lemp
☐ 1025 Dave Paveloff
☐ 1026 John Polasek
☐ 1027 Mark Smith
☐ 1028 Cesar Devarez
☐ 1029 Kris Gresham
☐ 1030 Troy Tallman
☐ 1031 Gregg Castaldo
☐ 1032 Scott McClain
☐ 1033 Doug McConathy
☐ 1034 Feliciano Mercedes
☐ 1035 Jose Millares
☐ 1036 Dam Ramirez
☐ 1037 Brad Seitzer
☐ 1038 Jason Alstead
☐ 1039 Curtis Goodwin
☐ 1040 Alex Ochoa
☐ 1041 Basillio Ortiz
☐ 1042 Pete MacKanin MG
☐ 1043 Joe Durham CO
☐ 1044 Larry McCall CO
☐ 1045 Checklist

1993 Fort Lauderdale Red Sox Fleer/ProCards

This 30-card standard-size set of the 1993 Ft. Lauderdale Red Sox, a Class A Florida State League affiliate of the Boston Red Sox, features white-bordered posed color player photos on its fronts. The player's name, team, and position appear near the bottom. The white horizontal back is framed by a blue line and carries the player's name at the top, followed by biography and statistics. A drawing of a ballplayer in action appears on the left.

	MINT	NRMT	EXC
COMPLETE SET (30)	5.00	2.20	.60

☐ 1587 Chad Amos
☐ 1588 Chris Davis
☐ 1589 Melvin Gonzalez
☐ 1590 Brent Hansen
☐ 1591 Peter Hoy
☐ 1592 Jeff Johnson
☐ 1593 David Klvac
☐ 1594 Randy Lawrence
☐ 1595 Cesar Martinez
☐ 1596 Ken Osterkamp
☐ 1597 Hillario Perez
☐ 1598 Silverio Santa Maria
☐ 1599 Alex Delgado
☐ 1600 Dana Levangie
☐ 1601 Emison Soto
☐ 1602 Todd Carye
☐ 1603 Tim Davis
☐ 1604 Marty Durkin
☐ 1605 Tony Ferreira
☐ 1606 Nick Ortiz
☐ 1607 Ed Perozo
☐ 1608 Brian Bright
☐ 1609 Bryan Brown
☐ 1610 Gino DiMare
☐ 1611 Derek Vinyard
☐ 1612 Jose Zambrano
☐ 1613 DeMario Hale MG
☐ 1614 Luis Dorante CO
☐ 1615 Lee Stange CO
☐ 1616 Checklist

1993 Geneva Cubs Classic/Best

This 30-card standard-size set of the 1993 Geneva Cubs, a Class A New York-Penn League affiliate of the Chicago Cubs, features white-bordered posed color player shots on its fronts. A team-color-coded stripe below the photo carries the player's name; another above, his position and team name. On a ghosted team-logo, the white back carries the player's name at the top, followed by biography and statistics.

	MINT	NRMT	EXC
COMPLETE SET (30)	5.00	2.20	.60

☐ 1 Jon Ratliff
☐ 2 Doug Alongi
☐ 3 Thomas Ball
☐ 4 Joe Biernat
☐ 5 Kevin Booker
☐ 6 Alexander Cabrera
☐ 7 Ricardo Cruz
☐ 8 Brendan Donnelly
☐ 9 Demetrius Dowler
☐ 10 Gabe Duross
☐ 11 James Farrow
☐ 12 Michael Gibson
☐ 13 Shawn Hill
☐ 14 Greg Hillman
☐ 15 Sean Hogan
☐ 16 Karun Jackson
☐ 17 Ken Jones
☐ 18 Stephen Kulpa
☐ 19 Tony Locey
☐ 20 Brett McCabe
☐ 21 Shane McGinnis
☐ 22 Emilio Mendez
☐ 23 Danny Montero
☐ 24 Jared Snyder
☐ 25 Greg Twiggs
☐ 26 Wade Walker
☐ 27 Brent Woodall
☐ 28 James Young
☐ 29 Jerry Weinstein
☐ 30 John Noce Checklist

1993 Geneva Cubs Fleer/ProCards

This 31-card standard-size set of the 1993 Geneva Cubs, a Class A New York-Penn League affiliate of the Chicago Cubs, features white-bordered posed color player photos on its fronts. The player's name, team, and position appear near the bottom. The white horizontal back is framed by a blue line and carries the player's name at the top, followed by biography and statistics. A drawing of a ballplayer in action appears on the left.

	MINT	NRMT	EXC
COMPLETE SET (31)	5.00	2.20	.60

☐ 3165 Tom Ball
☐ 3166 Brendan Donnelly
☐ 3167 Jim Farrow
☐ 3168 Shawn Hill
☐ 3169 Greg Hillman
☐ 3170 Sean Hogan
☐ 3171 Anthony Locey
☐ 3172 Jon Ratliff
☐ 3173 Greg Twiggs
☐ 3174 Wade Walker
☐ 3175 Brent Woodall
☐ 3176 Ricardo Cruz
☐ 3177 Danny Montero
☐ 3178 Jared Snyder
☐ 3179 J.J. Biernat
☐ 3180 Alex Cabrera
☐ 3181 Demetrius Dowler
☐ 3182 Gabe DuRoss
☐ 3183 Karun Jackson
☐ 3184 Steve Kulpa
☐ 3185 Brent McCabe
☐ 3186 Shane McGinnis
☐ 3187 Emilio Mendez
☐ 3188 Doug Alongi
☐ 3189 Kevin Booker
☐ 3190 Michael Gibson
☐ 3191 Kenneth Jones
☐ 3192 James Young
☐ 3193 Jerry Weinstein MG
☐ 3194 Alan Dunn CO
☐ 3195 Checklist

1993 Glens Falls Redbirds Classic/Best

This 30-card standard-size set of the 1993 Glens Falls Redbirds, a Class A New York-Penn League affiliate of the St. Louis Cardinals, features white-bordered posed color player shots on its fronts. A team-color-coded stripe below the photo carries the player's name; another above, his position and team name. On a ghosted team-logo, the white back carries the player's name at the top, followed by biography and statistics.

	MINT	NRMT	EXC
COMPLETE SET (30)	5.00	2.20	.60

☐ 1 Joe Jumonville
☐ 2 Eric Alexander
☐ 3 Greg Almond
☐ 4 Matt Arrandale
☐ 5 Sal Bando
☐ 6 Jeff Berblinger
☐ 7 Mike Borzello
☐ 8 Ken Britt
☐ 9 Chance Cain
☐ 10 Rick Croushore
☐ 11 Mark Dean
☐ 12 Greg Deares
☐ 13 Osmel Garcia
☐ 14 Craig Grasser
☐ 15 Antoine Henry
☐ 16 Joe Henson
☐ 17 Ed Kehrli
☐ 18 Joe Larson
☐ 19 Victor Llanos
☐ 20 Tony Magnelli
☐ 21 Mike Matvey
☐ 22 Marc Ottmers
☐ 23 Dan Pontes
☐ 24 Trey Ritz
☐ 25 Steve Santucci
☐ 26 John Stutz
☐ 27 Mike Taylor
☐ 28 Mark Williams
☐ 29 Mike Windham
☐ 30 Mauricio Nunez Steve Turco Checklist

1993 Glens Falls Redbirds Fleer/ProCards

This 31-card standard-size set of the 1993 Glens Falls Redbirds, a Class A New York-Penn League affiliate of the St. Louis Cardinals, features white-bordered posed color player photos on its fronts. The player's name, team, and position appear near the bottom. The white horizontal back is framed by a blue line and carries the player's name at the top, followed by biography and statistics. A drawing of a ballplayer in action appears on the left.

	MINT	NRMT	EXC
COMPLETE SET (31)	5.00	2.20	.60

☐ 3992 Eric Alexander
☐ 3993 Matt Arrandale
☐ 3994 Kenny Britt
☐ 3995 Chance Cain
☐ 3996 Rick Croushore
☐ 3997 Craig Grasser
☐ 3998 Eddie Kehrli
☐ 3999 Joe Larson
☐ 4000 Anthony Magnelli
☐ 4001 Marc Ottmers
☐ 4002 Daniel Pontes
☐ 4003 Mike Windham
☐ 4004 Greg Almond
☐ 4005 Mike Borzello
☐ 4006 Mark Williams
☐ 4007 Sal Bando Jr.
☐ 4008 Jeff Berblinger
☐ 4009 Mark Dean
☐ 4010 Joey Henson
☐ 4011 Joe Jumonville
☐ 4012 Victor Llanos
☐ 4013 Mike Matvey
☐ 4014 Trey Ritz
☐ 4015 John Stutz
☐ 4016 Mike Taylor
☐ 4017 Greg Deares
☐ 4018 Ozzie Garcia
☐ 4019 Antoine Henry
☐ 4020 Steve Santucci
☐ 4021 Steve Turco MG
☐ 4022 Checklist

1993 Great Falls Dodgers Sports Pro

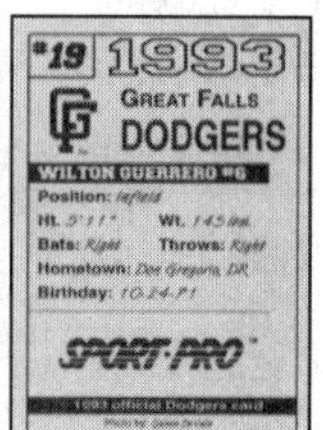

This issue includes the minor league card debut of Wilton Guerrero.

	MINT	NRMT	EXC
COMPLETE SET (30)	18.00	8.00	2.20

☐ 1 Craig Watts
☐ 2 Juan Hernaiz
☐ 3 Dan Markham
☐ 4 Kym Ashworth

☐ 5 Brian Clark
☐ 6 Mike Biltimier
☐ 7 Joshua Rash
☐ 8 Juan Rosario
☐ 9 Craig Scheffler
☐ 10 Eduardo Rios
☐ 11 Michael Kinney
☐ 12 Brian Rolocut
☐ 13 George Perez
☐ 14 Ken Sikes
☐ 15 Dave Steed
☐ 16 Ervan Wingate
☐ 17 Dan Sarmiento
☐ 18 Keith Troutman
☐ 19 Wilton Guerrero
☐ 20 Wilfredo Romero
☐ 21 Dan Hubbs
☐ 22 Daniel Camacho
☐ 23 Dwaine Bostic
☐ 24 Paul Wittig
☐ 25 Jason Kenady
☐ 26 Chris Costello
☐ 27 Brian Carpenter
☐ 28 Brian Richardson
☐ 29 James Breuer
☐ 30 Jon Debus MG

1993 Greensboro Hornets Classic/Best

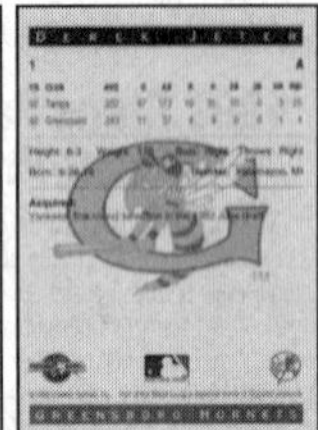

This 30-card standard-size set of the 1993 Greensboro Hornets, a Class A South Atlantic League affiliate of the New York Yankees, features white-bordered posed color player shots on its fronts. A team-color-coded stripe below the photo carries the player's name; another above, his position and team name. On a ghosted team-logo, the white back carries the player's name at the top, followed by biography and statistics. This issue includes a second year card of Derek Jeter.

	MINT	NRMT	EXC
COMPLETE SET(30)	25.00	11.00	3.10

☐ 1 Derek Jeter
☐ 2 Jeff Antolick
☐ 3 Mike Buddie
☐ 4 Jeff Cindrich
☐ 5 Billy Coleman
☐ 6 Abdiel Cumberbatch
☐ 7 Mike DeJean
☐ 8 Nick Delvecchio
☐ 9 Elston Hansen
☐ 10 Kraig Hawkins
☐ 11 Robert Hinds
☐ 12 Bert Inman
☐ 13 Ryan Karp
☐ 14 Blaise Kozeniewski
☐ 15 Joe Long
☐ 16 R.D. Long
☐ 17 Matt Luke
☐ 18 Bruce Pool
☐ 19 Scott Romano
☐ 20 Sandi Santiago
☐ 21 Shane Spencer
☐ 22 Ray Suplee
☐ 23 Jaime Torres
☐ 24 Bill Underwood
☐ 25 Kent Wallace
☐ 26 Jason Wuerch
☐ 27 Bill Evers MG
☐ 28 Ken Dominguez CO
☐ 29 Mascot logo
☐ 30 Checklist

1993 Greensboro Hornets Fleer/ProCards

This 31-card standard-size set of the 1993 Greensboro Hornets, a Class A South Atlantic League affiliate of the New York Yankees, features white-bordered posed color player photos on its fronts. The player's name, team, and position appear near the bottom. The white horizontal back is framed by a blue line and carries the player's name at the top, followed by biography and statistics. A drawing of a ballplayer in action appears on the left. This set includes a second year card of Derek Jeter.

	MINT	NRMT	EXC
COMPLETE SET(31)	25.00	11.00	3.10

☐ 876 Jeff Antolick
☐ 877 Mike Buddie
☐ 878 Jeff Cindrich
☐ 879 Billy Coleman
☐ 880 Mike DeJean
☐ 881 Bert Inman
☐ 882 Ryan Karp
☐ 883 Joe Long
☐ 884 Bruce Pool
☐ 885 Sandi Santiago
☐ 886 Bill Underwood
☐ 887 Kent Underwood
☐ 888 Jaime Torres
☐ 889 Tom Wilson
☐ 890 Nick Delvecchio
☐ 891 Elston Hansen
☐ 892 Robert Hinds
☐ 893 Derek Jeter
☐ 894 Blaise Kozeniewski
☐ 895 R.D. Long
☐ 896 Scott Romano
☐ 897 Abdiel Cumberbatch
☐ 898 Kraig Hawkins
☐ 899 Matt Luke
☐ 900 Shane Spencer
☐ 901 Ray Suplee
☐ 902 Jason Wuerch
☐ 903 Bill Evers MG
☐ 904 Gary Denbo CO
☐ 905 Mark Rose CO
☐ 906 Checklist

1993 Greenville Braves Fleer/ProCards

This 28-card standard-size set of the 1993 Greenville Braves, a Class AA Southern League affiliate of the Atlanta Braves, features white-bordered posed color player photos on its fronts. The player's name, team, and position appear near the bottom. The white horizontal back is framed by a blue line and carries the player's name at the top, followed by biography and statistics. A drawing of a ballplayer in action appears on the left.

	MINT	NRMT	EXC
COMPLETE SET (28)	5.00	2.20	.60

☐ 341 Brian Boltz
☐ 342 Dennis Burlingame
☐ 343 Vance Lovelace
☐ 344 Dale Polley
☐ 345 Mike Potts
☐ 346 Carlos Reyes
☐ 347 Blase Sparma
☐ 348 Don Strange
☐ 349 Lee Upshaw
☐ 350 Marcos Vasquez
☐ 351 Dave Williams
☐ 352 Tyler Houston
☐ 353 Ed Perez
☐ 354 Brad Ripplemeyer
☐ 355 Edwin Alicea
☐ 356 Tim Gillis
☐ 357 Ed Giovanola
☐ 358 Jose Olmeda
☐ 359 Hector Roa
☐ 360 Lee Heath
☐ 361 Troy Hughes
☐ 362 Brian Kowitz
☐ 363 Kevin O'Connor
☐ 364 Bruce Kimm MG
☐ 365 Dave Hilton CO
☐ 366 Bill Slack CO
☐ 367 Brian Snitker CO
☐ 368 Checklist

1993 Hagerstown Suns Classic/Best

This 30-card standard-size set of the 1993 Hagerstown Suns, a Class A South Atlantic League affiliate of the Toronto Blue Jays, features white-bordered posed color player shots on its fronts. A team-color-coded stripe below the photo carries the player's name; another above, his position and team name. The white back carries the player's name at the top, followed by statistics and biography. This issue includes Jose Silva's first Classic/Best team set appearance.

	MINT	NRMT	EXC
COMPLETE SET (30)	5.00	2.20	.60

☐ 1 Jose Herrera
☐ 2 Louis Benbow
☐ 3 D.J. Boston
☐ 4 Derek Brandow
☐ 5 Mike Coolbaugh
☐ 6 Brad Cornett
☐ 7 Ricky Cradle
☐ 8 Ned Darley
☐ 9 Roger Doman
☐ 10 Mariano Dotel
☐ 11 Tom Evans
☐ 12 Kris Harmes
☐ 13 Santiago Henry
☐ 14 Keith Hines
☐ 15 Aaron Jersild
☐ 16 Jeff Ladd
☐ 17 Levon Largusa
☐ 18 Trevor Mallory
☐ 19 Angel Martinez
☐ 20 Scot McCloughan
☐ 21 Steve Renko Jr.
☐ 22 Lonell Roberts
☐ 23 Ken Robinson
☐ 24 Jose Silva
☐ 25 Jim Nettles MG
☐ 26 Leroy Stanton CO
☐ 27 Darren Balsley CO
☐ 28 Dennis Brogna TR
☐ 29 Title Card
☐ 30 Checklist

1993 Hagerstown Suns Fleer/ProCards

This 30-card standard-size set of the 1993 Hagerstown Suns, a Class A South Atlantic League affiliate of the Toronto Blue Jays, features white-bordered posed color player photos on its fronts. The player's name, team, and position appear near the bottom. The white horizontal back is framed by a blue line and carries the player's name at the top, followed by biography and statistics. A drawing of a ballplayer in action appears on the left. This issue includes Jose Silva's first Fleer/ProCards team set appearance.

	MINT	NRMT	EXC
COMPLETE SET (30)	5.00	2.20	.60

☐ 1870 Derek Brandow
☐ 1871 Brad Cornett
☐ 1872 Ned Darley
☐ 1873 Andrew Dolson
☐ 1874 Roger Doman
☐ 1875 Aaron Jersild
☐ 1876 Levon Largusa
☐ 1877 Trevor Mallory
☐ 1878 Steve Renko Jr.
☐ 1879 Ken Robinson
☐ 1880 Jose Silva
☐ 1881 Kris Harmes
☐ 1882 Jeff Ladd
☐ 1883 Angel Martinez
☐ 1884 Lou Benbow
☐ 1885 D.J. Boston (Numbered SAL-24 on back)
☐ 1886 Mike Coolbaugh
☐ 1887 Mariano Dotel
☐ 1888 Tom Evans
☐ 1889 Santiago Henry
☐ 1890 Rick Cradle
☐ 1891 Jose Herrera
☐ 1892 Keith Hines
☐ 1893 Scot McCloughan
☐ 1894 Lonell Roberts
☐ 1895 Jim Nettles MG
☐ 1896 Darren Balsley CO
☐ 1897 Leroy Stanton CO
☐ 1898 Field Staff
☐ 1899 Checklist

1993 Harrisburg Senators Fleer/ProCards

This 28-card standard-size set of the 1993 Harrisburg Senators, a Class AA Eastern League affiliate of the Montreal Expos, features white-bordered posed color player photos on its fronts. The player's name, team, and position appear near the bottom. The white horizontal back is framed by a blue line and carries the player's name at the top, followed by biography and statistics. A drawing of a ballplayer in action appears on the left. This set includes Rondell White's third year team set card.

	MINT	NRMT	EXC
COMPLETE SET (28)	7.00	3.10	.85

☐ 260 Miguel Batista
☐ 261 Mario Brito
☐ 262 Archie Corbin
☐ 263 Reid Cornelius
☐ 264 Ralph Diaz
☐ 265 Joey Eischen
☐ 266 Heath Haynes
☐ 267 Chris Johnson
☐ 268 Yorkis Perez
☐ 269 Kirk Rueter
☐ 270 Gabe White
☐ 271 Miah Bradbury
☐ 272 Rob Fitzpatrick
☐ 273 Shane Andrews
☐ 274 Cliff Floyd
☐ 275 Ron Krause
☐ 276 Oreste Marrero
☐ 277 Chris Martin
☐ 278 Edgar Tovar
☐ 279 Glenn Murray
☐ 280 Curtis Pride
☐ 281 Rondell White
☐ 282 Tyrone Woods
☐ 283 Greg Fulton P/CO
☐ 284 Jim Tracy MG
☐ 285 Gomer Hodge CO
☐ 286 Chuck Kniffin CO
☐ 287 Checklist

1993 Helena Brewers Fleer/ProCards

This 31-card standard-size set of the 1993 Helena Brewers, a Class A Pioneer League affiliate of the Milwaukee Brewers, features white-bordered posed color player photos on its fronts. The player's name, team, and position appear near the bottom. The white horizontal back is framed by a blue line and carries the player's name at the top, followed by biography and statistics. A drawing of a ballplayer in action appears on the left.

	MINT	NRMT	EXC
COMPLETE SET (31)	5.00	2.20	.60

☐ 4084 Wagner Arias
☐ 4085 Jim Cole
☐ 4086 Jeff Droll
☐ 4087 Steve Duda
☐ 4088 Chad Kopitzke
☐ 4089 Sean Maloney
☐ 4090 Matt Murphy
☐ 4091 Gary Rhoda
☐ 4092 Frankie Rodriguez
☐ 4093 Fabian Salmon
☐ 4094 Chris Schmitt
☐ 4095 Rick Werner
☐ 4096 Judd Wilstead
☐ 4097 Rob Campillo
☐ 4098 Chris Carter
☐ 4099 Brad Gay
☐ 4100 Eduardo Acosta
☐ 4101 Todd Landry
☐ 4102 Ed Mackie
☐ 4103 Chris McInnes
☐ 4104 Mike Olexa
☐ 4105 Bobby Powers
☐ 4106 Jerry Salzano
☐ 4107 Brian Banks
☐ 4108 Ruben Cephas
☐ 4109 Hayland Hardy
☐ 4110 Clayton Hill
☐ 4111 Greg Martinez
☐ 4112 Harry Dunlop MG
☐ 4113 Mike Caldwell CO
☐ 4114 Checklist

1993 Helena Brewers Sports Pro

	MINT	NRMT	EXC
COMPLETE SET (28)	6.00	2.70	.75

☐ 1 Bobby Powers
☐ 2 Frank Rodriguez
☐ 3 Ruben Cephas
☐ 4 Rob Campillo
☐ 5 Craig Smith
☐ 6 Wagner Arias
☐ 7 Clayton Hill
☐ 8 Chris Thomas
☐ 9 Todd Landry
☐ 10 Jerry Salzano
☐ 11 Mike Olexa
☐ 12 Eduardo Acosta
☐ 13 Fabian Salmon
☐ 14 Judd Wilstead
☐ 15 Matt Murphy
☐ 16 Hayland Hardy
☐ 17 Sean Maloney
☐ 18 Ed Mackie
☐ 19 Jim Cole
☐ 20 Chris Carter
☐ 21 Chad Kopitske
☐ 22 Gary Rhoda
☐ 23 Chris Schmitt
☐ 24 Rick Werner
☐ 25 Chris McInnes
☐ 26 Roger Caplinger TR
☐ 27 Mike Epstein MG
☐ 28 Mike Caldwell CO

1993 Hickory Crawdads Classic/Best

This 30-card standard-size set of the 1993 Hickory Crawdads, a Class A South Atlantic League affiliate of the Chicago White Sox, features white-bordered posed color player shots on its fronts. A team-color-coded stripe below the photo carries the player's name; another above, his position and team name. On a ghosted team-logo, the white back carries the player's name at the top, followed by biography and statistics. This issue includes the minor league card debuts of Magglio Ordonez and Nerio Rodriguez.

	MINT	NRMT	EXC
COMPLETE SET (30)	8.00	3.60	1.00

☐ 1 Eddie Pearson
☐ 2 Rickey Bennett
☐ 3 Mike Bertotti
☐ 4 Mark Brincks
☐ 5 David Elsbernd
☐ 6 Jason Evans
☐ 7 Wayne Faircloth
☐ 8 David Fitzpatrick

☐ 9 Chris Gay
☐ 10 Marc Harris
☐ 11 Scot Hollrah
☐ 12 Toby Lehman
☐ 13 Wayne Lindemann
☐ 14 Chris Mader
☐ 15 Johnny Malaver
☐ 16 Mickey McKinion
☐ 17 Magglio Ordonez
☐ 18 Scott Patton
☐ 19 Wilfredo Polidor
☐ 20 Jimmy Reyes
☐ 21 Eric Richardson
☐ 22 Nerio Rodriguez
☐ 23 Fred Starks
☐ 24 Juan Thomas
☐ 25 Chris Tremie
☐ 26 Fred Kendall MG
☐ 27 Paul Casanova CO
Sic, Cassanova
☐ 28 Curtis Hasler CO
☐ 29 Mark Salas CO
☐ 30 Joseph Geck TR
Checklist

1993 Hickory Crawdads Fleer/ProCards

This 30-card standard-size set of the 1993 Hickory Crawdads, a Class A South Atlantic League affiliate of the Chicago White Sox, features white-bordered posed color player photos on its fronts. The player's name, team, and position appear near the bottom. The white horizontal back is framed by a blue line and carries the player's name at the top, followed by biography and statistics. A drawing of a ballplayer in action appears on the left. This set includes the first cards of Magglio Ordonez and Nerio Rodriguez.

	MINT	NRMT	EXC
COMPLETE SET (30)	8.00	3.60	1.00

☐ 1269 Ricky Bennett
☐ 1270 Mike Bertotti
☐ 1271 Mark Brincks
☐ 1272 David Elsbernd
☐ 1273 David Fitzpatrick
☐ 1274 Toby Lehman
☐ 1275 Wanye Lindermann
☐ 1276 Johnny Malaver
☐ 1277 Mickey McKinion
☐ 1278 Juan Soto
☐ 1279 Fred Starks
☐ 1280 Wayne Faircloth
☐ 1281 Nerio Rodriguez
☐ 1282 Chris Tremie
☐ 1283 Jason Evans
☐ 1284 Scot Hollrah
☐ 1285 Chris Mader
☐ 1286 Eddie Pearson
☐ 1287 Wilfredo Polidor
☐ 1288 Jimmy Reyes
☐ 1289 Juan Thomas
☐ 1290 Geronimo Aquino
☐ 1291 Marc Harris
☐ 1292 Magglio Ordonez
☐ 1293 Scott Patton
☐ 1294 Eric Richardson
☐ 1295 Fred Kendall MG
☐ 1296 Curt Hasler CO
☐ 1297 Mark Salas CO
☐ 1298 Checklist

1993 High Desert Mavericks Classic/Best

This 30-card standard-size set of the 1993 High Desert Mavericks, a Class A California League affiliate of the Florida Marlins, features white-bordered posed color player shots on its fronts. A team-color-coded stripe below the photo carries the player's name; another above, his position and team name. On a ghosted team-logo, the white back carries the player's name at the top, followed by biography and statistics.

	MINT	NRMT	EXC
COMPLETE SET (30)	5.00	2.20	.60

☐ 1 Carl Everett
☐ 2 Joel Adamson
☐ 3 Andres Berumen
☐ 4 Tim Clark
☐ 5 Sean Gousha
☐ 6 Ken Kendrena
☐ 7 George Kerfut
☐ 8 Bryn Kosco
☐ 9 Don Lemon
☐ 10 Jim Magill
☐ 11 Chris Malinoski
☐ 12 Ramon Martinez
☐ 13 Kerwin Moore
☐ 14 Tim North
☐ 15 Barry Parisotto
☐ 16 Jim Patterson
☐ 17 Robert Person
☐ 18 Mark Skeels
☐ 19 Randy Snyder
☐ 20 Stan Spencer
☐ 21 Jerry Stafford
☐ 22 Jesus Tavarez
☐ 23 John Toale
☐ 24 Tony Torres
☐ 25 Mike Whitten
☐ 26 Fredi Gonzalez MG
☐ 27 Marty DeMerritt CO
☐ 28 Carlos Ponce CO
☐ 29 Mike McGowan TR
☐ 30 Checklist

1993 High Desert Mavericks Fleer/ProCards

This 31-card standard-size set of the 1993 High Desert Mavericks, a Class A California League affiliate of the Florida Marlins, features white-bordered posed color player photos on its fronts. The player's name, team, and position appear near the bottom. The white horizontal back is framed by a blue line and carries the player's name at the top, followed by biography and statistics. A drawing of a ballplayer in action appears on the left.

	MINT	NRMT	EXC
COMPLETE SET (31)	5.00	2.20	.60

☐ 31 Joel Adamson
☐ 32 Andres Berumen
☐ 33 Kenny Kendrena
☐ 34 George Kerfut
☐ 35 Don Lemon
☐ 36 Jim Magill
☐ 37 Tom McGraw
☐ 38 Barry Parisotto
☐ 39 Jim Patterson
☐ 40 Robert Person
☐ 41 Stan Spencer
☐ 42 Gerry Stafford
☐ 43 Mike Whitten
☐ 44 Sean Gousha
☐ 45 Mark Skeels
☐ 46 Randy Snyder
☐ 47 Bryn Kosco
☐ 48 Chris Malinoski
☐ 49 Ramon Martinez
☐ 50 Tim North
☐ 51 John Toale
☐ 52 Tony Torres
☐ 53 Tim Clark
☐ 54 Carl Everett
☐ 55 Kerwin Moore
☐ 56 Jesus Tavarez
☐ 57 Fredi Gonzalez MG
☐ 58 Marty DeMerritt CO
☐ 59 Carlos Ponce CO
☐ 60 Checklist
☐ NNO Mike McGowan TR

1993 Huntington Cubs Classic/Best

This 30-card standard-size set of the 1993 Huntington Cubs, a Rookie Class Appalachian League affiliate of the Chicago Cubs, features white-bordered posed color player shots on its fronts. A team-color-coded stripe below the photo carries the player's name; another above, his position and team name. On a ghosted team-logo, the white back carries the player's name at the top, followed by biography and statistics. This issue includes the minor league card debuts of Pat Cline and Jeremi Gonzalez.

	MINT	NRMT	EXC
COMPLETE SET (30)	7.00	3.10	.85

☐ 1 Kevin Ellis
☐ 2 Greg Bobbitt
☐ 3 Britton Bonneau
☐ 4 Chris Bryant
☐ 5 Billy Childress
☐ 6 Pat Cline
☐ 7 Ralph Eusebio
☐ 8 Sean Fric
☐ 9 Geremis Gonzalez
☐ 10 Sean Hennessey
☐ 11 Artis Johnson
☐ 12 Tony Khoury
☐ 13 Anthony King
☐ 14 Thomas King
☐ 15 Rodd Kurtz
☐ 16 Mark Lavenia
☐ 17 Orlando Lopez
☐ 18 Ariel Martin
☐ 19 Jason Maxwell
☐ 20 Juan Mercedes
☐ 21 Bob Morris
☐ 22 Danny Ortiz
☐ 23 Jacob Serrato
☐ 24 Brad Sigler
☐ 25 Ronald Smith
☐ 26 David Weber
☐ 27 Gabe Whatley
☐ 28 Steve Kolinsky MG
☐ 29 Philip Hannon CO
☐ 30 Brian Phipps TR
Checklist

1993 Huntington Cubs Fleer/ProCards

This 30-card standard-size set of the 1993 Huntington Cubs, a Rookie Class Appalachian League affiliate of the Chicago Cubs, features white-bordered posed color player photos on its fronts. The player's name, team, and position appear near the bottom. The white horizontal back is framed by a blue line and carries the player's name at the top, followed by biography and statistics. A drawing of a ballplayer in action appears on the left. This set includes the first cards of Pat Cline and Jeremi Gonzalez.

	MINT	NRMT	EXC
COMPLETE SET (30)	7.00	3.10	.85

☐ 3227 Greg Bobbitt
☐ 3228 Chris Bryant
☐ 3229 Billy Childress
☐ 3230 Geremis Gonzalez
☐ 3231 Sean Hennessey
☐ 3232 Rodd Kurtz
☐ 3233 Mark Lavenia
☐ 3234 Orlando Lopez
☐ 3235 Danny Ortiz
☐ 3236 David Weber
☐ 3237 Pat Cline
☐ 3238 Tony Khoury
☐ 3239 Jacob Serrato
☐ 3240 Britt Bonneau
☐ 3241 K.J. Ellis
☐ 3242 Ariel Martin
☐ 3243 Jason Maxwell
☐ 3244 Juan Mercedes
☐ 3245 Bobby Morris
☐ 3246 Brad Sigler
☐ 3247 Ronald Smith
☐ 3248 Ralph Eusebio
☐ 3249 Sean Fric
☐ 3250 Artis Johnson
☐ 3251 Anthony King
☐ 3252 Thomas King
☐ 3253 Gabe Whatley
☐ 3254 Steve Kolinsky MG
☐ 3255 Phil Hannon CO
☐ 3256 Checklist

1993 Huntsville Stars Fleer/ProCards

This 26-card standard-size set of the 1993 Huntsville Stars, a Class AA Southern League affiliate of the Oakland Athletics, features white-bordered posed color player photos on its fronts. The player's name, team, and position appear near the bottom. The white horizontal back is framed by a blue line and carries the player's name at the top, followed by biography and statistics. A drawing of a ballplayer in action appears on the left.

	MINT	NRMT	EXC
COMPLETE SET (26)	5.00	2.20	.60

☐ 2074 Dana Allison
☐ 2075 Scott Baker
☐ 2076 John Briscoe
☐ 2077 Steve Chitren
☐ 2078 Miguel Jimenez
☐ 2079 Doug Johns
☐ 2080 Dave Latter
☐ 2081 Gavin Osteen
☐ 2082 Curtis Shaw
☐ 2083 Roger Smithberg
☐ 2084 Tanyon Sturtze
☐ 2085 Eric Helfand
☐ 2086 George Williams
☐ 2087 Jim Bowie
☐ 2088 Fabio Gomez
☐ 2089 John Kuehl
☐ 2090 Francisco Matos
☐ 2091 Jim Waggoner
☐ 2092 Jason Wood
☐ 2093 Kevin Dattola
☐ 2094 Chris Hart
☐ 2095 Damon Mashore
☐ 2096 Enoch Simmons
☐ 2097 Casey Parsons MG
☐ 2098 Glenn Abbott CO
☐ 2099 Checklist

1993 Idaho Falls Braves Fleer/ProCards

This 31-card standard-size set of the 1993 Idaho Falls Braves, a Class A Pioneer League affiliate of the Atlanta Braves, features white-bordered posed color player photos on its fronts. The player's name, team, and position appear near the bottom. The white horizontal back is framed by a blue line and carries the player's name at the top, followed by biography and statistics. A drawing of a ballplayer in action appears on the left.

	MINT	NRMT	EXC
COMPLETE SET (31)	5.00	2.20	.60

☐ 4023 James Blaine
☐ 4024 Alberto Evangelista
☐ 4025 Clint Gagnon
☐ 4026 Yves Martineau
☐ 4027 Earl Nelson
☐ 4028 Chris Rusciano
☐ 4029 Jason Simmons
☐ 4030 Tony Stoecklin
☐ 4031 Jason Thomas
☐ 4032 Aaron Turnier
☐ 4033 Marcus Tyner
☐ 4034 David Wells
☐ 4035 Casey Burrill
☐ 4036 Erik Moreno
☐ 4037 Jason Bugg
☐ 4038 David Catlett
☐ 4039 Mike Eaglin
☐ 4040 Charles McBride
☐ 4041 Darren Vazquetelles
☐ 4042 Cameron Browder
☐ 4043 Ralph Denman
☐ 4044 Anthony Dileso
☐ 4045 Marcel Johnson
☐ 4046 Bruce Newman
☐ 4047 Eddie Perez
☐ 4048 Anthony Rujff
☐ 4049 Miguel Valdez
☐ 4050 Paul Runge MG
☐ 4051 Steve Givins CO
☐ 4052 Mark Ross CO
☐ 4053 Checklist

1993 Idaho Falls Braves Sports Pro

	MINT	NRMT	EXC
COMPLETE SET (30)	7.00	3.10	.85

☐ 1 Alberto Evangelista
☐ 2 Eddie Perez
☐ 3 Yves Martineau
☐ 4 Charles McBride
☐ 5 Earl Nelson
☐ 6 Erik Moreno
☐ 7 Mike Eaglin
☐ 8 Anthony Ruff
☐ 9 Miguel Valdez
☐ 10 Jason Simmons
☐ 11 Tony Stoecklin
☐ 12 Darren Vazquetelles
☐ 13 Marcel Johnson
☐ 14 Ralph Denman
☐ 15 Chris Rusciano
☐ 16 James Blaine
☐ 17 Jose Rodriquez
☐ 18 Luis Garcia
☐ 19 Bruce Newman
☐ 20 Cameron Browder
☐ 21 Jason Thomas
☐ 22 Clint Gagnon
☐ 23 Casey Burrill
☐ 24 Jason Bugg
☐ 25 Anthony Dileso
☐ 26 David Wells
☐ 27 Marcus Tyner
☐ 28 Aaron Turnier
☐ 29 David Catlett
☐ 30 Paul Runge MG

1993 Indianapolis Indians Fleer/ProCards

This 25-card standard-size set of the 1993 Indianapolis Indians, a Class AAA American Association affiliate of the Cincinnati Reds, features white-bordered posed color player photos on its fronts. The player's name, team, and position appear near the bottom. The white horizontal back is framed by a blue line and carries the player's name at the top, followed by biography and statistics. A drawing of a ballplayer in action appears on the left.

	MINT	NRMT	EXC
COMPLETE SET (25)	5.00	2.20	.60

☐ 1482 Matt Grott
☐ 1483 Bo Kennedy
☐ 1484 Larry Luebbers
☐ 1485 David Lynch
☐ 1486 Ross Powell
☐ 1487 John Roper
☐ 1488 Scott Ruskin
☐ 1489 Scott Service
☐ 1490 Jerry Spradlin
☐ 1491 Troy Afenir
☐ 1492 Brian Dorsett
☐ 1493 Tom Costo
☐ 1494 Gary Green
☐ 1495 Willie Greene
☐ 1496 Tommy Gregg
☐ 1497 Frank Kremblas
☐ 1498 Gary Scott
☐ 1499 Jacob Brumfield
☐ 1500 Steve Carter
☐ 1501 Keith Hughes
☐ 1502 Greg Tubbs
☐ 1503 Marc Bombard MG
☐ 1504 Mike Griffin CO
☐ 1505 Razor Shines
☐ 1506 Checklist

1993 Iowa Cubs Fleer/ProCards

This 24-card standard-size set of the 1993 Iowa Cubs, a Class AAA American Association affiliate of the Chicago Cubs, features white-bordered posed color player photos on its fronts. The player's name, team, and position appear near the bottom. The white horizontal back is framed by a blue line and carries the player's name at the top, followed by biography and statistics. A drawing of a ballplayer in action appears on the left.

	MINT	NRMT	EXC
COMPLETE SET (24)	5.00	2.20	.60

- ☐ 2128 Shawn Boskie
- ☐ 2129 Jim Bullinger
- ☐ 2130 Michael Dyer
- ☐ 2131 Blaise Ilsley
- ☐ 2132 Heath Slocumb
- ☐ 2133 Steve Trachsel
- ☐ 2134 Ed Vosberg
- ☐ 2135 Turk Wendell
- ☐ 2136 Orlando Mercado
- ☐ 2137 George Pedre
- ☐ 2138 Kent Anderson
- ☐ 2139 Doug Jennings
- ☐ 2140 Dan Lewis
- ☐ 2141 Greg Lonigro
- ☐ 2142 Greg Smith
- ☐ 2143 Craig Worthington
- ☐ 2144 Tony Chance
- ☐ 2145 Fernando Ramsey
- ☐ 2146 Scott Wade
- ☐ 2147 Eddie Zambrano
- ☐ 2148 Marv Foley MG
- ☐ 2149 Bill Earley CO
- ☐ 2150 Stan Kyles CO
- ☐ 2151 Checklist

1993 Jackson Generals Fleer/ProCards

This 27-card standard-size set of the 1993 Jackson Generals, a Class AA Texas League affiliate of the Houston Astros, features white-bordered posed color player photos on its fronts. The player's name, team, and position appear near the bottom. The white horizontal back is framed by a blue line and carries the player's name at the top, followed by biography and statistics. A drawing of a ballplayer in action appears on the left. This set includes a fourth year card of Brian L. Hunter.

	MINT	NRMT	EXC
COMPLETE SET (27)	6.00	2.70	.75

- ☐ 2100 James Bruske
- ☐ 2101 Fred Costello
- ☐ 2102 James Dougherty
- ☐ 2103 Benjamin Gonzales
- ☐ 2104 Chris Hill
- ☐ 2105 Bob Hurta
- ☐ 2106 Doug Ketchen
- ☐ 2107 Terry Mathews
- ☐ 2108 Alvin Morman
- ☐ 2109 Mark Small
- ☐ 2110 Tony Gilmore
- ☐ 2111 Scott Makarewicz
- ☐ 2112 Mike Groppuso
- ☐ 2113 David Hajeck
- ☐ 2114 Frank Kellner
- ☐ 2115 Lance Madsen
- ☐ 2116 Thomas Nevers
- ☐ 2117 Roberto Petagine
- ☐ 2118 Fletcher Thompson
- ☐ 2119 Chris Hatcher
- ☐ 2120 Brian Hunter
- ☐ 2121 Ray Montgomery
- ☐ 2122 Gary Mota
- ☐ 2123 Sal Butera MG
- ☐ 2124 Dave Hudgens CO
- ☐ 2125 Charlie Taylor CO
- ☐ 2126 Checklist

1993 Jacksonville Suns Fleer/ProCards

This 22-card standard-size set of the 1993 Jacksonville Suns, a Class AA Southern League affiliate of the Seattle Mariners, features white-bordered posed color player photos on its fronts. The player's name, team, and position appear near the bottom. The white horizontal back is framed by a blue line and carries the player's name at the top, followed by biography and statistics. A drawing of a ballplayer in action appears on the left.

	MINT	NRMT	EXC
COMPLETE SET (22)	5.00	2.20	.60

- ☐ 2703 Greg Bicknell
- ☐ 2704 Jeff Darwin
- ☐ 2705 Kevin Foster
- ☐ 2706 George Glinatsis
- ☐ 2707 Reggie Harris
- ☐ 2708 Brett Knackert
- ☐ 2709 Jim Newlin
- ☐ 2710 Paul Perkins
- ☐ 2711 Erik Plantenberg
- ☐ 2712 LaGrande Russell
- ☐ 2713 Scott Schanz
- ☐ 2714 Jim Campanis
- ☐ 2715 Tony Kounas
- ☐ 2716 Eddy Diaz
- ☐ 2717 Lipso Nava
- ☐ 2718 Desi Relaford
- ☐ 2719 Ruben Santana
- ☐ 2720 Bubba Smith
- ☐ 2721 Darren Bragg
- ☐ 2722 Marc Newfeld
- ☐ 2723 Tony Scruggs
- ☐ 2724 Checklist

1993 Jamestown Expos Classic/Best

This 30-card standard-size set of the 1993 Jamestown Expos, a Class A New York-Penn League affiliate of the Montreal Expos, features white-bordered posed color player shots on its fronts. A team-color-coded stripe below the photo carries the player's name; another above, his position and team name. The white back carries the player's name at the top, followed by biography and statistics.

	MINT	NRMT	EXC
COMPLETE SET (30)	5.00	2.20	.60

- ☐ 1 Ramsey Koeyers
- ☐ 2 Antonio Alfonseca
- ☐ 3 Juan Batista
- ☐ 4 Josh Bullock
- ☐ 5 Jesus Campos
- ☐ 6 Fernando DaSilva
- ☐ 7 Christopher Grubb
- ☐ 8 Rich Haar
- ☐ 9 Matt Harrell
- ☐ 10 Scott Harrison
- ☐ 11 Bobby Henley
- ☐ 12 Aaron Knieper
- ☐ 13 Vincent LaChance
- ☐ 14 Mike Leon
- ☐ 15 Alex Pacheco
- ☐ 16 Tommy Phelps
- ☐ 17 Scott Quade
- ☐ 18 Matthew Raleigh
- ☐ 19 Mark Respondek
- ☐ 20 Jon Saffer
- ☐ 21 Tom Schneider
- ☐ 22 Dennis Stutts
- ☐ 23 Angelo Thompson
- ☐ 24 Joe Tosone
- ☐ 25 Neil Weber
- ☐ 26 Tim Torricelli MG
- ☐ 27 Pat Heiderscheit CO
- ☐ 28 Mike Haag TR
- ☐ 29 Title Card
- ☐ 30 Checklist

1993 Jamestown Expos Fleer/ProCards

This 28-card standard-size set of the 1993 Jamestown Expos, a Class A New York-Penn League affiliate of the Montreal Expos, features white-bordered posed color player photos on its fronts. The player's name, team, and position appear near the bottom. The white horizontal back is framed by a blue line and carries the player's name at the top, followed by biography and statistics. A drawing of a ballplayer in action appears on the left.

	MINT	NRMT	EXC
COMPLETE SET (28)	5.00	2.20	.60

- ☐ 3318 Josh Bullock
- ☐ 3319 Fernando DaSilva
- ☐ 3320 Scott Harrison
- ☐ 3321 Aaron Knieper
- ☐ 3322 Mike Leon
- ☐ 3323 Alex Pacheco
- ☐ 3324 Tommy Phelps
- ☐ 3325 Mark Respondek
- ☐ 3326 Tom Schneider
- ☐ 3327 Dennis Stutts
- ☐ 3328 Neil Weber
- ☐ 3329 Matt Harrell
- ☐ 3330 Bobby Henley
- ☐ 3331 Ramsey Koeyers
- ☐ 3332 Juan Batista
- ☐ 3333 Chris Grubb
- ☐ 3334 Rich Haar
- ☐ 3335 Scott Quade
- ☐ 3336 Matt Relaigh
- ☐ 3337 Jesus Campos
- ☐ 3338 Vince LaChance
- ☐ 3339 Jon Saffer
- ☐ 3340 Angelo Thompson
- ☐ 3341 Joe Tosone
- ☐ 3342 Tim Torricelli MG
- ☐ 3343 Pat Heiderscheit CO
- ☐ 3344 Herm Starrette DIR
- ☐ 3345 Checklist card

1993 Johnson City Cardinals Classic/Best

This 30-card standard-size set of the 1993 Johnson City Cardinals, a Rookie Class Appalachian League affiliate of the St. Louis Cardinals, features white-bordered posed color player shots on its fronts. A team-color-coded stripe below the photo carries the player's name; another above, his position and team name. On a ghosted team-logo, the white back carries the player's name at the top, followed by biography and statistics.

	MINT	NRMT	EXC
COMPLETE SET (30)	5.00	2.20	.60

- ☐ 1 Dee Dalton
- ☐ 2 Jeff Battles
- ☐ 3 Juan Bautista
- ☐ 4 Steve Biermann
- ☐ 5 Randy Bledsoe
- ☐ 6 Domingo Charles
- ☐ 7 Chris Christopher
- ☐ 8 Cory Corrigan
- ☐ 9 Rongie Dicken
- ☐ 10 Pat Donohue
- ☐ 11 Aaron Gerteisen
- ☐ 12 Jim Marchesi
- ☐ 13 Scott Marquardt
- ☐ 14 Tom McKinnon
- ☐ 15 Victor Pellot
- ☐ 16 Darek Robinson
- ☐ 17 Jamie Sailors
- ☐ 18 Ron Scott
- ☐ 19 Duane Stanton
- ☐ 20 Chris Stewart
- ☐ 21 Jason Stoppello
- ☐ 22 Bobby Strehlow Jr.
- ☐ 23 George Strus
- ☐ 24 Jamie Surratt
- ☐ 25 Danny Tatrow
- ☐ 26 Hector Ugueto
- ☐ 27 Dale Wagner
- ☐ 28 Joe Wallace
- ☐ 29 Jay Witasick
- ☐ 30 Joe Cunningham Jr. MG Checklist

1993 Johnson City Cardinals Fleer/ProCards

This 31-card standard-size set of the 1993 Johnson City Cardinals, a Rookie Class Appalachian League affiliate of the St. Louis Cardinals, features white-bordered posed color player photos on its fronts. The player's name, team, and position appear near the bottom. The white horizontal back is framed by a blue line and carries the player's name at the top, followed by biography and statistics. A drawing of a ballplayer in action appears on the left.

	MINT	NRMT	EXC
COMPLETE SET (31)	5.00	2.20	.60

- ☐ 3668 Jeff Battles
- ☐ 3669 Randy Bledsoe
- ☐ 3670 Domingo Charles
- ☐ 3671 Cory Corrigan
- ☐ 3672 Jim Marchesi
- ☐ 3673 Scott Marquardt
- ☐ 3674 Jamie Sailors
- ☐ 3675 Ron Scott
- ☐ 3676 Duane Stanton
- ☐ 3677 Chris Stewart
- ☐ 3678 Jason Stoppello
- ☐ 3679 Dale Wagner
- ☐ 3680 Jay Witasick
- ☐ 3681 Kevin Herde
- ☐ 3682 George Strus
- ☐ 3683 Joe Wallace
- ☐ 3684 Steve Biermann
- ☐ 3685 Dee Dalton
- ☐ 3686 Rongie Dicken
- ☐ 3687 Pat Donohue
- ☐ 3688 Tom McKinnon
- ☐ 3689 Darek Robinson
- ☐ 3690 Jamie Surratt
- ☐ 3691 Danny Tatrow
- ☐ 3692 Hector Ugueto
- ☐ 3693 Juan Bautista
- ☐ 3694 Chris Christopher
- ☐ 3695 Aaron Gerteisen
- ☐ 3696 Victor Pellot
- ☐ 3697 Robby Strehlow
- ☐ 3698 Checklist

1993 Kane County Cougars Classic/Best

This 30-card standard-size set of the 1993 Kane County Cougars, a Class A Midwest League affiliate of the Florida Marlins, features white-bordered posed color player shots on its fronts. A team-color-coded stripe below the photo carries the player's name; another above, his position and team name. On a ghosted team-logo, the white back carries the player's name at the top, followed by biography and statistics. This issue includes the minor league card debuts of Charles Johnson and Edgar Renteria.

	MINT	NRMT	EXC
COMPLETE SET (30)	25.00	11.00	3.10

- ☐ 1 Charles Johnson
- ☐ 2 Hector Carrasco
- ☐ 3 Eddie Christian
- ☐ 4 Chris Clapinski
- ☐ 5 Vic Darensbourg
- ☐ 6 Matt Donahue
- ☐ 7 Brad Frazier
- ☐ 8 Freddie Gamble
- ☐ 9 Jarod Juelsgaard
- ☐ 10 Pat Leahy
- ☐ 11 Lou Lucca
- ☐ 12 John Lynch
- ☐ 13 Reynol Mendoza
- ☐ 14 Matt Petersen
- ☐ 15 Doug Pettit
- ☐ 16 Todd Pridy
- ☐ 17 Mike Redmond
- ☐ 18 Edgar Renteria
- ☐ 19 Dan Robinson
- ☐ 20 Chris Sheff
- ☐ 21 Tony Sylvestri
- ☐ 22 Jim Vlcek
- ☐ 23 Matt Whisenant
- ☐ 24 Pookie Wilson
- ☐ 25 Eric Wulf
- ☐ 26 Carlos Tosca MG
- ☐ 27 Jose Castro CO
- ☐ 28 Brian Peterson CO
- ☐ 29 Todd Sorensen TR
- ☐ 30 Ozzie Cougar (Mascot) Checklist

1993 Kane County Cougars Fleer/ProCards

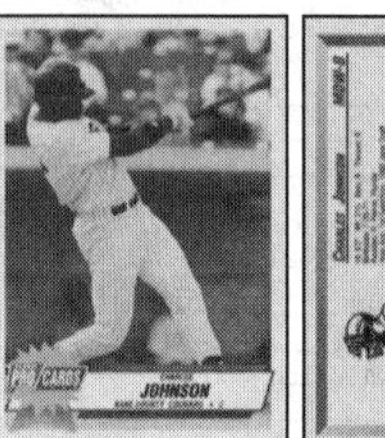

This 28-card standard-size set of the 1993 Kane County Cougars, a Class A Midwest League affiliate of the Florida Marlins, features white-bordered posed color player photos on its fronts. The player's name, team, and position appear near the bottom. The white horizontal back is framed by a blue line and carries the player's name at the top, followed by biography and statistics. A drawing of a ballplayer in action appears on the left. This set includes the first year cards of Charles Johnson and Edgar Renteria.

	MINT	NRMT	EXC
COMPLETE SET (28)	25.00	11.00	3.10

- ☐ 907 Hector Carrasco
- ☐ 908 Vic Darensbourg
- ☐ 909 Matt Donahue
- ☐ 910 Brad Frazier
- ☐ 911 Jarod Juelsgaard
- ☐ 912 Pat Leahy
- ☐ 913 Reynol Mendoza
- ☐ 914 Matt Petersen
- ☐ 915 Doug Pettit
- ☐ 916 Jim Vlcek
- ☐ 917 Matt Whisenant
- ☐ 918 Charles Johnson
- ☐ 919 Mike Redmond
- ☐ 920 Eric Wulf
- ☐ 921 Chris Clapinski
- ☐ 922 Freddie Gamble
- ☐ 923 Lou Lucca
- ☐ 924 Todd Pridy
- ☐ 925 Edgar Reneteria
- ☐ 926 Tony Sylvestri
- ☐ 927 Eddie Christian
- ☐ 928 Dan Robinson
- ☐ 929 Chris Sheff
- ☐ 930 Pookie Wilson
- ☐ 931 Carlos Tosca MG
- ☐ 932 Jose Castro CO
- ☐ 933 Brian Peterson CO
- ☐ 934 Checklist

1993 Kane County Cougars Team Issue

This 30-card standard-size set of the 1993 Kane County Cougars, a Class A Midwest League affiliate of the Florida Marlins, features the minor league card debuts of Charles Johnson and Edgar Renteria.

	MINT	NRMT	EXC
COMPLETE SET (30)	25.00	11.00	3.10

- ☐ 1 Hector Carrasco
- ☐ 2 Jose Castro

- ☐ 3 Eddie Christian
- ☐ 4 Chris Clapinski
- ☐ 5 Vic Darensbourg
- ☐ 6 Matt Donahue
- ☐ 7 Brad Frazier
- ☐ 8 Freddie Gamble
- ☐ 9 Charles Johnson
- ☐ 10 Jarod Juelsgaard
- ☐ 11 Pat Leahy
- ☐ 12 Lou Lucca
- ☐ 13 Rey Mendoza
- ☐ 14 Brian Peterson
- ☐ 15 Matt Peterson
- ☐ 16 Doug Pettit
- ☐ 17 Todd Pridy
- ☐ 18 Mike Redmond
- ☐ 19 Edgar Renteria
- ☐ 20 Daniel Robinson
- ☐ 21 Chris Sheff
- ☐ 22 Todd Sorensen
- ☐ 23 Tony Sylvestri
- ☐ 24 Jason Tidwell
- ☐ 25 Carlos Tosca
- ☐ 26 Jim Vlcek
- ☐ 27 Matt Whisenant
- ☐ 28 Pookie Wilson
- ☐ 29 Eric Wulf
- ☐ 30 Ozzie

1993 Kingsport Mets Classic/Best

This 30-card standard-size set of the 1993 Kingsport Mets, a Rookie Class Appalachian League affiliate of the New York Mets, features white-bordered posed color player shots on its fronts. A team-color-coded stripe below the photo carries the player's name; another above, his position and team name. On a ghosted team-logo, the white back carries the player's name at the top, followed by biography and statistics. This issue includes the minor league card debut of Preston Wilson.

	MINT	NRMT	EXC
COMPLETE SET (30)	6.00	2.70	.75

- ☐ 1 Preston Wilson
- ☐ 2 Jason Adams
- ☐ 3 Derek Baker
- ☐ 4 Bobby Carr
- ☐ 5 Slick Collier
- ☐ 6 Andrew Cotner
- ☐ 7 Bob Daly
- ☐ 8 Cesar Diaz
- ☐ 9 James Dorsey
- ☐ 10 Chad Epperson
- ☐ 11 Mike Farrell
- ☐ 12 Rob Gontkosky
- ☐ 13 Rafael Guerrero
- ☐ 14 Mike Johnson
- ☐ 15 Stephen Lackey
- ☐ 16 Brian Mast
- ☐ 17 Juan Moreno
- ☐ 18 Sandy Pichardo
- ☐ 19 Freddy Rojas
- ☐ 20 Rafael Roque
- ☐ 21 Derek Sutton
- ☐ 22 Ramon Tatis
- ☐ 23 Randy Warner
- ☐ 24 Tom Wolff
- ☐ 25 Ron Gideon MG
- ☐ 26 Jesus Hernaiz CO
- ☐ 27 Kevin Culpepper TR
- ☐ 28 Team Photo
- ☐ 29 Title Card
- ☐ 30 Checklist

1993 Kingsport Mets Fleer/ProCards

This 27-card standard-size set of the 1993 Kingsport Mets, a Rookie Class Appalachian League affiliate of the New York Mets, features white-bordered posed color player photos on its fronts. The player's name, team, and position appear near the bottom. The white horizontal back is framed by a blue line and carries the player's name at the top, followed by biography and statistics. A drawing of a ballplayer in action appears on the left. This set includes the first year card of Preston Wilson.

	MINT	NRMT	EXC
COMPLETE SET (27)	6.00	2.70	.75

- ☐ 3787 Derek Baker
- ☐ 3788 Bobby Carr
- ☐ 3789 Drvin Collier
- ☐ 3790 Andrew Cotner
- ☐ 3791 Rob Gontkosky
- ☐ 3792 Brian Mast
- ☐ 3793 Juan Moreno
- ☐ 3794 Rafael Roque
- ☐ 3795 Derek Sutton
- ☐ 3796 Ramon Tatis
- ☐ 3797 Tom Wolff
- ☐ 3798 Cesar Diaz
- ☐ 3799 Chad Epperson
- ☐ 3800 Bob Daly
- ☐ 3801 Mike Farrell
- ☐ 3802 Mike Johnson
- ☐ 3803 Stephen Lackey
- ☐ 3804 Sandy Pichardo
- ☐ 3805 Freddy Rojas
- ☐ 3806 Preston Wilson
- ☐ 3807 Jason Adams
- ☐ 3808 James Dorsey
- ☐ 3809 Rafael Guerrero
- ☐ 3810 Randy Warner
- ☐ 3811 Ron Gideon MG
- ☐ 3812 Jesus Hernaiz CO
- ☐ 3813 Checklist

1993 Kinston Indians Classic/Best

This 30-card standard-size set of the 1993 Kinston Indians, a Class A Carolina League affiliate of the Cleveland Indians, features white-bordered posed color player shots on its fronts. A team-color-coded stripe below the photo carries the player's name; another above, his position and team name. On a ghosted team-logo, the white back carries the player's name at the top, followed by biography and statistics.

	MINT	NRMT	EXC
COMPLETE SET (30)	5.00	2.20	.60

- ☐ 1 Pete Rose Jr.
- ☐ 2 Juan Andujar
- ☐ 3 Dickie Brown
- ☐ 4 Mark Charbonnet
- ☐ 5 John Cotton
- ☐ 6 Carlos Crawford
- ☐ 7 Mike Crosby
- ☐ 8 Ian Doyle
- ☐ 9 Joe Fleet
- ☐ 10 Jason Fronio
- ☐ 11 Ray Harvey
- ☐ 12 Fernando Hernandez
- ☐ 13 Kevin Logsdon
- ☐ 14 Marc Marini
- ☐ 15 Pat Maxwell
- ☐ 16 Rod McCall
- ☐ 17 Greg McCarthy
- ☐ 18 Paul Meade
- ☐ 19 Tony Mitchell
- ☐ 20 Scott Morgan
- ☐ 21 Cesar Perez
- ☐ 22 Chop Pough
- ☐ 23 Nick Sued
- ☐ 24 Julian Tavarez
- ☐ 25 David Welch
- ☐ 26 Matt Williams
- ☐ 27 Dave Keller MG
- ☐ 28 Dan Norman CO
- ☐ 29 Greg Booker CO
- ☐ 30 Dan DeVoe TR Checklist

1993 Kinston Indians Fleer/ProCards

This 30-card standard-size set of the 1993 Kinston Indians, a Class A Carolina League affiliate of the Cleveland Indians, features white-bordered posed color player photos on its fronts. The player's name, team, and position appear near the bottom. The white horizontal back is framed by a blue line and carries the player's name at the top, followed by biography and statistics. A drawing of a ballplayer in action appears on the left.

	MINT	NRMT	EXC
COMPLETE SET (30)	5.00	2.20	.60

- ☐ 2237 Dickie Brown
- ☐ 2238 Carlos Crawford
- ☐ 2239 Ian Doyle
- ☐ 2240 Joe Fleet
- ☐ 2241 Jason Fronio
- ☐ 2242 Fernando Hernandez
- ☐ 2243 Kevin Logsdon
- ☐ 2244 Greg McCarthy
- ☐ 2245 Scott Morgan
- ☐ 2246 Cesar Perez
- ☐ 2247 Julian Tavarez
- ☐ 2248 David Welch
- ☐ 2249 Matt Williams
- ☐ 2250 Mike Crosby
- ☐ 2251 Nick Sued
- ☐ 2252 Juan Andujar
- ☐ 2253 Pat Maxwell
- ☐ 2254 Rod McCall
- ☐ 2255 Paul Meade
- ☐ 2256 Chop Pough
- ☐ 2257 Pete Rose Jr.
- ☐ 2258 Mark Charbonnet
- ☐ 2259 John Cotton
- ☐ 2260 Ray Harvey
- ☐ 2261 Marc Marini
- ☐ 2262 Tony Mitchell
- ☐ 2263 Dave Keller MG
- ☐ 2264 Greg Booker CO
- ☐ 2265 Dan Norman CO
- ☐ 2266 Checklist

1993 Kinston Indians Team Issue

	MINT	NRMT	EXC
COMPLETE SET (30)	6.00	2.70	.75

- ☐ 1 Juan Andujar
- ☐ 2 Dickie Brown
- ☐ 3 Mark Charbonnet
- ☐ 4 John Cotton
- ☐ 5 Carlos Crawford
- ☐ 6 Mike Crosby
- ☐ 7 Ian Doyle
- ☐ 8 Joe Fleet
- ☐ 9 Jason Fronio
- ☐ 10 Ray Harvey
- ☐ 11 Fernando Hernandez
- ☐ 12 Dave Keller MG
- ☐ 13 Kevin Logsdon
- ☐ 14 Marc Marini
- ☐ 15 Pat Maxwell
- ☐ 16 Rod McCall
- ☐ 17 Greg McCarthy
- ☐ 18 Paul Meade
- ☐ 19 Tony Mitchell
- ☐ 20 Scott Morgan
- ☐ 21 Cesar Perez
- ☐ 22 Chop Pough
- ☐ 23 Pete Rose Jr.
- ☐ 24 Nick Sued
- ☐ 25 Juan Tavarez
- ☐ 26 David Welch
- ☐ 27 Matt Williams
- ☐ 28 Dan Norman CO
- ☐ 29 Dan DeVoe TR
- ☐ 30 Greg Booker CO

1993 Knoxville Smokies Fleer/ProCards

This 29-card standard-size set of the 1993 Knoxville Smokies, a Class AA Southern League affiliate of the Toronto Blue Jays, features white-bordered posed color player photos on its fronts. The player's name, team, and position appear near the bottom. The white horizontal back is framed by a blue line and carries the player's name at the top, followed by biography and statistics. A drawing of a ballplayer in action appears on the left. This set includes the second year cards of Alex Gonzalez and Shawn Green and a third year card of Carlos Delgado.

	MINT	NRMT	EXC
COMPLETE SET (29)	8.00	3.60	1.00

- ☐ 1240 Travis Baptist
- ☐ 1241 Scott Brow
- ☐ 1242 Daren Brown
- ☐ 1243 Tim Crabtree
- ☐ 1244 Nate Cromwell
- ☐ 1246 Huck Flener
- ☐ 1247 Joe Ganote
- ☐ 1248 Scott Grove
- ☐ 1249 Steve Karsay
- ☐ 1250 Daren Kizziah
- ☐ 1251 Aaron Small
- ☐ 1252 Carlos Delgado
- ☐ 1253 Anastacio Garcia
- ☐ 1254 Mike Morland
- ☐ 1255 Kyle Duey
- ☐ 1255 Sharnol Adriana
- ☐ 1256 Howard Battle
- ☐ 1257 Alex Gonzalez
- ☐ 1258 Derek Henderson
- ☐ 1259 Tim Hyers
- ☐ 1260 Joe Lis Jr.
- ☐ 1261 Brent Bowers
- ☐ 1262 Shawn Green
- ☐ 1263 Tim Hodge
- ☐ 1264 Ron Reams
- ☐ 1265 Garth Iorg MG
- ☐ 1266 Mike McAlpin CO
- ☐ 1267 Steve Mingori CO
- ☐ 1268 Checklist

1993 Lakeland Tigers Classic/Best

This 30-card standard-size set of the 1993 Lakeland Tigers, a Class A Florida State League affiliate of the Detroit Tigers, features white-bordered posed color player shots on its fronts. A team-color-coded stripe below the photo carries the player's name; another above, his position and team name. On a ghosted team-logo, the white back carries the player's name at the top, followed by biography and statistics.

	MINT	NRMT	EXC
COMPLETE SET (30)	5.00	2.20	.60

- ☐ 1 Justin Thompson
- ☐ 2 Pat Ahearne
- ☐ 3 Carlos Burguillos
- ☐ 4 Greg Coppetta
- ☐ 5 Brian DuBose
- ☐ 6 Brian Edmondson
- ☐ 7 Carlos Fermin
- ☐ 8 Pedro Gonzalez
- ☐ 9 Rick Greene
- ☐ 10 Michael Guilfoyle
- ☐ 11 Bob Higginson
- ☐ 12 Brent Killen
- ☐ 13 John Kosenski
- ☐ 14 Johnny LaMar
- ☐ 15 Justin Mashore
- ☐ 16 Tim McConnell
- ☐ 17 Casey Mendenhall
- ☐ 18 Darren Milne
- ☐ 19 Kevin Morgan
- ☐ 20 Kelley O'Neal III
- ☐ 21 Cecil Pettiford
- ☐ 22 Dan Ruff
- ☐ 23 Phil Stidham
- ☐ 24 Timothy Thomas
- ☐ 25 Dennis Walsh
- ☐ 26 Gerry Groninger MG
- ☐ 27 Kevin Bradshaw CO
- ☐ 28 Rich Bombard CO
- ☐ 29 Bryan Goike TR
- ☐ 30 Checklist

1993 Lakeland Tigers Fleer/ProCards

This 31-card standard-size set of the 1993 Lakeland Tigers, a Class A Florida State League affiliate of the Detroit Tigers, features white-bordered posed color player photos on its fronts. The player's name, team, and position appear near the bottom. The white horizontal back is framed by a blue line and carries the player's name at the top, followed by biography and statistics. A drawing of a ballplayer in action appears on the left. .

	MINT	NRMT	EXC
COMPLETE SET (31)	5.00	2.20	.60

- ☐ 1299 Pat Ahearne
- ☐ 1300 Greg Coppeta
- ☐ 1301 Brian Edmondson
- ☐ 1302 Rick Greene
- ☐ 1303 Mike Guilfoyle
- ☐ 1304 Rich Kelley
- ☐ 1305 John Kosenski
- ☐ 1306 Casey Mendenhall
- ☐ 1307 Cecil Pettiford
- ☐ 1308 Greg Raffo
- ☐ 1309 Tom Schwarber
- ☐ 1310 Phil Stidham
- ☐ 1311 Justin Thompson
- ☐ 1312 Dennis Walsh
- ☐ 1313 Pete Gonzalez
- ☐ 1314 Tim McConnell
- ☐ 1315 Rob Yelton
- ☐ 1316 Brian DuBose
- ☐ 1317 Carlos Fermin
- ☐ 1318 Kevin Morgan
- ☐ 1319 Kelley O'Neal
- ☐ 1320 Tim Thomas
- ☐ 1321 Carlos Burguillos
- ☐ 1322 Bob Higginson
- ☐ 1323 John LaMar
- ☐ 1324 Justin Mashore
- ☐ 1325 Dan Ruff
- ☐ 1326 Gerry Groninger MG
- ☐ 1327 Rich Bombard CO
- ☐ 1328 Kevin Bradshaw CO
- ☐ 1329 Checklist

1993 Las Vegas Stars Fleer/ProCards

This 29-card standard-size set of the 1993 Las Vegas Stars, a Class AAA Pacific Coast League affiliate of the San Diego Padres, features white-bordered posed color player photos on its fronts. The player's name, team, and position appear near the bottom. The white horizontal back is framed by a blue line and carries the player's name at the top, followed by biography and statistics. A drawing of a ballplayer in action appears on the left.

	MINT	NRMT	EXC
COMPLETE SET (29)	5.00	2.20	.60

- ☐ 935 Juan Agosto
- ☐ 936 Denis Boucher
- ☐ 937 Doug Brocail
- ☐ 938 Ricky Davis
- ☐ 939 Mark Ettles
- ☐ 940 Mike Linskey
- ☐ 941 Pedro Martinez
- ☐ 942 Jim Pena
- ☐ 943 Scott Sanders
- ☐ 944 Joe Strong
- ☐ 945 Tim Worrell

☐ 946 Ray Young
☐ 947 Mike Basso
☐ 948 Brian Johnson
☐ 949 Billy Bean
☐ 950 Steve Bethea
☐ 951 Kevin Higgins
☐ 952 Luis Lopez
☐ 953 Mike Simms
☐ 954 Matt Witkowski
☐ 955 Jarvis Brown
☐ 956 D.J. Dozier
☐ 957 Chris Jelic
☐ 958 Steve Pegues
☐ 959 Jim Vatcher
☐ 960 Russ Nixon MG
☐ 961 Marty Barrett CO
☐ 962 John Cumberland CO
☐ 963 Checklist

1993 Lethbridge Mounties Fleer/ProCards

This 26-card standard-size set of the 1993 Lethbridge Mounties, a Rookie Class Pioneer League Independent, features white-bordered posed color player photos on its fronts. The player's name, team, and position appear near the bottom. The white horizontal back is framed by a blue line and carries the player's name at the top, followed by biography and statistics. A drawing of a ballplayer in action appears on the left.

	MINT	NRMT	EXC
COMPLETE SET (26)	5.00	2.20	.60

☐ 4142 Dale Ballance
☐ 4143 Miguel Bonilla
☐ 4144 Rodney Davidson
☐ 4145 Elcilio DeLeon
☐ 4146 John Dillinger
☐ 4147 Merlin Kath
☐ 4148 Shawn Ohman
☐ 4149 Dan Roman
☐ 4150 Ray Solomon
☐ 4151 Ben Boka
☐ 4152 Jason Marshall
☐ 4153 Lee Reiber
☐ 4154 John Allen
☐ 4155 Gavin Baugh
☐ 4156 Matt Jones
☐ 4157 Juan Segura
☐ 4158 Anthony Bonifazio
☐ 4159 Adrian Brown
☐ 4160 Willie Brown
☐ 4161 Luis Cordova
☐ 4162 Corey Lea
☐ 4163 Pat Lussier
☐ 4164 Phil Wellman MG
☐ 4165 Juan Bustabad CO
☐ 4166 Bil Sizemore CO
☐ 4167 Checklist

1993 Lethbridge Mounties Sports Pro

	MINT	NRMT	EXC
COMPLETE SET (26)	6.00	2.70	.75

☐ 1 John Allen
☐ 2 Rodney Davidson
☐ 3 Ben Boka
☐ 4 Adrian Brown
☐ 5 Elcilio DeLeon
☐ 6 John Dillinger
☐ 7 Gavin Baugh
☐ 8 Anthony Bonifazio
☐ 9 Miguel Bonillia
☐ 10 Willie Brown
☐ 11 Merlin Kath
☐ 12 Jason Marshall
☐ 13 Matt Jones
☐ 14 Luis Cordova
☐ 15 Shawn Ohman
☐ 16 Dan Roman
☐ 17 Dale Ballance
☐ 18 Corey Lea
☐ 19 Ray Soloman
☐ 20 Juan Segura
☐ 21 Lee Reiber
☐ 22 Pat Lussier
☐ 23 Pat Laverty TR
☐ 24 Juan Bustabad CO
☐ 25 Phillip Wellman MG
☐ 26 Bill Sizemore CO

1993 London Tigers Fleer/ProCards

This 29-card standard-size set of the 1993 London Tigers, a Class AA Eastern League affiliate of the Detroit Tigers, features white-bordered posed color player photos on its fronts. The player's name, team, and position appear near the bottom. The white horizontal back is framed by a blue line and carries the player's name at the top, followed by biography and statistics. A drawing of a ballplayer in action appears on the left.

	MINT	NRMT	EXC
COMPLETE SET (29)	5.00	2.20	.60

☐ 2297 Ben Blomdahl
☐ 2298 Jeff Braley
☐ 2299 Ken Carlyle
☐ 2300 Mike Garcia
☐ 2301 Henrique Gomez
☐ 2302 Jim Henry
☐ 2303 Jose Limba
☐ 2304 Felipe Lira
☐ 2305 Jason Pfaff
☐ 2306 Tom Schwarber
☐ 2307 Bob Undorf
☐ 2308 Brian Warren
☐ 2309 Steve Wolf
☐ 2310 Joe Perona
☐ 2311 Brian Saltzgaber
☐ 2312 Rick Sellers
☐ 2313 Jimmy Alder
☐ 2314 Jim Givens
☐ 2315 Kirk Mendenhall
☐ 2316 Shannon Penn
☐ 2317 Evan Pratte
☐ 2318 Mike Rendina
☐ 2319 Dan Bautista
☐ 2320 Brian Cornelius
☐ 2321 Rudy Pemberton
☐ 2322 Tom Runnells MG
☐ 2323 Sid Monge CO
☐ 2324 Dan Raley CO
☐ 2325 Checklist

1993 Louisville Redbirds Fleer/ProCards

This 26-card standard-size set of the 1993 Louisville Redbirds, a Class AAA American Association affiliate of the St. Louis Cardinals, features white-bordered posed color player photos on its fronts. The player's name, team, and position appear near the bottom. The white horizontal back is framed by a blue line and carries the player's name at the top, followed by biography and statistics. A drawing of a ballplayer in action appears on the left.

	MINT	NRMT	EXC
COMPLETE SET (26)	5.00	2.20	.60

☐ 206 Gary Buckels
☐ 207 Fidel Compres
☐ 208 Steve Dixon
☐ 209 Paul Kilgus
☐ 210 Kevin Meier
☐ 211 Mike Milchin
☐ 212 Gabriel Ozuna
☐ 213 Bob Sebra
☐ 214 Tom Urbani
☐ 215 Allen Watson
☐ 216 Dennis Wiseman
☐ 217 Ed Fulton
☐ 218 Barry Lyons
☐ 219 Erik Pappas
☐ 220 Tripp Cromer
☐ 221 Bien Figueroa
☐ 222 Tim Jones
☐ 223 Keith Lockhard
☐ 224 Stan Royer
☐ 225 Jeff Shireman
☐ 226 Ozzie Canseco
☐ 227 Lonnie Maclin
☐ 228 John Morris
☐ 229 Van Snider
☐ 230 Skeets Thomas
☐ 231 Checklist

1993 LSU Tigers McDag

	MINT	NRMT	EXC
COMPLETE SET (16)	12.00	5.50	1.50

☐ 1 Team Photo
☐ 2 Skip Bertman CO
☐ 3 Jim Greely
☐ 4 Armando Rios
☐ 5 Mike Sirotka
☐ 6 Will Hunt
☐ 7 Kenny Jackson
☐ 8 Mike Neal
☐ 9 Adrian Antonini
☐ 10 Harry Berrios
☐ 11 Matt Chamberlain
☐ 12 Todd Walker
☐ 13 Russ Johnson
☐ 14 Jason Williams
☐ 15 Brett Laxton
☐ 16 Scott Schultz

1993 Lynchburg Red Sox Classic/Best

This 30-card standard-size set of the 1993 Lynchburg Red Sox, a Class A Carolina League affiliate of the Boston Red Sox, features white-bordered posed color player shots on its fronts. A team-color-coded stripe below the photo carries the player's name; another above, his position and team name. On a ghosted team-logo, the white back carries the player's name at the top, followed by biography and statistics.

	MINT	NRMT	EXC
COMPLETE SET (30)	5.00	2.20	.60

☐ 1 Diogenes Baez
☐ 2 Scott Bakkum
☐ 3 Joel Bennett
☐ 4 Randy Brown
☐ 5 Tim Carey
☐ 6 Felix Colon
☐ 7 Bret Donovan
☐ 8 John Eierman
☐ 9 Jeff Faino
☐ 10 Gettys Glaze
☐ 11 Doug Hecker
☐ 12 Rob Henkel
☐ 13 Joe Hudson
☐ 14 Bob Juday
☐ 15 Ron Mahay
☐ 16 Jose Malave
☐ 17 Ryan Maloney
☐ 18 Jeff Martin
☐ 19 Walt McKeel
☐ 20 Todd Miller
☐ 21 Tommy Niles
☐ 22 Steve Rodriguez
☐ 23 George Scott III
☐ 24 Bill Selby
☐ 25 Mark Meleski MG
☐ 26 Joe Marchese CO
☐ 27 Jim Bibby CO
☐ 28 David Duchin TR
☐ 29 Title Card
☐ 30 Checklist

1993 Lynchburg Red Sox Fleer/ProCards

This 29-card standard-size set of the 1993 Lynchburg Red Sox, a Class A Carolina League affiliate of the Boston Red Sox, features white-bordered posed color player photos on its fronts. The player's name, team, and position appear near the bottom. The white horizontal back is framed by a blue line and carries the player's name at the top, followed by biography and statistics. A drawing of a ballplayer in action appears on the left.

	MINT	NRMT	EXC
COMPLETE SET (29)	5.00	2.20	.60

☐ 2508 Scott Bakkum
☐ 2509 Joel Bennett
☐ 2510 Bret Donovan
☐ 2511 Jeff Faino
☐ 2512 Gettys Glaze
☐ 2513 Bob Henkel
☐ 2514 Joe Hudson
☐ 2515 Ryan Maloney
☐ 2516 Todd Miller
☐ 2517 Tommy Niles
☐ 2518 Tim Carey
☐ 2519 Jeff Martin
☐ 2520 Walt McKeel
☐ 2521 Randy Brown
☐ 2522 Felix Colon
☐ 2523 Doug Hecker
☐ 2524 Bob Juday
☐ 2525 Steve Rodriguez
☐ 2526 Dave Schmidt
☐ 2527 Bill Selby
☐ 2528 Diogunes Baez
☐ 2529 John Eierman
☐ 2530 Ron Mahay
☐ 2531 Jose Malave
☐ 2532 George Scott III
☐ 2533 Mark Meleski MG
☐ 2534 Jim Bibby CO
☐ 2535 Joe Marchese CO
☐ 2536 Checklist

1993 Macon Braves Classic/Best

This 30-card standard-size set of the 1993 Macon Braves, a Class A South Atlantic League affiliate of the Atlanta Braves, features white-bordered posed color player shots on its fronts. A team-color-coded stripe below the photo carries the player's name; another above, his position and team name. On a ghosted team-logo, the white back carries the player's name at the top, followed by biography and statistics.

	MINT	NRMT	EXC
COMPLETE SET(30)	6.00	2.70	.75

☐ 1 Terrell Wade
☐ 2 Jamie Arnold
☐ 3 Chris Brock
☐ 4 Terrell Buckley
☐ 5 Jason Butler
☐ 6 Mark Chambers
☐ 7 Miguel Correa
☐ 8 Michael D'Andrea
☐ 9 Adrian Garcia
☐ 10 Kenneth Giard
☐ 11 Kevin Grijak
☐ 12 Jason Keeline
☐ 13 John Knott
☐ 14 Marty Malloy
☐ 15 Darrell May
☐ 16 Jay Noel
☐ 17 Raymond Nunez
☐ 18 Nelson Paulino
☐ 19 Michael Place
☐ 20 Leo Ramirez
☐ 21 John Simmons
☐ 22 Kian Sly
☐ 23 Miguel Soto
☐ 24 Tom Thobe
☐ 25 David Toth
☐ 26 Thomas Waldrop
☐ 27 Randy Ingle MG
☐ 28 Joe Szekely CO
☐ 29 Larry Jaster CO
☐ 30 Willy Johnson TR

1993 Macon Braves Fleer/ProCards

This 30-card standard-size set of the 1993 Macon Braves, a Class A South Atlantic League affiliate of the Atlanta Braves, features white-bordered posed color player photos on its fronts. The player's name, team, and position appear near the bottom. The white horizontal back is framed by a blue line and carries the player's name at the top, followed by biography and statistics. A drawing of a ballplayer in action appears on the left. This set includes a second year card of Terrell Wade.

	MINT	NRMT	EXC
COMPLETE SET(30)	6.00	2.70	.75

☐ 1391 Jamie Arnold
☐ 1392 Chris Brock
☐ 1393 Jason Butler
☐ 1394 Mike D'Andrea
☐ 1395 Ken Giard
☐ 1396 Darrell May
☐ 1397 Mike Place
☐ 1398 Leo Ramirez
☐ 1399 John Simmons
☐ 1400 Tom Thobe
☐ 1401 Terrell Wade
☐ 1402 Adrian Garcia
☐ 1403 Miguel Soto
☐ 1404 David Toth
☐ 1405 Terrell Buckley
☐ 1406 Kevin Grijak
☐ 1407 Jason Keeline
☐ 1408 John Knott
☐ 1409 Marty Malloy
☐ 1410 Raymond Nunez
☐ 1411 Nelson Paulino
☐ 1412 Mark Chambers
☐ 1413 Miguel Correa
☐ 1414 Jay Noel
☐ 1415 Kian Sly
☐ 1416 Tom Waldrop
☐ 1417 Randy Ingle MG
☐ 1418 Larry Jaster CO
☐ 1419 Joe Szekely CO
☐ 1420 Checklist

1993 Madison Muskies Classic/Best

This 30-card standard-size set of the 1993 Madison Muskies, a Class A Midwest League affiliate of the Oakland Athletics, features white-bordered posed color player shots on its fronts. A team-color-coded stripe below the photo carries the player's name; another above, his position and team name. On a ghosted team-logo, the white back carries the player's name at the top, followed by biography and statistics.

	MINT	NRMT	EXC
COMPLETE SET (30)	5.00	2.20	.60

☐ 1 Don Wengert
☐ 2 Mark Acre
☐ 3 Luinis Aracena
☐ 4 James Banks
☐ 5 Carlos Belliard
☐ 6 Tim Bojan
☐ 7 D.T. Cromer
☐ 8 Brian Eldridge
☐ 9 Cliff Foster
☐ 10 David Francisco
☐ 11 Vincente Francisco
☐ 12 Creighton Gubanich
☐ 13 Jose Guillen
☐ 14 Gary Haught
☐ 15 Stacy Hollins
☐ 16 Gary Hust
☐ 17 Tim Killeen
☐ 18 Rob Leary
☐ 19 Brian Lesher
☐ 20 Julio Martinez
☐ 21 Troy Penix
☐ 22 Zack Sawyer
☐ 23 Scott Sheldon
☐ 24 Greg Smock
☐ 25 William Urbina
☐ 26 Jason White
☐ 27 Gary Jones MG

☐ 28 Gil Patterson CO
☐ 29 Title Card
☐ 30 Checklist

1993 Madison Muskies Fleer/ProCards

This 27-card standard-size set of the 1993 Madison Muskies, a Class A Midwest League affiliate of the Oakland Athletics, features white-bordered posed color player photos on its fronts. The player's name, team, and position appear near the bottom. The white horizontal back is framed by a blue line and carries the player's name at the top, followed by biography and statistics. A drawing of a ballplayer in action appears on the left.

	MINT	NRMT	EXC
COMPLETE SET (27)	5.00	2.20	.60

☐ 1814 James Banks
☐ 1815 Carlos Belliard
☐ 1816 Tim Bojan
☐ 1817 Cliff Foster
☐ 1818 Gary Haught
☐ 1819 Stacy Hollins
☐ 1820 Julio Martinez
☐ 1821 Zachary Sawyer
☐ 1822 William Urbina
☐ 1823 Don Wengert
☐ 1824 Creighton Gubanich
☐ 1825 Tim Killeen
☐ 1826 Brian Eldridge
☐ 1827 Vicente Francisco
☐ 1828 Jose Guillen
☐ 1829 Rob Leary
☐ 1830 Troy Penix
☐ 1831 Scott Sheldon
☐ 1832 Jason White
☐ 1833 Luinis Aracena
☐ 1834 David Cromer
☐ 1835 David Francisco
☐ 1836 Gary Hust
☐ 1837 Brian Lesher
☐ 1838 Gary Jones MG
☐ 1839 Gil Patterson CO
☐ 1840 Checklist

1993 Martinsville Phillies Classic/Best

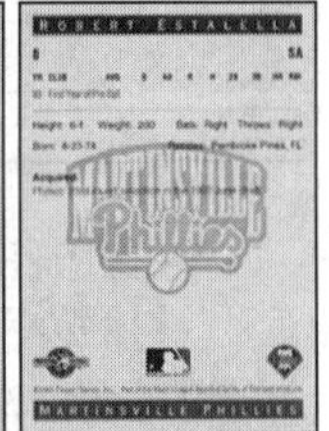

This 30-card standard-size set of the 1993 Martinsville Phillies, a Rookie Class Appalachian League affiliate of the Philadelphia Phillies, features white-bordered posed color player shots on its fronts. A team-color-coded stripe below the photo carries the player's name; another above, his position and team name. On a ghosted team-logo, the white back carries the player's name at the top, followed by biography and statistics. This issue includes the minor league card debuts of Bobby Estalella and Rich Hunter.

	MINT	NRMT	EXC
COMPLETE SET (30)	8.00	3.60	1.00

☐ 1 Josh Watts
☐ 2 Dell Allen
☐ 3 Manuel Amador
☐ 4 Scott Barstad
☐ 5 Tim Cornish
☐ 6 Brian Costello
☐ 7 Linardo Diaz
☐ 8 Robert Estalella
☐ 9 Barry Fitzgerald
☐ 10 Mark Foster
☐ 11 Todd Genke
☐ 12 Paul Hamilton
☐ 13 Shane Hobbs
☐ 14 Trevor Humphrey
☐ 15 Richard Hunter
☐ 16 Jeffrey Key
☐ 17 Bryan Lundberg
☐ 18 Thomas McGlawn
☐ 19 Fernando Mejias
☐ 20 Brian O'Connor
☐ 21 Chris Phipps
☐ 22 Danton Pierre-Louis
☐ 23 Jackie Rife
☐ 24 Nate Rodriguez
☐ 25 Lance Sanders
☐ 26 Michael Shipman
☐ 27 Derek Stingley
☐ 28 Andy Szarko
☐ 29 Charles Tinsley
☐ 30 Bryan Weigandt
Checklist

1993 Martinsville Phillies Fleer/ProCards

This 31-card standard-size set of the 1993 Martinsville Phillies, a Rookie Class Appalachian League affiliate of the Philadelphia Phillies, features white-bordered posed color player photos on its fronts. The player's name, team, and position appear near the bottom. The white horizontal back is framed by a blue line and carries the player's name at the top, followed by biography and statistics. A drawing of a ballplayer in action appears on the left. This set includes the first year cards of Bobby Estalella and Rich Hunter.

	MINT	NRMT	EXC
COMPLETE SET (31)	8.00	3.60	1.00

☐ 3463 Scott Barstad
☐ 3464 Mark Foster
☐ 3465 Todd Genke
☐ 3466 Bo Hamilton
☐ 3467 Trevor Humphry
☐ 3468 Rich Hunter
☐ 3469 Bryan Lundberg
☐ 3470 Fernando Mejias
☐ 3471 Brian O'Connor
☐ 3472 Chris Phipps
☐ 3473 Jackie Rife
☐ 3474 Lance Sanders
☐ 3475 Andy Szarko
☐ 3476 Robert Estalella
☐ 3477 Barry Fitzgerald
☐ 3478 Shane Hobbs
☐ 3479 Mike Shipman
☐ 3480 Dell Allen
☐ 3481 Manny Amador
☐ 3482 Tim Cornish
☐ 3483 Tom McGlawn
☐ 3484 Danton Pierre-Louis
☐ 3485 Nate Rodriquez
☐ 3486 Bryan Wiegandt
☐ 3487 Brian Costello
☐ 3488 Linardo Diaz
☐ 3489 Jeff Key
☐ 3490 Derek Stingley
☐ 3491 Charles Tinsley
☐ 3492 Josh Watts
☐ 3493 Checklist

1993 Medicine Hat Blue Jays Fleer/ProCards

This 27-card standard-size set of the 1993 Medicine Hat Blue Jays, a Class A Pioneer League affiliate of the Toronto Blue Jays, features white-bordered posed color player photos on its fronts. The player's name, team, and position appear near the bottom. The white horizontal back is framed by a blue line and carries the player's name at the top, followed by biography and statistics. A drawing of a ballplayer in action appears on the left. This set includes the first year card of Ryan Jones.

	MINT	NRMT	EXC
COMPLETE SET (27)	8.00	3.60	1.00

☐ 3729 Rob Adkins
☐ 3730 Brian Grant
☐ 3731 Scott Kennedy
☐ 3732 Jeff Leystra
☐ 3733 Rob Patterson
☐ 3734 Scott Jeffery
☐ 3735 Mark Sievert
☐ 3736 Steve Sinclair
☐ 3737 Kielan Smith
☐ 3738 Joe Vogelgesang
☐ 3739 Hector Martinez
☐ 3740 David Morgan
☐ 3741 Pete Polis
☐ 3742 Carlos Colmenares
☐ 3743 Willy Daunic
☐ 3744 Freddy Garcia
☐ 3745 Ryan Jones
☐ 3746 Jeff Patzke
☐ 3747 Eddy Vasquez
☐ 3748 Ben Candelaria
☐ 3749 Lorenzo De La Cruz
☐ 3750 Angel Ramirez
☐ 3751 Anthony Sanders
☐ 3752 Omar Malave MG
☐ 3753 Hal Dyer CO
☐ 3754 Scott Miller CO
☐ 3755 Checklist

1993 Medicine Hat Blue Jays Sports Pro

This 25-card standard-size set of the 1992 Medicine Hat Blue Jays, a Class A Pioneer League affiliate of the Toronto Blue Jays, features on its fronts white-bordered posed color player photos framed by a black line. The player's name and position appear in white lettering within a black stripe near the bottom. The blue-on-black team name appears near the left margin. The white back is framed by a black line and carries the year and team name at the top, followed by the player's name, uniform number, position, and hometown. The sponsor's name, One Hour Photo, appears near the bottom.

	MINT	NRMT	EXC
COMPLETE SET (25)	7.00	3.10	.85

☐ 1 Carlos Colmenares
☐ 2 Steve Sinclair
☐ 3 Angel Ramirez
☐ 4 Hector Martinez
☐ 5 Brian Grant
☐ 6 Scott Kennedy
☐ 7 Willie Daunic
☐ 8 Eddy Vasquez
☐ 9 Mike Toney
☐ 10 Joe Vogelgesang
☐ 11 Rob Adkins
☐ 12 Jeff Patzke
☐ 13 Ben Candelaria
☐ 14 Freddy Garcia
☐ 15 Mark Sievert
☐ 16 Anthony Sanders
☐ 17 Scott Jeffrey
☐ 18 Jeff Leystra
☐ 19 David Morgan
☐ 20 Lorenzo De La Cruz
☐ 21 Rob Patterson
☐ 22 Mike Wirsta TR
☐ 23 Omar Malave MG
☐ 24 Hal Dyer CO
☐ 25 Scott Miller CO

1993 Memphis Chicks Fleer/ProCards

This 25-card standard-size set of the 1993 Memphis Chicks, a Class AA Southern League affiliate of the Kansas City Royals, features white-bordered posed color player photos on its fronts. The player's name, team, and position appear near the bottom. The white horizontal back is framed by a blue line and carries the player's name at the top, followed by biography and statistics. A drawing of a ballplayer in action appears on the left.

	MINT	NRMT	EXC
COMPLETE SET (25)	5.00	2.20	.60

☐ 369 Brian Givens
☐ 370 Matt Karchner
☐ 371 Chris Limbach
☐ 372 Danny Miceli
☐ 373 Vladimir Perez
☐ 374 Doug Piatt
☐ 375 Eddie Pierce
☐ 376 Alex Sanchez
☐ 377 Jose Ventura
☐ 378 Carlos Diaz
☐ 379 Lance Jennings
☐ 380 Jeff Garber
☐ 381 Mike Guerrero
☐ 382 Domingo Mota
☐ 383 Joe Randa
☐ 384 Joe Vitiello
☐ 385 Adam Casillas
☐ 386 Butch Cole
☐ 387 Scott Jaster
☐ 388 Mark Johnson
☐ 389 Lee May Jr.
☐ 390 Les Norman
☐ 391 Tom Poquette MG
☐ 392 Mike Mason CO
☐ 393 Checklist

1993 Midland Angels Fleer/ProCards

This 27-card standard-size set of the 1993 Midland Angels, a Class AA Texas League affiliate of the California Angels, features white-bordered posed color player photos on its fronts. The player's name, team, and position appear near the bottom. The white horizontal back is framed by a blue line and carries the player's name at the top, followed by biography and statistics. A drawing of a ballplayer in action appears on the left.

	MINT	NRMT	EXC
COMPLETE SET (27)	5.00	2.20	.60

☐ 314 Erik Bennett
☐ 315 Ken Edenfield
☐ 316 John Fritz
☐ 317 Bobby Gamez
☐ 318 Chance Gledhill
☐ 319 Julian Heredia
☐ 320 David Holdridge
☐ 321 Jose Musset
☐ 322 Derek Stroud
☐ 323 Shad Williams
☐ 324 Jorge Fabregas
☐ 325 Fausto Tejero
☐ 326 Mark Brakebill
☐ 327 Kevin Davis
☐ 328 P.J. Forbes
☐ 329 Brian Grebeck
☐ 330 Chris Pritchett
☐ 331 Emmitt Cohick
☐ 332 John Jackson
☐ 333 Orlando Palmeiro
☐ 334 Luis Raven
☐ 335 Dan Rumsey
☐ 336 Mark Wasinger
☐ 337 Don Long MG
☐ 338 Nate Oliver CO
☐ 339 Kernan Ronan CO
☐ 340 Checklist

1993 Midland Angels One Hour Photo

This 33-card set of the 1993 Midland Angels, a Class AA Texas League affiliate of the California Angels, features color player photos. The set measures approximately 5 1/2" by 5". The backs are blank. The cards are unnumbered and checklisted below in alphabetical order. 500 sets were produced.

	MINT	NRMT	EXC
COMPLETE SET (33)	45.00	20.00	5.50

☐ 1 Brian Anderson
☐ 2 Mark Brakebill
☐ 3 Colin Charland
☐ 4 Todd Claus
☐ 5 Emmitt Cohick
☐ 6 Mark Dalesandro
☐ 7 Kevin Davis
☐ 8 Ken Edenfield
☐ 9 Jorge Fabregas
☐ 10 P.J. Forbes
☐ 11 John Fritz
☐ 12 Robert Gamez
☐ 13 Chance Gledhill
☐ 14 Brian Grebeck
☐ 15 Julian Heredia
☐ 16 David Holdridge
☐ 17 John Jackson
☐ 18 Jeff Kipila
☐ 19 Orlando Munoz
☐ 20 Jose Musset
☐ 21 Nate Oliver
☐ 22 Orlando Palmeiro
☐ 23 Chris Pritchett
☐ 24 Shawn Purdy
☐ 25 Mark Ratekin
☐ 26 Luis Raven
☐ 27 Dan Rumsey
☐ 28 Derek Stroud
☐ 29 Mark Sweeney
☐ 30 Fausto Tejero
☐ 31 Mark Wasinger
☐ 32 Ron Watson
☐ 33 Shaw Williams

1993 Midwest League All-Stars Fleer/ProCards

	MINT	NRMT	EXC
COMPLETE SET (56)	12.00	5.50	1.50

☐ 1 Tim Davis
☐ 2 Eddy Diaz
☐ 3 Danny Perez
☐ 4 Scott Talanoa
☐ 5 Anthony Byrd
☐ 6 Gus Gandarillas
☐ 7 Ken Tirpack
☐ 8 Charles Johnson
☐ 9 Reynol Mendoza
☐ 10 Chris Sheff
☐ 11 Mark Acre
☐ 12 David Francisco
☐ 13 Gary Haught
☐ 14 Troy Penis
☐ 15 Scott Sheldon
☐ 16 Don Wengert
☐ 17 Mel Bunch
☐ 18 Steve Sisco
☐ 19 Rodney Myers
☐ 20 Essex Burton
☐ 21 Michael Call
☐ 22 Troy Fryman
☐ 23 Sean Johnston
☐ 24 Robert Machado
☐ 25 Byron Mathews
☐ 26 Jason Pierson
☐ 27 Craig Wilson
☐ 28 Steve Worrell
☐ 29 Jolbert Cabrera
☐ 30 Chris Hmielewski
☐ 31 Javier Pages
☐ 32 Ugueth Urbina
☐ 33 Alberto Reyes
☐ 34 Tony Chavez
☐ 35 Larry Hingle
☐ 36 Chris Smith
☐ 37 Michael Wolff
☐ 38 Chad Fonville
☐ 39 Aaron Fultz
☐ 40 Marcus Jensen
☐ 41 Jim Rosenbohm
☐ 42 Amaury Telemaco
☐ 43 Hector Trinidad
☐ 44 Pedro Valdez
☐ 45 Jeff Ball
☐ 46 Tim Evans
☐ 47 Chris Holt
☐ 48 Joe Biasucci
☐ 49 Andy Bruce
☐ 50 Kirk Bullinger

☐ 51 Keith Johns
☐ 52 T.J. Mathews
☐ 53 Basil Shabazz
☐ 54 Dennis Slininger
☐ 55 Homer Bush
☐ 56 Checklist

1993 Mississippi State Bulldogs

	MINT	NRMT	EXC
COMPLETE SET (49)	10.00	4.50	1.25

☐ 1 Daryl Albro
☐ 2 Blake Anderson
☐ 3 Craig Bane
☐ 4 Tim Brickler
☐ 5 Ron Brown
☐ 6 Rex Buckner
☐ 7 Matt Carpenter
☐ 8 Brian Clark
☐ 9 Joe Clemente
☐ 10 Kyle Cook
☐ 11 Scott Davidson
☐ 12 Grant Davis
☐ 13 Brent Deweese
☐ 14 Jerry Dupuy
☐ 15 Justin Ewing
☐ 16 Hap Fleming
☐ 17 Nat Harden
☐ 18 Robbie Hayes
☐ 19 David Hayman
☐ 20 Steve Hegan
☐ 21 Carl Henderson
☐ 22 Tripp Hill
☐ 23 Steve Jaszczak
☐ 24 Steve Johnigan CO
☐ 25 Kyle Kennedy
☐ 26 Carlton Loewer
☐ 27 Eddie Lyons
☐ 28 Jeff Mackin
☐ 29 Joel Matthews
☐ 30 David Perkins
☐ 31 Jay Powell
☐ 32 David Marsland
☐ 33 Paul Newell
☐ 34 Niles Norris
☐ 35 Paul Petrulis
☐ 36 Ron Polk CO
☐ 37 Gary Rath
☐ 38 Ricky Joe Redd
☐ 39 Steve Smith CO
☐ 40 Todd Stanley
☐ 41 Scott Tanksley
☐ 42 Mitch Thompson CO
☐ 43 Larry Tomkins
☐ 44 Bryan Triche
☐ 45 Jason Van Every
☐ 46 Drew Williams
☐ 47 Diamond Girls
☐ 48 Managers - Trainers
Jason Ayers MG
Jay Bailey MG
Jon Burt MG
David Land MG
Joel Kennedy TR
David Chewning TR
☐ 49 Dudy Noble Field

1993 Modesto A's Classic/Best

This 30-card standard-size set of the 1993 Modesto A's, a Class A California League affiliate of the Oakland Athletics, features white-bordered posed color player shots on its fronts. A team-color-coded stripe below the photo carries the player's name; another above, his position and team name. On a ghosted team-logo, the white back carries the player's name at the top, followed by biography and statistics. This issue includes the minor league team set card debut of Jason Giambi.

	MINT	NRMT	EXC
COMPLETE SET(30)	12.00	5.50	1.50

☐ 1 Benji Grigsby
☐ 2 Jeff Barns
☐ 3 Garrett Beard
☐ 4 Russell Brock
☐ 5 Bobby Chouinard
☐ 6 Craig Connolly
☐ 7 Fausto Cruz
☐ 8 Lauro Felix
☐ 9 Ramon Fermin
☐ 10 Terance Frazier
☐ 11 Jason Giambi
☐ 12 Todd Ingram
☐ 13 Izzy Molina
☐ 14 Tom Myers
☐ 15 Rick Norton
☐ 16 Allen Plaster
☐ 17 Michael Rossiter
☐ 18 Scott Shockey
☐ 19 Mark Sobolewski
☐ 20 Ricky Strebeck
☐ 21 Craig Sudbury
☐ 22 Dane Walker
☐ 23 Steven Wojciechowski
☐ 24 Joel Wolfe
☐ 25 Ernie Young
☐ 26 Ted Kubiak MG
☐ 27 Pete Richert CO
☐ 28 Ric Moreno TR
☐ 29 Logo card
☐ 30 Checklist

1993 Modesto A's Fleer/ProCards

This 28-card standard-size set of the 1993 Modesto A's, a Class A California League affiliate of the Oakland Athletics, features white-bordered posed color player photos on its fronts. The player's name, team, and position appear near the bottom. The white horizontal back is framed by a blue line and carries the player's name at the top, followed by biography and statistics. A drawing of a ballplayer in action appears on the left. This set includes the first team set card of Jason Giambi.

	MINT	NRMT	EXC
COMPLETE SET(28)	12.00	5.50	1.50

☐ 790 Russell Brock
☐ 791 Bobby Chouinard
☐ 792 Craig Connolly
☐ 793 Ramon Fermin
☐ 794 Benji Grigsby
☐ 795 Todd Ingram
☐ 796 Thomas Myers
☐ 797 Allen Plaster
☐ 798 Michael Rossiter
☐ 799 Ricky Strebeck
☐ 800 Craig Sudbury
☐ 801 Steve Wojciechowski
☐ 802 Izzy Molina
☐ 803 Rick Norton
☐ 804 Jeff Barns
☐ 805 Garrett Beard
☐ 806 Fausto Cruz
☐ 807 Lauro Felix
☐ 808 Jason Giambi
☐ 809 Scott Shockey
☐ 810 Mark Sobolewski
☐ 811 Terance Frazier
☐ 812 Dane Walker
☐ 813 Joel Wolfe
☐ 814 Ernie Young
☐ 815 Ted Kubiak MG
☐ 816 Pete Richert CO
☐ 817 Checklist

1993 Nashville Sounds Fleer/ProCards

This 25-card standard-size set of the 1993 Nashville Sounds, a Class AAA American Association affiliate of the Chicago White Sox, features white-bordered posed color player photos on its fronts. The player's name, team, and position appear near the bottom. The white horizontal back is framed by a blue line and carries the player's name at the top, followed by biography and statistics. A drawing of a ballplayer in action appears on the left.

	MINT	NRMT	EXC
COMPLETE SET (25)	5.00	2.20	.60

☐ 563 Jason Bere
☐ 564 Jeff Carter
☐ 565 Fred Dabney
☐ 566 Brian Drahman
☐ 567 Ramon Garcia
☐ 568 Chris Howard
☐ 569 Barry Jones
☐ 570 Brian Keyser
☐ 571 Larry Thomas
☐ 572 Rick Wrona
☐ 573 Esteban Beltre
☐ 574 Scott Cepicky
☐ 575 Chris Cron
☐ 576 Drew Denson
☐ 577 Shawn Gilbert
☐ 578 Norberto Martin
☐ 579 Joe Hall
☐ 580 Shawn Jeter
☐ 581 Brad Komminsk
☐ 582 Scott Tedder
☐ 583 Rick Renick MG
☐ 584 Mark Haley CO
☐ 585 Roger LaFrancois CO
☐ 586 Rick Peterson CO
☐ 587 Checklist

1993 Nashville Xpress Fleer/ProCards

This 27-card standard-size set of the 1993 Nashville Xpress, a Class AA Southern League affiliate of the Minnesota Twins, features white-bordered posed color player photos on its fronts. The player's name, team, and position appear near the bottom. The white horizontal back is framed by a blue line and carries the player's name at the top, followed by biography and statistics. A drawing of a ballplayer in action appears on the left.

	MINT	NRMT	EXC
COMPLETE SET (27)	5.00	2.20	.60

☐ 394 Jayson Best
☐ 395 Eddie Guardado
☐ 396 Jason Klonoski
☐ 397 Dominic Konieczki
☐ 398 Jeff Mansur
☐ 399 Bob McCreary
☐ 400 Mike Misuraca
☐ 401 Oscar Munoz
☐ 402 Alan Newman
☐ 403 Todd Ritchie
☐ 404 Bill Wissler
☐ 405 Mike Durant
☐ 406 Pedro Grifol
☐ 407 Steve Dunn
☐ 408 Tom Houk
☐ 409 Dan Masteller
☐ 410 Brian Raabe
☐ 411 David Rivera
☐ 412 Scott Stahoviak
☐ 413 Rich Becker
☐ 414 Marty Cordova
☐ 415 Rex DeLaNuez
☐ 416 Mike McDonald
☐ 417 Phil Roof MG
☐ 418 Rick Anderson CO
☐ 419 Mark Funderburk CO
☐ 420 Checklist

1993 New Britain Red Sox Fleer/ProCards

This 28-card standard-size set of the 1993 New Britain Red Sox, a Class AA Eastern League affiliate of the Boston Red Sox, features white-bordered posed color player photos on its fronts. The player's name, team, and position appear near the bottom. The white horizontal back is framed by a blue line and carries the player's name at the top, followed by biography and statistics. A drawing of a ballplayer in action appears on the left.

	MINT	NRMT	EXC
COMPLETE SET (28)	5.00	2.20	.60

☐ 1212 Bernhard Dzafic
☐ 1213 Tom Fischer
☐ 1214 Peter Hoy
☐ 1215 Steve Mintz
☐ 1216 Gary Painter
☐ 1217 Ed Riley
☐ 1218 Frank Rodriguez
☐ 1219 John Shea
☐ 1220 Tim Smith
☐ 1221 Kevin Uhrhan
☐ 1222 Tim Vanegmond
☐ 1223 Brian Young
☐ 1224 Kevin Carroll
☐ 1225 Scott Hatteberg
☐ 1226 Scott Bethea
☐ 1227 Jim Crowley
☐ 1228 Colin Dixon
☐ 1229 Bill Norris
☐ 1230 Tony Rodriguez
☐ 1231 Les Wallin
☐ 1232 Mike Beams
☐ 1233 Boo Moore
☐ 1234 Jim Morrison
☐ 1235 Paul Rappoli
☐ 1236 Paul Thoutsis
☐ 1237 Jim Pankovits MG
☐ 1238 Dennis Burtt CO
☐ 1239 Checklist

1993 New Orleans Zephyrs Fleer/ProCards

This 26-card standard-size set of the 1993 New Orleans Zephyrs, a Class AAA American Association affiliate of the Milwaukee Brewers, features white-bordered posed color player photos on its fronts. The player's name, team, and position appear near the bottom. The white horizontal back is framed by a blue line and carries the player's name at the top, followed by biography and statistics. A drawing of a ballplayer in action appears on the left.

	MINT	NRMT	EXC
COMPLETE SET (26)	5.00	2.20	.60

☐ 964 Mike Farrell
☐ 965 Jim Hunter
☐ 966 Mike Ignasiak
☐ 967 Garland Kiser
☐ 968 Matt Maysey
☐ 969 Jamie McAndrew
☐ 970 Eric Nolte
☐ 971 Rafael Novoa
☐ 972 Steve Sparks
☐ 973 Jeff Tabaka
☐ 974 Rob Wishnevski
☐ 975 Mike Fitzgerald
☐ 976 Tom Lampkin
☐ 977 John Byington
☐ 978 Edgar Caceres
☐ 979 John Finn
☐ 980 Larry Sheets
☐ 981 Jose Valentin
☐ 982 Eddie Williams
☐ 983 Tony Piggs
☐ 984 Matt Mieske
☐ 985 Troy O'Leary
☐ 986 Chris Bando MG
☐ 987 Bill Campbell CO
☐ 988 Ron Jackson CO
☐ 989 Checklist

1993 Niagara Falls Rapids Fleer/ProCards

This 31-card standard-size set of the 1993 Niagara Falls Rapids, a Class A New York-Penn League affiliate of the Detroit Tigers, features white-bordered posed color player photos on its fronts. The player's name, team, and position appear near the bottom. The white horizontal back is framed by a blue line and carries the player's name at the top, followed by biography and statistics. A drawing of a ballplayer in action appears on the left.

	MINT	NRMT	EXC
COMPLETE SET (31)	5.00	2.20	.60

☐ 3377 Sam Arguto
☐ 3378 Eddie Gaillard
☐ 3379 Gary Goldsmith
☐ 3380 Rod Jackson
☐ 3381 Paul Magrini
☐ 3382 Toby McFarland
☐ 3383 Brian Moehler
☐ 3384 Joshua Neese
☐ 3385 Corey Reincke
☐ 3386 Mike Richardson
☐ 3387 David Rodriguez
☐ 3388 John Rosengren
☐ 3389 Mike Salazar
☐ 3390 Henry Santos
☐ 3391 Gabe Sollecito
☐ 3392 Corey Broome
☐ 3393 Del Marine
☐ 3394 Ken Marrero
☐ 3395 Shawn Brown
☐ 3396 Malvin DeJesus
☐ 3397 Duane Kinnon
☐ 3398 Kirk Ordway
☐ 3399 Jorge Valandia
☐ 3400 Glen Barker
☐ 3401 Eric Danapilis
☐ 3402 Robert Dickerson
☐ 3403 Tyrone Dixon
☐ 3404 Jorge Moreno
☐ 3405 Mike Wiseley
☐ 3406 Larry Parrish MG
☐ 3407 Checklist

1993 Norfolk Tides Fleer/ProCards

This 27-card standard-size set of the 1993 Norfolk Tides, a Class AAA International League affiliate of the New York Mets, features white-bordered posed color player photos on its fronts. The player's name, team, and position appear near the bottom. The white horizontal back is framed by a blue line and carries the player's name at the top, followed by biography and statistics. A drawing of a ballplayer in action appears on the left. This set includes a second year card of Bobby Jones.

	MINT	NRMT	EXC
COMPLETE SET (27)	6.00	2.70	.75

☐ 2562 Tom Filer
☐ 2563 Paul Gibson
☐ 2564 Mauro Gozzo
☐ 2565 Eric Hillman
☐ 2566 Bobby Jones
☐ 2567 Gregg Langbehn
☐ 2568 Dale Plummer
☐ 2569 Dave Telgheder
☐ 2570 Brandy Vann
☐ 2571 Tom Wegmann
☐ 2572 Dann Bilardello
☐ 2573 Brook Fordyce
☐ 2574 Kevin Baez
☐ 2575 Joe Delli Carri
☐ 2576 Tito Navarro
☐ 2577 Doug Saunders
☐ 2578 Steve Springer
☐ 2579 Mike Twardoski
☐ 2580 Eric Bullock
☐ 2581 Jeromy Burnitz
☐ 2582 Tim Howard
☐ 2583 Bert Hunter
☐ 2584 Ryan Thompson
☐ 2585 Clint Hurdle MG
☐ 2586 Bob Apodaca CO
☐ 2587 Marlin McPhail CO
☐ 2588 Checklist

1993 Oklahoma City 89ers Fleer/ProCards

This 26-card standard-size set of the 1993 Oklahoma City 89ers, a Class AAA American Association affiliate of the Texas Rangers, features white-bordered posed color player photos on its fronts. The player's name, team, and position appear near the bottom. The white horizontal back is framed by a blue line and carries the player's name at the top, followed by biography and statistics. A drawing of a ballplayer in action appears on the left.

	MINT	NRMT	EXC
COMPLETE SET (26)	5.00	2.20	.60

- ☐ 1617 Allan Anderson
- ☐ 1618 Jeff Bronkey
- ☐ 1619 Rob Brown
- ☐ 1620 Terry Burrows
- ☐ 1621 Steve Fireovid
- ☐ 1622 Mark Lee
- ☐ 1623 Danny Leon
- ☐ 1624 Francisco Oliveras
- ☐ 1625 Roger Pavlik
- ☐ 1626 Mike Schooler
- ☐ 1627 Cedric Shaw
- ☐ 1628 Doug Davis
- ☐ 1629 Ray Stephens
- ☐ 1630 Steve Balboni
- ☐ 1631 Mario Diez
- ☐ 1632 Larry Hanlon
- ☐ 1633 Keith Miller
- ☐ 1634 Luke Sable
- ☐ 1635 Jon Shave
- ☐ 1636 Benny Distefano
- ☐ 1637 Donald Harris
- ☐ 1638 Dan Peltier
- ☐ 1639 Bobby Jones MG
- ☐ 1640 Mike Berger CO
- ☐ 1641 Rick Knapp CO
- ☐ 1642 Checklist

1993 Omaha Royals Fleer/ProCards

This 29-card standard-size set of the 1993 Omaha Royals, a Class AAA American Association affiliate of the Kansas City Royals, features white-bordered posed color player photos on its fronts. The player's name, team, and position appear near the bottom. The white horizontal back is framed by a blue line and carries the player's name at the top, followed by biography and statistics. A drawing of a ballplayer in action appears on the left. This issue includes second year cards of Ruben Rivera and Ricky Ledee.

	MINT	NRMT	EXC
COMPLETE SET (29)	5.00	2.20	.60

- ☐ 1671 Brian Ahern
- ☐ 1672 Keith Brown
- ☐ 1673 Enrique Burgos
- ☐ 1674 Jim Campbell
- ☐ 1675 Dera Clark
- ☐ 1676 Chris Haney
- ☐ 1677 Mike Magnante
- ☐ 1678 Rick Reed
- ☐ 1679 Bill Sampen
- ☐ 1680 Steve Shifflett
- ☐ 1681 Mike Knapp
- ☐ 1682 Nelson Santovenia
- ☐ 1683 Kiki Diaz
- ☐ 1684 Bob Hamelin
- ☐ 1685 Russ McGinnis
- ☐ 1686 Jose Mota
- ☐ 1687 Rico Rossy
- ☐ 1688 Terry Shumpert
- ☐ 1689 Shawn Abner
- ☐ 1690 Mike Kingery
- ☐ 1691 Kevin Koslofski
- ☐ 1692 Kevin Long
- ☐ 1693 Kiki Diaz
- ☐ 1694 Karl Rhodes
- ☐ 1695 Dan Rohrmeier
- ☐ 1696 Jeff Cox MG
- ☐ 1697 Mike Alvarez CO
- ☐ 1698 Rich Dauer CO
- ☐ 1699 Checklist

1993 Oneonta Yankees Classic/Best

This 30-card standard-size set of the 1993 Oneonta Yankees, a Class A New York-Penn League affiliate of the New York Yankees, features white-bordered posed color player shots on its fronts. A team-color-coded stripe below the photo carries the player's name; another above, his position and team name. On a ghosted team-logo, the white back carries the player's name at the top, followed by biography and statistics. This issue includes second year cards of Ruben Rivera and Ricky Ledee.

	MINT	NRMT	EXC
COMPLETE SET (30)	18.00	8.00	2.20

- ☐ 1 Ruben Rivera
- ☐ 2 Shawn Alazaus
- ☐ 3 Steve Aldridge
- ☐ 4 Kurt Bierek
- ☐ 5 Abdiel Cumberbatch
- ☐ 6 Chris Cumberland
- ☐ 7 Al Drumheller
- ☐ 8 Elston Hansen
- ☐ 9 Mike Jerzembeck
- ☐ 10 Rich Josepher
- ☐ 11 Blaise Kozeniewski
- ☐ 12 Frank Lankford
- ☐ 13 Ricky Ledee
- ☐ 14 Brian Lewis
- ☐ 15 Brian McLamb
- ☐ 16 Silverio Navas
- ☐ 17 David Renteria
- ☐ 18 Greg Resz
- ☐ 19 Mike Schmitz
- ☐ 20 Scott Standish
- ☐ 21 Jim Thomforde
- ☐ 22 Jaime Torres
- ☐ 23 Rob Trimble
- ☐ 24 Joe Wharton
- ☐ 25 Clint Whitworth
- ☐ 26 Ernie Yaroshuk
- ☐ 27 Ken Dominguez MG
- ☐ 28 Bill Schmidt CO
- ☐ 29 Juan Nieves CO
- ☐ 30 John Nader GM Checklist

1993 Oneonta Yankees Fleer/ProCards

This 31-card standard-size set of the 1993 Oneonta Yankees, a Class A New York-Penn League affiliate of the New York Yankees, features white-bordered posed color player photos on its fronts. The player's name, team, and position appear near the bottom. The white horizontal back is framed by a blue line and carries the player's name at the top, followed by biography and statistics. A drawing of a ballplayer in action appears on the left. This set includes second year cards of Ruben Rivera and Ricky Ledee.

	MINT	NRMT	EXC
COMPLETE SET (31)	18.00	8.00	2.20

- ☐ 3494 Shawn Alazaus
- ☐ 3495 Chris Cumberland
- ☐ 3496 Al Drumheller
- ☐ 3497 Keith Heberling
- ☐ 3498 Blaise Kozeniewski
- ☐ 3499 Frank Lankford
- ☐ 3500 Jim Musselwhite
- ☐ 3501 Greg Resz
- ☐ 3502 Scott Standish
- ☐ 3503 Jim Thomforde
- ☐ 3504 Joe Wharton
- ☐ 3505 Clint Whitworth
- ☐ 3506 Jaime Torres
- ☐ 3507 Steve Aldridge
- ☐ 3508 Kurt Bierek
- ☐ 3509 Elston Hansen
- ☐ 3510 Rich Josepher
- ☐ 3511 Brian McLamb
- ☐ 3512 Silverio Navas
- ☐ 3513 David Renteria
- ☐ 3514 Mike Schmitz
- ☐ 3515 Abdiel Cumberbatch
- ☐ 3516 Ricky Ledee
- ☐ 3517 Brian Lewis
- ☐ 3518 Ruben Rivera
- ☐ 3519 Ernie Yaroshuk
- ☐ 3520 Ken Dominguez MG
- ☐ 3521 Steve Chandler CO
- ☐ 3522 Juan Nieves CO
- ☐ 3523 Bill Schmidt CO
- ☐ 3524 Checklist

1993 Orlando Cubs Fleer/ProCards

This 26-card standard-size set of the 1993 Orlando Cubs, a Class AA Southern League affiliate of the Chicago Cubs, features white-bordered posed color player photos on its fronts. The player's name, team, and position appear near the bottom. The white horizontal back is framed by a blue line and carries the player's name at the top, followed by biography and statistics. A drawing of a ballplayer in action appears on the left.

	MINT	NRMT	EXC
COMPLETE SET (26)	5.00	2.20	.60

- ☐ 2152 Checklist
- ☐ 2778 Tim Delgado
- ☐ 2779 Chris Johnson
- ☐ 2780 Earnie Johnson
- ☐ 2781 Bill Melvin
- ☐ 2782 John Salles
- ☐ 2783 Dave Stevens
- ☐ 2784 Aaron Taylor
- ☐ 2785 Jimmy Williams
- ☐ 2786 Travis Willis
- ☐ 2787 Brad Erdman
- ☐ 2788 Jack Johnson
- ☐ 2789 Jim Robinson
- ☐ 2790 Chris Ebright
- ☐ 2791 Matt Franco
- ☐ 2792 Mike Grace
- ☐ 2793 Jose Hernandez
- ☐ 2794 Greg Lonigro
- ☐ 2795 Darryl Vice
- ☐ 2796 Phil Dauphin
- ☐ 2797 Richie Grayum
- ☐ 2798 John Jensen
- ☐ 2799 Corey Kapano
- ☐ 2800 Ozzie Timmons
- ☐ 2801 Tommy Jones MG
- ☐ 2802 Rick Kranitz CO

1993 Osceola Astros Classic/Best

This 30-card standard-size set of the 1993 Osceola Astros, a Class A Florida State League affiliate of the Houston Astros, features white-bordered posed color player shots on its fronts. A team-color-coded stripe below the photo carries the player's name; another above, his position and team name. On a ghosted team-logo, the white back carries the player's name at the top, followed by biography and statistics. This issue includes a second year card of Bob Abreu.

	MINT	NRMT	EXC
COMPLETE SET (30)	7.00	3.10	.85

- ☐ 1 Buck McNabb
- ☐ 2 Bob Abreu
- ☐ 3 Tom Anderson
- ☐ 4 Perry Berry
- ☐ 5 Duane Brown
- ☐ 6 Mike Burns
- ☐ 7 Raul Chavez
- ☐ 8 Dennis Colon
- ☐ 9 Ruben Cruz
- ☐ 10 Jose Flores
- ☐ 11 Kevin Gallaher
- ☐ 12 Kyle Guerry
- ☐ 13 Al Harley
- ☐ 14 Brian Holliday
- ☐ 15 Kevin Lane
- ☐ 16 Doug Mlicki
- ☐ 17 Roy Nieto
- ☐ 18 Steve Powers
- ☐ 19 Rich Schulte
- ☐ 20 Kevin Scott
- ☐ 21 Joe Sewell
- ☐ 22 Kenny Wheeler
- ☐ 23 Chris White
- ☐ 24 Jimmy White
- ☐ 25 Todd Winston
- ☐ 26 Tim Tolman MG
- ☐ 27 Bob Robertson CO
- ☐ 28 Jack Billingham CO
- ☐ 29 Mike Freer TR
- ☐ 30 Checklist

1993 Osceola Astros Fleer/ProCards

This 29-card standard-size set of the 1993 Osceola Astros, a Class A Florida State League affiliate of the Houston Astros, features white-bordered posed color player photos on its fronts. The player's name, team, and position appear near the bottom. The white horizontal back is framed by a blue line and carries the player's name at the top, followed by biography and statistics. A drawing of a ballplayer in action appears on the left. This set includes a second year card of Bob Abreu.

	MINT	NRMT	EXC
COMPLETE SET (29)	7.00	3.10	.85

- ☐ 618 Tom Anderson
- ☐ 619 Duane Brown
- ☐ 620 Kevin Gallaher
- ☐ 621 Kyle Guerry
- ☐ 622 Brian Holliday
- ☐ 623 Kevin Lane
- ☐ 624 Doug Mlicki
- ☐ 625 Roy Nieto
- ☐ 626 Steve Powers
- ☐ 627 Joe Sewell
- ☐ 628 Kenny Wheeler
- ☐ 629 Chris White
- ☐ 630 Mike Burns
- ☐ 631 Raul Chavez
- ☐ 632 Kevin Scott
- ☐ 633 Perry Berry
- ☐ 634 Dennis Colon
- ☐ 635 Ruben Cruz
- ☐ 636 Jose Flores
- ☐ 637 Al Harley
- ☐ 638 Bob Abreu
- ☐ 639 Buck McNabb
- ☐ 640 Rich Schulte
- ☐ 641 Jimmy White
- ☐ 642 Todd Winston
- ☐ 643 Tim Tolman MG
- ☐ 644 Jack Billingham CO
- ☐ 645 Bob Robertson CO
- ☐ 646 Checklist

1993 Ottawa Lynx Fleer/ProCards

This 23-card standard-size set of the 1993 Ottawa Lynx, a Class AAA International League affiliate of the Montreal Expos, features white-bordered posed color player photos on its fronts. The player's name, team, and position appear near the bottom. The white horizontal back is framed by a blue line and carries the player's name at the top, followed by biography and statistics. A drawing of a ballplayer in action appears on the left.

	MINT	NRMT	EXC
COMPLETE SET (23)	5.00	2.20	.60

- ☐ 2428 Tavo Alvarez
- ☐ 2429 Tim Fortugno
- ☐ 2430 Gil Heredia
- ☐ 2431 Jonathan Hurst
- ☐ 2432 Mike Mathile
- ☐ 2433 Len Picota
- ☐ 2434 Bill Risley
- ☐ 2435 Doug Simons
- ☐ 2436 Sergio Valdez
- ☐ 2437 Pete Young
- ☐ 2438 Gary Hymel
- ☐ 2439 Joe Siddall
- ☐ 2440 Tim Barker
- ☐ 2441 Vince Castaldo
- ☐ 2442 Todd Haney
- ☐ 2443 Charlie Montoyo
- ☐ 2444 Hector Vargas
- ☐ 2445 Terrel Hansen
- ☐ 2445 Rick Hirtensteiner
- ☐ 2447 F.P. Santangelo
- ☐ 2448 Matt Stairs
- ☐ 2449 Mike Quade MG
- ☐ 2450 Checklist

1993 Palm Springs Angels Classic/Best

This 30-card standard-size set of the 1993 Palm Springs Angels, a Class A California League affiliate of the California Angels, features white-bordered posed color player shots on its fronts. A team-color-coded stripe below the photo carries the player's name; another above, his position and team name. On a ghosted team-logo, the white back carries the player's name at the top, followed by biography and statistics.

	MINT	NRMT	EXC
COMPLETE SET (30)	5.00	2.20	.60

- ☐ 1 Marquis Riley
- ☐ 2 Chris Anderson
- ☐ 3 Tyrone A. Boykin
- ☐ 4 Tim Burcham
- ☐ 5 Michael Butler
- ☐ 6 Todd Claus
- ☐ 7 Mark Dalesandro
- ☐ 8 Tommy Dodge
- ☐ 9 Gary Hagy
- ☐ 10 Pete Janicki
- ☐ 11 Dominick Johnson
- ☐ 12 Korey Keling
- ☐ 13 Dennis McCaffery
- ☐ 14 Keith Morrison
- ☐ 15 Orlando Munoz
- ☐ 16 Beban Perez
- ☐ 17 John Pricher
- ☐ 18 Mark Ratekin
- ☐ 19 Dallas Rinehart
- ☐ 20 Jay Simpson
- ☐ 21 Joel Smith
- ☐ 22 Jose Stela
- ☐ 23 Mark Sweeney
- ☐ 24 Joseph Urso
- ☐ 25 Pat Wernig
- ☐ 26 Mario Mendoza MG
- ☐ 27 Gene Richards CO
- ☐ 28 Howie Gershberg CO
- ☐ 29 Mike Twomey TR
- ☐ 30 Stadium Photo Checklist

1993 Palm Springs Angels Fleer/ProCards

This 29-card standard-size set of the 1993 Palm Springs Angels, a Class A California League affiliate of the California Angels, features white-bordered posed color player photos on its fronts. The player's name, team, and position appear near the bottom. The white horizontal back is framed by a blue line and carries the player's name at the top, followed by biography and statistics. A drawing of a ballplayer in action appears on the left.

	MINT	NRMT	EXC
COMPLETE SET (29)	5.00	2.20	.60

- ☐ 61 Tim Burcham
- ☐ 62 Mike Butler
- ☐ 63 Dominick Johnson
- ☐ 64 Korey Keling
- ☐ 65 Keith Morrison
- ☐ 66 Beban Perez
- ☐ 67 John Pricher
- ☐ 68 Mark Ratekin
- ☐ 69 Dallas Rinehart
- ☐ 70 Jose Trujillo
- ☐ 71 Pat Wernig
- ☐ 72 Mark Dalesandro
- ☐ 73 Jose Stela
- ☐ 74 Chris Anderson

☐ 75 Todd Claus
☐ 76 Tommy Dodge
☐ 77 Gary Hagy
☐ 78 Orlando Munoz
☐ 79 Joel Smith
☐ 80 Joe Urso
☐ 81 Tyrone Boykin
☐ 82 Dennis McCaffery
☐ 83 Marquis Riley
☐ 84 Jay Simpson
☐ 85 Mark Sweeney
☐ 86 Mario Mendoza MG
☐ 87 Howie Gershberg CO
☐ 88 Gene Richards CO
☐ 89 Checklist

1993 Pawtucket Red Sox Team Issue

	MINT	NRMT	EXC
COMPLETE SET (25)	6.00	2.70	.75

☐ 1 Buddy Bailey MG
☐ 2 Cory Bailey
☐ 3 Mike Beams
☐ 4 Greg Blosser
☐ 5 Jim Byrd
☐ 6 Joe Caruso
☐ 7 Joe Ciccarella
☐ 8 Brian Conroy
☐ 9 Gar Finnvold
☐ 10 John Flaherty
☐ 11 Don Florence
☐ 12 Cheo Garcia
☐ 13 Derek Livernois
☐ 14 John Malzone
☐ 15 Jeff McNeely
☐ 16 Dave Milstien
☐ 17 Nate Minchey
☐ 18 Luis Ortiz
☐ 19 Ruben Rodriguez
☐ 20 Sean Ross
☐ 21 Aaron Sele
☐ 22 Greg Sparks
☐ 23 Willie Tatum
☐ 24 Scott Taylor
☐ 25 Luis Aguayo CO
Rick Wise CO

1993 Pawtucket Red Sox Dunkin' Donuts

This 31-card set of the Pawtucket Red Sox, a Class AAA International League affiliate of the Boston Red Sox, was issued in one large sheet featuring six perforated five-card strips with a large team photo in the wide top strip. Sponsored by Channel 10 and Dunkin' Donuts, the fronts carry color player photos while the backs display player career statistics. The cards are unnumbered and checklisted below in alphabetical order.

	MINT	NRMT	EXC
COMPLETE SET (31)	40.00	18.00	5.00

☐ 1 Luis Aguayo
☐ 2 Buddy Bailey
☐ 3 Cory Bailey
☐ 4 Greg Blosser
☐ 5 Jim Byrd
☐ 6 Joe Caruso
☐ 7 Joe Ciccarella
☐ 8 Brian Conroy
☐ 9 Gar Finnvold
☐ 10 John Flaherty
☐ 11 Don Florence
☐ 12 Cheo Garcia
☐ 13 Derek Livernois
☐ 14 Steve Lyons
☐ 15 John Malzone
☐ 16 Jeff McNeely
☐ 17 Jose Melendez
☐ 18 Dave Milstien
☐ 19 Nate Minchey
☐ 20 Luis Ortiz
☐ 21 Jeff Plympton
☐ 22 Ruben Rodriguez
☐ 23 Ken Ryan
☐ 24 Aaron Sele
☐ 25 Greg Sparks
☐ 26 Franklin Stubbs
☐ 27 Scott Taylor
☐ 28 Herm Winningham
☐ 29 Rick Wise
☐ 30 Peter Youngman
☐ 31 Team Photo

1993 Pawtucket Red Sox Fleer/ProCards

This 29-card standard-size set of the 1993 Pawtucket Red Sox, a Class AAA International League affiliate of the Boston Red Sox, features white-bordered posed color player photos on its fronts. The player's name, team, and position appear near the bottom. The white horizontal back is framed by a blue line and carries the player's name at the top, followed by biography and statistics. A drawing of a ballplayer in action appears on the left. This set includes a second year card of Aaron Sele.

	MINT	NRMT	EXC
COMPLETE SET (29)	5.00	2.20	.60

☐ 2399 Cory Bailey
☐ 2400 Joe Caruso
☐ 2401 Joe Ciccarella
☐ 2402 Brian Conroy
☐ 2403 Gar Finnvoid
☐ 2404 Don Florence
☐ 2405 Derek Livernois
☐ 2406 Jose Melendez
☐ 2407 Nate Minchey
☐ 2408 Aaron Sele
☐ 2409 Scott Taylor
☐ 2410 John Flaherty
☐ 2411 Ruben Rodriguez
☐ 2412 Jim Byrd
☐ 2413 Cheo Garcia
☐ 2414 John Malzone
☐ 2415 Dave Milstien
☐ 2416 Luis Ortiz
☐ 2417 Jeff Richardson
☐ 2418 Greg Sparks
☐ 2419 Greg Blosser
☐ 2420 Steve Lyons
☐ 2421 Jeff McNeely
☐ 2422 Sean Ross
☐ 2423 Herm Winningham
☐ 2424 Buddy Bailey MG
☐ 2425 Luis Aguayo CO
☐ 2426 Rick Wise CO
☐ 2427 Checklist

1993 Peoria Chiefs Classic/Best

This 30-card standard-size set of the 1993 Peoria Chiefs, a Class A Midwest League affiliate of the Chicago Cubs, features white-bordered posed color player shots on its fronts. A team-color-coded stripe below the photo carries the player's name; another above, his position and team name. On a ghosted team-logo, the white back carries the player's name at the top, followed by biography and statistics.

	MINT	NRMT	EXC
COMPLETE SET (30)	5.00	2.20	.60

☐ 1 Pedro Valdez
☐ 2 Bill Bliss
☐ 3 London Bradley
☐ 4 Chuck Daniel
☐ 5 John Deutsch
☐ 6 Daryle Gavlick
☐ 7 Jay Hassel
☐ 8 Robin Jennings
☐ 9 Jack Johnson
☐ 10 Collin Kerley
☐ 11 Anthony Lee
☐ 12 Dan Madsen
☐ 13 Ricardo Medina
☐ 14 Emilio Mendez
☐ 15 Geno Morones
☐ 16 Richard Perez
☐ 17 Chris Rodriguez
☐ 18 Adam Schulhofer
☐ 19 Raphael Soto
☐ 20 Tim Stutheit
☐ 21 Amaury Telemaco
☐ 22 Hector Tinidad
☐ 23 Steve Walker
☐ 24 Vincent Zarate
☐ 25 Scott Krusinski GM
☐ 26 Jim O'Reilly TR
☐ 27 Ralph Rashid
☐ 28 Brien Taylor
Classic Best
Advertisement
☐ 29 Title Card
☐ 30 Checklist

1993 Peoria Chiefs Fleer/ProCards

This 27-card standard-size set of the 1993 Peoria Chiefs, a Class A Midwest League affiliate of the Chicago Cubs, features white-bordered posed color player photos on its fronts. The player's name, team, and position appear near the bottom. The white horizontal back is framed by a blue line and carries the player's name at the top, followed by biography and statistics. A drawing of a ballplayer in action appears on the left.

	MINT	NRMT	EXC
COMPLETE SET (27)	5.00	2.20	.60

☐ 1075 Bill Bliss
☐ 1076 Chuck Daniel
☐ 1077 Scott Gardner
☐ 1078 Daryle Gavlick
☐ 1079 Jay Hassel
☐ 1080 Collin Kerley
☐ 1081 Anthony Lee
☐ 1082 Geno Morones
☐ 1083 Chris Rodriguez
☐ 1084 Adam Schulhofer
☐ 1085 Amaury Telmaco
☐ 1086 Hector Tinidad
☐ 1087 Brad Erdman
☐ 1088 Jack Johnson
☐ 1089 London Bradley
☐ 1090 John Deutsch
☐ 1091 Ricardo Medina
☐ 1092 Emilio Mendez
☐ 1093 Richard Perez
☐ 1094 Raphael Soto
☐ 1095 Robin Jennings
☐ 1096 Dan Madsen
☐ 1097 Pedro Valdez
☐ 1098 Steve Walker
☐ 1099 Vince Zarate
☐ 1100 Steve Roadcap MG
☐ 1101 Checklist

1993 Peoria Chiefs Team Issue

This 30-card standard-size set of the 1993 Peoria Chiefs, a Class A Midwest League affiliate of the Chicago Cubs, features the minor league card debut of Kevin Orie.

	MINT	NRMT	EXC
COMPLETE SET (30)	12.00	5.50	1.50

☐ 1 Bill Bliss
☐ 2 London Bradley
☐ 3 Ben Burlingame
☐ 4 Earl Cunningham
☐ 5 Scott Gardner
☐ 6 Esmili Guerra
☐ 7 Daryle Gavlick
☐ 8 Jay Hassel
☐ 9 Vee Hightower
☐ 10 Dave Hutcheson
☐ 11 Robin Jennings
☐ 12 Collin Kerley
☐ 13 Mark Kingston
☐ 14 Anthony Lee
☐ 15 Dan Madsen
☐ 16 Ricardo Medina
☐ 18 Jim O'Reilly TR
☐ 19 Kevin Orie
☐ 20 Richard Perez
☐ 21 Glen Raasch
☐ 22 Steve Roadcap MG
☐ 23 John Rodgers
☐ 24 Adrian Sanchez
☐ 25 Josh Simmons
☐ 26 Rafael Soto
☐ 27 Amaury Telemaco
☐ 28 Hector Trinidad
☐ 30 Pedro Valdez
☐ 31 Steve Walker
☐ 32 Vincent Zarate

1993 Phoenix Firebirds Fleer/ProCards

This 29-card standard-size set of the 1993 Phoenix Firebirds, a Class AAA Pacific Coast League affiliate of the San Francisco Giants, features white-bordered posed color player photos on its fronts. The player's name, team, and position appear near the bottom. The white horizontal back is framed by a blue line and carries the player's name at the top, followed by biography and statistics. A drawing of a ballplayer in action appears on the left.

	MINT	NRMT	EXC
COMPLETE SET (29)	5.00	2.20	.60

☐ 1507 Terry Bross
☐ 1508 Kevin Brown
☐ 1509 Dan Carlson
☐ 1510 Larry Carter
☐ 1511 Brian Fisher
☐ 1512 Tim Layana
☐ 1513 Kevin McGehee
☐ 1514 Jim Myers
☐ 1515 Dan Rambo
☐ 1516 Rob Taylor
☐ 1517 Andy Allanson
☐ 1518 Jim McNamara
☐ 1519 Clay Bellinger
☐ 1520 Joel Chilmelis
☐ 1521 Adell Davenport
☐ 1522 Paul Faries
☐ 1523 Erik Johnson
☐ 1524 J.R. Phillips
☐ 1525 Mickey Brantley
☐ 1526 Rikkert Faneyte
☐ 1527 Steve Hosey
☐ 1528 Rob Katzaroff
☐ 1529 Andy Mota
☐ 1530 Reed Peters
☐ 1531 Reuben Smiley
☐ 1532 Carlos Alfonso MG
☐ 1533 Duane Espy CO
☐ 1534 Joel Horlen CO
☐ 1535 Checklist

1993 Pittsfield Mets Classic/Best

This 30-card standard-size set of the 1993 Pittsfield Mets, a Class A New York-Penn League affiliate of the New York Mets, features white-bordered posed color player shots on its fronts. A team-color-coded stripe below the photo carries the player's name; another above, his position and team name. On a ghosted team-logo, the white back carries the player's name at the top, followed by biography and statistics.

	MINT	NRMT	EXC
COMPLETE SET (30)	6.00	2.70	.75

☐ 1 Eric Ludwick
☐ 2 Benny Agbayani
☐ 3 Terry Childers
☐ 4 Gary Collum
☐ 5 Jeff Cosman
☐ 6 Tom Engle
☐ 7 Steve Grennan
☐ 8 Josh Haggas
☐ 9 Eric Harris
☐ 10 Rafael Hernandez
☐ 11 Jason Isringhausen
☐ 12 Scott Jones
☐ 13 Kevin Lewis
☐ 14 Rodney Mazion
☐ 15 Brandon Newell
☐ 16 Paul Petrulis
☐ 17 Travis Shaffer
☐ 18 Tad Smith
☐ 19 Charlie Sullivan
☐ 20 David Swanson
☐ 21 Jeff Tam
☐ 22 Matt Terrell
☐ 23 Mike Welch
☐ 24 David Zuniga
☐ 25 Howie Freiling MG
☐ 26 Jeff Edwards CO
☐ 27 Mark Stoughton TR
☐ 28 Brien Taylor
Classic Best
Advertisement
☐ 29 Title Card
☐ 30 Checklist

1993 Pittsfield Mets Fleer/ProCards

This 30-card standard-size set of the 1993 Pittsfield Mets, a Class A New York-Penn League affiliate of the New York Mets, features white-bordered posed color player photos on its fronts. The player's name, team, and position appear near the bottom. The white horizontal back is framed by a blue line and carries the player's name at the top, followed by biography and statistics. A drawing of a ballplayer in action appears on the left. This set includes a second year card of Jason Isringhausen.

	MINT	NRMT	EXC
COMPLETE SET (30)	6.00	2.70	.75

☐ 3699 Jeff Cosman
☐ 3700 Tom Engle
☐ 3701 Steve Grennan
☐ 3702 Jason Isringhausen
☐ 3703 Scott Jones
☐ 3704 Sean Kenny
☐ 3705 Eric Ludwick
☐ 3706 Allan McDill
☐ 3707 Brandon Newell
☐ 3708 Travis Shaffer
☐ 3709 David Swanson
☐ 3710 Jeff Tam
☐ 3711 Mike Welch
☐ 3712 Terry Childers
☐ 3713 Kevin Lewis
☐ 3714 David Maize
☐ 3715 Josh Haggas
☐ 3716 Eric Harris
☐ 3717 Rafael Hernandez
☐ 3718 Paul Petrulis
☐ 3719 Tad Smith
☐ 3720 Charlie Sullivan
☐ 3721 David Zuniga
☐ 3722 Benny Agbayani
☐ 3723 Gary Collum
☐ 3724 Rodney Mazion
☐ 3725 Matt Terrell
☐ 3726 Howie Freiling MG

□ 3727 Jeff Edwards CO
□ 3728 Checklist

1993 Pocatello Posse Fleer/ProCards

This 25-card standard-size set of the 1993 Pocatello Posse, a Rookie Class Pioneer League Independent, features white-bordered posed color player photos on its fronts. The player's name, team, and position appear near the bottom. The white horizontal back is framed by a blue line and carries the player's name at the top, followed by biography and statistics. A drawing of a ballplayer in action appears on the left.

	MINT	NRMT	EXC
COMPLETE SET (25)	5.00	2.20	.60

□ 3843 Checklist
□ 4199 Jason Atwood
□ 4200 Louis Birdt
□ 4201 Eugene Caruso
□ 4202 Steve Dempsey
□ 4203 Rafael Diaz
□ 4204 Mark Graham
□ 4205 Cory Lidle
□ 4206 Nick Lymberopoulos
□ 4207 Steve May
□ 4208 Tim Ploeger
□ 4209 Jeff Post
□ 4210 Chris Hunts
□ 4211 Todd Takayoshi
□ 4212 Jeff Boyle
□ 4213 Pedro Caranza
□ 4214 Will Fitzpatrick
□ 4215 Orlando Garcia
□ 4216 D.J. Harris
□ 4217 J.P. Postiff
□ 4218 Julian Salazar
□ 4219 Alonso Mendoza
□ 4220 Jason Pollock
□ 4221 Derek Vaughn
□ 4222 Ernie Rodriguez MG

1993 Pocatello Posse Sports Pro

	MINT	NRMT	EXC
COMPLETE SET (26)	6.00	2.70	.75

□ 1 Jeff Boyle
□ 2 Alonso Mendoza
□ 3 Gene Caruso
□ 4 Steve Dempsey
□ 5 Rafael Diaz
□ 6 Mark Graham
□ 7 J.P. Postiff
□ 8 Will Fitzpatrick
□ 9 Chris Hunt
□ 10 Cory Lidle
□ 11 Nick Lymberopoulos
□ 12 Orlando Garcia
□ 13 Jason Pollock
□ 14 Ron Matthews
□ 15 Todd Takayoshi
□ 16 Steve May
□ 17 Tim Ploeger
□ 18 Darren Greenlee
□ 19 D.J. Harris
□ 20 Derek Vaughn
□ 21 Jeff Post
□ 22 Julian Salazar
□ 23 Lou Birdt
□ 24 Ernie Rodriquez MG
□ 25 Adam Sanchez CO
□ 26 Dan Overman TR

1993 Portland Beavers Fleer/ProCards

This 21-card standard-size set of the 1993 Portland Beavers, a Class AAA Pacific Coast League affiliate of the Minnesota Twins, features white-bordered posed color player photos on its fronts. The player's name, team, and position appear near the bottom. The white horizontal back is framed by a blue line and carries the player's name at the top, followed by biography and statistics. A drawing of a ballplayer in action appears on the left.

	MINT	NRMT	EXC
COMPLETE SET (21)	5.00	2.20	.60

□ 2378 Tom Drees
□ 2379 Rich Garces
□ 2380 Jon Henry
□ 2381 Dave LaPoint
□ 2382 Jim Neidinger
□ 2383 Carlos Pulido
□ 2384 Mark Sims
□ 2385 Matt Stevens
□ 2386 Derek Parks
□ 2387 Chip Hale
□ 2388 David McCarty
□ 2389 Pat Meares
□ 2390 Paul Russo
□ 2391 Jerry Schunk
□ 2392 Bernardo Brito
□ 2393 Pat Howell
□ 2394 Derek Lee
□ 2395 Ray Ortiz
□ 2396 Scott Ullger MG
□ 2397 Gorman Heimueller CO
□ 2398 Checklist

1993 Prince William Cannons Classic/Best

This 30-card standard-size set of the 1993 Prince William Cannons, a Class A Carolina League affiliate of the New York Yankees, features white-bordered posed color player shots on its fronts. A team-color-coded stripe below the photo carries the player's name; another above, his position and team name. On a ghosted team-logo, the white back carries the player's name at the top, followed by biography and statistics.

	MINT	NRMT	EXC
COMPLETE SET (30)	5.00	2.20	.60

□ 1 Tate Seefried
□ 2 Roger Burnett
□ 3 Tommy Carter
□ 4 Jovino Carvajal
□ 5 Andy Croghan
□ 6 Bob Deller
□ 7 Matt Dunbar
□ 8 Greg Erickson
□ 9 Tim Flannelly
□ 10 Carlton Fleming
□ 11 Ron Frazier
□ 12 Keith Garagozzo
□ 13 Scott Gully
□ 14 Lew Hill IV
□ 15 Mark Hubbard
□ 16 Eric Knowles
□ 17 Jeff Motuzas
□ 18 Steve Munda
□ 19 Andy Pettitte
□ 20 Jorge Posada
□ 21 Curtis Ralph
□ 22 Keith Seiler
□ 23 Grant Sullivan
□ 24 Sean Twitty
□ 25 Jim Wiley
□ 26 Trey Hillman MG
□ 27 Rich Arena CO
□ 28 Brian Milner CO
□ 29 Mark Shiflett CO
□ 30 Tom Raynor TR Checklist

1993 Prince William Cannons Fleer/ProCards

This 30-card standard-size set of the 1993 Prince William Cannons, a Class A Carolina League affiliate of the New York Yankees, features white-bordered posed color player photos on its fronts. The player's name, team, and position appear near the bottom. The white horizontal back is framed by a blue line and carries the player's name at the top, followed by biography and statistics. A drawing of a ballplayer in action appears on the left.

	MINT	NRMT	EXC
COMPLETE SET (30)	5.00	2.20	.60

□ 647 Tom Carter
□ 648 Andy Croghan
□ 649 Matt Dunbar
□ 650 Ron Frazier
□ 651 Keith Garagozzo
□ 652 Scott Gully
□ 653 Steve Munda
□ 654 Curtis Ralph
□ 655 Kieth Seiler
□ 656 Grant Sullivan
□ 657 Jim Wiley
□ 658 Scott Epps
□ 659 Jeff Motuzas
□ 660 Jorge Posada
□ 661 Roger Burnett
□ 662 Greg Erickson
□ 663 Tim Flannelly
□ 664 Carltyon Fleming
□ 665 Eric Knowles
□ 666 Tate Seefried
□ 667 Jovino Carvajal
□ 668 Bob Deller
□ 669 Lew Hill
□ 670 Mark Hubbard
□ 671 Sean Twitty
□ 672 Trey Hillman MG
□ 673 Rich Arena CO
□ 674 Brian Milner CO
□ 675 Mark Shiflett CO
□ 676 Checklist

1993 Princeton Reds Classic/Best

This 30-card standard-size set of the 1993 Princeton Reds, a Rookie Class Appalachian League affiliate of the Cincinnati Reds, features white-bordered posed color player shots on its fronts. A team-color-coded stripe below the photo carries the player's name; another above, his position and team name. On a ghosted team-logo, the white back carries the player's name at the top, followed by biography and statistics. This issue includes the minor league card debut of Luis Ordaz.

	MINT	NRMT	EXC
COMPLETE SET (30)	6.00	2.70	.75

□ 1 Jhonney Carvajal
□ 2 Donald Broach
□ 3 Jason Chandler
□ 4 Yamil Concepcion
□ 5 Cobi Cradle
□ 6 Randy DeBruhl
□ 7 Joh Dold
□ 8 Robert Domino
□ 9 Roger Etheridge
□ 10 Luis Fernandez
□ 11 Joel Franklin
□ 12 Joe Fuccillo
□ 13 Danny Hagan
□ 14 Darran Hall
□ 15 Brad Keenan
□ 16 Argenis Labarca
□ 17 James Lofton
□ 18 Jackie McCroskey
□ 19 Armondo Morales
□ 20 Sam Mullins
□ 21 Jeff Murphy
□ 22 Luis Ordaz
□ 23 Sam Osorio
□ 24 Jeff Ramey
□ 25 Jason Robbins
□ 26 Trey Rutledge
□ 27 Rod Sanders
□ 28 Brian Silvia
□ 29 J'son Sullivan
□ 30 Maximo White Checklist

1993 Princeton Reds Fleer/ProCards

This 31-card standard-size set of the 1993 Princeton Reds, a Rookie Class Appalachian League affiliate of the Cincinnati Reds, features white-bordered posed color player photos on its fronts. The player's name, team, and position appear near the bottom. The white horizontal back is framed by a blue line and carries the player's name at the top, followed by biography and statistics. A drawing of a ballplayer in action appears on the left. This set includes the first year card of Luis Ordaz.

	MINT	NRMT	EXC
COMPLETE SET (31)	6.00	2.70	.75

□ 4168 Jason Chandler
□ 4169 Roger Etheridge
□ 4170 Luis Fernandez
□ 4171 Joel Franklin
□ 4172 Joe Fuccillo
□ 4173 Danny Hagan
□ 4174 Brad Keenan
□ 4175 Armando Morales
□ 4176 Sam Mullins
□ 4177 Jeff Murphy
□ 4178 Jason Robbins
□ 4179 Trey Rutledge
□ 4180 Jason Sullivan
□ 4181 Randy DeBruhl
□ 4182 Rob Domino
□ 4183 Brian Silvia
□ 4184 Jhonny Carvajal
□ 4185 Yamil Concepcion
□ 4186 Argenis LaBarca
□ 4187 James Lofton
□ 4188 Luis Ordaz
□ 4189 Jeff Ramey
□ 4190 Maximo White
□ 4191 Donald Broach
□ 4192 Cobi Cradle
□ 4193 Jon Dold
□ 4194 Darran Hall
□ 4195 Jackie McCroskey
□ 4196 Sam Osorio
□ 4197 Rod Sanders
□ 4198 Checklist

1993 Quad City River Bandits Classic/Best

This 30-card standard-size set of the 1993 Quad City River Bandits, a Class A Midwest League affiliate of the Houston Astros, features white-bordered posed color player shots on its fronts. A team-color-coded stripe below the photo carries the player's name; another above, his position and team name. On a ghosted team-logo, the white back carries the player's name at the top, followed by biography and statistics.

	MINT	NRMT	EXC
COMPLETE SET (30)	5.00	2.20	.60

□ 1 Chris Holt
□ 2 Jeff Ball
□ 3 Craig Bjornson
□ 4 Henri Centeno
□ 5 Dwayne Dawson
□ 6 Chris Durkin
□ 7 Jamie Evans
□ 8 Tim Evans
□ 9 Jimmy Gonzalez
□ 10 Anthony Gutierrez
□ 11 Mario Linares
□ 12 Mark Loughlin
□ 13 Brian McGlone
□ 14 Pat Murphy
□ 15 Ed Ponte
□ 16 Eddy Ramos
□ 17 Rob Rees
□ 18 Jeff Rhein
□ 19 Vince Roman
□ 20 Heath Rose
□ 21 Chuck Smith
□ 22 Damian Torino
□ 23 Jamie Walker
□ 24 Bryant Winslow
□ 25 Steve Dillard MG
□ 26 Cesar Cedeno CO
□ 27 Gary Lucas CO
□ 28 Kenny Crofford TR
□ 29 Title Card
□ 30 Checklist

1993 Quad City River Bandits Fleer/ProCards

This 30-card standard-size set of the 1993 Quad City River Bandits, a Class A Midwest League affiliate of the Houston Astros, features white-bordered posed color player photos on its fronts. The player's name, team, and position appear near the bottom. The white horizontal back is framed by a blue line and carries the player's name at the top, followed by biography and statistics. A drawing of a ballplayer in action appears on the left.

	MINT	NRMT	EXC
COMPLETE SET (30)	5.00	2.20	.60

□ 90 Craig Bjornson
□ 91 Dwayne Dawson
□ 92 Jamie Evans
□ 93 Anthony Gutierrez
□ 94 Chris Holt
□ 95 Mark Loughlin
□ 96 Jim McCutchen
□ 97 Pat Murphy
□ 98 Ed Ponte
□ 99 Rob Rees
□ 100 Chuck Smith
□ 101 Jamie Walker
□ 102 Jimmy Gonzalez
□ 103 Mario Linares
□ 104 Damian Torino
□ 105 Jeff Ball
□ 106 Ron Cancini
□ 107 Henri Centeno
□ 108 Brian McGlone
□ 109 Eddy Ramos
□ 110 Bryant Winslow
□ 111 Chris Durkin
□ 112 Tim Evans
□ 113 Jeff Rhein
□ 114 Vince Roman
□ 115 Steve Dillard MG
□ 116 Cesar Cedeno CO
□ 117 Gary Lucas CO
□ 118 Checklist
□ 130 Mario Linares

1993 Rancho Cucamonga Quakes Classic/Best

This 30-card standard-size set of the 1993 Rancho Cucamonga Quakes, a Class A California League affiliate of the San Diego Padres, features white-bordered posed color player shots on its fronts. A team-color-coded stripe below the photo carries the player's name; another above, his position and team name. On a ghosted team-logo, the white back carries the player's name at the top, followed by biography and statistics.

	MINT	NRMT	EXC
COMPLETE SET (30)	7.00	3.10	.85

□ 1 Julio Bruno
□ 2 Jared Baker
□ 3 Robbie Beckett
□ 4 Brent Bish
□ 5 Scott Bream
□ 6 Jeff Brown
□ 7 Cam Cairncross
□ 8 Clint Compton
□ 9 Sean Drinkwater
□ 10 Anito Encarnacion
□ 11 Luis Galindez
□ 12 Brad Gennero
□ 13 Ken Grzelaczyk
□ 14 Joey Hamilton
□ 15 Jason Hardtke
□ 16 Lee Henderson
□ 17 Jeff Huber
□ 18 Cole Hyson

☐ 19 Jason Kerr
☐ 20 Tom Martin
☐ 21 Sean Mulligan
☐ 22 Tom Paskievitch
☐ 23 Jeffrey Pearce
☐ 24 Scott Pugh
☐ 25 Bil Robbs
☐ 26 Ira Smith
☐ 27 Keith Champion MG
☐ 28 Bruce Tanner CO
☐ 29 Jim Daniel TR
☐ 30 Stadium
Checklist

1993 Rancho Cucamonga Quakes Fleer/ProCards

This 32-card standard-size set of the 1993 Rancho Cucamonga Quakes, a Class A California League affiliate of the San Diego Padres, features white-bordered posed color player photos on its fronts. The player's name, team, and position appear near the bottom. The white horizontal back is framed by a blue line and carries the player's name at the top, followed by biography and statistics. A drawing of a ballplayer in action appears on the left. This set includes a second year card of Joey Hamilton.

	MINT	NRMT	EXC
COMPLETE SET (32)	7.00	3.10	.85

☐ 818 Jared Baker
☐ 819 Robbie Beckett
☐ 820 Jeff Brown
☐ 821 Cam Cairncross
☐ 822 Clint Compton
☐ 823 Ron Dale
☐ 824 Luis Galindez
☐ 825 Ken Grzelaczyk
☐ 826 Joey Hamilton
☐ 827 Steve Hoeme
☐ 828 Jeff Huber
☐ 829 Cole Hyson
☐ 830 Jason Kerr
☐ 831 Tom Martin
☐ 832 Tom Paskievitch
☐ 833 Andy Rush
☐ 834 Anito Encarnacion
☐ 835 Lee Henderson
☐ 836 Sean Milligan
☐ 837 Brent Bish
☐ 838 Julio Bruno
☐ 839 Sean Drinkwater
☐ 840 Jason Hardtke
☐ 841 Scott Pugh
☐ 842 Scott Bream
☐ 843 Brad Gennaro
☐ 844 Jeff Pearce
☐ 845 Bill Robbs
☐ 846 Ira Smith
☐ 847 Keith Champion MG
☐ 848 Bruce Tanner CO
☐ 849 Checklist

1993 Reading Phillies Fleer/ProCards

This 26-card standard-size set of the 1993 Reading Phillies, a Class AA Eastern League affiliate of the Philadelphia Phillies, features white-bordered posed color player photos on its fronts. The player's name, team, and position appear near the bottom. The white horizontal back is framed by a blue line and carries the player's name at the top, followed by biography and statistics. A drawing of a ballplayer in action appears on the left.

	MINT	NRMT	EXC
COMPLETE SET (26)	5.00	2.20	.60

☐ 288 Ron Allen
☐ 289 Toby Borland
☐ 290 Mike Farmer
☐ 291 Robert Gaddy
☐ 292 Darrell Goedhart
☐ 293 Todd Goergen
☐ 294 Eric Hill
☐ 295 Mike Sullivan
☐ 296 Scott Wiegandt
☐ 297 Jose Fernandez
☐ 298 Ed Rosado
☐ 299 Carlo Colombino
☐ 300 John Escobar
☐ 301 Keith Kimberlin
☐ 302 Mica Lewis
☐ 303 Ron Lockett
☐ 304 Gene Schall
☐ 305 steve Bieser
☐ 306 Pat Brady
☐ 307 Mickey Hyde
☐ 308 Jeff Jackson
☐ 309 Sam Taylor
☐ 310 Don McCormack MG
☐ 311 Carlos Arroyo CO
☐ 312 Kelly Heath CO
☐ 313 Checklist

1993 Richmond Braves Bleacher Bums

This 26-card standard-size set of the 1993 Richmond Braves, a Class AAA International League affiliate of the Atlanta Braves features a third year card of Chipper Jones.

	MINT	NRMT	EXC
COMPLETE SET (26)	30.00	13.50	3.70
COMPLETE GOLD SET (26)	90.00	40.00	11.00

☐ 1 Ryan Klesko
☐ 2 Ramon Caraballo
☐ 3 Keith Mitchell
☐ 4 Napoleon Robinson
☐ 5 Melvin Nieves
☐ 6 Mike Mordecai
☐ 7 Mike Hostetler
☐ 8 Mike Kelly
☐ 9 Ron Jones
☐ 10 Brian Bark
☐ 11 Pedro Borbon Jr.
☐ 12 Tony Tarasco
☐ 13 Chipper Jones
☐ 14 Shawn Holman
☐ 15 Javy Lopez
☐ 16 Jose Oliva
☐ 17 Barry Jones
☐ 18 Donnie Elliott
☐ 19 Jerry Willard
☐ 20 Mark Wohlers
☐ 21 Mike Birkbeck
☐ 22 Judd Johnson
☐ 23 Bill Taylor
☐ 24 Boi Rodriguez
☐ 25 Grady Little MG
☐ NNO Team photo

1993 Richmond Braves Fleer/ProCards

This 30-card standard-size set of the 1993 Richmond Braves, a Class AAA International League affiliate of the Atlanta Braves, features white-bordered posed color player photos on its fronts. The player's name, team, and position appear near the bottom. The white horizontal back is framed by a blue line and carries the player's name at the top, followed by biography and statistics. A drawing of a ballplayer in action appears on the left. This set includes a third year card of Chipper Jones.

	MINT	NRMT	EXC
COMPLETE SET (30)	18.00	8.00	2.20

☐ 176 Brian Bark
☐ 177 Mike Birkbeck
☐ 178 Pedro Borbon Jr.
☐ 179 Donnie Elliott
☐ 180 Shawn Holman
☐ 181 Mike Hostetler
☐ 182 Judd Johnson
☐ 183 Napoleon Robinson
☐ 184 Randy St. Claire
☐ 185 Bill Taylor
☐ 186 Mark Wohlers
☐ 187 Javy Lopez
☐ 188 Jerry Willard
☐ 189 Ramon Caraballo
☐ 190 Chipper Jones
☐ 191 Ryan Klesko
☐ 192 Mike Mordecai
☐ 193 Jose Olivia
☐ 194 Boi Rodriguez
☐ 195 Barry Jones
☐ 196 Ron Jones
☐ 197 Mike Kelly
☐ 198 Keith Mitchell
☐ 199 Melvin Nieves
☐ 200 Tony Tarasco
☐ 201 Grady Little MG
☐ 202 Bruce Dal Canton CO
☐ 203 Glenn Hubbard CO
☐ 204 Jim Snyder CO
☐ 205 Checklist

1993 Richmond Braves Pepsi

This 25-card standard-size set of the 1993 Richmond Braves, a Class AAA International League affiliate of the Atlanta Braves features a third year card of Chipper Jones.

	MINT	NRMT	EXC
COMPLETE SET (25)	40.00	18.00	5.00

☐ 1 Ryan Klesko
☐ 2 Javy Lopez
☐ 3 Brian Bark
☐ 4 Mike Mordecai
☐ 5 Pedro Borbon
☐ 6 Chipper Jones
☐ 7 Jose Oliva
☐ 8 Donnie Elliott
☐ 9 Mike Birkbeck
☐ 10 Don Strange
☐ 11 Tony Tarasco
☐ 12 Ramon Caraballo
☐ 13 Mike Loynd
☐ 14 Ron Jones
☐ 15 Napoleon Robinson
☐ 16 Mike Kelly
☐ 17 Bill Taylor
☐ 18 Keith Mitchell
☐ 19 Dennis Burlingame
☐ 20 Boi Rodriguez
☐ 21 Melvin Nieves
☐ 22 Jerry Willard
☐ 23 Shawn Holman
☐ 24 Judd Johnson
☐ 25 Grady Little MG

1993 Richmond Braves Richmond Comix

This 30-card standard-size set of the 1993 Richmond Braves, a Class AAA International League affiliate of the Atlanta Braves features a third year card of Chipper Jones.

	MINT	NRMT	EXC
COMPLETE SET (30)	40.00	18.00	5.00

☐ 1 Grady Little MG
☐ 2 Bruce Dal Canton CO
☐ 3 Glenn Hubbard CO
☐ 4 Jim Snyder CO
☐ 5 Brian Bark
☐ 6 Mike Birkbeck
☐ 7 Pedro Borbon Jr.
☐ 8 Ramon Caraballo
☐ 9 Donnie Elliott
☐ 10 Shawn Holman
☐ 11 Mike Hostetler
☐ 12 Judd Johnson
☐ 13 Barry Jones
☐ 14 Chipper Jones
☐ 15 Ron Jones
☐ 16 Mike Kelly
☐ 17 Ryan Klesko
☐ 18 Javy Lopez
☐ 19 Jim Lovell TR
☐ 20 Keith Mitchell
☐ 21 Mike Mordecai
☐ 22 Melvin Nieves
☐ 23 Jose Oliva
☐ 24 Napoleon Robinson
☐ 25 Boi Rodriguez
☐ 26 ???
☐ 27 Bill Taylor
☐ 28 Jerry Willard
☐ 29 Mark Wohlers
☐ 30 Frank Miller
Jessica Miller

1993 Richmond Braves Richmond Camera

This 25-card team set of the 1993 Richmond Braves, a Class AA International League affiliate of the Atlanta Braves, measures approximately 4" by 4 7/8". The fronts feature borderless color player photos with sponsors' and team's logos in the wide bottom margin. The backs are blank. This set includes a third year card of Chipper Jones. 500 sets were produced.

	MINT	NRMT	EXC
COMPLETE SET (25)	90.00	40.00	11.00

☐ 1 Mike Mordecai
☐ 2 Ramon Caraballo
☐ 3 Napoleon Robinson
☐ 4 Boi Rodriguez
☐ 5 Mark Wohlers
☐ 6 Mike Birkbeck
☐ 7 Jose Oliva
☐ 8 Pedro Borbon Jr.
☐ 9 Shawn Holman
☐ 10 Javier Lopez
☐ 11 Donnie Elliott
☐ 12 Brian Bark
☐ 13 Mike Hostetler
☐ 14 Mike Kelly
☐ 15 Chipper Jones
☐ 16 Melvin Nieves
☐ 17 Ryan Klesko
☐ 18 Keith Mitchell
☐ 19 Tony Tarasco
☐ 20 Bill Taylor
☐ 21 Mike Loynd
☐ 22 Judd Johnson
☐ 23 Ron Jones
☐ 24 Don Strange
☐ 25 Grady Little

1993 Riverside Pilots Cal League Cards

	MINT	NRMT	EXC
COMPLETE SET (32)	6.00	2.70	.75

☐ 1 Ron Villone
☐ 2 Derek Lowe
☐ 3 David Adam
☐ 4 James Bonnici
☐ 5 Jeff Borski
☐ 6 Craig Clayton
☐ 7 Tim Furtado
☐ 8 Jim Gutierrez
☐ 9 Kevin King
☐ 10 Tow Maynard
☐ 11 Fred McNair
☐ 12 Jim Mecir
☐ 13 Tony Phillips
☐ 14 Arquimedez Pozo
☐ 15 Sean Rees
☐ 16 Tommy Robertson
☐ 17 Raul Rodarte
☐ 18 Andy Sheets
☐ 19 Greg Shockey
☐ 20 Dan Sullivan
☐ 21 Dave Waldenberger
☐ 22 Chris Widger
☐ 23 Willie Wilder
☐ 24 Chuck Wiley
☐ 25 Todd Youngblood
☐ 26 Jim Koehler
☐ 27 Craig Griffey
☐ 28 Dave Myers MG
☐ 29 Bryan Price CO
☐ 30 Manny Cervantes CO
☐ 31 Robert Nodine TR
☐ 32 Checklist

1993 Rochester Red Wings Fleer/ProCards

This 29-card standard-size set of the 1993 Rochester Red Wings, a Class AAA International League affiliate of the Baltimore Orioles, features white-bordered posed color player photos on its fronts. The player's name, team, and position appear near the bottom. The white horizontal back is framed by a blue line and carries the player's name at the top, followed by biography and statistics. A drawing of a ballplayer in action appears on the left. This set includes the first year minor league card of Jeffrey Hammonds.

	MINT	NRMT	EXC
COMPLETE SET (29)	7.00	3.10	.85

☐ 232 Pat Clements
☐ 233 Mike Cook
☐ 234 Jamie Moyer
☐ 235 John O'Donoghue
☐ 236 Mike Oquist
☐ 237 Brad Pennington
☐ 238 Don Schulze
☐ 239 Steve Searcy
☐ 240 Todd Stephan
☐ 241 Anthony Telford
☐ 242 Darrin Campbell
☐ 243 Rey Palacios
☐ 244 Mark Parent
☐ 245 Manny Alexander
☐ 246 Paul Carey
☐ 247 Scott Coolbaugh
☐ 248 Bobby Dickerson
☐ 249 Tommy Hinzo
☐ 250 Mel Wearing
☐ 251 Damon Buford
☐ 252 Jeffrey Hammonds
☐ 253 Mark Leonard
☐ 254 Mark Smith
☐ 255 Jack Voigt
☐ 256 Ed Yacopino
☐ 257 Bob Miscik MG
☐ 258 Steve Luebber CO
☐ 259 Joe Altobelli GM/CO
☐ 421 Checklist

1993 Rockford Royals Classic/Best

This 30-card standard-size set of the 1993 Rockford Royals, a Class A Midwest League affiliate of the Kansas City Royals, features white-bordered posed color player shots on its fronts. A team-color-coded stripe below the photo carries the player's name; another above, his position and team name. On a ghosted team-logo, the white back carries the player's name at the top, followed by biography and statistics. This issue includes the minor league card debuts of Johnny Damon, Rod Myers and Jim Pittsley.

	MINT	NRMT	EXC
COMPLETE SET(30)	20.00	9.00	2.50

☐ 1 Johnny Damon
☐ 2 Jeff Antoon

☐ 3 Michael Bovee
☐ 4 Ramy Brooks Jr.
☐ 5 Melvin Bunch Jr.
☐ 6 Rick Burley
☐ 7 Sherard Clinkscales
☐ 8 Chris Connolly
☐ 9 Bryan Currier
☐ 10 Sean Delaney
☐ 11 John Dickens
☐ 12 Aaron Dorlarque
☐ 13 Bart Evans
☐ 14 Jeff Haas II
☐ 15 Trentor Hauswirth
☐ 16 Ryan Long
☐ 17 Julio Montilla
☐ 18 Cesar Morillo
☐ 19 Rodney Myers
☐ 20 Steve Murphy
☐ 21 Roderick Myers
☐ 22 Andre Newhouse
☐ 23 Jim Pittsley
☐ 24 Chris Sheehen
☐ 25 Steve Sisco
☐ 26 Larry Sutton
☐ 27 John Weglarz
☐ 28 Mike Jirschele MG
☐ 29 Tom Burgmeier CO
☐ 30 Jim Thrift CO
Checklist

1993 Rockford Royals Fleer/ProCards

This 31-card standard-size set of the 1993 Rockford Royals, a Class A Midwest League affiliate of the Kansas City Royals, features white-bordered posed color player photos on its fronts. The player's name, team, and position appear near the bottom. The white horizontal back is framed by a blue line and carries the player's name at the top, followed by biography and statistics. A drawing of a ballplayer in action appears on the left. This set includes the first year cards of Johnny Damon, Jim Pittsley and Rod Myers.

	MINT	NRMT	EXC
COMPLETE SET (31)	20.00	9.00	2.50

☐ 704 Mike Bovee
☐ 705 Mel Bunch
☐ 706 Rick Burley
☐ 707 Sherard Clinkscales
☐ 708 Chris Connolly
☐ 709 Bryan Currier
☐ 710 John Dickens
☐ 711 Aaron Dorlarque
☐ 712 Bart Evans
☐ 713 Jeff Haas
☐ 714 Rodney Myers
☐ 715 Jim Pittsley
☐ 716 Chris Sheehen
☐ 717 John Weglarz
☐ 718 Rae Brooks
☐ 719 Sean Delaney
☐ 720 Trent Hauswirth
☐ 721 Jeff Antoon
☐ 722 Ryan Long
☐ 723 Julio Montilla
☐ 724 Cesar Morillo
☐ 725 Steve Sisco
☐ 726 Larry Sutton
☐ 727 Johnny Damon
☐ 728 Steve Murphy
☐ 729 Roderick Myers
☐ 730 Andre Newhouse
☐ 731 Mike Jirschele MG
☐ 732 Tom Burgmeier CO
☐ 733 Jim Thrift CO
☐ 734 Checklist

1993 Salem Buccaneers Classic/Best

This 30-card standard-size set of the 1993 Salem Buccaneers, a Class A Carolina League affiliate of the Pittsburgh Pirates, features white-bordered posed color player shots on its fronts. A team-color-coded stripe below the photo carries the player's name; another above, his position and team name. On a ghosted team-logo, the white back carries the player's name at the top, followed by biography and statistics.

	MINT	NRMT	EXC
COMPLETE SET (30)	5.00	2.20	.60

☐ 1 Kenneth Bonifay
☐ 2 Michael Brown II
☐ 3 Joe Calder
☐ 4 Jason Christiansen
☐ 5 Jeff Conger
☐ 6 Mariano De Los Santos
☐ 7 David Doorneweerd
☐ 8 Angelo Encarnacion
☐ 9 Sean Evans
☐ 10 Jon Farrell
☐ 11 Don Garvey
☐ 12 Marcus Hanel
☐ 13 Dennis Konuszewski
☐ 14 Esteban Loaiza
☐ 15 Jim Martin
☐ 16 Tim Marx
☐ 17 Jeff McCurry
☐ 18 Marty Neff
☐ 19 Trace Ragland
☐ 20 Matt Ruebel
☐ 21 Kevin Rychel
☐ 22 Chance Sanford
☐ 23 Michael Teich
☐ 24 Gary Wilson
☐ 25 Tony Womack
☐ 26 Scott Little MG
☐ 27 Dave Rajsich CO
☐ 28 Bill Zick TR
☐ 29 Sam Lazzaro GM/VP
☐ 30 Stu Paul ANN
Checklist

1993 Salem Buccaneers Fleer/ProCards

This 29-card standard-size set of the 1993 Salem Buccaneers, a Class A Carolina League affiliate of the Pittsburgh Pirates, features white-bordered posed color player photos on its fronts. The player's name, team, and position appear near the bottom. The white horizontal back is framed by a blue line and carries the player's name at the top, followed by biography and statistics. A drawing of a ballplayer in action appears on the left.

	MINT	NRMT	EXC
COMPLETE SET (29)	5.00	2.20	.60

☐ 422 Jason Christiansen
☐ 423 Mariano DeLosSantos
☐ 424 Dave Doorneweerd
☐ 425 Sean Evans
☐ 426 Dennis Konuszewski
☐ 427 Esteban Loaiza
☐ 428 Jim Martin
☐ 429 Jeff McCurry
☐ 430 Matt Ruebel
☐ 431 Kevin Rychel
☐ 432 Michael Teich
☐ 433 Gary Wilson
☐ 434 Angelo Encarnacion
☐ 435 Marcus Hanel
☐ 436 Tim Marx
☐ 437 Ken Bonifay
☐ 438 Mike Brown
☐ 439 Joe Calder
☐ 440 Don Garvey
☐ 441 Rich Juday
☐ 442 Chance Sanford
☐ 443 Tony Womack
☐ 444 Jeff Conger
☐ 445 Jon Farrell
☐ 446 Marty Neff
☐ 447 Trace Ragland
☐ 448 Scott Little MG
☐ 449 Dave Rajsich CO
☐ 450 Checklist

1993 San Antonio Missions Fleer/ProCards

This 28-card standard-size set of the 1993 San Antonio Missions, a Class AA Texas League affiliate of the Los Angeles Dodgers, features white-bordered posed color player photos on its fronts. The player's name, team, and position appear near the bottom. The white horizontal back is framed by a blue line and carries the player's name at the top, followed by biography and statistics. A drawing of a ballplayer in action appears on the left. This set includes the second year cards of Todd Hollandsworth and Roger Cedeno.

	MINT	NRMT	EXC
COMPLETE SET (28)	12.00	5.50	1.50

☐ 2996 Bill Bene
☐ 2997 Jamie Daspit
☐ 2998 Javier Delahoya
☐ 2999 Rick Gorecki
☐ 3000 Isidro Marquez
☐ 3001 Terric McFarlin
☐ 3002 Jose Parra
☐ 3003 Brian Piotrowicz
☐ 3004 Royal Thomas
☐ 3005 Ben VanRyn
☐ 3006 Joey Vierra
☐ 3007 Chris Abbe
☐ 3008 Hector Ortiz
☐ 3009 Jorge Alvarez
☐ 3010 Juan Castro
☐ 3011 Garey Ingram
☐ 3012 Ron Maurer
☐ 3013 Dan Melendez
☐ 3014 Murph Proctor
☐ 3015 Roger Cedeno
☐ 3016 Anthony Collier
☐ 3017 Todd Hollandsworth
☐ 3018 Billy Lott
☐ 3019 Vernon Spearman
☐ 3020 Glenn Hoffman MG
☐ 3021 Burt Hooton CO
☐ 3022 Brett Magnusson P/CO
☐ 3023 Checklist

1993 San Bernardino Spirit Classic/Best

This 30-card standard-size set of the 1993 San Bernardino Spirit, a Class A California League Independent, features white-bordered posed color player shots on its fronts. A team-color-coded stripe below the photo carries the player's name; another above, his position and team name. On a ghosted team-logo, the white back carries the player's name at the top, followed by biography and statistics.

	MINT	NRMT	EXC
COMPLETE SET (30)	6.00	2.70	.75

☐ 1 Rodney Pedraza
☐ 2 Steve Anderson
☐ 3 Shawn Buchanan
☐ 4 Michael Conte
☐ 5 Tim Cooper
☐ 6 Rick DeHart
☐ 7 Tim Demerson
☐ 8 Mike Figga
☐ 9 Ryan Freeburg
☐ 10 Bo Gilliam
☐ 11 Adin Lohry
☐ 12 Todd Malone
☐ 13 Manny Martinez
☐ 14 Tim Scott
☐ 15 Steve Shoemaker
☐ 16 Tim Smith
☐ 17 Rick Sutch
☐ 18 John Sutherland
☐ 19 Makoto Suzuki
☐ 20 Brian Turner
☐ 21 Gregory J. Mahlberg MG
☐ 22 Steve Livesey CO
☐ 23 Chuck Estrada CO
☐ 24 Chris Phillips TR
☐ 25 The Bug (Mascot)
☐ 26 Stadium
☐ 27 Chipper Jones
Classic Best
Advertisement
☐ 28 Brien Taylor
Classic Best
Advertisement
☐ 29 Title Card
☐ 30 Checklist

1993 San Bernardino Spirit Fleer/ProCards

This 26-card standard-size set of the 1993 San Bernardino Spirit, a Class A California League Independent, features white-bordered posed color player photos on its fronts. The player's name, team, and position appear near the bottom. The white horizontal back is framed by a blue line and carries the player's name at the top, followed by biography and statistics. A drawing of a ballplayer in action appears on the left.

	MINT	NRMT	EXC
COMPLETE SET (26)	6.00	2.70	.75

☐ 764 Michael Conte
☐ 765 Rick DeHart
☐ 766 Todd Malone
☐ 767 Rod Pedraza
☐ 768 Scott Rose
☐ 769 Steve Shoemaker
☐ 770 Tim Smith
☐ 771 Rick Sutch
☐ 772 John Sutherland
☐ 773 Mac Suzuki
☐ 774 Mike Figa
☐ 775 Adin Lohry
☐ 776 Steve Anderson
☐ 777 Tim Cooper
☐ 778 Ryan Freeburg
☐ 779 Tim Scott
☐ 780 Brian Turner
☐ 781 Shawn Buchanan
☐ 782 Tim Demerson
☐ 783 Rick Freehling
☐ 784 Sean Gilliam
☐ 785 Manny Martinez
☐ 786 Greg Mahlberg MG
☐ 787 Chuck Estrada CO
☐ 788 Steve Livesey CO
☐ 789 Checklist

1993 San Jose Giants Classic/Best

This 30-card standard-size set of the 1993 San Jose Giants, a Class A California League affiliate of the San Francisco Giants, features white-bordered posed color player shots on its fronts. A team-color-coded stripe below the photo carries the player's name; another above, his position and team name. On a ghosted team-logo, the white back carries the player's name at the top, followed by biography and statistics.

	MINT	NRMT	EXC
COMPLETE SET (30)	5.00	2.20	.60

☐ 1 Adam Hyzdu
☐ 2 Andrew Albrecht
☐ 3 Kevin Bellomo
☐ 4 Danny Calcagno
☐ 5 Tim Casper
☐ 6 Troy Clemens
☐ 7 Brent Cookson
☐ 8 Ricky Ward
☐ 9 Chuck Wanke
☐ 10 Brian Dour
☐ 11 Kurt Ehmann
☐ 12 Charlie Hicks
☐ 13 Richard Hyde
☐ 14 Brett Jenkins
☐ 15 Brian McLeod
☐ 16 Doug Mirabelli
☐ 17 Don Montgomery
☐ 18 Steven Whitaker
☐ 19 Kurt Peltzer
☐ 20 Mark Peterson
☐ 21 Ron Pezzoni
☐ 22 Chris Wimmer
☐ 23 Eric Stonecipher
☐ 24 Doug Vanderweele
☐ 25 Bill VanLandingham
☐ 26 Dick Dietz MG
☐ 27 Jim Davenport CO
☐ 28 Todd Oakes CO
☐ 29 John Pletsch
☐ 30 Ed Bautista
Checklist

1993 San Jose Giants Fleer/ProCards

This 30-card standard-size set of the 1993 San Jose Giants, a Class A California League affiliate of the San Francisco Giants, features white-bordered posed color player photos on its fronts. The player's name, team, and position appear near the bottom. The white horizontal back is framed by a blue line and carries the player's name at the top, followed by biography and statistics. A drawing of a ballplayer in action appears on the left.

	MINT	NRMT	EXC
COMPLETE SET (30)	5.00	2.20	.60

☐ 1 Brian Dour
☐ 2 Charlie Hicks
☐ 3 Rich Hyde
☐ 4 Brian McLeod
☐ 5 Kurt Peltzer
☐ 6 Mark Peterson
☐ 7 Eric Stonecipher
☐ 8 Doug Vanderweele
☐ 9 William VanLandingham
☐ 10 Chuck Wanke
☐ 11 Steve Whitaker
☐ 12 Danny Calcagno
☐ 13 Troy Clemens
☐ 14 Doug Mirabelli
☐ 15 Tim Casper
☐ 16 Chris Dotolo
☐ 17 Kurt Ehmann
☐ 18 Brett Jenkins
☐ 19 Don Montgomery
☐ 20 Ricky Ward
☐ 21 Chris Wimmer
☐ 22 Drew Albrecht
☐ 23 Kevin Bellomo
☐ 24 Brent Cookson
☐ 25 Adam Hyzdu
☐ 26 Ron Pezzoni
☐ 27 Dick Dietz MG
☐ 28 Jim Davenport CO
☐ 29 Todd Oakes CO
☐ 30 Checklist

1993 Sarasota White Sox Classic/Best

This 30-card standard-size set of the 1993 Sarasota White Sox, a Class A Florida State League affiliate of the Chicago White Sox, features white-bordered posed color player shots on its fronts. A team-color-coded stripe below the photo carries the player's name; another above, his position and team name. On a ghosted team-logo, the white back carries the player's name at the top, followed by biography and statistics.

	MINT	NRMT	EXC
COMPLETE SET (30)	5.00	2.20	.60

- ☐ 1 Glenn DiSarcina
- ☐ 2 Luis Andujar
- ☐ 3 Brian Boehringer
- ☐ 4 Mike Bradish
- ☐ 5 Doug Brady
- ☐ 6 Carmine Cappuccio
- ☐ 7 Ken Coleman
- ☐ 8 Kevin Coughlin
- ☐ 9 Robert Ellis
- ☐ 10 Steve Gajkowski
- ☐ 11 Tony Gordon
- ☐ 12 Mike Heathcott
- ☐ 13 Harold Henry
- ☐ 14 Randy Hood
- ☐ 15 Barry Johnson
- ☐ 16 David Keating
- ☐ 17 Alan Levine
- ☐ 18 Dean Locklear
- ☐ 19 Henry Manning
- ☐ 20 Jason Ogden
- ☐ 21 Charles Poe
- ☐ 22 Nilson Robledo
- ☐ 23 Olmedo Saenz
- ☐ 24 Shane Spry
- ☐ 25 Keith Strange
- ☐ 26 Kevin Tolar
- ☐ 27 Kerry Valrie
- ☐ 28 Dave Huppert MG
- ☐ 29 Jon Matlack CO
- ☐ 30 Checklist

1993 Sarasota White Sox Fleer/ProCards

This 30-card standard-size set of the 1993 Sarasota White Sox, a Class A Florida State League affiliate of the Chicago White Sox, features white-bordered posed color player photos on its fronts. The player's name, team, and position appear near the bottom. The white horizontal back is framed by a blue line and carries the player's name at the top, followed by biography and statistics. A drawing of a ballplayer in action appears on the left. This set includes the first year card of Tom Fordham.

	MINT	NRMT	EXC
COMPLETE SET (30)	6.00	2.70	.75

- ☐ 1360 Luis Andujar
- ☐ 1361 Brian Boehringer
- ☐ 1362 Tom Fordham
- ☐ 1363 Steve Gajkowski
- ☐ 1364 Robert Ellis
- ☐ 1365 Mike Heathcott
- ☐ 1366 David Keating
- ☐ 1367 Al Levine
- ☐ 1368 Hank Tagle
- ☐ 1369 Kevin Tolar
- ☐ 1370 Chris Woodfin
- ☐ 1371 Nilson Robledo
- ☐ 1372 Chris Tremie
- ☐ 1373 Mike Vogel
- ☐ 1374 Doug Brady
- ☐ 1375 Kevin Coughlin
- ☐ 1376 Glenn DiSarcina
- ☐ 1377 Troy Fryman
- ☐ 1378 Giovanni Miranda
- ☐ 1379 Olmedo Saenz
- ☐ 1380 Chris Snopek
- ☐ 1381 Shawn Buchanan
- ☐ 1382 Carmine Cappuccio
- ☐ 1383 Randy Hood
- ☐ 1384 Charles Poe
- ☐ 1385 Kerry Valrie
- ☐ 1386 Dave Huppert MG
- ☐ 1387 Jon Matlack CO
- ☐ 1388 Pat Roessler CO
- ☐ 1389 Checklist

1993 Savannah Cardinals Classic/Best

This 30-card standard-size set of the 1993 Savannah Cardinals, a Class A South Atlantic League affiliate of the St. Louis Cardinals, features white-bordered posed color player shots on its fronts. A team-color-coded stripe below the photo carries the player's name; another above, his position and team name. On a ghosted team-logo, the white back carries the player's name at the top, followed by biography and statistics.

	MINT	NRMT	EXC
COMPLETE SET (30)	5.00	2.20	.60

- ☐ 1 Aldo Pecorilli
- ☐ 2 Jeff Alkire
- ☐ 3 Charlie Anderson
- ☐ 4 Keith Black
- ☐ 5 Garrett Blanton
- ☐ 6 Mike Busby
- ☐ 7 Brian Carpenter
- ☐ 8 Joe Carrillo
- ☐ 9 Jamie Cochran
- ☐ 10 Hector Colon
- ☐ 11 Ray Davis
- ☐ 12 Darren Doucette
- ☐ 13 Steve Dudek
- ☐ 14 Ronnie French
- ☐ 15 Doug Goodman
- ☐ 16 Larry Lucchetti
- ☐ 17 Frankie Martinez
- ☐ 18 Joe McEwing
- ☐ 19 Jeff Murphy
- ☐ 20 John O'Brien
- ☐ 21 Brian Rupp
- ☐ 22 Karl Stanley
- ☐ 23 Chad Sumner
- ☐ 24 Mark Tranbarger
- ☐ 25 Jesus Ugueto
- ☐ 26 Chris Maloney MG
- ☐ 27 Ramon Ortiz CO
- ☐ 28 Steve Proctor TR
- ☐ 29 Tommy McCoy BB
- ☐ 30 Checklist

1993 Savannah Cardinals Fleer/ProCards

This 27-card standard-size set of the 1993 Savannah Cardinals, a Class A South Atlantic League affiliate of the St. Louis Cardinals, features white-bordered posed color player photos on its fronts. The player's name, team, and position appear near the bottom. The white horizontal back is framed by a blue line and carries the player's name at the top, followed by biography and statistics. A drawing of a ballplayer in action appears on the left.

	MINT	NRMT	EXC
COMPLETE SET (27)	5.00	2.20	.60

- ☐ 677 Jeff Alkire
- ☐ 678 Mike Busby
- ☐ 679 Brian Carpenter
- ☐ 680 Joe Carrillo
- ☐ 681 Jamie Cochran
- ☐ 682 Ray Davis
- ☐ 683 Doug Goodman
- ☐ 684 Larry Lucchetti
- ☐ 685 Frankie Martinez
- ☐ 686 Karl Stanley
- ☐ 687 Mike Tranbaerger
- ☐ 688 Jeff Murphy
- ☐ 689 Aldo Pecorilli
- ☐ 690 Charlie Anderson
- ☐ 691 Keith Black
- ☐ 692 Darren Doucette
- ☐ 693 John O'Brien
- ☐ 694 Brian Rupp
- ☐ 695 Chad Sumner
- ☐ 696 Jesus Ugueto
- ☐ 697 Garrett Blanton
- ☐ 698 Hector Colon
- ☐ 699 Steve Dudek
- ☐ 700 Ronnie French
- ☐ 701 Joe McEwing
- ☐ 702 Chris Maloney MG
- ☐ 703 Checklist

1993 Scranton-Wilkes-Barre Red Barons Team Issue

	MINT	NRMT	EXC
COMPLETE SET (30)	6.00	2.70	.75

- ☐ 1 Kyle Abbott
- ☐ 2 Ruben Amaro
- ☐ 3 Cliff Brantley
- ☐ 4 Brad Brink
- ☐ 5 Dave Cash CO
- ☐ 6 Pat Combs
- ☐ 7 George Culver MG
- ☐ 8 Bruce Dostal
- ☐ 9 Paul Fletcher
- ☐ 10 Tyler Green
- ☐ 11 Drew Hall
- ☐ 12 Greg Legg
- ☐ 13 Mike Lieberthal
- ☐ 14 Doug Lindsey
- ☐ 15 Tony Longmire
- ☐ 16 Jeff Manto
- ☐ 17 Tom Marsh
- ☐ 18 Tim Mauser
- ☐ 19 Joe Millette
- ☐ 20 Steve Parris
- ☐ 21 Jeff Patterson
- ☐ 22 Victor Rodriguez
- ☐ 23 Sean Ryan
- ☐ 24 Kevin Stocker
- ☐ 25 Craig Strobel TR
- ☐ 26 Casey Waller
- ☐ 27 Cary Williams
- ☐ 28 Mike Williams
- ☐ 29 Jim Wright CO
- ☐ 30 Title Card
  Re/Max Real Estate

1993 Scranton/Wilkes-Barre Red Barons Fleer/ProCards

This 25-card standard-size set of the 1993 Scranton/Wilkes-Barre Red Barons, a Class AAA International League affiliate of the Philadelphia Phillies, features white-bordered posed color player photos on its fronts. The player's name, team, and position appear near the bottom. The white horizontal back is framed by a blue line and carries the player's name at the top, followed by biography and statistics. A drawing of a ballplayer in action appears on the left.

	MINT	NRMT	EXC
COMPLETE SET (25)	5.00	2.20	.60

- ☐ 2537 Kyle Abbott
- ☐ 2538 Cliff Brantley
- ☐ 2539 Brad Brink
- ☐ 2540 Pat Combs
- ☐ 2541 Paul Fletcher
- ☐ 2542 Tyler Green
- ☐ 2543 Tim Mauser
- ☐ 2544 Jeff Patterson
- ☐ 2545 Mike Williams
- ☐ 2546 Mike Lieberthal
- ☐ 2547 Greg Legg
- ☐ 2548 Jeff Manto
- ☐ 2549 Joe Millette
- ☐ 2550 Victor Rodriguez
- ☐ 2551 Sean Ryan
- ☐ 2552 Kevin Stocker
- ☐ 2553 Casey Waller
- ☐ 2554 Steve Bieser
- ☐ 2555 Tony Longmire
- ☐ 2556 Tom Marsh
- ☐ 2557 Cary Williams
- ☐ 2558 George Culver MG
- ☐ 2559 Dave Cash CO
- ☐ 2560 Jim Wright CO
- ☐ 2561 Checklist

1993 Shreveport Captains Fleer/ProCards

This 27-card standard-size set of the 1993 Shreveport Captains, a Class AA Texas League affiliate of the San Francisco Giants, features white-bordered posed color player photos on its fronts. The player's name, team, and position appear near the bottom. The white horizontal back is framed by a blue line and carries the player's name at the top, followed by biography and statistics. A drawing of a ballplayer in action appears on the left.

	MINT	NRMT	EXC
COMPLETE SET (27)	5.00	2.20	.60

- ☐ 2702 Checklist
- ☐ 2752 Brian Griffiths
- ☐ 2753 Chris Hancock
- ☐ 2754 Carl Hanselman
- ☐ 2755 Dave Masters
- ☐ 2756 Jim Myers
- ☐ 2757 Lou Pote
- ☐ 2758 Richie Simon
- ☐ 2759 Shad Smith
- ☐ 2760 Salomon Torres
- ☐ 2761 Mark Yockey
- ☐ 2762 Bert Heffernan
- ☐ 2763 Dan Fernandez
- ☐ 2764 Adell Davenport
- ☐ 2765 Matt Davis
- ☐ 2766 Andres Duncan
- ☐ 2767 Tim Florez
- ☐ 2768 Steve Hecht
- ☐ 2769 Kevin Kasper
- ☐ 2770 Barry Miller
- ☐ 2771 Dax Jones
- ☐ 2772 Rob Katzaroff
- ☐ 2773 Calvin Murray
- ☐ 2774 Pete Weber
- ☐ 2775 Ron Wotus MG
- ☐ 2776 Steve Cline CO
- ☐ 2777 Bill Stein CO

1993 South Atlantic League All-Stars Fleer/ProCards

	MINT	NRMT	EXC
COMPLETE SET (57)	25.00	11.00	3.10

- ☐ 1 Clayton Byrne
- ☐ 2 Eric Chavez
- ☐ 3 Matt Jarvis
- ☐ 4 Billy Owens
- ☐ 5 B.J. Waszgis
- ☐ 6 Scott Eyre
- ☐ 7 Jack Kimel
- ☐ 8 Kerry Lacy
- ☐ 9 Mike Welch
- ☐ 10 Ted Blackwell
- ☐ 11 Mike Brown
- ☐ 12 Epi Cardenas
- ☐ 13 Derek Hacopian
- ☐ 14 Jonathan Nunnally
- ☐ 15 J.J. Thobe
- ☐ 16 Charles York
- ☐ 17 Roberto Rojas
- ☐ 18 Jeff Antolick
- ☐ 19 Nick Delvecchio
- ☐ 20 Bill Evers
- ☐ 21 Derek Jeter
- ☐ 22 Ryan Karp
- ☐ 23 Ray Suplee
- ☐ 24 D.J. Boston
- ☐ 25 Brad Cornett
- ☐ 26 Kris Harmes
- ☐ 27 Jose Herrera
- ☐ 28 Chris Mader
- ☐ 29 Greg Elliott
- ☐ 30 Richard Hidalgo
- ☐ 31 Melvin Mora
- ☐ 32 Danny Clyburn
- ☐ 33 Jason Kendall
- ☐ 34 Andy Beckerman
- ☐ 35 Guillermo Garcia
- ☐ 36 Miguel Correa
- ☐ 37 Randy Ingle
- ☐ 38 Willy Johnson
- ☐ 39 Marty Malloy
- ☐ 40 Darrell May
- ☐ 41 Raymond Nunez
- ☐ 42 Leo Ramirez
- ☐ 43 Terrell Wade
- ☐ 44 Jeff Alkire
- ☐ 45 Keith Black
- ☐ 46 Mike Busby
- ☐ 47 Jamie Cochran
- ☐ 48 Chris Maloney
- ☐ 49 John O'Brien
- ☐ 50 Aldo Percorilli
- ☐ 51 Brian Rupp
- ☐ 52 Stanley Evans
- ☐ 53 Mike Murphy
- ☐ 54 Mark Tranberg
- ☐ 55 Daniel Kopriva
- ☐ 56 David Tuttle
- ☐ 57 Checklist

1993 South Atlantic League All-Stars Play II

	MINT	NRMT	EXC
COMPLETE SET (42)	40.00	18.00	5.00

- ☐ 1 Shane Andrews
- ☐ 2 Joe Ayrault
- ☐ 3 Willie Canate
- ☐ 4 P.J. Carey MG
- ☐ 5 Giovanni Carrara
- ☐ 6 Dan Cholowsky
- ☐ 7 Manny Cora
- ☐ 8 John Courtright
- ☐ 9 Ian Doyle
- ☐ 10 Cliff Floyd
- ☐ 11 Omar Garcia
- ☐ 12 Benji Gil
- ☐ 13 K.C. Gillum
- ☐ 14 Tucker Hammargren
- ☐ 15 Lew Hill
- ☐ 16 Aaron Holbert
- ☐ 17 John Hrusovsky
- ☐ 18 Rich Kelly
- ☐ 19 Chris Kotes
- ☐ 20 Joe Lis
- ☐ 21 Scott Little MG
- ☐ 22 Albie Lopez
- ☐ 23 Marc Marini
- ☐ 24 Rod McCall
- ☐ 25 Antonio Mitchell
- ☐ 26 Gary Mota
- ☐ 27 Marty Neff
- ☐ 28 Ernie Nieves
- ☐ 29 Ricky Otero
- ☐ 30 Bobby Perna
- ☐ 31 Andy Pettitte
- ☐ 32 Evan Pratt
- ☐ 33 Elliot Quinones
- ☐ 34 Calvin Reese
- ☐ 35 Scott Robinson
- ☐ 36 Matt Ruebel
- ☐ 37 Paul Spoljaric
- ☐ 38 Nick Sued
- ☐ 39 Quilvio Veras
- ☐ 40 Matt Whisenant
- ☐ 41 John Wilder
- ☐ 42 Tom Wilson

1993 South Atlantic League All-Stars Inserts Play II

	MINT	NRMT	EXC
COMPLETE SET (18)	125.00	55.00	15.50

- ☐ 1 Cliff Floyd
  Aaron Holbert
  Shane Andrews
- ☐ 2 Aaron Holbert
- ☐ 3 Lew Hill
- ☐ 4 Quilvio Veras
- ☐ 5 Benji Gil
- ☐ 6 Matt Whisenant
- ☐ 7 Scott Robinson
- ☐ 8 Dan Cholowsky
- ☐ 9 Ricky Otero
- ☐ 10 Calvin Reese
- ☐ 11 Marc Marini
- ☐ 12 Manny Cora
- ☐ 13 Shane Andrews
- ☐ 14 Paul Spoljaric

□ 15 Willie Canate
□ 16 Gary Mota
□ 17 K.C. Gillum
□ 18 Cliff Floyd

1993 South Bend White Sox Classic/Best

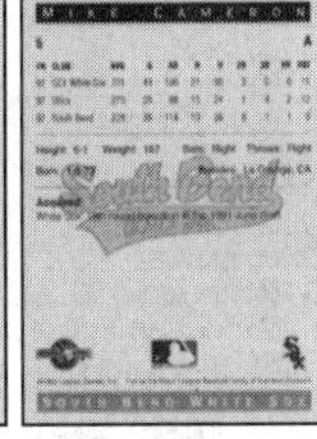

This 30-card standard-size set of the 1993 South Bend White Sox, a Class A Midwest League affiliate of the Chicago White Sox, features white-bordered posed color player shots on its fronts. A team-color-coded stripe below the photo carries the player's name; another above, his position and team name. On a ghosted team-logo, the white back carries the player's name at the top, followed by biography and statistics. This issue includes a second year card of Mike Cameron.

	MINT	NRMT	EXC
COMPLETE SET (30)	12.00	5.50	1.50

□ 1 Troy Fryman
□ 2 Ricky Bowrosen
□ 3 Essex Burton
□ 4 Mike Call
□ 5 Mike Cameron
□ 6 Carmine Cappuccio
□ 7 Don Culberson
□ 8 Edgar Devers
□ 9 Greg Fritz
□ 10 Ariel Garcia
□ 11 Jimmy Hurst
□ 12 Jon Jenkins
□ 13 Sean Johnston
□ 14 Robert Machado
□ 15 Byron Mathews
□ 16 Tim Moore
□ 17 Jason Pierson
□ 18 Wilfredo Polidor
□ 19 Ted Rich
□ 20 Chris Snopek
□ 21 Hank Tagle
□ 22 Julio Vinas
□ 23 Jason Watkins
□ 24 Craig Wilson
□ 25 Chip Winiarski
□ 26 Steve Worrell
□ 27 Jim Reinebold CO
□ 28 Jaime Garcia CO
□ 29 Von Joshua CO
□ 30 Scott Takao TR Checklist

1993 South Bend White Sox Fleer/ProCards

This 30-card standard-size set of the 1993 South Bend White Sox, a Class A Midwest League affiliate of the Chicago White Sox, features white-bordered posed color player photos on its fronts. The player's name, team, and position appear near the bottom. The white horizontal back is framed by a blue line and carries the player's name at the top, followed by biography and statistics. A drawing of a ballplayer in action appears on the left. This set includes a second year card of Mike Cameron.

	MINT	NRMT	EXC
COMPLETE SET (30)	12.00	5.50	1.50

□ 1421 Michael Call
□ 1422 Don Culberson
□ 1423 Greg Fritz
□ 1424 Ariel Garcia
□ 1425 Jon Jenkins
□ 1426 Sean Johnston
□ 1427 Jim McDermott
□ 1428 Tim Moore
□ 1429 Jason Pierson
□ 1430 Jason Watkins
□ 1431 Chip Winiarski
□ 1432 Steve Worrell
□ 1433 Robert Machado
□ 1434 Julio Vinas
□ 1435 Mike Vogel
□ 1436 Ricky Bowrosen
□ 1437 Essex Burton
□ 1438 Dan Fraraccio
□ 1439 Troy Fryman
□ 1440 Chris Snopek
□ 1441 Craig Wilson
□ 1442 Mike Cameron
□ 1443 Edgar Devers
□ 1444 Jimmy Hurst
□ 1445 Byron Mathews
□ 1446 Tony Franklin MG
□ 1447 Jaime Garcia CO
□ 1448 Von Joshua CO
□ 1449 Jim Reinebold CO
□ 1450 Checklist

1993 Southern Oregon A's Classic/Best

This 30-card standard-size set of the 1993 Southern Oregon A's, a Class A Northwest League affiliate of the Oakland Athletics, features white-bordered posed color player shots on its fronts. A team-color-coded stripe below the photo carries the player's name; another above, his position and team name. On a ghosted team-logo, the white back carries the player's name at the top, followed by biography and statistics. This issue includes the minor league card debuts of Scott Spiezio and Steve Cox.

	MINT	NRMT	EXC
COMPLETE SET (30)	7.00	3.10	.85

□ 1 Steve Cox
□ 2 Luini Aracena
□ 3 Scott Baldwin
□ 4 Tony Banks
□ 5 Brandy Bengoechea
□ 6 Mike Conte
□ 7 Juan Dilone
□ 8 Marcel Galligani
□ 9 Craig Gienger
□ 10 Eric Harris
□ 11 David Keel
□ 12 Richard King
□ 13 Steve Lemke
□ 14 Geoff Loomis
□ 15 Jason Lowe
□ 16 John MacCauley
□ 17 Derek Manning
□ 18 Chris Michalak
□ 19 Mark Moore
□ 20 Willie Morales
□ 21 Mathew Reese II
□ 22 Jeffrey Richardson
□ 23 Pat Sanders
□ 24 Scott Spiezio
□ 25 William Urbina
□ 26 Ryan Whitaker
□ 27 Steven Zongor
□ 28 Dick Scott MG
□ 29 Rick Rodriguez CO
□ 30 Bill Courtney GM Checklist

1993 Southern Oregon A's Fleer/ProCards

This 30-card standard-size set of the 1993 Southern Oregon A's, a Class A Northwest League affiliate of the Oakland Athletics, features white-bordered posed color player photos on its fronts. The player's name, team, and position appear near the bottom. The white horizontal back is framed by a blue line and carries the player's name at the top, followed by biography and statistics. A drawing of a ballplayer in action appears on the left. This set includes the first year cards of Scott Spiezio and Steve Cox.

	MINT	NRMT	EXC
COMPLETE SET (30)	7.00	3.10	.85

□ 4054 Scott Baldwin
□ 4055 Mike Conte
□ 4056 Craig Gierger
□ 4057 Richard King
□ 4058 Steve Lemke
□ 4059 Jason Lowe
□ 4060 John MacCauley
□ 4061 Derek Manning
□ 4062 Chris Michalak
□ 4063 William Urbina
□ 4064 Ryan Whitaker
□ 4065 Steve Zongor
□ 4066 Mark Moore
□ 4067 Willie Morales
□ 4068 Brandy Bergoechea
□ 4069 Steven Cox
□ 4070 Juan Dilone
□ 4071 Marcel Galligani
□ 4072 Geoff Loomis
□ 4073 Pat Sanders
□ 4074 Scott Spiezio
□ 4075 Luini Aracena
□ 4076 Tony Banks
□ 4077 Eric Harris
□ 4078 David Keel
□ 4079 Mathew Reese
□ 4080 Jeff Richardson
□ 4081 Dick Scott MG
□ 4082 Tony DeFrancesco CO
□ 4083 Checklist

1993 Spartanburg Phillies Classic/Best

This 30-card standard-size set of the 1993 Spartanburg Phillies, a Class A South Atlantic League affiliate of the Philadelphia Phillies, features white-bordered posed color player shots on its fronts. A team-color-coded stripe below the photo carries the player's name; another above, his position and team name. On a ghosted team-logo, the white back carries the player's name at the top, followed by biography and statistics.

	MINT	NRMT	EXC
COMPLETE SET (30)	5.00	2.20	.60

□ 1 Mark Tranberg
□ 2 Peter Agostinelli
□ 3 Kevin Alger
□ 4 Chad Anderson
□ 5 Gary Bennett
□ 6 Luis Brito
□ 7 E.J. Brophy
□ 8 Daniel Brown
□ 9 Alan Burke
□ 10 William Carmona
□ 11 Reynaldo DeLosSantos
□ 12 Blake Doolan
□ 13 Stanley Evans
□ 14 Scott Haws
□ 15 Ramon Hernandez
□ 16 Trevor Humphry
□ 17 Danny Larson
□ 18 Larry Mitchell
□ 19 Rob Mitchell
□ 20 Mike Murphy
□ 21 Steven Nutt
□ 22 Philip Romero
□ 23 Pat Ruth
□ 24 Andy Sallee
□ 25 Roy Majtyka MG
□ 26 Tony Scott CO
□ 27 Buzz Capra CO
□ 28 Clete Sigwart TR
□ 29 Title Card
□ 30 Checklist

1993 Spartanburg Phillies Fleer/ProCards

This 29-card standard-size set of the 1993 Spartanburg Phillies, a Class A South Atlantic League affiliate of the Philadelphia Phillies, features white-bordered posed color player photos on its fronts. The player's name, team, and position appear near the bottom. The white horizontal back is framed by a blue line and carries the player's name at the top, followed by biography and statistics. A drawing of a ballplayer in action appears on the left.

	MINT	NRMT	EXC
COMPLETE SET (29)	5.00	2.20	.60

□ 1046 Peter Agostinelli
□ 1047 Kevin Alger
□ 1048 Chad Anderson
□ 1049 Dan Brown
□ 1050 Blake Doolan
□ 1051 Trevor Humphry
□ 1052 Thomas Irwin
□ 1053 Larry Mitchell
□ 1054 Robert Mitchell
□ 1055 Steve Nuitt
□ 1056 Mark Tranberg
□ 1057 Gary Bennett
□ 1058 E.J. Brophy
□ 1059 Scott Haws
□ 1060 Luis Brito
□ 1061 Ramon Hernandez
□ 1062 Brian Lawler
□ 1063 Philip Romero
□ 1064 Andy Sallee
□ 1065 Alan Burke
□ 1066 Reynaldo DeLosSantos
□ 1067 Stanley Evans
□ 1068 Danny Larson
□ 1069 Mike Murphy
□ 1070 Shawn Wills
□ 1071 Roy Majtyka MG
□ 1072 Buzz Capra CO
□ 1073 Tony Scott CO
□ 1074 Checklist

1993 Spokane Indians Classic/Best

This 30-card standard-size set of the 1993 Spokane Indians, a Class A Northwest League affiliate of the San Diego Padres, features white-bordered posed color player shots on its fronts. A team-color-coded stripe below the photo carries the player's name; another above, his position and team name. On a ghosted team-logo, the white back carries the player's name at the top, followed by biography and statistics.

	MINT	NRMT	EXC
COMPLETE SET (30)	5.00	2.20	.60

□ 1 Glenn Dishman
□ 2 Jim Bostock
□ 3 Brad Dandridge
□ 4 Tommy Doyle
□ 5 Dan Drewien
□ 6 Darrick Duke
□ 7 Todd Erdos
□ 8 Hector Fargas
□ 9 Earl Johnson
□ 10 Brad Kaufman
□ 11 Gregory Keagle
□ 12 Alberto Matos
□ 13 Roy McKinnis
□ 14 Brian McLain
□ 15 Derek Mix
□ 16 Chris Prieto
□ 17 Santiago Rivera
□ 18 Melvin Rosario
□ 19 Britton Scheibe
□ 20 Jason Schlutt
□ 21 Jason Thompson
□ 22 Chris West
□ 23 Kyle White
□ 24 Marty Winchester
□ 25 Bryan Wolff
□ 26 Dickie Woodridge
□ 27 Dan Zanolla
□ 28 Tim Flannery MG
□ 29 Barry Moss CO
□ 30 Charlie Greene CO Checklist

1993 Spokane Indians Fleer/ProCards

This 27-card standard-size set of the 1993 Spokane Indians, a Class A Northwest League affiliate of the San Diego Padres, features white-bordered posed color player photos on its fronts. The player's name, team, and position appear near the bottom. The white horizontal back is framed by a blue line and carries the player's name at the top, followed by biography and statistics. A drawing of a ballplayer in action appears on the left. This set includes the first year card of Todd Erdos.

	MINT	NRMT	EXC
COMPLETE SET (27)	5.00	2.20	.60

□ 3581 Glenn Dishman
□ 3582 Tom Doyle
□ 3583 Dan Drewien
□ 3584 Todd Erdos
□ 3585 Hector Fargas
□ 3586 Brad Kaufman
□ 3587 Gregory Keagle
□ 3588 Alberto Matos
□ 3589 Brian McLain
□ 3590 Derek Mix
□ 3591 Jason Schulutt
□ 3592 Kyle White
□ 3593 Marty Winchester
□ 3594 Bryan Wolff
□ 3595 Leroy McKinnis
□ 3596 Melvin Rosario
□ 3597 Jim Bostock
□ 3598 Jason Thompson
□ 3599 Chris West
□ 3600 Dickie Woodridge
□ 3601 Dan Zanolla
□ 3602 Darrick Duke
□ 3603 Earl Johnson
□ 3604 Chris Prieto
□ 3605 Britton Scheibe
□ 3606 Tim Flannery MG
□ 3607 Checklist

1993 Springfield Cardinals Classic/Best

This 30-card standard-size set of the 1993 Springfield Cardinals, a Class A Midwest League affiliate of the St. Louis Cardinals, features white-bordered posed color player shots on its fronts. A team-color-coded stripe below the photo carries the player's name; another above, his position and team name. On a ghosted team-logo, the white back carries the player's name at the top, followed by biography and statistics.

	MINT	NRMT	EXC
COMPLETE SET (30)	5.00	2.20	.60

□ 1 Eddie Williams
□ 2 Joe Biasucci
□ 3 Todd Blake
□ 4 Andy Bruce
□ 5 Kirk Bullinger
□ 6 Tim DeGrasse
□ 7 Mike Difelice
□ 8 Mike Eicher
□ 9 Ben Ellsworth
□ 10 John Frascatore
□ 11 Mike Gulan
□ 12 Jonas Hamlin
□ 13 Keith Johns
□ 14 Steve Johnson
□ 15 Tim Jordan
□ 16 Greg Knowles
□ 17 carlos Landinez
□ 18 T.J. Mathews
□ 19 Eric Miller
□ 20 Dave Oehrlein
□ 21 Greg Rudolph
□ 22 Basil Shabazz
□ 23 Dennis Slininger

☐ 24 Chad Smith
☐ 25 Derron Spiller
☐ 26 DaRond Stovall
☐ 27 Gary Taylor
☐ 28 Mike Ramsey MG
☐ 29 Scott Melvin CO
☐ 30 Mike Evans TR Checklist

1993 Springfield Cardinals Fleer/ProCards

This 29-card standard-size set of the 1993 Springfield Cardinals, a Class A Midwest League affiliate of the St. Louis Cardinals, features white-bordered posed color player photos on its fronts. The player's name, team, and position appear near the bottom. The white horizontal back is framed by a blue line and carries the player's name at the top, followed by biography and statistics. A drawing of a ballplayer in action appears on the left.

	MINT	NRMT	EXC
COMPLETE SET (29)	5.00	2.20	.60

☐ 1841 Todd Blake
☐ 1842 Kirk Bullinger
☐ 1843 Tim DeGrasse
☐ 1844 John Frascatore
☐ 1845 Steve Johnson
☐ 1846 Greg Knowles
☐ 1847 T.J. Mathews
☐ 1848 Eric Miller
☐ 1849 Dave Oehlein
☐ 1850 Dennis Slininger
☐ 1851 Chad Smith
☐ 1852 Derron Spiller
☐ 1853 Mike DiFelice
☐ 1854 Eddie Williams
☐ 1855 Joe Biasucci
☐ 1856 Andy Bruce
☐ 1857 Ben Ellsworth
☐ 1858 Mike Gulan
☐ 1859 Jonas Hamlin
☐ 1860 Keith Johns
☐ 1861 Carlos Landinez
☐ 1862 Mike Eicher
☐ 1863 Tim Jordan
☐ 1864 Greg Rudolph
☐ 1865 Basil Shabazz
☐ 1866 DaRond Stovall
☐ 1867 Gary Taylor
☐ 1868 Mike Ramsey MG
☐ 1869 Checklist

1993 St. Catharines Blue Jays Classic/Best

This 30-card standard-size set of the 1993 St. Catharines Blue Jays, a Class A New York-Penn League affiliate of the Toronto Blue Jays, features white-bordered posed color player shots on its fronts. A team-color-coded stripe below the photo carries the player's name; another above, his position and team name. On a ghosted team-logo, the white back carries the player's name at the top, followed by biography and statistics. This set includes Shannon Stewart's first team set card.

	MINT	NRMT	EXC
COMPLETE SET (30)	7.00	3.10	.85

☐ 1 Shannon Stewart
☐ 2 Tim Adkins
☐ 3 Alonso Beltran
☐ 4 Chad Brown
☐ 5 Jeff Cheek
☐ 6 Brandon Cromer
☐ 7 Rafael Debrand
☐ 8 Joe Durso
☐ 9 Emanuel Hayes
☐ 10 Sean Hearn
☐ 11 Edwin Hurtado
☐ 12 Jay Maldonado
☐ 13 Doug Meiners
☐ 14 Adam Meinershagen
☐ 15 Adam Melhuse
☐ 16 Patrick Moultrie
☐ 17 Harry Muir
☐ 18 Rob Mummau
☐ 19 David Pearlman
☐ 20 Juan Querecuto
☐ 21 Kip Roggendorf
☐ 22 Rob Steinert
☐ 23 Dilson Torres
☐ 24 Craig Vaught
☐ 25 J.J. Cannon MG
☐ 26 Rolando Pino CO
☐ 27 Scott Breeden CO
☐ 28 Reggie Cleveland CO
☐ 29 Scott Shannon TR
☐ 30 Team Photo Checklist

1993 St. Catharines Blue Jays Fleer/ProCards

This 27-card standard-size set of the 1993 St. Catharines Blue Jays, a Class A New York-Penn League affiliate of the Toronto Blue Jays, features white-bordered posed color player photos on its fronts. The player's name, team, and position appear near the bottom. The white horizontal back is framed by a blue line and carries the player's name at the top, followed by biography and statistics. A drawing of a ballplayer in action appears on the left. This set includes Shannon Stewart's first team set card.

	MINT	NRMT	EXC
COMPLETE SET (27)	6.00	2.70	.75

☐ 3965 Tim Adkins
☐ 3966 Alonso Beltran
☐ 3967 Chad Brown
☐ 3968 Jeff Cheek
☐ 3969 Edwin Hurtado
☐ 3970 Jay Maldonado
☐ 3971 Doug Meiners
☐ 3972 Adam Meinershagen
☐ 3973 Harry Muir
☐ 3974 David Pearlman
☐ 3975 Rob Steinert
☐ 3976 Dilson Torres
☐ 3977 Joe Durso
☐ 3978 Juan Querecuto
☐ 3979 Brandon Cromer
☐ 3980 Emmanuel Hayes
☐ 3981 Adam Melhuse
☐ 3982 Rob Mummau
☐ 3983 Kip Roggendorf
☐ 3984 Craig Vaught
☐ 3985 Rafael Debrand
☐ 3986 Sean Hearn
☐ 3987 Patrick Moultrie
☐ 3988 Shannon Stewart
☐ 3989 J.J. Cannon MG
☐ 3990 Rolando Pino CO
☐ 3991 Checklist

1993 St. Lucie Mets Classic/Best

This 30-card standard-size set of the 1993 St. Lucie Mets, a Class A Florida State League affiliate of the New York Mets, features white-bordered posed color player shots on its fronts. A team-color-coded stripe below the photo carries the player's name; another above, his position and team name. On a ghosted team-logo, the white back carries the player's name at the top, followed by biography and statistics.

	MINT	NRMT	EXC
COMPLETE SET (30)	5.00	2.20	.60

☐ 1 Edgardo Alfonzo
☐ 2 Jeff Barry
☐ 3 Greg Beals
☐ 4 Rob Carpentier
☐ 5 Alberto Castillo
☐ 6 Joe Crawford
☐ 7 Randy Curtis
☐ 8 Todd Fiegel
☐ 9 Mark Fuller
☐ 10 Edward Fully
☐ 11 Omar Garcia
☐ 12 Robbie Guzik
☐ 13 Jason Jacome
☐ 14 Tripp Keister
☐ 15 Jason King
☐ 16 Tim McClinton
☐ 17 Jim McCready
☐ 18 Bernie Millan
☐ 19 Pat Miller
☐ 20 Chris Roberts
☐ 21 Mason Rudolph
☐ 22 Chris Saunders
☐ 23 Brad Schorr
☐ 24 John Smith
☐ 25 Ottis Smith
☐ 26 John Tamargo MG
☐ 27 Bill Latham CO
☐ 28 Larry Bennese TR
☐ 29 Title Card
☐ 30 Checklist

1993 St. Lucie Mets Fleer/ProCards

This 28-card standard-size set of the 1993 St. Lucie Mets, a Class A Florida State League affiliate of the New York Mets, features white-bordered posed color player photos on its fronts. The player's name, team, and position appear near the bottom. The white horizontal back is framed by a blue line and carries the player's name at the top, followed by biography and statistics. A drawing of a ballplayer in action appears on the left.

	MINT	NRMT	EXC
COMPLETE SET (28)	5.00	2.20	.60

☐ 2912 Rob Carpentier
☐ 2913 Andy Cotner
☐ 2914 Joe Crawford
☐ 2915 Todd Fiegel
☐ 2916 Mark Fuller
☐ 2917 Robbie Guzik
☐ 2918 Jason Jacome
☐ 2919 Jim McCready
☐ 2920 Chris Roberts
☐ 2921 Brad Schorr
☐ 2922 Ottis Smith
☐ 2923 Greg Beals
☐ 2924 Alberto Castillo
☐ 2925 Mason Rudolph
☐ 2926 Edgardo Alfonzo
☐ 2927 Omar Garcia
☐ 2928 Greg Graham
☐ 2929 Bernie Millan
☐ 2930 Chris Saunders
☐ 2931 Jeff Barry
☐ 2932 Randy Curtis
☐ 2933 Ed Fully
☐ 2934 Tim McClinton
☐ 2935 Tim Sandy
☐ 2936 John Smith
☐ 2937 John Tamargo
☐ 2938 Bill Latham
☐ 2939 Checklist

1993 St. Petersburg Cardinals Classic/Best

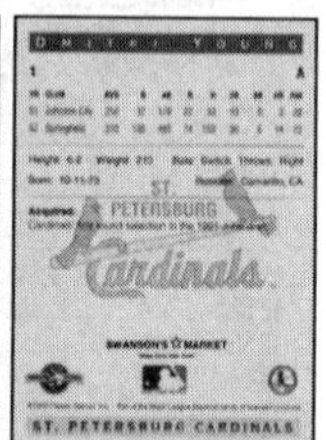

This 30-card standard-size set of the 1993 St. Petersburg Cardinals, a Class A Florida State League affiliate of the St. Louis Cardinals, features white-bordered posed color player shots on its fronts. A team-color-coded stripe below the photo carries the player's name; another above, his position and team name. On a ghosted team-logo, the white back carries the player's name at the top, followed by biography and statistics.

	MINT	NRMT	EXC
COMPLETE SET (30)	5.00	2.20	.60

☐ 1 Dmitri Young
☐ 2 Mike Badorek
☐ 3 Roy Bailey
☐ 4 Andy Beasley
☐ 5 Alan Botkin
☐ 6 Terry Bradshaw
☐ 7 Duff Brumley
☐ 8 Mike Cantu
☐ 9 Steve Cerio
☐ 10 Dan Cholowsky
☐ 11 John Corona
☐ 12 Clint Davis
☐ 13 Ed Gerald
☐ 14 Jason Hisey
☐ 15 Aaron Holbert
☐ 16 Keith Jones
☐ 17 Sean Lowe
☐ 18 Jeremy McGarity
☐ 19 Lorenzo Meza
☐ 20 Doug Radziewicz
☐ 21 Paul Romanoli
☐ 22 Marc Ronan
☐ 23 Scott Simmons
☐ 24 Joe Turvey
☐ 25 Jose Vazquez
☐ 26 Jose Velez
☐ 27 Ron Warner
☐ 28 Rich Folkers CO
☐ 29 Terry Kennedy MG
☐ 30 Pete Fagan TR Checklist

1993 St. Petersburg Cardinals Fleer/ProCards

This 30-card standard-size set of the 1993 St. Petersburg Cardinals, a Class A Florida State League affiliate of the St. Louis Cardinals, features white-bordered posed color player photos on its fronts. The player's name, team, and position appear near the bottom. The white horizontal back is framed by a blue line and carries the player's name at the top, followed by biography and statistics. A drawing of a ballplayer in action appears on the left.

	MINT	NRMT	EXC
COMPLETE SET (30)	5.00	2.20	.60

☐ 2617 Mike Badorek
☐ 2618 Roy Bailey
☐ 2619 Alan Botkin
☐ 2620 Duff Brumley
☐ 2621 John Corona
☐ 2622 Clint Davis
☐ 2623 Jason Hisey
☐ 2624 Sean Lowe
☐ 2625 Jeremy McGarity
☐ 2626 Paul Romanoli
☐ 2627 Scott Simmons
☐ 2628 Andy Beasley
☐ 2629 Steve Cerio
☐ 2630 Marc Ronan
☐ 2631 Joe Turvey
☐ 2632 Michael Cantu
☐ 2633 Dan Cholowsky
☐ 2634 Aaron Holbert
☐ 2635 Lorenzo Meza
☐ 2636 Doug Radziewicz
☐ 2637 Ron Warner
☐ 2638 Dmitri Young
☐ 2639 Terry Bradshaw
☐ 2640 Ed Gerald
☐ 2641 Keith Jones
☐ 2642 Jose Vazquez
☐ 2643 Jose Velez
☐ 2644 Terry Kennedy MG
☐ 2645 Rich Folkers CO
☐ 2646 Checklist

1993 Stockton Ports Classic/Best

This 30-card standard-size set of the 1993 Stockton Ports, a Class A California League affiliate of the Milwaukee Brewers, features white-bordered posed color player shots on its fronts. A team-color-coded stripe below the photo carries the player's name; another above, his position and team name. On a ghosted team-logo, the white back carries the player's name at the top, followed by biography and statistics.

	MINT	NRMT	EXC
COMPLETE SET (30)	5.00	2.20	.60

☐ 1 Tyrone Hill
☐ 2 Marshall Boze
☐ 3 Bryon Browne
☐ 4 Greg Carmona
☐ 5 Ramser Correa
☐ 6 Mike Couture
☐ 7 John Criminger
☐ 8 Tony Diggs
☐ 9 Bill Dobrolsky
☐ 10 Andy Fairman
☐ 11 Pat Fetty
☐ 12 Leon Glenn
☐ 13 Mark Hampton
☐ 14 Bubba Hardwick
☐ 15 Michael Harris
☐ 16 Brian Hostetler
☐ 17 Mike Huyler
☐ 18 Brian McKeon
☐ 19 Don Pruitt
☐ 20 Kevin Riggs
☐ 21 Sidney Roberson
☐ 22 Todd Samples
☐ 23 Mike Stefanski
☐ 24 Timothy Unroe
☐ 25 Derek Wachter
☐ 26 Eric Whitford
☐ 27 Lamar Johnson MG
☐ 28 Mick Kelleher CO
☐ 29 Mark Littell CO
☐ 30 Scott Meissner TR Checklist

1993 Stockton Ports Fleer/ProCards

This 29-card standard-size set of the 1993 Stockton Ports, a Class A California League affiliate of the Milwaukee Brewers, features white-bordered posed color player photos on its fronts. The player's name, team, and position appear near the bottom. The white horizontal back is framed by a blue line and carries the player's name at the top, followed by biography and statistics. A drawing of a ballplayer in action appears on the left.

	MINT	NRMT	EXC
COMPLETE SET (29)	5.00	2.20	.60

☐ 735 Marshall Boze
☐ 736 Byron Browne
☐ 737 John Criminger
☐ 738 Pat Fetty
☐ 739 Ron Gerstein
☐ 740 Mark Hampton
☐ 741 Bubba Hardwick
☐ 742 Tyrone Hill
☐ 743 Brian McKeon
☐ 744 Don Pruitt
☐ 745 Sidney Roberson
☐ 746 Bill Dobrolsky
☐ 747 Brian Hostetler
☐ 748 Mike Stefanski
☐ 749 Mark Cole
☐ 750 Andy Fairman
☐ 751 Leon Glenn
☐ 752 Mike Huyler
☐ 753 Kevin Riggs
☐ 754 Tim Unroe
☐ 755 Erie Chitford
☐ 756 Mike Couture
☐ 757 Michael Harris
☐ 758 Todd Samples

☐ 759 Derek Wachter
☐ 760 Lamar Johnson MG
☐ 761 Mike Kelleher CO
☐ 762 Mark Littell CO
☐ 763 Checklist

1993 Syracuse Chiefs Fleer/ProCards

This 27-card standard-size set of the 1993 Syracuse Chiefs, a Class AAA International League affiliate of the Toronto Blue Jays, features white-bordered posed color player photos on its fronts. The player's name, team, and position appear near the bottom. The white horizontal back is framed by a blue line and carries the player's name at the top, followed by biography and statistics. A drawing of a ballplayer in action appears on the left.

	MINT	NRMT	EXC
COMPLETE SET (27)	5.00	2.20	.60

☐ 990 Steve Adkins
☐ 991 Darrel Akerfelds
☐ 992 Pete Blohm
☐ 993 Tim Brown
☐ 994 Jesse Cross
☐ 995 Darren Hall
☐ 996 Doug Linton
☐ 997 Paul Menhart
☐ 998 Mark Ohlms
☐ 999 Woody Williams
☐ 1000 Jose Monzon
☐ 1001 Greg O'Halloran
☐ 1002 Domingo Cedeno
☐ 1003 Ray Giannelli
☐ 1004 Domingo Martinez
☐ 1005 Rob Montalvo
☐ 1006 Tom Quinlan
☐ 1007 Lee Stevens
☐ 1008 Julian Yan
☐ 1009 Robert Butler
☐ 1010 Juan DeLaRosa
☐ 1011 Robert Perez
☐ 1012 Shawn Scott
☐ 1013 Nick Leyva MG
☐ 1014 John Poloni CO
☐ 1015 Rocket Wheeler CO
☐ 1016 Checklist

1993 Tacoma Tigers Fleer/ProCards

This 27-card standard-size set of the 1993 Tacoma Tigers, a Class AAA Pacific Coast League affiliate of the Oakland Athletics, features white-bordered posed color player photos on its fronts. The player's name, team, and position appear near the bottom. The white horizontal back is framed by a blue line and carries the player's name at the top, followed by biography and statistics. A drawing of a ballplayer in action appears on the left.

	MINT	NRMT	EXC
COMPLETE SET (27)	5.00	2.20	.60

☐ 3024 Brad Arnsberg
☐ 3025 Kevin Campbell
☐ 3026 Johnny Guzman
☐ 3027 Bronswell Patrick
☐ 3028 Tim Peek
☐ 3029 Steve Phoenix
☐ 3030 Mike Raczka
☐ 3031 Larry Shikles
☐ 3032 Joe Slusarski
☐ 3033 Todd Van Poppel
☐ 3034 Dean Borrelli
☐ 3035 Henry Mercedes
☐ 3036 Doug Robbins
☐ 3037 Kurt Abbott
☐ 3038 Garrett Beard
☐ 3039 Webster Garrison
☐ 3040 Brent Gates
☐ 3041 Ron Witmeyer
☐ 3042 Mike Aldrete
☐ 3043 Marcos Armas
☐ 3044 Jim Buccheri
☐ 3045 Kevin Dattola
☐ 3046 Eric Fox
☐ 3047 Scott Lydy
☐ 3048 Troy Neel
☐ 3049 Mitchell Page CO
☐ 3050 Checklist

1993 Texas Longhorns

University of Texas college set

	MINT	NRMT	EXC
COMPLETE SET (9)	15.00	6.75	1.85

☐ 1 Cliff Gustafson CO
☐ 2 Tim Harkrider
☐ 3 Braxton Hickman
☐ 4 Brooks Kieschnick
☐ 5 Mark Prather
☐ 6 Jay Vaught
☐ 7 Taco Bell Ad
☐ 8 Taco Bell Ad
☐ 9 Taco Bell Ad

1993 Toledo Mud Hens Fleer/ProCards

This 28-card standard-size set of the 1993 Toledo Mud Hens, a Class AAA International League affiliate of the Detroit Tigers, features white-bordered posed color player photos on its fronts. The player's name, team, and position appear near the bottom. The white horizontal back is framed by a blue line and carries the player's name at the top, followed by biography and statistics. A drawing of a ballplayer in action appears on the left.

	MINT	NRMT	EXC
COMPLETE SET (28)	5.00	2.20	.60

☐ 1643 Sean Bergman
☐ 1644 Sherm Corbett
☐ 1645 John DeSilva
☐ 1646 Willie Fraser
☐ 1647 Frank Gonzales
☐ 1648 Mark Grater
☐ 1649 Buddy Groom
☐ 1650 John Hudek
☐ 1651 Dave Johnson
☐ 1652 Kurt Knudsen
☐ 1653 Mike Lumley
☐ 1654 Ron Rightnowar
☐ 1655 Wally Ritchie
☐ 1656 Rich Rowland
☐ 1657 Rico Brogna
☐ 1658 Ivan Cruz
☐ 1659 Chris Gomez
☐ 1660 Johnny Paredes
☐ 1661 Bob Reimink
☐ 1662 Rod Robertson
☐ 1663 Shawn Hare
☐ 1664 Jody Hurst
☐ 1665 Riccardo Ingram
☐ 1666 Ted Williams
☐ 1667 Joe Sparks MG
☐ 1668 Bruce Fields CO
☐ 1669 Jeff Jones CO
☐ 1670 Checklist

1993 Triple A All-Stars Fleer/ProCards

This 55-card standard-size set of the 1993 Triple A All-Stars features white-bordered posed color player photos on its fronts. The player's name, team, and position appear near the bottom. The white horizontal back is framed by a blue line and carries the player's name at the top, followed by biography and statistics. A drawing of a ballplayer in action appears on the left. This issue includes third year cards of Chipper Jones and Jim Thome.

	MINT	NRMT	EXC
COMPLETE SET (55)	20.00	9.00	2.50

☐ 1 Chipper Jones
☐ 2 Ryan Klseko
☐ 3 Javier Lopez
☐ 4 Bill Taylor
☐ 5 Kevin Roberson
☐ 6 Eddie Zambrano
☐ 7 Marc Bombard
☐ 8 Brian Dorsett
☐ 9 Scott Ruskin
☐ 10 Lance Painter
☐ 11 David Weathers
☐ 12 James Mouton
☐ 13 Billy Ashley
☐ 14 Stan Johnston
☐ 15 Bill Russell
☐ 16 Todd Williams
☐ 17 Todd Haney
☐ 18 Ryan Thompson
☐ 19 George Culver
☐ 20 Tony Longmire
☐ 21 Roy Smith
☐ 22 Tripp Cromer
☐ 23 Keith Lockhard
☐ 24 Allen Watson
☐ 25 Steve Pegues
☐ 26 Paul Faries
☐ 27 J.R. Phillips
☐ 28 Tommy Hinzo
☐ 29 John O'Donoghue
☐ 30 Mark Smith
☐ 31 Don Florence
☐ 32 Eduardo Perez
☐ 33 Darryl Scott
☐ 34 Drew Denson
☐ 35 Brian Drahman
☐ 36 Jerry DiPoto
☐ 37 Charlie Manuel
☐ 38 Jim Thome
☐ 39 Wally Ritchie
☐ 40 Rich Rowland
☐ 41 Jeff Cox
☐ 42 Rick Reed
☐ 43 Karl Rhodes
☐ 44 Terry Shumpert
☐ 45 Troy O'Leary
☐ 46 Bernardo Brito
☐ 47 Derek Parks
☐ 48 Scott Ullger
☐ 49 Billy Masse
☐ 50 Kurt Abbott
☐ 51 Walt Horn
☐ 52 Anthony Manahan
☐ 53 Rob Ducey
☐ 54 Lee Stevens
☐ 55 Checklist

1993 Tucson Toros Fleer/ProCards

This 29-card standard-size set of the 1993 Tucson Toros, a Class AAA Pacific Coast League affiliate of the Houston Astros, features white-bordered posed color player photos on its fronts. The player's name, team, and position appear near the bottom. The white horizontal back is framed by a blue line and carries the player's name at the top, followed by biography and statistics. A drawing of a ballplayer in action appears on the left.

	MINT	NRMT	EXC
COMPLETE SET (29)	5.00	2.20	.60

☐ 3051 Eric Bell
☐ 3052 Mike Capel
☐ 3053 Eddie Dixon
☐ 3054 Dean Hartgraves
☐ 3055 Bob Hurta
☐ 3056 Todd Jones
☐ 3057 Jeff Juden
☐ 3058 Shane Reynolds
☐ 3059 Dave Veres
☐ 3060 Donne Wall
☐ 3061 Tony Eusebio
☐ 3062 Scooter Tucker
☐ 3063 Tommy Barrett
☐ 3064 Mike Brumley
☐ 3065 Jack Daugherty
☐ 3066 Jim Lindeman
☐ 3067 Orlando Miller
☐ 3068 James Mouton
☐ 3069 Phil Nevin
☐ 3070 Luis Quinones
☐ 3071 Willie Ansley
☐ 3072 Braulio Castillo
☐ 3073 John Massarelli
☐ 3074 Joe Mikulik
☐ 3075 Rick Parker
☐ 3076 Rick Sweet MG
☐ 3077 Dave Engle CO
☐ 3078 Brent Strom CO
☐ 3079 Checklist

1993 Tulsa Drillers Fleer/ProCards

This 27-card standard-size set of the 1993 Tulsa Drillers, a Class AA Texas League affiliate of the Texas Rangers, features white-bordered posed color player photos on its fronts. The player's name, team, and position appear near the bottom. The white horizontal back is framed by a blue line and carries the player's name at the top, followed by biography and statistics. A drawing of a ballplayer in action appears on the left. .

	MINT	NRMT	EXC
COMPLETE SET (27)	5.00	2.20	.60

☐ 2725 Jose Alberro
☐ 2726 Mike Arner
☐ 2727 Steve Dreyer
☐ 2728 Chris Gies
☐ 2729 Barry Goetz
☐ 2730 James Hurst
☐ 2731 Kurt Miller
☐ 2732 Ritchie Moody
☐ 2733 Darren Oliver
☐ 2734 Brian Romero
☐ 2735 Roger Luce
☐ 2736 David Rolls
☐ 2737 Miguel Castellano
☐ 2738 Jim Clinton
☐ 2739 Cris Colon
☐ 2740 Benji Gil
☐ 2741 Rusty Greer
☐ 2742 Ever Magallanes
☐ 2743 Trey McCoy
☐ 2744 Frank Turco
☐ 2745 Benny Castillo
☐ 2746 Daren Epley
☐ 2747 Paul List
☐ 2748 Timmie Morrow
☐ 2749 Stan Cliburn MG
☐ 2750 Randy Whisler CO
☐ 2751 Checklist

1993 Tulsa Drillers Team Issue

	MINT	NRMT	EXC
COMPLETE SET (30)	6.00	2.70	.75

☐ 1 Jose Alberro
☐ 2 Mike Arner
☐ 3 Miguel Castellanos
☐ 4 Benny Castillo
☐ 5 Stan Cliburn
☐ 6 Cris Colon
☐ 7 Steve Dreyer
☐ 8 Daren Epley
☐ 9 Chris Gies
☐ 10 Barry Goetz
☐ 11 Rusty Greer
☐ 13 James Hurst
☐ 14 Paul List
☐ 15 Roger Luce
☐ 16 Ever Magallanes
☐ 17 Trey McCoy
☐ 18 Kurt Miller
☐ 19 Ritchie Moody
☐ 20 Timmie Morrow
☐ 21 Darren Oliver
☐ 22 Donna Papangellin
☐ 23 David Perez
☐ 24 David Rolls
☐ 25 Brian Romero
☐ 26 Jackson Todd
☐ 27 Frank Turco
☐ 28 Randy Whisler
☐ 29 Benji Gil
☐ 30 Sammy Sosa PS

1993 Utica Blue Sox Classic/Best

This 30-card standard-size set of the 1993 Utica Blue Sox, a Class A New York-Penn League affiliate of the Boston Red Sox, features white-bordered posed color player shots on its fronts. A team-color-coded stripe below the photo carries the player's name; another above, his position and team name. On a ghosted team-logo, the white back carries the player's name at the top, followed by biography and statistics. .

	MINT	NRMT	EXC
COMPLETE SET (30)	5.00	2.20	.60

☐ 1 Dan Collier
☐ 2 Victor Aguado
☐ 3 Diogenes Baez
☐ 4 Robb Berryman
☐ 5 Richie Borrero
☐ 6 Craig Bush
☐ 7 Eric Cormier
☐ 8 Juan Debrand
☐ 9 Joe DePastino
☐ 10 J.J. Johnson
☐ 11 Jeff Johnson
☐ 12 Donny Jones
☐ 13 Randy Lawrence
☐ 14 Leif McKinley
☐ 15 Ricky Milligan
☐ 16 Andy Moore
☐ 17 T.J. O'Donnell
☐ 18 Rafael Orellano
☐ 19 Nicholas Ortiz
☐ 20 Hilario Perez
☐ 21 Chad Renfroe
☐ 22 Mark Senkowitz
☐ 23 John Stratton
☐ 24 Jim Tyrrell
☐ 25 Dave Holt
☐ 26 Garry Roggenburk
☐ 27 Chipper Jones Classic Best Advertisement
☐ 28 Brien Taylor Classic Best Advertisement
☐ 29 Title Card
☐ 30 Checklist

1993 Utica Blue Sox Fleer/ProCards

This 26-card standard-size set of the 1993 Utica Blue Sox, a Class A New York-Penn League affiliate of the Boston Red Sox, features white-bordered posed color player photos on its fronts. The player's name, team, and position appear near the bottom. The white horizontal back is framed by a blue line and carries the player's name at the top, followed by biography and statistics. A drawing of a ballplayer in action appears on the left.

	MINT	NRMT	EXC
COMPLETE SET (26)	5.00	2.20	.60

☐ 3525 Robb Berryman
☐ 3526 Craig Bush
☐ 3527 Eric Cormier
☐ 3528 Danny Johnston
☐ 3529 Randy Lawrence
☐ 3530 Leif McKinley
☐ 3531 Rafael Orellano
☐ 3532 Hilario Perez
☐ 3533 Chad Renfroe
☐ 3534 Jim Tyrrell
☐ 3535 Richie Borrero
☐ 3536 Mark Senkowitz
☐ 3537 John Stratton
☐ 3538 Victor Aguado
☐ 3539 Juan Debrand
☐ 3540 Joe Depastino

☐ 3541 Andy Moore
☐ 3542 T.J. O'Donnell
☐ 3543 Nick Ortiz
☐ 3544 Diogenes Baez
☐ 3545 Daniel Collier
☐ 3546 J.J. Johnson
☐ 3547 Ricky Milligan
☐ 3548 Dave Holt MG
☐ 3549 Garry Roggenburk CO
☐ 3550 Checklist

1993 Vancouver Canadians Fleer/ProCards

This 28-card standard-size set of the 1993 Vancouver Canadians, a Class AAA Pacific Coast League affiliate of the California Angels, features white-bordered posed color player photos on its fronts. The player's name, team, and position appear near the bottom. The white horizontal back is framed by a blue line and carries the player's name at the top, followed by biography and statistics. A drawing of a ballplayer in action appears on the left. This set includes a fourth year card of Garret Anderson and a sixth year card of Jim Edmonds.

	MINT	NRMT	EXC
COMPLETE SET (28)	8.00	3.60	1.00

☐ 2589 Otis Green
☐ 2590 Hilly Hathaway
☐ 2591 Mark Holzemer
☐ 2592 Phil Leftwich
☐ 2593 Jerry Nielsen
☐ 2594 Steve Peck
☐ 2595 Troy Percival
☐ 2596 Darryl Scott
☐ 2597 Russ Springer
☐ 2598 Paul Swingle
☐ 2599 Julian Vasquez
☐ 2600 Mark Zappelli
☐ 2601 Larry Gonzales
☐ 2602 Chris Turner
☐ 2603 Rod Correia
☐ 2604 Ramon Martinez
☐ 2605 Eduardo Perez
☐ 2606 Ty Van Burkleo
☐ 2607 Jim Walewander
☐ 2608 Garret Anderson
☐ 2609 Jim Edmonds
☐ 2610 Jeff Kipila
☐ 2611 Jerome Walton
☐ 2612 Reggie Williams
☐ 2613 Max Oliveras MG
☐ 2614 Gary Ruby CO
☐ 2615 Lenn Sakata CO
☐ 2616 Checklist

1993 Vero Beach Dodgers Classic/Best

This 30-card standard-size set of the 1993 Vero Beach Dodgers, a Class A Florida State League affiliate of the Los Angeles Dodgers, features white-bordered posed color player shots on its fronts. A team-color-coded stripe below the photo carries the player's name; another above, his position and team name. On a ghosted team-logo, the white back carries the player's name at the top, followed by biography and statistics.

	MINT	NRMT	EXC
COMPLETE SET (30)	5.00	2.20	.60

☐ 1 Chris Demetral
☐ 2 Jason Brosnan
☐ 3 Michael Brown
☐ 4 Miguel Cairo
☐ 5 Angel Dotel
☐ 6 Steve Green
☐ 7 Ken Hamilton
☐ 8 Ryan Henderson
☐ 9 Ken Huckaby
☐ 10 Keith Johnson
☐ 11 Reggie Johnson
☐ 12 Kiki Jones
☐ 13 Tito Landrum
☐ 14 Eduardo Lantigua
☐ 15 Martin Lavigne
☐ 16 Richard Licursi
☐ 17 Rich Linares
☐ 18 Dwight Maness
☐ 19 Chris Morrow
☐ 20 Javier Puchales
☐ 21 Felix Rodriguez
☐ 22 Christopher Sinacori
☐ 23 Eric Vorbeck
☐ 24 Ronnie Walden
☐ 25 Brandon Watts
☐ 26 Lonnie Webb
☐ 27 Brandon White
☐ 28 Joe Vavra MG
☐ 29 Garett Teel CO
☐ 30 Dennis Lewallyn CO
Checklist

1993 Vero Beach Dodgers Fleer/ProCards

This 31-card standard-size set of the 1993 Vero Beach Dodgers, a Class A Florida State League affiliate of the Los Angeles Dodgers, features white-bordered posed color player photos on its fronts. The player's name, team, and position appear near the bottom. The white horizontal back is framed by a blue line and carries the player's name at the top, followed by biography and statistics. A drawing of a ballplayer in action appears on the left.

	MINT	NRMT	EXC
COMPLETE SET (31)	5.00	2.20	.60

☐ 2206 Jason Brosnan
☐ 2207 Edwin Correa
☐ 2208 Jamie Daspit
☐ 2209 Roberto Duran
☐ 2210 Scott Freeman
☐ 2211 Ken Hamilton
☐ 2212 Ryan Henderson
☐ 2213 Kiki Jones
☐ 2214 Martin Lavigne
☐ 2215 Rich Linares
☐ 2216 Kevin Pencavitch
☐ 2217 Felix Rodriguez
☐ 2218 Chris Sinacori
☐ 2219 Ron Walden
☐ 2220 Brandon Watts
☐ 2221 Brandon White
☐ 2222 Mike Brown
☐ 2223 Ken Huckaby
☐ 2224 Miguel Cairo
☐ 2225 Chris Demetral
☐ 2226 Angel Dotel
☐ 2227 Keith Johnson
☐ 2228 Reggie Johnson
☐ 2229 Eduardo Lantigua
☐ 2230 Steve Green
☐ 2231 Tito Landrum
☐ 2232 Dwight Maness
☐ 2233 Alton Pinkney
☐ 2234 Javier Puchales
☐ 2235 Eric Vorbeck
☐ 2236 Checklist

1993 Waterloo Diamonds Classic/Best

This 30-card standard-size set of the 1993 Waterloo Diamonds, a Class A Midwest League affiliate of the San Diego Padres, features white-bordered posed color player shots on its fronts. A team-color-coded stripe below the photo carries the player's name; another above, his position and team name. On a ghosted team-logo, the white back carries the player's name at the top, followed by biography and statistics.

	MINT	NRMT	EXC
COMPLETE SET (30)	5.00	2.20	.60

☐ 1 Bobby Bonds II
☐ 2 Greg Anthony
☐ 3 Luis Arroyo
☐ 4 LaRue Baber
☐ 5 Jon Barnes
☐ 6 Stoney Briggs
☐ 7 Homer Bush
☐ 8 German Carrion
☐ 9 Raul Casanova
☐ 10 Brian D'Amato
☐ 11 Roberto DeLeon
☐ 12 Keith Dunckel
☐ 13 Iggy Duran
☐ 14 Todd Erdos
☐ 15 John Fantauzzi
☐ 16 Charlie Greene
☐ 17 Craig Hanson
☐ 18 Mike Hermanson
☐ 19 Adrian Hollinger
☐ 20 Tom Kindler
☐ 21 Rich Loiselle
☐ 22 Joey Long
☐ 23 Kevin Minchk
☐ 24 John Roberts
☐ 25 Melvin Rosario
☐ 26 Todd Schmitt
☐ 27 Reggie Stewart
☐ 28 Ed Romero MG
☐ 29 Dean Treanor CO
☐ 30 Bill Murray TR
Checklist

1993 Waterloo Diamonds Fleer/ProCards

This 29-card standard-size set of the 1993 Waterloo Diamonds, a Class A Midwest League affiliate of the San Diego Padres, features white-bordered posed color player photos on its fronts. The player's name, team, and position appear near the bottom. The white horizontal back is framed by a blue line and carries the player's name at the top, followed by biography and statistics. A drawing of a ballplayer in action appears on the left. This set includes a second year card of Raul Casanova.

	MINT	NRMT	EXC
COMPLETE SET (29)	5.00	2.20	.60

☐ 1758 Pepper Anthony
☐ 1759 Jon Barnes
☐ 1760 Brian D'Amato
☐ 1761 Todd Erdos
☐ 1762 Craig Hanson
☐ 1763 Mike Hermanson
☐ 1764 Adrian Hollinger
☐ 1765 Tom Kindler
☐ 1766 Richard Loiselle
☐ 1767 Joey Long
☐ 1768 Todd Schmitt
☐ 1769 Joe Waldron
☐ 1770 Raul Casanova
☐ 1771 Charlie Greene
☐ 1772 Homer Bush
☐ 1773 Manny Cora
☐ 1774 Roberto DeLeon
☐ 1775 Iggy Duran
☐ 1776 John Fantauzzi
☐ 1777 Kevin Minchk
☐ 1778 Melvin Rosario
☐ 1779 Larue Baber
☐ 1780 Bobby Bonds II
☐ 1781 Stoney Briggs
☐ 1782 John Roberts
☐ 1783 Reggie Stewart
☐ 1784 Ed Romero MG
☐ 1785 Dean Treanor CO
☐ 1786 Checklist

1993 Watertown Indians Classic/Best

This 30-card standard-size set of the 1993 Watertown Indians, a Class A New York-Penn League affiliate of the Cleveland Indians, features white-bordered posed color player shots on its fronts. A team-color-coded stripe below the photo carries the player's name; another above, his position and team name. On a ghosted team-logo, the white back carries the player's name at the top, followed by biography and statistics.

	MINT	NRMT	EXC
COMPLETE SET (30)	5.00	2.20	.60

☐ 1 Casey Whitten
☐ 2 Robert Augustine
☐ 3 Gerad Cawhorn
☐ 4 Eric Chapman
☐ 5 Roland DeLaMaza
☐ 6 Dalton Dempsey
☐ 7 German Diaz
☐ 8 Travis Driskill
☐ 9 Bryan Garrett
☐ 10 Roberto Garza
☐ 11 Jeff Haag
☐ 12 Kris Hanson
☐ 13 Steven Hodson
☐ 14 Chuck Kulle
☐ 15 Robert Lewis
☐ 16 Jason Lyman
☐ 17 Pedro Marte
☐ 18 Michael Matthews
☐ 19 Mike Neal
☐ 20 Michael Neilson
☐ 21 Jon Oram
☐ 22 Chris Plumlee
☐ 23 Rick Prieto
☐ 24 Pat Schulz
☐ 25 Greg Sinner
☐ 26 Steve Soliz
☐ 27 Greg Thomas
☐ 28 Jeff Williams
☐ 29 Mike Young MG
☐ 30 Tony Arnold CO
Checklist

1993 Watertown Indians Fleer/ProCards

This 30-card standard-size set of the 1993 Watertown Indians, a Class A New York-Penn League affiliate of the Cleveland Indians, features white-bordered posed color player photos on its fronts. The player's name, team, and position appear near the bottom. The white horizontal back is framed by a blue line and carries the player's name at the top, followed by biography and statistics. A drawing of a ballplayer in action appears on the left.

	MINT	NRMT	EXC
COMPLETE SET (30)	5.00	2.20	.60

☐ 3551 Rob Augstine
☐ 3552 Roland De La Maza
☐ 3553 Wes Dempsey
☐ 3554 German Diaz
☐ 3555 Travis Driskill
☐ 3556 Roberto Garza
☐ 3557 Kris Hanson
☐ 3558 Mike Mathews
☐ 3559 Mike Neilson
☐ 3560 Chris Plumlee
☐ 3561 Greg Sinner
☐ 3562 Casey Whitten
☐ 3563 Jeff Williams
☐ 3564 Jef Haag
☐ 3565 Robert Lewis
☐ 3566 Steven Soliz
☐ 3567 Gerad Cawhorn
☐ 3568 Blair Hodson
☐ 3569 Jason Lyman
☐ 3570 Mike Neal
☐ 3571 Jon Oram
☐ 3572 Rick Prieto
☐ 3573 Greg Thomas
☐ 3574 Eric Chapman
☐ 3575 Bryan Garrett
☐ 3576 Chuck Kulle
☐ 3577 Pedro Marte
☐ 3578 Pat Schulz
☐ 3579 Mike Young MG
☐ 3580 Checklist

1993 Welland Pirates Classic/Best

This 30-card standard-size set of the 1993 Welland Pirates, a Class A New York-Penn League affiliate of the Pittsburgh Pirates, features white-bordered posed color player shots on its fronts. A team-color-coded stripe below the photo carries the player's name; another above, his position and team name. On a ghosted team-logo, the white back carries the player's name at the top, followed by biography and statistics. This set includes the first year card of Lou Collier.

	MINT	NRMT	EXC
COMPLETE SET (30)	5.00	2.20	.60

☐ 1 Mitch House
☐ 2 Brian Beck
☐ 3 Aaron Cannaday
☐ 4 Louis Collier
☐ 5 Kenny Fairfax
☐ 6 G.G. Harris
☐ 7 Riegal Hunt
☐ 8 Jeff Isom
☐ 9 Tom Johnston
☐ 10 Erskine Kelley
☐ 11 Richard Luna
☐ 12 Jeff Lutt
☐ 13 Sergio Mendez
☐ 14 Johnny Mitchell
☐ 15 Ramon Morel
☐ 16 Jamison Nuttle
☐ 17 Raul Paez
☐ 18 Brian Pelka
☐ 19 Gil Perez
☐ 20 Chris Peters
☐ 21 Jason Phillips
☐ 22 Jeff Pickich
☐ 23 Alan Purdy
☐ 24 Patrick Reed
☐ 25 Maximo Rivera
☐ 26 Joe Serna
☐ 27 Stanley Wiltz
☐ 28 John Yselonia
☐ 29 Larry Smith MG
☐ 30 Julio Garcia CO
Checklist

1993 Welland Pirates Fleer/ProCards

This 31-card standard-size set of the 1993 Welland Pirates, a Class A New York-Penn League affiliate of the Pittsburgh Pirates, features white-bordered posed color player photos on its fronts. The player's name, team, and position appear near the bottom. The white horizontal back is framed by a blue line and carries the player's name at the top, followed by biography and statistics. A drawing of a ballplayer in action appears on the left. This issue includes the debut of Jermaine Allensworth.

	MINT	NRMT	EXC
COMPLETE SET (31)	5.00	2.20	.60

☐ 3346 Jason Abramvicius
☐ 3347 Brian Beck
☐ 3348 Matt Chamberlain
☐ 3349 Kenny Fairfax
☐ 3350 Jeff Isom
☐ 3351 Jeff Lutt
☐ 3352 Ramon Morel
☐ 3353 Jamison Nuttle
☐ 3354 Brian Pelka
☐ 3355 Gil Perez
☐ 3356 Chris Peters
☐ 3357 Jason Phillips
☐ 3358 Jeff Pickich
☐ 3359 Aaron Cannaday
☐ 3360 Sergio Mendez
☐ 3361 Joel Williamson
☐ 3362 Lou Collier
☐ 3363 Pat Gosselin
☐ 3364 G.G. Harris
☐ 3365 Mitch House
☐ 3366 Tom Johnston
☐ 3367 Rich Luna
☐ 3368 Raul Paez
☐ 3369 Maximo Rivera
☐ 3370 Stan Wiltz

☐ 3371 Jermaine Allensworth
☐ 3372 Riegal Hunt
☐ 3373 Erskine Kelley
☐ 3374 Johnny Mitchell
☐ 3375 Pat Reed
☐ 3376 Checklist

1993 West Palm Beach Expos Classic/Best

This 30-card standard-size set of the 1993 West Palm Beach Expos, a Class A Florida State League affiliate of the Montreal Expos, features white-bordered posed color player shots on its fronts. A team-color-coded stripe below the photo carries the player's name; another above, his position and team name. On a ghosted team logo, the white back carries the player's name at the top, followed by statistics and biography.

	MINT	NRMT	EXC
COMPLETE SET (30)	5.00	2.20	.60

☐ 1 B.J. Wallace
☐ 2 Derek Aucoin
☐ 3 Jim Austin
☐ 4 Mike Daniel
☐ 5 Scott Gentile
☐ 6 Marc Griffin
☐ 7 Mark Grudzielanek
☐ 8 Mike Hardge
☐ 9 Rod Henderson
☐ 10 Tyrone Horne
☐ 11 Mark LaRosa
☐ 12 Brian Looney
☐ 13 Austin Manahan
☐ 14 Domingo Matos
☐ 15 Kevin McDonald
☐ 16 Joe Norris
☐ 17 Kevin Northrup
☐ 18 Claudio Ozario
☐ 19 Terry Powers
☐ 20 Raul Santana
☐ 21 Curtis Schmidt
☐ 22 Mitch Simons
☐ 23 Mike Thomas
☐ 24 Matt Allen
☐ 25 Randy Wilstead
☐ 26 Rob Leary MG
☐ 27 Rich Dubee CO
☐ 28 Lee Slagle TR
☐ 29 Sponsor Photo
☐ 30 Willie Bananas (Mascot) Checklist

1993 West Palm Beach Expos Fleer/ProCards

This 30-card standard-size set of the 1993 West Palm Beach Expos, a Class A Florida State League affiliate of the Montreal Expos, features white-bordered posed color player photos on its fronts. The player's name, team, and position appear near the bottom. The white horizontal back is framed by a blue line and carries the player's name at the top, followed by biography and statistics. A drawing of a ballplayer in action appears on the left.

	MINT	NRMT	EXC
COMPLETE SET (30)	5.00	2.20	.60

☐ 1330 Derek Aucoin
☐ 1331 Matt Connolly
☐ 1332 Scott Gentile
☐ 1333 Rod Henderson
☐ 1334 Mark LaRosa
☐ 1335 Brian Looney
☐ 1336 Kevin McDonald
☐ 1337 Joe Norris
☐ 1338 Terry Powers
☐ 1339 Curtis Schmidt
☐ 1340 Mike Thomas
☐ 1341 B.J. Wallace
☐ 1342 Matt Allen
☐ 1343 Mike Daniel
☐ 1344 Tim Hines
☐ 1345 Raul Santana
☐ 1346 Mark Grudzielanek
☐ 1347 Michael Hardge
☐ 1348 Austin Manahan
☐ 1349 Domingo Matos
☐ 1350 Mitch Simons
☐ 1351 Randy Wilstead
☐ 1352 Jim Austin
☐ 1353 Marc Griffin
☐ 1354 Tyrone Horne
☐ 1355 Kevin Northrup
☐ 1356 Claudio Ozario
☐ 1357 Rob Leary MG
☐ 1358 Rich Dubee CO
☐ 1359 Checklist

1993 West Virginia Wheelers Classic/Best

This 30-card standard-size set of the 1993 West Virginia Wheelers, a Class A South Atlantic League affiliate of the Cincinnati Reds, features white-bordered posed color player shots on its fronts. A team-color-coded stripe below the photo carries the player's name; another above, his position and team name. On a ghosted team logo, the white back carries the player's name at the top, followed by statistics and biography.

	MINT	NRMT	EXC
COMPLETE SET (30)	5.00	2.20	.60

☐ 1 Chad Fox
☐ 2 Johnny Bess
☐ 3 John Brothers
☐ 4 William Brunson
☐ 5 Roger Etheridge
☐ 6 Micah Franklin
☐ 7 Dan Frye
☐ 8 Fermin Garcia
☐ 9 Dee Jenkins
☐ 10 Bob Jesperson
☐ 11 Brad Keenan
☐ 12 Dan Kopriva
☐ 13 Jason Kummerfeldt
☐ 14 Rich Langford
☐ 15 Marty Lister
☐ 16 Louis Maberry
☐ 17 Ricky Magdaleno
☐ 18 Matt Martin
☐ 19 Mike Meggers
☐ 20 Jeff Nagy
☐ 21 James Nix
☐ 22 Todd Ruyak
☐ 23 Dave Tuttle
☐ 24 Waynbe Wilkerson
☐ 25 Tom Nieto MG
☐ 26 Mack Jenkins CO
☐ 27 Tom Iverson TR
☐ 28 Brien Taylor Classic Best Advertisement
☐ 29 Title Card
☐ 30 Checklist

1993 West Virginia Wheelers Fleer/ProCards

This 27-card standard-size set of the 1993 West Virginia Wheelers, a Class A South Atlantic League affiliate of the Cincinnati Reds, features white-bordered posed color player photos on its fronts. The player's name, team, and position appear near the bottom. The white horizontal back is framed by a blue line and carries the player's name at the top, followed by biography and statistics. A drawing of a ballplayer in action appears on the left.

	MINT	NRMT	EXC
COMPLETE SET (27)	5.00	2.20	.60

☐ 2856 John Brothers
☐ 2857 William Brunson
☐ 2858 Roger Etheridge
☐ 2859 Chad Fox
☐ 2860 Fermin Garcia
☐ 2861 Jason Kummerfeldt
☐ 2862 Rich Langford
☐ 2863 Marty Lister
☐ 2864 Louis Maberry
☐ 2865 James Nix
☐ 2866 Todd Ruyak
☐ 2867 David Tuttle
☐ 2868 Johnny Bess
☐ 2869 Toby Rumfield
☐ 2870 Dan Frye
☐ 2871 Dee Jenkins
☐ 2872 Brad Keenan
☐ 2873 Dan Kopriva
☐ 2874 Ricky Magdaleno
☐ 2875 Matt Martin
☐ 2876 Micah Franklin
☐ 2877 Bob Jesperson
☐ 2878 Mike Meggers
☐ 2879 Jeff Nagy
☐ 2880 Wayne Wilkerson
☐ 2881 Mack Jenkins CO
☐ 2882 Checklist

1993 Wichita Wranglers Fleer/ProCards

This 26-card standard-size set of the 1993 Wichita Wranglers, a Class AA Texas League affiliate of the San Diego Padres, features white-bordered posed color player photos on its fronts. The player's name, team, and position appear near the bottom. The white horizontal back is framed by a blue line and carries the player's name at the top, followed by biography and statistics. A drawing of a ballplayer in action appears on the left.

	MINT	NRMT	EXC
COMPLETE SET (26)	5.00	2.20	.60

☐ 2970 Renay Bryand
☐ 2971 Nate Cromwell
☐ 2972 Nick Felix
☐ 2973 Bryce Florie
☐ 2974 Don Heinkel
☐ 2975 Steve Hoeme
☐ 2976 Geoff Kellogg
☐ 2977 Kelly Lifgren
☐ 2978 William Wengert
☐ 2979 John Abercrombie
☐ 2980 Lee Henderson
☐ 2981 Jerrey Thurston
☐ 2982 Mark Gieseke
☐ 2983 Paul Gonzalez
☐ 2984 Billy Hall
☐ 2985 Ray Holbert
☐ 2986 Pablo Martinez
☐ 2987 Tookie Spann
☐ 2988 Darius Gash
☐ 2989 Vince Harris
☐ 2990 Dwayne Hosey
☐ 2991 Ray McDavid
☐ 2992 Tracy Sanders
☐ 2993 Dave Trembley MG
☐ 2994 Sonny Siebert CO
☐ 2995 Checklist

1993 Wilmington Blue Rocks Classic/Best

This 30-card standard-size set of the 1993 Wilmington Blue Rocks, a Class A Carolina League affiliate of the Kansas City Royals, features white-bordered posed color player shots on its fronts. A team-color-coded stripe below the photo carries the player's name; another above, his position and team name. On a ghosted team logo, the white back carries the player's name at the top, followed by statistics and biography. This set includes the minor league card debut of Michael Tucker.

	MINT	NRMT	EXC
COMPLETE SET (30)	12.00	5.50	1.50

☐ 1 Michael Tucker
☐ 2 Francisco Baez
☐ 3 Brian Bevil
☐ 4 Darren Burton
☐ 5 Gary Caraballo
☐ 6 Jim Chrisman
☐ 7 Pat Dando
☐ 8 John Dempsey Jr.
☐ 9 Chris Eddy
☐ 10 Mike Fyhrie
☐ 11 Raul Gonzalez
☐ 12 John Gross
☐ 13 Shane Halter
☐ 14 Brian Harrison
☐ 15 Steve Hinton
☐ 16 Roger Landress
☐ 17 Jon Lieber
☐ 18 Jason Marshall
☐ 19 Dario Perez
☐ 20 Jeff Smith
☐ 21 Tom Smith
☐ 22 Andy Stewart
☐ 23 Brady Stewart
☐ 24 Chad Strickland
☐ 25 Robert Toth
☐ 26 Hugh Walker
☐ 27 Ron Johnson MG
☐ 28 Gary Lance CO
☐ 29 Rafael Santana CO
☐ 30 Marty Yuhas TR Checklist

1993 Wilmington Blue Rocks Fleer/ProCards

This 30-card standard-size set of the 1993 Wilmington Blue Rocks, a Class A Carolina League affiliate of the Kansas City Royals, features white-bordered posed color player photos on its fronts. The player's name, team, and position appear near the bottom. The white horizontal back is framed by a blue line and carries the player's name at the top, followed by biography and statistics. A drawing of a ballplayer in action appears on the left. This set includes the first year minor league card of Michael Tucker.

	MINT	NRMT	EXC
COMPLETE SET (30)	12.00	5.50	1.50

☐ 1987 Francisco Baez
☐ 1988 Brian Bevil
☐ 1989 David Bladow
☐ 1990 Jim Chrisman
☐ 1991 Chris Eddy
☐ 1992 John Gross
☐ 1993 Brian Harrison
☐ 1994 Rogers Landress
☐ 1995 Jon Lieber
☐ 1996 Dario Perez
☐ 1997 Jeff Smith
☐ 1998 Robert Toth
☐ 1999 John Dempsey
☐ 2000 Andy Stewart
☐ 2001 Chad Strickland
☐ 2002 Gary Caraballo
☐ 2003 Pat Dando
☐ 2004 Shane Halter
☐ 2005 Steve Hinton
☐ 2006 Jason Marshall
☐ 2007 Brady Stewart
☐ 2008 Michael Tucker
☐ 2009 Darren Burton
☐ 2010 Raul Gonzalez
☐ 2011 Tom Smith
☐ 2012 Hugh Walker
☐ 2013 Ron Johnson MG
☐ 2014 Gary Lance CO
☐ 2015 Rafael Santana CO
☐ 2016 Checklist

1993 Winston-Salem Spirits Classic/Best

This 30-card standard-size set of the 1993 Winston-Salem Spirits, a Class A Carolina League affiliate of the Cincinnati Reds, features white-bordered posed color player shots on its fronts. A team-color-coded stripe below the photo carries the player's name; another above, his position and team name. On a ghosted team logo, the white back carries the player's name at the top, followed by statistics and biography.

	MINT	NRMT	EXC
COMPLETE SET (30)	5.00	2.20	.60

☐ 1 Chad Mottola
☐ 2 Jason Angel
☐ 3 Amador Arias
☐ 4 Tim Belk
☐ 5 Troy Buckley
☐ 6 Scott Duff
☐ 7 Greg Hammond
☐ 8 Mike Harrison
☐ 9 John Hrusovsky
☐ 10 Kevin Jarvis
☐ 11 MotorBoat Jones
☐ 12 Cleveland Laddell
☐ 13 Bo Loftin
☐ 14 Joe McCann
☐ 15 Charles McClain
☐ 16 Eric Owens
☐ 17 Mateo Ozuna
☐ 18 Bobby Perna
☐ 19 Craig Pueschner
☐ 20 Rene Quinones
☐ 21 Kevin Shaw
☐ 22 Rodney Steph
☐ 23 Carl Stewart
☐ 24 Chris Vasquez
☐ 25 Mark Berry MG
☐ 26 Derek Botelho CO
☐ 27 Tom Spencer TR
☐ 28 Brien Taylor Classic Best Advertisement
☐ 29 Title Card
☐ 30 Checklist

1993 Winston-Salem Spirits Fleer/ProCards

This 25-card standard-size set of the 1993 Winston-Salem Spirits, a Class A Carolina League affiliate of the Cincinnati Reds, features white-bordered posed color player photos on its fronts. The player's name, team, and position appear near the bottom. The white horizontal back is framed by a blue line and carries the player's name at the top, followed by biography and statistics. A drawing of a ballplayer in action appears on the left.

	MINT	NRMT	EXC
COMPLETE SET (25)	5.00	2.20	.60

☐ 1562 Jason Angel
☐ 1563 Scott Duff
☐ 1564 John Hrusovsky
☐ 1565 Kevin Jarvis
☐ 1566 Bo Loftin
☐ 1567 Joe McCann
☐ 1568 Charles McClain
☐ 1569 Rene Quinones
☐ 1570 Kevin Shaw
☐ 1571 Rodney Steph
☐ 1572 Troy Buckley
☐ 1573 Greg Hammond
☐ 1574 Mike Harrison
☐ 1575 Amador Arias
☐ 1576 Tim Belk
☐ 1577 Eric Owens
☐ 1578 Mateo Ozuna
☐ 1579 Bobby Perna
☐ 1580 Eugene Jones
☐ 1581 Cleveland Ladell
☐ 1582 Craig Pueschner
☐ 1583 Chris Vasquez
☐ 1584 Mark Berry
☐ 1585 Derek Botelho
☐ 1586 Checklist

1993 Yakima Bears Classic/Best

This 30-card standard-size set of the 1993 Yakima Bears, a Class A Northwest League affiliate of the Los Angeles Dodgers, features white-bordered posed color player shots on its fronts. A team-color-coded stripe below the photo carries the player's name; another above, his position and team name. On a ghosted team logo, the white back carries the player's name at the top, followed by statistics and biography.

	MINT	NRMT	EXC
COMPLETE SET (30)	5.00	2.20	.60

□ 1 Ryan Luzinski
□ 2 Herb Baxter
□ 3 Brett Binkley
□ 4 Nathan Bland
□ 5 Jake Botts
□ 6 Scott Compton
□ 7 Kenny Cook
□ 8 Roberto Duran
□ 9 Jose Garcia
□ 10 Frans Groot
□ 11 Rich Haley
□ 12 J.R. Hawkins
□ 13 Vince Jackson
□ 14 Joe Jacobsen
□ 15 Angel Jaime
□ 16 Joe LaGarde
□ 17 Chris Latham
□ 18 Doug Newstrom
□ 19 Kevin Pincavitch
□ 20 Kevin Pitts
□ 21 David Post
□ 22 David Ravitz
□ 23 David Spykstra
□ 24 Dilone Uribe
□ 25 Leroy Williams
□ 26 Bruce Yard
□ 27 Kevin Zahner
□ 28 John Shoemaker MG
□ 29 Luis Tiant CO
□ 30 Checklist

1993 Yakima Bears Fleer/ProCards

This 31-card standard-size set of the 1993 Yakima Bears, a Class A Northwest League affiliate of the Los Angeles Dodgers, features white-bordered posed color player photos on its fronts. The player's name, team, and position appear near the bottom. The white horizontal back is framed by a blue line and carries the player's name at the top, followed by biography and statistics. A drawing of a ballplayer in action appears on the left.

	MINT	NRMT	EXC
COMPLETE SET (31)	5.00	2.20	.60

□ 3873 Herb Baxter
□ 3874 Brett Binkley
□ 3875 Nathan Bland
□ 3876 Jake Botts
□ 3877 Kenny Cook
□ 3878 Roberto Duran
□ 3879 Jose Garcia
□ 3880 Franz Groot
□ 3881 Joe Jacobsen
□ 3882 Jayson Perez
□ 3883 Kevin Pincavitch
□ 3884 David Spykstra
□ 3885 Ryan Luzinski
□ 3886 Dilone Uribe
□ 3887 Kevin Zehner
□ 3888 Nathan Dunn
□ 3889 Doug Newstrom
□ 3890 David Post
□ 3891 David Ravitz
□ 3892 Leroy Williams
□ 3893 Bruce Yard
□ 3894 Scott Compton
□ 3895 Rich Haley
□ 3896 John Harris
□ 3897 J.R. Hawkins
□ 3898 Vince Jackson
□ 3899 Chris Latham
□ 3900 Kevin Pitts
□ 3901 John Shoemaker MG
□ 3902 Luis Tiant CO
□ 3903 Checklist

1994 Abany Yankees Fleer/ProCards

This 31-card standard size set of the 1994 Albany Yankees, a Class AA Eastern League affiliate of the New York Yankees, features white-bordered posed color player photos on its fronts with the player's name, position, team name and Fleer/ProCards logo across the bottom of each card. The white back with vertical light blue stripes carries the player's name at the top, followed by biography and statistics.

	MINT	NRMT	EXC
COMPLETE SET (31)	5.00	2.20	.60

□ 1430 Brian Boehringer
□ 1431 Tom Carter
□ 1432 Billy Coleman
□ 1433 Andy Croghan
□ 1434 Matt Dunbar
□ 1435 Brian Faw
□ 1436 Darren Hodges
□ 1437 Jhonny Pantoja
□ 1438 Andy Pettitte
□ 1439 Curtis Ralph
□ 1440 Tim Rumer
□ 1441 Keith Seiler
□ 1442 John Sutherland
□ 1443 Jim Wiley
□ 1444 Jeff Livesey
□ 1445 Tom Wilson
□ 1446 Roger Burnett
□ 1447 Greg Erickson
□ 1448 Carlton Fleming
□ 1449 Andy Fox
□ 1450 Tony Perezchica
□ 1451 Tate Seefried
□ 1452 Bubba Carpenter
□ 1453 Joe DeBerry
□ 1454 Lew Hill
□ 1455 Lyle Mouton
□ 1456 Jason Robertson
□ 1457 Bill Evers MG
□ 1458 Gary Denbo CO
□ 1459 David Schuler CO
□ 1539 Checklist

1994 Action Packed

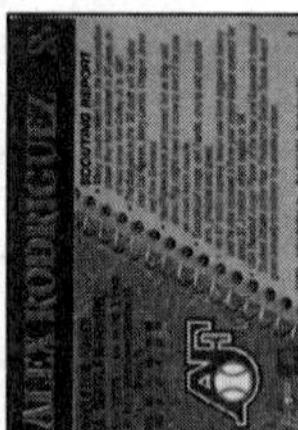

The 1994 Action Packed Scouting Report set consists of 72 standard-size cards featuring top AAA, AA, and A prospects picked by Action Packed's scouts. 24K gold versions of selected cards were randomly inserted in the foil packs as chase cards. The 12-card Franchise Gems subset feature a heat sensitive graphic that reveals Action Packed's prediction of the player's impact year. Special cards reveal a prize-winning message and become exchange cards which could be redemmed for genuine diamond-studded collector vesions of the card.

	MINT	NRMT	EXC
COMPLETE SET (72)	20.00	9.00	2.50
COMMON CARD (1-72)	.15	.07	.02
□ 1 Alex Rodriguez	5.00	2.20	.60
□ 2 Trot Nixon	.25	.11	.03
□ 3 Chan Ho Park	1.00	.45	.12
□ 4 Brooks Kieschnick	.50	.23	.06
□ 5 Matt Brunson	.15	.07	.02
□ 6 Wayne Gomes	.15	.07	.02
□ 7 Charles Johnson	.75	.35	.09
□ 8 Kirk Presley	.15	.07	.02
□ 9 Daron Kirkreit	.15	.07	.02
□ 10 Curtis Goodwin	.15	.07	.02
□ 11 Alex Ochoa	.75	.35	.09
□ 12 Midre Cummings	.15	.07	.02
□ 13 Russ Davis	.15	.07	.02
□ 14 Phil Nevin	.15	.07	.02
□ 15 J.R. Phillips	.15	.07	.02
□ 16 Jeff Granger	.15	.07	.02
□ 17 Mac Suzuki	.15	.07	.02
□ 18 Johnny Damon	1.00	.45	.12
□ 19 Chad Mottola	.15	.07	.02
□ 20 Scott Ruffcorn	.15	.07	.02
□ 21 Brian Barber	.15	.07	.02
□ 22 Frank Rodriguez	.15	.07	.02
□ 23 Michael Jordan	5.00	2.20	.60
□ 24 Michael Tucker	.30	.14	.04
□ 25 Rondell White	.60	.25	.07
□ 26 Ugueth Urbina	.15	.07	.02
□ 27 Tyrone Hill	.15	.07	.02
□ 28 Dmitri Young	.60	.25	.07
□ 29 Marshall Boze	.15	.07	.02
□ 30 Marc Newfield	.25	.11	.03
□ 31 James Baldwin	.25	.11	.03
□ 32 Terrell Wade	.25	.11	.03
□ 33 Curtis Pride	.15	.07	.02
□ 34 Gabe White	.15	.07	.02
□ 35 Derrek Lee	2.00	.90	.25
□ 36 Bill Pulsipher	.30	.14	.04
□ 37 Butch Huskey	.15	.07	.02
□ 38 Nigel Wilson	.15	.07	.02
□ 39 Tim Clark	.15	.07	.02
□ 40 Ozzie Timmons	.15	.07	.02
□ 41 Brien Taylor	.15	.07	.02
□ 42 J.T. Snow	.15	.07	.02
□ 43 Derek Jeter	2.50	1.10	.30
□ 44 Rick Krivda	.15	.07	.02
□ 45 Kevin Millar	.15	.07	.02
□ 46 Matt Franco	.15	.07	.02
□ 47 Jose Silva	.15	.07	.02
□ 48 Benji Gil	.15	.07	.02
□ 49 Calvin Reese	.15	.07	.02
□ 50 Todd Hollandsworth	.75	.35	.09
□ 51 Robert Ellis	.15	.07	.02
□ 52 Brian L. Hunter	.40	.18	.05
□ 53 Ryan Luzinski	.15	.07	.02
□ 54 Kurt Miller	.15	.07	.02
□ 55 Alex Rodriguez FG	5.00	2.20	.60
□ 56 Chan Ho Park FG	1.00	.45	.12
□ 57 Brooks Kieschnick FG	.50	.23	.06
□ 58 Charles Johnson FG	.75	.35	.09
□ 59 Alex Ochoa FG	.75	.35	.09
□ 60 Michael Tucker FG	.30	.14	.04
□ 61 Phil Nevin FG	.15	.07	.02
□ 62 Jose Silva FG	.15	.07	.02
□ 63 James Baldwin FG	.25	.11	.03
□ 64 Rondell White FG	.60	.25	.07
□ 65 Trot Nixon FG	.25	.11	.03
□ 66 Todd Hollandsworth FG	.75	.35	.09
□ 67 Roberto Clemente Hidden Talent	1.00	.45	.12
□ 68 Roberto Clemente Four-time batting champ	1.00	.45	.12
□ 69 Roberto Clemente 1966 NL MVP	1.00	.45	.12
□ 70 Roberto Clemente 3,000-Hit Club	1.00	.45	.12
□ 71 Roberto Clemente 1973 Hall of Fame	1.00	.45	.12
□ 72 Checklist (1-72)	.15	.07	.02
□ AU1 Frank Rodriguez AU/2500	25.00	11.00	3.10

1994 Action Packed 24K Gold

	MINT	NRMT	EXC
COMPLETE SET (13)	300.00	135.00	38.00
COMMON CARD (1G-13G)	10.00	4.50	1.25
DIAMOND VERSIONS: 5X VALUE			
□ 1G Alex Rodriguez	100.00	45.00	12.50
□ 2G Chan Ho Park	30.00	13.50	3.70
□ 3G Brooks Kieschnick	20.00	9.00	2.50
□ 4G Charles Johnson	30.00	13.50	3.70
□ 5G Alex Ochoa	30.00	13.50	3.70
□ 6G Michael Tucker	20.00	9.00	2.50
□ 7G Phil Nevin	10.00	4.50	1.25
□ 8G Jose Silva	10.00	4.50	1.25
□ 9G James Baldwin	20.00	9.00	2.50
□ 10G Rondell White	30.00	13.50	3.70
□ 11G Trot Nixon	20.00	9.00	2.50
□ 12G Todd Hollandsworth	30.00	13.50	3.70
□ 13G Checklist	10.00	4.50	1.25

1994 Albany Polecats Classic

This 30-card standard-size set of the 1994 Albany Polecats, a Class A South Atlantic League affiliate of the Baltimore Orioles, features white-bordered posed color player shots on its fronts with the player's name and position, team name, logo and Classic logo appearing across the bottom of each card. On a ghosted team logo, the white back carries the player's name at the top, followed by biography and statistics.

	MINT	NRMT	EXC
COMPLETE SET (30)	7.00	3.10	.85

□ 1 Jim Foster
□ 2 Matt Anderson
□ 3 Myles Barnden
□ 4 Harry Berrios
□ 5 Brian Brewer
□ 6 Brandon Bridgers
□ 7 Cory Brown
□ 8 Butch Burrough
□ 9 Rocco Cafaro
□ 10 Hector Castaneda
□ 11 Carlos Chavez
□ 12 Howie Clark
□ 13 Ryan Griffin
□ 14 Shane Hale
□ 15 Aaron Lane
□ 16 John Lombardi
□ 17 Miguel Mejia
□ 18 Angel Pagan
□ 19 Billy Percibal
□ 20 Kenny Reed
□ 21 Matt Riemer
□ 22 Francisco Saneaux
□ 23 Jose Serra
□ 24 Hut Smith
□ 25 Mike Trimarco
□ 26 Kyle Yeske
□ 27 Butch Wynegar MG
□ 28 Jeff Morris CO
□ 29 Peter Howell TR
□ 30 Scott Skadan GM
Checklist

1994 Albany Polecats Fleer/ProCards

This 30-card standard size set of the 1994 Albany Polecats, a Class A South Atlantic League affiliate of the Baltimore Orioles, features white-bordered posed color player photos on its fronts with the player's name, position, team name and Fleer/ProCards logo across the bottom of each card. The white back with vertical light blue stripes carries the player's name at the top, followed by biography and statistics.

	MINT	NRMT	EXC
COMPLETE SET (30)	5.00	2.20	.60

□ 2227 Matt Anderson
□ 2228 Brian Brewer
□ 2229 Cory Brown
□ 2230 Rocco Cafaro
□ 2231 Ryan Griffin
□ 2232 Shane Hale
□ 2233 Aaron Lane
□ 2234 John Lombardi
□ 2235 Billy Percibal
□ 2236 Francisco Saneaux
□ 2237 Hut Smith
□ 2238 Mike Trimarco
□ 2239 Hector Castaneda
□ 2240 Jim Foster
□ 2241 Myles Barnden
□ 2242 Howie Clark
□ 2243 David Lamb
□ 2244 Angel Pagan
□ 2245 Kenny Reed
□ 2246 Matt Riemer
□ 2247 Jose Serra
□ 2248 Brandon Bridgers
□ 2249 Butch Burrough
□ 2250 Wes Hawkins
□ 2251 Miguel Mejia
□ 2252 Trovin Valdez
□ 2253 Kyle Yeski
□ 2254 Butch Wynegar MG
□ 2255 Jeff Morris CO
□ 2256 Checklist

1994 Albany-Colonie Yankees Team Issue

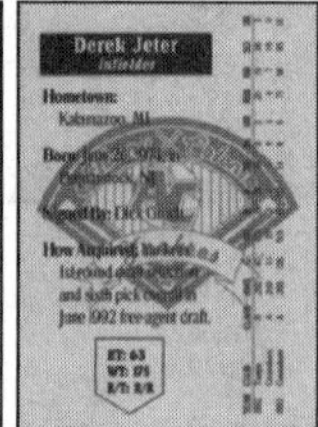

Issued as a three card panel in the 1994 Albany-Colonie Yankees Souvenir Yearbooks. This issue features a third year card of Derek Jeter.

	MINT	NRMT	EXC
COMPLETE SET (3)	40.00	18.00	5.00

□ 1 Andy Fox
□ 2 Derek Jeter
□ 3 Tate Seefried

1994 Albuquerque Dukes Fleer/ProCards

This 27-card standard size set of the 1994 Albuquerque Dukes, a Class AAA Pacific Coast League affiliate of the Los Angeles, features white-bordered posed color player photos on its fronts with the player's name, position, team name and Fleer/ProCards logo across the bottom of each card. The white back with vertical light blue stripes carries the player's name at the top, followed by biography and statistics.

	MINT	NRMT	EXC
COMPLETE SET (27)	12.00	5.50	1.50

□ 835 Bill Bene
□ 836 John DeSilva
□ 837 Rick Gorecki
□ 838 Greg Hansell
□ 839 Mark Mimbs
□ 840 Al Osuna
□ 841 Jose Parra
□ 842 Rudy Seanez
□ 843 Jody Treadwell
□ 844 Ben Van Ryn
□ 845 Hector Ortiz
□ 846 Don Barbara
□ 847 Rafael Bournigal
□ 848 Mike Busch
□ 849 Ron Coomer
□ 850 Matt Howard
□ 851 Ron Maurer
□ 852 Eddie Pye
□ 853 Kash Beauchamp
□ 854 Jerry Brooks
□ 855 Roger Cedeno
□ 856 Todd Hollandsworth
□ 857 Reggie Williams
□ 858 Rick Dempsey MG
□ 859 Glenn Gregson CO

☐ 860 Nate Oliver CO
☐ 861 Checklist

1994 Appleton Foxes Classic

This 30-card standard-size set of the 1994 Appleton Foxes, a Class A Midwest League affiliate of the Seattle Mariners, features white-bordered posed color player shots on its fronts with the player's name and position, team name and logo and Classic logo appearing across the bottom of each card. On a ghosted team logo, the white back carries the player's name at the top, followed by biography and statistics. This issue includes the minor league card debut of Alex Rodriguez.

	MINT	NRMT	EXC
COMPLETE SET (30)	200.00	90.00	25.00

☐ 1 Alex Rodriguez
☐ 2 Mike Barger
☐ 3 Tim Bruce
☐ 4 James Clifford
☐ 5 Giomar Guevara
☐ 6 Robin Cope
☐ 7 Jose Cueller
☐ 8 Brian Doughty
☐ 9 Ryan Franklin
☐ 10 Tim Harikkala
☐ 11 Brett Hinchliffe
☐ 12 Raul Ibanez
☐ 13 Robert Krueger
☐ 14 Ivan Montane
☐ 15 Manny Patel
☐ 16 Oscar Rivera
☐ 17 Marcus Sturdivant
☐ 18 Alex Sutherland
☐ 19 Greg Theron
☐ 20 Brian Wallace
☐ 21 Marty Winchester
☐ 22 Carlos Lezcano MG
☐ 23 Juan Eichelberger CO
☐ 24 Tommy Cruz CO
☐ 25 Allen Wirtala TR
☐ 26 Jason Cook UER
(Card back says 21, should be 26)
☐ 27 Logo Card UER
(Card back says 29, should be 27)
☐ 28 Logo Card UER
(Card back says 29, should be 28)
☐ 29 Logo Card
☐ 30 Checklist

1994 Appleton Foxes Fleer/ProCards

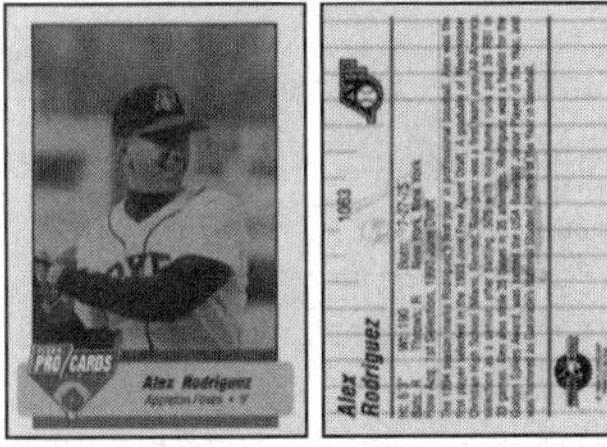

This 28-card standard size set of the 1994 Appleton Foxes, a Class A Midwest League affiliate of the Seattle Mariners, features white-bordered posed color player photos on its fronts with the player's name, position, team name and Fleer/ProCards logo across the bottom of each card. The white back with vertical light blue stripes carries the player's name at the top, followed by biography and statistics. This issue includes the minor league card debut of Alex Rodriguez.

	MINT	NRMT	EXC
COMPLETE SET (28)	35.00	16.00	4.40

☐ 1044 Tim Bruce
☐ 1045 Robin Cope
☐ 1046 Brian Doughty
☐ 1047 Ryan Franklin
☐ 1048 Tim Harikkala
☐ 1049 Brett Hinchliffe
☐ 1050 Robert Krueger
☐ 1051 Matt Mantei
☐ 1052 Ivan Montane
☐ 1053 Oscar Rivera
☐ 1054 Greg Theron
☐ 1055 Marty Winchester
☐ 1056 Jose Cuellar
☐ 1057 Raul Ibanez
☐ 1058 Alex Sutherland
☐ 1059 Jim Clifford
☐ 1060 Jason Cook
☐ 1061 Giomar Guevara
☐ 1062 Manny Patel
☐ 1063 Alex Rodriguez
☐ 1064 Brian Wallace
☐ 1065 Mike Barger
☐ 1066 Chad Dunavan
☐ 1067 David Lawson
☐ 1068 Marcus Sturdivant
☐ 1069 Carlos Lezcano MG
☐ 1070 Juan Eichelberger CO
☐ 1071 Checklist

1994 Arizona Fall League SplitSecond

Manufactured and distributed by Jessen Associates, Inc.

	MINT	NRMT	EXC
COMPLETE SET (21)	15.00	6.75	1.85

☐ 1 Cover Card
☐ 2 Doug Bochtler
☐ 3 Tony Clark
☐ 4 Marty Cordova
☐ 5 Andy Fox
☐ 6 Mark Grudzielanek
☐ 7 Bob Higginson
☐ 8 Stacy Hollins
☐ 9 Brian L. Hunter
☐ 10 Charles Johnson
☐ 11 Scott Karl
☐ 12 Brooks Kieschnick
☐ 13 Sean Mulligan
☐ 14 Alex Ochoa
☐ 15 Curtis Pride
☐ 16 Joe Randa
☐ 17 Desi Relaford
☐ 18 Ruben Rivera
☐ 19 Chris Snopek
☐ 20 Jim Tatum
☐ 21 Ron Villone

1994 Arkansas Travelers Fleer/ProCards

This 26-card standard size set of the 1994 Arkansas Travelers, a Class AA Texas League affiliate of the St. Louis Cardinals, features white-bordered posed color player photos on its fronts with the player's name, position, team name and Fleer/ProCards logo across the bottom of each card. The white back with vertical light blue stripes carries the player's name at the top, followed by biography and statistics.

	MINT	NRMT	EXC
COMPLETE SET (26)	5.00	2.20	.60

☐ 3081 Mike Badorek
☐ 3082 Rigo Beltran
☐ 3083 John Corona
☐ 3084 John Frascatore
☐ 3085 John Kelly
☐ 3086 Frankie Martinez
☐ 3087 Steve Montgomery
☐ 3088 Gabriel Ozuna
☐ 3089 Gerald Santos
☐ 3090 Scott Simmons
☐ 3091 Mike DiFelice
☐ 3092 Paul Ellis
☐ 3093 Joe Biasucci
☐ 3094 Andy Bruce
☐ 3095 Dan Cholowsky
☐ 3096 Aaron Holbert
☐ 3097 Jeff Shireman
☐ 3098 Ron Warner
☐ 3099 Dmitri Young
☐ 3100 Terry Bradshaw
☐ 3101 Tony Diggs
☐ 3102 Anthony Lewis
☐ 3103 Doug Radziewicz
☐ 3104 Chris Maloney MG
☐ 3105 Marty Mason CO
☐ 3106 Checklist

1994 Asheville Tourists Classic

This 30-card standard-size set of the 1994 Asheville Tourists, a Class A South Atlantic League affiliate of the Colorado Rockies, features white-bordered posed color player shots on its fronts with the player's name and position, team name and logo and Classic logo appearing across the bottom of each card. On a ghosted team logo, the white back carries the player's name at the top, followed by biography and statistics. This issue features the minor league card debuts of Edgar Velasquez and Jamey Wright.

	MINT	NRMT	EXC
COMPLETE SET (30)	20.00	9.00	2.50

☐ 1 Vicente Garcia
☐ 2 Keith Barnes
☐ 3 Pedro Carranza
☐ 4 Tony Dermendziev
☐ 5 Martin Dewett
☐ 6 Randy Edwards
☐ 7 Danny Figueroa
☐ 8 Neil Garrett
☐ 9 John Giudice
☐ 10 Keith Grunewald
☐ 11 Rick Hatfield
☐ 12 Mike Higgins
☐ 13 Nate Holdren
☐ 14 Bob Lasbury
☐ 15 Jose Matos
☐ 16 Dennis McAdams
☐ 17 Patrick McClinton
☐ 18 Chris Neier
☐ 19 Jason Smith
☐ 20 Jeff Sobkoviak
☐ 21 John Thomson
☐ 22 Edgard Velasquez
☐ 23 Jacob Viano
☐ 24 Doug Walls
☐ 25 Jamey Wright
☐ 26 Tony Torchia MG
☐ 27 Jack Lamabe CO
☐ 28 Bill McGuire CO
☐ 29 Marc Gustafson TR
☐ 30 Ron McKee GM
Checklist

1994 Asheville Tourists Fleer/ProCards

This 30-card standard size set of the 1994 Asheville Tourists, a Class A South Atlantic League affiliate of the Colorado Rockies, features white-bordered posed color player photos on its fronts with the player's name, position, team name and Fleer/ProCards logo across the bottom of each card. The white back with vertical light blue stripes carries the player's name at the top, followed by biography and statistics. This issue features the minor league card debuts of Edgar Velasquez and Jamey Wright.

	MINT	NRMT	EXC
COMPLETE SET (30)	14.00	6.25	1.75

☐ 1771 Keith Barnes
☐ 1772 Martin Dewett
☐ 1773 Neil Garrett
☐ 1774 Bob Lasbury
☐ 1775 Jose Matos
☐ 1776 Dennis McAdams
☐ 1777 Pat McClinton
☐ 1778 Chris Neier
☐ 1779 Jeff Sobkoviak
☐ 1780 John Thomson
☐ 1781 Jacob Viano
☐ 1782 Doug Walls
☐ 1783 Jamey Wright
☐ 1784 Rick Hatfield
☐ 1785 Mike Higgins
☐ 1786 Jason Smith
☐ 1787 Pedro Carranza
☐ 1788 Javier Diaz
☐ 1789 Danny Figueroa
☐ 1790 Vincente Garcia
☐ 1791 Keith Grunewald
☐ 1792 Nate Holdren
☐ 1793 Tony Dermendziev
☐ 1794 Randy Edwards
☐ 1795 John Giudice
☐ 1796 Edgard Velasquez
☐ 1797 Tony Torchia MG
☐ 1798 Jack Lamabe CO
☐ 1799 Bill McGuire CO
☐ 1800 Checklist

1994 Auburn Astros Classic

This 30-card standard size set of the 1994 Auburn Astros, a Class A New York-Penn League affiliate of the Houston Astros, features white-bordered posed color player shots on its fronts with the player's name and position, team name and logo and Classic logo appearing across the bottom of each card. On a ghosted team logo, the white back carries the player's name at the top, followed by biography and statistics.

	MINT	NRMT	EXC
COMPLETE SET (30)	7.00	3.10	.85

☐ 1 Randy Albaladejo
☐ 2 John Anderson
☐ 3 Terry Beyna
☐ 4 Mike Gunderson
☐ 5 John Halama
☐ 6 Josh Halemanu
☐ 7 Roy Marsh III
☐ 8 Bryant Nelson
☐ 9 Paul O'Malley
☐ 10 Jon Phillips
☐ 11 Wes Pratt
☐ 12 Kendall Rhine
☐ 13 Hassan Robinson
☐ 14 Tony Ross
☐ 15 Sean Runyan
☐ 16 Vic Sanchez
☐ 17 Troy Schulte
☐ 18 Don Scolaro
☐ 19 Dennis Shrum
☐ 20 Gary Trammell
☐ 21 Chris Truby
☐ 22 Julien Tucker
☐ 23 John Vindivich
☐ 24 Manny Acta MG
☐ 25 Don Alexander CO
☐ 26 Michael Ra TR
☐ 27 Shawn Smith GM
☐ 28 Mark Harrington
☐ 29 Logo Card
☐ 30 Checklist

1994 Auburn Astros Fleer/ProCards

This 29-card standard size set of the 1994 Auburn Astros, a Class A New York-Penn League affiliate of the Houston Astros, features white-bordered posed color player photos on its fronts with the player's name, position, team name and Fleer/ProCards logo across the bottom of each card. The white back with vertical light blue stripes carries the player's name at the top, followed by biography and statistics.

	MINT	NRMT	EXC
COMPLETE SET (29)	5.00	2.20	.60

☐ 3750 John Anderson
☐ 3751 Mike Gunderson
☐ 3752 John Halama
☐ 3753 Johann Lopez
☐ 3754 Paul O'Malley
☐ 3755 Jon Phillips
☐ 3756 Kendall Rhine
☐ 3757 Sean Runyan
☐ 3758 Troy Schulte
☐ 3759 Dennis Shrum
☐ 3760 Julien Tucker
☐ 3761 Randy Albaladejo
☐ 3762 Adan Amezcua
☐ 3763 Victor Sanchez
☐ 3764 Terry Beyna
☐ 3765 Josh Halemanu
☐ 3766 Bryant Nelson
☐ 3767 Donny Scolaro
☐ 3768 Gary Trammell
☐ 3769 Chris Truby
☐ 3770 Roy Marsh
☐ 3771 Wes Pratt
☐ 3772 Hassan Robinson
☐ 3773 Tony Ross
☐ 3774 John Vindivich
☐ 3775 Manny Acta MG
☐ 3776 Don Alexander CO
☐ 3777 Rusty Harris CO
☐ 3778 Checklist

1994 Augusta Greenjackets Classic

This 30-card standard size set of the 1994 Augusta GreenJackets, a Class A South Atlantic League affiliate of the Pittsburgh Pirates, features white-bordered posed color player shots on its fronts with the player's name and position, team name and logo and Classic logo appearing across the bottom of each card. On a ghosted team logo, the white back carries the player's name at the top, followed by biography and statistics.

	MINT	NRMT	EXC
COMPLETE SET (30)	7.00	3.10	.85

☐ 1 Lou Collier
☐ 2 Aaron Cannady
☐ 3 John Dillinger
☐ 4 Francisco Garcia-Luna
☐ 5 Mitch House
☐ 6 Jeff Isom
☐ 7 Jason Johnson
☐ 8 Jamie Keefe
☐ 9 Erskine Kelley
☐ 10 Jeff Lutt
☐ 11 Craig Mattson
☐ 12 Sergio Mendez
☐ 13 Ramon Morel
☐ 14 Primitivo Nunez
☐ 15 Chris Peters
☐ 16 Charles Peterson
☐ 17 Jason Phillips
☐ 18 Jeff Pickich
☐ 19 Felipe Polanco
☐ 20 Matt Pontbriant
☐ 21 Matt Ryan
☐ 22 Juan Segura
☐ 23 Jose Sosa
☐ 24 Dario Tena
☐ 25 Shon Walker
☐ 26 Joel Williamson
☐ 27 John Yselonia
☐ 28 Scott Little MG
☐ 29 Bruce Tanner CO
☐ 30 Todd Hoyt TR
Checklist

1994 Augusta GreenJackets Fleer/ProCards

This 28-card standard size set of the 1994 Augusta GreenJackets, a Class A South Atlantic League affiliate of the Pittsburgh Pirates, features white-bordered posed color player photos on its fronts with the player's name, position, team name and Fleer/ProCards logo across the bottom of each card. The white back with vertical light blue stripes carries the player's name at the top, followed by biography and statistics.

	MINT	NRMT	EXC
COMPLETE SET (28)	5.00	2.20	.60

☐ 2999 Jason Abramavicius
☐ 3000 John Dillinger
☐ 3001 Jason Johnson
☐ 3002 Jeff Lutt
☐ 3003 Craig Mattson
☐ 3004 Ramon Morel
☐ 3005 Chris Peters
☐ 3006 Jason Phillips
☐ 3007 Jeff Pickich
☐ 3008 Matt Pontbriant
☐ 3009 Matt Ryan
☐ 3010 Jose Sosa
☐ 3011 Aaron Cannaday
☐ 3012 Sergio Mendez
☐ 3013 Joel Williamson
☐ 3014 Lou Collier
☐ 3015 G.G. Harris
☐ 3016 Mitch House
☐ 3017 Rich Luna
☐ 3018 Felipe Polanco
☐ 3019 John Yselonia
☐ 3020 Erskine Kelley
☐ 3021 Charles Peterson
☐ 3022 Dario Tena
☐ 3023 Shon Walker
☐ 3024 Scott Little MG
☐ 3025 Bruce Tanner CO
☐ 3026 Checklist

1994 Bakersfield Dodgers Classic

This 30-card standard size set of the 1994 Bakersfield Dodgers, a Class A California League affiliate of the Los Angeles Dodgers, features white-bordered posed color player shots on its fronts with the player's name and position, team name and logo and Classic logo appearing across the bottom of each card. On a ghosted team logo, the white back carries the player's name at the top, followed by biography and statistics..

	MINT	NRMT	EXC
COMPLETE SET (30)	7.00	3.10	.85

☐ 1 Kym Ashworth
☐ 2 Mike Biltimier
☐ 3 Nathan Bland
☐ 4 Miguel Cairo
☐ 5 Daniel Camacho
☐ 6 Brian Carpenter
☐ 7 Nelson Castro
☐ 8 Kenny Cook
☐ 9 Roberto Duran
☐ 10 Ken Huckaby
☐ 11 Keith Johnson
☐ 12 Mike Kinney
☐ 13 Tito Landrum
☐ 14 Rich Linares
☐ 15 Paul LoDuca
☐ 16 Dwight Maness
☐ 17 Mike Metcalfe
☐ 18 Michael Moore
☐ 19 Kevin Pincavitch
☐ 20 Jose Prado
☐ 21 Willie Romero
☐ 22 Matt Schwenke
☐ 23 Carlos Thomas
☐ 24 Michael Walkden
☐ 25 Ervan Wingate
☐ 26 Dax Winslett
☐ 27 John Shelby MG
☐ 28 Guy Conti CO
☐ 29 Dino Ebel P/CO
☐ 30 Bart Dugger TR
Checklist

1994 Batavia Clippers Classic

This 30-card standard size set of the 1994 Batavia Clippers, a Class A New York-Penn League affiliate of the Philadelphia Phillies, features white-bordered posed color player shots on its fronts with the player's name and position, team name and logo and Classic logo appearing across the bottom of each card. On a ghosted team logo, the white back carries the player's name at the top, followed by biography and statistics.

	MINT	NRMT	EXC
COMPLETE SET (30)	7.00	3.10	.85

☐ 1 Adrian Antonini
☐ 2 Joe Barbao
☐ 3 Matt Beech
☐ 4 Jose Flores
☐ 5 Jeff Gyselman
☐ 6 Bronson Heflin
☐ 7 Jeff Jensen
☐ 8 Kris Kirkland
☐ 9 Brett Legrow
☐ 10 Bryan Lundberg
☐ 11 Joey Madden
☐ 12 Wendell Magee
☐ 13 Shaun McGinn
☐ 14 Bill Mobilia
☐ 15 Jamie Northeimer
☐ 16 Pete Nyari
☐ 17 Ryan Nye
☐ 18 Joe O'Brien
☐ 19 Steve Paasch
☐ 20 Torrey Pettiford
☐ 21 Mike Shipman
☐ 22 Scott Shores
☐ 23 David Stewart
☐ 24 Jason Valley
☐ 25 John Vandemark
☐ 26 James White
☐ 27 Al LeBoeuf MG
☐ 28 Floyd Rayford CO
☐ 29 Ken Westray CO
☐ 30 Troy McIntosh TR
Checklist

1994 Batavia Clippers Fleer/ProCards

This 32-card standard size set of the 1994 Batavia Clippers, a Class A New York-Penn League affiliate of the Philadelphia Phillies, features white-bordered posed color player photos on its fronts with the player's name, position, team name and Fleer/ProCards logo across the bottom of each card. The white back with vertical light blue stripes carries the player's name at the top, followed by biography and statistics.

	MINT	NRMT	EXC
COMPLETE SET (32)	6.00	2.70	.75

☐ 3435 Adrian Antonini
☐ 3436 Joe Barbao
☐ 3437 Matt Beech
☐ 3438 Bronson Heflin
☐ 3439 Kris Kirkland
☐ 3440 Brett LeGrow
☐ 3441 Bryan Lundberg
☐ 3442 Pete Nyari
☐ 3443 Ryan Nye
☐ 3444 Steve Paasch
☐ 3445 David Stewart
☐ 3446 Jason Valley
☐ 3447 John Vandemark
☐ 3448 Jeff Gyselman
☐ 3449 Adam Millan
☐ 3450 Jaime Northeimer
☐ 3451 Mike Shipman
☐ 3452 Jose Flores
☐ 3453 Jeff Jensen
☐ 3454 Shaun McGinn
☐ 3455 Bill Mobilia
☐ 3456 Joe O'Brien
☐ 3457 Matt Williamson
☐ 3458 Joey Madden
☐ 3459 Wendell Magee
☐ 3460 Scott Shores
☐ 3461 John Torok
☐ 3462 Josh Watts
☐ 3463 James White
☐ 3464 Field Staff
Ken Westray CO
Al LeBoeuf MG
Troy McIntosh TR
☐ 3464 Floyd Rayford CO
☐ 3749 Checklist

1994 Bellingham Mariners Classic

This 30-card standard size set of the 1994 Bellingham Mariners, a Class A Northwest League affiliate of the Seattle Mariners, features white-bordered posed color player shots on its fronts with the player's name and position, team name and logo and Classic logo appearing across the bottom of each card. On a ghosted team logo, the white back carries the player's name at the top, followed by biography and statistics.

	MINT	NRMT	EXC
COMPLETE SET (30)	7.00	3.10	.85

☐ 1 Dave Vanhof
☐ 2 Matthew Aminoff
☐ 3 Andy Augustine
☐ 4 Dario Batista
☐ 5 Chris Beck
☐ 6 Teddy Bishop
☐ 7 Shawn Buhner
☐ 8 Mike Collett
☐ 9 John Daniels
☐ 10 Scott Davison
☐ 11 Jose De Leon
☐ 12 Chris Dean
☐ 13 Santos Deleon
☐ 14 Chris Green
☐ 15 Jason Heath
☐ 16 Robert Ippolito
☐ 17 Rick Ladjevich
☐ 18 Mike Lanza
☐ 19 Joe Mathis
☐ 20 Geronimo Newton
☐ 21 Joe Pomierski
☐ 22 Joel Ramirez
☐ 23 Jason Ruskey
☐ 24 Marino Santana
☐ 25 Nestor Serrano
☐ 26 Thomas Szimanski
☐ 27 John Thompson
☐ 28 Kyle Towner
☐ 29 Brian Williams
☐ 30 Staff
Checklist

1994 Bellingham Mariners Fleer/ProCards

This 31-card standard size set of the 1994 Bellingham Mariners, a Class A Northwest League affiliate of the Seattle Mariners, features white-bordered posed color player photos on its fronts with the player's name, position, team name and Fleer/ProCards logo across the bottom of each card. The white back with vertical light blue stripes carries the player's name at the top, followed by biography and statistics.

	MINT	NRMT	EXC
COMPLETE SET (31)	5.00	2.20	.60

☐ 2663 Checklist
☐ 3223 Matt Aminoff
☐ 3224 Chris Beck
☐ 3225 Mike Collett
☐ 3226 John Daniels
☐ 3227 Scott Davison
☐ 3228 Chris Green
☐ 3229 Rob Ippolito
☐ 3230 Geronimo Newton
☐ 3231 Jason Ruskey
☐ 3232 Marino Santana
☐ 3233 Field Staff
Bryan Price CO
Mike Goff MG
Orlando Gomez CO
Spyder Webb TR
☐ 3234 Tom Szimanski
☐ 3235 John Thompson
☐ 3236 Dave Vanhof
☐ 3237 Brian Williams
☐ 3238 Andy Augustine
☐ 3239 Teddy Bishop
☐ 3240 Jason Heath
☐ 3241 Shawn Buhner
☐ 3242 Chris Dean
☐ 3243 Rick Ladjevich
☐ 3244 Mike Lanza
☐ 3245 Joe Pomierski
☐ 3246 Joel Ramirez
☐ 3247 Nestor Serrano
☐ 3248 Dario Batista
☐ 3249 Jose DeLeon
☐ 3250 Santo Deleon
☐ 3251 Joe Mathis
☐ 3252 Kyle Towner

1994 Beloit Brewers Classic

This 30-card standard size set of the 1994 Beloit Brewers, a Class A Midwest League affiliate of the Milwaukee Brewers, features white-bordered posed color player shots on its fronts with the player's name and position, team name and logo and Classic logo appearing across the bottom of each card. On a ghosted team logo, the white back carries the player's name at the top, followed by biography and statistics.

	MINT	NRMT	EXC
COMPLETE SET (30)	7.00	3.10	.85

☐ 1 Kelly Wunsch
☐ 2 Wagner Arias
☐ 3 Brian Banks
☐ 4 Stoney Burke
☐ 5 Jim Cole
☐ 6 Brian Dennison
☐ 7 Bill Dobrolsky
☐ 8 Michael Dumas
☐ 9 Todd Dunn
☐ 10 Will Fitzpatrick
☐ 11 Jonas Hamlin
☐ 12 Jim Hodge
☐ 13 Danny Klassen
☐ 14 Chad Kopitzke
☐ 15 Sean Maloney
☐ 16 Greg Martinez
☐ 17 Chris McInnes
☐ 18 John Morreale
☐ 19 George Preston
☐ 20 Cecil Rodriques
☐ 21 John Salamon
☐ 22 Fabian Salmon
☐ 23 Jerry Salzano
☐ 24 Chris Schmitt
☐ 25 Joe Wagner
☐ 26 Judd Wilstead
☐ 27 Wayne Krenchicki MG
☐ 28 Steve Foucault CO
☐ 29 Jon Pont CO
☐ 30 Jeff Paxson TR
Checklist

1994 Beloit Brewers Fleer/ProCards

This 30-card standard size set of the 1994 Beloit Brewers, a Class A Midwest League affiliate of the Milwaukee Brewers, features white-bordered posed color player photos on its fronts with the player's name, position, team name and Fleer/ProCards logo across the bottom of each card. The white back with vertical light blue stripes carries the player's name at the top, followed by biography and statistics.

	MINT	NRMT	EXC
COMPLETE SET (30)	5.00	2.20	.60

☐ 92 Wagner Arias
☐ 93 Jim Cole
☐ 94 Brian Dennison
☐ 95 Chad Kopitzke
☐ 96 Sean Maloney
☐ 97 George Preston
☐ 98 John Salamon
☐ 99 Fabian Salmon
☐ 100 Chris Schmitt
☐ 101 Joe Wagner
☐ 102 Judd Wilstead
☐ 103 Kelly Wunsch
☐ 104 Stoney Burke
☐ 105 Bill Dobrolsky
☐ 106 Mike Dumas
☐ 107 Will Fitzpatrick
☐ 108 Jonas Hamlin
☐ 109 Danny Klassen
☐ 110 Chris McInnes
☐ 111 John Morreale
☐ 112 Jerry Salzano
☐ 113 Brian Banks
☐ 114 Todd Dunn
☐ 115 Jim Hodge
☐ 116 Greg Martinez
☐ 117 Cecil Rodriques
☐ 118 Wayne Krenchicki MG
☐ 119 Steve Foucault CO
☐ 120 Jon Pont CO
☐ 121 Checklist

1994 Bend Rockies Classic

This 30-card standard size set of the 1994 Bend Rockies, a Class A Northwest League affiliate of the Colorado Rockies,features white-bordered posed color player shots on its fronts with the player's name and position, team name and logo and Classic logo appearing across the bottom of each card. On a ghosted team logo, the white back carries the player's name at the top, followed by biography and statistics. This issue features the minor league card debuts of Derrick Gibson and Doug Millon.

	MINT	NRMT	EXC
COMPLETE SET (30)	30.00	13.50	3.70

☐ 1 Mudcat Brewers
☐ 2 Matt Carpenter
☐ 3 Brent Crowther
☐ 4 Jason Dietrich
☐ 5 Bill Eden
☐ 6 Fernando Fernandez
☐ 7 Chad Gambill
☐ 8 Derrick Gibson
☐ 9 Kyle Houser
☐ 10 Chris Howard
☐ 11 Link Jarrett
☐ 12 Gary Jones
☐ 13 Pookie Jones
☐ 14 Scott LaRock
☐ 15 Jim Lezeau
☐ 16 Jon Mathews
☐ 17 John Meskauskas
☐ 18 Doug Million
☐ 19 Matt Pool
☐ 20 Brian Rose
☐ 21 Mike Saipe
☐ 22 Jeff Twist
☐ 23 Art Waldrep
☐ 24 Scott Warembourg
☐ 25 Kevin Wehn
☐ 26 Forry Wells
☐ 27 Mark Wells
☐ 28 Rudy Jaramillo
☐ 29 Al Bleser
☐ 30 Bill Slosson CL

1994 Bend Rockies Fleer/ProCards

This 31-card standard size set of the 1994 Bend Rockies, a Class A Northwest League affiliate of the Colorado Rockies, features white-bordered posed color player photos on its fronts with the player's name, position, team name and Fleer/ProCards logo across the bottom of each card. The white back with vertical light blue stripes carries the player's name at the top, followed by biography and statistics. This issue features the minor league card debuts of Derrick Gibson and Doug Millon.

	MINT	NRMT	EXC
COMPLETE SET (31)	20.00	9.00	2.50

☐ 3582 Morgan Burdick
☐ 3583 Brent Crowther
☐ 3584 Jason Dietrich
☐ 3585 Bill Eden
☐ 3586 Fernando Fernandez
☐ 3587 Chris Howard
☐ 3588 Scott LaRock
☐ 3589 Jose Matos
☐ 3590 Doug Million
☐ 3591 Matt Pool
☐ 3592 Brian Rose
☐ 3593 Mike Saipe
☐ 3594 Art Waldrep
☐ 3595 Scott Warembourg
☐ 3596 Kevin Wehn
☐ 3597 John Meskauskas
☐ 3598 Yohel Pozo
☐ 3599 Jeff Twist
☐ 3600 Mudcat Brewer
☐ 3601 Kyle Houser
☐ 3602 Link Jarrett
☐ 3603 Gary Jones
☐ 3604 John Mathews
☐ 3605 Forry Wells
☐ 3606 Chad Gambill
☐ 3607 Derrick Gibson
☐ 3608 Ronnie Hall
☐ 3609 Pookie Jones
☐ 3610 Jim Lezeau
☐ 3611 Mark Wells
☐ 3688 Checklist

1994 Billings Mustangs Fleer/ProCards

This 27-card standard size set of the 1994 Billings Mustangs, a Rookie Class Pioneer League affiliate of the Cincinnati Reds, features white-bordered posed color player photos on its fronts with the player's name, position, team name and Fleer/ProCards logo across the bottom of each card. The white back with vertical light blue stripes carries the player's name at the top, followed by biography and statistics. This issue features the minor league card debut of Aaron Boone.

	MINT	NRMT	EXC
COMPLETE SET (27)	12.00	5.50	1.50

☐ 3661 Adam Bryant
☐ 3662 Clay Caruthers
☐ 3663 Joel Franklin
☐ 3664 Clint Koppe
☐ 3665 Daniel Masse
☐ 3666 Tony Nieto
☐ 3667 Eddie Priest
☐ 3668 John Riedling
☐ 3669 Jason Robbins
☐ 3670 David Solomon
☐ 3671 Marc Weiss
☐ 3672 Jeff Andrews
☐ 3673 Rob Domino
☐ 3674 Aaron Boone
☐ 3675 Ray Brown
☐ 3676 Doug Durrwachter
☐ 3677 Denny Fussell
☐ 3678 Mike Hampton
☐ 3679 James Lofton
☐ 3680 Brian Wilson
☐ 3681 Donald Broach
☐ 3682 Nick Morrow
☐ 3683 Scott Savary
☐ 3684 Tony Terry
☐ 3685 Donnie Scott MG
☐ 3686 Steve Oliverio CO
☐ 3687 Checklist

1994 Billings Mustangs Sports Pro

This 27-card standard size set of the 1994 Billings Mustangs, a Rookie Class Pioneer League affiliate of the Cincinnati Reds features the minor league card debut of Aaron Boone.

	MINT	NRMT	EXC
COMPLETE SET (30)	16.00	7.25	2.00

☐ 1 Jeff Andrews
☐ 2 Rob Domino
☐ 3 Aaron Boone
☐ 4 Ray Brown

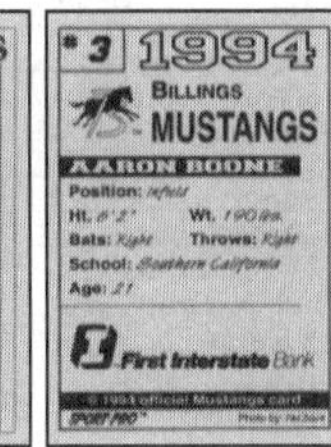

☐ 5 Doug Durrwachter
☐ 6 Denny Fussell
☐ 7 Mike Hampton
☐ 8 James Lofton
☐ 9 Brian Wilson
☐ 10 Donald Broach
☐ 11 Nick Morrow
☐ 12 Scott Savary
☐ 13 Tony Terry
☐ 14 Adam Bryant
☐ 15 Clay Caruthers
☐ 16 Joel Franklin
☐ 17 Clint Koppe
☐ 18 Tony Nieto
☐ 19 Eddie Priest
☐ 20 Jason Robbins
☐ 21 David Solomon
☐ 22 Marc Weiss
☐ 23 Donnie Scott MG
☐ 24 Steve Oliverio CO
☐ 25 Bill Maxwell TR
☐ 26 Blank Card
☐ 27 Blank Card
☐ 28 Blank Card
☐ 29 Blank Card
☐ 30 Blank Card

1994 Binghamton Mets Fleer/ProCards

This 28-card standard size set of the 1994 Binghamton Mets, a Class AA Eastern League affiliate of the New York Mets, features white-bordered posed color player photos on its fronts with the player's name, position, team name and Fleer/ProCards logo across the bottom of each card. The white back with vertical light blue stripes carries the player's name at the top, followed by biography and statistics.

	MINT	NRMT	EXC
COMPLETE SET (28)	6.00	2.70	.75

☐ 696 Andy Beckerman
☐ 697 Juan Castillo
☐ 698 Joe Crawford
☐ 699 Mark Fuller
☐ 700 Gregg Langbehn
☐ 701 Jim McCready
☐ 702 Robert Person
☐ 703 Bill Pulsipher
☐ 704 Chris Roberts
☐ 705 Joe Vitko
☐ 706 Alberto Castillo
☐ 707 Tony Tijerina
☐ 708 Edgardo Alfonzo
☐ 709 Omar Garcia
☐ 710 Greg Graham
☐ 711 Frank Jacobs
☐ 712 Chris Saunders
☐ 713 Doug Saunders
☐ 714 Jeff Barry
☐ 715 Jay Davis
☐ 716 Ed Fully
☐ 717 Pat Howell
☐ 718 Ricky Otero
☐ 719 Tracy Sanders
☐ 720 John Tamargo MG
☐ 721 Tom Allison CO
☐ 722 Randy Niemann CO
☐ 723 Checklist

1994 Birmingham Barons Classic

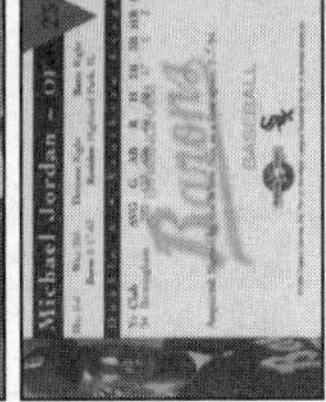

This 30-card standard size set of the 1994 Birmingham Barons, a Class AA Southern League affiliate of the Chicago White Sox, features white-bordered posed color player shots on its fronts with the player's name and position, team name and logo and Classic logo appearing across the bottom of each card. On a ghosted team logo, the white back carries the player's name at the top, followed by biography and statistics. This issue features the minor league card debut of Michael Jordan.

	MINT	NRMT	EXC
COMPLETE SET (30)	12.00	5.50	1.50

☐ 1 Chris Tremie
☐ 2 Luis Andujar
☐ 3 Mike Bertotti
☐ 4 Doug Brady
☐ 5 Ken Coleman
☐ 6 Kevin Coughlin
☐ 7 Glenn DiSarcina
☐ 8 Troy Fryman
☐ 9 Steve Gajkowski
☐ 10 Brian Givens
☐ 11 Atlee Hammaker
☐ 12 Mike Heathcott
☐ 13 Randy Hood
☐ 14 Barry Johnson
☐ 15 Matt Karchner
☐ 16 Al Levine
☐ 17 Rogelio Nunez
☐ 18 Steve Olsen
☐ 19 Mike Robertson
☐ 20 Chris Snopek
☐ 21 Scott Tedder
☐ 22 Larry Thomas
☐ 23 Michael Jordan
☐ 24 Kerry Valrie
☐ 25 Joey Vierra
☐ 26 Terry Francona MG
☐ 27 Kirk Champion CO
☐ 28 Mike Barnett CO
☐ 29 Sam Hairston CO
☐ 30 Steve Davis CL

1994 Birmingham Barons Fleer/ProCards

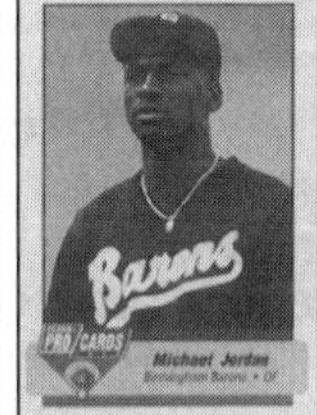

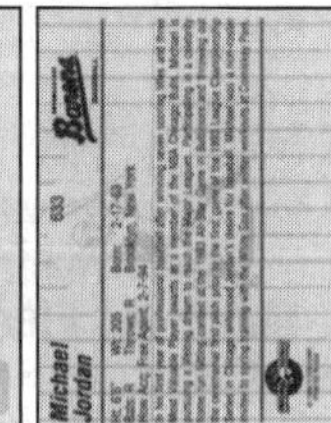

This 28-card standard size set of the 1994 Birmingham Barons, a Class AA Southern League affiliate of the Chicago White Sox, features white-bordered posed color player photos on its fronts with the player's name, position, team name and Fleer/ProCards logo across the bottom of each card. The white back with vertical light blue stripes carries the player's name at the top, followed by biography and statistics. This issue features the minor league card debut of Michael Jordan.

	MINT	NRMT	EXC
COMPLETE SET (28)	10.00	4.50	1.25

☐ 614 Luis Andujar
☐ 615 Steve Gajkowski
☐ 616 Brian Givens
☐ 617 Mike Heathcott
☐ 618 Barry Johnson
☐ 619 Matt Karchner
☐ 620 Al Levine
☐ 621 Steve Olson
☐ 622 Larry Thomas
☐ 623 Joey Vierra
☐ 624 Rogelio Nunez
☐ 625 Chris Tremie
☐ 626 Doug Brady
☐ 627 Ken Coleman
☐ 628 Glenn DiSarcina
☐ 629 Troy Fryman
☐ 630 Chris Snopek
☐ 631 Kevin Coughlin
☐ 632 Randy Hood
☐ 633 Michael Jordan
☐ 634 Mike Robertson
☐ 635 Scott Tedder
☐ 636 Kerry Valrie
☐ 637 Terry Francona MG
☐ 638 Mike Barnett CO
☐ 639 Kirk Champion CO
☐ 640 Sam Hairston CO
☐ 641 Checklist

1994 Bluefield Orioles Classic

This 30-card standard size set of the 1994 Bluefield Orioles, a Rookie Class Appalachian League affiliate of the Baltimore Orioles, features white-bordered posed color player shots on its fronts with the player's name and position, team name and logo and Classic logo appearing across the bottom of each card. On a ghosted team logo, the white back carries the player's name at the top, followed by biography and statistics. This issue includes the minor league card debut of Rocky Coppinger.

	MINT	NRMT	EXC
COMPLETE SET (30)	12.00	5.50	1.50

☐ 1 Rolando Avila
☐ 2 Jairo Cabrera
☐ 3 Carlos Chavez
☐ 4 Rocky Coppinger
☐ 5 Brad Crills
☐ 6 Tim Daigle
☐ 7 Tom D'Aquila
☐ 8 Joey Dawley
☐ 9 Michael Gargiulo
☐ 10 Ryan Griffin
☐ 11 Ryan Hendricks
☐ 12 Chris Kirgan
☐ 13 Matt Marenghi
☐ 14 Miguel Mejia
☐ 15 Michael Nadeau
☐ 16 Angel Pagan
☐ 17 Alex Pena
☐ 18 Jason Rogers
☐ 19 Rick Short
☐ 20 Rachaad Stewart
☐ 21 Trovin Valdez
☐ 22 Shane Ziegler
☐ 23 Andy Etchebarren MG
☐ 24 Charlie Puleo CO
☐ 25 Len Johnston CC
☐ 26 Dave Walker TR
☐ 27 Logo Card
☐ 28 Logo Card
☐ 29 Logo Card
☐ 30 Checklist

1994 Bluefield Orioles Fleer/ProCards

This 30-card standard size set of the 1994 Bluefield Orioles, a Rookie Class Appalachian League affiliate of the Baltimore Orioles, features white-bordered posed color player photos on its fronts with the player's name, position, team name and Fleer/ProCards logo across the bottom of each card. The white back with vertical light blue stripes carries the player's name at the top, followed by biography and statistics. This issue includes the minor league card debut of Rocky Coppinger.

	MINT	NRMT	EXC
COMPLETE SET (30)	10.00	4.50	1.25

☐ 3552 Carlos Chavez
☐ 3553 Rocky Coppinger
☐ 3554 Brad Crills
☐ 3555 Tim Daigle
☐ 3556 Joey Dawley
☐ 3557 Ryan Griffin
☐ 3558 Derek Gulledge
☐ 3559 Mike Lane
☐ 3560 Matt Marenghi
☐ 3561 Alex Pena
☐ 3562 Jason Rogers
☐ 3563 Richard Stewart
☐ 3564 Shane Ziegler
☐ 3565 Jairo Cabrera
☐ 3566 Mike Gargiulo
☐ 3567 Ryan Hendricks
☐ 3568 Chris Kirgan
☐ 3569 Mike Nadeau
☐ 3570 Angel Pagan
☐ 3571 Chris Sauritch
☐ 3572 Rich Short
☐ 3573 Rolando Avila
☐ 3574 Todd Brown
☐ 3575 Tom D'Aquila
☐ 3576 Miguel Mejia
☐ 3577 Trovin Valdez
☐ 3578 Andy Etchebarren MG
☐ 3579 Len Johnston CO
☐ 3580 Charlie Puleo CO
☐ 3581 Checklist

1994 Boise Hawks Classic

This 30-card standard size set of the 1994 Boise Hawks, a Class A Northwest League affiliate of the California Angels, features white-bordered posed color player shots on its fronts with the player's name and position, team name and logo and Classic logo appearing across the bottom of each card. On a ghosted team logo, the white back carries the player's name at the top, followed by biography and statistics.

	MINT	NRMT	EXC
COMPLETE SET (30)	7.00	3.10	.85

☐ 1 Bret Hemphill
☐ 2 Todd Blyleven
☐ 3 Rob Bonanno
☐ 4 Mathew Buckley
☐ 5 Jerry Carpenter
☐ 6 Jose Carrasco
☐ 7 Jose Cintron
☐ 8 Keith Coe
☐ 9 John Donati
☐ 10 Mike Freehill
☐ 11 Jim Greely
☐ 12 Kevin Ham

- ☐ 13 Keith Hattig
- ☐ 14 Jason Hill
- ☐ 15 Mike Holtz
- ☐ 16 Rodd Kelley
- ☐ 17 Jeff Knox
- ☐ 18 Brandon Markiewicz
- ☐ 19 Greg Morris
- ☐ 20 Don Nestor
- ☐ 21 Dan Petroff
- ☐ 22 David Sick
- ☐ 23 Nick Skuse
- ☐ 24 Demond Smith
- ☐ 25 Sammy Taylor Jr.
- ☐ 26 Travis Thurmond
- ☐ 27 Mike Vallarelli
- ☐ 28 Dennis Van Pelt
- ☐ 29 Ryan Wheeler
- ☐ 30 Tom Kotchman MG Checklist

1994 Boise Hawks Fleer/ProCards

This 31-card standard size set of the 1994 Boise Hawks, a Class A Northwest League affiliate of the California Angels, features white-bordered posed color player photos on its fronts with the player's name, position, team name and Fleer/ProCards logo across the bottom of each card. The white back with vertical light blue stripes carries the player's name at the top, followed by biography and statistics.

	MINT	NRMT	EXC
COMPLETE SET (31)	5.00	2.20	.60

- ☐ 3343 Todd Blyleven
- ☐ 3344 Rob Bonanno
- ☐ 3345 Jose Carrasco
- ☐ 3346 Jose Cintron
- ☐ 3347 Keith Coe
- ☐ 3348 Mike Freehill
- ☐ 3349 Jason Hill
- ☐ 3350 Mike Holtz
- ☐ 3351 Jeff Knox
- ☐ 3352 Don Nestor
- ☐ 3353 Dan Petroff
- ☐ 3354 David Sick
- ☐ 3355 Nick Skuse
- ☐ 3356 Travis Thurmond
- ☐ 3357 Jerry Carpenter
- ☐ 3358 Bret Hemphill
- ☐ 3359 Mike Vallarelli
- ☐ 3360 Mat Buckley
- ☐ 3361 John Donati
- ☐ 3362 Keith Hattig
- ☐ 3363 Rodd Kelley
- ☐ 3364 Brandon Markiewicz
- ☐ 3365 Greg Morris
- ☐ 3366 Ryan Wheeler
- ☐ 3367 Jim Greely
- ☐ 3368 Kevin Ham
- ☐ 3369 Demond Smith
- ☐ 3370 Sam Taylor
- ☐ 3371 Dennis Van Pelt
- ☐ 3372 Tom Kotchman MG
- ☐ 3373 Checklist

1994 Bowie Baysox Fleer/ProCards

This 27-card standard size set of the 1994 Bowie Baysox, a Class AA Eastern League affiliate of the Baltimore Orioles, features white-bordered posed color player photos on its fronts with the player's name, position, team name and Fleer/ProCards logo across the bottom of each card. The white back with vertical light blue stripes carries the player's name at the top, followed by biography and statistics.

	MINT	NRMT	EXC
COMPLETE SET (27)	5.00	2.20	.60

- ☐ 2404 Steve Adkins
- ☐ 2405 Armando Benitez
- ☐ 2406 Joe Borowski
- ☐ 2407 Steve Chitren
- ☐ 2408 Vaughn Eshelman
- ☐ 2409 Rick Forney
- ☐ 2410 Jimmy Haynes
- ☐ 2411 Scott Klingenbeck
- ☐ 2412 Dave Paveloff
- ☐ 2413 Kevin Ryan
- ☐ 2414 Brian Sackinsky
- ☐ 2415 Cesar Devarez
- ☐ 2416 Kris Gresham
- ☐ 2417 Edgar Alfonzo
- ☐ 2418 Ken Arnold
- ☐ 2419 Scott McClain
- ☐ 2420 Jose Millares
- ☐ 2421 Brent Miller
- ☐ 2422 Hector Vargas
- ☐ 2423 Curtis Goodwin
- ☐ 2424 Rob Lukachyk
- ☐ 2425 Alex Ochoa
- ☐ 2426 Bo Ortiz
- ☐ 2427 Pete Mackanin MG
- ☐ 2428 John O'Donoghue Sr. CO
- ☐ 2429 Al Bumbry CO
- ☐ 2430 Checklist

1994 Brevard County Manatees Classic

This 30-card standard size set of the 1994 Brevard County Manatees, a Class A Florida State League affiliate of the Florida Marlins, features white-bordered posed color player shots on its fronts with the player's name and position, team name and logo and Classic logo appearing across the bottom of each card. On a ghosted team logo, the white back carries the player's name at the top, followed by biography and statistics.

	MINT	NRMT	EXC
COMPLETE SET (30)	20.00	9.00	2.50

- ☐ 1 Edgar Renteria
- ☐ 2 Mitchel Bowen
- ☐ 3 Todd Carl
- ☐ 4 Daniel Chergey
- ☐ 5 Chris Clapinski
- ☐ 6 Kenny Kendrena
- ☐ 7 Pat Leahy
- ☐ 8 Lou Lucca
- ☐ 9 Greg Mix
- ☐ 10 Clemente Nunez
- ☐ 11 Matt Petersen
- ☐ 12 Doug Pettit
- ☐ 13 Todd Pridy
- ☐ 14 Dan Robinson
- ☐ 15 Scott Samuels
- ☐ 16 Tony Saunders
- ☐ 17 Mike Sims
- ☐ 18 Jerry Stafford
- ☐ 19 Tony Sylvestri
- ☐ 20 Jason Tidwell
- ☐ 21 Tony Torres
- ☐ 22 Matt Whisenant
- ☐ 23 Pookie Wilson
- ☐ 24 Fredi Gonzalez
- ☐ 25 Britt Burns
- ☐ 26 Carlos Ponce
- ☐ 27 Vinny Scavo
- ☐ 29A Brevard County Manatees Logo
- ☐ 29B Florida Marlins Logo
- ☐ 30 Brevard County Manatees Logo CL

1994 Brevard County Manatees Fleer/ProCards

This 30-card standard size set of the 1994 Brevard County Manatees, a Class A Florida State League affiliate of the Florida Marlins, features white-bordered posed color player photos on its fronts with the player's name, position, team name and Fleer/ProCards logo across the bottom of each card. The white back with vertical light blue stripes carries the player's name at the top, followed by biography and statistics.

	MINT	NRMT	EXC
COMPLETE SET (30)	10.00	4.50	1.25

- ☐ 1 Mitch Bowen
- ☐ 2 Daniel Chergey
- ☐ 3 Jim Corsi
- ☐ 4 Kenny Kendrena
- ☐ 5 Pat Leahy
- ☐ 6 Rey Mendoza
- ☐ 7 Greg Mix
- ☐ 8 Matt Petersen
- ☐ 9 Doug Pettit
- ☐ 10 Tony Saunders
- ☐ 11 Stan Spencer
- ☐ 12 Gerry Stafford
- ☐ 13 Jason Tidwell
- ☐ 14 Matt Whisenant
- ☐ 15 Mike Sims
- ☐ 16 Mark Skeels
- ☐ 17 Tony Turnbull
- ☐ 18 Chris Clapinski
- ☐ 19 Lou Lucca
- ☐ 20 Todd Pridy
- ☐ 21 Edgar Renteria
- ☐ 22 Tony Sylvestri
- ☐ 23 Tony Torres
- ☐ 24 Dan Robinson
- ☐ 25 Willie Romay
- ☐ 26 Scott Samuels
- ☐ 27 Chris Sheff
- ☐ 28 Pookie Wilson
- ☐ 29 Fredi Gonzales MG
- ☐ 30 Checklist

1994 Bristol Tigers Classic

This 30-card standard size set of the 1994 Bristol Tigers, a Rookie Class Appalachian League affiliate of the Detroit Tigers, features white-bordered posed color player shots on its fronts with the player's name and position, team name and logo and Classic logo appearing across the bottom of each card. On a ghosted team logo, the white back carries the player's name at the top, followed by biography and statistics. This issue includes the minor league card debuts of Juan Encarnacion and Willis Roberts.

	MINT	NRMT	EXC
COMPLETE SET (30)	10.00	4.50	1.25

- ☐ 1 Tomo Adachi
- ☐ 2 Eloy Arano
- ☐ 3 Ryan Balfe
- ☐ 4 Robert Balint
- ☐ 5 Justin Bettencourt
- ☐ 6 Jamie Borel
- ☐ 7 Candido Brazoban
- ☐ 8 Nick Constantinides
- ☐ 9 Elvis DeLaRosa
- ☐ 10 Dale Dolejsi
- ☐ 11 Juan Encarnacion
- ☐ 12 Tony Fuduric
- ☐ 13 Apostol Garcia
- ☐ 14 Generoso Gonzalez
- ☐ 15 Bobby 'BJ' Jones
- ☐ 16 Graham Koonce
- ☐ 17 Andy Kruger
- ☐ 18 Osvaldo Martinez
- ☐ 19 Rivers Mitchell
- ☐ 20 Brandon Reed
- ☐ 21 Willis Roberts
- ☐ 22 Cesar Ruiz
- ☐ 23 Kazu Shiotani
- ☐ 24 Trad Sobik
- ☐ 25 Chad Stevenson
- ☐ 26 Eric Weber
- ☐ 27 Tony Whiteman
- ☐ 28 Kevin Bradshaw MG
- ☐ 29 Shigeyuki Takahashi CO
- ☐ 30 Mark Gruesbeck TR Checklist

1994 Bristol Tigers Fleer/ProCards

This 30-card standard size set of the 1994 Bristol Tigers, a Rookie Class Appalachian League affiliate of the Detroit Tigers, features white-bordered posed color player photos on its fronts with the player's name, position, team name and Fleer/ProCards logo across the bottom of each card. The white back with vertical light blue stripes carries the player's name at the top, followed by biography and statistics. This issue includes the minor league card debuts of Juan Encarnacion, Daryle Ward and Willis Roberts.

	MINT	NRMT	EXC
COMPLETE SET (30)	8.00	3.60	1.00

- ☐ 3492 Justin Bettencourt
- ☐ 3493 Candido Brazoban
- ☐ 3494 Nick Constantinides
- ☐ 3495 Dale Dolejsi
- ☐ 3496 Tony Fuduric
- ☐ 3497 Generoso Gonzalez
- ☐ 3498 David Kauflin
- ☐ 3499 Osvaldo Martinez
- ☐ 3500 Brandon Reed
- ☐ 3501 Willis Roberts
- ☐ 3502 Trad Sobik
- ☐ 3503 Eric Weber
- ☐ 3504 Tony Whiteman
- ☐ 3505 Robert Balint
- ☐ 3506 Elvis De La Rosa
- ☐ 3507 Chad Stevenson
- ☐ 3508 Eloy Arano
- ☐ 3509 Ryan Balfe
- ☐ 3510 Apostol Garcia
- ☐ 3511 Kirk Hagge
- ☐ 3512 Cesar Ruiz
- ☐ 3513 Keith Smith
- ☐ 3514 Daryle Ward
- ☐ 3515 Jamie Borel
- ☐ 3516 Mike Darr
- ☐ 3517 Juan Encarnacion
- ☐ 3518 Bobby Jones
- ☐ 3519 Andy Kruger
- ☐ 3520 Rivers Mitchell
- ☐ 3521 Checklist

1994 Buffalo Bisons Fleer/ProCards

This 27-card standard size set of the 1994 Buffalo Bisons, a Class AAA American Association affiliate of the Pittsburgh Pirates, features white-bordered posed color player photos on its fronts with the player's name, position, team name and Fleer/ProCards logo across the bottom of each card. The white back with vertical light blue stripes carries the player's name at the top, followed by biography and statistics.

	MINT	NRMT	EXC
COMPLETE SET (28)	5.00	2.20	.60

- ☐ 1828 Archie Corbin
- ☐ 1829 Mike Dyer
- ☐ 1830 Lee Hancock
- ☐ 1831 John Hope
- ☐ 1832 Dan Miceli
- ☐ 1833 Paul Miller
- ☐ 1834 Rich Robertson
- ☐ 1835 Scott Scudder
- ☐ 1836 Brian Shouse
- ☐ 1837 Jeff Tabaka
- ☐ 1838 Tim Wakefield
- ☐ 1839 Travis Willis
- ☐ 1840 Keith Osik
- ☐ 1841 Mandy Romero
- ☐ 1842 Rich Aude
- ☐ 1843 Frank Bolick
- ☐ 1844 Dave Rohde
- ☐ 1845 Mike Simms
- ☐ 1846 John Wehner
- ☐ 1847 Tony Womack
- ☐ 1848 Midre Cummings
- ☐ 1849 Tim Leiper
- ☐ 1850 Darren Reed
- ☐ 1851 Greg Tubbs
- ☐ 1852 Doc Edwards MG
- ☐ 1853 Tom Dettore CO
- ☐ 1854 Julio Garcia CO

1994 Burlington Bees Classic

This 30-card standard size set of the 1994 Burlington Bees, a Class A Midwest League affiliate of the Montreal Expos, features white-bordered posed color player shots on its fronts with the player's name and position, team name and logo and Classic logo appearing across the bottom of each card. On a ghosted team logo, the white back carries the player's name at the top, followed by biography and statistics.

	MINT	NRMT	EXC
COMPLETE SET (30)	8.00	3.60	1.00

- ☐ 1 Matthew Raleigh
- ☐ 2 Juan Batista
- ☐ 3 Jim Boynewicz
- ☐ 4 Josh Bullock
- ☐ 5 Rick Clelland
- ☐ 6 Fernando DaSilva
- ☐ 7 Josue Estrada
- ☐ 8 Jeff Foster
- ☐ 9 Bobby Henley
- ☐ 10 Al Kermode
- ☐ 11 Aaron Knieper
- ☐ 12 Vincent LaChance
- ☐ 13 Charles Lee
- ☐ 14 Tony Marabella
- ☐ 15 Andy Markham
- ☐ 16 Shane McCubbin
- ☐ 17 Marc Niethammer
- ☐ 18 Alex Pacheco
- ☐ 19 John Pachot
- ☐ 20 Tomas Perez
- ☐ 21 Tom Phelps
- ☐ 22 Scott Pisciotta
- ☐ 23 Tom Schneider
- ☐ 24 Chris Schwab
- ☐ 25 Jason Woodring
- ☐ 26 Lorenzo Bundy MG
- ☐ 27 Jeff Fischer CO
- ☐ 28 Steven Alonzo CO
- ☐ 29 Ryan Richeal GM
- ☐ 30 Checklist

1994 Burlington Bees Fleer/ProCards

This 29-card standard size set of the 1994 Burlington Bees, a Class A Midwest League affiliate of the Montreal Expos, features white-bordered posed color player photos on its fronts with the player's name, position, team name and Fleer/ProCards logo across the bottom of each card. The white back with vertical light blue stripes carries the player's name at the top, followed by biography and statistics.

	MINT	NRMT	EXC
COMPLETE SET (29)	5.00	2.20	.60

- ☐ 1072 Jim Boynewicz
- ☐ 1073 Josh Bullock
- ☐ 1074 Rick Clelland
- ☐ 1075 Fernando DaSilva
- ☐ 1076 Russell Handy
- ☐ 1077 Al Kermode
- ☐ 1078 Aaron Knieper
- ☐ 1079 Andy Markham
- ☐ 1080 Alex Pacheco
- ☐ 1081 Tom Schneider
- ☐ 1082 Jason Woodring
- ☐ 1083 Bob Henley
- ☐ 1084 Shane McCubbin
- ☐ 1085 John Pachot
- ☐ 1086 Juan Batista
- ☐ 1087 Trace Coquillette
- ☐ 1088 John Mahalik
- ☐ 1089 Tony Marabella
- ☐ 1090 Marc Niethammer
- ☐ 1091 Tomas Perez
- ☐ 1092 Matt Raleigh
- ☐ 1093 Jesus Campos
- ☐ 1094 Josue Estrada
- ☐ 1095 Vince LaChance
- ☐ 1096 Chris Schwab
- ☐ 1097 Lorenzo Bundy MG
- ☐ 1098 Steve Alonzo CO
- ☐ 1099 Jeff Fischer CO
- ☐ 1100 Checklist

1994 Burlington Indians Classic

This 30-card standard size set of the 1994 Burlington Indians, a Rookie Class Appalachian League affiliate of the Cleveland Indians, features white-bordered posed color player shots on its fronts with the player's name and position, team name and logo and Classic logo appearing across the bottom of each card. On a ghosted team logo, the white back carries the player's name at the top, followed by biography and statistics. This issue includes the minor league card debut of Russ Branyan.

	MINT	NRMT	EXC
COMPLETE SET (30)	15.00	6.75	1.85

☐ 1 Carlos Arellano
☐ 2 Darnell Batiste
☐ 3 Russ Branyan
☐ 4 David Caldwell
☐ 5 Mack Chambers
☐ 6 Tyler Cheff
☐ 7 Matt Hobbie
☐ 8 Reggie Ignash
☐ 9 Blair Jensen
☐ 10 Andreaus Lewis
☐ 11 Elliot Lowry
☐ 12 Johnny Martinez
☐ 13 Michael Mastrullo
☐ 14 Pepe McNeal
☐ 15 Rafael Mesa
☐ 16 Quinn Murphy
☐ 17 Robert Oldham
☐ 18 Steve Ortiz
☐ 19 Walter Owens
☐ 20 Brett Palmer
☐ 21 Chan Perry
☐ 22 Arnold Santiago
☐ 23 Mike Stadler
☐ 24 Brad Tiller
☐ 25 Bryan Warner
☐ 26 Teddy Warrecker
☐ 27 Lenny Weber
☐ 28 Brian Wisler
☐ 29 Jim Gabella
☐ 30 David Lassiter

1994 Burlington Indians Fleer/ProCards

This 31-card standard size set of the 1994 Burlington Indians, a Rookie Class Appalachian League affiliate of the Cleveland Indians, features white-bordered posed color player photos on its fronts with the player's name, position, team name and Fleer/ProCards logo across the bottom of each card. The white back with vertical light blue stripes carries the player's name at the top, followed by biography and statistics. This issue includes the minor league card debuts of Russ Branyan and Bartolo Colon.

	MINT	NRMT	EXC
COMPLETE SET (31)	15.00	6.75	1.85

☐ 3783 Carlos Arellano
☐ 3784 David Caldwell
☐ 3785 Camp Campbell
☐ 3786 Bartolo Colon
☐ 3787 Johnny Martinez
☐ 3788 Rafael Mesa
☐ 3789 Gonzalo Mojica
☐ 3790 Bob Oldham
☐ 3791 Steve Ortiz
☐ 3792 Julio Perez
☐ 3793 Marvin Pierce
☐ 3794 Teddy Warrecker
☐ 3795 Lenny Weber
☐ 3796 Brian Wisler
☐ 3797 Tyler Cheff
☐ 3798 Pepe McNeal
☐ 3799 Mike Stadler
☐ 3800 Darnell Batiste
☐ 3801 Russell Branyan
☐ 3802 Mack Chambers
☐ 3803 Quinn Murphy
☐ 3804 Chan Perry
☐ 3805 Arnold Santiago
☐ 3806 Brad Tiller
☐ 3807 Matt Hobbie
☐ 3808 Reggie Ignash
☐ 3809 Andreaus Lewis
☐ 3810 Mike Mastrullo
☐ 3811 Walter Owens
☐ 3812 Bryan Warner
☐ 3813 Checklist

1994 Butte Copper Kings Sports Pro

	MINT	NRMT	EXC
COMPLETE SET (30)	7.00	3.10	.85

☐ 1 Terry Wright
☐ 2 Norman Williams
☐ 3 Tom Hutchinson
☐ 4 Nate Olmstead
☐ 5 Rob Linfante
☐ 6 Rich Howard
☐ 7 Scott Vatter
☐ 8 Brian Reed
☐ 9 Greg Rosar
☐ 10 Leigh Santos
☐ 11 Carl Grinstead
☐ 12 Frank Lesperance
☐ 13 Shane Hill
☐ 14 Cecil Aswegan
☐ 15 Toraino Golston
☐ 16 Kale Gilmore
☐ 17 Mike Moyle
☐ 18 Chris Plumlee
☐ 19 Gresham Fortune
☐ 20 J.J. Gottsch
☐ 21 Josh Montgomery
☐ 22 Darren Riley
☐ 23 Chris Spenrath
☐ 24 Doug Valdez
☐ 25 Matt Bragga
☐ 26 Mike Collins
☐ 27 Bruce Crabbe MG
☐ 28 Mark Sims CO
☐ 29 Stan Jefferson CO
☐ 30 Chris Tomashoff TR

1994 Calgary Cannons Fleer/ProCards

This 27-card standard size set of the 1994 Calgary Cannons, a Class AAA Pacific Coast League affiliate of the Seattle Mariners, features white-bordered posed color player photos on its fronts with the player's name, position, team name and Fleer/ProCards logo across the bottom of each card. The white back with vertical light blue stripes carries the player's name at the top, followed by biography and statistics.

	MINT	NRMT	EXC
COMPLETE SET (27)	5.00	2.20	.60

☐ 781 Todd Burns
☐ 782 Jim Converse
☐ 783 Jeff Darwin
☐ 784 Brad Holman
☐ 785 Bob MacDonald
☐ 786 Tony Phillips
☐ 787 Bill Risley
☐ 788 Roger Salkeld
☐ 789 Alex Sanchez
☐ 790 Weston Weber
☐ 791 Jeff Williams
☐ 792 Clint Zavaras
☐ 793 Chris Howard
☐ 794 Jerry Willard
☐ 795 Tommy Hinzo
☐ 796 Tommy LeVasseur
☐ 797 Anthony Manahan
☐ 798 Luis Quinones
☐ 799 Luis Sojo
☐ 800 Dale Sveum
☐ 801 Quinn Mack
☐ 802 Marc Newfield
☐ 803 John Tejcek
☐ 804 Steve Smith MG
☐ 805 Dave Brundage CO
☐ 806 Bobby Cuellar CO
☐ 807 Checklist

1994 Canton-Akron Indians Fleer/ProCards

This 30-card standard size set of the 1994 Canton-Akron Indians, a Class AA Eastern League affiliate of the Cleveland Indians, features white-bordered posed color player photos on its fronts with the player's name, position, team name and Fleer/ProCards logo across the bottom of each card. The white back with vertical light blue stripes carries the player's name at the top, followed by biography and statistics.

	MINT	NRMT	EXC
COMPLETE SET (30)	5.00	2.20	.60

☐ 3107 Paul Byrd
☐ 3108 John Carter
☐ 3109 Ramser Correa
☐ 3110 Carlos Crawford
☐ 3111 Fred Dabney
☐ 3112 Ian Doyle
☐ 3113 Alan Embree
☐ 3114 Jason Fronio
☐ 3115 Apolinar Garcia
☐ 3116 John Hrusovsky
☐ 3117 Kevin Logsdon
☐ 3118 Greg McCarthy
☐ 3119 Cesar Perez
☐ 3120 Mike Crosby
☐ 3121 Ryan Martindale
☐ 3122 Damian Jackson
☐ 3123 Pat Maxwell
☐ 3124 Paul Meade
☐ 3125 Rouglas Odor
☐ 3126 Clyde Pough
☐ 3127 Murph Proctor
☐ 3128 Mike Sarbaugh
☐ 3129 Pat Bryant
☐ 3130 Ray Harvey
☐ 3131 Marc Marini
☐ 3132 Tony Mitchell
☐ 3133 Ted Kubiak MG
☐ 3134 Mike Brown CO
☐ 3135 Ken Rowe CO
☐ 3136 Checklist

1994 Capital City Bombers Classic

This 30-card standard size set of the 1994 Capital City Bombers, a Class A South Atlantic affiliate of the New York Mets, features white-bordered posed color player shots on its fronts with the player's name and position, team name and logo and Classic logo appearing across the bottom of each card. On a ghosted team logo, the white back carries the player's name at the top, followed by biography and statistics.

	MINT	NRMT	EXC
COMPLETE SET (30)	8.00	3.60	1.00

☐ 1 Preston J.R. Wilson
☐ 2 Gary Collum
☐ 3 Jeff Cosman
☐ 4 Kirk Demyan
☐ 5 Cesar Diaz
☐ 6 Tom Engle
☐ 7 Rob Gontkosky
☐ 8 Steve Grennan
☐ 9 Rafael Guerrero
☐ 10 Al Hammell
☐ 11 Sean Kenny
☐ 12 Jeff Kiraly
☐ 13 Kevin Lewis
☐ 14 Allen McDill
☐ 15 Brandon Newell
☐ 16 J.J. Osentowski
☐ 17 Paul Petrulis
☐ 18 Sandy Pichardo
☐ 19 Al Shirley
☐ 20 Dave Swanson
☐ 21 Jeff Tam
☐ 22 Randy Warner
☐ 23 Mike Welch
☐ 24 Mark Wipf
☐ 25 David Zuniga
☐ 26 Ron Washington MG
☐ 27 Dave Jorn CO
☐ 28 John Gibbons CO
☐ 29 Logo Card
☐ 30 Checklist

1994 Capital City Bombers Fleer/ProCards

This 29-card standard size set of the 1994 Capital City Bombers, a Class A South Atlantic affiliate of the New York Mets, features white-bordered posed color player photos on its fronts with the player's name, position, team name and Fleer/ProCards logo across the bottom of each card. The white back with vertical light blue stripes carries the player's name at the top, followed by biography and statistics.

	MINT	NRMT	EXC
COMPLETE SET (29)	5.00	2.20	.60

☐ 1742 Jeff Cosman
☐ 1743 Kirk Demyan
☐ 1744 Tom Engle
☐ 1745 Robert Gontkowsky
☐ 1746 Steve Grennan
☐ 1747 Sean Kenny
☐ 1748 Allen McDill
☐ 1749 Brandon Newell
☐ 1750 David Swanson
☐ 1751 Jeff Tam
☐ 1752 Mike Welch
☐ 1753 Cesar Diaz
☐ 1754 Al Hammell
☐ 1755 Kevin Lewis
☐ 1756 Jeff Kiraly
☐ 1757 Jared Osentowski
☐ 1758 Paul Petrulis
☐ 1759 Sandy Pichardo
☐ 1760 Preston Wilson
☐ 1761 Dave Zuniga
☐ 1762 Gary Collum
☐ 1763 Rafael Guerrero
☐ 1764 Al Shirley
☐ 1765 Randy Warner
☐ 1766 Mark Wipf
☐ 1767 Ron Washington MG
☐ 1768 John Gibbons CO
☐ 1769 Dave Jorn CO
☐ 1770 Checklist

1994 Carolina League All-Stars Fleer/ProCards

	MINT	NRMT	EXC
COMPLETE SET (53)	15.00	6.75	1.85

☐ CAR1 Kimera Bartee
☐ CAR2 B.J. Waszgis
☐ CAR3 Pat Murphy
☐ CAR4 Trot Nixon
☐ CAR5 Bill Selby
☐ CAR6 Essex Burton
☐ CAR7 Michael Call
☐ CAR8 Jimmy Hurst
☐ CAR9 Sean Johnston
☐ CAR10 Eddie Pearson
☐ CAR11 Jason Pierson
☐ CAR12 Craig Wilson
☐ CAR13 Chris Woodfin
☐ CAR14 Mike Bovee
☐ CAR15 Johnny Damon
☐ CAR16 Bart Evans
☐ CAR17 Lance Jennings
☐ CAR18 Mike Jirschele MG
☐ CAR19 Gary Lance CO
☐ CAR20 Sixto Lezcano CO
☐ CAR21 Jim Pittsley
☐ CAR22 Kris Ralston
☐ CAR23 Chad Spaulding TR
☐ CAR24 Andy Stewart
☐ CAR25 Larry Sutton
☐ CAR26 Dilson Torres
☐ CAR27 Jamie Arnold
☐ CAR28 Damon Hollins
☐ CAR29 Darrell May
☐ CAR30 Carl Schultz
☐ CAR31 Robert Smith
☐ CAR32 Mike Warner
☐ CAR33 Juan Andujar
☐ CAR34 Daron Kirkreit
☐ CAR35 Jonathan Nunnally
☐ CAR36 Steve Soliz
☐ CAR37 Danny Clyburn
☐ CAR38 Jay Cranford
☐ CAR39 Sean Evans
☐ CAR40 Jason Kendall
☐ CAR41 Sean Lawrence
☐ CAR42 Marc Pisciotta
☐ CAR43 Chance Sanford
☐ CAR44 Mark Berry MG
☐ CAR45 Derek Botelho CO
☐ CAR46 William Brunson
☐ CAR47 Chad Fox
☐ CAR48 Bob Jesperson
☐ CAR49 Ricky Magdaleno
☐ CAR50 Toby Rumfield
☐ CAR51 Tom Spencer
☐ CAR52 Pat Watkins
☐ CAR53 Checklist

1994 Carolina Mudcats Fleer/ProCards

This 28-card standard size set of the 1994 Carolina Mudcats, a Class AA Southern League affiliate of the Pittsburgh Pirates, features white-bordered posed color player photos on its fronts with the player's name, position, team name and Fleer/ProCards logo across the bottom of each card. The white back with vertical light blue stripes carries the player's name at the top, followed by biography and statistics.

	MINT	NRMT	EXC
COMPLETE SET (28)	6.00	2.70	.75

☐ 1569 Brett Backlund
☐ 1570 Jason Christiansen
☐ 1571 Mariano De Los Santos
☐ 1572 Dennis Konuszewski
☐ 1573 Michel LaPlante
☐ 1574 Jon Lieber
☐ 1575 Steve Loaiza
☐ 1576 Jeff McCurry
☐ 1577 Mark Mesewicz
☐ 1578 Roberto Ramirez
☐ 1579 Matt Ruebel
☐ 1580 Kevin Rychel
☐ 1581 Mike Zimmerman
☐ 1582 Tim Edge
☐ 1583 Angel Encarnacion
☐ 1584 Michael Brown
☐ 1585 Mark Johnson
☐ 1586 Jim Krevokuch
☐ 1587 Kevin Polcovich
☐ 1588 Bruce Schreiber
☐ 1589 William Suero
☐ 1590 Jermaine Allensworth
☐ 1591 Trey Beamon
☐ 1592 Stanton Cameron
☐ 1593 Ramon Espinosa
☐ 1594 Bobby Meacham MG
☐ 1595 Wayne Garland CO
☐ 1596 Checklist

1994 Cedar Rapids Kernels Classic

This 30-card standard size set of the 1994 Cedar Rapids Kernels, a Class A Midwest League affiliate of the California Angels, features white-bordered posed color player shots on its fronts with the player's name and position, team name and logo and Classic logo appearing across the bottom of each card. On a ghosted team logo, the white back carries the player's name at the top, followed by biography and statistics. This issue includes the minor league card debut of Matt Perisho.

	MINT	NRMT	EXC
COMPLETE SET (30)	7.00	3.10	.85

☐ 1 DeShawn Warren
☐ 2 Jose Aguirre Jr.
☐ 3 Lyall Barwick
☐ 4 Willard Brown
☐ 5 Jamie Burke
☐ 6 Jovino Carvajal
☐ 7 Steve Cook
☐ 8 Derrin Doty
☐ 9 Brooks Drysdale
☐ 10 Geoff Edsell
☐ 11 Geoffrey Grenert
☐ 12 Aaron Guiel
☐ 13 Juan Henderson
☐ 14 Jason Herrick
☐ 15 Aaron Latarola
☐ 16 David Kessler
☐ 17 Jeff Knox
☐ 18 Tony Moeder
☐ 19 Matthew Perisho
☐ 20 Mark Simmons
☐ 21 Shawn Slade
☐ 22 Brian Willard
☐ 23 Tom Lawless MG
☐ 24 Joe Georger CO
☐ 25 Charlie Romero CO
☐ 26 Douglas Baker TR
☐ 27 Logo Card UER
(Card back says 29, should be 27)
☐ 28 Logo Card UER
(Card back says 29, should be 28)
☐ 29 Logo Card
☐ 30 Checklist

1994 Cedar Rapids Kernels Fleer/ProCards

This 27-card standard size set of the 1994 Cedar Rapids Kernels, a Class A Midwest League affiliate of the California Angels, features white-bordered posed color player photos on its fronts with the player's name, position, team name and Fleer/ProCards logo across the bottom of each card. The white back with vertical light blue stripes carries the player's name at the top, followed by biography and statistics. This issue includes the minor league card debut of Matt Perisho.

	MINT	NRMT	EXC
COMPLETE SET (27)	6.00	2.70	.75

☐ 1101 Jose Aguirre
☐ 1102 Willie Brown
☐ 1103 Brooks Drysdale
☐ 1104 Geoff Edsell
☐ 1105 Geoff Grenert
☐ 1106 John Lloyd
☐ 1107 Matt Perisho
☐ 1108 Shawn Slade
☐ 1109 Deshawn Warren
☐ 1110 Brian Williard
☐ 1111 Lyall Barwick
☐ 1112 Dave Kessler
☐ 1113 Jamie Burke
☐ 1114 Steve Cook
☐ 1115 Aaron Guiel
☐ 1116 Juan Henderson
☐ 1117 Tony Moeder
☐ 1118 Mark Simmons
☐ 1119 Julian Vizcaino
☐ 1120 Jovino Carvajal
☐ 1121 Derrin Doty
☐ 1122 Jason Herrick
☐ 1123 Aaron latarola
☐ 1124 Tom Lawless MG
☐ 1125 Joe Georger CO
☐ 1126 Charlie Romero CO
☐ 1127 Checklist

1994 Central Valley Rockies Classic

This 30-card standard size set of the 1994 Central Valley Rockies, a Class A California League affiliate of the Colorado Rockies, features white-bordered posed color player shots on its fronts with the player's name and position, team name and logo and Classic logo appearing across the bottom of each card. On a ghosted team logo, the white back carries the player's name at the top, followed by biography and statistics. .

	MINT	NRMT	EXC
COMPLETE SET (30)	10.00	4.50	1.25

☐ 1 Joel Moore
☐ 2 Garvin Alston
☐ 3 Steve Bernhardt
☐ 4 Curt Conley
☐ 5 Angel Echevarria
☐ 6 Mike Farmer
☐ 7 Ryan Freeburg
☐ 8 Mauricio Gonzales
☐ 9 Chris Henderson
☐ 10 Jason Hutchins
☐ 11 Jason Johnson
☐ 12 Terry Jones
☐ 13 John Myrow
☐ 14 Shigeki Noguchi
☐ 15 Erik O'Donnell
☐ 16 Mike Oakland
☐ 17 Ben Ortman
☐ 18 Neifi Perez
☐ 19 Mike Pineiro
☐ 20 Bryan Rekar
☐ 21 Kenichi Sasaki
☐ 22 Will Scalzitti
☐ 23 Tom Schmidt
☐ 24 Mark Voisard
☐ 25 Mike Zolecki
☐ 26 Bill Hayes MG
☐ 27 Chuck Estrada CO
☐ 28 Tomoyoshi Ohishi CO
☐ 29 Jim Eppard CO
☐ 30 Bill Borowski TR
Checklist

1994 Central Valley Rockies Fleer/ProCards

This 30-card standard size set of the 1994 Central Valley Rockies, a Class A California League affiliate of the Colorado Rockies, features white-bordered posed color player photos on its fronts with the player's name, position, team name and Fleer/ProCards logo across the bottom of each card. The white back with vertical light blue stripes carries the player's name at the top, followed by biography and statistics.

	MINT	NRMT	EXC
COMPLETE SET (30)	7.00	3.10	.85

☐ 3193 Garvin Alston
☐ 3194 Curt Conley
☐ 3195 Mike Farmer
☐ 3196 Chris Henderson
☐ 3197 Jason Hutchins
☐ 3198 J.J. Johnson
☐ 3199 Joel Moore
☐ 3200 Shigaki Noguchi
☐ 3201 Erik O'Donnell
☐ 3202 Bryan Rekar
☐ 3203 Kenishi Sasaki
☐ 3204 Mark Voisard
☐ 3205 Mike Zolecki
☐ 3206 Ryan Freeburg
☐ 3207 Mike Pineiro
☐ 3208 Will Scalzitti
☐ 3209 Steve Bernhardt
☐ 3210 Mauricio Gonzalez
☐ 3211 Mike Oakland
☐ 3212 Neifi Perez
☐ 3213 Tom Schmidt
☐ 3214 Angel Echevarria
☐ 3215 Terry Jones
☐ 3216 John Myrow
☐ 3217 Ben Ortman
☐ 3218 Bill Hayes MG
☐ 3219 Jim Eppard CO
☐ 3220 Chuck Estrada CO
☐ 3221 Tomoyoshi Ohishi CO
☐ 3222 Checklist

1994 Charleston Riverdogs Classic

This 30-card standard size set of the 1994 Charleston RiverDogs, a Class A South Atlantic League affiliate of the Texas Rangers, features white-bordered posed color player shots on its fronts with the player's name and position, team name and logo and Classic logo appearing across the bottom of each card. On a ghosted team logo, the white back carries the player's name at the top, followed by biography and statistics. This issue includes the minor league card debuts of Mike Bell and Edwin Diaz.

	MINT	NRMT	EXC
COMPLETE SET (30)	12.00	5.50	1.50

☐ 1 Mike Bell
☐ 2 Brian Blair
☐ 3 Jeffrey Davis
☐ 4 Domingo Delzine
☐ 5 Edwin Diaz
☐ 6 Larry Ephan
☐ 7 Bert Gerhart III
☐ 8 Mario Gonzalez
☐ 9 Larry Hanlon
☐ 10 Rob Kell
☐ 11 Toure' Knighton
☐ 12 Andreaus Lewis
☐ 13 Leland Macon
☐ 14 Joe Morvay
☐ 15 Cory Pearson
☐ 16 Querbin Reynoso
☐ 17 Jeff Runion
☐ 18 Julio Santana
☐ 19 Rodney Seip
☐ 20 Dan Smith
☐ 21 Chris Unrat
☐ 22 Andrew Vessel
☐ 23 Marty Watson
☐ 24 Beck Wells
☐ 25 Greg Wilming
☐ 26 Walt Williams
☐ 27 Allen Anderson
☐ 28 George Threadgill
☐ 29 Sponsor
☐ 30 Charlie the RiverDog CL

1994 Charleston RiverDogs Fleer/ProCards

This 29-card standard size set of the 1994 Charleston RiverDogs, a Class A South Atlantic League affiliate of the Texas Rangers, features white-bordered posed color player photos on its fronts with the player's name, position, team name and Fleer/ProCards logo across the bottom of each card. The white back with vertical light blue stripes carries the player's name at the top, followed by biography and statistics. This issue includes the minor league card debuts of Mike Bell and Edwin Diaz.

	MINT	NRMT	EXC
COMPLETE SET (29)	8.00	3.60	1.00

☐ 2664 Jeff Davis
☐ 2665 Domingo Delzine
☐ 2666 Bert Gerhart
☐ 2667 Rob Kell
☐ 2668 Toure Knighton
☐ 2669 Joe Morvay
☐ 2670 Querbin Reynoso
☐ 2671 Jeff Runion
☐ 2672 Julio Santana
☐ 2673 Rod Seip
☐ 2674 Dan Smith
☐ 2675 Greg Willming
☐ 2676 Larry Ephan
☐ 2677 Chris Unrat
☐ 2678 Beck Wells
☐ 2679 Mike Bell
☐ 2680 Brian Blair
☐ 2681 Edwin Diaz
☐ 2682 Mario Gonzalez
☐ 2683 Larry Hanlon
☐ 2684 A.D. Lewis
☐ 2685 Leland Macon
☐ 2686 Cory Pearson
☐ 2687 Andy Vessel
☐ 2688 Marty Watson
☐ 2689 Walt Williams MG
☐ 2690 Allan Anderson CO
☐ 2691 George Threadgill CO
☐ 2692 Checklist

1994 Charleston Wheelers Classic

This 30-card standard size set of the 1994 Charleston Wheelers, a Class A South Atlantic League affiliate of the Cincinnati Reds, features white-bordered posed color player shots on its fronts with the player's name and position, team name and logo and Classic logo appearing across the bottom of each card. On a ghosted team logo, the white back carries the player's name at the top, followed by biography and statistics.

	MINT	NRMT	EXC
COMPLETE SET (30)	8.00	3.60	1.00

☐ 1 Steve Gann
☐ 2 Chris Sexton
☐ 3 Chad Akers
☐ 4 Johnny Carvajal
☐ 5 Chad Connors
☐ 6 Cobi Cradle
☐ 7 Randy DeBruhl
☐ 8 Steve Eddie
☐ 9 Roger Etheridge
☐ 10 Todd Etler
☐ 11 Ricky Gonzalez
☐ 12 Danny Hagan
☐ 13 Pete Harvell
☐ 14 Jon Hebel
☐ 15 Bob Jesperson
☐ 16 Brad Keenan
☐ 17 Johnny LaMar
☐ 18 Luis Ordaz
☐ 19 Danny Oyas
☐ 20 Ricky Pickett
☐ 21 Chris Reed
☐ 22 Trey Rutledge
☐ 23 Rodney Thomas
☐ 24 Justin Towle
☐ 25 Steve Wilkerson
☐ 26 Mack Jenkins CO
☐ 27 Tom Iverson TR
☐ 28 Logo Card UER
Card back says 29 and should say 28
☐ 29 Logo Card
☐ 30 Checklist

1994 Charleston Wheelers Fleer/ProCards

This 28-card standard size set of the 1994 Charleston Wheelers, a Class A South Atlantic League affiliate of the Cincinnati Reds, features white-bordered posed color player photos on its fronts with the player's name, position, team name and Fleer/ProCards logo across the bottom of each card. The white back with vertical light blue stripes carries the player's name at the top, followed by biography and statistics.

	MINT	NRMT	EXC
COMPLETE SET (28)	5.00	2.20	.60

☐ 2693 Chad Connors
☐ 2694 Roger Etheridge
☐ 2695 Todd Etler
☐ 2696 Danny Hagan
☐ 2697 Pete Harvell
☐ 2698 Jon Hebel
☐ 2699 Brad Keenan
☐ 2700 Pete Magre
☐ 2701 Ricky Pickett
☐ 2702 Chris Reed
☐ 2703 Trey Rutledge
☐ 2704 Steve Wilkerson
☐ 2705 Randy DeBruhl
☐ 2706 Justin Towle
☐ 2707 Derek Valenzuela
☐ 2708 Chad Akers
☐ 2709 Jhonny Carvajal
☐ 2710 Steve Eddie
☐ 2711 Steve Gann
☐ 2712 Johnny LaMar
☐ 2713 Luis Ordaz
☐ 2714 Chris Sexton
☐ 2715 Cobi Cradle
☐ 2716 Danny Oyas
☐ 2717 Rod Thomas
☐ 2718 Tom Nieto MG
☐ 2719 Mac Jenkins CO
☐ 2720 Checklist

1994 Charlotte Knights Fleer/ProCards

This 26-card standard size set of the 1994 Charlotte Knights, a Class AAA International League affiliate of the Cleveland Indians, features white-bordered posed color player photos on its fronts with the player's name, position, team name and Fleer/ProCards logo across the bottom of each card. The white back with vertical light blue stripes carries the player's name at the top, followed by biography and statistics.

	MINT	NRMT	EXC
COMPLETE SET (26)	5.00	2.20	.60

☐ 887 Jason Grimsley
☐ 888 Jeff Johnson
☐ 889 Calvin Jones
☐ 890 Tom Kramer
☐ 891 Albie Lopez
☐ 892 David Lynch
☐ 893 Dave Mlicki
☐ 894 Chad Ogea
☐ 895 Julian Tavarez
☐ 896 Bill Wertz
☐ 897 Craig Colbert
☐ 898 Jesse Levis
☐ 899 David Bell
☐ 900 Chris Cron
☐ 901 Miguel Flores
☐ 902 Rene Gonzales
☐ 903 Tim Jones
☐ 904 Herb Perry
☐ 905 Ruben Amaro
☐ 906 Greg Briley
☐ 907 Brian Giles
☐ 908 Omar Ramirez
☐ 909 Brian Graham MG
☐ 910 Dyar Miller CO
☐ 911 Donell Nixon CO
☐ 912 Checklist

1994 Charlotte Rangers Fleer/ProCards

This 27-card standard size set of the 1994 Charlotte Rangers, a Class A Florida State League affiliate of the Texas Rangers, features white-bordered posed color player photos on its fronts with the player's name, position, team name and Fleer/ProCards logo across the bottom of each card. The white back with vertical light blue stripes carries the player's name at the top, followed by biography and statistics.

	MINT	NRMT	EXC
COMPLETE SET (27)	5.00	2.20	.60

☐ 2489 Mike Anderson
☐ 2490 Mark Brandenburg
☐ 2491 Mike Cather
☐ 2492 Pete Hartmann
☐ 2493 David Manning
☐ 2494 Jerry Martin
☐ 2495 Dave Pike
☐ 2496 Scotty Smith
☐ 2497 Earl Wheeler
☐ 2498 Chad Wiley
☐ 2499 Frank Charles
☐ 2500 Darryl Kennedy

☐ 2501 Jon Pitts
☐ 2502 Osmani Estrada
☐ 2503 Scott Malone
☐ 2504 Guillermo Mercedes
☐ 2505 Franklin Parra
☐ 2506 Wes Sims
☐ 2507 Jack Stanczak
☐ 2508 Malvin Matos
☐ 2509 Marc Sagmoen
☐ 2510 Jose Texidor
☐ 2511 Brian Thomas
☐ 2512 Tommy Thompson MG
☐ 2513 Darrin Garner CO
☐ 2514 Marvin White CO
☐ 2515 Checklist

1994 Chattanooga Lookouts Fleer/ProCards

This 27-card standard size set of the 1994 Chattanooga Lookouts, a Class AA Southern League affiliate of the Cincinnati Reds, features white-bordered posed color player photos on its fronts with the player's name, position, team name and Fleer/ProCards logo across the bottom of each card. The white back with vertical light blue stripes carries the player's name at the top, followed by biography and statistics.

	MINT	NRMT	EXC
COMPLETE SET (27)	5.00	2.20	.60

☐ 1350 Blaine Beatty
☐ 1351 John Burgos
☐ 1352 John Courtright
☐ 1353 Calvain Culberson
☐ 1354 Glen Cullop
☐ 1355 Eddie Dixon
☐ 1356 Tim Fortugno
☐ 1357 John Hrusovsky
☐ 1358 Scott Sullivan
☐ 1359 Marcos Vazquez
☐ 1360 Troy Buckley
☐ 1361 Jon Fuller
☐ 1362 Tim Belk
☐ 1363 Adam Hyzdu
☐ 1364 Frank Kremblas
☐ 1365 Eric Owens
☐ 1366 Bobby Perna
☐ 1367 Pokey Reese
☐ 1368 Bubba Smith
☐ 1369 Steve Gibralter
☐ 1370 Cleveland Ladell
☐ 1371 Mark Merchant
☐ 1372 Chad Mottola
☐ 1373 Pat Kelly MG
☐ 1374 Terry Abbott CO
☐ 1375 Tommy Dunbar CO
☐ 1376 Checklist

1994 Classic

	MINT	NRMT	EXC
COMPLETE SET (200)	15.00	6.75	1.85
COMMON CARD (1-200)	.05	.02	.01
☐ 1 Michael Jordan	3.00	1.35	.35
☐ 2 Felipe Lira	.05	.02	.01
☐ 3 Jose Silva	.05	.02	.01
☐ 4 Turi Sanchez	.05	.02	.01
☐ 5 Marcus Jensen	.05	.02	.01
☐ 6 Julio Santana	.05	.02	.01
☐ 7 Angel Martinez	.05	.02	.01
☐ 8 Jose Herrera	.05	.02	.01
☐ 9 D.J. Boston	.05	.02	.01
☐ 10 Trot Nixon	.15	.07	.02
☐ 11 Trey Beamon	.30	.14	.04
☐ 12 Danny Clyburn	.25	.11	.03
☐ 13 John Wasdin	.15	.07	.02
☐ 14 Vince Moore	.05	.02	.01
☐ 15 Vic Darensbourg	.05	.02	.01
☐ 16 Kevin Gallaher	.05	.02	.01
☐ 17 Julio Bruno	.05	.02	.01
☐ 18 Terrell Lowery	.05	.02	.01
☐ 19 Phil Geisler	.05	.02	.01
☐ 20 Chan Ho Park	.60	.25	.07
☐ 21 Chad McConnell	.05	.02	.01
☐ 22 Ricky Bottalico	.20	.09	.03
☐ 23 Jim Pittsley	.15	.07	.02
☐ 24 Gabe Martinez	.05	.02	.01
☐ 25 Johnny Damon	.60	.25	.07
☐ 26 Basil Shabazz	.05	.02	.01
☐ 27 Billy Ashley	.05	.02	.01
☐ 28 Andy Pettitte	1.25	.55	.16
☐ 29 Robert Ellis	.05	.02	.01
☐ 30 Mike Zolecki	.05	.02	.01
☐ 31 AS League Card #1	.05	.02	.01
☐ 32 John Burke	.05	.02	.01
☐ 33 Chris Snopek	.15	.07	.02
☐ 34 Mark Thompson	.05	.02	.01
☐ 35 Jimmy Haynes	.05	.02	.01
☐ 36 Ron Villone	.05	.02	.01
☐ 37 Curtis Goodwin	.05	.02	.01
☐ 38 Tim Belk	.05	.02	.01
☐ 39 Rod Henderson	.05	.02	.01
☐ 40 Butch Huskey	.05	.02	.01
☐ 41 Chris Smith	.05	.02	.01
☐ 42 B.J. Wallace	.05	.02	.01
☐ 43 Guillermo Mercedes	.05	.02	.01
☐ 44 Ugueth Urbina	.05	.02	.01
☐ 45 Fausto Cruz	.05	.02	.01
☐ 46 Julian Tavarez	.05	.02	.01
☐ 47 Scott Lydy	.05	.02	.01
☐ 48 Darren Burton	.05	.02	.01
☐ 49 Mac Suzuki	.05	.02	.01
☐ 50 Kirk Presley	.15	.07	.02
☐ 51 Alex Rodriguez CL	.50	.23	.06
☐ 52 Armando Benitez	.05	.02	.01
☐ 53 Rodney Pedraza	.05	.02	.01
☐ 54 LaTroy Hawkins	.05	.02	.01
☐ 55 Rick Forney	.05	.02	.01
☐ 56 Tripp Cromer	.05	.02	.01
☐ 57 Andres Berumen	.05	.02	.01
☐ 58 Terry Bradshaw	.05	.02	.01
☐ 59 Omar Ramirez	.05	.02	.01
☐ 60 Derek Jeter	1.50	.70	.19
☐ 61 Kerwin Moore	.05	.02	.01
☐ 62 Andy Larkin	.15	.07	.02
☐ 63 Neifi Perez	.20	.09	.03
☐ 64 Casey Whitten	.05	.02	.01
☐ 65 Jon Ratliff	.05	.02	.01
☐ 66 J.J. Johnson	.05	.02	.01
☐ 67 Preston Wilson	.20	.09	.03
☐ 68 Jason Isringhausen	.40	.18	.05
☐ 69 Adam Meinershagen	.05	.02	.01
☐ 70 Rondell White	.40	.18	.05
☐ 71 Shannon Stewart	.15	.07	.02
☐ 72 Keith Heberling	.05	.02	.01
☐ 73 Ruben Rivera	2.50	1.10	.30
☐ 74 Mike Lieberthal	.15	.07	.02
☐ 75 Damon Hollins	.15	.07	.02
☐ 76 Jason Jacome	.05	.02	.01
☐ 77 Amaury Telemaco	.05	.02	.01
☐ 78 Scott Talanoa	.05	.02	.01
☐ 79 Dave Stevens	.05	.02	.01
☐ 80 Brien Taylor	.05	.02	.01
☐ 81 AS League Card #2	.05	.02	.01
☐ 82 Brian Barber	.05	.02	.01
☐ 83 Ray Durham	.75	.35	.09
☐ 84 Brent Bowers	.05	.02	.01
☐ 85 Shane Andrews	.05	.02	.01
☐ 86 Gabe White	.05	.02	.01
☐ 87 Midre Cummings	.05	.02	.01
☐ 88 Brad Radke	.15	.07	.02
☐ 89 Joe Randa	.05	.02	.01
☐ 90 Phil Nevin	.05	.02	.01
☐ 91 Joe Vitiello	.05	.02	.01
☐ 92 Ray McDavid	.05	.02	.01
☐ 93 Robbie Beckett	.05	.02	.01
☐ 94 Frank Rodriguez	.05	.02	.01
☐ 95 Marc Newfield	.15	.07	.02
☐ 96 Joey Eischen	.05	.02	.01
☐ 97 Manny Alexander	.05	.02	.01
☐ 98 Jeff McNeely	.05	.02	.01
☐ 99 Mark Smith	.05	.02	.01
☐ 100 Alex Rodriguez	3.00	1.35	.35
☐ 101 Todd Hollandsworth	.50	.23	.06
☐ 102 Scott Ruffcorn	.05	.02	.01
☐ 103 Kurt Miller	.05	.02	.01
☐ 104 Justin Mashore	.05	.02	.01
☐ 105 Garret Anderson	.40	.18	.05
☐ 106 Nigel Wilson	.05	.02	.01
☐ 107 Howard Battle	.05	.02	.01
☐ 108 Calvin Reese	.05	.02	.01
☐ 109 Orlando Miller	.05	.02	.01
☐ 110 Bill Pulsipher	.20	.09	.03
☐ 111 Edgar Renteria	.75	.35	.09
☐ 112 Steve Gibralter	.05	.02	.01
☐ 113 Gene Schall	.05	.02	.01
☐ 114 John Roper	.05	.02	.01
☐ 115 Alvin Morman	.05	.02	.01
☐ 116 Doug Glanville	.05	.02	.01
☐ 117 Mark Hutton	.05	.02	.01
☐ 118 Glenn Murray	.05	.02	.01
☐ 119 Curtis Shaw	.05	.02	.01
☐ 120 Alex Ochoa	.50	.23	.06
☐ 121 Michael Moore	.05	.02	.01
☐ 122 Joey Hamilton	.15	.07	.02
☐ 123 James Baldwin	.15	.07	.02
☐ 124 Chad Ogea	.05	.02	.01
☐ 125 Rikkert Faneyte	.05	.02	.01
☐ 126 Benji Gil	.05	.02	.01
☐ 127 Kenny Felder	.05	.02	.01
☐ 128 Brant Brown	.05	.02	.01
☐ 129 Eddie Pearson	.05	.02	.01
☐ 130 Derrek Lee	1.25	.55	.16
☐ 131 AS League Card #3	.05	.02	.01
☐ 132 Dan Serafini	.05	.02	.01
☐ 133 Ramon Caraballo	.05	.02	.01
☐ 134 Derek Wallace	.05	.02	.01
☐ 135 Jamie Arnold	.05	.02	.01
☐ 136 Domingo Jean	.05	.02	.01
☐ 137 Jose Malave	.05	.02	.01
☐ 138 Derek Lowe	.05	.02	.01
☐ 139 Marshall Boze	.05	.02	.01
☐ 140 Billy Wagner	.25	.11	.03
☐ 141 Matt Franco	.05	.02	.01
☐ 142 Roger Cedeno	.20	.09	.03
☐ 143 Russ Davis	.05	.02	.01
☐ 144 Kevin Flora	.05	.02	.01
☐ 145 Rick Gorecki	.05	.02	.01
☐ 146 Rick Greene	.05	.02	.01
☐ 147 Brian L. Hunter	.25	.11	.03
☐ 148 Rich Aurilia	.05	.02	.01
☐ 149 Jason Moler	.05	.02	.01
☐ 150 Michael Tucker	.20	.09	.03
☐ 151 Alex Rodriguez CL	.50	.23	.06
☐ 152 Chad Mottola	.05	.02	.01
☐ 153 Calvin Murray	.05	.02	.01
☐ 154 Melvin Nieves	.15	.07	.02
☐ 155 Luis Ortiz	.05	.02	.01
☐ 156 Chris Roberts	.05	.02	.01
☐ 157 Todd Williams	.05	.02	.01
☐ 158 Tony Phillips	.05	.02	.01
☐ 159 DeShawn Warren	.05	.02	.01
☐ 160 Paul Shuey	.05	.02	.01
☐ 161 Dmitri Young	.40	.18	.05
☐ 162 Jermaine Allensworth	.05	.02	.01
☐ 163 Daron Kirkreit	.05	.02	.01
☐ 164 Scott Christman	.05	.02	.01
☐ 165 Steve Soderstrom	.05	.02	.01
☐ 166 J.R. Phillips	.05	.02	.01
☐ 167 Karim Garcia	2.00	.90	.25
☐ 168 Marc Acre	.05	.02	.01
☐ 169 Jose Paniagua	.05	.02	.01
☐ 170 Terrell Wade	.15	.07	.02
☐ 171 Mike Bell	.40	.18	.05
☐ 172 Alan Benes	.60	.25	.07
☐ 173 Jeff D'Amico	.15	.07	.02
☐ 174 Tate Seefried	.05	.02	.01
☐ 175 Wayne Gomes	.05	.02	.01
☐ 176 Chris Singleton	.05	.02	.01
☐ 177 Marc Valdes	.05	.02	.01
☐ 178 Jamey Wright	.40	.18	.05
☐ 179 Jay Powell	.05	.02	.01
☐ 180 Charles Johnson	.50	.23	.06
☐ 181 Mitch House	.05	.02	.01
☐ 182 Torii Hunter	.20	.09	.03
☐ 183 Jeff Suppan	.60	.25	.07
☐ 184 Roberto Petagine	.05	.02	.01
☐ 185 Ryan McGuire	.05	.02	.01
☐ 186 Andrew Lorraine	.05	.02	.01
☐ 187 Matt Brunson	.05	.02	.01
☐ 188 Eduardo Perez	.05	.02	.01
☐ 189 Jay Witasick	.05	.02	.01
☐ 190 Shawn Green	.05	.02	.01
☐ 191 Cleveland Ladell	.05	.02	.01
☐ 192 Paul Bako	.05	.02	.01
☐ 193 Brook Fordyce	.05	.02	.01
☐ 194 Kym Ashworth	.15	.07	.02
☐ 195 Tony Mitchell	.05	.02	.01
☐ 196 Tony Clark	.75	.35	.09
☐ 197 Curtis Pride	.05	.02	.01
☐ 198 Arquimedez Pozo	.15	.07	.02
☐ 199 Rey Ordonez	.75	.35	.09
☐ 200 Brooks Kieschnick	.30	.14	.04
☐ AU1 Alex Rodriguez AU/2100	90.00	40.00	11.00
☐ AU2 Terrell Wade AU/2080	20.00	9.00	2.50
☐ AU3 Brooks Kieschnick AU/3400	20.00	9.00	2.50
☐ AU4 Rondell White AU/2880	25.00	11.00	3.10
☐ AU5 Michael Tucker AU/2400	20.00	9.00	2.50
☐ AU6 Kirk Presley AU/1300	25.00	11.00	3.10

1994 Classic Bonus Baby

	MINT	NRMT	EXC
COMPLETE SET (5)	18.00	8.00	2.20
COMMON CARD (BB1-BB5)	1.00	.45	.12
☐ BB1 Trot Nixon	1.00	.45	.12
☐ BB2 Kirk Presley	1.00	.45	.12
☐ BB3 Alex Rodriguez	15.00	6.75	1.85
☐ BB4 Brooks Kieschnick	1.50	.70	.19
☐ BB5 Michael Tucker	1.00	.45	.12

1994 Classic Cream of the Crop

One per Classic pack insert.

	MINT	NRMT	EXC
COMPLETE SET (25)	12.00	5.50	1.50
COMMON CARD (C1-C25)	.10	.05	.01

	MINT	NRMT	EXC
☐ C1 Trot Nixon	.20	.09	.03
☐ C2 Kirk Presley	.20	.09	.03
☐ C3 Mac Suzuki	.10	.05	.01
☐ C4 Brooks Kieschnick	.40	.18	.05
☐ C5 Johnny Damon	.75	.35	.09
☐ C6 Howard Battle	.10	.05	.01
☐ C7 Michael Tucker	.25	.11	.03
☐ C8 Todd Hollandsworth	.60	.25	.07
☐ C9 J.R. Phillips	.10	.05	.01
☐ C10 Shannon Stewart	.20	.09	.03
☐ C11 Alex Rodriguez	4.00	1.80	.50
☐ C12 Terrell Wade	.20	.09	.03
☐ C13 Rondell White	.50	.23	.06
☐ C14 James Baldwin	.20	.09	.03
☐ C15 Shane Andrews	.20	.09	.03
☐ C16 Chan Ho Park	.75	.35	.09
☐ C17 Derek Jeter	2.00	.90	.25
☐ C18 Charles Johnson	.60	.25	.07
☐ C19 Bill Pulsipher	.25	.11	.03
☐ C20 Phil Nevin	.10	.05	.01
☐ C21 Scott Ruffcorn	.10	.05	.01
☐ C22 Midre Cummings	.20	.09	.03
☐ C23 Frank Rodriguez	.20	.09	.03
☐ C24 Dmitri Young	.50	.23	.06
☐ C25 Shawn Green	.20	.09	.03

1994 Classic Update Cream of the Crop

One per Classic Update pack insert.

	MINT	NRMT	EXC
COMPLETE SET (20)	30.00	13.50	3.70
COMMON CARD (CC1-CC20)	.30	.14	.04
☐ CC1 Paul Wilson	1.00	.45	.12
☐ CC2 Ben Grieve	3.00	1.35	.35
☐ CC3 Dustin Hermanson	.30	.14	.04
☐ CC4 Antone Williamson	1.25	.55	.16
☐ CC5 Josh Booty	1.00	.45	.12
☐ CC6 Doug Million	.75	.35	.09
☐ CC7 Todd Walker	6.00	2.70	.75
☐ CC8 C.J. Nitkowski	.30	.14	.04
☐ CC9 Jaret Wright	1.50	.70	.19
☐ CC10 Mark Farris	.30	.14	.04
☐ CC11 Nomar Garciaparra	3.00	1.35	.35
☐ CC12 Paul Konerko	4.00	1.80	.50
☐ CC13 Jayson Peterson	.30	.14	.04
☐ CC14 Matt Smith	.30	.14	.04
☐ CC15 Ramon Castro	.40	.18	.05
☐ CC16 Cade Gaspar	.30	.14	.04
☐ CC17 Terrence Long	1.25	.55	.16
☐ CC18 Hiram Bocachica	1.00	.45	.12
☐ CC19 Dante Powell	3.00	1.35	.35
☐ CC20 Brian Buchanan	.40	.18	.05
☐ CR1 Cal Ripken Special	8.00	3.60	1.00
☐ AU1 Cal Ripken AU/2000	150.00	70.00	19.00

1994 Classic #1 Draft Pick Mail-In

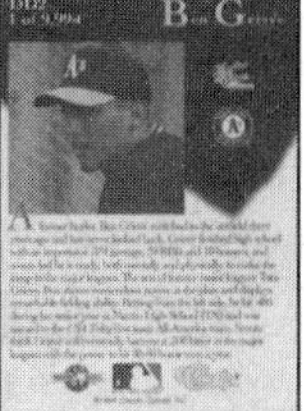

One set per mail-in wrapper offer.

	MINT	NRMT	EXC
COMPLETE SET (5)	15.00	6.75	1.85
COMMON CARD (DD1-DD5)	2.00	.90	.25

□ DD1 Paul Wilson	2.50	1.10	.30
□ DD2 Ben Grieve	8.00	3.60	1.00
□ DD3 Dustin Hermanson	2.00	.90	.25
□ DD4 Antone Williamson	3.00	1.35	.35
□ DD5 Josh Booty	2.50	1.10	.30

1994 Classic Tri-Cards

	MINT	NRMT	EXC
COMPLETE SET (28)	100.00	45.00	12.50
COMMON CARD (T1-T84)	2.00	.90	.25
□ T1 Jamie Arnold	2.00	.90	.25
T2 Terrell Wade			
T3 Ramon Caraballo			
□ T4 Jay Powell	3.00	1.35	.35
T5 Alex Ochoa			
T6 Manny Alexander			
□ T7 Trot Nixon	4.00	1.80	.50
T8 Jose Malave			
T9 Frank Rodriguez			
□ T10 DeShawn Warren	2.00	.90	.25
T11 Chris Smith			
T12 Andrew Lorraine			
□ T13 Jon Ratliff	3.00	1.35	.35
T14 Brooks Kieschnick			
T15 Matt Franco			
□ T16 Eddie Pearson	5.00	2.20	.60
T17 Chris Snopek			
T18 James Baldwin			
□ T19 Paul Bako	2.00	.90	.25
T20 Chad Mottola			
T21 John Roper			
□ T22 Daron Kirkreit	2.00	.90	.25
T23 Tony Mitchell			
T24 Chad Ogea			
□ T25 Mike Zolecki	2.00	.90	.25
T26 Rodney Pedraza			
T27 Mark Thompson			
□ T28 Matt Brunson	5.00	2.20	.60
T29 Tony Clark			
T30 Felipe Lira			
□ T31 Edgar Renteria	15.00	6.75	1.85
T32 Charles Johnson			
T33 Kurt Miller			
□ T34 Billy Wagner	2.50	1.10	.30
T35 Kevin Gallaher			
T36 Phil Nevin			
□ T37 Johnny Damon	10.00	4.50	1.25
T38 Darren Burton			
T39 Michael Tucker			
□ T40 Kym Ashworth	12.00	5.50	1.50
T41 Chan Ho Park			
T42 Todd Hollandsworth			
□ T43 Gabe Martinez	2.00	.90	.25
T44 Scott Talanoa			
T45 Marshall Boze			
□ T46 LaTroy Hawkins	2.00	.90	.25
T47 Brad Radke			
T48 Dave Stevens			
□ T49 Jose Paniagua	6.00	2.70	.75
T50 Ugueth Urbina			
T51 Rondell White			
□ T52 Bill Pulsipher	12.00	5.50	1.50
T53 Butch Huskey			
T54 Kirk Presley			
□ T55 Derek Jeter	20.00	9.00	2.50
T56 Brien Taylor			
T57 Russ Davis			
□ T58 Jose Herrera	2.00	.90	.25
T59 Curtis Shaw			
T60 Mark Acre			
□ T61 Wayne Gomes	2.00	.90	.25
T62 Jason Moler			
T63 Phil Geisler			
□ T64 Mitch House	2.00	.90	.25
T65 Jermaine Allensworth			
T66 Midre Cummings			
□ T67 Derrek Lee	5.00	2.20	.60
T68 Robbie Beckett			
T69 Ray McDavid			
□ T70 Chris Singleton	2.00	.90	.25
T71 Calvin Murray			
T72 J.R. Phillips			
□ T73 Alex Rodriguez	30.00	13.50	3.70
T74 Mac Suzuki			
T75 Marc Newfield			
□ T76 Basil Shabazz	2.00	.90	.25
T77 Dmitri Young			
T78 Brian Barber			
□ T79 Mike Bell	3.00	1.35	.35
T80 Terrell Lowery			
T81 Benji Gil			
□ T82 Jose Silva	3.00	1.35	.35
T83 Brent Bowers			
T84 Shawn Green			

1994 Classic/Best Gold

These 200 standard-size cards of the 1994 Classic Best Minor League Gold set feature players from Triple A, Double A, Single A, Short Season, and the Rookie League. Randomly inserted in the foil packs were a 19-card #1 Picks set, five acetate cards, and autographed cards by David Justice. The fronts feature borderless color player photos, with the player's name appearing vertically in gold foil at the upper right. The player's team name appears vertically up the right side. The back carries an oblique, horizontally oriented color player photo. To its right are the player's name, team name, position, and stats; all vertically oriented and stamped in gold foil. The player's biography appears horizontally oriented to the photo's left.

	MINT	NRMT	EXC
COMPLETE SET (200)	15.00	6.75	1.85
COMMON CARD (1-200)	.05	.02	.01
□ 1 Brien Taylor	.05	.02	.01
□ 2 Jeff D'Amico	.40	.18	.05
□ 3 Trot Nixon	.15	.07	.02
□ 4 Clayton Byrne	.05	.02	.01
□ 5 Eric Chavez	.05	.02	.01
□ 6 Matt Jarvis	.05	.02	.01
□ 7 Billy Owens	.05	.02	.01
□ 8 Jay Powell	.05	.02	.01
□ 9 Robert Eenhoorn	.05	.02	.01
□ 10 Trey Beamon	.30	.14	.04
□ 11 Todd Williams	.05	.02	.01
□ 12 Tim Davis	.05	.02	.01
□ 13 Brian Barber	.05	.02	.01
□ 14 Jeff Shireman	.05	.02	.01
□ 15 Melvin Mora	.05	.02	.01
□ 16 Phil Nevin	.05	.02	.01
□ 17 Kendall Rhine	.05	.02	.01
□ 18 Billy Wagner	.25	.11	.03
□ 19 Jason Kendall	.50	.23	.06
□ 20 Kelly Wunsch	.05	.02	.01
□ 21 D.J. Boston	.05	.02	.01
□ 22 Shannon Stewart	.15	.07	.02
□ 23 Anthony Manahan	.05	.02	.01
□ 24 Dwight Robinson	.05	.02	.01
□ 25 Alan Benes	.60	.25	.07
□ 26 Dennis Slininger	.05	.02	.01
□ 27 John Burke	.05	.02	.01
□ 28 Jamey Wright	.40	.18	.05
□ 29 Scott Eyre	.05	.02	.01
□ 30 Jack Kimel	.05	.02	.01
□ 31 Kerry Lacy	.05	.02	.01
□ 32 Rich Aurilia	.05	.02	.01
□ 33 Dave Giberti	.05	.02	.01
□ 34 Daryl Henderson	.05	.02	.01
□ 35 Stanley Evans	.05	.02	.01
□ 36 Wayne Gomes	.05	.02	.01
□ 37 Rob Grable	.05	.02	.01
□ 38 Mike Juhl	.05	.02	.01
□ 39 Jason Moler	.05	.02	.01
□ 40 Jon Zuber	.05	.02	.01
□ 41 Chad Fonville	.05	.02	.01
□ 42 Mark Thompson	.05	.02	.01
□ 43 Billy Masse	.05	.02	.01
□ 44 Derek Hacopian	.05	.02	.01
□ 45 J.J. Thobe	.05	.02	.01
□ 46 Charles York	.05	.02	.01
□ 47 Jamie Howard	.05	.02	.01
□ 48 Andre King	.05	.02	.01
□ 49 Tim Delgado	.05	.02	.01
□ 50 Mike Hubbard	.05	.02	.01
□ 51 Bernie Nunez	.05	.02	.01
□ 52 Jon Ratliff	.05	.02	.01
□ 53 Pedro Valdez	.15	.07	.02
□ 54 Rich Butler	.05	.02	.01
□ 55 Felipe Crespo	.05	.02	.01
□ 56 Randy Phillips	.05	.02	.01
□ 57 Todd Steverson	.05	.02	.01
□ 58 Chris Stynes	.05	.02	.01
□ 59 Ben Weber	.05	.02	.01
□ 60 Chris Weinke	.05	.02	.01
□ 61 Rob Lukachyk	.05	.02	.01
□ 62 Brett King	.05	.02	.01
□ 63 Chris Singleton	.05	.02	.01
□ 64 Brian Bright	.05	.02	.01
□ 65 Brent Brede	.05	.02	.01
□ 66 Steve Hazlett	.05	.02	.01
□ 67 Dan Serafini	.15	.07	.02
□ 68 Matt Farner	.05	.02	.01
□ 69 Jeremy Lee	.15	.07	.02
□ 70 Anthony Medrano	.05	.02	.01
□ 71 Josue Estrada	.05	.02	.01
□ 72 Martin Mainville	.05	.02	.01
□ 73 Chris Schwab	.15	.07	.02
□ 74 John Roskos	.05	.02	.01
□ 75 Charles Peterson	.25	.11	.03
□ 76 Kevin Pickford	.05	.02	.01
□ 77 Charles Rice	.05	.02	.01
□ 78 Mike Bell	.40	.18	.05
□ 79 Ed Diaz	.50	.23	.06
□ 80 Torii Hunter	.20	.09	.03
□ 81 Kelcey Mucker	.05	.02	.01
□ 82 Nick Delvecchio	.05	.02	.01
□ 83 Derek Jeter	1.50	.70	.19
□ 84 Ryan Karp	.05	.02	.01
□ 85 Matt Luke	.05	.02	.01
□ 86 Ray Suplee	.05	.02	.01
□ 87 Tyler Houston	.05	.02	.01
□ 88 Brad Cornett	.05	.02	.01
□ 89 Kris Harmes	.05	.02	.01
□ 90 Shane Andrews	.05	.02	.01
□ 91 Ugueth Urbina	.05	.02	.01
□ 92 Chris Mader	.05	.02	.01
□ 93 Eddie Pearson	.05	.02	.01
□ 94 Tim Clark	.05	.02	.01
□ 95 Chris Malinoski	.05	.02	.01
□ 96 John Toale	.05	.02	.01
□ 97 Mark Acre	.05	.02	.01
□ 98 Ernie Young	.15	.07	.02
□ 99 Jeff Schmidt	.05	.02	.01
□ 100 Roberto Petagine	.05	.02	.01
□ 101 Eddy Diaz	.05	.02	.01
□ 102 Ruben Santana	.05	.02	.01
□ 103 Ron Villone	.05	.02	.01
□ 104 Nate Dishington	.05	.02	.01
□ 105 Charles Johnson	.50	.23	.06
□ 106 Preston Wilson	.20	.09	.03
□ 107 Paul Shuey	.05	.02	.01
□ 108 Howard Battle	.05	.02	.01
□ 109 Tim Hyers	.05	.02	.01
□ 110 Rick Greene	.05	.02	.01
□ 111 Justin Thompson	.05	.02	.01
□ 112 Frank Rodriguez	.05	.02	.01
□ 113 Jamie Arnold	.05	.02	.01
□ 114 Marty Malloy	.05	.02	.01
□ 115 Darrell May	.05	.02	.01
□ 116 Leo Ramirez	.05	.02	.01
□ 117 Tom Thobe	.05	.02	.01
□ 118 Terrell Wade	.15	.07	.02
□ 119 Marc Valdes	.05	.02	.01
□ 120 Scott Rolen	4.00	1.80	.50
□ 121 Les Norman	.05	.02	.01
□ 122 Michael Tucker	.20	.09	.03
□ 123 Joe Vitiello	.05	.02	.01
□ 124 Chris Roberts	.05	.02	.01
□ 125 Jason Giambi	.50	.23	.06
□ 126 Izzy Molina	.05	.02	.01
□ 127 Scott Shockey	.05	.02	.01
□ 128 John Wasdin	.15	.07	.02
□ 129 Joel Wolfe	.05	.02	.01
□ 130 Brooks Kieschnick	.30	.14	.04
□ 131 Kennie Steenstra	.05	.02	.01
□ 132 Hector Trinidad	.05	.02	.01
□ 133 Derek Wallace	.05	.02	.01
□ 134 Kevin Lane	.05	.02	.01
□ 135 Buck McNabb	.05	.02	.01
□ 136 James Mouton	.05	.02	.01
□ 137 Joey Eischen	.05	.02	.01
□ 138 Todd Haney	.05	.02	.01
□ 139 John Pricher	.05	.02	.01
□ 140 Jeff Brown	.05	.02	.01
□ 141 Jason Hardtke	.05	.02	.01
□ 142 Derrek Lee	1.25	.55	.16
□ 143 Ira Smith	.05	.02	.01
□ 144 Mike Kelly	.05	.02	.01
□ 145 Mark Smith	.05	.02	.01
□ 146 Sherard Clinkscales	.05	.02	.01
□ 147 Ben Van Ryn	.05	.02	.01
□ 148 Tim Cooper	.05	.02	.01
□ 149 Manny Martinez	.05	.02	.01
□ 150 Kurt Ehmann	.05	.02	.01
□ 151 Doug Mirabelli	.05	.02	.01
□ 152 Chris Wimmer	.05	.02	.01
□ 153 Scott Christman	.05	.02	.01
□ 154 Kevin Coughlin	.05	.02	.01
□ 155 Troy Fryman	.05	.02	.01
□ 156 Sean Johnston	.05	.02	.01
□ 157 Jeff Alkire	.05	.02	.01
□ 158 Mike Busby	.05	.02	.01
□ 159 John O'Brien	.05	.02	.01
□ 160 Brian Rupp	.05	.02	.01
□ 161 Steve Soderstrom	.05	.02	.01
□ 162 Craig Wilson	.05	.02	.01
□ 163 Alan Burke	.05	.02	.01
□ 164 Mike Murphy	.05	.02	.01
□ 165 T.J. Mathews	.05	.02	.01
□ 166 Edgardo Alfonzo	.05	.02	.01
□ 167 Randy Curtis	.05	.02	.01
□ 168 Bernie Millan	.05	.02	.01
□ 169 Mike Cantu	.05	.02	.01
□ 170 Clint Davis	.05	.02	.01
□ 171 Jason Hisey	.05	.02	.01
□ 172 Aldo Pecorilli	.15	.07	.02
□ 173 Dmitri Young	.40	.18	.05
□ 174 Marshall Boze	.05	.02	.01
□ 175 Bill Hardwick	.05	.02	.01
□ 176 Kevin Riggs	.05	.02	.01
□ 177 Lee Stevens	.05	.02	.01
□ 178 Webster Garrison	.05	.02	.01
□ 179 Wally Ritchie	.05	.02	.01
□ 180 Cris Colon	.05	.02	.01
□ 181 Rick Helling	.05	.02	.01
□ 182 Trey McCoy	.05	.02	.01
□ 183 Marc Barcelo	.05	.02	.01
□ 184 Chris Demetral	.05	.02	.01
□ 185 Rich Linares	.05	.02	.01
□ 186 Daron Kirkreit	.05	.02	.01
□ 187 Casey Whitten	.05	.02	.01
□ 188 Shon Walker	.05	.02	.01
□ 189 Rod Henderson	.05	.02	.01
□ 190 Tyrone Horne	.05	.02	.01
□ 191 B.J. Wallace	.05	.02	.01
□ 192 Louis Maberry	.05	.02	.01
□ 193 Brian Boehringer	.05	.02	.01
□ 194 Glenn DiSarcina	.05	.02	.01
□ 195 Melvin Bunch	.05	.02	.01
□ 196 Chad Mottola	.05	.02	.01
□ 197 Ryan Luzinski	.05	.02	.01
□ 198 Tom Wilson	.05	.02	.01
□ 199 Checklist (1-100)	.05	.02	.01
□ 200 Checklist (101-200)	.05	.02	.01
□ AU1 David Justice AU/4000	35.00	16.00	4.40

1994 Classic/Best Gold Acetates

These Glow-in-the-dark illustrated acetate cards. "Renowned comic artist Neal Adams illustrated five minor league players with a common background ... Each illustrated card will glow in the dark. An average of 4 per case. The cards are numbered on the back with a "SH" prefix.

	MINT	NRMT	EXC
COMPLETE SET (5)	25.00	11.00	3.10
COMMON CARD (SH1-SH5)	2.50	1.10	.30
□ SH1 Brien Taylor	2.50	1.10	.30
□ SH2 Dmitri Young	5.00	2.20	.60
□ SH3 Derek Jeter	20.00	9.00	2.50
□ SH4 Phil Nevin	2.50	1.10	.30
□ SH5 Frank Rodriguez	2.50	1.10	.30

1994 Classic/Best Gold #1 Pick LPs

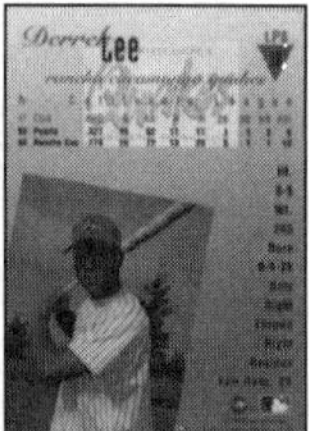

Limited-print, chromium effect (reflective texture, shiny/glossy glass look) featuring 19 first round picks from the 1993 June Major League Baseball Draft. An average of 30 per case. The cards are numbered on the back with an "LP" prefix.

	MINT	NRMT	EXC
COMPLETE SET (19)	50.00	22.00	6.25
COMMON CARD (LP1-LP19)	2.00	.90	.25
□ LP1 Alan Benes	8.00	3.60	1.00
□ LP2 Scott Christman	2.00	.90	.25
□ LP3 Jeff D'Amico	5.00	2.20	.60
□ LP4 Wayne Gomes	2.00	.90	.25
□ LP5 Torii Hunter	2.50	1.10	.30
□ LP6 Brooks Kieschnick	4.00	1.80	.50
□ LP7 Daron Kirkreit	2.00	.90	.25
□ LP8 Derrek Lee	15.00	6.75	1.85
□ LP9 Trot Nixon	2.00	.90	.25
□ LP10 Charles Peterson	2.00	.90	.25
□ LP11 Jay Powell	2.00	.90	.25
□ LP12 Jon Ratliff	2.00	.90	.25
□ LP13 Chris Schwab	2.00	.90	.25
□ LP14 Steve Soderstrom	2.00	.90	.25
□ LP15 Marc Valdes	2.00	.90	.25
□ LP16 Billy Wagner	3.00	1.35	.35
□ LP17 John Wasdin	2.00	.90	.25
□ LP18 Jamey Wright	5.00	2.20	.60
□ LP19 Kelly Wunsch	2.00	.90	.25

1994 Classic/Best Gold Rookie Express

	MINT	NRMT	EXC
COMPLETE SET (20)	8.00	3.60	1.00
COMMON CARD (RE1-RE20)	.25	.11	.03
□ RE1 Alan Benes	1.00	.45	.12
□ RE2 Scott Ruffcorn	.25	.11	.03
□ RE3 Jeff D'Amico	.60	.25	.07
□ RE4 Wayne Gomes	.25	.11	.03
□ RE5 Torii Hunter	.30	.14	.04
□ RE6 Brooks Kieschnick	.50	.23	.06
□ RE7 Daron Kirkreit	.25	.11	.03
□ RE8 Derrek Lee	2.00	.90	.25
□ RE9 Trot Nixon	.25	.11	.03
□ RE10 Charles Peterson	.25	.11	.03
□ RE11 Jay Powell	.25	.11	.03
□ RE12 Jon Ratliff	.25	.11	.03
□ RE13 Chris Schwab	.25	.11	.03
□ RE14 Steve Soderstrom	.25	.11	.03
□ RE15 Marc Valdes	.25	.11	.03
□ RE16 Billy Wagner	.40	.18	.05
□ RE17 John Wasdin	.25	.11	.03
□ RE18 Jamey Wright	.60	.25	.07
□ RE19 Kelly Wunsch	.25	.11	.03
□ RE20 Brooks Kieschnick GLOW	.50	.23	.06

1994 Clearwater Phillies Classic

This 30-card standard size set of the 1994 Clearwater Phillies, a Class A Florida State League affiliate of the Philadelphia Phillies, features white-bordered posed color player shots on its fronts with the player's name and position, team name and logo and Classic logo appearing across the bottom of each card. On a ghosted team logo, the white back carries the player's name at the top, followed by biography and statistics.

	MINT	NRMT	EXC
COMPLETE SET (30)	7.00	3.10	.85

☐ 1 David Doster
☐ 2 Peter Agostinelli
☐ 3 Kevin Alger
☐ 4 Gary Bennett
☐ 5 Jeff Bigler
☐ 6 Kent Blasingame
☐ 7 Ron Blazier
☐ 8 Luis Brito
☐ 9 E.J. Brophy
☐ 10 Dan Brown
☐ 11 Alan Burke
☐ 12 Blake Doolan
☐ 13 Tommy Eason
☐ 14 Stanley Evans
☐ 15 Wayne Gomes
☐ 16 Scott Haws
☐ 17 Laurence Heisler
☐ 18 Gary Herrmann
☐ 19 Chad McConnell
☐ 20 Nelson Metheney
☐ 21 Ron Ollison
☐ 22 Kevin Sefcik
☐ 23 Jamie Sepeda
☐ 24 Eric Smith
☐ 25 Steve Solomon
☐ 26 John Trisler
☐ 27 Don McCormack MG
☐ 28 Darold Knowles CO
☐ 29 Greg Legg CO
☐ 30 Clete Sigwart TR
Checklist

1994 Clearwater Phillies Fleer/ProCards

This 30-card standard size set of the 1994 Clearwater Phillies, a Class A Florida State League affiliate of the Philadelphia Phillies, features white-bordered posed color player photos on its fronts with the player's name, position, team name and Fleer/ProCards logo across the bottom of each card. The white back with vertical light blue stripes carries the player's name at the top, followed by biography and statistics.

	MINT	NRMT	EXC
COMPLETE SET (30)	5.00	2.20	.60

☐ 2331 Scott Haws
☐ 2516 Pete Agostinelli
☐ 2517 Kevin Alger
☐ 2518 Ron Blazier
☐ 2519 Dan Brown
☐ 2520 Dom DeSantis
☐ 2521 Blake Doolan
☐ 2522 Wayne Gomes
☐ 2523 Laurence Heisler
☐ 2524 Gary Herrmann
☐ 2525 Nelson Metheney
☐ 2526 Jamie Sepeda
☐ 2527 Eric Smith
☐ 2528 John Trisler
☐ 2529 Gary Bennett
☐ 2530 E.J. Brophy
☐ 2532 Jeff Bigler
☐ 2533 Luis Brito
☐ 2534 Dave Doster
☐ 2535 Tommy Eason
☐ 2536 Ron Ollison
☐ 2537 Kevin Sefcik
☐ 2538 Kent Blasingame
☐ 2539 Alan Burke
☐ 2540 Stan Evans
☐ 2541 Chad McConnell
☐ 2542 Steve Solomon
☐ 2543 Darold Knowles CO
☐ 2544 Greg Legg CO
☐ 2545 Checklist

1994 Clinton Lumberkings Classic

This 30-card standard size set of the 1994 Clinton LumberKings, a Class A Midwest League affiliate of the San Francisco Giants, features white-bordered posed color player shots on its fronts with the player's name and position, team name and logo and Classic logo appearing across the bottom of each card. On a ghosted team logo, the white back carries the player's name at the top, followed by biography and statistics.

	MINT	NRMT	EXC
COMPLETE SET (30)	7.00	3.10	.85

☐ 1 Benji Simonton
☐ 2 Jose Alguacil
☐ 3 Charles Alimena
☐ 4 Heath Altman
☐ 5 Steven Bourgeois
☐ 6 Isbel Cardona
☐ 7 Mike Cavanagh
☐ 8 Melvin Davis
☐ 9 Steven Day
☐ 10 Chris Gambs
☐ 11 Ed Hartwell
☐ 12 Dan Henrikson
☐ 13 Jeff Locklear
☐ 14 Jeff Martin
☐ 15 Raul Marval
☐ 16 Craig Mayes
☐ 17 Jason Myers
☐ 18 Gary Phillips
☐ 19 Armando Rios
☐ 20 Jim Rosenbohm
☐ 21 John Sbrocco
☐ 22 Jason Sievers
☐ 23 David Tessicini
☐ 24 D.J. Thielen
☐ 25 Brian Zaletel
☐ 26 Jack Mull
☐ 27 Steve Lienhard
☐ 28 Glenn Tufts
☐ 29 Steve Dietzman
☐ 30 Robert Boyd CL
Brian Eggers

1994 Clinton LumberKings Fleer/ProCards

This 30-card standard size set of the 1994 Clinton LumberKings, a Class A Midwest League affiliate of the San Francisco Giants, features white-bordered posed color player photos on its fronts with the player's name, position, team name and Fleer/ProCards logo across the bottom of each card. The white back with vertical light blue stripes carries the player's name at the top, followed by biography and statistics.

	MINT	NRMT	EXC
COMPLETE SET (30)	5.00	2.20	.60

☐ 1970 Heath Altman
☐ 1971 Steve Bourgeois
☐ 1972 Isbel Cardona
☐ 1973 Steve Day
☐ 1974 Chris Gambs
☐ 1975 Dan Henrikson
☐ 1976 Jeff Locklear
☐ 1977 Jeff Martin
☐ 1978 Jason Myers
☐ 1979 Jim Rosenbohm
☐ 1980 Dave Soult
☐ 1981 Brett Tucker
☐ 1982 Mike Cavanagh
☐ 1983 Craig Mayes
☐ 1984 Jason Sievers
☐ 1985 Jose Alguacil
☐ 1986 Charles Alimena
☐ 1987 Raul Marval
☐ 1988 Gary Phillips
☐ 1989 Jon Sbrocco
☐ 1990 David Tessicini
☐ 1991 D.J. Thielen
☐ 1992 Brian Zaletel
☐ 1993 Melvin Davis
☐ 1994 Eddie Hartwell
☐ 1995 Armando Rios
☐ 1996 Benji Simonton
☐ 1997 Jack Mull MG
☐ 1998 Field Staff
Steve Leinhard CO
Steve Dietzman TR
Glenn Tufts CO
☐ 1999 Checklist

1994 Colorado Springs Sky Sox Fleer/ProCards

This 28-card standard size set of the 1994 Colorado Springs Sky Sox, a Class AAA Pacific Coast League affiliate of the Colorado Rookies, features white-bordered posed color player photos on its fronts with the player's name, position, team name and Fleer/ProCards logo across the bottom of each card. The white back with vertical light blue stripes carries the player's name at the top, followed by biography and statistics.

	MINT	NRMT	EXC
COMPLETE SET (28)	5.00	2.20	.60

☐ 724 Steve Allen
☐ 725 John Burke
☐ 726 Jim Czajkowski
☐ 727 Ryan Hawblitzel
☐ 728 Curtis Leskanic
☐ 729 Randy Marshall
☐ 730 Kevin Meier
☐ 731 Lance Painter
☐ 732 Kevin Ritz
☐ 733 Keith Shepherd
☐ 734 Mark Thompson
☐ 735 Bruce Walton
☐ 736 Scott Bradley
☐ 737 Jayhawk Owens
☐ 738 Jason Bates
☐ 739 Pedro Castellano
☐ 740 Stu Cole
☐ 741 Jay Gainer
☐ 742 Webster Garrison
☐ 743 Ty Van Burkleo
☐ 744 Trent Hubbard
☐ 745 Andy Mota
☐ 746 Darrell Sherman
☐ 747 Jim Tatum
☐ 748 Brad Mills MG
☐ 749 Frank Funk CO
☐ 750 Amos Otis CO
☐ 751 Checklist

1994 Columbus Clippers Fleer/ProCards

This 30-card standard size set of the 1994 Columbus Clippers, a Class AAA International League affiliate of the New York Yankees, features white-bordered posed color player photos on its fronts with the player's name, position, team name and Fleer/ProCards logo across the bottom of each card. The white back with vertical light blue stripes carries the player's name at the top, followed by biography and statistics.

	MINT	NRMT	EXC
COMPLETE SET (30)	5.00	2.20	.60

☐ 2940 Joe Ausanio
☐ 2941 Mark Carper
☐ 2942 Royal Clayton
☐ 2943 Andy Cook
☐ 2944 Matt Dunbar
☐ 2945 Dave Eiland
☐ 2946 Ron Frazier
☐ 2947 Keith Garagozzo
☐ 2948 Sterling Hitchcock
☐ 2949 Mark Hutton
☐ 2950 Sam Militello
☐ 2951 Jose Musset
☐ 2952 Kirt Ojala
☐ 2953 Rafael Quirico
☐ 2954 Kiki Hernandez
☐ 2955 Jorge Posada
☐ 2956 Russ Davis
☐ 2957 Bobby DeJardin
☐ 2958 Robert Eenhoorn
☐ 2959 Sam Horn
☐ 2960 Dave Silvestri
☐ 2961 Don Sparks
☐ 2962 Rich Barnwell
☐ 2963 Mike Humphreys
☐ 2964 Jalal Leach
☐ 2965 Chito Martinez
☐ 2966 Billy Masse
☐ 2967 Stump Merrill MG
☐ 2968 Coaching Staff
Tom Spencer CO
Nardi Contreras CO
Hop Cassady CO
Darren London TR
☐ 2969 Checklist

1994 Columbus Clippers Police

	MINT	NRMT	EXC
COMPLETE SET (25)	6.00	2.70	.75

☐ 1 Joe Ausanio
☐ 2 Mark Carper
Keith Garagozzo
☐ 3 Hop Cassady CO
Nardi Contreras CO
Tom Spencer CO
Daren London TR
☐ 4 Royal Clayton
☐ 5 Andy Cook
☐ 6 Russ Davis
☐ 7 Bobby DeJardin
☐ 8 Robert Eenhoorn
☐ 9 Dave Eiland
☐ 10 Ron Frazier
Matt Dunbar
☐ 11 Kiki Hernandez
Sic, Kirk
☐ 12 Rich Hines
☐ 13 Sterling Hitchcock
☐ 14 Sam Horn
☐ 15 Mike Humphreys
☐ 16 Mark Hutton
☐ 17 Jalal Leach
Rich Barnwell
☐ 18 Chito Martwez
☐ 19 Billy Masse
☐ 20 Stump Merrill MG
Ken Schnacke GM
☐ 21 Kirt Ojala
☐ 22 Jorge Posada
☐ 23 Rafael Quirico
☐ 24 Dave Silvestri
☐ 25 Don Sparks

1994 Columbus Redstixx Classic

This 30-card standard size set of the 1994 Columbus RedStixx, a Class A South Atlantic League affiliate of the Cleveland Indians, features white-bordered posed color player shots on its fronts with the player's name and position, team name and logo and Classic logo appearing across the bottom of each card. On a ghosted team logo, the white back carries the player's name at the top, followed by biography and statistics. This issue includes second year cards of Enrique Wilson and and Richie Sexson.

	MINT	NRMT	EXC
COMPLETE SET (30)	15.00	6.75	1.85

☐ 1 Enrique Wilson
☐ 2 Jesus Azuaje
☐ 3 Daniel Brabant
☐ 4 Camp Campbell
☐ 5 Gerad Cawhorn
☐ 6 Roland de la Maza
☐ 7 Maximo de la Rosa
☐ 8 Einar Diaz
☐ 9 Travis Driskill
☐ 10 Bryan Garrett
☐ 11 Blair Hodson
☐ 12 Steve Kline
☐ 13 Rich Lemons
☐ 14 Rob Lewis
☐ 15 Jason Lyman
☐ 16 Rick Prieto
☐ 17 Alex Ramirez
☐ 18 Cesar Ramos
☐ 19 Tony Runion
☐ 20 Richie Sexson
☐ 21 Leroy (Boo) Thompson
☐ 22 Eric White
☐ 23 Greg Williams
☐ 24 Jeff Williams
☐ 25 Jon Zubiri
☐ 26 Mike Young MG
☐ 27 Fred Gladding CO
☐ 28 Dan Williams CO
☐ 29 Rick Jameyson TR
☐ 30 Tim Straus
Checklist

1994 Columbus RedStixx Fleer/ProCards

This 31-card standard size set of the 1994 Columbus RedStixx, a Class A South Atlantic League affiliate of the Cleveland Indians, features white-bordered posed color player photos on its fronts with the player's name, position, team name and Fleer/ProCards logo across the bottom of each card. The white back with vertical light blue stripes carries the player's name at the top, followed by biography and statistics. This issue includes second year cards of Enrique Wilson and Richie Sexson.

	MINT	NRMT	EXC
COMPLETE SET (31)	12.00	5.50	1.50

☐ 433 Dan Brabant
☐ 434 Camp Campbell
☐ 435 Roland De La Maza
☐ 436 Maximo De La Rosa
☐ 437 Travis Driskill
☐ 438 Kris Hanson
☐ 439 Steven Kline
☐ 440 Mike Matthews
☐ 441 Cesar Ramos
☐ 442 Greg Williams
☐ 443 Jeff Williams
☐ 444 Jon Zubiri
☐ 445 Einar Diaz
☐ 446 Rob Lewis
☐ 447 Jesus Azuaje
☐ 448 Gerad Cawhorn
☐ 449 Blair Hodson
☐ 450 Jason Lyman
☐ 451 Richie Sexson
☐ 452 Eric White
☐ 453 Enrique Wilson
☐ 454 Bryan Garrett
☐ 455 Richard Lemons
☐ 456 Pedro Marte
☐ 457 Rick Prieto
☐ 458 Alex Ramirez
☐ 459 Leroy Thompson
☐ 460 Mike Young MG
☐ 461 Fred Gladding CO
☐ 462 Dan Williams CO
☐ 463 Checklist

1994 Danville Braves Classic

This 30-card standard size set of the 1994 Danville Braves, a Class A Appalachian League affiliate of the Atlanta Braves, features white-bordered posed color player shots on its fronts with the player's name and position, team name and logo and Classic logo appearing across the bottom of each card. On a ghosted team logo, the white back carries the player's name at the top, followed by biography and statistics. This issue includes the minor league card debut of Damian Moss.

	MINT	NRMT	EXC
COMPLETE SET (30)	15.00	6.75	1.85

☐ 1 Jacob Shumate
☐ 2 Keith Bolognese
☐ 3 Doug Brewer
☐ 4 Travis Cain
☐ 5 Wes Culp
☐ 6 Jose Delgado
☐ 7 Ralph Denman
☐ 8 Alberto Evangelista
☐ 9 Jim Felch
☐ 10 Derek Foote
☐ 11 Jason Garcia
☐ 12 Chris Gobert
☐ 13 Christopher Gongora
☐ 14 Steve Graham
☐ 15 Jason Green
☐ 16 Gus Kennedy
☐ 17 Ryan Martin
☐ 18 Raymond McWhite
☐ 19 Damian Moss
☐ 20 Brett Newell
☐ 21 Bruce Newman
☐ 22 John Rocker
☐ 23 Anthony Ruff
☐ 24 Rich Spiegel
☐ 25 Mark Thompson
☐ 26 Craig Zedalis
☐ 27 Kevin Millwood
☐ 28 Jason "J.T" Thomas
☐ 29 Miguel Valdez
☐ 30 Paul Runge MG
Checklist

1994 Danville Braves Fleer/ProCards

This 30-card standard size set of the 1994 Danville Braves, a Class A Appalachian League affiliate of the Atlanta Braves, features white-bordered posed color player photos on its fronts with the player's name, position, team name and Fleer/ProCards logo across the bottom of each card. The white back with vertical light blue stripes carries the player's name at the top, followed by biography and statistics. This issue includes the minor league card debut of Damian Moss.

	MINT	NRMT	EXC
COMPLETE SET (30)	12.00	5.50	1.50

☐ 3522 Travis Cain
☐ 3523 Wes Culp
☐ 3524 Alberto Evangelista
☐ 3525 Chris Gobert
☐ 3526 Chris Gongora
☐ 3527 Jason Green
☐ 3528 Kevin Millwood
☐ 3529 Damian Moss
☐ 3530 John Rocker
☐ 3531 Jason Thomas
☐ 3532 Mark Thompson
☐ 3533 Craig Zedalis
☐ 3534 Derek Foote
☐ 3535 Ryan Martin
☐ 3536 Rich Spiegel
☐ 3537 Keith Bolognese
☐ 3538 Jose Delgado
☐ 3539 Ralph Denman
☐ 3540 Jason Garcia
☐ 3541 Ray McWhite
☐ 3542 Brett Newell
☐ 3543 Brett Brewer
☐ 3544 Jim Felch
☐ 3545 Jesse Kennedy
☐ 3546 Bruce Newman
☐ 3547 Miguel Valdez
☐ 3548 Paul Runge MG
☐ 3549 Jerry Nyman CO
☐ 3550 Brian Snitker CO
☐ 3551 Checklist

1994 David Lipscomb Bisons

This 25-card standard-size set features the 1994 Bisons. On a light blue background, the fronts feature posed color player photos with rounded corners. The team name appears above the picture, while the player's name and position, and the team logo are printed under the picture. The white backs carry the player's name, number, and position, a short biography and a summary of accomplishments. The cards are unnumbered and checklisted below in alphabetical order.

	MINT	NRMT	EXC
COMPLETE SET (25)	10.00	4.50	1.25

☐ 1 Chad Blasingim
Jonathan Burns
☐ 2 John Boatman
☐ 3 Paul Bobo
☐ 4 Randy Bostic ACO
☐ 5 Brad Buher
☐ 6 Brian Cromwell
J.D. Blackburn
☐ 7 Ken Dugan CO
☐ 8 Kurt Dugan
☐ 9 Chad Estep
☐ 10 Brad Frasier
V.H. Pickle
☐ 11 Chris Gainer
☐ 12 Lynn Griffith
☐ 13 Scott Grissom
Andy Lane
J.J. Dillingham
Bison Radio Crew
☐ 14 Hunter Henson
☐ 15 Brent High
☐ 16 Kolin Holladay ACO
☐ 17 Gary Johnson
Brad Buther
☐ 18 Gary Johnson
☐ 19 Tim Lewis
Richie Estep
☐ 20 Roy Pardue ACO
☐ 21 Craig Portwood TR
Kenn Niebrugge TR
Brent Oliver TR
☐ 22 Bryan Skelton
☐ 23 Adam Sullivan
☐ 24 Michael Wells
Scott Blair
☐ 25 David Wray
David Cloud

1994 Daytona Cubs Classic

This 30-card standard size set of the 1994 Daytona Cubs, a Class A Florida State League affiliate of the Chicago Cubs, features white-bordered posed color player shots on its fronts with the player's name and position, team name and logo and Classic logo appearing across the bottom of each card. On a ghosted team logo, the white back carries the player's name at the top, followed by biography and statistics.

	MINT	NRMT	EXC
COMPLETE SET (30)	14.00	6.25	1.75

☐ 1 Amaury Telemaco
☐ 2 Terry Adams
☐ 3 London Bradley
☐ 4 Demetrius Dowler
☐ 5 Brad Erdman
☐ 6 Jay Franklin
☐ 7 Daryle Gavlick
☐ 8 Andy Hartung
☐ 9 Ben Howze
☐ 10 Dave Hutcheson
☐ 11 Robin Jennings
☐ 12 Collin Kerley
☐ 13 Mark Kingston
☐ 14 Eddie Larregui
☐ 15 Anthony Lee
☐ 16 Jason Maxwell
☐ 17 Danny Montero
☐ 18 Kevin Orie
☐ 19 Richard Perez
☐ 20 Jon Ratliff
☐ 21 Chris Rodriguez
☐ 22 Dan Smith
☐ 23 Joey Terilli
☐ 24 Hector Trinidad
☐ 25 Greg Twiggs
☐ 26 Steve Walker
☐ 27 Ken Bolek MG
☐ 28 Oscar Acosta CO
☐ 29 Esteban Melendez TR
☐ 30 Ira Penner DIR
Checklist

1994 Daytona Cubs Fleer/ProCards

This 29-card standard size set of the 1994 Daytona Cubs, a Class A Florida State League affiliate of the Chicago Cubs, features white-bordered posed color player photos on its fronts with the player's name, position, team name and Fleer/ProCards logo across the bottom of each card. The white back with vertical light blue stripes carries the player's name at the top, followed by biography and statistics.

	MINT	NRMT	EXC
COMPLETE SET (29)	8.00	3.60	1.00

☐ 2343 Terry Adams
☐ 2344 Jay Franklin
☐ 2345 Daryle Gavlick
☐ 2346 Ben Howze
☐ 2347 Dave Hutcheson
☐ 2348 Collin Kerley
☐ 2349 Tony Lee
☐ 2350 Jon Ratliff
☐ 2351 Chris Rodriguez
☐ 2352 Amaury Telemaco
☐ 2353 Hector Trindad
☐ 2354 Greg Twiggs
☐ 2355 Brad Erdman
☐ 2356 Danny Montero
☐ 2357 Byron Bradley
☐ 2358 Andy Hartung
☐ 2359 Mark Kingston
☐ 2360 Jason Maxwell
☐ 2361 Kevin Orie
☐ 2362 Richard Perez
☐ 2363 Dan Smith
☐ 2364 Dee Dowler
☐ 2365 Robin Jennings
☐ 2366 Ed Larregui
☐ 2367 Joey Terilli
☐ 2368 Steve Walker
☐ 2369 Ken Bolek MG
☐ 2370 Oscar Acosta CO
☐ 2371 Checklist

1994 Dunedin Blue Jays Classic

This 30-card standard size set of the 1994 Dunedin Blue Jays, a Class A Florida State League affiliate of the Toronto Blue Jays, features white-bordered posed color player shots on its fronts with the player's name and position, team name and logo and Classic logo appearing across the bottom of each card. On a ghosted team logo, the white back carries the player's name at the top, followed by biography and statistics.

	MINT	NRMT	EXC
COMPLETE SET (30)	7.00	3.10	.85

☐ 1 D.J. Boston
☐ 2 Alonso Beltran
☐ 3 Lou Benbow
☐ 4 Derek Brandow
☐ 5 Chad Brown
☐ 6 Mike Coolbaugh
☐ 7 Rickey Cradle
☐ 8 Lee Daniels
☐ 9 Andy Dolson
☐ 10 Roger Doman
☐ 11 Kris Harmes
☐ 12 Sean Hearn
☐ 13 Santiago Henry
☐ 14 Aaron Jersild
☐ 15 Matt Johnson
☐ 16 Chris Kotes
☐ 17 Marc Loeb
☐ 18 Angel Martinez
☐ 19 Adam Meinershagen
☐ 20 Rob Montalvo
☐ 21 Mike Murphy
☐ 22 Juan Querecuto
☐ 23 Lonell Roberts
☐ 24 Jose Silva
☐ 25 Tom Singer
☐ 26 Ben Weber
☐ 27 Jim Nettles MG
☐ 28 Bill Monbouquette CO
☐ 29 Rocket Wheeler CO
☐ 30 Dennis Brogna TR
Checklist

1994 Dunedin Blue Jays Fleer/ProCards

This 30-card standard size set of the 1994 Dunedin Blue Jays, a Class A Florida State League affiliate of the Toronto Blue Jays, features white-bordered posed color player photos on its fronts with the player's name, position, team name and Fleer/ProCards logo across the bottom of each card. The white back with vertical light blue stripes carries the player's name at the top, followed by biography and statistics.

	MINT	NRMT	EXC
COMPLETE SET (30)	5.00	2.20	.60

☐ 2546 Alonso Beltran
☐ 2547 Derek Brandow
☐ 2548 Chad Brown
☐ 2549 Lee Daniels
☐ 2550 Andy Dolson
☐ 2551 Roger Doman
☐ 2552 Aaron Jersild
☐ 2553 Chris Kotes
☐ 2554 Levon Largusa
☐ 2555 Adam Meinershagen
☐ 2556 Jose Silva
☐ 2557 Tom Singer
☐ 2558 Ben Weber
☐ 2559 Kris Harmes
☐ 2560 Marc Loeb
☐ 2561 Angel Martinez
☐ 2562 Lou Benbow
☐ 2563 Mike Coolbaugh
☐ 2564 Santiago Henry
☐ 2565 Matt Johnson
☐ 2566 Juan Querecuto
☐ 2567 D.J. Boston
☐ 2568 Rickey Cradle
☐ 2569 Sean Hearn
☐ 2570 Mike Murphy
☐ 2571 Lonell Roberts
☐ 2572 Jim Nettles MG
☐ 2573 Bill Monbouquette CO
☐ 2574 Rocket Wheeler CO
☐ 2575 Checklist

1994 Durham Bulls Classic

This 30-card standard size set of the 1994 Durham Bulls, a Class A Carolina League affiliate of the Atlanta Braves, features white-bordered posed color player shots on its fronts with the player's name and position, team name and logo and Classic logo appearing across the bottom of each card. On a ghosted team logo, the white back carries the player's name at the top, followed by biography and statistics. This issue includes the minor league card debut of Robert Smith.

	MINT	NRMT	EXC
COMPLETE SET (30)	10.00	4.50	1.25

☐ 1 Damon Hollins
☐ 2 Jamie Arnold
☐ 3 Jeff Bock
☐ 4 Jason Butler
☐ 5 Matt Byrd
☐ 6 Mike D'Andrea
☐ 7 Adrian Garcia
☐ 8 Ken Giard
☐ 9 Kevin Grijak
☐ 10 Jason Keeline
☐ 11 Marty Malloy
☐ 12 Matt Murray
☐ 13 Ramon Nunez
☐ 14 Nelson Paulino
☐ 15 Brad Rippelmeyer
☐ 16 Keith Schmidt
☐ 17 Carl Schutz
☐ 18 John Simmons
☐ 19 Robert Smith
☐ 20 Blase Sparma
☐ 21 Anthony Stoecklin
☐ 22 David Toth
☐ 23 Julio Trapaga
☐ 24 Tom Waldrop
☐ 25 Mike Warner
☐ 26 Juan Wiliams
☐ 27 Matt West MG
☐ 28 Bill Slack CO
☐ 29 Rick Albert CO
☐ 30 Jay Williams TR
Checklist

1994 Durham Bulls Fleer/ProCards

This 30-card standard size set of the 1994 Durham Bulls, a Class A Carolina League affiliate of the Atlanta Braves, features white-bordered posed color player photos on its fronts with the player's name, position, team name and Fleer/ProCards logo across the bottom of each card. The white back with vertical light blue stripes carries the player's name at the top, followed by biography and statistics. This issue includes the minor league card debut of Robert Smith.

	MINT	NRMT	EXC
COMPLETE SET (30)	8.00	3.60	1.00

☐ 319 Jamie Arnold
☐ 320 Jeff Bock
☐ 321 Jason Butler
☐ 322 Matt Byrd
☐ 323 Mike D'Andrea
☐ 324 Ken Giard
☐ 325 Matt Murray
☐ 326 Carl Schutz
☐ 327 John Simmons
☐ 328 Blase Sparma
☐ 329 Tony Stoecklin
☐ 330 Adrian Garcia
☐ 331 Brad Ripplemeyer
☐ 332 Dave Toth
☐ 333 Jason Keeline
☐ 334 Marty Malloy
☐ 335 Ramon Nunez
☐ 336 Nelson Paulino
☐ 337 Bobby Smith
☐ 338 Julio Trapaga
☐ 339 Kevin Grijak
☐ 340 Damon Hollins
☐ 341 Keith Schmidt
☐ 342 Tom Waldrop
☐ 343 Mike Warner
☐ 344 Juan Williams
☐ 345 Matt West
☐ 346 Rick Albert MG
☐ 347 Bill Slack CO
☐ 348 Checklist CO

1994 Durham Bulls Team Issue

The cards are unnumbered and checklisted below in alphabetical order. This issue includes the minor league card debut of Robert Smith.

	MINT	NRMT	EXC
COMPLETE SET (32)	8.00	3.60	1.00

☐ 1 Rick Albert CO
☐ 2 Jamie Arnold
☐ 3 Jeff Bock
☐ 4 Matt Byrd
☐ 5 Mike D'Andrea
☐ 6 Adrian Garcia
☐ 7 Ken Giard
☐ 8 Kevin Grijak
☐ 9 Damon Hollins

☐ 10 Jason Keeline
☐ 11 Marty Malloy
☐ 12 Darrell May
☐ 13 Matt Murray
☐ 14 Raymond Nunez
☐ 15 Nelson Paulino
☐ 16 Brad Rippelmeyer
☐ 17 Keith Schmidt
☐ 18 Carl Schutz
☐ 19 John Simmons
☐ 20 Bill Slack CO
☐ 21 Robert Smith
☐ 22 Blase Sparma
☐ 23 Anthony Stoecklin
☐ 24 David Toth
☐ 25 Julio Trapaga
☐ 26 Tom Waldrop
☐ 27 Mike Warner
☐ 28 Matt West MG
☐ 29 Jay Williams TR
☐ 30 Juan Williams
☐ 31 Willie Wilson BB
☐ 32 Blank Card

1994 Edmonton Trappers Fleer/ProCards

This 27-card standard size set of the 1994 Edmonton Trappers, a Class AAA Pacific Coast League affiliate of the Florida Marlins, features white-bordered posed color player photos on its fronts with the player's name, position, team name and Fleer/ProCards logo across the bottom of each card. The white back with vertical light blue stripes carries the player's name at the top, followed by biography and statistics.

	MINT	NRMT	EXC
COMPLETE SET (27)	5.00	2.20	.60

☐ 2867 Darrin Chapin
☐ 2868 Brian Drahman
☐ 2869 Willie Fraser
☐ 2870 Mike Jeffcoat
☐ 2871 John Johnstone
☐ 2872 Steve Long
☐ 2873 Terry Mathews
☐ 2874 Kurt Miller
☐ 2875 Dana Ridenour
☐ 2876 Rich Scheid
☐ 2877 Mitch Lyden
☐ 2878 Bob Natal
☐ 2879 Joe Millette
☐ 2880 Russ Morman
☐ 2881 Al Pedrique
☐ 2882 Vic Rodriguez
☐ 2883 Jim Walewander
☐ 2884 Nick Capra
☐ 2885 Carl Everett
☐ 2886 Monty Fariss
☐ 2887 John Massarelli
☐ 2888 Darrell Whitmore
☐ 2889 Nigel Wilson
☐ 2890 Sal Rende MG
☐ 2891 Rich Dubee CO
☐ 2892 Adrian Garrett CO
☐ 2893 Checklist

1994 El Paso Diablos Fleer/ProCards

This 28-card standard size set of the 1994 El Paso Diablos, a Class AA Texas League affiliate of the Milwaukee Brewers, features white-bordered posed color player photos on its fronts with the player's name, position, team name and Fleer/ProCards logo across the bottom of each card. The white back with vertical light blue stripes carries the player's name at the top, followed by biography and statistics.

	MINT	NRMT	EXC
COMPLETE SET (28)	5.00	2.20	.60

☐ 3137 Kurt Archer
☐ 3138 Greg Bicknell
☐ 3139 Francisco Gamez
☐ 3140 Chris George
☐ 3141 Ron Gerstein
☐ 3142 Tony Gordon
☐ 3143 Steve Peck
☐ 3144 Tom Popplewell
☐ 3145 Sid Roberson
☐ 3146 John Shea
☐ 3147 Mike Thomas
☐ 3148 Dan Calcagno
☐ 3149 Bob Kappesser
☐ 3150 Mike Stefanski
☐ 3151 Matt Davis
☐ 3152 Rod Lofton
☐ 3153 Mark Loretta
☐ 3154 Kevin Riggs
☐ 3155 Scott Talanoa
☐ 3156 Tim Unroe
☐ 3157 Leon Glenn
☐ 3158 Mike Harris
☐ 3159 Danny Perez
☐ 3160 Todd Samples
☐ 3161 Tim Ireland MG
☐ 3162 Rob Derksen CO
☐ 3163 Bob Mariano CO
☐ 3164 Checklist

1994 Elizabethton Twins Classic

This 30-card standard size set of the 1994 Elizabethton Twins, a Rookie Class Appalachian League affiliate of the Minnesota Twins, features white-bordered posed color player shots on its fronts with the player's name and position, team name and logo and Classic logo appearing across the bottom of each card. On a ghosted team logo, the white back carries the player's name at the top, followed by biography and statistics. This issue includes the minor league card debut of Jose Valentin.

	MINT	NRMT	EXC
COMPLETE SET (30)	12.00	5.50	1.50

☐ 1 Guillermo Abreu
☐ 2 Luis Alvarado
☐ 3 Eric Anderson
☐ 4 Ruben Castro
☐ 5 Trevor Cobb
☐ 6 Deron Dowhower
☐ 7 Darren Fidge
☐ 8 Troy Fortin
☐ 9 Adrian Gordon
☐ 10 Ryan Lane
☐ 11 Matthew Leach
☐ 12 Jim McCalmont
☐ 13 Jason Meyhoff
☐ 14 Paul Morse
☐ 15 Kelcey Mucker
☐ 16 Jake Patterson
☐ 17 Paul Pavicich
☐ 18 Kevin Pearson
☐ 19 Dan Perkins
☐ 20 John Peters
☐ 21 Rob Ruch
☐ 22 Aaron Schooler
☐ 23 Marcus Starling
☐ 24 Jose Valentin
☐ 25 Romulo Vizcaino
☐ 26 Juan Williams
☐ 27 Logo Card
☐ 28 Logo Card
☐ 29 Logo Card
☐ 30 Checklist

1994 Elizabethton Twins Fleer/ProCards

This 29-card standard size set of the 1994 Elizabethton Twins, a Rookie Class Appalachian League affiliate of the Minnesota Twins, features white-bordered posed color player photos on its fronts with the player's name, position, team name and Fleer/ProCards logo across the bottom of each card. The white back with vertical light blue stripes carries the player's name at the top, followed by biography and statistics. This issue includes the minor league card debut of Jose Valentin.

	MINT	NRMT	EXC
COMPLETE SET (29)	8.00	3.60	1.00

☐ 3720 Luis Alvarado
☐ 3721 Eric Anderson
☐ 3722 Trevor Cobb
☐ 3723 Deron Dowhower
☐ 3724 Darren Fidge
☐ 3725 Matthew Leach
☐ 3726 Jason Meyhoff
☐ 3727 Paul Morse
☐ 3728 Paul Pavicich
☐ 3729 Dan Perkins
☐ 3730 John Peters
☐ 3731 Rob Ruch
☐ 3732 Aaron Schooler
☐ 3733 Marcus Starling
☐ 3734 Juan Williams
☐ 3735 Troy Fortin
☐ 3736 Jose Valentin
☐ 3737 Guillermo Abreu
☐ 3738 Ruben Castro
☐ 3739 Ryan Lane
☐ 3740 Jim McCalmont
☐ 3741 Jake Patterson
☐ 3742 Adrian Gordon
☐ 3743 Kelcey Mucker
☐ 3744 Kevin Pearson
☐ 3745 Romulo Vizcaino
☐ 3746 Ray Smith MG
☐ 3747 Dwight Bernard CO
☐ 3748 Checklist

1994 Elmira Pioneers Classic

This 29-card standard size set of the 1994 Elmira Pioneers, a Class A New York-Penn League affiliate of the Florida Marlins, features white-bordered posed color player shots on its fronts with the player's name and position, team name and logo and Classic logo appearing across the bottom of each card. On a ghosted team logo, the white back carries the player's name at the top, followed by biography and statistics.

	MINT	NRMT	EXC
COMPLETE SET (29)	10.00	4.50	1.25

☐ 1 Fritz Allison
☐ 2 Todd Cady
☐ 3 Todd Carl
☐ 4 Justin Charles
☐ 5 Antonio Darden
☐ 6 Mark Gugino
☐ 7 Lionel Hastings
☐ 8 Allan Hebbert
☐ 9 Ryan Jackson
☐ 10 Scott Johnson
☐ 11 Andrew Linehan
☐ 12 Sommer McCartney
☐ 13 Chad Miles
☐ 14 Scott Pace
☐ 15 Mike Parisi
☐ 16 Greg Press
☐ 17 Michael Reyes
☐ 18 John Roskos
☐ 19 Randy Shagena
☐ 20 Robby Stanifer
☐ 21 Sean Touchet
☐ 22 Don Tynon
☐ 23 Walt White
☐ 24 Jim Hendry
☐ 25 Bill Long
☐ 26 Steve Tolly
☐ 29A Florida Marlins Logo
☐ 29B Elmira Pioneers Logo
☐ 30 Elmira Pioneers Logo CL

1994 Elmira Pioneers Fleer/ProCards

This 27-card standard size set of the 1994 Elmira Pioneers, a Class A New York-Penn League affiliate of the Florida Marlins, features white-bordered posed color player photos on its fronts with the player's name, position, team name and Fleer/ProCards logo across the bottom of each card. The white back with vertical light blue stripes carries the player's name at the top, followed by biography and statistics.

	MINT	NRMT	EXC
COMPLETE SET (27)	5.00	2.20	.60

☐ 3465 Todd Carl
☐ 3466 Allan Hebbert
☐ 3467 Scott Johnson
☐ 3468 Andy Linehan
☐ 3469 Chad Miles
☐ 3470 Scott Pace
☐ 3471 Mike Parisi
☐ 3472 Greg Press
☐ 3473 Randy Shagena
☐ 3474 Robby Stanifer
☐ 3475 Sean Touchet
☐ 3476 Don Tynon
☐ 3477 Todd Cady
☐ 3478 Sommer McCartney
☐ 3479 John Roskos
☐ 3480 Fritz Allison
☐ 3481 Justin Charles
☐ 3482 Tony Darden
☐ 3483 Lionel Hastings
☐ 3484 Rich Seminoff
☐ 3485 Walt White
☐ 3486 Mark Gugino
☐ 3487 Ryan Jackson
☐ 3488 Mike Reyes
☐ 3489 Jim Hendry MG
☐ 3490 Bill Long CO
☐ 3491 Checklist

1994 Eugene Emeralds Classic

This 30-card standard size set of the 1994 Eugene Emeralds, a Class A Northwest League affiliate of the Kansas City Royals, eatures white-bordered posed color player shots on its fronts with the player's name and position, team name and logo and Classic logo appearing across the bottom of each card. On a ghosted team logo, the white back carries the player's name at the top, followed by biography and statistics.

	MINT	NRMT	EXC
COMPLETE SET (30)	10.00	4.50	1.25

☐ 1 Jaime Bluma
☐ 2 Jelani Brandon
☐ 3 Carlos Burgos
☐ 4 Tim Byrdak
☐ 5 Lance Carter
☐ 6 Malcolm Cepeda
☐ 7 Shannon Coulter
☐ 8 Donovan Delaney
☐ 9 Dan Dillingham
☐ 10 Javier Gamboa
☐ 11 Tim Grieve
☐ 12 Andres Lopez
☐ 13 Sean McNally
☐ 14 Eric Mooney
☐ 15 Kortney Paul
☐ 16 Marc Phillips
☐ 17 Scott Pinoni
☐ 18 Jason Ritter
☐ 19 Ray Roberts
☐ 20 Jeff Scarpitti
☐ 21 Rodney Sparks
☐ 22 Brian Teeters
☐ 23 D. Wayne Upchurch
☐ 24 Tyler Williamson
☐ 25 Ken Winkle
☐ 26 Eddie Cedeno
☐ 27 Jason Huffman
☐ 28 Brian Poldberg MG UER
No picture--just Logo
☐ 29 Theo Shaw CO UER
No picture--just Logo
☐ 30 Rafael Santana CO UER
No picture--just Logo
Checklist

1994 Eugene Emeralds Fleer/ProCards

This 28-card standard size set of the 1994 Eugene Emeralds, a Class A Northwest League affiliate of the Kansas City Royals, features white-bordered posed color player photos on its fronts with the player's name, position, team name and Fleer/ProCards logo across the bottom of each card. The white back with vertical light blue stripes carries the player's name at the top, followed by biography and statistics.

	MINT	NRMT	EXC
COMPLETE SET (28)	5.00	2.20	.60

☐ 3701 Jaime Bluma
☐ 3702 Tim Byrdak
☐ 3703 Lance Carter
☐ 3704 Javier Gamboa
☐ 3705 Tim Grieve
☐ 3706 Jason Huffman
☐ 3707 Andres Lopez
☐ 3708 Eric Mooney
☐ 3709 Marc Phillips
☐ 3710 Jason Ritter
☐ 3711 Ray Roberts
☐ 3712 Jeff Scarpitti
☐ 3713 David Upchurch
☐ 3714 Ken Winkle
☐ 3715 Carlos Burgos
☐ 3716 Kortney Paul
☐ 3717 Tyler Williamson
☐ 3718 Eduardo Cedeno
☐ 3719 Malcolm Cepeda
☐ 3720 Shannon Coulter
☐ 3721 Sean McNally
☐ 3722 Scott Pinoni
☐ 3723 Rodney Sparks
☐ 3724 Jelani Brandon
☐ 3725 Donovan Delaney
☐ 3726 Dan Dillingham
☐ 3727 Brian Teeters
☐ 3728 Checklist

1994 Everett Giants Classic

This 30-card standard size set of the 1994 Everett Giants, a Class A Northwest League affiliate of the San Francisco Giants, features white-bordered posed color player shots on its fronts with the player's name and position, team name and logo and Classic logo appearing across the bottom of each card. On a ghosted team logo, the white back carries the player's name at the top, followed by biography and statistics.

	MINT	NRMT	EXC
COMPLETE SET (30)	7.00	3.10	.85

☐ 1 Jamie Apicella
☐ 2 Isbel Cardona
☐ 3 Alberto Castillo
☐ 4 Kevin Watson
☐ 5 Scott Cook
☐ 6 Don Denbow
☐ 7 Keith Foulke
☐ 8 Chad Frontera
☐ 9 Mike Giardi
☐ 10 Dennys Gomez
☐ 11 Chad Hartvigson
☐ 12 Ryan Hornbeck
☐ 13 Bobby Howry
☐ 14 Jesse Ibarra
☐ 15 Greg Keifer
☐ 16 Jeff Keith
☐ 17 Kevin Lake
☐ 18 Cory Lintern
☐ 19 Mike Villano
☐ 20 Eric Martin
☐ 21 Raul Marval
☐ 22 Tony Mattos
☐ 23 Pete Prater
☐ 24 Melvin Roman
☐ 25 Mike Schiefelbein
☐ 26 Danny Schneider
☐ 27 Chris Stasio
☐ 28 David Tessicini
☐ 29 Keith Comstock CO
☐ 30 Juan Lopez CO
Checklist

1994 Everett Giants Fleer/ProCards

This 31-card standard size set of the 1994 Everett Giants, a Class A Northwest League affiliate of the San Francisco Giants, features white-bordered posed color player photos on its fronts with the player's name, position, team name and Fleer/ProCards logo across the bottom of each card. The white back with vertical light blue stripes carries the player's name at the top, followed by biography and statistics. This issue includes the minor league card debut of Dante Powell.

	MINT	NRMT	EXC
COMPLETE SET (31)	15.00	6.75	1.85

☐ 3641 Isbel Cardona
☐ 3642 Scott Cook
☐ 3643 Keith Foulke
☐ 3644 Chad Frontera
☐ 3645 Dennys Gomez
☐ 3646 Chad Hartvigson
☐ 3647 Ryan Hornbeck
☐ 3648 Bobby Howry
☐ 3649 Jeff Keith
☐ 3650 Kevin Lake
☐ 3651 Cory Lintern
☐ 3652 Pete Prater
☐ 3653 Mike Schiefelbein
☐ 3654 Danny Schneider
☐ 3655 Brian Shepherd
☐ 3656 Mike Villano
☐ 3657 Alberto Castillo
☐ 3658 Mike Giardi
☐ 3659 Jesse Ibarra
☐ 3660 Raul Marval
☐ 3661 Melvin Roman
☐ 3662 Chris Stasio
☐ 3663 David Tessicini
☐ 3664 Todd Wilson
☐ 3665 Jamie Apicella
☐ 3666 Don Denbow
☐ 3667 Greg Keifer
☐ 3668 Eric Martin
☐ 3669 Dante Powell
☐ 3670 Kevin Watson
☐ 3671 Checklist

1994 Excel

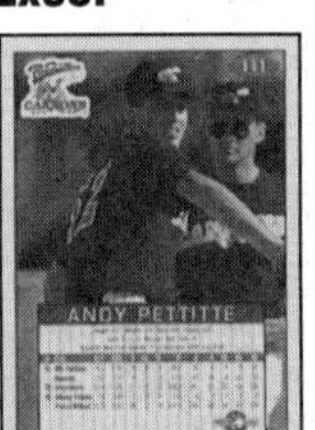

The 1994 Excel Minor League set consists of 300 cards featuring minor league players from AAA, AA and A teams. The fronts display color player photos bordered in white. The player's name, the team's city, and his position appear in a bar at the bottom of the picture. The backs carry a large color close-up photo with the team logo superimposed at the upper left corner. Overlaying the photo toward the bottom is a colorful player information panel displaying biographical and statistical information. The cards are numbered on the back and checklisted below alphabetically within and according to major league teams for the NL and AL.

	MINT	NRMT	EXC
COMPLETE SET (300)	30.00	13.50	3.70
COMMON CARD (1-300)	.05	.02	.01

Card	MINT	NRMT	EXC
☐ 1 Armando Benitez	.05	.02	.01
☐ 2 Stanton Cameron	.05	.02	.01
☐ 3 Eric Chavez	.05	.02	.01
☐ 4 Rick Forney	.05	.02	.01
☐ 5 Jim Foster	.05	.02	.01
☐ 6 Curtis Goodwin	.05	.02	.01
☐ 7 Jimmy Haynes	.05	.02	.01
☐ 8 Scott Klingenbeck	.05	.02	.01
☐ 9 Rick Krivda	.05	.02	.01
☐ 10 T.R. Lewis	.05	.02	.01
☐ 11 Brian Link	.05	.02	.01
☐ 12 Scott McClain	.05	.02	.01
☐ 13 Alex Ochoa	.75	.35	.09
☐ 14 Jay Powell	.05	.02	.01
☐ 15 Brian Sackinsky	.05	.02	.01
☐ 16 Brad Tyler	.05	.02	.01
☐ 17 Gregg Zaun	.05	.02	.01
☐ 18 Joel Bennett	.05	.02	.01
☐ 19 Felix Colon	.05	.02	.01
☐ 20 Ryan McGuire	.05	.02	.01
☐ 21 Frankie Rodriguez	.05	.02	.01
☐ 22 Tim Vanegmond	.05	.02	.01
☐ 23 Garret Anderson	.60	.25	.07
☐ 24 Jorge Fabregas	.05	.02	.01
☐ 25 P.J. Forbes	.05	.02	.01
☐ 26 John Fritz	.05	.02	.01
☐ 27 Todd Greene	.75	.35	.09
☐ 28 Jose Musset	.05	.02	.01
☐ 29 Orlando Palmeiro	.05	.02	.01
☐ 30 Jon Pricher	.05	.02	.01
☐ 31 Chris Pritchett	.05	.02	.01
☐ 32 Marquis Riley	.05	.02	.01
☐ 33 Luis Andujar	.05	.02	.01
☐ 34 James Baldwin	.15	.07	.02
☐ 35 Brian Boehringer	.05	.02	.01
☐ 36 Ron Coomer	.05	.02	.01
☐ 37 Ray Durham	1.25	.55	.16
☐ 38 Robert Ellis	.05	.02	.01
☐ 39 Jeff Pierce	.05	.02	.01
☐ 40 Olmedo Saenz	.05	.02	.01
☐ 41 Brandon Wilson	.05	.02	.01
☐ 42 Ian Doyle	.05	.02	.01
☐ 43 Jason Fronio	.05	.02	.01
☐ 44 Derek Hacopian	.05	.02	.01
☐ 45 Daron Kirkreit	.05	.02	.01
☐ 46 Mike Neal	.05	.02	.01
☐ 47 Chad Ogea	.15	.07	.02
☐ 48 Cesar Perez	.05	.02	.01
☐ 49 Omar Ramirez	.05	.02	.01
☐ 50 J.J. Thobe	.05	.02	.01
☐ 51 Casey Whitten	.05	.02	.01
☐ 52 Eric Danapilis	.05	.02	.01
☐ 53 Brian Edmondson	.05	.02	.01
☐ 54 Tony Fuduric	.05	.02	.01
☐ 55 Ricky Greene	.05	.02	.01
☐ 56 Bob Higginson	.75	.35	.09
☐ 57 Felipe Lira	.05	.02	.01
☐ 58 Joshua Neese	.05	.02	.01
☐ 59 Shannon Penn	.05	.02	.01
☐ 60 John Rosengren	.05	.02	.01
☐ 61 Phil Stidham	.05	.02	.01
☐ 62 Justin Thompson	.15	.07	.02
☐ 63 Shawn Wooten	.05	.02	.01
☐ 64 Brian Bevil	.05	.02	.01
☐ 65 Mel Bunch	.05	.02	.01
☐ 66 Johnny Damon	1.00	.45	.12
☐ 67 Chris Eddy	.05	.02	.01
☐ 68 Jon Lieber	.15	.07	.02
☐ 69 Les Norman	.05	.02	.01
☐ 70 Jim Pittsley	.15	.07	.02
☐ 71 Kris Ralston	.05	.02	.01
☐ 72 Joe Randa	.05	.02	.01
☐ 73 Kevin Rawitzer	.05	.02	.01
☐ 74 Chris Sheehan	.05	.02	.01
☐ 75 Robert Toth	.05	.02	.01
☐ 76 Michael Tucker	.30	.14	.04
☐ 77 Brian Banks	.05	.02	.01
☐ 78 Marshall Boze	.05	.02	.01
☐ 79 Jeff Cirillo	.15	.07	.02
☐ 80 Bo Dodson	.05	.02	.01
☐ 81 Bobby Hughes	.05	.02	.01
☐ 82 Scott Karl	.05	.02	.01
☐ 83 Mike Matheny	.05	.02	.01
☐ 84 Kevin Riggs	.05	.02	.01
☐ 85 Sid Roberson	.05	.02	.01
☐ 86 Charlie Rogers	.05	.02	.01
☐ 87 Mike Stefanski	.05	.02	.01
☐ 88 Scott Talanoa	.05	.02	.01
☐ 89 Derek Wachter	.05	.02	.01
☐ 90 Wes Weger	.05	.02	.01
☐ 91 Anthony Byrd	.05	.02	.01
☐ 92 Marty Cordova	1.00	.45	.12
☐ 93 Steve Dunn	.15	.07	.02
☐ 94 Gus Gandarillos	.05	.02	.01
☐ 95 LaTroy Hawkins	.05	.02	.01
☐ 96 Oscar Munoz	.05	.02	.01
☐ 97 Dan Perkins	.15	.07	.02
☐ 98 Dan Serafini UER Name spelled Ken on card	.15	.07	.02
☐ 99 Ken Tirpack	.05	.02	.01
☐ 100 Russell Davis	.15	.07	.02
☐ 101 Nick Delvecchio	.05	.02	.01
☐ 102 Robert Eenhoorn	.05	.02	.01
☐ 103 Ron Frazier	.05	.02	.01
☐ 104 Kraig Hawkins	.05	.02	.01
☐ 105 Keith Heberling	.05	.02	.01
☐ 106 Derek Jeter	2.50	1.10	.30
☐ 107 Kevin Jordan	.05	.02	.01
☐ 108 Ryan Karp	.05	.02	.01
☐ 109 Matt Luke	.05	.02	.01
☐ 110 Lyle Mouton	.05	.02	.01
☐ 111 Andy Pettitte	2.00	.90	.25
☐ 112 Jorge Posada	.15	.07	.02
☐ 113 Ruben Rivera	4.00	1.80	.50
☐ 114 Tate Seefried	.05	.02	.01
☐ 115 Brien Taylor	.05	.02	.01
☐ 116 Mark Acre	.05	.02	.01
☐ 117 Jim Bowie	.05	.02	.01
☐ 118 Russ Brock	.05	.02	.01
☐ 119 Fausto Cruz	.05	.02	.01
☐ 120 Jason Giambi	.75	.35	.09
☐ 121 Izzy Molina	.05	.02	.01
☐ 122 George Williams	.15	.07	.02
☐ 123 Joel Wolfe	.05	.02	.01
☐ 124 Ernie Young	.15	.07	.02
☐ 125 Tim Davis	.05	.02	.01
☐ 126 Jackie Nickell	.05	.02	.01
☐ 127 Ruben Santana	.05	.02	.01
☐ 128 Mac Suzuki	.05	.02	.01
☐ 129 Ron Villone	.05	.02	.01
☐ 130 Rich Aurilia	.05	.02	.01
☐ 131 John Dettmer	.05	.02	.01
☐ 132 Scott Eyre	.05	.02	.01
☐ 133 Dave Geeve	.05	.02	.01
☐ 134 Rick Helling	.05	.02	.01
☐ 135 Kerry Lacy	.05	.02	.01
☐ 136 Trey McCoy	.05	.02	.01
☐ 137 Wes Shook	.05	.02	.01
☐ 138 Howard Battle	.05	.02	.01
☐ 139 D.J. Boston	.05	.02	.01
☐ 140 Rick Butler	.05	.02	.01
☐ 141 Brad Cornett	.05	.02	.01
☐ 142 Jesse Cross	.05	.02	.01
☐ 143 Alex Gonzalez	.15	.07	.02
☐ 144 Kurt Heble	.05	.02	.01
☐ 145 Jose Herrera	.15	.07	.02
☐ 146 Ryan Jones	.75	.35	.09
☐ 147 Robert Perez	.05	.02	.01
☐ 148 Jose Silva	.15	.07	.02
☐ 149 Shannon Stewart	.15	.07	.02
☐ 150 Chris Weinke	.05	.02	.01
☐ 151 Jamie Arnold	.05	.02	.01
☐ 152 Chris Brock	.05	.02	.01
☐ 153 Tony Graffagnino	.05	.02	.01
☐ 154 Damon Hollins	.25	.11	.03
☐ 155 Mike Hostetler	.05	.02	.01
☐ 156 Mike Kelly	.05	.02	.01
☐ 157 Andre King	.05	.02	.01
☐ 158 Darrell May	.05	.02	.01
☐ 159 Vince Moore	.05	.02	.01
☐ 160 Don Strange	.05	.02	.01
☐ 161 Dominic Therrien	.05	.02	.01
☐ 162 Terrell Wade	.05	.02	.01
☐ 163 Brant Brown	.05	.02	.01
☐ 164 Matt Franco	.05	.02	.01
☐ 165 Brooks Kieschnick	.50	.23	.06
☐ 166 Jon Ratliff	.05	.02	.01
☐ 167 Kennie Steenstra	.05	.02	.01
☐ 168 Amaury Telemaco	.05	.02	.01
☐ 169 Ozzie Timmons	.05	.02	.01
☐ 170 Hector Trinidad	.05	.02	.01
☐ 171 Travis Willis	.05	.02	.01
☐ 172 Tim Belk	.05	.02	.01
☐ 173 Jamie Dismuke	.05	.02	.01
☐ 174 Mike Ferry	.05	.02	.01
☐ 175 Chris Hook	.05	.02	.01
☐ 176 John Hrusovsky	.05	.02	.01
☐ 177 Cleveland Ladell	.05	.02	.01
☐ 178 Martin Lister	.05	.02	.01
☐ 179 Chad Mottola	.05	.02	.01
☐ 180 Eric Owens	.05	.02	.01
☐ 181 Scott Sullivan	.05	.02	.01
☐ 182 Pat Watkins	.15	.07	.02
☐ 183 Jason Bates	.05	.02	.01
☐ 184 John Burke	.05	.02	.01
☐ 185 Quinton McCracken	.05	.02	.01
☐ 186 Neifi Perez	.40	.18	.05
☐ 187 Bryan Rekar	.05	.02	.01
☐ 188 Mark Thompson	.05	.02	.01
☐ 189 Tim Clark	.05	.02	.01
☐ 190 Vic Darensbourg	.05	.02	.01
☐ 191 Charles Johnson	.75	.35	.09
☐ 192 Bryn Kosco	.05	.02	.01
☐ 193 Reynol Mendoza	.05	.02	.01
☐ 194 Kerwin Moore	.05	.02	.01
☐ 195 John Toale	.05	.02	.01
☐ 196 Bob Abreu	.75	.35	.09
☐ 197 Jim Bruske	.05	.02	.01
☐ 198 Jim Dougherty	.05	.02	.01
☐ 199 Tony Eusebio	.05	.02	.01
☐ 200 Kevin Gallaher	.05	.02	.01
☐ 201 Chris Holt	.05	.02	.01
☐ 202 Brian L. Hunter	.40	.18	.05
☐ 203 Orlando Miller	.05	.02	.01
☐ 204 Donovan Mitchell	.05	.02	.01
☐ 205 Alvin Morman	.05	.02	.01
☐ 206 James Mouton	.05	.02	.01
☐ 207 Phil Nevin	.05	.02	.01
☐ 208 Roberto Petagine	.05	.02	.01
☐ 209 Billy Wagner	.40	.18	.05
☐ 210 Mike Busch	.05	.02	.01
☐ 211 Roger Cedeno	.30	.14	.04
☐ 212 Chris Demetral	.05	.02	.01
☐ 213 Rick Gorecki	.05	.02	.01
☐ 214 Ryan Henderson	.05	.02	.01
☐ 215 Todd Hollandsworth	.75	.35	.09
☐ 216 Ken Huckaby	.05	.02	.01
☐ 217 Rich Linares	.05	.02	.01
☐ 218 Ryan Luzinski	.05	.02	.01
☐ 219 Doug Newstrom	.05	.02	.01
☐ 220 Ben VanRyn	.05	.02	.01
☐ 221 Todd Williams	.05	.02	.01
☐ 222 Shane Andrews	.05	.02	.01
☐ 223 Reid Cornelius	.05	.02	.01
☐ 224 Joey Eischen	.05	.02	.01
☐ 225 Heath Haynes	.05	.02	.01
☐ 226 Rod Henderson	.05	.02	.01
☐ 227 Mark LaRosa	.05	.02	.01
☐ 228 Glenn Murray	.05	.02	.01
☐ 229 Ugueth Urbina	.05	.02	.01
☐ 230 B.J. Wallace	.05	.02	.01
☐ 231 Gabe White	.05	.02	.01
☐ 232 Edgardo Alfonzo	.05	.02	.01
☐ 233 Randy Curtis	.05	.02	.01
☐ 234 Omar Garcia	.05	.02	.01
☐ 235 Jason Isringhausen	.60	.25	.07
☐ 236 Eric Ludwick	.05	.02	.01
☐ 237 Bill Pulsipher	.30	.14	.04
☐ 238 Chris Roberts	.05	.02	.01
☐ 239 Quilvio Veras	.15	.07	.02
☐ 240 Pete Walker	.05	.02	.01
☐ 241 Mike Welch	.05	.02	.01
☐ 242 Preston Wilson	.30	.14	.04
☐ 243 Ricky Bottalico	.30	.14	.04
☐ 244 Alan Burke	.05	.02	.01
☐ 245 Phil Geisler	.05	.02	.01
☐ 246 Mike Lieberthal	.15	.07	.02
☐ 247 Jason Moler	.05	.02	.01
☐ 248 Gene Schall	.05	.02	.01
☐ 249 Mark Tranberg	.05	.02	.01
☐ 250 Jermaine Allensworth	.05	.02	.01
☐ 251 Michael Brown	.05	.02	.01
☐ 252 Jason Kendall	.75	.35	.09
☐ 253 Jeff McCurry	.05	.02	.01
☐ 254 Jeff Alkire	.05	.02	.01
☐ 255 Mike Badorek	.05	.02	.01
☐ 256 Brian Barber	.05	.02	.01
☐ 257 Alan Benes	1.00	.45	.12
☐ 258 Jeff Berblinger	.05	.02	.01
☐ 259 Joe Biasucci	.05	.02	.01
☐ 260 Terry Bradshaw	.05	.02	.01
☐ 261 Duff Brumley	.05	.02	.01
☐ 262 Kirk Bullinger	.05	.02	.01
☐ 263 Mike Busby	.05	.02	.01
☐ 264 Jamie Cochran	.05	.02	.01
☐ 265 Clint Davis	.05	.02	.01
☐ 266 Mike Gulan	.05	.02	.01
☐ 267 Aaron Holbert	.05	.02	.01
☐ 268 John Kelly	.05	.02	.01
☐ 269 John Mabry	.15	.07	.02
☐ 270 Frankie Martinez	.05	.02	.01
☐ 271 T.J. Mathews	.05	.02	.01
☐ 272 Aldo Pecorilli	.15	.07	.02
☐ 273 Doug Radziewicz	.05	.02	.01
☐ 274 Brian Rupp	.05	.02	.01
☐ 275 Gerald Witasick	.05	.02	.01
☐ 276 Dmitri Young	.60	.25	.07
☐ 277 Homer Bush	.05	.02	.01
☐ 278 Glenn Dishman	.05	.02	.01
☐ 279 Sean Drinkwater	.05	.02	.01
☐ 280 Bryce Florie	.05	.02	.01
☐ 281 Billy Hall	.05	.02	.01
☐ 282 Jason Hardtke	.05	.02	.01
☐ 283 Ray Holbert	.05	.02	.01
☐ 284 Brian Johnson	.05	.02	.01
☐ 285 Ray McDavid	.05	.02	.01
☐ 286 Ira Smith	.05	.02	.01
☐ 287 Steve Day	.05	.02	.01
☐ 288 Kurt Ehmann	.05	.02	.01
☐ 289 Chad Fonville	.05	.02	.01
☐ 290 Kris Franko	.05	.02	.01
☐ 291 Aaron Fultz	.05	.02	.01
☐ 292 Marcus Jensen	.05	.02	.01
☐ 293 Calvin Murray	.05	.02	.01
☐ 294 Jeff Richey	.05	.02	.01
☐ 295 Bill VanLandingham	.05	.02	.01
☐ 296 Keith Williams	.05	.02	.01
☐ 297 Chris Wimmer	.05	.02	.01
☐ 298 Checklist	.05	.02	.01
☐ 299 Checklist	.05	.02	.01
☐ 300 Checklist	.05	.02	.01

1994 Excel All-Stars

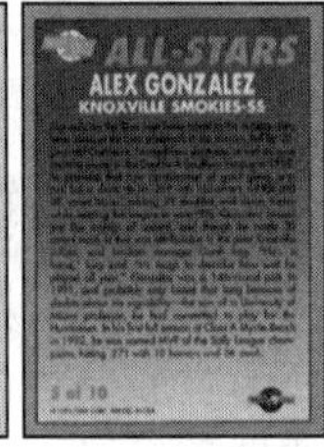

	MINT	NRMT	EXC
COMPLETE SET (10)	10.00	4.50	1.25
COMMON CARD (1-10)	.75	.35	.09

Card	MINT	NRMT	EXC
☐ 1 Charles Johnson	2.00	.90	.25
☐ 2 Roberto Petagine	.75	.35	.09
☐ 3 James Mouton	.75	.35	.09
☐ 4 Russ Davis	1.00	.45	.12
☐ 5 Alex Gonzalez	1.00	.45	.12
☐ 6 Johnny Damon	2.50	1.10	.30
☐ 7 Garret Anderson	1.50	.70	.19
☐ 8 Brian L. Hunter	1.25	.55	.16
☐ 9 D.J. Boston	.75	.35	.09
☐ 10 Terrell Wade	1.00	.45	.12

1994 Excel First Year Phenoms

	MINT	NRMT	EXC
COMPLETE SET (10)	8.00	3.60	1.00
COMMON CARD (1-10)	1.00	.45	.12

Card	MINT	NRMT	EXC
☐ 1 Jim Foster	1.00	.45	.12
☐ 2 Brian Link	1.00	.45	.12
☐ 3 Jeff Berblinger	1.00	.45	.12
☐ 4 Doug Newstrom	1.00	.45	.12

	MINT	NRMT	EXC
☐ 5 Mike Neal	1.00	.45	.12
☐ 6 Jermaine Allensworth	1.00	.45	.12
☐ 7 Todd Greene	2.00	.90	.25
☐ 8 Keith Williams	1.00	.45	.12
☐ 9 Shawn Wooten	1.00	.45	.12
☐ 10 Joshua Neese	1.00	.45	.12

1994 Excel League Leaders

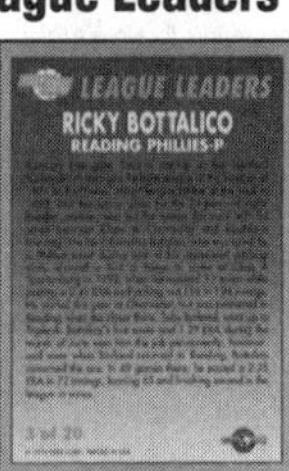

	MINT	NRMT	EXC
COMPLETE SET (20)	15.00	6.75	1.85
COMMON CARD (1-20)	.50	.23	.06
☐ 1 James Baldwin	.75	.35	.09
☐ 2 Joel Bennett	.50	.23	.06
☐ 3 Ricky Bottalico	1.00	.45	.12
☐ 4 Mike Busch	.50	.23	.06
☐ 5 Duff Brumley	.50	.23	.06
☐ 6 Jamie Cochran	.50	.23	.06
☐ 7 John Dettmer	.50	.23	.06
☐ 8 Joey Eischen	.50	.23	.06
☐ 9 LaTroy Hawkins	.50	.23	.06
☐ 10 Derek Jeter	8.00	3.60	1.00
☐ 11 Ryan Karp	.50	.23	.06
☐ 12 Rick Krivda	.50	.23	.06
☐ 13 Trey McCoy	.50	.23	.06
☐ 14 Jason Moler	.50	.23	.06
☐ 15 Chad Mottola	.50	.23	.06
☐ 16 Jose Silva	.75	.35	.09
☐ 17 Brien Taylor	.50	.23	.06
☐ 18 Michael Tucker	1.00	.45	.12
☐ 19 Ugueth Urbina	.75	.35	.09
☐ 20 Ben Van Ryn	.50	.23	.06

1994 Fayetteville Generals Classic

This 30-card standard size set of the 1994 Fayetteville Generals, a Class A South Atlantic League affiliate of the Detroit Tigers, features white-bordered posed color player shots on its fronts with the player's name and position, team name and logo and Classic logo appearing across the bottom of each card. On a ghosted team logo, the white back carries the player's name at the top, followed by biography and statistics. This issue includes the minor league card debut of Juan Encarnacion.

	MINT	NRMT	EXC
COMPLETE SET (30)	8.00	3.60	1.00

☐ 1 Matt Brunson
☐ 2 Sam Arguto
☐ 3 Glen Barker
☐ 4 Alvin Brown
☐ 5 Frank Catalanotto
☐ 6 Drew Christmon
☐ 7 Eric Danapilis
☐ 8 Malvin DeJesus
☐ 9 Bobby Dickerson
☐ 10 Steve Dietz
☐ 11 Juan Encarnacion
☐ 12 Chris Facione
☐ 13 Greg Granger
☐ 14 Will Hunt
☐ 15 Del Marine
☐ 16 Toby McFarland
☐ 17 Jorge Moreno
☐ 18 Scott Norman
☐ 19 Corey Parker
☐ 20 Adam Rodriguez
☐ 21 Mike Salazar
☐ 22 Henry Santos
☐ 23 Cam Smith
☐ 24 Gabe Sollecito
☐ 25 Mike Wilson
☐ 26 Shawn Wooten
☐ 27 Dwight Lowry MG
☐ 28 Jim Van Scoyoc CO
☐ 29 Basilio Cabrera CO
☐ 30 Matt Lewis TR Checklist

1994 Fayetteville Generals Fleer/ProCards

This 29-card standard size set of the 1994 Fayetteville Generals, a Class A South Atlantic League affiliate of the Detroit Tigers, features white-bordered posed color player photos on its fronts with the player's name, position, team name and Fleer/ProCards logo across the bottom of each card. The white back with vertical light blue stripes carries the player's name at the top, followed by biography and statistics. This issue includes the minor league card debut of Juan Encarnacion.

	MINT	NRMT	EXC
COMPLETE SET (29)	5.00	2.20	.60

☐ 2138 Sam Arguto
☐ 2139 Greg Granger
☐ 2140 Will Hunt
☐ 2141 Toby McFarland
☐ 2142 Scott Norman
☐ 2143 Steve Nowak
☐ 2144 Mike Salazar
☐ 2145 Henry Santos
☐ 2146 Cam Smith
☐ 2147 Gabe Sollecito
☐ 2148 Corey Broome
☐ 2149 Del Marine
☐ 2150 Adam Rodriguez
☐ 2151 Matt Brunson
☐ 2152 Frank Catalanotto
☐ 2153 Eric Danapilis
☐ 2154 Malvin DeJesus
☐ 2155 Steve Dietz
☐ 2156 Jorge Moreno
☐ 2157 Corey Parker
☐ 2158 Shawn Wooten
☐ 2159 Glen Barker
☐ 2160 Drew Christmon
☐ 2161 Bobby Dickerson
☐ 2162 Juan Encarnacion
☐ 2163 Chris Facione
☐ 2164 Dwight Lowry MG
☐ 2165 Jim Van Scoyoc CO
☐ 2166 Checklist

1994 Florida State League All-Stars Fleer/ProCards

	MINT	NRMT	EXC
COMPLETE SET (52)	30.00	13.50	3.70

☐ FSL1 Mark Bradenburg
☐ FSL2 Darryl Kennedy
☐ FSL3 Jerry Martin
☐ FSL4 Brian Thomas
☐ FSL5 Lee Daniels
☐ FSL6 Aaron Jersild
☐ FSL7 Angel Martinez
☐ FSL8 Gus Gandarillas
☐ FSL9 Andy Kontorinis
☐ FSL10 Matt Lawton
☐ FSL11 Scott Moten
☐ FSL12 Chad Roper
☐ FSL13 Tarrik Brock
☐ FSL14 John Rosengren
☐ FSL15 Clint Sodowsky
☐ FSL16 Tim Thomas
☐ FSL17 Jason Friedman
☐ FSL18 Mike DeJean
☐ FSL19 Mike Figga
☐ FSL20 Keith Heberling
☐ FSL21 Rob Hinds
☐ FSL22 Derek Jeter
☐ FSL23 Matt Luke
☐ FSL24 Jim Musselwhite
☐ FSL25 Scott Romano
☐ FSL26 Dan Chergey
☐ FSL27 Pat Leahy
☐ FSL28 Matt Petersen
☐ FSL29 Doug Pettit
☐ FSL30 Edgar Renteria
☐ FSL31 Kent Blasingame
☐ FSL32 Dave Doster
☐ FSL33 Brad Erdman
☐ FSL34 Amaury Telemaco
☐ FSL35 Hector Mercado
☐ FSL36 Jim Waring
☐ FSL37 Benny Agbayani
☐ FSL38 Guillermo Garcia
☐ FSL39 Jason Isringhausen
☐ FSL40 Rey Ordonez
☐ FSL41 Alan Benes
☐ FSL42 T.J.Mathews
☐ FSL43 Eric Miller
☐ FSL44 Basil Shabazz
☐ FSL45 DaRond Stovall
☐ FSL46 Karim Garcia
☐ FSL47 Ryan Luzinski
☐ FSL48 Doug Newstrom
☐ FSL49 Willie Otanez
☐ FSL50 Hugo Pivaral
☐ FSL51 Dick Dehart
☐ FSL52 Checklist

1994 Fort Myers Miracle Classic

This 30-card standard size set of the 1994 Fort Myers Miracle, a Class A Florida State League affiliate of the Minnesota Twins, features white-bordered posed color player shots on its fronts with the player's name and position, team name and logo and Classic logo appearing across the bottom of each card. On a ghosted team logo, the white back carries the player's name at the top, followed by biography and statistics.

	MINT	NRMT	EXC
COMPLETE SET (30)	8.00	3.60	1.00

☐ 1 LaTroy Hawkins
☐ 2 David Bigham
☐ 3 Brent Brede
☐ 4 Ron Caridad
☐ 5 Marc Claus
☐ 6 Jose Correa
☐ 7 Gus Gandarillas
☐ 8 David Garrow
☐ 9 Jeff Horn
☐ 10 Dominic Konieczki
☐ 11 Andrew Kontorinis
☐ 12 Matt Lawton
☐ 13 Kevin Legault
☐ 14 Rene Lopez
☐ 15 Scott Moten
☐ 16 Dan Naulty
☐ 17 Ken Norman
☐ 18 Jamie Ogden
☐ 19 Chris Phillips
☐ 20 Brett Roberts
☐ 21 Chad Roper
☐ 22 Craig Saccavino
☐ 23 Dan Serafini
☐ 24 Rich Tunison
☐ 25 Ramon Valette
☐ 26 Steve Liddle MG
☐ 27 Rick Tomlin CO
☐ 28 Jerry White CO
☐ 29 Lanning Tucker TR
☐ 30 Kenny Agacinski BB Checklist

1994 Fort Myers Miracle Fleer/ProCards

This 28-card standard size set of the 1994 Fort Myers Miracle, a Class A Florida State League affiliate of the Minnesota Twins, features white-bordered posed color player photos on its fronts with the player's name, position, team name and Fleer/ProCards logo across the bottom of each card. The white back with vertical light blue stripes carries the player's name at the top, followed by biography and statistics.

	MINT	NRMT	EXC
COMPLETE SET (28)	5.00	2.20	.60

☐ 1158 Dave Bigham
☐ 1159 Ron Caridad
☐ 1160 Jose Correa
☐ 1161 Aaron Fultz
☐ 1162 Gus Gandarillas
☐ 1163 LaTroy Hawkins
☐ 1164 Dom Konieczki
☐ 1165 Kevin Legault
☐ 1166 Scott Moten
☐ 1167 Dan Naulty
☐ 1168 Brett Roberts
☐ 1169 Craig Saccavino
☐ 1170 Jeff Horn
☐ 1171 Rene Lopez
☐ 1172 Marc Claus
☐ 1173 Andy Kontorinis
☐ 1174 Chris Phillips
☐ 1175 Chad Roper
☐ 1176 Rich Tunison
☐ 1177 Ramon Vallette
☐ 1178 Brent Brede
☐ 1179 Dave Garrow
☐ 1180 Matt Lawton
☐ 1181 Ken Norman
☐ 1182 Jamie Ogden
☐ 1183 Steve Liddle MG
☐ 1184 Rick Tomlin CO
☐ 1185 Checklist

1994 Fort Wayne Wizards Classic

This 30-card standard size set of the 1994 Fort Wayne Wizards, a Class A Midwest League affiliate of the Minnesota Twins, features white-bordered posed color player shots on its fronts with the player's name , position, team name , logo and Classic logo appearing across the bottom of each card. On a ghosted team logo, the white back carries the player's name at the top, followed by biography and statistics. The cards are numbered on the back.

	MINT	NRMT	EXC
COMPLETE SET (30)	7.00	3.10	.85

☐ 1 Benj Sampson
☐ 2 Jason Baker
☐ 3 Shane Bowers
☐ 4 Armann Brown
☐ 5 Troy Carrasco
☐ 6 Tim Costic
☐ 7 Rob Debrino
☐ 8 Javi DeJesus
☐ 9 Tom Gourdin
☐ 10 Ben Jones
☐ 11 Grier Jones
☐ 12 Tom Knauss
☐ 13 Russell Lehoisky
☐ 14 Keith Linebarger
☐ 15 Shawn Miller
☐ 16 James Motte
☐ 17 Brian O'Brien
☐ 18 Dan Perkins
☐ 19 Ryan Radmanovich
☐ 20 Chad Rupp
☐ 21 Aaron Santini
☐ 22 Scott Stricklin
☐ 23 Jason Tatar
☐ 24 Danny Venezia
☐ 25 Romulo Vizcaino
☐ 26 Jim Dwyer MG
☐ 27 Stu Cliburn CO
☐ 28 Wayne the Wizard (Mascot)
☐ 29 Eric Margenau PR
☐ 30 Dan Fox TR Checklist

1994 Fort Wayne Wizards Fleer/ProCards

This 28-card standard size set of the 1994 Fort Wayne Wizards, a Class A Midwest League affiliate of the Minnesota Twins, features white-bordered posed color player photos on its fronts with the player's name, position, team name and Fleer/ProCards logo across the bottom of each card. The white back with vertical light blue stripes carries the player's name at the top, followed by biography and statistics.

	MINT	NRMT	EXC
COMPLETE SET (28)	5.00	2.20	.60

☐ 2000 Shane Bowers
☐ 2001 Troy Carrasco
☐ 2002 Rob Debrino
☐ 2003 Javi DeJesus
☐ 2004 Tom Gourdin
☐ 2005 Russ Lehoisky
☐ 2006 Keith Linebarger
☐ 2007 Shawn Miller
☐ 2008 Brian O'Brien
☐ 2009 Dan Perkins
☐ 2010 Ben Sampson
☐ 2011 Jason Tater
☐ 2012 Grier Jones
☐ 2013 Scott Stricklin
☐ 2014 Tim Costic
☐ 2015 James Motte
☐ 2016 Ryan Radmanovich
☐ 2017 Chad Rupp
☐ 2018 Aaron Santini
☐ 2019 Dan Venezia
☐ 2020 Jason Baker
☐ 2021 Armann Brown
☐ 2022 Ben Jones
☐ 2023 Tom Knauss
☐ 2024 Romulo Vizcaino
☐ 2025 Jim Dwyer MG
☐ 2026 Stu Cliburn CO
☐ 2027 Checklist

1994 Frederick Keys Classic

This 30-card standard size set of the 1994 Frederick Keys, a Class A Carolina League affiliate of the Baltimore Orioles, features white-bordered posed color player shots on its fronts with the player's name and position, team name and logo and Classic logo appearing across the bottom of each card. On a ghosted team logo, the white back carries the player's name at the top, followed by biography and statistics.

	MINT	NRMT	EXC
COMPLETE SET (30)	7.00	3.10	.85

☐ 1 Kimera Bartee
☐ 2 Matt Anderson
☐ 3 Harry Berrios
☐ 4 Clayton Byrne
☐ 5 Paul Carey
☐ 6 Gregg Castaldo
☐ 7 Eric Chavez
☐ 8 Scott Conner
☐ 9 Charles Devereaux
☐ 10 Scott Emerson
☐ 11 Roy Hodge
☐ 12 Matt Jarvis
☐ 13 Chris Lemp
☐ 14 Bryan Link
☐ 15 Calvin Maduro
☐ 16 Marco Manrique
☐ 17 Lincoln Martin
☐ 18 Jeff Michael
☐ 19 Jay Powell
☐ 20 Larry Shenk
☐ 21 Garrett Stephenson
☐ 22 Tommy Taylor
☐ 23 Jim Walker
☐ 24 B.J. Waszgis
☐ 25 Mike O'Berry
☐ 26 Larry McCall
☐ 27 Joe Durham
☐ 28 Dan Eaves
☐ 29 Mark Schumaker
☐ 30 Frederick Keys Logo CL

1994 Frederick Keys Fleer/ProCards

This 29-card standard size set of the 1994 Frederick Keys, a Class A Carolina League affiliate of the Baltimore Orioles, features white-bordered posed color player photos on its fronts with the player's name, position, team name and Fleer/ProCards logo across the bottom of each card. The white back with vertical light blue stripes carries the player's name at the top, followed by biography and statistics.

	MINT	NRMT	EXC
COMPLETE SET (29)	5.00	2.20	.60

□ 2605 Scott Conner
□ 2606 Chad Devereux
□ 2607 Scott Emerson
□ 2608 Matt Jarvis
□ 2609 Chris Lemp
□ 2610 Calvin Maduro
□ 2611 Tom Myers
□ 2612 Jay Powell
□ 2613 Larry Shenk
□ 2614 Garrett Stephenson
□ 2615 Tommy Taylor
□ 2616 Jim Walker
□ 2617 Marco Manrique
□ 2618 B.J. Waszgis
□ 2619 Gregg Castaldo
□ 2620 Eric Chavez
□ 2621 Lincoln Martin
□ 2622 Feliciano Mercedes
□ 2623 Jeff Michael
□ 2624 Billy Owens
□ 2625 Kimera Bartee
□ 2626 Clayton Byrne
□ 2627 Keith Eaddy
□ 2628 Roy Hodge
□ 2629 Bryan Link
□ 2630 Mike O'Berry MG
□ 2631 Joe Durham CO
□ 2632 Larry McCall CO
□ 2633 Checklist

1994 Great Falls Dodgers Sports Pro

	MINT	NRMT	EXC
COMPLETE SET (30)	10.00	4.50	1.25

□ 1 Freddy Agramonte
□ 2 Julio Aquino
□ 3 Fernando Ayala
□ 4 Nate Bland
□ 5 Julio Colon
□ 6 Bryan Coyle
□ 7 Alex Asencio
□ 8 Francisco Castro
□ 9 Brian Harmon
□ 10 Johnny Hilo
□ 11 Brian Majeski
□ 12 Travis Barbary
□ 13 Kyle Cooney
□ 14 Dennis Hedspeth
□ 15 Rafael Gross
□ 16 Scott Hunter
□ 17 Tony Mellan
□ 18 Nate Rasmussen
□ 19 Adam Riggs
□ 20 J.P. Roberge
□ 21 Ryan Sowards
□ 22 Brad Eaddy
□ 23 Jeff Eddings
□ 24 Elias Tapia
□ 25 Tom Price
□ 26 Dennis Reyes
□ 27 Carl South
□ 28 Ricky Stone
□ 29 Luis Tiant CO
□ 30 Ron Roenicke MG

1994 Greensboro Bats Classic

This 30-card standard size set of the 1994 Greensboro Bats, a Class A South Atlantic League affiliate of the New York Yankees, features white-bordered posed color player shots on its fronts with the player's name and position, team name and logo and Classic logo appearing across the bottom of each card. On a ghosted team logo, the white back carries the player's name at the top, followed by biography and statistics. This issue includes a third year card of Ruben Rivera.

	MINT	NRMT	EXC
COMPLETE SET (30)	12.00	5.50	1.50

□ 1 Ruben Rivera
□ 2 Steve Aldridge
□ 3 Kurt Bierek
□ 4 Vick Brown
□ 5 Chris Cumberland
□ 6 Will Delafield
□ 7 Al Drumheller
□ 8 Marcus Gipner
□ 9 Mark Hubbard
□ 10 Eric Knowles
□ 11 Blaise Kozeniewski
□ 12 Frank Lankford
□ 13 Ricky Ledee
□ 14 Donnie Leshnock
□ 15 Brian McLamb
□ 16 Jason Rathbun
□ 17 David Renteria
□ 18 Danny Rios
□ 19 Alexis Santaella
□ 20 Mike Schmitz
□ 21 Sloan Smith
□ 22 Scott Standish
□ 23 Jim Thomforde
□ 24 Jaime Torres
□ 25 Rob Trimble
□ 26 Joe Wharton
□ 27 Trey Hillman
□ 28 Juan Nieves
□ 29 Brian Milner
□ 30 Chris DeLucia CL

1994 Greensboro Bats Fleer/ProCards

This 31-card standard size set of the 1994 Greensboro Bats, a Class A South Atlantic League affiliate of the New York Yankees, features white-bordered posed color player photos on its fronts with the player's name, position, team name and Fleer/ProCards logo across the bottom of each card. The white back with vertical light blue stripes carries the player's name at the top, followed by biography and statistics. This issue includes a third year card of Ruben Rivera.

	MINT	NRMT	EXC
COMPLETE SET (31)	10.00	4.50	1.25

□ 464 Chris Cumberland
□ 465 Al Drumheller
□ 466 Mike Gordon
□ 467 Mark Hubbard
□ 468 Blaise Kozeniewski
□ 469 Frank Lankford
□ 470 Donnie Leshnock
□ 471 Jason Rathbun
□ 472 Greg Resz
□ 473 Alexis Santaella
□ 474 Scott Standish
□ 475 Jim Thomforde
□ 476 Joe Wharton
□ 477 Steve Aldridge
□ 478 Mark Gipner
□ 479 Jaime Torres
□ 480 Rob Trimble
□ 481 Kurt Bierek
□ 482 Vick Brown
□ 483 Eric Knowles
□ 484 Brian McLamb
□ 485 Dave Renteria
□ 486 Mike Schmitz
□ 487 Wil Delafield
□ 488 Ricky Ledee
□ 489 Ruben Rivera
□ 490 Sloan Smith
□ 491 Trey Hillman MG
□ 492 Brian Milner CO
□ 493 Juan Neives CO
□ 494 Checklist

1994 Greenville Braves Team Issue

Sponsored by Super Stars and Rock 101 (WROQ), this 30-card set was issued as an uncut, perforated sheet. It consists of three panels (each measuring approximately 10 5/8" by 9 3/8") joined together to form one continuous sheet. The first panel features sponsors' logos and a game photo. The second panel features 15 player cards, while the third panel has 13 player cards and two logo cards. After perforation, the cards measure approximately 2 1/8" by 3 1/8". On a white card face, the fronts have color player portraits with red and blue borders. The player's name and position appear below the picture with the sponsor logos immediately below. The horizontal backs carry a short player biography and career stats. The cards are unnumbered and arranged alphabetical, with the manager and coaches listed before the players.

	MINT	NRMT	EXC
COMPLETE SET (30)	7.00	3.10	.85

□ 1 Bruce Benedict MG
□ 2 Bruce Dal Canton CO
□ 3 Brian Snitker CO
□ 4 Randy Ingle CO
□ 5 Joe Ayrault
□ 6 Dirk Blair
□ 7 Chris Brock
□ 8 Ramon Caraballo
□ 9 Brad Clontz
□ 10 Tim Gillis
□ 11 Tony Graffanino
□ 12 Kevin Grijak
□ 13 Brad Hassinger
□ 14 Manny Jimenez
□ 15 Jerry Koller
□ 16 Thomas Martin
□ 17 Kevin O'Connor
□ 18 Hector Roa
□ 19 Don Robinson
□ 20 Jason Schmidt
□ 21 Chris Seelbach
□ 22 Steve Swail
□ 23 Pedro Swann
□ 24 Thomas Thobe
□ 25 Royal Thomas
□ 26 Terrell Wade
□ 27 Aubrey Waggoner
□ 28 Doug Wollenburg
□ 29 Logo Card
□ 30 Logo Card

1994 Greenville Braves Fleer/ProCards

This 28-card standard size set of the 1994 Greenville Braves, a Class AA Southern League affiliate of the Atlanta Braves, features white-bordered posed color player photos on its fronts with the player's name, position, team name and Fleer/ProCards logo across the bottom of each card. The white back with vertical light blue stripes carries the player's name at the top, followed by biography and statistics.

	MINT	NRMT	EXC
COMPLETE SET (28)	5.00	2.20	.60

□ 405 Dirk Blair
□ 406 Chris Brock
□ 407 Brad Clontz
□ 408 Brad Hassinger
□ 409 Jerry Koller
□ 410 Tom Martin
□ 411 Jason Schmidt
□ 412 Chris Seelbach
□ 413 Tom Thobe
□ 414 Royal Thomas
□ 415 Terrell Wade
□ 416 Joe Ayrault
□ 417 Steve Swail
□ 418 Tim Gillis
□ 419 Ed Giovanola
□ 420 Tony Graffanino
□ 421 Manuel Jimenez
□ 422 Hector Roa
□ 423 Doug Wollenburg
□ 424 Miguel Correa
□ 425 Kevin O'Connor
□ 426 Don Robinson
□ 427 Pedro Swann
□ 428 Bruce Benedict MG
□ 429 Bruce Dal Canton CO
□ 430 Randy Ingle CO
□ 431 Brian Snitker CO
□ 432 Checklist

1994 Hagerstown Suns Classic

This 30-card standard size set of the 1994 Hagerstown Suns, a Class A South Atlantic League affiliate of the Toronto Blue Jays, features white-bordered posed color player shots on its fronts with the player's name and position, team name and logo and Classic logo appearing across the bottom of each card. On a ghosted team logo, the white back carries the player's name at the top, followed by biography and statistics.

	MINT	NRMT	EXC
COMPLETE SET (30)	7.00	3.10	.85

□ 1 Shannon Stewart
□ 2 Tim Adkins
□ 3 Carlos Cabrera
□ 4 Brandon Cromer
□ 5 Victor Davila
□ 6 Lorenzo De La Cruz
□ 7 Joe Durso
□ 8 Edwin Hurtado
□ 9 Ryan Jones
□ 10 Jeff Ladd
□ 11 Mark Lukasiewicz
□ 12 Jay Maldonado
□ 13 Trevor Mallory
□ 14 Doug Meiners
□ 15 Adam Melhuse
□ 16 Patrick Moultrie
□ 17 Harry Muir Jr.
□ 18 Jeff Patzke
□ 19 Angel Ramirez
□ 20 Ken Robinson
□ 21 Mike Romano
□ 22 Steve Sinclair
□ 23 David Sinnes
□ 24 Rob Steinert
□ 25 Gene Vaninetti
□ 26 Omar Malave MG
□ 27 Reggie Cleveland CO
□ 28 Leroy Stanton CO
□ 29 Pat McMorran TR
□ 30 Checklist

1994 Hagerstown Suns Fleer/ProCards

This 29-card standard size set of the 1994 Hagerstown Suns, a Class A South Atlantic League affiliate of the Toronto Blue Jays, features white-bordered posed color player photos on its fronts with the player's name, position, team name and Fleer/ProCards logo across the bottom of each card. The white back with vertical light blue stripes carries the player's name at the top, followed by biography and statistics.

	MINT	NRMT	EXC
COMPLETE SET (29)	5.00	2.20	.60

□ 2721 Tim Adkins
□ 2722 Edwin Hurtado
□ 2723 Mark Lukasiewicz
□ 2724 Jay Maldonado
□ 2725 Trevor Mallory
□ 2726 Doug Meiners
□ 2727 Harry Muir
□ 2728 Ken Robinson
□ 2729 Mike Romano
□ 2730 Steve Sinclair
□ 2731 Dave Sinnes
□ 2732 Rob Steinert
□ 2733 Joe Durso
□ 2734 Jeff Ladd
□ 2735 Adam Melhuse
□ 2736 Carlos Cabrera
□ 2737 Brandon Cromer
□ 2738 Vic Davila
□ 2739 Ryan Jones
□ 2740 Jeff Patzke
□ 2741 Geno Vaninetti
□ 2742 Lorenzo De La Cruz
□ 2743 Pat Moultrie
□ 2744 Angel Ramirez
□ 2745 Shannon Stewart
□ 2746 Omar Malave MG
□ 2747 Reggie Cleveland CO
□ 2748 Leroy Stanton CO
□ 2749 Checklist

1994 Harrisburg Senators Fleer/ProCards

This 29-card standard size set of the 1994 Harrisburg Senators, a Class AA Eastern League affiliate of the Montreal Expos, features white-bordered posed color player photos on its fronts with the player's name, position, team name and Fleer/ProCards logo across the bottom of each card. The white back with vertical light blue stripes carries the player's name at the top, followed by biography and statistics.

	MINT	NRMT	EXC
COMPLETE SET (29)	5.00	2.20	.60

□ 1096 Gary Hymel
□ 2082 Miguel Batista
□ 2083 Bob Baxter
□ 2084 Scott Gentile
□ 2085 Rod Henderson
□ 2086 Steve Hoeme
□ 2087 Mike Mimbs
□ 2088 Carlos Perez
□ 2089 Al Reyes
□ 2090 Curt Schmidt
□ 2091 J.J. Thobe
□ 2092 Ugueth Urbina
□ 2093 B.J. Wallace
□ 2094 Darrin Winston
□ 2095 Rob Fitzpatrick
□ 2097 Mark Grudzielanek
□ 2098 Mike Hardge
□ 2099 Jeff Kipila
□ 2100 Matt Rundels
□ 2101 George Virgilio
□ 2102 Randy Wilstead
□ 2103 Yamil Benitez
□ 2104 Marc Griffin
□ 2105 Tyrone Horne
□ 2106 Kevin Northrup
□ 2107 Dave Jauss MG
□ 2108 Lance Rice CO
□ 2109 Dave Tomlin CO
□ 2110 Checklist

1994 Helena Brewers Fleer/ProCards

This 27-card standard size set of the 1994 Helena Brewers, a Rookie Class Pioneer League affiliate of the Milwaukee Brewers, features white-bordered posed color player photos on its fronts with the player's name, position, team name and Fleer/ProCards logo across the bottom of each card. The white back with vertical light blue stripes carries the player's name at the top, followed by biography and statistics.

	MINT	NRMT	EXC
COMPLETE SET (27)	5.00	2.20	.60

□ 3604 Greg Beck
□ 3605 Chris Burt

☐ 3606 Brian Dalton
☐ 3607 Derek Gaskill
☐ 3608 Steve Gold
☐ 3609 Juan Gonzalez
☐ 3610 Jon Hillis
☐ 3611 Jeff Kramer
☐ 3612 Shane Moses
☐ 3613 Scott Perkins
☐ 3614 Tano Tijerina
☐ 3615 Brian Titus
☐ 3616 Rob Campillo
☐ 3617 Rob Snook
☐ 3618 Josh Zwisler
☐ 3619 Junior Betances
☐ 3620 Domingo Carrasquel
☐ 3621 Roberto Escalet
☐ 3622 Michael Pritchard
☐ 3623 Spanky Floyd
☐ 3624 Jim Hodge
☐ 3625 Allen Mealing
☐ 3626 Darrell Nicholas
☐ 3627 Chris Wilson
☐ 3628 Dub Kilgo MG
☐ 3629 Mike Caldwell CO
☐ 3630 Checklist

1994 Helena Brewers Sports Pro

	MINT	NRMT	EXC
COMPLETE SET (30)	7.00	3.10	.85

☐ 1 Roberto Escalet
☐ 2 Michael Pritchard
☐ 3 Domingo Carrasquel
☐ 4 Junior Betances
☐ 5 Steve Gold
☐ 6 Tano Tijerina
☐ 7 Chris Burt
☐ 8 George Preston
☐ 9 Shane Moses
☐ 10 Brian Dalton
☐ 11 Scott Perkins
☐ 12 Josh Zwisler
☐ 13 Robert Campillo
☐ 14 Rob Snook
☐ 15 Jim Hodge
☐ 16 Chris Wilson
☐ 17 Allen Mealing
☐ 18 Darrell Nicholas
☐ 19 Jon Hillis
☐ 20 Derek Gaskill
☐ 21 Brian Titus
☐ 22 Greg Beck
☐ 23 Juan Gonzalez
☐ 24 Jeff Kramer
☐ 25 Dub Kilgo MG
☐ 26 Mike Caldwell CO
☐ 27 Doug Michlovitz TR
☐ 28 John Emmett ANN
☐ 29 Jeff Nelson GM
☐ 30 Blank Card

1994 Hickory Crawdads Classic

This 30-card standard size set of the 1994 Hickory Crawdads, a Class A South Atlantic League affiliate of the Chicago White Sox, features white-bordered posed color player shots on its fronts with the player's name and position, team name and logo and Classic logo appearing across the bottom of each card. On a ghosted team logo, the white back carries the player's name at the top, followed by biography and statistics.

	MINT	NRMT	EXC
COMPLETE SET (30)	7.00	3.10	.85

☐ 1 Jeff Droll
☐ 2 Eddy Beltre
☐ 3 Dave Bingham
☐ 4 Kevin Booker
☐ 5 Ben Boulware
☐ 6 Curtis Broome
☐ 7 Rick Carone
☐ 8 Jim Dixon
☐ 9 David Elsbernd
☐ 10 Tom Fordham
☐ 11 Jason Goligoski
☐ 12 Augustine Gomez
☐ 13 Andres Levias
☐ 14 David Lundquist
☐ 15 Chris Mader
☐ 16 Mickey McKinion
☐ 17 Magglio Ordonez
☐ 18 John Quirk
☐ 19 Eric Richardson
☐ 20 Pete Rose Jr.
☐ 21 Shane Spry
☐ 22 Robert Theodile
☐ 23 Archie Vazquez
☐ 24 Scott Vollmer
☐ 25 Harold Williams
☐ 26 Fred Kendall MG
☐ 27 Curt Hasler CO
☐ 28 Mark Haley CO
☐ 29 Paul Cassanova CO
☐ 30 Joe Geck TR
Checklist

1994 Hickory Crawdads Fleer/ProCards

This 30-card standard size set of the 1994 Hickory Crawdads, a Class A South Atlantic League affiliate of the Chicago White Sox, features white-bordered posed color player photos on its fronts with the player's name, position, team name and Fleer/ProCards logo across the bottom of each card. The white back with vertical light blue stripes carries the player's name at the top, followed by biography and statistics.

	MINT	NRMT	EXC
COMPLETE SET (30)	5.00	2.20	.60

☐ 2167 Curtis Broome
☐ 2168 Jim Dixon
☐ 2169 Jeff Droll
☐ 2170 Dave Elsbernd
☐ 2171 Tom Fordham
☐ 2172 Augustine Gomez
☐ 2173 David Lundquist
☐ 2174 Mickey McKinion
☐ 2175 Richard Pratt
☐ 2176 John Quirk
☐ 2177 Robert Theodile
☐ 2178 Archie Vazquez
☐ 2179 Dave Bingham
☐ 2180 Rick Carone
☐ 2181 Scott Vollmer
☐ 2182 Eddy Beltre
☐ 2183 Ben Boulware
☐ 2184 Jason Goligoski
☐ 2185 Pete Rose Jr.
☐ 2186 Harold Williams
☐ 2187 Kevin Booker
☐ 2188 Andres Levias
☐ 2189 Magglio Ordonez
☐ 2190 Eric Richardson
☐ 2191 Shane Spry
☐ 2192 Fred Kendall MG
☐ 2193 Paul Casanova CO
☐ 2194 Mark Haley CO
☐ 2195 Curt Hasler CO
☐ 2257 Checklist

1994 High Desert Mavericks Classic

This 30-card standard size set of the 1994 High Desert Mavericks, a Class A California League Independent, features white-bordered posed color player shots on its fronts with the player's name , position, team name , logo and Classic logo appearing across the bottom of each card. On a ghosted team logo, the white back carries the player's name at the top, followed by biography and statistics.

	MINT	NRMT	EXC
COMPLETE SET (30)	8.00	3.60	1.00

☐ 1 Darren Paxton
☐ 2 Rob Augustine
☐ 3 Scott Bethea
☐ 4 Jamie Bethke
☐ 5 Ray Brooks
☐ 6 Dickie Brown
☐ 7 Jason Bugg
☐ 8 Kurt Burgess
☐ 9 Dennis Burlingame
☐ 10 Brian D'Amato
☐ 11 Hanley Frias
☐ 12 Tim Graham
☐ 13 Joe Hayward
☐ 14 Lee Heath
☐ 15 Dean Hinson
☐ 16 Jeff Hostetler
☐ 17 Donny Jones
☐ 18 Brian Knowles
☐ 19 Rich Licursi
☐ 20 Tim Ploeger
☐ 21 Oscar Resendez
☐ 22 Raul Santana
☐ 23 David Sartain
☐ 24 Mark Saugstad
☐ 25 Mike Smith
☐ 26 Chad Townsend
☐ 27 Phil Hannon MG
☐ 28 Tim Conroy CO
☐ 29 Billy Gardner Jr. CO
☐ 30 Chris Felix TR
Checklist

1994 High Desert Mavericks Fleer/ProCards

This 30-card standard size set of the 1994 High Desert Mavericks, a Class A California League Independent, features white-bordered posed color player photos on its fronts with the player's name, position, team name and Fleer/ProCards logo across the bottom of each card. The white back with vertical light blue stripes carries the player's name at the top, followed by biography and statistics.

	MINT	NRMT	EXC
COMPLETE SET (30)	5.00	2.20	.60

☐ 2778 Rob Augustine
☐ 2779 Dickie Brown
☐ 2780 Kurt Burgess
☐ 2781 Dennis Burlingame
☐ 2782 Brian D'Amato
☐ 2783 Dean Hinson
☐ 2784 Jeff Hostetler
☐ 2785 Rich Licursi
☐ 2786 Darrin Paxton
☐ 2787 Tim Ploeger
☐ 2788 Oscar Resendez
☐ 2789 David Sartain
☐ 2790 Mark Saugstad
☐ 2791 Jamie Bethke
☐ 2792 Ray Brooks
☐ 2793 Raul Santana
☐ 2794 Scott Bethea
☐ 2795 Jason Bugg
☐ 2796 Hanley Frias
☐ 2797 Mike Smith
☐ 2798 Chad Townsend
☐ 2799 Tim Graham
☐ 2800 Joe Hayward
☐ 2801 Lee Heath
☐ 2802 Brian Knowles
☐ 2803 Donny Jones
☐ 2804 Phil Hannon MG
☐ 2805 Tim Conroy CO
☐ 2806 Billy Gardner Jr. CO
☐ 2807 Checklist

1994 Hudson Valley Renegades Classic

This 30-card standard size set of the 1994 Hudson Valley Renegades, a Class A New York-Penn League affiliate of the Texas Rangers, features white-bordered posed color player shots on its fronts with the player's name and position, team name and logo and Classic logo appearing across the bottom of each card. On a ghosted team logo, the white back carries the player's name at the top, followed by biography and statistics. This issue includes the minor league card debut of Kevin Brown.

	MINT	NRMT	EXC
COMPLETE SET (30)	10.00	4.50	1.25

☐ 1 Matt Bokemeier
☐ 2 Kevin Brown
☐ 3 Eddie Comeaux
☐ 4 Jaime Escamilla
☐ 5 Dom Gatti
☐ 6 Mike Hill
☐ 7 Dan Hower
☐ 8 Joe Kail
☐ 9 Joe Keusch
☐ 10 Steve Larkin
☐ 11 Mark Little
☐ 12 Mike Manning
☐ 13 Kevin Millican
☐ 14 Eric Moody
☐ 15 Mike Mortimer
☐ 16 Mark O'Brien
☐ 17 Gardner O'Flynn
☐ 18 Luis Perez
☐ 19 John Pyle
☐ 20 Ryan Rutz
☐ 21 Reid Ryan
☐ 22 Roberto Santa
☐ 23 Erik Sauve
☐ 24 Shawn Shugars
☐ 25 Ray Williams
☐ 26 Doug Sisson
☐ 27 Marc Del Piano
☐ 28 Kevin Andrews ERR #29
☐ 29 Texas Rangers Logo
☐ 30 Hudson Valley Renegades Logo CL

1994 Hudson Valley Renegades Fleer/ProCards

This 30-card standard size set of the 1994 Hudson Valley Renegades, a Class A New York-Penn League affiliate of the Texas Rangers, features white-bordered posed color player photos on its fronts with the player's name, position, team name and Fleer/ProCards logo across the bottom of each card. The white back with vertical light blue stripes carries the player's name at the top, followed by biography and statistics. This issue includes the minor league card debut of Kevin Brown.

	MINT	NRMT	EXC
COMPLETE SET (30)	8.00	3.60	1.00

☐ 3374 James Brower
☐ 3375 David Chavarria
☐ 3376 Jaime Escamilla
☐ 3377 Dan Hower
☐ 3378 Joe Keusch
☐ 3379 Mike Manning
☐ 3380 Eric Moody
☐ 3381 Mike Mortimer
☐ 3382 Mark O'Brien
☐ 3383 Gardner O'Flynn
☐ 3384 Luis Perez
☐ 3385 Reid Ryan
☐ 3386 Kevin Brown
☐ 3387 Tim Cossins
☐ 3388 Kevin Millican
☐ 3389 John Pyle
☐ 3390 Matt Bokemeier
☐ 3391 Mike Hill
☐ 3392 Joe Kail
☐ 3393 Ryan Rutz
☐ 3394 Roberto Santa
☐ 3395 Erik Sauve
☐ 3396 Ray Williams
☐ 3397 Edward Comeaux
☐ 3398 Dom Gatti
☐ 3399 Steve Larkin
☐ 3400 Mark Little
☐ 3401 Shawn Shugars
☐ 3402 Doug Sisson MG
☐ 3403 Checklist

1994 Huntington Cubs Classic

This 30-card standard size set of the 1994 Huntington Cubs, a Rookie Class Appalachian League affiliate of the Chicago Cubs, features white-bordered posed color player shots on its fronts with the player's name and position, team name and logo and Classic logo appearing across the bottom of each card. On a ghosted team logo, the white back carries the player's name at the top, followed by biography and statistics.

	MINT	NRMT	EXC
COMPLETE SET (30)	7.00	3.10	.85

☐ 1 Jayson Peterson
☐ 2 Richard Barker
☐ 3 Bryan Bogle
☐ 4 Ryan Casey
☐ 5 Mark D'Ambrosia
☐ 6 Andy Devries
☐ 7 Mike Dieguez
☐ 8 Neal Faulkner
☐ 9 Ricky Freeman
☐ 10 Alfredo Garcia
☐ 11 Eduard Garcia
☐ 12 Danny Gil
☐ 13 Andrew Holin
☐ 14 James Huntley
☐ 15 Elinton Jasco
☐ 16 Artis Johnson
☐ 17 Jason Kelley
☐ 18 Michael Lauterhahn
☐ 19 Mark Lavenia
☐ 20 Javier Martinez
☐ 21 Ryan Opatkiewicz
☐ 22 Troy Ormonde
☐ 23 Josh Putrich
☐ 24 Steve Rain
☐ 25 Steve Ryder
☐ 26 Jason Stevenson
☐ 27 Jules Van Landuyt
☐ 28 Steve Kolinsky
☐ 29 Ray Korn
☐ 30 John Noce CL

1994 Huntington Cubs Fleer/ProCards

This 31-card standard size set of the 1994 Huntington Cubs, a Rookie Class Appalachian League affiliate of the Chicago Cubs, features white-bordered posed color player photos on its fronts with the player's name, position, team name and Fleer/ProCards logo across the bottom of each card. The white back with vertical light blue stripes carries the player's name at the top, followed by biography and statistics.

	MINT	NRMT	EXC
COMPLETE SET (31)	5.00	2.20	.60

☐ 3542 Richard Barker
☐ 3543 Ryan Casey
☐ 3544 Andy Devries
☐ 3545 Neal Faulkner
☐ 3546 Alfredo Garcia
☐ 3547 Jason Kelley
☐ 3548 Mark Lavenia
☐ 3549 Javier Martinez
☐ 3550 Troy Ormonde
☐ 3551 Jayson Peterson
☐ 3552 Josh Putrich
☐ 3553 Steve Rain
☐ 3554 Jason Stevenson
☐ 3555 Jules Van Landuyt
☐ 3556 Andy Holin
☐ 3557 Mark D'Ambrosia
☐ 3558 Mike Dieguez
☐ 3559 Ricky Freeman
☐ 3560 James Huntley
☐ 3561 Elinton Jasco
☐ 3562 Ryan Opatkiewicz
☐ 3563 Steve Ryder
☐ 3564 Bryan Bogle
☐ 3565 Eduard Garcia
☐ 3566 Danny Gil

- ☐ 3567 Artis Johnson
- ☐ 3568 Mike Lauterhahn
- ☐ 3569 Steve Kolinsky MG
- ☐ 3570 Ray Korn CO
- ☐ 3571 John Noce CO
- ☐ 3572 Checklist

1994 Huntsville Stars Fleer/ProCards

This 27-card standard size set of the 1994 Huntsville Stars, a Class AA Southern League affiliate of the Oakland Athletics, features white-bordered posed color player photos on its fronts with the player's name, position, team name and Fleer/ProCards logo across the bottom of each card. The white back with vertical light blue stripes carries the player's name at the top, followed by biography and statistics.

	MINT	NRMT	EXC
COMPLETE SET (27)	8.00	3.60	1.00

- ☐ 1323 Scott Baker
- ☐ 1324 Russ Brock
- ☐ 1325 Todd Ingram
- ☐ 1326 Doug Johns
- ☐ 1327 Bronswell Patrick
- ☐ 1328 Steve Phoenix
- ☐ 1329 Rob Pierce
- ☐ 1330 Scott Rose
- ☐ 1331 Curtis Shaw
- ☐ 1332 Steve Shoemaker
- ☐ 1333 Steve Wojciechowski
- ☐ 1334 Garrett Beard
- ☐ 1335 Izzy Molina
- ☐ 1336 Jason Giambi
- ☐ 1337 Scott Sheldon
- ☐ 1338 Scott Shockey
- ☐ 1339 Mark Sobolewski
- ☐ 1340 Jim Waggoner
- ☐ 1341 Joel Wolfe
- ☐ 1342 Jason Wood
- ☐ 1343 Chris Hart
- ☐ 1344 Damon Mashore
- ☐ 1345 Kerwin Moore
- ☐ 1346 Ernie Young
- ☐ 1347 Gary Jones MG
- ☐ 1348 Glenn Abbott CO
- ☐ 1349 Checklist

1994 Idaho Falls Braves Fleer/ProCards

This 31-card standard size set of the 1994 Idaho Falls Braves, a Rookie Class Pioneer League affiliate of the Atlanta Braves, features white-bordered posed color player photos on its fronts with the player's name, position, team name and Fleer/ProCards logo across the bottom of each card. The white back with vertical light blue stripes carries the player's name at the top, followed by biography and statistics.

	MINT	NRMT	EXC
COMPLETE SET (31)	5.00	2.20	.60

- ☐ 3573 Shawn Brennan
- ☐ 3574 Anthony Briggs
- ☐ 3575 Darold Brown
- ☐ 3576 Zach Collins
- ☐ 3577 Chuck Fritz
- ☐ 3578 Chuck Gann
- ☐ 3579 Brandon Hoalton
- ☐ 3580 Tony Mazzone
- ☐ 3581 Jerrod Miller
- ☐ 3582 Eric Olszewski
- ☐ 3583 Ken Raines
- ☐ 3584 Chris Rusciano
- ☐ 3585 Marcus Tyner
- ☐ 3586 Paul Wollins
- ☐ 3587 Charles Dawson
- ☐ 3588 Pascual Matos
- ☐ 3589 Jose Rodriguez
- ☐ 3590 Colby Weaver
- ☐ 3591 David Catlett
- ☐ 3592 Ray Hofer
- ☐ 3593 Gerald Roberson
- ☐ 3594 Rob Sasser
- ☐ 3595 Ben Utting
- ☐ 3596 Roosevelt Brown
- ☐ 3597 Jason Dailey
- ☐ 3598 Bo Franklin
- ☐ 3599 Dwight Lewis
- ☐ 3600 Wilton Person
- ☐ 3601 Bennie Tillman
- ☐ 3602 Andrew Tolbert
- ☐ 3603 Checklist

1994 Idaho Falls Braves Sports Pro

	MINT	NRMT	EXC
COMPLETE SET (30)	8.00	3.60	1.00

- ☐ 1 Roosevelt Brown
- ☐ 2 Jason Dailey
- ☐ 3 Dwight Lewis
- ☐ 4 Wilton Person
- ☐ 5 Bennie Tillman
- ☐ 6 Andrew Tolbert
- ☐ 7 Shawn Brennan
- ☐ 8 Darold Brown
- ☐ 9 Zach Collins
- ☐ 10 Charles Fritz
- ☐ 11 Charlie Gann
- ☐ 12 Brandon Hoalton
- ☐ 13 Tony Mazzone
- ☐ 14 Charles Dawson
- ☐ 15 Pascual Matos
- ☐ 16 David Catlett
- ☐ 17 Ray Hofer
- ☐ 18 Gerald Roberson
- ☐ 19 Jerrod Miller
- ☐ 20 Eric Olszewski
- ☐ 21 Ken Raines
- ☐ 22 Chris Rusciano
- ☐ 23 Marcus Tyner
- ☐ 24 Robert Sasser
- ☐ 25 Jose Rodriguez
- ☐ 26 Ben Utting
- ☐ 27 Max Venable MG
- ☐ 28 Dave Hilton CO
- ☐ 29 Mark Ross CO
- ☐ 30 Allen Morales TR

1994 Indianapolis Indians Fleer/ProCards

This 27-card standard size set of the 1994 Indianapolis Indians, a Class AAA American Association League affiliate of the Cincinnati Reds, features white-bordered posed color player photos on its fronts with the player's name, position, team name and Fleer/ProCards logo across the bottom of each card. The white back with vertical light blue stripes carries the player's name at the top, followed by biography and statistics.

	MINT	NRMT	EXC
COMPLETE SET (27)	5.00	2.20	.60

- ☐ 1801 Terry Bross
- ☐ 1802 Rich DeLucia
- ☐ 1803 Mike Ferry
- ☐ 1804 Matt Grott
- ☐ 1805 Kevin Jarvis
- ☐ 1806 Rusty Kilgo
- ☐ 1807 Mike Mathile
- ☐ 1808 Ross Powell
- ☐ 1809 John Roper
- ☐ 1810 Rich Sauveur
- ☐ 1811 Scott Service
- ☐ 1812 Jerry Spradlin
- ☐ 1813 Brian Warren
- ☐ 1814 Barry Lyons
- ☐ 1815 Gary Cooper
- ☐ 1816 Jamie Dismuke
- ☐ 1817 Keith Kessinger
- ☐ 1818 Brian Koelling
- ☐ 1819 Kurt Stillwell
- ☐ 1820 Casey Candaele
- ☐ 1821 Doug Jennings
- ☐ 1822 Jim Olander
- ☐ 1823 Steve Pegues
- ☐ 1824 Marc Bombard MG
- ☐ 1825 Mike Griffin CO
- ☐ 1826 Jim Thrift CO
- ☐ 1827 Checklist

1994 Iowa Cubs Fleer/ProCards

This 26-card standard size set of the 1994 Iowa Cubs, a Class AAA American Association affiliate of the Chicago Cubs, features white-bordered posed color player photos on its fronts with the player's name, position, team name and Fleer/ProCards logo across the bottom of each card. The white back with vertical light blue stripes carries the player's name at the top, followed by biography and statistics.

	MINT	NRMT	EXC
COMPLETE SET (26)	5.00	2.20	.60

- ☐ 1269 Mike Anderson
- ☐ 1270 Bill Brennan
- ☐ 1271 Lance Dickson
- ☐ 1272 Mark Lee
- ☐ 1273 Larry Luebbers
- ☐ 1274 Rafael Novoa
- ☐ 1275 Dave Swartzbaugh
- ☐ 1276 Randy Veres
- ☐ 1277 Mike Walker
- ☐ 1278 Darron Cox
- ☐ 1279 Mike Maksudian
- ☐ 1280 Cris Colon
- ☐ 1281 Matt Franco
- ☐ 1282 Todd Haney
- ☐ 1283 Tommy Shields
- ☐ 1284 Craig Worthington
- ☐ 1285 Scott Bullett
- ☐ 1286 Mike Carter
- ☐ 1287 Kevin Roberson
- ☐ 1288 Ozzie Timmons
- ☐ 1289 Eric Yelding
- ☐ 1290 Rick Patterson MG
- ☐ 1291 Bill Earley CO
- ☐ 1292 Mark Johnston CO
- ☐ 1293 Rick Wilson CO
- ☐ 1294 Checklist

1994 Jackson Generals Fleer/ProCards

This 27-card standard size set of the 1994 Jackson Generals, a Class AA Texas League affiliate of the Houston Astros, features white-bordered posed color player photos on its fronts with the player's name, position, team name and Fleer/ProCards logo across the bottom of each card. The white back with vertical light blue stripes carries the player's name at the top, followed by biography and statistics.

	MINT	NRMT	EXC
COMPLETE SET (27)	5.00	2.20	.60

- ☐ 208 Jamie Daspit
- ☐ 209 Kevin Gallaher
- ☐ 210 Dave Gandolph
- ☐ 211 Chris Gardner
- ☐ 212 Chris Hill
- ☐ 213 Chris Holt
- ☐ 214 Rick Huisman
- ☐ 215 Doug Ketchen
- ☐ 216 Doug Mlicki
- ☐ 217 Mark Small
- ☐ 218 Chris White
- ☐ 219 Raul Chavez
- ☐ 220 Tony Gilmore
- ☐ 221 Jeff Ball
- ☐ 222 Dennis Colon
- ☐ 223 Jose Flores
- ☐ 224 Mike Groppuso
- ☐ 225 Tom Nevers
- ☐ 226 Fletcher Thompson
- ☐ 227 Bob Abreu
- ☐ 228 Tim Evans
- ☐ 229 Buck McNabb
- ☐ 230 Gary Mota
- ☐ 231 Sal Butera MG
- ☐ 232 Don Reynolds CO
- ☐ 233 Charley Taylor CO
- ☐ 234 Checklist

1994 Jacksonville Suns Fleer/ProCards

This 27-card standard size set of the 1994 Jacksonville Suns, a Class AA Southern League affiliate of the Seattle Mariners, features white-bordered posed color player photos on its fronts with the player's name, position, team name and Fleer/ProCards logo across the bottom of each card. The white back with vertical light blue stripes carries the player's name at the top, followed by biography and statistics.

	MINT	NRMT	EXC
COMPLETE SET (27)	6.00	2.70	.75

- ☐ 1403 Dave Adam
- ☐ 1404 Travis Buckley
- ☐ 1405 Craig Clayton
- ☐ 1406 Dave Evans
- ☐ 1407 Jim Gutierrez
- ☐ 1408 Derek Lowe
- ☐ 1409 Jim Mecir
- ☐ 1410 Erik Plantenberg
- ☐ 1411 Scott Schanz
- ☐ 1412 Mac Suzuki
- ☐ 1413 Ron Villone
- ☐ 1414 Tony Kounas
- ☐ 1415 Chris Widger
- ☐ 1416 Eddy Diaz
- ☐ 1417 Danny Lewis
- ☐ 1418 Fred McNair
- ☐ 1419 Arquimedez Pozo
- ☐ 1420 Desi Relaford
- ☐ 1421 Raul Rodarte
- ☐ 1422 Ruben Santana
- ☐ 1423 Tony Barron
- ☐ 1424 Craig Griffey
- ☐ 1425 Terrel Hansen
- ☐ 1426 Marc Hill MG
- ☐ 1427 Jeff Andrews CO
- ☐ 1428 Jerry Royster CO
- ☐ 1429 Checklist

1994 Jamestown Jammers Classic

This 30-card standard size set of the 1994 Jamestown Jammers, a Class A New York-Penn League affiliate of the Detroit Tigers, features white-bordered posed color player shots on its fronts with the player's name and position, team name and logo and Classic logo appearing across the bottom of each card. On a ghosted team logo, the white back carries the player's name at the top, followed by biography and statistics. This issue includes the minor league card debut of Bubba Trammell.

	MINT	NRMT	EXC
COMPLETE SET (30)	15.00	6.75	1.85

- ☐ 1 Bubba Trammell
- ☐ 2 Mike Bajda
- ☐ 3 Jeff Barker
- ☐ 4 Jayson Bass
- ☐ 5 Javier Cordona
- ☐ 6 Brian Corey
- ☐ 7 Eric Dinyar
- ☐ 8 Jeff Driskell
- ☐ 9 Sean Freeman
- ☐ 10 Luis Garcia
- ☐ 11 Ismael Guzman
- ☐ 12 Jason Jordan
- ☐ 13 Lonny Landry
- ☐ 14 Kenny Marrero
- ☐ 15 Mike Martin
- ☐ 16 Dalvis Martinez
- ☐ 17 Darryl Monroe
- ☐ 18 Chris Newton
- ☐ 19 Shawn Pagee
- ☐ 20 Dave Roberts
- ☐ 21 Mitch Root
- ☐ 22 Matt Ruess
- ☐ 23 Matt Skrmetta
- ☐ 24 Rob Welles
- ☐ 25 Mac White
- ☐ 26 Greg Whiteman
- ☐ 27 Dave Anderson MG
- ☐ 28 Sid Monge CO
- ☐ 29 Tim Torcelli CO
- ☐ 30 Doug Teter TR

1994 Jamestown Jammers Fleer/ProCards

This 30-card standard size set of the 1994 Jamestown Jammers, a Class A New York-Penn League affiliate of the Detroit Tigers, features white-bordered posed color player photos on its fronts with the player's name, position, team name and Fleer/ProCards logo across the bottom of each card. The white back with vertical light blue stripes carries the player's name at the top, followed by biography and statistics. This issue includes the minor league card debut of Bubba Trammell.

	MINT	NRMT	EXC
COMPLETE SET (30)	10.00	4.50	1.25

- ☐ 3956 Mike Bajda
- ☐ 3957 Jeff Barker
- ☐ 3958 Eric Dinyar
- ☐ 3959 Jason Jordan
- ☐ 3960 Kenny Marrero
- ☐ 3961 Chris Newton
- ☐ 3962 Steve Nowak
- ☐ 3963 Matt Ruess
- ☐ 3964 Matt Skrmetta
- ☐ 3965 Greg Whiteman
- ☐ 3966 Javier Cordona
- ☐ 3967 Jeff Driskell
- ☐ 3968 Neil Garcia
- ☐ 3969 Shawn Pagee
- ☐ 3970 Bryan Corey
- ☐ 3971 Sean Freeman
- ☐ 3972 Luis Garcia
- ☐ 3973 Michael Martin
- ☐ 3974 Dalvis Martinez
- ☐ 3975 Mitch Root
- ☐ 3976 Rob Welles
- ☐ 3977 Jason Bass
- ☐ 3978 Ismael Guzman
- ☐ 3979 Lonny Landry
- ☐ 3980 Darryl Monroe
- ☐ 3981 Dave Roberts
- ☐ 3982 Bubba Trammell
- ☐ 3983 Kelly White
- ☐ 3984 Dave Anderson MG
- ☐ 3985 Checklist

1994 Johnson City Cardinals Classic

This 30-card standard size set of the 1994 Johnson City Cardinals, a Rookie Class Appalachian League affiliate of the St. Louis Cardinals, features white-bordered posed color player shots on its fronts with the player's name and position, team name and logo and Classic logo appearing across the bottom of each card. On a ghosted team logo, the white back carries the player's name at the top, followed by biography and statistics. This issue includes the minor league card debut of Blake Stein.

	MINT	NRMT	EXC
COMPLETE SET (30)	8.00	3.60	1.00

- ☐ 1 Steve Abbs
- ☐ 2 Pete Ambrosina
- ☐ 3 Juan Bautista
- ☐ 4 Joe Bowen
- ☐ 5 Domingo Charles
- ☐ 6 Calvin Coach
- ☐ 7 Mark Cruise
- ☐ 8 Jody Crump
- ☐ 9 Tighe Curran
- ☐ 10 Kevin Folcerero
- ☐ 11 Bert Green
- ☐ 12 Ryan Hall
- ☐ 13 Robert Helvey

☐ 14 Ruben Jimenez
☐ 15 Clarence Johns
☐ 16 Bo Johnson
☐ 17 Scott Lair
☐ 18 Rich Lopez
☐ 19 Mike Martin
☐ 20 Keith McDonald
☐ 21 Kevin McNeill
☐ 22 Jorge Millan
☐ 23 Isaias Nunez
☐ 24 Christian Reinheimer
☐ 25 Miquel Rivera
☐ 26 B.J. Stanley
☐ 27 Blake Stein
☐ 28 Travis Welch
☐ 29 Curtis Williams
☐ 30 Aaron Bruns CL

1994 Johnson City Cardinals Fleer/ProCards

This 31-card standard size set of the 1994 Johnson City Cardinals, a Rookie Class Appalachian League affiliate of the St. Louis Cardinals, features white-bordered posed color player photos on its fronts with the player's name, position, team name and Fleer/ProCards logo across the bottom of each card. The white back with vertical light blue stripes carries the player's name at the top, followed by biography and statistics. This issue includes the minor league card debut of Blake Stein.

	MINT	NRMT	EXC
COMPLETE SET (31)	6.00	2.70	.75

☐ 3617 Rich Lopez
☐ 3618 Curtis Williams
☐ 3619 Checklist
☐ 3689 Domingo Charles
☐ 3690 Mark Cruise
☐ 3691 Jody Crump
☐ 3692 Tighe Curran
☐ 3693 Kevin Foderaro
☐ 3694 Rob Helvey
☐ 3695 Clarence Johns
☐ 3696 Bo Johnson
☐ 3697 Scott Lair
☐ 3698 Julio Manon
☐ 3699 Mike Martin
☐ 3700 Kevin McNeill
☐ 3701 Christian Reinheimer
☐ 3702 Blake Stein
☐ 3703 Travis Welch
☐ 3704 Joe Bowen
☐ 3705 Ryan Hall
☐ 3706 Keith McDonald
☐ 3707 Pete Ambrosina
☐ 3708 Bert Green
☐ 3709 Ruben Jimenez
☐ 3710 Jorge Millan
☐ 3711 Isaias Nunez
☐ 3712 Miguel Rivera
☐ 3713 Brian Stanley
☐ 3714 Steve Abbs
☐ 3715 Juan Bautista
☐ 3716 Calvin Coach

1994 Kane County Cougars Classic

This 30-card standard size set of the 1994 Kane County Cougars, a Class A Midwest League affiliate of the Florida Marlins, features white-bordered posed color player shots on its fronts with the player's name and position, team name and logo and Classic logo appearing across the bottom of each card. On a ghosted team logo, the white back carries the player's name at the top, followed by biography and statistics. This issue includes the minor league card debut of Felix Heredia.

	MINT	NRMT	EXC
COMPLETE SET (30)	8.00	3.60	1.00

☐ 1 Marc Valdes
☐ 2 Antonio Alfonseca
☐ 3 Alex Aranzamendi
☐ 4 Gavin Baugh
☐ 5 Dave Berg
☐ 6 Ron Brown
☐ 7 Willie Brown
☐ 8 William Cunnane
☐ 9 Dan Ehler
☐ 10 Ryan Filbeck
☐ 11 Felix Heredia
☐ 12 Brendan Kingman
☐ 13 Andy Larkin
☐ 14 Marcus Mays
☐ 15 Billy McMillon
☐ 16 Kevin Millar
☐ 17 Ralph Milliard
☐ 18 Robbie Moen
☐ 19 Andrew Prater
☐ 20 Mike Redmond
☐ 21 Glenn Reeves
☐ 22 Bart Rich
☐ 23 Scott Southard
☐ 24 Paul Thornton
☐ 25 Alan Walania
☐ 26 Bryan Ward
☐ 27 Lynn Jones MG
☐ 28 Brian Peterson CO
☐ 29 Rod Allen CO
☐ 30 Mike McGowan TR
Checklist

1994 Kane County Cougars Fleer/ProCards

This 30-card standard size set of the 1994 Kane County Cougars, a Class A Midwest League affiliate of the Florida Marlins, features white-bordered posed color player photos on its fronts with the player's name, position, team name and Fleer/ProCards logo across the bottom of each card. The white back with vertical light blue stripes carries the player's name at the top, followed by biography and statistics. This issue includes the minor league card debut of Felix Heredia.

	MINT	NRMT	EXC
COMPLETE SET (30)	6.00	2.70	.75

☐ 152 Antonio Alfonseca
☐ 153 Will Cunnane
☐ 154 Dan Ehler
☐ 155 Ryan Filbeck
☐ 156 Felix Heredia
☐ 157 Andy Larkin
☐ 158 Marcus Mays
☐ 159 Tom Paskievitch
☐ 160 Paul Thornton
☐ 161 Marc Valdes
☐ 162 Al Walania
☐ 163 Bryan Ward
☐ 164 Brendan Kingman
☐ 165 Andrew Prater
☐ 166 Mike Redmond
☐ 167 Alex Aranzamendi
☐ 168 Gavin Baugh
☐ 169 Dave Berg
☐ 170 Kevin Millar
☐ 171 Ralph Milliard
☐ 172 Scott Southard
☐ 173 Ron Brown
☐ 174 Willie Brown
☐ 175 Billy McMillon
☐ 176 Robbie Moen
☐ 177 Glenn Reeves
☐ 178 Lynn Jones MG
☐ 179 Rod Allen CO
☐ 180 Brian Peterson CO
☐ 181 Checklist

1994 Kane County Cougars Team Issue

This 30-card standard size set of the 1994 Kane County Cougars, a Class A Midwest League affiliate of the Florida Marlins, features the minor league card debut of Felix Heredia.

	MINT	NRMT	EXC
COMPLETE SET (30)	6.00	2.70	.75

☐ 1 Antonio Alfonseca
☐ 2 Rod Allen CO
☐ 3 Alex Aranzamendi
☐ 4 Gavin Baugh
☐ 5 Dave Berg
☐ 6 Ron Brown
☐ 7 Willie Brown
☐ 8 William Cunnane
☐ 9 Dan Ehler
☐ 10 Ryan Filbeck
☐ 11 Felix Heredia
☐ 12 Lynn Jones MG
☐ 13 Brendan Kingman
☐ 14 Andy Larkin
☐ 15 Marcus Mays
☐ 16 Mike McGowan TR
☐ 17 Billy McMillon
☐ 18 Kevin Millar
☐ 19 Ralph Milliard
☐ 20 Ozzie (Mascot)
☐ 21 Thomas Paskievitch
☐ 22 Brian Peterson CO
☐ 23 Andrew Prater
☐ 24 Mike Redmond
☐ 25 Glenn Reeves
☐ 26 Scott Southard
☐ 27 Paul Thornton
☐ 28 Marc Valdes
☐ 29 Al Walania
☐ 30 Bryan Ward

1994 Kingsport Mets Classic

This 30-card standard size set of the 1994 Kingsport Mets, a Rookie Class Appalachian League affiliate of the New York Mets, features white-bordered posed color player shots on its fronts with the player's name and position, team name and logo and Classic logo appearing across the bottom of each card. On a ghosted team logo, the white back carries the player's name at the top, followed by biography and statistics. This issue includes the minor league card debut of Terrence Long.

	MINT	NRMT	EXC
COMPLETE SET (30)	15.00	6.75	1.85

☐ 1 Roberto Alfonzo
☐ 2 Thomas Arvelo
☐ 3 Paul Bowman
☐ 4 Jerry Hiraldo
☐ 5 Scott Kindell
☐ 6 Matt Koenig
☐ 7 Justin Krablin
☐ 8 Paul John LeClair
☐ 9 Joseph Lisio
☐ 10 Terrence Deon Long
☐ 11 Ethan McEntire
☐ 12 Eric Morales
☐ 13 Guillermo Mota
☐ 14 Steve Pack
☐ 15 Jarrod Patterson
☐ 16 Juan Ramirez
☐ 17 Jesus Sanchez
☐ 18 David Sanderson
☐ 19 Don Spingola
☐ 20 Ramon Tatis
☐ 21 Dale Torborg
☐ 22 Andy Trumpour
☐ 23 John Turlais
☐ 24 Tom Wolff
☐ 25 Ron Gideon MG
☐ 26 Jesus Hernaiz CO
☐ 27 John Stephenson CO
☐ 28 Kevin Culpepper TR
☐ 29 Logo Card
☐ 30 Checklist

1994 Kingsport Mets Fleer/ProCards

This 29-card standard size set of the 1994 Kingsport Mets, a Rookie Class Appalachian League affiliate of the New York Mets, features white-bordered posed color player photos on its fronts with the player's name, position, team name and Fleer/ProCards logo across the bottom of each card. The white back with vertical light blue stripes carries the player's name at the top, followed by biography and statistics. This issue includes the minor league card debut of Terrence Long.

	MINT	NRMT	EXC
COMPLETE SET (29)	8.00	3.60	1.00

☐ 3814 Paul Bowman
☐ 3815 Scott Kindell
☐ 3816 Matt Koenig
☐ 3817 Justin Krablin
☐ 3818 Joe Lisio
☐ 3819 Ethan McEntire
☐ 3820 Steve Pack
☐ 3821 Jesus Sanchez
☐ 3822 Don Spingola
☐ 3823 Ramon Tatis
☐ 3824 Andy Trumpour
☐ 3825 Tom Wolff
☐ 3826 Eric Morales
☐ 3827 John Turlais
☐ 3828 Robert Alfonzo
☐ 3829 Thomas Arvelo
☐ 3830 Steve Lackey
☐ 3831 Guillermo Mota
☐ 3832 Jarrod Patterson
☐ 3833 Dale Torborg
☐ 3834 Jerry Hiraldo
☐ 3835 Paul LeClair
☐ 3836 Terrence Long
☐ 3837 Juan Ramirez
☐ 3838 David Sanderson
☐ 3839 Ron Gideon MG
☐ 3840 Jesus Hernaiz CO
☐ 3841 John Stephenson CO
☐ 3842 Checklist

1994 Kinston Indians Classic

This 30-card standard size set of the 1994 Kinston Indians, a Class A Carolina League affiliate of the Cleveland Indians, features white-bordered posed color player shots on its fronts with the player's name and position, team name and logo and Classic logo appearing across the bottom of each card. On a ghosted team logo, the white back carries the player's name at the top, followed by biography and statistics.

	MINT	NRMT	EXC
COMPLETE SET (30)	10.00	4.50	1.25

☐ 1 Casey Whitten
☐ 2 Jose Cabrera
☐ 3 Epi Cardenas
☐ 4 Patricio Claudio
☐ 5 Jason Fronio
☐ 6 Derek Hacopian
☐ 7 Pep Harris
☐ 8 Sam Hence
☐ 9 Carl Johnson
☐ 10 Todd Johnson
☐ 11 Bo Magee
☐ 12 Rod McCall
☐ 13 Mitch Meluskey
☐ 14 Michael Neal
☐ 15 Jonathan Nunnally
☐ 16 Todd Ruyak
☐ 17 Steve Soliz
☐ 18 Jamie Taylor
☐ 19 Greg Thomas
☐ 20 David Welch
☐ 21 Andre White
☐ 22 Charles York
☐ 23 Dave Keller MG
☐ 24 Greg Booker CO
☐ 25 Dan Norman CO
☐ 26 Teddy Blackwell TR
☐ 27 Bob McElligott ANN
☐ 28 Logo Card
☐ 29 Logo Card
☐ 30 Checklist

1994 Kinston Indians Fleer/ProCards

This 29-card standard size set of the 1994 Kinston Indians, a Class A Carolina League affiliate of the Cleveland Indians, features white-bordered posed color player photos on its fronts with the player's name, position, team name and Fleer/ProCards logo across the bottom of each card. The white back with vertical light blue stripes carries the player's name at the top, followed by biography and statistics.

	MINT	NRMT	EXC
COMPLETE SET (29)	5.00	2.20	.60

☐ 2634 Jose Cabrera
☐ 2635 Jason Fronio
☐ 2636 Pep Harris
☐ 2637 Carl Johnson
☐ 2638 Daron Kirkreit
☐ 2639 Bo Magee
☐ 2640 Todd Ruyak
☐ 2641 Paul Shuey
☐ 2642 David Welch
☐ 2643 Casey Whitten
☐ 2644 Matt Williams
☐ 2645 Charles York
☐ 2646 Todd Johnson
☐ 2647 Mitch Meluskey
☐ 2648 Steve Soliz
☐ 2649 Juan Andujar
☐ 2650 Epi Cardenas
☐ 2651 Rod McCall
☐ 2652 Mike Neal
☐ 2653 Jamie Taylor
☐ 2654 Greg Thomas
☐ 2655 Patricio Claudio
☐ 2656 Derek Hacopian
☐ 2657 Sam Hence
☐ 2658 Jonathon Nunnally
☐ 2659 Andre White
☐ 2660 Dave Keller MG
☐ 2661 Greg Booker CO
☐ 2662 Checklist

1994 Knoxville Smokies Fleer/ProCards

This 28-card standard size set of the 1994 Knoxville Smokies, a Class AA Southern League affiliate of the Toronto Blue Jays, features white-bordered posed color player photos on its fronts with the player's name, position, team name and Fleer/ProCards logo across the bottom of each card. The white back with vertical light blue stripes carries the player's name at the top, followed by biography and statistics.

	MINT	NRMT	EXC
COMPLETE SET (28)	5.00	2.20	.60

☐ 1295 Giovanni Carrara
☐ 1296 Brad Cornett
☐ 1297 Joe Ganote
☐ 1298 Dennis Gray
☐ 1299 Kurt Heble
☐ 1300 Ricardo Jordan
☐ 1301 Al Montoya
☐ 1302 Mark Ohlms
☐ 1303 Randy Phillips
☐ 1304 Aaron Small
☐ 1305 Eric Brooks
☐ 1306 Brent Lutz
☐ 1307 Mike Morland
☐ 1308 Tilson Brito
☐ 1309 Felipe Crespo
☐ 1310 Derek Henderson
☐ 1311 Liriano Rosario
☐ 1312 Chris Stynes
☐ 1313 Chris Weinke
☐ 1314 Brent Bowers
☐ 1315 Rich Butler
☐ 1316 Rick Holifield
☐ 1317 Don Sheppard
☐ 1318 Todd Steverson
☐ 1319 Garth Iorg MG
☐ 1320 Mark Connor CO
☐ 1321 Scott Miller CO
☐ 1322 Checklist

1994 Lake Elsinore Storm Classic

This 30-card standard size set of the 1994 Lake Elsinore Storm, a Class A California League affiliate of the California Angels, features white-bordered posed color player shots on its fronts with the player's name and position, team name and logo and Classic logo appearing across the bottom of each card. On a ghosted team logo, the white back carries the player's name at the top, followed by biography and statistics.

	MINT	NRMT	EXC
COMPLETE SET (30)	12.00	5.50	1.50

☐ 1 Todd Greene
☐ 2 George Arias
☐ 3 Mike Butler
☐ 4 Anthony Chavez
☐ 5 Earl Cunningham
☐ 6 Moe Daniels
☐ 7 Freddie Diaz
☐ 8 Ryan Hancock
☐ 9 Bryan Harris
☐ 10 Larry Hingle
☐ 11 Hank King
☐ 12 Brandon Markiewicz
☐ 13 Shawn Purdy
☐ 14 Thomas Redington
☐ 15 Jeff Schmidt
☐ 16 Kyle Sebach
☐ 17 Billy Simas
☐ 18 Jay Simpson
☐ 19 Demond Smith
☐ 20 John Snyder
☐ 21 Todd Takayoshi
☐ 22 John Thibert
☐ 23 Robert Tucker
☐ 24 Joseph Urso
☐ 25 Derek Vaughn
☐ 26 Mitch Seoane MG
☐ 27 Howie Gershberg CO
☐ 28 Bruce Hines CO
☐ 29 Mike Twomey TR
☐ 30 Alan Gordon
Checklist

1994 Lake Elsinore Storm Fleer/ProCards

This 29-card standard size set of the 1994 Lake Elsinore Storm, a Class A California League affiliate of the California Angels, features white-bordered posed color player photos on its fronts with the player's name, position, team name and Fleer/ProCards logo across the bottom of each card. The white back with vertical light blue stripes carries the player's name at the top, followed by biography and statistics.

	MINT	NRMT	EXC
COMPLETE SET (29)	8.00	3.60	1.00

☐ 1655 Mike Butler
☐ 1656 Tony Chavez
☐ 1657 Ryan Hancock
☐ 1658 Bryan Harris
☐ 1659 Larry Hingle
☐ 1660 Shawn Purdy
☐ 1661 Jeff Schmidt
☐ 1662 Kyle Sebach
☐ 1663 Bill Simas
☐ 1664 John Snyder
☐ 1665 John Thibert
☐ 1666 Todd Greene
☐ 1667 Todd Takayoshi
☐ 1668 Rob Tucker
☐ 1669 George Arias
☐ 1670 Freddie Diaz
☐ 1671 Hank King
☐ 1672 Brandon Markiewicz
☐ 1673 Tom Redington
☐ 1674 Joe Urso
☐ 1675 Earl Cunningham
☐ 1676 Moe Daniels
☐ 1677 Jay Simpson
☐ 1678 Demond Smith
☐ 1679 Derek Vaugn
☐ 1680 Mitch Seoane MG
☐ 1681 Howie Gershberg CO
☐ 1682 Bruce Hines CO
☐ 1683 Checklist

1994 Lakeland Tigers Classic

This 30-card standard size set of the 1994 Lakeland Tigers, a Class A Florida State League affiliate of the Detroit Tigers, features white-bordered posed color player shots on its fronts with the player's name and position, team name and logo and Classic logo appearing across the bottom of each card. On a ghosted team logo, the white back carries the player's name at the top, followed by biography and statistics.

	MINT	NRMT	EXC
COMPLETE SET (30)	10.00	4.50	1.25

☐ 1 Tarrik Brock
☐ 2 Mike Berlin
☐ 3 Shawn Brown
☐ 4 Carlos Burguillos
☐ 5 Todd Bussa
☐ 6 Matt Evans
☐ 7 Carlos Fermin
☐ 8 Eddie Gaillard
☐ 9 Gary Goldsmith
☐ 10 John Grimm
☐ 11 Rich Kelley
☐ 12 Brent Killen
☐ 13 Keith Kimsey
☐ 14 Kevin Lidle
☐ 15 Tim McConnell
☐ 16 Brian Moehler
☐ 17 Rick Navarro
☐ 18 Roberto Rojas
☐ 19 John Rosengren
☐ 20 Yuri Sanchez
☐ 21 Clint Sodowsky
☐ 22 Timothy Thomas
☐ 23 Billy Thompson
☐ 24 Jorge Velandia
☐ 25 Sean Whiteside
☐ 26 Mike Wiseley
☐ 27 Mark Wagner MG
☐ 28 Brian Allard CO
☐ 29 Daniel Raley CO
☐ 30 Bryan Goike TR
Checklist

1994 Lakeland Tigers Fleer/ProCards

This 28-card standard size set of the 1994 Lakeland Tigers, a Class A Florida State League affiliate of the Detroit Tigers, features white-bordered posed color player photos on its fronts with the player's name, position, team name and Fleer/ProCards logo across the bottom of each card. The white back with vertical light blue stripes carries the player's name at the top, followed by biography and statistics.

	MINT	NRMT	EXC
COMPLETE SET (28)	5.00	2.20	.60

☐ 3027 Alvin Brown
☐ 3028 Blas Cedeno
☐ 3029 Ed Gaillard
☐ 3030 Gary Goldsmith
☐ 3031 John Grimm
☐ 3032 Rich Kelley
☐ 3033 Brian Moehler
☐ 3034 Rich Navarro
☐ 3035 John Rosengren
☐ 3036 Clint Sodowsky
☐ 3037 Sean Whiteside
☐ 3038 Kevin Lidle
☐ 3039 Tim McConnell
☐ 3040 Billy Thompson
☐ 3041 Brett Wyngarden
☐ 3042 Shawn Brown
☐ 3043 Matt Evans
☐ 3044 Brent Killen
☐ 3045 Yuri Sanchez
☐ 3046 Tim Thomas
☐ 3047 Jorge Velandia
☐ 3048 Tarrik Brock
☐ 3049 Carlos Burguillos
☐ 3050 Roberto Rojas
☐ 3051 Mike Wiseley
☐ 3052 Brian Allard CO
☐ 3053 Dan Raley CO
☐ 3954 Checklist

1994 Las Vegas Stars Fleer/ProCards

This 25-card standard size set of the 1994 Las Vegas Stars, a Class AAA Pacific Coast League affiliate of the San Diego Padres, features white-bordered posed color player photos on its fronts with the player's name, position, team name and Fleer/ProCards logo across the bottom of each card. The white back with vertical light blue stripes carries the player's name at the top, followed by biography and statistics.

	MINT	NRMT	EXC
COMPLETE SET (25)	6.00	2.70	.75

☐ 862 Andres Berumen
☐ 863 Doug Bochtler
☐ 864 Mike Campbell
☐ 865 Scott Chiamparino
☐ 866 Fidel Compres
☐ 867 Mike Draper
☐ 868 Bryce Florie
☐ 869 Joey Hamilton
☐ 870 Denny Harriger
☐ 871 Hilly Hathaway
☐ 872 Kerry Taylor
☐ 873 Brian Deak
☐ 874 Kevin Higgins
☐ 875 John Ramos
☐ 876 Julio Bruno
☐ 877 Eddie Williams
☐ 878 Matt Witkowski
☐ 879 Randy Curtis
☐ 880 Ray McDavid
☐ 881 Melvin Nieves
☐ 882 Harvey Pulliam
☐ 883 Russ Nixon MG
☐ 884 Marty Barrett CO
☐ 885 Dan Warthen CO
☐ 886 Checklist

1994 Lethbridge Mounties Fleer/ProCards

This 30-card standard size set of the 1994 Lethbridge Mounties, a Rookie Class Pioneer League Independent, features white-bordered posed color player photos on its fronts with the player's name, position, team name and Fleer/ProCards logo across the bottom of each card. The white back with vertical light blue stripes carries the player's name at the top, followed by biography and statistics.

	MINT	NRMT	EXC
COMPLETE SET (30)	5.00	2.20	.60

☐ 3868 Dale Ballance
☐ 3869 Jason Carruth
☐ 3870 Dave Dudeck
☐ 3871 Curtis Falls
☐ 3872 Craig Farmer
☐ 3873 Jess Gonzalez
☐ 3874 Chris Gunnett
☐ 3875 John Henrickson
☐ 3876 Mark McGinn
☐ 3877 John Nape
☐ 3878 Art Ontiveros
☐ 3879 Clayton Premack
☐ 3880 Ricardo Trevino
☐ 3881 Marty Boryczewski
☐ 3882 John Liepa
☐ 3883 Corey Woinarowicz
☐ 3884 Drew Brown
☐ 3885 Mark Duncan
☐ 3886 Kevin Holt
☐ 3887 Robbie Ryan
☐ 3888 Ronnie Shankle
☐ 3889 Brett Bakner
☐ 3890 Mike Lynch
☐ 3891 John Pallino
☐ 3892 Chris Priest
☐ 3893 Thurston Rockmore
☐ 3894 Phillip Wellman MG
☐ 3895 Rodney McCray CO
☐ 3896 Bill Sizemore CO
☐ 3897 Checklist

1994 Lethbridge Mounties Sports Pro

	MINT	NRMT	EXC
COMPLETE SET (30)	7.00	3.10	.85

☐ 1 Brett Bakner
☐ 2 Mike Lynch
☐ 3 John Pallino
☐ 4 Chris Priest
☐ 5 Thurston Rockmore
☐ 6 Dale Ballance
☐ 7 Jason Carruth
☐ 8 Dave Dudeck
☐ 9 Curtis Falls
☐ 10 Craig Farmer
☐ 11 Jess Gonzalez
☐ 12 Chris Gunnett
☐ 13 John Henrickson
☐ 14 Robbie Ryan
☐ 15 John Nape
☐ 16 Art Ontiveros
☐ 17 Clayton Premack
☐ 18 Ricardo Trevino
☐ 19 Marty Boryczewski
☐ 20 John Liepa
☐ 21 Ron Shankle
☐ 22 Corey Woinarowicz
☐ 23 Drew Brown
☐ 24 Mark Duncan
☐ 25 Kevin Holt
☐ 26 Phillip Wellman MG
☐ 27 Hamlin Smith TR
☐ 28 Bill Sizemore CO
☐ 29 Rodney 'Crash' McCray CO
☐ 30 Blank Card

1994 Louisville Redbirds Fleer/ProCards

This 29-card standard size set of the 1994 Louisville Redbirds, a Class AAA American Association affiliate of the St. Louis Cardinals, features white-bordered posed color player photos on its fronts with the player's name, position, team name and Fleer/ProCards logo across the bottom of each card. The white back with vertical light blue stripes carries the player's name at the top, followed by biography and statistics.

	MINT	NRMT	EXC
COMPLETE SET (29)	5.00	2.20	.60

☐ 2970 Paul Anderson
☐ 2971 Brian Barber
☐ 2972 Rich Batchelor
☐ 2973 Rigo Beltran
☐ 2974 Gary Buckels
☐ 2975 Frank Cimorelli
☐ 2976 Doug Creek
☐ 2977 Steve Dixon
☐ 2978 Jeff Hartsock
☐ 2979 Kerry Knox
☐ 2980 Jim Neidlinger
☐ 2981 Omar Olivares
☐ 2982 Rob Wishnevski
☐ 2983 Jose Fernandez
☐ 2984 Marc Ronan
☐ 2985 Scott Coolbaugh
☐ 2986 Tripp Cromer
☐ 2987 Darrell Deak
☐ 2988 Steve Fanning
☐ 2989 Howard Prager
☐ 2990 Jeff Richardson
☐ 2991 Phil Stephenson
☐ 2992 Allen Battle
☐ 2993 John Mabry
☐ 2994 Skeets Thomas
☐ 2995 Gerald Young
☐ 2996 Joe Pettini MG
☐ 2997 Mark Riggins CO
☐ 2998 Checklist

1994 LSU Tigers

These 16 standard-size cards feature on their fronts posed color player photos of the 1994 LSU Tigers. The cards' white borders are highlighted by diagonal purple lines. Most cards carry the players name at the top of the photo and the team name at the bottom, but a few have this arrangement reversed. The white horizontal back carries the player's name, position, and uniform number at the top, followed below by biography and career highlights. All text is in purple lettering.

	MINT	NRMT	EXC
COMPLETE SET (16)	10.00	4.50	1.25

☐ 1 Skip Bertman CO
☐ 2 Todd Walker
☐ 3 Russ Johnson
☐ 4 Jason Williams
☐ 5 Adrian Antonini
☐ 6 Matt Malejko
☐ 7 Brian Winders
☐ 8 Brett Laxton
☐ 9 Scott Schultz
☐ 10 Ryan Huffman
☐ 11 Chad Cooley
☐ 12 Scott Berardi
☐ 13 Chris Pearce
☐ 14 Jeremy Tyson
☐ 15 Eric Berthelot
☐ 16 Jeramie Moore

1994 LSU Tigers McDag Purple

	MINT	NRMT	EXC
COMPLETE SET (16)	10.00	4.50	1.25

☐ 1 Todd Walker
☐ 2 Kenny Jackson
☐ 3 Russ Johnson
☐ 4 Tom Lanier
☐ 5 Brett Laxton
☐ 6 Jim Greely
☐ 7 Adrian Antonini
☐ 8 Harry Berrios
☐ 9 Matt Chamberlain
☐ 10 Chad Cooley
☐ 11 Mike Neal
☐ 12 Armando Rios
☐ 13 Trey Rutledge
☐ 14 Mike Sirotka
☐ 15 Scott Schultz
☐ 16 Jason Williams

1994 Lynchburg Red Sox Classic

This 30-card standard size set of the 1994 Lynchburg Red Sox, a Class A Carolina League affiliate of the Boston Red Sox, features white-bordered posed color player shots on its fronts with the player's name and position, team name and logo and Classic logo appearing across the bottom of each card. On a ghosted team logo, the white back carries the player's name at the top, followed by biography and statistics. This issue includes the minor league card debut of Trot Nixon.

	MINT	NRMT	EXC
COMPLETE SET (30)	8.00	3.60	1.00

☐ 1 Trot Nixon
☐ 2 Ron Allen
☐ 3 Mike Blais
☐ 4 Wesley Brooks
☐ 5 Todd Carey
☐ 6 Dan Collier
☐ 7 Jim Crowley
☐ 8 Bernie Dzafic

- ☐ 9 John Eierman
- ☐ 10 Jeff Faino
- ☐ 11 Gettys Glaze
- ☐ 12 Steve Hayward
- ☐ 13 J.J. Johnson
- ☐ 14 Bob Juday
- ☐ 15 Gregg Kennedy
- ☐ 16 Dana LeVangie
- ☐ 17 Jeff Martin
- ☐ 18 Ryan McGuire
- ☐ 19 Boo Moore
- ☐ 20 Pat Murphy
- ☐ 21 Chad Renfroe
- ☐ 22 Bill Selby
- ☐ 23 Shawn Senior
- ☐ 24 John Stratton
- ☐ 25 Brian Young
- ☐ 26 Mark Meleski MG
- ☐ 27 Jim Bibby CO
- ☐ 28 Joe Marchese CO
- ☐ 29 Chris Correnti TR
- ☐ 30 Checklist

1994 Lynchburg Red Sox Fleer/ProCards

This 29-card standard size set of the 1994 Lynchburg Red Sox, a Class A Carolina League affiliate of the Boston Red Sox, features white-bordered posed color player photos on its fronts with the player's name, position, team name and Fleer/ProCards logo across the bottom of each card. The white back with vertical light blue stripes carries the player's name at the top, followed by biography and statistics. This issue includes the minor league card debut of Trot Nixon.

	MINT	NRMT	EXC
COMPLETE SET (29)	7.00	3.10	.85

- ☐ 1883 Ron Allen
- ☐ 1884 Mike Blais
- ☐ 1885 Wes Brooks
- ☐ 1886 Bernie Dzafic
- ☐ 1887 Jeff Faino
- ☐ 1888 Gettys Glaze
- ☐ 1889 Steve Hayward
- ☐ 1890 Greg Kennedy
- ☐ 1891 Chad Renfroe
- ☐ 1892 Shawn Senior
- ☐ 1893 Brian Young
- ☐ 1894 Dana LeVangie
- ☐ 1895 Jeff Martin
- ☐ 1896 John Stratton
- ☐ 1897 Todd Carey
- ☐ 1898 Jim Crowley
- ☐ 1899 Bob Juday
- ☐ 1900 Ryan McGuire
- ☐ 1901 Pat Murphy
- ☐ 1902 Bill Selby
- ☐ 1903 Dan Collier
- ☐ 1904 John Eierman
- ☐ 1905 J.J. Johnson
- ☐ 1906 Boo Moore
- ☐ 1907 Trot Nixon
- ☐ 1908 Mark Meleski MG
- ☐ 1909 Jim Bibby CO
- ☐ 1910 Joe Marchese CO
- ☐ 1911 Checklist

1994 Macon Braves Classic

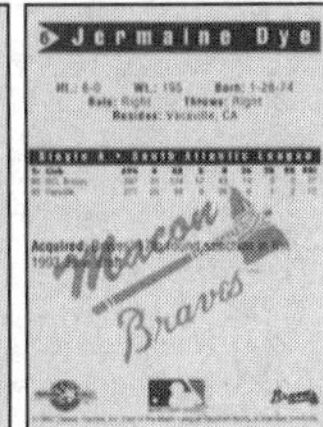

This 30-card standard size set of the 1994 Macon Braves, a Class A South Atlantic League affiliate of the Atlanta Braves, features white-bordered posed color player shots on its fronts with the player's name and position, team name and logo and Classic logo appearing across the bottom of each card. On a ghosted team logo, the white back carries the player's name at the top, followed by biography and statistics. This issue includes the minor league card debut of Jermaine Dye.

	MINT	NRMT	EXC
COMPLETE SET (30)	30.00	13.50	3.70

- ☐ 1 Andre King
- ☐ 2 David Catlett
- ☐ 3 Maurice Christmas
- ☐ 4 Jose Columna
- ☐ 5 Brian Cruz
- ☐ 6 Jermaine Dye
- ☐ 7 Mike Eaglin
- ☐ 8 Marcus Hostetler
- ☐ 9 Ryan Jacobs
- ☐ 10 John Knott
- ☐ 11 Danny Magee
- ☐ 12 Del Mathews
- ☐ 13 Pascual Matos
- ☐ 14 Kevin Millwood
- ☐ 15 Wonderful Monds
- ☐ 16 Carey Paige
- ☐ 17 Chris Rusciano
- ☐ 18 Sherton Saturnino
- ☐ 19 Bill Shafer
- ☐ 20 Randall Simon
- ☐ 21 Sean Smith
- ☐ 22 Jason Thomas
- ☐ 23 Aaron Turnier
- ☐ 24 Miguel Valdez
- ☐ 25 David Wells
- ☐ 26 Esteban Yan
- ☐ 27 Leon Roberts MG
- ☐ 28 Larry Jaster CO
- ☐ 29 Glenn Hubbard CO
- ☐ 30 Dave Hilton CO
  Checklist

1994 Macon Braves Fleer/ProCards

This 31-card standard size set of the 1994 Macon Braves, a Class A South Atlantic League affiliate of the Atlanta Braves, features white-bordered posed color player photos on its fronts with the player's name, position, team name and Fleer/ProCards logo across the bottom of each card. The white back with vertical light blue stripes carries the player's name at the top, followed by biography and statistics. This issue includes the minor league card debut of Jermaine Dye.

	MINT	NRMT	EXC
COMPLETE SET (31)	16.00	7.25	2.00

- ☐ 2196 Maurice Christmas
- ☐ 2197 Marcus Hostetler
- ☐ 2198 Ryan Jacobs
- ☐ 2199 Del Mathews
- ☐ 2200 Kevin Millwood
- ☐ 2201 Carey Paige
- ☐ 2202 Chris Rusciano
- ☐ 2203 Bill Shafer
- ☐ 2204 Jason Thomas
- ☐ 2205 Aaron Turnier
- ☐ 2206 David Wells
- ☐ 2207 Esteban Yan
- ☐ 2208 Brian Cruz
- ☐ 2209 Pascual Matos
- ☐ 2210 Sean Smith
- ☐ 2211 David Catlett
- ☐ 2212 Jose Columna
- ☐ 2213 Mike Eaglin
- ☐ 2214 John Knott
- ☐ 2215 Danny Magee
- ☐ 2216 Randall Simon
- ☐ 2217 Jermaine Dye
- ☐ 2218 Andre King
- ☐ 2219 Wonderful Monds
- ☐ 2220 Sherton Saturnino
- ☐ 2221 Miguel Valdez
- ☐ 2222 Leon Roberts MG
- ☐ 2223 Dave Hilton CO
- ☐ 2224 Glenn Hubbard CO
- ☐ 2225 Larry Jaster CO
- ☐ 2226 Checklist

1994 Madison Hatters Classic

This 30-card standard size set of the 1994 Madison Hatters, a Class A Midwest League affiliate of the St. Louis Cardinals, features white-bordered posed color player shots on its fronts with the player's name and position, team name and logo and Classic logo appearing across the bottom of each card. On a ghosted team logo, the white back carries the player's name at the top, followed by biography and statistics.

	MINT	NRMT	EXC
COMPLETE SET (30)	7.00	3.10	.85

- ☐ 1 Greg Almond
- ☐ 2 Charlie Anderson
- ☐ 3 Chance Cain
- ☐ 4 David Carroll
- ☐ 5 Hector Colon
- ☐ 6 Keith Conway
- ☐ 7 Rick Croushore
- ☐ 8 Dee Dalton
- ☐ 9 Ray Davis
- ☐ 10 Darren Doucette
- ☐ 11 Aaron Gerteisen
- ☐ 12 Keith Jones
- ☐ 13 Dave Madsen
- ☐ 14 Andy Martin
- ☐ 15 Jeff Matulevich
- ☐ 16 Joe McEwing
- ☐ 17 Jeremy McGarity
- ☐ 18 Santo Mota
- ☐ 19 Marc Ottmers
- ☐ 20 Jamie Sailors
- ☐ 21 Steve Santucci
- ☐ 22 Duane Stanton
- ☐ 23 Jesus Ugueto
- ☐ 24 Joe Wallace
- ☐ 25 Mike Windham
- ☐ 26 Jay Witasick
- ☐ 27 Joe Cunningham Jr. MG
- ☐ 28 Ray Searage CO
- ☐ 29 Steve Proctor TR
- ☐ 30 Checklist

1994 Madison Hatters Fleer/ProCards

This 30-card standard size set of the 1994 Madison Hatters, a Class A Midwest League affiliate of the St. Louis Cardinals, features white-bordered posed color player photos on its fronts with the player's name, position, team name and Fleer/ProCards logo across the bottom of each card. The white back with vertical light blue stripes carries the player's name at the top, followed by biography and statistics.

	MINT	NRMT	EXC
COMPLETE SET (30)	5.00	2.20	.60

- ☐ 122 Chance Cain
- ☐ 123 Dave Carroll
- ☐ 124 Keith Conway
- ☐ 125 Rick Croushore
- ☐ 126 Ray Davis
- ☐ 127 Jeff Matulevich
- ☐ 128 Jeremy McGarity
- ☐ 129 Marc Ottmers
- ☐ 130 Jamie Sailors
- ☐ 131 Duane Stanton
- ☐ 132 Mike Windham
- ☐ 133 Jay Witasick
- ☐ 134 Greg Almond
- ☐ 135 Blaine Milne
- ☐ 136 Joe Wallace
- ☐ 137 Charlie Anderson
- ☐ 138 Hector Colon
- ☐ 139 Dee Dalton
- ☐ 140 Darren Doucette
- ☐ 141 Dave Madsen
- ☐ 142 Andy Martin
- ☐ 143 Santo Mota
- ☐ 144 Jesus Ugueto
- ☐ 145 Aaron Gerteisen
- ☐ 146 Keith Jones
- ☐ 147 Joe McEwing
- ☐ 148 Steve Santucci
- ☐ 149 Joe Cunningham Jr. MG
- ☐ 150 Ray Searage CO
- ☐ 151 Checklist

1994 Martinsville Phillies Classic

This 30-card standard size set of the 1994 Martinsville Phillies, a Class A Appalachian League affiliate of the Philadelphia Phillies, features white-bordered posed color player shots on its fronts with the player's name and position, team name and logo and Classic logo appearing across the bottom of each card. On a ghosted team logo, the white back carries the player's name at the top, followed by biography and statistics.

	MINT	NRMT	EXC
COMPLETE SET (30)	7.00	3.10	.85

- ☐ 1 Lawrence Huff Jr.
- ☐ 2 Luis Andino
- ☐ 3 Johnny Beck
- ☐ 4 Jason Boyd
- ☐ 5 Domingo Brito
- ☐ 6 Linardo Diaz
- ☐ 7 Matt Guiliano
- ☐ 8 Paul 'Bo' Hamilton
- ☐ 9 Richard Hunter
- ☐ 10 Kyle Karvala
- ☐ 11 Len Manning
- ☐ 12 Clint McClurg
- ☐ 13 Courtney Mitchell
- ☐ 14 Bear Nitschke
- ☐ 15 Leonardo Oliveros
- ☐ 16 Chris Phipps
- ☐ 17 Danton Pierre-Louis
- ☐ 18 Shane Pullen
- ☐ 19 Kenny Reed
- ☐ 20 Winston Reyes
- ☐ 21 Jackie Rife
- ☐ 22 Aaron Royster
- ☐ 23 Jake Russell
- ☐ 24 Eric Shreimann
- ☐ 25 Jason Sikes
- ☐ 26 Brian Stumpf
- ☐ 27 Charles Tinsley
- ☐ 28 Sam Wampler
- ☐ 29 Matt Williamson
- ☐ 30 Larry Wimberly
  Checklist

1994 Martinsville Phillies Fleer/ProCards

This 31-card standard size set of the 1994 Martinsville Phillies, a Class A Appalachian League affiliate of the Philadelphia Phillies, features white-bordered posed color player photos on its fronts with the player's name, position, team name and Fleer/ProCards logo across the bottom of each card. The white back with vertical light blue stripes carries the player's name at the top, followed by biography and statistics.

	MINT	NRMT	EXC
COMPLETE SET (31)	6.00	2.70	.75

- ☐ 3282 Johnny Beck
- ☐ 3283 Jason Boyd
- ☐ 3284 Bo Hamilton
- ☐ 3285 Rich Hunter
- ☐ 3286 Kyle Karvala
- ☐ 3287 Len Manning
- ☐ 3288 Clint McClurg
- ☐ 3289 Chic Mitchell
- ☐ 3290 Chris Phipps
- ☐ 3291 Kenny Reed
- ☐ 3292 Jackie Rife
- ☐ 3293 Jason Sikes
- ☐ 3294 Brian Stumpf
- ☐ 3295 Larry Wimberly
- ☐ 3296 Bear Nitschke
- ☐ 3297 Leonaldo Oliveros
- ☐ 3298 Eric Schreimann
- ☐ 3299 Sam Wampler
- ☐ 3300 Domingo Brito
- ☐ 3301 Matt Guiliano
- ☐ 3302 Larry Huff
- ☐ 3303 Danton Pierre-Louis
- ☐ 3304 Winston Reyes
- ☐ 3305 Jake Russell
- ☐ 3306 Luis Andino
- ☐ 3307 Linardo Diaz
- ☐ 3308 Chad Kearny
- ☐ 3309 Shane Pullen
- ☐ 3310 Aaron Royster
- ☐ 3311 Charles Tinsley
- ☐ 3312 Checklist

1994 Medicine Hat Blue Jays Fleer/ProCards

This 29-card standard size set of the 1994 Medicine Hat Blue Jays, a Rookie Class Pioneer League affiliate of the Toronto Blue Jays, features white-bordered posed color player photos on its fronts with the player's name, position, team name and Fleer/ProCards logo across the bottom of each card. The white back with vertical light blue stripes carries the player's name at the top, followed by biography and statistics. This issue includes the minor league card debuts of Chris Carpenter, Kevin Witt and Joe Young.

	MINT	NRMT	EXC
COMPLETE SET (29)	10.00	4.50	1.25

- ☐ 3672 Carlos Almanzar
- ☐ 3673 Chris Carpenter
- ☐ 3674 Thomas Davey
- ☐ 3675 Narciso De La Cruz
- ☐ 3676 Lester Henderson
- ☐ 3677 Eric Horton
- ☐ 3678 Mike Johnson
- ☐ 3679 Brian Smith
- ☐ 3680 Mason Smith
- ☐ 3681 Ramon Smith
- ☐ 3682 Sean Strade
- ☐ 3683 Mike Toney
- ☐ 3684 Oreste Volkert
- ☐ 3685 Joe Young
- ☐ 3686 David Becker
- ☐ 3687 Julio Mosquera
- ☐ 3688 Mark Landers
- ☐ 3689 Steve Soper
- ☐ 3690 Craig Stone
- ☐ 3691 Gene Vaninetti
- ☐ 3692 Kevin Witt
- ☐ 3693 Damon Johnson
- ☐ 3694 Dagoberto Prensi
- ☐ 3695 Jonathan Rivers
- ☐ 3696 Felix Rosario
- ☐ 3697 Darren Balsley MG
- ☐ 3698 Hal Dyer CO
- ☐ 3699 Julian Yan CO
- ☐ 3700 Checklist

1994 Medicine Hat Blue Jays Sports Pro

This 30-card standard size set of the 1994 Medicine Hat Blue Jays, a Rookie Class Pioneer League affiliate of the Toronto Blue Jays, features the minor league card debuts of Chris Carpenter, Kevin Witt and Joe Young.

	MINT	NRMT	EXC
COMPLETE SET (30)	15.00	6.75	1.85

- ☐ 1 Mark Landers
- ☐ 2 Steve Soper
- ☐ 3 Craig Stone
- ☐ 4 Gene Vaninetti
- ☐ 5 Kevin Witt
- ☐ 6 Damon Johnson
- ☐ 7 Dagoberto Prensi
- ☐ 8 Jonathan Rivers

☐ 9 Felix Rosario
☐ 10 David Becker
☐ 11 Julio Mosquera
☐ 12 Carlos Almanzar
☐ 13 Chris Carpenter
☐ 14 Thomas Davey
☐ 15 Narciso De La Cruz
☐ 16 Lester Henderson
☐ 17 Eric Horton
☐ 18 Mike Johnson
☐ 19 Brian Smith
☐ 20 Mason Smith
☐ 21 Ramon Smith
☐ 22 Sean Strade
☐ 23 Mike Toney
☐ 24 Oreste Volkert
☐ 25 Joe Young
☐ 26 Darren Balsley MG
☐ 27 Julian Yan CO
☐ 28 Hal Dyer CO
☐ 29 Mike Wirsta TR
☐ 30 Blank Card

1994 Memphis Chicks Fleer/ProCards

This 28-card standard size set of the 1994 Memphis Chicks, a Class AA Southern League affiliate of the Kansas City Royals, features white-bordered posed color player photos on its fronts with the player's name, position, team name and Fleer/ProCards logo across the bottom of each card. The white back with vertical light blue stripes carries the player's name at the top, followed by biography and statistics.

	MINT	NRMT	EXC
COMPLETE SET (28)	5.00	2.20	.60

☐ 349 Brian Bevil
☐ 350 Aaron Dorlarque
☐ 351 Chris Eddy
☐ 352 Jeff Granger
☐ 353 Doug Harris
☐ 354 Brian Harrison
☐ 355 Jimmy Myers
☐ 356 Tim Peek
☐ 357 Vladimir Perez
☐ 358 Ed Pierce
☐ 359 Robert Toth
☐ 360 Carlos Diaz
☐ 361 Chad Strickland
☐ 362 George Canale
☐ 363 Gary Caraballo
☐ 364 Kevin Davis
☐ 365 Jeff Garber
☐ 366 Shane Halter
☐ 367 Brady Stewart
☐ 368 Darren Burton
☐ 369 Kevin Long
☐ 370 Bobby Moore
☐ 371 Dan Rohrmeier
☐ 372 Hugh Walker
☐ 373 Ron Johnson MG
☐ 374 Mike Mason CO
☐ 375 U.L. Washington CO
☐ 376 Checklist

1994 Midland Angels Fleer/ProCards

This 27-card standard size set of the 1994 Midland Angels, a Class AA Texas League affiliate of the California Angels, features white-bordered posed color player photos on its fronts with the player's name, position, team name and Fleer/ProCards logo across the bottom of each card. The white back with vertical light blue stripes carries the player's name at the top, followed by biography and statistics.

	MINT	NRMT	EXC
COMPLETE SET (27)	5.00	2.20	.60

☐ 2431 David Holdridge
☐ 2432 Pete Janicki
☐ 2433 Dom Johnson
☐ 2434 Korey Keling
☐ 2435 Keith Morrison
☐ 2436 Jerry Nielsen
☐ 2437 John Pricher
☐ 2438 Shawn Purdy
☐ 2439 Ron Watson
☐ 2440 Shad Williams
☐ 2441 Jose Monzon
☐ 2442 Fausto Tejero
☐ 2443 Ty Boykin
☐ 2444 Brian Grebeck
☐ 2445 Tim Harkrider
☐ 2446 Chris Pritchett
☐ 2447 J.D. Ramirez
☐ 2448 Luis Raven
☐ 2449 Chris Smith
☐ 2450 Emmitt Cohick
☐ 2451 Marquis Riley
☐ 2452 Mike Wolff
☐ 2453 Mario Mendoza MG
☐ 2454 Jeff Barns P/CO
☐ 2455 Kernan Ronan CO
☐ 2456 John Morris CO
☐ 2457 Checklist

1994 Midland Angels One Hour Photo

This 33-card set of the 1994 Midland Angels, a Class AA Texas League affiliate of the California Angels, features color player photos. The set measures approximately 5 1/2" by 5". The backs are blank. The cards are unnumbered and checklisted below in alphabetical order. 500 sets were produced.

	MINT	NRMT	EXC
COMPLETE SET (33)	45.00	20.00	5.50

☐ 1 Jeff Barns
☐ 2 Ty Boykin
☐ 3 Emmitt Cohick
☐ 4 John Fritz
☐ 5 Larry Gonzales
☐ 6 Brian Grebeck
☐ 7 Ryan Hancock
☐ 8 Tim Harkrider
☐ 9 Julian Heredia
☐ 10 David Holdridge
☐ 11 Pete Janicki
☐ 12 Dom Johnson
☐ 13 Rob Katzaroff
☐ 14 Korey Keling
☐ 15 Dean Locklear
☐ 16 Mario Mendoza
☐ 17 Jose Monzon
☐ 18 John Morris
☐ 19 Keith Morrison
☐ 20 Jerry Nielsen
☐ 21 John Pricher
☐ 22 Chris Pritchett
☐ 23 J.D. Ramirez
☐ 24 Mark Ratekin
☐ 25 Luis Raven
☐ 26 Marquis Riley
☐ 27 Kernan Ronan
☐ 28 Kyle Sebach
☐ 29 Chris Smith
☐ 30 Fausto Tejero
☐ 31 Ron Watson
☐ 32 Shad Williams
☐ 33 Mike Wolff

1994 Midwest League All-Stars Fleer/ProCards

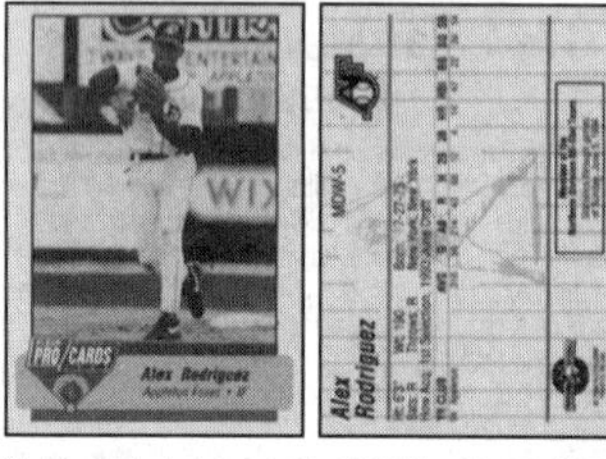

This 59-card standard size set of the 1994 Midwest League All-Stars features white-bordered posed color player photos on its fronts with the player's name, position, team name and Fleer/ProCards logo across the bottom of each card. The white back with vertical light blue stripes carries the player's name at the top, followed by biography and statistics. This issue includes a first year card of Alex Rodriguez.

	MINT	NRMT	EXC
COMPLETE SET (59)	40.00	18.00	5.00

☐ MDW1 Giomar Guevara
☐ MDW2 Tim Harikkala
☐ MDW3 Raul Ibanez
☐ MDW4 Matt Mantei
☐ MDW5 Alex Rodriguez
☐ MDW6 Brian Banks
☐ MDW7 Jim Cole
☐ MDW8 Will Fitzpatrick
☐ MDW9 Sean Maloney
☐ MDW10 John Salamon
☐ MDW11 Jason Baker
☐ MDW12 Javi DeJesus
☐ MDW13 James Motte
☐ MDW14 Ryan Radmanovich
☐ MDW15 Scott Stricklin
☐ MDW16 Andy Larkin
☐ MDW17 Billy McMillon
☐ MDW18 Kevin Millar
☐ MDW19 Ralph Milliard
☐ MDW20 Rick Burley
☐ MDW21 Lino Diaz
☐ MDW22 Sal Fasano
☐ MDW23 Phil Grundy
☐ MDW24 Kevin Rawitzer
☐ MDW25 Mike Sweeney
☐ MDW26 Jason Evans
☐ MDW27 Frank Menechino
☐ MDW28 Mike Sirotka
☐ MDW29 Julio Vinas
☐ MDW30 Scott Baldwin
☐ MDW31 Steve Lemke
☐ MDW32 Bob Henley
☐ MDW33 John Pachot
☐ MDW34 Tomas Perez
☐ MDW35 Willie Brown
☐ MDW36 Derrin Doty
☐ MDW37 Brooks Drysdale
☐ MDW38 Geoff Edsell
☐ MDW39 Tony Moeder
☐ MDW40 Gary Philips
☐ MDW41 Benji Simonton
☐ MDW42 Chance Cain
☐ MDW43 Ray Davis
☐ MDW44 Joe McEwing
☐ MDW45 Jay Witasick
☐ MDW46 Greg Bobbit
☐ MDW47 Gabe Duross
☐ MDW48 Shawn Hill
☐ MDW49 Bobby Morris
☐ MDW50 Brandon Pico
☐ MDW51 Tim Forkner
☐ MDW52 Richard Hidalgo
☐ MDW53 Alan Probst
☐ MDW54 Billy Wagner
☐ MDW55 Luis Arroyo
☐ MDW56 Erick Corps
☐ MDW57 Dan Drewien
☐ MDW58 John Fantauzzi
☐ MDW59 Checklist

1994 Modesto A's Classic

This 30-card standard size set of the 1994 Modesto A's, a Class A California League affiliate of the Oakland Athletics, features white-bordered posed color player shots on its fronts with the player's name and position, team name and logo and Classic logo appearing across the bottom of each card. On a ghosted team logo, the white back carries the player's name at the top, followed by biography and statistics.

	MINT	NRMT	EXC
COMPLETE SET (30)	7.00	3.10	.85

☐ 1 Jose Herrera
☐ 2 Willie Adams
☐ 3 James Banks
☐ 4 Tony Batista
☐ 5 Carlos Belliard
☐ 6 Robert Chouinard
☐ 7 Brian Eldridge
☐ 8 Lauro Felix
☐ 9 Ramon Fermin
☐ 10 David Francisco
☐ 11 Terance Frazier
☐ 12 Benji Grigsby
☐ 13 Creighton Gubanich
☐ 14 Gary Haught
☐ 15 Stacy Hollins
☐ 16 Gary Hust
☐ 17 Tim Killeen
☐ 18 Brian Lesher
☐ 19 Allen Plaster
☐ 20 Greg Smock
☐ 21 Fred Soriano
☐ 22 Scott Spiezio
☐ 23 John Wasdin
☐ 24 Don Wengert
☐ 25 Jason White
☐ 26 Dick Scott MG
☐ 27 Pete Richert CO
☐ 28 Ric Moreno TR
☐ 29 Logo Card
☐ 30 Checklist

1994 Modesto A's Fleer/ProCards

This 26-card standard size set of the 1994 Modesto A's, a Class A California League affiliate of the Oakland Athletics, features white-bordered posed color player photos on its fronts with the player's name, position, team name and Fleer/ProCards logo across the bottom of each card. The white back with vertical light blue stripes carries the player's name at the top, followed by biography and statistics.

	MINT	NRMT	EXC
COMPLETE SET (26)	5.00	2.20	.60

☐ 3055 Willie Adams
☐ 3056 Jim Banks
☐ 3057 Bob Bennett
☐ 3058 Bobby Chouinard
☐ 3059 Ramon Fermin
☐ 3060 Benji Grigsby
☐ 3061 Gary Haught
☐ 3062 Stacy Hollins
☐ 3063 Allen Plaster
☐ 3064 Don Wengert
☐ 3065 Creighton Gubanich
☐ 3066 Tim Killeen
☐ 3067 Tony Batista
☐ 3068 Brian Eldridge
☐ 3069 Lauro Felix
☐ 3070 David Francisco
☐ 3071 Fred Soriano
☐ 3072 Scott Spiezio
☐ 3073 Jason White
☐ 3074 Terance Frazier
☐ 3075 Jose Herrera
☐ 3076 Gary Hust
☐ 3077 Brian Lesher
☐ 3078 Dick Scott MG
☐ 3079 Pete Richert CO
☐ 3080 Checklist

1994 Nashville Sounds Fleer/ProCards

This 27-card standard size set of the 1994 Nashville Sounds, a Class AAA American Association League affiliate of the Chicago White Sox, features white-bordered posed color player photos on its fronts with the player's name, position, team name and Fleer/ProCards logo across the bottom of each card. The white back with vertical light blue stripes carries the player's name at the top, followed by biography and statistics.

	MINT	NRMT	EXC
COMPLETE SET (27)	6.00	2.70	.75

☐ 1242 James Baldwin
☐ 1243 Rod Bolton
☐ 1244 Chris Bushing
☐ 1245 Robert Ellis
☐ 1246 Dane Johnson
☐ 1247 Brian Keyser
☐ 1248 Isidrio Marquez
☐ 1249 Mike Mongiello
☐ 1250 Dennis Powell
☐ 1251 Scott Ruffcorn
☐ 1252 Steve Schrenk
☐ 1253 Clemente Alvarez
☐ 1254 Doug Lindsey
☐ 1255 Drew Denson
☐ 1256 Ray Durham
☐ 1257 Norberto Martin
☐ 1258 Domingo Martinez
☐ 1259 Olmedo Saenz
☐ 1260 Brandon Wilson
☐ 1261 Dann Howitt
☐ 1262 Javier Ortiz
☐ 1263 Gary Thurman
☐ 1264 Jerry Wolak
☐ 1265 Rick Renick
☐ 1266 Roger LaFrancois MG
☐ 1267 Rick Peterson CO
☐ 1268 Checklist CO

1994 Nashville Xpress Fleer/ProCards

This 28-card standard size set of the 1994 Nashville Xpress, a Class AA Southern League affiliate of the Minnesota Twins, features white-bordered posed color player photos on its fronts with the player's name, position, team name and Fleer/ProCards logo across the bottom of each card. The white back with vertical light blue stripes carries the player's name at the top, followed by biography and statistics.

	MINT	NRMT	EXC
COMPLETE SET (28)	5.00	2.20	.60

☐ 377 Narc Barcelo
☐ 378 Rich Garces
☐ 379 Sean Gavaghan
☐ 380 Jon Henry
☐ 381 Jeff Mansur
☐ 382 Mike Misuraca
☐ 383 Joe Norris
☐ 384 Brad Radke
☐ 385 Todd Ritchie
☐ 386 Erik Schullstrom
☐ 387 Denny Sweeney
☐ 388 Scott Watkins
☐ 389 Pedro Grifol
☐ 390 Damian Miller
☐ 391 Ted Corbin
☐ 392 Adell Davenport
☐ 393 Andres Duncan
☐ 394 Mike Fernandez
☐ 395 Ken Tirpack
☐ 396 Ricky Ward
☐ 397 Tony Byrd
☐ 398 Ed Gerald
☐ 399 Steve Hazlett
☐ 400 Tim Moore
☐ 401 Phil Roof MG
☐ 402 Rick Anderson CO
☐ 403 Mark Funderburk CO
☐ 404 Checklist

1994 New Britain Red Sox Fleer/ProCards

This 27-card standard size set of the 1994 New Britain Red Sox, a Class AA Eastern League affiliate of the Boston Red Sox, features white-bordered posed color player photos on its fronts with the player's name, position, team name and Fleer/ProCards logo across the bottom of each card. The white back with vertical light blue stripes carries the player's name at the top, followed by biography and statistics.

	MINT	NRMT	EXC
COMPLETE SET (27)	5.00	2.20	.60

- ☐ 642 Joel Bennett
- ☐ 643 Glenn Carter
- ☐ 644 Joe Caruso
- ☐ 645 Joe Ciccarella
- ☐ 646 Dan Gakeler
- ☐ 647 Jeff Pierce
- ☐ 648 Mike Raczka
- ☐ 649 Ed Riley
- ☐ 650 Tim Smith
- ☐ 651 Pete Young
- ☐ 652 Javier Gonzalez
- ☐ 653 Scott Hatteberg
- ☐ 654 Randy Brown
- ☐ 655 Jim Byrd
- ☐ 656 Felix Colon
- ☐ 657 Pat Lennon
- ☐ 658 John Malzone
- ☐ 659 Bill Norris
- ☐ 660 Steve Rodriguez
- ☐ 661 Bruce Chick
- ☐ 662 Wayne Housie
- ☐ 663 Jose Malave
- ☐ 664 Matt Stairs
- ☐ 665 Jim Pankovits
- ☐ 666 Tommy Barrett
- ☐ 667 Dennis Burtt
- ☐ 668 Checklist

1994 New Haven Ravens Fleer/ProCards

This 29-card standard size set of the 1994 New Haven Ravens, a Class AA Eastern League affiliate of the Colorado Rockies, features white-bordered posed color player photos on its fronts with the player's name, position, team name and Fleer/ProCards logo across the bottom of each card. The white back with vertical light blue stripes carries the player's name at the top, followed by biography and statistics.

	MINT	NRMT	EXC
COMPLETE SET (29)	5.00	2.20	.60

- ☐ 1540 Juan Acevedo
- ☐ 1541 Ivan Arteaga
- ☐ 1542 Roger Bailey
- ☐ 1543 Kyle Duke
- ☐ 1544 Mike Ericson
- ☐ 1545 Mike Kotarski
- ☐ 1546 Rod Pedraza
- ☐ 1547 Lloyd Peever
- ☐ 1548 Phil Schneider
- ☐ 1549 Larry Stanford
- ☐ 1550 David Tellers
- ☐ 1551 Jorge Brito
- ☐ 1552 Mark Strittmatter
- ☐ 1553 Mike Case
- ☐ 1554 Alan Cockrell
- ☐ 1555 Craig Counsell
- ☐ 1556 Fabio Gomez
- ☐ 1557 Bryn Kosco
- ☐ 1558 Lamarr Rogers
- ☐ 1559 Greg Sparks
- ☐ 1560 Billy White
- ☐ 1561 Lew List
- ☐ 1562 Quinton McCracken
- ☐ 1563 J.D. Noland
- ☐ 1564 Ryan Turner
- ☐ 1565 Paul Zuvella MG
- ☐ 1566 P.J. Carey CO
- ☐ 1567 Billy Champion CO
- ☐ 1568 Checklist

1994 New Jersey Cardinals Classic

This 30-card standard size set of the 1994 New Jersey Cardinals, a Class A New York-Penn League affiliate of the St. Louis Cardinals, features white-bordered posed color player shots on its fronts with the player's name and position, team name and logo and Classic logo appearing across the bottom of each card. On a ghosted team logo, the white back carries the player's name at the top, followed by biography and statistics.

	MINT	NRMT	EXC
COMPLETE SET (30)	7.00	3.10	.85

- ☐ 1 Sal Bando Jr.
- ☐ 2 Troy Barrick
- ☐ 3 Randy Bledsoe
- ☐ 4 Efrain Contreras
- ☐ 5 Scott Cunningham
- ☐ 6 Carl Dale
- ☐ 7 Steve Frascatore
- ☐ 8 Ossie Garcia
- ☐ 9 Sean Garman
- ☐ 10 Mike Gautreau
- ☐ 11 Aaron Gerteisen
- ☐ 12 Keith Glauber
- ☐ 13 Matt Golden
- ☐ 14 Yates Hall
- ☐ 15 Rich Hartmann
- ☐ 16 Curtis King
- ☐ 17 Marcus Logan
- ☐ 18 Kevin Lovingier
- ☐ 19 Tommy Minor
- ☐ 20 Darek Robinson
- ☐ 21 Rafael Robles
- ☐ 22 Hector Rodriguez
- ☐ 23 Steve Santucci
- ☐ 24 Brian Silvia
- ☐ 25 Byron Taylor
- ☐ 26 Mike Taylor
- ☐ 27 Bret Wagner
- ☐ 28 Mark Williams
- ☐ 29 Roy Silver MG
- ☐ 30 Orlando Thomas CO
  Checklist

1994 New Jersey Cardinals Fleer/ProCards

This 31-card standard size set of the 1994 New Jersey Cardinals, a Class A New York-Penn League affiliate of the St. Louis Cardinals, features white-bordered posed color player photos on its fronts with the player's name, position, team name and Fleer/ProCards logo across the bottom of each card. The white back with vertical light blue stripes carries the player's name at the top, followed by biography and statistics.

	MINT	NRMT	EXC
COMPLETE SET (31)	5.00	2.20	.60

- ☐ 3404 Troy Barrick
- ☐ 3405 Randy Bledsoe
- ☐ 3406 Scott Cunningham
- ☐ 3407 Carl Dale
- ☐ 3408 Steve Frascatore
- ☐ 3409 Mike Gautreau
- ☐ 3410 Keith Glauber
- ☐ 3411 Matt Golden
- ☐ 3412 Yates Hall
- ☐ 3413 Rich Hartmann
- ☐ 3414 Curtis King
- ☐ 3415 Marcus Logan
- ☐ 3416 Kevin Lovinger
- ☐ 3417 Tommy Minor
- ☐ 3418 Brady Raggio
- ☐ 3419 Bret Wagner
- ☐ 3420 Brian Silvia
- ☐ 3421 Mark Williams
- ☐ 3422 Sal Bando
- ☐ 3423 Mark Dean
- ☐ 3424 Sean Garman
- ☐ 3425 Darek Robinson
- ☐ 3426 Rafael Robles
- ☐ 3427 Hector Rodriguez
- ☐ 3428 Mike Taylor
- ☐ 3429 Efrain Contreras
- ☐ 3430 Ossie Garcia
- ☐ 3431 Aaron Gerteisen
- ☐ 3432 Steve Santucci
- ☐ 3433 Byron Taylor
- ☐ 3434 Checklist

1994 New Orleans Zephyrs Fleer/ProCards

This 27-card standard size set of the 1994 New Orleans Zephyrs, a Class AAA American Association affiliate of the Milwaukee Brewers, features white-bordered posed color player photos on its fronts with the player's name, position, team name and Fleer/ProCards logo across the bottom of each card. The white back with vertical light blue stripes carries the player's name at the top, followed by biography and statistics.

	MINT	NRMT	EXC
COMPLETE SET (27)	5.00	2.20	.60

- ☐ 1460 Scott Anderson
- ☐ 1461 Marshall Boze
- ☐ 1462 Mike Ignasiak
- ☐ 1463 Barry Jones
- ☐ 1464 Scott Karl
- ☐ 1465 Jamie McAndrew
- ☐ 1466 Ron Rightnowar
- ☐ 1467 Charlie Rogers
- ☐ 1468 Steve Sparks
- ☐ 1469 Scott Taylor
- ☐ 1470 Steve Wilson
- ☐ 1471 Rob Campillo
- ☐ 1472 Jimmy Kremers
- ☐ 1473 Tim Barker
- ☐ 1474 John Byington
- ☐ 1475 Jeff Cirillo
- ☐ 1476 Bo Dodson
- ☐ 1477 Greg Smith
- ☐ 1478 Wes Weger
- ☐ 1479 Mike Basse
- ☐ 1480 Ozzie Canseco
- ☐ 1481 Scott Pose
- ☐ 1482 Troy O'Leary
- ☐ 1483 Chris Bando MG
- ☐ 1484 Bill Campbell CO
- ☐ 1485 Ron Jackson CO
- ☐ 1486 Checklist

1994 Norfolk Tides Fleer/ProCards

This 27-card standard size set of the 1994 Norfolk Tides, a Class AAA International League affiliate of the New York Mets, features white-bordered posed color player photos on its fronts with the player's name, position, team name and Fleer/ProCards logo across the bottom of each card. The white back with vertical light blue stripes carries the player's name at the top, followed by biography and statistics.

	MINT	NRMT	EXC
COMPLETE SET (27)	5.00	2.20	.60

- ☐ 2913 Mauro Gozzo
- ☐ 2914 Kenny Greer
- ☐ 2915 Jason Jacome
- ☐ 2916 Gregg Langbehn
- ☐ 2917 Josias Manzanillo
- ☐ 2918 Kevin Morton
- ☐ 2919 Mike Remlinger
- ☐ 2920 Bryan Rogers
- ☐ 2921 Frank Seminara
- ☐ 2922 Dave Telgheder
- ☐ 2923 Brook Fordyce
- ☐ 2924 Joe Kmak
- ☐ 2925 Rico Brogna
- ☐ 2926 Butch Huskey
- ☐ 2927 Aaron Ledesma
- ☐ 2928 Jeff Manto
- ☐ 2929 Pablo Martinez
- ☐ 2930 Quilvio Veras
- ☐ 2931 Jeromy Burnitz
- ☐ 2932 Pat Howell
- ☐ 2933 Jim Lindeman
- ☐ 2934 Rick Parker
- ☐ 2935 Jim Vatcher
- ☐ 2936 Bobby Valentine MG
- ☐ 2937 Bob Apodaca CO
- ☐ 2938 Martin McPhail CO
- ☐ 2939 Checklist

1994 Ogden Raptors Fleer/ProCards

This 24-card standard size set of the 1994 Ogden Raptors, a Rookie Class Pioneer League Independent, features white-bordered posed color player photos on its fronts with the player's name, position, team name and Fleer/ProCards logo across the bottom of each card. The white back with vertical light blue stripes carries the player's name at the top, followed by biography and statistics.

	MINT	NRMT	EXC
COMPLETE SET (24)	5.00	2.20	.60

- ☐ 3729 Jason Evenhus
- ☐ 3730 Jeff Garrett
- ☐ 3731 Steve Gay
- ☐ 3732 Edson Hoffman
- ☐ 3733 John Homan
- ☐ 3734 Josh Kirtlan
- ☐ 3735 Danny Miller
- ☐ 3736 Paul O'Hearn
- ☐ 3737 Tim Salado
- ☐ 3738 Brett Smith
- ☐ 3739 Chris Amos
- ☐ 3740 Mike Carrigg
- ☐ 3741 Tommy Johnston
- ☐ 3742 Shane Jones
- ☐ 3743 Brett Mandel
- ☐ 3744 Jeremy Winget
- ☐ 3745 Dan Zanola
- ☐ 3746 Brad Dandridge
- ☐ 3747 Tim Gavello
- ☐ 3748 Doug O'Neill
- ☐ 3749 Jason Pollock
- ☐ 3750 Chris Simmons
- ☐ 3751 Rich Morales CO
  Willy Ambos MG
- ☐ 3752 Checklist

1994 Ogden Raptors Sports Pro

	MINT	NRMT	EXC
COMPLETE SET (30)	7.00	3.10	.85

- ☐ 1 Chris Amos
- ☐ 2 Mike Carrigg
- ☐ 3 Tommy Johnston
- ☐ 4 Shane Jones
- ☐ 5 Jason Evanhus
- ☐ 6 Jeff Garrett
- ☐ 7 Steve Gay
- ☐ 8 Edson Hoffman
- ☐ 9 John Homan
- ☐ 10 Troy Doezie
- ☐ 11 Brett Smith
- ☐ 12 Brett Mandell
- ☐ 13 Jeremy Winget
- ☐ 14 Dan Zanola
- ☐ 15 Brad Dandridge
- ☐ 16 Tim Gavello
- ☐ 17 Doug O'Neill
- ☐ 18 Jason Pollock
- ☐ 19 Chris Simmons
- ☐ 20 Josh Kirtlan
- ☐ 21 Tim Salado
- ☐ 22 Danny Miller
- ☐ 23 Paul O'Hearn
- ☐ 24 Willy Ambos MG
- ☐ 25 Rich Morales CO
- ☐ 26 Dan Overman TR
- ☐ 27 Craig Holmes
  Pictured with son
- ☐ 28 Todd Nuttall BB
  Ty Doezie BB
  Peter Kline BB
  Brandon Crandell BB
- ☐ 29 Dave Baggott GM
- ☐ 30 Blank Card

1994 Oklahoma City 89ers Fleer/ProCards

This 25-card standard size set of the 1994 Oklahoma City 89ers, a Class AAA American Association affiliate of the Texas Rangers, features white-bordered posed color player photos on its fronts with the player's name, position, team name and Fleer/ProCards logo across the bottom of each card. The white back with vertical light blue stripes carries the player's name at the top, followed by biography and statistics.

	MINT	NRMT	EXC
COMPLETE SET (25)	5.00	2.20	.60

- ☐ 1487 Jose Alberro
- ☐ 1488 Brian Bohanon
- ☐ 1489 Duff Brumley
- ☐ 1490 Terry Burrows
- ☐ 1491 Steve Dreyer
- ☐ 1492 Barry Goetz
- ☐ 1493 James Hurst
- ☐ 1494 Ritchie Moody
- ☐ 1495 David Perez
- ☐ 1496 Doug Davis
- ☐ 1497 Jim McNamara
- ☐ 1498 Benji Gil
- ☐ 1499 Chuck Jackson
- ☐ 1500 Rob Maurer
- ☐ 1501 Jon Shave
- ☐ 1502 Butch Davis
- ☐ 1503 Rob Ducey
- ☐ 1504 Rusty Greer
- ☐ 1505 Donald Harris
- ☐ 1506 Trey McCoy
- ☐ 1507 Dan Peltier
- ☐ 1508 Bobby Jones MG
- ☐ 1509 Mike Berger CO
- ☐ 1510 Rick Knapp CO
- ☐ 1511 Checklist

1994 Omaha Royals Fleer/ProCards

This 27-card standard size set of the 1994 Omaha Royals, a Class AAA American Association affiliate of the Kansas City Royals, features white-bordered posed color player photos on its fronts with the player's name, position, team name and Fleer/ProCards logo across the bottom of each card. The white back with vertical light blue stripes carries the player's name at the top, followed by biography and statistics. This issue includes a second year card of Michael Tucker.

	MINT	NRMT	EXC
COMPLETE SET (27)	8.00	3.60	1.00

- ☐ 1215 Paul Abbott
- ☐ 1216 Enrique Burgos
- ☐ 1217 Jose DeJesus
- ☐ 1218 Mike Fyhrie
- ☐ 1219 Jerry Kutzler
- ☐ 1220 Rusty Meacham
- ☐ 1221 Bob Milacki
- ☐ 1222 Dennis Moeller
- ☐ 1223 Steve Shifflett
- ☐ 1224 Doug Simons
- ☐ 1225 Mike Knapp
- ☐ 1226 Russ McGinnis
- ☐ 1227 Nelson Santovenia
- ☐ 1228 Edgar Caceres
- ☐ 1229 Glenn Davis
- ☐ 1230 Jose Mota
- ☐ 1231 Joe Randa
- ☐ 1232 Joe Vitiello
- ☐ 1233 Curtis Wilkerson
- ☐ 1234 Tom Goodwin
- ☐ 1235 Dwayne Hosey
- ☐ 1236 Les Norman
- ☐ 1237 Michael Tucker
- ☐ 1238 Jeff Cox MG
- ☐ 1239 Mike Alvarez CO
- ☐ 1240 Tom Poquette CO
- ☐ 1241 Checklist

1994 Oneonta Yankees Classic

This 30-card standard size set of the 1994 Oneonta Yankees, a Class A New York-Penn League affiliate of the New York Yankees, features white-bordered posed color player shots on its fronts with the player's name and position, team name and logo and Classic logo appearing across the bottom of each card. On a ghosted team logo, the white back carries the player's name at the top, followed by biography and statistics. This issue includes the minor league card debut of Matt Drews.

	MINT	NRMT	EXC
COMPLETE SET (30)	10.00	4.50	1.25

☐ 1 Matt Drews
☐ 2 Ryan Beeney
☐ 3 Jeremy Benson
☐ 4 Jason Berry
☐ 5 Brian Binversie
☐ 6 Charlie Brown
☐ 7 Derek Dukart
☐ 8 Dwaine Edgar
☐ 9 Mark Gipner
☐ 10 Jason Jarvis
☐ 11 Jose Lobaton
☐ 12 Brian McLamb
☐ 13 Rafael Medina
☐ 14 David Meyer
☐ 15 Casey Mittauer
☐ 16 Trey Nelson
☐ 17 John Picollo
☐ 18 Ray Ricken
☐ 19 Cody Samuel
☐ 20 Fernando Seguignol
☐ 21 Steve Shoemaker
☐ 22 Derek Shumpert
☐ 23 Sloan Smith
☐ 24 Rob Trimble
☐ 25 Carlos Yedo
☐ 26 Ken Dominguez MG
☐ 27 Mark Rose CO
☐ 28 Paul Faulk CO
☐ 29 Rob Thompson CO
☐ 30 Carl Randolph TR Checklist

1994 Oneonta Yankees Fleer/ProCards

This 31-card standard size set of the 1994 Oneonta Yankees, a Class A New York-Penn League affiliate of the New York Yankees, features white-bordered posed color player photos on its fronts with the player's name, position, team name and Fleer/ProCards logo across the bottom of each card. The white back with vertical light blue stripes carries the player's name at the top, followed by biography and statistics. This issue includes the minor league card debut of Matt Drews.

	MINT	NRMT	EXC
COMPLETE SET (31)	8.00	3.60	1.00

☐ 3779 Jeremy Benson
☐ 3780 Jason Berry
☐ 3781 Brian Binversie
☐ 3782 Charlie Brown
☐ 3783 Chris Corn
☐ 3784 Matt Drews
☐ 3785 Dwaine Edgar
☐ 3786 Jason Jarvis
☐ 3787 Rafael Medina
☐ 3788 David Meyer
☐ 3789 Casey Mittauer
☐ 3790 Ray Ricken
☐ 3791 Tony Rush
☐ 3792 Steve Shoemaker
☐ 3793 Mark Gipner
☐ 3794 John Picollo
☐ 3795 Jon Strauss
☐ 3796 Jason Troilo
☐ 3797 Ryan Beeney
☐ 3798 Derek Dukart
☐ 3799 Julio Garcia
☐ 3800 Jose Lobaton
☐ 3801 Brian McLamb
☐ 3802 Mike Mitchell
☐ 3803 Cody Samuel
☐ 3804 Tray Nelson
☐ 3805 Fernando Seguignol
☐ 3806 Derek Shumpert
☐ 3807 Sloan Smith
☐ 3808 Ken Dominguez MG
☐ 3809 Checklist

1994 Orlando Cubs Fleer/ProCards

This 26-card standard size set of the 1994 Orlando Cubs, a Class AA Southern League affiliate of the Chicago Cubs, features white-bordered posed color player photos on its fronts with the player's name, position, team name and Fleer/ProCards logo across the bottom of each card. The white back with vertical light blue stripes carries the player's name at the top, followed by biography and statistics. This issue includes the minor league card debut of Brooks Kieschnick.

	MINT	NRMT	EXC
COMPLETE SET (26)	8.00	3.60	1.00

☐ 1377 Tony Bradford
☐ 1378 Ben Burlingame
☐ 1379 Darren Dreyer
☐ 1380 Doug Harrah
☐ 1381 Chris Johnson
☐ 1382 Greg Perschke
☐ 1383 Ottis Smith
☐ 1384 Kennie Steenstra
☐ 1385 Dave Swartzbaugh
☐ 1386 Derek Wallace
☐ 1387 Adam Brown
☐ 1388 Ricardo Galvez
☐ 1389 Mike Hubbard
☐ 1390 Brant Brown
☐ 1391 Rudy Gomez
☐ 1392 Chris Peterson
☐ 1393 Rod Robertson
☐ 1394 Ed Smith
☐ 1395 Chad Tredaway
☐ 1396 Doug Glanville
☐ 1397 Richie Grayum
☐ 1398 Brooks Kieschnick
☐ 1399 Paul Torres
☐ 1400 Pedro Valdez
☐ 1401 Dave Trembley MG
☐ 1402 Checklist

1994 Osceola Astros Classic

This 30-card standard size set of the 1994 Osceola Astros, a Class A Florida State League affiliate of the Houston Astros, features white-bordered posed color player shots on its fronts with the player's name and position, team name and logo and Classic logo appearing across the bottom of each card. On a ghosted team logo, the white back carries the player's name at the top, followed by biography and statistics.

	MINT	NRMT	EXC
COMPLETE SET (30)	7.00	3.10	.85

☐ 1 Jimmy White
☐ 2 Tom Anderson
☐ 3 Marvin Billingsley
☐ 4 Brett Callan
☐ 5 Henri Centeno
☐ 6 Chris Durkin
☐ 7 Greg Elliott
☐ 8 Jamie Evans
☐ 9 Sean Fesh
☐ 10 Jimmy Gonzalez
☐ 11 Billy Hartnett
☐ 12 Tim Kester
☐ 13 Jim Lewis UER (Card back says Doug McGraw, has his stats)
☐ 14 Shawn Livsey
☐ 15 Hector Mercado
☐ 16 Donovan Mitchell
☐ 17 Melvin Mora
☐ 18 Tyrone Narcisse
☐ 19 Corey Powell
☐ 20 Jose Santana
☐ 21 Chuck Smith
☐ 22 Steve Verduzco
☐ 23 Jim Waring
☐ 24 Chad White
☐ 25 Todd Winston
☐ 26 Tim Tolman MG
☐ 27 Jack Billingham CO
☐ 28 Ivan DeJesus CO
☐ 29 Mike Cerame TR
☐ 30 Checklist UER (#13 says Doug McGraw, should be Jim Lewis)

1994 Osceola Astros Fleer/ProCards

This 30-card standard size set of the 1994 Osceola Astros, a Class A Florida State League affiliate of the Houston Astros, features white-bordered posed color player photos on its fronts with the player's name, position, team name and Fleer/ProCards logo across the bottom of each card. The white back with vertical light blue stripes carries the player's name at the top, followed by biography and statistics.

	MINT	NRMT	EXC
COMPLETE SET (30)	5.00	2.20	.60

☐ 1128 Tom Anderson
☐ 1129 Marvin Billingsley
☐ 1130 Jamie Evans
☐ 1131 Sean Fesh
☐ 1132 Billy Hartnett
☐ 1133 Tim Kester
☐ 1134 Jimmy Lewis
☐ 1135 Doug McGraw
☐ 1136 Hector Mercado
☐ 1137 Tyrone Narcisse
☐ 1138 Chuck Smith
☐ 1139 Jim Waring
☐ 1140 Brett Callan
☐ 1141 Jimmy Gonzalez
☐ 1142 Todd Winston
☐ 1143 Henri Centeno
☐ 1144 Greg Elliott
☐ 1145 Donovan Mitchell
☐ 1146 Corey Powell
☐ 1147 Jose Santana
☐ 1148 Steve Verduzco
☐ 1149 Chris Durkin
☐ 1150 Shawn Livsey
☐ 1151 Melvin Mora
☐ 1152 Chad White
☐ 1153 Jimmy White
☐ 1154 Tim Tolman MG
☐ 1155 Jack Billingham CO
☐ 1156 Ivan DeJesus CO
☐ 1157 Checklist

1994 Ottawa Lynx Fleer/ProCards

This 19-card standard size set of the 1994 Ottawa Lynx, a Class AAA International League affiliate of the Montreal Expos, features white-bordered posed color player photos on its fronts with the player's name, position, team name and Fleer/ProCards logo across the bottom of each card. The white back with vertical light blue stripes carries the player's name at the top, followed by biography and statistics.

	MINT	NRMT	EXC
COMPLETE SET (19)	5.00	2.20	.60

☐ 2894 Reid Cornelius
☐ 2895 Ralph Diaz
☐ 2896 Joey Eischen
☐ 2897 Heath Haynes
☐ 2898 Shawn Holman
☐ 2899 Benny Puig
☐ 2900 Darrin Winston
☐ 2901 Joe Siddall
☐ 2902 Shane Andrews
☐ 2903 Bien Figueroa
☐ 2904 Oreste Marrero
☐ 2905 Chris Martin
☐ 2906 F.P. Santangelo
☐ 2907 Derrick White
☐ 2908 Derek Lee
☐ 2909 Rondell White
☐ 2910 Ted Wood
☐ 2911 Tyrone Woods
☐ 2912 Checklist

1994 Pawtucket Red Sox Dunkin' Donuts

This 31-card set of the Pawtucket Red Sox, a Class AAA International League affiliate of the Boston Red Sox, was issued in one large sheet featuring six perforated five-card strips with a large team photo in the wide top strip. Sponsored by Channel 10 and Dunkin' Donuts, the fronts carry color player photos while the backs display player career statistics. The cards are unnumbered and checklisted below in alphabetical order.

	MINT	NRMT	EXC
COMPLETE SET (31)	50.00	22.00	6.25

☐ 1 Luis Aguayo
☐ 2 Buddy Bailey
☐ 3 Cory Bailey
☐ 4 Greg Blosser
☐ 5 Glenn Carter
☐ 6 Gar Finnvold
☐ 7 Don Florence
☐ 8 Scott Hatteberg
☐ 9 Chris Howard
☐ 10 Greg Litton
☐ 11 Jeff McNeely
☐ 12 Jose Melendez
☐ 13 Nate Minchey
☐ 14 Jose Munoz
☐ 15 Glenn Murray
☐ 16 Luis Ortiz
☐ 17 George Pedre
☐ 18 Carlos Rodriguez
☐ 19 Frank Rodriguez
☐ 20 Ruben Rodriguez
☐ 21 Steve Rodriguez
☐ 22 Tony Rodriguez
☐ 23 Jim Rowe
☐ 24 Paul Thoutsis
☐ 25 Andy Tomberlin
☐ 26 Mike Twardoski
☐ 27 Sergio Valdez
☐ 28 Tim Vanegmond
☐ 29 Eric Wedge
☐ 30 Rick Wise
☐ 31 Team Photo

1994 Pawtucket Red Sox Fleer/ProCards

This 25-card standard size set of the 1994 Pawtucket Red Sox, a Class AAA International League affiliate of the Boston Red Sox, features white-bordered posed color player photos on its fronts with the player's name, position, team name and Fleer/ProCards logo across the bottom of each card. The white back with vertical light blue stripes carries the player's name at the top, followed by biography and statistics.

	MINT	NRMT	EXC
COMPLETE SET (25)	5.00	2.20	.60

☐ 939 Cory Bailey
☐ 940 Brian Conroy
☐ 941 Gar Finnvold
☐ 942 Don Florence
☐ 943 Todd Frohwirth
☐ 944 Chris Howard
☐ 945 Jose Melendez
☐ 946 Nate Minchey
☐ 947 Frank Rodriguez
☐ 948 Tim Vanegmond
☐ 949 Ruben Rodriguez
☐ 950 Greg Litton
☐ 951 Jose Munoz
☐ 952 Luis Ortiz
☐ 953 Carlos Rodriguez
☐ 954 Mike Twardoski
☐ 955 Jeff McNeely
☐ 956 Glenn Murray
☐ 957 Paul Thoutsis
☐ 958 Andy Tomberlin
☐ 959 Bob Zupcic
☐ 960 Buddy Bailey MG
☐ 961 Luis Aguayo CO
☐ 962 Rick Wise CO
☐ 963 Checklist

1994 Peoria Chiefs Classic

This 30-card standard size set of the 1994 Peoria Chiefs, a Class A Midwest League affiliate of the Chicago Cubs, features white-bordered posed color player shots on its fronts with the player's name and position, team name and logo and Classic logo appearing across the bottom of each card. On a ghosted team logo, the white back carries the player's name at the top, followed by biography and statistics.

	MINT	NRMT	EXC
COMPLETE SET (30)	7.00	3.10	.85

☐ 1 Bobby Morris
☐ 2 Gilbert Avalos
☐ 3 Joe Biernat
☐ 4 Greg Bobbitt
☐ 5 Alex Cabrera
☐ 6 Gabe Duross
☐ 7 Kevin Ellis
☐ 8 Sean Fric
☐ 9 Danny Gil
☐ 10 Jeremi Gonzalez
☐ 11 Jason Hart
☐ 12 Shawn Hill
☐ 13 Greg Hillman
☐ 14 Rodd Kurtz
☐ 15 Tony Locey
☐ 16 Orlando Lopez
☐ 17 Dan Madsen
☐ 18 Shawn McDonnell
☐ 19 Emilio Mendez
☐ 20 Jose Molina
☐ 21 Brandon Pico
☐ 22 Roberto Rivera
☐ 23 Coleman Smith
☐ 24 Wade Walker
☐ 25 Brent Woodall
☐ 26 Steven Roadcap MG
☐ 27 Alan Dunn CO
☐ 28 Joe Tanner CO
☐ 29 Logo Card
☐ 30 Checklist

1994 Peoria Chiefs Fleer/ProCards

This 29-card standard size set of the 1994 Peoria Chiefs, a Class A Midwest League affiliate of the Chicago Cubs, features white-bordered posed color player photos on its fronts with the player's name, position, team name and Fleer/ProCards logo across the bottom of each card. The white back with vertical light blue stripes carries the player's name at the top, followed by biography and statistics.

	MINT	NRMT	EXC
COMPLETE SET (29)	5.00	2.20	.60

☐ 2258 Greg Bobbitt
☐ 2259 Jeremi Gonzalez
☐ 2260 Jason Hart
☐ 2261 Shawn Hill
☐ 2262 Greg Hillman
☐ 2263 Rodd Kurtz
☐ 2264 Tony Locey
☐ 2265 Orlando Lopez
☐ 2266 Roberto Rivera
☐ 2267 Wade Walker
☐ 2268 Brent Woodall
☐ 2269 Shawn McDonnell
☐ 2270 Jose Molina

☐ 2271 Gilbert Avalos
☐ 2272 Joe Biernat
☐ 2273 Alex Cabrera
☐ 2274 Gabe Duross
☐ 2275 Kevin Ellis
☐ 2276 Emilio Mendez
☐ 2277 Bobby Morris
☐ 2278 Sean Fric
☐ 2279 Danny Gil
☐ 2280 Dan Madsen
☐ 2281 Brandon Pico
☐ 2282 Coleman Smith
☐ 2283 Steve Roadcap MG
☐ 2284 Alan Dunn CO
☐ 2285 Joe Tanner CO
☐ 2286 Checklist

1994 Phoenix Firebirds Fleer/ProCards

This 27-card standard size set of the 1994 Phoenix Firebirds, a Class AAA Pacific Coast League affiliate of the San Francisco Giants, features white-bordered posed color player photos on its fronts with the player's name, position, team name and Fleer/ProCards logo across the bottom of each card. The white back with vertical light blue stripes carries the player's name at the top, followed by biography and statistics.

	MINT	NRMT	EXC
COMPLETE SET (27)	5.00	2.20	.60

☐ 1512 Brad Brink
☐ 1513 Dan Carlson
☐ 1514 Fred Costello
☐ 1515 Bob Gamez
☐ 1516 Chris Hook
☐ 1517 Tony Menendez
☐ 1518 Dennis Rasmussen
☐ 1519 Scott Robinson
☐ 1520 Rob Taylor
☐ 1521 Mike Walker
☐ 1522 Dan Fernandez
☐ 1523 Tom Lampkin
☐ 1524 Clay Bellinger
☐ 1525 Paul Faries
☐ 1526 Erik Johnson
☐ 1527 Ray Ortiz
☐ 1528 J.R. Phillips
☐ 1529 Gary Scott
☐ 1530 Shane Turner
☐ 1531 Rikkert Faneyte
☐ 1532 Dax Jones
☐ 1533 Mark Leonard
☐ 1534 Rueben Smiley
☐ 1535 Carlos Alfonso MG
☐ 1536 Duane Espy CO
☐ 1537 Joel Horlen CO
☐ 1538 Checklist

1994 Pittsfield Mets Classic

This 30-card standard size set of the 1994 Pittsfield Mets, a Class A New York-Penn League affiliate of the New York Mets, features white-bordered posed color player shots on its fronts with the player's name and position, team name and logo and Classic logo appearing across the bottom of each card. On a ghosted team logo, the white back carries the player's name at the top, followed by biography and statistics. This issue includes the minor league card debut of Jay Payton.

	MINT	NRMT	EXC
COMPLETE SET (30)	25.00	11.00	3.10

☐ 1 Jay Payton
☐ 2 Jason Adams
☐ 3 Steve Arffa
☐ 4 Joe Atwater
☐ 5 Derek Baker
☐ 6 Ben Boka
☐ 7 James Dorsey
☐ 8 Ross Ferrier
☐ 9 Mark Guerra
☐ 10 Bo Haley
☐ 11 Wicho Hernandez
☐ 12 John Kelly
☐ 13 Toby Larson
☐ 14 Dave Leonhart
☐ 15 Ryan Miller
☐ 16 Jared Osentowski
☐ 17 Kirk Presley
☐ 18 Ty Quillin
☐ 19 Scott Sauerbeck
☐ 20 Brandon Smith
☐ 21 Derek Sutton
☐ 22 Rocky Turner
☐ 23 Todd Whitehurst
☐ 24 Vance Wilson
☐ 25 Howie Freiling MG
☐ 26 Dave LaRoche CO
☐ 27 Jeff Weems TR
☐ 28 Yudith Ozorio
☐ 29 Logo Card
☐ 30 Checklist

1994 Pittsfield Mets Fleer/ProCards

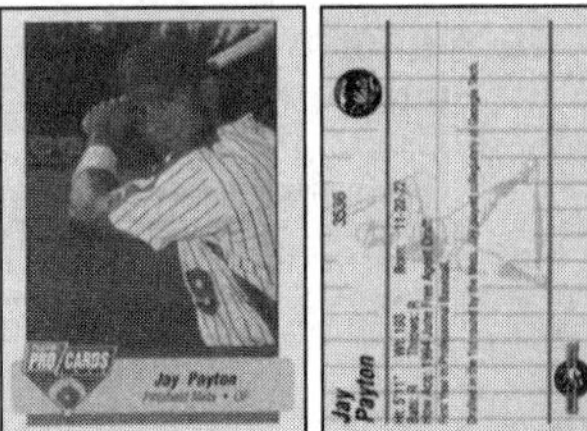

This 27-card standard size set of the 1994 Pittsfield Mets, a Class A New York-Penn League affiliate of the New York Mets, features white-bordered posed color player photos on its fronts with the player's name, position, team name and Fleer/ProCards logo across the bottom of each card. The white back with vertical light blue stripes carries the player's name at the top, followed by biography and statistics. This issue includes the minor league card debut of Jay Payton.

	MINT	NRMT	EXC
COMPLETE SET (27)	18.00	8.00	2.20

☐ 3514 Steve Arffa
☐ 3515 Joe Atwater
☐ 3516 Derek Baker
☐ 3517 Mark Guerra
☐ 3518 John Kelly
☐ 3519 Toby Larson
☐ 3520 Dave Leonhart
☐ 3521 Kirk Presley
☐ 3522 Ty Quillen
☐ 3523 Scott Sauerbeck
☐ 3524 Derek Sutton
☐ 3525 Ben Boka
☐ 3526 Vance Wilson
☐ 3527 Bo Haley
☐ 3528 Wicho Hernandez
☐ 3529 Ryan Miller
☐ 3530 Jared Osentowski
☐ 3531 Todd Whitehurst
☐ 3532 Jason Adams
☐ 3533 Jim Dorsey
☐ 3534 Ross Ferrier
☐ 3535 Yudith Ozario
☐ 3536 Jay Payton
☐ 3537 Rocky Turner
☐ 3538 Howie Freiling MG
☐ 3539 Dave LaRoche CO
☐ 3540 Checklist

1994 Portland Sea Dogs Fleer/ProCards

This 27-card standard size set of the 1994 Portland Sea Dogs, a Class AA Eastern League affiliate of the Florida Marlins, features white-bordered posed color player photos on its fronts with the player's name, position, team name and Fleer/ProCards logo across the bottom of each card. The white back with vertical light blue stripes carries the player's name at the top, followed by biography and statistics. This issue includes a second year card of Charles Johnson.

	MINT	NRMT	EXC
COMPLETE SET (27)	7.00	3.10	.85

☐ 669 Joel Adamson
☐ 670 Rafael Chaves
☐ 671 Vic Darensbourg
☐ 672 Javier De La Hoya
☐ 673 Jarod Juelsgaard
☐ 674 Don Lemon
☐ 675 Jim Newlin
☐ 676 Don Perigny
☐ 677 Mike Whitten
☐ 678 Kip Yaughn
☐ 679 Mark Yockey
☐ 680 Sean Gousha
☐ 681 Charles Johnson
☐ 682 Greg O'Halloran
☐ 683 Jorge Alvarez
☐ 684 Tim Clark
☐ 685 Terry Jorgensen
☐ 686 Chris Malinoski
☐ 687 Ramon Martinez
☐ 688 Edinson Renteria
☐ 689 Eddie Christian
☐ 690 Rick Hirtensteiner
☐ 691 Jesus Tavarez
☐ 692 Carlos Tosca MG
☐ 693 Jose Castro CO
☐ 694 Marty DeMerritt CO
☐ 695 Checklist

1994 Portland Sea Dogs Team Issue

This 31-card standard size set of the 1994 Portland Sea Dogs, a Class AA Eastern League affiliate of the Florida Marlins, features a second year card of Charles Johnson.

	MINT	NRMT	EXC
COMPLETE SET (31)	7.00	3.10	.85

☐ 1 Cover Card
☐ 2 Team Photo
☐ 3 Carlos Tosca
☐ 4 Marty Demerritt
☐ 5 Jose Castro
☐ 6 Todd Sorensen
☐ 7 Joel Adamson
☐ 8 Jorge Alvarez
☐ 9 Rafael Chavez
☐ 10 Eddie Christian
☐ 11 Tim Clark
☐ 12 Vic Darensbourg
☐ 13 Javier De La Hoya
☐ 14 Sean Gousha
☐ 15 Rick Hirtensteiner
☐ 16 Charles Johnson
☐ 17 Terry Jorgensen
☐ 18 Jarod Juelsgaard
☐ 19 Don Lemon
☐ 20 Chris Malinoski
☐ 21 Slugger
☐ 22 Ramon Martinez
☐ 23 Jim Newlin
☐ 24 Greg O'Halloran
☐ 25 Thomas Paskievitch
☐ 26 Don Perigny
☐ 27 Jerry A. Schunk
☐ 28 Jesus Tavarez
☐ 29 Mike Whitten
☐ 30 Kip Yaughn
☐ 31 Mark Yockey

1994 Prince William Cannons Classic

This 30-card standard size set of the 1994 Prince William Cannons, a Class A Carolina League affiliate of the Chicago White Sox, features white-bordered posed color player shots on its fronts with the player's name and position, team name and logo and Classic logo appearing across the bottom of each card. On a ghosted team logo, the white back carries the player's name at the top, followed by biography and statistics.

	MINT	NRMT	EXC
COMPLETE SET (30)	12.00	5.50	1.50

☐ 1 Jimmy Hurst
☐ 2 Mike Bertotti
☐ 3 Mike Bradish
☐ 4 Essex Burton
☐ 5 Mike Call
☐ 6 Mike Cameron
☐ 7 Carmine Cappuccio
☐ 8 Scott Christman
☐ 9 Dan Fraraccio
☐ 10 Jack Johnson
☐ 11 Sean Johnston
☐ 12 David Keating
☐ 13 Dean Locklear
☐ 14 Robert Machado
☐ 15 Henry Manning
☐ 16 Geovany Miranda
☐ 17 Tim Moore
☐ 18 Eddie Pearson
☐ 19 Jason Pierson
☐ 20 Charles Poe
☐ 21 Jason Watkins
☐ 22 Craig Wilson
☐ 23 Chris Woodfin
☐ 24 Steve Worrell
☐ 25 Dave Huppert MG
☐ 26 Jon Matlack CO
☐ 27 Von Joshua CO
☐ 28 Logo Card UER
(Card back says 29, should be 28)
☐ 29 Logo Card
☐ 30 Checklist

1994 Prince William Cannons Fleer/ProCards

This 28-card standard size set of the 1994 Prince William Cannons, a Class A Carolina League affiliate of the Chicago White Sox, features white-bordered posed color player photos on its fronts with the player's name, position, team name and Fleer/ProCards logo across the bottom of each card. The white back with vertical light blue stripes carries the player's name at the top, followed by biography and statistics.

	MINT	NRMT	EXC
COMPLETE SET (28)	7.00	3.10	.85

☐ 1912 Mike Bertotti
☐ 1913 Mike Call
☐ 1914 Scott Christman
☐ 1915 Sean Johnston
☐ 1916 Dave Keating
☐ 1917 Dean Locklear
☐ 1918 Tim Moore
☐ 1919 Jason Pierson
☐ 1920 Jason Watkins
☐ 1921 Chris Woodfin
☐ 1922 Steve Worrell
☐ 1923 Jack Johnson
☐ 1924 Robert Machado
☐ 1925 Henry Manning
☐ 1926 Mike Bradish
☐ 1927 Essex Burton
☐ 1928 Dan Fraraccio
☐ 1929 Geovany Miranda
☐ 1930 Eddie Pearson
☐ 1931 Craig Wilson
☐ 1932 Mike Cameron
☐ 1933 Carmine Cappuccio
☐ 1934 Jimmy Hurst
☐ 1935 Charles Poe
☐ 1936 Dave Huppert MG
☐ 1937 Von Joshua CO
☐ 1938 Jon Matlack CO
☐ 1939 Checklist

1994 Princeton Reds Classic

This 30-card standard size set of the 1994 Princeton Reds, a Rookie Class Appalachian League affiliate of the Cincinnati Reds, features white-bordered posed color player shots on its fronts with the player's name and position, team name and logo and Classic logo appearing across the bottom of each card. On a ghosted team logo, the white back carries the player's name at the top, followed by biography and statistics. This issue includes the minor league card debut of Darron Ingram.

	MINT	NRMT	EXC
COMPLETE SET (30)	10.00	4.50	1.25

☐ 1 Decomba Conner
☐ 2 Cedric Allen
☐ 3 Marlon Allen
☐ 4 Tony Boyette
☐ 5 Damon Callahan
☐ 6 Williams Carmona
☐ 7 John DiFilippo
☐ 8 Wayne Ennis
☐ 9 Eddy Garcia
☐ 10 Emiliano Giron
☐ 11 Darran Hall
☐ 12 Darron Ingram
☐ 13 Argenis LaBarca
☐ 14 Rick Lapka
☐ 15 Brian Lott
☐ 16 Jackie McCroskey
☐ 17 Pat Meier
☐ 18 Sal Mepri
☐ 19 Luis Ordaz
☐ 20 Christian Rojas
☐ 21 Paul Runyan
☐ 22 Rod Sanders
☐ 23 Scott Sharp
☐ 24 Justin Smith
☐ 25 Jay Sorg
☐ 26 John Stearns MG
☐ 27 Jim Holland GM
☐ 28 Brad Kelley CO
☐ 29 Dan Siegel TR
☐ 30 Checklist

1994 Princeton Reds Fleer/ProCards

This 29-card standard size set of the 1994 Princeton Reds, a Rookie Class Appalachian League affiliate of the Cincinnati Reds, features white-bordered posed color player photos on its fronts with the player's name, position, team name and Fleer/ProCards logo across the bottom of each card. The white back with vertical light blue stripes carries the player's name at the top, followed by biography and statistics. This issue includes the minor league card debut of Darron Ingram.

	MINT	NRMT	EXC
COMPLETE SET (29)	5.00	2.20	.60

☐ 3253 Cedric Allen
☐ 3254 Damon Callahan
☐ 3255 Williams Carmona
☐ 3256 Eddy Garcia
☐ 3257 Emiliano Giron
☐ 3258 Rick Lapka
☐ 3259 Brian Lott
☐ 3260 Pat Meier
☐ 3261 Paul Runyan
☐ 3262 Justin Smith
☐ 3263 Tony Boyette
☐ 3264 Sal Mepri
☐ 3265 Scott Sharp

☐ 3266 Marlon Allen
☐ 3267 John DiFilippo
☐ 3268 Wayne Ennis
☐ 3269 Argenis LaBarca
☐ 3270 Luis Ordaz
☐ 3271 Doyle Preston
☐ 3272 Christian Rojas
☐ 3273 Rod Sanders
☐ 3274 Jay Sorg
☐ 3275 Decomba Conner
☐ 3276 Darran Hall
☐ 3277 Darron Ingram
☐ 3278 Jackie McCroskey
☐ 3279 John Stearns MG
☐ 3280 Brad Kelley CO
☐ 3281 Checklist

1994 Quad City River Bandits Classic

This 30-card standard size set of the 1994 Quad City River Bandits, a Class A Midwest League affiliate of the Houston Astros, features white-bordered posed color player shots on its fronts with the player's name and position, team name and logo and Classic logo appearing across the bottom of each card. On a ghosted team logo, the white back carries the player's name at the top, followed by biography and statistics. This issue includes second year cards of Billy Wagner and Richard Hidalgo.

	MINT	NRMT	EXC
COMPLETE SET (30)	12.00	5.50	1.50

☐ 1 Billy Wagner
☐ 2 Randy Albaladejo
☐ 3 Manuel Barrios
☐ 4 Alberto Blanco
☐ 5 R.J. Bowers
☐ 6 Kary Bridges
☐ 7 Ryan Creek
☐ 8 Tom Czanstkowski
☐ 9 Mark Dorencz
☐ 10 Tim Forkner
☐ 11 Mike Grzanich
☐ 12 Richard Hidalgo
☐ 13 Eddie Lewis
☐ 14 Bryant Nelson
☐ 15 Nate Peterson
☐ 16 Alan Probst
☐ 17 Eddie Ramos
☐ 18 Edgar Ramos
☐ 19 Mike Rennhack
☐ 20 Noel Rodriguez
☐ 21 Chris Truby
☐ 22 Jamie Walker
☐ 23 Mike Walter
☐ 24 Destry Westbrook
☐ 25 Steve Dillard MG
☐ 26 Gary Lucas CO
☐ 27 Cesar Cedeno CO
☐ 28 Kenny Crofford TR
☐ 29 Logo Card
☐ 30 Checklist

1994 Quad City River Bandits Fleer/ProCards

This 29-card standard size set of the 1994 Quad City River Bandits, a Class A Midwest League affiliate of the Houston Astros, features white-bordered posed color player photos on its fronts with the player's name, position, team name and Fleer/ProCards logo across the bottom of each card. The white back with vertical light blue stripes carries the player's name at the top, followed by biography and statistics. This issue includes second year cards of Billy Wagner and Richard Hidalgo.

	MINT	NRMT	EXC
COMPLETE SET (29)	8.00	3.60	1.00

☐ 525 Manual Barrios
☐ 526 Alberto Blanco
☐ 527 Ryan Creek
☐ 528 Tom Czanstkowski
☐ 529 Mike Grzanich
☐ 530 Eddie Lewis
☐ 531 Edgar Ramos
☐ 532 Billy Wagner
☐ 533 Jamie Walker
☐ 534 Mike Walter
☐ 535 Destry Westbrook
☐ 536 Randy Albaladejo
☐ 537 Nate Peterson
☐ 538 Alan Probst
☐ 539 Kary Bridges
☐ 540 Mark Dorencz
☐ 541 Tim Forkner
☐ 542 Dave Landaker
☐ 543 Bryant Nelson
☐ 544 Eddie Ramos
☐ 545 Chris Truby
☐ 546 R.J. Bowers
☐ 547 Richard Hidalgo
☐ 548 Mike Rennhack
☐ 549 Noel Rodriguez
☐ 550 Steve Dillard MG
☐ 551 Cesar Cedeno CO
☐ 552 Gary Lucas CO
☐ 553 Checklist

1994 Rancho Cucamonga Quakes Classic

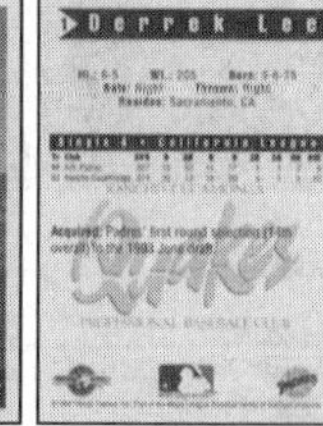

This 30-card standard size set of the 1994 Rancho Cucamonga Quakes, a Class A California League affiliate of the San Diego Padres, features white-bordered posed color player shots on its fronts with the player's name and position, team name and logo and Classic logo appearing across the bottom of each card. On a ghosted team logo, the white back carries the player's name at the top, followed by biography and statistics. This issue includes the minor league card debut of Derrek Lee.

	MINT	NRMT	EXC
COMPLETE SET (30)	25.00	11.00	3.10

☐ 1 Derrek Lee
☐ 2 Larue Baber
☐ 3 Jared Baker
☐ 4 Jon Barnes
☐ 5 Mike Basso
☐ 6 Bobby Bonds II
☐ 7 Stoney Briggs
☐ 8 Homer Bush
☐ 9 Cam Cairncross
☐ 10 Raul Casanova
☐ 11 Roberto DeLeon
☐ 12 Luis Galindez
☐ 13 Ken Grzelaczyk
☐ 14 Craig Hanson
☐ 15 Mike Hermanson
☐ 16 Adrian Hollinger
☐ 17 Greg Keagle
☐ 18 Marc Kroon
☐ 19 Rich Loiselle
☐ 20 Joey Long
☐ 21 Sean Mulligan
☐ 22 Chris Prieto
☐ 23 Todd Schmitt
☐ 24 Jason Thompson
☐ 25 Dario Veras
☐ 26 Tim Flannery MG
☐ 27 Dean Treanor CO
☐ 28 Jim Daniel TR
☐ 29 Logo Card
☐ 30 Checklist

1994 Rancho Cucamonga Quakes Fleer/ProCards

This 29-card standard size set of the 1994 Rancho Cucamonga Quakes, a Class A California League affiliate of the San Diego Padres, features white-bordered posed color player photos on its fronts with the player's name, position, team name and Fleer/ProCards logo across the bottom of each card. The white back with vertical light blue stripes carries the player's name at the top, followed by biography and statistics. This issue includes the minor league card debut of Derrek Lee.

	MINT	NRMT	EXC
COMPLETE SET (29)	15.00	6.75	1.85

☐ 1626 Jared Baker
☐ 1627 Jon Barnes
☐ 1628 Cam Cairncross
☐ 1629 Luis Galindez
☐ 1630 Ken Grzelaczyk
☐ 1631 Craig Hanson
☐ 1632 Mike Hermanson
☐ 1633 Adrian Hollinger
☐ 1634 Greg Keagle
☐ 1635 Marc Kroon
☐ 1636 Rich Loiselle
☐ 1637 Joey Long
☐ 1638 Rob Mallicoat
☐ 1639 Todd Schmitt
☐ 1640 Dario Veras
☐ 1641 Papo Casanova
☐ 1642 Sean Mulligan
☐ 1643 Homer Bush
☐ 1644 Roberto DeLeon
☐ 1645 Derrek Lee
☐ 1646 Austin Manahan
☐ 1647 Jason Thompson
☐ 1648 LaRue Baber
☐ 1649 Stoney Briggs
Bobby Bonds
☐ 1650 Chris Prieto
☐ 1651 Tim Flannery MG
☐ 1652 Mike Basso P/CO
☐ 1653 Dean Treanor CO
☐ 1654 Checklist

1994 Reading Phillies Fleer/ProCards

This 27-card standard size set of the 1994 Reading Phillies, a Class AA Eastern League affiliate of the Philadelphia Phillies, features white-bordered posed color player photos on its fronts with the player's name, position, team name and Fleer/ProCards logo across the bottom of each card. The white back with vertical light blue stripes carries the player's name at the top, followed by biography and statistics.

	MINT	NRMT	EXC
COMPLETE SET (27)	5.00	2.20	.60

☐ 2055 Greg Brown
☐ 2056 Eric Hill
☐ 2057 Craig Holman
☐ 2058 Ryan Karp
☐ 2059 Larry Mitchell
☐ 2060 J.J. Munoz
☐ 2061 Chuck Ricci
☐ 2062 Mark Tranberg
☐ 2063 Bob Wells
☐ 2064 Scott Wiegandt
☐ 2065 Jason Moler
☐ 2066 Troy Rusk
☐ 2067 David Fisher
☐ 2068 Mike Gomez
☐ 2069 Rob Grable
☐ 2070 David Hayden
☐ 2071 Keith Kimberlin
☐ 2072 John Kupsey
☐ 2073 Jon Zuber
☐ 2074 Jay Edwards
☐ 2075 Jeff Jackson
☐ 2076 Tom Nuneviller
☐ 2077 Dave Tokheim
☐ 2078 Bill Dancy MG
☐ 2079 Carlos Arroyo CO
☐ 2080 Bill Robinson CO
☐ 2081 Checklist

1994 Richmond Braves Fleer/ProCards

This 30-card standard size set of the 1994 Richmond Braves, a Class AAA International League affiliate of the Atlanta Braves, features white-bordered posed color player photos on its fronts with the player's name, position, team name and Fleer/ProCards logo across the bottom of each card. The white back with vertical light blue stripes carries the player's name at the top, followed by biography and statistics.

	MINT	NRMT	EXC
COMPLETE SET (30)	5.00	2.20	.60

☐ 2837 Brian Bark
☐ 2838 Mike Birkbeck
☐ 2839 Pedro Borbon
☐ 2840 Dera Clark
☐ 2841 Terry Clark
☐ 2842 Mike Hostetler
☐ 2843 Judd Johnson
☐ 2844 Kevin Lomon
☐ 2845 Mike Potts
☐ 2846 Anthony Telford
☐ 2847 Brad Woodall
☐ 2850 Eddie Perez
☐ 2851 Ramon Caraballo
☐ 2852 Pat Kelly
☐ 2853 Luis Lopez
☐ 2854 Mike Mordecai
☐ 2855 Jose Oliva
☐ 2856 Jose Olmeda
☐ 2857 Beau Allred
☐ 2858 Jarvis Brown
☐ 2859 Troy Hughes
☐ 2860 Mike Kelly
☐ 2861 Brian Kowitz
☐ 2862 Grady Little MG
☐ 2863 Bill Fischer CO
☐ 2864 Bruce Kimm CO
☐ 2865 Tack Wilson CO
☐ 2866 Checklist
☐ 2948 Tyler Houston
☐ 2949 John Orton

1994 Riverside Pilots Cal League Cards

	MINT	NRMT	EXC
COMPLETE SET (32)	6.00	2.70	.75

☐ 1 Matt Apana
☐ 2 Craig Clayton
☐ 3 Desi Relaford
☐ 4 Manny Cora
☐ 5 George Glinatsis
☐ 6 Mike Hickey
☐ 7 Roy Miller
☐ 8 James Bonnici
☐ 9 Sal Urso
☐ 10 Charles Gipson
☐ 11 Randy Jorgensen
☐ 12 Osvaldo Fernandez
☐ 13 Keifer Rackley
☐ 14 Bob Wolcott
☐ 15 John Tejcek
☐ 16 Andy Sheets
☐ 17 Rafael Carmona
☐ 18 Dan Sullivan
☐ 19 Jackie Nickell
☐ 20 Roberto Ramirez
☐ 21 Ryan Franklin
☐ 22 John Cardenas
☐ 23 Trey Witte
☐ 24 Bob Worley
☐ 25 Mike Triessl
☐ 26 Jim Koehler
☐ 27 Doug Fitzer
☐ 28 Sam August
☐ 29 Dave Myers MG
☐ 30 Ron Romanick CO
☐ 31 Manny Cervantes CO
☐ 32 Robert Nodine TR

1994 Rochester Red Wings Team Issue

	MINT	NRMT	EXC
COMPLETE SET (30)	8.00	3.60	1.00

☐ 1 Steve Adkins
☐ 2 Manny Alexander
☐ 3 Kevin Baez
☐ 4 Damon Buford
☐ 5 Paul Carey
☐ 6 Jim Dedrick
☐ 7 Bruce Dostal
☐ 8 Craig Faulkner
☐ 9 Rick Krivda
☐ 10 T.R. Lewis
☐ 11 Steve Luebber
☐ 12 Jeff Manto
☐ 13 Barry Manuel
☐ 14 Kevin McGehee
☐ 15 Bob Miscik
☐ 16 Sherman Obando
☐ 17 John O'Donoghue
☐ 18 Brad Pennington
☐ 19 Arthur Rhodes
☐ 20 Jason Satre
☐ 21 Mark Smith
☐ 22 Brad Tyler
☐ 23 Jim Wawruck
☐ 24 Jim Weaver
☐ 25 Tom Wegmann
☐ 26 Gregg Zaun
☐ 27 Sponsor Card
Wegmans
Coupon
☐ 28 Sponsor Card
Wegmans
Coupon
☐ 29 Sponsor Card
Wegmans
Coupon
☐ 30 Sponsor Card
Wegmans
Coupon

1994 Rochester Red Wings Fleer/ProCards

This 27-card standard size set of the 1994 Rochester Red Wings, a Class AAA International League affiliate of the Baltimore Orioles, features white-bordered posed color player photos on its fronts with the player's name, position, team name and Fleer/ProCards logo across the bottom of each card. The white back with vertical light blue stripes carries the player's name at the top, followed by biography and statistics.

	MINT	NRMT	EXC
COMPLETE SET (27)	8.00	3.60	1.00

☐ 990 Tom Bolton
☐ 991 Jim Dedrick
☐ 992 Brian DuBois
☐ 993 Rick Krivda
☐ 994 Barry Manuel
☐ 995 Kevin McGehee
☐ 996 John O'Donoghue
☐ 997 Brad Pennington
☐ 998 Jason Satre
☐ 999 Tom Wegmann
☐ 1000 Craig Faulkner
☐ 1001 Gregg Zaun
☐ 1002 Manny Alexander
☐ 1003 Kevin Baez
☐ 1004 T.R. Lewis
☐ 1005 Brad Tyler
☐ 1006 Mel Wearing
☐ 1007 Tracy Woodson
☐ 1008 Damon Buford

- ☐ 1009 Bruce Dostal
- ☐ 1010 Sherman Obando
- ☐ 1011 Mark Smith
- ☐ 1012 Jim Wawruck
- ☐ 1013 Bob Miscik MG
- ☐ 1014 Steve Luebber CO
- ☐ 1015 Ed Napoleon CO
- ☐ 1016 Checklist

1994 Rockford Royals Classic

This 30-card standard size set of the 1994 Rockford Royals, a Class A Midwest League affiliate of the Kansas City Royals, features white-bordered posed color player shots on its fronts with the player's name and position, team name and logo and Classic logo appearing across the bottom of each card. On a ghosted team logo, the white back carries the player's name at the top, followed by biography and statistics. This issue includes the minor league card debut of Glendon Rusch.

	MINT	NRMT	EXC
COMPLETE SET (30)	10.00	4.50	1.25

- ☐ 1 Sal Fasano
- ☐ 2 Neil Atkinson
- ☐ 3 Nevin Brewer
- ☐ 4 Rick Burley
- ☐ 5 Jimmie Byington
- ☐ 6 Jeremy Carr
- ☐ 7 Eduardo Cedeno
- ☐ 8 Lino Diaz
- ☐ 9 Kenny Fitzpatrick
- ☐ 10 Pat Flury
- ☐ 11 Phil Grundy
- ☐ 12 Braxton Hickman
- ☐ 13 Kevin Hodges
- ☐ 14 Jason Huffman
- ☐ 15 Oscar Jimenez
- ☐ 16 Carlos Mendez
- ☐ 17 Luke Oglesby
- ☐ 18 Kevin Rawitzer
- ☐ 19 Ken Ray
- ☐ 20 O.J. Rhone
- ☐ 21 Glendon Rusch
- ☐ 22 Toby Ray Smith
- ☐ 23 Carlos Subero
- ☐ 24 Mike Sweeney
- ☐ 25 Ryan Towns
- ☐ 26 Paul Vindivich
- ☐ 27 Eric Walls
- ☐ 28 John Mizerock MG
- ☐ 29 Tom Burgmeier CO
- ☐ 30 Cliff Pastornicky CO Checklist

1994 Rockford Royals Fleer/ProCards

This 31-card standard size set of the 1994 Rockford Royals, a Class A Midwest League affiliate of the Kansas City Royals, features white-bordered posed color player photos on its fronts with the player's name, position, team name and Fleer/ProCards logo across the bottom of each card. The white back with vertical light blue stripes carries the player's name at the top, followed by biography and statistics. This issue includes the minor league card debut of Glendon Rusch.

	MINT	NRMT	EXC
COMPLETE SET (31)	7.00	3.10	.85

- ☐ 554 Neil Atkinson
- ☐ 555 Nevin Brewer
- ☐ 556 Rick Burley
- ☐ 557 Kenny Fitzpatrick
- ☐ 558 Pat Flury
- ☐ 559 Phil Grundy
- ☐ 560 Kevin Hodges
- ☐ 561 Jason Huffman
- ☐ 562 Kevin Rawitzer
- ☐ 563 Ken Ray
- ☐ 564 Glendon Rusch
- ☐ 565 Toby Smith
- ☐ 566 Ryan Towns
- ☐ 567 Sal Fasano
- ☐ 568 Carlos Mendez
- ☐ 569 Mike Sweeney
- ☐ 570 Jimmie Byington
- ☐ 571 Jeremy Carr
- ☐ 572 Eduardo Cedeno
- ☐ 573 Lino Diaz
- ☐ 574 Braxton Hickman
- ☐ 575 Carlos Subero
- ☐ 576 Oscar Jimenez
- ☐ 577 Luke Oglesby
- ☐ 578 O.J. Rhone
- ☐ 579 Paul Vindivich
- ☐ 580 Eric Walls
- ☐ 581 John Mizerock MG
- ☐ 582 Tom Burgmeier CO
- ☐ 583 Cliff Pastornicky CO
- ☐ 584 Checklist

1994 Salem Buccaneers Classic

This 30-card standard size set of the 1994 Salem Buccaneers, a Class A Carolina League affiliate of the Pittsburgh Pirates, features white-bordered posed color player shots on its fronts with the player's name and position, team name and logo and Classic logo appearing across the bottom of each card. On a ghosted team logo, the white back carries the player's name at the top, followed by biography and statistics.

	MINT	NRMT	EXC
COMPLETE SET (30)	12.00	5.50	1.50

- ☐ 1 Danny Clyburn
- ☐ 2 Jason Abramavicius
- ☐ 3 Jake Austin
- ☐ 4 Matt Chamberlain
- ☐ 5 Jeff Conger
- ☐ 6 Jay Cranford
- ☐ 7 David Dooneweerd
- ☐ 8 John Ericks
- ☐ 9 Sean Evans
- ☐ 10 Jon Farrell
- ☐ 11 Marcus Hanel
- ☐ 12 Jason Kendall
- ☐ 13 Ted Klamm
- ☐ 14 Sean Lawrence
- ☐ 15 Marc Pisciotta
- ☐ 16 Alan Purdy
- ☐ 17 Daryl Ratliff
- ☐ 18 Chance Sanford
- ☐ 19 Manuel Santana
- ☐ 20 Reed Secrist
- ☐ 21 Juan Segura
- ☐ 22 Rich Townsend
- ☐ 23 Marc Wilkins
- ☐ 24 Gary Wilson
- ☐ 25 Ramon Zapata
- ☐ 26 Trent Jewett MG
- ☐ 27 Dave Rajsich CO
- ☐ 28 Sam Lazzaro GM/VP
- ☐ 29 Dennis Robarge AGM
- ☐ 30 Long Ball Siver (Mascot) Checklist

1994 Salem Buccaneers Fleer/ProCards

This 28-card standard size set of the 1994 Salem Buccaneers, a Class A Carolina League affiliate of the Pittsburgh Pirates, features white-bordered posed color player photos on its fronts with the player's name, position, team name and Fleer/ProCards logo across the bottom of each card. The white back with vertical light blue stripes carries the player's name at the top, followed by biography and statistics.

	MINT	NRMT	EXC
COMPLETE SET (28)	8.00	3.60	1.00

- ☐ 2315 Jason Abramavicius
- ☐ 2316 Matt Chamberlain
- ☐ 2317 Dave Doorneweerd
- ☐ 2318 John Ericks
- ☐ 2319 Ted Klamm
- ☐ 2320 Sean Lawrence
- ☐ 2321 Marc Pisciotta
- ☐ 2322 Manuel Santana
- ☐ 2323 Rich Townsend
- ☐ 2324 Marc Wilkins
- ☐ 2325 Gary Wilson
- ☐ 2326 Marcus Hanel
- ☐ 2327 Jason Kendall
- ☐ 2328 Jay Cranford
- ☐ 2329 Raul Paez
- ☐ 2330 Alan Purdy
- ☐ 2331 Chance Sanford
- ☐ 2332 Reed Secrist
- ☐ 2333 Juan Segura
- ☐ 2334 Ramon Zapata
- ☐ 2335 Jake Austin
- ☐ 2336 Danny Clyburn
- ☐ 2337 Jeff Conger
- ☐ 2338 Jon Farrell
- ☐ 2339 Trent Jewett MG
- ☐ 2340 Jay Bluthardt CO
- ☐ 2341 Dave Rajsich CO
- ☐ 2342 Checklist

1994 Salt Lake Buzz Fleer/ProCards

This 27-card standard size set of the 1994 Salt Lake Buzz, a Class AAA Pacific Coast League affiliate of the Minnesota Twins, features white-bordered posed color player photos on its fronts with the player's name, position, team name and Fleer/ProCards logo across the bottom of each card. The white back with vertical light blue stripes carries the player's name at the top, followed by biography and statistics.

	MINT	NRMT	EXC
COMPLETE SET (27)	5.00	2.20	.60

- ☐ 808 Greg Brummett
- ☐ 809 Shawn Bryant
- ☐ 810 Kevin Cambell
- ☐ 811 Andy Cook
- ☐ 812 Eddie Guardado
- ☐ 813 Brett Merriman
- ☐ 814 Oscar Munoz
- ☐ 815 Mo Sanford
- ☐ 816 Dave Stevens
- ☐ 817 Matt Stevens
- ☐ 818 Bill Wissler
- ☐ 819 Mike Durant
- ☐ 820 Tim McIntosh
- ☐ 821 Jeff Carter
- ☐ 822 Steve Dunn
- ☐ 823 Denny Hocking
- ☐ 824 Brian Raabe
- ☐ 825 Paul Russo
- ☐ 826 Scott Stahoviak
- ☐ 827 Bernardo Brito
- ☐ 828 J.T. Bruett
- ☐ 829 Juan De La Rosa
- ☐ 830 Dan Masteller
- ☐ 831 Scott Ullger MG
- ☐ 832 Gorman Heimueller CO
- ☐ 833 Dan Rohn CO
- ☐ 834 Checklist

1994 San Antonio Missions Fleer/ProCards

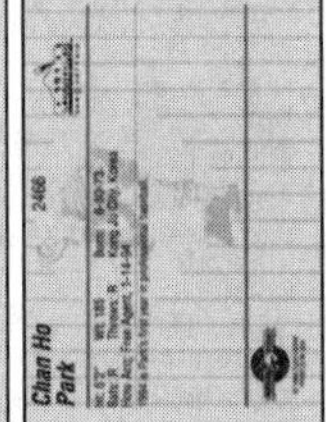

This 31-card standard size set of the 1994 San Antonio Missions, a Class AA Texas League affiliate of the Los Angeles Dodgers, features white-bordered posed color player photos on its fronts with the player's name, position, team name and Fleer/ProCards logo across the bottom of each card. The white back with vertical light blue stripes carries the player's name at the top, followed by biography and statistics. This issue includes the minor league card debut of Chan Ho Park.

	MINT	NRMT	EXC
COMPLETE SET (31)	10.00	4.50	1.25

- ☐ 2458 John Barfield
- ☐ 2459 Jason Brosnan
- ☐ 2460 Albert Bustillos
- ☐ 2461 Nelson Castro
- ☐ 2462 Dan Hubbs
- ☐ 2463 Joe Jacobsen
- ☐ 2464 Chris Nichting
- ☐ 2465 Pedro Osuna
- ☐ 2466 Chan Ho Park
- ☐ 2467 Dave Pyc
- ☐ 2468 Felix Rodriguez
- ☐ 2469 Carlos Thomas
- ☐ 2470 Ismael Valdez
- ☐ 2471 Chris Abbe
- ☐ 2472 Ken Huckaby
- ☐ 2473 Noe Munoz
- ☐ 2474 Henry Blanco
- ☐ 2475 Juan Castro
- ☐ 2476 Chris Demetral
- ☐ 2477 Garey Ingram
- ☐ 2478 Jay Kirkpatrick
- ☐ 2479 Steve Kliafas
- ☐ 2480 Kash Beauchamp
- ☐ 2481 Billy Lott
- ☐ 2482 Dwight Maness
- ☐ 2483 Mike Moore
- ☐ 2484 Javier Puchales
- ☐ 2485 Vernon Spearman
- ☐ 2486 Tom Beyers MG
- ☐ 2487 Brett Magnusson CO
- ☐ 2488 Checklist

1994 San Bernardino Spirit Classic

This 30-card standard size set of the 1994 San Bernardino Spirit, a Class A California League Independent, features white-bordered posed color player shots on its fronts with the player's name and position, team name and logo and Classic logo appearing across the bottom of each card. On a ghosted team logo, the white back carries the player's name at the top, followed by biography and statistics.

	MINT	NRMT	EXC
COMPLETE SET (30)	10.00	4.50	1.25

- ☐ 1 Colin Dixon
- ☐ 2 Ray Cervantes
- ☐ 3 Manny Gagliano
- ☐ 4 Jeff Grotewold
- ☐ 5 Elston Hansen
- ☐ 6 Brian Harrison
- ☐ 7 Kenneth Howell
- ☐ 8 Bert Inman
- ☐ 9 Adin Lohry
- ☐ 10 Steve Maye
- ☐ 11 Jeff Motuzas
- ☐ 12 Steve Munda
- ☐ 13 Eric Nolte
- ☐ 14 Rob Parkins
- ☐ 15 Jim Patterson
- ☐ 16 Jose Peguero
- ☐ 17 Jim Pena
- ☐ 18 Steven Phillips
- ☐ 19 Derek Reid
- ☐ 20 Sandi Santiago
- ☐ 21 Joe Strong
- ☐ 22 Toni Tajima
- ☐ 23 Edgar Tovar
- ☐ 24 Jason Wuerch
- ☐ 25 Gregory Mahlberg MG
- ☐ 26 Warren Brusstar CO
- ☐ 27 Steve Livesey CO
- ☐ 28 Crystal Phillips TR
- ☐ 29 The Spirit Bug (Mascot)
- ☐ 30 Fiscalini Field Checklist

1994 San Bernardino Spirit Fleer/ProCards

This 28-card standard size set of the 1994 San Bernardino Spirit, a Class A California League Independent, features white-bordered posed color player photos on its fronts with the player's name, position, team name and Fleer/ProCards logo across the bottom of each card. The white back with vertical light blue stripes carries the player's name at the top, followed by biography and statistics.

	MINT	NRMT	EXC
COMPLETE SET (28)	5.00	2.20	.60

- ☐ 2750 Greg Bicknell
- ☐ 2751 Bert Inman
- ☐ 2752 Tim Layana
- ☐ 2753 Eric Nolte
- ☐ 2754 Chad O'Laughlin
- ☐ 2755 Rob Parkins
- ☐ 2756 Jim Patterson
- ☐ 2757 Jim Pena
- ☐ 2758 Sandi Santiago
- ☐ 2759 Joe Strong
- ☐ 2760 Tony Tajima
- ☐ 2761 Andy Allanson
- ☐ 2762 Adin Lohry
- ☐ 2763 Jeff Motuzas
- ☐ 2764 Ray Cervantes
- ☐ 2765 Colin Dixon
- ☐ 2766 Manny Gagliano
- ☐ 2767 Elston Hansen
- ☐ 2768 Jose Peguero
- ☐ 2769 Edgar Tovar
- ☐ 2770 Abdiel Cumberbatch
- ☐ 2771 Steve Phillips
- ☐ 2772 Derek Reid
- ☐ 2773 Jason Wuerch
- ☐ 2774 Greg Mahlberg MG
- ☐ 2775 Warren Brusstar CO
- ☐ 2776 Steve Livesey CO
- ☐ 2777 Checklist

1994 San Jose Giants Classic

This 30-card standard size set of the 1994 San Jose Giants, a Class A California League affiliate of the San Francisco Giants, features white-bordered posed color player shots on its fronts with the player's name and position, team name and logo and Classic logo appearing across the bottom of each card. On a ghosted team logo, the white back carries the player's name at the top, followed by biography and statistics.

	MINT	NRMT	EXC
COMPLETE SET (30)	10.00	4.50	1.25

- ☐ 1 Steve Soderstrom
- ☐ 2 Jay Canizaro
- ☐ 3 Marino Castillo
- ☐ 4 Troy Clemens
- ☐ 5 Edwin Corps
- ☐ 6 Chris Dotolo
- ☐ 7 Tracey Ealy
- ☐ 8 Kris Franko
- ☐ 9 Andy Heckman
- ☐ 10 Charlie Hicks
- ☐ 11 Marcus Jensen
- ☐ 12 Andre Keene
- ☐ 13 Brett King
- ☐ 14 Clay King
- ☐ 15 Jeff Locklear
- ☐ 16 Mike McLain
- ☐ 17 Roger Miller
- ☐ 18 Bill Mueller
- ☐ 19 Mark Peterson
- ☐ 20 Jeff Richey
- ☐ 21 Chris Singleton

☐ 22 D.J. Thielen
☐ 23 Carlos Valdez
☐ 24 Doug VanderWeele
☐ 25 Keith Willimas
☐ 26 Kenny Woods
☐ 27 Dick Dietz MG
☐ 28 Todd Oakes CO
☐ 29 Jim Davenport CO
☐ 30 Dan Dodson TR
Checklist

1994 San Jose Giants Fleer/ProCards

This 29-card standard size set of the 1994 San Jose Giants, a Class A California League affiliate of the San Francisco Giants, features white-bordered posed color player photos on its fronts with the player's name, position, team name and Fleer/ProCards logo across the bottom of each card. The white back with vertical light blue stripes carries the player's name at the top, followed by biography and statistics.

	MINT	NRMT	EXC
COMPLETE SET (29)	5.00	2.20	.60

☐ 2808 Marino Castillo
☐ 2809 Edwin Corps
☐ 2810 Kris Franko
☐ 2811 Andy Heckman
☐ 2812 Jeff Locklear
☐ 2813 Mike McLain
☐ 2814 Mark Peterson
☐ 2815 Jeff Richey
☐ 2816 Steve Soderstrom
☐ 2817 Carlos Valdez
☐ 2818 Doug Vanderweele
☐ 2819 Troy Clemens
☐ 2820 Marcus Jensen
☐ 2821 Roger Miller
☐ 2822 Jay Canizaro
☐ 2823 Chris Dotolo
☐ 2824 Andre Keene
☐ 2825 Brett King
☐ 2826 Clay King
☐ 2827 Bill Mueller
☐ 2828 Tracey Ealy
☐ 2829 Chris Singleton
☐ 2830 D.J. Thielen
☐ 2831 Keith Williams
☐ 2832 Kenny Woods
☐ 2833 Dick Dietz MG
☐ 2834 Jim Davenport CO
☐ 2835 Todd Oakes CO
☐ 2836 Checklist

1994 Sarasota Red Sox Classic

This 30-card standard size set of the 1994 Sarasota Red Sox, a Class A Florida State League affiliate of the Boston Red Sox, features white-bordered posed color player shots on its fronts with the player's name and position, team name and logo and Classic logo appearing across the bottom of each card. On a ghosted team logo, the white back carries the player's name at the top, followed by biography and statistics. This issue includes the minor league card debut of Jeff Suppan.

	MINT	NRMT	EXC
COMPLETE SET (30)	14.00	6.25	1.75

☐ 1 Jeff Suppan
☐ 2 Andy Abad
☐ 3 Scott Bakkum
☐ 4 Jeff Berry
☐ 5 Brian Bright
☐ 6 Gerry Creamer
☐ 7 Rocky Elli
☐ 8 Jason Friedman
☐ 9 Aaron Fuller
☐ 10 David Gibraltar
☐ 11 Brent Hansen
☐ 12 Doug Hecker
☐ 13 Rob Henkel
☐ 14 Daren Hobson
☐ 15 Joe Hudson
☐ 16 Gavin Jackson
☐ 17 Ron Mahay
☐ 18 Walt McKeel
☐ 19 Lou Merloni
☐ 20 T.J. O'Donnell
☐ 21 Rafael Orellano
☐ 22 Gary Painter
☐ 23 Paul Rappoli
☐ 24 Tony Rodriguez
☐ 25 Ken Ryan
☐ 26 Dave Smith
☐ 27 Jim Telgheder
☐ 28 Sergio Valdez
☐ 29 DeMarlo Hale MG
☐ 30 Al Nipper CO
Checklist

1994 Sarasota Red Sox Fleer/ProCards

This 30-card standard size set of the 1994 Sarasota Red Sox, a Class A Florida State League affiliate of the Boston Red Sox, features white-bordered posed color player photos on its fronts with the player's name, position, team name and Fleer/ProCards logo across the bottom of each card. The white back with vertical light blue stripes carries the player's name at the top, followed by biography and statistics. This issue includes the minor league card debut of Jeff Suppan.

	MINT	NRMT	EXC
COMPLETE SET (30)	10.00	4.50	1.25

☐ 1940 Chad Amos
☐ 1941 Scott Bakkum
☐ 1942 Gerry Creamer
☐ 1943 Rocky Elli
☐ 1944 Brent Hansen
☐ 1945 Daren Hobson
☐ 1946 Joe Hudson
☐ 1947 Raphael Orellano
☐ 1948 Gary Painter
☐ 1949 Silverio Santa Maria
☐ 1950 Jeff Suppan
☐ 1951 James Telgheder
☐ 1952 Sergio Valdez
☐ 1953 Jeff Berry
☐ 1954 Walt McKeel
☐ 1955 Jason Friedman
☐ 1956 David Gibralter
☐ 1957 Doug Hecker
☐ 1958 Gavin Jackson
☐ 1959 Lou Merloni
☐ 1960 T.J. O'Donnell
☐ 1961 Tony Rodriguez
☐ 1962 Dave Smith
☐ 1963 Andy Abad
☐ 1964 Brian Bright
☐ 1965 Aaron Fuller
☐ 1966 Ron Mahay
☐ 1967 Paul Rappoli
☐ 1968 DeMarlo Hale MG
☐ 1969 Checklist

1994 Savannah Cardinals Classic

This 30-card standard size set of the 1994 Savannah Cardinals, a Class A South Atlantic League affiliate of the St. Louis Cardinals, features white-bordered posed color player shots on its fronts with the player's name and position, team name and logo and Classic logo appearing across the bottom of each card. On a ghosted team logo, the white back carries the player's name at the top, followed by biography and statistics. This issue includes the minor league card debut of Eli Marrero and Alan Benes.

	MINT	NRMT	EXC
COMPLETE SET (30)	14.00	6.25	1.75

☐ 1 Alan Benes
☐ 2 Eric Alexander
☐ 3 Matt Arrandale
☐ 4 Troy Barrick
☐ 5 Jeff Battles
☐ 6 Jeff Berblinger
☐ 7 Steve Biermann
☐ 8 Todd Blake
☐ 9 Mike Borzello
☐ 10 Chris Christopher
☐ 11 Cory Corrigan
☐ 12 Ben Ellsworth
☐ 13 Craig Grasser
☐ 14 Antoine Henry
☐ 15 Joe Jumonville
☐ 16 Victor Llanos
☐ 17 Scott Marquardt
☐ 18 Elieser Marrero
☐ 19 Mike Matvey
☐ 20 Eric Mediavilla
☐ 21 Plinio Morel
☐ 22 Chris Norton
☐ 23 Dave Oehrlein
☐ 24 Ron Scott
☐ 25 Chris Stewart
☐ 26 Hector Ugueto
☐ 27 Chris Vlasis
☐ 28 Eddie Williams
☐ 29 Luis Melendez MG
☐ 30 Ramon Ortiz CO
Checklist

1994 Savannah Cardinals Fleer/ProCards

This 31-card standard size set of the 1994 Savannah Cardinals, a Class A South Atlantic League affiliate of the St. Louis Cardinals, features white-bordered posed color player photos on its fronts with the player's name, position, team name and Fleer/ProCards logo across the bottom of each card. The white back with vertical light blue stripes carries the player's name at the top, followed by biography and statistics. The cards are numbered on the back. This issue includes the minor league card debut of Eli Marrero and Alan Benes.

	MINT	NRMT	EXC
COMPLETE SET (31)	10.00	4.50	1.25

☐ 495 Eric Alexander
☐ 496 Matt Arrandale
☐ 497 Troy Barrick
☐ 498 Jeff Battles
☐ 499 Alan Benes
☐ 500 Todd Blake
☐ 501 Cory Corrigan
☐ 502 Craig Grasser
☐ 503 Scott Marquardt
☐ 504 Dave Oehrlein
☐ 505 Ron Scott
☐ 506 Chris Stewart
☐ 507 Mike Borzello
☐ 508 Elieser Marrero
☐ 509 Plinio Morel
☐ 510 Chris Norton
☐ 511 Eddie Williams
☐ 512 Jeff Berblinger
☐ 513 Steve Biermann
☐ 514 Ben Ellsworth
☐ 515 Joe Jumonville
☐ 516 Victor Llanos
☐ 517 Mike Matvey
☐ 518 Hector Ugueto
☐ 519 Chris Christopher
☐ 520 Antoine Henry
☐ 521 Eric Mediavilla
☐ 522 Chris Vlasis
☐ 523 Luis Melendez MG
☐ 524 Ramon Ortiz CO
☐ 1882 Checklist

1994 Scranton/Wilkes-Barre Red Barons Fleer/ProCards

This 26-card standard size set of the 1994 Scranton/Wilkes-Barre Red Barons, a Class AAA International League affiliate of the Philadelphia Phillies, features white-bordered posed color player photos on its fronts with the player's name, position, team name and Fleer/ProCards logo across the bottom of each card. The white back with vertical light blue stripes carries the player's name at the top, followed by biography and statistics.

	MINT	NRMT	EXC
COMPLETE SET (26)	5.00	2.20	.60

☐ 913 Toby Borland
☐ 914 Ricky Bottalico
☐ 915 Don Carman
☐ 916 Pat Combs
☐ 917 Mike Dunne
☐ 918 Paul Fletcher
☐ 919 Robert Gaddy
☐ 920 Tyler Green
☐ 921 Jeff Patterson
☐ 922 Mike Lieberthal
☐ 923 John Marzano
☐ 924 Shawn Gilbert
☐ 925 Kevin Jordan
☐ 926 Keith Kimberlin
☐ 927 Charlie Montoyo
☐ 928 Tom Quinlan
☐ 929 Gene Schall
☐ 930 Steve Bieser
☐ 931 Pat Brady
☐ 932 Phil Geisler
☐ 933 Ron Lockett
☐ 934 Cary Williams
☐ 935 Mike Quade MG
☐ 936 Dave Cash CO
☐ 937 Jim Wright CO
☐ 938 Checklist

1994 Shreveport Captains Fleer/ProCards

This 29-card standard size set of the 1994 Shreveport Captains, a Class AA Texas League affiliate of the San Francisco Giants, features white-bordered posed color player photos on its fronts with the player's name, position, team name and Fleer/ProCards logo across the bottom of each card. The white back with vertical light blue stripes carries the player's name at the top, followed by biography and statistics.

	MINT	NRMT	EXC
COMPLETE SET (29)	5.00	2.20	.60

☐ 1597 Mike Gardella
☐ 1598 Doug Gogolewski
☐ 1599 Chris Hancock
☐ 1600 Stacy Jones
Stacey
☐ 1601 Steve Mintz
☐ 1602 Kurt Peltzer
☐ 1603 Lou Pote
☐ 1604 Joe Rosselli
☐ 1605 Richie Simon
☐ 1606 Shad Smith
☐ 1607 Steve Whitaker
☐ 1608 Bill VanLandingham
☐ 1609 Eric Christopherson
☐ 1610 Doug Mirabelli
☐ 1611 Joel Chimelis
☐ 1612 Kurt Ehmann
☐ 1613 Tim Florez
☐ 1614 Steve Hecht
☐ 1615 Barry Miller
☐ 1616 Chris Wimmer
☐ 1617 Marvin Benard
☐ 1618 Brent Cookson
☐ 1619 Jason McFarlin
☐ 1620 Calvin Murray
☐ 1621 Ron Pezzoni
☐ 1622 Ron Wotus MG
☐ 1623 Frank Cacciatore CO
☐ 1624 Steve Cline CO
☐ 1625 Checklist

1994 Signature Rookies

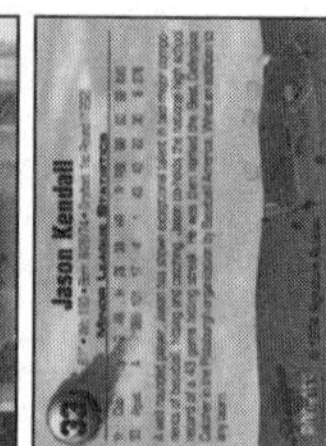

	MINT	NRMT	EXC
COMPLETE SET (50)	12.00	5.50	1.50
COMMON CARD (1-50)	.10	.05	.01
☐ 1 Russ Davis	.20	.09	.03
☐ 2 Brant Brown	.10	.05	.01
☐ 3 Ricky Bottalico	.20	.09	.03
☐ 4 Brian Bevil	.10	.05	.01
☐ 5 Garret Anderson	.60	.25	.07
☐ 6 Rod Henderson	.10	.05	.01
☐ 7 Keith Herling	.10	.05	.01
☐ 8 Scott Hatteberg UER Spelled Hatteburg on front	.10	.05	.01
☐ 9 Brook Fordyce	.10	.05	.01
☐ 10 Joey Eischen	.10	.05	.01
☐ 11 Orlando Miller	.10	.05	.01
☐ 12 Ray McDavid	.10	.05	.01
☐ 13 Andre King	.10	.05	.01
☐ 14 Todd Hollandsworth	.75	.35	.09
☐ 15 Tyrone Hill	.10	.05	.01
☐ 16 Paul Spoljaric	.10	.05	.01
☐ 17 Todd Ritchie	.10	.05	.01
☐ 18 Herbert Perry	.10	.05	.01
☐ 19 Alex Ochoa	.75	.35	.09
☐ 20 Mike Neill	.10	.05	.01
☐ 21 John Burke	.10	.05	.01
☐ 22 Alan Benes	1.00	.45	.12
☐ 23 Robbie Beckett	.10	.05	.01
☐ 24 Brian Barber	.10	.05	.01
☐ 25 Justin Thompson	.20	.09	.03
☐ 26 Joey Hamilton	.30	.14	.04
☐ 27 Rick Greene	.10	.05	.01
☐ 28 Wayne Gomes	.10	.05	.01
☐ 29 Matt Drews	.40	.18	.05
☐ 30 Jeff D'Amico	.60	.25	.07
☐ 31 Bryn Kosco	.10	.05	.01
☐ 32 Brooks Kieschnick	.50	.23	.06
☐ 33 Jason Kendall	.75	.35	.09
☐ 34 Mike Kelly	.10	.05	.01
☐ 35 Derek Jeter	2.50	1.10	.30
☐ 36 Jay Powell	.10	.05	.01
☐ 37 Phil Nevin	.10	.05	.01
☐ 38 Kurt Miller	.10	.05	.01
☐ 39 Chad McConnell	.10	.05	.01
☐ 40 Sean Lowe	.10	.05	.01
☐ 41 Michael Tucker	.30	.14	.04
☐ 42 Paul Shuey	.10	.05	.01
☐ 43 Dan Smith	.10	.05	.01
☐ 44 Calvin Reese	.20	.09	.03
☐ 45 Kirk Presley	.20	.09	.03
☐ 46 Jamey Wright	.60	.25	.07

☐ 47 Gabe White	.10	.05	.01
☐ 48 John Wasdin	.20	.09	.03
☐ 49 Billy Wagner	.40	.18	.05
☐ 50 Joe Vitiello	.10	.05	.01

1994 Signature Rookies Signatures

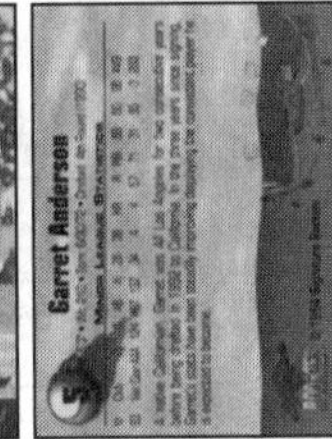

Each card is numbered out of 8650.

	MINT	NRMT	EXC
COMPLETE SET (50)	275.00	125.00	34.00
COMMON SIGNATURE (1-50)	4.00	1.80	.50
☐ 1 Russ Davis	6.00	2.70	.75
☐ 2 Brant Brown	5.00	2.20	.60
☐ 3 Ricky Bottalico	6.00	2.70	.75
☐ 4 Brian Bevil	4.00	1.80	.50
☐ 5 Garret Anderson	8.00	3.60	1.00
☐ 6 Rod Henderson	4.00	1.80	.50
☐ 7 Keith Herling	4.00	1.80	.50
☐ 8 Scott Hatteberg UER Name spelled Hatteburg on front	4.00	1.80	.50
☐ 9 Brook Fordyce	4.00	1.80	.50
☐ 10 Joey Eischen	4.00	1.80	.50
☐ 11 Orlando Miller	4.00	1.80	.50
☐ 12 Ray McDavid	4.00	1.80	.50
☐ 13 Andre King	4.00	1.80	.50
☐ 14 Todd Hollandsworth	12.00	5.50	1.50
☐ 15 Tyrone Hill	4.00	1.80	.50
☐ 16 Paul Spoljaric	4.00	1.80	.50
☐ 17 Todd Ritchie	4.00	1.80	.50
☐ 18 Herbert Perry	5.00	2.20	.60
☐ 19 Alex Ochoa	10.00	4.50	1.25
☐ 20 Mike Neill	4.00	1.80	.50
☐ 21 John Burke	4.00	1.80	.50
☐ 22 Alan Benes	12.00	5.50	1.50
☐ 23 Robbie Beckett	4.00	1.80	.50
☐ 24 Brian Barber	4.00	1.80	.50
☐ 25 Justin Thompson	6.00	2.70	.75
☐ 26 Joey Hamilton	10.00	4.50	1.25
☐ 27 Rick Greene	5.00	2.20	.60
☐ 28 Wayne Gomes	5.00	2.20	.60
☐ 29 Matt Drews	6.00	2.70	.75
☐ 30 Jeff D'Amico	10.00	4.50	1.25
☐ 31 Bryn Kosco	4.00	1.80	.50
☐ 32 Brooks Kieschnick	6.00	2.70	.75
☐ 33 Jason Kendall	12.00	5.50	1.50
☐ 34 Mike Kelly	4.00	1.80	.50
☐ 35 Derek Jeter	30.00	13.50	3.70
☐ 36 Jay Powell	4.00	1.80	.50
☐ 37 Phil Nevin	5.00	2.20	.60
☐ 38 Kurt Miller	4.00	1.80	.50
☐ 39 Chad McConnell	4.00	1.80	.50
☐ 40 Sean Lowe	4.00	1.80	.50
☐ 41 Michael Tucker	6.00	2.70	.75
☐ 42 Paul Shuey	4.00	1.80	.50
☐ 43 Dan Smith	4.00	1.80	.50
☐ 44 Calvin Reese	6.00	2.70	.75
☐ 45 Kirk Presley	6.00	2.70	.75
☐ 46 Jamey Wright	10.00	4.50	1.25
☐ 47 Gabe White	4.00	1.80	.50
☐ 48 John Wasdin	6.00	2.70	.75
☐ 49 Billy Wagner	7.00	3.10	.85
☐ 50 Joe Vitiello	5.00	2.20	.60

1994 Signature Rookies Bonus Signatures

Randomly inserted in packs, this five-card set measures the standard size. The fronts feature glossy color player photos that are full-bleed except at the bottom where the picture is edged by a black stripe carrying the player's name. The words "Tuff Stuff Promo" and the production figures "1 of 10,000" are stamped in gold foil and run down the left edge. The cards are signed on the front in blue ink, with each card individually numbered out of 1,562. A gold foil "Bonus Signature" logo in the lower left rounds out the front. On a background consisting of a blue sky, green grass and a baseball stadium, the horizontal backs present biography, statistics and player profile. Unsigned promo versions of these cards were also issued.

	MINT	NRMT	EXC
COMPLETE SET (5)	80.00	36.00	10.00
COMMON SIGNATURE (P1-P5)	15.00	6.75	1.85
☐ P1 Rick Helling	15.00	6.75	1.85
☐ P2 Charles Johnson/1000	40.00	18.00	5.00
☐ P3 Chad Mottola	15.00	6.75	1.85
☐ P4 J.R. Phillips	15.00	6.75	1.85
☐ P5 Glenn Williams UER Name spelled Glen on card	15.00	6.75	1.85

1994 Signature Rookies Cliff Floyd

Randomly inserted in packs, this five-card set measures the standard size. The fronts feature glossy color player photos that are full-bleed, except at the bottom where the picture is edged by a black stripe carrying the player's name. The production figures "1 of 10,000" is stamped in gold foil and runs down the left edge. A gold foil "Hottest Rookie" logo in the lower left rounds out the front. On a background consisting of a blue sky, green grass and a baseball stadium, the horizontal backs present player profile, statistics, and other information. Floyd also signed 225 of each cards which were randomly inserted into packs..

	MINT	NRMT	EXC
COMPLETE SET (5)	2.00	.90	.25
COMMON CARD (BB1-BB5)	.40	.18	.05
*SIGNATURES: 100X BASIC CARDS ..			
☐ B1 Cliff Floyd Defensive posture in field	.40	.18	.05
☐ B2 Cliff Floyd Signing autographs	.40	.18	.05
☐ B3 Cliff Floyd Awaiting pitch, bat behind head	.40	.18	.05
☐ B4 Cliff Floyd Side shot, holding bat	.40	.18	.05
☐ B5 Cliff Floyd Bat behind back after swinging	.40	.18	.05

1994 Signature Rookies Hottest Prospects

Randomly inserted in packs, this 12-card set measures the standard size. The fronts feature glossy color player photos that are full-bleed except at the bottom, where the picture is edged by a black stripe carrying the player's name. The production figures "1 of 5,000" is stamped in gold foil and runs down the left edge. A gold foil "Hottest Prospect" logo in the lower left rounds out the front. On a background consisting of a blue sky, green grass and a baseball stadium, the horizontal backs present biography, statistics and player profile.

	MINT	NRMT	EXC
COMPLETE SET (12)	12.00	5.50	1.50
COMMON CARD (S1-S12)	.50	.23	.06
*STGNATURES: 8X BASIC CARDS......			
☐ S1 John Burke	.50	.23	.06
☐ S2 Russ Davis	.75	.35	.09
☐ S3 Todd Hollandsworth	2.50	1.10	.30
☐ S4 Derek Jeter	10.00	4.50	1.25
☐ S5 Mike Kelly	.50	.23	.06
☐ S6 Ray McDavid	.50	.23	.06
☐ S7 Kurt Miller	.50	.23	.06
☐ S8 Phil Nevin	.50	.23	.06
☐ S9 Alex Ochoa	2.50	1.10	.30
☐ S10 Justin Thompson	.75	.35	.09
☐ S11 Michael Tucker	1.00	.45	.12
☐ S12 Gabe White	.50	.23	.06

1994 Signature Rookies Draft Picks

The 1994 Signature Rookies Draft Picks set consists of 100 standard-size cards. The fronts feature full-bleed color action shots. Marbleized green stripes accent the pictures on the left and bottom. In these green stripes appear the production figures ("of 7,750") and the player's name, both in gold foil. On a background consisting of a ghosted version of the front photo, the backs have a color headshot in the upper left corner, with the remainder of the back filled with biography, statistics, and player profile.

	MINT	NRMT	EXC
COMPLETE SET (100)	15.00	6.75	1.85
COMMON CARD (1-100)	.15	.07	.02
☐ 1 Josh Booty	.50	.23	.06
☐ 2 Paul Wilson	.75	.35	.09
☐ 3 Ben Grieve	2.50	1.10	.30
☐ 4 Dustin Hermanson	.15	.07	.02
☐ 5 Antone Williamson	.60	.25	.07
☐ 6 McKay Christensen	.15	.07	.02
☐ 7 Doug Million	.50	.23	.06
☐ 8 Todd Walker	3.00	1.35	.35
☐ 9 C.J. Nitkowski	.15	.07	.02
☐ 10 Jaret Wright	1.00	.45	.12
☐ 11 Mark Farris	.15	.07	.02
☐ 12 Nomar Garciaparra	2.50	1.10	.30
☐ 13 Paul Konerko	3.00	1.35	.35
☐ 14 Jason Varitek	.25	.11	.03
☐ 15 Jayson Peterson	.25	.11	.03
☐ 16 Matt Smith	.15	.07	.02
☐ 17 Ramon Castro	.25	.11	.03
☐ 18 Cade Gaspar	.25	.11	.03
☐ 19 Bret Wagner	.15	.07	.02
☐ 20 Terrence Long	1.00	.45	.12
☐ 21 Hiram Bocachica	.50	.23	.06
☐ 22 Dante Powell	2.50	1.10	.30
☐ 23 Brian Buchanan	.25	.11	.03
☐ 24 Scott Elarton	.75	.35	.09
☐ 25 Mark Johnson	.25	.11	.03
☐ 26 Jacob Shumate	.15	.07	.02
☐ 27 Kevin Witt	.50	.23	.06
☐ 28 Jay Payton	2.00	.90	.25
☐ 29 Mike Thurman	.15	.07	.02
☐ 30 Jacob Cruz	1.00	.45	.12
☐ 31 Chris Clemons	.15	.07	.02
☐ 32 Travis Miller	.15	.07	.02
☐ 33 Sean Johnston	.15	.07	.02
☐ 34 Brad Rigby	.15	.07	.02
☐ 35 Doug Webb	.15	.07	.02
☐ 36 John Ambrose	.15	.07	.02
☐ 37 Cletus Davidson	.15	.07	.02
☐ 38 Tony Terry	.15	.07	.02
☐ 39 Jason Camilli	.15	.07	.02
☐ 40 Roger Goedde	.15	.07	.02
☐ 41 Corey Pointer	.15	.07	.02
☐ 42 Trey Moore	.15	.07	.02
☐ 43 Brian Stephenson	.15	.07	.02
☐ 44 Dan Lock	.15	.07	.02
☐ 45 Mike Darr	.25	.11	.03
☐ 46 Carl Dale	.15	.07	.02
☐ 47 Tommy Davis	.15	.07	.02
☐ 48 Kevin Brown	.75	.35	.09
☐ 49 Ryan Nye	.40	.18	.05
☐ 50 Rodriguez Smith	.15	.07	.02
☐ 51 Andy Taulbee	.15	.07	.02
☐ 52 Jerry Whittaker	.15	.07	.02
☐ 53 John Crowther	.15	.07	.02
☐ 54 Bryon Gainey	.15	.07	.02
☐ 55 Bill King	.15	.07	.02
☐ 56 Heath Murray	.25	.11	.03
☐ 57 Larry Barnes	.15	.07	.02
☐ 58 Todd Cadey	.15	.07	.02
☐ 59 Paul Failla	.15	.07	.02
☐ 60 Brian Meadows	.15	.07	.02
☐ 61 A.J. Pierzynski	.30	.14	.04
☐ 62 Aaron Boone	.75	.35	.09
☐ 63 Mike Metcalfe	.15	.07	.02
☐ 64 Matt Wagner	.15	.07	.02
☐ 65 Jaime Bluma	.15	.07	.02
☐ 66 Oscar Robles	.15	.07	.02
☐ 67 Greg Whiteman	.15	.07	.02
☐ 68 Roger Worley	.15	.07	.02
☐ 69 Paul Ottavinia	.15	.07	.02
☐ 70 Joe Giuliano	.15	.07	.02
☐ 71 Chris McBride	.15	.07	.02
☐ 72 Jason Beverlin	.15	.07	.02
☐ 73 Gordon Amerson	.25	.11	.03
☐ 74 Tom Mott	.15	.07	.02
☐ 75 Rob Welch	.15	.07	.02
☐ 76 Jason Kelly	.15	.07	.02
☐ 77 Matt Treanor	.15	.07	.02
☐ 78 Jason Sikes	.15	.07	.02
☐ 79 Steve Shoemaker	.15	.07	.02
☐ 80 Troy Brohawn	.15	.07	.02
☐ 81 Jeff Abbott	.50	.23	.06
☐ 82 Steve Woodard	.15	.07	.02
☐ 83 Greg Morris	.15	.07	.02
☐ 84 John Slamka	.15	.07	.02
☐ 85 John Schroeder	.15	.07	.02
☐ 86 Clay Caruthers	.15	.07	.02
☐ 87 Eddie Brooks	.15	.07	.02
☐ 88 Tim Byrdak	.15	.07	.02
☐ 89 Bob Howry	.15	.07	.02
☐ 90 Midre Cummings	.15	.07	.02
☐ 91 John Dettmer	.15	.07	.02
☐ 92 Gar Finnvold	.15	.07	.02
☐ 93 Dwayne Hosey	.15	.07	.02
☐ 94 Jason Jacome	.15	.07	.02
☐ 95 Doug Jennings	.15	.07	.02
☐ 96 Luis Lopez	.15	.07	.02
☐ 97 John Mabry	.25	.11	.03
☐ 98 Rondell White	.50	.23	.06
☐ 99 J.T. Snow	.25	.11	.03
☐ 100 Vic Darensbourg	.15	.07	.02

1994 Signature Rookies Signatures Draft Picks

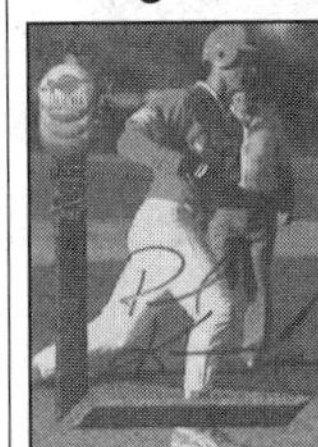

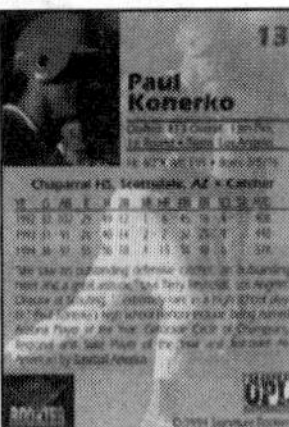

The 1994 Signature Rookies Draft Picks Signature set consists of 100 standard-size cards. An autographed card or a trade coupon was seeded in each pack. The trade coupon could be mailed in and redeemed for an autograph card. The card design is identical to the regular issue series. These cards differ in that an autograph in blue ink is inscribed across the picture and the cards are individually numbered out "of 7,750."

	MINT	NRMT	EXC
COMPLETE SET (100)	300.00	135.00	38.00
COMMON SIGNATURE (1-100)	2.00	.90	.25
☐ 1 Josh Booty	8.00	3.60	1.00
☐ 2 Paul Wilson	10.00	4.50	1.25
☐ 3 Ben Grieve	20.00	9.00	2.50
☐ 4 Dustin Hermanson	2.00	.90	.25
☐ 5 Antone Williamson	8.00	3.60	1.00
☐ 6 McKay Christensen	2.00	.90	.25
☐ 7 Doug Million	7.00	3.10	.85
☐ 8 Todd Walker	25.00	11.00	3.10
☐ 9 C.J. Nitkowski	2.00	.90	.25
☐ 10 Jaret Wright	12.00	5.50	1.50
☐ 11 Mark Farris	2.00	.90	.25
☐ 12 Nomar Garciaparra	20.00	9.00	2.50
☐ 13 Paul Konerko	25.00	11.00	3.10
☐ 14 Jason Varitek	5.00	2.20	.60
☐ 15 Jayson Peterson	3.00	1.35	.35
☐ 16 Matt Smith	2.00	.90	.25
☐ 17 Ramon Castro	3.00	1.35	.35
☐ 18 Cade Gaspar	3.00	1.35	.35
☐ 19 Bret Wagner	2.00	.90	.25
☐ 20 Terrence Long	12.00	5.50	1.50
☐ 21 Hiram Bocachica	5.00	2.20	.60
☐ 22 Dante Powell	20.00	9.00	2.50
☐ 23 Brian Buchanan	3.00	1.35	.35
☐ 24 Scott Elarton	7.00	3.10	.85
☐ 25 Mark Johnson	3.00	1.35	.35
☐ 26 Jacob Shumate	2.00	.90	.25
☐ 27 Kevin Witt	5.00	2.20	.60
☐ 28 Jay Payton	15.00	6.75	1.85
☐ 29 Mike Thurman	2.00	.90	.25
☐ 30 Jacob Cruz	10.00	4.50	1.25
☐ 31 Chris Clemons	2.00	.90	.25
☐ 32 Travis Miller	2.00	.90	.25
☐ 33 Sean Johnston	2.00	.90	.25
☐ 34 Brad Rigby	2.00	.90	.25
☐ 35 Doug Webb	2.00	.90	.25
☐ 36 John Ambrose	2.00	.90	.25
☐ 37 Cletus Davidson	2.00	.90	.25
☐ 38 Tony Terry	2.00	.90	.25
☐ 39 Jason Camilli	2.00	.90	.25
☐ 40 Roger Goedde	2.00	.90	.25
☐ 41 Corey Pointer	2.00	.90	.25
☐ 42 Trey Moore	2.00	.90	.25
☐ 43 Brian Stephenson	2.00	.90	.25
☐ 44 Dan Lock	2.00	.90	.25
☐ 45 Mike Darr	2.00	.90	.25
☐ 46 Carl Dale	2.00	.90	.25
☐ 47 Tommy Davis	2.00	.90	.25
☐ 48 Kevin Brown	8.00	3.60	1.00
☐ 49 Ryan Nye	5.00	2.20	.60
☐ 50 Rodriguez Smith	2.00	.90	.25
☐ 51 Andy Taulbee	2.00	.90	.25
☐ 52 Jerry Whittaker	2.00	.90	.25
☐ 53 John Crowther	2.00	.90	.25
☐ 54 Bryon Gainey	2.00	.90	.25
☐ 55 Bill King	2.00	.90	.25
☐ 56 Heath Murray	5.00	2.20	.60
☐ 57 Larry Barnes	2.00	.90	.25
☐ 58 Todd Cadey	2.00	.90	.25
☐ 59 Paul Failla	2.00	.90	.25
☐ 60 Brian Meadows	2.00	.90	.25
☐ 61 A.J. Pierzynski	5.00	2.20	.60
☐ 62 Aaron Boone	7.00	3.10	.85
☐ 63 Mike Metcalfe	2.00	.90	.25
☐ 64 Matt Wagner	2.00	.90	.25
☐ 65 Jaime Bluma	2.00	.90	.25
☐ 66 Oscar Robles	2.00	.90	.25
☐ 67 Greg Whiteman	2.00	.90	.25
☐ 68 Roger Worley	2.00	.90	.25
☐ 69 Paul Ottavinia	2.00	.90	.25
☐ 70 Joe Giuliano	2.00	.90	.25
☐ 71 Chris McBride	2.00	.90	.25
☐ 72 Jason Beverlin	2.00	.90	.25
☐ 73 Gordon Amerson	3.00	1.35	.35
☐ 74 Tom Mott	2.00	.90	.25
☐ 75 Rob Welch	2.00	.90	.25
☐ 76 Jason Kelly	2.00	.90	.25
☐ 77 Matt Treanor	2.00	.90	.25
☐ 78 Jason Sikes	2.00	.90	.25
☐ 79 Steve Shoemaker	2.00	.90	.25
☐ 80 Troy Brohawn	2.00	.90	.25
☐ 81 Jeff Abbott	6.00	2.70	.75
☐ 82 Steve Woodard	2.00	.90	.25
☐ 83 Greg Morris	2.00	.90	.25
☐ 84 John Slamka	2.00	.90	.25
☐ 85 John Schroeder	2.00	.90	.25
☐ 86 Clay Caruthers	2.00	.90	.25
☐ 87 Eddie Brooks	2.00	.90	.25
☐ 88 Tim Byrdak	2.00	.90	.25
☐ 89 Bob Howry	2.00	.90	.25
☐ 90 Midre Cummings	2.00	.90	.25
☐ 91 John Dettmer	2.00	.90	.25
☐ 92 Gar Finnvold	2.00	.90	.25
☐ 93 Dwayne Hosey	2.00	.90	.25
☐ 94 Jason Jacome	2.00	.90	.25
☐ 95 Doug Jennings	2.00	.90	.25
☐ 96 Luis Lopez	2.00	.90	.25
☐ 97 John Mabry	5.00	2.20	.60
☐ 98 Rondell White	15.00	6.75	1.85
☐ 99 J.T. Snow	8.00	3.60	1.00
☐ 100 Vic Darensbourg	2.00	.90	.25

1994 Signature Rookies Bonus Signatures Draft Picks

Randomly inserted in packs, this 10-card standard-size set features on its fronts full-bleed color action shots. Marbleized green stripes accent the pictures on the left and bottom. In the bottom green stripe appears the player's name in gold foil. The autograph is inscribed across the picture in blue ink. On a background consisting of a ghosted version of the front photo, the backs have a color headshot in the upper left corner, with the remainder of the back filled with biography, statistics, and player profile.

	MINT	NRMT	EXC
COMPLETE SET (10)	70.00	32.00	8.75
COMMON SIGNATURE (1-10)	6.00	2.70	.75
☐ 1 Matt Beaumont	8.00	3.60	1.00
☐ 2 Yates Hall	6.00	2.70	.75
☐ 3 Jed Hansen	6.00	2.70	.75
☐ 4 Ryan Helms	6.00	2.70	.75
☐ 5 Russ Johnson/3250	12.00	5.50	1.50
☐ 6 Carlton Loewer	8.00	3.60	1.00
☐ 7 Darrell Nicholas	6.00	2.70	.75
☐ 8 Paul O'Malley	6.00	2.70	.75
☐ 9 Jeremy Powell	10.00	4.50	1.25
☐ 10 Scott Shores	6.00	2.70	.75

1994 Signature Rookies Flip Cards Draft Picks

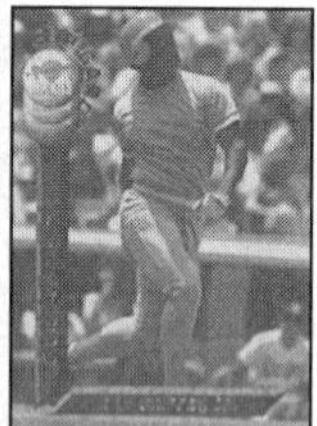

Randomly inserted in packs, this five-card standard-size set features full-bleed color action shots on both sides. Marbleized green stripes accent the pictures on the left and bottom. In these green stripes appear the production figures ("1 of 15,000") and the player's name, both in gold foil. The cards are unnumbered and checklisted below alphabetically according to the first player listed.

	MINT	NRMT	EXC
COMPLETE SET (5)	10.00	4.50	1.25
COMMON CARD (1-5)	.75	.35	.09
☐ 1 Craig Griffey Ken Griffey Sr.	.75	.35	.09
☐ 2 Craig Griffey Ken Griffey Jr.	3.00	1.35	.35
☐ 3 Ken Griffey Jr. Ken Griffey Sr.	4.00	1.80	.50
☐ 4 Reid Ryan Nolan Ryan	2.50	1.10	.30
☐ 5 Paul Wilson Phil Nevin	1.00	.45	.12

1994 Signature Rookies Flip Card Signatures Draft Picks

Randomly inserted in Signature Rookie Draft Picks baseball packs, this nine-card standard-size, autograph set features full-bleed color action shots on both sides. Marbleized green stripes accent the pictures on the left and bottom. In these green stripes appear the production figures ("1 of 15,000") and the player's name, both in gold foil. Individually autographs appear across the photo. Instead of inserting an autographed card, a individually numbered certificate was inserted to be redeemed for those cards featuring the autographs of Nolan Ryan and Ken Griffey Jr. Ryan signed 1,000 of the Nolan/Reid cards and Ken Jr. signed 500 picturing him with Ken Sr.and 500 with brother Craig. Phil Nevin signed 1,050 cards, Reid Ryan 2,100, Craig Griffey signed 2,000 (1000 with Ken Jr. and 1000 with Ken Sr.) and Ken Sr. signed 2000 (1000 with Craig and 1000 with Ken Jr.). The cards are unnumbered and checklisted below alphabetically according to the first player listed.

	MINT	NRMT	EXC
COMPLETE SET (9)	900.00	400.00	110.00
COMMON SIGNATURE (1-9)	18.00	8.00	2.20
☐ AU1 Craig Griffey AU2000 Ken Griffey Sr.	18.00	8.00	2.20
☐ AU2 Craig Griffey AU1000 Ken Griffey Jr.	18.00	8.00	2.20
☐ AU3 Ken Griffey Sr. AU1000 Craig Griffey	18.00	8.00	2.20
☐ AU4 Ken Griffey Sr. AU1000 Ken Griffey Jr.	18.00	8.00	2.20
☐ AU5 Ken Griffey Jr. AU500 Craig Griffey	300.00	135.00	38.00
☐ AU6 Ken Griffey Jr. AU500 Ken Griffey Sr.	300.00	135.00	38.00
☐ AU7 Nolan Ryan AU1000 Reid Ryan	350.00	160.00	45.00
☐ AU8 Reid Ryan AU2100 Nolan Ryan	18.00	8.00	2.20
☐ AU9 Phil Nevin AU1050 Paul Wilson	18.00	8.00	2.20

1994 Signature Rookies Top Prospects Draft Picks

These five standard-size cards feature on their fronts color player action shots that are borderless, except at the bottom where the black border carries the player's name in red lettering. The player's signature appears in blue ink across the card face. The words "Authentic Signature" appear in gold-foil lettering to the left. Each card is also hand numbered out of 5,250. On a cartoonlike background of a baseball rocketing skyward from a ballpark, the horizontal backs carry the player's name, biography, statistics and highlights in black lettering.

	MINT	NRMT	EXC
COMPLETE SET (5)	6.00	2.70	.75
COMMON CARD (T1-T5)	1.00	.45	.12
☐ T1 Scott Ruffcorn	1.00	.45	.12
☐ T2 Brad Woodall	1.00	.45	.12
☐ T3 Andrew Lorraine	1.00	.45	.12
☐ T4 LaTroy Hawkins	1.00	.45	.12
☐ T5 Alan Benes	2.50	1.10	.30

1994 Signature Rookies Top Prospects Signatures Draft Picks

Randomly inserted in packs, this five-card standard-size set features on its fronts full-bleed color action shots. Marbleized green stripes accent the pictures on the left and bottom. In these green stripes appear the production figures ("1 of 2,100") and the player's name, both in gold foil. The autograph is inscribed across the picture in blue ink. On a background consisting of a ghosted version of the front photo, the backs have a color headshot in the upper left corner, with the remainder of the back filled with biography, statistics, and player profile.

	MINT	NRMT	EXC
COMPLETE SET (5)	70.00	32.00	8.75
COMMON SIGNATURE (T1-T5)	12.00	5.50	1.50
☐ T1 Scott Ruffcorn	12.00	5.50	1.50
☐ T2 Brad Woodall	12.00	5.50	1.50
☐ T3 Andrew Lorraine	12.00	5.50	1.50
☐ T4 LaTroy Hawkins	12.00	5.50	1.50
☐ T5 Alan Benes	30.00	13.50	3.70

1994 Stadium Club Draft Picks

This 90-card standard-size set features players chosen in the June 1994 MLB draft and photographed in their major league uniforms. Each 24-pack box included four First Day Issue Draft Pick cards randomly packed, one in every six packs. The fronts display full-bleed color player photos. A "94 Draft Pick" emblem in the shape of a home plate appears in an upper corner. The player's name is printed vertically in gold foil on a line extending down from this emblem. On a colorful screened background, the horizontal backs present a color closeup cutout, biography, scouting report, and a short list of other first round draft picks.

	MINT	NRMT	EXC
COMPLETE SET (90)	15.00	6.75	1.85
COMMON CARD (1-90)	.15	.07	.02
☐ 1 Jacob Shumate	.15	.07	.02
☐ 2 C.J. Nitkowski	.15	.07	.02
☐ 3 Doug Million	.50	.23	.06
☐ 4 Matt Smith	.15	.07	.02
☐ 5 Kevin Lovinger	.15	.07	.02
☐ 6 Alberto Castillo	.15	.07	.02
☐ 7 Mike Russell	.15	.07	.02
☐ 8 Dan Lock	.15	.07	.02
☐ 9 Tom Szimanski	.15	.07	.02
☐ 10 Aaron Boone	.75	.35	.09
☐ 11 Jayson Peterson	.25	.11	.03
☐ 12 Mark Johnson	.25	.11	.03
☐ 13 Cade Gaspar	.25	.11	.03
☐ 14 George Lombard	1.25	.55	.16
☐ 15 Russ Johnson	.25	.11	.03
☐ 16 Travis Miller	.15	.07	.02
☐ 17 Jay Payton	2.00	.90	.25
☐ 18 Brian Buchanan	.25	.11	.03
☐ 19 Jacob Cruz	1.00	.45	.12
☐ 20 Gary Rath	.15	.07	.02
☐ 21 Ramon Castro	.25	.11	.03
☐ 22 Tommy Davis	.15	.07	.02
☐ 23 Tony Terry	.15	.07	.02
☐ 24 Jerry Whittaker	.15	.07	.02
☐ 25 Mike Darr	.25	.11	.03
☐ 26 Doug Webb	.15	.07	.02
☐ 27 Jason Camilli	.15	.07	.02
☐ 28 Brad Rigby	.15	.07	.02
☐ 29 Ryan Nye	.40	.18	.05
☐ 30 Carl Dale	.15	.07	.02
☐ 31 Andy Taulbee	.15	.07	.02
☐ 32 Trey Moore	.15	.07	.02
☐ 33 John Crowther	.15	.07	.02
☐ 34 Joe Giuliano	.15	.07	.02
☐ 35 Brian Rose	.50	.23	.06
☐ 36 Paul Failla	.15	.07	.02
☐ 37 Brian Meadows	.15	.07	.02
☐ 38 Oscar Robles	.15	.07	.02
☐ 39 Mike Metcalfe	.15	.07	.02
☐ 40 Larry Barnes	.15	.07	.02
☐ 41 Paul Ottavinia	.15	.07	.02
☐ 42 Chris McBride	.15	.07	.02
☐ 43 Ricky Stone	.15	.07	.02
☐ 44 Billy Blythe	.15	.07	.02
☐ 45 Eddie Priest	.15	.07	.02
☐ 46 Scott Forster	.15	.07	.02
☐ 47 Eric Pickett	.15	.07	.02
☐ 48 Matt Beaumont	.60	.25	.07
☐ 49 Darrell Nicholas	.15	.07	.02
☐ 50 Mike Hampton	.15	.07	.02
☐ 51 Paul O'Malley	.15	.07	.02
☐ 52 Steve Shoemaker	.15	.07	.02
☐ 53 Jason Sikes	.15	.07	.02
☐ 54 Bryan Farson	.15	.07	.02
☐ 55 Yates Hall	.15	.07	.02
☐ 56 Troy Brohawn	.15	.07	.02
☐ 57 Dan Hower	.15	.07	.02
☐ 58 Clay Caruthers	.15	.07	.02
☐ 59 Pepe McNeal	.15	.07	.02
☐ 60 Ray Ricken	.15	.07	.02
☐ 61 Scott Shores	.15	.07	.02
☐ 62 Eddie Brooks	.15	.07	.02
☐ 63 Dave Kauflin	.15	.07	.02
☐ 64 David Meyer	.15	.07	.02
☐ 65 Geoff Blum	.25	.11	.03
☐ 66 Roy Marsh	.15	.07	.02
☐ 67 Ryan Beeney	.15	.07	.02
☐ 68 Derek Dukart	.15	.07	.02
☐ 69 Nomar Garciaparra	2.50	1.10	.30
☐ 70 Jason Kelly	.15	.07	.02
☐ 71 Jesse Ibarra	.15	.07	.02
☐ 72 Bucky Buckles	.15	.07	.02
☐ 73 Mark Little	.15	.07	.02
☐ 74 Heath Murray	.25	.11	.03
☐ 75 Greg Morris	.15	.07	.02
☐ 76 Mike Halperlin	.15	.07	.02
☐ 77 Wes Helms	2.50	1.10	.30
☐ 78 Ray Brown	.15	.07	.02
☐ 79 Kevin Brown	.75	.35	.09
☐ 80 Paul Konerko	3.00	1.35	.35
☐ 81 Mike Thurman	.15	.07	.02
☐ 82 Paul Wilson	.75	.35	.09
☐ 83 Terrence Long	1.00	.45	.12
☐ 84 Ben Grieve	2.50	1.10	.30
☐ 85 Mark Farris	.15	.07	.02
☐ 86 Bret Wagner	.15	.07	.02
☐ 87 Dustin Hermanson	.15	.07	.02
☐ 88 Kevin Witt	.50	.23	.06
☐ 89 Corey Pointer	.15	.07	.02
☐ 90 Tim Grieve	.15	.07	.02

1994 Stadium Club Draft Picks First Day Issue

Randomly inserted in packs, this 90-card standard-size set is identical in design with the regular Stadium Club Draft Picks cards except for a holographic "1st Day Issue" emblem on the fronts.

	MINT	NRMT	EXC
COMPLETE SET (90)	225.00	100.00	28.00
COMMON CARD (1-90)	3.00	1.35	.35
*STARS: 9X TO 15X BASIC CARDS			

1994 South Atlantic League All-Stars Fleer/ProCards

	MINT	NRMT	EXC
COMPLETE SET (57)	20.00	9.00	2.50

☐ SAL1 Brandon Bridgers
☐ SAL2 Jim Foster
☐ SAL3 Mike Bell
☐ SAL4 Bert Gerhart
☐ SAL5 Julio Santana
☐ SAL6 Gerad Cawhorn
☐ SAL7 Maximo De La Rosa
☐ SAL8 Einar Diaz
☐ SAL9 Steve Kline
☐ SAL10 Richie Sexson
☐ SAL11 Frank Catalanotto
☐ SAL12 Vick Brown
☐ SAL13 Chris Cumberland
☐ SAL14 Eric Knowles
☐ SAL15 Ricky Ledee
☐ SAL16 Ruben Rivera
☐ SAL17 Omar Malave MG
☐ SAL18 Mike Romano
☐ SAL19 Dave Sinnes
☐ SAL20 Shannon Stewart
☐ SAL21 Tom Fordham
☐ SAL22 Joe Geck
☐ SAL23 Jason Goligoski
☐ SAL24 Fred Kendall MG
☐ SAL25 Magglio Ordonez
☐ SAL26 Archie Vazquez
☐ SAL27 Scott Vollmer
☐ SAL28 Harold Williams
☐ SAL29 John Giudice
☐ SAL30 Jason Smith
☐ SAL31 Tony Torchia MG
☐ SAL32 Jacob Viano
☐ SAL33 Lou Collier
☐ SAL34 Sergio Mendez
☐ SAL35 Matt Pontbriant
☐ SAL36 Cesar Diaz
☐ SAL37 Sandy Pichardo
☐ SAL38 Jeff Tam
☐ SAL39 Cobi Cradle
☐ SAL40 Todd Etler
☐ SAL41 Steve Gann
☐ SAL42 Danny Oyas
☐ SAL43 Jermaine Dye
☐ SAL44 Willy Johnson
☐ SAL45 Carey Paige
☐ SAL46 Matt Arrandale
☐ SAL47 Jeff Berblinger
☐ SAL48 Chris Christopher
☐ SAL49 Craig Grasser
☐ SAL50 Elieser Marrero
☐ SAL51 Mike Matvey
☐ SAL52 Luis Melendez MG
☐ SAL53 Dave Oehrlein
☐ SAL54 Dan Held
☐ SAL55 Jeremey Kendall
☐ SAL56 Tyrone Swan
☐ SAL57 Checklist

1994 South Bend Silver Hawks Classic

This 30-card standard size set of the 1994 South Bend Silver Hawks, a Class A Midwest League affiliate of the Chicago White Sox, features white-bordered posed color player shots on its fronts with the player's name and position, team name and logo and Classic logo appearing across the bottom of each card. On a ghosted team logo, the white back carries the player's name at the top, followed by biography and statistics.

	MINT	NRMT	EXC
COMPLETE SET (30)	7.00	3.10	.85

☐ 1 Hank Tagle
☐ 2 Mike Bailey
☐ 3 Ricky Bennett
☐ 4 Shawn Buchanan
☐ 5 Jason Evans
☐ 6 David Fitzpatrick
☐ 7 Toby Lehman
☐ 8 Wayne Lindemann
☐ 9 Byron Mathews
☐ 10 Andy McCormack
☐ 11 Sandy McKinnon
☐ 12 Frank Menechino
☐ 13 Bob Mumma
☐ 14 Andre Newhouse
☐ 15 Greg Norton
☐ 16 Jason Ogden
☐ 17 Wil Polidor
☐ 18 Bill Proctor
☐ 19 Jimmy Reyes
☐ 20 Nilson Robledo
☐ 21 Mike Sirotka
☐ 22 Juan Thomas
☐ 23 Julio Vinas
☐ 24 Brian Woods
☐ 25 Mike Gellinger MG
☐ 26 Jaime Garcia CO
☐ 27 Jim Reinebold CO
☐ 28 Scott Takao TR
☐ 29 Logo Card
☐ 30 Checklist

1994 South Bend Silver Hawks Fleer/ProCards

This 29-card standard size set of the 1994 South Bend Silver Hawks, a Class A Midwest League affiliate of the Chicago White Sox, features white-bordered posed color player photos on its fronts with the player's name, position, team name and Fleer/ProCards logo across the bottom of each card. The white back with vertical light blue stripes carries the player's name at the top, followed by biography and statistics.

	MINT	NRMT	EXC
COMPLETE SET (29)	5.00	2.20	.60

☐ 585 Mike Bailey
☐ 586 Ricky Bennett

☐ 587 Dave Fitzpatrick
☐ 588 Toby Lehman
☐ 589 Wayne Lindemann
☐ 590 Andy McCormack
☐ 591 Jason Ogden
☐ 592 Bill Proctor
☐ 593 Mike Sirotka
☐ 594 Hank Tagle
☐ 595 Brian Woods
☐ 596 Wayne Faircloth
☐ 597 Nilson Robledo
☐ 598 Julio Vinas
☐ 599 Frank Menechino
☐ 600 Bob Mumma
☐ 601 Greg Norton
☐ 602 Wil Polidor
☐ 603 Jimmy Reyes
☐ 604 Juan Thomas
☐ 605 Shawn Buchanan
☐ 606 Jason Evans
☐ 607 Byron Mathews
☐ 608 Sandy McKinnon
☐ 609 Andre Newhouse
☐ 610 Mike Gellinger MG
☐ 611 Jaime Garcia CO
☐ 612 Jim Reinebold CO
☐ 613 Checklist

1994 Southern Oregon Athletics Classic

This 30-card standard size set of the 1994 Southern Oregon Athletics, a Class AAA International League affiliate of the Montreal Expos, features white-bordered posed color player shots on its fronts with the player's name and position, team name and logo and Classic logo appearing across the bottom of each card. On a ghosted team logo, the white back carries the player's name at the top, followed by biography and statistics. This issue includes the minor league card debut of Ben Grieve.

	MINT	NRMT	EXC
COMPLETE SET (30)	30.00	13.50	3.70

☐ 1 Brandy Bengoechea
☐ 2 Chris Cochrane
☐ 3 Brian Darwin
☐ 4 Manny DaSilva
☐ 5 Rob DeBoer
☐ 6 Brian Domenico
☐ 7 Ben Grieve
☐ 8 Leon Hamburg
☐ 9 Eric Harris
☐ 10 Brendan Hause
☐ 11 Chris Helfrich
☐ 12 Aaron Huber
☐ 13 John Jones
☐ 14 Bill King
☐ 15 Skye Leibee
☐ 16 Jason Lowe
☐ 17 Eric Martins
☐ 18 Mike Maurer
☐ 19 Alex Miranda
☐ 20 Mike Moschetti
☐ 21 Damon Newman
☐ 22 Jeff Richardson
☐ 23 Chad Rolish
☐ 24 Pat Sanders
☐ 25 Andy Smith
☐ 26 John Smith
☐ 27 Jose Soriano
☐ 28 Mike Stamison
☐ 29 Leonardo Ventura
☐ 30 Todd Weinberg Checklist

1994 Southern Oregon Athletics Fleer/ProCards

This 29-card standard size set of the 1994 Southern Oregon Athletics, a Class AAA International League affiliate of the Montreal Expos, features white-bordered posed color player photos on its fronts with the player's name, position, team name and Fleer/ProCards logo across the bottom of each card. The white back with vertical light blue stripes carries the player's name at the top, followed by biography and statistics. This issue includes the minor league card debut of Ben Grieve.

	MINT	NRMT	EXC
COMPLETE SET (29)	18.00	8.00	2.20

☐ 3612 Chris Cochrane
☐ 3613 Brian Domenico
☐ 3614 Brendan Hause
☐ 3615 Chris Helfrich
☐ 3616 Aaron Huber
☐ 3617 Bill King
☐ 3618 Skye Leibee
☐ 3619 Jason Lowe
☐ 3620 Mike Maurer
☐ 3621 Chad Rolish
☐ 3622 Andy Smith
☐ 3623 John Smith
☐ 3624 Todd Weinberg
☐ 3625 Manny DaSilva
☐ 3626 Rob DeBoer
☐ 3627 Leonardo Ventura
☐ 3628 Brandy Bengoechea
☐ 3629 John Jones
☐ 3630 Eric Martins
☐ 3631 Alex Miranda
☐ 3632 Mike Moschetti
☐ 3633 Pat Sanders
☐ 3634 Mike Stamison
☐ 3635 Brian Darwin
☐ 3636 Ben Grieve
☐ 3637 Leon Hamburg
☐ 3638 Eric Harris
☐ 3639 Jeff Richardson
☐ 3640 Checklist

1994 Spartanburg Phillies Classic

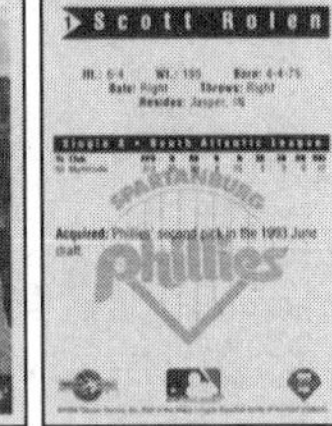

This 30-card standard size set of the 1994 Spartanburg Phillies, a Class A South Atlantic League affiliate of the Philadelphia Phillies, features white-bordered posed color player shots on its fronts with the player's name and position, team name and logo and Classic logo appearing across the bottom of each card. On a ghosted team logo, the white back carries the player's name at the top, followed by biography and statistics. This issue includes the minor league card debut of Scott Rolen and a second year card of Bobby Estalella.

	MINT	NRMT	EXC
COMPLETE SET (28)	40.00	18.00	5.00

☐ 1 Scott Rolen
☐ 2 Doug Angeli
☐ 3 Matthew Brainard
☐ 4 Tony Costa
☐ 5 Brian Costello
☐ 6 Scott Eggleston
☐ 7 Robert Estalella
☐ 8 Tony Fiore
☐ 9 Mark Foster
☐ 10 Tom Franek
☐ 11 Santy Gallone
☐ 12 Todd Genke
☐ 13 Dan Held
☐ 14 Jeremey Kendall
☐ 15 Mac McMullen
☐ 16 Steven Nutt
☐ 17 Shelby Rama
☐ 18 Lance Sanders
☐ 19 Derek Stingley
☐ 20 Tyrone Swan
☐ 21 David Waco
☐ 22 Bryan Weigandt
☐ 23 Shawn Wills
☐ 24 Mike Wood
☐ 25 Roy Majtyka
☐ 26 Buzz Capra
☐ 27 Tony Scott
☐ 28 Troy Hoffert
☐ 29 Philadelphia Phillies Logo
☐ 30 Spartanburg Phillies Logo CL

1994 Spartanburg Phillies Fleer/ProCards

This 30-card standard size set of the 1994 Spartanburg Phillies, a Class A South Atlantic League affiliate of the Philadelphia Phillies, features white-bordered posed color player photos on its fronts with the player's name, position, team name and Fleer/ProCards logo across the bottom of each card. The white back with vertical light blue stripes carries the player's name at the top, followed by biography and statistics. This issue includes the minor league card debut of Scott Rolen and a second year card of Bobby Estalella.

	MINT	NRMT	EXC
COMPLETE SET (30)	25.00	11.00	3.10

☐ 1712 Tony Costa
☐ 1713 Scott Eggleston
☐ 1714 Tony Fiore
☐ 1715 Mark Foster
☐ 1716 Tom Franek
☐ 1717 Todd Genke
☐ 1718 Laurence Heisler
☐ 1719 Steve Nutt
☐ 1720 Christopher Olsen
☐ 1721 Shelby Rama
☐ 1722 Lance Sanders
☐ 1723 Tyrone Swan
☐ 1724 Mike Wood
☐ 1725 Matt Brainard
☐ 1726 Bobby Estalella
☐ 1727 Dan Held
☐ 1728 Doug Angeli
☐ 1729 Santy Gallone
☐ 1730 Jon McMullen
☐ 1731 Scott Rolen
☐ 1732 David Waco
☐ 1733 Bryan Wiegandt
☐ 1734 Brian Costello
☐ 1735 Jeremey Kendall
☐ 1736 Derek Stingley
☐ 1737 Shawn Wills
☐ 1738 Roy Majtyka MG
☐ 1739 Buzz Capra CO
☐ 1740 Tony Scott CO
☐ 1741 Checklist

1994 Spokane Indians Classic

This 30-card standard size set of the 1994 Spokane Indians, a Class A Northwest League affiliate of the San Diego Padres, features white-bordered posed color player shots on its fronts with the player's name and position, team name and logo and Classic logo appearing across the bottom of each card. On a ghosted team logo, the white back carries the player's name at the top, followed by biography and statistics.

	MINT	NRMT	EXC
COMPLETE SET (30)	7.00	3.10	.85

☐ 1 Bubba Dixon
☐ 2 Mark Barrett
☐ 3 Pete Bifone
☐ 4 Jeff Conway
☐ 5 Keith Davis
☐ 6 Shane Dennis
☐ 7 Francisco Derotal
☐ 8 Devohn 'Sport' Duncan
☐ 9 Antonio Fernandez
☐ 10 Darren Grass
☐ 11 Kenya Hunt
☐ 12 Arthur Jenkins
☐ 13 Jay Johnson
☐ 14 Jeff Jones
☐ 15 Shawn Knight
☐ 16 Greg LaRocca
☐ 17 Jumaane Leach
☐ 18 Chris Logan
☐ 19 Erik Martinez
☐ 20 Mark Merilia
☐ 21 Derek Mix
☐ 22 Scott Singleton
☐ 23 Jason Tyrus
☐ 24 Dave Ullan
☐ 25 Tye Waller MG
☐ 26 Tim McWilliam CO
☐ 27 Jerry Fragasso TR
☐ 28 Logo Card
☐ 29 Logo Card
☐ 30 Checklist

1994 Spokane Indians Fleer/ProCards

This 30-card standard size set of the 1994 Spokane Indians, a Class A Northwest League affiliate of the San Diego Padres, features white-bordered posed color player photos on its fronts with the player's name, position, team name and Fleer/ProCards logo across the bottom of each card. The white back with vertical light blue stripes carries the player's name at the top, followed by biography and statistics.

	MINT	NRMT	EXC
COMPLETE SET (30)	6.00	2.70	.75

☐ 3313 Mark Barrett
☐ 3314 Keith Davis
☐ 3315 Shane Dennis
☐ 3316 Bubba Dixon
☐ 3317 DeVohn Duncan
☐ 3318 Arthur Jenkins
☐ 3319 Jeff Jones
☐ 3320 Jarman Leach
☐ 3321 Chris Logan
☐ 3322 Derek Mix
☐ 3323 Heath Murray
☐ 3324 Scott Singleton
☐ 3325 Darren Grass
☐ 3326 Dave Ullan
☐ 3327 Pete Bifone
☐ 3328 Antonio Fernandez
☐ 3329 Kenya Hunt
☐ 3330 Shawn Knight
☐ 3331 Greg LaRocca
☐ 3332 Erik Martinez
☐ 3333 Mark Merila
☐ 3334 Jeff Conway
☐ 3335 Francisco Derotal
☐ 3336 Jay Johnson
☐ 3337 Gary Matthews Jr.
☐ 3338 Jason Tyrus
☐ 3339 Tye Waller MG
☐ 3340 Tim McWilliam CO
☐ 3341 Dave Smith CO
☐ 3342 Checklist

1994 Springfield Sultans Classic

This 30-card standard size set of the 1994 Springfield Sultans, a Class A Midwest League affiliate of the San Diego Padres, features white-bordered posed color player shots on its fronts with the player's name and position, team name and logo and Classic logo appearing across the bottom of each card. On a ghosted team logo, the white back carries the player's name at the top, followed by biography and statistics.

	MINT	NRMT	EXC
COMPLETE SET (30)	8.00	3.60	1.00

☐ 1 John Fantauzzi
☐ 2 Luis Arroyo
☐ 3 Jim Baron
☐ 4 Erick Corps
☐ 5 Eduardo Cuevas
☐ 6 Dan Drewien
☐ 7 Darrick Duke
☐ 8 Iggy Duran
☐ 9 Juan Espinal
☐ 10 Hector Fargas
☐ 11 Hal Garrett
☐ 12 Lee Henderson
☐ 13 Earl Johnson
☐ 14 Brad Kaufman
☐ 15 Tom Kindler
☐ 16 Matt LaChappa
☐ 17 Leroy McKinnis
☐ 18 David Mowry
☐ 19 Santiago Rivera
☐ 20 John Roberts
☐ 21 Jason Schlutt
☐ 22 Mike Thomas
☐ 23 Jorge Velandia
☐ 24 Darell White
☐ 25 Kyle White
☐ 26 Bryan Wolff
☐ 27 Dickie Woodridge
☐ 28 Ed Romero MG
☐ 29 Saul Soltero CO
☐ 30 Bob Packard TR Checklist

1994 Springfield Sultans Fleer/ProCards

This 27-card standard size set of the 1994 Springfield Sultans, a Class A Midwest League affiliate of the San Diego Padres, features white-bordered posed color player photos on its fronts with the player's name, position, team name and Fleer/ProCards logo across the bottom of each card. The white back with vertical light blue stripes carries the player's name at the top, followed by biography and statistics.

	MINT	NRMT	EXC
COMPLETE SET (27)	6.00	2.70	.75

☐ 2028 Luis Arroyo
☐ 2029 Jim Baron
☐ 2030 Dan Drewien
☐ 2031 Hal Garrett
☐ 2032 Brad Kaufman
☐ 2033 Tom Kindler
☐ 2034 Matt LaChappa
☐ 2035 Jason Schlutt
☐ 2036 Darell White
☐ 2037 Kyle White
☐ 2038 Bryan Wolff
☐ 2039 Lee Henderson
☐ 2040 Leroy McKinnis
☐ 2041 Erick Corps
☐ 2042 Eduardo Cuevas
☐ 2043 Juan Espinal
☐ 2044 John Fantauzzi
☐ 2045 Dave Mowry
☐ 2046 Santiago Rivera
☐ 2047 Dickie Woodridge
☐ 2048 John Cotton
☐ 2049 Darrick Duke
☐ 2050 Earl Johnson
☐ 2051 John Roberts
☐ 2052 Ed Romero MG
☐ 2053 Saul Soltero CO
☐ 2054 Checklist

1994 St. Catharines Blue Jays Classic

This 30-card standard size set of the 1994 St. Catherines Blue Jays, a Class A New York-Penn League affiliate of the Toronto Blue Jays, features white-bordered posed color player shots on its fronts with the player's name and position, team name and logo and Classic logo appearing across the bottom of each card. On a ghosted team logo, the white back carries the player's name at the top, followed by biography and statistics.

	MINT	NRMT	EXC
COMPLETE SET (30)	10.00	4.50	1.25

☐ 1 Chris McBride
☐ 2 Alfredo Arias

- ☐ 3 Brent Bearden
- ☐ 4 Ed Budz
- ☐ 5 Carlos Cabrera
- ☐ 6 Ben Candelaria
- ☐ 7 John Crowther
- ☐ 8 Willy Daunic
- ☐ 9 Freddy Garcia
- ☐ 10 Brian Grant
- ☐ 11 Michael Halperin
- ☐ 12 Battle Holley
- ☐ 13 Wayne Hoy
- ☐ 14 Jeff Ladd
- ☐ 15 Jeremy Lee
- ☐ 16 Jeff Leystra
- ☐ 17 John Reilly
- ☐ 18 Omar Sanchez
- ☐ 19 Anthony Sanders
- ☐ 20 Jeff Schneider
- ☐ 21 Mark Sievert
- ☐ 22 Keilan Smith
- ☐ 23 Randy Smith
- ☐ 24 Fausto Solano
- ☐ 25 Shayne Timmons
- ☐ 26 Eddy Vasquez
- ☐ 27 J.J. Cannon MG
- ☐ 28 Kip Roggendorf
- ☐ 29 Rolando Pino CO
- ☐ 30 Al Widmar CO Checklist

1994 St. Catharines Blue Jays Fleer/ProCards

This 30-card standard size set of the 1994 St. Catherines Blue Jays, a Class A New York-Penn League affiliate of the Toronto Blue Jays, features white-bordered posed color player photos on its fronts with the player's name, position, team name and Fleer/ProCards logo across the bottom of each card. The white back with vertical light blue stripes carries the player's name at the top, followed by biography and statistics.

	MINT	NRMT	EXC
COMPLETE SET (30)	6.00	2.70	.75

- ☐ 3631 Alfredo Arias
- ☐ 3632 Brent Bearden
- ☐ 3633 Ed Budz
- ☐ 3634 Jeff Cheek
- ☐ 3635 John Crowther
- ☐ 3636 Brian Grant
- ☐ 3637 Michael Halperin
- ☐ 3638 Wayne Hoy
- ☐ 3639 Jeremy Lee
- ☐ 3640 Jeff Leystra
- ☐ 3641 Chris McBride
- ☐ 3642 Jeff Schneider
- ☐ 3643 Mark Sievert
- ☐ 3644 Keilan Smith
- ☐ 3645 Randy Smith
- ☐ 3646 Jeff Ladd
- ☐ 3647 John Reilly
- ☐ 3648 Shayne Timmons
- ☐ 3649 Carlos Cabrera
- ☐ 3650 Willie Daunic
- ☐ 3651 Freddy Garcia
- ☐ 3652 Battle Holley
- ☐ 3653 Kip Roggendorf
- ☐ 3654 Fausto Solano
- ☐ 3655 Eddy Vasquez
- ☐ 3656 Ben Candelaria
- ☐ 3657 Omar Sanchez
- ☐ 3658 Tony Sanders
- ☐ 3659 J.J. Cannon MG
- ☐ 3660 Checklist

1994 St. Lucie Mets Classic

This 30-card standard size set of the 1994 St. Lucie Mets, a Class A Florida State League affiliate of the New York Mets, features white-bordered posed color player shots on its fronts with the player's name and position, team name and logo and Classic logo appearing across the bottom of each card. On a ghosted team logo, the white back carries the player's name at the top, followed by biography and statistics.

	MINT	NRMT	EXC
COMPLETE SET (30)	16.00	7.25	2.00

- ☐ 1 Rey Ordonez
- ☐ 2 Benny Agbayani
- ☐ 3 Lou Benbow
- ☐ 4 Craig Bullock
- ☐ 5 Joe Crawford
- ☐ 6 Brian Daubach
- ☐ 7 Chad Epperson
- ☐ 8 Mike Farrell
- ☐ 9 Mark Fuller
- ☐ 10 Guillermo Garcia
- ☐ 11 Robbie Guzik
- ☐ 12 Al Hammell
- ☐ 13 Erik Hiljus
- ☐ 14 Jason Isringhausen
- ☐ 15 Tripp Keister
- ☐ 16 Eric Ludwick
- ☐ 17 Steve Lyons
- ☐ 18 Kevin Morgan
- ☐ 19 Hector Ramirez
- ☐ 20 Dwight Robinson
- ☐ 21 Brad Schorr
- ☐ 22 Travis Shaffer
- ☐ 23 John Smith
- ☐ 24 Matt Terrell
- ☐ 25 Donnie White
- ☐ 26 Larry Bennese TR
- ☐ 27 Rafael Landestoy MG
- ☐ 28 Bill Latham CO
- ☐ 29 Andre David CO
- ☐ 30 Checklist UER (#26 says Paul Bennese, should be Larry Bennese)

1994 St. Lucie Mets Fleer/ProCards

This 29-card standard size set of the 1994 St. Lucie Mets, a Class A Florida State League affiliate of the New York Mets, features white-bordered posed color player photos on its fronts with the player's name, position, team name and Fleer/ProCards logo across the bottom of each card. The white back with vertical light blue stripes carries the player's name at the top, followed by biography and statistics.

	MINT	NRMT	EXC
COMPLETE SET (29)	12.00	5.50	1.50

- ☐ 1186 Craig Bullock
- ☐ 1187 Todd Fiegel
- ☐ 1188 Robbie Guzik
- ☐ 1189 Erik Hiljus
- ☐ 1190 Jason Isringhausen
- ☐ 1191 Eric Ludwick
- ☐ 1192 Steve Lyons
- ☐ 1193 Joe Petcka
- ☐ 1194 Hector Ramirez
- ☐ 1195 Brad Schorr
- ☐ 1196 Travis Shaffer
- ☐ 1197 Chad Epperson
- ☐ 1198 Guillermo Garcia
- ☐ 1199 Charlie Greene
- ☐ 1200 Brian Daubach
- ☐ 1201 Mike Farrell
- ☐ 1202 Kevin Morgan
- ☐ 1203 Tito Navarro
- ☐ 1204 Rey Ordonez
- ☐ 1205 Dwight Robinson
- ☐ 1206 Benny Agbayani
- ☐ 1207 Tripp Keister
- ☐ 1208 John Smith
- ☐ 1209 Matt Terrell
- ☐ 1210 Don White
- ☐ 1211 Rafael Landestoy MG
- ☐ 1212 Andre David CO
- ☐ 1213 Bill Latham CO
- ☐ 1214 Checklist

1994 St. Petersburg Cardinals Classic

This 30-card standard size set of the 1994 St. Petersburg Cardinals, a Class A Florida State League affiliate of the St. Louis Cardinals, features white-bordered posed color player shots on its fronts with the player's name and position, team name and logo and Classic logo appearing across the bottom of each card. On a ghosted team logo, the white back carries the player's name at the top, followed by biography and statistics. This issue includes the minor league card debut of Alan Benes.

	MINT	NRMT	EXC
COMPLETE SET (30)	14.00	6.25	1.75

- ☐ 1 Alan Benes
- ☐ 2 Joe Aversa
- ☐ 3 Juan Ballara
- ☐ 4 Keith Black
- ☐ 5 Kirk Bullinger
- ☐ 6 Mike Busby
- ☐ 7 Mike Cantu
- ☐ 8 Brian Carpenter
- ☐ 9 Steve Cerio
- ☐ 10 Mike Gulan
- ☐ 11 Keith Johns
- ☐ 12 Steve Johnson
- ☐ 13 Greg Knowles
- ☐ 14 Sean Lowe
- ☐ 15 Larry Lucchetti
- ☐ 16 T.J. Mathews
- ☐ 17 Jeff Matranga
- ☐ 18 Larry Meza
- ☐ 19 Eric Miller
- ☐ 20 Jeff Murphy
- ☐ 21 Aldo Pecorilli
- ☐ 22 Wander Pimentel
- ☐ 23 Brian Rupp
- ☐ 24 Basil Shabazz
- ☐ 25 Derron Spiller
- ☐ 26 DaRond Stovall
- ☐ 27 Jose Velez
- ☐ 28 Mike Ramsey MG
- ☐ 29 Rich Folkers CO
- ☐ 30 Brad Bluestone TR Checklist

1994 St. Petersburg Cardinals Fleer/ProCards

This 29-card standard size set of the 1994 St. Petersburg Cardinals, a Class A Florida State League affiliate of the St. Louis Cardinals, features white-bordered posed color player photos on its fronts with the player's name, position, team name and Fleer/ProCards logo across the bottom of each card. The white back with vertical light blue stripes carries the player's name at the top, followed by biography and statistics.

	MINT	NRMT	EXC
COMPLETE SET (29)	5.00	2.20	.60

- ☐ 2576 Kirk Bullinger
- ☐ 2577 Mike Busby
- ☐ 2578 Brian Carpenter
- ☐ 2579 Steve Johnson
- ☐ 2580 Greg Knowles
- ☐ 2581 Sean Lowe
- ☐ 2582 Larry Lucchetti
- ☐ 2583 T.J. Mathews
- ☐ 2584 Jeff Matranga
- ☐ 2585 Eric Miller
- ☐ 2586 Derron Spiller
- ☐ 2587 Juan Ballara
- ☐ 2588 Jeff Murphy
- ☐ 2589 Joe Aversa
- ☐ 2590 Keith Black
- ☐ 2591 Mike Cantu
- ☐ 2592 Mike Gulan
- ☐ 2593 Keith Johns
- ☐ 2594 Larry Meza
- ☐ 2595 Aldo Pecorilli
- ☐ 2596 Wander Pimentel
- ☐ 2597 Steve Cerio
- ☐ 2598 Brian Rupp
- ☐ 2599 Basil Shabazz
- ☐ 2600 DaRond Stovall
- ☐ 2601 Jose Velez
- ☐ 2602 Mike Ramsey MG
- ☐ 2603 Rich Folkers CO
- ☐ 2604 Checklist

1994 Stockton Ports Classic

This 30-card standard size set of the 1994 Stockton Ports, a Class A California League affiliate of the Milwaukee Brewers, features white-bordered posed color player shots on its fronts with the player's name , position, team name , logo and Classic logo appearing across the bottom of each card. On a ghosted team logo, the white back carries the player's name at the top, followed by biography and statistics.

	MINT	NRMT	EXC
COMPLETE SET (30)	7.00	3.10	.85

- ☐ 1 Bobby Hughes
- ☐ 2 Kurt Archer
- ☐ 3 Donny Blair
- ☐ 4 Gene Caruso
- ☐ 5 Steve Duda
- ☐ 6 Andy Fairman
- ☐ 7 Ken Felder
- ☐ 8 Brad Gay
- ☐ 9 Brian Hancock
- ☐ 10 Tyrone Hill
- ☐ 11 Brian Hostetler
- ☐ 12 Bobby Jones
- ☐ 13 Dan Kyslinger
- ☐ 14 Todd Landry
- ☐ 15 Cory Lidle
- ☐ 16 Gabe Martinez
- ☐ 17 Bernie Millan
- ☐ 18 Andy Paul
- ☐ 19 Danny Perez
- ☐ 20 Scott Richardson
- ☐ 21 Frank Rodriguez
- ☐ 22 Roman Rodriguez
- ☐ 23 Jose Salcedo
- ☐ 24 Todd Samples
- ☐ 25 T.J. Schenbeck
- ☐ 26 Craig Smith
- ☐ 27 Lamar Johnson MG
- ☐ 28 Mark Littell CO
- ☐ 29 Fred Patek CO
- ☐ 30 Richard Stark TR Checklist

1994 Stockton Ports Fleer/ProCards

This 28-card standard size set of the 1994 Stockton Ports, a Class A California League affiliate of the Milwaukee Brewers, features white-bordered posed color player photos on its fronts with the player's name, position, team name and Fleer/ProCards logo across the bottom of each card. The white back with vertical light blue stripes carries the player's name at the top, followed by biography and statistics.

	MINT	NRMT	EXC
COMPLETE SET (28)	5.00	2.20	.60

- ☐ 1684 Donnie Blair
- ☐ 1685 Gino Caruso
- ☐ 1686 Steve Duda
- ☐ 1687 Brian Hancock
- ☐ 1688 Tyrone Hill
- ☐ 1689 Bobby Jones
- ☐ 1690 Dan Kyslinger
- ☐ 1691 Cory Lidle
- ☐ 1692 Andy Paul
- ☐ 1693 Frank Rodriguez
- ☐ 1694 Jose Salcedo
- ☐ 1695 Tom Schenbeck
- ☐ 1696 Brad Gay
- ☐ 1697 Brian Hostetler
- ☐ 1698 Bobby Hughes
- ☐ 1699 Andy Fairman
- ☐ 1700 Todd Landry
- ☐ 1701 Gabe Martinez
- ☐ 1702 Bernie Millan
- ☐ 1703 Roman Rodriguez
- ☐ 1704 Craig Smith
- ☐ 1705 Ken Felder
- ☐ 1706 Scott Richardson
- ☐ 1707 Todd Samples
- ☐ 1708 Lamar Johnson MG
- ☐ 1709 Mark Littell CO
- ☐ 1710 Fred Patek CO
- ☐ 1711 Checklist

1994 Syracuse Chiefs Team Issue

Sponsored by Kool-Aid, Post and WIXT, this 30-card set was issued as an uncut, perforated sheet. It consists of three panels (each measuring approximately 10 5/8" by 9 3/8") joined together to form one continuous sheet. The first panel features sponsors' logos and a large player photo. The second and third panels feature 15 player cards each. After perforation, the cards measure approximately 2 1/8" by 3 1/8". On a red card face, the fronts have posed color player photos. The player's name and position appear in a blue bar below the picture with the sponsor logos immediately below. The horizontal backs carry a short player biography and career stats.

	MINT	NRMT	EXC
COMPLETE SET (30)	8.00	3.60	1.00

- ☐ 1 Sharnol Adriana
- ☐ 2 Travis Baptist
- ☐ 3 Howard Battle
- ☐ 4 Rob Butler
- ☐ 5 Willie Canate
- ☐ 6 Brad Cornett
- ☐ 7 Tim Crabtree
- ☐ 8 Jesse Cross
- ☐ 9 Jack Daugherty
- ☐ 10 Bob Didier MG
- ☐ 11 Kyle Duey
- ☐ 12 Huck Flener
- ☐ 13 Ray Giannelli
- ☐ 14 Alex Gonzalez
- ☐ 15 Shawn Green
- ☐ 16 Les Lancaster
- ☐ 17 Joe Lis Jr.
- ☐ 18 Rob Montalvo
- ☐ 19 Robert Perez
- ☐ 20 Jose Pett
- ☐ 21 Marty Pevey
- ☐ 22 John Poloni CO
- ☐ 23 Jim Rogers
- ☐ 24 Paul Spoljaric
- ☐ 25 Randy St. Claire
- ☐ 26 Hector Torres CO
- ☐ 27 Jason Townley
- ☐ 28 Anthony Ward
- ☐ 29 Julian Yan
- ☐ 30 Eddie Zosky

1994 Syracuse Chiefs Fleer/ProCards

This 26-card standard size set of the 1994 Syracuse Chiefs, a Class AAA International League affiliate of the Toronto Blue Jays, features white-bordered posed color player photos on its fronts with the player's name, position, team name and Fleer/ProCards logo across the bottom of each card. The white back with vertical light blue stripes carries the player's name at the top, followed by biography and statistics.

	MINT	NRMT	EXC
COMPLETE SET (26)	5.00	2.20	.60

- ☐ 964 Travis Baptist
- ☐ 965 Tim Crabtree
- ☐ 966 Jesse Cross
- ☐ 967 Kyle Duey
- ☐ 968 Huck Flener
- ☐ 969 Les Lancaster
- ☐ 970 Jim Rogers
- ☐ 971 Randy St. Claire
- ☐ 972 Anthony Ward
- ☐ 973 Marty Pevey
- ☐ 974 Jason Townley
- ☐ 975 Sharnol Adriana
- ☐ 976 Howard Battle
- ☐ 977 Jack Daugherty
- ☐ 978 Ray Giannelli
- ☐ 979 Joe Lis Jr.
- ☐ 980 Julian Yan

☐ 981 Eddie Zosky
☐ 982 Rob Butler
☐ 983 Willie Canate
☐ 984 Shawn Green
☐ 985 Robert Perez
☐ 986 Bob Didier MG
☐ 987 John Poloni CO
☐ 988 Hector Torres CO
☐ 989 Checklist

1994 Tacoma Tigers Fleer/ProCards

This 28-card standard size set of the 1994 Tacoma Tigers, a Class AAA Pacific Coast League affiliate of the Oakland Athletics, features white-bordered posed color player photos on its fronts with the player's name, position, team name and Fleer/ProCards logo across the bottom of each card. The white back with vertical light blue stripes carries the player's name at the top, followed by biography and statistics.

	MINT	NRMT	EXC
COMPLETE SET (28)	5.00	2.20	.60

☐ 3165 Mark Acre
☐ 3166 Dana Allison
☐ 3167 Russ Brock
☐ 3168 Doug Johns
☐ 3169 Dave Leiper
☐ 3170 Carlos Maldonado
☐ 3171 Gavin Osteen
☐ 3172 Bronswell Patrick
☐ 3173 Curtis Shaw
☐ 3174 Tim Smith
☐ 3175 Roger Smithberg
☐ 3176 Ed Vosberg
☐ 3177 Dean Borrelli
☐ 3178 Eric Helfand
☐ 3179 Henry Mercedes
☐ 3180 Marcos Armas
☐ 3181 Jim Bowie
☐ 3182 Fausto Cruz
☐ 3183 Francisco Matos
☐ 3184 Craig Paquette
☐ 3185 Jim Buccheri
☐ 3186 Eric Fox
☐ 3187 Scott Lydy
☐ 3188 Manny Martinez
☐ 3189 Enoch Simmons
☐ 3190 Casey Parsons MG
☐ 3191 Bert Bradley CO
☐ 3192 Checklist

1994 Tampa Yankees Classic

This 30-card standard size set of the 1994 Tampa Yankees, a Class A Florida State League affiliate of the New York Yankees, features white-bordered posed color player shots on its fronts with the player's name , position, team name , logo and Classic logo appearing across the bottom of each card. On a ghosted team logo, the white back carries the player's name at the top, followed by biography and statistics. The cards are numbered on the back. This issue includes a third year card of Derek Jeter.

	MINT	NRMT	EXC
COMPLETE SET (30)	25.00	11.00	3.10

☐ 1 Derek Jeter
☐ 2 Jeff Antolick
☐ 3 Mike Buddie
☐ 4 Jeff Cindrich
☐ 5 Billy Coleman
☐ 6 Tim Cooper
☐ 7 Mike DeJean
☐ 8 Nick Delvecchio
☐ 9 Scott Epps
☐ 10 Greg Erickson
☐ 11 Mike Figga
☐ 12 Kraig Hawkins
☐ 13 Keith Heberling
☐ 14 Robert Hinds
☐ 15 Mike Jerzembeck
☐ 16 Joe Long
☐ 17 R.D. Long
☐ 18 Matt Luke
☐ 19 Jim Musselwhite
☐ 20 Mariano Rivera
☐ 21 Scott Romano
☐ 22 Yamil Salcedo
☐ 23 Gordon Sanchez
☐ 24 Shane Spencer
☐ 25 Grant Sullivan
☐ 26 Ray Suplee
☐ 27 Brian Turner
☐ 28 Sean Twitty
☐ 29 Kent Wallace
☐ 30 Checklist

1994 Tampa Yankees Fleer/ProCards

This 32-card standard size set of the 1994 Tampa Yankees, a Class A Florida State League affiliate of the New York Yankees, features white-bordered posed color player photos on its fronts with the player's name, position, team name and Fleer/ProCards logo across the bottom of each card. The white back with vertical light blue stripes carries the player's name at the top, followed by biography and statistics. This issue includes a third year card of Derek Jeter.

	MINT	NRMT	EXC
COMPLETE SET (32)	15.00	6.75	1.85

☐ 2372 Jeff Antolick
☐ 2373 Mike Buddie
☐ 2374 Jeff Cindrich
☐ 2375 Billy Coleman
☐ 2376 Mike DeJean
☐ 2377 Keith Heberling
☐ 2378 Mike Jerzembeck
☐ 2379 Joe Long
☐ 2380 Steve Munda
☐ 2381 Jim Musselwhite
☐ 2382 Mariano Rivera
☐ 2383 Grant Sullivan
☐ 2384 Kent Wallace
☐ 2385 Scott Epps
☐ 2386 Mike Figga
☐ 2387 Edwin Salcedo
☐ 2388 Gordon Sanchez
☐ 2389 Tim Cooper
☐ 2390 Nick Delvecchio
☐ 2391 Greg Erickson
☐ 2392 Rob Hinds
☐ 2393 Derek Jeter
☐ 2394 R.D. Long
☐ 2395 Scott Romano
☐ 2396 Kraig Hawkins
☐ 2397 Matt Luke
☐ 2398 Shane Spencer
☐ 2399 Ray Suplee
☐ 2400 Brian Turner
☐ 2401 Sean Twitty
☐ 2402 Jake Gibbs MG
☐ 2403 Checklist

1994 Toledo Mud Hens Fleer/ProCards

This 27-card standard size set of the 1994 Toledo Mud Hens, a Class AAA International League affiliate of the Detroit Tigers, features white-bordered posed color player photos on its fronts with the player's name, position, team name and Fleer/ProCards logo across the bottom of each card. The white back with vertical light blue stripes carries the player's name at the top, followed by biography and statistics.

	MINT	NRMT	EXC
COMPLETE SET (27)	5.00	2.20	.60

☐ 1017 Sean Bergman
☐ 1018 Ben Blomdahl
☐ 1019 Mike Christopher
☐ 1020 Wayne Edwards
☐ 1021 Greg Gohr
☐ 1022 Frank Gonzales
☐ 1023 Buddy Groom
☐ 1024 John Kiely
☐ 1025 Kurt Knudsen
☐ 1026 Jose Lima
☐ 1027 Felipe Lira
☐ 1028 John Flaherty
☐ 1029 Ed Fulton
☐ 1030 Ivan Cruz
☐ 1031 Jim Givens
☐ 1032 Jeff Kunkel
☐ 1033 Shannon Penn
☐ 1034 Steve Springer
☐ 1035 Alan Zinter
☐ 1036 Skeeter Barnes
☐ 1037 Shawn Hare
☐ 1038 Bob Higginson
☐ 1039 Riccardo Ingram
☐ 1040 Joe Sparks MG
☐ 1041 Bruce Fields CO
☐ 1042 Jeff Jones CO
☐ 1043 Checklist

1994 Trenton Thunder Fleer/ProCards

This 27-card standard size set of the 1994 Trenton Thunder, a Class AA Eastern League affiliate of the Detroit Tigers, features white-bordered posed color player photos on its fronts with the player's name, position, team name and Fleer/ProCards logo across the bottom of each card. The white back with vertical light blue stripes carries the player's name at the top, followed by biography and statistics.

	MINT	NRMT	EXC
COMPLETE SET (27)	5.00	2.20	.60

☐ 2111 Pat Ahearne
☐ 2112 Matt Bauer
☐ 2113 Ken Carlyle
☐ 2114 Blas Cedeno
☐ 2115 Brian Edmondson
☐ 2116 Rick Greene
☐ 2117 Mike Guilfoyle
☐ 2118 Trever Miller
☐ 2119 Dave Mysel
☐ 2120 Cecil Pettiford
☐ 2121 Shannon Withem
☐ 2122 Tim McConnell
☐ 2123 Joe Perona
☐ 2124 Tony Clark
☐ 2125 Dean Decillis
☐ 2126 Joe Dellicarri
☐ 2127 Kirk Mendenhall
☐ 2128 Kelley O'Neal
☐ 2129 Mike Rendina
☐ 2130 Brian DuBose
☐ 2131 Justin Mashore
☐ 2132 Darren Milne
☐ 2133 Brian Saltzgaber
☐ 2134 Tom Runnells MG
☐ 2135 Rich Bombard CO
☐ 2136 Kevin Bradshaw CO
☐ 2137 Checklist

1994 Triple A All-Stars Fleer/ProCards

	MINT	NRMT	EXC
COMPLETE SET (47)	12.00	5.50	1.50

☐ AAA1 Chris Howard
☐ AAA2 Herb Perry
☐ AAA3 Julian Tavarez
☐ AAA4 Kirt Ojala
☐ AAA5 Drew Denson
☐ AAA6 Ray Durham
☐ AAA7 Scott Ruffcorn
☐ AAA8 Ron Rightnowar
☐ AAA9 Rob Ducey
☐ AAA10 Dwayne Hosey
☐ AAA11 Rico Rossy
☐ AAA12 Luis Ortiz
☐ AAA13 Rick Krivda
☐ AAA14 Sherman Obando
☐ AAA15 Bernardo Brito
☐ AAA16 Tim McIntosh
☐ AAA17 Brian Raabe
☐ AAA18 Alex Gonzalez
☐ AAA19 Robert Perez
☐ AAA20 Ed Vosberg
☐ AAA21 Sean Bergman
☐ AAA22 Garret Anderson
☐ AAA23 Andrew Lorraine
☐ AAA24 Billy Ashley
☐ AAA25 Ron Coomer
☐ AAA26 Rich Aude
☐ AAA27 Rich Robertson
☐ AAA28 Trent Hubbard
☐ AAA29 Carl Everett
☐ AAA30 Rich Scheid
☐ AAA31 Doug Jennings
☐ AAA32 Barry Lyons
☐ AAA33 MarK Lee
☐ AAA34 Kevin Higgins
☐ AAA35 Allen Battle
☐ AAA36 Scott Coolbaugh
☐ AAA37 Steve Dixon
☐ AAA38 Quilvio Veras
☐ AAA39 Tim Laker
☐ AAA40 Paul Faries
☐ AAA41 Terry Clark
☐ AAA42 Luis Lopez
☐ AAA43 Brad Woodall
☐ AAA44 Gene Schall
☐ AAA45 Jim Dougherty
☐ AAA46 Craig McMurtry
☐ AAA47 Checklist

1994 Tucson Toros Fleer/ProCards

This 29-card standard size set of the 1994 Tucson Toros, a Class AAA Pacific Coast affiliate of the Houston Astros, features white-bordered posed color player photos on its fronts with the player's name, position, team name and Fleer/ProCards logo across the bottom of each card. The white back with vertical light blue stripes carries the player's name at the top, followed by biography and statistics.

	MINT	NRMT	EXC
COMPLETE SET (29)	5.00	2.20	.60

☐ 752 Eric Bell
☐ 753 Jim Bruske
☐ 754 Jim Dougherty
☐ 755 Dean Hartgraves
☐ 756 Domingo Jean
☐ 757 Craig McMurtry
☐ 758 Gino Minutelli
☐ 759 Al Morman
☐ 760 Mark Petkovsek
☐ 761 Ross Powell
☐ 762 Dave Veres
☐ 763 Donne Wall
☐ 764 Scott Makarewicz
☐ 765 Scooter Tucker
☐ 766 Juan Guerrero
☐ 767 Dave Hajek
☐ 768 Frank Kellner
☐ 769 Lance Madsen
☐ 770 Orlando Miller
☐ 771 Phil Nevin
☐ 772 Roberto Petagine
☐ 773 Chris Hatcher
☐ 774 Brian Hunter
☐ 775 Ray Montgomery
☐ 776 Ken Ramos
☐ 777 Rick Sweet MG
☐ 778 Dave Engle CO
☐ 779 Brent Strom CO
☐ 780 Checklist

1994 Tulsa Drillers Fleer/ProCards

This 27-card standard size set of the 1994 Tulsa Drillers, a Class AA Texas League affiliate of the Texas Rangers, features white-bordered posed color player photos on its fronts with the player's name, position, team name and Fleer/ProCards logo across the bottom of each card. The white back with vertical light blue stripes carries the player's name at the top, followed by biography and statistics.

	MINT	NRMT	EXC
COMPLETE SET (27)	5.00	2.20	.60

☐ 235 Chris Curtis
☐ 236 John Dettmer
☐ 237 Dave Geeve
☐ 238 Dave Giberti
☐ 239 Wilson Heredia
☐ 240 Jack Kimel
☐ 241 Kerry Lacy
☐ 242 Ramiro Martinez
☐ 243 Steve Rowley
☐ 244 Steve Sadecki
☐ 245 Lance Schuermann
☐ 246 Roger Luce
☐ 247 David Rolls
☐ 248 Rich Aurilia
☐ 249 Jim Clinton
☐ 250 Mike Edwards
☐ 251 Todd Guggiana
☐ 252 Ever Magallanes
☐ 253 Frank Turco
☐ 254 Sergio Cairo
☐ 255 Terrell Lowery
☐ 256 Timmie Morrow
☐ 257 Desi Wilson
☐ 258 Stan Cliburn MG
☐ 259 Jackson Todd CO
☐ 260 Randy Whisler CO
☐ 261 Checklist

1994 Tulsa Drillers Team Issue

	MINT	NRMT	EXC
COMPLETE SET (30)	6.00	2.70	.75

☐ 1 Rich Aurilia
☐ 2 Sergio Cairo
☐ 3 Jim Clinton
☐ 4 Chris Curtis
☐ 5 John Dettmer
☐ 6 Mike Edwards
☐ 7 Dave Geeve
☐ 8 Dave Giberti
☐ 9 Todd Guggiana
☐ 10 Wilson Heredia
☐ 11 Jack Kimel
☐ 12 Kerry Lacy
☐ 13 Terrell Lowery
☐ 14 Roger Luce
☐ 15 Ever Magallanes
☐ 16 Ramiro Martinez
☐ 17 Timmie Morrow
☐ 18 Danny Patterson
☐ 19 David Rolls
☐ 20 Steve Rowley
☐ 21 Steve Sadecki
☐ 22 Lance Schuermann
☐ 23 Timmie Morrow
☐ 24 Frank Turco
☐ 25 Desi Wilson
☐ 26 Stan Cliburn MG
☐ 27 Jackson Todd CO
☐ 28 Randy Whisler CO
☐ 29 Donna Papangellin TR
☐ 30 Vince and Larry
Crash Dummies

1994 Upper Deck

	MINT	NRMT	EXC
COMPLETE SET (270)	40.00	18.00	5.00
COMMON CARD (1-270)	.10	.05	.01
☐ 1 Alex Gonzalez	.25	.11	.03
☐ 2 Brooks Kieschnick	.60	.25	.07
☐ 3 Michael Tucker	.40	.18	.05
☐ 4 Trot Nixon	.25	.11	.03
☐ 5 Brien Taylor	.10	.05	.01
☐ 6 Quinton McCracken	.10	.05	.01
☐ 7 Terrell Wade	.25	.11	.03
☐ 8 Brandon Wilson	.10	.05	.01
☐ 9 Roberto Petagine	.10	.05	.01

☐ 10 Chad Mottola	.10	.05	.01
☐ 11 T.R. Lewis	.10	.05	.01
☐ 12 Hebert Perry	.10	.05	.01
☐ 13 Bob Abreu	1.00	.45	.12
☐ 14 Jorge Fabregas	.10	.05	.01
☐ 15 Mike Kelly	.10	.05	.01
☐ 16 Ryan McGuire	.10	.05	.01
☐ 17 Alan Zinter	.10	.05	.01
☐ 18 Troy Hughes	.10	.05	.01
☐ 19 Brook Fordyce	.10	.05	.01
☐ 20 Alex Ochoa	1.00	.45	.12
☐ 21 Chris Wimmer	.10	.05	.01
☐ 22 Alan Embree	.10	.05	.01
☐ 23 Richard Hidalgo	1.25	.55	.16
☐ 24 Greg Zaun	.10	.05	.01
☐ 25 Roger Cedeno	.40	.18	.05
☐ 26 Curtis Shaw	.10	.05	.01
☐ 27 Brian Giles	.10	.05	.01
☐ 28 Matt Murray	.10	.05	.01
☐ 29 Motor-Boat Jones	.10	.05	.01
☐ 30 Dmitri Young	.75	.35	.09
☐ 31 Justin Mashore	.10	.05	.01
☐ 32 Curtis Goodwin	.10	.05	.01
☐ 33 Marquis Riley	.10	.05	.01
☐ 34 Les Norman	.10	.05	.01
☐ 35 Billy Hall	.10	.05	.01
☐ 36 Jamie Arnold	.10	.05	.01
☐ 37 Mike Farmer	.10	.05	.01
☐ 38 Brent Bowers	.10	.05	.01
☐ 39 Chad McConnell	.10	.05	.01
☐ 40 Mike Robertson	.10	.05	.01
☐ 41 Brent Cookson	.10	.05	.01
☐ 42 Dan Cholowsky	.10	.05	.01
☐ 43 Justin Thompson	.20	.09	.03
☐ 44 Joe Vitiello	.10	.05	.01
☐ 45 Todd Steverson	.10	.05	.01
☐ 46 Brian Bevil	.10	.05	.01
☐ 47 Paul Shuey	.10	.05	.01
☐ 48 Scott Eyre	.10	.05	.01
☐ 49 Rick Greene	.10	.05	.01
☐ 50 Jose Silva	.20	.09	.03
☐ 51 Kurt Miller	.10	.05	.01
☐ 52 Ron Villone	.10	.05	.01
☐ 53 Darren Bragg	.10	.05	.01
☐ 54 Mike Lieberthal	.25	.11	.03
☐ 55 Gabe White	.10	.05	.01
☐ 56 Vince Moore	.10	.05	.01
☐ 57 Tony Clark	1.25	.55	.16
☐ 58 Chris Eddy	.10	.05	.01
☐ 59 Ray Durham	1.50	.70	.19
☐ 60 Todd Hollandsworth	1.00	.45	.12
☐ 61 Andres Berumen	.10	.05	.01
☐ 62 Quilvio Veras	.25	.11	.03
☐ 63 Wayne Gomes	.20	.09	.03
☐ 64 Ryan Karp	.10	.05	.01
☐ 65 Randy Curtis	.10	.05	.01
☐ 66 Steve Rodriguez	.10	.05	.01
☐ 67 Jason Schmidt	.25	.11	.03
☐ 68 Mark Acre	.10	.05	.01
☐ 69 B.J. Wallace	.10	.05	.01
☐ 70 Alvin Morman	.10	.05	.01
☐ 71 Travis Baptist	.10	.05	.01
☐ 72 Jim Wawruck	.10	.05	.01
☐ 73 Marty Cordova	1.25	.55	.16
☐ 74 Jamie Dismuke	.10	.05	.01
☐ 75 Joe Randa	.25	.11	.03
☐ 76 Danny Clyburn	.50	.23	.06
☐ 77 Joey Eischen	.10	.05	.01
☐ 78 Chris Seelbach	.10	.05	.01
☐ 79 Izzy Molina	.10	.05	.01
☐ 80 Chris Roberts	.10	.05	.01
☐ 81 Rod Henderson	.10	.05	.01
☐ 82 Kennie Steenstra	.10	.05	.01
☐ 83 Ugueth Urbina	.20	.09	.03
☐ 84 Stanton Cameron	.10	.05	.01
☐ 85 Doug Glanville	.10	.05	.01
☐ 86 Billy Wagner	.50	.23	.06
☐ 87 Tate Seefried	.10	.05	.01
☐ 88 Tyler Houston	.25	.11	.03
☐ 89 Derek Lowe	.10	.05	.01
☐ 90 Alan Benes	1.25	.55	.16
☐ 91 Terrell Wade AS FOIL	.25	.11	.03
☐ 92 Rod Henderson AS FOIL	.10	.05	.01
☐ 93 Charles Johnson AS FOIL	1.00	.45	.12
☐ 94 D.J. Boston AS FOIL	.10	.05	.01
☐ 95 Ruben Santana AS FOIL	.10	.05	.01
☐ 96 Joe Randa AS FOIL	.25	.11	.03
☐ 97 Alex Gonzalez AS FOIL	.25	.11	.03
☐ 98 Tim Clark AS FOIL	.10	.05	.01
☐ 99 Randy Curtis AS FOIL	.10	.05	.01
☐ 100 Brian L. Hunter AS FOIL	.50	.23	.06
☐ 101 Jose Lima	.10	.05	.01
☐ 102 Ray Holbert	.10	.05	.01
☐ 103 Karim Garcia	4.00	1.80	.50
☐ 104 Chris Martin	.10	.05	.01
☐ 105 David Bell	.10	.05	.01
☐ 106 Tim Clark	.10	.05	.01
☐ 107 Matt Drews	.50	.23	.06
☐ 108 Dan Serafini	.10	.05	.01
☐ 109 Demetrish Jenkins	.20	.09	.03
☐ 110 Charles Johnson	1.00	.45	.12
☐ 111 Jason Moler	.10	.05	.01
☐ 112 Bret Backlund	.10	.05	.01
☐ 113 Kevin Jordan	.10	.05	.01
☐ 114 Jesus Tavarez	.10	.05	.01
☐ 115 Frank Rodriguez	.25	.11	.03
☐ 116 Derrek Lee	2.50	1.10	.30
☐ 117 Calvin Reese	.20	.09	.03
☐ 118 Dave Stevens	.10	.05	.01
☐ 119 Julio Bruno	.10	.05	.01
☐ 120 D.J. Boston	.10	.05	.01
☐ 121 Jim Dougherty	.10	.05	.01
☐ 122 Daron Kirkreit	.10	.05	.01
☐ 123 Kerwin Moore	.10	.05	.01
☐ 124 Jason Kendall	1.00	.45	.12
☐ 125 Johnny Damon	1.25	.55	.16
☐ 126 Andre King	.10	.05	.01
☐ 127 Raul Gonzalez	.10	.05	.01
☐ 128 Eddie Pearson	.10	.05	.01
☐ 129 Yuri Sanchez	.10	.05	.01
☐ 130 Russ Davis	.25	.11	.03
☐ 131 Arquimedez Pozo	.20	.09	.03
☐ 132 Jon Lieber	.25	.11	.03
☐ 133 Glenn Murray	.10	.05	.01
☐ 134 Brant Brown	.10	.05	.01
☐ 135 Brian L. Hunter	.50	.23	.06
☐ 136 Mike Gulan	.10	.05	.01
☐ 137 Tim Vanegmond	.10	.05	.01
☐ 138 Will VanLandingham	.10	.05	.01
☐ 139 Robert Ellis	.10	.05	.01
☐ 140 Calvin Murray	.10	.05	.01
☐ 141 Kurt Ehmann	.10	.05	.01
☐ 142 Brian DuBose	.10	.05	.01
☐ 143 Robert Eenhoorn	.10	.05	.01
☐ 144 Howard Battle	.10	.05	.01
☐ 145 Jason Giambi	1.00	.45	.12
☐ 146 James Baldwin MLE FOIL	.25	.11	.03
☐ 147 Rick Helling MLE FOIL	.10	.05	.01
☐ 148 Ricky Bottalico MLE FOIL	.25	.11	.03
☐ 149 Paul Spoljaric MLE FOIL	.10	.05	.01
☐ 150 Alex Gonzalez MLE FOIL	.25	.11	.03
☐ 151 Tavo Alvarez MLE FOIL	.10	.05	.01
☐ 152 Joey Eischen MLE FOIL	.10	.05	.01
☐ 153 Shane Andrews MLE FOIL	.25	.11	.03
☐ 154 James Mouton MLE FOIL	.10	.05	.01
☐ 155 Russ Davis MLE FOIL	.25	.11	.03
☐ 156 Phil Nevin MLE FOIL	.10	.05	.01
☐ 157 Garret Anderson MLE FOIL	.75	.35	.09
☐ 158 Gabe White MLE FOIL	.10	.05	.01
☐ 159 Brian L. Hunter MLE FOIL	.50	.23	.06
☐ 160 Ray McDavid MLE FOIL	.10	.05	.01
☐ 161 Mike Durant	.10	.05	.01
☐ 162 Eric Owens	.10	.05	.01
☐ 163 Rick Gorecki	.10	.05	.01
☐ 164 Lyle Mouton	.10	.05	.01
☐ 165 Ray McDavid	.10	.05	.01
☐ 166 Tony Graffanino	.10	.05	.01
☐ 167 Todd Ritchie	.10	.05	.01
☐ 168 Jose Herrera	.20	.09	.03
☐ 169 Steve Dunn	.20	.09	.03
☐ 170 Tavo Alvarez	.10	.05	.01
☐ 171 Jon Farrell	.10	.05	.01
☐ 172 Omar Ramirez	.10	.05	.01
☐ 173 Ruben Santana	.10	.05	.01
☐ 174 Dan Smith	.10	.05	.01
☐ 175 Shane Andrews	.10	.05	.01
☐ 176 Rob Henkel	.10	.05	.01
☐ 177 Joel Wolfe	.10	.05	.01
☐ 178 Chris Schwab	.10	.05	.01
☐ 179 Chris Weinke	.10	.05	.01
☐ 180 Ozzie Timmons	.10	.05	.01
☐ 181 Jason Bates	.10	.05	.01
☐ 182 Matt Brunson	.10	.05	.01
☐ 183 Garret Anderson	.75	.35	.09
☐ 184 Brian Rupp	.10	.05	.01
☐ 185 Derek Jeter	3.00	1.35	.35
☐ 186 Desi Relaford	.20	.09	.03
☐ 187 Darren Burton	.10	.05	.01
☐ 188 David Mysel	.10	.05	.01
☐ 189 Steve Soderstrom	.10	.05	.01
☐ 190 Steve Gibralter	.20	.09	.03
☐ 191 Brian Sackinsky	.10	.05	.01
☐ 192 Marc Pisciotta	.10	.05	.01
☐ 193 Gene Schall	.10	.05	.01
☐ 194 Jimmy Haynes	.10	.05	.01
☐ 195 Shannon Stewart	.20	.09	.03
☐ 196 Neifi Perez	.50	.23	.06
☐ 197 Chris Colon	.10	.05	.01
☐ 198 Trey Beamon	.60	.25	.07
☐ 199 Jon Zuber	.10	.05	.01
☐ 200 John Burke	.10	.05	.01
☐ 201 Derek Wallace	.10	.05	.01
☐ 202 Chad Ogea	.25	.11	.03
☐ 203 Ernie Young	.25	.11	.03
☐ 204 Jose Malave	.10	.05	.01
☐ 205 Bill Pulsipher	.40	.18	.05
☐ 206 Leon Glenn	.10	.05	.01
☐ 207 Scott Sullivan	.10	.05	.01
☐ 208 Orlando Miller	.10	.05	.01
☐ 209 John Wasdin	.25	.11	.03
☐ 210 Paul Spoljaric	.10	.05	.01
☐ 211 Charles Peterson	.50	.23	.06
☐ 212 Ben Van Ryn	.10	.05	.01
☐ 213 Chris Sexton	.10	.05	.01
☐ 214 Bobby Bonds Jr	.10	.05	.01
☐ 215 James Mouton	.10	.05	.01
☐ 216 Terrell Lowery	.10	.05	.01
☐ 217 Oscar Munoz	.10	.05	.01
☐ 218 Mike Bell	.75	.35	.09
☐ 219 Preston Wilson	.40	.18	.05
☐ 220 Mark Thompson	.10	.05	.01
☐ 221 Aaron Holbert	.10	.05	.01
☐ 222 Tommy Adams	.10	.05	.01
☐ 223 Ramon D. Martinez	.10	.05	.01
☐ 224 Tim Davis	.10	.05	.01
☐ 225 Ricky Bottalico	.40	.18	.05
☐ 226 Rick Krivda	.10	.05	.01
☐ 227 Troy Percival	.10	.05	.01
☐ 228 Mark Sweeney	.10	.05	.01
☐ 229 Joey Hamilton	.40	.18	.05
☐ 230 Phil Nevin	.10	.05	.01
☐ 231 Jon Ratliff	.10	.05	.01
☐ 232 Mark Smith	.10	.05	.01
☐ 233 Tyrone Hill	.10	.05	.01
☐ 234 Kevin Riggs	.10	.05	.01
☐ 235 John Dettmer	.10	.05	.01
☐ 236 Brian Barber	.10	.05	.01
☐ 237 Hector Trinidad	.10	.05	.01
☐ 238 Jeff Alkire	.10	.05	.01
☐ 239 Phil Geisler	.10	.05	.01
☐ 240 Rick Helling	.10	.05	.01
☐ 241 Edgardo Alfonzo	.20	.09	.03
☐ 242 Matt Franco	.10	.05	.01
☐ 243 Chad Roper	.10	.05	.01
☐ 244 Basil Shabazz	.10	.05	.01
☐ 245 James Baldwin	.25	.11	.03
☐ 246 Scott Hatteberg	.10	.05	.01
☐ 247 Glenn DiSarcina	.10	.05	.01
☐ 248 LaTroy Hawkins	.10	.05	.01
☐ 249 Marshall Boze	.10	.05	.01
☐ 250 Michael Moore	.10	.05	.01
☐ 251 Brien Taylor SP FOIL	.10	.05	.01
☐ 252 Johnny Damon SP FOIL	1.25	.55	.16
☐ 253 Curtis Goodwin SP FOIL	.10	.05	.01
☐ 254 Jose Silva SP FOIL	.20	.09	.03
☐ 255 Terrell Wade SP FOIL	.25	.11	.03
☐ 256 Dmitri Young SP FOIL	.75	.35	.09
☐ 257 Roger Cedeno SP FOIL	.40	.18	.05
☐ 258 Alex Ochoa SP FOIL	1.00	.45	.12
☐ 259 D.J. Boston SP FOIL	.10	.05	.01
☐ 260 Michael Tucker SP FOIL	.40	.18	.05
☐ 261 Calvin Murray SP FOIL	.10	.05	.01
☐ 262 Frank Rodriguez SP FOIL	.25	.11	.03
☐ 263 Michael Moore SP FOIL	.10	.05	.01
☐ 264 Ugueth Urbina SP FOIL	.25	.11	.03
☐ 265 Chad Mottola SP FOIL	.10	.05	.01
☐ 266 Todd Hollandsworth SP FOIL	1.00	.45	.12
☐ 267 Rod Henderson SP FOIL	.10	.05	.01
☐ 268 Roberto Petagine SP FOIL	.10	.05	.01
☐ 269 Charles Johnson SP FOIL	1.00	.45	.12
☐ 270 Trot Nixon SP FOIL	.25	.11	.03
☐ MJ23 Michael Jordan Gold	70.00	32.00	8.75
☐ MJ23 Michael Jordan Silver	20.00	9.00	2.50
☐ TC1 Alex Rodriguez	70.00	32.00	8.75
☐ TC2 Kirk Presley	10.00	4.50	1.25
☐ NNO Expired Trade Card 2	.25	.11	.03
☐ NNO Expired Trade Card 1	.25	.11	.03

1994 Upper Deck Player of the Year

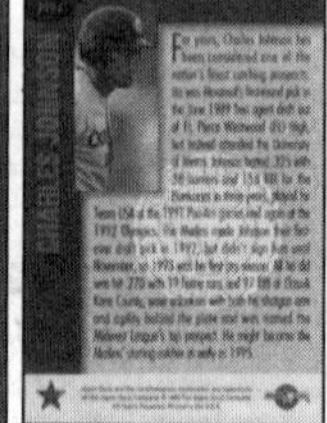

	MINT	NRMT	EXC
COMPLETE SET (28)	80.00	36.00	10.00
COMMON CARD (PY1-PY28)	2.50	1.10	.30
☐ PY1 Marquis Riley	2.50	1.10	.30
☐ PY2 Roberto Petagine	2.50	1.10	.30
☐ PY3 Ernie Young	3.00	1.35	.35
☐ PY4 Alex Gonzalez	3.00	1.35	.35
☐ PY5 Terrell Wade	3.00	1.35	.35
☐ PY6 Marshall Boze	2.50	1.10	.30
☐ PY7 Mike Gulan	2.50	1.10	.30
☐ PY8 Brant Brown	2.50	1.10	.30
☐ PY9 Roger Cedeno	4.00	1.80	.50
☐ PY10 Rod Henderson	2.50	1.10	.30
☐ PY11 Calvin Murray	2.50	1.10	.30
☐ PY12 Omar Ramirez	2.50	1.10	.30
☐ PY13 Ruben Santana	2.50	1.10	.30
☐ PY14 Charles Johnson	10.00	4.50	1.25
☐ PY15 Bill Pulsipher	4.00	1.80	.50
☐ PY16 Alex Ochoa	10.00	4.50	1.25
☐ PY17 Ray McDavid	2.50	1.10	.30
☐ PY18 Jason Moler	2.50	1.10	.30
☐ PY19 Danny Clyburn	5.00	2.20	.60
☐ PY20 Rick Helling	2.50	1.10	.30
☐ PY21 Frank Rodriguez	3.00	1.35	.35
☐ PY22 Chad Mottola	2.50	1.10	.30
☐ PY23 John Burke	2.50	1.10	.30
☐ PY24 Michael Tucker	4.00	1.80	.50
☐ PY25 Brian DuBose	2.50	1.10	.30
☐ PY26 LaTroy Hawkins	2.50	1.10	.30
☐ PY27 James Baldwin	3.00	1.35	.35
☐ PY28 Ryan Karp	2.50	1.10	.30

1994 Upper Deck Top 10 Prospect Jumbos

One jumbo per box.

	MINT	NRMT	EXC
COMPLETE SET (10)	35.00	16.00	4.40
COMMON CARD (TP1-TP10)	1.00	.45	.12
☐ TP1 Roger Cedeno	2.50	1.10	.30
☐ TP2 Johnny Damon	8.00	3.60	1.00
☐ TP3 Alex Gonzalez	2.00	.90	.25
☐ TP4 Charles Johnson	6.00	2.70	.75
☐ TP5 Chad Mottola	1.00	.45	.12
☐ TP6 Phil Nevin	1.00	.45	.12
☐ TP7 Alex Ochoa	6.00	2.70	.75
☐ TP8 1993 No. 1 Draft Pick	1.00	.45	.12
☐ TP9 Jose Silva	1.00	.45	.12
☐ TP10 Michael Tucker	2.50	1.10	.30

1994 Upper Deck Top 10 Prospect Mail-In

	MINT	NRMT	EXC
COMPLETE SET (10)	50.00	22.00	6.25
COMMON CARD (1-10)	2.00	.90	.25
☐ 1 Roger Cedeno	2.50	1.10	.30
☐ 2 Johnny Damon	8.00	3.60	1.00
☐ 3 Alex Gonzalez	2.00	.90	.25
☐ 4 Charles Johnson	6.00	2.70	.75
☐ 5 Chad Mottola	2.00	.90	.25
☐ 6 Phil Nevin	2.00	.90	.25
☐ 7 Alex Ochoa	6.00	2.70	.75
☐ 8 Alex Rodriguez	35.00	16.00	4.40
☐ 9 Jose Silva	2.00	.90	.25
☐ 10 Michael Tucker	2.50	1.10	.30

1994 Utica Blue Sox Classic

This 29-card standard size set of the 1994 Utica Blue Sox, a Class A New York-Penn League affiliate of the Boston Red Sox, features white-bordered posed color player shots on its fronts with the player's name and position, team name and logo and Classic logo appearing across the bottom of each card. On a ghosted team logo, the white back carries the player's name at the top, followed by biography and statistics.

	MINT	NRMT	EXC
COMPLETE SET (30)	8.00	3.60	1.00

☐ 1 Marc Albarado
☐ 2 Chris Allison
☐ 3 Diogenes Baez
☐ 4 Kevin Becker
☐ 5 Jeff Berry
☐ 6 John Bowles
☐ 7 Craig Bush
☐ 8 Kevin Clark
☐ 9 Joe DePastino
☐ 10 Jared Fernandez
☐ 11 Eric Ford
☐ 12 David Gibralter
☐ 13 Joe Hamilton
☐ 14 Jeff Huffman
☐ 15 Chris Kurek
☐ 16 Charles Malloy
☐ 17 Joe Mamott
☐ 18 Denis McLaughlin
☐ 19 Carlos Mejia
☐ 20 Ethan Merrill
☐ 21 Alvin Mitchell
☐ 22 Hilario Perez
☐ 23 John Raifstanger
☐ 24 Willie Rivera
☐ 25 Tony Sheffield
☐ 26 Nate Tebbs
☐ 27 Jim Tyrrell
☐ 28 Dave Holt
☐ 29 Garry Roggenburk
☐ 30 Robert Bill CL

1994 Utica Blue Sox Fleer/ProCards

This 29-card standard size set of the 1994 Utica Blue Sox, a Class A New York-Penn League affiliate of the Boston Red Sox, features white-bordered posed color player photos on its fronts with the player's name, position, team name and Fleer/ProCards logo across the bottom of each card. The white back with vertical light blue stripes carries the player's name at the top, followed by biography and statistics.

	MINT	NRMT	EXC
COMPLETE SET (29)	6.00	2.70	.75

☐ 3810 Kevin Becker
☐ 3811 Craig Bush
☐ 3812 Lyle Hartgrove
☐ 3813 Jeff Huffman
☐ 3814 Charles Malloy
☐ 3815 Joe Mamott
☐ 3816 Denis McLaughlin
☐ 3817 Carlos Mejia
☐ 3818 Alvin Mitchell
☐ 3819 Hilario Perez
☐ 3820 Jim Tyrrell
☐ 3821 Jeff Berry
☐ 3822 Kevin Clark
☐ 3823 Joe DePastino
☐ 3824 Marc Albarado
☐ 3825 Chris Allison
☐ 3826 John Bowles
☐ 3827 David Gibralter
☐ 3828 Jim Larkin
☐ 3829 Nate Tebbs
☐ 3830 Johnnie Walker
☐ 3831 Raul Baez
☐ 3832 Eric Ford
☐ 3833 Joe Hamilton
☐ 3834 Willie Rivera
☐ 3835 Tony Sheffield
☐ 3836 Dave Holt MG
☐ 3837 Gary Roggenburk CO
☐ 3838 Checklist

1994 Vancouver Canadians Fleer/ProCards

This 26-card standard size set of the 1994 Vancouver Canadians, a Class AAA Pacific Coast League affiliate of the California Angels, features white-bordered posed color player photos on its fronts with the player's name, position, team name and Fleer/ProCards logo across the bottom of each card. The white back with vertical light blue stripes carries the player's name at the top, followed by biography and statistics.

	MINT	NRMT	EXC
COMPLETE SET (26)	7.00	3.10	.85

☐ 1856 Erik Bennett
☐ 1857 Ken Edenfield
☐ 1858 John Farrell
☐ 1859 John Fritz
☐ 1860 David Holdridge
☐ 1861 Mark Holzemer
☐ 1862 Mike James
☐ 1863 Andrew Lorraine
☐ 1864 Troy Percival
☐ 1865 Russ Springer
☐ 1866 Mark Dalesandro
☐ 1867 Jorge Fabregas
☐ 1868 Rod Correia
☐ 1869 P.J. Forbes
☐ 1870 Orlando Munoz
☐ 1871 Ernie Riles
☐ 1872 J.T. Snow
☐ 1873 Garret Anderson
☐ 1874 Steve Hosey
☐ 1875 John Jackson
☐ 1876 Orlando Palmeiro
☐ 1877 Mark Sweeney
☐ 1878 Don Long MG
☐ 1879 Gary Ruby CO
☐ 1880 Lenn Sakata CO
☐ 1881 Checklist

1994 Vermont Expos Classic

This 28-card standard size set of the 1994 Vermont Expos, a Class A New York-Penn League affiliate of the Montreal Expos, features white-bordered posed color player shots on its fronts with the player's name and position, team name and logo and Classic logo appearing across the bottom of each card. On a ghosted team logo, the white back carries the player's name at the top, followed by biography and statistics. This issue includes the minor league card debut of Jason Baker.

	MINT	NRMT	EXC
COMPLETE SET (28)	8.00	3.60	1.00

☐ 1 Carlos Adolfo
☐ 2 Kurt Alderman
☐ 3 Ed Bady
☐ 4 Jason Baker
☐ 5 Jacob Benz
☐ 6 Jose Centeno
☐ 7 Xavier Civit
☐ 8 Jason Cole
☐ 9 Trace Coquillette
☐ 10 Cary Fenton
☐ 11 Brady Frost
☐ 12 Matt Haas
☐ 13 Carl Hall
☐ 14 Russell Handy
☐ 15 Robert Hughes
☐ 16 Mark Lewis
☐ 17 Jason McCommon
☐ 18 Shane McCubbin
☐ 19 Jon Saffer
☐ 20 Jerry Stubbs
☐ 21 Terry Kennedy
☐ 22 Pat Heiderscheit
☐ 23 Lee Slagle
☐ 24 Geoff Blum
☐ 25 Jeff Peer
☐ 29A Vermont Expos Logo
☐ 29B Montreal Expos Logo
☐ 30 Vermont Expos Logo CL

1994 Vermont Expos Fleer/ProCards

This 28-card standard size set of the 1994 Vermont Expos, a Class A New York-Penn League affiliate of the Montreal Expos, features white-bordered posed color player photos on its fronts with the player's name, position, team name and Fleer/ProCards logo across the bottom of each card. The white back with vertical light blue stripes carries the player's name at the top, followed by biography and statistics. This issue includes the minor league card debut of Jason Baker.

	MINT	NRMT	EXC
COMPLETE SET (28)	6.00	2.70	.75

☐ 3898 Jason Baker
☐ 3899 Jacob Benz
☐ 3900 Jose Centeno
☐ 3901 Xavier Civit
☐ 3902 Jason Cole
☐ 3903 Jason Durocher
☐ 3904 Benjamin Fleetham
☐ 3905 Scott Forster
☐ 3906 Brady Frost
☐ 3907 Russell Handy
☐ 3908 Jason McCommon
☐ 3909 Jerald Stubbs
☐ 3910 Michael Thurman
☐ 3911 Kurt Alderman
☐ 3912 Matt Haas
☐ 3913 Shane McCubbin
☐ 3914 Geoffery Blum
☐ 3915 Trace Coquillette
☐ 3916 Cary Fenton
☐ 3917 Mark Lewis
☐ 3918 Jeff Peer
☐ 3919 Carlos Adolfo
☐ 3920 Edward Bady
☐ 3921 Carl Hall
☐ 3922 Jon Saffer
☐ 3923 Terry Kennedy MG
☐ 3924 Pat Heiderscheit CO
☐ 3925 Checklist

1994 Vero Beach Dodgers Classic

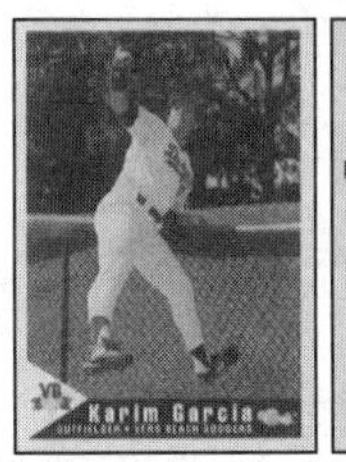

This 30-card standard size set of the 1994 Vero Beach Dodgers, a Class A Florida State League affiliate of the Los Angeles Dodgers, features white-bordered posed color player shots on its fronts with the player's name and position, team name and logo and Classic logo appearing across the bottom of each card. On a ghosted team logo, the white back carries the player's name at the top, followed by biography and statistics. This issue includes the second year cards of Karim Garcia and Wilton Guerrero.

	MINT	NRMT	EXC
COMPLETE SET (30)	35.00	16.00	4.40

☐ 1 Ryan Luzinski
☐ 2 William Adams
☐ 3 Clifford Anderson
☐ 4 Herb Baxter
☐ 5 Brett Binkley
☐ 6 Chris Costello
☐ 7 Karim Garcia
☐ 8 Wilton Guerrero
☐ 9 Matt Herges
☐ 10 Michael Iglesias
☐ 11 Angel Jaime
☐ 12 Doug Newstrom
☐ 13 Willis Otanez
☐ 14 Kevin Pitts
☐ 15 Dennis Reyes
☐ 16 Brian Richardson
☐ 17 Eduardo Rios
☐ 18 Wilfredo Romero
☐ 19 Craig Scheffler
☐ 20 Christopher Sinacori
☐ 21 Frank Smith
☐ 22 Keith Troutman
☐ 23 Eric Weaver
☐ 24 Paul Wittig
☐ 25 Kevin Zahner
☐ 26 Chad Zerbe
☐ 27 Jon Debus MG
☐ 28 Dennis Lewallyn CO
☐ 29 John Shoemaker CO
☐ 30 Robert Giesecke TR
Checklist

1994 Vero Beach Dodgers Fleer/ProCards

This 31-card standard size set of the 1994 Vero Beach Dodgers, a Class A Florida State League affiliate of the Los Angeles Dodgers, features white-bordered posed color player photos on its fronts with the player's name, position, team name and Fleer/ProCards logo across the bottom of each card. The white back with vertical light blue stripes carries the player's name at the top, followed by biography and statistics. This issue includes the second year cards of Karim Garcia and Wilton Guerrero.

	MINT	NRMT	EXC
COMPLETE SET (31)	20.00	9.00	2.50

☐ 61 Herb Baxter
☐ 62 Brett Binkley
☐ 63 Bubba Costello
☐ 64 Jose Garcia
☐ 65 Matt Herges
☐ 66 Mike Iglesias
☐ 67 Jesus Martinez
☐ 68 Hugo Pivaral
☐ 69 Dennis Reyes
☐ 70 Craig Scheffler
☐ 71 Chris Sinacori
☐ 72 Keith Troutman
☐ 73 Eric Weaver
☐ 74 Chad Zerbe
☐ 75 Ryan Luzinski
☐ 76 Paul Wittig
☐ 77 Kevin Zahner
☐ 78 Cliff Anderson
☐ 79 Wilton Guerrero
☐ 80 Doug Newstrom
☐ 81 Willie Otanez
☐ 82 Brian Richardson
☐ 83 Eduardo Rios
☐ 84 Frank Smith
☐ 85 Billy Adams
☐ 86 Karim Garcia
☐ 87 Angel Jaime
☐ 88 Kevin Pitts
☐ 89 Wil Romero
☐ 90 Jon Debus MG
☐ 91 Checklist

1994 Watertown Indians Classic

This 30-card standard size set of the 1994 Watertown Indians, a Class A New York-Penn League affiliate of the Cleveland Indians, features white-bordered posed color player shots on its fronts with the player's name and position, team name and logo and Classic logo appearing across the bottom of each card. On a ghosted team logo, the white back carries the player's name at the top, followed by biography and statistics.

	MINT	NRMT	EXC
COMPLETE SET (30)	8.00	3.60	1.00

☐ 1 Bruce Aven
☐ 2 Todd Betts
☐ 3 James Betzsold
☐ 4 Jonathan Choate
☐ 5 J.J. Done
☐ 6 Scott Donovan
☐ 7 Tony Dougherty
☐ 8 Brian Duva
☐ 9 Patrick Evans
☐ 10 Mark Gapski
☐ 11 Miguel Garcia
☐ 12 Chip Glass
☐ 13 Chris Granata
☐ 14 Ricky Gutierrez
☐ 15 Jeff Haag
☐ 16 Robin Harriss
☐ 17 Heath Hayes
☐ 18 Scott Kramer
☐ 19 Julius Matos
☐ 20 Wilmer Montoya
☐ 21 Noe Najera
☐ 22 Jon Oram
☐ 23 Igor Oropeza
☐ 24 Jeff Sexton
☐ 25 Darren Stumberger
☐ 26 Jay Vaught
☐ 27 Jason Walker
☐ 28 Jeff Datz MG
☐ 29 Tony Arnold CO
☐ 30 Billy Williams CO
Checklist

1994 Watertown Indians Fleer/ProCards

This 30-card standard size set of the 1994 Watertown Indians, a Class A New York-Penn League affiliate of the Cleveland Indians, features white-bordered posed color player photos on its fronts with the player's name, position, team name and Fleer/ProCards logo across the bottom of each card. The white back with vertical light blue stripes carries the player's name at the top, followed by biography and statistics.

	MINT	NRMT	EXC
COMPLETE SET (30)	5.00	2.20	.60

☐ 3926 J.J. Done
☐ 3927 Scot Donovan
☐ 3928 Tony Dougherty
☐ 3929 Mark Gapski
☐ 3930 Chris Granata
☐ 3931 Rick Heiserman
☐ 3932 Scott Karner
☐ 3933 Wilmer Montoya
☐ 3934 Noe Najera
☐ 3935 Igor Oropeza
☐ 3936 Jeff Sexton
☐ 3937 Jay Vaught
☐ 3938 Jason Walker
☐ 3939 Patrick Evans
☐ 3940 Jeff Haag
☐ 3941 Robin Harriss
☐ 3942 Todd Betts
☐ 3943 Ricky Gutierrez
☐ 3944 Heath Hayes
☐ 3945 Julius Matos
☐ 3946 Jon Oram
☐ 3947 Darren Stumberger
☐ 3948 Bruce Aven
☐ 3949 Jim Betzsold
☐ 3950 Jon Choate
☐ 3951 Brian Duva
☐ 3952 Miguel Garcia
☐ 3953 Chip Glass
☐ 3954 Jeff Datz MG
☐ 3955 Checklist

1994 Welland Pirates Classic

This 30-card standard size set of the 1994 Welland Pirates, a Class A New York-Penn League affiliate of the Pittsburgh Pirates, features white-bordered posed color player shots on its fronts with the player's name and position, team name and logo and Classic logo appearing across the bottom of each card. On a ghosted team logo, the white back carries the player's name at the top, followed by biography and statistics.

	MINT	NRMT	EXC
COMPLETE SET (30)	8.00	3.60	1.00

☐ 1 Mark Farris
☐ 2 Matt Amman
☐ 3 Mike Asche
☐ 4 Richie Blackwell
☐ 5 Keith Breitenstein
☐ 6 Greg Chew
☐ 7 Kane Davis
☐ 8 Elcilio de Leon
☐ 9 Aaron France
☐ 10 Ramon Garcia
☐ 11 Jonnie Gendron
☐ 12 Tim Leger
☐ 13 Joseph Maskivish Jr.
☐ 14 Tonka Maynor
☐ 15 Rick Paugh
☐ 16 Brian Pelka
☐ 17 Gil Perez
☐ 18 Kevin Pickford
☐ 19 Felipe Polanco
☐ 20 Shannon Puttmann
☐ 21 Miguel Ojeda
☐ 22 Trevor Skjerpen
☐ 23 Matthew Spade
☐ 24 T.J. Staton
☐ 25 Derek Swafford
☐ 26 Jonathan Sweet
☐ 27 Steven Thobe
☐ 28 Rich Venezia
☐ 29 Jeff Banister MG
☐ 30 Larry Smith CO
Checklist

1994 Welland Pirates Fleer/ProCards

This 31-card standard size set of the 1994 Welland Pirates, a Class A New York-Penn League affiliate of the Pittsburgh Pirates, features white-bordered posed color player photos on its fronts with the player's name, position, team name and Fleer/ProCards logo across the bottom of each card. The white back with vertical light blue stripes carries the player's name at the top, followed by biography and statistics.

	MINT	NRMT	EXC
COMPLETE SET (31)	5.00	2.20	.60

☐ 3483 Richie Blackwell
☐ 3484 Keith Brietenstein
☐ 3485 Greg Chew
☐ 3486 Kane Davis
☐ 3487 Elcilio DeLeon
☐ 3488 Aaron France
☐ 3489 Ramon Garcia
☐ 3490 Jon Gendron
☐ 3491 Joe Maskivish
☐ 3492 Rick Paugh
☐ 3493 Brian Pelka
☐ 3494 Gil Perez
☐ 3495 Kevin Pickford
☐ 3496 Shannon Puttmann
☐ 3497 Trevor Skjerpen
☐ 3498 Matthew Spade
☐ 3499 Miguel Ojeda
☐ 3500 Jonathan Sweet
☐ 3501 Mike Asche
☐ 3502 Mark Farris
☐ 3503 Felipe Polanco
☐ 3504 Steven Thobe
☐ 3505 Derek Swafford
☐ 3506 Richard Venezia
☐ 3507 Matt Amman
☐ 3508 Tim Leger
☐ 3509 Tonka Maynor
☐ 3510 Tarrence Staton
☐ 3511 Jeff Banister MG
☐ 3512 Larry Smith CO
☐ 3513 Checklist

1994 West Michigan Whitecaps Classic

This 30-card standard size set of the 1994 West Michigan Whitecaps, a Class A Midwest League affiliate of the Oakland Athletics, features white-bordered posed color player shots on its fronts with the player's name and position, team name and logo and Classic logo appearing across the bottom of each card. On a ghosted team logo, the white back carries the player's name at the top, followed by biography and statistics.

	MINT	NRMT	EXC
COMPLETE SET (30)	8.00	3.60	1.00

☐ 1 Bob Bennett
☐ 2 Scott Baldwin
☐ 3 Tony Banks
☐ 4 Tim Bojan
☐ 5 Steven Cox
☐ 6 D.T. Cromer
☐ 7 Juan Dilone
☐ 8 Vincente Francisco
☐ 9 Marcel Galligani
☐ 10 Jose Guillen
☐ 11 David Keel
☐ 12 Tim Kubinski
☐ 13 Steve Lemke
☐ 14 Derek Manning
☐ 15 Jason McDonald
☐ 16 Chris Michalak
☐ 17 Mark Moore
☐ 18 Willie Morales
☐ 19 Randy Ortega
☐ 20 Mat Reese
☐ 21 Zack Sawyer
☐ 22 William Urbina
☐ 23 Matt Walsh
☐ 24 Ryan Whitaker
☐ 25 Steve Zongor
☐ 26 Jim Colborn MG
☐ 27 Gil Patterson CO
☐ 28 Crash the River Rascal (Mascot)
☐ 29 Logo Card
☐ 30 Checklist

1994 West Michigan Whitecaps Fleer/ProCards

This 28-card standard size set of the 1994 West Michigan Whitecaps, a Class A Midwest League affiliate of the Oakland Athletics, features white-bordered posed color player photos on its fronts with the player's name, position, team name and Fleer/ProCards logo across the bottom of each card. The white back with vertical light blue stripes carries the player's name at the top, followed by biography and statistics.

	MINT	NRMT	EXC
COMPLETE SET (28)	6.00	2.70	.75

☐ 2287 Scott Baldwin
☐ 2288 Bob Bennett
☐ 2289 Tim Bojan
☐ 2290 Tim Kubinski
☐ 2291 Steve Lemke
☐ 2292 Derek Manning
☐ 2293 Chris Michalak
☐ 2294 Zack Sawyer
☐ 2295 William Urbina
☐ 2296 Matt Walsh
☐ 2297 Ryan Whitaker
☐ 2298 Steve Zongor
☐ 2299 Mark Moore
☐ 2300 Willie Morales
☐ 2301 Randy Ortega
☐ 2302 Steve Cox
☐ 2303 Juan Dilone
☐ 2304 Vicente Francisco
☐ 2305 Jose Guillen
☐ 2306 Jason McDonald
☐ 2307 Tony Banks
☐ 2308 D.T. Cromer
☐ 2309 Marcel Galligani
☐ 2310 David Keel
☐ 2311 Mat Reese
☐ 2312 Jim Colborn MG
☐ 2313 Gil Patterson CO
☐ 2314 Checklist

1994 West Palm Beach Expos Classic

This 30-card standard size set of the 1994 West Palm Beach Expos, a Class A Florida State League affiliate of the Montreal Expos, features white-bordered posed color player shots on its fronts with the player's name and position, team name and logo and Classic logo appearing across the bottom of each card. On a ghosted team logo, the white back carries the player's name at the top, followed by biography and statistics.

	MINT	NRMT	EXC
COMPLETE SET (30)	7.00	3.10	.85

☐ 1 Isreal Alcantara
☐ 2 Matt Allen
☐ 3 Juan Bell
☐ 4 Jolbert Cabrera
☐ 5 Mark Charbonnet
☐ 6 Rick DeHart
☐ 7 David duPlessis
☐ 8 David Eggert
☐ 9 Steve Falteisek
☐ 10 Steve Gill
☐ 11 Antonio Grissom
☐ 12 Rich Haar
☐ 13 Chris Hmielewski
☐ 14 Ramsey Koeyers
☐ 15 Dan Lane
☐ 16 Charles Lee
☐ 17 Domingo Matos
☐ 18 Claudio Ozoria
☐ 19 Javier Pages
☐ 20 Jose Paniagua
☐ 21 Scott Pisciotta
☐ 22 Terry Powers
☐ 23 James Rushworth
☐ 24 Everett Stull
☐ 25 Jose Vidro
☐ 26 Joe Waldron
☐ 27 Neil Weber
☐ 28 Rob Leary MG
☐ 29 Chuck Kniffin CO
☐ 30 Alex Ochoa TR Checklist

1994 West Palm Beach Expos Fleer/ProCards

This 30-card standard size set of the 1994 West Palm Beach Expos, a Class A Florida State League affiliate of the Montreal Expos, features white-bordered posed color player photos on its fronts with the player's name, position, team name and Fleer/ProCards logo across the bottom of each card. The white back with vertical light blue stripes carries the player's name at the top, followed by biography and statistics.

	MINT	NRMT	EXC
COMPLETE SET (30)	5.00	2.20	.60

☐ 31 Rick Dehart
☐ 32 David Eggert
☐ 33 Steve Falteisek
☐ 34 Chris Hmielewski
☐ 35 Jose Paniagua
☐ 36 Scott Pisciotta
☐ 37 Terry Powers
☐ 38 Jim Rushworth
☐ 39 Everett Stull
☐ 40 Joe Waldron
☐ 41 Neil Weber
☐ 42 Matt Allen
☐ 43 Ramsey Koeyers
☐ 44 Javier Pages
☐ 45 Isreal Alcantara
☐ 46 Juan Bell
☐ 47 Jolbert Cabrera
☐ 48 Dave DuPlessis
☐ 49 Rich Haar
☐ 50 Dan Lane
☐ 51 Domingo Matos
☐ 52 Jose Vidro
☐ 53 Mark Charbonnet
☐ 54 Steve Gill
☐ 55 Antonio Grissom
☐ 56 Charles Lee
☐ 57 Claudio Ozoria
☐ 58 Rob Leary MG
☐ 59 Chuck Kniffin CO
☐ 60 Checklist

1994 Wichita Wranglers Fleer/ProCards

This 26 card standard size set of the 1994 Wichita Wranglers, a Class AA Texas League affiliate of the San Diego Padres, features white-bordered posed color player photos on its fronts with the player's name, position, team name and Fleer/ProCards logo across the bottom of each card. The white back with vertical light blue stripes carries the player's name at the top, followed by biography and statistics.

	MINT	NRMT	EXC
COMPLETE SET (26)	5.00	2.20	.60

☐ 182 Robbie Beckett
☐ 183 Nate Cromwell
☐ 184 Glenn Dishman
☐ 185 Jeff Huber
☐ 186 Jose Martinez
☐ 187 Terric McFarlin
☐ 188 Steve Renko
☐ 189 Mike Schooler
☐ 190 Bill Wengert
☐ 191 Ryan Whitman
☐ 192 Pedro Lopez
☐ 193 Jerrey Thurston
☐ 194 Scott Bream
☐ 195 Sean Drinkwater
☐ 196 Paul Gonzalez
☐ 197 Billy Hall
☐ 198 Jason Hardtke
☐ 199 Kevin Maas
☐ 200 Scott Pugh
☐ 201 Brad Gennaro
☐ 202 Vince Moore
☐ 203 Ira Smith
☐ 204 Keith Thomas
☐ 205 Keith Champion MG
☐ 206 Rick Adair CO
☐ 207 Checklist

1994 Williamsport Cubs Classic

This 30-card standard size set of the 1994 Williamsport Cubs, a Class A New York-Penn League affiliate of the Chicago Cubs, features white-bordered posed color player shots on its fronts with the player's name and position, team name and logo and Classic logo appearing across the bottom of each card. On a ghosted team logo, the white back carries the player's name at the top, followed by biography and statistics.

	MINT	NRMT	EXC
COMPLETE SET (30)	7.00	3.10	.85

☐ 1 Jesse Armendariz
☐ 2 Alex Barylak
☐ 3 John Broome
☐ 4 Saul Bustos
☐ 5 Brian Dennis
☐ 6 Larry Edens
☐ 7 Sean Fric
☐ 8 Marty Gazarek
☐ 9 Jeremi Gonzalez
☐ 10 Sean Hogan
☐ 11 Roy Hurst
☐ 12 Tom King
☐ 13 Kevin Krause
☐ 14 Emilio Mendez
☐ 15 Mike Micucci
☐ 16 Joe Montelongo
☐ 17 Chad Olinde
☐ 18 Keith Pelatowski
☐ 19 Rob Rehkopf
☐ 20 Jerry Salzano
☐ 21 Joe Scopio
☐ 22 Brian Stephenson
☐ 23 Terry Vaske
☐ 24 Gabe Whatley
☐ 25 Cortez Wyatt
☐ 26 Jerry Weinstein MG
☐ 27 Butch Hughes CO
☐ 28 Mike Melhuse CO
☐ 29 Jacques Bolton CO
☐ 30 Dan Lovelace TR Checklist

1994 Williamsport Cubs Fleer/ProCards

This 30-card standard size set of the 1994 Williamsport Cubs, a Class A New York-Penn League affiliate of the Chicago Cubs, features white-bordered posed color player photos on its fronts with the player's name, position, team name and Fleer/ProCards logo across the bottom of each card. The white back with vertical light blue stripes carries the player's name at the top, followed by biography and statistics.

	MINT	NRMT	EXC
COMPLETE SET (30)	5.00	2.20	.60

☐ 3753 Jesse Armendariz
☐ 3754 Alex Barylak
☐ 3755 Sean Bogle
☐ 3756 John Broome
☐ 3757 Jeremi Gonzalez
☐ 3758 Jeff Havens
☐ 3759 Sean Hogan
☐ 3760 Kevin Krause
☐ 3761 Joe Montclongo
☐ 3762 Keith Pelatowski
☐ 3763 Rob Rehkopf
☐ 3764 Brian Stephenson
☐ 3765 Dave Weber
☐ 3766 Cortez Wyatt
☐ 3767 Brian Dennis
☐ 3768 Roy Hurst
☐ 3769 Mike Micucci
☐ 3770 Saul Bustos
☐ 3771 Emilio Mendez
☐ 3772 Chad Olinde
☐ 3773 Jerry Salzano
☐ 3774 Terry Vaske
☐ 3775 Gabe Whatley
☐ 3776 Larry Edens
☐ 3777 Sean Fric
☐ 3778 Marty Gazarek
☐ 3779 Tom King
☐ 3780 Joe Scopio
☐ 3781 Jerry Weinstein MG
☐ 3782 Checklist

1994 Wilmington Blue Rocks Classic

This 30-card standard size set of the 1994 Wilmington Blue Rocks, a Class A Carolina League affiliate of the Kansas City Royals, features white-bordered posed color player shots on its fronts with the player's name and position, team name and logo and Classic logo appearing across the bottom of each card. On a ghosted team logo, the white back carries the player's name at the top, followed by biography and statistics. This issue includes a second year card of Johnny Damon.

	MINT	NRMT	EXC
COMPLETE SET (30)	16.00	7.25	2.00

☐ 1 Michael Bovee
☐ 2 Melvin Bunch
☐ 3 Chris Connolly
☐ 4 Johnny Damon
☐ 5 John Dempsey
☐ 6 John Dickens
☐ 7 John Downs
☐ 8 Travis Dunlap
☐ 9 Bart Evans
☐ 10 Raul Gonzalez
☐ 11 Lance Jennings
☐ 12 Ryan Long
☐ 13 Felix Martinez
☐ 14 Ramon Martinez
☐ 15 Cesar Morillo
☐ 16 Steve Murphy
☐ 17 Roderick Myers
☐ 18 Rodney Myers
☐ 19 Dario Perez
☐ 20 Jim Pittsley
☐ 21 Kris Ralston
☐ 22 Jeff Smith
☐ 23 Larry Sutton
☐ 24 Mike Jirschele MG
☐ 25 Gary Lance CO
☐ 26 Sixto Lezcano CO
☐ 27 Rocky Bluewinkle UER (Mascot) (Card back says #29, should be #27)
☐ 28 Logo Card UER (Card back says #29, should be #28)
☐ 29 Logo Card
☐ 30 Checklist

1994 Wilmington Blue Rocks Fleer/ProCards

This 29-card standard size set of the 1994 Wilmington Blue Rocks, a Class A Carolina League affiliate of the Kansas City Royals, features white-bordered posed color player photos on its fronts with the player's name, position, team name and Fleer/ProCards logo across the bottom of each card. The white back with vertical light blue stripes carries the player's name at the top, followed by biography and statistics. This issue includes a second year card of Johnny Damon.

	MINT	NRMT	EXC
COMPLETE SET (29)	10.00	4.50	1.25

☐ 290 Mike Bovee
☐ 291 Mel Bunch
☐ 292 Chris Connolly
☐ 293 John Dickens
☐ 294 John Downs
☐ 295 Travis Dunlap
☐ 296 Bart Evans
☐ 297 Rodney Myers
☐ 298 Dario Perez
☐ 299 Jim Pittsley

- ☐ 300 Kris Ralston
- ☐ 301 Jeff Smith
- ☐ 302 John Dempsey
- ☐ 303 Lance Jennings
- ☐ 304 Andy Stewart
- ☐ 305 Ryan Long
- ☐ 306 Jason Marshall
- ☐ 307 Felix Martinez
- ☐ 308 Ramon Martinez
- ☐ 309 Cesar Morillo
- ☐ 310 Larry Sutton
- ☐ 311 Johnny Damon
- ☐ 312 Raul Gonzalez
- ☐ 313 Steve Murphy
- ☐ 314 Rod Myers
- ☐ 315 Mike Jirschele MG
- ☐ 316 Gary Lance CO
- ☐ 317 Sixto Lescano CO
- ☐ 318 Checklist

1994 Winston-Salem Spirits Classic

This 30-card standard size set of the 1994 Winston-Salem Spirits, a Class A Carolina League affiliate of the Cincinnati Reds, features white-bordered posed color player shots on its fronts with the player's name and position, team name and logo and Classic logo appearing across the bottom of each card. On a ghosted team logo, the white back carries the player's name at the top, followed by biography and statistics.

	MINT	NRMT	EXC
COMPLETE SET (30)	7.00	3.10	.85

- ☐ 1 Micah Franklin
- ☐ 2 Jason Angel
- ☐ 3 Amador Arias
- ☐ 4 Paul Bako
- ☐ 5 Johnny Bess
- ☐ 6 John Brothers
- ☐ 7 William Brunson
- ☐ 8 Chad Fox
- ☐ 9 Dan Frye
- ☐ 10 Mike Harrison
- ☐ 11 Dee Jenkins
- ☐ 12 Dan Kopriva
- ☐ 13 Jason Kummerfeldt
- ☐ 14 Marty Lister
- ☐ 15 Ricky Magdaleno
- ☐ 16 Matt Martin
- ☐ 17 Mike Meggers
- ☐ 18 James Nix
- ☐ 19 Rene Quinones
- ☐ 20 Toby Rumfield
- ☐ 21 Mark Tranbarger
- ☐ 22 Dave Tuttle
- ☐ 23 Brad Tweedlie
- ☐ 24 Chris Vasquez
- ☐ 25 Pat Watkins
- ☐ 26 Mark Berry MG
- ☐ 27 Derek Botelho CO
- ☐ 28 Tom Spencer TR
- ☐ 29 Logo Card
- ☐ 30 Checklist

1994 Winston-Salem Spirits Fleer/ProCards

This 28-card standard size set of the 1994 Winston-Salem Spirits, a Class A Carolina League affiliate of the Cincinnati Reds, features white-bordered posed color player photos on its fronts with the player's name, position, team name and Fleer/ProCards logo across the bottom of each card. The white back with vertical light blue stripes carries the player's name at the top, followed by biography and statistics.

	MINT	NRMT	EXC
COMPLETE SET (28)	6.00	2.70	.75

- ☐ 262 Jason Angel
- ☐ 263 John Brothers
- ☐ 264 Will Brunson
- ☐ 265 Chad Fox
- ☐ 266 Jason Kummerfeldt
- ☐ 267 Marty Lister
- ☐ 268 Jim Nix
- ☐ 269 Rene Quinones
- ☐ 270 Mark Tranbarger
- ☐ 271 Dave Tuttle
- ☐ 272 Brad Tweedlie
- ☐ 273 Paul Bako
- ☐ 274 Johnny Bess
- ☐ 275 Mike Harrison
- ☐ 276 Amador Arias
- ☐ 277 Dan Frye
- ☐ 278 Dee Jenkins
- ☐ 279 Dan Kopriva
- ☐ 280 Ricky Magdaleno
- ☐ 281 Matt Martin
- ☐ 282 Toby Rumfield
- ☐ 283 Micah Franklin
- ☐ 284 Mike Meggers
- ☐ 285 Chris Vasquez
- ☐ 286 Pat Watkins
- ☐ 287 Mark Berry MG
- ☐ 288 Derek Botelho CO
- ☐ 289 Checklist

1994 Yakima Bears Classic

This 30-card standard size set of the 1994 Yakima Bears, a Class A Northwest League affiliate of the Los Angeles Dodgers, features white-bordered posed color player shots on its fronts with the player's name and position, team name and logo and Classic logo appearing across the bottom of each card. On a ghosted team logo, the white back carries the player's name at the top, followed by biography and statistics. This issue includes the minor league card debut of Paul Konerko.

	MINT	NRMT	EXC
COMPLETE SET (30)	35.00	16.00	4.40

- ☐ 1 Jerry Berteotti
- ☐ 2 Jim Breuer
- ☐ 3 Jason Butcher
- ☐ 4 John Challinor
- ☐ 5 Kevin Faircloth
- ☐ 6 Ron Hollis
- ☐ 7 Jake Kenady
- ☐ 8 Paul Konerko
- ☐ 9 Chris Latham
- ☐ 10 Charlie Nelson
- ☐ 11 Jeff Paluk
- ☐ 12 David Post
- ☐ 13 Josh Rash
- ☐ 14 Jason Reed
- ☐ 15 Dan Ricabal
- ☐ 16 Brian Richardson
- ☐ 17 Brian Rolocut
- ☐ 18 Bob Scafa
- ☐ 19 Bob Schaaf
- ☐ 20 Craig Scheffler
- ☐ 21 Chip Sell
- ☐ 22 Ken Sikes
- ☐ 23 David Spykstra
- ☐ 24 David Steed
- ☐ 25 Eric Stuckenschneider
- ☐ 26 Greg Thompson
- ☐ 27 David Valdes
- ☐ 28 John Vukson
- ☐ 29 Kevin Zellers
- ☐ 30 Joe Vavra MG Checklist

1994 Yakima Bears Fleer/ProCards

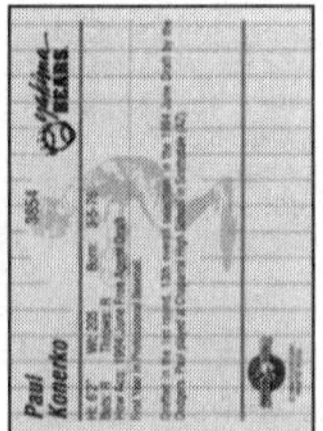

This 30-card standard size set of the 1994 Yakima Bears, a Class A Northwest League affiliate of the Los Angeles Dodgers, features white-bordered posed color player photos on its fronts with the player's name, position, team name and Fleer/ProCards logo across the bottom of each card. The white back with vertical light blue stripes carries the player's name at the top, followed by biography and statistics. This issue includes the minor league card debut of Paul Konerko.

	MINT	NRMT	EXC
COMPLETE SET (30)	20.00	9.00	2.50

- ☐ 3541 Checklist
- ☐ 3839 Jason Butcher
- ☐ 3840 John Challinor
- ☐ 3841 Ron Hollis
- ☐ 3842 Jake Kenady
- ☐ 3843 Jeff Paluk
- ☐ 3844 Jason Reed
- ☐ 3845 Dan Ricabal
- ☐ 3846 Petie Roach
- ☐ 3847 Brian Rolocut
- ☐ 3848 Craig Scheffler
- ☐ 3849 Ken Sikes
- ☐ 3850 Dave Spykstra
- ☐ 3851 Greg Thompson
- ☐ 3852 John Vukson
- ☐ 3853 Jerry Berteotti
- ☐ 3854 Paul Konerko
- ☐ 3855 Dave Steed
- ☐ 3856 Kevin Faircloth
- ☐ 3857 Mike Hernandez
- ☐ 3858 Dave Post
- ☐ 3859 Brian Richardson
- ☐ 3860 Bob Schaaf
- ☐ 3861 Kevin Zellers
- ☐ 3862 Chris Latham
- ☐ 3863 Charlie Nelson
- ☐ 3864 Josh Rash
- ☐ 3865 Chip Sell
- ☐ 3866 Eric Stuckenschneider
- ☐ 3867 Joe Vavra MG

1995 Action Packed

The 1995 Action Packed Scouting Report set consists of standard-size cards featuring top AAA, AA, and A prospects picked by Action Packed's scouts. 24K gold versions of selected cards were randomly inserted in the foil packs as chase cards. The 12-card Franchise Gems subset feature a heat sensitive graphic that reveals Action Packed's prediction of the player's impact year. Hobby foil packs were randomly seeded with autographed 24K Gold and Diamond version Franchise Gem cards of minor league Player of the Year Derek Jeter. Hot packs, which contained six 24K Gold cards, were seeded one per 480 packs. Topical subsets featured include No. 1 Draft Picks (52-61) and Franchise Gems (62-79). Each card in the second subset was highlighted with gold foil accents in every groove and die cut. Also each card features a scouting report of each player's strengths and weaknesses.

	MINT	NRMT	EXC
COMPLETE SET (83)	20.00	9.00	2.50
COMMON CARD (1-83)	.10	.05	.01
☐ 1 Derek Jeter POY	1.50	.70	.19
☐ 2 Trot Nixon	.20	.09	.03
☐ 3 Charles Johnson	.40	.18	.05
☐ 4 Chan Ho Park	.60	.25	.07
☐ 5 Terrell Wade	.20	.09	.03
☐ 6 Carlos Delgado	.40	.18	.05
☐ 7 Brian L. Hunter	.10	.05	.01
☐ 8 Tony Clark	1.00	.45	.12
☐ 9 Russ Davis	.10	.05	.01
☐ 10 Derek Jeter	1.50	.70	.19
☐ 11 Alex Gonzalez	.10	.05	.01
☐ 12 Scott Ruffcorn	.10	.05	.01
☐ 13 Todd Hollandsworth	.20	.09	.03
☐ 14 Phil Nevin	.10	.05	.01
☐ 15 Marc Newfield	.10	.05	.01
☐ 16 Jose Silva	.10	.05	.01
☐ 17 Willie Greene	.10	.05	.01
☐ 18 Billy Ashley	.10	.05	.01
☐ 19 James Baldwin	.10	.05	.01
☐ 20 Jeff Granger	.10	.05	.01
☐ 21 Michael Tucker	.20	.09	.03
☐ 22 Johnny Damon	.50	.23	.06
☐ 23 Roger Cedeno	.10	.05	.01
☐ 24 Mac Suzuki	.10	.05	.01
☐ 25 Curtis Goodwin	.10	.05	.01
☐ 26 Frank Rodriguez	.10	.05	.01
☐ 27 Roberto Mejia	.10	.05	.01
☐ 28 LaTroy Hawkins	.10	.05	.01
☐ 29 Alex Ochoa	.20	.09	.03
☐ 30 Jose Oliva	.10	.05	.01
☐ 31 Ruben Rivera	2.00	.90	.25
☐ 32 Ray Durham	.40	.18	.05
☐ 33 Eduardo Perez	.10	.05	.01
☐ 34 Jose Malave	.10	.05	.01
☐ 35 Jeromy Burnitz	.10	.05	.01
☐ 36 Brad Woodall	.10	.05	.01
☐ 37 Joe Vitiello	.10	.05	.01
☐ 38 Daron Kirkreit	.10	.05	.01
☐ 39 Jimmy Haynes	.10	.05	.01
☐ 40 Andrew Lorraine	.10	.05	.01
☐ 41 Arquimedez Pozo	.10	.05	.01
☐ 42 Armando Benitez	.10	.05	.01
☐ 43 Alan Benes	.50	.23	.06
☐ 44 Julian Tavarez	.10	.05	.01
☐ 45 Curtis Pride	.10	.05	.01
☐ 46 Homer Bush	.10	.05	.01
☐ 47 Calvin Reese	.10	.05	.01
☐ 48 Billy Wagner	.10	.05	.01
☐ 49 Richard Hidalgo	.50	.23	.06
☐ 50 Allen Battle	.10	.05	.01
☐ 51 Kevin Millar	.10	.05	.01
☐ 52 Paul Wilson FDP	.50	.23	.06
☐ 53 Ben Grieve FDP	2.50	1.10	.30
☐ 54 Dustin Hermanson FDP	.10	.05	.01
☐ 55 Antone Williamson FDP	.60	.25	.07
☐ 56 Josh Booty FDP	.40	.18	.05
☐ 57 Doug Million FDP	.25	.11	.03
☐ 58 Jaret Wright FDP	.50	.23	.06
☐ 59 Todd Walker FDP	3.00	1.35	.35
☐ 60 Nomar Garciaparra FDP	2.50	1.10	.30
☐ 61 C.J. Nitkowski FDP	.10	.05	.01
☐ 62 Charles Johnson FG	.40	.18	.05
☐ 63 Marc Newfield FG	.10	.05	.01
☐ 64 Ray Durham FG	.40	.18	.05
☐ 65 Carlos Delgado FG	.40	.18	.05
☐ 66 Alex Gonzalez FG	.10	.05	.01
☐ 67 Derek Jeter FG	1.50	.70	.19
☐ 68 Jose Oliva FG	.10	.05	.01
☐ 69 Billy Ashley FG	.10	.05	.01
☐ 70 Brian L. Hunter FG	.10	.05	.01
☐ 71 Ruben Rivera FG	2.00	.90	.25
☐ 72 Alan Benes FG	.50	.23	.06
☐ 73 Willie Greene FG	.10	.05	.01
☐ 74 Russ Davis FG	.10	.05	.01
☐ 75 Jose Malave FG	.10	.05	.01
☐ 76 LaTroy Hawkins FG	.10	.05	.01
☐ 77 Frank Rodriguez FG	.10	.05	.01
☐ 78 Scott Ruffcorn FG	.10	.05	.01
☐ 79 Ben Grieve FG	2.50	1.10	.30
☐ 80 Max Patkin With Glove	.25	.11	.03
☐ 81 Max Patkin Grinning	.25	.11	.03
☐ 82 Max Patkin Tounge Sticking Out	.25	.11	.03
☐ 83 Checklist	.10	.05	.01

1995 Action Packed 24K Gold

	MINT	NRMT	EXC
COMPLETE SET (18)	275.00	125.00	34.00
COMMON CARD (1G-18G)	10.00	4.50	1.25
☐ 1G Charles Johnson	25.00	11.00	3.10
☐ 2G Marc Newfield	15.00	6.75	1.85
☐ 3G Ray Durham	20.00	9.00	2.50
☐ 4G Carlos Delgado	20.00	9.00	2.50
☐ 5G Alex Gonzalez	15.00	6.75	1.85
☐ 6G Derek Jeter	60.00	27.00	7.50
☐ 7G Jose Oliva	10.00	4.50	1.25
☐ 8G Billy Ashley	10.00	4.50	1.25
☐ 9G Brian L. Hunter	18.00	8.00	2.20
☐ 10G Ruben Rivera	40.00	18.00	5.00
☐ 11G Alan Benes	25.00	11.00	3.10
☐ 12G Willie Greene	10.00	4.50	1.25
☐ 13G Russ Davis	10.00	4.50	1.25
☐ 14G Jose Malave	10.00	4.50	1.25
☐ 15G LaTroy Hawkins	10.00	4.50	1.25
☐ 16G Frank Rodriguez	15.00	6.75	1.85
☐ 17G Scott Ruffcorn	10.00	4.50	1.25
☐ 18G Ben Grieve	50.00	22.00	6.25
☐ AU1 Derek Jeter 1G	125.00	55.00	15.50
☐ AU2 Derek Jeter 1D	350.00	160.00	45.00

1995 Arizona Fall League SplitSecond

This 22-card set of the Arizona Fall League honors some of the all-stars of the League's 1995 season. These cards were manufactured and distributed by Jessen Associates, Inc. The fronts feature color action player photos with clouds over a mountain top as the bottom border. The backs carry player biographical information and career statistics. The cards are unnumbered and checklisted below in alphabetical order. This issue features the first year cards of Todd Walker and Darin Erstad.

	MINT	NRMT	EXC
COMPLETE SET (22)	25.00	11.00	3.10

- ☐ 1 David Bell
- ☐ 2 Alan Benes
- ☐ 3 Doug Brady
- ☐ 4 Darin Erstad
- ☐ 5 Shawn Estes
- ☐ 6 Chad Fonville
- ☐ 7 Ed Giovanola
- ☐ 8 Todd Greene
- ☐ 9 LaTroy Hawkins
- ☐ 10 Dustin Hermanson
- ☐ 11 Chan Ho Park
- ☐ 12 Jason Kendall
- ☐ 13 Derrek Lee
- ☐ 14 Quinton McCracken
- ☐ 15 Jon Nunnally
- ☐ 16 Pokey Reese
- ☐ 17 Mac Suzuki
- ☐ 18 Michael Tucker
- ☐ 19 Jason Varitek
- ☐ 20 Todd Walker
- ☐ NNO Back Card
- ☐ NNO Cover Card

1995 Arkansas Travelers Team Issue

This 30-card set was produced by Multi-Ad Services and sponsored by Sonic Drive-Ins and features borderless color player photos of the 1995 Arkansas Travelers, a Class AA Texas League affiliate of the St. Louis Cardinals. The backs carry player biographical information and career statistics. The cards are unnumbered and checklisted below in alphabetical order. 500 sets were produced.

	MINT	NRMT	EXC
COMPLETE SET (29)	18.00	8.00	2.20

☐ 1 Charlie Anderson
☐ 2 Paul Anderson
☐ 3 Matt Arrandale
☐ 4 Mike Badorek
☐ 5 Jeff Berblinger
☐ 6 Mike Busby
☐ 7 Dan Cholowsky
☐ 8 Doug Creek
☐ 9 Ray Davis
☐ 10 Mike Defelice
☐ 11 Pete Fagan TR
☐ 12 Paul Ellis
☐ 13 Ty Griffin
☐ 14 Mike Gulan
☐ 15 Keith Johns
☐ 16 Greg Jones
Also Known as Keith
☐ 17 Anthony Lewis
☐ 18 Tony Long
☐ 19 Sean Lowe
☐ 20 Marty Mason CO
☐ 21 Steve Montgomery
☐ 22 Dave Oehrlein
☐ 23 Mike Ramsey MGR
☐ 24 Jeff Shireman CO
☐ 25 Scott Simmons
☐ 26 Jose Velez
☐ 27 Ron Warner
☐ 28 Dmitri Young
☐ NNO Ray Winder Field
☐ NNO Sponsor Card

1995 Asheville Tourists Team Issue

This 30-card set of the 1995 Asheville Tourists, a Class A South Atlantic League affiliate of the Colorado Rockies, features color player photos with a white border and thin gold inner border. The backs carry player information and career statistics. The cards are unnumbered and checklisted below according to the player's jersey number. This issue features the minor league card debuts of Arnold Gooch and Mike Kusiewicz and a second year card of Derrick Gibson.

	MINT	NRMT	EXC
COMPLETE SET (30)	15.00	6.75	1.85

☐ 2 Elvis Pena
☐ 3 Danny Figueroa
☐ 5 Link Jarrett
☐ 7 Art Waldrep
☐ 9 Chan Mayber
☐ 10 Mike Kusiewicz
☐ 11 Joe Marchese CO
☐ 12 Johnny Gonzales
☐ 14 Kyle Houser
☐ 15 Arnold Gooch
☐ 17 Mark Brownson
☐ 18 Rogelio Arias
☐ 19 Luis Colmenares
☐ 21 Morgan Burdick
☐ 22 Luther Hackman
☐ 23 Pedro Carranza
☐ 24 Chad Gambill
☐ 25 Ronnie Hall
☐ 26 Ken Grundt
☐ 29 John Fantauzzi
☐ 30 Jason Smith
☐ 31 Brent Crowther
☐ 32 Bill McGuire
☐ 33 Yohel Pozo
☐ 34 Derrick Gibson
☐ 36 Jack Lamabe CO
☐ NNO R.J. Martino
☐ NNO Bill Slosson TR
☐ NNO Ron McKee GM
☐ NNO Terry Cole

1995 Asheville Tourists Update Team Issue

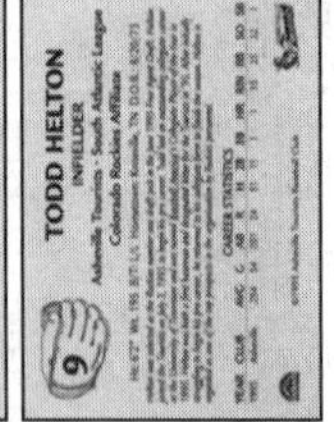

This 15-card set is an update of the 30-card 1995 Asheville Tourists team set, A Class A South Atlantic League affiliate of the Colorado Rockies, features the same format and design as the original set. The cards are unnumbered and checklisted below according to the player's jersey number. This issue features the minor league card debut of Todd Helton.

	MINT	NRMT	EXC
COMPLETE SET (15)	25.00	11.00	3.10

☐ 7 Mike Vavrek
☐ 8 Brian Rose
☐ 9 Todd Helton
☐ 13 Chris Henderson
☐ 16 Bill Eden
☐ 18 Fred Ocasio
☐ 20 Mike Zolecki
☐ 21 Pat McClinton
☐ 26 Tal Light
☐ 27 John Meskauskas
☐ 28 John Slamka
☐ 30 Mark Wells
☐ 31 Keith Barnes
☐ 34 Derrick Gibson
☐ NNO Team Photo

1995 Auburn Astros Team Issue

This 30-card set of the Auburn Astros, a Class A New York-Penn League affiliate of the Houston Astros, was sponsored by Multi-Ad Services Inc. and features borderless posed color player photos on the fronts. The backs carry player information. 750 sets were produced.

	MINT	NRMT	EXC
COMPLETE SET (30)	14.00	6.25	1.75

☐ 1 Shawn Smith GM
☐ 2 Ron Buzzell
☐ 3 Derek Root
☐ 4 Scott Tribolet
☐ 5 Andy Bovender
☐ 6 Don Scolaro
☐ 7 Josh Halemanu
☐ 8 Julio Lugo
☐ 9 Jose Barron TR
☐ 10 Wes Pratt
☐ 11 Mike Brunner
☐ 12 Oscar Robles
☐ 13 Chad Alexander
☐ 14 Brian Sikorski
☐ 15 Eric Smith
☐ 16 Jim Rosenbohm
☐ 17 Troy Schulte
☐ 18 Mike Corominas
☐ 19 Jon Phillips
☐ 20 Jason Green
☐ 21 Gregg Smyth
☐ 22 Eric Stachler
☐ 23 Brian Tickell
☐ 24 Steve Fuller
☐ 25 Jason Adams
☐ 26 Don Alexander CO
☐ 27 Hassan Robinson
☐ 28 Manny Acta MG
☐ 29 Mark Harrington AGM
☐ 30 Ramon Castro
Randy Albaladejo

1995 Bakersfield Blaze Team Issue

This 32-card set of the 1995 Bakersfield Blaze, a Class A California League Independent, features color player photos in a blue outer border with a thin white inner border. The backs carry player information and statistics. 8,000 sets were produced and each checklist is sequentially numbered. This issue includes the minor league card debut of Hideo Nomo.

	MINT	NRMT	EXC
COMPLETE SET (32)	18.00	8.00	2.20

☐ 1 Lonny Stare
☐ 2 Rod McCall
☐ 3 Alex Ramirez
☐ 4 Hideo Nomo
☐ 5 Cesar Morillo
☐ 6 Jeremy Carr
☐ 7 Rick Prieto
☐ 8 Ervan Wingate
☐ 9 Paul Wittig
☐ 10 Kevin Zahner
☐ 11 Nathan Bland
☐ 12 Brad Eaddy
☐ 13 Wayne Edwards
☐ 14 Mike Iglesias
☐ 15 Kevin Zellers
☐ 16 Jake Kenady
☐ 17 Rich Linares
☐ 18 Kendrick Mitchell
☐ 19 Bob Scafa
☐ 20 Craig Scheffler
☐ 21 Charles York
☐ 22 Bruce Yard
☐ 23 Rob Thomas
☐ 24 Elias Tapia
☐ 25 Jamie Jaye
☐ 26 Steve Soliz
☐ 27 Buck McNabb
☐ 28 Paul Meade
☐ 29 Hideo Nomo
☐ 30 John Moncier CO
☐ 31 Greg Mahlberg MG
☐ 32 Team Photo CL

1995 Batavia Clippers Team Issue

This 33-card set of the Batavia Clippers, a Class A New York-Penn League of the Philadelphia Phillies, was produced by Multi-Ad Services Inc. and features color player posed photos with a two-sided white triangular border. The backs display player information and career statistics. The cards are unnumbered and checklisted below in alphabetical order. This issue includes the minor league card debuts of Marlon Anderson and Steve Carver. 1,500 sets were produced.

	MINT	NRMT	EXC
COMPLETE SET (33)	9.00	4.00	1.10

☐ 1 Marlon Anderson
☐ 2 Adrian Antonini
☐ 3 Marty Barnett
☐ 4 Domingo Brito
☐ 5 Steve Carver
☐ 6 Chang Yang Choi
☐ 7 Jon Cornelius
☐ 8 Chuck Cox
☐ 9 Todd Crane
☐ 10 Walter Dawkins
☐ 11 Alberto Fana
☐ 12 Brian Ford
☐ 13 Rob Gaiko
☐ 14 Chris Gambs
☐ 15 Todd Genke
☐ 16 Paul Hamilton
☐ 17 Kyle Karvala
☐ 18 Kyle Kawabata
☐ 19 Tyson Kimm
☐ 20 Jeff Leaman
☐ 21 Clint McClurg
☐ 22 Jaime Mendes
☐ 23 Brian Mensink
☐ 24 Courtney Mitchell
☐ 25 Torrey Pettiford
☐ 26 Kirk Pierce
☐ 27 Mark Raynor
☐ 28 David Robinson
☐ 29 Jake Russell
☐ 30 Anthony Shumaker
☐ 31 Justin Smith
☐ 32 Chris Snusz
☐ 33 Gary Yeager Jr.

1995 Bellingham Giants Team Issue

This 36-card set of the 1995 Bellingham Giants, A Class A Northwest League affiliate of the San Francisco Giants, features posed color player photos by Greenleaf Photography with a black, white, and orange border. The backs carry player information. The cards are unnumbered and checklisted below according to the player's jersey number as listed on the card back. This issue includes the minor league card debuts of Joe Fontenot, Darin Blood, Russ Ortiz and Jason Brester.

	MINT	NRMT	EXC
COMPLETE SET (36)	18.00	8.00	2.20

☐ 2 Teo Prospero
☐ 3 Pedro Felix
☐ 6 Jonathan Watson
☐ 7 Deivi Cruz
☐ 8 Bruce Thompson
☐ 9 Alex Morales
☐ 10 Rey Corujo
☐ 11 Joseph Nathan
☐ 12 Joe Fontenot
☐ 13 Juan Lopez CO
☐ 14 Lorenzo Barcelo
☐ 15 Luis Rodriguez
☐ 16 Darin Blood
☐ 20 Russell Ortiz
☐ 21 Yolvit Torrealba
☐ 23 Marc Mosman
☐ 24 Ian Rand
☐ 25 Andy Norton
☐ 26 Jason Brester
☐ 27 Jim Stoops
☐ 28 Dan Topping
☐ 29 Brian Knoll
☐ 30 Mike Schiefelbein
☐ 31 Terry Weaver
☐ 33 Alberto Castillo
☐ 34 Elias Sosa CO
☐ 35 Kurt Takahashi
☐ 36 James Woodrow
☐ 37 Joe Blasingim
☐ 39 Manuel Bermudez
☐ 40 Benjamin Tucker
☐ 41 Phillip Bailey
☐ 44 Ricardo Calderon
☐ 48 Glenn Tufts MGR
☐ NNO Jerry Walker
Bill Tucker
☐ NNO Benjamin Potenziano TR

1995 Beloit Snappers Team Issue

This 31-card set of the 1995 Beloit Snappers, a Class A Midwest League affiliate of the Milwaukee Brewers, features borderless color action player photos on the fronts. The backs carry player information and career statistics. This issue includes the minor league card debut of Ron Belliard. 1,000 sets were produced.

	MINT	NRMT	EXC
COMPLETE SET (31)	9.00	4.00	1.10

☐ 1 Josh Tyler
☐ 2 Steve Woodard
☐ 3 John Smith
☐ 4 Yfrain Linares
☐ 5 Brian Dalton
☐ 6 Josh Zwisler
☐ 7 Gabby Mercado
☐ 8 Drew Williams
☐ 9 Jeff D'Amico
☐ 10 Greg Beck
☐ 11 Ruben Felix
☐ 12 Derek Hacopian
☐ 13 Cah Kopitzke
☐ 14 Chris Burt
☐ 15 Brian Tollberg
☐ 16 Gregory Mullins
☐ 17 Scott Krause
☐ 18 Juan Gonzalez
☐ 19 Junior Betances
☐ 20 Dan Klassen
☐ 21 Toby Kominek
☐ 22 Scott Nate
☐ 23 Scott Huntsman
☐ 24 Alex Andreopoulos
☐ 25 Ronnie Belliard
☐ 26 David Montiel
☐ 27 Jeff Paxson TR
☐ 28 Jon Pont CO
☐ 29 Dub Kilgo MG
☐ 30 Mike Caldwell
Jim Colborn
☐ 31 Team Photo CL

1995 Best

This 135-card set was issued in two parts; the first part (1-100) featured the Top 100 Prospects with the second part featuring the Top Draft Picks (101-135) from the 1995 Draft. The first series of cards was available in both hobby and retail packs while the final 34 cards were only available in retail packs. The cards feature color player photo shots with a white border. The player's name and position appear across the bottom of the card. The back carry a color photo along with player information.

	MINT	NRMT	EXC
COMPLETE SET (135)	30.00	13.50	3.70
COMPLETE SET (101)	20.00	9.00	2.50
COMMON CARD (1-135)	.05	.02	.01
☐ 1 Rocky Coppinger	.40	.18	.05
☐ 2 Rafael Orellano	.05	.02	.01
☐ 3 Nomar Garciaparra	2.00	.90	.25
☐ 4 Ryan McGuire	.05	.02	.01
☐ 5 Pork Chop Pough	.05	.02	.01
☐ 6 Trot Nixon	.05	.02	.01
☐ 7 Donnie Sadler	.60	.25	.07
☐ 8 Chris Allison	.05	.02	.01
☐ 9 Todd Greene	.30	.14	.04
☐ 10 George Arias	.40	.18	.05
☐ 11 Matt Beaumont	.20	.09	.03
☐ 12 Jeff Abbott	.20	.09	.03
☐ 13 Tom Fordham	.05	.02	.01
☐ 14 Damian Jackson	.05	.02	.01
☐ 15 Richie Sexson	1.00	.45	.12
☐ 16 Bartolo Colon	.60	.25	.07
☐ 17 David Roberts	.05	.02	.01
☐ 18 Daryle Ward	.20	.09	.03
☐ 19 Brandon Reed	.05	.02	.01
☐ 20 Juan Encarnacion	.25	.11	.03
☐ 21 Eddy Gaillard	.05	.02	.01
☐ 22 Derek Hacopian	.05	.02	.01
☐ 23 Glendon Rusch	.40	.18	.05
☐ 24 Lino Diaz	.05	.02	.01
☐ 25 Tim Byrdak	.05	.02	.01
☐ 26 Antone Williamson	.40	.18	.05
☐ 27 Jonas Hamlin	.05	.02	.01
☐ 28 Todd Walker	3.00	1.35	.35
☐ 29 Dan Serafini	.05	.02	.01
☐ 30 Kim Bartee	.05	.02	.01
☐ 31 Shane Bowers	.05	.02	.01
☐ 32 Tyrone Horne	.05	.02	.01
☐ 33 Nick DelVecchio	.05	.02	.01
☐ 34 Mike Figga	.05	.02	.01

☐ 35 Matt Drews	.05	.02	.01
☐ 36 Ray Ricken	.05	.02	.01
☐ 37 Ben Grieve	2.00	.90	.25
☐ 38 Steve Cox	.40	.18	.05
☐ 39 Scott Spiezio	.15	.07	.02
☐ 40 Desi Relaford	.05	.02	.01
☐ 41 Matt Wagner	.05	.02	.01
☐ 42 James Bonnici	.05	.02	.01
☐ 43 Osvaldo Fernandez	.05	.02	.01
☐ 44 Marino Santana	.05	.02	.01
☐ 45 Julio Santana	.05	.02	.01
☐ 46 Jeff Davis	.05	.02	.01
☐ 47 Trey Beamon	.20	.09	.03
☐ 48 Jose Pett	.05	.02	.01
☐ 49 Chris Carpenter	.30	.14	.04
☐ 50 Andruw Jones	8.00	3.60	1.00
☐ 51 Damon Hollins	.05	.02	.01
☐ 52 Jermaine Dye	2.00	.90	.25
☐ 53 Aldo Pecorilli	.15	.07	.02
☐ 54 Corey Paige	.05	.02	.01
☐ 55 Damian Moss	1.00	.45	.12
☐ 56 Ron Wright	2.00	.90	.25
☐ 57 Brooks Kieschnick	.20	.09	.03
☐ 58 Pedro Valdes	.05	.02	.01
☐ 59 Scott Samuels	.05	.02	.01
☐ 60 Bobby Morris	.05	.02	.01
☐ 61 Amaury Telemaco	.05	.02	.01
☐ 62 Steve Gibralter	.05	.02	.01
☐ 63 Calvin Reese	.05	.02	.01
☐ 64 Pat Watkins	.15	.07	.02
☐ 65 Aaron Boone	.50	.23	.06
☐ 66 Jamey Wright	.15	.07	.02
☐ 67 Derrick Gibson	2.00	.90	.25
☐ 68 Brent Crowther	.05	.02	.01
☐ 69 Ralph Millard	.05	.02	.01
☐ 70 Edgar Renteria	.30	.14	.04
☐ 71 Billy McMillon	.05	.02	.01
☐ 72 Clemente Nunez	.05	.02	.01
☐ 73 Bob Abreu	.30	.14	.04
☐ 74 Eric Ludwick	.05	.02	.01
☐ 75 Tony Mounce	.05	.02	.01
☐ 76 Chris Latham	.05	.02	.01
☐ 77 Wilton Guerrero	.60	.25	.07
☐ 78 Adam Riggs	.05	.02	.01
☐ 79 Paul Konerko	2.50	1.10	.30
☐ 80 Vladimir Guerrero	5.00	2.20	.60
☐ 81 Brad Fullmer	.30	.14	.04
☐ 82 Hiram Bocachica	.25	.11	.03
☐ 83 Paul Wilson	.50	.23	.06
☐ 84 Jay Payton	1.50	.70	.19
☐ 85 Rey Ordonez	.25	.11	.03
☐ 86 Wendell Magee	.05	.02	.01
☐ 87 Wayne Gomes	.05	.02	.01
☐ 88 Carlton Loewer	.05	.02	.01
☐ 89 Scott Rolen	3.00	1.35	.35
☐ 90 Rich Hunter	.05	.02	.01
☐ 91 Jason Kendall	.05	.02	.01
☐ 92 Micah Franklin	.05	.02	.01
☐ 93 Elmer Dessens	.05	.02	.01
☐ 94 Matt Ruebel	.05	.02	.01
☐ 95 Mike Gulan	.05	.02	.01
☐ 96 Jay Witasick	.05	.02	.01
☐ 97 Bret Wagner	.05	.02	.01
☐ 98 Greg LaRocca	.05	.02	.01
☐ 99 Jason Thompson	.05	.02	.01
☐ 100 Derrek Lee	.75	.35	.09
☐ 101 Jason Kendall BB	.15	.07	.02
☐ 102 Derrek Lee BB	.40	.18	.05
☐ 103 Todd Walker BB	2.00	.90	.25
☐ 104 Edgar Renteria BB	.15	.07	.02
☐ 105 Scott Rolen BB	2.00	.90	.25
☐ 106 Andruw Jones BB	5.00	2.20	.60
☐ 107 Jay Payton BB	1.00	.45	.12
☐ 108 Derrick Gibson BB	1.25	.55	.16
☐ 109 Paul Wilson BB	.30	.14	.04
☐ 110 Brandon Reed BB	.05	.02	.01
☐ 111 Ben Davis	1.00	.45	.12
☐ 112 Chad Hermansen	1.25	.55	.16
☐ 113 Corey Jenkins	.40	.18	.05
☐ 114 Geoff Jenkins	.75	.35	.09
☐ 115 Ryan Jaroncyk	.05	.02	.01
☐ 116 Andy Yount	.20	.09	.03
☐ 117 Reggie Taylor	.60	.25	.07
☐ 118 Joe Fontenot	.25	.11	.03
☐ 119 Mike Drumright	.20	.09	.03
☐ 120 David Yocum	.05	.02	.01
☐ 121 Jonathan Johnson	.20	.09	.03
☐ 122 Jaime Jones	1.00	.45	.12
☐ 123 Tony McKnight	.05	.02	.01
☐ 124 Michael Barrett	.20	.09	.03
☐ 125 Roy Halladay	.50	.23	.06
☐ 126 Todd Helton	2.50	1.10	.30
☐ 127 Juan LeBron	.40	.18	.05
☐ 128 Darin Erstad	4.00	1.80	.50
☐ 129 Jose Cruz Jr.	4.00	1.80	.50
☐ 130 Kerry Wood	.60	.25	.07
☐ 131 Shea Morenz	.05	.02	.01
☐ 132 Mark Redman	.05	.02	.01
☐ 133 Matt Morris	.40	.18	.05
☐ AU1 Todd Greene	8.00	3.60	1.00
☐ AU2 Andruw Jones	60.00	27.00	7.50
☐ AU3 Jay Payton	20.00	9.00	2.50
☐ AU4 Paul Wilson	12.00	5.50	1.50
☐ NNO Checklist (1-100)	.05	.02	.01
☐ NNO Checklist (101-133)	.05	.02	.01

1995 Best Franchise

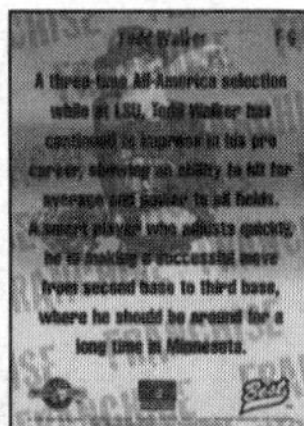

Inserted at an average of one per four boxes. The first six-cards were available only in retail packs with the remaining six available only in hobby packs.

	MINT	NRMT	EXC
COMPLETE SET (12)	250.00	110.00	31.00
COMMON CARD (1-12)	10.00	4.50	1.25
☐ F1 Darin Erstad	50.00	22.00	6.25
☐ F2 Nomar Garciaparra	30.00	13.50	3.70
☐ F3 Rocky Coppinger	12.00	5.50	1.50
☐ F4 Matt Drews	10.00	4.50	1.25
☐ F5 Ben Grieve	30.00	13.50	3.70
☐ F6 Todd Walker	40.00	18.00	5.00
☐ F7 Edgar Renteria	25.00	11.00	3.10
☐ F8 Derrick Gibson	30.00	13.50	3.70
☐ F9 Andruw Jones	90.00	40.00	11.00
☐ F10 Derrek Lee	25.00	11.00	3.10
☐ F11 Jason Kendall	15.00	6.75	1.85
☐ F12 Paul Wilson	12.00	5.50	1.50

1995 Billings Mustangs Team Issue

This 29-card set of the 1995 Billings Mustangs, a Rookie Class Pioneer League affiliate of the Cincinnati Reds, was sponsored by First Interstate Bank and features borderless black-and-white player photos by Dennis R. Clark. The backs carry player information.

	MINT	NRMT	EXC
COMPLETE SET (29)	40.00	18.00	5.00

☐ 1 Andy Burress
☐ 2 Justin Atchley
☐ 3 Jason LaRue
☐ 4 Andre Montgomery
☐ 5 Rick Lapka
☐ 6 Christian Rojas
☐ 7 Jay Sorg
☐ 8 Ben Bailey
☐ 9 Herbert Goodman
☐ 10 Todd Fehrenbach
☐ 11 Adam Bryant
☐ 12 Scott Wright
☐ 13 Brian Wilson
☐ 14 Jason Parsons
☐ 15 John Riedling
☐ 16 Damon Callahan
☐ 17 Steve Goodhart
☐ 18 Tom Scott
☐ 19 Steve Claybrook
☐ 20 Eddy Garcia
☐ 21 Raymond King
☐ 22 Doyle Preston
☐ 23 Scott MacRae
☐ 24 Marc Weiss
☐ 25 Justin Marine
☐ 26 Richard Lawrence
☐ 27 Donnie Scott
☐ 28 Steve Oliverio
☐ 29 Matt Martin

1995 Binghamton Mets Team Issue

This 28-card set of the 1995 Binghamton Mets, a Class AA Eastern League affiliate of the New York Mets, features color player photos in a wide blue border with red and thin white inner borders. The backs carry player information and career statistics. The cards are unnumbered and checklisted below according to the player's jersey number. 2,500 sets were produced.

	MINT	NRMT	EXC
COMPLETE SET (28)	12.00	5.50	1.50

☐ 8 Brian Daubach
☐ 10 Tony Tijerina
☐ 11 John Mahalik
☐ 15 Kevin Morgan
☐ 16 Robert Person
☐ 17 Jim McCready
☐ 20 Jason Hardtke
☐ 21 Charlie Greene
☐ 22 Jay Davis
☐ 23 Don White
☐ 24 Jay Payton
☐ 25 Joe Delli Carri CO
☐ 27 Jeff Barry
☐ 28 Ed Fully
☐ 29 Mark Fuller
☐ 31 Hector Ramirez
☐ 32 John Tamargo MGR
☐ 34 Brent Knackert
☐ 35 Chris Saunders
☐ 38 Eric Ludwick
☐ 39 Bill Latham CO
☐ 40 Paul Wilson
☐ 43 Joe Crawford
☐ 44 Jason Isringhausen
☐ 46 Tom Engle
☐ 47 Frank Jacobs
☐ NNO Ballwinkle(Mascot)
☐ NNO Buddy the Bee(Mascot)

1995 Boise Hawks Team Issue

This 35-card set of the 1995 Boise Hawks, a Class A Northwest League affiliate of the California Angels, features color player photos in a marblized blue border. The backs carry player information and career statistics. The cards are unnumbered and checklisted below alphabetically. This issue inlcudes the minor league card debut of Jarrod Washburn. 1,000 sets were produced.

	MINT	NRMT	EXC
COMPLETE SET (35)	14.00	6.25	1.75

☐ 1 Daniel Alzualde
☐ 2 Edwin Avila
☐ 3 Justin Baughman
☐ 4 Jim Bennett CO
☐ 5 Randy Betten
☐ 6 Tyler Bilderback
☐ 7 Danny Buxbaum
☐ 8 Leonardo Bryan
☐ 9 Ray Choi
☐ 10 Todd Claus CO
☐ 11 Keith Coe
☐ 12 Chad Crossley
☐ 13 Kekoa Dafun
☐ 14 Jed Dalton
☐ 15 Josh Deakman
☐ 16 Trent Durrington
☐ 17 David Farfan
☐ 18 Bryan Graves
☐ 19 Kevin Ham
☐ 20 Ryan Kane
☐ 21 Tom Kotchman MGR
☐ 22 Aaron Mayer
☐ 23 John McAninch
☐ 24 Alfonso Mota
☐ 25 James O'Quinn
☐ 26 Brian Scutero
☐ 27 Kevin Sumter
☐ 28 Travis Thurmond
☐ 29 Ken Valdez
☐ 30 Gar Vallone
☐ 31 Jon Vandergriend
☐ 32 Grant Vermillion
☐ 33 Kyle Wagner
☐ 34 Jarrod Washburn
☐ 35 Team Photo CL

1995 Bowie Baysox Team Issue

This 31-card set of the 1995 Bowie Baysox, a Class AA Eastern League affiliate of the Baltimore Orioles, was produced by Choice Marketing, Inc. and features posed borderless color player photos by Ben Koeber and Greg L'Heureux. The backs carry player information and career statistics. The cards are unnumbered and checklisted below according to the player's jersey number. 4,000 sets were produced.

	MINT	NRMT	EXC
COMPLETE SET (31)	10.00	4.50	1.25

☐ 1 George Virgilio
☐ 4 Jarvis Brown
☐ 9 Jim Wawruck
☐ 10 Bob Miscik MGR
☐ 12 Joe Borowski
☐ 13 Kim Batiste
☐ 14 Jose Millares
☐ 18 Kimera Bartee
☐ 19 Aaron Lane
☐ 22 Matt Howard
☐ 23 Gregg Castaldo
☐ 24 Sean Hugo
☐ 25 Chris Lein
☐ 26 Billy Owens
☐ 27 Hector Castaneda
☐ 28 Jim Dedrick
☐ 29 Jeff Faino
☐ 31 Tom Wegmann
☐ 32 Scott Conner
☐ 34 Jim Newlin
☐ 35 Greg Knowles
☐ 36 Garrett Stephenson
☐ 37 Matt Jarvis
☐ 39 Jason Friedman
☐ 40 Kevin Ryan
☐ 41 B.J. Waszgis
☐ 43 Rick Forney
☐ 44 T.R. Lewis
☐ 45 Rocky Coppinger
☐ 47 Craig Faulkner CO
☐ NNO Mitch Bibb TR

1995 Brevard County Manatees Fleer/ProCards

This 30-card set of the 1995 Brevard County Manatees, a Class A Florida State League affiliate of the Florida Marlins, was produced by the Fleer Corp and features posed color player photos in a white border on the card fronts. The backs carry player information and career statistics.

	MINT	NRMT	EXC
COMPLETE SET (30)	9.00	4.00	1.10

☐ 236 Mark Andersen
☐ 237 Mitch Bowen
☐ 238 Todd Carl
☐ 239 Dan Ehler
☐ 240 Felix Heredia
☐ 241 Adrian Hollinger
☐ 242 Bill Hurst
☐ 243 Mike Lewis
☐ 244 Clemente Nunez
☐ 245 Rob Stanifer
☐ 246 Paul Thornton
☐ 247 Mike Whitten
☐ 248 Brendan Kingman
☐ 249 Andrew Prater
☐ 250 Mike Sims
☐ 251 Brady Babin
☐ 252 Gavin Baugh
☐ 253 Dave Berg
☐ 254 Lionel Hastings
☐ 255 Kevin Millar
☐ 256 Scott Southard
☐ 257 Ron Brown
☐ 258 Willie Brown
☐ 259 Glenn Reeves
☐ 260 Daniel Robinson
☐ 261 Fredi Gonzalez MG
☐ 262 Britt Burns CO
☐ 263 Jose Castro CO
☐ 264 Vinny Scavo TR
☐ 265 Ken Lehner GM

1995 Burlington Bees Team Issue

This 36-card set of the 1995 Burlington Bees, a Class A Midwest League affiliate of the San Francisco Giants, features color action player photos on the fronts. The backs carry a small black-and-white player head photo with player information and career statistics. This issue includes the only minor league card ever issued of Paul Molitor. 2,000 sets were produced.

	MINT	NRMT	EXC
COMPLETE SET (36)	15.00	6.75	1.85

☐ 1 Wilson Delgado
☐ 2 Don Denbow
☐ 3 Darrin Glenn
☐ 4 Mark Gulseth
☐ 5 Santos Hernandez
☐ 6 Jesse Ibarra
☐ 7 Jeff Keith
☐ 8 Kevin Lake
☐ 9 Cory Lintern
☐ 10 Raul Marval
☐ 11 Tony Mattos
☐ 12 Leonard McMillan
☐ 13 Mike McMullen
☐ 14 Jason Myers
☐ 15 Jeff Poor
☐ 16 Pete Prater
☐ 17 Bobby Rector
☐ 18 Chris Ratliff
☐ 19 Derek Reid
☐ 20 Dan Schneider
☐ 21 Paul Molitor
☐ 22 Ryan Richeal GM
☐ 23 Jose Abreu
☐ 24 Heath Altman
☐ 25 Aaron Charlton
☐ 26 Pablo Cordero
☐ 27 Eric Dantzler
☐ 28 Brook Smith
☐ 29 Scott Swift
☐ 30 Brian Wallace
☐ 31 Kevin Watson
☐ 32 Mike Hart MGR
☐ 33 Keith Comstock CO
☐ 34 Mickey Brantley CO
☐ 35 Sy Katcher TR
☐ NNO Title Card CL

1995 Butte Copper Kings Team Issue

This 32-card set of the 1995 Butte Copper Kings, a Rookie Class Pioneer League Independent, features posed color photos of the players each sitting beside his locker with his name and jersey number printed on the locker shelf. A facsimile autograph is printed in a red bar down the left. The backs carry player information. 2,000 sets were produced.

	MINT	NRMT	EXC
COMPLETE SET (32)	7.00	3.10	.85

☐ 1 Cover Card
☐ 2 Juan Abreu
☐ 3 Courtney Arrollado
☐ 4 Brian Benner
☐ 5 Welnis Bonilla
☐ 6 Scott Johnson
☐ 7 Chad Dillon
☐ 8 Jamie Fernandes
☐ 9 Jason Grote
☐ 10 Brook Holding
☐ 11 Matt Jones
☐ 12 Rene Justiniano
☐ 13 Phil Kernan
☐ 14 Andre LeVias
☐ 15 J.T. Messick
☐ 16 Roy Padilla
☐ 17 Nelson Perez
☐ 18 Cliff Shanks
☐ 19 Tony Shapiro
☐ 20 Devin Underwood
☐ 21 Rusty Zumwalt
☐ 22 Billy Gardner
☐ 23 George Threadgill
☐ 24 Steve Lienhard
☐ 25 Chris Tomashoff
☐ 26 Notorris Bray
☐ 27 Steve Waites
☐ 28 Craig DeSensi
☐ 29 Brian Giallella
☐ 30 Andy Barkett
☐ 31 Team Photo
☐ 32 Alumni Coliseum CL

1995 Carolina Mudcats Fleer/ProCards

This 30-card set of the1995 Carolina Mudcats, a Class AA Southern League affiliate of the Pittsburgh Pirates, was produced by the Fleer Corp. and feature posed color player photos in a white border on the card fronts. The backs carry player information and career statistics.

	MINT	NRMT	EXC
COMPLETE SET (30)	7.00	3.10	.85

☐ 148 Elmer Dessens
☐ 149 Sean Evans
☐ 150 Milt Hill
☐ 151 Dennis Konuszewski
☐ 152 Steve Parris
☐ 153 Marc Pisciotta
☐ 154 Matt Ruebel
☐ 155 Matt Ryan
☐ 156 Kevin Rychel
☐ 157 Brian Shouse
☐ 158 Marc Wilkins
☐ 159 Tim Edge
☐ 160 Marcus Hanel
☐ 161 Jason Kendall
☐ 162 Tony Beasley
☐ 163 Mike Brown
☐ 164 George Canale
☐ 165 Jay Cranford
☐ 166 Jim Krevokuch
☐ 167 Omer Munoz
☐ 168 Kevin Polcovich
☐ 169 Jermaine Allensworth
☐ 170 Jake Austin
☐ 171 Ramon Espinosa
☐ 172 Jon Farrell
☐ 173 Trent Jewett MG
☐ 174 Dave Rajsich CO
☐ 175 Don Werner CO
☐ 176 Sandy Krum TR
☐ 177 Title Card CL

1995 Cedar Rapids Kernels Team Issue

This 32-card set of the 1995 Cedar Rapids Kernels, a Class A Midwest League affiliate of the California Angels, was sponsored by McDonald's and features borderless color action player photos by Jim Tevis. The backs carry player information and statistics. The cards are unnumbered and checklisted below according to the player's jersey number printed on the card back. This issue inlcudes the minor league card debut of Jason Dickson.

	MINT	NRMT	EXC
COMPLETE SET (32)	12.00	5.50	1.50

☐ 4 David Davalillo
☐ 9 Shawn Slade
☐ 10 Jose Cintron
☐ 11 Juan Henderson
☐ 12 Jose Aguirre
☐ 13 Paul Failla
☐ 14 Jason Herrick
☐ 15 Lance Robbins
☐ 16 Aaron Iatarola
☐ 17 Kevin Young
☐ 19 Jason Hill
☐ 20 Derek Ryder
☐ 21 Geoff Grenert
☐ 23 Michael Freehill
☐ 24 Demond Smith
☐ 25 John Donati
☐ 26 Anito Encarnacion
☐ 27 Ben Molina
☐ 28 Dave Sick
☐ 29 Jason Dickson
☐ 30 Nate Olmstead
☐ 31 Bret Hemphill
☐ 32 DeShawn Warren
☐ 33 John Bushart
☐ 35 Jeffery Knox
☐ 36 Greg Morris
☐ 37 Travis Thurmond
☐ 38 Nick Skuse
☐ 39 Dan Petroff
☐ NNO Mr. Shucks(Mascot)
☐ NNO Field Staff
☐ NNO Batboys CL

1995 Charleston Riverdogs Team Issue

This 30-card set of the 1995 Charleston Riverdogs, a Class A South Atlantic League affiliate of the Texas Rangers, was produced by Multi-Ad Services Inc. and sponsored by Kinko's, Charleston Classic Rock and Roll Radio Station 98ROCK. The fronts feature borderless color player photos with the player's name and team's name in team colored bars at the bottom. The backs carry player information and career statistics. This issue includes the minor league card debut of Fernando Tatis. 2,000 sets were produced.

	MINT	NRMT	EXC
COMPLETE SET (30)	9.00	4.00	1.10

☐ 1 Reid Ryan
☐ 2 Scott Stewart
☐ 3 Matt Pauls
☐ 4 Rodney Cook
☐ 5 Lonnie Goldberg
☐ 6 Stephen Larkin
☐ 7 Joe Perez
☐ 8 Fernando Tatis
☐ 9 Jamie Escamilla
☐ 10 Chris Gogolewski
☐ 11 Toure' Knighton
☐ 12 Gardner O'Flynn
☐ 13 Ryan Rutz
☐ 14 Kevin Millican
☐ 15 Dan Vasquez
☐ 16 Brad Heller
☐ 17 Jeff Runion
☐ 18 David Chavarria
☐ 19 Nelson Perpetuo
☐ 20 Dan Hower
☐ 21 Juan Veras
☐ 22 Roberto Santa
☐ 23 Dom Gatti
☐ 24 Jim Cooney
☐ 25 Eddie Comeaux
☐ 26 Virgilio Luciano
☐ 27 Shawn Shugars
☐ 28 Brad Arnsberg CO
☐ 29 Mike Berger MG
☐ 30 Charlie the RiverDog (Mascot)

1995 Charleston Riverdogs Update Team Issue

This 9-card set is an update of the 30-card 1995 Charleston Riverdogs team set and features the same format and design as the original set with a continuation of the card numbers. 1,000 sets were produced.

	MINT	NRMT	EXC
COMPLETE SET (9)	8.00	3.60	1.00

☐ 31 Donald Morillo
☐ 32 Ted Silva
☐ 33 Rob Kell
☐ 34 Cory Pearson
☐ 35 Donald Morillo
☐ 36 Fernando Tatis
Ryan Rutz
☐ 37 Brandon Knight
☐ 38 Tim Cossins
☐ 39 Team Photo CL

1995 Charlotte Knights Team Issue

This 30-card set of the 1995 Charlotte Knights, a Class AAA International League affiliate of the Florida Marlins, was produced by Coastal Forms and Data Products and features color player photos with a white outside border and team colored inner borders. The backs carry player career statistics. 5,000 sets were produced.

	MINT	NRMT	EXC
COMPLETE SET (30)	13.00	5.75	1.60

☐ 1 Sal Rende MGR
☐ 2 Smokey Garrett CO
☐ 3 Mike Parrott CO
☐ 4 Mike Leon TR
☐ 5 Joel Adamson
☐ 6 Miguel Batista
☐ 7 Nick Capra
☐ 8 Jeff Carter
☐ 9 Brian Drahman
☐ 10 Curt Ford
☐ 11 Kiki Hernandez
☐ 12 Terry Jorgensen
☐ 13 Steve Long
☐ 14 John Massarelli
☐ 15 Kurt Miller
☐ 16 Joe Millette
☐ 17 Russ Morman
☐ 18 Jeff Mutis
☐ 19 Mike Myers
☐ 20 Bob Natal
☐ 21 Erik Pappas
☐ 22 Rich Scheid
☐ 23 Jerry Schunk
☐ 24 Stan Spencer
☐ 25 Jerry Spradlin
☐ 26 Jesus Tavarez
☐ 27 Marc Valdes
☐ 28 Mike Zimmerman
☐ 29 Eddie Zosky
☐ 30 Cover Card CL

1995 Chattanooga Lookouts Team Issue

This 31-card set of the 1995 Chattanooga Lookouts, a Class AA Southern League affiliate of the Cincinnati Reds, features posed color player photos with empty stadium seats as the background and a black border. The backs carry player information and career statistics.

	MINT	NRMT	EXC
COMPLETE SET (31)	10.00	4.50	1.25

☐ 1 Amador Arias
☐ 2 Adam Brown
☐ 3 John Burgos
☐ 4 Jamie Dismuke
☐ 5 Mike Ferry
☐ 6 Chad Fox
☐ 7 Adam Hyzdu
☐ 8 Rusty Kilgo
☐ 9 Brian Koelling
☐ 10 Dan Kopriva
☐ 11 Tommy Kramer
☐ 12 Cleveland Ladell
☐ 13 Larry Luebbers
☐ 14 Mark Merchant
☐ 15 Chad Mottola
☐ 16 James Nix
☐ 17 Ricky Pickett
☐ 18 Dan Rohrmeier
☐ 19 Toby Rumfield
☐ 20 Ruben Santana
☐ 21 Rick Sellers
☐ 22 Mark Tranbarger
☐ 23 David Tuttle
☐ 24 Marcos Vasquez
☐ 25 Pat Watkins
☐ 26 Terry Abbott
☐ 27 Jim Knudtson TR
☐ 28 Dave Miley MGR
☐ 29 Larry Ward
☐ 30 Rocky Raccoon(Mascot)
☐ 31 Title Card CL

1995 Clearwater Phillies Fleer/ProCards

This 30-card set of the 1995 Clearwater Phillies, a Class A Florida State League affiliate of the Philadelphia Phillies, was produced by the Fleer Corp. and features posed and action color player photos in a white border on the card fronts. The backs carry player information and career statistics. This issue includes the minor league card debut of Carlton Loewer.

	MINT	NRMT	EXC
COMPLETE SET (30)	7.00	3.10	.85

☐ 207 Peter Agostinelli
☐ 208 Matt Beech
☐ 209 Tony Costa
☐ 210 Robert Dodd
☐ 211 Tony Fiore
☐ 212 Bronson Heflin
☐ 213 Gary Herrmann
☐ 214 Carlton Loewer
☐ 215 Nelson Metheney
☐ 216 Ryan Nye
☐ 217 John Vandemark
☐ 218 Robert Estalella
☐ 219 Jeff Gyselman
☐ 220 Manuel Amador
☐ 221 Luis Brito
☐ 222 Jose Flores
☐ 223 Santy Gallone
☐ 224 Dan Held
☐ 225 Jon McMullen
☐ 226 David Waco
☐ 227 Brian Costello
☐ 228 Stan Evans
☐ 229 Wendell Magee
☐ 230 Scott Shores
☐ 231 Don McCormack MC
☐ 232 Darold Knowles CO
☐ 233 Greg Legg CO
☐ 234 Clete Sigwart TR
☐ 235 Cover Card CL
☐ NNO Logo Card

1995 Columbus Clippers Milk Caps Team Issue

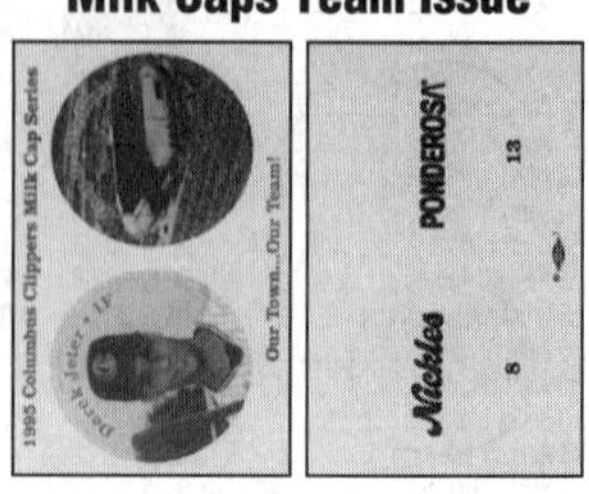

This 12-card set featuring 24 Milk Caps of 1995 Columbus Clippers. One card was given out to children 12 and under at each Monday home game during the1995 season. The set includes milk caps of Derek Jeter and Andy Pettitte. 2,750 sets were produced.

	MINT	NRMT	EXC
COMPLETE SET (12)	40.00	18.00	5.00

☐ 1 Bill Evers MGR
☐ 2 Jorge Posada
☐ 3 Rafael Quirico
☐ 4 Tim Rumer
☐ 5 Rich Hines
☐ 6 Jose Musset
☐ 7 Mark Carper
☐ 8 Copper Stadium
☐ 10 Kirt Ojala
☐ 11 Yankees Logo
☐ 12 Andy Pettitte
☐ 13 Derek Jeter
☐ 14 Mark Hutton
☐ 15 Russ Davis
☐ 16 Tony Perezchica
☐ 17 Clippers Logo
☐ 18 Andy Cook
☐ 19 Billy Masse
☐ 20 Lyle Mouton
☐ 21 Jalal Leach
☐ 23 Bubba Carpenter
☐ 24 Don Sparks

1995 Columbus Clippers Police

This 32-card set of the 1995 Columbus Clippers, a Class AAA International League affiliate of the New York Yankees, was sponsored by the Columbus Police Department and features color player photos in a blue border. The backs carry player statistics and various messages from area elementary school students about the dangers of using drugs. The cards are unnumbered and checklisted below in alphabetical order. 1,500 sets were produced.

	MINT	NRMT	EXC
COMPLETE SET (32)	15.00	6.75	1.85

☐ 1 Joe Ausanio
☐ 2 Brian Boehringer
☐ 3 Bubba Carpenter
☐ 4 Mark Carper
☐ 5 Andy Cook
☐ 6 Matt Dunbar
☐ 7 Robert Eenhoorn
☐ 8 Dave Eiland
☐ 9 Bill Evers MG
☐ 10 Andy Fox
☐ 11 Ron Frazier
☐ 12 Lew Hill
☐ 13 Mark Hutton
☐ 14 Derek Jeter
☐ 15 Jalal Leach
☐ 16 Jeff Livesey
☐ 17 Kevin Maas
☐ 18 Billy Masse
☐ 19 Kirt Ojala
☐ 20 Jeff Patterson
☐ 21 Dave Pavlas
☐ 22 Tony Perezchica
☐ 23 Andy Pettitte
☐ 24 Jorge Posada
☐ 25 Rafael Quirico
☐ 26 Ruben Rivera
☐ 27 Tim Rumer
☐ 28 Don Sparks
☐ 29 Darryl Strawberry
☐ 30 Paul Thoutsis
☐ 31 Kent Wallace
☐ NNO Coaching Staff

1995 Columbus Clippers Team Issue

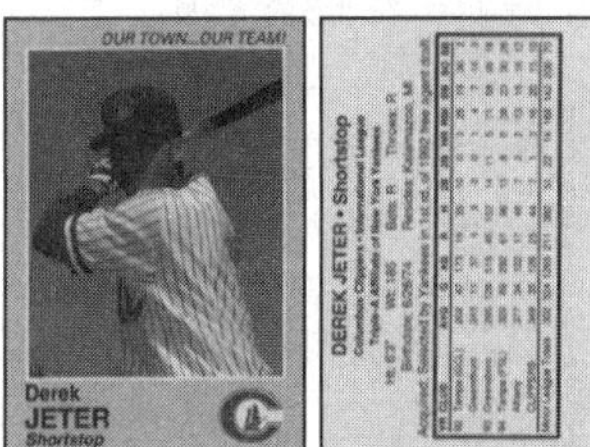

This 32-card set of the 1995 Columbus Clippers, a Class AAA International League affiliate of the New York Yankees, features color player photos in a gray border. The backs carry player information and career statistics. The cards are unnumbered and checklisted below alphabetically. 2,500 sets were produced.

	MINT	NRMT	EXC
COMPLETE SET (32)	15.00	6.75	1.85

□ 1 Joe Ausanio
□ 2 Brian Boehringer
□ 3 Bubba Carpenter
□ 4 Mark Carper
□ 5 Andy Cook
□ 6 Matt Dunbar
□ 7 Robert Eenhoorn
□ 8 Dave Eiland
□ 9 Bill Evers MG
□ 10 Andy Fox
□ 11 Ron Frazier
□ 12 Lew Hill
□ 13 Mark Hutton
□ 14 Derek Jeter
□ 15 Jalal Leach
□ 16 Jeff Livesey
□ 17 Kevin Maas
□ 18 Billy Masse
□ 19 Kirt Ojala
□ 20 Jeff Patterson
□ 21 Dave Pavlas
□ 22 Tony Perezchica
□ 23 Andy Pettitte
□ 24 Jorge Posada
□ 25 Rafael Quirico
□ 26 Ruben Rivera
□ 27 Tim Rumer
□ 28 Don Sparks
□ 29 Darryl Strawberry
□ 30 Paul Thoutsis
□ 31 Kent Wallace
□ NNO Coaching Staff

1995 Danville Braves Team Issue

This 30-card set of the Danville Braves, a Rookie Class Appalachian League affiliate of the Atlanta Braves, was issued in six strips of six perforated cards each and was distributed by McDonald's restaurants. Each strip features five player cards with a sixth card being a "buy one get one free" coupon for a Big Mac Sandwich redeemable at a specific McDonald's. The fronts feature color player photos with player information and statistics on the backs. The cards are unnumbered and checklisted below in alpabetical order. This issue includes the minor league card debuts of Bruce Chen, Jimmy Osting and Jayson Bass. Only 1,000 sets were produced.

	MINT	NRMT	EXC
COMPLETE SET (30)	25.00	11.00	3.10

□ 1 Winston Abreu
□ 2 Toby Anglen
□ 3 Jason Bass
□ 4 Bruce Chen
□ 5 Andrew Cochran
□ 6 Kenneth Collins
□ 7 Adam Cross
□ 8 Robert Duncan
□ 9 Keith Daugherty
□ 10 Angel Espada
□ 11 James Franklin
□ 12 Joe Giuliano
□ 13 Chris Gobert
□ 14 Sam Knowland
□ 15 P.K. Koehler
□ 16 Kevin Lowe
□ 17 Ryan Martin
□ 18 Raymond McWhite
□ 19 Adam Mullen
□ 20 Jimmy Osting
□ 21 Eric Pickett
□ 22 Corey Pointer
□ 23 Kenneth Raines
□ 24 Walker Reynolds Jr.
□ 25 Robert Sasser
□ 26 Curt Schnur
□ 27 Ben Utting
□ 28 Max Venable
□ 29 James Wise
□ 30 Will Wise

1995 David Lipscomb Bisons

The cards are unnumbered and checklisted below in alphabetical order.

	MINT	NRMT	EXC
COMPLETE SET (25)	10.00	4.50	1.25

□ 1 J.D. Blackburn
□ 2 John Boatman
□ 3 Josh Bostic
□ 4 Randy Bostic P/ACO
□ 5 Mark Cardin
□ 6 David Cloud
□ 7 Brian Cromwell
□ 8 Ken Dugan CO
□ 9 Kurt Dugan
□ 10 Chad Estep P/CO
□ 11 Richie Estep
□ 12 Brad Frasier
□ 13 Chris Gainer
□ 14 Hunter Henson
□ 15 Kolin Holladay ACO
□ 16 Tim Lewis
□ 17 Seth Massey
□ 18 Roy Pardue CO
□ 19 V.H. Pickle
□ 20 Corey Redding
□ 21 Bryan Skelton
□ 22 Adam Sullivan
□ 23 Jeremy Townes
□ 24 Michael Wells
□ 25 David Wray

1995 Dunedin Blue Jays Team Issue

This 30-card set of the 1995 Dunedin Blue Jays, a Class A Florida State League affiliate of the Toronto Blue Jays, features color player portraits in a white border. The player's name and position are printed in white in a bottom black bar. The backs carry player information, career statistics, and sponsor logos. The cards are unnumbered and checklisted below in alphabetical order.

	MINT	NRMT	EXC
COMPLETE SET (30)	100.00	45.00	12.50

□ 1 Tim Adkins
□ 2 Dennis Brogna TR
□ 3 Ben Candelaria
□ 4 Chris Carpenter
□ 5 Brandon Cromer
□ 6 Vic Davila
□ 7 Tom Evans
□ 8 Mike Halperin
□ 9 D.J. Harris
□ 10 Ryan Jones
□ 11 Levon Largusa
□ 12 Marc Loeb
□ 13 Mark Lukasiewicz
□ 14 Trevor Mallory
□ 15 Adam Melhuse
□ 16 Jim Nettles MG
□ 17 Jeff Patzke
□ 18 Rolando Pino CO
□ 19 John Poloni CO
□ 20 Juan Querecuto
□ 21 Angel Ramirez
□ 22 Mike Romano
□ 23 Omar Sanchez
□ 24 Chris Sinacori
□ 25 Steve Sinclair
□ 26 Keilan Smith
□ 27 Fausto Solano
□ 28 Joshua Spring
□ 29 Rob Steinert
□ 30 Mike Toney

1995 Durham Bulls Team Issue

This 42-card set of the 1995 Durham Bulls, a Class A Carolina League affiliate of the Atlanta Braves, was sponsored by Crystal Springs and the Herald-Sun Newpapers. The fronts feature color player photos in a thin maroon, gold, or brown frame with the player's name and position printed in white in the wide maroon, gold, or brown margin at the top. The backs carry player information and career statistics. The cards are unnumbered and checklisted below in alphabetical order. This issue includes the minor league card debut of John LeRoy. 2,000 set were produced.

	MINT	NRMT	EXC
COMPLETE SET (42)	10.00	4.50	1.25

□ 1 Jamie Arnold
□ 2 Lou Benbow
□ 3 Brett Binkley
□ 4 Jeff Bock
□ 5 Micah Bowie
□ 6 Kurt Burgess
□ 7 Matt Byrd
□ 8 Maurice Christmas
□ 9 Miguel Correa
□ 10 Jason Green
□ 11 Tommy Harrison
□ 12 Jamie Hicks
□ 13 Ryan Jacobs
□ 14 Evan Jackson BB
□ 15 Manny Jimenez
□ 16 Andre King
□ 17 John Knott
□ 18 John LeRoy
□ 19 Danny Magee
□ 20 Del Mathews
□ 21 Gator McBride
□ 22 Wonderful Monds
□ 23 Raymond Nunez
□ 24 Scott Pagano
□ 25 Carey Paige
□ 26 Ken Raines
□ 27 Randall Simon
□ 28 Bill Slack CO
□ 29 Sean Smith
□ 30 Brian Snitker CO
□ 31 David Toth
□ 32 Ken Warner
□ 33 Colby Weaver
□ 34 Kevin Webb
□ 35 Matt West MG
□ 36 Mike Wieser
□ 37 Jay Williams TR
□ 38 Willie Wilson BB
□ NNO Checklist
□ NNO Durham Bulls Stadium
□ NNO Wool E. Bull(Mascot)
□ NNO Cover Card

1995 Edmonton Trappers Team Issue

This 30-card set of the 1995 Edmonton Trappers, a Class AAA Pacific Coast League affiliate of the Oakland Athletics, was produced by Macri Photographic Design and features borderless color player portraits with the player's name and position printed in a white bar at the bottom. The backs carry player information and career statistics. The cards are unnumbered and checklisted below in alphabetical order.

	MINT	NRMT	EXC
COMPLETE SET (30)	13.00	5.75	1.60

□ 1 Scott Baker
□ 2 Jim Bowie
□ 3 Russ Brock
□ 4 Scott Bryant
□ 5 Fausto Cruz
□ 6 Paul Faries
□ 7 Orv Franchuk CO
□ 8 Jason Giambi
□ 9 Heath Haynes
□ 10 Walt Horn
□ 11 Miguel Jimenez
□ 12 Doug Johns
□ 13 Gary Jones MGR
□ 14 Scott Lydy
□ 15 Mike Maksudian
□ 16 Damon Mashore
□ 17 Mike Mohler
□ 18 Steve Phoenix
□ 19 Todd Revenig
□ 20 Pete Richert CO
□ 21 Curtis Shaw
□ 22 Scott Sheldon
□ 23 Russ Swan
□ 24 John Wasdin
□ 25 Don Wengert
□ 26 George Williams
□ 27 Steve Wojciechowski
□ 28 Jason Wood
□ 29 Ernie Young
□ NNO Cover Card CL

1995 El Paso Diablos Team Issue

This 24-card set of the 1995 El Paso Diablos, a Class AA Texas League affiliate of the Milwaukee Brewers, was produced by Multi-Ad Services Inc. and features borderless color player photos with the player's name printed across the small gold and red bars at the bottom. The backs carry player information and career statistics. The cards are unnumbered and checklisted below in alphabetical order. This issue includes the minor league card debut of Antone Williamson. 1,000 sets were produced.

	MINT	NRMT	EXC
COMPLETE SET (24)	15.00	6.75	1.85

□ 1 Brian Banks
□ 2 Byron Browne
□ 3 Gene Caruso
□ 4 Robert Derksen
□ 5 Bo Dodson
□ 6 Kenny Felder
□ 7 Lauro Felix
□ 8 Francisco Gamez
□ 9 Ron Gerstein
□ 10 Tim Ireland
□ 11 Bryan Jaquette TR
□ 12 Bob Kappesser
□ 13 Kevin Kloek
□ 14 Todd Landry
□ 15 Cory Lidle
□ 16 Pedro Lopez
□ 17 Roberto Lopez
□ 18 Sean Maloney
□ 19 Norm Montoya
□ 20 Scott Richardson
□ 21 Frank Rodriguez
□ 22 Glenn Sutko
□ 23 Wes Weger
□ 24 Antone Williamson

1995 Elmira Pioneers Team Issue

This 30-card set of the 1995 Elmira Pioneers, a Class A New York-Penn League affiliate of the Florida Marlins, was produced by Multi-Ad Services Inc. and features color player portraits with the player's name printed in a bar down the left. The backs carry player information and career statistics. The cards are unnumbered and checklisted below in alphabetical order. This issue inlcudes the minor league card debut of Josh Booty. 1,000 sets were produced.

	MINT	NRMT	EXC
COMPLETE SET (30)	35.00	16.00	4.40

□ 1 Josh Booty
□ 2 Travis Burgus
□ 3 Tony Enard
□ 4 Mat Erwin
□ 5 Mark Farr
□ 6 Joe Funaro
□ 7 Amaury Garcia
□ 8 Ricky Garcia
□ 9 Jason Garrett
□ 10 Steve Goodell
□ 11 Rob Hernandez
□ 12 Thomas Howard
□ 13 Paul Kirsch MG
□ 14 Justin Long
□ 15 Sommer McCartney
□ 16 Steve McFarland CO
□ 17 Steve Micknich
□ 18 Chad Miles
□ 19 Kumandae Miller
□ 20 Sam Moore
□ 21 Bob Pailthorpe
□ 22 Rene Rascon
□ 23 Derek Reichstein
□ 24 Jeremy Ross
□ 25 Gary Santoro
□ 26 Jason Shanahan
□ 27 Bill Sizemore
□ 28 Shannon Stephens
□ 28 Pat Treend
□ 30 Randy Winn

1995 Elmira Pionners Update Team Issue

This 31-card set of the 1995 Elmira Pioneers, a Class A New York-Penn League affiliate of the Florida Marlins, was produced by Multi-Ad Services Inc. and features color player portraits with the player's name printed in a bar down the left. The backs carry player information and career statistics. The cards are unnumbered and checklisted below in alphabetical order. This issue inlcudes the minor league card debut of Jaime Jones. 500 sets were produced.

	MINT	NRMT	EXC
COMPLETE SET (31)	50.00	22.00	6.25

□ 1 Josh Booty
□ 2 Travis Burgus
□ 3 Tony Enard
□ 4 Mat Erwin
□ 5 Mark Farr
□ 6 Joe Funaro
□ 7 Amaury Garcia
□ 8 Ricky Garcia
□ 9 Jason Garrett
□ 10 Steve Goodell
□ 11 Rob Hernandez
□ 12 Thomas Howard
□ 13 Paul Kirsch MG
□ 14 Justin Long
□ 15 Sommer McCartney
□ 16 Steve McFarland CO
□ 17 Steve Micknich
□ 18 Chad Miles
□ 19 Kumandae Miller
□ 20 Sam Moore
□ 21 Bob Pailthorpe

☐ 22 Rene Rascon
☐ 23 Derek Reichstein
☐ 24 Jeremy Ross
☐ 25 Gary Santoro
☐ 26 Jason Shanahan
☐ 27 Bill Sizemore
☐ 28 Pat Treend
☐ 30 Randy Winn
☐ NNO Jaime Jones

1995 Eugene Emeralds Team Issue

This 32-card set of the 1995 Eugene Emeralds, a Class A Northwest League affiliate of the Atlanta Braves, features color player photos in a white border. The backs carry player information and career statistics along with a police safety message printed at the bottom. This issue includes the minor league card debut of George Lombard. 3,000 sets were produced.

	MINT	NRMT	EXC
COMPLETE SET (32)	12.00	5.50	1.50

☐ 1 George Lombard
☐ 2 Fernando Lunar
☐ 3 Ken Giard
☐ 4 Billy Blythe
☐ 5 Charlie Cruz
☐ 6 Matt McWilliams
☐ 7 Roosevelt Brown
☐ 8 Brian Rust
☐ 9 Joe Trippy
☐ 10 Chris McKnight
☐ 11 Jose Garcia
☐ 12 Antone Brooks
☐ 13 Wilton Person
☐ 14 Mike Mahoney
☐ 15 Jason Shy
☐ 16 Zachary'Pooh' Hines
☐ 17 John Rocker
☐ 18 Jerry McMullen
☐ 19 Reymundo DeLeon
☐ 20 Randy Hodges
☐ 21 Thad Chrismon
☐ 22 Adam Butler
☐ 23 Greg Gerland
☐ 24 Keith Mayhew
☐ 25 Tony Mazzone
☐ 26 Robert Sasser
☐ 27 Todd Tocco
☐ 28 Glenn Williams
☐ 29 Paul Runge MG
☐ 30 Jerry Nyman CO
☐ 31 Wallace Johnson CO
☐ 32 Cover Card CL

1995 Everett Aquasox Team Issue

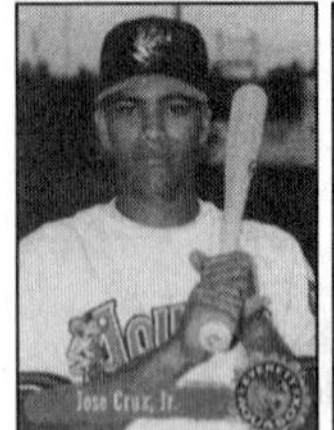
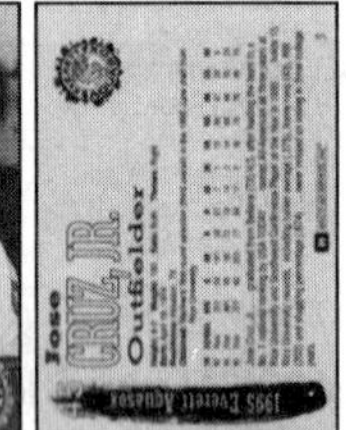

This 30-card set of the 1995 Everett Aquasox, a Class A Northwest League affiliate of the Seattle Mariners, was produced by Multi-Ad Services Inc. and features borderless color player portaits with the player's name in an orange bar at the bottom. The backs carry player information and career statistics. This issue includes the minor league card debut of Jose Cruz Jr. 2,000 sets were produced.

	MINT	NRMT	EXC
COMPLETE SET (30)	40.00	18.00	5.00

☐ 1 Jose Amado
☐ 2 Andy Bottin CO
☐ 3 Mike Burrows
☐ 4 Eric Clifford
☐ 5 Dave Cooper
☐ 6 Jose Cruz Jr.
☐ 7 Orlando Gomez MG
☐ 8 Chad Griffin
☐ 9 Kevin Gryboski
☐ 10 Shane Hearns
☐ 11 Brent Iddon
☐ 12 Damaso Marte
☐ 13 Kelvin Mitchell
☐ 14 Todd Niemeier
☐ 15 Joe Pomierski
☐ 16 Bryan Price CO
☐ 17 Joel Ramirez
☐ 18 Javier Rodriguez
☐ 19 Matt Sachse
☐ 20 Greg Scheer
☐ 21 Aaron Scheffer
☐ 22 Chad Sheffer
☐ 23 Cy Simonton
☐ 24 Chad Soden
☐ 25 Shane Thomasson
☐ 26 Karl Thompson
☐ 27 Luis Tinoco
☐ 28 Tim Trawick
☐ 29 Randy Vickers
☐ 30 Dusty Wathan

1995 Excel

The 1995 Excel Minor League set consists of 300 cards featuring minor league players from AAA, AA and A teams. The fronts display color player photos bordered in white. The player's name, the team's city, and his position appear on the righthand side. The backs carry a large color photo. Overlaying the photo is player information displaying statistical information. The cards are numbered on the back and checklisted below alphabetically within and according to major league teams for the NL and AL.

	MINT	NRMT	EXC
COMPLETE SET (300)	30.00	13.50	3.70
COMMON CARD (1-300)	.05	.02	.01
☐ 1 Kim Bartee	.05	.02	.01
☐ 2 Harry Berrios	.05	.02	.01
☐ 3 Tommy Davis	.05	.02	.01
☐ 4 Cesar Devarez	.05	.02	.01
☐ 5 Curtis Goodwin	.05	.02	.01
☐ 6 Jimmy Haynes	.05	.02	.01
☐ 7 Chris Lemp	.05	.02	.01
☐ 8 Alex Ochoa	.15	.07	.02
☐ 9 B.J. Waszgis	.05	.02	.01
☐ 10 Nomar Garciaparra	2.50	1.10	.30
☐ 11 Jose Malave	.05	.02	.01
☐ 12 Glenn Murray	.05	.02	.01
☐ 13 Trot Nixon	.15	.07	.02
☐ 14 Frank Rodriguez	.05	.02	.01
☐ 15 Bill Selby	.05	.02	.01
☐ 16 Jeff Suppan	.50	.23	.06
☐ 17 George Arias	.50	.23	.06
☐ 18 Todd Blyleven	.05	.02	.01
☐ 19 John Donati	.05	.02	.01
☐ 20 Todd Greene	.40	.18	.05
☐ 21 Bret Hemphill	.05	.02	.01
☐ 22 Michael Holtz	.05	.02	.01
☐ 23 Troy Percival	.15	.07	.02
☐ 24 Luis Raven	.05	.02	.01
☐ 25 James Baldwin	.15	.07	.02
☐ 26 Mike Bertotti	.05	.02	.01
☐ 27 Ben Boulware	.05	.02	.01
☐ 28 Ray Durham	.40	.18	.05
☐ 29 Jimmy Hurst	.05	.02	.01
☐ 30 Rich Pratt	.05	.02	.01
☐ 31 Mike Sirotka	.05	.02	.01
☐ 32 Archie Vazquez	.05	.02	.01
☐ 33 Harold Williams	.05	.02	.01
☐ 34 Chris Woodfin	.05	.02	.01
☐ 35 David Bell	.05	.02	.01
☐ 36 Todd Betts	.05	.02	.01
☐ 37 Jim Betzsold	.05	.02	.01
☐ 38 Einar Diaz	.05	.02	.01
☐ 39 Travis Driskill	.05	.02	.01
☐ 40 Damian Jackson	.15	.07	.02
☐ 41 Daron Kirkreit	.05	.02	.01
☐ 42 Steve Kline	.15	.07	.02
☐ 43 Tony Mitchell	.05	.02	.01
☐ 44 Enrique Wilson	.60	.25	.07
☐ 45 Jaret Wright	.75	.35	.09
☐ 46 Matt Brunson	.05	.02	.01
☐ 47 Tony Clark	1.00	.45	.12
☐ 48 Cade Gaspar	.05	.02	.01
☐ 49 John Grimm	.05	.02	.01
☐ 50 Bob Higginson	.15	.07	.02
☐ 51 Shannon Penn	.05	.02	.01
☐ 52 John Rosengren	.05	.02	.01
☐ 53 Jaime Bluma	.05	.02	.01
☐ 54 Mike Bovee	.05	.02	.01
☐ 55 Nevin Brewer	.05	.02	.01
☐ 56 Johnny Damon	.50	.23	.06
☐ 57 Lino Diaz	.05	.02	.01
☐ 58 Bart Evans	.05	.02	.01
☐ 59 Sal Fasano	.05	.02	.01
☐ 60 Tim Grieve	.05	.02	.01
☐ 61 Jim Pittsley	.05	.02	.01
☐ 62 Joe Randa	.05	.02	.01
☐ 63 Ken Ray	.05	.02	.01
☐ 64 Glendon Rusch	.50	.23	.06
☐ 65 Larry Sutton	.05	.02	.01
☐ 66 Dilson Torres	.05	.02	.01
☐ 67 Michael Tucker	.15	.07	.02
☐ 68 Joe Vitiello	.05	.02	.01
☐ 69 James Cole	.05	.02	.01
☐ 70 Danny Klassen	.05	.02	.01
☐ 71 Jeff Kramer	.05	.02	.01
☐ 72 Mark Loretta	.05	.02	.01
☐ 73 Danny Perez	.05	.02	.01
☐ 74 Sid Roberson	.05	.02	.01
☐ 75 Scott Talanoa	.05	.02	.01
☐ 76 Tim Unroe	.05	.02	.01
☐ 77 Antone Williamson	.60	.25	.07
☐ 78 Marc Barcelo	.05	.02	.01
☐ 79 Trevor Cobb	.05	.02	.01
☐ 80 Marty Cordova	.25	.11	.03
☐ 81 Javier DeJesus	.05	.02	.01
☐ 82 Darren Fidge	.05	.02	.01
☐ 83 Troy Fortin	.05	.02	.01
☐ 84 Gus Gandarillas	.05	.02	.01
☐ 85 Adrian Gordon	.05	.02	.01
☐ 86 LaTroy Hawkins	.05	.02	.01
☐ 87 Jake Patterson	.05	.02	.01
☐ 88 Brad Radke	.05	.02	.01
☐ 89 Todd Walker	4.00	1.80	.50
☐ 90 Brian Boehringer	.05	.02	.01
☐ 91 Brian Buchanan	.15	.07	.02
☐ 92 Andy Croghan	.05	.02	.01
☐ 93 Chris Cumberland	.05	.02	.01
☐ 94 Matt Drews	.05	.02	.01
☐ 95 Keith Heberling	.05	.02	.01
☐ 96 Jason Jarvis	.05	.02	.01
☐ 97 Derek Jeter	1.50	.70	.19
☐ 98 Ricky Ledee	1.25	.55	.16
☐ 99 Matt Luke	.05	.02	.01
☐ 100 James Musselwhite	.05	.02	.01
☐ 101 Andy Pettitte	.75	.35	.09
☐ 102 Mariano Rivera	.25	.11	.03
☐ 103 Ruben Rivera	2.00	.90	.25
☐ 104 Tate Seefried	.05	.02	.01
☐ 105 Scott Standish	.05	.02	.01
☐ 106 Jim Banks	.05	.02	.01
☐ 107 Tony Batista	.15	.07	.02
☐ 108 Ben Grieve	2.50	1.10	.30
☐ 109 Jose Herrera	.05	.02	.01
☐ 110 Steve Lemke	.05	.02	.01
☐ 111 Eric Martins	.05	.02	.01
☐ 112 Scott Spiezio	.15	.07	.02
☐ 113 John Wasdin	.05	.02	.01
☐ 114 Scott Davison	.05	.02	.01
☐ 115 Chris Dean	.05	.02	.01
☐ 116 Giomar Guevara	.05	.02	.01
☐ 117 Tim Harikkala	.05	.02	.01
☐ 118 Brett Hinchliffe	.05	.02	.01
☐ 119 Matt Mantei	.05	.02	.01
☐ 120 Arquimedez Pozo	.05	.02	.01
☐ 121 Marino Santana	.05	.02	.01
☐ 122 John Vanhof	.05	.02	.01
☐ 123 Chris Widger	.05	.02	.01
☐ 124 Mike Bell	.05	.02	.01
☐ 125 Mark Brandenburg	.05	.02	.01
☐ 126 Kevin Brown	.50	.23	.06
☐ 127 Bucky Buckles	.05	.02	.01
☐ 128 Jaime Escamilla	.05	.02	.01
☐ 129 Terrell Lowery	.05	.02	.01
☐ 130 Jerry Martin	.05	.02	.01
☐ 131 Reid Ryan	.05	.02	.01
☐ 132 Julio Santana	.05	.02	.01
☐ 133 Howard Battle	.05	.02	.01
☐ 134 D.J. Boston	.05	.02	.01
☐ 135 Chris Carpenter	.60	.25	.07
☐ 136 Freddy Garcia	.15	.07	.02
☐ 137 Aaron Jersild	.05	.02	.01
☐ 138 Ricardo Jordan	.05	.02	.01
☐ 139 Angel Martinez	.05	.02	.01
☐ 140 Jose Pett	.30	.14	.04
☐ 141 Jose Silva	.05	.02	.01
☐ 142 David Sinnes	.05	.02	.01
☐ 143 Rob Steinert	.05	.02	.01
☐ 144 Chris Stynes	.05	.02	.01
☐ 145 Mike Toney	.05	.02	.01
☐ 146 Chris Weinke	.05	.02	.01
☐ 147 Kevin Witt	.25	.11	.03
☐ 148 Brad Clontz	.05	.02	.01
☐ 149 Jermaine Dye	3.00	1.35	.35
☐ 150 Tony Graffanino	.05	.02	.01
☐ 151 Kevin Grijak	.05	.02	.01
☐ 152 Damon Hollins	.05	.02	.01
☐ 153 Marcus Hostetler	.05	.02	.01
☐ 154 Darrell May	.05	.02	.01
☐ 155 Wonderful Monds	.05	.02	.01
☐ 156 Carl Schutz	.05	.02	.01
☐ 157 Chris Seelbach	.05	.02	.01
☐ 158 Jacob Shumate	.05	.02	.01
☐ 159 Terrell Wade	.15	.07	.02
☐ 160 Glenn Williams	.30	.14	.04
☐ 161 Alex Cabrera	.05	.02	.01
☐ 162 Gabe Duross	.05	.02	.01
☐ 163 Shawn Hill	.05	.02	.01
☐ 164 Mike Hubbard	.05	.02	.01
☐ 165 Dave Hutcheson	.05	.02	.01
☐ 166 Brooks Kieschnick	.25	.11	.03
☐ 167 Bobby Morris	.05	.02	.01
☐ 168 Jayson Peterson	.05	.02	.01
☐ 169 Jason Ryan	.05	.02	.01
☐ 170 Ozzie Timmons	.05	.02	.01
☐ 171 Cedric Allen	.05	.02	.01
☐ 172 Aaron Boone	.60	.25	.07
☐ 173 Ray Brown	.40	.18	.05
☐ 174 Damon Callahan	.05	.02	.01
☐ 175 Decomba Conner	.15	.07	.02
☐ 176 Emiliano Giron	.05	.02	.01
☐ 177 James Lofton	.05	.02	.01
☐ 178 Nick Morrow	.05	.02	.01
☐ 179 C.J. Nitkowski	.05	.02	.01
☐ 180 Eddie Priest	.05	.02	.01
☐ 181 Pokey Reese	.05	.02	.01
☐ 182 Jason Robbins	.05	.02	.01
☐ 183 Scott Sullivan	.05	.02	.01
☐ 184 Pat Watkins	.15	.07	.02
☐ 185 Juan Acevedo	.05	.02	.01
☐ 186 Derrick Gibson	2.50	1.10	.30
☐ 187 Pookie Jones	.05	.02	.01
☐ 188 Terry Jones	.05	.02	.01
☐ 189 Doug Million	.15	.07	.02
☐ 190 Lloyd Peever	.05	.02	.01
☐ 191 Jacob Viano	.05	.02	.01
☐ 192 Mark Voisard	.05	.02	.01
☐ 193 Josh Booty	.40	.18	.05
☐ 194 Will Cunnane	.05	.02	.01
☐ 195 Andy Larkin	.05	.02	.01
☐ 196 Billy McMillon	.05	.02	.01
☐ 197 Kevin Millar	.05	.02	.01
☐ 198 Marc Valdes	.05	.02	.01
☐ 199 Bob Abreu	.40	.18	.05
☐ 200 Jamie Daspit	.05	.02	.01
☐ 201 Scott Elarton	.50	.23	.06
☐ 202 Kevin Gallaher	.05	.02	.01
☐ 203 Richard Hidalgo	.50	.23	.06
☐ 204 Chris Holt	.05	.02	.01
☐ 205 Rick Huisman	.05	.02	.01
☐ 206 Doug Mlicki	.05	.02	.01
☐ 207 Julien Tucker	.05	.02	.01
☐ 208 Billy Wagner	.15	.07	.02
☐ 209 Juan Castro	.05	.02	.01
☐ 210 Roger Cedeno	.20	.09	.03
☐ 211 Ron Coomer	.05	.02	.01
☐ 212 Karim Garcia	1.50	.70	.19
☐ 213 Todd Hollandsworth	.25	.11	.03
☐ 214 Paul Konerko	4.00	1.80	.50
☐ 215 Antonio Osuna	.05	.02	.01
☐ 216 Willis Otanez	.05	.02	.01
☐ 217 Dan Ricabal	.05	.02	.01
☐ 218 Ken Sikes	.05	.02	.01
☐ 219 Yamil Benitez	.50	.23	.06
☐ 220 Geoff Blum	.05	.02	.01
☐ 221 Scott Gentile	.05	.02	.01
☐ 222 Mark Grudzielanek	.05	.02	.01
☐ 223 Kevin Northrup	.05	.02	.01
☐ 224 Carlos Perez	.15	.07	.02
☐ 225 Matt Raleigh	.05	.02	.01
☐ 226 Al Reyes	.05	.02	.01
☐ 227 Everett Stull	.05	.02	.01
☐ 228 Ugueth Urbina	.05	.02	.01
☐ 229 Neil Weber	.20	.09	.03
☐ 230 Edgardo Alfonzo	.05	.02	.01
☐ 231 Jason Isringhausen	.30	.14	.04
☐ 232 Terrence Long	.60	.25	.07
☐ 233 Rey Ordonez	1.00	.45	.12
☐ 234 Ricky Otero	.05	.02	.01
☐ 235 Jay Payton	2.00	.90	.25
☐ 236 Kirk Presley	.15	.07	.02
☐ 237 Bill Pulsipher	.20	.09	.03
☐ 238 Chris Roberts	.05	.02	.01
☐ 239 Jeff Tam	.05	.02	.01
☐ 240 Paul Wilson	.50	.23	.06
☐ 241 David Doster	.05	.02	.01
☐ 242 Wayne Gomes	.05	.02	.01
☐ 243 Jeremey Kendall	.05	.02	.01
☐ 244 Ryan Nye	.30	.14	.04
☐ 245 Shane Pullen	.05	.02	.01
☐ 246 Scott Rolen	5.00	2.20	.60
☐ 247 Gene Schall	.05	.02	.01
☐ 248 Brian Stumpf	.05	.02	.01
☐ 249 Jake Austin	.05	.02	.01
☐ 250 Trey Beamon	.25	.11	.03
☐ 251 Danny Clyburn	.20	.09	.03
☐ 252 Louis Collier	.05	.02	.01
☐ 253 Mark Farris	.05	.02	.01
☐ 254 Mark Johnson	.05	.02	.01
☐ 255 Jason Kendall	.15	.07	.02
☐ 256 Esteban Loaiza	.15	.07	.02
☐ 257 Joe Maskivish	.05	.02	.01
☐ 258 Ramon Morel	.05	.02	.01
☐ 259 Gary Wilson	.05	.02	.01
☐ 260 Matt Arrandale	.05	.02	.01
☐ 261 Allen Battle	.05	.02	.01
☐ 262 Alan Benes	.50	.23	.06
☐ 263 Jeff Berblinger	.05	.02	.01
☐ 264 Terry Bradshaw	.05	.02	.01
☐ 265 Darrell Deak	.05	.02	.01
☐ 266 Criag Grasser	.05	.02	.01
☐ 267 Yates Hall	.05	.02	.01
☐ 268 Kevin Lovingier	.05	.02	.01
☐ 269 Elieser Marrero	.30	.14	.04
☐ 270 Jeff Matulevich	.05	.02	.01
☐ 271 Joe McEwing	.05	.02	.01
☐ 272 Eric Miller	.05	.02	.01
☐ 273 Tom Minor	.05	.02	.01
☐ 274 Scott Simmons	.05	.02	.01
☐ 275 Chris Stewart	.05	.02	.01
☐ 276 Bret Wagner	.05	.02	.01
☐ 277 Travis Welch	.05	.02	.01
☐ 278 Jay Witasick	.05	.02	.01

Card	MINT	NRMT	EXC
☐ 279 Homer Bush	.05	.02	.01
☐ 280 Raul Casanova	.40	.18	.05
☐ 281 Glenn Dishman	.05	.02	.01
☐ 282 Gary Dixon	.05	.02	.01
☐ 283 Devohn Duncan	.05	.02	.01
☐ 284 Dustin Hermanson	.05	.02	.01
☐ 285 Earl Johnson	.05	.02	.01
☐ 286 Derrek Lee	1.00	.45	.12
☐ 287 Todd Schmitt	.05	.02	.01
☐ 288 Ira Smith	.05	.02	.01
☐ 289 Jason Thompson	.05	.02	.01
☐ 290 Bryan Wolff	.05	.02	.01
☐ 291 Jeff Martin	.05	.02	.01
☐ 292 Dante Powell	2.50	1.10	.30
☐ 293 Jeff Richey	.05	.02	.01
☐ 294 Joe Rosselli	.05	.02	.01
☐ 295 Benji Simonton	.05	.02	.01
☐ 296 Steve Whitaker	.05	.02	.01
☐ 297 Keith Williams	.05	.02	.01
☐ 298 Checklist 1-113	.05	.02	.01
☐ 299 Checklist 114-226	.05	.02	.01
☐ 300 Checklist 227-300	.05	.02	.01

1995 Excel All-Stars

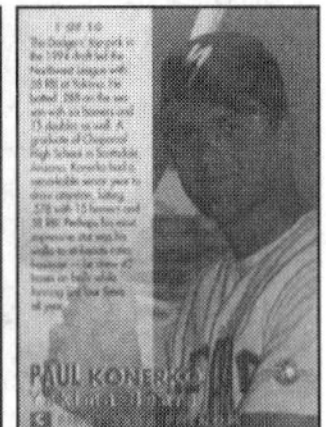

	MINT	NRMT	EXC
COMPLETE SET (10)	15.00	6.75	1.85
COMMON CARD (1-10)	.50	.23	.06

Card	MINT	NRMT	EXC
☐ 1 Raul Casanova	1.25	.55	.16
☐ 2 Tony Clark	2.00	.90	.25
☐ 3 Ray Durham	1.25	.55	.16
☐ 4 Ron Coomer	.50	.23	.06
☐ 5 Derek Jeter	5.00	2.20	.60
☐ 6 Trey Beamon	.75	.35	.09
☐ 7 Johnny Damon	1.50	.70	.19
☐ 8 Ruben Rivera	4.00	1.80	.50
☐ 9 Todd Greene	1.00	.45	.12
☐ 10 Alan Benes	2.00	.90	.25

1995 Excel First Year Phenoms

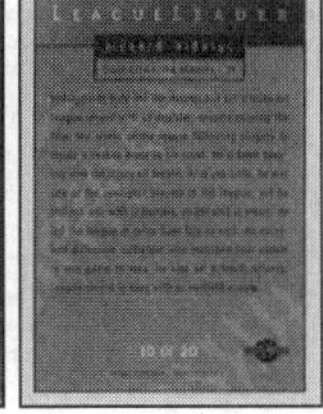

	MINT	NRMT	EXC
COMPLETE SET (10)	25.00	11.00	3.10
COMMON CARD (1-10)	.75	.35	.09

Card	MINT	NRMT	EXC
☐ 1 Paul Konerko	8.00	3.60	1.00
☐ 2 Ray Brown	1.50	.70	.19
☐ 3 Chris Dean	.75	.35	.09
☐ 4 Aaron Boone	2.50	1.10	.30
☐ 5 Rey Ordonez	2.00	.90	.25
☐ 6 Decomba Conner	.75	.35	.09
☐ 7 Ben Grieve	6.00	2.70	.75
☐ 8 Jay Payton	5.00	2.20	.60
☐ 9 Dante Powell	6.00	2.70	.75
☐ 10 Dustin Hermanson	.75	.35	.09

1995 Excel League Leaders

	MINT	NRMT	EXC
COMPLETE SET (20)	12.00	5.50	1.50
COMMON CARD (1-20)	.40	.18	.05

Card	MINT	NRMT	EXC
☐ 1 Juan Acevedo	.40	.18	.05
☐ 2 James Baldwin	.60	.25	.07
☐ 3 Allen Battle	.40	.18	.05
☐ 4 Harry Berrios	.40	.18	.05
☐ 5 Brad Clontz	.40	.18	.05
☐ 6 Will Cunnane	.40	.18	.05
☐ 7 Glenn Dishman	.40	.18	.05
☐ 8 LaTroy Hawkins	.40	.18	.05
☐ 9 Jimmy Haynes	.40	.18	.05
☐ 10 Richard Hidalgo	3.00	1.35	.35
☐ 11 Earl Johnson	.40	.18	.05
☐ 12 Jim Pittsley	1.00	.45	.12
☐ 13 Bill Pulsipher	.75	.35	.09
☐ 14 Benji Simonton	.40	.18	.05
☐ 15 Larry Sutton	.40	.18	.05
☐ 16 Michael Tucker	.75	.35	.09
☐ 17 Tim Unroe	.40	.18	.05
☐ 18 Joe Vitiello	.40	.18	.05
☐ 19 Billy Wagner	.60	.25	.07
☐ 20 Harold Williams	.40	.18	.05

1995 Fayetteville Generals Team Issue

This 30-card set of the 1995 Fayetteville Generals, a Class South Atlantic League affiliate of the Detroit Tigers, was produced by Multi-Ad Services Inc. and features borderless color player photos with the player's name printed on an orange bar at the bottom. The backs carry player information and career statistics. 4,000 sets were produced with 3,600 given away at the ballpark.

	MINT	NRMT	EXC
COMPLETE SET (30)	15.00	6.75	1.85

☐ 1 Ryan Balfe
☐ 2 Rob Balint
☐ 3 Jayson Bass
☐ 4 Jamie Borel
☐ 5 Matt Brunson
☐ 6 Basilio Cabrera CO
☐ 7 Javier Cardona
☐ 8 Mike Darr
☐ 9 Eric Dinyar
☐ 10 Juan Encarnacion
☐ 11 Neil Garcia
☐ 12 Scott Gardner
☐ 13 Kelton Jacobson
☐ 14 Jason Jordan
☐ 15 Matt Lewis TR
☐ 16 Dwight Lowry MG
☐ 17 Sid Monge CO
☐ 18 Darryl Monroe
☐ 19 Santiago Perez
☐ 20 Brandon Reed
☐ 21 Sherron Rives
☐ 22 Willie Roberts
☐ 23 Matt Skrmetta
☐ 24 Cameron Smith
☐ 25 Trad Sobik
☐ 26 Daryle Ward
☐ 27 Greg Whiteman
☐ 28 Tony Whiteman
☐ 29 Mike Wilson
☐ 30 Taylor Carr ANN

1995 Fort Myers Miracle Team Issue

This 32-card set of the 1995 Fort Myers Miracle, a Class A Florida State League affiliate of the Minnesota Twins, features color player photos in a white border with the player's name and team name printed in a vertical bar down the left. The backs carry player information and statistics. This issue includes the minor league card debuts of Torii Hunter, Mark Redman and Troy Carrasco. 1,000 sets were produced.

	MINT	NRMT	EXC
COMPLETE SET (32)	12.00	5.50	1.50

☐ 1 Jason Baker
☐ 2 Shane Bowers
☐ 3 Gary Caraballo
☐ 4 Lee County Sports Complex
☐ 5 Troy Carrasco
☐ 6 Jim Champion
☐ 7 Aaron Fultz
☐ 8 Rob Debrino
☐ 9 Mark Redman
☐ 10 Jeff Horn
☐ 11 Torii Hunter
☐ 12 Ben Jones
☐ 13 Tom Knauss
☐ 14 Russ Lehoisky
☐ 15 Keith Linebarger
☐ 16 Shawn Miller
☐ 17 Paul Morse
☐ 18 James Motte
☐ 19 James McCalmont
☐ 20 Marlo Nava
☐ 21 Brian O'Brien
☐ 22 Ryan Radmanovich
☐ 23 Chad Rupp
☐ 24 Benj Sampson
☐ 25 Bubba Smith
☐ 26 Scott Stricklin
☐ 27 Jason Tatar
☐ 28 Rick Tomlin CO
☐ 29 Jose Marzan CO
☐ 30 Al Newman MGR
☐ 31 Lanning Tucker TR
☐ 32 Doug Mientkiewicz

1995 Fort Wayne Wizards Team Issue

This 32-card set of the 1995 Fort Wayne Wizards, a Class A Midwest League affiliate of the Minnesota Twins, features borderless color player photos with the player's name and position printed on a small blue triangle in the bottom left corner. The backs carry player information and career statistics. This issue includes the minor league card debut of A.J. Pierzynski and a second year card of Jose Valentin. 1,000 sets were produced.

	MINT	NRMT	EXC
COMPLETE SET (32)	9.00	4.00	1.10

☐ 1 Luis Alvarado
☐ 2 Doug Bedinger
☐ 3 Walker Chapman
☐ 4 Deron Dowhower
☐ 5 Darren Fidge
☐ 6 Tom Gourdin
☐ 7 Jason Meyhoff
☐ 8 Tom Mott
☐ 9 Paul Pavicich
☐ 10 Dan Perkins
☐ 11 Brannon Peters
☐ 12 Robert Radlosky
☐ 13 Troy Fortin
☐ 14 A.J. Pierzynski
☐ 15 Jose J. Valentin
☐ 16 Carlos Garcia
☐ 17 Corey Koskie
☐ 18 Ryan Lane
☐ 19 Israel Paez
☐ 20 Jake Patterson
☐ 21 Rafael Alvarez
☐ 22 Adrian Gordon
☐ 23 Kelcey Mucker
☐ 24 Kevin Pearson
☐ 25 Romulo Vizcaino
☐ 26 Dan Rohn MG
☐ 27 Stu Cliburn CO
☐ 28 Jose Baez CO
☐ 29 Dan Overman TR
☐ 30 Wayne the Wizard(Mascot)
☐ 31 Eric Margenau OWN
☐ 32 Team Photo CL

1995 Great Falls Dodgers Team Issue

This 40-card set of the 1995 Great Falls Dodgers, a Rookie Class Pioneer League affiliate of the Los Angeles Dodgers, features black-and-white borderless player photos and measures approximately 3 5/8" by 6". The team's logo, player's name, and player's position are printed in the wide bottom margin. The backs carry a postcard format with player information printed in the top left corner. Only 200 complete collated sets were produced.

	MINT	NRMT	EXC
COMPLETE SET (40)	70.00	32.00	8.75

☐ 1 Jackson Torres
☐ 2 Pedro Feliciano
☐ 3 Jose Flores
☐ 4 John Davis
☐ 5 Oscar Rivera
☐ 6 Toni Nakashima
☐ 7 Omar Fernandez
☐ 8 Juan Sangeado
☐ 9 Javier Chapa
☐ 10 Michael Bourbakis
☐ 11 Craig Taczy
☐ 12 Joel Manfredi
☐ 13 Marc Charbonneau
☐ 14 Bobby Meyer
☐ 15 Chris Ochsenfeld
☐ 16 Luke Prokopec
☐ 17 Gary Sweezey
☐ 18 Angel Pena
☐ 19 Jason Reed
☐ 20 Dennis Mauch
☐ 21 Jason Baker
☐ 22 Jose Mateo
☐ 23 Manny Gonzalez
☐ 24 Brett Illig
☐ 25 Larry Bethea
☐ 26 Eric Flores
☐ 27 Jeff Bramlett
☐ 28 Rafael Ozuna
☐ 29 Todd Barlok
☐ 30 Rafael Martinez
☐ 31 John Shoemaker
☐ 32 Mickey Hatcher
☐ 33 Eric Stuckenschneider
☐ 34 Ruben Barrera
☐ 35 Greg Morrison
☐ 36 Edwin Correa
☐ 37 Miquel Garcia
☐ 38 Dodger Rabbit
☐ 39 Eric Brown
☐ 40 Cover Card

1995 Greensboro Bats Team Issue

This 33-card set of the 1995 Greensboro Bats, a Class A South Atlantic League affiliate of the New York Yankees, was produced by Multi-Ad Services Inc. and features color player photos with a black outside border and thin red inside border. The backs carry player information and career statistics. This issue includes the minor league card debut of Rafael Medina.

	MINT	NRMT	EXC
COMPLETE SET (33)	9.00	4.00	1.10

☐ 1 Shawn Alvarez
☐ 2 Chris Ashby
☐ 3 Dan Donato
☐ 4 Brian Binversie
☐ 5 Charlie Brown
☐ 6 Vick Brown
☐ 7 Brian Buchanan
☐ 8 Chris Corn
☐ 9 Wil Delafield
☐ 10 Derek Dukart
☐ 11 Grant Fithian
☐ 12 Mike Giardi
☐ 13 Jason Jarvis
☐ 14 Ricky Ledee
☐ 15 Jose Lobaton
☐ 16 Brian McLamb
☐ 17 Rafael Medina
☐ 18 Casey Mittauer
☐ 19 Frisco Parotte
☐ 20 Ray Ricken
☐ 21 Brett Schlomann
☐ 22 Anthony Shelby
☐ 23 Steve Shoemaker
☐ 24 Carlos Yedo
☐ 25 Rod Smith
☐ 26 Sean Twitty
☐ 27 Jason Wuerch
☐ 28 Pete Filson CO
☐ 29 Trey Hillman MG
☐ 30 Brian Milner CO
☐ 31 Chris DeLucia CL
☐ 32 Rafael Rojano
☐ 33 Dale Torborg

1995 Greenville Braves Team Issue

This 28-card set of the 1995 Greenville Braves, a Class AA Southern League affiliate of the Atlanta Braves, features color player photos in a blue-and-white border with the player's last name running continuously down one side. The Coca-Cola logo is printed in a red-framed blue bar at the bottom. The backs carry player information and career statistics. The cards are unnumbered and checklisted below according to the player's jersey number printed in red in a blue circle at the bottom on the card's front.

	MINT	NRMT	EXC
COMPLETE SET (28)	14.00	6.25	1.75

☐ 2 Bobby Smith
☐ 5 Pablo Martinez
☐ 7 Damon Hollins
☐ 8 Ray Nunez
☐ 9 Brad Rippelmeyer
☐ 10 Troy Hughes
☐ 12 Randy Ingle CO
☐ 15 Aldo Pecorilli
☐ 16 Pedro Swann
☐ 18 Roger Etheridge
☐ 20 Bruce Benedict MG
☐ 22 Doug Wollenburg
☐ 24 Jermaine Dye
☐ 25 Darrell May
☐ 28 Bill Shafer
☐ 30 Jerry Koller
☐ 33 Mike Hostetler
☐ 34 Jamie Arnold
☐ 37 Juan Williams
☐ 39 Bruce Dal Canton CO
☐ 42 Joe Ayrault
☐ 43 Dirk Blair
☐ 46 Mike D'Andrea
☐ 48 Aaron Turnier
☐ 49 Carl Schutz
☐ 50 John Simmons
☐ 51 Marcus Hostetler
☐ TR Dave Tomchek TR

1995 Hagerstown Suns Fleer/ProCards

This 30-card set of the 1995 Hagerstown Suns, a Class A South Atlantic League affiliate of the Toronto Blue Jays, was produced by the Fleer Corp. and features posed color player photos in a white border on the card fronts. The backs carry player information and career statistics.

	MINT	NRMT	EXC
COMPLETE SET (30)	9.00	4.00	1.10

☐ 59 Alfredo Arias
☐ 60 John Crowther
☐ 61 Joe Davenport
☐ 62 Tyson Hartshorn
☐ 63 Billy Hibbard
☐ 64 Jeremy Lee
☐ 65 Chris McBride
☐ 66 Maximo Nunez
☐ 67 Scotty Pace
☐ 68 Kendall Rhine
☐ 69 Mark Sievert
☐ 70 Brian Smith
☐ 71 Jeff Ladd
☐ 72 Dave Morgan
☐ 73 Julio Mosquera
☐ 74 Battle Holley
☐ 75 Rob Mummau
☐ 76 Craig Stone
☐ 77 Mike Strange
☐ 78 Andy Thompson
☐ 79 Kevin Witt
☐ 80 Aurelio Llanos
☐ 81 Dagoberto Prensi
☐ 82 Jonathan Rivers
☐ 83 Anthony Sanders
☐ 84 Omar Malave MG
☐ 85 Reggie Cleveland CO
☐ 86 Scott Miller CO
☐ 87 Cover Card CL
☐ NNO Hagerstown Logo

1995 Hardware City Rock Cats Team Issue

This 29-card set of the 1995 Hardware City Rock Cats, a Class AA Eastern League affiliate of the Minnesota Twins, was produced by Multi-Ad Services Inc. and features color player photos in a white pin-striped frame. The backs carry player information and career statistics. This issue includes the minor league card debut of Todd Walker. 1,000 sets were produced.

	MINT	NRMT	EXC
COMPLETE SET (29)	40.00	18.00	5.00

☐ 1 Brent Brede
☐ 2 Sal Butera MG
☐ 3 Anthony Byrd
☐ 4 Andres Duncan
☐ 5 Jim Dwyer CO
☐ 6 Gus Gandarillas
☐ 7 Pedro Grifol
☐ 8 Gorman Heimueller CO
☐ 9 Dom Konieczki
☐ 10 Matt Lawton
☐ 11 Kevin LeGault
☐ 12 Keith LeGree
☐ 13 Rene Lopez
☐ 14 Travis Miller
☐ 15 Tim Moore
☐ 16 Scott Moten
☐ 17 Joe Norris
☐ 18 Jamie Ogden
☐ 19 Kevin Ohme
☐ 20 Todd Ritchie
☐ 21 Brett Roberts
☐ 22 Chad Roper
☐ 23 Dan Serafini
☐ 24 Bubba Smith
☐ 25 Hector Trinidad
☐ 26 Ramon Valette
☐ 27 Todd Walker (Batting)
☐ 28 Todd Walker
☐ 29 Rick McWane TR

1995 Harrisburg Senators Team Issue

This 28-card set of the 1995 Harrisburg Senators, a Class AA Eastern League affiliate of the Montreal Expos, features color player photos in a blue border with thin red and thinner white inner borders. The player's name, team name, and position are printed in a light yellow bar at the bottom. The backs carry player information and career statistics. The cards are unnumbered and checklisted below according to the player's jersey number printed on the back of the card. 2,000 sets were produced.

	MINT	NRMT	EXC
COMPLETE SET (28)	10.00	4.50	1.25

☐ 2 Damon Pollard
☐ 4 Matt Rundels
☐ 5 Israel Alcantara
☐ 6 Gary Louis Hymel
☐ 7 Dan Lane
☐ 10 Neil Weber
☐ 13 Edgar Tovar
☐ 14 Rob Fitzpatrick
☐ 15 George Virgilio
☐ 16 Alex Pacheco
☐ 17 Steve Falteisek
☐ 18 Scott Gentile
☐ 19 Tyrone Horne
☐ 20 Tony Kounas
☐ 22 Phil Dauphin
☐ 23 Jose Vidro
☐ 27 Mark Charbonnet
☐ 28 Darrin Paxton
☐ 29 Everett Stull
☐ 30 Pat Kelly MGR
☐ 32 Ken Kendrena
☐ 33 Rick DeHart
☐ 36 Aris Tirado
☐ 37 Lincoln Mikkelsen
☐ 38 Antonio Grissom
☐ 45 Collin Kerley
☐ 46 Kirk Bullinger
☐ NNO Alex Ochoa TR

1995 Helena Brewers Team Issue

This 32-card set of the 1995 Helena Brewers, a Rookie Class Pioneer League affiliate of the Milwaukee Brewers, features borderless color player photos with the player's name and position printed on purple mountains at the bottom. The backs carry player information. This issue includes the minor league card debut of Mike Pasqualicchio.

	MINT	NRMT	EXC
COMPLETE SET (32)	13.00	5.75	1.60

☐ 1 Brooke Knight
☐ 2 Anthony Iopoce
☐ 3 Jared Camp
☐ 4 Ryan Arrevalos
☐ 5 Dave Elliott
☐ 6 Mike Kinkade
☐ 7 Sergio Guerrero
☐ 8 Darren Berninger
☐ 9 Allen Mealing
☐ 10 Brian Johnson
☐ 11 Travis Smith
☐ 12 Rick Smith
☐ 13 Ledowick Johnson
☐ 14 Shawn Miller
☐ 15 Ryan Ritter
☐ 16 Jason Dawsey
☐ 17 Mickey Lopez
☐ 18 Alex Morales
☐ 19 Bernie Moncallo
☐ 20 Edward Collins
☐ 21 Derrick Caskill
☐ 22 David Gooda
☐ 23 Greg Mullins
☐ 24 Shane Sheldon
☐ 25 Robinson Cancel
☐ 26 Peter Benny
☐ 27 Brian Hommel
☐ 28 Jesse Richardson
☐ 29 Tobias Kominek
☐ 30 Jerry Parent
☐ 31 Mike Pasqualicchio
☐ 32 Team Photo CL

1995 Hudson Valley Renegades Team Issue

This 30-card set of the 1995 Hudson Valley Renegades, a Class A New York-Penn League affiliate of the Texas Rangers, was produced by Multi-Ad Services Inc. and features color player photos framed at the top in violet and at the bottom in green with a thin gray inner border. The backs display player information. 1,500 sets were produced.

	MINT	NRMT	EXC
COMPLETE SET (30)	10.00	4.50	1.25

☐ 1 Cliff Brumbaugh
☐ 2 Scott Podsednik
☐ 3 Kyle Evans
☐ 4 Scott Mudd
☐ 5 Billy Reed
☐ 6 Nate Vopata
☐ 7 Ryan Gorecki
☐ 8 Mandell Echols
☐ 9 Joey Goodwin
☐ 10 Danny Vasquez
☐ 11 Bobby Kahlon
☐ 12 Bryan Link
☐ 13 Mike Venafro
☐ 14 Tim Codd
☐ 15 Chris Briones
☐ 16 Dave Martinez
☐ 17 Charles Bauer
☐ 18 Kelly Stratton
☐ 19 Brian Martineau
☐ 20 Jason Johnson
☐ 21 Mike McHugh
☐ 22 John McAulay
☐ 23 Ryan Glynn
☐ 24 Rod Walker
☐ 25 Brent Sagedal
☐ 26 Mark Draeger
☐ 27 Bobby Moore
☐ 28 Bump Wills MG
☐ 29 Steve Foucault CO
☐ 30 Rookie and Rene(Mascots) CL

1995 Huntsville Stars Team Issue

This 29-card set of the 1995 Huntsville Stars, a Class AA Southern League affiliate of the Oakland Athletics, was sponsored by Burger King and features color player portraits in a thin red border and a red, white, blue, and black or yellow wider outside border. The backs carry player information and statistics. The cards are unnumbered and checklisted below in alphabetical order.

	MINT	NRMT	EXC
COMPLETE SET (29)	13.00	5.75	1.60

☐ 1 Glenn Abbott CO
☐ 2 Willie Adams
☐ 3 James Banks
☐ 4 Tony Batista
☐ 5 Garrett Beard
☐ 6 Bob Bennett
☐ 7 Bobby Chouinard
☐ 8 Ramon Fermin
☐ 9 David Francisco
☐ 10 Benji Grigsby
☐ 11 Creighton Gubanich
☐ 12 Chris Hart
☐ 13 Jose Herrera
☐ 14 Dave Hollenback TR
☐ 15 Stacy Hollins
☐ 16 Dave Joppie CO
☐ 17 Steve Lemke
☐ 18 Brian Lesher
☐ 19 Izzy Molina
☐ 20 Rob Pierce
☐ 21 Allen Plaster
☐ 22 Scott Rose
☐ 23 Dick Scott MGR
☐ 24 Steve Shoemaker
☐ 25 Mark Sobolewski
☐ 26 Scott Spiezio
☐ 27 Jim Waggoner
☐ 28 Dane Walker
☐ 29 Joel Wolfe

1995 Idaho Falls Braves Team Issue

This 29-card set of the 1995 Idaho Falls Braves, a Rookie Class Pioneer League affiliate of the San Diego Padres, was sponsored by Hardee's, the Post Register, and KIFI-TV. The fronts feature color player portraits with various shades and widths of red, white, and blue borders. The backs display player information and statistics. The set also contains two smaller cards of first round draft pick Ben Davis, which were issued later as singles. The backs of these two cards carry a message from Ben Davis to Little Leaguers along with player information. The cards are unnumbered and checklisted below according to the jersey number of the player printed on the card front. 2,000 sets were produced.

	MINT	NRMT	EXC
COMPLETE SET (29)	24.00	11.00	3.00

☐ 1 Ricky Gama
☐ 2 Eliezer Rosario
☐ 5 Carmen Bucci
☐ 6 Russell Spear
☐ 7 Rodney Lindsey
☐ 11 Michael Irvine
☐ 13 Ben Davis
☐ 16 Kenya Hunt
☐ 17 Rich Hills
☐ 18 Matt Abernathy
☐ 19 Gary Roenicke CO
☐ 20 Jim Baron
☐ 21 Jake Remington
☐ 22 Mark Merila
☐ 23 Daniel Bales
☐ 25 Todd Erdos
☐ 26 Obed Martinez
☐ 28 Gordon Amerson
☐ 29 Tim Campbell
☐ 30 Eric Newman
☐ 31 Matt Clement
☐ 32 Domingo Guzman
☐ 33 Sean Watkins
☐ 34 Marcos Sanchez
☐ 35 Mike Basso MG
☐ 36 Scipio Spinks CO
☐ NNO Ben Davis (Batting)
☐ NNO Ben Davis (Catching)
☐ NNO John Maxwell TR

1995 Indianapolis Indians Fleer/ProCards

This 30-card set of the 1995 Indianapolis Indians, a Class AAA American Association affiliate of the Cincinnati Reds, was produced by the Fleer Corp. and features posed color player photos in a white border on the card fronts. The backs carry player information and career statistics.

	MINT	NRMT	EXC
COMPLETE SET (30)	8.00	3.60	1.00

☐ 88 Blaine Beatty
☐ 89 Tim Belcher
☐ 90 Travis Buckley
☐ 91 Mike Mathile
☐ 92 Rick Steed
☐ 93 Johnny Ruffin
☐ 94 Rich Sauveur
☐ 95 Scott Service
☐ 96 Brian Warren
☐ 97 Jerry Brooks
☐ 98 Brian Dorsett
☐ 99 Tim Belk
☐ 100 Drew Denson
☐ 101 Willie Greene
☐ 102 Eric Owens
☐ 103 Pokey Reese
☐ 104 Kurt Stillwell
☐ 105 Craig Worthington
☐ 106 Greg Briley
☐ 107 Steve Gibralter
☐ 108 Keith Gordon
☐ 109 Nigel Wilson
☐ 110 Kris Kremblas P/CO
☐ 111 Marc Bombard MG
☐ 112 Mike Griffin CO
☐ 113 Jim Thrift CO
☐ 114 John Young TR
☐ 115 J.D. Cannon
☐ 116 Bush Stadium
☐ 117 Cover Card CL

1995 Iowa Cubs Team Issue

This 25-card set of the 1995 Iowa Cubs, a Class AAA American Association affiliate of the Chicago Cubs, was produced by Multi-Ad Services Inc. and features borderless color player photos with the player's name. The backs carry player information and career statistics. The cards are unnumbered and checklisted below in alphabetical order. 1,000 sets were produced.

	MINT	NRMT	EXC
COMPLETE SET (25)	12.00	5.50	1.50

☐ 1 Paul Abbott
☐ 2 Glenn Adams CO
☐ 3 Mike Anderson
☐ 4 Freddie Benavides
☐ 5 Mike Campbell
☐ 6 Mike Carter
☐ 7 Ron Clark MGR
☐ 8 Cris Colon
☐ 9 Fred Dabney
☐ 10 Steve Dixon
☐ 11 Bill Earley CO
☐ 12 Matt Franco
☐ 13 Doug Glanville
☐ 14 Mark Grant
☐ 15 Todd Haney
☐ 16 Mike Hubbard
☐ 17 Keith Kessinger
☐ 18 Brooks Kieschnick
☐ 19 Joe Kmak
☐ 20 Bryn Kosco
☐ 21 Manny Martinez
☐ 22 Kevin Morton
☐ 23 Kennie Steenstra
☐ 24 Dave Swartzbaugh
☐ 25 Rob Taylor

1995 Jackson Generals Team Issue

This 27-card set of the 1995 Jackson Generals, a Class AA Texas League affiliate of the Houston Astros, was produced by Multi-Ad Services Inc. and features borderless color player photos. The backs carry player information and career statistics. This issue includes the minor league card debut of Russ Johnson. 1,000 sets were produced.

	MINT	NRMT	EXC
COMPLETE SET (27)	15.00	6.75	1.85

☐ 1 Ryan Creek
☐ 2 David Evans
☐ 3 Mike Grzanich
☐ 4 Chris Holt
☐ 5 Martin Lister
☐ 6 Doug Mlicki
☐ 7 Tyrone Narcisse
☐ 8 Billy Wagner
☐ 9 Joe Waldron
☐ 10 Jamie Walker
☐ 11 Jim Waring
☐ 12 Chris White

- ☐ 13 Raul Chavez
- ☐ 14 Tony Gilmore
- ☐ 15 Richard Hidalgo
- ☐ 16 Melvin Mora
- ☐ 17 Tony Mitchell
- ☐ 18 Ray Montgomery
- ☐ 19 Kary Bridges
- ☐ 20 Henri Centeno
- ☐ 21 Dennis Colon
- ☐ 22 Mike Groppuso
- ☐ 23 Russ Johnson
- ☐ 24 Tom Nevers
- ☐ 25 Tim Tolman MG
- ☐ 26 Charley Taylor CO
- ☐ 27 Mike Freer TR

1995 Jacksonville Suns Team Issue

This 28-card set of the 1995 Jacksonville Suns, a Class AA Southern League affiliate of the Detroit Tigers, features color player photos in white borders. The backs carry player information and career statistics. The cards are unnumbered and checklisted below in alphabetical order. 700 sets were produced.

	MINT	NRMT	EXC
COMPLETE SET (28)	9.00	4.00	1.10

- ☐ 1 Glen Barker
- ☐ 2 Rich Bombard CO
- ☐ 3 Frank Catalanotto
- ☐ 4 Blas Cedeno
- ☐ 5 Gary Cooper
- ☐ 6 Ivan Cruz
- ☐ 7 Eric Danapilis
- ☐ 8 Rex De La Nuez
- ☐ 9 Carlos Fermin
- ☐ 10 Daniel Fernandez
- ☐ 11 Bryan Goike TR
- ☐ 12 Gary Goldsmith
- ☐ 13 Rick Greene
- ☐ 14 Michael Guilfoyle
- ☐ 15 Jim Gutierrez
- ☐ 16 Terrel Hansen
- ☐ 17 John Kelly
- ☐ 18 Tim Leiper
- ☐ 19 Kevin Lidle
- ☐ 20 Mark Meleski CO
- ☐ 21 Trever Miller
- ☐ 22 Brian Moehler
- ☐ 23 Bill Plummer MG
- ☐ 24 John Rosengren
- ☐ 25 Yuri Sanchez
- ☐ 26 Clint Sodowsky
- ☐ 27 Sean Whiteside
- ☐ 28 Shannon Withem

1995 Kane County Cougars Legends Team Issue

This 15-card set features borderless color player photos of some of the 1993, 1994, and 1995 Cougars Alumni and Prospects. The backs carry information about the player and career statistics. The cards are unnumbered and checklisted below in alphabetical order. 2,000 sets were produced.

	MINT	NRMT	EXC
COMPLETE SET (15)	10.00	4.50	1.25

- ☐ 1 Josh Booty
- ☐ 2 Hector Carrasco
- ☐ 3 Luis Castillo
- ☐ 4 Will Cunnane
- ☐ 5 Vic Darensbourg
- ☐ 6 Ryan Jackson
- ☐ 7 Charles Johnson
- ☐ 8 Andy Larkin
- ☐ 9 Billy McMillon
- ☐ 10 Brian Meadows
- ☐ 11 Ralph Milliard
- ☐ 12 Edgar Renteria
- ☐ 13 Victor Rodriguez
- ☐ 14 Marc Valdes
- ☐ 15 Matt Whisenant

1995 Kane County Cougars Team Issue

This 32-card set of the 1995 Kane County Cougars, a Class A Midwest League affiliate of the Florida Marlins, features color player photos with a thin gold inner border around the player's image. The backs carry information about the player and career statistics. 3,000 regular sets and 1,000 sponsor sets by Eckrich were produced. The cards are unnumbered and checklisted below according to the player's jersey number. This issue includes the minor league card debuts of Todd Dunwoody and Luis Castillo.

	MINT	NRMT	EXC
COMPLETE SET (32)	12.00	5.50	1.50
COMPLETE SPONSOR SET (32)	25.00	11.00	3.10

- ☐ 4 Luis Castillo
- ☐ 8 Tony Darden
- ☐ 9 Aaron Harvey
- ☐ 10 Lynn Jones MG
- ☐ 11 Maximo Rodriguez
- ☐ 13 Michael Reyes
- ☐ 17 Ryan Jackson
- ☐ 18 Michael Parisi
- ☐ 19 Brian Peterson CO
- ☐ 20 Abdul Cole
- ☐ 21 Walter White
- ☐ 22 John Roskos
- ☐ 24 Victor Rodriguez
- ☐ 25 Todd Cady
- ☐ 26 Greg Press
- ☐ 27 Lionel Pineda
- ☐ 28 Chad Miles
- ☐ 29 Dan Zanolla
- ☐ 31 Nigel Zlejo
- ☐ 32 Allan Hebbert
- ☐ 34 Zachary Stark
- ☐ 35 Josh Booty
- ☐ 37 Todd Dunwoody
- ☐ 38 Jamie Ybarra
- ☐ 39 Todd Bussa
- ☐ 41 Jon Farmer
- ☐ 42 Hayward Cook
- ☐ 43 Walter Miranda
- ☐ 44 Brian Meadows
- ☐ 46 Rod Allen CO
- ☐ NNO Pat Laverty TR
- ☐ NNO Ozzie(Mascot)

1995 Kinston Indians Team Issue

This 30-card set of the 1995 Kinston Indians, a Class A Carolina League affiliate of the Cleveland Indians, was produced by Multi-Ad Services Inc. and features borderless color player photos. The backs carry player information and career statistics. The cards are unnumbered and checklisted below in alphabetical order. This issue includes the minor league card debut of Danny Graves.

	MINT	NRMT	EXC
COMPLETE SET (30)	15.00	6.75	1.85

- ☐ 1 Tony Arnold CO
- ☐ 2 Bruce Aven
- ☐ 3 Todd Betts
- ☐ 4 James Betzsold
- ☐ 5 Dan Brabant
- ☐ 6 Gerald Cawhorn
- ☐ 7 Bartolo Colon
- ☐ 8 Roland De La Maza
- ☐ 9 Maximo De La Rosa
- ☐ 10 Einar Diaz
- ☐ 11 Dan Graves
- ☐ 12 Ricky Gutierrez
- ☐ 13 Gary Hagy
- ☐ 14 Kris Hanson
- ☐ 15 Rick Heiserman
- ☐ 16 Todd Johnson
- ☐ 17 Gordy MacKenzie MG
- ☐ 18 Bob McElligott ANN
- ☐ 19 Rafael Mesa
- ☐ 20 Michael Murphy
- ☐ 21 Igor Oropeza
- ☐ 22 Rick Prieto
- ☐ 23 Tony Runion
- ☐ 24 Mike Sarbaugh CO
- ☐ 25 Richie Sexson
- ☐ 26 Greg Thomas
- ☐ 27 Jay Vaught
- ☐ 28 Greg Williams
- ☐ 29 Enrique Wilson
- ☐ 30 Kinston Indians Logo CL

1995 Knoxville Smokies Fleer/ProCards

This 29-card set of the 1995 Knoxville Smokies, a Class AA Southern League affiliate of the Toronto Blue Jays, was produced by the Fleer Corp. and features posed color player photos in a white border on the card fronts. The backs carry player information and career statistics.

	MINT	NRMT	EXC
COMPLETE SET (29)	8.00	3.60	1.00

- ☐ 31 Carlos Almanzar
- ☐ 32 Alonso Beltran
- ☐ 33 Derek Brandow
- ☐ 34 Chad Brown
- ☐ 35 Roger Doman
- ☐ 36 Chris Freeman
- ☐ 37 Kurt Heble
- ☐ 38 Todd Ingram
- ☐ 39 Aaron Jersild
- ☐ 40 Chris Kotes
- ☐ 41 Jose Pett
- ☐ 42 Rick Steed
- ☐ 43 Kris Harmes
- ☐ 44 Angel Martinez
- ☐ 45 Sharnol Adriana
- ☐ 46 D.J. Boston
- ☐ 47 Mike Coolbaugh
- ☐ 48 Santiago Henry
- ☐ 49 Matt Johnson
- ☐ 50 Rickey Cradle
- ☐ 51 Lorenzo De La Cruz
- ☐ 52 Lonell Roberts
- ☐ 53 Warren Sawkiw
- ☐ 54 Shannon Stewart
- ☐ 55 Garth Iorg MG
- ☐ 56 Mark Connor CO
- ☐ 57 Pat McMorran TR
- ☐ 58 Checklist
- ☐ NNO Logo Card

1995 Lake Elsinore Storm Team Issue

This 30-card set of the 1995 Lake Elsinore Storm, a Class A California League affiliate of the California Angels, was produced by Multi-Ad Services Inc. and features color player photos with blue borders. The backs carry player information and career statistics. This issue includes the minor league card debut of Darin Erstad. 2,000 sets were produced.

	MINT	NRMT	EXC
COMPLETE SET (30)	35.00	16.00	4.40

- ☐ 1 Jose Aguirre
- ☐ 2 Andy Allanson
- ☐ 3 Matt Beaumont
- ☐ 4 Todd Blyleven
- ☐ 5 Rob Bonanno
- ☐ 6 Jamie Burke
- ☐ 7 Carlos Castillo
- ☐ 8 Anthony Chavez
- ☐ 9 Earl Cunningham
- ☐ 10 Moe Daniels
- ☐ 11 Alfredo Diaz
- ☐ 12 Derrin Doty
- ☐ 13 Geoff Edsell
- ☐ 14 Darin Erstad
- ☐ 15 Aaron Guiel
- ☐ 16 Mike Holtz
- ☐ 17 Pete Janicki
- ☐ 18 Keith Luuloa
- ☐ 19 Tom Redington
- ☐ 20 Mitch Seoane MG
- ☐ 21 Greg Shockey
- ☐ 22 Mark Simmons
- ☐ 23 Joel Smith
- ☐ 24 Todd Takayoshi
- ☐ 25 Joe Urso
- ☐ 26 Derek Vaughn
- ☐ 27 Brian Williard
- ☐ 28 Hamlet(Mascot)
- ☐ 29 The Lake Elsinore Diamond
- ☐ 30 Team Photo CL

1995 Louisville Redbirds Fleer/ProCards

This 30-card set of the 1995 Louisville Redbirds, a Class AAA American Association affiliate of the St. Louis Cardinals, was produced by the Fleer Corp. and features posed color player photos in a white border on the card fronts. The backs carry player information and career statistics.

	MINT	NRMT	EXC
COMPLETE SET (30)	18.00	8.00	2.20

- ☐ 266 Cory Bailey
- ☐ 267 Brian Barber
- ☐ 268 Richard Batchelor
- ☐ 269 Rigo Beltran
- ☐ 270 Alan Benes
- ☐ 271 Cris Carpenter
- ☐ 272 Francisco De La Rosa
- ☐ 273 John Frascatore
- ☐ 274 T.J. Mathews
- ☐ 275 Nate Minchey
- ☐ 276 Mike Raczka
- ☐ 277 Brian Deak
- ☐ 278 Marc Ronan
- ☐ 279 Joe Aversa
- ☐ 280 Ramon Caraballo
- ☐ 281 Darrel Deak
- ☐ 282 Aaron Holbert
- ☐ 283 Domingo Martinez
- ☐ 284 Howard Prager
- ☐ 285 Tracy Woodson
- ☐ 286 Allen Battle
- ☐ 287 Terry Bradshaw
- ☐ 288 Ray Giannelli
- ☐ 289 Jeff McNeely
- ☐ 290 Skeets Thomas
- ☐ 291 Joe Pettini MG
- ☐ 292 Joe Cunningham Jr. CO
- ☐ 293 Dyar Miller CO
- ☐ 294 Mark O'Neal TR
- ☐ 295 Cover Card CL

1995 Lynchburg Hillcats Team Issue

This 30-card set of the 1995 Lynchburg Hillcats, a Class A Carolina League affiliate of the Pittsburgh Pirates, was produced by Multi-Ad Services Inc. and features borderless color player photos. The backs carry player information and Minor League statistics. The cards are unnumbered and checklisted below in alphabetical order.

	MINT	NRMT	EXC
COMPLETE SET (30)	8.00	3.60	1.00

- ☐ 1 Jim Bibby CO
- ☐ 2 Ken Bonifay
- ☐ 3 Rafael Chaves
- ☐ 4 Lou Collier
- ☐ 5 Jeff Conger
- ☐ 6 Mike Daniel
- ☐ 7 John Dillinger
- ☐ 8 Bryan Farson
- ☐ 9 Cullen Hartzog
- ☐ 10 Marc Hill MG
- ☐ 11 Jay Knoblauh
- ☐ 12 Sean Lawrence
- ☐ 13 Rob Leary
- ☐ 14 Rod Lich TR
- ☐ 15 Sergio Mendez
- ☐ 16 Mark Mesewicz
- ☐ 17 Ramon Morel
- ☐ 18 Paul Perkins
- ☐ 19 Chris Peters
- ☐ 20 Charles Peterson
- ☐ 21 Jason Pfaff
- ☐ 22 Matt Pontbriant
- ☐ 23 Jeff Richardson
- ☐ 24 Tommy Robertson
- ☐ 25 Raul Rodarte
- ☐ 26 Roman Rodriguez
- ☐ 27 Redd Secrist
- ☐ 28 Kevin Tolar
- ☐ 29 Danny Young
- ☐ 30 Ramon Zapata

1995 Macon Braves Team Issue

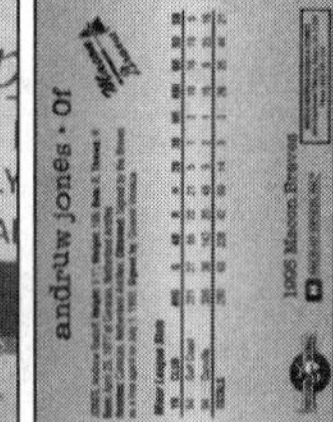

This 30-card set of the 1995 Macon Braves, a Class A South Atlantic League affiliate of the Atlanta Braves, was produced by Multi-Ad Services and features borderless color player photos. The backs carry player information and career statistics. The cards are unnumbered and checklisted below in alphabetical order. This issue includes the minor league card debuts of Andruw Jones, Wes Helms and Ron Wright. 1,000 sets were produced.

	MINT	NRMT	EXC
COMPLETE SET (30)	200.00	90.00	25.00

- ☐ 1 Brett Brewer
- ☐ 2 Anthony Briggs
- ☐ 3 Travis Cain
- ☐ 4 Wes Culp
- ☐ 5 Charlie Dawson
- ☐ 6 Jose Delgado
- ☐ 7 Mike Eaglin
- ☐ 8 Derrin Ebert
- ☐ 9 Alberto Evangelista
- ☐ 10 Wes Helms
- ☐ 11 Dave Hilton CO
- ☐ 12 Larry Jaster CO
- ☐ 13 Willy Johnson TR
- ☐ 14 Andruw Jones
- ☐ 15 Gus Kennedy
- ☐ 16 Mark Lavenia
- ☐ 17 Fernando Lunar
- ☐ 18 Pascual Matos
- ☐ 19 Kevin Millwood
- ☐ 20 Damian Moss
- ☐ 21 Brett Newell
- ☐ 22 Nelson Norman MG
- ☐ 23 Eric Olszewski
- ☐ 24 John Rocker
- ☐ 25 Mark Thompson
- ☐ 26 Marcus Tyner
- ☐ 27 Jacob Shumate
- ☐ 28 Terry Vaske

☐ 29 Tom Waldrop
☐ 30 Ron Wright

1995 Macon Braves Update Team Issue

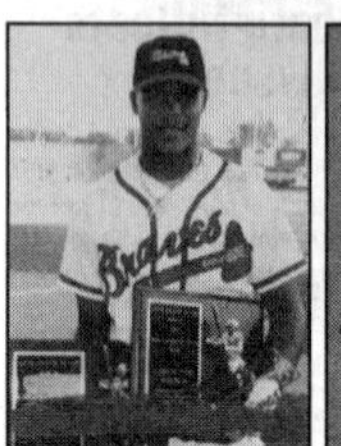

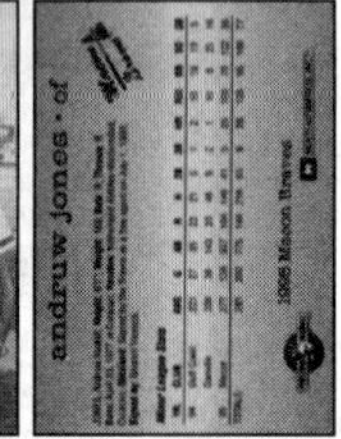

This six-card set Macon Braves Update was produced by Multi-Ad Services Inc. and carried a retail price of $5, features borderless color player photos of Macon Braves 1995 All-Stars with a limited addition Andruw Jones Player of the Year card. The backs carry player information and career statistics. The cards are unnumbered and checklisted below in alphabetical order.

	MINT	NRMT	EXC
COMPLETE SET (6)	70.00	32.00	8.75

☐ 1 Brett Brewer
☐ 2 Derrin Ebert
☐ 3 Andruw Jones
☐ 4 Gus Kennedy
☐ 5 Damian Moss
☐ 6 Ron Wright

1995 Martinsville Phillies Team Issue

This 30-card set of the Martinsville Phillies, a Rookie Class Appalachian League affiliate of the Philadelphia Phillies, was issued in six strips of five perforated cards each and was produced by Multi-Ad Services Inc. and sponsored by Nabisco and Acme Markets. Each card features color action player photos on the front with player information and statistics on the back. The cards are unnumbered and checklisted below in alphabetical order. This issue includes the minor league card debuts of Reggie Taylor, Dave Coggin and Texas Longhorns' running back Ricky Williams. 1,000 sets were produced.

	MINT	NRMT	EXC
COMPLETE SET (30)	50.00	22.00	6.25

☐ 1 Douglas Aguiar
☐ 2 Luis Andino
☐ 3 Robert Bowser
☐ 4 Domingo Brito
☐ 5 Matthew Buckles
☐ 6 Dave Coggin
☐ 7 Brian Dunne
☐ 8 Zach Elliott
☐ 9 Kevin Hooker
☐ 10 Jared Janke
☐ 11 Chad Kearney
☐ 12 Justin Kennedy
☐ 13 Jason Kershner
☐ 14 Kory Kosek
☐ 15 Clyde Livingston
☐ 16 Brian Miller
☐ 17 Alberto Mosquea
☐ 18 Richard O'Connor
☐ 19 Leonardo Oliveros
☐ 20 Melvin Pizarro
☐ 21 Kenny Reed
☐ 22 Eric Schreimann
☐ 23 Ricardo Serafin
☐ 24 Anthony Shumaker
☐ 25 Jason Sikes
☐ 26 Matthew Stone
☐ 27 Reggie Taylor
☐ 28 Scott Tebbetts
☐ 29 Samuel Wampler
☐ 30 Errick Williams

1995 Memphis Chicks Team Issue

This 27-card set of the 1995 Memphis Chicks, A Class AA Southern League affiliate of the San Diego Padres, was produced by Multi-Ad Services Inc. and features borderless color player photos. The backs carry player information and career statistics. 1,000 sets were produced.

	MINT	NRMT	EXC
COMPLETE SET (27)	10.00	4.50	1.25

☐ 1 Jerry Royster MG
☐ 2 Dean Treanor CO
☐ 3 Quentin Harley
☐ 4 Jason Thompson
☐ 5 Jorge Velandia
☐ 6 Stoney Briggs
☐ 7 John Cotton
☐ 8 Brad Gennaro
☐ 9 Ira Smith
☐ 10 Keith Thomas
☐ 11 Robbie Beckett
☐ 12 Mike Freitas
☐ 13 Brian Harrison
☐ 14 Brad Kaufman
☐ 15 Greg Keagle
☐ 16 Marc Kroon
☐ 17 Rich Loiselle
☐ 18 Rob Mattson
☐ 19 Craig Hanson
☐ 20 Todd Schmitt
☐ 21 Dario Veras
☐ 22 Raul Casanova
☐ 23 Tim Killeen
☐ 24 Homer Bush
☐ 25 Roberto Deleon
☐ 26 Sean Drinkwater
☐ 27 Paul Russo

1995 Michigan Battle Cats Team Issue

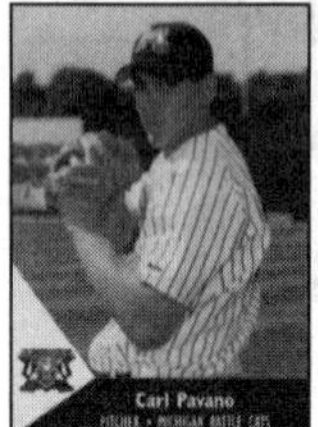

This 30-card set of the 1995 Michigan Battle Cats, a Class A Midwest League affiliate of the Boston Red Sox, features borderless color player photos with the player's name and position printed in a black bar at the bottom. The backs carry player information and career statistics. The cards are unnumbered and checklisted below in alphabetical order. This issue includes the minor league card debuts of Carl Pavano, Brian Rose and Donnie Sadler. 10,000 sets were produced.

	MINT	NRMT	EXC
COMPLETE SET (30)	18.00	8.00	2.20

☐ 1 Chris Allison
☐ 2 Joey Barksdale
☐ 3 Mike Blais
☐ 4 John Bowles
☐ 5 Craig Bush
☐ 6 Michael Coleman
☐ 7 Jake Cook
☐ 8 Joe Depastino
☐ 9 Tony DeRosso
☐ 10 John Dutch Jr.
☐ 11 Ethan Faggett
☐ 12 Jim Farrell
☐ 13 David Gibralter
☐ 14 Chad Hale Jr.
☐ 15 Joe Hamilton
☐ 16 Chris Kurek
☐ 17 Alvin Mitchell
☐ 18 Greg Patton
☐ 19 Carl Pavano
☐ 20 Bill Moloney CO
☐ 21 Brian Moore TR
☐ 22 Chad Renfroe
☐ 23 Brian Rose
☐ 24 Donnie Sadler
☐ 25 David Smith
☐ 26 Chris Stasio
☐ 27 Jim Telgheder
☐ 28 Darrell Tillmon
☐ 29 Jim Tyrell
☐ NNO Cover Card CL

1995 Midland Angels Team Issue

This 30-card set of the 1995 Midland Angels, a Class AA Texas League affiliate of the California Angels, was produced by Multi-Ad Services Inc. and features borderless color player portraits. The backs carry player information and career statistics. The cards are unnumbered and checklisted below in alphabetical order. 1,000 sets were produced.

	MINT	NRMT	EXC
COMPLETE SET (30)	12.00	5.50	1.50

☐ 1 Darrel Akerfelds
☐ 2 George Arias
☐ 3 Jeff Barns CO
☐ 4 Rob Bonanno
☐ 5 Ty Boykin
☐ 6 Willard Brown
☐ 7 Mike Butler
☐ 8 Jovino Carvajal
☐ 9 Emmitt Cohick
☐ 10 Leon Glenn
☐ 11 Todd Greene
☐ 12 Pedro Guerrero
☐ 13 Ryan Hancock
☐ 14 Tim Harkrider
☐ 15 Bryan Harris
☐ 16 David Holdridge
☐ 17 Steve Hosey
☐ 18 Korey Keling
☐ 19 Mario Mendoza MG
☐ 20 Jose Monzon
☐ 21 Orlando Munoz
☐ 22 Basilio Ortiz
☐ 23 J.D. Ramirez
☐ 24 Kernan Ronan CO
☐ 25 Jeff Schmidt
☐ 26 Mike Schooler
☐ 27 John Snyder
☐ 28 Joe Urso
☐ 29 Michael Wolff
☐ 30 Juice the Moose(Mascot)

1995 Midland Angels One Hour Photo

This 36-card set of the 1995 Midland Angels, a Class AA Texas League affiliate of the California Angels, features color player photos. The set measures approximately 5 1/2" by 5". The backs are blank. The cards are unnumbered and checklisted below in alphabetical order. 500 sets were produced.

	MINT	NRMT	EXC
COMPLETE SET (36)	80.00	36.00	10.00

☐ 1 Darrel Akerfelds
☐ 2 George Arias
☐ 3 Jeff Barns
☐ 4 Todd Blyleven
☐ 5 Ty Boykin
☐ 6 Willard Brown
☐ 7 Mike Butler
☐ 8 Jovino Carvajal
☐ 9 Emmit Cohick
☐ 10 Moe Daniels
☐ 11 Freddy Diaz
☐ 12 Leon Glenn
☐ 13 Todd Greene
☐ 14 Pedro Guerrero
☐ 15 Ryan Hancock
☐ 16 Tim Harkrider
☐ 17 Bryan Harris
☐ 18 David Holdridge
☐ 19 Steve Hosey
☐ 20 Korey Keling
☐ 21 Mario Mendoza
☐ 22 Jose Monzon
☐ 23 Orlando Munoz
☐ 24 Ernie Nieves
☐ 25 Basilio Ortiz
☐ 26 J.D. Ramirez
☐ 27 Mark Ratekin
☐ 28 Luis Raven
☐ 29 Kernan Ronan
☐ 30 Jeff Schmidt
☐ 31 Mike Schooler
☐ 32 John Snyder
☐ 33 Fausto Tejero
☐ 34 John Thibert
☐ 35 Joe Urso
☐ 36 Mike Wolff

1995 Midwest League All-Stars

This 58-card set honors the Midwest Minor League's 1995 All-Stars and features color player photos in a pastel star-design border. The backs carry player information and career statistics with the player's team logo. The cards are unnumbered and checklisted below in alphabetical order.

	MINT	NRMT	EXC
COMPLETE SET (58)	15.00	6.75	1.85

☐ 1 Nigel Alejo
☐ 2 Chris Allison
☐ 3 Alberto Blanco
☐ 4 R.J. Bowers
☐ 5 Emil Brown
☐ 6 Chris Burt
☐ 7 Todd Bussa
☐ 8 Todd Cady
☐ 9 Pat Cline
☐ 10 Carl Dale
☐ 11 Jeff D'Amico
☐ 12 John Donati
☐ 13 Todd Dunwoody
☐ 14 Ethan Faggett
☐ 15 Paul Failla
☐ 16 Michael Freehill
☐ 17 Alejandro Freire
☐ 18 Javier Gamboa
☐ 19 Ariel Garcia
☐ 20 Derek Hacopian
☐ 21 Billy Hall
☐ 22 Jed Hansen
☐ 23 Brendan Hause
☐ 24 Aaron Iatarola
☐ 25 Ryan Jackson
☐ 26 Tim Kester
☐ 27 Bill King
☐ 28 Corey Koskie
☐ 29 Mike MacDonald
☐ 30 Sean McNally
☐ 31 Brian Meadows
☐ 32 Rodolfo Mendez
☐ 33 Donovan Mitchell
☐ 34 Ben Molina
☐ 35 Tony Mounce
☐ 36 Greg Morris
☐ 37 Tom Mott
☐ 38 Jake Patterson
☐ 39 Carl Pavano
☐ 40 Jeff Poor
☐ 41 Greg Press
☐ 42 Brady Raggio
☐ 43 Steve Rain
☐ 44 Nilson Robledo
☐ 45 Victor Rodriguez
☐ 46 Mitch Root
☐ 47 Pete Rose Jr.
☐ 48 John Roskos
☐ 49 Tony Ross
☐ 50 Donnie Sadler
☐ 51 Mariano Santana
☐ 52 Demond Smith
☐ 53 Gary Trammell
☐ 54 Brett Walters
☐ 55 DeShawn Warren
☐ NNO Old Kent Park
☐ NNO Checklist
☐ NNO Cover Card

1995 Modesto A's Team Issue

This 32-card set of the 1995 Modesto A's, a Class A California League affiliate of the Oakland Athletics, was sponsored by McDonalds Restaurants and features black-and-white player portraits. The backs carry player information and career statistics. The cards are unnumbered and checklisted below in alphabetical order. This issue includes a second year card of Ben Grieve.

	MINT	NRMT	EXC
COMPLETE SET (32)	13.00	5.75	1.60

☐ 1 Tony Banks
☐ 2 Herb Baxter
☐ 3 Brandy Bengoechea
☐ 4 Steve Cox
☐ 5 D.T. Cromer
☐ 6 Kirk Dressendorfer
☐ 7 Glenn Ezell MGR
☐ 8 Ben Grieve
☐ 9 Jose Guillen
☐ 10 Gary Haught
☐ 11 Gary Hust
☐ 12 Tim Kubinski
☐ 13 Derek Manning
☐ 14 Eric Martins
☐ 15 Mike Maurer
☐ 16 Jason McDonald
☐ 17 Chris Michalak
☐ 18 Mark Moore
☐ 19 Willie Morales
☐ 20 Mike Neill
☐ 21 Randy Ortega
☐ 22 Rich Ramirez
☐ 23 Matt Reese
☐ 24 Brad Rigby
☐ 25 Rick Rodriguez CO
☐ 26 Mike Rossiter
☐ 27 Matthew Santos CO
☐ 28 Zach Sawyer
☐ 29 Matt Walsh
☐ 30 Ryan Whitaker
☐ 31 Jason White
☐ 32 Steve Zongor

1995 Nashville Sounds Team Issue

This 30-card set of the Nashville Sounds, a Class AAA American Association affiliate of the Chicago White Sox, was issued in one large sheet measuring approximately 14 3/8" by 24 1/2" and was sponsored by Nabisco and H.G. Hill Food Stores. Each sheet consists of five perforated six-card player strips with the sponsors' names and team logo printed in a wide strip at the top. The fronts feature color player photos with the backs displaying player information printed over a very light team logo as background.

	MINT	NRMT	EXC
COMPLETE SET (30)	8.00	3.60	1.00

☐ 1 James Baldwin
☐ 2 Rodney Bolton
☐ 3 Tom Bolton
☐ 4 Doug Brady
☐ 5 Carmine Cappuccio
☐ 6 Tim Howard
☐ 7 Dane Johnson
☐ 8 Brian Keyser
☐ 9 Roger LaFrancois CO
☐ 10 Greg Latta TR
☐ 11 Andrew Lorraine

☐ 12 Barry Lyons
☐ 13 Isidro Marquez
☐ 14 Mike Mongiello
☐ 15 Junior Ortiz
☐ 16 Donn Pall
☐ 17 Fernando Ramsey
☐ 18 Rick Renick MGR
☐ 19 Dave Righetti
☐ 20 Mike Robertson
☐ 21 Olmedo Saenz
☐ 22 Larry Schmittou
☐ 23 Bill Simas
☐ 24 Mike Sirotka
☐ 25 Chris Snopek
☐ 26 Chris Tremie
☐ 27 Kerry Valrie
☐ 28 Joey Vierra
☐ 29 Steve Wilson CO
☐ 30 Jerry Wolak

1995 New Haven Ravens Team Issue

This 34-card set of the 1995 New Haven Ravens, a Class AA Eastern League affiliate of the Colorado Rockies, was produced by Choice Marketing and features color player portraits. The backs carry player information and career statistics. 3,000 sets were produced.

	MINT	NRMT	EXC
COMPLETE SET (34)	15.00	6.75	1.85

☐ 1 Quinton McCracken
☐ 3 Neifi Perez
☐ 4 Maurico Gonzalez
☐ 5 Lamarr Rogers
☐ 6 Greg Gross
☐ 7 Joe List
☐ 8 John Myrow
☐ 10 Terry Jones
☐ 11 Billy White
☐ 12 David Tellers
☐ 13 Joel Moore
☐ 14 Paul Zuvella MG
☐ 15 Will Scalzitti
☐ 16 Garvin Alston
☐ 17 Jacob Viano
☐ 18 Phil Schneider
☐ 19 Mark Strittmatter
☐ 20 John Thomson
☐ 22 Ivan Arteaga
☐ 23 Chuck Estrada
☐ 24 Mike Case
☐ 25 Ken Grundt
☐ 27 Mike Farmer
☐ 28 Chris Neier
☐ 29 Angel Echevarria
☐ 31 David Kennedy
☐ 32 Jason Johnson
☐ 33 Bobby Jones
☐ 34 Tom Schmidt
☐ 35 Bryan Rekar
☐ NNO Rally(Mascot)
☐ NNO Mark Voisard
☐ NNO Marc Gustafson TR
☐ NNO Charlie Dowd GM

1995 New Jersey Cardinals Team Issue

This 30-card set of the 1995 New Jersey Cardinals, a Class A New York-Penn League affiliate of the St. Louis Cardinals, was produced by Multi-Ad Services Inc. and features color player photos with a thin white border around the player's image. The backs carry player information and career statistics. The cards are unnumbered and checklisted below in alphabetical order. This issue includes the minor league card debut of Matt Morris. 3,000 sets were produced.

	MINT	NRMT	EXC
COMPLETE SET (30)	15.00	6.75	1.85

☐ 1 Adam Benes
☐ 2 Matt Bennett
☐ 3 Darrell Betts
☐ 4 Ken Cameron
☐ 5 Ruben Cardona
☐ 6 Lou Deman
☐ 7 Troy Doezie
☐ 8 Robert Donnelly
☐ 9 Steve Frascatore
☐ 10 Sean Garman
☐ 11 Andy Hall
☐ 12 Rob Helvey
☐ 13 Miguel Inzunza
☐ 14 Nick Kast
☐ 15 Hub Kittle
☐ 16 Jason Lariviere
☐ 17 Travis McClendon
☐ 18 Shawn McNally
☐ 19 Luis Melendez
☐ 20 Kevin Miedreich
☐ 21 Bret Mueller
☐ 22 Matt Morris
☐ 23 Britt Reames
☐ 24 Tim Redman
☐ 25 Chris Richard
☐ 26 Jose Severino
☐ 27 Scott Spaulding
☐ 28 Mike Swenson
☐ 29 Hector Ugueto
☐ 30 Jose Villafana

1995 Norfolk Tides Team Issue

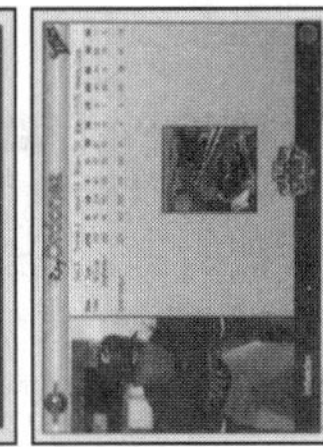

This 30-card set of the 1995 Norfolk Tides, a Class AAA International League affiliate of the New York Mets, features color player photos in a white frame with a blue inner border. The backs carry another player photo at the side of the player information and career statistics box. 10,000 sets were produced.

	MINT	NRMT	EXC
COMPLETE SET (30)	12.00	5.50	1.50

☐ 1 Toby Harrah MG
☐ 2 Bob Apodaca CO
☐ 3 Ron Washington CO
☐ 4 Joe Hawkins TR
☐ 5 Ed Alicea
☐ 6 Mike Birkbeck
☐ 7 Paul Byrd
☐ 8 Alberto Castillo
☐ 9 Reid Cornelius
☐ 10 Carl Everett
☐ 11 Dan Florence
☐ 12 Omar Garcia
☐ 13 Greg Graham
☐ 14 Butch Huskey
☐ 15 Jason Isringhausen
☐ 16 Jason Jacome
☐ 17 Aaron Ledesma
☐ 18 Derek Lee
☐ 19 Rey Ordonez
☐ 20 John Orton
☐ 21 Al Osuna
☐ 22 Ricky Otero
☐ 23 Bill Pulsipher
☐ 24 Chris Roberts
☐ 25 Bryan Rogers
☐ 26 Tracy Sanders
☐ 27 Phil Stidham
☐ 28 Dave Telgheder
☐ 29 Pete Walker
☐ 30 Jimmy Williams

1995 Norwich Navigators Team Issue

This 42-card set of the 1995 Norwich Navigators, a Class AA Eastern League affiliate of the New York Yankees, was produced by Choice Marketing. The fronts feature borderless color player photos. The backs carry player information and career statistics. The cards are checklisted below according to the players' jersey numbers printed on the backs of the cards.

	MINT	NRMT	EXC
COMPLETE SET (42)	10.00	4.50	1.25

☐ 11 Kraig Hawkins
☐ 11 Scott Epps
☐ 14 Jimmy Johnson MG
☐ 17 Joe DeBerry
☐ 18 Ramiro Mendoza
☐ 19 Carlton Fleming
☐ 20 Keith Seiler
☐ 21 Robert Hinds
☐ 22 Jason Robertson
☐ 22 Brian Faw
☐ 23 John Sutherland
☐ 23 Alexis Cabreja
☐ 24 Ruben Rivera
☐ 24 R.D. Long
☐ 25 James Musselwhite
☐ 26 Roger Burnett
☐ 27 Jhonny Pantoja
☐ 28 Steve Phillips
☐ 30 Kent Wallace
☐ 33 Mike DeJean
☐ 34 Scott Romano
☐ 34 Grant Sullivan
☐ 35 Brian Turner
☐ 36 Mike Buddie
☐ 38 Scott Standish
☐ 39 Rich Hines
☐ 40 Jeff Antolick
☐ 41 Kevin Riggs
☐ 43 Joe Long
☐ 45 Yamil Salcedo
☐ 46 Mike Figga
☐ 47 Nick DelVecchio
☐ 48 Matt Luke
☐ 48 Gordon Sanchez
☐ 49 Juan Nieves CO
☐ 50 Tom Nieto CO
☐ 51 Andy Fox
☐ 52 Billy Coleman
☐ 53 Tommy Carter
☐ 54 Tom Wilson
☐ NNO Norwich Navigators Logo CL
☐ NNO Greg Spratt TR

1995 Norwich Navigators Update Team Issue

These 11 cards are an update to the original 1995 Norwich Navigators Team Set and feature the same design as the original set. The cards are checklisted below according to the player's jersey number as listed on the back of the card.

	MINT	NRMT	EXC
COMPLETE SET (11)	8.00	3.60	1.00

☐ 2 Dave Renteria
☐ 21 Robert Hinds
☐ 22 Jason Robertson
☐ 24 Ruben Rivera
☐ 31 Tate Seefried
☐ 38 Mark Hubbard
☐ 39 Blaise Kozeniewski
☐ 45 Jose Musset
☐ 47 Nick DelVecchio
☐ 48 Matt Luke
☐ NNO Jimmy Johnson and Sons

1995 Ogden Raptors Team Issue

This 30-card set of the 1995 Ogden Raptors, a Rookie Class Pioneer League Independent, was produced by Multi-Ad Services Inc. and features borderless color player photos. The backs carry player information. The cards are unnumbered and checklisted below in alphabetical order.

	MINT	NRMT	EXC
COMPLETE SET (30)	16.00	7.25	2.00

☐ 1 Don Alexander
☐ 2 Willy'Bull' Ambos MG
☐ 3 Mark Coca
☐ 4 Alan Cook
☐ 5 Tim Cornish
☐ 6 Scott Demetral
☐ 7 Rene Gamez
☐ 8 Mark Hindy
☐ 9 Craig Holmes
☐ 10 Shane Jones
☐ 11 Yuhito Kazama
☐ 12 Chris Keighley
☐ 13 Jason Kline
☐ 14 Calvin Lee
☐ 15 John Lindquist VP
☐ 16 Jamie Lopiccolo
☐ 17 Louis Lopez
☐ 18 Erik Martinez
☐ 19 Rich Morales CO
☐ 20 Troy Novak
☐ 21 Paul O'Hearn
☐ 22 Kelly Phair
☐ 23 Mike Porzio
☐ 24 Keith Sayers TR
☐ 25 Lawrence Scheffer
☐ 26 Matt Schultea
☐ 27 Rich Vallero
☐ 28 Eric Whitson
☐ 29 Kurt Wilson ANN
☐ 30 Bat Boys CL

1995 Omaha Royals Team Issue

This 29-card set of the 1995 Omaha Royals, a Class AAA American Association affiliate of the Kansas City Royals, was produced by Multi-Ad Services Inc. and features color player photos with a thin white border around the player's image. The backs carry player information and career statistics.

	MINT	NRMT	EXC
COMPLETE SET (29)	12.00	5.50	1.50

☐ 1 Joe Adams
☐ 2 Mike Alvarez CO
☐ 3 Scott Anderson
☐ 4 J.T. Bruett
☐ 5 Melvin Bunch
☐ 6 Brent Cookson
☐ 7 Jose DeJesus
☐ 8 Chris Eddy
☐ 9 Mark Farnsworth TR
☐ 10 Bill Gorman VP/GM
☐ 11 Gary Green
☐ 12 Shane Halter
☐ 13 Dwayne Hosey
☐ 14 Keith Hughes
☐ 15 Mike Jirschele MG
☐ 16 Jerry Kutzler
☐ 17 Doug Linton
☐ 18 Mitch Lyden
☐ 19 Mike Magnante
☐ 20 Jose Melendez
☐ 21 Henry Mercedes
☐ 22 Bob Milacki
☐ 23 J.J. Munoz
☐ 24 Rod Myers
☐ 25 Tom Poquette CO
☐ 26 Chris Stynes
☐ 27 Michael Tucker
☐ 28 Joe Vitiello
☐ 29 Casey(Mascot)

1995 Orlando Cubs Fleer/ProCards

This 30-card set of the 1995 Orlando Cubs, a Class AA Southern League affiliate of the Chicago Cubs, was produced by the Fleer Corp. and features posed color player photos in a white border on the card fronts. The backs carry player information and career statistics.

	MINT	NRMT	EXC
COMPLETE SET (30)	8.00	3.60	1.00

☐ 1 Terry Adams
☐ 2 Ben Burlingame
☐ 3 Doug Harrah
☐ 4 David Hutcheson
☐ 5 Chris Johnson
☐ 6 Kevin Meier
☐ 7 Matt Petersen
☐ 8 Jon Ratliff
☐ 9 Roberto Rivera
☐ 10 Ottis Smith
☐ 11 David Swaetzbaugh
☐ 12 Amaury Telemaco
☐ 13 Darron Cox
☐ 14 Hector Ortiz
☐ 15 Brant Brown
☐ 16 Ken Coleman
☐ 17 Gabe Duross
☐ 18 Rudy Gomez
☐ 19 Austin Manahan
☐ 20 Chris Petersen
☐ 21 Robin Jennings
☐ 22 Ed Larregui
☐ 23 Paul Torres
☐ 24 Pedro Valdes
☐ 25 Bruce Kimm MG
☐ 26 Marty DeMerritt CO
☐ 27 Chris Speier CO
☐ 28 Steve Melendez TR
☐ 29 Spike(Mascot)
☐ 30 Checklist

1995 Pawtucket Red Sox Team Issue

This 30-card set of the 1995 Pawtucket Red Sox, a Class AAA International League affiliate of the Boston Red Sox, features color player portraits on the front with a fading yellow border of various widths. The backs carry player information and career statistics. 4,500 sets were produced.

	MINT	NRMT	EXC
COMPLETE SET (30)	10.00	4.50	1.25

☐ 2 Tony Rodriguez
☐ 7 Steve Rodriguez
☐ 10 Mike Hardge
☐ 11 Tim Howard
☐ 12 Scott Hatteberg
☐ 16 Luis Aguayo CO
☐ 17 Brian Looney
☐ 18 Joel Bennett
☐ 19 Dale Plummer
☐ 20 Alex Delgado
☐ 22 Pat Lennon
☐ 23 Juan Bell
☐ 24 Matt Stairs
☐ 25 Randy Brown
☐ 26 Buddy Bailey MG
☐ 27 Mike Hartley
☐ 30 Frank Rodriguez
☐ 32 Joe Ciccarella
☐ 33 Greg Blosser
☐ 34 Glenn Murray
☐ 35 Eric Wedge
☐ 36 Calvin Jones
☐ 37 Don Barbara
☐ 38 Bill Wertz
☐ 39 Steve Hoeme
☐ 40 Rick Wise CO
☐ 41 Jose Malave
☐ NNO Kent Qualls TR
☐ NNO Gar Finnvold
☐ NNO Tim Wakefield

1995 Pawtucket Red Sox Dunkin' Donuts

This 31-card Pawtucket Red Sox set, a Class AAA International League affiliate of the Boston Red Sox, was issued in one large sheet featuring six perforated five-card strips with a large team photo in the wide top strip. Sponsored by WJAR Newschannel 10 and Dunkin' Donuts, the fronts carry color player photos while the backs display player career statistics. The cards are unnumbered and checklisted below in alphabetical order.

	MINT	NRMT	EXC
COMPLETE SET (31)	50.00	22.00	6.25

☐ 1 Luis Aguayo CO
☐ 2 Buddy Bailey MG
☐ 3 Don Barbara
☐ 4 Juan Bell
☐ 5 Joel Bennett
☐ 6 Greg Blosser
☐ 7 Randy Brown
☐ 8 Joe Ciccarella
☐ 9 Alex Delgado
☐ 10 Gar Finnvold
☐ 11 Mike Hardge
☐ 12 Mike Hartley
☐ 13 Scott Hatteberg
☐ 14 Steve Hoeme
☐ 15 Tim Howard
☐ 16 Calvin Jones
☐ 17 Pat Lennon
☐ 18 Brian Looney
☐ 19 Jose Malave
☐ 20 Glenn Murray
☐ 21 Dale Plummer
☐ 22 Kent Qualls TR
☐ 23 Frank Rodriguez
☐ 24 Steve Rodriguez
☐ 25 Tony Rodriguez
☐ 26 Matt Stairs
☐ 27 Tim Wakefield
☐ 28 Eric Wedge
☐ 29 Bill Wertz
☐ 30 Rick Wise CO
☐ 31 Team Photo

1995 Peoria Chiefs Team Issue

This 31-card set of the 1995 Peoria Chiefs, a Class A Midwest League affiliate of the St. Louis Cardinals, was sponsored by Kitchen Cooked Potato Chips and Kroger Food Stores. The fronts feature color player photos with a fading blue to red border on two sides. The backs carry player information and career statistics.

	MINT	NRMT	EXC
COMPLETE SET (31)	10.00	4.50	1.25

☐ 1 Steve Biermann
☐ 3 Darek Robinson
☐ 5 Mark Dean
☐ 7 Keith McDonald
☐ 9 Tighe Curran
☐ 10 Placido Polanco
☐ 11 Efrain Contreras
☐ 15 Juan Ballara
☐ 16 Ryan Hall
☐ 18 Anton French
☐ 19 Ron Scott
☐ 21 Brian Reed
☐ 22 Joe Jumonville
☐ 23 Cory Corrigan
☐ 24 Victor Llanos
☐ 25 David Carroll
☐ 26 Bo Johnson
☐ 27 Dan Pontes
☐ 28 Juan Bautista
☐ 29 Travis Welch
☐ 30 Keith Smith
☐ 31 Mike Gautreau
☐ 32 Jesus Lugo
☐ 33 Isaias Nunez
☐ 34 Blake Stein
☐ 36 Steve Grandizio
☐ 37 Bardy Raggio
☐ 38 Roy Silver MG
☐ 39 Ray Searage CO
☐ 40 Carl Dale
☐ NNO Bert Boyd TR

1995 Phoenix Firebirds Team Issue

This 30-card set of the 1995 Phoenix Firebirds, a Class AAA Pacific Coast League affiliate of the San Francisco Giants, was sponsored by Keebler, Smitty's and KVRY 104.7 FM. The fronts feature color player photos with a blue border imprinted with the team logo. The backs carry sponsor logos and a small black-and-white player head photo with player information and career statistics. 4,000 sets were produced.

	MINT	NRMT	EXC
☐ 0 Phineas T. Firebird(Mascot)			
COMPLETE SET (30)	8.00	3.60	1.00

☐ 4 Marvin Benard
☐ 6 Kurt Ehmann
☐ 7 Kurt Knudsen
☐ 8 Chris Wimmer
☐ 10 Brad Brink
☐ 11 Joel Chimelis
☐ 12 Brent Cookson
☐ 14 Scott Robinson
☐ 16 Eric Christopherson
☐ 18 Shawn Barton
☐ 19 Dan Carlson
☐ 20 Clay Bellinger
☐ 21 Gary Scott
☐ 22 Bob Gamez
☐ 23 Barry Miller
☐ 24 Dax Jones
☐ 26 Randy Phillips
☐ 27 Mark Leonard
☐ 29 Ray Ortiz
☐ 31 Keith Bodie MG
☐ 32 Steve Cline CO
☐ 34 Sergio Valdez
☐ 35 Rick Trlicek
☐ 36 Tony Menendez
☐ 39 Rikkert Faneyte
☐ 44 Ken Greer
☐ 47 Enrique Burgos
☐ NNO Team Photo CL
☐ NNO Bill Carpine TR

1995 Piedmont Phillies Fleer/ProCards

This 28-card set of the 1995 Piedmont Phillies, a Class A South Atlantic League affiliate of the Philadelphia Phillies, was produced by the Fleer Corp. and features posed color player photos in a white border on the card fronts. The backs carry player information and career statistics.

	MINT	NRMT	EXC
COMPLETE SET (28)	8.00	3.60	1.00

☐ 178 Joe Barbao
☐ 179 Jason Boyd
☐ 180 Silvio Censale
☐ 181 Mauricio Estavil
☐ 182 Bo Hamilton
☐ 183 Trevor Humphry
☐ 184 Rich Hunter
☐ 185 Len Manning
☐ 186 Pete Nyari
☐ 187 Brian Stumpf
☐ 188 Larry Wimberly
☐ 189 Jamie Northeimer
☐ 190 Adan Millan
☐ 191 Matt Guiliano
☐ 192 Larry Huff
☐ 193 Bill Mobilia
☐ 194 Joe O'Brien
☐ 195 Shane Pullen
☐ 196 Matt Williamson
☐ 197 Jeffrey Key
☐ 198 Aaron Royster
☐ 199 Derek Stingley
☐ 200 John Torok
☐ 201 Josh Watts
☐ 202 Roy Majtyka MG
☐ 203 John Martin CO
☐ 206 Cover Card CL
☐ NNO Piedmont Phillies Logo

1995 Pittsfield Mets Team Issue

This 32-card set of the 1995 Pittsfield Mets, a Class A New York-Penn League affiliate of the New York Mets, was produced by Multi-Ad Services Inc. and features color player photos with a thin white border around the player's image. The backs carry player information and career statistics. The cards are unnumbered and checklisted below according to the player's jersey number. 1,000 sets were produced. This issue includes a second year card of Terrence Long.

	MINT	NRMT	EXC
COMPLETE SET (32)	12.00	5.50	1.50

☐ 7 Ramon Tatis
☐ 9 Jeff Parsons
☐ 11 Stan Jefferson CO
☐ 12 Roger Martinez
☐ 13 Ron Gideon MG
☐ 17 Bob Daly
☐ 18 Jeffry Motes
☐ 20 Paul Yoder
☐ 21 Thomas Arvelo
☐ 23 Terrence Long
☐ 24 Tom Wolff
☐ 25 Joe Pyrtle
☐ 26 Steve Lackey
☐ 27 Osvaldo Coronado
☐ 29 Dan Murray
☐ 30 Casey Patterson
☐ 31 Eric Morales
☐ 32 Gleydel Mota
☐ 33 Michael Parker
☐ 34 Andy Trumpour
☐ 35 Paul LeClair
☐ 38 Buzz Capra CO
☐ 39 Fletcher Bates
☐ 40 Ethan McEntire
☐ 42 Joe Lisio
☐ 43 Mike Dieguez
☐ 44 Matt Koenig
☐ 45 Scott Kindell
☐ 46 Jeff Howatt
☐ 47 Matt Ferullo
☐ NNO Charles Leddon TR
☐ NNO Skip Donald

1995 Port City Roosters Team Issue

This 29-card set of the 1995 Port City Roosters, a Class AA Southern League affiliate of the Seattle Mariners, was produced by Multi-Ad Services Inc. and features color player photos with a thin white border around the player's image. The backs carry player information and career statistics. The cards are unnumbered and checklisted below in alphabetical order. This issue includes the minor league card debut of Jason Varitek.

	MINT	NRMT	EXC
COMPLETE SET (29)	9.00	4.00	1.10

☐ 1 David Adam
☐ 2 James Bonnici
☐ 3 Johnny Cardenas
☐ 4 Manny Cora
☐ 5 Scott Davison
☐ 6 Eddy Diaz
☐ 7 Osvaldo Fernandez
☐ 8 Ryan Franklin
☐ 9 Darrin Garner CO
☐ 10 Charles Gipson
☐ 11 George Glinatsis
☐ 12 Craig Griffey
☐ 13 Paul Harker TR
☐ 14 Mike Hickey
☐ 15 Dave Myers MG
☐ 16 Jackie Nickell
☐ 17 Julio Peguero
☐ 18 Keifer Rackley
☐ 19 Roberto Ramirez
☐ 20 Desi Relaford
☐ 21 Rowdy the Rooster(Mascot)
☐ 22 Ron Romanick CO
☐ 23 Lagrande Russell
☐ 24 Sal(Salvy) Urso
☐ 25 Jason Varitek
☐ 26 Matt Wagner
☐ 27 Trey White
☐ 28 Bob Wolcott
☐ 29 Bob Worley

1995 Portland Sea Dogs Team Issue

This 30-card set of the 1995 Portland Sea Dogs, a Class AA Eastern League affiliate of the Florida Marlins, features color player photos in a black border. The backs carry a small color player head photo with player information and career statistics. The cards are unnumbered and checklisted below in alphabetical order.

	MINT	NRMT	EXC
COMPLETE SET (30)	8.00	3.60	1.00

☐ 1 Antonio Alfonseca
☐ 2 Daniel Chergey
☐ 3 Chris Clapinski
☐ 4 Tim Clark
☐ 5 Will Cunnane
☐ 6 Rich Gale CO
☐ 7 Jarod Juelsgaard
☐ 8 Robbie Katzaroff
☐ 9 Jimmy Kremers
☐ 10 Andy Larkin
☐ 11 Pat Leahy
☐ 12 Lou Lucca
☐ 13 Mike McGowan TR
☐ 14 Tom McGraw
☐ 15 Bill McMillon
☐ 16 Reynol Mendoza
☐ 17 Ralph Milliard
☐ 18 Greg Mix
☐ 19 Jeff Pentland CO
☐ 20 Doug Pettit
☐ 21 Jay Powell
☐ 22 Mike Redmond
☐ 23 Edgar Renteria
☐ 24 Mason Rudolph
☐ 25 Chris Sheff
☐ 26 Carlos Tosca MG
☐ 27 Casey Waller
☐ 28 Bryan Ward
☐ 29 Pookie Wilson
☐ 30 Team Photo

1995 Prince William Cannons Team Issue

This 30-card set of the 1995 Prince William Cannons, a Class A Carolina League affiliate of the Chicago White Sox, was produced by Multi-Ad Services Inc. and features borderless color player photos. The backs carry player information and career statistics. This issue includes the minor league card debut of Jeff Abbott.

	MINT	NRMT	EXC
COMPLETE SET (30)	14.00	6.25	1.75

☐ 1 Jeff Abbott
☐ 2 Sandy McKinnon
☐ 3 Andre Newhouse
☐ 4 Magglio Ordonez
☐ 5 Shawn Buchanan
☐ 6 Dan Fraraccio
☐ 7 Jason Goligoski
☐ 8 Paul Gonzalez
☐ 9 Frank Menechino
☐ 10 Wil Polidor
☐ 11 Juan Thomas
☐ 12 Harold Williams
☐ 13 Joe Durso
☐ 14 Robert Machado
☐ 15 Joe Spinello
☐ 16 Micheal Call
☐ 17 Chris Clemons
☐ 18 Tom Fordham
☐ 19 Mike Heathcott
☐ 20 Wayne Lindemann
☐ 21 Jason Pierson
☐ 22 Rich Pratt
☐ 23 Todd Rizzo
☐ 24 Hank Tagle
☐ 25 Archie Vazquez
☐ 26 Brian Woods
☐ 27 Steve Worrell
☐ 28 Dave Huppert MG
☐ 29 Jay Ward CO
☐ 30 Jaime Garcia CO

1995 Quad City River Bandits Team Issue

This 30-card set of the 1995 Quad City River Bandits, a Class A Midwest League affiliate of the Houston Astros, features color player photos over a background of baseballs. The backs carry player information and career statistics. The cards are unnumbered and checklisted below in alphabetical order. This issue includes the minor league card debut of Scott Elarton. 500 sets were produced.

	MINT	NRMT	EXC
COMPLETE SET (30)	16.00	7.25	2.00

☐ 1 Manuel Barrios
☐ 2 Alberto Blanco
☐ 3 R.J. Bowers
☐ 4 Mike Diorio
☐ 5 Scott Elarton
☐ 6 Alejandro Freire
☐ 7 Jimmy Gonzalez
☐ 8 John Halama
☐ 9 Billy Hall
☐ 10 Carlos Hernandez
☐ 11 Jim Hickey
☐ 12 Tim Kester
☐ 13 Dan Lock
☐ 14 Nate Lucero TR
☐ 15 Donovan Mitchell
☐ 16 Tony Mounce
☐ 17 Jim Pankovits MG
☐ 18 Wes Pratt
☐ 19 Alan Probst
☐ 20 Edgar Ramos
☐ 21 Mike Rennhack
☐ 22 Noel Rodriguez
☐ 23 Tony Ross
☐ 24 Victor Sanchez
☐ 25 Jose Santana
☐ 26 Tony Shaver
☐ 27 Gary Trammell
☐ 28 Chris Truby
☐ 29 Chad White
☐ 30 Checklist

1995 Rancho Cucamonga Quakes Team Issue

This 30-card set of the 1995 Rancho Cucamonga Quakes, a Class A California League affiliate of the San Diego Padres, was produced by Sport Shots and features borderless color player photos with the player's name, jersey number, and position in a bar near the bottom. The backs carry information about the player and career statistics. The cards are unnumbered and checklisted below according to the player's jersey number. This issue includes a second year card of Derrek Lee. 1,000 sets were produced.

	MINT	NRMT	EXC
COMPLETE SET (30)	15.00	6.75	1.85

☐ 1 Chris Prieto
☐ 3 Earl Johnson
☐ 5 Erick Corps
☐ 9 Chad Tredaway
☐ 10 Dickie Woodridge
☐ 12 Francisco Derotal
☐ 14 Ryan Whitman
☐ 15 Matt LaChappa

☐ 16 Bubba Dixon
☐ 17 Marty Barrett MG
☐ 18 Greg LaRocca
☐ 19 Eduardo Cuevas
☐ 20 Mike Hermanson
☐ 21 Luis Arroyo
☐ 22 Darell White
☐ 23 John Roberts
☐ 24 Leroy McKinnis
☐ 26 Santiago Rivera
☐ 27 Jason Schlutt
☐ 28 Heath Murray
☐ 29 Bryan Wolff
☐ 31 Matt Clement
☐ 33 Dave Mowry
☐ 34 Derrek Lee
☐ 35 Darren Grass
☐ 36 Jared Baker
☐ 37 Dave Smith CO
☐ NNO Dan Drewien
☐ NNO Cover Card CL
☐ NNO Jim Daniel TR

1995 Reading Phillies Eastern League Champions Team Issue

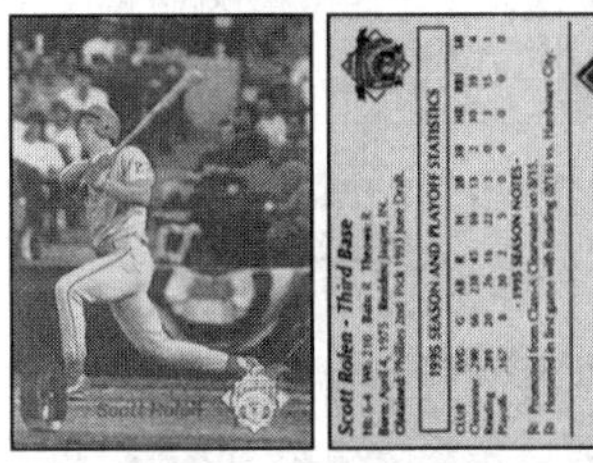

This 36-card set of the 1995 Reading Phillies, a Class AA Eastern League affiliate of the Philadelphia Phillies, honors the 1996 Easter League Champions and was sponsored by Nabisco. The fronts feature borderless player photos. The backs carry player information and career statistics. The cards are unnumbered and checklisted below in alphabetical order. This issue includes a second year card of Scott Rolen.

	MINT	NRMT	EXC
COMPLETE SET (36)	70.00	32.00	8.75

☐ 1 Doug Angeli
☐ 2 Larry Andersen CO
☐ 3 Matt Beech
☐ 4 Gary Bennett
☐ 5 Kent Blasingame
☐ 6 Ron Blazier
☐ 7 Bill Dancy MG
☐ 8 Robert Dodd
☐ 9 Blake Doolan
☐ 10 David Doster
☐ 11 Tommy Eason
☐ 12 Bobby Estalella
☐ 13 David Fisher
☐ 14 Wayne Gomes
☐ 15 Rob Grable
☐ 16 Mike Grace
☐ 17 Bronson Heflin
☐ 18 Dan Held
☐ 19 Rick Holifield
☐ 20 Craig Holman
☐ 21 Rich Hunter
☐ 22 Mike Juhl
☐ 23 Ryan Karp
☐ 24 Brent Leiby
☐ 25 Carlton Loewer
☐ 26 Wendell Magee
☐ 27 Chad McConnell
☐ 28 Fred McNair
☐ 29 Larry Mitchell
☐ 30 Bill Robinson CO
☐ 31 Scott Rolen
☐ 32 Kevin Sefcik
☐ 33 Steve Solomon
☐ 34 John Trisler
☐ NNO Team Photo
☐ NNO Trophy Card

1995 Reading Phillies Team Issue

This 28-card set of the 1995 Reading Phillies, a Class AA Eastern League affiliate of the Philadelphia Phillies, features color player action photos in a blue border with thin red and thinner white inner borders. The backs carry player information and career statistics. The cards are unnumbered and checklisted below in alphabetical order.

	MINT	NRMT	EXC
COMPLETE SET (28)	15.00	6.75	1.85

☐ 3 David Doster
☐ 6 David Fisher
☐ 8 Gary Mota
☐ 9 Kevin Sefcik
☐ 10 Blake Doolan
☐ 11 Ryan Karp
☐ 12 Mark Foster
☐ 13 Samuel Eason
☐ 14 Chad McConnell
☐ 15 Michael Juhl
☐ 16 David Hayden
☐ 17 Gary Bennett
☐ 18 Craig Holman
☐ 19 Fred McNair
☐ 21 Wayne Gomes
☐ 22 Jason Moler
☐ 23 Carl Hanselman
☐ 26 Mark Tranberg
☐ 27 Steven Solomon
☐ 29 Kent Blasingame
☐ 30 Eric Hill
☐ 33 Larry Andersen
☐ 34 Robert Grable
☐ 35 Michael Grace
☐ 37 Larry Mitchell
☐ 38 Joel Gilmore
☐ 39 John Trisler
☐ 40 Ron Blazier

1995 Richmond Braves Richmond Camera

This 29-card team set of the 1995 Richmond Braves, a Class AAA International League affiliate of the Atlanta Braves, was sponsored by Richmond Camera and measures approximately 4" by 4 7/8". The fronts feature borderless color player photos with sponsors' and team's logos in the wide bottom margin. The backs are blank. The cards are unnumbered and checklisted below in alphabetical order. 500 sets were produced.

	MINT	NRMT	EXC
COMPLETE SET (29)	60.00	27.00	7.50

☐ 1 Brian Bark
☐ 2 Chris Brock
☐ 3 Ed Giovanola
☐ 4 Kevin Grijak
☐ 5 Tyler Houston
☐ 6 Mike Kelly
☐ 7 Pat Kelly
☐ 8 Brian Kowitz
☐ 9 Grady Little
☐ 10 Kevin Lomon
☐ 11 Darrell May
☐ 12 Bobby Moore
☐ 13 Jose Munoz
☐ 14 Matt Murray
☐ 15 Kevin O'Connor
☐ 16 Jose Olmeda
☐ 17 Aldo Pecorilli
☐ 18 Eddie Perez
☐ 19 Dave Polley
☐ 20 Michael Potts
☐ 21 Hector Roa
☐ 22 Jason Schmidt
☐ 23 Chris Seelbach
☐ 24 Mike Sharperson
☐ 25 Tom Thobe
☐ 26 Royal Thomas
☐ 27 Terrell Wade
☐ 28 Juan Williams
☐ 29 Brad Woodall

1995 Richmond Braves Team Issue

This 30-card set of the 1995 Richmond Braves, a Class AAA International League affiliate of the Atlanta Braves, was sponsored by Pepsi Cola and features color art work of the players. The backs carry the player's name, postion, and statistics with the sponsor logo printed at the bottom. 7,500 sets were produced.

	MINT	NRMT	EXC
COMPLETE SET (30)	8.00	3.60	1.00

☐ 1 Grady Little MG
☐ 2 Chris Brock
☐ 3 Ed Giovanola
☐ 4 Tony Graffanino
☐ 5 Kevin Grijak
☐ 6 Tyler Houston
☐ 7 Brian Kowitz
☐ 8 Kevin Lomon
☐ 9 Bobby Moore
☐ 10 Jose Munoz
☐ 11 Matt Murray
☐ 12 Rod Nichols
☐ 13 Kevin O'Connor
☐ 14 Jose Olmeda
☐ 15 Eddie Perez
☐ 16 Dale Polley
☐ 17 Mike Potts
☐ 18 Darren Reed
☐ 19 Hector Roa
☐ 20 Jason Schmidt
☐ 21 Chris Seelbach
☐ 22 Mike Sharperson
☐ 23 Tom Thobe
☐ 24 Royal Thomas
☐ 25 Terrell Wade
☐ 26 Brad Woodall
☐ 27 Bill Fischer CO
☐ 28 Glenn Hubbard CO
☐ 29 Max Venable CO
☐ 30 Jim Lovell TR

1995 Rochester Red Wings Team Issue

This 48-card set of the 1995 Rochester Red Wings, a Class AAA International League affiliate of the Baltimore Orioles, was produced by Bill Pucko Cards and features borderless color player photos by Barbara Jean Germano. The backs carry player information and career statistics.

	MINT	NRMT	EXC
COMPLETE SET (48)	9.00	4.00	1.10

☐ 1 1995 Red Wings CL
☐ 2 Opening Day
☐ 3 Silver Stadium
☐ 4 New Frontier
☐ 5 Stadiumstock
☐ 6 Edgar Alphonzo
☐ 7 Kimera Bartee
☐ 8 Joe Borowski
☐ 9 Paul Carey
☐ 10 Steve Chitren
☐ 11 Jim Dedrick
☐ 12 Bobby Dejardin
☐ 13 John DeSilva
☐ 14 Cesar Devarez
☐ 15 Rick Forney
☐ 16 Curtis Goodwin
☐ 17 Kris Gresham
☐ 18 Jimmy Haynes
☐ 19 Jeff Huson
☐ 20 Scott Klingenbeck
☐ 21 Rick Krivda
☐ 22 Mark Lee
☐ 23 T.R. Lewis
☐ 24 Scott McClain
☐ 25 Kevin McGehee
☐ 26 Jimmy Myers
☐ 27 Junior Noboa
☐ 28 Alex Ochoa
☐ 29 Billy Owens
☐ 30 Rod Robertson
☐ 31 Kevin Ryan
☐ 32 Brian Sackinsky
☐ 33 Frank Seminara
☐ 34 John Shea
☐ 35 Mark Smith
☐ 36 Brad Tyler
☐ 37 Jim Wawruck
☐ 38 Tom Wegmann
☐ 39 Tyrone Woods
☐ 40 Greg Zaun
☐ 41 Marv Foley MG
☐ 42 Claude Osteen CO
☐ 43 Butch Davis CO
☐ 44 Dan Mason GM
☐ 45 Glenn Geffner ANN
☐ 46 Hall of Fame
☐ 47 Wild Fang(Mascot)
☐ 48 Kevin Harmon TR

1995 Rockford Cubs Team Issue

This 32-card set of the 1995 Rockford Cubs, a Class A Midwest League affiliate of the Chicago Cubs, was sponsored by AM radio station WROK 1440 and Eagle Country Market. The fronts feature color player photos with the player's name and position in a red bar at the bottom. The backs carry player information and career statistics with the sponsor logos printed below. 1,000 sets were produced.

	MINT	NRMT	EXC
COMPLETE SET (32)	15.00	6.75	1.85

☐ 2 Gilbert Avalos
☐ 3 Joseph Montelongo
☐ 6 Earl Byrne
☐ 8 Kevin Krause
☐ 9 Steve Walker
☐ 11 Saul Bustos
☐ 12 Shawn Livesy
☐ 14 Chad Olinde
☐ 18 Gabe Whatley
☐ 19 Ryan Casey
☐ 20 Jeremi Gonzales
☐ 21 Alfredo Garcia
☐ 22 Alger Medina
☐ 23 Pat Cline
☐ 24 Brian Dennis
☐ 25 Tony Khoury
☐ 26 Jason Stevenson
☐ 27 Richard Barker
☐ 28 Steve Rain
☐ 29 Jack Johnson
☐ 30 Doug Kimber
☐ 31 Richard Freeman
☐ 32 Javier Martinez
☐ 33 Marty Gazarek
☐ 34 Neil Faulkner
☐ 35 Troy Ormonde
☐ NNO Alan Dunn CO
☐ NNO Greg Keuter TR
☐ NNO Steve Dillard CO
☐ NNO Steve Roadcap MG
☐ NNO Michael Holmes GM
☐ NNO Casey the Cub(Mascot)

1995 Salem Avalanche Team Issue

This 30-card set of the 1995 Salem Avalanche, a Class A Carolina League affiliate of the Colorado Rockies, was produced by Multi-Ad Services Inc. and features borderless color player photos. The backs carry player information and career statistics.

	MINT	NRMT	EXC
COMPLETE SET (30)	20.00	9.00	2.50

☐ 1 Randy Snyder
☐ 2 Colin Dixon
☐ 3 Jeff Sobkoviak
☐ 4 Keith Barnes
☐ 5 Mark Voisard
☐ 6 John Giudice
☐ 7 Doug Walls
☐ 8 Matt Aminoff
☐ 9 Chris Sexton
☐ 10 Jamey Wright
☐ 11 Edgard Velazquez
☐ 12 Curt Conley
☐ 13 Brian Culp
☐ 14 Nate Holdren
☐ 15 Mike Higgins
☐ 16 Keith Grunewald
☐ 17 Steven Bernhardt
☐ 18 Vincente Garcia
☐ 19 Michael Saipe
☐ 20 Scott LaRock
☐ 21 Mark Wells
☐ 22 Doug Million
☐ 23 Matt Pool
☐ 24 Forry Wells
☐ 25 Bill Bliss
☐ 26 Bill Borowski TR
☐ 27 Tony Torchia CO
☐ 28 Billy Champion CO
☐ 29 Bill Hayes MG
☐ 30 Sam Lazzaro VP/GM

1995 San Antonio Missions Team Issue

This 30-card set of the 1995 San Antonio Missions, a Class AA Texas League affiliate of the Los Angeles Dodgers, was produced by Multi-Ad Services Inc. and features borderless color player photos. The backs carry player information and career statistics. The cards are unnumbered and checklisted below according to the player's jersey number as listed on the card back. This issue includes a third year card of Wilton Guerrero.

	MINT	NRMT	EXC
COMPLETE SET (30)	15.00	6.75	1.85

☐ 4 Wilton Guerrero
☐ 17 Paul LoDuca
☐ 19 Gary Rath
☐ 20 Dwight Maness
☐ 21 Eddie Rios
☐ 23 Angel Jaime
☐ 26 Jose Garcia
☐ 27 Nelson Castro
☐ 28 Oreste Marrero
☐ 30 Miguel Cairo
☐ 31 John Shelby
☐ 32 Tito Landrum
☐ 33 Javier Puchales
☐ 34 Dan Hubbs
☐ 35 Willie Romero
☐ 36 Keith Troutman
☐ 41 Chris Butterfield
☐ 42 Ryan Luzinski
☐ 44 Eric Weaver
☐ 45 James Martin
☐ 46 Dan Melendez
☐ 47 Jesus Martinez
☐ 48 Henry Blanco
☐ 50 Ramser Correa
☐ 53 Matt Herges
☐ 54 Eddie Oropesa
☐ 55 Jose Prado
☐ 57 David Pyc
☐ NNO Matt Wilson TR
☐ NNO Puffy Taco(Mascot)

1995 San Bernardino Spirit Team Issue

This 32-card set of the 1995 San Bernardino Spirit, a Class A California League affiliate of the Los Angeles Dodgers, was produced by Multi-Ad Services Inc. and features borderless color player posed and action photos. The backs carry player information and career statistics. This issue includes a second year card of Paul Konerko.

	MINT	NRMT	EXC
COMPLETE SET (32)	30.00	13.50	3.70

☐ 1 Julio Aquino
☐ 2 Will Brunson
☐ 3 Dan Camacho
☐ 4 Julio Colon
☐ 5 Brad Dandridge
☐ 6 Kevin Faircloth
☐ 7 Johnny Hilo
☐ 8 Scott Hunter
☐ 9 Keith Johnson
☐ 10 Jay Kirkpatrick
☐ 11 Paul Konerko
☐ 12 Joe Lagarde
☐ 13 Doug Newstrom
☐ 14 Jeff Paluk
☐ 15 Hugo Pivaral
☐ 16 Tom Price
☐ 17 Dan Ricabal
☐ 18 Brian Richardson
☐ 19 Adam Riggs
☐ 20 Petie Roach
☐ 21 J.P. Roberge
☐ 22 Brian Rolocut
☐ 23 Bob Schaaf
☐ 24 Frank Smith
☐ 25 Vernon Spearman
☐ 26 Eric Stuckenschneider
☐ 27 Chad Zerbe
☐ 28 Mike Collins TR
☐ 29 Dino Ebel CO
☐ 30 Dennis Lewallyn CO
☐ 31 Ron Roenicke MG
☐ 32 The Bug(Mascot)

1995 Scranton/Wilkes-Barre Red Barons Team Issue

This 30-card set of the 1995 Scranton/Wilkes-Barre Red Barons, a Class AAA International League affiliate of the Philadelphia Phillies, features color player photos in a blue frame with thin red outside and inside borders. The teams name is printed in white around the frame with the player's name and position at the bottom. The backs carry player information and career statistics. The cards are unnumbered and checklisted below in alphabetical order.

	MINT	NRMT	EXC
COMPLETE SET (30)	20.00	9.00	2.50

☐ 1 Steve Bieser
☐ 2 E.J. Brophy
☐ 3 Rob Butler
☐ 4 Andy Carter
☐ 5 Dave Cash CO
☐ 6 Jim Deshaies
☐ 7 Brian DuBois
☐ 8 Paul Fletcher
☐ 9 Robert Gaddy
☐ 10 Phil Geisler
☐ 11 Shawn Gilbert
☐ 12 Eric Hill
☐ 13 Rick Holifield
☐ 14 Blaise Ilsley
☐ 15 Kevin Jordan
☐ 16 Jeff Juden
☐ 17 Ryan Karp
☐ 18 Mike Lieberthal
☐ 19 Anthony Manahan
☐ 20 Tom Marsh
☐ 21 Charlie Montoyo
☐ 22 Mike Quade MG
☐ 23 Chuck Ricci
☐ 24 Gene Schall
☐ 25 Dennis Springer
☐ 26 Craig Strobel TR
☐ 27 David Tokheim
☐ 28 Scott Wiegandt
☐ 29 Jim Wright CO
☐ 30 Jon Zuber

1995 Signature Rookies

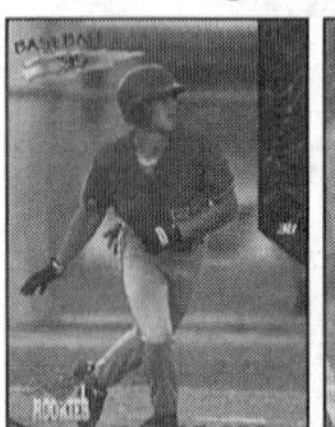

	MINT	NRMT	EXC
COMPLETE SET (50)	5.00	2.20	.60
COMMON CARD (1-50)	.10	.05	.01
☐ 1 Mark Acre	.10	.05	.01
☐ 2 Edgar Alfonzo	.10	.05	.01
☐ 3 Ivan Arteaga	.10	.05	.01
☐ 4 Rich Aude	.10	.05	.01
☐ 5 Joe Ausanio	.10	.05	.01
☐ 6 Marc Barcelo	.10	.05	.01
☐ 7 Allen Battle	.10	.05	.01
☐ 8 Rigo Beltran	.10	.05	.01
☐ 9 Darren Bragg	.10	.05	.01
☐ 10 Rico Brogna	.15	.07	.02
☐ 11 Mike Busch	.10	.05	.01
☐ 12 Juan Castillo	.10	.05	.01
☐ 13 Joe Ciccarella	.10	.05	.01
☐ 14 Darrell Deak	.10	.05	.01
☐ 15 Steve Dunn	.15	.07	.02
☐ 16 Vaughn Eshelman	.10	.05	.01
☐ 17 Bart Evans	.10	.05	.01
☐ 18 Rikkert Faneyte	.10	.05	.01
☐ 19 Kenny Felder	.10	.05	.01
☐ 20 Micah Franklin	.15	.07	.02
☐ 21 Brad Fullmer	.50	.23	.06
☐ 22 Willie Greene	.15	.07	.02
☐ 23 Greg Hansell	.10	.05	.01
☐ 24 Phil Hiatt	.10	.05	.01
☐ 25 Todd Hollandsworth	.40	.18	.05
☐ 26 Damon Hollins	.15	.07	.02
☐ 27 Chris Hook	.10	.05	.01
☐ 28 Kerry Lacy	.10	.05	.01
☐ 29 Todd LaRocca	.10	.05	.01
☐ 30 Sean Lawrence	.10	.05	.01
☐ 31 Aaron Ledesma	.10	.05	.01
☐ 32 Esteban Loaiza	.15	.07	.02
☐ 33 Albie Lopez	.10	.05	.01
☐ 34 Luis Lopez	.10	.05	.01
☐ 35 Marc Marini	.10	.05	.01
☐ 36 Nate Minchey	.10	.05	.01
☐ 37 Doug Mlicki	.10	.05	.01
☐ 38 Glenn Murray	.10	.05	.01
☐ 39 Troy O'Leary	.15	.07	.02
☐ 40 Eric Owens	.10	.05	.01
☐ 41 Orlando Palmeiro	.10	.05	.01
☐ 42 Todd Pridy	.10	.05	.01
☐ 43 Joe Randa	.15	.07	.02
☐ 44 Jason Schmidt	.30	.14	.04
☐ 45 Basil Shabazz	.10	.05	.01
☐ 46 Paul Spoljaric	.10	.05	.01
☐ 47 J.J. Thobe	.10	.05	.01
☐ 48 Sean Whiteside	.10	.05	.01
☐ 49 Gary Wilson	.10	.05	.01
☐ 50 Shannon Withem	.10	.05	.01

1995 Signature Rookies Signatures

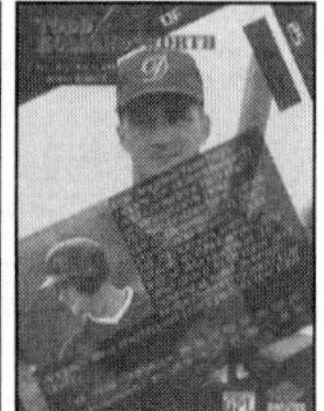

#28 Kerry Lacy and #45 Basil Shabazz did not sign/return their cards.

	MINT	NRMT	EXC
COMPLETE SET (47)	175.00	80.00	22.00
COMMON SIGNATURE (1-49)	3.00	1.35	.35
☐ 1 Mark Acre	3.00	1.35	.35
☐ 2 Edgar Alfonzo	3.00	1.35	.35
☐ 3 Ivan Arteaga	3.00	1.35	.35
☐ 4 Rich Aude	3.00	1.35	.35
☐ 5 Joe Ausanio	3.00	1.35	.35
☐ 6 Marc Barcelo	3.00	1.35	.35
☐ 7 Allen Battle	3.00	1.35	.35
☐ 8 Rigo Beltran	3.00	1.35	.35
☐ 9 Darren Bragg	3.00	1.35	.35
☐ 10 Rico Brogna	5.00	2.20	.60
☐ 11 Mike Busch	3.00	1.35	.35
☐ 12 Juan Castillo	3.00	1.35	.35
☐ 13 Joe Ciccarella	3.00	1.35	.35
☐ 14 Darrell Deak	3.00	1.35	.35
☐ 15 Steve Dunn	5.00	2.20	.60
☐ 16 Vaughn Eshelman	3.00	1.35	.35
☐ 17 Bart Evans	3.00	1.35	.35
☐ 18 Rikkert Faneyte	3.00	1.35	.35
☐ 19 Kenny Felder	3.00	1.35	.35
☐ 20 Micah Franklin	5.00	2.20	.60
☐ 21 Brad Fullmer	15.00	6.75	1.85
☐ 22 Willie Greene	5.00	2.20	.60
☐ 23 Greg Hansell	3.00	1.35	.35
☐ 24 Phil Hiatt	3.00	1.35	.35
☐ 25 Todd Hollandsworth	12.00	5.50	1.50
☐ 26 Damon Hollins	7.00	3.10	.85
☐ 27 Chris Hook	3.00	1.35	.35
☐ 29 Todd LaRocca	3.00	1.35	.35
☐ 30 Sean Lawrence	3.00	1.35	.35
☐ 31 Aaron Ledesma	3.00	1.35	.35
☐ 32 Esteban Loaiza	5.00	2.20	.60
☐ 33 Albie Lopez	3.00	1.35	.35
☐ 34 Luis Lopez	3.00	1.35	.35
☐ 35 Marc Marini	3.00	1.35	.35
☐ 36 Nate Minchey	3.00	1.35	.35
☐ 37 Doug Mlicki	3.00	1.35	.35
☐ 38 Glenn Murray	3.00	1.35	.35
☐ 39 Troy O'Leary	6.00	2.70	.75
☐ 40 Eric Owens	3.00	1.35	.35
☐ 41 Orlando Palmeiro	3.00	1.35	.35
☐ 42 Todd Pridy	3.00	1.35	.35
☐ 43 Joe Randa	6.00	2.70	.75
☐ 44 Jason Schmidt	8.00	3.60	1.00
☐ 46 Paul Spoljaric	3.00	1.35	.35
☐ 47 J.J. Thobe	3.00	1.35	.35
☐ 48 Sean Whiteside	3.00	1.35	.35
☐ 49 Gary Wilson	3.00	1.35	.35
☐ 50 Shannon Withem	3.00	1.35	.35

1995 Signature Rookies Draft Day Stars

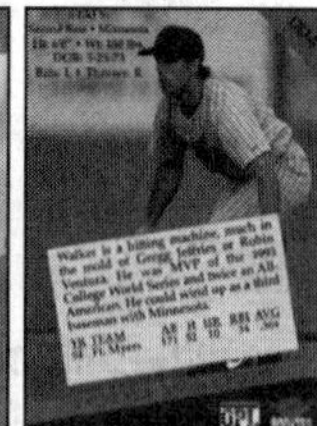

	MINT	NRMT	EXC
COMPLETE SET (5)	6.00	2.70	.75
COMMON CARD (DD1-DD5)	.75	.35	.09
☐ DD1 Matt Beaumont	.75	.35	.09
☐ DD2 Josh Booty	1.25	.55	.16
☐ DD3 Russ Johnson	.75	.35	.09
☐ DD4 Todd Walker	2.50	1.10	.30
☐ DD5 Jaret Wright	1.50	.70	.19

1995 Signature Rookies Draft Day Stars Signatures

Each card numbered out of 2100.

	MINT	NRMT	EXC
COMPLETE SET (5)	100.00	45.00	12.50
COMMON SIGNATURE (DD1-DD5)	15.00	6.75	1.85
☐ DD1 Matt Beaumont	15.00	6.75	1.85
☐ DD2 Josh Booty	20.00	9.00	2.50
☐ DD3 Russ Johnson	15.00	6.75	1.85
☐ DD4 Todd Walker	40.00	18.00	5.00
☐ DD5 Jaret Wright	25.00	11.00	3.10

1995 Signature Rookies Future Dynasty

	MINT	NRMT	EXC
COMPLETE SET (5)	4.00	1.80	.50
COMMON CARD (FD1-FD5)	.50	.23	.06
☐ FD1 Billy Ashley	.50	.23	.06
☐ FD2 Ben Grieve	1.50	.70	.19
☐ FD3 Derek Jeter	1.50	.70	.19
☐ FD4 Ruben Rivera	1.25	.55	.16
☐ FD5 Antone Williamson	1.00	.45	.12

1995 Signature Rookies Future Dynasty Signatures

Each card numbered out of 1000.

	MINT	NRMT	EXC
COMPLETE SET (5)	125.00	55.00	15.50
COMMON CARD (FD1-FD5)	15.00	6.75	1.85
☐ FD1 Billy Ashley	15.00	6.75	1.85
☐ FD2 Ben Grieve	40.00	18.00	5.00
☐ FD3 Derek Jeter	40.00	18.00	5.00
☐ FD4 Ruben Rivera	30.00	13.50	3.70
☐ FD5 Antone Williamson	20.00	9.00	2.50

1995 Signature Rookies Major Rookies

	MINT	NRMT	EXC
COMPLETE SET (5)	7.00	3.10	.85
COMMON CARD (MR1-MR5)	1.25	.55	.16
☐ MR1 Marty Cordova	2.00	.90	.25
☐ MR2 Benji Gil	1.25	.55	.16

	MINT	NRMT	EXC
☐ MR3 Charles Johnson	1.50	.70	.19
☐ MR4 Manny Ramirez	2.00	.90	.25
☐ MR5 Alex Rodriguez	5.00	2.20	.60

1995 Signature Rookies Major Rookies Signatures

Each card numbered out of 750.

	MINT	NRMT	EXC
COMPLETE SET (5)	175.00	80.00	22.00
COMMON CARD (MR1-MR5)	25.00	11.00	3.10
☐ MR1 Marty Cordova	40.00	18.00	5.00
☐ MR2 Benji Gil	25.00	11.00	3.10
☐ MR3 Charles Johnson	30.00	13.50	3.70
☐ MR4 Manny Ramirez	50.00	22.00	6.25
☐ MR5 Alex Rodriguez	80.00	36.00	10.00

1995 Signature Rookies Organizational Player of the Year

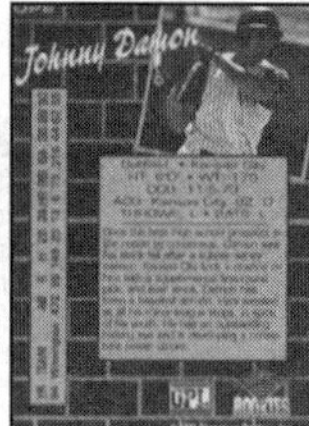

	MINT	NRMT	EXC
COMPLETE SET (5)	4.00	1.80	.50
COMMON CARD (OP1-OP5)	.75	.35	.09
☐ OP1 Juan Acevedo	.75	.35	.09
☐ OP2 Johnny Damon	1.50	.70	.19
☐ OP3 Ray Durham	1.50	.70	.19
☐ OP4 LaTroy Hawkins	.75	.35	.09
☐ OP5 Brad Woodall	.75	.35	.09

1995 Signature Rookies Organizational Player of the Year Signatures

Each card numbered out of 1000. #OP2 Johnny Damon did not sign or return his cards.

	MINT	NRMT	EXC
COMPLETE SET (4)	60.00	27.00	7.50
COMMON CARD (OP1-OP5)	15.00	6.75	1.85
☐ OP1 Juan Acevedo	15.00	6.75	1.85
☐ OP3 Ray Durham	25.00	11.00	3.10
☐ OP4 LaTroy Hawkins	15.00	6.75	1.85
☐ OP5 Brad Woodall	15.00	6.75	1.85

1995 Signature Rookies Old Judge

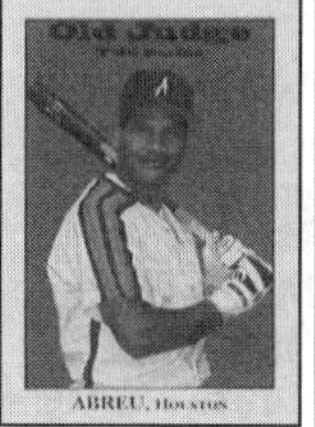
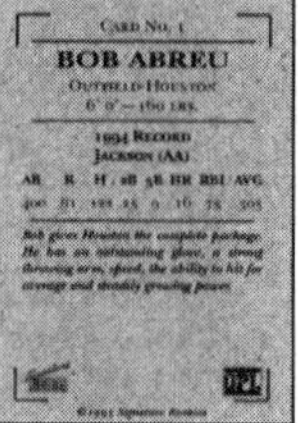

6 cards per pack--4 Old Judge, 1 chase set card, 1 autographed card; classic tobacco style settings on regular T-95 set, brings together a great old name with some of baseball's greatest new names; each player had signed 3,750 cards.[from press release] This specially designed series emulates the original size and styling of the early 1900's Old Judge Tobacco cards and features 35 of today's top minor league baseball players. Each player hand signed 3,750 cards.

	MINT	NRMT	EXC
COMPLETE SET (36)	5.00	2.20	.60
COMMON CARD (1-36)	.05	.02	.01

☐ 1 Bob Abreu	.40	.18	.05
☐ 2 Kym Ashworth	.20	.09	.03
☐ 3 Jared Baker	.05	.02	.01
☐ 4 Paul Bako	.05	.02	.01
☐ 5 Jason Bates	.05	.02	.01
☐ 6 Yamil Benitez	.30	.14	.04
☐ 7 Marshall Boze	.05	.02	.01
☐ 8 Rich Butler	.05	.02	.01
☐ 9 John Carter	.05	.02	.01
☐ 10 Jeff Cirillo	.15	.07	.02
☐ 11 Randy Curtis	.05	.02	.01
☐ 12 Sal Fasano	.05	.02	.01
☐ 13 Aaron Fultz	.05	.02	.01
☐ 14 Karim Garcia	2.00	.90	.25
☐ 15 Kevin Grijak	.05	.02	.01
☐ 16 Wilton Guerrero	.60	.25	.07
☐ 17 Stacy Hollins	.05	.02	.01
☐ 18 Bobby Hughes	.05	.02	.01
☐ 19 Jimmy Hurst	.05	.02	.01
☐ 20 Jason Isringhausen	.30	.14	.04
☐ 21 Ryan Karp	.05	.02	.01
☐ 22 Derek Lowe	.05	.02	.01
☐ 23 Matt Luke	.05	.02	.01
☐ 24 Lyle Mouton	.05	.02	.01
☐ 25 David Mysel	.05	.02	.01
☐ 26 Marc Newfield	.25	.11	.03
☐ 27 Jim Pittsley	.15	.07	.02
☐ 28 Chris Scheff	.05	.02	.01
☐ 29 Tate Seefried	.05	.02	.01
☐ 30 Shawn Senior	.05	.02	.01
☐ 31 Andy Stewart	.05	.02	.01
☐ 32 Ozzie Timmons	.05	.02	.01
☐ 33 Quilvio Veras	.15	.07	.02
☐ 34 Donny White	.05	.02	.01
☐ 35 Mike Zimmerman	.05	.02	.01
☐ 36 Ruben Rivera CL	1.00	.45	.12
☐ JD1 Joe DiMaggio	10.00	4.50	1.25

1995 Signature Rookies Old Judge Signatures

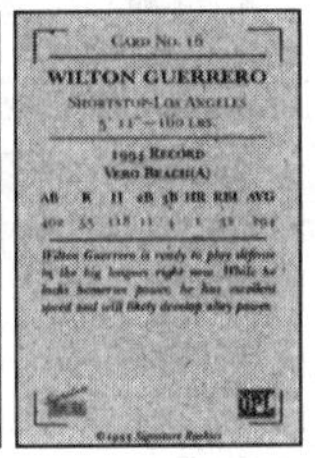

Each card numbered out of 5750.

	MINT	NRMT	EXC
COMPLETE SET (35)	125.00	55.00	15.50
COMMON CARD (1-35)	2.00	.90	.25
☐ 1 Bob Abreu	10.00	4.50	1.25
☐ 2 Kym Ashworth	4.00	1.80	.50
☐ 3 Jared Baker	2.00	.90	.25
☐ 4 Paul Bako	2.00	.90	.25
☐ 5 Jason Bates	2.00	.90	.25
☐ 6 Yamil Benitez	7.00	3.10	.85
☐ 7 Marshall Boze	2.00	.90	.25
☐ 8 Rich Butler	2.00	.90	.25
☐ 9 John Carter	2.00	.90	.25
☐ 10 Jeff Cirillo	4.00	1.80	.50
☐ 11 Randy Curtis	2.00	.90	.25
☐ 12 Sal Fasano	2.00	.90	.25
☐ 13 Aaron Fultz	2.00	.90	.25
☐ 14 Karim Garcia	20.00	9.00	2.50
☐ 15 Kevin Grijak	2.00	.90	.25
☐ 16 Wilton Guerrero	12.00	5.50	1.50
☐ 17 Stacy Hollins	2.00	.90	.25
☐ 18 Bobby Hughes	2.00	.90	.25
☐ 19 Jimmy Hurst	4.00	1.80	.50
☐ 20 Jason Isringhausen	8.00	3.60	1.00
☐ 21 Ryan Karp	2.00	.90	.25
☐ 22 Derek Lowe	2.00	.90	.25
☐ 23 Matt Luke	2.00	.90	.25
☐ 24 Lyle Mouton	2.00	.90	.25
☐ 25 David Mysel	2.00	.90	.25
☐ 26 Marc Newfield	8.00	3.60	1.00
☐ 27 Jim Pittsley	5.00	2.20	.60
☐ 28 Chris Scheff	2.00	.90	.25
☐ 29 Tate Seefried	2.00	.90	.25
☐ 30 Shawn Senior	2.00	.90	.25
☐ 31 Andy Stewart	2.00	.90	.25
☐ 32 Ozzie Timmons	3.00	1.35	.35
☐ 33 Quilvio Veras	3.00	1.35	.35
☐ 34 Donny White	2.00	.90	.25
☐ 35 Mike Zimmerman	2.00	.90	.25
☐ JD1 Joe DiMaggio AU/250	400.00	180.00	50.00

1995 Signature Rookies Old Judge All-Stars

Unsigned ratio 1:12; signed ratio 1:24; only 2,250 unsigned sets produced; each player signed 1,500 cards

	MINT	NRMT	EXC
COMPLETE SET (5)	3.00	1.35	.35
COMMON CARD (AS1-AS5)	.50	.23	.06
☐ AS1 Trey Beamon	1.50	.70	.19
☐ AS2 Tim Belk	.50	.23	.06
☐ AS3 Jimmy Haynes	.50	.23	.06
☐ AS4 Mark Johnson	.50	.23	.06
☐ AS5 Chris Stynes	.50	.23	.06

1995 Signature Rookies Old Judge All-Stars Signatures

Each card numbered out of 2100

	MINT	NRMT	EXC
COMPLETE SET (5)	30.00	13.50	3.70
COMMON CARD (AS1-AS5)	5.00	2.20	.60
☐ AS1 Trey Beamon	15.00	6.75	1.85
☐ AS2 Tim Belk	5.00	2.20	.60
☐ AS3 Jimmy Haynes	5.00	2.20	.60
☐ AS4 Mark Johnson	5.00	2.20	.60
☐ AS5 Chris Stynes	5.00	2.20	.60

1995 Signature Rookies Old Judge Hot Prospects

Unsigned ratio 1:10; signed ratio 1:30; only 2,750 unsigned sets produced; each player signed 1,000 of his cards.

	MINT	NRMT	EXC
COMPLETE SET (5)	6.00	2.70	.75
COMMON CARD (HP1-HP5)	.50	.23	.06
☐ HP1 Billy Ashley	.50	.23	.06
☐ HP2 Brad Clontz	.50	.23	.06
☐ HP3 Andrew Lorraine	.50	.23	.06
☐ HP4 Ruben Rivera	4.00	1.80	.50
☐ HP5 Jason Thompson	.50	.23	.06

1995 Signature Rookies Old Judge Hot Prospects Signatures

Each card numbered out of 1550.

	MINT	NRMT	EXC
COMPLETE SET (5)	50.00	22.00	6.25
COMMON CARD (HP1-HP5)	8.00	3.60	1.00
☐ HP1 Billy Ashley	8.00	3.60	1.00
☐ HP2 Brad Clontz	8.00	3.60	1.00
☐ HP3 Andrew Lorraine	8.00	3.60	1.00
☐ HP4 Ruben Rivera	30.00	13.50	3.70
☐ HP5 Jason Thompson	8.00	3.60	1.00

1995 Signature Rookies Old Judge Preview '95

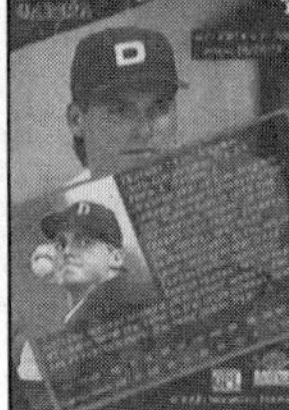

Featuring 35 of today's top minor league baseball players, the Old Judge T-95 series emulates the original size (2" by 3") and styling of the early 1900's Old Judge Tobacco cards. This preview set differs from the regular Old Judge T-95 in gold stamping, multiple photos and UV coating. Just 500 of these are signed, ratio 1:14.

	MINT	NRMT	EXC
COMPLETE SET (35)	25.00	11.00	3.10
COMMON CARD (1-35)	.15	.07	.02
☐ 1 Bob Abreu	2.00	.90	.25
☐ 2 Kym Ashworth	.60	.25	.07
☐ 3 Jared Baker	.15	.07	.02
☐ 4 Paul Bako	.15	.07	.02
☐ 5 Jason Bates	.15	.07	.02
☐ 6 Yamil Benitez	1.25	.55	.16
☐ 7 Marshall Boze	.15	.07	.02
☐ 8 Rich Butler	.15	.07	.02
☐ 9 John Carter	.15	.07	.02
☐ 10 Jeff Cirillo	.60	.25	.07
☐ 11 Randy Curtis	.15	.07	.02
☐ 12 Sal Fasano	.15	.07	.02
☐ 13 Aaron Fultz	.15	.07	.02
☐ 14 Karim Garcia	7.00	3.10	.85
☐ 15 Kevin Grijak	.15	.07	.02
☐ 16 Wilton Guerrero	2.50	1.10	.30
☐ 17 Stacy Hollins	.15	.07	.02
☐ 18 Bobby Hughes	.15	.07	.02
☐ 19 Jimmy Hurst	.60	.25	.07
☐ 20 Jason Isringhausen	1.50	.70	.19
☐ 21 Ryan Karp	.15	.07	.02
☐ 22 Derek Lowe	.15	.07	.02
☐ 23 Matt Luke	.15	.07	.02
☐ 24 Lyle Mouton	.15	.07	.02
☐ 25 David Mysel	.15	.07	.02
☐ 26 Marc Newfield	.75	.35	.09
☐ 27 Jim Pittsley	.75	.35	.09
☐ 28 Chris Scheff	.15	.07	.02
☐ 29 Tate Seefried	.15	.07	.02
☐ 30 Shawn Senior	.15	.07	.02
☐ 31 Andy Stewart	.15	.07	.02
☐ 32 Ozzie Timmons	.15	.07	.02
☐ 33 Quilvio Veras	.25	.11	.03
☐ 34 Donny White	.15	.07	.02
☐ 35 Mike Zimmerman	.15	.07	.02

1995 Signature Rookies Old Judge Preview '95 Signatures

Each card numbered out of 500.

	MINT	NRMT	EXC
COMPLETE SET (35)	600.00	275.00	75.00
COMMON CARD (1-35)	10.00	4.50	1.25
☐ 1 Bob Abreu	40.00	18.00	5.00
☐ 2 Kym Ashworth	20.00	9.00	2.50
☐ 3 Jared Baker	10.00	4.50	1.25
☐ 4 Paul Bako	10.00	4.50	1.25
☐ 5 Jason Bates	10.00	4.50	1.25
☐ 6 Yamil Benitez	30.00	13.50	3.70
☐ 7 Marshall Boze	10.00	4.50	1.25
☐ 8 Rich Butler	10.00	4.50	1.25
☐ 9 John Carter	10.00	4.50	1.25
☐ 10 Jeff Cirillo	20.00	9.00	2.50
☐ 11 Randy Curtis	10.00	4.50	1.25
☐ 12 Sal Fasano	10.00	4.50	1.25
☐ 13 Aaron Fultz	10.00	4.50	1.25
☐ 14 Karim Garcia	80.00	36.00	10.00
☐ 15 Kevin Grijak	10.00	4.50	1.25
☐ 16 Wilton Guerrero	50.00	22.00	6.25
☐ 17 Stacy Hollins	10.00	4.50	1.25
☐ 18 Bobby Hughes	10.00	4.50	1.25
☐ 19 Jimmy Hurst	20.00	9.00	2.50
☐ 20 Jason Isringhausen	30.00	13.50	3.70
☐ 21 Ryan Karp	10.00	4.50	1.25
☐ 22 Derek Lowe	10.00	4.50	1.25
☐ 23 Matt Luke	10.00	4.50	1.25
☐ 24 Lyle Mouton	10.00	4.50	1.25
☐ 25 David Mysel	10.00	4.50	1.25
☐ 26 Marc Newfield	30.00	13.50	3.70
☐ 27 Jim Pittsley	25.00	11.00	3.10
☐ 28 Chris Scheff	10.00	4.50	1.25
☐ 29 Tate Seefried	10.00	4.50	1.25
☐ 30 Shawn Senior	10.00	4.50	1.25
☐ 31 Andy Stewart	10.00	4.50	1.25
☐ 32 Ozzie Timmons	10.00	4.50	1.25
☐ 33 Quilvio Veras	15.00	6.75	1.85
☐ 34 Donny White	10.00	4.50	1.25
☐ 35 Mike Zimmerman	10.00	4.50	1.25

1995 Signature Rookies Old Judge Star Squad

	MINT	NRMT	EXC
COMPLETE SET (10)	20.00	9.00	2.50
COMMON CARD (1-10)	.75	.35	.09
☐ 1 Ruben Rivera	3.00	1.35	.35
☐ 2 Charles Johnson	2.50	1.10	.30
☐ 3 Derek Jeter	5.00	2.20	.60
☐ 4 Todd Hollandsworth	2.50	1.10	.30
☐ 5 Billy Ashley	.75	.35	.09
☐ 6 Benji Gil	.75	.35	.09
☐ 7 Vaughn Eshelman	.75	.35	.09

☐ 8 Ray Durham	2.00	.90	.25
☐ 9 Marty Cordova	3.00	1.35	.35
☐ 10 Manny Ramirez	4.00	1.80	.50

1995 Signature Rookies Old Judge Star Squad Signatures

Each card numbered out of 525.

	MINT	NRMT	EXC
COMPLETE SET (10)	350.00	160.00	45.00
COMMON CARD (1-10)	15.00	6.75	1.85
☐ 1 Ruben Rivera	60.00	27.00	7.50
☐ 2 Charles Johnson	40.00	18.00	5.00
☐ 3 Derek Jeter	80.00	36.00	10.00
☐ 4 Todd Hollandsworth	50.00	22.00	6.25
☐ 5 Billy Ashley	15.00	6.75	1.85
☐ 6 Benji Gil	15.00	6.75	1.85
☐ 7 Vaughn Eshelman	15.00	6.75	1.85
☐ 8 Ray Durham	30.00	13.50	3.70
☐ 9 Marty Cordova	60.00	27.00	7.50
☐ 10 Manny Ramirez	60.00	27.00	7.50

1995 SP

This 165-card set with 140 silver metallic die-cut cards features the top prospects in the minors. The set includes two subsets; Top Ten Prospects (1-10) featuring the cream of the crop and 1995 Draft Class subset (100-114) featuring 15-players who were selected in the 1995 amateur draft.

	MINT	NRMT	EXC
COMPLETE SET (165)	125.00	55.00	15.50
COMMON CARD (1-165)	.15	.07	.02
☐ 1 Andruw Jones	20.00	9.00	2.50
☐ 2 Brooks Kieschnick	.30	.14	.04
☐ 3 Nomar Garciaparra	3.00	1.35	.35
☐ 4 Adam Riggs	.40	.18	.05
☐ 5 Paul Wilson	.75	.35	.09
☐ 6 Trey Beamon	.30	.14	.04
☐ 7 Vladimir Guerrero	12.00	5.50	1.50
☐ 8 Ben Grieve	3.00	1.35	.35
☐ 9 Jay Payton	2.50	1.10	.30
☐ 10 Todd Walker	5.00	2.20	.60
☐ 11 Jermaine Dye	4.00	1.80	.50
☐ 12 Damon Hollins	.25	.11	.03
☐ 13 Wonderful Monds	.15	.07	.02
☐ 14 Damian Moss	1.25	.55	.16
☐ 15 Andruw Jones	20.00	9.00	2.50
☐ 16 Danny Clyburn	.30	.14	.04
☐ 17 Billy Percibal	.15	.07	.02
☐ 18 Rocky Coppinger	1.00	.45	.12
☐ 19 Tommy Davis	.15	.07	.02
☐ 20 Nomar Garciaparra	3.00	1.35	.35
☐ 21 Trot Nixon	.25	.11	.03
☐ 22 Jose Malave	.15	.07	.02
☐ 23 Ryan McGuire	.15	.07	.02
☐ 24 Rafael Orellano	.15	.07	.02
☐ 25 Darin Erstad	10.00	4.50	1.25
☐ 26 George Arias	.50	.23	.06
☐ 27 Matt Beaumont	.30	.14	.04
☐ 28 Jason Dickson	.50	.23	.06

Card	MINT	NRMT	EXC
☐ 29 Greg Shockey	.15	.07	.02
☐ 30 Brooks Kieschnick	.30	.14	.04
☐ 31 Jon Ratliff	.15	.07	.02
☐ 32 Amaury Telemaco	.15	.07	.02
☐ 33 Bob Morris	.15	.07	.02
☐ 34 Charles Poe	.15	.07	.02
☐ 35 Harold Williams	.15	.07	.02
☐ 36 Jeff Abbott	.30	.14	.04
☐ 37 Tom Fordham	.25	.11	.03
☐ 38 Calvin Reese	.15	.07	.02
☐ 39 Pat Watkins	.25	.11	.03
☐ 40 Aaron Boone	.75	.35	.09
☐ 41 Chad Mottola	.15	.07	.02
☐ 42 Jason Robbins	.15	.07	.02
☐ 43 Jaret Wright	1.00	.45	.12
☐ 44 Casey Whitten	.15	.07	.02
☐ 45 Bartolo Colon	1.50	.70	.19
☐ 46 Richie Sexson	2.00	.90	.25
☐ 47 Enrique Wilson	.75	.35	.09
☐ 48 Doug Million	.60	.25	.07
☐ 49 Joel Moore	.15	.07	.02
☐ 50 Derrick Gibson	2.50	1.10	.30
☐ 51 Neifi Perez	.30	.14	.04
☐ 52 Jamey Wright	.60	.25	.07
☐ 53 Juan Encarnacion	.40	.18	.05
☐ 54 Cade Gaspar	.15	.07	.02
☐ 55 Justin Thompson	.15	.07	.02
☐ 56 Bubba Trammell	1.50	.70	.19
☐ 57 Daryle Ward	.30	.14	.04
☐ 58 Clemente Nunez	.15	.07	.02
☐ 59 Will Cunnane	.15	.07	.02
☐ 60 Billy McMillon	.15	.07	.02
☐ 61 Matt Whisenant	.15	.07	.02
☐ 62 Edgar Renteria	1.50	.70	.19
☐ 63 Josh Booty	.60	.25	.07
☐ 64 Bob Abreu	.50	.23	.06
☐ 65 Richard Hidalgo	1.00	.45	.12
☐ 66 Ramon Castro	.25	.11	.03
☐ 67 Scott Elarton	.60	.25	.07
☐ 68 Jhonny Perez	.15	.07	.02
☐ 69 Mendy Lopez	.25	.11	.03
☐ 70 Glendon Rusch	.60	.25	.07
☐ 71 Sal Fasano	.15	.07	.02
☐ 72 Sergio Nunez	.15	.07	.02
☐ 73 Matt Smith	.15	.07	.02
☐ 74 Chris Latham	.15	.07	.02
☐ 75 Adam Riggs	.40	.18	.05
☐ 76 Wilton Guerrero	1.25	.55	.16
☐ 77 Paul Konerko	5.00	2.20	.60
☐ 78 Gary Rath	.15	.07	.02
☐ 79 Jim Cole	.15	.07	.02
☐ 80 Jeff D'Amico	.40	.18	.05
☐ 81 Antone Williamson	.75	.35	.09
☐ 82 Todd Dunn	.15	.07	.02
☐ 83 Brian Banks	.15	.07	.02
☐ 84 Shane Bowers	.15	.07	.02
☐ 85 Todd Walker	5.00	2.20	.60
☐ 86 Troy Carrasco	.15	.07	.02
☐ 87 Travis Miller	.15	.07	.02
☐ 88 Kim Bartee	.15	.07	.02
☐ 89 Dan Serafini	.15	.07	.02
☐ 90 Vladimir Guerrero	12.00	5.50	1.50
☐ 91 Hiram Bocachica	1.00	.45	.12
☐ 92 Brad Fullmer	1.00	.45	.12
☐ 93 Geoff Blum	.15	.07	.02
☐ 94 Israel Alcantara	.15	.07	.02
☐ 95 Jay Payton	2.50	1.10	.30
☐ 96 Rey Ordonez	1.25	.55	.16
☐ 97 Paul Wilson	.75	.35	.09
☐ 98 Preston Wilson	.15	.07	.02
☐ 99 Terrence Long	.75	.35	.09
☐ 100 Darin Erstad	10.00	4.50	1.25
☐ 101 Gabe Alvarez	.40	.18	.05
☐ 102 Jonathan Johnson	.40	.18	.05
☐ 103 Adam Benes	.40	.18	.05
☐ 104 Dennis Martinez Jr.	.15	.07	.02
☐ 105 Jaime Jones	1.50	.70	.19
☐ 106 Chad Hermansen	2.00	.90	.25
☐ 107 Geoff Jenkins	1.25	.55	.16
☐ 108 Juan LeBron	.50	.23	.06
☐ 109 Mark Redman	.40	.18	.05
☐ 110 Jose Cruz Jr.	10.00	4.50	1.25
☐ 111 Carlos Beltran	.50	.23	.06
☐ 112 Todd Helton	5.00	2.20	.60
☐ 113 Andy Yount	.50	.23	.06
☐ 114 Ryan Jaroncyk	.30	.14	.04
☐ 115 Sean Johnston	.30	.14	.04
☐ 116 Scott Romano	.15	.07	.02
☐ 117 Brian Buchanan	.25	.11	.03
☐ 118 Nick Delvecchio	.15	.07	.02
☐ 119 Ramiro Mendoza	.15	.07	.02
☐ 120 Matt Drews	.15	.07	.02
☐ 121 Shane Spencer	.15	.07	.02
☐ 122 Jason McDonald	.15	.07	.02
☐ 123 Scott Spiezio	.50	.23	.06
☐ 124 Brad Rigby	.15	.07	.02
☐ 125 Ben Grieve	3.00	1.35	.35
☐ 126 Steve Cox	.60	.25	.07
☐ 127 Willie Morales	.15	.07	.02
☐ 128 Wayne Gomes	.15	.07	.02
☐ 129 Larry Wimberly	.30	.14	.04
☐ 130 Scott Rolen	8.00	3.60	1.00
☐ 131 Carlton Loewer	.15	.07	.02
☐ 132 Wendell Magee	.25	.11	.03
☐ 133 Charles Peterson	.30	.14	.04
☐ 134 Lou Collier	.25	.11	.03
☐ 135 Trey Beamon	.30	.14	.04
☐ 136 Micah Franklin	.15	.07	.02
☐ 137 Jason Kendall	.60	.25	.07
☐ 138 Homer Bush	.15	.07	.02
☐ 139 Dickie Woodridge	.15	.07	.02
☐ 140 Derrek Lee	1.25	.55	.16
☐ 141 Raul Casanova	.50	.23	.06
☐ 142 Greg LaRocca	.15	.07	.02
☐ 143 Jason Thompson	.15	.07	.02
☐ 144 Jacob Cruz	1.00	.45	.12
☐ 145 Jesus Ibarra	.15	.07	.02
☐ 146 Jay Canizaro	.15	.07	.02
☐ 147 Steve Soderstrom	.15	.07	.02
☐ 148 Dante Powell	3.00	1.35	.35
☐ 149 James Bonnici	.15	.07	.02
☐ 150 Raul Ibanez	.15	.07	.02
☐ 151 Trey Moore	.15	.07	.02
☐ 152 Desi Relaford	.15	.07	.02
☐ 153 Jason Varitek	.50	.23	.06
☐ 154 Jay Witasick	.15	.07	.02
☐ 155 Bret Wagner	.15	.07	.02
☐ 156 Aaron Holbert	.15	.07	.02
☐ 157 Fernando Tatis	.40	.18	.05
☐ 158 Mike Bell	.25	.11	.03
☐ 159 Jeff Davis	.15	.07	.02
☐ 160 Julio Santana	.15	.07	.02
☐ 161 Kevin Brown	.50	.23	.06
☐ 162 Felipe Crespo	.15	.07	.02
☐ 163 Kevin Witt	.40	.18	.05
☐ 164 Mark Sievert	.15	.07	.02
☐ 165 Jose Pett	.40	.18	.05

1995 SP Autographs

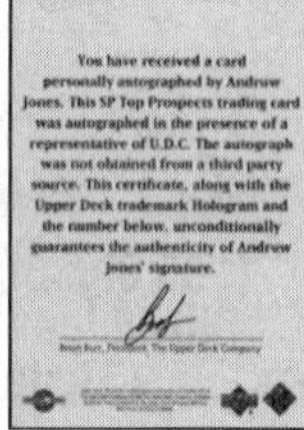

You have received a card personally autographed by Andruw Jones. This SP Top Prospects trading card was autographed in the presence of a representative of U.D.C. The autograph was not obtained from a third party source. This certificate, along with the Upper Deck trademark Hologram and the number below, unconditionally guarantees the authenticity of Andruw Jones' signature.

This 26-card insert set features autographs of the top prospects in the minors and a rare Michael Jordan. The autographs are inserted at a rate of one per box.

	MINT	NRMT	EXC
COMPLETE SET (26)	5000.00	2200.00	600.00
COMMON CARD (1-26)	20.00	9.00	2.50
☐ 1 Bob Abreu	40.00	18.00	5.00
☐ 2 Gabe Alvarez	25.00	11.00	3.10
☐ 3 George Arias	25.00	11.00	3.10
☐ 4 Trey Beamon	25.00	11.00	3.10
☐ 5 Aaron Boone	25.00	11.00	3.10
☐ 6 Raul Casanova	25.00	11.00	3.10
☐ 7 Bartolo Colon	60.00	27.00	7.50
☐ 8 Jermaine Dye	80.00	36.00	10.00
☐ 9 Nomar Garciaparra	80.00	36.00	10.00
☐ 10 Ben Grieve	80.00	36.00	10.00
☐ 11 Vladimir Guerrero	150.00	70.00	19.00
☐ 12 Richard Hidalgo	40.00	18.00	5.00
☐ 13 Andruw Jones	225.00	100.00	28.00
☐ 14 Michael Jordan	4000.00	1800.00	500.00
☐ 15 Jason Kendall	40.00	18.00	5.00
☐ 16 Brooks Kieschnick	25.00	11.00	3.10
☐ 17 Derrek Lee	60.00	27.00	7.50
☐ 18 Wonderful Monds	20.00	9.00	2.50
☐ 19 Rey Ordonez	50.00	22.00	6.25
☐ 20 Jay Payton	70.00	32.00	8.75
☐ 21 Adam Riggs	20.00	9.00	2.50
☐ 22 Scott Rolen	125.00	55.00	15.50
☐ 23 Jason Thompson	20.00	9.00	2.50
☐ 24 Paul Wilson	30.00	13.50	3.70
☐ 25 Jaret Wright	40.00	18.00	5.00
☐ 26 Todd Greene	25.00	11.00	3.10

1995 SP Destination the Show

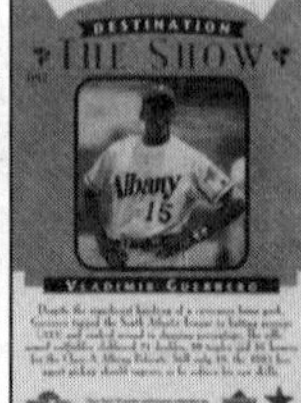

This 20-card insert set features the high-profile Minor League players expected to make their major league debut by 1996. The Destination the Show inserts were inserted at a rate of one in 63 packs.

	MINT	NRMT	EXC
COMPLETE SET (20)	1400.00	650.00	180.00
COMMON CARD (DS1-DS20)	20.00	9.00	2.50
☐ DS1 Andruw Jones	225.00	100.00	28.00
☐ DS2 Richard Hidalgo	40.00	18.00	5.00
☐ DS3 Paul Wilson	30.00	13.50	3.70
☐ DS4 Brooks Kieschnick	25.00	11.00	3.10
☐ DS5 Ben Grieve	80.00	36.00	10.00
☐ DS6 Adam Riggs	20.00	9.00	2.50
☐ DS7 Vladimir Guerrero	150.00	70.00	19.00
☐ DS8 Paul Konerko	100.00	45.00	12.50
☐ DS9 Jose Cruz Jr.	150.00	70.00	19.00
☐ DS10 Todd Walker	100.00	45.00	12.50
☐ DS11 Darin Erstad	150.00	70.00	19.00
☐ DS12 Derrek Lee	60.00	27.00	7.50
☐ DS13 Scott Rolen	125.00	55.00	15.50
☐ DS14 Trey Beamon	25.00	11.00	3.10
☐ DS15 Nomar Garciaparra	80.00	36.00	10.00
☐ DS16 Jason Kendall	40.00	18.00	5.00
☐ DS17 Aaron Boone	25.00	11.00	3.10
☐ DS18 Matt Drews	20.00	9.00	2.50
☐ DS19 Derrick Gibson	80.00	36.00	10.00
☐ DS20 Jay Payton	70.00	32.00	8.75

1995 SP Michael Jordan Time Capsule

This four-card set recaps Michael Jordan's Minor League career. Time Capsules are inserted at a rate of one per nine packs.

	MINT	NRMT	EXC
COMPLETE SET (4)	30.00	13.50	3.70
COMMON CARD (TC1-TC4)	8.00	3.60	1.00
☐ TC1 Michael Jordan Throwing	8.00	3.60	1.00
☐ TC2 Michael Jordan Batting	8.00	3.60	1.00
☐ TC3 Michael Jordan	8.00	3.60	1.00
☐ TC4 Michael Jordan	8.00	3.60	1.00

1995 Spokane Indians Team Issue

This 32-card set of the 1995 Spokane Indians, a Class A Northwest League affiliate of the Kansas City Royals, was sponsored by First Seafirst Bank and features color player photos with a thin red inner border and blue marblized frame. The backs carry player information and career statistics with the sponsor's logo printed at the bottom. The cards are unnumbered and checklisted below in alphabetical order.

	MINT	NRMT	EXC
COMPLETE SET (32)	14.00	6.25	1.75

☐ 1 Cover Card CL
☐ 2 Justin Adam
☐ 3 Jon Albrecht
☐ 4 Emiliano Escandon
☐ 5 Tyrone Frazier
☐ 6 Patrick Hallmark
☐ 7 Hal Hodge
☐ 8 Bryan Judice
☐ 9 Brent Kaysner
☐ 10 Scott Kortmeyer
☐ 11 Dwayne Lewis
☐ 12 Jesus Liz
☐ 13 Mark Melito
☐ 14 Tony Miranda
☐ 15 Joel Nations
☐ 16 Otto(Mascot)
☐ 17 Randy Paulin
☐ 18 Al Pedrique MG
☐ 19 Stephen Prihoda
☐ 20 Mark Quinn
☐ 21 Jason Ritter
☐ 22 William Roland
☐ 23 Matt Saier
☐ 24 Allen Sanders
☐ 25 Craig Sanders
☐ 26 Jose Santiago
☐ 27 Brett Schafer
☐ 28 James Vida
☐ 29 Modesto Villarreal
☐ 30 Leon Weathersby
☐ 31 Jeremy Williamson
☐ 32 Seafirst Stadium

1995 Syracuse Chiefs Team Issue

	MINT	NRMT	EXC
COMPLETE SET (29)	10.00	4.50	1.25

☐ 1 Travis Baptist
☐ 2 Howard Battle
☐ 3 Brent Bowers
☐ 4 Eric Brooks
☐ 5 Scott Brow
☐ 6 Tim Brown
☐ 7 Rich Butler
☐ 8 Willie Canate
☐ 9 Giovanni Carrara
☐ 10 Tim Crabtree
☐ 11 Felipe Crespo
☐ 12 Carlos Delgado
☐ 13 Huck Flener
☐ 14 Richie Hebner MGR
☐ 15 Joe Lis Jr.
☐ 16 Paul Menhart
☐ 17 Steve McInerney TR
☐ 18 Bill Monbouquette CO
☐ 19 Robert Perez
☐ 20 John Ramos
☐ 21 Ken Robinson
☐ 22 Jimmy Rogers
☐ 23 Paul Spoljaric
☐ 24 Hector Torres
☐ 25 Jason Townley
☐ 26 Jeff Ware
☐ 27 Ben Weber
☐ 28 Chris Weinke
☐ NNO Cover Card CL

1995 Springfield Sultans Team Issue

This 30-card set of the 1995 Springfield Sultans, a Class A Midwest League affiliate of the Kansas City Royals, was produced by Multi-Ad Services Inc. and features borderless color player photos. The backs carry player information and career statistics. 1,500 sets were produced.

	MINT	NRMT	EXC
COMPLETE SET (30)	14.00	6.25	1.75

☐ 1 Eric Anderson
☐ 2 Jelani Brandon
☐ 3 Dustin Brixey
☐ 4 Carlos Burgos Jr.
☐ 5 Lance Carter
☐ 6 Eduardo Cedeno
☐ 7 Sean Delaney
☐ 8 Ken Fitzpatrick
☐ 9 Pat Flury
☐ 10 Javier Gamboa
☐ 11 Jed Hansen
☐ 12 Mike MacDonald
☐ 13 Mike Mason
☐ 14 Sean McNally
☐ 15 Rodolfo Mendez
☐ 16 Francisco Mendoza
☐ 17 Blaine Mull
☐ 18 Rodney Nelson
☐ 19 Marc Phillips
☐ 20 Brian Poldberg
☐ 21 Chris Price
☐ 22 Alejandro Prieto
☐ 23 Ray Roberts
☐ 24 Juan Rocha
☐ 25 Rafael Santana
☐ 26 Matt Smith
☐ 27 Rodney Sparks
☐ 28 Ryan Towns
☐ 29 Matt Treanor
☐ 30 Eric Walls

1995 St. Catherines Stompers Team Issue

This 36-card set of the 1995 St. Catherines Stompers, a Class A New York-Penn League affiliate of the Toronto Blue Jays, features color player photos with a thin yellow inner border and a purple frame with yellow corner stripes. The backs carry player information and a team safety tip.

	MINT	NRMT	EXC
COMPLETE SET (36)	10.00	4.50	1.25

☐ 1 Tom Davey
☐ 2 Joe Young
☐ 3 Tyson Hartshorn
☐ 4 Benny Lowe
☐ 5 John Crowther
☐ 6 Rusty Volkert
☐ 7 Wayne Hoy
☐ 8 Randy Smith
☐ 9 Eric Horton
☐ 10 Narcisco Delacruz
☐ 11 Jose Peguero
☐ 12 Scott Fitterer
☐ 13 Ernie Peterman
☐ 14 Luis Rodriguez
☐ 15 John Reilly
☐ 16 Bryan Williams
☐ 17 Ryan Freel
☐ 18 Battle Holley
☐ 19 Chris Hayes
☐ 20 Mark Landers
☐ 21 Fausto Solano
☐ 22 Damon Johnson
☐ 23 Felix Rosario
☐ 24 Tim Bourne
☐ 25 Omar Sanchez
☐ 26 J.J. Cannon MG
☐ 27 Al Widmar CO
☐ 28 Bat Boys CL
☐ 29 Mark Spridzans

- ☐ 30 John Belford GM
- ☐ 31 Ernie Whitt OWN
- ☐ 32 Paul Pettipiece
- ☐ 33 Chris Marotta
- ☐ 34 Jaycees Logo
- ☐ 35 Timbit Safety License
- ☐ 36 Stompers logo CL

1995 St. Lucie Mets Team Issue

This 36-card set of the 1995 St. Lucie Mets, a Class A Florida State League affiliate of the New York Mets, was sponsored by Publix Super Markets and features color player photos with different colored borders. The backs carry player information, career statistics, and the sponsor's logo.

	MINT	NRMT	EXC
COMPLETE SET (36)	9.00	4.00	1.10

- ☐ 1 Rafael Landestoy
- ☐ 2 Randy Niemann
- ☐ 3 Larry Bennese TR
- ☐ 4 Benny Agbayani
- ☐ 5 Steve Arffa
- ☐ 6 Jesus Azuaje
- ☐ 7 Lou Benbow
- ☐ 8 Craig Bullock
- ☐ 9 Jeff Cosman
- ☐ 10 Cobi Cradle
- ☐ 11 Cesar Diaz
- ☐ 12 Chad Epperson
- ☐ 13 Ross Ferrier
- ☐ 14 Steve Grennan
- ☐ 15 Mark Guerra
- ☐ 16 Al Hammel
- ☐ 17 Erik Hiljus
- ☐ 18 Tripp Keister
- ☐ 19 Sean Kenny
- ☐ 20 Toby Larson
- ☐ 21 Allen McDill
- ☐ 22 Ryan Miller
- ☐ 23 Jeff Motes
- ☐ 24 Brandon Newell
- ☐ 25 Joe Petcka
- ☐ 26 Paul Petrulis
- ☐ 27 Sandy Pichardo
- ☐ 28 Rafael Roque
- ☐ 29 Scott Sauerbeck
- ☐ 30 Al Shirley
- ☐ 31 Matt Terrell
- ☐ 32 Randy Warner
- ☐ 33 Mike Welch
- ☐ 34 Todd Whitehurst
- ☐ 35 Mark Wipf
- ☐ 36 Slider(Mascot)

1995 Tacoma Rainers Team Issue

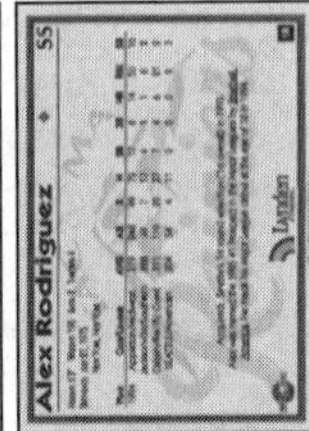

This 30-card set of the 1995 Tacoma Raniers, a Class AAA Pacific Coast League affiliate of the Seattle Mariners, was sponsored by Lynden Farms and features color player photos in a white frame with a red inner border. The backs carry player information and 1994 season statistics. This issue includes a second year card of Alex Rodriguez. 5,000 sets were produced.

	MINT	NRMT	EXC
COMPLETE SET (30)	40.00	18.00	5.00

- ☐ 1 Steve Smith MG
- ☐ 2 Jeff Andrews CO
- ☐ 3 Terry Kennedy CO
- ☐ 4 Matt Apana
- ☐ 5 Darren Bragg
- ☐ 6 Jim Converse
- ☐ 7 Jeff Darwin
- ☐ 8 Tim Harikkala
- ☐ 9 Chris Howard
- ☐ 10 Greg Litton
- ☐ 11 Quinn Mack
- ☐ 12 Jim Mecir
- ☐ 13 Marc Newfield
- ☐ 14 J.D. Noland
- ☐ 15 Tony Phillips
- ☐ 16 Greg Pirkl
- ☐ 17 Arquimedez Pozo
- ☐ 18 Alex Rodriguez
- ☐ 19 Doug Sanders
- ☐ 20 Andy Sheets
- ☐ 21 Darrell Sherman
- ☐ 22 Gary Thurman
- ☐ 23 Salomon Torres
- ☐ 24 Brian Turang
- ☐ 25 Ron Villone
- ☐ 26 Weston Weber
- ☐ 27 Chris Widger
- ☐ 28 Jerry Willard
- ☐ 29 Bob Wolcott
- ☐ 30 Rhubarb(Mascot)

1995 Tampa Yankees Team Issue

This 30-card set of the 1995 Tampa Yankees, a Class A Florida State League affiliate of the New York Yankees, was sponsored by Multi-Ad Services Inc. and features borderless color player photos by Cliff Welch. The backs carry player information and career statistics.

	MINT	NRMT	EXC
COMPLETE SET (30)	8.00	3.60	1.00

- ☐ 1 Kurt Bierek
- ☐ 2 Jeff Cindrich
- ☐ 3 Tim Cooper
- ☐ 4 Joe DeBerry
- ☐ 5 Matt Drews
- ☐ 6 Albert Drumheller
- ☐ 7 Jake Gibbs MG
- ☐ 8 Mike Gordon
- ☐ 9 Elston Hansen
- ☐ 10 Kraig Hawkins
- ☐ 11 Mark Hubbard
- ☐ 12 Marty Janzen
- ☐ 13 Scott Kamieniecki
- ☐ 14 Pat Kelly
- ☐ 15 Eric Knowles
- ☐ 16 Frank Lankford
- ☐ 17 Donnie Leshnock
- ☐ 18 R.D. Long
- ☐ 19 Mike Mitchell
- ☐ 20 Jeff Motuzas
- ☐ 21 Jason Rathbun
- ☐ 22 Ray Ricken
- ☐ 23 Danny Rios
- ☐ 24 Sandi Santiago
- ☐ 25 Sloan Smith
- ☐ 26 Shane Spencer
- ☐ 27 Darryl Strawberry
- ☐ 28 Ray Suplee
- ☐ 29 Jaime Torres
- ☐ 30 Dave Howard CO
  Mark Shiflett CO#(Ken Dominguez CO

1995 Tennessee Volunteers Wendy's

The cards are unnumbered and checklisted below in alphabetical order. Issued in two eight-card sheets.

	MINT	NRMT	EXC
COMPLETE SET (16)	25.00	11.00	3.10

- ☐ 1 Rod Delmonico CO
- ☐ 2 Chris Freeman
- ☐ 3 Bronson Heflin
- ☐ 4 Todd Helton (Batting)
- ☐ 5 Todd Helton (USA)
- ☐ 6 Ed Lewis
- ☐ 7 Ryan Meyers
- ☐ 8 James Northeimer
- ☐ 9 Allan Parker
- ☐ 10 Adam Priest
- ☐ 11 Bubba Trammell
- ☐ 12 Richie Wyman
- ☐ 13 Smokey (Mascot)
- ☐ 14 Lindsey Nelson Stadium
- ☐ 15 1994 Team Picture
- ☐ 16 1993 Division
  Champions Card

1995 Toledo Mud Hens Team Issue

This 30-card team set of the 1995 Toledo Mud Hens, a Class AAA International League affiliate of the Detroit Tigers, features posed color player photos with blue, white, and two-sided thin red borders. The backs carry player biographical information and career statistics. 5,000 sets were produced.

	MINT	NRMT	EXC
COMPLETE SET (30)	8.00	3.60	1.00

- ☐ 1 Tom Runnells MGR
- ☐ 2 Skeeter Barnes CO
- ☐ 3 Rick Adair CO
- ☐ 4 Lon Pinhey TR
- ☐ 5 Pat Ahearne
- ☐ 6 Kevin Baez
- ☐ 7 Ben Blomdahl
- ☐ 8 Kent Bottenfield
- ☐ 9 Ken Carlyle
- ☐ 10 Mike Christopher
- ☐ 11 Tony Clark
- ☐ 12 Milt Cuyler
- ☐ 13 Jim Givens
- ☐ 14 Frank Gonzales
- ☐ 15 Joe Hall
- ☐ 16 Dwayne Henry
- ☐ 17 Jose Lima
- ☐ 18 Rob Lukachyk
- ☐ 19 Randy Marshall
- ☐ 20 Justin Mashore
- ☐ 21 Terry McGriff
- ☐ 22 Rudy Pemberton
- ☐ 23 Shannon Penn
- ☐ 24 Jeff Tackett
- ☐ 25 Mickey Weston
- ☐ 26 Derrick White
- ☐ 27 Kevin Wickander
- ☐ 28 Craig Wilson
- ☐ 29 Alan Zinter
- ☐ 30 Muddy(Mascot)

1995 Trenton Thunder Team Issue

This 31-card set of the Trenton Thunder, a Class AA Eastern League affiliate of the Boston Red Sox, features posed color player portraits with a white and thin green-striped border. The team logo and player's name and position are printed in the wide bottom margin. The backs carry player biographical information and career statistics. This issue includes the minor league card set debut of Nomar Garciaparra.

	MINT	NRMT	EXC
COMPLETE SET (31)	30.00	13.50	3.70

- ☐ 1 Ken Macha MGR
- ☐ 2 Al Nipper CO
- ☐ 3 Rico Petrocelli CO
- ☐ 4 Chris Correnti TR
- ☐ 5 Steve Hoeme
- ☐ 6 Scott Bakkum
- ☐ 7 Wes Brooks
- ☐ 8 Tim Cain
- ☐ 9 Brent Hansen
- ☐ 10 Joe Hudson
- ☐ 11 Todd Ingram
- ☐ 12 Rafael Orellano
- ☐ 13 Dean Peterson
- ☐ 14 Shawn Senior
- ☐ 15 Jeff Suppan
- ☐ 16 Joe Ciccarella
- ☐ 17 Dana Levangie
- ☐ 18 Jeff Martin
- ☐ 19 Nomar Garciaparra
- ☐ 20 Ryan McGuire
- ☐ 21 Lou Merloni
- ☐ 22 Clyde "Pork Chop" Pough
- ☐ 23 Bill Selby
- ☐ 24 Andy Abad
- ☐ 25 Ron Mahay
- ☐ 26 Patrick Lennon
- ☐ 27 Greg Blosser
- ☐ 28 Todd Carey
- ☐ 29 Mike Hardge
- ☐ 30 Boomer(Mascot)
- ☐ NNO Title Card CL

1995 Tucson Toros Team Issue

This 29-card team set of the 1995 Tucson Toros, a Class AAA Pacific Coast League affiliate of the Houston Astros, features color player images on a transparent light gray background over a wood simulated background with the team's name and logo running througout. The backs display a black-and-white player's head photo with biographical information and career statistics. The cards are unnumbered and checklisted below in alphabetical order. 3,000 sets were produced.

	MINT	NRMT	EXC
COMPLETE SET (29)	8.00	3.60	1.00

- ☐ 1 Bob Abreu
- ☐ 2 Jeff Ball
- ☐ 3 Mike Brumley
- ☐ 4 Jamie Daspit
- ☐ 5 Chris Gardner
- ☐ 6 Jerry Goff
- ☐ 7 Juan Guerrero
- ☐ 8 Ricky Gutierrez
- ☐ 9 Dave Hajek
- ☐ 10 Chris Hatcher
- ☐ 11 Chris Holt
- ☐ 12 Rick Huisman
- ☐ 13 Brian L. Hunter
- ☐ 14 Scott Makarewicz
- ☐ 15 Craig McMurtry
- ☐ 16 Ray Montgomery
- ☐ 17 Alvin Morman
- ☐ 18 Phil Nevin
- ☐ 19 Bronswell Patrick
- ☐ 20 Ron Porterfield TR
- ☐ 21 Ken Ramos
- ☐ 22 Don Reynolds CO
- ☐ 23 Dave Rohde
- ☐ 24 Mike Simms
- ☐ 25 Mark Small
- ☐ 26 Brent Strom
- ☐ 27 Rick Sweet MGR
- ☐ 28 Billy Wagner
- ☐ 29 Donne Wall

1995 Tulsa Drillers Team Issue

This 30-card set of the 1995 Tulsa Drillers, a Class AA Texas League affiliate of the Texas Rangers, features borderless color player photos on the fronts with the player's name, position, and team logo printed in a red bar across the bottom. The backs carry player information and career statistics with sponsor logo and an Oklahoma Highway Safety message printed at the bottom..

	MINT	NRMT	EXC
COMPLETE SET (30)	10.00	4.50	1.25

- ☐ 1 James Byrd P/CO
- ☐ 2 Julio Santana
- ☐ 3 Mike Cather
- ☐ 4 Frank Charles
- ☐ 5 Jim Clinton
- ☐ 6 Chip Duncan
- ☐ 7 Mike Edwards
- ☐ 8 Osmani Estrada
- ☐ 9 Darryl Kennedy
- ☐ 10 Jack Kimel
- ☐ 11 Kerry Lacy
- ☐ 12 Jerry Martin
- ☐ 13 Ramiro Martinez
- ☐ 14 Guillermo Mercedes
- ☐ 15 Johnny Monell
- ☐ 16 Joe Morvay
- ☐ 17 Rogelio Nunez
- ☐ 18 Franklin Parra
- ☐ 19 Danny Patterson
- ☐ 20 John Powell
- ☐ 21 Mike Smith
- ☐ 22 Scott Smith
- ☐ 23 Jose Texidor
- ☐ 24 Brian Thomas
- ☐ 25 Tom Tisdale
- ☐ 26 Frank Turco
- ☐ 27 Chad Wiley
- ☐ 28 Bobby Jones MGR
- ☐ 29 Jackson Todd CO
- ☐ 30 Vince and Larry
  (Crash Dummies)

1995 Upper Deck

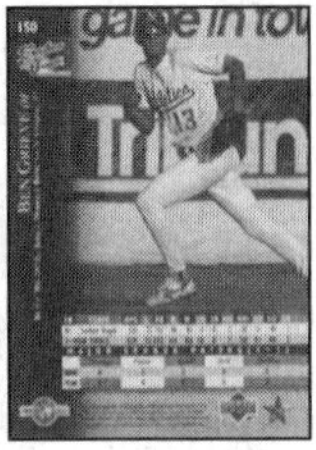

The set can be subdivided into regular cards (1-100), Season Highlights (101-106), International Flavor (107-160), Road To The Show (161-214), and Draft Class (215-225).

	MINT	NRMT	EXC
COMPLETE SET (225)	35.00	16.00	4.40
COMMON CARD (1-225)	.10	.05	.01
☐ 1 Derek Jeter	2.00	.90	.25
☐ 2 Michael Tucker	.20	.09	.03
☐ 3 Alex Ochoa	.20	.09	.03
☐ 4 Bill Pulsipher	.10	.05	.01
☐ 5 Terrell Wade	.10	.05	.01
☐ 6 Johnny Damon	.60	.25	.07
☐ 7 LaTroy Hawkins	.10	.05	.01
☐ 8 Ruben Rivera	2.00	.90	.25
☐ 9 Jason Giambi	.25	.11	.03
☐ 10 Todd Hollandsworth	.25	.11	.03
☐ 11 Alan Benes	.60	.25	.07
☐ 12 John Wasdin	.10	.05	.01
☐ 13 Roger Cedeno	.10	.05	.01
☐ 14 Karim Garcia	2.00	.90	.25
☐ 15 Brooks Kieschnick	.25	.11	.03
☐ 16 David Bell	.10	.05	.01
☐ 17 Trot Nixon	.20	.09	.03
☐ 18 Jose Malave	.10	.05	.01
☐ 19 Rey Ordonez	1.00	.45	.12
☐ 20 Raul Casanova	.50	.23	.06

☐ 21 Chad Mottola .10 .05 .01
☐ 22 Phil Nevin .10 .05 .01
☐ 23 Jim Pittsley .10 .05 .01
☐ 24 Frank Rodriguez .10 .05 .01
☐ 25 Todd Greene .40 .18 .05
☐ 26 Mike Bell .20 .09 .03
☐ 27 Jason Kendall .40 .18 .05
☐ 28 Calvin Reese .10 .05 .01
☐ 29 Jose Silva .10 .05 .01
☐ 30 Kirk Presley .10 .05 .01
☐ 31 Joe Randa .10 .05 .01
☐ 32 Shannon Stewart .10 .05 .01
☐ 33 Danny Clyburn .25 .11 .03
☐ 34 Glenn Williams .30 .14 .04
☐ 35 Terry Bradshaw .10 .05 .01
☐ 36 Jimmy Hurst .10 .05 .01
☐ 37 Scott Spiezio .20 .09 .03
☐ 38 Richard Hidalgo .60 .25 .07
☐ 39 Matt Brunson .10 .05 .01
☐ 40 Jaun Acevedo .10 .05 .01
☐ 41 Trey Beamon .40 .18 .05
☐ 42 Kim Bartee .10 .05 .01
☐ 43 James Baldwin .10 .05 .01
☐ 44 Matt Arrandale .10 .05 .01
☐ 45 Michael Jordan 4.00 1.80 .50
☐ 46 Tony Graffanino .10 .05 .01
☐ 47 Wonderful Monds .10 .05 .01
☐ 48 Bob Abreu .50 .23 .06
☐ 49 Edgardo Alfonzo .10 .05 .01
☐ 50 Damon Hollins .10 .05 .01
☐ 51 Marc Barcelo .10 .05 .01
☐ 52 D.J. Boston .10 .05 .01
☐ 53 Einar Diaz .10 .05 .01
☐ 54 Matt Drews .10 .05 .01
☐ 55 Benji Simonton .10 .05 .01
☐ 56 Bart Evans .10 .05 .01
☐ 57 Micah Franklin .10 .05 .01
☐ 58 Curtis Goodwin .10 .05 .01
☐ 59 Craig Griffey .10 .05 .01
☐ 60 Billy Wagner .10 .05 .01
☐ 61 Jimmy Haynes .10 .05 .01
☐ 62 Jose Herrera .10 .05 .01
☐ 63 Greg Keagle .10 .05 .01
☐ 64 Andy Larkin .10 .05 .01
☐ 65 Jason Isringhausen .40 .18 .05
☐ 66 Derrek Lee 1.00 .45 .12
☐ 67 Terrell Lowery .10 .05 .01
☐ 68 Ryan Luzinski .10 .05 .01
☐ 69 Angel Martinez .10 .05 .01
☐ 70 Tony Clark 1.00 .45 .12
☐ 71 Ryan McGuire .10 .05 .01
☐ 72 Damian Moss 1.00 .45 .12
☐ 73 Hugo Pivaral .25 .11 .03
☐ 74 Arquimedez Pozo .10 .05 .01
☐ 75 Daron Kirkreit .10 .05 .01
☐ 76 Luis Raven .10 .05 .01
☐ 77 Desi Relaford .10 .05 .01
☐ 78 Scott Rolen 5.00 2.20 .60
☐ 79 Joe Rosselli .10 .05 .01
☐ 80 Chris Roberts .10 .05 .01
☐ 81 Giomar Guevara .10 .05 .01
☐ 82 Gene Schall .10 .05 .01
☐ 83 Jeff Suppan .60 .25 .07
☐ 84 Mac Suzuki .10 .05 .01
☐ 85 Jason Thompson .10 .05 .01
☐ 86 Marc Valdes .10 .05 .01
☐ 87 Pat Watkins .10 .05 .01
☐ 88 Jay Witasick .10 .05 .01
☐ 89 Ray Durham .50 .23 .06
☐ 90 Brad Fullmer .60 .25 .07
☐ 91 Roger Bailey .10 .05 .01
☐ 92 DeShawn Warren .10 .05 .01
☐ 93 Jermaine Dye 3.00 1.35 .35
☐ 94 Scott Romano .10 .05 .01
☐ 95 Aaron Boone .60 .25 .07
☐ 96 Tate Seefried .10 .05 .01
☐ 97 Chris Stynes .10 .05 .01
☐ 98 Chris Widger .10 .05 .01
☐ 99 Desi Wilson .10 .05 .01
☐ 100 Dante Powell 2.50 1.10 .30
☐ 101 Neifi Perez SH .10 .05 .01
☐ 102 Alex Ochoa SH .10 .05 .01
☐ 103 Kelly Wunsch SH .10 .05 .01
☐ 104 Jason Robbins SH .10 .05 .01
☐ 105 Kevin Coughlin SH .10 .05 .01
☐ 106 Bill Pulsipher SH .10 .05 .01
☐ 107 Roger Cedeno IF .10 .05 .01
☐ 108 Jose Herrera IF .10 .05 .01
☐ 109 Andre King IF .10 .05 .01
☐ 110 Rey Ordonez IF .50 .23 .06
☐ 111 Jose Pett IF .10 .05 .01
☐ 112 Ruben Rivera IF 1.00 .45 .12
☐ 113 Jose Silva IF .10 .05 .01
☐ 114 Mac Suzuki IF .10 .05 .01
☐ 115 Glenn Williams IF .10 .05 .01
☐ 116 Will Cunnane .10 .05 .01
☐ 117 Neifi Perez .25 .11 .03
☐ 118 Andre King .10 .05 .01
☐ 119 Quinton McCracken .10 .05 .01
☐ 120 Brian Giles .10 .05 .01
☐ 121 Kenny Felder .10 .05 .01
☐ 122 Jermaine Allensworth .10 .05 .01
☐ 123 Allen Battle .10 .05 .01
☐ 124 Howard Battle .10 .05 .01
☐ 125 Doug Million .50 .23 .06
☐ 126 Geoff Blum .10 .05 .01
☐ 127 Vladimir Guerrero 6.00 2.70 .75
☐ 128 Torii Hunter .25 .11 .03
☐ 129 Doug Glanville .10 .05 .01
☐ 130 Dustin Hermanson .10 .05 .01
☐ 131 Mark Grudzielanek .50 .23 .06
☐ 132 Phil Geisler .10 .05 .01
☐ 133 Chris Carpenter .60 .25 .07
☐ 134 Brain Sackinsky .10 .05 .01
☐ 135 Josh Booty .50 .23 .06
☐ 136 Shane Andrews .10 .05 .01
☐ 137 Scott Eyre .10 .05 .01
☐ 138 Chad Fox .10 .05 .01
☐ 139 George Arias .60 .25 .07
☐ 140 Scott Sullivan .10 .05 .01
☐ 141 Todd Dunn .10 .05 .01
☐ 142 Nate Holdren .10 .05 .01
☐ 143 Gus Gandarillas .10 .05 .01
☐ 144 Scott Talanoa .10 .05 .01
☐ 145 Sal Fasano .10 .05 .01
☐ 146 Stoney Briggs .10 .05 .01
☐ 147 Yamil Benitez .50 .23 .06
☐ 148 Chris Wimmer .10 .05 .01
☐ 149 Mariano De los Santos .20 .09 .03
☐ 150 Ben Grieve 2.50 1.10 .30
☐ 151 Homer Bush .10 .05 .01
☐ 152 Wilton Guerrero .75 .35 .09
☐ 153 Benji Grigsby .10 .05 .01
☐ 154 Cade Gaspar .10 .05 .01
☐ 155 Hiram Bocachica .40 .18 .05
☐ 156 Dave Vanhof .10 .05 .01
☐ 157 Frank Catalanotto .40 .18 .05
☐ 158 Marcus Jensen .10 .05 .01
☐ 159 Jamie Arnold .10 .05 .01
☐ 160 Cesar Devarez .10 .05 .01
☐ 161 Alan Benes RTS .30 .14 .04
☐ 162 Johnny Damon RTS .30 .14 .04
☐ 163 LaTroy Hawkins RTS .10 .05 .01
☐ 164 Dustin Hermanson RTS .10 .05 .01
☐ 165 Derek Jeter RTS 1.00 .45 .12
☐ 166 Terrell Wade RTS .10 .05 .01
☐ 167 Todd Walker RTS 1.50 .70 .19
☐ 168 John Wasdin RTS .10 .05 .01
☐ 169 Paul Wilson RTS .25 .11 .03
☐ 170 Todd Walker 4.00 1.80 .50
☐ 171 Danny Klassen .10 .05 .01
☐ 172 Bob Morris .10 .05 .01
☐ 173 Kelly Wunsch .10 .05 .01
☐ 174 Fletcher Thompson .10 .05 .01
☐ 175 Terrence Long .60 .25 .07
☐ 176 Andy Pettitte 1.00 .45 .12
☐ 177 Lou Pote .10 .05 .01
☐ 178 Steve Kline .20 .09 .03
☐ 179 Damian Jackson .20 .09 .03
☐ 180 Matt Smith .10 .05 .01
☐ 181 Tim Unroe .10 .05 .01
☐ 182 Jim Cole .10 .05 .01
☐ 183 Bill McMillon .10 .05 .01
☐ 184 Matt Luke .10 .05 .01
☐ 185 Sergio Nunez .10 .05 .01
☐ 186 Edgar Renteria .40 .18 .05
☐ 187 Bill Selby .10 .05 .01
☐ 188 Jamey Wright .40 .18 .05
☐ 189 Steve Whitaker .10 .05 .01
☐ 190 Joe Vitiello .10 .05 .01
☐ 191 Jacob Shumate .10 .05 .01
☐ 192 C.J. Nitkowski .10 .05 .01
☐ 193 Mark Johnson .10 .05 .01
☐ 194 Paul Konerko 4.00 1.80 .50
☐ 195 Jay Payton 2.00 .90 .25
☐ 196 Jayson Peterson .10 .05 .01
☐ 197 Brian Buchanan .20 .09 .03
☐ 198 Ramon Castro .20 .09 .03
☐ 199 Antone Williamson .60 .25 .07
☐ 200 Paul Wilson .50 .23 .06
☐ 201 Jaret Wright .75 .35 .09
☐ 202 Carlton Loewer .10 .05 .01
☐ 203 Jon Zuber .10 .05 .01
☐ 204 Ugueth Urbina .10 .05 .01
☐ 205 Nomar Garciaparra 2.50 1.10 .30
☐ 206 Yuri Sanchez .10 .05 .01
☐ 207 Jason Moler .10 .05 .01
☐ 208 Lyle Mouton .10 .05 .01
☐ 209 Mark P. Johnson .10 .05 .01
☐ 210 Matt Raleigh .10 .05 .01
☐ 211 Julio Santana .10 .05 .01
☐ 212 Willis Ontanez .10 .05 .01
☐ 213 Ozzie Timmons .10 .05 .01
☐ 214 Victor Rodriguez .10 .05 .01
☐ 215 Paul Wilson DC .25 .11 .03
☐ 216 Ben Grieve DC 1.25 .55 .16
☐ 217 Dustin Hermanson DC .10 .05 .01
☐ 218 Antone Williamson DC .30 .14 .04
☐ 219 Josh Booty DC .30 .14 .04
☐ 220 Todd Walker DC 2.00 .90 .25
☐ 221 Jaret Wright DC .40 .18 .05
☐ 222 Paul Konerko DC 2.00 .90 .25
☐ 223 Doug Million DC .20 .09 .03
☐ 224 Hiram Bocachica DC .20 .09 .03
☐ 225 Durham Athletic Park .25 .11 .03

1995 Upper Deck Future Stock

	MINT	NRMT	EXC
COMPLETE SET (225)	100.00	45.00	12.50
COMMON CARD (1-225)	.20	.09	.03
*STARS: 1.5X to 3X BASIC CARDS			

1995 Upper Deck Minor League Autographs

Autographed cards were issued to the first dealers who ordered the 1995 Upper Deck Minor League product. The fronts feature full-bleed color action photos, with the player's autograph inscribed across the picture. The backs carry a congratulatory message. Each player signed 1,000 of his cards. Depending on the size of the order, dealers received from one to four cards.

	MINT	NRMT	EXC
COMPLETE SET (10)	300.00	135.00	38.00
COMMON CARD (1-10)	15.00	6.75	1.85
☐ 1 Mike Bell	25.00	11.00	3.10
☐ 2 Alan Benes	40.00	18.00	5.00
☐ 3 Johnny Damon	40.00	18.00	5.00
☐ 4 Jason Giambi	25.00	11.00	3.10
☐ 5 LaTroy Hawkins	15.00	6.75	1.85
☐ 6 Todd Hollandsworth	25.00	11.00	3.10
☐ 7 Derek Jeter	125.00	55.00	15.50
☐ 8 Alex Ochoa	25.00	11.00	3.10
☐ 9 Terrell Wade	25.00	11.00	3.10
☐ 10 Paul Wilson	30.00	13.50	3.70

1995 Upper Deck Michael Jordan One On One

	MINT	NRMT	EXC
COMPLETE SET (10)	10.00	4.50	1.25
COMMON CARD (1-10)	1.00	.45	.12
☐ 1 Michael Jordan (Throwing)	1.00	.45	.12
☐ 2 Michael Jordan (Fielding)	1.00	.45	.12
☐ 3 Michael Jordan (Hitting)	1.00	.45	.12
☐ 4 Michael Jordan (Speed)	1.00	.45	.12
☐ 5 Michael Jordan (Overall Skills)	1.00	.45	.12
☐ 6 Michael Jordan ('94 Spring)	1.00	.45	.12
☐ 7 Michael Jordan ('94 Season)	1.00	.45	.12
☐ 8 Michael Jordan (First Homer)	1.00	.45	.12
☐ 9 Michael Jordan ('94 Autumn)	1.00	.45	.12
☐ 10 Michael Jordan (The Future)	1.00	.45	.12

1995 Upper Deck Michael Jordan Season Highlights Jumbos

	MINT	NRMT	EXC
COMPLETE SET (5)	25.00	11.00	3.10
COMMON CARD (MJ1-MJ5)	5.00	2.20	.60
☐ MJ1 Michael Jordan White Sox welcome Jordan to Spring Training	5.00	2.20	.60
☐ MJ2 Michael Jordan Jordan supplies offense at Classic!	5.00	2.20	.60
☐ MJ3 Michael Jordan Jordan extends hitting streak to 13	5.00	2.20	.60
☐ MJ4 Michael Jordan Jordan hits first home run	5.00	2.20	.60
☐ MJ5 Michael Jordan Jordan does extracurricular baseball	5.00	2.20	.60

1995 Upper Deck Michael Jordan's Scrapbook

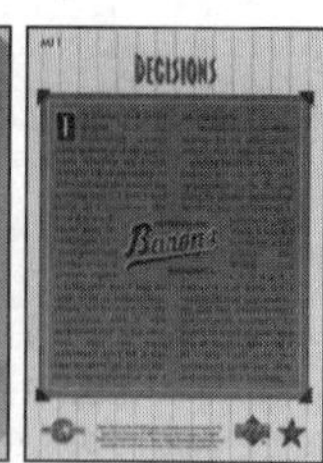

	MINT	NRMT	EXC
COMPLETE SET (10)	180.00	80.00	22.00
COMMON CARD (MJ1-MJ10)	18.00	8.00	2.20
☐ MJ1 Michael Jordan Decisions	18.00	8.00	2.20
☐ MJ2 Michael Jordan Practice	18.00	8.00	2.20
☐ MJ3 Michael Jordan Spring Training and Assignment	18.00	8.00	2.20
☐ MJ4 Michael Jordan Windy City Classic	18.00	8.00	2.20
☐ MJ5 Michael Jordan Firsts	18.00	8.00	2.20
☐ MJ6 Michael Jordan The Hitting Streak	18.00	8.00	2.20
☐ MJ7 Michael Jordan Struggles	18.00	8.00	2.20
☐ MJ8 Michael Jordan Life on the Road	18.00	8.00	2.20
☐ MJ9 Michael Jordan First Home Run	18.00	8.00	2.20
☐ MJ10 Michael Jordan Arizona Fall League	18.00	8.00	2.20

1995 Upper Deck Organizational Profiles

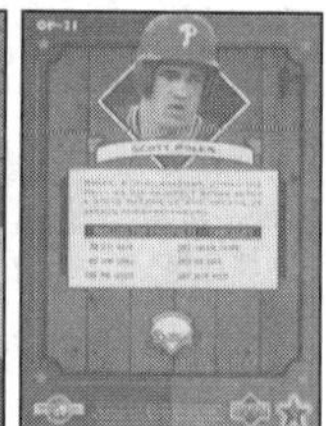

	MINT	NRMT	EXC
COMPLETE SET (28)	125.00	55.00	15.50
COMMON CARD (OP1-OP28)	3.00	1.35	.35
☐ OP1 Terrell Wade	4.00	1.80	.50
☐ OP2 Alex Ochoa	4.00	1.80	.50
☐ OP3 Nomar Garciaparra	12.00	5.50	1.50
☐ OP4 Todd Greene	4.00	1.80	.50
☐ OP5 Brooks Kieschnick	4.00	1.80	.50
☐ OP6 Michael Jordan	25.00	11.00	3.10
☐ OP7 C.J. Nitkowski	3.00	1.35	.35
☐ OP8 Daron Kirkreit	3.00	1.35	.35
☐ OP9 Juan Acevedo	3.00	1.35	.35
☐ OP10 Tony Clark	8.00	3.60	1.00
☐ OP11 Josh Booty	5.00	2.20	.60
☐ OP12 Billy Wagner	4.00	1.80	.50
☐ OP13 Johnny Damon	6.00	2.70	.75
☐ OP14 Paul Konerko	15.00	6.75	1.85
☐ OP15 Antone Williamson	6.00	2.70	.75
☐ OP16 Todd Walker	15.00	6.75	1.85
☐ OP17 Ugueth Urbina	3.00	1.35	.35
☐ OP18 Bill Pulsipher	5.00	2.20	.60
☐ OP19 Ruben Rivera	10.00	4.50	1.25
☐ OP20 John Wasdin	3.00	1.35	.35
☐ OP21 Scott Rolen	25.00	11.00	3.10
☐ OP22 Trey Beamon	4.00	1.80	.50
☐ OP23 Alan Benes	8.00	3.60	1.00
☐ OP24 Raul Casanova	3.00	1.35	.35
☐ OP25 Dante Powell	12.00	5.50	1.50
☐ OP26 Arquimedez Pozo	3.00	1.35	.35
☐ OP27 Julio Santana	3.00	1.35	.35
☐ OP28 Jose Silva	3.00	1.35	.35

1995 Upper Deck Top 10 Prospect

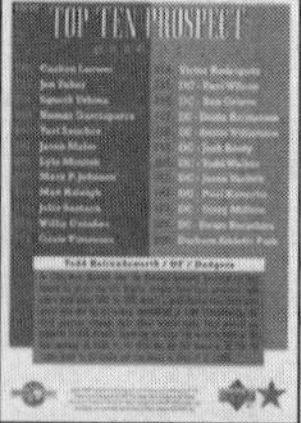

	MINT	NRMT	EXC
COMPLETE SET (10)	30.00	13.50	3.70
COMMON CARD (1-10)	1.50	.70	.19
☐ 1 Derek Jeter	12.00	5.50	1.50
☐ 2 James Baldwin	1.50	.70	.19
☐ 3 Johnny Damon	4.00	1.80	.50
☐ 4 Ruben Rivera	6.00	2.70	.75
☐ 5 Bill Pulsipher	2.00	.90	.25
☐ 6 Jose Silva	1.50	.70	.19

☐ 7 Roger Cedeno	2.00	.90	.25
☐ 8 Alan Benes	2.00	.90	.25
☐ 9 Michael Tucker	2.00	.90	.25
☐ 10 Todd Hollandsworth	3.00	1.35	.35

1995 Vero Beach Dodgers Team Issue

This 30-card set of the Vero Beach Dodgers, a Class A Florida State League affiliate of the Los Angeles Dodgers, was issued in one sheet consisting of five perforated six-card strips. The fronts feature color player photos while the backs carry player information and career statistics. The cards are unnumbered and checklisted below in alphabetical order. 750 sets were produced.

	MINT	NRMT	EXC
COMPLETE SET (30)	25.00	11.00	3.10

☐ 1 Cliff Anderson
☐ 2 Kym Ashworth
☐ 3 Mike Biltimier
☐ 4 Quincy Boyd
☐ 5 John Challinor
☐ 6 Kyle Cooney
☐ 7 Roberto Duran
☐ 8 Rob Giesecke TR
☐ 9 Frans Groot
☐ 10 Tony Harris CO
☐ 11 Ryan Henderson
☐ 12 Juan Hernaiz
☐ 13 Ron Hollis
☐ 14 Chris Latham
☐ 15 Mike Metcalfe
☐ 16 Brian Majeski
☐ 17 Charlie Nelson
☐ 18 Willie Otanez
☐ 19 Julio Parra
☐ 20 Kevin Pincavitch
☐ 21 David Post
☐ 22 Jason Reed
☐ 23 Chip Sell
☐ 24 Dave Steed
☐ 25 Ryan Sowards
☐ 26 Ken Sikes
☐ 27 Dan Urbina
☐ 28 Brandon Watts
☐ 29 Mike Walkden
☐ 30 Jon Debus MG
Guy Conti CO#(Tony Harris CO#(D.J. Kim CO

1995 Watertown Indians Team Issue

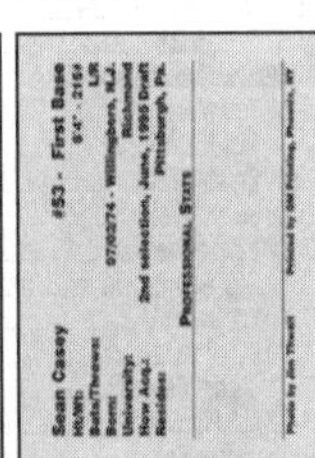

This 30-card set of the 1995 Watertown Indians, a Class A New York-Penn League affiliate of the Cleveland Indians, features color player action photos by Jim Thwaits in a white border. The backs carry player information and career statistics. The cards are unnumbered and checklisted below in alphabetical order. This issue includes the minor league card debut of Sean Casey.

	MINT	NRMT	EXC
COMPLETE SET (30)	25.00	11.00	3.10

☐ 1 Jason Adge
☐ 2 Tom Afenir
☐ 3 Ross Atkins
☐ 4 Mark Baker
☐ 5 Jason Bennett
☐ 6 Mark Budzinski
☐ 7 Matt Carpenter
☐ 8 Sean Casey
☐ 9 John Choate
☐ 10 James Crowell
☐ 11 Matt Culp
☐ 12 Marc Deschenes
☐ 13 Rich Gonzalez
☐ 14 Terry Harvey
☐ 15 Keith Horn
☐ 16 Derrick Hritz
☐ 17 Tim Jorgensen
☐ 18 Sammie Mathis
☐ 19 Brett Merrick
☐ 20 Jason Minici
☐ 21 Scott Morgan
☐ 22 Richard Negrette
☐ 23 Walter Owens
☐ 24 Jason Rakers
☐ 25 Ken Rowe CO
☐ 26 Scott Schultz
☐ 27 Joel Skinner MGR
☐ 28 Chad Thornhil
☐ 29 Willy Valera
☐ 30 Scott Winchester

1995 West Michigan Whitecaps Team Issue

This 30-card set of the 1995 West Mighigan Whitecaps, a Class A Midwest League affiliate of the Oakland Athletics, features color player photos with a team color and logo border. The backs carry a small black-and-white player head photo with biographical information and career statistics. The cards are unnumbered and checklisted below according to the player's jersey number. This issue includes a second year card of Ben Grieve.

	MINT	NRMT	EXC
COMPLETE SET (30)	10.00	4.50	1.25

☐ 4 Juan Castro
☐ 6 Fred Soriano
☐ 9 Rich Juday
☐ 11 Juan Perez
☐ 13 Vinny Francisco
☐ 14 Jose Soriano
☐ 15 Jason Beverlin
☐ 16 Brendan Hause
☐ 17 Bert Bradley CO
☐ 18 Rob DeBoer
☐ 19 Damon Newman
☐ 20 Jason Rajotte
☐ 21 Skye Leibee
☐ 22 Ben Grieve
☐ 23 Leon Hamburg
☐ 24 Luis Silva
☐ 25 Manny DaSilva
☐ 26 Pat Sanders
☐ 27 Helpis Sosa
☐ 28 Alex Rondon
☐ 29 Ian Espstein
☐ 30 Jeff D'Amico
☐ 31 Andy Smith
☐ 32 Emil Brown
☐ 33 Alex Miranda
☐ 34 Bill King
☐ 35 Todd Weinberg
☐ 36 Chris Cochrane
☐ 48 Jim Colborn MGR
☐ 99 Crash the River Rascal (Mascot)

1995 Wichita Wranglers Team Issue

This 30-card set of the 1995 Wichita Wranglers, a Class AA Texas League affiliate of the Kansas City Royals, was produced by Multi-Ad Services Inc. and features borderless color player photos on the fronts. The backs carry player biographical information and career statistics. The cards are unnumbered and checklisted below according to the player's jersey number.

	MINT	NRMT	EXC
COMPLETE SET (30)	12.00	5.50	1.50

☐ 3 Steve Murphy
☐ 6 Jason Marshall
☐ 7 Rod Myers
☐ 8 Larry Sutton
☐ 9 Ryan Long
☐ 11 Gary Lance
☐ 13 Robert Toth
☐ 15 Ramon Martinez
☐ 16 Felix Martinez
☐ 17 Aaron Dorlarque
☐ 18 Johnny Damon
☐ 19 Jaime Bluma
☐ 21 Ron Johnson
☐ 22 Don Strange
☐ 23 Derek Wallace
☐ 25 Mike Fyhrie
☐ 26 Steve Sisco
☐ 27 Chad Strickland
☐ 28 Andy Stewart
☐ 29 Mandy Romero
☐ 30 U.L. Washington
☐ 31 Neil Atkinson
☐ 32 Geno Morones
☐ 33 Sal Fasano
☐ 34 Jeff Granger
☐ 35 Kris Ralston
☐ 36 Chris Sheehan
☐ 37 Bart Evans
☐ 38 Mike Bovee
☐ 95 Wilbur T. Wrnagler(Mascot)

1995 Wilmington Blue Rocks Team Issue

This 30-card set of the 1995 Wilmington Blue Rocks, a Class A Carolina League affiliate of the Kansas City Royals, was produced by Choice Marketing Inc. and features color player photos on the fronts. The backs carry player biographical information and career statistics. The cards are unnumbered and checklisted below according to the player's jersey number. This issue includes the minor league card debut of Jose Rosado.

	MINT	NRMT	EXC
COMPLETE SET (30)	20.00	9.00	2.50

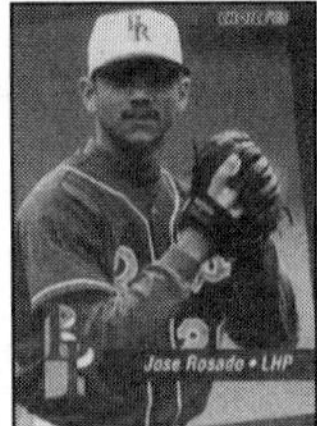

☐ 1 Luke Oglesby
☐ 4 Anthony Medrano
☐ 7 John Mizerock MGR
☐ 8 Brian Teeters
☐ 9 Jimmie Byington
☐ 12 Tim Byrdak
☐ 14 Raul Gonzalez
☐ 15 Tom Burgmeier CO
☐ 16 Sixto Lezcano CO
☐ 17 Oscar Jimenez
☐ 18 Glendon Rusch
☐ 19 Bart Evans
☐ 21 Michael Evans
☐ 22 Ramy Brooks
☐ 23 David Sinnes
☐ 24 Ken Ray
☐ 25 John Dickens
☐ 26 Jose Rosado
☐ 27 Mendy Lopez
☐ 28 Carlos Mendez
☐ 30 Chris Connolly
☐ 31 Kevin Hodges
☐ 32 Phil Grundy
☐ 33 Mike Sweeney
☐ 34 Toby Smith
☐ 35 Sergio Nunez
☐ 36 Kevin Rawitzer
☐ 37 Nevin Brewer
☐ 38 Chris Sheehan
☐ 40 Donovan Delaney

1995 Yakima Bears Team Issue

This 36-card set of the 1995 Yakima Bears, a Class A Northwest League affiliate of the Los Angeles Dodgers, features color player photos on the fronts with a white and thin-gold border. The backs carry player information and career statistics. The cards are unnumbered and checklisted below in alphabetical order. 1,500 sets were produced.

	MINT	NRMT	EXC
COMPLETE SET (36)	15.00	6.75	1.85

☐ 1 Darrin Babineaux
☐ 2 Lance Backowski
☐ 3 Mike Carpentier
☐ 4 Pedro Cervantes
☐ 5 Scott Chambers
☐ 6 Bryan Coyle
☐ 7 Trent Cuevas
☐ 8 Eddie Davis
☐ 9 Kris Foster
☐ 10 Kevin Gibbs
☐ 11 Judd Granzow
☐ 12 Rafael Gross
☐ 13 Brian Harmon
☐ 14 Juan Hernaiz
☐ 15 Johnny Hilo
☐ 16 Jeff Keppen
☐ 17 Jaime Malave
☐ 18 Josh Markert
☐ 19 Onan Masaoka
☐ 20 Terrence McClain
☐ 21 Mitch McNeely
☐ 22 Travis Meyer
☐ 23 Ken Morimoto
☐ 24 Andy Owen
☐ 25 J.J. Pearsall
☐ 26 Nate Rasmussen
☐ 27 Mike Sanchez
☐ 28 Juan Sosa
☐ 29 Seferino Soto
☐ 30 Carl South
☐ 31 Ricky Stone
☐ 32 Elias Tapia
☐ 33 Jon Tucker
☐ 34 Joe Vavra
☐ 35 John Vukson
☐ 36 A.J. Walkanoff

1996 Appalachian League All-Stars Best

	MINT	NRMT	EXC
COMPLETE SET (30)	18.00	8.00	2.20

☐ 1 Chipper Alley
Bluefield Orioles
☐ 2 Carlos Casimiro
Bluefield Orioles
☐ 3 Darrell Dent
Bluefield Orioles
☐ 4 Scott Eibey
Bluefield Orioles
☐ 5 Jason Lakman
Bristol Sox
☐ 6 Craig McClure
Bristol Sox
☐ 7 James Nichols
Bristol Sox
☐ 8 Jimmy Hamilton
Cleveland Indians
☐ 9 Ryan McDermott
Cleveland Indians
☐ 10 Grant Sharpe
Cleveland Indians
☐ 11 Jewell Williams
Cleveland Indians
☐ 12 Kevin McGlinchy
Danville Braves
☐ 13 Shawn Onley
Danville Braves
☐ 14 Jim Scharrer
Danville Braves
☐ 15 Jeff Spencer
Danville Braves
☐ 16 Damon Irvis
Elizabethton Twins
☐ 17 Chad Moeller
Elizabethton Twins
☐ 18 Freddy Reyes
Elizabethton Twins
☐ 19 Brent Butler
Johnson City Cardinals
☐ 20 Billy Deck
Johnson City Cardinals
☐ 21 Luis Saturria
Johnson City Cardinals
☐ 22 Brett Herbison
Kingsport Mets
☐ 23 Ryan Jaroncyk
Kingsport Mets
☐ 24 Rafael "Pee Wee" Lopez
Kingsport Mets
☐ 25 Jimmy Rollins
Martinsville Phillies
☐ 26 B.J. Schlicher
Martinsville Phillies
☐ 27 Kristopher Stevens
Martinsville Phillies
☐ 28 Carl Caddell
Princeton Reds
☐ 29 Randi Mallard
Princeton Reds
☐ 30 Johnny Oliver
Princeton Reds

1996 Arkansas Travelers Best

This 29-card set of the 1996 Arkansas Travellers, a Class AA Texas League affiliate of the St. Louis Cardinals, was produced by Best Cards, Inc. and features color action player photos in a white border. The backs carry player information and career statistics.This issue includes the minor league card debuts of Manuel Aybar and Kris Detmers.

	MINT	NRMT	EXC
COMPLETE SET (29)	15.00	6.75	1.85

☐ 1 Rick Mahler MG
☐ 2 Jeff Shireman CO
☐ 3 Marty Mason CO
☐ 4 Pete Fagan TR
☐ 5 Manuel Aybar
☐ 6 Jeff Berblinger
☐ 7 Brian Carpenter
☐ 8 Rich Croushore
☐ 9 Dee Dalton
☐ 10 Ray Davis
☐ 11 Kris Detmers
☐ 12 Tony Diggs
☐ 13 Paul Ellis
☐ 14 Chris Fick
☐ 15 Keith Johns
☐ 16 Kevin Lovinger
☐ 17 Elieser Marrero
☐ 18 Jeff Matranga
☐ 19 Jeff Matulevich
☐ 20 Joe McEwing
☐ 21 Matt Morris
☐ 22 Jeff Murphy
☐ 23 Brady Raggio
☐ 24 Brian Rupp
☐ 25 Paul Torres
☐ 26 Jose Velez
☐ 27 Ron Warner
☐ 28 Joel Wolfe
☐ 29 Ray Lankford

1996 Asheville Tourists Best

This 30-card set of the 1996 Asheville Tourists, a Class A South Atlantic League affiliate of the Colorado Rockies, was produced by Best Cards, Inc. and features color action player photos in a white border. The backs carry player information and career statistics. This issue includes the minor leagur card debut of Ben Petrick.

	MINT	NRMT	EXC
COMPLETE SET (30)	10.00	4.50	1.25

☐ 1 Ron McKee GM
☐ 2 P.J. Carey MG
☐ 3 Stu Cole CO
☐ 4 Stan Kyles CO
☐ 5 Bill Slosson TR
☐ 6 Rogelio Arias
☐ 7 Bobby Bevel
☐ 8 Heath Bost
☐ 9 John Clifford
☐ 10 Earl Cunningham
☐ 11 Marc D'Allessandro
☐ 12 Jason Dietrich
☐ 13 Justin Drizos
☐ 14 Salvador Duverge
☐ 15 Brett Elam
☐ 16 James Emiliano
☐ 17 David Feuerstein
☐ 18 Neil Garrett
☐ 19 Laril Gonzalez
☐ 20 David Groseclose
☐ 21 John Hallead
☐ 22 James Kammerer
☐ 23 Tal Light
☐ 24 Chris Macca
☐ 25 Chandler Martin
☐ 26 Sean Murphy
☐ 27 Garrett Neubart
☐ 28 Ben Petrick
☐ 29 Scott Randall
☐ 30 Matt Whitley

1996 Auburn Doubledays Best

This 30-card set of the 1996 Auburn Doubledays, a Class A New York-Penn League affiliate of the Houston Astros, was produced by Best Cards, Inc. and features color action player photos in a white border. The backs carry player information and career statistics.

	MINT	NRMT	EXC
COMPLETE SET (30)	10.00	4.50	1.25

☐ 1 Bryan Braswell
☐ 2 Jason Green
☐ 3 Wes Pratt
☐ 4 Jason Turley
☐ 5 Steve Fuller
☐ 6 Brian Dallimore
☐ 7 Jesus Farraez
☐ 8 Marlon Mejia
☐ 9 Luis Yanez
☐ 10 Jose Rijo
☐ 11 David Bernhard
☐ 12 Jay Mansavage
☐ 13 Chris McFerrin
☐ 14 Matt Hyers
☐ 15 Derek Dace
☐ 16 Jim Reeder
☐ 17 John Cook
☐ 18 Barry Wesson
☐ 19 Kevin Burns
☐ 20 Randy Young
☐ 21 Eric Cole
☐ 22 Esteban Maldonado
☐ 23 Mike Rose
☐ 24 Manny Acta
☐ 25 Bill Ballou
☐ 26 Kevin Stein
☐ 27 Ron Buzzell
☐ 28 Jose Barron
☐ 29 Oliver Gordon ASST GM
☐ 30 Mark Harrington GM

1996 Augusta Greenjackets Best

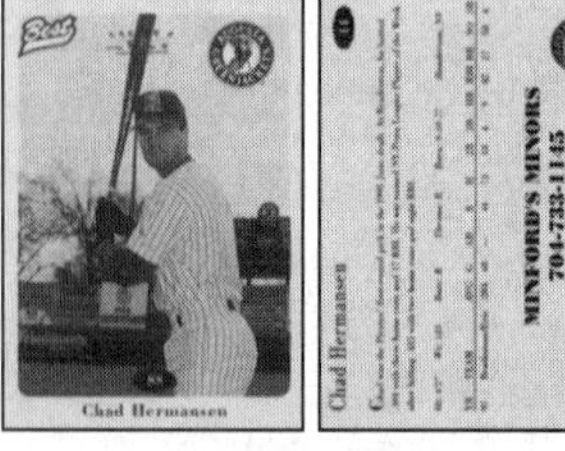

This 29-card set of the 1996 Augusta Greenjackets, a Class A South Atlantic League affiliate of the Pittsburgh Pirates, was produced by Best Cards, Inc. and features color action player photos in a white border. The backs carry player information and career statistics.This issue includes the minor league team set card debuts of Chad Hermansen, Bronson Arroyo and Elvin Hernandez.

	MINT	NRMT	EXC
COMPLETE SET (29)	30.00	13.50	3.70

☐ 1 Jay Loviglio MGR
☐ 2 Doc Watson CO
☐ 3 Mike Sandoval TR
☐ 4 Bronson Arroyo
☐ 5 Jeff Bigler
☐ 6 Tim Collie
☐ 7 David Daniels
☐ 8 Mark Farris
☐ 9 Jason Farrow
☐ 10 Ryan Fisher
☐ 11 Steve Flanigan
☐ 12 Wiklenman Gonzalez
☐ 13 Jeff Havens
☐ 14 Chad Hermansen
☐ 15 Elvin Hernandez
☐ 16 Jeff Kelly
☐ 17 Freddy May
☐ 18 Paul McSparin
☐ 19 Chris Miyake
☐ 20 Brian O'Connor
☐ 21 Alex Pena
☐ 22 Jason Phillips
☐ 23 Elton Pollock
☐ 24 Rayon Reid
☐ 25 Jose Reyes
☐ 26 Charlie Rice
☐ 27 Stan Schreiber
☐ 28 Boomer Whipple
☐ NNO Logo Card CL

1996 Batavia Clippers Team Issue

This 34-card set of the 1996 Batavia Clippers, a Class A New York-Penn League affiliate of the Philadelphia Phillies, features color player portraits with white borders. The backs carry player information and career statistics.

	MINT	NRMT	EXC
COMPLETE SET (34)	10.00	4.50	1.25

☐ 1 Jason Knupfer
☐ 2 David Tober
☐ 3 Todd Crane
☐ 4 Kyle Kawabata
☐ 5 Kris Stevens
☐ 6 Brandon Marsters
☐ 7 Brian Miller
☐ 8 Kirby Clark
☐ 9 Joe Cotton
☐ 10 Evan Thomas
☐ 11 Shannon Cooley
☐ 12 Adam Shadburne
☐ 13 Jason Cafferty
☐ 14 Mike Torti
☐ 15 Leonardo Oliveros
☐ 16 Courtney Mitchell
☐ 17 Rodney Batts
☐ 18 Brandon Allen
☐ 19 Marty Crawford
☐ 20 Ira Tilton
☐ 21 Ryan Frace
☐ 22 Greg Taylor
☐ 23 David Francia
☐ 24 John Crane
☐ 25 Jason Wesemann
☐ 26 Brad Crede
☐ 27 Shawn Smith GM
☐ 28 Drew McCarthy
☐ 29 Rebecca Mullen
☐ 30 Wayne Fuller ANN
☐ 31 Joe Henderson
☐ 32 Tom Doody
☐ 33 Daniel Hoffman
☐ 34 Jason Smorol AGM

1996 Bellingham Giants Team Issue

This 36-card set of the 1996 Bellingham Giants, a Class A Northwest League affiliate of the San Francisco Giants, was produced by Grandstand Cards and sponsored by various area companies. The fronts feature color player photos with white frames and a two-sided fading orange inner border. The backs carry player information and interesting player notes with a sponsor name at the bottom.

	MINT	NRMT	EXC
COMPLETE SET (36)	15.00	6.75	1.85

☐ 1 Matt Wells
☐ 2 Guillermo Rodriguez
☐ 3 Tony Zuniga
☐ 4 Chris Van Rossum
☐ 5 Yolvit Torrealba
☐ 6 Tom Topaum
☐ 7 Ian Rand
☐ 8 Teodoro Prospero
☐ 9 Levi Miskolczi
☐ 10 Damon Minor
☐ 11 Matt McGuire
☐ 12 Brian Manning
☐ 13 David Kenna
☐ 14 Mike Glendenning
☐ 15 Paul Galloway
☐ 16 Mike Caruso
☐ 17 Ricardo Calderon
☐ 18 Mike Riley
☐ 19 James Woodrow
☐ 20 Kurt Takahashi
☐ 21 Jeff Pohl
☐ 22 Michael Pageler
☐ 23 Bill Malloy
☐ 24 Brandon Leese
☐ 25 Guillermo Larreal
☐ 26 Ryan Jensen
☐ 27 Ivan Herrera
☐ 28 Luis Estrella
☐ 29 Robert Crabtree
☐ 30 Joie Blasingim
☐ 31 Jose Abreu
☐ 32 Bill Tucker
Jerry Walker
☐ 33 Shane Turner CO
☐ 34 Ozzie Virgil MG
☐ 35 Elias Sosa CO
☐ 36 David Groeschner TR

1996 Beloit Snappers Team Issue

This 36-card set of the 1996 Beloit Snappers, a Class A Midwest League affiliate of the Milwaukee Brewers, was produced by Raging Color Classics and sponsored by radio station 97ZOK and the Beloit Memorial Hospital. The fronts feature color player photos in white borders. The backs carry a small black-and-white player portrait with player information and career statistics. The cards are unnumbered and checklisted below in alphabetical order. This issue includes the minor league card debut of Valerio De Los Santos.

	MINT	NRMT	EXC
COMPLETE SET (36)	25.00	11.00	3.10

☐ 1 Peter Benny
☐ 2 Darren Berninger
☐ 3 Carrie Bieniek
Keith Michlig#{Daniel Cleland
☐ 4 Josh Bishop
☐ 5 Jered Camp
☐ 6 Bill Campbell CO
☐ 7 Carlos Campusano
☐ 8 Robinson Cancel
☐ 9 Domingo Carrasquel
☐ 10 Edward Collins
☐ 11 Jason Dawsey
☐ 12 Valerio De Los Santos
☐ 13 Brett Dolan ANN
☐ 14 David Elliot
☐ 15 Pamela Graves
☐ 16 Matt Harris AGM
☐ 17 Adam Housley
☐ 18 Anthony Iapoce
☐ 19 Michael Kinkade
☐ 20 Mickey Lopez
☐ 21 Jamie Lopiccolo
☐ 22 John Mallee CO
☐ 23 Allen Mealing
☐ 24 Jeff Nelson GM
☐ 25 Tracie Nelson
☐ 26 Kevin Noriega
☐ 27 Troy O'Neal
☐ 28 Gerald Parent
☐ 29 Tony Pavlovich
☐ 30 Jeffrey Paxson TR
☐ 31 Anthony Peters
☐ 32 Ryan Ritter
☐ 33 Luis Salazar MG
☐ 34 Richard Smith
☐ 35 John Sortedahl
☐ 36 Team Photo CL

1996 Best Autograph Series

This 100-card set features color player photo shots on white borders. The team logo, player's name and position appear across the bottom of the card. The back carry a color photo along with player information.

	MINT	NRMT	EXC
COMPLETE SET (100)	10.00	4.50	1.25
COMMON CARD (1-100)	.05	.02	.01
☐ 1 Winston Abreu	.25	.11	.03
☐ 2 Antonio Alfonseca	.05	.02	.01
☐ 3 Richard Almanzar	.15	.07	.02
☐ 4 Gabe Alvarez	.20	.09	.03
☐ 5 Marlon Anderson	.05	.02	.01
☐ 6 Kym Ashworth	.05	.02	.01
☐ 7 Marc Barcelo	.05	.02	.01
☐ 8 Brian Barkley	.20	.09	.03
☐ 9 Mike Bell	.15	.07	.02
☐ 10 Carlos Beltran	.30	.14	.04
☐ 11 Shayne Bennett	.05	.02	.01
☐ 12 Jeremy Blevins	.25	.11	.03
☐ 13 Kevin Brown	.20	.09	.03
☐ 14 Ray Brown	.05	.02	.01
☐ 15 Homer Bush	.05	.02	.01
☐ 16 Jay Canizaro	.05	.02	.01
☐ 17 Troy Carrasco	.05	.02	.01
☐ 18 Raul Casanova	.25	.11	.03
☐ 19 Luis Castillo	.50	.23	.06
☐ 20 Ramon Castro	.05	.02	.01
☐ 21 Gary Coffee	.05	.02	.01
☐ 22 Decomba Conner	.05	.02	.01
☐ 23 Kevin Coughlin	.05	.02	.01
☐ 24 Jacob Cruz	.50	.23	.06
☐ 25 Jeff D'Amico	.20	.09	.03
☐ 26 Tommy Davis	.05	.02	.01
☐ 27 Edwin Diaz	.20	.09	.03
☐ 28 Einar Diaz	.05	.02	.01
☐ 29 David Doster	.05	.02	.01
☐ 30 Derrin Ebert	.20	.09	.03
☐ 31 Bobby Estalella	.50	.23	.06
☐ 32 Alex Gonzalez	.25	.11	.03
☐ 33 Kevin Grijak	.05	.02	.01
☐ 34 Jose Guillen	2.00	.90	.25
☐ 35 Tim Harkrider	.05	.02	.01
☐ 36 Dan Held	.05	.02	.01
☐ 37 Wes Helms	1.50	.70	.19
☐ 38 Erik Hiljus	.05	.02	.01
☐ 39 Aaron Holbert	.05	.02	.01
☐ 40 Raul Ibanez	.05	.02	.01
☐ 41 Jesse Ibarra	.05	.02	.01
☐ 42 Marty Janzen	.05	.02	.01
☐ 43 Robin Jennings	.05	.02	.01
☐ 44 Sean Johnston	.20	.09	.03
☐ 45 Randy Jorgensen	.05	.02	.01
☐ 46 Marc Kroon	.05	.02	.01
☐ 47 Mike Kusiewicz	.25	.11	.03
☐ 48 Carlos Lee	1.00	.45	.12
☐ 49 Brian Lesher	.05	.02	.01
☐ 50 George Lombard	1.00	.45	.12
☐ 51 Roberto Lopez	.05	.02	.01
☐ 52 Fernando Lunar	.05	.02	.01
☐ 53 Len Manning	.05	.02	.01
☐ 54 Eddy Martinez	.05	.02	.01
☐ 55 Jesus Martinez	.05	.02	.01
☐ 56 Onan Masaoka	.40	.18	.05
☐ 57 Joe Maskavish	.05	.02	.01
☐ 58 Jeff Matulevich	.05	.02	.01
☐ 59 Brian Meadows	.05	.02	.01
☐ 60 Mike Metcalfe	.05	.02	.01
☐ 61 Doug Mlick	.05	.02	.01
☐ 62 Steve Montgomery	.05	.02	.01
☐ 63 Trey Moore	.05	.02	.01
☐ 64 Nick Morrow	.05	.02	.01
☐ 65 Bryant Nelson	.05	.02	.01
☐ 66 Sergio Nunez	.05	.02	.01
☐ 67 Hector Ortega	.05	.02	.01
☐ 68 Russell Ortiz	.05	.02	.01
☐ 69 Eric Owens	.05	.02	.01
☐ 70 Billy Percibal	.05	.02	.01
☐ 71 Charles Peterson	.05	.02	.01
☐ 72 A.J. Pierzynski	.20	.09	.03
☐ 73 Charles Poe	.05	.02	.01
☐ 74 Dante Powell	.75	.35	.09
☐ 75 Kenny Pumphrey	.05	.02	.01
☐ 76 Angel Ramirez	.05	.02	.01
☐ 77 Julio Ramirez	.20	.09	.03
☐ 78 Gary Rath	.05	.02	.01
☐ 79 Jon Ratliff	.05	.02	.01
☐ 80 Brad Rigby	.05	.02	.01
☐ 81 Benj Sampson	.20	.09	.03
☐ 82 Greg Shockey	.05	.02	.01
☐ 83 Steve Shoemaker	.05	.02	.01
☐ 84 Demond Smith	.05	.02	.01
☐ 85 Robert Smith	.25	.11	.03
☐ 86 Steve Soderstrom	.05	.02	.01
☐ 87 Fernando Tatis	.15	.07	.02
☐ 88 Jose Texidor	.05	.02	.01
☐ 89 Brett Tomko	.15	.07	.02
☐ 90 Jose Valentin	.50	.23	.06
☐ 91 Jason Varitek	.15	.07	.02
☐ 92 Andrew Vessel	.15	.07	.02
☐ 93 Casey Whitten	.05	.02	.01
☐ 94 Enrique Wilson	.20	.09	.03
☐ 95 Preston Wilson	.15	.07	.02
☐ 96 Larry Wimberly	.20	.09	.03
☐ 97 Jaret Wright	.30	.14	.04
☐ 98 Dmitri Young	.25	.11	.03
☐ 99 Joe Young	.25	.11	.03
☐ 100 Checklist	.05	.02	.01

1996 Best Autograph Series Autographs

This 91-card set features signed color player photos on a white background. The autographs were inserted at a rate of one per pack.

	MINT	NRMT	EXC
COMPLETE SET (91)	400.00	180.00	50.00
COMMON AUTOGRAPGH	3.00	1.35	.35

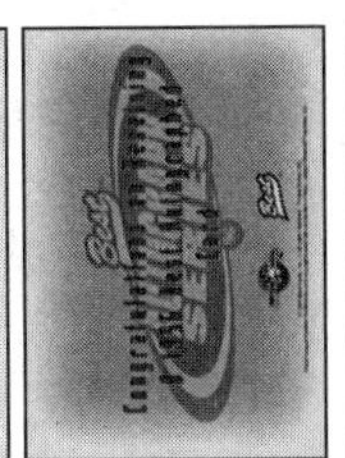

Card	MINT	NRMT	EXC
☐ 1 Israel Alcantera	3.00	1.35	.35
☐ 2 Richard Almanzar	4.00	1.80	.50
☐ 3 Brian Banks	3.00	1.35	.35
☐ 4 Marc Barcelo	3.00	1.35	.35
☐ 5 Kimera Bartee	3.00	1.35	.35
☐ 6 Jeremy Blevins	3.00	1.35	.35
☐ 7 Jamie Bluma	3.00	1.35	.35
☐ 8 D.J. Boston	3.00	1.35	.35
☐ 9 Kevin Brown	8.00	3.60	1.00
☐ 10 Homer Bush	3.00	1.35	.35
☐ 11 Jay Canizaro	3.00	1.35	.35
☐ 12 Luis Castillo	10.00	4.50	1.25
☐ 13 Dave Coggin	5.00	2.20	.60
☐ 14 Bartolo Colon	15.00	6.75	1.85
☐ 15 Jacob Cruz	10.00	4.50	1.25
☐ 16 Lino Diaz	3.00	1.35	.35
☐ 17 Todd Dunn	3.00	1.35	.35
☐ 18 Jermaine Dye	25.00	11.00	3.10
☐ 19 Bobby Estalella	10.00	4.50	1.25
☐ 20 Tom Fordham	4.00	1.80	.50
☐ 21 Karim Garcia	20.00	9.00	2.50
☐ 22 Todd Greene	8.00	3.60	1.00
☐ 23 Ben Grieve	25.00	11.00	3.10
☐ 24 Mike Gulan	3.00	1.35	.35
☐ 25 Derek Hacopian	3.00	1.35	.35
☐ 26 Wes Helms	30.00	13.50	3.70
☐ 27 Brett Herbison	5.00	2.20	.60
☐ 28 Chad Hermansen	20.00	9.00	2.50
☐ 29 Aaron Holbert	3.00	1.35	.35
☐ 30 Damon Hollins	4.00	1.80	.50
☐ 31 Ryan Jaroncyk	3.00	1.35	.35
☐ 32 Geoff Jenkins	10.00	4.50	1.25
☐ 33 Earl Johnson	3.00	1.35	.35
☐ 34 Andruw Jones	50.00	22.00	6.25
☐ 35 Jason Kendall	12.00	5.50	1.50
☐ 36 Brooks Kieschnick	6.00	2.70	.75
☐ 37 Andre King	3.00	1.35	.35
☐ 38 Paul Konerko	30.00	13.50	3.70
☐ 39 Todd Landry	3.00	1.35	.35
☐ 40 Mendy Lopez	4.00	1.80	.50
☐ 41 Roberto Lopez	3.00	1.35	.35
☐ 42 Eric Ludwick	3.00	1.35	.35
☐ 43 Mike Maurer	3.00	1.35	.35
☐ 44 Brian Meadows	3.00	1.35	.35
☐ 45 Ralph Milliard	3.00	1.35	.35
☐ 46 Doug Mlicki	3.00	1.35	.35
☐ 47 Julio Mosquera	3.00	1.35	.35
☐ 48 Tony Mounce	3.00	1.35	.35
☐ 49 Sergio Nunez	3.00	1.35	.35
☐ 50 Russell Ortiz	3.00	1.35	.35
☐ 51 Carey Paige	3.00	1.35	.35
☐ 52 Jay Payton	20.00	9.00	2.50
☐ 53 Charles Peterson	4.00	1.80	.50
☐ 54 Tommy Phelps	3.00	1.35	.35
☐ 55 Hugo Pivaral	4.00	1.80	.50
☐ 56 Dante Powell	20.00	9.00	2.50
☐ 57 Angel Ramirez	3.00	1.35	.35
☐ 58 Gary Rath	3.00	1.35	.35
☐ 59 Mark Redman	3.00	1.35	.35
☐ 60 Adam Riggs	3.00	1.35	.35
☐ 61 Lonell Roberts	3.00	1.35	.35
☐ 62 Scott Rolen	30.00	13.50	3.70
☐ 63 Glendon Rusch	4.00	1.80	.50
☐ 64 Matt Sachse	3.00	1.35	.35
☐ 65 Donnie Sadler	10.00	4.50	1.25
☐ 66 William Santamaria	3.00	1.35	.35
☐ 67 Todd Schmidt	3.00	1.35	.35
☐ 68 Richie Sexson	12.00	5.50	1.50
☐ 69 Alvie Shepherd	3.00	1.35	.35
☐ 70 Steve Shoemaker	3.00	1.35	.35
☐ 71 Brian Sikorski	3.00	1.35	.35
☐ 72 Randall Simon	5.00	2.20	.60
☐ 73 Matt Smith	3.00	1.35	.35
☐ 74 Scott Spiezio	4.00	1.80	.50
☐ 75 Everett Stull	3.00	1.35	.35
☐ 76 Jose Texidor	3.00	1.35	.35
☐ 77 Mike Thurman	3.00	1.35	.35
☐ 78 Brett Tomko	5.00	2.20	.60
☐ 79 Hector Trinidad	3.00	1.35	.35
☐ 80 Pedro Valdes	4.00	1.80	.50
☐ 81 Andrew Vessel	4.00	1.80	.50
☐ 82 Jacob Viano	3.00	1.35	.35
☐ 83 Terrell Wade	5.00	2.20	.60
☐ 84 Bret Wagner	3.00	1.35	.35
☐ 85 Todd Walker	30.00	13.50	3.70
☐ 86 Travis Welch	3.00	1.35	.35
☐ 87 Casey Whitten	3.00	1.35	.35
☐ 88 Paul Wilson	12.00	5.50	1.50
☐ 89 Preston Wilson	5.00	2.20	.60
☐ 90 Kevin Witt	5.00	2.20	.60
☐ 91 Jamey Wright	12.00	5.50	1.50

1996 Best Autograph Series 1st Round Picks

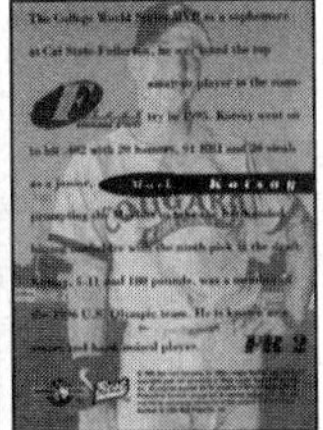

	MINT	NRMT	EXC
COMPLETE SET (16)	80.00	36.00	10.00
COMMON CARD (FR1-FR16)	5.00	2.20	.60
☐ FR1 Chad Green	10.00	4.50	1.25
☐ FR2 Mark Kotsay	15.00	6.75	1.85
☐ FR3 Robert Stratton	6.00	2.70	.75
☐ FR4 Dermal Brown	6.00	2.70	.75
☐ FR5 Matt Halloran	8.00	3.60	1.00
☐ FR6 Joe Lawrence	8.00	3.60	1.00
☐ FR7 Todd Noel	5.00	2.20	.60
☐ FR8 Jake Westbrook	8.00	3.60	1.00
☐ FR9 Gil Meche	5.00	2.20	.60
☐ FR10 Damian Rolls	10.00	4.50	1.25
☐ FR11 John Oliver	6.00	2.70	.75
☐ FR12 Josh Garrett	10.00	4.50	1.25
☐ FR13 A.J. Zapp	6.00	2.70	.75
☐ FR14 Danny Peoples	6.00	2.70	.75
☐ FR15 Paul Wilder	6.00	2.70	.75
☐ FR16 Nick Bierbrodt	6.00	2.70	.75

1996 Best Player of the Year Andruw Jones

Inserted one per retail box.

	MINT	NRMT	EXC
COMPLETE SET (5)	25.00	11.00	3.10
COMMON CARD (1-5)	5.00	2.20	.60
☐ 1 Andruw Jones (Macon Braves)	5.00	2.20	.60
☐ 2 Andruw Jones (Durham Bulls)	5.00	2.20	.60
☐ 3 Andruw Jones (Greenville Braves)	5.00	2.20	.60
☐ 4 Andruw Jones (Richmond Braves)	5.00	2.20	.60
☐ 5 Andruw Jones (Player of the Year)	5.00	2.20	.60

1996 Best Player of the Year Andruw Jones Autographs

	MINT	NRMT	EXC
COMPLETE SET (5)	200.00	90.00	25.00
COMMON AUTOGRAPH (1-5)	40.00	18.00	5.00
☐ 1 Andruw Jones (Macon Braves)	40.00	18.00	5.00
☐ 2 Andruw Jones (Durham Bulls)	40.00	18.00	5.00
☐ 3 Andruw Jones (Greenville Braves)	40.00	18.00	5.00
☐ 4 Andruw Jones (Richmond Braves)	40.00	18.00	5.00
☐ 5 Andruw Jones (Player of the Year)	40.00	18.00	5.00

1996 Billings Mustangs Team Issue

This 31-card set of the 1996 Billings Mustangs, a Rookie Class Pioneer League affiliate of the Cincinnati Reds, was sponsored by the First Interstate Bank and features black-and-white borderless color player photos by Dennis Clark. The backs carry player information and statistics. The cards are unnumbered and checklisted below in alphabetical order.

	MINT	NRMT	EXC
COMPLETE SET (31)	40.00	18.00	5.00

- ☐ 1 Chad Angerhofer
- ☐ 2 Matt Buckley
- ☐ 3 Andy Burress
- ☐ 4 Wylie Campbell
- ☐ 5 Tony Cloud
- ☐ 6 Lance Davis
- ☐ 7 Michael Dresch
- ☐ 8 Chad Fonceca
- ☐ 9 Scott Garrett
- ☐ 10 Rod Griggs
- ☐ 11 David Guthrie
- ☐ 12 Josh Harris
- ☐ 13 Desmond Herrera
- ☐ 14 Darron Ingram
- ☐ 15 Daniel Jenkins
- ☐ 16 Jeremy Keller
- ☐ 17 Doug Kirby
- ☐ 18 Eric Mapp
- ☐ 19 Justin Marine
- ☐ 20 Kevin Marn
- ☐ 21 Matt Martin
- ☐ 22 Philip Merrell
- ☐ 23 Kevin Needham
- ☐ 24 Steve Oliverio CO
- ☐ 25 Anthony Patellis
- ☐ 26 Nick Presto
- ☐ 27 Corey Price
- ☐ 28 David Shepard
- ☐ 29 Stephen Smith
- ☐ 30 Tom Spencer TR
- ☐ 31 Bryan Zwemke

1996 Binghamton Bees Best

This 30-card set of the 1996 Binghamton Bees, a Class AA Eastern League affiliate of the New York Mets, was produced by Best Cards, Inc. and features color action player photos in a white border. The backs carry player information and career statistics.

	MINT	NRMT	EXC
COMPLETE SET (30)	10.00	4.50	1.25

- ☐ 1 Benny Agbayani
- ☐ 2 Jesus Azuaje
- ☐ 3 Ballwinkle and Buddy the Bee(Mascot)
- ☐ 4 Joe Crawford
- ☐ 5 Brian Daubach
- ☐ 6 Brian Edmondson
- ☐ 7 Mark Fuller
- ☐ 8 Philip Geisler
- ☐ 9 Charlie Greene
- ☐ 10 Pedro Grifol
- ☐ 11 Mark Guerra
- ☐ 12 Jason Hardtke
- ☐ 13 Michael Herbst
- ☐ 14 Bill Latham
- ☐ 15 Tim Leiper
- ☐ 16 Cory Lidle
- ☐ 17 Terrell Lowery
- ☐ 18 John Mahalik
- ☐ 19 Dwight Maness
- ☐ 20 Kevin Morgan
- ☐ 21 Scott Pagano
- ☐ 22 Jason Pierson
- ☐ 23 Hector Ramirez
- ☐ 24 Rafael Roque
- ☐ 25 Chris Saunders
- ☐ 26 Jeff Tam
- ☐ 27 John Tamargo
- ☐ 28 Mike Welch
- ☐ 29 Donnie White
- ☐ 30 Shannon Withem

1996 Birmingham Barons Best

This 30-card set of the 1996 Birmingham Barons, a Class AA Southern League affiliate of the Chicago White Sox, was produced by Best Cards, Inc. and features color action player photos in a white border. The backs carry player information and career statistics.

	MINT	NRMT	EXC
COMPLETE SET (30)	8.00	3.60	1.00

- ☐ 1 Eddie Pearson
- ☐ 2 Mike Cameron
- ☐ 3 Troy Fryman
- ☐ 4 Jimmy Hurst
- ☐ 5 Magglio Ordonez
- ☐ 6 Frank Menechino
- ☐ 7 Greg Norton
- ☐ 8 Glenn DiSarcina
- ☐ 9 Harold Williams
- ☐ 10 Robert Machado
- ☐ 11 Scott Vollmer
- ☐ 12 Pete Rose Jr.
- ☐ 13 Tom Fordham
- ☐ 14 Scott Eyre
- ☐ 15 Tim Moore
- ☐ 16 Barry Johnson
- ☐ 17 John Snyder
- ☐ 18 Rich Pratt
- ☐ 19 Steve Worrell
- ☐ 20 Archie Vasquez
- ☐ 21 Brian Woods
- ☐ 22 Mike Heath MG
- ☐ 23 Luis Andujar
- ☐ 24 Kevin Coughlin
- ☐ 25 Charles Poe
- ☐ 26 Mike Sirotka
- ☐ 27 Larry Thomas
- ☐ 28 Craig Wilson
- ☐ 29 Julio Vinas
- ☐ 30 Terry Francona MG

1996 Bluefield Orioles Best

This 27-card set of the 1996 Bluefield Orioles, a Rookie Class Appalachian League affiliate of the Baltimore Orioles, was produced by Best Cards, Inc. and features color action player photos in a white border. The backs carry player information and career statistics. This issue includes the minor league card debut of Calvin Pickering.

	MINT	NRMT	EXC
COMPLETE SET (30)	12.00	5.50	1.50

- ☐ 1 Bobby Dickerson MG
- ☐ 2 Dan Simonds CO
- ☐ 3 Charlie Puleo CO
- ☐ 4 Carlos Akins
- ☐ 5 Chipper Alley
- ☐ 6 Chris Bray
- ☐ 7 Carlos Casimiro
- ☐ 8 Curtis Charles
- ☐ 9 Tim DeCinces
- ☐ 10 Darrell Dent
- ☐ 11 Scott Eibey
- ☐ 12 Louis Fisher
- ☐ 13 Maleke Fowler
- ☐ 14 Abraham Hacen
- ☐ 15 Jason Hackett
- ☐ 16 Brandon Huntsman
- ☐ 17 Chip Lawrence
- ☐ 18 Adam McCollough
- ☐ 19 Carlos Mercedes
- ☐ 20 Gabe Molina
- ☐ 21 Bobby O'Toole
- ☐ 22 Chad Paronto
- ☐ 23 Richard Paz
- ☐ 24 Alex Pedrosa
- ☐ 25 Americo Peguero
- ☐ 26 Calvin Pickering
- ☐ 27 Juan Carlos Santos Perez
- ☐ 28 Joel Stephens
- ☐ 29 Josh Towers
- ☐ 30 Checklist

1996 Boise Hawks Best

This 30-card set of the 1996 Boise Hawks, a Class A Northwest League affiliate of the California Angels, was produced by Best Cards, Inc. and features color action player photos in a white border. The backs carry player information and career statistics.

	MINT	NRMT	EXC
COMPLETE SET (30)	12.00	5.50	1.50

- ☐ 1 Tom Kotchman MG
- ☐ 2 Todd Claus CO
- ☐ 3 Jim Bennett CO
- ☐ 4 Chuck Abbott
- ☐ 5 Jeremy Blevins
- ☐ 6 Scott Byers
- ☐ 7 Brendon Cowsill
- ☐ 8 Matt Curtis
- ☐ 9 Tommy Darrell
- ☐ 10 Fernando Delacruz
- ☐ 11 Trent Durrington
- ☐ 12 Eduardo Ferrer
- ☐ 13 Eric Gillespie
- ☐ 14 Mark Harriger
- ☐ 15 Matt Hobbie
- ☐ 16 Michael Hughes
- ☐ 17 Kevin Humphreys
- ☐ 18 Wade Jackson
- ☐ 19 Aaron Mayer
- ☐ 20 Nate Murphy
- ☐ 21 Rob Neal
- ☐ 22 Leonardo Patino
- ☐ 23 Eric Plooy
- ☐ 24 Jerrod Riggan
- ☐ 25 Hector Rodriguez
- ☐ 26 Juan Rodriguez
- ☐ 27 Jason Stockstill
- ☐ 28 Richard Stuart
- ☐ 29 Brian Ussery
- ☐ 30 Keith Volkman

1996 Bowie Baysox Best

This 27-card set of the 1996 Bowie Baysox, a Class AA Eastern League affiliate of the Baltimore Orioles, was produced by Best Cards, Inc. and features color action player photos in a white border. The backs carry player information and career statistics.

	MINT	NRMT	EXC
COMPLETE SET (27)	8.00	3.60	1.00

- ☐ 1 Tim Blackwell MG
- ☐ 2 Chris Lein CO
- ☐ 3 Dan Simonds CO
- ☐ 4 Mitch Bibb TR
- ☐ 5 Juan Bautista

□ 6 Harry Berrios
□ 7 Brent Bowers
□ 8 Brian Brewer
□ 9 Rocco Cafaro
□ 10 Carlos Chavez
□ 11 Howie Clark
□ 12 Danny Clyburn
□ 13 Kevin Curtis
□ 14 Tommy Davis
□ 15 Kris Gresham
□ 16 Shane Hale
□ 17 Marcus Hostetler
□ 18 Matt Jarvis
□ 19 Chris Lemp
□ 20 Calvin Maduro
□ 21 Jose Millares
□ 22 John O'Donoghue
□ 23 Willis Otanez
□ 24 Lance Rice
□ 25 Lance Schuermann
□ 26 Fletcher Thompson
□ 27 Esteban Yan

1996 Brevard County Manatees Best

This 30-card set of the 1996 Brevard County Manatees, a Class A Florida State League affiliate of the Florida Marlins, was produced by Best Cards, Inc. and features color action player photos in a white border. The backs carry player information and career statistics.

	MINT	NRMT	EXC
COMPLETE SET (30)	10.00	4.50	1.25

□ 1 Fredi Gonzalez MG
□ 2 Jose Castro CO
□ 3 Randy Hennis CO
□ 4 Nigel Alejo
□ 5 Heath Altman
□ 6 Mitch Bowen
□ 7 Matt Brunson
□ 8 Todd Cady
□ 9 Michael Caravelli
□ 10 Dennis Castro
□ 11 Hayward Cook
□ 12 Tony Darden
□ 13 Dan Ehler
□ 14 Tony Enard
□ 15 Dan Fagley
□ 16 Gabe Gonzalez
□ 17 Juan Gonzalez
□ 18 Aaron Harvey
□ 19 Brian Meadows
□ 20 Chad Miles
□ 21 David Miller
□ 22 Walter Miranda
□ 23 Tom Owen
□ 24 Michael Parisi
□ 25 Scott Podesednik
□ 26 Gregg Press
□ 27 Glenn Reeves
□ 28 Maximo Rodriguez
□ 29 Victor Rodriguez
□ 30 Jason Shanahan

1996 Bristol White Sox Best

This 30-card set of the 1996 Bristol White Sox, a Rookie Class Appalachian League affiliate of the Chicago White Sox, was produced by Best Cards, Inc. and features color action player photos in a white border. The backs carry player information and career statistics.

	MINT	NRMT	EXC
COMPLETE SET (30)	10.00	4.50	1.25

□ 1 Nick Capra MG
□ 2 Greg Ritchie CO
□ 3 Steve Wilson CO
□ 4 Matt Bekkedal TR
□ 5 Todd Stranghoner CO
□ 6 Aaron McCready(Clubhouse MG)
□ 7 Boyce Cox(President)
□ 8 Rashad Albert
□ 9 Joe Bales
□ 10 Doug Bearden Jr.
□ 11 Tom Buckman
□ 12 Garret Carlson
□ 13 Sean Connolly
□ 14 Pete DeMorejon
□ 15 Joe Farley
□ 16 Rick Heineman
□ 17 Chris Heintz
□ 18 Reid Hodges
□ 19 Mario Iglesias
□ 20 Jeff Inglin
□ 21 Chuck Klee
□ 22 Jason Lakman
□ 23 Omar Lopez
□ 24 Manuel Lutz
□ 25 Craig McClure
□ 26 Jamie Nichols
□ 27 Robinson Romero
□ 28 Steve Schorzman
□ 29 Clay Stevens
□ 30 Checklist

1996 Buffalo Bisons Best

This 24-card set of the 1996 Buffalo Bisons, a Class AAA American Association affiliate of the Cleveland Indians, was produced by Best Cards, Inc. and features color action player photos in a white border. The backs carry player information and career statistics.

	MINT	NRMT	EXC
COMPLETE SET (24)	10.00	4.50	1.25

□ 1 Brian Graham MG
□ 2 Brian Anderson
□ 3 Greg Cadaret
□ 4 Casey Candaele
□ 5 Reid Cornelius
□ 6 Tim Costo
□ 7 Steve Dunn
□ 8 Brian Giles
□ 9 Danny Graves
□ 10 Eric Helfand
□ 11 Damian Jackson
□ 12 Jim Lewis
□ 13 Joe Lis
□ 14 Albie Lopez
□ 15 Tom Marsh
□ 16 Herbert Perry
□ 17 Joe Roa
□ 18 Darryl Scott
□ 19 Paul Shuey
□ 20 Don Sparks
□ 21 Ryan Thompson
□ 22 Jimmy Williams
□ 23 Nigel Wilson
□ 24 Tom Wilson

1996 Burlington Bees Team Issue

This 33-card set of the 1996 Burlington Bees, a Class A Midwest League affiliate of the San Francisco Giants, features borderless color player photos. The backs carry a small black-and-white player portrait with player information and career statistics. The cards are unnumbered and checklisted below according to the way they are listed on the checklist card.

	MINT	NRMT	EXC
COMPLETE SET (33)	15.00	6.75	1.85

□ 1 Lorenzo Barcelo
□ 2 Manuel Bermudz
□ 3 Jason Brester
□ 4 Jason Grote
□ 5 Santos Hernandez
□ 6 Jeff Hutzler
□ 7 Jeff Keith
□ 8 Brian Knoll
□ 9 Kevin Lake
□ 10 Jim Stoops
□ 11 Mike McMullen
□ 12 Jeff Poor
□ 13 Pete Ramirez
□ 14 Dan Topping
□ 15 Malcom Cepeda
□ 16 Delvi Cruz
□ 17 Mark Gulseth
□ 18 John Watson
□ 19 Terry Weaver
□ 20 Pedro Felix
□ 21 Raul Marval
□ 22 Alex Morales
□ 23 Pablo Cordero
□ 24 Don Denbow
□ 25 Bruce Thompson
□ 26 Kevin Watson
□ 27 Glenn Tufts
□ 28 Keith Comstock CO
□ 29 Tom Newell TR
□ 30 Beesley(Mascot)
□ 31 Team Photo CL
□ 32 Team Logo
□ 33 Staff Card

1996 Burlington Indians Best

This 30-card set of the 1996 Burlington Indians, a Rookie Class Appalachian League affiliate of the Cleveland Indians, was produced by Best Cards, Inc. and features color action player photos in a white border. The backs carry player information and career statistics.

	MINT	NRMT	EXC
COMPLETE SET (30)	10.00	4.50	1.25

□ 1 Juan Aracena
□ 2 Mike Bacsik
□ 3 Sean DePaula
□ 4 Alberto Garza
□ 5 Jimmy Hamilton
□ 6 Scott Harrison
□ 7 Joe Horgan
□ 8 Richard Negrette
□ 9 Matt Koeman
□ 10 Darren Loudermilk
□ 11 Ryan McDermott
□ 12 Gonzalo Mojica
□ 13 Brad Pelton
□ 14 Robert Reichow
□ 15 Mike Spiegel
□ 16 Eric Weber
□ 17 Cody Allison
□ 18 Rob Landstad
□ 19 Mike Edwards
□ 20 Bryan Hardy
□ 21 Christian Mota
□ 22 Eddie Perez
□ 23 Aurelio Rodriguez
□ 24 Grant Sharpe
□ 25 Frank Taveras
□ 26 Jake Messner
□ 27 Jesus Hernandez
□ 28 William Jackson
□ 29 Jewell Williams
□ 30 Harry Spilman MG

1996 Butte Copper Kings Best

This 30-card set of the 1996 Butte Copper Kings, a Class Rookie Class Pioneer League affiliate of the Tampa Bay Devil Rays, was produced by Best Cards, Inc. and features color action player photos in a white border. The backs carry player information and career statistics.

	MINT	NRMT	EXC
COMPLETE SET (30)	8.00	3.60	1.00

□ 1 Checklist
□ 2 Bill Murray(Co-Owner)
□ 3 Tom Foley MG
□ 4 Howard Johnson CO
□ 5 Dennis Rasmussen CO
□ 6 Mike Klein TR
□ 7 Chris Tomashoff ASST TR
□ 8 Donkey-Hotey(Mascot)
□ 9 Hernando Arredondo
□ 10 Tyler Bain
□ 11 Mickey Callaway
□ 12 Michael DeCelle
□ 13 Everard Griffiths
□ 14 Mark Hale
□ 15 R.J. Howerton
□ 16 Matt Kastelic
□ 17 John Kaufman
□ 18 Jim Kerr
□ 19 Mike Kimbrell
□ 20 Mike King
□ 21 Scott Madison
□ 22 Jim Manias
□ 23 Leo Martinez
□ 24 Mike McGehee
□ 25 Denis Pujals
□ 26 Matt Quatraro
□ 27 Trey Salinas
□ 28 Shawn Stutz
□ 29 Jared Verrall
□ 30 Kyle Whitley

1996 Canton-Akron Indians Best

This 30-card set of the 1996 Canton-Akron Indians, a Class AA Eastern League affiliate of the Cleveland Indians, was produced by Best Cards, Inc. and features color action player photos in a white border. The backs carry player information and career statistics.

	MINT	NRMT	EXC
COMPLETE SET (30)	12.00	5.50	1.50

□ 1 Jeff Datz MG
□ 2 Tony Arnold CO
□ 3 Minnie Mendoza CO
□ 4 Bruce Aven
□ 5 Todd Betts
□ 6 Jim Betzsold
□ 7 Pat Bryant
□ 8 Bartolo Colon
□ 9 Roland De La Maza
□ 10 Maximo De La Rosa
□ 11 Einar Diaz
□ 12 Travis Driskill
□ 13 Ricky Gutierrez
□ 14 Steve Kline
□ 15 Johnny Martinez
□ 16 Rod McCall
□ 17 Andy McCormack
□ 18 Mike Matthews
□ 19 Mike Neal
□ 20 Erik Plantenberg
□ 21 Alex Ramirez
□ 22 Richie Sexson
□ 23 Jeff Sexton
□ 24 Steve Soliz
□ 25 Greg Thomas
□ 26 Kevin Tolar
□ 27 Jay Vaught
□ 28 Casey Whitten
□ 29 Enrique Wilson
□ 30 Dan DeVoe

1996 Carolina League All-Stars 1 Best

This 24-card set of the 1996 Carolina League's All-Star team was produced by Best Cards, Inc. and sponsored by Minford's Minors. The cards are printed on thin card stock. The fronts feature color player photos in a white border. The backs carry player information. The features first year cards of Jose Guillen and Jaret Wright and second year cards of Andruw Jones, Wes Helms and Ron Wright. 1, 582 sets were produced.

	MINT	NRMT	EXC
COMPLETE SET (24)	20.00	9.00	2.50

□ 1 Chris Fussell
□ 2 Jaret Wright
□ 3 Damian Moss
□ 4 Jimmy Anderson
□ 5 Steve Prihoda
□ 6 Noe Najera
□ 7 John LeRoy
□ 8 Russ Herbert
□ 9 Doug Million
□ 10 Michael Moyle
□ 11 Carlos Mendez
□ 12 Ron Wright
□ 13 Mike Eaglin
□ 14 Kyle Houser
□ 15 Wes Helms
□ 16 Lincoln Martin
□ 17 Amador Arias
□ 18 Andruw Jones
□ 19 Johnny Isom
□ 20 Jose Guillen
□ 21 Chip Glass
□ 22 Sean Casey
□ 23 Minford's Minors
□ 24 Team Photo CL

1996 Carolina League All-Stars 2 Best

This 26-card set of the 1996 Carolina League's All-Star team was produced by Best Cards, Inc. and sponsored by Minford's Minors. The fronts feature color player photos in white borders. The backs carry player information. This set was printed on a thicker card stock. The features first year cards of Jose Guillen, Miquel Tejada and Jaret Wright and second year cards of Andruw Jones, Wes Helms and Ron Wright. 1,110 sets were produced.

	MINT	NRMT	EXC
COMPLETE SET (26)	40.00	18.00	5.00

□ 1 Chris Fussell
□ 2 Jaret Wright
□ 3 Damian Moss
□ 4 Jimmy Anderson
□ 5 Steve Prihoda
□ 6 Noe Najera
□ 7 John LeRoy
□ 8 Russ Herbert
□ 9 Doug Million
□ 10 Michael Moyle
□ 11 Carlos Mendez
□ 12 Ron Wright
□ 13 Mike Eaglin
□ 14 Kyle Houser
□ 15 Wes Helms
□ 16 Lincoln Martin
□ 17 Amador Arias
□ 18 Andruw Jones
□ 19 Johnny Isom
□ 20 Jose Guillen
□ 21 Chip Glass
□ 22 Sean Casey MVP
□ 23 Minford's Minors
Rich and Mitchell
□ 24 Team Photo CL
□ 25 Ron Wright
Sean Casey
□ 26 Miguel Tejada

1996 Carolina League All-Stars Insert Best

This 10-card set was produced by Best Cards, Inc. and sponsored by Minford's Minors. The fronts feature borderless color player photos of some of the most notable All-Stars of the 1996 Carolina League's All-Star team. The backs carry a statement about why the player was picked for this set. Only a limited number of this set was produced and each set is sequentially numbered.

	MINT	NRMT	EXC
COMPLETE SET (10)	125.00	55.00	15.50

- ☐ B1 Wes Helms
  Ron Wright#(Andruw Jones
- ☐ B2 Damian Moss
  Michael Moyle
- ☐ B3 Ron Wright
  Home Run Leader
- ☐ B4 Wes Helms
  Most Hits
- ☐ B5 Andruw Jones
  Runs Scored Leader
- ☐ B6 Andruw Jones
  Slugging Percentage Lader
- ☐ B7 Andruw Jones
  Minor League POY
- ☐ B8 Marc Lewis
  (Carolina League Trivia Card)
- ☐ B9 Jose Guillen
- ☐ B10 Miguel Tejada

1996 Carolina Mudcats Best

This 30-card set of the 1996 Carolina Mudcats, a Class AA Southern League affiliate of the Pittsburgh Pirates, was produced by Best Cards, Inc. and features color action player photos in a white border. The backs carry player information and career statistics.

	MINT	NRMT	EXC
COMPLETE SET (30)	10.00	4.50	1.25

- ☐ 1 Blaine Beatty
- ☐ 2 Mariano Delossantos
- ☐ 3 Dennis Konuszewski
- ☐ 4 Sean Lawrence
- ☐ 5 Adrian Brown
- ☐ 6 Chris Peters
- ☐ 7 Steve Phoenix
- ☐ 8 Matt Pontbriant
- ☐ 9 Kevin Rychel
- ☐ 10 Scott Taylor
- ☐ 11 Dave Wainhouse
- ☐ 12 Marc Wilkins
- ☐ 13 Tim Edge
- ☐ 14 Marcus Hanel
- ☐ 15 Chance Reynolds
- ☐ 16 Tony Beasley
- ☐ 17 Ken Bonifay
- ☐ 18 D.J. Boston
- ☐ 19 Lou Collier
- ☐ 20 Jay Cranford
- ☐ 21 Chance Sanford
- ☐ 22 Jon Farrell
- ☐ 23 Jeff Conger
- ☐ 24 Charles Peterson
- ☐ 25 T.J. Staton
- ☐ 26 Marc Hill MG
- ☐ 27 Bruce Tanner CO
- ☐ 28 Mark Rogow TR
- ☐ 29 Muddy the Mudcat(Mascot)
- ☐ 30 Checklist

1996 Cedar Rapids Kernels Team Issue

This 32-card set of the 1996 Cedar Rapids Kernels, a Class A Midwest League affiliate of the California Angels, was sponsored by McDonald's Restaurants and features color player photos by Jim Tevis. The backs carry player information and statistics. The cards are unnumbered and checklisted below according to the way they are listed on the checklist card.

	MINT	NRMT	EXC
COMPLETE SET (32)	12.00	5.50	1.50

- ☐ 1 Stevenson Agosto
- ☐ 2 Juan Alvarez
- ☐ 3 Justin Baughman
- ☐ 4 Larry Barnes
- ☐ 5 Jose Cintron
- ☐ 6 Jed Dalton
- ☐ 7 David Davalillo
- ☐ 8 Fernando Dela Cruz
- ☐ 9 Bryan Graves
- ☐ 10 Geoff Grenert
- ☐ 11 Kevin Ham
- ☐ 12 Jason Hill
- ☐ 13 Norm Hutchins
- ☐ 14 Ryan Kane
- ☐ 15 John Lloyd
- ☐ 16 John McAninch
- ☐ 17 Alfonso Mota
- ☐ 18 Jimmy O'Quinn
- ☐ 19 Dan Petroff
- ☐ 20 Derek Ryder
- ☐ 21 Brian Scutero
- ☐ 22 David Sick
- ☐ 23 Nick Skuse
- ☐ 24 Gar Vallone
- ☐ 25 Jon Vander Griend
- ☐ 26 Grant Vermillion
- ☐ 27 Tom Lawless MG
- ☐ 28 Steve Renko CO
- ☐ 29 Charlie Romero CO
- ☐ 30 Jamie Macias TR
- ☐ 31 Team Photo
- ☐ 32 Title Card CL

1996 Charleston Riverdogs Team Issue

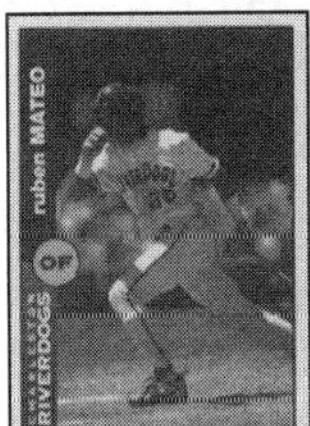

This 32-card set of the 1996 Charleston Riverdogs, a Class A South Atlantic League affiliate of the Texas Rangers, features color player photos in white borders. The backs carry player information and career statistics. This issue includes the minor league card debuts of Ruben Mateo, Dan Kolb and Ryan Dempster.

	MINT	NRMT	EXC
COMPLETE SET (32)	15.00	6.75	1.85

- ☐ 9601 Gary Allenson MG
- ☐ 9602 Frank Velasquez TR
- ☐ 9603 Brad Arnsberg CO
- ☐ 9604 Shamrock the Riverdog(Mascot)
- ☐ 9605 Charlie the Riverdog(Mascot)
- ☐ 9606 Chuck Bauer Jr.
- ☐ 9607 Chris Briones
- ☐ 9608 Cliff Brumbaugh
- ☐ 9609 Tim Codd
- ☐ 9610 Miguel De La Rosa
- ☐ 9611 Ryan Dempster
- ☐ 9612 Mark Draeger
- ☐ 9613 Shawn Gallagher
- ☐ 9614 Joey Goodwin
- ☐ 9615 Jason Johnson
- ☐ 9616 Cesar King
- ☐ 9617 Dan Kolb
- ☐ 9618 Jose Martinez
- ☐ 9619 Ruben Mateo
- ☐ 9620 Mike McHugh
- ☐ 9621 Craig Monroe
- ☐ 9622 Bobby Moore
- ☐ 9623 Scott Mudd
- ☐ 9624 Juan Nunez
- ☐ 9625 Asbel Ortiz
- ☐ 9626 Jose Parra
- ☐ 9627 Jose Santo
- ☐ 9628 Carlos Simmons
- ☐ 9629 Mike Venafro
- ☐ 9630 Nate Vopata
- ☐ 9631 Charleston Riverdogs Logo
- ☐ 9632 Checklist

1996 Charlotte Knights Best

This 29-card set of the 1996 Charlotte Knights, a Class AAA International League affiliate of the Florida Marlins, was produced by Best Cards, Inc. and features color action player photos in a white border. The backs carry player information and career statistics. This issue includes the minor league card debut Livan Hernandez.

	MINT	NRMT	EXC
COMPLETE SET (29)	10.00	4.50	1.25

- ☐ 1 Sal Rende MG
- ☐ 2 Jeff Pentland CO
- ☐ 3 Mike Parrott CO
- ☐ 4 Mike Leon TR
- ☐ 5 Homer the Dragon(Mascot)
- ☐ 6 Joel Adamson
- ☐ 7 Antonio Alfonseca
- ☐ 8 Miguel Batista
- ☐ 9 Mario Brito
- ☐ 10 Jerry Brooks
- ☐ 11 Dan Chergey
- ☐ 12 Tommy Gregg
- ☐ 13 Shane Halter
- ☐ 14 Livan Hernandez
- ☐ 15 Jarold Juelsgaard
- ☐ 16 Lou Lucca
- ☐ 17 Billy McMillon
- ☐ 18 Kurt Miller
- ☐ 19 Ralph Milliard
- ☐ 20 Russ Morman
- ☐ 21 Jose Olmeda
- ☐ 22 Yorkis Perez
- ☐ 23 Edgar Renteria
- ☐ 24 Jason Robertson
- ☐ 25 Marc Ronan
- ☐ 26 Chris Seelbach
- ☐ 27 Marc Valdes
- ☐ 28 Matt Whisenant
- ☐ 29 Darrell Whitmore

1996 Chattanooga Lookouts Best

This 30-card set of the 1996 Chattanooga Lookouts, a Class AA Southern League affiliate of the Cincinnati Reds, was produced by Best Cards, Inc. and features color action player photos in a white border. The backs carry player information and career statistics. This issue includes the minor league card debut of Brett Tomko.

	MINT	NRMT	EXC
COMPLETE SET (30)	12.00	5.50	1.50

- ☐ 1 Mark Berry MG
- ☐ 2 Mack Jenkins CO
- ☐ 3 Mark Wagner CO
- ☐ 4 Jim Knudtson TR
- ☐ 5 Larry Ward DIR
- ☐ 6 Paul Bako
- ☐ 7 Aaron Boone
- ☐ 8 Donald Broach
- ☐ 9 Ray Brown
- ☐ 10 Travis Buckley
- ☐ 11 Brendan Donnelly
- ☐ 12 Tom Doyle
- ☐ 13 Ronald Frazier
- ☐ 14 Billy Hall
- ☐ 15 Domingo Jean
- ☐ 16 Cleveland Ladell
- ☐ 17 Larry Luebbers
- ☐ 18 Curt Lyons
- ☐ 19 Ricky Magdaleno
- ☐ 20 Scott McKenzie
- ☐ 21 Mike Meggers
- ☐ 22 James Nix
- ☐ 23 Chris Reed
- ☐ 24 Jason Robbins
- ☐ 25 John Roper
- ☐ 26 Toby Rumfield
- ☐ 27 Ruben Santana
- ☐ 28 Brett Tomko
- ☐ 29 Pat Watkins
- ☐ 30 Checklist

1996 Clinton Lumber Kings Team Issue

This 29-card set of lthe 1996 Clinton Lumber Kings, a Class A Midwest League affiliate of the San Diego Padres, features color player photos with a vertical green bar on the left. The backs carry a small black-and-white head photo with player information and career statistics. The cards are unnumbered and checklisted below in alphabetical order.

	MINT	NRMT	EXC
COMPLETE SET (29)	25.00	11.00	3.10

- ☐ 1 Matt Abernathy
- ☐ 2 Dusty Allen
- ☐ 3 Gordon Amerson
- ☐ 4 Carmen Bucci
- ☐ 5 Tim Campbell
- ☐ 6 Cesarin Carmona
- ☐ 7 Chris Clark
- ☐ 8 Craig Clayton
- ☐ 9 Matt Clement
- ☐ 10 Eduardo Cuevas
- ☐ 11 Chad Ebbert
- ☐ 12 Hal Garrett
- ☐ 13 Jason Haeussinger TR
- ☐ 14 Kenny Henderson
- ☐ 15 Rich Hills
- ☐ 16 James Johnson
- ☐ 17 Brandon Kolb
- ☐ 18 Curt Lowry
- ☐ 19 Mike Martin
- ☐ 20 Eric Newman
- ☐ 21 Mike Ramsey MG
- ☐ 22 Jake Remington
- ☐ 23 James Sak
- ☐ 24 Marcos Sanchez
- ☐ 25 Russell Spear
- ☐ 26 Scipio Spinks CO
- ☐ 27 Luis Torres
- ☐ 28 Jason Totman
- ☐ 29 Mark Wulfert

1996 Colorado Springs Sky Sox Team Issue

This 33-card set of the 1996 Colorado Springs Sky Sox, a Class AAA Pacific Coast League affiliate of the Colorado Rockies, features borderless color player photos with the player's name and position printed in a black bar at the bottom. The backs carry player information and career statistics.

	MINT	NRMT	EXC
COMPLETE SET (33)	12.00	5.50	1.50

- ☐ 1 Garvin Alston
- ☐ 2 Roger Bailey
- ☐ 3 Jorge Brito
- ☐ 4 John Burke
- ☐ 5 Albert Bustillos
- ☐ 6 Jeff Carter
- ☐ 7 Pedro Castellano
- ☐ 8 Alan Cockrell
- ☐ 9 Craig Counsell
- ☐ 10 Mike DeJean
- ☐ 11 Keith Dugger TR
- ☐ 12 Angel Echevarria
- ☐ 13 Scott Fredrickson
- ☐ 14 Jay Gainer
- ☐ 15 Ray Giannelli
- ☐ 16 Pedro Gonzalez
- ☐ 17 Ryan Hawblitzel
- ☐ 18 Trenidad Hubbard
- ☐ 19 Bobby Jones
- ☐ 20 Terry Jones
- ☐ 21 David Kennedy
- ☐ 22 Tom Kramer
- ☐ 23 Brad Mills MGR
- ☐ 24 David Nied
- ☐ 25 Neifi Perez
- ☐ 26 Harvey Pulliam
- ☐ 27 Bryan Rekar
- ☐ 28 Sonny Siebert CO
- ☐ 29 Mark Strittmatter
- ☐ 30 Tony Torchia CO
- ☐ 31 Billy White
- ☐ 32 Jamey Wright
- ☐ NNO Cover Card CL

1996 Columbus Clippers Best

This 30-card set of the 1996 Columbus Clippers, a Class AAA International League affiliate of the New York Yankees, was produced by Best Cards, Inc. and features color action player photos in a white border. The backs carry player information and career statistics.

	MINT	NRMT	EXC
COMPLETE SET (30)	8.00	3.60	1.00

- ☐ 1 Stump Merrill MG
  Jim Johnson CO#(Oscar Acosta CO#(Hop Cassady#(Rob Thomson CO
- ☐ 2 Tim Barker
- ☐ 3 Brian Boehringer
- ☐ 4 Bubba Carpenter
- ☐ 5 Mark Carper
- ☐ 6 Ivan Cruz
- ☐ 7 Chris Cumberland
- ☐ 8 Mark Dalesandro
- ☐ 9 Nick Delvecchio
- ☐ 10 Mario Diaz
- ☐ 11 Matt Drews
- ☐ 12 Robert Eenhoorn
- ☐ 13 Mike Figga
- ☐ 14 Paul Gibson
- ☐ 15 Rich Hines
- ☐ 16 Matt Howard
- ☐ 17 Matt Luke
- ☐ 18 Marc Marini
- ☐ 19 Tim McIntosh
- ☐ 20 Jim Mecir
- ☐ 21 Ramiro Mendoza
- ☐ 22 Rich Monteleone
- ☐ 23 Kevin Northrup
- ☐ 24 Dave Pavlas
- ☐ 25 Dale Polley
- ☐ 26 Jorge Posada
- ☐ 27 Ruben Rivera
- ☐ 28 Jaime Torres
- ☐ 29 Kent Wallace
- ☐ 30 Tracy Woodson

1996 Danville Braves Best

This 30-card set of the 1996 Danville Braves, a Rookie Class Appalachian League affiliate of the Atlanta Braves, was produced by Best Cards, Inc. and features color action player photos in a white border. The backs carry player information and career statistics. This issue includes the minor league card debuts of Kevin McGlinchy and Delvis Pacheco.

	MINT	NRMT	EXC
COMPLETE SET (30)	10.00	4.50	1.25

- ☐ 1 Brian Snitker MG
- ☐ 2 Steve Bedrosian CO
- ☐ 3 Nelson Norman CO
- ☐ 4 Jayson Bass
- ☐ 5 Joe Bauldree
- ☐ 6 Ray Beasley
- ☐ 7 Simon Birrell
- ☐ 8 Anthony Brooks
- ☐ 9 Eric Castaldo
- ☐ 10 Skeeter Ellison
- ☐ 11 Ben Fowler
- ☐ 12 Jason Katz
- ☐ 13 Yan Lagrandeur
- ☐ 14 Kevin McGlinchy
- ☐ 15 Shawn Onley
- ☐ 16 Delvis Pacheco
- ☐ 17 Tyrone Pendergrass
- ☐ 18 Jason Ross
- ☐ 19 Jim Scharrer
- ☐ 20 Ryan Schurman
- ☐ 21 Jason Shiell
- ☐ 22 Jason Shy
- ☐ 23 Jeff Spencer

- ☐ 24 Aaron Strangfeld
- ☐ 25 Mike Terhune
- ☐ 26 Jerry Vecchioni
- ☐ 27 Corey Walker
- ☐ 28 Joe Winkelsas
- ☐ 29 Will Wise
- ☐ 30 Ben Wyatt

1996 Daytona Cubs Best

This 30-card set of the 1996 Daytona Cubs, a Class A Florida State League affiliate of the Chicago Cubs, was produced by Best Cards, Inc. and features color action player photos in a white border. The backs carry player information and career statistics. This issue includes the minor league card debut of Kerry Wood.

	MINT	NRMT	EXC
COMPLETE SET (30)	15.00	6.75	1.85

- ☐ 1 Kerry Wood
- ☐ 2 Gilbert Avalos
- ☐ 3 Dennis Bair
- ☐ 4 Richard Barker
- ☐ 5 Shawn Box
- ☐ 6 Saul Bustos
- ☐ 7 Todd Carl
- ☐ 8 Pat Cline
- ☐ 9 Kevin Ellis
- ☐ 10 Trey Forkerway
- ☐ 11 Ricky Freeman
- ☐ 12 Chris Gambs
- ☐ 13 Alfredo Garcia
- ☐ 14 Marty Gazarek
- ☐ 15 Shawn Livsey
- ☐ 16 John McNeese
- ☐ 17 Brian McNichol
- ☐ 18 Mike MiCucci
- ☐ 19 Brandon Pico
- ☐ 20 Bo Porter
- ☐ 21 Jared Snyder
- ☐ 22 Justin Speier
- ☐ 23 Jason Stevenson
- ☐ 24 Steve Walker
- ☐ 25 Gabe Whatley
- ☐ 26 Dave Trembley MG
- ☐ 27 Jim Slaton CO
- ☐ 28 Richie Zisk CO
- ☐ 29 Jim O'Reilly TR
- ☐ 30 Jarrod Scholan
Tom Morgan

1996 Delmarva Shorebirds Best

This 30-card set of the 1996 Delmarva Shorebirds, a Class A South Atlantic League affiliate of the Montreal Expos, was produced by Best Cards, Inc. and features color action player photos in a white border. The backs carry player information and career statistics.

	MINT	NRMT	EXC
COMPLETE SET (30)	8.00	3.60	1.00

- ☐ 1 Doug Sisson MG
- ☐ 2 Dean Treanor CO
- ☐ 3 Ed Sardinha CO
- ☐ 4 Eddie Acosta
- ☐ 5 Carlos Adolfo
- ☐ 6 Basilio Alvarado
- ☐ 7 Jason Baker
- ☐ 8 Michael Barrett
- ☐ 9 Michael Bell
- ☐ 10 Orlando Cabrera
- ☐ 11 Jason Camilli
- ☐ 12 Jose Centeno
- ☐ 13 Xavier Civit
- ☐ 14 Jason Cole
- ☐ 15 Wes Denning
- ☐ 16 Jose Fernandez
- ☐ 17 Ben Fleetham
- ☐ 18 Jaime Garcia
- ☐ 19 Sean Leslie
- ☐ 20 Jose Macias
- ☐ 21 Robert Marquez
- ☐ 22 Troy Mattes
- ☐ 23 Scott Mitchell
- ☐ 24 D.C. Olsen
- ☐ 25 Jeremy Powell
- ☐ 26 Chris Schwab
- ☐ 27 Fernando Seguignol
- ☐ 28 J.D. Smart
- ☐ 29 Javier Vazquez
- ☐ 30 Jason Woodring

1996 Dunedin Blue Jays Best

This 30-card set of the 1996 Dunedin Blue Jays, a Class A Florida State League affiliate of the Toronto Blue Jays, was produced by Best Cards, Inc. and features color action player photos in a white border. The backs carry player information and career statistics. This issue includes the minor league card debuts of Roy Halladay and Kelvim Escobar.

	MINT	NRMT	EXC
COMPLETE SET (30)	15.00	6.75	1.85

- ☐ 1 Tim Adkins
- ☐ 2 Kurt Bogott
- ☐ 3 John Curl
- ☐ 4 Vic Davila
- ☐ 5 Roger Doman
- ☐ 6 Roberto Duran
- ☐ 7 Kelvin Escobar
- ☐ 8 Scott Fitterer
- ☐ 9 Ryan Freel
- ☐ 10 Herman Gordon
- ☐ 11 Mike Gordon
- ☐ 12 Roy Halladay
- ☐ 13 D.J. Harris
- ☐ 14 Jason Jarvis
- ☐ 15 Mark Lukasiewicz
- ☐ 16 Andrew McCormick
- ☐ 17 Adam Melhuse
- ☐ 18 Rob Mummau
- ☐ 19 Scott Pace
- ☐ 20 Kendall Rhine
- ☐ 21 Jonathan Rivers
- ☐ 22 Anthony Sanders
- ☐ 23 Steve Sinclair
- ☐ 24 Andy Thompson
- ☐ 25 Bryan Williams
- ☐ 26 Kevin Witt
- ☐ 27 Dennis Holmberg MG
- ☐ 28 Scott Breeden CO
- ☐ 29 Rolando Pino CO
- ☐ 30 Dennis Brogna TR

1996 Dunedin Blue Jays Team Issue

This 30-card set of the 1996 Dunedin Blue Jays, a Class A Florida State League affiliate of the Toronto Blue Jays, was sponsored by the Times, Perkins Family Restaurant and Bakery, and ABC Station 28. The fronts feature color player portraits in a white border. The player's name and position is printed in a black bar at the bottom. The backs carry player information and career statistics. The cards are unnumbered and checklisted below in alphabetical order. This issue includes the minor league card debuts of Roy Halladay and Kelvim Escobar.

	MINT	NRMT	EXC
COMPLETE SET (30)	40.00	18.00	5.00

- ☐ 1 Tim Adkins
- ☐ 2 Kurt Bogott
- ☐ 3 Scott Breeden CO
- ☐ 4 Dennis Brogna TR
- ☐ 5 John Curl
- ☐ 6 Vic Davila
- ☐ 7 Roger Doman
- ☐ 8 Roberto Duran
- ☐ 9 Kelvim Escobar
- ☐ 10 Scott Fitterer
- ☐ 11 Ryan Freel
- ☐ 12 Herman Gordon
- ☐ 13 Mike Gordon
- ☐ 14 Roy Halladay
- ☐ 15 D.J. Harris
- ☐ 16 Dennis Holmberg MG
- ☐ 17 Jason Jarvis
- ☐ 18 Mark Lukasiewicz
- ☐ 19 Andrew McCormick
- ☐ 20 Adam Melhuse
- ☐ 21 Rob Mummau
- ☐ 22 Scott Pace
- ☐ 23 Rolando Pino CO
- ☐ 24 Kendall Rhine
- ☐ 25 Jonathan Rivers
- ☐ 26 Anthony Sanders
- ☐ 27 Steve Sinclair
- ☐ 28 Andy Thompson
- ☐ 29 Bryan Williams
- ☐ 30 Kevin Witt

1996 Dunedin Blue Jays Update Team Issue

This 18-card set is an update to the regular 1996 Dunedin Blue Jays team and features color player photos in a white border. The backs carry player information. The cards are unnumbered and checklisted below in alphabetical order.

	MINT	NRMT	EXC
COMPLETE SET (18)	50.00	22.00	6.25

- ☐ 1 Kelvim Escobar
- ☐ 2 Miguel Gomez
- ☐ 3 Roy Halladay
- ☐ 4 Chris Hayes
- ☐ 5 Brion King
- ☐ 6 Selwyn Langaigne
- ☐ 7 Jeremy Lee
- ☐ 8 Doug Meiners
- ☐ 9 Adam Melhuse
- ☐ 10 Dave Morgan
- ☐ 11 Omar Sanchez
- ☐ 12 Anthony Sanders
- ☐ 13 Keilan Smith
- ☐ 14 Craig Stone
- ☐ 15 Mike Strange
- ☐ 16 Jay Veniard
- ☐ 17 Kevin Witt
- ☐ NNO Cover Card CL

1996 Durham Bulls (Blue) Best

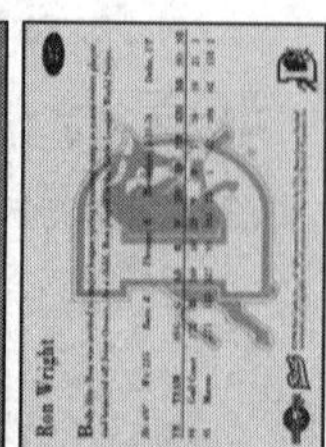

This 30-card set of the 1996 Durham Bulls, a Class A Carolina League affiliate of the Atlanta Braves, was produced by Best Cards, Inc. and features color action player photos in a blue border. The backs carry player information and career statistics. This issue features the second year cards of Andruw Jones, Ron Wright and Wes Helms.

	MINT	NRMT	EXC
COMPLETE SET (30)	35.00	16.00	4.40

- ☐ 1 Andruw Jones
- ☐ 2 Micah Bowie
- ☐ 3 Ken Giard
- ☐ 4 Anthony Briggs
- ☐ 5 Erie Olszewski
- ☐ 6 Derrin Ebert
- ☐ 7 Gator McBride
- ☐ 8 John LeRoy
- ☐ 9 Willy Johnson TR
- ☐ 10 Del Mathews
- ☐ 11 Willie Wilson(Batboy)
- ☐ 12 Kevin Millwood
- ☐ 13 Randy Ingle MG
- ☐ 14 Damian Moss
- ☐ 15 Anton French
- ☐ 16 Kerry Ligtenberg
- ☐ 17 Gus Kennedy
- ☐ 18 Evan Jackson
- ☐ 19 Chris Schmitt
- ☐ 20 Bruce Dal Canton
- ☐ 21 Mike Mahoney
- ☐ 22 Tony Wood
- ☐ 23 Sean Smith
- ☐ 24 Pascual Matos
- ☐ 25 Max Venable CO
- ☐ 26 Edward Cordero
- ☐ 27 Ron Wright
- ☐ 28 Danny Magee
- ☐ 29 Mike Eaglin
- ☐ 30 Wes Helms

1996 Durham Bulls (Brown) Best

This 30-card set of the 1996 Durham Bulls, a Class A Carolina League affiliate of the Atlanta Braves, honors the Carolina League's Southern Division First Half Champions and the team's All-Star players. The set was produced by Best Cards, Inc. and features color action player photos in a brown border. The backs carry player information and career statistics. This issue features the second year cards of Andruw Jones, Ron Wright and Wes Helms.

	MINT	NRMT	EXC
COMPLETE SET (30)	30.00	13.50	3.70

- ☐ 1 1996 Durham Bulls
Carolina League Champions
- ☐ 2 Andruw Jones AS
- ☐ 3 Ray King
- ☐ 4 Ken Giard
- ☐ 5 Anthony Briggs
- ☐ 6 Eric Olszewski
- ☐ 7 Derrin Ebert
- ☐ 8 Gator McBride
- ☐ 9 John Leroy AS
- ☐ 10 Terry Wright
- ☐ 11 Del Mathews
- ☐ 12 Mickey Correa
- ☐ 13 Kevin Millwood
- ☐ 14 Damian Moss AS
- ☐ 15 Ray Nunez
- ☐ 16 Kerry Ligtenberg
- ☐ 17 Gus Kennedy
- ☐ 18 Wes Helms AS
- ☐ 19 Marc Lewis
- ☐ 20 Chris Schmitt
- ☐ 21 Max Venable CO
Randy Ingle MG#(Bruce Dal Canton CO
- ☐ 22 Mike Mahoney
- ☐ 23 Tony Wood
- ☐ 24 Sean Smith
- ☐ 25 Pascual Matos
- ☐ 26 Luis Brito
- ☐ 27 Edward Cordero
- ☐ 28 Danny Magee
- ☐ 29 Mike Eaglin AS
- ☐ 30 Ron Wright AS

1996 El Paso Diablos Best

This 30-card set of the 1996 El Paso Diablos, a Class AA Texas League affiliate of the Milwaukee Brewers, was produced by Best Cards, Inc. and features color player photos in a white border. The backs carry player information and career statistics. This issue includes the minor league card debut of Geoff Jenkins.

	MINT	NRMT	EXC
COMPLETE SET (30)	12.00	5.50	1.50

- ☐ 1 Geoff Jenkins
- ☐ 2 Mike Caldwell CO
- ☐ 3 Jon Pont CO
- ☐ 4 Dave Machemer MG
- ☐ 5 Bryan Jaquette TR
- ☐ 6 Ronnie Belliard
- ☐ 7 Jeff D'Amico
- ☐ 8 Bill Dobrolsky
- ☐ 9 Todd Dunn
- ☐ 10 Lauro Felix
- ☐ 11 Jonas Hamlin
- ☐ 12 Mike Harris
- ☐ 13 Kevin Kloek
- ☐ 14 Jeff Kramer
- ☐ 15 Scott Krause
- ☐ 16 Pedro Lopez
- ☐ 17 Sean Maloney
- ☐ 18 Gabby Martinez
- ☐ 19 Norm Montoya
- ☐ 20 Greg Mullins
- ☐ 21 Darrell Nicholas
- ☐ 22 Hector Ortega
- ☐ 23 Andy Paul
- ☐ 24 Cecil Rodriques
- ☐ 25 Henry Santos
- ☐ 26 Brad Seitzer
- ☐ 27 Doug Webb
- ☐ 28 Steve Whitaker
- ☐ 29 Judd Wilstead
- ☐ 30 Checklist

1996 Erie Seawolves Best

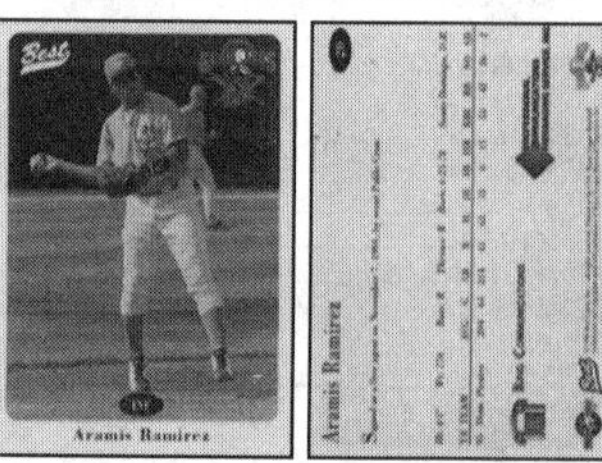

This 25-card set of the 1996 Erie Seawolves, a Class A New York-Penn League affiliate of the Pittsburgh Pirates, was produced by Best Cards, Inc. and features color player photos in a white border. The backs carry player information and career statistics. This issue includes the minor league card debut of Aramis Ramirez and Alex Hernandez.

	MINT	NRMT	EXC
COMPLETE SET (25)	15.00	6.75	1.85

- ☐ 1 Jeff(Whitey) Richardson MG
- ☐ 2 Larry Smith CO
- ☐ 3 Brian Lancaster TR
- ☐ 4 Nilson Antigua
- ☐ 5 Jose Avila
- ☐ 6 Butch Bellenger
- ☐ 7 Tedde Campbell
- ☐ 8 Michael Chaney
- ☐ 9 David Daniels
- ☐ 10 Jason Elmore
- ☐ 11 Luis Gonzalez
- ☐ 12 Jason Haynie
- ☐ 13 Alex Hernandez
- ☐ 14 Garrett Long
- ☐ 15 Scott May
- ☐ 16 Neal McDade
- ☐ 17 Brian O'Connor
- ☐ 18 Adelis Pena
- ☐ 19 Jesus Pena
- ☐ 20 Armis Ramirez
- ☐ 21 Charlies Rice
- ☐ 22 Skip Shipp
- ☐ 23 Jess Siciliano
- ☐ 24 Maximo Villar
- ☐ 25 Checklist

1996 Eugene Emeralds Best

This 27-card set of the 1996 Eugene Emeralds, a Class A Northwest League affiliate of the Atlanta Braves, was produced by Best Cards, Inc. and features color player photos in a white border. The backs carry player information and career statistics.

	MINT	NRMT	EXC
COMPLETE SET (27)	10.00	4.50	1.25

- ☐ 1 Corey Pointer
- ☐ 2 Rob Bell
- ☐ 3 Gavin Brown

☐ 4 Bruce Chen
☐ 5 Andrew Cochran
☐ 6 Adam Cross
☐ 7 Mark DeRosa
☐ 8 Angel Espada
☐ 9 Joe Giuliano
☐ 10 Steve Hacker
☐ 11 Pooh Hines
☐ 12 Adam Johnson
☐ 13 Mike Jones
☐ 14 P.K. Koehler
☐ 15 Adam Milburn
☐ 16 Joe Nelson
☐ 17 Dax Norris
☐ 18 Jimmy Osting
☐ 19 Odalis Perez
☐ 20 Eric Pickett
☐ 21 John Arnold
☐ 22 Brian Rust
☐ 23 Jason Flach
☐ 24 Rodney Allen
☐ 25 Jim Saul MG
☐ 26 Rick Albert CO
☐ 27 Jerry Nyman CO

1996 Everett Aquasox Best

This 30-card set of the 1996 Everett Aquasox, a Class A Northwest League affiliate of the Seattle Mariners, was produced by Best Cards, Inc. and features color player photos in a white border. The backs carry player information and career statistics.

	MINT	NRMT	EXC
COMPLETE SET (30)	10.00	4.50	1.25

☐ 1 Rob Zachmann
☐ 2 Julio Ayala
☐ 3 Roger Blanco
☐ 4 Jason Bond
☐ 5 Mike Burrows
☐ 6 Cirilo Cruz
☐ 7 Jeff Farnsworth
☐ 8 Brian Fitzgerald
☐ 9 Brian Fuentes
☐ 10 Javier Gutierrez
☐ 11 Jhonny Jimenez
☐ 12 Duan Johnson
☐ 13 Kyle Kennison
☐ 14 Brian Lindner
☐ 15 Robert Luce
☐ 16 Brian Nelson
☐ 17 Brandon Nogowski
☐ 18 Rafael Rivera
☐ 19 James Rowson
☐ 20 Matt Sachse
☐ 21 Cy Simonton
☐ 22 David Skeels
☐ 23 Scott Steinmann
☐ 24 Keith Stewart
☐ 25 Ramon Vazquez
☐ 26 Joe Victery
☐ 27 Marty Weymouth
☐ 28 Roger Hansen MG
☐ 29 Andy Bottin CO
☐ 30 Gil Meche

1996 Excel

The 1996 Excel Minor League set consists of 250 cards featuring minor league players from AAA, AA and A teams. The fronts display full color borderless player photos. The player's name and team name appear across the bottom of the picture in gold foil. The backs carry a large color close-up photo. Overlaying the photo toward the bottom is a colorful player information panel displaying biographical and statistical information. The cards are numbered on the back and checklisted below alphabetically within and according to major league teams for the NL and AL.

	MINT	NRMT	EXC
COMPLETE SET (250)	40.00	18.00	5.00
COMMON CARD (1-250)	.05	.02	.01

	MINT	NRMT	EXC
☐ 1 Kim Bartee	.05	.02	.01
☐ 2 Carlos Chavez	.05	.02	.01
☐ 3 Rocky Coppinger	.50	.23	.06
☐ 4 Tommy Davis	.05	.02	.01
☐ 5 Eddy Martinez	.05	.02	.01
☐ 6 Billy Owens	.05	.02	.01
☐ 7 Billy Percibal	.05	.02	.01
☐ 8 Garrett Stephenson	.05	.02	.01
☐ 9 Rachaad Stewart	.05	.02	.01
☐ 10 Chris Allison	.05	.02	.01
☐ 11 Virgil Chevalier	.05	.02	.01
☐ 12 Nomar Garciaparra	1.25	.55	.16
☐ 13 Jose Malave	.05	.02	.01
☐ 14 Ryan McGuire	.05	.02	.01
☐ 15 Trot Nixon	.05	.02	.01
☐ 16 Rafael Orellano	.05	.02	.01
☐ 17 Pork Chop Pough	.05	.02	.01
☐ 18 Donnie Sadler	.75	.35	.09
☐ 19 Bill Selby	.05	.02	.01
☐ 20 Nathan Tebbs	.05	.02	.01
☐ 21 George Arias	.25	.11	.03
☐ 22 Matt Beaumont	.25	.11	.03
☐ 23 Danny Buxbaum	.05	.02	.01
☐ 24 Jovino Carvajal	.05	.02	.01
☐ 25 Geoff Edsell	.05	.02	.01
☐ 26 Darin Erstad	6.00	2.70	.75
☐ 27 Aaron Guiel	.05	.02	.01
☐ 28 Mike Holtz	.05	.02	.01
☐ 29 Ryan Kane	.30	.14	.04
☐ 30 Jeff Abbott	.25	.11	.03
☐ 31 Kevin Coughlin	.05	.02	.01
☐ 32 Tom Fordham	.15	.07	.02
☐ 33 Carlos Lee	1.50	.70	.19
☐ 34 Frank Menechino	.05	.02	.01
☐ 35 Charles Poe	.05	.02	.01
☐ 36 Nilson Robledo	.05	.02	.01
☐ 37 Juan Thomas	.05	.02	.01
☐ 38 Archie Vazquez	.05	.02	.01
☐ 39 Bruce Aven	.15	.07	.02
☐ 40 Russ Branyan	3.00	1.35	.35
☐ 41 Bartolo Colon	1.00	.45	.12
☐ 42 Einar Diaz	.05	.02	.01
☐ 43 Mike Glavine	.15	.07	.02
☐ 44 Ricky Gutierrez	.05	.02	.01
☐ 45 Rick Heiserman	.05	.02	.01
☐ 46 Richie Sexson	1.50	.70	.19
☐ 47 Enrique Wilson	.30	.14	.04
☐ 48 Jaret Wright	.40	.18	.05
☐ 49 Bryan Corey	.05	.02	.01
☐ 50 Mike Drumright	.25	.11	.03
☐ 51 Juan Encarnacion	.30	.14	.04
☐ 52 Brandon Reed	.05	.02	.01
☐ 53 Bubba Trammell	.40	.18	.05
☐ 54 Daryle Ward	.25	.11	.03
☐ 55 Jaime Bluma	.05	.02	.01
☐ 56 Tim Byrdak	.05	.02	.01
☐ 57 Gary Coffee	.25	.11	.03
☐ 58 Lino Diaz	.05	.02	.01
☐ 59 Sal Fasano	.05	.02	.01
☐ 60 Jed Hansen	.05	.02	.01
☐ 61 Juan LeBron	.40	.18	.05
☐ 62 Sean McNally	.05	.02	.01
☐ 63 Anthony Medrano	.05	.02	.01
☐ 64 Rodolfo Mendez	.05	.02	.01
☐ 65 Sergio Nunez	.05	.02	.01
☐ 66 Mandy Romero	.05	.02	.01
☐ 67 Glendon Rusch	.25	.11	.03
☐ 68 Brian Banks	.05	.02	.01
☐ 69 Jeff D'Amico	.30	.14	.04
☐ 70 Jonas Hamlin	.05	.02	.01
☐ 71 Geoff Jenkins	1.00	.45	.12
☐ 72 Roberto Lopez	.05	.02	.01
☐ 73 Gerald Parent	.05	.02	.01
☐ 74 Doug Webb	.05	.02	.01
☐ 75 Antone Williamson	.30	.14	.04
☐ 76 Shane Bowers	.05	.02	.01
☐ 77 Shane Gunderson	.05	.02	.01
☐ 78 Corey Koskie	.05	.02	.01
☐ 79 Jake Patterson	.05	.02	.01
☐ 80 A.J. Pierzynski	.30	.14	.04
☐ 81 Mark Redman	.30	.14	.04
☐ 82 Dan Serafini	.05	.02	.01
☐ 83 Todd Walker	2.50	1.10	.30
☐ 84 Chris Corn	.05	.02	.01
☐ 85 Nick Delvecchio	.05	.02	.01
☐ 86 Dan Donato	.05	.02	.01
☐ 87 Matt Drews	.05	.02	.01
☐ 88 Mike Figga	.05	.02	.01
☐ 89 Ben Ford	.05	.02	.01
☐ 90 Marty Janzen	.05	.02	.01
☐ 91 Shea Morenz	.25	.11	.03
☐ 92 Ray Ricken	.05	.02	.01
☐ 93 Shane Spencer	.05	.02	.01
☐ 94 Bob St.Pierre	.20	.09	.03
☐ 95 Jay Tessmer	.05	.02	.01
☐ 96 Chris Wilcox	.05	.02	.01
☐ 97 Steve Cox	.50	.23	.06
☐ 98 Ben Grieve	1.25	.55	.16
☐ 99 Jason McDonald	.05	.02	.01
☐ 100 Brad Rigby	.05	.02	.01
☐ 101 Demond Smith	.05	.02	.01
☐ 102 Jim Bonnici	.05	.02	.01
☐ 103 Jose Cruz Jr.	6.00	2.70	.75
☐ 104 Osvaldo Fernandez	.05	.02	.01
☐ 105 Raul Ibanez	.05	.02	.01
☐ 106 Desi Relaford	.05	.02	.01
☐ 107 Marino Santana	.05	.02	.01
☐ 108 Kevin Brown	.25	.11	.03
☐ 109 Jeff Davis	.05	.02	.01
☐ 110 Edwin Diaz	.30	.14	.04
☐ 111 Jonathan Johnson	.25	.11	.03
☐ 112 Fernando Tatis	.30	.14	.04
☐ 113 Andrew Vessel	.30	.14	.04
☐ 114 John Curl	.05	.02	.01
☐ 115 Ryan Jones	.50	.23	.06
☐ 116 Julio Mosquera	.05	.02	.01
☐ 117 Jeff Patzke	.20	.09	.03
☐ 118 Mike Peeples	.25	.11	.03
☐ 119 Mark Sievert	.05	.02	.01
☐ 120 Joe Young	.40	.18	.05
☐ 121 Winston Abreu	.40	.18	.05
☐ 122 Athony Briggs	.05	.02	.01
☐ 123 Matt Byrd	.05	.02	.01
☐ 124 Jermaine Dye	1.50	.70	.19
☐ 125 Derrin Ebert	.30	.14	.04
☐ 126 Wes Helms	2.50	1.10	.30
☐ 127 Damon Hollins	.05	.02	.01
☐ 128 Ryan Jacobs	.05	.02	.01
☐ 129 Andruw Jones	12.00	5.50	1.50
☐ 130 Gus Kennedy	.05	.02	.01
☐ 131 George Lombard	1.50	.70	.19
☐ 132 Damian Moss	1.00	.45	.12
☐ 133 Robert Smith	.40	.18	.05
☐ 134 Pedro Swann	.05	.02	.01
☐ 135 Ron Wright	2.50	1.10	.30
☐ 136 Pat Cline	.60	.25	.07
☐ 137 Robin Jennings	.05	.02	.01
☐ 138 Brooks Kieschnick	.15	.07	.02
☐ 139 Ed Larregui	.05	.02	.01
☐ 140 Jason Maxwell	.05	.02	.01
☐ 141 Bobby Morris	.05	.02	.01
☐ 142 Amaury Telemaco	.05	.02	.01
☐ 143 Pedro Valdes	.05	.02	.01
☐ 144 Cedric Allen	.05	.02	.01
☐ 145 Justin Atchley	.05	.02	.01
☐ 146 Aaron Boone	.30	.14	.04
☐ 147 Steve Goodhart	.05	.02	.01
☐ 148 Chris Murphy	.05	.02	.01
☐ 149 Christian Rojas	.25	.11	.03
☐ 150 Terry Wright	.05	.02	.01
☐ 151 Brent Crowther	.05	.02	.01
☐ 152 Angel Echevarria	.05	.02	.01
☐ 153 Derrick Gibson	1.25	.55	.16
☐ 154 Todd Helton	2.50	1.10	.30
☐ 155 Terry Jones	.05	.02	.01
☐ 156 David Kennedy	.05	.02	.01
☐ 157 Mike Kusiewicz	.40	.18	.05
☐ 158 Joel Moore	.05	.02	.01
☐ 159 Jacob Viano	.05	.02	.01
☐ 160 Jamey Wright	.40	.18	.05
☐ 161 Todd Dunwoody	1.00	.45	.12
☐ 162 Ryan Jackson	.05	.02	.01
☐ 163 Billy McMillon	.05	.02	.01
☐ 164 Ralph Millard	.05	.02	.01
☐ 165 Clemente Nunez	.05	.02	.01
☐ 166 Edgar Renteria	.40	.18	.05
☐ 167 Chris Sheff	.05	.02	.01
☐ 168 Matt Whisenant	.05	.02	.01
☐ 169 Bob Abreu	.25	.11	.03
☐ 170 Ramon Castro	.05	.02	.01
☐ 171 Richard Hidalgo	.25	.11	.03
☐ 172 Tony McKnight	.05	.02	.01
☐ 173 Tony Mounce	.30	.14	.04
☐ 174 Roberto Duran	.05	.02	.01
☐ 175 Wilton Guerrero	.75	.35	.09
☐ 176 Joe Jacobsen	.05	.02	.01
☐ 177 Paul Konerko	2.50	1.10	.30
☐ 178 Chris Latham	.05	.02	.01
☐ 179 Onan Masaoka	.60	.25	.07
☐ 180 Mike Metcalfe	.05	.02	.01
☐ 181 Kevin Pincavitch	.05	.02	.01
☐ 182 Adam Riggs	.20	.09	.03
☐ 183 David Yocum	.25	.11	.03
☐ 184 Jake Benz	.05	.02	.01
☐ 185 Hiram Bocachica	.30	.14	.04
☐ 186 Brad Fullmer	.30	.14	.04
☐ 187 Vladimir Guerrero	8.00	3.60	1.00
☐ 188 Eric Ludwick	.05	.02	.01
☐ 189 Carlos Mendoza	.05	.02	.01
☐ 190 Jarrod Patterson	.05	.02	.01
☐ 191 Jay Payton	1.00	.45	.12
☐ 192 Paul Wilson	.25	.11	.03
☐ 193 Julio Zorrilla	.20	.09	.03
☐ 194 Marlon Anderson	.25	.11	.03
☐ 195 Ron Blazier	.05	.02	.01
☐ 196 Steve Carver	.25	.11	.03
☐ 197 Blake Doolan	.05	.02	.01
☐ 198 David Doster	.05	.02	.01
☐ 199 Tommy Eason	.05	.02	.01
☐ 200 Zach Elliott	.05	.02	.01
☐ 201 Bobby Estalella	.75	.35	.09
☐ 202 Rob Grable	.05	.02	.01
☐ 203 Bronson Heflin	.05	.02	.01
☐ 204 Dan Held	.05	.02	.01
☐ 205 Kevin Hooker	.05	.02	.01
☐ 206 Rich Hunter	.25	.11	.03
☐ 207 Carlton Loewer	.20	.09	.03
☐ 208 Wendell Magee	.15	.07	.02
☐ 209 Len Manning	.05	.02	.01
☐ 210 Fred McNair	.05	.02	.01
☐ 211 Ryan Nye	.05	.02	.01
☐ 212 Scott Rolen	3.00	1.35	.35
☐ 213 Brian Stumpf	.05	.02	.01
☐ 214 Reggie Taylor	.60	.25	.07
☐ 215 Larry Wimberly	.20	.09	.03
☐ 216 Micah Franklin	.05	.02	.01
☐ 217 Chad Hermansen	1.25	.55	.16
☐ 218 Jason Kendall	.05	.02	.01
☐ 219 Garrett Long	.25	.11	.03
☐ 220 Joe Maskivish	.05	.02	.01
☐ 221 Chris Peters	.05	.02	.01
☐ 222 Charles Peterson	.20	.09	.03
☐ 223 Charles Rice	.25	.11	.03
☐ 224 Reed Secrist	.05	.02	.01
☐ 225 Derek Swafford	.20	.09	.03
☐ 226 Mike Busby	.05	.02	.01
☐ 227 Mike Gulan	.05	.02	.01
☐ 228 Chris Haas	.40	.18	.05
☐ 229 Jeff Matulevich	.05	.02	.01
☐ 230 Steve Montgomery	.05	.02	.01
☐ 231 Matt Morris	.50	.23	.06
☐ 232 Bret Wagner	.05	.02	.01
☐ 233 Gabe Alvarez	.15	.07	.02
☐ 234 Raul Casanova	.40	.18	.05
☐ 235 Ben Davis	1.00	.45	.12
☐ 236 Bubba Dixon	.05	.02	.01
☐ 237 Greg LaRocca	.05	.02	.01
☐ 238 Derrek Lee	.50	.23	.06
☐ 239 Jason Thompson	.05	.02	.01
☐ 240 Darin Blood	.75	.35	.09
☐ 241 Jay Canizaro	.05	.02	.01
☐ 242 Edwin Corps	.05	.02	.01
☐ 243 Jacob Cruz	.75	.35	.09
☐ 244 Joe Fontenot	.40	.18	.05
☐ 245 Jesse Ibarra	.05	.02	.01
☐ 246 Dante Powell	1.25	.55	.16
☐ 247 Keith Williams	.05	.02	.01
☐ 248 Checklist	.05	.02	.01
☐ 249 Checklist	.05	.02	.01
☐ 250 Checklist	.05	.02	.01

1996 Excel All-Stars

	MINT	NRMT	EXC
COMPLETE SET (10)	30.00	13.50	3.70
COMMON CARD (1-10)	.75	.35	.09

	MINT	NRMT	EXC
☐ 1 Jason Kendall	1.00	.45	.12
☐ 2 Steve Cox	1.25	.55	.16
☐ 3 Adam Riggs	.75	.35	.09
☐ 4 George Arias	.75	.35	.09
☐ 5 Wilton Guerrero	3.00	1.35	.35
☐ 6 Vladimir Guerrero	12.00	5.50	1.50
☐ 7 Andruw Jones	20.00	9.00	2.50
☐ 8 Jay Payton	2.50	1.10	.30
☐ 9 Raul Ibanez	.75	.35	.09
☐ 10 Paul Wilson	1.00	.45	.12

1996 Excel Climbing

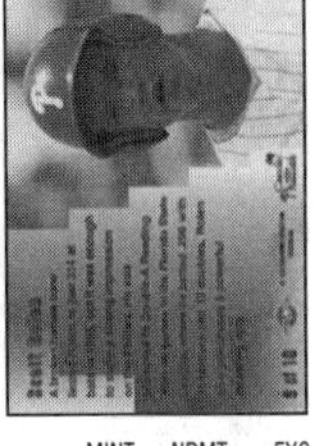

	MINT	NRMT	EXC
COMPLETE SET (10)	12.00	5.50	1.50
COMMON CARD (1-10)	.75	.35	.09

	MINT	NRMT	EXC
☐ 1 Jeff Abbott	1.25	.55	.16
☐ 2 Rocky Coppinger	2.00	.90	.25
☐ 3 Brent Crowther	.75	.35	.09
☐ 4 Rich Hunter	1.00	.45	.12
☐ 5 Chris Latham	.75	.35	.09
☐ 6 Wendell Magee	1.00	.45	.12
☐ 7 Jay Payton	2.50	1.10	.30
☐ 8 Ray Ricken	.75	.35	.09
☐ 9 Scott Rolen	8.00	3.60	1.00
☐ 10 Paul Wilson	1.00	.45	.12

1996 Excel First Year Phenoms

	MINT	NRMT	EXC
COMPLETE SET (10)	25.00	11.00	3.10
COMMON CARD (1-10)	.50	.23	.06

	MINT	NRMT	EXC
☐ 1 Gabe Alvarez	.60	.25	.07
☐ 2 Jose Cruz Jr.	10.00	4.50	1.25
☐ 3 Ben Davis	2.00	.90	.25
☐ 4 Darin Erstad	10.00	4.50	1.25
☐ 5 Todd Helton	5.00	2.20	.60
☐ 6 Chad Hermansen	3.00	1.35	.35

	MINT	NRMT	EXC
☐ 7 Geoff Jenkins	2.50	1.10	.30
☐ 8 Carlton Loewer	.50	.23	.06
☐ 9 Shea Morenz	.75	.35	.09
☐ 10 Matt Morris	1.25	.55	.16

1996 Excel Season Crowns

	MINT	NRMT	EXC
COMPLETE SET (10)	20.00	9.00	2.50
COMMON CARD (1-10)	.75	.35	.09
☐ 1 Matt Beaumont	.75	.35	.09
☐ 2 Bartolo Colon	2.50	1.10	.30
☐ 3 Matt Drews	.75	.35	.09
☐ 4 Derrick Gibson	3.00	1.35	.35
☐ 5 Vladimir Guerrero	8.00	3.60	1.00
☐ 6 Andruw Jones	15.00	6.75	1.85
☐ 7 Brandon Reed	.75	.35	.09
☐ 8 Glendon Rusch	1.00	.45	.12
☐ 9 Richie Sexson	4.00	1.80	.50
☐ 10 Shane Spencer	.75	.35	.09

1996 Excel Season Team Leaders

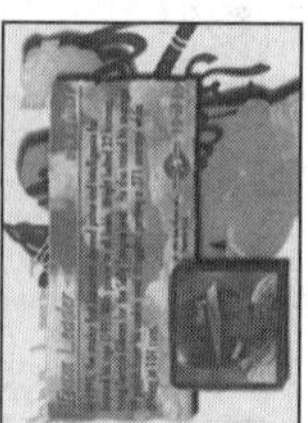

	MINT	NRMT	EXC
COMPLETE SET (10)	40.00	18.00	5.00
COMMON CARD (1-10)	2.50	1.10	.30
☐ 1 George Arias	4.00	1.80	.50
☐ 2 Kevin Coughlin	2.50	1.10	.30
☐ 3 Wilton Guerrero	12.00	5.50	1.50
☐ 4 Dan Held	2.50	1.10	.30
☐ 5 Brooks Kieschnick	5.00	2.20	.60
☐ 6 Wendell Magee	3.00	1.35	.35
☐ 7 Jason McDonald	3.00	1.35	.35
☐ 8 Adam Riggs	4.00	1.80	.50
☐ 9 Juan Thomas	2.50	1.10	.30
☐ 10 Ron Wright	30.00	13.50	3.70

1996 Fayeteville Generals Best

This 30-card set of the 1996 Fort Myers Miracle, a Class A South Atlantic League affiliate of the Detroit Tigers, was produced by Best Cards, Inc. and features color player photos in a white border. The backs carry player information and career statistics. This issue includes the minor league card debuts of Gabe Kapler and David Borkowski.

	MINT	NRMT	EXC
COMPLETE SET (30)	15.00	6.75	1.85

☐ 1 Dwight Lowry MG
☐ 2 Sid Monge CO
☐ 3 Shawn Pagee CO
☐ 4 Matt Lewis TR
☐ 5 Jayson Bass
☐ 6 Justin Bettencourt
☐ 7 David Borkowski
☐ 8 Clayton Bruner
☐ 9 Javier Cardona
☐ 10 Bryan Corey
☐ 11 Carlos De La Cruz
☐ 12 Peter Durkovic
☐ 13 Michael Eby
☐ 14 Matt Engleka
☐ 15 John Foran
☐ 16 Brian Fuller
☐ 17 Apostol Garcia
☐ 18 Generoso Gonzalez
☐ 19 Gabe Kapler
☐ 20 Graham Koonce
☐ 21 Derek Kopacz
☐ 22 Steve Lackey
☐ 23 David Melendez
☐ 24 Bill Perusek
☐ 25 Jose Ramirez
☐ 26 Cesar Ruiz
☐ 27 Franklin Sosa
☐ 28 Brent Stentz
☐ 29 Scott Weaver
☐ 30 B.C.(Mascot)

1996 Fort Myers Miracle Best

This 30-card set of the 1996 Fort Myers Miracle, a Class A Florida State League affiliate of the Minnesota Twins, was produced by Best Cards, Inc. and features color player photos in a white border. The backs carry player information and career statistics.

	MINT	NRMT	EXC
COMPLETE SET (30)	12.00	5.50	1.50

☐ 1 John Russell MG
☐ 2 Jerry White CO
☐ 3 Eric Rasmussen CO
☐ 4 Jason Bell
☐ 5 Jose Valentin
☐ 6 Dan Perkins
☐ 7 Rob Radlosky
☐ 8 Mark Redman
☐ 9 Will Rushing
☐ 10 Jason Tatar
☐ 11 Mike Moriarty
☐ 12 Paul Morse
☐ 13 Kelcey Mucker
☐ 14 Tom Mott
☐ 15 Paul Pavicich
☐ 16 Dom Konieczki
☐ 17 Corey Koskie
☐ 18 Ryan Lane
☐ 19 Jim McCalmont
☐ 20 Doug Mientkiewicz
☐ 21 Tom Gourdin
☐ 22 Shane Gunderson
☐ 23 Ben Jones
☐ 24 Ivory Jones
☐ 25 Tom Knauss
☐ 26 Rafael Alvarez
☐ 27 Armann Brown
☐ 28 Trevor Cobb
☐ 29 Deron Dowhower
☐ 30 Troy Fortin

1996 Fort Wayne Wizards Best

This 31-card set of the 1996 Fort Wayne Wizards, a Class A Midwest League affiliate of the Minnesota Twins, was produced by Best Cards, Inc. and features color player photos in a white border. The backs carry player information and career statistics.

	MINT	NRMT	EXC
COMPLETE SET (31)	10.00	4.50	1.25

☐ 1 Jamie Splittorff
☐ 2 Rafael Alvarez
☐ 3 Todd Bartels
☐ 4 Robert Boggs
☐ 5 Antuan Bunkley
☐ 6 Cleatus Davidson
☐ 7 Joe Fraser
☐ 8 Carlos Garcia
☐ 9 Adrian Gordon
☐ 10 Jeff Harris
☐ 11 Travis Johnson
☐ 12 Raul Juarez
☐ 13 Greg Lakovic
☐ 14 Alan Mahaffey
☐ 15 Rodney McBride
☐ 16 Jason McKenzie
☐ 17 Brad Niedermaier
☐ 18 Israel Paez
☐ 19 Tim Peters
☐ 20 A.J. Pierzynski
☐ 21 Fred Rath
☐ 22 Kasey Richardson
☐ 23 John Schroeder
☐ 24 Jeff Smith
☐ 25 Scott Tanksley
☐ 26 Matt Vanderbush
☐ 27 Dan Rohn MG
☐ 28 Stu Cliburn CO
☐ 29 Jose Baez CO
☐ 30 Eric Margenau(Owner)
☐ 31 Wayne the Wizard(Mascot)

1996 Frederick Keys Best

This 30-card set of the 1996 Frederick Keys, a Class A Carolina League affiliate of the Baltimore Orioles, was produced by Best Cards, Inc. and features color player photos in a white border. The backs carry player information and career statistics. This issue includes the minor league card debut of Chris Fussell and Eugene Kingsale.

	MINT	NRMT	EXC
COMPLETE SET (30)	12.00	5.50	1.50

☐ 1 Alvie Shepherd
☐ 2 Wady Almonte
☐ 3 Eric Chavez
☐ 4 Scott Conner
☐ 5 Tom D'Aquila
☐ 6 David Dellucci
☐ 7 Todd Dyess
☐ 8 Radhames Dykhoff
☐ 9 Chris Fussell
☐ 10 Jim Foster
☐ 11 Mike Gargiulo
☐ 12 Eugene Kingsale
☐ 13 Lincoln Martin
☐ 14 Eddy Martinez
☐ 15 Julio Moreno
☐ 16 Robert Morseman
☐ 17 Nerio Rodriguez
☐ 18 Jason Rogers
☐ 19 Matt Raleigh
☐ 20 Johnny Isom
☐ 21 Rick Short
☐ 22 Mike Trimarco
☐ 23 Mike Wolff
☐ 24 Julio Garcia MG
☐ 25 Jeff Morris CO
☐ 26 Francis Hernandez
Dave Bigham
☐ 27 Chris Bryant
Tom Russin
☐ 28 Denio Gabriel
Rudy Higgins
☐ 29 Keyote(Mascot)
☐ 30 1996 Frederick Keys Checklist

1996 Great Falls Dodgers Team Issue

This 36-card set of the 1996 Great Falls Dodgers, a Rookie Class Pioneer League affiliate of the Los Angeles Dodgers, features color player photos with a black shadow in gray and blue borders. The backs carry a small black-and-white player head photo with player information and career highlights. The cards are unnumbered and checklisted below according to the way they are listed on the checklist.

	MINT	NRMT	EXC
COMPLETE SET (36)	25.00	11.00	3.10

☐ 1 Craig Allen
☐ 2 John Bohman
☐ 3 Michael Bourbakis
☐ 4 Adrian Burnside
☐ 5 Pedro Cervantes
☐ 6 Elvis Correa
☐ 7 Toby Dollar
☐ 8 Pedro Feliciano
☐ 9 Pedro Flores
☐ 10 Miguel Garcia
☐ 11 Brian Jacobson
☐ 12 Mike Sanchez
☐ 13 Ed Sordo
☐ 14 Seferino Soto
☐ 15 Brad Thomas
☐ 16 Frank Thompson
☐ 17 Bobby Cripps
☐ 18 Edwin Falcon
☐ 19 Casey Snow
☐ 20 Jeff Bramlett
☐ 21 Trent Cuevas
☐ 22 Brett Lllig
☐ 23 Nick Leach
☐ 24 Monte Marshall
☐ 25 Ken Morimoto
☐ 26 Jon Tucker
☐ 27 Jeff Auterson
☐ 28 Brian Foulks
☐ 29 Matt McCarty
☐ 30 Mikal Richey
☐ 31 Cash Riley
☐ 32 Jason Weekley
☐ 33 Mickey Hatcher MG
☐ 34 Mark Brewer CO
☐ 35 Tom Thomas CO
☐ NNO Team Photo CL

1996 Great Falls Dodgers Best

This Minor Miracles 30-card set of the 1996 Great Falls Dodgers team was produced by Best Cards, Inc. and features color player photos in a blue border. The backs carry player information and career statistics. Each set is numbered out of 1,000 and indicated on Card #30.

	MINT	NRMT	EXC
COMPLETE SET (30)	25.00	11.00	3.10

☐ 1 Mickey Hatcher
Tom Thomas#(Homer Zulaica#(Mark Brewer CL
☐ 2 Craig Allen
☐ 3 Jeff Auterson
☐ 4 Mike Bourbakis
☐ 5 Jeff Bramlett
☐ 6 Adrian Burnside
☐ 7 Elvis Correa
☐ 8 Bobby Cripps
☐ 9 Trent Cuevas
☐ 10 Toby Dollar
☐ 11 Pedro Feliciano
☐ 12 Pedro Flores
☐ 13 Brian Foulks
☐ 14 Miguel Garcia
☐ 15 Brett Illig
☐ 16 Taisuke Ishimaru
☐ 17 Brian Jacobson
☐ 18 Nick Leach
☐ 19 Matt McCarty
☐ 20 Bobby Meyer
☐ 21 Ken Morimoto
☐ 22 Mikal Richey
☐ 23 Cash Riley
☐ 24 Mike Sanchez
☐ 25 Casey Snow
☐ 26 Seferino Soto
☐ 27 Brad Thomas
☐ 28 Frank Thompson
☐ 29 Jon Tucker
☐ 30 Jason Weekley

1996 Greensboro Bats Best

This 30-card set of the 1996 Greensboro Bats, a Class A South Atlantic League affiliate of the New York Yankees, was produced by Best Cards, Inc. and features color player photos in a white border. The backs carry player information and career statistics. This issue includes the minor league card debut of D'Angelo Jimenez.

	MINT	NRMT	EXC
COMPLETE SET (30)	10.00	4.50	1.25

☐ 1 Jimmy Johnson MG
☐ 2 Tom Nieto CO
☐ 3 Juan Nieves CO
☐ 4 Chris DeLucia TR
☐ 5 Tom Becker
☐ 6 Alejandro Bracho
☐ 7 Eric Camfield
☐ 8 Les Dennis
☐ 9 Darrell Einerston
☐ 10 Ben Ford
☐ 11 Mike Giardi
☐ 12 D'Angelo Jimenez
☐ 13 Mike Judd
☐ 14 Mike Lowell
☐ 15 Cody McCormick
☐ 16 Shea Morenz
☐ 17 Richard Olivier
☐ 18 Frisco Parotte
☐ 19 Rene Pinto
☐ 20 Steve Randolph
☐ 21 Jake Robbins
☐ 22 Marty Robinson
☐ 23 Jeffery Saffer
☐ 24 Cody Samuel
☐ 25 Eric Schaffner
☐ 26 Anthony Shelby
☐ 27 Derek Shumpert
☐ 28 Rod Smith
☐ 29 Jason Troilo
☐ 30 Jose Velazquez

1996 Greenville Braves Best

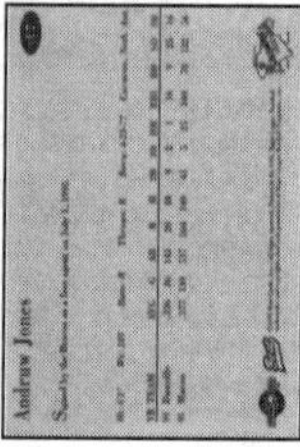

This 30-card set of the 1996 Greenville Braves, a Class AA Southern League affiliate of the Atlanta Braves, was produced by Best Cards, Inc. and features color player photos in a white border. The backs carry player information and career statistics. This issue features the second year cards of Andruw Jones, Ron Wright and Wes Helms.

	MINT	NRMT	EXC
COMPLETE SET (30)	30.00	13.50	3.70

☐ 1 Jeff Cox
☐ 2 Bill Slack
☐ 3 Mel Roberts
☐ 4 Jay Williams
☐ 5 Jamie Arnold

- ☐ 6 Jeff Bock
- ☐ 7 Adam Butler
- ☐ 8 Matt Byrd
- ☐ 9 Mike Cather
- ☐ 10 Lee Daniels
- ☐ 11 John Dettmer
- ☐ 12 Roger Etheridge
- ☐ 13 Tommy Harrison
- ☐ 14 Wes Helms
- ☐ 15 Ryan Jacobs
- ☐ 16 Manny Jimenez
- ☐ 17 Andruw Jones
- ☐ 18 Marty Malloy
- ☐ 19 Gator McBride
- ☐ 20 Jason McFarlin
- ☐ 21 Damian Moss
- ☐ 22 Brett Newell
- ☐ 23 Raul Rodarte
- ☐ 24 Randall Simon
- ☐ 25 Rick Steed
- ☐ 26 Rachaad Stewart
- ☐ 27 Scott Stricklin
- ☐ 28 David Toth
- ☐ 29 Mike Warner
- ☐ 30 Ron Wright

1996 Greenville Braves Team Issue

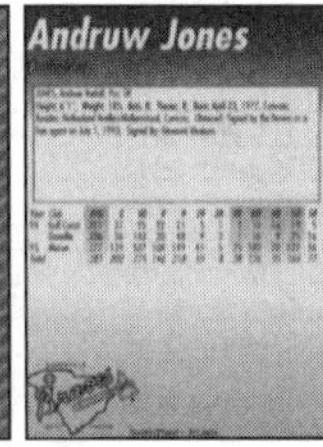

This 30-card set of the 1996 Greenville Braves, a Class AA Southern League affiliate of the Atlanta Braves, was sponsored by Coca-Cola and features color player photos in a blue striped frame with a thin red inner border. The backs carry player information and career statistics. This issue features the second year cards of Andruw Jones, Ron Wright and Wes Helms.

	MINT	NRMT	EXC
COMPLETE SET (30)	40.00	18.00	5.00

- ☐ 2 Gator McBride
- ☐ 4 Marty Malloy
- ☐ 6 Andruw Jones
- ☐ 7 Mike Warner
- ☐ 9 Raul Rodarte
- ☐ 10 Damian Moss
- ☐ 10 Lee Daniels
- ☐ 12 Manny Jimenez
- ☐ 15 Brett Newell
- ☐ 16 Ron Wright
- ☐ 18 Randall Simon
- ☐ 24 Mike Cather
- ☐ 25 Scott Stricklin
- ☐ 27 Bill Slack CO
- ☐ 30 Mel Roberts CO
- ☐ 33 Wes Helms
- ☐ 34 Matt Byrd
- ☐ 36 Tommy Harrison
- ☐ 39 Jeff Bock
- ☐ 42 David Toth
- ☐ 43 Jeff Cox MGR
- ☐ 43 Roger Etheridge
- ☐ 46 Jamie Arnold
- ☐ 48 Ryan Jacobs
- ☐ 49 Rick Steed
- ☐ 50 Jason McFarlin
- ☐ 51 Rachaad Stewart
- ☐ 58 Adam Butler
- ☐ GM Steve DeSalvo GM
- ☐ TR Jay Williams TR

1996 Hagerstown Suns Best

This 30-card set of the 1996 Hagerstwon Suns, a Class A South Atlantic League affiliate of the Toronto Blue Jays, was produced by Best Cards, Inc. and features color player photos in a white border. The backs carry player information and career statistics. This issue includes the minor league card debuts of Craig Wilson and Mike Whitlock.

	MINT	NRMT	EXC
COMPLETE SET (30)	10.00	4.50	1.25

- ☐ 1 Ruben Corral
- ☐ 2 John Crowther
- ☐ 3 Tom Davey
- ☐ 4 Ernesto Delgado
- ☐ 5 Scott Fitterer
- ☐ 6 Herman Gordon
- ☐ 7 Tyson Hartshorn
- ☐ 8 Chris Hayes
- ☐ 9 Eric Horton
- ☐ 10 Mike Johnson
- ☐ 11 John Kehoe
- ☐ 13 Benny Lowe
- ☐ 14 Andy McCormick
- ☐ 15 Patrick Moultrie
- ☐ 16 Tom Peck
- ☐ 17 Mike Peeples
- ☐ 18 Luis Rodriguez
- ☐ 19 Omar Sanchez
- ☐ 20 Fausto Solano
- ☐ 21 Craig Stone
- ☐ 22 Rusty Volkert
- ☐ 23 Mike Whitlock
- ☐ 24 Craig Wilson
- ☐ 25 Chris Woodward
- ☐ 26 Joe Young
- ☐ 27 J.J. Cannon
- ☐ 28 Darren Balsley
- ☐ 29 Paul Elliott
- ☐ 30 1996 Hagerstown Suns(Bat Boys)

1996 Hardware City Rock Cats Best

This 30-card set of the 1996 Hardware City Rock Cats, a Class AA Eastern League affiliate of the Minnesota Twins, was produced by Best Cards, Inc. and features color player photos in a white border. The backs carry player information and career statistics.

	MINT	NRMT	EXC
COMPLETE SET (30)	10.00	4.50	1.25

- ☐ 1 Rock Cats Team Photo
- ☐ 2 Al Newman MG
- ☐ 3 Jim Dwyer CO
- ☐ 4 Gorman Heimueller CO
- ☐ 5 Bill Sandillo(Baseball Executive)
- ☐ 6 Lanning Tucker TR
- ☐ 7 Jason Bell
- ☐ 8 Shane Bowers
- ☐ 9 Anthony Byrd
- ☐ 10 Gary Caraballo
- ☐ 11 Troy Carrasco
- ☐ 12 Jeff Ferguson
- ☐ 13 Sean Gavaghan
- ☐ 14 Scott Hilt
- ☐ 15 Torii Hunter
- ☐ 16 J.J. Johnson
- ☐ 17 Dom Konieczki
- ☐ 18 Anthony Lewis
- ☐ 19 Keith Linebarger
- ☐ 20 Rene Lopez
- ☐ 21 Paul Morse
- ☐ 22 Tom Nevers
- ☐ 23 Kevin Ohme
- ☐ 24 Ryan Radmanovich
- ☐ 25 Mark Redman
- ☐ 26 Todd Ritchie
- ☐ 27 Chad Roper
- ☐ 28 Chad Rupp
- ☐ 29 Hector Trinidad
- ☐ 30 Radio Team

1996 Harrisburg Senators Best

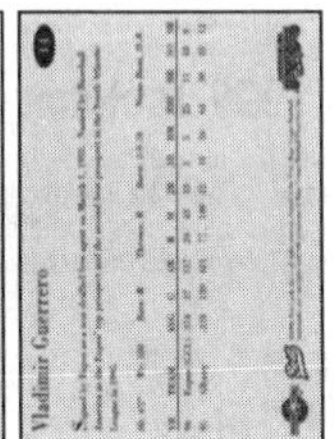

This 29-card set of the 1996 Harrisburg Senators, a Class AA Eastern League affiliate of the Montreal Expos, was produced by Best Cards, Inc. and features color player photos in a white border. The backs carry player information and career statistics. This issue includes the minor league team set card debut of Vladimir Guerrero.

	MINT	NRMT	EXC
COMPLETE SET (29)	25.00	11.00	3.10

- ☐ 1 Pat Kelly MG
- ☐ 2 Jeff Livesey CO
- ☐ 3 Alex Ochoa TR
- ☐ 4 Israel Alcantara
- ☐ 5 Tony Barron
- ☐ 6 Shayne Bennett
- ☐ 7 Jake Benz
- ☐ 8 Geoff Blum
- ☐ 9 Kirk Bullinger
- ☐ 10 Jolbert Cabrera
- ☐ 11 Rick DeHart
- ☐ 12 Scott Forster
- ☐ 13 Dennis Gray
- ☐ 14 Vladimir Guerrero
- ☐ 15 Robert Henley
- ☐ 16 Ramsey Koeyers
- ☐ 17 Jalal Leach
- ☐ 18 Rob Lukachyk
- ☐ 19 Jason McCommon
- ☐ 20 Charlie Montoyo
- ☐ 21 Jose Paniagua
- ☐ 22 Scott Pisciotta
- ☐ 23 Lou Pote
- ☐ 24 Jon Saffer
- ☐ 25 DaRond Stovall
- ☐ 26 Everett Stull
- ☐ 27 Jose Vidro
- ☐ 28 Neil Weber
- ☐ 29 Checklist

1996 Helena Brewers Team Issue

This 34-card set of the 1996 Helena Brewers, a Rookie Class Pioneer League affiliate of the Milwaukee Brewers, was sponsored by TV station KTVH Channel 12 and Shodair Children's Hospital. The fronts feature borderless color player photos with the player's name and position printed in red at the bottom above purple snow-capped mountain tops. The backs carry a small black-and-white player portrait with player information and sponsors' logos.

	MINT	NRMT	EXC
COMPLETE SET (34)	35.00	16.00	4.40

- ☐ 1 Ledowick Johnson
- ☐ 2 Cio Cafaro
- ☐ 3 Mick Fieldbinder
- ☐ 4 Mark Fink
- ☐ 5 Jose Garcia
- ☐ 6 Sergio Guerrero
- ☐ 7 Jonathan Guzman
- ☐ 8 Brian Hedley
- ☐ 9 James Hemphill
- ☐ 10 Phil Kendall
- ☐ 11 Scott Kirby
- ☐ 12 Josh Klimek
- ☐ 13 Maney Leshay
- ☐ 14 Allen Levrault
- ☐ 15 Martin Lorenzo
- ☐ 16 MacKenzie Norris
- ☐ 17 Garrett Osilka
- ☐ 18 Roberto Paredes
- ☐ 19 Brian Passini
- ☐ 20 Lyle Prempas
- ☐ 21 Francisco Roque
- ☐ 22 Greg Schaub
- ☐ 23 Ignacio Suero
- ☐ 24 Travis Tank
- ☐ 25 Dan Thompson
- ☐ 26 Tano Tijerina
- ☐ 27 Mark Watson
- ☐ 28 Jason Washam
- ☐ 29 Michael Wetmore
- ☐ 30 Alex Morales MG
- ☐ 31 Jim Merrick CO
- ☐ 32 Javier Gonzales CO
- ☐ 33 Paul Anderson TR
- ☐ NNO Team Photo CL

1996 Hickory Crawdads Best

This 30-card set of the 1996 Hickory Crawdads team was produced by Best Cards, Inc. and features color player photos. The backs carry player information and statistics. Only 1,000 of this set were produced and is sequentially numbered on Card #30. This issue includes the minor league card debuts of Carlos Lee, Josh Paul and Mario Valdez.

	MINT	NRMT	EXC
COMPLETE SET (30)	20.00	9.00	2.50

- ☐ 1 Team Logo CL
- ☐ 2 Darren Baugh
- ☐ 3 Chad Bradford
- ☐ 4 Brian Downs
- ☐ 5 Joe Farley
- ☐ 6 Josh Fauske
- ☐ 7 Joel Garber
- ☐ 8 Ramon Gomez
- ☐ 9 John Hunt
- ☐ 10 Marlo Iglesias
- ☐ 11 Carlos Lee
- ☐ 12 Maximo Nunez
- ☐ 13 Dan Olson
- ☐ 14 Josh Paul
- ☐ 15 Pete Pryor
- ☐ 16 Tom Reimers
- ☐ 17 Mark Roberts
- ☐ 18 Liu Rodriguez
- ☐ 19 Rafael Ruiz
- ☐ 20 Rich Sauget
- ☐ 21 Brian Schmack
- ☐ 22 Barry Shelton
- ☐ 23 John Strasser
- ☐ 24 Allen Thomas
- ☐ 25 Mario Valdez
- ☐ 26 Adam Virchis
- ☐ 27 Sean Snedeker CO
- ☐ 28 Chris Cron MG
Mike Barnett CO
- ☐ 29 Hickory Crawdads Inaugural Little League Clinic
- ☐ 30 Carlos Lee

1996 High Desert Mavericks Best

This 30-card set of the 1996 High Desert Mavericks, a Class A California League affiliate of the Baltimore Orioles, was produced by Best Cards, Inc. and features color player photos in a white border. The backs carry player information and career statistics.

	MINT	NRMT	EXC
COMPLETE SET (30)	10.00	4.50	1.25

- ☐ 1 Joe Ferguson MG
- ☐ 2 Larry McCall CO
- ☐ 3 Dave Walker TR
- ☐ 4 Wooly Bully(Mascot)
- ☐ 5 Rolando Avila
- ☐ 6 Mike Berry
- ☐ 7 Bryan Bogle
- ☐ 8 Brad Crills
- ☐ 9 Ned Darley
- ☐ 10 Greg Dean
- ☐ 11 Jesse Garcia
- ☐ 12 Ryan Hendricks
- ☐ 13 Roy Hodge
- ☐ 14 Brandon Huntsman
- ☐ 15 Chris Kirgan
- ☐ 16 David Lamb
- ☐ 17 Jason LeCronier
- ☐ 18 Toby Lehman
- ☐ 19 Matt Marenghi
- ☐ 20 Steve Montgomery
- ☐ 21 Doug Newstrom
- ☐ 22 Tim Olszewski
- ☐ 23 Joey Rhodes
- ☐ 24 Melvin Rosario
- ☐ 25 Chris Sauritch
- ☐ 26 Matt Snyder
- ☐ 27 Ray Suplee
- ☐ 28 Fletcher Thompson
- ☐ 29 Gary White
- ☐ 30 The Maverick Girls

1996 Hilo Stars Hawaii Winter Ball

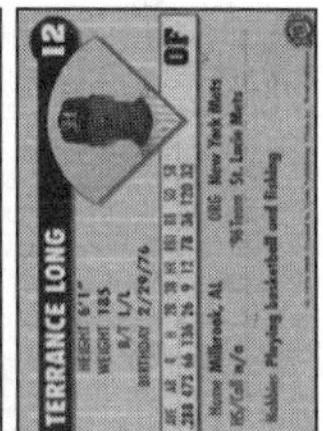

This 36-card set of the 1996 Hilo Stars team was produced by Trade Publishing and features borderless color player portraits by Reed Takaaze. The backs carry player information and player statistics.

	MINT	NRMT	EXC
COMPLETE SET (36)	20.00	9.00	2.50

- ☐ 1 Tsuyoshi Shinjyo
- ☐ 3 Yasuo Yoshida CO
- ☐ 6 Scott Hunter
- ☐ 7 Myung Ju Cha
- ☐ 8 Antonio Fernandez
- ☐ 9 Gavin Jackson
- ☐ 10 Hirotoshi Kitagawa
- ☐ 11 Brent Butler
- ☐ 12 Terrence Long
- ☐ 13 Howie Gershberg CO
- ☐ 14 Bong Kuen Kim CO
- ☐ 15 Yukiyasu Nakanose
- ☐ 16 Kazuharu Yamazaki
- ☐ 17 Michael Coleman
- ☐ 20 Chris Haas
- ☐ 21 Robert Bonnano
- ☐ 22 Jimmy Baron
- ☐ 23 Yoshiya Takeuchi
- ☐ 24 Jerrod Riggan
- ☐ 25 Tony Derosso
- ☐ 26 John Gibbons CO
- ☐ 27 Kevin Young
- ☐ 28 Sang Hyun Kim
- ☐ 29 Tae Seok Kim
- ☐ 30 Brandon Villafuerte
- ☐ 31 Soo Hyuk Lim
- ☐ 32 Virgil Chevalier
- ☐ 32 Ben Agbayani
- ☐ 33 Matt Beaumont
- ☐ 34 Demarlo Hale MG
- ☐ 35 Jon Vander Griend
- ☐ 38 Dan Murray
- ☐ NNO Dan Ricabal
- ☐ NNO Lance Cacanindin TR
- ☐ NNO Clucky Star(Mascot)
- ☐ NNO Team Photo CL

1996 Honolulu Sharks Hawaii Winter Ball

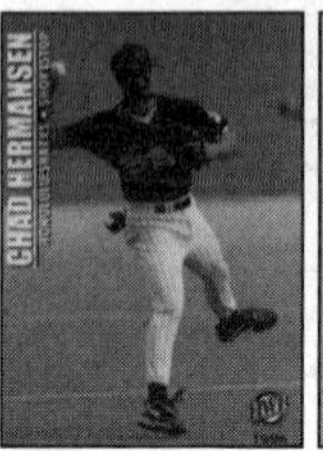

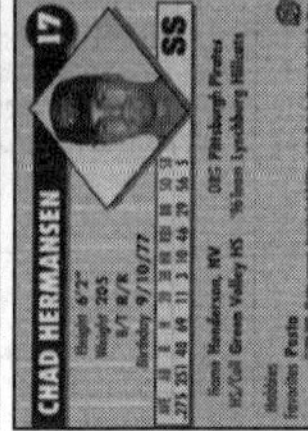

This 36-card set of the 1996 Honolulu Sharks team was produced by Trade Publishing and features borderless action color player photos by Jay Metzger. The backs carry a small black-and-white player headshot by Ray Wong with player information and statistics. This issue includes first year cards of Chad Hermansen and Brad Fullmer.

	MINT	NRMT	EXC
COMPLETE SET (36)	20.00	9.00	2.50

☐ 2 Shunsuke Hara
☐ 3 Toyokazu Ohba
☐ 4 Takayuki Saitoh
☐ 6 Jason Conti
☐ 7 Mike Asche
☐ 8 Hideki Okajima
☐ 10 Mark Farris
☐ 11 Jeremy Carr
☐ 12 Takuichi Koike
☐ 14 Katsuyoshi Murata
☐ 15 Michael Barrett
☐ 16 Hideki Satoh
☐ 17 Chad Hermansen
☐ 18 Masao Teramae
☐ 19 Mike McCutcheon
☐ 20 Brad Fullmer
☐ 21 Jeff Martin
☐ 22 John Kelly
☐ 23 Matt Smith
☐ 24 Geoff Blum
☐ 25 Kazuya Shibata
☐ 26 Dennis Lewallyn CO
☐ 27 Yoshihiro Seo
☐ 28 Jeff Banister MG
☐ 30 Keith Hughes CO
☐ 30 Donovan Delaney
☐ 31 Russell Jacob
☐ 32 Kevin Sweeney
☐ 33 Kaoru Nimura CO
☐ 34 Pat Flury
☐ 35 Joe Verplancke
☐ 36 Steve Thobe
☐ NNO Megabyte (Mascot)
☐ NNO Mark Rogow TR
☐ NNO Sharkettes
☐ NNO Team Photo CL

1996 Hudson Valley Renegades Best

This 30-card set of the 1996 Hudson Valley Renegades, a Class A New Yok-Penn League Co-op, was produced by Best Cards, Inc. and features color player photos in a white border. The backs carry player information and career statistics.

	MINT	NRMT	EXC
COMPLETE SET (30)	10.00	4.50	1.25

☐ 1 Joe Pomierski
☐ 2 Kelly Dransfeldt
☐ 3 Rowan Richards
☐ 4 Mark Draeger
☐ 5 Brandon Knight
☐ 6 John Ellis
☐ 7 Chris Anderson
☐ 8 Manny Vazquez
☐ 9 Ken Raines
☐ 10 Jose Martinez
☐ 11 Adrian Myers
☐ 12 Scott Leon
☐ 13 Eric Whitson
☐ 14 Marc Niethammer
☐ 15 Luke Owens-Bragg
☐ 16 Justin Siegel
☐ 17 Travis Cain
☐ 18 Jason Berry
☐ 19 Matt Majcherek
☐ 20 Aaron Horton
☐ 21 Michael Raymondi
☐ 22 Julio Aquino
☐ 23 Anthony Dellamano
☐ 24 Bump Wills MG
☐ 25 Greg Harris CO
☐ 26 Steve Livesay CO
☐ 27 Gene Basham TR
☐ 28 Rene Gades(Mascot)
☐ 29 Rookie the Renegade(Mascot)
☐ 30 1996 Hudson Valley Renegades

1996 Huntsville Stars Team Issue

This 28-card set of the 1996 Huntsville Stars, a Class AA Southern League affiliate of the Oakland Athletics, was sponsored by Burger King and features color player portraits with a thin red and a wider blue border. The backs carry player information and career statistics. The cards are unnumbered and checklisted below in alphabetical order.

	MINT	NRMT	EXC
COMPLETE SET (28)	40.00	18.00	5.00

☐ 1 Glenn Abbott CO
☐ 2 Bob Bennett
☐ 3 Mark Bellhorn
☐ 4 Rod Correia
☐ 5 Steve Cox
☐ 6 Rob DeBoer
☐ 7 David Francisco
☐ 8 Ben Grieve
☐ 9 Gary Haught
☐ 10 Dave Hollenback TR
☐ 11 Stacy Hollins
☐ 12 Gary Hust
☐ 13 Dave Joppie CO
☐ 14 Tim Kubinski
☐ 15 Derek Manning
☐ 16 Eric Martins
☐ 17 Mike Maurer
☐ 18 Chris Michalak
☐ 19 Willie Morales
☐ 20 Charles Poe
☐ 21 Brad Rigby
☐ 22 Mike Rossiter
☐ 23 Dick Scott MG
☐ 24 Demond Smith
☐ 25 Bret Wagner
☐ 26 Jason Wood
☐ 27 Dave Zancanaro
☐ NNO Burger King Cover Card

1996 Idaho Falls Braves Team Issue

This 32-card set of the 1996 Idaho Falls Braves, a Rookie Class Pioneer League affiliate of the San Diego Padres, was sponsored by C-A-L Ranch Stores, United Furniture Warehouse, Radio Station Z103 and KIFI-TV Channel 8. The fronts feature color player portraits in a fading blue, white, and salmon border. The backs carry player information, career statistics, and sponsor logos. The cards are unnumbered and checklisted below in alphabetical order.

	MINT	NRMT	EXC
COMPLETE SET (32)	10.00	4.50	1.25

☐ 1 Scott Adair
☐ 2 Tyler Boulo
☐ 3 Steven Chavez
☐ 4 Daniel Conroy
☐ 5 Joshua Davis
☐ 6 Mark D. Desabrais
☐ 7 Chad Ebbert
☐ 8 Kent Ervin
☐ 9 Domingo S. Guzman
☐ 10 Andy Hunter
☐ 11 Roderick Jackson
☐ 12 Robert Kent
☐ 13 Rodney L. Lindsey
☐ 14 Rodrigo Lopez
☐ 15 Obed R. Martinez
☐ 16 John Maxwell TR
☐ 17 Brian McClure
☐ 18 Pascual Nova
☐ 19 Peter S. Paciorek
☐ 20 Ben Reynoso
☐ 21 Daryl Rutherford
☐ 22 Scott A. Schroeder
☐ 23 Brendan Sullivan
☐ 24 Rick Sutcliffe CO
☐ 25 Thomas Szymborski
☐ 26 Ryan Thomas
☐ 27 Kevin Walker
☐ 28 Don Werner MG
☐ 29 Dominic Witte
☐ 30 Widd Workman
☐ 31 Team Logo
☐ 32 Team Logo

1996 Indianapolis Indians Best

This 30-card set of the 1996 Indianapolis Indians, a Class AAA American Association affiliate of the Cincinnati Reds, was produced by Best Cards, Inc. and features color player photos in a white border. The backs carry player information and career statistics.

	MINT	NRMT	EXC
COMPLETE SET (30)	8.00	3.60	1.00

☐ 1 1996 Indianapolis Indians Team
☐ 2 Dave Miley MG
☐ 3 Jim Thrift CO
☐ 4 Grant Jackson CO
☐ 5 John Young TR
☐ 6 Tim Belk
☐ 7 Hector Carrasco
☐ 8 Brook Fordyce
☐ 9 Steve Gibralter
☐ 10 Curtis Goodwin
☐ 11 Kevin Jarvis
☐ 12 Mike Kelly
☐ 13 Joe Kmak
☐ 14 Roberto Majia
☐ 15 Keith Mitchell
☐ 16 Chad Mottola
☐ 17 Kirt Ojala
☐ 18 Eric Owens
☐ 19 Eduardo Perez
☐ 20 Ross Powell
☐ 21 Pokey Reese
☐ 22 Mike Remlinger
☐ 23 Scott Service
☐ 24 Jerry Spradlin
☐ 25 Scott Sullivan
☐ 26 Brian Warren
☐ 27 Gabe White
☐ 28 Brandon Wilson
☐ 29 Rowdie(Mascot)
☐ 30 Q95 Morning Crew

1996 Iowa Cubs Best

This 30-card set of the 1996 Iowa Cubs, a Class AAA American Association affiliate of the Chicago Cubs, was produced by Best Cards, Inc. and features color player photos in a white border. The backs carry player information and career statistics.

	MINT	NRMT	EXC
COMPLETE SET (30)	8.00	3.60	1.00

☐ 1 Brooks Kieschnick
☐ 2 Ron Clark
☐ 3 Glenn Adams
☐ 4 Bill Earley
☐ 5 Bob Grimes
☐ 6 Bret Barberie
☐ 7 Kent Bottenfield
☐ 8 Brant Brown
☐ 9 Ben Burlingame
☐ 10 Mike Campbell
☐ 11 Mike Carter
☐ 12 Brad Erdman
☐ 13 Paul Faries
☐ 14 Doug Glanville
☐ 15 Mike Hubbard
☐ 16 Robin Jennings
☐ 17 Keith Kessinger
☐ 18 Bryn Kosco
☐ 19 Matt Merullo
☐ 20 Scott Moten
☐ 21 Carlos Pulido
☐ 22 Roberto Rivera
☐ 23 Terry Shumpert
☐ 24 Kennie Steenstra
☐ 25 Tanyon Sturtze
☐ 26 Dave Swartzbaugh
☐ 27 Amaury Telemaco
☐ 28 Pedro Valdes
☐ 29 Cubbie(Mascot)
☐ 30 Jon Ratliff

1996 Jackson Generals Best

This 27-card set of the 1996 Jackson Generals, a Class AA Texas League affiliate of the Houston Astros, was produced by Best Cards, Inc. and features color player photos in a white border. The backs carry player information and career statistics.

	MINT	NRMT	EXC
COMPLETE SET (27)	10.00	4.50	1.25

☐ 1 Dave Engle MG
☐ 2 Rusty Harris CO
☐ 3 Jim Hickey CO
☐ 4 Manuel Barrios
☐ 5 Kary Bridges
☐ 6 Dennis Colon
☐ 7 Ryan Creek
☐ 8 Tim Forkner
☐ 9 Mike Grzanich
☐ 10 John Halama
☐ 11 Chris Hatcher
☐ 12 Richard Hidalgo
☐ 13 Rich Humphrey
☐ 14 Russ Johnson
☐ 15 Tim Kester
☐ 16 Rich Loiselle
☐ 17 Roger Luce
☐ 18 Tom Martin
☐ 19 Donovan Mitchell
☐ 20 Melvin Mora
☐ 21 Tyrone Narcisse
☐ 22 Nate Peterson
☐ 23 Alan Probst
☐ 24 Vic Sanchez
☐ 25 Doug Simons
☐ 26 Jamie Walker
☐ 27 Mike Freer

1996 Jacksonville Suns Best

This 30-card set of the 1996 Jacksonville Suns, a Class AA Southern League affiliate of the Detroit Tigers, was produced by Best Cards, Inc. and features color player photos in a white border. The backs carry player information and career statistics. This issue includes the minor league card debut of Mike Drumright.

	MINT	NRMT	EXC
COMPLETE SET (30)	8.00	3.60	1.00

☐ 1 Peter Bragan OWNER
☐ 2 Bill Plummer MG
☐ 3 Jeff Jones CO
☐ 4 Mark Meleski CO
☐ 5 Glen Barker
☐ 6 Kenny Carlyle
☐ 7 Frank Catalanotto
☐ 8 Blas Cedeno
☐ 9 John Cotton
☐ 10 Mike Drumright
☐ 11 Ramon Fermin
☐ 12 Sean Freeman
☐ 13 Eddie Gaillard
☐ 14 Luis Garcia
☐ 15 Rick Greene
☐ 16 Jim Gutierrez
☐ 17 Terrel Hansen
☐ 18 Scott Makarewicz
☐ 19 Justin Mashore
☐ 20 Antonio Mitchell
☐ 21 Brian Moehler
☐ 22 Phil Nevin
☐ 23 Scott Norman
☐ 24 Brandon Reed
☐ 25 John Rosengren
☐ 26 Tom Schmidt
☐ 27 William Thompson
☐ 28 Bubba Trammell
☐ 29 Sean Whiteside
☐ 30 Frank Bray
Card Collector

1996 Johnson City Cardinals Team Issue

This 35-card set of the 1996 Johnson City Cardinals, a Rookie Class Pioneer League affiliate of the St. Louis Cardinals, was produced and sponsored by Interstate Graphics, Inc. and co-sponsored by Fox TV station, WEMT-TV 39. The fronts feature color player portraits in a white border. The backs carry information about the player. The cards are unnumbered and checklisted below in alphabetical order. This issue includes the minor league card debut of Brent Butler.

	MINT	NRMT	EXC
COMPLETE SET (35)	12.00	5.50	1.50

☐ 1 Antonio Abell
☐ 2 Brian Barfield
☐ 3 Aaron Bruns TR
☐ 4 Brent Butler
☐ 5 Isaac Byrd
☐ 6 Stubby Clapp
☐ 7 Billy Deck
☐ 8 Jose DeLeon
☐ 9 Matt DeWitt
☐ 10 Chris Dooley
☐ 11 Brad Evans
☐ 12 Cordell Farley
☐ 13 Jimmy Gargiulo
☐ 14 Toribio Guzman
☐ 15 Rodger Harris
☐ 16 Todd Hogan
☐ 17 Shawn Hogge
☐ 18 Ryan Kritscher
☐ 19 Jason Lee
☐ 20 Jose Leon
☐ 21 Jesus Lugo
☐ 22 Pepe McNeal
☐ 23 Richard Mear
☐ 24 Steve Norris
☐ 25 Tim Onofrei
☐ 26 Steve Reed
☐ 27 Tim Riegert
☐ 28 Ruben Rosario
☐ 29 Luis Saturria
☐ 30 Paul Tanner
☐ 31 Steve Turco MG
☐ 32 John Tuttle
☐ 33 Clint Weibl
☐ NNO Logo Card
☐ NNO Checklist

1996 Kane County Cougars Team Issue

This 31-card set of the 1996 Kane County Cougars, a Class A Midwest League affiliate of the Florida Marlins, features color player photos with the player's name and team logo printed in a green vertical bar on the left. The backs carry a small black-and-white player head photo with player information and career statistics. A parallel set was produced that was a little bit larger in size and printed on heavier card stock. The team logo was printed in gold foil. A limited number of this set was produced and each card is sequentially numbered. A second parallel set was produced for a Connies Pizza Giveaway and was printed on somewhat thinner card stock. The cards are unnumbered and checklisted below in alphabetical order. 3,500 regular sets, 1,500 gold foil and1,100 sponsor Connie's Pizza sets were produced. This issue includes a second year card of Jaime Jones.

	MINT	NRMT	EXC
COMPLETE SET (31)	10.00	4.50	1.25
COMPLETE GOLD SET (31)	15.00	6.75	1.85
COMPLETE SPONSOR SET (31)	30.00	13.50	3.70

☐ 1 Earl Agnoly
☐ 2 Josh Booty
☐ 3 Travis Burgus
☐ 4 Antonio Castro
☐ 5 Scott DeWitt
☐ 6 Michael Duvall
☐ 7 Tony Enard
☐ 8 Joe Funaro
☐ 9 Amaury Garcia
☐ 10 Rick Garcia
☐ 11 Rod Getz
☐ 12 Steve Goodell
☐ 13 Victor Hurtado
☐ 14 Jake the Diamond Dog(Mascot)
☐ 15 Jaime Jones
☐ 16 Lynn Jones
☐ 17 Hector Kuilan
☐ 18 Sommer McCartney
☐ 19 Ozzie Cougar(Mascot)
☐ 20 Bob Pailthorpe
☐ 21 Brian Peterson
☐ 22 Rene Rascon
☐ 23 Ryan Robertson
☐ 24 Nate Rolison
☐ 25 Gary Santoro
☐ 26 Shannon Stephens
☐ 27 Dan Vardijan
☐ 28 Walter White
☐ 29 Harold Williams TR
☐ 30 Randy Winn
☐ 31 Matt Winters CO

1996 Kane County Cougars Update Team Issue

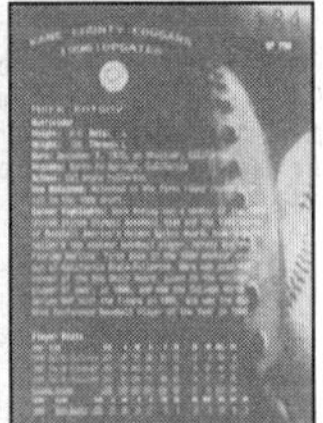

This 13-card set is printed on heavy card stock and features color player images on a simulated wood background with the words "Pro Stock" made to look burned into the background. The backs carry player information with career highlights and statistics. Only 750 of this set were produced and each card is sequentially numbered. The cards are unnumbered and checklisted below in alphabetical order. This set includes the minor league card debuts of Mark Kotsay and Alex Gonzalez. 750 sets were produced.

	MINT	NRMT	EXC
COMPLETE SET (13)	35.00	16.00	4.40

☐ 1 Josh Booty
☐ 2 Josh Booty
Jaime Jones#(Mark Kotsay
☐ 3 Roosevelt Brown
☐ 4 Ryan Dempster
☐ 5 Amaury Garcia
☐ 6 Alex Gonzalez
☐ 7 Victor Hurtado
☐ 8 Jaime Jones
☐ 9 Mark Kotsay
☐ 10 Hector Kuilan
☐ 11 Nate Rolison
☐ 12 Dan Vardijan
☐ 13 Randy Winn

1996 Kinston Indians Best

This 30-card set of the 1996 Kinston Indians, a Class A Carolina League affiliate of the Cleveland Indians, was produced by Best Cards, Inc. and features color player photos in a white border. The backs carry player information and career statistics. This issue includes the minor league card debut of Jaret Wright.

	MINT	NRMT	EXC
COMPLETE SET (30)	12.00	5.50	1.50

☐ 1 Dan Brabant
☐ 2 David Caldwell
☐ 3 Sean Casey
☐ 4 Gerad Cawhorn
☐ 5 Patricio Claudio
☐ 6 Scot Donovan
☐ 7 Pat Evans
☐ 8 Chip Glass
☐ 9 Chris Granata
☐ 10 Gary Hagy
☐ 11 Kris Hanson
☐ 12 Robin Harriss
☐ 13 Terry Harvey
☐ 14 Tim Jorgensen
☐ 15 Guillermo Mercedes
☐ 16 Rafael Mesa
☐ 17 David Miller
☐ 18 Michael Moyle
☐ 19 Noe Najera
☐ 20 Julio Perez
☐ 21 Chan Perry
☐ 22 Tony Runion
☐ 23 Jerry Taylor
☐ 24 Teddy Warrecker
☐ 25 Lenny Weber
☐ 26 Eric White
☐ 27 Jaret Wright
☐ 28 Jack Mull MG
☐ 29 Ken Rowe CO
☐ 30 Carlo Colombino CO

1996 Kissimmee Cobras Best

This 30-card set of the 1996 Kissimmee Cobras, a Class A Florida State League affiliate of the Houston Astros, was produced by Best Cards, Inc. and features color player photos in a white border. The backs carry player information and career statistics.

	MINT	NRMT	EXC
COMPLETE SET (30)	10.00	4.50	1.25

☐ 1 Alan Ashby MG
☐ 2 Jack Billingham CO
☐ 3 Ivan DeJesus CO
☐ 4 Adan Amezcua
☐ 5 Donnie Dault
☐ 6 Mike Diorio
☐ 7 Scott Elarton
☐ 8 Alejandro Freire
☐ 9 Jimmy Gonzalez
☐ 10 Billy Hall
☐ 11 Oscar Henriquez
☐ 12 David Landaker
☐ 13 Dan Lock
☐ 14 Johan Lopez
☐ 15 Marc Manwarren
☐ 16 Mitch Meluskey
☐ 17 Hector Mercado
☐ 18 Tony Mounce
☐ 19 Bryant Nelson
☐ 20 Jhonny Perez
☐ 21 Edgar Ramos
☐ 22 Oscar Robles
☐ 23 Noel Rodriguez
☐ 24 Tony Ross
☐ 25 Nelson Samboy
☐ 26 Tony Shaver
☐ 27 Eric Stachler
☐ 28 Brock Steinke
☐ 29 Gary Trammell
☐ 30 Julien Tucker

1996 Knoxville Smokies Best

This 30-card set of the 1996 Knoxville Smokies, a Class AA Southern League affiliate of the Toronto Blue Jays, was produced by Best Cards, Inc. and features color player photos in a white border. The backs carry player information and career statistics.

	MINT	NRMT	EXC
COMPLETE SET (25)	10.00	4.50	1.25

☐ 1 Omar Malave MG
☐ 2 Rick Langford CO
☐ 3 Scott Shannon TR
☐ 4 Carlos Almanzar
☐ 5 Kurtiss Bogott
☐ 6 Chad Brown
☐ 7 Ben Candelaria
☐ 8 Chris Carpenter
☐ 9 Rickey Cradle
☐ 10 Brandon Cromer
☐ 11 Lorenzo De La Cruz
☐ 12 Tom Evans
☐ 13 Chris Freeman
☐ 14 Mike Halperin
☐ 15 Kris Harmes
☐ 16 Santiago Henry
☐ 17 Ryan Jones
☐ 18 Julio Mosquera
☐ 19 Jeff Patzke
☐ 20 Jose Pett
☐ 21 Lonell Roberts
☐ 22 Mike Romano
☐ 23 Mark Sievert
☐ 24 Brian Smith
☐ 25 Chris Weinke

1996 Lake Elsinore Storm Best

This 30-card set of the 1996 Lake Elsinore Storm, a Class A California League affiliate of the California Angels, was produced by Best Cards, Inc. and features color player photos in a white border. The backs carry player information and career statistics.

	MINT	NRMT	EXC
COMPLETE SET (30)	10.00	4.50	1.25

☐ 1 Carlos Castillo
☐ 2 Brian Cooper
☐ 3 Josh Deakman
☐ 4 Dave Doorneweerd
☐ 5 Heath Haynes
☐ 6 Mike Hermanson
☐ 7 Jason Hill
☐ 8 Korey Keling
☐ 9 Matt Perisho
☐ 10 Kyle Sebach
☐ 11 Scott Schoeneweis
☐ 12 Bret Hemphill
☐ 13 Todd Takayoshi
☐ 14 Randy Betten
☐ 15 Danny Buxbaum
☐ 16 Paul Failla
☐ 17 Juan Henderson
☐ 18 Tony Moeder
☐ 19 Greg Morris
☐ 20 Allan Parker
☐ 21 Chris Smith
☐ 22 Joe Urso
☐ 23 Cale Carter
☐ 24 Jason Herrick
☐ 25 Kevin Young
☐ 26 Mitch Seoane
☐ 27 Ty Van Burkleo
☐ 28 Leon Durham
☐ 29 Howie Gershberg
☐ 30 Hamlet(Mascot)

1996 Lakeland Tigers Best

This 30-card set of the 1996 Lakeland Tigers, a Class A Florida State League affiliate of the Detroit Tigers, was produced by Best Cards, Inc. and features color player photos in a white border. The backs carry player information and career statistics. This issue includes the minor league card debut of Richard Almanzar.

	MINT	NRMT	EXC
COMPLETE SET (30)	10.00	4.50	1.25

☐ 1 Dave Anderson MGR
☐ 2 Rich Bombard CO
☐ 3 Basilio Cabrera CO
☐ 4 Doug Teter TR
☐ 5 Richard Almanzar
☐ 6 Ryan Balfe
☐ 7 Jamie Borel
☐ 8 Marty Boryczewski
☐ 9 Tarrik Brock
☐ 10 Blas Cedeno
☐ 11 Mike Darr
☐ 12 Eric Dinyar
☐ 13 Juan Encarnacion
☐ 14 Kelton Jacobson
☐ 15 Lonny Landry
☐ 16 Kevin Lidle
☐ 17 Kenny Marrero
☐ 18 Santiago Perez
☐ 19 Brian Powell
☐ 20 Willis Roberts
☐ 21 Adam Rodriguez
☐ 22 Mike Salazar
☐ 23 Jerry Salzano
☐ 24 Jeff Siler
☐ 25 Matt Skrmetta
☐ 26 Cameron Smith
☐ 27 Trad Sobik
☐ 28 Jay Waggoner
☐ 29 Daryle Ward
☐ 30 Greg Whiteman

1996 Lancaster Jethawks Best

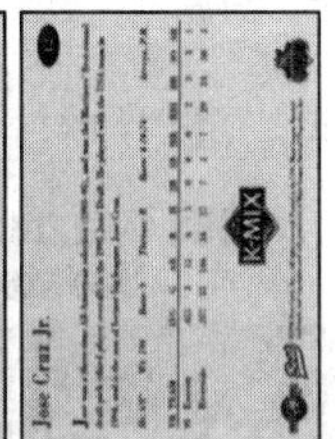

This 30-card set of the 1996 Lancaster Jethawks, a Class A California League affiliate of the Seattle Mariners, was produced by Best Cards, Inc. and features color player photos in a white border. The backs carry player information and career statistics. This issue includes the minor league card debut of Ken Cloude and a second year card of Jose Cruz Jr.

	MINT	NRMT	EXC
COMPLETE SET (30)	20.00	9.00	2.50

☐ 1 Dave Brundage MGR
☐ 2 Delwyn Young CO
☐ 3 Juan Eichelberger CO
☐ 4 Rob Nodine TR
☐ 5 Andy Augustine
☐ 6 Chris Beck
☐ 7 Chris Bosio
☐ 8 Shawn Buhner
☐ 9 James Clifford
☐ 10 Ken Cloude
☐ 11 Jason Cook
☐ 12 Jose Cruz Jr.
☐ 13 John Daniels
☐ 14 Clint Gould
☐ 15 Brett Hinchliffe
☐ 16 Mike Lanza
☐ 17 Jesus Marquez
☐ 18 Luis Molina
☐ 19 Shane Monahan
☐ 20 Ivan Montane
☐ 21 Todd Niemeier
☐ 22 Jeff Pearce
☐ 23 Marino Santana
☐ 24 Scot Sealy
☐ 25 Marcus Sturdivant
☐ 26 Tom Szimanski
☐ 27 John Thompson
☐ 28 Tim Trawick
☐ 29 Carlos Villalobos
☐ 30 Dusty Wathan

1996 Lansing Lugnuts Best

This 30-card set of the 1996 Lansing Lugnuts, a Class A Midwest League affiliate of the Kansas City Royals, was produced by Best Cards, Inc. and features color player photos in a white border. The backs carry player information and career statistics. This Issue includes the minor league card debut of Carlos Beltran.

	MINT	NRMT	EXC
COMPLETE SET (30)	12.00	5.50	1.50

☐ 1 Brian Poldberg MG
☐ 2 Curtis Wilkerson CO
☐ 3 Mike Mason CO
☐ 4 Justin Adam
☐ 5 Carlos Beltran
☐ 6 Manuel Bernal
☐ 7 Doug Blosser
☐ 8 Jose Cepeda
☐ 9 Gary Coffee
☐ 10 Emiliano Escandon
☐ 11 Carlos Febles
☐ 12 Adam R. Finnieston
☐ 13 Patrick Hallmark
☐ 14 Brent Kaysner
☐ 15 Scott Key
☐ 16 Mark Melito
☐ 17 Blaine Mull
☐ 18 Carlos Paredes
☐ 19 Mark Quinn
☐ 20 Jason Ritter
☐ 21 Mike Robbins
☐ 22 Juan Robles
☐ 23 Juan Rocha
☐ 24 Craig Sanders
☐ 25 Jose Santiago
☐ 26 Brett Schafer
☐ 27 Todd Thorn
☐ 28 Matthew Treanor
☐ 29 Modesto Villarreal
☐ 30 Jeff Wallace

1996 Las Vegas Stars Best

This 30-card set of the 1996 Las Vegas Stars, a Class AAA Pacific Coast League affiliate of the San Diego Padres, was produced by Best Cards, Inc. and features color player photos in a white border. The backs carry player information and career statistics.

	MINT	NRMT	EXC
COMPLETE SET (30)	10.00	4.50	1.25

☐ 1 Mike Sharperson
☐ 2 Jerry Royster MG
☐ 3 Galen Cisco CO
☐ 4 Eric Bullock CO
☐ 5 Paul Abbott
☐ 6 Andres Berumen
☐ 7 Julio Bruno
☐ 8 Homer Bush
☐ 9 Craig Colbert
☐ 10 Doug Dascenzo
☐ 11 Rob Deer
☐ 12 Glenn Dishman
☐ 13 Denny Harriger
☐ 14 Dustin Hermanson
☐ 15 Riccardo Ingram
☐ 16 Scott Lewis
☐ 17 Joey Long
☐ 18 Sean Mulligan
☐ 19 Mike Oquist
☐ 20 Rico Rossy
☐ 21 Paul Russo
☐ 22 Matt Schwenke
☐ 23 Ira Smith
☐ 24 Pete Smith
☐ 25 Todd Steverson
☐ 26 Russ Swan

☐ 27 Jason Thompson
☐ 28 Chad Tredaway
☐ 29 Pete Walker
☐ 30 Weston Weber

1996 Lethbridge Black Diamonds Best

This 33-card set of the 1996 Lethbridge Black Diamonds, a Rookie Class Pioneer League affiliate of the Arizona Diamondbacks, was produced by Best Cards, Inc. and features color player photos in a white border. The backs carry player information and career statistics. This issue includes the minor league card debuts of Vladimir Nunez and Larry Rodriguez.

	MINT	NRMT	EXC
COMPLETE SET (33)	12.00	5.50	1.50

☐ 1 Chris Speier MG
☐ 2 Dennis Lewallyn CO
☐ 3 Jim Presley CO
☐ 4 Gord Watt
☐ 5 Brad Allison
☐ 6 Dallas Anderson
☐ 7 Beau Baltzell
☐ 8 Rod Barajas
☐ 9 Justin Bice
☐ 10 Mike Boughton
☐ 11 Mark Chavez
☐ 12 Jason Conti
☐ 13 Jason Crews
☐ 14 Clay Crossan
☐ 15 Reggie Davis
☐ 16 Johnny Done
☐ 17 Ryan Duffy
☐ 18 Jamie Gann
☐ 19 Javier Gomez
☐ 20 Ron Hartmen Jr.
☐ 21 David Hayman
☐ 22 Jason Moore
☐ 23 Jose Nunez
☐ 24 Vladimir Nunez
☐ 25 George Oleksik
☐ 26 Chip Rhea
☐ 27 Larry Rodriguez
☐ 28 Rob Ryan
☐ 29 Erik Sabel
☐ 30 Javier Samboy
☐ 31 Mike Stoner
☐ 32 Kevin Sweeney
☐ 33 Joe Verplancke

1996 Louisville Redbirds Best

This 30-card set of the 1996 Louisville Redbirds, a Class AAA American Association affiliate of the St. Louis Cardinals, was produced by Best Cards, Inc. and features color player photos in a white border. The backs carry player information and career statistics.

	MINT	NRMT	EXC
COMPLETE SET (28)	12.00	5.50	1.50

☐ 1 Joe Pettini
☐ 2 Joe Cunningham Jr.
☐ 3 Dyar Miller
☐ 4 Mark O'Neal
☐ 5 Billy Bird
☐ 6 Matt Arrandale
☐ 7 Mike Badorek
☐ 8 Brian Barber
☐ 9 Rich Batchelor
☐ 10 Rigo Beltran
☐ 11 Terry Bradshaw
☐ 12 Mike Busby
☐ 13 Tripp Cromer
☐ 14 Darrel Deak
☐ 15 Mike Defelice
☐ 16 Tony Diggs
☐ 17 Dave Eiland
☐ 18 John Frascatore
☐ 19 Mike Gulan
☐ 20 Shawn Hare
☐ 21 Scott Hemond
☐ 22 Aaron Holbert
☐ 23 Jeff Mutis
☐ 24 Jose Oliva
☐ 25 Scott Simmons
☐ 26 Mike Stefanski
☐ 27 Chris Wimmer
☐ 28 Dmitri Young

1996 Lowell Spinners Best

This 30-card set of the 1996 Lowell Spinners, a Class A New York-Penn League affiliate of the Boston Red Sox, was produced by Best Cards, Inc. and features color player photos in a white border. The backs carry player information and career statistics. This issue includes the minor league card debut of Corey Jenkins.

	MINT	NRMT	EXC
COMPLETE SET (30)	10.00	4.50	1.25

☐ 1 Billy Gardner Jr.
☐ 2 Dan Gakeler
☐ 3 Frank Mahon
☐ 4 Elvis Alayon
☐ 5 Charles Beale
☐ 6 John Duffy
☐ 7 Chris Festa
☐ 8 Javier Fuentes
☐ 9 Shea Hillenbrand
☐ 10 Steve Hine
☐ 11 Corey Jenkins
☐ 12 Jeff Keaveney
☐ 13 Matt Kinney
☐ 14 Tim Kratochvil
☐ 15 Ruben Lebron
☐ 16 Steve Lomasney
☐ 17 Joe Mamott
☐ 18 Michael McKinley
☐ 19 Erik Metzger
☐ 20 Steve Morgan
☐ 21 Scott Musgrave
☐ 22 Bob Rodgers
☐ 23 Steve Smetana
☐ 24 Maika Symmonds
☐ 25 Andre Thompson
☐ 26 Chris Thompson
☐ 27 Wilton Veras
☐ 28 Robb Welch
☐ 29 Andy Yount
☐ 30 Checklist

1996 Lynchburg Hillcats Best

This 30-card set of the 1996 Lynchburg Hillcats, a Class A Carolina League affiliate of the Pittsburgh Pirates, was produced by Best Cards, Inc. and features color player photos in a white border. The backs carry player information and career statistics. This issue includes the minor league card debuts of Jose Guillen and Jimmy Anderson.

	MINT	NRMT	EXC
COMPLETE SET (30)	30.00	13.50	3.70

☐ 1 Jimmy Anderson
☐ 2 Mike Asche
☐ 3 Eddie Brooks
☐ 4 Adrian Brown
☐ 5 Michael Brown
☐ 6 Stoney Burke
☐ 7 Kane Davis
☐ 8 John Dillinger
☐ 9 Aaron France
☐ 10 Freddy Garcia
☐ 11 Jose Guillen
☐ 12 Jason Johnson
☐ 13 Erskine Kelley
☐ 14 Ramon Martinez
☐ 15 Joe Maskivish
☐ 16 Craig Mattson
☐ 17 Rick Paugh
☐ 18 Kevin Pickford
☐ 19 Tony Robinson
☐ 20 Matt Spade
☐ 21 Derek Swafford
☐ 22 Jonathan Sweet
☐ 23 Jason Temple
☐ 24 Steve Thobe
☐ 25 Shon Walker
☐ 26 Matt Williams
☐ 27 Jeff Banister MG
☐ 28 Jim Bibby CO
☐ 29 Omer Munoz CO
☐ 30 Bryan Butz TR

1996 Lynchburg Hillcats Update Best

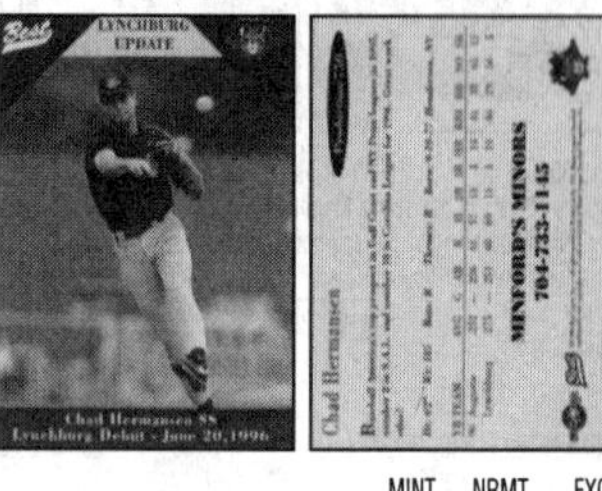

	MINT	NRMT	EXC
COMPLETE SET (1)	10.00	4.50	1.25

☐ 1 Chad Hermansen

1996 Macon Braves Best

This 30-card set of the 1996 Macon Braves, a Class A South Atlantic League affiliate of the Atlanta Braves, was produced by Best Cards, Inc. and features color player photos in a white border. The backs carry player information and career statistics. This issue includes the minor league card debut of Marc Lewis.

	MINT	NRMT	EXC
COMPLETE SET (30)	12.00	5.50	1.50

☐ 1 Winston Abreu
☐ 2 Billy Blythe
☐ 3 Antone Brooks
☐ 4 Christopher Case
☐ 5 Maurice Christmas
☐ 6 Charlie Cruz
☐ 7 Jose Garcia
☐ 8 Dwayne Jacobs
☐ 9 Ray King
☐ 10 Aquiles Pinales
☐ 11 John Rocker
☐ 12 Martin Sanchez
☐ 13 Derek Foote
☐ 14 Jamie Hicks
☐ 15 Fernando Lunar
☐ 16 Keith Daugherty
☐ 17 Jose Delgado
☐ 18 Randy Hodges
☐ 19 Robert Sasser
☐ 20 Ben Utting
☐ 21 Glenn Williams
☐ 22 Roosevelt Brown
☐ 23 Marc Lewis
☐ 24 George Lombard
☐ 25 Joe Trippy
☐ 26 Paul Runge
☐ 27 Wallace Johnson
☐ 28 Mark Ross CO
☐ 29 Mike Graus TR
☐ 30 Checklist

1996 Martinsville Phillies Best

This 30-card set of the 1996 Martinsville Phillies, a Rookie Class Appalachian League affiliate of the Philadelphia Phillies, was produced by Best Cards, Inc. and features color player photos in a white border. The backs carry player information and career statistics.

	MINT	NRMT	EXC
COMPLETE SET (30)	10.00	4.50	1.25

☐ 1 Douglas Aguiar
☐ 2 Jose Arias
☐ 3 Terry Bishop
☐ 4 Matthew Buckles
☐ 5 Matthew Buczkowski
☐ 6 Lamont Edwards
☐ 7 Justin Fenus
☐ 8 Ryan Ferguson
☐ 9 Thomas Ferrand
☐ 10 Ben Jenkins
☐ 11 Jason Johnson
☐ 12 Manny Mata
☐ 13 Javier Mejia
☐ 14 Juan Mejia
☐ 15 Sal Molta
☐ 16 Francisco Montero
☐ 17 Alberto Mosquea
☐ 18 Kevin Nichols
☐ 19 Ramon Portillo
☐ 20 Urbano Quintana
☐ 21 Jimmy Rollins
☐ 22 B.J. Schlicher
☐ 23 Ricardo Serafin
☐ 24 Keith Shockley
☐ 25 Carlos Silva
☐ 26 Kristopher Stevens
☐ 27 Nick Thompson
☐ 28 Robert Van Iten
☐ 29 Tim Walton
☐ 30 Tommy Worthy

1996 Maui Stingrays Hawaii Winter Ball

This 36-card set of the 1996 Maui Stingrays team was produced by Trade Publishing and features borderless color player portraits by Wayne Tanaka. The backs carry a small circular black-and-white player head photo with player information and statistics. This issue includes a first year card of Mark Kotsay and a second year card of Jaime Jones.

	MINT	NRMT	EXC
COMPLETE SET (36)	20.00	9.00	2.50

☐ 1 Minoru Yano CO
☐ 2 Shinya Miyamoto
☐ 3 Mitsuru Honma
☐ 6 Ben Petrick
☐ 7 Akira Matsumoto
☐ 8 Kenji Johjima
☐ 9 Mark Kotsay
☐ 10 Kevin Pincavitch

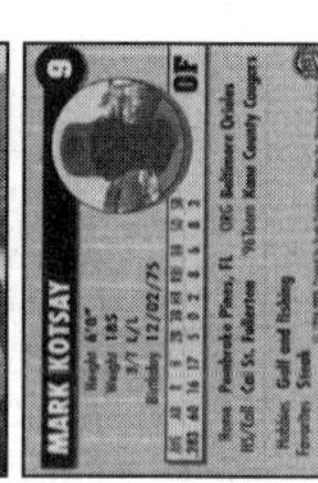

☐ 11 Orin Kawahara
☐ 14 Chris Macca
☐ 15 Keith Johnson
☐ 16 Masahiro Sakumoto
☐ 17 Shintaroh Yoshitake
☐ 18 Anthony Sanders
☐ 19 Matt Snyder
☐ 20 Danny Clyburn
☐ 21 Kyle Cooney
☐ 22 Josh Booty
☐ 23 Chad Brown
☐ 24 Keisaburoh Tanoue
☐ 25 Luther Hackman
☐ 26 Kenichi Wakatabe
☐ 27 Jaime Jones
☐ 28 Chris Fussell
☐ 29 Nate Rolison
☐ 30 Doug Million
☐ 31 Jon Debus CO
☐ 32 P.J. Carey MG
☐ 33 Jeff Morris CO
☐ 34 Derrick Gibson
☐ 35 Mike Iglesias
☐ 36 Mark Seaver
☐ NNO Ray the Rookie(Mascot)
☐ NNO Tim Abraham TR
☐ NNO Stingrayettes
☐ NNO Team Photo CL

1996 Medicine Hat Blue Jays Team Issue

This 33-card set of the 1996 Medicine Hat Blue Jays, a Rookie Class Pioneer League affiliate of the Toronto Blue Jays, was sponsored by CSC Collectables and Prime Printing. The fronts feature color player posed photos in a white border. The backs carry player information. The cards are unnumbered and checklisted below in alphabetical order.

	MINT	NRMT	EXC
COMPLETE SET (33)	50.00	22.00	6.25

☐ 1 Randy Albaral
☐ 2 Clayton Andrews
☐ 3 Lorenzo Bagley
☐ 4 Stanley Baston
☐ 5 David Bleaszard
☐ 6 Brian Bowles
☐ 7 Kyle Burchart
☐ 8 Tim Giles
☐ 9 Gary Glover
☐ 10 Samuel Goure
☐ 11 Matthew Gourlay
☐ 12 Jonathan Herring
☐ 13 Roberta Higuchi
☐ 14 Davan Keathley
☐ 15 Selwyn Langaigne
☐ 16 Jeffrey Maloney
☐ 17 Sean McClellan
☐ 18 Chris McKenna GM
☐ 19 Robert Medina
☐ 20 Bradley Moon
☐ 21 Omar Moreno CO
☐ 22 Marty Pevey
☐ 23 Joshua Phelps
☐ 24 Jeremi Rudolph
☐ 25 Jeremy Satterfield
☐ 26 Jaron Seabury
☐ 27 Pablo Sencion
☐ 28 Eddy Severino
☐ 29 Ryan Stromsborg
☐ 30 Jose Umbria
☐ 31 Bruce Walton CO
☐ 32 Symmion Willis
☐ 33 Mike Wirsta TR

1996 Memphis Chicks Best

This 30-card set of the 1996 Memphis Chicks, a Class AA Southern League affiliate of the San Diego Padres, was produced by Best Cards, Inc. and features color player photos in a white border. The backs carry player information and career statistics. This issue includes the minor league card debut of Gabe Alvarez and a third year card of Derrek Lee.

	MINT	NRMT	EXC
COMPLETE SET (30)	15.00	6.75	1.85

☐ 1 Ed Romero MG
☐ 2 Jackson Todd CO
☐ 3 George Poulis TR
☐ 4 Jeff Capriotti MG

☐ 5 Chief Chickasaw(Mascot)
☐ 6 Gabe Alvarez
☐ 7 Jeff Barry
☐ 8 Stoney Briggs
☐ 9 Julio Bruno
☐ 10 Dera Clark
☐ 11 Shane Dennis
☐ 12 Bubba Dixon
☐ 13 Mike Freitas
☐ 14 Fernando Hernandez
☐ 15 Earl Johnson
☐ 16 Brad Kaufman
☐ 17 Jamie Keefe
☐ 18 Rusty Kilgo
☐ 19 Tim Killeen
☐ 20 Marc Kroon
☐ 21 Greg LaRocca
☐ 22 Derrek Lee
☐ 23 Rob Mattson
☐ 24 Vince Moore
☐ 25 Heath Murray
☐ 26 Dan Rohrmeier
☐ 27 Mandy Romero
☐ 28 Jorge Velandia
☐ 29 Dario Veras
☐ 30 Checklist

1996 Michigan Battle Cats Best

This 29-card set of the 1996 Michigan Battle Cats, a Class A Midwest League affiliate of the Boston Red Sox, was produced by Best Cards, Inc. and features color player photos in a white border. The backs carry player information and career statistics. This issue includes the minor card debuts of Damian Sapp and Cole Liniak.

	MINT	NRMT	EXC
COMPLETE SET (30)	16.00	7.25	2.00

☐ 1 Tommy Barrett MG
☐ 2 Nehamas(Pookie) Bernstine CO
☐ 3 Bill Maloney CO
☐ 4 Brian Moore TR
☐ 5 Rafael Betancourt
☐ 6 Kevan Cannon
☐ 7 Jim Chamblee
☐ 8 Virgil Chevalier
☐ 9 Kevin Clark
☐ 10 Paxton Crawford
☐ 11 Keith Goodwin
☐ 12 Joe Hamilton
☐ 13 Scott Jones
☐ 14 Ruben Lebron
☐ 15 Cole Liniak
☐ 16 Denis McLaughlin
☐ 17 Andy Noffke
☐ 18 Nick Ortiz
☐ 19 Roy Padilla
☐ 20 Juan Pena
☐ 21 John Raifstanger
☐ 22 Willie Rivera
☐ 23 Curt Romboli
☐ 24 Damian Sapp
☐ 25 Jeff Sauve
☐ 26 Michael Spinelli
☐ 27 Greg Tippin
☐ 28 Larry Wimberley
☐ 29 Jay Yennaco
☐ 30 Rally Cat(Mascot)

1996 Midwest League All-Stars Best

	MINT	NRMT	EXC
COMPLETE SET (58)	12.00	5.50	1.50

☐ 1 Karl Thompson
Wisconsin Timber Rattlers
☐ 2 David Arias
Wisconsin Timber Rattlers
☐ 3 Jose Amado
Wisconsin Timber Rattlers
☐ 4 Brent Iddon
Wisconsin Timber Rattlers
☐ 5 Joel Ramirez
Wisconsin Timber Rattlers
☐ 6 Scott Smith
Wisconsin Timber Rattlers
☐ 7 Luis Tinoco
Wisconsin Timber Rattlers
☐ 8 Greg Wooten
Wiscon Timber Rattlers
☐ 9 Peter Benny
Beloit Snappers
☐ 10 Valerio de los Santos
Beloit Snappers
☐ 11 Mike Kinkade
Beloit Snappers
☐ 12 Lorenzo Barcelo
Burlington Bees
☐ 13 Don Denbow
Burlington Bees
☐ 14 Santos Hernandez
Burlington Bees
☐ 15 Larry Barnes
Cedar Rapids Kernels
☐ 16 Jose Cintron
Cedar Rapids Kernels
☐ 17 David Davalillo
Cedar Rapids Kernels
☐ 18 Matt Clement
Clinton Lumber Kings
☐ 19 Andy Hall
Peoria Chiefs
☐ 20 Juan Munoz
Peoria Chiefs
☐ 21 Cliff Politte
Peoria Chiefs
☐ 22 Britt Reames
Peoria Chiefs
☐ 23 Kerry Robinson
Peoria Chiefs
☐ 24 Travis Welch
Peoria Chiefs
☐ 25 R.J. Bowers
Quad City River Bandits
☐ 26 Ramon Castro
Quad City River Bandits
☐ 27 Ryan Coe
Quad City River Bandits
☐ 28 Brian Sikorski
Quad City River Bandits
☐ 29 Mike Walter
Quad City River Bandits
☐ 30 Adrian Gordon
Fort Wayne Wizards
☐ 31 Fred Rath
Fort Wayne Wizards
☐ 32 Amaury Garcia
Kane County Cougars
☐ 33 Victor Hurtado
Kane County Cougars
☐ 34 Shannon Stephens
Kane County Cougars
☐ 35 Walter White
Kane County Cougars
☐ 36 Jose Cepeda
Lansing Lugnuts
☐ 37 Mark Melito
Lansing Lugnuts
☐ 38 Blaine Mull
Lansing Lugnuts
☐ 39 Mark Quinn
Lansing Lugnuts
☐ 40 Juan Rocha
Lansing Lugnuts
☐ 41 Todd Thorn
Lansing Lugnuts
☐ 42 Virgil Chevalier
Michigan Battle Cats
☐ 43 Kevin Clark
Michigan Battle Cats
☐ 44 Scott Jones
Michigan Battle Cats
☐ 45 Roy Padilla
Michigan Battle Cats
☐ 46 Juan Pena
Michigan Battle Cats
☐ 47 Curt Romboli
Michigan Battle Cats
☐ 48 Brandon Hammack
Rockford Cubbies
☐ 49 Carlos Castillo
South Bend Silver Hawks
☐ 50 Steve Friedrich
South Bend Silver Hawks
☐ 51 Derek Hasselhoff
South Bend Silver Hawks
☐ 52 Mark Johnson
South Bend Silver Hawks
☐ 53 Jeff Liefer
South Bend Silver Hawks
☐ 54 Jason Olsen
South Bend Silver Hawks
☐ 55 Brian Simmons
South Bend Silver Hawks
☐ 56 Mario Valdez
South Bend Silver Hawks
☐ 57 Duane Filchner
West Michigan Whitecaps
☐ 58 Chris Nelson
West Michigan Whitecaps

1996 Midland Angels Best

This 29-card set of the 1996 Midland Angels, a Class AA Texas League affiliate of the California Angels, was produced by Best Cards, Inc. and features color player photos in a white border. The backs carry player information and career statistics.

	MINT	NRMT	EXC
COMPLETE SET (30)	10.00	4.50	1.25

☐ 1 Mario Mendoza MG
☐ 2 Kernan Ronan CO
☐ 3 Jeff Barns CO
☐ 4 Scott Sowell TR
☐ 5 Edgar Alfonzo
☐ 6 Matt Beaumont
☐ 7 Ty Boykin
☐ 8 Ralph Bryant
☐ 9 Jamie Burke
☐ 10 Carlos Castillo
☐ 11 Jon DeClue
☐ 12 Jason Dickson
☐ 13 Dave Doorneweerd
☐ 14 Derrin Doty
☐ 15 Geoff Edsell
☐ 16 Mike Freehill
☐ 17 Aaron Guiel
☐ 18 Pep Harris
☐ 19 Mike Holtz
☐ 20 Korey Keling
☐ 21 Keith Luuloa
☐ 22 Tony Moeder
☐ 23 Ben Molina
☐ 24 Jose Monzon
☐ 25 Basilio Ortiz
☐ 26 Tracy Sanders
☐ 27 Kyle Sebach
☐ 28 Greg Shockey
☐ 29 Checklist

1996 Midland Angels One Hour Photo

This 23-card set of the 1996 Midland Angels, a Class AA Texas League affiliate of the California Angels, was sponsored by the Leukemia Society of America and features color player photos. The set measures approximately 5 1/2" by 5". The backs are blank. The cards are unnumbered and checklisted below in alphabetical order. 500 sets were produced.

	MINT	NRMT	EXC
COMPLETE SET (23)	70.00	32.00	8.75

☐ 1 Edgar Alfonzo
☐ 2 Jeff Barns
☐ 3 Matt Beaumont
☐ 4 Rob Bonanno
☐ 5 Ty Boykin
☐ 6 Willard Brown
☐ 7 Ralph Bryant
☐ 8 Eddie Christian
☐ 9 Jon DeClue
☐ 10 Geoff Edsell
☐ 11 Mike Freehill
☐ 12 Leon Glenn
☐ 13 Aaron Guiel
☐ 14 Mike Holtz
☐ 15 Korey Keling
☐ 16 Keith Luuloa
☐ 17 Mario Mendoza
☐ 18 Jeff McNeely
☐ 19 Ben Molina
☐ 20 Jose Monzon
☐ 21 Basilio Ortiz
☐ 22 Kernan Ronan
☐ 23 Greg Shockey

1996 Modesto A's Best

This 30-card set of the 1996 Modesto A's team was produced by Best Cards, Inc. and sponsored by Krier's Cards and Comics. The fronts feature black-and-white player portraits in a white border. The backs carry player information and career statistics. This Issue includes the minor league card debut of Miquel Tejada and a third year card of Ben Grieve. 1,000 sets were produced.

	MINT	NRMT	EXC
COMPLETE SET (30)	20.00	9.00	2.50

☐ 1 Miguel Tejada
☐ 2 Fred Soriano
☐ 3 Dan Ardoin
☐ 4 Ben Grieve
☐ 5 Juan Dilone
☐ 6 Carl Dale
☐ 7 D.T. Cromer
☐ 8 Rob DeBoer
☐ 9 Chris Cochrane
☐ 10 Jason Rajotte
☐ 11 Matt Walsh
☐ 12 Steve Karsay
☐ 13 Dave Zancanaro
☐ 14 Curtis Shaw
☐ 15 Brendan Hause
☐ 16 Emil Brown
☐ 17 Dave Newhan
☐ 18 Jeff D'Amico
☐ 19 Ryan Whitaker
☐ 20 Dave Madsen
☐ 21 Chris Michalak
☐ 22 Bill King
☐ 23 Mike Neill
☐ 24 Steve Connelly
☐ 25 Rick Rodriguez CO
☐ 26 Juan Perez
☐ 27 Jim Colborn MG
☐ 28 Jeffrey Leonard CO
☐ 29 Rich Ramirez TR
☐ 30 Kevin McClatchy PRES

1996 Nashville Sounds Best

This 30-card set of the 1996 Nashville Sounds, a Class AAA American Association affiliate of the Chicago White Sox, was produced by Best Cards, Inc. and features color player photos in a white border. The backs carry player information and career statistics.

	MINT	NRMT	EXC
COMPLETE SET (30)	8.00	3.60	1.00

☐ 1 Rick Renick MG
☐ 2 Don Cooper CO
☐ 3 Roger LaFrancois CO
☐ 4 Greg Latta TR
☐ 5 Jeff Abbott
☐ 6 Luis Andujar
☐ 7 James Baldwin
☐ 8 Mike Bertotti
☐ 9 Doug Brady
☐ 10 Carmine Cappuccio
☐ 11 Jeff Darwin
☐ 12 Glenn DiSarcina
☐ 13 Robert Ellis
☐ 14 Steve Gajkowski
☐ 15 Alan Levine
☐ 16 Mark Merchant
☐ 17 Fernando Ramsey
☐ 18 Mike Robertson
☐ 19 Scott Ruffcorn
☐ 20 Olmedo Saenz
☐ 21 Rich Sauveur
☐ 22 Steve Schrenk
☐ 23 Mike Sirotka
☐ 24 Bobby Thigpen
☐ 25 Chris Tremie
☐ 26 Kerry Valrie
☐ 27 Julio Vinas
☐ 28 Craig Wilson
☐ 29 Champ(Mascot)
☐ 30 Checklist

1996 New Haven Raven Uncut Sheet Team Issue

This nine-card set of the 1996 New Haven Ravens, a Class AA Eastern League affiliate of the Colorado Rockies, was issued in one perforated sheet measuring approximately 8 1/2" by 11 1/2" and sponsored by the Herlin Press. The fronts feature color player portraits, while the backs display player information and career statistics. The ninth card was a raffle card that could be sent into the team with a dollar donation to be eligible for a drawing for prizes. This issue includes a second year card of Todd Helton.

	MINT	NRMT	EXC
COMPLETE UNCUT SHEET (9)	12.00	5.50	1.50

☐ 12 Edgar Velazquez
Sic, Valazquez
☐ 13 Roger Miller
☐ 16 Chris Sexton
☐ 19 Rodney Pedraza
☐ 21 Jamey Wright
☐ 22 Todd Helton
☐ 23 John Thomson
☐ 34 Derrick Gibson
☐ NNO Donation Card

1996 New Haven Ravens Best

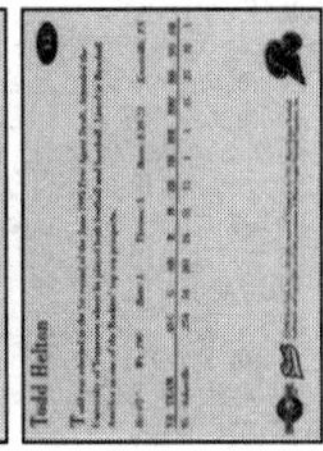

This 30-card set of the 1996 New Haven Ravens, a Class AA Eastern League affiliate of the Colorado Rockies, was produced by Best Cards, Inc. and features color player photos in a white border. The backs carry player information and career statistics. This issue includes a second year card of Todd Helton.

	MINT	NRMT	EXC
COMPLETE SET (31)	18.00	8.00	2.20

☐ 1 Bill Hayes MG
☐ 2 Greg Gross CO
☐ 3 Jack Lamabe CO
☐ 4 Marc Gustafson TR
☐ 5 Robbie Beckett
☐ 6 Mark Brownson
☐ 7 Brent Crowther
☐ 8 Mike DeJean
☐ 9 Bill Eden
☐ 10 Derrick Gibson
☐ 11 Jason Goligoski
☐ 12 Keith Grunewald
☐ 13 Todd Helton
☐ 14 Mike Higgins
☐ 15 Link Jarrett
☐ 16 Michael Kusiewicz
☐ 17 Roger Miller
☐ 18 John Myrow

☐ 19 Chris Neier
☐ 20 Rodney Pedraza
☐ 21 Mike Saipe
☐ 22 Chris Sexton
☐ 23 Jamie Taylor
☐ 24 John Thomson
☐ 25 Edgar Velazquez
☐ 26 Jacob Viano
☐ 27 Forry Wells
☐ 28 Jamey Wright
☐ 29 Mike Zolecki
☐ 30 Charlie Dowd MG
☐ 31 Ian Bethune MG

1996 New Jersey Cardinals Best

This 30-card set of the 1996 New Jersey Cardinals, a Class A New York-Penn League affiliate of the St. Louis Cardinals, was produced by Best Cards, Inc. and features color player photos in a white border. The backs carry player information and career statistics.

	MINT	NRMT	EXC
COMPLETE SET (30)	8.00	3.60	1.00

☐ 1 Scott Melvin MG
☐ 2 Darrell Betts
☐ 3 Bryan Britt
☐ 4 Ken Cameron
☐ 5 Bryan Clark
☐ 6 Kevin Crafton
☐ 7 Lou Deman
☐ 8 Tony Falciglia
☐ 9 Keith Finnerty
☐ 10 Joe Freitas
☐ 11 Keith Gallagher
☐ 12 Andrew Gordon
☐ 13 Greg Hefferman
☐ 14 Ruben Jimenez
☐ 15 Brad Kennedy
☐ 16 Stacy Kleiner
☐ 17 Jeff Love
☐ 18 Brian Mazurek
☐ 19 Mike McDougal
☐ 20 Mark Nussbeck
☐ 21 Jason Pollock
☐ 22 Jay Reames
☐ 23 Jorge Roque
☐ 24 Dave Schmidt
☐ 25 Andy Schofield
☐ 26 Gene Stechschulte
☐ 27 Hector Ugueto
☐ 28 Jon Ward
☐ 29 Adam West
☐ 30 Paul Wilders

1996 Norfolk Tides Best

This 30-card set of the 1996 Norfolk Tides, a Class AAA International League affiliate of the New York Mets, was produced by Best Cards, Inc. and features color player photos in a white border. The backs carry player information and career statistics.

	MINT	NRMT	EXC
COMPLETE SET (30)	12.00	5.50	1.50

☐ 1 Bobby Valentine MG
☐ 2 Bob Apodaca CO
☐ 3 Bruce Benedict CO
☐ 4 Joe Hawkins TR
☐ 5 Juan Acevedo
☐ 6 Benny Agbayani
☐ 7 Joe Ausanio
☐ 8 Brian Bark
☐ 9 Jason Bullard
☐ 10 Alberto Castillo
☐ 11 Joe Crawford
☐ 12 Kevin Flora
☐ 13 Matt Franco
☐ 14 Mike Fyhrie
☐ 15 Mike Gardiner
☐ 16 Shawn Gilbert
☐ 17 Jason Hardtke
☐ 18 Chris Howard
☐ 19 Mark Lee
☐ 20 Pedro Martinez
☐ 21 Alex Ochoa
☐ 22 Jay Payton
☐ 23 Robert Person
☐ 24 Roberto Petagine
☐ 25 Rick Reed
☐ 26 Luis Rivera
☐ 27 Gary Thurman
☐ 28 Andy Tomberlin
☐ 29 Rick Trlicek
☐ 30 Derek Wallace

1996 Norwich Navigators Best

This 28-card set of the 1996 Norwich Navigators, a Class AA Eastern League affiliate of the New York Yankees, was produced by Best Cards, Inc. and features color player photos in a white border. The backs carry player information and career statistics.

	MINT	NRMT	EXC
COMPLETE SET (28)	8.00	3.60	1.00

☐ 1 Jim Essian MG
☐ 2 Gary Denbo CO
☐ 3 Rich Tomlin CO
☐ 4 Greg Spratt TR
☐ 5 Mike Buddie
☐ 6 Joe DeBerry
☐ 7 Dan Donato
☐ 8 Matt Dunbar
☐ 9 Mike Figga
☐ 10 Grant Fithian
☐ 11 Carlton Fleming
☐ 12 Mike Jerzembeck
☐ 13 Eric Knowles
☐ 14 Mike Kotarski
☐ 15 Frank Lankford
☐ 16 Ricky Ledee
☐ 17 Rafael Medina
☐ 18 Kinnis Pledger
☐ 19 Ray Ricken
☐ 20 Kevin Riggs
☐ 21 Danny Rios
☐ 22 Tim Rumer
☐ 23 Tate Seefried
☐ 24 Sloan Smith
☐ 25 Shane Spencer
☐ 26 John Sutherland
☐ 27 Brien Taylor
☐ 28 Jaime Torres

1996 Ogden Raptors Team Issue

This 39-card set of the 1996 Ogden Raptors, a Rookie Class Pioneer League affiliate of the Milwaukee Brewers, was sponsored by Warrens Restaurant and features color action player photos in a gray border. The backs carry player information and sponsor logo. The cards are checklisted below according to the player's jersey number.

	MINT	NRMT	EXC
COMPLETE SET (39)	12.00	5.50	1.50

☐ 2 Adam Faurot
☐ 3 Gabe Ishee
☐ 4 Kevin Barker
☐ 5 Tom Houk CO
☐ 6 Jeff Alfano
☐ 7 Kelly Phair
☐ 8 David Martinez
☐ 9 Ross Parmenter
☐ 20 David Glick
☐ 22 Gabby Mercado
☐ 23 John Boker
☐ 24 Bernie Moncallo MG
☐ 25 Miguel Rodriguez
☐ 26 Jason Glover
☐ 27 Jerry Parent
☐ 28 Brad Richardson
☐ 29 Juan Zapata
☐ 30 Jesse Perez
☐ 32 Steve Cline CO
☐ 33 John Fulcher
☐ 34 Alfredo Gutierrez
☐ 35 Shawn Miller
☐ 36 Bobby Darula
☐ 37 Jay Arnold
☐ 38 Ramon Fernandez
☐ 39 Jon Macalutas
☐ 40 DeShawn Warren
☐ 42 Chris Walther
☐ 43 Larry Barnes
☐ 44 Donnie Moore
☐ 45 Jim Podjan
☐ 46 John O'Reilly
☐ 47 Paul Stewart
☐ 48 Pete Jenkins
☐ 49 Richard Ledeit
☐ 50 Al Hawkins
☐ NNO Jed Cowan ANN
☐ NNO Keith Sayers TR
☐ NNO Warrens Restaurant

1996 Oklahoma City 89ers Best

This 28-card set of the 1996 Oklahoma City 89ers, a Class AAA American Association affiliate of the Texas Rangers, was produced by Best Cards, Inc. and features color player photos in a white border. The backs carry player information and career statistics.

	MINT	NRMT	EXC
COMPLETE SET (28)	8.00	3.60	1.00

☐ 1 Greg Biagini MG
☐ 2 Tom Brown CO
☐ 3 Greg Harrel TR
☐ 4 Jose Alberro
☐ 5 Johnny Cardenas
☐ 6 Chris Curtis
☐ 7 Steven Dreyer
☐ 8 Osmani Estrada
☐ 9 Bryan Eversgerd
☐ 10 Rikkert Faneyte
☐ 11 Rick Helling
☐ 12 Kerry Lacy
☐ 13 Derek Lee
☐ 14 Luis Ortiz
☐ 15 Erik Pappas
☐ 16 Danny Patterson
☐ 17 Mo Sanford
☐ 18 Julio Santana
☐ 19 Jon Shave
☐ 20 Alex Smith
☐ 21 Lee Stevens
☐ 22 Brian Thomas
☐ 23 Jack Voigt
☐ 24 Matt Whiteside
☐ 25 Vince,
Crash Test Dummy
☐ 26 Larry
Crash Test Dummy
☐ 27 Trooper Charlie Hanger
☐ 28 Title Card

1996 Omaha Royals Best

This 30-card set of the 1996 Omaha Royals, a Class AAA American Association affiliate of the Kansas City Royals, was produced by Best Cards, Inc. and features color player photos in a white border. The backs carry player information and career statistics.

	MINT	NRMT	EXC
COMPLETE SET (30)	15.00	6.75	1.85

☐ 1 Mike Jirschele MG
☐ 2 Sixto Lezcano CO
☐ 3 Mike Alvarez CO
☐ 4 Mark Farnsworth TR
☐ 5 Casey(Mascot)
☐ 6 Joe Adams, President
☐ 7 Bill Gorman GM
☐ 8 Jaime Bluma
☐ 9 Melvin Bunch
☐ 10 Darren Burton
☐ 11 Lino Diaz
☐ 12 Jeff Granger
☐ 13 Jeff Grotewold
☐ 14 Rick Huisman
☐ 15 Doug Linton
☐ 16 Felix Martinez
☐ 17 Ramon Martinez
☐ 18 Rusty Meacham
☐ 19 Henry Mercedes
☐ 20 Jose Mota
☐ 21 Jon Nunnally
☐ 22 Craig Paquette
☐ 23 Kris Ralston
☐ 24 Rich Rodriguez
☐ 25 Jose Rosado
☐ 26 Glendon Rusch
☐ 27 Chris Stynes
☐ 28 Robert Toth
☐ 29 Scooter Tucker
☐ 30 Kevin Young

1996 Orlando Cubs Best

This 30-card set of the 1996 Orlando Cubs, a Class AA Southern League affiliate of the Chicago Cubs, was produced by Best Cards, Inc. and features color player photos in a white border. The backs carry player information and career statistics.

	MINT	NRMT	EXC
COMPLETE SET (30)	10.00	4.50	1.25

☐ 1 Bruce Kimm MG
☐ 2 Marty DeMerritt CO
☐ 3 Barry Moss CO
☐ 4 Steve Melendez TR
☐ 5 Joe Ciccarella
☐ 6 Matt Connolly
☐ 7 Dee Dowler
☐ 8 Gabe Duross
☐ 9 Jeremi Gonzalez
☐ 10 Jason Hart
☐ 11 Vee Hightower
☐ 12 Troy Hughes
☐ 13 David Hutcheson
☐ 14 Mark Kingston
☐ 15 Ed Larregui
☐ 16 Jason Maxwell
☐ 17 Bobby Morris
☐ 18 Kevin Orie
☐ 19 Hector Ortiz
☐ 20 Richard Perez
☐ 21 Chris Petersen
☐ 22 Steve Rain
☐ 23 Jason Ryan
☐ 24 Scott Samuels
☐ 25 Brian Stephenson
☐ 26 Greg Twiggs
☐ 27 Wade Walker
☐ 28 Dax Winslett
☐ 29 Spike(Mascot)
☐ 30 Checklist

1996 Pawtucket Red Sox Dunkin' Donuts

This 30-card set of the Pawtucket Red Sox, a Class AAA International League affiliate of the Boston Red Sox, was issued in one large sheet featuring six perforated five-card strips with a large team photo in the wide top strip. Sponsored by Channel 10 and Dunkin' Donuts, the fronts carry color player photos while the backs display player career statistics. The cards are unnumbered and checklisted below in alphabetical order.

	MINT	NRMT	EXC
COMPLETE SET (30)	50.00	22.00	6.25

☐ 1 Buddy Bailey MG
☐ 2 Phil Clark
☐ 3 Alex Cole
☐ 4 Brent Cookson
☐ 5 John Cumberland CO
☐ 6 John DeSilva
☐ 7 Bo Dodson
☐ 8 John Doherty
☐ 9 Gar Finnvold
☐ 10 Ken Grundt
☐ 11 Scott Hatteberg
☐ 12 Dwayne Hosey
☐ 13 Joe Hudson
☐ 14 Gavin Jackson
☐ 15 Brent Knackert
☐ 16 T.R. Lewis
☐ 17 Brian Looney
☐ 18 Nate Minchey
☐ 19 Ric Moreno TR
☐ 20 Rafael Orellano
☐ 21 Rudy Pemberton
☐ 22 Rico Petrocelli CO
☐ 23 Pork Chop Pough
☐ 24 Chuck Ricci
☐ 25 Tony Rodriguez
☐ 26 Erik Schullstrom
☐ 27 Bill Selby
☐ 28 Jeff Suppan
☐ 29 Alan Zinter
☐ 30 Team Photo

1996 Peoria Chiefs Best

This 30-card set of the 1996 Peoria Chiefs, a Class A Midwest League affiliate of the St. Louis Cardinals, was produced by Best Cards, Inc. and features color player photos in a white border. The backs carry player information and career statistics.

	MINT	NRMT	EXC
COMPLETE SET (30)	18.00	8.00	2.20

☐ 1 Roy Silver MG
☐ 2 Ray Searage CO
☐ 3 Bert Boyd TR
☐ 4 Armando Almanza
☐ 5 Greg Almond
☐ 6 Corey Avrard
☐ 7 Adam Benes
☐ 8 Nate Dishington
☐ 9 Robert Donnelly
☐ 10 Kevin Foderaro
☐ 11 Ossie Garcia
☐ 12 Keith Glauber
☐ 13 Chris Haas
☐ 14 Andy Hall
☐ 15 Miguel Inzunza
☐ 16 Jose Jimenez
☐ 17 Nick Kast
☐ 18 Jason Lariviere
☐ 19 Travis McClendon
☐ 20 Shawn McNally
☐ 21 Bret Mueller
☐ 22 Juan Munoz
☐ 23 Isaias Nunez
☐ 24 Cliff Politte
☐ 25 Britt Reames
☐ 26 Miguel Rivera
☐ 27 Kerry Robinson
☐ 28 Mark Roettgen
☐ 29 Travis Welch
☐ 30 Jason Woolf

1996 Phoenix Firebirds Best

This 30-card set of the 1996 Phoenix Firebirds, a Class AAA Pacific Coast League affiliate of the San Francisco Giants, was produced by Best Cards, Inc. and features color player photos in a white border. The backs carry player information and career statistics.

	MINT	NRMT	EXC
COMPLETE SET (30)	10.00	4.50	1.25

☐ 1 1996 Phoenix Firebirds
☐ 2 Ron Wotus MG
☐ 3 Joel Horlen CO
☐ 4 Joe Lefebvre CO
☐ 5 Bill Carpine
☐ 6 Rich Aurilia
☐ 7 Shawn Barton
☐ 8 Jose Bautista
☐ 9 Marvin Benard

☐ 10 Jamie Brewington
☐ 11 Jay Canizaro
☐ 12 Dan Carlson
☐ 13 Andy Carter
☐ 14 Jacob Cruz
☐ 15 Kurt Ehmann
☐ 16 Shawn Estes
☐ 17 Julian Heredia
☐ 18 Marcus Jensen
☐ 19 Dax Jones
☐ 20 Steve Mintz
☐ 21 Bill Mueller
☐ 22 Dan Peltier
☐ 23 Ricky Pickett
☐ 24 Steve Soderstrom
☐ 25 Carlos Valdez
☐ 26 Doug Vanderweele
☐ 27 Keith Williams
☐ 28 Desi Wilson
☐ 29 Phineas T. Firebird(Mascot)
☐ 30 Checklist

1996 Piedmont Boll Weevils Best

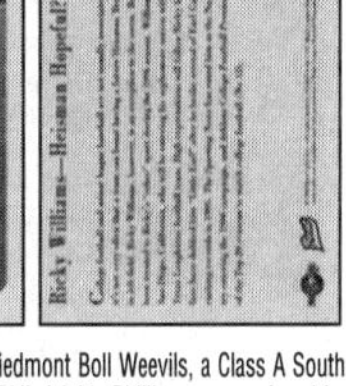

This 30-card set of the 1996 Piedmont Boll Weevils, a Class A South Atlantic League affiliate of the Philadelphia Phillies, was produced by Best Cards, Inc. and features color player photos in a white border. The backs carry player information and career statistics. This issue includes two cards of Texas Longhorns' runningback Ricky Williams; including a posed Heisman shot.

	MINT	NRMT	EXC
COMPLETE SET (30)	30.00	13.50	3.70

☐ 1 Roy Majtyka MGR
☐ 2 John Martin CO
☐ 3 Troy Hoffert TR
☐ 4 Joe Barbao
☐ 5 Rob Burger
☐ 6 Todd Coburn
☐ 7 David Coggin
☐ 8 Jon Cornelius
☐ 9 Chuck Cox
☐ 10 Todd Crane
☐ 11 Zach Elliott
☐ 12 Brian Ford
☐ 13 Jared Janke
☐ 14 Jason Kershner
☐ 15 Tyson Kimm
☐ 16 Randy Knoll
☐ 17 Jaime Mendes
☐ 18 Rick O'Connor
☐ 19 Torrey Pettiford
☐ 20 Kirk Pierce
☐ 21 Shane Pullen
☐ 22 Mark Raynor
☐ 23 David Robinson
☐ 24 Eric Schreimann
☐ 25 Anthony Shumaker
☐ 26 Jason Sikes
☐ 27 Reggie Taylor
☐ 28 Ricky Williams
☐ 29 Gary Yeager Jr.
☐ 30 Ricky Williams (Heisman)

1996 Pittsfield Mets Best

This 30-card set of the 1996 Pittsfield Mets, a Class A New York-Penn League affiliate of the New York Mets, was produced by Best Cards, Inc. and features color player photos in a white border. The backs carry player information and career statistics. This issue includes the minor league card debut of Corey Erickson.

	MINT	NRMT	EXC
COMPLETE SET (30)	12.00	5.50	1.50

☐ 1 Doug Davis MG
☐ 2 Buzz Capra CO
☐ 3 Juan Lopez CO
☐ 4 Gary Borges TR
☐ 5 Hans Beebe
☐ 6 Ryan Bennett
☐ 7 Corey Brittan
☐ 8 Todd Cutchins
☐ 9 Corey Erickson
☐ 10 Matt Ferulio
☐ 11 Garrick Haltiwanger
☐ 12 B.J. Huff
☐ 13 Kyle Kessel
☐ 14 Roger Martinez
☐ 15 Ryan Morrison
☐ 16 Brandon Naples
☐ 17 Jeff Parsons
☐ 18 Casey Patterson
☐ 19 Melvin Poupart
☐ 20 Kirk Presley
☐ 21 Ken Pumphrey
☐ 22 Danny Ramirez
☐ 23 Sammy Rodriguez
☐ 24 Jim Rosenbohm
☐ 25 Matt Splawn
☐ 26 John Tamargo Jr.
☐ 27 Randy Vickers
☐ 28 Brandon Villafuerte
☐ 29 P.J. Yoder
☐ 30 Bruce Nolte

1996 Port City Roosters Best

This 29-card set of the 1996 Port City Roosters, a Class AA Southern League affiliate of the Seattle Mariners, was produced by Best Cards, Inc. and features color player photos in a white border. The backs carry player information and career statistics.

	MINT	NRMT	EXC
COMPLETE SET (29)	8.00	3.60	1.00

☐ 1 Orlando Gomez MG
☐ 2 Henry Cotto CO
☐ 3 Bryan Price CO
☐ 4 Paul Harker TR
☐ 5 Matt Apana
☐ 6 Mike Barger
☐ 7 Jason Brosnan
☐ 8 Johnny Cardenas
☐ 9 Dean Crow
☐ 10 Ryan Franklin
☐ 11 Jason Friedman
☐ 12 Charles Gipson Jr.
☐ 13 Craig Griffey
☐ 14 Giomar Guevara
☐ 15 Craig Hanson
☐ 16 Michael Hickey
☐ 17 Randy Jorgensen
☐ 18 Rick Ladjevich
☐ 19 Derek Lowe
☐ 20 Trey Moore
☐ 21 Geronimo Newton
☐ 22 Manish Patel
☐ 23 Roberto Ramirez
☐ 24 LaGrande Russell
☐ 25 Ryan Smith
☐ 26 Makato Suzuki
☐ 27 Jason Varitek
☐ 28 Bob Worley
☐ 29 Rowdy the Rooser(Mascot)

1996 Portland Rockies Best

This 30-card set of the 1996 Portland Rockies, a Class A Northwest League affiliate of the Colorado Rockies, was produced by Best Cards, Inc. and features color player photos in a white border. The backs carry player information and career statistics.

	MINT	NRMT	EXC
COMPLETE SET (30)	10.00	4.50	1.25

☐ 1 Ron Gideon MG
☐ 2 Al Bleser CO
☐ 3 Pete Filson CO
☐ 4 Blake Anderson
☐ 5 Brian Anthony
☐ 6 Rogelio Arias
☐ 7 Rod Bair
☐ 8 Dean Brueggeman
☐ 9 Marc Brzozoski
☐ 10 Angel Cespedes
☐ 11 Tim Christman
☐ 12 John Clark
☐ 13 Jason Ford
☐ 14 John Hallead
☐ 15 Mark Hamlin
☐ 16 Bernard Hutchison
☐ 17 Brian Keck
☐ 18 David Lee
☐ 19 John Lindsey
☐ 20 Doug Livingston
☐ 21 John Mahlberg
☐ 22 Dean Marnell
☐ 23 Steven Matcuk
☐ 24 Aaron Myers
☐ 25 Jason Romine
☐ 26 Donnie Schmidt
☐ 27 Scott Schroeffel
☐ 28 Jeff Sebring
☐ 29 Tom Stepka
☐ 30 Gilbert Vidal

1996 Portland Sea Dogs Best

This 29-card set of the 1996 Portland Sea Dogs, a Class AA Eastern League affiliate of the Florida Marlins, was produced by Best Cards, Inc. and features color player photos in a white border. The backs carry player information and career statistics.

	MINT	NRMT	EXC
COMPLETE SET (29)	40.00	18.00	5.00

☐ 1 Carlos Tosca MG
☐ 2 Britt Burns CO
☐ 3 Ken Joyce CO
☐ 4 Timothy Abraham TR
☐ 5 Slugger(Mascot)
☐ 6 Jeff Alkire
☐ 7 Robbie Beckett
☐ 8 Dave Berg
☐ 9 Ron Brown
☐ 10 Luis Castillo
☐ 11 Chris Clapinski
☐ 12 Will Cunnane
☐ 13 Todd Dunwoody
☐ 14 Lionel Hastings
☐ 15 Felix Heredia
☐ 16 Bill Hurst
☐ 17 Rey Mendoza
☐ 18 Kevin Millar
☐ 19 Greg Mix
☐ 20 Clemente Nunez
☐ 21 Doug O'Neill
☐ 22 Mike Redmond
☐ 23 John Roskos
☐ 24 Tony Saunders
☐ 25 Chris Sheff
☐ 26 Paul Thornton
☐ 27 Tony Torres
☐ 28 Bryan Ward
☐ 29 Pookie Wilson

1996 Prince William Cannons Best

This 30-card set of the 1996 Prince William Cannons, a Class A Carolina League affiliate of the Chicago White Sox, was produced by Best Cards, Inc. and features color player photos in a white border. The backs carry player information and career statistics.

	MINT	NRMT	EXC
COMPLETE SET (30)	10.00	4.50	1.25

☐ 1 Dave Huppert MG
☐ 2 Jaime Garcia CO
☐ 3 Mark Haley CO
☐ 4 Mark Avery
☐ 5 Ben Boulware
☐ 6 Curtis Broome
☐ 7 Chris Clemons
☐ 8 Erik Desrosiers
☐ 9 Jim Dixon
☐ 10 Jason Evans
☐ 11 Jack Ford
☐ 12 Dan Fraraccio
☐ 13 Allen Halley
☐ 14 Darren Hayes
☐ 15 Russell Herbert
☐ 16 Dan Kopriva
☐ 17 Andres Levias
☐ 18 Sandy McKinnon
☐ 19 Brandon Moore
☐ 20 Mike Place
☐ 21 Alex Portillo
☐ 22 John Quirk
☐ 23 Nilson Robledo
☐ 24 Chuck Smith
☐ 25 John Strasser
☐ 26 Robert Theodile
☐ 27 Juan Thomas
☐ 28 Joe Walker
☐ 29 Jerry Whitaker
☐ 30 Rick Carone

1996 Quad City River Bandits Best

This 29-card set of the 1996 Quad City River Bandits, a Class A Midwest League affiliate of the Houston Astros, was produced by Best Cards, Inc. and features color player photos in a white border. The backs carry player information and career statistics.

	MINT	NRMT	EXC
COMPLETE SET (29)	10.00	4.50	1.25

☐ 1 Jim Pankovits MG
☐ 2 Joe Pittman CO
☐ 3 Don Alexander CO
☐ 4 Nathan Lucero TR
☐ 5 The Crew
☐ 6 Jason Adams
☐ 7 Chad Alexander
☐ 8 Alberto Blanco
☐ 9 Andy Bovender
☐ 10 R.J. Bowers
☐ 11 Ramon Castro
☐ 12 Arnie Chavera
☐ 13 Ryan Coe
☐ 14 Freddy Garcia
☐ 15 Mike Gunderson
☐ 16 Carlos Hernandez
☐ 17 Ric Johnson
☐ 18 Niuman Loiz
☐ 19 Julio Lugo
☐ 20 Jim Lynch
☐ 21 Paul O'Malley
☐ 22 Hassan Robinson
☐ 23 Marlon Roche
☐ 24 Derek Root
☐ 25 Sean Runyan
☐ 26 Brian Sikorski
☐ 27 Eric Smith
☐ 28 Chris Truby
☐ 29 Mike Walter

1996 Rancho Cucamonga Quakes Best

This 30-card set of the 1996 Rancho Cucamonga Quakes, a Class A California League affiliate of the San Diego Padres, was produced by Best Cards, Inc. and features color player photos in a white border. The backs carry player information and career statistics. This issue includes the minor league card debut of Juan Melo.

	MINT	NRMT	EXC
COMPLETE SET (30)	10.00	4.50	1.25

☐ 1 Title Card
☐ 2 Mike Basso MG
☐ 3 Dan Norman CO
☐ 4 Saul Soltero CO
☐ 5 Jim Daniel TR
☐ 6 Jim Baron
☐ 7 Darryl Brinkley
☐ 8 Randy Curtis
☐ 9 Keith Davis
☐ 10 Ben Davis
☐ 11 Shane Dennis
☐ 12 Todd Erdos
☐ 13 Antonio Fernandez
☐ 14 Sean Fesh
☐ 15 Rick Gama
☐ 16 Cade Gaspar
☐ 17 Andy Hammerschmidt
☐ 18 Chris Logan
☐ 19 Gary Matthews
☐ 20 Leroy McKinnis Jr.
☐ 21 Juan Melo
☐ 22 Chris Prieto
☐ 23 John Roberts
☐ 24 James Sak
☐ 25 Matt Schwenke
☐ 26 Ryan Van De Weg
☐ 27 Brett Walters
☐ 28 Sean Watkins
☐ 29 Darell White
☐ 30 1996 Rancho Cucamonga Quakes

1996 Reading Phillies Best

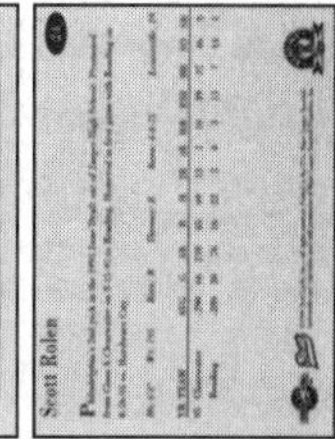

This 29-card set of the 1996 Reading Phillies, a Class AA Eastern League affiliate of the Philadelphia Phillies, was produced by Best Cards, Inc. and features color player photos in a white border. The backs carry player information and career statistics. This issue includes a third year card of Scott Rolen.

	MINT	NRMT	EXC
COMPLETE SET (29)	20.00	9.00	2.50

☐ 1 Matt Beech
☐ 2 Tony Costa
☐ 3 Robert Dodd
☐ 4 Mark Foster
☐ 5 Wayne Gomes
☐ 6 Bronson Heflin
☐ 7 Gary Herrmann
☐ 8 Carlton Loewer
☐ 9 Larry Mitchell
☐ 10 Ryan Nye
☐ 11 Rafael Quirico
☐ 12 Keith Troutman
☐ 13 Bobby Estalella
☐ 14 Jeff Gyselman
☐ 15 Doug Angeli
☐ 16 Essex "Gas" Burton
☐ 17 David Fisher
☐ 18 Matt Guiliano
☐ 19 Dan Held
☐ 20 Jason Moler
☐ 21 Scott Rolen
☐ 22 Jeremey Kendall
☐ 23 Wendell Magee Jr.
☐ 24 Chad McConnell
☐ 25 Scott Shores
☐ 26 Bill Robinson MGR
☐ 27 Larry Andersen CO
☐ 28 Kelly Heath CO
☐ 29 Brent Leiby TR

1996 Richmond Braves Best

This 30-card set of the 1996 Richmond Braves, a Class AAA International League affiliate of the Atlanta Braves, was produced by Best Cards, Inc. and features color player photos in a white border. The backs carry player information and career statistics.

	MINT	NRMT	EXC
COMPLETE SET (30)	10.00	4.50	1.25

☐ 1 Bill Dancy MG
☐ 2 Bill Fischer CO
☐ 3 Glenn Hubbard CO
☐ 4 Jim Lovell TR
☐ 5 Joe Ayrault
☐ 6 Lou Benbow
☐ 7 Joe Borowski
☐ 8 Chris Brock
☐ 9 Darron Cox
☐ 10 Jermaine Dye
☐ 11 Chad Fox
☐ 12 Omar Garcia
☐ 13 Ed Giovanola
☐ 14 Tony Graffanino
☐ 15 Tom Harrison
☐ 16 Damon Hollins
☐ 17 Mike Hostetler
☐ 18 Kevin Lomon
☐ 19 Marty Malloy
☐ 20 Pablo Martinez
☐ 21 Bobby Moore
☐ 22 Rod Nichols
☐ 23 Aldo Pecorilli
☐ 24 Jason Schmidt
☐ 25 Carl Schutz
☐ 26 Robert Smith
☐ 27 Rodney Steph
☐ 28 Tom Thobe
☐ 29 Juan Williams
☐ 30 Brad Woodall

1996 Richmond Braves Update Best

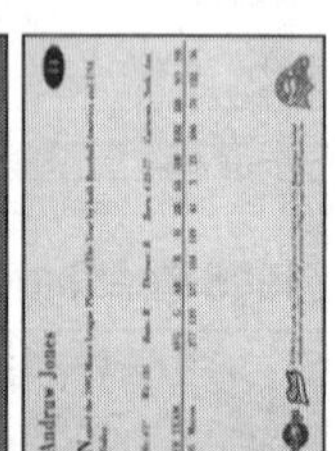

This 30-card set of the 1996 Richmond Braves team features color player photos in red borders. The backs carry player information and career statistics. This issue includes a second year card of Andruw Jones. Card #1 of Andruw Jones is numbered out of 1,000.

	MINT	NRMT	EXC
COMPLETE SET (30)	50.00	22.00	6.25

☐ 1 Andruw Jones/1000
☐ 2 Joe Ayrault
☐ 3 Lou Benbow
☐ 4 Joe Borowski
☐ 5 Chris Brock
☐ 6 John Detmer
☐ 7 Jermaine Dye
☐ 8 Ed Giovanola
☐ 9 Tony Graffanino
☐ 10 Kevin Grijak
☐ 11 Dean Hartgraves
☐ 12 Damon Hollins
☐ 13 Mike Hostetler
☐ 14 Andruw Jones
☐ 15 Andruw Jones
☐ 16 Mark Lee
☐ 17 Kevin Loman
☐ 18 Pablo Martinez
☐ 19 Matt Murray
☐ 20 Rod Nichols
☐ 21 Aldo Pecorilli
☐ 22 Steve Pegues
☐ 23 Raul Rodarte
☐ 24 Jason Schmidt
☐ 25 Carl Schutz
☐ 26 Robert Smith
☐ 27 Pedro Swann
☐ 28 Tom Thobe
☐ 29 Juan Williams
☐ 30 Brad Woodall

1996 Richmond Braves Richmond Camera

This 26-card team set of the 1996 Richmond Braves, a Class AAA International League affiliate of the Atlanta Braves, was sponsored by Richmond Camera and Benjamin Moore Paints and measures approximately 4" by 4 7/8". The fronts feature borderless color player photos with sponsors' and team's logos in the wide bottom margin. This issue includes a second year card of Andruw Jones. The backs are blank. 500 sets were produced.

	MINT	NRMT	EXC
COMPLETE SET (26)	125.00	55.00	15.50

☐ 1 Kevin Lomon
☐ 2 Aldo Pecorilli
☐ 3 Darrell May
☐ 4 Tony Graffanino
☐ 5 Bobby Moore
☐ 6 Chris Brock
☐ 6 Carl Schutz
☐ 7 Chad Fox
☐ 8 Robert Smith
☐ 9 Jermaine Dye
☐ 10 Omar Garcia
☐ 11 Mike Hostetler
☐ 12 Ed Giovanola
☐ 13 Damon Hollins
☐ 14 Joe Ayrault
☐ 15 Juan Williams
☐ 16 Rod Nichols
☐ 17 Tom Thobe
☐ 18 Pablo Martinez
☐ 20 Raul Rodarte
☐ 21 Darron Cox
☐ 22 Steve Pegues
☐ 23 Andruw Jones
☐ 24 Bill Dancy MG
☐ 25 Lou Benbow
☐ NNO Pedro Swann

1996 Rochester Red Wings Best

This 30-card set of the 1996 Rochester Red Wings, a Class AAA International League affiliate of the Baltimore Orioles, was produced by Best Cards, Inc. and features color player photos in a white border. The backs carry player information and career statistics.

	MINT	NRMT	EXC
COMPLETE SET (30)	10.00	4.50	1.25

☐ 1 Silver Stadium
☐ 2 Marv Foley MG
☐ 3 Ross Grimsley CO
☐ 4 Butch Davis CO
☐ 5 Clay Bellinger
☐ 6 Greg Blosser
☐ 8 Rocky Coppinger
☐ 9 Archie Corbin
☐ 10 Jim Dedrick
☐ 11 Cesar Devarez
☐ 12 Steve Dixon
☐ 13 Tom Edens
☐ 14 Don Florence
☐ 15 Joe Hall
☐ 16 Doug Harris
☐ 17 Aaron Lane
☐ 18 Scott McClain
☐ 19 Oscar Munoz
☐ 20 Jimmy Myers
☐ 21 Billy Owens
☐ 23 Brian Sackinsky
☐ 24 Keith Shepherd
☐ 25 Mark Smith
☐ 26 Garrett Stephenson
☐ 27 Brad Tyler
☐ 28 B.J. Waszgis
☐ 29 Jim Wawruck
☐ 30 Eddie Zosky

1996 Rockford Cubs Team Issue

This 32-card set of the 1996 Rockford Cubs, a Class A Midwest League affiliate of the Chicago Cubs, was sponsored by AM radio station WROK 1440 and TV station WREX channel 13. The fronts feature color player photos with a red side and a blue bottom border. The backs carry player information and sponsor logos. The cards are unnumbered and checklisted below in alphabetical order.

	MINT	NRMT	EXC
COMPLETE SET (32)	15.00	6.75	1.85

☐ 1 Kelvin Barnes
☐ 2 Sean Bogle
☐ 3 Chris Brynt
☐ 4 Casey the Cub(Mascot)
☐ 5 David Catlett
☐ 6 Jairo Diaz
☐ 7 Alan Dunn CO
☐ 8 Kyle Farnsworth
☐ 9 Brandon Hammack
☐ 10 Matthew Hammons
☐ 11 Michael Holmes MG
☐ 12 Elinton Jasco
☐ 13 David Jefferson
☐ 14 Terry Joseph
☐ 15 Greg Keuter TR
☐ 16 Jeremy Lewis
☐ 17 Orlando Lopez
☐ 18 Gary Marshall
☐ 19 Ashanti McDonald
☐ 20 Jose Molina
☐ 21 Tim Mosley
☐ 22 Jose Nieves
☐ 23 Richard Perez
☐ 24 Jayson Peterson
☐ 25 John Pierson CO
☐ 26 Bo Porter
☐ 27 Chad Ricketts
☐ 28 Steve Roadcap MG
☐ 29 Ryan Seidel
☐ 30 Scott Vieira
☐ 31 Ismael Villegas
☐ 32 Jeff Yoder

1996 Salem Avalanche Best

This 30-card set of the 1996 Salem Avalanche, a Class A Carolina League affiliate of the Colorado Rockies, was produced by Best Cards, Inc. and features color player photos in a white border. The backs carry player information and career statistics.

	MINT	NRMT	EXC
COMPLETE SET (30)	10.00	4.50	1.25

☐ 1 Doug Million
☐ 2 Keith Barnes
☐ 3 Blake Barthol
☐ 4 Steven Bernhardt
☐ 5 Luis Colmenares
☐ 6 Brent Crowther
☐ 7 Brian Culp
☐ 8 John Fantauzzi
☐ 9 Chad Gambill
☐ 10 Todd Genke
☐ 11 John Giudice
☐ 12 Luther Hackman
☐ 13 Ronnie Hall
☐ 14 Mike Higgins
☐ 15 Nate Holdren
☐ 16 Kyle Houser
☐ 17 Pookie Jones
☐ 18 Scott LaRock
☐ 19 Chan Mayber
☐ 20 Patrick McClinton
☐ 21 Elvis Pena
☐ 22 Matt Pool
☐ 23 John Burke
☐ 24 Stephen Shoemaker
☐ 25 Michael Vavrek
☐ 26 Bill McGuire MG
☐ 27 Billy Champion CO
☐ 28 Joe Marchese CO
☐ 29 Bill Borowski TR
☐ NNO Checklist

1996 San Antonio Missions Best

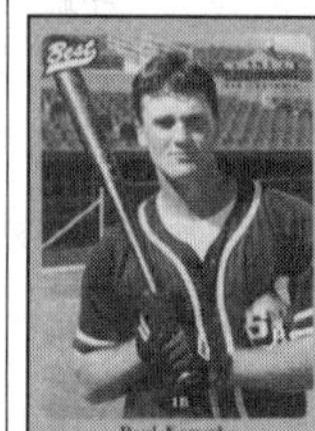

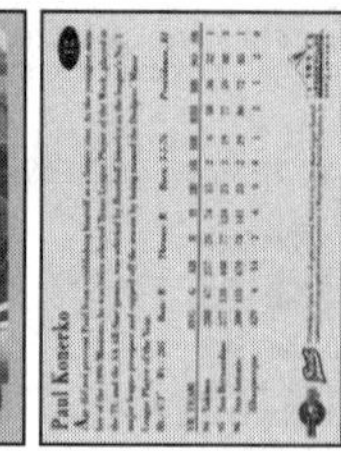

This 30-card set of the 1996 San Antonio Missions, a Class AA Texas League affiliate of the Los Angeles Dodgers, was produced by Best Cards, Inc. and features color player photos with a yellow border. The backs carry player information and career statistics. This issue includes a third year card of Paul Konerko.

	MINT	NRMT	EXC
COMPLETE SET (30)	12.00	5.50	1.50

☐ 1 Henry Blanco
☐ 2 Will Brunson
☐ 3 Ramser Correa
☐ 4 Brad Dandridge
☐ 5 Karim Garcia
☐ 6 Ryan Henderson
☐ 7 Matt Herges
☐ 8 Ron Hollis
☐ 9 Joe Jacobsen
☐ 10 Keith Johnson
☐ 11 Jay Kirkpatrick
☐ 12 Paul Konerko
☐ 13 Jesus Martinez
☐ 14 Ramon Martinez
☐ 15 Dan Melendez
☐ 16 Michael Moore
☐ 17 David Pyc
☐ 18 Adam Riggs
☐ 19 Eduardo Rios
☐ 20 Petie Roach
☐ 21 J.P. Roberge
☐ 22 Willie Romero
☐ 23 Vernon Spearman
☐ 24 Brandon Watts
☐ 25 Eric Weaver
☐ 26 Bruce Yard
☐ 27 Mike Collins TR
☐ 28 Dino Ebel CO
☐ 29 Claude Osteen CO
☐ 30 John Shelby MGR

1996 San Bernardino Stampede Best

This 30-card set of the 1996 San Bernardino Stampede, a Class A California League affiliate of the Los Angeles Dodgers, was produced by Best Cards, Inc. and features color player photos in a white border. The backs carry player information and career statistics.

	MINT	NRMT	EXC
COMPLETE SET (30)	8.00	3.60	1.00

☐ 1 Del Crandall MG
☐ 2 Charlie Hough CO
☐ 3 Alan Lewis CO
☐ 4 San Bernardino Stadium
☐ 5 Cliff Anderson
☐ 6 Mike Carpentier
☐ 7 Kyle Cooney
☐ 8 Eddie Davis
☐ 9 Kris Foster
☐ 10 Manny Gonzalez
☐ 11 Rafael Gross
☐ 12 Jake Kenady
☐ 13 Jeff Keppen
☐ 14 Tito Landrum
☐ 15 Ty Lewis
☐ 16 Rich Linares
☐ 17 Matt McCarty
☐ 18 Claudio Moreno
☐ 19 Eddie Oropesa
☐ 20 Jeff Paluk
☐ 21 Dennis Reyes
☐ 22 Scott Richardson
☐ 23 Mike Sanchez
☐ 24 Chip Sell
☐ 25 Ken Sikes
☐ 26 David Steed
☐ 27 Chad Townsend
☐ 28 Dan Urbina
☐ 29 Ervan Wingate
☐ 30 The Bug (Mascot)

1996 San Jose Giants Best

This 30-card set of the 1996 San Jose Giants, a Class A California League affiliate of the San Francisco Giants, was produced by Best Cards, Inc. and features color player photos in a white border. The backs carry player information and career statistics.

	MINT	NRMT	EXC
COMPLETE SET (30)	10.00	4.50	1.25

☐ 1 Jesus Ibarra
☐ 2 Jose Alguacil
☐ 3 Jon Sbrocco
☐ 4 Wilson Delgado
☐ 5 Edwards Guzman
☐ 6 Todd Wilson
☐ 7 Rey Corujo
☐ 8 Tim Garland
☐ 9 Derek Reid
☐ 10 Bobby Bonds Jr.
☐ 11 Craig Mayes
☐ 12 Joel Galarza
☐ 13 Russell Ortiz
☐ 14 Jeff Martin
☐ 15 Dennys Gomez
☐ 16 Joe Fontenot
☐ 17 Darin Blood
☐ 18 Aaron Fultz
☐ 19 Chad Hartvigson
☐ 20 Jason Myers
☐ 21 Mike Villano
☐ 22 Phillip Bailey
☐ 23 Carl Schramm
☐ 24 Ben Tucker
☐ 25 Bobby Rector
☐ 26 Darrin Glenn
☐ 27 Carlos Lezcano MG
☐ 28 Sonny Jackson CO
☐ 29 Dave Schuler CO
☐ 30 Ben Potenziano TR

1996 Sarasota Red Sox Best

This 30-card set of the 1996 Sarasota Red Sox, a Class A Florida State League affiliate of the Boston Red Sox, was produced by Best Cards, Inc. and features color player photos in a white border. The backs carry player information and career statistics.

	MINT	NRMT	EXC
COMPLETE SET (30)	10.00	4.50	1.25

☐ 1 DeMarlo Hale MG
☐ 2 Jeff Gray CO
☐ 3 Victor Rodriguez CO
☐ 4 Tom Lichtenberger TR
☐ 5 Andy Abad

☐ 6 Joe Barksdale
☐ 7 Matt Bazzani
☐ 8 Richard Betti
☐ 9 John Bowles
☐ 10 Junior Braddy
☐ 11 Michael Coleman
☐ 12 Joe DePastino
☐ 13 Tony DeRosso
☐ 14 Ethan Faggett
☐ 15 Aaron Fuller
☐ 16 David Gibralter
☐ 17 Rich Graham
☐ 18 Chad Hale
☐ 19 Lyle Hartgrove
☐ 20 Doug Hecker
☐ 21 Gavin Jackson
☐ 22 Cesar Martinez
☐ 23 Ethan Merrill
☐ 24 Peter Munro
☐ 25 Greg Patton
☐ 26 Dean Peterson
☐ 27 Tony Rodriguez
☐ 28 Nathan Tebbs
☐ 29 Larry Wimberly
☐ 30 Socko (Mascot)

1996 Savannah Sandgnats Best

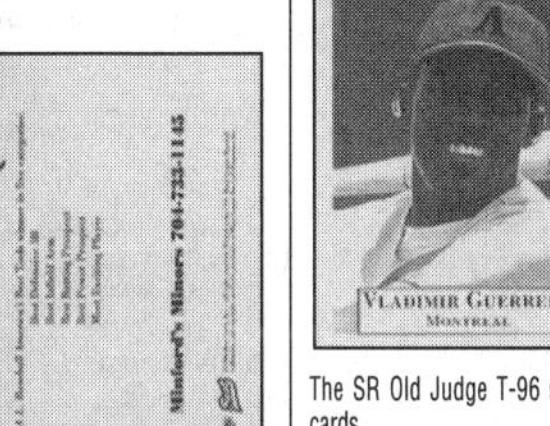

This 30-card set features color player photos of the 1996 Savannah Sandgnats team. The backs carry player information and career statistics. Card #30 in each set is individually numbered out of 750. This issue includes the minor league card debut of Adrian Beltre.

	MINT	NRMT	EXC
COMPLETE SET (30)	30.00	13.50	3.70

☐ 1 Checklist
John Shoemaker MG#(Ed Correa CO#(Travis Barbary CO
☐ 2 Adrian Beltre
☐ 3 Marc Charbonneau
☐ 4 Manuel Gonzalez
☐ 5 Brian Harmon
☐ 6 Lance Backowski
☐ 7 Luke Prokopee
☐ 8 Greg Morrison
☐ 9 Eric Stuckenschneider
☐ 10 Geronimo Gil
☐ 11 David Spykstra
☐ 12 Eric Gagne
☐ 13 Dan Ricabal
☐ 14 Chris Ochsenfeld
☐ 15 John Davis
☐ 16 Jackson Torres
☐ 17 Gwynne (J.J.) Pearsall
☐ 18 Onan Masaoka
☐ 19 Juan Hernaiz
☐ 20 Jeff Keppen
☐ 21 Juan Sosa
☐ 22 Toni Nakashima
☐ 23 Carl South
☐ 24 Jose Pimentel
☐ 25 Jose Mateo
☐ 26 Mike Judd
☐ 27 Matt McDonald
☐ 28 Rafael Ozuna
☐ 29 Eric Stuckenschneider
Juan Hernaiz#(Jose Pimentel
☐ 30 Adrian Beltre

1996 Scranton/Wilkes-Barre Red Barons Best

This 30-card set of the 1996 Scranton/Wilkes-Barre Red Barons, a Class AAA International League affiliate of the Philadelphia Phillies, was produced by Best Cards, Inc. and features color player photos in a white border. The backs carry player information and career statistics.

	MINT	NRMT	EXC
COMPLETE SET (30)	10.00	4.50	1.25

☐ 1 Butch Hobson MGR
☐ 2 Jim Wright CO
☐ 3 Greg Legg CO
☐ 4 Craig Strobel TR
☐ 5 Howard Battle
☐ 6 Gary Bennett
☐ 7 Ron Blazier
☐ 8 Duff Brumley
☐ 9 Rob Butler
☐ 10 Carlos Crawford
☐ 11 Blake Doolan
☐ 12 David Doster
☐ 13 Donnie Elliott
☐ 14 David Fisher
☐ 15 Matt Grott
☐ 16 Craig Holman
☐ 17 Ricardo Jordan
☐ 18 Ryan Karp
☐ 19 Anthony Manahan
☐ 20 Glenn Murray
☐ 21 Matt Murray
☐ 22 Ricky Otero
☐ 23 Gene Schall
☐ 24 Kevin Sefcik
☐ 25 David Tokheim
☐ 26 Scott Wiegandt
☐ 27 Rick Wrona
☐ 28 Jon Zuber
☐ 29 Bob Zupcic
☐ 30 The Grump (Mascot)

1996 Signature Rookies Old Judge

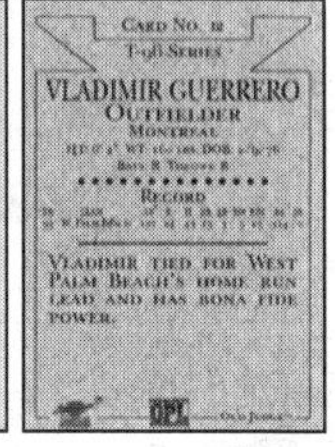

The SR Old Judge T-96 set was issued in one series totalling 38 cards.

	MINT	NRMT	EXC
COMPLETE SET (38)	7.00	3.10	.85
COMMON CARD (1-38)	.10	.05	.01
☐ 1 Tommy Adams	.10	.05	.01
☐ 2 Travis Baptist	.10	.05	.01
☐ 3 Mike Birkbeck	.10	.05	.01
☐ 4 Jim Bowie	.10	.05	.01
☐ 5 Duff Brumley	.10	.05	.01
☐ 6 Scott Bullett	.10	.05	.01
☐ 7 Frank Catalanotto	.50	.23	.06
☐ 8 Chris Cumberland	.10	.05	.01
☐ 9 Travis Driskill	.10	.05	.01
☐ 10 John Frascatore	.10	.05	.01
☐ 11 Brian Giles	.15	.07	.02
☐ 12 Vladimir Guerrero	4.00	1.80	.50
☐ 13 Butch Huskey	.25	.11	.03
☐ 14 Greg Keagle	.10	.05	.01
☐ 15 Jay Kirkpatrick	.10	.05	.01
☐ 16 Ed Larregui	.10	.05	.01
☐ 17 Mitch Lyden	.10	.05	.01
☐ 18 T.J. Mathews	.10	.05	.01
☐ 19 Brian Maxcy	.10	.05	.01
☐ 20 Jeff McNeely	.10	.05	.01
☐ 21 Tony Mitchell	.10	.05	.01
☐ 22 Kerwin Moore	.10	.05	.01
☐ 23 Oscar Munoz	.10	.05	.01
☐ 24 Les Norman	.10	.05	.01
☐ 25 Jayhawk Owens	.10	.05	.01
☐ 26 Mark Petkovsek	.10	.05	.01
☐ 27 Hugo Pivaral	.30	.14	.04
☐ 28 Chad Renfroe	.10	.05	.01
☐ 29 Victor Rodriguez	.15	.07	.02
☐ 30 Matt Rundels	.10	.05	.01
☐ 31 Willie Smith	.10	.05	.01
☐ 32 Amaury Telemaco	.30	.14	.04
☐ 33 Robert Toth	.10	.05	.01
☐ 34 Ben Van Ryn	.10	.05	.01
☐ 35 Wes Weger	.10	.05	.01
☐ 36 Don Wengert	.10	.05	.01
☐ 37 Kelly Wunsch	.10	.05	.01
☐ NNO Checklist	.10	.05	.01

1996 Signature Rookies Old Judge Signatures

Each card is numbered out of 6000. Vladimir Guerrero and Victor Rodriguez did not sign/return their cards.

	MINT	NRMT	EXC
COMPLETE SET (35)	100.00	45.00	12.50
COMMON CARD (1-35)	2.00	.90	.25
☐ 1 Tommy Adams	2.00	.90	.25
☐ 2 Travis Baptist	2.00	.90	.25
☐ 3 Mike Birkbeck	2.00	.90	.25
☐ 4 Jim Bowie	2.00	.90	.25
☐ 5 Duff Brumley	2.00	.90	.25
☐ 6 Scott Bullett	2.00	.90	.25
☐ 7 Frank Catalanotto	10.00	4.50	1.25
☐ 8 Chris Cumberland	2.00	.90	.25
☐ 9 Travis Driskill	2.00	.90	.25
☐ 10 John Frascatore	2.00	.90	.25
☐ 11 Brian Giles	3.00	1.35	.35
☐ 13 Butch Huskey	10.00	4.50	1.25
☐ 14 Greg Keagle	2.00	.90	.25
☐ 15 Jay Kirkpatrick	2.00	.90	.25
☐ 16 Ed Larregui	2.00	.90	.25
☐ 17 Mitch Lyden	2.00	.90	.25
☐ 18 T.J. Mathews	2.00	.90	.25
☐ 19 Brian Maxcy	2.00	.90	.25
☐ 20 Jeff McNeely	2.00	.90	.25
☐ 21 Tony Mitchell	2.00	.90	.25
☐ 22 Kerwin Moore	2.00	.90	.25
☐ 23 Oscar Munoz	2.00	.90	.25
☐ 24 Les Norman	2.00	.90	.25
☐ 25 Jayhawk Owens	2.00	.90	.25
☐ 26 Mark Petkovsek	2.00	.90	.25
☐ 27 Hugo Pivaral	7.00	3.10	.85
☐ 28 Chad Renfroe	2.00	.90	.25
☐ 30 Matt Rundels	2.00	.90	.25
☐ 31 Willie Smith	2.00	.90	.25
☐ 32 Amaury Telemaco	7.00	3.10	.85
☐ 33 Robert Toth	2.00	.90	.25
☐ 34 Ben Van Ryn	2.00	.90	.25
☐ 35 Wes Weger	2.00	.90	.25
☐ 36 Don Wengert	2.00	.90	.25
☐ 37 Kelly Wunsch	2.00	.90	.25

1996 Signature Rookies Old Judge Marty Cordova

	MINT	NRMT	EXC
COMPLETE SET (5)	3.00	1.35	.35
COMMON CARD (RY1-RY5)	.60	.25	.07
☐ RY1 Marty Cordova	.60	.25	.07
☐ RY2 Marty Cordova	.60	.25	.07
☐ RY3 Marty Cordova	.60	.25	.07
☐ RY4 Marty Cordova	.60	.25	.07
☐ RY5 Marty Cordova	.60	.25	.07

1996 Signature Rookies Old Judge Ken Griffey Jr.

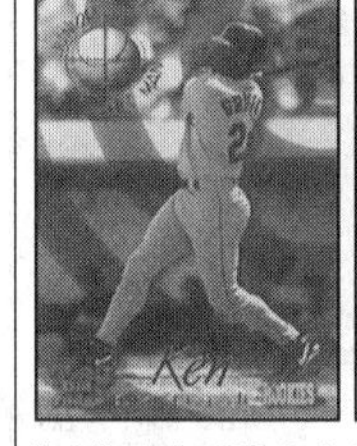
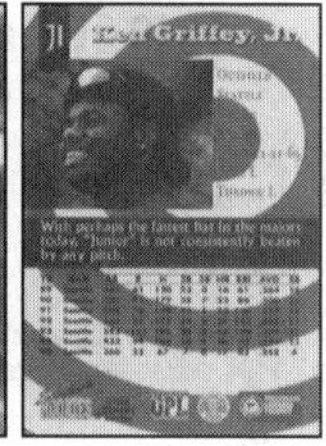

Ken Griffey Jr. signed 250 of each of the cards.

	MINT	NRMT	EXC
COMPLETE SET (5)	10.00	4.50	1.25
COMMON CARD (J1-J5)	2.00	.90	.25
*SIGNATURES: 90X to 150X BASIC CARDS			
☐ J1 Ken Griffey, Jr.	2.00	.90	.25
☐ J2 Ken Griffey, Jr.	2.00	.90	.25
☐ J3 Ken Griffey, Jr.	2.00	.90	.25
☐ J4 Ken Griffey, Jr.	2.00	.90	.25
☐ J5 Ken Griffey, Jr.	2.00	.90	.25

1996 Signature Rookies Old Judge Major Respect

	MINT	NRMT	EXC
COMPLETE SET (5)	8.00	3.60	1.00
COMMON CARD (M1-M5)	.75	.35	.09
☐ M1 Alex Rodriguez	5.00	2.20	.60
☐ M2 Johnny Damon	1.25	.55	.16
☐ M3 Karim Garcia	4.00	1.80	.50
☐ M4 Garret Anderson	.75	.35	.09
☐ M5 Bill Pulsipher	.75	.35	.09

1996 Signature Rookies Old Judge Peak Picks

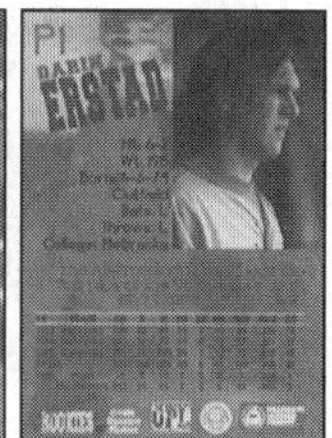

	MINT	NRMT	EXC
COMPLETE SET (10)	25.00	11.00	3.10
COMMON CARD (P1-P10)	.75	.35	.09
*SIGNATURES: 10X BASIC CARDS			
☐ P1 Darin Erstad	10.00	4.50	1.25
☐ P2 Jose Cruz, Jr.	10.00	4.50	1.25
☐ P3 Jonathan Johnson	1.00	.45	.12
☐ P4 Todd Helton	6.00	2.70	.75
☐ P5 Matt Morris	1.25	.55	.16
☐ P6 Tony McKnight	.75	.35	.09
☐ P7 Reggie Taylor	1.50	.70	.19
☐ P8 David Yocum	.75	.35	.09
☐ P9 Shea Morenz	1.00	.45	.12
☐ P10 Ben Davis	2.50	1.10	.30

1996 Signature Rookies Old Judge Rising Stars

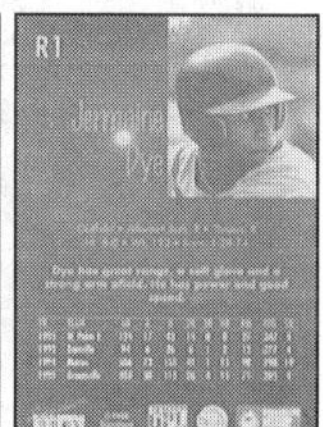

	MINT	NRMT	EXC
COMPLETE SET (5)	6.00	2.70	.75
COMMON CARD (R1-R5)	.50	.23	.06
*SIGNATURES: 10X BASIC CARDS			
☐ R1 Jermaine Dye	4.00	1.80	.50
☐ R2 Ben Grieve	3.00	1.35	.35
☐ R3 Ryan Helms	.50	.23	.06
☐ R4 Jeff Darwin	.50	.23	.06
☐ R5 Alan Benes	1.00	.45	.12

1996 Signature Rookies Old Judge Top Prospect

	MINT	NRMT	EXC
COMPLETE SET (10)	6.00	2.70	.75
COMMON CARD (T1-T10)	.50	.23	.06
☐ T1 Juan Acevedo	.50	.23	.06
☐ T2 Mike Bovee	.50	.23	.06
☐ T3 Mark Hubbard	.50	.23	.06
☐ T4 Luis Raven	.50	.23	.06
☐ T5 Desi Relaford	.75	.35	.09
☐ T6 Antone Williamson	1.25	.55	.16
☐ T7 Nick Delvecchio	.50	.23	.06
☐ T8 Andy Larkin	.75	.35	.09
☐ T9 Kris Ralston	.50	.23	.06
☐ T10 Jeff Suppan	2.00	.90	.25

1996 South Bend Silver Hawks Best

This 28-card set of the 1996 South Bend Silver Hawks, a Class A Midwest League affiliate of the Chicago White Sox, was produced by Best Cards, Inc. and features color player photos in a white border. The backs carry player information and career statistics. This issue includes the minor league card debuts of Jeff Liefer and Mario Valdez.

	MINT	NRMT	EXC
COMPLETE SET (28)	12.00	5.50	1.50

☐ 1 Dave Keller MG
☐ 2 Curt Hasler CO
☐ 3 Greg Barber TR
☐ 4 Franklin Anderson
☐ 5 Kevin Beirne
☐ 6 Brian Bowness
☐ 7 Shane Buteaux
☐ 8 David Cancel
☐ 9 Carlos Castillo
☐ 10 Brian Drent

☐ 11 Sean Duncan
☐ 12 Steve Friedrich
☐ 13 Joel Garber
☐ 14 Ariel Garcia
☐ 15 Derek Hasselhoff
☐ 16 Jeffrey Johnson
☐ 17 Mark Johnson
☐ 18 Tim Kraus
☐ 19 Kelly Kruse
☐ 20 Jeff Liefer
☐ 21 Jason Olsen
☐ 22 Jason Secoda
☐ 23 Greg Shepard
☐ 24 Brian Simmons
☐ 25 Ryan Topham
☐ 26 Mario Valdez
☐ 27 Mike Vota
☐ 28 Brent Wilhelm

1996 Southern Oregon Timberjacks Team Issue

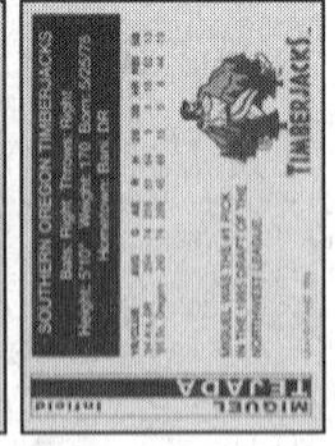

This 28-card set of the 1996 Southern Oregon Timberjacks, a Class A Northwest League affiliate of the Oakland Athletics, was produced by Grandstand Cards and sponsored by various area companies. The fronts feature color player photos with white frames and a two-sided fading green inner border. The backs carry player notes with a sponsor name at the bottom. This issue includes the minor league card debut of Miguel Tejada.

	MINT	NRMT	EXC
COMPLETE SET (28)	50.00	22.00	6.25

☐ 1 Miguel Tejada
☐ 2 Tim Jones
☐ 3 Todd Mensik
☐ 4 Troy Rauer
☐ 5 Cody McKay
☐ 6 Juan Polanco
☐ 7 Rico Lagattuta
☐ 8 MacGregor Byers
☐ 9 Doug Robertson
☐ 10 T.R. Marcinczyk
☐ 11 Ray Noriega
☐ 12 Brad Blumenstock
☐ 13 Flint Wallace
☐ 14 Randy Glaze
☐ 15 Ryan Kjos
☐ 16 T.J. Costello
☐ 17 Alex Rondon
☐ 18 Pete DellaRatta
☐ 19 Elton Gogolin
☐ 20 Brett Laxton
☐ 21 Justin Bowles
☐ 22 Terrance Freeman
☐ 23 Jake O'Dell
☐ 24 Jose Paulino
☐ 25 Jace Johnson
☐ 26 Dionys Cesar
☐ 27 Willy Hilton
☐ 28 Joe Espada

1996 Spokane Indians Best

This 30-card set of the 1996 Spokane Indians, a Class A Northwest League affiliate of the Kansas City Royals, was produced by Best Cards, Inc. and features color player photos in a white border. The backs carry player information and career statistics. This issue includes the minor league card debut of Carlos Beltran.

	MINT	NRMT	EXC
COMPLETE SET (30)	12.00	5.50	1.50

☐ 1 Bob Herold
☐ 2 Rick "Buster" Keeton CO
Jeff Garber CO
☐ 3 Alonso Aguilar
☐ 4 Courtney Arrollado
☐ 5 Carlos Beltran
☐ 6 Brandon Berger
☐ 7 Jaime Burton
☐ 8 Enrique Calero
☐ 9 Jake Chapman
☐ 10 Kristopher Didion
☐ 11 Roman Escamilla
☐ 12 Jeremy Giambi
☐ 13 Scott Harp
☐ 14 Steve Hueston
☐ 15 Jason Layne
☐ 16 Aaron Lineweaver
☐ 17 Tony Miranda
☐ 18 Kenderick Moore
☐ 19 Scott Mullen
☐ 20 Kit Pellow
☐ 21 Rick Pitts
☐ 22 Donald Quigley
☐ 23 Juan Robles
☐ 24 Allen Sanders
☐ 25 Eric Sees
☐ 26 Jason Simontacchi
☐ 27 Ethan Stein
☐ 28 Brett Taft
☐ 29 Modesto Villarreal
☐ 30 Otto the Spokaneasaurus (Mascot)

1996 St. Catharines Stompers Best

This 30-card set of the 1996 St. Catherines Stompers, a Class A New York-Penn League affiliate of the Toronto Blue Jays, was produced by Best Cards, Inc. and features color player photos in a white border. The backs carry player information and career statistics. This issue includes the minor league card debut of Abraham Nunez.

	MINT	NRMT	EXC
COMPLETE SET (30)	15.00	6.75	1.85

☐ 1 Rocket Wheeler MG
☐ 2 Neil Allen CO
☐ 3 Mike Frostad TR
☐ 4 John Bale
☐ 5 Josh Bradford
☐ 6 Steve Charles
☐ 7 Joe Davenport
☐ 8 Blaine Fortin
☐ 9 Derek Gaskill
☐ 10 Beiker Graterol
☐ 11 Robbie Hampton
☐ 12 Alejandro Hueda
☐ 13 Damon Johnson
☐ 14 Jason Koehler
☐ 15 Yan LaChapelle
☐ 16 Clint Lawrence
☐ 17 Luis Lopez
☐ 18 Jim Mann
☐ 19 Chris McBride
☐ 20 Ryan Meyers
☐ 21 Chad Needle
☐ 22 Abraham Nunez
☐ 23 Mike Rodriguez
☐ 24 Victor Rodriguez
☐ 25 Andy Shatley
☐ 26 Will Skett
☐ 27 Allen Snelling
☐ 28 Paxton Stewart
☐ 29 Mike Zavershnik
☐ 30 Team Card CL

1996 St. Lucie Mets Team Issue

This 34-card set of the St. Luice Mets, a Class A Florida State League affiliate of the New York Mets, was issued in six perforated strips with four strips containing six player cards and two strips containing five player cards and a sponsor ad card. The set was sponsored by Publix Super Markets. The player cards feature color player portraits on the fronts and player information and statistics on the backs. This issue includes the minor league card debut of Jose Lopez.

	MINT	NRMT	EXC
COMPLETE SET (34)	15.00	6.75	1.85

☐ 1 John Gibbons
☐ 2 Paul Gomez
☐ 3 Arnold Gooch
☐ 4 Dan Murray
☐ 5 Barry Short
☐ 6 Luis Arroyo
☐ 7 Rafael Guerrero
☐ 8 Sean Johnston
☐ 9 Phil Olson
☐ 10 Jeramie Simpson
☐ 11 Field Staff
☐ 12 Joe Atwater
☐ 13 John Kelly
☐ 14 Steve Pack
☐ 15 Ramon Tatis
☐ 16 Randy Warner
☐ 17 Craig Bullock
☐ 18 Scott Hunter
☐ 19 Jose Lopez
☐ 20 Jarrod Patterson
☐ 21 Tony Tijerina
☐ 22 Preston Wilson
☐ 23 Cesar Diaz
☐ 24 Angel Jaime
☐ 25 Ryan Miller
☐ 26 Jesus Sanchez
☐ 27 Brian Turner
☐ 28 Vance Wilson
☐ 29 Slider
☐ 30 Steve Arffa
☐ 31 Guillermo Mota
☐ 32 Scott Sauerbeck
☐ 33 Rich Turrentine
☐ 34 Julio Zorrilla

1996 St. Petersburg Cardinals Best

This 30-card set of the 1996 St. Petersburg Cardinals, a Class A Florida State League affiliate of the St. Louis Cardinals, was produced by Best Cards, Inc. and features color player photos in a white border. The backs carry player information and career statistics. This issue includes the minor league card debut of Luis Ordaz.

	MINT	NRMT	EXC
COMPLETE SET (30)	10.00	4.50	1.25

☐ 1 Chris Maloney MG
☐ 2 Rich Folkers CO
☐ 3 Matt Morris
☐ 4 Alan Benes
☐ 5 Steve Bierman
☐ 6 Efrain Contreras
☐ 7 Keith Conway
☐ 8 Frank Garcia
☐ 9 Matt Golden
☐ 10 Scarborough Green
☐ 11 Ryan Hall
☐ 12 Yates Hall
☐ 13 Rick Heiserman
☐ 14 Joe Jumonville
☐ 15 Marcus Logan
☐ 16 Jesus Lugo
☐ 17 Mike Matvey
☐ 18 Keith McDonald
☐ 19 Kevin McNeill
☐ 20 John Mendez
☐ 21 Francisco Morales
☐ 22 Luis Ordaz
☐ 23 Yudith Ozorio
☐ 24 Placido Polanco
☐ 25 Dan Pontes
☐ 26 Brian Reed
☐ 27 Chris Richard
☐ 28 Steve Santucci
☐ 29 Blake Stein
☐ 30 Mike Windham

1996 Stockton Ports Best

This 30-card set of the 1996 Stockton Ports, a Class A California League affiliate of the Milwaukee Brewers, was produced by Best Cards, Inc. and features color player photos in a white border. The backs carry player information and career statistics.

	MINT	NRMT	EXC
COMPLETE SET (30)	10.00	4.50	1.25

☐ 1 Dan Klassen
☐ 2 Steve Woodard
☐ 3 Toby Kominek
☐ 4 Mike Pasqualicchio
☐ 5 Greg Martinez
☐ 6 Scott Huntsman
☐ 7 Drew Williams
☐ 8 Tyrone Hill
☐ 9 Scott Krause
☐ 10 Luis Salazar
☐ 11 Jermaine Swinton
☐ 12 Greg Beck
☐ 13 Joe DeBerry
☐ 14 Travis Smith
☐ 15 Mike Rennhack
☐ 16 Scott Gardner
☐ 17 Alex Andreopoulos
☐ 18 Joe Wagner
☐ 19 John Morreale
☐ 20 Josh Tyler
☐ 21 Nelson Cana
☐ 22 Bill McGonigle
☐ 23 Chris Burt
☐ 24 Rob Campillo
☐ 25 Junior Betances
☐ 26 Brooks Drysdale
☐ 27 Greg Mahlberg
☐ 28 Randy St. Clair
☐ 29 Theron Todd
☐ 30 Richard Stark

1996 Syracuse Chiefs Team Issue

This 30-card set of the 1996 Syracuse Chiefs, a Class AAA International League affiliate of the Toronto Blue Jays, features color player photos on a facsimile stone background with a black border. The backs carry player information and career statistics. The cards are unnumbered and checklisted below in alphabetical order.

	MINT	NRMT	EXC
COMPLETE SET (30)	10.00	4.50	1.25

☐ 1 Sharnol Adriana
☐ 2 Travis Baptist
☐ 3 D.J. Boston
☐ 4 Derek Brandow
☐ 5 Tilson Brito
☐ 6 Scott Brow
☐ 7 Miguel Cairo
☐ 8 Giovanni Carrara
☐ 9 Wes Chamberlain
☐ 10 Felipe Crespo
☐ 11 Jim Czajkowski
☐ 12 Huck Flener
☐ 13 Richie Hebner MG
☐ 14 Vince Horsman
☐ 15 Michael Huff
☐ 16 Marty Janzen
☐ 17 Dane Johnson
☐ 18 Felix Jose
☐ 19 Brian Kowitz
☐ 20 Terry McGriff
☐ 21 Bill Monbouquette CO
☐ 22 Jose Pett
☐ 23 Scott Pose
☐ 24 John Ramos
☐ 25 Ken Robinson
☐ 26 Jimmy Rogers
☐ 27 Rich Rowland
☐ 28 Paul Spoljaric
☐ 29 Shannon Stewart
☐ 30 Hector Torres CO

1996 Tacoma Rainiers Best

This 30-card set of the 1996 Tacoma Rainers, a Class AAA Pacific Coast League affiliate of the Seattle Mariners, was produced by Best Cards, Inc. and features color player photos in a white border. The backs carry player information and career statistics.

	MINT	NRMT	EXC
COMPLETE SET (30)	8.00	3.60	1.00

☐ 1 Dave Myers MG
☐ 2 Terry Kennedy CO
☐ 3 Jeff Andrews CO
☐ 4 Randy Roetter TR
☐ 5 James Bonnici
☐ 6 Darren Bragg
☐ 7 Mike Butcher
☐ 8 Tim Davis
☐ 9 Scott Davison
☐ 10 Alex Diaz
☐ 11 Eddy Diaz
☐ 12 Lee Guetterman
☐ 13 Tim Harikkala
☐ 14 Brian Hunter
☐ 15 Raul Ibanez
☐ 16 Mike Knapp
☐ 17 Manny Martinez
☐ 18 Bob Milacki
☐ 19 Julio Peguero
☐ 20 Tony Phillips
☐ 21 Greg Pirkl
☐ 22 Arquimedez Pozo
☐ 23 Desi Relaford
☐ 24 Andy Sheets
☐ 25 Salomon Torres
☐ 26 Sal Urso
☐ 27 Matt Wagner
☐ 28 Chris Widger
☐ 29 Trey Witte
☐ 30 Rhubarb(Mascot)

1996 Tampa Yankees Best

This 29-card set of the 1996 Tampa Yankees, a Class A Florida State League affiliate of the New York Yankees, was produced by Best Cards, Inc. and features color player photos in a white border. The backs carry player information and career statistics.

	MINT	NRMT	EXC
COMPLETE SET (29)	12.00	5.50	1.50

☐ 1 Trey Hillman MG
☐ 2 Rich Arena CO
Dave Howard CO#(Mark Shiflett CO#(Carl Randolph CO
☐ 3 Christopher Ashby
☐ 4 Ryan Beeney
☐ 5 Charlie Brown
☐ 6 Vick Brown
☐ 7 Brian (Buck) Buchanan
☐ 8 Eric Camfield
☐ 9 Chris Corn
☐ 10 Abert Drumheller
☐ 11 Derek Dukart
☐ 12 Kraig Hawkins
☐ 13 Kevin Henthorne
☐ 14 Kurt Bierek
☐ 15 Jason Imrisek
☐ 16 Jose Lobaton
☐ 17 Brian McLamb
☐ 18 David Meyer
☐ 19 Casey Mittauer
☐ 20 Sandy Pichardo
☐ 21 Greg Resz
☐ 22 Brett Schlomann
☐ 23 Michael Spence
☐ 24 Stanley Stewart
☐ 25 Jay Tessmer
☐ 26 Jason Troilo
☐ 27 Luke Wilcox
☐ 28 Carlos Yedo
☐ 29 Checklist

1996 Texas League All-Stars Best

	MINT	NRMT	EXC
COMPLETE SET (36)	15.00	6.75	1.85

☐ 1 Manuel Barrios
Jackson Generals
☐ 2 Jeff Berblinger
Arkansas Travelers
☐ 3 Kevin Brown
Tulsa Drillers
☐ 4 Edwin Diaz
Tulsa Drillers
☐ 5 Tim Forkner
Jackson Generals
☐ 6 Keith Foulke
Shreveport Captains
☐ 7 Mike Grzanich
Jackson Generals
☐ 8 Richard Hidalgo
Jackson Generals
☐ 9 Jonathan Johnson
Tulsa Drillers
☐ 10 Russ Johnson
Jackson Generals
☐ 11 Mark Little
Tulsa Drillers
☐ 12 Eli Marrero
Arkansas Travelers
☐ 13 Dante Powell
Shreveport Captains
☐ 14 Brady Raggio
Arkansas Travelers
☐ 15 Doug Simons
Jackson Generals
☐ 16 Chris Singleton
Shreveport Captains
☐ 17 Bubba Smith
Tulsa Drillers
☐ 18 Andy Taulbee
Shreveport Captains
☐ 19 Matt Beaumont
Midland Angels
☐ 20 Ronnie Belliard
El Paso Diablos
☐ 21 Brian Bevil
Wichita Wranglers
☐ 22 Jeremy Carr
Wichita Wranglers
☐ 23 Mike Freehill
Midland Angels
☐ 24 Aaron Guiel
Midland Angels
☐ 25 Jonas Hamlin
El Paso Diablos
☐ 26 Jed Hansen
Wichita Wranglers
☐ 27 Paul Konerko
San Antonio Missions
☐ 28 Mendy Lopez
Wichita Wranglers
☐ 29 Keith Luuloa
Midland Angels
☐ 30 Sean Maloney
El Paso Diablos
☐ 31 Jesus Martinez
San Antonio Missions
☐ 32 Anthony Medrano
Wichita Wranglers
☐ 33 Ben Molina
Midland Angels
☐ 34 Bo Ortiz
Midland Angels
☐ 35 Greg Shockey
Midland Angels
☐ 36 Mike Sweeney
Wichita Wranglers

1996 Toledo Mud Hens Best

This 30-card set of the 1996 Toledo Mud Hens, a Class AAA International League affiliate of the Detroit Tigers, was produced by Best Cards, Inc. and features color player photos in a white border. The backs carry player information and career statistics.

	MINT	NRMT	EXC
COMPLETE SET (30)	8.00	3.60	1.00

☐ 1 Justin Thompson
☐ 2 Tom Runnells MG
☐ 3 Skeeter Barnes CO
☐ 4 Brian Allard CO
☐ 5 Kevin Baez
☐ 6 Ben Blomdahl
☐ 7 Raul Casanova
☐ 8 Tony Clark
☐ 9 John Cotton
☐ 10 Fausto Cruz
☐ 11 Micah Franklin
☐ 12 Mike Guilfoyle
☐ 13 Phil Hiatt
☐ 14 Tim Hyers
☐ 15 Brian Kowitz
☐ 16 Jose Lima
☐ 17 Randy Marshall
☐ 18 Brian Maxcy
☐ 19 Jeff McCurry
☐ 20 Trever Miller
☐ 21 C.J. Nitkowski
☐ 22 Shannon Penn
☐ 23 Curtis Pride
☐ 24 Steve Rodriguez
☐ 25 A.J. Sager
☐ 26 Duane Singleton
☐ 27 Clint Sodowsky
☐ 28 Jeff Tackett
☐ 29 Mike Walker
☐ 30 Eric Wedge

1996 Trenton Thunder Best

This 30-card set of the 1996 Trenton Thunder, a Class AA Eastern League affiliate of the Boston Red Sox, was produced by Best Cards, Inc. and features color player photos in a white border. The backs carry player information and career statistics.

	MINT	NRMT	EXC
COMPLETE SET (30)	15.00	6.75	1.85

☐ 1 Ken Macha MG
☐ 2 Harold(Gomer) Hodge CO
☐ 3 Ralph Treuel CO
☐ 4 Terry Smith TR
☐ 5 Brian Barkley
☐ 6 Rich Betti
☐ 7 Mike Blais
☐ 8 Brett Cederblad
☐ 9 John Doherty
☐ 10 Jared Fernandez
☐ 11 Ken Grundt
☐ 12 Carl Pavano
☐ 13 Brian Rose
☐ 14 Shawn Senior
☐ 15 Erik Schullstrom
☐ 16 Alex Delgado
☐ 17 Dana Levangie
☐ 18 Walt McKeel
☐ 19 Chris Allen
☐ 20 Randy Brown
☐ 21 Todd Carey
☐ 22 Lou Merloni
☐ 23 Dan Collier
☐ 24 Kevin Coughlin
☐ 25 Paul Rappoli
☐ 26 Rick Holifield
☐ 27 Adam Hyzdu
☐ 28 Trot Nixon
☐ 29 Donnie Sadler
☐ 30 Boomer(Mascot)

1996 Tucson Toros Best

This 29-card set of the 1996 Tucson Toros, a Class AAA Pacific Coast League affiliate of the Houston Astros, was produced by Best Cards, Inc. and features color player photos in a white border. The backs carry player information and career statistics.

	MINT	NRMT	EXC
COMPLETE SET (29)	10.00	4.50	1.25

☐ 1 Bob Abreu
☐ 2 Jeff Ball
☐ 3 Eric Bell
☐ 4 Kary Bridges
☐ 5 Mike Brumley
☐ 6 Jim Dougherty
☐ 7 Dave Evans
☐ 8 Kevin Gallaher
☐ 9 Jerry Goff
☐ 10 Dave Hajek
☐ 11 Dean Hartgraves
☐ 12 Chris Hatcher
☐ 13 Chris Holt
☐ 14 Frank Kellner
☐ 15 Roger Luce
☐ 16 Doug Mlicki
☐ 17 Ray Montgomery
☐ 18 Melvin Mora
☐ 19 Bronswell Patrick
☐ 20 Jay Davis
Eddie Pye
☐ 21 Ken Ramos
☐ 22 Mark Small
☐ 23 Jeff Tabaka
☐ 24 Billy Wagner
☐ 25 Donne Wall
☐ 26 Tim Tolman
☐ 27 Don Reynolds
☐ 28 Charley Taylor
☐ 29 Ron Porterfield TR

1996 Tulsa Drillers Team Issue

This 30-card set of the 1996 Tulsa Drillers, a Class AA Texas League affiliate of the Texas Rangers, was sponsored by radio station K95FM and the Oklahoma Highway Patrol. The fronts feature borderless color player photos. The backs carry player information and career statistics.

	MINT	NRMT	EXC
COMPLETE SET (30)	10.00	4.50	1.25

☐ 1 Ken Arnold
☐ 2 Mike Bell
☐ 3 Brian Blair
☐ 4 Kevin Brown
☐ 5 Juan Castillo
☐ 6 Frank Charles
☐ 7 Julio Cruz
☐ 8 Jeff Davis
☐ 9 Edwin Diaz
☐ 10 Hanley Frias
☐ 11 Dave Geeve
☐ 12 Hornsby(Mascot)
☐ 13 Jonathan Johnson
☐ 14 Bobby Jones MG
☐ 15 Mark Little
☐ 16 David Manning
☐ 17 Jerry Martin
☐ 18 Eric Moody
☐ 19 Joe Morway
☐ 20 John O'Donoghue
☐ 21 John Powell
☐ 22 Marc Sagmoen
☐ 23 Tracy Sanders
☐ 24 Bubba Smith
☐ 25 Scott Terry CO
☐ 26 Jose Texidor
☐ 27 Chris Uurat
☐ 28 Guido Van Ryssegem TR
☐ 29 Vince and Larry
Crash Dummies
☐ 30 Team Logo

1996 Vancouver Canadians Best

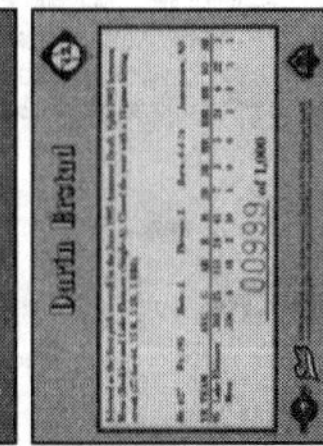

This 30-card set of the 1996 Vancouver Canadians, a Class AAA Pacific Coast League affiliate of the California Angels, was produced by Best Cards, Inc. and features color player photos in a blue border. The backs carry player information and career statistics. This issue includes a second year card of Darin Erstad. Each set is numbered out of 1,000.

	MINT	NRMT	EXC
COMPLETE SET (30)	20.00	9.00	2.50

☐ 1 Don Long MG
☐ 2 Frank Reberger CO
☐ 3 John Morris CO
☐ 4 Jim Abbott
☐ 5 George Arias
☐ 6 Jamie Burke
☐ 7 Vince Coleman
☐ 8 Alfredo Diaz
☐ 9 Jason Dickson
☐ 10 Geoff Edsell
☐ 11 Robert Ellis
☐ 12 Darin Erstad
☐ 13 P.J. Forbes
☐ 14 Brian Grebeck
☐ 15 Todd Greene
☐ 16 Ryan Hancock
☐ 17 Pep Harris
☐ 18 Pete Janicki
☐ 19 Aaron Ledesma
☐ 20 Orlando Palmeiro
☐ 21 Brad Pennington
☐ 22 Will Pennyfeather
☐ 23 Chris Pritchett
☐ 24 Joe Rosselli
☐ 25 Jeff Schmidt
☐ 26 Paul Swingle
☐ 27 Fausto Tejero
☐ 28 Chris Turner
☐ 29 Shad Williams
☐ 30 Michael Wolff

1996 Vermont Expos Best

This 30-card set of the 1996 Vermont Expos, a Class A New York-Penn League affiliate of the Montreal Expos, was produced by Best Cards, Inc. and features color player photos in a white border. The backs carry player information and career statistics.

	MINT	NRMT	EXC
COMPLETE SET (30)	10.00	4.50	1.25

☐ 1 Kevin Higgins MG
☐ 2 Stan Fansler CO
☐ 3 Brian McArn CO
☐ 4 Julian Yan CO
☐ 5 Tim Swift TR
☐ 6 Phil Schelzo MG
☐ 7 Basilio Alvarado
☐ 8 Ethan Barlow
☐ 9 Paul Blandford
☐ 10 Matt Buirley
☐ 11 Jamey Carrol
☐ 12 Karl Chatman
☐ 13 Julio Figueroa
☐ 14 Brian Garsky
☐ 15 Giovanni Lara
☐ 16 Sean Leslie
☐ 17 Brian Matz
☐ 18 Tripp McKay
☐ 19 Chad Morris
☐ 20 Willie Oropeza
☐ 21 Christian Parker
☐ 22 Simon Pond
☐ 23 Edward Quezada
☐ 24 Juan Rosado
☐ 25 Rodney Stevenson
☐ 26 Chris Stowers
☐ 27 Shannon Swaino
☐ 28 Andy Tracy
☐ 29 Richard Westover
☐ 30 Tim Young

1996 Vero Beach Dodgers Best

This 30-card set of the 1996 Vero Beach Dodgers, a Class A Florida State League affiliate of the Los Angeles Dodgers, was produced by Best Cards, Inc. and features color player photos in a white border. The backs carry player information and career statistics.

	MINT	NRMT	EXC
COMPLETE SET (30)	15.00	6.75	1.85

☐ 1 Jon Debus MG
☐ 2 Tony Harris CO
☐ 3 Field Staff
☐ 4 Rob Giesecke TR
☐ 5 Alex Asencio
☐ 6 Todd Barlok
☐ 7 Nathan Bland
☐ 8 Dan Camacho
☐ 9 Mike Carpentier
☐ 10 Scott Chambers
☐ 11 Julio Colon
☐ 12 Chris Durkin
☐ 13 Kevin Gibbs
☐ 14 Ron Hollis
☐ 15 Mike Iglesias
☐ 16 Joe Lagarde
☐ 17 Paul LoDuca
☐ 18 Brian Majeski
☐ 19 Rafael Martinez
☐ 20 Kendrick Mitchell
☐ 21 Billy Neal
☐ 22 Andy Owen
☐ 23 Rafael Ozuna
☐ 24 Petie Roach
☐ 25 Brian Rolocut
☐ 26 Bob Schaaf
☐ 27 Craig Scheffler
☐ 28 A.J. Walkanoff
☐ 29 Bruce Yard
☐ 30 David Yocum

1996 Watertown Indians Team Issue

This 36-card set of the 1996 Watertown Indians, a Class A New York-Penn League affiliate of the Cleveland Indians, was sponsored by Cablesystems of Watertown and features color player action photos by Jim Thwaits in a white border. The backs carry player information and career statistics. The cards are unnumbered and checklisted below in alphabetical order. This issue includes the minor league card debut of Willie Martinez.

	MINT	NRMT	EXC
COMPLETE SET (36)	12.00	5.50	1.50

☐ 1 Tom Afenir
☐ 2 Mark Baker
☐ 3 John Brammer
☐ 4 Lance Calmus
☐ 5 Jared Camp
☐ 6 Nathan Coats
☐ 7 Jon Edwards
☐ 8 Bienvenido Feliz
☐ 9 Tony Fleetwood
☐ 10 Mike Huelsmann
☐ 11 Troy Kent
☐ 12 Dennis Konrady
☐ 13 Ted Kubiak
☐ 14 Jarrod Mays
☐ 15 Dennis Martinez Jr.
☐ 16 Willie Martinez
☐ 17 John McDonald
☐ 18 Dave Miller CO
☐ 19 Matthew Minter
☐ 20 Bud Moore
☐ 21 Mel Motley

☐ 22 Nick Paparesta TR
☐ 23 Danny Peoples
☐ 24 Jonathan Petke
☐ 25 Paul Rigdon
☐ 26 Chris Rodriguez
☐ 27 Gary Rodriguez
☐ 28 Rob Stanton
☐ 29 Adam Taylor
☐ 30 Mark Taylor
☐ 31 Brad Tiller
☐ 32 Ken Wagner
☐ 33 Brian Whitlock
☐ NNO Blizzard(Mascot)
☐ NNO Interns
☐ NNO Bat Boys

1996 West Michigan Whitecaps Best

This 30-card set of the 1996 West Michigan Whitecaps, a Class A Midwest League affiliate of the Oakland Athletics, was produced by Best Cards, Inc. and features color player photos in a white border. The backs carry player information and career statistics.

	MINT	NRMT	EXC
COMPLETE SET (30)	10.00	4.50	1.25

☐ 1 Mike Quade MG
☐ 2 Bert Bradley CO
☐ 3 Gil Lopez CO
☐ 4 Crash the River Rascal(Mascot)
☐ 5 Todd Abbott
☐ 6 Benito Baez
☐ 7 Jeff DaVanon
☐ 8 Mario Encarnacion
☐ 9 Duane Filchner
☐ 10 Kevin Gunther
☐ 11 Ramon Hernandez
☐ 12 Bob Kazmirski
☐ 13 Eddie Lara
☐ 14 Alex Miranda
☐ 15 Kevin Mlodik
☐ 16 Juan Moreno
☐ 17 Chris Morrison
☐ 18 Chris Nelson
☐ 19 Randy Ortega
☐ 20 Arturo Paulino
☐ 21 Jamey Price
☐ 22 Troy Rauer
☐ 23 Scott Rivette
☐ 24 Alex Rondon
☐ 25 Andy Smith
☐ 26 Jose Soriano
☐ 27 Jon Valenti
☐ 28 Dane Walker
☐ 29 Todd Weinberg
☐ 30 Derrick White

1996 West Oahu Canefires Hawaii Winter Ball

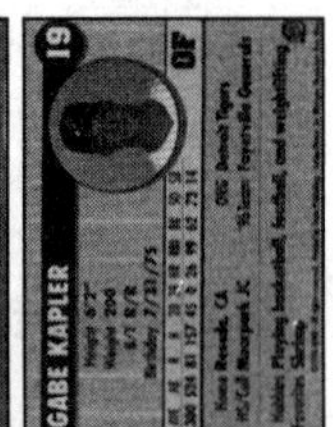

This 36-card set of the 1996 West Oahu Canefires team was produced by Trade Publishing and features borderless color action player photos by Jay Metzger. The backs carry a small black-and-white player headshot by Ray Wong with player information and statistics. The cards are unnumbered and checklisted below according to the player's jersey number. This issue includes a first year card of Gabe Kapler.

	MINT	NRMT	EXC
COMPLETE SET (36)	20.00	9.00	2.50

☐ 2 Luke Owens-Bragg
☐ 7 Pil Sung Kong
☐ 11 Manny Vazquez
☐ 15 Marty Gazarek
☐ 16 Cam Smith
☐ 17 David Schuler CO
☐ 18 Aaron Fultz
☐ 19 Gabe Kapler
☐ 20 Terry Harvey
☐ 21 Jim Betzsold
☐ 23 Matt Skrmetta
☐ 24 Sam Voita
☐ 25 Brad Tiller
☐ 26 Sang Soo Kang
☐ 27 Atsunori Inaba
☐ 28 Travis Cain
☐ 29 Craig Mayes
☐ 30 Steve Livesey CO
☐ 31 Dong Hee Park
☐ 32 Tony Dougherty
☐ 33 Andrew Vessel
☐ 34 Jason Berry
☐ 36 Justin Speier
☐ 36 Russell Ortiz
☐ 37 Sang Moon Yang CO
☐ 39 Ji Chol Park
☐ 40 Kevin Lidle
☐ 41 Matt Bokemeier
☐ 42 Chad Hartvigson
☐ 43 Jason Myers
☐ 44 Scott Morgan
☐ 45 Jeff Datz MG
☐ NNO Sugarcanes
☐ NNO Mark Gruesbeck TR
☐ NNO Team Photo CL
☐ NNO Caneman(Mascot)

1996 West Palm Beach Expos Best

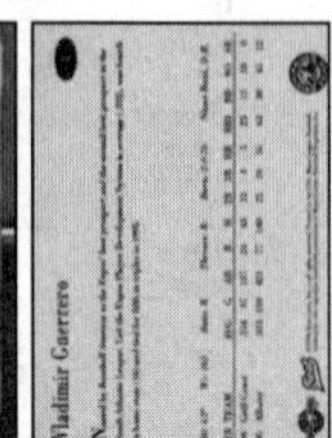

This 31-card set of the 1996 West Palm Beach Expos, a Class A Florida State League affiliate of the Montreal Expos, was produced by Best Cards, Inc. and features color player photos with red top borders and bottom blue ones. The backs carry player information and career statistics. Card #31 in each set is individually numbered out of 2,000. This issue includes the minor league team set card debuts of Vladimir Guerrero, Brad Fullmer and Hiram Bocachica.

	MINT	NRMT	EXC
COMPLETE SET (31)	30.00	13.50	3.70

☐ 1 Vladimir Guerrero (Batting)
☐ 2 Rick Sofield MGR
☐ 3 Jeff Fischer CO
☐ 4 Kash Beauchamp CO
☐ 5 Jose Centeno
☐ 6 Jason Cole
☐ 7 Fernando DaSilva
☐ 8 Tim Dixon
☐ 9 Jayson Durocher
☐ 10 Ben Fleetham
☐ 11 David Moraga
☐ 12 Tommy Phelps
☐ 13 Rory Rhodriquez
☐ 14 Jerry Stubbs
☐ 15 Mike Thurman
☐ 16 Chris Weidert
☐ 17 Josh Brinkley
☐ 18 Matt Haas
☐ 19 Francisco Morales
☐ 20 John Pachot
☐ 21 Hiram Bocachica
☐ 22 Danny Bravo
☐ 23 Nate Brown
☐ 24 Jhonny Carvajal
☐ 25 Trace Coquillette
☐ 26 Mike Giardi
☐ 27 David Post
☐ 28 Ed Bady
☐ 29 Brad Fullmer
☐ 30 Paul Ottavinia
☐ 31 Vladimir Guerrero
Follow Through Pose

1996 Wichita Wranglers Best

This 30-card set of the 1996 Wichita Wranglers, a Class AA Texas League affiliate of the Kansas City Royals, was produced by Best Cards, Inc. and features color player photos in a white border. The backs carry player information and career statistics.

	MINT	NRMT	EXC
COMPLETE SET (30)	15.00	6.75	1.85

☐ 1 Mike Sweeney
☐ 2 Mike Bovee
☐ 3 Kevin Long
☐ 4 Tim Byrdak
☐ 5 Larry Sutton
☐ 6 Jeremy Carr
☐ 7 Brian Harrison
☐ 8 Allen McDill
☐ 9 Anthony Medrano
☐ 10 Kevin Rawitzer
☐ 11 Ken Ray
☐ 12 Jose Rosado
☐ 13 Ryan Long
☐ 14 Dilson Torres
☐ 15 Sean Delaney
☐ 16 Andy Stewart
☐ 17 Brian Bevil
☐ 18 Jed Hansen
☐ 19 Mendy Lopez
☐ 20 Steve Olsen
☐ 21 Cesar Morillo
☐ 22 Steve Sisco
☐ 23 Chris Eddy
☐ 24 Bart Evans
☐ 25 Toby Smith
☐ 26 Raul Gonzalez
☐ 27 Ron Johnson MG
☐ 28 U.L. Washington CO
☐ 29 Gary Lance CO
☐ 30 Wilbur T. Wrangler(Mascot)

1996 Wilmington Blue Rocks Best

This 30-card set of the 1996 Wilmington Blue Rocks, a Class A Carolina League affiliate of the Kansas City Royals, was produced by Best Cards, Inc. and features color player photos in a white border. The backs carry player information and career statistics.

	MINT	NRMT	EXC
COMPLETE SET (30)	10.00	4.50	1.25

☐ 1 Matt Smith
☐ 2 Carlos Mendez
☐ 3 Michael Evans
☐ 4 Ramy Brooks
☐ 5 Steve Prihoda
☐ 6 Phil Grundy
☐ 7 Javier Gamboa
☐ 8 Brian Teeters
☐ 9 Donovan Delaney
☐ 10 Sergio Nunez
☐ 11 Sean McNally
☐ 12 Eduardo Cedeno
☐ 13 Jimmie Byington
☐ 14 Jeff Martin
☐ 15 Eric Anderson
☐ 16 Geno Morones
☐ 17 Al Shirley
☐ 18 Lance Carter
☐ 19 Pat Flury
☐ 20 Bryan Wolff
☐ 21 Keifer Rackley
☐ 22 Alejandro Prieto
☐ 23 Dustin Brixey
☐ 24 Julio Montilla
☐ 25 Marc Phillips
☐ 26 Matt Saier
☐ 27 Jim Telgheder
☐ 28 John Mizerock MG
☐ 29 Tom Burgmeier CO
☐ 30 Keith Hughes CO

1996 Wisconsin Timber Rattlers Best

This 30-card set of the 1996 Wisconsin Timber Rattlers, a Class A Midwest League affiliate of the Seattle Mariners, was produced by Best Cards, Inc. and features color player photos in a white border. The backs carry player information and career statistics. This issue includes the minor league card debut of David Arias.

	MINT	NRMT	EXC
COMPLETE SET (30)	12.00	5.50	1.50

☐ 1 Mike Goff MG
☐ 2 Pat Rice CO
☐ 3 Joaquin Contreras CO
☐ 4 Jeff Carr TR
☐ 5 Jose Amado
☐ 6 David Arias
☐ 7 Denny Bonilla
☐ 8 Faruq Darcuiel
☐ 9 Chris Dean
☐ 10 Kevin Gryboski
☐ 11 Brent Iddon
☐ 12 Russell Jacobs
☐ 13 Dan Kurtz
☐ 14 Damaso Marte
☐ 15 Joe Mathis
☐ 16 Theodoro Medrano
☐ 17 Joel Ramirez
☐ 18 Ed Randolph
☐ 19 Greg Scheer
☐ 20 Aaron Scheffer
☐ 21 Chad Sheffer
☐ 22 Roy Smith
☐ 23 Scott Smith
☐ 24 Chad Soden
☐ 25 Karl Thompson
☐ 26 Luis Tinoco
☐ 27 John Vanhof
☐ 28 Randy Vickers
☐ 29 Greg Wooten
☐ 30 Checklist

1996 Yakima Bears Team Issue

This 35-card set of lthe 1996 Yakima Bears, a Class A Northwest League affiliate of the Los Angeles Dodgers, was sponsored by TV station KIMA channel 29 and features color player action photos in a white border. The backs carry a small black-and-white player head photo with player information and statistics. The cards are unnumbered and checklisted below according to the player's jersey number as printed on the c--d back. This issue includes the minor league card debuts of Damian Rolls and Peter Bergeron.

	MINT	NRMT	EXC
COMPLETE SET (35)	15.00	6.75	1.85

☐ 4 Rich Saitta
☐ 5 Bobby Meyer
☐ 8 Randy Stearns
☐ 10 Ted Lilly
☐ 11 Tony Mota
☐ 12 Eric Brown
☐ 14 Dean Mitchell
☐ 16 Wayne Franklin
☐ 17 Brian Sankey
☐ 18 Matt Meyer
☐ 19 Kevin Culmo
☐ 21 Scott Morrison
☐ 23 Eric Flores
☐ 24 Matt Kramer
☐ 25 Peter Bergeron
☐ 26 Kimani Newton
☐ 27 Neal Hannah
☐ 29 Damian Rolls
☐ 30 Jaime Malave
☐ 31 Jay O'Shaughnessy
☐ 33 Steve Wilson
☐ 35 Mickey Maestas
☐ 37 Jeff Kubenka
☐ 41 Ben Simon
☐ 43 Blake Mayo
☐ 44 C.D. Stover
☐ 45 Josh Glassey
☐ 46 Craig Taczy
☐ 47 Brian Paluk
☐ 50 Casey Deskins
☐ 55 Willie King
☐ NNO Jason Mahnke TR
☐ NNO Dave Osteen CO
☐ NNO Joe Vavra MG
☐ NNO Mitch Webster CO

1956 Big League Statues

These 3" bronze colored plastic statues were issued in bubble packs. The backing of the package is actually a card of the featured player. Prices below are for statues only. Unopened bubble packs are valued 3 to 5 times the listed prices below. Prices for single cards are listed under Big League in the card section. Players are listed alphabetically.

	NRMT	VG-E	GOOD
COMPLETE SET (18)	700.00	325.00	140.00
COMMON STATUE (1-18)	20.00	9.00	4.00
☐ 1 John Antonelli	20.00	9.00	4.00
☐ 2 Bobby Avila	20.00	9.00	4.00
☐ 3 Yogi Berra	50.00	22.00	10.00
☐ 4 Roy Campanella	50.00	22.00	10.00
☐ 5 Larry Doby	30.00	13.50	6.00
☐ 6 Del Ennis	20.00	9.00	4.00
☐ 7 Jim Gilliam	30.00	13.50	6.00
☐ 8 Gil Hodges	40.00	18.00	8.00
☐ 9 Harvey Kuenn	20.00	9.00	4.00
☐ 10 Bob Lemon	35.00	16.00	7.00
☐ 11 Mickey Mantle	250.00	110.00	50.00
☐ 12 Eddie Mathews	40.00	18.00	8.00
☐ 13 Minnie Minoso	30.00	13.50	6.00
☐ 14 Stan Musial	50.00	22.00	10.00
☐ 15 Pee Wee Reese	50.00	22.00	10.00
☐ 16 Al Rosen	20.00	9.00	4.00
☐ 17 Duke Snider	40.00	18.00	8.00
☐ 18 Mickey Vernon	25.00	11.00	5.00

1955 Dairy Queen Statues

This 18-statue set was available in Dairy Queen stores. The white statues measure around 3" in height. The player selection is identical to the 1956 Big League statues, as is the design.

	NRMT	VG-E	GOOD
COMPLETE SET (18)	850.00	375.00	170.00
COMMON STATUE (1-18)	25.00	11.00	5.00
☐ 1 Johnny Antonelli	25.00	11.00	5.00
☐ 2 Bob Avila	25.00	11.00	5.00
☐ 3 Yogi Berra	60.00	27.00	12.00
☐ 4 Roy Campanella	60.00	27.00	12.00
☐ 5 Larry Doby	35.00	16.00	7.00
☐ 6 Del Ennis	25.00	11.00	5.00
☐ 7 Jim Gilliam	35.00	16.00	7.00
☐ 8 Gil Hodges	60.00	27.00	12.00
☐ 9 Harvey Kuenn	25.00	11.00	5.00
☐ 10 Bob Lemon	50.00	22.00	10.00
☐ 11 Mickey Mantle	300.00	135.00	60.00
☐ 12 Ed Mathews	60.00	27.00	12.00
☐ 13 Minnie Minoso	35.00	16.00	7.00
☐ 14 Stan Musial	60.00	27.00	12.00
☐ 15 Pee Wee Reese	60.00	27.00	12.00
☐ 16 Al Rosen	25.00	11.00	5.00

☐ 17 Duke Snider	60.00	27.00	12.00
☐ 18 Mickey Vernon	25.00	11.00	5.00

1963 Hall of Fame Busts

These 20 statues meaure 6" high and are made of plastic. The player's face is in white and it is set against a brown base. The statues in sealed boxes in cellophane is worth two to four times the prices listed below.

	NRMT	VG-E	GOOD
COMPLETE SET	1000.00	450.00	200.00
COMMON STATUE	50.00	22.00	10.00
☐ 1 Grover Cleveland Alexander	60.00	27.00	12.00
☐ 2 Cap Anson	50.00	22.00	10.00
☐ 3 Ty Cobb	90.00	40.00	18.00
☐ 4 Eddie Collins	50.00	22.00	10.00
☐ 5 Joe DiMaggio	75.00	34.00	15.00
☐ 6 Johnny Evers	50.00	22.00	10.00
☐ 7 Jimmie Foxx	75.00	34.00	15.00
☐ 8 Lou Gehrig	90.00	40.00	18.00
☐ 9 Charlie Gehringer	50.00	22.00	10.00
☐ 10 Rogers Hornsby	60.00	27.00	12.00
☐ 11 Walter Johnson	60.00	27.00	12.00
☐ 12 Willie Keeler	50.00	22.00	10.00
☐ 13 Nap Lajoie	50.00	22.00	10.00
☐ 14 Christy Mathewson	60.00	27.00	12.00
☐ 15 Babe Ruth	100.00	45.00	20.00
☐ 16 Al Spalding	50.00	22.00	10.00
☐ 17 Tris Speaker	50.00	22.00	10.00
☐ 18 Pie Traynor	50.00	22.00	10.00
☐ 19 Honus Wagner	60.00	27.00	12.00
☐ 20 Cy Young	60.00	27.00	12.00

1958-63 Hartland Statues

During the years 1958 to 1963 the Hartland Plastics Company of Hartland, Wisconsin, produced a series of baseball, football and TV western star plastic statues which have become highly collectible. The statues bear an excellent resemblence (particularly the facial features of the baseball and western characters) to the personalities portrayed. We shall concern ourselves here with the 10 baseball statues; however, mention will be made of the football and western statues as they too are quite popular. Of the 20 baseball Hartland statues, 18 are full sized (8") replicas of popular major league baseball players. Each is posed in a stance for which he is well known. In addition to the standard-sized baseball statues, two others were produced -- the Little Leaguer and the 4" batter. The 6" Little Leaguer, sometimes called the "batboy", was produced for a short period of time by the Hartland Company unitl legal problems with Little League, Inc., of Williamsport, PA, over the use of the name Little League curtailed production. The 4" batter, which is supposedly part of a miniature set including a golfer, a bowler, and a tennis player, is a nameless replica of a batter attached to a black base. It is quite inferior aesthetically to the larger statues; however, because of its relative scarcity and the fact that it is a Hartland statue portraying a baseball player, it has merited collector attention. Originally, the statues could be purchase at department stores, five and dime stores and similar retail establishments for between $2 - $4 in a box with the picture of the player inside printed on the box. The boxes themselves have also become a sought after collectible. The statues were issued in the order listed in the checklist below. Many of the statues included a removable piece (bat, mask) or a standing aide (toe plate, pitching rubber, base) in addition to the player himself. The bats came in a small and large size and the toe plate is either white or purple. At least three of the statues are known to exist in more than one form. The Mays statue has either an orange or light brown glove. The Aparicio statue comes with or without a toe plate (to aid the figure in standing). The Aaron statue variations are the only one's known where there appears to be a definite change or alteration made to the statue mold. One style has the right foot flat on the surface on which it stood. This style also has the hands configured in a manner to give the impression that the bat is tilted toward's Aaron's head. The other style of Aaron has, in its most stable standing position, the toe of the right foot raised considerably from the surface and has the hands of the of Aaron configured so that the bat is parallel to Aaron's head. The facial color of this variation is noticeably lighter (More brown than black) than the first variation. Additional versions of the Fox and Aparicio statues have been reported; however, the reports can not be confirmed. Supposedly, the red border around the word "Sox" was omitted to save painting time for a "Hurry-up" promotional event at a Chicago ball park. Condition grades for Hartland statues are somewhat different from condition grades for cards. The prime determinants of a statue's condition are boldness and clarity of the the painted parts, number and scarcity of scratches, yellowing, and the ability of the statue to stand by itself. All missing parts (bats, masks, toe plates, etc.) and broken parts (arms, heads, hats) should be described in addition to the condition grade. Repaired statues should be noted as such. An Ex-Mt or better Hartland staute should have boldly painted markings which have shown little fading; very minor, if any, scratches; little of no yellowing; and the ability to stand by itself without the aid of bracing or adhesive additions. Collectibles statues with noticable wear, fading, yellowing and such statues are normally held only as fillers until a better condition replacement can be found. Each statue came with a red 2" circular name tag. Below values are for statues out of the box. Statues and all accessories in sealed boxes are valued significantly higher.

	NRMT	VG-E	GOOD
COMPLETE SET (20)	7500.00	3400.00	1500.00
☐ 1 Mickey Mantle	400.00	180.00	80.00
Large bat			
☐ 2 Babe Ruth	300.00	135.00	60.00
Large bat			
☐ 3 Hank Aaron	350.00	160.00	70.00
Large bat			
☐ 4 Eddie Mathews	200.00	90.00	40.00
☐ 5 Ted Williams	350.00	160.00	70.00
Large bat, toe plate			
☐ 6 Stan Musial	300.00	135.00	60.00
Large bat			
☐ 7 Warren Spahn	225.00	100.00	45.00
☐ 8 Yogi Berra	275.00	125.00	55.00
Mask			
☐ 9 Willie Mays	300.00	135.00	60.00
☐ 10 Nellie Fox	350.00	160.00	70.00
☐ 11 Ernie Banks	350.00	160.00	70.00
☐ 12 Duke Snider	600.00	275.00	120.00
Large bat			
☐ 13 Don Drysdale	500.00	220.00	100.00
Pitching rubber, toe plate			
☐ 14 Rocky Colavito	1200.00	550.00	240.00
Large bat; toe plate			
☐ 15 Luis Aparicio	400.00	180.00	80.00
With or without toe plate			
☐ 16 Harmon Killebrew	600.00	275.00	120.00
Small bat, standing base			
☐ 17 Dick Groat	1800.00	800.00	350.00
Small bat			
☐ 18 Roger Maris	600.00	275.00	120.00
☐ 19 Minor Leaguer (4")	300.00	135.00	60.00
☐ 20 Little Leaguer	250.00	110.00	50.00
Bat Boy			

1997 Headliners by Corinthian

This series of figures was produced by Corinthian Marketing. Each figures is 3 1/4" tall and comes with a cap. Also in the blister package the pieces comes in is a "Headliners Collector's Catalog." At press time Corinthian had released 20 of the confirmed 33 pieces they intended on releasing in 1997. The checklist below has been confirmed by Corinthian officals and doesn't match the one found in the Collector's Catalog that comes with the figure. Due to contracts and agreements some of the players were dropped that was on the original list. The figures were primarily sold through mass market retail outlets at a suggested retail price of $3.99. The values listed below refer to unopened packages. The figures are unnumbered and checklisted below in alphabetical order.

	MINT	NRMT	EXC
☐ 1 Roberto Alomar	6.00	4.50	2.70
☐ 2 Albert Belle			
☐ 3 Wade Boggs	6.00	4.50	2.70
☐ 4 Barry Bonds	6.00	4.50	2.70
☐ 5 Ken Caminiti			
☐ 6 Jose Canseco	6.00	4.50	2.70
☐ 7 Lenny Dykstra	6.00	4.50	2.70
☐ 8 Andres Galarraga	6.00	4.50	2.70
☐ 9 Juan Gonzalez			
☐ 10 Ken Griffey Jr.			
☐ 11 Tony Gwynn			
☐ 12 Orel Hershiser			
☐ 13 Derek Jeter			
☐ 14 Randy Johnson			
☐ 15 Chipper Jones	12.00	9.00	5.50
☐ 16 Dave Justice	6.00	4.50	2.70
☐ 17 Eric Karros	6.00	4.50	2.70
☐ 18 Barry Larkin	6.00	4.50	2.70
☐ 19 Kenny Lofton			
☐ 20 Fred McGriff	6.00	4.50	2.70
☐ 21 Mark McGwire			
☐ 22 Paul Molitor	6.00	4.50	2.70
☐ 23 Raul Mondesi	6.00	4.50	2.70
☐ 24 Hideo Nomo	6.00	4.50	2.70
☐ 25 Paul O'Neill	6.00	4.50	2.70
☐ 26 Mike Piazza	6.00	4.50	2.70
☐ 27 Cal Ripken	12.00	9.00	5.50
☐ 28 Ivan Rodriguez			
☐ 29 Ryne Sandberg	6.00	4.50	2.70
☐ 30 Gary Sheffield			
☐ 31 Frank Thomas			
☐ 32 Mo Vaughn	6.00	4.50	2.70
☐ 33 Matt Williams	6.00	4.50	2.70

1988 Kenner Starting Lineup

This 124-piece set was issued by Cincinnati-based Kenner Toy Company. The statues feature top Major League Baseball stars in action poses and are accompanied by a standard-size card of each player. The card front has either a posed or action color shot. The

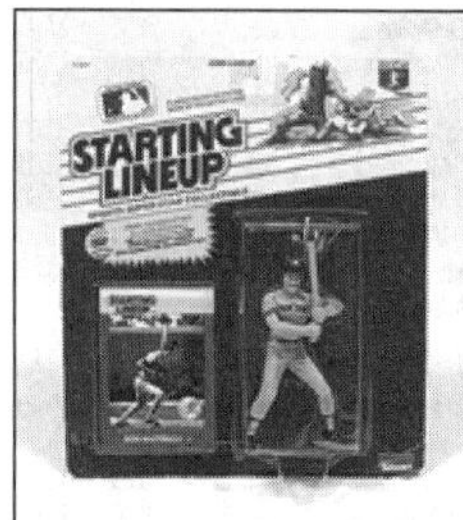

back has biographical and statistical information along with a facsimile signature. This was the first set produced under the Starting Lineup brand. The four modes of distribution for the '88 Baseball set were regionally issued team cases (24 pieces), nationally distributed All-Star cases (24 pieces), via a 1-800 number that offered team sets and complete sets, and through the J.C. Penney and Sears catalogs. The retail catalogs offered 72 of the figures in 36 different 2-player combinations. Each player was teamed with another player from their respective team. The Montreal Expos and Toronto Blue Jays were the only teams not to offer 2 player hook-ups due to Tim Raines and George Bell being each of the Canadian teams sole representative in the set. There were two Nationally distributed All-Star cases, an American League and a National League. The American League case consisted of the following 11 players: George Bell, Wade Boggs, George Brett, Roger Clemens, Rickey Henderson, Wally Joyner, Don Mattingly, Eddie Murray, Kirby Puckett, Alan Trammell and Dave Winfield. The 13 players featured in the National League case were Gary Carter, Eric Davis, Andre Dawson, Dwight Gooden, Pedro Guerrero, Tony Gwynn, Dale Murphy, Tim Raines, Mike Schmidt, Mike Scott, Ozzie Smith, Darryl Strawberry and Fernando Valenzuela. Each package that the figure came in also was issued in two variations, one with and one without the All-Star baseball offer. This offer was part of the front of the packaging. This ad wasnit a sticker; it was a part of the cardboard. The offer that appeared in a yellow starburst type ad right where the cardboard turns into the blue area was for a facsimile autographed baseball of all 24 of the nationally issued All-Star players. The baseball has a current retail value of $15-$35 but was available in 1988 for only five proofs of purchase and $3.99. Some of the key figures in the set include Barry Bonds, Cal Ripken and Nolan Ryan. The values listed below refer to unopened packages. The figures are unnumbered and checklisted below in alphabetical order.

	NRMT	EXC	DIS
COMPLETE SET (124)	2800.00	1400.00	700.00
BLUE DISPLAY STAND	60.00	30.00	15.00
☐ 1 Alan Ashby	24.00	12.00	6.00
☐ 2 Harold Baines	14.00	7.00	3.50
☐ 3 Kevin Bass	14.00	7.00	3.50
☐ 4 Steve Bedrosian	16.00	8.00	4.00
☐ 5 Buddy Bell	24.00	12.00	6.00
☐ 6 George Bell	14.00	7.00	3.50
☐ 7 Mike Boddicker	24.00	12.00	6.00
☐ 8 Wade Boggs	25.00	12.50	6.25
☐ 9 Barry Bonds	100.00	50.00	25.00
☐ 10 Bobby Bonilla	20.00	10.00	5.00
☐ 11 Sid Bream	14.00	7.00	3.50
☐ 12 George Brett	75.00	38.00	19.00
☐ 13 Chris Brown	14.00	7.00	3.50
☐ 14 Tom Brunansky	24.00	12.00	6.00
☐ 15 Ellis Burks	40.00	20.00	10.00
☐ 16 Jose Canseco	35.00	17.50	8.75
☐ 17 Gary Carter	20.00	10.00	5.00
☐ 18 Joe Carter	40.00	20.00	10.00
☐ 19 Jack Clark	18.00	9.00	4.50
☐ 20 Will Clark	30.00	15.00	7.50
☐ 21 Roger Clemens	30.00	15.00	7.50
☐ 22 Vince Coleman	14.00	7.00	3.50
☐ 23 Kal Daniels	16.00	8.00	4.00
☐ 24 Alvin Davis	14.00	7.00	3.50
☐ 25 Eric Davis	12.00	6.00	3.00
☐ 26 Glenn Davis	14.00	7.00	3.50
☐ 27 Jody Davis	16.00	8.00	4.00
☐ 28 Andre Dawson	24.00	12.00	6.00
☐ 29 Rob Deer	16.00	8.00	4.00
☐ 30 Brian Downing	14.00	7.00	3.50
☐ 31 Mike Dunne	12.00	6.00	3.00
☐ 32 Shawon Dunston	18.00	9.00	4.50
☐ 33 Leon Durham	14.00	7.00	3.50
☐ 34 Lenny Dykstra	25.00	12.50	6.25
☐ 35 Dwight Evans	20.00	10.00	5.00
☐ 36 Carlton Fisk	75.00	38.00	19.00
☐ 37 John Franco	20.00	10.00	5.00
☐ 38 Julio Franco	18.00	9.00	4.50
☐ 39 Gary Gaetti	16.00	8.00	4.00
☐ 40 Dwight Gooden	14.00	7.00	3.50
☐ 41 Ken Griffey Sr.	25.00	12.50	6.25
☐ 42 Pedro Guerrero	12.00	6.00	3.00
☐ 43 Ozzie Guillen	18.00	9.00	4.50
☐ 44 Tony Gwynn	100.00	50.00	25.00
☐ 45 Mell Hall	14.00	7.00	3.50
☐ 46 Billy Hatcher	16.00	8.00	4.00
☐ 47 Von Hayes	20.00	10.00	5.00
☐ 48 Rickey Henderson	24.00	12.00	6.00
☐ 49 Keith Hernandez	16.00	8.00	4.00
☐ 50 Willie Hernandez	14.00	7.00	3.50
☐ 51 Tom Herr	14.00	7.00	3.50
☐ 52 Ted Higuera	16.00	8.00	4.00
☐ 53 Charlie Hough	20.00	10.00	5.00
☐ 54 Kent Hrbek	16.00	8.00	4.00
☐ 55 Pete Incaviglia	16.00	8.00	4.00
☐ 56 Howard Johnson	20.00	10.00	5.00
☐ 57 Wally Joyner	14.00	7.00	3.50
☐ 58 Terry Kennedy	14.00	7.00	3.50
☐ 59 John Kruk	25.00	12.50	6.25
☐ 60 Mark Langston	25.00	12.50	6.25
☐ 61 Carney Lansford	24.00	12.00	6.00
☐ 62 Jeffrey Leonard	14.00	7.00	3.50
☐ 63 Fred Lynn	20.00	10.00	5.00
☐ 64 Candy Maldonado	16.00	8.00	4.00
☐ 65 Mike Marshall	16.00	8.00	4.00
☐ 66 Don Mattingly	25.00	12.50	6.25
☐ 67 Willie McGee	18.00	9.00	4.50
☐ 68 Mark McGwire	40.00	20.00	10.00
☐ 69 Kevin McReynolds	16.00	8.00	4.00
☐ 70 Paul Molitor	50.00	25.00	12.50
☐ 71 Donnie Moore	18.00	9.00	4.50
☐ 72 Jack Morris	25.00	12.50	6.25
☐ 73 Dale Murphy	14.00	7.00	3.50
☐ 74 Eddie Murray	55.00	28.00	14.00
☐ 75 Matt Nokes	14.00	7.00	3.50
☐ 76 Pete O'Brien	16.00	8.00	4.00
☐ 77 Ken Oberkfell	14.00	7.00	3.50
☐ 78 Dave Parker	25.00	12.50	6.25
☐ 79 Larry Parrish	14.00	7.00	3.50
☐ 80 Ken Phelps	14.00	7.00	3.50
☐ 81 Jim Presley	14.00	7.00	3.50
☐ 82 Kirby Puckett	60.00	30.00	15.00
☐ 83 Dan Quisenberry	20.00	10.00	5.00
☐ 84 Tim Raines	16.00	8.00	4.00
☐ 85 Willie Randolph	16.00	8.00	4.00
☐ 86 Shane Rawley	14.00	7.00	3.50
☐ 87 Jeff Reardon	24.00	12.00	6.00
☐ 88 Gary Redus	14.00	7.00	3.50
☐ 89 Rick Reuschel	16.00	8.00	4.00
☐ 90 Jim Rice	24.00	12.00	6.00
☐ 91 Dave Righetti	16.00	8.00	4.00
☐ 92 Cal Ripken	400.00	200.00	100.00
☐ 93 Pete Rose	55.00	28.00	14.00
☐ 94 Nolan Ryan	325.00	160.00	80.00
☐ 95 Bret Saberhagen	18.00	9.00	4.50
☐ 96 Juan Samuel	14.00	7.00	3.50
☐ 97 Ryne Sandberg	70.00	35.00	17.50
☐ 98 Benito Santiago	16.00	8.00	4.00
☐ 99 Steve Sax	14.00	7.00	3.50
☐ 100 Mike Schmidt	50.00	25.00	12.50
☐ 101 Mike Scott	12.00	6.00	3.00
☐ 102 Kevin Seitzer	14.00	7.00	3.50
☐ 103 Ruben Sierra	20.00	10.00	5.00
☐ 104 Ozzie Smith	60.00	30.00	15.00
☐ 105 Zane Smith	14.00	7.00	3.50
☐ 106 Cory Snyder	14.00	7.00	3.50
☐ 107 Darryl Strawberry	12.00	6.00	3.00
☐ 108 Franklin Stubbs	14.00	7.00	3.50
☐ 109 B.J. Surhoff	20.00	10.00	5.00
☐ 110 Rick Sutcliffe	16.00	8.00	4.00
☐ 111 Pat Tabler	14.00	7.00	3.50
☐ 112 Danny Tartabull	16.00	8.00	4.00
☐ 113 Alan Trammell	20.00	10.00	5.00
☐ 114 Fernando Valenzuela	12.00	6.00	3.00
☐ 115 Andy Van Slyke	25.00	12.50	6.25
☐ 116 Frank Viola	18.00	9.00	4.50
☐ 117 Ozzie Virgil	14.00	7.00	3.50
☐ 118 Greg Walker	14.00	7.00	3.50
☐ 119 Lou Whitaker	25.00	12.50	6.25
☐ 120 Devon White	25.00	12.50	6.25
☐ 121 Dave Winfield	45.00	22.00	11.00
☐ 122 Mike Witt	14.00	7.00	3.50
☐ 123 Todd Worrell	16.00	8.00	4.00
☐ 124 Robin Yount	75.00	38.00	19.00

1989 Kenner Starting Lineup

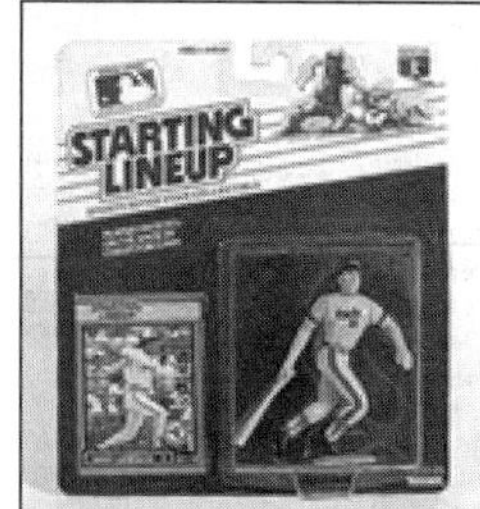

This 168-piece set was issued by Cincinnati-based Kenner Toy Company. The statues feature top baseball stars in action poses and are accompanied by a standard-size card of each player. The front of each card has either a posed or action color shot. The back has biographical and statistical information and a facsimile signature. At 168 pieces, this is the largest set issued under the Starting Lineup brand. The three modes of distribution for these figures were regionally issued team cases (24 pieces), nationally distributed All-Star cases (24 pieces) and a 1-800 number. The 1-800 number was through a fulfillment house in conjunction with Kenner and offered team sets and complete sets. The regionally issued team cases were 24 count but each player in the team case was not equally distributed. This caused some figures to be shorter than others. The 24 count All-Star cases were divided into American League and National League.

The 14 American League players in the 24-piece AL cases were George Bell, Wade Boggs, Jose Canseco, Roger Clemens, Mike Greenwell, Rickey Henderson, Wally Joyner, Don Mattingly, Mark McGwire, Paul Molitor, Kirby Puckett, Alan Trammell, Frank Viola and Dave Winfield. The 13 National League players that were featured in the 24-piece NL cases were Bobby Bonilla, Will Clark, Vince Coleman, Eric Davis, Andre Dawson, Kirk Gibson, Dwight Gooden, Dale Murphy, Tim Raines, Ryne Sandberg, Mike Scott, Ozzie Smith and Darryl Strawberry. The key first appearances include Roberto Alomar, Ron Gant, and Greg Maddux. The figures of the California Angels team, except for Wally Joyner, are the toughest pieces to find. The values listed below refer to unopened packages. The figures are unnumbered and checklisted below in alphabetical order.

	NRMT	EXC	DIS
COMPLETE SET (168)	4500.00	2200.00	1100.00
☐ 1 Roberto Alomar	450.00	220.00	110.00
☐ 2 Brady Anderson	180.00	90.00	45.00
☐ 3 Harold Baines	14.00	7.00	3.50
☐ 4 Marty Barrett	16.00	8.00	4.00
☐ 5 Kevin Bass	12.00	6.00	3.00
☐ 6 Steve Bedrosian	10.00	5.00	2.50
☐ 7 George Bell	12.00	6.00	3.00
☐ 8 Damon Berryhill	12.00	6.00	3.00
☐ 9 Wade Boggs	24.00	12.00	6.00
☐ 10 Barry Bonds	90.00	45.00	22.00
☐ 11 Bobby Bonilla	18.00	9.00	4.50
☐ 12 Phil Bradley	20.00	10.00	5.00
☐ 13 Glenn Braggs	14.00	7.00	3.50
☐ 14 Mickey Brantley	14.00	7.00	3.50
☐ 15 George Brett	70.00	35.00	17.50
☐ 16 Tom Brookens	12.00	6.00	3.00
☐ 17 Tom Brunansky	14.00	7.00	3.50
☐ 18 Steve Buechele	16.00	8.00	4.00
☐ 19 Ellis Burks	16.00	8.00	4.00
☐ 20 Brett Butler	20.00	10.00	5.00
☐ 21 Ivan Calderon	18.00	9.00	4.50
☐ 22 Jose Canseco	16.00	8.00	4.00
☐ 23 Gary Carter	18.00	9.00	4.50
☐ 24 Joe Carter	20.00	10.00	5.00
☐ 25 Will Clark	24.00	12.00	6.00
☐ 26 Roger Clemens	30.00	15.00	7.50
☐ 27 Vince Coleman	10.00	5.00	2.50
☐ 28 David Cone	35.00	17.50	8.75
☐ 29 Kal Daniels	14.00	7.00	3.50
☐ 30 Alvin Davis	18.00	9.00	4.50
☐ 31 Chili Davis	120.00	60.00	30.00
☐ 32 Eric Davis	10.00	5.00	2.50
☐ 33 Glenn Davis	12.00	6.00	3.00
☐ 34 Mark Davis	20.00	10.00	5.00
☐ 35 Andre Dawson	20.00	10.00	5.00
☐ 36 Rob Deer	12.00	6.00	3.00
☐ 37 Bo Diaz	14.00	7.00	3.50
☐ 38 Bill Doran	20.00	10.00	5.00
☐ 39 Doug Drabek	30.00	15.00	7.50
☐ 40 Shawon Dunston	18.00	9.00	4.50
☐ 41 Lenny Dykstra	30.00	15.00	7.50
☐ 42 Dennis Eckersley	90.00	45.00	22.00
☐ 43 Kevin Elster	12.00	6.00	3.00
☐ 44 Scott Fletcher	12.00	6.00	3.00
☐ 45 John Franco	14.00	7.00	3.50
☐ 46 Gary Gaetti	14.00	7.00	3.50
☐ 47 Ron Gant	225.00	110.00	55.00
☐ 48 Kirk Gibson	14.00	7.00	3.50
☐ 49 Dan Gladden	14.00	7.00	3.50
☐ 50 Dwight Gooden	12.00	6.00	3.00
☐ 51 Mark Grace	30.00	15.00	7.50
☐ 52 Mike Greenwell	12.00	6.00	3.00
☐ 53 Mark Gubicza	12.00	6.00	3.00
☐ 54 Pedro Guerrero	12.00	6.00	3.00
☐ 55 Ozzie Guillen	25.00	12.50	6.25
☐ 56 Tony Gwynn	250.00	125.00	60.00
☐ 57 Albert Hall	12.00	6.00	3.00
☐ 58 Mel Hall	10.00	5.00	2.50
☐ 59 Billy Hatcher	12.00	6.00	3.00
☐ 60 Von Hayes	12.00	6.00	3.00
☐ 61 Rickey Henderson	18.00	9.00	4.50
☐ 62 Mike Henneman	12.00	6.00	3.00
☐ 63 Keith Hernandez	12.00	6.00	3.00
☐ 64 Orel Hershiser	18.00	9.00	4.50
☐ 65 Ted Higuera	20.00	10.00	5.00
☐ 66 Jack Howell	110.00	55.00	28.00
☐ 67 Kent Hrbek	12.00	6.00	3.00
☐ 68 Pete Incaviglia	12.00	6.00	3.00
☐ 69 Bo Jackson	25.00	12.50	6.25
☐ 70 Danny Jackson	12.00	6.00	3.00
☐ 71 Brook Jacoby	12.00	6.00	3.00
☐ 72 Chris James	12.00	6.00	3.00
☐ 73 Dion James	14.00	7.00	3.50
☐ 74 Gregg Jefferies	30.00	15.00	7.50
☐ 75 Doug Jones	16.00	8.00	4.00
☐ 76 Wally Joyner	12.00	6.00	3.00
☐ 77 John Kruk	30.00	15.00	7.50
☐ 78 Mark Langston	25.00	12.50	6.25
☐ 79 Carney Lansford	20.00	10.00	5.00
☐ 80 Barry Larkin	60.00	30.00	15.00
☐ 81 Tim Laudner	20.00	10.00	5.00
☐ 82 Mike LaValliere	12.00	6.00	3.00
☐ 83 Al Leiter	12.00	6.00	3.00
☐ 84 Chet Lemon	14.00	7.00	3.50
☐ 85 Jose Lind	20.00	10.00	5.00
☐ 86 Greg Maddux	400.00	200.00	100.00
☐ 87 Candy Maldonado	12.00	6.00	3.00
☐ 88 Mike Marshall	12.00	6.00	3.00
☐ 89 Don Mattingly	25.00	12.50	6.25
☐ 90 Willie McGee	14.00	7.00	3.50
☐ 91 Mark McGwire	25.00	12.50	6.25
☐ 92 Kevin McReynolds	16.00	8.00	4.00
☐ 93 Kevin Mitchell	18.00	9.00	4.50
☐ 94 Paul Molitor	40.00	20.00	10.00
☐ 95 Jack Morris	25.00	12.50	6.25
☐ 96 Dale Murphy	12.00	6.00	3.00
☐ 97 Randy Myers	16.00	8.00	4.00
☐ 98 Matt Nokes	10.00	5.00	2.50
☐ 99 Mike Pagliarulo	10.00	5.00	2.50
☐ 100 Dave Parker	20.00	10.00	5.00
☐ 101 Dan Pasqua	18.00	9.00	4.50
☐ 102 Tony Pena	20.00	10.00	5.00
☐ 103 Terry Pendleton	25.00	12.50	6.25
☐ 104 Melido Perez	20.00	10.00	5.00
☐ 105 Gerald Perry	14.00	7.00	3.50
☐ 106 Dan Plesac	10.00	5.00	2.50
☐ 107 Kirby Puckett	50.00	25.00	12.50
☐ 108 Rey Quinones	20.00	10.00	5.00
☐ 109 Tim Raines	10.00	5.00	2.50
☐ 110 Johnny Ray	110.00	55.00	28.00
☐ 111 Jeff Reardon	40.00	20.00	10.00
☐ 112 Harold Reynolds	20.00	10.00	5.00
☐ 113 Jim Rice	18.00	9.00	4.50
☐ 114 Dave Righetti	18.00	9.00	4.50
☐ 115 Cal Ripken	400.00	200.00	100.00
☐ 116 Jeff Russell	20.00	10.00	5.00
☐ 117 Bret Saberhagen	16.00	8.00	4.00
☐ 118 Chris Sabo	18.00	9.00	4.50
☐ 119 Luis Salazar	12.00	6.00	3.00
☐ 120 Juan Samuel	12.00	6.00	3.00
☐ 121 Ryne Sandberg	40.00	20.00	10.00
☐ 122 Benito Santiago	20.00	10.00	5.00
☐ 123 Mike Schmidt	50.00	25.00	12.50
☐ 124 Dick Schofield	110.00	55.00	28.00
☐ 125 Mike Scioscia	24.00	12.00	6.00
☐ 126 Mike Scott	10.00	5.00	2.50
☐ 127 Kevin Seitzer	12.00	6.00	3.00
☐ 128 Larry Sheets	16.00	8.00	4.00
☐ 129 John Shelby	12.00	6.00	3.00
☐ 130 Ruben Sierra	24.00	12.00	6.00
☐ 131 Don Slaught	12.00	6.00	3.00
☐ 132 Dave Smith	12.00	6.00	3.00
☐ 133 Lee Smith	75.00	38.00	19.00
☐ 134 Ozzie Smith	50.00	25.00	12.50
☐ 135 Zane Smith	12.00	6.00	3.00
☐ 136 Cory Snyder	12.00	6.00	3.00
☐ 137 Pete Stanicek	16.00	8.00	4.00
☐ 138 Terry Steinbach	20.00	10.00	5.00
☐ 139 Dave Stewart	25.00	12.50	6.25
☐ 140 Kurt Stillwell	10.00	5.00	2.50
☐ 141 Darryl Strawberry	12.00	6.00	3.00
☐ 142 B.J. Surhoff	20.00	10.00	5.00
☐ 143 Rick Sutcliffe	16.00	8.00	4.00
☐ 144 Bruce Sutter	30.00	15.00	7.50
☐ 145 Greg Swindell	20.00	10.00	5.00
☐ 146 Pat Tabler	12.00	6.00	3.00
☐ 147 Danny Tartabull	12.00	6.00	3.00
☐ 148 Bobby Thigpen	30.00	15.00	7.50
☐ 149 Milt Thompson	20.00	10.00	5.00
☐ 150 Robby Thompson	18.00	9.00	4.50
☐ 151 Alan Trammell	18.00	9.00	4.50
☐ 152 Jeff Treadway	30.00	15.00	7.50
☐ 153 Jose Uribe	12.00	6.00	3.00
☐ 154 Fernando Valenzuela	12.00	6.00	3.00
☐ 155 Andy Van Slyke	16.00	8.00	4.00
☐ 156 Frank Viola	12.00	6.00	3.00
☐ 157 Bob Walk	12.00	6.00	3.00
☐ 158 Greg Walker	16.00	8.00	4.00
☐ 159 Walt Weiss	30.00	15.00	7.50
☐ 160 Bob Welch	24.00	12.00	6.00
☐ 161 Lou Whitaker	25.00	12.50	6.25
☐ 162 Devon White	120.00	60.00	30.00
☐ 163 Dave Winfield	25.00	12.50	6.25
☐ 164 Mike Witt	110.00	55.00	28.00
☐ 165 Todd Worrell	14.00	7.00	3.50
☐ 166 Marvell Wynne	25.00	12.50	6.25
☐ 167 Gerald Young	14.00	7.00	3.50
☐ 168 Robin Yount	75.00	38.00	19.00

1989 Kenner Starting Lineup Baseball Greats

This 10-piece set was issued by Cincinnati-based Kenner Toy Company. There are two legendary Major League Baseball players per package along with a collectors card for each player. The fronts of the cards feature an action or posed shot. The backs of the carfeature biographical and statistical information. The packages usually feature two of the greatest players from a particular organization. The only piece that doesn't is the Hank Aaron and Carl Yastrzemski package. There are also three variations of the Babe Ruth/Lou Gehrig piece. The common version has Ruth in a gray uniform and Gehrig in a white uniform. The second version has the uniform colors reversed and the third version has both wearing a white uniform. The third version is the scarest. The complete set price only reflects the common version. The pieces came in 2 different 12-piece case assortments. The values listed below refer to unopened packages. The cards and figures are unnumbered and checklisted below.

	NRMT	EXC	DIS
COMPLETE SET (10)	375.00	190.00	95.00
☐ 1 Johnny Bench	50.00	25.00	12.50
Pete Rose			
☐ 2 Don Drysdale	45.00	22.00	11.00
Reggie Jackson			
☐ 3 Mickey Mantle	80.00	40.00	20.00
Joe DiMaggio			
☐ 4 Eddie Mathews	40.00	20.00	10.00
Hank Aaron			
☐ 5 Willie Mays	40.00	20.00	10.00
Willie McCovey			
☐ 6 Stan Musial	40.00	20.00	10.00
Bob Gibson			
☐ 7A Babe Ruth	40.00	20.00	10.00
Gray Jersey			
Lou Gehrig			
White Jersey			
☐ 7B Babe Ruth	45.00	22.00	11.00
White Jersey			
Lou Gehrig			
Gray Jersey			
☐ 7C Babe Ruth	60.00	30.00	15.00
White Jersey			
Lou Gehrig			
White Jersey			
☐ 8 Willie Stargell	45.00	22.00	11.00
Roberto Clemente			
☐ 9 Billy Williams	40.00	20.00	10.00
Ernie Banks			
☐ 10 Carl Yastrzemski	60.00	30.00	15.00
Hank Aaron			

1990 Kenner Starting Lineup

This 92-piece set was issued by Cincinnati-based Kenner Toy Company. The statues feature top Major League Baseball stars in action poses and are accompanied by two cards. There is a regular card which features a posed or action color shot on front. The back has biographical and statistical information along with a facsimile signature. The second card is titled a "Rookie" card. The front has an action or posed shot along with a banner in the upper part that has the "Rookie Year" for that particular player. The back features biographical information. Figures were distributed through regionally issued team cases (16 pieces), nationally issued All-Star cases (24 pieces), via a 1-800 number and through extended series cases (24 pieces). This was the last year that the baseball series had the distribution through the regional team cases. The All-Star cases were divided into American and National League. The 15 players included in the American League All-Star cases were Wade Boggs, Jose Canseco, Roger Clemens, Mike Greenwell, Ken Griffey Jr. (Sliding), Rickey Henderson, Bo Jackson, Don Mattingly (Bat in Hand), Fred McGriff, Mark McGwire, Paul Molitor, Kirby Puckett, Cal Ripken, Nolan Ryan and Steve Sax. The 16 players included in the National League cases were Will Clark (Batting), Vince Coleman, Eric Davis, Andre Dawson, Andres Galarraga, Kirk Gibson, Dwight Gooden, Mark Grace (Batting), Orel Hershiser, Gregg Jefferies, Kevin Mitchell, Chris Sabo, Ryne Sandberg, Mike Scott, Ozzie Smith and Darryl Strawberry (Batting). This was also the first year of the Extend series release. The extended case had five new figures and four previously released figures. The breakdown for the extended case is Sandy Alomar (2), Jim Abbott (3), Jose Canseco (4), Joe Carter, Ken Griffey Jr. Jumping (4), Bo Jackson (4), Ben McDonald (2), Nolan Ryan (2) and Jerome Walton (2). The key first pieces are both of the Ken Griffey Jr. poses. The most valuable, Greg Maddux was available only in Chicago regional cases and is tougher to find than his 1989 figure. The values listed below refer to unopened packages. The figures are unnumbered and checklisted below in alphabetical order.

	NRMT	EXC	DIS
COMPLETE SET (92)	1500.00	750.00	375.00
☐ 1 Jim Abbott EXT	18.00	9.00	4.50
☐ 2 Sandy Alomar Jr. EXT	12.00	6.00	3.00
☐ 3 Allan Anderson	12.00	6.00	3.00
☐ 4 Wally Backman	14.00	7.00	3.50
☐ 5 Jeff Ballard	10.00	5.00	2.50
☐ 6 Jesse Barfield	10.00	5.00	2.50
☐ 7 Steve Bedrosian	10.00	5.00	2.50
☐ 8 Todd Benzinger	12.00	6.00	3.00
☐ 9 Damon Berryhill	12.00	6.00	3.00
☐ 10 Wade Boggs	25.00	12.50	6.25
☐ 11 Barry Bonds	60.00	30.00	15.00
☐ 12 Bobby Bonilla	14.00	7.00	3.50
☐ 13 Chris Bosio	14.00	7.00	3.50
☐ 14 Ellis Burks	14.00	7.00	3.50
☐ 15 Jose Canseco	12.00	6.00	3.00
☐ 16 Joe Carter EXT	35.00	17.50	8.75
☐ 17 Will Clark	18.00	9.00	4.50
Batting Pose			
☐ 18 Will Clark	20.00	10.00	5.00
Power Pose			
☐ 19 Roger Clemens	25.00	12.50	6.25
☐ 20 Vince Coleman	10.00	5.00	2.50
☐ 21 Ron Darling	10.00	5.00	2.50
☐ 22 Eric Davis	10.00	5.00	2.50
☐ 23 Andre Dawson	20.00	10.00	5.00
☐ 24 Rob Dibble	14.00	7.00	3.50
☐ 25 Lenny Dykstra	20.00	10.00	5.00
☐ 26 Dennis Eckersley	45.00	22.00	11.00
☐ 27 Nick Esasky	20.00	10.00	5.00
☐ 28 Gary Gaetti	12.00	6.00	3.00
☐ 29 Andres Galarraga	30.00	15.00	7.50
☐ 30 Kirk Gibson	10.00	5.00	2.50
☐ 31 Dwight Gooden	10.00	5.00	2.50
☐ 32 Mark Grace	14.00	7.00	3.50
Batting Pose			
☐ 33 Mark Grace	20.00	10.00	5.00
Power Pose			
☐ 34 Mike Greenwell	10.00	5.00	2.50
☐ 35 Ken Griffey Jr.	110.00	55.00	28.00
Sliding Pose			
☐ 36 Ken Griffey Jr. EXT	110.00	55.00	28.00
Jumping Pose			
☐ 37 Pedro Guerrero	10.00	5.00	2.50
☐ 38 Von Hayes	10.00	5.00	2.50
☐ 39 Dave Henderson	12.00	6.00	3.00
☐ 40 Rickey Henderson	14.00	7.00	3.50
☐ 41 Tom Herr	10.00	5.00	2.50
☐ 42 Orel Hershiser	18.00	9.00	4.50
☐ 43 Kent Hrbek	10.00	5.00	2.50
☐ 44 Bo Jackson EXT	10.00	5.00	2.50
☐ 45 Gregg Jefferies	12.00	6.00	3.00
☐ 46 Howard Johnson	12.00	6.00	3.00
☐ 47 Ricky Jordan	12.00	6.00	3.00
☐ 48 Roberto Kelly	16.00	8.00	4.00
☐ 49 Barry Larkin	30.00	15.00	7.50
☐ 50 Greg Maddux	550.00	275.00	140.00
☐ 51 Joe Magrane	12.00	6.00	3.00
☐ 52 Don Mattingly	14.00	7.00	3.50
Bat in Hand Pose			
☐ 53 Don Mattingly	20.00	10.00	5.00
Power Pose			
☐ 54 Ben McDonald EXT	18.00	9.00	4.50
☐ 55 Fred McGriff	50.00	25.00	12.50
☐ 56 Mark McGwire	16.00	8.00	4.00
☐ 57 Kevin McReynolds	10.00	5.00	2.50
☐ 58 Kevin Mitchell	10.00	5.00	2.50
☐ 59 Paul Molitor	25.00	12.50	6.25
☐ 60 Eddie Murray	125.00	60.00	31.00
☐ 61 Matt Nokes	12.00	6.00	3.00
☐ 62 Paul O'Neill	25.00	12.50	6.25
☐ 63 Jose Oquendo	12.00	6.00	3.00
☐ 64 Gary Pettis	18.00	9.00	4.50
☐ 65 Kirby Puckett	35.00	17.50	8.75
☐ 66 Willie Randolph	12.00	6.00	3.00
☐ 67 Jody Reed	12.00	6.00	3.00
☐ 68 Rick Reuschel	12.00	6.00	3.00
☐ 69 Dave Righetti	10.00	5.00	2.50
☐ 70 Cal Ripken	160.00	80.00	40.00
☐ 71 Nolan Ryan	50.00	25.00	12.50
☐ 72 Chris Sabo	12.00	6.00	3.00
☐ 73 Juan Samuel	12.00	6.00	3.00
☐ 74 Ryne Sandberg	30.00	15.00	7.50
☐ 75 Steve Sax	10.00	5.00	2.50
☐ 76 Mike Scott	10.00	5.00	2.50
☐ 77 Gary Sheffield	25.00	12.50	6.25
☐ 78 John Smiley	12.00	6.00	3.00
☐ 79 Ozzie Smith	35.00	17.50	8.75
☐ 80 Dave Stewart	14.00	7.00	3.50
☐ 81 Darryl Strawberry	10.00	5.00	2.50
Batting Pose			
☐ 82 Darryl Strawberry	16.00	8.00	4.00
Fielding Pose			
☐ 83 Rick Sutcliffe	12.00	6.00	3.00
☐ 84 Mickey Tettleton	14.00	7.00	3.50
☐ 85 Alan Trammell	12.00	6.00	3.00
☐ 86 Andy Van Slyke	16.00	8.00	4.00
☐ 87 Frank Viola	10.00	5.00	2.50
☐ 88 Jerome Walton EXT	10.00	5.00	2.50
☐ 89 Lou Whitaker	12.00	6.00	3.00
☐ 90 Mitch Williams	14.00	7.00	3.50
☐ 91 Dave Winfield	30.00	15.00	7.50
☐ 92 Robin Yount	60.00	30.00	15.00

1991 Kenner Starting Lineup

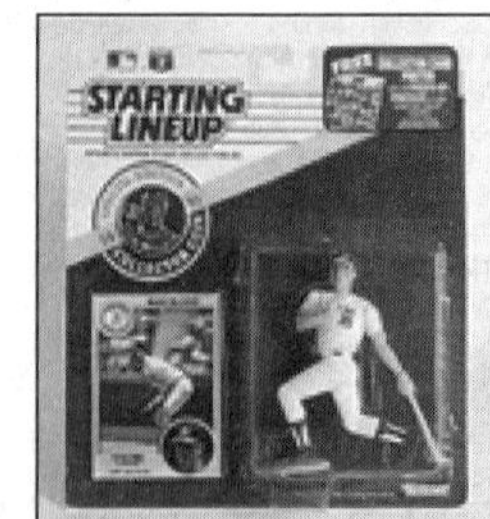

This 55-piece set was issued by Cincinnati-based Kenner Toy Company. The statues feature top Major League Baseball stars in action poses and are accompanied by a standard-size card and a collector coin of each player. The card front has either a posed or action color shot. The back has biographical and statistical information and a facsimile signature. The coin features a embossed player portrait and came in two different variations, steel and aluminum. This was the first year for distribution to be only through American League and National League case assortments. There were at least two 16-piece case assortments for each league that made up the distribution for the 46 original pieces. Later in the year a nine-piece extended series was released. The 16-piece case assortment that the extended series came in had 10 different players. Nolan Ryan was the only figure that was previously released. The only difference in the two Ryans is that the UPC number on the back was different on the second version. Collectors have deemed the difference too insignificant to make any difference in price. The key first pieces are Dave Justice and Matt Williams. The values listed below refer to unopened packages. The figures are unnumbered and checklisted below in alphabetical order.

	MINT	NRMT	EXC
COMPLETE SET (55)	500.00	375.00	220.00
☐ 1 Jim Abbott	12.00	9.00	5.50
☐ 2 Sandy Alomar Jr.	10.00	7.50	4.50
☐ 3 Jack Armstrong	10.00	7.50	4.50
☐ 4 George Bell EXT	10.00	7.50	4.50
☐ 5 Barry Bonds	40.00	30.00	18.00
☐ 6 Bobby Bonilla	14.00	10.50	6.25
☐ 7 Tom Browning	10.00	7.50	4.50
☐ 8 Jose Canseco	10.00	7.50	4.50
☐ 9 Will Clark	14.00	10.50	6.25
☐ 10 Vince Coleman EXT	10.00	7.50	4.50
☐ 11 Eric Davis	10.00	7.50	4.50
☐ 12 Glenn Davis EXT	10.00	7.50	4.50
☐ 13 Andre Dawson	16.00	12.00	7.25
☐ 14 Delino DeShields	14.00	10.50	6.25
☐ 15 Doug Drabek	14.00	10.50	6.25
☐ 16 Shawon Dunston	10.00	7.50	4.50
☐ 17 Lenny Dykstra	14.00	10.50	6.25
☐ 18 Cecil Fielder	14.00	10.50	6.25
☐ 19 John Franco	10.00	7.50	4.50
☐ 20 Dwight Gooden	10.00	7.50	4.50
☐ 21 Mark Grace	12.00	9.00	5.50
☐ 22 Ken Griffey Jr. Batting Pose	24.00	18.00	11.00
☐ 23 Ken Griffey Jr. EXT Running Pose	28.00	21.00	12.50
☐ 24 Ken Griffey Sr. EXT	20.00	15.00	9.00
☐ 25 Kelly Gruber	10.00	7.50	4.50
☐ 26 Ozzie Guillen	10.00	7.50	4.50
☐ 27 Rickey Henderson	10.00	7.50	4.50
☐ 28 Bo Jackson Royals Uniform	10.00	7.50	4.50
☐ 29 Bo Jackson EXT White Sox Uniform	14.00	10.50	6.25
☐ 30 Gregg Jefferies	10.00	7.50	4.50
☐ 31 Howard Johnson	10.00	7.50	4.50
☐ 32 Dave Justice EXT	25.00	19.00	11.00
☐ 33 Roberto Kelly	10.00	7.50	4.50
☐ 34 Barry Larkin	16.00	12.00	7.25
☐ 35 Kevin Maas	10.00	7.50	4.50
☐ 36 Dave Magadan	10.00	7.50	4.50
☐ 37 Ramon Martinez	10.00	7.50	4.50
☐ 38 Don Mattingly	16.00	12.00	7.25
☐ 39 Ben McDonald	12.00	9.00	5.50
☐ 40 Mark McGwire	16.00	12.00	7.25
☐ 41 Kevin Mitchell	10.00	7.50	4.50
☐ 42 Kirby Puckett	25.00	19.00	11.00
☐ 43 Tim Raines EXT	12.00	9.00	5.50
☐ 44 Nolan Ryan	50.00	38.00	22.00
☐ 45 Chris Sabo	10.00	7.50	4.50
☐ 46 Ryne Sandberg	25.00	19.00	11.00
☐ 47 Benito Santiago	10.00	7.50	4.50
☐ 48 Steve Sax	10.00	7.50	4.50
☐ 49 Dave Stewart	10.00	7.50	4.50
☐ 50 Darryl Strawberry Mets Uniform	10.00	7.50	4.50
☐ 51 Darryl Strawberry EXT Dodgers Uniform	10.00	7.50	4.50
☐ 52 Alan Trammell	10.00	7.50	4.50
☐ 53 Frank Viola	10.00	7.50	4.50
☐ 54 Matt Williams	35.00	26.00	16.00
☐ 55 Todd Zeile	16.00	12.00	7.25

1991 Kenner Starting Lineup Baseball Headline Collection

This seven-piece set was the first of the Headline Collection brand issued by Cincinnati-based Kenner Toy Company. The pieces feature Top Major League Kenner Starting Lineup players in action poses. The figures are accompanied by an authentic newspaper article and a high gloss, black base used to insert the article and display the figure. The article is framed and describes a memorable moment from the previous season. The pieces came in 12-count case assortments. Will Clark and Don Mattingly are the known short prints. The values listed below refer to unopened packages. The figures are unnumbered and listed below in alphabetical order.

	MINT	NRMT	EXC
COMPLETE SET (7)	200.00	150.00	90.00
☐ 1 Jose Canseco	18.00	13.50	8.00
☐ 2 Will Clark	25.00	19.00	11.00
☐ 3 Ken Griffey Jr.	45.00	34.00	20.00
☐ 4 Rickey Henderson	18.00	13.50	8.00
☐ 5 Bo Jackson	16.00	12.00	7.25
☐ 6 Don Mattingly	40.00	30.00	18.00
☐ 7 Nolan Ryan	60.00	45.00	27.00

1992 Kenner Starting Lineup

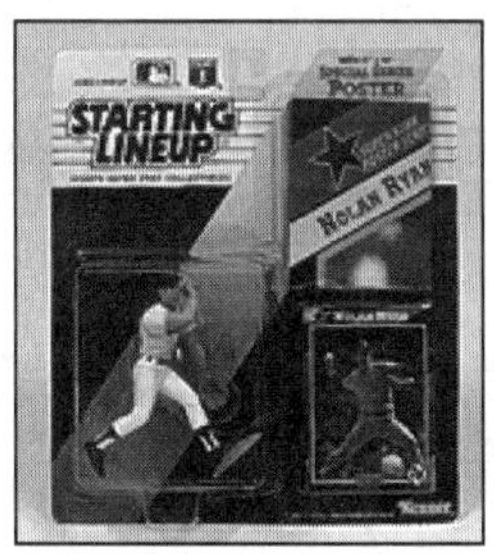

This 46-piece set was issued by Cincinnati-based Kenner Toy Company. The statues feature top Major League Baseball stars in action poses and are accompanied by a standard-size card and a poster of each player. The card front has either a posed or action color shot. The back has biographical and statistical information and a facsimile signature. The poster folds out to be a 11" X 14" shot of the player. The figures came in 16-piece cases and each case was either American League or National League player specific. A nine-piece extended series was released later in the year. The 16-piece case assortment that the extended series came in had nine different players. Bret Saberhagen and Danny Tartabull were the only players in the extended case that came one per case while the other seven players were two per case. Some of the key first pieces include Steve Avery, Albert Belle, Tom Glavine, Juan Gonzalez and the two poses of Frank Thomas. The values listed below refer to unopened packages. The figures are unnumbered and checklisted below in alphabetical order.

	MINT	NRMT	EXC
COMPLETE SET (46)	500.00	375.00	220.00
☐ 1 Roberto Alomar	20.00	15.00	9.00
☐ 2 Steve Avery EXT	18.00	13.50	8.00
☐ 3 George Bell	10.00	7.50	4.50
☐ 4 Albert Belle	45.00	34.00	20.00
☐ 5 Craig Biggio	10.00	7.50	4.50
☐ 6 Barry Bonds	25.00	19.00	11.00
☐ 7 Bobby Bonilla EXT	10.00	7.50	4.50
☐ 8 Ivan Calderon	10.00	7.50	4.50
☐ 9 Jose Canseco	10.00	7.50	4.50
☐ 10 Will Clark	16.00	12.00	7.25
☐ 11 Roger Clemens	16.00	12.00	7.25
☐ 12 Eric Davis EXT	10.00	7.50	4.50
☐ 13 Rob Dibble	10.00	7.50	4.50
☐ 14 Scott Erickson	10.00	7.50	4.50
☐ 15 Cecil Fielder	12.00	9.00	5.50
☐ 16 Chuck Finley	10.00	7.50	4.50
☐ 17 Tom Glavine	30.00	22.00	13.50
☐ 18 Juan Gonzalez	35.00	26.00	16.00
☐ 19 Ken Griffey Jr. Regular Uniform	20.00	15.00	9.00
☐ 20 Ken Griffey Jr. Spring Uniform	25.00	19.00	11.00
☐ 21 Tony Gwynn	24.00	18.00	11.00
☐ 22 Dave Henderson	10.00	7.50	4.50
☐ 23 Rickey Henderson	10.00	7.50	4.50
☐ 24 Bo Jackson Regular Uniform	10.00	7.50	4.50
☐ 25 Bo Jackson Spring Uniform	10.00	7.50	4.50
☐ 26 Howard Johnson	10.00	7.50	4.50
☐ 27 Felix Jose	10.00	7.50	4.50
☐ 28 Dave Justice	16.00	12.00	7.25
☐ 29 Kevin Maas	10.00	7.50	4.50
☐ 30 Ramon Martinez	10.00	7.50	4.50
☐ 31 Fred McGriff	16.00	12.00	7.25
☐ 32 Brian McRae	10.00	7.50	4.50
☐ 33 Kirby Puckett EXT	30.00	22.00	13.50
☐ 34 Cal Ripken	65.00	50.00	29.00
☐ 35 Nolan Ryan	35.00	26.00	16.00
☐ 36 Bret Saberhagen EXT	10.00	7.50	4.50
☐ 37 Chris Sabo	10.00	7.50	4.50
☐ 38 Ryne Sandberg	16.00	12.00	7.25
☐ 39 Tom Seaver EXT	35.00	26.00	16.00
☐ 40 Ruben Sierra	10.00	7.50	4.50
☐ 41 Darryl Strawberry	10.00	7.50	4.50
☐ 42 Danny Tartabull EXT	10.00	7.50	4.50
☐ 43 Frank Thomas Fielding Pose	40.00	30.00	18.00
☐ 44 FrankThomas EXT Batting Pose	50.00	38.00	22.00
☐ 45 Todd Van Poppel EXT	10.00	7.50	4.50
☐ 46 Matt Williams	14.00	10.50	6.25

1992 Kenner Starting Lineup Baseball Headline Collection

This seven-piece set was the first of the Headline Collection brand issued by Cincinnati-based Kenner Toy Company. The pieces feature Top Major League Baseball players in action poses. The figures are accompanied by an authentic newspaper article and a high gloss, black base used to insert the article and display the figure. The article is framed and describes a memorable moment from the previous season. The pieces came in 12-count case assortments. The values listed below refer to unopened packages. The figures are unnumbered and listed below in alphabetical order.

	MINT	NRMT	EXC
COMPLETE SET (7)	150.00	110.00	70.00
☐ 1 George Brett	40.00	30.00	18.00
☐ 2 Cecil Fielder	15.00	11.00	6.75
☐ 3 Ken Griffey Jr.	30.00	22.00	13.50
☐ 4 Rickey Henderson	15.00	11.00	6.75
☐ 5 Bo Jackson	14.00	10.50	6.25
☐ 6 Nolan Ryan	35.00	26.00	16.00
☐ 7 Ryne Sandberg	35.00	26.00	16.00

1993 Kenner Starting Lineup

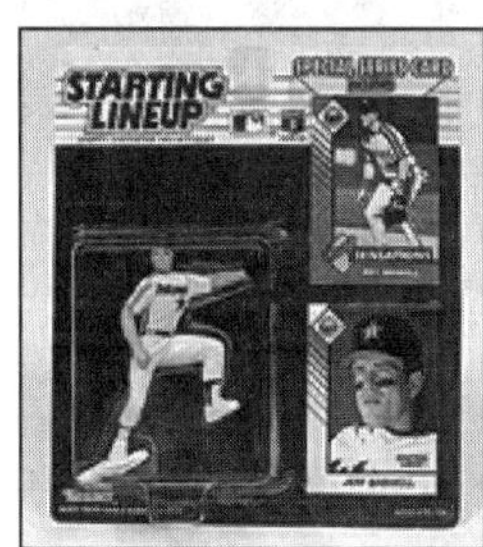

This 45-piece set was issued by Cincinnati-based Kenner Toy Company. The statues feature top Major League Baseball stars in action poses and are accompanied by two cards of each player. The regular card front has either a posed or action color shot. The back has biographical and statistical information and a facsimile signature. The second card is one of a titled subset. The front feature either a posed or action color shot. The back features a paragraph about the accomplishments of that player. The figures came in 16-piece case. Ken Griffey Jr. and Frank Thomas were the widest distributed figures even being included in cases that primarily contained National League players. A seven-piece extended series was released later in the year. The 16-piece case assortment that the extended series came in had seven different players. Nolan Ryan Retirement figure was the only piece to appear more than twice in the extended cases, showing up four per case. The David Neid and Benito Santiago extend series pieces were the first Starting Lineup figures to feature a player in the Colorado Rockies and Florida Marlin uniform respectively. Key first pieces include Carlos Baerga, Jeff Bagwell and Mike Mussina. The values listed below refer to unopened packages. The figures are unnumbered and checklisted below in alphabetical order. The set price does not include the two without eyeblack variations on Ken Griffey and Cal Ripken.

	MINT	NRMT	EXC
COMPLETE SET (45)	600.00	450.00	275.00
☐ 1 Roberto Alomar	12.00	9.00	5.50
☐ 2 Carlos Baerga	15.00	11.00	6.75
☐ 3 Jeff Bagwell	45.00	34.00	20.00
☐ 4 Barry Bonds Pirates Uniform	24.00	18.00	11.00
☐ 5 Barry BondsEXT Giants Uniform	25.00	19.00	11.00
☐ 6 Kevin Brown	10.00	7.50	4.50
☐ 7 Jose Canseco	10.00	7.50	4.50
☐ 8 Will Clark	10.00	7.50	4.50
☐ 9 Roger Clemens	10.00	7.50	4.50
☐ 10 David Cone	10.00	7.50	4.50
☐ 11 Carlton Fisk EXT	25.00	19.00	11.00
☐ 12 Travis Fryman	10.00	7.50	4.50
☐ 13 Tom Glavine	18.00	13.50	8.00
☐ 14 Juan Gonzalez	18.00	13.50	8.00
☐ 15 Ken Griffey Jr.	20.00	15.00	9.00
☐ 15B Ken Griffey Jr. Without Eyeblack	30.00	22.00	13.50
☐ 16 Marquis Grissom	10.00	7.50	4.50
☐ 17 Juan Guzman	10.00	7.50	4.50
☐ 18 Bo Jackson EXT	10.00	7.50	4.50
☐ 19 Eric Karros	15.00	11.00	6.75
☐ 20 Roberto Kelly	10.00	7.50	4.50
☐ 21 John Kruk	10.00	7.50	4.50
☐ 22 Ray Lankford	10.00	7.50	4.50
☐ 23 Barry Larkin	12.00	9.00	5.50
☐ 24 Shane Mack	10.00	7.50	4.50
☐ 25 Greg Maddux EXT	150.00	110.00	70.00
☐ 26 Jack McDowell	10.00	7.50	4.50
☐ 27 Fred McGriff	10.00	7.50	4.50
☐ 28 Mark McGwire	12.00	9.00	5.50
☐ 29 Mike Mussina	20.00	15.00	9.00
☐ 30 David Nied EXT	15.00	11.00	6.75
☐ 31 Dean Palmer	10.00	7.50	4.50
☐ 32 Terry Pendleton	10.00	7.50	4.50
☐ 33 Kirby Puckett	16.00	12.00	7.25
☐ 34 Cal Ripken	35.00	26.00	16.00
☐ 34B Cal Ripken Without Eyeblack	35.00	26.00	16.00
☐ 35 Bip Roberts	10.00	7.50	4.50
☐ 36 Nolan Ryan	30.00	22.00	13.50
☐ 37 Nolan Ryan EXT Retirement Pose	160.00	120.00	70.00
☐ 38 Ryne Sandberg	12.00	9.00	5.50
☐ 39 Benito Santiago EXT	10.00	7.50	4.50
☐ 40 Gary Sheffield	10.00	7.50	4.50
☐ 41 John Smoltz	40.00	30.00	18.00
☐ 42 Frank Thomas	20.00	15.00	9.00
☐ 43 Andy Van Slyke	10.00	7.50	4.50
☐ 44 Robin Ventura	10.00	7.50	4.50
☐ 45 Larry Walker	12.00	9.00	5.50

1993 Kenner Starting Lineup Baseball Headline Collection

This eight-piece set was the last in the Headline Collection series to be issued by Cincinnati-based Kenner Toy Company. The pieces feature top Major League Baseball players in action poses. The figures are accompanied by an authentic newspaper article and a high gloss, black base used to insert the article and display the figure. The article is framed and describes a memorable moment from the previous season. The pieces came in 12 count case assortments. The values listed below refer to unopened packages. The figures are unnumbered and listed below in alphabetical order.

	MINT	NRMT	EXC
COMPLETE SET (8)	175.00	130.00	80.00
☐ 1 Jim Abbott	16.00	12.00	7.25
☐ 2 Roberto Alomar	18.00	13.50	8.00
☐ 3 Tom Glavine	18.00	13.50	8.00
☐ 4 Mark McGwire	18.00	13.50	8.00
☐ 5 Cal Ripken	45.00	34.00	20.00
☐ 6 Nolan Ryan	50.00	38.00	22.00
☐ 7 Deion Sanders	18.00	13.50	8.00
☐ 8 Frank Thomas	30.00	22.00	13.50

1993 Kenner Starting Lineup Stadium Stars

This six-piece set was issued by the Cincinnati-based Kenner Toy Company. This was the first release of the Stadium Star brand. The figures are 25% larger than the typical Starting Lineup pieces. Each player is featured on top of a replica of their respective home stadium. The figures are also packaged in a window style display box. There were at least two different case assortments and eight figures in each case. A special case that featured only Nolan Ryan was issued late in the production release cycle. These cases were mainly distributed in the Southwest region of the U.S. The values listed below refer to unopened packages. The pieces are unnumbered and checklisted below in alphabetical order.

	MINT	NRMT	EXC
COMPLETE SET (6)	175.00	130.00	80.00
☐ 1 Roger Clemens	25.00	19.00	11.00
☐ 2 Cecil Fielder	20.00	15.00	9.00
☐ 3 Ken Griffey Jr.	32.00	24.00	14.50
☐ 4 Nolan Ryan	40.00	30.00	18.00
☐ 5 Ryne Sandberg	32.00	24.00	14.50
☐ 6 Frank Thomas	50.00	38.00	22.00

1994 Kenner Starting Lineup

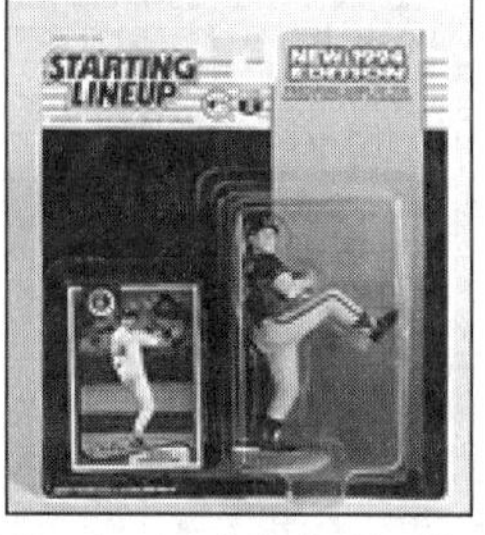

This 65-piece set was issued by Cincinnati-based Kenner Toy Company. The statues feature top Major League Baseball stars in action poses and are accompanied by a standard-size card of each player. The card front has either a posed or action color shot. The back has biographical and statistical information. The figures came in 16-piece cases and each case was either American League or National League. An eight-piece extended series was released later in the year. The extended figures also came in a 16-piece case assortment. Key first pieces include Randy Johnson, Kenny Lofton and Mike Piazza. The values listed below refer to unopened packages. The figures are unnumbered and checklisted below in alphabetical order.

	MINT	NRMT	EXC
COMPLETE SET (65)	550.00	400.00	250.00
☐ 1 Kevin Appier	8.00	6.00	3.60
☐ 2 Steve Avery	10.00	7.50	4.50
☐ 3 Carlos Baerga	10.00	7.50	4.50
☐ 4 Jeff Bagwell	18.00	13.50	8.00
☐ 5 Derek Bell	10.00	7.50	4.50
☐ 6 Jay Bell	10.00	7.50	4.50
☐ 7 Albert Belle	15.00	11.00	6.75
☐ 8 Wade Boggs	10.00	7.50	4.50
☐ 9 Barry Bonds	12.00	9.00	5.50
☐ 10 John Burkett	10.00	7.50	4.50
☐ 11 Steve Carlton EXT	30.00	22.00	13.50
☐ 12 Joe Carter	10.00	7.50	4.50
☐ 13 Will Clark EXT	14.00	10.50	6.25
☐ 14 Roger Clemens	12.00	9.00	5.50
☐ 15 David Cone	10.00	7.50	4.50

□ 16 Chad Curtis	10.00	7.50	4.50
□ 17 Darren Daulton	14.00	10.50	6.25
□ 18 Delino DeShields	10.00	7.50	4.50
□ 19 Lenny Dykstra EXT	12.00	9.00	5.50
□ 20 Alex Fernandez	12.00	9.00	5.50
□ 21 Cecil Fielder	10.00	7.50	4.50
□ 22 Andres Galarraga	14.00	10.50	6.25
□ 23 Juan Gonzalez EXT	18.00	13.50	8.00
□ 24 Tommy Greene	10.00	7.50	4.50
□ 25 Ken Griffey Jr.	20.00	15.00	9.00
□ 26 Mark Grace	10.00	7.50	4.50
□ 27 Brian Harper	10.00	7.50	4.50
□ 28 Bryan Harvey	10.00	7.50	4.50
□ 29 Charlie Hayes	10.00	7.50	4.50
□ 30 Chris Hoiles	10.00	7.50	4.50
□ 31 Dave Hollins	10.00	7.50	4.50
□ 32 Gregg Jefferies	10.00	7.50	4.50
□ 33 Randy Johnson	25.00	19.00	11.00
□ 34 Dave Justice	10.00	7.50	4.50
□ 35 Eric Karros	10.00	7.50	4.50
□ 36 Jimmy Key	14.00	10.50	6.25
□ 37 Darryl Kile	10.00	7.50	4.50
□ 38 Chuck Knoblauch	18.00	13.50	8.00
□ 39 Mark Langston	10.00	7.50	4.50
□ 40 Kenny Lofton EXT	45.00	34.00	20.00
□ 41 Don Mattingly	14.00	10.50	6.25
□ 42 Fred McGriff EXT	14.00	10.50	6.25
□ 43 Orlando Merced	10.00	7.50	4.50
□ 44 Paul Molitor	12.00	9.00	5.50
□ 45 Mike Mussina	12.00	9.00	5.50
□ 46 John Olerud	12.00	9.00	5.50
□ 47 Rafael Palmeiro EXT	14.00	10.50	6.25
□ 48 Tony Phillips	10.00	7.50	4.50
□ 49 Mike Piazza	45.00	34.00	20.00
□ 50 Jose Rijo	10.00	7.50	4.50
□ 51 Cal Ripken	30.00	22.00	13.50
□ 52 Ivan Rodriguez	15.00	11.00	6.75
□ 53 Tim Salmon	15.00	11.00	6.75
□ 54 Ryne Sandberg	20.00	15.00	9.00
□ 55 Curt Schilling	10.00	7.50	4.50
□ 56 Gary Sheffield	10.00	7.50	4.50
□ 57 Gary Sheffield EXT Power Pose	12.00	9.00	5.50
□ 58 J.T. Snow	15.00	11.00	6.75
□ 59 Frank Thomas	15.00	11.00	6.75
□ 60 Robby Thompson	10.00	7.50	4.50
□ 61 Greg Vaughn	10.00	7.50	4.50
□ 62 Mo Vaughn	18.00	13.50	8.00
□ 63 Robin Ventura	10.00	7.50	4.50
□ 64 Matt Williams	12.00	9.00	5.50
□ 65 Dave Winfield	12.00	9.00	5.50

1994 Kenner Starting Lineup Cooperstown Collection

This eight-piece set is the first in the Cooperstown Collection line to be released by Cincinnati-based Kenner Toy Company. Each figure is a Hall of Fame player in an action pose and is accompanied by a standard size card. Each card features a posed or an action shot on the front. The back has biographical and statistical information. The figures came in 16 count case assortments with Babe Ruth being the most prolific figure at three per case. One of the most valuable Starting Lineup figures is the #44 jersey variation of the Jackie Robinson figure. The values listed below refer to unopened packages. The figures are unnumbered and checklisted below in alphabetical order.

	MINT	NRMT	EXC
COMPLETE SET (8)	130.00	100.00	57.50
□ 1 Ty Cobb	15.00	11.00	6.75
□ 2 Lou Gehrig	15.00	11.00	6.75
□ 3 Reggie Jackson	30.00	22.00	13.50
□ 4 Willie Mays	15.00	11.00	6.75
□ 5A Jackie Robinson Number 42 on back of jersey	15.00	11.00	6.75
□ 5B Jackie Robinson Number 44 on back of jersey	550.00	400.00	250.00
□ 6 Babe Ruth	15.00	11.00	6.75
□ 7 Honus Wagner	30.00	22.00	13.50
□ 8 Cy Young	15.00	11.00	6.75

1994 Kenner Starting Lineup Stadium Stars

This eight-piece set was issued by the Cincinnati-based Kenner Toy Company. The figures are 25% larger than the typical Starting Lineup pieces. Each player is featured on top of a replica of their respective home stadium. The figures are also packaged in a window style display box. The figures came in at least three different eight count case assortments. The Bo Jackson figure is the shortest piece in the series. The values listed below refer to unopened packages. The pieces are unnumbered and checklisted below in alphabetical order.

	MINT	NRMT	EXC
COMPLETE SET (8)	200.00	150.00	90.00
□ 1 Barry Bonds	24.00	18.00	11.00
□ 2 Will Clark	24.00	18.00	11.00
□ 3 Dennis Eckersley	24.00	18.00	11.00
□ 4 Tom Glavine	24.00	18.00	11.00
□ 5 Juan Gonzalez	26.00	19.50	11.50
□ 6 Bo Jackson	60.00	45.00	27.00
□ 7 Kirby Puckett	24.00	18.00	11.00
□ 8 Deion Sanders	40.00	30.00	18.00

1995 Kenner Starting Lineup

This 67-piece set was issued by Cincinnati-based Kenner Toy Company. The statues feature top Major League Baseball stars in action poses and are accompanied by a standard-size card of each player. The card front has either a posed or action color shot. The back has biographical and statistical information. The figures came in 16-piece cases and each case was either American League or National League. A nine-piece extended series was released later in the year. The extended figures also came in a 16-piece case assortment. The extended series was highlighted by the Cal Ripken figure that features him in a 1982 Orioles uniform and has a sticker on the packaging that pays tribute to his breaking Lou Gehrig's streak. The first Alex Rodriguez piece was in the extended series. There was also a special release of Mike Schmidt 16-count cases to the Eastern region of the U.S. These figures were released in conjunction with his induction into the Hall-of-Fame. Key first pieces include Dante Bichette, Ryan Klesko, Javier Lopez, Raul Mondesi and Manny Ramirez. The values listed below refer to unopened packages. The figures are unnumbered and checklisted below in alphabetical order.

	MINT	NRMT	EXC
COMPLETE SET (67)	750.00	550.00	350.00
□ 1 Jim Abbott	10.00	7.50	4.50
□ 2 Moises Alou	12.00	9.00	5.50
□ 3 Carlos Baerga	10.00	7.50	4.50
□ 4 Jeff Bagwell	12.00	9.00	5.50
□ 5 Albert Belle	12.00	9.00	5.50
□ 6 Geronimo Berroa	10.00	7.50	4.50
□ 7 Dante Bichette	18.00	13.50	8.00
□ 8 Barry Bonds	12.00	9.00	5.50
□ 9 Jay Buhner	12.00	9.00	5.50
□ 10 Jose Canseco	10.00	7.50	4.50
□ 11 Jose Canseco EXT	10.00	7.50	4.50
□ 12 Chuck Carr	10.00	7.50	4.50
□ 13 Joe Carter	10.00	7.50	4.50
□ 14 Andujar Cedeno	10.00	7.50	4.50
□ 15 Will Clark	10.00	7.50	4.50
□ 16 Roger Clemens	10.00	7.50	4.50
□ 17 Jeff Conine	10.00	7.50	4.50
□ 18 Scott Cooper	10.00	7.50	4.50
□ 19 Darren Daulton	10.00	7.50	4.50
□ 20 Carlos Delgado	12.00	9.00	5.50
□ 21 Cecil Fielder	10.00	7.50	4.50
□ 22 Cliff Floyd	10.00	7.50	4.50
□ 23 Julio Franco	10.00	7.50	4.50
□ 24 Juan Gonzalez	12.00	9.00	5.50
□ 25 Rusty Greer EXT	15.00	11.00	6.75
□ 26 Ken Griffey Jr.	15.00	11.00	6.75
□ 27 Tony Gwynn	12.00	9.00	5.50
□ 28 Bob Hamelin	10.00	7.50	4.50
□ 29 Jeffery Hammonds	10.00	7.50	4.50
□ 30 Randy Johnson	14.00	10.50	6.25
□ 31 Jeff Kent	10.00	7.50	4.50
□ 32 Jeff King	10.00	7.50	4.50
□ 33 Ryan Klesko	40.00	30.00	18.00
□ 34 Chuck Knoblauch	12.00	9.00	5.50
□ 35 John Kruk	10.00	7.50	4.50
□ 36 Ray Lankford	10.00	7.50	4.50
□ 37 Barry Larkin	12.00	9.00	5.50
□ 38 Kenny Lofton EXT	40.00	30.00	18.00
□ 39 Javier Lopez	35.00	26.00	16.00
□ 40 Al Martin	10.00	7.50	4.50
□ 41 Brian McRae	10.00	7.50	4.50
□ 42 Paul Molitor	10.00	7.50	4.50
□ 43 Raul Mondesi	30.00	22.00	13.50
□ 44 Mike Mussina	10.00	7.50	4.50
□ 45 Troy Neel	10.00	7.50	4.50
□ 46 Dave Nilsson	10.00	7.50	4.50
□ 47 John Olerud	10.00	7.50	4.50
□ 48 Paul O'Neill	10.00	7.50	4.50
□ 49 Tom Pagnozzi EXT	10.00	7.50	4.50
□ 50 Mike Piazza	18.00	13.50	8.00
□ 51 Mike Piazza EXT Hitting Pose	20.00	15.00	9.00
□ 52 Kirby Puckett	12.00	9.00	5.50
□ 53 Manny Ramirez EXT	50.00	38.00	22.00
□ 54 Cal Ripken	25.00	19.00	11.00
□ 55 Cal Ripken EXT In 1982 Orioles Uniform	70.00	52.50	32.00
□ 56 Alex Rodriguez EXT	90.00	70.00	40.00
□ 57 Tim Salmon	10.00	7.50	4.50
□ 58 Deion Sanders	12.00	9.00	5.50
□ 59 Reggie Sanders	10.00	7.50	4.50
□ 60 Mike Schmidt EXT	15.00	11.00	6.75
□ 61 Sammy Sosa	12.00	9.00	5.50
□ 62 Mickey Tettleton	10.00	7.50	4.50
□ 63 Frank Thomas	15.00	11.00	6.75
□ 64 Andy Van Slyke	10.00	7.50	4.50
□ 65 Mo Vaughn	12.00	9.00	5.50
□ 66 Rick Wilkins	10.00	7.50	4.50
□ 67 Matt Williams	10.00	7.50	4.50

1995 Kenner Starting Lineup Cooperstown Collection

This 10-piece set was issued by Cincinnati-based Kenner Toy Company. Each figure is a Hall of Fame player in an action pose and is accompanied by a standard size card. Each card features a posed or an action shot on the front. The back has biographical and statistical information. The figures came in 16-count case assortments with Babe Ruth being available at a rate of three per case. Harmon Killebrew and Eddie Mathews are the toughest, being inserted only one per case respectively. The values listed below refer to unopened packages. Since the cards are unnumbered, we have listed this set in alphabetical order.

	MINT	NRMT	EXC
COMPLETE SET (10)	110.00	80.00	50.00
□ 1 Rod Carew	12.00	9.00	5.50
□ 2 Dizzy Dean	12.00	9.00	5.50
□ 3 Don Drysdale	12.00	9.00	5.50
□ 4 Bob Feller	12.00	9.00	5.50
□ 5 Whitey Ford	12.00	9.00	5.50
□ 6 Bob Gibson	12.00	9.00	5.50
□ 7 Harmon Killebrew	20.00	15.00	9.00
□ 8 Eddie Mathews	20.00	15.00	9.00
□ 9 Satchel Paige	12.00	9.00	5.50
□ 10 Babe Ruth	20.00	15.00	9.00

1995 Kenner Starting Lineup Stadium Stars

This nine-piece set was issued by the Cincinnati-based Kenner Toy Company. The figures are 25% larger than the typical Starting Lineup pieces. Each player is featured on top of a replica of their respective home stadium. The figures are also packaged in a window style display box. The figures came in at least three different eight count case assortments. Darren Daulton, Randy Johnson and Mark McGwire appear to be the shortest pieces in the series. The values listed below refer to unopened packages. The pieces are unnumbered and checklisted below in alphabetical order.

	MINT	NRMT	EXC
COMPLETE SET (9)	240.00	180.00	110.00
□ 1 Darren Daulton	35.00	26.00	16.00
□ 2 Lenny Dykstra	26.00	19.50	11.50
□ 3 Ken Griffey Jr.	30.00	22.00	13.50
□ 4 Randy Johnson	45.00	34.00	20.00
□ 5 Dave Justice	26.00	19.50	11.50
□ 6 Greg Maddux	45.00	34.00	20.00
□ 7 Mark McGwire	30.00	22.00	13.50
□ 8 Frank Thomas	30.00	22.00	13.50
□ 9 Mo Vaughn	26.00	19.50	11.50

1996 Kenner Starting Lineup

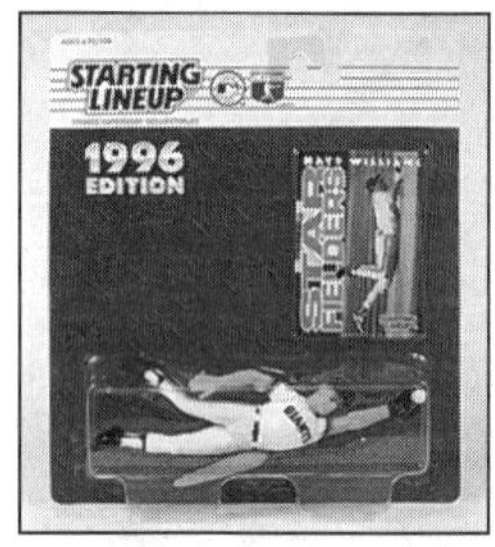

This 69-piece set was issued by Cincinnati-based Kenner Toy Company. The statues feature top Major League Baseball stars in action poses and are accompanied by a standard-size card of each player. The card front has either a posed or action color shot. The back has biographical and statistical information. The figures came in 16-piece cases and each case was either American League or National League. Cal Ripken and Hideo Nomo appear in two different poses in the set. There was a 16 piece extended set that is part of the listing below. Key first pieces are Derek Jeter, Chipper Jones and both Hideo Nomos. The Ken Griffey Jr. and Don Mattingly pieces from the extended series were the most popular extended figures. The values listed below refer to unopened packages. The figures are unnumbered and checklisted below in alphabetical order.

	MINT	NRMT	EXC
COMPLETE SET (69)	750.00	550.00	350.00
□ 1 Roberto Alomar	10.00	7.50	4.50
□ 2 Moises Alou EXT	12.00	9.00	5.50
□ 3 Garret Anderson FP EXT	12.00	9.00	5.50
□ 4 Carlos Baerga EXT	10.00	7.50	4.50
□ 5A Jeff Bagwell Black Bat	12.00	9.00	5.50
□ 5B Jeff Bagwell Tan Bat	12.00	9.00	5.50
□ 6 Albert Belle	12.00	9.00	5.50
□ 7 Dante Bichette EXT	12.00	9.00	5.50
□ 8 Craig Biggio	10.00	7.50	4.50
□ 9 Barry Bonds	12.00	9.00	5.50
□ 10 Ricky Bones	10.00	7.50	4.50
□ 11 Rico Brogna	10.00	7.50	4.50
□ 12 Ken Caminiti	12.00	9.00	5.50
□ 13 Joe Carter EXT	10.00	7.50	4.50
□ 14 Vinny Castilla	10.00	7.50	4.50
□ 15 Will Clark	10.00	7.50	4.50
□ 16 David Cone	10.00	7.50	4.50
□ 17 Jeff Conine EXT	10.00	7.50	4.50
□ 18 Marty Cordova	12.00	9.00	5.50
□ 18 Wil Cordero	10.00	7.50	4.50
□ 20 Chad Curtis EXT	10.00	7.50	4.50
□ 21 Shawon Dunston	10.00	7.50	4.50
□ 22 Lenny Dykstra	10.00	7.50	4.50
□ 23 Jim Edmonds	10.00	7.50	4.50
□ 24 Jim Eisenreich	10.00	7.50	4.50
□ 25 Gary Gaetti	10.00	7.50	4.50
□ 26 Ron Gant	10.00	7.50	4.50
□ 27 Juan Gonzalez EXT	15.00	11.00	6.75
□ 28 Ken Griffey Jr.	18.00	13.50	8.00
□ 29 Ken Griffey Jr. EXT	30.00	22.00	13.50
□ 30 Marquis Grissom	10.00	7.50	4.50
□ 31 Ozzie Guillen	10.00	7.50	4.50
□ 32 Brian L. Hunter	10.00	7.50	4.50
□ 33 Derek Jeter	50.00	38.00	22.00
□ 34 Charles Johnson	12.00	9.00	5.50
□ 35 Chipper Jones	120.00	90.00	55.00
□ 36 David Justice EXT	15.00	11.00	6.75
□ 37 Eric Karros EXT	10.00	7.50	4.50
□ 38 Barry Larkin EXT	12.00	9.00	5.50
□ 39 Greg Maddux	35.00	26.00	16.00
□ 40 Jeff Manto	10.00	7.50	4.50
□ 41 Edgar Martinez	12.00	9.00	5.50
□ 42 Don Mattingly EXT	20.00	15.00	9.00
□ 43 Fred McGriff	10.00	7.50	4.50
□ 44 Mark McGwire	12.00	9.00	5.50
□ 45 Raul Mondesi	10.00	7.50	4.50
□ 46 Hal Morris EXT	10.00	7.50	4.50
□ 47 Eddie Murray	12.00	9.00	5.50
□ 48 Denny Neagle EXT	14.00	10.50	6.25
□ 49 Hideo Nomo White Uniform	55.00	40.00	25.00
□ 50 Hideo Nomo Gray Uniform	55.00	40.00	25.00
□ 51 Paul O'Neill	10.00	7.50	4.50
□ 52 Rafael Palmeiro EXT	12.00	9.00	5.50
□ 53 Mike Piazza	12.00	9.00	5.50
□ 54 Kirby Puckett	10.00	7.50	4.50
□ 55 Cal Ripken Fielding Pose	25.00	19.00	11.00
□ 56 Cal Ripken Sliding Pose	25.00	19.00	11.00
□ 57 Ivan Rodriguez	10.00	7.50	4.50
□ 58 Deion Sanders	10.00	7.50	4.50
□ 59 Ozzie Smith	12.00	9.00	5.50
□ 60 Sammy Sosa	10.00	7.50	4.50
□ 61 Terry Steinbach	10.00	7.50	4.50
□ 62 Frank Thomas	15.00	11.00	6.75
□ 63 Jim Thome	20.00	15.00	9.00
□ 64 Ryan Thompson	10.00	7.50	4.50
□ 65 John Valentin	10.00	7.50	4.50
□ 66 Mo Vaughn	10.00	7.50	4.50
□ 67 Larry Walker	10.00	7.50	4.50
□ 68 Rondell White	10.00	7.50	4.50
□ 69 Matt Williams	10.00	7.50	4.50

1996 Kenner Starting Lineup Cooperstown Collection

This 10-piece set was issued by Cincinnati-based Kenner Toy Company. Each figure is a Hall of Fame player in an action pose and is accompanied by a standard size card. Each card features a posed or an action shot on the front. The back has biographical and statistical information. The figures came in two 16-count case assortments. There are two special figures that were produced in the Cooperstown Collection packaging but are not part of the 10-piece set. Those two figures are Richie Ashburn and Rod Carew. The Richie Ashburn figure was available through a Clover stores, a retail chain. The second figure, Rod Carew, was available for $10 to attendees of the 1996 National Sports Collectors Convention in Anaheim. These two piece are not valued in the complete set price. The values listed below refer to unopened packages. Since the figures are unnumbered, we have listed this set in alphabetical order.

	MINT	NRMT	EXC
COMPLETE SET (10)	125.00	95.00	55.00
□ 1 Hank Aaron	15.00	11.00	6.75
□ 2 Richie Ashburn Clover Retail Special	20.00	15.00	9.00
□ 3 Rod Carew National Sports Collectors Convention	35.00	26.00	16.00
□ 4 Grover Cleveland Alexander	12.00	9.00	5.50
□ 5 Roberto Clemente	15.00	11.00	6.75
□ 6 Jimmie Foxx	12.00	9.00	5.50
□ 7 Hank Greenberg	12.00	9.00	5.50
□ 8 Rogers Hornsby	12.00	9.00	5.50
□ 9 Joe Morgan	12.00	9.00	5.50
□ 10 Mel Ott	12.00	9.00	5.50
□ 11 Robin Roberts	12.00	9.00	5.50
□ 12 Jackie Robinson	15.00	11.00	6.75

1996 Kenner Starting Lineup Cooperstown Collection 12" Figures

This series of six figures was Kenner's first entry into the 12" figure market. The figures featued Hall of Fame players from the early part of the 20th century. Each figure was done with actual cloth uniforms and simiulated wood bats and gloves. Two of the pieces were exclusive to mass market retailers. The Babe Ruth Red Sox piece was only available at Kay Bee Toys and the Honus Wagner was only available at Toys-R-Us. These pieces carried an original retail price between $24.95 and $29.95.

	MINT	NRMT	EXC
COMPLETE SET (6)	150.00	110.00	70.00
☐ 1 Ty Cobb	30.00	22.00	13.50
☐ 2 Lou Gehrig	30.00	22.00	13.50
☐ 3 Babe Ruth Red Sox Uniform Kay Bee Toys	30.00	22.00	13.50
☐ 4 Babe Ruth Yankees	30.00	22.00	13.50
☐ 5 Honus Wagner Toys-R-Us Exclusive	30.00	22.00	13.50
☐ 6 Cy Young	30.00	22.00	13.50

1996 Kenner Starting Lineup Stadium Stars

This 11-piece set was issued by the Cincinnati-based Kenner Toy Company. The figures are 25% larger than the typical Starting Lineup pieces. Most players are featured on top of a replica of their respective home stadium. Due to contractual problems, Albert Belle, Mike Piazza, and Cal Ripken appear on top of Veteran Stadium. Veteran Stadium was chosen as a replacement since that was were the 1996 All-Star game was held. The figures are also packaged in a window style display box. The figures came in at least two different eight count case assortments. The values listed below refer to unopened packages. The pieces are unnumbered and checklisted below in alphabetical order.

	MINT	NRMT	EXC
COMPLETE SET (11)	300.00	220.00	135.00
☐ 1 Albert Belle	26.00	19.50	11.50
☐ 2 Jay Buhner	26.00	19.50	11.50
☐ 3 Jose Canseco	26.00	19.50	11.50
☐ 4 Darren Daulton	26.00	19.50	11.50
☐ 5 Mark Grace	26.00	19.50	11.50
☐ 6 Chuck Knoblauch	26.00	19.50	11.50
☐ 7 Javier Lopez	30.00	22.00	13.50
☐ 8 Mike Piazza	30.00	22.00	13.50
☐ 9 Cal Ripken	50.00	38.00	22.00
☐ 10 Robin Ventura	26.00	19.50	11.50
☐ 11 Matt Williams	26.00	19.50	11.50

1997 Kenner Starting Lineup

This 48-piece set was issued by Cincinnati-based Kenner Toy Company. The statues feature top Major League Baseball stars in action poses and are accompanied by a standard-size card of each player. The card front has either a posed or action color shot. The back has biographical and statistical information. The figures came in 16-piece cases and each case was either American League or National League. Tino Martinez and Bernie Williams both of the Yankees were amoung the key First Pieces. Brady Anderson first piece since 1989, the second Chipper Jones piece, and the second Alex Rodriguez piece are some of the most desirable in the set. The values listed below refer to unopened packages. The figures are unnumbered and checklisted below in alphabetical order.

	MINT	NRMT	EXC
COMPLETE SET (48)	600.00	450.00	275.00
☐ 1 Roberto Alomar	12.00	9.00	5.50
☐ 2 Brady Anderson	28.00	21.00	12.50
☐ 3 Jeff Bagwell	12.00	9.00	5.50
☐ 4 Derek Bell	10.00	7.50	4.50
☐ 5 Albert Belle	12.00	9.00	5.50
☐ 6 Dante Bichette	12.00	9.00	5.50
☐ 7 Barry Bonds	12.00	9.00	5.50
☐ 8 Scott Brosius	10.00	7.50	4.50
☐ 9 Ellis Burks	16.00	12.00	7.25
☐ 10 Roger Clemens	14.00	10.50	6.25
☐ 11 Johnny Damon	12.00	9.00	5.50
☐ 12 Steve Finley	16.00	12.00	7.25
☐ 13 Tom Glavine	14.00	10.50	6.25
☐ 14 Rusty Greer	10.00	7.50	4.50
☐ 15 Ken Griffey Jr.	18.00	13.50	8.00
☐ 16 Todd Hundley	20.00	15.00	9.00
☐ 17 Jason Isringhausen	12.00	9.00	5.50
☐ 18 John Jaha	10.00	7.50	4.50
☐ 19 Randy Johnson	14.00	10.50	6.25
☐ 20 Chipper Jones	40.00	30.00	18.00
☐ 21 Brian Jordan	15.00	11.00	6.75
☐ 22 Wally Joyner	10.00	7.50	4.50
☐ 23 Jason Kendall	16.00	12.00	7.25
☐ 24 Ryan Klesko	14.00	10.50	6.25
☐ 25 Javier Lopez	12.00	9.00	5.50
☐ 26 Tino Martinez	24.00	18.00	11.00
☐ 27 Brian McRae	10.00	7.50	4.50
☐ 28 Jose Mesa	10.00	7.50	4.50
☐ 29 Paul Molitor	12.00	9.00	5.50
☐ 30 Raul Mondesi	12.00	9.00	5.50
☐ 31 Hideo Nomo	18.00	13.50	8.00
☐ 32 Rey Ordonez	20.00	15.00	9.00
☐ 33 Chan Ho Park	20.00	15.00	9.00
☐ 34 Mike Piazza	12.00	9.00	5.50
☐ 35 Manny Ramirez	15.00	11.00	6.75
☐ 36 Cal Ripken	15.00	11.00	6.75
☐ 37 Alex Rodriguez	25.00	19.00	11.00
☐ 38 Henry Rodriguez	16.00	12.00	7.25
☐ 39 Ivan Rodriguez	12.00	9.00	5.50
☐ 40 Ryne Sandberg	12.00	9.00	5.50
☐ 41 Reggie Sanders	10.00	7.50	4.50
☐ 42 John Smoltz	20.00	15.00	9.00
☐ 43 J.T. Snow	12.00	9.00	5.50
☐ 44 Frank Thomas	14.00	10.50	6.25
☐ 45 Ismael Valdez	14.00	10.50	6.25
☐ 46 Devon White	12.00	9.00	5.50
☐ 47 Bernie Williams	24.00	18.00	11.00
☐ 48 Matt Williams	10.00	7.50	4.50

1997 Kenner Starting Lineup 12" Figures

This will be the second year that Kenner has produced 12" figures. This time Kenner did four modern players and one retired Hall of Famer. The Jackie Robinson piece will be a Target only retail special scheduled to hit in September. At press time none of the 12" figures were not live.

	MINT	NRMT	EXC
COMPLETE SET (4)			
☐ 1 Ken Griffey Jr.			
☐ 2 Greg Maddux			
☐ 3 Mike Piazza			
☐ 4 Cal Ripken			
☐ 5 Jackie Robinson Target Spec.			

1997 Kenner Starting Lineup Classic Doubles

This is the first time that Kenner has produced the Classic Doubles brand line. The figures feature a two figures to a package and inlcude such notable names as Mickey Mantle, Nolan Ryan and Roger Maris. There are 10 two-piece packages slated to be in this set. The series is due for release in July and at our deadline none of the figures were live.

	MINT	NRMT	EXC
COMPLETE SET (10)			
☐ 1 Hank Aaron Jackie Robinson			
☐ 2 Barry Bonds Bobby Bonds			
☐ 3 Don Drysdale Hideo Nomo			
☐ 4 Ken Griffey Ken Griffey Jr.			
☐ 5 Randy Johnson Nolan Ryan			
☐ 6 Greg Maddux Cy Young			
☐ 7 Mickey Mantle Roger Maris			
☐ 8 Roger Maris Mark McGwire			
☐ 9 Cal Ripken Brooks Robinson			
☐ 10 Babe Ruth Frank Thomas			

1997 Kenner Starting Lineup Cooperstown Collection

For the fourth consecutive year Kenner again plans to release its Cooperstown Collection. This years series will be 10 figures and include Mickey Mantle, Josh Gibson and Dottie Kamenshek. This is the first time Kenner has done a woman baseball player. At press time the only piece that was live was a special Cincinnati convention Johnny Bench figure. The figure only differentiated in that it had a sticker that mentioned its origin.The rest of the series is scheduled for release in June.

	MINT	NRMT	EXC
COMPLETE SET (10)			
☐ 1 Johnny Bench			
☐ 2 Rollie Fingers			
☐ 3 Josh Gibson			
☐ 4 Walter Johnson			
☐ 5 Dottie Kamenshek			
☐ 6 Mickey Mantle			
☐ 7 Brooks Robinson			
☐ 8 Duke Snider			
☐ 9 Hoyt Wilhelm			
☐ 10 Carl Yastrzemski			

1997 Kenner Starting Lineup Cooperstown Stadium Stars

Kenner decided to combine its Stadium Star line with Cooperstown players in 1997. The series features such notables as Babe Ruth and Mickey Mantle atop Yankee Stadium. Each figure comes with them standing on top of their respective home stadium.

	MINT	NRMT	EXC
COMPLETE SET (7)			
☐ 1 Hank Aaron	25.00	19.00	11.00
☐ 2 Ferguson Jenkins	22.00	16.50	10.00
☐ 3 Al Kaline	22.00	16.50	10.00
☐ 4 Mickey Mantle	50.00	37.50	22.50
☐ 5 Babe Ruth	30.00	22.50	13.50
☐ 6 Mike Schmidt	30.00	22.50	13.50
☐ 7 Carl Yastrzemski	22.00	16.50	10.00

1997 Kenner Starting Lineup Microverse

This is the first year that Kenner released the Mircoverse line. The figures are approximately 1" in heighth. There is two different series. The first released was the Swinging Stars. These pieces started hitting the shelves in late April. The next series is the Living Legends. They are scheduled to hit the market in July.

	MINT	NRMT	EXC
COMPLETE SET (12)			
☐ 1 Jeff Bagwell LL			
☐ 2 Barry Bonds SS	8.00	6.00	3.60
☐ 3 Joe Carter LL			
☐ 4 Ken Griffey Jr. SS	10.00	7.50	4.50
☐ 5 Tony Gwynn LL			
☐ 6 Barry Larkin LL			
☐ 7 Fred McGriff LL			
☐ 8 Mark McGwire LL			
☐ 9 Mike Piazza SS	8.00	6.00	3.60
☐ 10 Cal Ripken LL			
☐ 11 Frank Thomas SS	8.00	6.00	3.60
☐ 12 Mo Vaughn LL			

VINTAGE AUTOGRAPH PRICE GUIDE

( ) H.O.F. Induction Year
d. Deceased
Campanella- Pre-Accident

BASEBALL

Aaron, Hank-(1982)
3 X 5 12.00
8 X 10 Photo 25.00
Gold HOF Signed Postcard 25.00
Perez-Steele Signed Postcard 25.00
Single Signed Ball 50.00

Alexander, Grover Clev. (1938) d. 1950
3 X 5 350.00
8 X 10 Photo 700.00
B&W HOF Signed Postcard 1500.00
Single Signed Ball 3500.00

Alston, Walter-(1983) d. 1984
3 X 5 25.00
8 X 10 Photo 100.00
Cancelled Check 75.00
Gold HOF Signed Postcard 150.00
Single Signed Ball 850.00

Anson, Cap-(1939) d. 1922
3 X 5 1500.00
Signed Document 2500.00

Aparicio, Luis-(1984)
3 X 5 8.00
8 X 10 Photo 15.00
Gold HOF Signed Postcard 15.00
Perez-Steele Signed Postcard 15.00
Single Signed Ball 20.00

Appling, Luke-(1964) d. 1991
3 X 5 10.00
8 X 10 Photo 25.00
Gold HOF Signed Postcard 15.00
Perez-Steele Signed Postcard 50.00
Single Signed Ball 75.00

Ashburn, Richie-(1995)
3 X 5 5.00
8 X 10 Photo 15.00
Cancelled Check 25.00
Gold HOF Signed Postcard 15.00
Perez-Steele Signed Postcard 20.00
Single Signed Ball 25.00

Averill, Earl-(1975) d. 1983
3 X 5 15.00
8 X 10 Photo 50.00
Gold HOF Signed Postcard 25.00
Single Signed Ball 400.00

Baker, Frank-(1955) d. 1963
3 X 5 200.00
8 X 10 Photo 600.00
B&W HOF Signed Postcard 1200.00
Single Signed Ball 3500.00

Bancroft, Dave-(1971) d. 1972
3 X 5 150.00
8 X 10 Photo 300.00
Gold HOF Signed Postcard 600.00
Single Signed Ball 3500.00

Banks, Ernie-(1977)
3 X 5 10.00
8 X 10 Photo 15.00
Gold HOF Signed Postcard 15.00
Perez-Steele Signed Postcard 30.00
Single Signed Ball 35.00

Barlick, Al-(1989) d. 1995
3 X 5 5.00
8 X 10 Photo 15.00
Gold HOF Signed Postcard 15.00
Perez-Steele Signed Postcard 15.00
Single Signed Ball 25.00

Barrow, Ed-(1953) d. 1953
3 X 5 75.00
8 X 10 Photo 250.00
Cancelled Check 150.00
Single Signed Ball 3500.00

Beckley, Jake-(1971) d. 1918
3 X 5 1500.00
Signed Document 3500.00

Bell, Cool Papa-(1974) d. 1991
3 X 5 15.00
8 X 10 Photo 50.00
Gold HOF Signed Postcard 30.00
Perez-Steele Signed Postcard 75.00
Single Signed Ball 350.00

Bench, Johnny-(1989)
3 X 5 10.00
8 X 10 Photo 25.00
Gold HOF Signed Postcard 25.00
Perez-Steele Signed Postcard 30.00
Single Signed Ball 40.00

Bender, Chief-(1953) d. 1954
3 X 5 150.00
8 X 10 Photo 350.00
Cancelled Check 750.00
Single Signed Ball 3000.00

Berg, Moe d. 1972
3 X 5 100.00
8 X 10 Photo 350.00
Single Signed Ball 1200.00

Berra, Yogi-(1972)
3 X 5 8.00
8 X 10 Photo 15.00
Gold HOF Signed Postcard 20.00
Perez-Steele Signed Postcard 25.00
Single Signed Ball 50.00

Bottomley, Jim-(1974) d. 1959
3 X 5 200.00
8 X 10 Photo 400.00
Single Signed Ball 3500.00

Boudreau, Lou-(1970)
3 X 5 5.00
8 X 10 Photo 10.00
Cancelled Check 40.00
Gold HOF Signed Postcard 10.00
Perez-Steele Signed Postcard 25.00
Single Signed Ball 25.00

Bresnahan, Roger-(1945) d. 1944
3 X 5 400.00
Signed Document 1500.00
Single Signed Ball 5000.00

Brock, Lou-(1985)
3 X 5 5.00
8 X 10 Photo 15.00
Gold HOF Signed Postcard 15.00
Perez-Steele Signed Postcard 15.00
Single Signed Ball 25.00

Brouthers, Dan-(1945) d. 1932
3 X 5 1500.00
Signed Document 3000.00

Brown, Three-Finger-(1949) d. 1948
3 X 5 300.00
8 X 10 Photo 1000.00
Cancelled Check 750.00
Single Signed Ball 4000.00

Bunning, Jim (1996)
3 X 5 5.00
8 X 10 Photo 10.00
Gold HOF Signed Postcard 15.00
Single Signed Ball 25.00

Burkett, Jesse-(1946) d. 1953
3 X 5 450.00
8 X 10 Photo 1200.00
B&W HOF Signed Postcard 1500.00
Single Signed Ball 4000.00

Campanella, Roy-(1969) d. 1993
3 X 5 300.00
8 X 10 Photo 750.00
Single Signed Ball 3500.00

Carew, Rod-(1991)
3 X 5 5.00
8 X 10 Photo 15.00
Gold HOF Signed Postcard 20.00
Perez-Steele Signed Postcard 25.00
Single Signed Ball 35.00

Carey, Max-(1961) d. 1976
3 X 5 15.00
8 X 10 Photo 125.00
B&W HOF Signed Postcard 75.00
Cancelled Check 75.00
Gold HOF Signed Postcard 60.00
Single Signed Ball 500.00

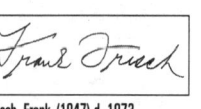

Carlton, Steve-(1994)
3 X 5 5.00
8 X 10 Photo 15.00
Gold HOF Signed Postcard 20.00
Perez-Steele Signed Postcard 35.00
Single Signed Ball 40.00

Cartwright, Alexander-(1938) d. 1892
3 X 5 750.00
Signed Document 2500.00

Chadwick, Henry-(1938) d. 1908
3 X 5 1500.00
Signed Document 3500.00

Chance, Frank-(1946) d. 1924
3 X 5 600.00
Signed Document 1800.00
Single Signed Ball 5000.00

Chandler, Happy-(1982) d. 1991
3 X 5 10.00
8 X 10 Photo 25.00
Gold HOF Signed Postcard 15.00
Perez-Steele Signed Postcard 25.00
Single Signed Ball 75.00

Charleston, Oscar-(1976) d. 1954
3 X 5 1000.00
Signed Document 3000.00
Single Signed Ball 5000.00

Chesbro, Jack-(1946) d. 1931
3 X 5 1000.00
Signed Document 3000.00

Clarke, Fred-(1945) d. 1960
3 X 5 150.00
8 X 10 Photo 400.00
B&W HOF Signed Postcard 650.00
Single Signed Ball 3000.00

Clarkson, John-(1963) d. 1909
3 X 5 1500.00
Signed Document 3500.00

Clemente, Roberto-(1973) d. 1972
3 X 5 250.00
8 X 10 Photo 600.00
Cancelled Check 1200.00
Single Signed Ball 3200.00

Cobb, Ty-(1936) d. 1961
3 X 5 300.00
8 X 10 Photo 1500.00
B&W HOF Signed Postcard 1200.00
Cancelled Check 350.00
Single Signed Ball 3500.00

Cochrane, Mickey-(1947) d. 1962
3 X 5 75.00
8 X 10 Photo 400.00
B&W HOF Signed Postcard 350.00
Cancelled Check 150.00
Single Signed Ball 2000.00

Collins, Eddie-(1939) d. 1951
3 X 5 100.00
8 X 10 Photo 400.00
B&W HOF Signed Postcard 1200.00
Single Signed Ball 3500.00

Collins, Jimmie-(1945) d. 1943
3 X 5 800.00
8 X 10 Photo 2000.00
Single Signed Ball 5000.00

Combs, Earle-(1970) d. 1976
3 X 5 20.00
8 X 10 Photo 125.00
Cancelled Check 10.00
Gold HOF Signed Postcard 35.00
Single Signed Ball 2000.00

Comiskey, Charles-(1939) d. 1931
3 X 5 450.00
8 X 10 Photo 1200.00
Single Signed Ball 6000.00

Conlan, Jocko-(1974) d. 1989
3 X 5 15.00
8 X 10 Photo 35.00
Gold HOF Signed Postcard 15.00
Perez-Steele Signed Postcard 50.00
Single Signed Ball 150.00

Connolly, Tom-(1953) d. 1963
3 X 5 350.00
8 X 10 Photo 750.00
B&W HOF Signed Postcard 1200.00
Single Signed Ball 3500.00

Connor, Roger-(1976) d. 1931
3 X 5 1000.00
Signed Document 3000.00
Single Signed Ball 6000.00

Coveleski, Stan-(1969) d. 1984
3 X 5 15.00
8 X 10 Photo 50.00
Gold HOF Signed Postcard 25.00
Single Signed Ball 450.00

Crawford, Sam-(1957) d. 1968
3 X 5 125.00
8 X 10 Photo 450.00
B&W HOF Signed Postcard 300.00
Gold HOF Signed Postcard 350.00
Single Signed Ball 2000.00

Cronin, Joe-(1956) d. 1984
3 X 5 20.00
8 X 10 Photo 100.00
B&W HOF Signed Postcard 40.00
Cancelled Check 125.00
Gold HOF Signed Postcard 30.00
Single Signed Ball 750.00

Cummings, Candy-(1939) d. 1924
3 X 5 1800.00
Signed Document 5000.00

Cuyler, Kiki-(1968) d. 1950
3 X 5 250.00
8 X 10 Photo 600.00
Single Signed Ball 3000.00

Dandridge, Ray-(1987) d. 1994
3 X 5 10.00
8 X 10 Photo 20.00
Cancelled Check 35.00
Gold HOF Signed Postcard 20.00
Perez-Steele Signed Postcard 15.00
Single Signed Ball 75.00

Day, Leon-(1995) d. 1995
3 X 5 10.00
8 X 10 Photo 45.00
Cancelled Check 100.00
Single Signed Ball 150.00

Dean, Dizzy-(1953) d. 1974
3 X 5 75.00
8 X 10 Photo 200.00
B&W HOF Signed Postcard 150.00
Gold HOF Signed Postcard 175.00
Single Signed Ball 800.00

Delahanty, Ed-(1945) d. 1903
3 X 5 1800.00
Signed Document 5000.00

Dickey, Bill-(1954) d. 1993
3 X 5 15.00
8 X 10 Photo 45.00
B&W HOF Signed Postcard 50.00
Cancelled Check 200.00
Gold HOF Signed Postcard 30.00
Perez-Steele Signed Postcard 75.00
Single Signed Ball 300.00

Dihigo, Martin-(1977) d. 1971
3 X 5 650.00
Signed Document 2000.00
Single Signed Ball 4000.00

DiMaggio, Joe-(1955)
3 X 5 75.00
8 X 10 Photo 125.00
B&W HOF Signed Postcard 175.00
Gold HOF Signed Postcard 125.00
Perez-Steele Signed Postcard 250.00
Single Signed Ball 250.00

Doerr, Bobby-(1986)
3 X 5 5.00
8 X 10 Photo 15.00
Cancelled Check 25.00
Gold HOF Signed Postcard 7.00
Perez-Steele Signed Postcard 10.00
Single Signed Ball 25.00

Drysdale, Don-(1984) d. 1993
3 X 5 15.00
8 X 10 Photo 40.00
Gold HOF Signed Postcard 35.00
Perez-Steele Signed Postcard 40.00
Single Signed Ball 125.00

Duffy, Hugh-(1945) d. 1954
3 X 5 300.00
8 X 10 Photo 900.00
B&W HOF Signed Postcard 1500.00
Single Signed Ball 2500.00

Durocher, Leo-(1994) d. 1991
3 X 5 25.00
8 X 10 Photo 40.00
Single Signed Ball 150.00

Evans, Billy-(1973) d. 1956
3 X 5 200.00
8 X 10 Photo 700.00
Single Signed Ball 3000.00

Evers, Johnny-(1946) d. 1947
3 X 5 400.00
8 X 10 Photo 1000.00
Single Signed Ball 4500.00

Ewing, Buck-(1939) d. 1906
3 X 5 1500.00
Signed Document 5000.00

Faber, Red-(1964) d. 1976
3 X 5 40.00
8 X 10 Photo 125.00
Gold HOF Signed Postcard 100.00
Single Signed Ball 1500.00

Feller, Bob-(1962)
3 X 5 5.00
8 X 10 Photo 10.00
B&W HOF Signed Postcard 20.00
Gold HOF Signed Postcard 10.00
Perez-Steele Signed Postcard 20.00
Single Signed Ball 25.00

Ferrell, Rick-(1984) d. 1995
3 X 5 8.00
8 X 10 Photo 20.00
Cancelled Check 30.00
Gold HOF Signed Postcard 10.00
Perez-Steele Signed Postcard 15.00
Single Signed Ball 75.00

Fingers, Rollie-(1992)
3 X 5 5.00
8 X 10 Photo 15.00
Gold HOF Signed Postcard 15.00
Perez-Steele Signed Postcard 20.00
Single Signed Ball 25.00

Flick, Elmer-(1963) d. 1971
3 X 5 50.00
8 X 10 Photo 150.00
B&W HOF Signed Postcard 350.00
Gold HOF Signed Postcard 500.00
Single Signed Ball 1500.00

Ford, Whitey-(1974)
3 X 5 8.00
8 X 10 Photo 15.00
Cancelled Check 35.00
Gold HOF Signed Postcard 20.00
Perez-Steele Signed Postcard 25.00
Single Signed Ball 30.00

Foster, Rube-(1981) d. 1930
3 X 5 2500.00
Signed Document 8000.00

Fox, Nellie-(1997) d. 1975
3 X 5 150.00
8 X 10 Photo 400.00
Cancelled Check 600.00
Single Signed Ball 1800.00

Foxx, Jimmie-(1951) d. 1967
3 X 5 250.00
8 X 10 Photo 700.00
B&W HOF Signed Postcard 800.00
Single Signed Ball 3000.00

Frick, Ford-(1970) d. 1978
3 X 5 50.00
8 X 10 Photo 150.00
Gold HOF Signed Postcard 125.00
Single Signed Ball 1500.00

Frisch, Frank-(1947) d. 1973
3 X 5 50.00
8 X 10 Photo 150.00
B&W HOF Signed Postcard 250.00
Cancelled Check 250.00
Gold HOF Signed Postcard 250.00
Single Signed Ball 1500.00

Furillo, Carl d. 1989
3 X 5 20.00
8 X 10 Photo 60.00
Single Signed Ball 350.00

Galvin, Pud-(1965) d. 1902
3 X 5 1250.00
Signed Document 3000.00

Gehrig, Lou-(1939) d. 1941
3 X 5 1000.00
8 X 10 Photo 4500.00
Single Signed Ball 8000.00

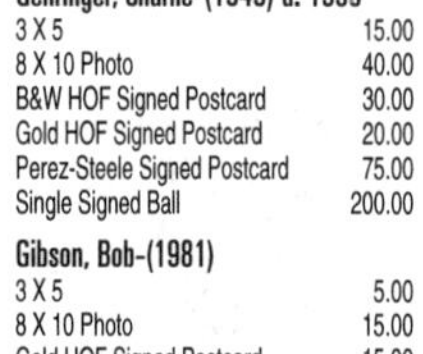

Gehringer, Charlie-(1949) d. 1993
3 X 5 15.00
8 X 10 Photo 40.00
B&W HOF Signed Postcard 30.00
Gold HOF Signed Postcard 20.00
Perez-Steele Signed Postcard 75.00
Single Signed Ball 200.00

Gibson, Bob-(1981)
3 X 5 5.00
8 X 10 Photo 15.00
Gold HOF Signed Postcard 15.00
Perez-Steele Signed Postcard 20.00
Single Signed Ball 25.00

Gibson, Josh-(1972) d. 1947
3 X 5 600.00
Signed Document 1500.00
Single Signed Ball 5000.00

Giles, Warren-(1979) d. 1979
3 X 5 30.00
8 X 10 Photo 100.00
Single Signed Ball 200.00

Gilliam, Jim d. 1978
3 X 5 20.00
8 X 10 Photo 60.00
Single Signed Ball 600.00

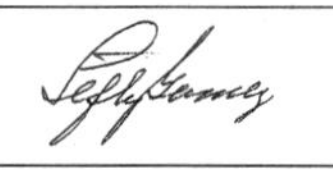

Gomez, Lefty-(1972) d. 1988
3 X 5 15.00
8 X 10 Photo 50.00
Gold HOF Signed Postcard 20.00
Perez-Steele Signed Postcard 75.00
Single Signed Ball 200.00

Goslin, Goose-(1968) d. 1971
3 X 5 100.00
8 X 10 Photo 300.00
Gold HOF Signed Postcard 400.00
Single Signed Ball 2000.00

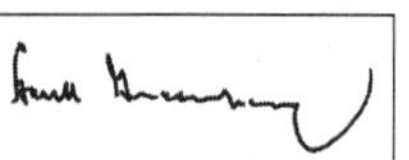

Greenberg, Hank-(1956) d. 1986
3 X 5 50.00
8 X 10 Photo 150.00
B&W HOF Signed Postcard 150.00
Gold HOF Signed Postcard 125.00
Perez-Steele Signed Postcard 300.00
Single Signed Ball 800.00

Griffith, Clark-(1946) d. 1955
3 X 5 200.00
8 X 10 Photo 600.00
B&W HOF Signed Postcard 750.00
Single Signed Ball 3500.00

Grimes, Burleigh-(1964) d. 1985
- 3 X 5 15.00
- 8 X 10 Photo 75.00
- Cancelled Check 60.00
- Gold HOF Signed Postcard 20.00
- Perez-Steele Signed Postcard 200.00
- Single Signed Ball 250.00

Grove, Lefty-(1947) d. 1975
- 3 X 5 40.00
- 8 X 10 Photo 150.00
- B&W HOF Signed Postcard 150.00
- Cancelled Check 100.00
- Gold HOF Signed Postcard 125.00
- Single Signed Ball 2000.00

Hafey, Chick-(1971) d. 1973
- 3 X 5 50.00
- 8 X 10 Photo 150.00
- Gold HOF Signed Postcard 400.00
- Single Signed Ball 2000.00

Haines, Jesse-(1970) d. 1978
- 3 X 5 25.00
- 8 X 10 Photo 125.00
- Cancelled Check 100.00
- Gold HOF Signed Postcard 100.00
- Single Signed Ball 1200.00

Hamilton, Billy-(1961) d. 1940
- 3 X 5 800.00
- 8 X 10 Photo 2000.00
- Single Signed Ball 5000.00

Harridge, Will-(1972) d. 1971
- 3 X 5 40.00
- 8 X 10 Photo 200.00
- Single Signed Ball 2500.00

Harris, Bucky-(1975) d. 1977
- 3 X 5 40.00
- 8 X 10 Photo 150.00
- Gold HOF Signed Postcard 150.00
- Single Signed Ball 1500.00

Hartnett, Gabby-(1955) d. 1972
- 3 X 5 60.00
- 8 X 10 Photo 150.00
- B&W HOF Signed Postcard 250.00
- Cancelled Check 250.00
- Gold HOF Signed Postcard 400.00
- Single Signed Ball 2000.00

Heilmann, Harry-(1952) d. 1951
- 3 X 5 350.00
- 8 X 10 Photo 800.00
- Single Signed Ball 3000.00

Herman, Billy-(1975) d. 1992
- 3 X 5 10.00
- 8 X 10 Photo 40.00
- Gold HOF Signed Postcard 10.00
- Perez-Steele Signed Postcard 25.00
- Single Signed Ball 150.00

Hodges, Gil d. 1972
- 3 X 5 75.00
- 8 X 10 Photo 250.00
- Single Signed Ball 1000.00

Hooper, Harry-(1971) d. 1974
- 3 X 5 25.00
- 8 X 10 Photo 125.00
- Cancelled Check 75.00
- Gold HOF Signed Postcard 150.00
- Single Signed Ball 750.00

Hornsby, Rogers-(1942) d. 1963
- 3 X 5 200.00
- 8 X 10 Photo 500.00
- B&W HOF Signed Postcard 450.00
- Single Signed Ball 2500.00

Howard, Elston d. 1980
- 3 X 5 100.00
- 8 X 10 Photo 350.00
- Single Signed Ball 1000.00

Hoyt, Waite-(1969) d. 1984
- 3 X 5 20.00
- 8 X 10 Photo 75.00
- Cancelled Check 125.00
- Gold HOF Signed Postcard 50.00
- Single Signed Ball 450.00

Hubbard, Cal-(1976) d. 1977
- 3 X 5 40.00
- 8 X 10 Photo 150.00
- Single Signed Ball 1000.00

Hubbell, Carl-(1947) d. 1988
- 3 X 5 15.00
- 8 X 10 Photo 50.00
- B&W HOF Signed Postcard 40.00
- Cancelled Check 75.00
- Gold HOF Signed Postcard 20.00
- Perez-Steele Signed Postcard 75.00
- Single Signed Ball 200.00

Hubbs, Ken d. 1964
- 3 X 5 25.00
- 8 X 10 Photo 150.00
- Single Signed Ball 700.00

Huggins, Miller-(1964) d. 1929
- 3 X 5 600.00
- 8 X 10 Photo 1800.00
- Single Signed Ball 4000.00

Hunter, Catfish-(1987)
- 3 X 5 5.00
- 8 X 10 Photo 15.00
- Gold HOF Signed Postcard 7.00
- Perez-Steele Signed Postcard 10.00
- Single Signed Ball 25.00

Irvin, Monte-(1973)
- 3 X 5 5.00
- 8 X 10 Photo 10.00
- Cancelled Check 25.00
- Gold HOF Signed Postcard 7.00
- Perez-Steele Signed Postcard 15.00
- Single Signed Ball 20.00

Jackson, Joe d. 1951
- 3 X 5 5000.00

Jackson, Reggie-(1993)
- 10.00
- 8 X 10 Photo 25.00
- Gold HOF Signed Postcard 50.00
- Perez-Steele Signed Postcard 50.00
- Single Signed Ball 65.00

Jackson, Travis-(1982) d. 1987
- 3 X 5 25.00
- 8 X 10 Photo 75.00
- Gold HOF Signed Postcard 40.00
- Perez-Steele Signed Postcard 75.00
- Single Signed Ball 300.00

Jenkins, Ferguson-(1991)
- 3 X 5 5.00
- 8 X 10 Photo 10.00
- Gold HOF Signed Postcard 10.00
- Perez-Steele Signed Postcard 15.00
- Single Signed Ball 25.00

Jennings, Hughie-(1945) d. 1928
- 3 X 5 700.00
- 8 X 10 Photo 2000.00
- Single Signed Ball 6000.00

Jensen, Jackie d. 1982
- 3 X 5 20.00
- 8 X 10 Photo 50.00
- Cancelled Check 100.00
- Single Signed Ball 150.00

Johnson, Ban-(1937) d. 1931
- 3 X 5 350.00
- 8 X 10 Photo 1000.00
- Single Signed Ball 3000.00

Johnson, Judy-(1975) d. 1989
- 3 X 5 15.00
- 8 X 10 Photo 35.00
- Gold HOF Signed Postcard 40.00
- Perez-Steele Signed Postcard 60.00
- Single Signed Ball 225.00

Johnson, Walter-(1936) d. 1946
- 3 X 5 400.00
- 8 X 10 Photo 1000.00
- B&W HOF Signed Postcard 1200.00
- Cancelled Check 1000.00
- Single Signed Ball 4000.00

Joss, Addie-(1978) d. 1911
- 3 X 5 1500.00
- Signed Document 4000.00

Kaline, Al-(1980)
- 3 X 5 8.00
- 8 X 10 Photo 15.00
- Gold HOF Signed Postcard 15.00
- Perez-Steele Signed Postcard 20.00
- Single Signed Ball 30.00

Keefe, Tim-(1964) d. 1933
- 3 X 5 1000.00
- Signed Document 2500.00
- Single Signed Ball 5500.00

Keeler, Willie-(1939) d. 1923
- 3 X 5 1000.00
- Signed Document 2500.00
- Single Signed Ball 6500.00

Kell, George-(1983)
- 3 X 5 5.00
- 8 X 10 Photo 10.00
- Gold HOF Signed Postcard 7.00
- Perez-Steele Signed Postcard 15.00
- Single Signed Ball 20.00

Kelley, Joe-(1971) d. 1943
- 3 X 5 1200.00
- 8 X 10 Photo 3000.00
- Single Signed Ball 6000.00

Kelly, George-(1973) d. 1984
- 3 X 5 10.00
- 8 X 10 Photo 50.00
- Cancelled Check 60.00
- Gold HOF Signed Postcard 25.00
- Perez-Steele Signed Postcard 300.00
- Single Signed Ball 250.00

Kelly, Mike "King"-(1945) d. 1894
- 3 X 5 1800.00
- Signed Document 4500.00

Killebrew, Harmon-(1984)
- 3 X 5 8.00
- 8 X 10 Photo 15.00
- Gold HOF Signed Postcard 15.00
- Perez-Steele Signed Postcard 20.00
- Single Signed Ball 30.00

Kiner, Ralph-(1975)
- 3 X 5 5.00
- 8 X 10 Photo 15.00
- Gold HOF Signed Postcard 7.00
- Perez-Steele Signed Postcard 15.00
- Single Signed Ball 25.00

Klein, Chuck-(1980) d. 1958
- 3 X 5 250.00
- 8 X 10 Photo 750.00
- Single Signed Ball 2500.00

Klem, Bill-(1953) d. 1951
- 3 X 5 300.00
- 8 X 10 Photo 750.00
- Single Signed Ball 2500.00

Kluszewski, Ted d. 1988
- 3 X 5 20.00
- 8 X 10 Photo 50.00
- Cancelled Check 100.00
- Single Signed Ball 150.00

Koufax, Sandy-(1972)
- 3 X 5 12.00
- 8 X 10 Photo 35.00
- Gold HOF Signed Postcard 50.00
- Perez-Steele Signed Postcard 50.00
- Single Signed Ball 75.00

Lajoie, Nap-(1937) d. 1959
- 3 X 5 300.00
- 8 X 10 Photo 1000.00
- B&W HOF Signed Postcard 750.00
- Single Signed Ball 4000.00

Landis, Kenesaw-(1939) d. 1944
- 3 X 5 250.00
- 8 X 10 Photo 750.00
- Single Signed Ball 3500.00

Lazzeri, Tony-(1991) d. 1946
- 3 X 5 325.00
- 8 X 10 Photo 850.00
- Single Signed Ball 3500.00

Lemon, Bob-(1976)
- 3 X 5 5.00
- 8 X 10 Photo 10.00
- Gold HOF Signed Postcard 7.00
- Perez-Steele Signed Postcard 15.00
- Single Signed Ball 20.00

Leonard, Buck-(1972)
- 3 X 5 15.00
- 8 X 10 Photo 30.00
- Cancelled Check 25.00
- Gold HOF Signed Postcard 20.00
- Perez-Steele Signed Postcard 35.00
- Single Signed Ball 50.00

Lindstrom, Fred-(1976) d. 1981
- 3 X 5 25.00
- 8 X 10 Photo 100.00
- Gold HOF Signed Postcard 50.00
- Single Signed Ball 500.00

Lloyd, John Henry-(1977) d. 1964
- 3 X 5 750.00
- 8 X 10 Photo 2500.00
- Single Signed Ball 5000.00

Lombardi, Ernie-(1986) d. 1977
- 3 X 5 50.00
- 8 X 10 Photo 125.00
- Single Signed Ball 1000.00

Lopez, Al-(1977)
- 3 X 5 15.00
- 8 X 10 Photo 30.00
- Gold HOF Signed Postcard 20.00
- Perez-Steele Signed Postcard 75.00
- Single Signed Ball 75.00

Lyons, Ted-(1955) d. 1986
- 3 X 5 20.00
- 8 X 10 Photo 50.00
- B&W HOF Signed Postcard 30.00
- Cancelled Check 60.00
- Gold HOF Signed Postcard 30.00
- Perez-Steele Signed Postcard 200.00
- Single Signed Ball 200.00

Mack, Connie-(1937) d. 1956
- 3 X 5 150.00
- 8 X 10 Photo 350.00
- B&W HOF Signed Postcard 750.00
- Single Signed Ball 1800.00

MacPhail, Larry-(1978) d. 1975
- 3 X 5 100.00
- 8 X 10 Photo 250.00
- Single Signed Ball 1500.00

Mantle, Mickey-(1974) d. 1995
- 3 X 5 50.00
- 8 X 10 Photo 100.00
- Gold HOF Signed Postcard 150.00
- Perez-Steele Signed Postcard 250.00
- Single Signed Ball 200.00

Manush, Heinie-(1964) d. 1971
- 3 X 5 50.00
- 8 X 10 Photo 200.00
- Gold HOF Signed Postcard 200.00
- Single Signed Ball 1500.00

Maranville, Rabbit-(1954) d. 1954
- 3 X 5 200.00
- 8 X 10 Photo 500.00
- B&W HOF Signed Postcard 700.00
- Single Signed Ball 1500.00

Marichal, Juan-(1983)
- 3 X 5 5.00
- 8 X 10 Photo 15.00
- Gold HOF Signed Postcard 10.00
- Perez-Steele Signed Postcard 10.00
- Single Signed Ball 30.00

Maris, Roger d. 1985
- 3 X 5 150.00
- 8 X 10 Photo 450.00
- Single Signed Ball 1200.00

Marquard, Rube-(1971) d. 1980
- 3 X 5 40.00
- 8 X 10 Photo 100.00
- Gold HOF Signed Postcard 40.00
- Single Signed Ball 750.00

Martin, Billy d. 1989
- 3 X 5 15.00
- 8 X 10 Photo 50.00
- Single Signed Ball 150.00

Mathews, Eddie-(1978)
- 3 X 5 8.00
- 8 X 10 Photo 15.00
- Gold HOF Signed Postcard 10.00
- Perez-Steele Signed Postcard 15.00
- Single Signed Ball 30.00

Mathewson, Christy-(1936) d. 1925
- 3 X 5 1000.00
- 8 X 10 Photo 3500.00
- Single Signed Ball 10000.00

Mays, Willie-(1979)
- 3 X 5 20.00
- 8 X 10 Photo 35.00
- Gold HOF Signed Postcard 30.00
- Perez-Steele Signed Postcard 50.00
- Single Signed Ball 50.00

McCarthy, Joe-(1957) d. 1978
- 3 X 5 40.00
- 8 X 10 Photo 150.00
- B&W HOF Signed Postcard 75.00
- Gold HOF Signed Postcard 50.00
- Single Signed Ball 1200.00

McCarthy, Tom-(1946) d. 1922
- 3 X 5 1200.00
- 8 X 10 Photo 4000.00

McCovey, Willie-(1986)
- 3 X 5 8.00
- 8 X 10 Photo 15.00
- Cancelled Check 40.00
- Gold HOF Signed Postcard 15.00
- Perez-Steele Signed Postcard 15.00
- Single Signed Ball 40.00

McGinnity, Joe-(1946) d. 1929
- 3 X 5 1000.00
- Signed Document 4500.00
- Single Signed Ball 6000.00

McGowan, Bill-(1992) d. 1954
- 3 X 5 350.00
- 8 X 10 Photo 1200.00
- Single Signed Ball 3000.00

McGraw, John-(1937) d. 1934
- 3 X 5 650.00
- 8 X 10 Photo 1500.00
- Single Signed Ball 5500.00

McKechnie, Bill-(1962) d. 1965
- 3 X 5 125.00
- 8 X 10 Photo 350.00
- B&W HOF Signed Postcard 400.00
- Single Signed Ball 2500.00

Medwick, Joe-(1968) d. 1975
- 3 X 5 40.00
- 8 X 10 Photo 150.00
- Gold HOF Signed Postcard 150.00
- Single Signed Ball 750.00

Mize, Johnny-(1981) d. 1993
- 3 X 5 10.00
- 8 X 10 Photo 20.00
- Gold HOF Signed Postcard 15.00
- Perez-Steele Signed Postcard 25.00
- Single Signed Ball 50.00

Morgan, Joe-(1990)
- 3 X 5 8.00
- 8 X 10 Photo 15.00
- Gold HOF Signed Postcard 15.00
- Perez-Steele Signed Postcard 20.00
- Single Signed Ball 30.00

Munson, Thurman d. 1979
- 3 X 5 175.00
- 8 X 10 Photo 400.00
- Single Signed Ball 1500.00

Musial, Stan-(1969)
- 3 X 5 15.00
- 8 X 10 Photo 25.00
- Gold HOF Signed Postcard 25.00
- Perez-Steele Signed Postcard 50.00
- Single Signed Ball 50.00

Newhouser, Hal-(1992)
- 3 X 5 5.00
- 8 X 10 Photo 15.00
- Gold HOF Signed Postcard 7.00
- Perez-Steele Signed Postcard 25.00
- Single Signed Ball 30.00

Nichols, Kid-(1949) d. 1953
- 3 X 5 300.00
- 8 X 10 Photo 600.00
- B&W HOF Signed Postcard 1500.00
- Single Signed Ball 3000.00

O'Rourke, Jim-(1945) d. 1914
- 3 X 5 1200.00
- Signed Document 3500.00

Ott, Mel-(1951) d. 1958
- 3 X 5 250.00
- 8 X 10 Photo 750.00
- B&W HOF Signed Postcard 700.00
- Cancelled Check 350.00
- Single Signed Ball 3500.00

Paige, Satchel-(1971) d. 1982
- 3 X 5 75.00
- 8 X 10 Photo 250.00
- Gold HOF Signed Postcard 175.00
- Single Signed Ball 1200.00

Palmer, Jim-(1990)
- 3 X 5 5.00
- 8 X 10 Photo 15.00
- Gold HOF Signed Postcard 15.00
- Perez-Steele Signed Postcard 20.00
- Single Signed Ball 25.00

Pennock, Herb-(1948) d. 1948
- 3 X 5 200.00
- 8 X 10 Photo 600.00
- Single Signed Ball 2500.00

Perry, Gaylord-(1991)
- 3 X 5 5.00
- 8 X 10 Photo 15.00
- Gold HOF Signed Postcard 7.00
- Perez-Steele Signed Postcard 15.00
- Single Signed Ball 25.00

Plank, Eddie-(1946) d. 1926
- 3 X 5 1000.00
- 8 X 10 Photo 3500.00
- Single Signed Ball 7000.00

Radbourne, Hoss-(1939) d. 1897
- 3 X 5 1200.00
- Signed Document 3500.00

Reese, Pee Wee-(1984)
- 3 X 5 10.00
- 8 X 10 Photo 25.00
- Gold HOF Signed Postcard 30.00
- Perez-Steele Signed Postcard 25.00
- Single Signed Ball 50.00

Rice, Sam-(1963) d. 1974
- 3 X 5 30.00
- 8 X 10 Photo 175.00
- B&W HOF Signed Postcard 125.00
- Gold HOF Signed Postcard 150.00
- Single Signed Ball 1500.00

Rickey, Branch-(1967) d. 1965
- 3 X 5 150.00
- 8 X 10 Photo 400.00
- Single Signed Ball 1500.00

Rixey, Eppa-(1963) d. 1963
- 3 X 5 150.00
- 8 X 10 Photo 500.00
- Cancelled Check 150.00
- Single Signed Ball 2500.00

Rizzuto, Phil-(1994)
- 3 X 5 8.00
- 8 X 10 Photo 15.00
- Gold HOF Signed Postcard 20.00
- Perez-Steele Signed Postcard 25.00
- Single Signed Ball 30.00

Roberts, Robin-(1976)
- 3 X 5 5.00
- 8 X 10 Photo 10.00
- Gold HOF Signed Postcard 7.00
- Perez-Steele Signed Postcard 15.00
- Single Signed Ball 20.00

Robinson, Brooks-(1983)
- 3 X 5 5.00
- 8 X 10 Photo 15.00
- Gold HOF Signed Postcard 10.00
- Perez-Steele Signed Postcard 15.00
- Single Signed Ball 25.00

Robinson, Frank-(1982)
- 3 X 5 10.00
- 8 X 10 Photo 25.00
- Gold HOF Signed Postcard 15.00
- Perez-Steele Signed Postcard 15.00
- Single Signed Ball 30.00

Robinson, Jackie-(1962) d. 1972	
3 X 5	250.00
8 X 10 Photo	600.00
B&W HOF Signed Postcard	750.00
Cancelled Check	400.00
Gold HOF Signed Postcard	300.00
Single Signed Ball	3200.00

Robinson, Wilbert-(1945) d. 1934	
3 X 5	750.00
8 X 10 Photo	2000.00
Single Signed Ball	5500.00

Roush, Edd-(1962) d. 1988	
3 X 5	15.00
8 X 10 Photo	35.00
B&W HOF Signed Postcard	30.00
Gold HOF Signed Postcard	20.00
Perez-Steele Signed Postcard	75.00
Single Signed Ball	300.00

Ruffing, Red-(1967) d. 1986	
3 X 5	25.00
8 X 10 Photo	100.00
Gold HOF Signed Postcard	75.00
Single Signed Ball	500.00

Rusie, Amos-(1977) d. 1942	
3 X 5	700.00
8 X 10 Photo	2000.00
Single Signed Ball	5000.00

Ruth, Babe-(1936) d. 1948	
3 X 5	750.00
8 X 10 Photo	2500.00
Cancelled Check	1500.00
Single Signed Ball	5000.00

Schalk, Ray-(1955) d. 1970	
3 X 5	50.00
8 X 10 Photo	150.00
B&W HOF Signed Postcard	250.00
Gold HOF Signed Postcard	450.00
Single Signed Ball	1200.00

Schmidt, Mike-(1995)	
3 X 5	10.00
8 X 10 Photo	20.00
Gold HOF Signed Postcard	50.00
Perez-Steele Signed Postcard	60.00
Single Signed Ball	50.00

Schoendienst, Red-(1989)	
3 X 5	5.00
8 X 10 Photo	15.00
Gold HOF Signed Postcard	10.00
Perez-Steele Signed Postcard	15.00
Single Signed Ball	25.00

Seaver, Tom-(1992)	
3 X 5	8.00
8 X 10 Photo	15.00
Gold HOF Signed Postcard	20.00
Perez-Steele Signed Postcard	40.00
Single Signed Ball	40.00

Sewell, Joe-(1977) d. 1990	
3 X 5	15.00
8 X 10 Photo	40.00
Cancelled Check	30.00
Gold HOF Signed Postcard	20.00
Perez-Steele Signed Postcard	50.00
Single Signed Ball	100.00

Simmons, Al-(1953) d. 1956	
3 X 5	200.00
8 X 10 Photo	500.00
B&W HOF Signed Postcard	600.00
Cancelled Check	175.00
Single Signed Ball	2000.00

Sisler, George-(1939) d. 1973	
3 X 5	50.00
8 X 10 Photo	150.00
B&W HOF Signed Postcard	125.00
Gold HOF Signed Postcard	150.00
Single Signed Ball	1500.00

Slaughter Enos-(1985)	
3 X 5	5.00
8 X 10 Photo	15.00
Cancelled Check	30.00
Gold HOF Signed Postcard	7.00
Perez-Steele Signed Postcard	15.00
Single Signed Ball	25.00

Snider, Duke-(1980)	
3 X 5	10.00
8 X 10 Photo	15.00
Cancelled Check	50.00
Gold HOF Signed Postcard	10.00
Perez-Steele Signed Postcard	25.00
Single Signed Ball	30.00

Spahn, Warren-(1973)	
3 X 5	8.00
8 X 10 Photo	15.00
Gold HOF Signed Postcard	10.00
Perez-Steele Signed Postcard	20.00
Single Signed Ball	30.00

Spalding, Al-(1939) d. 1915	
3 X 5	1000.00
Signed Document	3000.00

Speaker, Tris-(1937) d. 1958	
3 X 5	250.00
8 X 10 Photo	700.00
B&W HOF Signed Postcard	800.00
Single Signed Ball	3000.00

Stargell, Willie-(1988)	
3 X 5	5.00
8 X 10 Photo	15.00
Gold HOF Signed Postcard	7.00
Perez-Steele Signed Postcard	15.00
Single Signed Ball	25.00

Stengel, Casey-(1966) d. 1975	
3 X 5	60.00
8 X 10 Photo	200.00
Gold HOF Signed Postcard	150.00
Single Signed Ball	1000.00

Terry, Bill-(1954) d. 1989	
3 X 5	15.00
8 X 10 Photo	35.00
B&W HOF Signed Postcard	30.00
Cancelled Check	75.00
Gold HOF Signed Postcard	20.00
Perez-Steele Signed Postcard	75.00
Single Signed Ball	350.00

Thompson, Sam-(1974) d. 1922	
3 X 5	1500.00
Signed Document	4000.00

Tinker, Joe-(1946) d. 1948	
3 X 5	450.00
8 X 10 Photo	1200.00
Single Signed Ball	3500.00

Traynor, Pie-(1948) d. 1972	
3 X 5	100.00
8 X 10 Photo	400.00
B&W HOF Signed Postcard	300.00
Gold HOF Signed Postcard	500.00
Single Signed Ball	1500.00

Vance, Dazzy-(1955) d. 1961	
3 X 5	200.00
8 X 10 Photo	500.00
Single Signed Ball	2000.00

Vaughan, Arky-(1985) d. 1952	
3 X 5	300.00
8 X 10 Photo	600.00
Single Signed Ball	3000.00

Veeck, Bill-(1991) d. 1987	
3 X 5	10.00
8 X 10 Photo	50.00
Single Signed Ball	750.00

Waddell, Rube-(1946) d. 1914	
3 X 5	1250.00
Signed Document	4000.00

Wagner, Honus-(1936) d. 1955	
3 X 5	350.00
8 X 10 Photo	1000.00
Cancelled Check	2000.00
Single Signed Ball	3500.00

Wallace, Bobby-(1953) d. 1960	
3 X 5	300.00
8 X 10 Photo	1200.00
B&W HOF Signed Postcard	1500.00
Single Signed Ball	2500.00

Walsh, Ed-(1946) d. 1959	
3 X 5	250.00
8 X 10 Photo	750.00
B&W HOF Signed Postcard	400.00
Single Signed Ball	3000.00

Waner, Lloyd-(1967) d. 1982	
3 X 5	25.00
8 X 10 Photo	75.00
Gold HOF Signed Postcard	30.00
Single Signed Ball	500.00

Waner, Paul-(1952) d. 1965	
3 X 5	150.00
8 X 10 Photo	300.00
B&W HOF Signed Postcard	350.00
Single Signed Ball	2000.00

Ward, John-(1964) d. 1925	
3 X 5	2000.00
Signed Document	4000.00

Weaver, Earl (1996)	
3 X 5	5.00
8 X 10 Photo	15.00
Gold HOF Signed Postcard	15.00
Single Signed Ball	25.00

Welch, Mickey-(1973) d. 1941	
3 X 5	1200.00
8 X 10 Photo	3500.00
Single Signed Ball	6000.00

Wheat, Zack-(1959) d. 1972	
3 X 5	50.00
8 X 10 Photo	150.00
B&W HOF Signed Postcard	250.00
Cancelled Check	650.00
Gold HOF Signed Postcard	350.00
Single Signed Ball	1500.00

Wilhelm, Hoyt-(1985)	
3 X 5	5.00
8 X 10 Photo	12.00
Cancelled Check	25.00
Gold HOF Signed Postcard	7.00
Perez-Steele Signed Postcard	10.00
Single Signed Ball	25.00

Williams, Billy-(1987)	
3 X 5	5.00
8 X 10 Photo	12.00
Gold HOF Signed Postcard	7.00
Perez-Steele Signed Postcard	10.00
Single Signed Ball	25.00

Williams, Ted-(1966)	
3 X 5	60.00
8 X 10 Photo	125.00
Gold HOF Signed Postcard	125.00
Perez-Steele Signed Postcard	200.00
Single Signed Ball	175.00

Willis, Vic-(1995) d. 1947	
3 X 5	1000.00
Signed Document	2500.00

Wilson, Hack-(1979) d. 1948	
3 X 5	400.00
8 X 10 Photo	1000.00
Cancelled Check	650.00
Single Signed Ball	4000.00

Wright, George-(1937) d. 1937	
3 X 5	700.00
8 X 10 Photo	2500.00
Single Signed Ball	6000.00

Wright, Harry-(1953) d. 1895	
3 X 5	1000.00
Signed Document	4000.00

Wynn, Early-(1972)	
3 X 5	5.00
8 X 10 Photo	15.00
Cancelled Check	35.00
Gold HOF Signed Postcard	7.00
Perez-Steele Signed Postcard	20.00
Single Signed Ball	25.00

Yastrzemski, Carl-(1989)	
3 X 5	8.00
8 X 10 Photo	20.00
Gold HOF Signed Postcard	20.00
Perez-Steele Signed Postcard	20.00
Single Signed Ball	40.00

Young, Cy-(1937) d. 1955	
3 X 5	350.00
8 X 10 Photo	1250.00
B&W HOF Signed Postcard	1000.00
Single Signed Ball	4500.00

Youngs, Ross-(1972) d. 1927	
3 X 5	700.00
Signed Document	2500.00

Modern Autograph Price Guide

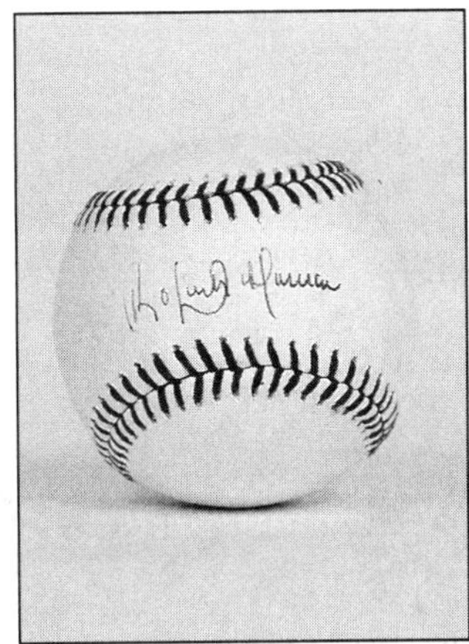

Roberto Alomar ball

Chipper Jones photo

Don Mattingly ball

Pete Rose ball

Player	BB Card	8X10 Photo	AL/NL Ball	Bat	Wool Cap	Authen. Jersey
Roberto Alomar	10.00	20.00	30.00	75.00	55.00	200.00
Brady Anderson	7.00	16.00	25.00	65.00	45.00	180.00
Carlos Baerga	6.00	15.00	22.00	60.00	40.00	170.00
Jeff Bagwell	12.00	22.00	35.00	90.00	60.00	220.00
Albert Belle	16.00	28.00	40.00	100.00	65.00	240.00
Dante Bichette	8.00	18.00	28.00	70.00	50.00	190.00
Craig Biggio	7.00	16.00	25.00	65.00	45.00	180.00
Wade Boggs	10.00	20.00	30.00	75.00	55.00	200.00
Barry Bonds	15.00	25.00	40.00	100.00	65.00	240.00
Bobby Bonilla	6.00	15.00	22.00	60.00	40.00	170.00
George Brett	18.00	30.00	48.00	120.00	75.00	280.00
Ken Caminiti	8.00	18.00	28.00	70.00	50.00	190.00
Jose Canseco	8.00	18.00	28.00	70.00	50.00	190.00
Joe Carter	8.00	18.00	28.00	70.00	50.00	190.00
Tony Clark	7.00	16.00	25.00	65.00	45.00	180.00
Will Clark	8.00	18.00	28.00	70.00	50.00	190.00
Roger Clemens	16.00	28.00	45.00	110.00	70.00	260.00
David Cone	8.00	18.00	28.00	70.00	50.00	190.00
Andre Dawson	8.00	18.00	28.00	70.00	50.00	190.00
Dennis Eckersley	8.00	18.00	28.00	70.00	50.00	190.00
Cecil Fielder	7.00	16.00	25.00	65.00	45.00	180.00
Carlton Fisk	15.00	25.00	40.00	100.00	65.00	240.00
Andres Galarraga	10.00	20.00	30.00	75.00	55.00	200.00
Nomar Garciaparra	7.00	16.00	25.00	65.00	45.00	180.00
Tom Glavine	7.00	16.00	25.00	65.00	45.00	180.00
Juan Gonzalez	10.00	20.00	30.00	75.00	55.00	200.00
Mark Grace	8.00	18.00	28.00	70.00	50.00	190.00
Ken Griffey Jr.	25.00	40.00	60.00	150.00	95.00	350.00
Vladimir Guerrero	7.00	16.00	25.00	65.00	45.00	180.00
Tony Gwynn	10.00	20.00	30.00	75.00	55.00	200.00
Rickey Henderson	10.00	20.00	30.00	75.00	55.00	200.00
Pat Hentgen	6.00	15.00	22.00	60.00	40.00	170.00
Orel Hershiser	8.00	18.00	28.00	70.00	50.00	190.00
Todd Hundley	6.00	15.00	22.00	60.00	40.00	170.00
Derek Jeter	18.00	30.00	48.00	120.00	75.00	280.00
Randy Johnson	16.00	28.00	45.00	110.00	70.00	260.00
Andruw Jones	12.00	22.00	35.00	90.00	60.00	220.00
Chipper Jones	15.00	25.00	40.00	100.00	65.00	240.00
David Justice	10.00	20.00	30.00	75.00	55.00	200.00
Eric Karros	6.00	15.00	22.00	60.00	40.00	170.00
Jimmy Key	6.00	15.00	22.00	60.00	40.00	170.00
Ryan Klesko	8.00	18.00	28.00	70.00	50.00	190.00

Player	BB Card	8X10 Photo	AL/NL Ball	Bat	Wool Cap	Authen. Jersey
Chuck Knoblauch	7.00	16.00	25.00	65.00	45.00	180.00
Barry Larkin	8.00	18.00	28.00	70.00	50.00	190.00
Kenny Lofton	10.00	20.00	30.00	75.00	55.00	200.00
Javier Lopez	6.00	15.00	22.00	60.00	40.00	170.00
Greg Maddux	20.00	32.00	50.00	130.00	85.00	300.00
Edgar Martinez	8.00	18.00	28.00	70.00	50.00	190.00
Tino Martinez	7.00	16.00	25.00	65.00	45.00	180.00
Don Mattingly	18.00	30.00	48.00	120.00	75.00	280.00
Fred McGriff	10.00	20.00	30.00	75.00	55.00	200.00
Mark McGwire	15.00	25.00	40.00	100.00	65.00	240.00
Paul Molitor	12.00	22.00	35.00	90.00	60.00	220.00
Raul Mondesi	10.00	20.00	30.00	75.00	55.00	200.00
Dale Murphy	8.00	18.00	28.00	70.00	50.00	190.00
Eddie Murray	18.00	30.00	48.00	120.00	75.00	280.00
Mike Mussina	8.00	18.00	28.00	70.00	50.00	190.00
Denny Neagle	6.00	15.00	22.00	60.00	40.00	170.00
Hideo Nomo	18.00	30.00	48.00	120.00	75.00	280.00
Paul O'Neill	8.00	18.00	28.00	70.00	50.00	190.00
Rafael Palmeiro	7.00	16.00	25.00	65.00	45.00	180.00
Andy Pettitte	15.00	25.00	40.00	100.00	65.00	240.00
Mike Piazza	18.00	30.00	48.00	120.00	75.00	280.00
Kirby Puckett	15.00	25.00	40.00	100.00	65.00	240.00
Manny Ramirez	8.00	18.00	28.00	70.00	50.00	190.00
Cal Ripken	25.00	40.00	60.00	150.00	95.00	350.00
Alex Rodriguez	18.00	30.00	48.00	120.00	75.00	280.00
Ivan Rodriguez	10.00	20.00	30.00	75.00	55.00	200.00
Pete Rose	15.00	25.00	40.00	100.00	65.00	240.00
Nolan Ryan	20.00	32.00	50.00	130.00	85.00	300.00
Tim Salmon	7.00	16.00	25.00	65.00	45.00	180.00
Ryne Sandberg	16.00	28.00	45.00	110.00	70.00	260.00
Gary Sheffield	6.00	15.00	22.00	60.00	40.00	170.00
Ozzie Smith	12.00	22.00	35.00	90.00	60.00	220.00
John Smoltz	8.00	18.00	28.00	70.00	50.00	190.00
Sammy Sosa	8.00	18.00	28.00	70.00	50.00	190.00
Frank Thomas	25.00	40.00	60.00	150.00	95.00	350.00
Mo Vaughn	10.00	20.00	30.00	75.00	55.00	200.00
Robin Ventura	7.00	16.00	25.00	65.00	45.00	180.00
Larry Walker	8.00	18.00	28.00	70.00	50.00	190.00
Bernie Williams	10.00	20.00	30.00	75.00	55.00	200.00
Matt Williams	10.00	20.00	30.00	75.00	55.00	200.00
Dave Winfield	12.00	22.00	35.00	90.00	60.00	220.00
Robin Yount	15.00	25.00	40.00	100.00	65.00	240.00

UDA PRICE GUIDE

UDA Roger Clemens

AL Baseball	80.00
16x20 Photo Framed	180.00
16x20 Photo Unframed	140.00
Cap With Display	150.00
'93 UD 8 1/2x11 card blowup/500	70.00
16x20 Pitching Photo Framed/300*	180.00
16x20 Pitching Photo Unframed/300*	140.00
'91 UD 8 1/2x11 card blowup/500	80.00

UDA Ken Griffey Jr.

Mariners Jersey Unframed (White)	450.00
AL Baseball	100.00
SI Cover 'The Natural' 5/7/90 Framed	130.00
Mariners White Jersey Framed	700.00
Mini Batting Helmet	130.00
Mini Glove	130.00
Glove	450.00
8x10 Photo Sliding Home/ALCS vs NY	100.00

UDA Reggie Jackson

SI Cover 'A's Superstar' 6/17/24 Framed	100.00
Batting Helmet/563	160.00
Yankees Jersey Unframed/563	300.00
16x20 Leifer Photo Framed/250*	300.00
16x20 Leifer Photo Unframed/250*	250.00

UDA Misc Baseball

Whitey Ford AL Baseball	70.00
Joe Morgan NL Baseball	50.00
Frank Robinson Triple Crown: '66 Baseball	60.00
Lou Brock NL Baseball	60.00
Yogi Berra AL Baseball	70.00
Doerr/Feller/Gaylord Perry AL Baseball	50.00
Frank Robinson Triple Crown: '66 8x10 Photo Framed	70.00
F. Robinson Triple Crown: '66 8x10 Photo Unframed	60.00
Tom Glavine 16x20 Photo Framed/500*	120.00
Tom Glavine 16x20 Photo Unframed/500*	70.00
Billy Williams NL Baseball	45.00
Ted Williams 16x20 Photo 'Dugout' Framed/500	500.00
Tom Glavine 1991 2-card set/1000	40.00
Orel Hershiser '93 UD 8 1/2x11 card blowup/500	35.00
Bobby Bonds NL Baseball	40.00
Orel Hershiser '93 UD 2-card set/500	30.00
Luis Tiant 8x10 Photo Unframed	30.00
Rico Petrocelli AL Baseball	35.00
Steve Garvey NL Baseball	35.00
Tony Gwynn NL Baseball	65.00
Tim Salmon 1993 looss 2-card set/1500	35.00
Jack McDowell 1993 2-card set/1000	30.00
Tim Salmon AL Baseball	35.00
Roberto Alomar AL Baseball	50.00
Roberto Alomar 1993 Future Heroes 2-card set	45.00
Paul Molitor 1993 2-card set/1000 (NC)	50.00
Raul Mondesi NL Baseball	40.00
Raul Mondesi '94 SP #59 2-card set/1000	40.00
Ted Williams Alan Studt art 2-card set	200.00
Ted Williams 8x10 Photo All-Star Home Run	300.00
George Foster NL Baseball	35.00
Brian Jordan NL Baseball	45.00
Ivan Rodriguez AL Baseball	60.00
Tino Martinez AL Baseball	50.00
Robin Ventura AL Baseball	45.00

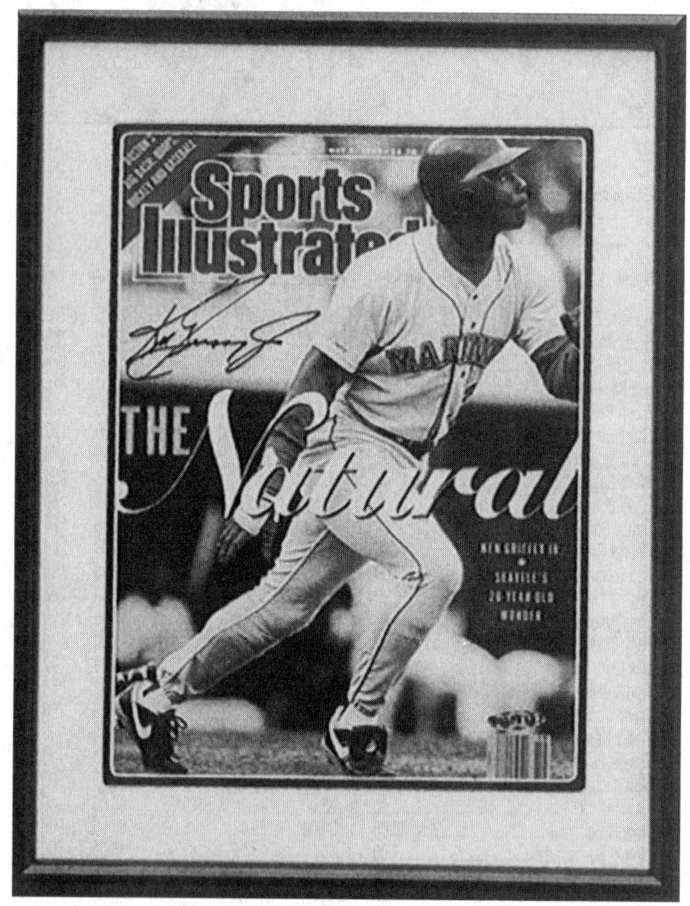

Cereal Box Price Guide

Kellogg's Corn Flakes Baseball

1970 Willie Mays	50.00
1983 San Diego Chicken	25.00
1983 Fernando Valenzuela (12/18)	40.00
1983 Mike Reilly (umpire)	20.00
1991 Hank Aaron	40.00
1991 Ernie Banks	25.00
1991 Yogi Berra	25.00
1991 Lou Brock	25.00
1991 Steve Carlton	25.00
1991 Bob Gibson	25.00
1991 Aaron/Berra/Mays/Spahn	30.00
1992 Mike Schmidt	30.00
1993 Roberto Clemente portrait	35.00
1993 Nolan Ryan (18/24)	25.00
1993 Nolan Ryan farewell	25.00
1994 R.Clemente batting English	18.00
1994 R.Clemente batting Spanish	75.00

Kellogg's Frosted Flakes Baseball

1991 Atlanta Braves NL Champs	35.00
1991 Atl.Braves WS (phantom)	75.00
1991 Minnesota Twins WS Champs	35.00
1992 Toronto Blue Jays WS Champs (Can.)	35.00
1992 Atlanta Braves NL Champs	35.00
1992 St. Louis Cardinals	35.00
1993 Ken Griffey Jr. (20/25)	25.00
1993 Florida Marlins inaugural	18.00
1993 Colorado Rockies inaugural	18.00
1995 Carlos Baerga (Spanish; 10/15)	15.00
1995 Colorado Rockies (Spanish)	15.00

Wheaties Baseball

1985 Pete Rose (8/12/18)	35.00
1987 Minn. Twins WS Champs R	45.00
1987 Twins WS Champs w/19 autos R	75.00
1989 Johnny Bench HOF R	30.00
1990 Jim Palmer HOF R	50.00
1990 Cincinnati Reds R	30.00
1991 Rod Carew R	100.00
1991 Joe Morgan HOF R	50.00
1991 Minn. Twins WS Champs (.75 oz) R	100.00
1991 Minn. Twins WS Champs R	30.00
1993 Lou Gehrig	12.00
1993 Willie Mays	12.00
1993 Babe Ruth	12.00
1993 Phillies WS Champs phantom R	50.00
1995 Cal Ripken no O's logo R	18.00
1995 Cal Ripken w/O's logo	12.00
1995 Atlanta Braves WS Champs R	25.00
1995 Cleveland Indians AL Champs R	18.00
1996 Ken Griffey Jr. (HF 1)	5.00
1996 Ken Griffey Jr. (HF 14.75)	8.00
1996 Ken Griffey Jr. gold emboss (HF 18)	8.00
1996 Ken Griffey Jr. (HF 38)	12.00
1996 Kirby Puckett R	18.00
1996 Atlanta Braves NL Champs R	18.00
1996 St.Louis Cards NL Champs phantom R	50.00
1996 Negro Leagues 75th Ann.	12.00
1996 NY Yankees WS Champs R	12.00
1997 Jackie Robinson (12/18/CW 18/HF 14.75)	8.00

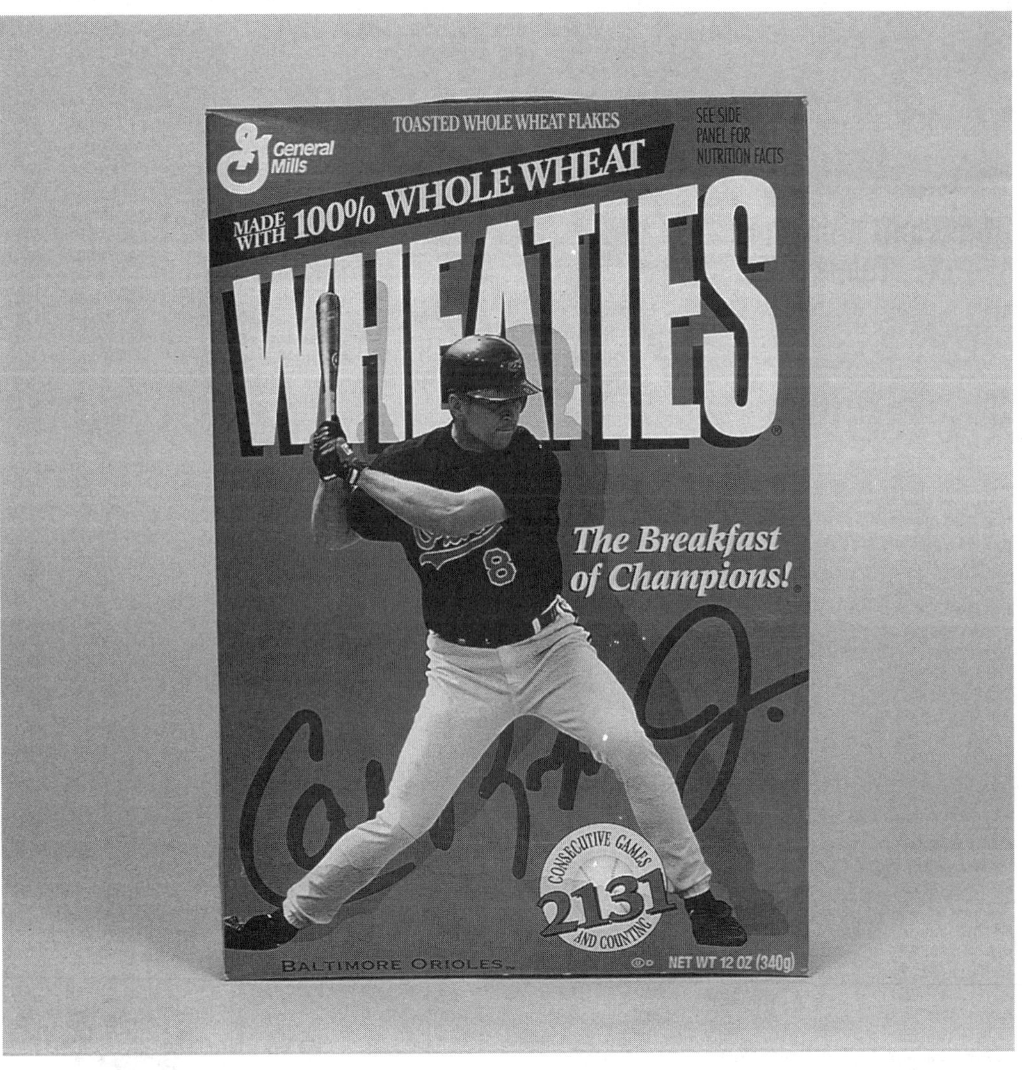

Highland Mint Price Guide

Baseball Mint-Cards Topps

Roberto Alomar 88/S/214	175.00	225.00
Roberto Alomar 88/B/928	35.00	50.00
Ernie Banks 54/S/437	150.00	200.00
Ernie Banks 54/B/920	35.00	50.00
Johnny Bench 69/S/500	175.00	225.00
Johnny Bench 69/B/1384	35.00	50.00
Barry Bonds 86/S/596	150.00	200.00
Barry Bonds 86/B/2677	35.00	50.00
George Brett 75/S/999	150.00	200.00
George Brett 75/B/3560	50.00	65.00
Will Clark 86/S/150	250.00	325.00
Will Clark 86/B/1044	45.00	60.00
Roger Clemens 85/S/432	200.00	250.00
Roger Clemens 85/B/1789	45.00	60.00
Juan Gonzalez 90/S/365	175.00	225.00
Juan Gonzalez 90/B/1899	35.00	50.00
Ken Griffey Jr. 92/G/500	475.00	600.00
Ken Griffey Jr. 92/S/1000	325.00	400.00
Ken Griffey Jr. 92/B/5000	65.00	90.00
David Justice 90/S/265	175.00	225.00
David Justice 90/B/1396	45.00	60.00
Don Mattingly 84/S/414	175.00	225.00
Don Mattingly 84/B/1550	65.00	90.00
Paul Molitor 79/S/260	175.00	225.00
Paul Molitor 79/B/639	65.00	90.00
Mike Piazza 93/G/374	400.00	500.00
Mike Piazza 93/S/750	175.00	225.00
Mike Piazza 93/B/2500	55.00	75.00
Kirby Puckett 85/S/359	175.00	225.00
Kirby Puckett 85/B/1723	65.00	90.00
Cal Ripken 92/S/1000	275.00	350.00
Cal Ripken 92/B/4065	90.00	125.00
Brooks Robinson 57/S/796	175.00	225.00
Brooks Robinson 57/B/2043	35.00	50.00
Nolan Ryan 92/S/999	400.00	500.00
Nolan Ryan 92/B/5000	120.00	160.00
Tim Salmon 93/S/264	175.00	225.00
Tim Salmon 93/B/768	45.00	60.00
Ryne Sandberg 92/S/430	175.00	225.00
Ryne Sandberg 92/B/1932	45.00	60.00
Deion Sanders 89/S/187	175.00	225.00
Deion Sanders 89/B/668	35.00	50.00
Mike Schmidt 74/S/500	175.00	225.00
Mike Schmidt 74/B/1641	35.00	50.00
Ozzie Smith 79/S/211	200.00	250.00
Ozzie Smith 79/B/1088	65.00	90.00
Frank Thomas 92/G/500	500.00	650.00
Frank Thomas 92/S/1000	275.00	350.00
Frank Thomas 92/B/5000	65.00	90.00
Dave Winfield 74/S/266	175.00	225.00
Dave Winfield 74/B/1216	35.00	50.00
Carl Yastrzemski 60/S/500	175.00	225.00
Carl Yastrzemski 60/B/1072	45.00	60.00
Robin Yount 75/S/349	175.00	225.00
Robin Yount 75/B/1564	45.00	60.00

Baseball Mint-Cards Pinnacle/UD

Jeff Bagwell 92/S/750	150.00	200.00
Jeff Bagwell 92/B/2500	35.00	50.00
Michael Jordan 94/G/500	550.00	700.00
Michael Jordan 94/S/1000	400.00	500.00
Michael Jordan 94/B/5000	75.00	100.00
Greg Maddux 92/S/750	175.00	225.00
Greg Maddux 92/B/2500	45.00	60.00
Mickey Mantle 92/G/500	550.00	700.00
Mickey Mantle 92/S/1000	400.00	500.00
Mickey Mantle 92/B/5000	75.00	100.00
Nolan Ryan 92/G/500	550.00	700.00
Nolan Ryan 92/S/1000	240.00	300.00
Nolan Ryan 92/B/5000	90.00	125.00

Baseball Mini Mint-Cards

K.Griffey Jr./F.Thomas S/1000	135.00	180.00
K.Griffey Jr./F.Thomas B/5000	65.00	90.00
R.Johnson/N.Ryan S/500	110.00	150.00
R.Johnson/N.Ryan B/2500	55.00	75.00
G.Maddux/C.Young G/375	240.00	300.00
G.Maddux/C.Young S/500	110.00	150.00
G.Maddux/C.Young B/2500	55.00	75.00
M.Piazza/R.Campanella S/500	110.00	150.00
M.Piazza/R.Campanella B/2500	55.00	75.00
C.Ripken/L.Gehrig G/375	325.00	400.00
C.Ripken/L.Gehrig S/500	200.00	250.00
C.Ripken/L.Gehrig B/2500	90.00	125.00

Baseball Mint-Coins

Jeff Bagwell S/5000	15.00	20.00
Jeff Bagwell B/25000	9.00	12.00
Barry Bonds Gold Sig./1000	35.00	50.00
Barry Bonds S/5000	15.00	20.00
Roger Clemens S/5000	20.00	25.00
Roger Clemens Gold Sig./1500	35.00	50.00
Ken Griffey Jr. Gold Sig./1500	65.00	90.00
Ken Griffey Jr. S/5000	35.00	50.00
Ken Griffey Jr. B/25000	11.00	14.00
Greg Maddux Gold Sig./1500	45.00	60.00
Greg Maddux S/5000	20.00	25.00
Greg Maddux B/25000	9.00	12.00
Don Mattingly S/5000	20.00	25.00
Don Mattingly B/25000	9.00	12.00
Hideo Nomo Gold Sig./1500	45.00	60.00
Hideo Nomo S/5000	15.00	20.00
Mike Piazza Gold Sig./1500	45.00	60.00
Mike Piazza S/5000	15.00	20.00
Mike Piazza B/25000	9.00	12.00
Cal Ripken Gold Sig./1500	55.00	75.00
Cal Ripken S/5000	35.00	50.00
Cal Ripken B/25000	12.00	15.00
Frank Thomas Gold Sig./1500	50.00	65.00
Frank Thomas S/5000	35.00	50.00
Frank Thomas B/25000	9.00	12.00
Albert Belle S/5000	15.00	20.00
Wade Boggs S/5000	15.00	20.00
Jose Canseco S/5000	15.00	20.00
Will Clark S/5000	15.00	20.00
Cecil Fielder S/5000	15.00	20.00
Tony Gwynn S/5000	15.00	20.00
Chipper Jones S/5000	24.00	30.00
Chipper Jones B/25000	9.00	12.00
Eddie Murray S/5000	15.00	20.00
Kirby Puckett S/5000	15.00	20.00
Ozzie Smith S/5000	15.00	20.00
Derek Jeter Gold Sig./1500	50.00	65.00
Derek Jeter S/5000	20.00	25.00
Andruw Jones S/5000	20.00	25.00
Chipper Jones Gold Sig./1500	50.00	65.00
Raul Mondesi S/5000	15.00	20.00
Kirby Puckett Gold Sig./1500	45.00	60.00
Cal Ripken B/15000	12.00	15.00
Alex Rodriguez Gold Sig./1500	50.00	65.00
Alex Rodriguez S/5000	24.00	30.00
Alex Rodriguez B/25000	9.00	12.00
Mo Vaughn S/5000	15.00	20.00

Baseball Magnum Series Medallions

Ken Griffey Jr. Gold Sig./375	200.00	250.00
Ken Griffey Jr. S/750	120.00	160.00
Ken Griffey Jr. B/3000	50.00	65.00
Cal Ripken Gold Sig./375	240.00	300.00
Cal Ripken S/750	135.00	180.00
Cal Ripken B/3000	50.00	65.00
Alex Rodriguez S/750	120.00	160.00
Alex Rodriguez B/3000	35.00	50.00
Babe Ruth S/750	120.00	160.00
Babe Ruth B/3500	35.00	50.00
Nolan Ryan S/750	120.00	160.00
Nolan Ryan B/3500	35.00	50.00
Frank Thomas S/7500	120.00	160.00
Frank Thomas B/3000	50.00	65.00

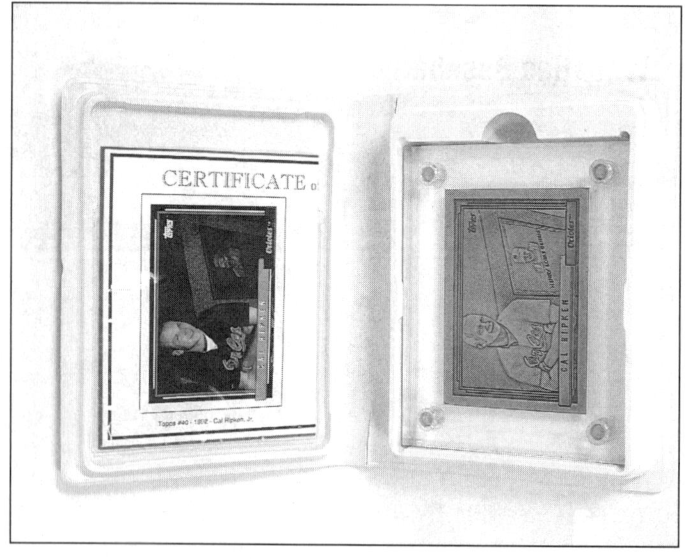

Sports Illustrated Baseball

How to Use

The majority of Sports Illustrateds on the market are subscription copies that were distributed with mailing labels or inkjetted addresses. SI switched from labeling to inkjetting in the early '90s; the exact date varied by region.

The Price Guide refers to magazine in ExMt condition. ExMt magazines may have mailing labels or inkjetted addresses if they are otherwise flawless. Magazines without mailing labels or inkjetted addresses can still be considered ExMt if they have minor flaws such as dinged/frayed corners, light creases, fingerprints, scratches or scuffing.

Magazines with labels or addresses and minor flaws are valued at 50-75% the listed prices depending on severity. Flawless magazines without labels or addresses are considered Mint and are valued at 150% the listed prices. Magazines with major flaws such as heavy creases, stains, tears or writing are valued at 10-25% the listed prices depending on severity.

Cover Subjects and First Covers

Magazines are listed by main cover subject(s). In cases of covers with multiple subjects, only the most famous and/or prominent may be listed depending on space limitations.

For popular athletes with multiple cover appearances, a First Cover (FC) may be designated. This is generally applied to the first issue that the player was intentionally featured on the cover; he/she may have appeared in a small photo or in the background of an earlier cover. For instance, the "Baseball Salaries" issue (4/20/87) features mugshots of 43 players, but these are not considered FCs.

Issue Dates and Special Issues

Magazines are listed in order of issue date, which normally appears on the cover. However, special issues may list the date inside, or list only a season or year rather than a specific date. For the latter, the magazine is listed by the approximate date of release.

SI usually combines two weeks into one with a double issue at the end of the year; for these issues, the date is followed by an asterisk. Other designations used are SOY for SI's annual Sportsman of the Year issue, and PV for various event or season preview issues.

	EXMT	VGEX	G-VG
☐ 8/16/54 Eddie Mathews	200.00	90.00	25.00
☐ 4/11/55 Willie Mays (FC)	125.00	55.00	15.50
☐ 4/18/55 Al Rosen	75.00	34.00	9.50
☐ 5/30/55 Herb Score	15.00	6.75	1.85
☐ 6/27/55 Duke Snider	50.00	22.00	6.25
☐ 7/11/55 Yogi Berra (FC)	30.00	13.50	3.70
☐ 8/1/55 Ted Williams (FC)	100.00	45.00	12.50
☐ 8/15/55 1st Anniversary Issue	12.00	5.50	1.50
☐ 9/26/55 Walter Alston	15.00	6.75	1.85
☐ 1/2/56 Johnny Podres	20.00	9.00	2.50
☐ 3/5/56 Cardinals: Musial (FC) etc.	20.00	9.00	2.50
☐ 4/9/56 Spring Training Issue	15.00	6.75	1.85
☐ 4/23/56 Billy Martin	12.00	5.50	1.50
☐ 5/14/56 A. Kaline/H. Kuenn	30.00	13.50	3.70
☐ 6/18/56 Mickey Mantle (FC)	75.00	34.00	9.50
☐ 6/25/56 Warren Spahn	25.00	11.00	3.10
☐ 7/9/56 All-Star Game Issue	12.00	5.50	1.50
☐ 7/16/56 Ted Kluszewski	25.00	11.00	3.10
☐ 7/30/56 Joe Adcock	9.00	4.00	1.10

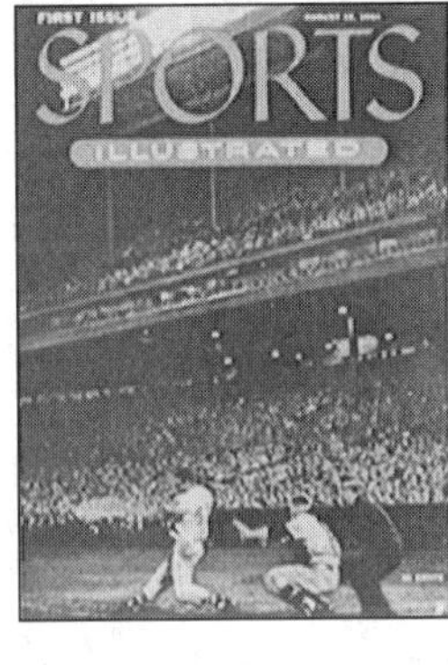

	EXMT	VGEX	G-VG
☐ 8/20/56 2nd Anniversary Issue	9.00	4.00	1.10
☐ 9/10/56 Whitey Ford	30.00	13.50	3.70
☐ 10/1/56 WS: Mickey Mantle	75.00	34.00	9.50
☐ 3/4/57 Mickey Mantle	60.00	27.00	7.50
☐ 4/15/57 Spring Training Issue	20.00	9.00	2.50
☐ 4/22/57 Wally Moon	9.00	4.00	1.10
☐ 5/13/57 Billy Pierce	9.00	4.00	1.10
☐ 6/3/57 Clem Labine	6.00	2.70	.75
☐ 7/8/57 AS: Musial/Williams	50.00	22.00	6.25
☐ 7/22/57 Hank Bauer	9.00	4.00	1.10
☐ 9/9/57 Roy McMillian	9.00	4.00	1.10
☐ 9/30/57 World Series Issue	9.00	4.00	1.10
☐ 10/7/57 Ollie Matson	9.00	4.00	1.10
☐ 12/23/57 Stan Musial	18.00	8.00	2.20
☐ 3/3/58 Spring Training Issue	9.00	4.00	1.10
☐ 3/17/58 Sal Maglie	9.00	4.00	1.10
☐ 3/31/58 Roy Sievers	12.00	5.50	1.50
☐ 4/14/58 Baseball Issue	18.00	8.00	2.20
☐ 4/21/58 Del Crandall	9.00	4.00	1.10
☐ 5/5/58 Gil McDougald	9.00	4.00	1.10

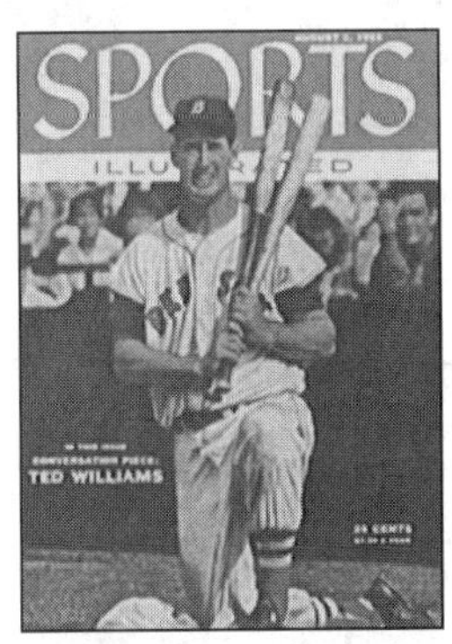

	EXMT	VGEX	G-VG
☐ 5/19/58 Richie Ashburn	12.00	5.50	1.50
☐ 6/2/58 Eddie Mathews	25.00	11.00	3.10
☐ 6/23/58 Jackie Jensen	9.00	4.00	1.10
☐ 7/7/58 All-Star Game Issue	15.00	6.75	1.85
☐ 7/28/58 Frank Thomas	9.00	4.00	1.10
☐ 9/29/58 World Series Issue	9.00	4.00	1.10
☐ 3/2/59 Spring Train. (Stengel)	12.00	5.50	1.50
☐ 4/13/59 Baseball Issue (Mays)	30.00	13.50	3.70
☐ 5/4/59 Bob Turley	9.00	4.00	1.10
☐ 6/15/59 Dodgers Crowd	6.00	2.70	.75
☐ 8/10/59 N. Fox/L. Aparicio	50.00	22.00	6.25
☐ 9/28/59 White Sox Team	18.00	8.00	2.20
☐ 3/7/60 Spring Train.: Phillies cartoon	6.00	2.70	.75
☐ 4/11/60 Baseball Issue	15.00	6.75	1.85
☐ 6/6/60 Red Schoendienst	12.00	5.50	1.50
☐ 7/4/60 Comiskey Park	6.00	2.70	.75
☐ 7/18/60 Candlestick Park	6.00	2.70	.75
☐ 8/8/60 Dick Groat	12.00	5.50	1.50
☐ 10/10/60 Vern Law	9.00	4.00	1.10
☐ 3/6/61 Spring Training Issue	9.00	4.00	1.10
☐ 4/10/61 Baseball Issue	12.00	5.50	1.50
☐ 6/26/61 Cardinals	9.00	4.00	1.10
☐ 7/31/61 Home Run Record	9.00	4.00	1.10
☐ 10/2/61 Roger Maris	30.00	13.50	3.70
☐ 10/9/61 Joey Jay	12.00	5.50	1.50
☐ 4/9/62 Baseball Issue	15.00	6.75	1.85

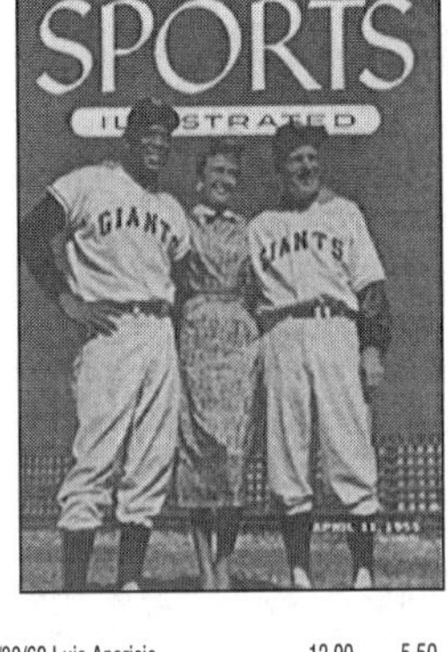

	EXMT	VGEX	G-VG
☐ 4/30/62 Luis Aparicio	12.00	5.50	1.50
☐ 6/4/62 Willie Mays	18.00	8.00	2.20
☐ 7/2/62 Mickey Mantle	50.00	22.00	6.25
☐ 7/30/62 Ken Boyer	9.00	4.00	1.10
☐ 8/20/62 Don Drysdale	9.00	4.00	1.10
☐ 10/1/62 World Series Issue	6.00	2.70	.75
☐ 3/4/63 Sandy Koufax (FC)	20.00	9.00	2.50
☐ 4/8/63 Baseball (Killebrew)	15.00	6.75	1.85
☐ 4/29/63 Art Mahaffey	9.00	4.00	1.10
☐ 6/24/63 Roy Face	12.00	5.50	1.50
☐ 7/22/63 Dick Groat	12.00	5.50	1.50
☐ 9/2/63 Ron Fairly	5.00	2.20	.60
☐ 9/30/63 Whitey Ford	18.00	8.00	2.20
☐ 3/2/64 C. Stengel/Y. Berra	15.00	6.75	1.85
☐ 4/13/64 Baseball (Koufax)	18.00	8.00	2.20
☐ 5/11/64 Al Kaline	20.00	9.00	2.50
☐ 5/25/64 Frank Howard	6.00	2.70	.75
☐ 7/6/64 Alvin Dark	5.00	2.20	.60
☐ 8/10/64 Johnny Callison	15.00	6.75	1.85
☐ 8/31/64 Brooks Robinson (FC)	18.00	8.00	2.20
☐ 3/1/65 J.Bunning/B. Belinsky	9.00	4.00	1.10
☐ 4/19/65 Baseball Issue	12.00	5.50	1.50
☐ 5/17/65 Bill Veeck	4.00	1.80	.50
☐ 6/21/65 Mickey Mantle	40.00	18.00	5.00
☐ 7/12/65 Maury Wills	4.00	1.80	.50
☐ 8/9/65 Juan Marichal	12.00	5.50	1.50

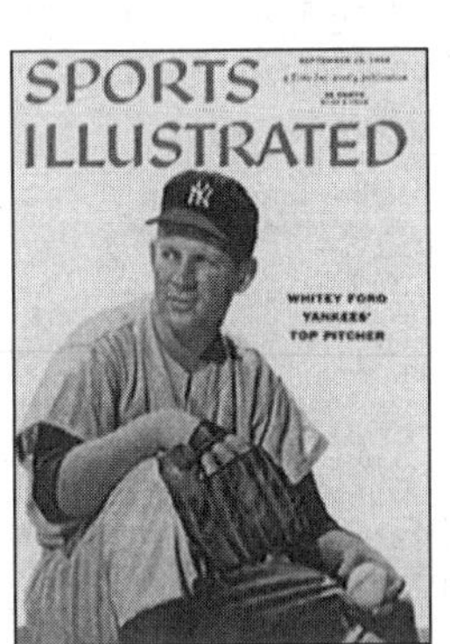

	EXMT	VGEX	G-VG
☐ 8/23/65 Tony Oliva	6.00	2.70	.75
☐ 10/4/65 WS PV: Zoilo Versailles	9.00	4.00	1.10
☐ 12/20/65 Sandy Koufax	18.00	8.00	2.20
☐ 2/28/66 L. Durocher/E. Stanky	6.00	2.70	.75
☐ 4/18/66 Baseball Issue (Groat)	12.00	5.50	1.50
☐ 5/23/66 Sam McDowell	6.00	2.70	.75
☐ 6/6/66 Joe Morgan (FC)	12.00	5.50	1.50
☐ 7/11/66 Andy Etchebarren	5.00	2.20	.60
☐ 9/5/66 Harry Walker	4.00	1.80	.50
☐ 9/26/66 Gaylord Perry	9.00	4.00	1.10
☐ 10/10/66 Brooks/F.Robinson (FC)	20.00	9.00	2.50
☐ 3/13/67 Jim Nash	4.00	1.80	.50
☐ 4/17/67 Baseball Issue (Wills)	12.00	5.50	1.50
☐ 5/8/67 K. Berry/M. Mantle	20.00	9.00	2.50
☐ 5/15/67 L.A. Dodgers	4.00	1.80	.50
☐ 6/5/67 Al Kaline	18.00	8.00	2.20

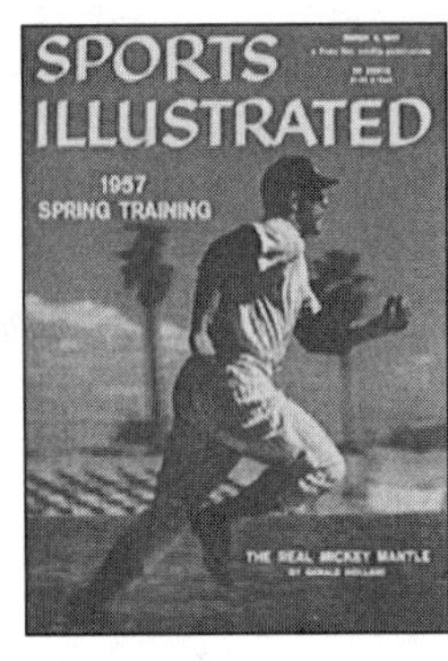

	EXMT	VGEX	G-VG
☐ 7/3/67 Roberto Clemente	30.00	13.50	3.70
☐ 7/31/67 Spitball	4.00	1.80	.50
☐ 8/21/67 Carl Yastrzemski (FC)	18.00	8.00	2.20
☐ 9/4/67 Tim McCarver	6.00	2.70	.75
☐ 10/15/67 Lou Brock	12.00	5.50	1.50
☐ 12/25/67 Carl Yastzemski	18.00	8.00	2.20
☐ 3/11/68 Johnny Bench (FC)	12.00	5.50	1.50
☐ 4/15/68 Baseball Issue (Brock)	12.00	5.50	1.50
☐ 5/6/68 Ron Swoboda	5.00	2.20	.60
☐ 5/27/68 Pete Rose (FC)	15.00	6.75	1.85
☐ 6/17/68 Don Drysdale	8.00	3.60	1.00
☐ 7/8/68 Ted Williams	6.00	2.70	.75
☐ 7/29/68 Denny McLain	9.00	4.00	1.10
☐ 8/19/68 Curt Flood	5.00	2.20	.60
☐ 9/2/68 Ken Harrelson	6.00	2.70	.75
☐ 9/23/68 Denny McLain	15.00	6.75	1.85
☐ 10/7/68 Maris/Gibson/Brock	15.00	6.75	1.85
☐ 3/17/69 Ted Williams	9.00	4.00	1.10
☐ 4/14/69 Baseball (B. Freehan)	12.00	5.50	1.50
☐ 5/19/69 Walter Alston	4.00	1.80	.50
☐ 6/30/69 Ron Santo	9.00	4.00	1.10
☐ 7/7/69 Reggie Jackson (FC)	15.00	6.75	1.85
☐ 7/21/69 Billy Martin	5.00	2.20	.60
☐ 8/18/69 Hank Aaron (FC)	12.00	5.50	1.50
☐ 9/8/69 P. Rose/E. Banks	20.00	9.00	2.50
☐ 10/6/69 Frank Robinson	5.00	2.20	.60
☐ 10/20/69 Brooks Robinson	18.00	8.00	2.20
☐ 12/22/69 Tom Seaver (FC)	15.00	6.75	1.85
☐ 2/23/70 Denny McLain	9.00	4.00	1.10
☐ 3/23/70 Richie Allen	5.00	2.20	.60
☐ 4/13/70 Baseball PV: J.Koosman	15.00	6.75	1.85

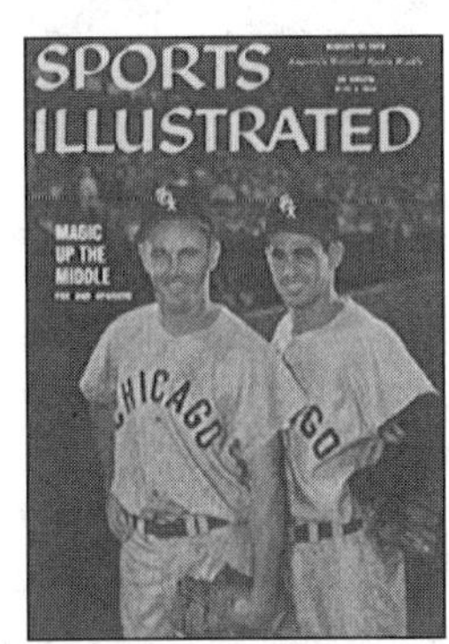

	EXMT	VGEX	G-VG
☐ 5/25/70 Henry Aaron	12.00	5.50	1.50
☐ 6/22/70 Tony Conigliaro	6.00	2.70	.75
☐ 7/13/70 Johnny Bench	9.00	4.00	1.10
☐ 7/27/70 Willie Mays	9.00	4.00	1.10
☐ 9/7/70 Bud Harrelson	5.00	2.20	.60
☐ 9/28/70 Danny Murtaugh	5.00	2.20	.60
☐ 10/19/70 WS: B.Robinson	5.00	2.20	.60
☐ 3/22/71 Wes Parker	4.00	1.80	.50
☐ 4/12/71 BB PV: Boog Powell	9.00	4.00	1.10
☐ 5/3/71 D. Duncan/J. Fregosi	4.00	1.80	.50
☐ 5/31/71 Vida Blue	5.00	2.20	.60
☐ 6/21/71 Jerry Grote	4.00	1.80	.50
☐ 7/5/71 Alex Johnson	4.00	1.80	.50

Issue			
☐ 8/2/71 Willie Stargell	6.00	2.70	.75
☐ 8/30/71 Ferguson Jenkins	6.00	2.70	.75
☐ 9/27/71 Maury Wills	4.00	1.80	.50
☐ 10/18/71 Frank Robinson	5.00	2.20	.60
☐ 3/13/72 Johnny Bench	9.00	4.00	1.10
☐ 3/27/72 Vida Blue	3.00	1.35	.35
☐ 4/10/72 Baseball Issue (Torre)	8.00	3.60	1.00
☐ 5/1/72 Willie Davis	3.00	1.35	.35
☐ 5/22/72 Willie Mays	12.00	5.50	1.50
☐ 6/12/72 Dick Allen	5.00	2.20	.60
☐ 7/3/72 Steve Blass	3.00	1.35	.35
☐ 8/21/72 Sparky Lyle	3.00	1.35	.35
☐ 9/25/72 Carlton Fisk	9.00	4.00	1.10
☐ 10/23/72 Jim Hunter	6.00	2.70	.75
☐ 3/12/73 Bill Melton	4.00	1.80	.50
☐ 4/9/73 BB PV: S.Carlton	9.00	4.00	1.10
☐ 4/30/73 Chris Speier	3.00	1.35	.35
☐ 6/4/73 Wilbur Wood	5.00	2.20	.60
☐ 7/2/73 B. Murcer/R. Blomberg	6.00	2.70	.75
☐ 7/30/73 Carlton Fisk	9.00	4.00	1.10
☐ 8/20/73 C. Osteen/B. Russell	4.00	1.80	.50
☐ 9/24/73 Danny Murtaugh	4.00	1.80	.50
☐ 10/22/73 WS: Campaneris/Milner	8.00	3.60	1.00
☐ 3/18/74 Babe Ruth	6.00	2.70	.75
☐ 4/8/74 BB PV: Pete Rose	9.00	4.00	1.10
☐ 4/15/74 Henry Aaron #715!	15.00	6.75	1.85
☐ 5/27/74 Jim Wynn	3.00	1.35	.35
☐ 6/17/74 Reggie Jackson	6.00	2.70	.75
☐ 7/1/74 Rod Carew (FC)	6.00	2.70	.75
☐ 7/22/74 Lou Brock	5.00	2.20	.60
☐ 8/12/74 Mike Marshall	3.00	1.35	.35
☐ 10/7/74 Jim Hunter	6.00	2.70	.75
☐ 10/21/74 WS: Fingers etc	6.00	2.70	.75
☐ 3/3/75 Spring Training Issue	5.00	2.20	.60
☐ 4/7/75 BB PV: Garvey	6.00	2.70	.75
☐ 6/2/75 Billy Martin	3.00	1.35	.35
☐ 6/16/75 Nolan Ryan (FC)	15.00	6.75	1.85
☐ 7/7/75 Fred Lynn	4.00	1.80	.50
☐ 7/21/75 J. Palmer/T. Seaver	9.00	4.00	1.10
☐ 8/11/75 Baseball Boom	3.00	1.35	.35
☐ 10/6/75 Reggie Jackson	5.00	2.20	.60
☐ 10/20/75 L. Tiant/J. Bench	6.00	2.70	.75
☐ 11/3/75 WS: Johnny Bench	6.00	2.70	.75
☐ 12/22/75 Pete Rose SOY	9.00	4.00	1.10
☐ 4/12/76 Joe Morgan	5.00	2.20	.60
☐ 5/3/76 Mike Schmidt (FC)	12.00	5.50	1.50
☐ 5/31/76 C.Fisk/L.Pinella	5.00	2.20	.60
☐ 6/21/76 George Brett (FC)	12.00	5.50	1.50
☐ 6/28/76 Bowie Kuhn	3.00	1.35	.35
☐ 7/12/76 Randy Jones	3.00	1.35	.35
☐ 8/30/76 Reggie Jackson	5.00	2.20	.60
☐ 10/11/76 George Foster	3.00	1.35	.35
☐ 11/1/76 Johnny Bench	6.00	2.70	.75
☐ 3/14/77 Tom Lasorda	5.00	2.20	.60
☐ 3/28/77 Bump Wills	3.00	1.35	.35
☐ 4/11/77 BB PV: Joe Rudi	3.00	1.35	.35
☐ 5/2/77 Reggie Jackson	10.00	4.50	1.25
☐ 5/30/77 Dave Parker	3.00	1.35	.35
☐ 6/6/77 Mark Fidrych	3.00	1.35	.35
☐ 6/27/77 Tom Seaver	10.00	4.50	1.25
☐ 7/18/77 R.Carew/T.Williams	12.00	5.50	1.50
☐ 8/15/77 Sadaharu Oh	15.00	6.75	1.85
☐ 8/29/77 Greg Luzinski	3.00	1.35	.35
☐ 10/24/77 Thurman Munson	10.00	4.50	1.25
☐ 3/20/78 Clint Hurdle	3.00	1.35	.35

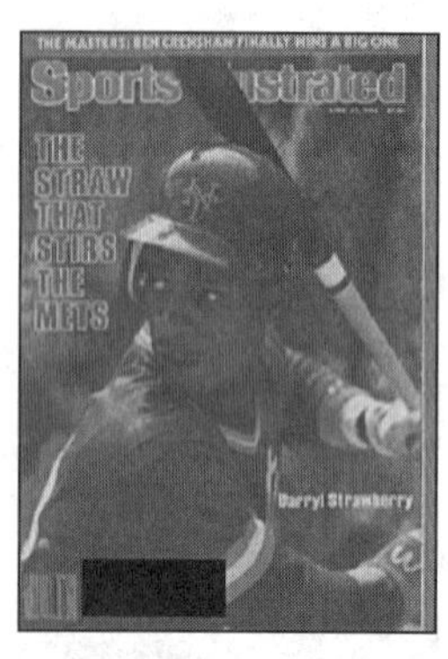

Issue			
☐ 4/10/78 BB PV: G.Foster/R.Carew	6.00	2.70	.75
☐ 4/24/78 Mark Fidrych	3.00	1.35	.35
☐ 7/31/78 Billy Martin	4.00	1.80	.50
☐ 8/7/78 Pete Rose	12.00	5.50	1.50
☐ 10/23/78 L.Lacy/B.Doyle	3.00	1.35	.35
☐ 3/5/79 Spring Training	3.00	1.35	.35
☐ 3/19/79 Harry Chappas	3.00	1.35	.35
☐ 4/9/79 BB PV: J.Rice/D.Parker	4.00	1.80	.50
☐ 4/30/79 George Bamberger	3.00	1.35	.35
☐ 5/28/79 Pete Rose	10.00	4.50	1.25
☐ 6/18/79 Earl Weaver	5.00	2.20	.60
☐ 7/23/79 Nolan Ryan	20.00	9.00	2.50
☐ 8/27/79 BB Golden Oldies	3.00	1.35	.35
☐ 10/22/79 D.DeCinces/Garner	3.00	1.35	.35
☐ 12/24/79* Stargell/Bradshaw SOY	10.00	4.50	1.25

Issue			
☐ 3/24/80 Kirk Gibson	5.00	2.20	.60
☐ 4/7/80 BB PV: Keith Hernandez	4.00	1.80	.50
☐ 6/9/80 Darrell Porter	3.00	1.35	.35
☐ 7/21/80 Steve Carlton	8.00	3.60	1.00
☐ 8/4/80 Reggie Jackson	8.00	3.60	1.00
☐ 8/18/80 J.R.Richard	3.00	1.35	.35
☐ 8/25/80 Yankees vs. Orioles	3.00	1.35	.35
☐ 10/6/80 Gary Carter	5.00	2.20	.60

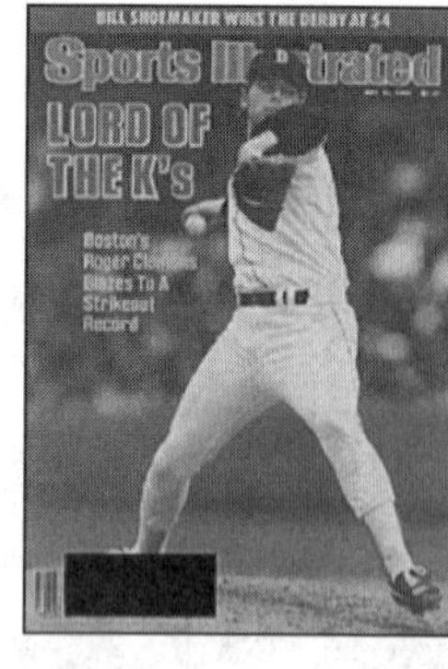

Issue			
☐ 10/27/80 Mike Schmidt	12.00	5.50	1.50
☐ 1/5/81 Dave Winfield (FC)	10.00	4.50	1.25
☐ 3/2/81 J.R. Richard	3.00	1.35	.35
☐ 3/16/81 Rollie Fingers	5.00	2.20	.60
☐ 4/13/81 BB PV: Brett/Schmidt	12.00	5.50	1.50
☐ 4/27/81 Oakland A's pitchers	3.00	1.35	.35
☐ 5/18/81 Fernando Valenzuela	5.00	2.20	.60
☐ 6/8/81 Greg Luzinski	3.00	1.35	.35
☐ 6/22/81 Baseball strike	3.00	1.35	.35
☐ 7/27/81 Tom Seaver	8.00	3.60	1.00
☐ 8/10/81 G.Brett/M.Schmidt	12.00	5.50	1.50
☐ 8/17/81 G.Carter/D.Williams	5.00	2.20	.60
☐ 10/26/81 Graig Nettles	4.00	1.80	.50
☐ 11/2/81 Davey Lopes	3.00	1.35	.35
☐ 3/15/82 Reggie Jackson	8.00	3.60	1.00
☐ 4/12/82 BB PV: Steve Garvey	4.00	1.80	.50
☐ 5/17/82 Gaylord Perry	5.00	2.20	.60
☐ 7/5/82 Kent Hrbek	5.00	2.20	.60
☐ 7/19/82 Rose/Yastrzemski	8.00	3.60	1.00
☐ 8/9/82 Dale Murphy	5.00	2.20	.60
☐ 9/6/82 Rickey Henderson (FC)	10.00	4.50	1.25
☐ 10/11/82 Robin Yount (FC)	10.00	4.50	1.25
☐ 10/25/82 Robin Yount	8.00	3.60	1.00
☐ 3/14/83 Rose/Morgan/Perez	10.00	4.50	1.25
☐ 4/4/83 BB PV: Gary Carter	5.00	2.20	.60
☐ 4/18/83 Tom Seaver	8.00	3.60	1.00
☐ 4/25/83 Steve Garvey	4.00	1.80	.50
☐ 6/13/83 Rod Carew	6.00	2.70	.75
☐ 7/4/83 Dale Murphy	5.00	2.20	.60
☐ 7/18/83 A.Dawson/D.Stieb	5.00	2.20	.60
☐ 10/3/83 Steve Carlton	6.00	2.70	.75
☐ 10/24/83 Rick Dempsey	3.00	1.35	.35
☐ 3/12/84 George Brett	10.00	4.50	1.25
☐ 4/2/84 BB PV: Yogi Berra	6.00	2.70	.75
☐ 4/16/84 G.Nettles/R.Gossage	4.00	1.80	.50
☐ 4/23/84 Darryl Strawberry (FC)	5.00	2.20	.60
☐ 5/28/84 Alan Trammell (FC)	6.00	2.70	.75
☐ 6/11/84 Leon Durham	3.00	1.35	.35
☐ 8/27/84 Pete Rose	6.00	2.70	.75
☐ 9/24/84 D.Gooden/R.Sutcliffe	5.00	2.20	.60
☐ 10/22/84 Alan Trammell	6.00	2.70	.75
☐ 3/4/85 BB salaries: M.Schmidt	6.00	2.70	.75
☐ 3/18/85 Fred Lynn	3.00	1.35	.35
☐ 3/25/85 Ueberroth/Mays/Mantle	15.00	6.75	1.85
☐ 4/15/85 BB PV: Dwight Gooden	5.00	2.20	.60
☐ 5/6/85 Billy Martin	4.00	1.80	.50
☐ 7/8/85 Fernando Valenzuela	4.00	1.80	.50
☐ 8/5/85 Pedro Guerrero	3.00	1.35	.35
☐ 8/19/85 Pete Rose	6.00	2.70	.75
☐ 9/2/85 Dwight Gooden	4.00	1.80	.50
☐ 9/23/85 Ozzie Smith (FC)	8.00	3.60	1.00
☐ 10/28/85 Ozzie Smith	8.00	3.60	1.00
☐ 11/4/85 Royals Team	6.00	2.70	.75
☐ 12/10/85 Kirk Gibson	3.00	1.35	.35
☐ 4/14/86 BB PV: Wade Boggs (FC)	5.00	2.20	.60
☐ 5/12/86 Roger Clemens (FC)	8.00	3.60	1.00
☐ 7/14/86 Bo Jackson BB	6.00	2.70	.75
☐ 7/28/86 Rickey Henderson	5.00	2.20	.60
☐ 8/4/86 Oil Can Boyd	2.00	.90	.25
☐ 8/25/86 Ron Darling	2.00	.90	.25
☐ 10/6/86 Darryl Strawberry	4.00	1.80	.50
☐ 10/20/86 B.Grich/D.DeCinces	2.00	.90	.25
☐ 10/27/86 G.Carter/J.Rice	4.00	1.80	.50
☐ 11/3/86 Ray Knight	2.00	.90	.25
☐ 3/9/87 Cal Jr.(FC)/Cal Sr./Bill Ripken	15.00	6.75	1.85
☐ 4/6/87 BB PV: J.Carter (FC)/Snyder	5.00	2.20	.60
☐ 4/20/87 Baseball salaries	2.00	.90	.25
☐ 4/27/87 Rob Deer	2.00	.90	.25
☐ 5/11/87 Reggie Jackson	5.00	2.20	.60
☐ 5/25/87 Eric Davis	2.00	.90	.25
☐ 7/6/87 One Day in Baseball	2.00	.90	.25
☐ 7/13/87 Mattingly (FC)/Strawberry	8.00	3.60	1.00

Issue			
☐ 7/20/87 Andre Dawson	4.00	1.80	.50
☐ 8/17/87 Alan Trammell	4.00	1.80	.50
☐ 9/28/87 Ozzie Smith	5.00	2.20	.60
☐ 10/5/87 Lloyd Moseby	2.00	.90	.25
☐ 10/19/87 Greg Gagne	2.00	.90	.25
☐ 10/26/87 Dan Gladden	2.00	.90	.25
☐ 11/2/87 Twins Team	6.00	2.70	.75
☐ 12/14/87 Bo Jackson BB/FB	6.00	2.70	.75
☐ 12/21/87 Athletes Who Care SOY: Murphy etc	5.00	2.20	.60
☐ 3/7/88 Kirk Gibson	3.00	1.35	.35
☐ 3/14/88 Pam Postema	2.00	.90	.25
☐ 4/4/88 BB PV: W.Clark/McGwire (both FC)	6.00	2.70	.75
☐ 5/2/88 Billy Ripken	2.00	.90	.25
☐ 5/9/88 Pete Rose	5.00	2.20	.60
☐ 7/11/88 Darryl Strawberry	3.00	1.35	.35
☐ 7/18/88 Casey at the Bat	2.00	.90	.25
☐ 9/26/88 Dwight Evans	2.00	.90	.25
☐ 10/17/88 Jose Canseco (FC)	5.00	2.20	.60
☐ 10/31/88 Hershiser/R.Dempsey	4.00	1.80	.50
☐ 12/19/88 Orel Hershiser SOY	4.00	1.80	.50
☐ 3/6/89 Wade Boggs	4.00	1.80	.50
☐ 4/3/89 Pete Rose	5.00	2.20	.60

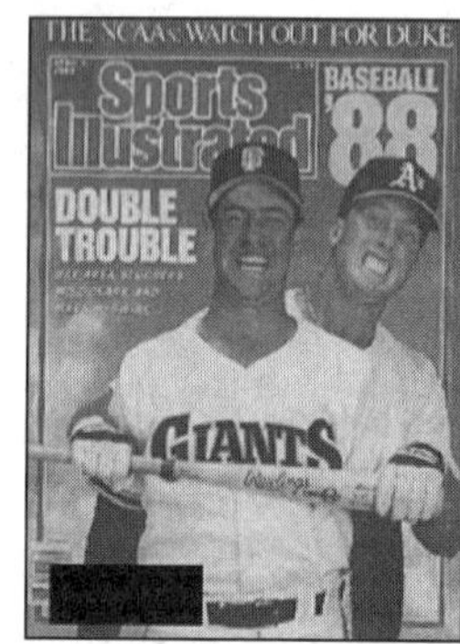

Issue			
☐ 4/5/89 BB PV: Benito Santiago	3.00	1.35	.35
☐ 5/1/89 Nolan Ryan	10.00	4.50	1.25
☐ 5/8/89 Jon Peters	2.00	.90	.25
☐ 6/12/89 Bo Jackson BB	4.00	1.80	.50
☐ 7/3/89 Pete Rose	5.00	2.20	.60
☐ 7/10/89 Rick Reuschel	2.00	.90	.25
☐ 7/24/89 Gregg Jefferies	3.00	1.35	.35
☐ 10/16/89 Rickey Henderson	5.00	2.20	.60
☐ 10/30/89 Kelly Downs	2.00	.90	.25
☐ 11/13/89 Deion Sanders (FC)	6.00	2.70	.75
☐ 3/12/90 Tony LaRussa	3.00	1.35	.35
☐ 4/16/90 BB PV: Ted Williams	8.00	3.60	1.00
☐ 5/7/90 Ken Griffey Jr. (FC)	10.00	4.50	1.25
☐ 5/28/90 Will Clark	4.00	1.80	.50
☐ 6/4/90 Lenny Dykstra	2.00	.90	.25
☐ 6/18/90 Nicklaus/Seles (FC)/Steinbr.	4.00	1.80	.50
☐ 7/9/90 Darryl Strawberry	3.00	1.35	.35
☐ 7/23/90 Minor league BB	2.00	.90	.25
☐ 8/20/90 Jose Canseco	4.00	1.80	.50
☐ 10/1/90 Bobby Bonilla	2.00	.90	.25
☐ 10/22/90 Dennis Eckersley	3.00	1.35	.35
☐ 10/29/90 Chris Sabo	2.00	.90	.25
☐ 3/4/91 Darryl Strawberry	3.00	1.35	.35
☐ 4/15/91 BB PV: Nolan Ryan	10.00	4.50	1.25
☐ 5/13/91 Roger Clemens	4.00	1.80	.50
☐ 5/27/91 M.Mantle/R.Maris	10.00	4.50	1.25

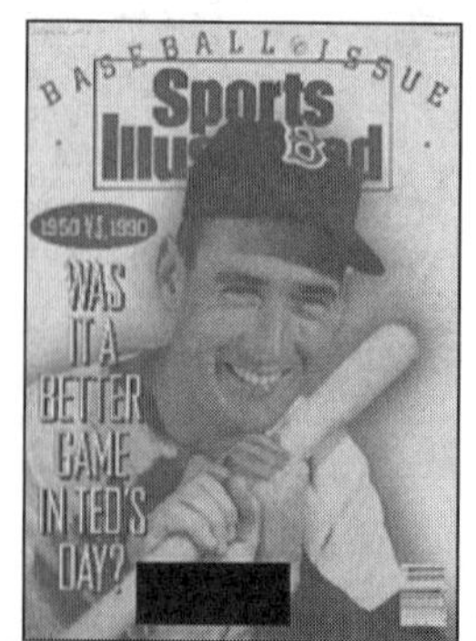

Issue			
☐ 7/1/91 Orel Hershiser	3.00	1.35	.35
☐ 7/29/91 Cal Ripken	12.00	5.50	1.50
☐ 9/30/91 Ramon Martinez	3.00	1.35	.35
☐ 10/21/91 Kirby Puckett (FC)	8.00	3.60	1.00
☐ 10/28/91 D.Gladden/G.Olson	3.00	1.35	.35
☐ 11/4/91 Twins Team	5.00	2.20	.60

Issue			
☐ 3/16/92 Ryne Sandberg (FC)	5.00	2.20	.60
☐ 4/6/92 BB PV: Kirby Puckett	5.00	2.20	.60
☐ 4/27/92 Deion Sanders BB	4.00	1.80	.50
☐ 5/4/92 Barry Bonds (FC)	5.00	2.20	.60
☐ 5/18/92 Baseball errors	2.00	.90	.25
☐ 6/1/92 Mark McGwire	4.00	1.80	.50
☐ 7/6/92 Steve Palermo	2.00	.90	.25

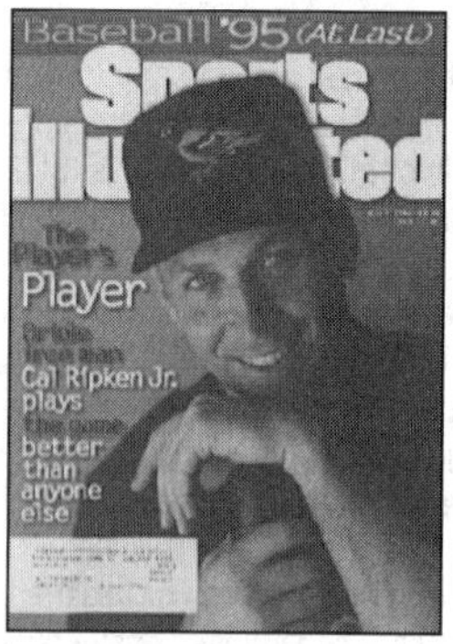

Issue			
☐ 8/24/92 Deion Sanders BB/FB	4.00	1.80	.50
☐ Fall '92 Classic SI: Willie Mays	8.00	3.60	1.00
☐ 10/5/92 George Brett	5.00	2.20	.60
☐ 10/19/92 Dave Winfield	3.00	1.35	.35
☐ 10/26/92 R.Alomar/Smoltz (both FC)	6.00	2.70	.75
☐ 11/2/92 Blue Jays Team	5.00	2.20	.60
☐ 3/1/93 George Steinbrenner	3.00	1.35	.35
☐ 3/22/93 Dwight Gooden	3.00	1.35	.35
☐ 4/5/93 BB PV: David Cone	3.00	1.35	.35
☐ 5/3/93 Joe DiMaggio	10.00	4.50	1.25
☐ 5/24/93 Barry Bonds	4.00	1.80	.50
☐ 7/5/93 Mike Piazza (FC)	8.00	3.60	1.00
☐ 7/12/93 Crews/Olin widows	2.00	.90	.25
☐ 7/19/93 B.Gibson/D.McLain	4.00	1.80	.50
☐ 9/27/93 Ron Gant	3.00	1.35	.35
☐ 11/1/93 Joe Carter	4.00	1.80	.50
☐ 3/14/94 Michael Jordan BB	6.00	2.70	.75
☐ 4/4/94 BB PV: Griffey/Piazza foldout	8.00	3.60	1.00

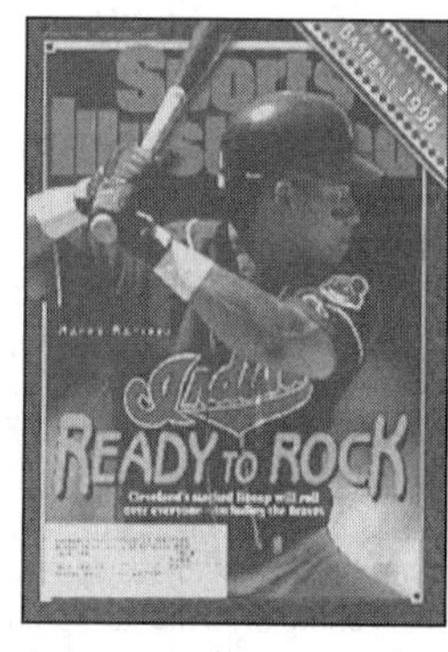

Issue			
☐ 4/18/94 Mickey Mantle	8.00	3.60	1.00
☐ 5/23/94 C.O'Brien/Cangelosi	2.00	.90	.25
☐ 6/6/94 Ken Griffey Jr.	6.00	2.70	.75
☐ 7/18/94 Mussina/McDonald	3.00	1.35	.35
☐ 8/8/94 F.Thomas (FC)/K.Griffey	8.00	3.60	1.00
☐ 8/16/94 Eddie Mathews SI 40th ann.	5.00	2.20	.60
☐ 8/22/94 Cubs-Red Sox fake WS	2.00	.90	.25
☐ 10/31/94 Hisanobu Watanabe	3.00	1.35	.35
☐ 2/27/95 Strawberry/Gooden	3.00	1.35	.35
☐ 5/1/95 BB PV: Cal Ripken	6.00	2.70	.75
☐ 5/15/95 Erickson/Moeller/Cox	2.00	.90	.25
☐ 6/5/95 Matt Williams	3.00	1.35	.35
☐ 7/10/95 Hideo Nomo	6.00	2.70	.75
☐ 8/7/95 Cal Ripken	6.00	2.70	.75
☐ 8/14/95 Greg Maddux (FC)	10.00	4.50	1.25
☐ 8/21/95 Mickey Mantle	10.00	4.50	1.25
☐ 9/11/95 Cal Ripken	6.00	2.70	.75
☐ 10/2/95 Mo Vaughn	3.00	1.35	.35
☐ 10/16/95 Ken Griffey Jr.	6.00	2.70	.75
☐ 10/30/95 Bo Jackson	3.00	1.35	.35
☐ 11/6/95 Braves Team: Maddux etc	6.00	2.70	.75
☐ 12/18/95 Cal Ripken SOY	8.00	3.60	1.00
☐ 3/18/96 Jay/Chase Buhner	3.00	1.35	.35
☐ 4/1/96 BB PV: Manny Ramirez	4.00	1.80	.50
☐ 5/6/96 Albert Belle	4.00	1.80	.50
☐ 5/20/96 Marge Schott	2.00	.90	.25
☐ 7/8/96 Alex Rodriguez (FC)	6.00	2.70	.75
☐ 8/19/96 Al Simmons	2.00	.90	.25
☐ 10/14/96 Roberto Alomar	3.00	1.35	.35
☐ 10/21/96 Derek Jeter (FC)	5.00	2.20	.60
☐ 11/4/96 Yankees: Wetteland/Girardi	5.00	2.20	.60
☐ 11/25/96 Ted Williams	4.00	1.80	.50

VINTAGE MEMORABILIA PRICE GUIDE

World Series Programs

World Series programs are the most popular item in the publication field. Programs prior to 1920 are difficult to find and command a premium in top condition. Programs prior to 1910 are quite scarce; only a few copies from 1903 are known to exist.

	Nr-Mt	Nr-Mt-Mt
1 1903 Boston Red Sox	18000.00	30000.00
2 1903 Pittsburgh Pirates	15000.00	25000.00
3 1904 No Series		
4 1905 New York Giants	7500.00	10000.00
5 1905 Philadelphia Athletics	9000.00	12000.00
6 1906 Chicago White Sox	7500.00	10000.00
7 1906 Chicago Cubs	8000.00	11000.00
8 1907 Detroit Tigers	7500.00	10000.00
9 1908 Chicago Cubs	7500.00	10000.00
10 1909 Detroit Tigers	7500.00	10000.00
11 1909 Pittsburgh Pirates	7500.00	10000.00
12 1910 Philadelphia Athletics	6500.00	9000.00
13 1910 Chicago Cubs	6000.00	8000.00
14 1911 Philadelphia Athletics	3000.00	5000.00
15 1911 New York Giants	2500.00	4000.00
16 1912 Boston Red Sox	2000.00	3500.00
17 1912 New York Giants	2500.00	4000.00
18 1913 Philadelphia Athletics	2500.00	4000.00
19 1913 New York Giants	2000.00	3500.00
20 1914 Philadelphia Athletics	2000.00	3500.00
21 1914 Boston Braves	1800.00	3000.00
22 1915 Boston Red Sox	2000.00	3500.00
23 1915 Philadelphia Phillies	7500.00	10000.00
24 1916 Boston Red Sox	2500.00	4000.00
25 1916 Brooklyn Dodgers	3500.00	6000.00
26 1917 Chicago White Sox	6000.00	8000.00
27 1917 New York Giants	2000.00	3500.00
28 1918 Boston Red Sox	9000.00	12000.00
29 1918 Chicago Cubs	7500.00	10000.00
30 1919 Chicago White Sox	9000.00	12000.00
31 1919 Cincinnati Reds	2500.00	4000.00
32 1920 Cleveland Indians	3500.00	6000.00
33 1920 Brooklyn Dodgers	6000.00	8000.00
34 1921 New York Yankees	1200.00	2000.00
35 1921 New York Giants	1200.00	2000.00
36 1922 New York Yankees	1200.00	2000.00
37 1922 New York Giants	1200.00	2000.00
38 1923 New York Yankees	1200.00	2000.00
39 1923 New York Giants	1200.00	2000.00
40 1924 Washington Senators	800.00	1200.00
41 1924 New York Giants	900.00	1500.00
42 1925 Washington Senators	800.00	1200.00
43 1925 Pittsburgh Pirates	3000.00	5000.00
44 1926 New York Yankees	900.00	1500.00
45 1926 St. Louis Cardinals	800.00	1200.00
46 1927 New York Yankees	2000.00	3500.00
47 1927 Pittsburgh Pirates	3000.00	5000.00
48 1928 New York Yankees	900.00	1500.00
49 1928 St. Louis Cardinals	800.00	1200.00
50 1929 Philadelphia Athletics	800.00	1200.00
51 1929 Chicago Cubs	700.00	1000.00
52 1930 Philadelphia Athletics	700.00	1000.00
53 1930 St. Louis Cardinals	500.00	750.00
54 1931 Philadelphia Athletics	500.00	750.00
55 1931 St. Louis Cardinals	300.00	600.00
56 1932 New York Yankees	700.00	1000.00
57 1932 Chicago Cubs	300.00	600.00
58 1933 Washington Senators	300.00	600.00
59 1933 New York Giants	250.00	500.00
60 1934 St. Louis Cardinals	250.00	500.00
61 1934 Detroit Tigers	300.00	600.00
62 1935 Detroit Tigers	350.00	700.00
63 1935 Chicago Cubs	250.00	500.00
64 1936 New York Yankees	250.00	500.00
65 1936 New York Giants	200.00	400.00
66 1937 New York Yankees	250.00	500.00
67 1937 New York Giants	200.00	400.00
68 1938 New York Yankees	200.00	400.00
69 1938 Chicago Cubs	175.00	350.00
70 1939 New York Yankees	200.00	400.00
71 1939 Cincinnati Reds	175.00	350.00
72 1940 Cincinnati Reds	175.00	350.00
73 1940 Detroit Tigers	200.00	400.00
74 1941 New York Yankees	175.00	350.00
75 1941 Brooklyn Dodgers	250.00	500.00
76 1942 St. Louis Cardinals	125.00	250.00
77 1942 New York Yankees	150.00	300.00
78 1943 New York Yankees	125.00	250.00
79 1943 St. Louis Cardinals	150.00	300.00
80 1944 St. Louis Browns	200.00	400.00
81 1944 St. Louis Cardinals	125.00	250.00
82 1945 Detroit Tigers	200.00	400.00
83 1945 Chicago Cubs	100.00	200.00
84 1946 St. Louis Cardinals	100.00	200.00
85 1946 Boston Red Sox	100.00	200.00
86 1947 New York Yankees	150.00	300.00
87 1947 Brooklyn Dodgers	200.00	400.00
88 1948 Cleveland Indians	75.00	125.00
89 1948 Boston Braves	90.00	150.00
90 1949 New York Yankees	125.00	250.00
91 1949 Brooklyn Dodgers	150.00	300.00
92 1950 New York Yankees	90.00	150.00
93 1950 Philadelphia Phillies	75.00	125.00
94 1951 New York Yankees	90.00	150.00
95 1951 New York Giants	75.00	125.00
96 1952 New York Yankees	75.00	125.00
97 1952 Brooklyn Dodgers	150.00	300.00
98 1953 New York Yankees	75.00	125.00
99 1953 Brooklyn Dodgers	150.00	300.00
100 1954 New York Giants	125.00	250.00
101 1954 Cleveland Indians	100.00	200.00
102 1955 Brooklyn Dodgers	175.00	350.00
103 1955 New York Yankees	90.00	150.00
104 1956 New York Yankees	100.00	175.00
105 1956 Brooklyn Dodgers	125.00	250.00
106 1957 Milwaukee Braves	100.00	175.00
107 1957 New York Yankees	75.00	125.00
108 1958 New York Yankees	75.00	125.00
109 1958 Milwaukee Braves	100.00	175.00
110 1959 Los Angeles Dodgers	75.00	125.00
111 1959 Chicago White Sox	125.00	225.00
112 1960 Pittsburgh Pirates	60.00	100.00
113 1960 New York Yankees	50.00	75.00
114 1961 New York Yankees	75.00	150.00
115 1961 Cincinnati Reds	60.00	100.00
116 1962 New York Yankees	60.00	100.00
117 1962 San Francisco Giants	75.00	150.00
118 1963 Los Angeles Dodgers	40.00	60.00
119 1963 New York Yankees	40.00	60.00
120 1964 St. Louis Cardinals	75.00	125.00
121 1964 New York Yankees	50.00	75.00
122 1965 Los Angeles Dodgers	25.00	40.00
123 1965 Minnesota Twins	60.00	100.00
124 1966 Baltimore Orioles	60.00	100.00
125 1966 Los Angeles Dodgers	25.00	40.00
126 1967 St. Louis Cardinals	60.00	100.00
127 1967 Boston Red Sox	75.00	125.00
128 1968 Detroit Tigers	125.00	225.00
129 1968 St. Louis Cardinals	60.00	100.00
130 1969 New York Mets	90.00	150.00
131 1969 Baltimore Orioles	25.00	40.00
132 1970 Baltimore Orioles	25.00	40.00
133 1970 Cincinnati Reds	50.00	75.00
134 1971 Pittsburgh Pirates	60.00	100.00
135 1971 Baltimore Orioles	25.00	40.00
136 1972 Oakland Athletics	30.00	60.00
137 1972 Cincinnati Reds	30.00	60.00
138 1973 Oakland Athletics	30.00	60.00
139 1973 New York Mets	20.00	35.00
140 1974 Oakland Athletics	15.00	25.00
141 1974 Los Angeles Dodgers	15.00	25.00
142 1975 Boston Red Sox	18.00	30.00
143 1975 Cincinnati Reds	15.00	25.00
144 1976 New York Yankees	12.00	20.00
145 1976 Cincinnati Reds	12.00	20.00
146 1977 New York Yankees	8.00	15.00
147 1977 Los Angeles Dodgers	8.00	15.00
148 1978 New York Yankees	8.00	15.00
149 1978 Los Angeles Dodgers	8.00	15.00
150 1979 Baltimore Orioles	8.00	15.00
151 1979 Pittsburgh Pirates	8.00	15.00
152 1980 Kansas City Royals	8.00	15.00
153 1980 Philadelphia Phillies	8.00	15.00
154 1981 New York Yankees	8.00	15.00
155 1981 Los Angeles Dodgers	8.00	15.00
156 1982 Milwaukee Brewers	12.00	20.00
157 1982 St. Louis Cardinals	8.00	15.00
158 1983 Baltimore Orioles	8.00	15.00
159 1983 Philadelphia Phillies	12.00	20.00
160 1984 Detroit Tigers	8.00	15.00
161 1984 San Diego Padres	7.00	12.00
162 1985 Kansas City Royals	7.00	12.00
163 1985 St. Louis Cardinals	7.00	12.00
164 1986 Boston Red Sox	8.00	15.00
165 1986 New York Mets	8.00	15.00
166 1987 Minnesota Twins	7.00	12.00
167 1987 St. Louis Cardinals	7.00	12.00
168 1988 Oakland Athletics	7.00	12.00
169 1988 Los Angeles Dodgers	7.00	12.00
170 1989 Oakland Athletics	8.00	15.00
171 1989 San Francisco Giants	8.00	15.00
172 1990 Oakland Athletics	6.00	10.00
173 1990 Cincinnati Reds	6.00	10.00
174 1991 Minnesota Twins	6.00	10.00
175 1991 Atlanta Braves	6.00	10.00
176 1992 Toronto Blue Jays	6.00	10.00
177 1992 Atlanta Braves	6.00	10.00
178 1993 Toronto Blue Jays	6.00	10.00
179 1993 Philadelphia Phillies	6.00	10.00
180 1994 No Series	6.00	10.00
181 1995 Cleveland Indians	6.00	10.00
182 1995 Atlanta Braves	6.00	10.00

World Series Ticket Stubs

Note * The value for complete World Series tickets is generally double that of a stub. Complete World Series tickets prior to 1920 are valued even higher. Ticket stubs for historic World Series games, such as Don Larsen's 1956 perfect World Series game, or Babe Ruth's famous called shot game, can command anywhere from 3 to 6 times that of a regular stub.

	Nr-Mt	Nr-Mt-Mt
1 1903 Boston Red Sox	2000.00	3500.00
2 1903 Pittsburgh Pirates	1500.00	2500.00
3 1904 No Series		
4 1905 New York Giants	1200.00	1800.00
5 1905 Philadelphia Athletics	900.00	1500.00
6 1906 Chicago White Sox	700.00	1200.00
7 1906 Chicago Cubs	700.00	1200.00
8 1907 Detroit Tigers	600.00	1000.00
9 1908 Chicago Cubs	600.00	1000.00
10 1909 Detroit Tigers	600.00	1000.00
11 1909 Pittsburgh Pirates	500.00	800.00
12 1910 Philadelphia Athletics	500.00	800.00
13 1910 Chicago Cubs	500.00	800.00
14 1911 Philadelphia Athletics	500.00	800.00
15 1911 New York Giants	500.00	800.00
16 1912 Boston Red Sox	700.00	1000.00
17 1912 New York Giants	500.00	800.00
18 1913 Philadelphia Athletics	400.00	700.00
19 1913 New York Giants	500.00	800.00
20 1914 Philadelphia Athletics	400.00	700.00
21 1914 Boston Braves	500.00	800.00
22 1915 Boston Red Sox	500.00	800.00
23 1915 Philadelphia Phillies	400.00	700.00
24 1916 Boston Red Sox	500.00	800.00
25 1916 Brooklyn Dodgers	600.00	900.00
26 1917 Chicago White Sox	400.00	700.00
27 1917 New York Giants	400.00	700.00
28 1918 Boston Red Sox	500.00	800.00
29 1918 Chicago Cubs	400.00	700.00
30 1919 Chicago White Sox	900.00	1500.00
31 1919 Cincinnati Reds	500.00	800.00
32 1920 Cleveland Indians	350.00	600.00
33 1920 Brooklyn Dodgers	400.00	700.00
34 1921 New York Yankees	350.00	600.00
35 1921 New York Giants	300.00	500.00
36 1922 New York Yankees	350.00	600.00
37 1922 New York Giants	300.00	500.00
38 1923 New York Yankees	350.00	600.00
39 1923 New York Giants	300.00	500.00
40 1924 Washington Senators	250.00	400.00
41 1924 New York Giants	250.00	400.00
42 1925 Washington Senators	250.00	400.00
43 1925 Pittsburgh Pirates	250.00	400.00
44 1926 New York Yankees	250.00	400.00
45 1926 St. Louis Cardinals	200.00	350.00
46 1927 New York Yankees	300.00	500.00
47 1927 Pittsburgh Pirates	175.00	300.00
48 1928 New York Yankees	200.00	350.00
49 1928 St. Louis Cardinals	175.00	300.00
50 1929 Philadelphia Athletics	150.00	250.00
51 1929 Chicago Cubs	150.00	250.00
52 1930 Philadelphia Athletics	150.00	250.00
53 1930 St. Louis Cardinals	150.00	250.00
54 1931 Philadelphia Athletics	150.00	250.00
55 1931 St. Louis Cardinals	150.00	250.00
56 1932 New York Yankees	125.00	200.00
57 1932 Chicago Cubs	125.00	200.00
58 1933 Washington Senators	125.00	200.00
59 1933 New York Giants	90.00	150.00
60 1934 St. Louis Cardinals	90.00	150.00
61 1934 Detroit Tigers	125.00	175.00
62 1935 Detroit Tigers	125.00	200.00
63 1935 Chicago Cubs	125.00	200.00
64 1936 New York Yankees	90.00	150.00
65 1936 New York Giants	90.00	150.00
66 1937 New York Yankees	90.00	150.00
67 1937 New York Giants	90.00	150.00
68 1938 New York Yankees	90.00	150.00
69 1938 Chicago Cubs	100.00	175.00
70 1939 New York Yankees	90.00	150.00
71 1939 Cincinnati Reds	90.00	150.00
72 1940 Cincinnati Reds	75.00	125.00
73 1940 Detroit Tigers	125.00	200.00
74 1941 New York Yankees	75.00	125.00
75 1941 Brooklyn Dodgers	125.00	200.00
76 1942 St. Louis Cardinals	75.00	125.00
77 1942 New York Yankees	90.00	150.00
78 1943 New York Yankees	90.00	150.00
79 1943 St. Louis Cardinals	75.00	125.00
80 1944 St. Louis Browns	90.00	150.00
81 1944 St. Louis Cardinals	90.00	150.00
82 1945 Detroit Tigers	125.00	200.00
83 1945 Chicago Cubs	90.00	150.00
84 1946 St. Louis Cardinals	90.00	150.00
85 1946 Boston Red Sox	125.00	200.00
86 1947 New York Yankees	90.00	150.00
87 1947 Brooklyn Dodgers	125.00	200.00
88 1948 Cleveland Indians	75.00	125.00
89 1948 Boston Braves	75.00	125.00
90 1949 New York Yankees	75.00	125.00
91 1949 Brooklyn Dodgers	100.00	175.00
92 1950 New York Yankees	75.00	125.00
93 1950 Philadelphia Phillies	90.00	150.00
94 1951 New York Yankees	75.00	125.00
95 1951 New York Giants	60.00	90.00
96 1952 New York Yankees	75.00	125.00
97 1952 Brooklyn Dodgers	100.00	175.00
98 1953 New York Yankees	75.00	125.00
99 1953 Brooklyn Dodgers	100.00	175.00
100 1954 New York Giants	75.00	125.00
101 1954 Cleveland Indians	60.00	90.00
102 1955 Brooklyn Dodgers	150.00	250.00
103 1955 New York Yankees	50.00	75.00
104 1956 New York Yankees	50.00	75.00
105 1956 Brooklyn Dodgers	75.00	125.00
106 1957 Milwaukee Braves	50.00	75.00
107 1957 New York Yankees	50.00	75.00
108 1958 New York Yankees	50.00	75.00
109 1958 Milwaukee Braves	50.00	75.00
110 1959 Los Angeles Dodgers	50.00	75.00
111 1959 Chicago White Sox	50.00	75.00
112 1960 Pittsburgh Pirates	50.00	75.00
113 1960 New York Yankees	45.00	70.00
114 1961 New York Yankees	60.00	90.00
115 1961 Cincinnati Reds	45.00	70.00
116 1962 New York Yankees	50.00	75.00
117 1962 San Francisco Giants	50.00	75.00
118 1963 Los Angeles Dodgers	40.00	60.00
119 1963 New York Yankees	40.00	60.00
120 1964 St. Louis Cardinals	40.00	60.00
121 1964 New York Yankees	45.00	70.00
122 1965 Los Angeles Dodgers	40.00	60.00
123 1965 Minnesota Twins	40.00	60.00
124 1966 Baltimore Orioles	40.00	60.00
125 1966 Los Angeles Dodgers	40.00	60.00
126 1967 St. Louis Cardinals	40.00	60.00
127 1967 Boston Red Sox	50.00	75.00
128 1968 Detroit Tigers	50.00	75.00
129 1968 St. Louis Cardinals	50.00	75.00
130 1969 New York Mets	50.00	75.00
131 1969 Baltimore Orioles	45.00	60.00
132 1970 Baltimore Orioles	45.00	60.00
133 1970 Cincinnati Reds	45.00	60.00
134 1971 Pittsburgh Pirates	45.00	60.00
135 1971 Baltimore Orioles	45.00	60.00
136 1972 Oakland Athletics	45.00	60.00
137 1972 Cincinnati Reds	45.00	60.00
138 1973 Oakland Athletics	45.00	60.00
139 1973 New York Mets	50.00	70.00
140 1974 Oakland Athletics	35.00	50.00
141 1974 Los Angeles Dodgers	35.00	50.00
142 1975 Boston Red Sox	40.00	55.00
143 1975 Cincinnati Reds	30.00	45.00
144 1976 New York Yankees	30.00	45.00
145 1976 Cincinnati Reds	30.00	45.00
146 1977 New York Yankees	30.00	45.00
147 1977 Los Angeles Dodgers	30.00	45.00
148 1978 New York Yankees	30.00	45.00
149 1978 Los Angeles Dodgers	30.00	45.00
150 1979 Baltimore Orioles	25.00	40.00
151 1979 Pittsburgh Pirates	25.00	40.00
152 1980 Kansas City Royals	25.00	40.00
153 1980 Philadelphia Phillies	25.00	40.00
154 1981 New York Yankees	25.00	40.00
155 1981 Los Angeles Dodgers	25.00	40.00
156 1982 Milwaukee Brewers	25.00	40.00
157 1982 St. Louis Cardinals	25.00	40.00
158 1983 Baltimore Orioles	25.00	40.00
159 1983 Philadelphia Phillies	25.00	40.00
160 1984 Detroit Tigers	30.00	45.00
161 1984 San Diego Padres	25.00	40.00
162 1985 Kansas City Royals	25.00	40.00
163 1985 St. Louis Cardinals	25.00	40.00
164 1986 Boston Red Sox	30.00	45.00
165 1986 New York Mets	30.00	45.00
166 1987 Minnesota Twins	25.00	40.00
167 1987 St. Louis Cardinals	25.00	40.00
168 1988 Oakland Athletics	25.00	40.00
169 1988 Los Angeles Dodgers	20.00	35.00
170 1989 Oakland Athletics	20.00	35.00
171 1989 San Francisco Giants	25.00	40.00
172 1990 Oakland Athletics	25.00	40.00
173 1990 Cincinnati Reds	20.00	35.00
174 1991 Minnesota Twins	20.00	35.00
175 1991 Atlanta Braves	20.00	35.00
176 1992 Toronto Blue Jays	20.00	35.00
177 1992 Atlanta Braves	20.00	35.00
178 1993 Toronto Blue Jays	20.00	35.00
179 1993 Philadelphia Phillies	20.00	35.00
180 1994 No Series		
181 1995 Cleveland Indians	20.00	35.00
182 1995 Atlanta Braves	20.00	35.00

World Series Press Pins

World Series press pins were first introduced by the Philadelphia Athletics during the 1911 Fall Classic. The press pin was intended to keep non-press personnel out of the press box. Today, World Seres press pins are given to members of the media more as a symbolic gesture. 1911-1919 graded Ex-Mt, 1920-1995 graded Nr-Mt-Mt.

14 1911 Philadelphia Athletics	15000.00
16 1912 Boston Red Sox	5000.00
17 1912 New York Giants	9000.00
18 1913 Philadelphia Athletics	6000.00
19 1913 New York Giants	8000.00
20 1914 Philadelphia Athletics	10000.00
21 1914 Boston Braves	5000.00
22 1915 Boston Red Sox	6000.00
23 1915 Philadelphia Phillies	10000.00
24 1916 Boston Red Sox	4500.00
25 1916 Brooklyn Dodgers	4000.00
26 1917 Chicago White Sox	8000.00
27 1917 New York Giants	7500.00
28 1918 Boston Red Sox	5000.00
30 1919 Chicago White Sox	10000.00
31 1919 Cincinnati Reds	4000.00
32 1920 Cleveland Indians	3000.00
33 1920 Brooklyn Dodgers	3200.00
34 1921 New York Yankees	3500.00
35 1921 New York Giants	3000.00
36 1922 New York Yankees	3000.00
37 1922 New York Giants	2500.00
38 1923 New York Yankees	3000.00
40 1924 Washington Senators	2000.00
41 1924 New York Giants	1500.00
42 1925 Washington Senators	2000.00
43 1925 Pittsburgh Pirates	2000.00
44 1926 New York Yankees	1250.00
45 1926 St. Louis Cardinals	1000.00
46 1927 New York Yankees	2400.00
47 1927 Pittsburgh Pirates	1000.00
48 1928 New York Yankees	1500.00
49 1928 St. Louis Cardinals	800.00
50 1929 Philadelphia Athletics	800.00
51 1929 Chicago Cubs	2000.00
52 1930 Philadelphia Athletics	4000.00
53 1930 St. Louis Cardinals	700.00
54 1931 Philadelphia Athletics	1000.00
55 1931 St. Louis Cardinals	800.00
56 1932 New York Yankees	1000.00
57 1932 Chicago Cubs	2000.00
58 1933 Washington Senators	1000.00
59 1933 New York Giants	800.00
60 1934 St. Louis Cardinals	700.00
61 1934 Detroit Tigers	750.00
62 1935 Detroit Tigers	750.00
63 1935 Chicago Cubs	2000.00
64 1936 New York Yankees	800.00
65 1936 New York Giants	400.00
66 1937 New York Yankees	800.00
67 1937 New York Giants	400.00
68 1938 New York Yankees	800.00
69 1938 Chicago Cubs	2000.00
70 1939 New York Yankees	750.00
71 1939 Cincinnati Reds	450.00
72 1940 Cincinnati Reds	400.00
73 1940 Detroit Tigers	500.00
74 1941 New York Yankees	800.00

75 1941 Brooklyn Dodgers	1000.00
76 1942 St. Louis Cardinals	2500.00
77 1942 New York Yankees	600.00
78 1943 New York Yankees	600.00
79 1943 St. Louis Cardinals	2500.00
80 1944 St. Louis Browns	500.00
81 1944 St. Louis Cardinals	600.00
82 1945 Detroit Tigers	600.00
83 1945 Chicago Cubs	600.00
84 1946 St. Louis Cardinals	500.00
85 1946 Boston Red Sox	600.00
86 1947 New York Yankees	800.00
87 1947 Brooklyn Dodgers	900.00
88 1948 Cleveland Indians	400.00
89 1948 Boston Braves	500.00
90 1949 New York Yankees	600.00
91 1949 Brooklyn Dodgers	750.00
92 1950 New York Yankees	350.00
93 1950 Philadelphia Phillies	300.00
94 1951 New York Yankees	300.00
95 1951 New York Giants	200.00
96 1952 New York Yankees	300.00
97 1952 Brooklyn Dodgers	700.00
98 1953 New York Yankees	300.00
99 1953 Brooklyn Dodgers	400.00
100 1954 New York Giants	200.00
101 1954 Cleveland Indians	250.00
102 1955 Brooklyn Dodgers	500.00
103 1955 New York Yankees	300.00
104 1956 New York Yankees	300.00
105 1956 Brooklyn Dodgers	1500.00
106 1957 Milwaukee Braves	175.00
107 1957 New York Yankees	200.00
108 1958 New York Yankees	200.00
109 1958 Milwaukee Braves	175.00
110 1959 Los Angeles Dodgers	250.00
111 1959 Chicago White Sox	200.00
112 1960 Pittsburgh Pirates	275.00
113 1960 New York Yankees	175.00
114 1961 New York Yankees	250.00
115 1961 Cincinnati Reds	150.00
116 1962 New York Yankees	175.00
117 1962 San Francisco Giants	300.00
118 1963 Los Angeles Dodgers	225.00
119 1963 New York Yankees	200.00
120 1964 St. Louis Cardinals	150.00
121 1964 New York Yankees	200.00
122 1965 Los Angeles Dodgers	100.00
123 1965 Minnesota Twins	100.00
124 1966 Baltimore Orioles	200.00
125 1966 Los Angeles Dodgers	100.00
126 1967 St. Louis Cardinals	100.00
127 1967 Boston Red Sox	175.00
128 1968 Detroit Tigers	200.00
129 1968 St. Louis Cardinals	100.00
130 1969 New York Mets	400.00
131 1969 Baltimore Orioles	150.00
132 1970 Baltimore Orioles	100.00
133 1970 Cincinnati Reds	100.00
134 1971 Pittsburgh Pirates	125.00
135 1971 Baltimore Orioles	150.00
136 1972 Oakland Athletics	300.00
137 1972 Cincinnati Reds	100.00
138 1973 Oakland Athletics	300.00
139 1973 New York Mets	150.00
140 1974 Oakland Athletics	400.00
141 1974 Los Angeles Dodgers	150.00
142 1975 Boston Red Sox	250.00
143 1975 Cincinnati Reds	150.00
144 1976 New York Yankees	150.00
145 1976 Cincinnati Reds	150.00
146 1977 New York Yankees	150.00
147 1977 Los Angeles Dodgers	100.00
148 1978 New York Yankees	100.00
149 1978 Los Angeles Dodgers	75.00
150 1979 Baltimore Orioles	100.00
151 1979 Pittsburgh Pirates	100.00
152 1980 Kansas City Royals	150.00
153 1980 Philadelphia Phillies	125.00
154 1981 New York Yankees	100.00
155 1981 Los Angeles Dodgers	75.00
156 1982 Milwaukee Brewers	100.00
157 1982 St. Louis Cardinals	60.00
158 1983 Baltimore Orioles	60.00
159 1983 Philadelphia Phillies	60.00
160 1984 Detroit Tigers	75.00
161 1984 San Diego Padres	60.00
162 1985 Kansas City Royals	100.00
163 1985 St. Louis Cardinals	75.00
164 1986 Boston Red Sox	75.00
165 1986 New York Mets	100.00
166 1987 Minnesota Twins	50.00
167 1987 St. Louis Cardinals	50.00
168 1988 Oakland Athletics	50.00
169 1988 Los Angeles Dodgers	75.00
170 1989 Oakland Athletics	75.00
171 1989 San Francisco Giants	75.00
172 1990 Oakland Athletics	125.00
173 1990 Cincinnati Reds	125.00
174 1991 Minnesota Twins	100.00
175 1991 Atlanta Braves	100.00
176 1992 Toronto Blue Jays	125.00
177 1992 Atlanta Braves	100.00
178 1993 Toronto Blue Jays	125.00
179 1993 Philadelphia Phillies	125.00
180 1994 No Series	
181 1995 Cleveland Indians	150.00
182 1995 Atlanta Braves	150.00

All-Star Game Programs

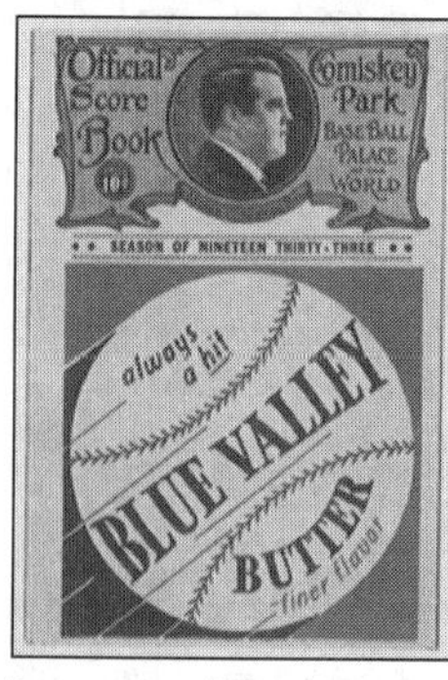

Pre-war programs are difficult to obtain in top condition and are graded Ex-Mt and Vg-Ex below.

	Nr-Mt	Ex-Mt
1933 Chicago	4500.00	3000.00
1934 New York	6000.00	4500.00
1935 Cleveland	1500.00	600.00
1936 Boston	4000.00	2500.00
1937 Washington	2500.00	1500.00
1938 Cincinnati	2500.00	1500.00
1939 New York	3000.00	1800.00
1940 St. Louis	1500.00	900.00
1941 Detroit	1500.00	900.00
1942 New York	3500.00	2000.00
1943 Philadelphia	1000.00	700.00
1944 Pittsburgh	1500.00	900.00
1945 War Year - No Game		
1946 Boston	1500.00	900.00
1947 Chicago	600.00	450.00
1948 St. Louis	600.00	450.00
1949 Brooklyn	1000.00	700.00
1950 Chicago	400.00	300.00
1951 Detroit	300.00	200.00
1952 Philadelphia	250.00	175.00
1953 Cincinnati	300.00	200.00
1954 Cleveland	250.00	175.00
1955 Milwaukee	250.00	175.00
1956 Washington	250.00	175.00
1957 St. Louis	300.00	200.00
1958 Baltimore	250.00	175.00
1959 Pittsburgh	300.00	200.00
1959 Los Angeles	300.00	200.00
1960 Kansas City	200.00	150.00
1960 New York	150.00	100.00
1961 Boston	400.00	300.00
1961 San Francisco	425.00	325.00
1962 Washington	250.00	175.00
1962 Chicago	200.00	150.00
1963 Cleveland	200.00	150.00
1964 New York	200.00	150.00
1965 Minnesota	100.00	70.00
1966 St. Louis	175.00	125.00
1967 Anaheim	150.00	100.00
1968 Houston	125.00	80.00
1969 Washington	125.00	80.00
1970 Cincinnati	150.00	100.00
1971 Detroit	175.00	125.00
1972 Atlanta	75.00	50.00
1973 Kansas City	150.00	100.00
1974 Pittsburgh	50.00	30.00
1975 Milwaukee	50.00	30.00
1976 Philadelphia	35.00	20.00
1977 New York	20.00	12.00
1978 San Diego	50.00	30.00
1979 Seattle	25.00	15.00
1980 Los Angeles	35.00	20.00
1981 Cleveland	20.00	12.00
1982 Montreal	35.00	20.00
1983 Chicago	20.00	12.00
1984 San Francisco	10.00	7.00
1985 Minnesota	10.00	7.00
1986 Houston	10.00	7.00
1987 Oakland	15.00	9.00
1988 Cincinnati	15.00	9.00
1989 California	15.00	9.00
1990 Chicago	15.00	9.00
1991 Toronto	20.00	12.00
1992 San Diego	15.00	9.00
1993 Baltimore	15.00	9.00
1994 Pittsburgh	12.00	8.00
1995 Arlington	10.00	7.00
1996 Philadelphia	10.00	7.00

All-Star Game Ticket Stubs

Pre-war ticket stubs are difficult to obtain in top condition and are graded Ex-Mt and Vg-Ex below. Complete tickets are valued 2 to 5 times that of a stub.

	Nr-Mt	Ex-Mt
1933 Chicago	700.00	500.00
1934 New York	800.00	600.00
1935 Cleveland	250.00	175.00
1936 Boston	500.00	350.00
1937 Washington	425.00	325.00
1938 Cincinnati	300.00	200.00
1939 New York	250.00	175.00
1940 St. Louis	350.00	250.00
1941 Detroit	250.00	175.00
1942 New York	300.00	200.00
1943 Philadelphia	250.00	175.00
1944 Pittsburgh	250.00	175.00
1945 War Year - No Game		
1946 Boston	200.00	150.00
1947 Chicago	125.00	80.00
1948 St. Louis	150.00	100.00
1949 Brooklyn	175.00	125.00
1950 Chicago	125.00	80.00
1951 Detroit	100.00	70.00
1952 Philadelphia	150.00	100.00
1953 Cincinnati	125.00	80.00
1954 Cleveland	75.00	50.00
1955 Milwaukee	100.00	70.00
1956 Washington	150.00	100.00
1957 St. Louis	100.00	70.00
1958 Baltimore	100.00	70.00
1959 Los Angeles	75.00	50.00
1959 Pittsburgh	125.00	80.00
1960 Kansas City	125.00	80.00
1960 New York	100.00	70.00
1961 San Francisco	100.00	70.00
1961 Boston	125.00	80.00
1962 Chicago	100.00	70.00
1962 Washington	75.00	50.00
1963 Cleveland	60.00	40.00
1964 New York	60.00	40.00
1965 Minnesota	50.00	30.00
1966 St. Louis	60.00	40.00
1967 Anaheim	50.00	30.00
1968 Houston	50.00	30.00
1969 Washington	50.00	30.00
1970 Cincinnati	50.00	30.00
1971 Detroit	60.00	40.00
1972 Atlanta	50.00	30.00
1973 Kansas City	60.00	40.00
1974 Pittsburgh	35.00	20.00
1975 Milwaukee	35.00	20.00
1976 Philadelphia	25.00	15.00
1977 New York	25.00	15.00
1978 San Diego	30.00	18.00
1979 Seattle	25.00	15.00
1980 Los Angeles	25.00	15.00
1981 Cleveland	25.00	15.00
1982 Montreal	30.00	18.00
1983 Chicago	25.00	15.00
1984 San Francisco	20.00	12.00
1985 Minnesota	20.00	12.00
1986 Houston	20.00	12.00
1987 Oakland	20.00	12.00
1988 Cincinnati	20.00	12.00
1989 California	20.00	12.00
1990 Chicago	20.00	12.00
1991 Toronto	25.00	15.00
1992 San Diego	20.00	12.00
1993 Baltimore	25.00	15.00
1994 Pittsburgh	20.00	12.00
1995 Arlington	20.00	12.00
1996 Philadelphia	20.00	12.00

All-Star Game Press Pins

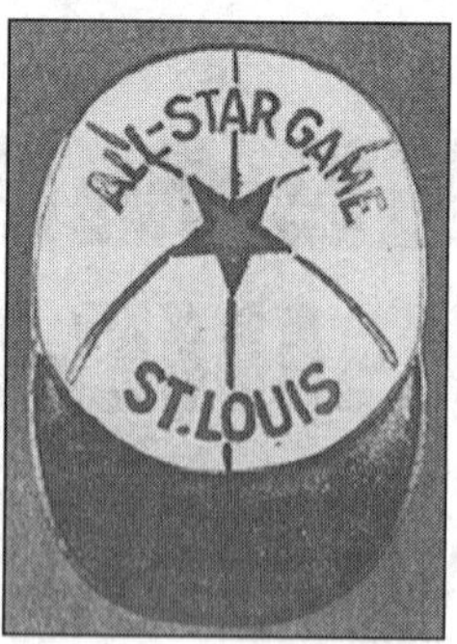

	Nr-Mt	Ex-Mt
1933 No Pin Issued		
1934 No Pin Issued		
1935 No Pin Issued		
1936 No Pin Issued		
1937 No Pin Issued		
1938 Cincinnati	4500.00	3000.00
1939 No Pin Issued		
1940 No Pin Issued		
1941 Detroit	1500.00	900.00
1942 No Pin Issued		
1943 Philadelphia	1500.00	900.00
1944 No Pin Issued		
1945 War Year - No Game		
1946 Boston	800.00	600.00
1947 Chicago	1800.00	1000.00
1948 St. Louis	2000.00	1200.00
1949 Brooklyn	425.00	325.00
1950 Chicago	300.00	200.00
1951 Detroit	350.00	250.00
1952 Philadelphia	400.00	300.00
1953 Cincinnati	400.00	300.00
1954 Cleveland	300.00	200.00
1955 Milwaukee	350.00	250.00
1956 Washington	300.00	200.00
1957 St. Louis	300.00	200.00
1958 Baltimore	600.00	450.00
1959 Los Angeles	250.00	175.00
1959 Pittsburgh	250.00	175.00
1960 Kansas City	300.00	200.00
1960 New York	350.00	250.00
1961 Boston	300.00	200.00
1961 San Francisco	500.00	350.00
1962 Chicago	300.00	200.00
1962 Washington	250.00	175.00
1963 Cleveland	125.00	80.00
1964 New York	200.00	150.00
1965 Minnesota	125.00	80.00
1966 St. Louis	100.00	70.00
1967 Anaheim	75.00	50.00
1968 Houston	125.00	80.00
1969 Washington	100.00	70.00
1970 Cincinnati	100.00	70.00
1971 Detroit	100.00	70.00
1972 Atalnta	125.00	80.00
1973 Kansas City	75.00	50.00
1974 Pittsburgh	250.00	175.00
1975 Milwaukee	75.00	50.00
1976 Philadelphia	100.00	70.00
1977 New York	75.00	50.00
1978 San Diego	75.00	50.00
1979 Seattle	50.00	30.00
1980 Los Angeles	50.00	30.00
1981 Cleveland	50.00	30.00
1982 Montreal	75.00	50.00
1983 Chicago	35.00	20.00
1984 San Francisco	30.00	18.00
1985 Minnesota	50.00	30.00
1986 Houston	150.00	100.00
1987 Oakland	100.00	70.00
1988 Cincinnati	125.00	80.00
1989 California	50.00	30.00
1990 Chicago	125.00	80.00
1991 Toronto	100.00	70.00
1992 San Diego	75.00	50.00
1993 Baltimore	100.00	70.00
1994 Pittsburgh	125.00	80.00
1995 Arlington	125.00	80.00
1996 Philadelphia	125.00	80.00

American League Championship Series Programs

	Nr-Mt	Ex-Mt
1969 Minnesota	125.00	80.00
1969 Baltimore	75.00	50.00
1970 Minnesota	125.00	80.00
1970 Baltimore	35.00	20.00
1971 Baltimore	35.00	20.00
1971 Oakland	30.00	18.00
1972 Detroit	100.00	70.00
1972 Oakland	35.00	20.00
1973 Oakland	25.00	15.00
1973 Baltimore	35.00	20.00
1974 Oakland	425.00	325.00
1974 Baltimore	35.00	20.00
1975 Oakland	40.00	25.00
1975 Boston	50.00	30.00
1976 New York	15.00	9.00
1976 Kansas City	20.00	12.00
1977 New York	15.00	9.00
1977 Kansas City	20.00	12.00
1978 Kansas City	20.00	12.00
1978 New York	15.00	9.00
1979 Baltimore	50.00	30.00
1979 California	15.00	9.00
1980 New York	15.00	9.00
1980 Kansas City	15.00	9.00
1981 New York	15.00	9.00
1981 Oakland	15.00	9.00
1982 Milwaukee	50.00	30.00
1982 California	15.00	9.00
1983 Baltimore	15.00	9.00
1983 Chicago	15.00	9.00
1984 Detroit	10.00	7.00
1984 Kansas City	15.00	9.00
1985 Toronto	25.00	15.00
1985 Kansas City	20.00	12.00
1986 California	20.00	12.00
1986 California	10.00	7.00
1987 Detroit	15.00	9.00
1987 Minnesota	10.00	7.00
1988 Boston	10.00	7.00
1988 Oakland	30.00	18.00
1989 Toronto	10.00	7.00
1989 Oakland	15.00	9.00
1990 Oakland	10.00	7.00
1990 Boston	10.00	7.00
1991 Minnesota	10.00	7.00
1991 Toronto	15.00	9.00
1992 Oakland	10.00	7.00
1992 Toronto	15.00	9.00
1993 Chicago	10.00	7.00
1993 Toronto	15.00	9.00
1994 No Series		
1994 No Series		
1995 Cleveland	10.00	7.00
1995 Seattle	10.00	7.00
1996 Baltimore	10.00	7.00
1996 New York	10.00	7.00

American League Championship Series Ticket Stubs

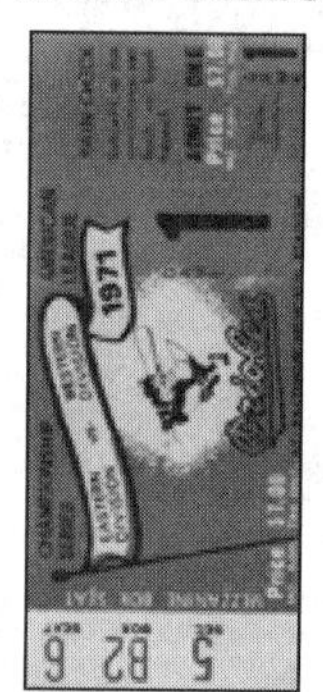

Ticket stubs from historic ALCS Championship games such as 1986's game #5 are valued higher. Complete unused tickets are valued 2 times that of a stub.

	Nr-Mt	Ex-Mt
1969 Baltimore	25.00	15.00
1969 Minnesota	25.00	15.00
1970 Minnesota	25.00	15.00
1970 Baltimore	25.00	15.00
1971 Oakland	20.00	12.00
1971 Baltimore	20.00	12.00
1972 Oakland	20.00	12.00
1972 Detroit	25.00	12.00
1973 Oakland	20.00	12.00
1973 Baltimore	20.00	12.00
1974 Baltimore	20.00	12.00
1974 Oakland	20.00	12.00
1975 Boston	25.00	15.00
1975 Oakland	20.00	12.00
1976 Kansas City	15.00	9.00
1976 New York	20.00	12.00
1977 New York	15.00	9.00
1977 Kansas City	15.00	9.00
1978 New York	15.00	9.00
1978 Kansas City	15.00	9.00
1979 California	15.00	9.00
1979 Baltimore	15.00	9.00
1980 Kansas City	15.00	9.00
1980 New York	15.00	9.00
1981 Oakland	15.00	9.00
1981 New York	18.00	10.00
1982 California	18.00	10.00
1982 Milwaukee	15.00	9.00
1983 Chicago	15.00	9.00
1983 Baltimore	15.00	9.00
1984 Kansas City	12.00	7.00
1984 Detroit	15.00	9.00

1985 Toronto	15.00	9.00
1985 Kansas City	12.00	7.00
1986 California	15.00	9.00
1986 Boston	15.00	9.00
1987 Minnesota	12.00	7.00
1987 Detroit	15.00	9.00
1988 Oakland	12.00	7.00
1988 Boston	15.00	9.00
1989 Oakland	12.00	7.00
1989 Toronto	15.00	9.00
1990 Boston	12.00	7.00
1990 Oakland	10.00	6.00
1991 Minnesota	10.00	6.00
1991 Toronto	12.00	7.00
1992 Toronto	12.00	7.00
1992 Oakland	10.00	6.00
1993 Chicago	10.00	6.00
1993 Toronto	10.00	6.00
1994 No Series		
1994 No Series		
1995 Cleveland	10.00	6.00
1995 Seattle	10.00	6.00
1996 Baltimore	10.00	6.00
1996 New York	10.00	6.00

National League Championship Series Programs

Complete tickets are valued 2 times that of a stub.

	Nr-Mt	Ex-Mt
1969 Atlanta	30.00	18.00
1969 New York	300.00	200.00
1970 Cincinnati	100.00	70.00
1970 Pittsburgh	250.00	175.00
1971 San Francisco	500.00	350.00
1971 Pittsburgh	250.00	175.00
1972 Pittsburgh	40.00	25.00
1972 Cincinnati	35.00	20.00
1973 Cincinnati	175.00	125.00
1973 New York	100.00	70.00
1974 Los Angeles	250.00	175.00
1974 Pittsburgh	175.00	125.00
1975 Cincinnati	15.00	9.00
1975 Pittsburgh	20.00	12.00
1976 Philadelphia	15.00	9.00
1976 Cincinnati	60.00	40.00
1977 Los Angeles	50.00	30.00
1977 Philadelphia	15.00	9.00
1978 Los Angeles	15.00	9.00
1978 Philadelphia	15.00	9.00
1979 Cincinnati	10.00	7.00
1979 Pittsburgh	15.00	9.00
1980 Houston	40.00	25.00
1980 Philadelphia	15.00	9.00
1981 Los Angeles	15.00	9.00
1981 Montreal	25.00	15.00
1982 Atlanta	10.00	7.00
1982 St. Louis	10.00	7.00
1983 Los Angeles	50.00	30.00
1983 Philadelphia	10.00	7.00
1984 San Diego	25.00	15.00
1984 Chicago	15.00	9.00
1985 St. Louis	25.00	15.00
1985 Los Angeles	50.00	30.00
1986 Houston	15.00	9.00
1986 New York	25.00	15.00
1987 St. Louis	20.00	12.00
1987 San Francisco	10.00	7.00
1988 Los Angeles	10.00	7.00
1988 New York	10.00	7.00
1989 Chicago	10.00	7.00
1989 San Francisco	15.00	9.00
1990 Pittsburgh	10.00	7.00
1990 Cincinnati	10.00	7.00
1991 Atlanta	20.00	12.00
1991 Pittsburgh	10.00	7.00
1992 Pittsburgh	10.00	7.00
1992 Atlanta	20.00	12.00
1993 Atlanta	15.00	9.00
1993 Philadelphia	10.00	7.00
1994 No Series		
1994 No Series		
1995 Atlanta	10.00	6.00
1995 Cincinnati	10.00	6.00
1996 Atlanta	10.00	6.00
1996 St. Louis	10.00	6.00

National League Championship Series Ticket Stubs

Ticket stubs from historic NLCS Championship games such as 1992's game #7 are valued higher. Complete unused tickets are valued 2 times that of a stub.

	Nr-Mt	Ex-Mt
1969 New York	50.00	35.00
1969 Atlanta	25.00	15.00
1970 Cincinnati	25.00	15.00
1970 Pittsburgh	25.00	15.00
1971 Pittsburgh	20.00	12.00
1971 San Francisco	25.00	15.00
1972 Cincinnati	20.00	12.00
1972 Pittsburgh	20.00	12.00
1973 Cincinnati	20.00	12.00
1973 New York	25.00	15.00
1974 Pittsburgh	20.00	12.00
1974 Los Angeles	20.00	12.00
1975 Cincinnati	25.00	15.00
1975 Pittsburgh	20.00	12.00
1976 Cincinnati	15.00	9.00
1976 Philadelphia	15.00	9.00
1977 Philadelphia	15.00	9.00
1977 Los Angeles	15.00	9.00
1978 Philadelphia	15.00	9.00
1978 Los Angeles	15.00	9.00
1979 Pittsburgh	15.00	9.00
1979 Cincinnati	15.00	9.00
1980 Houston	15.00	9.00
1980 Philadelphia	15.00	9.00
1981 Montreal	15.00	9.00
1981 Los Angeles	15.00	9.00
1982 Atlanta	15.00	9.00
1982 St. Louis	15.00	9.00
1983 Los Angeles	15.00	9.00
1983 Philadelphia	15.00	9.00
1984 San Diego	12.00	7.00
1984 Chicago	18.00	9.00
1985 Los Angeles	12.00	7.00
1985 St. Louis	12.00	7.00
1986 New York	15.00	9.00
1986 Houston	12.00	7.00
1987 San Francisco	12.00	7.00
1987 St. Louis	12.00	7.00
1988 New York	12.00	7.00
1988 Los Angeles	10.00	6.00
1989 San Francisco	10.00	6.00
1989 Chicago	15.00	9.00
1990 Cincinnati	10.00	6.00
1990 Pittsburgh	10.00	6.00
1991 Atlanta	10.00	6.00
1991 Pittsburgh	10.00	6.00
1992 Atlanta	10.00	6.00
1992 Pittsburgh	10.00	6.00
1993 Atlanta	10.00	6.00
1993 Philadelphia	10.00	6.00
1994 No Series		
1994 No Series		
1995 Cincinnati	10.00	6.00
1995 Atlanta	10.00	6.00
1996 Atlanta	10.00	6.00
1996 St. Louis	10.00	6.00

Famous Slugger Yearbook

The Famous Slugger Yearbook was created as an advertising tool for the company to sell its products. Each booklet contains information highlighted with player photos.

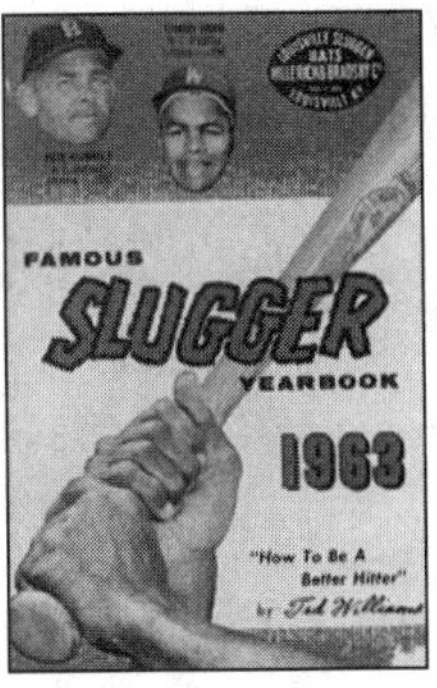

	Nr-Mt	Ex-Mt
1921 Art Illustration	250.00	175.00
1927 Art Illustration	100.00	70.00
1928 Art Illustration	100.00	70.00
1929 Art Illustration	100.00	70.00
1930 Art Illustration	75.00	50.00
1931 Art Illustration	75.00	50.00
1932 Art Illustration	75.00	50.00
1933 Jimmy Foxx/Chuck Klein	60.00	40.00
1934 Lou. Gehrig/Paul Waner	75.00	50.00
1935 Arky Vaughn/Buddy Myer	60.00	40.00
1936 Lou Gehrig/Mel Ott	75.00	50.00
1937 C. Gehringer/J. Medwick	60.00	40.00
1938 Art Illustration	60.00	40.00
1939 J. Foxx/E. Lombardi	50.00	30.00
1940 Joe DiMaggio	50.00	30.00
1941 Joe DiMaggio	50.00	30.00
1942 J. DiMaggio/T. Williams	50.00	30.00
1943 T. Williams/E. Lombardi	50.00	30.00
1944 Stan Musial	50.00	30.00
1945 D. Walker/L. Boudreau	40.00	25.00
1946 Art Illustration	40.00	25.00
1947 S. Musial/M. Vernon	40.00	25.00
1948 Lefty O'Doul	30.00	18.00
1949 T. Williams/S. Musial	35.00	20.00
1950 J. Robinson/T. Williams	35.00	20.00
1951 Ralph Kiner	30.00	18.00
1952 Art Illustration	25.00	15.00
1953 Art Illustration	25.00	15.00
1954 Art Illustration	20.00	12.00
1955 Ted Williams	25.00	15.00
1956 A. Kaline/R. Ashburn	25.00	15.00
1957 Mantle/Aaron/Kluszewski	30.00	18.00
1958 Ted Williams	25.00	15.00
1959 Stan Musial	25.00	15.00
1960 Rocky Colavito	20.00	12.00
1961 Ernie Banks	20.00	12.00
1962 Roger Maris	25.00	15.00
1963 T.Davis/P. Runnels	18.00	10.00
1964 T.Davis/Yazstremski	20.00	12.00
1965 R.Clemente/T. Oliva	25.00	15.00
1966 R. Clemente/T. Oliva	25.00	15.00
1967 F.Robinson/M.Alou	15.00	9.00
1968 R Clemente/Yazstremski	20.00	12.00
1969 P. Rose/Yazstremski	15.00	9.00
1970 P. Rose/R. Carew	15.00	9.00
1971 J. Bench/A.Johnson	15.00	9.00
1972 Willie Stargell	10.00	7.00
1973 Dick Allen	10.00	7.00
1974 Hank Aaron	12.00	8.00
1975 Johnny Bench	10.00	7.00
1976 National League Salute	10.00	7.00
1977 Yankee Stadium	10.00	7.00
1978 Art Illustration	10.00	7.00

Reach Baseball Guides

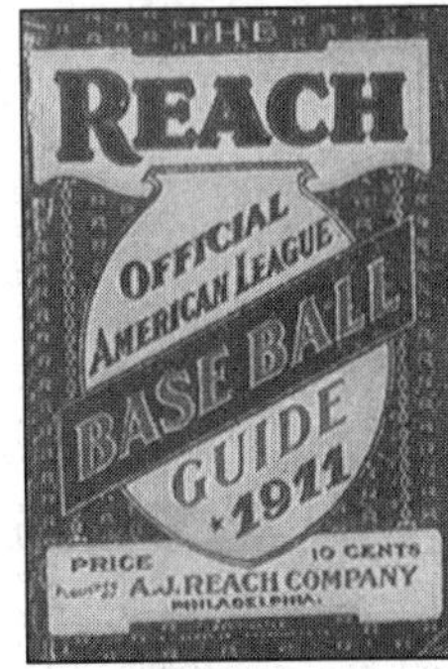

The Reach guide was the official guide of the American League. Spalding's parent, American Sports Publishing Company, retained the rights to the Reach guide after its 1934 edition, producing both from 1935 through 1939. Spalding combined both baseball guides in 1940 and 1941. The Sporting News Baseball guide became the official baseball guide beginning in 1942. The majority of Reach covers feature a non-player design except the years 1935 through 1938 when it was produced by Spalding. Reach guides from 1883 through 1929 are graded in Excellent and Vg-Ex condition respectively.

	Ex-Mt	Ex
1883 Non-Player	1500.00	900.00
1884 Non-Player	1200.00	800.00
1885 Non-Player	750.00	550.00
1886 Non-Player	500.00	350.00
1887 Non-Player	500.00	350.00
1888 Non-Player	500.00	350.00
1889 Non-Player	500.00	350.00
1890 Non-Player	500.00	350.00
1891 Non-Player	425.00	325.00
1892 Non-Player	425.00	325.00
1893 Non-Player	400.00	300.00
1894 Non-Player	400.00	300.00
1895 Non-Player	400.00	300.00
1896 Non-Player	400.00	300.00
1897 Non-Player	400.00	300.00
1898 Non-Player	400.00	300.00
1899 Non-Player	400.00	300.00
1900 Non-Player	350.00	250.00
1901 Non-Player	350.00	225.00
1902 Non-Player	350.00	250.00
1903 Non-Player	350.00	250.00
1904 Non-Player	425.00	325.00
1905 Non-Player	300.00	200.00
1906 Non-Player	325.00	225.00
1907 Non-Player	325.00	225.00
1908 Non-Player	300.00	200.00
1909 Non-Player	300.00	200.00
1910 Non-Player	300.00	200.00
1911 Non-Player	300.00	200.00
1912 Non-Player	350.00	250.00
1913 Non-Player	350.00	250.00
1914 Non-Player	350.00	250.00
1915 Non-Player	350.00	250.00
1916 Non-Player	300.00	200.00
1917 Non-Player	300.00	200.00
1918 Non-Player	300.00	200.00
1919 Non-Player	300.00	200.00
1920 Non-Player	300.00	200.00
1921 Non-Player	250.00	175.00
1922 Non-Player	250.00	175.00
1923 Non-Player	350.00	250.00
1924 Non-Player	350.00	250.00
1925 Non-Player	350.00	250.00
1926 Non-Player	300.00	200.00
1927 Non-Player	300.00	200.00
1928 Non-Player	250.00	175.00
1929 Non-Player	250.00	175.00
1930 Non-Player	200.00	150.00
1931 Non-Player	200.00	150.00
1932 Non-Player	200.00	150.00
1933 Non-Player	250.00	175.00
1934 Non-Player	200.00	150.00
1935 Lou Gehrig	250.00	175.00
1936 Mickey Cochrane	150.00	100.00
1937 Lou Gehrig	200.00	150.00
1938 Hank Greenberg	150.00	100.00
1939 Centenial Logo	150.00	100.00
1940 Spalding/Reach Combo	100.00	70.00
1941 Spalding/Reach Combo	100.00	70.00

Spalding Baseball Guides

Spalding claimed to be the official guide of Major League Baseball. Except for a few issues in the 1930's, most of the Spalding guides cover subjects featured a portraiture of an 18th century ballplayer, or in some cases, a generic baseball scene. Spalding guides from 1876 through 1929 are graded Excellent and Vg-Ex respectively.

	Ex-Mt	Ex
1876 Generic Ballplayer	2500.00	1500.00
1877 Generic Ballplayer	2000.00	1200.00
1878 Generic Ballplayer	1500.00	900.00
1879 Generic Ballplayer	1500.00	900.00
1880 Generic Ballplayer	1000.00	700.00
1881 Generic Ballplayer	1000.00	700.00
1882 Generic Ballplayer	750.00	550.00
1883 Generic Ballplayer	750.00	550.00
1884 Generic Ballplayer	750.00	550.00
1885 Generic Ballplayer	600.00	450.00
1886 Generic Ballplayer	600.00	450.00
1887 Generic Ballplayer	600.00	450.00
1888 Generic Ballplayer	600.00	450.00
1889 Generic Ballplayer	600.00	450.00
1890 Generic Ballplayer	600.00	450.00
1891 Generic Ballplayer	500.00	350.00
1892 Generic Ballplayer	500.00	350.00
1893 Generic Ballplayer	500.00	350.00
1894 Generic Ballplayer	500.00	350.00
1895 Generic Ballplayer	500.00	350.00
1896 Generic Ballplayer	400.00	300.00
1897 Generic Ballplayer	400.00	300.00
1898 Generic Ballplayer	400.00	300.00
1899 Generic Ballplayer	400.00	300.00
1900 Generic Ballplayer	350.00	250.00
1901 Generic Ballplayer	350.00	250.00
1902 Generic Ballplayer	350.00	250.00
1902 Generic Ballplayer	350.00	250.00
1903 Generic Ballplayer	350.00	250.00
1904 Generic Ballplayer	400.00	300.00
1905 Generic Ballplayer	300.00	200.00
1906 Generic Ballplayer	300.00	200.00
1907 Generic Ballplayer	300.00	200.00
1908 Generic Ballplayer	300.00	200.00
1909 Generic Ballplayer	250.00	175.00
1910 Generic Ballplayer	250.00	175.00
1911 Generic Ballplayer	250.00	175.00
1912 Generic Ballplayer	250.00	175.00
1913 Generic Ballplayer	200.00	150.00
1914 Generic Ballplayer	200.00	150.00
1915 Generic Ballplayer	200.00	150.00
1916 Generic Ballplayer	200.00	150.00
1917 Generic Ballplayer	200.00	150.00
1918 Generic Ballplayer	200.00	150.00
1919 Generic Ballplayer	250.00	175.00
1920 Generic Ballplayer	300.00	200.00
1921 Generic Ballplayer	300.00	200.00
1922 Generic Ballplayer	250.00	175.00
1923 Generic Ballplayer	150.00	100.00
1924 Generic Ballplayer	150.00	100.00
1925 Generic Ballplayer	150.00	100.00
1926 Generic Ballplayer	150.00	100.00
1927 Generic Ballplayer	150.00	100.00
1928 Generic Player	150.00	100.00
1929 Generic Ballplayer	150.00	100.00
1930 Generic Ballplayer	150.00	100.00
1931 Generic Ballplayer	150.00	100.00
1932 Generic Ballplayer	150.00	100.00
1933 Generic Ballplayer	150.00	100.00
1934 Generic Ballplayer	150.00	100.00
1935 Dizzy Dean	175.00	125.00
1936 Generic Ballplayer	150.00	100.00
1937 Carl Hubbell	175.00	125.00
1938 Joe Medwick	150.00	100.00
1939 Centenial Logo	125.00	80.00
1940 Spalding/Reach Combo	100.00	70.00
1941 Spalding/Reach Combo	100.00	70.00

The Sporting News Baseball Guide

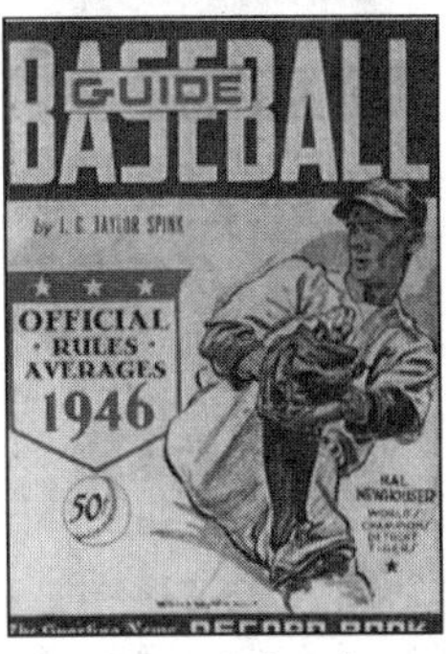

This publication began as The Sporting News Record Book until 1948 when it changed its name to The Sporting News Official Baseball Guide. A radio edition was published during the 1940's war years. The thinner radio editions are valued slightly less than the regular guides. Hardcover versions were produced for distribution to the baseball media. Hardcover versions are valued slightly higher.

	Nr-Mt	Ex-Mt
1942 Art Illustration	250.00	175.00
1943 Serviceman	125.00	80.00
1944 B. Newsom/ B. Dahlgren	100.00	70.00
1945 M. Marion/H. Newhouser	100.00	70.00
1946 Hal Newhouser	100.00	70.00
1947 Harry Brecheen	100.00	70.00
1948 Ewell Blackwell	100.00	70.00
1949 Lou Boudreau	75.00	50.00
1950 P. Ruzzuto/P. Reese	100.00	70.00
1951 Red Schoendist	75.00	50.00
1952 Stan Musial	100.00	70.00
1953 Robin Roberts	75.00	50.00
1954 Casey Stengel	60.00	40.00
1955 Game Play	75.00	50.00
1956 J. Coleman/B. Martin	75.00	50.00
1957 Mickey Mantle/Yogi Berra	100.00	70.00
1958 Ted Williams	100.00	70.00
1959 Spalding Advertisment	60.00	40.00
1960 Dodger Bum Mascot	60.00	40.00
1961 Relief Pitcher Award	50.00	30.00
1962 Babe Ruth/ Roger Maris	50.00	30.00
1963 Willard Mullin Artwork	50.00	30.00
1964 Stan Musial	50.00	30.00
1965 B. Robinson/Boyer/Chance	40.00	25.00
1966 Willie Mays/SandyKoufax	40.00	25.00
1967 Clemente/Koufax/F. Robinson	35.00	20.00

1968 Cepeda/Lonborg/Yaz	35.00	20.00
1969 Rose/McLain/Gibson	30.00	18.00
1970 McCovey/Killebrew	30.00	18.00
1971 Bench/Gibson/Killebrew	25.00	15.00
1972 Jenkins/Blue/Torre	25.00	15.00
1973 Carlton/Bench/Perry	20.00	12.00
1974 Palmer/Bonds/R. Jackson	20.00	12.00
1975 Lou Brock/Jim Hunter	20.00	12.00
1976 Morgan/Palmer/Seaver	15.00	9.00
1977 T. Munson/J. Palmer	15.00	9.00
1978 Carew/Carlton/Ryan	15.00	9.00
1979 Rice/Guidry/Parker	15.00	9.00
1980 K. Hernandez/ D. Baylor	10.00	7.00
1981 Steve Carlton	12.00	8.00
1982 Tom Seaver	12.00	8.00
1983 Robin Yount	12.00	8.00
1984 Ryne Sandberg	12.00	8.00
1985 Cal Ripken Jr.	15.00	9.00
1986 Willie McGee	10.00	7.00
1987 Roger Clemens	12.00	8.00
1988 Andre Dawson	10.00	7.00
1989 Jose Canseco	10.00	7.00
1990 Bret Saberhagen	10.00	7.00
1991 Bob Welch	10.00	7.00
1992 Will Clark	10.00	7.00
1993 Kirby Puckett	12.00	8.00
1994 Jack McDowell	10.00	7.00
1995 Ken Griffey Jr.	15.00	9.00
1996 Hideo Nomo	10.00	7.00
John Smoltz	10.00	7.00

The Sporting News Baseball Record Book

In 1941 the pocket-sized Sporting News Record Book was replaced by The Sporting News Dope Book, later renamed One For The Book.

	Nr-Mt	Ex-Mt
1909 Null	125.00	75.00
1910 Ty Cobb/H. Wagner	100.00	60.00
1911 Null	75.00	50.00
1912 Eddie Collins	75.00	50.00
1913 Null	75.00	50.00
1914 Null	75.00	50.00
1915 Null	75.00	50.00
1916 Joseph Lannin	60.00	40.00
1917 Null	50.00	35.00
1918 Null	50.00	35.00
1919 Lt. Col. T.L. Huston	40.00	25.00
1920 Null	50.00	35.00
1921 Babe Ruth/Geo. Sisler	60.00	40.00
1922 Rogers Hornsby	40.00	25.00
1923 George Sisler	40.00	25.00
1924 Everett Scott	35.00	20.00
1925 Walter Johnson	40.00	25.00
1926 Max Carey	30.00	18.00
1927 Bob O'Farrell	30.00	18.00
1928 Lou Gehrig	50.00	35.00
1929 L. Gehrig/B. Ruth	60.00	40.00
1930 Mickey Cochrane	40.00	25.00
1931 Hack Wilson	40.00	25.00
1932 Lefty Grove	40.00	25.00
1933 Jimmy Foxx	40.00	25.00
1934 Carl Hubbell	35.00	20.00
1935 Dizzy Dean	35.00	20.00
1936 Hank Greenberg	30.00	18.00
1937 Joe McCarthy	25.00	15.00
1938 Joe Medwick	25.00	15.00
1939 Abner Doubleday	25.00	15.00
1940 Bucky Walters	25.00	15.00

The Sporting News Baseball Register

The Sporting News Baseball Register became popular with autograph enthusiasts because it contained facsimile autographs for most current-day ballplayers. The Register ceased featuring sample signatures in the late 1960's. Hardcover

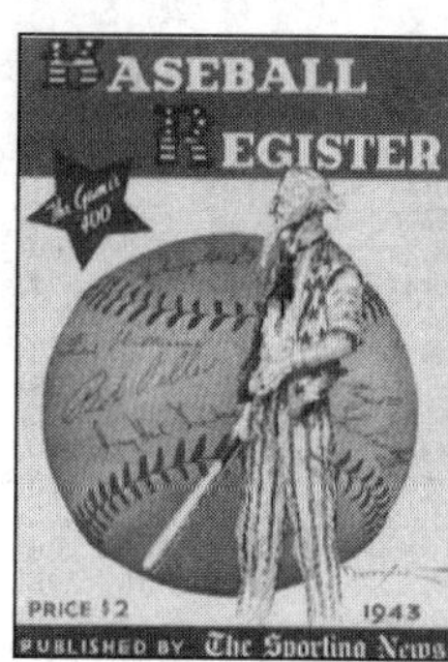

versions were produced for distribution to the baseball media and are valued slightly higher.

	Nr-Mt	Ex-Mt
1940 Ty Cobb	200.00	150.00
1941 Paul Derringer	100.00	70.00
1942 Joe DiMaggio	150.00	100.00
1943 Uncle Sam	100.00	70.00
1944 Rube Waddell	125.00	80.00
1945 Billy Southworth	100.00	70.00
1946 Art Illustration	100.00	70.00
1947 Walter Johnson	100.00	70.00
1948 Art Illustration	75.00	50.00
1949 Art Illustration	75.00	50.00
1950 Joe DiMaggio	100.00	70.00
1951 Art Illustration	75.00	50.00
1952 Art Illustration	60.00	40.00
1953 Art Illustration	60.00	40.00
1955 Art Illustration	60.00	40.00
1956 Art Illustration	60.00	40.00
1957 Art Illustration	60.00	40.00
1958 Art Illustration	50.00	30.00
1959 Art Illustration	50.00	30.00
1960 Art Illustration	50.00	30.00
1961 Art Illustration	50.00	30.00
1962 Art Illustration	50.00	30.00
1963 Art Illustration	40.00	25.00
1964 Yankee Stadium	40.00	25.00
1965 Kenny Boyer	30.00	18.00
1966 Sandy Koufax	40.00	25.00
1967 B. Robinson/F. Robinson	30.00	18.00
1968 Jim Lonborg	25.00	15.00
1969 Willie Horton	25.00	15.00
1970 Tom Seaver	30.00	18.00
1971 Willie Mays	30.00	18.00
1972 Joe Torre	25.00	15.00
1973 Wilbur Wood	20.00	12.00
1974 Pete Rose	25.00	15.00
1975 Jim Hunter	20.00	12.00
1976 Jim Palmer	20.00	12.00
1977 Joe Morgan	20.00	12.00
1978 Rod Carew	20.00	12.00
1979 Ron Guidry	15.00	9.00
1980 Carl Yastrzemski	15.00	9.00
1981 George Brett	20.00	12.00
1982 Tom Seaver	15.00	9.00
1982 Fernando Valenzuela	15.00	9.00
1983 Robin Yount	15.00	9.00
1984 Cal Ripken Jr.	20.00	12.00
1984 John Denny	15.00	9.00
1985 Willie Hernandez	12.00	8.00
1985 Eyne Sandberg	12.00	8.00
1986 Don Mattingly	15.00	9.00
1986 Willie McGee	10.00	7.00
1987 Roger Clemens	10.00	7.00
1987 Mike Schmidt	12.00	8.00
1988 Andre Dawson	10.00	7.00
1988 George Bell	10.00	7.00
1989 Jose Canseco	10.00	7.00
1989 Frank Viola	10.00	7.00
1990 Kevin Mitchell	10.00	7.00
1991 Barry Bonds	10.00	7.00
1992 Frank Thomas	15.00	9.00
1993 Gary Sheffield	10.00	7.00
1994 Lenny Dykstra	10.00	7.00
1995 Bret Saberhagen	10.00	7.00
1996 Greg Maddux	10.00	7.00
Ken Griffey Jr.	15.00	9.00

Street & Smith Baseball Yearbook

Early Street and Smith Baseball Yearbooks are popular with uniform collectors and researchers because they were one of the few sources that provided player's uniform numbers. Street & Smith began publishing regional covers in 1963.

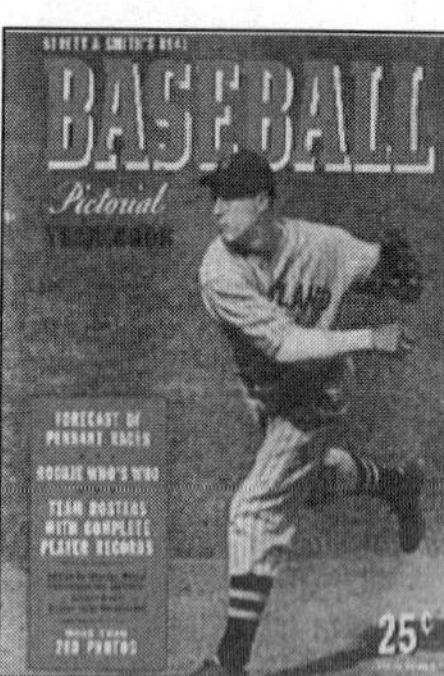

	Nr-Mt	Ex-Mt
1941 Bob Feller	300.00	200.00
1942 Howard Pollett	200.00	150.00
1943 N.Y. Giants Game Play	200.00	150.00
1944 Joe McCarthy	150.00	100.00
1945 N.Y. Giants Spring Training	175.00	125.00
1946 Dick Fowler	150.00	100.00
1947 Leo Durocher	175.00	125.00
1948 Joe DiMaggio	200.00	150.00
1949 Lou Boudreau	125.00	80.00
1950 Ted Williams/Joe DiMaggio	200.00	150.00
1951 Joe DiMaggio/Ralph Kiner	175.00	125.00
1952 Stan Musial	150.00	100.00
1953 Mickey Mantle	200.00	150.00
1954 Eddie Mathews	125.00	80.00
1955 Yogi Berra	150.00	100.00
1956 Duke Snider/Mickey Mantle	175.00	125.00
1957 Mantle/Larsen/Berra	150.00	100.00
1958 Bob Buhl/Lew Burdette	125.00	80.00
1959 Burdette/Mantle/Spahn	125.00	80.00
1960 Nellie Fox/Luis Aparicio	100.00	70.00
1961 Dick Groat	75.00	50.00
1962 Roger Maris	100.00	70.00
1963 Don Drysdale	75.00	50.00
1963 Stan Musial	75.00	50.00
1963 Tom Tresh	60.00	40.00
1964 Mickey Mantle	75.00	50.00
1964 Sandy Koufax	60.00	40.00
1964 Warren Spahn	60.00	40.00
1965 Brooks Robinson	60.00	40.00
1965 Dean Chance	50.00	30.00
1965 Ken Boyer	50.00	30.00
1966 Sandy Koufax	40.00	25.00
1966 Rocky Colavito	50.00	30.00
1966 Ron Swoboda	40.00	25.00
1967 Andy Etchebarren	40.00	25.00
1967 Harmon Killebrew	40.00	25.00
1967 Juan Marichal	40.00	25.00
1968 Orlando Cepeda	40.00	25.00
1968 Jim McGlothin	35.00	20.00
1968 Jim Lonborg	40.00	25.00
1969 Denny McClain/Bob Gibson	35.00	20.00
1970 Tom Seaver	40.00	25.00
1970 Bill Singer	35.00	20.00
1970 Harmon Killebrew	35.00	20.00
1971 Johnny Bench	40.00	25.00
1971 Gaylord Perry	30.00	18.00
1971 Boog Powell	30.00	18.00
1972 Joe Torre	30.00	18.00
1972 Roberto Clemente	50.00	30.00
1972 Vida Blue	30.00	18.00
1973 Steve Carlton	35.00	20.00
1973 Johnny Bench	30.00	18.00
1973 Reggie Jackson	35.00	20.00
1974 Hank Aaron	35.00	20.00
1974 Pete Rose	35.00	20.00
1974 Nolan Ryan	50.00	30.00
1975 Catfish Hunter	30.00	18.00
1975 Mike Marshall	25.00	15.00
1975 Lou Brock	25.00	15.00
1976 Davey Lopes	20.00	12.00
1976 Joe Morgan	25.00	15.00
1976 Fred Lynn	25.00	15.00
1977 Mark Fidrych	25.00	15.00
1977 Randy Jones	20.00	12.00
1977 Thurman Munson	25.00	15.00
1978 Rod Carew	20.00	12.00
1978 Steve Garvey	20.00	12.00
1978 Reggie Jackson	20.00	12.00
1979 Ron Guidry	20.00	12.00
1979 J.R. Richard	20.00	12.00
1979 Burt Hooten	20.00	12.00
1980 Mike Flanagan	20.00	12.00
1980 Brian Downing	20.00	12.00
1980 Joe Niekro	12.00	8.00
1981 Mike Schmidt	20.00	12.00
1981 Rickey Henderson	20.00	12.00
1981 George Brett	20.00	12.00
1982 Rollie Fingers/Tom Seaver	20.00	12.00
1982 Pete Rose/Goose Gossage	20.00	12.00
1982 Nolan Ryan	35.00	20.00
1983 Steve Carlton	20.00	12.00
1983 Robin Yount	20.00	12.00
1983 Phil Niekro	15.00	9.00
1983 Doug DeCinces	15.00	9.00
1984 Pedro Guerrero	15.00	9.00
1984 Dale Murphy	15.00	9.00
1984 Scott McGregor/Rick Dempsey	15.00	9.00
1984 Carlton Fisk	15.00	9.00
1985 Tigers Celebrate	15.00	9.00
1985 Steve Garvey	15.00	9.00
1985 Dwight Gooden	20.00	12.00
1986 Jesse Barfield/Ernie Whitt	15.00	9.00
1986 Dwight Gooden/Don Mattingly	20.00	12.00
1986 Royals Celebrate	15.00	9.00
1987 Joe Carter	15.00	9.00
1987 Wally Joyner	15.00	9.00
1987 Mike Scott	15.00	9.00
1987 Gary Carter/Jesse Orosco	15.00	9.00
1987 Roger Clemens	20.00	12.00
1988 Benito Santiago/Mark McGwire	20.00	12.00
1988 Dale Murphy	15.00	9.00
1988 Jeff Reardon	15.00	9.00
1988 Ozzie Smith	15.00	9.00
1988 Don Mattingly	20.00	12.00
1989 Andres Galarraga/Fred McGriff	15.00	9.00
1989 Orel Hershiser	15.00	9.00
1989 Mark Grace/Chris Sabo	15.00	9.00
1989 Kevin McReynolds	15.00	9.00
1990 50th Anniversary Issue	20.00	12.00
1991 Ryne Sandberg	15.00	9.00
1991 Lou Piniella	15.00	9.00
1992 Roger Clemens	15.00	9.00
1992 Kirby Puckett	15.00	9.00
1992 Bobby Bonilla	10.00	7.00
1993 To Present	10.00	7.00

Who's Who in Major League Baseball

The 1933 oversized hardback version (various colors) was edited by Speed Johnson. The publication was edited by John Carmichael from 1938 through 1952. Hardcover versions of the smaller format also were available and are valued slightly higher.

	Nr-Mt	Ex-Mt
1933 Speed Johnson Edition	400.00	300.00
1935 Mickey Cochrane/Charlie Grimm	150.00	100.00
1936 Non-Player	125.00	80.00
1937 Carl Hubbell/Luke Appling	100.00	70.00
1938 Joe DiMaggio	125.00	80.00
1939 Pitcher	100.00	70.00
1940 Joe DiMaggio	125.00	80.00
1941 Non-Player	75.00	50.00
1942 Non-Player	75.00	50.00
1943 Ted Williams	100.00	70.00
1944 Three players	75.00	50.00
1945 Hal Newhouser	75.00	50.00
1946 Various Players	75.00	50.00
1947 Stan Musial	75.00	50.00
1948 Ted Williams/Joe DiMaggio	100.00	70.00
1949 Non-Player	60.00	40.00
1950 Ralph Kiner	60.00	40.00
1951 Non-Player	60.00	40.00
1952 Joe DiMaggio/Ford Frick	75.00	50.00

Who's Who in Baseball

Who's Who in Baseball contains lifetime records (including minor league) and personal photos for most current-day major leaguers. Editions from 1912 through 1929 are graded in Ex and Vg-Ex condition respectively. Hardcover versions were produced for distribution to the baseball media. Hardcover versions are valued slightly higher.

	Nr-Mt	Ex-Mt
1912 Ty Cobb	2000.00	1200.00
1916 Athletics Outfielder	800.00	600.00
1916 Ty Cobb	1200.00	800.00
1917 Tris Speaker	1200.00	800.00
1918 George Sisler	1000.00	700.00
1919 Grover C. Alexander	700.00	500.00
1920 Babe Ruth	750.00	550.00
1921 Babe Ruth	800.00	600.00
1922 Rogers Hornsby	425.00	325.00
1923 George Sisler	300.00	200.00
1924 Walter Johnson	300.00	200.00
1925 Dizzy Vance	250.00	175.00
1926 Max Carey	250.00	175.00
1927 Frankie Frisch	250.00	175.00
1928 Hack Wilson	200.00	150.00
1929 Bob O'Farrell	150.00	100.00
1930 Burleigh Grimes	150.00	100.00
1931 Lefty Grove	150.00	100.00
1932 Al Simmons	125.00	80.00
1933 Chuck Klein	125.00	80.00
1934 Bill Terry	100.00	70.00
1935 Dizzy Dean	100.00	70.00
1936 Hank Greenberg	100.00	70.00
1937 Lou Gehrig	150.00	100.00
1938 Joe Medwick	75.00	50.00
1939 Jimmie Foxx	100.00	70.00
1940 Bucky Walters	75.00	50.00
1941 Bob Feller	75.00	50.00
1942 Joe DiMaggio	100.00	70.00
1943 Ted Williams	75.00	50.00
1944 Stan Musial	75.00	50.00
1945 Hal Newhouser/Dizzy Trout	50.00	30.00
1946 Hal Newhouser	50.00	30.00
1947 Eddie Dyer	40.00	25.00
1948 Johnny Mize/Ralph Kiner	50.00	30.00
1949 Lou Boudreau	40.00	25.00
1950 Mel Parnell	35.00	20.00
1951 Jim Konstanty	35.00	20.00
1952 Stan Musial	40.00	25.00
1953 Hank Sauer/Bobby Shantz	30.00	18.00
1954 Al Rosen	25.00	15.00
1955 Alvin Dark	25.00	15.00
1956 Duke Snider	35.00	20.00
1957 Mickey Mantle	75.00	50.00
1958 Warren Spahn	40.00	25.00
1959 Bob Turley	30.00	18.00
1960 Don Drysdale	30.00	18.00
1961 Roger Maris	35.00	20.00
1962 Whitey Ford	30.00	18.00
1963 Don Drysdale	25.00	15.00
1964 Sandy Koufax	30.00	18.00
1965 Ken Boyer	25.00	15.00
1966 Willie Mays/Sandy Koufax	25.00	15.00
1967 Roberto Clemente/Sandy Koufax	35.00	20.00
1968 Carl Yastrzemski	25.00	15.00
1969 Denny McLain	20.00	12.00
1970 Tom Seaver Blue Cover	20.00	12.00
1970 Tom Seaver	20.00	12.00
1971 Johnny Bench	20.00	12.00
1971 Johnny Bench Blue Cover	20.00	12.00
1972 Joe Torre Blue Cover	15.00	9.00
1972 Joe Torre	15.00	9.00
1973 Steve Carlton Blue Cover	15.00	9.00
1973 Steve Carlton	15.00	9.00
1974 Ryan/R. Jackson/Rose	25.00	15.00
1975 Lou Brock	15.00	9.00
1976 Fred Lynn/Joe Morgan	15.00	9.00
1977 Thurman Munson/Joe Morgan	15.00	9.00
1978 George Foster/Rod Carew	15.00	9.00
1979 Ron Guidry	15.00	9.00
1980 Stargell/D. Baylor/K. Hernandez	10.00	7.00
1981 George Brett	15.00	9.00
1982 Fernando Valenzuela/Mike Schmidt	10.00	7.00
1983 Robin Yount	10.00	7.00
1984 Cal Ripken	15.00	9.00
1985 Ryne Sandberg	10.00	7.00
1986 Gooden/Mattingly/W. McGee	10.00	7.00
1987 Roger Clemens/Mike Schmidt	10.00	7.00
1989 Joe Canseco/Kirk Gibson	10.00	7.00
1990 Robin Yount/Kevin Mitchell	10.00	7.00
1991 Ryan/Sandberg/Fielder	10.00	7.00
1992 To Present	8.00	6.00

Anaheim Angels Yearbooks

The Angels did not issue Yearbooks between 1968 and 1982. Also, there was no Yearbook issued for the 1986 through 1991 seasons. The team was named the Los Angeles Angels from 1961 through 1965, and the California Angels between 1966 and 1995.

	Nr-Mt	Ex-Mt
1 1961 (First Year)	125.00	80.00
1A 1962	75.00	50.00
2 1963	40.00	25.00
3 1964	25.00	15.00
4 1965	25.00	15.00
5 1966	40.00	25.00
6 1967	15.00	9.00
7 1983	10.00	6.00
8 1984	10.00	6.00
9 1985	7.00	4.00
10 1992-Present	10.00	6.00

Atlanta Braves Yearbooks

The Atlanta Braves did not issue a Yearbook for the 1989, 1991 or 1993 seasons.

	Nr-Mt	Ex-Mt
1 1966 (First Year)	25.00	15.00
2 1967	15.00	9.00
3 1968	10.00	6.00
4 1969	10.00	6.00
5 1970	15.00	9.00
6 1971	10.00	6.00
7 1972	10.00	6.00
8 1973	15.00	9.00
9 1974	10.00	6.00
10 1975	12.00	7.00
11 1976	12.00	7.00
12 1977	10.00	6.00
13 1978	10.00	6.00
14 1979	12.00	7.00
15 1980	12.00	7.00
16 1981	12.00	7.00
17 1982	10.00	6.00
18 1983	10.00	6.00
19 1984	10.00	6.00
20 1985	10.00	6.00

21 1986	10.00	6.00
22 1987	10.00	6.00
23 1988	7.00	4.00
24 1990	7.00	4.00
25 1992-Present	10.00	6.00

Baltimore Orioles Yearbooks

The Orioles did not issue a Yearbook between 1976 and 1979.

	Nr-Mt	Ex-Mt
1 1954 (First Year)	250.00	150.00
2 1955	150.00	90.00
3 1956	150.00	90.00
4 1957	125.00	80.00
5 1958	125.00	80.00
6 1959	125.00	80.00
7 1960	125.00	80.00
8 1961	75.00	50.00
9 1962	100.00	70.00
10 1963 (Oversized)	75.00	50.00
11 1964 (Oversized)	75.00	50.00
12 1965 (Oversized)	75.00	50.00
13 1966	50.00	30.00
13A 1966 (Revised)	50.00	30.00
14 1967	50.00	30.00
15 1968	35.00	20.00
16 1969	35.00	20.00
17 1970	25.00	15.00
18 1971	20.00	12.00
19 1972	20.00	12.00
20 1973	15.00	9.00
21 1974	15.00	9.00
22 1975	15.00	9.00
23 1980	10.00	6.00
24 1981	10.00	6.00
25 1982	12.00	7.00
26 1983	10.00	6.00
27 1984	10.00	6.00
28 1986	10.00	6.00
29 1983-Present	10.00	6.00

Boston Braves Yearbooks

The team did not issue Yearbooks during the 1948, 1949, 1953 or 1954 seasons.

	Nr-Mt	Ex-Mt
1 1946 (First Year)	325.00	225.00
2 1947	175.00	100.00
3 1950	150.00	90.00
4 1951	125.00	80.00

Boston Red Sox Yearbooks

There were Yearbook-style publications issued for the Red Sox in 1912, 1936 and 1946. The team did not issue Yearbooks for the 1953 or 1954 seasons.

	Nr-Mt	Ex-Mt
1 1951* (First Year)	250.00	150.00
2 1952	125.00	80.00
3 1955	125.00	80.00
4 1956	100.00	70.00
5 1957	100.00	70.00
6 1958	75.00	50.00
7 1959	75.00	50.00
8 1960	75.00	50.00
9 1961	75.00	50.00
10 1962	50.00	30.00
11 1963	50.00	30.00
12 1964	50.00	30.00
12A 1964 (Revised)	60.00	40.00
13 1965	35.00	20.00
14 1966	35.00	20.00
15 1967	100.00	70.00
16 1968	35.00	20.00
17 1969	35.00	20.00
18 1970	35.00	20.00
19 1971	15.00	9.00
20 1972	15.00	9.00
21 1973	25.00	15.00
22 1974	10.00	6.00
23 1975	10.00	6.00
24 1976	10.00	6.00
24A 1976 (Revised)	10.00	6.00
25 1977	10.00	6.00
25A 1977 (Revised)	10.00	6.00
26 1978	10.00	6.00
26A 1978 (Revised)	10.00	6.00
27 1979	10.00	6.00
27A 1979 (Revised)	12.00	6.00
28 1980	10.00	6.00
29 1981	10.00	6.00
30 1982	10.00	6.00
31 1983	10.00	6.00
32 1984	7.00	4.00
33 1985	7.00	4.00
34 1986	7.00	4.00
35 1987	7.00	4.00
36 1988	7.00	4.00
37 1989	10.00	6.00
41 1989-Present	10.00	6.00

Brooklyn Dodgers Yearbooks

There was no Yearbook issued for the 1948 season. The Dodgers also had unofficial Yearbook-style publications published in 1888, 1940, 1941, 1942 and 1947.

	Nr-Mt	Ex-Mt
1 1947 (First Year)	125.00	80.00
2 1949	250.00	150.00
3 1950	200.00	125.00
4 1951	150.00	90.00
5 1952	150.00	90.00
6 1953	150.00	90.00
7 1954	150.00	90.00
8 1955	350.00	250.00
9 1955 (Revised)	400.00	300.00
10 1956	125.00	80.00
11 1957	125.00	80.00

Chicago Cubs Yearbooks

The Cubs did not issue Yearbooks between 1958 and 1984. There were unofficial Yearbook-style publications published in 1919, 1934, 1935, 1936, 1937, 1938, 1939, 1940,1941,1942 and 1946.

	Nr-Mt	Ex-Mt
1 1948* (First Year)	125.00	80.00
2 1949	50.00	30.00
3 1950	50.00	30.00
4 1951	75.00	50.00
5 1952	50.00	30.00
6 1953	50.00	30.00
7 1954	50.00	30.00
8 1955	50.00	30.00
9 1956	75.00	50.00
10 1957	125.00	80.00
11 1985	10.00	6.00
12 1986	7.00	4.00
13 1987	7.00	4.00
14 1988	7.00	4.00
15 1989	7.00	4.00
16 1990	10.00	6.00
17 1991	10.00	6.00
18 1992	10.00	6.00
19 1990-Present	10.00	6.00

Chicago White Sox Yearbooks

The White Sox failed to issue Yearbooks from 1971 thru 1981 and again in 1985, 1987 and 1989. There were unofficial Yearbook-style publications issued for the 1947, 1948, 1949 1nd 1950 seasons.

	Nr-Mt	Ex-Mt
1 1951* (First Year)	275.00	175.00
2 1952	150.00	90.00
3 1953	125.00	80.00
4 1953 (Revised)	150.00	90.00
5 1954	125.00	80.00
6 1954 (Revised)	150.00	90.00
7 1955	100.00	70.00
8 1956	75.00	50.00
9 1957	75.00	50.00
10 1957 (Revised)	100.00	70.00
11 1958	75.00	50.00
12 1959	150.00	90.00
13 1960	75.00	50.00
14 1961	50.00	30.00
15 1962	35.00	20.00
16 1963	20.00	12.00
17 1964	25.00	15.00
18 1965	25.00	15.00
19 1966	35.00	20.00
20 1967	25.00	15.00
21 1968	25.00	15.00
22 1969	25.00	15.00
23 1970	35.00	20.00
24 1982	10.00	6.00
25 1983	10.00	6.00
26 1984	5.00	3.00
27 1986	10.00	6.00
28 1988	10.00	6.00
29 1990	10.00	6.00
30 1991	10.00	6.00
31 1986-Present	10.00	6.00

Cincinnati Reds Yearbooks

The Reds failed to issue a Yearbook in 1950 and 1986. Unofficial Yearbook-style publications were issued in 1919 (2-diff.) and 1930.

	Nr-Mt	Ex-Mt
1 1948* (First Year)	150.00	90.00
2 1949	250.00	150.00
3 1951	125.00	80.00
4 1952	125.00	80.00
5 1953	100.00	70.00
6 1954	100.00	70.00
7 1955 (Red Cover)	75.00	50.00
7B 1955 (Orange Cover)	75.00	50.00
8 1956	75.00	50.00
9 1957	75.00	50.00
10 1957 (Revised)	75.00	50.00
11 1958	50.00	30.00
11A 1958 (Revised)	50.00	30.00
12 1959	50.00	30.00
12A 1959 (Spring)	50.00	30.00
13 1960	35.00	20.00
14 1961	35.00	20.00
15 1962	35.00	20.00
15A 1962 (Spring)	50.00	30.00
15B 1962 (Apr.- May Edt.)	60.00	40.00
16 1963	60.00	40.00
16A 1963 (Revised)	75.00	50.00
17 1964	35.00	20.00
18 1965	35.00	20.00
19 1966	35.00	20.00
20 1967	25.00	15.00
21 1968	25.00	15.00
22 1969	20.00	12.00
23 1970	25.00	15.00
24 1971	15.00	9.00
25 1972	15.00	9.00
26 1973	15.00	9.00
27 1974	10.00	6.00
28 1975	15.00	9.00
29 1976	20.00	12.00
30 1977	10.00	6.00
31 1977 (Revised)	10.00	6.00
32 1978	10.00	6.00
33 1979	10.00	6.00
34 1980	10.00	6.00
35 1981	10.00	6.00
36 1982	10.00	6.00
37 1983	10.00	6.00
38 1984	10.00	6.00
39 1985	7.00	4.00
40 1987	7.00	4.00
41 1988	7.00	4.00
42 1989	7.00	4.00
43 1990	7.00	4.00
44 1991	7.00	4.00
45 1992-Present	10.00	6.00

Cleveland Indians Yearbooks

The Indians did not issue a Yearbook between 1974 and 1983. and again between 1985 thru 1988 and the strike season of 1993.

	Nr-Mt	Ex-Mt
1 1948 (First Year)	150.00	90.00
2 1949	60.00	40.00
3 1950	60.00	40.00
4 1951	75.00	50.00
5 1952	75.00	50.00
6 1953	100.00	70.00
7 1954	100.00	70.00
8 1955	75.00	50.00
9 1956	75.00	50.00
10 1957	100.00	70.00
11 1958	250.00	150.00
12 1959	150.00	90.00
13 1960	100.00	70.00
14 1961	100.00	70.00
15 1962	75.00	50.00
16 1963	100.00	70.00
17 1964	75.00	50.00
18 1965	75.00	50.00
19 1966	60.00	40.00
20 1967	60.00	40.00
21 1968	35.00	20.00
22 1969	25.00	15.00
23 1970	25.00	15.00
24 1971	15.00	9.00
25 1972	10.00	6.00
26 1973	10.00	6.00
27 1984	7.00	4.00
28 1989	10.00	6.00
29 1990	10.00	6.00
30 1991	10.00	6.00
31 1989-Present	10.00	6.00

Detroit Tigers Yearbooks

The Tigers failed to issue a Yearbook for the 1956 and 1993 seasons. There were Yearbook-style publications published for the Tigers in 1912, 1934, 1935 and 1939.

	Nr-Mt	Ex-Mt
1 1955* (First Year)	275.00	175.00
2 1957	150.00	90.00
3 1958	150.00	90.00
4 1959	125.00	80.00
5 1960	125.00	80.00
6 1961	100.00	70.00
7 1962	100.00	70.00
8 1963	100.00	70.00
9 1964	75.00	50.00
10 1965	75.00	50.00
11 1966	50.00	30.00
12 1967	50.00	30.00
13 1968	75.00	50.00
14 1969	50.00	30.00
15 1970	15.00	9.00
16 1971	20.00	12.00
17 1972	10.00	6.00
18 1973	10.00	6.00
19 1974	10.00	6.00
20 1975	10.00	6.00
21 1976	10.00	6.00
22 1977	10.00	6.00
23 1978	10.00	6.00
24 1979	10.00	6.00
25 1980	10.00	6.00
26 1981	10.00	6.00
27 1982	7.00	4.00
28 1983	7.00	4.00
29 1984	10.00	6.00
30 1985	10.00	6.00
31 1986	10.00	6.00
32 1987	10.00	6.00
33 1988	10.00	6.00
34 1989	10.00	6.00
35 1990	10.00	6.00
36 1991	10.00	6.00
37 1984-Present	10.00	6.00

Houston Astros Yearbooks

The Houston franchise was known as the Colt 45's between 1962 and 1964. The Astros did not issue a Yearbook for the 1967, 1980 or 1981 seasons. Also, no Yearbook was issued between 1969-1971, 1973-1976 and 1983-1991.

	Nr-Mt	Ex-Mt
1 1962 (First Year)	150.00	90.00
2 1963	150.00	90.00
3 1964	125.00	80.00
4 1965	125.00	80.00
5 1966	60.00	40.00
6 1968	50.00	30.00
7 1972	35.00	20.00
8 1977	15.00	9.00
9 1978	15.00	9.00
10 1979	15.00	9.00
11 1982	15.00	9.00
12 1992-Present	10.00	6.00

Kansas City A's Yearbooks

	Nr-Mt	Ex-Mt
1 1955 (First Year)	150.00	90.00
1A 1955 (Yellow Cover)	125.00	80.00
2 1956	125.00	80.00
2A 1956 (Revised)	150.00	90.00
3 1957	125.00	80.00
3A 1957 (Revised)	150.00	90.00
4 1958	125.00	80.00
5 1959	125.00	80.00
6 1960	100.00	70.00
7 1961	100.00	70.00
8 1962	100.00	70.00
9 1963	100.00	70.00
10 1964	100.00	70.00
11 1965	75.00	50.00
12 1966	75.00	50.00
13 1967	50.00	30.00
14 1967 (Revised)	60.00	40.00

Kansas City Royals Yearbooks

The Royals failed to issue Yearbooks from 1976 through 1982.

	Nr-Mt	Ex-Mt
1 1969 (First Year)	25.00	15.00
2 1970	15.00	9.00
3 1971	15.00	9.00
4 1972	10.00	6.00
5 1973	10.00	6.00
6 1974	10.00	6.00
7 1975	15.00	9.00
8 1983	10.00	6.00
9 1984	10.00	6.00
10 1985	10.00	6.00
11 1986	10.00	6.00
12 1987	10.00	6.00
13 1988	10.00	6.00
14 1989	10.00	6.00
15 1990	10.00	6.00
16 1991	10.00	6.00
17 1983-Present	10.00	6.00

Los Angeles Dodgers Yearbooks

	Nr-Mt	Ex-Mt
1 1958 (First Year)	150.00	90.00
2 1959	75.00	50.00
3 1960	50.00	30.00
4 1961	50.00	30.00
5 1962	25.00	15.00
6 1963	50.00	30.00
7 1964	10.00	6.00
8 1965	25.00	15.00
9 1966	20.00	12.00
10 1967	10.00	6.00
11 1968	10.00	6.00
12 1969	10.00	6.00
13 1970	10.00	6.00
14 1971	10.00	6.00
15 1972	15.00	9.00
16 1973	10.00	6.00
17 1974	10.00	6.00
18 1975	10.00	6.00
19 1976	10.00	6.00
20 1977	10.00	6.00
21 1978	10.00	6.00
22 1979	10.00	6.00
23 1980	10.00	6.00
24 1981	10.00	6.00
25 1982	10.00	6.00
26 1983	10.00	6.00
27 1984	10.00	6.00
28 1985	10.00	6.00
29 1986	10.00	6.00
30 1987	10.00	6.00
31 1988	10.00	6.00
32 1989	10.00	6.00
33 1990	10.00	6.00
34 1991	10.00	6.00
35 1973-Present	10.00	6.00

Milwaukee Braves Yearbooks

	Nr-Mt	Ex-Mt
1 1953 (First Year)	150.00	90.00
2 1954	100.00	70.00
2A 1954 (Revised)	125.00	80.00
3 1955	100.00	70.00
4 1956	125.00	80.00
5 1957	125.00	80.00
6 1958	125.00	80.00
7 1959	75.00	50.00
8 1960	75.00	50.00
9 1961	60.00	40.00
9A 1961 (Bob Allen Edt.)	75.00	50.00
10 1962	50.00	30.00
11 1963	50.00	30.00
12 1964	50.00	30.00
13 1965	50.00	30.00

Milwaukee Brewers Yearbooks

The Brewers failed to issue a Yearbook between 1971-1978, and in 1993.

	Nr-Mt	Ex-Mt
1 1970 (First Year)	50.00	30.00
2 1979	10.00	6.00
3 1980	10.00	6.00
4 1981	10.00	6.00
5 1982	15.00	9.00
6 1983	10.00	6.00
7 1984	10.00	6.00
8 1985	10.00	6.00
9 1986	10.00	6.00
10 1987	10.00	6.00
11 1988	10.00	6.00
12 1989	10.00	6.00
13 1990	10.00	6.00
14 1991	10.00	6.00
15 1983-Present	10.00	6.00

Minnesota Twins Yearbooks

The Twins failed to issue Yearbooks in 1983, 1984 and 1993.

	Nr-Mt	Ex-Mt
1 1961 (First Year)	150.00	90.00
2 1962	125.00	80.00
3 1963	100.00	70.00
4 1964	50.00	30.00
5 1965	50.00	30.00
6 1966	50.00	30.00
7 1967	25.00	15.00
8 1968	25.00	15.00
9 1969	20.00	12.00
10 1970	15.00	9.00
11 1971	15.00	9.00
12 1972	15.00	9.00
13 1973	10.00	6.00
14 1974	20.00	12.00
15 1975	15.00	9.00
16 1976	20.00	12.00
17 1977	10.00	6.00
18 1978	10.00	6.00
19 1979	10.00	6.00
20 1980	10.00	6.00
21 1981	10.00	6.00
22 1982	10.00	6.00
23 1985	10.00	6.00
24 1986	10.00	6.00
25 1987	10.00	6.00
26 1988	10.00	6.00
27 1989	10.00	6.00
28 1990	10.00	6.00
29 1991	10.00	6.00
30 1977-Present	10.00	6.00

Montreal Expos Yearbooks

The Expos revised its Yearbook three times each during the 1969 thru 1972 seasons. All revisions have equal value. The team did not issue a Yearbook in 1973 through 1981, and again during the 1987 through 1993 seasons.

	Nr-Mt	Ex-Mt
1 1969 (First Year)	40.00	25.00
2 1970	50.00	30.00
3 1971	35.00	20.00
4 1972	35.00	20.00
5 1982	10.00	6.00
6 1983	10.00	6.00
7 1984	10.00	6.00
8 1985	10.00	6.00
9 1986	10.00	6.00
10 1982-Present	10.00	6.00

New York Giants Yearbooks

The Giants did not issue a Yearbook for the 1948, 1949 or 1950 seasons. There were Yearbook-style publications issued for the Giants in 1887, 1888, and 1889.

	Nr-Mt	Ex-Mt
1 1947 (First Year)	150.00	90.00
2 1951	125.00	80.00
3 1952	100.00	70.00
4 1953	100.00	70.00
5 1954	100.00	70.00
6 1955	125.00	80.00
7 1956	100.00	70.00
8 1957	100.00	70.00

New York Mets Yearbooks

	Nr-Mt	Ex-Mt
1 1962 (First Year)	300.00	200.00
2 1963	150.00	90.00
3 1963 (Revised #2)	125.00	80.00
4 1963 (Revised #3)	150.00	90.00
5 1964	50.00	30.00
6 1964 (Revised #2)	50.00	30.00
7 1964 (Revised #3)	60.00	40.00
8 1965	50.00	30.00
9 1965 (Revised #2)	60.00	40.00
10 1965 (Revised #3)	60.00	40.00
11 1966	50.00	30.00
12 1966 (Revised #2)	50.00	30.00
13 1966 (Revised #3)	60.00	40.00
14 1967	50.00	30.00
15 1967 (Revised #2)	50.00	30.00
16 1967 (Revised #3)	60.00	40.00
17 1968	50.00	30.00
18 1968 (Revised)	50.00	30.00
19 1969	100.00	70.00
20 1970	35.00	20.00
21 1971	25.00	15.00
22 1971 (Revised)	35.00	20.00
23 1972	15.00	9.00
24 1972 (Revised)	15.00	9.00
25 1973	15.00	9.00
26 1973 (Revised)	15.00	9.00
27 1974	15.00	9.00
28 1974 (Revised)	15.00	9.00
29 1975	15.00	9.00
30 1975 (Revised)	15.00	9.00
31 1976	15.00	9.00
32 1976 (Revised)	15.00	9.00
33 1977	10.00	6.00
34 1977 (Revised)	10.00	6.00
35 1978	10.00	6.00
36 1979	10.00	6.00
37 1980	20.00	12.00
38 1981	15.00	9.00
39 1982	10.00	6.00
40 1982 (Revised)	15.00	9.00
41 1983	10.00	6.00
42 1983 (Revised)	15.00	9.00
43 1984	20.00	12.00
44 1984 (Revised)	20.00	12.00
45 1985	20.00	12.00
46 1985 (Revised)	20.00	12.00
47 1986	20.00	12.00
48 1986 (Revised)	20.00	12.00
49 1987	10.00	6.00
50 1988	10.00	6.00
51 1989	10.00	6.00
52 1990	10.00	6.00
53 1991	10.00	6.00
54 1987-Present	10.00	6.00

New York Yankees Yearbooks

Jay Publishing issued unofficial Yankee's Yearbooks between 1952 and 1965. The Jay Yearbooks were available through various mail order sources and souvenir outlets outside Yankee Stadium.

	Nr-Mt	Ex-Mt
1 1950 (First Year)	300.00	200.00
2 1951	200.00	125.00
3 1952	150.00	90.00
4 1952 (Jay)	100.00	70.00
5 1953	150.00	90.00
6 1953 (Jay)	100.00	70.00
7 1954	150.00	90.00
8 1954 (Jay)	100.00	70.00
9 1955	250.00	150.00
10 1955 (Revised)	250.00	150.00
11 1955 (Jay)	100.00	70.00
12 1956	125.00	80.00
13 1956 (Revised)	125.00	80.00
14 1956 (Jay)	75.00	50.00
15 1957	200.00	125.00
16 1957 (Revised)	200.00	125.00
17 1957 (Jay)	75.00	50.00
18 1958	150.00	90.00
19 1958 (Revised)	150.00	90.00
20 1958 (Jay)	75.00	50.00
21 1959	150.00	90.00
22 1959 (Revised)	150.00	90.00
23 1959 (Jay)	75.00	50.00
24 1960	150.00	90.00
25 1960 (Revised)	150.00	90.00
26 1960 (Jay)	75.00	50.00
27 1961	150.00	90.00
28 1961 (Revised)	150.00	90.00
29 1961 (Jay)	75.00	50.00
30 1962	100.00	70.00
31 1962 (Revised)	100.00	70.00
32 1962 (Revised #2)	100.00	70.00
33 1962 (Revised #3)	100.00	70.00
34 1962 (Jay)	60.00	35.00
35 1963	75.00	50.00
36 1963 (Revised)	75.00	50.00
37 1963 (Jay)	40.00	25.00
38 1964	75.00	50.00
38A 1964 (Revised)	75.00	50.00
40 1964 (Revised #2)	75.00	50.00
41 1964 (Revised #3)	75.00	50.00
42 1964 (Jay)	35.00	20.00
43 1965	60.00	40.00
44 1965 (Revised)	60.00	40.00
45 1965 (Jay)	35.00	20.00
46 1966	50.00	30.00
46A 1966 (Revised)	50.00	30.00
47 1966 (Revised #2)	50.00	30.00
48 1966 (Revised #3)	50.00	30.00
49 1967	50.00	30.00
50 1967 (Revised)	50.00	30.00
51 1968	25.00	15.00
52 1969	40.00	25.00
53 1970	60.00	40.00
54 1971	7.00	4.00
55 1972	15.00	9.00
56 1973	15.00	9.00
57 1974	15.00	9.00
58 1975	15.00	9.00
59 1976	20.00	12.00
60 1977	10.00	6.00
61 1978	10.00	6.00
62 1979	10.00	6.00
63 1980	10.00	6.00
64 1981	15.00	9.00
65 1982	7.00	4.00
66 1983	7.00	4.00
67 1984	10.00	6.00
68 1985	7.00	4.00
69 1986	7.00	4.00
70 1987	7.00	4.00
71 1988	10.00	6.00
72 1989	10.00	6.00
73 1990	10.00	6.00
74 1991	10.00	6.00
75 1988-Present	10.00	6.00

Oakland Athletics Yearbooks

The Athletics did not issue a Yearbook during the 1978, 1980, or 1981seasons. There also were no A's Yearbook issued between 1984 and 1993.

	Nr-Mt	Ex-Mt
1 1968 (First Year)	35.00	20.00
2 1969	20.00	12.00
3 1970	20.00	12.00
4 1971	20.00	12.00
5 1972	20.00	12.00
6 1973	20.00	12.00
7 1974	15.00	9.00
8 1975	15.00	9.00
9 1976	15.00	9.00
10 1977	10.00	6.00
11 1979	10.00	6.00
12 1982	10.00	6.00
13 1983	10.00	6.00
14 1977-Present	10.00	6.00

Philadelphia Athletics Yearbooks

	Nr-Mt	Ex-Mt
1 1949 (First Year)	60.00	40.00
2 1950	50.00	30.00
3 1951	50.00	30.00
4 1952	50.00	30.00
5 1953	20.00	12.00
6 1954	35.00	20.00

Philadelphia Phillies Yearbooks

	Nr-Mt	Ex-Mt
1 1949 (First Year)	250.00	150.00
2 1950	200.00	125.00
3 1951	450.00	325.00
4 1952	100.00	70.00
5 1953	25.00	15.00
6 1954	100.00	70.00
7 1955	125.00	80.00
8 1956	150.00	90.00
9 1957	100.00	70.00
10 1958	100.00	70.00
11 1959	75.00	50.00
12 1960	75.00	50.00
13 1961	125.00	80.00
14 1961 (Revised)	150.00	90.00
15 1962	100.00	70.00
16 1963	100.00	70.00
17 1964	75.00	50.00
18 1964 (Revised #2)	100.00	70.00
19 1964 (Revised #3)	100.00	70.00
20 1965	60.00	40.00
21 1966	50.00	30.00
22 1967	50.00	30.00
23 1968	50.00	30.00
24 1969	50.00	30.00
25 1970	40.00	25.00
26 1971	40.00	25.00
27 1972	25.00	15.00
28 1973	35.00	20.00
29 1974	20.00	12.00
30 1975	25.00	15.00
31 1976	10.00	6.00
32 1977	10.00	6.00
33 1978	10.00	6.00
34 1979	10.00	6.00
35 1980	20.00	12.00
36 1981	20.00	12.00
37 1982	10.00	6.00
38 1983	10.00	6.00
39 1984	7.00	4.00
40 1985	7.00	4.00
41 1986	10.00	6.00
42 1987	7.00	4.00
43 1988	10.00	6.00
44 1989	10.00	6.00
45 1990	10.00	6.00
46 1991	10.00	6.00
47 1988-Present	10.00	6.00

Pittsburgh Pirates Yearbooks

	Nr-Mt	Ex-Mt
1 1951 (First Year)	250.00	150.00
2 1952	150.00	90.00
3 1953	100.00	70.00
4 1954	100.00	70.00
5 1955	125.00	80.00
6 1956	100.00	70.00
7 1957	100.00	70.00
8 1958	75.00	50.00
9 1959	75.00	50.00
10 1960	75.00	50.00
11 1961	50.00	30.00
12 1962	35.00	20.00
12A 1962 (Revised)	50.00	30.00
13 1963	35.00	20.00
14 1964	20.00	12.00
15 1965	25.00	15.00
16 1966	25.00	15.00
17 1967	25.00	15.00
18 1968	20.00	12.00
19 1969	20.00	12.00
20 1970	60.00	40.00
21 1971	60.00	40.00
22 1972	15.00	9.00
23 1973	15.00	9.00
24 1974	15.00	9.00
25 1975	10.00	6.00
26 1976	7.00	4.00
27 1977	7.00	4.00
28 1978	7.00	4.00
29 1979	15.00	9.00
30 1980	7.00	4.00
31 1981	7.00	4.00
32 1982	7.00	4.00
33 1983	7.00	4.00
34 1984	7.00	4.00
35 1985	7.00	4.00
36 1986	10.00	6.00
37 1987	10.00	6.00
38 1988	5.00	3.00
39 1989	10.00	6.00
40 1990	10.00	6.00
41 1991	10.00	6.00
42 1989-Present	10.00	6.00

San Diego Padres Yearbooks

The Padres did not issue Yearbooks for the years 1970 through 1978, 1981 or 1987 through 1991.

	Nr-Mt	Ex-Mt
1 1969 (First Year)	75.00	50.00
2 1979	7.00	4.00
3 1980	7.00	4.00
4 1983	10.00	6.00
5 1984	10.00	6.00
6 1985	10.00	6.00
7 1986	10.00	6.00
8 1983-Present	10.00	6.00

San Francisco Giants Yearbooks

The Giants did not issue a Yearbook during 1977, 1978 or 1979, nor the 1986 through 1993 seasons.

	Nr-Mt	Ex-Mt
1 1958 (First Year)	275.00	175.00
2 1959	100.00	70.00
2A 1959 (Revised)	125.00	80.00
3 1960	60.00	40.00
4 1961	60.00	40.00
5 1962	50.00	30.00
6 1963	50.00	30.00
7 1964	35.00	20.00
8 1965	35.00	20.00
9 1966	35.00	20.00
10 1967	35.00	20.00
11 1968	25.00	15.00
12 1969	25.00	15.00
13 1970	25.00	15.00
14 1971	15.00	9.00
15 1972	10.00	6.00
16 1973	10.00	6.00
17 1974	10.00	6.00
18 1975	10.00	6.00
19 1976	15.00	9.00
20 1980	10.00	6.00
21 1981	15.00	9.00
22 1982	10.00	6.00
23 1983	10.00	6.00
24 1984	10.00	6.00
26 1985	10.00	6.00
27 1982-Present	10.00	6.00

Seattle Mariners Yearbooks

All Mariners Yearbooks are listed below.

	Nr-Mt	Ex-Mt
1 1977 (First Year)	50.00	30.00
2 1985	15.00	9.00
3 1994-Present	10.00	6.00

Seattle Pilots Yearbooks

	Nr-Mt	Ex-Mt
1 1969	175.00	100.00

St. Louis Browns Yearbooks

	Nr-Mt	Ex-Mt
1 1944 (First Year)	300.00	200.00
2 1945	250.00	150.00
3 1946	250.00	150.00
4 1947	250.00	150.00
5 1948	200.00	125.00
6 1949	200.00	125.00
7 1950	250.00	150.00
8 1951	200.00	125.00
9 1952	250.00	150.00
10 1953	250.00	150.00

St. Louis Cardinals Yearbooks

The Cardinals did not issue a Yearbook in 1978 nor the 1981 through 1988 seasons.

	Nr-Mt	Ex-Mt
1 1951 (First Year)	250.00	150.00
2 1952	150.00	90.00
3 1953	150.00	90.00
4 1954	125.00	80.00
5 1955	100.00	70.00
6 1956	75.00	50.00
7 1957	75.00	50.00
8 1958	75.00	50.00
9 1959	60.00	40.00
10 1960	60.00	40.00
11 1961	50.00	30.00
12 1962	50.00	30.00
13 1963	50.00	30.00
14 1964	40.00	25.00
15 1965	40.00	25.00
16 1966	40.00	25.00
17 1967	60.00	40.00
18 1968	35.00	20.00
19 1969	25.00	15.00
20 1970	15.00	9.00
21 1971	15.00	9.00
22 1973	15.00	9.00
23 1974	15.00	9.00
24 1975	15.00	9.00
25 1976	15.00	9.00
26 1977	15.00	9.00
27 1979	10.00	6.00
28 1980	10.00	6.00
29 1988	10.00	6.00
30 1989	10.00	6.00
31 1990	10.00	6.00
32 1991	10.00	6.00
33 1979-Present	10.00	6.00

Texas Rangers Yearbooks

The Rangers did not issue a Yearbook for the 1983, 1986, 1987, 1988 or 1989 seasons.

	Nr-Mt	Ex-Mt
1 1976 (First Year)	20.00	12.00
2 1977	15.00	9.00
3 1978	15.00	9.00
4 1979	10.00	6.00
5 1980	15.00	9.00
6 1981	10.00	6.00
7 1982	10.00	6.00
8 1984	10.00	6.00
9 1985	10.00	6.00
10 1988	10.00	6.00
11 1990	10.00	6.00
12 1991	10.00	6.00
13 1981-Present	10.00	6.00

Toronto Blue Jays Yearbooks

The Blue Jay's did not release a Yearbook during the 1978 season.

	Nr-Mt	Ex-Mt
1 1977 (First Year)	15.00	9.00
2 1979	10.00	6.00
3 1980	10.00	6.00
4 1981	10.00	6.00
5 1982	10.00	6.00
6 1983	10.00	6.00
7 1984	10.00	6.00
8 1985	10.00	6.00
9 1986	10.00	6.00
10 1987	10.00	6.00
11 1988	10.00	6.00
12 1989	10.00	6.00
13 1990	10.00	6.00
14 1991	12.00	7.00
15 1979-Present	10.00	6.00

Washington Senators Yearbooks

The Washington team was also known as the Nationals in the 1940's and early 1950's. The team did not issue a Yearbook in 1948, 1951, 1970 or 1971.

	Nr-Mt	Ex-Mt
1 1947 (First Year)	350.00	225.00
2 1949	300.00	200.00
3 1950	300.00	200.00
4 1952	125.00	80.00
5 1953	25.00	15.00
6 1954	75.00	50.00
7 1955	75.00	50.00
8 1956	100.00	70.00
9 1957	100.00	70.00
10 1958	75.00	50.00
10A 1958 (Revised)	100.00	70.00
11 1959	50.00	30.00
12 1960	50.00	30.00
13 1961	125.00	80.00
14 1962	60.00	40.00
15 1963	25.00	15.00
15A 1963 (Revised)	35.00	20.00
16 1964	20.00	12.00
17 1965	20.00	12.00
18 1966	20.00	12.00
19 1967	25.00	15.00
20 1968	20.00	12.00

VINTAGE COMIC PRICE GUIDE

1913 Oh Skin-Nay

Published by P.F. Volland & Co.

	Ex-Mt	Ex
The Days of Real Sport	150.00	90.00

1934-39 Famous Funnies

The Famous Funnies series was the first comic book sold directly to the public. Published by Eastern Color Printing Co.

	Ex-Mt	Ex
Football Cover (#4, Nov.,1934)	750.00	500.00
Football Cover (#15, Oct.,1935)	300.00	200.00
Baseball Cover (#21, April,1936)	300.00	200.00
Baseball Cover (#22, May,1936)	300.00	200.00
Baseball Cover (#58, May,1939)	200.00	125.00

1937-39 Feature Funnies

Joe Palooka made his debut in issue No.1 of Feature Funnies. The Feature Funnies series changed its name to Feature Comics after issue No. 18. Published by Harry A. Chesler.

	Ex-Mt	Ex
Joe Palooka Cover (#1, Oct., 1937)	1200.00	800.00
Joe Palooka Story (#4, Jan., 1938)	350.00	250.00
Joe Palooka Story (#5, Feb., 1938)	350.00	252.00
Joe Palooka Cover (#6, Mar., 1938)	300.00	200.00
Joe Palooka Cover (#9, June, 1938)	300.00	200.00
Joe Palooka Cover (#12, Sept., 1938)	250.00	150.00
World Series Cover (#13, Oct., 1938)	250.00	150.00
Joe Palooka Cover (#15, Dec., 1938)	200.00	125.00
Joe Palooka Cover (#18, Mar., 1939)	200.00	125.00

1939 Feature Comics

The Feature Funnies series became know as Feature Comics beginning with issue No. 21. Published by Quality Comics Group.

	Ex-Mt	Ex
Joe Palooka Cover (#21, June)	300.00	200.00
Joe Palooka Cover (#24, Sept.)	250.00	150.00
Joe Palooka Cover (#27, Dec.)	1500.00	900.00

1939-62 Four Color

This title had great success churning out many one-shot comics that lasted 23 years. Published by Dell Publishing Co.

	Ex-Mt	Ex
Ozark Ike Baseball Fan (#180, 1948)	30.00	20.00
All-American Cotton Woods (#837, 1957)	20.00	12.00

1940-46 Big Shot Comics

The Big Shot Comics title carried strips of the popular Joe Palooka character during its nine-year run. Published by Columbia Comics Group.

	Ex-Mt	Ex
Joe Palooka Cover (#4, Aug.,1940)	200.00	125.00
Joe Palooka Cover (#5, Sept.,1940)	200.00	125.00
Joe Palooka Cover (#6, Oct.,1940)	200.00	125.00
Joe Palooka Cover (#7, Nov.,1940)	200.00	125.00
Joe Palooka Cover (#8, Dec.,1940)	200.00	125.00
Joe Palooka Cover (#22, 1942)	150.00	90.00
Joe Palooka Cover (#40,1944)	75.00	50.00
Joe Palooka Story (#41, 1944)	60.00	40.00
Joe Palooka Story (#42, 1944)	60.00	40.00
Joe Palooka Story (#60, 1945)	50.00	30.00
Joe Palooka Story (#68, 1946)	25.00	15.00
Joe Palooka Cover (#70, 1946)	25.00	15.00

1940-54 Fight Comics

Fight Comics began as a sports title, but changed to a war theme and later a jungle theme before ceasing publication with the Summer 1954 issue. Published by Fiction House Magazines.

	Ex-Mt	Ex
Jack Dempsey Story (#1, 1940)	600.00	450.00
Joe Louis Story (#2, 1940)	300.00	200.00

1940-41 Sport Comics

This real-life drama series depicted modern-day athletes. The title was changed to True Sport Picture Stories after the fourth issue. Published by Street & Smith Publications.

	Ex-Mt	Ex
Lou Gehrig Story (#1, Oct.,1940)	200.00	125.00
Gene Tunney Story (#2, Oct.,1940)	100.00	60.00
Phil Rizzuto Story (#3, Oct.,1940)	75.00	50.00
Frank Leahy Story (#4, Nov.,1941)	75.00	50.00

1941-49 Foremost Boys Comics

The Foremost Boys series launched the popular Dick Cole character. Issue Nos. 5 - 36 are valued the same. Published by Funnies, Inc.

	Ex-Mt	Ex
Dick Cole Story (#1, Winter,1941)	50.00	30.00
Dick Cole Story (#2, Spring,1942)	30.00	20.00
Dick Cole Story (#3, Summer,1942)	25.00	15.00
Dick Cole Story (#4, Fall,1942)	25.00	15.00
Dick Cole Stories (#5 - #6, 1942 thru 1949)	25.00	15.00

1941-46 Real Heroes Comics

Published by Parents' Institute.

	Ex-Mt	Ex
Lou Gehrig Story (#6)	100.00	60.00
Pete Gray Story (#14)	25.00	15.00

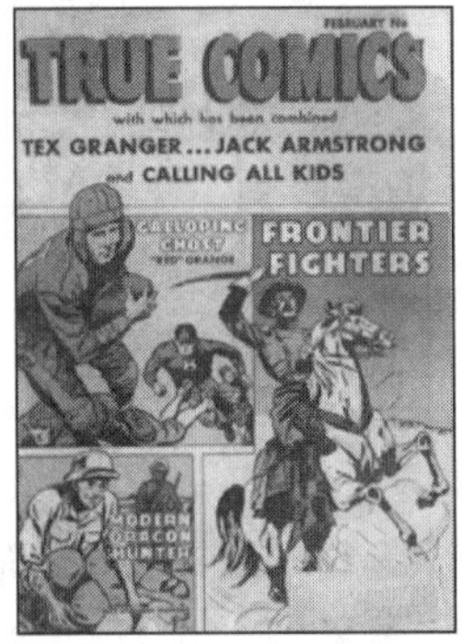

1941-50 True Comics

The True Comics series was based on real-life stories. The series lasted nine years. Published by True Comics/Parents' Magazine Press.

	Ex-Mt	Ex
Marathon Run Story (#1, April,1941)	100.00	60.00
Baseball Hall of Fame Story (#3, Aug.,1941)	60.00	40.00
Joe Louis Story (#5, Oct.,1941)	40.00	25.00
World Series Story (#6, Nov.,1941)	50.00	30.00
Football Stars (#7, Dec.,1941)	30.00	20.00
Basketball's Origin (#11, April,1942)	30.00	20.00
Bob Feller Story (#15, Aug.,1942)	30.00	20.00
Brooklyn Dodgers Story (#17, Oct.,1942)	30.00	20.00
Barney Ross Story (#24, May,1943)	20.00	12.00
Walt & Walker Cooper (#30, Dec.,1943)	20.00	12.00
Red Grange Story (#31, Dec.,1943)	20.00	12.00
Rube Waddell Story (#37, July,1944)	20.00	12.00
Rube Marquard Story (#49, May,1946)	20.00	12.00
Dixie Walker Story (#50, July,1946)	20.00	12.00
Jim Jeffries Story (#58, Mar.,1947)	20.00	12.00
Indianapolis Speedway (#60, May,1947)	20.00	12.00
Bob Feller Story (#61, June,1947)	20.00	12.00
Wally Butts Story (#65, Oct.,1947)	20.00	12.00
Guide to Football Formations (#66, Nov.,1947)	20.00	12.00
Univ. of Michigan Basketball (#70, Mar.,1948)	20.00	12.00
Joe DiMaggio Cover (#71, May,1948)	125.00	75.00
Jackie Robinson Story (#72, July,1948)	40.00	25.00
Story of the Marathon (#73, Sept.,1948)	15.00	9.00
Special Football Tips (#74, Nov.,1948)	15.00	9.00
Stan Musial Cover (#78, Aug.,1949)	100.00	60.00
Red Grange Story (#81, Feb.,1950)	75.00	50.00

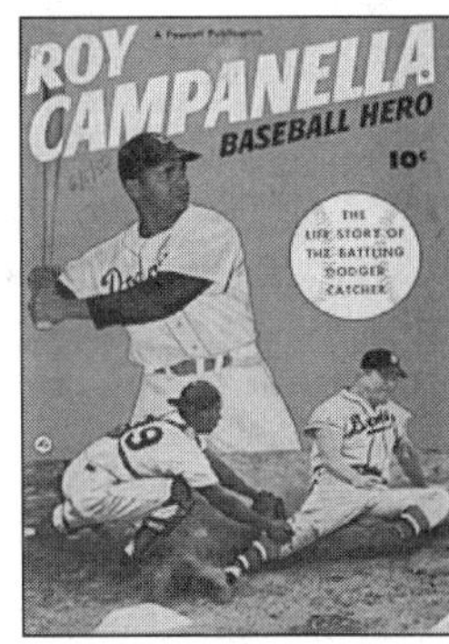

1941 World Famous Heroes Magazine

World Famous Heroes Magazine lasted four issues. Lou Gehrig was its sole sports personality. Published by Comic Corp. of America

	Ex-Mt	Ex
Lou Gehrig Story (#2, 1941)	300.00	200.00

1942-44 Joe Palooka

Due to his popularity in the Big Shot comic book series, the Joe Palooka character got his big break and became a star in this, his very own title. Published by Columbia Comic Corp.

	Ex-Mt	Ex
Joe Palooka Cover (#1, 1942)	250.00	150.00
Joe Palooka Cover (#2, 1943)	150.00	90.00
Joe Palooka Cover (#3, 1943)	100.00	60.00
Joe Palooka Cover (#4, 1944)	100.00	60.00

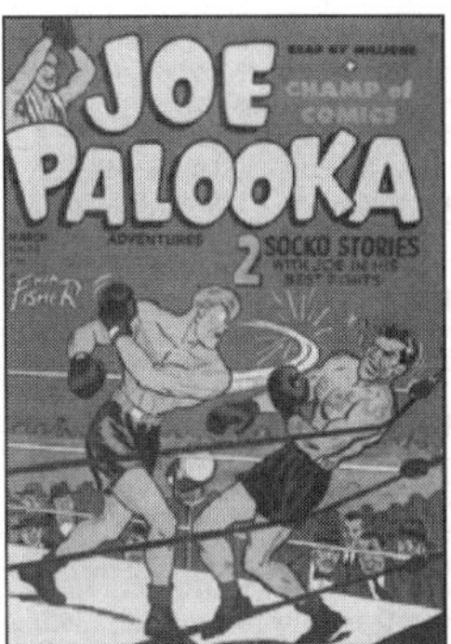

1942-49 True Sport Picture Stories

This real-life drama series depicted modern-day athletes. The title was changed from Sport Comics after that series' fourth issue. Published by Street & Smith Publications.

	Ex-Mt	Ex
Joe DiMaggio Cover (#5, Feb.,1942)	200.00	125.00
Billy Conn Cover (#6, Apr.,1942)	60.00	40.00
Mel Ott Cover (#7, June,1942)	60.00	40.00
Lou Ambers Cover (#8, Aug.,1942)	50.00	30.00
Pete Reiser Cover (#9, Oct.,1942)	60.00	40.00
Frankie Sinkwich Cover (#10, Dec.,1942)	50.00	30.00
Red Grange Cover (#11, Feb.,1943)	60.00	40.00
Jack Dempsey Cover (#12, Apr.,1943)	60.00	40.00
Willie Pep Cover (Vol.2 #1, June,1943)	50.00	30.00
Mort Cooper Cover (Vol.2 #2,Aug.,1943)	40.00	25.00
Carl Hubbell Cover (Vol.2 #3, Oct.,1943)	40.00	25.00
Baseball of Tomorrow (Vol.2 #4, Dec.,1943)	40.00	25.00
Don Hutson Cover (Vol.2 #5, Feb.,1944)	40.00	25.00
Dixie Walker Cover (Vol.2 #6, Apr.,1944)	40.00	25.00
Stan Musial Cover (Vol.2 #7, June,1944)	60.00	40.00
Famous Boxers Cover (Vol.2 #8, Aug.1944)	50.00	30.00
Negro Leagues Stars Cover (Vol.2 #9 ,Oct.,1944)	100.00	60.00
Connie Mack Cover (Vol.2 #10, Dec.,1944)	60.00	40.00
Winning Basketball Plays (Vol.2 #11, Feb.,1945)	40.00	25.00
Eddie Gottlieb Cover (Vol.2 #12, Apr.,1945)	40.00	25.00
Bill Conn Cover (Vol.3 #1, June,1945)	40.00	25.00
Philadelphia A's Cover (Vol.3 #2, Aug.,1945)	50.00	30.00
Leo Durocher Cover (Vol.3 #3, Oct.,1945)	50.00	30.00
Football Plays (Vol.3 #4, Nov.,1945)	40.00	25.00
Curley Lambeau Cover (Vol.3 #5, Jan.1946)	40.00	25.00
Bowling with Ned Day (Vol.3 #6, Mar.,1946)	40.00	25.00

Home From War/DiMaggio (Vol.3 #7, May,1946)	75.00	50.00
Billy Conn vs. Joe Lous (Vol.3 #8, July,1946)	75.00	50.00
Mexican Baseball (Vol.3 #9, Sept.1946)	50.00	30.00
Don "Dopey" Dillock (Vol.3 #10, Nov.,1946)	40.00	25.00
Death Scores a Touchdown (Vol.3 #11, Jan.,1947)	40.00	25.00
Red Sox vs. Senators (Vol.3 #12, March,1947)	50.00	30.00
Spring Training (Vol4 #1, May,1947)	40.00	25.00
How To Pitch (Vol.4 #2, July,1947)	40.00	25.00
Joe Fulks Cover (Vol.4 #3, Sept.,1947)	40.00	25.00
Get Ready for Olympics (Vol.4 #4, Nov.,1947)	40.00	25.00
Hugh Casey Cover (Vol.4 #5, Jan.,1948)	40.00	25.00
Jackie Robinson Cover (Vol.4 #6, Mar.,1948)	75.00	50.00
How to Bowl Better (Vol.4 #7, May,1948)	30.00	20.00
Joe Wolcott & Joe Louis (Vol.4 #8, July,1948)	50.00	30.00
Bill McCahan Cover (Vol.4 #9, Sept.,1948)	30.00	20.00
Great Football Plays (Vol.4 #10, Nov.,1948)	30.00	20.00
Steve Van Buren Cover (Vol.4 #11, Jan.,1949)	40.00	25.00
Basketball Cover (Vol.4 #12, Mar.,1949)	30.00	20.00
Satchel Paige Cover (Vol.5 #1, May,1949)	75.00	50.00
History of Boxing (Vol.5 #2, July,1949)	30.00	20.00

1943-55 Ha Ha Comics

Published by Creston Publications.

	Ex-Mt	Ex
Baseball Cover (May,1949)	20.00	12.00

1944 Dick Cole Blue Bolt

Published by Novelty Press.

	Ex-Mt	Ex
Boxing Cover (Vol.5 #2, Nov.1944)	50.00	30.00

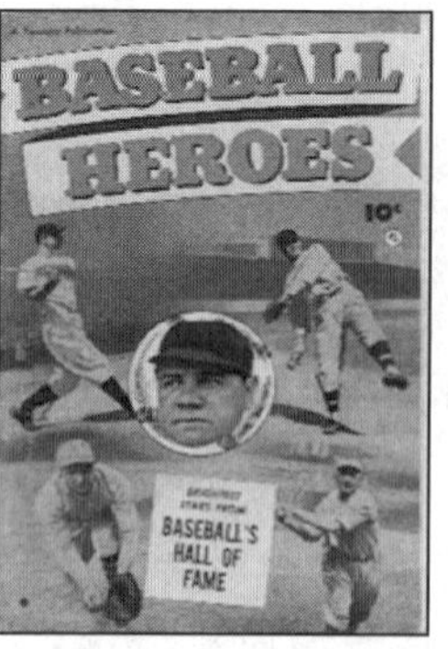

1944-47 It Really Happend

Published by William H. Wise/Visual Editions.

	Ex-Mt	Ex
Lou Gehrig Story (#5)	60.00	40.00
Man O'War Story (#8)	75.00	50.00
Honus Wagner Story (#10)	30.00	20.00

1945-61 Joe Palooka

Harvey Comics began publishing the Joe Palooka series beginning in 1945. The Harvey Comics run lasted 118 issues.

	Ex-Mt	Ex
Joe Palooka Cover (#1, 1945)	250.00	150.00
Joe Palooka Cover (#2, 1946)	100.00	60.00
Joe Palooka Cover (#3-#4, 1946)	75.00	50.00
Joe Palooka Cover (#5, 1946)	100.00	60.00
Joe Palooka Cover (#6-#15, 1946-47)	30.00	20.00
Joe Palooka Cover (#16-#29, 1948-49)	25.00	15.00
Joe Palooka Cover (#30-#44, 1949-50)	20.00	12.00
Joe Palooka Cover (#45-#62, 1950-52)	25.00	15.00
Joe Palooka Cover (#63-#118, 1952-61)	15.00	8.00
Joe Palooka Fights His Way Back (1945)	100.00	60.00
Joe Palooka Special Issue (1945)	40.00	25.00
Joe Palooka Special Issue (1949)	40.00	25.00
Joe Palooka Special Issue (1958)	40.00	25.00

1946-47 All-New Comics

Joe Palooka made an appearnce in the final three issues of this series. Published by Harvey Publications.

	Ex-Mt	Ex
Joe Palooka Cover (#13, July, 1946)	250.00	150.00
Joe Palooka Cover (#14, Nov, 1946)	250.00	150.00
Joe Palooka Cover (#15, Mar., 1947)	300.00	200.00

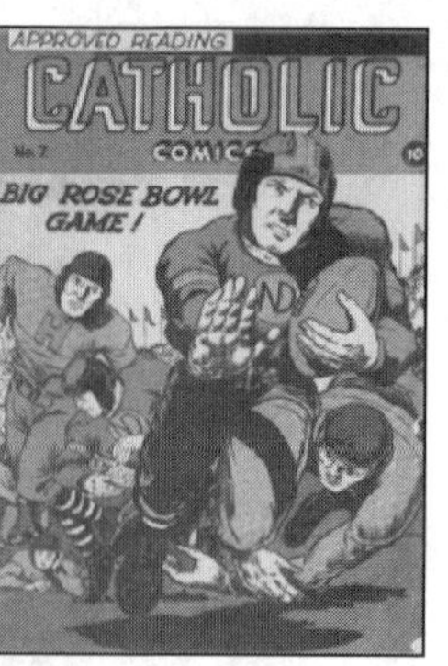

1946-49 Catholic Comics

Published by Catholic Publications.

	Ex-Mt	Ex
Rose Bowl Game (Vol.1 #7, Dec.,1946)	60.00	40.00

1946 First Love Illustrated

Published by Harvey Enterprises Inc.

	Ex-Mt	Ex
Baseball Cover (#65, June, 1946)	15.00	9.00

1946-47 Picture News in Color and Action

Published by 299 Lafayette Street Corporation.

	Ex-Mt	Ex
America's 1st Girl Boxer (#2, Feb., 1946)	50.00	30.00
Jackie Robinson Story (#4, Apr., 1946)	60.00	40.00
Hank Greenberg Story (#5, May, 1946)	40.00	25.00
Joe Louis Cover (#6, June, 1946)	50.00	30.00
Joe DiMaggio Story (#9, Nov.- Dec., 1946)	75.00	50.00

1946-49 Real Fact Comics

Published by National Periodical Publications.

	Ex-Mt	Ex
Jackie Robinson Story (#2, 1946)	150.00	90.00
Joe DiMaggio Story (#4, 1946	150.00	90.00

1946-48 Sports Stars

Published by Sports Stars Inc./Parents' Institute.

	Ex-Mt	Ex
Johnny Weissmuller Cover (#1, Feb., 1946)	125.00	75.00
Mel Ott Story (#2, April, 1946)	75.00	50.00
Joe DiMaggio Cover (#3, June, 1946)	125.00	75.00
Pepper Martin Story (#4, August, 1946)	75.00	50.00

1946 Vic Verity Magazine

Published by Vic Verity Publications.

	Ex-Mt	Ex
Baseball Fiction (#5, June, 1946)	20.00	12.00

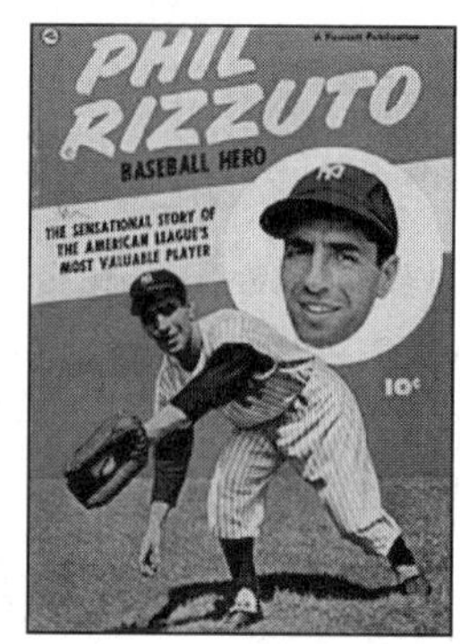

1947-49 Jack Armstrong

Published by Parents' Institute.

	Ex-Mt	Ex
Baffling Mystery of the Diamond (#7, June,1948)	30.00	20.00

1947-48 Negro Heroes

Published by Parents' Institute.

	Ex-Mt	Ex
Jackie Robinson Story (Summer, 1948)	350.00	250.00

1948-49 All Sports Comics

The title was changed From Real Sports Comics to All Sports Comics beginning with Issue No. 2. Published by Hillman Periodicals.

	Ex-Mt	Ex
Fictional Cover (#2, Dec., 1948)	125.00	75.00
Fictional Cover (#3, Feb., 1949)	75.00	50.00
Fictional Cover (Vol.2 #4, Apr.-May,1949)	60.00	40.00
Ty Cobb Story (Vol.2 #5, Jun.- Jul.,1949)	50.00	30.00
Fictional Cover (Vol.2 #6, Aug.- Sep.,1949)	50.00	30.00
W.Johnson/K.Rockne (Vol.2 #7, Oct.- Nov.,1949)	50.00	30.00

1948-50 Babe, Darling of the Hills

The adventures of Babe, a fictional female athlete. Published by Prize Publications.

	Ex-Mt	Ex
Female Fictional Cover (#1,June,1948)	60.00	40.00
Female Fictional Cover (#2,1948)	50.00	30.00
Female Fictional Cover (#3,1948)	30.00	20.00
Female Fictional Cover (#4,1949)	30.00	20.00
Female Fictional Cover (#5 - #11,1949-50)	25.00	15.00

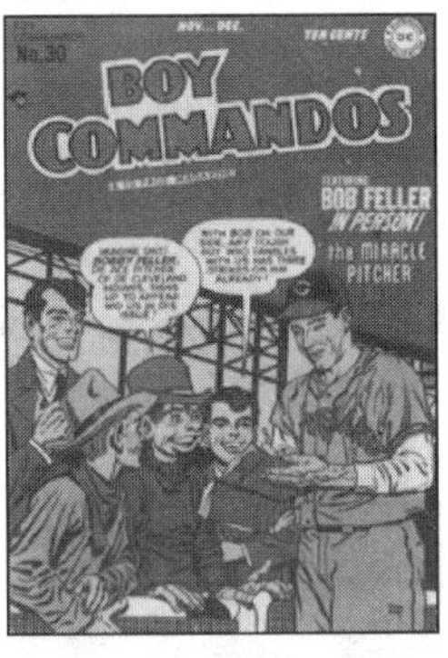

1948-51 Dick Cole

The popular Dick Cole character was later picked-up and featured in Sport Thrills beginning with issue No.11. Published by Curtis Publications/Star Publications.

	Good	Poor
All Sports Cover Dick Cole (#1, Dec.,1948)	75.00	50.00
All Sports Cover Dick Cole (#2, Dec.,1948)	60.00	40.00
All Sports Cover Dick Cole (#3, Dec.,1948)	50.00	30.00
Rowing Cover (#4, Dec.,1948)	50.00	30.00
Rowing Cover (#5, Dec.,1948)	50.00	30.00
Rodeo Cover (#6, Dec.,1948)	40.00	25.00
Rodeo Cover (#7, Dec.,1948)	40.00	25.00
Football Cover (#8, Dec.,1948)	40.00	25.00
Basketball Cover (#9, Dec.,1948)	40.00	25.00
Joe Louis Story (#10, July,1950)	40.00	25.00

1948-49 Ozark Ike

The Adventures of Ozark Ike. Published by Dell Publishing Co.

	Ex-Mt	Ex
Sports Fiction (#11/15,1948-49)	25.00	15.00
Sports Fiction (#16/23,1949-51)	20.00	12.00
Sports Fiction (#24,Dec.,1951)	20.00	12.00
Sports Fiction (#25,Sept.,1952)	20.00	12.00

1948 Real Sports Comics

This title's name was changed to All Sports Comics after issue No. 1. Published by Hillman Periodicals.

	Ex-Mt	Ex
Joe Louis Cover (#1, 1948)	100.00	60.00

1949-53 A-1 Comics

The title of this listing is "Home Run". This title is actually No. 89 in the A-1 comic book series. Published by Magazine Enterprises

	Ex-Mt	Ex
Stan Musial Cover (#3, 1953)	250.00	150.00

1949-51 Babe Ruth Sports Comics

The popular series was launched shortly after Babe Ruth's death in 1948 and lasted 11 issues. Published by Harvey Publications

	Ex-Mt	Ex
Basketball Cover (April,1949)	75.00	50.00
Baseball Cover (June,1949)	75.00	50.00
Joe DiMaggio Cover (Aug.,1949)	100.00	60.00
Bob Feller Cover (Oct.,1949)	75.00	50.00
Football Cover (Dec.,1949)	50.00	30.00
George Mikan Cover (Feb.,1950)	40.00	25.00
Sugar Ray Robinson (May,1950)	30.00	20.00
Yogi Berra (Aug.,1950)	60.00	40.00
Stan Musial Cover (Oct.,1950)	60.00	40.00
Kyle Rote (Dec.,1950)	30.00	20.00
Basketball Cover (Feb.,1951)	30.00	20.00

1949 Baseball Comics

Published by Will Eisner Productions

	Ex-Mt	Ex
Rube Rooky Story (#1, Spring, 1949)	300.00	200.00

1949-50 Mel Allen Sports Comics

Published by Standard Comics/Visual Editions

	Ex-Mt	Ex
Sports Cover (#5, Nov.,1949)	100.00	60.00
Sports Cover (#6, June,1950)	75.00	50.00

1949 Smash Hits Sports Comics

Published by Essankay Publications

	Ex-Mt	Ex
Multi-Sports Cover (Vol.1 #2, Jan. 1949)	100.00	60.00

1949 Sport Stars

Published by Marvel/Animirth Comics

	Ex-Mt	Ex
Life of Knute Rockne (#1, Nov. 1949)	125.00	75.00

1949 The Pride of the Yankees

The Lou Gehrig Story. Published by Magazine Enterprises.

	Ex-Mt	Ex
Lou Gehrig Cover (1949)	250.00	150.00

1950 Baltimore Colts

Published by American Visuals Corp.

	Ex-Mt	Ex
Baltimore Colts Logo Cover (1950)	200.00	125.00

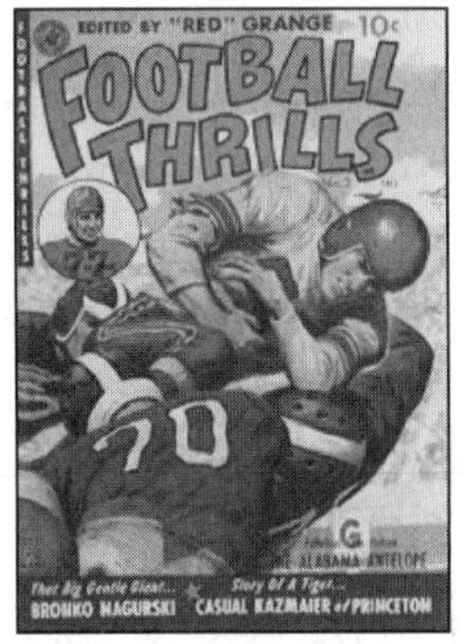

1950 Don Newcombe Baseball Star

Published by Fawcett Publications

	Ex-Mt	Ex
Don Newcombe Cover (1950)	125.00	75.00

1950 Eddie Stanky Baseball Hero

Published by Fawcett Publications

	Ex-Mt	Ex
Eddie Stanky Cover (1950)	125.00	75.00

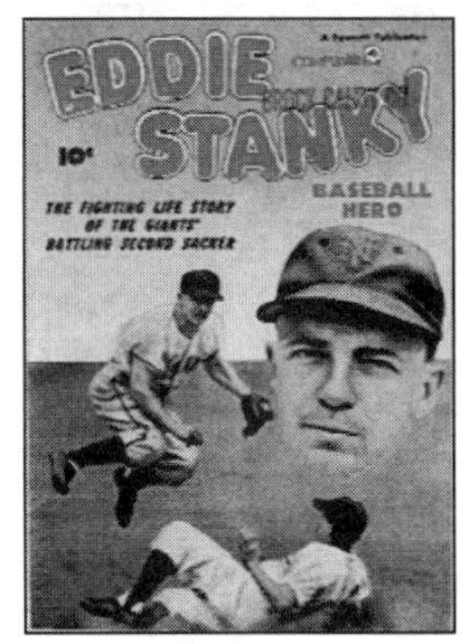

1950 Foremost Boy's Comics

Published by Star Publications

	Ex-Mt	Ex
Jim Braddock (#38, Jan.,1950)	150.00	90.00

1950-52 Jackie Robinson

Published by Fawcett Publications

	Ex-Mt	Ex
Jackie Robinson Cover (#1, May,1950)	150.00	90.00
Jackie Robinson Cover (#2, July,1950)	275.00	175.00
Jackie Robinson Cover (#3, Sept.,1950)	200.00	125.00
Jackie Robinson Cover (#4, Nov.,1950)	150.00	90.00
Jackie Robinson Cover (#5, May,1951)	150.00	90.00
Jackie Robinson Cover (#6, May,1952)	150.00	90.00

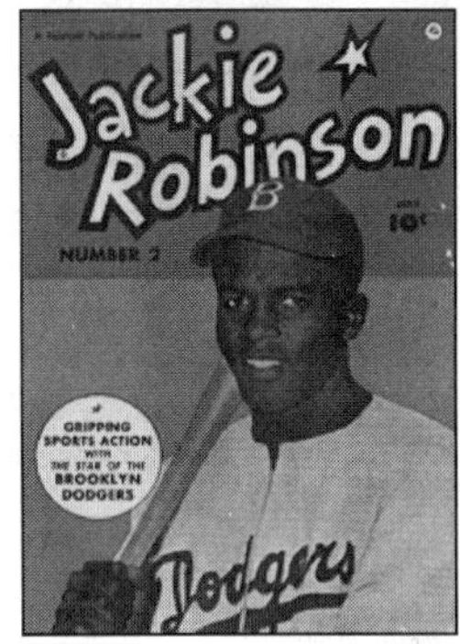

1950 Joe Louis

Published by Fawcett Publications

	Ex-Mt	Ex
Joe Louis Cover (#1, Sept.,1950)	200.00	125.00
Joe Louis Cover (#2, Nov.,1950)	150.00	90.00

1950 Larry Doby Baseball Hero

Published by Fawcett Publications

	Ex-Mt	Ex
Larry Doby Cover (1950)	225.00	150.00

1950 Ralph Kiner Home Run King

Published by Fawcett Publications

	Ex-Mt	Ex
Ralph Kiner Cover (1950)	125.00	75.00

1950-51 Sport Thrills

Published by Curtis Publications/Star Publications.

	Ex-Mt	Ex
T. Williams/T. Cobb Stories (#11, Nov.,1950)	100.00	60.00
J. DiMaggio/P. Rizzuto Stories (#12, Nov.,1950)	75.00	50.00
J. Robinson/P. Reese Cover (#13, May,1951)	100.00	60.00
J. Weismuller Story (#14, May,1951	50.00	30.00
Yankees Cover (#15, Nov.,1951)	75.00	50.00

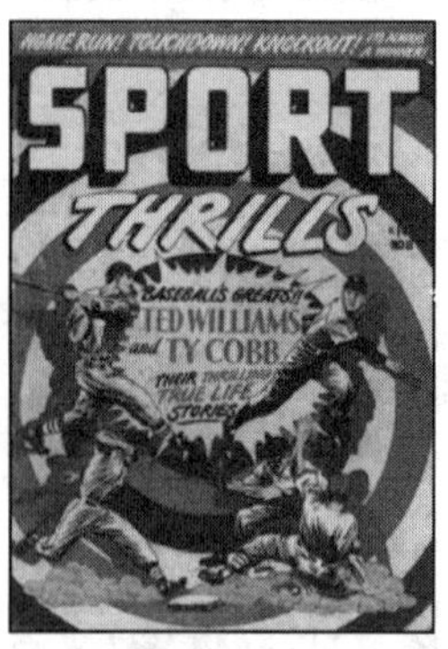

1950-52 Sports Action

This title changed its name from Sport Stars beginning with issue No. 2. Published by Marvel Comics

	Ex-Mt	Ex
Life of George Gipp (#2, Feb.,1950)	125.00	75.00
Hack Wilson (#3, June,1950)	100.00	60.00
Art Houtteman (#4, Oct.,1950)	75.00	50.00
Nile Kinnick (#5, Jan.,1951)	75.00	50.00
Warren Gun (#6, Mar.,1951)	60.00	40.00
Jim Konstanty (#7, May,1951)	75.00	50.00
Ralph Kiner (#8, May,1951)	75.00	50.00
Ed "Strangler" Lewis (#9, Oct.,1951)	50.00	30.00
"The Yella-Belly" (#10, Oct.,1951)	50.00	30.00
"The Killers" (#11, Mar.,1952)	50.00	30.00
"Man Behind the Mask" (#12, May,1952)	50.00	30.00
Lew Andrews (#13, July,1952)	50.00	30.00
Ken Roper (#14, Sept.,1952)	50.00	30.00

1951-52 Baseball Thrills

Published by Ziff-Davis Publishing Co.

	Ex-Mt	ExBob
Feller Predicts Pennant (#1, Summer,1951)	150.00	90.00
Yogi Berra Story (#2, Summer,1951)	100.00	60.00
Joe DiMaggio Story (#3, Summer,1952)	100.00	60.00

1951-52 Bill Stern's Sports Book

	Ex-Mt	Ex
Ewell Blackwell Cover (#1, 1951)	75.00	50.00
Sporting Cover (#2, 1952)	60.00	40.00
Giant Issue (Vol.2 #2, 1952)	75.00	50.00

1951-52 Football Thrills

Published by Approved Comics (Ziff-Davis Publishing)

	Ex-Mt	Ex
Red Grange Story (#1, Fall/Winter, 1952)	40.00	25.00
Bronco Nagurski Story (#2, Fall, 1952)	30.00	20.00

1951 Phil Ruzzuto Baseball Hero

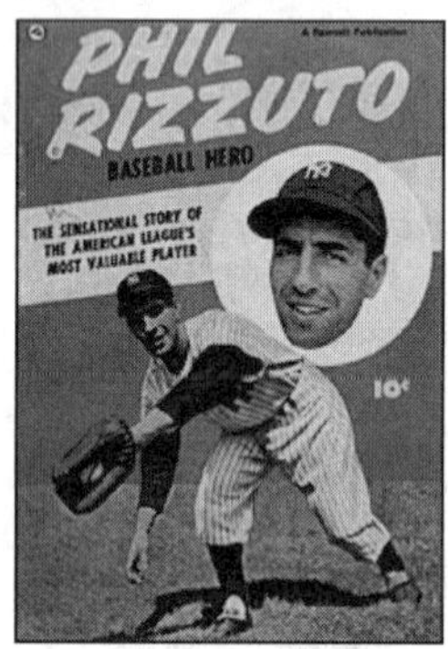

Published by Fawcett Publications

	Ex-Mt	Ex
Phil Ruzzuto Cover (1951)	150.00	90.00

1951 Roy Campanella Baseball Hero

Published by Fawcett Publications

	Ex-Mt	Ex
Roy Campanella Cover (1951)	175.00	100.00

1951 Yogi Berra Baseball Hero

Published by Fawcett Publications

	Ex-Mt	Ex
Yogi Berra Cover (1951)	175.00	100.00

1952 Baseball Heroes

Published by Fawcett Publications

	Ex-Mt	Ex
Ruth, others on Cover (1952)	200.00	125.00

1952 Thrilling True Story of Baseball

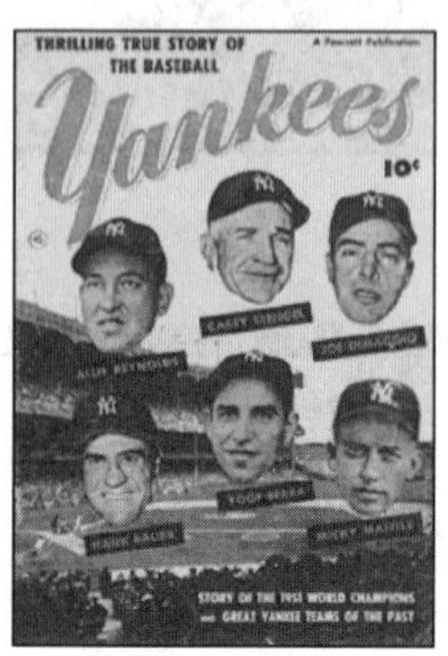

Published by Fawcett Publications

	Ex-Mt	Ex
Giants Players on Cover (1952)	250.00	150.00
Yankees Players on Cover (1952)	275.00	175.00

1952 The Amaizin Willie Mays

Published by Famous Funnies

	Ex-Mt	Ex
Willie Mays Cover (Sept., 1954)	250.00	150.00

1955-70 Charlton Sport Library

Published by Charlton Comics

	Ex-Mt	Ex
Football Cover (#1, Jan., 1970)	10.00	7.50

1955-56 Frank Merriwell at Yale

Published by Charlton Comics

	Ex-Mt	Ex
Frank Merriwell Cover (#1, June,1955)	20.00	12.00
Frank Merriwell Cover (#2, Aug.,1955)	20.00	12.00
Frank Merriwell Cover (#3, Oct.,1955)	20.00	12.00
Frank Merriwell Cover (#4, Jan.,1956)	20.00	12.00

1955 Swatt Malone Home Run Hero

Published by Swat Malone Enterprises

	Ex-Mt	Ex
Jim Thorpe Cover (#1, Sept.,1955)	250.00	150.00

1956 Championship Basketball

Published by Pennsylvania Athletic Products

	Ex-Mt	Ex
Paul Arizin Cover (1956)	40.00	25.00

1959-72 Three Stooges

Published by Dell Publications/Gold Key

	Ex-Mt	Ex
Baseball Cover (#13,1963)	40.00	25.00

1962 Baltimore Colts

Published by George Wright Hawkins

	Ex-Mt	Ex
Baltimore Colt Logo Cover (May,1962)	30.00	20.00

1962-63 The Brave and the Bold

Published by DC Comics

	Ex-Mt	Ex
Strangest Sports Stories (#45, April,1970)	30.00	20.00
Strange Sports Stories (#46, April,1970)	30.00	20.00
Strange Sports Stories (#47, Dec.,1962)	30.00	20.00
Strange Sports Stories (#48, Feb.,1963)	30.00	20.00
Strange Sports Stories (#49, April,1963)	30.00	20.00

1967 All-American Sports

Published by Charlton Comics

	Ex-Mt	Ex
Sporting Cover (#1, Oct., 1967)	10.00	7.50

1967 Estrellas Del Deporte

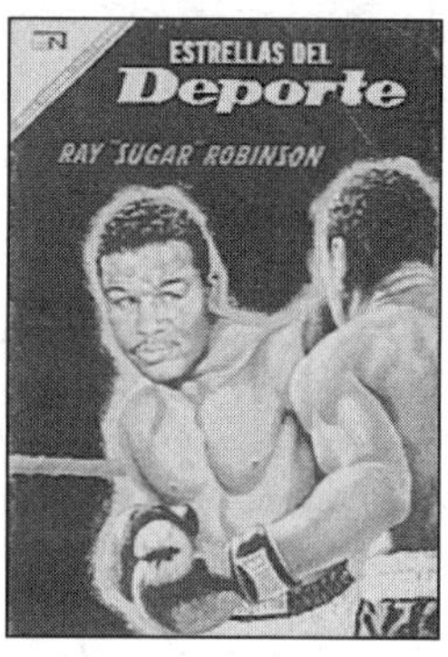

Published by Organizacion Editorial Novaro

	Ex-Mt	Ex
Sugar Ray Robinson Cover (Vol.11 #12, May, 1967)	125.00	75.00

1973-74 Champion Sports

Published by National Periodical Publication

	Ex-Mt	Ex
Fictional Cover (#1, 1973)	5.00	3.00
Fictional Cover (#2, 1973)	5.00	3.00
Fictional Cover (#3, 1974)	5.00	3.00

1973-74 Strange Sport Stories

Published by National Periodical Publication

	Ex-Mt	Ex
Wierd Fiction (#1, Sept.1973)	5.00	3.00
Wierd Fiction (#2, Nov.,1973)	3.50	2.50
Wierd Fiction (l#3, Jan.,1974)	3.50	2.50
Wierd Fiction (#4, March,1974)	3.50	2.50
Wierd Fiction (#5, May,1974)	3.50	2.50
Wierd Fiction (#6, July,1974)	3.50	2.50

1973 Tom Landry & Dallas Cowboys

Published by Fleming H. Revell Co.

	Ex-Mt	Ex
Tom Landry Cover (#1)	2.50	1.50
Tom Landry Cover (#2)	2.50	1.50

1973 Walt Disney Showcase

Published by Dell Publications
1973 Walt Disney Showcase ™ 1

	Ex-Mt	Ex
Baseball Cover (#14, 1973)	10.00	7.50

Acknowledgments

Each year we refine the process of developing the most accurate and up-to-date information for this book. I believe this year's Price Guide is our best yet. Thanks again to all the contributors nationwide (listed below) as well as our staff here in Dallas.

Those who have worked closely with us on this and many other books have again proven themselves invaluable: David Berman, Levi Bleam and Jim Fleck (707 Sportscards), Peter Brennan, Ray Bright, Card Collectors Co., Cartophilium (Andrew Pywowarczuk), Dwight Chapin, Barry Colla, Bill and Diane Dodge, Donruss/Leaf (Shawn Heilbron, Eric Tijerina), David Festberg, Fleer/SkyBox (Rich Bradley, Doug Drotman and Ted Taylor), Steve Freedman, Gervise Ford, Larry and Jeff Fritsch, Tony Galovich, Georgia Music and Sports (Dick DeCourcey), Dick Gilkeson, Steve Gold (AU Sports), Bill Goodwin (St. Louis Baseball Cards), Mike and Howard Gordon, George Grauer, John Greenwald, Greg's Cards, Wayne Grove, Bill Henderson, Jerry and Etta Hersh, Mike Hersh, Neil Hoppenworth, Jay and Mary Kasper (Jay's Emporium), David Kohler (SportsCards Plus), Paul Lewicki, Lew Lipset (Four Base Hits), Mike Livingston (University Trading Cards), Mark Macrae, Bill Madden, Bill Mastro, Michael McDonald (The Sports Page), Mid-Atlantic Sports Cards (Bill Bossert), Gary Mills, Brian Morris, Mike Mosier (Columbia City Collectibles Co.), B.A. Murry, Ralph Nozaki, Mike O'Brien, Oldies and Goodies (Nigel Spill), Pacific Trading Cards (Mike Cramer and Mike Monson), Pinnacle (Laurie Goldberg, Kurt Iverson), Jack Pollard, Jeff Prillaman, Pat Quinn, Jerald Reichstein (Fabulous Cardboard), Tom Reid, Gavin Riley, Clifton Rouse, John Rumierz, San Diego Sport Collectibles (Bill Goepner and Nacho Arredondo), Kevin Savage (Sports Gallery), Gary Sawatski, Mike Schechter, Scoreboard (Brian Cahill), Barry Sloate, John E. Spalding, Phil Spector, Frank Steele, Murvin Sterling, Lee Temanson, Topps (Marty Appel, Sy Berger and Melissa Rosen), Treat (Harold Anderson), Ed Twombly (New England Bullpen), Upper Deck (Steve Ryan, Marilyn Van Dyke), Wayne Varner, Bill Vizas, Bill Wesslund (Portland Sports Card Co.), Kit Young and Bob Ivanjack (Kit Young Cards), Rick Young, Ted Zanidakis, Robert Zanze (Z-Cards and Sports), Bill Zimpleman and Dean Zindler. Finally we give a special acknowledgment to the late Dennis W. Eckes, "Mr. Sport Americana." The success of the Beckett Price Guides has always been the result of a team effort.

It is very difficult to be "accurate" — one can only do one's best. But this job is especially difficult since we're shooting at a moving target: Prices are fluctuating all the time. Having several full-time pricing experts has definitely proven to be better than just one, and I thank all of them for working together to provide you, our readers, with the most accurate prices possible.

Many people have provided price input, illustrative material, checklist verifications, errata, and/or background information. We should like to individually thank AbD Cards (Dale Wesolewski), Action Card Sales, Jerry Adamic, Johnny and Sandy Adams, Alex's MVP Cards & Comics, Doug Allen (Round Tripper Sportscards), Will Allison, Dennis Anderson, Ed Anderson, Shane Anderson, Bruce W. Andrews, Ellis Anmuth, Tom Antonowicz, Alan Applegate, Ric Apter, Jason Arasate, Clyde Archer, Randy Archer, Matt Argento, Burl Armstrong, Neil Armstrong (World Series Cards), Todd Armstrong, Ara Arzoumanian, B and J Sportscards, Shawn Bailey, Ball Four Cards (Frank and Steve Pemper), Frank and Vivian Barning, Bob Bartosz, Nathan Basford, Carl Berg, Beulah Sports (Jeff Blatt), Brian Bigelow, George Birsic, B.J. Sportscollectables, David Boedicker (The Wild Pitch Inc.), Bob Boffa, Louis Bollman, Tim Bond (Tim's Cards & Comics), Andrew Bosarge, Brian W. Bottles, Kenneth Braatz, Bill Brandt, Jeff Breitenfield, John Brigandi, John Broggi, Chuck Brooks, Dan Bruner, Lesha Bundrick, Michael Bunker, John E. Burick, Ed Burkey Jr., Bubba Burnett, Virgil Burns, California Card Co., Capital Cards, Danny Cariseo, Carl Carlson (C.T.S.), Jim Carr, Patrick Carroll, Ira Cetron, Don Chaffee, Michael Chan, Sandy Chan, Ric Chandgie, Ray Cherry, Bigg Wayne Christian, Josh Chidester, Dick Cianciotto, Michael and Abe Citron, Dr. Jeffrey Clair, Derrick F. Clark, Bill Cochran, Don Coe, Michael Cohen, Tom Cohoon (Cardboard Dreams), Collection de Sport AZ (Ronald Villaneuve), Gary Collett, Andrew T. Collier, Charles A. Collins, Curt Cooter, Steven Cooter, Pedro Cortes, Rick Cosmen (RC Card Co.), Lou Costanzo (Champion Sports), Mike Coyne, Paul and Ryan Crabb, Tony Craig (T.C. Card Co.), Kevin Crane, Taylor Crane, Chad Cripe, Brian Cunningham, Allen Custer, Donald L. Cutler, Eugene C. Dalager, Dave Dame, Brett Daniel, Tony Daniele III, Scott Dantio, Roy Datema, John Davidson, Travis Deaton, Dee's Baseball Cards (Dee Robinson), Joe Delgrippo, Tim DelVecchio, Steve Dempski, John Derossett, Mark Diamond, Gilberto Diaz Jr., Ken Dinerman (California Cruizers), Frank DiRoberto, Cliff Dolgins, Discount Dorothy, Walter J. Dodds Sr., Bill Dodson, Richard Dolloff (Dolloff Coin Center), Ron Dorsey, Double Play Baseball Cards, Richard Duglin (Baseball Cards-N-More), The Dugout, Kyle Dunbar, B.M. Dungan, Ken Edick (Home Plate of Utah), Randall Edwards, Rick Einhorn, Mark Ely, Todd Entenman, Doak Ewing, Bryan Failing, R.J. Faletti, Terry Falkner, Mike and Chris Fanning, John Fedak, Stephen A. Ferradino, Tom Ferrara, Dick Fields, Louis Fineberg, Jay Finglass, L.V. Fischer, Bob Flitter, Fremont Fong, Perry Fong, Craig Frank, Mark Franke, Walter Franklin, Tom Freeman, Bob Frye, Chris Gala, Richard Galasso, Ray Garner, David Garza, David Gaumer, Georgetown Card Exchange, Richard Gibson Jr., Glenn A. Giesey, David Giove, Dick Goddard, Alvin Goldblum, Brian Goldner, Jeff Goldstein, Ron Gomez, Rich Gove, Joseph Griffin, Mike Grimm, Neil Gubitz (What-A-Card), Hall's Nostalgia, Hershell Hanks, Gregg Hara, Zac Hargis, Floyd Haynes (H and H Baseball Cards), Ben Heckert, Kevin Heffner, Kevin Heimbigner, Dennis Heitland, Joel Hellman, Arthur W. Henkel, Kevin Hense, Hit and Run Cards (Jon, David, and Kirk Peterson), Gary Holcomb, Lyle Holcomb, Rich Hovorka, John Howard, Mark Hromalik, H.P. Hubert, Dennis Hughes, Harold Hull, Johnny Hustle Card Co., Tom Imboden, Chris Imbriaco, Vern Isenberg, Dale Jackson, Marshall Jackson, Mike Jardina, Hal Jarvis, Paul Jastrzembski, Jeff's Sports Cards, David Jenkins, Donn Jennings Cards, George Johnson, Robe Johnson, Stephen Jones, Al Julian, Chuck Juliana, Dave Jurgensmeier, John Just, Robert Just, Nick Kardoulias, Scott Kashner, Frank J. Katen, Jerry Katz (Bottom of the Ninth), Mark Kauffman, Allan Kaye, Rick Keplinger, Sam Kessler, Kevin's Kards, Larry B. Killian, Kingdom Collectibles, Inc., John Klassnik, Philip C. Klutts, Don Knutsen, Steven Koenigsberg, Bob & Bryan Kornfield, Blake Krier, Neil Krohn, Scott Ku, Thomas Kunnecke, Gary Lambert, Matthew Lancaster (MC's Card and Hobby), Jason Lassic, Allan Latawiec, Howard Lau, Gerald A. Lavelle, Dan Lavin, Richard S. Lawrence, William Lawrence, Brent Lee, W.H. Lee, Morley Leeking, Ronald Lenhardt, Brian Lentz, Tom Leon, Leo's Sports Collectibles, Irv Lerner, Larry and Sally Levine, Lisa Licitra, James Litopoulos, Larry Loeschen (A and J Sportscards), Neil Lopez, Allan Lowenberg, Kendall Loyd (Orlando Sportscards South), Robert Luce, David Macaray, Jim Macie, Joe Maddigan, David Madison, Rob Maerten, Frank Magaha, Pierre Marceau, Paul Marchant, Jim Marsh, Rich Markus, Bob Marquette, Brad L. Marten, Ronald L. Martin, Scott Martinez, Frank J. Masi, Duane Matthes, James S. Maxwell Jr., Dr. William McAvoy, Michael McCormick, Paul McCormick, McDag Productions Inc., Tony McLaughlin, Mendal Mearkle, Carlos Medina, Ken Melanson, William Mendel, Eric Meredith, Blake Meyer (Lone Star Sportscards), Tim Meyer, Joe Michalowicz, Lee Milazzo, Jimmy Milburn, Cary S. Miller, David (Otis) Miller, Eldon Miller, George Miller, Wayne Miller, Dick Millerd, Mitchell's Baseball Cards, Perry Miyashita, Douglas Mo, John Morales, William Munn, Mark Murphy, John Musacchio,

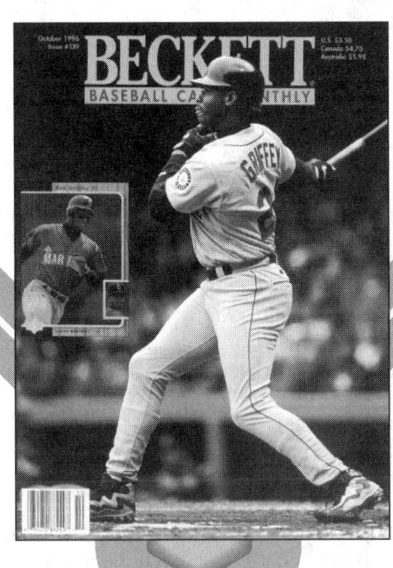

Robert Nappe, National Sportscard Exchange, Roger Neufeldt, Bud Obermeyer, Francisco Ochoa, John O'Hara, Glenn Olson, Mike Orth, Ron Oser, Luther Owen, Earle Parrish, Clay Pasternack, Mickey Payne, Michael Perrotta, Doug and Zachary Perry, Tom Pfirrmann, Bob Pirro, George Pollitt, Don Prestia, Coy Priest, Loran Pulver, Bob Ragonese, Richard H. Ranck, Bryan Rappaport, Robert M. Ray, R.W. Ray, Phil Regli, Glenn Renick, Rob Resnick, John Revell, Carson Ritchey, Bill Rodman, Craig Roehrig, David H. Rogers, Michael H. Rosen, Martin Rotunno, Michael Runyan, Mark Rush, George Rusnak, Mark Russell, Terry Sack, Joe Sak, Jennifer Salems, Barry Sanders, Everett Sands, Jon Sands, Tony Scarpa, John Schad, Dave Schau (Baseball Cards), Bruce M. Schwartz, Keith A. Schwartz, Charlie Seaver, Tom Shanyfelt, Steven C. Sharek, Eddie Silard, Art Smith, Ben Smith, Michael Smith, Jerry Sorice, Don Spagnolo, Carl Specht, Sports Card Fan-Attic, The Sport Hobbyist, Dauer Stackpole, Norm Stapleton, Bill Steinberg, Bob Stern, Lisa Stellato, Jason Stern, Andy Stoltz, Bill Stone, Tim Strandberg (East Texas Sports Cards), Edward Strauss, Strike Three, Richard Strobino, Superior Sport Card, Dr. Richard Swales, Paul Taglione, George Tahinos, Ian Taylor, Lyle Telfer, The Thirdhand Shoppe, Scott A. Thomas, Paul Thornton, Carl N. Thrower, Jim Thurtell, John Tomko, Bud Tompkins (Minnesota Connection), Philip J. Tremont, Ralph Triplette, Mike Trotta, Umpire's Choice Inc., Eric Unglaub, Hoyt Vanderpool, Rob Veres, Nathan Voss, Steven Wagman, Jonathan Waldman, Terry Walker, T. Wall, Gary A. Walter, Mark Weber, Joe and John Weisenburger (The Wise Guys), Brian Wentz, Richard West, Mike Wheat, Richard Wiercinski, Don Williams (Robin's Nest of Dolls), Jeff Williams, John Williams, Kent Williams, Craig Williamson, Opry Winston, Brandon Witz, Rich Wojtasick, John Wolf Jr., Jay Wolt (Cavalcade of Sports), Carl Womack, Pete Wooten, Peter Yee, Wes Young, Dean Zindler, Mark Zubrensky and Tim Zwick.

Every year we make active solicitations for expert input. We are particularly appreciative of help (however extensive or cursory) provided for this volume. We receive many inquiries, comments and questions regarding material within this book. In fact, each and every one is read and digested. Time constraints, however, prevent us from personally replying. But keep sharing your knowledge. Your letters and input are part of the "big picture" of hobby information we can pass along to readers in our books and magazines. Even though we cannot respond to each letter, you are making significant contributions to the hobby through your interest and comments.

The effort to continually refine and improve this book also involves a growing number of people and types of expertise on our home team. Our company boasts a substantial Sports Data Publishing team, which strengthens our ability to provide comprehensive analysis of the marketplace. SDP capably handled numerous technical details and provided able assistance in the preparation of this edition.

Our baseball analysts played a major part in compiling this year's book, traveling thousands of miles during the past year to attend sports card shows and visit card shops around the United States and Canada. The Beckett baseball specialists are Theo Chen (Assistant Manager, Hobby Information), Ben Ecklar, Mike Jaspersen, Rich Klein and Grant Sandground (Senior Price Guide Editor). Their pricing analysis and careful proofreading were key contributions to the accuracy of this annual.

Grant Sandground's coordination and reconciling of prices as Beckett Baseball Card Monthly Price Guide Editor helped immeasurably. Rich Klein, as research analyst, contributed detailed pricing analysis and hours of proofing.

Ben Ecklar contributed his time and efforts to produce our first comprehensive listing of minor league cards, a resource of unparalled quality. Mike Jaspersen contributed his knowledge of both vintage and modern issues to help insure the excellence in both checklisting and pricing. Theo Chen and Eddie Kelly added to the effort with information about the industry's finest listings of figurines and autographs.

They were ably assisted by Jeany Finch and Beverly Mills, who helped enter new sets and pricing information, and ably handled administration of our contributor Price Guide surveys. Card librarian Gabriel Rangel handled the ever-growing quantity of cards we need organized for efforts such as this.

The effort was led by SDP Senior Manager Pepper Hastings and Manager of SDP Dan Hitt. They were ably assisted by the rest of the Price Guide analysts: Pat Blandford, Steven Judd, Eddie Kelly, Lon Levitan, Allan Muir, Rob Springs and William Sutherland.

The price gathering and analytical talents of this fine group of hobbyists have helped make our Beckett team stronger, while making this guide and its companion monthly Price Guide more widely recognized as the hobby's most reliable and relied upon sources of pricing information.

The IS (Information Services) department, ably headed by Airey Baringer, played a critical role in technology. Working with software designed by assistant manager David Schneider and Yvonne Yeung, they spent countless hours programming, testing, and implementing it to simplify the handling of thousands of prices that must be checked and updated for each edition.

In the Production Department, Paul Kerutis, Marlon DePaula and Belinda Cross were responsible for the typesetting and for the card photos you see throughout the book.

Loretta Gibbs and Don Pendergraft spent tireless hours on the phone attending to the wishes of our dealer advertisers. Once the ad specifications were delivered to our offices, Phaedra Strecher used her computer skills to turn raw copy into attractive display advertisements.

In the years since this guide debuted, Beckett Publications has grown beyond any rational expectation. A great many talented and hard working individuals have been instrumental in this growth and success. Our whole team is to be congratulated for what we together have accomplished. Our Beckett Publications team is led by President Jeff Amano, Vice Presidents Claire Backus and Joe Galindo, Directors Mark Harwell, Reed Poole and Dave Stock, and Senior Managers Jeff Anthony, Beth Harwell and Pepper Hastings. They are ably assisted by Pete Adauto, Dana Alecknavage, Kaye Ball, Airey Baringer, Rob Barry, Therese Bellar, Andrea Bergeron, Eric Best, Julie Binion, Louise Bird, Amy Brougher, Bob Brown, Angie Calandro, Randall Calvert, Emily Camp, Mary Campana, Cara Carmichael, Eric Cash, Susan Catka, Jud Chappell, Albert Chavez, Marty Click, C.R. Conant, Andy Costilla, Belinda Cross, Randy Cummings, Von Daniel, Aaron Derr, Gary Doughty, Lauren Drews, Ryan Duckworth, Amy Durrett, Kandace Elmore, Eric Evans, Craig Ferris, Gean Paul Figari, Carol Fowler, Mary Gonzalez-Davis, Rosanna Gonzalez-Oleachea, Jeff Greer, Mary Gregory, Robert Gregory, Jenifer Grellhesl, Julie Grove, Tracy Hackler, Patti Harris, Steve Harris, Becky Hart, Mark Hartley, Joanna Hayden, Chris Hellem, Melissa Herzog, Yexin Huang, Tim Jaska, Julia Jernigan, Wendy Kizer, Gayle Klancnik, Rudy J. Klancnik, Brian Kosley, Michael Lallemont, Tom Layberger, Jane Ann Layton, Sara Leeman, Benedito Leme, Lori Lindsey, Stanley Lira, Kirk Lockhart, Sara Maneval, Louis Marroquin, John Marshall, Mike McAllister, Teri McGahey, Matt McGuire, Omar Mediano, Sherry Monday, Mila Morante, Terrence Morawski, Daniel Moscoso Jr., Mike Moss, Randy Mosty, Allan Muir, Hugh Murphy, Shawn Murphy, Bridget Norris, Mike Obert, Stacy Olivieri, Lisa O'Neill, Clark Palomino, Mike Pagel, Clark Palomino, Wendy Pallugna, Laura Patterson, Missy Patton, Mike Payne, Susan Plonka, Tim Polzer, John Randall, Bob Richardson, Tina Riojas, Lisa Runyon, Susan Sainz, David Schneider, Christine Seibert, Brett Setter (Special thanks for his Ryan information), Len Shelton, Dave Sliepka, Judi Smalling, Sheri Smith, Jeff Stanton, Margaret Steele, Marcia Stoesz, Mark Stokes, Dawn Sturgeon, Doree Tate, Jim Tereschuk, Roz Theesfeld, Doug Williams, Steve Wilson, Ed Wornson, Bryan Winstead, David Yandry, Mark Zeske and Jay Zwerner. The whole Beckett Publications team has my thanks for jobs well done. Thank you, everyone.

I also thank my family, especially my wife, Patti, and our daughters, Christina, Rebecca, and Melissa, for putting up with me again.

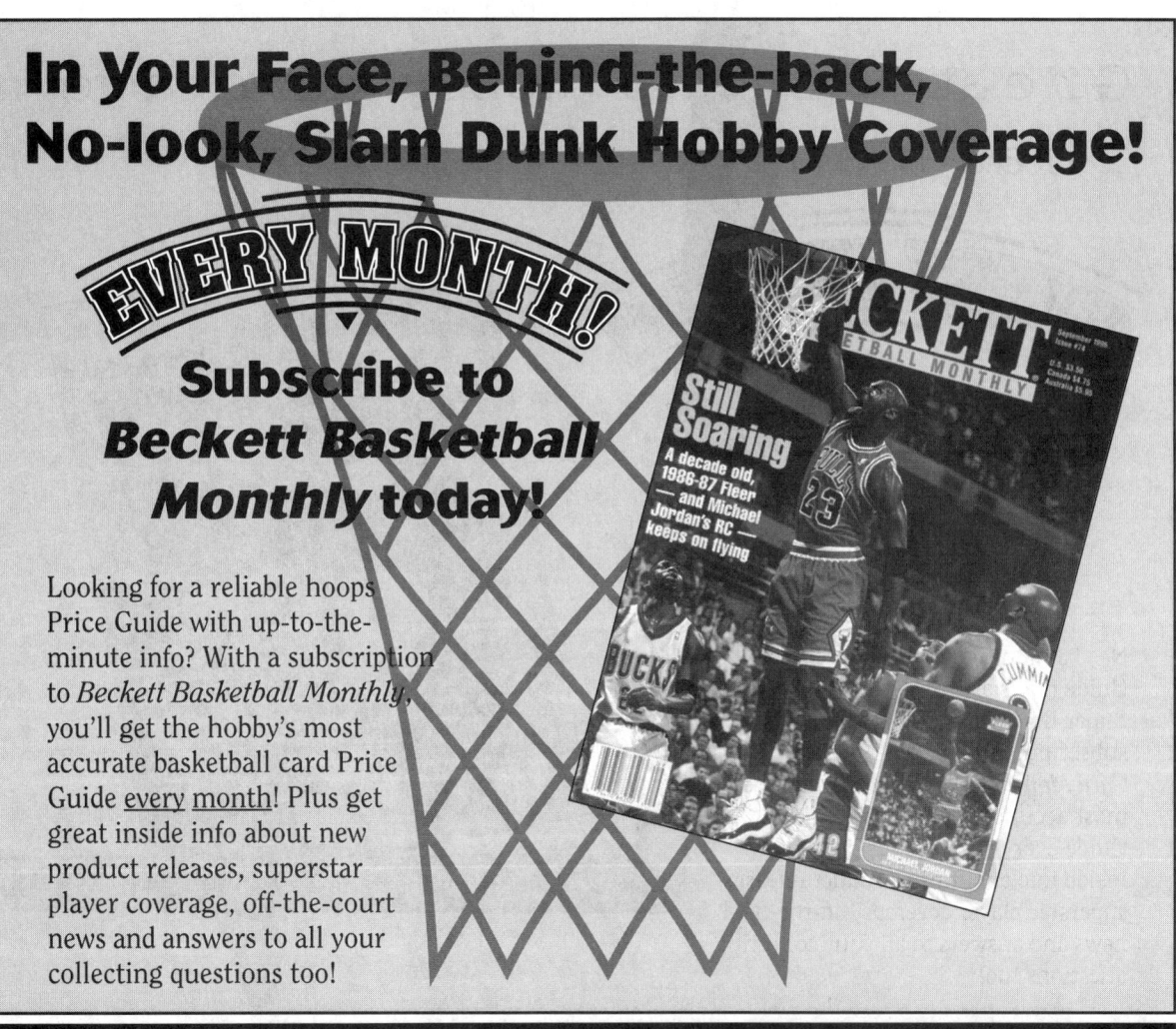

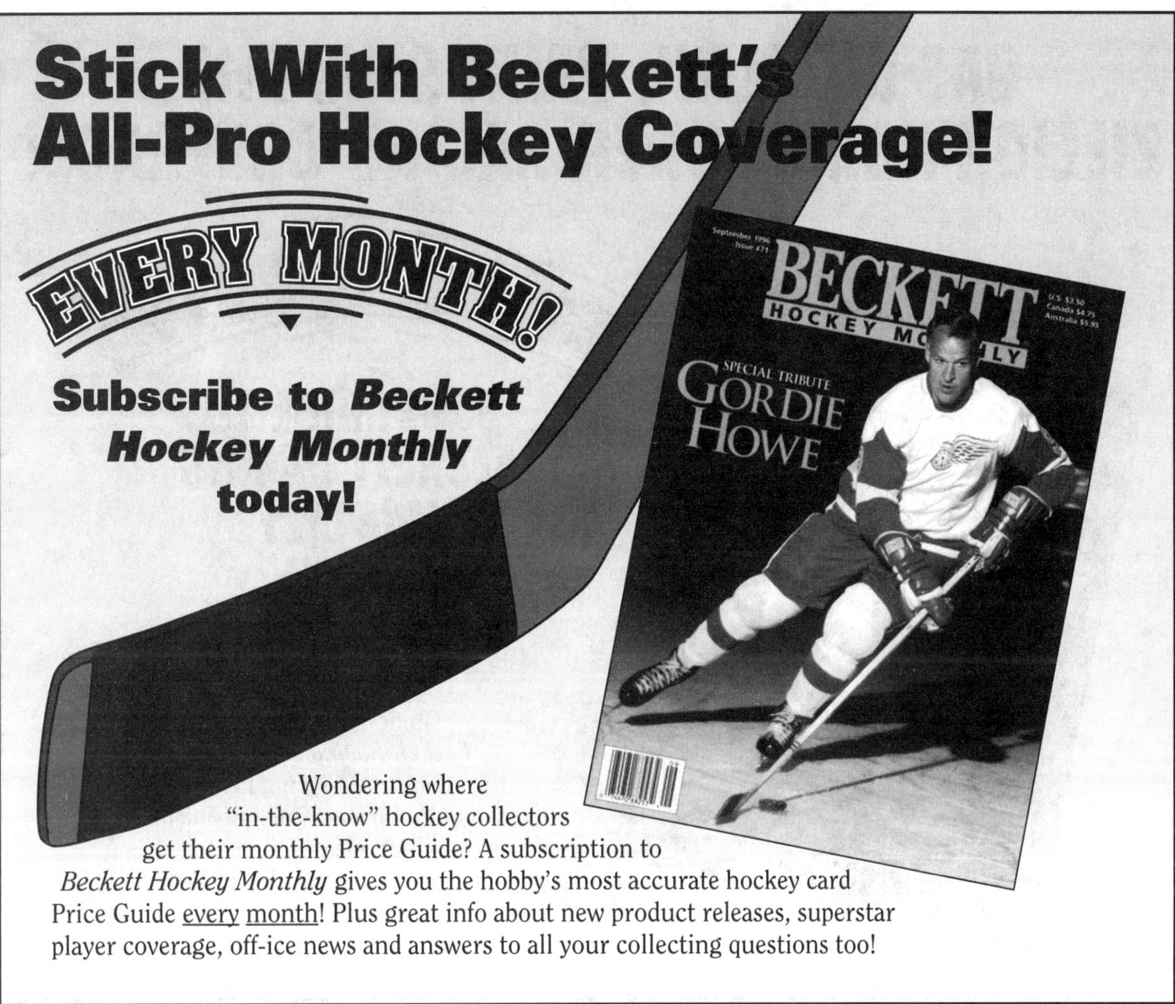
Stick With Beckett's
All-Pro Hockey Coverage!
EVERY MONTH!
Subscribe to Beckett Hockey Monthly today!
BECKETT
HOCKEY MONTHLY
SPECIAL TRIBUTE
GORDIE HOWE
Wondering where "in-the-know" hockey collectors get their monthly Price Guide? A subscription to Beckett Hockey Monthly gives you the hobby's most accurate hockey card Price Guide every month! Plus great info about new product releases, superstar player coverage, off-ice news and answers to all your collecting questions too!